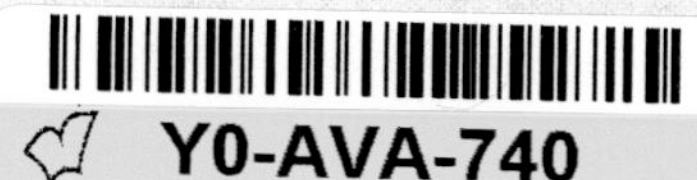

Books Out Loud™

Bowker's Guide to Audiobooks 2011

This edition of

BOOKS OUT LOUD™ 2011

was prepared by R.R. Bowker's Database Publishing Group
in collaboration with the Information Technology Department.

Annie Callanan, Chief Operating Officer
Philip Evans, Chief Financial Officer
Sy Inwentarz, Senior Vice President
Gary Aiello, Senior Vice President
Angela D'Agostino, Vice President Business Development

International Standard Book Number/Standard Address Number Agency
Beat Barblan, Director Identifier Services
Louise Timko, Director Publisher Relations, Identifier Services
Heidi Weber, Publisher Relations Representatives
Cheryl Russo, Publisher Relations Representative
Patrick David, User Interface Designer

Data Integration
Lisa Heft, Senior Director
Adrene Allen, Director Data Integration and Quality Control
Ila Joseph, John Litzenberger, Jesse Ricablanca and Tom Lucas, Senior Analysts
Steve Zaffuto, Cheryl Patrick, Associate Analysts
Marissa Hubbard and Melissa Overby, Analysts
Jenny Marie DeJesus and Mervaine Ricks, Senior Data Quality Analysts
Suzanne Franks, Data Quality Analysts
Roy Crego, Product Manager Title Linking
Rhonda McKendrick, Beverly Palacio, Senior Analysts

Syndetics
Mark Tullos, Senior Product Manager
Kathleen Cunningham, Director
Stacey Stegmann, Product Specialist
Lynda Keller, Fiction Profiler
Mark Ahmad, Children's Profiler
Rosemary Walker, Non-Fiction Profiler
Ron Butkiewicz, Data Specialist

Publisher Relations
Patricia Payton, Senior Director
Tricia McCraney, Jack Tipping, Ralph Coviello, Publisher Relations Managers
Rebecca Albani, Publisher Liaison

Data Distribution
Doreen Gravesande, Senior Director
Andy Haramasz, Manager Raw Data and Data Distribution
Patrick Gibbons, Production Sales Engineer
Stephanie Halpern, Production Key Accounts Manager
Myriam Nunez and Brittany Hartman, Production Project Managers

Business Analyst Group
Misty Poush, Evelyn Nicholas, Michael Olenick

Editorial Systems Group
Mark Heinzelman, Chief Data Architect
Dr. Lan Ho, Director Application Development
Steve Gorski, Programmer Analyst

Computer Operations Group
John Nesselt, UNIX Administrator

CONTENTS

FOREWORD

This 2011 edition is the 26th of **Books Out Loud™: Bowker's Guide to Audiobooks**. The growing popularity of audio books, as evidenced by the jump in audio titles output over the last decade, is reflected in the increase in the number of titles since the first edition of *Words On Tape,* published by Meckler Corporation in 1985. It contained 11,500 titles from 200 producers. In 1991, R. R. Bowker acquired *Words On Tape* and combined it with its own directory, *Books On Cassette,* to form **Words On Cassette (WOC)** database. The 2011 edition of **Books Out Loud™** lists approximately 174,350 audiobooks including some 69,100 audiobooks on compact disk, from over 6,400 producers and 1,790 distributors and wholesalers, making it the most comprehensive and authoritative bibliography of its kind.

In the 13th edition we add the section, **Best-selling Audiobooks & Audie Winners,** which highlighted the best of the best in audiobooks. The section received rave reviews from our users and is now a permanent feature of the directory. The listees are audio bestsellers as identified by *Publishers Weekly* and Audie Award Winners. The Audies are awarded annually by the Audio Publishers Association.

Some comments on prior editions are:

> "Selectors who have hitherto relied on *Schwann's Record and Tape Guide* and on such sources as Irene Iwan's *Words On Tape* (Meckler) will welcome *On Cassette,* which does for spoken-word audiocassettes what *Books In Print* does for books ... a revelation of the quantity and range of spoken-word cassettes currently available ... as a selection, acquisition, cataloging, reference, and advisory tool it should be acquired by school, public and academic libraries interested in this expanding medium."
>
> ***-Booklist/Reference Books Bulletin***
>
> " ... the definitive bibliography of audiocassettes ... "
>
> ***–U.S. News & World Report***
>
> "In the tradition of *Books In Print,* Bowker's *Words On Cassette* offers extensive and authoritative information on what is available in the medium of spoken-word audiocassettes, who produces them, and where they can be found ... an excellent tool for acquisitions work."
>
> ***- Wilson Library Bulletin***
>
> In citing *Words On Cassette* as one of the top reference books of the year, *Library Journal* commented:
>
> *"On Cassette* gives librarians an excellent tool to build spoken-word audio collections. The strength of this work is in thorough entries. Access is aptly provided ... an essential new tool for public, school, and academic libraries."
>
> Recognized as the **Most Comprehensive New Directory** by Morgan Directory Reviews.

Works in this publication represent a comprehensive look at the contemporary marketplace of spoken-word audiocassettes and compact disks, the importance of which is apparent from the size of this year's Title Index. Major book publishing houses have developed separate departments that produce and distribute audiobooks, and "The Book of the Month Club" now offers audiobooks to its members. Bowker's editors have kept abreast of all the latest developments and activity in the audiobook industry and provide a new and up-to-date record of the current market for research, acquisition, and reference.

HOW TO USE BOOKS OUT LOUD:

Bowker's Guide to Audiobooks

GENERAL EDITORIAL POLICIES

In order to ensure that the essential information in these listings is uniform, complete, and easy to find, the following editorial policies have been maintained:

- Every effort is made by most contributing producers to prepare their material with consideration for its accuracy throughout the life of this edition of **Books Out Loud™: Bowker's Guide to Audiobooks.**
- Many producers anticipate price changes when they submit their material, list forthcoming tapes even if publication dates and prices are not set, and for the most part, try not to list cassettes that may shortly become unavailable. In spite of these efforts, a number of changes in price will occur and a number of titles in this edition will become unavailable before the new edition is produced. All prices are subject to change without notice.
- Prices are list prices. Information is generally supplied by producers to Bowker for each product. However, all publishers do not uniformly supply this information, and Bowker makes its best effort to utilize all the information when it is provided.
- Producers' names in most cases are abbreviated. A key to these abbreviations will be found in the Producer Name Index.

INFORMATION INCLUDED IN AN ENTRY

Books Out Loud™: Bowker's Guide to Audiobooks is divided into six indexes in two volumes: Volume 1: Titles, A-S; Volume 2: Titles, T-Z, Author, Reader/Performer, Subject, Producer Name index, and Wholesaler & Distributor Name Index.

Within each index entries are filed alphabetically by word, with the following exceptions:

- Initial articles (e.g., The, A) of titles in English, French, German, Italian, and Spanish are omitted from the Title Index.
- Entries beginning with an asterisk (*) indicate titles added to this publication since last year's edition.
- M', Mc and Mac are filed as if they were Mac and are interfiled with other names beginning with Mac; for example, Macan, McAnally, Macardle, McAree, McArthur, Macarthur, M'Aulay, Macaulay, McAuley. Within a specific name grouping Mc and Mac are interfiled according to the given name of the author; for example, Macdonald, Agnes; McDonald, Alexander; MacDonald, Anne L.; McDonald, Austin F.; MacDonald, Betty.
- Compound names are listed under the first part of the name, and cross-references appear under the last part of the name.
- Entries beginning with initial letters (whether author's given names or titles) are filed first, e.g., Smith, H. C., comes before Smith, Harold A.; B E A M A Directory comes before Baal, Babylon

- When provided by the publisher as such, numerals are written out, and therefore filed alphabetically. For example:

  Seven Years In Tibet
  Seventeen Favorite Operas
  Seventeen Fifteen to the Present
  Seventeenth Century

- Entries beginning with numeric characters (such as 748 Italian Sentences) may be found at the conclusion of the Title Index after the letter "Z", and are sorted by specific beginning digit.
- Dr., Mr., and St. are filed as though they were spelled out.

TITLE INDEX

The Title Index lists each cassette alphabetically by title. The full bibliographic record is found in this index and will include the following elements when provided: title, subtitle, title volume number, edition (whether a work is abridged or unabridged), author, reader/performer, number of cassettes, running time, whether a work is a dramatization as opposed to a reading, series title and volume number, original title, original language, audience, grade level, publication date, price, ISBN (International Standard Book Number), order number, publisher imprint, publisher, and description.

When a cassette is available from the distributor rather than the publisher, the publisher is distinguished with the label "Pub:" and the distributor with the label "Dist(s):".

Foreign publishers are followed by their three-character ISO (International Standard Organization) code ("GBR," "CAN," etc.).

Poems, speeches, short stories, and other collective works brought together by one title may be found under the collective title while the name of the specific work appears as a cross-reference to the main entry.

TITLE INDEX SAMPLE ENTRY

1 Pinocchio: 2 Truth Lives. 3 Vol. 1. 4 unabr. ed. 5 Cynthia L. Daley. 6 Read by Lorraine Parker. 7 Performed by Kate Kendall. 8 4 cass. 9 (Running Time: 1 hr. 30 min. per cass.). 10 Dramatization. 11 (Puppet Ser.). 12 No. 1 13 The Mischievous Puppet 14 (GER.). 15 Juv. 16 (ps-3). 17 2000. 18 38.95 19 (978-0-89926-124-8(6)), 20 125, 21 Audio Magazine) 22 **Audio Bk.**
23 **Dist(s): New Leaf Dist.**
24 *Pinocchio begins to lead a life of his own & sets out to explore the world. He stumbles from one adventure into the next, always choosing the right path.*

KEY

1 Title
2 Subtitle
3 Title Volume Number
4 Edition
5 Author
6 Read by
7 Performed by
8 Number of Cassettes
9 Running Time
10 Dramatization
11 Series Title
12 Series Volume Number
13 Original Title
14 Original Language
15 Audience
16 Grade Level
17 Publication Date
18 Price
19 International Standard Book Number (ISBN)
20 Order Number
21 Publisher Imprint
22 Publisher
23 Distributor(s)
24 Description

OTHER NOTES

Unabridged Titles

Unabridged titles have been noted when indicated by the producer. Major producers of these works are: Audio Partners, Blackstone Audio, Books in Motion, Books on Tape, Brilliance Corporation, Random House, Recorded Books, The Reader's Chair, and Sounds True.

Rentals

While the majority of these works are for sale, there are also a large number for rent. These works are generally delivered to the patron via U.S. mail, complete with return postage and box. Major producers of these works are Books on Tape and Recorded Books.

Dramatizations

Dramatizations of works have also been noted. Only the first two key cast members are listed in the Reader/Performer Index. Other cast members (when information is furnished) may be found in the annotation. Major producers of these works are HarperAudio (Caedmon) and Listening Library.

Old Time Radio Shows

Old Time Radio shows, e.g., Burns & Allen, Abbott & Costello, are listed by Title with guest stars listed as performers. A major producer of these works is Metacom, Inc.

AUTHOR INDEX

The Author Index consists of truncated entries and is in alphabetical sequence by author. Other elements in the entry are the title and producer. At the end of each entry, there is a page number that refers the user to the page in the Title Index on which the full entry can be found. See the example listed below:

> **Albee, Edward.** The Zoo Story. Spoken Arts (pg. 3416).

When two authors are responsible for a work, the main entry is indexed under the primary author's name, and a cross-reference directs the user from the second author to the primary entry. See the example listed below:

> Wilson, **Robert** E., jt. auth, *see* Fench, E.A.

If more than two authors are responsible for a work, only the name of the primary one is given followed by the notation *"et al."*

READER/PERFORMER INDEX

The Reader/Performer Index is in alphabetical sequence by names of readers or key cast members of dramatized works. It, too, consists of truncated entries, noting the reader/performer, title, and producer. Each entry concludes with a page number cross-reference that refers the user to the full Title Index entry. See the example below:

> Caruso, **Barbara.** Anne of Green Gables. Recorded Bks. (pg. 119).

Entries follow the same cross-referencing policies found in the Author Index. Those performing in their own shows are not listed in this index, as this material is not consistently styled by the producers.

SUBJECT INDEX

The Subject Index arranges entries alphabetically by author within subject. If no author is given, the entry is filed alphabetically by title within the author arrangement. A complete listing of all subjects can be found in this index. Note that annotations are not included, although they are available in the Title Index.

PRODUCER NAME INDEX

Entries in the Producer Name Index are arranged alphabetically by the publisher's abbreviated name used in the bibliographic entries. They contain each publisher's name, followed by its ISBN prefix(es), business affiliation when available (e.g., "Div. of International Publishing"), ordering address(es), SAN (Standard Address Number), telephone number(s), fax and toll-free numbers. Editorial address(es) (and associated contact numbers) follows. E-mail and Web site addresses are then supplied. A listing of distributors associated with the publisher concludes each entry; each distributor name is in bold type.

Full information on these distributors and wholesalers can be found in the Wholesaler & Distributor Name Index (also in Vol. 2). Note that publishers who also serve as distributors may be listed both here and in the Producer Name Index.

ISBN AGENCY

Many titles included in **Books Out Loud™: Bowker's Guide to Audiobooks** have been assigned an International Standard Book Number by the publishers. All ISBNs listed in this volume have been validated by using the check digit control, ensuring accuracy. ISBNs allow information updating using the Book Industry Study Group (BISG) standard format for data transmission.

Note that the ISBN prefix 0-615 is for decentralized use by the U.S. ISBN Agency and has been assigned to many publishers. It's not unique to one publisher.

Publishers not currently participating in the ISBN system may request the assignment of an ISBN Publisher Prefix from the ISBN Agency by calling 888-269-5372, faxing 908-219-0188, or through the ISBN Website at www.myidentifiers.com.

SAN AGENCY

Another listing feature in **Books Out Loud™: Bowker's Guide to Audiobooks** is the Standard Address Number (SAN). The SAN is a unique identification number assigned to each address of an organization in or served by the publishing industry; it facilitates communications and repetitive transactions such as purchasing, billing, shipping, receiving, paying, crediting, and refunding, with other members of the industry.

To obtain an application or further information on the SAN system, please visit the ISBN/SAN Web site at http://www.isbn.org.

SAMPLE ENTRY PRODUCER NAME INDEX

1 † 2 **Mosby Inc.** 3 *(0-323; 0-7234; 0-8016; 0-8151; 0-88416; 0-941158;1-55664; 1-56815),*
4 Div. of Harcourt, Inc., A Harcourt Health Sciences Co., 5 Orders Addr.: 6227 Sea Harbor Dr., Orlando, FL 32887 6 Toll Free Fax: 800-235-0256 7 Toll Free: 800-545-2522
8 Edit Addr.: 11830 Westline Industrial Dr., Saint Louis, MO 63146 9 (SAN 200-2280)
10 Tel: 314-872-8370 11 Toll Free: 800-325-4177
12 Web site: http://www.mosby.com/
13 Dist(s): **PennWell Corp** 14 *CIP.*

KEY

1 CIP Identifier
2 Publisher Name
3 ISBN Prefixes
4 Division of
5 Orders Address
6 Orders Fax
7 Orders Toll-Free
8 Editorial Address
9 SAN
10 Telephone
11 Toll-Free
12 Web site
13 Distributors
14 Cataloging in Publication

SAMPLE ENTRY WHOLESALER & DISTRIBUTOR NAME INDEX

1 **New Leaf Dist.,** 2 *(0-9627209),* 3 Div. of Al-Wali Corp., 4 401 Thornton Rd., Lithia Springs, GA 30122-1557 5 (SAN 169-1449) 6 Tel: 770-948-7845; 7 Fax: 770-944-2313; 8 Toll Free Fax: 800-326-1066; 9 Toll Free: 800-326-2665
10 Email: NewLeaf@NewLeaf-dist.com
11 Web site: http://www.NewLeaf-dist.com

KEY

1 Distributor Name
2 ISBN Prefixes
3 Division of
4 Editorial Address
5 SAN
6 Telephone
7 Fax
8 Toll Free Fax
9 Toll Free
10 E-mail
11 Web site

PUBLISHER COUNTRY CODES

Foreign Publishers are listed with the three letter International Standards Organization (ISO) code for their country of domicile. This is the complete list of ISO codes though not all countries may be represented. The codes are mnemonic in most cases. The country names here may be shortened to a more common usage form.

AFG	AFGHANISTAN
AGO	ANGOLA
ALB	ALBANIA
AND	ANDORRA
ANT	NETHERLANDS ANTILLES
ARE	UNITED ARAB EMIRATES
ARG	ARGENTINA
ARM	ARMENIA
ASM	AMERICAN SAMOA
ATA	ANTARCTICA
ATG	ANTIGUA & BARBUDA
AUS	AUSTRALIA
AUT	AUSTRIA
AZE	AZERBAIJAN
BDI	BURUNDI
BEL	BELGIUM
BEN	BENIN
BFA	BURKINA FASO
BGD	BANGLADESH
BGR	BULGARIA
BHR	BAHRAIN
BHS	BAHAMAS
BIH	BOSNIA & HERZEGOVINA
BLR	BELARUS
BLZ	BELIZE
BMU	BERMUDA
BOL	BOLIVIA
BRA	BRAZIL
BRB	BARBADOS
BRN	BRUNEI DARUSSALAM
BTN	BHUTAN
BWA	BOTSWANA
BWI	BRITISH WEST INDIES
CAF	CENTRAL AFRICAN REP
CAN	CANADA
CH2	CHINA
CHE	SWITZERLAND
CHL	CHILE
CHN	CHINA
CIV	IVORY COAST
CMR	CAMEROON
COD	ZAIRE
COG	CONGO (BRAZZAVILLE)
COL	COLOMBIA
COM	COMOROS
CPV	CAPE VERDE
CRI	COSTA RICA
CS	CZECHOSLOVAKIA
CUB	CUBA
CYM	CAYMAN ISLANDS
CYP	CYPRUS
CZE	CZECH REPUBLIC
DEU	GERMANY
DJI	DJIBOUTI
DMA	DOMINICA
DNK	DENMARK
DOM	DOMINICAN REPUBLIC
DZA	ALGERIA
ECU	ECUADOR
EG	EAST GERMANY
EGY	EGYPT
EI	EUROPEAN UNION
EN	ENGLAND
ESP	SPAIN
EST	ESTONIA
ETH	ETHIOPIA
FIN	FINLAND
FJI	FIJI
FLK	FALKLAND ISLANDS
FRA	FRANCE
FRO	FAEROE ISLANDS
FSM	MICRONESIA
GAB	GABON
GBR	UNITED KINGDOM
GEO	GEORGIA
GHA	GHANA
GIB	GIBRALTAR
GIN	GUINEA
GLP	GUADELOUPE
GMB	GAMBIA
GNB	GUINEA-BISSAU
GNQ	EQUATORIAL GUINEA
GRC	GREECE
GRD	GRENADA
GRL	GREENLAND
GTM	GUATEMALA
GUF	FRENCH GUIANA
GUM	GUAM
GUY	GUYANA
HKG	HONG KONG
HND	HONDURAS
HRV	CROATIA
HTI	HAITI
HUN	HUNGARY
IDN	INDONESIA
IND	INDIA
IRL	IRELAND
IRN	IRAN
IRQ	IRAQ
ISL	ICELAND
ISR	ISRAEL
ITA	ITALY
JAM	JAMAICA
JOR	JORDAN
JPN	JAPAN
KAZ	KAZAKSTAN
KEN	KENYA
KGZ	KYRGYZSTAN
KHM	CAMBODIA
KNA	ST. KITTS-NEVIS
KO	KOREA
KOR	SOUTH KOREA
KOS	KOSOVA
KWT	KUWAIT
LAO	LAOS
LBN	LEBANON
LBR	LIBERIA
LBY	LIBYA
LCA	ST. LUCIA
LIE	LIECHTENSTEIN
LKA	SRI LANKA
LSO	LESOTHO
LTU	LITHUANIA
LUX	LUXEMBOURG
LVA	LATVIA
MAC	MACAO
MAR	MOROCCO
MCO	MONACO
MDA	MOLDOVA
MDG	MALAGASY REPUBLIC
MDV	MALDIVE ISLANDS
MEX	MEXICO
MHL	MARSHALL ISLANDS
MKD	MACEDONIA
MLI	MALI
MLT	MALTA
MMR	UNION OF MYANMAR
MNE	MONTENEGRO
MNG	MONGOLIA
MOZ	MOZAMBIQUE
MRT	MAURITANIA
MSR	MONTESERRAT
MTQ	MARTINIQUE
MUS	MAURITIUS
MWI	MALAWI
MYS	MALAYSIA
NAM	NAMIBIA
NCL	NEW CALEDONIA
NER	NIGER
NGA	NIGERIA
NIC	NICARAGUA
NLD	THE NETHERLANDS
NOR	NORWAY
NPL	NEPAL
NRU	NAURU
NZL	NEW ZEALAND
OMN	SULTANATE OF OMAN
PAK	PAKISTAN
PAN	PANAMA
PER	PERU
PHL	PHILIPPINES
PNG	PAPUA NEW GUINEA
POL	POLAND
PRI	PUERTO RICO
PRK	NORTH KOREA
PRT	PORTUGAL
PRY	PARAGUAY
PYF	FRENCH POLYNESIA
REU	REUNION
ROM	RUMANIA
RUS	RUSSIA
RWA	RWANDA
SAU	SAUDI ARABIA
SC	SCOTLAND
SCG	SERBIA & MONTENEGRO
SDN	SUDAN
SEN	SENEGAL
SGP	SINGAPORE
SLB	SOLOMON ISLANDS
SLE	SIERRA LEONE
SLV	EL SALVADOR
SMR	SAN MARINO
SOM	SOMALIA

PUBLISHER COUNTRY CODES

STP	SAO TOME E PRINCIPE
SU	SOVIET UNION
SUR	SURINAM
SVK	SLOVAKIA
SVN	SLOVENIA
SWE	SWEDEN
SWZ	SWAZILAND
SYC	SEYCHELLES
SYN	SYNDETICS
SYR	SYRIA
TCA	TURKS NDS
TCD	CHAD
TGO	TOGO
THA	THAILAND
TKM	TURKMENISTAN
TON	TONGA
TTO	TRINIDAD AND TOBAGO
TUN	TUNISIA
TUR	TURKEY
TWN	TAIWAN
TZA	TANZANIA
UGA	UGANDA
UI	UNITED KINGDOM
UKR	UKRAINE
UN	UNITED NATIONS
URY	URUGUAY
USA	UNITED STATES
UZB	UZBEKISTAN
VAT	VATICAN CITY
VCT	ST. VINCENT
VEN	VENEZUELA
VGB	BRITISH VIRGIN ISLANDS
VIR	U.S. VIRGIN ISLANDS
VNM	VIETNAM
VUT	VANUATU
WA	WALES
WSM	WESTERN SAMOA
YEM	REPUBLIC OF YEMEN
YUG	YUGOSLAVIA
ZAF	SOUTH AFRICA
ZMB	ZAMBIA
ZWE	ZIMBABWE

COUNTRY SEQUENCE

AFGHANISTAN AFG
ALBANIA ALB
ALGERIA DZA
AMERICAN SAMOA ASM
ANDORRA AND
ANGOLA AGO
ANGUILLA AIA
ANTARCTICA ATA
ANTIGUA & BARBUDA ATG
ARGENTINA ARG
ARMENIA ARM
ARUBA ABW
AUSTRALIA AUS
AUSTRIA AUT
AZERBAIJAN AZE
BAHAMAS BHS
BAHRAIN BHR
BANGLADESH BGD
BARBADOS BRB
BELARUS BLR
BELGIUM BEL
BELIZE BLZ
BENIN BEN
BERMUDA BMU
BHUTAN BTN
BOLIVIA BOL
BOSNIA & HERZEGOVINA BIH
BOTSWANA BWA
BOUVET ISLAND BVT
BRAZIL BRA
BRITISH INDIAN OCEAN TERRITORY IOT
BRITISH WEST INDIES BWI
BRUNEI DARUSSALAM BRN
BULGARIA BGR
BURKINA FASO BFA
BURUNDI BDI
CAMBODIA KHM
CAMEROON CMR
CANADA CAN
CAPE VERDE CPV
CAYMAN ISLANDS CYM
CENTRAL AFRICAN REPUBLIC CAF
CHAD TCD
CHILE CHL
CHINA CHN
CHRISTMAS ISLAND CXR
COCOS (KEELING) ISLANDS CCK
COLOMBIA COL
COMOROS COM
CONGO COG
CONGO, THE DEMOCRATIC REPUBLIC OF THE CONGO COD
COOK ISLANDS COK
COSTA RICA CRI
COTE' D' IVOIRE CIV
CROATIA HRV
CUBA CUB
CYPRUS CYP
CZECH REPUBLIC CZE
CZECHOSLOVAKIA CSK
DENMARK DNK
DJIBOUTI DJI
DOMINICA DMA
DOMINICAN REPUBLIC DOM
EAST TIMOR TMP
ECUADOR ECU
EGYPT (ARAB REPUBLIC OF EGYPT) EGY
EL SALVADOR SLV
EQUATORIAL GUINEA GNQ
ERITREA ERI
ESTONIA EST
ETHIOPIA ETH
EAST GERMANY DDR
FALKLAND ISLANDS FLK
FAROE ISLANDS FRO
FEDERATED STATES OF MICRONESIA FSM
FIJI FJI
FINLAND FIN
FRANCE FRA
FRENCH GUIANA GUF
FRENCH POLYNESIA PYF
FRENCH SOUTHERN TERRITORIES ATF
GABON GAB
GAMBIA GMB
GEORGIA GEO
GERMANY DEU
GHANA GHA
GIBRALTAR GIB
GREECE GRC
GREENLAND GRL
GRENADA GRD
GUADELOUPE GLP
GUAM GUM
GUATEMALA GTM
GUINEA GIN
GUINEA-BISSAU GNB
GUYANA GUY
HAITI HTI
HEARD ISLAND & MCDONALD ISLANDS HMD
HONDURAS HND
HONG KONG HKG
HUNGARY HUN
ICELAND ISL
INDIA IND
INDONESIA IDN
IRAN, ISLAMIC REPUBLIC OF IRN
IRAQ IRQ
IRELAND IRL
ISRAEL ISR
ITALY ITA
JAMAICA JAM
JAPAN JPN
JORDAN JOR
KAZAKSTAN KAZ
KENYA KEN
KIRIBATI KIR
KOREA, DEMOCRATIC PEOPLE'S REPUBLIC OF PRK
KOREA, REPUBLIC OF KOR
KUWAIT KWT
KYRGYZSTAN KGZ
KOSOVA KOS
LAO PEOPLE'S DEMOCRATIC REPUBLIC LAO
LATVIA LVA
LEBANON LBN
LESOTHO LSO
LIBERIA LBR
LIBYAN ARAB JAMAHIRIYA LBY
LIECHTENSTEIN LIE
LITHUANIA LTU
LUXEMBOURG LUX
MACAU MAC
MACEDONIA, THE FORMER YUGOSLAV REPUBLIC OF MKD
MADAGASCAR MDG
MALAWI MWI
MALAYSIA MYS
MALDIVE ISLANDS MDV
MALI MLI
MALTA MLT
MARSHALL ISLANDS MHL
MARTINIQUE MTQ
MAURITANIA MRT
MAURITIUS MUS
MAYOTTE MYT
MEXICO MEX
MOLDOVA, REPUBLIC OF MDA
MONACO MCO

COUNTRY SEQUENCE

Country	Code
MONGOLIA	MNG
MONTENEGRO	MNE
MONTSERRAT	MSR
MOROCCO	MAR
MOZAMBIQUE	MOZ
MYANMAR	MMR
NAMIBIA	NAM
NAURU	NRU
NEPAL	NPL
NETHERLANDS	NLD
NETHERLANDS ANTILLES	ANT
NEW CALEDONIA	NCL
NEW ZEALAND	NZL
NICARAGUA	NIC
NIGER	NER
NIGERIA	NGA
NIUE	NIU
NORFOLK ISLAND	NFK
NORTHERN MARIANA ISLANDS	MNP
NORWAY	NOR
OMAN	OMN
OCCUPIED PALESTINIAN TERRITORY	PSE
PAKISTAN	PAK
PALAU	PLW
PANAMA	PAN
PAPUA NEW GUINEA	PNG
PARAGUAY	PRY
PERU	PER
PHILIPPINES	PHL
PITCAIRN	PCN
POLAND	POL
PORTUGAL	PRT
PUERTO RICO	PRI
QATAR	QAT
REUNION	REU
ROMANIA	ROM
RUSSIAN FEDERATION	RUS
RWANDA	RWA
SAINT HELENA	SHN
SAINT KITTS & NEVIS	KNA
SAINT PIERRE & MIQUELON	SPM
SAINT VINCENT & THE GRENADINES	VCT
SAMOA	WSM
SAN MARINO	SMR
SAO TOME E PRINCIPE	STP
SAUDI ARABIA	SAU
SENEGAL	SEN
SERBIA	SRB
SERBIA & MONTENEGRO	SCG
SEYCHELLES	SYC
SIERRA LEONE	SLE
SINGAPORE	SGP
SLOVAKIA	SVK
SLOVENIA	SVN
SOLOMON ISLANDS	SLB
SOMALIA	SOM
SOUTH AFRICA	ZAF
SOUTH GEORGIA & THE SANDWICH ISLANDS	SGS
SPAIN	ESP
SRI LANKA	LKA
ST. LUCIA	LCA
SUDAN	SDN
SURINAME	SUR
SVALBARD & JAN MAYEN	SJM
SWAZILAND	SWZ
SWEDEN	SWE
SWITZERLAND	CHE
SYRIAN ARAB REPUBLIC	SYR
TAIWAN, REPUBLIC OF CHINA	TWN
TAJIKISTAN	TJK
TANZANIA, UNITED REPUBLIC OF	TZA
THAILAND	THA
TOGO	TGO
TOKELAU	TKL
TONGA	TON
TRINIDAD & TOBAGO	TTO
TUNISIA	TUN
TURKEY	TUR
TURKMENISTAN	TKM
TURKS & CAICOS ISLANDS	TCA
TUVALU	TUV
U.S.S.R.	SUN
UGANDA	UGA
UKRAINE	UKR
UNITED ARAB EMIRATES	UAE
UNITED KINGDOM	GBR
UNITED STATES	USA
UNITED STATES MINOR OUTLYING ISLANDS	UMI
URUGUAY	URY
UZBEKISTAN	UZB
VANUATU	VUT
VATICAN CITY STATE (HOLY SEE)	VAT
VENEZUELA	VEN
VIET NAM	VNM
VIRGIN ISLANDS, BRITISH	VGB
VIRGIN ISLANDS, U. S.	VIR
WALLIS & FUTUNA	WLF
WESTERN SAHARA	ESH
WEST GERMANY	BRD
YEMEN	YEM
YUGOSLAVIA	YUG
ZAMBIA	ZMB
ZIMBABWE	ZWE
ZAIRE	ZAR

LANGUAGE CODES

Code	Language
ACE	Achioli
AFA	Afro-Asiatic
AFR	Afrikaans
AKK	Akkadian
ALB	Albanian
ALE	Aleut
ALG	Algonquin
AMH	Amharic
ANG	Anglo-Saxon
APA	Apache
ARA	Arabic
ARC	Aramaic
ARM	Armenian
ARN	Araucanian
ARP	Arapaho
ARW	Arawak
ASM	Assamese
AVA	Avar
AVE	Avesta
AYM	Aymara
AZE	Azerbaijani
BAK	Bashkir
BAL	Baluchi
BAM	Bambara
BAQ	Basque
BAT	Baltic
BEJ	Beja
BEL	Belorussian
BEM	Bemba
BEN	Bengali
BER	Berber Group
BIH	Bihari
BLA	Blackfoot
BRE	Breton
BUL	Bulgarian
BUR	Burmese
CAD	Caddo
CAI	Central American
CAM	Cambodian
CAR	Carib
CAT	Catalan
CAU	Caucasian
CEL	Celtic Group
CHB	Chibcha
CHE	Chechen
CHI	Chinese
CHN	Chinook
CHO	Choctaw
CHR	Cherokee
CHU	Church Slavic
CHV	Chuvash
CHY	Cheyenne
COP	Coptic
COR	Cornish
CRE	Cree
CRO	Croatian
CRP	Creoles and Pidgins
CUS	Cushitic
CZE	Czech
DAK	Dakota
DAN	Danish
DEL	Delaware
DIN	Dinka
DOI	Dogri
DRA	Dravidian
DUA	Duala
DUT	Dutch
EFI	Efik
EGY	Egyptian
ELX	Elamite
ENG	English
ENM	English, Middle
ESK	Eskimo
RUM	Romanian
RUN	Rundi
RUS	Russian
SAD	Sandawe
SAG	Sango
SAI	South American
SAM	Samaritan
SAN	Sanskrit
SAO	Sampan
SBC	Serbo-Croatian
SCO	Scots
SEL	Selkup
SEM	Semitic
SER	Serbian
SHN	Shan
SHO	Shona
SID	Sidamo
SIO	Siouan Languages
SIT	Sino-Tibetan
SLA	Slavic
SLO	Slovak
SLV	Slovenian
SMO	Samoan
SND	Sindhi
SNH	Singhalese
SOG	Sogdian
SOM	Somali
SON	Songhai
ESP	Esperanto
EST	Estonian
ETH	Ethiopic
EWE	Ewe
FAN	Fang
FAR	Faroese
FEM	French, Middle
FIJ	Fijian
FIN	Finnish
FIU	Finno-Ugrian
FLE	Flemish
FON	Fon
FRE	French
FRI	Frisian
FRO	French, Old
GAA	Ga
GAE	Gaelic
GAG	Gallegan
GAL	Galla
GEC	Greek, Classical
GEH	German, Middle
GEM	Germanic
GEO	Georgian
GER	German
GLG	Galician
GOH	German, Old High
GON	Gondi
GOT	Gothic
GRE	Greek
GUA	Guarani
GUJ	Gujarati
HAU	Hausa
HAW	Hawaiian
HEB	Hebrew
HER	Herero
HIL	Hiligaynon
HIN	Hindi
HUN	Hungarian
HUP	Hupa
IBA	Iban
IBO	Igbo
ICE	Icelandic
IKU	Inuktitut
ILO	Ilocano
INC	Indic
IND	Indonesian
INE	Indo-European
INT	Interlingua
IRA	Iranian
IRI	Irish
IRO	Iroquois
ITA	Italian
JAV	Javanese
JPN	Japanese
KAA	Karakalpak
KAC	Kachin
KAM	Kamba
KAN	Kannada
KAR	Karen
KAS	Kashmiri
KAU	Kanuri
KAZ	Kazakh
KHA	Khasi
KHM	Khmer, Central
KIK	Kikuyu
KIN	Kinyarwanda
KIR	Kirghiz
KOK	Konkani
KON	Kongo
KOR	Korean
KPE	Kpelle
KRO	Kru
KRU	Kurukh
SOT	Sotho, Southern
SPA	Spanish

LANGUAGE CODES

Code	Language
SRD	Sardinian
SRR	Serer
SSA	Sub-Saharan
SUK	Sukuma
SUN	Sundanese
SUS	Susu
SUX	Sumerian
SWA	Swahili
SWE	Swedish
SYR	Syriac
TAG	Tagalog
TAJ	Tajik
TAM	Tamil
TAR	Tatar
TEL	Telugu
TEM	Temne
TER	Tereno
THA	Thai
TIB	Tibetan
TIG	Tigre
TIR	Tigrinya
TOG	Tonga, Nyasa
TON	Tonga, Tonga
TSI	Tsimshian
TSO	Tsonga
TSW	Tswana
KUA	Kwanyama
KUR	Kurdish
LAD	Ladino
LAH	Lahnda
LAM	Lamba
LAO	Laotian
LAP	Lapp
LAT	Latin
LAV	Latvian
LIN	Lingala
LIT	Lithuanian
LOL	Lolo
LUB	Luba
LUG	Luganda
LUI	Luiseno
MAC	Macedonian
MAI	Maithili
MAL	Malayalam
MAN	Mandingo
MAO	Maori
MAP	Malayo-Polynesian
MAR	Marathi
MAS	Masai
MAY	Malay
MEN	Mende
MIC	Micmac
MIS	Miscellaneous
MLA	Malagasy
MLT	Malteses
MNO	Manobo
MOL	Moldavian
MON	Mongol
MOS	Mossi
MUL	Multiple Languages
MUS	Muskogee
MYN	Mayan
NAI	North American
NAV	Navaho
NBL	Ndebele, Southern
NDE	Ndebele, Northern
NEP	Nepali
NEW	Newari
NIC	Niger-Congo
NNO	Norwegian
NOB	Norwegian Bokmal
NOR	Norwegian
NSO	Sotho, Northern
NUB	Nubian
NYA	Nyanja
NYM	Nyamwezi
NYO	Nyoro Group
OES	Ossetic
OJI	Ojibwa
ORI	Oriya
OSA	Osage
OTO	Otomi
PAA	Papuan-Australian
PAH	Pahari
PAL	Pahlavi
PAN	Panjabi
PEO	Persian, Old
PER	Persian, Modern
PLI	Pali
POL	Polish
POR	Portuguese
PRA	Prakrit
PRO	Provencal
PUS	Pushto
QUE	Quechua
RAJ	Rajasthani
ROA	Romance
ROH	Romanish
ROM	Romany
TUK	Turkmen
TUR	Turkish
TUT	Turko-Tataric
TWI	Twi
UGA	Ugaritic
UIG	Uigur
UKR	Ukrainian
UMB	Umbundu
UND	Undetermined
URD	Urdu
UZB	Uzbek
VIE	Vietnamese
VOT	Votic
WAL	Walamo
WAS	Washo
WEL	Welsh
WEN	Wendic
WOL	Wolof
XHO	Xhosa
YAO	Yao
YID	Yiddish
YOR	Yoruba
ZAP	Zapotec
ZEN	Zenaga
ZUL	Zulu
ZUN	Zuni

LIST OF ABBREVIATIONS

Abr.	abridged
act. bk.	activity book
adapt.	adapted
aft.	afterword
alt.	alternate
Amer.	American
anniv.	anniversary
anno.	annotated by
annot.	annotation(s)
ans.	answer(s)
app.	appendix
Apple II	Apple II disk
approx.	approximately
assn.	association
audio	analog audio cassette
auth.	author
bd.	bound
bdg.	binding
bds.	boards
bibl(s).	bibliography(ies)
bk(s).	book(s)
bklet(s).	booklet(s)
boxed	boxed set, slipcase or caseboard
Bro.	Brother
C	college audience level
co.	company
comm.	commission, committee
comment.	commentaries
comp.	complied
cond.	condensed
contrib.	contributed
corp.	corporation
dept.	department
des	designed
diag(s).	diagram(s)
digital audio	digital audio cassette
dir.	director
disk	software disk or diskette
dist.	distributed
Div.	Division
doz.	dozen
ea.	each
ed.	edited, edition, editor
eds.	editions, editors
educ.	education
elem.	elementary
ency.	encyclopedia
ENG	English
enl.	enlarged
epil.	epilogue
exp.	expanded
expr.	experiments
expurg.	expurgated
fac.	facsimile
fasc.	fascicule
fict.	fiction
fig(s).	figure(s)
flmstrp.	filmstrip
footn.	footnote
for.	foreign
frwd.	foreword
gen.	general
gr.	grade(s)
hndbk.	handbook
illus.	Illustrated, illustration(s), Illustrator(s)
in prep.	in preparation
incl.	includes, including
info.	information
inst.	institute
intro.	introduction
ISBN	International Standard Book Number
ISO	International Standards Organization
ITA	Italian
i.t.a.	initial teaching alphabet
J.	juvenile audience level
JPN	Japanese
Jr.	Junior
jt. auth.	joint author
jt. ed.	joint editor
k	kindergarten audience level
lab	laboratory
lang(s).	language(s)
LC	Library of Congress
lea.	leather
lib.	library
lib. bdg.	library binding
lit.	literature, literary
lp	record, album, long playing
l.t.	large type
ltd.	limited
ltd. ed.	limited edition
mac hd	144M, Mac
mac ld	800K, Mac
mass mkt.	mass market paperbound
math.	mathematics
mic. film	microfilm
mic form	microform
mod.	modern
MS(S)	manuscript(s)
natl.	national
net	net price
no(s).	number(s)
o.p.	out of print
orig.	original text, not a reprint (paperback)
o.s.i.	out of stock indefinitely
p.	pages
pap.	paper
per.	perfect binding
photos	photographer, photographs
pop. ed.	Popular edition
prep.	preparation
probs.	problems
prog. bk.	programmed books
ps.	preschool audience level
pseud.	pseudonym
pt(s).	part(s)
pub.	published, publisher publishing
pubn.	publication
ref(s).	reference(s)
rep.	reprint
reprod(s).	reproduction(s)
ret.	retold by
rev.	revised
rpm.	revolution per minute (phono records)
SAN	Standard Address Number
S&L	signed and limited
sec.	section
sel.	selected
ser.	series
Soc.	society
sols.	solutions
s.p.	school price
Sr. (after given name)	Senior
Sr. (before given name	Sister
St.	Saint
stu.	student manual, study guide, etc.
subs.	subsidiary
subsc.	subscription
suppl.	supplement
tech.	technical
text ed.	text edition
tr.	translated, translation translator
trans.	transparencies
unabr.	unabridged
unexpurg.	unexpurgated
univ.	university
var.	variorum
vdisk	videodisk
VHS	video, VHS format
vol(s).	volume(s)
wkbk.	workbook
YA	Young adult audience level
yrbk.	yearbook
3.5 hd	1.44M, 3.5 disk, DOS
3.5 ld	720, 3.5 Disk, DOS
5.25 hd	1.2M, 5.25 Disk, DOS
5.25 ld	360K, 5.25 Disk, DOS

BESTSELLING AUDIOBOOKS & AUDIE WINNERS 2005-2010

The audiobooks listed in this section appeared on the bestseller lists of PUBLISHERS WEEKLY for the years 2005-2010 or were chosen as winners of the Audie Awards by the Audio Publisher's Association (APA). The Audie Awards were started by the APA in 1996 and the initial presentation was made at the American Bookseller's Association (ABA) convention.

This section is arranged alphabetically by subjects that are assigned by the editorial staff of the R.R. Bowker Company and are consistent with those used in Books Out Loud. Within the subject categories, titles are listed alphabetically. The entries are abbreviated and include these elements: Title, primary author or reader/performer, and publisher name. "Audie Winners" are identified as such. New entries since the last edition begin with an asterisk (*). Complete bibliographic information can be found in the Title Index and ordering information in the Producers' Index.

Biography

The Age of Turbulence: Adventures in a New World. *Alan Greenspan.* Penguin Audio

***Anne Frank Remembered.** *Miep Gies & Alison Leslie Gold.* Oasis Audio/Springwater, Audie Winner 2010

The Audacity of Hope: Thoughts on Reclaiming the American Dream. *Barack Obama.* Random House Audio

Audition: A Memoir. *Barbara Walters.* Random House Audio

The Beatles. *Robert Spitz.* Simon & Schuster Audio, Audie Winner 2007

Benjamin Franklin: An American Life. *Walter Isaacson.* Simon & Schuster Audio

Big Russ & Me. *Tim Russert.* Hyperion Audio

***The Blind Side.** *Michael Lewis.* Random House Audio

A Bold Fresh Piece of Humanity: A Memoir. *Bill O'Reilly.* Penguin Audio

Born Standing Up. *Steve Martin.* Simon & Schuster Audio

Change We Can Believe In: Barack Obama's Plan to Renew America's Promise. *Barack Obama.* Random House Audio

Chronicles: Volume 1. *Bob Dylan.* Simon & Schuster Audio, Audie Winner 2005

Clapton: The Autobiography. *Eric Clapton.* Random House Audio

***Committed.** *Elizabeth Gilbert.* Penguin Audio

***Courage and Consequence.** *Karl Rove.* Simon & Schuster Audio

Dispatches from the Edge. *Anderson Cooper.* HarperAudio.

Dreams from My Father: A Story of Race and Inheritance. *Barack Obama.* Random House Audio

Eat, Pray, Love: One Woman's Search for Everything Across Italy, India and Indonesia. *Elizabeth Gilbert.* Penguin Audio

Einstein: His Life and Universe. *Walter Isaacson.* Simon & Schuster Audio, Audie Winner 2008

The Essential Barack Obama. *Barack Obama.* Random House Audio

Founding Fathers. *Arthur M. Schlesinger.* Macmillan Audio, Audie Winner 2009

Garlic & Sapphires. *Ruth Reichl.* Random House Audio, Audie Winner 2006

***Going Rogue.** *Sarah Palin.* Harper Audio

His Excellency: George Washington. *Joseph Ellis.* Recorded Books

Home: A Memoir of My Early Years. *Julie Andrews.* Hyperion Audio

I Shouldn't Even Be Doing This! *Bob Newhart.* Hyperion Audio

***The Immortal Life of Henrietta Lacks.** *Rebecca Skloot.* Random House Audio

The Innocent Man. *Craig Wasson.* Random House Audio

Into the Wild. *Jon Krakauer.* Random House Audio

John Adams. *David McCullough.* Simon & Schuster Audio

Julie and Julia. *Julie Powell.* Hachette Audio

Luckiest Man. *Jonathan Eig.* Simon & Schuster Audio, Audie Winner 2006

Me of Little Faith. *Lewis Black.* Penguin Audio

A Million Little Pieces. *James Frey.* HighBridge Audio

My Life in France. *Julia Child.* Random House Audio

My Stroke of Insight. *Jill Bolte Taylor.* Penguin Audio

Obama Nation: Leftist Politics and the Cult of Personality. *Jerome R. Corsi.* Simon & Schuster Audio

Official Book Club Selection. *Kathy Griffin.* Random House Audio

***The Politician.** *Andrew Young.* Tantor Media

Rise, Let Us Be On Our Way. *Pope John Paul II.* Time Warner AudioBooks

Roots: The Saga of an American Family. *Alex Haley.* BBC Audiobooks America, Audie Winner 2008

Running with Scissors. *Augusten Burroughs.* Audio Renaissance

The Snowball: Warren Buffett and the Business of Life. *Alice Schroeder.* Random House Audio

***Spoken from the Heart.** *Laura Bush.* Simon & Schuster Audio

Teacher Man. *Frank McCourt.* Simon & Schuster Audio, Audie Winner 2007

Team of Rivals. *Doris Kearns Goodwin.* Simon & Schuster Audio

The Tender Bar. *J.R. Moehringer.* Hyperion AudioBooks, Audie Winner 2006

Things I Overheard While Talking to Myself. *Alan Alda.* Random House Audio

Think Big and Kick Ass in Business and Life. *Donald Trump & Bill Zanker.* HarperAudio

***Three Cups of Tea.** *Greg Mortenson & David Oliver Relin.* Tantor Media

The Time of My Life. *Patrick Swayze & Lisa Niemi.* Simon & Schuster Audio

Too Fat to Fish. *Artie Lange.* Random House Audio

True Compass. *Edward M. Kennedy.* Hachette Audio

Tuesdays with Morrie. *Mitch Albom.* Random House Audio

A Wolf at the Table: A Memoir of My Father. *Augusten Burroughs.* Macmillan Audio

Zodiac. *Robert Graysmith.* Blackstone Audio

Business, Economics, Personal Finance

The Age of Turbulence: Adventures in a New World. *Alan Greenspan.* Penguin Audio

The Automatic Millionaire Homeowner. *David Bach.* Random House Audio

***The Big Short.** *Michael Lewis.* Simon & Schuster Audio

Blink. *Malcolm Gladwell.* Hachette Audio

Death by Meeting. *Patrick Lencioni.* Audio Renaissance, Audie Winner 2005

***Drive.** *Daniel H. Pink.* Penguin Audio

Freakonomics. *Steven D. Levitt.* HarperAudio

Good to Great: Why Some Companies Make the Leap...and Others Don't. *Jim Collins.* Harper Audio, Audie Winner 2006

How to Talk to Anyone. *Leil Lowndes.* Listen & Live Audio

Jim Cramer's Stay Mad for Life: Get Rich, Stay Rich (Make Your Kids Even Richer). *Jim Cramer.* Simon & Schuster Audio

***Linchpin.** *Seth Godin.* Random House Audio

The Little Red Book of Selling. *Jeffrey Gitomer.* Simon & Schuster Audio, Audie Winner 2009

The Long Tail: Why the Future of Business Is Selling Less of More. *Chris Anderson.* Hyperion Audio, Audie Winner 2007

***On the Brink.** *Henry M. Paulson.* Hachette Audio

Peaks and Valleys. *Spencer Johnson.* Simon & Schuster Audio

***The Quants.** *Scott Patterson.* Random House Audio

***Rain.** *Jeffrey J. Fox.* Brilliance Audio, Audie Winner 2010

The Snowball: Warren Buffett and the Business of Life. *Alice Schroeder.* Random House Audio

Start Late, Finish Rich: A No-Fail Plan for Achieving Freedom at Any Age. *David Bach.* Random House Audio

***SuperFreakonomics.** *Steven D. Levitt &*

Stephen J. Dubner. Harper Audio

Suze Orman's 2009 Action Plan. *Suze Orman.* Random House Audio

Think Big and Kick Ass in Business and Life. *Donald Trump & Bill Zanker.* HarperAudio

***13 Bankers.** *Simon Johnson & James Kwak.* Tantor Media

***Too Big to Fall.** *Andrew Ross Sorkin.* Penguin Audio

Trump: Think Like a Billionaire. *Donald Trump.* Simon & Schuster Audio

***What the Dog Saw.** *Malcolm Gladwell.* Hachette Audio

Why We Want You to Be Rich: Two Men, One Message. *Donald J. Trump & Robert T. Kiyosaki.* Simon & Schuster Audio

Winning. *Jack Welch.* HarperAudio

Composer

What Charlie Heard. *Mordicai Gerstein.* Live Oak Media, Audie Winner 2005

Cookery

Julie and Julia. *Julie Powell.* Hachette Audio

My Life in France. *Julia Child.* Random House Audio

Drama (General)

Sweeney Todd and the String of Pearls. *Yuri Rasovsky.* Blackstone Audio, Audie Winner 2008

Education

Teacher Man. *Frank McCourt.* Simon & Schuster Audio

***Three Cups of Tea.** *Greg Mortenson & David Oliver Relin.* Tantor Media

---

English Language

Words That Work: It's Not What You Say, It's What People Hear. *Frank Luntz.* Hyperion Audiobooks, Audie Winner 2008

Family & Interpersonal Relationships

The Five Love Languages. *Gary Chapman.* Oasis Audio, Audie Winner 2006

The Happiest Toddler on the Block. *Harvey Karp & Paula Spencer.* Recorded Books, Audie Winner 2005

Love Smart. *Phillip McGraw.* Simon & Schuster Audio

Wisdom of Our Fathers. *Tim Russert.* Random House Audio

Foreign Language Instruction (General)

Instant Immersion Hawaiian. *Kaliko Beamer-Trapp & Kiele Akama Gooch.* Topics Entertainment, Audie Winner 2005

Health & Fitness

***Born to Run.** *Christopher McDougall* Random House Audio

***Change Your Brain, Change Your Body.** *Daniel G. Amen.* Random House Audio

Fit to Live: The 5-Point Plan to Be Lean, Strong, and Fearless for Life. *Pamela Peeke.* Macmillan Audio, Audie Winner 2008

Healthy Aging. *Andrew Weil.* Random House Audio

***The Skinnygirl Rules.** *Bethenny Franke.l* Simon & Schuster Audio

***Women, Food, and God.** *Geneen Roth.* Simon & Schuster Audio

You: Being Beautiful. *Michael F. Roizen & Mehmet C. Oz.* Simon & Schuster Audio

You: Staying Young: The Owner's Manual for Extending Your Warranty. *Michael F. Roizen & Mehmet C. Oz.* Recorded Books, Audie Winner 2009

You on a Walk: Listen as You Walk for a Leaner, Healthier Life. *Michael F. Roizen & Mehmet C. Oz.* Simon & Schuster Audio

History (United States)

1776. *David McCullough.* Simon & Schuster Audio

Boom!: Voices of the Sixties. *Tom Brokaw.* Random House Audio

Flags of Our Fathers. *James Bradley.* Random House Audio

***Flyboys.** *James Bradley.* Hachette Audio

Founding Fathers. *Arthur M. Schlesinger.* Macmillan Audio, Audie Winner 2009

Hubris: The Inside Story of Spin, Scandal, and the Selling of the Iraq War. *Michael Isikoff & David Corn.* Blackstone Audio, Incorporated, Audie Winner 2007

The Island at the Center of the World. *Russell Shorto.* Recorded Books, Audie Winner 2005

Mayflower. *Nathaniel Philbrick.* Penguin Audio

Midnight in the Garden of Good and Evil. *John Berendt.* Random House Audio

The One Percent Doctrine. *Ron Suskind.* Simon & Schuster Audio

The War: An Intimate History, 1941-1945. *Geoffrey C. Ward & Ken Burns.* Simon & Schuster Audio

The War Within: A Secret White House History, 2006-2008. *Bob Woodward.* Simon & Schuster Audio

What Happened: Inside the Bush White House and Washington's Culture of Deception. *Scott McClellan.* Blackstone Audio

History (World)

Fiasco. *Thomas E. Ricks.* Penguin Audio

Gandhi and Churchill. *Arthur Herman.* Recorded Books, Audie Winner 2009

***The Imperial Cruise.** *James Bradley.* Hachette Audio

The Monster of Florence: A True Story. *Douglas Preston & Mario Spezi.* Hachette Audio

The Murder of King Tut. *James Patterson & Martin Dugard.* Hachette Audio

***Tears in the Darkness.** *Elizabeth M. Norman & Michael Norman.* Tantor Audio, Audie Winner 2010

The World Is Flat. *Thomas L. Friedman.* Audio Renaissance, Audie Winner 2006

Humor

***Church People.** *Garrison Keillor.* HighBridge Audio, Audie Winner 2010

David Sedaris Live at Carnegie Hall. *David Sedaris.* Time Warner AudioBooks

English Majors. *Garrison Keillor.* HighBridge, Audie Winner 2009

He's Just Not That Into You. *Greg Behrendt.* Simon & Schuster Audio

Holidays on Ice. *David Sedaris.* Hachette Audio

I Am America (and So Can You!) *Stephen Colbert.* Hachette Audio, Audie Winner 2008

Marley & Me. *John Grogan.* Harper Audio

New Rules. *Bill Maher.* Phoenix Audio

Nothing's Sacred. *Lewis Black.* Simon & Schuster Audio

***The Obama Diaries.** *Laura Ingraham.* Simon & Schuster Audio

Spoiled Rotten America: Outrages of Everyday Life. *Larry Miller.* Harper Audio, Audie Winner 2007

The Truth (with Jokes). *Al Franken.* Brilliance Audio, Audie Winner 2006

When You Are Engulfed in Flames. *David Sedaris.* Hachette Audio, Audie Winner 2009

Why We Suck. *Denis Leary.* Penguin Audio

Literature & Fiction (Action & Adventure)

The Afghan. *Frederick Forsyth.* Penguin Audio

The Ambler Wa nrning. *Robert Ludlum.* Audio Renaissance

Arctic Drift. *Clive Cussler & Dirk Cussler.* Penguin Audio

Around the World in 80 Days. *Jules Verne.* Listening Library, Audie Winner 2006

Black Ops. *W.E.B. Griffin.* Penguin Audio

Black Wind. *Clive Cussler.* Penguin Audio Books

*** The Bourne Objective.** *Eric Lustbader.* Hachette Audio

The Bourne Ultimatum. *Robert Ludlum.* Random House Audio Publishing Group

The Camel Club. *David Baldacci.* Time Warner AudioBooks

Chill Factor. *Sandra Brown.* Simon & Schuster Audio

Corsair. *Clive Cussler & Jack DuBrul.* Penguin Audio

The Dangerous Days of Daniel X. *James Patterson & Michael Ledwidge.* Hachette Audio

Devil May Care. *Sebastian Faulks.* Random House Audio

Hour Game. *David Baldacci.* Time Warner. AudioBooks

Indiana Jones and the Kingdom of the Crystal Skull. *James Rollins.* HarperAudio

The Lincoln Lawyer. *Michael Connelly.* Time Warner AudioBooks

***Lost Empire.** *Clive Cussler & Grant Blackwood.* Penguin Audio

Medusa. *Clive Cussler & Paul Kemprecos.* Penguin Audio

Moby Dick. *Herman Melville.* Naxos AudioBooks Ltd., Audie Winner 2006

***Pirate Latitudes.** *Michael Crichton.* Harper Audio

Robert Ludlum's The Bourne Betrayal. *Eric Van Lustbader.* Hachette Audio

Robert Ludlum's The Bourne Sanction. *Eric Van Lustbader.* Hachette Audio

Robert Ludlum's The Moscow Vector. *Patrick Larkin.* Audio Renaissance

***The Silent Sea.** *Clive Cussler & Jack Du Bruhl.* Penguin Audio

Spartan Gold. *Clive Cussler & Grant Blackwood.* Penguin Audio

***The Spy.** *Clive Cussler & Justin Scott.* Penguin Audio

Twelve Sharp. *Janet Evanovich.* Audio Renaissance

***The Wrecker.** *Clive Cussler & Justin Scott.* Penguin Audio

Literature & Fiction (Fantasy & Science Fiction)

Airborn. *Kenneth Oppel.* Full Cast Audio, Audie Winner 2007

At the Back of the North Wind. *George MacDonald.* Tyndale-Focus on the Family, Audie Winner 2006

***Backlash.** *Aaron Allston.* Random House Audio

***Bellwether.** *Connie Willis.* Blackstone Audiobooks, Audie Winner 2010

A Breath of Snow & Ashes. *Diana Gabaldon.* Recorded Books, LLC, Audie Winner 2006

Calculating God. *Robert J. Sawyer.* Audible, Audie Winner 2009

Chronicles of Narnia Box Set. *C.S. Lewis.* HarperChildren's Audio, Audie Winner 2005

The Dangerous Days of Daniel X. *James Patterson & Michael Ledwidge.* Hachette Audio

Dune. *Frank Herbert.* Macmillan Audio, Audie Winner 2008

The Golden Compass. *Philip Pullman.* Random House Audio Publishing Group, Audie Winner 2007

The Hitchhiker's Guide to the Galaxy: Quintessential Phase. *Douglas Adams.* BBC Audiobooks America, Audie Winner 2007

The Hitchhiker's Guide to the Galaxy: The Tertiary Phase. *Douglas Adams.* BBC Audiobooks America, Audie Winner 2006

The Hitchhiker's Guide to the Universe. *Douglas Adams.* Random House Audio

The Host. *Stephenie Meyer.* Hachette Audio

I Am Legend. *Richard Matheson.* Blackstone Audio

***Impact.** *Douglas Preston.* Macmillan Audio

Market Forces. *Richard K. Morgan.* Tantor Media, Inc., Audie Winner 2006

Phantom. *Terry Goodkind.* Brilliance Audio

Serpent on the Crown. *Elizabeth Peters.* HarperCollins Publishers, Audie Winner 2006

Skeleton Man. *Tony Hillerman.* HarperAudio

Star Wars: Episode III Revenge of the Sith. *Matthew Stover.* Random House Audio

Star Wars: Labyrinth of Evil. *James Luceno.* Random House Audio

The Stolen Child. *Keith Donohue.* Recorded Books, LLC, Audie Winner 2007

Wicked. *Gregory Maguire.* HarperAudio

World War Z. *Max Brooks.* Random House Audio Publishing Group, Audie Winner 2007

Literature & Fiction (Foreign Languages)

Angeles y Demonios. *Dan Brown.* FonoLibro, Inc., Audie Winner 2007

El Codigo Da Vinci. *Dan Brown.* FonoLibro Inc., Audie Winner 2006

Malinche. *Laura Esquivel.* FonoLibro, Audie Winner 2008

Por un Día Más. *Mitch Albom.* FonoLibro, Audie Winner 2009

***La Traversia de Enrique/ Enrique's Journey.** *Sonia Nazario.* Recorded Books/AudioLibros, Audie Winner 2010

Literature & Fiction (General)

The Angels of Morgan Hill. *Donna VanLiere.* Macmillan Audio, Audie Winner 2007

At First Sight. *Nicholas Sparks.* Time Warner AudioBooks

Atonement. *Ian McEwan.* Recorded Books

Best Friends Forever. *Jennifer Weiner.* Simon & Schuster Audio

The Broker. *John Grisham.* Random House Audio

Can't Wait to Get to Heaven. *Fannie Flagg.* Random House Audio

Change of Heart. *Jodi Picoult.* Random House Audio

The Chase. *Clive Cussler.* Penguin AudioBooks

The Christmas Sweater. *Glenn Beck.* Simon & Schuster Audio

The Christmas Thief. *Mary Higgins Clark & Carol Higgins Clark.* Simon & Schuster Audio

The Count of Monte Cristo. *Alexandre Dumas.* Blackstone Audio, Audie Winner 2009

Daddy's Girl. *Lisa Scottoline.* HarperAudio

The Darling. *Russell Banks.* BBC Audiobooks America, Audie Winner 2005

Dashing Through the Snow. *Mary Higgins Clark & Carol Higgins Clark.* Simon &

Schuster Audio

The Devil Wears Prada. *Lauren Weisberger.* Random House Audio

The Divide. *Nicholas Evans.* Penguin Audio Books

The Double Bind. *Chris Bohjalian.* Random House Audio Publishing Group

Elmer Gantry. *Sinclair Lewis.* Blackstone Audio, Audie Winner 2009

For One More Day. *Mitch Albom.* Hyperion Audiobooks

4th of July. *James Patterson & Maxine Paetro.* Time Warner AudioBooks

***Freedom.** *Jonathan Franzen.* Macmillan Audio

Great Expectations. *Charles Dickens.* Tantor Media, Audie Winner 2009

***Great Expectations.** *Charles Dickens.* Audio Connoisseur, Audie Winner 2010

Handle with Care. *Jodi Picoult.* Recorded Books

Heart and Soul. *Maeve Binchy.* Random House Audio

Heart-Shaped Box. *Joe Hill.* HarperAudio, Audie Winner 2008

High Noon. *Nora Roberts.* Brilliance Audio

The Historian. *Elizabeth Kostova.* Time Warner AudioBooks

Honeymoon. *James Patterson.* Time Warner AudioBooks

***House Rules.** *Jodi Picoult.* Recorded Books

Impossible. *Danielle Steel.* Random House Audio

The Interruption of Everything. *Terry McMillan.* Penguin Audio Books

The Kite Runner. *Khaled Hosseini.* Simon & Schuster Audio

Last Song. *Nicholas Sparks.* Hachette Audio

The Lazarus Vendetta. *Patrick Larkin.* Audio Renaissance

Life Expectancy. *Dean Koontz.* Random House Audio

Life of Pi. *Yann Martel.* HighBridge Audio

***The Lovely Bones.** *Alice Sebold.* Hachette Audio

***Man Riding West; Grub Line Rider; Down the Pogonip Trail.** *Louis L'Amour.* Random House Audio

Memoirs of a Geisha. *Arthur Golden.* Random House Audio

The Memory Keeper's Daughter. *Kim Edwards.* HarperAudio

The Mermaid Chair. *Sue Monk Kidd.* Penguin Audio Books

Miracle. *Danielle Steel.* Random House Audio

***A Month of Summer.** *Lisa Wingate.* Recorded Books/Lone Star Audio, Audie Winner 2010

My Sister's Keeper. *Jodi Picoult.* Recorded Books, Audie Winner 2005

Nights of Rain and Stars. *Maeve Binchy.* Penguin Audio Books

Nineteen Minutes. *Jodi Picoult.* Recorded Books, LLC

The Odyssey. *Homer.* BBC Audiobooks

America, Audie Winner 2009

On the Road. *Jack Kerouac.* HarperAudio

On the Run. *Iris Johansen.* Random House Audio Publishing Group

Playing for Pizza. *John Grisham.* Random House Audio Publishing Group

Polar Shift. *Clive Cussler.* Penguin Audio Books

Pontoon: A Novel of Lake Wobegon. *Garrison Keillor.* HighBridge Company, Audie Winner 2008

Por un Día Más. *Mitch Albom.* FonoLibro, Audie Winner 2009

The Princess of Ireland. *Edward Rutherfurd.* Random House Audio

Q&A. *Vikas Swarup.* The Audio Partners Publishing Corp., Audie Winner 2006

The Quickie. *James Patterson & Michael Ledwidge.* Hachette Audio

The Reader. *Bernhard Schlink.* Random House Audio

Remember Me? *Sophie Kinsella.* Random House Audio

Restless. *William Boyd.* Macmillan Audio, Audie Winner 2007

Revolutionary Road. *Richard Yates.* Random House Audio

Ricochet. *Sandra Brown.* Simon & Schuster Audio

Rise and Shine. *Anna Quindlen.* Recorded Books, LLC, Audie Winner 2007

River Rising. *Athol Dickson.* Recorded Books, Audie Winner 2008

The Sanctuary. *Raymond Khoury.* Penguin AudioBooks

School Days. *Robert B. Parker.* Random House Audio

South of Broad. *Pat Controy.* Random House Audio

***Star Island.** *Carl Hiaasen.* Random House Audio

***State of the Union.** *Brad Thor.* Simon & Schuster Audio

The Story of Edgar Sawtelle. *David Wroblewski.* Recorded Books

***The Swan Thieves.** *Elizabeth Kostova.* Hachette Audio

Sweet Revenge. *Diane Mott Davidson.* Harper Audio

Swine Not?: A Novel Pig Tale. *Jimmy Buffett.* Hachette Audio

Telegraph Days. *Larry McMurtry.* Simon & Schuster Audio, Audie Winner 2007

Thirteen Moons. *Charles Frazier.* Random House Audio

The Thirteenth Tale. *Diane Setterfield.* Simon & Schuster Audio, Audie Winner 2007

A Thousand Splendid Suns. *Khaled Hosseini.* Simon & Schuster Audio

The Time Traveler's Wife. *Audrey Niffenegger.* HighBridge

To Kill a Mockingbird. *Harper Lee.* HarperCollins Publishers, Audie Winner

2007

Treasure of Stonewycke. *Michael Phillips & Judith Pella.* Recorded Books, Audie Winner 2004

True Believer. *Nicholas Sparks.* Time Warner AudioBooks

The Undomestic Goddess. *Sophie Kinsella.* Random House Audio

Upstate. *Kalisha Buckhanon.* Audio Renaissance, Audie Winner 2006

You've Been Warned. *James Patterson & Howard Roughan.* Hachette Audio

---

Literature & Fiction (Historical Fiction)

A Breath of Snow & Ashes. *Diana Gabaldon.* Recorded Books, LLC, Audie Winner 2006

***Conspirata.** *Robert Harris.* Simon & Schuster Audio

***An Echo in the Bone.** *Diana Gabaldon.* Recorded Books

The Good German. *Joseph Kanon.* Simon & Schuster Audio

A Good Woman. *Danielle Steel.* Brilliance Audio

***The Help.** *Kathryn Stockett.* Penguin Audio, Audie Winner 2010

Malinche. *Laura Esquivel.* FonoLibro, Audie Winner 2008

The March. *E.L. Doctorow.* Random House Audio

A Mercy. *Toni Morrison.* Random House Audio

Mudbound. *Hillary Jordan.* Recorded Books, Audie Winner 2009

The Other Boleyn Girl. *Philippa Gregory.* Simon & Schuster Audio

The Other Queen. *Philippa Gregory.* Simon & Schuster Audio

The Pillars of the Earth. *Ken Follett.* Penguin AudioBooks

***The Postmistress.** *Sarah Blake.* Penguin Audio

Prague Counterpoint. *Bodie Thoene & Brock Thoene.* FamilyAudioLibrary, Audie Winner 2009

The Templar Legacy. *Steve Berry.* Random House Audio

Tree of Smoke. *Denis Johnson.* Macmillan Audio, Audie Winner 2008

The White Queen. *Philippa Gregory.* Simon & Schuster Audio

***Wolf Hall.** *Hilary Mantel.* Macmillan Audio/BBC Audiobooks, Audie Winner 2010

World Without End. *Ken Follett.* Penguin AudioBooks

Literature & Fiction (Horror & Ghost Stories)

Cell. *Stephen King.* Simon & Schuster

Duma Key. *Stephen King.* Simon & Schuster Audio, Audie Winner 2009

***The Eyes of Darkness.** *Dean Koontz.* Brilliance Audio

From a Buick 8. *Stephen King.* Simon & Schuster Audio

The Gingerbread Girl. *Stephen King.* Simon & Schuster Audio

Just After Sunset. *Stephen King.* Simon & Schuster Audio

Stationary Bike. *Stephen King.* Simon & Schuster Audio

20th Century Ghosts. *Joe Hill.* HarperAudio, Audie Winner 2008

Twisted: Selected Stories of Jeffery Deaver. *Jeffery Deaver.* Recorded Books, Audie Winner 2005

***Ur.** *Stephen King.* Simon & Schuster Audio

Literature & Fiction (Juvenile)

Airborn. *Kenneth Oppel.* Full Cast Audio, Audie Winner 2007

Arnie the Doughnut. *Laurie Keller.* Weston Woods Studios, Audie Winner 2006

Bloody Jack: Being an Account of the Curious Adventures of Mary "Jacky" Faber, Ship's Boy. *L.A. Meyer.* Listen & Live Audio, Audie Winner 2008

Breaking Dawn. *Stephenie Meyer.* Listening Library/Random House Audio

Brisingr. *Christopher Paolini.* Listening Library/Random House Audio

Buddha Boy. *Kathe Koja.* Full Cast Audio, Audie Winner 2005

Chato and the Party Animals. *Gary Soto.* Weston Woods Studios, Audie Winner 2004

***The Chosen One.** *Carol Lynch Williams.* Macmillan Audio/BBC Audiobooks America, Audie Winner 2010

A Christmas Carol. *Charles Dickens.* HighBridge Company

A Christmas Carol. *Charles Dickens.* Listening Library, Audie Winner 2005

A Christmas Carol. *Charles Dickens.* Simon & Schuster Audio

Chronicles of Narnia Box Set. *C.S. Lewis.* HarperChildren's Audio, Audie Winner 2005

Clementine. *Sara Pennypacker.* Recorded Books, Audie Winner 2008

Curse of the Blue Tattoo. *L.A. Meyer.* Listen & Live Audio, Audie Winner 2009

Eldest. *Christopher Paolini.* Random House Audio Publishing Group

Eragon. *Christopher Paolini.* Listening Library

Famous Composers. *Darren Henley.* Naxos AudioBooks Ltd., Audie Winner 2006

The Golden Compass. *Philip Pullman.* Random House Audio Publishing Group, Audie Winner 2007

The Goose Girl. *Shannon Hale.* Full Cast Audio, Audie Winner 2007

The Graveyard Book. *Neil Gaiman.* HarperAudio, Audie Winner 2009

Harry Potter and the Deathly Hallows. *J.K. Rowling.* Random House Audio Publishing Group, Audie Winner 2008

Harry Potter and the Order of the Phoenix. *J.K. Rowling.* Random House Audio Publishing Group

The Harry Potter Audiobook Series. *J.K. Rowling.* Listening Library, Audie Winner 2006

Horton Hears a Who! and Other Sounds of Dr. Seuss. *Dr. Seuss.* Listening Library/Random House Audio

James Herriot's Treasury for Children. *James Herriot.* Macmillan Audio, Audie Winner 2009

Knuffle Bunny. *Mo Willems.* Weston Woods Studios, Incorporated, Audie Winner 2007

The Last Battle. *C.S. Lewis.* HarperCollins Publishers, Audie Winner 2005

Listening for Lions. *Gloria Whelan.* Recorded Books, LLC, Audie Winner 2007

***Louise: The Adventures of a Chicken.** *Kate DiCamillo.* Live Oak Media, Audie Winner 2010

More About Paddington. *Michael Bond.* HarperChildren's Audio, Audie Winner 2008

***Odd and the Frost Giants.** *Neil Gaiman.* Harper Audio, Audie Winner 2010

***Operation Yes.** *Sara Lewis Holmes.* Audible, Inc., Audie Winner 2010

***Peace, Locomotion.** *Jacqueline Woodson.* Brilliance Audio, Audie Winner 2010

Peter and the Shadow Thieves. *Dave Barry & Ridley Pearson.* Brilliance Audio, Audie Winner 2007

Peter and the Starcatchers. *Dave Barry & Ridley Pearson.* Brilliance Audio, Audie Winner 2005

The Spiderwick Chronicles Box Set. *Tony DiTerlizzi & Holly Black.* Listening Library/Random House Audio

Star of Kazan. *Eva Ibbotson.* Recorded Books, LLC, Audie Winner 2006

The Story of Classical Music. *Darren Henley.* Naxos AudioBooks, Audie Winner 2005

The Tale of Despereaux. *Kate DiCamillo.* Listening Library/Random House Audio

***Tell Me a Story.** *Amy Friedman.* Listen & Live Audio, Audie Winner 2010

Treasure Island. *Robert Louis Stevenson.* Listening Library/Random House Audio, Audie Winner 2008

Twilight. *Stephenie Meyer.* Listening Library/Random House Audio

---

Literature & Fiction (Mystery & Suspense)

***Act of Treason.** *Vince Flynn.* Simon & Schuster Audio

Alex Cross's Trial. *James Patterson & Richard DiLallo.* Hachette Audio

The Alexandria Link. *Steve Berry.* Random House Audio Publishing Group

The Alibi Man. *Tami Hoag.* Random House Audio Publishing Group

Angeles and Demonios. Dan Brown. Fonolibro, Audie Winner 2007

Angels and Demons. *Dan Brown.* Simon & Schuster Audio

The Appeal. *John Grisham.* Random House Audio

The Associate. *John Grisham.* Random House Audio

At Risk. *Patricia Cornwell.* Penguin Audio

Bad Luck and Trouble. *Lee Child.* Random House Audio Publishing Group

The Beach Road. *James Patterson & Peter deJonge.* Time Warner AudioBooks

Black Ops. *W.E.B. Griffin.* Penguin Audio

Blue Shoes & Happiness. *Alexander McCall Smith.* Recorded Books

Bones. *Jonathan Kellerman.* Random House Audio

Bones to Ashes. *Kathy Reichs.* Simon & Schuster Audio

The Book of Fate. *Brad Meltzer.* Hachette Audio

The Book of Lies. *Brad Meltzer.* Hachette Audio

Book of the Dead. *Patricia Cornwell.* Penguin AudioBooks

The Brass Verdict. *Michael Connelly.* Penguin Audio

Break No Bones. *Kathy Reichs.* Simon & Schuster Audio

Brimstone. *Douglas Preston & Lincoln Child.* Time Warner AudioBooks, Audie Winner 2005

The Broken Window. *Jeffery Deaver.* Simon & Schuster Audio

The Broker. *John Grisham.* Random House Audio

***Caught.** *Harlan Coben.* Random House Audio

The Cat Who Dropped a Bombshell. *Lilian Jackson Braun.* Penguin Audio

The Cat Who Had 60 Whiskers. *Lilian Jackson Braun.* Penguin AudioBooks

The Charlemagne Pursuit. *Steve Berry.* Random House Audio

Chasing Darkness. *Robert Crais.* Brilliance Audio

Child 44. *Tom Rob Smith.* Hachette Audio, Audie Winner 2009

The Chopin Manuscript. *Jeffery Deaver, Lisa Scottoline, Lee Child, et al.* Audible, Audie Winner 2008

The Closers. *Michael Connelly.* Time Warner AudioBooks

El Codigo Da Vinci. *Dan Brown.* FonoLibro Inc., Audie Winner 2006

Cold Service. *Robert B. Parker.* Random House Audio

Compulsion. *Jonathan Kellerman.* Random House Audio

Creation in Death. *J.D. Robb.* Brilliance Audio

Crisis. *Robin Cook.* Penguin Audio

Cross Country. *James Patterson.* Hachette Audio

Dark of the Moon. *John Sandford.* Penguin AudioBooks

The Darkest Evening of the Year. *Dean Koontz.* Random House Audio Publishing Group

***Jim Darling.** *Christian Moerk.* Tantor Audio, Audie Winner 2010

Dead Heat. *Dick Francis & Felix Francis.* Penguin AudioBooks

Dead Watch. *John Sandford.* Penguin Audio

The Dead Yard. *Adrian McKinty.* Blackstone Audio, Incorporated, Audie Winner 2007

***Deception.** *Jonathan Kellerman.* Random House Audio

Deception Point. *Dan Brown.* Simon & Schuster Audio

The Defector. *Daniel Silva.* Brilliance Audio

***Deliver Us from Evil.** *David Baldacci.* Hachette Audio

Devil Bones. *Kathy Reichs.* Simon & Schuster Audio

***Devil in a Blue Dress.** *Walter Mosley.* Audible, Inc., Audie Winner 2010

Divine Justice. *David Baldacci.* Hachette Audio

Double Cross. *James Patterson.* Hachette Audio

Double Homicide. *Faye Kellerman.* Time Warner Audio

Double Take: An FBI Thriller. *Catherine Coulter.* Brilliance Audio

Echo Park. *Michael Connelly.* Hachette Audio, Audie Winner 2007

Eleven on Top. *Janet Evanovich.* Audio Renaissance

Extreme Measures. *Vince Flynn.* Simon & Schuster Audio

***Fantasy in Death.** *J. D. Robb.* Brilliance Audio

Fearless Fourteen. *Janet Evanovich.* Macmillan Audio

***Fever Dream.** *Lincoln Child & Douglas Preston.* Hachette Audio

The 5th Horseman. *James Patterson & Maxine Paetro.* Time Warner AudioBooks

Finger Lickin' Fifteen. *Janet Evanovich.* Macmillan Audio

First Family. *David Baldacci.* Hachette Audio

Foreign Body. *Robin Cook.* Penguin Audio

Forever Odd. *Dean Koontz.* Random House Audio

The Forgotten Man. *Robert Crais.* Brilliance Audio

Fresh Disasters: A Stone Barrington Novel. *Stuart Woods.* Penguin AudioBooks

Friends, Lovers, Chocolate. *Alexander McCall Smith.* Recorded Books

The Front. *Patricia Cornwell.* Penguin Audio

The Gate House. *Nelson Demille.* Hachette Audio

***The Girl Who Kicked the Hornet's Nest.** *Stieg Larsson.* Random House Audio

The Girl Who Played with Fire. *Stieg Larsson.* Random House Audio

The Girl with the Dragon Tattoo. *Stieg Larsson.* Random House Audio

***The Glass Rainbow.** *James Lee Burke.* Simon & Schuster Audio

Gone. *Lisa Gardner.* Random House Audio Publishing Group

Gone. *Jonathan Kellerman.* Random House Audio

The Good Guy. *Dean Koontz.* Random House Audio Publishing Group

The Good Husband of Zebra Drive. *Alexander McCall Smith.* Recorded Books, LLC

Hannibal Rising. *Thomas Harris.* Random House Audio Publishing Group

HeartSick. *Chelsea Cain.* Macmillan Audio

Heat Lightning. *John Sandford.* Penguin Audio

Hidden Prey. *John Sandford.* Penguin Audio

High Profile. *Robert B. Parker.* Random House. Audio Publishing Group

Hold Tight. *Harlan Coben.* Brilliance Audio

The Hollow. *Nora Roberts.* Brilliance Audio

Hollywood Crows. *Joseph Wambaugh.* Hachette Audio

Hot Mahogany. *Stuart Woods.* Penguin Audio

Hothouse Orchid. *Stuart Woods.* Penguin Audio

The Husband. *Dean Koontz.* Random House Audio

***I, Alex Cross.** *James Patterson.* Hachette Audio

I Heard That Song Before. *Mary Higgins Clark.* Simon & Schuster Audio

Icebound. *Dean Koontz.* Random House Audio Publishing Group

In the Company of Cheerful Ladies. *Alexander McCall Smith.* Recorded Books

***Innocent.** *Scott Turow.* Hachette Audio

Innocent in Death. *J.D. Robb.* Brilliance Audio

Invisible Prey. *John Sandford.* Penguin AudioBooks

Judge & Jury. *James Patterson & Andrew Gross.* Hachette Audio

***Kindred in Death.** *J. D. Robb.* Brilliance Audio

Kiss Me While I Sleep. *Linda Howard.* Brilliance Audio, Audie Winner 2005

***Kisser.** *Stuart Woods.* Penguin Audio

Lady Killer. *Lisa Scottoline.* HarperAudio

The Last Juror. *John Grisham.* Random House Audio

The Last Oracle. *James Rollins.* HarperAudio

Lean Mean Thirteen. *Janet Evanovich.* Macmillan Audio

The Lighthouse. *P.D. James.* Random House Audio

***The Lion.** *Nelson DeMille.* Hachette Audio

Lost Boys. *Orson Scott Card.* Blackstone Audio Books, Audie Winner 2005

Lost Light. *Michael Connelly.* Time Warner Audio, Audie Winner 2004

The Lost Symbol. *Dan Brown.* Random House Audio

***The Maltese Falcon.** *Dashiell Hammett.* Blackstone Audiobooks, Audie Winner 2010

Mary, Mary. *James Patterson.* Time Warner AudioBooks

Memory in Death. *J.D. Robb.* Brilliance Audio

The Messenger. *Daniel Silva.* Brilliance Audio

Metro Girl. *Janet Evanovich.* HarperAudio

***The Midnight House.** *Alex Berenson.* Penguin Audio

The Miracle at Speedy Motors. *Alexander McCall Smith.* Recorded Books

Moscow Rules. *Daniel Silva.* Brilliance Audio

Mounting Fears. *Stuart Woods.* Penguin Audio

Nature Girl. *Carl Hiaasen.* Random House Audio Publishing Group

Next. *Michael Crichton.* HarperAudio

Night Fall. *Nelson DeMille.* Time Warner AudioBooks

Nights in Rodanthe. *Nicholas Sparks.* Hachette Audio

***Nine Dragons.** *Michael Connelly.* Hachette Audio

***The 9th Judgment.** *James Patterson & Maxine Paetro.* Hachette Audio

No Place Like Home. *Mary Higgins Clark.* Simon & Schuster Audio

Now and Then. *Robert B. Parker.* Random House Audio Publishing Group

Obsession. *Jonathan Kellerman.* Random House Audio Publishing Group

Odd Hours. *Dean Koontz.* Brilliance Audio

Origin in Death. *J.D. Robb.* Brilliance Audio, Audie Winner 2006

The Overlook. *Michael Connelly.* Hachette Audio

***The Overton Window.** *Glenn Beck.* Simon & Schuster Audio

Pegasus Descending. *James Lee Burke.* Simon & Schuster Audio

Phantom Prey. *John Sandford.* Penguin Audio

Plague Ship. *Clive Cussler with Jack Du Brul.* Penguin Audio

Play Dirty. *Sandra Brown.* Simon & Schuster Audio

Plum Lovin'. *Janet Evanovich.* Macmillan Audio

Plum Lucky. *Janet Evanovich.* Macmillan Audio

Plum Spooky. *Janet Evanovich.* Macmillan Audio

***The Postcard Killers.** *James Patterson & Liza Marklund.* Hachette Audio

Predator. *Patricia Cornwell.* Penguin Audio

A Prisoner of Birth. *Jeffrey Archer.* Macmillan Audio

***Private.** *James Patterson & Maxine Paetro.* Hachette Audio

***The Professional.** *Robert B. Parker.* Random House Audio

Promise Me. *Harlan Coben.* Brilliance Audio

Promises in Death. *J.D. Robb.* Brilliance Audio

Protect and Defend. *Vince Flynn.* Simon & Schuster Audio

***Pursuit of Honor.** *Vince Flynn.* Simon & Schuster Audio

The Race. *Richard North Patterson.* Macmillan Audio, Audie Winner 2008

Rage. *Jonathan Kellerman.* Random House Audio

Raymond & Hannah. *Stephen Marche.* HighBridge Audio, Audie Winner 2006

The Romanov Prophecy. *Steve Berry.* Random House Audio

Rough Country. *John Sandford.* Penguin Audio

Rough Weather. *Robert B. Parker.* Random House Audio

The Rule of Four. *Ian Caldwell.* Simon & Schuster Audio

Run for Your Life. *James Patterson & Michael Ledwidge.* Hachette Audio

S Is for Silence. *Sue Grafton.* Random House Audio

Sail. *James Patterson & Howard Roughan.* Hachette Audio

A Salty Piece of Land. *Jimmy Buffett.* Time Warner AudioBooks

Salvation in Death. *J.D. Robb.* Brilliance Audio

Santa Fe Dead. *Stuart Woods.* Penguin Audio

Scarpetta. *Patricia Cornwell.* Penguin Audio

***The Scarpetta Factor.** *Patricia Cornwell.* Penguin Audio

The Secret Servant. *Daniel Silva.* Brilliance Audio

7th Heaven. *James Patterson & Maxine Paetro.* Hachette Audio

The Shack: Where Tragedy Confronts Eternity. *William P. Young.* Oasis Audio

The Sherlock Holmes Theatre. *Arthur Conan Doyle, William Gillette & Yuri Rasovsky.* Blackstone Audiobooks, Audie Winner 2006

Shoot Him If He Runs. *Stuart Woods.* Penguin AudioBooks

Simple Genius. *David Baldacci.* Hachette Audio

The 6th Target. *James Patterson & Maxine Paetro.* Hachette Audio

***61 Hours.** *Lee Child.* Random House Audio

***Sizzling Sixteen.** *Janet Evanovich.* Macmillan Audio

A Slight Trick of the Mind. *Mitch Cullin* HighBridge Audio, Audie Winner 2006

Smoke Screen. *Sandra Brown.* Simon & Schuster Audio

***Spider Bones.** *Kathy Reichs.* Simon & Schuster Audio

***Split Image.** *Robert B. Parker.* Random House Audio

State of Fear. *Michael Crichton.* HarperAudio

Step on a Crack. *James Patterson & Michael Ledwidge.* Hachette Audio

Stone Cold. *David Baldacci.* Hachette Audio

***Storm Prey.** *John Sandford.* Penguin Audio

Strangers in Death. *J.D. Robb.* Brilliance Audio

The Sunday Philosophy Club. *Alexander McCall Smith.* Recorded Books

Sundays at Tiffany's. *James Patterson & Gabrielle Charbonnet.* Hachette Audio

Swan Peak. *James Lee Burke.* Simon & Schuster Audio

Swimsuit. *James Patterson & Maxine Paetro.* Hachette Audio

T Is for Trespass. *Sue Grafton.* Random House Audio Publishing Group

Tallgrass. *Sandra Dallas.* Macmillan Audio, Audie Winner 2008

The Templar Legacy. *Steve Berry.* Random House Audio

3rd Degree. *James Patterson & Andrew Gross.* Hachette Audio

The Tin Roof Blowdown. *James Lee Burke.* Simon & Schuster Audio, Audie Winner 2008

The Tortilla Curtain. *T.C. Boyle.* Blackstone Audio, Incorporated, Audie Winner 2007

Treasure of Khan: A Dirk Pitt Novel. *Clive Cussler & Dirk Cussler.* Penguin AudioBooks

***True Blue.** *David Baldacci.* Hachette Audio

206 Bones. *Kathy Reichs.* Simon & Schuster Audio

Two Little Girls in Blue. *Mary Higgins Clark.* Simon & Schuster Audio

***U Is for Undertow.** *Sue Grafton.* Random House Audio

Under Orders. *Dick Francis.* Penguin Audio

***Under the Dome.** *Stephen King.* Simon & Schuster Audio

An Unpardonable Crime. *Andrew Taylor.* Hyperion AudioBooks, Audie Winner 2005

Velocity. *Dean Koontz.* Random House Audio

The Venetian Betrayal. *Steve Berry.* Random House Audio

Voice of the Violin. *Andrea Camilleri.* Blackstone Audio, Audie Winner 2009

The Watchman. *Robert Crais.* Brilliance Audio

The Wheel of Darkness. *Douglas Preston & Lincoln Child.* Hachette Audio

Where Are You Now? *Mary Higgins Clark.* Simon & Schuster Audio

The Whole Truth. *David Baldacci.* Hachette Audio

***Wicked Appetite.** *Janet Evanovich.* Macmillan Audio

The Woods. *Harlan Coben.* Brilliance Audio

***Worst Case.** *James Patterson & Michael Ledwidge.* Hachette Audio

The Yiddish Policemen's Union. *Michael Chabon.* HarperAudio

Your Heart Belongs to Me. *Dean Koontz.* Brilliance Audio

Literature & Fiction (Romance)

Angels Fall. *Nora Roberts.* Brilliance Audio

Belong to Me. *Marisa de los Santos.* HarperAudio

Blue Smoke. *Nora Roberts.* Brilliance Audio

The Choice. *Nicholas Sparks.* Hachette Audio

The Dark Highlander. *Karen Marie Moning.* Brilliance Audio, Audie Winner 2009

***Dear John.** *Nicholas Sparks.* Hachette Audio

Echo Park. *Michael Connelly.* Hachette Audio

The Good German. *Joseph Kanon.* Simon & Schuster Audio

The Host. *Stephenie Meyer.* Hachette Audio

***Hot Rocks.** *Nora Roberts.* Brilliance Audio

If You Could See Me Now. *Cecelia Ahern.* Hyperion Audio, Audie Winner 2007

Kiss Me While I Sleep. *Linda Howard.* Brilliance Audio, Audie Winner 2005

The Lucky One. *Nicholas Sparks.* Hachette Audio

Motor Mouth. *Janet Evanovich.* HarperAudio

Natural Born Charmer. *Susan Elizabeth Phillips.* HarperAudio, Audie Winner 2008

The Notebook. *Nicholas Sparks.* Time Warner Audio

Origin in Death. *J.D. Robb.* Brilliance Audio, Audie Winner 2006

Survivor in Death. *J.D. Robb.* Brilliance Audio

TailSpin. *Catherine Coulter.* Brilliance Audio

Tribute. *Nora Roberts.* Brilliance Audio

Twenties Girl. *Sophie Kinsella.* Random House Audio

***The Untamed Bride.** *Stephanie Laurens.* Harper Audio/ Blackstone Audiobooks, Audie Winner 2010

Literature & Fiction (Short Stories & Essays)

Armageddon in Retrospect. *Kurt Vonnegut.* Penguin Audio, Audie Winner 2009

***Black Mask Audio Magazine, Vol. 1.** *Dashiell Hammett, et al.* Blackstone Audiobooks, Audie Winner 2010

***Ford County.** *John Grisham.* Random House Audio

Holidays on Ice. *David Sedaris.* Hachette Audio

***Nelson Mandela's Favorite African Folktales.** *Nelson Mandela.* Hachette Audio, Audie Winner 2010

Runaway. *Alice Munro.* BBC Audiobooks America, Audie Winner 2006

Medicine & Medical Care

Against Medical Advice. *James Patterson & Hal Friedman.* Hachette Audio

***The Checklist Manifesto.** *Atul Gawande.* Macmillan Audio

***The Immortal Life of Henrietta Lacks.** *Rebecca Skloot.* Random House Audio

My Stroke of Insight. *Jill Bolte Taylor.* Penguin Audio

Movies & Television

The Time of My Life. *Patrick Swayze & Lisa Niemi.* Simon & Schuster Audio

Music

The Christmas Companion. *Garrison Keillor.* HighBridge Audio

Nature

Hot, Flat, and Crowded: Why We Need a Green Revolution--and How It Can Renew America. *Thomas L. Friedman.* Macmillan Audio, Audie Winner 2009

New Age Movement

Ask and It Is Given: The Law of Attraction. *Esther & Jerry Hicks.* Hay House Audio

Change Your Thoughts--Change Your Life: Living the Wisdom of the Tao. *Wayne W. Dyer.* Hay House

Change Your Thoughts Meditation: Do the Tao Now! *Wayne W. Dyer.* Hay House

The Law of Attraction: The Basics of the Teachings of Abraham. *Esther & Jerry Hicks.* Hay House

The Law of Attraction CD Collection. *Esther & Jerry Hicks.* Hay House

Money, and the Law of Attraction: Learning to Attract Wealth, Health, and Happiness. *Esther & Jerry Hicks.* Hay House

***The Vortex.** *Esther & Jerry Hicks.* Hay House

Personal Growth & Achievement

Bad Childhood Good Life. *Laura Schlessinger.* Harper Audio

Be the Pack Leader: Use Cesar's Way to Transform Your Dog... and Your Life. *Cesar Millan.* Random House Audio

Become a Better You: 7 Keys to Improving Your Life Every Day. *Joel Osteen.* Simon & Schuster Audio

Change Your Thoughts--Change Your Life: Living the Wisdom of the Tao. *Wayne W. Dyer.* Hay House

The 8th Habit. *Stephen R. Covey.* Simon & Schuster Audio

Excuses Begone. *Wayne Dwyer.* Hay House

Fear the Fear and Do It Anyway. *Susan Jeffries.* Simon & Schuster Audio

The Five Love Languages. *Gary Chapman.* Oasis Audio, Audie Winner 2006

For the Love of a Dog: Understanding Emotion in You and Your Best Friend. *Patricia McConnell.* Tantor Media, Incorporated, Audie Winner 2007

Giving: How Each of Us Can Change the World. *Bill Clinton.* Random House Audio

How to Meditate with Pema Chodron: A Practical Guide to Making Friends with Your Mind. *Pema Chodron.* Sounds True Audio

How to Talk to Anyone. *Leil Lowndes.* Listen & Live Audio

Inspiration. *Wayne W. Dyer.* Hay Hou

The Last Lecture. *Randy Pausch.* Hyperion Audio, Audie Winner 2009

Law of Attraction: The Science of Attracting More of What You Want and Less of What You Don't. *Michael Losier.* Hachette Audio

Maximum Confidence: 10 Secrets of Extreme Self-Esteem. *James Canfield.* Simon & Schuster Audio

The Missing Secret. *Joe Vitale.* Nightingale-Conant

A New Earth: Awakening to Your Life's Purpose. *Eckhart Tolle.* Penguin Audio

Peaks and Valleys. *Spencer Johnson.* Simon & Schuster Audio

The Secret. *Rhonda Byrne.* Simon & Schuster Audio

The Secret Universal Mind Meditation. *Kelly Howell.* Brain Sync Corporation

The Secret Universal Mind Meditation II. *Kelly Howell.* Brain Sync Corporation

The 7 Habits of Highly Effective People. *Stephen R. Covey.* Covey Leadership Center

Stop Whining, Start Living. *Laura Schlessinger.* HarperAudio

Sylvia Browne's Tools for Life. *Sylvia Browne.* Hay House

This I Believe: The Personal Philosophies of Remarkable Men and Women. *Jay Allison & Dan Gediman.* Macmillan Audio, Audie Winner 2007

The World According to Mister Rogers. *Fred Rogers.* Simon & Schuster Audio, Audie Winner 2005

Political Science

Against All Enemies. *Richard Clarke.* Simon & Schuster Audio, Audie Winner 2005

Arguing with Idiots. *Glenn Beck.* Simon & Schuster Audio

The Audacity of Hope: Thoughts on Reclaiming the American Dream. *Barack Obama.* Random House Audio

Bush at War. *Bob Woodward.* Simon & Schuster Audio

Bushworld. *Maureen Dowd.* Penguin Audio

Change We Can Believe In: Barack Obama's Plan to Renew America's Promise. *Barack Obama.* Random House Audio

Collapse: How Societies Choose to Fail or Succeed. *Jared Diamond.* Penguin Audio Books

Culture of Corruption. *Michelle Malkin.* Tantor Media

Culture Warrior. *Bill O'Reilly.* Random House Audio

The Essential Barack Obama. *Barack Obama.* Random House Audio

***Game Change.** *John Heilemann & Mark Halperin.* Harper Audio

Glenn Beck's Common Sense. *Glenn Beck.* Simon & Schuster Audio

Godless. *Ann Coulter.* Random House Audio

Guilty. *Ann Coulter.* Random House Audio

Hot, Flat, and Crowded: Why We Need a Green Revolution--and How It Can Renew America. *Thomas L. Friedman.* Macmillan Audio, Audie Winner 2009

Hubris: The Inside Story of Spin, Scandal, and the Selling of the Iraq War. *Michael Isikoff & David Corn.* Blackstone Audio, Incorporated, Audie Winner 2007

***Idiots Unplugged.** *Glenn Beck.* Simon & Schuster Audio

Liberty and Tyranny. *Mark Levin.* Simon & Schuster Audio

Lies: And the Lying Liars Who Tell Them. *Al Franken.* HighBridge Audio

Longitudes & Attitudes. *Thomas L. Friedman.* Audio Renaissance

My FBI. *Louis J. Freeh.* Audio Renaissance

Naked in Baghdad. *Anne Garrels.* Audio Renaissance, Audie Winner 2004

Obama Nation: Leftist Politics and the Cult of Personality. *Jerome R. Corsi.* Simon & Schuster Audio

100 People Who Are Screwing Up America. *Bernie Goldberg.* HarperAudio

Our Endangered Values. *Jimmy Carter.* Simon & Schuster Audio

Plan of Attack. *Bob Woodward.* Simon & Schuster Audio

***The Politician.** *Andrew Young.* Tantor Media

The Price of Loyalty. *Ron Suskind.* Simon & Schuster Audio

***The Promise**. *Jonathan Alter.* Simon & Schuster Audio

State of Denial: Bush at War, Part III. *Bob Woodward.* Simon & Schuster

True Compass. *Edward M. Kennedy.* Hachette Audio

The War Within: A Secret White House History, 2006-2008. *Bob Woodward.* Simon & Schuster Audio

What Happened: Inside the Bush White House and Washington's Culture of Deception. *Scott McClellan.* Blackstone Audio

---

Psychology

***Nurtureshock.** *Po Bronson & Ashley Merryman.* Hachette Audio, Audie Winner 2010

Outliers. *Malcolm Gladwell.* Hachette Audio

***The Tipping Point.** *Malcolm Gladwell.* Hachette Audio

***The Upside of Irrationality.** *Dan Ariely.* Harper Audio

The World According to Mister Rogers. *Fred Rogers.* Simon & Schuster Audio, Audie Winner 2005

Radio Broadcasts

Lost and Found Sound and Beyond. *Kitchen Sisters.* HighBridge Audio, Audie Winner 2005

The Twilight Zone Radio Dramas: Collection 11. Blackstone Audio, Audie Winner 2008

Religious & Inspirational

Become a Better You: 7 Keys to Improving Your Life Every Day. *Joel Osteen.* Simon & Schuster Audio

The 8th Habit. *Stephen R. Covey.* Simon & Schuster Audio

Finding God in Unexpected Places. *Philip Yancey.* Brilliance Audio, Audie Winner 2006

Good, Better, Blessed. *Joel Osteen.* Simon & Schuster Audio

Have a Little Faith. *Mitch Albom.* Hachette Audio

Inside My Heart. *Robin McGraw.* Thomas Nelson Audio

Inspired by…the Bible Experience: The Complete Bible. Zondervan

Inspired by...the Bible Experience: New Testament. *Angela Bassett, Cuba Gooding, Jr. & Samuel L. Jackson, et al.* Zondervan, Audie Winner 2007

Inspired by...the Bible Experience: Old Testament. Zondervan, Audie Winner 2008

***It's Your Time.** *Joel Osteen.* Simon & Schuster Audio

The Life of Jesus: Dramatic Eyewitness Accounts from the Luke Reports. *Paul McClusker.* Focus on the Family Publishing, Audie Winner 2007

Love Your Life. *Victoria Osteen.* Simon & Schuster Audio

A New Earth: Awakening to Your Life's Purpose. *Eckhart Tolle.* Penguin Audio Books

***The Power of Now.** *Eckhart Tolle.* New World Audio.

Reposition Yourself: Living Life Without Limits. *T.D. Jakes.* Simon & Schuster Audio

Rise, Let Us Be On Our Way. *Pope John Pau. II.* Time Warner AudioBooks

***Tao I.** *Zhi Gang Sha.* Simon & Schuster Audio

The Third Jesus: The Christ We Cannot Ignore. *Deepak Chopra.* Random House Audio

Tuesdays with Morrie. *Mitch Albom.* Random House Audio

Walking the Bible. *Bruce Feiler.* HarperAudio

Where God Was Born. *Bruce Feiler.* HarperAudio

***The Word of Promise Audio Bible.** Thomas Nelson, Audie Winner 2010

The Word of Promise: New Testament. Thomas Nelson

The Word of Promise Next Generation—New Testament. Thomas Nelson, Audie Winner 2009

Your Best Life Now. *Joel Osteen.* Time Warner AudioBooks

Science & Technology

Einstein: His Life and Universe. *Walter Isaacson.* Simon & Schuster Audio, Audie Winner 2008

***The Grand Design.** *Stephen W. Hawking & Leonard Mlodinow.* Random House Audio

***Packing for Mars.** *Mary Roach.* Brilliance Audio

Social Sciences

Chasing the Devil: My Twenty-Year Quest to Capture the Green River Killer. *Sheriff David Reichert.* Time Warner AudioBooks, Audie Winner 2005

Giving: How Each of Us Can Change the World. *Bill Clinton.* Random House Audio

Guns, Germs and Steel: The Fates of Human Societies. *Jared Diamond.* HighBridge Audio

Our Endangered Values. *Jimmy Carter.* Simon & Schuster Audio

***The Tipping Point.** *Malcolm Gladwell.* Hachette Audio

Who's Looking Out For You? *Bill O'Reilly.* Random Audio Books

The World Is Flat. *Thomas L. Friedman.* Audio Renaissance, Audie Winner 2006

Zodiac. *Robert Graysmith.* Blackstone Audio

Travel & Geography

The City of Falling Angels. *John Berendt.* Random House Audio

Into the Wild. *Jon Krakauer.* Random House Audio

Louis Vuitton Soundwalk: Beijing. *Stephan Crasneanscki.* Soundwalk, Audie Winner 2009

Narrow Dog to Carcassonne. *Terry Darlington.* ISIS Audio Books, Audie Winner 2007

***The National Parks.** *Ken Burns & Dayton Duncan.* Books on Tape, Audie Winner 2010

BOOKS OUT LOUD™

Volume 1

Title Index
A – S

A

A. A. & the Self-Help Group Movement. 1 cass. (Running Time: 90 min.). (Introduction to Chemical Dependency Ser.). 1980. 8.95 (1501G) Hazelden.

A. A. Milne's Pooh Classics Boxed Set: Winnie-the-Pooh; the House at Pooh Corner; When We Were Very Young; & Now We Are Six. unabr. ed. A. A. Milne. Read by Peter Dennis. (Running Time: 10 hrs.). (J). 2007. audio compact disk 24.95 (978-0-7861-7095-1(6)) Blckstn Audio.

A. Alvarez. Interview with A. Alvarez. 1 cass. (Running Time: 25 min.). 1972. 11.95 (L003) TFR.
Alvarez talks about the savage God: A study of suicide, which describes recent literary figures who have taken their own lives. He speaks particularly of the poet, Sylvia Plath to whom he was both friend & editor.

A+ Audio Study Guide Box 1. unabr. ed. William Shakespeare et al. (ENG.). 2009. 29.98 (978-1-60788-164-3(0)) Pub: Hachet Audio. Dist(s): HachBkGrp

A-Cappella Praise. 1 cass. (Running Time: 90 mins.). 6.98 (978-1-57908-454-7(0)) Platinm Enter.

A-Cappella Praise. 1 CD. (Running Time: 90 mins.). 1999. audio compact disk 9.98 (978-1-57908-449-3(4), 5334) Platinm Enter.

A+ Certification CertTrainer 2001. Syngress Staff. 2001. 69.99 (978-0-07-213472-8(0)) McGraw-Hill Osborne.

A. D. after the Death of Christ. Scripts. Glenn Kimball & Chase Kimball. Prod. by John Fassett. Engineer Robert Karp. Music by Steve Millet. 1 CD. (Running Time: 01:14:18). 2005. audio compact disk 15.00 (978-1-59772-040-3(2), Your Own Wrld Bks) Your Own Wrld.
A. D. After the death of Jesus, Christianity exploded onto the world. However, few would have guessed in our day that most of ?Smoking Guns? came from ancient Britannia.For example, twenty seven years after the death of Jesus, the spear that lanced the side of Jesus was carried into battle by the rich British Queen Bodicea in defense of the "Hides of Glastonbury," a gift given by her rich uncle Aviragus to the Biblical Joseph of Arimathea. Nineteen years after the death of Jesus, the rich Christian British King Cardoc, or Caractacus, was held hostage in his home, the Paladicum Britanicum, across the street from what is now the Vatican, by Caesar Claudius. This ancient palace of Prudentia, the cousin of Bodicea, survives today facing the Vatican.The year Nero burnt Rome to the ground, Bodicea burnt the thriving ancient city of London to the ground. Historians say in our day that Nero blamed the burning of Rome on an obscure sect from the Roman Eastern Province. Nothing could be farther from the truth. The Christian Bodicea slaughtered 40,000 Roman soldiers in that battle. Two years later, she became the only general in history whose death on the battle field so affected both sides that all the soldiers sheathed their weapons and went home.This story, filled with enigma, finally makes sense when we take into account all the artifacts, documents and buildings, which survive today to tell the tale. The apostles Paul, Peter, Phillip and others lived with the Britons in their home in Rome as they launched Christianity into the world.The personalities that played a role in this saga exceed any Playbill ever written. This story survives in the histories of famous kings, Caesars, dictators, martyrs and villains to this day.

A. D. D. A Positive Perspective on Attention Deficit Disorder. Cynthia Calvert-Phillips. Read by Cynthia Calvert-Phillips. Read by Phil Phillips. Told to Phil Phillips. (ENG.). 2006. audio compact disk 24.99 (978-1-930034-99-0(7)) Casscomm.

A. D. D. Audio Coach: Step-by-Step Audio Program for Adults with Attention Deficit Disorder/Attention Deficit Hyperactivity Disorder. 4th ed. Short Stories. Linda Hillger & Richard Carlson. 3 CDs. (Running Time: 83 mins.). 2004. spiral bd. 59.99 (978-0-9761963-6-5(0)) Lifelifters.
Are you tired of struggling with organizational issues because of ADD / ADHD? This 87-minute 3-CD audio course - with companion 120-page workbook - will help you regain control over your time, home environment, and personal finances The CDs function like coaching sessions, guiding you past your roadblocks and offering new ways of approaching old problems. And the workbook includes exercises and forms that will help you put these principles into practice every day. Designed specifically for adults with ADD / ADHD, this program has been called the "what to do" for balancing different responsibilities and overcoming that constant feeling of overwhelm. Even if you've never been able to get organized before, this system will create awareness of your specific challenges, provide tools for you to rely on, and help build a plan for your future success.

A. D. D. in Childhood: An Overview. John F. Taylor. 1 cass. (Running Time: 52 mins.). (Answers to ADD Ser.). 1993. 9.95 (978-1-883963-02-6(8)) ADD Plus.
Lecture tape.

A. D. D. Is Really Bugging Me. John F. Taylor. 1 cass. (Running Time: 5 mins.). 1993. 3.95 (978-1-883963-13-2(3)) ADD Plus.

A. D. D., the Natural Approach Vol. 1: Help for Attention Deficit Disorder & Hyperactivity. unabr. ed. Nina Anderson & Howard Peiper. Perf. by Roy Howard. 1 cass. (Running Time: 90 mins.). 1997. 9.95 (978-1-884820-25-0(5)) Safe Goods.
Natural help for attention deficit disorder & hyperactivity. Alternative healing methods without drugs.

A. D. Two Thousand... the End? Jack Van Impe. 1 cass. (Running Time: 90 mins.). 1990. 7.00 J Van Impe.
Dr. & Mrs. Van Impe share the time table for the final events of the world.

A. E. I. O. U. Ahora Cantastu. 2 cass. (Running Time: 2 hrs. 30 min.). 1990. cass. & flmstrp 19.95 (Natl Textbk Co) M-H Contemporary.
Features a selection of two line verses on filmstrip & cassette.

A. Elite Minds-Elite Minds & Who Are the Elected Ones?/B. Soul at Death: Volume 9, Vol. 9. Speeches. Bhagat Singh Thind. (Running Time: 60 mins.). (ENG.). 2003. audio compact disk 12.00 (978-1-932630-10-7(4)) Pub: Dr Bhagat Sin. Dist(s): Baker Taylor

A-Files: Alien Songs. 1 cass., 1 CD. (Running Time: 90 mins.). (J). 1999. 7.98 (SME 63463); audio compact disk 11.18 CD Jewel box. (SME 63463) NewSound.
Alien-Space oriented repertoire featuring tracks from the X-Files, Men in Black & Star Wars as well as out of this world pop songs sung by Alvin & the Chipmunks.

A Is for Aargh! collector's ed. Narrated by William J. Brooke. 5 cass. (Running Time: 6 hrs.). (J). 2004. 32.95 (978-0-7887-8390-6(4)) Recorded Bks.

A Is for AARRGH! abr. ed. William J. Brooke. Narrated by William J. Brooke. 5 cass. (Running Time: 6 hrs.). (gr. 5 up). 2001. 36.00 (978-0-7887-4722-9(3), 96396E7) Recorded Bks.
In prehistoric times, people pointed to what they wanted & grunted. But when one young man invented words, even the sun seemed to stop & listen.

A Is for AARRGH! unabr. ed. William J. Brooke. 5 cass. (Running Time: 6 hrs.). (J). 2003. 36.00 Recorded Bks.
In prehistoric times, people pointed to what they wanted and grunted. But when one young man invented words, even the sun seemed to stop and listen.

A Is for Alibi. abr. ed. Sue Grafton. Read by Judy Kaye. (Running Time: 10800 sec.). (Kinsey Millhone Mystery Ser.). (ENG.). 2007. audio compact disk 14.99 (978-0-7393-5734-7(4), Random AudioBks) Pub: Random Audio Pubg. Dist(s): Random

A Is for Alibi. unabr. collector's ed. Sue Grafton. Read by Mary Peiffer. 8 cass. (Running Time: 8 hrs.). (Kinsey Millhone Mystery Ser.). 1993. 64.00 (978-0-7366-2455-8(4), 3219) Books on Tape.
When Laurence Fife was murdered, plenty of people had reason for wanting him dead, but the police thought his wife, Nikki, was the #1 suspect. Now, eight years later, Nikki hires P.I. Kinsey Millhone to seek out the real killer. She's 32, twice divorced, no kids, an ex-cop & a loner who knows how to work the system.

A la Recherche du Temps Perdu, Pts. 1 & 2, set. unabr. ed. Marcel Proust. Read by Andre Dussollier. 8 cass. (FRE.). 1992. 69.95 (1600-01); 39.95 Olivia & Hill.
"Longtemps, je me suis couche de bonne heure." With this famous sentence noted actor Andre Dussollier launches into the haunting reading of the unabridged text of "Du cote de chez Swann" & "Combray.".

À L'Aventure: An Introduction to French Language & Francophone Cultures. Anne C. Cummings & Evelyne Charvier-Berman. (ENG.). (C). 1998. 32.95 (978-0-471-17488-2(2), JWiley) Wiley US.

A. Lincoln: A Biography. Ronald C. White, Jr. Read by Bill Weideman. (Playaway Adult Nonfiction Ser.). (ENG.). 2009. 69.99 (978-1-60812-699-6(4)) Find a World.

A. Lincoln: A Biography. unabr. ed. Ronald C. White, Jr. Read by Bill Weideman. (Running Time: 28 hrs.). 2009. 44.97 (978-1-4233-7727-6(3), 9781423377276, BADLE); 44.97 (978-1-4233-7725-2(7), 9781423377252, Brlnc Audio MP3 Lib); 29.99 (978-1-4233-7724-5(9), 9781423377245, Brilliance MP3); 29.99 (978-1-4233-7726-9(5), 9781423377269, BAD); audio compact disk 99.99 (978-1-4233-7723-8(0), 9781423377238, BriAudCD Unabrid); audio compact disk 49.99 (978-1-4233-7722-1(2), 9781423377221, Bril Audio CD Unabri) Brilliance Audio.

A l'Ombre des Jeunes Filles en Fleurs, Pt. 1. Marcel Proust. Read by Lambert Wilson. 4 cass. (FRE.). 1995. 39.95 (1714-TH) Olivia & Hill.
This second volume of A la recherche du temps perdu won Proust the Prix Goncourt (1920).

A l'Ombre des Jeunes Filles en Fleurs, Pt. 2. Marcel Proust. Read by Lambert Wilson. 4 cass. (FRE.). 1995. 39.95 (1715-TH) Olivia & Hill.

A l'Ombre des Jeunes Filles en Fleurs, Pt. 3. Marcel Proust. Read by Lambert Wilson. 4 cass. (FRE.). 1995. 39.95 (1769-TH) Olivia & Hill.

A l'Ombre des Jeunes Filles en Fleurs, Pt. 4. Marcel Proust. Read by Lambert Wilson. 4 cass. (FRE.). 1995. 39.95 (1770-TH) Olivia & Hill.

A l'Ombre des Jeunes Filles en Fleurs, Pts. 1-2. Marcel Proust. Read by Lambert Wilson. 8 cass. (FRE.). 1995. 69.95 (1714/5-TH) Olivia & Hill.

A l'Ombre des Jeunes Filles en Fleurs, Pts. 3-4. Marcel Proust. Read by Lambert Wilson. 8 cass. (FRE.). 1995. 69.95 (1769/70-TH) Olivia & Hill.

A. M. Yoga Meditations Vol. 1: Guided Meditations to Start Your Day with Calm, Clarity & Vitality. Gael Chiarella. 1 CD. (Running Time: 1 hrs.). 2001. audio compact disk 12.00 (93-0213) Relaxtn Co.
Frame your day with healing music and sound. Start your day with calm, clarity and vitality. Each CD consists of four 15-minute programs. Offers programs for energizing, creativity, chakra balance and physical balance.

A. Meditation Manuscripts B. the Sub-conscious Mind: Volume 23, Vol. 23. Speeches. Bhagat Singh Thind. (Running Time: 60 mins.). (ENG., 2003. audio compact disk 12.00 (978-1-932630-24-4(4)) Pub: Dr Bhagat Sin. Dist(s): Baker Taylor

A Orillas del Río Piedra Me Senté y Lloré. Paulo Coelho. 2 cass. (Running Time: 2 hrs.).Tr. of By the River Piedra I Sat down & Wept. (SPA.). 2001. 20.00 (978-970-05-1296-9(7)) Pub: Grijalbo Edit MEX. Dist(s): Lectorum Pubns
Travel with two lovers on a spirtual search and discover the profound secrets of love and life in this new magically written novel by the acclaimed author of El Alquimista.

A. P. Hill: Lee's Forgotten General. unabr. ed. William Woods Hassler. Narrated by George Wilson. 7 cass. (Running Time: 9 hrs. 15 mins.). 1999. 60.00 (978-1-55690-769-2(9), 92412E7) Recorded Bks.
Biography of the Confederacy's long neglected general, A.P. Hill, veteran of the battles of Second Manassas, Chancellorsville, Gettysburg, the Wilderness & Petersburg among others & one of Robert E. Lee's most valued commanders.

A. Progress Thru Ego-Centered - B. Planned Chaos: Volume 10, Vol. 10. Speeches. As told by Bhagat Singh Thind. Clark Walker. (Running Time: 60 mins.). (ENG., 2003. audio compact disk 12.00 (978-1-932630-11-4(2)) Pub: Dr Bhagat Sin. Dist(s): Baker Taylor

A. R. Ammons: Collected Poems, 1951-1971. unabr. ed. Read by A. R. Ammons. 1 cass. (Running Time: 29 min.). 1985. 10.00 New Letters.
National Book Award winning poet reads from "Lake Effect Country" & "A Coast of Trees.".

***A-Rod.** abr. ed. Selena Roberts. Read by L. J. Ganser. (ENG.). 2009. (978-0-06-193891-7(2), Harper Audio); (978-0-06-195168-8(4), Harper Audio) HarperCollins Pubs.

A-Rod: The Many Lives of Alex Rodriguez. Selena Roberts. Read by L. J. Ganser. (ENG.). 2009. 59.99 (978-1-61574-925-6(X)) Find a World.

A-Rod: The Many Lives of Alex Rodriguez. abr. ed. Selena Roberts. Read by L. J. Ganser. 2009. audio compact disk 29.99 (978-0-06-194089-7(5), Harper Audio) HarperCollins Pubs.

A. T. C. Communications of a Typical V. F. R. Cross Country Flight. Aviation Language School, Inc. Staff. 1 cass. (Running Time: 1 hr. 30 mins.). 1997. pap. bk. 40.00 (978-0-941456-17-3(X)) Aviation Lang Sch.

A to Z Mysteries: Books A to C. Ron Roy. Read by David Pittu. 2 CDs. (Running Time: 2 hrs. 29 mins.). (A to Z Mysteries Ser.: Nos. 1-3). (J). (gr. k-3). 2004. audio compact disk 24.00 (978-0-8072-1774-0(3), Listening Lib) Random Audio Pubg.

A to Z Mysteries: Books H to J. unabr. ed. Ron Roy. Read by David Pittu. 3 CDs. (Running Time: 2 hrs. 45 mins.). (A to Z Mysteries Ser.: Nos. 8-10). (J). (gr. 1-3). 2007. audio compact disk 24.00 (978-0-7393-5140-6(0), Listening Lib) Pub: Random Audio Pubg. Dist(s): Random

A to Z Mysteries Vol. 1: Books A to H. Ron Roy. 2 cass. (Running Time: 2 hrs. 29 mins.). (A to Z Mysteries Ser.: Nos. 1-8). (J). (gr. k-3). 2004. 23.00 (978-0-8072-1632-3(1), Listening Lib) Pub: Random Audio Pubg. Dist(s): Random

A to Z Mysteries Vol. 2: Books D to G. unabr. ed. Ron Roy. 2 cass. (Running Time: 3 hrs. 15 mins.). (A to Z Mysteries Ser.: Nos. 4-7). (J). 2003. 23.00 (978-0-8072-1635-4(6), Listening Lib) Pub: Random Audio Pubg. Dist(s): Random

A to Z Mysteries Vol. 2: D-G. unabr. ed. Prod. by Listening Library Staff. 3 CDs. (Running Time: 3 hrs. 15 mins.). 2005. audio compact disk 30.00 (978-0-307-20735-7(8), Listening Lib) Pub: Random Audio Pubg. Dist(s): Random

An Asterisk (*) at the beginning of an entry indicates that the title is appearing for the first time.

A to Z, the Animals & Me. Jill Gallina & Michael Gallina. 1 cass. (Running Time: 1 hr.). (J). (ps). 2001. pap. bk. 10.95 (KIM 9136C); pap. bk. 14.95 (KIM 9136CD); pap. bk. 11.95 (KIM 9136) Kimbo Educ.
Teach kids the alphabet in a creative way. Each letter is represented by an animal & reinforced with a movement activity, such as the Aerobic Armadillo, the Skiing Sheep & the Weight-lifting Walrus. Includes lyric sheet & activity guide.

¡A Trabajar! Spanish for Construction Classroom Set. Tara Bradley Williams. (SPA.). 2007. per. 34.95 (978-1-934467-08-4(1)) Pronto Spanish.

¡A Trabajar! Spanish for Educators Classroom Set. Tara Bradley Williams. (SPA.). 2007. per. 34.95 (978-1-934467-09-1(X)) Pronto Spanish.

¡A Trabajar! Spanish for Food Service Classroom Set. Tara Bradley Williams. (SPA.). 2007. per. 34.95 (978-1-934467-10-7(3)) Pronto Spanish.

¡A Trabajar! Spanish for Health Care Classroom Set. Tara Bradley Williams. (SPA.). 2007. per. 34.95 (978-1-934467-11-4(1)) Pronto Spanish.

¡A Trabajar! Spanish for Hospitality Classroom Set. Tara Bradley Williams. (SPA.). 2007. per. 34.95 (978-1-934467-12-1(X)) Pronto Spanish.

¡A Trabajar! Spanish for Human Resources Classroom Set. Tara Bradley Williams. (SPA.). 2007. per. 34.95 (978-1-934467-13-8(8)) Pronto Spanish.

¡A Trabajar! Classroom Set. Compiled by Tara Bradley Williams. Pronto Spanish. (ENG & SPA.). 2007. per. 32.95 (978-1-934467-26-8(X)) Pronto Spanish.

A-U-M. George King. 2005. audio compact disk 12.50 (978-0-937249-24-6(6)) Aetherius Soc.

A. W. ESL Demo Cassette. Addison-Wesley Publishing Staff. Perf. by Addison-Wesley Publishing Staff. 1 cass. (Running Time: 40 mins.). (J). (gr. k-5). 1989. 12.95 (978-0-201-94462-4(6)) Longman.
A selection of songs & stories from each level of the A-W ESL series.

A-ware: Multilingual Simulation Software for Anesthesiology. (GER, ENG & FRE.). (C). 2001. stu. ed. 197.00 (978-3-540-14866-1(3)) Spri.

A-Z of Classical Music. Hugh Griffith. 2 CDs. (Running Time: 2 hrs. 30 min.). 2003. pap. bk. (978-962-634-210-7(2), Naxos AudioBooks) Naxos.
Details the lives of all the great composers as well as many less known, but equally fascinating, musical masters.

A-Z of Classical Music. 2nd exp. ed. 2 CDs. (Running Time: 2 hrs. 30 min.). 2001. pap. bk. 12.99 (978-1-930838-01-7(8), Naxos AudioBooks) Naxos.
Includes an extensive glossary of Musical Terms plus a unique guide to classical music used in acclaimed films.

A-Z of Opera. 2 CDs. (Running Time: 2 hrs. 30 min.). 2001. pap. bk. 12.99 (978-1-930838-02-4(6)) Naxos.
Features plot synopses, background details and cast lists for hundreds of operas including well known standards and opera rarities.

A-Z of Opera. 2 CDs. (Running Time: 2 hrs. 30 min.). 2003. pap. bk. (978-962-634-710-2(4), Naxos AudioBooks) Naxos.

A-Z Sort of Thing. abr. ed. Lily Savage. Read by Lily Savage. 1 cass. (Running Time: 1 hr.). 1998. pap. bk. (978-1-84032-185-2(7), HoddrStoughton) Hodder General GBR.
From her childhood on the streets of Birkenhead, through her unconventional education.

AA Classic Issues. 3 cass. (Running Time: 90 mins. per cass.). Incl. AA Classic Issues: More Articles from Classic Issues. 1986.; AA Classic Issues: Selected Articles from Classic Issues. 1986.; 1986. 5.50 Hazelden.
Selected articles from the "A.A. Grapevine," the monthly, international journal of Alcoholics Anonymous.

AA Classic Issues: More Articles from Classic Issues see AA Classic Issues

AA Classic Issues: Selected Articles from Classic Issues see AA Classic Issues

AA Classical Issues: Not for Newcomers Only. A. A. Staff. 1 cass. (Running Time: 90 min.). 1986. 5.50 (2950) Hazelden.

AAA+ Credit Repair Made Easy-2009: How to Restore Your AAA+ Credit Rating! Speeches. Mervin L. Evans. 1-Audio CD. (Running Time: 1 Hours). 2004. 14.99 (978-0-914391-35-7(6)) Comm People Pr.

AACE's Professional Practice Guide to Earned Value. Ed. by George R. Stumpp. 1999. bk. 43.50 (978-1-885517-18-0(1)) AACE Intl.

Aardvark Is Ready for War. abr. ed. James Blinn. Read by Dorian Harwood. (ENG.). 2006. 9.99 (978-1-59483-836-1(4)) Pub: Hachet Audio. Dist(s): HachBkGrp

Aardvark Who Wasn't Sure: And the Gorilla Who Wanted to Grow Up. Read by Maureen Lipman. (Running Time: 7680 sec.). (J). 2001. audio compact disk 21.95 (978-0-7540-6737-5(8)) AudioGo GBR.

Aaron & Me. Short Stories. 1 cass. (Running Time: 45 min.). 1999. 10.00 Esstee Audios.
Dreams come to a man in which he is a friend of Alexander Hamilton. As a result, he becomes an enemy of Aaron Burr. The dreams invade his real life with tragic results. Taken from a Thurber short story.

Aaron Copland & Virgil Thomson: Sacred & Secular Choral Music. Perf. by Gloriae Dei Cantores. 1 CD. (Running Time: 90 min.). 2000. audio compact disk 16.95 (978-1-55725-274-6(2), GDCD029) Paraclete MA.

Aaron's Rod. unabr. ed. D. H. Lawrence. Read by Flo Gibson. 8 cass. (Running Time: 11 hrs. 30 min.). 1994. 26.95 (978-1-55685-592-4(3)) Audio Bk Con.
In this original & uncensored version Aaron abandons his wife & children to travel with his flute to London & through Italy where he observes & explores relationships between men & women.

Aaron's Rod. unabr. collector's ed. D. H. Lawrence. Read by Richard Brown. 8 cass. (Running Time: 12 hrs.). 1987. 64.00 (978-0-7366-1233-3(5), 2151) Books on Tape.
Semi-autobiographical novel of a working-class Englishman who leaves his home & family to become a musician.

AB. unabr. ed. 1 CD. (Running Time: 46 mins.). (J). 2001. audio compact disk 13.00 (978-0-9662994-2-7(6)) Adven Meadow.
Educational sing along CD helps little ones to learn the alphabet.

AB Variant GM2-Gangliosidosis - A Bibliography & Dictionary for Physicians, Patients, & Genome Researchers. Compiled by Icon Group International, Inc. Staff. 2007. ring bd. 28.95 (978-0-497-11225-7(6)) Icon Grp.

Abandon. unabr. ed. Blake Crouch. Read by Luke Daniels. (Running Time: 12 hrs.). 2009. 24.99 (978-1-4233-9471-6(2), 9781423394716, Brilliance MP3); 39.97 (978-1-4233-9472-3(0), 9781423394723, Brlnc Audio MP3 Lib); 24.99 (978-1-4233-9473-0(9), 9781423394730, BAD); 39.97 (978-1-4233-9474-7(7), 9781423394747, BADLE); audio compact disk 36.99 (978-1-4233-9469-3(0), 9781423394693, Bril Audio CD Unabri); audio compact disk 97.97 (978-1-4233-9470-9(4), 9781423394709, BriAudCD Unabrid) Brilliance Audio.

Abandon Ship! The Saga of the U. S. S. Indianapolis, the Navy's Greatest Sea Disaster. Richard F. Newcomb. Afterword by Peter Maas. Intro. by Peter Maas. Narrated by Richard M. Davidson. 8 cass. (Running Time: 10 hrs. 30 mins.). 2001. 74.00 (978-0-7887-8850-5(7), 96743) Recorded Bks.
As World War Ii was winding down, the U.S.S. Indianapolis was sunk by a Japanese submarine. Three hundred men went down with the ship and 900 more went into the shark-infested waters. When the wreckage was discovered, only 316 sailors still lived.

Abandoned. Jennie L. Hansen. 3 cass. 2004. 14.95 (978-1-59156-071-5(3)) Covenant Comms.

Abandoned. unabr. ed. Cody McFadyen. Read by Joyce Bean. (Running Time: 12 hrs.). (Smoky Barrett Ser.: No. 4). 2009. 24.99 (978-1-4418-0417-4(X), 9781441804174, Brilliance MP3); 39.97 (978-1-4418-0418-1(8), 9781441804181, Brlnc Audio MP3 Lib); 24.99 (978-1-4418-0419-8(6), 9781441804198, BAD); 39.97 (978-1-4418-0420-4(X), 9781441804204, BADLE); audio compact disk 34.99 (978-1-4418-0265-1(7), 9781441802651, Bril Audio CD Unabri); audio compact disk 87.97 (978-1-4418-0266-8(5), 9781441802668, BriAudCD Unabrid) Brilliance Audio.

Abandoned Outlaw. unabr. ed. Max Brand. Read by William Dufris. 5 cass. (Running Time: 7 hrs. 30 min.). (Sagebrush Western Ser.). (J). 2005. 54.95 (978-1-57490-297-6(0)) Pub: ISIS Lrg Prnt GBR. Dist(s): Ulverscroft US

Abandoning the Child. James Hillman. Read by James Hillman. 2 cass. (Running Time: 2 hrs.). 1992. pap. bk. 17.95 (978-1-879816-06-0(7)) Pub: Spring Audio. Dist(s): Daimon Verlag
Who is this "inner child" that now demands attention in all the schools of therapy and in the recovery movement? And in what lost nursery of the soul do we dream the dream of childhood? Hillman tries to answer these questions in an elegant and remarkable analysis of the child myth as it misbehaves today.

Abandonment to Divine Providence. Jean-Pierre De Causade. Read by Mark Taheny. 4 cass. 19.95 Set. (908-C) Ignatius Pr.
Spiritual classic.

***Abandonment to Divine Providence.** Jean-Pierre de Caussade. Read by Tedd Lovett. Patrick Reis. (ENG.). 2009. audio compact disk 17.95 (978-1-936231-00-3(X)) Cath Audio.

Abandonment to Divine Providence. Jean-Pierre de Caussade. 4 CDs. (Running Time: 4 hrs.). 2003. audio compact disk 26.95 (978-1-57058-512-8(1)) St Joseph Communs.
Although recognized as a work of profound spirituality, Abandonment to Divine Providence is a book that gifted 18th century cleric Jean-Pierre de Caussade did not even know he had written! It was actually compiled and published over a century after his death by Visitation nuns who, fortunately for the world, saved his writings on how to determine God's Will for your life. Written to help those who despair of ever becoming holy, Abandonment to Divine Providence shows how God is to be found amidst the simplest of daily activities-but especially through total surrender to His Will. Newly re-mastered on four CDs you can experience timeless lessons of practical spiritual counsel on conformity to the Will of God, interior direction, overcoming temptations and trials, prayer and much more. A treasure of inspiration and direction that you'll listen to again and again as steady guide for your journey of faith.

Abandonment to Joy. Swami Amar Jyoti. 1 cass. 1984. 9.95 (M-49) Truth Consciousness.
The way to true abandonment, not degradation. Practical & intense life in religion.

Abarat. Clive Barker. audio compact disk (978-1-4025-8302-5(8)) Recorded Bks.

***Abarat.** abr. ed. Clive Barker. Read by Richard Ferrone. (ENG.). 2005. (978-0-06-083472-2(2)); (978-0-06-083471-5(4)) HarperCollins Pubs.

Abarat. unabr. abr. ed. Clive Barker. Read by Richard Ferrone. 8 cass. (Running Time: 12 hrs.). (J). (gr. 9-12). 2002. 39.95 (978-0-06-051075-6(7)) HarperCollins Pubs.

***Abarat: Days of Magic, Nights of War.** unabr. ed. Clive Barker. Read by Richard Ferrone. (ENG.). 2005. (978-0-06-082058-9(6)); (978-0-06-082059-6(4)) HarperCollins Pubs.

Abba Eban Reads from Psalms & Ecclesiastes. Read by Abba Eban. 1 CD. (Running Time: 56 mins.). (HEB.). 2006. audio compact disk 16.95 (978-1-57970-377-6(1), CHE001D, Audio-For) J Norton Pubs.
Read in English and Hebrew. "Ambassador Eban reads the passages in English and Hebrew. A knowledge of the latter language isn't necessary for appreciation of these portions, because his voice is so lyrical that it takes the form of music. The English sections are gems and are read with rare insight." - Variety.

Abba Father. Contrib. by Carey Landry. 2005. audio compact disk 17.00 (978-5-559-49086-1(5)) OR Catholic.

Abba Padre. unabr. ed. 2000. audio compact disk 11.99 (978-0-8297-2761-6(2)) Zondervan.

Abba Padre. unabr. ed. Luis Mellado & Zondervan Publishing Staff. (SPA.). 2000. 7.99 (978-0-8297-2760-9(4)) Pub: Vida Pubs. Dist(s): Zondervan

***Abba's Child: The Cry of the Heart for Intimate Belonging.** unabr. ed. Brennan Manning. Narrated by Dan Cashman. (ENG.). 2005. 14.98 (978-1-59644-128-6(3), Hovel Audio) christianaud.

Abba's Child: The Cry of the Heart for Intimate Belonging. unabr. ed. Brennan Manning. Narrated by Dan Cashman. 1 MP3 CD. (Running Time: 6 hrs. 12 mins. 0 sec.). (ENG.). 2005. lp 19.98 (978-1-59644-129-3(1), Hovel Audio); audio compact disk 23.98 (978-1-59644-130-9(5), Hovel Audio) christianaud.
Is an imposter robbing you of God's love? Many Christians have bought into the lie that we are worthy of God's love only when our lives are going well. If our families are happy or our jobs are meaningful, life is a success. But when life begins to fall through the cracks and embarrassing sins threaten to reveal our less-than-perfect identity, we scramble to keep up a good front to present to the world- and God. We cower and hide until we can rearrange the mask of perfection and look good again. Sadly, it is then that we wonder why we lack intimate relationships and a passionate faith. Yes all this time God is calling us to take the mask off and come openly to Him. God longs for us to know in the depth of our being that He loves us and accepts us as we are. When we are true selves, we can finally claim our identity as God's child-Abba's child-and experience His pleasure in who we are. Brennan Manning encourages readers to let go of the imposter lifestyle and freely accept our belovedness as a child of the heavenly Father. In Him there is life, our passion is rekindled, and our union with Him is His greatest pleasure.

Abba's Child - DELETE: The Cry of the Heart for the Intimate Belonging. unabr. ed. Brennan Manning. Read by Dan Cashman. 5 CD's. (Running Time: 6 hours and 12 minutes). (ENG.). 2005. 14.98 (978-1-59644-131-6(3)) christianaud.
Is an imposter robbing you of God?s love? Many Christians have bought into the lie that we are worthy of God?s love only when our lives are going well. If our families are happy or our jobs are meaningful, life is a success. But when life begins to fall through the cracks and embarrassing sins threaten to reveal our less-than-perfect identity, we scramble to keep up a good front to present to the world- and God. We cower and hide until we can rearrange the mask of perfection and look good again. Sadly, it is then that we wonder why we lack intimate relationships and a passionate faith. Yes all this time God is calling us to take the mask off and come openly to Him. God longs for us to know in the depth of our being that He loves us and accepts us as we are. When we are true selves, we can finally claim our identity as God?s child-Abba?s child-and experience His pleasure in who we are. Brennan Manning encourages readers to let go of the imposter lifestyle and freely accept our belovedness as a child of the heavenly Father. In Him there is life, our passion is rekindled, and our union with Him is His greatest pleasure.

Abbe Pierre. 1 cass. (Running Time: 45 min.). (FRE.). 1995. 16.95 (1539-RF) Olivia & Hill.
Priest, champion of the homeless. Radio interview with Jacques Chancel.

Abbey Actors Read from the Legends of the Fianna. unabr. ed. Poems. 1 cass. (Running Time: 60 min.). (Abbey Theatre Reads Ser.). 1988. 114.95 (978-0-88432-278-8(5), ABB 005) J Norton Pubs.
More poetry & prose readings including a chapter from the ancient saga of Diarmuid & Grainne.

Abbey Actors Read Poetry, Stories, & Songs in Irish. unabr. ed. 1 cass. (Running Time: 1 hr. 08 min.). (Abbey Theatre Reads Ser.). 1988. 14.95 (978-0-88432-274-0(2), ABB 003) J Norton Pubs.
Features poetry, songs, & stories which are read & sung in Irish.

Abbey Grange see Return of Sherlock Holmes

Abbey Grange. 1981. (S-36) Jimcin Record.
Two more classic Sherlock Holmes mysteries.

Abbey Grange. Arthur Conan Doyle. 1 cass. (Running Time: 1 hr. 30 min.). 1998. 7.95 (S-76) Jimcin Record.
Holmes faces a dilemma of conscience.

Abbey Reads: Kavanagh Back to Keats. Perf. by Abbey Theatre Company Staff. 1 cass. (Running Time: 60 mins.). (IRI.). 2001. 14.95 (ABB004) J Norton Pubs.
Barry McGovern's reading of Edward Lear's "The Dong with the Long Nose" & Brendan Behan's short story "The Confirmation Suit" are some of the highlights.

Abbey Reads: Poetry, Stories & Songs in Irish. Perf. by Abbey Theatre Company Staff. 1 cass. (Running Time: 60 mins.). (IRI.). 2001. 14.95 (ABB003) J Norton Pubs.
Poetry ranges from works of modern writers to old poems which have survived through the ages.

Abbey Reads: The Legends of Fianna. Perf. by Abbey Theatre Company Staff. 1 cass. (Running Time: 60 mins.). (IRI.). 2001. 14.95 (ABB005) J Norton Pubs.
More poetry & prose including the reading of a chapter from the ancient sage of Diarmuid & Grainne.

Abbey Theatre Reads: Plus the Confirmation Suit by Brendan Behan: Poetry, Kavanagh back to Keats. Poems. Patrick Kavanagh et al. Read by Barry McGovern et al. Prod. by Kathleen Barrington. Music by Jim Doherty. 1 CD. (Running Time: 58 mins.). (Abbey Theatre Reads Ser.). 2006. audio compact disk 15.95 (978-1-57970-376-9(3), ABB004D, Audio-For) J Norton Pubs.
Abbey Theatre actors read poems by Kavanagh, Yeats, MacNeice, Spender, burns, Tennyson, Campbell, Betjeman, Keats, Auden, De La Mare, Lear, Mangan, DeVere, Byron, Belloc, Hopkins, Wordsworth, and Thomas. Also read is Brendan Behan's short story, "The Confirmation Suit.".

Abbey's Road: Take the Other. unabr. collector's ed. Edward Abbey. Read by Paul Shay. 6 cass. (Running Time: 9 hrs.). 1990. 48.00 (978-0-7366-1814-4(7), 2650) Books on Tape.
A journey with the celebrated environmentalist to those parts of the world he loved & feared for. Timely & relevant.

Abbott & Costello. 1 cass. (Running Time: 60 min.). (Old Time Radio Classic Singles Ser.). 1997. 4.95 (978-1-57816-085-3(5), AC101) Audio File.
Their best comedy routines including "Who's on First," "Income Tax Refund," "Sanitorium Skit," "Vitamin Routine," "The Salesman." Plus Escape: "Leinengen vs. the Ants.".

Abbott & Costello. 1 cass. (Running Time: 1 hr.). 1999. 4.99 (978-1-57019-235-7(9), 4999); audio compact disk 6.99 (978-1-57019-236-4(7), 3999D) Radio Spirits.
Side A) Costello confides in Abbott about a gal he calls his pilot light... she's his old flame that has stayed it! In true Abbott & Costello form, a hilarious misunderstanding results. Entertainment at its best! Side B) Costello lists all the girls he wants to kiss. Abbott believes he should stop worrying about girls & get a job. A telegram request from Joe Di Maggio just happens to arrive which leads Costello into a new career. Can you guess which profession? Includes everyone's favorite comedy routing, "Who's on first?".

Abbott & Costello. Read by Bud Abbott & Lou Costello. 8 cass. (Running Time: 12 hrs.). 2002. 39.98 (978-1-57019-532-7(3), 4466) Radio Spirits.

Abbott & Costello. Read by Bud Abbott & Lou Costello. 4 vols. (Running Time: 6 hrs.). (Smithsonian Legendary Performers Ser.). 2003. bk. 24.98 (978-1-57019-608-9(7), OTR50424) Pub: Radio Spirits. Dist(s): AudioGO

Abbott & Costello. Old Radio Staff. 1995. audio compact disk (978-0-88676-747-1(4)) Metacom Inc.

Abbott & Costello. Radio Spirits Staff. Read by Bud Abbott. 12 CDs. (Running Time: 12 hrs.). 2005. audio compact disk 39.98 (978-1-57019-531-0(5), 4467) Radio Spirits.

Abbott & Costello: Buck Privates. 1 cass. (Running Time: 60 min.). 1941. 7.95 (CC-5000) Natl Recrd Co.
Abbott & Costello portray characters in an army camp. Also included are popular skits: "Shooting Craps," "Money Loaning," & "You Can Play the Radio".

Abbott & Costello: Costello Buys Horse, Peanut Butter & Costello in School Play. unabr. ed. Perf. by Bud Abbott et al. 1 cass. (Running Time: 1 hr.). 6.98 (1600) Radio Spirits.

Abbott & Costello: Costello the Cowboy & Andrew Brothers & Andrew Sisters? unabr. ed. Perf. by Bud Abbott et al. 1 cass. (Running Time: 1 hr.). 2001. 6.98 (2001) Radio Spirits.

Abbott & Costello: Costello's Big Inheritance & Costello Wants to Learn to Swim. unabr. ed. Perf. by Bud Abbott & Lou Costello. 1 cass. (Running Time: 1 hrs.). 2001. 6.98 (1603) Radio Spirits.

Abbott & Costello: Costello's Math Abilities & Gold Mine Investment. unabr. ed. Perf. by Bud Abbott & Lou Costello. 1 cass. (Running Time: 1 hr.). 2001. 6.98 (1861) Radio Spirits.

Abbott & Costello: Elsa Maxwell & Lou Wants to Join the Circus. unabr. ed. Perf. by Lou Costello et al. 1 cass. (Running Time: 1 hr.). 2001. 6.98 (1841) Radio Spirits.

Abbott & Costello: Frank Sinatra & The Andrew Sisters. unabr. ed. Perf. by Bud Abbott et al. 1 cass. (Running Time: 1 hr.). 2001. 6.98 (1539) Radio Spirits.

Abbott & Costello: Harold Peary & Janet Blair. unabr. ed. Perf. by Bud Abbott et al. 1 cass. (Running Time: 1 hr.). 2001. 6.98 (2151) Radio Spirits.

***Abbott & Costello: It's Time to Smile.** Perf. by Bud Abbott & Lou Costello. 2010. audio compact disk 18.95 (978-1-57019-953-0(1)) Radio Spirits.

Abbott & Costello: Lou Promises His Girlfriend a Job & Lou Has to Pay Income Tax. unabr. ed. Perf. by Lou Costello & Bud Abbott. 1 cass. (Running Time: 1 hr.). 2001. 6.98 (2491) Radio Spirits.

Abbott & Costello: Lou Replacing Joe DiMaggio! 1 cass. (Running Time: 1 hr.). 1945. 7.95 (CC8400) Natl Recrd Co.

In the first sketch Lou has been invited to join the N.Y. Yankees as a temporary replacement for the injured Joe DiMaggio. They go into a sports store to get some baseball equipment & run into a smart-alec salesman. The cast also includes Skinny Ennis. In the second sketch Charlie & his gang are selling "no-soap" stickers even though it is near Thanksgiving. Edgar Bergen is upset about this. He has Richard Widmark throw a scare into Charlie to get him to stop. Mortimer Snerd also has a skit where he's stuck in the steam bath.

Abbott & Costello: Marlene Dietrich & Merle Oberon. unabr. ed. Perf. by Lou Costello et al. 1 cass. (Running Time: 1 hr.). 2001. 6.98 (2391) Radio Spirits.

Abbott & Costello: Marriage Bureau & Looking for a Job. unabr. ed. Perf. by Bud Abbott & Lou Costello. 1 cass. (Running Time: 1 hr.). 2001. 6.98 (2271) Radio Spirits.

Abbott & Costello: Masters of Comedy. Perf. by Bud Abbott & Lou Costello. 2009. audio compact disk 31.95 (978-1-57019-882-3(9)) Radio Spirits.

Abbott & Costello: Mrs. Niles Gives Boys Job & Costello Has 24 Hours to Raise Rent. unabr. ed. Perf. by Bud Abbott et al. 1 cass. (Running Time: 1 hrs.). 2001. 6.98 (1602) Radio Spirits.

Abbott & Costello: Sam Shovel: Case of the Russian Diplomat & Case of the Curbstone Murder. unabr. ed. Perf. by Bud Abbott & Lou Costello. 1 cass. (Running Time: 1 hr.). 2001. 6.98 (2591) Radio Spirits.

Abbott & Costello: Their Best Comedy Routines. 1 cass. (Running Time: 60 min). 1987. 7.95 (CD-4736) Natl Recrd Co.

Comics Bud Abbott & Lou Costello in five of their routines, includes Peter Lorre & Mr. Kitzel. "Leinengen vs. the Ants" takes place on an isolated plantation in the Amazon jungle where an immense army of ravenous ants are closing in to eat them alive.

Abbott & Costello: Veronica Lake & Mrs. Beanbag vs. Costello. unabr. ed. Perf. by Bud Abbott et al. 1 cass. (Running Time: 1 hr.). 2001. 6.98 (2451) Radio Spirits.

Abbott & Costello: 1945 Christmas Show & Lou Buys a Beauty Shop. unabr. ed. Perf. by Lou Costello et al. 1 cass. (Running Time: 1 hr.). 6.98 (1601) Radio Spirits.

Abbott & Costello Show. Perf. by Alan Ladd. 1 CD. (Running Time: 1 hr.). (Old-Time Radio Blockbusters Ser.). 2002. audio compact disk 4.98 (978-1-57019-389-7(4), OTR7700) Pub: Radio Spirits. Dist(s): AudioGO

Incl. "Who's on First?".

Abbott & Costello Show. unabr. ed. Perf. by Marilyn Maxwell et al. 1 cass. (Running Time: 60 min.). Dramatization. 1994. 7.95 Norelco box. (CC-5010) Natl Recrd Co.

Marilyn Maxwell & Skinny Ennis: The boys go on a hunting trip. They meet the game warden who tells them of a mean mountain lion with a 1,000 dollar price on its head. They trap the lion in a cave, & then Lou Costello has to go in & bring out the lion's skin. Yeah! Camels, 1946. Lucille Ball & Mel Blanc: Bud & Lou go to a department store to get a pair of nylons (very hard to find during the war) for singer Connie Haines. The store has one pair on sale, & Lucille Ball gets them. The fun starts when they try to get the nylons from Lucille Ball. Abbott & Costello Extra: The boys do their famous "Moby Dick" routine. Camels, 1943.

Abbott & Costello Show: Heyaaaaabbott!! Perf. by Bud Abbott & Lou Costello. 6 cass. (Running Time: 9 hrs.). 2002. 34.98 (4687) Radio Spirits.

Abbott & Costello Show: Who's on First & Alan Ladd. Perf. by Bud Abbott et al. 1 CD. (Running Time: 1 hr.). (Old-Time Radio Blockbusters Ser.). 2001. audio compact disk 4.98 (7700) Radio Spirits.

Abbott & Costello Show Vol. 1: Who's on First? Perf. by Bud Abbott & Lou Costello. 6 cass. (Running Time: 9 hrs.). 2001. 34.98 (4141) Radio Spirits.

Starting in vaudeville, their slapstick brand of comedy was perfect for radio and their broadcast antics quickly propelled them to national fame. These collections are filled with their classic verbal routines.

Abbott & Costello Show Vol. 2: The Lost Shows!, collector's ed. Perf. by Bud Abbott et al. 6 cass. (Running Time: 9 hrs.). 2000. bk. 34.98 (4197) Radio Spirits.

18 broadcasts.

***Abby Carnelia's One & Only Magical Power.** unabr. ed. David Pogue. Read by David Pogue. 1 MP3-CD. (Running Time: 6 hrs.). 2010. 14.99 (978-1-4418-6435-2(0), 9781441864352, Brilliance MP3); 19.99 (978-1-4418-6443-7(1), 9781441864437, BAD); 39.97 (978-1-4418-6436-9(9), 9781441864369, Brinc Audio MP3 Lib); 39.97 (978-1-4418-6444-4(X), 9781441864444, BADLE); audio compact disk 19.99 (978-1-4418-6427-7(X), 9781441864277, Bril Audio CD Unabri); audio compact disk 54.97 (978-1-4418-6428-4(8), 9781441864284, BriAudCD Unabrid) Brilliance Audio.

ABC: Rock, Rap, Tap & Learn. Lyrics by Jan Z. Olsen. Music by Emily Knapton. Emily Knapton. Voice by Cathy Fink & Marcy Marxer. Lyrics by Monica Hawpetoss. Music by Monica Hawpetoss. 2007. tchr. ed. 12.95 (978-1-891627-84-2(8)) Handwriting.

ABC (Active Basic Communication), Program 1. Pace International Research, Inc. Staff. 1 cass. (Running Time: 60 min.). (ABC Video Ser.). 1984. 4.00 (978-0-89209-327-4(7)) Pace Grp Intl.

ABC (Active Basic Communication), Program 2. Pace International Research, Inc. Staff. 1 cass. (Running Time: 60 min.). (ABC Video Ser.). 1984. 4.00 (978-0-89209-329-8(3)) Pace Grp Intl.

ABC (Active Basic Communication), Program 3. Pace International Research, Inc. Staff. (ABC Video Ser.). 1984. 4.00 (978-0-89209-331-1(5)) Pace Grp Intl.

ABC (Active Basic Communication), Program 4. Pace International Research, Inc. Staff. 1 cass. (Running Time: 60 min.). (ABC Video Ser.). 1984. 4.00 (978-0-89209-333-5(1)) Pace Grp Intl.

ABC (Active Basic Communication), Program 5. Pace International Research, Inc. Staff. 1 cass. (Running Time: 60 min.). (ABC Video Ser.). 1984. 4.00 (978-0-89209-335-9(8)) Pace Grp Intl.

ABC (Active Basic Communication), Program 6. Pace International Research, Inc. Staff. (ABC Video Ser.). 1984. 4.00 (978-0-89209-337-3(4)) Pace Grp Intl.

ABC (Active Basic Communication), Program 7. Pace International Research, Inc. Staff. 1 cass. (Running Time: 60 min.). (ABC Video Ser.). 1984. 4.00 (978-0-89209-339-7(0)) Pace Grp Intl.

ABC (Active Basic Communication), Program 8. Pace International Research, Inc. Staff. 1 cass. (Running Time: 60 min.). (ABC Video Ser.). 1984. 4.00 (978-0-89209-341-0(2)) Pace Grp Intl.

ABC (Active Basic Communication), Program 9. Pace International Research, Inc. Staff. (ABC Video Ser.). 1984. 4.00 (978-0-89209-343-4(9)) Pace Grp Intl.

ABC (Active Basic Communication), Program 10. Pace International Research, Inc. Staff. (ABC Video Ser.). 1984. 4.00 (978-0-89209-345-8(5)) Pace Grp Intl.

ABC (Active Basic Communication), Program 11. Pace International Research, Inc. Staff. (ABC Video Ser.). 1984. 4.00 (978-0-89209-347-2(1)) Pace Grp Intl.

ABC (Active Basic Communication), Program 12. Pace International Research, Inc. Staff. (ABC Video Ser.). 1984. 4.00 (978-0-89209-349-6(8)) Pace Grp Intl.

ABC (Active Basic Communication), Program 13. Pace International Research, Inc. Staff. (ABC Video Ser.). 1984. 4.00 (978-0-89209-376-2(5)) Pace Grp Intl.

ABC (Active Basic Communication), Program 14. Pace International Research, Inc. Staff. (ABC Video Ser.). 1984. 4.00 (978-0-89209-378-6(1)) Pace Grp Intl.

ABC (Active Basic Communication), Program 15. Pace International Research, Inc. Staff. (ABC Video Ser.). 1984. 4.00 (978-0-89209-380-9(3)) Pace Grp Intl.

ABC (Active Basic Communication), Program 16. Pace International Research, Inc. Staff. (ABC Video Ser.). 1984. 4.00 (978-0-89209-382-3(X)) Pace Grp Intl.

ABC Animales de la Biblia. (J). 1996. (978-1-57697-492-6(8)) Untd Bible Amrcas Svce.

ABC Chicka Boom with Me & Other Phonemic Awareness/Phonics Songs & Activities. John Archambault & David Plummer. Ed. by Kim Cernek. Illus. by Marek-Janci Design Staff. 1 cass. (ps). 2002. pap. bk. & tchr. ed. 13.99 (2360) Creat Teach Pr.

ABC Chicka Boom with Me & Other Phonemic Awareness/Phonics Songs & Activities, Grades Preschool-2. John Archambault & David Plummer. Ed. by Kim Cernek. Illus. by Marek-Janci Design Staff. (Happy Song Sing-Alongs Ser.: Vol. 2355). 1999. pap. bk. & tchr. ed. 13.99 (978-1-57471-636-8(0), 2355) Creat Teach Pr.

ABC de los Angeles: Como Comenzar a Conectarse, Trabajar y Sanarse con los Angeles see Angels 101: An Introduction to Connecting, Working, & Healing with the Angels

ABC Feelings. Alexandra Delis-Abrams. 1 cass. (Running Time: 1 hr.). (J). 1999. pap. bk. 17.95 (30422); 10.95 (30421) Courage-to-Change.

Using the alphabet to help children explore & communicate feelings.

ABC Feelings. abr. ed. Alexandra Delis-Abrams. Read by Alexandra Delis-Abrams. Read by Julia Blythe & Riley Marshall. Contrib. by Bob Mills. 1 cass. (Running Time: 1 hr.). (J). (ps-4). 1990. 10.95 (978-1-879889-01-9(3)) Adage Pubns.

A fun adventure into music & sound for children of all ages to explore 26 different feelings. "The communication tool of the 90s.".

ABC Feelings: A Learning/Coloring Book & Companion 60 Minute Audio Tape. 5th rev. ed. Alexandra Delis-Abrams. Ed. by Joan Follendore. Illus. by Shari Scott. 1 cass. (Running Time: 1 hr.). (ABC Feelings Ser.). (J). (ps-3). 1989. pap. bk. 16.95 (978-1-879889-04-0(8)) Adage Pubns.

ABC Murders. unabr. ed. Agatha Christie. Read by Hugh Fraser. 4 cass. (Running Time: 6 hrs.). (Hercule Poirot Mystery Ser.). 2003. 25.95 (978-1-57270-326-1(1)) Pub: Audio Partners. Dist(s): PerseuPGW

A serial killer is on the loose, murdering his victims in alphabetical order, leaving an ABC Railway Guide beside each body... and also playing a game with Hercule Poirot, alerting him in advance to the location of the murders, but Poirot always arrives too late. Intrigued by the psychopath's mind and methodology, Poirot travels the length and breadth of England - determined to track down the ruthless killer.

ABC Murders. unabr. ed. Agatha Christie. Narrated by Hugh Fraser. 5 CDs. (Running Time: 6 hrs.). (Hercule Poirot Mystery Ser.). (ENG.). 2003. audio compact disk 27.95 (978-1-57270-327-8(X)) Pub: AudioGO. Dist(s): Perseus Dist

There is a serial killer on the loose, murdering his victims in alphabetical order.

***ABC Murders: A BBC Full-Cast Radio Drama.** Agatha Christie. Narrated by Full Cast Production Staff & John Moffatt. 2 CDs. (Running Time: 1 hr. 30 mins. 0 sec.). (ENG., 2010. audio compact disk 24.95 (978-0-563-51050-5(1)) Pub: AudioGO. Dist(s): Perseus Dist

ABC of Hindi, Panjabi, Urdu. Harinder J. Dhillon. Read by Harinder J. Dhillon. 1 cass. (Running Time: 1 hr. 30 min.). 1986. pap. bk. 16.00; 16.00 H J Dhillon.

Based on a book of the same name. Intended to aid in developing listening skills & the correct pronunciation of the words.

ABC of Imagery (with Cassette) Akhter Ahsen. 1987. pap. bk. 19.95 (978-0-913412-33-6(3)) Brandon Hse.

ABC Personajes de la Biblia (Audiocasete para Ninos) (SPA.). (J). 2003. (978-1-931952-37-8(X)) Untd Bible Amrcas Svce.

***ABC Phonics: Using American Sign Language: Sing, Sign, & Read! (Book/CD Combo)** Nellie Edge. Illus. by Gaelan Kelly. Created by Sign2Me. (ENG.). (J). 2010. spiral bd. 23.95 (978-1-932354-27-0(1), Sign Two Me) Northlight Commns.

ABC Pronunciary: American English Pronunciation Dictionary. Perf. by Mary G. Iorio. Directed By Charles E. Beyer. 1 cass. (Running Time: 50 mins.). 1998. per. 34.95 (978-0-9665743-0-2(3), ABC-BAV, Vocalis) Vocalis Ltd.

ABC Pronunciary: American English Pronunciation Dictionary. Perf. by Mary G. Iorio & Charles E. Beyer. 1 cass. (Running Time: 49 min.). bk. 29.95 Vocalis Ltd.

ABC Pronunciary: American English Pronunciation Dictionary. Created by Vocalis Ltd. (Running Time: 3000 sec.). 2004. 34.95 (978-1-932653-16-8(3), ABC-DVD, Vocalis) Vocalis Ltd.

ABC Short Story Book. unabr. ed. Short Stories. Herman Melville et al. Read by Grover Gardner et al. 3 cass. (Running Time: 4 hrs. 30 min.). (gr. 8 up). 1991. 16.95 (978-1-55685-222-0(3)) Audio Bk Con.

"Bartleby the Scrivener," "The Truth about Piecroft," "The Angel Child," "The Journey" & "Phyllis & Rosamund.".

ABC Short Story Collection. Herman Melville et al. Narrated by Grover Gardner et al. (ENG.). 2009. audio compact disk 19.95 (978-1-60646-105-1(2)) Audio Bk Con.

ABC Songs. 1 cass. (Running Time: 1 hr.). (J). (ps-2). 2001. 10.95 (THR 107C) Kimbo Educ.

Teach children the sounds of each letter of the alphabet. Performed by children & adults & reinforced by an included coloring book. Catchy lyrics & melodies. Includes reproducible coloring book & lyrics.

ABC Songs. Kidzup Productions Staff. 1 CD. (Running Time: 1 hr.). (Learning Beat Ser.). (J). 2003. cass. & audio compact disk 13.99 (978-1-894677-39-4(0)) Pub: Kidzup Prodns. Dist(s): Penton Overseas

ABC Theater. 1 cass. (Running Time: 1 hr.). (J). 2000. 8.99 Kidzup Prodns.

ABC Theater. Kidzup Productions Staff. 1 cass. (Running Time: 1 hr.). (Interactive Learning Kits Ser.). (J). (gr. k-2). 2000. pap. bk. 8.99 (978-1-894281-45-4(4)) Pub: Kidzup CAN. Dist(s): Penton Overseas

Join Melody & meet an intriguing cast of characters ready to help you learn your ABC's.

ABC Theater. Kidzup Productions Staff. 1 cass. (Running Time: 1 hr.). (Interactive Learning Kits Ser.). (J). (gr. k-2). 2003. bk. 13.99 (978-1-894281-00-3(4)) Pub: Kidzup Prodns. Dist(s): Penton Overseas

ABCelebramos. 90.00 (978-0-7635-9691-0(4)) Rigby Educ.

ABC's & Much More Home Connection Kit. Created by Music. 2009. spiral bd. 19.95 (978-1-935572-07-7(5)) MMnM Bks.

ABC's & Much More Home Connection Kit - Bilingual. Created by Music. 2009. spiral bd. 19.95 (978-1-935572-08-4(3)) MMnM Bks.

ABC's & Much More Supplemental Curriculum Kit. 2nd rev. ed. Created by Music Movement and Magination. (ENG.). 2009. spiral bd. 179.95 (978-1-935572-02-2(4)) MMnM Bks.

ABC's & 123's. Prod. by Twin Sisters Productions Staff. 1 CD. (Running Time: 30 mins). (J). 2005. audio compact disk 4.99 (978-1-57583-801-4(X)) Twin Sisters.

Music makes learning essential skills fun and easy! Jumpstart or reinforce the learning of letters, numbers and basic counting with this new collection of learning songs! Perfect for home and travel, preschool and kindergarten, and childcare programs. BONUS! Includes 50 fun things to do with kids!.

ABCs for Lifestyle Wellness: Eliminate the Stress of Day-to-Day Living. abr. ed. Featuring Tim Connor. Interview with Angela Brown. Prod. by Les Lingle. 2 cass. (Running Time: 3 hrs.). (Words of Wellness Ser.: 311). 2000. 12.95 (978-1-930995-02-4(4), LLP311) Life Long Pubg.

Stop struggling with the day-to-day details of life. Learn handy tips for instant use that are easy to remember.

ABC's in Song. Francine M. O'Connor. Perf. by Monica Bonfe-Erikson. Music by Curtis Bell. 1 cass. (Running Time: 62 mins.). (J). (ps-3). 1996. 9.95 (978-0-89243-893-8(2)) Liguori Pubns.

Francine's short stories of faith, love, & God have entertained children of all ages for years in the "Liguorian" magazine. Now 15 of her most popular stories have been turned into songs on tape. Songs include: "Jesus - The Greatest Story Teller," "I Saw Jesus Today," & "A Thanksgiving Prayer".

ABC's of ABG's. Kristi E. Brookshire. Read by Kristi E. Brookshire. 1 cass. (Running Time: 30 mins.). 1998. pap. bk. 19.95 (978-0-9702296-0-1(7)) Know Quest Unltd.

Discusses the laboratory test, Arterial Blood Gasses. It explains each item within a set of these results.

ABCs of Bible Faith. Kenneth E. Hagin. 6 cass. 24.00 (59H) Faith Lib Pubns.

ABC's of Black History. unabr. ed. Olivia Ward. Read by Olivia Ward. Perf. by Lionel Hampton Orchestra. Ed. by Judith Keith. 1 cass. (Running Time: 45 min.). (J). (gr. k-6). 1974. bk. 9.95 incl. flashcards. Tandem Pr.

26 original songs describing African-Americans and their achievements. Lively jazz-rock music.

ABC's of Black History, Set. unabr. ed. Olivia Ward. Read by Olivia Ward. Perf. by Lionel Hampton Orchestra. Ed. by Judith Keith. 1 cass. (Running Time: 45 min.). (J). (gr. k-6). 1974. bk. 9.95 (978-0-913024-04-1(X)) Tandem Pr.

ABC's of Building a Business Team That Wins: The Invisible Code of Honor That Takes Ordinary People & Turns Them into a Championship Team. abr. ed. Blair Singer. Read by Jim Ward. (Running Time: 3 hrs.). (ENG.). 2006. 14.98 (978-1-59483-495-0(4)) Pub: Hachet Audio. Dist(s): HachBkGrp

ABC's of Building a Business Team That Wins: The Invisible Code of Honor That Takes Ordinary People & Turns Them into a Championship Team. abr. ed. Blair Singer. Read by Blair Singer. Read by Jim Ward. Frwd. by Robert T. Kiyosaki. 3 CDs. (Running Time: 3 hrs.). (ENG.). 2006. audio compact disk 24.98 (978-1-59483-075-4(4)) Pub: Hachet Audio. Dist(s): HachBkGrp

ABC's of Choosing a Good Husband: How to Find & Marry a Great Guy. Stephen Wood. 3 cass. (Running Time: 4 hrs. 30 min.). 2001. 12.95 (978-0-9658582-7-4(8)) Family Life Ctr.

ABC's of Credit Repair: Credit Repair Made Easy-the DVD. Mervin Evans & Lynette Bigelow. 5 CDs. (Running Time: 300 min.). 2006. audio compact disk 19.99 (978-0-914391-59-3(3)) Comm People Pr.

ABC's of Criminal Defense. Prod. by Advantage Legal Seminars. (ENG.). 2008. audio compact disk 177.00 (978-0-9795737-6-7(9)) Anzman Publg.

ABCs of Dating Safely. Virgil B. Smith. 1 cass. (Running Time: 15 min.). 1972. 5.95 (978-1-878507-05-1(2), 24C) Human Grwth Services.

Basic human needs; sensible advance preparation to keep emotions under control; the non-relationship of science to moral values.

ABCs of Eating Disorders. Gloria Arenson. 1 cass. (Running Time: 60 min.). 1988. 9.95 (978-0-9621942-0-7(4)) Brockart Bks.

Describes the symptoms, medical dangers, social & personal issues of Anorexia Nervosa, Bulimia & compulsive overeating. Suggests a treatment plan for effectively overcoming eating disorders.

ABC's of Financial Wellness: Winning Keys to Financial Wellness. abr. ed. Perf. by Angela Brown et al. 1 cass. (Running Time: 60 mins.). (Words of Wellness Ser.: Vol. 8). 2000. 14.95 (978-0-9673451-8-5(9), LLP308) Life Long Pubg.

How to go from broke to balance in your finances, includes planning, forecasting, budgeting, investing, educating yourself on the basics of money management.

ABC'S of Hydration & Breathing: Listen to Fitness? Scripts. Patty Kondub. Executive Producer Patty Kondub. 2002. audio compact disk 9.95 (978-0-9721802-0-7(6)) P Kondub.

A revolutionary idea in fitness! A spoken word CD or tape of tips, techniques & facts to breathe correctly and drink water for your better health! Informative, motivating and fun! Everyone can gain insight and be motivated toward a healthier lifestyle.

ABC's of Lifestyle Wellness Pt. 2: Eliminate the Stress of Day-to-Day Living. Illus. by Angela Brown. Voice by Tim Connor. Prod. by Les Lingle. 1 cass. (Running Time: 30 mins.). (Words of Wellness Ser.: Vol. 312). 2000. 12.95 (978-1-930995-03-1(2), LLP312) Life Long Pubg.

Stop struggling with the day-to-day details of life. With the ABC's of lifestyle wellness you'll learn handy tips for instant use that will bring results today.

ABCs of Liquor Law. 1996. bk. 99.00 (ACS-1037) PA Bar Inst.

The authors include attorneys from the agencies & private practioners who practice before the state agencies responsible for regulating the alcoholic beverage licensee.

ABCs of Love. E. J. Gold. 2 cass. (Running Time: 3 hrs.). 18.98 set. (TP145) Union Label.

Love in the shamanistic view is discussed: opening to the breath of love; using attention to mold the force of love; nondependency & risk of real love; difference between love, God, & lightning handlers.

ABCs of Numerology. unabr. ed. Jackie Suggs. Read by Jackie Suggs. 1 cass. (Running Time: 40 min.). (Life Improvement Programs Ser.). 1994. pap. bk. 9.95 (978-0-914295-47-1(0)) Top Mtn Pub.
A step-by-step mini-course leading to a better understanding of yourself through the use of Numerology.

ABC's of Property Management: What You Need to Know to Maximize Your Money Now. abr. ed. Ken McElroy. Read by Ken McElroy. 3 CDs. (Running Time: 3 hrs.). (ENG.). 2004. audio compact disk 24.98 (978-1-58621-735-8(6)) Pub: Hachet Audio. Dist(s): HachBkGrp

ABC's of Property Management: What You Need to Know to Maximize Your Money Now. abr. ed. Ken McElroy. Read by Dave Mallow. (Running Time: 3 hrs. 30 mins.). (Rich Dad's Advisors Ser.). (ENG.). 2008. 16.98 (978-1-60024-290-8(1)); audio compact disk 24.98 (978-1-60024-289-2(8)) Pub: Hachet Audio. Dist(s): HachBkGrp

ABCs of Reg D Funding: How to Find Private Investors. Speeches. Mervin Evans. 3 CDs. (Running Time: 180). 2006. audio compact disk 39.99 (978-0-914391-89-0(5)) Comm People Pr.

ABCs of Success... & If You Can Count to Five - Success Is Yours. Paul Stanyard. 1 cass. 12.50 Alpha Tape.

ABC's of Taxes: A Poor Man's Primer. Eulalia Cain. (J). 1978. 23.95 (978-0-89420-197-4(2), 481004) Natl Book.

ABC's of the Lessons of Love: For Children. Francine M. O'Connor. 1 cass. (Running Time: 22 min.). (Sermon on the Mount Ser.). (J). (ps-3). 1993. 9.95 (978-0-89243-570-8(4)) Liguori Pubns.
Francine M. O'Connor selected Matthew's Sermon on the Mount for two reasons. First, the entire Gospel of Matthew is essentially a teaching gospel. A more important persuasion, however, comes from the discovery that Matthew had already compiled Christ's teachings into one remarkable sermon. As children learn about Jesus, we hope they will have a bit of fun in the process.

ABCs of the Old Testament... for Children. Francine M. O'Connor. 1 cass. (Running Time: 19 min.). (J). (ps-3). 1993. pap. bk. 9.95 (978-0-89243-568-5(2)) Liguori Pubns.
Favorite Old Testament stories tailored to young imaginations. This audio introduces little ones to the stories of Creation, Noah, Abraham, Moses, & more.

ABC's of Vocal Harmony - Also Known as Music Reading & Hearing, Singing Harmony. unabr. ed. Howard Austin & Elisabeth Howard. 2 cass. (Running Time: 1 hr. 30 min. per cass.). (J). (gr. 7 up). 1989. pap. bk. 29.95 (978-0-934419-24-6(8), BTS-HD) Vocal Power Inc.
No prior music knowledge required. Music theory course with hundreds of ear-training exercises. Scales, intervals, 4 part chords, rhythm, & meter.

ABC's of Vocal Harmony, Music Reading, Sight-Singing, Singing Harmony, Ear-Training. unabr. ed. Howard Austin & Elisabeth Howard. Perf. by Howard Austin. 4 CDs. (Running Time: 1 hr. 30 min. per cass.). 1999. pap. bk. 39.95 (978-0-934419-35-2(3), BTS-HD-CD) Vocal Power Inc.

ABC's of Writing Winning Business Plans: How to Prepare a Business Plan That Others Will Want to Read - & Invest In. abr. unabr. ed. Garrett Sutton. Read by Garrett Sutton. Contrib. by Robert T. Kiyosaki. (Running Time: 6 hrs.). (ENG.). 2010. 16.98 (978-1-60024-881-8(0)) Pub: Hachet Audio. Dist(s): HachBkGrp

Abdominal Wall & Back. D. Hastings-Nield. (Anatomy Project). 1999. audio compact disk 199.95 (978-1-85070-860-5(6), Parthenon Pbng) Pub: CRC Pr. Dist(s): Taylor and Fran

Abduction. abr. ed. Mark Gimenez. Read by Buck Schirner. (Running Time: 6 hrs.). 2008. audio compact disk 14.99 (978-1-4233-4464-3(2), 9781423344643, BCD Value Price) Brilliance Audio.

Abduction. unabr. ed. Mark Gimenez. Read by Buck Schirner. (Running Time: 13 hrs.). 2007. 39.25 (978-1-4233-4462-9(6), 9781423344629, BADLE); 24.95 (978-1-4233-4461-2(8), 9781423344612, BAD); 87.25 (978-1-4233-4456-8(1), 9781423344568, BrilAudUnabridg); audio compact disk 36.95 (978-1-4233-4457-5(X), 9781423344575); audio compact disk 24.95 (978-1-4233-4459-9(6), 9781423344599, Brilliance MP3); audio compact disk 102.25 (978-1-4233-4458-2(8), 9781423344582, BriAudCD Unabrid); audio compact disk 39.25 (978-1-4233-4460-5(X), 9781423344605, Brinc Audio MP3 Lib) Brilliance Audio.

Abduction. unabr. ed. James Grippando. Narrated by Paul Hecht. 9 cass. (Running Time: 12 hrs. 45 mins.). 1998. 78.00 (978-0-7887-2172-4(0), 95468E7) Recorded Bks.
One candidate's granddaughter has been kidnapped & it is the job of the other, as U.S. attorney general, to find her.

Abduction. unabr. ed. James Grippando. Narrated by Paul Hecht. 9 cass. (Running Time: 12 hrs. 45 mins.). 2002. 42.95 (978-0-7887-8259-6(2), RD740) Recorded Bks.
In this fast-paced political thriller, bestselling author James Grippando exposes the ultimate election nightmare. Filled with electrifying suspense, The Abduction delivers the edge-of-your-seat excitement Grippando fans have come to expect. Allison Leahy is the U.S. attorney general and the highly touted Democratic presidential nominee. She is running neck and neck with her opponent, Lincoln Howe, a prestigious African-American and former general, when his granddaughter is kidnapped. Allison's motives for finding the girl become more personal than political, especially since her own baby daughter was taken years ago, and now it seems likely there is some connection between the two abductions. A former trial lawyer, Grippando is known for his insider's knowledge of Capitol Hill politics and the workings of government agencies. With his involving narrative style, Paul Hecht captures the fine sense of tension and authenticity Grippando so skillfully portrays.

Abduction. unabr. ed. Gordon Korman. Read by Andrew Rannels & Christie Moreau. (Kidnapped Ser.). (J). 2007. 34.99 (978-1-60252-686-0(9)) Find a World.

***Abduction Low Price.** abr. ed. James Grippando. Read by Allison Janney. (ENG.). 2004. (978-0-06-082400-6(X), Harper Audio); (978-0-06-082401-3(8), Harper Audio) HarperCollins Pubs.

Abductors. unabr. ed. Tom E. Neet. Read by Lynda Evans. 6 cass. (Running Time: 7 hrs.). 2001. 39.95 (978-1-55686-794-1(8)) Books in Motion.
Evidence points to Fotopolus, when heiress Abigail Witherspoon is abducted. Mel teams up with former KGB agent Lumpkin for her rescue.

Abe Lincoln: The War Years. Read by Raymond Massey. 1 cass. 10.00 (MC1009) Esstee Audios.
Radio drama.

Abe Lincoln & the Muddy Pig. abr. ed. Stephen Krensky. Narrated by Ed Sala. 1 cass. (Running Time: 15 mins.). (gr. k up). 2002. 10.00 (978-1-4025-1418-0(2)) Recorded Bks.
Young Abe Lincoln is all dressed up in his best suit and on his way to deliver an important speech. But as he walks along, he finds a pig stuck in a mudhole. Abe hates to see any animal suffer, but if he helps the pig, his clothes will get muddy. Based on an old folk tale.

Abe Lincoln Grows Up. Carl Sandburg. (J). (gr. 5-6). 2001. 8.00 (2653, Hewitt Homeschl Res) Hewitt Res Fnd.

Abe Lincoln in Illinois. Read by Raymond Massey. 1 cass. 10.00 (MC1008) Esstee Audios.
Radio drama.

Abe Lincoln in Song & Story. Ailene Goodman. 1 cass. (Running Time: 40 min.). (J). (gr. 4-12). 1989. bk. 14.98 (978-0-9620704-0-2(8), Eliza Records) A S Goodman.
Anecdotes, toe-tapping tunes, and authentic ballads from American history and folklore during the period of westward expansion, the growing-up years of Abraham Lincoln, his Presidency, and the Civil War.

Abe Lincoln Speaks. Alan Venable. (Step into History Ser.). 2005. pap. bk. 69.00 (978-1-4105-0670-2(3)); audio compact disk 18.95 (978-1-4105-0668-9(1)) D Johnston Inc.

Abecedario de los Animales. Alma Flor Ada.Tr. of Animal Alphabet. (SPA.). (J). 2001. 13.95 (978-1-58186-201-0(6)) Pub: Del Sol Pub. Dist(s): Lectorum Pubns

Abecedario de los Animales. Alma Flor Ada. Perf. by Suni Paz. 1 CD.Tr. of Animal Alphabet. (SPA.). 2001. audio compact disk 15.95 (978-1-58186-226-3(1)) Del Sol Pub.
A companion to Abecedario de los animales. Suni Paz has turned each of the alphabet poems into a delightful song. Includes an original Spanish ABC song.

Abeille see Coquerico

Abel & the Difficult Task. unabr. ed. 1 cass. (Running Time: 20 min.). Dramatization. (Magic Looking Glass Ser.). (J). (gr. 2-6). 1989. 9.95 (978-0-7810-0040-6(8), NIM-CW-129-5-C) NIMCO.
A Dutch folk tale.

Abelard's Loving Criticism. Thomas Merton. 1 cass. (Running Time: 54 min.). 1993. 8.95 (AA2621) Credence Commun.
Abelard insisted on critical thinking. He insisted that all Christians understand what they were being asked to believe.

Abel's Daughter. unabr. ed. Meg Hutchinson. Read by Marie McCarthy. 8 cass. (Running Time: 10 hrs. 35 min.). 1998. 83.95 Set. (978-1-85903-193-3(5)) Pub: Magna Story GBR. Dist(s): Ulverscroft US
Wrongfully arrested, due to the scheming of her jealous Aunt Annie, Phoebe Pardoe finds it hard to adjust to the harsh cruelty of life in the infamous Handsworth Prison. She has a guardian angel in the form of Sir William Dartmouth, but even when he engineers her release, Phoebe must struggle to make a living for herself in a man's world. Annie has not given up her own perverse quest for revenge, & Phoebe must rise above adversity to enable her to grasp happiness at last.

Abel's Island see Isla de Abel

Abel's Island, unabr. ed. William Steig. Narrated by George Guidall. 2 pieces. (Running Time: 2 hrs. 15 mins.). (gr. 3 up). 1995. 19.00 (978-0-7887-0143-6(6), 94368E7) Recorded Bks.
Abel, a fastidious Edwardian mouse whose inherited wealth ensures the leisurely comforts of the idle rich, is snatched up by a hurricane & deposited on a desert island in the middle of a river where he must come to grips with survival & loneliness.

***Aberation & the Handling Of.** L. Ron Hubbard. 2010. audio compact disk 15.00 (978-1-4031-7297-6(8)); audio compact disk 15.00 (978-1-4031-7295-2(1)); audio compact disk 15.00 (978-1-4031-7291-4(9)); audio compact disk 15.00 (978-1-4031-7288-4(9)); audio compact disk 15.00 (978-1-4031-7299-0(4)); audio compact disk 15.00 (978-1-4031-7300-3(1)); audio compact disk 15.00 (978-1-4031-7287-7(0)); audio compact disk 15.00 (978-1-4031-7285-3(4)); audio compact disk 15.00 (978-1-4031-7289-1(7)); audio compact disk 15.00 (978-1-4031-7293-8(5)); audio compact disk 15.00 (978-1-4031-7290-7(0)); audio compact disk 15.00 (978-1-4031-7298-3(6)); audio compact disk 15.00 (978-1-4031-7294-5(3)); audio compact disk 15.00 (978-1-4031-7296-9(X)); audio compact disk 15.00 (978-1-4031-7292-1(7)) Bridge Pubns Inc.

Aberjaber. Prod. by Sain Recordiau. 1 CD. (Running Time: 50 mins.). (WEL.). 2006. audio compact disk 12.95 (978-1-57970-366-0(6), C11058D, Audio-For) J Norton Pubs.
An analysis of our present knowledge of ancient Greek life, especially the contributions of the city-states to art, poetry, science, philosophy, and war. An excellent opportunity to hear the legendary Toynbee speak in his own voice!.

Aberjaber: Welsh Music. unabr. ed. 1 cass. 12.95 (C11058) J Norton Pubs.
Instrumental folk music from Wales & other Celtic countries.

***Aberration & the Handling Of.** L. Ron Hubbard. 2010. audio compact disk 15.00 (978-1-4031-8685-0(5)); audio compact disk 15.00 (978-1-4031-1312-2(2)) Bridge Pubns Inc.

***Abe's Honest Words.** Doreen Rappaport. Narrated by Christopher King. Illus. by Kadir Nelson. 1 cass. (Running Time: 13 mins.). (J). (gr. 2-4). 2009. bk. 27.95 (978-0-8045-6984-2(3)); bk. 29.95 (978-0-8045-4209-8(0)) Spoken Arts.

Abetalipoproteinemia - A Bibliography & Dictionary for Physicians, Patients, & Genome Researchers. Compiled by Icon Group International, Inc. Staff. 2007. ring bd. 28.95 (978-0-497-11316-2(3)) Icon Grp.

Abhorsen. Garth Nix. Read by Tim Curry. 7 vols. (Running Time: 11 hrs. 13 mins.). (Old Kingdom Ser.: No. 3). (J). (gr. 7 up). 2004. pap. bk. 54.00 (978-1-4000-9011-2(3), Listening Lib); audio compact disk 65.00 (978-1-4000-8611-5(6), Listening Lib) Random Audio Pubg.

Abhorsen. unabr. ed. Garth Nix. Read by Tim Curry. 7 cass. (Running Time: 11 hrs. 13 mins.). (Old Kingdom Ser.: No. 3). (J). (gr. 7 up). 2004. 46.00 (978-0-8072-0560-0(5), S YA 420 CX, Listening Lib) Random Audio Pubg.

Abide as the Self: The Essential Teachings of Ramana Maharshi. Interview with Ram Dass & H. W. Poonja. 1 cass. (Running Time: 1 hrs. 2 min.). 1996. (978-1-878019-04-2(X)) Inner Drctns.
The life & teachings of Ramana Maharshi, taken from the video production of the same name.

Abide in Him. Francis Frangipane. 1 cass. (Running Time: 90 mins.). (Abide in Him Ser.: Vol. 1). 2000. 5.00 (FF08-001) Morning NC.
A subject Francis teaches on with great gifting, this series deals with the advantages of walking in the "abiding principle".

Abide in Him Series. Francis Frangipane. 4 cass. (Running Time: 6 hrs.). 2000. 20.00 (FF08-000) Morning NC.

Abide with Me. Perf. by Bob Thomas. 1 cass. (Running Time: 45 min.). (New Covenant Ser.). 1988. 5.98 (978-0-570-09662-7(6), 79-7904) Family Films.
The sweet, singular sound of acoustic guitar creates a soulful atmosphere for reflection during personal devotions, drive time, & group Bible study.

Abiding: John 15:1-11, 645. Ed Young. 1988. 4.95 (978-0-7417-1645-3(3), 645) Win Walk.

Abiding Darkness. unabr. ed. John Aubrey Anderson. Read by Lillian Thayer. (Running Time: 41400 sec.). (Black or White Chronicles Ser.). 2006. audio compact disk 81.00 (978-0-7861-6427-1(1)) Blckstn Audio.

Abiding Darkness. unabr. ed. John Aubrey Anderson. Read by Lillian Thayer. (Running Time: 41400 sec.). (Black or White Chronicles: No. 1). 2006. audio compact disk 29.95 (978-0-7861-7574-1(5)) Blckstn Audio.

Abiding Darkness: Black or White Chronicles, Book 1. abr. unabr. ed. John Aubrey Anderson. Read by Lillian Thayer. 8 cass. (Running Time: 41400 sec.). 2006. 25.95 (978-0-7861-4543-0(9)); audio compact disk 25.95 (978-0-7861-7135-4(9)) Blckstn Audio.

Abiding Darkness: Black or White Chronicles, Book 1. unabr. ed. John Aubrey Anderson. Read by Lillian Thayer. (Running Time: 41400 sec.). 2006. 65.95 (978-0-7861-4713-7(X)) Blckstn Audio.

Abiding in Christ. 6 cass. 19.95 (20132, HarperThor) HarpC GBR.

Abiding in Jesus. Gloria Copeland. 1 cass. 1986. 5.00 (978-0-88114-783-4(4)) K Copeland Pubns.
Biblical teaching on walking with Jesus.

Abiding in the Anointing. Kenneth Copeland. 4 cass. 1995. 20.00 (978-0-88114-982-1(9)) K Copeland Pubns.
Biblical teaching on the Anointing.

Abiding under the Shadow. Bobby Hilton. 4 cass. 2000. 22.00 (978-1-930766-15-0(7)) Pub: Bishop Bobby. Dist(s): STL Dist NA

Abie's Irish Rose. unabr. ed. Anne Nichols. Read by Flo Gibson. 2 cass. (Running Time: 2 hrs. 30 mins.). 1998. 14.95 (978-1-55685-505-4(2)) Audio Bk Con.
About religious tolerance. For 14 years it was Broadway's longest running play as love conquers all for a Jewish boy & Irish girl.

***Abigail Adams.** unabr. ed. Woody Holton. Narrated by Cassandra Campbell. (Running Time: 19 hrs. 30 mins.). 2009. 23.99 (978-1-4001-8421-7(5)) Tantor Media.

Abigail Adams: A Life. unabr. ed. Woody Holton. Narrated by Cassandra Campbell. 2 MP3-CDs. (Running Time: 19 hrs. 30 mins. 0 sec.). (ENG.). 2009. 29.99 (978-1-4001-6421-9(4)); audio compact disk 39.99 (978-1-4001-1421-4(7)); audio compact disk 79.99 (978-1-4001-4421-1(3)) Pub: Tantor Media. Dist(s): IngramPubServ

Abigail Adams: A Revolutionary Woman. unabr. ed. Jacqueline Ching. Read by Suzy Myers. (Running Time: 2 hrs.). (Library of American Lives & Times Ser.). 2009. 19.99 (978-1-4233-9427-3(5), 9781423394273, Brilliance MP3); 39.97 (978-1-4233-9428-0(3), 9781423394280, Brinc Audio MP3 Lib); 39.97 (978-1-4233-9429-7(1), 9781423394297, BADLE); audio compact disk 19.99 (978-1-4233-9425-9(9), 9781423394259, Bril Audio CD Unabri) Brilliance Audio.

Abigail Adams: A Revolutionary Woman. unabr. ed. Jacqueline Ching. Read by Suzy Myers. 2 CDs. (Running Time: 2 hrs.). (Library of American Lives & Times Ser.). (J). (gr. 4-8). 2009. audio compact disk 39.97 (978-1-4233-9426-6(7), 9781423394266, BriAudCD Unabrid) Brilliance Audio.

Abilene. Hank Mitchum. Read by Charlie O'Dowd. 4 vols. No. 10. 2004. 25.00 (978-1-58807-193-4(6)); (978-1-58807-594-9(X)) Am Pubng Inc.

Abilene Trail: Traildrive Series. unabr. abr. ed. Ralph Compton Novel & Dusty Richards. 3 CDs. (Running Time: 4 hrs. 45 mins.). (ENG.). 2003. audio compact disk 22.95 (978-1-56511-808-9(1), 1565118081) Pub: HighBridge. Dist(s): Workman Pub

Ability to Abide Assured. Elbert Willis. 1 cass. (Because of Calvary Ser.). 4.00 Fill the Gap.

Ability to Live Contented. Elbert Willis. 1 cass. (Outcome of Abiding in Jesus Ser.). 4.00 Fill the Gap.

Abingdon Press Choral Club 17. 1 Demo CD Set. 2007. audio compact disk 4.00 (978-0-687-33577-0(9)) Abingdon.

Abingdon Worship Photos 4, Vol. 4. Mary Whitmer. 2004. audio compact disk 35.00 (978-0-687-05842-6(2)) Abingdon.

Abinger Harvest. unabr. collector's ed. E. M. Forster. Read by Stuart Langton. 9 cass. (Running Time: 13 hrs. 30 min.). 1995. 72.00 (978-0-7366-3022-1(8), 3705) Books on Tape.
Forster, author of "A Passage to India" & "A Room with a View," offers a collection of his articles, essays, reviews & poems.

Abiyoyo & Other Story Songs for Children. Perf. by Pete Seeger. 1 cass. (Running Time: 41 min.). (J). (ps-7). 1989. Incl. bklet. (0-9307-450010-9307-45001-2-5); audio compact disk (0-9307-45001-2-5) Smithsonian Folkways.
Includes the famous saga of the giant Abiyoyo.

Abkhazian Newspaper Reader. George Hewitt & Zaira Khiba. 3 cass. (Running Time: 90 mins. per cass.). (MIS.). 1998. 24.00 (3145) Dunwoody Pr.
Fifty-eight selections for learners of the language at the low intermediate to advanced level. Read by a native Abkhaz.

Able One. unabr. ed. Ben Bova. (Running Time: 13 hrs. 30 mins.). 2010. 29.95 (978-1-4417-2534-9(2)); 79.95 (978-1-4417-2530-1(X)); audio compact disk 109.00 (978-1-4417-2531-8(8)) Blckstn Audio.

***Ableton Live 6 Csi Master.** 2007. audio compact disk 49.99 (978-1-59863-324-5(4)) Pub: Course Tech. Dist(s): CENGAGE Learn

Abnormal Psychology. 4th ed. David L. Rosenhan. (C). Date not set. audio compact disk (978-0-393-10380-9(3)) Norton.

Abnormal Uterine Bleeding - Evaluation & Treatment. Contrib. by David L. Olive et al. 1 cass. (American College of Obstetrics & Gynecologists UPDATE: Vol. 24, No. 5). 1998. 20.00 Am Coll Obstetric.

Abolish Anxiety. 2 CDs. 2004. audio compact disk 25.50 (978-1-55841-135-7(6)) Emmett E Miller.
A complete self-healing program, compatible with all medical, herbal and spiritual therapies. This program presents a new view on anxiety delivered in the form of a heart-to-heart talk. CD #2 offers a graduated series of guided imagery experiences to rescript your deeper mind and nervous system.

Abolition of Man & the Great Divorce. unabr. ed. C. S. Lewis. Read by Robert Whitfield. 4 cass. (Running Time: 5 hrs. 30 mins.). 2000. 32.95 (978-0-7861-1812-0(1), 2611); audio compact disk 32.00 (978-0-7861-9819-1(2), 2611) Blckstn Audio.
In "The Abolition of Man," the author looks at the curriculum of the English "prep school" & begins to wonder if this subliminal teaching has indeed produced a generation who discount such a nature. In "The Great Divorce," the narrator boards a bus on a drizzly English afternoon & embarks on an incredible voyage through Heaven & Hell. He meets a host of supernatural beings far removed from his expectations & comes to some significant realizations about the nature of good & evil.

Abominable Man. unabr. ed. Maj Sjöwall & Per Wahlöö. Read by Tom Weiner. (Running Time: 1 hr. 0 mins.). (ENG.). 2009. 29.95 (978-1-4332-6327-9(0)); 34.95 (978-1-4332-6323-1(8)); audio compact disk 55.00 (978-1-4332-6324-8(6)) Blckstn Audio.

Abominable Snowmen. Doctor Who. 2 CDs. 2001. cd-rom 15.99 (978-0-563-47856-0(X)) London Brdge.

Abomination. unabr. ed. Robert Swindells. Read by Amanda Hulme. 3 cass. (Running Time: 3 hrs. 30 mins.). 2004. 28.00 (978-1-74030-493-1(4)); audio compact disk 54.95 (978-1-74030-909-7(X)) Pub: Bolinda Pubng AUS. Dist(s): Bolinda Pub Inc

Abondance Dans la Simplicitee. Sarah Ban Breathnach. 2 CDs. (Running Time: 2 hrs.). (French Audiobooks Ser.).Tr. of Simple Abundance. (FRE.).

2002. pap. bk. 21.95 (978-2-89558-096-6(0)) Pub: Coffragants CAN. Dist(s): Penton Overseas

Abortion. Barrie Konicov. 1 cass. 11.98 (978-0-87082-312-1(4), 001) Potentials.
Addresses the after-effects of abortion: weight gain, headaches, depression, anger, high blood pressure & sexual disfunction. The program takes no side on abortion but is designed to help you heal.

Abortion. Contrib. by Lee P. Shulman et al. 1 cass. (American College of Obstetrics & Gynecologists UPDATE: Vol. 22, No. 7). 1998. 20.00 Am Coll Obstetric.

Abortion: Commentaries by Rod MacLeish. 1 cass. (Running Time: 15 mins.). 1987. 9.95 (I0430B090, HarperThor) HarpC GBR.

Abortion: The Best We Can Do Is Agree to Disagree. 1 cass. (Care Cassettes Ser.: Vol. 17, No. 7). 1990. 10.80 Assn Prof Chaplains.

Abortion: The Slaughter of the Innocents. 2 cass. 7.95 (22-2, HarperThor) HarpC GBR.

Abortion - Personal Reflections. 1 cass. (Running Time: 30 mins.). 9.95 (I0500B090, HarperThor) HarpC GBR.

Abortion & Euthanasia. unabr. ed. David James. Read by Robert Guillaume. Ed. by John Lachs & Mike Hassell. Prod. by Pat Childs. (Running Time: 10800 sec.). (Morality in Our Age Ser.). 2006. audio compact disk 25.95 (978-0-7861-6628-2(2)) Pub: Blckstn Audio. Dist(s): NetLibrary CO

Abortion & Euthanasia. unabr. ed. David James. Read by Robert Guillaume. Ed. by John Lachs & Mike Hassell. 2 cass. (Running Time: 3 hrs.). Dramatization. (Morality in Our Age Ser.). 1995. 17.95 (978-1-56823-033-7(8), 10511) Knowledge Prod.
The beginning & ending of life are deeply controversial moral topics with enormous stakes. Most people agree that it is wrong to kill humans - but are fetuses, or people in a deep coma, fully human? Does a person have the moral discretion or "right" to take his or her own life, or to aid another person who does so? And who should bear the cost for those who cannot afford to extend their life, or to pay for ending an unwanted pregnancy?.

Abortion & Healing: Counseling the Aborted Woman. unabr. ed. Michael T. Mannion. 1 cass. (Running Time: 60 mins.). 1986. 6.95 (978-1-55612-012-1(5), LL7012, SheWard) Rowman.
This is a presentation of Father Mannion at the Maryland Right to Life Conference in late 1985.

Abortion & Human Life: The Hard Questions. J. C. Willke & Willke. Read by J. C. Willke & Willke. 2 cass. (Running Time: 2 hrs. 2 mins.). 1987. 65.00 set, incl. 2 bklets with both cass.; 35.00 ea. cass. incl. bklet. Hayes.
Discusses facts of human life, abortion & questions concerning the abortion issues.

Abortion & the Breast Cancer Link. 1 cass. (Running Time: 1 hr.). 2003. 13.95 (978-1-932631-51-7(8)); audio compact disk 13.95 (978-1-932631-52-4(6)) Ascensn Pr.

Abortion, Capital Punishment & the Ecumenical Movement. Jack Van Impe. 1977. 7.00 (978-0-934803-31-1(5)) J Van Impe.
Features three sermons in one & what God's Word has to say about these subjects.

Abortion under Siege. Hosted by Leonard Peikoff. 1 cass. (Philosophy: Who Needs It? Ser.). 1998. 12.95 (LPXXC47) Second Renaissance.

Abortionist's Daughter. unabr. ed. Elisabeth Hyde. Read by Beth McDonald. (YA). 2006. 44.99 (978-1-59895-636-8(1)) Find a World.

About a Boy. collector's ed. Nick Hornby. Read by David Case. 6 cass. (Running Time: 9 hrs.). 1999. 48.00 (978-0-7366-4732-8(5), 5070) Books on Tape.
Will Freeman may have discovered the key to dating success. If the simple fact that they were single mothers meant that gorgeous women, women who would not ordinarily look twice at Will, might not only be willing, but enthusiastic about dating him, then he was really onto something. Single mothers, bright, attractive, available women, thousands of them, were all over London. He just had to find them.

About Alice. unabr. ed. Calvin Trillin. Read by Calvin Trillin. 1 CD. (Running Time: 1 hr.). 2006. audio compact disk 23.80 (978-1-4159-3547-7(5)) Pub: Books on Tape. Dist(s): NetLibrary CO

About Alice. unabr. ed. Calvin Trillin. Read by Calvin Trillin. 1 CD. (Running Time: 4500 sec.). (ENG.). 2006. audio compact disk 19.95 (978-0-7393-4216-9(9), Random AudioBks) Pub: Random Audio Pubg. Dist(s): Random

***About as Long as a Hare's Tale.** Anonymous. 2009. (978-1-60136-589-7(6)) Audio Holding.

About Cancer. Cynthia Moritz. (For Your Information Ser.). 1993. 16.00 (978-1-56420-032-7(9)) New Readers.

About Face. unabr. ed. Donna Leon. Read by David Colacci. 8 CDs. (Running Time: 9 hrs.). (Commissario Guido Brunetti Mystery Ser.: Bk. 18). (ENG.). 2009. audio compact disk 29.95 (978-1-60283-566-5(7)) Pub: AudioGO. Dist(s): Perseus Dist

About Faces: The essentials of makeup & Skincare 101. Speeches. Georgia Donovan. 2 CD's. (Running Time: 2 hours). 2007. audio compact disk 27.00 (978-0-9786891-1-7(9)) Austin Bay.

About Grace: A Novel. unabr. ed. Anthony Doerr. Narrated by Henry Strozier. 10 cass. (Running Time: 14 hrs. 30 mins.). 2004. 89.75 (978-1-4193-0525-2(5), 97848MC) Recorded Bks.

About Grace: A Novel. unabr. ed. Anthony Doerr. 13 CDs. (Running Time: 16 hrs.). 2004. audio compact disk 39.99 (978-1-4025-9776-3(2), 01842) Recorded Bks.
Anthony Doerr received waves of accolades for his short story collection, The Shell Collector, a New York Times Notable Book, a Publishers Weekly Best Book, and an American Library Association Book of the Year. This is his eagerly anticipated first novel.

About Learning. Bernice McCurthy. Ed. by Mary McNamara. Illus. by Carol Keene. 2 cass. (Running Time: 2 hrs.). 1997. 19.95 (978-0-9608992-8-9(6)) About Learning.

About Love: Reinventing Romance for Our Times. Robert C. Solomon. 1993. 18.95 (978-0-8226-3027-2(3)) Pub: Littlefield. Dist(s): Natl Bk Netwk

About Me Audio CD. Adapted by Benchmark Education Company Staff. Based on a work by Jeffrey B. Fuerst. (My First Reader's Theater Ser.). (J). (gr. k-1). 2008. audio compact disk 10.00 (978-1-60634-094-3(8)) Benchmark Educ.

About My Father's Business. 1 cass. (Running Time: 36 mins.). 7.95 (978-1-58169-000-2(2), GDS101) Genesis Comm Inc.
Includes 24 sets of scriptures, reflections & prayers with musical backgrounds. Designed to help prepare for the workday which will become more productive with focus on the Lord.

About Schmidt. Louis Begley. 5 cass. (Running Time: 8 hrs. 45 mins.). 2004. 29.99 (978-0-7887-9027-0(7), 00494) Recorded Bks.

About Schmidt. unabr. ed. Louis Begley. Narrated by George Guidall. 6 cass. (Running Time: 8 hrs. 45 mins.). 1997. 51.00 (978-0-7887-0876-3(7), 95011E7) Recorded Bks.
Attorney Albert Schmidt is suddenly widowed, forcibly retired from his firm & faced with mixed feelings about his daughter's impending marriage.

About the New Yorker & Me: A Sentimental Journal. unabr. ed. Heywood Hale Broun & E. J. Kahn. 1 cass. (Running Time: 56 mins.). (Broun Radio Ser.). 12.95 (40373) J Norton Pubs.

About This Life. abr. ed. Barry Lopez. Read by Barry Lopez. 4 cass. (Running Time: 6 hrs.). 2001. 25.00 (978-1-59040-156-9(5), Phoenix Audio) Pub: Amer Intl Pub. Dist(s): PerseuPGW

About Time: A Hypnotic Journey in Time. Nick Kemp. (Running Time: 1 hr.). 2005. audio compact disk 25.95 (978-0-9545993-8-6(1)) Crown Hse Pub GBR.

About Tomorrow's Mileage. Perf. by Traindodge. 1 CD. 1999. audio compact disk 16.98 (978-1-57908-478-3(8), 5324) Platinm Enter.

Above & Beyond. unabr. ed. Erin St. Claire, pseud. Narrated by Jack Garrett. 7 cass. (Running Time: 9 hrs. 30 mins.). 2004. 69.75 (978-1-4025-6370-6(1)) Recorded Bks.
The letters Kyla sent to her husband, Sergeant Richard Stroud, spoke of a love that stretched across the ocean, but it wasn?t enough to keep tragedy from striking. Trevor Rule, Richard?s best friend, returned home from military duty carrying with him the letters Kyla had sent. Now he needed to convince Kyla of his feelings. But Trevor was harboring a secret with the power to destroy the love he was trying so hard to protect.

Above Suspicion. Betsy Green. 3 cass. 2004. 14.95 (978-1-59156-311-2(9)); audio compact disk 15.95 (978-1-59156-320-4(8)) Covenant Comms.

Above Suspicion, Set. Helen MacInnes. Read by Christine Dawe. 6 cass. 1999. 54.95 (61403) Pub: Soundings Ltd GBR. Dist(s): ISIS Pub

Above the Bright Blue Sky. unabr. ed. Margaret Thornton. Read by Maggie Mash. 11 cass. (Running Time: 14 hrs. 35 mins.). (Story Sound Ser.). Orig. Title: Allison & Busby. 2007. 89.95 (978-1-85903-978-6(2)); audio compact disk 99.95 (978-1-84652-093-8(2)) Pub: Mgna Lrg Print GBR. Dist(s): Ulverscroft US

Above the Law. unabr. ed. J. F. Freedman. Read by Dick Hill. (Running Time: 18 hrs.). 2008. 44.97 (978-1-4233-4012-6(4), 9781423340126, BADLE); 44.97 (978-1-4233-4010-2(8), 9781423340102, Brinc Audio MP3 Lib); 29.99 (978-1-4233-4009-6(4), 9781423340096, Brilliance MP3); 29.99 (978-1-4233-4011-9(6), 9781423340119, BAD) Brilliance Audio.

Above the Law. unabr. ed. Tim Green. Narrated by Bernadette Dunne. 7 CDs. (Running Time: 8 hrs. 30 mins.). (Casey Jordan Ser.: Bk. 2). 2009. audio compact disk 90.00 (978-1-4159-6206-0(5), BksonTape) Pub: Random Audio Pubg. Dist(s): Random

Abracadabra. Joe Scruggs. 1 cass. (Running Time: 34 mins.). (J). (ps-2). 1986. 9.95 (978-0-916123-07-9(3), KJS-621) Ed Graphics Pr.
Presents 13 activity & listening songs for kindergarten & elementary school age children & their parents & teachers.

Abracadabra Boys see Carl Sandburg's Poems for Children

Abracadabra Kid: A Writer's Life. unabr. ed. Sid Fleischman. Narrated by Nelson Runger. 4 pieces. (Running Time: 4 hrs. 45 mins.). (gr. 6 up). 1997. 35.00 (978-0-7887-1588-4(7), 95200E7) Recorded Bks.
Author recounts his first career as a magician, his years as a journalist & screen writer, & his success as an author of children's books. It is filled with the joy of the unexpected.

***Abraham.** unabr. ed. Bruce Feiler. Read by Bruce Feiler. (ENG.). 2003. (978-0-06-079914-4(5), Harper Audio) HarperCollins Pubs.

Abraham. unabr. ed. Bruce S. Feiler. Read by Bruce S. Feiler. 4 vols. (Running Time: 6 hrs.). 2002. bk. 39.95 (978-0-7927-2703-3(7), CSL 489, Chivers Sound Lib); audio compact disk 49.95 (978-0-7927-2728-6(2), SLD 489, Chivers Sound Lib) AudioGO.
At a moment when world peace has been shattered in the name of religion, one figure stands out as the shared ancestor of the Jews, Christians, and Muslims. One man holds the key to our deepest fears - and our possible reconciliation: Abraham.

Abraham. unabr. ed. Bruce S. Feiler. Read by Bruce S. Feiler. (YA). 2007. 44.99 (978-1-60252-738-6(5)) Find a World.

Abraham, Vol. 7. 1 cass. (Running Time: 1 hr.). (Sabio Y Prudente Ser.). (SPA.). 2001. 7.99 (978-0-8254-0896-0(2), Edit Portavoz) Kregel.
The 7th Spanish musical production from Sabio y Prudente is a delightful collection inspired by the Bible's story of Abraham. A choir of children sings such well-known choruses as "Padre Abraham" (Father Abraham)" and introduces such fun-filled songs as "Cuantas estrellas hay" (How Many Stars are There?") and "Dios Proveera" (God Will Provide).

***Abraham: A Journey to the Heart of Three Faiths.** unabr. ed. Bruce Feiler. Read by Bruce Feiler. (ENG.). 2003. (978-0-06-073557-9(0), Harper Audio) HarperCollins Pubs.

Abraham: A Journey to the Heart of Three Faiths. unabr. ed. Bruce S. Feiler. Read by Bruce S. Feiler. 5 CDs. (Running Time: 6 hrs.). 2005. audio compact disk 14.95 (978-0-06-087275-5(9)) HarperCollins Pubs.

Abraham: The Friend of God. unabr. ed. Charles R. Swindoll. 12 cass. (Running Time: 10 hrs). 1998. 57.95 (978-1-57972-293-7(8)) Insight Living.

Abraham & Faith: Romans 4:1-12. Ed Young. 1984. 4.95 (978-0-7417-1359-9(4), 359) Win Walk.

Abraham & the Idols. unabr. ed. (Running Time: 1800 sec.). 2007. 15.95 (978-1-4332-1051-8(7)); audio compact disk 17.00 (978-1-4332-1052-5(5)) Blckstn Audio.

Abraham & the Idols. unabr. ed. A. C. Fellner. (Running Time: 0 mins. 30 sec.). 2007. audio compact disk 19.95 (978-1-4332-1053-2(3)) Blckstn Audio.

Abraham, Enoch & You! Life-Changing Lessons from the Heroes of Faith. Mac Hammond. 6 cass. (Running Time: 6 hrs). (Faith Ser.: Vol. 1). 2005. 15.00 (978-1-57399-231-2(3)) Mac Hammond.
Faith. It's not a message or a movement. It's the only way to please God. In this series, you'll learn practical principles of faith building from the Bible's "Hall of Famers.".

Abraham, Enoch & You! Life-Changing Lessons from the Heroes of Faith. Mac Hammond. 6 CDs. (Faith Ser.: Vol. 1). 2006. audio compact disk 30.00 (978-1-57399-312-8(3)) Mac Hammond.
Faith. It's not a message or a movement. It's the only way to please God. In this series, you'll learn practical principles of faith building from the Bible's "Hall of Famers.".

Abraham-Hicks G-Series Cd's - G-SERIES FALL, 2001 WHATEVER YOU LIKE IS APPROPRIATE. 2001. audio compact disk 117.00 (978-1-935063-25-4(1)) Abraham-Hicks Pubns.

Abraham-Hicks G-Series Cd's - G-SERIES FALL, 2002 SYOUR WELL-BEING IS NATURAL. 2002. audio compact disk 117.00 (978-1-935063-21-6(9)) Abraham-Hicks Pubns.

Abraham-Hicks G-Series Cd's - G-SERIES FALL, 2003 EVERY PREFERENCE SUMMONS SOURCE. 2004. audio compact disk 117.00 (978-1-935063-17-9(0)) Abraham-Hicks Pubns.

Abraham-Hicks G-Series Cd's - G-SERIES FALL, 2004 NOW, IS ALWAYS on the LEADING EDGE. (ENG.). 2005. audio compact disk 117.00 (978-1-935063-13-1(8)) Abraham-Hicks Pubns.

Abraham-Hicks G-Series Cd's - G-SERIES FALL, 2005 LIFE IS SUPPOSED to FEEL GOOD. (ENG.). 2006. audio compact disk 117.00 (978-1-935063-07-0(3)) Abraham-Hicks Pubns.

Abraham-Hicks G-Series Cd's - G-SERIES FALL, 2006 RELAX & LET GO of the OARS. 2008. audio compact disk 117.00 (978-1-935063-10-0(3)) Abraham-Hicks Pubns.

Abraham-Hicks G-Series Cd's - G-SERIES SPRING, 2001 GOOD FEELS GOOD & BAD FEELS BAD. 2001. audio compact disk 117.00 (978-1-935063-27-8(8)) Abraham-Hicks Pubns.

Abraham-Hicks G-Series Cd's - G-SERIES SPRING, 2002 VIRTUAL REALITY PROCESS REFINED. 2002. audio compact disk 117.00 (978-1-935063-23-0(5)) Abraham-Hicks Pubns.

Abraham-Hicks G-Series Cd's - G-SERIES SPRING, 2003 ETHERE IS NO VALUE in SUFFERING. 2004. audio compact disk 117.00 (978-1-935063-19-3(7)) Abraham-Hicks Pubns.

Abraham-Hicks G-Series Cd's - G-SERIES SPRING, 2004 REACH for DESIRE¿S EMOTIONAL ESSENCE. 2005. audio compact disk Rental 117.00 (978-1-935063-15-5(4)) Abraham-Hicks Pubns.

Abraham-Hicks G-Series Cd's - G-SERIES SPRING, 2005 MAKE PEACE with WHERE YOU ARE. 2006. audio compact disk 117.00 (978-1-935063-09-4(X)) Abraham-Hicks Pubns.

Abraham-Hicks G-Series Cd's - G-SERIES SUMMER, 2001 LOCK on to YOUR RECEIVING MODE. 2001. audio compact disk 117.00 (978-1-935063-26-1(X)) Abraham-Hicks Pubns.

Abraham-Hicks G-Series Cd's - G-SERIES SUMMER, 2002 CREATIVE CONTROL IS YOURS. 2002. audio compact disk 117.00 (978-1-935063-22-3(7)) Abraham-Hicks Pubns.

Abraham-Hicks G-Series Cd's - G-SERIES SUMMER, 2004 TAKE the EMOTIONAL JOURNEY FIRST. 2005. audio compact disk 117.00 (978-1-935063-14-8(6)) Abraham-Hicks Pubns.

Abraham-Hicks G-Series Cd's - G-SERIES SUMMER, 2005 IT¿S ALL about VIBRATIONAL RELATIVITY. 2006. audio compact disk 117.00 (978-1-935063-08-7(1)) Abraham-Hicks Pubns.

Abraham-Hicks G-Series Cd's - G-SERIES WINTER, 2001 LIMITING BELIEFS & the ART of ALLOWING. 2001. audio compact disk 117.00 (978-1-935063-28-5(6)) Abraham-Hicks Pubns.

Abraham-Hicks G-Series Cd's - G-SERIES WINTER, 2001 PRACTICE YOUR VIRTUAL REALITY. 2002. audio compact disk 117.00 (978-1-935063-24-7(3)) Abraham-Hicks Pubns.

Abraham-Hicks G-Series Cd's - G-SERIES WINTER, 2002 SAVOR the MOMENT! 2003. audio compact disk 117.00 (978-1-935063-20-9(0)) Abraham-Hicks Pubns.

Abraham-Hicks G-Series Cd's - G-SERIES WINTER, 2003 VIBRATION, IT¿S ALL about VIBRATION. 2004. audio compact disk 117.00 (978-1-935063-16-2(2)) Abraham-Hicks Pubns.

Abraham-Hicks G-Series Cd's - G-SERIES WINTER, 2004 FEAR to HOPE an EMOTIONAL JOURNEY. 2005. audio compact disk Rental 117.00 (978-1-935063-12-4(X)) Abraham-Hicks Pubns.

Abraham-Hicks G-Series Cd's - G-SERIES WINTER, 2005 the VALUE in UNDERSTANDING the LAW of ATTRACTION. 2006. audio compact disk 117.00 (978-1-935063-06-3(5)) Abraham-Hicks Pubns.

Abraham-Hicks G-Series Cd's - G-SERIES WINTER, 2006 JUST TURNING AROUND IS ENOUGH. 2008. audio compact disk 117.00 (978-1-935063-11-7(1)) Abraham-Hicks Pubns.

Abraham-Hicks G-Series Cd's - Spring 2006 YOUR DESIRES HAVE ALREADY BECOME A REALITY. 2008. audio compact disk 117.00 (978-1-935063-05-6(7)) Abraham-Hicks Pubns.

Abraham-Hicks G-Series Cd's - Summer 2006 Going with the Flow. 2008. audio compact disk 117.00 (978-1-935063-04-9(9)) Abraham-Hicks Pubns.

Abraham-Hicks Special Subjects Vol. One - CD's, Vol. 1. 2004. audio compact disk 80.00 (978-1-935063-01-8(4)) Abraham-Hicks Pubns.

Abraham-Hicks Special Subjects Vol. One - Tapes, Vol. 1. 1989. 80.00 (978-1-935063-00-1(6)) Abraham-Hicks Pubns.

Abraham-Hicks Special Subjects Vol. Two - CD's, Vol.2. 2007. audio compact disk 80.00 (978-1-935063-03-2(0)) Abraham-Hicks Pubns.

Abraham-Hicks Special Subjects Vol. Two - Tapes, Vol.2. 1989. 80.00 (978-1-935063-02-5(2)) Abraham-Hicks Pubns.

Abraham Lincoln see Great American Essays: A Collection

Abraham Lincoln. John Drinkwater. 10.00 Esstee Audios.
Drama of the rise of a great politician to the presidency & the saving of a nation.

Abraham Lincoln. H. G. Pitt. Read by William Hope. 2 cass. (Running Time: 3 hrs.). 2001. 24.95 (990217) Pub: ISIS Audio GBR. Dist(s): Ulverscroft US

Abraham Lincoln. abr. ed. Jean F. Blashfield. 1 cass. (Running Time: 22 mins.). Incl. Abraham Lincoln: First Inaugural Address. (SAC 7033C); Abraham Lincoln: Letter to Mary Owens. (SAC 7033C); Abraham Lincoln: Letter to Mrs. Bixby. (SAC 7033C); Abraham Lincoln: Second Inaugural Address. (SAC 7033C); 10.95 (978-0-8045-0806-3(2), SAC 7033C) Spoken Arts.

Abraham Lincoln. unabr. ed. Robert Hogrogian. 1 cass. (Running Time: 16 mins.). (People to Remember Ser.: Set I). (J). (gr. 4-7). 1979. bk. 16.99 (978-0-934898-46-1(4)); pap. bk. 9.95 (978-0-934898-05-8(7)) Jan Prods.
The engrossing story of a poor boy who grew to be one of his country's greatest leaders.

Abraham Lincoln. unabr. ed. Ingri Parin D'Aulaire & Edgar Parin D'Aulaire. 1 cass. (Running Time: 6 mins.). (J). (gr. 3-5). 1989. pap. bk. 10.00 (978-0-8045-6619-3(4), 6512-G) Spoken Arts.
Young Abe faced many challenges before becoming President.

Abraham Lincoln. unabr. ed. Ingri Parin D'Aulaire & Edgar Parin D'Aulaire. 1 cass. (Running Time: 15 min.). (J). (gr. 3-5). 2001. pap. bk. 20.00 (978-0-8045-6719-0(0), 6512G/6) Spoken Arts.
Young Abe faced many challenges before becoming President. Includes 6 books.

Abraham Lincoln. unabr. ed. H. G. Pitt. Read by William Hope. 2 CDs. (Running Time: 2 hrs. 7 min.). (Isis Ser.). (J). 2003. audio compact disk 34.95 (978-0-7531-2240-2(5)) Pub: ISIS Lrg Prnt GBR. Dist(s): Ulverscroft US
Tells the story of how this man, born in a log cabin and almost entirely self-educated, rose, in the nation's gravest hour, to determine it's fate, only to die at the hands of an assassin in the moment of victory.

Abraham Lincoln. unabr. ed. H. G. Pitt. Read by William Hope. 2 cass. (Running Time: 2 hrs. 20 mins.). 1999. 24.95 (978-0-7531-0573-3(X), 990216) Ulverscroft US.
This short biography tells the story of how this man, born in a log cabin & almost entirely self-educated, rose, in the nation's gravest hour, to determine its fate, only to die at the hands of an assassin in the moment of victory.

Abraham Lincoln: A Biography. Brand Whitlock. Read by Jim Killavey. 4 cass. (Running Time: 3 hrs. 50 mins.). 28.00 (C-215) Jimcin Record.
Short biography - Good introduction to more detailed studies.

Abraham Lincoln: A Biography & Ann Rutledge. 1 cass. 16.95 (CART005) CA Artists.

Abraham Lincoln: A Man of Faith & Courage - Stories of Our Most Admired President. unabr. ed. Joe Wheeler. Narrated by Grover Gardner. (Running Time: 9 hrs. 21 mins. 11 sec.). (ENG.). 2008. audio compact disk 29.99 (978-1-59859-365-5(X)) Oasis Audio.

Abraham Lincoln: First Inaugural Address see Abraham Lincoln

Abraham Lincoln: His Last Day. (CC7940) Natl Recrd Co.

Abraham Lincoln: In His Words. David Zarefsky. audio compact disk 69.95 (978-1-59803-301-4(8)) Teaching Co.

Abraham Lincoln: Letter to Mary Owens see Abraham Lincoln

Abraham Lincoln: Letter to Mrs. Bixby see Abraham Lincoln

Abraham Lincoln: Letters from a Slave Girl. 2 vols. (Running Time: 30 mins.). (J). (gr. 4-7). 2002. bk. 25.95 (978-0-87499-983-9(9)) Live Oak Media.
Fictionalized letters between a 12-year-old slave girl living on a South Carolina plantation and President Lincoln. Includes hardcover book.

***Abraham Lincoln: Redeemer President.** unabr. ed. Allen C. Guelzo. Read by Edward Lewis. (Running Time: 19 hrs. NaN mins.). (ENG.). 2011. 44.95 (978-1-4417-8406-3(3)); audio compact disk 123.00 (978-1-4417-8404-9(7)) Blckstn Audio.

Abraham Lincoln: Redeemer President. unabr. ed. Allen Guezlo. Read by Edward Lewis. 13 cass. (Running Time: 19 hrs.). 2001. 85.95 (978-0-7861-2016-1(9), 2784) Blckstn Audio.
Allen C. Guelzo's unique intellectual portrait explores the role of ideas in Lincoln's life, treating him for the first time in any Lincoln biography as a serious thinker deeply involved in the struggles of nineteenth-century ideas, including those of classical liberalism, the Lockean Enlightenment, Victorian unbelief and Calvinist spirituality.

Abraham Lincoln: Second Inaugural Address see Abraham Lincoln

Abraham Lincoln: The Great Emancipator. unabr. ed. Augusta Stevenson. Read by Lloyd James. 2 cass. (Running Time: 5 hrs. 30 mins.). 2001. 17.95 (978-0-7861-2028-4(2), 2795) Blckstn Audio.
Focuses on Lincoln's childhood, with events that children can understand and relate to. Living on the frontier, standing up to his father for the right to attend school, and a visit from Johnny Appleseed are a few of the events from the childhood years of the man who was to play such a pivotal role in the abolishment of slavery.

Abraham Lincoln: The 16th President, 1860-1865. unabr. ed. George S. McGovern. Read by William Dufris. Ed. by Arthur M. Schlesinger, Jr. & Sean Wilentz. 5 CDs. (Running Time: 5 hrs. 30 mins. 0 sec.). (American Presidents Ser.). (ENG.). 2008. audio compact disk 29.95 (978-1-4272-0613-8(9)) Pub: Macmill Audio. Dist(s): Macmillan

***Abraham Lincoln: Vampire Hunter.** unabr. ed. Seth Grahame-Smith. Narrated by Scott Holst. 9 CDs. (Running Time: 11 hrs.). 2010. audio compact disk 69.99 (978-1-60788-354-8(6)) Pub: Hachet Audio. Dist(s): HachBkGrp

Abraham Lincoln: Vampire Hunter. unabr. ed. Seth Grahame-Smith. Read by Scott Holst. (Running Time: 10 hrs. 30 mins.). (ENG.). 2010. 18.98 (978-1-60788-174-2(8)); audio compact disk 26.98 (978-1-60788-173-5(X)) Pub: Hachet Audio. Dist(s): HachBkGrp

Abraham Lincoln: Will You Ever Give Up? Loyd Uglow. Illus. by Kennon James. 1cass. Dramatization. (Another Great Achiever Ser.). (J). 2003. lib. bdg. 23.95 (978-1-57537-790-2(X)); 16.95 (978-1-57537-590-8(7)) Advance Pub.

Abraham Lincoln Pts. I-II: In His Own Words. Instructed by David Zarefsky. 12 cass. (Running Time: 12 hrs.). 1999. 54.95 (978-1-56585-262-4(1), 877) Teaching Co.

Abraham Lincoln Pts. I-II, Vol. 1: In His Own Words. Instructed by David Zarefsky. 12 CDs. (Running Time: 12 hrs.). 1999. audio compact disk 179.95 (978-1-56585-723-0(2)) Teaching Co.

Abraham Lincoln Vol. I: The Prairie Years. unabr. collector's ed. Carl Sandburg. Read by Dick Estell. 13 cass. (Running Time: 19 hrs. 30 mins.). 1993. 104.00 (978-0-7366-2505-0(4), 3262) Books on Tape.
"The all-time best biography of Lincoln ever written." (B-O-T Editorial Review Board).

Abraham Lincoln Vol. 1, Pt. 1: The War Years. unabr. collector's ed. Carl Sandburg. Read by Dick Estell. 13 cass. (Running Time: 19 hrs. 30 mins.). 1994. 104.00 (978-0-7366-2660-6(3), 3398A) Books on Tape.
Covers the period from president-elect's journey to Washington (1861) through end of 1862.

Abraham Lincoln Vol. 1, Pt. 2: The War Years. unabr. collector's ed. Carl Sandburg. Read by Dick Estell. 13 cass. (Running Time: 19 hrs. 30 mins.). 1994. 104.00 (978-0-7366-2661-3(1), 3398-B) Books on Tape.

Abraham Lincoln Vol. 2: In His Own Words. Instructed by David Zarefsky. 6 cass. (Running Time: 6 hrs.). 1999. 129.95 (978-1-56585-263-1(X)); audio compact disk 179.95 (978-1-56585-724-7(0)) Teaching Co.

Abraham Lincoln Vol. II: The Prairie Years. unabr. collector's ed. Carl Sandburg. Read by Dick Estell. 12 cass. (Running Time: 18 hrs.). 1994. 96.00 (978-0-7366-2609-5(3), 3351) Books on Tape.
Second volume in Sandburg's epic biography takes Lincoln to the White House to begin his presidency.

Abraham Lincoln Vol. 2, Pt. 1: The War Years. unabr. collector's ed. Carl Sandburg. Perf. by Dick Estell. 13 cass. (Running Time: 19 hrs. 30 mins.). 1994. 104.00 (978-0-7366-2707-8(3), 3440A) Books on Tape.
Lincoln as Commander-in-chief.

Abraham Lincoln Vol. 2, Pt. 2: The War Years. unabr. collector's ed. Carl Sandburg. Read by Dick Estell. 13 cass. (Running Time: 19 hrs. 30 mins.). 1994. 104.00 (978-0-7366-2708-5(1), 3440-B) Books on Tape.
Lincoln's titanic proclamation & ends in 1864 amidst presidential election politics & his bid for re-election.

Abraham Lincoln Vol. 3, Pt. 1: The War Years. unabr. collector's ed. Carl Sandburg. Read by Dick Estell. 15 cass. (Running Time: 22 hrs. 30 mins.). 1994. 120.00 (978-0-7366-2763-4(4), 3485-A) Books on Tape.
Chronicles the military & political battles of 1864, including Lincoln's reelection.

Abraham Lincoln Vol. 3, Pt. 2: The War Years. unabr. collector's ed. Carl Sandburg. Read by Dick Estell. 12 cass. (Running Time: 18 hrs.). 1994. 96.00 (978-0-7366-2764-1(2), 3845-B) Books on Tape.

Abraham Lincoln Vol. 4, Pt. 1: The War Years. unabr. collector's ed. Carl Sandburg. Read by Dick Estell. 8 cass. (Running Time: 12 hrs.). 1994. 64.00 (978-0-7366-2801-3(0), 3516-A) Books on Tape.
1865: Lincoln's last year. Second inaugural, visits to the front, assassination...a loss more vivid with the passage of time.

Abraham Lincoln Vol. 4, Pt. 2: The War Years. unabr. collector's ed. Carl Sandburg. Read by Dick Estell. 8 cass. (Running Time: 12 hrs.). 1994. 64.00 (978-0-7366-2802-0(9), 3516-B) Books on Tape.
This is from the second inaugural, Lee's surrender at Appomattox & Booth's fatal attack at Ford's Theatre.

Abraham Lincoln - A Man of Faith & Courage: Stories of Our Most Admired President. unabr. ed. Joe Wheeler. Narrated by Grover Gardner. (Running Time: 9 hrs. 21 mins. 11 sec.). (ENG.). 2008. 20.99 (978-1-60814-028-2(8)) Oasis Audio.

Abraham Lincoln: A Life 1809-1837: Lincoln's Frontier Background Shapes the Future President. unabr. ed. Michael Burlingame. Read by Sean Pratt. (Running Time: 8 hrs.). (ENG.). 2009. 14.98 (978-1-59659-422-7(5), GildAudio) Pub: Gildan Media. Dist(s): HachBkGrp

Abraham Lincoln: A Life 1837-1842: A Righteous Lawyer Deals with an Unhappy Marriage. unabr. ed. Michael Burlingame. Read by Sean Pratt. (Running Time: 5 hrs. 30 mins.). (ENG.). 2009. 24.98 (978-1-59659-423-4(3), GildAudio) Pub: Gildan Media. Dist(s): HachBkGrp

Abraham Lincoln: A Life 1843-1849: A Win in Congress & a Battle Against Slavery. unabr. ed. Michael Burlingame. Read by Sean Pratt. (Running Time: 6 hrs.). (ENG.). 2009. 24.98 (978-1-59659-424-1(1), GildAudio) Pub: Gildan Media. Dist(s): HachBkGrp

Abraham Lincoln: A Life 1849-1855: A Mid-Life Crisis & a Re-Entry to Politics. unabr. ed. Michael Burlingame. Read by Sean Pratt. (Running Time: 6 hrs. 30 mins.). (ENG.). 2009. 24.98 (978-1-59659-425-8(X), GildAudio) Pub: Gildan Media. Dist(s): HachBkGrp

Abraham Lincoln: A Life 1855-1858: Building a New Party, a House Divided & the Lincoln Douglas Debates. unabr. ed. Michael Burlingame. Read by Sean Pratt. (Running Time: 10 hrs.). (ENG.). 2009. 29.98 (978-1-59659-426-5(8), GildAudio) Pub: Gildan Media. Dist(s): HachBkGrp

Abraham Lincoln: A Life 1859-1860: The Rail Splitter Fights for & Wins the Republican Nomination. unabr. ed. Michael Burlingame. Read by Sean Pratt. (Running Time: 4 hrs. 30 mins.). (ENG.). 2009. 24.98 (978-1-59659-428-9(4), GildAudio) Pub: Gildan Media. Dist(s): HachBkGrp

Abraham Lincoln: A Life 1860-1861: An Election Victory, Threats of Secession, & Appointing a Cabinet. unabr. ed. Michael Burlingame. Read by Sean Pratt. (Running Time: 8 hrs. 30 mins.). (ENG.). 2009. 24.98 (978-1-59659-437-1(3), GildAudio) Pub: Gildan Media. Dist(s): HachBkGrp

Abraham Lincoln & the Heart of America. 1 CD. (Running Time: 1 hr. 10 mins.). (YA). (gr. 12 up). 2004. audio compact disk 14.95 (978-1-882513-84-0(3)) Greathall Prods.

Abraham Lincoln & the Second American Revolution. unabr. collector's ed. James M. McPherson. Read by Wolfram Kandinsky. 7 cass. (Running Time: 7 hrs.). 1992. 42.00 (978-0-7366-2131-1(8), 2932) Books on Tape.
Pulitzer-Prize winning author interprets Lincoln & the Civil War. Fascinating & insightful.

Abraham Lincoln Books. Abraham Lincoln. 2004. audio compact disk 25.00 (978-0-917466-18-2(7)) B & R Samizdat.

***Abraham Lincoln Comes Home.** Robert Burleigh. Illus. by Wendell Minor. 1 cass. (Running Time: 7 mins.). (J). (gr. 3-5). 2009. bk. 27.95 (978-0-8045-6977-4(0)); bk. 29.95 (978-0-8045-4202-9(3)) Spoken Arts.

Abraham Lincoln Logues. unabr. ed. Joe Loesch. Ed. by Cheryl J. Hutchinson. Illus. by Brian T. Cox. (Backyard Adventure Ser.). (J). (gr. k-6). 2000. pap. bk. 16.95 (978-1-887729-77-2(1)); pap. bk. 14.95 (978-1-887729-76-5(3)) Toy Box Prods.

Abraham Lincoln, the Prairie Years & Abraham Lincoln, the War Years. Carl Sandburg. 1 cass. (Running Time: 60 mins.). (Radiobook Ser.). 1987. 4.98 (978-0-929541-06-8(5)) Radiola Co.
Two complete stories.

***Abraham Lincoln: Vampire Hunter.** Seth Grahame-Smith. Read by Scott Holst. (Running Time: 10 hrs. 30 mins.). (ENG.). 2011. audio compact disk & audio compact disk 19.98 (978-1-60941-998-1(7)) Pub: Hachet Audio. Dist(s): HachBkGrp

Abraham Lincoln Walks at Midnight see Poetry of Vachel Lindsay

Abraham Lincoln's Writings & Speeches. unabr. ed. Abraham Lincoln. Read by Raymond Massey. 6 cass. 35.70 Audio Bk.
The most significant historical works of our 16th President.

Abraham Maslow-Humanistic Psychology. Robert Stone. 1 cass. 1986. 10.00 Listen & Learn.
Focuses on: mental health; deficiency vs. being needs; heirarchy of needs - physiological, safety, love & belongingness; esteem; self-actualization; characteristics of the self-actualizing person; peak experiences; causes of psychopathology.

Abraham the Alligator. Paula Allene Stark. (J). 2007. audio compact disk 9.99 (978-1-60247-220-4(3)) Tate Pubng.

***Abraham's Boys.** unabr. ed. Joe Hill. (ENG.). 2007. (978-0-06-155210-6(0)); (978-0-06-155212-0(7)) HarperCollins Pubs.

Abraham's Sacrifice. Jack Deere. 1 cass. (Running Time: 90 mins.). (Cross Ser.: Vol. 3). 2000. 5.00 (JD01-003) Morning NC.
These are outstanding messages on the work & power of the most important truths of our faith.

Abraham's Staggering Task: Genesis 22:1-24. Ed Young. 1994. 4.95 (978-0-7417-2038-2(8), 1038) Win Walk.

***Abram's Daughters.** abr. ed. Beverly Lewis. Narrated by Aimee Lilly. (Running Time: 15 hrs. 0 mins. 0 sec.). (Abram's Daughters Ser.). (ENG.). 2010. audio compact disk 28.98 (978-1-59644-932-9(2), christaudio) christianaud.

Abran Paso a los Patitos. 1 cass. (Running Time: 35 min.).Tr. of Make Way for Ducklings. (SPA.). (J). 2001. 15.95 (VXS-43C) Kimbo Educ.

Abran Paso a los Patitos. Robert McCloskey. 11 vols. (Running Time: 13 mins.).Tr. of Make Way for Ducklings. (SPA., (J). (gr. k-3). 2000. pap. bk. 16.95 (978-0-87499-659-3(7)); pap. bk. & tchr. ed. 37.95 Reading Chest. (978-0-87499-661-6(9)) Live Oak Media.
The tale of the famous Mallard ducks of Boston.

Abran Paso a los Patitos. Robert McCloskey. Tr. by Osvaldo Blanco. 11 vols. (Running Time: 13 mins.).Tr. of Make Way for Ducklings. (SPA., (J). (gr. k-3). 2000. bk. 25.95 (978-0-87499-660-9(0)) Live Oak Media.

Abran Paso a los Patitos. Robert McCloskey. Illus. by Robert McCloskey. 11 vols. (Running Time: 13 mins.).Tr. of Make Way for Ducklings. 2000. bk. 28.95 (978-1-59519-122-9(4)); pap. bk. 39.95 (978-1-59519-121-2(6)); 9.95 (978-0-87499-658-6(9)); audio compact disk 12.95 (978-1-59519-119-9(4)) Live Oak Media.

Abran Paso a los Patitos. Robert McCloskey. Illus. by Robert McCloskey. 11 vols. (Running Time: 13 mins.).Tr. of Make Way for Ducklings. (SPA.). (J). 2000. pap. bk. 18.95 (978-1-59519-120-5(8)) Pub: Live Oak Media. Dist(s): AudioGO

Abre Tu Corazón. unabr. ed. Carlos Cintrón. (SPA.). 1999. 9.99 (978-0-8297-2237-6(8)) Pub: Vida Pubs. Dist(s): Zondervan

Abre Tu Corazón. unabr. ed. Carlos Cintrón. 1999. audio compact disk 14.99 (978-0-8297-2238-3(6)) Zondervan.

Abroad. unabr. collector's ed. Paul Fussell. Read by Christopher Hurt. 10 cass. (Running Time: 10 hrs.). 1985. 60.00 (978-0-7366-0710-0(2), 1673) Books on Tape.
A collection of the greatest travel writing of the 20's & 30's.

Abs Diet: The Six-Week Plan to Flatten Your Stomach & Keep You Lean for Life. unabr. ed. David Zinczenko. Told to Ted Spiker. 4 CDs. (Running Time: 4 hrs.). (ENG.). 2006. audio compact disk 19.98 (978-1-59659-039-7(4), GildAudio) Pub: Gildan Media. Dist(s): HachBkGrp

Absalom, Absalom! William Faulkner. Read by Grover Gardner. 2002. 72.00 (978-0-7366-8955-7(9)); audio compact disk 80.00 (978-0-7366-9123-9(5)) Books on Tape.

Absalom, Absalom! unabr. ed. William Faulkner. Read by Wolfram Kandinsky. 11 cass. (Running Time: 16 hrs. 30 mins.). 1993. 88.00 (978-0-7366-2456-5(2), 3220) Books on Tape.
In 1830s Mississippi a ruthless stranger wrests a fabulous plantation out of the muddy swamplands.

Absalom & Achitophel see Poetry of John Dryden

Absence of Fault-Finding. Swami Jyotirmayananda. 1 cass. (Running Time: 1 hr.). 1990. 12.99 Yoga Res Foun.

Absence of Fault-Finding Nature. 1 cass. (Running Time: 60 mins.). (710) Yoga Res Foun.

Absence of Fickleness. Swami Jyotirmayananda. 1990. (711) Yoga Res Foun.

Absence of Fickleness. Swami Jyotirmayananda. 1 cass. (Running Time: 1 hr.). 1990. 12.99 (711) Yoga Res Foun.

Absence of Greed. 1 cass. (Running Time: 90 mins.). 1990. (711) Yoga Res Foun.

Absence of Greed. Swami Jyotirmayananda. 1 cass. (Running Time: 1 hr.). 1990. 12.99 Yoga Res Foun.

Absence of Light. abr. ed. David Lindsey. Read by Dick Hill. 2 cass. (Running Time: 3 hrs.). 2000. 7.95 (978-1-57815-035-9(3), 1025, Media Bks Audio) Media Bks NJ.
Murder mystery deep within the Houston's PD's intelligence division.

Absence of Light. unabr. ed. David Lindsey. Read by Dick Hill. (Running Time: 18 hrs.). 2007. 44.25 (978-1-4233-3143-8(5), 9781423331438, BADLE) Brilliance Audio.

Absence of Light. unabr. ed. David Lindsey. Read by Dick Hill. (Running Time: 18 hrs.). 2007. 44.25 (978-1-4233-3141-4(9), 9781423331414, Brinc Audio MP3 Lib); 29.95 (978-1-4233-3140-7(0), 9781423331407, Brilliance MP3) Brilliance Audio.

Absence of Light. unabr. ed. David Lindsey. Read by Dick Hill. (Running Time: 18 hrs.). 2007. 29.95 (978-1-4233-3142-1(7), 9781423331421, BAD) Brilliance Audio.

Absence of Nectar. Kathy Hepinstall. Narrated by Carine Montbertrand. 7 cass. (Running Time: 10 hrs. 15 mins.). 2001. 66.00 (978-1-4025-4505-4(3)) Recorded Bks.

Absence of the 'Me' J. Krishnamurti. 1 cass. (Running Time: 1 hr.). (Ojai Public Talks - 1984 Ser.: No. 4). 8.50 (AJT844) Krishnamurti.
In the idyllic setting of the oak grove in Ojai, California, Krishnamurti began giving talks in 1922. Over the years, hundreds of thousands of people have heard Krishnamurti explore every aspect of our lives, his language & expression constantly changing, as he strove to communicate to each successive generation those profound truths which he had come upon, & which he maintained were accessible to all.

Absent Author. unabr. ed. Ron Roy. Illus. by John Steven Gurney. (Running Time: 50 mins.). (A to Z Mysteries Ser.: No. 1). (J). (gr. k-3). 2004. pap. bk. 17.00 (978-0-8072-1703-0(4), S FTR 269 SP, Listening Lib) Random Audio Pubg.

Absent Friends. unabr. ed. Read by Barbara McCulloh. 10 cass. 84.95 (978-0-7927-3300-3(2)); audio compact disk 110.95 (978-0-7927-3301-0(0)) AudioGO.

Absent in the Spring. unabr. ed. Agatha Christie. Contrib. by Mary Westmacott. 6 CDs. (Running Time: 9 hrs.). 2002. audio compact disk 64.95 (978-0-7540-5479-5(9), CCD 170) AudioGO.
This is the story of a woman returning from a visit to her daughter in Iraq who is immobilized in an isolated railway rest house by flooding of the railway tracks. Enforced solitude compels Joan Scudamore to face up to many of the truths about herself and about her relationships, which she has striven to hide, and in doing so to reevaluate her life.

Absent in the Spring. unabr. ed. Mary Westmacott, pseud. Read by Ann Beach. 4 cass. (Running Time: 6 hrs.). 2001. 24.95 (978-1-57270-199-1(4), M41199u) Pub: Audio Partners. Dist(s): PerseuPGW
Delayed in her return to England, Joan Scudamore finds that solitude forces her to review her life. Much of the story comes from Joan's inner thoughts and reflections, allowing Beach to deliver the story like a soliloquy.

Absent-Minded Coterie see Classic Detective Stories, Vol. I, A Collection

Absent-Minded Coterie. unabr. ed. Robert Barr. Read by Walter Covell. 1 cass. (Running Time: 76 mins.). Dramatization. 1981. 7.95 (S-7) Jimcin Record.
Famous French detective story from the book, "The Triumphs of Eugene Valmont".

Absentee. unabr. ed. Maria Edgeworth. Read by Flo Gibson. 7 cass. (Running Time: 10 hrs.). 1994. 25.95 (978-1-55685-324-1(6)) Audio Bk Con.
A comic novel of Irish life on the serious consequences of absentee ownership. While his ambitious mother leads an extravagant life in London, Lord Colambre visits his family's estates & investigates the background of the woman he loves.

Absolute Abba. Chrome Dreams. 1 CD. (Running Time: 0 hr. 30 mins. 0 sec.). (ENG.). 2001. audio compact disk 9.95 (978-1-84240-112-5(2)) Pub: Chrome Dreams GBR. Dist(s): IPG Chicago

Absolute & Manifestation. unabr. ed. Vivekananda. Read by Alan Arkin. 1 cass. (Running Time: 33 mins.). 1988. 7.95 (978-1-882915-05-7(4)) Vedanta Ctr Atlanta.
The absolute divinity of the individual person & the manifestation of the absolute as the world.

Absolute Beginners: Alto Saxaphone. Steve Taxton. (Absolute Beginners Ser.). 2004. bk. 12.95 (978-0-7119-7432-6(2), AM92620) Music Sales.

Absolute Beginners: Bass Guitar. Phil Mulford. (Absolute Beginners Ser.). 2004. audio compact disk 12.95 (978-0-7119-7427-2(6), AM92616) Music Sales.

Absolute Beginners: Complete Guitar Course. Amsco Music Staff. 2 CDs. (ENG., 2003. DVD & audio compact disk 29.95 (978-0-8256-2796-5(6), 0825627966, Schirmer Trade Bks) Pub: Music Sales. Dist(s): H Leonard

Absolute Beginners: Guitar Scales. Cliff Douse. 1 cd. 2004. audio compact disk 12.95 (978-0-7119-8772-2(6), AM969672) Music Sales.

Absolute Beginners: Harmonica. Steve Jennings. (Absolute Beginners Ser.). 2004. audio compact disk 12.95 (978-0-7119-7431-9(4), AM92619) Music Sales.

Absolute Beginners: Keyboard. Arranged by Jeff Hammer. (Absolute Beginners Ser.). 2004. pap. bk. 12.95 (978-0-7119-7430-2(6), AM92618) Music Sales.

***Absolute Beginners - Ukulele.** Steven Sproat. 2010. pap. bk. 19.99 (978-0-8256-3740-7(6), 0825637406) Pub: Music Sales. Dist(s): H Leonard

Absolute Beginners Bodhran. Contrib. by Conor Long. (Running Time: 40 mins.). (ENG.). 2006. 32.95 (978-5-558-08918-9(0)) Waltons Manu IRL.

Absolute Beginners Drums. Music Sales Staff. 2005. DVD & audio compact disk 24.95 (978-0-8256-2971-6(3), AM980969, Amsco Music) Pub: Music Sales. Dist(s): H Leonard

Absolute Beginners Guitar: Omnibus Edition. Music Sales Publishing Staff. 2004. audio compact disk 19.95 (978-0-8256-2764-4(8), AM974468) Pub: Music Sales. Dist(s): H Leonard

Absolute Beginners' Guitar Book, Vol. 2. John Bennett. 2004. audio compact disk 12.95 (978-0-7119-8121-8(3), AM963622) Music Sales.

Absolute Beginners Keyboard. Jeff Hammer. 2005. DVD & audio compact disk 24.95 (978-0-8256-2969-3(1), AM980947, Amsco Music) Pub: Music Sales. Dist(s): H Leonard

Absolute Britney. Chrome Dreams Staff. 1 CD. (Running Time: 45 min.). (ENG.). 2001. audio compact disk 9.95 (978-1-84240-101-9(7)) Pub: Chrome Dreams GBR. Dist(s): IPG Chicago

Absolute Certainty. Rose Connors. Narrated by Bernadette Dunne. (Running Time: 7 hrs.). 2003. 27.95 (978-1-59912-400-1(9)) Iofy Corp.

Absolute Certainty: A Crime Novel. unabr. ed. Rose Connors. Read by Bernadette Dunne. 5 cass. (Running Time: 7 hrs.). 2003. 39.95 (978-0-7861-2459-6(8), 3094); audio compact disk 24.95 (978-0-7861-8923-6(1), 3094); audio compact disk 48.00 (978-0-7861-9188-8(0), 3094) Blckstn Audio.

Martha Nickerson, an assistant district attorney on Cape Cod, speaks for victims of crime and their families and sees the system as a means for doing right. After she wins a murder case, a suspect is put behind bars. But soon another body turns up in disturbingly similar circumstances. Did Marty and her colleagues target the wrong man? If so, Marty fears that the real killer will strike again. With her career on the line and lives at stake, Marty must rely on her own moral compass, legal savvy, and gut instinct as she matches wits with a twisted killer.

Absolute Certainty: A Crime Novel. unabr. ed. Rose Connors. Read by Bernadette Dunne. 5 pieces. 2004. reel tape 29.95 (978-0-7861-2466-4(0)); audio compact disk 32.95 (978-0-7861-9094-2(9)) Blckstn Audio.

Absolute Christina Aguilera. Chrome Dreams. (ENG.). 2001. audio compact disk 9.95 (978-1-84240-110-1(6)) Pub: Chrome Dreams GBR. Dist(s): IPG Chicago

Absolute Corrs. abr. ed. Chrome Dreams. (ENG.). 2001. audio compact disk 9.95 (978-1-84240-111-8(4)) Pub: Chrome Dreams GBR. Dist(s): IPG Chicago

Absolute Elizabeth. Joanna Dessau. 5 cass. (Running Time: 6 hrs. 30 mins.). (Soundings Ser.). (J). 2004. 49.95 (978-1-84283-747-4(8)) Pub: ISIS Lrg Prnt GBR. Dist(s): Ulverscroft US

Absolute Essentials. Charles R. Swindoll. 2008. audio compact disk 24.00 (978-1-57972-814-4(6)) Insight Living.

Absolute Existence. Swami Amar Jyoti. 1 cass. 1983. 9.95 (R-49) Truth Consciousness.

Essential Existence, the central idea of eternity. Answering the only valid question, getting back to the soul space. Signs of His working.

Absolute Experience in Medical Transcription: Family Medicine, General Surgery, Neurology, Radiology, Urology, Gastroenterology, Cardiology, ESL Internal Medicine, Otolaryngology. 3 CDs .wav. (Running Time: 965 mins.). 2004. cd-rom 269.00 (978-0-9763966-3-5(7)) HomEx Medical.

Three practice medical transcription CD-ROMs in .wav format. This 3-CD set contains 965 minutes of real physician dictation in the fields of Family Medicine, General Surgery, Neurology, Radiology, Urology, Gastroenterology, Cardiology, ESL Internal Medicine, and Otolaryngology. Transcript booklet included for self evaluation.

Absolute Experience in Medical Transcription CD #1: Family Medicine, General Surgery, Neurology. 1 CD. (Running Time: 300 mins.). 2004. cd-rom 99.00 (978-0-9763966-0-4(2)) HomEx Medical.

Practice medical transcription CD in .wav format. CD#1 contains 300+ minutes of real physician dictation in the fields of Family Medicine, General Surgery, and Neurology. Transcript booklet included for self evaluation.

Absolute Experience in Medical Transcription CD #2: Radiology, Urology, Gastroenterology. 1 CD .wav. (Running Time: 360 mins.). 2004. cd-rom 99.00 (978-0-9763966-1-1(0)) HomEx Medical.

Practice medical transcription CD-ROM in .wav format. CD#2 contains 360+ minutes of real physician dictation in the fields of Radiology, Urology, and Gastroenterology. Transcript booklet included for self evaluation.

Absolute Experience in Medical Transcription CD #3: Cardiology, ESL Internal Medicine, Otolaryngology. 1 CD .wav. (Running Time: 305 mins.). 2004. cd-rom 99.00 (978-0-9763966-2-8(9)) HomEx Medical.

Practice medical transcription CD-ROM in .wav format. CD#3 contains 305+ minutes of real physician dictation in the fields of Cardiology, ESL Internal Medicine, and Otolaryngology. Transcript booklet included for self evaluation.

Absolute Fear. Lisa Jackson. Read by Joyce Bean. (Playaway Adult Fiction Ser.). 2008. 84.99 (978-1-60640-919-0(0)) Find a World.

Absolute Fear. abr. ed. Lisa Jackson. Read by Joyce Bean. (Running Time: 21600 sec.). (New Orleans Ser.: Bk. 4). 2008. audio compact disk 14.99 (978-1-4233-1522-3(7), 9781423315223, BCD Value Price) Brilliance Audio.

Absolute Fear. unabr. ed. Lisa Jackson. (Running Time: 15 hrs.). (New Orleans Ser.: Bk. 4). 2007. 39.25 (978-1-4233-1518-6(9), 9781423315186, Brlnc Audio MP3 Lib); 24.95 (978-1-4233-1517-9(0), 9781423315179, Brilliance MP3); 97.25 (978-1-4233-1514-8(6), 9781423315148, BrilAudUnabridg); audio compact disk 117.25 (978-1-4233-1516-2(2), 9781423315162, BriAudCD Unabrid); audio compact disk 38.95 (978-1-4233-1515-5(4), 9781423315155, Bril Audio CD Unabri) Brilliance Audio.

Absolute Fear. unabr. ed. Lisa Jackson. Read by Joyce Bean. (Running Time: 15 hrs.). (New Orleans Ser.: Bk. 4). 2007. 39.25 (978-1-4233-1520-9(0), 9781423315209, BADLE); 24.95 (978-1-4233-1519-3(7), 9781423315193, BAD) Brilliance Audio.

Absolute French: Complete Learning Guide & Tapescript. Mark Frobose. 8 cass. (Running Time: 8 hrs.). (FRE.). 1999. stu. ed. 59.00 (978-1-893564-18-3(5)) Macmill Audio.

Absolute Friends. abr. ed. John Le Carre. (ENG.). 2005. 14.98 (978-1-59483-307-6(9)) Pub: Hachet Audio. Dist(s): HachBkGrp

Absolute Friends. abr. ed. John Le Carre. (Running Time: 7 hrs. 30 mins.). (ENG.). 2009. 49.98 (978-1-60024-560-2(9)) Pub: Hachet Audio. Dist(s): HachBkGrp

Absolute Friends. unabr. ed. John Le Carre. 9 cass. (Running Time: 13 hrs. 30 min.). 2004. 90.00 (978-0-7366-9853-5(1)) Books on Tape.

Absolute Green Day. Chrome Dreams. (ENG.). 2001. audio compact disk 9.95 (978-1-84240-115-6(7)) Pub: Chrome Dreams GBR. Dist(s): IPG Chicago

Absolute Italian: Complete Learning Guide & Tapescript. 6 cass. (Running Time: 6 hrs.). 2000. stu. ed. 19.99 (978-1-893564-36-7(3)) Macmill Audio.

Absolute Life. Kenneth Copeland. 6 cass. 1983. bk. & stu. ed. 30.00 (978-0-938458-42-5(6)) K Copeland Pubns.

How to lead a full life in Christ.

Absolute Light Healing. Christopher Love. Read by Christopher Love. 1 cass. (Running Time: 30 min.). 1997. 10.95 (978-1-891820-04-5(4)) World Sangha Pubg.

Self-hypnosis meditation for healing, self-improvement & realizing our full & powerful potential as spiritual beings.

Absolute Madonna. Chrome Dreams. (Running Time: 0 hr. 30 mins. 0 sec.). (ENG.). 2001. audio compact disk 9.95 (978-1-84240-114-9(9)) Pub: Chrome Dreams GBR. Dist(s): IPG Chicago

Absolute Power. David Baldacci. Read by Michael Kramer. 1996. audio compact disk 112.00 (978-0-7366-8516-0(2)) Books on Tape.

Absolute Power. David Baldacci. 2001. 17.00 (978-1-57042-763-3(1)) Hachet Audio.

Absolute Power. David Baldacci. Narrated by George Guidall. 15 CDs. (Running Time: 17 hrs.). 2001. audio compact disk 134.00 (978-0-7887-5179-0(4), C1341E7) Recorded Bks.

Tightly-woven, fast-paced political thriller that is as fascinating as it is relentlessly suspenseful.

Absolute Power. abr. ed. David Baldacci. (Running Time: 2 hrs.). (ENG.). 2006. 14.98 (978-1-59483-769-2(4)) Pub: Hachet Audio. Dist(s): HachBkGrp

Absolute Power, unabr. ed. David Baldacci. Read by Michael Kramer. 11 cass. (Running Time: 16 hrs. 30 mins.). 1996. 88.00 (978-0-913369-16-6(0), 3991) Books on Tape.

A cat burglar sees a murder approved by the President of the United States & runs for his life. Can he trust anyone?.

Absolute Power. unabr. ed. David Baldacci. Read by Scott Brick. (Running Time: 19 hrs.). (ENG.). 2010. 19.98 (978-1-60788-323-4(6)); audio compact disk 24.98 (978-1-60788-321-0(X)) Pub: Hachet Audio. Dist(s): HachBkGrp

Absolute Power, unabr. ed. David Baldacci. Narrated by George Guidall. 12 cass. (Running Time: 17 hrs.). 1997. 97.00 (978-0-7887-0524-3(5), 94719E7) Recorded Bks.

Tightly-woven, fast-paced political thriller that is as fascinating as it is relentlessly suspenseful.

Absolute Rage. Robert K. Tanenbaum. Read by Lee Sellars. 2004. 15.95 (978-0-7435-4088-9(3)) Pub: S&S Audio. Dist(s): S and S Inc

Absolute Rage. unabr. ed. Lee Sellars. Read by Nick Sullivan. 12 vols. (Running Time: 18 hrs.). 2002. bk. 96.95 (978-0-7927-2721-7(5), CSL 507, Chivers Sound Lib); audio compact disk 115.95 (978-0-7927-2749-1(5), SLD 507, Chivers Sound Lib) AudioGO.

What's at stake for the incorruptible prosecutor Butch Karp is nothing less than his personal code of honor - the imperative that drives him to protect his family above all else. A fast-rising, blue-collar Teamster with designs on the union presidency has been murdered in the mountains of West Virginia, along with his wife and youngest child. Karp is wary from the start about wading into such a politically dicey situation - and his fears are chillingly justified when killers target his own beloved family.

Absolute S Club 7. Chrome Dreams. (Running Time: 0 hr. 30 mins. 0 sec.). (ENG.). 2001. audio compact disk 9.95 (978-1-84240-103-3(3)) Pub: Chrome Dreams GBR. Dist(s): IPG Chicago

Absolute Spanish: Complete Learning Guide & Tapescript. Mark Frobose. 8 cass. (Running Time: 8 hrs.). (SPA.). 1999. stu. ed. 69.00 (978-1-893564-17-6(7)) Macmill Audio.

Absolute Spice. Chrome Dreams. (Running Time: 0 hr. 30 mins. 0 sec.). (ENG.). 2001. audio compact disk 9.95 (978-1-84240-117-0(3)) Pub: Chrome Dreams GBR. Dist(s): IPG Chicago

Absolute Steps. Chrome Dreams. (Running Time: 0 hr. 30 mins. 0 sec.). (ENG.). 2001. audio compact disk 9.95 (978-1-84240-113-2(0)) Pub: Chrome Dreams GBR. Dist(s): IPG Chicago

Absolute Sting. Chrome Dreams. (Running Time: 0 hr. 30 mins. 0 sec.). (ENG.). 2001. audio compact disk 9.95 (978-1-84240-118-7(1)) Pub: Chrome Dreams GBR. Dist(s): IPG Chicago

Absolute Surrender. Andrew Murray. Narrated by Charlie Glaize. 2008. 19.99 (978-1-4245-0826-6(6)) Tre Med Inc.

Absolute Surrender. unabr. ed. Andrew Murray. 2 CDs. (Running Time: 3 hrs. 30 mins. 0 sec.). (ENG.). 2006. audio compact disk 18.98 (978-1-59644-346-4(4), Hovel Audio) christianaud.

***Absolute Surrender.** unabr. ed. Andrew Murray. Narrated by Simon Vance. (ENG.). 2006. 10.98 (978-1-59644-347-1(2), Hovel Audio) christianaud.

Absolute Travis. Chrome Dreams. 1 CD. (Running Time: 0 hr. 30 mins. 0 sec.). (ENG.). 2001. audio compact disk 9.95 (978-1-84240-102-6(5)) Pub: Chrome Dreams GBR. Dist(s): IPG Chicago

Five scruffs from Glasgow, hardly the recipe for superstar success. But these are no normal scruffs, as Travis they've torn up the rule book all over the world and touched the masses with their brilliant melodies and poetic lyrics.

***Absolute Truth in Relative Terms.** Featuring Ravi Zacharias. 2003. audio compact disk 9.00 (978-1-61256-024-3(5)) Ravi Zach.

Absolute Truths. Susan Howatch. Read by Robert Whitfield. (Running Time: 73800 sec.). 2005. cass., cass., DVD 105.95 (978-0-7861-3496-0(8)); DVD & audio compact disk 44.95 (978-0-7861-8067-7(6)); DVD, audio compact disk, audio compact disk 120.00 (978-0-7861-7884-1(1)) Blckstn Audio.

Absolute Westlife. Chrome Dreams. (Running Time: 0 hr. 30 mins. 0 sec.). (ENG.). 2001. audio compact disk 9.95 (978-1-84240-116-3(5)) Pub: Chrome Dreams GBR. Dist(s): IPG Chicago

***Absolute Zero.** abr. ed. Chuck Logan. Read by J. K. Simmons. (ENG.). 2004. (978-0-06-078323-5(0), Harper Audio) HarperCollins Pubs.

***Absolute Zero.** abr. ed. Chuck Logan. Read by J. K. Simmons. (ENG.). 2004. (978-0-06-082422-8(0), Harper Audio) HarperCollins Pubs.

Absolute Zero. abr. ed. Chuck Logan. Read by J. K. Simmons. 2005. audio compact disk 14.95 (978-0-06-076360-2(4)) HarperCollins Pubs.

Absolutely Fabulous. unabr. ed. Jennifer Saunders et al. (Ab Fab Ser.). (ENG.). 2008. audio compact disk 14.95 (978-1-60283-363-0(X)) Pub: AudioGO. Dist(s): Perseus Dist

Absolutely Fabulous, Vols. 1-2. Jennifer Saunders. 2004. audio compact disk 29.95 (978-0-563-52452-6(9)) AudioGO.

Absolutely Fabulous 2. abr. ed. Read by J. Saunder & J. S. P. Lumley. 1 cass. (Running Time: 1 hr.). 1999. 11.25 (978-0-563-55710-4(9)) BBC WrldWd GBR.

Edina's father's death makes her aware of her own mortality. Will purchasing modern art help to ease her guilt & ease her conscience.

Absolutely Normal Chaos. Sharon Creech. Narrated by Kate Forbes. 5 CDs. (Running Time: 5 hrs. 30 mins.). (YA). (gr. 7 up). audio compact disk 48.00 (978-0-7887-4664-2(2)) Recorded Bks.

Absolutely Normal Chaos. Sharon Creech. Read by Kate Forbes. 4 cass. (Running Time: 5 hrs. 30 mins.). (J). 1999. pap. bk. 50.20 (978-0-7887-2994-2(2), 40876) Recorded Bks.

A journal kept by 13-year-old Mary Lou starts as a boring school project, but becomes a record of the most outrageously exciting summer of her life - so exciting that Mary Lou begs her teacher not to read it! Available to libraries only.

Absolutely Normal Chaos. Sharon Creech. Read by Kate Forbes. 2000. audio compact disk 48.00 Recorded Bks.

Absolutely Normal Chaos, unabr. ed. Sharon Creech. Narrated by Kate Forbes. 4 pieces. (Running Time: 5 hrs. 30 mins.). (YA). (gr. 7 up). 37.00 (978-0-7887-2964-5(0), 95738E7) Recorded Bks.

Absolutely Normal Chaos, Class Set. Sharon Creech. Read by Kate Forbes. 4 cass. (Running Time: 5 hrs. 30 mins.). (J). 1999. pap. bk. & wbk. ed. 107.30 (978-0-7887-3024-5(X), 46841) Recorded Bks.

Absolutely, Positively. Jayne Ann Krentz. Narrated by Richard Ferrone. 9 cass. (Running Time: 12 hrs. 30 mins.). 82.00 (978-1-4025-3350-1(0)) Recorded Bks.

Absolutely, Positively. unabr. ed. Jayne Ann Krentz. Read by Mary Peiffer. 8 cass. (Running Time: 12 hrs.). 1996. 64.00 (978-0-7366-3436-6(3), 104621) Books on Tape.

A scientist treats his girlfriend like a project, & the synergy is all wrong. Can he find a breakthrough.

Absolutely True Diary of a Part-Time Indian. unabr. ed. Sherman Alexie. 5 CDs. (Running Time: 5 hrs.). (YA). (gr. 8 up). 2008. audio compact disk 46.75 (978-1-4281-8297-4(7)); 33.75 (978-1-4281-8292-9(6)) Recorded Bks.

National Book Award winner Sherman Alexie delivers a captivating, semi-autobiographical account of one Spokane Indian's struggle against incredible obstacles. Born poor and hydrocephalic, Arnold Spirit survives brain surgery. But his enormous skull, lopsided eyes, profound stuttering, and frequent seizures target him for abuse on his Indian reservation. Protected by a formidable friend, the book-loving artist survives childhood. And then - convinced his future lies off the rez - the bright 14-year-old enrolls in an all-white high school 22 miles away.

Absolutes. Perf. by Stavesacre. 1 cass. 1997. audio compact disk 15.99 (D1081) Diamante Music Grp.

The four members of Stavesacre all come from other bands, including the likes of Mortal, The Crucified, Focused & Scaterd Few. Stavesacre claims a completely different sound than any of those previous groups, as each of the members as changed & matured accordingly since their days in those other bands. The lyrical content of Stavesacre reflects that change & maturity as well. The songs are catchy, the beats are solid, the musicianship is phenomenal & the ministry value is invaluable.

Absolutes & Negotiables: Acts 11:1-30. Ed Young. 1998. 4.95 (978-0-7417-2169-3(4), A1169) Win Walk.

Absolutes & Other Stories. unabr. ed. Robert Stanek, pseud. Read by Karl Fehr. (YA). 2008. 34.99 (978-1-60514-550-1(5)) Find a World.

Absolutes & Other Stories. unabr. ed. Robert Stanek, pseud. Narrated by Karl Fehr. (Running Time: 1 hr. 50 mins.). (ENG.). 2007. 14.95 (978-1-57545-311-8(8), RP Audio Pubng) Pub: Reagent Press. Dist(s): OverDrive Inc

Absolution Gap. unabr. ed. Alastair Reynolds. Narrated by John Lee. (Running Time: 27 hrs. 0 mins. 0 sec.). (Revelation Space Ser.). (ENG.). 2009. 44.99 (978-1-4001-5958-1(X)); audio compact disk 129.99 (978-1-4001-3958-3(9)) Pub: Tantor Media. Dist(s): IngramPubServ

Absolution Gap. unabr. ed. Alastair Reynolds. Read by John Lee. (Running Time: 27 hrs. 0 mins. 0 sec.). (Revelation Space Ser.). (ENG.). 2009. audio compact disk 64.99 (978-1-4001-0958-6(2)) Pub: Tantor Media. Dist(s): IngramPubServ

Absorptive Capacity of the Arab Members of OPEC. unabr. ed. Farid Abolfathi. 1985. (455) J Norton Pubs.

Abstinence Teacher. unabr. ed. Tom Perrotta. Read by Campbell Scott. (Running Time: 11 hrs. 30 mins. 0 sec.). (ENG.). 2007. audio compact disk 39.95 (978-1-4272-0191-1(9)) Pub: Macmill Audio. Dist(s): Macmillan

Abstraction from Abstractions. Harry Binswanger. 5 cass. (Running Time: 5 hrs.). 1997. 69.95 (978-1-56114-327-6(8), CB44D) Second Renaissance.

An examination of concept-formation & the means by which the range & power of man's conceptual faculty is expanded.

Abuelas Weave. unabr. ed. Omar S. Castañeda. 1 cass. (Running Time: 12 mins.). (J). (gr. k-4). 1994. bk. 25.90 (978-0-8045-6810-4(3), 6810); pap. bk. 16.90 (6810S) Spoken Arts.

Abuelita's Paradise. unabr. ed. Carmen Santiago Nodar. Illus. by Diane Paterson. 1 cass. (Running Time: 15 min.). (J). (gr. k-3). 2001. bk. 25.90 (978-0-8045-6847-0(2), 6847) Spoken Arts.

Share with Marita the memories of Abuelita's Puerto Rican childhood - the lush forests and evening sunsets - a true paradise.

Abundance. abr. ed. Marianne Williamson. 4 cass. (Running Time: 4 hrs.). 1998. 25.00 (978-1-56170-582-5(9), M863) Hay House.

Lectures on bringing abundance into your life.

Abundance: A Novel of Marie Antoinette. abr. ed. Sena Jeter Naslund. Read by Susanna Burney. 10 CDs. (Running Time: 43200 sec.). 2006. audio compact disk 39.95 (978-0-06-115091-3(6)) HarperCollins Pubs.

Abundance: A Novel of Marie Antoinette. unabr. ed. Sena Jeter Naslund. Narrated by Susanna Burney. 15 CDs. (Running Time: 66000 sec.). 2006. audio compact disk 117.95 (978-0-7927-4517-4(5), SLD 1047); audio compact disk 74.95 (978-0-7927-4562-4(0), CMP 1047) AudioGO.

***Abundance: A Novel of Marie Antoinette.** unabr. ed. Sena Jeter Naslund. Read by Susanna Burney. 2006. (978-0-06-123065-3(0), Harper Audio); (978-0-06-123066-0(9), Harper Audio) HarperCollins Pubs.

Abundance: A Sack of Polished Emeralds. Stuart Wilde. 1 cass. (Running Time: 1 hr.). 11.95 (978-0-930603-28-1([illegible])) White Dove NM.

A subliminal tape. Abundance is so m[illegible] matter of how you feel. In order for you to pull more money into your li[illegible] your intellect & the inner you have to agree to accept more abundanc[illegible]

Abundance - Staying Healthy Getting Wealthy. Patricia O'Malley. Perf. by Barry Weiss. 1 cass. (Running Time: 50 mins.). 1998. 11.95 (978-1-892450-06-7(2), 112) Pub: Promo Music. Dist(s): Penton Overseas

Learn how to develop the life & energy you need so you can create all the abundance your life can hold for you.

Abundance Hypnosis. Ormond McGill. 1989. (978-1-933332-02-4(6)) Hypnotherapy Train.

Abundance Hypnosis. Ormond McGill. 1 cass. 2005. audio compact disk (978-1-933332-31-4(X)) Hypnotherapy Train.

Abundance of Katherines. unabr. ed. John Green. Read by Jeff Woodman. (Running Time: 7 hrs.). 2006. 39.25 (978-1-4233-2455-3(2), 9781423324553, BADLE); 24.95 (978-1-4233-2454-6(4), 9781423324546,

BAD); 39.25 (978-1-4233-2453-9(6), 9781423324539, Brlnc Audio MP3 Lib) Brilliance Audio.
From the acclaimed author of Looking for Alaska, a witty novel about an aging child prodigy in search of relevance and a relationship he can count on. When it comes to relationships, Colin Singleton's type happens to be girls named Katherine. And when it comes to girls named Katherine, Colin is always getting dumped. Nineteen times, to be exact. He's also a washed-up child prodigy with ten thousand dollars in his pocket, a passion for anagrams, and an overweight, Judge Judy-obsessed best friend. Colin's on a mission to prove The Theorem of Underlying Katherine Predictability, which will predict the future of all relationships, transform him from a fading prodigy into a true genius, and finally win him the girl. Letting expectations go and love in are at the heart of Colin's hilarious quest to find his missing piece and avenge dumpees everywhere.

Abundance of Katherines. unabr. ed. John Green. Read by Jeff Woodman. 6 CDs. (Running Time: 7 hrs.). (YA). (gr. 9-12). 2006. audio compact disk 82.25 (978-1-4233-2451-5(X), 9781423324515, BriAudCD Unabrid); audio compact disk 24.95 (978-1-4233-2452-2(8), 9781423324522, Brilliance MP3); audio compact disk 29.95 (978-1-4233-2450-8(1), 9781423324508, Bril Audio CD Unabri) Brilliance Audio.

***Abundance of Valor: Resistance, Liberation, & Survival: 1944-45.** unabr. ed. Will Irwin. Narrated by Michael Prichard. (Running Time: 14 hrs. 0 mins.). 2010. 19.99 (978-1-4001-8423-1(1)) Tantor Media.

***Abundance of Valor: Resistance, Liberation, & Survival: 1944-45.** unabr. ed. Will Irwin. Narrated by Michael Prichard. (Running Time: 13 hrs. 30 mins. 0 sec.). (ENG.). 2010. 29.99 (978-1-4001-6423-3(0)); audio compact disk 79.99 (978-1-4001-4423-5(X)); audio compact disk 39.99 (978-1-4001-1423-8(3)) Pub: Tantor Media. Dist(s): IngramPubServ

Abundance Principle Audio. Thompson Leroy. 2004. 10.00 (978-1-931804-18-9(4)) Ever Increase Wd Min.

***Abundance Triggers: A Journey of Self-Discovery.** Kanta Bosniak. Composed by Kanta Bosniak. Composed by Joshua Bosniak. 2010. 16.99 (978-0-9843447-1-0(3)) K Bosniak.

Abundantly Wild: Collecting & Cooking Wild Edibles in the Upper Midwest. Teresa Marrone. 2004. per. 22.95 (978-1-59193-034-1(0)) Adventure Pubns.

Abuse Healed Through Forgiveness. Barrie Konicov. 2 CDs. 2003. audio compact disk 27.98 (978-1-56001-967-1(0)) Potentials.
Forgiveness is a quiet, inner action. It requires courage and a willingness on your part to take the first step. This program is gentle and loving in its approach and will lead you to the peace that you seek.This 2-CD program from our Super Consciousness series is our newest, most powerful format. On the self-hypnosis CD, SC programs have the Subliminal Persuasion soundtrack added under Barrie?s voice. And the 17th Century Baroque music on the Subliminal CD has the same beat as your body's natural rhythm, thereby allowing the suggestions to enter deeply and effortlessly.

Abuse of Power. unabr. ed. Nancy Taylor Rosenberg. Read by Frances Cassidy. 9 cass. (Running Time: 13 hrs. 30 min.). 1997. 72.00 (978-0-913369-73-9(X), 4326) Books on Tape.
A cop blows the whistle on a violent colleague & higher-ups recriminate. A tale of danger & betrayal.

Abuse of Power, unabr. ed. Nancy Taylor Rosenberg. Narrated by Barbara Rosenblat. 9 cass. (Running Time: 12 hrs. 45 mins.). 1997. 78.00 (978-0-7887-0916-6(X), 94957E7) Recorded Bks.
Rachel Simmons is a young widow, the mother of two children & a police officer. When she is caught in a perilous web of blackmail & corruption, she must decide which role is most important.

Abuse of Power: The New Nixon Tapes. abr. ed. Stanley I. Kutler. Perf. by David Ackroyd et al. 6 cass. (Running Time: 9 hrs.). 2001. 32.00 (978-1-59040-026-5(7), Phoenix Audio) Pub: Amer Intl Pub. Dist(s): PerseuPGW
Packed with revelations, this dramatic reconstruction of the Nixon tapes is a spellbinding portrait of raw power and a Shakespearean depiction of a king and his court. The personalities of Haldeman, Ehrlichman, Colson, Haig, Kissinger and Dean are vividly captured and the full story of Nixon's downfall is told.

Abused No More: A Survivor's Story of Courage. Interview. Carol Pierce. Interview with Monica Pierre. 1 cassette. (Running Time: 55 minutes). 1998. 19.95 (978-0-9662717-4-4(2), 1002) Success Now LA.
See domestic violence through the eyes of a victim who is now a highly successful survivor. Listen as Carol Pierce reveals the real reasons why breaking free from an abusive relationship is so difficult. Learn about the deep inner turmoil the victims, their families, and everyone in their presence experiences. Understand how you can truly help victims of abuse break those chains. Discover the powerful steps and superb resources guaranteed to help individuals become survivors leading successful lives, no matter how dark their present situation may seem. This audiotape gives hope to victims and creates a better understanding for those who so desperately want to help them.

Abusive Family & Treating Violent Families. unabr. ed. Walter Kempler. 1 cass. 8.50 Kempler Inst.
The nature of abusiveness in families, its meaning & the basic way to meet violence therapeutically.

Abyss. unabr. ed. Troy Denning. Read by Marc Thompson. (Star Wars Ser.). (ENG.). 2009. audio compact disk 40.00 (978-0-7393-7665-2(9), Random AudioBks) Pub: Random Audio Pubg. Dist(s): Random

Abyssinia. unabr. ed. Ursula Dubosarsky. Read by Rebecca Macauley. 3 CDs. (Running Time: 13500 sec.). (YA). (gr. 7-13). 2005. audio compact disk 54.95 (978-1-74093-686-6(8)) Pub: Bolinda Pubng AUS. Dist(s): Bolinda Pub Inc

Abyssinian Proof. Jenny White. Read by Nadia May. (Playaway Adult Fiction Ser.). (ENG.). 2008. 69.99 (978-1-60640-754-7(6)) Find a World.

Abyssinian Proof. unabr. ed. Jenny White. Read by Nadia May. (Running Time: 46800 sec.). 2008. 29.95 (978-1-4332-0945-1(4)); 65.95 (978-1-4332-0943-7(8)); audio compact disk 29.95 (978-1-4332-0946-8(2)); audio compact disk & audio compact disk 29.95 (978-1-4332-0947-5(0)); audio compact disk & audio compact disk 81.00 (978-1-4332-0944-4(6)) Blckstn Audio.

Ac-cent-tchu-ate the Positive. Music by Johnny Mercer & Harold Arlen. Arranged by Paula Foley Tillen. 1 CD. (Running Time: 5 mins.). 2000. audio compact disk 19.95 (08201242) H Leonard.
This standard is one of the top swing tunes of the '40s & this SSA setting will show your girl group at their finest!.

Acacia: Book One: the War with the Mein. unabr. ed. David Anthony Durham. Read by Dick Hill. (Running Time: 29 hrs. 30 mins. 0 sec.). (Acacia Ser.). (ENG.). 2007. audio compact disk 59.99 (978-1-4001-0488-8(2)) Pub: Tantor Media. Dist(s): IngramPubServ

Acacia Bk. 1: The Acclaimed New Fantasy. unabr. ed. David Anthony Durham. Narrated by Dick Hill. (Running Time: 29 hrs. 30 mins. 0 sec.). (War with the Mein Ser.). 2007. audio compact disk 39.99 (978-1-4001-5488-3(X)); audio compact disk 119.99 (978-1-4001-3488-5(9)) Pub: Tantor Media. Dist(s): IngramPubServ

Academic Advising & Support in Residential Learning Communities: NACADA Webinar Series 10. Featuring Derek Jackson & Nick Lander. 2008. audio compact disk 140.00 (978-1-935140-52-8(3)) Nat Acad Adv.

Academic Advising Delivery Models: Foundations of Academic Advising CD 2. (ENG.). 2006. audio compact disk 65.00 (978-1-935140-41-2(8)) Nat Acad Adv.

Academic Advising Syllabus: NACADA Webinar Series 02. Featuring Karen Thurmond. Charlie Nutt. (ENG.). 2007. audio compact disk 140.00 (978-1-935140-44-3(2)) Nat Acad Adv.

Academic Advising's Integral Role in the Academic Success & Persistence of Students: NACADA Webinar Series 06. Featuring Susan Campbell & Charlie Nutt. (ENG.). 2007. audio compact disk 140.00 (978-1-935140-48-1(5)) Nat Acad Adv.

Academic Listening Encounters: Listening, Note Taking, & Discussion. Miriam Espeseth. (Running Time: 3 hrs. 45 mins.). (Academic Encounters Ser.). (ENG., 1999. 69.00 (978-0-521-57819-6(1)) Cambridge U Pr.

Academic Listening Encounters: American Studies Class Audio CDs: Listening, Note Taking, & Discussion. Kim Sanabria & Carlos Sanabria. (Running Time: 3 hrs. 42 mins.). (Academic Encounters Ser.). (ENG.). 2007. audio compact disk 56.00 (978-0-521-68433-0(1)) Cambridge U Pr.

Academic Listening Encounters Human Behavior: Listening, Note Taking & Discussion. Miriam Espeseth. (Running Time: 3 hrs. 45 mins.). (Academic Encounters Ser.). (ENG., 2001. audio compact disk 69.00 (978-0-521-78357-6(7)) Cambridge U Pr.

Academic Listening Encounters: Life in Society: Listening, Note Taking & Discussion. Kim Sanabria. (Running Time: 2 hrs. 58 mins.). (Academic Encounters Ser.). (ENG.). 2004. 56.00 (978-0-521-75485-9(2)); audio compact disk 56.00 (978-0-521-75486-6(0)) Cambridge U Pr.

Academic Listening Encounters: the Natural World Class Audio CDs (3) Yoneko Kanaoka. (Running Time: 3 hrs. 42 mins.). (ENG.). 2009. audio compact disk 56.00 (978-0-521-71640-6(3)) Cambridge U Pr.

Academic Vocabulary: Study Wizard. 2nd rev. ed. Olsen. audio compact disk 14.97 (978-0-321-14261-0(6)) PH School.

Academ's Fury. unabr. ed. Jim Butcher. (Running Time: 21 hrs.). Bk. 2. (ENG.). (gr. 8). 2008. audio compact disk 49.95 (978-0-14-314377-2(8), PengAudBks) Penguin Grp USA.

Academy. unabr. ed. Ridley Pearson. Read by William Dufris. 1 MP3-CD. (Running Time: 8 hrs.). 2010. 24.99 (978-1-4418-3041-8(3), 9781441830418, Brilliance MP3); 24.99 (978-1-4418-3043-2(X), 9781441830432, BAD); 39.97 (978-1-4418-3042-5(1), 9781441830425, Brlnc Audio MP3 Lib); 39.97 (978-1-4418-3044-9(8), 9781441830449, BADLE); audio compact disk 26.99 (978-1-4418-3039-5(1), 9781441830395, Bril Audio CD Unabri); audio compact disk 74.97 (978-1-4418-3040-1(5), 9781441830401, BriAudCD Unabrid) Brilliance Audio.

Academy Award: Maltese Falcon. Perf. by Humphrey Bogart et al. 1 cass. (Running Time: 60 mins.). (Old Time Radio Classic Singles Ser.). 4.95 (978-1-57816-114-0(2), MA102) Audio File.
The radio version of the classic film. House of Squibb (7/31/46). Plus Screen Guild Players: "Arsenic & Old Lace".

Academy Award Theatre: Enchanted Cottage & Lost Angel with Margaret O'Brien. unabr. ed. Perf. by Bud Abbott et al. 1 cass. (Running Time: 1 hr.). 2001. 6.98 (1605) Radio Spirits.

Academy Award Theatre: Night Train & Devil & Miss Jones with Virginia Mayo. unabr. ed. Perf. by Bud Abbott et al. 1 cass. (Running Time: 1 hr.). 2001. 6.98 (1604) Radio Spirits.

Academy of Master Closing. Tom Hopkins. 12 cass. (Running Time: 12 hrs.). 1993. 169.95 (779PA) Nightingale-Conant.

Academy of Master Closing. Tom Hopkins. Read by Tom Hopkins. 12 cass. (Running Time: 12 hrs.). 1992. 195.00 (978-0-938636-28-1(6), 1085) T Hopkins Intl.
Advanced selling strategies for salespeople who have mastered the basics.

Acappella Praise. 2004. audio compact disk 9.99 (978-0-8474-1916-6(9)) Back to Bible.

Acappella Praise. Perf. by Liberty Voices, The. 9.95 (QA2385CS); audio compact disk 12.95 (QA2385CD) Questar CA.
The artistry & harmony of the famous Liberty Voices of Orlando's Disney World create the feeling of a down home revival meeting. Celebrate the spirit of the Lord in this musical jubilee featuring twenty-five gospel classics.

ACCEL. Ed. by Sylvan L. Weinberg. 12 cass. (Running Time: 90 mins. per cass.). 150.00 Am Coll Cardiology.
Monthly audiocassette subscription product (12 cassettes per year) features 8-10 interviews with leaders in the field of cardiovascular medicine every month.

Accelerate Healing Forces, Vol. 2. Jonathan Parker. Read by Jonathan Parker. 1 CD. (Running Time: 1 hr.). (Subliminal Ser.: Vol. 4). 1999. audio compact disk (978-1-58400-043-3(0)) QuantumQuests Intl.
Positive subliminal messages with classical music on compact disc.

Accelerate Healing Forces with Mind Power, Vol. 35, Set. Jonathan Parker. Read by Jonathan Parker. 2 CDs. (Running Time: 2 hrs.). (Success Ser.: Vol. 3). 1999. audio compact disk (978-1-58400-034-1(1)) QuantumQuests Intl.
Disc 1 contains several guided visualizations. Disc 2 contains audible & subliminal positive affirmations with music.

Accelerate Learning. Dick Sutphen. 1 cass. (Running Time: 1 hr.). (Only Subliminals Ser.). 1990. 12.98 (978-0-87554-448-9(7), T208) Valley Sun.
One hour of soothing, digitally mastered stereo music with positive subliminal suggestions phrased for maximum acceptance by your subconscious mind.

Accelerate Natural Healing with Tropical Ocean, Vol. 12. Jonathan Parker. Read by Jonathan Parker. 1 CD. (Running Time: 1 hr.). (Subliminal Ser.: Vol. 4). 1999. audio compact disk (978-1-58400-068-6(6)) QuantumQuests Intl.
1 compact disc with subliminal affirmations & tropical ocean.

Accelerate Your Healing. 1998. 24.95 (978-1-58557-018-8(4)) Dynamic Growth.

Accelerate Your Learning. 3 cass. cass. & video 99.95 Set, 8 bklets. OptimaLearning.
Become an accelerated learner & discover ways of learning that suit you. Read & absorb information faster, improve writing skills, improve memory, study more effectively, get the best possible results in exams, use your preferred way of learning. This program improves motivation, confidence & results.

Accelerated Healing & Well Being. Eldon Taylor. 1 CD. (Running Time: 52 mins.). (Whole Brain Innertalk Ser.). 1998. audio compact disk (978-1-55978-871-7(2)) Progress Aware Res.

Accelerated Healing & Well Being. Eldon Taylor. 1 CD. (Running Time: 52 mins.). (Whole Brain Innertalk Ser.). 1999. audio compact disk (978-1-55978-946-2(8)) Progress Aware Res.

Accelerated High Speed Learning. 1 cass. (Running Time: 60 min.). (Dick Sutphen Ser.). 1989. 9.95 Valley Sun.

Accelerated Learning. Dick Sutphen. 5 cass. (Self-Change Programming Ser.). cass. & video 59.95 set, incl. 4 audio cass. & 1 video cass. (978-0-87554-331-4(6), PK104) Valley Sun.
Includes: Accelerated Learning Video Hypnosis; Instruction - Motivation Tape; 25 Best Ways to Boost Your Brainpower; Do More in Less Time; Speed Reading. The Accelerated Learning 5-Tape Power Package is the ultimate approach to "power boosting" your brain.

Accelerated Learning: Memory Enhancement. unabr. ed. Inna Segal. Read by Inna Segal. (Running Time: 1 hr.). (ENG.). 2009. 12.98 (978-1-59659-326-8(1), GildAudio) Pub: Gildan Media. Dist(s): HachBkGrp

Accelerated Learning: OZO. Eldon Taylor. Read by Eldon Taylor. Ed. by Leslie Brice. 1 cass. (Running Time: 1 hr.). 1992. 19.95 (978-1-56705-012-7(3)) Gateways Inst.
Self improvement.

Accelerated Learning: Whispers. Eldon Taylor. Read by Eldon Taylor. Ed. by Leslie Brice. 1 cass. (Running Time: 1 hr.). 1992. 16.95 (978-1-56705-201-5(0)) Gateways Inst.

Accelerated Learning & Comprehension. Norman J. Caldwell. Read by Norman J. Caldwell. Ed. by Achieve Now Institute Staff. 1 cass. (Running Time: 20 mins.). (Academic Achievement Ser.). 1988. 9.97 (978-1-56273-080-2(0)) My Mothers Pub.
New ideas about how fast your mind can learn & comprehend.

Accelerated Learning & Study: Classic. Eldon Taylor. Read by Eldon Taylor. Ed. by Leslie Brice. 1 cass. (Running Time: 1 hr.). 1992. 16.95 (978-1-56705-071-4(9)) Gateways Inst.
Self improvement.

Accelerated Learning & Study: Easy. Eldon Taylor. Read by Eldon Taylor. Ed. by Leslie Brice. 1 cass. (Running Time: 1 hr.). 1992. 16.95 (978-1-56705-072-1(7)) Gateways Inst.

Accelerated Learning & Study: Ocean. Eldon Taylor. Read by Eldon Taylor. Ed. by Leslie Brice. 1 cass. (Running Time: 1 hr.). 1992. 16.95 (978-1-56705-073-8(5)) Gateways Inst.

Accelerated Learning & Study: Stream. Eldon Taylor. Read by Eldon Taylor. Ed. by Leslie Brice. 1 cass. (Running Time: 1 hr.). 1992. 16.95 (978-1-56705-074-5(3)) Gateways Inst.

Accelerated Learning & Studying. Eldon Taylor. 1 cass. (Running Time: 62 mins.). (Inner Talk Ser.). 16.95 (978-1-55978-093-3(2), 5310A) Progress Aware Res.
Soundtrack - Tropical Lagoon with underlying subliminal affirmations.

Accelerated Learning & Studying: Babbling Brook. Eldon Taylor. 1 cass. 16.95 (978-1-55978-459-7(8), 5310F) Progress Aware Res.

Accelerated Learning & Studying: Music Theme. Eldon Taylor. 1 cass. 16.95 (978-1-55978-095-7(9), 5310C) Progress Aware Res.

Accelerated Learning Language Courses - French. Ivan Barzakov. 12 cass. (Running Time: 1 hr. per cass.). 199.00 Set, incl. large format textbk., word cards. (ALS100) OptimaLearning.
Utilize numerous accelerated learning techniques & provides an excellent foundation for language learning with over 2,000 words & phrases.

Accelerated Learning Language Courses - German. Ivan Barzakov. 12 cass. (Running Time: 1 hr. per cass.). 199.00 Set, incl. large format textbk., word cards. (ALS200) OptimaLearning.

Accelerated Learning Language Courses - Italian. Ivan Barzakov. 12 cass. (Running Time: 1 hr. per cass.). 199.00 Set, incl. large format textbk., word cards. (ALS400) OptimaLearning.

Accelerated Learning Language Courses - Spanish. Ivan Barzakov. 12 cass. (Running Time: 1 hr. per cass.). 199.00 Set, incl. large format textbk., word cards. (ALS300) OptimaLearning.

Accelerated Learning Language Series. Colin Rose. 12 cass. 199.95 Set, Spanish Version. (11450AV); 199.95 Set, German Version. (11440AV); 199.95 Set, French Version. (11430AV); 199.95 Set, Italian Version. (11420AV) Nightingale-Conant.
Utilizing the revolutionary technique of accelerated learning, these foreign language courses allow anyone to converse comfortably in a new language within 30 days! Developed by the acclaimed learning expert Colin Rose, accelerated learning is based on the premise of involving both hemispheres of the brain, using music to "unstress" the learning process. The best way to realize our potential is by using all our brain - not just the analytical left half. Old style, repetitive teaching only uses the "logic" of the left half of the brain & neglects the more powerful, imaginative right half. Using these untapped mental capacities of your learning ability is the basis of this unique, highly effective course. Includes a comprehensive action guidebook & physical learning video, a fun & helpful packet filled with word games & cards & an informative booklet entitled, "The Secrets of Learning a Language".

Accelerated Learning Techniques. Brian S. Tracy & Colin Rose. 6 cass. (Running Time: 6 hrs.). wbk. ed. (978-1-55525-028-7(9), 11970A); wbk. ed. 69.95 (978-1-55525-029-4(7), 11970cd) Nightingale-Conant.
Access your genius potential.

Accelerated Learning Techniques. Brian S. Tracy & Colin Rose. 6 cass. (Running Time: 6 hrs.). 1995. wbk. ed. 59.95 Set incl. bonus cass. (11970AM) Nightingale-Conant.
This landmark program - based on Nobel Prize-winning research - offers the most effective system of learning ever developed for releasing your potential & exercising your capacity for thinking, learning & memorizing.

Accelerated Reader Quizzes. (McGraw-Hill. Lectura Ser.). (SPA & ENG.). (gr. 1 up). 2001. audio compact disk (978-0-02-186376-1(8)); audio compact disk (978-0-02-187860-4(9)) Macmillan McGraw-Hill Schl Div.

Accelerated Reader Quizzes. (McGraw-Hill. Lectura Ser.). (SPA & ENG.). (gr. 2 up). 2001. audio compact disk (978-0-02-186377-8(6)); audio compact disk (978-0-02-187861-1(7)) Macmillan McGraw-Hill Schl Div.

Accelerated Reader Quizzes. (McGraw-Hill. Lectura Ser.). (SPA & ENG.). (gr. 3 up). 2001. audio compact disk (978-0-02-186378-5(4)); audio compact disk (978-0-02-187862-8(5)) Macmillan McGraw-Hill Schl Div.

Accelerated Reader Quizzes. (McGraw-Hill. Lectura Ser.). (SPA & ENG.). (gr. 4 up). 2001. audio compact disk (978-0-02-186379-2(2)); audio compact disk (978-0-02-187863-5(3)) Macmillan McGraw-Hill Schl Div.

Accelerated Reader Quizzes. (McGraw-Hill. Lectura Ser.). (SPA & ENG.). (gr. 5 up). 2001. audio compact disk (978-0-02-186380-8(6)); audio compact disk (978-0-02-187864-2(1)) Macmillan McGraw-Hill Schl Div.

Accelerated Reader Quizzes. (McGraw-Hill. Lectura Ser.). (SPA & ENG.). (gr. 6 up). 2001. audio compact disk (978-0-02-186381-5(4)); audio compact disk (978-0-02-187865-9(X)) Macmillan McGraw-Hill Schl Div.

Accelerated Transition: Fast Forward Through Corporate Change. Mark L. Feldman & Michael F. Spratt. Read by Mark L. Feldman & Michael F. Spratt. 1 cass. (Running Time: 60 mins.). 1997. 12.00 (978-1-888232-29-5(3)) Knowldge Exchange.

Accelerating Learning. Steven Halpern. 1 cass. (Soundwave Two Thousand, the Audio Active Subliminal Ser.). 1990. (2003) Inner Peace Mus.
Relaxing music with subliminal affirmations.

Accelerating Profitability: Unlocking the Secrets to Intelligent Growth. Liz Lynch. Created by Liz Lynch. 6 CDs. (Running Time: 4 hrs. 40 mins). 2004. bk. (978-0-9724239-1-5(5)) Consult Ad.
Accelerating Profitability is a practical program designed specifically to help business leaders run their companies more profitability and effectively. Lean what it takes to build profit-making habits that increase margins, improve performance and expand your ability to lead a growing company. This product includes 6 audio CDs and a 120-page companion guide enclosed in a white vinyl case.

Accelerating Self-Healing. Steven Halpern. 1 cass. (Soundwave Two Thousand, the Audio Active Subliminal Ser.). 1990. (2016) Inner Peace Mus.
Relaxing music with subliminal affirmations.

Accelerating Soul Evolution - Personal & Planetary: Expedition Field Guide & Reference Book for the Interdimensional Adventurer. Scripts. Ralph Genter. 1 CD. (Running Time: 45 minutes). 2003. per. 25.00 (978-0-9640829-1-5(8)) Pub: Pleiadian Connect. Dist(s): New Leaf Dist
Basic Consciousness Raising Meditation.

Accelerating Student Learning & Motivation in Your Social Studies Classes: Hand-on Activities & Engaging Projects. Betty Ziskovsky. 2008. 95.00 (978-1-886397-87-3(2)) Bureau of Educ.

Accelerating the Healing Process: The Geometry of Being - Geometry in Motion. Eldon Taylor. Read by Eldon Taylor. 1 cass. (Running Time: 30 mins.). (Sacred Geometry Ser.). 1997. cass. & video 29.95 (978-1-55978-696-6(5), V103) Progress Aware Res.
Geometry in motion developing from fractals, forming mandalas, absolutely mesmerizing with tones & frequencies.

Accelerating Your Spiritual Progress Through Kriya Yoga. Kriyananda, pseud. (Running Time: 105 mins.). 14.95 (ST-36) Crystal Clarity.
Topics include: Gaining outward control of your life as a condition of spiritual progress; the role of the guru; Kriya as a process of magnetization; spiritual progress & the unfolding of the heart.

Acceleration. unabr. ed. Graham McNamee. 4 cass. (Running Time: 5 hrs. 39 mins.). (J). 2005. 35.00 (978-0-307-20732-6(3), Listening Lib); audio compact disk 45.00 (978-0-307-20733-3(1), Listening Lib) Random Audio Pubg.

Accent. unabr. ed. 4 cass. bk. 89.50 Set, incl. 42 visual aid cards & mirror. J Norton Pubs.
Spanish Speakers (SEN180); Tagalog Speakers (SEN210); Thai Speakers (SEN255); Vietnamese Speakers (SEN185).

Accent English: Arabic. 4 cass. (Running Time: 6 hrs.). 2001. pap. bk. 89.50 (SEN125) J Norton Pubs.
For the advanced foreign-born learner, this program provides a proven method for perfecting the pronunciation of American English. Teaches appropriate lip & mouth positions, stress, pause & intonation patterns. Includes 42 visual-aid cards, mirror & additional introductory cassette with helpful pre- & post-test.

Accent English: Chinese. 4 cass. (Running Time: 6 hrs.). 2001. pap. bk. 89.50 (SEN150) J Norton Pubs.

Accent English: French. 4 cass. (Running Time: 6 hrs.). (FRE & ENG.). 2001. pap. bk. 89.50 (SEN165) J Norton Pubs.

Accent English: Greek. 4 cass. (Running Time: 6 hrs.). 2001. pap. bk. 89.50 (SEN245) J Norton Pubs.

Accent English: Indonesian. 4 cass. (Running Time: 6 hrs.). 2001. pap. bk. 89.50 (SEN190) J Norton Pubs.

Accent English: Japanese. 4 cass. (Running Time: 6 hrs.). 2001. pap. bk. 89.50 (SEN170) J Norton Pubs.

Accent English: Korean. 4 cass. (Running Time: 6 hrs.). 2001. pap. bk. 89.50 (SEN175) J Norton Pubs.

Accent English: Russian. 4 cass. (Running Time: 6 hrs.). 2001. pap. bk. 89.50 (SEN195) J Norton Pubs.

Accent English: Sound of American Speech for Spanish Speakers. unabr. ed. Harold Stearns. Illus. by Jaime Servine. 4 cass. (Running Time: 6 hrs.). (Accent English Ser.). (YA). (gr. 10-12). 1990. spiral bd. 79.50 (978-0-924799-00-6(5)) Am Articulat.
Teaches foreign speakers of English the sounds of American speech with precise instructions on how to form the sounds through training of the mechanics and training the ear hear the sounds. Uses a mirror, pictures and drawings of mouth positions and audio tapes with drills of sounds, phrases, words and sentences.

Accent English: Sounds of American Speech for Arabic Speakers. unabr. ed. Harold Stearns. Illus. by Jaime Servine. 4 cass. (Running Time: 6 hrs.). (Accent English Ser.). (YA). (gr. 10-12). 1988. spiral bd. 79.50 (978-0-924799-03-7(X)) Am Articulat.

Accent English: Sounds of American Speech for Chinese Speakers. unabr. ed. Harold Stearns. Illus. by Jaime Servine. 4 cass. (Running Time: 6 hrs.). (Accent English Ser.). (YA). (gr. 10-12). 1988. spiral bd. 79.50 (978-0-924799-04-4(8)) Am Articulat.

Accent English: Sounds of American Speech for French Speakers. unabr. ed. Harold Stearns. Illus. by Jaime Servine. 4 cass. (Running Time: 6 hrs.). (Accent English Ser.). (YA). (gr. 10-12). 1988. spiral bd. 79.50 (978-0-924799-06-8(4)) Am Articulat.

Accent English: Sounds of American Speech for Greek Speakers. unabr. ed. Harold Stearns. 4 cass. (Running Time: 6 hrs.). (Accent English Ser.). 1993. pap. bk. 79.50 Set. (978-0-924799-12-9(9)) Am Articulat.
Teaches foreign speakers of English the sounds of American Speech with precise instruction how to form the sounds through training of the mechanics and training the ear to hear the sounds. Uses a mirror, pictures and drawings of mouth positions and audio tapes with drills of sounds, phrases, words and sentences.

Accent English: Sounds of American Speech for Indonesian Speakers. unabr. ed. Harold Stearns. Illus. by Jaime Servine. 4 cass. (Running Time: 6 hrs.). (Accent English Ser.). (YA). (gr. 10-12). 1988. spiral bd. 79.50 Set. (978-0-924799-07-5(2)) Am Articulat.
Teaches foreign speakers of English the sounds of American speech with precise instructions how to form the sounds through training of the mechanics and training the ear to hear the sounds. Uses a mirror, pictures and drawings of mouth positions and audio tapes with drills of sounds, phrases, words and sentences.

Accent English: Sounds of American Speech for Japanese Speakers. unabr. ed. Harold Stearns. Illus. by Jaime Servine. 4 cass. (Running Time: 6 hrs.). (Accent English Ser.). (YA). (gr. 10-12). 1988. spiral bd. 79.50 Set. (978-0-924799-01-3(3)) Am Articulat.

Accent English: Sounds of American Speech for Korean Speakers. unabr. ed. Harold Stearns. Illus. by Jaime Servine. 4 cass. (Running Time: 6 hrs.). (Accent English Ser.). (YA). (gr. 10-12). 1988. spiral bd. 79.50 Set. (978-0-924799-05-1(6)) Am Articulat.

Accent English: Sounds of American Speech for Russian Speakers. Harold Stearns. Illus. by Jaime Servine. 4 cass. (Running Time: 6 hrs.). (Accent English Ser.). 1989. spiral bd. 79.50 (978-0-924799-09-9(9)) Am Articulat.

Accent English: Sounds of American Speech for Tagalog Speakers. unabr. ed. Harold Stearns. Read by Harold Stearns. Illus. by Jaime Servine. 4 cass. (Running Time: 6 hrs.). (Accent English Ser.). 1989. spiral bd. 79.50 Set. (978-0-924799-10-5(2)) Am Articulat.
Teaches foreign speakers of English the sounds of American speech with precise instructions on how to form the sounds through training of the mechanics and training the ear hear the sounds. Uses a mirror, pictures and drawings of mouth positions and audio tapes with drills of sounds, phrases, words and sentences.

Accent English: Sounds of American Speech for Thai Speakers. unabr. ed. Harold Stearns. Illus. by Jaime Servine. 4 cass. (Running Time: 6 hrs.). (Accent English Ser.). 1989. pap. bk. 79.50 Set. (978-0-924799-08-2(0)) Am Articulat.
Teaches foreign speakers of English the sounds of American speech with precise instructions how to form the sounds through training of the mechanics and training the ear to hear the sounds. Uses a mirror, pictures and drawings of mouth positions and audio tapes with drills of sounds, phrases, words and sentences.

Accent English: Sounds of American Speech for Vietnamese Speakers. unabr. ed. Harold Stearns. Illus. by Jaime Servine. 4 cass. (Running Time: 6 hrs.). (Accent English Ser.: SEN185). (YA). (gr. 10-12). 1988. spiral bd. 79.50 Set. (978-0-924799-02-0(1)) Am Articulat.

Accent English: Spanish. 4 cass. (Running Time: 6 hrs.). 2001. pap. bk. 89.50 (SEN180) J Norton Pubs.
For the advanced foreign-born learner, this program provides a proven method for perfecting the pronunciation of American English. Teaches appropriate lip & mouth positions, stress, pause & intonation patterns. Includes 42 visual-aid cards, mirror & additional introductory cassette with helpful pre- & post-test.

Accent English: Tagalog. 4 cass. (Running Time: 6 hrs.). 2001. pap. bk. 89.50 (SEN210) J Norton Pubs.

Accent English: Thai. 4 cass. (Running Time: 6 hrs.). 2001. pap. bk. 89.50 (SEN255) J Norton Pubs.

Accent English: Vietnamese. 4 cass. (Running Time: 6 hrs.). 2001. pap. bk. 89.50 (SEN185) J Norton Pubs.

Accent Modification Audiotapes. 1 cass. 1995. 49.95 (978-1-56593-454-2(7), Singular) Delmar.

Accent on Achievement, Bk. 1. John O'Reilly & Mark Williams. (Accent on Achievement Ser.). (ENG.). 1997. audio compact disk 14.95 (978-0-7390-0483-8(2), 17144) Alfred Pub.

Accent on Achievement, Bk. 2. Steve Bach et al. 2 CDs. (Accent on Achievement Ser.). (ENG.). 1998. audio compact disk 14.95 (978-0-7390-0295-7(3), 08278) Alfred Pub.

Accent Reduction: How to Make Your Message the Focus, Not Your Accent. Narrated by T. J. Walker. 2003. audio compact disk 39.00 (978-1-932642-16-2(1)) Media Training.

Accent Your Character, Volume 1: Cockney & the Queen's English. Paul Meier. Perf. by Paul Meier. Intro. by Derek Rex & Don Dehm. Music by Al Roeder. Prod. by Don Dehm. (ENG.). 2007. audio compact disk 13.95 (978-0-9798255-0-7(4)) Pulp Gamer.

Accent Your Character, Volume 2: Irish & Scottish. Paul Meier. Perf. by Paul Meier. Intro. by Derek Rex & Deon Dehm. Music by Al Roeder. Prod. by Don Dehm. (ENG.). 2007. audio compact disk 13.95 (978-0-9798255-1-4(2)) Pulp Gamer.

Accents for Actors. abr. ed. 1 cass. (Running Time: 55 min.). 11.95 (978-0-8045-1027-1(X), SAC 1027) Spoken Arts.
Accents of Britain & Ireland for those seeking authentic pronunciation, with excerpts from famous plays & comparative reading of Shakespeare's sonnet "Shall I compare thee to a summer's day".

Accents for Actors. unabr. ed. 1 cass. pap. bk. 16.95 incl. transcripts. (SEN430) J Norton Pubs.
Of special interest to linguistics & actors.

Accents for Actors CD & Booklet. 1 CD. 2005. audio compact disk 19.95 (978-1-57970-273-1(2), SEN431, Audio-For) J Norton Pubs.

Accents of English, Vol. 1. John C. Wells. 1 cass. (ENG.). (C). 1982. 35.99 (978-0-521-24648-4(2)) Cambridge U Pr.

Accents on Artists. Barbara Toohil & Peter Toohil. Read by Mary Beth Evans & Erica Junke. Ed. by Kara Parmelee. 1 cass. (Running Time: 60 min.). 1996. 7.95 (978-0-9655152-1-4(4)) Art N Facts.
Easy phonetic pronounciation of over 800 artists' full names.

Accents on Artists. Barbara Toohil & Peter Toohil. Read by Mary Beth Evans & Erica Junke. Ed. by Barbara Toohil & Kara Parmelee. Illus. by Peter Toohil. 1 cass. (Running Time: 60 min.). 1996. pap. bk. 21.90 (978-0-9655152-2-1(2)) Art N Facts.

Accept the Challenge. Elbert Willis. 1 cass. (Moving Life's Mountains Ser.). 4.00 Fill the Gap.

Acceptable Risk. unabr. ed. Robin Cook. Read by Frances Cassidy. 10 cass. (Running Time: 15 hr.). 1995. 80.00 (978-0-7366-3038-2(4), 3720) Books on Tape.
Kimberly Stewart wants to kill development of shaky anti-depressant drug. A thriller with medicine & pharmaceuticals as backgrounds.

Acceptable Time. unabr. ed. Madeleine L'Engle. Read by Ann Marie Lee. 8 CDs. (Running Time: 9 hrs. 42 mins.). (YA). (gr. 6 up). 2008. audio compact disk 55.00 (978-0-7393-7203-6(3), Listening Lib) Pub: Random Audio Pubg. Dist(s): Random

Acceptable Time. unabr. ed. Madeleine L'Engle. Read by Ann Marie Lee. (ENG.). (J). (gr. 5). 2008. audio compact disk 40.00 (978-0-7393-7201-2(7), Listening Lib) Pub: Random Audio Pubg. Dist(s): Random

Acceptance. Vincent P. Collins. 1 cass. 1986. 7.95 (1539) Hazelden.
"Acceptance" comments on the formula for contentment - the Serenity Prayer. "Me, Myself & You" describes a philosophy for being happier with oneself & growing intellectually & spiritually.

Acceptance: The Gateway to Transformation. unabr. ed. Carol Howe. 3 cass. (Running Time: 4 hrs. 15 min.). 1995. 24.95 Set. (978-1-889642-05-5(3)) C Howe.
Do you feel trapped & upset by situations that seem endlessly unresolved? Discover the transforming power of true acceptance & precisely how it applies in even the most "hopeless" cases. Using the rich visual imagery of a new teaching aid, this workshop: Clarifies the difference between true acceptance & resignation or "selling out." Explores what we resist & why & reveals the process by which difficulties are automatically transformed. Proves it's never too late for change! The opportunities for a happy life never end.

Acceptance Breeds... Power! Set: How to Stop Railing Against Reality & Move On. David Grudermeyer & Rebecca Grudermeyer. 2 cass. (Running Time: 3 hrs.). 1999. 18.95 (T-15) Willingness Wrks.

Acceptance; Good Friday Inspirations. Jonathan Murro & Ann Ree Colton. 1 cass. 1990. 7.95 A R Colton Fnd.

Acceptance of Ambivalence, Vol. III. 1 cass. (Running Time: 50 min.). 12.95 Comn Studies.
Discusses the difficult & often misunderstood topic of ambivalence, what it is like to feel a number of conflicting feelings at the same time. Learn how the battles within can be resolved.

Accepting Change. Eldon Taylor. 1 cass. (Running Time: 62 min.). (Inner Talk Ser.). 16.95 (978-1-55978-373-6(7), 5380A) Progress Aware Res.
Soundtrack - Tropical Lagoon with underlying subliminal affirmations.

Accepting Change: Easy. Eldon Taylor. Read by Eldon Taylor. Ed. by Leslie Brice. 1 cass. (Running Time: 1 hr.). 1992. 16.95 (978-1-56705-212-1(6)) Gateways Inst.
Self improvement.

Accepting Change: Music Theme. Eldon Taylor. 1 cass. 16.95 (978-0-940699-58-8(3), 5380C) Progress Aware Res.

Accepting Change: Ocean. Eldon Taylor. Read by Eldon Taylor. Ed. by Leslie Brice. 1 cass. (Running Time: 1 hr.). 1992. 16.95 (978-1-56705-214-5(2)) Gateways Inst.

Accepting Change: Peaceful Ocean. Eldon Taylor. 1 cass. 16.95 (978-1-55978-440-5(7), 5380O) Progress Aware Res.

Accepting Change & Moving On: Loss & Letting Go. 1 cassette. (Running Time: 58:24 mins.). 1981. 12.95 (978-1-55841-048-0(1)) Emmett E Miller.
Dealing with loss is one of our most difficult challenges - the loss of possessions, social status, a loved one or even your own life - may be difficult to accept. Dr. Miller's wise guidance and soothing voice are layered into a bed of beautiful music creating a thoroughly serene experience to enable mind and body to let go.

Accepting Change & Moving On: Loss & Letting Go. 1 CD. 1981. audio compact disk 16.95 (978-1-55841-124-1(0)) Emmett E Miller.

Accepting Christ As Saviour. Theodore H. Epp & Dave Breese. 1 cass. 4.95 (978-0-8474-2222-7(4)) Back to Bible.
Series of messages to share with a loved one or friend.

Accepting Healthy Criticism. Eldon Taylor. 1 CD. (Running Time: 52 min.). (Whole Brain Innertalk Ser.). 1998. audio compact disk (978-1-55978-862-5(3)) Progress Aware Res.

Accepting Healthy Criticism. Eldon Taylor. 1 CD. (Running Time: 52 min.). (Whole Brain Innertalk Ser.). 1999. audio compact disk (978-1-55978-912-7(3)) Progress Aware Res.

Accepting My Own Authority - Getting Rid of Self-Condemnation & Guilt. unabr. ed. Lilburn S. Barksdale. Read by Mark Denis. 1 cass. (Running Time: 42 min.). 1977. 9.95 (978-0-918588-29-6(4), 123) NCADD.
Side one helps you take conscious charge of your life. Side two explains why guilt is irrational despite the fact that each of us is inescapably responsible for everything we think, say & do.

Accepting Myself Totally & Unconditionally: Accepting Others Totally & Unconditionally. unabr. ed. Lilburn S. Barksdale. Read by Mark Denis. 1 cass. (Running Time: 48 min.). 1980. 9.95 (978-0-918588-32-6(4), 166) NCADD.
Exercises begin with noticing how bad you feel when finding fault with yourself & others, then go on to show how to change your attitude by realizing that we are all precious beings doing the best we can with the awareness we have at the time.

Accepting Others & Making Friends. unabr. ed. Trenna Daniells. 2 cass. (Running Time: 80 mins.). Dramatization. (One to Grow On Ser.). (J). (gr. k-8). 1999. 19.95 (978-0-918519-23-8(3)) Trenna Prods.
Four stories that teach children how to accept others as themselves & ideas for making friends. These action-packed stories promote high self-esteem, self-responsibility, morals & values.

Accepting Others As They Are: Travis & the Dragon. Trenna Daniells. Read by Trenna Daniells. 1 cass. (Running Time: 30 mins.). (One to Grow On! Ser.). (J). (gr. 4 up). 9.95 (978-0-918519-07-8(1), 12006) Trenna Prods.

Accepting Others As They Are - Travis & the Dragon. Trenna Daniells. Narrated by Trenna Daniells. (ENG.). (J). 2009. (978-0-918519-55-9(1)) Trenna Prods.

Accepting People & Truth & Consequence. Marianne Williamson. Read by Marianne Williamson. 1 cass. (Running Time: 90 mins.). (Lectures on a Course in Miracles). 1999. 10.00 (978-1-56170-222-0(6), M700) Hay House.

Accepting Unwanted Realities: I Am My Own Authority. unabr. ed. Lilburn S. Barksdale. Read by Mark Denis. 1 cass. (Running Time: 27 mins.). 1980. 9.95 (978-0-918588-33-3(2), 167) NCADD.
Side one teaches how to drop your resistance to unwanted realities so you can cope with them calmly & rationally. Side two shows that you alone are responsible for your own life & explains how to exercise your innate freedom & authority to fulfill that responsibility.

Access: Fundamentals of Literacy & Communication. Steven J. Molinsky & Bill Bliss. 2002. 40.80 (978-0-13-004250-7(1)) Longman.

Access Accents: Geordie (Newcastle) an Accent Training Resource for Actors. Gwyneth Strong & Penny Dyer. (Access Accents Ser.). (ENG., 2007. audio compact disk 29.95 (978-0-7136-8535-0(2)) Pub: A and C Blk GBR. Dist(s): Macmillan

Access Accents: London (Cockney) an Accent Training Resource for Actors. Gwyneth Strong & Penny Dyer. (Access Accents Ser.). (ENG., 2007. audio compact disk 29.95 (978-0-7136-8518-3(2)) Pub: A and C Blk GBR. Dist(s): Macmillan

Access Accents: Received Pronunciation (RP) an Accent Training Resource for Actors. Gwyneth Strong & Penny Dyer. (Access Accents Ser.). (ENG., 2007. audio compact disk 29.95 (978-0-7136-8504-6(2)) Pub: A and C Blk GBR. Dist(s): Macmillan

Access Accents: Yorkshire (North, West & South) an Accent Training Resource for Actors. Gwyneth Strong & Penny Dyer. (Access Accents Ser.). (ENG., 2007. audio compact disk 29.95 (978-0-7136-8519-0(0)) Pub: A and C Blk GBR. Dist(s): Macmillan

Access Control Equipment in France: A Strategic Reference 2006. Compiled by Icon Group International, Inc. Staff. 2007. ring bd. 195.00 (978-0-497-35942-3(1)) Icon Grp.

Access Control Equipment in Hong Kong: A Strategic Reference 2007. Compiled by Icon Group International, Inc. Staff. 2007. ring bd. 195.00 (978-0-497-35997-3(9)) Icon Grp.

Access New York City. Richard Saul Wurman. 1999. 29.95 (978-0-694-52158-6(2)) HarperCollins Pubs.

Access San Francisco. Richard Saul Wurman. 1999. 29.95 (978-0-694-52157-9(4)) HarperCollins Pubs.

Access the Akashic Records. Bruce Goldberg. (ENG.). 2005. audio compact disk 17.00 (978-1-57968-064-0(X)) Pub: B Goldberg. Dist(s): Baker Taylor

Access the Akashic Records. Bruce Goldberg. Read by Bruce Goldberg. 1 cass. (Running Time: 25 mins.). (ENG.). 2006. 13.00 (978-1-885577-89-4(3)) Pub: B Goldberg. Dist(s): Baker Taylor
Through self-hypnosis tap into the karmic files of one's past/future lives, or that of the universe.

Access the Light Body. Nancy A. Clark. Read by Nancy A. Clark. 1 cass. (Running Time: 60 mins.). (Journeys of Rememberance Audio Ser.). 1999. 9.95 (A5003) Lghtwrks Aud & Vid.
"Light Bodies & The Fourth Dimension" (side A) is for anyone interested in ascension & the future of their physical body. Learn clear, precise information about Fourth Dimensional density & how it differs from our present density. The "Light Body Meditation" will lead you on a trip into the future where many breathtaking "Gardens of Eden" exist on Earth. Learn to put on your "garment of light" (the Biblical "Gematrian" body) & as the highlight of this meditation, meet the Cosmic Christ & receive a special gift. Also gain an understanding of the meaning of crop circles & how to anchor heightened energy vibrations into the planet.

Access the Light Body. Nancy A. Clark. Read by Nancy A. Clark. 1 cass. (Running Time: 1 hr.). (Journeys of Remembrance Ser.). 1975. 16.00 (978-0-9648307-0-7(1)) Violet Fire Pubns.
Side A: Clear information on the 4th dimension & the process of ascension. Side B: "Light Body Meditation" takes you on a trip to the future of earth & future humanity.

Access the Zone: A Mental Strategy to Maximize Your Golf Game for Men. Marianne Hill & Mike Allen. 4 cass. (Running Time: 4 hrs.). 1999. bk. 79.95 (978-1-930326-50-7(5)) Subconscious Sol.
Introduction to use of hypnosis for achieving enhanced golf performance. Includes seven 30 minute hypnosis sessions that will teach relaxation, visualization & self-hypnosis.

Access the Zone: A Mental Strategy to Maximize Your Golf Game for Women. Marianne Hill & Mike Allen. 4 cass. (Running Time: 4 hrs.). 1999. bk. 79.95 (978-1-930326-00-2(9)) Subconscious Sol.

Access to English. unabr. ed. Michael Coles & Basil Lord. 8 cass. (Running Time: 12 hrs.). 1999. 251.95 (978-0-19-454060-5(X)) OUP.

Access to English As a Second Language, Vol. 2. Robert G. Breckenridge. 1 cass. 1975. 104.00 (978-0-07-007404-0(6)) McGraw.

Accessing God's Benefits. Mark Crow. 2 cass. (Running Time: 3 hrs.). 2001. (978-1-931537-29-2(1)) Vision Comm Creat.

Accessing the Spiritual Dimension. Hal Stone & Sidra Stone. 1 cass. (Running Time: 1 hrs.). (Mendocino Ser.: Vol. 16). 1997. 10.95 (978-1-56557-056-6(1), T16) Delos Inc.
The spiritual dimension is the golden strand in the tapestry of life. It gives depth & meaning to everything we do. Learn how Voice Dialogue & the Psychology of Selves can contribute new ways of weaving its soul-based reality into the totality of our lives.

Accessing Your Inherent Talent & Creative Inner Wisdom for All Musicians. Christopher Love. Read by Christopher Love. 1 cass. (Running Time: 30 mins.). 1997. 10.95 (978-1-891820-28-1(1)) World Sangha Pubg.
Self-hypnosis meditation for healing, self-improvement & realizing our full & powerful potential as spiritual beings.

Accessors of His Power, Dispensers of His Glory. Lynne Hammond. 3 CDs. (Running Time: 3 hours). 2005. audio compact disk 15.00 (978-1-57399-198-8(8)) Mac Hammond.
Lynne points out the biblical laws that govern the working of God's supernatural power. And she reveals how, by degrees, a last days' outpouring of the Lord's glory can fill us, change us and the world.

Accident see Widdershins: The First Book of Ghost Stories

Accident. unabr. ed. Elie Wiesel. Narrated by George Guidall. 3 cass. (Running Time: 3 hrs. 45 mins.). 1999. 26.00 (978-1-55690-833-0(4), 93201E7) Recorded Bks.
A young man, survivor of the German death camps, struggles to understand the many catastrophes of his past in the aftermath of a life-threatening accident.

Accident Investigation. Delmar Learning Staff & NATMI Staff. 2009. audio compact disk 91.95 (978-1-4354-9747-4(3)) Pub: Delmar. Dist(s): CENGAGE Learn

Accident Man. Tom Cain. Read by John Lee. (Running Time: 13 hrs.). (ENG.). (gr. 12 up). 2008. audio compact disk 39.95 (978-0-14-314300-0(X), PengAudBks) Penguin Grp USA.

Accidental. unabr. ed. Ali Smith. (YA). 2006. 49.99 (978-1-59895-210-0(2)) Find a World.

Accidental. unabr. ed. Ali Smith. 8 CDs. (Running Time: 9 hrs.). (ENG.). 2006. audio compact disk 34.95 (978-1-59887-013-8(0), 1598870130) Pub: Penguin-HghBrdg. Dist(s): Penguin Grp USA

accidental American. Alex Carr. Read by Caroline Lee. (Running Time: 8 hrs. 35 mins.). 2009. 74.99 (978-1-74214-199-2(4), 9781742141992) Pub: Bolinda Pubng AUS. Dist(s): Bolinda Pub Inc

Accidental American. unabr. ed. Alex Carr. Read by Caroline Lee. (Running Time: 8 hrs. 35 mins.). 2007. audio compact disk 83.95 (978-1-74093-923-2(9), 9781740939232) Pub: Bolinda Pubng AUS. Dist(s): Bolinda Pub Inc

accidental American. unabr. ed. Alex Carr. Read by Caroline Lee. (Running Time: 8 hrs. 35 mins.). 2009. 43.95 (978-1-74214-397-2(0), 9781742143972) Pub: Bolinda Pubng AUS. Dist(s): Bolinda Pub Inc

Accidental Billionaires: The Founding of Facebook - A Tale of Sex, Money, Genius & Betrayal. unabr. ed. Ben Mezrich. Read by Mike Chamberlain. (ENG.). 2009. audio compact disk 35.00 (978-0-7393-8358-2(2), Random AudioBks) Pub: Random Audio Pubg. Dist(s): Random

***Accidental Billionaires: The Founding of Facebook - A Tale of Sex, Money, Genius & Betrayal.** unabr. ed. Ben Mezrich. Read by Mike Chamberlain. 6 CDs. 2009. audio compact disk 70.00 (978-1-4159-6565-8(X), BksonTape) Pub: Random Audio Pubg. Dist(s): Random

Accidental Crimes. unabr. collector's ed. John Hutton. Read by Richard Brown. 6 cass. (Running Time: 9 hrs.). 1987. 48.00 (978-0-7366-1107-7(X), 2033) Books on Tape.
A school administrator alters truth, to his great regret.

***Accidental Detective.** unabr. ed. Laura Lippman. Read by Linda Emond & Francois Battiste. (ENG.). 2008. (978-0-06-176289-5(X), Harper Audio); (978-0-06-176288-8(1), Harper Audio) HarperCollins Pubs.

Accidental Life. unabr. ed. Titia Sutherland. Read by Carole Boyd. 6 cass. (Running Time: 7 hrs. 30 mins.). 1998. 54.95 (978-0-7531-0402-6(4), 980608) Pub: ISIS Audio GBR. Dist(s): Ulverscroft US
On a cold day in January, Philip Stavely, successful actor & family man, was killed during a shooting party, leaving behind his wife Ellie & their children. Although the inquest determined that the death was accidental, his wife is convinced it was suicide & she is determined to discover the cause.

Accidental Life. unabr. ed. Titia Sutherland. Read by Carole Boyd. 6 CDs. (Running Time: 9 hrs.). 2001. audio compact disk 64.95 (978-0-7531-1251-9(5), 1251-5) Pub: ISIS Audio GBR. Dist(s): ISIS Pub

Accidental Sorcerer. unabr. ed. K. E. Mills. Narrated by Stephen Hoye. (Running Time: 16 hrs. 0 mins. 0 sec.). (Rogue Agent Ser.). (ENG.). 2009. audio compact disk 79.99 (978-1-4001-4319-1(5)); audio compact disk 39.99 (978-1-4001-1319-4(9)); audio compact disk 29.99 (978-1-4001-6319-9(6)) Pub: Tantor Media. Dist(s): IngramPubServ

Accidental Tourist. Anne Tyler. Read by George Guidall. 8 Cass. (Running Time: 13.5 Hours). 34.95 (978-1-4025-2802-6(7)) Recorded Bks.

Accidental Tourist. unabr. ed. Anne Tyler. Read by Ruth Stokesberry. 8 cass. (Running Time: 12 hrs.). 1989. 64.00 (978-0-7366-1657-7(8), 2508) Books on Tape.
A man who looses his son & wife.

Accidental Tourist. unabr. ed. Anne Tyler. Narrated by George Guidall. 12 CDs. (Running Time: 13 hrs. 15 mins.). 2001. audio compact disk 116.00 (978-0-7887-7185-9(X), C1435) Recorded Bks.
When Muriel Pritchett falls into travel writer Macon Leary's life, her eccentric, disorderly world becomes his gentle reprieve.

Accidental Tourist. unabr. ed. Anne Tyler. Narrated by George Guidall. 9 cass. (Running Time: 13 hrs. 15 mins.). 1991. 78.00 (978-1-55690-000-6(7), 91404E7) Recorded Bks.
Muriel Pritchett overturns Macon Leary's carefully organized life with a free spirit & open heart.

***Accidental Vampire.** unabr. ed. Lynsay Sands. (ENG.). 2009. (978-0-06-196143-4(4), Harper Audio) HarperCollins Pubs.

***Accidental Vampire: An Argeneau Novel.** unabr. ed. Lynsay Sands. (ENG.). 2009. (978-0-06-195863-2(8), Harper Audio) HarperCollins Pubs.

Accidental Woman. abr. ed. Barbara Delinsky. Read by Jennifer Wiltsie. 2007. 17.95 (978-0-7435-6102-0(3)) Pub: S&S Audio. Dist(s): S and S Inc

Accidents of Nature. unabr. ed. Harriet McBryde Johnson. Read by Jenna Lamia. 5 CDs. (Running Time: 5 hrs. 41 mins.). (YA). (gr. 9 up). 2006. audio compact disk 45.00 (978-0-7393-3562-8(6), Listening Lib); 35.00 (978-0-7393-3571-0(5), Listening Lib) Pub: Random Audio Pubg. Dist(s): Random
Seventeen-year-old Jean has cerebral palsy and gets around in a wheelchair, but she's always believed she's just the same as everyone else. She goes to normal school and has normal friends. She's never really known another disabled person before she arrives at Camp Courage. But there Jean meets Sara, who welcomes her to "Crip Camp" and nicknames her Spazzo. Sara has radical theories about how people fit into society. She's full of rage and revolution against pitying insults and the lack of respect for people with disabilities. As Jean joins a community unlike any she has ever imagined, she comes to question her old beliefs and look at the world in a new light. The camp session is only ten days long, but that may be all it takes to change a life forever.

Accolay - Concerto No. 1 for Violin & Piano in A Minor: Concerto No. 1 for Violin & Piano in A Minor. Composed by Jean-Baptiste Accolay. 2006. pap. bk. 19.95 (978-3-905479-98-0(2), 3905479982) Pub: Dowani Intl LIE. Dist(s): H Leonard

Accompaniment Piano-by-Ear: Piano "By Ear" unabr. ed. David W. Lawrence. 6 cass. (Running Time: 2 hrs.). (Rapid Music Development Ser.: Vol. 101). 1994. 199.95 (978-1-890122-03-4(3)) Kingdom Ent.

Accompaniments for Anthology of Spanish Song: High Voice. Ed. by Richard Walters & Maria DiPalma. (Vocal Library). 2006. pap. bk. 16.95 (978-1-4234-1835-1(2), 1423418352) H Leonard.

Accompaniments for the Lieder Anthology: High Voice. Ed. by Virginia Saya & Richard Walters. Contrib. by Laura Ward. (Vocal Library). (ENG.). 2006. audio compact disk 16.95 (978-1-4234-1305-9(9), 1423413059) H Leonard.

Accomplish Your Goals: Do More in Less Time. Dick Sutphen. 1 cass. (Running Time: 1 hr.). (Only Subliminals Ser.). 1990. 12.98 (978-0-87554-451-9(7), T211) Valley Sun.
One hour of soothing, digitally mastered stereo music with positive subliminal suggestions phrased for maximum acceptance by your subconscious mind.

***Accomplished Teaching: The Key to National Board Certification - Cd.** 2nd rev. ed. Jennings. (ENG.). 2010. audio compact disk 42.45 (978-0-7575-5189-5(0)) Kendall-Hunt.

Accomplishment: The Science & Practice. Peter Thomson. 6 cass. (Running Time: 9 hrs.). 1996. 59.95 Set incl. bonus cass. (10890UKM) Nightingale-Conant.
Peter Thomson, one of Great Britain's most electrifying speakers, shares more than 500 methods, ideas & techniques that have helped the world's greatest achievers rise to the top. Discover how to develop a "photographic memory"...turn every problem into a golden opportunity...& use the power within you to achieve your objectives. With this captivating collection of ideas, anecdotes & opinions, you'll become more enthusiastic about how you live & more accomplished in what you do.

According To. Perf. by James Hall & Worship and Praise. 1 cass. 10.98 (978-1-57908-134-8(7)); audio compact disk 15.98 (978-1-57908-133-1(9)) Platinm Enter.

According to Queeney. unabr. ed. Beryl Bainbridge. Read by Miriam Margolyes. 6 cass. (Running Time: 9 hrs.). 2002. 49.95 (978-0-7540-0777-7(4), CAB 2199, Chivers Sound Lib) AudioGO.

According to Queeney. unabr. ed. Beryl Bainbridge. Read by Miriam Margolyes. 12 CDs. (Running Time: 18 hrs.). 2002. audio compact disk 64.95 (978-0-7540-5489-4(6), CCD 180) AudioGO.

According to Tradition. Short Stories. Perf. by Medicine Story et al. 1 cass. (Running Time: 1 hr.). 1984. 9.95 (978-0-938756-12-5(5), 001) Yellow Moon.
A collection of four "tellers" that represent the rich tradition of storytelling in New England.

Accordion Crimes. Annie Proulx & Annie Proulx. 2004. 15.95 (978-0-7435-4089-6(1)) Pub: S&S Audio. Dist(s): S and S Inc

Accordion Crimes. unabr. ed. Annie Proulx & Annie Proulx. Read by Anna Fields. 12 cass. (Running Time: 18 hrs.). 1996. 96.00 (978-0-913369-21-0(7), 4172) Books on Tape.
An accordion travels with immigrants in a new world. Its music is their last link with the past & voice of their dreams.

Account of Brother William Branham's Accident. unabr. ed. Pearry Green. (ENG.). 1966. audio compact disk (978-0-9700955-9-6(7)) Tucson Taber.

Account of Hope: Christian Faith in an Age of Relative Truth & Religious Pluralism. John Billington. (Running Time: 32340 sec.). 2007. audio compact disk 37.99 (978-1-60462-054-2(4)) Tate Pubng.

Accountability in Action. 2nd ed. Douglas B. Reeves. 2005. audio compact disk 30.00 (978-0-9747343-5-4(7)) Pub: LeadplusLrn. Dist(s): Natl Bk Netwk

Accountability Packet: Putting off Old Self & Putting on the New. Richard D. Dobbins. 1 cass., bklet. (Running Time: 90 mins.). 1999. pap. bk. 35.00 (978-1-890329-72-3(X)) Totally Alive.

Accountable to God: Romans 3:1-20. Ed Young. 1996. 4.95 (978-0-7417-2108-2(2), 1108) Win Walk.

Accountants' Liability. 1991. 65.00 (AC-620) PA Bar Inst.

Accountants' Liability Litigation. 10 cass. (Running Time: 13 hrs. 30 min.). 1998. 275.00 Set; incl. study guide. (MC46) Am Law Inst.
Provides an overview of the various & rapidly changing principles.

Accountant's Role in Litigation. 1987. bk. 90.00; 45.00 PA Bar Inst.

Accountant's Role in Planning for the Older Client. Tony Allessandra. 6 cass. (Running Time: 8 hrs.). 1995. 99.00 set, incl. wkbk. (740102EZ) Am Inst CPA.
For many middle-income clients, potential medical costs, including nursing home care, are major financial & estate planning concerns. They want to protect their assets & provide for their future medical needs. With this course, you'll be able to help them do both.

Accountant's Role in Planning for the Older Client. rev. ed. Ezra Huber. 2 cass. (Running Time: 3 hrs.). 1994. 99.00 incl. wkbk. set. (740102VC) Am Inst CPA.

Accountant's Story: Inside the Violent World of the Medellin Cartel. abr. unabr. ed. Roberto Escobar. Read by Ruben Diaz. Told to David Fisher. (Running Time: 10 hrs.). (ENG.). 2009. 24.98 (978-1-60024-476-6(9)) Pub: Hachet Audio. Dist(s): HachBkGrp

Accountant's Story: Inside the Violent World of the Medellin Cartel. unabr. ed. Roberto Escobar & David Fisher. Read by Ruben Diaz. 8 CDs. (Running Time: 10 hrs.). (ENG.). 2009. audio compact disk 34.98 (978-1-60024-475-9(0)) Pub: Hachet Audio. Dist(s): HachBkGrp

***Accounting.** abr. ed. John A. Tracy. Read by Brett Barry. (ENG.). 2007. (978-0-06-155602-9(5)) HarperCollins Pubs.

***Accounting.** 3rd abr. ed. John A. Tracy. Read by Brett Barry. (ENG.). 2007. (978-0-06-155601-2(7)) HarperCollins Pubs.

Accounting. 3rd abr. ed. John A. Tracy. Read by Brett Barry. (Running Time: 12600 sec.). 2007. audio compact disk 14.95 (978-0-06-137434-0(2), Harper Audio) HarperCollins Pubs.

Accounting & Auditing for Certain Nonprofit Organizations. rev. ed. Eugene G. Geiser & Clifford D. Brown. 2 cass. (Running Time: 10 hrs.). 1995. 129.00 set, incl. wkbk. (743409EZ) Am Inst CPA.
This course meets the needs of both the nonprofit client & the auditor. It contains practical new cases that help you in day-to-day situations. These concern the internal control environment, planning an audit to meet the requirements of Government Auditing Standards, & compliance auditing under OMB A-133.

Accounting & Auditing Report. Totaltape Editorial Board. Prod. by Paul Munter & Thomas A. Ratcliffe. 12 cass. 225.00 incl. 1-Year Subscription, monthly transcripts, yearly album, indes & quizzers. (CPE0020) Bisk Educ.
Explores constantly changing accounting & auditing developments.

Accounting & Auditing Report (Two Years) 24 cass. 395.00 set, incl. monthly written transcripts. (CPE0021) Bisk Educ.

Accounting & Auditing Update. Paul Munter & Thomas A. Ratcliffe. 6 cass. 129.00 set, incl. wkbk. & quizzer. (CPE0110) Bisk Educ.
All recent FASB, AICPA, SEC & GASB pronouncements are outlined, explained & analyzed.

Accounting for Lawyers. (Running Time: 6 hrs.). 1995. 92.00 Incl. 148p. coursebk. (20631) NYS Bar.
Practical, basic-level set of presentations designed to provide a fundamental understanding of the terms, principles, standards & issues involved in accounting, auditing & financial matters.

Accounting for Lawyers. Read by William D. Kilbourn, Jr. & Charles Meyer. 135.00 incl. workbook. (1003) Natl Prac Inst.
A solid background in the basics of accounting & finance.

Accounting for Lawyers. Charles Meyer & W. Douglas Kilbourn, Jr. 1994. 135.00 (978-1-55917-000-0(X)) Natl Prac Inst.

Accounting for Lawyers 1988. unabr. ed. Contrib. by Dan L. Goldwasser & Samuel P. Gunther. 4 cass. (Running Time: 5 hrs. 30 min.). 1988. pap. bk. 60.00 (T6-9089) PLI.
Designed to introduce attorneys to the accounting principles & concepts needed for understanding financial & corporate statements, these tapes serve as a review & update for those who deal with accounting problems & financial statements in their practices. In Addition, auditing & the meaning of auditors' reports, are covered in this recording of PLI's November 1988 satellite program.

Accounting for Nonprofits: Contributions & Financial Statements (How to Comply with FAS 116 & 117) Eugene G. Geiser & Clifford D. Brown. 2 cass. (Running Time: 10 hrs.). 1995. 129.00 set, incl. wkbk. (743257EZ) Am Inst CPA.
Don't let your nonprofit clients or employer get caught in a compliance bind! This course includes full texts of FAS 116 & 117, plus illustrative statements in compliance with them. It also includes the full text of AICPA's proposed Audit & Accounting Guide, "Not-for-Profit Organizations".

Accounting for Restaurant Operations. Phyllis A. Webster. 1 cass. 119.00 incl. wkbk. (749758KQ) Am Inst CPA.
Designed for the accountant who has little or no experience in restaurant accounting, this course will teach you how to install a set of accounting records for a small restaurant &/or bar.

Accounting Standards Update Audiocourse. 2 cass. (Bottom Line Ser.). 59.00 set incl. study guide. (730522KQ) Am Inst CPA.
This course covers the most recent pronouncements of the Financial Accounting Standards Board (FASB) & the AICPA's Accounting Standards Executive Committee (AcSEC) & pinpoints their practical applications. Also discussed is SAS No. 69 which makes significant changes in the GAAP hierarchy of accounting pronouncements.

Accounting Standards Update Audiocourse: 1994 Edition. 2 cass. 1994. 79.00 set incl. study guide. (730523VC) Am Inst CPA.

Accounting System for Small Business. unabr. ed. Egon Van den Berg. 6 cass. 89.95 incl. binder, sample forms. (S13559) J Norton Pubs.
Shows you, step-by-step, how to keep accurate records. No special knowledge or bookkeeping experience is required. Learn disbursements, receipts, summaries, balancing & closing for sales, distribution, personal service or retail businesses.

Accurate English Set: A Complete Course in Pronunciation. Rebecca M. Dauer. 2001. 86.85 (978-0-13-007287-0(7)) Longman.

Accused see Your Own World

Accuser of the Brethren. Francis Frangipane. 1 cass. (Running Time: 90 mins.). (Pulling Down Strongholds Ser.: Vol. 9). 2000. 5.00 (FF05-009) Morning NC.
Some of Francis' most famous life-changing messages are contained in this comprehensive 10-tape series.

Accuser of the Brethren 569: Rev. 11:19-12:17. Ed Young. 1986. 4.95 (978-0-7417-1569-2(4), 569) Win Walk.

Accusers. Lindsey Davis. Read by Jamie Glover. 7 cass. (Marcus Didius Falco Ser.). 59.95 (978-0-7927-3375-1(4), CSL 716); audio compact disk 79.95 (978-0-7927-3376-8(2), SLD 716) AudioGO.

AC/DC: The Savage Tale of the First Standards War. unabr. ed. Tom McNichol. Read by Malcolm Hillgartner. (Running Time: 23400 sec.). 2008. 44.95 (978-1-4332-4469-8(1)); audio compact disk 29.95 (978-1-4332-4473-5(X)); audio compact disk & audio compact disk 60.00 (978-1-4332-4470-4(5)) Blckstn Audio.

AC/DC: The Unauthorized Biography of AC/DC. Andrea Thorn. (Maximum Ser.). (ENG.). 2001. audio compact disk 14.95 (978-1-84240-088-3(6)) Pub: Chrome Dreams GBR. Dist(s): IPG Chicago

Ace. unabr. ed. Jack D. Hunter. Read by Paul Michael Garcia. (Running Time: 11 hrs. 0 mins.). (ENG.). 2009. 29.95 (978-1-4332-7764-1(6)); 65.95 (978-1-4332-7760-3(3)); audio compact disk 100.00 (978-1-4332-7761-0(1)) Blckstn Audio.

Ace: The Very Important Pig. Contrib. by Dick King-Smith. 2 cass. (J). 1995. 14.95 Set. (978-0-86220-092-3(X)) AudioGO.

Ace Ghosts; Ghouls Rule. unabr. ed. Karen Wallace. Read by Eve Karpf. 2 cass. (Running Time: 3 hrs.). (J). (gr. 1-8). 1999. 18.95 (CCA 3496, Chivers Child Audio) AudioGO.

***Ace in the Hole: A Selection from the John Updike Audio Collection.** unabr. ed. John Updike. Read by John Updike. (ENG.). 2009. (978-0-06-196230-1(9), Caedmon); (978-0-06-196229-5(5), Caedmon) HarperCollins Pubs.

ACE Inhibitors in Heart Failure. Read by James F. Spann. 1 cass. (Running Time: 90 min.). 1985. 12.00 (C8561) Amer Coll Phys.

Ace the Exam. unabr. ed. Greg McPhee et al. Read by Jane Briggs et al. (YA). 2008. 54.99 (978-1-60252-911-3(6)) Find a World.

***Acerca de mi Audio CD.** Jeffrey B. Fuerst. Adapted by Benchmark Education Company, LLC. (My First Reader's Theater Ser.). (SPA.). (J). 2009. audio compact disk 10.00 (978-1-935470-61-8(2)) Benchmark Educ.

Aces & Eights. unabr. ed. Loren D. Estleman. Narrated by Joel Fabiani. 5 cass. (Running Time: 6 hrs. 45 mins.). 1991. 44.00 (978-1-55690-639-8(0), 91418E7) Recorded Bks.
Jack McCall is on trial for the murder of Wild Bill Hickok.

Aces' Wild. Ed. by Marco A. V. Bitetto. 1 cass. 2000. (978-1-58578-068-6(5)) Inst of Cybernetics.

Ach Est Plng & Incm Tx Ppt Cd. Ed. by Kaplan Publishing Staff. 2005. (978-1-4195-1941-3(7)) Dearborn Financial.

Ach Gen Prin Fin Plnng Ppt Cd. Ed. by Kaplan Publishing Staff. 2005. (978-1-4195-1866-9(6)) Dearborn Financial.

Ach Retirement Needs Ppt Cd 1. Ed. by Kaplan Publishing Staff. 2005. (978-1-4195-1863-8(1)) Dearborn Financial.

Ach Retirement Needs Ppt Cd 2. Ed. by Kaplan Publishing Staff. 2005. (978-1-4195-1862-1(3)) Dearborn Financial.

Ach Ya! Traditional German-American Music from Wisconsin. Ed. by Phillip Martin & James P. Leary. 2 vols. 2005. audio compact disk 16.00 (978-0-924119-14-9(4)) Pub: Max Kade. Dist(s): Chicago Distribution Ctr
Now available as a double CD, Ach Ya! was selected in 1985 as an outstanding American folk music recording by the Library of Congress American Folklife Center.nbsp; Featuring acapella singers, yodelers, zither players, button accordionists, and full-fledged "Dutchman" bands from Watertown to Wausau, from Cedar Grove to Birnamwood, this compilation’s nearly 50 performances were chosen by folklorists Philip Martin and James P. Leary following a year of intensive field and archival research.nbsp; Accompanied by an extensively annotated booklet, the CD’s tracks follow four themes: Around the Table, Children’s Songs and Rites of Passage, Across the Generations, and Dance Melodies and Marches. A valuable resource for teachers of German, especially in the Badger State, the lives, lyrics, and melodies captured on Ach Ya! help reflect and define the German American experience in Wisconsin and the Upper Midwest. Originally released as a 1985 double LP, Wisconsin Folklife Center Distributed for the Center for the Study of Upper Midwestern Cultures.

Acheron. abr. unabr. ed. Sherrilyn Kenyon. Narrated by Holter Graham. 19 CDs. (Running Time: 23 hrs. 30 mins. 0 sec.). Bk. 12. (ENG.). 2008. audio compact disk 39.95 (978-1-4272-0472-1(1)) Pub: Macmill Audio. Dist(s): Macmillan

Aches & Pains. unabr. ed. Maeve Binchy. Read by Kate Binchy. 1 cass. (Running Time: 1 hr. 15 min.). 2001. 10.95 (978-1-57270-240-0(0), L11240u) Pub: Audio Partners. Dist(s): PerseuPGW
Based on the author's own experience as a hip replacement patient, she provides funny insider advice about coping with the ordeals of surgery, a hospital stay & at-home convalescence.

Achieve Excellence. Betty L. Randolph. Read by Betty L. Randolph. Read by Leonard Baron. Ed. by Success Education Institute International. 1 cass. (Success Ser.). 1989. bk. 14.98 Ocean Format. (978-1-55909-229-6(7), 180P); bk. 14.98 Music Format. (978-1-55909-230-2(0), 180PM) Randolph Tapes.
Includes 60,000 messages with the left-right brain.

Achieve Goals. 1 cass. (Running Time: 45 min.). (Success Ser.). 9.98 (978-1-55909-003-2(0), 21S); 9.98 90 min. extended length stereo music. (21X) Randolph Tapes.
No limitations, no unobtainable goals. Teaches you to focus on your goals. Subliminal messages are heard 3-5 minutes before becoming ocean sounds or music.

Achieve Permanent Weight Control. Eldon Taylor. Read by Eldon Taylor. Ed. by Leslie Brice. 8 cass. (Running Time: 8 hrs.). 1992. 89.95 set. (978-1-56705-365-4(3)) Gateways Inst.
Self improvement.

Achieve Sound Sleep. Barry Tesar. 2 cass. 1998. 14.95 Set. (978-1-889800-13-4(9)) TNT Media Grp.

Achieve Weight Mastery. Created by Zoilita Grant. 2001. audio compact disk 15.95 (978-1-890575-33-5(X)) Zoilita Grant.

Achieve Your Dreams: A Complete Program to Help You Attain Overall Abundance. unabr. ed. Bette St. Laurence. Read by Bette St. Laurence. Illus. by Roy Rezentes, II. 3 cass. 1996. pap. bk. & wbk. ed. 29.95 (978-1-891023-00-2(4)) Starfound Direct.
Combines the step-by-step instruction for goal setting & achievement with the support of meditation & hypnosis.

Achieve Your Full Potential in Life. (Running Time: 48 mins.). audio compact disk (978-1-59076-203-5(7)) DscvrHlpPubng.

Achieve Your Goals: Guided Meditation. Concept by Vicky Thurlow. Voice by Vicky Thurlow. (ENG.). 2008. audio compact disk 14.95 (978-0-9817055-1-4(0)) DVT Invest.

Achieve Your Ideal Weight Auto-Matically. Bob Griswold & Deirdre Griswold. (Running Time: 3480 sec.). (While-U-Drive Ser.). 2004. audio compact disk 15.98 (978-1-55848-706-2(9)) EffectiveMN.

Achieve Your Ideal Weight Auto-maticallyTM. Read by Bob Griswold & Deirdre Griswold. 1 cass. (Running Time: 60 mins.). (While-U-Drive Ser.). 1996. 11.98 (978-1-55848-900-4(2)) EffectiveMN.
How to win the mental game of weight control.

Achievements of Love. Elbert Willis. 1 cass. (Developing Ability to Love Ser.). 4.00 Fill the Gap.

Achiever: The Power of the Enneagram Individual Type Audio Recording. Scripts. Based on a work by Enneagram Institute Staff. 1 CD. (Running Time: 60 mins.). 2004. audio compact disk 10.00 (978-0-9755222-2-6(1)) Enneagr.
Type Three Individual Type Audio Recording (ITAR) in CD format from the audio tapeset The Power of the Enneagram. Includes a 25 minute introduction to the system as a whole, as well as a 35 minute exposition on Type Three. An excellent way for therapists or business consultants to introduce the Enneagram to clients, or to work with the Enneagram in ongoing situations.

Achieving Career Fulfillment. Hosted by Leonard Peikoff. 1 cass. (Philosophy: Who Needs It? Ser.). 1998. 12.95 (LPXXC53) Second Renaissance.

Achieving Comfortable Flight. R. Reid Wilson & T. W. Cummings. Read by T. W. Cummings & Reid Wilson. 4 cass. (Running Time: 2 hrs. 41 mins.). 1991. pap. bk. 45.95 Set with 2 booklets, 60 pgs. each. (978-0-9630683-0-9(X)) Pathway Systs.
Self-help tape & booklet package for the fear of flying.

Achieving Credibility: The Key to Effective Leadership. James M. Kouzes. 6 cass. (Running Time: 6 hrs.). 1995. bk. (12820AP) Nightingale-Conant.
You will discover the 6 disciplines of leadership & credibility, how to foster trust, how to increase productivity & why commitment to credibility begins with clarity, unity & understanding yourself.

Achieving emotional literacy: A personal prog increase emotnl intellgnc Cst: A Personal Program to Increase Your Emotional Intelligence. George A. Steiner. 2004. 7.95 (978-0-7435-4090-2(5)) Pub: S&S Audio. Dist(s): S and S Inc

Achieving Emotional Maturity. 1 cass. (Running Time: 85 mins.). (Personal Growth Ser.). 9.95 (ST-108) Crystal Clarity.
Topics include: Moods as one of the main obstacles to emotional maturity; how to get out of a mood; why feeling guilty is always self-defeating; the difference between positive & wishful thinking.

Achieving Excellence. Lou Heckler. 4 cass. (Running Time: 3 hrs. 57 mins.). 49.95 CareerTrack Pubns.
Discusses how to implement the new excellence oriented management. Explains how principles in your department or company 1) gain productivity through people, 2) create quality, 3) "make things happen" & 4) achieve personal excellence.

Achieving Excellence: The Performance Appraisal Process. 4 cass. 155.00 Set, incl. wkbk. & 2 multiple choice tests. (80212NQ1) AMACOM.
This program shows you how to use ongoing performance appraisals to boost productivity & morale, decrease turnover & absenteeism, & improve work quality, efficiency, & job satisfaction. You'll learn how to: Conduct formal & informal performance evaluations; Monitor & direct employee performance; Set priorities, formulate goal statements, & write job descriptions; Ensure effective communication during formal appraisal interviews by using a proven six-point method & much more.

Achieving Flawless Auditions & Performances. Created by Laura Boynton King. 2 CD's. 2003. audio compact disk 50.00 (978-0-9748885-9-0(1)) Summit Dynamics.
A 2-CD Self-Hypnosis mini-series designed to guide performers to improved memory, increased concentration and relieve performance anxiety.

Achieving Goals & Removing Blocks to Success. Scott Sulak. 1998. 15.00 (978-1-932659-02-3(1)) Change For Gd.

Achieving Goals for Successful Sales. Created by Ellen Chernoff Simon. 1 CD. (Running Time: 70 min.). 2004. audio compact disk 18.00 (978-0-9765587-5-0(0)) Imadulation.
This Audio CD will guided you into a deeply relaxed and confident state using the same method that Olympic athletes, professional musicians, and actors do to prepare for a successful performance. you will experience a level of competency in gaining entry, developing customer connections and dealing with resistance.

Achieving Peace, Relieving Depression. Patricia O'Malley. Perf. by Barry Weiss. 1 cass. (Running Time: 50 mins.). 1998. (978-1-892450-09-8(7), 151) Promo Music.
Guided imagery.

Achieving Results with Electional Astrology. Elayne J. Manago. 1 cass. 8.95 (557) Am Fed Astrologers.
Rules of electional & horary - examples.

Achieving Sales Excellence. Tom Hopkins. Read by Tom Hopkins. 6 cass. (Running Time: 6 hrs.). 1995. 95.00 (978-0-938636-34-2(0), 1475) T Hopkins Intl.
Nuts & bolts of selling. Where to find prospects, how to qualify & get the sale.

Achieving Success: Success World Hypnotic & Subliminal Learning. David Illig. 1999. 14.99 (978-0-86580-011-3(1)) Success World.

Achieving Super Sales. Shad Helmstetter. 1 cass. (Self-Talk Cassettes Ser.). 10.95 (978-0-937065-09-9(9)) Grindle Pr.

Achieving Super Success: OZO. Eldon Taylor. Read by Eldon Taylor. Ed. by Leslie Brice. 1 cass. (Running Time: 1 hr.). 1992. 19.95 (978-1-56705-017-2(4)) Gateways Inst.
Self improvement.

Achieving Your Ideal Weight. Steven Halpern. 1 cass. (Soundwave Two Thousand, the Audio Active Subliminal Ser.). 1990. (2009) Inner Peace Mus.
Beautiful, relaxing music with subliminal affirmations.

Achilles' Heel. unabr. ed. Sean Flannery. Read by Edward Lewis. 8 cass. (Running Time: 11 hrs. 30 mins.). 1999. 56.95 (978-0-7861-1652-2(8), 2480) Blckstn Audio.
Ex-KGB agent Valeri Yernin, known as "The Surgeon" for the accuracy of his hits, is supposed to be dead. but at the National Security Intercept Center they identify a telephone call originating from Karachi as a ninety-eight percent voice match. In the call, Yernin vows to finally get even with military intelligence analyst Bill Lane.

Achilles' Heel. unabr. ed. Sean Flannery. Read by Edward Lewis. (Running Time: 37800 sec.). 2008. audio compact disk & audio compact disk 80.00 (978-1-4332-3440-8(8)); audio compact disk & audio compact disk 29.95 (978-1-4332-3441-5(6)) Blckstn Audio.

Achondrogenesis - A Bibliography & Dictionary for Physicians, Patients, & Genome Researchers. Compiled by Icon Group International, Inc. Staff. 2007. ring bd. 28.95 (978-0-497-11317-9(1)) Icon Grp.

Achondroplasia - A Bibliography & Dictionary for Physicians, Patients, & Genome Researchers. Compiled by Icon Group International, Inc. Staff. 2007. ring bd. 28.95 (978-0-497-11318-6(X)) Icon Grp.

Acid Bath: To Earth Ever Triumphant. Garson Vaseleos. Perf. by Max Bollinger. Adapted by Max Bollinger. Prod. by Progres et Declin SA. (ENG.). 2009. cd-rom 24.00 (978-0-9561165-3-6(1), Fantastica) Max Bollinger GBR.

Acid Rain. 1 cass. (Running Time: 30 mins.). 9.95 (NJ-82-02-23, HarperThor) HarpC GBR.

Acid Rain. Hosted by Nancy Pearlman. 1 cass. (Running Time: 29 mins.). 10.00 (111) Educ Comm CA.

Acid Rain - A United States-Canadian Controversy. Hosted by Nancy Pearlman. 1 cass. (Running Time: 27 mins.). 10.00 (605) Educ Comm CA.

Acid Row. unabr. ed. Minette Walters. Read by Gerard Doyle. 6 cass. (Running Time: 10 hrs. 30 mins.). 2004. 29.99 (978-1-4025-2482-0(X), 01714) Recorded Bks.
When a young girl disappears without a trace, a furious vigilante mob focuses its violent outbursts on the home of a known pedophile. Into this madness comes Dr. Sophie Morrison, who soon finds herself trapped as the fury rages out of control-and everyone is powerless to stop it.

Acid Row. unabr. ed. Minette Walters & M. K. Wren. Narrated by Gerard Doyle & Myra Lucretia Taylor. 7 cass. (Running Time: 10 hrs.). 1999. 69.00 (978-1-4025-2838-5(8)) Recorded Bks.

Acid Test. unabr. ed. Ross LaManna. Narrated by George Guidall. 11 cass. (Running Time: 14 hrs.). 2002. 91.00 (978-0-7887-9950-1(9), 96854) Recorded Bks.
What if the world was suddenly rocked by widespread murder, political chaos, and the peril of nuclear attack? The ruthless Batu Khan has forged an empire across Mongolia and central Asia. He has developed a frightening arsenal of weaponry and uses mind-altering drugs to give his minions superhuman strength. When Khan invades the Ukraine, the president of the United States issues an ultimatum - get out or else. But the president harbors a dark and deadly secret that may put countless lives at risk.

Acing the Interview: How to Ask & Answer the Questions That Will Get You the Job! unabr. ed. Tony Beshara. Read by Tony Beshara. (Running Time: 10 hrs.). (ENG.). 2008. 29.98 (978-1-59659-268-1(0), GildAudio) Pub: Gildan Media. Dist(s): HachBkGrp

Acing the Interview: How to Ask & Answer the Questions That Will Get You the Job! unabr. ed. Tony Beshara. Read by Tony Beshara. 7 CDs. (Running Time: 10 hrs.). (ENG.). 2009. audio compact disk 39.98 (978-1-59659-214-8(1), GildAudio) Pub: Gildan Media. Dist(s): HachBkGrp

Acknowledging God in the Decisions of State: A Biblically Informed Treatise on Public Policy for the Integration of Knowledge, Action, & Faith in the Exercise of Biblical Statesmanship. Olivia M. McDonald. Olivia M. McDonald. 2006. (978-0-9778294-4-6(8), CADIPS) Grace Hse USA.

ACL Proceedings: Coling. COLING Staff & ACL Staff. (ENG.). 2003. audio compact disk 125.00 (978-1-55860-899-3(0)) Sci Tech Bks.
Proceedings of the biennial International Conferences on Computational Linguistics. Also see ACL Proceedings.

Acland's Video Atlas of Human Anatomy. Robert D. Acland. (978-0-7817-5822-2(X)) Lppncott W W.

ACLS Essentials: Basics & More. Kim McKenna. 2008. audio compact disk (978-0-07-312094-2(4)) McGraw.

ACLS Survival Hymns. Vital Signs Unlimited staff. Read by Michael Richmond. Ed. by David Doernbach. 1 cass. (Running Time: 30 mins.). 1994. 15.00 (978-0-9638043-2-7(4)) Vital Signs.
Songs to assist with learning all the medical protocols for Advanced Cardiac Life Support courses taken by nurses & physicians.

***Acne Prescription.** abr. ed. Nicholas Perricone. Read by Robb Webb. (ENG.). 2005. (978-0-06-084293-2(8), Harper Audio); (978-0-06-084294-9(6), Harper Audio) HarperCollins Pubs.

ACOA's Guide to Raising Healthy Children. unabr. ed. Jim Mastrich & Bill Birnes. Narrated by George Guidall. 8 cass. (Running Time: 11 hrs.). 1995. 70.00 (978-0-7887-0302-7(1), 94495E7) Recorded Bks.
Mastrich, a psychologist & substance abuse counselor, aims this child-rearing manual at adult children of alcoholics (ACOAs). His premise is that ACOAs come from dysfunctional & atypical families & thus may need help in acquiring parenting skills. He strives to provide guidance & support for ACOAs' lack of positive family experiences.

ACOA's Guide to Raising Healthy Children. unabr. ed. Jim Mastrich & Bill Birnes. Read by George Guidall. 8 cass. (Running Time: 11 hrs.). 1995. Rental 16.50 (94495) Recorded Bks.

Acorna: The Unicorn Girl. unabr. ed. Anne McCaffrey & Margaret Ball. Read by Anna Fields. 7 cass. (Running Time: 10 hrs. 30 min.). (Acorna Ser.). 1999. 56.00 (978-0-7366-4340-5(0), 4835) Books on Tape.
Three space miners, Gill, Calu, & Rafik, find a survival pod drifting in space: inside sleeps Acorna, a furry, unicorn-like humanoid infant. Young Acorna soon manifests special powers such as the ability to purify water & air, to make plants grow & to heal injuries. When Acorna is almost snatched by scientists who want to study her as an anomaly, the miners must flee & whisk Acorna away to the planet Kezdet, a planet known to deal in child slave labor, & the last place they wanted to go.

Acorna's People: The Further Adventures of the Unicorn Girl. Anne McCaffrey & Elizabeth Ann Scarborough. Read by Anna Fields. (Acorna Ser.). 2000. 56.00 (978-0-7366-4847-9(X)); audio compact disk 64.00 (978-0-7366-5216-2(7)) Books on Tape.

Acorna's People: The Further Adventures of the Unicorn Girl. unabr. ed. Anne McCaffrey & Elizabeth Ann Scarborough. Read by Anna Fields. 7 cass. (Running Time: 10 hrs. 30 min.). (Acorna Ser.). 2000. 56.00 Books on Tape.
The Unicorn Girl finds her people but must still battle evil before enjoying peace.

Acorna's People: The Further Adventures of the Unicorn Girl. unabr. ed. Anne McCaffrey & Elizabeth Ann Scarborough. Read by Anna Fields. 8 CDs. (Running Time: 9 hrs. 30 mins.). (Acorna Ser.). (YA). 2000. audio compact disk 64.00 Books on Tape.
Acorna has found her people at last. Abandoned in space as a baby after the evil Khleevi destroyed her planet, rescued & raised by gruff human asteroid miners, she is at last among her own. The beautiful healing horn in the center of her forehead that once set her apart now makes her one with the telepathic Linyaari. But Acorna still has much to do before she can enjoy her peaceful home. The legendary resting place of the lost Linyaari ancestors has yet to be found.

Acorna's Quest. unabr. ed. Anne McCaffrey & Margaret Ball. Read by Anna Fields. (Acorna Ser.). 1999. 56.00 (978-0-7366-4353-5(2), 4836) Books on Tape.
Acorna, now a young adult desperately needing questions answered about her heritage, embarks on a search for her ancestry. Accompanied by one of the miners who raised her, she begins a journey across the universe. Her trek temporarily aborts when her ship malfunctions, forcing her to land on Rushima. There she finds the populace starving. Even as Acorna is caught up in their plight, a strange people with telepathic powers appear in the sector who are seeking the whereabouts of a missing person lost as an infant several years ago.

Acorna's Search. unabr. ed. Anne McCaffrey & Elizabeth Ann Scarborough. Read by Anna Fields. 6 cass. (Running Time: 9 hrs.). (Acorna Ser.). 2002. 48.00 (978-0-7366-8566-5(9)) Books on Tape.
Acorna, the unicorn girl, must find a way to save her people's home planet from menacing alien foes. Now she has been reunited with her own people, the telepathic Linyaari. Her task now is to restore her home planet, devastated decades ago by the Khleevi, to its original state of beauty and spiritual purity. But to do so, she must fight the evil Khleevi, dire enemies of both her human and unicoid families, who are not willing to relinquish their grip on the precious planet. The insectoid Khleevi race has no compunctions about doing away with other races, as they regard them as fodder, and they have already committed genocide on numerous worlds.

Acorna's Triumph. unabr. ed. Anne McCaffrey & Elizabeth Ann Scarborough. Read by Anna Fields. 6 cass. (Running Time: 9 hrs.). (Acorna Ser.). (YA). 2004. 72.00 (978-1-4159-0160-1(0)) Books on Tape.
Acorna, the Unicom Girl, must save her mate and fend off vicious aliens.

Acorna's World. Anne McCaffrey & Elizabeth Ann Scarborough. Read by Anna Fields. (Acorna Ser.). 2000. 48.00 (978-0-7366-5599-6(9)); audio compact disk 56.00 (978-0-7366-6299-4(5)) Books on Tape.

Acorna's World. unabr. collector's ed. Anne McCaffrey & E. Scarborough. Read by Anna Fields. 7 CDs. (Running Time: 10 hrs. 30 mins.). (Acorna Ser.). 2001. audio compact disk 56.00 Books on Tape.
Although she has made peace with her Linyaari heritage, Acorna knows that only by returning to the frozen stillness of space will she ever truly feel at home. Answering a faint distress signal leads Acorna to a strange, perfumed world where plants are sentient and think. There she finds a burned-out ship with all the signs of a Khleevi attack. Facing the annihilation of her entire race, Acorna must discover the Khleevi's weakness. Setting off with the salvager Becker; his ship's cat, Roadkill; and Aari, a young man of her own race, she knows they must strike first.

Acoustic Christmas. Perf. by David Grisman et al. 1 cass. 9.98 (446); audio compact disk 17.98 (D446) MFLP CA.
This acoustic mixture with exotic instruments such as hurdy gurdy, crumhorn, mandocello & recorders provides unique festive listening.

Acoustic Dreams. Jack Jezzro. Transcribed by Lenny Carlson. 1998. pap. bk. 32.95 (978-0-7866-2939-8(8), 96728CDP) Mel Bay.

Acoustic Ep: Seattle Sessions. Contrib. by Classic Crime. Prod. by Matt Bayles. 2007. audio compact disk 9.99 (978-5-557-56807-4(7)) Tooth & Nail.

Acoustic Guitar. Contrib. by Helmut Zehe & Uli Turk. 2006. pap. bk. 19.95 (978-3-8024-0567-9(6)) Mel Bay.

Acoustic Guitar Basics. Georg Wolf. 2007. pap. bk. 12.95 (978-3-8024-0606-5(0)) Voggenreiter Pubs DEU.

Acoustic Guitar Bible. Eric Roche. 2 CDs. 2004. audio compact disk 29.95 (978-1-84492-063-1(1), SMT1408) Pub: Sanctuary Pubng GBR. Dist(s): H Leonard

Acoustic Guitar Manual. Brett Duncan. (Complete Learn to Play Ser). 2006. pap. bk. 29.95 (978-1-86469-336-2(3)) Kolala Music SGP.

Acoustic Holidays. 2002. audio compact disk Rounder Records.

Acoustic Praise Collection. 2 CDs. audio compact disk 15.98 (978-1-57908-441-7(9)) Platinm Enter.

Acoustic Sunday. Perf. by Jack Jezzro. 9.98; audio compact disk 14.98 Pub: Brentwood Music. Dist(s): Provident Mus Dist
Performed with simple acoustic instruments. Includes "Holy, Holy, Holy," "Blessed Assurance," "Amazing Grace," & many more.

Acoustic Worship, Vol. 2. 1 cass. (Running Time: 90 min.). (America's Twenty Five Favorite Ser.). 1999. 8.99 (978-0-7601-2675-2(5), 83061-0495-483061-0505-483061-0495-283061-0505-2); 10.98 Stereo, Split-Trax. (978-0-7601-2677-6(1), 83061-0505-483061-0495-283061-0505-2); audio compact disk 13.99 (978-0-7601-2676-9(3), 83061-0495-283061-0505-2); audio compact disk 15.98 Stereo, Split-Trax. (978-0-7601-2678-3(X), 83061-0505-2) Brentwood Music.
Features 25 more of America's favorite praise & worship choruses recorded in a relaxed, unplugged style with acoustic instruments & a small vocal ensemble.

Acoustic Worship, Vol. 3. 1 cass. (Running Time: 90 mins.). 1999. (978-0-7601-2916-6(9)); (978-0-7601-2920-3(7)) Brentwood Music.
Features 25 more of America's choruses recorded in a relaxed, unplugged style with acoustic instruments & a small vocal ensemble.

Acoustic Worship, Vol. 3. 1 CD. (Running Time: 90 min.). 1999. audio compact disk (978-0-7601-2915-9(0)) Brentwood Music.

Acoustic Worship, Vol. 4. 1 CD. 2000. audio compact disk 13.99 (978-0-7601-3233-3(X), SO33439) Pub: Brentwood Music. Dist(s): Provident Mus Dist
A whole new way of singing God's praises. Includes: "I Will Celebrate," "His Name Is Wonderful," "Our Heart" & Twenty-two other songs.

Acoustic Worship: Twenty-five of Your Favorite Praise & Worship Songs. 1 cass., 1 CD. 1998. 10.98 split-trax. Provident Mus Dist.
Reflective of a modern church service that will lead you in a time of personal worship.

Acoustic Worship: Twenty-Five of Your Favorite Praise & Worship Songs. 1 cass., 1 CD. 1998. audio compact disk 15.98 split-trax. (978-0-7601-2260-0(1)) Provident Mus Dist.

Acoustic Worship: Twenty-Five of Your Favorite Praise & Worship Songs. 1 cass. 1998. 10.98 (978-0-7601-1937-2(6)); audio compact disk (978-0-7601-1938-9(4)) Provident Music.

Acoustic Worship: Volume 3, Vol. 3. Prod. by Brentwood Records. 1 CD. (Running Time: 90 mins.). (Acoustic Worship (Brentwood) Ser.). 1999. audio compact disk (978-0-7601-2919-7(3)) Brentwood Music.
Features 25 more of America's choruses recorded in a relaxed, unplugged style with acoustic instruments & a small vocal ensemble.

Acoustic '90s: Guitar Play-along Volume 72. Created by Hal Leonard Corporation Staff. 2007. pap. bk. 14.95 (978-1-4234-1444-5(6), 1423414446) H Leonard.

Acoustics & Architecture. unabr. ed. Frank Lloyd Wright. 1 cass. (Running Time: 30 mins.). 1951. 12.95 (C11021) J Norton Pubs.
An informal, non-technical discussion of the physical requirements & psychological aspects of acoustics in architecture.

Acoustitherapy. 2 cass., 2 CDs. (Running Time: 1 hr. per cass.). 1999. 9.98 Regeneration. (45750); 9.98 Relaxation. (45752); audio compact disk 13.98 CD Regeneration. (45749); audio compact disk 13.98 CD Relaxation. (45751) Courage-to-Change.
Music to change state of mind, body & spirit.

ACP & Dimelo Tu. 4th ed. Fabián A. Samaniego. 1 CD. (Running Time: 1 hr.). 2002. bk. 93.20 (978-0-8384-6443-4(2)) Heinle.
A communication-based program designed for a short or intensive Introductory Spanish course.

ACP & Invitation Au Monde Francophone. Ana C. Jarvis. (C). bk. 88.53 (978-0-8384-6446-5(7)) Heinle.

Acqua Alta. unabr. ed. Donna Leon. Read by Anna Fields. 6 cass. (Running Time: 8 hrs. 30 mins.). (Commissario Guido Brunetti Mystery Ser.: Bk. 5). 2001. 44.95 (978-0-7861-2014-7(2), 2781); audio compact disk 64.00 (978-0-7861-9720-0(X), 2781) Blckstn Audio.
Brunetti heard a siren shriek out and shatter the tranquility of the night... It was the siren at San Marco, calling out to the sleeping city the news that the waters were rising: aqua alta had begun." Commissario Guido Brunetti of the Venice Questura is shocked to hear that Brett Lynch, a friend since a murder case at La Fenice, has suffered a savage beating.

Acqua Alta. unabr. collector's ed. Donna Leon. Read by Anna Fields. 6 cass. (Running Time: 9 hrs.). (Commissario Guido Brunetti Mystery Ser.: Bk. 5). 1998. 48.00 (978-0-7366-4294-1(3), 4787) Books on Tape.
When Brett Lynch, an American archaeologist, is savagely beaten on the doorstep of her Venice flat, few besides Brunetti are outraged. Lynch is, after all, a foreigner as well as a lesbian. Later, Brunetti connects the beating to a murder & starts an investigation which his adversaries want to bring to an end.

Acquaintances. unabr. collector's ed. Arnold J. Toynbee. Read by David Case. 8 cass. (Running Time: 12 hrs.). 1989. 64.00 (978-0-7366-1567-9(9), 2433) Books on Tape.
Toynbee knew most of the memorable figures of our century & gives his recollection of them in this compelling memoir.

Acquainted with the Night see Gathering of Great Poetry for Children

Acquainted with the Night see Robert Frost Reads

Acquainted with the Night see Twentieth-Century Poetry in English, No. 6, Recordings of Poets Reading Their Own Poetry

Acquire Contentment. Swami Jyotirmayananda. Read by Swami Jyotirmayananda. 1 cass. (Running Time: 45 mins.). 10.00 (804) Yoga Res Foun.

Acquired Immunodeficiency Syndrome. Read by Anthony S. Fauci. 1 cass. (Running Time: 90 min.). 1986. 12.00 (C8670) Amer Coll Phys.

Acquiring or Selling the Privately Held Company. 8 cass. (Running Time: 11 hrs.). 1990. bk. 95.00 Set incl. course handbook. (T6-9153) PLI.

Acquisition of Alaska. Kenneth Bruce. 1 cass. (Running Time: 1 hr.). Dramatization. (Excursions in History Ser.). 12.50 Alpha Tape.

Acquisitions of Physician Practices. 1997. bk. 99.00 (ACS-1317) PA Bar Inst.
Acquisitions of physcian practices are occurring in record numbers. When a physician contacts you, will you be prepared to represent him or her throughout the entire acquisition? Now is the most critical time to learn the essentials of these transactions. Written with the nonspecialist in mind. You learn the steps of an acquisition by going through a model acquisition agreement.

Acres of Diamonds. Russell H. Conwell. Read by Charlie Tremendous Jones. (Life-Changing Classics Ser.). (ENG.). 2007. audio compact disk 19.95 (978-1-933715-39-1(1)) Executive Bks.

Acres of Diamonds. unabr. ed. Russel H. Conwell. Read by Kevin T. Norris. (Running Time: 1 hr.). (ENG.). 2008. 9.98 (978-1-59659-052-6(1), GildAudio) Pub: Gildan Media. Dist(s): HachBkGrp

Acres of Diamonds: All Good Things Are Possible. Russell H. Conwell. Ed. by Bianca Leonardo. 1 cass. (Running Time: 1 hr. 30 mins.). 1998. 10.95 (978-0-930852-36-8(2)) Prog Press.

Acres of Diamonds: All Good Things Are Possible. deluxe ed. Russell H. Conwell. Ed. by Bianca Leonardo. Intro. by Bianca Leonardo. 1 cass. (Running Time: 1 hrs. 30 mins.). 1998. pap. bk. 20.00 Deluxe wrapping. (978-0-930852-38-2(9)) Prog Press.
Russell Conwell was a humanitarian & founder of Temple University. He gave his lecture "Acres of Diamonds" over 6,000 times, earning millions of dollars, all of which went to youth & education.

Acres of Diamonds: Bonus the Work of Russell Conwell. Russell H. Conwell. Narrated by Ross M. Armetta. 1 CD. (Running Time: 70 Mins. Aprox.). 2005. audio compact disk 12.99 (978-1-59733-002-2(7), Trans Greats) InfoFount.
?It is your duty to get rich.? ?Money is power, and you ought to be reasonably ambitious to have it. You ought because you can do more good with it than you could without it. You never knew an exception to it in your life. The person who gets the largest salary can do the most good with the power that is furnished to them by it.GET AHEAD! BECOME WEALTHY, WELL-LIKED AND FULLFILLEDAcres of Diamonds by Russell Conwell has been universally recognized for almost 100 years as one of, if not the, most inspiring and powerful books ever written for wealth creation. Written in simple, clear, and complete terms it describes how DO-IT-NOW, DO-IT-HERE thinking will directly influence and alter your life. It provides powerful suggestions on how you may influence and better your life by ALTERING your actions and circumstances by what you think and taking common-sense yet insightful action. It also provides practical, proven methods to become wealthy. There are thousands of people who have dramatically benefited from this information. Acres of Diamonds is not an overwhelming, complex treatise of useless theories. It is a concise inspiring and imminently useful audiobook. It will provide the keys for you to change yourself in relation to yourself and external forces. The ideas in Acres of Diamonds are tested and PROVEN.A man in Michigan who was on the verge of bankruptcy, having lost heavily in real estate, heard "Acres of Diamonds" and began?as the lecture advises? right at home to rebuild his fortunes. Instead of giving up, he went into the same business again, fought a courageous fight and is now president of the bank and a leading financier of the town. In Clinton, Massachusetts, a young man just out of prison on probation heard the lecture and wrote Doctor Conwell the next day asking if he thought there was any chance for him, with the stigma of prison attached to him, to make a success of life. Doctor Conwell replied in his usual practical fashion, and further told the man to stay right at home and live down the disgrace. The man acted upon the advice; became an honored member of the community and was a member of Congress for sixteen years.A man in Ohio who has today, clear of all indebtedness, factories valued at $700,000 (1917 Dollars) was not worth a cent when he heard "Acres of Diamonds." He went from the lecture hall determined to find some diamonds right at home. His present business attests the success of his search. The man who invented the turn-out switch system for electric cars received his ?suggestion? from "Acres of Diamonds."These are but a few of the thousands upon thousands of similar incidents. In every state in the Union and in many countries abroad are hundreds and hundreds of men and women whose lives have been directly affected by hearing "Acres of Diamonds." Such results show it to be a lecture out of the ordinary. Rarely, if ever, has any other lecture produced such practical effects in such an almost incalculable number of instances. The lecture is the outcome of Doctor Conwell""""s practical view of life. He follows his own motto, "Supply a need." Could you be making more? In a rut? What will you do knowing the key secrets to finding control in your life, the ability to realize your dreams, obtain wealth, spiritual health, and peace with yourself? The Transformational Greats? Acres of Diamonds is made in a light-hearted, joyful, friendly and inspiring style with music. It includes (partial listing) WHERE TO FIND WEALTH: RIGHT HERE, RIGHT NOW, Riches Surround You Here and Now; MISCONCEPTIONS ABOUT MONEY AND THE POOR AND RICH, You Have No Right to be Poor , There are Some Things More Valuable than Money, The Foundation of Your Faith is Altogether False, The Number of Sympathetic Poor is Very Small: Sympathize with the Rich, Pity the Rich Man?s Son; HOW TO BECOME WEALTHY, You Don?t Need Capital You Need Common Sense, You Can Measure Your Good by What You are Paid, The Royal Road to Wealth Proven by Thousands of Millionaires, Discouragement Prevents People From Getting Rich: That is All There is to it, Great Opportunities are Waiting to be Seized, True Greatness. The Bonus Audiobook The Work of Russell Conwell is included. It is complimentary and synergistic to the Acres of Diamonds lecture. It focuses on Conwell?s optimistic philosophy, lectures, and respect for education and how it changed many people?s lives for the better.This audiobook is also available as part of the ?7 Motivational Greats? audiobook combo pack that includes this and 6 other audiobooks on CD for under $23.More information is available at www.InfoFount.com.

Acres of Diamonds: The Magic Story. Russell H. Conwell. Read by Billy Nash. 2 cass. 1998. 17.95 (978-1-57949-007-2(7)) Destination Success.

Acres of Diamonds: The Magic Story. Russell H. Conwell. (5171) Meyer Res Grp.

Acrogems... Key to Motivation & Memory. Paul Stanyard. 1 cass. 12.50 Alpha Tape.

Acrophonology-Applied Techniques. Shirlee Kiley. 1 cass. 8.95 (742) Am Fed Astrologers.

Acrophonology for the Student Astrologer. Shirlee Kiley. 1 cass. 8.95 (429) Am Fed Astrologers.

Across All the Barriers. Swami Amar Jyoti. 1 cass. 1983. 9.95 (R-50) Truth Consciousness.
Crossing the barriers to Perfection, our own true nature. The beautiful space of our true life, joy & oneness. Dharma gives us eyes.

Across America on an Emigrant Train. unabr. ed. Jim Murphy. Narrated by Richard M. Davidson. 2 pieces. (Running Time: 2 hrs. 45 mins.). (gr. 6 up). 1998. 21.00 (978-0-7887-2269-1(7), 95531E7) Recorded Bks.
Robert Louis Stevenson left his home in Scotland in 1879 & sailed to New York. He then traveled to Monterey, California & this records his lively 24-day journey.

Across America on an Emigrant Train, Class Set. unabr. ed. Jim Murphy. Read by Richard M. Davidson. 2 cass., 10 bks. (Running Time: 2 hrs. 45 mins.). (YA). (gr. 7 up). 1998. bk. 198.80 (978-0-7887-2559-3(9), 46729) Recorded Bks.

Across America on an Emigrant Train, Homework Set. unabr. ed. Jim Murphy. Read by Richard M. Davidson. 2 cass. (Running Time: 2 hrs. 45 mins.). (YA). (gr. 7 up). 1998. bk. 44.95 (978-0-7887-2272-1(7), 40739) Recorded Bks.

Across Five Aprils. unabr. ed. Irene Hunt. Narrated by Terry Bregy. 5 CDs. (Running Time: 6 hrs.). (J). 2002. audio compact disk 44.95 (978-1-883332-75-4(3), CD1-02) Audio Bkshelf.
The compelling classic of a boy's coming of age during the Civil War is based on stories the author's grandfather told her about his own life.

Across Five Aprils. unabr. ed. Irene Hunt. Narrated by Terry Bregy. 4 cass. (Running Time: 6 hrs.). (YA). (gr. 7 up). 2002. 34.95 (978-1-883332-48-8(6)) Audio Bkshelf.

Across Five Aprils. unabr. ed. Irene Hunt. Read by Terry Bregy. (J). 2008. 64.99 (978-1-60252-944-1(2)) Find a World.

Across Five Aprils. unabr. ed. Irene Hunt. Narrated by Tom Stechschulte. 6 CDs. (Running Time: 6 hrs. 30 mins.). (gr. 6 up). 1964. audio compact disk 64.00 (978-1-4025-1484-5(0), C1609) Recorded Bks.
Southern Illinois is a place of mixed emotions as the Civil War erupts. For the Creightons, the war lures two sons to the Union army and one to the Confederacy, leaving 10-year-old Jethro to care for the family farm. As the war rages on, Jethro is forced to grow up in a hurry and provide for his loved ones amidst the turmoil of a state torn by conflicting loyalties.

Across Five Aprils. unabr. ed. Irene Hunt. Narrated by Tom Stechschulte. 5 pieces. (Running Time: 6 hrs. 30 mins.). (gr. 6 up). 2002. 52.00 (978-1-4025-0182-1(X)) Recorded Bks.
Southern Illinois is a place of mixed emotions as the American Civil War erupts. For the Creightons, the war lures two sons to the Union army and one to the Confederacy, leaving 10-year-old Jethro to care for the family farm. As the war rages, Jethro does whatever he can to learn about the fates of his brothers, while the Creighton family faces its own danger. Some townspeople can't forgive the Creightons for having a rebel son - and they're willing to use violence to make their feelings known. In a state torn by conflicting loyalties, Jethro is forced to grow up quickly to preserve his family and their home.

Across the Barricades. unabr. ed. Joan Lingard. Read by Gerard Murphy. 4 cass. (Running Time: 4 hrs. 10 mins.). 2002. (978-1-85549-755-9(7)) Cover To Cover GBR.
Kevin and Sadie are made for each other, but it is a bitter, cruel path they take when they continue their meetings.

Across the Border. Paul Sybert. 1 CD. (Running Time: 15 mins). 2005. audio compact disk 15.00 (978-0-9767842-2-7(X)) Paul Syb.

Across the Brooklyn Bridge: An Engineered Work of Art. unabr. ed. Gerald J. Morse. Read by Brooks Baldwin. 1 cass. (Running Time: 85 mins.). (Talk-A-Walk Tours on Cassette Ser.). 1983. 9.95 (978-0-939969-03-6(3), BB7) Talk-a-Walk.
A walk from Brooklyn to Manhattan reporting on the history of the bridge, exploring the politics at the time of its construction & describing the city as seen from the bridge. Detailed street map included.

Across the Limpopo. unabr. ed. Michael Nicholson. Read by Ian Craig. 6 cass. (Running Time: 7 hrs. 15 mins.). (Isis Ser.). (J). 2004. 54.95 (978-1-85695-443-3(9), 90042) Pub: ISIS Lrg Prnt GBR. Dist(s): Ulverscroft US

Across the Moor see Secret Garden: A Young Reader's Edition of the Classic Story

Across the Narrow Seas. James Pattinson & James Pattinson. 2008. 54.95 (978-1-84559-620-0(X)); audio compact disk 71.95 (978-1-84559-677-4(3)) Pub: Soundings Ltd GBR. Dist(s): Ulverscroft US

Across the Nightingale Floor. abr. unabr. ed. Lian Hearn. Read by Kevin Gray & Aiko Nakasone. 8 CDs. (Running Time: 8 hrs. 30 mins.). Bk. 1. (ENG.). 2002. audio compact disk 36.95 (978-1-56511-711-2(5), 1565117115) Pub: HighBridge. Dist(s): Workman Pub

Across the Rio Colorado. abr. ed. Ralph Compton. Read by Jim Gough. 4 cass. (Running Time: 6 hrs.). (Sundown Riders Ser.). 1999. Rental 24.95 (978-1-890990-30-5(2)) Otis Audio.
Wagon boss Chance McQuade struggles to lead a wagon train of a hundred families from Missouri across the frontier to Texas as he does battle with Kiowa Indians, lightning storms & killers on his trail.

Across the River & into the Trees. unabr. ed. Ernest Hemingway. Read by Alexander Adams. 6 cass. (Running Time: 9 hrs.). 2001. 29.95 (978-0-7366-5670-2(7)) Books on Tape.
The poignant story of Richard Cantwell, an American officer haunted by his experience in WW II & a young Italian countess.

Across the River & into the Trees. unabr. ed. Ernest Hemingway. Read by Boyd Gaines. 2006. 17.95 (978-0-7435-6517-2(7), Audioworks); 69.75 (978-0-7435-6603-2(3)); audio compact disk 29.95 (978-0-7435-6443-4(X)) Pub: S&S Audio. Dist(s): S and S Inc

Across the River & into the Trees. unabr. collector's ed. Ernest Hemingway. Read by Wolfram Kandinsky. 6 cass. (Running Time: 9 hrs.). 1990. 48.00 (978-0-7366-1731-4(0), 2571) Books on Tape.

Across the Sea of Stars. unabr. collector's ed. Arthur C. Clarke. Read by Dan Lazar. 8 cass. (Running Time: 8 hrs.). 1980. 48.00 (978-0-7366-0259-4(3), 1254) Books on Tape.
Eighteen of Clarke's finest short stories including "Encounter at Dawn", "The Sentinel", "Jupiter Five", & "Time's Arrow".

Across the Straits: 22 Miniscripts for Developing Advanced Listening Skills. Jianhua Bai & Hesheng Zhang. 3 cass. (CHI & ENG.). (C). (gr. k up). 1998. 41.95 (978-0-88727-306-3(8)) Cheng Tsui.

Across the Straits: 22 Miniscripts for Developing Advanced Listening Skills. Jianhua Bai et al. 3 cass. (Running Time: 2 hrs. 40 mins.). 1998. 75.00 (978-0-88727-310-0(6)) Cheng Tsui.

***Across the Universe.** Beth Revis. (Running Time: 10 hrs.). (ENG.). 2011. audio compact disk 34.95 (978-0-14-242899-3(X), PengAudBks) Penguin Grp USA.

Across the Universe: John Lennon Forever. Geoffrey Giuliano. 2009. (978-1-60136-138-7(6)) Audio Holding.

Across the Wide & Lonesome Prairie: The Oregon Trail Diary of Hattie Campbell. unabr. ed. Kristiana Gregory. 3 cass. (Running Time: 3 hrs. 30 mins.). (Dear America Ser.). (J). (gr. 4-7). 2005. bk. 36.95 (978-1-59519-458-9(4)); bk. 39.95 (978-1-59519-464-0(9)); 25.95 (978-1-59519-457-2(6)) Live Oak Media.
At first, 13-year-old Hattie and her family find the wagon train adventure exciting, but as time passes, death, disease, weather, and the terrain make it a tedious and dangerous trip. Through Hattie's diary, the rigors - and the joys - of this fascinating era in history are deftly chronicled.

Across the Wide & Lonesome Prairie: The Oregon Trail Diary of Hattie Campbell 1847. Kristiana Gregory. Read by Barbara Rosenblat & Stina Nielsen. Directed By Robin Miles. (Running Time: 12600 sec.). (Dear America Ser.). (YA). (gr. 8). 2006. audio compact disk 28.95 (978-1-59519-463-3(0)) Live Oak Media.

Across the Wide Missouri. unabr. ed. Bernard A. De Voto. Read by Larry McKeever. 11 cass. (Running Time: 16 hrs. 30 min.). 1983. 88.00 (978-0-7366-0375-1(1), 1354) Books on Tape.
A Pulitzer prize book. How explorers opened the far west.

Across the Years. abr. ed. Tracie Peterson. Read by Sandra Burr. (Running Time: 10800 sec.). (Desert Roses Ser.: Vol. 2). 2003. audio compact disk 24.95 (978-1-4233-0389-3(X), 9781423303893, Brilliance MP3) Brilliance Audio.
Disowned by her parents for marrying a man they disapproved of, Ashley Reynolds faces even greater hardship when she loses her husband in a tragic accident - and she's left alone with a baby on the way. Working as a Harvey Girl in Winslow, Arizona, provides the element of peace she has sought. But despite her young daughter's desire for a father, Ashley finds her heart still attached to the man she lost so long ago. When circumstances force Ashley to confront the past, she finds herself torn between her desire for love and the pain she harbors in her heart.

Across the Years. abr. ed. Tracie Peterson. Read by Sandra Burr. 2 cass. (Running Time: 3 hrs.). (Desert Roses Ser.: Vol. 2). 2003. 17.95 (978-1-59086-818-8(8), 1590868188); 44.25 (978-1-59086-819-5(6), 1590868196); audio compact disk 24.95 (978-1-59086-820-1(X), 159086820X); audio compact disk 62.25 (978-1-59086-821-8(8), 1590868218) Brilliance Audio.

Across the Years. abr. ed. Tracie Peterson. Read by Sandra Burr. (Running Time: 3 hrs.). (Desert Roses Ser.: Vol. 2). 2006. 39.25 (978-1-4233-0392-3(X), 9781423303923, BADLE); 24.95 (978-1-4233-0391-6(1), 9781423303916, BAD); audio compact disk 39.25 (978-1-4233-0390-9(3), 9781423303909, Brlnc Audio MP3 Lib) Brilliance Audio.

Across 5 Aprils. Irene Hunt. (J). 1988. 21.33 (978-0-394-76922-6(8)) SRA McGraw.

ACS Patient Education Guidelines to Oncology Drugs. ACS Staff. (C). 1999. audio compact disk 36.95 (978-0-7637-1221-1(3), 1221-3) Jones Bartlett.

Act I. (LifeLight Bible Studies: Course 13). bk. & stu. ed. 0.55 (978-0-570-09285-8(X), 20-2307) Concordia.

Act Interaction, Set. Edwin T. Cornelius. Illus. by John Odam. (New Technology English Ser.: Vol. 12). 1984. 36.00 (978-0-89209-162-1(2)) Pace Grp Intl.

Act Normal: A Stan Turner Mystery, bk. 8. William Manchee. Read by William Timnick. (ENG.). 2009. 12.00 (978-1-929976-60-7(7)) Top Pubns.

Act Now: End Procrastination. Eldon Taylor. 2 cass. 29.95 Set. (978-1-55978-746-8(5), 4411) Progress Aware Res.

Act of Betrayal. unabr. ed. Edna Buchanan. Narrated by Barbara Caruso. 7 cass. (Running Time: 10 hrs. 15 mins.). (Britt Montero Mystery Ser.). 2000. 60.00 (978-0-7887-0488-8(5), 94681E7) Recorded Bks.

Act of Betrayal. unabr. collector's ed. Edna Buchanan. Read by Anna Fields. 7 cass. (Running Time: 10 hrs. 30 min.). (Britt Montero Mystery Ser.). 1996. 56.00 (978-0-7366-3306-2(5), 3960) Books on Tape.
Britt Montero tracks the man who betrayed her father. Can she find him in a hurricane.

Act of Betrayal, Set. unabr. ed. Edna Buchanan. Read by Sandra Burr. 6 cass. (Britt Montero Mystery Ser.). 1999. 57.25 (FS9-34253) Highsmith.

Act of Faith. unabr. ed. Erica James. Read by Eve Matheson. 12 cass. (Running Time: 59520 sec.). (Church of England Ser.). 2000. 96.95 (978-0-7540-0485-1(6), CAB1980) AudioGO.
Ali Anderson has always been a loose cannon. While she's still trying to come to terms with the death of her baby son & subsequent divorce from Elliot, she takes it upon herself to play God with her best friend's incomprehensible marriage. Ali's meddling has disastrous results & when she finds herself cut off from those she loves, Ali realizes that a little forgiveness can go a long way.

Act of Love. unabr. ed. Nancy Thayer. Narrated by Barbara Caruso. 7 cass. (Running Time: 10 hrs. 15 mins.). 1997. 66.00 (978-0-7887-1743-7(X), 95221E7) Recorded Bks.
A deeply moving portrait of a family torn apart by a search for truth.

Act of Marriage Pt. 1: Gen. 2:24-25. Ed Young. 1991. 4.95 (978-0-7417-1843-3(X), 843) Win Walk.

Act of Marriage after 40: Making Love for Life. abr. ed. Tim LaHaye & Beverly LaHaye. 2 cass. (Running Time: 2 hrs.). 2000. 16.99 (978-0-310-23483-8(2)) Zondervan.
Help on such topics as nutrition (how do nutritional supplements affect your sex life?), fitness, sexual desire (does sexual desire actually reverse with age?), male impotence (psychological & physical causes, including a discussion of Viagra), female hormone drugs (the effect on desire), menopause and hysterectomy sex, first-time marriage, & much more.

Act of Marriage the $64,000 Question Pt. 2: Heb. 13:4. Ed Young. 1991. 4.95 (978-0-7417-1845-7(6), 845) Win Walk.

Act of Revenge. unabr. ed. Robert K. Tanenbaum. Read by Arthur Addison. 11 cass. (Running Time: 16 hrs. 30 min.). (Butch Karp Mystery Ser.). 1999. 88.00 (978-0-7366-4742-7(2), 5080) Books on Tape.
Chief Assistant D.A. Butch Karp heads what must be the most unconventional family in crime fiction.

Act of Terror. Richard Woodman. Read by Terry W. Pearson. 10 cass. (Running Time: 15 hrs.). 2001. 84.95 (978-1-86042-827-2(4), 28274) Pub: Soundings Ltd GBR. Dist(s): Ulverscroft US

Act of Terror. Richard Woodman & Richard Woodman. (Soundings (CDs) Ser.). 2006. audio compact disk 89.95 (978-1-84559-372-8(3)) Pub: ISIS Lrg Prnt GBR. Dist(s): Ulverscroft US

ACT of Treachery. unabr. ed. Ann Widdecombe. Read by Carole Boyd. 8 cass. (Running Time: 10 hrs.). 2003. 69.95 (978-0-7540-0969-6(6), CAB 2391) AudioGO.

Act of Treason. abr. ed. Vince Flynn. Read by Armand Schultz. (Mitch Rapp Ser.: No. 7). 2006. 17.95 (978-0-7435-6346-8(8)) Pub: S&S Audio. Dist(s): S and S Inc

Act of Treason. abr. ed. Vince Flynn. Read by Armand Schultz. (Running Time: 6 hrs. 0 mins. 0 sec.). No. 7. (ENG.). 2008. audio compact disk 14.99 (978-0-7435-7611-6(X)) Pub: S&S Audio. Dist(s): S and S Inc

Act of Treason. unabr. ed. Vince Flynn. Read by George Guidall. 10 cass. (Running Time: 11 hrs.). (Mitch Rapp Ser.: No. 7). 2006. 89.75 (978-1-4281-1584-2(6)); audio compact disk 119.75 (978-1-4281-1586-6(2)) Recorded Bks.
With two weeks to go in the presidential election, Vice President Sherman Baxter is trailing in the polls by more than five points. After delivering a speech at Georgetown University, Baxter's motorcade is ambushed by a group of terrorists. The vice president narrowly escapes, but his wife and a half dozen Secret Service agents are killed in the assault. Two weeks later Baxter is carried to victory by a sympathy vote. On the surface the terrorist attack appears to be an open and shut case. That is, until a package appears on the doorstep of Special Agent Skip McMahon, the FBI's lead investigator of the terrorist attack. The contents of the package are so toxic that the veteran law enforcement officer seriously considers destroying the evidence, that is until he thinks of Mitch Rapp, the one man who's reckless enough to follow the evidence to its explosive conclusion.

Act of Treason. unabr. ed. Vince Flynn. Read by George Guidall. (Mitch Rapp Ser.: No. 7). 2006. 29.95 (978-0-7435-6347-5(6)); audio compact disk 49.95 (978-0-7435-5591-3(0)) Pub: S&S Audio. Dist(s): S and S Inc

Act of War. abr. ed. Dale Brown. Read by Larry Pressman. 2005. audio compact disk 29.95 (978-0-06-075643-7(8)) HarperCollins Pubs.

Act of War. abr. ed. Dale Brown. Read by Larry Pressman. (Running Time: 21600 sec.). 2007. audio compact disk 14.95 (978-0-06-128450-2(5), Harper Audio) HarperCollins Pubs.

***Act of War.** abr. ed. Dale Brown. (ENG.). 2005. (978-0-06-079683-9(9), Harper Audio) HarperCollins Pubs.

***Act of War.** abr. ed. Dale Brown. Read by Larry Pressman. (ENG.). 2005. (978-0-06-085452-2(9), Harper Audio) HarperCollins Pubs.

Act of War. unabr. ed. Dale Brown. Read by William Dufris. 2 pieces. 2005. 49.95 (978-0-7927-3653-0(2), CMP 807); 79.95 (978-0-7927-3651-6(6), CSL 807); audio compact disk 99.95 (978-0-7927-3652-3(4), SLD 807) AudioGO.

Act of War. unabr. ed. Dale Brown. 2005. audio compact disk 39.95 (978-0-06-075929-2(1)) HarperCollins Pubs.

Act of Will. unabr. ed. Barbara Taylor Bradford. Read by Diana Bishop. 12 cass. (Running Time: 15 hrs.). (Isis Ser.). (J). 1994. 94.95 (978-1-85695-715-1(2), 940605) Pub: ISIS Lrg Prnt GBR. Dist(s): Ulverscroft US

Act of Will. unabr. ed. Barbara Taylor Bradford. Read by Diana Bishop. 14 CDs. (Running Time: 14 hrs.). (Isis Ser.). (J). 2001. audio compact disk 104.95 (978-0-7531-0974-8(3), 109743) Pub: ISIS Lrg Prnt GBR. Dist(s): Ulverscroft US
A sparkling compulsive story of three generations of women that moves from the bleak Yorkshire Dales to London & the glamorous world of New York haute couture.

Acteur Celebre, Le Demarcheur. Eric Naggar. Read by Jean Rochefort & Jean-Pierre Marielle. 1 cass. (FRE.). 1991. 16.95 (1267-RF) Olivia & Hill.

Acting As If Life Mattered: The Theatre of Life. Michael Toms. Interview with Arleen Lorrance & Diane K. Pike. 1 cass. (Running Time: 60 min.). 9.95 Teleos Inst.

Acting on the Good News. 6 cass. 19.95 (20143, HarperThor) HarpC GBR.

Acting Psychic: How to Spot a Fake. abr. ed. Sally Atman. Read by Sally Atman. 1 cass. (Running Time: 1 hr. 26 min.). 1999. bk. 8.95 (978-1-928843-06-1(9)) Ad Lib Res.
Explains how insincere psychics use nonverbal communication & acting skills to give a convincing "reading".

Acting Strangely. unabr. ed. Martin Jarvis. Read by Martin Jarvis. 6 cass. (Running Time: 9 hrs.). 2000. 54.95 (978-0-7540-0455-4(4), CAB 1878) Pub: Chivers Audio Bks GBR. Dist(s): AudioGO
Martin Jarvis tells about a distinguished acting career. With numerous roles to his credit, Jarvis populates his autobiography with amusing tales of fellow actors such as Sir John Gielgud, Dame Judy Dench & Leonardo DiCaprio.

Acting Strangely: A Funny Kind of Life. unabr. ed. Martin Jarvis. 6 CDs. (Running Time: 9 hrs.). 2002. audio compact disk 64.95 (978-0-7540-5529-7(9), CCD 220) Pub: Chivers Audio Bks GBR. Dist(s): AudioGO

Acting with an Accent. David A. Stern. Read by David A. Stern. 16 cass. Incl. Cockney. 1979. 16.95; Essential Verbs! French: No Sentence Is Complete without that One Key Word: the VERBS! Penton Overseas, Inc. Staff. 1979. 16.95; Essential Verbs! German: No Sentence Is Complete Without That One Key Word: the VERBS! Penton Overseas, Inc. Staff. 1979. 16.95; Irish. 1979. 16.95; Italian. Lonely Planet Publications Staff. 1979. 16.95; New York. Ed. by Lonely Planet Publications Staff. 1979. 16.95; Russian. Penton Overseas, Inc. Staff. 1979. 16.95; Scottish. 1979. 16.95; Southern U. S. 1979. 16.95; Spanish. 1979. 16.95 (C99); Standard British. 1979. 16.95; Yiddish. 1979. 16.95; 1979. 16.95 ea. incl. bklt. Meriwether Pub.
One hour instructional cassettes by a master dialectician. David A. Stern, Ph.D. of Hollywood is the teacher of film & TV actors. He doesn't use dialect "tricks", but teaches the basics of convincing dialects, the resonance, the lilt & the pace. He explains pronunciations, word choice & touches on idioms.

Acting with Atman's Pyramid. abr. ed. Sally Atman. Read by Sally Atman. 1 cass. (Running Time: 1 hr. 32 min.). 1999. 10.95 (978-1-928843-05-4(0)) Ad Lib Res.
Re-edited version of "Pyramid Acting," which teaches basic structure. Based on the L.A. workshop.

Action! A Novel. unabr. ed. Robert Cort. Read by Grover Gardner. 12 CDs. (Running Time: 14 hrs. 30 mins.). 2003. audio compact disk 96.00 (978-0-7861-9143-7(0), 3147); 76.95 (978-0-7861-2514-2(4), 3147) Blckstn Audio.
A family saga in which five decades of Hollywood history are embodied in the lives of three generations of a movie dynasty, with each generation reflecting the changing values of the motion-picture industry.

***Action Bible.** unabr. ed. David C. Cook. Ed. by Doug Mauss. (Running Time: 10 hrs. 20 mins. 18 sec.). (ENG.). 2010. audio compact disk 29.99 (978-1-59859-792-9(2)) Oasis Audio.

***Action Bible.** unabr. ed. Ed. by Doug Mauss. (Running Time: 10 hrs. 20 mins. 18 sec.). (ENG.). 2010. 20.99 (978-1-60814-729-8(0)) Oasis Audio.

Action Bible Songs. 1 CD. (Running Time: 30 min.). (J). 2001. pap. bk. 9.99 (978-1-894677-03-5(X)); pap. bk. 7.99 (978-1-894677-04-2(8)) Kidzup Prodns.
Features children's favorite Christian songs performed by kids.

Action Bible Songs. Prod. by Twin Sisters Productions Staff. 1 CD. (Running Time: 30 mins). (J). 2005. audio compact disk 4.99 (978-1-57583-804-5(4)) Twin Sisters.
Encourage child-like faith and worship with this new contemporary collection of classic church school songs kids love! Sing and celebrate together at home, church, preschool and school. BONUS! Includes 50 fun things to do with kids!.

Action French! A Lively Activity Starter Pack for Adults & Children. Catherine Bruzzone & Clare Beaton. 1 cass. (Running Time: 45 mins.). (J). (ps-5). 2000. pap. bk. & suppl. ed. 14.95 (978-0-658-00448-3(4), 004484) M-H Contemporary.
Combines activities from the workbook with words, phrases, rhymes & songs on the audiotape.

Action Is Essential. George King. 2009. audio compact disk (978-0-937249-53-6(X)) Aetherius Soc.

Action Jackson. Sandra Jordan & Jan Greenberg. Illus. by Robert Andrew Parker. 11 vols. pap. bk. 16.95 (978-1-59112-959-2(1)); pap. bk. (978-1-59112-961-5(3)); pap. bk. 18.95 (978-1-59112-963-9(X)); pap. bk. (978-1-59112-965-3(6)); 9.95 (978-1-59112-958-5(3)); audio compact disk 12.95 (978-1-59112-962-2(1)) Live Oak Media.

Action Jackson. Sandra Jordan & Jan Greenberg. Illus. by Robert Andrew Parker. 11 vols. (J). 2005. bk. 25.95 (978-1-59112-960-8(5)); bk. 28.95 (978-1-59112-964-6(8)) Pub: Live Oak Media. Dist(s): AudioGO

Action Plan for IELTS. abr. ed. Vanessa Jakeman & Clare McDowell. (Running Time: 1 hr. 17 mins.). (ENG.). 2006. 25.00 (978-0-521-61532-7(1)); audio compact disk 25.00 (978-0-521-61533-4(X)) Cambridge U Pr.

Action Reading Fast Track. Jeanie Eller. Read by Jeanie Eller. 6 cass. (Running Time: 9 hrs. 31 mins.). 1992. (978-1-928606-65-9(2)) Action Readg.
Systematic learn to read program.

Action Songs. Perf. by Cedarmont Kids. 1 cass. 1999. 3.99 (978-0-00-546332-1(7)); audio compact disk 5.99 (978-0-00-507227-1(1)) Provident Music.

Action Spanish! A Lively Activity Starter Pack for Adults & Children. Catherine Bruzzone et al. 1 cass. (Running Time: 45 min.). (ENG & SPA., (J). (ps-5). 2000. pap. bk. 14.95 (978-0-658-00443-8(3), 004433) M-H Contemporary.

Action Strategies for Those at Risk. Read by Bertie Ryan Synowiec. 1 cass. (Running Time: 1 hr. 10 min.). 1989. 9.97 (978-1-885335-11-1(3)) Positive Support.
Self-esteem, good example & healthy choices.

Actionlogues. JoAnne Robinson Klopp. 1 cass. (Running Time: 30 min.). (FRE.). 1985. 10.95 (978-0-940296-54-1(3)) Sky Oaks Prodns.
Features a native speaker uttering directions in French to lead students photograph by photograph through the Actionlogues.

Actionlogues. JoAnne Robinson Klopp. 1 cass. (Running Time: 30 min.). (GER.). 1989. 10.95 (978-0-940296-74-9(8)); 10.95 (978-0-940296-52-7(7)) Sky Oaks Prodns.
Features 25 TPR lessons, such as getting ready for work, making a sandwich, working in the yard, driving a car, & more.

Actionlogues. unabr. ed. JoAnne Robinson Klopp. Illus. by Laura Clark & Stephen Klopp. Photos by Stephen Klopp. 1 cass. (Running Time: 30 min.). (FRE.). (J). (gr. 7-12). 1988. pap. bk. 10.95 (978-0-940296-53-4(5), 232) Sky Oaks Prodns.
Features a native speaker uttering directions in French to lead students photograph by photograph through the Actionlogues.

Actitud de un Vencedor. Hugo Martinez. 6 cass. (SPA.). 2003. 29.99 (978-0-89985-405-2(2)); audio compact disk 35.00 (978-0-89985-423-6(0)) Christ for the Nations.

Actitud Mental Positiva. unabr. ed. Camilo Cruz. 2 cass. (Running Time: 2 hrs.).Tr. of Positive Mental Attitude. (SPA.). 2003. 18.00 (978-1-931059-00-8(4)) Taller del Exito.
You become what you think about. The thoughts that you allow to occupy your mind shape the person that you will become. Motivating oneself and motivating others begins with developing a positive outlook in life. This program will teach you how to identify the different sources of motivation, a key component of every success plan.

Actitudes Positivas. Cesar Lozano.Tr. of Positive Thinking. (SPA.). 2009. audio compact disk 17.00 (978-1-935405-46-7(2)) Hombre Nuevo.

Activa Tu Fe. unabr. ed. Michael Rodriguez. (SPA.). 2002. 9.99 (978-0-8297-3234-4(9)) Pub: Vida Pubs. Dist(s): Zondervan

Activa Tu Fe. unabr. ed. Michael Rodriguez. 2002. audio compact disk 14.99 (978-0-8297-3232-0(2)) Zondervan.

Activate Your English Intermediate Class: A Short Course for Adults. Barbara Sinclair & Philip Prowse. 1. (Running Time: hrs. mins.). (ENG.). 1997. 23.00 (978-0-521-48417-6(0)) Cambridge U Pr.

Activate Your English Intermediate Self-Study: A Short Course for Adults. Barbara Sinclair & Philip Prowse. (Running Time: hrs. mins.). (ENG.). 1997. wbk. ed. 24.15 (978-0-521-48416-9(2)) Cambridge U Pr.

Activate Your English Intermediate Self-Study: A Short Course for Adults. Barbara Sinclair & Philip Prowse. (Running Time: hrs. mins.). (ENG.). 1997. wbk. ed. 24.15 (978-0-521-48415-2(4)) Cambridge U Pr.

Activate Your English Pre-Intermediate: A Short Course for Adults. Barbara Sinclair. 1 cass. (ENG., 1996. 23.00 (978-0-521-42571-1(9)) Cambridge U Pr.

Activate Your English Pre-Intermediate Self Study: A Short Course for Adults. Barbara Sinclair. 1 cass. (ENG., 1996. wbk. ed. 24.15 (978-0-521-42572-8(7)) Cambridge U Pr.

Activate Your Genius. Megan Sillito. Intro. by Denver Robbins. Prod. by Dark Sun Productions. 2007. audio compact disk 39.95 (978-0-9801727-2-0(1)) Lifeworks Str.

Activating an Astrological Practice. John L. Ahern. 1 cass. (Workshop Ser.). 8.95 (017) Am Fed Astrologers.

Activating God's Power. Elbert Willis. 1 cass. (Miracle Land Ser.). 4.00 Fill the Gap.

Activating the Law of Attraction: Visualise & attain the future of your Dreams. Created by Christine Sherborne. (ENG.). (YA). 2007. audio compact disk 19.95 (978-0-9804155-3-7(5)) Pub: Colourstory AUS. Dist(s): APG

Active Directory Infrastructure Classroom-to-Go: Self-paced Instructional Training Course. abr. ed. William Stanek. Narrated by Ron Knowles. (Running Time: 1 hr. 35 mins.). (ENG.). 2007. 14.99 (978-1-57545-312-5(6), Classroom) Pub: Reagent Press. Dist(s): OverDrive Inc

Active Directory Sites, Trusts, & Troubleshooting Classroom-to-Go: Self-paced Instructional Training Course. abr. ed. William Stanek. Narrated by Ron Knowles. (Running Time: 1 hr. 33 mins.). (ENG.). 2007. 14.99 (978-1-57545-313-2(4), Classroom) Pub: Reagent Press. Dist(s): OverDrive Inc

Active Imagination. Read by Joan Chodorow. 1 cass. (Running Time: 90 min.). 1990. 10.95 (978-0-7822-0035-5(4), 415) C G Jung IL.
An examination of the uses of active imagination in therapy, with particular attention given to dance & movement.

Active Imagination: The Waking Dream. Read by Garey Malek. 2 cass. (Running Time: 4 hrs.). 1986. 21.95 Set. (978-0-7822-0152-9(0), 212) C G Jung IL.

Active Korean: A Functional Approach. Scripts. Namgui Chang & Yong-chol Kim. 2 cass. (C). 1995. bk. 52.50 (978-1-56591-050-8(8)) Hollym Intl.

Active Learning: Truths, Tips, & Tricks. 2001. (978-1-928843-09-2(3)) Ad Lib Res.

Active Liberty: Interpreting Our Democratic Constitution. Stephen Breyer. (Running Time: 13500 sec.). 2006. audio compact disk 19.99 (978-1-4281-0003-9(2)) Recorded Bks.

Active Listening 1: Class Audio CDs. 2nd rev. ed. Steve Brown & Dorolyn Smith. (Active Listening Second Edition Ser.). (ENG., 2006. audio compact disk 59.00 (978-0-521-67815-5(3)) Cambridge U Pr.

Active Listening 2. 2nd rev. ed. Steve Brown & Dorolyn Smith. (ENG., 2006. audio compact disk 59.00 (978-0-521-67819-3(6)) Cambridge U Pr.

Active Listening 3: Class Audio CDs. 2nd rev. ed. Steve Brown & Dorolyn Smith. (Active Listening Second Edition Ser.). (ENG.). 2007. audio compact disk 59.00 (978-0-521-67823-0(4)) Cambridge U Pr.

Active Management of Labor. Contrib. by Alan M. Peaceman et al. 1 cass. (American College of Obstetrics & Gynecologists UPDATE: Vol. 24, No. 1). 1998. 20.00 Am Coll Obstetric.

***Active Methods of Spiritual Growth.** Ira Progoff. 2010. audio compact disk 15.00 (978-1-935859-06-2(4)) Dialogue Assoc.

Active Parenting. Michael Popkin. 6 cass. (Running Time: 5 hrs.). 39.95 (K1042) Active Parenting.
The tapes include case studies, commentary & real-life vignettes. The sixth tape, dealing with drug & alcohol abuse by children & teens, is an excellent stand-alone session for every parent.

Active Parenting. Michael Popkin. Read by Michael Popkin. 6 cass. 49.95 Set. (447AD) Nightingale-Conant.

Active Parenting Review: Mind Maps. 1 cass. (Running Time: 64 min.). 9.95 (C7010) Active Parenting.
The accompanying mind maps of this audiocassette are fun, creative visualizations of AP principles. By following the mind maps as the audiocassette plays, the positive parenting principles emphasized in the Active Parenting programs are reinforced & enhanced.

Active Parenting USA. Michael H. Popkin. 4 vols. (Running Time: 296 mins.). 2004. audio compact disk 19.95 (978-1-880283-89-9(1)) Pub: Active Parenting. Dist(s): Natl Bk Netwk

Active Participation of the Disciple. Swami Amar Jyoti. 1 cass. 1982. 9.95 (E-23) Truth Consciousness.
Aspiration opens us to receive from the Master. Need for faith & sincerity. Letting go of all that preserves self-image.

Active Relaxation. Narrated by Dick Lutz. 1 cass. (Running Time: 15 min.). 1981. 7.95 (978-0-931625-02-2(5), 2) DIMI Pr.
Contains instructions to tense & then relax specific muscle groups. For physical symptoms of tension such as high blood pressure, headaches, muscle spasms. Reversible.

Active Relaxation: Female Voice. Narrated by Mary Lutz. 1 cass. (Running Time: 15 min.). 7.95 (978-0-931625-12-1(2), 12) DIMI Pr.
Contains instructions to tense & then relax specific muscles-uses a woman narrator.

Active Service. Stephen Crane. Read by John Bolen. (Running Time: 8 hrs.). 2001. 27.95 (978-1-60083-605-3(4), Audiofy Corp) Iofy Corp.

Active Service. Stephen Crane. Read by John Bolen. (ENG.). 2005. audio compact disk 78.00 (978-1-4001-3034-4(4)) Pub: Tantor Media. Dist(s): IngramPubServ

Active Service. unabr. ed. Stephen Crane. Narrated by John Bolen. 7 CDs. (Running Time: 7 hrs. 59 mins.). (ENG.). 2001. audio compact disk 39.00 (978-1-4001-0034-7(8)); audio compact disk 20.00 (978-1-4001-5034-2(5)) Pub: Tantor Media. Dist(s): IngramPubServ

Active Service. unabr. ed. Stephen Crane. Narrated by John Bolen. (Running Time: 8 hrs. 0 mins. 0 sec.). (ENG.). 2009. audio compact disk 55.99 (978-1-4001-4104-3(4)); audio compact disk 27.99 (978-1-4001-1104-6(8)); audio compact disk 19.99 (978-1-4001-6104-1(5)) Pub: Tantor Media. Dist(s): IngramPubServ

Active Skills for Reading. Neil J. Anderson. 1 CD. (Running Time: 1 hr.). 2002. audio compact disk 23.95 (978-0-8384-2609-8(3)) Heinle.

Active Skills for Reading, Bk. 2. 1 cass. (Running Time: 1 hr.). 2002. 23.95 (978-0-8384-2610-4(7)) Heinle.

Active Skills for Reading, Bk. 2. Jacob Ornstein-Galicia et al. 1 cass. (Running Time: 1 hr.). (Language & the Teacher Ser.). 2002. 23.95 (978-0-8384-2629-6(8)) Heinle.
Reading series that uses thematicallly organized nonfiction reading passages to teach reading comprehension and vocabulary skills.

Active Skills for Reading, Bk.3. Neil J. Anderson. 1 CD. (Running Time: 1 hr.). 2002. audio compact disk 23.95 (978-0-8384-2625-8(5)) Heinle.

Active Time. Perf. by Rob Evans. (J). (ps-3). 1996. cass. & video 11.95 (978-84-7200-027-8(3)) Integrity Music.

Active Time Songs. (Donut Man Ser.). (J). cass. & video 12.99 (1006) Vision Vid PA.

Active Vocabulary: Study Wizard. 2nd rev. ed. Olsen. audio compact disk 14.97 (978-0-321-14245-0(4)) PH School.

Activities for the Substitute Teacher. (gr. k-8). 2000. audio compact disk 43.40 (978-0-382-34140-3(6)) Silver.

Activity Based Cost Management: Understanding Frozen Food Profitability. 1 cass. (America's Supermarket Showcase '96 Ser.). 1996. 11.00 (NGA96-008) Sound Images.

Activity Songs. unabr. ed. 1 cass. (Running Time: 90 min.). (My First Sing-Alongs Ser.). (J). 1998. 7.99 (978-1-55723-605-0(4)) W Disney Records.

***Actor Retires.** Bruce Norris. Contrib. by Lucy Childs et al. (Running Time: 3420 sec.). (L. A. Theatre Works Audio Theatre Collections). (ENG.). 2010. audio compact disk 18.95 (978-1-58081-686-1(X)) L A Theatre.

Actor Retires. unabr. ed. Bruce Norris. Perf. by D. W. Moffett et al. 1 cass. (Running Time: 58 min.). 1992. 25.95 (978-1-58081-019-7(5)) Pub: L A Theatre. Dist(s): NetLibrary CO
Comedy in which an actor decides to end his career, throw out his resumes & become a funiture maker.

Actors Jessica Tandy & Hume Cronyn. unabr. ed. Read by Jessica Tandy & Hume Cronyn. 1 cass. (Running Time: 90 min.). 1988. 12.95 (AF1725) J Norton Pubs.
Discover what the creative life means to an older person & how aging can nourish creativity. The artists tell how they overcame career frustrations & personal tragedies & talk about the sources of their artistic inspiration.

ACTOR's JOURNEY for KIDS (10 Volume Audio CD Set) 100 Distinguished Entertainment Industry Professionals Help Parents Launch the Acting Career of Their Child or Teen. Created by Stanley Livingston. 801. audio compact disk 159.00 (978-0-9825167-3-7(8)) CinergyEntpri.

ACTOR's JOURNEY (16 Volume Audio CD Set) 100 Distinguished Entertainment Industry Professionals Help You Launch Your Acting Career. Created by Stanley Livingston. 811. audio compact disk 229.00 (978-0-9825167-2-0(X)) CinergyEntpri.

Acts. T. Evans. Read by Tenniel Evans. 2 cass. (Running Time: 0 hr. 60 mins. 0 sec.). (Hodder Christian Audiobooks Ser.). (ENG., 1979. 16.99 (978-1-85998-200-6(X), HoddrStoughton) Pub: Hodder General GBR. Dist(s): IPG Chicago

Acts Commentary. collector's ed. Chuck Missler. 1 MP3 CD-ROM. (Running Time: 16 hours). (Chuck Missler Commentaries). 2001. cd-rom 39.95 (978-1-57821-146-3(8)) Koinonia Hse.
Explore Acts verse-by-verse with Chuck Missler. This is a 2 volume set with eight audios in each volume including notes.Volume One:Tape One: Acts 1 - Introduction. Ascension. Election of Matthias.Tape Two: Acts 2 - Pentecost. Peter's first sermon.Tape Three: Acts 3 - Lame man healed. Peter's second sermon. Jubilee year.Tape Four: Acts 4-6 - Peter before the Sanhedrin. Ananias & Sapphira.Tape Five: Acts 7 - Stephen addresses the Sanhedrin. First martyr.Tape Six: Acts 8-9 - Philip and Ethiopian. Saul's conversion.Tape Seven: Acts 10-12 - Peter's vision. Ministry to the GentilesTape Eight: Acts 13-14 - Paul's first missionary journey. Paul turns to Gentiles.Volume Two:Tape One: Acts 15 - Council at Jerusalem. Paul and Barnabas separate.Tape Two: Acts 16 - 17:15 - Paul's second missionary journey. Galatia. Philippi.Tape Three: Acts 17:16 - 18 - Athens and Paul on Mars Hill. Corinth.Tape Four: Acts 19 - 20 - Third missionary journey. Galatia, Ephesus.Tape Five: Acts 21 - 24 - Tyre. Paul in Jerusalem. Paul's defense.Tape Six: Acts 25 - 28 - Paul before Festus, Agrippa. Shipwreck. Rome.EpliogueTape Seven: 7 Letters to 7 Churches (part 1) - Letters to Ephesus, Smyrna, and Pergamos.Tape Eight: 7 Letters to 7 Churches (part 2) - Letters to Thyatira, Sardis, Philadelphia, Laodicea.

Acts, Epistles & Revelation: King James Version, unabr. ed. Narrated by James Hamilton. 8 cass. (Running Time: 11 hrs. 30 mins.). 1999. 70.00 (978-1-55690-372-4(3), 80140E7) Recorded Bks.

Acts II. (LifeLight Bible Studies: Course 14). 13.95 Set. (20-2313) Concordia.

Acts of God. James BeauSeigneur. Narrated by Pete Bradbury. 9 cass. (Running Time: 13 hrs. 30 mins.). (Christ Clone Trilogy: Bk. 3). 98.00 (978-1-4025-2119-5(7)) Recorded Bks.

Acts of King Arthur & His Noble Knights. unabr. ed. John Steinbeck. Read by Robert Fass. (YA). 2008. 84.99 (978-1-60514-551-8(3)) Find a World.

***Acts of Love.** abr. ed. Judith Michael. Read by Buck Schirner. (Running Time: 3 hrs.). 2010. audio compact disk 9.99 (978-1-4418-6706-3(6), 9781441867063, BCD Value Price) Brilliance Audio.

Acts of Love. unabr. ed. Elia Kazan. Read by Michael Owens. 9 cass. (Running Time: 9 hrs.). 1984. 54.00 (978-0-7366-0461-1(8), 1433) Books on Tape.
The dilemma of a young woman who tries to live her life through others.

Acts of Love. unabr. ed. Judith Michael. Read by Buck Schirner. (Running Time: 16 hrs.). 2008. 24.95 (978-1-4233-5443-7(5), 9781423354437, Brilliance MP3); 24.95 (978-1-4233-5445-1(1), 9781423354451, BAD); 39.25 (978-1-4233-5444-4(3), 9781423354444, Brinc Audio MP3 Lib); 49.97 (978-1-4233-5446-8(X), 9781423354468, BADLE) Brilliance Audio.

***Acts of Love.** unabr. ed. Judith Michael. Read by Buck Schirner. (Running Time: 15 hrs.). 2010. audio compact disk 29.99 (978-1-4418-4109-4(1), 9781441841094, Bril Audio CD Unabri); audio compact disk 89.97 (978-1-4418-4110-0(5), 9781441841100, BriAudCD Unabrid) Brilliance Audio.

Acts of Malice. abr. ed. Perri O'Shaughnessy. Read by Laural Merlington. 3 CDs. (Running Time: 3 hrs.). 2003. audio compact disk 14.99 (978-1-59086-534-7(0), 1590865340, BAU); audio compact disk 62.25 (978-1-59086-564-4(2), 1590865642) Brilliance Audio.

Acts of Malice. unabr. ed. Read by Laural Merlington. (Running Time: 39600 sec.). (Nina Reilly Ser.). 2007. audio compact disk 39.25 (978-1-4233-1421-9(2), 9781423314219, Brinc Audio MP3 Lib); audio compact disk 102.25 (978-1-4233-1419-6(0), 9781423314196, BriAudCD Unabrid); audio compact disk 38.95 (978-1-4233-1418-9(2), 9781423314189, Bril Audio CD Unabri); audio compact disk 24.95 (978-1-4233-1420-2(4), 9781423314202, Brilliance MP3) Brilliance Audio.

Acts of Malice. unabr. ed. Perri O'Shaughnessy. Read by Laural Merlington. 8 cass. (Running Time: 11 hrs.). 1999. 73.25 (978-1-56740-668-9(8), 1567406688, Unabridge Lib Edns) Brilliance Audio.

Acts of Malice. unabr. ed. Perri O'Shaughnessy. Read by Laural Merlington. (Running Time: 11 hrs.). (Nina Reilly Ser.). 2007. 39.25 (978-1-4233-1423-3(9), 9781423314233, BADLE); 24.95 (978-1-4233-1422-6(0), 9781423314226, BAD) Brilliance Audio.

Acts of Malice, Set. abr. ed. Perri O'Shaughnessy. Read by Laural Merlington. 2 cass. 1999. 17.95 (FS9-51006) Highsmith.

Acts of Malice, Set. unabr. ed. Perri O'Shaughnessy. Read by Laural Merlington. 8 cass. 1999. 73.25 (FS9-51028) Highsmith.

***Acts of Mercy.** unabr. ed. Mariah Stewart. (Running Time: 10 hrs.). (Mercy Street Ser.: No. 3). 2010. 24.99 (978-1-4418-4305-0(1), 9781441843050, BAD); 39.97 (978-1-4418-4306-7(X), 9781441843067, BADLE) Brilliance Audio.

***Acts of Mercy.** unabr. ed. Mariah Stewart. Read by Joyce Bean. (Running Time: 9 hrs.). (Mercy Street Ser.: No. 3). 2010. 39.97 (978-1-4418-4304-3(3), 9781441843043, Brinc Audio MP3 Lib); audio compact disk 79.97 (978-1-4418-4299-2(3), 9781441842992, BriAudCD Unabrid) Brilliance Audio.

***Acts of Mercy: A Mercy Street Novel.** unabr. ed. Mariah Stewart. Read by Joyce Bean. (Running Time: 9 hrs.). (Mercy Street Foundation Ser.). 2010. 24.99 (978-1-4418-4303-6(5), 9781441843036, Brilliance MP3); audio compact disk 29.99 (978-1-4418-4283-1(7), 9781441842831, Bril Audio CD Unabri) Brilliance Audio.

Acts of Nature. unabr. ed. Jonathon King. Read by Mel Foster. (Running Time: 7 hrs.). (Max Freeman Ser.). 2007. 39.25 (978-1-4233-3001-1(3), 9781423330011, BADLE); 24.95 (978-1-4233-3000-4(5), 9781423330004, BAD); 69.25 (978-1-4233-2995-4(3), 9781423329954, BrilAudUnabridg); audio compact disk 29.95 (978-1-4233-2996-1(1), 9781423329961, Bril Audio CD Unabri); audio compact disk 24.95 (978-1-4233-2998-5(8), 9781423329985, Brilliance MP3); audio compact disk 82.25 (978-1-4233-2997-8(X), 9781423329978, BriAudCD Unabrid); audio compact disk 39.25 (978-1-4233-2999-2(6), 9781423329992, Brinc Audio MP3 Lib) Brilliance Audio.

Acts of the Apostles. Scott Hahn. Read by Scott Hahn. 3 cass. 19.95 Set. (5258-C) Ignatius Pr.
Hahn believes Catholics should pay particular attention to Acts because of its importance in understanding the foundation & mission of the Church in the world. A "how-to" manual for Cathoic evangelization.

Acts of the Apostles. John A. Hardon. 10 cass. (Running Time: 90 min. per cass.). 40.00 Set. (95I) IRL Chicago.

Acts of the Apostles. Ellen G. White. 2 MP3 disks. 2004. audio compact disk 39.95 (978-1-883012-14-4(7)); audio compact disk 99.95 (978-1-883012-13-7(9)) Remnant Pubns.

Acts of the Apostles: A Biblical Interpretation. Concept by Ermance Rejebian. (ENG.). 2007. 5.99 (978-1-60339-143-6(6)); audio compact disk 5.99 (978-1-60339-144-3(4)) Listenr Digest.

Acts of the Apostles: Volume 2 of Luke. Eugene LaVerdiere. Perf. by Eugene LaVerdiere. 3 cass. (Running Time: 4 hrs.). 1997. (AA3047) Credence Commun.
Paul & Barnabus as real people, the urgent concerns of Luke, how important it was that Christians called themselves "the Way", & why Antioch was so important.

Acts of the Apostles: 8 Cassette Dramatized Audio Stories. 2006. 30.00 (978-1-60079-019-5(4)) YourStory.

Acts of the Apostles: 8 CD Dramatized Audio Stories. 2006. 30.00 (978-1-60079-042-3(9)) YourStory.

Acts Through Revelation Bible. Ty Fischer & Emily Fischer. Perf. by Steve Scheffler. 1998. 6.95 (978-1-930710-89-4(5)) Veritas Pr PA.

Actual Messages from Angels, U. F. O's, (Extra-Terrestrials) & Nature Spirits. unabr. ed. Dean Marshall & Marie Kirkendoll. 1 cass. (Running Time: 60 mins.). 1986. 9.95 (978-1-55585-076-0(6)) Quest NW Pub.
Messages from a higher intelligence. Discover what they are trying to tell mankind.

Actualism & Inner Alchemy. unabr. ed. Ralph Metzner. 1 cass. (Running Time: 1hr. 21min.). 1978. 11.00 (01604) Big Sur Tapes.
Alchemy is a metaphor for personal transformation. Metzner shows how it can be applied as a working, practical system. He introduces Actualism, a Western practice based on Agni Yoga - the yoga of fire - as a usable tool for channeling energy to dissolve blocks in consciousness, thereby enacting alchemical transformation.

Actually, It Is Your Parents' Fault: Why Your Romantic Relationship Isn't Working, & How to Fix It. Philip Van Munching & Bernie Katz. Read by Philip Van Munching. (Running Time: 23400 sec.). 2007. 44.95 (978-0-7861-4781-6(4)); audio compact disk 55.00 (978-0-7861-6249-9(X)) Blckstn Audio.

Actually, It Is Your Parents' Fault: Why Your Romantic Relationship Isnt Working, & How to Fix It. unabr. ed. Philip Van Munching & Bernie Katz. Read by Philip Van Munching. (Running Time: 23400 sec.). 2007. 26.95 (978-0-7861-4787-8(3)); audio compact disk 26.95 (978-0-7861-6280-2(5)) Blckstn Audio.

Actually, It Is Your Parent's Fault: Why Your Romantic Relationship Isn't Working & How to Fix It. unabr. ed. Philip Van Munching & Bernie Katz. Read by Philip Van Munching. (Running Time: 23400 sec.). 2007. audio compact disk 29.95 (978-0-7861-7207-8(X)) Blckstn Audio.

Actue y Hagase Rico: Cuatro estrategias para ir del deseo a la Accion. Napoleon Hill. Taller del Exito. 2009. audio compact disk 19.95 (978-1-60738-012-2(9)) Taller del Exito.

Acupressure, Vol. 1. Jonathan Parker. 2 cass. (Running Time: 2 hrs.). 1998. 17.00 (978-1-58400-006-7(7)) QuantumQuests Intl.

Acupuncture: An Introduction to Basic Principles. unabr. ed. Jack Worsley. 1 cass. (Running Time: 1 hr. 24 mins.). 1971. 11.00 (08201) Big Sur Tapes.
Worlsey describes acupuncture as the oldest system of medicine known to mankind, continually practiced for over 5,000 years. He gives a general outline of this ancient Eastern method of maintaining health & curing illness & disease.

Acupuncture & Herbal Medicine. Verena J. Smith. Read by Verena J. Smith. 4 cass. (Running Time: 5 hrs.). (Gift of Health Ser.). 1999. 29.95 (978-1-893565-00-5(9)) Inner Gate.
Designed for medical practitioners, healthcare providers, individuals & families to enhance health care treatment & promote a wholistic approach to health. Learn about eastern medicine's history; ponder explanations of Qi, the Life Force & discover the concepts of Yin & Yang & the Five Transformational Phases.

Acupuncture As Holistic Practice. Ralph Alan Dale. Read by Ralph Alan Dale. 1 cass. (Running Time: 90 mins.). 1980. 9.00 (15) Dialectic Pubng.
Holism in relation to the changing nature of health care & social transformation.

Acupuncture As Physical Therapy. Ralph Alan Dale. Read by Ralph Alan Dale. 1 cass. (Running Time: 90 min.). 1981. pap. bk. 14.00; 9.00 (17) Dialectic Pubng.
The use of acupuncture in physical therapy, the physiology of acupuncture, a practical primer of cardinal acupoints for physical therapists.

Acustico: el Sonido del Silencio. Contrib. by Alex Campos. (SPA.). 2009. audio compact disk 14.99 (978-0-8297-6118-4(7)) CanZion.

Acute Abdomen: Current Management. 3 cass. (Gynecology & Obstetrics Ser.: C84-GO3). 1984. 22.50 (8434) Am Coll Surgeons.

Acute Abdomen in Infancy. Moderated by H. Biemann Othersen, Jr. 2 cass. (Pediatric Surgery Ser.: PE-1). 1986. 19.00 (8659) Am Coll Surgeons.

Acute Management of Sports Injuries - Sexual Abuse. John Gregg & Joyce Carol Thomas. (Pediatric Emergencies: The National Conference for Practioners Ser.). 1986. 9.00 (978-0-932491-77-0(4)) Res Appl Inc.

***Acute Respiratory Disorders: Complete Series.** Concept Media Staff. (ENG.). (C). 2006. 970.00 (978-1-60232-300-1(3), ConceptMedia) Pub: Delmar. Dist(s): CENGAGE Learn

Ada & You. Marco A. V. Bitetto. Read by Marco A. V. Bitetto. 1 cass. 2000. (978-1-58578-023-5(5)) Inst of Cybernetics.

***ADA Update 2009.** PUEI. 2009. audio compact disk 199.00 (978-1-935041-58-0(4), CareerTrack) P Univ E Inc.

Adaline Falling Star. unabr. ed. Mary Pope Osborne. Read by Elaina Erika Davis. 2 vols. (Running Time: 2 hrs. 41 mins.). (Middle Grade Cassette Librariestm Ser.). (J). (gr. 3-7). 2004. pap. bk. 29.00 (978-0-8072-1195-3(8), S YA 319 SP, Listening Lib); 23.00 (978-0-8072-0522-8(2), Listening Lib) Random Audio Pubg.

Adaline Falling Star. unabr. ed. Mary Pope Osborne. Narrated by Elaine Erika Davis. 2 cass. (Running Time: 2 hrs. 45 min.). 2003. 27.00 Recorded Bks.
When her Arapaho mother dies, Adaline is sent to live with relatives in St. Louis while her father, famous explorer, Kit Carson, treks through the West. But when Adaline is treated unfairly, she runs off to make her own adventure in the wilderness - and befriends a stray dog along the way.

Adam. unabr. ed. Ted Dekker. Narrated by Tim Gregory. (ENG.). 2008. 24.49 (978-1-60814-029-9(6)); audio compact disk 34.99 (978-1-59859-381-5(1)) Oasis Audio.

Adam: God's Beloved. Henri J. M. Nouwen. Read by Dan Anderson. 3 CDs. (Running Time: 12600 sec.). 2007. audio compact disk 24.95 (978-0-86716-829-7(3)) St Anthony Mess Pr.

Adam Again. Perf. by Adam Again. 1 CD. 1999. audio compact disk 16.98 (KMGD 8693) Provident Mus Dist.

Adam Again: Classic Archives. 1 CD. (Running Time: 60 mins.). 1999. audio compact disk (978-0-7601-3524-2(X)) Brentwood Music.
Songs include: "Homeboys," "The Fine Line," "Hide Away," "Save Me," "Dig" & more.

Adam & Eve. 1 cass. (Running Time: 60 mins.). (Mother Angelica Live Ser.). 10.00 (978-1-55794-085-8(1), T36) Eternal Wrd TV.

***Adam & Eve.** unabr. ed. Sena Jeter Naslund. Read by Karen White. 2010. (978-0-06-200702-5(5), Harper Audio); (978-0-06-204204-0(1), Harper Audio) HarperCollins Pubs.

Adam & Eve DVD CD Combo. (J). 2006. DVD & audio compact disk (978-0-9792640-5-4(7)) GSP Players.

Adam & Eve Sound Effects CD. (J). 2006. audio compact disk (978-0-9792640-3-0(0)) GSP Players.

Adam & Evil. unabr. ed. Gillian Roberts. Narrated by Christina Moore. 6 cass. (Running Time: 8 hrs. 15 mins.). (Amanda Pepper Mystery Ser.). 2000. 54.00 (978-0-7887-4311-5(2), 96107E7) Recorded Bks.
When a class trip to the library coincides with a murder, Amanda's concerns over the behavior of one of her students makes him the prime suspect, To clear him, she'll have to fend off a pompous principal, rebuff an romantic reference librarian & sift through enough suspects to stuff a cheese steak sandwich.

Adam Bede. George Eliot. Read by Flo Gibson. 14 cass. (Running Time: 19 hrs. 30 mins.). 1997. 42.95 (978-1-55685-199-5(5)) Audio Bk Con.
The heartrending tale of carpenter Adam Bede's love for pretty, superficial Hetty Sorrel; her trial for the murder of her illegitimate child; the plight of her seducer, squire Arthur Donnithorne; & Adam's growing affection for Dinah Morris, a Methodist preacher.

Adam Bede. George Eliot. Read by Nadia May. 18 CDs. (Running Time: 20 hrs. 30 mins.). 2004. audio compact disk 130.00 (978-0-7861-8176-6(1), 1555) Blckstn Audio.

Adam Bede. George Eliot. Read by Nadia May. (Running Time: 20 hrs. 30 mins.). 1995. 50.95 (978-1-59912-401-8(7)) Iofy Corp.

Adam Bede. George Eliot. Read by David Case. (Running Time: 75600 sec.). (Unabridged Classics in Audio Ser.). (ENG.). 1994. audio compact disk 49.99 (978-1-4001-0212-9(X)); audio compact disk 99.99 (978-1-4001-3212-6(6)) Pub: Tantor Media. Dist(s): IngramPubServ

Adam Bede. George Eliot. Narrated by Flo Gibson. (ENG.). 2008. audio compact disk 48.95 (978-1-60646-025-2(0)) Audio Bk Con.

Adam Bede. unabr. ed. George Eliot. Read by Nadia May. 14 cass. (Running Time: 20 hrs. 30 mins.). 1995. 89.95 (978-0-7861-0659-2(X), 1555) Blckstn Audio.
Set in the English Midlands at the turn of the eighteenth century, this is the moving story of three people troubled by unwise love. Adam Bede, a young man possessing dignity & character, loves too blindly; Hetty Sorrel, pretty, vain & self-centered, loves too recklessly; & Arthur Donnithorne, a dashing young squire, loves too carelessly. Betrayed by their naivete, vanity & impulsiveness, their foolishness leads them into a calamitous triangle of seduction, retribution & murder.

Adam Bede. unabr. collector's ed. George Eliot. Read by David Case. 15 cass. (Running Time: 22 hrs. 30 mins.). 1994. 120.00 (978-0-7366-2803-7(7), 3517) Books on Tape.
Seduction, murder & retribution in the English midlands of the early 1800s.

Adam Bede, with EBook. unabr. ed. George Eliot. Narrated by David Case. (Running Time: 21 hrs. 0 mins. 0 sec.). (ENG.). 2009. 29.99 (978-1-4001-5894-2(X)); audio compact disk 39.99 (978-1-4001-0894-7(2)) Pub: Tantor Media. Dist(s): IngramPubServ

Adam Bede, with eBook. unabr. ed. George Eliot. Narrated by David Case. (Running Time: 21 hrs. 0 mins. 0 sec.). (ENG.). 2009. audio compact disk 79.99 (978-1-4001-3894-4(9)) Pub: Tantor Media. Dist(s): IngramPubServ

Adam Canfield of the Slash. unabr. ed. Michael Winerip. Read by Patrick G. Lawlor. (Running Time: 6 hrs.). (Slash Ser.). 2005. 24.95 (978-1-59737-093-6(2), 9781597370936, Brilliance MP3); 39.25 (978-1-59737-096-7(7), 9781597370967, BADLE); 24.95 (978-1-59737-095-0(9), 9781597370950, BAD); 39.25 (978-1-59737-094-3(0), 9781597370943, Brlnc Audio MP3 Lib); 62.25 (978-1-59737-090-5(8), 9781597370905, BrilAudUnabridg); 24.95 (978-1-59737-089-9(4), 9781597370899, BAU); audio compact disk 74.25 (978-1-59737-092-9(4), 9781597370929, BriAudCD Unabrid); audio compact disk 26.95 (978-1-59737-091-2(6), 9781597370912, Bril Audio CD Unabri) Brilliance Audio.
For years, Adam Canfield has been the number-one star reporter for the Harris Elementary/Middle School paper, the Slash. Nowadays he's also the most overprogrammed kid in America. Gladiator quiz bowl, jazz band, statewide test prep class - he's always running somewhere, and nine times out of ten, running late. When does a guy get time to just shoot some baskets anymore? Then his friend Jennifer talks him into being co-editor of the Slash. Between supervising know-it-all cub reporters and arguing with Principal Marris about which articles will "propel the Good Ship Harris forward," Adam worries he might lose it altogether. But then a third grader delivers a scoop bigger than any of Adam's career, and only Adam can dig deep enough to crack through a cover-up that will rock the very foundations of Harris itself. From Pulitzer Prize-winning New York Times columnist Michael Winerip, here is a first novel that delivers the rush of the newsroom, the adrenaline of a reporter on the trail of a hot story, and some keen insights into human nature - all with a lot of laughs.

Adam Canfield, the Last Reporter. unabr. ed. Michael Winerip. (Running Time: 6 hrs.). (Slash Ser.). 2007. 69.25 (978-1-59737-106-3(8), 9781597371063, BrilAudUnabridg) Brilliance Audio.
Please enter a Synopsis.

Adam Canfield, the Last Reporter. unabr. ed. Michael Winerip. Read by Patrick G. Lawlor. (Running Time: 8 hrs.). (Slash Ser.). 2009. 39.97 (978-1-59737-112-4(2), 9781597371124, BADLE); 24.99 (978-1-59737-111-7(4), 9781597371117, BAD); 39.97 (978-1-59737-110-0(6), 9781597371100, Brlnc Audio MP3 Lib); 24.99 (978-1-59737-109-4(2), 9781597371094, Brilliance MP3); audio compact disk 74.97 (978-1-59737-108-7(4), 9781597371087, BriAudCD Unabrid); audio compact disk 26.99 (978-1-59737-107-0(6), 9781597371070, Bril Audio CD Unabri) Brilliance Audio.

Adam Canfield, Watch Your Back! unabr. ed. Michael Winerip. Read by Patrick G. Lawlor. (Running Time: 8 hrs.). (Slash Ser.). 2007. 39.25 (978-1-59737-104-9(1), 9781597371049, BADLE); 24.95 (978-1-59737-103-2(3), 9781597371032, BAD); 39.25 (978-1-59737-102-5(5), 9781597371025, Brlnc Audio MP3 Lib); 74.25 (978-1-59737-098-1(3), 9781597370981, BrilAudUnabridg) Brilliance Audio.

Adam Canfield, Watch Your Back! unabr. ed. Michael Winerip. Read by Patrick G. Lawlor. 1 MP3-CD. (Running Time: 8 hrs.). (Slash Ser.). (J). (gr. 4-7). 2007. audio compact disk 24.95 (978-1-59737-101-8(7), 9781597371018, Brilliance MP3); audio compact disk 26.95 (978-1-59737-099-8(1), 9781597370998, Bril Audio CD Unabri) Brilliance Audio.

Adam Canfield, Watch Your Back! unabr. ed. Michael Winerip. Read by Patrick G. Lawlor. 6 CDs. (Running Time: 8 hrs.). (Slash Ser.). (J). (ps). 2007. audio compact disk 74.25 (978-1-59737-100-1(9), 9781597371001, BriAudCD Unabrid) Brilliance Audio.

Adam Gann, Outlaw. unabr. ed. Ray Hogan. Read by William Dufris. 4 cass. (Sagebrush Western Ser.). (J). 1999. 44.95 (978-1-57490-231-0(8)) Pub: ISIS Lrg Prnt GBR. Dist(s): Ulverscroft US

Adam of the Road. abr. ed. Elizabeth J. Gray. 1 cass. (Running Time: 1 hr. 1 min.). Dramatization. (J). 1980. 24.95 incl. cloth bk. in bag.; 15.95 incl. pap. bk. in bag. Live Oak Media.
Life in 13th century England - its color & excitement as well as its discomforts & hard times.

Adam of the Road. abr. ed. Elizabeth J. Gray. 1 cass. (Running Time: 1 hr. 1 min.). Dramatization. (J). (gr. 4-7). 1980. 9.95 (978-0-670-10437-6(X)) Live Oak Media.

Adam of the Road, Set. abr. ed. Ed. by Elizabeth J. Gray. Illus. by Robert Lawson. 11 vols. (Running Time: 1 hr. 1 min.). Dramatization. (J). (gr. 4-7). 1980. bk. 24.95 (978-0-670-10439-0(6)); pap. bk. 15.95 (978-0-670-10438-3(8)) Live Oak Media.
Adventures of a thirteenth-century minstrel boy. Newbery Medal winner, 1943.

Adam Resurrected. unabr. ed. Yoram Kaniuk. Tr. by Seymour Simckes. (Running Time: 55800 sec.). 2007. 85.95 (978-1-4332-0766-2(4)); audio compact disk 29.95 (978-1-4332-0768-6(0)); audio compact disk 99.00 (978-1-4332-0767-9(2)) Blckstn Audio.

Adam Resurrected. unabr. ed. Yoram Kaniuk. Read by Stefan Rudnicki. (Running Time: 15 hrs. 50 mins.). 2008. audio compact disk & audio compact disk 24.95 (978-1-4332-5108-5(6)) Blckstn Audio.

Adam Smith & the Founding of Capitalism. John Ridpath. 1 cass. (Running Time: 90 mins.). 1988. 12.95 (978-1-56114-125-8(9), CR02C) Second Renaissance.

Adam Smith & Today's World. Ernest Yaniger. Read by Tim O'Connor. 1 cass. (Running Time: 43 mins. per cass.). 1981. 10.00 (HT1051) Esstee Audios.
Examines the theoretical laws & procedures of Smith's free marketplace.

Adam! Where Are You? Why Most Black Men Don't Go to Church. Jawanza Kunjufu. 1994. 5.95 (978-0-318-19120-1(2)) African Am Imag.

Adam! Where Are You? Why Most Black Men Don't Go to Church. Jawanza Kunjufu. 1 cass. (Running Time: 60 mins.). 1999. 5.95 (AT15) African Am Imag.
Why is the church 75 percent female? What are 21 reasons why "he' is not there? How can we bring the Black man back to God?.

Adam's Curse: A Future Without Men. unabr. ed. Bryan Sykes. Read by Christopher Kay. 10 CDs. (Running Time: 12 hrs. 30 mins.). 2004. audio compact disk 109.75 (978-1-4025-8995-9(6)); 79.75 (978-1-4025-8993-5(X)) Recorded Bks.
In his astonishing New York Times best-seller, The Seven Daughters of Eve (H1345), Oxford University geneticist Bryan Sykes showed that nearly all Europeans are descended from seven women. Now Sykes tackles what may be the most provocative question geneticists have ever considered: Are we facing a future where men become extinct? Bold, controversial, and endlessly fascinating, Adam?s Curse is certain to spark discussion and provoke debate.

Adam's Curse: A Future Without Men. unabr. ed. Bryan Sykes & Christopher Kay. 10 CDs. (Running Time: 12 hrs. 30 mins.). 2004. audio compact disk 29.99 (978-1-4025-8219-6(6), 01612) Recorded Bks.

Adam's Dream see Twentieth-Century Poetry in English, No. 23, Recordings of Poets Reading Their Own Poetry

Adam's Return: The Five Promises of Male Initiation. unabr. ed. Richard Rohr. Read by Richard Rohr. 7 CDs. (Running Time: 28800 sec.). 2006. audio compact disk 41.95 (978-0-86716-769-6(6)) St Anthony Mess Pr.

Adam's Rib. Perf. by Adam Arkin & Anne Heche. Sreenplay by Garson Kanin & Ruth Gordon. Adapted by David Rambo. 2 CDs. (Running Time: 1 hr. 14 mins.). 2005. audio compact disk 25.95 (978-1-58081-283-2(X), CDTPT191) Pub: L A Theatre. Dist(s): NetLibrary CO

Adams vs. Jefferson: The Tumultuous Election of 1800. John Ferling. 8 CDs. (Running Time: 12 hrs. 75 min.). 2004. audio compact disk 34.99 (978-1-4193-0480-4(1)) Recorded Bks.

Adams vs Jefferson: The Tumultuous Election Of 1800. unabr. ed. John Ferling. Narrated by Jack Garrett. 8 cass. (Running Time: 11 hrs. 30 mins.). 2004. 79.75 (978-1-4193-1262-5(6), 97893MC) Recorded Bks.

Adaptability: How to Survive Change You Didn't Ask For. unabr. ed. M. J. Ryan. Read by M. J. Ryan. (Running Time: 5 hrs. 30 mins.). (ENG.). 2009. 24.98 (978-1-59659-430-2(6), GildAudio) Pub: Gildan Media. Dist(s): HachBkGrp

Adaptability: How to Survive Change You Didn't Ask For. unabr. ed. M. J. Ryan. Read by M. J. Ryan. (Running Time: 5 hrs. 30 mins.). (ENG.). 2010. audio compact disk 29.98 (978-1-59659-356-5(3), GildAudio) Pub: Gildan Media. Dist(s): HachBkGrp

Adaptation. Compiled by Benchmark Education Staff. 2005. audio compact disk 10.00 (978-1-4108-5505-3(8)) Benchmark Educ.

Adapted Classics Short Stories, Vol. 1. unabr. ed. Ed. by Marybeth Hageman. 5 cass. (Running Time: 6 hrs. 30 mins.). 1998. pap. bk. 69.95 Set, incl. 5 student texts, carrying case. (48101) Recorded Bks.
Includes: "The Tell-Tale Heart" by E.A. Poe, "The Cask of Amontillado" by E.A. Poe, "How Much Land Does a Man Need? by L. Tolstoy, "The Revolt of Mother" by M. W. Freeman, "The Story of an Hour" by K. Chopin. A short author's biography follows each story. Text includes vocabulary & activities supporting the stories.

Adapted Classics Short Stories, Vol. 2. unabr. ed. Ed. by Marybeth Hageman. 5 cass. (Running Time: 6 hrs. 30 mins.). 1998. 69.95 Set, incl. 5 student texts, carrying case. (48102) Recorded Bks.
Includes: "The Gift of the Magi" by O. Henry, "The Diamond Necklace" by G. de Maupassant, "Rip van Winkle" by W. Irving, "The Lady or the Tiger?" by F. Stockton, "The Monkey's Paw" by W.W. Jacobs. A short author's biography follows each story. Text includes vocabulary & activities supporting the stories.

Adapting Bible Lessons Booklet. Jane Mose. 2000. (978-0-9679793-3-5(1)) JCM Pub WI.

Adapting Math Curriculum: Money Skills. Judi Kinney. 2003. spiral bd. 59.00 (978-1-57861-479-0(1), IEP Res) Attainment.

ADD: The Ritalin Controversy. Joan Andrews. 1 cass. 1993. (978-1-881618-01-0(3)) Coastline Couns.
Medication for the ADD individual.

ADD & Adult Relationships. Jonathan Halvestadt. 1 cass. (Running Time: 1 hr. 29 mins.). 1998. bk. 20.00 (978-1-58111-068-5(5)) Contemporary Medical.
Personal insights into ADD, defines ADD & subtypes, "Hallmarks" of ADD.

ADD & Hyperactivity. unabr. ed. Don Colbert. Read by Greg Wheatley. 1 cass. (Running Time: 1 hr.). (Bible Cure for...Ser.). 2003. 7.99; audio compact disk 9.99 Oasis Audio.

Add to the Beauty. Contrib. by Sara Groves. Prod. by Brown Bannister. Contrib. by Troy Groves. 2005. audio compact disk 17.98 (978-5-558-78759-7(7)) INO Rec.

Add up to Three Hundred Points to Your SAT. Gary R. Gruber. 2 cass. (YA). (gr. 9-12). 2007. pap. bk. 14.95 (978-1-55569-258-2(3), EDU-6025) Great Am Audio.
Features information necessary to raise scores.

Add/adhd. Speeches. 1 CD. (Running Time: 2 hrs.). 2003. audio compact disk 14.95 (978-0-9743448-2-9(6)) NMA Media Pr.

Addicted. abr. ed. Tony Adams. Read by Jasper Britton. 2 cass. (Running Time: 3 hrs.). 1999. 16.85 (978-0-00-105564-3(X)) Ulvrscrft Audio.
The author is one of the legends of English football. This account of his playing days & descent into alcoholism is a human interest story as well as a footbal story, of a player & a person willing to go to any lengths to succeed.

Addicted Society: Pleasure-Seeking & Punishment Revisited. unabr. collector's ed. Joel Fort. Read by Michael Prichard. 5 cass. (Running Time: 5 hrs.). 1985. 30.00 (978-0-7366-1026-1(X), 1956) Books on Tape.
Dr. Fort argues that drugs are not our greatest problem, but that alcohol, tranquilizers, coffee, tobacco are.

Addicted to Hurry: Spiritual Strategies for Slowing Down. Read by Kirk Byron Jones. (ENG.). 2009. audio compact disk 17.00 (978-0-8170-1547-3(7)) Judson.

Addicted to Love. Lewis Grizzard. Read by Lewis Grizzard. Ed. by Bill Anderson. 1 cass. 1989. 9.98 (978-0-945258-22-3(4), STC-0011); audio compact disk 9.98 (978-0-945258-03-2(8), STCD-0011) Sthrn Tracks.

Addicted to Mediocrity: 20th Century Christians & the Arts. unabr. ed. Frank Schaeffer. Read by Nick Bernard. 2 cass. (Running Time: 2 hrs. 30 mins.). 1993. 17.95 (978-0-7861-0389-8(2), 1341) Blckstn Audio.
Shows how Christians today have sacrificed the artistic prominence they enjoyed for centuries and settled instead for mediocrity. The evidence for this sad state of affairs abounds. We are flooded with "Christian" doodads, trinkets, tee shirts, bumper stickers, etc., that use God's name as an advertising slogan - "Things Go Better with Jesus" - putting the Creator of the universe on the same level as soda pop! Schaeffer offers not only an unflinching critique, but specific and practical direction for becoming "unaddicted.".

Addiction: Program from the Award Winning Public Radio Series. Interview. Hosted by Fred Goodwin. Comment by John Hockenberry. Contrib. by Alan Leshner et al. 1 CD. (Running Time: 1 hr.). (Infinite Mind Ser.). 1998. audio compact disk 21.95 (978-1-888064-37-7(4), LCM 18) Lichtenstein Creat.
We now know more than ever before about addiction and its neurobiological effects on the brain. Drug and alcohol dependence can stunt personality development so that people in recovery have to cope with maturing, as well as staying sober. The price, availability and supply of a particular drug can contribute to an epidemic of addiction. New medications make it easier to kick addictions, but unlike diabetes or schizophrenia, recovery still depends on free will: the daily personal decision to stay clean. However, there's still much to learn about how to support that process.

Addiction: The Neurobiology of Dependency. Speeches. Narrated by Carlton Erickson. 4 CDs. (Running Time: 5 hrs. 9 mins). 2003. audio compact disk 59.00 (978-1-932609-04-2(0)) Cortext.
This seminar is designed to enhance and expand on participants' understanding of addictive disorders - integrating discussion of the most current research, theories and controversies in the field. Participants will learn how to assess and evaluate the effectiveness of various treatments and interventions for addiction. Also discussed are up-to-date findings on the pharmacological qualities of euphoria, cravings and "drug need.".

Addiction & Spiritual Quest. unabr. ed. David Steindl-Rast. 1 cass. (Running Time: 1 hr. 28 mins.). 1987. 11.00 (05110) Big Sur Tapes.
Using poetry & soulful questioning in an engaging interactive format, Brother David explores experiences that are often beyond our control or understanding.

Addiction II. rev. ed. Mary Blakely. 1 cass. (Rap Pack Ser.). (978-1-882995-05-9(8)) Azuray Learn.
Multi-sensory education workbooklet incl.

Addiction to Perfection. unabr. ed. Marion Woodman. 4 cass. (Running Time: 6 hrs.). 1990. 36.00 (OC71W) Sound Horizons AV.

Addictions: A Banquet in the Grave - Finding Hope in the Power of the Gospel. Edward T. Welch. (ENG.). 2001. audio compact disk 49.95 (978-1-934885-63-5(0)) New Growth Pr.

Addictive Personalities. Albert Ellis. 3 cass. (Running Time: 3 hrs. 30 mins.). 28.95 (PC11) A Ellis Institute.
For professionals focusing on addictive personalities & behavioral excesses. These tapes include the basics of REBT, its application to addictions, use of humor, three live demonstrations (on weight control, personal betrayal & procastination) & a question & answer session.

Addictive Personalities. Albert Ellis. 3 cass. (Running Time: 3 hrs. 30 mins.). 28.95 (PC11) Inst Rational-Emotive.
For professionals on addictive personalities & behavioral excesses. Includes the basics of REBT, its application to addictions, use of humor, three live demonstrations (on weight control, personal betrayal & procrastination) & a question & answer session.

Addictive Process: The Development of an Addictive Personality. Craig Hakken. 2 cass. (Running Time: 60 mins. per cass.). (Explore, Strengthen & Renew Ser.). 16.00 (978-0-89486-665-4(6), 5633G) Hazelden.

An Asterisk (*) at the beginning of an entry indicates that the title is appearing for the first time.

Addie. Lee Thompson. Read by Johanna Ward. (Running Time: 8 hrs. 18 mins.). 2005. audio compact disk 63.00 (978-0-7861-7886-5(8)) Blckstn Audio.

Addie. Lee Thompson. Narrated by Johanna Ward. (Running Time: 8 hrs. 30 mins.). 2005. 27.95 (978-1-59912-402-5(5)) Iofy Corp.

Addie. Lee Thompson. Read by Johanna Ward. (Running Time: 30600 sec.). 2005. cass., cass., DVD 54.95 (978-0-7861-3494-6(1)); DVD & audio compact disk 29.95 (978-0-7861-8069-1(2)) Blckstn Audio.

Addie: A Memoir. unabr. ed. Mary Lee Settle. Narrated by Sally Darling. 8 cass. (Running Time: 11 hrs.). 2001. 71.00 (978-0-7887-5473-9(4), 96608x7) Recorded Bks.
As Mary Lee Settle begins the story of her grandmother's life, she also traces the path of her own years. Rich with local color & the touching details of southern life, Addie is filled with humor, wisdom & power.

Adding Animals. Sundance/Newbridge, LLC Staff. (Early Math Ser.). (gr. k-1). 2000. 12.00 (978-1-58273-307-4(4)) Sund Newbrdge.

Adding at the Baseball Field Audio CD. Adapted by Benchmark Education Company Staff. Based on a work by Jeffrey B. Fuerst. (My First Reader's Theater Ser.). (J). (gr. k-1). 2008. audio compact disk 10.00 (978-1-60634-105-6(7)) Benchmark Educ.

Adding to Your Faith. John MacArthur, Jr. 4 cass. 15.95 (20155, HarperThor) HarpC GBR.

Addison Road. Contrib. by Addison Road. 2008. audio compact disk 11.99 (978-5-557-51562-7(3)) INO Rec.

Addison-Wesley Big Book Programs. 2 cass. (Running Time: 40 mins. per cass.). Dramatization. (J). (gr. k-2). 1990. 18.36 ea. AddisonWesley.

Addition. Kim Mitzo Thompson & Karen Mitzo Hilderbrand. Arranged by Hal Wright. (J). 2000. pap. bk. 13.99 (978-1-57583-332-3(8), Twin 443CD); audio compact disk 12.99 (978-1-57583-310-1(7), Twin 143CD) Twin Sisters.

Addition & Subtraction. Kidzup Productions Staff. 1 cass. (Running Time: 1 hr.). (Interactive Learning Kits Ser.). (J). (gr. k-2). 2003. cass. & audio compact disk 13.99 (978-1-894281-01-0(2)) Pub: Kidzup Prodns. Dist(s): Penton Overseas
Join Melody on a magical numbers journey and meet the Math Wizard. Along the way, discover the wonders of adding and subtracting through fun interactive games and activities.

Addition & Subtraction. Contrib. by Scholastic, Inc. Staff. 1 cass. (Running Time: 1 hr.). (Interactive Learning Kits Ser.). (J). (gr. k-2). 2000. pap. bk. 8.99 (978-1-894281-46-1(2)) Pub: Kidzup CAN. Dist(s): Penton Overseas
Join Melody on a magical numbers journey & meet the Math Wizard. Along the way, discover the wonders of adding & subtracting through fun interactive games & activities.

Addition & Subtraction. Contrib. by Scholastic, Inc. Staff. 1 cass. (Running Time: 1 hr.). 2000. 8.99 Kidzup Prodns.

Addition & Subtraction Country. Brad Caudle & Richard Caudle. Perf. by Brad Caudle & Todd Golden. Illus. by Bart Harlan. 1 cass. (Running Time: 30 mins.). (Rock 'N Learn Ser.). (J). (gr. 1 up). 1995. pap. bk. 12.99 (978-1-878489-33-3(X), RL933) Rock N Learn.
Original country songs with educational lyrics teach addition & subtraction facts through 18. Includes activity book with reproducible worksheets.

Addition & Subtraction Rap. Created by Rock 'N Learn. (Rock 'n Learn Ser.). (J). 2010. pap. bk. 12.99 (978-1-878489-18-0(6)) Rock N Learn.

Addition & Subtraction Rock. unabr. ed. Brad Caudle & Richard Caudle. Perf. by Brad Caudle et al. 1 cass. (Running Time: 40 mins.). (Rock 'N Learn Ser.). (J). (gr. 1 up). 1993. pap. bk. 12.99 (978-1-878489-06-7(2), RL906) Rock N Learn.
"Top 40" type songs with educational lyrics teach addition & subtraction facts through 18. Includes activity book with reproducible worksheets.

Addition Rap. Brad Caudle. 1 cass. (Running Time: 1 hr.). (J). (gr. 2-10). 2001. pap. bk. 11.95 (RL 910C); pap. bk. 13.95 (RL 909CD) Kimbo Educ.
An absolute "must add" teaching/learning resource for the classroom & home! Facts with sums through 18. Includes activity book.

Addition Rap. unabr. ed. Brad Caudle & Richard Caudle. Perf. by D. J. Doc Roc and the Get Smart Crew Staff. 1 cass. (Running Time: 30 mins.). (Rock 'N Learn Ser.). (J). (gr. 1 up). 1992. bk. 12.99 (978-1-878489-09-8(7), RL909) Rock N Learn.
"Top 40"-type rap songs with educational lyrics teach addition facts through 18. Includes activity book with reproducible worksheets.

Addition Songs. 1 CD. (Running Time: 1 hr.). 2001. pap. bk., tchr. ed., wbk. ed. 12.95 (11CD) Audio Memory.
Begins by counting 1-20, sings facts from 1+1 to 9+9.

Addition Songs. 2004. audio compact disk 12.95 (978-1-883028-15-2(9)) Audio Memory.

Addition Songs. 1 cass. (Running Time: 1 hr.). (YA). (gr. k up). 2001. pap. bk. 10.95 (THR 106C) Kimbo Educ.
Learning to add has never been more fun when it's done with T-Rex & other friends. Catchy songs teach children addition facts through 18. Reproducible activity book included.

Addition Songs. Kidzup Productions Staff. (Learning Beat Ser.). (J). 2003. cass. & audio compact disk 13.99 (978-1-894677-38-7(2)) Pub: Kidzup Prodns. Dist(s): Penton Overseas

Addition Songs, Grades K-2. Kathy Troxel. 1 cass. (Running Time: 1 hr.). (J). 1994. tchr. ed. 9.95 (978-1-883028-02-2(7), 11) Audio Memory.
Counting 1-20, addition facts.

Addition Unplugged. Emad Girgis. Prod. by Sara Jordan. Composed by Sara Jordan. Prod. by Mark Shannon. Composed by Mark Shannon. Illus. by Glen Wyand. 1 cass. (Running Time: 51 min. 34 secs.). (Math Unplugged Ser.). (J). 1997. pap. bk. 14.95 (978-1-895523-53-9(2), JMP112K) Jordan Music.
Nine catchy songs teaching students addition facts with sums up to 18. A complement of self-quizzing tracks allows students to quiz themselves.

Addition Unplugged. abr. ed. Emad Girgis. Prod. by Sara Jordan. Composed by Sara Jordan. 1 CD. (Running Time: 30 min.). (Songs that Teach Math Ser.). (ENG.). (J). (gr. 4-7). 1997. audio compact disk 13.95 (978-1-895523-65-2(6), JMP 112CD) Pub: S Jordan Publ. Dist(s): CrabtreePubCo

Addition Workbook & Music CD. Twin Sisters Productions Staff. 2009. pap. bk. & wbk. ed. 10.99 (978-1-57583-892-2(3)) Twin Sisters.

Addition Wrap-up Rap: Audio CD. Rick Blair. 1 cass. (ENG.). (J). (gr. 1-6). 1985. audio compact disk 9.99 (978-0-943343-21-1(6), LWU201CD) Lrn Wrap-Ups.
Learning aid.

Additional Dialogue: The Letters of Dalton Trumbo. unabr. ed. Christopher Trumbo. Perf. by Jeff Corey et al. 1 cass. (Running Time: 1 hrs. 28 min.). 1998. 19.95 (978-1-58081-117-0(5)) L A Theatre.
In 1947, Dalton Trumbo became one of the blacklisted Hollywood Ten & went to prison for defying the House Committee on Un-American Activities. Explore the inner workings of Hollywood through the witty & passionate correspondence of the Oscar-winning author of "Roman Holiday" & "Spartacus".

Address to Congress after Pearl Harbor. unabr. ed. Read by Winston L. S. Churchill. 1 cass. (Running Time: 36 min.). 12.95 (AF0124) J Norton Pubs.
The British prime minister reviewed the nature of the next few years of war, the U.S. role & the need for unity against the foe.

Address to Congress after Pearl Harbor: Wintson Churchill. (ENG.). 2008. audio compact disk 12.95 (978-1-57970-521-3(9), Audio-For) J Norton Pubs.

Address to the First Montgomery Improvement Association (MIA) Mass Meeting: An Unabridged Selection from A Call to Conscience - the Landmark Speeches of Dr. Martin Luther King, Jr. unabr. ed. Read by Rosa Parks et al. (Running Time: 30 mins.). (ENG.). 2006. 1.98 (978-1-59483-484-4(9)) Pub: Hachet Audio. Dist(s): HachBkGrp

Address to the U. S. Congress, Feb. 19 1943: Madame Chiang Kai-Shek. (ENG.). 2008. audio compact disk 12.95 (978-1-57970-520-6(0), Audio-For) J Norton Pubs.

***Addressing Mental Health Concerns in Primary Care: A Clinician's Toolkit.** Created by American Academy of Pediatrics. (ENG.). 2009. audio compact disk (978-1-58110-348-9(4)) Am Acad Pediat.

Addy: An American Girl. unabr. ed. Connie Rose Porter. Read by Cynthia Adams. 6 cass. (Running Time: 6 hrs.). (J). 2006. 59.75 (978-1-4193-5917-0(7), 98186) Recorded Bks.
Meet Addy Walker, a courageous nine-year-old girl growing up during the Civil War. When her poppa and brother are sold to another plantation, Addy and her mother take the terrible risk of escaping to freedom in the North. To get away safely, they must leave Addy¿s baby sister behind in the slave quarters - her cries could cost them their freedom. As Addy and Momma slowly build a new life in Philadelphia and struggle to bring their family together again, Addy comes to realize a powerful truth - freedom has great costs.

Adelante. 3rd ed. Holt, Rinehart and Winston Staff. 2002. audio compact disk 195.73 (978-0-03-065951-5(5)) Holt McDoug.

Adelante & En Camino: Sampler. Holt, Rinehart and Winston Staff. 1999. 8.20 (978-0-03-054044-8(5)) Holt McDoug.

¡Adelante! Más Práctico (Internacional) CCOE Libro1 1 libro por nivel Prueba de Comprensión Auditiva CD: Curso de comunicaciÓn oral y escrita / spanish language Teaching. (SPA.). 2006. audio compact disk (978-0-7428-1635-0(4)) CCLS Pubg Hse.
!Adelante! Mas PracticoCCOE (Curso de Comunicacion Oral y Escrita) Beginner to high Intermediate?Principiante a Intermedio altoIn this interactive multimedia Spanish course, teenage and adult students experience up-to-date, real-life situations drawn from the cultural diversity and richness of the Spanish-speaking world. The 8-book version is for learners with no significant Romance Language background and the 7-book version is specially geared to the needs of learners with Portuguese or other significant Romance Language backgrounds. The learning process is enriched through:10 lessons per bookAverage of 45 hours of instruction per bookCALL (Computer-Assisted Language Learning) Workbook with CD-ROM for each level, which allows students to do and correct written exercises on the computer and listen to lesson textsTV shows and high-interest, authentic commercialsGenuine selections from Spanish language comic stripsContextualized sound and image on the Interactive Classroom Program presented on a TV from a CD-ROM or DVDContent, characters and situations that reflect the daily lives of Spanish speakers at work, at home, shopping or enjoying their leisure timeObjective, practical and systematic presentation of Spanish grammarContinuous practice of spoken and written Spanish with models from Latin AmericaGradual and progressive development of solid skills in listening, speaking, reading and writingEn este curso interactivo de espa?ol multimedios, los estudiantes adolescentes y adultos se enfrentan a situaciones de la vida real actual, deducidas de la diversidad cultural y riqueza del mundo hispanohablante. La version de 8 libros es para estudiantes sin informacion previa significativa de un idioma romance, y la version de 7 libros se integra especialmente a las necesidades de estudiantes con portugues u otros antecedentes significativos de idioma romance. El proceso de aprendizaje se enriquece a traves de:? 10 lecciones por libro? Un promedio de 45 horas de instruccion por libro? Libro de Ejercicios CALL (Computer-Assisted Language Learning) con CD-ROM para cada nivel, que les permite a los estudiantes hacer y corregir los ejercicios escritos en la computadora y escuchar los textos de las lecciones? Exhibicion de autenticos e interesantes comerciales y shows de TV? Seleccion de tiras comicas autenticos en idioma espa?ol? Sonido e imagen contextualizados del Programa Interactivo de Sala de Clase, presentados en un televisor desde un CD-ROM o DVD? Contenido, personajes y situaciones que reflejan la vida diaria de hablantes de espa?ol en el trabajo, en casa, yendo de compras o disfrutando de su tiempo libre? Presentacion objetiva, practica y sistematica de la gramatica del espa?ol? Practica continua de la expresion oral y escrita del espa?ol, con modelos de Hispanoamerica? Desarrollo gradual y progresivo de solidas destrezas en comprension, habla, lectura y escriturateacher?s resourcesICP ? Interactive Classroom Program with digitalized audio and colorful, contextualized artwork and media materials. The ICP is available on CD-ROM or DVD. The DVD includes all video materials.Videos: TV shows, commercials, clips, etc.Lesson Plan: step-by-step instructions for each lesson. A foolproof resource to eliminate guesswork and reduce time-consuming class planningOral and written exams and correction keysSchedulesrecursos del profesorPISC - Programa Interactivo de Sala de Clase con audio digital y animado, trabajo artistico contextualizado y materiales de medios de comunicacion masiva. El PISC esta disponible en CD-ROM o DVD. El DVD incluye todos los materiales en videoVideos: shows de TV, comerciales, clips, etc.Libro del Profesor: instrucciones paso a paso para cada leccion. Un recurso seguro para eliminar conjeturas y reducir el tiempo usado en la planificacion de la clasePrueba oral y prueba escrita y clave de correccionSugerencia de cronogramastudent?s materialTextbooks 1?8 or 1-2, 2-3, 4?8Listening Comprehension Practice Books 1?8 or 1-2, 2-3, 4?8CALL Workbook with CD-ROM 1?8 or 1-2, 2-3, 4?8Mas !Adelante! Booklet + CD or !Mas! Adelante Booklet + CD-ROM with Listening Comprehension Practice (optional)material del alumnoLibro de Textos 1?8 o 1-2, 2-3, 4?8Libro de Practica de Comprension Auditiva 1?8 o 1-2, 2-3, 4?8Libro de Ejercicios CALL con CD-ROM 1?8 o 1-2, 2-3, 4?8Folleto Mas !Adelante! + CD, o Folleto Mas !Adelante! + CD-ROM con Practica de Comprension Auditiva (opcionales).

¡Adelante! Más Práctico (Internacional) CCOE Libro2 1 libro por nivel Prueba de Comprensión Auditiva CD: Curso de comunicaciÓn oral y escrita / spanish language Teaching. (SPA.). 2006. audio compact disk (978-0-7428-1636-7(2)) CCLS Pubg Hse.

¡Adelante! Más Práctico (Internacional) CCOE Libro3 1 libro por nivel Prueba de Comprensión Auditiva CD: Curso de comunicaciÓn oral y escrita / spanish language Teaching. (SPA.). 2006. audio compact disk (978-0-7428-1637-4(0)) CCLS Pubg Hse.

¡Adelante! Más Práctico (para Hablantes de Portugués) CCOE Libro 1-2 hasta 4 11/2 libro por nivel Prueba de Comprensión Auditiva CD: Curso de comunicaciÓn oral y escrita / spanish language Teaching. (SPA.). 2006. audio compact disk (978-0-7428-1583-4(8)) CCLS Pubg Hse.

Adelante! Más Práctico (para hablantes de Portugués) CCOE Libro 1-2 Prueba de Comprensión Auditiva CD-A: Spanish Language Teaching. (SPA.). 2003. audio compact disk (978-0-7428-0950-5(1)) CCLS Pubg Hse.

Adelante! Más Práctico (para Hablantes de Portugués) CCOE Libro 2-3 Prueba de Comprensión Auditiva CD: Spanish Language Teaching / Curso de Comunicación Oral y Escrita. (SPA.). 1998. audio compact disk (978-0-7428-0951-2(X)) CCLS Pubg Hse.

Adelante! Más Práctico (para Hablantes de Portugués) CCOE Libro 4 Prueba de Comprensión Auditiva CD: Spanish Language Teaching / Curso de Comunicación Oral y Escrita. (SPA.). 2003. audio compact disk (978-0-7428-0952-9(8)) CCLS Pubg Hse.
In this interactive multimedia Spanish course, teenage and adult students experience up-to-date, real-life situations drawn from the cultural diversity and richness of the Spanish-speaking world. The 8-book version is for learners with no significant Romance Language background and the 7-book version is specially geared to the needs of learners with Portuguese or other significant Romance Language backgrounds. The learning process is enriched through:10 lessons per bookAverage of 45 hours of instruction per bookCALL (Computer-Assisted Language Learning) Workbook with CD-ROM for each level, which allows students to do and correct written exercises on the computer and listen to lesson textsTV shows and high-interest, authentic commercialsGenuine selections from Spanish language comic stripsContextualized sound and image on the Interactive Classroom Program presented on a TV from a CD-ROM or DVDContent, characters and situations that reflect the daily lives of Spanish speakers at work, at home, shopping or enjoying their leisure timeObjective, practical and systematic presentation of Spanish grammarContinuous practice of spoken and written Spanish with models from Latin AmericaGradual and progressive development of solid skills in listening, speaking, reading and writing.

Adelante! Más Práctico (para Hablantes de Portugués) CCOE Libro 5 Prueba de Comprensión Auditiva CD: Spanish Language Teaching / Curso de Comunicación Oral y Escrita. (SPA.). 2003. audio compact disk (978-0-7428-0953-6(6)) CCLS Pubg Hse.

¡Adelante! Más Práctico (para Hablantes de Portugués) CCOE Libro 5 y 6 11/2 libro por nivel Prueba de Comprensión Auditiva CD: Curso de comunicaciÓn oral y escrita / spanish language Teaching. (SPA.). 2006. audio compact disk (978-0-7428-1584-1(6)) CCLS Pubg Hse.
!Adelante! Mas PracticoCCOE (Curso de Comunicacion Oral y Escrita) Beginner to high Intermediate?Principiante a Intermedio altoIn this interactive multimedia Spanish course, teenage and adult students experience up-to-date, real-life situations drawn from the cultural diversity and richness of the Spanish-speaking world. The 8-book version is for learners with no significant Romance Language background and the 7-book version is specially geared to the needs of learners with Portuguese or other significant Romance Language backgrounds. The learning process is enriched through:10 lessons per bookAverage of 45 hours of instruction per bookCALL (Computer-Assisted Language Learning) Workbook with CD-ROM for each level, which allows students to do and correct written exercises on the computer and listen to lesson textsTV shows and high-interest, authentic commercialsGenuine selections from Spanish language comic stripsContextualized sound and image on the Interactive Classroom Program presented on a TV from a CD-ROM or DVDContent, characters and situations that reflect the daily lives of Spanish speakers at work, at home, shopping or enjoying their leisure timeObjective, practical and systematic presentation of Spanish grammarContinuous practice of spoken and written Spanish with models from Latin AmericaGradual and progressive development of solid skills in listening, speaking, reading and writingEn este curso interactivo de espa?ol multimedios, los estudiantes adolescentes y adultos se enfrentan a situaciones de la vida real actual, deducidas de la diversidad cultural y riqueza del mundo hispanohablante. La version de 8 libros es para estudiantes sin informacion previa significativa de un idioma romance, y la version de 7 libros se integra especialmente a las necesidades de estudiantes con portugues u otros antecedentes significativos de idioma romance. El proceso de aprendizaje se enriquece a traves de:? 10 lecciones por libro? Un promedio de 45 horas de instruccion por libro? Libro de Ejercicios CALL (Computer-Assisted Language Learning) con CD-ROM para cada nivel, que les permite a los estudiantes hacer y corregir los ejercicios escritos en la computadora y escuchar los textos de las lecciones? Exhibicion de autenticos e interesantes comerciales y shows de TV? Seleccion de tiras comicas autenticos en idioma espa?ol? Sonido e imagen contextualizados del Programa Interactivo de Sala de Clase, presentados en un televisor desde un CD-ROM o DVD? Contenido, personajes y situaciones que reflejan la vida diaria de hablantes de espa?ol en el trabajo, en casa, yendo de compras o disfrutando de su tiempo libre? Presentacion objetiva, practica y sistematica de la gramatica del espa?ol? Practica continua de la expresion oral y escrita del espa?ol, con modelos de Hispanoamerica? Desarrollo gradual y progresivo de solidas destrezas en comprension, habla, lectura y escriturateacher?s resourcesICP ? Interactive Classroom Program with digitalized audio and colorful, contextualized artwork and media materials. The ICP is available on CD-ROM or DVD. The DVD includes all video materials.Videos: TV shows, commercials, clips, etc.Lesson Plan: step-by-step instructions for each lesson. A foolproof resource to eliminate guesswork and reduce time-consuming class planningOral and written exams and correction keysSchedulesrecursos del profesorPISC - Programa Interactivo de Sala de Clase con audio digital y animado, trabajo artistico contextualizado y materiales de medios de comunicacion masiva. El PISC esta disponible en CD-ROM o DVD. El DVD incluye todos los materiales en videoVideos: shows de TV, comerciales, clips, etc.Libro del Profesor: instrucciones paso a paso para cada leccion. Un recurso seguro para eliminar conjeturas y reducir el tiempo usado en la planificacion de la clasePrueba oral y prueba escrita y clave de correccionSugerencia de cronogramastudent?s materialTextbooks 1?8 or 1-2, 2-3, 4?8Listening Comprehension Practice Books 1?8 or 1-2, 2-3, 4?8CALL Workbook with CD-ROM 1?8 or 1-2, 2-3, 4?8Mas !Adelante! Booklet + CD or !Mas! Adelante Booklet + CD-ROM with Listening Comprehension Practice (optional)material del alumnoLibro de Textos 1?8 o 1-2, 2-3, 4?8Libro de Practica de Comprension Auditiva 1?8 o 1-2, 2-3, 4?8Libro de Ejercicios CALL con CD-ROM 1?8 o 1-2, 2-3, 4?8Folleto Mas !Adelante! + CD, o Folleto Mas !Adelante! + CD-ROM con Practica de Comprension Auditiva (opcionales).

Adelante! Más Práctico (para Hablantes de Portugués) CCOE Libro 6 Prueba de Comprensión Auditiva CD: Spanish Language Teaching / Curso de Comunicación Oral y Escrita. (SPA.). 2003. audio compact disk (978-0-7428-0954-3(4)) CCLS Pubg Hse.

¡Adelante! Más Práctico (para Hablantes de Portugués) CCOE Libro 6 y 7 11/2 libro por nivel Prueba de Comprensión Auditiva CD: Curso de comunicaciÓn oral y escrita / spanish language Teaching. (SPA.). 2006. audio compact disk (978-0-7428-1585-8(4)) CCLS Pubg Hse.

Adelante! Más Práctico (para Hablantes de Portugués) CCOE Libro 7 Prueba de Comprensión Auditiva CD: Spanish Language Teaching / Curso de Comunicación Oral y Escrita. (SPA.). 2003. audio compact disk (978-0-7428-0955-0(2)) CCLS Pubg Hse.

Adelante! Más Práctico (para Hablantes de Portugués) CCOE Libro 8 Prueba de Comprensión Auditiva CD: Spanish Language Teaching / Curso de Comunicación Oral y Escrita. (SPA.). 2003. audio compact disk (978-0-7428-0956-7(0)) CCLS Pubg Hse.

Adelgace. Betty L. Randolph. 1 cass. (Health Ser.). (SPA.). 1989. bk. 9.98 (978-1-55909-181-7(9), 20E) Randolph Tapes.
Presents a program in spanish. Features male-female voice tracks with the right-left brain.

Adept Tradition in Modern Living. Instructed by Manly P. Hall. 8.95 (978-0-89314-000-7(7), C820411) Philos Res.

Adequate: 11 Cor. 3:1-6. Ed Young. 1990. 4.95 (978-0-7417-1778-8(6), 778) Win Walk.

Adesso. 2nd ed. Danesi. (C). lab manual ed. 42.95 (978-0-8384-6709-1(1)) Heinle.

Adesso Lab Audio CDs. 3rd ed. DANESI. (C). 2005. audio compact disk 44.95 (978-1-4130-0356-7(7)) Pub: Heinle. Dist(s): CENGAGE Learn

Adesso 3e- Text Aud Cd-Stand. 3rd ed. Marcel Danesi. (ITA & ENG., 2005. audio compact disk (978-1-4130-1408-2(9)) Course Tech.

ADHD: Diagnosis, Causes & Treatment. Contrib. by Michael Levin. 1 cass. (Running Time: 1 hrs. 15 min.). 17.00 (19-002A) J W Wood.
Overview of the child with ADHD. Compares ADHD to bipolar depressive disorders & generalized anxiety disorder, describes the types & core characteristics of ADHD, discusses the function of attention.

ADHD (Attention Deficit Hyperactive Disorder) Eldon Taylor. 1 cass. (Running Time: 62 min.). (Inner Talk Ser.). 16.95 incl. script. (978-1-55978-613-3(2), 53862F) Progress Aware Res.
Soundtrack - Babbling Brook with underlying subliminal affirmations.

Adhesion & Adhesives. Alphonsus V. Pocius & Carl Dahlquist. 8 cass. (Running Time: 7 hrs. 36 min.). 655.00 incl. manual. (978-0-8412-1044-8(6), 86); 50.00 manual. (978-0-8412-1045-5(4)) Am Chemical.
Develop an overall understanding of the fundamentals of surface science, polymer science & mechanics - & the role each plays in the successful design of adhesive bonds.

Adios: The Greatest Hits. Contrib. by Audio Adrenaline & Brad O'Donnell. 2006. audio compact disk 16.99 (978-5-558-33250-6(6)) FF Rcds.

Adios a las Armas. abr. ed. Ernest Hemingway. Read by Hernando Iván Cano. 3 CDs.Tr. of Farewell to Arms. (SPA.). 2003. audio compact disk 17.00 (978-958-43-0201-4(9)) YoYoMusic.

Adios, Mr. Chips. abr. ed. James Hilton. Read by Santiago Munevar. 3 CDs. (SPA.). 2002. audio compact disk 17.00 (978-958-9494-78-3(1)) YoYoMusic.

***Adirondack Murray.** Harry Radford. (Running Time: 54). (ENG.). 2010. audio compact disk 9.95 (978-0-9830742-1-2(6)) AABks.

***Adirondack Stories.** Philander Deming. Read by Randall Young. Prod. by Adirondack Audio Books. (Running Time: 220). (ENG.). 2010. audio compact disk 19.95 (978-0-9830742-0-5(8)) AABks.

Adjunct Staff Program. Don Gum et al. 1986. 10.80 (0708) Assn Prof Chaplains.

Adjunctive Methods for the Treatment of Facial Aging. Moderated by Melvin Spira. 2 cass. (Plastic & Maxillofacial Surgery Ser.: PL-3). 1986. 19.00 (8662) Am Coll Surgeons.

Adjusting the Mind the Victory! Creflo A. Dollar. 3 cass. (Running Time: 4 hrs. 30 mins.). 2000. 15.00 (978-1-931172-82-0(X), 9210, Kidz Faith) Pub: Creflo Dollar. Dist(s): STL Dist NA

Adjusting to a New Baby. Martha B. Beveridge. 1 cass. (Running Time: 60 min.). 1994. 9.95 (978-1-889237-35-0(3)) Options Now.
An experienced panel of parents helps you understand the concerns that arise for parents as they welcome a new baby. You'll be relieved to find you are not alone when you feel overwhelmed, exhausted & neglected as well as joyous, devoted & incredibly blessed.

Adjustment of Nature see Favorite Stories by O. Henry

Adlai Stevenson on Democracy. Read by Adlai Stevenson. 10.00 Esstee Audios.
A talk by a major figure on a much debated concept.

Administering Prophecy. Steve Thompson. 1 cass. (Running Time: 90 mins.). (Prophetic Ministry Ser.: Vol. 4). 2000. 5.00 (ST01-004) Morning NC.
Now updated & expanded, this popular series combines insights from the Scriptures & personal experience to explain how we can more effectively hear from God & minister prophetically.

Administering the Inner Journey of God's Forgiveness, Set. Scripts. George Aschenbrenner. 2 cass. (Running Time: 2 hrs. 22 min.). (Spirituality of Diocesan Priesthood Ser.). 1998. 19.95 (TAH406) Alba Hse Comns.
To be an administrator of forgiveness, the diocesan priest must understand its profoundly transforming nature & the necessary stages & attitudes that lead to full comprehension of this mystery.

Administration of Difficult Estates. 1 cass. 1989. bk. 45.00 (AC-512) PA Bar Inst.

Administration of Estates. 1987. bk. 90.00 cass. only.; 45.00 PA Bar Inst.

Administration of the Small & Medium Size Estate. Read by William E. Miller, Jr. 1 cass. 1990. 20.00 (AL-91) PA Bar Inst.

Administrative Due Process: Walls of Division. 1995. bk. 99.00 (ACS-966) PA Bar Inst.
Agencies with both prosecutorial & adjudicative functions have been reevaluating their procedures since the Supreme Court decision in "Lyness." Many have made dramatic changes.

Administrative Law. Steven Finz. 4 cass. (Running Time: 4 hrs. 30 mins.). (Outstanding Professors Ser.). 1995. 63.00 (978-0-940366-63-3(0), 28387, West Lglwrks) West.
Lecture by a prominent American law school professor.

Administrative Law. Glen H. Reynolds. 3 cass. (Blond's Audio Lectures). 1994. 39.99 (978-0-945819-71-4(4)) Sulzburger & Graham Pub.
Audio lectures summarizing the laws of administrative law for law students.

Administrative Law. 2nd ed. Steven Finz. 1999. Sum & Substance.

Administrative Law. 3rd rev. ed. Patrick J. Borchers. (Law School Legends Audio Ser.). 2008. 52.00 (978-0-314-19880-8(6)) West.

Administrative Law Practice. Contrib. by Mary A. Burgess et al. (Running Time: 4 hrs.). 1984. 70.00 incl. Administrative Law Skills Text. NJ Inst CLE.
Covers the overview of O.A.L., jurisdiction, procedural rules, handling a contested case, N.J. Administrative code & Register provisions, plus more.

Administrative Law, 2005 ed. (Law School Legends Audio Series) 2005th rev. ed. Patrick J. Borchers. 2005. audio compact disk 47.95 (978-0-314-16068-3(X), gilbert) West.

Administrative Law, 2005 ed. (Law School Legends Audio Series) 2005th rev. ed. Patrick J. Borchers & Thomas L. Evans. 2005. 47.95 (978-0-314-16067-6(1), gilbert) West.

Administrative Rule Making. 1 cass. (Running Time: 1 hr.). (Advocacy Before Administrative Agencies Ser.). 1984. 20.00 PA Bar Inst.

Admirable. Danilo Montero. 1 CD. (Running Time: 90 min.). 2003. audio compact disk 14.99 (978-0-8297-4302-9(2)) Zondervan.
Recorded in Toronto, Canada and produce by Juan Salinas. It has songs that reflect a personal and intimate relationship with the Lord.

Admiral Hornblower in the West Indies. unabr. ed. C. S. Forester. Read by Richard Green. 8 cass. (Running Time: 8 hrs.). (Hornblower Ser.: No. 10). (J). 1980. 48.00 (1347-C) Books on Tape.
Napoleon is finally defeated, but far from falling into an easy rhythm of peace, the world seethes. France's empire is ripe for plucking, her citizens for revenge. Out of retirement & into this maelstrom comes Hornblower, assigned military & diplomatic chores for which only he is suited.

Admiral Hornblower in the West Indies. unabr. ed. C. S. Forester. Read by Richard Green. 8 cass. (Running Time: 12 hrs.). (Hornblower Ser.). 2001. 29.95 (978-0-7366-6761-6(X)) Books on Tape.
Napoleon is defeated as Hornblower prowls the waters of the Caribbean.

Admiral Hornblower in the West Indies, Pt. 1. unabr. collector's ed. C. S. Forester. Read by Richard Green. 8 cass. (Running Time: 8 hrs.). (Hornblower Ser.: No. 10). 1980. 56.00 (978-0-7366-0361-4(1)) Books on Tape.
The Commodore sailed to Russian waters with a bid for the Czar's alliance.

Admiral Hornblower in the West Indies, Pt. 2. collector's ed. C. S. Forester. Read by Richard Green. 8 cass. (Running Time: 8 hrs.). 1980. 48.00 (978-0-7366-0363-8(8)) Books on Tape.

Admiral Jerauld Wright: Warrior among Diplomats. unabr. ed. David M. Key, Jr. Narrated by Erik Synnestvedt. (Running Time: 13 hrs. 38 mins.). 44.95 (978-1-55685-747-8(0)) Audio Bk Con.

Admiral Jerauld Wright: Warrior among Diplomats. unabr. ed. David M. Key, Jr. Narrated by Erik Synnestvedt. 10 cass. (Running Time: 14 hrs. 30 mins.). 2003. 71.95 Audio Bk Con.
The biography follows the life and adventures of Admiral Wright from the Naval Academy through World Wars I and II and beyond. The stories and recollections are told in the Admiral's own words and are full of his sharp and observant wit.

Admiral of the Ocean Sea: A Life of Christopher Columbus. unabr. ed. Samuel Eliot Morison. Read by John MacDonald. 16 cass. (Running Time: 24 hr.). Incl. Pt. I. Admiral of the Ocean Sea: A Life of Christopher Columbus. 9 cass. (Running Time: 13 hrs. 30 mins.). Samuel Eliot Morison. Read by John MacDonald. 1985. 72.00 (1954-A); Pt. II. Admiral of the Ocean Sea: A Life of Christopher Columbus. 7 cass. (Running Time: 10 hrs. 30 mins.). Samuel Eliot Morison. Read by John MacDonald. 1985. 56.00 (1954-B); 1985. 128.00 (978-0-7366-1023-0(5), 1954A/B) Books on Tape.
A fascinating story of Columbus' life & struggle. A Pulitzer Prize biography.

Admiral of the Ocean Sea Pt. 1: A Life of Christopher Columbus. unabr. ed. Samuel Eliot Morison. Read by Frederick Davidson. 10 cass. (Running Time: 25 hrs. 30 mins.). 1995. 69.95 (978-0-7861-0723-0(5), 1599A,B) Blckstn Audio.
A classic biography of the greatest sailor of them all, Christopher Columbus. It is written with the insight, energy, & authority that only someone who had himself sailed in Columbus's path to the New World could muster. Morison undertook this expedition in a 147-foot schooner & a 47-foot ketch, the dimensions of these craft roughly matching those of Columbus's "Santa Maria" & "Nina." The result is this vivid & definitive biography, detailing the voyages that, for better or worse, changed the world.

Admiral of the Ocean Sea Pt. 2: A Life of Christopher Columbus. unabr. ed. Samuel Eliot Morison. Read by Frederick Davidson. 8 cass. (Running Time: 25 hrs. 30 mins.). 1995. 56.95 (978-0-7861-0724-7(3), 1599A,B) Blckstn Audio.

Admit to Murder. Margaret Yorke. Read by David Collins. 8 cass. (Running Time: 12 hrs.). 2002. 69.95 (978-0-7540-0702-9(2), CAB 2124) AudioGO.

Adolescent: 11 Sam. 15:1-12; Heb. 5:12-14. Ed Young. 1999. 4.95 (978-0-7417-2214-0(3), 1214) Win Walk.

Adolescent d'Autrefois, Set. Francois Mauriac. Ed. by J.E. Flower. Intro. by J.E. Flower. 4 cass. (Textes Français Classiques et Modernes Ser.). (FRE.). 1991. 34.95 (1366-VSL) Olivia & Hill.
Mauriac's last novel is a nostalgic reminiscence of the past, more or less autobiographical, of a young man growing up in the Bordelais region at the turn of the century.

Adolescent Owner's Manual: A Guide to Parenting Prodigal Teenagers. William H. Glover. 2007. audio compact disk 29.99 (978-1-60247-616-5(0)) Tate Pubng.

Adolescent Rites of Passage: Honoring the Transitions from Child to Adult. William G. DeFoore. (ENG.). 2006. audio compact disk 29.99 (978-0-9785244-6-3(2)) Halcyon Life.

Adolescents & Abuse, Pt. 2. 1990. (D035AB090) Natl Public Radio.

Adolescent's Christmas. Short Stories. Read by Carol Bly. Prod. by Scott Beyers. 1 CD. (Running Time: 67 mins.). 2002. audio compact disk 15.00 (978-0-9665212-8-3(5), 5, EssayAudiocom) EssayAudio.

Adolescents in Adult Bodies. Charles R. Swindoll. 1 cass. 1986. 10.99 (978-2-01-022273-3(3)) Nelson.
Since biblical times, society has been faced with a particular developmental condition that more recently has been labeled the "Peter Pan Syndrome." Swindoll traces this phenomenon from the fall of man in the Garden of Eden to modern congregations & analyzes three biblical characters who deliberately chose to act out attitudes & lifestyles that reflected an unwillingness to grow up.

Adolf Hitler. unabr. ed. John Toland. Read by John MacDonald. 2 pts. on 27 cass. (Running Time: 1 hr. 30 min. per cass.). 1992. 216.00 Set. (2933 A/B) Books on Tape.
WW II, the Holocaust, 50 million deaths, famine & suffering unimaginable...who could have dreamed such a Wagnerian scene in the mid-20th century? Only one man - Adolf Hitler.

Adolf Hitler, Pt. 1. collector's unabr. ed. John Toland. Read by John MacDonald. 12 cass. (Running Time: 18 hrs.). 1992. 96.00 (978-0-7366-2132-8(6), 2933-A) Books on Tape.
He staged the takeover of a great nation, all its resources, largely with the consent & approbation of its people, in their full knowledge of what he stood for & intended to do.

Adolf Hitler, Pt. 2. collector's ed. John Toland. Read by John MacDonald. 15 cass. (Running Time: 22 hrs. 30 min.). 1992. 120.00 (978-0-7366-2133-5(4), 2933-B) Books on Tape.

Adolf Hitler: My Part in His Downfall. unabr. ed. Spike Milligan. Read by Spike Milligan. 3 cass. (Running Time: 4 hrs. 30 min.). 1993. 34.95 (978-1-85089-693-7(3), 88031) Pub: ISIS Audio GBR. Dist(s): Ulverscroft US
Milligan's on the march, blitzing friend & foe alike with his uproarious recollections of army life from enlistment to the landing at Algiers in 1943. This is the first book in a series of autobiographies written by Spike Milligan.

Adolphe. Benjamin Constant. Read by Monique Lebreton-Savigny. 4 cass. (Running Time: 4 hrs.). (FRE.). 1996. pap. bk. 49.50 incl. plastic box & text. (978-1-58085-352-1(8)) Interlingua VA.

Adolphe, Set. Benjamin Constant. Read by Anne Wiazemsky. 2 cass. (FRE.). 1991. 38.95 (1469-EF) Olivia & Hill.
The love & subsequent torment of young Adolphe for Ellenore, an older woman, who leaves her protector & two children to follow him.

Adonai. Perf. by Avalon Staff. 1 cass. 1998. 7.98 HiLo Plus. (978-0-7601-2577-9(5)) Brentwood Music.

Adonai. Perf. by Avalon Staff. 1 CD. 1999. audio compact disk (978-7-5132-6339-9(6), 751-326-3396) Brentwood Music.

Adonai. Composed by Don Koch et al. Contrib. by Bradley Knight & Regi Stone. 2007. audio compact disk 24.98 (978-5-557-49192-1(9), Word Music) Word Enter.

Adonais see Treasury of Percy Bysshe Shelley

Adonais see Poetry of Shelley

Adonde? pap. bk. 18.95 (978-88-536-0951-9(6)) EMC-Paradigm.

Adopted Child's Search for Meaning: A Journey Through Fear to Friendship. Illus. by Angela Brown & Cheryle Timbrook Jennings. Prod. by Les Lingle. 1 cass. (Running Time: 30 mins.). (Words of Wellness - Your Show for Simple Solutions Ser.: Vol. 316). 2000. 12.95 (978-1-930995-08-6(3), LLP316) Life Long Pubg.
Adopted children seek their birthparents in order to find their roots. Their insecurities & fears mirror those in us all.

***Adopted for Life: The Priority of Adoption for Christian Families & Churches.** unabr. ed. Russell Moore. (ENG.). 2010. 14.98 (978-1-59644-852-0(0)) christianaud.

***Adopted for Life: The Priority of Adoption for Christian Families & Churches.** unabr. ed. Russell D. Moore & Russell Moore. (Running Time: 7 hrs. 30 mins. 0 sec.). (ENG.). 2010. audio compact disk 24.98 (978-1-59644-851-3(2)) christianaud.

Adopting Children from the United States: A Basic Guide. Karen Jean Matsko Hood. 2006. 29.95 (978-1-59434-675-0(5)); audio compact disk 24.95 (978-1-59434-676-7(3)) Whsprng Pine.

Adoption: A Basic Guide. 2005. 29.95 (978-1-59808-018-6(0)); audio compact disk 24.95 (978-1-59808-017-9(2)) Whsprng Pine.

Adoption Help for Miltary Families. Hosted by Mardie Caldwell. (ENG.). 2008. audio compact disk 12.95 (978-1-935176-03-9(X)) Pub: Am Carrage Hse Pubng. Dist(s): STL Dist NA

Adoption Practice, Procedure & Pitfalls. 1997. bk. 99.00 (ACS-1274) PA Bar Inst.
If you handle only the occasional adoption & have always considered them to be "simple cases," please pause for a moment. The reality of adoptions today is a multitude of complex legal issues requiring a thorough knowledge of the latest developments & strategies. Attorneys who fail to fully understand their ethical & legal duties are susceptible to liability for wrongful adoption. These & other emerging issues require you to be fully prepared when the next client walks through the door.

Adoración Instrumental. unabr. ed. 2001. audio compact disk 11.99 (978-0-8297-3252-8(7)); audio compact disk 11.99 (978-0-8297-3262-7(4)) Zondervan.

Adoracion Instrumental. unabr. ed. Zondervan Publishing Staff. 1 cass. (Running Time: 30 min.). 2001. 4.99 (978-0-8297-3254-2(3)); 4.99 (978-0-8297-3264-1(0)) Zondervan.

Adoracion Instrumental, No. 1. unabr. ed. Jeff McKenzie. (SPA.). 2000. 4.99 (978-0-8297-2512-4(1)) Pub: Vida Pubs. Dist(s): Zondervan

Adoracion Instrumental, No. 2. unabr. ed. Jeff McKenzie. (SPA.). 2000. 4.99 (978-0-8297-2518-6(0)) Pub: Vida Pubs. Dist(s): Zondervan

Adoracion sin reservas see Extravagant Worship

Adorar: Cantos de Alabanza y Adoracion. Prod. by Phil Sillas. 2005. audio compact disk 13.99 (978-5-558-84564-8(3)) Sprg Hill Music Group.

Adoration. 1 cass. 10.98 (978-1-57908-247-5(5), 1306); audio compact disk 15.98 (978-1-57908-246-8(7)) Platinm Enter.

Adoration. 1 CD. 1999. audio compact disk 16.98 (978-1-57908-501-8(6), 5344) Platinm Enter.

Adoration Eucharistic Hymns. Jerry Barnes. audio compact disk 10.95 (978-0-8198-0773-1(7), 332-009) Pauline Bks.

Adoration Eucharistic Hymns. Jerry Barnes. 2000. audio compact disk 16.95 (978-0-8198-0772-4(9), 332-008) Pauline Bks.

Adoration II. FSP Staff. 2004. audio compact disk 16.95 (978-0-8198-0776-2(1), 332-011) Pauline Bks.

Adoration of Jenna Fox. unabr. ed. Mary E. Pearson. Read by Jenna Lamia. 6 CDs. (Running Time: 7 hrs. 30 mins. 0 sec.). (ENG.). (YA). (gr. 9 up). 2008. audio compact disk 29.95 (978-1-4272-0443-1(8)) Pub: Macmill Audio. Dist(s): Macmillan

Adorations to Divine Mother. Yogi Hari. 1 cass. (Running Time: 45 mins.). (Adoration Ser.). 9.95 (ADM) Nada Prodns.
Bara Sarasvati Sa Ma; Jai Jai Devi; Bhavani Daiyani; Adi Divya Jyoti Maha; Sri Saraswati Namostute; De Maja Divya Mati; Dheeno Dharenee.

Adorations to Krishna. Yogi Hari. 1 cass. (Running Time: 1 hr.). (Adoration Ser.). 9.95 (ADK) Nada Prodns.
Krishna Mantra; Maha Mantra; Govinda Narayana; Sri Krishna Govinda; Govinda Jai Jai; Radhay Shyam; Gopala; Bhajo Radhay Govinda.

Adorations to Rama. Yogi Hari. 1 cass. (Running Time: 45 min.). (Adoration Ser.). 9.95 (ADR) Nada Prodns.
Suddha Brahma Parat Para Ram (Balakanda); Khelati Mama Hridaye; Pibare Rama Rasam; Rama Ratan Dhan Payo; Bhaja Man Rama Charan Sukha Dayi; Aiye Raghu Veera Dheera; Shri Rama Chandra; Tarana & Prema Mudita.

Adorations to Siva. Yogi Hari. 1 cass. (Running Time: 45 mins.). (Adoration Ser.). 9.95 (ADS) Nada Prodns.
Om Namah Sivaya; Brahmamurari Surachita Lingam; He Chandra Mouli; Shankar Maha Deva Deva; Namamisam Isana Nirvanaroopam.

Adorations to Vishnu. Yogi Hari. 1 cass. (Running Time: 45 mins.). (Adoration Ser.). 9.95 (ADV) Nada Prodns.
Om Namo Narayanaya Mantra; Narayana Ka Naam Neerala; Narayana Shri Man Narayana; Rama Krishna Govinda.

Adore Him: A Christmas Worship Experience. Created by Lillenas Publishing Company. 2007. audio compact disk 60.00 (978-5-557-70006-1(4)) Lillenas.

Adored. abr. ed. Tilly Bagshawe. Read by Sonya Walger. (ENG.). 2005. 14.98 (978-1-59483-238-3(2)) Pub: Hachet Audio. Dist(s): HachBkGrp

Adored. abr. ed. Tilly Bagshawe. Read by Sonya Walger. (Running Time: 6 hrs. 30 mins.). (ENG.). 2009. 49.98 (978-1-60788-054-7(7)) Pub: Hachet Audio. Dist(s): HachBkGrp

Adored. unabr. ed. Tilly Bagshawe. Narrated by Barbara Rosenblat. 14 cass. (Running Time: 20 hrs.). 2005. 109.75 (978-1-4193-4472-5(2), 98061) Recorded Bks.
Adored is right at home alongside the best fiction from Danielle Steel and Jackie Collins. Bold and beautiful Siena McMahon wants to be a movie star like her grandfather. But her father, a bigshot producer, wants Siena to be a doctor. So Siena sets out on her own in this epic romance filled with glamourous characters and locales.

Adoremos. Marcos Witt. 1 cass. CanZion.
Teacher on praise & worship.

Adoremos. Marcos Witt. 2 cass. (Running Time: 3 hrs.). (SPA.). 1999. 10.99 (978-0-88113-214-4(4)) Grupo Nelson.

Adoremos. unabr. ed. Marcos Witt. 2003. 9.99 (978-0-8297-4314-2(6)) Pub: Vida Pubs. Dist(s): Zondervan

Adra. unabr. ed. Deanna Durbin. Read by Lynda Evans. 6 cass. (Running Time: 7 hrs. 30 min.). 2001. 39.95 (978-1-55686-743-9(3)) Books in Motion.
Alliance Academy cadet Adra is under suspicion of being a spy for the Alliance's arch-enemy, the Sesans. With her amazing mental powers, Adra sets out to find her past.

Adrenal Exhaustion. Ingrid Naiman. 2 cass. (Running Time: 3 hrs.). 20.00 (978-1-882834-93-8(3)) Seventh Ray.
How to deal with fatigue. The roll of support & relationship to the feminine in maintaining stamina.

Adrenal Thyroid Connection. 2003. audio compact disk 14.95 (978-0-9743448-5-0(0)) NMA Media Pr.

***Adrenaline.** unabr. ed. Jeff Abbott. (Running Time: 11 hrs. 30 mins.). (ENG.). 2011. 26.98 (978-1-60941-371-2(7)) Pub: Hachet Audio. Dist(s): HachBkGrp

Adrenaline to Go! Lets Hurry Up. Brainstore Inc. Staff. 2002. 15.00 (978-1-890460-15-0(X)) Pub: Corwin Pr. Dist(s): SAGE

Adrian Louis. unabr. ed. Ed. by Jim McKinley. Prod. by Rebekah Presson. 1 cass. (Running Time: 29 mins.). (New Letters on the Air Ser.). 1994. 10.00 (040993) New Letters.
Louis is an award-winning poet who has worked as editor of four tribal newspapers. He is enrolled in the Lovelock Pauite Tribe & teaches at the Oglata Lakota College on the Pine Ridge reservation in South Dakota. His poems are tough, funny & biting as he paints portraits of a hard-fought, sometimes hard-drinking life.

Adrian Mole: The Cappuccino Years. unabr. ed. Sue Townsend. Narrated by Paul Daintry. 7 cass. (Running Time: 9 hrs. 15 mins.). 1999. 60.00 (978-0-7887-4054-1(7), 96160E7) Recorded Bks.
It's 1997. Adrian, is a chef at an up-market restaurant, selling down-market food for ridiculous prices. The only person who seems to notice he can't cook is AA Gill. But problems abound when, in a fit of madness, he agrees to become a TV chef on the show "Offally Good".

Adrian Mole: The Cappuccino Years. unabr. ed. Sue Townsend. Narrated by Paul Daintry. 8 CDs. (Running Time: 9 hrs. 15 mins.). 2000. audio compact disk 82.00 (978-1-84197-136-0(7), C1246E7) Recorded Bks.

Adrift. unabr. collector's ed. Steven Callahan. Read by Dick Estell. 6 cass. (Running Time: 9 hrs.). 1987. 48.00 (978-0-7366-1091-9(X), 2015) Books on Tape.
The author's boat sank. He spent 2-1/2 months by himself in a rubber raft alone at sea.

Adrift: 76 Days Lost at Sea. unabr. ed. Steven Callahan. Read by Steven Callahan. (Running Time: 7 hrs.). 2007. 39.25 (978-1-4233-3647-1(X), 9781423336471, BADLE); 24.95 (978-1-4233-3646-4(1), 9781423336464, BAD); audio compact disk 29.95 (978-1-4233-3642-6(9), 9781423336426, Bril Audio CD Unabri); audio compact disk 24.95 (978-1-4233-3644-0(5), 9781423336440, Brilliance MP3); audio compact disk 39.25 (978-1-4233-3645-7(3), 9781423336457, Brinc Audio MP3 Lib); audio compact disk 82.25 (978-1-4233-3643-3(7), 9781423336433, BriAudCD Unabrid) Brilliance Audio.

Adrift on a Raft. E. A. Olsen. Illus. by L. Le Blanc. (Oceanography Ser.). (J). (gr. 3 up). 1970. pap. bk. 10.60 (978-0-87783-176-1(9)) Oddo.

Adrift on an Ice Pan. Wilfred T. Grenfell. Read by Chris Brookes et al. 1 CD. (Running Time: 3720 sec.). 2004. audio compact disk 14.99 (978-0-9734223-4-4(3)) Pub: Rattling Bks CAN. Dist(s): Hse Anansi
How does a man save his own life? In 1908 Dr. Wilfred Grenfell, a medical missionary in northern Newfoundland, was traveling by dog team to treat a patient. In his haste Grenfell took a short cut across the sea ice. A change of wind and ice conditions left the doctor and his dogs stranded on an ice pan, their komatik and provisions lost. Grenfell came close to perishing. This is his account of this near fatal misadventure.

***Adsense Code 2nd Edition: The Definitive Guide to Making Money with Adsense.** unabr. ed. Joel Comm. Read by Sean Pratt. (Running Time: 7 hrs.). (ENG.). 2010. 27.98 (978-1-59659-576-7(0), GildAudio) Pub: Gildan Media. Dist(s): HachBkGrp

Adult ADD: Program from the Award Winning Public Radio Series. Hosted by Fred Goodwin. Comment by John Hockenberry. Contrib. by Edward M. Hallowell et al. 1 cass. (Running Time: 1 hr.). (Infinite Mind Ser.). 1998. audio compact disk 21.95 (978-1-888064-51-3(X), LCM 4) Lichtenstein Creat.
Common signs of ADD in adults sound like the normal side effects of life in the 90s: difficulty getting organized, chronic procrastination, handling too many projects at once, impatience, restlessness and worry. You might ask yourself: Who hasn't experienced this? That's part of the problem. ADD is not obvious and it is often over-looked. But it can have profound influence, both good and bad, on those it affects. Guests include ADD expert Dr. Edward Hallowell, Dr. Marc Grossman, a developmental behavioral optometrist, and performance artist, Reno, who has ADD herself and puts it into her act. We are also joined by Mike Faenza, campaigner for mentally ill young people behind bars.

***Adult Bible Studies CD Winter 2009-10.** 2009. 12.00 (978-0-687-65965-4(5), Cokebury) Abingdon.

Adult Children from Alcoholic Homes. Heather Lawn. 1 cass. 8.95 (208) Am Fed Astrologers.
Unlearn patterns of dysfunction.

Adult Children of ... Parents. Judith Black. (YA). 13.00 (978-0-9701073-3-6(1)) J Black Storyteller.

Adult Children of Alcoholics. Hunt. 1 cass. (Running Time: 1 hr.). 1990. 9.00 (OC98) Sound Horizons AV.

Adult Children of Alcoholics & Struggle for Intimacy. unabr. collector's ed. Janet Geringer Woititz. Read by Ruth Stokesberry. 8 cass. (Running Time: 8 hrs.). 1988. 48.00 (978-0-7366-1325-5(0), 2229) Books on Tape.
Alcoholics wreck their own lives & the lives of those around them. These books helps heal problems in the family.

Adult Children of Dysfunctional Families. 6 cass. (Family & Friends Discussion Tape Ser.). 44.95 (8150) Hazelden.

Adult Children of Dysfunctional Families. John E. Bradshaw. (Running Time: 7200 sec.). 2008. audio compact disk 70.00 (978-1-57388-082-4(5)) J B Media.

Adult Greatest Hits, No. 2. Ed. by E. L. Lancaster & Morton Manus. (Alfred's Basic Adult Piano Course Ser.). (ENG.). 2001. audio compact disk 10.95 (978-0-7390-1663-3(6), 19666) Alfred Pub.

***Adult Piano Adventures All-in-One Lesson Book 2.** Composed by Nancy Faber & Randall Faber. (ENG.). 2004. pap. bk. 26.95 (978-1-61677-332-8(4), 1616773324) Pub: Faber. Dist(s): H Leonard

Adult Relationships & Stages of Growth. 1 cass. (Hazelden Guidebooks Ser.). 8.95 (5627G) Hazelden.

Adult Resources Quarterly. Created by Standard Publishing. (Standard Lesson Quarterly KJV Ser.). 2006. audio compact disk 13.99 (978-0-7847-5865-6(4)) Standard Pub.

Adulterous Woman. abr. ed. Reinhard Bonnke. (Running Time: Approx: 1 hr.). 2001. audio compact disk 7.00 (978-1-933106-06-9(9)) E-R-Productions.

Adultery & Other Choices. unabr. collector's ed. Andre Dubus. Read by Dan Lazar. 7 cass. (Running Time: 7 hrs.). 1981. 42.00 (978-0-7366-0464-2(2), 1436) Books on Tape.
Lonesome boy reaches manhood via USMC.

Adultry: Exodus 20:15. Ed Young. 1985. 4.95 (978-0-7417-1434-3(5), 434) Win Walk.

Adultry Defined: Exodus 20:14. Ed Young. 1999. 4.95 (978-0-7417-2224-9(0), 1224) Win Walk.

***Adults.** Alison Espach. 2011. audio compact disk 39.99 (978-1-61120-013-3(X)) Dreamscap OH.

Adults Only. unabr. ed. Morris Gleitzman. 2 cass. (Running Time: 3 hrs. 11 mins.). (YA). 2002. 24.00 (978-1-74030-734-5(8)) Pub: Bolinda Pubng AUS. Dist(s): Bolinda Pub Inc

Adults Only. unabr. ed. Morris Gleitzman. Read by Morris Gleitzman. 3 CDs. (Running Time: 3 hrs. 11 mins.). (YA). 2003. audio compact disk 54.95 (978-1-74093-116-8(5)) Pub: Bolinda Pubng AUS. Dist(s): Bolinda Pub Inc

Adv of Philip Marlowe, Vol. 2. Radio Spirits Staff. Read by Gerald Mohr. 2005. audio compact disk 39.98 (978-1-57019-602-7(8)) Radio Spirits.

Adv of Sam Spade Detective, Vol. 2. Contrib. by Radio Spirits Publishing Staff. 2007. audio compact disk 17.98 (978-1-57019-838-0(1)) Radio Spirits.

Advance Directives: Legal, Pastoral, & Clinical Dimensions. 1 cass. (Care Cassettes Ser.: Vol. 18, No. 3). 1993. 10.80 Assn Prof Chaplains.

Advance Memory Research Module 1. 4 cass. (Running Time: 60 mins. per cass.). bk. Oasis Audio.
Contains short dialogues centered around travel situations.

Advance Your English: A Short Course for Advanced Learners. Annie Broadhead. (Running Time: hrs. mins.). (ENG.). 2000. wbk. ed. 24.99 (978-0-521-59775-3(7)); 26.24 (978-0-521-59777-7(3)) Cambridge U Pr.

***Advance Your English Class Audio CD: A Short Course for Advanced Learners.** Annie Broadhead. (Running Time: 1 hr. 7 mins.). (ENG.). 2009. audio compact disk 23.00 (978-0-521-16890-8(2)) Cambridge U Pr.

***Advance Your English Workbook Audio CD: A Short Course for Advanced Learners.** Annie Broadhead. (Running Time: 47 mins.). (ENG.). 2010. audio compact disk 24.00 (978-0-521-14770-5(0)) Cambridge U Pr.

Advanced Accounting: Syllabus. W. R. Singleton & E. R. Johansson. (J). 1977. bk. 250.85 (978-0-89420-124-0(7)) Natl Book.

Advanced Alto Sax Solos - Vol. 1. Created by Hal Leonard Corporation Staff. Paul Brodie. 2008. pap. bk. 24.98 (978-1-4234-5938-5(5), 1423459385) Pub: Music Minus. Dist(s): H Leonard

Advanced Alto Sax Solos - Volume 2. Created by Hal Leonard Corporation Staff. 2008. pap. bk. 24.98 (978-1-4234-5939-2(3), 1423459393) Pub: Music Minus. Dist(s): H Leonard

Advanced Anecdotes in American English. Leslie A. Hill. (Anecdotes in American English Ser.). 1981. bk. 17.50 (978-0-19-502830-0(9)) OUP.

Advanced Arabic Composition. 2 cass. 34.07 Set. U MI Lang Res.
Readings of articles.

Advanced Astrodynes. Lee V. Johnson. 1 cass. 8.95 (179) Am Fed Astrologers.
Calculation of major progressed astrodynes.

Advanced Bird Language: Reading the Concentric Rigs of Nature. unabr. ed. Jon Young. 6 cass. (Running Time: 9 hrs.). (YA). (gr. 9 up). 1999. 49.95 (978-1-57994-007-2(2), A1202) Owlink.
Through exciting stories & examples this explains the hidden worlds of nature that await discovery & unlocks the secrets to learning the language of the forest. Learn to interpret the voices of birds & more!.

Advanced Bird Language: Reading the Concentric Rings of Nature. Jon Young. 1999. audio compact disk 74.95 (978-1-57994-018-8(8)) Owlink.

Advanced Bulgarian I. Charles E. Gribble & Lyubomira P. Gribble. 1 cass. 1987. 5.00 (978-0-87415-113-8(9), 47B) Foreign Lang.

Advanced Bulgarian 2. Lyubomira P. Gribble & Charles Gribble. 1 cass. 1987. 5.00 (978-0-87415-116-9(3), 48B) Foreign Lang.

Advanced Chakra Wisdom: Insights & Practices for Transforming Your Life. abr. ed. Cyndi Dale. (Running Time: 25200 sec.). 2008. audio compact disk 69.95 (978-1-59179-896-5(5)) Sounds True.

Advanced Chinese Newspaper Readings. 2 cass. 1985. 8.95 ea. incl. suppl. materials. (978-0-88710-128-1(3)) Yale Far Eastern Pubns.

Advanced Clarinet Solos - Volume I. Stanley Drucker. 2008. pap. bk. 24.98 (978-1-4234-6150-0(9), 1423461509) Pub: Music Minus. Dist(s): H Leonard

Advanced Computer Applications: An Information Technology Approach; Instructor Resources; Instructor Resources CD. Daphne Press. 2005. audio compact disk 69.00 (978-0-7638-2163-0(2)) EMC-Paradigm.

Advanced Consultant Selling. Charles D. Brennan, Jr. 6 cass. 1996. wbk. ed. 99.00 (978-1-928821-01-4(4), 330) Brennan Sales Inst.
Presents advanced selling & communication skills to develop stronger relationships with perspective & existing customers.

Advanced Cross-Examination Techniques DVD 2E. Larry S. Pozner & Roger J. Dodd. 1905. audio compact disk 359.00 (978-1-4224-4674-4(3)) Pub: LexisNexis Matthew Bender. Dist(s): LEXIS Pub

Advanced Custody Issues. 1997. bk. 99.00 (ACS-1242) PA Bar Inst.
Under what circumstances should you seek to transfer a custody case? How should a transfer be timed? When does a non-parent have standing to seek primary custody? Does Gancas v. Schultz change the criteria for relocation? A team of experienced family lawyers join together in this advanced-level book with hypothetical problems to illustrate these & other issues related to jurisdiction, standing, & relocation. You may also receive the latest information on legislation & recent cases from family law judges.

Advanced Czech 1. Charles E. Townsend & Tanya McAuley. 4 cass. 1986. 20.00 (978-0-87415-119-0(8), 49B) Foreign Lang.

Advanced Czech 2. Charles E. Townsend & Tanya McAuley. 3 cass. 1986. 15.00 (978-0-87415-122-0(8), 50B) Foreign Lang.

Advanced Employment Law & Litigation. 11 cass. (Running Time: 16 hrs. 30 min.). 1998. 395.00 Set; incl. study guide 1241p. (MD34) Am Law Inst.
Advanced course discusses the latest developments, including the four recent U.S. Supreme Court sexual harassment cases; the first two U.S. Supreme Court disabilities cases under the Americans with Disabilities Act (ADA); EEOC policy guidance on mental disabilities, releases under the Older Workers Benefit Protection Act, & alternative dispute resolution, which may or may notbe adopted by the courts.

Advanced Energy Anatomy. unabr. ed. Caroline Myss. Read by Caroline Myss. 9 CDs. (Running Time: 9 hrs. 30 min.). 2001. audio compact disk 69.95 (978-1-56455-917-3(3), AW00581D) Sounds True.
The energy of creation is real. According to Dr. Caroline Myss, this unlimited power source is available to you right now - if you know the science of how to access it. Now, for the first time, the author and medical intuitive reveals a bold, all-new program for excavating the deep unconscious forces that block the flow of energy through your life - with Advanced Energy Anatomy.

Advanced English for Spanish Speakers. unabr. ed. Conversa-Phone Institute Staff. 3 cass. (Running Time: 2 hrs. 30 mins.). (Modern Method Language Ser.). 23.95 (978-1-56752-079-8(0)) Conversa-phone.
English conversation for Spanish speakers that have a basic knowledge of English. Includes 96 page instruction manual.

Advanced English Language. Ilona Davydova. 12 cass. 1990. 179.00 (978-0-9675296-2-2(X)) Express Method.

Advanced Estate Planning: Recent Trends & Techniques. Georgetown University Law Center Staff & NAEPC Staff. 6 cass. 159.00 set, incl. textbk. & quizzer. (CPE2430) Bisk Educ.

Advanced Estate Planning Techniques. 11 cass. (Running Time: 15 hrs. 30 mins.). 1999. 395.00 Set; incl. study guide 974p. (MD51) Am Law Inst.
Examines some of the most important issues with emphasis on the practical "how to do it" aspects.

***Advanced Excel Tips for the Power User.** PUEI. 2009. audio compact disk 199.00 (978-1-935041-73-3(8), CareerTrack) P Univ E Inc.

Advanced Feng Shui of the LAND. 6 CD's. 2004. audio compact disk (978-1-932616-12-5(8)) Feng Shui Para.
Capitalize on the Power & Energy of the land.Learn how Architects, Builders and Realtors? are outsmarting and outselling their competition, while creating safe and healthy environments for people.This Series includes the following 5 TeleSeminars:CAPITALIZE on Feng Shui in 2004 and Beyond!LIKE GRAVITY... You Don't Have to Believe in Feng Shui for it to Work! READY or NOT, LET'S FENG SHUI!!!! CHI WIZ.... Feng Shui and the LAND THE LAND... GUA BY GUA!!!.

Advanced Flute Solos, Vol. 1. Murray Panitz. 2007. pap. bk. 24.98 (978-1-59615-301-1(6), 1596153016) Pub: Music Minus. Dist(s): H Leonard

Advanced Flute Solos - Volume 4: Julius Baker. Julius Baker. 2009. pap. bk. 24.98 (978-1-4234-7392-3(2), 1423473922) Pub: Music Minus. Dist(s): H Leonard

Advanced Focus Ten. unabr. ed. Robert A. Monroe. Read by Robert A. Monroe. (Running Time: 45 mins.). (Gateway Experience - Discovery Ser.). 1981. 14.95 (978-1-56113-252-2(7)) Monroe Institute.
Expand the perception & gain better control.

Advanced French, Module 3. AMR Staff. 4 cass. (Running Time: 4 hrs.). (AMR Language Ser.). bk. 46.95 (978-1-55536-287-4(7)) Oasis Audio.
The equivalent of four years college conversational language instruction. Subject material business related, poltics, family relations, health care, schooling, traffic accident & more. A concentration on grammar instruction.

Advanced French - Module Four. AMR Staff. 4 cass. (Running Time: 4 hrs.). (AMR Language Ser.). bk. 46.95 (978-1-55536-288-1(5)) Oasis Audio.

Advanced German. Ed. by Berlitz Publishing Staff. 3 CDs. (ADVANCED Ser.). 2009. audio compact disk 34.95 (978-981-268-431-8(X)) Pub: Berlitz Pubng. Dist(s): Langenscheidt

Advanced German, Set. AMR Staff. 4 cass. (Running Time: 4 hrs.). (AMR Language Ser.: Vol. 3). bk. 46.95 (978-1-55536-314-7(8)) Oasis Audio.
The equivalent of four years of college conversational language instruction. Subject material business related, politics, family relations, health care, schooling, traffic accidents & more. A concentration on grammar instruction.

Advanced Grammar & Writing. Susan Kesner Bland. (Grammar Sense Ser.). 2007. audio compact disk 39.95 (978-0-19-449024-5(6)) OUP.

Advanced Graph Analysis, Vol. 1. Sanford G. Kulkin. 8 cass. (Running Time: 12 hrs.). 1992. ring bd. & wbk. ed. 195.00 (978-1-58034-009-0(1)) IML Pubns.
An in-depth course of study of the DISC graphs & how to apply them in pastoral & counseling situations.

Advanced Graph Analysis Vol. 2: Making High Touch... High Tech. Sanford G. Kulkin. 8 cass. (Running Time: 12 hrs.). 1994. ring bd. 445.00 Set. (978-1-58034-003-8(2)) IML Pubns.
How to apply the DISC Personality System in business to resolve tough behavioral management issues. How to use twenty different computer reports.

Advanced Guide to Bankruptcy. Nathan Bisk & Richard M. Feldheim. 3 cass. bk. 159.00 (CPE4380) Bisk Educ.
This comprehensive program explains the IRS collection system, the bankruptcy process & how to work effectively within both.

Advanced Guide to Real Estate Investing: How to Identify the Hottest Markets & Secure the Best Deals. abr. ed. Ken McElroy. Read by Dave Mallow. (Running Time: 3 hrs. 30 mins.). (ENG.). 2008. 16.98 (978-1-60024-286-1(3)) Pub: Hachet Audio. Dist(s): HachBkGrp

Advanced Guide to Real Estate Investing: How to Identify the Hottest Markets & Secure the Best Deals. abr. ed. Ken McElroy. Read by Dave Mallow. Frwd. by Robert T. Kiyosaki. 3 CDs. (Running Time: 3 hrs. 30 mins.). (ENG.). 2008. audio compact disk 24.98 (978-1-60024-285-4(5)) Pub: Hachet Audio. Dist(s): HachBkGrp

Advanced Guided Reading Strategies: New Practical Ideas to Maximize the Effectiveness of Your Guided Reading Instruction. Hosted by Pamela Haack. 4 CDs. (Running Time: 4 hrs 10 mins). (J). (gr. 3-6). 2008. audio compact disk 95.00 (978-1-886397-88-0(0)) Bureau of Educ.

Advanced Home Schooling Workshop. unabr. ed. Gregg Harris. 8 cass. 1992. 39.95 Set. (978-0-923463-80-9(1)) Noble Pub Assocs.
The next step in home schooling answers; for the home schooling household that needs to progress to the next level of encouragement.

Advanced Hypnotherapy Course. 1995. (978-1-932163-28-5(X)) Infinity Inst.

Advanced Hypnotherapy Course. 10 CDs. 2003. audio compact disk (978-1-932163-42-1(5)) Infinity Inst.

Advanced Improvising. Duane Shinn. 19.95 ea. Jazz. (WC-2) Duane Shinn.
Discusses advance improvising - make up music as one goes along.

Advanced Inorganic Fibrous Composites V. Ed. by P. Vincenzini & M. Singh. (Advances in Science & Technology Ser.: Vol. 50). audio compact disk 113.00 (978-3-908158-06-6(0)) Trans T Pub CHE.

Advanced Intuition Training. unabr. ed. Helen Palmer. 2 cass. (Running Time: 2 hrs. 52 mins.). 1991. 18.00 (08604) Big Sur Tapes.
Presents her perspective on the training for the development of intuition & then teaches the practices that support that frame of mind. She describes intuition as when you perceive information that is beyond the boundaries of personal thoughts & emotions, beyond the thinking/feeling life.

Advanced Issues in Estate Administration. 1998. bk. 99.00 (ACS-2033) PA Bar Inst.
Designed for more seasoned practitioners, this concentrates on complex estate administration issues. The experienced authors use a hypothetical case study to show how to deal with difficult questions.

Advanced Issues in Estate Administration. 1991. 65.00 (AC-649) PA Bar Inst.

Advanced Issues in Land Use Practice. 1 cass. 1990. 75.00 (AC-569) PA Bar Inst.

Advanced Issues in Medical Malpractice. 1990. 145.00 (AC-563) PA Bar Inst.

Advanced Jazz Conception for Saxophone, Vol. 4. Composed by Lennie Niehaus. 1964. audio compact disk 19.95 (978-1-934638-03-3(X), try1004) Try Publg Co.

Advanced Lessons: Volume 22, Vol. 22. Speeches. Bhagat Singh Thind. (Running Time: 60 mins.). (ENG., 2003. audio compact disk 12.00 (978-1-932630-23-7(6)) Pub: Dr Bhagat Sin. Dist(s): Baker Taylor

Advanced Lessons: Volume 22, Vol. 22. Speeches. As told by Bhagat Singh Thind. (Running Time: 60 mins.). (ENG., 2003. 6.50 (978-1-932630-46-6(5)) Pub: Dr Bhagat Sin. Dist(s): Baker Taylor

Advanced Listening Comprehension. 2nd ed. Patricia A. Dunkel & Frank Pialorsi. 5 cass. 54.00 (978-0-8384-4843-4(7), 6321269, Newbury) Heinle.
Designed to develop student confidence & skills for listening to & taking notes from extended spoken discourse at the advanced listening level.

***Advanced Listening Comprehension.** 3rd ed. LIM & DUNKEL. (ENG.). (C). 2004. 168.95 (978-1-4130-0602-5(7)) Pub: Heinle. Dist(s): CENGAGE Learn

Advanced Manifestation Program: Shaping Your Reality with the Power of Your Desire. Rick Jarow. 6 CDs. (Running Time: 7 hrs 30 mins). 2006. audio compact disk & audio compact disk 69.95 (978-1-59179-349-6(1), F950D) Sounds True.

Advanced Meditation. Pat Carroll. Read by Pat Carroll. Ed. by Tony Carroll. 1 cass. (Running Time: 30 mins.). 10.00 Inner-Mind Concepts.
Explains how to communicate with teachers & guides through the subconcious mind & visualization techniques.

Advanced Meditation. Steven S. Sadleir. 3. (Running Time: 3 hrs.). 2005. 15.00 (978-1-883544-11-9(4)) Self Awareness.
For the more advanced students of yoga and meditation. It includes: Thuriyateeth Meditation, Sahaj Meditation, Kriya Meditation, Crown Chakra Meditation, Aura Expansion Meditation, and Jhana or Non-duality Meditation.

Advanced Meditation Exercises: Exercises & Guided Meditations for the High Intermediate to Expert Meditator. Robert Morgen. 1 CD. (Running Time: 74:40). 2006. audio compact disk 49.95 (978-0-9773801-9-0(X)) MysticWolf.

Advanced Mega Memory. Kevin Trudeau. 6 cass. (Running Time: 6 hrs.). 79.95 (2060AVX) Nightingale-Conant.
In this exciting program for enthusiastic learners, Kevin Trudeau builds on the foundation laid in Mega Memory to provide you what is truly a "graduate-level" course in mind & memory power. Kevin offers listeners a greatly expanded, all-new presentation of memory applications. Advanced Mega Memory further explores the revolutionary techniques & skill-building exercises that made Mega Memory the most utilized self-improvement series of all time. Includes 54-minute bonus videocassette, interactive workbook plus pocket guide.

Advanced Mega Memory. Kevin Trudeau. 6 cass. (Running Time: 6 hrs.). 1992. wbk. ed. 79.95 (978-1-55525-030-0(0), 2060AV) Nightingale-Conant.
You've surprised your friends... amazed your colleagues impressed the important people who can boost your career.

Advanced Memory Skills: Babbling Brook. Eldon Taylor. 1 cass. 16.95 (978-1-55978-461-0(X), 5312F) Progress Aware Res.

Advanced Memory Skills: Classic. Eldon Taylor. Read by Eldon Taylor. Ed. by Leslie Brice. 1 cass. (Running Time: 1 hr.). 1992. 16.95 (978-1-56705-078-3(6)) Gateways Inst.
Self improvement.

Advanced Memory Skills: Easy. Eldon Taylor. Read by Eldon Taylor. Ed. by Leslie Brice. 1 cass. (Running Time: 1 hr.). 1992. 16.95 (978-1-56705-079-0(4)) Gateways Inst.

Advanced Memory Skills: Ocean. Eldon Taylor. Read by Eldon Taylor. Ed. by Leslie Brice. 1 cass. (Running Time: 1 hr.). 1992. 16.95 (978-1-56705-080-6(8)) Gateways Inst.

Advanced Memory Skills: Soundtrack: Leisure Listening. Eldon Taylor. 1 cass. (Running Time: 62 mins.). 16.95 (978-0-940699-20-5(6), 5312B) Progress Aware Res.
Musical soundtrack with underlying subliminal affirmations.

Advanced Memory Skills: Soundtrack: Musical Themes. Eldon Taylor. 1 cass. (Running Time: 62 mins.). 16.95 incl. script. (978-0-940699-21-2(4), 5312C) Progress Aware Res.

Advanced Memory Skills: Soundtrack: Synthesized Moments. Eldon Taylor. 1 cass. (Running Time: 62 mins.). 16.95 (978-0-940699-84-7(2), 5312D) Progress Aware Res.

Advanced Memory Skills: Soundtrack: Tropical Lagoon. Eldon Taylor. 1 cass. (Running Time: 62 mins.). 16.95 (978-0-940699-85-4(0), 5312A) Progress Aware Res.
Ocean soundtract with underlying subliminal affirmations.

Advanced Memory Skills: Stream. Eldon Taylor. Read by Eldon Taylor. Ed. by Leslie Brice. 1 cass. (Running Time: 1 hr.). 1992. 15.95 (978-1-56705-081-3(6)) Gateways Inst.
Self improvement.

Advanced Metaphor Demonstrations: Enchantment & Intervention. Stephen R. Lankton & Carol H. Lankton. 1 cass. (Running Time: 90 mins.). 1987. 22.50 (978-0-87630-467-9(6)) Pub: Brunner-Routledge. Dist(s): Taylor and Fran
Presents examples of advanced metaphor protocols & group hypnotic induction taught & demonstrated in the authors' book. "Enchantment & Intervention in Family Therapy".

Advanced Microsoft Word 2000: Desktop Publishing; Instructor Resources; Test Generator CD. Joanne Arford et al. (Signature Ser.). audio compact disk 78.95 (978-0-7638-0290-5(5)) EMC-Paradigm.

Advanced Modeling. John Grinder. Read by John Grinder. Read by Viola Legere. 14 cass. (Running Time: 21 hrs.). 1988. 150.00 Metamorphous Pr.
Created on the occasion of John Grinder's modeling of the highly acclaimed French Canadian actress, Viola Legere, this set of tapes is rich with material, both metaphoric & literal, focusing on the core organizing definition of NLP, modeling.

Advanced Modern Rock Guitar Improvisation. (ENG.). 2004. pap. bk. 29.95 (978-0-7866-6866-3(0), 98053SET) Mel Bay.

Advanced of Tom Sawyer. unabr. ed. Mark Twain. 2002. audio compact disk 29.95 (978-0-7607-3518-3(2)) Barnes & Noble Inc.

Advanced Online Research Skills Series: Course 1: What to Do Before You Start Your Research. Peggy Garvin. Prod. by TheCapitol.Net. (ENG.). 2008. 47.00 (978-1-58733-113-8(6)) TheCapitol.

Advanced Online Research Skills Series: Course 2: Online Search Techniques: Faster Searching, Better Results. Peggy Garvin. Prod. by TheCapitol.Net. (ENG.). 2008. 47.00 (978-1-58733-112-1(8)) TheCapitol.

Advanced Online Research Skills Series: Course 3: U. S. Legislative Branch Research. Peggy Garvin. Prod. by TheCapitol.Net. (ENG.). 2008. 47.00 (978-1-58733-111-4(X)) TheCapitol.

Advanced Online Research Skills Series: Course 4: U. S. Judicial Branch Research. Peggy Garvin. Prod. by TheCapitol.Net. (ENG.). 2008. 47.00 (978-1-58733-110-7(1)) TheCapitol.

Advanced Online Research Skills Series: Course 5: U. S. Executive Branch Research. Peggy Garvin. Prod. by TheCapitol.Net. (ENG.). 2008. 47.00 (978-1-58733-109-1(8)) TheCapitol.

Advanced Online Research Skills Series: Course 6: State-Level & International Research. Peggy Garvin. Prologue by TheCapitol.Net. (ENG.). 2008. 47.00 (978-1-58733-108-4(X)) TheCapitol.

Advanced Online Research Skills Series: Course 7: Offline: People Resources. Peggy Garvin. Prod. by TheCapitol.Net. (ENG.). 2008. 47.00 (978-1-58733-107-7(1)) TheCapitol.

Advanced Out-of-Body Experiences. Bruce Goldberg. (ENG.). 2005. audio compact disk 17.00 (978-1-57968-061-9(5)) Pub: B Goldberg. Dist(s): Baker Taylor

Advanced Out-of-Body Experiences. Bruce Goldberg. Read by Bruce Goldberg. 1 cass. (Running Time: 25 mins.). (ENG.). 2006. 13.00 (978-1-885577-75-7(3)) Pub: B Goldberg. Dist(s): Baker Taylor
Be prepared for the ultimate journey to other dimensions beyond the physical plane in a safe, yet fascinating self-hypnosis trip.

Advanced Phonics. Kim Mitzo Thompson & Karen Mitzo Hilderbrand. Arranged by Hal Wright. (J). 1995. pap. bk. 13.99 (978-1-57583-330-9(1), Twin 419CD); audio compact disk 12.99 (978-1-57583-308-8(5), Twin 119CD) Twin Sisters.

Advanced Phonics. Kim Mitzo Thompson et al. Illus. by Mark Paskiet. 1 cass. (Running Time: 30 min.). (Early Childhood Ser.). (J). (gr. k-3). 1995. pap. bk. 9.98 (978-1-882331-87-1(7), TWIN 419) Twin Sisters.

Advanced Phonics Two. 1 cass. (Learn to Read Ser.: No. 2). (J). bk. Incl. 24p. bk. (TWIN 419) NewSound.
Teach initial consonant sounds, the hard & soft sound of "c" & "g", & short & long vowel sounds - including "y" as a vowel, with animated characters, rhyming lyrics & rhythmic sounds.

Advanced Placement* French: Preparing for the Language Examination. 2nd ed. Ladd & Girard. audio compact disk 49.97 (978-0-13-165907-0(3)) PH School.

Advanced Placement Spanish: Preparing for the Language Examination. 2nd ed. José M. Díaz et al. (SPA.). (J). 1996. 46.97 (978-0-8013-1533-6(6), LM5336) Longman.

Advanced Placement* Spanish, Preparing for the Language Examination: Audio Program on CDs. 2nd ed. Diaz et al. audio compact disk 46.97 (978-0-13-165906-3(5)) PH School.

Advanced Polish 1. Jerzy R. Krzyzanowski. 6 cass. (Running Time: 9 hrs.). 1984. 30.00 (978-0-87415-006-3(X), 9B) Foreign Lang.

Advanced Polish 2. Jerzy R. Krzyzanowski. 5 cass. 1984. 25.00 (978-0-87415-009-4(4), 10B) Foreign Lang.

Advanced Psychology of the East. unabr. ed. Idries Shah. Read by Idries Shah. Read by London College of Storytellers Staff. 2 vols. (Running Time: 3 hrs.). (Idries Shah Live on Tape Ser.). 1996. bk. 17.00 (978-1-883536-02-2(2), ADPE1, Hoopoe Books) ISHK.
A lecture delivered before a live audience, plus teaching stories & narratives selected from two of Shah's works: "The Way of the Sufi" & "The Magic Monastery".

Advanced Relationship Selling. Rick Crandall. 1 CD, 1 Cass. 2000. audio compact disk 69.95 Personal Quest.
This tape doesn't contain a discussion of closing or overcoming objections, instead it covers the relationship building, needs analysis methods used by the top 20 percent of all sales professionals. Whether you're a sales professional, or someone who needs to sell but doesn't want to use hard-sell tactics, here are proven, but little used ways to improve your customer relationships & sales success.

Advanced Reproductive Technologies in Bulgaria: A Strategic Reference 2007. Compiled by Icon Group International, Inc. Staff. 2007. ring bd. 195.00 (978-0-497-35846-4(8)) Icon Grp.

Advanced Rock Guitar Technique. Steve Griffin & Neil Griffin. 1982. spiral bd. 18.95 (978-0-7866-0931-4(1), 93764P); 9.98 (978-1-56222-599-5(5), 93764C) Mel Bay.

Advanced Russian 1. Anelya Rugaleva. 1 cass. 1980. 5.00 (978-0-87415-075-9(2), 37B) Foreign Lang.

Advanced S Corporation Taxation. Robert H. Ginsburgh. 6 cass. 199.00 set, incl. textbk. & quizzer. (CPE2360) Bisk Educ.
Tax planning for S Corporations.

Advanced S Corporations. William J. Lindquist & William H. Olson. 1 cass. pap. bk. & wbk. ed. 119.00 (752302KQ) Am Inst CPA.
This course explores in-depth the tax planning opportunities that exist for small businesses that elect, maintain or terminate S corporation status. It takes off where the related AICPA course, S Corporations ends. In addition, the course provides helpful insights into estate tax planning opportunities.

Advanced Sales Skills Certificate Program: Sales Skills Development in a Series of 8 Useful & Humorous Courses, Including Sales Body Language, Sales Humor Delivery & Writing Skills, the Laugh & Learn Series on Sales Letters, Sales Time Management, Sales Territory Management, Internet Searches to Help in Sales, & Writing Clearly, for Introductory to Advanced Levels. Daniel Farb & Bruce Gordon. 2004. audio compact disk 299.95 (978-0-9743674-3-9(5)) Pub: UnivofHealth. Dist(s): AtlasBooks

Advanced Sales Survival Training. Tom Hopkins. Read by Tom Hopkins. 4 cass. (Running Time: 4 hrs.). 1992. 49.95 (978-0-938636-23-6(5), 1325) T Hopkins Intl.
How to handle stresses common to the selling profession.

Advanced Secretarial Seminar. unabr. ed. 6 cass. (Running Time: 6 hrs.). (Seminars on Tape Ser.). 1980. pap. bk. 49.95 Prof Train TX.
Discusses how to organize one's manager, handling crisis & conflicts, arranging travel & meetings, learning to delegate, updates on issues affecting the secretarial profession, diversifying communication skills, dealing with difficult people, planning the future.

Advanced Selling Strategies: The Proven System Practiced by Top Salespeople. Brian Tracy. 2004. 11.95 (978-0-7435-3916-6(8)) Pub: S&S Audio. Dist(s): S and S Inc

Advanced Selling Strategies: The Proven System Practiced by Top Salespeople. abr. ed. Brian Tracy. Read by Brian Tracy. 2 CDs. (Running Time: 13 hrs. 0 mins. 0 sec.). (ENG.). 2004. audio compact disk 20.00 (978-0-7435-3727-8(0), Sound Ideas) Pub: S&S Audio. Dist(s): S and S Inc
GAIN THE EDGE YOU NEED! Strategy, tactics, and mental preparedness separate superior salespeople from the average - and with technological advances leveling the competition, the selling edge is more important than ever. Drawing on his own successful sales career, and on his extensive experience as a sales consultant and seminar leader, Brian Tracy has developed the most comprehensive and effective approach to selling ever created. Advanced Selling Strategies provides you with the techniques and tools used by top sales people in every industry - methods that net immediate and spectacular results. This audiobook explains how to: • Develop the self-image to give you the edge in every sales situation • Concentrate on the customer's emotional factors to ensure better sales results • Identify your customer's most pressing concerns and position your product or service to fill those needs.

Advanced Selling Techniques. Brian S. Tracy. 6 cass. (Running Time: 6 hrs.). 1994. wbk. ed. (978-1-55525-031-7(9), 10660A); wbk. ed. (978-1-55525-032-4(7), 10660cd) Nightingale-Conant.
Shatter sales records with Brian Tracy's revolutionary selling tactics.

Advanced Seminar for Supervisors. unabr. ed. Read by George Varchola. 6 cass. (Running Time: 6 hrs.). (Seminars on Tape Ser.). 1981. pap. bk. 49.95 Prof Train TX.
Explains how to change people's work habits, get employees to want to do better, unlock people's potential & deepen their sense of commitment.

Advanced Serbo-Croatian 1. Biljana Sljivic-Simsic & Robert Price. 2 cass. 1987. 10.00 (978-0-87415-131-2(7), 53B) Foreign Lang.

Advanced Serbo-Croatian 2. Biljana Sljivic-Simsic & Robert Price. 3 cass. 1987. 15.00 (978-0-87415-134-3(1), 54B) Dragonhawk Pub.

Advanced Social Security Disability Practice. 1996. bk. 99.00 (ACS-1108) PA Bar Inst.
Experienced Social Security disability practitioners are finding claims frequently involve many related areas including Veterans Administration benefits, long term disability insurance, the use of trusts to preserve eligibility for SSI & Medicaid & any number of elder law issues.

Advanced Spanish, Module 3 2nd ed. AMR Staff. 4 cass. (Running Time: 5 hrs.). (Instant Language Courses Ser.). (SPA.). 1999. pap. bk. 46.99 (978-1-886463-58-5(1)) Oasis Audio.

Advanced Spanish - Module Four, Set. AMR Staff. 4 cass. (Running Time: 4 cass.). (AMR Language Ser.). bk. 46.95 (978-1-55536-261-4(3)) Oasis Audio.
The equivalent of four year college conversational language instruction. Subject material business related, politics, family relation, health care, schooling, traffic accidents & more. A concentration on grammar instruction.

Advanced Spanish - Module Three, Set. 4 cass. (Running Time: 4 hrs.). (Instant Language Courses Ser.). 1998. bk. 46.95 (978-1-55536-260-7(5)) Oasis Audio.

Advanced Steps. David Yount & Paul DeKock. (YA). (gr. 7-10). 2001. wbk. ed. 5.00 (978-1-57336-304-4(9), 7123) Interactn Pubs.

Advanced Strategies for Option Trading Success. Instructed by James Bittman. (Trade Secrets Audio Ser.). 2002. 19.95 (978-1-931611-57-2(2)) Marketplace Bks.

Advanced Strategies for Recruiters. Bill Radin. 2 audio CDs. (Running Time: 105 minutes). 2003. audio compact disk 79.95 (978-1-929836-10-9(4)) Innovative Consulting.
Sales, marketing and technical information for executive recruiters and search consultants.

Advanced Surgery for Prolapse & Incontinence. Contrib. by John O. DeLancey et al. 1 cass. (American College of Obstetrics & Gynecologists UPDATE: Vol. 21, No. 1). 1998. 20.00 Am Coll Obstetric.

Advanced Swaps & Derivative Financial Products. 4 cass. (Running Time: 5 hrs.). 1991. 125.00 Set. (T7-9339) PLI.
Intended for the sophisticated practitioner, this June 1991 program examines: documentation of advanced swaps including swap options, caps, floors & regulatory options state law regulatory issues CFTC & other commodity regulatory issues the status of rate swap agreements tax & accounting issues.

Advanced Tenor Solos. George Shirley. 2008. pap. bk. 24.98 (978-1-4234-5929-3(6), 1423459296) Pub: Music Minus. Dist(s): H Leonard

***Advanced Tips & Techniques for Microsoft Word Users.** PUEI. 2009. audio compact disk 199.00 (978-1-935041-83-2(5), CareerTrack) P Univ E Inc.

Advanced Tonal Dictation. Thomas L. Durham. (C). 2004. pap. bk. 26.95 (978-1-57766-355-3(1)) Waveland Pr.

Advanced Training. Swami Amar Jyoti. 1 cass. 1976. 9.95 (E-6) Truth Consciousness.
Discipleship as a 24-hour job. Master gives when disciple is ready. Coming in tune at deeper levels.

Advanced Training for Microsoft Excel 7 for Windows 95. unabr. ed. B. Alan August. Read by Lee McFadden. Contrib. by Natalie B. Young. 4 cass. (Running Time: 5 hrs. 20 mins.). 1996. pap. bk. 225.00 set. (978-1-56562-073-5(9), 294) OneOnOne Comp Trng.

Advanced Training for Word for Windows 95. unabr. ed. Linda K. Schwartz. Read by Lee McFadden. Ed. by Deborah Paulsen & Paulsen and Associates Staff. 4 cass. (Running Time: 5 hrs. 15 min.). 1996. pap. bk. 225.00 set. (978-1-56562-072-8(0), 476) OneOnOne Comp Trng.

Advanced Training for WordPerfect for Windows: Modular. unabr. ed. Sally Hargrave. Read by Lee McFadden. Ed. by Christine Reid. 4 cass. 1992. 225.00 (978-1-56562-079-7(8), 466) OneOnOne Comp Trng.

Advanced Trial Techniques in Medical Malpractice Cases. 60.00 (T7-9138) PLI.

***Advanced Trombone Solos, Volume 1: For Trombone.** Keith Brown. 2009. pap. bk. 24.98 (978-1-59615-473-5(X), 159615473X) Pub: Music Minus. Dist(s): H Leonard

***Advanced Trumpet Solos, Volume II: For Trumpet.** Robert Nagel. 2009. pap. bk. 24.98 (978-1-59615-433-9(0), 1596154330) Pub: Music Minus. Dist(s): H Leonard

Advanced Ukranian 1. Assya Humesky & Kateryna Dowbenko. 2 cass. 1987. (978-0-87415-137-4(6), 55B) Foreign Lang.

Advanced Ukranian 2. Assya Humesky & Kateryna Dowbenko. 2 cass. 1987. 10.00 (978-0-87415-140-4(6), 56B) Foreign Lang.

Advanced Yoga Relaxations. Rolf Sovik. audio compact disk 18.95 (978-0-89389-249-4(1), CD270MO) Himalayan Inst.

Advancement of Learning. unabr. ed. Fr[illegible] Bacon. Read by Robert L. Halvorson. 2 cass. (Running Time: 18[illegible]). 14.95 (4) Halvorson Assocs.

Advancement of Learning. unabr. ed. Reginald Hill. Read by Brian Glover. 8 cass. (Running Time: 12 hrs.). (Dalziel & Pascoe Ser.). 2000. 59.95

(978-0-7451-6688-9(1), CAB 1304) Pub: Chivers Audio Bks GBR. Dist(s): AudioGO
Superintendent Dalziel was very cynical about college administrations. But when he and Sergeant Pascoe are sent to investigate a disinterred corpse at Holm Coultram College, he didn't count on a rash of killings. While Pascoe rekindled an old flame on the staff, protesting students identified Dalziel as a fascist pig! Dalziel smiled with satisfaction, if that's how they wanted to play it.

Advances in Agricultural Economic History, Vol. 2. Ed. by Kyle Dean Kauffman. (Advances in Agricultural Economic History Ser.). 2003. 120.95 (978-0-7623-1001-2(4)) Pub: E G Pubng GBR. Dist(s): TurpinDistUSA

Advances in Ophthalmology, Vol. 2. Garg. 2005. bk. 100.00 (978-81-8061-390-6(9)) Jaypee Brothers IND.

Advances in the Management of Cancer Pain. Moderated by David L. Kasdon. 2 cass. (Neurological Surgery Ser.: NS-2). 1986. 19.00 (8648) Am Coll Surgeons.

Advancing Beyond the Confinements of Your Mindset see Avanzando Mas Alla del Confinamento de la Mente

Advancing Jazz-Rock-Pop Guitarist. Don Coffman et al. 2 cass. (Complete Guide for the Guitar Ser.: Vol. 1). 1995. 35.95 (978-1-879542-43-3(9)) Ellis Family Mus.
Primarily for the guitar classroom, can be used by schools. Includes all the exercises to practice with split mix for deleting lead or rhythm. Participants include all professional name musicians.

Advancing Your Spirit: Finding Meaning in Your Life's Journey. unabr. ed. Wayne W. Dyer & Marianne Williamson. 4 CDs. 2008. audio compact disk 23.95 (978-1-4019-2176-7(0)) Hay House.

Advantages of Poverty. Andrew Carnegie. Read by Charlie Tremendous Jones. (Life-Changing Classics Ser.). (ENG.). 2007. audio compact disk 19.95 (978-1-933715-36-0(7)) Executive Bks.

Advent. Perf. by Monte Mason. Gregorian Singers. 1. 2000. audio compact disk 18.00 (978-0-89869-433-8(7)) Church Pub Inc.

Advent, Christmas & New Year. Read by Mother Basilea Schlink. 1 cass. (Running Time: 30 mins.). 1985. (0206) Evang Sisterhood Mary.
Topics are: When He Appears; The Most Important Thing in the Old & New Year; A Christmas Like Never Before.

***Advent Conspiracy: Can Christmas Still Change the World?** unabr. ed. Rick McKinley et al. (Running Time: 1 hr. 53 mins. 0 sec.). (ENG.). 2009. 12.99 (978-0-310-40052-3(X)) Zondervan.

Advent of Our God. James Hansen. Read by James Hansen. 1 cass. 1990. 14.95 DIR EDITION. (9217); 10.95 (9218); audio compact disk 15.95 (10903) OR Catholic.
A service for the Advent season containing easy SAB arrangements of traditional Advent carols and psalm settings along with readings.

Adventues in Japanese: Set of 6 Audio CD's. Hiromi Peterson & Naomi Omizo. 2007. stu. ed. 56.95 (978-0-88727-445-9(5)) Cheng Tsui.

Adventure According to Humphrey. unabr. ed. Betty G. Birney. (Running Time: 4 hrs.). (ENG.). (J). 2010. audio compact disk 24.95 (978-0-14-314557-8(6), PengAudBks) Penguin Grp USA.

Adventure Album. unabr. ed. Robert A. Monroe. Read by Robert A. Monroe. 6 cass. (Running Time: 45 mins.). (Gateway Experience - Adventure Ser.). 1983. 72.00 (978-1-56113-283-6(7)) Monroe Institute.
Album for Adventure Series.

Adventure Begins: The Early Classics. AIO Team Staff. Created by Focus on the Family Staff. 4 CDs. (Running Time: 6 hrs.). (Adventures in Odyssey Ser.: Vol. 1). (ENG.). (J). 2005. audio compact disk 24.99 (978-1-58997-070-0(5)) Pub: Focus Family. Dist(s): Tyndale Hse

Adventure Capitalist: The Ultimate Investor's Road Trip. unabr. ed. Jim Rogers. 11 CDs. (Running Time: 13 hrs.). 2003. audio compact disk 74.80 (978-0-7366-9333-2(5)) Pub: Books on Tape. Dist(s): NetLibrary CO

Adventure-Cise with Suzy Prudden. unabr. ed. Suzy Prudden & Joan Meier-Hirschland. 1 cass. (Running Time: 51 mins.). (J). 1987. 9.95 (978-0-89845-659-2(2), CPN 1801) HarperCollins Pubs.
Teaches a child to exercise the body & imagination at the same time.

Adventure Collection 1-3. unabr. ed. (J). 2006. 39.99 (978-1-59895-625-2(6)) Find a World.

Adventure Collection 3-5. unabr. ed. (J). 2006. 39.99 (978-1-59895-722-8(8)) Find a World.

Adventure in Space: The Flight to Fix the Hubble. unabr. ed. Elaine Scott. Narrated by Nelson Runger. 1 cass. (Running Time: 1 hr. 15 min.). (J). 2003. 10.00 Recorded Bks.
The exciting story of the Endeavour's bold mission, and the five historic space walks it took to repair the Hubble Telescope.

Adventure in the Bitter Lost, Vol. 1. unabr. ed. Chief Little Summer. Interview with Warm Night Rain. 2 CDs. (J). (gr. 6-12). 1999. audio compact disk 14.95 CD Set. (978-1-880440-14-8(8)) Piqua Pr.
Humorous, educational Indian philosophy concerning children's adventure & fun during the great depression.

Adventure of Becoming an Airline Pilot: My Story as a High School Dropout & Succeeding in Doing What I Dreamed. George Flavell. Narrated by Eric Kramer. (ENG.). 2008. audio compact disk 24.95 (978-1-60031-029-4(X)) Spoken Books.

Adventure of Black Peter see Return of Sherlock Holmes

Adventure of Black Peter. unabr. ed. Arthur Conan Doyle. Read by Walter Covell. 1 cass. (Running Time: 48 mins.). Dramatization. 1989. 7.95 (S-34) Jimcin Record.
Sherlock Holmes tracks down a sinister villain.

Adventure of Charles Augustus Milverton see Return of Sherlock Holmes

Adventure of Charles Augustus Milverton. Arthur Conan Doyle. 1 cass. 1989. 7.95 (S-35) Jimcin Record.

Adventure of Charles Augustus Milverton. unabr. ed. Arthur Conan Doyle. Read by Walter Covell. 1 cass. (Running Time: 50 mins.). Dramatization. 1981. 7.95 (S-35) Jimcin Record.
A blackmailed woman seeks Sherlock Holmes' help.

Adventure of Six Napoleons. Arthur Conan Doyle. Narrated by Edward Raleigh. (Running Time: 2 hrs. 30 mins.). 2006. 14.95 (978-1-60083-001-3(3)) Iofy Corp.

Adventure of the Beryl Coronet. unabr. ed. Arthur Conan Doyle. Read by Walter Covell. 1 cass. (Running Time: 52 mins.). Dramatization. 1981. 7.95 (N-71) Jimcin Record.
Sherlock Holmes defends a man caught with stolen jewels.

Adventure of the Blue Carbuncle see Adventures of Sherlock Holmes

Adventure of the Blue Carbuncle see Selections from the Adventures of Sherlock Holmes

Adventure of the Blue Carbuncle. Arthur Conan Doyle. 1 cass. (Running Time: 48 mins.). 1999. (978-0-7588-0003-9(7), Acme Record); audio compact disk (978-0-7588-0004-6(5), Acme Record) Goss Commns.

Adventure of the Blue Carbuncle. unabr. ed. Arthur Conan Doyle. Read by Walter Covell. 1 cass. (Running Time: 47 mins.). Dramatization. 7.95 (N-70) Jimcin Record.
Sherlock Holmes discovers a mysterious hiding place - a goose's gullet!.

Adventure of the Cardboard Box. unabr. ed. Arthur Conan Doyle. Read by Walter Covell. 1 cass. (Running Time: 46 min.). Dramatization. 1989. 7.95 (S-41) Jimcin Record.
This story was considered so shocking at the time of its first publication that it was left out of the original collection of Sherlock Holmes stories.

***Adventure of the Christmas Pudding.** Agatha Christie. Narrated by Full Cast Production Staff. (Running Time: 1 hr. 0 mins. 0 sec.). (ENG., 2011. audio compact disk 24.95 (978-0-563-51051-2(X)) Pub: AudioGO. Dist(s): Perseus Dist

Adventure of the Christmas Pudding & The Mystery of the Spanish Chest. unabr. ed. Agatha Christie. Read by Hugh Fraser. 2 cass. (Running Time: 3 hrs.). 2001. 18.95 (978-1-57270-230-1(3), N61236U) Pub: Audio Partners. Dist(s): PerseuPGW
These two stories showcase Hercule Poirot at the top of his form. One story is set in a 14th-century English manor house, the other involves beautiful women & jealous husbands.

Adventure of the Clapham Cook see Aventure de la Cuisiniere

Adventure of the Copper Beeches. unabr. ed. Arthur Conan Doyle. Read by Walter Covell. 1 cass. (Running Time: 48 min.). Dramatization. 1989. 7.95 (S-30) Jimcin Record.
A governess hired under mysterious circumstances goes to Sherlock Holmes for help.

Adventure of the Crooked Man see Memoirs of Sherlock Holmes

Adventure of the Dancing Men. Arthur Conan Doyle. 1 cass. 1989. 7.95 (S-33) Jimcin Record.

Adventure of the Dancing Men. unabr. ed. Arthur Conan Doyle. Read by Walter Covell. 1 cass. (Running Time: 50 min.). Dramatization. 1981. 7.95 (S-33) Jimcin Record.
Sherlock Holmes faces one of his greatest challenges in trying to unscramble the mysterious messages of the dancing men in time to prevent a murder.

Adventure of the Empty House see Classic Detective Stories, Vol. I, A Collection

Adventure of the Empty House. unabr. ed. Arthur Conan Doyle. Read by Walter Covell. 1 cass. (Running Time: 48 min.). Dramatization. 1981. 7.95 (N-17) Jimcin Record.
Sherlock Holmes returns from the dead.

Adventure of the Engineer's Thumb. unabr. ed. Arthur Conan Doyle. Read by Walter Covell. 1 cass. (Running Time: 52 min.). Dramatization. 1989. 7.95 (S-38) Jimcin Record.
A man who has lost a thumb comes to Sherlock Holmes with a grisley tale - & a plea for help.

Adventure of the German Student see Tales of Terror & the Supernatural: A Collection

Adventure of the Gloria Scott see Memoirs of Sherlock Holmes

Adventure of the Golden Lenses - Adventures of Sherlock Holmes see Aventura de los Lentes de Oro - Aventuras de Sherlock Holmes

Adventure of the Golden Lenses - Adventures of Sherlock Holmes. Arthur Conan Doyle. Read by Hernando Iván Cano. (Running Time: 1 hr.). 2002. 14.95 (978-1-60083-145-4(1), Audiofy Corp) Iofy Corp.

Adventure of the Golden Pince-Nez. unabr. ed. Arthur Conan Doyle. Read by Walter Covell. 1 cass. (Running Time: 46 min.). Dramatization. 1989. 7.95 (S-31) Jimcin Record.
Sherlock Holmes tracks down a missing person.

Adventure of the Greek Interpreter see Memoirs of Sherlock Holmes

Adventure of the Greek Philosopher see Selected Cases of Sherlock Holmes

Adventure of the Mason. (J). 1977. (N-16) Jimcin Record.

Adventure of the Musgrave Ritual see Memoirs of Sherlock Holmes

Adventure of the Musgrave Ritual. unabr. ed. Arthur Conan Doyle. Read by Walter Zimmerman & Jack Benson. 1 cass. (Running Time: 48 min.). Dramatization. 1979. 7.95 (N-26) Jimcin Record.
Sherlock Holmes solves a puzzles that leads to an ancient treasure.

Adventure of the Naval Treaty see Memoirs of Sherlock Holmes

Adventure of the Naval Treaty see Classic Detective Stories, Vol. III, A Collection

Adventure of the Noble Bachelor see Classic Detective Stories, Vol. II, A Collection

Adventure of the Noble Bachelor. unabr. ed. Arthur Conan Doyle. 1 cass. (Running Time: 48 min.). Dramatization. 1978. 7.95 (D-13); 9.95 incl. follow along script. Jimcin Record.
Sherlock Holmes solves the case of the disappearing bride.

Adventure of the Norwood Builder. unabr. ed. Arthur Conan Doyle. Read by Walter Covell. 1 cass. (Running Time: 51 min.). Dramatization. 1989. 7.95 (S-28) Jimcin Record.
Sherlock Holmes foils the plot of a man bent on revenge.

Adventure of the Priory School. unabr. ed. Arthur Conan Doyle. Read by Walter Covell. (Running Time: 48 min.). Dramatization. 1989. 7.95 (S-29) Jimcin Record.
Very strange goings on in a very proper school. Only Sherlock Holmes can provide an explanation.

Adventure of the Red-Headed League. unabr. ed. Arthur Conan Doyle. 1 cass. (Running Time: 48 min.). Dramatization. 1978. 7.95 (D-14); 9.95 incl. follow along script. Jimcin Record.
Sherlock Holmes' most famous case.

Adventure of the Reigate Squire see Memoirs of Sherlock Holmes

Adventure of the Reigate Squire. unabr. ed. Arthur Conan Doyle. Read by Walter Covell. 1 cass. (Running Time: 87 min.). Dramatization. 1981. 7.95 (S-40) Jimcin Record.
Sherlock Holmes' brother, Mycroft, makes a rare appearance.

Adventure of the Resident Patient see Memoirs of Sherlock Holmes

Adventure of the Second Stain. unabr. ed. Arthur Conan Doyle. Read by Walter Covell. 1 cass. (Running Time: 48 min.). Dramatization. 1989. 7.95 (S-32) Jimcin Record.
Another classic Sherlock Holmes adventure.

Adventure of the Silver Blaze. unabr. ed. Arthur Conan Doyle. Read by Walter Zimmerman & Jack Benson. 1 cass. (Running Time: 48 min.). Dramatization. 1979. 7.95 (N-25) Jimcin Record.
Sherlock Holmes solves the mystery of a stolen thoroughbred.

Adventure of the Six Napoleons see Classic Detective Stories, Vol. I, A Collection

Adventure of the Six Napoleons see Return of Sherlock Holmes

Adventure of the Six Napoleons see Selected Cases of Sherlock Holmes

Adventure of the Six Napoleons. unabr. ed. Arthur Conan Doyle. Read by Walter Covell. 1 cass. (Running Time: 49 min.). Dramatization. 1979. 7.95 (N-18) Jimcin Record.
Holmes solves the mystery of the broken statues.

Adventure of the Speckled Band see Selected Cases of Sherlock Holmes

Adventure of the Speckled Band see Sherlock Holmes No. 2

Adventure of the Speckled Band. Arthur Conan Doyle. Retold by John Bergez. (Sherlock Holmes Mysteries Ser.). 2000. audio compact disk 18.95 (978-1-4105-0155-4(8)) D Johnston Inc.

Adventure of the Speckled Band. Arthur Conan Doyle. Ed. by Jerry Stemach. Retold by John Bergez. Narrated by Nick Sandys. 2000. audio compact disk 200.00 (978-1-58702-494-8(2)) D Johnston Inc.

Adventure of the Speckled Band. Arthur Conan Doyle. Ed. by Jerry Stemach et al. Retold by John Bergez. Illus. by Michael Letwenko & Edward Letwenko. Narrated by Nick Sandys. Contrib. by Ted S. Hasselbring. (Start-to-Finish Books). 2000. 35.00 (978-1-58702-495-5(0)) D Johnston Inc.

Adventure of the Speckled Band. unabr. ed. Arthur Conan Doyle. 1 cass. (Running Time: 48 min.). Dramatization. 1977. 7.95 (D-12); 9.95 incl. follow along script. Jimcin Record.
Sherlock Holmes faces a sinister plot & a deadly snake!.

Adventure of the Speckled Band, Vol. 2. abr. ed. Arthur Conan Doyle. Ed. by Nick Sandys et al. Retold by John Bergez. Illus. by Michael Letwenko & Edward Letwenko. Contrib. by Ted S. Hasselbring. 1 cass. (Running Time: 1 hr.). (Start-to-Finish Books). (J). (gr. 2-3). 2000. (978-1-58702-326-2(1), F28) D Johnston Inc.
The night Julia Stoner died, Miss Helen Stoner heard a scream and rushed to her twin sister's bedroom. The door flew open and Julia Stoner was standing in the doorway, swaying back and forth. She screamed, "it was the band! The speckled band!" Then she fell over and died. Julia Stoner died just after becoming engaged to be married. After the marriage, she was to receive a large inheritance. Now, her sister is next in line.

Adventure of the Stockbroker's Clerk see Memoirs of Sherlock Holmes

Adventure of the Yellow Face see Memoirs of Sherlock Holmes

Adventure of the Yellow Face. unabr. ed. Arthur Conan Doyle. Read by Walter Covell. 1 cass. (Running Time: 82 min.). Dramatization. 1981. 7.95 (S-39) Jimcin Record.
Two classic Sherlock Holmes mysteries.

Adventure Radio: Grade 1-6. (Stereo Boom Box Ser.: Vol. 3). 1998. tchr. ed. & ring bd. 164.99 (978-1-57405-050-9(8)) CharismaLife Pub.

Adventure Travel Northwest Mini-trips for Families with Children. Karen Jean Matsko Hood. (J). 2003. 24.95 (978-1-59210-044-6(9)) Whsprng Pine.

Adventure Travel Northwest Mini-trips for Families with Children, Vol. 1. Karen Jean Matsko Hood. 2003. audio compact disk 29.95 (978-1-59210-173-3(9)) Whsprng Pine.

Adventurers Wanted Bk. 1: Slathbog's Gold. M. L. Forman. 2009. audio compact disk 39.95 (978-1-60641-059-2(8), Shadow Mount) Deseret Bk.

Adventures. (Dovetales Ser.: Tape 8). pap. bk. 6.95 (978-0-944391-43-3(5)); 4.95 (978-0-944391-23-5(0)) DonWise Prodns.

Adventures: Breathtaking Stories from Nature's Extremes. unabr. ed. Narrated by Jon Hamilton. 1 CD. (Running Time: 1 hr.). (ENG.). 2010. audio compact disk 14.95 (978-1-61573-064-3(8), 1615730648) Pub: HighBridge. Dist(s): Workman Pub

Adventures: In Search Of. Barry Layton & Diane Layton. 1 cass. 10.00 (978-1-56043-881-6(9)) Destiny Image Pubs.

Adventures: Seeker. Barry Layton & Diane Layton. 1 cass. 10.00 (978-1-56043-880-9(0)) Destiny Image Pubs.

Adventures: Tower. Barry Layton & Diane Layton. 1 cass. 10.00 (978-1-56043-882-3(7)) Destiny Image Pubs.

Adventures at Catfish Pond. (Running Time: 40 mins.). 9.98; audio compact disk 15.98 MFLP CA.
Catfish Hodge's rolicking collection of dynamic songs.

Adventures Beyond the Solar System: Planetron & Me. (J). 2005. cass. & cd-rom 24.95 (978-0-9771381-5-9(1)) Geoffrey Williams.

***Adventures by Morse, Volume 1.** RadioArchives.com. (Running Time: 600). (ENG.). 2006. audio compact disk 29.98 (978-1-61081-051-7(1)) Radio Arch.

***Adventures by Morse, Volume 2.** RadioArchives.com. (Running Time: 600). (ENG.). 2007. audio compact disk 29.98 (978-1-61081-056-2(2)) Radio Arch.

***Adventures by Morse, Volume 3.** RadioArchives.com. (Running Time: 360). (ENG.). 2007. audio compact disk 17.98 (978-1-61081-063-0(5)) Radio Arch.

Adventures in Accelerated Learning. Patrick K. Porter. 2 cass. Set. (978-1-887630-05-4(8)) Renaissnce Pub.
Psychology self-help.

Adventures in Acts: CD Set. Jeff Cavins. 2006. audio compact disk 139.99 (978-1-932927-73-3(5)) Ascensn Pr.

Adventures in Christian Parenting! Christian Fatherhood. 2002. 29.95 (978-0-9701911-3-7(8)) Safe At Home.

Adventures in Christian Parenting! Christian Motherhood. 2002. 29.95 (978-0-9701911-2-0(X)) Safe At Home.

Adventures in Christian Parenting: Foundation Stones for Thriving Families. Hosted by Rick Arndt & Cathy Arndt. Photos by Mark Arndt. 6 cassettes. (Running Time: 6 hours total). 2002. 29.95 (978-0-9701911-1-3(1)) Safe At Home.

Adventures in Darkness: Memoirs of an Eleven-Year-Old Blind Boy. abr. ed. Tom Sullivan. (Running Time: 3 hrs. 30 mins.). 2007. audio compact disk 24.99 (978-0-7852-2395-5(9)) Nelson.

Adventures in Exodus CD Set: Called to Freedom. Timothy Gray. 2007. audio compact disk 39.95 (978-1-934217-20-7(4)) Ascensn Pr.

Adventures in Food & Nutrition! Carol Byrd-Bredbenner. (gr. 6-9). 2003. tchr. ed. 62.00 (978-1-56637-837-6(0)) Goodheart.

Adventures in Japanese. 4 CDs. 2004. audio compact disk 108.00 (978-0-88727-558-6(3)); audio compact disk 100.00 (978-0-88727-556-2(7)); audio compact disk 162.00 (978-0-88727-559-3(1)) Cheng Tsui.

Adventures in Japanese, Level 1. Hiromi Peterson & Naomi Omizo. 5 cass. (JPN., 2004. 69.95 (978-0-88727-303-2(3)) Cheng Tsui.

Adventures in Japanese, Vol. 1. Hiromi Peterson & Naomi Omizo. 5 CDs. (Running Time: 6 hrs.). (JPN & ENG., (gr. 6-9). 2005. audio compact disk 53.95 (978-0-88727-361-2(0)) Cheng Tsui.

Adventures in Japanese, Vol. 2. 5 CDs. 2004. audio compact disk 135.00 (978-0-88727-557-9(5)) Cheng Tsui.

Adventures in Japanese, Vol. 2. Hiromi Peterson & Naomi Omizo. 6 cass. (JPN., 2004. 79.95 (978-0-88727-323-0(8)) Cheng Tsui.

Adventures in Japanese, Vol. 2. Hiromi Peterson & Naomi Omizo. 5 CDs. (Running Time: 7 hrs. 30 mins.). (JPN & ENG., (gr. 7-10). 2006. stu. ed. 53.95 (978-0-88727-362-9(9)) Cheng Tsui.

Adventures in Japanese, Vol. 3. Hiromi Peterson & Naomi Omizo. 4 CDs. (JPN & ENG., (gr. 9-11). 2007. stu. ed. 51.95 (978-0-88727-395-7(5)) Cheng Tsui.

Adventures in Japanese: Level 4 Language Lab. Hiromi Peterson & Naomi Omizo. 2005. audio compact disk 199.95 (978-0-88727-446-6(3)) Cheng Tsui.

Adventures in Life, Vol. 8. 2004. 45.00 (978-0-01-208136-5(1)) Your Story.

Adventures in Life, Vol. 9. 2004. 45.00 (978-0-01-208137-2(X)) Your Story.

Adventures in Life, Vol. 10. 2004. 45.00 (978-0-01-208138-9(8)) Your Story.

Adventures in Life, Vol. 11. 2004. 45.00 (978-0-01-208139-6(6)) Your Story.

Adventures in Life Series Album 10: 12 Cassette Dramatized Audio Stories. 2006. 45.00 (978-1-60079-009-6(7)) YourStory.

Adventures in Life Series Album 10: 12 CD Dramatized Audio Stories. 2006. 45.00 (978-1-60079-032-4(1)) YourStory.

Adventures in Life Series Album 11: 12 Cassette Dramatized Audio Stories. 2006. 45.00 (978-1-60079-010-2(0)) YourStory.

Adventures in Life Series Album 11: 12 CD Dramatized Audio Stories. 2006. 45.00 (978-1-60079-033-1(X)) YourStory.

Adventures in Life Series Album 8: 12 Cassette Dramatized Audio Stories. 2006. 45.00 (978-1-60079-007-2(0)) YourStory.

Adventures in Life Series Album 8: 12 CD Dramatized Audio Stories. 2006. 45.00 (978-1-60079-030-0(5)) YourStory.

Adventures in Life Series Album 9: 12 Cassette Dramatized Audio Stories. 2006. 45.00 (978-1-60079-008-9(9)) YourStory.

Adventures in Life Series Album 9: 12 CD Dramatized Audio Stories. 2006. 45.00 (978-1-60079-031-7(3)) YourStory.

Adventures in Music, Cass. 1. Roy Bennett. (Running Time: 1 hr. 3 mins.). (Adventures in Music Ser.). (ENG.). 1986. 46.00 (978-0-521-56943-9(5)) Cambridge U Pr.

Adventures in Music, Cass. 2. Roy Bennett. (Running Time: 45 mins.). (Adventures in Music Ser.). (ENG.). 1986. 46.00 (978-0-521-56942-2(7)) Cambridge U Pr.

Adventures in Music, Cass. 3. Roy Bennett. (Running Time: 1 hr.). (Adventures in Music Ser.). (ENG.). 1988. 46.00 (978-0-521-56940-8(0)) Cambridge U Pr.

Adventures in Music, Cass. 4. Roy Bennett. (Running Time: 58 mins.). (Adventures in Music Ser.). (ENG.). 1989. 46.00 (978-0-521-56938-5(9)) Cambridge U Pr.

Adventures in Odyssey: Chronicles, Kings & Crosses. Tommy Nelson. Prod. by Focus on the Family Staff. 6 cass. (Running Time: 360 mins.). (Adventures in Odyssey Ser.). 1994. 24.99 (978-1-56179-245-0(4)) Pub: Focus Family. Dist(s): Nelson
Adventures in Odyssey gives your family hours of entertainment with values straight out of God's Word! This special edition contains some of the best Bible stories ever told. . .so pull up to the edge of your seat and get ready for amazing things to happen! This album includes: The Imagination Station I & II, Elijah I & II, Bernard and Joseph and others.

Adventures in Odyssey: Imagination Station. 1 cass. (Running Time: 1 hr.). (J). 1999. 16.99 Gospel Lght.
Two episodes from "Focus on the Family" radio drama. Reproducible.

Adventures in Odyssey: In Your Wildest Dreams. 4 CDs. (Running Time: 6 hrs.). (J). 2000. audio compact disk 24.99 Nelson.
12 episodes of the popular radio drama, which feature lessons for kids.

Adventures in Odyssey: In Your Wildest Dreams. 4 cass. (Running Time: 6 hrs.). (J). (gr. 3). 2000. 24.99 Nelson.

Adventures in Odyssey: The Imagination Station. 1 cass. (Running Time: 60 mins.). (J). 16.99 (Regal Bks) Gospel Lght.
Two episodes of focus on the family's hit radio drama. Reproducible.

Adventures in Odyssey Vol. 31: Days to Remember. 6 cass. (Running Time: 50 mins. per cass.). (J). (gr. 1 up). 25.00 (AIO31) Nelson.
Experience the havoc & hilarious happenings with favorite characters - like Eugene at his engagement party, Connie at her graduation & the whole gang's wacky New Year's Eve. Each episode is an important reminder of thankfulness, God's faithfulness & His love for all of us.

Adventures in Odyssey Vol. 31: Days to Remember, 4 CDs. (Running Time: 50 mins. per cass.). (J). (gr. 1 up). audio compact disk 25.00 Nelson.

Adventures in Odyssey Christmas Sampler. (Adventures in Odyssey Samplers Ser.). 0.99 (978-1-56179-818-6(5)) Focus Family.

Adventures in Odyssey Live! AIO Team Staff. Created by Focus Staff. (Adventures in Odyssey Ser.). (ENG.). (J). 2009. audio compact disk 19.99 (978-1-58997-576-7(6), Tyndale Ent) Tyndale Hse.

Adventures in Odyssey Platinum Collection: Producers' Picks Showcasing Our First 20 Years. AIO Team Staff. Created by Focus on the Family Staff. (Running Time: 15 hrs.). (Adventures in Odyssey Ser.). (ENG.). (J). (gr. 1-7). 2007. audio compact disk 39.97 (978-1-58997-383-1(6), Tyndale Ent) Tyndale Hse.

Adventures in Old-Time Radio: Dracula. Perf. by Orson Welles et al. 1 cass. (Running Time: 1 hr.). Dramatization. (Halloween at Radio Spirits Ser.). 2002. 4.98 (978-1-57019-427-6(0), OTR7030) Pub: Radio Spirits. Dist(s): AudioGO

Adventures in Revelation CD Set. Jeff Cavins & Thomas Smith. 2007. audio compact disk 79.95 (978-1-934217-03-0(4)) Ascensn Pr.

Adventures in Rhythm. Ella Jenkins. 1 CD. (Running Time: 1 hr.). (J). 2001. audio compact disk 15.00 (FC 45007CD) Kimbo Educ.

Adventures in Rhythm. Perf. by Ella Jenkins. 1 cass. (Running Time: 23 mins.). (J). (gr. 1-4). 1989. (0-9307-450070-9307-45007-2-9); audio compact disk (0-9307-45007-2-9) Smithsonian Folkways.
Progression of simple to complex rhythmic concepts with Rhythm Workshop participants. Appropriate for children with learning difficulties. Includes "Caney Mi Macaro," "I've Been Working on the Railroad," "Hambone" & more.

Adventures in Self Discovery. Patrick K. Porter. 2 cass. (978-1-887630-04-7(X)) Renaissnce Pub.
Psychology self-help.

Adventures in Singing. Clifton Ware. 2 cass. 1995. 17.81 (978-0-07-068273-3(9)) McGraw.

Adventures in Singing: A Process for Exploring, Discovering, & Developing Vocal Potential. 3rd ed. Clifton Ware. 2005. spiral bd. 80.25 (978-0-07-299850-4(4), Mc-H Human Soc) McGrw-H Hghr Educ.

Adventures in Sound with Max Axiom, Super Scientist. Emily Sohn & Anne Timmons. Illus. by Cynthia Martin. (Graphic Science Ser.). (ENG.). (gr. 3-4). 2007. audio compact disk 6.95 (978-1-4296-1124-4(3)) CapstoneDig.

Adventures in Space: The Flight to Fix the Hubble. unabr. ed. Elaine Scott. Narrated by Nelson Runger. 1 cass. (Running Time: 1 hr. 15 mins.). (gr. 2 up). 2001. 10.00 (978-0-7887-0533-5(4), 94728E7) Recorded Bks.
In the longest & most difficult mission in NASA's history, seven space shuttle astronauts travel into space to repair the Hubble Space Telescope. Learn what it is like to live, sleep & eat in outer space.

Adventures in SportsLand - the Soccer Bully (with accompanying CD) Charles Hellman. Illus. by Robert Tiritilli. (Adventures in SportsLand: the Bully Ser.). (J). (ps-3). 2009. bk. 19.95 (978-0-935938-26-5(5), Sport Cartoon Bks) LuckySports.

Adventures in the Air. unabr. ed. Edgar Allan Poe. Read by Samuel W. Griffin. 2 cass. (Running Time: 3 hrs.). (Science Fiction Library). 1997. pap. bk. 16.95 (978-1-55656-196-2(2)) Pub: Dercum Audio. Dist(s): APG
Includes "The Unparalleled Adventure of Hans Pfall" & "Mellonta Tauta" (1849) which takes the form of a letter dated April Fool's Day, 2849, written by a woman aboard a doomed trans-Atlantic super-blimp.

Adventures in the Alaskan Skin Trade. John Hawkes. Interview with John Hawkes. 1 cass. (Running Time: 30 mins.). 8.95 (AMF-21) Am Audio Prose.
The author reads from his novel & talks about the Alaska of his youth & imagination.

Adventures in the Solar System: Planetron & Me. (J). 2005. cass. & cd-rom 24.95 (978-0-9771381-4-2(3)) Geoffrey Williams.

Adventures in the Unknown Interior of America. unabr. ed. Alvar Núñez Cabeza de Vaca. Narrated by George Guidall. 3 cass. (Running Time: 4 hrs. 30 mins.). 1994. 26.00 (978-1-55690-970-2(5), 94203E7) Recorded Bks.
The 16th century odyssey of Cabeza de Vaca, as the first European to cross the North American continent. The account of the journey is a glimpse into the pre-European Southwest, the climate, the customs of its natives & a portrait of an exceptional, suprisingly modern man.

***Adventures in the Wilderness: Camp Life in the Adirondacks.** William Murray. Prod. by Adirondack Audio Books. (Running Time: 285). (ENG.). 2010. audio compact disk 19.95 (978-0-9830742-2-9(4)) AABks.

Adventures in Theology. Charles R. Swindoll. 2007. audio compact disk 199.00 (978-1-57972-746-8(8)) Insight Living.

Adventures in Theology: Bible Stories & Holidays. Charles R. Swindoll. 2007. audio compact disk 79.00 (978-1-57972-769-7(7)) Insight Living.

Adventures in Time & Space with Max Merriwell. Pat Murphy & Johanna Ward. 2002. 49.95 (978-0-7861-2857-0(7)) Blckstn Audio.

Adventures in Time & Space with Max Merriwell. Pat Murphy. Narrated by Johanna Ward. (Running Time: 10 hrs.). 2004. 30.95 (978-1-59912-403-2(3)) Iofy Corp.

Adventures in 1 Corinthians. Tim Gray. 2007. audio compact disk 44.95 (978-1-934217-29-0(8)) Ascensn Pr.

Adventures of a Psychic: The Fascinating & Inspiring True-Life Story of One of America's Most Successful Clairvoyants. abr. ed. Sylvia Browne & Antoinette May. 2 x CDs. 2005. audio compact disk 19.95 (978-1-4019-0438-8(4)) Hay House.

Adventures of Albert, the Running Bear. unabr. ed. Barbara Isenberg & Susan Wolf. Illus. by Dick Gackenbach. 1 cass. (Running Time: 17 mins.). (J). (gr. k-3). 1985. pap. bk. 15.95 (978-0-941078-88-7(4)) Live Oak Media.
A former circus bear escapes from a zoo and overcomes his passion for "junk" food by stumbling into a marathon.

Adventures of Ali Baba Bernstein. Johanna Hurwitz. Narrated by George Guidall. 2 CDs. (Running Time: 1 hr. 30 mins.). (gr. 1 up). audio compact disk 20.00 (978-1-4025-2284-0(3)) Recorded Bks.

Adventures of Ali Baba Bernstein. unabr. ed. Johanna Hurwitz. Narrated by George Guidall. 1 cass. (Running Time: 1 hr. 30 mins.). (gr. 1 up). 1995. 10.00 (978-0-7887-0214-3(9), 94439E7) Recorded Bks.
Eight year old David Bernstein hopes changing his name to a more exciting one will make his life more exciting too.

Adventures of Arthur Gordon PYM see Aventuras de Arturo Gordon PYM

Adventures of Arthur Gordon Pym. Edgar Allan Poe. Read by Carlos J. Vega. (Running Time: 3 hrs.). 2002. 16.95 (978-1-60083-221-5(0), Audiofy Corp) Iofy Corp.

Adventures of Artie Eco: The Problem with Greed, Vol. 12. rev. ed. Billie Seaon Ducote. Illus. by Billie Seaon Ducote. (ENG.). (J). 2007. audio compact disk 18.95 (978-0-9787597-2-8(9)) PureLight Pubns.

Adventures of Artie Eco/Part One & Part Two: The Problem with Greed. Short Stories. Billie Seaon Ducote. Narrated by Billie Seaon Ducote. Music by Paul Alaniz. Paul Alaniz. e.g., 2 cds. (Running Time: e.g., 35 min). Dramatization. (J). 2006. audio compact disk 12.95 (978-0-9787597-0-4(2)) PureLight Pubns.

Adventures of Augie March. unabr. ed. Saul Bellow. Read by Tom Parker. 16 cass. (Running Time: 23 hrs. 30 mins.). 1992. 99.95 (978-0-7861-0344-7(2), 1301) Blckstn Audio.
Augie, the exuberant narrator-hero, is a poor Chicago boy growing up during the Depression. He latches on to a wild succession of occupations, then proudly rejects each one as too limiting. It is not until he tangles with a glamorous perfectionist named Thea, a huntress with a trained eagle, that his independence is seriously threatened. Luckily, his nature (like the eagle's) breaks down under the strain. He goes on to recruit himself to even more outlandish projects, but always ducks out in time to continue improvising his unconventional career.

Adventures of Augie March. unabr. ed. Saul Bellow. Read by Tom Parker. 2 pieces. (Running Time: 79200 sec.). 2008. audio compact disk 39.95 (978-0-7861-8659-4(3), 1301); audio compact disk & audio compact disk 130.00 (978-0-7861-6254-3(6)) Blckstn Audio.

Adventures of Augie March, Set. unabr. ed. Saul Bellow. Read by Tom Parker. 16 cass. 1999. 99.95 (FS9-51122) Highsmith.

Adventures of Basie, the Electric Bass Guitar, Bk. 1. Cathy Ellis. Perf. by Eric Bradley. Interview with Patricia Moya. 1 cass. (Complete Guide for the Guitar Ser.). (J). (ps-2). 1993. 12.95 (978-1-879542-33-4(1), EFMBS1TP) Ellis Family Mus.
Can be used in conjunction with "The Adventures of Gilly, the Guitar". Learn the basics along with "Basie" 500 Ellis Family Mus.

Adventures of Bertie & Jeeves. unabr. ed. P. G. Wodehouse. 3 cass/. (Running Time: 3 hrs. 2 min.). 2000. 24.00 (978-1-929718-02-3(0)) Audio Conn.
Five selections in volume one.

Adventures of Big Foot Wallace. unabr. ed. John C. Duval. Read by Jack Sondericker. 6 cass. (Running Time: 8 hrs.). 39.95 (978-1-55686-235-9(0), 235) Books in Motion.
Real-life adventures of a Texas pioneer who fought in the Mexican War.

Adventures of Big Shot & Teeny Weeny. Ed. by Via Page et al. Illus. by Norman Arinsberg. 2 CDs. (Running Time: 4 hrs.). (J). (gr. 2-4). 2002. pap. bk. 15.00 (978-0-9667442-1-7(7)) Curen Enterp.

Adventures of Billy Butterfly. Perf. by R. B. Lehnert. Created by R. B. Lehnert. Illus. by Marc Khayam Garcia. 1 cd. (Running Time: 16 mins., 38 sec.). Dramatization. (J). 2003. audio compact disk (978-0-9747628-0-7(6), BBB) BKB Grp.
This CD is the audio production of "The Adventures of Billy Butterfly" picture book performed in music, original songs and voice characterizations by the author.

Adventures of Blue Avenger. unabr. ed. Norma Howe. Read by John Beach. 3 vols. (Running Time: 4 hrs. 20 mins.). (Blue Avenger Ser.). (J). (gr. 6 up). 2004. pap. bk. 36.00 (978-0-8072-8423-0(8), YA167SP, Listening Lib); 30.00 (978-0-8072-8418-6(1), YA167CX, Listening Lib) Random Audio Pubg.
Could David be anything other than a "secret champion of the underdog, modest seeker of truth, fearless innovator of the unknown?" To know all that & to solve questions large & small - you'll just have to listen.

Adventures of Boo: The Journey Begins. Julie Cox. Illus. by Stephen Ortland. (J). 1990. (978-0-9627586-1-4(2)) Mango Entrps.

Adventures of Brian, Set. Eric Thompson. Read by Richard Wilson. 2 cass. (Running Time: 2 hrs.). (J). 1999. (978-1-84032-104-3(0), HoddrStoughton) Hodder General GBR.
Here once again are Dougal, Brian the snail, Florence, Zebedee & Ermintrude the cow.

Adventures of Brother Cadfael. abr. ed. Ellis Peters, pseud. Read by Derek Jacobi. 12 cass. (Running Time: 18 hrs.). 2001. 53.00 (978-1-59040-095-1(X), Phoenix Audio) Pub: Amer Intl Pub. Dist(s): PerseuPGW

Adventures of Buster Bear. Thornton W. Burgess. 2 cass. (Running Time: 3 hrs.). (J). (gr. k-2). 20.95 Audio Bk Con.
Princess Daffodil's gift of spreading flowers wherever she goes had its drawback until the king finds the magic hill. The adventure stories bring us into the warm whimsical world of the Green Forest, the Smiling Pool & the Purple Mountains where the Merry Little Breezes, Reddy fox, Johnny Chuck, Buster Bear & Peter Cottontail among others romp & tease each other through many escapades.

Adventures of Captain Hudson: The Lost Mines of Paradise. Short Stories. 4 cass. (Running Time: 5 hrs). Dramatization. 2004. 24.99 (978-0-9758605-0-2(X)); audio compact disk 29.99 (978-0-9758605-1-9(8)) Audio Cinema Ent.
The Adventures of Captain Hudson: The lost mines of Paradise2004 USADistributor/Production Company: Audio Cinema EntertainmentAudio Format: StereoProduct: Episodic Audio Adventure ProgramAvailable on 4 CDs or 4 Cassettes - Running Time: Approx. 5 hoursIncludes 8 page booklet with artwork and liner notesThe Producers at Audio Cinema Entertainment have created a feature lengthAudio Adventure produced and digitally mastered in stereo. Reminiscent ofthe 'Golden Age of Radio', this audio production is quite a bit more thanthat. It boasts an original script laced with nostalgia and excitement froma bygone era. It is brought to life with a terrific cast and the use ofmovie quality digital sound effects as well as a fully orchestratedmusical score. It's a real treat for the imagination, It is 'Cinema of themind'.In this pilot episode, we are introduced to our reluctant hero, Captain JimHudson and the crew of his state of the art DC-3 aircraft or (cargo plane). In addition, we get to know a colorful cast of regulars who become friends and allies and part of their lives forever. (or "we meet a terrific cast of regulars who"...)The majority of the story takes place in 1936 where we find that CaptainHudson is just a regular guy trying to make an honest buck. From MercuryAirfield in the Coastal town of Crescent Cove, California, Hudson and hispals embark on unexpected adventures as they journey into the forgottenregions of the Arizona desert. As one thing leads to another things beginto go terribly wrong. You'll find the whole story waiting for you in thisfun filled Audio Adventure from Audio Cinema Entertainment.

Adventures of Clyde & Camille, Vol. 1. Rev. by Todd Liebenow et al. (J). 1997. audio compact disk 15.00 (978-1-58302-177-4(9)) One Way St.
Contains all six pre-recorded scripts.

Adventures of Clyde & Camille, Vol. 2. Rev. by Todd Liebenow et al. 1997. audio compact disk 15.00 (978-1-58302-178-1(7)) One Way St.

Adventures of Connie & Diego - Las a Venturasde Connie y Diego. Read by Harriet Rohmer et al. Ed. by Anna Olivarez. Illus. by Malaquias Montoya. 1 cass. (Running Time: 30 mins.). (Tales of the Americas Ser.). (ENG & SPA.). (J). (ps-3). 1982. 9.95 (978-0-89239-051-9(4)) Pub: Childrens Book Pr. Dist(s): PerseuPGW
Mexican-American twins from the California farmworking community. In order to escape teasing for being different, Connie and Diego try to find a new home among their animal friends.

Adventures of Connie & Diego Read-Along. Maria Garcia. Illus. by Malaquias Montoya. (J). 1988. bk. 22.95 (978-0-89239-033-5(6)) Childrens Book Pr.

Adventures of Cowboy Bob. David Canterbury. (J). 2007. audio compact disk 9.99 (978-1-60247-185-6(1)) Tate Pubng.

Adventures of Don Quixote de la Mancha (Part 1), Vol. 1. unabr. ed. Miguel de Cervantes Saavedra. Narrated by Flo Gibson. 16 cass. (Running Time: 24 hrs.). 2003. 46.95 (978-1-55685-710-2(1)) Audio Bk Con.
A gentleman's mind is crazed by reading romances of chivalry. He believes himself to be a knight-errant and persuades rustic Sancho Panza to accompany him as his squire during his travels to right the wrongs of the world.

Adventures of Don Quixote de la Mancha (Part 2), Vol. 2. unabr. ed. Miguel de Cervantes Saavedra. Narrated by Flo Gibson. (Running Time: 13 hrs. 35 mins.). 2002. 28.95 (978-1-55685-784-3(5)) Audio Bk Con.

Adventures of Don Quixote de la Mancha (Parts 1 And 2) unabr. ed. Miguel de Cervantes Saavedra. Narrated by Flo Gibson. (Running Time: 37 hrs. 35 mins.). 2002. 65.95 (978-1-55685-785-0(3)) Audio Bk Con.

Adventures of Dougal. Eric Thompson. Read by Richard Wilson. 2 cass. (Running Time: 2 hrs.). 1999. (978-1-84032-128-9(8), HoddrStoughton) Hodder General GBR.
The Magic Roundabout is well loved for its gentle & intelligent humour.

Adventures of Dusty Sourdough: The Trail to Wrangell. Glen E. Guy. 1 cass. 1995. 14.95 (978-0-9644491-4-5(5)) Old Alaska.

Adventures of Dylan. Eric Thompson. Read by Richard Wilson. 2 cass. (Running Time: 2 hrs.). (J). 1999. (978-1-84032-114-2(8), HoddrStoughton) Hodder General GBR.
Whether you are coming to the stories for the first time or revisiting the characters as childhood friends, this will be a treat.

Adventures of Elizabeth Rugen. unabr. ed. Elizabeth von Arnim. 5 cass. (Running Time: 7 hrs. 30 min.). 2002. 20.95 (978-1-55685-727-0(6)) Audio Bk Con.
A tour of a beautiful Baltic island with glowing descriptions of the countryside.

Adventures of Ellery Queen. collector's ed. Perf. by Lee Bowman et al. 1 DVD. (Running Time: 3 hrs.). (TV from Yesteryear Ser.). 2001. bk. 9.98 (7800) Radio Spirits.
Contains three classic television shows and three complete old time radio shows.

Adventures of Ellery Queen: World Series Crime & Number 31. unabr. ed. 1 cass. (Running Time: 1 hr.). 2001. 6.98 (1557) Radio Spirits.

Adventures of Elmo in Grouchland, Set. Perf. by Vanessa Williams et al. 1 cass. (Running Time: 50 min.). 1999. 9.98 CASS. (Sony Wonder) Sony Music Ent.
Elmo returns to Grouchland to sing some of his favorite songs with his new friend Grizzy. However, there's one problem, Grouches aren't supposed to cooperate so Grizzy won't sing along. Never discouraged, Elmo starts

singing his favorite songs and before long Grizzy finds a way to join in while staying true to her grouchy self.

Adventures of Ermintrude. Eric Thompson. Read by Richard Wilson. 2 cass. (Running Time: 2 hrs.). (J). 1999. (978-1-84032-109-8(1), HoddrStoughton) Hodder General GBR.
The Magic Roundabout is an institution, well loved for its gentle & intelligent humour that is as much for adults as children.

Adventures of Flash Jackson. William Kowalski. Narrated by Julie Dretzin. 8 cass. (Running Time: 11 hrs.). 2003. 76.00 (978-1-4025-1818-8(8)) Recorded Bks.

Adventures of Flumpa & Friends Bk. 1: Someday... Someday. Wendy Whitten. Read by Wendy Whitten. Contrib. by Herb McCullough. Illus. by Mike Swerda. 1 cass. (Running Time: 30 mins.). (Adventures of Flumpa & Friends Ser.). (J). (ps-3). 1995. bk. 24.95 (978-1-886184-00-8(3)) Ion Imagination.
A large, imaginative picture book & cassette tape with something to teach about imagination, discovery & respect. Colorful, detailed illustrations, six original "story songs" & narration with sound effects put the fun into learning to read.

***Adventures of Frank Merriwell.** RadioArchives.com. (Running Time: 600). (ENG.). 2007. audio compact disk 29.98 (978-1-61081-101-9(1)) Radio Arch.

Adventures of Frank Merriwell: Promise & The Mystery Man. unabr. ed. Perf. by Lawson Zerbe. 1 cass. (Running Time: 1 hr.). (J). 2001. 6.98 (2071) Radio Spirits.

Adventures of Frank Merriwell: Tap Day & The Thunderstorm Mystery. unabr. ed. Perf. by Lawson Zerbe. 1 cass. (Running Time: 1 hr.). (J). 2001. 6.98 (2051) Radio Spirits.

Adventures of Fraser the Yellow Dog: Rescue on Snowmass Mountain. Jill Sheeley & Al Lyons. Perf. by Katy Hall et al. Contrib. by Bobby Mason & Polly Whitcomb. 1 cass. (Running Time: 20 mins.). (J). (ps-4). 1997. bk. 10.95 (978-0-9609108-4-7(0)) Courtney Pr.
Great sound effects & a song throughout.

Adventures of Gerard. Arthur Conan Doyle. Contrib. by John Bolen. (Playaway Young Adult Ser.). (ENG.). 2009. 69.99 (978-1-60775-782-5(6)) Find a World.

Adventures of Gerard. Arthur Conan Doyle. Read by John Bolen. (Running Time: 6 hrs. 30 mins.). 2001. 27.95 (978-1-60083-587-2(2), Audiofy Corp) Iofy Corp.

Adventures of Gerard. Arthur Conan Doyle. Read by John Bolen. (ENG.). 2001. audio compact disk 72.00 (978-1-4001-3014-6(X)) Pub: Tantor Media. Dist(s): IngramPubServ

Adventures of Gerard. unabr. ed. Arthur Conan Doyle. Read by John Bolen. 1 CD. (Running Time: 6 hrs. 30 mins.). 2001. audio compact disk 25.00; audio compact disk 51.00 Books on Tape.

Adventures of Gerard. unabr. ed. Arthur Conan Doyle. Read by John Bolen. 1 CD (MP3). (Running Time: 6 hrs. 28 mins.). (ENG.). 2001. audio compact disk 20.00 (978-1-4001-5014-4(0)) Pub: Tantor Media. Dist(s): IngramPubServ

Adventures of Gerard. unabr. ed. Arthur Conan Doyle. Read by John Bolen. 6 CDs. (Running Time: 6 hrs. 28 mins.). (ENG.). 2001. audio compact disk 36.00 (978-1-4001-0014-9(3)) Pub: Tantor Media. Dist(s): IngramPubServ

Adventures of Gerard. unabr. ed. Arthur Conan Doyle. Narrated by John Bolen. (Running Time: 6 hrs. 30 mins. 0 sec.). (ENG.). 2009. audio compact disk 19.99 (978-1-4001-6096-9(0)); audio compact disk 55.99 (978-1-4001-4096-1(X)); audio compact disk 27.99 (978-1-4001-1096-4(3)) Pub: Tantor Media. Dist(s): IngramPubServ

Adventures of Gilly, the Guitar. Cathy Ellis. Illus. by Patricia Moya. 1 cass. (J). (ps-2). 1991. 15.95 (978-1-879542-04-4(8)) Ellis Family Mus.

Adventures of Guy Noir: Radio Private Eye. unabr. ed. Contrib. by Garrison Keillor. 2 CDs. (Running Time: 2 hrs.). (ENG.). 2005. audio compact disk 24.95 (978-1-56511-956-7(8), 1565119568) Pub: HighBridge. Dist(s): Workman Pub

Adventures of Hajji Baba of Ispahan. James Morier. Read by Anais 9000. 2008. 33.95 (978-1-60112-077-9(X)) Babblebooks.

Adventures of Harry Nile, Vol. 1. 8 episodes on 2 cas. (Running Time: 90 min. per cass.). 1998. 14.98 Boxed set. (4267) Radio Spirits.
Detective stories with a complete cast of characters & great sound effects.

Adventures of Harry Nile, Vol. 2. 8 episodes on 2 cas. (Running Time: 90 min. per cass.). 1998. 14.98 Boxed set. (4268) Radio Spirits.

Adventures of Harry Nile, Vol. 3. 8 episodes on 2 cas. (Running Time: 90 min. per cass.). 1998. 14.98 Boxed set. (4343) Radio Spirits.

Adventures of Harry Nile, Vol. 4. 8 episodes on 2 cas. (Running Time: 90 min. per cass.). 1998. 14.98 Boxed set. (4344) Radio Spirits.

Adventures of Harry Nile, Vol. 5. 8 episodes on 2 cas. (Running Time: 90 min. per cass.). 1998. 14.98 Boxed set. (4402) Radio Spirits.

Adventures of Harry Nile, Vol. 6. 8 episodes on 2 cas. (Running Time: 90 min. per cass.). 1998. 14.98 Boxed set. (4403) Radio Spirits.

Adventures of Harry Nile, Vol. 7. 8 episodes on 2 cas. (Running Time: 90 min. per cass.). 1998. 14.98 Boxed set. (4404) Radio Spirits.

Adventures of Harry Nile, Vol. 8. 8 episodes on 2 cas. (Running Time: 90 min. per cass.). 1998. 14.98 Boxed set. (4405) Radio Spirits.

Adventures of Harry Nile Vol. 1: Private Investigator. 2 cass. (Running Time: 3 hrs.). 2001. 19.95 (COUN001) Lodestone Catalog.
Chicago cop Harry Nile quits the force to become a private investigator in L.A. You will meet some interesting people within the eight detective capers in each episode.

Adventures of Harry Nile Vol. 2: Private Investigator. 2 cass. (Running Time: 3 hrs.). 2001. 19.95 (COUN002) Lodestone Catalog.

Adventures of Harry Nile Vol. 3: Private Investigator. 2 cass. (Running Time: 3 hrs.). 2001. 19.95 (COUN003) Lodestone Catalog.

Adventures of Harry Nile Vol. 4: Private Investigator. 2 cass. (Running Time: 3 hrs.). 2001. 19.95 (COUN004) Lodestone Catalog.

Adventures of Harry Nile Vols. 1- 4: Private Investigator. 8 cass. (Running Time: 12 hrs.). 2001. 69.95 (COUN124) Lodestone Catalog.
Chicago cop Harry Nile quits the force to become a private investigator in L.A. You will meet some interesting people & the money's lousy & the days are long.

Adventures of Harry Nile Complete Collection Volume 1. Short Stories. 8 CDs. Dramatization. 2006. audio compact disk 39.95 (978-1-60245-084-4(6)) GDL Multimedia.

Adventures of Harry Nile Complete Collection Volume 2. Short Stories. 8 CDs. Dramatization. 2006. audio compact disk 39.99 (978-1-60245-085-1(4)) GDL Multimedia.

Adventures of Harry Nile Complete Collection Volume 3. Short Stories. 8 CDs. Dramatization. 2006. audio compact disk 39.99 (978-1-60245-086-8(2)) GDL Multimedia.

Adventures of Harry Nile Complete Collection Volume 4. Short Stories. 8 CDs. Dramatization. 2006. audio compact disk 39.99 (978-1-60245-087-5(0)) GDL Multimedia.

Adventures of Harry Nile Complete Collection Volume 5. Jim French. (ENG.). 2008. audio compact disk 39.95 (978-1-60245-163-6(X)) GDL Multimedia.

Adventures of Harry Nile Volume 1. Short Stories. 2 CDs. (Running Time: 2 hrs.). 2006. audio compact disk 9.95 (978-1-60245-000-4(5)) GDL Multimedia.

Adventures of Harry Nile Volume 10. Jim French. (ENG.). 2008. audio compact disk 9.95 (978-1-60245-132-2(X)) GDL Multimedia.

Adventures of Harry Nile Volume 11. Jim French. (ENG.). 2008. audio compact disk 9.95 (978-1-60245-133-9(8)) GDL Multimedia.

Adventures of Harry Nile Volume 12. Jim French. (ENG.). 2008. audio compact disk 9.95 (978-1-60245-134-6(6)) GDL Multimedia.

Adventures of Harry Nile Volume 13. Jim French. (ENG.). 2008. audio compact disk 9.95 (978-1-60245-135-3(4)) GDL Multimedia.

Adventures of Harry Nile Volume 14. Jim French. (ENG.). 2008. audio compact disk 9.95 (978-1-60245-136-0(2)) GDL Multimedia.

Adventures of Harry Nile Volume 15. Jim French. (ENG.). 2008. audio compact disk Rental 9.95 (978-1-60245-137-7(0)) GDL Multimedia.

Adventures of Harry Nile Volume 16. Jim French. (ENG.). 2008. audio compact disk 9.95 (978-1-60245-138-4(9)) GDL Multimedia.

Adventures of Harry Nile Volume 17. Jim French. (ENG.). 2008. audio compact disk 9.95 (978-1-60245-139-1(7)) GDL Multimedia.

Adventures of Harry Nile Volume 18. Jim French. (ENG.). 2008. audio compact disk 9.95 (978-1-60245-140-7(0)) GDL Multimedia.

Adventures of Harry Nile Volume 19. Jim French. (ENG.). 2008. audio compact disk 9.95 (978-1-60245-141-4(9)) GDL Multimedia.

Adventures of Harry Nile Volume 2. Short Stories. 2 CDs. (Running Time: 2 hrs.). Dramatization. (ENG.). 2006. audio compact disk 9.95 (978-1-60245-001-1(3)) GDL Multimedia.

Adventures of Harry Nile Volume 20. Jim French. (ENG.). 2008. audio compact disk 9.95 (978-1-60245-142-1(7)) GDL Multimedia.

Adventures of Harry Nile Volume 3. Short Stories. 2 CDs. (Running Time: 2 hrs.). Dramatization. (ENG.). 2006. audio compact disk 9.95 (978-1-60245-002-8(1)) GDL Multimedia.

Adventures of Harry Nile Volume 4. (ENG.). 2008. audio compact disk 9.95 (978-1-60245-098-1(6)) GDL Multimedia.

Adventures of Harry Nile Volume 5. Jim French. (ENG.). 2008. audio compact disk 9.95 (978-1-60245-127-8(3)) GDL Multimedia.

Adventures of Harry Nile Volume 6. Jim French. (ENG.). 2008. audio compact disk 9.95 (978-1-60245-128-5(1)) GDL Multimedia.

Adventures of Harry Nile Volume 7. Jim French. (ENG.). 2008. audio compact disk 9.95 (978-1-60245-129-2(X)) GDL Multimedia.

Adventures of Harry Nile Volume 8. Jim French. (ENG.). 2008. audio compact disk 9.95 (978-1-60245-130-8(3)) GDL Multimedia.

adventures of Harry Nile Volume 9. Jim French. (ENG.). 2008. audio compact disk 9.95 (978-1-60245-131-5(1)) GDL Multimedia.

Adventures of Honey Bear. Carolyn Hobbs. Illus. by Larry Beard. 1 cass. (Running Time: 30 mins.). (Aunt Carolyn's Collection). (J). (gr. k-6). 2000. pap. bk. 8.95 (978-0-929291-61-1(1)) Gospel Projects Pr.

***Adventures of Honey Collection.** Tom Greer. (ENG.). (J). 2010. audio compact disk 8.95 (978-0-9789227-6-4(X)) Weeping Willow Pub.

Adventures of Huckleberry Finn. Retold by John Matern. Mark Twain. (Classic Adventures Ser.). 1999. audio compact disk 18.95 (978-1-4105-0133-2(7)) D Johnston Inc.

Adventures of Huckleberry Finn. Mark Twain. Narrated by Grover Gardner. (ENG.). 2008. audio compact disk 29.95 (978-1-60646-028-3(5)) Audio Bk Con.

Adventures of Huckleberry Finn. Mark Twain. Read by Tom Parker. 8 CDs. (Running Time: 10 hrs.). 2000. audio compact disk 64.00 (978-0-7861-9891-7(5), 1336) Blckstn Audio.
Huck Finn is a homeless rebel who loved freedom more than respectability. He isn't above lying & stealing, but he faces a battle with his conscience when he meets up with a runaway slave named Jim. Jim is trying to escape to a free state in the North while his owner wants to sell him to a slave trader down-river. Huck knows that helping Jim will bring trouble, but can he turn in a man who only wants to be free?.

Adventures of Huckleberry Finn. Mark Twain. 4 CDs. (Running Time: 6 hrs.). 2005. audio compact disk 24.95 (978-0-660-18922-2(4)) Pub: Canadian Broadcasting CAN. Dist(s): Georgetown Term

Adventures of Huckleberry Finn. Mark Twain. Ed. by Jerry Stemach et al. Retold by John Matern. Illus. by Joe Schwajkowski. Contrib. by Ed Smaron & Ted S. Hasselbring. (Start-to-Finish Books: Vol. 3). (J). (gr. 2-3). 2000. 35.00 (978-1-58702-435-1(7)) D Johnston Inc.

Adventures of Huckleberry Finn. Mark Twain. 2 cass. 19.95 (8116Q) Filmic Archives.
A great classic by America's foremost humorist. Young Huck fakes his own death & with runaway slave Jim, escapes to freedom & adventure on a raft down the Mississippi.

Adventures of Huckleberry Finn. Mark Twain. Retold by Frances Justice. Illus. by Alfredo Belli. (Green Apple Step One Ser.). (J). (gr. 3-7). 2005. pap. bk. 21.95 (978-88-530-0397-3(9), BlackCat) Grove-Atltic.

Adventures of Huckleberry Finn. Mark Twain. Narrated by Mike McShane. 2000. 17.99 (978-0-00-104757-0(4), HarpColl UK) Pub: HarpC GBR. Dist(s): Trafalgar

Adventures of Huckleberry Finn. Mark Twain. Narrated by Jim Killavey. (Running Time: 9 hrs. 30 mins.). 1979. 30.95 (978-1-59912-146-8(8)) Iofy Corp.

Adventures of Huckleberry Finn. Mark Twain. Read by Tom Parker. (Running Time: 9 hrs. 30 mins.). 1997. 30.95 (978-1-59912-620-3(6)) Iofy Corp.

Adventures of Huckleberry Finn. Mark Twain. Read by Yadira Sánchez. (Running Time: 3 hrs.). 2001. 16.95 (978-1-60083-156-0(7), Audiofy Corp) Iofy Corp.

Adventures of Huckleberry Finn. Mark Twain. Read by Jim Killavey. 7 cass. (Running Time: 10 hrs.). 1989. 44.00 incl. album. (C-32) Jimcin Record.
One of the greatest American novels.

Adventures of Huckleberry Finn. Mark Twain. Read by Ray Verna. 7 cass. (Running Time: 9 hrs. 30 min.). 1993. 47.20 Set. (978-1-56544-030-2(7), 350039); Rental 9.10 30 day rental Set. (350039) Literate Ear.
Huckleberry Finn is every boy who ever lived. Not to have known Huck is like being deprived of July 4th picnics & baseball. Along the Mississippi River, Huck grapples with grown-up issues of life & death, freedom & slavery, the individual versus society, & the ever-present theme of brotherhood.

Adventures of Huckleberry Finn. Mark Twain. Perf. by St. Charles Players. 2 cass. (Running Time: 3 hrs.). (Audio Theatre Ser.). (J). (gr. 3). 2000. 16.95 (Monterey SoundWorks) Monterey Media Inc.

Adventures of Huckleberry Finn. Mark Twain. Perf. by Jackie Cooper & Orson Welles. (Running Time: 60 min.). (J). 1940. 7.95 (DD-8410) Natl Recrd Co.

Adventures of Huckleberry Finn. Mark Twain. Contrib. by Jennifer Basset et al. (Oxford Bookworms Ser.). 1998. 13.75 (978-0-19-422782-7(0)) OUP.

Adventures of Huckleberry Finn. Mark Twain. Narrated by Norman Dietz. 10 CDs. (Running Time: 11 hrs. 45 mins.). audio compact disk 97.00 (978-1-4025-1973-4(7)) Recorded Bks.

Adventures of Huckleberry Finn. Mark Twain. (Illustrated Classics Ser.). (YA). 2005. audio compact disk (978-1-56254-907-7(3)) Saddleback Edu.

Adventures of Huckleberry Finn. Mark Twain. Narrated by Thomas Becker. (Running Time: 37140 sec.). (Unabridged Classics in MP3 Ser.). (ENG.). 2008. audio compact disk 26.00 (978-1-58472-521-3(4), In Aud); audio compact disk 14.95 (978-1-58472-520-6(6), In Aud) Sound Room.

Adventures of Huckleberry Finn. Mark Twain. 2001. audio compact disk 21.45 (978-1-903342-13-8(9)) Wordsworth Educ GBR.

Adventures of Huckleberry Finn. abr. ed. Mark Twain. Ed. by Jerry Stemach et al. Retold by John Matern. Illus. by Joe Schwajkowski. Contrib. by Ed Smaron & Ted S. Hasselbring. 1 cass.1 hr. (Start-to-Finish Books: Vol. 3). 2000. 7.00 (978-1-893376-11-3(7), F06) D Johnston Inc.
Sometime before the Civil War, Huck Finn is the motherless son of a derelict father. Fleeing abuse, Huck leaves home in Hannibal, Missouri, and joins forces with Jim, an adult slave who is trying to avoid being sold to owners in the Deep South. By misadventure, Huck and Jim find themselves on a raft drifting south down the Mississippi. As they float into the heart of slavery, Huck develops new respect for Jim and realizations about slavery and human nature.

Adventures of Huckleberry Finn. abr. ed. Mark Twain. Read by Garrison Keillor. (Running Time: 3 hrs.). (ENG.). 2003. audio compact disk 24.95 (978-1-56511-813-3(8), 1565118138) Pub: HighBridge. Dist(s): Workman Pub

Adventures of Huckleberry Finn. abr. ed. Mark Twain. Read by St. Charles Players. 2 cass. (Running Time: 2 hrs. 35 mins.). 2000. 16.95 (978-1-56994-528-5(4), 300044) Monterey Media Inc.
Cast off on a raft with a runaway slave down the great Mississippi & a boy couldn't dream of a greater adventure. With each bend of the river, each town, comes a chance encounter. Perhaps with a king or duke wrapped in the schemes of scoundrels, or a young girl caught amidst a family feud. On a journey with a friend dreaming of freedom, it's full of mischief, full of fun & the adventures of a lifetime.

Adventures of Huckleberry Finn. abr. ed. Mark Twain. Read by Garrick Hagon. 4 CDs. bk. 28.98 (978-962-634-262-6(5), NAX26212) Naxos.

Adventures of Huckleberry Finn. abr. ed. Mark Twain. Read by Garrick Hagon. 2 cass. (Running Time: 2 hrs. 38 mins.). (J). 1995. 13.98 (978-962-634-573-3(X), NA207314, Naxos AudioBooks) Naxos.
Floating down the Mississippi on their raft, Huck and Jim, a runaway slave, find life filled with excitement and the spirit of adventure. Join Huck, Jim and their old friend, Tom Sawyer on a trip you'll never tire of.

Adventures of Huckleberry Finn. abr. ed. Mark Twain. Read by Garrick Hagon. 2 CDs. (Running Time: 2 hrs. 38 mins.). (Junior Classics Ser.). 1995. audio compact disk 17.98 (978-962-634-073-8(8), NA207312, Naxos AudioBooks) Naxos.

Adventures of Huckleberry Finn. abr. ed. Mark Twain. Perf. by Wil Wheaton. 2 cass. (Running Time: 3 hrs.). (Ultimate Classics Ser.). (gr. 6-12). 2004. 18.00 (978-1-931056-70-0(6), N Millennium Audio) New Millenn Enter.
Huck Finn is a homeless waif, a liar & thief on occasion & a casual rebel against respectability. But when he encounters another fugitive from trouble, a runaway slave named Jim, Huck finds, for the first time in his life, a sense of responsibility, acceptance and love. Fleecing down the Mississippi on a raft, the boy nobody wants becomes a human being with a sense of his own destiny and the courage to choose between violating the conventions of his day and betraying the one person who needs him the most.

Adventures of Huckleberry Finn. abr. ed. Mark Twain. 2 cass. (Running Time: 3 hrs.). Dramatization. (Children's Classics Ser.). (J). (gr. 4-7). 1998. 13.95 (978-1-55935-162-1(4), 392886) Soundelux.
Huckleberry, who runs away to escape his drunken father, joins up with a runaway slave, Jim. Together they travel down the Mississippi on a make-shift raft, taking us through some of the most remarkable adventures in American literature.

Adventures of Huckleberry Finn. abr. ed. Mark Twain. 3 CDs. (SPA.). 2001. audio compact disk 17.00 (978-958-9494-21-9(8)) YoYoMusic.

Adventures of Huckleberry Finn. abr. adpt. ed. Mark Twain. (Bring the Classics to Life: Level 1 Ser.). 2008. audio compact disk 12.95 (978-1-55576-416-6(9)) EDCON Pubng.

***Adventures of Huckleberry Finn.** unabr. ed. Mark Twain. Read by Dick Hill. (Running Time: 11 hrs.). 2010. 19.99 (978-1-4418-7661-4(8), 9781441876614, Brilliance MP3); audio compact disk 29.99 (978-1-4418-7659-1(6), 9781441876591, Bril Audio CD Unabri); audio compact disk 69.97 (978-1-4418-7660-7(X), 9781441876607, BriAudCD Unabrid) Brilliance Audio.

***Adventures of Huckleberry Finn.** unabr. ed. Mark Twain. Read by Don Hagen. (Running Time: 11 hrs.). (ENG.). 2010. 12.98 (978-1-59659-672-6(4), GildAudio) Pub: Gildan Media. Dist(s): HachBkGrp

Adventures of Huckleberry Finn, unabr. ed. Mark Twain. Read by Grover Gardner. 6 cass. (Running Time: 9 hrs.). 1965. 24.95 (978-1-55685-353-1(X)) Audio Bk Con.
Twain's classic tale of a young boy & his runaway-slave friend is still one of the best novels about human nature ever written. Readers will delight in the many wonderful episodes including a deadly feud, the comic grumblings of the Duke & the King, & Tom Sawyer's grand scheme to release Jim from captivity.

Adventures of Huckleberry Finn. unabr. ed. Mark Twain. Read by Patrick Fraley. 6 CDs. (Running Time: 11 hrs. 20 mins.). (gr. 6-12). 1999. 29.95 (978-1-57270-111-3(0), F71111u) Pub: Audio Partners. Dist(s): PerseuPGW
Huck, in flight from his father & Jim, in flight from slavery, float down the Mississippi. They survive a crash with a steamboat, betrayal by rogues & the final threat from the bourgeoisie.

Adventures of Huckleberry Finn. unabr. ed. Mark Twain. Narrated by Patrick Fraley. (Running Time: 40800 sec.). (ENG.). 2008. audio compact disk 29.95 (978-1-60283-429-3(6)) Pub: AudioGO. Dist(s): Perseus Dist

Adventures of Huckleberry Finn. unabr. ed. Mark Twain. 3 vols. (Running Time: 4 hrs.). Dramatization. 2003. audio compact disk 39.95 (978-0-563-49688-5(6), BBCD 034) BBC Worldwide.

Adventures of Huckleberry Finn. unabr. ed. Mark Twain. Read by Tom Parker. 7 cass. (Running Time: 10 hrs.). 2003. 49.95 (978-0-7861-0383-6(3), 1336) Blckstn Audio.
Huck Finn was a homeless rebel who loved freedom more than respectability. He wasn't above lying & stealing, but he faces a battle with his conscience when he meets up with a runaway slave named Jim. Jim is trying to escape to a free state in the North while his owner wants to sell him to a slave trader down-river. Huck knows that helping Jim will bring trouble, but can he turn in a man who only wants to be free?.

Adventures of Huckleberry Finn. unabr. ed. Mark Twain. Read by Tom Parker. 7 cass. (Running Time: 34200 sec.). 2005. 23.95

(978-0-7861-3460-1(7), E1336); audio compact disk 23.95 (978-0-7861-8037-0(4), ZE1336); audio compact disk 24.95 (978-0-7861-9615-9(7), 1336) Blckstn Audio.

Adventures of Huckleberry Finn. unabr. ed. Mark Twain. Read by Tim Behrens. 8 cass. (Running Time: 11 hrs. 15 min.). Dramatization. (J). 1990. 49.95 (978-1-55686-348-6(9), 102578) Books in Motion.
Published in 1885, this sequel to Tom Sawyer tells a purely entrancing tale of two mischievous boys who travel down the Mississippi on a make-shift raft during the old river boat days, taking us through some wild adventures.

Adventures of Huckleberry Finn. unabr. ed. Mark Twain. Read by Jack Lemmon. 7 CDs. (Running Time: 10 hrs. 30 mins.). 2001. audio compact disk Books on Tape.
Recounts the adventures of a boy growing up in the half-settled Missouri of the 1840s. Hucks's father was an irresponsible drunk & Huck was left to shift for himself at an early age. He lived by his wits & set in motion projects of great imagination.

Adventures of Huckleberry Finn. unabr. ed. Mark Twain. Read by Michael Prichard. 7 cass. (Running Time: 10 hrs.). 2001. 29.95 (978-0-7366-6796-8(2)) Books on Tape.
Recounts the adventures of a young boy & an escaped slave as they travel down the Mississippi River on a raft.

Adventures of Huckleberry Finn. unabr. ed. Mark Twain. 8 cass. (Running Time: 12 hrs.). 2002. 64.00 (978-0-7366-8639-6(8)) Books on Tape.
Huck is sick and tired of the "civilizing" influence of the Widow Douglas, not to mention regular beatings from his father, a drunk. So he and Jim, a runaway slave, set off on their great adventure: floating to freedom on a Mississippi raft. The Mississippi of Twain's day was another frontier: a place to lose your identity, to start over, to make your fortune.

Adventures of Huckleberry Finn. unabr. ed. Mark Twain. 10 CDs. (Running Time: 12 hrs.). 2002. audio compact disk 80.00 (978-0-7366-8640-2(1)) Books on Tape.
Huckleberry Finn and runaway slave Jim light out on the Mississippi River, seeking freedom.

Adventures of Huckleberry Finn. unabr. ed. Mark Twain. Read by Dick Hill. 8 cass. (Running Time: 11 hrs.). 2002. 29.95 (978-1-59086-150-9(7), 1590861507, BAU) Brilliance Audio.
When we first met "the pariah of the village . . .the son of the drunkard" in "The Adventures of Tom Sawyer", Tom was "under strict orders not to play with him", so he played with him every time he got the chance. Twain took his most outrageous and outcast character (and perhaps the one he loved the most), Huckleberry Finn, from the book and wrote his own Adventures. This giant work, in addition to entertaining boys and girls for generations, has defined the first-person novel in America, and continues to demand study, inspire reverence and stir controversy in our time.

Adventures of Huckleberry Finn. unabr. ed. Mark Twain. Read by Dick Hill & Susie Breck. (Running Time: 11 hrs.). 2004. 39.25 (978-1-59335-992-8(6), 1593359926, Brlnc Audio MP3 Lib) Brilliance Audio.

Adventures of Huckleberry Finn. unabr. ed. Mark Twain. Read by Dick Hill. (Running Time: 11 hrs.). 2004. 39.25 (978-1-59710-005-2(6), 1597100056, BADLE); 24.95 (978-1-59710-004-5(8), 1597100048, BAD) Brilliance Audio.

Adventures of Huckleberry Finn. unabr. ed. Mark Twain. Read by Thomas Becker. (YA). 2006. 64.99 (978-1-59895-169-1(6)) Find a World.

Adventures of Huckleberry Finn. unabr. ed. Mark Twain. Read by Tom Parker. 7 cass. (J). 1999. 49.95 (FS9-31974) Highsmith.

Adventures of Huckleberry Finn. unabr. ed. Mark Twain. 2 cass. (Read-along Ser.). bk. 34.95 Set, incl. learner's guide & exercises. (S23927) J Norton Pubs.

Adventures of Huckleberry Finn. unabr. ed. Mark Twain. Read by Garrick Hagon. 9 CDs. (Running Time: 41040 sec.). 2006. audio compact disk 59.98 (978-962-634-360-9(5), Naxos AudioBooks) Naxos.

Adventures of Huckleberry Finn. unabr. ed. Mark Twain. Narrated by Norman Dietz. 10 CDs. (Running Time: 11.75 hrs.). audio compact disk 11.25 (978-1-4193-2355-3(5)) Recorded Bks.

Adventures of Huckleberry Finn. unabr. ed. Mark Twain. Narrated by Norman Dietz. 8 cass. (Running Time: 11 hrs. 45 min.). 2003. audio compact disk 97.00 Recorded Bks.

Adventures of Huckleberry Finn, unabr. ed. Mark Twain. Narrated by Norman Dietz. 8 cass. (Running Time: 11 hrs. 45 mins.). (gr. 8). 1999. 72.00 (978-1-55690-001-3(5), 91327E7) Recorded Bks.
Huck Finn & the runaway, Jim, take off down the Mississippi on a raft.

Adventures of Huckleberry Finn. unabr. ed. Mark Twain. 9 CDs. (Running Time: 10 hrs. 19 mins.). (YA). (gr. 7 up). 2002. audio compact disk 88.00 (978-1-58472-160-4(X), Commuters Library) Sound Room.

Adventures of Huckleberry Finn. unabr. ed. Mark Twain. Read by Thomas Becker. 8 cds. (Running Time: 10 hrs 19 mins). (YA). 2002. pap. bk. (978-1-58472-261-8(4), In Aud) Sound Room.
Huck Finn, an orphan, who lives a life of independence, goes from one adventure to another in this greatest of American novels.

Adventures of Huckleberry Finn. unabr. ed. Mark Twain. Read by Thomas Becker. 8 cds. (Running Time: 8 hrs 10 mins). (YA). 2002. audio compact disk 39.95 (978-1-58472-259-5(2), 076, In Aud) Pub: Sound Room. Dist(s): Baker Taylor
Twain's story of an orphan is often cited as one of the best American novels.

Adventures of Huckleberry Finn. unabr. ed. Mark Twain. Narrated by William Dufris. (Running Time: 10 hrs. 0 mins. 0 sec.). (Unabridged Classics in Audio Ser.). (ENG.). 2008. audio compact disk 34.99 (978-1-4001-0631-8(1)); audio compact disk 69.99 (978-1-4001-3631-5(8)); audio compact disk 24.99 (978-1-4001-5631-3(9)) Pub: Tantor Media. Dist(s): IngramPubServ

Adventures of Huckleberry Finn. unabr. collector's ed. Mark Twain. Read by Michael Prichard. 7 cass. (Running Time: 10 hrs. 30 min.). (J). 1977. 56.00 (978-0-7366-0050-7(7), 1062) Books on Tape.
Recounts the adventures of a boy growing up in the half-settled Missouri of the 1840s. Hucks's father was an irresponsible drunk & Huck was left to shift for himself at an early age. He lived by his wits & set in motion projects of great imagination.

Adventures of Huckleberry Finn, Set. abr. ed. Mark Twain. Read by Ed Begley. 2 cass. (Running Time: 3 hrs.). 1992. 17.00 (978-1-55994-630-8(X), DCN 2038) HarperCollins Pubs.

Adventures of Huckleberry Finn, Vol. 1. abr. ed. Mark Twain. Read by Hiram Sherman. (Running Time: 34 min.). 10.95 (978-0-8045-1008-0(3), SAC 1008) Spoken Arts.
Includes "Civilizing Huck," "The Boys Escape Jim," "A Good Goin'-Over," & "The Judge".

Adventures of Huckleberry Finn, Vol. 2. abr. ed. Mark Twain. Read by Hiram Sherman. (Running Time: 54 min.). 10.95 (978-0-8045-1009-7(1), SAC 1009) Spoken Arts.
Includes "Slow Navigation," "Escaping from the Wreck," "A General Good Time," & "Huck Loses the Raft".

Adventures of Huckleberry Finn: An A+ Audio Study Guide. unabr. ed. Mark Twain. Read by John O'Connell. (Running Time: 1 hr.). (ENG.). 2006. 5.98 (978-1-59483-550-6(0)) Pub: Hachet Audio. Dist(s): HachBkGrp

Adventures of Huckleberry Finn: An A+ Audio Study Guide. unabr. ed. Mark Twain. Read by John O'Connell. (Running Time: 1 hr.). (ENG.). 2009. 14.98 (978-1-60788-261-9(2)) Pub: Hachet Audio. Dist(s): HachBkGrp

Adventures of Huckleberry Finn: Tom Sawyer's Comrade. Mark Twain. Illus. by Edward Kemble. Narrated by Dick Hill. Prod. by Ralph LaBarge. (ENG.). (YA). 2007. DVD 14.95 (978-0-9798626-0-1(4)) Alpha DVD.

Adventures of Huckleberry Finn Audiobook. Mark Twain. Read by Christopher Graybill. 6 cass. 2005. 14.95 (978-1-56585-986-9(3)); audio compact disk 19.95 (978-1-59803-002-0(7)) Teaching Co.

Adventures of Huckleberry Finn, Unabridged: Narrated by Richard Henzel. Ed. by Richard Henzel. Narrated by Richard Henzel. (ENG.). 2008. 29.99 (978-0-9747237-5-4(4)) R Henzel.

Adventures of King Midas. unabr. ed. Lynne Reid Banks. Read by Lynne Reid Banks. 3 cass. (Running Time: 2 hrs. 53 min.). (J). (gr. 3-5). 1995. pap. bk. 28.98 Set. (978-0-8072-7516-0(6), Listening Lib); 23.98 Set. (978-0-8072-7515-3(8), YA869CX, Listening Lib) Random Audio Pubg.

Adventures of Lana Ladybug in Europe. Lynn Cagney & Scott May. Perf. by Scott May & Cathy Braaten. 1 CD. (Running Time: 32 min.). (Adventures of Lana Ladybug Ser.: Vol. 1). (J). 1999. audio compact disk 14.98 (978-1-893967-02-1(6), EKCD5006, Emphasis on Kids) Emphasis Ent.
Follow Lana as she travels through Europe. At each of her stops, Lana learns a little history & folklore from a local resident as told in story & song.

Adventures of Lana Ladybug in Europe. Lynn Cagney & Scott May. Read by Scott May. Perf. by Cathy Braaten. 1 cass. (Running Time: 32 min.). (Adventures of Lana Ladybug Ser.: Vol. 1). (J). (gr. k-3). 1999. 9.98 (978-1-893967-03-8(4), EKCT5006, Emphasis on Kids) Emphasis Ent.

Adventures of Little David. Baldwin Betzer. 1 cass. (J). (gr. 1-5). 1992. (978-1-882491-00-1(9)) Paceset Pub Grp.
Children's Bible stories.

Adventures of Little Prince. unabr. ed. 1 cass. (Running Time: 20 min.). Dramatization. (Magic Looking Glass Ser.). (J). (gr. 2-6). 1989. 9.95 (978-0-7810-0029-1(7), NIM-CW-128-1-C) NIMCO.
A French folk story.

Adventures of Little Proto: A Musical Dinosaur Story. unabr. ed. Read by Odds Bodkin Storytelling Library Staff. 1 cass. (Running Time: 52 mins.). Dramatization. (Odds Bodkin Musical Story Collection). (ps-3). 2003. bk. 9.95 (978-1-882412-13-6(3)) Pub: Rivertree. Dist(s): Penton Overseas
It is 67 million years ago. Little Proto is on his first of many adventures, to Magnolia Island, where an old Triceratops lives. A heart-warming story with four original songs & exciting dinosaur sound effects.

Adventures of Maisie: The Efficiency Expert & Blondes in Politics. unabr. ed. Perf. by Ann Sothern. 1 cass. (Running Time: 1 hr.). 2001. 6.98 (1941) Radio Spirits.

Adventures of Makui. Amanda Vanderdoes & T. J. Ratcliffe, Jr. Read by Amanda Vanderdoes & T. J. Ratcliffe, Jr. 1 CD. (Running Time: 20 min.). (J). (gr. 2-5). 1999. pap. bk. 12.95 (978-1-928632-17-7(3)) Writers Mrktpl.
A young girl tries to save her village in the rainforest.

Adventures of Makui. l.t. ed. Amanda Vanderdoes & T. J. Ratcliffe, Jr. Read by Amanda Vanderdoes & T. J. Ratcliffe, Jr. 1 cass. (Running Time: 20 min.). (J). (gr. k-5). 1999. pap. bk. 8.95 (978-1-928632-18-4(1)) Writers Mrktpl.

***Adventures of Marco Polo, Volume 1.** RadioArchives.com. (Running Time: 360). (ENG.). 2010. audio compact disk 17.98 (978-1-61081-179-8(8)) Radio Arch.

***Adventures of Marco Polo, Volume 2.** RadioArchives.com. (Running Time: 300). (ENG.). 2010. audio compact disk 17.98 (978-1-61081-181-1(X)) Radio Arch.

Adventures of Minnie & Max Series. Patricia Reilly Giff. Read by Dana Lubotsky. Illus. by Lynne W. Cravath. 4 cass. (Running Time: 3 hrs. 6 mins.). (J). (gr. 4-6). 2000. 34.95 (978-0-87499-708-8(9)) Live Oak Media.
Includes: "Mary Moon Is Missing' & "Kidnap at the Catfish Cafe".

Adventures of Na Uh & Na Huh: The Super Rockin' Rollin' Roller Coaster Ride & No Ordinary Sandwich. unabr. ed. Jerry Piasecki. Perf. by Chenille Sister & Chenille Sisters. Illus. by Kevin Skinner. Composed by Wendy Rollin. Contrib. by Brian Brill. 1 cass. (Running Time: 20 min.). Dramatization. (J). (gr. k-3). 1997. pap. bk. 12.00 (978-0-9659936-0-9(4), CTR-02) Cantoo Recs.

Adventures of Nero Wolfe. Perf. by Francis X. Bushman, Jr. & Elliott Lewis. 10 CDs. (Running Time: 10 hrs.). 2002. audio compact disk 39.98 (47022); 34.98 (47024) Radio Spirits.
Though he only took clients grudgingly and never left his office, radio's most eccentric detective could always crack the case. And even though it was his partner, Archive Goodwin who did all the legwork, it was nero wolfe, the "gargantuan gourmet" who put the pieces together.

Adventures of Nero Wolfe: Case of the Calculated Risk & Case of The Phantom Fingers. unabr. ed. Perf. by Sydney Greenstreet. 1 cass. (Running Time: 1 hr.). 2001. 6.98 (1882) Radio Spirits.

Adventures of Nero Wolfe: Case of the Dear Dead Lady & Case of the Vanishing Shells. unabr. ed. Perf. by Sydney Greenstreet. 1 cass. (Running Time: 1 hr.). 2001. 6.98 (2471) Radio Spirits.

Adventures Of Nero Wolfe: Impolite Corpse & The Girl Who Cried Wolf. unabr. ed. Perf. by Sydney Greenstreet. 1 cass. (Running Time: 1 hr.). 2001. 6.98 (1519) Radio Spirits.

Adventures of Nero Wolfe: Party for Death & The Case of the Benevolent Medic. unabr. ed. Perf. by Sydney Greenstreet. 1 cass. (Running Time: 1 hr.). 2001. 6.98 (1942) Radio Spirits.

Adventures of Nero Wolfe: Shakespeare & The Case of the Hasty Will. unabr. ed. Perf. by Sydney Greenstreet & Francis X. Bushman, Jr. 1 cass,. (Running Time: 1 hr.). 2001. 6.98 (1921) Radio Spirits.

Adventures of Nero Wolfe: Stamped for Murder & The Case of Room 304. unabr. ed. Perf. by Sydney Greenstreet. 1 cass. (Running Time: 1 hr.). 2001. 6.98 (1842) Radio Spirits.

Adventures of Nero Wolfe: The Case of the Careless Cleaner & The Case of the Friendly Rabbit. unabr. ed. Perf. by Sydney Greenstreet. 1 cass. (Running Time: 1 hr.). 2001. 6.98 (2452) Radio Spirits.

Adventures of Nero Wolfe: The Disappearing Diamonds & The Midnight Ride. unabr. ed. Perf. by Sydney Greenstreet. 1 cass. (Running Time: 1 hr.). 2001. 6.98 (1728) Radio Spirits.

Adventures of Nero Wolfe: The Final Page & The Tell Tale Ribbon. unabr. ed. Perf. by Sydney Greenstreet. 1 cass. (Running Time: 1 hr.). 2001. 6.98 (1729) Radio Spirits.

Adventures of Nikko No-Tail. unabr. ed. Chief Little Summer. Contrib. by Warm Night Rain. 1 CD. (Nikko No-Tail - The Adventures of). (J). (gr. k-4). 1999. audio compact disk 11.95 CD. (978-1-880440-20-9(2)) Piqua Pr.
A kitten born without a tail teaches a little boy & girl about growing up.

Adventures of Odysseus. Benedict Flynn. Read by Benjamin Soames. (Running Time: 2 hrs. 30 mins.). 2001. 20.95 (978-1-60083-564-3(3)) Iofy Corp.

Adventures of Odysseus. Benedict Flynn. Read by Benjamin Soames. 2 cass. (Running Time: 2 hrs. 26 mins.). (YA). 1997. 13.98 (978-962-634-614-3(0), NA211414, Naxos AudioBooks) Naxos.
The story of what happened after the Trojan War when Odysseus, the most cunning of all Greek heroes, left Troy and made his way back home.

Adventures of Odysseus. Hugh Lupton et al. (Running Time: 3 mins. 19 sec.). (ENG., (J). 2007. audio compact disk 19.99 (978-1-84686-099-7(7)) BarefootBksMA.

Adventures of Odysseus. unabr. ed. Benedict Flynn. Read by Benjamin Soames. 2 CDs. (Running Time: 2 hrs. 26 mins.). (J). 1997. audio compact disk 17.98 (978-962-634-114-8(9), NA211412, Naxos AudioBooks) Naxos.

Adventures of Odysseus: The Greatest Hero of Them All. unabr. ed. Tony Robinson & Richard Curtis. Read by Tony Robinson. 2 cass. (Running Time: 2 hrs.). 2001. 18.95 (CCA3121, Chivers Child Audio) AudioGO.

Adventures of Odysseus & the Tale of Troy. Padraic Colum. Read by Sean Pratt. (Playaway Young Adult Ser.). 2008. 79.99 (978-1-60640-838-4(0)) Find a World.

Adventures of Odysseus & the Tale of Troy. Padraic Colum. Narrated by Sean Pratt. (Running Time: 22740 sec.). (Unabridged Classics in MP3 Ser.). (ENG.). (J). 2008. audio compact disk 24.00 (978-1-58472-530-5(3), In Aud) Sound Room.

Adventures of Old Bear. Clair LeBear. Perf. by Clair LeBear. 1 CD. (Running Time: 1 hr.). (J). 2001. audio compact disk 14.95 (978-0-9706321-8-0(5), SBR001) Cozy Cottage.
Stories & music for children featuring 3 stories of Old Bear Adventures.

Adventures of Ozzie & Harriet. collector's ed. Perf. by Ozzie Nelson et al. 1 DVD. (Running Time: 3 hrs.). (TV from Yesteryear Ser.). 2001. bk. 9.98 (7801) Radio Spirits.
Contains three classic television shows and three complete old time radio shows.

Adventures of Peter Cottontail, Set. Thornton W. Burgess. 1 cass. (J). 1996. bk. & pap. bk. 5.95 (29101-4) Dover.

Adventures of Peter Cottontail & The Adventures of Buster Bear. unabr. ed. Thornton W. Burgess. Read by Flo Gibson. 2 cass. (Running Time: 2 hrs. 9 mins.). (J). (gr. k-2). 2000. 20.95 Audio Bk Con.
Escapades of the animal inhabitants of Green Forest.

Adventures of Philip Marlowe. Radio Spirits Publishing Staff. (Running Time: 9 hrs.). 2002. 39.98 (978-1-57019-192-3(1)) Radio Spirits.

Adventures of Philip Marlowe, Vol. 1. collector's ed. Raymond Chandler. Perf. by Gerald Mohr. 6 cass. (Running Time: 9 hrs.). 1999. bk. 34.98 (4189) Radio Spirits.
Those who travel crime's road end up in the gutter, in prison or an early grave, thanks to the hard-boiled detective work of Philip Marlowe (a real blood, guts and thunder kind of tough detective).

Adventures of Philip Marlowe, Vol. 2. collector's ed. Raymond Chandler. Perf. by Gerald Mohr. 6 cass. (Running Time: 9 hrs.). 2000. bk. 34.98 (4685) Radio Spirits.

Adventures of Philip Marlowe: Collector's Item & The White Carnation. unabr. ed. Perf. by Gerald Mohr. 1 cass. (Running Time: 1 hr.). 2001. 6.98 (1862) Radio Spirits.

Adventures of Philip Marlowe: Covered Bridge & The Bid for Freedom. unabr. ed. Perf. by Gerald Mohr. 1 cass. (Running Time: 1 hr.). 2001. 6.98 (1951) Radio Spirits.

Adventures of Philip Marlowe: Tale of the Mermaid & Monkey's Uncle. unabr. ed. Perf. by Gerald Mohr. 1 cass. (Running Time: 1 hr.). 2001. 6.98 (2002) Radio Spirits.

Adventures of Philip Marlowe: The Birds on the Wing & The Kid on the Corner. unabr. ed. Perf. by Gerald Mohr. 1 cass. (Running Time: 1 hr.). 2001. 6.98 (2111) Radio Spirits.

Adventures of Philip Marlowe: The Dark Tunnel & The Anniversary Gift. unabr. ed. Perf. by Gerald Mohr. 1 cass. (Running Time: 1 hr.). 2001. 6.98 (1843) Radio Spirits.

Adventures of Philip Marlowe: The Dear, Dead Days & Life Can Be Murder. unabr. ed. Perf. by Gerald Mohr. 1 cass. (Running Time: 1 hr.). 2001. 6.98 (2272) Radio Spirits.

Adventures of Philip Marlowe: The Deep Shadow & The Face to Forget. unabr. ed. Perf. by Gerald Mohr. 1 cass. (Running Time: 1 hr.). 2001. 6.98 (1922) Radio Spirits.

Adventures of Philip Marlowe: The Headless Peacock & the August Lion. unabr. ed. Perf. by Gerald Mohr. 1 cass. (Running Time: 1 hr.). 2001. 6.98 (1570) Radio Spirits.

Adventures of Philip Marlowe: The Key Man & The Dude from Manhattan. unabr. ed. Perf. by Gerald Mohr. 1 cass. (Running Time: 1 hr.). 2001. 6.98 (2411) Radio Spirits.

Adventures of Philip Marlowe: The Rustin Hickory & The Long Arm. unabr. ed. Perf. by Gerald Mohr. 1 cass. (Running Time: 1 hr.). 2001. 6.98 (1883) Radio Spirits.

Adventures of Philip Marlowe: The Sword of Sabu & The Burn's Rush. unabr. ed. Perf. by Gerald Mohr. 1 cass. (Running Time: 1 hr.). 2001. 6.98 (1830) Radio Spirits.

***Adventures of Philip Marlowe, Volume 1.** RadioArchives.com. (Running Time: 600). (ENG.). 2004. audio compact disk 29.98 (978-1-61081-029-6(5)) Radio Arch.

Adventures of Phokey the Sea Otter: Based on a True Story. Marianne Riedman. Marianne Riedman. 1 cass. (Running Time: 63 min.). (ENG.). (J). (ps-7). 1996. 9.95 (978-0-9648600-1-8(5)) Sequoyah Pub.
Also includes music, sound effects & sea otter sounds rarely heard before, as well as a "Fun Facts" section about sea otters at end of tape. The story is based on true events of a young sea otter released at an island off Southern California, his many adventures with the island seals & sea lions, & his amazing long-distance journeys along the California coast.

Adventures of Pinocchio. unabr. ed. Carlo Collodi. Read by Marvin Miller. 5 cass. (J). 29.75 (D-303); 6.95 rental. Audio Bk.
Original story of the puppet who becomes a live boy.

Adventures of Pinocchio. unabr. ed. Carlo Collodi. Read by Donna Collette. 3 cass. (Running Time: 4 hrs. 30 min.). (J). 1985. 21.00 (C-25) Jimcin Record.
Classic tale of the puppet who became a boy.

Adventures of Red Cloud. 2 CDs. (Running Time: 1 hr. 40 mins.). Dramatization. 2004. audio compact disk 24.95 (978-0-9660392-9-0(7)) Pub: Radio Repertory. Dist(s): Timberwolf Pr
Hurls us into a web of intrigue swirling around an ancient temple, a mysterious ring - and a legend that offers the chance for someone to actually become a god.

Adventures of Red Ryder. collector's ed. Created by Fred Harman. 6 cass. (Running Time: 9 hrs.). (J). 2000. bk. 34.98 (4555) Radio Spirits.
18 western adventures.

Adventures of Robin Hood. Benedict Flynn. Read by Sean Bean. 2 cass. (Running Time: 2 hrs. 30 mins.). (J). 2000. 13.98 (978-962-634-692-1(2), NA219114) Naxos.
In this bright re-telling, Robin Hood steals from the rich and gives to the poor, faces and overcomes the Sheriff of Nottingham, is supported by Little John & Alan 'a' Bales and meets Maid Marian.

Adventures of Robin Hood. Howard Pyle. Read by David Case. (Running Time: 42540 sec.). (ENG.). 2004. audio compact disk 22.99 (978-1-4001-5103-5(1)) Pub: Tantor Media. Dist(s): IngramPubServ

Adventures of Robin Hood. Howard Pyle. Read by David Case. (ENG.). 2005. audio compact disk 79.99 (978-1-4001-3103-7(0)) Pub: Tantor Media. Dist(s): IngramPubServ

Adventures of Robin Hood. unabr. ed. Benedict Flynn. Read by John McAndrew. 2 CDs. (Running Time: 3 hrs.). (J). 2000. audio compact disk 17.98 (978-962-634-192-6(0), NA219212, Naxos AudioBooks) Naxos.

Adventures of Robin Hood, unabr. ed. E. Charles Vivian. Narrated by Dan Elsea. 3 cass. (Running Time: 3 hrs. 30 mins.). (gr. 6 up). 1980. 26.00 (978-1-55690-003-7(1), 80160E7) Recorded Bks.
The legendary outlaw & his band of followers outwit the dastardly Sheriff of Nottingham in a score of exploits.

Adventures of Robin Hood, Set. unabr. ed. Sbc109 Cae. 4 cass., bklet. (Running Time: 6 hrs.). Incl. Adventures of Robin Hood: How Robin Became an Outlaw. (YA). (SBC 109); Adventures of Robin Hood: Robin & His Merry Men. (YA). (SBC 109); Adventures of Robin Hood: Robin's Adventures with Little John. (YA). (SBC 109); Adventures of Robin Hood: The Outlaw Band of Sherwood Forest. (YA). (SBC 109); (YA). 1985. 29.95 (978-0-89845-040-8(3), SBC 109) HarperCollins Pubs.

Adventures of Robin Hood, Set unabr. ed. Benedict Flynn. Read by Sean Bean. 2 CD. (Running Time: 2 hr. 30 min.). (J). 2000. audio compact disk 15.98 (NA219112) Naxos.
In this bright re-telling, Robin Hood steals from the rich & gives to the poor, faces & overcomes the Sheriff of Nottingham, is supported by Little John & Alan 'a' Bales, & meets Maid Marian.

Adventures of Robin Hood: How Robin Became an Outlaw see Adventures of Robin Hood

Adventures of Robin Hood: Robin & His Merry Men see Adventures of Robin Hood

Adventures of Robin Hood: Robin's Adventures with Little John see Adventures of Robin Hood

Adventures of Robin Hood: The Outlaw Band of Sherwood Forest see Adventures of Robin Hood

***Adventures of Roscoe Sharpei, Dog Detective: An Audio Film Noir in XIV Acts.** Based on a story by Brian Swartz. (ENG.). 2009. 4.49 (978-0-9725911-9-5(2)) NE Key.

Adventures of Rowdy Raccoon. (J). 2006. per. 5.99 (978-0-9766823-8-7(9)) Pub: Sa Creek. Dist(s): STL Dist NA

Adventures of Sailor Steve Costigan. Violet Crown Radio Players. Based on a story by Robert E. Howard. 2007. audio compact disk 12.99 (978-1-934814-03-1(2)) Red Planet Au.

Adventures of Sally. unabr. ed. P. G. Wodehouse. Read by Frederick Davidson. 6 cass. (Running Time: 8 hrs. 30 mins.). 1998. 44.95 (978-0-7861-1281-4(6), 2176) Blckstn Audio.
Pretty, impecunious Sally Nicholas never dreamed a fortune could prove a disadvantage, until she becomes an heiress & watches in bewilderment as her orderly existence goes haywire. Coping first with her brother's wild theatrical ambitions, then with the defection of her fiance & his immediate replacement by a much more appropriate but strangely unattractive suitor, Sally finds that life in New York is becoming altogether too complicated & a trip to England only makes the whole situation worse.

Adventures of Sally. unabr. ed. P. G. Wodehouse. Read by Frederick Davidson. (Running Time: 27000 sec.). 2007. audio compact disk 29.95 (978-0-7861-6158-4(2)); audio compact disk 55.00 (978-0-7861-6157-7(4)) Blckstn Audio.

Adventures of Sam Spade. Radio Spirits Publishing Staff. Read by Howard Duff. 2005. audio compact disk 9.98 (978-1-57019-808-3(X)) Radio Spirits.

Adventures of Sam Spade: Dick Foley Caper & Farmer's Daughter Caper. unabr. ed. Perf. by Howard Duff. 1 cass. (Running Time: 1 hr.). 2001. 6.98 (1844) Radio Spirits.

Adventures of Sam Spade: The Wheel of Life Caper & The Missing News-Hawk Caper. unabr. ed. Perf. by Howard Duff. 1 cass. (Running Time: 1 hr.). 2001. 6.98 (1731) Radio Spirits.

***Adventures of Sexton Blake: Full-Cast BBC Radio Dramatization.** Dirk Maggs. Narrated by Simon Jones & June Whitfield. (Running Time: 2 hrs. 0 mins. 0 sec.). (ENG.). 2010. audio compact disk 24.95 (978-1-4084-1054-7(0)) Pub: AudioGO. Dist(s): Perseus Dist

Adventures of Shedoobee: Searching for the Good Life. Shanta Nurullah. Read by Shanta Nurullah. 1 cass. (Running Time: 29 mins.). (J). (ps-6). 1988. 10.00 (978-0-9623929-0-0(1), AS-1) Storywiz.
A recording of lively music, rhythmic poetry & stories through which the character of Shedoobee learns about health, nutrition, friendship, staying clean of drugs & loving herself.

Adventures of Sherlock Holmes see Ten All Time Favorite Stories

Adventures of Sherlock Holmes see Aventures de Sherlock Holmes

Adventures of Sherlock Holmes see Aventuras de Sherlock Holmes

Adventures of Sherlock Holmes. Arthur Conan Doyle. Read by Carlos Zambrano. (Running Time: 3 hrs.). 2002. 16.95 (978-1-60083-192-8(3), Audiofy Corp) Iofy Corp.

Adventures of Sherlock Holmes. Arthur Conan Doyle. Narrated by Walter Covell. (Running Time: 10 hrs. 30 mins.). 2006. 46.95 (978-1-59912-136-9(0)) Iofy Corp.

Adventures of Sherlock Holmes. Ed. by Arthur Conan Doyle. Narrated by Basil Rathbone. 2 cass. (Running Time: 2 hrs. 44 mins.). Incl. Red-Headed League. Arthur Conan Doyle. (813); Scandal in Bohemia. Arthur Conan Doyle. (813); Speckled Band. (813); 12.95 (978-0-89926-125-6(6), 813) Audio Bk.
Three classic Holmes adventures.

Adventures of Sherlock Holmes. Perf. by Basil Rathbone & Nigel Bruce. Ed. by Arthur Conan Doyle. 1 cass. (Running Time: 60 mins.). Incl. Great Gondolfo. (MM-7060); Scandal in Bohemia. Arthur Conan Doyle. (MM-7060); 7.95 (MM-7060) Natl Recrd Co.

Adventures of Sherlock Holmes, abr. ed. Arthur Conan Doyle. Read by John Whitaker. 4 cass. (Running Time: 6 hrs.). (Great Mysteries - Louis L'Amour Ser.). 2000. 12.99 (978-1-57815-157-8(0), 4406, Media Bks Audio) Media Bks NJ.

Adventures of Sherlock Holmes. abr. ed. Read by Edward Hardwicke. 1 cass. 1994. 12.00 (978-1-878427-38-0(5), XC422) Cimino Pub Grp.
Contains: "The Adventure of the Empty House," "The Adventure of the Devil's Foot," "The Adventure of the Abby Grange".

Adventures of Sherlock Holmes, abr. ed. Read by St. Charles Players. Ed. by Arthur Conan Doyle. 4 cass. (Running Time: 240 mins.). Dramatization. (National Public Radio Ser.). 1998. 24.95 (978-1-56994-503-2(9), Monterey SoundWorks) Monterey Media Inc.
Four of Doyle's original stories are presented: "The Adventure of the Engineer's Thumb," "The Adventure of the Copper Beeches," "The Adventure of the Noble Bachelor," & "The Adventure of the Beryl Coronet.".

Adventures of Sherlock Holmes. abr. ed. Read by John Whitaker. Ed. by Arthur Conan Doyle. 5 CDs. (Running Time: 6 hrs.). (Great Mystery Ser.). 2001. audio compact disk 14.99 (978-1-57815-530-9(4), Media Bks Audio) Media Bks NJ.

Adventures of Sherlock Holmes. abr. collector's ed. Edith Meiser. Perf. by John Stanley & Alfred Shirley. Characters created by Arthur Conan Doyle. Frwd. by Cy Harrice. 4 vols. (Running Time: 6 hrs.). (Smithsonian Historical Performances Ser.). 1998. bk. 24.98 (978-1-57019-034-6(8), OTR5016) Pub: Radio Spirits. Dist(s): AudioGO
John Stanley stars as Sherlock Holmes in 12 never-before-released episodes. Written by Edith Meiser and based on the stories by Sir Arthur Conan Doyle, these classic broadcasts were performed before a live theater audience.

Adventures of Sherlock Holmes. adpt. ed. Arthur Conan Doyle. (Bring the Classics to Life Ser.). (ENG.). 2008. audio compact disk 12.95 (978-1-55576-581-1(5)) EDCON Pubng.

Adventures of Sherlock Holmes. collector's ed. Edith Meiser. Perf. by John Stanley & Alfred Shirley. Characters created by Arthur Conan Doyle. Frwd. by Cy Harrice. 6 CDs. (Running Time: 6 hrs.). (Smithsonian Historical Performances Ser.). 1998. bk. 39.98 (978-1-57019-035-3(6), OTR5017) Pub: Radio Spirits. Dist(s): AudioGO

Adventures of Sherlock Holmes. unabr. ed. Read by John Brewster. Ed. by Arthur Conan Doyle. 2 cass. (Running Time: 1 hr. 40 mins.). (Cassette Bookshelf Ser.). 1985. 15.98 (978-0-8072-3415-0(X), CB 105CX, Listening Lib) Random Audio Pubg.
Features "The Speckled Band" & "The Red-Headed League".

Adventures of Sherlock Holmes. unabr. ed. Read by Walter Covell & Walter Zimmerman. Ed. by Arthur Conan Doyle. 7 cass. (Running Time: 10 hrs.). 39.00 incl. album. (C-43) Jimcin Record.
All twelve of the original Sherlock Holmes adventures: "A Scandal in Bohemia," "Red-Headed League," "A Case of Identity," "Boscombe Valley Mystery," "Five Orange Pips," "The Man with Twisted Lips," "Adventure of the Blue Carbuncle," "The Adventure of the Speckled Band," "Adventure of the Engineers Thumb," "The Adventure of the Noble Bachelor," "The Adventure of the Beryl Coronet," "Adventure of the Copper Beeches".

Adventures of Sherlock Holmes. unabr. ed. Arthur Conan Doyle. Read by Ralph Cosham. (Running Time: 9 hrs.). 2009. audio compact disk 32.95 (978-1-4417-1121-2(X)) Blckstn Audio.

Adventures of Sherlock Holmes. unabr. ed. Arthur Conan Doyle. Read by Ralph Cosham. (Running Time: 9 hrs. 0 mins.). 2009. 29.95 (978-1-4417-1122-9(8)); 59.95 (978-1-4417-1118-2(X)); audio compact disk 90.00 (978-1-4417-1119-9(8)) Blckstn Audio.

Adventures of Sherlock Holmes. unabr. ed. Arthur Conan Doyle. Read by Edward Hardwicke. 6 CDs. (Running Time: 5 hrs. 43 mins. 38 sec.). (Adventures of Sherlock Holmes Ser.). (ENG.). 2009. audio compact disk 31.95 (978-1-934997-22-2(6)) Pub: CSAWord. Dist(s): PerseuPGW

***Adventures of Sherlock Holmes.** unabr. ed. Arthur Conan Doyle. Narrated by Simon Prebble. (Running Time: 8 hrs. 30 mins. 0 sec.). (ENG.). 2010. 19.99 (978-1-4001-6517-9(2)); 15.99 (978-1-4001-8517-7(3)); audio compact disk 55.99 (978-1-4001-4517-1(1)); audio compact disk 27.99 (978-1-4001-1517-4(5)) Pub: Tantor Media. Dist(s): IngramPubServ

Adventures of Sherlock Holmes. unabr. ed. Ed. by Arthur Conan Doyle. 7 cass. 1999. 49.95 (FS9-34232) Highsmith.

Adventures of Sherlock Holmes. unabr. ed. Read by Richard Lancelyn Green. Ed. by Arthur Conan Doyle. 7 cass. (Running Time: 10 hrs.). 2001. 29.95 (978-0-7366-6801-9(2)) Books on Tape.
Contains twelve classic stories, including "A Scandal in Bohemia".

Adventures of Sherlock Holmes. unabr. ed. Read by Basil Rathbone. Ed. by Arthur Conan Doyle. 14 cass. 23.80 (E-401) Audio Bk.
Four complete unabridged stories of the greatest detective of all times.

Adventures of Sherlock Holmes. unabr. abr. ed. Arthur Conan Doyle. Read by Ben Kingsley. (Running Time: 16200 sec.). 2007. audio compact disk 24.00 (978-1-4332-0541-5(6)) Blckstn Audio.

Adventures of Sherlock Holmes. unabr. abr. ed. Arthur Conan Doyle. Read by Ben Kingsley. (Running Time: 16200 sec.). 2007. audio compact disk 19.95 (978-1-4332-0542-2(4)) Blckstn Audio.

Adventures of Sherlock Holmes. unabr. collector's ed. Read by Richard Lancelyn Green. Ed. by Arthur Conan Doyle. 7 cass. (Running Time: 10 hrs. 30 mins.). Incl. Adventure of the Blue Carbuncle. Arthur Conan Doyle. 1984. (1109); Beryl Coronet. 1984. (1109); Boscombe Valley Mystery. 1984. (1109); Case of Identity. 1984. (1109); Case of the Five Orange Pips. Arthur Conan Doyle. 1984. (1109); Copper Beeches. Jeremy Brett. 1984. (1109); Engineer's Thumb. 1984. (1109); Man with the Twisted Lip. Arthur Conan Doyle. 1984. (1109); Noble Bachelor. 1984. (1109); Red-Headed League. Arthur Conan Doyle. 1984. (1109); Scandal in Bohemia. Arthur Conan Doyle. 1984. (1109); Speckled Band. 1984. (1109); (Sherlock Holmes Ser.). (J). 1978. 56.00 (978-0-7366-0101-6(5), 1109) Books on Tape.
First published in 1891-92. Contains twelve classic stories, including "A Scandal in Bohemia".

Adventures of Sherlock Holmes, Episode 2. Read by Edward Hardwicke. Ed. by Arthur Conan Doyle. 1 cass. 12.00 (978-1-878427-42-7(3), XC436) Cimino Pub Grp.
"The Adventure of the Cardboard Box" tells the gruesome tale of a parcel containing two severed ears arriving at the home of a reclusive spinster who had no enemies in the world. Who sent them, for whom were they intended & why? "The Man with the Twisted Lip" tells about the disappearance of a city commuter. What did he do in the city, why did he disappear & what was his connection with an opium den? In "The Adventure of the Bruce-Partington Plans," a man's body is found on the rails of the underground with no ticket in his pocket. Why was he carrying top secret papers & why were three of them missing? Three exciting stories full of mystery & suspense with the inevitable Conan Doyle coup de theatre at the conclusion of each.

Adventures of Sherlock Holmes, No. 3. Ed. by Arthur Conan Doyle. 1 cass. 1998. 16.85 (978-1-901768-14-5(7)) Pub: CSA Telltapes GBR. Dist(s): Ulverscroft US

Adventures of Sherlock Holmes, Set. abr. ed. Perf. by St. Charles Players. Ed. by Arthur Conan Doyle. 4 cass. Dramatization. 1999. 24.95 (FS9-42731) Highsmith.

Adventures of Sherlock Holmes, Vol. 1. Arthur Conan Doyle. Read by Douglas Wilmer. 4 CDs. (ENG., 2002. audio compact disk (978-0-14-180388-3(6)) Pnguin Bks Ltd GBR.

Adventures of Sherlock Holmes, Vol. 2. unabr. ed. Arthur Conan Doyle. Narrated by Edward Hardwicke. 6 CDs. (Running Time: 5 hrs. 9 mins. 42 sec.). (Adventures of Sherlock Holmes Ser.). (ENG.). 2009. audio compact disk 31.95 (978-1-934997-34-5(X)) Pub: CSAWord. Dist(s): PerseuPGW

Adventures of Sherlock Holmes, Vol. 3. Arthur Conan Doyle. Narrated by Edward Hardwicke. (Running Time: 5 hrs. 0 mins. 0 sec.). (Adventures of Sherlock Holmes Ser.). (ENG.). 2009. audio compact disk 31.95 (978-1-934997-59-8(5)) Pub: CSAWord. Dist(s): PerseuPGW

Adventures of Sherlock Holmes, Vols. 1 - 6. unabr. ed. Arthur Conan Doyle. Read by David Timson. 18 CDs. bk. 107.98 (978-962-634-353-1(2), NAX35312) Naxos.

Adventures of Sherlock Holmes: A Sherlock Holmes Mystery. unabr. ed. Ed. by Arthur Conan Doyle. Narrated by Patrick Tull. 7 cass. (Running Time: 10 hrs. 30 mins.). (Sherlock Holmes Mystery Ser.). 1986. 60.00 (978-1-55690-004-4(X), 86950E7) Recorded Bks.
The Red-Headed League, A Scandal in Bohemia, A Case of Identity, The Speckled Band, The Five Orange Pips, The Man with the Twisted Lip, The Bascombe Valley Mystery, The Blue Carbuncle.

***Adventures of Sherlock Holmes: Bring the Classics to Life.** adpt. ed. Arthur Conan Doyle. (Bring the Classics to Life Ser.). 2008. pap. bk. 21.95 (978-1-55576-651-1(X)) EDCON Pubng.

Adventures of Sherlock Holmes: Episodes 1 & 2. unabr. ed. Arthur Conan Doyle. Read by Edward Hardwicke. 4 cass. (Running Time: 6 hrs.). 2002. (978-1-901768-63-3(5)) CSA Telltapes GBR.

Adventures of Sherlock Holmes: The Napoleon of Crime. Perf. by Orson Welles et al. 1 cass. (Running Time: 60 mins.). 7.95 (MM-3394) Natl Recrd Co.

Adventures of Sherlock Holmes Episode 1: The Adventure of the Empty House; The Adventure of the Devil's Foot; the Adventure of the Abbey Grange. unabr. ed. Arthur Conan Doyle. Read by Edward Hardwicke. 2 cass. (Running Time: 3 hrs.). 2002. (978-1-873859-22-3(8)) CSA Telltapes GBR.

Adventures of Sherlock Holmes Episode 2: The Adventure of the Bruce Partington Plans; The Man with the Twisted Lip; The Adventure of the Cardboard Box. Arthur Conan Doyle. Read by Edward Hardwicke. (Running Time: 3 hrs.). 2002. pap. bk. (978-1-873859-36-0(8)) CSA Telltapes GBR.

Adventures of Sherlock Holmes Episode 4: The Crooked Man; The Greek Interpreter; The Naval Treaty. Arthur Conan Doyle. Read by Edward Hardwicke. 2 cass. (Running Time: 3 hrs.). 2002. (978-1-901768-41-1(4)) CSA Telltapes GBR.

Adventures of Sherlock Holmes Vol. 2: A Scandal in Bohemia; the Five Orange Pips; the Adventure of the Engineer's Thumb; Silver Blaze. Arthur Conan Doyle. Read by David Timson. 3 cass. (Running Time: 3 hrs. 30 mins.). (Sherlock Holmes Stories). 1999. 17.98 (978-962-634-670-9(1), NA317014, Naxos AudioBooks) Naxos.
In this collection are four of the finest cases of Mr. Sherlock Holmes. What was the mystery of the engineer's thumb? What was behind the disappearance of the racehorse? Why did masked royalty walk up to see Holmes in Baker Street? These and other puzzles are solved by this bloodhound of a genius. Includes "The Engineer's Thumb," "The Silver Band," "The Scandal in Bohemia" and "The Five Orange Pips".

Adventures of Sherlock Holmes Vol. 2: A Scandal in Bohemia; the Five Orange Pips; the Adventure of the Engineer's Thumb; Silver Blaze. unabr. ed. Arthur Conan Doyle. Read by David Timson. 3 CDs. (Running Time: 3 hrs. 30 mins.). (YA). 1999. audio compact disk 22.98 (978-962-634-170-4(X), NA317012, Naxos AudioBooks) Naxos.

Adventures of Sherlock Holmes Vol. 3: The Man with the Twisted Lip; The Musgrave Ritual; The Adventure of the Cardboard Box; The Adventure of the Blue Carbuncle. Arthur Conan Doyle. Read by David Timson. 3 cass. (Running Time: 3 hrs. 30 mins.). (Sherlock Holmes Stories). 2000. 17.98 (978-962-634-691-4(4), NA319114, Naxos AudioBooks) Naxos.
Narrated by his faithful friend and admirer, Dr. Watson, the famous bloodhound of a genius, Sherlock Holmes sets out to solve four individual cases.

Adventures of Sherlock Holmes Vol. 3: The Man with the Twisted Lip; The Musgrave Ritual; The Adventure of the Cardboard Box; The Adventure of the Blue Carbuncle. unabr. ed. Arthur Conan Doyle. Read by David Timson. 3 CDs. (Running Time: 3 hrs. 30 mins.). (Sherlock Holmes Stories). 2000. audio compact disk 22.98 (978-962-634-191-9(2), NA319112, Naxos AudioBooks) Naxos.

Adventures of Sherlock Holmes Vol. 4: The Naval Treaty & Other Stories. Arthur Conan Doyle. Read by David Timson. 3 cass. (Running Time: 3 hrs. 31 mins.). (YA). (gr. 9 up). 2001. 17.98 (978-962-634-713-3(9), NA321314, Naxos AudioBooks) Naxos.
"A Case of Identity," "The Adventure of the Crooked Man," "The Naval Treaty" and "The Greek Interpreter" are all tales in which the appearances of those with whom Holmes must deal, in order to assist his various clients with their problems, are most deceiving.

Adventures of Sherlock Holmes Vol. 4: The Naval Treaty & Other Stories, Vol. 4. Arthur Conan Doyle. Read by David Timson. 3 CDs. (Running Time: 3 hrs. 31 mins.). (YA). (gr. 9 up). 2001. audio compact disk 22.98 (978-962-634-213-8(7), NA321312, Naxos AudioBooks) Naxos.

Adventures of Sherlock Holmes I: The Speckled Band; the Adventure of Copper Beeches; the Stock-Broker's Clerk; the Red-Headed League. Arthur Conan Doyle. Read by David Timson. 3 cass. (Running Time: 3 hrs. 30 mins.). (Sherlock Holmes Stories). (YA). 1998. 17.98 (978-962-634-652-5(3), NA315214, Naxos AudioBooks) Naxos.
Sherlock Holmes is a calculating, rational sleuth who also exudes an almost hypnotic sense of otherness. He is more than a mere detective, he is rather an enigmatic mix of folklore and science, with a knowledge and wisdom which seems mysterious and even, at times, unearthly.

Adventures of Sherlock Holmes I: The Speckled Band; the Adventure of Copper Beeches; the Stock-Broker's Clerk; the Red-Headed League. Arthur Conan Doyle. Read by David Timson. 3 CDs. (Running Time: 3 hrs. 30 mins.). (Sherlock Holmes Stories). (YA). 1999. audio compact disk 22.98 (978-962-634-152-0(1), NA315212, Naxos AudioBooks) Naxos.

Adventures of Sherlock Holmes V. unabr. ed. Arthur Conan Doyle. Read by David Timson. 3 CDs. (Running Time: 3 hrs. 30 mins.). 2002. audio compact disk 19.98 (NA326612) Naxos.
The ever-popular adventure is a calculating, rational sleuth who also exudes an almost hypnotic sense of otherness. He is more than a mere detective, he is rather an enigmatic mix of folklore and science, with a knowledge and wisdom, which seems mysterious and even at times, unearthly. Join the bloodhound of a genius and his faithful admirer and able assistant Dr. Watson, as they set out to solve the puzzles presented in this book.

Adventures of Sherlock Holmes V, Vol. 5. Read by David Timson. Ed. by Arthur Conan Doyle. 3 CDs. (Running Time: 3 hrs. 30 min.). 2003. audio compact disk 22.98 (978-962-634-266-4(8)) Naxos.

Adventures of Sherlock Holmes V, Vol. 5. unabr. ed. Arthur Conan Doyle. Read by David Timson. 3 cass. (Running Time: 3 hrs. 30 mins.). 2002. 17.98 (978-962-634-766-9(X), NA326614, Naxos AudioBooks) Naxos.

Adventures of Sherlock Holmes VI, Vol. 6. Read by David Timson. Ed. by Arthur Conan Doyle. 3 cass. (Running Time: 3 hrs. 30 min.). 2003. 17.98 (978-962-634-780-5(5), Naxos AudioBooks) Naxos.
In The Final Problem, the English detective encounters his most formidable rival, Professor Moriarty. "The Napoleon of Crime" is how Holmes describes his adversary to his faithful companion, Dr. Watson, as they move to the ultimate confrontation at the Reichenbach Falls. Also in this collection is the intriguing mystery of the disappearing bride in The Noble Bachelor, and two threats from the past in "Gloria Scott" and The Resident Patient.

Adventures of Sherlock Holmes VI, Vol. 6. Read by David Timson. Ed. by Arthur Conan Doyle. 3 CDs. (Running Time: 3 hrs. 30 min.). (Sherlock Holmes Stories). (YA). 2003. audio compact disk 22.98 (978-962-634-280-0(3), Naxos AudioBooks) Naxos.

Adventures of Silver Blaze see Memoirs of Sherlock Holmes

Adventures of Superman. Created by Radio Spirits. (Running Time: 10800 sec.). 2004. 9.98 (978-1-57019-632-4(X)) Radio Spirits.

Adventures of Superman: Doomsday & Beyond. BBC Audio Staff. 2006. audio compact disk (978-1-84607-072-3(4)) AudioGo GBR.

Adventures of Terence O'Rourke. unabr. ed. Louis J. Vance. Read by Gene Engene. 6 cass. (Running Time: 5 hrs. 30 mins.). 39.95 (978-1-55686-133-8(8), 133) Books in Motion.
O'Rourke, an Irish soldier of fortune, finds himself in Paris with barely the means to pay his rent & no real prospects for improving the situation. Through a sequence of circumstances, he finds himself allied with a beautiful princess & her weakling brother in a scheme to conquer the Sahara.

Adventures of the Hansom Cab see Suicide Club & Other Stories

Adventures of the Hi-Tech Shaman. E. J. Gold. 1 cass. (Running Time: 1 hr.). 15.00 (MT012) Union Label.
Contemporary teaching stories with humor & background music.

Adventures of the Missing Three Quarter. unabr. ed. Arthur Conan Doyle. Read by Walter Covell. 1 cass. (Running Time: 84 mins.). Dramatization. 1981. 7.95 (S-36) Jimcin Record.
Two more classic Sherlock Holmes mysteries.

Adventures of the Reigate Squire & the Greek Interpreter. Arthur Conan Doyle. 1 cass. 1989. 7.95 (S-40) Jimcin Record.

Adventures of the Speckled Band see Sherlock Holmes: Selected Stories

Adventures of the Superkids: CD #1. (J). 2005. audio compact disk (978-1-59833-965-9(6)) Rowland Reading.

Adventures of the Superkids: CD #2. (J). 2005. audio compact disk (978-1-59833-966-6(4)) Rowland Reading.

Adventures of the Superkids: CD #3 Songs (or other material) extracted from CDs 1 or 2 for reinforcement Activities. (J). 2005. audio compact disk (978-1-59833-967-3(2)) Rowland Reading.

Adventures of the Yellow Face & the Stockbroker's Clerk. Arthur Conan Doyle. 1 cass. 1989. 7.95 (S-39) Jimcin Record.

Adventures of Tick-i-ty Ted: The Search for the Peanut Butter King. unabr. ed. Jane Norman & Frank Beazley. Read by Jane Norman. 2 cass. (Running Time: 1 hr. 10 mins. per cass.). Dramatization. (Tick-i-ty Ted Adventure Ser.). (J). (ps-3). 1993. pap. bk. 4.95 (978-1-883585-00-6(7)); pap. bk. 6.95 ea. Pixanne Ent.
A continuous serialized, cliff-hanging adventure story about two bears, Tick-i-ty Ted & Toni, & their search for the Peanut Butter King (with music).

Adventures of Tom Sawyer see Aventuras de Tom Sawyer

Adventures of Tom Sawyer. Perf. by Steve Cook. Abr. by Steve Cook. Prod. by Steve Cook. (ENG.). (YA). 2009. audio compact disk 14.95 (978-0-9821616-2-3(X)) Five Talents.

Adventures of Tom Sawyer. Retold by Molly Jackel. Mark Twain. (Classic Adventures Ser.). 2002. audio compact disk 18.95 (978-1-4105-0189-9(2)) D Johnston Inc.

Adventures of Tom Sawyer. Mark Twain. Narrated by Christopher Hurt. (ENG.). 2007. audio compact disk 27.95 (978-1-55685-954-0(6)) Audio Bk Con.

Adventures of Tom Sawyer. Mark Twain. 4 cass. (Running Time: 6 hrs. 40 mins.). 26.95 (978-1-885546-05-0(X)) Big Ben Audio.

Adventures of Tom Sawyer. Mark Twain. Ed. by Jerry Stemach et al. Retold by Molly Jackel. Contrib. by Ted S. Hasselbring. (Start-to-Finish Books). (J). (gr. 2-3). 2002. (978-1-58702-807-6(7)) D Johnston Inc.

Adventures of Tom Sawyer. Mark Twain. Ed. by Jerry Stemach et al. Retold by Molly Jackel. Contrib. by Ted S. Hasselbring. (Start-to-Finish Books). (J). (gr. 2-3). 2002. 100.00 (978-1-58702-076-6(9)) D Johnston Inc.

Adventures of Tom Sawyer. Mark Twain. 2 cass. 19.95 set. (8125Q) Filmic Archives.
Tom & his friends, Huck Finn & Becky Thatcher, begin by playing pranks, but their sense of adventure leads to real danger as they discover a den of thieves & must use ingenuity to survive.

Adventures of Tom Sawyer. Mark Twain. (J). 1985. 12.95 (HarperChildAud) HarperCollins Pubs.

Adventures of Tom Sawyer. Mark Twain. Read by Pat Bottino. (Running Time: 8 hrs.). 1994. 27.95 (978-1-59912-621-0(4)) Iofy Corp.

Adventures of Tom Sawyer. Mark Twain. Read by Garrick Hagon. (Running Time: 2 hrs. 30 mins.). 2000. 20.95 (978-1-60083-668-8(2)) Iofy Corp.

Adventures of Tom Sawyer. Mark Twain. Read by Yadira Sánchez. (Running Time: 3 hrs.). 2001. 16.95 (978-1-60083-155-3(9), Audiofy Corp) Iofy Corp.

Adventures of Tom Sawyer. Mark Twain. Read by Garrick Hagon. 2 cass. (Running Time: 2 hrs. 38 mins.). (J). 1996. 13.98 (978-962-634-580-1(2), NA208014, Naxos AudioBooks) Naxos.
A boy's adventures growing up in a small town on the banks of the Mississippi River over a hundred years ago. The cheerful, adventurous hero plays truant to form a pirate band, together with his best friend Huckleberry Finn.

Adventures of Tom Sawyer. Mark Twain. Read by Garrick Hagon. 2 CDs. (Running Time: 2 hrs. 38 mins.). (YA). 1996. audio compact disk 17.98 (978-962-634-080-6(0), NA208012, Naxos AudioBooks) Naxos.

***Adventures of Tom Sawyer.** Mark Twain. Read by Matt Armstrong. (ENG.). (J). 2010. 9.95 (978-1-936455-03-4(X)) Open Bk Aud.

Adventures of Tom Sawyer. Mark Twain. Narrated by Dick Hill. (ENG.). 2007. 12.95 (978-0-9801087-3-6(X)) Alpha DVD.

Adventures of Tom Sawyer. Mark Twain. Read by Thomas Becker. (Running Time: 8 hrs.). 2002. 27.95 (978-1-59912-125-3(5), Audiofy Corp) Iofy Corp.

Adventures of Tom Sawyer. Mark Twain. Read by Robby Benson. 2 cass. (Running Time: 2 hrs.). (J). (gr. k-7). 16.98 Set. (343) MFLP CA.
Robby Benson delivers Twain's marvelous language in a manner that makes each vignette come to life.

Adventures of Tom Sawyer. Mark Twain. Narrated by Thomas Becker. (Running Time: 29400 sec.). (Unabridged Classics in MP3 Ser.). 2008. audio compact disk 14.95 (978-1-58472-554-1(0), In Aud); audio compact disk 24.00 (978-1-58472-555-8(9), In Aud) Sound Room.

Adventures of Tom Sawyer. abr. ed. Mark Twain. Read by Jeff Chandler. 2 cass. 10.95 (978-0-89926-133-1(7)) Audio Bk.
Twain's immortal life on the Mississippi.

Adventures of Tom Sawyer. abr. ed. Mark Twain. Ed. by Jerry Stemach et al. Retold by Molly Jackel. Contrib. by Ted S. Hasselbring. 1 cass. (Running Time: 1 hr.). (Start-to-Finish Books). (J). (gr. 2-3). 2002. (978-1-58702-792-5(5)) D Johnston Inc.
Mark Twain captures a boyhood summer on the Mississippi River, complete with haunted houses, rogue bandits, hidden treasure and schoolyard crushes. It is a simple, rural, dreamlike world, seen through the eyes of a boy who may have been based on the young Mark Twain himself. Tom Sawyer is an adventuresome prankster whose good-hearted and unpretentious nature is infectious and timelessly appealing.

Adventures of Tom Sawyer. abr. ed. Mark Twain. 2002. 7.95 (978-1-57815-268-1(2)) Media Bks NJ.

Adventures of Tom Sawyer. abr. ed. Mark Twain. Perf. by St. Charles Players. 2 cass. (Running Time: 3 hrs.). Dramatization. (Story Theatre for Young Readers Ser.). (J). (gr. 4-7). 1998. 16.95 (978-1-56994-508-7(X), 329934, Monterey SoundWorks) Monterey Media Inc.
Life along the Mississippi River is full of excitement & adventure for mischievous Tom Sawyer. If he's not playing pirates or witnessing a murder in the graveyard, he is busy whitewashing Aunt Polly's fence or falling in love with Becky Thatcher.

Adventures of Tom Sawyer. abr. ed. Mark Twain. Perf. by Wil Wheaton. 2 cass. (Running Time: 3 hrs.). (Ultimate Classics Ser.). 2004. 18.00 (978-1-931056-69-4(2), N Millennium Audio) New Millenn Enter.
An excursion into boyhood, a return to the simple rural Missouri world of Tom Sawyer, his friends Huck Finn, Becky Thacher, & Aunt Polly. It is a world of summertime and hooky, of pranks and punishments, of villains and adventure, seen through the eyes of a boy who might have been the young Mark Twain himself.

Adventures of Tom Sawyer. abr. ed. Mark Twain. Read by Paul Newman. 2 cass. (Running Time: 2 hrs.). 2000. 18.00 S&S Audio.

Adventures of Tom Sawyer. abr. ed. Mark Twain. Read by Hiram Sherman. (Running Time: 44 min.). Incl. Adventures of Tom Sawyer: Preface. (SAC 967); Adventures of Tom Sawyer: The Cat & the Pain Killer. (SAC 967); 10.95 (SAC 967) Spoken Arts.
The most famous episodes from Twain's immortal classic.

Adventures of Tom Sawyer. unabr. ed. 8 CDs. (Running Time: 8 hrs. 10 mins.). 2002. audio compact disk 79.00 (978-1-58472-159-8(6), Commuters Library) Sound Room.

Adventures of Tom Sawyer. unabr. ed. Mark Twain. Read by Jeff Chandler. 6 cass. (J). 35.70 (C-301) Audio Bk.
A nostalgic classic about one boy's adventures.

Adventures of Tom Sawyer. unabr. ed. Mark Twain. Read by Patrick Fraley. 5 cass. (Running Time: 7 hrs. 42 min.). (J). (gr. 6-12). 2004. 22.95 (978-1-57270-010-9(6), H90010u) Pub: Audio Partners. Dist(s): PerseuPGW
Storytelling genius, beloved by generations of readers, portrays an idyllic boyhood life in the mid-1800s along the Mississippi River.

Adventures of Tom Sawyer. unabr. ed. Mark Twain. Narrated by Patrick Fraley. 6 CDs. (Running Time: 7 hrs. 42 mins.). (ENG.). (J). 2003. audio compact disk 29.95 (978-1-57270-307-0(5)) Pub: AudioGO. Dist(s): Perseus Dist

Adventures of Tom Sawyer. unabr. ed. Mark Twain. Read by Grover Gardner. 1 MP3-CD. (Running Time: 8 hrs. 30 mins.). 2008. 29.95 (978-1-4332-1592-6(6)); 54.95 (978-1-4332-1590-2(X)); audio compact disk 70.00 (978-1-4332-1591-9(8)) Blckstn Audio.

Adventures of Tom Sawyer. unabr. ed. Mark Twain. Read by Tim Behrens. 6 cass. (Running Time: 8 hrs.). (J). 39.95 (978-1-55686-110-9(9), 752418) Books in Motion.
First published in 1875, this classic excursion into Mark Twain's Mississippi River country is full of affection, wit & adventure.

Adventures of Tom Sawyer. unabr. ed. Mark Twain. Read by Paul Newman. 6 CDs. (Running Time: 9 hrs.). 2001. audio compact disk Books on Tape.
Boyhood memories on the Mississippi, in the river town of Hannibal, Missouri. Many of the story's characters & episodes are constructed from the author's early adventures & Tom Sawyer is probably Mark Twain in mufti.

Adventures of Tom Sawyer. unabr. ed. Mark Twain. Read by Michael Prichard. 6 cass. (Running Time: 9 hrs.). 2001. 29.95 (978-0-7366-6797-5(0)) Books on Tape.
An amusing & nostalgic look of boyhood on the Mississippi River in the mid-nineteenth century.

Adventures of Tom Sawyer. unabr. ed. Mark Twain. Read by Dick Hill. 6 cass. (Running Time: 9 hrs.). 2002. 29.95 (978-1-59086-295-7(3), 1590862953, BAU) Brilliance Audio.
Generations of readers have enjoyed the ingenuous triumphs and feckless mishaps of boyhood days on the Mississippi. This classic of American wit and storytelling introduced Tom Sawyer, Becky Thatcher, Aunt Polly, the Widow Douglas, and many other characters to the world; including, of course, the boy who "was cordially hated and dreaded by all the mothers of the town, because he was idle and lawless and vulgar and bad - and because all their children admired him so," Huckleberry Finn.

Adventures of Tom Sawyer. unabr. ed. Mark Twain. Read by Dick Hill. (Running Time: 9 hrs.). 2004. 39.25 (978-1-59335-579-1(3), 1593355793, Brlnc Audio MP3 Lib) Brilliance Audio.

Adventures of Tom Sawyer. unabr. ed. Mark Twain. Read by Dick Hill. (Running Time: 9 hrs.). 2004. 39.25 (978-1-59710-007-6(2), 1597100072, BADLE); 24.95 (978-1-59710-006-9(4), 1597100064, BAD) Brilliance Audio.

***Adventures of Tom Sawyer.** unabr. ed. Mark Twain. Read by Dick Hill. (Running Time: 9 hrs.). 2010. 19.99 (978-1-4418-7658-4(8), 9781441876584, Brilliance MP3); audio compact disk 29.99 (978-1-4418-7656-0(1), 9781441876560, Bril Audio CD Unabri); audio compact disk 69.97 (978-1-4418-7657-7(X), 9781441876577, BriAudCD Unabrid) Brilliance Audio.

Adventures of Tom Sawyer. unabr. ed. Mark Twain. Read by Garrick Hagon. (Running Time: 29725 sec.). (Complete Classics Ser.). 2008. audio compact disk 34.98 (978-962-634-868-0(2), Naxos AudioBooks) Naxos.

Adventures of Tom Sawyer. unabr. ed. Mark Twain. Narrated by Norman Dietz. 5 CDs. (Running Time: 7 hrs.). 2003. audio compact disk 69.00 Recorded Bks.

Adventures of Tom Sawyer, unabr. ed. Mark Twain. Narrated by Norman Dietz. 5 cass. (Running Time: 7 hrs.). (gr. 5). 1986. 44.00 (978-1-55690-005-1(8), 86890E7) Recorded Bks.
The classic adventures & misadventures of Tom Sawyer, a young boy with age-old problems.

Adventures of Tom Sawyer. unabr. ed. Mark Twain. Narrated by William Dufris. (Running Time: 7 hrs. 30 mins. 0 sec.). (ENG.). 2008. audio compact disk 19.99 (978-1-4001-5685-6(8)); audio compact disk 55.99 (978-1-4001-3685-8(7)) Pub: Tantor Media. Dist(s): IngramPubServ

Adventures of Tom Sawyer. unabr. ed. Mark Twain. Read by William Dufris. (Running Time: 7 hrs. 30 mins. 0 sec.). (ENG.). 2008. audio compact disk 27.99 (978-1-4001-0685-1(0)) Pub: Tantor Media. Dist(s): IngramPubServ

Adventures of Tom Sawyer. unabr. ed. Mark Twain. Read by Thomas Becker. (YA). 2006. 49.99 (978-1-59895-186-8(6)) Find a World.

Adventures of Tom Sawyer. unabr. ed. Mark Twain. Read by Bob Hollands. 6 cass. (Running Time: 7 hrs. 30 min.). (J). 1980. 34.00 (C-33) Jimcin Record.
Adventures along the Mississippi in this juvenile classic.

Adventures of Tom Sawyer. unabr. ed. Mark Twain. Read by Thomas Becker. 7 cds. (Running Time: 8 hrs 10 mins). (YA). 2002. pap. bk. (978-1-58472-341-7(6), In Aud) Sound Room.

Adventures of Tom Sawyer. unabr. ed. Mark Twain. Read by Thomas Becker. 7 cds. (Running Time: 10 hrs 19 mins). (YA). 2002. audio compact disk 37.95 (978-1-58472-339-4(4), 077, In Aud) Pub: Sound Room. Dist(s): Baker Taylor
The delightful adventures of an independent, savvy boy.

Adventures of Tom Sawyer. unabr. collector's ed. Mark Twain. Read by Michael Prichard. 6 cass. (Running Time: 9 hrs.). (J). (gr. 4-7). 1979. 48.00 (978-0-7366-0158-0(9), 1158) Books on Tape.
Boyhood memories in the river town of Hannibal, Missouri. Many of the story's characters & episodes are constructed from the author's early adventures & Tom Sawyer is probably Mark Twain in mufti.

Adventures of Tom Sawyer, Set. Mark Twain. Read by Christopher Hurt. 5 cass. (Running Time: 7 hrs. 30 min.). (J). (gr. 5-7). 1986. 20.95 (978-1-55685-070-7(0)) Audio Bk Con.
Tells how Tom whitewashes the fence, meets convict Injun Joe, escapes from the cave & wins the love of Becky Thatcher.

Adventures of Tom Sawyer, Set. abr. ed. Mark Twain. Perf. by St. Charles Players. 2 cass. Dramatization. 1999. 16.95 (FS9-42729) Highsmith.

Adventures of Tom Sawyer: Classic Collection. unabr. ed. Mark Twain. Read by Grover Gardner. (Running Time: 8.5 hrs. 0 mins.). 2009. audio compact disk 19.95 (978-1-4332-1032-7(0)) Blckstn Audio.

Adventures of Tom Sawyer: Narrated by Richard Henzel. Narrated by Richard Henzel. (ENG.). (YA). 2009. audio compact disk 29.99 (978-0-9747237-7-8(0)) R Henzel.

Adventures of Tom Sawyer: Preface see Adventures of Tom Sawyer

Adventures of Tom Sawyer: The Cat & the Pain Killer see Adventures of Tom Sawyer

Adventures of Tom Sawyer: The Mark Twain Classic. Short Stories. As told by Jim Weiss. 1. (Running Time: 1 hour). Dramatization. (J). 2003. 10.95 (978-1-882513-57-4(6), 1124-33); audio compact disk 14.95 (978-1-882513-82-6(7), 1124-033) Greathall Prods.
The Mark Twain Classic comes alive in the Adventures of Tom Sawyer.

Adventures of Uki, the Ukelele, Tape 1. Cathy Ellis. 1993. pap. bk. 16.95 (978-1-879542-28-0(5)) Ellis Family Mus.

Adventures of Ulysses. Bernard Evslin. Read by George Guidall. 3 cass. (Running Time: 4 hrs.). (YA). 2000. pap. bk. 39.75 (978-0-7887-4155-5(1), 41117) Recorded Bks.
As Ulysses & his brave men sail to Greece, they encounter deadly Sirens, the man-eating Cyclops & other nightmarish creatures.

Adventures of Ulysses. Charles Lamb. Narrated by Nita Moyer. 1 CD. (Running Time: 3 hrs. 13 mins.). (J). 2005. audio compact disk 19.95 (978-0-9748692-1-6(X)) Access Dig Des.

Adventures of Ulysses. unabr. ed. Bernard Evslin. Narrated by John McDonough. 3 pieces. (Running Time: 4 hrs.). (gr. 7 up). 2000. 27.00 (978-0-7887-4029-9(6), 96148E7) Recorded Bks.

Adventures of Ulysses, Class Set. Bernard Evslin. Read by George Guidall. 3 cass. (Running Time: 4 hrs.). (YA). 1999. 92.80 (978-0-7887-4156-2(X), 47110) Recorded Bks.

Adventures of Uncle Tom. Thomas H. Jones. 2006. audio compact disk 29.95 (978-0-9779883-3-4(3)) Legacy Audio Bks.

Adventures of Vincent Marlow. Perf. by Van Heflin. 6 cass. (Running Time: 9 hrs.). 1999. 34.98 (4189) Radio Spirits.

Adventures of Well Being Now. Nick Kemp. (Running Time: 1 hr.). audio compact disk 24.95 (978-0-9545993-0-0(6)) Pub: Human Alchemy GBR. Dist(s): Crown Hse

Adventures on Air Cycle. Perf. by Banana Slug String Band Staff. 1 cass. (J). 1989. 9.98 incl. Norelco pkg. (978-1-877737-31-2(3), MLP 2159) MFLP CA.
Ecological-Science information expressed in children's music.

Adventures While Preaching the Gospel of Beauty. Poems. Joshua Beckman & Matthew Rohrer. 1. 2004. audio compact disk 10.00 (978-0-9723487-8-2(6), VersPr) Pub: WaveBks. Dist(s): Consort Bk Sales

Adventures with Family & Friends. Read by Joanie Bartels. 1 cass. (Running Time: 40 mins.). (Childhood Adventure Ser.: Vol. 1). (J). (ps-4). 1996. 10.98 (978-0-945267-29-4(0), YM-060-CM); lp 13.98 (978-0-945267-28-7(2)); audio compact disk 13.98 (YM-060-CD) Youngheart Mus.
A fine mix of original & top 40 hits.

Adventures with God: Experiencing the Supernatural Side of Prayer. Lynne Hammond. 4 CDs. 2005. audio compact disk 20.00 (978-1-57399-285-5(2)) Mac Hammond.
Why settle for more mundane times of prayer when the miraculous awaits you? Step out of the ordinary and into the amazing. Experience the supernatural side of prayer.

Adventures with Kazmir the Flying Camel: The Five Skies. (ENG., (J). 2008. 12.00 (978-0-9725180-0-0(2)) Camel Back Pubng.

Adventures with Kid Heroes: Night of the Homework Zombies/Jimmy Sniffles: Dognapped/Tigher Moth, Insect Ninja. Scott Nickel & Aaron Reynolds. Read by Full Cast Production Staff. (Playaway Children Ser.). (J). (gr. 3-7). 2008. 39.99 (978-1-60640-688-5(4)) Find a World.

Adventures with the Thrift Store Bears. Olive Evans. Narrated by Olive Evans. Illus. by Patricia Woolley. Composed by David/James Furmston. David/James Furmston. (ENG.). (J). 2007. bk. 18.95 (978-0-9748954-1-3(5)) Teddy Trvlr.

Adventuresome Kids Activities. (J). 2004. audio compact disk 29.95 (978-1-886441-54-5(5)) Zoo-phonics.

Adventuring with God. 2002. 16.95 (978-1-57972-514-3(7)); audio compact disk 25.00 (978-1-57972-515-0(5)) Insight Living.

Adverbs. unabr. ed. Daniel Handler. Read by Oliver Wyman. (Running Time: 27000 sec.). 2006. audio compact disk 34.95 (978-0-06-114984-9(5)) HarperCollins Pubs.

***Adverbs.** unabr. ed. Daniel Handler. Read by Oliver Wyman. (ENG.). 2006. (978-0-06-115434-8(2), Harper Audio); (978-0-06-115433-1(4), Harper Audio) HarperCollins Pubs.

Adverse Report. Gerald Hammond. Read by Gordon Griffin. 5 cass. 1999. 49.95 (66634) Pub: Soundings Ltd GBR. Dist(s): ISIS Pub

Adverse Report. Gerald Hammond. Read by Gordon Griffin. 5 cass. (Running Time: 7 hrs. 30 mins.). (Sound Ser.). 2004. 49.95 (978-1-85496-663-6(4), 66634) Pub: UlverLrgPrint GBR. Dist(s): Ulverscroft US

Adversity Advantage: Seven Steps Toward Everyday Greatness. unabr. ed. Paul Stoltz & Erik Weihenmayer. (Running Time: 9 hrs. 30 mins. 0 sec.).

(ENG.). 2007. audio compact disk 34.99 (978-1-4001-0358-4(4)) Pub: Tantor Media. Dist(s): IngramPubServ

Adversity Advantage: Turning Everyday Struggles into Everyday Greatness. Paul G. Stoltz & Erik Weihenmayer. Read by Lloyd James. Frwd. by Stephen R. Covey. (Playaway Adult Nonfiction Ser.). (ENG.). 2009. 65.00 (978-1-60775-639-2(0)) Find a World.

Adversity Advantage: Turning Everyday Struggles into Everyday Greatness. unabr. ed. Paul G. Stoltz & Erik Weihenmayer. (Running Time: 9 hrs. 30 mins. 0 sec.). (ENG.). 2007. audio compact disk 69.99 (978-1-4001-3358-1(0)) Pub: Tantor Media. Dist(s): IngramPubServ

Adversity Advantage: Turning Everyday Struggles into Everyday Greatness. unabr. ed. Erik Weihenmayer & Paul G. Stoltz. (Running Time: 9 hrs. 30 mins. 0 sec.). (ENG.). 2007. audio compact disk 24.99 (978-1-4001-5358-9(1)) Pub: Tantor Media. Dist(s): IngramPubServ

***Adversity Quotient Work.** abr. ed. Paul G. Stoltz. Read by Paul G. Stoltz. (ENG.). 2006. (978-0-06-114201-7(8), Harper Audio); (978-0-06-114200-0(X), Harper Audio) HarperCollins Pubs.

Advertising Agency Business: Your Guide to Ideas & Possibilities. 1 cass. (Running Time: 23 mins.). 32.95 (CFSS/CS23) Ctr Self Suff.

Advertising Creativity Dialogue. Alfreda C. Doyle. Read by Sell Out Recordings Staff. 1 cass. (Running Time: 15 mins.). 1991. 21.00 (S.O.R. 4001) Sell Out Recordings.

Ideas on creative advertising.

Advertising in America: What Works, Doesn't & Why. Featuring Roy H. Williams, 3rd. 5 CDs. 2003. audio compact disk 34.95 (978-1-932226-01-0(X)) Wizard Acdmy.

A seminar by Roy H. WilliamsAdvertising in America: What Works, What Doesn?t, and Why, featuring Roy H. Williams. Using 52-week radio schedules, the Wizard has been turning advertisers into millionaires with amazing results. In this series, the Wizard shares with you exactly how it?s done. In these CDs, you will hear the Wizard as he speaks to business owners, and private sessions in which he speaks directly to your staff. The Wizard says things that can only be said behind closed doors. Deep training. Things you?ve never heard about copy writing, scheduling, and comparative media analysis. He also explains how, why, and when to have those hard conversations with clients.Chosen by editor Eric Rhoads to be a permanent, featured columnist in Radio Ink, the Wizard brings a truly unique perspective to radio. Though his firm currently has 52-week schedules airing on more than 550 radio stations, his company does not specialize in radio. So why do they use newspaper only for classified ads and why do they buy TV schedules on less than 40 stations in America? Because radio advertising usually represents the highest and best use of his clients? ad dollars, that?s why!Contains 5 CDs also includes Radio as Taught by Wizard Academy CD.

Advertising Now. Online. Julius Wiedemann. (FRE, GER, ENG & SPA., 2006. 39.99 (978-3-8228-4956-9(1)) Pub: Taschen DEU. Dist(s): IngramPubServ

Advertising Sales Solution. Helen Berman. 8 cass. (Running Time: 8 hrs.). 195.00 (978-0-9649716-3-9(1)) Berman Pubng.

How to sell magazine advertising space.

Advertising Services in Germany: A Strategic Reference 2006. Compiled by Icon Group International, Inc. Staff. 2007. ring bd. 195.00 (978-0-497-35962-1(6)) Icon Grp.

Advertising Services in Indonesia: A Strategic Reference 2006. Compiled by Icon Group International, Inc. Staff. 2007. ring bd. 195.00 (978-0-497-36025-2(X)) Icon Grp.

Advertising Your Business. Ed. by Socrates Media Editors. 2005. audio compact disk 29.95 (978-1-59546-091-2(8)) Pub: Socrates Med LLC. Dist(s): Midpt Trade

Advice for Securing Clients. John L. Ahern. 1 cass. 8.95 (824) Am Fed Astrologers.

Advice from the World's Richest Man: Ecc. 5:8-20. Ed Young. 1993. 4.95 (978-0-7417-1986-7(X), 986) Win Walk.

Advice on Dying: And Living a Better Life. abr. ed. Dalai Lama XIV. Read by Jeffrey Hopkins. 2004. 15.95 (978-0-7435-4091-9(3)) Pub: S&S Audio. Dist(s): S and S Inc

Advice to a Prophet see Richard Wilbur Readings

Advice to Aspiring Advocates. James W. Jeams, Sr. 1999. (978-0-943380-72-8(3)) PEG MN.

Advise & Consent, Pt. 1. unabr. collector's ed. Allen Drury. Read by Dan Lazar. 9 cass. (Running Time: 13 hrs. 30 min.). 1978. 72.00 (978-0-7366-0138-2(4), 1142-A) Books on Tape.

A study of political animals in their natural habitat. It begins with the opening of Senate confirmation hearings on the nomination of Robert A. Leffingwell for Secretary of State. Supported by liberal politicians & press, the President's choice is bitterly opposed by Seab Cooley, a wily & worldly Southern Senator. Two weeks of furious debate & maneuvering expand the controversy to a major crisis.

Advise & Consent, Pt. 2. collector's ed. Allen Drury. Read by Dan Lazar. 11 cass. (Running Time: 16 hrs. 30 min.). 1978. 88.00 (978-0-7366-0139-9(2), 1142-B) Books on Tape.

Any one who recalls the Bork & Tower confirmation hearings will revel in this novel of Washington political infighting.

Advising as Teaching: NACADA Webinar Series 01. Featuring Nancy King. (ENG.). 2007. audio compact disk 140.00 (978-1-935140-43-6(4)) Nat Acad Adv.

Advising Clients on Powers of Attorney for Property. Edward S. Schlesinger. 1 cass. (Running Time: 90 mins.). 1992. 17.40 (M912) Am Law Inst.

This estate planning tool can raise complicated & unforeseen questions about the principal's selection of an agent, the specific powers granted & the effect of the power of attorney on the overall estate plan.

Advising Student-Athletes on a College Campus: NACADA Webinar Series 16. Featuring Derek Van Rheenen. (ENG.). 2008. audio compact disk 140.00 (978-1-935140-58-0(2)) Nat Acad Adv.

Advising Students on Academic Probation: NACADA Webinar No. 29. Moderated by Marsha Miller. (ENG.). 2010. audio compact disk 140.00 (978-1-935140-71-9(X)) Nat Acad Adv.

Advising Undecided/Undeclared Students for Success: NACADA Webinar No. 27. Featuring Kathleen Smith & David Spight. 2009. audio compact disk 140.00 (978-1-935140-69-6(8)) Nat Acad Adv.

Advising Your Clients on International Business Deals. 1988. 90.00 (AC-465) PA Bar Inst.

Advising Your Clients on Making Gifts. Contrib. by Edward S. Schlesinger. 1 cass. (Running Time: 1 hrs. 30 mins.). 1998. 22.40 (M211) Am Law Inst.

Understand the tax consequences of making lifetime gifts as compared to testamentary transfers, to enable easier explanation to clients. In a conversational format, discusses not only relative advantages & disadvantages, but also the background, development & impact of relevant Internal Revenus Code provisions.

Advising Your Clients on Nursing Home Issues. 2 cass. (Running Time: 2 hrs.). 1997. 25.00 Set; incl. study outline. (M209) Am Law Inst.

Prepares the listener to advise both elders & adult children about quality, access, payment sources, & liability of family members at three stages: planning in a non-crisis situation (no placement needed); choosing a placement (crisis time); & protecting the patient after placement. Live recording from the three-part teleseminar series, "Counseling the Older Client on Trusts & Nursing Home Issues".

Advisors Help Students SOAR to Academic Success: NACADA Webinar Series 12. Featuring Kenneth Kiewra. 2008. audio compact disk Rental 140.00 (978-1-935140-54-2(X)) Nat Acad Adv.

Advocacy & the Art of Storytelling. 1 cass. (Running Time: 47 mins.). (Complete Audiotape Ser.). 1990. 29.95 (FAZ060S) Natl Inst Trial Ad.

Advocacy & the Art of Storytelling. John D. Mooy. 1 cass. (Running Time: 47 mins.). 1990. 29.95 Incls. course bklet. in dust-proof album. (AUDZO6OS) NITA.

Shares the secrets of preparing & presenting compelling arguments & jury summations & shows their uses.

Advocacy Before Administrative Agencies. 1 cass. (Running Time: 1 hr.). (Advocacy Before Administrative Agencies Ser.). 1984. 20.00 PA Bar Inst.

Advocacy Campaigns for Nonprofits: Capitol Learning Audio Course. Michael Shannon. Prod. by TheCapitol.Net. (ENG.). 2007. 47.00 (978-1-58733-056-8(3)) TheCapitol.

Advocacy in Writing. 1 cass. (Running Time: 2 hrs. 30 mins.). 1986. 20.00 PA Bar Inst.

Advocating for Older Adults. 1998. bk. 99.00 (ACS-2125) PA Bar Inst.

The second highest percentage of older persons in the United States lives in Pennsylvania. This large segment of our population is growing each year & presents both an opportunity & a challenge to lawyers & other professionals who provide services to the elderly. Lawyers are increasingly called upon to guide the elderly through these critical issues as they prepare for failing health, disposition of assets & the infirmities of old age.

Advocating for the Individual with Nonverbal Learning Disorders. Contrib. by Sarah Clarke & Maria Antoniadis. 1 cass. (Running Time: 1 hr. 30 mins.). 20.00 (19-005A) J W Wood.

Eligibility for special education, eligibility under Section 504 of the Rehabilitation Act of 1973, Individualized Educational Plan (IEP), implementing & monitoring the student program.

***Aenarion.** Gav Thorpe. (ENG.). 2010. 17.00 (978-1-84416-843-9(3), Black Library) Pub: BL Pubng GBR. Dist(s): S and S Inc

Aeneid. Virgil. Tr. by Cecil Lewis. 4 cass. (Running Time: 5 hrs.). (C). 2002. 22.98 (978-962-634-778-2(3), NA427814, Naxos AudioBooks) Naxos.

Considered to be the Roman's version of Homer's the Iliad and the Odyssey. This poem is the story of Aeneas' survival of the siege of Troy and his destined-to-be-successful journey toward the founding of Rome.

Aeneid. Virgil. Read by Paul Scofield. (Running Time: 5 hrs.). 2006. 28.95 (978-1-60083-669-5(0)) Iofy Corp.

Aeneid. unabr. ed. Virgil. Read by Frederick Davidson. 10 cass. (Running Time: 14 hrs. 30 mins.). (gr. 9-12). 1992. 69.95 (978-0-7861-0316-4(7), 1277) Blckstn Audio.

"The Aeneid" describes Aeneas' adventures at sea following the capture of Troy by the Greeks during the Trojan War. As the story begins, a storm shipwrecks Aeneas & his Trojan followers near Carthage in North Africa. There, Aeneas falls in love with Dido, queen of Carthage. But the gods order thim to leave for Italy. In despair, Dido commits suicide. Upon finally reaching Italy, Aeneas goes down into the lower world & learns about his future descendants, the Romans.

Aeneid. unabr. ed. Virgil. Read by Frederick Davidson. Tr. by W. F. Jackson Knight. (Running Time: 50400 sec.). 2008. audio compact disk 19.95 (978-1-4332-1536-0(5)) Blckstn Audio.

Aeneid. unabr. ed. Virgil. Read by Simon Callow. Tr. by Robert Fagles. Intro. by Bernard Knox. (Running Time: 13 hrs.). (ENG.). (gr. 12 up). 2006. audio compact disk 49.95 (978-0-14-305902-8(5), PengAudBks) Penguin Grp USA.

Aeneid. unabr. ed. Virgil & Frederick Davidson. Tr. by W. F. Jackson Knight. (Running Time: 14 hrs. NaN mins.). 2008. 29.95 (978-1-4332-1535-3(7)); audio compact disk 99.00 (978-1-4332-1534-6(9)) Blckstn Audio.

***Aeneid.** unabr. ed. null Virgil. Narrated by Michael Page. (Running Time: 13 hrs. 0 mins. 0 sec.). (ENG.). 2010. 24.99 (978-1-4001-6600-8(4)); 18.99 (978-1-4001-8600-6(5)); audio compact disk 69.99 (978-1-4001-4600-0(3)); audio compact disk 34.99 (978-1-4001-1600-3(7)) Pub: Tantor Media. Dist(s): IngramPubServ

Aeneid of Virgil. Instructed by Elizabeth Vandiver. 6 CDs. (Running Time: 6 hrs.). bk. 39.95 (978-1-56585-319-5(9), 303); 29.95 (978-1-56585-068-2(8), 303) Teaching Co.

Aeolus! see Aeolus!

Aeolus! Donald Macintyre, Sr. Tr. by Bill Innes, 1st. Bill Innes, 1st. Composed by Sandy Stanage, II. Sandy Stanage, II.Tr. of Aeolus!. (ENG & GAE., 2008. audio compact disk 30.00 (978-0-9552326-2-6(7)) GraceN Pub GBR.

Aequanimitas, Set. unabr. ed. William Osler. Read by Robert L. Halvorson. 3 cass. (Running Time: 270 min.). 21.95 (71) Halvorson Assocs.

Aerial Warfare: Raspers & Scrapers. unabr. ed. David Attenborough. 1 cass. (Running Time: 54 mins.). (Animal Language Ser.). 12.95 (ECN19F) J Norton Pubs.

Aerobic Express for Kids. 1 cass. (Running Time: 1 hr.). (J). (gr. 2-5). 2001. pap. bk. 10.95 (KIM 9092C) Kimbo Educ.

All aboard teachers & kids! It's the Aerobic Express to fitness via music & rhythmic routines. Ideal for co-ed classes. Easy to learn activities for classroom or gymnasium. Includes guide.

Aerobic Fitness. 1 cass. (Running Time: 1 hr.). (J). 2001. pap. bk. 10.95 (KIM 6035C); pap. bk. 10.95 (KIM 6036); pap. bk. 10.95 (6036C) Kimbo Educ.

Aerobic routines with easy-to-follow steps. Fame, Eye of the Tiger, Abracadabra, Why Do Fools Fall in Love & more. Includes Intermediate version manual.

Aerobic Fitness. 1 cass. (Running Time: 45 mins.). (Sports Ser.). 9.98 (978-1-55909-080-3(4), 67S) Randolph Tapes.

Upbeat music selection provides stretching & cool-down time, plus messages to get you into shape. Subliminal messages are heard 3-5 minutes before becoming ocean sounds or music.

Aerobic Nutrition. Don Mannerberg & June Roth. 1 cass. (Running Time: 51 mins.). 11.00 (978-0-89811-211-5(7), 9425) Meyer Res Grp.

Use these tips from Dr. Don Mannerberg to combine good nutrition with an effective exercise program to achieve good health & long life.

Aerobic Nutrition. Don Mannerberg & June Roth. 1 cass. 10.00 (SP100050) SMI Intl.

New research reveals that you can combine good nutrition with an effective exercise program to achieve good health & long life. Measure living in quality as well as quantity; use these tips to maintain glowing vitality for all the years of your life.

Aerobic Power for Kids. 1 cass. (Running Time: 1 hr.). (J). (gr. k-4). 2001. pap. bk. 10.95 (KIM 9148C); pap. bk. 14.95 (KIM 9148CD) Kimbo Educ.

Collection of songs that everyone will enjoy listening, singing & exercising to. You'll shake & twist & power up with these easy but fun routines. Includes guide.

Aerobics for Fiddlers. Carol Ann Wheeler. 1994. pap. bk. 15.95 (978-0-7866-1222-2(3), 95166P); 9.98 (978-0-7866-0001-4(2), 95166C) Mel Bay.

Aerobics for Kids. 1 cass. (Running Time: 18 mins.). (J). 2001. pap. bk. 10.95 (KIM 7043C); pap. bk. 11.95 (KIM 7043); pap. bk. 14.95 (KIM 7043CD) Kimbo Educ.

Kimbo Fitness Made Fun!!! The first step toward aerobic fitness. A vigorous 18 minute program for lower & middle elementary grade children. Includes warm-up, conditioning exercises, endurance activities & cool down. Fun, invigorating & challenging. Slow down Mama, Funky Fiesta, Bouncing Back to You & more. Includes manual.

Aerobics U. S. A. Georgiana Stewart. Music by Bruce Springsteen. 1 LP. (Running Time: 1 hr.). 2001. pap. bk. & pupil's gde. ed. 11.95 (KIM 8065) Kimbo Educ.

Warm-up & workout to the music of Bruce Springsteen. Today's most exciting new sounds help you jog, jump, stretch & skip your way across the U.S.A. Simple exercise patterns can be followed by all ages. Born in the USA, Glory Days, Born to Run, Be All That You Can Be & more. Inlcudes guide.

Aerobics U. S. A. Georgiana Stewart. Music by Bruce Springsteen. 1 cass. (Running Time: 1 hr.). (J). 2001. pap. bk. 10.95 (KIM 8065C) Kimbo Educ.

Aerodrame. Emile De Harven. 108.95 (978-0-8219-3629-0(8)) EMC-Paradigm.

Aerodrome. unabr. collector's ed. Rex Warner. Read by Rodney Lay. 6 cass. (Running Time: 9 hrs.). 1987. 48.00 (978-0-7366-1173-2(8), 2095) Books on Tape.

An allegory that contrasts martial order with civilian muddle. Set in England, pre WW II. Unusual & gripping.

Aeroport, Autoroute. Short Stories. Patrick Liegibel. 1 cass. (FRE.). 1991. 16.95 (1249-RF) Olivia & Hill.

Two short stories.

Aerospace Equipment & Services in Belgium: A Strategic Reference 2006. Compiled by Icon Group International, Inc. Staff. 2007. ring bd. 195.00 (978-0-497-35822-8(0)) Icon Grp.

Aeschylus & the Death of Tragedy. unabr. ed. Narrated by Walter Kaufmann. 1 cass. (Running Time: 1 hr. 12 mins.). (Sound Seminars Lectures on the Classics). 1963. 14.95 (C23113) J Norton Pubs.

Although he is generally considered the creator of tragedy, his world view contains central elements that are usually associated with the death of tragedy in our time. "Oresteia" trilogy & "Prometheus Unbound" are examined.

Aesock's Travels/Los Viajes de Aesock: Lights, Camera, Edison!/¡Luz, Cámara, Edison! Gretchen McMasters. Narrated by Daniel Jennings. 1 cass. (Running Time: 1 hr. 20 mins.). (SPA & ENG.). (J). 2004. 7.99 (978-0-9758990-0-7(7)) Broad Reach Ent.

Benjamin is devastated when his science project fails in front of his second grade class - but help is on the way from a mysterious creature with an affinity for attracting lost socks: Aesock. Join Benjamin, Olivia and Aesock as they travel back in time to meet Thomas Edison as a seven-year-old boy plagued by a hearing deficit and struggling with self-doubt in school. Lights, Camera, Edison! & !Luz, Camara, Edison! is the first story in the series written primarily for ages seven to ten.

Aesop: Alive & Well. Short Stories. 1 CD. (Running Time: 53 Minutes). (J). 2001. audio compact disk 15.00 (978-0-9760432-4-9(6)) D Ferlatte.

Aesop: From City. abr. ed. Clifford Simak. Perf. by Clifford Simak. 1 cass. 1984. 8.98 (CP 1649) HarperCollins Pubs.

***Aesop Adventure: Fables, Songs & Activities.** Composed by Cristi Cary Miller & Sally Raymond. (ENG.). 2005. pap. bk. 59.99 (978-1-4234-9541-3(1), 1423495411) H Leonard.

Aesop Goes Modern. Scripts. 1 CD. (Running Time: 1 hrs. 10 mins). Dramatization. (J). 2004. audio compact disk 16.95 (978-0-9753782-0-5(1)) Virtual Theatre.

Timeless stories of the great Greek storyteller Aesop come to life through the magic of children's audio theater. Originating in folklore - often with animal protagonists - this collection features 25 fables scripted to create a rich tapestry of music and drama intended to stimulate children's imaginations.

Aesop Smarts by Dancing Beetle. Perf. by Eugene Ely. 1 cass. (Running Time: 86 mins.). (J). 1992. 10.00 Erthviibz.

Science, ecology, nature sounds & Aesop come together when Ms. Aardvark & the spunky musical humans read & sing with Dancing Beetle.

Aesop's Fables. Perf. by Daisy Anderson & Gene Ganssle. (ENG.). (J). 2006. audio compact disk 9.95 (978-0-9815788-1-1(0)) Amer Two.

Aesop's Fables. Jake Eberle. Composed by Paul Rabjohns. Illus. by Melanie Stimmell. (J). 2000. audio compact disk 15.00 (978-0-9700810-0-1(6)) Imagilot.

Aesop's Fables. S. A. Handford. Read by Wanda Mccaddon. (Running Time: 2 hrs. 30 mins.). (J). 2002. 16.95 (978-1-59912-038-6(0), Audiofy Corp) Iofy Corp.

Aesop's Fables. S. A. Handford. Read by Anton Lesser. (Running Time: 1 hr. 15 mins.). 2004. 16.95 (978-1-60083-670-1(4)) Iofy Corp.

Aesop's Fables. S. A. Handford. Read by Walter Covell. 5 cass. (Running Time: 5 hrs.). (J). 1989. 29.00 incl. album. (C-186) Jimcin Record.

Famous fables.

Aesop's Fables. S. A. Handford. Read by Anton Lesser. 1 CD. (Running Time: 1 hr. 15 mins.). (J). 2000. audio compact disk 14.98 (978-962-634-207-7(2), NA120712, Naxos AudioBooks) Naxos.

Fables by definition, are brief, allegorical narrative, in verse or prose, illustrating a moral thesis or satirizing human behavior. Among the most famous moral fables are those by Aesop.

Aesop's Fables. S. A. Handford. Read by Anton Lesser. 1 cass. (Running Time: 1 hr. 15 mins.). (J). (ps-3). 2000. 9.98 (978-962-634-707-2(4), NA120714, Naxos AudioBooks) Naxos.

Aesop's Fables. S. A. Handford. Read by Jonathan Kent. (Running Time: 9000 sec.). (ENG.). (J). (ps-3). 2005. audio compact disk 16.99 (978-1-4001-5119-6(8)) Pub: Tantor Media. Dist(s): IngramPubServ

Aesop's Fables. Maude Heurtelou. Tr. by Maude Heurtelou. Tr. by Z. Zeong et al. Illus. by G. Gautier et al. 1 cass. (Running Time: 1 hr.). (CRP & SPA.). (J). (gr. 3-5). 1999. pap. bk. 16.00 (978-1-881839-93-4(1)) Educa Vision.

Aesop's Fables. Michael Mish. Interview with Barry Caldwell. Based on a story by Aesop. 1 cass. (Running Time: 30 mins.). (J). (gr. 1-6). 1989. 9.95 (978-0-9622465-0-0(6)); audio compact disk 9.95 CD. Mish Mash Music.

Features various Aesop's fables, narrated with song reflecting the moral of each fable.

Aesops Fables. unabr. ed. Aesop. Read by Jonathan Kent. (J). 2007. 39.99 (978-1-59895-785-3(6)) Find a World.

Aesop's Fables. unabr. ed. S. A. Handford. Read by Mary Woods. 4 cass. (Running Time: 16200 sec.). (ps-2). 2002. 32.00 (978-0-7861-2185-4(8), 2936); audio compact disk 32.00 (978-0-7861-9584-8(3), 2936) Blckstn Audio.
A Storyteller who used cunning foxes, surly dogs, clever mice, fearsome lions, and foolish humans to describe the reality of a harsh world.

Aesop's Fables. unabr. ed. Short Stories. Read by Wanda McCaddon. 2 cds. (Running Time: 2 hrs. 21 mins.). (J). 2002. audio compact disk 18.95 (978-1-58472-200-7(2), 062, In Aud) Pub: Sound Room. Dist(s): Baker Taylor
119 of the best loved fables by Aesop.

Aesop's Fables. unabr. collector's ed. S. A. Handford. Read by Jonathan Kent. 3 cass. (Running Time: 3 hrs.). (J). 1996. 18.00 (978-0-7366-3529-5(7), 9186) Books on Tape.
A grand collection of morality tales that underline our civilization.

Aesop's Fables: 119 of Aesop's Best-Loved Stories. Aesop. Narrated by Wanda McCaddon. (Running Time: 8460 sec.). (Unabridged Classics in MP3 Ser.). (ENG.). (J). 2008. audio compact disk 24.00 (978-1-58472-632-6(6), In Aud) Sound Room.

***Aesop's Fables - Selected Stories & the Adventures of Poor Mrs. Quack.** Aesop & Thornton W. Burgess. Narrated by Flo Gibson. (ENG.). (J). 2010. audio compact disk 16.95 (978-1-60646-147-1(8)) Audio Bk Con.

Aesop's Fables & the Adventures of Poor Mrs. Quack. unabr. ed. Aesop. Read by Flo Gibson. Contrib. by Thornton W. Burgess. 2 cass. (Running Time: 2 hrs. 30 mins.). (J). (gr. 1 up). 1994. 14.95 (978-1-55685-309-8(2)) Audio Bk Con.
"The Fox & the Grapes", "The Goose That Laid the Golden Eggs", "The Hare & the Tortoise", & "The Town Mouse & the Country Mouse" are among these fifty fables that abound in manners & morals. In the companion piece poor Mrs. Quack's life is turned upside down by the men with the "terrible guns" until Peter Rabbit, Sammy Jay & other friends from the Smiling Pond come to her aid.

Aesop's Fables Deluxe. Scripts. 1 cass. (Running Time: 20 mins.). (J). (gr. k-3). 1999. pap. bk. & tchr. ed. 29.95 Bad Wolf Pr.
The songs are simple & playful, encouraging students to delight in the sounds of language while they practice basic word-building skills. Uniquely designed so that teachers can choose to have their kids do the entire show or merely perform any number of individual scenes/songs. Sheet music available.

Aesop's Fables the Smothers Brothers Way. Smothers Brothers. Perf. by Smothers Brothers. Based on a story by Aesop. 1 cass. (Running Time: 37 mins.). (J). (ps-6). 1990. 9.98 (978-1-877737-46-6(1), MLP 2178); audio compact disk 12.98 (978-1-877737-47-3(X), MLP D2178) MFLP CA.
Humorous storytelling & musical presentations of seven stories by Aesop.

Aesop's Fables, with EBook. unabr. ed. Aesop. Narrated by Jonathan Kent. (Running Time: 2 hrs. 30 mins. 0 sec.). (ENG.). (J). (ps-3). 2008. 17.99 (978-1-4001-5891-1(5)); audio compact disk 17.99 (978-1-4001-0891-6(8)) Pub: Tantor Media. Dist(s): IngramPubServ

Aesop's Fables, with eBook. unabr. ed. Aesop. Narrated by Jonathan Kent. (Running Time: 2 hrs. 30 mins. 0 sec.). (ENG.). (J). (ps-3). 2008. audio compact disk 35.99 (978-1-4001-3891-3(4)) Pub: Tantor Media. Dist(s): IngramPubServ

Affabel: Ventana de la Eternidad. Prod. by John Bevere. 2009. audio compact disk 29.99 (978-1-933185-48-4(1)) Messengr Intl.

Affabel: Window of Eternity. John Bevere. (Running Time: 2 hrs. 30 mins.). 2007. audio compact disk 19.99 (978-1-933185-06-4(6)) Pub: Bethany Hse. Dist(s): Baker Pub Grp

Affabel: Window of Eternity. John Bevere. (RUS.). 2009. audio compact disk 29.99 (978-1-933185-53-8(8)) Messengr Intl.

Affair. unabr. ed. Amanda Quick, pseud. Read by Mary Peiffer. 8 cass. (Running Time: 12 hrs.). 1997. 64.00 (978-0-7366-3756-5(7), 4431) Books on Tape.
Regency England is the setting for this tale of romance, mystery & murder. Fast-paced, charmingly told & filled with suspense.

Affair. unabr. ed. Amanda Quick, pseud. Narrated by Barbara Rosenblat. 8 cass. (Running Time: 11 hrs. 45 mins.). 70.00 (978-0-7887-0920-3(8), 95060E7) Recorded Bks.
In Regency England, the glamorous marriage broker Charlotte Arkendale has a flawless reputation for separating the suitable from the second rate. But when one of her clients is murdered, Charlotte fears for her own life. Can she trust her new, darkly handsome assistant? Available to libraries only.

Affair. unabr. ed. C. P. Snow. Read by John MacDonald. 8 cass. (Running Time: 12 hrs.). (Strangers & Brothers Ser.: Vol. 8). 1985. 64.00 (978-0-7366-0443-7(X), 1417) Books on Tape.
Eighth in Strangers & Brothers series. A young helper falsifies data, Eliot finds against him.

***Affair Before Christmas.** unabr. ed. Eloisa James. Read by Susan Duerden. (ENG.). 2010. (978-0-06-204849-3(X), Harper Audio); (978-0-06-202543-2(0), Harper Audio) HarperCollins Pubs.

Affair of the Heart: Fidelity & Commitment over the Course of the Life Cycle. Sean Sammon. 5 cass. (Running Time: 5 hrs. 30 mins.). 1987. 39.95 (TAH179) Alba Hse Comns.
Dealing with & understanding commitment & fidelity over the course of our life cycle.

Affair of the Tortoise see Classic Detective Stories, Vol. II, A Collection

Affair-Proof Marriage: 1 John 4:7-11. Ed Young. 1986. 4.95 (978-0-7417-1541-8(4), 541) Win Walk.

Affair Proof Your Marriage: Eph. 5:22-25. Ed Young. 1991. 4.95 (978-0-7417-1837-2(5), 837) Win Walk.

***Affair-Proofing Your Marriage.** 2010. audio compact disk (978-0-9826360-3-9(2)) Mid A Bks & Tapes.

Affair to Remember: The Remarkable Love Story of Katharine Hepburn & Spencer Tracy. abr. ed. Christopher Andersen. Read by Sandra Burr. (Running Time: 3 hrs.). 2008. 39.25 (978-1-4233-5782-7(5), 9781423357827, BADLE); 24.95 (978-1-4233-5779-7(5), 9781423357797, Brilliance MP3); 39.25 (978-1-4233-5780-3(9), 9781423357803, Brlnc Audio MP3 Lib); 24.95 (978-1-4233-5781-0(7), 9781423357810, BAD) Brilliance Audio.

Affair: Why? 11 Samuel 11:4-5. Ed Young. 1986. 4.95 (978-0-7417-1538-8(4), 538) Win Walk.

Affair with Africa. Alzada Carlisle Kistner. Narrated by C.M. Hébert. (Running Time: 10 hrs.). 2000. 30.95 (978-1-59912-409-4(2)) Iofy Corp.

Affair with Africa: Expeditions & Adventures Across a Continent. unabr. ed. Alzada Carlisle Kistner. Read by C. M. Herbert. 7 cass. (Running Time: 10 hrs.). 2001. 49.95 (978-0-7861-1935-6(7), 2706); audio compact disk 64.00 (978-0-7861-9783-5(8), 2706) Blckstn Audio.
The author & her husband, a promising entomologist, left their 18-month-old daughter in the care of relatives & began what was to be a four-month expedition in the Belgian Congo. Three weeks after their arrival, the country was gripped by a violent revolution, trapping the Kistners in its midst.

Affaire Dreyfus. Henri Guillemin. 1 cass. (FRE.). 1991. 22.95 (1203-VSL) Olivia & Hill.

Affairs & Attractions. Hal Stone & Sidra Stone. 1 cass. (Running Time: 1 hr.). (Mendocino Ser.). 1993. 10.95 (978-1-56557-014-6(6), T11) Delos Inc.
How does one handle attractions & affairs? For people in a committed relationship, even the thought of these can be threatening. Based on their understanding of relationship & their theory of the Psychology of Selves, Hal & Sidra Stone use a new way of thinking about this often painful topic.

Affairs at Thrush Green. unabr. ed. Miss Read. Read by Gwen Watford. 6 CDs. (Thrush Green Chronicle Ser.). 2000. audio compact disk 64.95 (978-0-7540-5365-1(2), CCD 056) Pub: Chivers Audio Bks GBR. Dist(s): AudioGO
Charles Henstock, rector of Thrush Green, is quite happy about his recent promotion. But an unfortunate skirmish with one of his wealthy new parishioners disheartens him. The return of Kit Armitage to Thrush Green also causes a stir. Could he be contemplating a second marriage?.

Affection, Love & Sex at the University of Maine. Harvey Jackins. 1 cass. 10.00 (978-1-885357-75-5(3)) Rational Isl.
A lecture given at the University of Maine.

Affirmaciones Basicas Para una Aceptacion Total e Incondicional. unabr. ed. Lilburn S. Barksdale. Read by Betty Teague. Tr. by George Teague. 1 cass. (Running Time: 36 mins.). (SPA.). 1994. 9.95 (978-0-918588-42-5(1), 122S) NCADD.
Accepting yourself & others totally & unconditionally is the key to loving relationships. This cassette shows how aligning your awareness with the truth about the human condition makes this acceptance possible.

Affirmation & Meditation: Effortless Prosperity Affirmations for Everyone. 1 cass. (Running Time: 1 hr.). 1999. 10.00 (978-1-930455-14-6(3)) E P Inc Pubng Co.
An absolutely great affirmation to bring everyone to light & joy.

Affirmation & Meditation: Effortless Prosperity Laughter with Subliminal Affirmation. 1 cass. (Running Time: 30 mins.). 1997. 10.00 (978-1-930455-13-9(5)) E P Inc Pubng Co.
A wonderful way of laughter for 30 minutes.

Affirmation of Identity. Read by Wayne Monbleau. 3 cass. 1993. 15.00 (978-0-944648-27-8(4), LGT-1214) Loving Grace Pubns.
Religious.

Affirmation Power: The Secrets of Success Through the Power of Your Mind. Michele Blood. Illus. by Musivation International Staff. 6 cass. (Running Time: 6 hrs.). 1995. audio compact disk 69.95 (978-1-890679-20-0(8), M015) Micheles.
Motivational program to help improve one'sto the positive & life towards success.

Affirmations. Belleruth Naparstek. Composed by Steven Mark Kohn. 1 CD. (Running Time: 1 hr.). (Health Journeys Ser.). 1995. audio compact disk 16.98 (978-1-881405-42-9(7)) Hlth Jrnys.
Positive statements, spoken in the first person, designed to combat negative thinking. Repeated listening can result in profound personal changes.

Affirmations. Instructed by Stuart Wilde. 2 cass. (Self-Help Tape Ser.). 21.95 (978-0-930603-15-1(X)) White Dove NM.
Most of the orgnizations & structures in the world are designed to take away your power. This highly successful two-tape series serves not as a way to give you nice words to say to yourself but rather as a magnificent battleplan whereby you learn to expand the power you already have in order to win back absolute control.

Affirmations & Meditation: Meditation. 1 cass. (Running Time: 30 mins.). 1998. 8.00 (978-1-930455-15-3(1)) E P Inc Pubng Co.
Peaceful and healing meditation.

Affirmations for Building Self-Esteem. unabr. ed. Lilburn S. Barksdale. Read by Phil Reed. 1 cass. (Running Time: 1 hr. 7 mins.). 1990. 9.95 (978-0-918588-35-7(9), 101) NCADD.
These affirmations & action statements from the book "Building Self-Esteem" are a great tool for changing destructive, negative inner dialogue to the loving words you deserve to hear from yourself.

Affirmations for Change, Confidence & Success: What You Think, You Become. Diane L. Tusek. Read by Diane L. Tusek. (ENG.). 2009. 39.99 (978-1-61574-702-3(8)) Find a World.

Affirmations for Healing. Created by Ellen Chernoff Simon. 1. (Running Time: 70 minutes). 2004. audio compact disk 18.00 (978-0-9765587-4-3(2)) Imadulation.

Affirmations for Living an Empowered Life. unabr. ed. Denise Lynch. Read by Denise Lynch. (Running Time: 45 mins.). (ENG.). 2008. 12.98 (978-1-59659-309-1(1), GildAudio) Pub: Gildan Media. Dist(s): HachBkGrp

Affirmations for Mind, Body & Spirit. unabr. ed. Belleruth Naparstek. Read by Steven Mark Kohn. Composed by Steven Mark Kohn. 1 CD. (Running Time: 15 Minutes). (Health Journeys Ser.). 1995. audio compact disk 17.98 (978-1-881405-21-4(4), 20) Hlth Jrnys.
These affirmations are positive statements, spoken in the first person, designed to combat negative thinking and set the stage for first attitude and then behavioral change. Repeated listening over time can result in profound personal changes.

Affirmations from the Prayers of Silent Unity: For Healing, Guidance, Prosperity, Inner Peace. (ENG.). 2009. audio compact disk 9.95 (978-0-87159-900-1(7), Unity Hse) Unity Schl Christ.

Affirmative Reaction. unabr. ed. Aileen Schumacher. Read by Stephanie Brush. 8 cass. (Running Time: 10 hrs. 12 min.). (Tory Travers Mystery Ser.: Bk. 3). 2001. 49.95 (978-1-55686-994-5(0)) Books in Motion.
A storm sewer system inspection turns dicey when Structural Engineer Tory Travers finds a decidedly dead businessman in the storm water pipe. The death has the marks of a gangland slaying, and according to Detective David Avarez, is not the first murder at this site.

Affliction. Russell Banks. Read by Russell Banks. 1 cass. (Running Time: 30 mins.). 1999. 8.95 (AMF-215) Am Audio Prose.
The author reads from his novel "Affliction" & talks about working class heroes.

Affliction. unabr. ed. Fay Weldon. Read by Fay Weldon. 6 cass. (Running Time: 7 hrs.). 1995. 54.95 (978-1-85695-932-2(5), 950501) Pub: ISIS Audio GBR. Dist(s): Ulverscroft US
Annette & Spicer make a perfect pair, he's thirty-nine, wide shouldered & square jawed & she's slight, fair & delicately featured. He has a twelve-year old son from a previous marriage & she a thirteen-year old daughter. After ten years they are expecting their own baby. But on this, the first day of the rest of their blissful lives, Spicer fails to kiss Annette goodbye as he leaves for the office. The years of marriage shift & change, the rock of Annette's marriage may only be sand. As psychiatrists, fortune tellers & hypnotherapists enter the game, one might wonder whether it's worth the effort, except there's the baby.

Affluence Technology Vol. 1: Mind over Money. Dennis B. Stevenson. 1 CD. 1999. audio compact disk 49.95 (978-1-892479-02-0(8)) Focus Educ.

Affluent Spirit: Lessons in Spiritual & Material Abundance. unabr. ed. Barbara Dershowitz. Read by Barbara Dershowitz. Read by Tony Florentino & Morgan Williams. 1 cass. (Running Time: 1 hr. 43 mins.). 1995. 16.00 (978-0-9647619-2-6(0)) BDCI.
A full-length reading of the lessons contained in the spiritual guidebook to practical living.

Affordable Singing Lessons: Fast & Funky Warm-Up. Yvonne DeBandi. 2002. cd-rom & audio compact disk 19.99 (978-0-9715793-7-8(7)) Pub: LOTI Pubng. Dist(s): C Dumont

Affordable Singing Lessons: Featuring the Fast & Funky Singers' Warmup. Yvonne DeBandi. 2001. audio compact disk 179.95 (978-0-9715793-2-3(6)) LOTI Pubng.

Affordable Store Remodels - Expanding Space to Preserve Your Market Share. 1 cass. (America's Supermarket Showcase '96 Ser.). 1996. 11.00 (NGA96-019) Sound Images.

Afghan. unabr. ed. Frederick Forsyth. Read by Robert Powell. (Running Time: 11 hrs.). (ENG.). (gr. 8). 2007. audio compact disk 19.95 (978-0-14-314267-6(4), PengAudBks) Penguin Grp USA.

Afghanada Vol. 1. Created by Canadian Broadcasting Corporation. 6 CDs. (Running Time: 21600 sec.). Dramatization. 2007. audio compact disk 44.95 (978-0-660-19684-8(0), CBC Audio) Pub: Canadian Broadcasting CAN. Dist(s): Georgetown Term
This spellbinding 6-CD set is a series of dramas based on Canada?s involvement in Afghanistan. Four Canadian soldiers ship out to Afghanistan. They are immediately sent deep into the heart of the conflict - Kandahar Province, where the Taliban insurgency is fiercest. Afghanada gives a grunt's eye view of the conflict. Every day these Canadian soldiers on the ground confront the chaos and violence of life "outside the wire". They don't have the big picture - they're not interest in the policy. They're just trying to help the people protect each other.

Afghanada, Vol. 2. Adam Pettle et al. (Running Time: 18000 sec.). (ENG.). 2007. audio compact disk 39.95 (978-0-660-19735-7(9)) Canadian Broadcasting CAN.

Afghanistan. Stephen Tanner. Narrated by Raymond Todd. (Running Time: 14 hrs. 30 mins.). 2000. 41.95 (978-1-59912-405-6(X)) Iofy Corp.

Afghanistan. unabr. ed. Stephen Tanner. Read by Raymond Todd. 10 pieces. 2004. reel tape 39.95 (978-0-7861-2357-5(5)) Blckstn Audio.

Afghanistan: A Military History from Alexander the Great to the Present. unabr. ed. Stephen Tanner. Read by Raymond Todd. 12 CDs. (Running Time: 14 hrs. 30 mins.). 2002. audio compact disk 96.00 (978-0-7861-9476-6(6), 2983); audio compact disk 24.95 (978-0-7861-9170-3(8), 2983); 69.95 (978-0-7861-2294-3(3), 2983) Blckstn Audio.
For more than 2,500 years, the forbidding territory of Afghanistan has served as a vital crossroads not only for armies but also for clashes between civilizations. As a result of the United States' engaging in armed conflict with the Afghan regime, an understanding of the military history of that blood-soaked land has become essential to every American.

Afghanistan Penetration. Axel Kilgore. Read by Carol Eason. 2 vols. No. 15. 2004. 18.00 (978-1-58807-171-2(5)); (978-1-58807-662-5(8)) Am Pubng Inc.

Afiches Amigos por Siempre. (SPA.). (J). 2004. audio compact disk (978-1-933218-03-8(7)) Untd Bible Amrcas Svce.

***Afirmaciones para Tu Poder Interior: Programa de Meditacion.** abr. ed. Vicente Passariello. (SPA.). 2010. audio compact disk 12.95 (978-1-933499-89-5(3)) Fonolibro Inc.

Afirmaciones Positivas. Carlos Gonzalez. Read by Carlos Gonzalez. Ed. by Dina Gonzalez. 1 cass. (Running Time: 32 mins.).Tr. of Positive Affirmations. (SPA.). 1991. 10.00 (978-1-56491-023-3(7)) Imagine Pubs.
In Spanish. Drill on assertions to become more causative in life.

Afirmaciones Positivas. Carlos Gonzalez. 1 CD. (Running Time: 32 mins). (SPA.). 2003. audio compact disk 15.00 (978-1-56491-118-6(7)) Imagine Pubs.

AFP Service Codes. 1993. audio compact disk (978-0-9746708-2-9(0)) Assn Finan Prof.

Afraid. unabr. ed. Jack Kilborn. Read by Phil Gigante. 1 MP3-CD. (Running Time: 10 hrs.). 2009. 39.97 (978-1-4233-8311-6(7), 9781423383116, Brlnc Audio MP3 Lib); 24.99 (978-1-4233-8310-9(9), 9781423383109, Brilliance MP3); 39.97 (978-1-4233-8313-0(3), 9781423383130, BADLE); 24.99 (978-1-4233-8312-3(5), 9781423383123, BAD); audio compact disk 82.97 (978-1-4233-8309-3(5), 9781423383093, BriAudCD Unabrid); audio compact disk 24.99 (978-1-4233-8308-6(7), 9781423383086, Bril Audio CD Unabri) Brilliance Audio.

Africa. 3 cass. 1994. 29.95 (978-1-55961-252-4(5)) Relaxtn Co.

Africa, Vol. 1. Perf. by Machete Ensemble. 1 cass. 1989. 9.98 incl. Norelco pkg. (978-1-877737-38-1(0), EB 2501); audio compact disk (978-1-877737-51-0(8)) MFLP CA.
Afro-Latin musical traditions dedicated to the continent of Africa.

Africa & Middle East. Compiled by John Armstrong. 2008. audio compact disk 14.95 (978-1-906063-03-0(6)) Pub: Rough Guides GBR. Dist(s): PerseuPGW

Africa & You. Dahia Shabaka. (Living & Working Together Ser.). (J). (gr. k). 2000. 7.98 (978-1-58120-836-8(7)) Metro Teaching.

Africa House. unabr. ed. Christina Lamb. Narrated by Erick Graham. 9 cass. (Running Time: 12 hrs. 30 mins.). 2001. 82.00 (978-1-84197-195-7(2), H1178E7) Recorded Bks.
Stewart Gore-Brown fell unconventionally in love with Africa. On the shores of Shiwa Ngandu, The Lake of Royal Crocodiles in remote Northern Rhodesia, he strove to create his own Utopia, a place he couldn't find in his native Britain. To share his vision, he brought with him the daughter of his first love, an orphan less than half his age, to be his wife. However, reality was soon to encroach, &, as it had been for the explorer Livingstone, Shiwa Ngandu was to become a place of tragedy.

Africa Smarts by Dancing Beetle. Perf. by Eugene Ely. 1 cass. (Running Time: 82 mins.). (J). 1994. 10.00 Shoofly.
African science, myth, ecology & nature sounds come together when Ms. Gazelle & the spunky musical humans read & sing with Dancing Beetle.

Africa Stories: A Storyteller's Version of "Bubble Gum," "A Lion a Day," "Oh, Look, It's a Nosserus" Kate Noble. Narrated by Jim Weiss. Contrib. by Rachel Bass. 1 cass. (J). (ps-4). 1998. 9.95 (978-0-9631798-7-6(X)) Silver Seahorse.
In a game park, engaging animals learn from their remarkable adventures. Some of the author's safari experiences are also included. Side 2 is a read-along version of the two published books with a signal for page turning.

African. unabr. ed. Harold Courlander. Read by Peter Francis James. 10 cass. (Running Time: 13 hrs. 15 mins.). 1995. 85.00 (978-0-7887-0567-0(9), 94543) Recorded Bks.
Story of the slave trade - from the perils of the Middle Passage & piracy to the always dangerous quest for freedom - as seen through the eyes of an enslaved African.

African Adventures. Bernie Krause. 1 cass. (Running Time: 50 mins.). (Wild Sanctuary Ser.). 1994. audio compact disk 15.95 (2328, Creativ Pub) Quayside.
Ark of the Waterhole, wildlife bustling around a water hole in Kenya. The Mighty, Great Gorilla, fragile rhythm of gorilla family life in the mountains of east central Africa.

African Adventures. Bernie Krause. 1 cass. (Running Time: 50 mins.). (Wild Sanctuary Ser.). 1994. 9.95 (2327, NrthWrd Bks) TandN Child.

African American Folk Songs & Rhythms. Perf. by Ella Jenkins & Goodwill Spiritual Choir of Chicago. 1 cass., 1 CD. (Running Time: 42 mins.). (J). (gr. 1-4). 1992. (0-9307-450030-9307-45003-23); audio compact disk (0-9307-45003-23) Smithsonian Folkways.
Simple work songs, rhythmic chants & inspiring spirituals. Includes "Did You Feed My Cow," "Cotton-Eyed Joe" & "Old Time Religion".

African-American History Facts, Vols. 1 & 2. P. Hilton Taylor & Prince Zaire. Read by P. Hilton Taylor & Prince Zaire. 2 cass. (Running Time: 60 mins.). 1991. pap. bk. 15.99 (978-0-9638528-4-7(1)); 7.99 (978-0-9638528-0-9(9)) Brainpower Pubng.
For the time period 1619 through 1974, this tape provides an audio timeline of African-Americans' achievements in the United States & a record of important dates & events.

African-American Inventors. Rex A. Barnett. (Running Time: 30 mins.). (YA). 1990. 16.99 Hist Video.
Review of the contributions of black inventors.

African-American Males & Initiation: Hopes, Dreams & Frustrations. Charles Payne. Read by Charles Payne. 1 cass. (Running Time: 1 hr. 40 mins.). 1994. 10.95 (978-0-7822-0470-4(8), 547) C G Jung IL.

African-American Migration. Rex A. Barnett. (Running Time: 23 mins.). (YA). 1990. 16.99 (978-0-924198-03-8(6)) Hist Video.
Discusses the historic journey from the south to the north in the 1940's.

African American Music in Minnesota: From Spirituals to Rap. Judy Henderson. Perf. by Leonard 'Baby Doo' Caston et al. 1 CD. (Running Time: 57 min.). 1994. bk. 16.95 (C-005A) Minn Hist.
A rich & wide-ranging anthology of sacred & secular music performed in Minnesota by African Americans today & in the past. Included with the recording is a book that explores the history of the state's African-American community & its thriving musical life. Drawing on oral interviews & written sources, Henderson traces the development of African-American music from the seminal spiritual to the explosive blending & the transformation of musical elements that produced gospel, blues, jazz, rock & rap. Rarely seen historical photographs feature Minnesota events, performers, listeners & community scenes. Performers also include Drumpac as well as children doing street rhymes & home music.

African-American Playbook for a Successful Career in Sports. Andre Taylor. 2001. audio compact disk 29.95 (978-0-9708388-2-7(4), 1002) Taylor Insight Grp.

African American Truth, Vol. 3. James T. Meeks. 1998. 69.99 (978-1-931500-00-5(2)) J T M Minist.

African Americans & the Color Line in Ohio, 1915-1930. William Wayne Giffin. 2005. audio compact disk 9.95 (978-0-8142-9081-1(7)) Pub: Ohio St U Pr. Dist(s): Chicago Distribution Ctr

African Americans & the Public Agenda: The Paradoxes of Public Policy. unabr. ed. Ed. by Cedric Herring. 2 cassettes. (Running Time: 3 hours). 1999. 24.95 (978-0-9660180-5-9(2)) Scholarly Audio.
Provides an analysis of affirmative action, racial differentials in health, crime & punishment, education & access to jobs & other policy issues that have paradoxical effects.

African & African-American Religion. unabr. ed. Victor Anderson. Read by Ben Kingsley. Ed. by Walter Harrelson & Mike Hassell. 2 cass. (Running Time: 3 hrs.). Dramatization. (Religion, Scriptures & Spirituality Ser.). 1994. 17.95 (978-1-56823-018-4(4), 10461) Knowledge Prod.
The religious ideas & practices of African peoples have much in common with each other, & with related religions in the Caribbean & the Americas. African Islam & African Christianity have developed separately since their earliest times in Ethiopia, Egypt & the Sudan.

African & African-American Religions. unabr. ed. Victor Anderson. Read by Ben Kingsley. (Running Time: 10800 sec.). (Religion, Scriptures, & Spirituality Ser.). 2006. audio compact disk 25.95 (978-0-7861-6493-6(X)) Pub: Blckstn Audio. Dist(s): NetLibrary CO

African-Cherokee Connections: Reconstructed Families from the Miller Roll A. Billy Dubois Edgington. 2002. audio compact disk 39.95 (978-0-7884-2207-2(3)) Heritage Bk.

African Dream. Shaman's Dream. 1 CD. (Running Time: 3660 sec.). 2006. audio compact disk 16.98 (978-1-59179-430-1(7), M1014D) Sounds True.
When Los Angeles' Shaman's Dream gets ready to perform live or in the studio, its members callupon the powers of nature to bring healing and positive transformation to their music. Like the shamans who take us into the spirit world to enlist the help of guides, animals, and nature, these prolific musicians use the same sounds, chants, and rhythms to take listeners on a musical pilgrimage to the mystical, primal heart of Africa. Here they serve up a deliciousethno-jammin blend of chant, fusion, and deep groove for bodycentered movement, dance, or serious trans-dimensional drifting. Features Amani Friend, well-established multi-instrumentalist from the international underground electronic scene, and Jason Hann, accomplished percussionist/drummer who has accompanied Grammy? Award-winners Isaac Hayes and Rickie Lee Jones, among others. Also available by Shaman's Dream: Kerala Dream.

African Drum: Four African Tales. unabr. ed. Sandra Robbins. 1 cass. (Running Time: 50 mins.). Dramatization. (See-More Ser.). (J). (ps-4). 1978. 9.95 (978-1-882601-01-1(7)) See-Mores Wrkshop.
Created for children based on Shadow Box Theatre's Production. Soundtrack of complete show.

African Environmental Education Experience. Hosted by Nancy Pearlman. 1 cass. (Running Time: 28 mins.). 10.00 (505) Educ Comm CA.

African Experience: From ¿Lucy¿ to Mandela. Instructed by Kenneth P. Vickery. 18 cass. (Running Time: 18 hrs.). 79.95 (978-1-59803-223-9(2)) Teaching Co.

African Experience: From ¿Lucy¿ to Mandela. Instructed by Kenneth P. Vickery. 18 CDs. (Running Time: 18 hrs.). 2006. audio compact disk 99.95 (978-1-59803-224-6(0)) Teaching Co.

African History Facts One B. C., Vol. I. abr. ed. Shomari Taylor et al. Read by Shomari Taylor et al. Ed. by Prince Zaire. 1 cass. (Running Time: 1 hr.). (Brainstorm Ser.). 1994. 7.99 (978-0-9638528-6-1(8)) Brainpower Pubng.
Audio history timeline. African facts, inventions, culture etc. 1 B.C. to present Egyptian-Nubian overview. Science, geography briefs.

African History Facts One B. C., Vol. 1. abr. ed. Shomari Taylor et al. Read by Shomari Taylor et al. Ed. by Prince Zaire. 1 cass. (Running Time: 1 hr.). (Brainstorm Ser.). 1994. pap. bk. 10.99 (978-0-9638528-7-8(6)) Brainpower Pubng.

African History on File#153;, Revised Edition, CD-ROM. (gr. 6-12). 2004. audio compact disk 149.95 (978-0-8160-5401-5(0)) Facts On File.

African Hunter. unabr. ed. James Mellon. Read by Michael Prichard. 7 cass. (Running Time: 10 hrs. 30 mins.). 1977. 56.00 (978-0-7366-0075-0(2), 1085) Books on Tape.
A banker's son takes on big game in the African bush.

African Islam. Interview with Ray Heffner. Featuring Joseph Abraham Levi. 1 cass. (Running Time: 30 mins.). 1998. 10.00 (978-0-9703261-1-9(4)) PanRomance.

African Mercenary. abr. ed. Barry Sadler. Read by Charlton Griffin. 2 vols. (Casca Ser.: No. 12). 2003. 18.00 (978-1-58807-112-5(X)); (978-1-58807-543-7(5)) Am Pubng Inc.

African Mercenary. abr. ed. Barry Sadler. Read by Charlton Griffin. 2 vols. (Running Time: 6 hrs.). (Casca Ser.: No. 12). 2004. audio compact disk 25.00 (978-1-58807-286-3(X)); audio compact disk (978-1-58807-717-2(9)) Am Pubng Inc.

African Names Audio Book Vol. 1: Swahili Names. Created by Darryl Patrick Wood. Narrated by Darryl Patrick Wood. 2002. 12.95 (978-0-9718491-0-5(2)) Wood Comm LLC.

African Poison Murders. unabr. collector's ed. Elspeth Huxley. Read by Donada Peters. 8 cass. (Running Time: 8 hrs.). 1988. 48.00 (978-0-7366-1252-4(1), 2166) Books on Tape.
A double murder leads to a treacherous Nazi bund & a deadly arrow poison.

African Queen. C. S. Forester. Perf. by Humphrey Bogart et al. 1 cass. (Running Time: 60 min.). 1952. 7.95 (DD-8000) Natl Recrd Co.

African Queen. C. S. Forester. Voice by Humphrey Bogart. 1 cass. (Running Time: 60 mins.). 2000. 14.98 Radio Spirits.

African Queen. unabr. ed. C. S. Forester. Read by Richard Green. 5 cass. (Running Time: 8 hrs.). 2001. 24.95 (978-0-7366-6752-4(0)) Books on Tape.
The action takes place in World War I far from the European stage where the war boiled over in equatorial colonies. Rose Sayer, sister of an English preacher on a mission in German Central Africa, seems an unlikely heroine until her brother's death & the press of events move her to center stage. With a gin drinking engineer, Allnutt & The African Queen, a leaky thirty foot river boat, the reconstituted Miss Sayer sets out to strike a blow for England & avenge her brother's death.

African Queen. unabr. collector's ed. C. S. Forester. Read by Richard Green. 6 cass. (Running Time: 6 hrs.). 1980. 36.00 (978-0-7366-0366-9(2), 1350) Books on Tape.
Action in Africa in WW I. Leaky river boat threatens German naval might.

African Rhythm & African Sensibility: Aesthetics & Social Action in African Musical Idioms. John Miller Chernoff. 1 cass. 1981. 26.00 (978-0-226-10346-4(3)) Pub: U Ch Pr. Dist(s): Chicago Distribution Ctr

African Rhythms & Instruments Morocco, Algeria, Tunisia, Libya. unabr. ed. 1 cass. 12.95 (7328) J Norton Pubs.

African Safari. Prod. by Laraim Associates. (Barclay Family Adventure Ser.). (J). 2005. audio compact disk (978-1-56254-988-6(X)) Saddleback Edu.

African Silences. unabr. ed. Peter Matthiessen. Read by John MacDonald. 8 cass. (Running Time: 8 hrs.). 1993. 48.00 (978-0-7366-2369-8(8), 3142) Books on Tape.
African expeditions illustrate crisis facing the continent's environment & wildlife.

African Songs & Rhythms for Children. 1 cass. (Running Time: 60 mins.). (J). 1999. 12.95 (SF-45011) African Am Imag.

African Village Folktales, Vol. 3. 1 cass. (Running Time: 30 mins.). 1999. 19.95 (CDL5-1312) African Am Imag.

African Voices. (Running Time: 60 mins.). 2002. audio compact disk 15.99 (978-1-904972-55-6(1)) Global Jrny GBR GBR.

Africans. unabr. ed. David Lamb & Harold Courlander. Narrated by Nelson Runger & Peter Francis James. 13 cass. (Running Time: 18 hrs. 30 mins.). 1996. 104.00 (978-0-7887-0351-5(X), 94744E7) Recorded Bks.
Personal commentary of the people of this vast continent. It offers colorful, close-up views of presidents, peasants, guerrilla leaders & merchants while tracing a vivid history of one of the most varied populations on earth.

Africa's Plea see Poems from Black Africa

Afro-American Blues & Games Songs. unabr. ed. 1 cass. 1994. 12.95 (978-0-88421-366-6(8), S11240) J Norton Pubs.
Includes 10-page booklet.

Afro-American Tales & Games. 1 cass. (Running Time: 60 mins.). 1999. 12.95 (SF-45031) African Am Imag.

Afro-Brazilian Candomble As a Form of Modern Sacred Dance in Europe. Renato Berger. 1 cass. 9.00 (A0223-87) Sound Photosyn.
ICSS '87 with An Painter on tape.

Afro-Cuban Grooves for Bass & Drums: Funkifying the Clave. Lincoln Goines & Robby Ameen. Ed. by Daniel Thress. Contrib. by Ricardo Bentancourt & Emily Moorefield. 1 cass. pap. bk. 24.95 DCI Music Video.
Afro-Cuban Grooves for Bass & Drums is a guide to applying Afro-Cuban grooves to jazz, funk & rock for bass & drums. Rhythms covered are clave, tumbao, songo, guaguanco, Afro-Cuban 6/8, cha-cha & Mozambique.

Afro-Cuban Percussion Play-along. Trevor Sallum. (ENG.). 2009. pap. bk. 9.99 (978-0-7866-7948-5(4)) Mel Bay.

Afro-Cuban Rhythms for Drumset. Frank Malabe & Bob Weiner. Ed. by Daniel Thress. 1 cass. (Drummers Collective Ser.). pap. bk. 24.95 (BD070) DCI Music Video.
Introduction to Afro-Cuban rhythms including history, traditional instruments & basic styles of Afro-Cuban music. Styles covered include: Songo, Mozambique, cascara, conga, merengue, bembe, guaguanco, clave & cha-cha-cha.

Afro-Latin Polyrhythms. Trevor Salloum. Ed. by Trevor Salloum. 2001. pap. bk. 14.95 (978-0-7866-5422-2(8), 98926BCD) Mel Bay.

After. unabr. ed. Amy Efaw. 9 CDs. (Running Time: 10 hrs.). (ENG.). (YA). (gr. 7 up). 2009. audio compact disk 34.95 (978-0-14-314505-9(3), PengAudBks) Penguin Grp USA.

After: How America Confronted the September 12 Era. Steven Brill. Read by Dennis Boutsikaris. 2004. 21.95 (978-0-7435-4092-6(1)) Pub: S&S Audio. Dist(s): S and S Inc

After a Journey see Poetry of Thomas Hardy

***After All These Years.** abr. ed. Susan Isaacs. Read by Christine Baranski. (ENG.). 2005. (978-0-06-089335-4(4), Harper Audio); (978-0-06-089334-7(6), Harper Audio) HarperCollins Pubs.

***After America.** unabr. ed. John Birmingham. Narrated by Kevin Foley. (Running Time: 20 hrs. 0 mins. 0 sec.). (ENG.). 2010. 34.99 (978-1-4001-6858-3(9)); 23.99 (978-1-4001-8858-1(X)); audio compact disk 119.99 (978-1-4001-4858-5(8)); audio compact disk 49.99 (978-1-4001-1858-8(1)) Pub: Tantor Media. Dist(s): IngramPubServ

After America: Narratives for the Next Global Age. unabr. ed. Paul Starobin. Read by Lloyd James. 2 MP3-CDs. (Running Time: 14 hrs. 30 mins. 0 sec.). (ENG.). 2009. 29.99 (978-1-4001-6315-1(3)); audio compact disk 79.99 (978-1-4001-4315-3(2)); audio compact disk 39.99 (978-1-4001-1315-6(6)) Pub: Tantor Media. Dist(s): IngramPubServ

After Apple-Picking see Robert Frost Reads

After Apple-Picking see Caedmon Treasury of Modern Poets Reading Their Own Poetry

After Caroline. unabr. ed. Kay Hooper. Read by Valerie Leonard. 8 vols. (Running Time: 12 hrs.). 2000. bk. 69.95 (978-0-7927-2358-5(9), CSL 247, Chivers Sound Lib) AudioGO.
Two women who look like twins. Both are involved in car wrecks at the same time, one survives, one doesn't. Now, plagued by a bewildering connection to a woman she never knew, Joanna Flynn travels across the country to the town where Caroline McKenna lived & mysteriously died. But Joanna runs into a wall of suspicion as she searches for the truth: Was Caroline's death an accident?.

After Chancellorsville. unabr. ed. Judith Bailey & Robert I. Cottom. Read by Brian Emerson. 6 cass. (Running Time: 8 hrs. 30 mins.). 2001. 44.95 (978-0-7861-2092-5(4), 2854); audio compact disk 56.00 (978-0-7861-9681-4(5), 2854) Blckstn Audio.
"I reckon I sympathize with you deeply Dear Walt and I wish I could be with you, if it would help you any. I would be the best nurse you ever had, I'll bet you. I would laugh and sing and read to you and if we both felt like it I could cry too, and not half try." So wrote Emma Randolph, a young woman not yet twenty, to her distant cousin, Private Walter G. Dunn of the 11th New Jersey Infantry, as he lay in a crowded, filthy hospital ward. They corresponded when Walter went off to war, but their real story began when he was carried from the smoke and carnage of Chancellorsville to a hospital in Baltimore. There, barely recovered, bloodied and dazed with ether, he aided overworked surgeons when the Gettysburg wounded poured into the city, and he regularly took up his pen to relay everyday events that became history.

After Chancellorsville: The Civil War Letters of Private Walter G. Dunn & Emma Randolph. unabr. ed. Read by Grover Gardner & Megan Anderson. (Running Time: 28800 sec.). 2007. audio compact disk 29.95 (978-0-7861-5959-8(6)) Blckstn Audio.

After College: The Business of Getting Jobs. unabr. ed. Jack Falvey. Read by Thomas H. Middleton. 5 cass. (Running Time: 5 hrs.). 1987. 30.00 (978-0-7366-1153-4(3), 2077) Books on Tape.
College doesn't provide the job, the graduate does. Here's how he can get a better one.

After Cumae see Poetry of Geoffrey

After Dark. abr. ed. Jayne Castle, pseud. Read by Joyce Bean. (Running Time: 5 hrs.). (Harmony Ser.: No. 2). 2010. audio compact disk 14.99 (978-1-4418-2596-4(7), 9781441825964, BCD Value Price) Brilliance Audio.

After Dark. unabr. ed. Jayne Castle, pseud. Read by Joyce Bean. (Running Time: 8 hrs.). (Harmony Ser.: No. 2). 2009. 24.99 (978-1-4233-8516-5(0), 9781423385165, BAD); 24.99 (978-1-4233-8514-1(4), 9781423385141, Brilliance MP3); 39.97 (978-1-4233-8515-8(2), 9781423385158, Brinc Audio MP3 Lib); 39.97 (978-1-4233-8517-2(9), 9781423385172, BADLE); audio compact disk 29.99 (978-1-4233-8512-7(8), 9781423385127, Bril Audio CD Unabri); audio compact disk 92.97 (978-1-4233-8513-4(6), 9781423385134, BriAudCD Unabrid) Brilliance Audio.

After Dark. unabr. ed. Phillip Margolin. Read by Michael Russotto. 8 cass. (Running Time: 12 hrs.). 1996. 64.00 (978-0-7366-3200-3(X), 3864) Books on Tape.
Someone murders a judge & his clerk & police tag the judge's wife. Do they have the real killer.

After Dark. unabr. ed. Haruki Murakami. Read by Janet K. Song. Tr. by Jay Rubin. (ENG.). 2007. audio compact disk 29.95 (978-0-7393-4306-7(8), Random AudioBks) Pub: Random Audio Pubg. Dist(s): Random

After Death - What? Job 14:10-14. Ed Young. 1983. 4.95 (978-0-7417-1320-9(9), 320) Win Walk.

After Death Meditation. Bruce Goldberg. (ENG.). 2005. audio compact disk 17.00 (978-1-57968-039-8(9)) Pub: B Goldberg. Dist(s): Baker Taylor

After Death Meditation. Bruce Goldberg. Read by Bruce Goldberg. 1 cass. (Running Time: 25 mins.). (ENG.). 2006. 13.00 (978-1-885577-25-2(7)) Pub: B Goldberg. Dist(s): Baker Taylor
This meditation is to be played after someone has made the transition from the physical body.

***After Ever After.** unabr. ed. Jordan Sonnenblick. (Running Time: 5 hrs.). 2011. 24.99 (978-1-61106-138-3(5), 9781611061383, BAD); 39.97 (978-1-61106-139-0(3), 9781611061390, BADLE); 24.99 (978-1-61106-136-9(9), 9781611061369, Brilliance MP3); 39.97 (978-1-61106-137-6(7), 9781611061376, Brinc Audio MP3 Lib); audio compact disk 24.99 (978-1-61106-134-5(2), 9781611061345, Bril Audio CD Unabri); audio compact disk 54.97 (978-1-61106-135-2(0), 9781611061352, BriAudCD Unabrid) Brilliance Audio.

After Fidel. unabr. ed. Brian Latell. Read by Stefan Rudnicki. (Running Time: 39600 sec.). 2006. 72.95 (978-0-7861-4842-4(X)); audio compact disk 90.00 (978-0-7861-6129-4(9)) Blckstn Audio.

After Fidel: The Inside Story of Castro's Regime & Cuba's Next Leader. unabr. ed. Brian Latell. Read by Stefan Rudnicki. (Running Time: 39600 sec.). 2006. 29.95 (978-0-7861-4843-1(8)); audio compact disk 29.95 (978-0-7861-6128-7(0)); audio compact disk 29.95 (978-0-7861-7163-7(4)) Blckstn Audio.

After Glow. abr. ed. Jayne Castle, pseud. Read by Joyce Bean. (Running Time: 6 hrs.). (Harmony Ser.: No. 3). 2009. audio compact disk 26.99 (978-1-4418-0712-0(8), 9781441807120, BACD) Brilliance Audio.

After Glow. abr. ed. Jayne Castle, pseud. Read by Joyce Bean. (Running Time: 6 hrs.). (Harmony Ser.: No. 3). 2010. audio compact disk 14.99 (978-1-4418-2606-0(8), 9781441826060, BCD Value Price) Brilliance Audio.

After Glow. unabr. ed. Jayne Castle, pseud. Read by Joyce Bean. (Running Time: 10 hrs.). (Harmony Ser.: No. 3). 2009. 24.99 (978-1-4233-8522-6(5), 9781423385226, BAD); 39.97 (978-1-4233-8521-9(7), 9781423385219, Brinc Audio MP3 Lib); 24.99 (978-1-4233-8520-2(9), 9781423385202, Brilliance MP3); 39.97 (978-1-4233-8523-3(3), 9781423385233, BADLE); audio compact disk 34.99 (978-1-4233-8518-9(7), 9781423385189, Bril Audio CD Unabri); audio compact disk 92.97 (978-1-4233-8519-6(5), 9781423385196, BriAudCD Unabrid) Brilliance Audio.

After God's Own Heart: Lessons from the Life of David. Sam Laing. 4 cass. (Running Time: 4 hrs.). 1998. 21.99 (978-1-57782-052-9(5)) Discipleshp.
Showing today's disciples what they can learn from David's intensely personal walk with God. Those who listen will learn to love God even more.

After Great Pain a Formal Feeling Comes see Poems & Letters of Emily Dickinson

***after Hours.** 2010. audio compact disk (978-1-59171-155-1(X)) Falcon Picture.

After Hours. Perf. by Andre Previn et al. 1 cass., 1 CD. 7.98 (TA 33302); audio compact disk 12.78 CD Jewel box. (TA 83302) NewSound.

After House. Mary Roberts Rinehart. Read by Rebecca Burns. (Playaway Adult Fiction Ser.). (ENG.). 2009. 49.99 (978-1-60775-762-7(1)) Find a World.

After House. Mary Roberts Rinehart. Read by Rebecca C. Burns. (ENG.). 2005. audio compact disk 49.99 (978-1-4001-3122-8(7)); audio compact disk 24.99 (978-1-4001-0122-1(0)); audio compact disk 19.99 (978-1-4001-5122-6(8)) Pub: Tantor Media. Dist(s): IngramPubServ

After House. collector's ed. Mary Roberts Rinehart. Read by Rebecca C. Burns. 4 cass. (Running Time: 6 hrs.). 1999. 32.00 (978-0-7366-4785-4(6), 5132) Books on Tape.

A dream voyage aboard the super-yacht "Ella" suddenly becomes a nightmare of blood & terror. Only one hand aboard, ex-landlubber Leslie, seemed enough in control to stay the bloody hand of the murderer. But he'd have to stay alive to do it & that wasn't going to be easy.

After House. unabr. ed. Mary Roberts Rinehart. Read by Kristen Underwood. 4 cass. (Running Time: 5 hrs. 30 mins.). 1995. 32.95 (978-0-7861-0811-4(8), 1634) Blckstn Audio.

Newly out of the hospital & totally out of funds, young Ralph Leslie longed for a long sea voyage. So he jumped at the chance to sign aboard millionaire Marshall Turner's luxurious super-yacht as steward to the passengers lodged in its after house. His job was easy sailing - until, one sultry summer night, the dream voyage suddenly became a nightmare of blood & terror.

After House. unabr. ed. Mary Roberts Rinehart. Read by Jim Killavey. 5 cass. (Running Time: 7 hrs. 30 mins.). 1993. 29.00 Set, in vinyl album. Jimcin Record.

A summer cruise leads to murder, mystery & madness in the afterhouse.

After House. unabr. ed. Mary Roberts Rinehart. Narrated by Rebecca Burns. (Running Time: 5 hrs. 0 mins. 0 sec.). (ENG.). 2009. audio compact disk 39.99 (978-1-4001-4126-5(5)) Pub: Tantor Media. Dist(s): IngramPubServ

After House, with EBook. unabr. ed. Mary Roberts Rinehart. Narrated by Rebecca Burns. (Running Time: 5 hrs. 0 mins. 0 sec.). (ENG.). 2009. 19.99 (978-1-4001-6126-3(6)); audio compact disk 19.99 (978-1-4001-1126-8(9)) Pub: Tantor Media. Dist(s): IngramPubServ

***After House, with EBook.** unabr. ed. Mary Roberts Rinehart. Narrated by Rebecca Burns. (Running Time: 5 hrs. 0 mins.). 2009. 13.99 (978-1-4001-8126-1(7)); 19.99 (978-1-4001-9126-0(2)) Tantor Media.

After Innocence. abr. ed. Brenda Joyce. Read by Alana Windsor. 1 cass. (Running Time: 90 mins.). 1995. 5.99 (978-1-57096-023-9(2), RAZ 923) Romance Alive Audio.

Wealthy but reclusive artist Sofie O'Neil is resigned to spinsterhood until she meets dazzling rogue, diamond smuggler & libertine, Edward Delanza. Determined to help her blossom into womanhood, Edward must heal Sofie's wounded past before they can enjoy a priceless future together.

After Jihad. unabr. ed. Oliver North. (Running Time: 10 hrs.). 2010. 39.97 (978-1-4233-5463-5(X), 9781423354635, Brlnc Audio MP3 Lib); 24.99 (978-1-4233-5462-8(1), 9781423354628, Brilliance MP3); 24.99 (978-1-4233-5464-2(8), 9781423354642, BAD); 39.97 (978-1-4233-5465-9(6), 9781423354659, BADLE); audio compact disk 36.99 (978-1-4233-5460-4(5), 9781423354604, Bril Audio CD Unabri); audio compact disk 97.97 (978-1-4233-5461-1(3), 9781423354611, BriAudCD Unabrid) Brilliance Audio.

After Job Loss - Moving On see Bounce Back from Job Loss in Six Days - Guaranteed!: Create the Career Comeback of Your Dreams with Mental Imagery Technology

After Long Silence: A Memoir. unabr. ed. Helen Fremont. Narrated by Suzanne Toren. 8 cass. (Running Time: 10 hrs. 30 mins.). 1999. 72.00 (978-0-7887-3750-3(3), 95934E7) Recorded Bks.

Raised as a Roman Catholic in America, Helen Fremont was stunned to discover her parents were Jews & Holocaust survivors. In this memoir, she searches for the explanation of this extraordinary secret. This is a journey through suffering, love & healing. Includes an exclusive interview with the author.

After Long Silence: A Memoir. unabr. ed. Helen Fremont. Narrated by Suzanne Toren. 9 CDs. (Running Time: 10 hrs. 30 mins.). 2000. audio compact disk 81.00 (978-0-7887-3985-9(9), C1148E7) Recorded Bks.

After Many Days. unabr. ed. Isobel Neill. Read by Margaret Sircom. 7 cass. (Running Time: 9 hrs. 15 mins.). 1998. 76.95 (978-1-85903-238-1(9)) Pub: Magna Story GBR. Dist(s): Ulverscroft US

The tender saga of a woman's search for love and happiness.

After Midnight. unabr. ed. Susan Sallis. Read by Hilary Neville. 12 cass. (Running Time: 14 hrs.). (Soundings Ser.). (J). 2005. 94.95 (978-1-84559-178-6(X)); audio compact disk 99.95 (978-1-84559-302-5(2)) Pub: ISIS Lrg Prnt GBR. Dist(s): Ulverscroft US

After Rain. unabr. collector's ed. William Trevor. Read by Edward Lewis. 7 cass. (Running Time: 7 hrs.). 1997. 42.00 (978-0-7366-3654-4(4), 4321) Books on Tape.

From the winner of the most prestigious prizes in English literature comes 12 short stories.

After St. Theresa see Twentieth-Century Poetry in English, No. 10, Recordings of Poets Reading Their Own Poetry

***After the Affair.** abr. ed. Janis A. Spring. Read by Janis A. Spring. (ENG.). 2007. (978-0-06-157296-8(9)); (978-0-06-157297-5(7)) HarperCollins Pubs.

After the Affair: Healing the Pain & Rebuilding Trust When a Partner Has Been Unfaithful. unabr. abr. ed. Janis A. Spring. Read by Janis A. Spring. Told to Michael Spring. (Running Time: 10800 sec.). 2008. audio compact disk 14.95 (978-0-06-144183-7(X), Harper Audio) HarperCollins Pubs.

After the Ball. unabr. collector's ed. Ian Whitcomb. Read by Ian Whitcomb. 9 cass. (Running Time: 13 hrs. 30 min.). 1988. 72.00 (978-0-7366-1253-1(X), 2167) Books on Tape.

A look at popular music from the 1890's to the 1960's.

After the Buffalo Jump: A Story of the Blackfoot Nation. Godwin Chu. (Step into History Ser.). 2001. audio compact disk 18.95 (978-1-4105-0170-7(1)) D Johnston Inc.

After the Buffalo Jump Vol. 10: A Story of the Blackfoot Nation. Godwin Chu. Ed. by Jerry Stemach et al. Illus. by Jeff Ham. Narrated by Jim DeNomie. Contrib. by Ted S. Hasselbring. (Start-to-Finish Books). (J). (gr. 2-3). 2001. 35.00 (978-1-58702-729-1(1)) D Johnston Inc.

After the Buffalo Jump Vol. 10: A Story of the Blackfoot Nation. unabr. ed. Godwin Chu. Ed. by Jerry Stemach et al. Illus. by Jeff Ham. Narrated by Jim DeNomie. Contrib. by Ted S. Hasselbring. 1 cass. (Running Time: 1 hr.). (Start-to-Finish Books). (J). (gr. 2-3). 2001. (978-1-58702-678-2(3), F43) D Johnston Inc.

Three Blackfoot tribes the North Blackfoot, the Bloods and the Peigan comprise the Blackfoot Nation in the lands that today include southern Alberta and Montana. For centuries, these tribes shared a common language, culture, and purpose in preserving their territory against attack from neighboring tribes. The blackfoot way of life was intimately associated with the great herds of buffalo that lived by the thousands throughout the grassy plains.

After the Cross. Contrib. by Bruce Greer. 1997. audio compact disk 90.00 (978-0-7601-2028-6(5), 75700083) Pub: Brentwood Music. Dist(s): H Leonard

After the Cross. Contrib. by Bruce Greer. 1997. 4.00 (978-0-7601-2032-3(3), 75700091) Pub: Brentwood Music. Dist(s): H Leonard

After the Ecstasy, the Laundry. Jack Kornfield. 8 CDs. (Running Time: 9 hrs 30 min). 2005. audio compact disk 49.95 (978-1-59179-394-6(7), AW00471D) Sounds True.

When does enlightenment come? At the end of the spiritual journey? Or the beginning? On After the Ecstasy, the Laundry, Jack Kornfield - author of the modern classic on American Buddhism, A Path with Heart - brings into focus the truth about satori, the awakened state of consciousness, and enlightenment practices today. Perfect enlightenment appears in many texts, Kornfield begins. But how is it viewed among Western teachers and practitioners? To find out, Kornfield talked to more than one hundred Zen masters, rabbis, nuns, lamas, monks, and senior meditation students from all walks of life. The result is this extraordinary look at the hard work we all must do - the laundry - no matter how often we experience ecstatic states of consciousness through meditation and other disciplines. Sweeping in its scope, and warmly told by one of American Buddhism's most trusted voices, After the Ecstasy, the Laundry is both a work of deep inspiration and daily instruction that cuts through the confusion about what enlightenment really is, who it comes to, and how it continues to inform and guide our spiritual lives.

After the Fall. unabr. ed. Arthur Miller. Perf. by Amy Brenneman et al. 2 CDs. (Running Time: 2 hrs. 6 mins.). Dramatization. (L. A. Theatre Works). 2001. audio compact disk 25.95 (978-1-58081-205-4(8), CDTPT128) Pub: L A Theatre. Dist(s): NetLibrary CO

This play, which takes place in the imaginal world of the character Quentin, is in a sense an ongoing self-analysis as he bravely re-collects how he has chosen to live, love & relate to people. But beneath all the idealistic frenzy he discovers an "angel" who "brings us back exactly what we want to lose & so you must love him, because he keeps truth in the world.".

After the Fall. unabr. ed. Arthur Miller. Read by Amy Brenneman & Anthony LaPaglia. 2 cass. (Running Time: 2 hrs.). Dramatization. 2001. 22.95 L A Theatre.

***After the Fall: A Novel.** unabr. ed. Kylie Ladd. (Running Time: 8 hrs. 30 mins.). 2010. 15.99 (978-1-4001-8741-6(9)) Tantor Media.

***After the Fall: A Novel.** unabr. ed. Kylie Ladd. Narrated by John Lee & Anne Flosnik. (Running Time: 9 hrs. 0 mins. 0 sec.). (ENG.). 2010. 19.99 (978-1-4001-6741-8(8)) Pub: Tantor Media. Dist(s): IngramPubServ

***After the Fall: A Novel.** unabr. ed. Kylie Ladd. Narrated by Anne Flosnik. (Running Time: 9 hrs. 0 mins. 0 sec.). (ENG.). 2010. audio compact disk 71.99 (978-1-4001-4741-0(7)) Pub: Tantor Media. Dist(s): IngramPubServ

***After the Fall: A Novel.** unabr. ed. Kylie Ladd. Narrated by Anne Flosnik & John Lee. (Running Time: 9 hrs. 0 mins. 0 sec.). (ENG.). 2010. audio compact disk 29.99 (978-1-4001-1741-3(0)) Pub: Tantor Media. Dist(s): IngramPubServ

After the Fire. 2 cass. (Running Time: 6480 sec.). 2005. 24.95 (978-0-7927-3786-5(5), CSL 859); audio compact disk 29.95 (978-0-7927-3787-2(3), SLD 859) AudioGO.

After the Fire. unabr. ed. Belva Plain. Read by Kate Harper. 12 CDs. (Running Time: 18 hrs.). 2001. audio compact disk 110.95 (978-0-7927-9986-3(0), SLD 037, Chivers Sound Lib) AudioGO.

What happens when the picture-perfect marriage dissolves? A marriage between a naive young artist & her handsome physician husband, when one terrible night she commits an act she will regret for the rest of her life.

After the Fire. unabr. ed. Belva Plain. Read by Kate Harper. 10 vols. (Running Time: 15 hrs.). 2001. bk. 84.95 (978-0-7927-2429-2(1), CSL 318, Chivers Sound Lib) AudioGO.

An ideal marriage between a naive young artist & her handsome physician husband, seemed ideal. Then one terrible night she commits an act she will regret for the rest of life. An act that gives her husband the ultimate weapon: blackmail. The price of his silence is uncontested custody of their two children. She alone knows or believes she knows, what really happened on that fateful night.

After the Fire: A True Story of Love & Survival. unabr. ed. Robin Gaby Fisher. (Running Time: 6 hrs. NaN mins.). 2008. 29.95 (978-1-4332-4438-4(1)); 44.95 (978-1-4332-4434-6(9)); cass. & cass. 29.95 (978-1-4332-4436-0(5)); cass. & audio compact disk 29.95 (978-1-4332-4437-7(3)); audio compact disk 50.00 (978-1-4332-4435-3(7)) Blckstn Audio.

After the Funeral see Dylan Thomas Reading On the Marriage of a Virgin, Over Sir John's Hill, In Country Sleep & Others

After the Funeral see Dylan Thomas Reading His Poetry

***After the Funeral.** Agatha Christie. Narrated by Full Cast Production Staff & John Moffatt. 2 CDs. (Running Time: 1 hr. 30 mins. 0 sec.). (ENG., 2010. audio compact disk 24.95 (978-0-563-51060-4(9)) Pub: AudioGO. Dist(s): Perseus Dist

After the Funeral: A Hercule Poirot Mystery. Agatha Christie. Read by Hugh Fraser. 2007. 27.95 (978-1-57270-847-1(6)) Pub: Audio Partners. Dist(s): PerseuPGW

After the Funeral: A Hercule Poirot Mystery. unabr. ed. Agatha Christie. Narrated by Hugh Fraser. (Running Time: 25200 sec.). (Mystery Masters Ser.). (ENG.). 2007. audio compact disk 29.95 (978-1-57270-846-4(8)) Pub: AudioGO. Dist(s): Perseus Dist

After the Honeymoon... & Forever. Douglas A. Brinley. 1 cass. 2004. 7.98 (978-1-55503-700-0(3), 06004954) Covenant Comms.

Improving marriage one step at a time.

After the New Testament: The Writings of the Apostolic Fathers, I-II. Instructed by Bart D. Ehrman. 12 cass. (Running Time: 12 hrs.). 54.95 (978-1-59803-062-4(0), 6537) Teaching Co.

After the New Testament: The Writings of the Apostolic Fathers, Vol. I-II. Instructed by Bart D. Ehrman. 12 CDs. (Running Time: 12 hrs.). 2005. audio compact disk 69.95 (978-1-59803-064-8(7), 6537) Teaching Co.

***After the Night.** abr. ed. Linda Howard. Read by Natalie Ross. (Running Time: 6 hrs.). 2010. audio compact disk 14.99 (978-1-4418-2560-5(6), 9781441825605, BACD) Brilliance Audio.

After the Night. unabr. ed. Linda Howard. Read by Natalie Ross. (Running Time: 12 hrs.). 2010. 39.97 (978-1-4233-6322-4(1), 9781423363224, Brlnc Audio MP3 Lib); 24.99 (978-1-4233-6321-7(3), 9781423363217, Brilliance MP3); 24.99 (978-1-4233-6323-1(X), 9781423363231, BAD); audio compact disk 92.97 (978-1-4233-6320-0(5), 9781423363200, BriAudCD Unabrid); audio compact disk 29.99 (978-1-4233-6319-4(1), 9781423363194, Bril Audio CD Unabri) Brilliance Audio.

***After the Night.** unabr. ed. Linda Howard. Read by Natalie Ross. (Running Time: 13 hrs.). 2010. 39.97 (978-1-4418-5024-9(4), 9781441850249, BADLE) Brilliance Audio.

After the Parade. unabr. ed. Dorothy Garlock. Read by Kate Forbes. 8 vols. (Running Time: 12 hrs.). 2000. bk. 69.95 (978-0-7927-2404-9(6), CSL 293, Chivers Sound Lib) AudioGO.

Johnny Henry is coming home from the Pacific & his estranged wife, Kathleen, secretly watches him step off the train to a hero's welcome.

After the Plague. T. C. Boyle. Read by Scott Brick. 2001. audio compact disk 88.00 (978-0-7366-8531-3(6)) Books on Tape.

After the Plague. unabr. ed. T. C. Boyle. 1 cass. (Running Time: 1 hr. 30 mins.). 2001. 72.00 (978-0-7366-7631-1(7)) Books on Tape.

Speaks of contemporary social issues in a range of emotional keys. The sixteen stories gathered here address everything from air rage to abortion doctors to first love and its consequences. The collection ends with the brilliant title story, a whimsical and imaginative vision of a disease-ravaged Earth.

After the Quake. Tina Dillion. 1 cass. (Running Time: 1 hr.). (Ten-Minute Thrillers Ser.). (YA). (gr. 6-12). 1995. pap. bk. 12.95 (978-0-7854-1073-7(2), 40798) Am Guidance.

After the Quake. unabr. ed. Haruki Murakami. Read by Rupert Degas et al. (Running Time: 15592 sec.). 2007. audio compact disk 28.98 (978-962-634-432-3(6), Naxos AudioBooks) Naxos.

***After the Rain.** abr. ed. Chuck Logan. Read by Kevin Conway. (ENG.). 2004. (978-0-06-078269-6(2), Harper Audio) HarperCollins Pubs.

***After the Rain.** abr. ed. Chuck Logan. Read by Kevin Conway. (ENG.). 2004. (978-0-06-081483-0(7), Harper Audio) HarperCollins Pubs.

After the Rain... The Cure. Richard Fargier. Tr. by Stephen Martin. (ENG.). 2009. bk. 19.98 (978-0-9636193-6-5(5)) Cleopatra Rec.

After the Rain-Music. 2007. audio compact disk 19.95 (978-1-56136-407-7(X)) Master Your Mind.

After the Rapture. Perf. by Institutional Radio Mass Choir. 1 cass., 1 CD. 10.98 (978-1-57908-317-5(X), 1326); audio compact disk 15.98 CD. (978-1-57908-316-8(1)) Platinm Enter.

After the Storm. Alma Flor Ada. (Stories for the Year 'Round Ser.). (J). (gr. k-3). 4.95 (978-1-58105-321-0(5)) Santillana.

After the Trial of Your Faith. Bernell Christensen. 1 cass. 7.98 (978-1-55503-133-6(1), 06003648) Covenant Comms.

Motivating & comforting message.

After the Wreck, I Picked Myself Up, Spread My Wings, & Flew Away. Joyce Carol Oates. 6. (Running Time: 6 hrs. 75 mins.). 2006. audio compact disk 66.75 (978-1-4281-2223-9(0)) Recorded Bks.

After the Wreck, I Picked Myself Up, Spread My Wings, & Flew Away. Joyce Carol Oates. Read by Jennifer Ikeda. 6. (Running Time: 6 hrs. 75 mins.). 2006. 49.75 (978-1-4281-2218-5(4)) Recorded Bks.

After This. unabr. ed. Alice McDermott. 9 CDs. (Running Time: 36540 sec.). 2006. audio compact disk 89.95 (978-0-7927-4355-2(5), SLD 989) AudioGO.

After This. unabr. ed. Alice McDermott. Narrated by Martha Plimpton. 6 cass. (Running Time: 36540 sec.). (Sound Library). 2006. 59.95 (978-0-7927-4537-2(X), CSL 989) AudioGO.

After This. unabr. ed. Alice McDermott. Read by Martha Plimpton. 9 CDs. (Running Time: 10 hrs. 30 mins. 0 sec.). (ENG.). 2006. audio compact disk 39.95 (978-1-59397-967-6(3)) Pub: Macmill Audio. Dist(s): Macmillan

After Tupac & D Foster. unabr. ed. Jacqueline Woodson. Read by Susan Spain. (Running Time: 3 hrs.). 2009. 39.97 (978-1-4233-9807-3(6), 9781423398073, Brlnc Audio MP3 Lib); 19.99 (978-1-4233-9806-6(8), 9781423398066, Brilliance MP3); 39.97 (978-1-4233-9809-7(2), 9781423398097, BADLE); 19.99 (978-1-4233-9808-0(4), 9781423398080, BAD); audio compact disk 19.99 (978-1-4233-9804-2(1), 9781423398042, Bril Audio CD Unabri) Brilliance Audio.

After Tupac & D Foster. unabr. ed. Jacqueline Woodson. Read by Susan Spain. 3 CDs. (Running Time: 3 hrs. 13 mins.). (YA). (gr. 6-10). 2009. audio compact disk 39.97 (978-1-4233-9805-9(X), 9781423398059, BriAudCD Unabrid) Brilliance Audio.

After Twenty Years see O. Henry Favorites

After Twenty Years see Best of O. Henry

After Twenty Years see Favorite Stories by O. Henry

After Twenty Years see Sredni Vashtar

After Yalta. unabr. collector's ed. Lisle A. Rose. Read by Justin Hecht. 6 cass. (Running Time: 9 hrs.). 1982. 48.00 (978-0-7366-0349-2(2), 1335) Books on Tape.

Consequences of the fatal wartime conference that gave Stalin all he wanted in eastern Europe.

After You. unabr. ed. Annie Garrett. Read by Mary Beth Quillin Gregor. (Running Time: 6 hrs.). 2009. 39.97 (978-1-4233-8607-0(8), 9781423386070, Brlnc Audio MP3 Lib); 24.99 (978-1-4233-8606-3(X), 9781423386063, Brilliance MP3); 39.97 (978-1-4233-8609-4(4), 9781423386094, BADLE); 24.99 (978-1-4233-8608-7(6), 9781423386087, BAD) Brilliance Audio.

***After You Believe.** unabr. ed. N. T. Wright. Read by Antony Ferguson. (ENG.). 2010. (978-0-06-197744-2(6), Harper Audio) HarperCollins Pubs.

***After You Believe: Why Christian Character Matters.** unabr. ed. N. T. Wright. Read by Antony Ferguson. (ENG.). 2010. (978-0-06-195365-1(2), Harper Audio) HarperCollins Pubs.

After You with a Pistol. unabr. ed. Kyril Bonfiglioli. Read by Simon Prebble. (Running Time: 25200 sec.). (Charlie Mortdecai Mysteries Ser.). 2006. audio compact disk 29.95 (978-0-7861-7762-2(4)) Blckstn Audio.

After You with the Pistol. Kyril Bonfiglioli. Read by Simon Prebble. (Running Time: 25200 sec.). (Charlie Mortdecai Mysteries Ser.). 2006. 44.95 (978-0-7861-4497-6(1)); audio compact disk 55.00 (978-0-7861-7233-7(9)) Blckstn Audio.

After You with the Pistol. unabr. ed. Kyril Bonfiglioli. Read by Simon Prebble. 5 cass. (Running Time: 25200 sec.). (Charlie Mortdecai Mysteries Ser.). 2006. 24.95 (978-0-7861-4411-2(4)); audio compact disk 25.95 (978-0-7861-7425-6(0)) Blckstn Audio.

After Your Mission. Ed Pinegar. 1 cass. 2004. 9.95 (978-1-57734-483-4(9), 06006019) Covenant Comms.

A valuable tool for all returned missionaries.

***After You've Blown It: Reconnecting with God & Others.** unabr. ed. Erwin Lutzer. Narrated by Lloyd James. (ENG.). 2005. 9.98 (978-1-59644-229-0(8), Hovel Audio) christianaud.

After You've Blown It: Reconnecting with God & Others. unabr. ed. Erwin W. Lutzer. Narrated by Lloyd James. 2 CDs. (Running Time: 2 hrs. 0 mins. 0 sec.). (ENG.). 2005. audio compact disk 15.98 (978-1-59644-228-3(X), Hovel Audio) christianaud.

After You've Gone. Alice Adams. Read by Alice Adams. Interview with Rebekah Presson. 1 cass. (Running Time: 29 min.). 1990. 10.00 (100590) New Letters.

Best-selling author of "Superior Women" reads the title story from her latest collection, "After You've Gone".

Afterburn. Colin Harrison. Narrated by Pete Bradbury. 15 CDs. (Running Time: 17 hrs. 30 mins.). audio compact disk 142.00 (978-1-4025-2111-9(1)) Recorded Bks.

Afterburn. unabr. ed. Keith Douglass. Read by David Hilder. 8 cass. (Running Time: 12 hrs.). (Carrier Ser.: No. 7). 2001. 29.95 (978-0-7366-6793-7(8)) Books on Tape.
A Carrier Battle Group is placed in harm's way during a civil war in Russia.

Afterburn. unabr. ed. Colin Harrison. Narrated by Pete Bradbury. 12 cass. (Running Time: 17 hrs. 30 mins.). 2001. 98.00 (978-0-7887-5317-6(7)) Recorded Bks.
A riveting thriller that whirls through the world of global commerce and scours the New York underworld. When the high-flying Charlie Ravich and mob boss Tony V. collide, a chain of betrayals breeds danger, and anyone caught in the middle will be lucky to survive.

Afterburn. unabr. collector's ed. Keith Douglass. Read by Edward Lewis. 8 cass. (Running Time: 12 hrs.). (Carrier Ser.: No. 7). 1998. 64.00 (978-0-7366-4125-8(4), 106025) Books on Tape.
In the not-so-distant future a Russian Civil War breaks out. Carrier Battle Group Fourteen is ordered into the Black Sea in a show of American strength.

Afterglow of the Rose see Savagery of Love: Brother Antoninus Reads His Poetry

Afterlife. unabr. ed. 3 cass. (Running Time: 4 hrs. 15 min.). 2004. 28.75 (978-1-4025-8477-0(6)) Recorded Bks.
After an East Fresno student is murdered, his mind leaves his body. Now he must get used to being an invisible spirit?one who watches his friends and family deal with his death.

***Afterlives of the Rich & Famous.** unabr. ed. Sylvia Browne. (ENG.). 2011. (978-0-06-202734-4(4), Harper Audio) HarperCollins Pubs.

Aftermath. Peter Robinson. Narrated by Ron Keith. 12 cass. (Running Time: 16 hrs. 30 mins.). (Inspector Banks Mystery Ser.). 98.00 (978-0-7887-9497-1(3)) Recorded Bks.

Aftermath, Bk. 4. Ben Bova. (978-1-59397-503-6(1)) Macmill Audio.

Aftermath, Pt. 1. unabr. collector's ed. Ladislas Farago. Read by Wolfram Kandinsky. 8 cass. (Running Time: 12 hrs.). 1984. 64.00 (978-0-7366-0750-6(1), 1708-A) Books on Tape.
The author tells how Hitler's vast fortune found it's way to South America, of Peron's complicity in aiding the Nazi war criminals, & of the FBI's search for Bormann in 1948.

Aftermath, Pt. 2. collector's ed. Ladislas Farago. Read by Wolfram Kandinsky. 7 cass. (Running Time: 10 hrs. 30 mins.). 1984. 56.00 (978-0-7366-0751-3(X), 1704-B) Books on Tape.
Story of the author's confrontation with Martin Bormann, former secretary to Hitler.

***Aftermath: A Snapped Novel.** unabr. ed. Tracy Brown. (Running Time: 12 hrs. 5 mins.). (ENG.). 2011. 29.95 (978-1-4417-7420-0(3)); 72.95 (978-1-4417-7417-0(3)); audio compact disk 29.95 (978-1-4417-7419-4(X)); audio compact disk 105.00 (978-1-4417-7418-7(1)) Blckstn Audio.

Afternoon: Amagansett Beach see Twentieth-Century Poetry in English, No. 25, Recordings of Poets Reading Their Own Poetry

Afternoon for Lizards. Dorothy Eden. Read by Angela Down. 5 cass. (Running Time: 7 hrs. 30 mins.). 1999. 49.95 (65395) Pub: Soundings Ltd GBR. Dist(s): Ulverscroft US

Afternoon for Lizards. unabr. ed. Dorothy Eden. Read by Angela Down. 5 cass. (Sound Ser.). 2004. 49.95 (978-1-85496-539-4(5)) Pub: UlverLrgPrint GBR. Dist(s): Ulverscroft US

Afternoon of the Elves. unabr. ed. Janet Taylor Lisle. Narrated by Christina Moore. 3 pieces. (Running Time: 3 hrs. 15 mins.). (gr. 4 up). 27.00 (978-0-7887-0386-7(2), 94577E7) Recorded Bks.
Hillary works in the imaginary village built by elves in Sara-Kate's backyard. She is very curious about Sara-Kate's real life with her mysterious silent mother who lives inside their big and gloomy house. Available to libraries only.

Afternoon on the Amazon. unabr. ed. Mary Pope Osborne. 1 cass. (Running Time: 37 mins.). (Magic Tree House Ser.: No. 6). (J). (gr. k-3). 2004. pap. bk. 17.00 (978-0-8072-0339-2(4), S FTR 217 SP, Listening Lib) Random Audio Pubg.
Jack and Annie journey back in time to a South American rain forest to search for new clues to the whereabouts of Morgan le Fay.

Afternoon Ragas. Music by Rajan Mishra. 1 cass. (From Dawn to Midnight Ser.: Vol. 4). 1990. (A90008); audio compact disk (CD A92079) Multi-Cultural Bks.

Afternoon Ragas, Vol. 1. Music by Amjad Ali Khan. 1 cass. (From Dawn to Midnight Ser.). 1990. (A90005); audio compact disk (CD A92076) Multi-Cultural Bks.

Afternoon Ragas, Vol. 2. Music by Hariprasad Chaurasia. 1 cass. (From Dawn to Midnight Ser.). 1990. (A90006); audio compact disk (CD A92077) Multi-Cultural Bks.

Afternoon Ragas, Vol. 3. Music by Mallikarjun Mansur. 1 cass. (From Dawn to Midnight Ser.). 1990. (A90007); audio compact disk (CD A92078) Multi-Cultural Bks.

Afternoon Tea Serenade: Recipes from Famous Tea Rooms, Classical Chamber Music. Sharon O'Connor. (Sharon O'Connor's Menus & Music Ser.). 1997. bk. 24.95 (978-1-883914-18-9(3)) Menus & Music.

Afternoon Tea Serenade: Recipes from Famous Tea Rooms, Classical Chamber Music. Sharon O'Connor. (Sharon O'Connor's Menus & Music Ser.: Vol. XII). 1999. pap. bk. 24.95 (978-1-883914-30-1(2)) Menus & Music.

Afternoon Walk. unabr. ed. Dorothy Eden. Read by Diana Bishop. 5 cass. (Running Time: 7 hrs.). 1999. 49.95 (978-1-86042-267-6(5), 22675) Pub: Soundings Ltd GBR. Dist(s): Ulverscroft US
A woman has been kidnapped & is believed to have been driven through the streets of the tidy little suburban town of Collingham. This & police questioning sets the neighborhood by the ears during these hot, brooding days of early summer. But it was the atmosphere in her own home that most upset Ella; threats from an unknown telephone caller, the feeling of being under surveillance & above all, her distant husband's contention that she was becoming increasingly fanciful, forgetful & not careful enough of Kitty, their little daughter. Rising doubts & fears force Ella into the confidence of her neighbor, Booth Bramwell. Maybe the heat was affecting her, but surely she hadn't imagined the dustcloud up at the the deserted house on the day of the kidnapping? It seemed that more than Ella's memory was failing her.

Afternoon with the Sage. Franklyn M. Wolff. 2 cass. 18.00 (A0154-82) Sound Photosyn.
Jonh Lilly says this philosopher-mathematician-metaphysician has had the greatest impact on his life of any man. Faustin interviews him at his home when he was 94 years old.

Afternoon with Timothy Leary. Christopher S. Hyatt & Timothy Leary. Ed. by Nick Tharcher. (ENG.). 2008. audio compact disk 14.95 (978-1-935150-07-7(3)) Orig Falcon.

Afternoons with Emily. Rose MacMurray. Narrated by Flo Gibson. (ENG.). 2008. 41.95 (978-1-55685-991-5(0)); audio compact disk 46.95 (978-1-60646-020-7(X)) Audio Bk Con.

Aftershock. Quintin Jardine. 2008. 84.95 (978-0-7531-3239-5(7)); audio compact disk 99.95 (978-0-7531-3240-1(0)) Pub: Isis Pubng Ltd GBR. Dist(s): Ulverscroft US

Aftershock. unabr. ed. Collin Wilcox. Read by Larry McKeever. 8 cass. (Running Time: 8 hrs.). (Frank Hastings Ser.). 1997. 48.00 (978-0-7366-3554-7(8), 4199) Books on Tape.
While a twisted teen stalks Frank Hastings's sweetheart, Hastings gets wrapped up in what seemed like a clear-cut case.

***Aftershocks.** unabr. ed. Harry Turtledove. Narrated by Patrick Lawlor. (Running Time: 27 hrs. 0 mins.). (Colonization Ser.). 2010. 59.99 (978-1-4001-9400-1(8)); audio compact disk 119.99 (978-1-4001-4400-6(0)) Pub: Tantor Media. Dist(s): IngramPubServ

Afterward see Selected Short Stories by Edith Wharton

Afterward. Based on a story by Edith Wharton. 2007. 5.00 (978-1-60339-089-7(8)); audio compact disk 5.00 (978-1-60339-090-3(1)) Listenr Digest.

Again I Say Rejoice. Contrib. by Israel Houghton. (iWorship Ser.). 2005. audio compact disk 9.98 (978-5-558-78682-8(5)) Integrity Music.

Again I Say, Rejoice! Contrib. by Robert Sterling. Created by Israel Houghton & Aaron Lindsey. 2007. audio compact disk 24.98 (978-5-557-53101-6(7), Word Music) Word Enter.

Again to Carthage. unabr. ed. John L. Parker, Jr. Read by Patrick G. Lawlor. (Running Time: 11 hrs.). 2010. 39.97 (978-1-4418-0096-1(4), 9781441800961, Brlnc Audio MP3 Lib); 39.97 (978-1-4418-0098-5(0), 9781441800985, BADLE); 24.99 (978-1-4418-0097-8(2), 9781441800978, BAD); 24.99 (978-1-4418-0095-4(6), 9781441800954, Brilliance MP3); audio compact disk 87.97 (978-1-4418-0094-7(8), 9781441800947, BriAudCD Unabrid); audio compact disk 29.99 (978-1-4418-0093-0(X), 9781441800930, Bril Audio CD Unabri) Brilliance Audio.

Against All Enemies: Inside America's War on Terror. abr. ed. Richard Clarke. 2004. 15.95 (978-0-7435-3932-6(X)) Pub: S&S Audio. Dist(s): S and S Inc

Against All Enemies: Inside America's War on Terror. unabr. ed. Richard A. Clarke. Narrated by Alan Nebelthau. 9 cass. (Running Time: 12 hrs.). 2005. 79.75 (978-1-4193-1506-0(4), 97900) Recorded Bks.
Terrorism expert and 30-year national security veteran Richard A. Clarke served as the counterterrorism czar for both Bill Clinton and George W. Bush. No one in America is more qualified to talk about terrorism and policy. This searing indictment of the Bush administration - from its deceptive use of long-discredited data, to its failure to seize vital opportunities - is an essential listen for every American.

Against All Hope. unabr. ed. Armando Valladares. Read by Grover Gardner. 12 cass. (Running Time: 17 hrs. 30 mins.). 1989. 83.95 (978-0-7861-0075-0(3), 1069) Blckstn Audio.
Armando Valladares describes his twenty-two years of torment & triumph in Castro's prison. Arrested at the age of twenty-two for being philosophically opposed to Communism, he gives a dramatic & harrowing account of the regular beatings, the hunger, the humiliation & psychological "experimentation" to which the Cuban Revolution subjected its unrepentant enemies.

Against All Hope: The Prison Memoirs of Armando Valladares. unabr. ed. Armando Valladares. Read by Grover Gardner. Tr. by Andrew Hurley. (Running Time: 63000 sec.). 2008. audio compact disk & audio compact disk 120.00 (978-0-7861-8990-8(8)) Blckstn Audio.

Against All Odds. 10.00 Esstee Audios.
The story of how one man brought the oil industry to Louisiana.

Against All Odds. Mark Chironna. 1 cass. 1992. 7.00 (978-1-56043-923-3(8)) Destiny Image Pubs.

Against All Odds. Marie Hutchinson Eichler. (J). 1991. 36.95 (978-0-8384-2856-6(8)) Heinle.

Against All Odds. unabr. ed. Julie Bell. Read by Stephanie Brush. 8 cass. (Running Time: 10 hrs.). 2001. 49.95 (978-1-58116-032-1(1)) Books in Motion.
After the Oklahoma City bombing, the once patriotic private militias have become the single largest threat to the stability of the U.S. government, When a list containing the names of government agents who have infiltrated the groups falls in the hands of a vagrant, both government agents and the militias begin a frantic search for the man.

***Against All Odds: A Life of Beating the Odds.** unabr. ed. Scott Brown. (ENG.). 2011. (978-0-06-206450-9(9), Harper Audio); (978-0-06-206451-6(7), Harper Audio) HarperCollins Pubs.

***Against All Odds: A Life of Beating the Odds.** unabr. ed. Scott Brown. (ENG.). 2011. audio compact disk 39.99 (978-0-06-202714-6(X), Harper Audio) HarperCollins Pubs.

Against All Odds: Hebrews 11:21-22. Ed Young. 1992. 4.95 (978-0-7417-1923-2(1), 923) Win Walk.

Against All Odds: My Story. abr. ed. Chuck Norris & Ken Abraham. (ENG.). 2004. 20.99 (978-1-60814-030-5(X)) Oasis Audio.

Against All Odds: My Story. unabr. ed. Chuck Norris & Ken Abraham. 5 cass. (Running Time: 6 hrs.). 2004. 27.99 (978-1-58926-737-4(0)) Oasis Audio.

Against All Odds: My Story. unabr. ed. Chuck Norris & Ken Abraham. Read by Michael Norris. 6 CDs. (Running Time: 6 hrs.). (ENG.). 2004. audio compact disk 29.99 (978-1-58926-738-1(9)) Oasis Audio.

Against All Odds Part 1. Elizabeth Moon. 2009. audio compact disk 19.99 (978-1-59950-594-7(0)) GraphicAudio.

Against All the Odds: George Washington & the Fight for American Independence. John Bergez. (Step into History Ser.). 2002. audio compact disk 18.95 (978-1-4105-0187-5(6)) D Johnston Inc.

Against All the Odds: George Washington & the Fight for American Independence. John Bergez & Noe Venable. Ed. by Jerry Stemach et al. Illus. by Rick Clubb. Narrated by Joe Sikora. Contrib. by Ted S. Hasselbring. (Start-to-Finish Books). (J). (gr. 2-3). 2002. 35.00 (978-1-58702-783-3(6)) D Johnston Inc.

Against All the Odds: George Washington & the Fight for American Independence. abr. ed. John Bergez & Noe Venable. Ed. by Jerry Stemach et al. Illus. by Rick Clubb. Narrated by Joe Sikora. Contrib. by Ted S. Hasselbring. 1 cass. (Running Time: 1 hr.). (Start-to-Finish Books). (J). (gr. 2-3). 2002. 7.00 (978-1-58702-768-0(2), H06) D Johnston Inc.
Just about everyone has heard of George Washington, but not many people know very much about him. Who was this man who commanded the American army during the war for independence and later became America's first President? What was he rally like? How did he become the one indispensable figure in the birth of the United States? And how could Washington fight for liberty when he himself owned slaves.

Against Christianity AudioBook. Peter J. Leithart. Read by Aaron Wells. (ENG.). 2007. audio compact disk 20.00 (978-1-59128-380-5(9)) Canon Pr ID.

Against Christianity (2007 Ministerial Conference) The Church As Politics. Peter J. Leithart et al. (ENG.). 2007. audio compact disk 40.00 (978-1-59128-392-8(2)) Canon Pr ID.

Against Depression. Peter D. Kramer. (Running Time: 6 hrs.). (ENG.). 2005. audio compact disk 34.95 (978-0-14-305761-1(8), PengAudBks) Penguin Grp USA.

Against Medical Advice: One Family's Struggle with an Agonizing Medical Mystery. unabr. ed. James Patterson & Hal Friedman. Read by Kevin T. Collins. (Running Time: 6 hrs.). (ENG.). 2008. 24.98 (978-1-60024-366-0(5)) Pub: Hachet Audio. Dist(s): HachBkGrp

Against Medical Advice: One Family's Struggle with an Agonizing Medical Mystery. unabr. ed. James Patterson & Hal Friedman. Read by Kevin T. Collins. (Running Time: 6 hrs.). (ENG.). 2009. audio compact disk 14.98 (978-1-60024-662-3(1)) Pub: Hachet Audio. Dist(s): HachBkGrp

Against Medical Advice: One Family's Struggle with an Agonizing Medical Mystery. unabr. ed. James Patterson & Hal Friedman. Read by Hal Friedman & Kevin Collins. 3 cass. 2008. 80.00 (978-1-4159-5956-5(0), BksonTape); audio compact disk 80.00 (978-1-4159-5421-8(6), BksonTape) Pub: Random Audio Pubg. Dist(s): Random

Against the Brotherhood. Quinn Fawcett. Narrated by Simon Prebble. 9 CDs. (Running Time: 11 hrs.). 2001. audio compact disk 94.00 (978-0-7887-3981-1(6), C1143E7) Recorded Bks.
Features Mycroft, Sherlock Holme's older brother. Mycroft is acknowledged by Sherlock himself as the smarter of the two & gifted with even greater powers of observation that the famous consulting detective.

Against the Brotherhood. unabr. ed. Quinn Fawcett. Narrated by Simon Prebble. 8 cass. (Running Time: 11 hrs.). 1999. 71.00 (978-0-7887-4079-4(2), H1073E7) Recorded Bks.
Who was this man, who at times seemed to control the British government even though he rarely left his home in Pall Mall or the comfortable environs of The Diogenes Club? Now the secrets of Mycroft Holmes, Sherlock's older brother are coming to the light, revealed in the carefully kept diaries of his secretary, Patterson Guthrie. Mycroft is acknowledged by Sherlock himself as the smarter of the two & gifted with even greater powers of observation.

Against the Cold (Sonnets Fourteen, Eighteen, & Twenty) see Twentieth-Century Poetry in English, No. 10, Recordings of Poets Reading Their Own Poetry

Against the Day. unabr. ed. Thomas Pynchon. Read by Dick Hill. (YA). 2008. 184.99 (978-1-60514-868-7(7)) Find a World.

Against the Day. unabr. ed. Thomas Pynchon. Read by Dick Hill. 42 CDs. (Running Time: 54 hrs. 30 mins. 0 sec.). (ENG.). 2006. audio compact disk 99.99 (978-1-4001-0370-6(3)); audio compact disk 59.99 (978-1-4001-5370-1(0)); audio compact disk 199.99 (978-1-4001-3370-3(X)) Pub: Tantor Media. Dist(s): IngramPubServ

Against the Flow. Perf. by American Made Staff. 1 cass. (J). 1999. 10.98 (978-5-553-70625-8(4), KMGC8696) Provident Mus Dist.
Melds equal parts punk, pop, hard rock & rap. Songs include: "American Made"; "Earth Girls"; "Kick It"; "Against the Flow"; "This Road"; "That Thing I Do"; "Nintendo"; "Enough"; "Nate"; "How We Roll"; "Live & Learn.".

Against the Flow. Perf. by American Made Staff. 1 CD. (YA). 1999. audio compact disk 16.98 (978-5-553-70599-2(1), KMGD8696) Provident Mus Dist.

Against the Law. unabr. ed. Michael C. Eberhardt. 11 cass. 1998. 103.95 Set. (978-1-85903-122-3(6)) Pub: Magna Story GBR. Dist(s): Ulverscroft US

Against the Odds Part 2. Based on a novel by Elizabeth Moon. 2009. audio compact disk 19.99 (978-1-59950-607-4(6)) GraphicAudio.

Against the Tide of Years. unabr. ed. S. M. Stirling. Read by Todd McLaren. Narrated by Todd McLaren. (Running Time: 22 hrs. 0 mins. 0 sec.). (Nantucket Ser.). (ENG.). 2008. audio compact disk 99.99 (978-1-4001-3680-3(6)); audio compact disk 49.99 (978-1-4001-0680-6(X)); audio compact disk 34.99 (978-1-4001-5680-1(7)) Pub: Tantor Media. Dist(s): IngramPubServ

Against the Wind. unabr. ed. J. F. Freedman. Read by David Colacci. (Running Time: 15 hrs.). 2009. 24.99 (978-1-4418-0730-4(6), 9781441807304, Brilliance MP3); 39.97 (978-1-4418-0731-1(4), 9781441807311, Brlnc Audio MP3 Lib); 24.99 (978-1-4418-0732-8(2), 9781441807328, BAD); 39.97 (978-1-4418-0733-5(0), 9781441807335, BADLE) Brilliance Audio.

Against the World. abr. ed. Kerry Eggers & Dwight Jaynes. Read by Willie Harris. 2 cass. (Running Time: 3 hrs.). Dramatization. bk. 15.95 set. (978-1-56703-030-3(0)) High-Top Sports.
Uncovers what went wrong with the Portland Trailblazer's 1991-1992 season.

Agapanthus Hum & Major Bark. unabr. ed. Joy Cowley. Narrated by Christina Moore. 1 cass. (Running Time: 15 mins.). (gr. 1 up). 2002. 10.00 (978-1-4025-1499-9(9)) Recorded Bks.
When Agapanthus is happy or excited, she hums. One day, her parents drive her to the animal shelter to find a nice kitten. But when Agapanthus sees a wiggly little dog, she likes it best of all. Holding her new pet in her arms, Agapanthus hums all the way home. Because he barks so well, the dog is named Major Bark. He isn't beautiful, but he is a very frisky pup, so Agapanthus takes him to the dog show. What will happen when Major Bark meets all the purebred dogs?.

Agapanthus Hum & the Eyeglasses. Joy Cowley. Read by Christina Moore. 1 cass. (Running Time: 15 mins.). (YA). 1999. pap. bk. 30.99 (978-0-7887-3788-6(0), 41032) Recorded Bks.
Agapanthus loves nothing better than kicking up into handstands. The problem is remembering to take off her glasses first. How will she ever become an acrobat? Luckily she gets some valuable mentoring from a beautiful lady acrobat.

Agapanthus Hum & the Eyeglasses. unabr. ed. Joy Cowley. Narrated by Christina Moore. 1 cass. (Running Time: 15 mins.). (J). 2000. pap. bk. & stu. ed. 30.99 (41032X4) Recorded Bks.

Agapanthus Hum & the Eyeglasses. unabr. ed. Joy Cowley. Narrated by Christina Moore. 1 cass. (Running Time: 15 mins.). (gr. k up). 2000. 10.00 (978-0-7887-3814-2(3), 96059E7) Recorded Bks.

Agapanthus Hum & the Eyeglasses, Class set. Joy Cowley. Read by Christina Moore. 1 cass. (Running Time: 15 mins.). (YA). 1999. 158.20 (978-0-7887-3859-3(3), 46999) Recorded Bks.

Agape - Gospel Hard Rock. ed. Music by Fred Caban. Prod. by David Di Sabatino. 1994. 19.99 (978-0-9790740-2-8(9)) D DiSabatino.

Agape - Victims of Tradition. ed. Music by Fred Caban. Prod. by David Di Sabatino. 1994. 19.99 (978-0-9790740-3-5(7)) D DiSabatino.

Agatha Christie. Radio Spirits Staff. Read by Orson Welles. 2007. audio compact disk 17.98 (978-1-57019-826-7(8)) Pub: Radio Spirits. Dist(s): AudioGO

Agatha Christie: The Woman & Her Mysteries. unabr. collector's ed. Gillian Gill. Read by Donada Peters. 7 cass. (Running Time: 10 hrs. 30 mins.). 1991. 56.00 (978-0-7366-2000-0(1), 2817) Books on Tape.
The private woman behind the all-time queen of mystery writers. Fascinating biography.

Agatha Christie a Pocket Full of Rye. Agatha Christie. Contrib. by June Whitfield. 2 CDs. (Running Time: 1 hr. 30 mins.). 2005. audio compact disk 29.95 (978-0-7927-3736-0(9), BBCD 128) AudioGO.

Agatha Christie Assortment 4. Agatha Christie. 2004. 155.40 (978-1-59397-507-4(4)) Pub: Macmill Audio. Dist(s): Macmillan

Agatha Christie Mystery Collection. Agatha Christie. Read by David Suchet & Robin Bailey. (Running Time: 20 hrs.). 2005. 67.95 (978-1-59912-392-9(4)) Iofy Corp.

Agatha Christie Series. Agatha Christie. 6 cass. 1998. 37.45 Box set. (978-0-563-55801-9(6)) BBC WrldWd GBR.
Contains "Murder on the Orient Express," "Death on the Nile," & "Mystery of the Blue Train".

Agatha Christie 450 from Paddington. Agatha Christie. Contrib. by June Whitfield. 2 CDs. (Running Time: 1 hr. 30 mins.). 2005. audio compact disk 29.95 (978-0-7927-3734-6(2), BBCD 126) AudioGO.

***Agatha H & the Airship City.** unabr. ed. Phil and Kaja Foglio. (Running Time: 10 hrs.). (Girl Genuis Ser.). 2011. audio compact disk 29.99 (978-1-4418-7846-5(7), 9781441878465, Bril Audio CD Unabri) Brilliance Audio.

***Agatha H & the Airship City.** unabr. ed. Phil And Kaja Foglio & Phil and Kaja Foglio. (Running Time: 10 hrs.). 2011. 24.99 (978-1-4418-7848-9(3), 9781441878489, Brilliance MP3) Brilliance Audio.

Agatha Raisin: The Quiche of Death & the Vicious Vet - A BBC Radio Full-Cast Dramatization. M. C. Beaton, pseud. (Running Time: 1 hr. 45 mins. 0 sec.). (Agatha Raisin Mystery Ser.: Bks. 1& 2). (ENG.). 2009. audio compact disk 24.95 (978-1-60283-733-1(3)) Pub: AudioGO. Dist(s): Perseus Dist

***Agatha Raisin: The Terrible Tourist; The Fairies of Fryfam.** M. C. Beaton, pseud. Narrated by Full Cast Production Staff & Penelope Keith. (Running Time: 2 hrs. 0 mins. 0 sec.). (ENG.). 2010. audio compact disk 24.95 (978-1-4084-2615-9(3)) Pub: AudioGO. Dist(s): Perseus Dist

Agatha Raisin: The Wizard of Evesham; The Murderous Marriage. M. C. Beaton, pseud. (Running Time: 1 hr. 45 mins. 0 sec.). (ENG.). 2009. audio compact disk 24.95 (978-1-60283-735-5(X)) Pub: AudioGO. Dist(s): Perseus Dist

Agatha Raisin & the Fairies of Fryfam. M. C. Beaton, pseud. (Agatha Raisin Mystery Ser.: Bk. 10). 2001. 32.00 (978-0-7366-7052-4(1)) Books on Tape.
Agatha's search for her destiny is postponed when a prominent resident is murdered and no one is blaming the fairies.

Agatha Raisin & the Haunted House. unabr. ed. M. C. Beaton, pseud. 4 cass. (Running Time: 6 hrs.). (Agatha Raisin Mystery Ser.: Bk. 14). 2003. 36.00 (978-1-4159-9995-0(3)) Books on Tape.

Agatha Raisin & the Love from Hell. unabr. ed. M. C. Beaton, pseud. Read by Donada Peters. 5 cass. (Running Time: 7 hrs. 30 mins.). (Agatha Raisin Mystery Ser.: Bk. 11). 2001. 40.00 (978-0-7366-8481-1(6)) Books on Tape.
Faced with the disappearance of her husband and the death of his mistress, Agatha must summon her own ex-lover to solve all.

Agatha Raisin & the Murderous Marriage. collector's ed. M. C. Beaton, pseud. Read by Donada Peters. 4 cass. (Running Time: 6 hrs.). (Agatha Raisin Mystery Ser.: Bk. 5). 2000. 32.00 (978-0-7366-5536-1(0)) Books on Tape.
Agatha Raisin is tying the knot with James Lacey before he can have second thoughts. After all, her first husband must be long dead of alcohol poisoning but Jimmy Raisin hears the news in his cardboard residence in London & reaches the village of Carsely just in time to stop Agatha from committing bigamy. Promptly jilted by her groom, Agatha pushes Jimmy in a ditch, where he is later found strangled. Even the Local Ladies Society believes her, or James, to be the killer. Soon the unhappy couple, thrown together again by their investigation of Jimmy's insalubrious past, are risking life & limb, not to mention love, as they ferret out dark doings that make Carsley the multiple murder capital of the english Cotswolds.

Agatha Raisin & the Potted Gardener. M. C. Beaton, pseud. Read by Donada Peters. (Agatha Raisin Mystery Ser.: Bk. 3). 2000. audio compact disk 32.00 (978-0-7366-7502-4(7)) Books on Tape.

Agatha Raisin & the Potted Gardener. collector's ed. M. C. Beaton, pseud. Read by Donada Peters. 4 cass. (Running Time: 6 hrs.). (Agatha Raisin Mystery Ser.: Bk. 3). 2000. 32.00 (978-0-7366-4998-8(0)) Books on Tape.
Agatha Raisin's latest plan to catch bachelor James Lacey is to take up gardening & enter the prestigious Carsley Horticultural Contest. Unfortunately, a hard freeze kills all of her seedlings just as her former assistant, Roy, arrives to persuade her to return to work at the PR agency. He promises to restore her garden but as the contest approaches, the plants are mysteriously being uprooted, poisoned & burned, as are plants in gardens throughout the Cotswold town where she lives. When the prime suspect, a beautiful blonde newcomer named Mary Fortune, who has her eye on James, turns up murdered in a particularly nasty way, he & Agatha must put aside their differences to solve the puzzle.

Agatha Raisin & the Terrible Tourist. collector's ed. M. C. Beaton, pseud. Read by Donada Peters. 4 cass. (Running Time: 6 hrs.). (Agatha Raisin Mystery Ser.: Bk. 6). 2000. 32.00 (978-0-7366-5641-2(3)) Books on Tape.
Agatha Raisin's marriage was put off when her ex-husband showed up, unfortunately alive. Fortunately, he was murdered & Agatha solved the crime. Now she is off to Cyprus to track down her ex-fiance. Instead of enjoying their planned honeymoon, however, they witness the murder of an obnoxious tourist. Two sets of terrible tourists surround the unhappy couple, arousing Agatha's suspicions & much to James' Chargrin, she wont rest until she finds the killer. Unfortunately, it seems the killer also won't rest until Agatha is out of the picture. Agatha is forced to track down the murderer, try to rekindle her romance with James & fend off a suave baronet, all while coping with the fact that it's always bathing suit season in Cyprus.

Agatha Raisin & the Walkers of Dembley. M. C. Beaton, pseud. Read by Donada Peters. (Agatha Raisin Mystery Ser.: Bk. 4). 2001. audio compact disk 40.00 (978-0-7366-8055-4(1)) Books on Tape.

Agatha Raisin & the Walkers of Dembley. collector's ed. M. C. Beaton, pseud. Read by Donada Peters. 4 cass. (Running Time: 6 hrs.). (Agatha Raisin Mystery Ser.: Bk. 4). 2000. 32.00 (978-0-7366-5537-8(9)) Books on Tape.
When Sir Charles Fraith, a kindly baronet, receives a letter from Jessica Tartinck, president of the Dembley Walkers Association, his life is thrown into chaos. Ms.Tartinck, as part of her campaign against landowners over the use of public footpaths, has chosen Fraith for her latest attack. Although he suggests a reasonable counteroffer to her demands, Jessica ignores him. Jessica's protest march turns into a death march & she ends up murdered in Sir Charles' field. Agatha is only too willing to try to help clear Sir Charles' name, especially since it means playing the "wife" of her attractive & elusive neighbor, James Lacey. Toward murder & romance, Agatha takes an agreeably direct approach.

Agatha Raisin & the Witch of Wyckhadden. M. C. Beaton, pseud. 4 cass. (Running Time: 6 hrs.). (Agatha Raisin Mystery Ser.: Bk. 9). 2001. 32.00 (978-0-7366-6204-8(9)) Books on Tape.
Agatha Raisin travels to an old-fashioned hotel in order to repair the damage away from the neighbors in her Cotswolds village. Unhappy about the slow recovery & prompted by the elderly residents of the resort, she consults the local witch for help. Agatha purchases a hair tonic & is soon sprouting hair & capturing the fancy of the village police inspector. But the quiet town is stunned by the murder of the witch.

Agatha Raisin & the Wizard of Evesham. collector's unabr. ed. M. C. Beaton, pseud. Read by Donada Peters. 4 cass. (Running Time: 6 hrs.). (Agatha Raisin Mystery Ser.: Bk. 8). 2000. 32.00 (978-0-7366-5931-4(5)) Books on Tape.
When a charming Evesham beautician, Mr. John, collapses from a fatal poisoning, Agatha has a murder case in her hair.

Age & Guile Beat Youth, Innocence, & a Bad Haircut. unabr. ed. P. J. O'Rourke. Read by Rob McQuay. 8 cass. (Running Time: 12 hrs.). 56.95 (1855) Blckstn Audio.
A quarter century of previously uncollected Fulminations, Philippics, Bullyrags, Middle-Finger Flag Downs & Licks with the Rough Side of the Tongue.

Age & Guile Beat Youth, Innocence, & a Bad Haircut. unabr. ed. P. J. O'Rourke. Read by Rob McQuay. 8 cass. (Running Time: 11 hrs. 30 mins.). 2006. 56.95 (978-0-7861-1083-4(X), 1855) Blckstn Audio.

Age & Guile Beat Youth, Innocence, & a Bad Haircut. unabr. ed. P. J. O'Rourke. Narrated by Norman Dietz. 10 cass. (Running Time: 13 hrs. 30 mins.). 1997. 85.00 (978-0-7887-1291-3(8), 94840E7) Recorded Bks.
Whether you are conservative, liberal, or somewhere in between, you will find something genuinely funny & thought-provoking in this previously uncollected series of articles by the award-winning & nationally-accaimed writer. O'Rourke's biting wit & insightful glimpses span a 25-year panorama of American culture.

Age Curve: How to Profit from the Coming Demographic Storm. unabr. ed. Kenneth W. Gronbach. Read by Max Bloomquist. (Running Time: 6 hrs.). 2008. 24.95 (978-1-4233-6453-5(8), 9781423364535, BAD); 39.25 (978-1-4233-6452-8(X), 9781423364528, Brlnc Audio MP3 Lib); 24.95 (978-1-4233-6451-1(1), 9781423364511, Brilliance MP3); 39.25 (978-1-4233-6454-2(6), 9781423364542, BADLE); audio compact disk 82.25 (978-1-4233-6450-4(3), 9781423364504, BriAudCD Unabrid); audio compact disk 29.95 (978-1-4233-6449-8(X), 9781423364498, Bril Audio CD Unabri) Brilliance Audio.

Age in Search of Security. 10.00 (HD420) Esstee Audios.

Age Is Just a Number: Achieve Your Dreams at Any Stage in Your Life. unabr. ed. Dara Torres & Elizabeth Weil. Read by Rebecca Lowman. (ENG.). 2009. audio compact disk 34.95 (978-0-7393-8405-3(8), Random AudioBks) Pub: Random Audio Pubg. Dist(s): Random

Age of American Unreason. unabr. ed. Susan Jacoby. Read by Cassandra Campbell. (YA). 2008. 64.99 (978-1-60514-859-5(8)) Find a World.

Age of American Unreason. unabr. ed. Susan Jacoby. Narrated by Cassandra Campbell. (Running Time: 15 hrs. 0 mins. 0 sec.). (ENG.). 2008. audio compact disk 39.99 (978-1-4001-0732-2(6)); audio compact disk 29.99 (978-1-4001-5732-7(3)); audio compact disk 79.99 (978-1-4001-3732-9(2)) Pub: Tantor Media. Dist(s): IngramPubServ

Age of Anxiety: McCarthyism to Terrorism. abr. ed. Haynes Johnson. Read by Kristoffer Tabori. 4 CDs. (Running Time: 10 hrs.). (ENG.). 2005. audio compact disk 34.95 (978-1-56511-997-0(5), 1565119975) Pub: Penguin-HghBrdg. Dist(s): Penguin Grp USA

Age of Chivalry. unabr. ed. Thomas Bulfinch. Read by Mary Woods. 10 cass. (Running Time: 14 hrs. 30 mins.). 1997. 69.95 (978-0-7861-1216-6(6), 1994) Blckstn Audio.
Recounts the tales of Arthur & the Round Table, explains the historical events & the mindset of the people during the period of their creation.

Age of Chivalry. unabr. ed. Thomas Bulfinch. Read by Mary Woods. (Running Time: 48600 sec.). 2008. audio compact disk 29.95 (978-0-7861-6217-8(1)); audio compact disk & audio compact disk 99.00 (978-0-7861-6216-1(3)) Blckstn Audio.

Age of Discontinuity: Guidelines to Our Changing Society. unabr. ed. Peter F. Drucker. Read by Michael Prichard. 11 cass. (Running Time: 16 hr. 30 min.). 1982. 88.00 (978-0-7366-0351-5(4), 1337) Books on Tape.
This predicted the new technology-based industries & the rise of world markets. Filled with timeless insights.

Age of Empathy: Nature's Lessons for a Kinder Society. unabr. ed. Frans de Waal. Narrated by Alan Sklar. 1 MP3-CD. (Running Time: 10 hrs. 0 mins. 0 sec.). (ENG.). 2009. 19.99 (978-1-4001-6355-7(2)); audio compact disk 29.99 (978-1-4001-1355-2(5)); audio compact disk 59.99 (978-1-4001-4355-9(1)) Pub: Tantor Media. Dist(s): IngramPubServ

***Age of Empathy: Nature's Lessons for a Kinder Society.** unabr. ed. Frans de Waal. Narrated by Alan Sklar. (Running Time: 10 hrs. 0 mins.). 2009. 16.99 (978-1-4001-8355-5(3)) Tantor Media.

Age of Entanglement: When Quantum Physics was Reborn. unabr. ed. Louisa Gilder. Read by Walter Dixon. (Running Time: 14 hrs.). (ENG.). 2009. 39.98 (978-1-59659-431-9(4), GildAudio) Pub: Gildan Media. Dist(s): HachBkGrp

Age of Fable. unabr. ed. Thomas Bulfinch. Read by Mary Woods. 10 cass. (Running Time: 14 hrs. 30 mins.). 1992. 69.95 (978-0-7861-0378-2(7), 1333) Blckstn Audio.
In this classic work you will find the stories of Cupid & Psyche, Venus & Adonis, The Golden Fleece, Hero & Leander, Hercules, Theseus, Midas, The Apple of Discord & many others - all those ancient myths that form a great timeless literature of the past.

Age of Fable. unabr. ed. Thomas Bulfinch. Read by Mary Woods. (Running Time: 46800 sec.). 2006. audio compact disk 55.00 (978-0-7861-6291-8(0)); audio compact disk 29.95 (978-0-7861-7214-6(2)) Blckstn Audio.

Age of Fable, Part. 1. unabr. ed. Thomas Bulfinch. Read by George Guidall. 5 cass. (Running Time: 6 hrs 30 min.). 2003. 49.00 Recorded Bks.
Includes tales of Prometheus, Hercules and Ulysses.

Age of Fable, Part. 2. unabr. ed. Thomas Bulfinch. Read by George Guidall. 5 cass. (Running Time: 6 hrs 15 min.). 2003. 44.00 Recorded Bks.
Includes Aeneas, Thor, Beowolf, and other heroes.

Age of Fable, Pt. 1. unabr. ed. Thomas Bulfinch. Narrated by George Guidall. 6 cass. (Running Time: 9 hrs.). 1995. 49.00 (978-0-7887-0423-9(0), 94615E7) Recorded Bks.
Includes tales of Prometheus, Hercules & Ulysses.

Age of Fable, Pt. 2. unabr. ed. Thomas Bulfinch. Narrated by George Guidall. 5 cass. (Running Time: 6 hrs. 15 mins.). 2001. 44.00 (978-0-7887-0442-0(7), 94634E7) Recorded Bks.
Includes adventures of Aeneas, Thor, Beowulf & other heroes.

Age of Faith, Pt. 2. unabr. collector's ed. Ariel Durant & Will Durant. Read by Alexander Adams. 13 cass. (Running Time: 19 hrs. 30 min.). (Story of Civilization Ser.). 1995. 104.00 (978-0-7366-3091-7(0), 3768-B) Books on Tape.
Here's a look at the Middle Ages through a wide angle lens. Will Durant blends stories of saints, martyrs, kings, knights, popes & poets to tell the story of three cultures: Christian, Islamic & Judaic. Christian civilization, rooted in Jewish philosophy, sits against the backdrop of a complex Islamic tradition.

Age of Fighting Sail: The Story of the Naval War of 1812. unabr. collector's ed. C. S. Forester. Read by Bill Kelsey. 8 cass. (Running Time: 8 hrs.). 1986. 48.00 (978-0-7366-0660-8(2), 1622) Books on Tape.
On June 18, 1812, the U.S. declared war on Britain. The avowed purpose of the war was to put an end to interference with American trade & shipping. It remained to be seen how the U.S. government proposed to bring it about.

Age of Gold: The California Gold Rush & the New American Dream. unabr. ed. H. W. Brands. 13 cass. (Running Time: 19 hrs. 30 mins.). 2002. 104.00 (978-0-7366-8761-4(0)) Books on Tape.
When gold was discovered at Sutter's Mill on the American River, it completely transformed the territory of California. Hundreds of thousands of people sped to California by any means possible, and small cities sprung up to service their needs as they sought the precious metal. By 1850, California had become a state; it had also become a symbol of where the nation was going. Great fortunes were made by such memorable figures as John Fremont, Leland Stanford, and George Hearst; great fortunes were lost by those who are now along history's wayside. The Gold Rush had a profound effect on the way Americans viewed their destinies, as the new get-rich-quick ethos prevailed over the old Puritan mores of hard work.

Age of Henry VIII, Parts I-II. Instructed by Dale Hoak. 12 CDs. (Running Time: 12 hrs.). 2003. bk. 69.95 (978-1-56585-777-3(1), 8467) Teaching Co.

Age of Henry VIII, Pts. I-II. Instructed by Dale Hoak. 12 cass. (Running Time: 12 hrs.). bk. 54.95 (978-1-56585-776-6(3), 8467) Teaching Co.

Age of Heroes. Teaching Co.

***Age of Innocence.** Ed. by Oxford University Press Staff. (Oxford Bookworms ELT Ser.). 2008. audio compact disk 23.75 (978-0-19-479213-4(7)) Pub: OUP-CN CAN. Dist(s): OUP

Age of Innocence. Edith Wharton. Read by David Horovitch. 10 CDs. (Running Time: 12 hrs. 0 mins. 0 sec.). (Cover to Cover Ser.). (ENG.). 2010. audio compact disk 29.95 (978-1-60283-877-2(1)) Pub: AudioGO. Dist(s): Perseus Dist

Age of Innocence. Edith Wharton. 4 cass. (Running Time: 6 hrs. 40 mins.). 26.95 (978-1-885546-08-1(4)) Big Ben Audio.
A tale of thwarted love which is both exuberantly comic & profoundly moving, a marvelous treatise of the manners & morals of the late 19th century in America. In the highest circle of New York social life during the 1870's, Newland Archer, a young lawyer prepares to marry the docile May Welland. Before their engagement is formally announced, he is introduced to May's cousin, the mysterious & nonconformist Countess Ellen Olenska, returning to New York after a long absence. This meeting alters Archer's world forever.

Age of Innocence. Edith Wharton. Read by Nadia May. (Running Time: 6 mins. 30 sec.). 2005. audio compact disk 45.00 (978-0-7861-7633-5(4)) Blckstn Audio.

Age of Innocence. Edith Wharton. Read by Flo Gibson. 8 cass. (Running Time: 12 hrs.). 2001. 29.95 (978-0-7366-6768-5(7)) Books on Tape.
A brilliant portrayal of New York society in the 1870s where money was important but counted for less than manners & morals.

Age of Innocence. Edith Wharton. Read by Dick Hill. (Playaway Young Adult Ser.). (ENG.). 2009. 69.99 (978-1-60775-874-7(1)) Find a World.

Age of Innocence. abr. ed. Edith Wharton. Read by J. Woodward. 4 cass. (Running Time: 6 hrs.). 2004. 25.00 (978-1-931056-83-0(8), N Millennium Audio) New Millenn Enter.
As Newland Archer prepares to marry the docile May Welland, the mysterious, intensely nonconformist Countess Ellen Olenska returns to New York after a long absence. In a dramatic portrait of desire & betrayal, Newland's corner of his conventional world is changed forever.

Age of Innocence. unabr. ed. Edith Wharton. Read by Flo Gibson. 7 cass. (Running Time: 9 hrs. 30 mins.). (Classic Books on Cassettes). 1998. bk. 25.95 (978-1-55685-533-7(8)) Audio Bk Con.
Newland Arther's marriage to docile May Welland is disturbed by the beautiful Countess Olenska, & the manners & morals of N.Y. society.

Age of Innocence. unabr. ed. Edith Wharton. Read by David Horovitch. 8 cass. (Running Time: 12 hrs.). 2004. 34.95 (978-1-57270-116-8(1), F81116u) Pub: Audio Partners. Dist(s): PerseuPGW
Set in the exclusive world of upper-class New York in the 1870's (where people "dread scandal more than disease"), Newland Archer is about to settle down & marry a girl from a suitable family, May Welland. His life is thrown into turmoil when he meets May's cousin, an exotic Countess & finds that he is falling in love with her.

Age of Innocence. unabr. ed. Edith Wharton. Read by Raver Lorna. (Running Time: 12 hrs. 0 mins.). 2009. audio compact disk & audio compact disk 19.95 (978-1-4332-5140-5(X)) Blckstn Audio.

Age of Innocence. unabr. ed. Edith Wharton. Read by Nadia May. 8 cass. (Running Time: 11 hrs. 30 mins.). 2000. 56.95 (978-0-7861-0443-7(0), 1395) Blckstn Audio.
An elegant portrait of desire & betrayal in Old New York. In the highest circle of New York social life during the 1870s, Newland Archer, a young lawyer, prepares to marry the docile May Welland. Before their engagement is announced, he meets May's cousin, the mysterious, nonconformist Countess Ellen Olenska, who has returned to New York after a long absence. Archer's world is always changing. A marvelous comedy of manners & morals, A literary achievement of the highest order, it is a tale of thwarted love which is both exuberantly comic & profoundly moving.

Age of Innocence. unabr. ed. Edith Wharton. Read by Nadia May. (Running Time: 6 mins. 30 sec.). 2005. 29.95 (978-0-7861-7900-8(7)) Blckstn Audio.

Age of Innocence. unabr. ed. Edith Wharton. Read by Lorna Raver. 9 cass. (Running Time: 12 hrs.). 2008. 72.95 (978-1-4332-1423-3(7)); audio compact disk 90.00 (978-1-4332-1424-0(5)) Blckstn Audio.

Age of Innocence. unabr. ed. Edith Wharton. Read by Lorna Raver. 1 MP3-CD. (Running Time: 12 hrs.). 2008. 29.95 (978-1-4332-1425-7(3)) Blckstn Audio.

Age of Innocence. unabr. ed. Edith Wharton. Read by Flo Gibson. 8 cass. (Running Time: 12 hrs.). 2001. 64.00 (978-0-7366-8309-8(7)) Books on Tape.
A brilliant portrayal of New York society in the 1870's where money was important but counted for less than manners and morals.

Age of Innocence. unabr. ed. Edith Wharton. Read by Flo Gibson. 10 CDs. (Running Time: 12 hrs.). 2001. audio compact disk 80.00 (978-0-7366-8460-6(3)) Books on Tape.

Age of Innocence. unabr. ed. Edith Wharton. Read by Dick Hill. 8 cass. (Running Time: 10 hrs.). (Bookcassette Classic Collection). 1997. 59.25 (978-1-56100-818-6(4), 1561008184, Unabridge Lib Edns) Brilliance Audio.
Newland Archer is a young lawyer, a member of New York's high society, and engaged to be married to May Welland. Countess Ellen Olenska is May's cousin, and wants a divorce from the Polish nobleman she married. Intelligent and beautiful, she comes back to New York where she tries to fit into the high society life she had before her marriage. Her family and former friends, however, are shocked by the idea of divorce within their social circle, and she finds herself snubbed by her own class. Ellen and Newland fall in love and must choose between passion and conventions.

Age of Innocence. unabr. ed. Edith Wharton. Read by Dick Hill. (Running Time: 10 hrs.). 2006. 39.25 (978-1-4233-1117-1(5), 9781423311171, BADLE); 24.95 (978-1-4233-1116-4(7), 9781423311164, BAD); audio compact disk 97.25 (978-1-4233-1113-3(2), 9781423311133, BriAudCD Unabrid); audio compact disk 39.25 (978-1-4233-1115-7(9), 9781423311157, Brlnc Audio MP3 Lib); audio compact disk 36.95 (978-1-4233-1112-6(4), 9781423311126, Bril Audio CD Unabri); audio compact disk 24.95 (978-1-4233-1114-0(0), 9781423311140, Brilliance MP3) Brilliance Audio.

Age of Innocence. unabr. ed. Edith Wharton. Read by Nadia May. (YA). 2008. 64.99 (978-1-60514-706-2(0)) Find a World.

Age of Innocence. unabr. ed. Edith Wharton. Read by Nadia May. 8 cass. 1999. 56.95 (FS9-26020) Highsmith.

Age of Innocence. unabr. ed. Edith Wharton. Narrated by Laural Merlington. 1 MP3-CD. (Running Time: 10 hrs. 30 mins. 0 sec.). (ENG.). 2008. 24.99 (978-1-4001-6013-6(8)); audio compact disk 34.99 (978-1-4001-1013-1(0)); audio compact disk 69.99 (978-1-4001-4013-8(7)) Pub: Tantor Media. Dist(s): IngramPubServ

Age of Innocence. unabr. collector's ed. Edith Wharton. Read by Flo Gibson. 8 cass. (Running Time: 12 hrs.). 1982. 64.00 (978-0-7366-0406-2(5), 1382) Books on Tape.
Pulitzer prize-winner of the manners & morals of New York society in the later 1800's.

Age of Jackson. Kenneth Bruce. 1 cass. (Excursions in History Ser.). 12.50 Alpha Tape.

Age of Lincoln. unabr. ed. Orville Vernon Burton. Read by Richard Mock. 12 CDs. (Running Time: 54000 sec.). 2007. audio compact disk 32.95 (978-0-7861-5779-2(8)) Blckstn Audio.
Distinguished historian Orville Vernon Burton suggests that, while abolishing slavery was the age's most extraordinary accomplishment, it was the inscribing of personal liberty into the nation's millennial aspirations that was its most profound. America had always perceived providence in its progress, but in the 1840s and 1850s, a pessimism accompanied a marked extremism. Even amidst historic political compromises, the middle ground collapsed. Burton shows how the president's authentic Southernness empowered him to conduct a civil war that redefined freedom as a personal right to be expanded to all Americans. In the violent decades to follow, while the extent of that freedom would be contested, its centrality to the definition of the country would not.

Age of Lincoln. unabr. ed. Orville Vernon Burton. Read by Richard Mock. (Running Time: 54000 sec.). 2007. 32.95 (978-0-7861-4984-1(1)) Blckstn Audio.

Age of Lincoln. unabr. ed. Orville Vernon Burton. Read by Richard Mock. (Running Time: 54000 sec.). 2007. audio compact disk 29.95 (978-0-7861-6953-5(2)) Blckstn Audio.

Age of Lincoln. unabr. ed. Orville Vernon Burton. Read by Richard Mock. (Running Time: 54000 sec.). 2007. 85.95 (978-0-7861-6772-2(6)); audio compact disk 99.00 (978-0-7861-6771-5(8)) Blckstn Audio.

Age of Louis the Fourteenth. Kenneth Bruce. 1 cass. (Running Time: 65 min.). Dramatization. (Excursions in History Ser.). 12.50 Alpha Tape.

Age of Mediocrity. Ayn Rand. Read by Ayn Rand. 1 cass. (Running Time: 60 mins.). 12.95 (978-1-56114-007-7(4), AR18C) Second Renaissance.
Here is the fascinating opportunity to hear Ayn Rand's predictions - & to judge, in retrospect, their accuracy - made about the Reagan Administration just after it took office.

Age of Mediocrity. Comment by Ayn Rand. 1 cass. (Running Time: 60 mins.). (Ford Hall Forum Ser.). 1981. 12.95 (AR18C) Second Renaissance.
Rand's predictions about Ronald Reagan ("a pragmatist who leans to the right") just after he took office. Her final Ford Hall address is a case-study in prognostication by philosophy. Includes Q&A.

Age of Miracles: Embracing the New Middle Age. unabr. ed. Marianne Williamson. 4 CDs. (Running Time: 4 hrs. 15 mins.). 2008. audio compact disk 23.95 (978-1-4019-1721-0(6)) Hay House.

Age of Miracles: Embracing the New Midlife. Marianne Williamson. (Playaway Adult Nonfiction Ser.). 2008. 59.99 (978-1-60640-618-2(3)) Find a World.

Age of Miracles: Stories. unabr. collector's ed. Ellen Gilchrist. Read by Mary Peiffer. 7 cass. (Running Time: 10 hrs. 30 min.). 1995. 56.00 (978-0-7366-3201-0(8), 3865) Books on Tape.
Piquant premises: three adult children kidnap their mother to keep her from getting a face lift; a writer who lives on Xanax, Evian & Donna Karan contemplates the pursuit by women of wealthy, self-made men; a socialite in search of a health cure finds romance but no rest. In these 16 amusing, sometimes bittersweet stories, Gilchrist's high-spirited heroines know better. Still, they often find themselves in situations with outrageous complications.

Age of Mountaineering. unabr. collector's ed. James R. Ullman. Read by Bob Erickson. 9 cass. (Running Time: 13 hrs. 30 min.). 1983. 72.00 (978-0-7366-0387-4(5), 1364) Books on Tape.
Except for white water rafting, this is the most rapidly growing outdoor sport.

Age of Napoleon, Pt. 1. collector's unabr. ed. Will Durant & Ariel Durant. Read by Alexander Adams. 9 cass. (Running Time: 13 hrs. 30 min.). (Story of Civilization Ser.). 2000. 72.00 (978-0-7366-5077-9(6)) Books on Tape.
Takes us from a feudal peasantry in revolt to the beginnings of the Industrial Revolution.

Age of Napoleon, Pt. 2. unabr. collector's ed. Will Durant & Ariel Durant. Read by Alexander Adams. 10 cass. (Running Time: 15 hrs.). (Story of Civilization Ser.). 2000. 80.00 (978-0-7366-5101-1(2)) Books on Tape.
Takes us from a feudal peasantry in revolt to the beginnings of the Industrial Revolution.

Age of Napoleon, Pts. I & II. Kenneth Bruce. 2 cass. (Running Time: 2 hrs.). Dramatization. (Excursions in History Ser.). 12.50 Set. Alpha Tape.

Age of Napoleon: A Modern Library Chronicles Book. unabr. ed. Alistair Horne. Narrated by Paul Hecht. 5 cass. (Running Time: 6 hrs. 15 mins.). 2004. 49.75 (978-1-4025-9645-2(6), 97794MC, Griot Aud) Recorded Bks.

Age of Opportunity. Paul David Tripp. (ENG.). 2001. audio compact disk 49.95 (978-1-934885-62-8(2)) New Growth Pr.

Age of Pericles, I-II. Instructed by Jeremy McInerney. 12 cass. (Running Time: 12 hrs.). bk. 54.95 (978-1-56585-904-3(9), 3317) Teaching Co.

Age of Pericles, I-II. Instructed by Jeremy McInerney. 12 CDs. (Running Time: 12 hrs.). 2004. bk. 69.95 (978-1-56585-906-7(5), 3317) Teaching Co.

Age of Reagan: A History, 1974-2008. unabr. ed. Sean Wilentz. Narrated by Dick Hill. (Running Time: 23 hrs. 0 mins. 0 sec.). (ENG.). 2008. audio compact disk 39.99 (978-1-4001-5758-7(7)) Pub: Tantor Media. Dist(s): IngramPubServ

Age of Reagan: A History, 1974-2008. unabr. ed. Sean Wilentz. Narrated by Dickie Hill. (Running Time: 23 hrs. 0 mins. 0 sec.). (ENG.). 2008. audio compact disk 109.99 (978-1-4001-3758-9(6)) Pub: Tantor Media. Dist(s): IngramPubServ

Age of Reagan: A History, 1974-2008. unabr. ed. Sean Wilentz. Narrated by Dick Hill. (Running Time: 23 hrs. 0 mins. 0 sec.). (ENG.). 2008. audio compact disk 54.99 (978-1-4001-0758-2(X)) Pub: Tantor Media. Dist(s): IngramPubServ

***Age of Reason.** unabr. ed. Thomas Paine. Narrated by Robin Field. (ENG.). 2010. 14.98 (978-1-59644-953-4(5), MissionAud); audio compact disk 24.98 (978-1-59644-952-7(7), MissionAud) christianaud.

Age of Reason, Set. unabr. ed. Thomas Paine. Read by Robert L. Halvorson. 2 cass. (Running Time: 180 min.). 14.95 (85) Halvorson Assocs.

Age of Reason Begins, Pt. 1. unabr. collector's ed. Will Durant & Ariel Durant. Read by Alexander Adams. 10 cass. (Running Time: 15 hrs.). (Story of Civilization Ser.). 1997. 80.00 (978-0-7366-3717-6(6), 4400-A) Books on Tape.
The Durants take on the linchpin of modern European history, the religious strife & scientific progress between the 1550's & 1650's.

Age of Reason Begins, Pt. 2. unabr. collector's ed. Will Durant & Ariel Durant. Read by Alexander Adams. 11 cass. (Running Time: 16 hrs. 30 min.). (Story of Civilization Ser.). 1997. 88.00 (978-0-7366-3718-3(4), 4400-B) Books on Tape.
Authors bring together a network of stories in their discussion of the bumpy road Towards the Enlightenment.

Age of Sacred Terror: Radical Islam's War Against America. Daniel K. Benjamin & Steven Simon. Read by Jonathan Marosz. 2002. audio compact disk 104.00 (978-0-7366-8830-7(7)) Books on Tape.

Age of Sacred Terror: Radical Islam's War Against America. unabr. ed. Steven Simon. Read by Philip Bosco. 13 cass. (Running Time: 19 hrs. 30 mins.). 2002. 88.00 (978-0-7366-8829-1(3)) Books on Tape.
Two top terrorism experts explain 9/11 - its past, and what it means for the future.

Age of Shiva. unabr. ed. Manil Suri. Narrated by Josephine Bailey. 16 CDs. (Running Time: 16 hrs. 0 mins. 0 sec.). (ENG.). 2008. audio compact disk 39.99 (978-1-4001-0621-9(4)); audio compact disk 29.99 (978-1-4001-5621-4(1)); audio compact disk 79.99 (978-1-4001-3621-6(0)) Pub: Tantor Media. Dist(s): IngramPubServ

***Age of Speed.** Vince Poscente. Read by Sean Mangan. (Running Time: 3 hrs. 55 mins.). 2010. 54.99 (978-1-74214-617-1(1), 9781742146171) Pub: Bolinda Pubng AUS. Dist(s): Bolinda Pub Inc

Age of Speed. unabr. ed. Vince Poscente. Read by Sean Mangan. 3 CDs. (Running Time: 3 hrs. 55 mins.). 2009. audio compact disk 54.95 (978-1-74214-462-7(4), 9781742144627) Pub: Bolinda Pubng AUS. Dist(s): Bolinda Pub Inc

***Age of Speed.** unabr. ed. Vince Poscente. Read by Sean Mangan. 1 MP3-CD. (Running Time: 3 hrs. 55 mins.). 2010. 43.95 (978-1-74214-694-2(5), 9781742146942) Pub: Bolinda Pubng AUS. Dist(s): Bolinda Pub Inc

***Age of Speed: Learning to Thrive in a More-Faster-Now World.** unabr. ed. Vince Poscente. Read by Sean Mangan. 3 CDs. (Running Time: 3 hrs. 55 mins.). 2009. audio compact disk 54.95 (978-1-74233-315-1(X), Bolinda Audio Bks) Bolinda Pub Inc.

Age of the Unthinkable: Why the New World Disorder Constantly Surprises Us & What We Can Do about It. unabr. ed. Joshua Cooper Ramo. Read by Joshua Cooper Ramo. (Running Time: 8 hrs. 30 mins.). (ENG.). 2009. 19.98 (978-1-60024-721-7(0)) Pub: Hachet Audio. Dist(s): HachBkGrp

Age of the Unthinkable: Why the New World Disorder Constantly Surprises Us & What We Can Do about It. unabr. ed. Joshua Cooper Ramo. Read by Joshua Cooper Ramo. (Running Time: 8 hrs. 30 mins.). (ENG.). 2010. audio compact disk 19.98 (978-1-60788-216-9(7)) Pub: Hachet Audio. Dist(s): HachBkGrp

Age of Turbulence: Adventures in a New World. abr. ed. Alan Greenspan. Read by Robertson Dean. Contrib. by Robertson Dean. 8 CDs. (Running Time: 11 hrs.). (ENG.). (gr. 12 up). 2007. audio compact disk 34.95 (978-0-14-314260-7(7), PengAudBks) Penguin Grp USA.

Age of Turbulence: Adventures in a New World. unabr. ed. Alan Greenspan. Contrib. by Robertson Dean. 17 CDs. (Running Time: 20 hrs.). (ENG.). (gr. 12 up). 2007. audio compact disk 44.95 (978-0-14-314259-1(3), PengAudBks) Penguin Grp USA.

Age of Turbulence: Adventures in a New World. unabr. ed. Alan Greenspan. Read by Robertson Dean. 18 CDs. (Running Time: 20 hrs.). 2007. audio compact disk 129.00 (978-1-4159-4420-2(2)) Random.

Age of Voltaire, Pt. 1. unabr. collector's ed. Will Durant & Ariel Durant. Read by Alexander Adams. 13 cass. (Running Time: 19 hrs. 30 min.). (Story of Civilization Ser.). 1998. 104.00 (978-0-7366-4177-7(7), 4676-A) Books on Tape.
The biography of a great man as well as the story of ideas & events that culminated in the French Revolution. But the revolution turned inward & set the stage for Napoleon, a disaster for Europe in general & for the French in particular.

Age of Voltaire, Pt. 2. unabr. collector's ed. Will Durant & Ariel Durant. Read by Alexander Adams. 13 cass. (Running Time: 19 hrs. 30 min.). (Story of Civilization Ser.). 1998. 104.00 (978-0-7366-4178-4(5), 4676-B) Books on Tape.

Age Regression. Bruce Goldberg. (ENG.). 2005. audio compact disk 17.00 (978-1-57968-030-5(5)) Pub: B Goldberg. Dist(s): Baker Taylor

Age Regression. Bruce Goldberg. 1 cass. (Hypnotic Time Travel Ser.). (ENG.). 2006. 13.00 (978-1-885577-02-3(8)) Pub: B Goldberg. Dist(s): Baker Taylor
Self hypnosis cassette that guides you back into the earlier ages of your current life.

Age Specific Competence: JCAHO Compliance Tool for Hospitals, Health Systesm, & Healthcare Organizations to Teach about & Document Competencies of Doctors, Nurses, & Clinical Care & Allied Health Staff in Treatment for Different Age Groups. M. Daniel Farb. 2004. audio compact disk 49.95 (978-1-59491-110-1(X)) Pub: UnivofHealth. Dist(s): AtlasBooks

Age Specific Competence 10 Users. Daniel Farb. 2005. audio compact disk 149.95 (978-1-59491-197-2(5)) Pub: UnivofHealth. Dist(s): AtlasBooks

Age Specific Competence 5 Users. Daniel Farb. 2005. audio compact disk 99.95 (978-1-59491-196-5(7)) Pub: UnivofHealth. Dist(s): AtlasBooks

Age to Age: Digitally Remastered. Contrib. by Amy Grant. Prod. by Brown Bannister. 2007. audio compact disk 13.99 (978-5-557-62609-5(3)) Pt of Grace Ent.

Aged Care Nursing: A Guide to Practice. Ed. by Susan Carmody & Sue Forster. 2 vols. (Running Time: 2 hrs). (Guide to Practice Ser.). 2004. audio compact disk 59.95 (978-0-9750445-8-2(3)) Pub: Ausmed AUS. Dist(s): MPHC

Aged to Perfection - Skin: Creative Visualization to Perfect Your Skin & Reverse the Aging Process. Donna R. Erickson. 2 cass. (Running Time: 30 min. per cass.). 1997. 19.95 Set. (978-1-890679-16-3(X)) Micheles.

Aged to Perfection - Weight: Creative Visualization to Perfect Your Weight & Reverse the Aging Process. Donna R. Erickson. 2 cass. (Running Time: 30 min. per cass.). 1997. 19.95 Set. (978-1-890679-02-6(X)) Micheles.

AgeLess: Take Control of Your Age & Stay Youthful for Life. abr. ed. Edward Schneider & Elizabeth Miles. Read by Greg Wheatley. (Smart Tapes Ser.). 2004. 25.99 (978-1-58926-104-4(6)); audio compact disk 27.99 (978-1-58926-105-1(4)) Oasis Audio.

Ageless Body, Timeless Mind see Mente Sin Tiempo/Cuerpo Sin Edad

Ageless Body, Timeless Mind: The Quantum Alternative to Growing Old. Deepak Chopra. 6 cass. (Running Time: 6 hrs.). 1993. 59.95 set. (1071A) Nightingale-Conant.
In this rejuvenation program, Dr. Deepak Chopra leads you to your true fountain of youth - your mind. You have the power to defy the aging process & improve with each passing year. You'll learn the 14 factors which retard the aging process, how "perceiving" yourself to be young can directly influence the aging process, exercises that reverse 10 biological effects of aging, & 7 traits of people who keep growing & evolving.

Ageless Body, Timeless Mind: The Quantum Alternative to Growing Old. abr. ed. Deepak Chopra. 2 cass. 14.95 Set. (42431) Books on Tape.
Goes beyond current anti-aging research & ancient mind/body wisdom to demonstrate that we do not have to grow old! Dr. Chopra shows that we can direct the way our bodies & minds metabolize time & reverse the aging process - retaining vitality, creativity, memory & self-esteem.

Ageless Body, Timeless Mind: The Quantum Alternative to Growing Old. abr. unabr. ed. Deepak Chopra. Read by Deepak Chopra. Perf. by George Harrison. 3 CDs. (Running Time: 3 hrs.). (Deepak Chopra Ser.). (ENG.). 2002. audio compact disk 19.95 (978-0-553-71373-2(6), Random AudioBks) Pub: Random Audio Pubg. Dist(s): Random

Ageless Face, Ageless Mind: Erase Wrinkles & Rejuvenate the Brain. unabr. ed. Nicholas Perricone. Narrated by Dick Hill. 9 CDs. (Running Time: 10 hrs. 30 mins. 0 sec.). (ENG.). 2007. audio compact disk 34.99 (978-1-4001-0579-3(X)); audio compact disk 69.99 (978-1-4001-3579-0(6)); audio compact disk 24.99 (978-1-4001-5579-8(7)) Pub: Tantor Media. Dist(s): IngramPubServ

Ageless in the Lord. Richard P. Johnson. Read by Richard P. Johnson. Ed. by Kenneth Daust. 4 cass. (Running Time: 2 hrs. 49 min.). 1995. 29.95 set. (978-0-89243-848-8(7), T8075) Liguori Pubns.
Dr. Johnson offers ways to resolve the challenges of aging on a spiritual level.

Ageless Memory: Simple Secrets for Keeping Your Brain Young: Foolproof Methods for People Over 50. abr. ed. Harry Lorayne. Read by Harry Lorayne. (Running Time: 14400 sec.). (ENG.). 2007. audio compact disk 19.95 (978-0-7393-2891-0(3), Random Hse Audible) Pub: Random Audio Pubg. Dist(s): Random

Agency. unabr. ed. Ally O'Brien. (Running Time: 7 hrs. NaN mins.). 2009. 29.95 (978-1-4332-6100-8(6)); audio compact disk 19.95 (978-1-4332-6099-5(9)); audio compact disk 44.95 (978-1-4332-6096-4(4)) Blckstn Audio.

Agency. unabr. ed. Ally O'Brien. Narrated by Kate Reading. 7 CDs. (Running Time: 9 hrs.). 2009. audio compact disk 60.00 (978-1-4332-6097-1(2)) Blckstn Audio.

Agency. 2nd ed. Christopher H. Munch. 4 cass. (Running Time: 5 hrs.). (Outstanding Professors Ser.). 1997. 55.00 (978-1-57793-011-2(8), 28389, West Lglwrks) West.
Lecture given by a prominent American law school professor.

Agency & Partnership. Thomas L. Evans. 4 cass. (Running Time: 4 hrs.). (Gilbert Law Summaries Ser.). (C). 2000. 45.95 (978-0-15-900351-0(2)) Barbri Grp.

Agency & Partnership. Michael J. Kaufman. 47.95 (978-0-314-16069-0(8), gilbert) West.

Agency & Partnership. unabr. ed. Christopher H. Munch. 8 cass. (Running Time: 10 hrs. 25 mins.). (Outstanding Professors Ser.). 1997. 63.00 (978-1-57793-012-9(6), 28388, West Lglwrks) West.
Lecture by a prominent American law school professor.

Agency & Partnership 2006. Michael J. Kaufman & Thomas L. Evans. (Law School Legends Audio Ser.). 52.00 (978-0-314-16070-6(1), gilbert) West.

Agency, Spiritual Progression & the Mighty Change. Blaine Yorgason & Brenton Yorgason. Read by Marvin Payne. 1 cass. (Gospel Power Ser.). 6.95 (978-0-929985-48-0(6)) Jackman Pubng.
A father's letter to his son regarding understanding the route to spiritual success.

***Agency 1, the: A Spy in the House: A Spy in the House.** unabr. ed. Y. S. Lee. (Running Time: 8 hrs.). 2010. 39.97 (978-1-4418-9041-2(6), 9781441890412, Candlewick Bril); 19.99 (978-1-4418-9040-5(8), 9781441890405, Candlewick Bril) Brilliance Audio.

***Agency 1, the: A Spy in the House: A Spy in the House.** unabr. ed. Y. S. Lee. Read by Justine Eyre. (Running Time: 8 hrs.). 2010. audio compact disk 19.99 (978-1-4418-9036-8(X), 9781441890368, Candlewick Bril); audio compact disk 19.99 (978-1-4418-9038-2(6), 9781441890382, Candlewick Bril); audio compact disk 54.97 (978-1-4418-9037-5(8), 9781441890375, Candlewick Bril); audio compact disk 39.97 (978-1-4418-9039-9(4), 9781441890399, Candlewick Bril) Brilliance Audio.

***Agency 2, the: the Body at the Tower: The Body at the Tower.** unabr. ed. Y. S. Lee. (Running Time: 8 hrs.). 2010. 19.99 (978-1-4418-9046-7(7), 9781441890467, Candlewick Bril); 39.97 (978-1-4418-9047-4(5), 9781441890474, Candlewick Bril) Brilliance Audio.

***Agency 2, the: the Body at the Tower: The Body at the Tower.** unabr. ed. Y. S. Lee. Read by Justine Eyre. (Running Time: 8 hrs.). 2010. audio compact disk 19.99 (978-1-4418-9044-3(0), 9781441890443, Candlewick Bril); audio compact disk 19.99 (978-1-4418-9042-9(4), 9781441890429, Candlewick Bril); audio compact disk 39.97 (978-1-4418-9045-0(9), 9781441890450, Candlewick Bril); audio compact disk 54.97 (978-1-4418-9043-6(2), 9781441890436, Candlewick Bril) Brilliance Audio.

Agenda del Estudiante - Full Color. Sara Mejia Castaings. 2005. audio compact disk 12.95 (978-1-881744-48-1(5)) Edit Panamericana.

***Agenda for Change: A Global Call for Spiritual & Social Transformation.** Joel Edwards. (Running Time: 2 hrs. 39 mins. 0 sec.). (ENG.). 2009. 14.99 (978-0-310-77236-1(2)) Zondervan.

Agent GCP & the Bloody Consent Form 10 Users. Daniel Farb & Bruce Gordon. 2005. audio compact disk 599.95 (978-1-59491-181-1(9)) Pub: UnivofHealth. Dist(s): AtlasBooks

Agent GCP & the Bloody Consent Form 5 Users. Daniel Farb & Bruce Gordon. 2005. audio compact disk 499.95 (978-1-59491-151-4(7)) Pub: UnivofHealth. Dist(s): AtlasBooks

Agent GXP FDA Part 11 Five Users. Daniel Farb & Bruce Gordon. 2005. audio compact disk 399.95 (978-1-59491-152-1(5)) Pub: UnivofHealth. Dist(s): AtlasBooks

Agent GXP FDA Part 11 Ten Users. Daniel Farb & Bruce Gordon. 2005. audio compact disk 499.95 (978-1-59491-182-8(7)) Pub: UnivofHealth. Dist(s): AtlasBooks

Agent in Place. unabr. collector's ed. Helen MacInnes. Read by Wanda McCaddon. 9 cass. (Running Time: 13 hrs. 30 min.). 1982. 72.00 (978-0-7366-0397-3(2), 1374) Books on Tape.
Sophisticated narrative of spy/counterspy set in Washington of the 1970's.

Agent Orange: A Novel. unabr. ed. George Hay. Read by William Shatner. (Running Time: 11 hrs.). 2004. 19.95 (978-0-9740926-0-7(6)) AV Bks Pubs.

Agent Z Meets the Masked Crusader. Mark Haddon. Read by Rory McGrath. 6 cass. (Running Time: 4 hrs., 30 min.). (J). 2001. 24.95 (CCA3360, Chivers Child Audio) AudioGO.

Agent 146. unabr. ed. Erich Gimpel. Read by Simon Vance. 6 cass. (Running Time: 8 hrs. 30 mins.). 2004. 44.95 (978-0-7861-2803-7(8), 3330); audio compact disk 56.00 (978-0-7861-8490-3(6), 3330) Blckstn Audio.

Ages of Initiation: The First Two Christian Millennia. Paul Turner. 2005. pap. bk. 14.95 (978-0-8146-2711-2(0)) Liturgical Pr.

***Ages of Man.** abr. ed. William Shakespeare. Read by Sir John Gielgud. (ENG.). 2006. (978-0-06-112611-6(X), Caedmon); (978-0-06-088663-9(3), Caedmon) HarperCollins Pubs.

Ages of Man. unabr. ed. William Shakespeare. Read by John Gielgud. 1 cass. (Running Time: 1 hr. 16 min.). 1996. 12.00 (978-0-89845-905-0(2), CPN 200) HarperCollins Pubs.

Ages 1-2. Ed. by Strang Communications Company Staff. 1 cass. (Running Time: 1 hr.). (J). 2001. 6.99 (978-1-57405-772-0(3), TOMC) CharismaLife Pub.
Introduce your 1-2 year olds to simple action songs that will capture their attention and their hearts. Teach them about God's love with easy praise and worship songs. They will quickly pick up the words, actions and melodies as you play these cassettes again and again.

Ages 1-2: Spring 2002. Ed. by Strang Communications Company Staff. 1 cass. (Running Time: 1 hr.). (J). 2002. 11.99 (978-1-57405-917-5(3)) CharismaLife Pub.

Ages 1-2: Summer 2000. Ed. by Strang Communications Company Staff. 1 cass. (Running Time: 1 hr.). (J). 2001. 6.99 (978-1-57405-812-3(6), TOMC) CharismaLife Pub.

Ages 1-2: Summer 2002. Ed. by Strang Communications Company Staff. 1 cass. (Running Time: 1 hr.). (J). 2002. 6.99 (978-1-57405-955-7(6)) CharismaLife Pub.

Ages 1-2 Activities: Winter 2001/2002. Ed. by Strang Communications Company Staff. 1 cass. (Running Time: 1 hr.). (J). 2002. 6.99 (978-1-57405-888-6(6)) CharismaLife Pub.

Ages 1-2 Cassette: Summer 2000. 1 cass. (J). (ps). 2000. 6.99 (978-1-57405-657-0(3)) CharismaLife Pub.

Ages 1-2 Cassette Winter 2002-2003. 2002. 6.99 (978-1-59185-090-8(8)) CharismaLife Pub.

Ages 1-2 CD Fall 2002. 2002. audio compact disk 6.99 (978-1-59185-003-8(7)) CharismaLife Pub.

AgeWiseLiving Expert Series: Elder Law Expert. Compiled by AgeWiseLiving LLC. (ENG.). 2008. 9.95 (978-0-9796879-2-1(6)) AgeWiseLiving.

AgeWiseLiving Expert Series: Family Relationship Expert. Compiled by AgeWiseLiving LLC. (ENG.). 2008. 9.95 (978-0-9796879-4-5(2)) AgeWiseLiving.

AgeWiseLiving Expert Series: Personal Financial Planning. Compiled by AgeWiseLiving LLC. (ENG.). 2008. 9.95 (978-0-9796879-3-8(4)) AgeWiseLiving.

AgeWiseLiving Expert Series: 3-CD Boxed Set. Compiled by AgeWiseLiving LLC. 2008. 24.95 (978-0-9796879-5-2(0)) AgeWiseLiving.

Aggressive Management of Acute Myocardial Infarction. Moderated by Eugene Braunwald. Contrib. by J. Ward Kenedy & K. Peter Rentrop. 1 cass. (Running Time: 90 min.). 1986. 12.00 (A8659) Amer Coll Phys.
This topic is discussed by a moderator & experts who offer differing opinions.

Aggressive Reconstruction of the Urinary Tract in Children. 2 cass. (Urologic Surgery Ser.: C85-UR4). 1985. 15.00 (8591) Am Coll Surgeons.

Aggressive Surgical Treatment of Locally Advanced Lung Cancer: Symposium. Moderated by Martin F. McKneally. 3 cass. (Thoracic Surgery Ser.: TH-1). 1986. 28.50 (8665) Am Coll Surgeons.

Agile Project Management Using Scrum. Speeches. Kevin Aguanno. 1 CD. (Running Time: 68 mins). 2005. audio compact disk 14.87 (978-1-895186-13-0(7)) Multi-Media ON CAN.
In recent years, the Internet revolution has caused a shift in how fast technology is developed and marketed. We have seen the appearance of ?Web Years? as a measure of time, and the widespread adoption of Rapid Application Development (RAD) as a standard software development method used in even our largest organizations. There has been a parallel shift in how projects are managed. First appearing in software development projects, Agile Development methods are now a very hot topic in software development conferences and magazines. These are methods that stress the speed of development and close interaction with the customer over traditional, more bureaucratic, practices.This recording will outline the underlying principles of Agile Development and details of how it differs from traditional development projects. Then, using an agile project management method called Scrum, it will illustrate how agile management methods used in software development may be extended to projects from other application areas outside of I/T. Listeners will come away from the session with a high-level understanding of the Agile Development philosophy and how it differs from traditional development approaches, enough of an understanding of Scrum to be able to determine if and how it could be implemented on a project, and a list of resources for further information on Agile Development and Scrum.

Agincourt. unabr. ed. Bernard Cornwell. Read by Charles Keating. 2009. audio compact disk 39.99 (978-0-06-078096-8(7), Harper Audio) HarperCollins Pubs.

***Agincourt.** unabr. ed. Bernard Cornwell. Read by Charles Keating. (ENG.). 2009. (978-0-06-172980-5(9), Harper Audio) HarperCollins Pubs.

Agincourt. unabr. ed. Christopher Hibbert. Read by David Case. 3 cass. (Running Time: 4 hrs. 30 mins.). 15.95 (978-0-7366-6017-4(8)) Books on Tape.
This is one of the great triumphs of British warfare. There have been few victories so complete, or achieved against such heavy odds, as that won by Henry V on October 14, 1415. In a pitched battle which lasted barely three hours, a depleted & exhausted British force of some 5,000 routed a French army four or five times its size.

Agincourt. unabr. ed. Christopher Hibbert. Narrated by Patrick Tull. 3 cass. (Running Time: 4 hrs. 45 mins.). 1990. 26.00 (978-1-55690-006-8(6), 90093E7) Recorded Bks.
In 1415 Henry the Fifth of England led a small force of English against the flower of French knighthood & triumphed.

***Agincourt: A Novel.** unabr. ed. Bernard Cornwell. Read by Charles Keating. (ENG.). 2009. (978-0-06-172976-8(0), Harper Audio) HarperCollins Pubs.

Aging: Pains to Youthful Thinking. 1 cass. (Running Time: 60 min.). 10.95 (0.19) Psych Res Inst.
Designed to promote a sense of fullness of life regardless of age.

Aging & Spirituality. Kathy Shaw. 1 cass. (Running Time: 41 mins.). 1997. bk. 15.00 (978-1-58111-005-0(7)) Contemporary Medical.
Impacting the health of older adults by integrating spirituality, ways to nurture & support spirituality, determining the meaning of spirituality for different people.

Aging Answers Audio Series: Secrets to Successful Long-Term Care Planning, Caregiving, & Crisis Management. Interview. As told by Valerie VanBooven. Interview with Valerie VanBooven & Althea West. Interview with Althea West. 6 cassettes. (Running Time: 3 hrs 30 mins). 2003. 40.00 (978-0-9743373-1-9(5)); audio compact disk 40.00 (978-0-9743373-2-6(3)) LTC Expert Pubns.
Aging Answers Series.

Aging As a Sacred Path: Hallowing Our Diminishments. 1 cass. (Care Cassettes Ser.: Vol. 22, No. 2). 1995. 10.80 Assn Prof Chaplains.

Aging Gratefully: Being Your Best for the Rest of Your Life. unabr. ed. Naomi Judd. Read by Renée Raudman. 1 MP3-CD. (Running Time: 7 hrs. 30 mins. 0 sec.). (ENG.). 2007. audio compact disk 19.99 (978-1-4001-5329-9(8)) Pub: Tantor Media. Dist(s): IngramPubServ

Aging Gratefully: Facts, Myths, & Good News for Boomers. unabr. ed. Naomi Judd. Read by Renée Raudman. 6 CDs. (Running Time: 7 hrs. 30 mins. 0 sec.). (ENG.). 2007. audio compact disk 29.99 (978-1-4001-0329-4(0)) Pub: Tantor Media. Dist(s): IngramPubServ
In Naomi's Guide to Aging Gratefully, Judd debunks society's myth s about aging. She helps us define ourselves from within, find our real beauty, and enjoy the benefits that come with growing older. With fifteen important life choices, she shows how to find freedom and simplicity in the latter half of life. Each chapter offers vital, proactive suggestions for developing a healthier body, mind, and spirit at every age.

Aging in America Pt. 1: Introduction. 1 cass. (Running Time: 1 hr.). 11.50 (I071AB090, HarperThor) HarpC GBR.

Aging in America Pt. 2: The Income of the Elderly. 1 cass. (Running Time: 1 hr.). 11.50 (I071BB090, HarperThor) HarpC GBR.

Aging in America Pt. 3: Retirement, the Financial Aspects. 1 cass. (Running Time: 1 hr.). 11.50 (I071CB090, HarperThor) HarpC GBR.

Aging in America Pt. 4: Retirement, Emotional & Identity Aspects. 1 cass. (Running Time: 1 hr.). 11.50 (I071DB090, HarperThor) HarpC GBR.

Aging in America Pt. 5: Nursing Homes, Segment A. 1 cass. (Running Time: 1 hr.). 11.50 (I071EB090, HarperThor) HarpC GBR.

Aging in America Pt. 6: Nursing Homes, Segment B. 1 cass. (Running Time: 1 hr.). 11.50 (I071FB090, HarperThor) HarpC GBR.

Aging in America Pt. 7: Physical Health & Health Care Programs. 1 cass. (Running Time: 1 hr.). 11.50 (SP-80-11-14, HarperThor) HarpC GBR.

Aging in America Pt. 8: Mental Health. 1 cass. (Running Time: 1 hr.). 11.50 (I0714B090, HarperThor) HarpC GBR.

Aging in America Pt. 9: Sex & Aging. 1 cass. (Running Time: 1 hr.). 11.50 (I0711B090, HarperThor) HarpC GBR.

Aging in America Pt. 10: Facing Death. 1 cass. (Running Time: 1 hr.). 11.50 (SP-80-12-05, HarperThor) HarpC GBR.

Aging in America Pt. 11: Special Circumstances of Older Women. 1 cass. (Running Time: 1 hr.). 11.50 (I071KB090, HarperThor) HarpC GBR.

Aging in America Pt. 12: Media Attitudes Toward Older People. 1 cass. (Running Time: 1 hr.). 11.50 (I071LB090, HarperThor) HarpC GBR.

Aging in America Pt. 13: Conclusion. 1 cass. (Running Time: 1 hr.). 11.50 (I071MB090, HarperThor) HarpC GBR.

Aging Process: Medical Facts for Women & Men. unabr. ed. Mercedes Leidlich. Read by Mercedes Leidlich. 1 cass. (Running Time: 1 hr.). 1992. 10.95 in Norelco box. (978-1-882174-12-6(7), MLL-013) UFD Pub.
This tape teaches the Baby Boom generation, who is now middle-aged, all about the physiology of aging. It covers age-related illnesses such as cancer, heart disease, osteoarthritis, osteoporosis, etc. Filled with valuable information & hints for holistic health care in middle age & beyond.

Aging to Saging. Zalman Schachter. 1 cass. 9.00 (A0615-90) Sound Photosyn.
Growing old with strength & conviction.

Aging with Joy. abr. ed. Ruth Morrison & Dawn Radtke. 3 cass. (Running Time: 3 hrs. 10 mins.). 1989. 5.95 pap. bk. (978-0-89622-751-4(0)) Twenty-Third.
Aging with Joy offers practical, workable & effective ways to take charge of our aging years. They offer rewarding alternatives to facing old age with resignation.

Agnes & the Hitman. Jennifer Crusie, pseud & Bob Mayer. Read by Sandra Burr. (Playaway Adult Fiction Ser.). 2008. 74.99 (978-1-60640-582-6(9)) Find a World.

Agnes & the Hitman. abr. ed. Jennifer Crusie, pseud & Bob Mayer. Read by Sandra Burr. (Running Time: 6 hrs.). 2008. audio compact disk 14.99 (978-1-4233-3656-3(9), 9781423336563, BCD Value Price) Brilliance Audio.

Agnes & the Hitman. abr. ed. Jennifer Crusie, pseud & Bob Mayer. Read by Sandra Burr. (Running Time: 6 hrs.). 2009. audio compact disk 9.99 (978-1-4418-2644-2(0), 9781441826442, BCD Value Price) Brilliance Audio.

Agnes & the Hitman. unabr. ed. Jennifer Crusie, pseud & Bob Mayer. Read by Sandra Burr. (Running Time: 12 hrs.). 2007. 39.25 (978-1-4233-3654-9(2), 9781423336549, BADLE); 24.95 (978-1-4233-3653-2(4), 9781423336532, BAD); 87.25 (978-1-4233-3648-8(8), 9781423336488, BrilAudUnabridg); audio compact disk 36.95 (978-1-4233-3649-5(6), 9781423336495, Bril Audio CD Unabri); audio compact disk 24.95 (978-1-4233-3651-8(8), 9781423336518, Brilliance MP3); audio compact disk 102.25 (978-1-4233-3650-1(X), 9781423336501, BriAudCD Unabrid); audio compact disk 39.25 (978-1-4233-3652-5(6), 9781423336525, Brlnc Audio MP3 Lib) Brilliance Audio.

Agnes' Cardboard Piano - Book & Audio Cassette. 1 read-along cass. (J). (ps-3). 1986. bk. 9.98 (978-0-89544-154-6(3), NO. 154) Silbert Bress.
Learns to play the piano & the meaning of friendship.

Agnes Grey. Anne Brontë. Read by Anais 9000. 2008. 27.95 (978-1-60112-187-5(3)) Babblebooks.

Agnes Grey. unabr. ed. Anne Brontë. Read by Flo Gibson. 5 cass. (Running Time: 7 hrs.). (gr. 9-12). 1987. 20.95 (978-1-55685-087-5(5)) Audio Bk Con.
The trials & tribulations of a governess in mid-nineteenth century England.

Agnes Grey. unabr. ed. Anne Brontë. Read by Emilia Fox. 6 CDs. (Running Time: 9 hrs.). 2003. audio compact disk 64.95 (978-0-7540-5537-2(X), CCD 228) AudioGO.

Agnes Grey, unabr. ed. Anne Brontë. Read by Nadia May. 5 cass. (Running Time: 7 hrs.). 1995. 39.95 (978-0-7861-0856-5(8), 1654) Blckstn Audio.
Written when she was twenty-six, this is Anne Bronte's first novel. It tells the story of a rector's daughter who has to earn her living as a governess. Drawing directly from her own experiences, Anne Bronte set out to describe the immense pressures that the governess's life involved - the frustration, the isolation & the insensitive & cruel treatment on the part of employers & their families.

Agnes Grey. unabr. ed. Anne Brontë. Read by Nadia May. (Running Time: 23400 sec.). 2007. audio compact disk 29.95 (978-0-7861-6156-0(6)); audio compact disk 45.00 (978-0-7861-6155-3(8)) Blckstn Audio.

Agnes Grey. unabr. ed. Anne Brontë. Read by Nadia May. (YA). 2008. 39.99 (978-1-60514-707-9(9)) Find a World.

Agnes Grey. unabr. ed. Anne Brontë. Read by Rosemary Davis. 6 cass. (Running Time: 7 hrs. 45 mins.). 2001. 54.95 (978-1-85089-766-8(2), 89064) Pub: ISIS Audio GBR. Dist(s): Ulverscroft US
She wrote this novel out of an urgent need to inform her contemporaries about the desperate position of unmarried, educated women driven to take up the only 'respectable' career open to them - that of a governess.

***Agnes Grey.** unabr. ed. Anne Bronte. Narrated by Anne Flosnik. (Running Time: 7 hrs. 30 mins.). 2010. 27.99 (978-1-4526-0059-8(7)); 66.99 (978-1-4526-3059-5(3)); 19.99 (978-1-4526-5059-3(4)); 14.99 (978-1-4526-7059-1(5)) Tantor Media.

***Agnes Grey (Library Edition)** unabr. ed. Anne Bronte. Narrated by Anne Flosnik. (Running Time: 7 hrs. 30 mins.). 2010. 27.99 (978-1-4526-2059-6(8)) Tantor Media.

Agnes Moorehead: First Lady of Suspense. 2 cass. (Running Time: 2 hrs.). vinyl bd. 10.95 (978-1-57816-040-2(5), AM2401) Audio File.
Includes: "Sorry, Wrong Number" (2-23-44) The classic study in terror as a woman overhears a phone conversation about death! "The Yellow Wallpaper" (7-29-48) The famous short story about a doctor's wife who keeps a journal about a haunted summer home. "The Signal Man" (3-23-53) Charles Dickens' terrifying story about a man mysteriously drawn to a railroad crossing from his childhood. "Don't Call Me Mother (1-4-59) A young man's mother is not very pleased when he brings home a lady friend for dinner.

Agnes of God. unabr. ed. John Pielmeier. Perf. by Barbara Bain et al. 2 CDs. (Running Time: 1 hr. 31 mins.). 2001. audio compact disk 25.95 (978-1-58081-178-1(7), CDTPT136) Pub: L A Theatre. Dist(s): NetLibrary CO

Agnes of God. unabr. ed. John Pielmeier. Read by Barbara Bain et al. 1 cass. (Running Time: 1 hr. 31 mins.). 2001. 20.95 (978-1-58081-159-0(0), TPT136) L A Theatre.

Agnes Parker - Girl in Progress. unabr. ed. Prod. by Listening Library Staff. 3 cass. (Running Time: 4 hrs.). 2005. 30.00 (978-0-307-20704-3(8), Listening Lib) Pub: Random Audio Pubg. Dist(s): Random

Agnes Parker... Happy Camper? unabr. ed. Kathleen O'Dell. Read by Cassandra Campbell. 3 cass. (Running Time: 3 hrs. 43 mins.). (J). (gr. 4-7). 2005. 30.00 (978-0-307-20706-7(4)) Books on Tape.
Agnes Parker is back! The first thing Agnes and her best friend Prejean learn at science camp is that they won't be sharing the same cabin. Being apart gives Agnes a different perspective, and a few worries, about what others think of her longtime friend. Everyone seems to be going on and on about how beautiful Prejean is. A beauty queen? What if Prejean starts acting like one? Soil studies, camp pranks, and a weird bunkmate all play a role in this funny, insightful story of the everyday casualties and payoffs of growing up.

Agnes's Jacket: A Psychologist's Search for the Meanings of Madness. unabr. ed. Gail A. Hornstein. Read by Marguerite Gavin. (Running Time: 14 hrs. 30 mins.). (ENG.). 2009. 31.98 (978-1-59659-436-4(5), GildAudio) Pub: Gildan Media. Dist(s): HachBkGrp

Agni: The Vedic Ritual of the Fire Altar, Set. Fritz Stall. (Hinduism & Its Sources Ser.). 2001. bk. 210.00 (978-81-208-1660-2(9)) Motilal Banarsidass IND.

Agni Lectures. frank eickermann. (ENG.). 2009. 19.80 (978-1-936060-25-2(6)) CLP FLorida.

Agnus Dei. Contrib. by Michael W. Smith. (Worship Tracks (Word Tracks) Ser.). 2006. audio compact disk 8.99 (978-5-558-26930-7(8), Word Music) Word Enter.

Agony & the Ecstasy: A Biographical Novel of Michelangelo see Agony & the Ecstasy, Pts. 1 & 2, A Biographical Novel of Michelangelo

Agony & the Ecstasy Pts. 1 & 2: A Biographical Novel of Michelangelo. unabr. ed. Irving Stone. Read by Daniel Grace. 21 cass. (Running Time: 31 hrs. 30 mins.). Incl. Pt. 1. Agony & the Ecstasy: A Biographical Novel of Michelangelo. 10 cass. (Running Time: 15 hrs.). Irving Stone. Read by Daniel Grace. 1977. 80.00 (1061-A); Pt. 2. Agony & the Ecstasy: A Biographical Novel of Michelangelo. 11 cass. (Running Time: 16 hrs. 30 mins.). Irving Stone. Read by Daniel Grace. 1977. 88.00 (1061-B); 1977. 168.00 (978-0-7366-0048-4(5), 1061-A/B) Books on Tape.
We meet Michelangelo's contemporaries, his benefactors, & the important personages of Renaissance art & politics.

Agony of Alice; The Keeper. abr. ed. Phyllis Reynolds Naylor. Read by Phyllis Reynolds Naylor. (Running Time: 1 hr. 1 min.). (Alice Ser.). (YA). (gr. 5-9). 13.95 (978-1-55644-190-5(8), 7062) Am Audio Prose.
Author reads from two of her novels for younger readers which deal with "real life" topics in a sensitive but unflinchingly honest manner.

Agony of Defeat: Joshua 7:13. Ed Young. 1985. 4.95 (978-0-7417-1450-3(7), 450) Win Walk.

Agony of Love. Chuck Missler & Mark Eastman. 2 CD's. (Running Time: 120 mins.). (Briefing Packages by Chuck Missler). 1997. audio compact disk 19.95 (978-1-57821-309-2(6)) Koinonia Hse.
What really happened at the crucifixion?How can one who is immortal die?How can eternity be compressed into six hours?What really held Jesus' body to the cross? Chuck explores the hyperdimensional aspects of a love letter written in blood on a wooden cross erected in Judea almost two thousand years ago.Dr. Mark Eastman highlights the medical and forensic aspects of the crucifixion.

Agoraphobia. unabr. ed. 1 cass. (Running Time: 60 min.). 1992. 10.95 (054) Psych Res Inst.
Designed to eliminate "panic attacks" by inducing a feeling of control in any public encounter.

Agoraphobia. unabr. ed. Barrie Konicov. 1 cass. 1987. 11.98 (978-0-87082-304-6(3), 002) Potentials.
Explains that when fears begin to control our minds we become a slave to them. This program unlocks the chains that bind your mind & places you into a deep state of relaxation.

Agreeing with God. Derek Prince. 2 cass. 11.90 (112-113) Derek Prince.
God invites us to fellowship with Him, but to do this we must bring our ways & thoughts into line with His.

Agricultural Chemicals in China: A Strategic Reference 2007. Compiled by Icon Group International, Inc. Staff. 2007. ring bd. 195.00 (978-0-497-35858-7(1)) Icon Grp.

Agricultural Machinery in Australia: A Strategic Reference 2007. Compiled by Icon Group International, Inc. Staff. 2007. ring bd. 195.00 (978-0-497-35805-1(0)) Icon Grp.

Agricultural Mechanics: Fundamentals & Applicati. (C). 2005. audio compact disk 69.95 (978-1-4180-1973-0(9)) Pub: Delmar. Dist(s): CENGAGE Learn

Agrochemical & Pesticide Desk Reference. Michael A. Kamrin & John H. Montgomery. 1999. audio compact disk 334.95 (978-0-8493-2179-5(4), 2179) Pub: CRC Pr. Dist(s): Taylor and Fran

Aground. unabr. collector's ed. Charles Williams. Read by Michael Russotto. 6 cass. (Running Time: 6 hrs.). 1993. 36.00 (978-0-7366-2414-5(7), 3181) Books on Tape.
Every man's dream - a beautiful blond, a schooner & an outlying island - becomes one man's nightmare.

Agua. 1 cass. (Primeros Pasos en Ciencia Ser.).Tr. of Water. (SPA.). (J). 12.00 (Natl Textbk Co) M-H Contemporary.
Helps children in grades 1-4 discover the process of scientific investigation. Part of the First Steps in Science Program.

Aguila Vuela Alto: Level 10, Vol. 11. 2003. 11.50 (978-0-7652-0998-6(5)) Modern Curr.

Aguja: Live at Cleveland Public Theatre. John M. Bennett. Perf. by John M. Bennett. Perf. by Byron Smith & Jim Wiese. 1 cass. (Running Time: 45 mins.). 1989. 5.00 (978-0-935350-25-8(X)) Luna Bisonte.
Live performance of avant-guard poetry to sound art.

***Ah-Choo! The Uncommon Life of Your Common Cold.** unabr. ed. Jennifer Ackerman. (Running Time: 8 hrs. 0 mins.). 2010. 15.99 (978-1-4001-8873-4(3)); 19.99 (978-1-4001-6873-6(2)); audio compact disk 29.99 (978-1-4001-1873-1(5)); audio compact disk 71.99 (978-1-4001-4873-8(1)) Pub: Tantor Media. Dist(s): IngramPubServ

Ah-Ha Phenomena. unabr. ed. Read by Robert Lorick. 1 cass; 1 CD. (Running Time: 70 mins.). Dramatization. 1977. 9.00 (978-1-881137-36-8(8)); audio compact disk 14.95 (978-1-881137-77-1(5), AHACD) ZBS Found.
Trolls, wizards, demons & beasts are encountered by Jack Flanders as he searches for the ancient archives that hold all the great past, present & future Ah-Has.

Ah, Treachery!, unabr. ed. Ross Thomas. Narrated by Frank Muller. 6 cass. (Running Time: 7 hrs. 45 mins.). 51.00 (978-0-7887-0260-0(2), 94469E7) Recorded Bks.

Ah, Wilderness! Eugene O'Neill. 1 cass. (Running Time: 60 min.). (Radiobook Ser.). 1987. 4.98 (978-0-929541-07-5(3)) Radiola Co.

Ahab's Wife: Or, the Star-Gazer. Sena Jeter Naslund. Read by Maryann Plunkett. 2004. 15.95 (978-0-7435-4093-3(X)) Pub: S&S Audio. Dist(s): S and S Inc

Ahab's Wife: Or, the Star-Gazer. unabr. ed. Sena Jeter Naslund. Read by Laura Hicks. 3 CDs. (Running Time: 6 hrs.). 2002. audio compact disk 69.95 (978-0-7927-2761-3(4), CMP 493, Chivers Sound Lib) AudioGO.
Disguised as a boy, Una earns a berth on a whaling ship where she encounters the power of nature, death, and madness, and gets her first glimpse of Captain Ahab.

Ahead of the Curve: Two Years at Harvard Business School. unabr. ed. Philip Delves Broughton. Narrated by Patrick G. Lawlor & Simon Vance. 8 CDs. (Running Time: 10 hrs. 30 mins. 0 sec.). (ENG.). 2008. audio compact disk 69.99 (978-1-4001-3713-8(6)); audio compact disk 24.99 (978-1-4001-5713-6(7)); audio compact disk 34.99 (978-1-4001-0713-1(X)) Pub: Tantor Media. Dist(s): IngramPubServ

AHIMSA. Eldon Taylor. Read by Eldon Taylor. 1 cass. (Running Time: 62 min.). (Inner Talk Ser.). 16.95 incl. script. (978-1-55978-619-5(1), 53864F) Progress Aware Res.
Soundtrack - Brook with underlying subliminal affirmations.

AHISMA, a Sect Dedicated to Harmlessness. Manly P. Hall. 1 cass. 8.95 (978-0-89314-001-4(5), C880508) Philos Res.
Explains philosophy & religion.

AHLA the Complete Connected Civil False Claims Act Laws & Cases CD-ROM (AHLA Members) American Health Lawyers Association & Robert S. Salcido. 2007. audio compact disk 285.00 (978-1-4224-3648-6(9)) Pub: Am Hlth Lawyers. Dist(s): LEXIS Pub

AHLA the Complete Connected Civil False Claims Act Laws & Cases CD-ROM (Non-members) American Health Lawyers Association & Robert S. Salcido. 2007. audio compact disk 400.00 (978-1-4224-3649-3(7)) Pub: Am Hlth Lawyers. Dist(s): LEXIS Pub

Ahlan wa Sahlan: An Introduction to Modern Standard Arabic. Mahdi Alosh. 10 cass. (Running Time: 15 hrs.). 2000. 125.00 (978-0-300-08060-5(3)) Yale U Pr.

Ahmad Karrimi Hakkak/ Yeki boud Yeki naboud/ Mohamad ali Jamalzadeh. Poems. Prod. by Nasser Farrokh. Based on a book by Ahmad Karimi-Hakkak. 2CD. 2005. DVD & audio compact disk 32.99 (978-1-933429-03-8(8)) Ket Goo Pub.

A$$hole: How I Got Rich & Happy by Not Giving a Damn about Anyone & How You Can, Too. unabr. ed. Martin Kihn. Read by Malcolm Hillgartner. (Running Time: 21600 sec.). 2008. 29.95 (978-1-4332-1246-8(3)); 44.95 (978-1-4332-1244-4(7)); audio compact disk 29.95 (978-1-4332-1248-2(X)); audio compact disk & audio compact disk 63.00 (978-1-4332-1245-1(5)) Blckstn Audio.

Ahora Puedo Leer. Betty L. Randolph. 1 cass. (Success Ser.). 1989. bk. 9.98 (978-1-55909-262-3(9), 112E) Randolph Tapes.
Presents a program in spanish. Features male-female voice tracks with the right-left brain.

Ahsahta Cassette Sampler. Norman Macleod et al. 1 cass. (Running Time: 90 min.). 1983. 6.00 (978-0-916272-22-7(2)) Ahsahta Pr.
Norman Macleod, Peggy Pond Church, Marnie Walsh, Robert Krieger, Carolyne Wright, Conger Beasley, Jr., Hildegarde Flanner, Susan Strayer Deal, Gretel Enrlich, Leo Romero, David Baker, Richard Speakes, Thomas Hornsby Ferril & Judson Crews read & comment on their poetry.

Ai. Ai. Read by Ai. 1 cass. (Running Time: 29 min.). 1988. 10.00 (020588) New Letters.
Interview with poet. She reads from her poems about her mixed racial heritage.

Ai! Pedrito! When Intelligence Goes Wrong. L. Ron Hubbard. 4 cass. (Running Time: 5 hrs.). 2001. 31.95 (LRON003) Lodestone Catalog.

Ai! Pedrito! When Intelligence Goes Wrong. abr. ed. L. Ron Hubbard & Kevin J. Anderson. 4 cass. (Running Time: 5 hrs.). 1998. 25.00 (978-1-59212-002-4(4)) Gala Pr LLC.
Takes Lt. Tom Smith and the reader on a rollicking and unpredictable adventure through the world of spies and double agents, lovers and enemies (often one and the same).

Ai! Pedrito! Set: When Intelligence Goes Wrong. abr. ed. L. Ron Hubbard & Kevin J. Anderson. 4 cass. (Running Time: 4 hrs.). 1998. 25.00 (978-1-57318-155-6(2), LRON003) Bridge Pubns Inc.
Full-cast reading opens with a musical flourish & bird sound effects to evoke the setting, the Cuban jungle outside of Havana. Here, in a dark fortress by the sea, Russian military operatives are scheming to switch the "vile" Latin American revolutionary & spy Pedrito Miraflores for his exact look-alike, Tom Smith, a bland U. S. Navy intelligence officer.

'Ai'ai. Kawika Napoleon. Ed. by William Wilson & Hokulani Cleeland. Illus. by Brook Parker. (HAW.). (J). (gr. 3-5). 1993. pap. bk. 3.95 (978-0-9645646-9-5(6)) Aha Punana Leo.

Aic Claims Envrnmnt Ppt Cd. Ed. by Kaplan Publishing Staff. 2005. (978-1-4195-1964-2(6)) Dearborn Financial.

Aic Claims Envrnmnt Terms Cd. Ed. by Kaplan Publishing Staff. 2005. (978-1-4195-1951-2(4)) Dearborn Financial.

Aic Lblty Clms Prac Ppt Cd. Ed. by Kaplan Publishing Staff. 2005. (978-1-4195-1955-0(7)) Dearborn Financial.

Aic Lblty Clms Prac Terms Cd. Ed. by Kaplan Publishing Staff. 2005. (978-1-4195-1982-6(4)) Dearborn Financial.

Aic Prprty Loss Adj Ppt Cd. Ed. by Kaplan Publishing Staff. 2005. (978-1-4195-1959-8(X)) Dearborn Financial.

Aic Prprty Loss Adj Terms Cd. Ed. by Kaplan Publishing Staff. 2005. (978-1-4195-1960-4(3)) Dearborn Financial.

Aic 34 - Wrkrs Comp Audio Cd. Ed. by Kaplan Publishing Staff. 2005. cd-rom 10.00 (978-1-4195-2490-5(9)) Dearborn Financial.

Aic 35 - Propty Loss Audio Cd. Ed. by Kaplan Publishing Staff. 2005. cd-rom 10.00 (978-1-4195-2400-4(3)) Dearborn Financial.

Aic 36 - Lblty Clms Audio Cd. Ed. by Kaplan Publishing Staff. 2005. cd-rom 10.00 (978-1-4195-2404-2(6)) Dearborn Financial.

AICPA Audit & Accounting Guide: Health Care Organizations. Aicpa. 2007. audio compact disk 106.25 (978-0-87051-687-0(6)) Am Inst CPA.

Aid to Successful Meditation. Swami Amar Jyoti. 1 cass. 1979. 9.95 (I-8) Truth Consciousness.
Removing the blocks to meditation, not fighting with the mind. Opening the door of ego to go within. Lord Krishna's flute.

Aida. rev. ed. Composed by Giuseppe Verdi. Comment by William Berger. Text by David Foil. 2 vols. (ENG., 2005. audio compact disk 19.95 (978-1-57912-506-6(9), 1579125069) Pub: Blck Dog & Leventhal. Dist(s): Workman Pub

Aida: An Introduction to Verdi's Opera. Thomson Smillie. Read by David Timson. 1 CD. (Running Time: 1 hr. 30 min.). (Opera Explained Ser.). 2003. audio compact disk 8.99 (978-1-84379-096-9(3)) NaxMulti GBR.
One of the most popular operas ever written.

Aiding & Abetting. unabr. ed. Muriel Spark. Narrated by Davina Porter. 3 cass. (Running Time: 4 hrs. 30 mins.). 2002. 34.00 (978-0-7887-8854-3(X)); audio compact disk 43.00 (978-1-4025-1533-0(2)) Recorded Bks.
Lord Lucan disappeared in 1974, shortly after murdering his children's nanny in a botched attempt to kill his wife. Despite reports of sightings, no one knows for sure where the crafty fugitive is. Noted psychiatrist Dr. Hildegard Wolf is intrigued when two patients begin therapy with her - both claiming to be the notorious Lord Lucan. It's not just the patients who have secrets, however. The good doctor has also abandoned a previous life.

AIDS. William A. Check. 1 cass. (Running Time: 2 hrs. 40 min.). 1995. 16.95 (978-1-879557-34-5(7)) Audio Scholar.

AIDS: A Positive Approach. Louise L. Hay. Read by Louise L. Hay. 1 cass. (Running Time: 1 hr. 04 mins.). 1988. 10.95 (978-0-937611-05-0(0), 206) Hay House.
Explains how people with AIDS can help themselves through positive, holistic thinking.

AIDS: A Self Healing Process. Read by Mary Richards. (Subliminal - Self Hypnosis Ser.). 12.95 (814) Master Your Mind.

AIDS: Hope, Hoax & Hoopla on Something's Happening! Mike Culbert & Spiro Diamantidis. 1 cass. (Roy Tuckman Interview Ser.). 9.00 (A0631-90) Sound Photosyn.
The world famous Greek homeopathic & allopathic physician with a medical freedom fighter & author of "AIDS: Hope, Hoax & Hoopla" hidden & suppressed by the mass media, includes cures.

AIDS: Kids, Prostitutes & Drug Abusers. Laurie Garrett. Read by Laurie Garrett. 1 cass. (Running Time: 65 mins.). 11.95 (I0460B090, HarperThor) HarpC GBR.

AIDS: The Relationship of Immune Dysfunction to Pathogenesis. Susan Zollar-Pazner. (AIDS: The National Conference for Practitioners). 1986. 9.00 (978-0-932491-46-6(4)) Res Appl Inc.

AIDS: Touching Deep with Music. Howard Richman. 1 cass. (Running Time: 12 mins.). (Entrainment Music Ser.). 15.95 (978-0-929060-61-3(X)) Sound Feelings.
Rejection & fear are expressed musically. The composition then transforms to express strength & confidence.

AIDS - Diagnosis & Management. Contrib. by Richard H. Schwarz et al. 1 cass. (American College of Obstetrics & Gynecologists UPDATE: Vol. 23, No. 5). 1998. 20.00 Am Coll Obstetric.

AIDS... A Self Healing Process. Read by Mary Richards & Dennis MacMillan. 1 cass. (Running Time: 93 mins.). (Series Two Thousand). 2007. audio compact disk 19.95 (978-1-56136-103-8(0)) Master Your Mind.

AIDS & Astrology. Lynne Palmer. 1 cass. (Running Time: 90 mins.). 1986. 8.95 (574) Am Fed Astrologers.

AIDS & Black America: Breaking the Silence. (Running Time: 3 hrs.). 1989. 49.95 Natl Public Radio.

AIDS & Its Implications for the Surgeon. 2 cass. (General Sessions Ser.: C84-SP10). 1984. 15.00 (8426) Am Coll Surgeons.

AIDS & Malignancy. Richard Leavitt. (AIDS: The National Conference for Practitioners). 1986. 9.00 (978-0-932491-48-0(0)) Res Appl Inc.

AIDS & Radical Healing. Marianne Williamson. Read by Marianne Williamson. 1 cass. (Running Time: 90 mins.). (Lectures on a Course in Miracles). 1999. 10.00 (978-1-56170-223-7(4), M701) Hay House.

AIDS & the Church: Equipping the Laity for AIDS. 1 cass. (Care Cassettes Ser.: Vol. 16, No. 6). 1989. 10.80 Assn Prof Chaplains.

AIDS Cover-Up. Jack Van Impe. 1 cass. 7.00 J Van Impe.
Dr. Van Impe links this killer epidemic to specific Bible prophecies & scriptural warnings.

AIDS Epidemic & Your Local Church: National Association of Evangelicals, 47th Annual Convention, March 7-9, 1989. Lon Solomon & Jeffrey A. Collins. 1 cass. (Open Forum Ser.: No. 116). 1989. 4.25 ea. 1-8 tapes.; 4.00 ea. 9 tapes or more. Nat Assn Evan.

AIDS in Africa. Laurie Garrett. 1 cass. (Running Time: 45 mins.). 10.95 (I0300B090, HarperThor) HarpC GBR.

AIDS in Prisons. Isabel Guerrero. (AIDS: The National Conference for Practitioners). 1986. 9.00 (978-0-932491-58-9(8)) Res Appl Inc.

AIDS Meditation. 1 cass. (Holistic Support Meditations Ser.). 14.98 (978-0-87554-585-1(8), MH104) Valley Sun.

AIDS Primer. Harry Haverkos. (AIDS: The National Conference for Practitioners). 1986. 9.00 (978-0-932491-44-2(8)) Res Appl Inc.

AIDSgate: Everything You Know Is Wrong. Robert Strecker. 3 cass. (Roy Tuckman Interview Ser.). 27.00 Set. (A0188-87) Sound Photosyn.

Ailerona. Short Stories. Paul Berge. 1. (Running Time: 53 mins.). 2003. audio compact disk 19.95 (978-0-9728150-0-0(7)) Ahquabi Hse.
Ailerona contains stories of flight is written and narrated by Paul Berge.

***Aill Uaithne.** Padraig Tom Photch. (ENG.). 1990. 11.95 (978-0-8023-7028-0(4)) Pub: Clo Iar-Chonnachta IRL. Dist(s): Dufour

Aim High: An Olympic Decathlete's Inspiring Story. Dave Johnson & Verne Becker. 2 cass. (Running Time: 60 mins. per cass.). 1994. 14.99 (978-0-310-46198-2(7)) Zondervan.
The inspiring story of Olympic decathlete Dave Johnson's quest to become the world's greatest athlete.

Aim of a Lady. unabr. ed. Laura Matthews. Read by Alicia Snow. 3 cass. (Running Time: 6 hrs.). 1999. 30.00 (978-0-9660643-8-4(0)) Belgrave Hse.
Regency romance.

Aim Was Song see Robert Frost in Recital

Aims of Education. unabr. ed. Eknath Easwaran. 1 cass. (Running Time: 60 mins.). 1992. 7.95 (978-1-58638-500-2(3), AE) Nilgiri Pr.
In an appreciative description of the ashrams of ancient India & his village school, Easwaran presents the long-range goals of education in terms of three harmonies: with oneself, with others & with the environment.

Ain't It Cool? Hollywood's Redheaded Stepchild Speaks Out. abr. ed. Harry Knowles et al. 2 cass. (Running Time: 3 hrs.). 2002. 17.98 (978-1-58621-208-7(7)) Hachet Audio.

Ain't Misbehavin: Understanding the Ups & Downs of Early Childhood. Tim Jordan. Read by Tim Jordan. 1 cass. (Running Time: 1 hr.). 1999. 12.00 (978-0-9705335-3-1(5)); audio compact disk 12.00 (978-0-9705335-8-6(6)) Child & Families.
Teaches parents & teaches about normal developmental stages for 0-7 year olds.

Ain't No Bugs on Me. unabr. ed. Perf. by Jerry Garcia & David Grisman. Illus. by Bruce Whatley. 1 cass. (Running Time: 30 mins.). (J). 2000. bk. 15.95 (T 6546 SH, Listening Lib) Random Audio Pubg.

***Ain't She Sweet?** abr. ed. Susan Elizabeth Phillips. Read by Melissa Leo. (ENG.). 2006. (978-0-06-085306-8(9), Harper Audio); (978-0-06-085305-1(0), Harper Audio) HarperCollins Pubs.

Ain't She Sweet? unabr. ed. Susan Elizabeth Phillips. Read by Kate Fleming. 8 cass. 2005. 69.95 (978-0-7927-3127-6(1), CSL 627); audio compact disk 89.95 (978-0-7927-3128-3(X), SLD 627); audio compact disk 29.95 (978-0-7927-3129-0(8), CMP 627) AudioGO.

***Ain't She Sweet?** unabr. ed. Susan Elizabeth Phillips. Read by Kate Flemming. (ENG.). 2004. (978-0-06-078444-7(X), Harper Audio); (978-0-06-081495-3(0), Harper Audio) HarperCollins Pubs.

Ain't That the Truth. Prod. by Connell Lewis. Arranged by Connell Lewis & Jelford Wade. (ENG.). 2009. (978-0-9729876-5-3(7)) Resurrecting Faith.

AIO Encore Collection: Fan's Picks Celebrating Our Favorite Stories & Characters. AIO Team Staff. (Adventures in Odyssey Ser.). (ENG.). (J). 2009. audio compact disk 49.97 (978-1-58997-545-3(6), Tyndale Ent) Tyndale Hse.

***AIO Sampler: Mystery.** AIO Team. (Adventures in Odyssey Ser.). (ENG.). (J). 2011. audio compact disk 2.99 (978-1-58997-647-4(9)) Tyndale Hse.

AIO Sampler: the Triangle. AIO Team Staff. Created by Focus on the Family Staff. (Adventures in Odyssey Ser.). (ENG.). (J). 2008. audio compact disk 2.99 (978-1-58997-546-0(4), Tyndale Ent) Tyndale Hse.

***AIO Sampler: Underground Railroad.** AIO Team. (Adventures in Odyssey Ser.). (ENG.). (J). 2010. audio compact disk 2.99 (978-1-58997-616-0(9)) Tyndale Hse.

AIO Sampler: Welcome to Whit's End. AIO Team. (Adventures in Odyssey Ser.). (ENG.). (J). 2010. audio compact disk 2.99 (978-1-58997-610-8(X)) Pub: Focus Family. Dist(s): Tyndale Hse

***Air Almanac.** Created by U S Government Printing Office. (ENG.). 2009. audio compact disk 54.00 (978-0-16-082848-5(1)) USGPO.

Air Battle Force. abr. ed. Dale Brown. Read by David McCallum. 2003. audio compact disk 29.95 (978-0-06-052246-9(1)) HarperCollins Pubs.

***Air Battle Force.** abr. ed. Dale Brown. Read by David Mccallum. (ENG.). 2005. (978-0-06-085675-5(0), Harper Audio); (978-0-06-085674-8(2), Harper Audio) HarperCollins Pubs.

Air Battle Force. unabr. ed. Dale Brown. Read by William Dufris. 11 cass. (Running Time: 17 hrs.). 2003. 89.95 (978-0-7927-2927-3(7), CSL 568, Chivers Sound Lib); audio compact disk 112.95 (978-0-7927-2928-0(5), SLD 568, Chivers Sound Lib) AudioGO.

***Air Battle Force.** unabr. ed. Dale Brown. (ENG.). 2005. (978-0-06-085668-7(8), Harper Audio); (978-0-06-085667-0(X), Harper Audio) HarperCollins Pubs.

Air Brakes Test. unabr. ed. Robert M. Calvin. Read by Jericho Productions, Inc. Staff. Ed. by Marilyn Martin. 3 cass. (Running Time: 31 mins.). (Truck & Bus Driver's CDL Audio Tape Ser.). 1991. pap. bk. 15.99 (978-0-89262-266-5(0), CDLBABTAT-731); 15.99 Set, Spanish Version. (978-0-89262-289-4(X), 1) Career Pub.
All questions & answers to the CDL Air Brakes Test drivers of trucks & buses with air brakes must take. Easy-to-understand explanations of the answers included. Test Study Book supports & enhances the tape.

Air Bridge. unabr. collector's ed. Hammond Innes. Read by Ron Shoop. 7 cass. (Running Time: 10 hrs. 30 mins.). 1984. 56.00 (978-0-7366-0850-3(8), 1801) Books on Tape.
Two WW II pilots team up to build an air fleet.

Air Conditioning & Refrigeration Equipment in Brazil: A Strategic Reference 2006. Compiled by Icon Group International, Inc. Staff. 2007. ring bd. 195.00 (978-0-497-35830-3(1)) Icon Grp.

Air Conditioning & Refrigeration Equipment in Uruguay: A Strategic Reference 2007. Compiled by Icon Group International, Inc. Staff. 2007. ring bd. 195.00 (978-0-497-82460-0(4)) Icon Grp.

Air Conditioning Equipment in Panama: A Strategic Reference 2006. Compiled by Icon Group International, Inc. Staff. 2007. ring bd. 195.00 (978-0-497-82378-8(0)) Icon Grp.

Air Conditioning Equipment in United Arab Emirates: A Strategic Reference 2006. Compiled by Icon Group International, Inc. Staff. 2007. ring bd. 195.00 (978-0-497-82449-5(3)) Icon Grp.

Air Guitar: Songs for Kids. Perf. by Cathy Fink & Marcy Marxer. 1 cass. (Running Time: 36 min.). (J). (gr. k up). 1993. 9.98 (978-0-942303-31-5(8), HW1254) Pub: High Windy Audio. Dist(s): August Hse
Rock & roll, blues, swing, folk-it's all here. These rollicking happy singalongs are just waiting for you to join in. So grab your air guitar & let the fun begin. Parents Choice Silver.

Air on a g String: Favorite encores with Orchestra (easy-medium) Geoffrey Applegate. 1997. pap. bk. 34.98 (978-1-59615-148-2(X), 586-001) Pub: Music Minus. Dist(s): Bookworld

Air on a G String: Favorite Encores with Orchestra: Violin Play-along Pack. Created by Hal Leonard Corporation Staff. 2006. pap. bk. 24.98 (978-1-59615-144-4(7), 1596151447) Pub: Music Minus. Dist(s): H Leonard

Air Pollution. Hosted by Nancy Pearlman. 1 cass. (Running Time: 28 mins.). 10.00 (113) Educ Comm CA.

Air Pollution Control Equipment & Services in Brazil: A Strategic Reference 2006. Compiled by Icon Group International, Inc. Staff. 2007. ring bd. 195.00 (978-0-497-35831-0(X)) Icon Grp.

Air Pollution Control Equipment & Services in China: A Strategic Reference 2006. Compiled by Icon Group International, Inc. Staff. 2007. ring bd. 195.00 (978-0-497-35859-4(X)) Icon Grp.

Air Pollution Control Equipment & Services in China: A Strategic Reference 2007. Compiled by Icon Group International, Inc. Staff. 2007. ring bd. 195.00 (978-0-497-35860-0(3)) Icon Grp.

Air Quality Update. Hosted by Nancy Pearlman. 1 cass. (Running Time: 29 mins.). 10.00 (106) Educ Comm CA.

Air Traffic Control Communications: I. F. R. Directives with Explanations. 1 cass. (Running Time: 1 hr. 30 mins.). 1992. pap. bk. 50.00 (978-0-941456-15-9(3)) Aviation Lang Sch.

Air Traffic Control Communications V. F. R. Directives with Explanations, Vol. 1. J. Deborah Balter. 2 cass. (Running Time: 3 hrs.). 1997. pap. bk. 100.00 (978-0-941456-13-5(7)) Aviation Lang Sch.

***Air Transportation Cd.** 15th rev. ed. Kane. (ENG.). 2010. audio compact disk 71.78 (978-0-7575-4142-1(9)) Kendall-Hunt.

Air We Breathe. unabr. ed. Andrea Barrett. Read by Jeff Woodman. (YA). 2008. 64.99 (978-1-60252-947-2(7)) Find a World.

***Air We Breathe: Unabridged Value-Priced Edition.** Andrea Barrett. Narrated by Jeff Woodman. (Running Time: 10 hrs. 20 mins. 0 sec.). (ENG.). 2010. audio compact disk 14.95 (978-1-60283-986-1(7)) Pub: AudioGO. Dist(s): Perseus Dist

Airborn. unabr. ed. Kenneth Oppel. Read by Full Cast Production Staff. (YA). 2007. 54.99 (978-1-60252-492-7(0)) Find a World.

Airborne: A Sentimental Journey. unabr. collector's ed. William F. Buckley, Jr. Read by Dan Lazar. 8 cass. (Running Time: 8 hrs.). 1980. 48.00 (978-0-7366-0337-9(9), 1323) Books on Tape.
A sailing trip across the Atlantic with Buckley & his buddies.

Aircraft. unabr. ed. Peter M. Spizzirri. Read by Charles Fuller. Ed. by Linda Spizzirri. 1 cass. (Running Time: 15 mins.). Dramatization. (Educational Coloring Book & Cassette Ser.). (J). (gr. 1-8). pap. bk. 6.95 (978-0-86545-109-4(5)) Spizzirri.
Aircraft developed quickly from the Moran-Saulnier Monoplane to the Boeing 747 jumbo jet.

Aircraft Flight Simulators. Ed. by Marco A. V. Bitetto. 1 cass. 2000. (978-1-58578-080-8(4)) Inst of Cybernetics.

Aircraft in Australia: A Strategic Reference 2006. Compiled by Icon Group International, Inc. Staff. 2007. ring bd. 195.00 (978-0-497-35806-8(9)) Icon Grp.

Aircraft Navigational Equipment in India: A Strategic Reference 2007. Compiled by Icon Group International, Inc. Staff. 2007. ring bd. 195.00 (978-0-497-36006-1(3)) Icon Grp.

Aire: Afuera, adentro y en todos Lados. Darlene R. Stille. Tr. by Sol Robledo. Illus. by Sheree Boyd. (Ciencia Asombrosa Ser.).Tr. of The Air: Outside, Inside & all Around. (MUL & SPA.). (gr. k-4). 2008. audio compact disk 14.60 (978-1-4048-4536-7(4)) CapstoneDig.

Aire de Nocturno see Poesia y Drama de Garcia Lorca

Airframe. unabr. ed. Michael Crichton. Read by Frances Cassidy. 10 CDs. (Running Time: 14 hrs.). 2001. audio compact disk 80.00 Books on Tape.
Disaster, or something close to it, strikes an airliner en route from Hong Kong to Denver.Three passengers dead, 56 injured , the interior cabin destroyed. Whether through luck or skill, the pilot gets the plane down, more or less in one piece. But to what end?.

Airframe. unabr. ed. Michael Crichton. Read by Frances Cassidy. 8 cass. (Running Time: 12 hrs.). 1996. 64.00 (978-0-913369-22-7(5), 4173) Books on Tape.
Disaster, or something close to it, strikes an airliner en route from Hong Kong to Denver. Three passengers dead, 56 injured, the interior cabin destroyed. Whether through luck or skill, the pilot gets the plane down, more or less in one piece.But to what end.

Airhead. unabr. ed. Meg Cabot. Narrated by Stina Nielsen. 7 CDs. (Running Time: 8 hrs. 15 mins.). (Airhead Ser.: No. 1). (YA). (gr. 7 up). 2008. audio compact disk 77.75 (978-1-4361-0674-0(5)); 61.75 (978-1-4361-0669-6(9)) Recorded Bks.
Airhead begins a series of books featuring Emerson Watts (Em, please). She doesn't want to go, but Em must chaperone her little sister to the grand opening of a new Stark Megastore. Her sister can't wait to see the heartthrobs and supermodels that will make an appearance, including hunky Gabriel Luna and beautiful Nikki Howard. Em couldn't care less. Then disaster strikes, and after a bizarre accident, it seems that Em just isn't herself any more - literally.

Airline & Railroad Labor & Employment Law: A Comprehensive Analysis Set: Thursday-Saturday, October 23-25, 1997, Madison Hotel, Washington, D. C. 11 cass. (Running Time: 15 hrs.). 1997. 275.00 Incl. course materials. (MA31) Am Law Inst.
Emphasis is placed on the Railway Labor Act (RLA), & on the rules & regulations of the National Mediation Board. Coverage of employment, civil rights, disability, & work force environment laws relating to airline & railroad labor & employment issues.

Airman. unabr. ed. Eoin Colfer. Read by John Keating. 9 CDs. (Running Time: 11 hrs. 22 mins.). (YA). (gr. 7 up). 2007. audio compact disk 55.00 (978-0-7393-6126-9(0), Listening Lib) Pub: Random Audio Pubg. Dist(s): Random

Airman. unabr. ed. Eoin Colfer. Read by John Keating. 9 CDs. (Running Time: 11 hrs. 30 mins.). (ENG.). (J). (gr. 9-7). 2007. audio compact disk 44.00 (978-0-7393-5974-7(6), Listening Lib) Pub: Random Audio Pubg. Dist(s): Random

Airman Mortensen. unabr. ed. Michael Blake. Read by Michael Blake. 4 cass. (Running Time: 6 hrs.). 24.00 (978-1-56508-000-3(9)) Seven Wolves.

Airman's Odyssey see Terre des Hommes

Airman's War. unabr. ed. Albert Marrin. Narrated by Johnny Heller. 3 cass. (Running Time: 4 hrs. 30 mins.). (gr. 4 up). 2003. 29.00 (978-1-4025-2767-8(5)) Recorded Bks.
Albert Marrin, noted historian and author, traces the importance of airplanes in World War II. Each battle in the sky comes to life in this exciting audio production.

Airmen & the Headhunters: A True Story of Lost Soldiers, Heroic Tribesmen & the Unlikeliest Rescue of World War II. unabr. ed. Judith M. Heimann. Read by Susan Ericksen. (Running Time: 9 hrs. 0 mins. 0 sec.). (ENG.). 2007. audio compact disk 34.99 (978-1-4001-0509-0(9)); audio compact disk 24.99 (978-1-4001-5509-5(6)); audio compact disk 69.99 (978-1-4001-3509-7(5)) Pub: Tantor Media. Dist(s): IngramPubServ

***Airplane Adventure.** Cari Meister. Illus. by Marilyn Janovitz. (My First Graphic Novel Ser.). (ENG.). 2010. audio compact disk 14.60 (978-1-4342-2583-2(6)) CapstoneDig.

Airport & Ground Support Equipment in Peru: A Strategic Reference 2007. Compiled by Icon Group International, Inc. Staff. 2007. ring bd. 195.00 (978-0-497-82380-1(2)) Icon Grp.

Airport, Maritime, & Ports Security in Bulgaria: A Strategic Reference 2007. Compiled by Icon Group International, Inc. Staff. 2007. ring bd. 195.00 (978-0-497-35851-8(4)) Icon Grp.

Airport Security & Ground Handling Equipment in Jordan: A Strategic Reference 2007. Compiled by Icon Group International, Inc. Staff. 2007. ring bd. 195.00 (978-0-497-82337-5(3)) Icon Grp.

Airport Services in Barbados: A Strategic Reference 2006. Compiled by Icon Group International, Inc. Staff. 2007. ring bd. 195.00 (978-0-497-35819-8(0)) Icon Grp.

Airport Services in Czech Republic: A Strategic Reference 2007. Compiled by Icon Group International, Inc. Staff. 2007. ring bd. 195.00 (978-0-497-35903-4(0)) Icon Grp.

Airs & Graces. unabr. ed. Erica James. Read by Eve Matheson. 10 cass. (Running Time: 10 hrs.). 1998. 84.95 (978-0-7540-0197-3(0), CAB 1620) AudioGO.
Based on a young widow struggling to make ends meet & her determination to re-marry for money.

Aisteoirí na Mainistreach ag Léamh see Irish Poetry, Stories & Songs

Ajamila Saved from Death (A); Ambarisa vs Durvasa (B) 1 cass. (Spiritual Stories Ser.). 5.00 Bhaktivedanta.

Ajanta see Twentieth-Century Poetry in English, No. 12, Recordings of Poets Reading Their Own Poetry

Ajapa Japa: Breath Mantra Consciousness. Swami Shankardev Saraswati & Jayne Stevenson. (ENG.). 2007. audio compact disk 33.00 (978-0-9803496-1-0(3)) Big Shakti AUS.

Ajoy Chakraborty Vol. 3: Patiala. 1 cass. (Gharana Ser.). 1994. (A94017) Multi-Cultural Bks.

Ajoy Chakraborty Vol. 4: Patiala. 1 cass. (Gharana Ser.). 1994. (A94018) Multi-Cultural Bks.

AKA Jane. abr. ed. Maureen Tan. Read by Mia Sara. 4 cass. (Running Time: 4 hrs. 30 min.). 1998. 23.00 Set. (978-1-56876-070-4(1)) Soundlines Ent.

Akashic Journey. Christopher Love. Read by Christopher Love. 1 cass. (Running Time: 30 mins.). 1997. 10.95 (978-1-891820-06-9(0)) World Sangha Pubg.
Self-hypnosis meditation for healing, self-improvement & realizing our full & powerful potential as spiritual beings.

Akashic Records: All Is He. Swami Amar Jyoti. 1 cass. 1991. 9.95 (R-106) Truth Consciousness.
The eternal, vibrational records. The seat of judgement. Only He is happening, in one interdependent Totality.

Akashic Records: Guided Meditation. Yana L. Freeman. Music by Thaddeus Music LuminEssence Production. (Running Time: 36 mins. 48 sec.). (ENG.). 2006. audio compact disk 15.00 (978-0-9768728-4-9(6), 72849) Sacred Path.
The Akashic Records is where every thought, word, emotion, intention and life of every soul is stored. By accessing the records you can identify addictive patterns, release blocks to knowledge, your life path, purpose, growth and prosperity. Identify self-defeating relationships and behaviors to rFind effective ways to create balance and a better alignment in your life.

Akashic Records Meditation. 1 cass. (Tara Sutphen Meditation Tapes Ser.). 11.98 (978-0-87554-569-1(6), TS207) Valley Sun.

Akathist Pt. 3: Glory to God for All Things & Akathist to the Resurrection of Christ. Perf. by Jane M. deVyver. 1 cass. (Running Time: 1 hr.). (Treasury of Orthodox Christian Prayers Ser.: Vol. 1). 1994. 6.95 (978-1-881211-14-3(2)) Firebird Videos.
Side 1: Akathist: Glory to God for All Things. Side 2: Akathist to the Resurrection of Christ.

Akathist for Holy Communion & Akathist to Jesus Christ, Pt. 4. Perf. by Jane M. deVyver. 1 cass. (Running Time: 1 hr.). (Treasury of Orthodox Christian Prayers Ser.: Vol. 1). 1994. 6.95 (978-1-881211-15-0(0)) Firebird Videos.
Side 1: Akathist for Holy Communion; Side 2: Akathist to Jesus Christ.

Akathist Service to St. Alexis Toth. St Tikhon's Seminary Choir. 2009. (978-1-878997-85-2(8)) St Tikhons Pr.

Akathist to St. Herman of Alaska & Akathist to St. Innocent of Alaska, Pt. 3. Perf. by Jane M. deVyver. 1 cass. (Running Time: 1 hr. 10 mins.). (Treasury of Orthodox Christian Prayers Ser.: Vol. 2). 1998. 6.95 (978-1-881211-48-8(7)) Firebird Videos.
Two Akathists (extended hymns) glorifying the lives of 2 Russian-American saints, most beloved by native Alaskans.

Akathist to St. John the Theologian & Akathist to St. Nicholas of Myra, Pt. 4. Perf. by Jane M. deVyver. 1 cass. (Running Time: 1 hrs.). (Treasury of Orthodox Christian Prayers Ser.: Vol. 2). 1998. 6.95 (978-1-881211-49-5(5)) Firebird Videos.
Two Akathists (extended hymns) glorifying the lives of 2 early Christian saints: the Apostle & Evangelist St. John the Theologian & St. Nicholas the Wonderworker, Bishop of Myra in Lycia.

Akathist to St. Xenia & Akathist to St. Seraphim, Pt. 1. Perf. by Jane M. deVyver. 1 cass. (Running Time: 1 hr. 9 mins.). (Treasury of Orthodox Christian Prayers Ser.: Vol. 2). 1998. 6.95 (978-1-881211-47-1(9)) Firebird Videos.
Akathists (extended hymns) to beloved Russian saints. Side 1: Akathist to St. Xenia; Side 2: Akathist to St. Seraphim.

Akenfield: Portrait of an English Village. Ronald Blythe. Read by Michael Tudor Barnes. 10 cass. (Soundings Ser.). 2006. 84.95 (978-1-84559-177-9(1)) Pub: ISIS Lrg Prnt GBR. Dist(s): Ulverscroft US

Akhenaten Adventure. P. B. Kerr. Narrated by Ron Keith. 7 cass. (Running Time: 10 hrs. 15 mins.). (Children of the Lamp Ser.: Vol. 1). (J). 2004. 66.75 (978-1-4193-0827-7(0)) Recorded Bks.

Akhenaten Adventure. unabr. ed. P. B. Kerr. Narrated by Ron Keith. 9 CDs. (Running Time: 10 hrs). (Children of the Lamp Ser.: Vol. 1). 2004. audio compact disk 34.99 (978-1-4193-0608-2(1)) Recorded Bks.

Akhmatova Reads Akhmatova. Anna Andreevena Akhmatova. Read by Anna Andreevena Akhmatova. Read by Igor Dmitriev. 1 cass. (Running Time: 1 hrs.). 1996. pap. bk. 19.50 Interlingua VA.

Akimbo & the Elephants. unabr. ed. Alexander McCall Smith. 1 CD. (Running Time: 1 hr.). 2006. audio compact disk 12.75 (978-1-4193-7033-5(2), C3538); 12.75 (978-1-4193-7028-1(6), 98263) Recorded Bks.
Born in Zimbabwe, New York Times best-selling author Alexander McCall Smith uses his first-hand knowledge of Africa to connect with his young audience and supply his Akimbo chapter books with vivid details. In a central African animal sanctuary, young Akimbo sees the carcass of a mother elephant rotting in the sun. Hearing that his ranger father rarely catches these killers, Akimbo hatches a secret plan to apprehend these villains himself. But are the dangers too daunting for this aspiring hero?.

Akita Warnings. Perf. by John F. O'Connor. 1 cass. (Running Time: 1 hr.). 7.00 (20132) Cath Treas.
In 1973, in Akita, Japan, Our Blessed Lady came weeping with the announcement to a humble Japanese nun that God is about to punish the world.

Akshara Vidya Upasana. Swami Jyotirmayananda. Read by Swami Jyotirmayananda. 1 cass. (Running Time: 60 mins.). 12.99 (718) Yoga Res Foun.

Aktuelle Texte: Die Deutschen bei der Arbeit - Berufswuensche - Arbeitsalltag - Stars - Satiren Level 4 (1994) Textbuch. U. Gibitz. (GER.). (C). 1994. 34.50 (978-3-12-675254-1(3)) Pub: Klett Ernst Verlag DEU. Dist(s): Intl Bk Import

Aktuelle Texte: Portraits der Deutschen - Politik und Argbeitswelt - aus dem Alltag Auslaender in der Bundesrepublik Level 1 (1977) Textbuch. H. Seeger & H. Zuleeg. (GER., (C). 1979. 33.50 (978-3-12-559610-8(6)) Pub: Klett Ernst Verlag DEU. Dist(s): Intl Bk Import

Aktuelle Texte: Zwischen Gestern und Morgen - Mann und Frau - Jugend - Im Alter - Randgruppen Level 3 (1979) Textbuch. H. Seeger & H. Zuleeg. (GER.). (C). 1979. 33.50 (978-3-12-559630-6(0)) Pub: Klett Ernst Verlag DEU. Dist(s): Intl Bk Import

Al. Lleucu Roberts. (Nofelau A Storiau I'R Arddegau Novels & Stories for Young Adults Ser.). 2005. 5.90 (978-0-00-067986-4(0)) Zondervan.

Al Capone Does My Shirts. Gennifer Choldenko. Narrated by Johnny Heller. 5 CDs. (Running Time: 5 hrs. 45 mins.). (J). 2004. audio compact disk 48.75 (978-1-4193-1789-7(X)) Recorded Bks.

Al Capone Does My Shirts. unabr. ed. Gennifer Choldenko. Read by Kirby Heyborne. (J). (gr. 5). 2009. audio compact disk 30.00 (978-0-307-58235-5(3), Listening Lib) Pub: Random Audio Pubg. Dist(s): Random

Al Capone Does My Shirts. unabr. ed. Gennifer Choldenko. 6 cass. (Running Time: 8 hrs. 45 min.). (J). (gr. 3-6). 2004. 54.75 (978-1-4025-6409-3(0)) Recorded Bks.

***Al Capone Shines My Shoes.** unabr. ed. Gennifer Choldenko. Read by Kirby Heyborne. 7 CDs. (J). (gr. 4-7). 2009. audio compact disk 55.00 (978-0-7393-8006-2(0), BksonTape) Pub: Random Audio Pubg. Dist(s): Random

Al Capone Shines My Shoes. unabr. ed. Gennifer Choldenko. Read by Kirby Heyborne. (J). (gr. 5). 2009. audio compact disk 37.00 (978-0-7393-8004-8(4), Listening Lib) Pub: Random Audio Pubg. Dist(s): Random

Al Corriente: Student Program. 3rd ed. Robert J. Blake et al. 1 cass. (Running Time: 90 min.). (C). 1998. stu. ed. 59.37 (978-0-07-913148-5(4), Mc-H Human Soc) Pub: McGrw-H Hghr Educ. Dist(s): McGraw

Al Franken Show Party Album. Al Franken. 2005. audio compact disk 18.98 (978-0-9745992-8-1(X)) Artemis Class.

Al Granum in Concert: Best Performance Strategy. Alfred Granum. Read by Alfred Granum. 6 cass. (Running Time: 7 hrs. 38 mins.). 1979. 64.00 Ntl Underwriter.
The author demonstrates how he teaches his agents to use Six-Three Prospecting & Promotion (of prospective buyers) pre-approach, telephone, approach fact find, close deliver. He presents his original concepts: One Card System, One Thousand Clients & discusses the problems of agent productivity & how to cope with inflation.

Al Jolson. 2 cass. (Running Time: 2 hrs.). vinyl bd. 10.95 (978-1-57816-041-9(3), AJ2401) Audio File.
The "World's Greatest Entertainer" in four broadcasts from the Kraft Music Hall, co-starring pianist Oscar Levant & special guests. "October 16, 1947" Guest Bing Crosby joins Al & Oscar for some nostalgia humor & a great medley of Gershwin songs. "September 30, 1948" Guest Judy Garland pays a visit to the Music Hall as Jolson begins his second season on the air. "October 21, 1948" There's no guest in the Music Hall tonight so Al turns up the house lights to take requests from the audience. "April 21, 1949" Guest JimmyDurante arrives in his usual dynamic style making for some great fun as he & Jolie musically travel around the world.

Al Petteway/Midsummer Moon. Al Petteway. 1997. pap. bk. 26.95 (978-0-7866-0584-2(7), 95552CDP) Mel Bay.

Al Petteway/Waters & the Wild. Al Petteway. 1996. pap. bk. 19.95 (978-0-7866-0797-6(1), 95608P); pap. bk. 24.95 (978-0-7866-0796-9(3), 95608CDP) Mel Bay.

Al Petteway/Whispering Stones. Al Petteway. 1995. pap. bk. 19.95 (978-0-7866-1303-8(3), 95381P) Mel Bay.

Al Que Vencio. Contrib. by Jaime Murrell. (SPA.). (gr. 13). 2009. audio compact disk 14.99 (978-0-8297-6136-8(5)) Pub: Vida Pubs. Dist(s): Zondervan

Al Read Show, Vol. 3. Al Read. Read by Al Read. 2 cass. (Running Time: 1 hr. 30 mins.). 1999. 16.85 (978-0-563-55843-9(1)) BBC WrldWd GBR.
Al started in comedy, working on his roots to come up with catchphrases such as 'Right Monkey' & 'You'll be lucky, I'll say, you'll be lucky.'.

Al Scates: Talking Volleyball. unabr. ed. Read by Al Scates. 4 cass. (Running Time: 2 hrs.). (Exceptional Teachers in Sports Ser.). 39.95 Lets Talk Assocs.
Coach Al Scates explains his approach to volleyball. His UCLA teams have won more NCAA championships than any other college in the history of the sport.

Al Taller del Maestros. unabr. ed. (SPA.). 2004. 9.99 (978-0-8297-4544-3(0)) Pub: Vida Pubs. Dist(s): Zondervan

Al Young. unabr. ed. Ed. by Jim McKinley. Prod. by Rebekah Presson. 1 cass. (Running Time: 29 mins.). (New Letters on the Air Ser.). 1994. 10.00 (112293) New Letters.
Young's newly-published book, "Heaven," collects the authors' poems written between 1956-1990. In his five novels & five collections of poetry, Young has consistently bucked the conventional wisdom regarding African Americans. When "Black Power" was all the rage, Young wrote "A Dance for Militant Dilettantes;" later, he became one of the foremost writers on jazz & blues music.

Al Young: Interview with Al Young & Kay Bonetti. 1 cass. (Running Time: 1 hr.). 1981. 13.95 (978-1-55644-032-8(4), 1172) Am Audio Prose.
Young, one of the founders of "Yardbird Press," discusses the question of "Black Literature" & the larger tradition, racism in publishing & criticism & problems of making a living solely as a writer.

Alabama Moon. unabr. ed. Watt Key. Read by Nick Landrum. 8 cass. (Running Time: 8 hrs. 45 mins.). (YA). (gr. 5-8). 2007. 67.75 (978-1-4281-3387-7(9)); audio compact disk 87.75 (978-1-4281-3392-1(5)) Recorded Bks.

Alabama Seminar. Michael Pearl. 2 cass. 1999. (978-1-892112-18-7(3)) No Greater Joy.

Alabanza Como Instrumento de la Gracia. Heriberto Hermosillo. 6 cass. (SPA.). 2003. 29.99 (978-0-89985-411-3(7)); audio compact disk 35.00 (978-0-89985-410-6(9)) Christ for the Nations.

Alabanza de Resurrection. Greg Skipper & Gail Skipper. 1993. 10.98 (978-0-7673-1838-9(2)) LifeWay Christian.

Alabanza y Adoracion. Prod. by Randy Ray. 1 cass. (Running Time: 60 mins.). (SPA.). 1990. 9.98 (978-1-57919-000-2(6)) Randolf Prod.
Twenty two songs of praise & worship.

Alabanza y Adoración Moderna. unabr. ed. 2004. audio compact disk 11.99 (978-0-8297-4702-7(8)) Zondervan.

Alabemos a Dios. Music by Eleazar Cortes. 2001. 11.11 (978-1-58459-095-8(5)); audio compact disk 16.00 (978-1-58459-094-1(7)) Wrld Lib Pubns.

Aladdin see Aladino

Aladdin. Illus. by Elisa Squillace. 1 cass. (FRE.). (J). (gr. 4 up). 1991. bk. 14.95 (1AD037) Olivia & Hill.
Aladdin & the Magic Lamp.

Aladdin. unabr. ed. Illus. by Elisa Squillace. 1 cass. (Running Time: 90 mins.). (Read-Along Ser.). (J). (ps-3). 1993. bk. 7.99 (978-1-55723-362-2(4)) W Disney Records.

Aladdin: Here Comes a Parade. unabr. ed. 1 cass. (Running Time: 90 mins.). (My First Read Along Ser.). (J). bk. 7.99 (978-1-55723-748-4(4)) W Disney Records.

Aladdin: King of Thieves Soundtrack. Prod. by Walt Disney Company Staff. 1 cass., 1 CD. 1996. audio compact disk 12.95 CD. (978-0-7634-0158-0(7)) W Disney Records.

Aladdin: King of Thieves Soundtrack. Prod. by Walt Disney Company Staff. 1 cass., 1 CD. (J). 1996. 8.95 (978-0-7634-0157-3(9)) W Disney Records.

Aladdin: The Story Teller. 1 cass. 24.95 1 tape, 10 bks. (Natl Textbk Co) M-H Contemporary.
Designed for students to experience the fairy tale with sound & music, helping to develop skills in another language.

Aladdin & His Lamp. 1 cass. (J). 3.98 Clamshell. (978-1-55886-113-8(0), BP/PT 440) Smarty Pants.

Aladdin & the Enchanted Lamp. Philip Pullman. Read by James Goode. 2 cds. (Running Time: 1 hr.). audio compact disk 15.75 (978-1-4281-4719-5(5)) Recorded Bks.

Aladdin & the Enchanted Lamp. abr. ed. Read by Souad Faress. Tr. by N. J. Dawood. 1 cass. (Running Time: 90 mins.). (Children's Classics Ser.). (J). 1996. 10.95 (PengAudBks) Penguin Grp USA.
Full of magic and trickery, genies & sorcerers, this masterpiece of Aladdin's adventures with the magic lamp has endured for over a thousand years.

Aladdin & the Magic Lamp. Illus. by Greg Couch. As told by John Hurt. Music by Mickey Hart. 1 cass. (Running Time: 1 hr.). 9.95 Weston Woods.
Enchanting tale of a young rogue & the genie who helps him win the love of the Sultan's daughter.

Aladdin & the Magic Lamp. Composed by Mickey Hart. Narrated by John Hurt. Contrib. by Greg Couch. (Running Time: 30 mins.). (Rabbit Ears Collection). Orig. Title: A Thousand & One Nights. (J). (gr. 1-5). 1998. 9.95 (PRE001AC) Weston Woods.

Aladdin Soundtrack. 1 cass. (J). (ps-3). 1992. 12.98 (978-1-55723-333-2(0)) W Disney Records.

Aladdin's Lamp. Read by Lou Diamond Phillips. 1 cass. (Running Time: 30 min.). (J). 1992. 8.95 incl. poster to color & crayons. (978-1-55800-662-1(1)) Olive Brnch.

Aladino. 1 cass. (Running Time: 1 hr. 30 min.).Tr. of Aladdin. (SPA., (J). 2000. 12.95 (978-84-207-6726-0(3)) Pub: Grupo Anaya ESP. Dist(s): Distribks Inc

Alagille Syndrome - A Bibliography & Dictionary for Physicians, Patients, & Genome Researchers. Compiled by Icon Group International, Inc. Staff. 2007. ring bd. 28.95 (978-0-497-11319-3(8)) Icon Grp.

Alamo. Perf. by Colonial Radio Theatre Staff. 1 cass. (Running Time: 1 hr. 30 mins.). 2001. 12.95 (COLR009) Lodestone Catalog.
History in the making as the heroic band attempts to hold the crumbling Alamo against a Mexican army nearly twenty times the size of their own forces.

Alamo. unabr. ed. John Myers. Read by Robert Morris. 5 cass. (Running Time: 7 hrs.). 1995. 39.95 (978-0-7861-0850-3(9), 1648) Blckstn Audio.
Poet, novelist and historian, John Myers gives us a fascinating account of an American symbol. Reveals the chronicle of the siege of the Alamo in an entirely different light... his story will stand as the best that has yet been written on the subject.

Alamo. unabr. ed. Wyman Windsor. Narrated by Rick Lance. Prod. by Joe Loesch. 1 cass. (Running Time: 1 hr.). (Wild West Ser.). (YA). 1999. 12.95 (978-1-887729-65-9(8)) Toy Box Prods.
People said it was "Thirteen Days to Glory" & for generations to come, it would be revered. Books would be written, songs would be sung, movies would be made. The legend of the Alamo would brow until it became bigger than life.

Alamo: Colonial Radio Theatre. Jerry Robbins. Perf. by Colonial Radio Theatre Staff. Prod. by Mark VanderBerg. 1 cass. (Running Time: 1 hr. 27 mins.). Dramatization. (J). 1999. 12.98 (978-1-929244-05-8(3), AT9901) Pub: Colonial Radio. Dist(s): Penton Overseas
The most dramatic thirteen days in American history. The defenders face impossible odds as they attempt to hold the old-mission-turned-fortress from a Mexican Army nearly ten times their size.

Alamo Journals. Steck-Vaughn Staff. 2003. (978-0-7398-8432-4(8)) SteckVau.

Alamos. unabr. ed. Joseph Kanon. Read by Michael Kramer. 11 cass. (Running Time: 16 hrs. 30 min.). 1997. 88.00 (978-0-7366-3785-5(0), 4457) Books on Tape.
Spring 1945. As work on the first atom bomb nears completion, someone kills a Manhattan project security officer in nearby Santa Fe. Is it random violence, or something more sinister? Michael Connolly, a government intelligence officer, takes over the investigation. Where to start? In a community so secret it has no acknowledged existence, deception is a way of the dark heart of Los Alamos, into a dramatic story of divided loyalties & espionage.

Alamuhan. 1 cass. (Running Time: 44 mins.). audio compact disk 16.95 (978-1-57606-351-4(8)) Pub: Wind Recs. Dist(s): Shens Bks

Alan Arkin see Movie Makers Speak: Actors

Alan Bennett. abr. ed. Alan Bennett. 6 cass. (Running Time: 8 hrs.). (J). 1998. lib. bdg. Box set. (978-0-563-55895-8(4)) BBC WrldWd GBR.
Set contains "Winnie The Pooh," "Wind in the Willows," & "Alice in Wonderland".

Alan Bennett: Three Plays. Alan Bennett. Contrib. by Nigel Anthony et al. 5 CDs. (Running Time: 4 hrs. 5 mins.). 2006. audio compact disk 59.95 (978-0-7927-4330-9(X), BBCD 157) AudioGO.

Alan Cheuse. Alan Cheuse. Read by Alan Cheuse. 1 cass. (Running Time: 29 min.). 1987. 10.00 (101687) New Letters.
Fiction writer & book reviewer for National Public Radio's "All Things Considered," Cheuse reads from his memoir, "Fall Out of Heaven".

Alan Landsburg: President, Alan Landsburg Productions see Scene Behind the Screen: The Business Realities of the TV Industry

Alan Munde: Festival Favorites Revisited. Alan Munde. 2001. audio compact disk 15.98 (978-0-7866-4785-9(X), 97296CD) Mel Bay.

***Alan Partridge in Knowing Me Knowing You.** British Broadcasting Corporation Staff. Created by Steve Coogan. (Running Time: 3 hrs. 0 mins. 0 sec.). (ENG.). 2010. audio compact disk 29.95 (978-1-4084-1001-1(X)) Pub: AudioGO. Dist(s): Perseus Dist

Alan Paton: A Profile. Interview with Alan Paton. 1 cass. (Running Time: 25 min.). 1978. 12.95 (L062) TFR.
Paton tells why he could never leave South Africa despite his pessimistic feelings about the future of his country, noting that "Cry, the Beloved Country" provided him with enough money for the rest of his life.

Alanna: The First Adventure. unabr. ed. Tamora Pierce. 3 vols. (Running Time: 5 hrs. 13 mins.). (Song of the Lioness Ser.: Bk. 1). (J). (gr. 6 up). 2004. pap. bk. 36.00 (978-0-8072-8772-9(5), YA263SP, Listening Lib) Random Audio Pubg.

Alanna: The First Adventure. unabr. ed. Tamora Pierce. Read by Trini Alvarado. 3 cass. (Running Time: 5 hrs. 13 mins.). (Song of the Lioness Ser.: Bk. 1). (J). (gr. 6 up). 2004. 30.00 (978-0-8072-8771-2(7), LL0225, Listening Lib) Random Audio Pubg.
Young Alanna knows she isn't meant to become some proper lady cloistered in a convent. She wants to be a great warrior maiden, a female knight. But in the land of Tortall, women aren't allowed to be warriors. So Alanna switches places with her twin, Thom & takes his place as a knight in training at the palace of King Roald. Disguised as a boy, Alanna begins her training as a page in the royal court. Soon, she is gaining the admiration of all around her, including the crown prince... But, she is haunted by the recurring vision of an evil black stone city & she knows it must be rid of its wickedness. But how will she find it? How can she keep her gender a secret?.

Alanna: The First Adventure. unabr. ed. Tamora Pierce. Read by Trini Alvarado. (Song of the Lioness Ser.: Bk. 1). (ENG.). (J). (gr. 6). 2008. audio compact disk 30.00 (978-0-7393-7196-1(7), Listening Lib) Pub: Random Audio Pubg. Dist(s): Random

Alarm Call. Quintin Jardine. Read by Joe Dunlop. 8 cass. (Soundings Ser.). (J). 2005. 69.95 (978-1-84559-098-7(8)) Pub: ISIS Lrg Prnt GBR. Dist(s): Ulverscroft US

Alarm Call. unabr. ed. Quintin Jardine. Read by Joe Dunlop. 9 CDs. (Running Time: 10 hrs.). (Soundings (CDs) Ser.). (J). 2005. audio compact disk 84.95 (978-1-84559-217-2(4)) Pub: ISIS Lrg Prnt GBR. Dist(s): Ulverscroft US

Alarms & Diversions. unabr. collector's ed. James Thurber. Read by Wolfram Kandinsky. 8 cass. (Running Time: 12 hrs.). 1983. 64.00 (978-0-7366-2088-8(5), 2894) Books on Tape.
Thirty-two gently humorous stories including "The Psychosemanticist Will See You Now, Mr. Thurber" & "Get Thee to a Monastery".

Alaska. unabr. ed. James A. Michener. Read by Larry McKeever. 14 cass. (Running Time: 21 hrs.).Tr. of Alaska. 1994. 112.00 (978-0-7366-2710-8(3), 3441-B) Books on Tape.
A stirring portrait of a community, set against the background of Alaska's emotional & at times violent history.

Alaska. unabr. ed. James A. Michener. Read by Larry McKeever. 40 cass. (Running Time: 60 hrs.).Tr. of Alaska. 1999. 112.00 (978-0-7366-2709-2(X)) Books on Tape.

Alaska: A Place of Grace & Beauty. Charles R. Swindoll. 2006. audio compact disk 30.00 (978-1-57972-732-1(8)) Insight Living.

Alaska: An Audio Portrait. 2 cass. (Running Time: 2 hrs.). 20.95 (G0080B090, HarperThor) HarpC GBR.

Alaskan. unabr. ed. James Oliver Curwood. Read by Maynard Villers. 6 cass. (Running Time: 8 hrs. 12 min.). 1996. 39.95 (978-1-55686-724-8(7)) Books in Motion.
An action story of mystery, intrigue & romance in Alaska during the first quarter of the twentieth century. Mary Standish is the mystery woman whose past & purpose is hidden to Alan Holt.

Albanian: Learn to Speak & Understand Albanian with Pimsleur Language Programs. Pimsleur Staff & Pimsleur. (Running Time: 500 hrs. 0 mins. NaN sec.). (Compact Ser.). (ENG.). 2004. audio compact disk 115.00 (978-0-7435-3686-8(X), Pimsleur) Pub: S&S Audio. Dist(s): S and S Inc

Albanian: Scientifically Proven Method - Interactive Lessons - Only 30 Minutes a Day. unabr. ed. Pimsleur. Created by Pimsleur. 5 CDs. (Running Time: 50 hrs. 0 mins. 0 sec.). (Compact Ser.). (ALB & ENG.). 2006. audio compact disk 49.95 (978-0-7435-5058-1(7), Pimsleur) Pub: S&S Audio. Dist(s): S and S Inc

Albanian: Short Course, Set. Paul Pimsleur. 5 cass. (Running Time: 7 hrs. 30 min.). (Pimsleur Language Learning Ser.). 1994. pap. bk. & stu. ed. 149.95 (0671-57909-6) SyberVision.

Albanian: World Citizen Edition. unabr. ed. 2003. audio compact disk 115.00 (978-0-7887-9766-8(2)); 95.00 (978-0-7887-9699-9(2)) Recorded Bks.
Original and unique method enables you to acquire another language as easily as you learned English-by listening. With the Pimsleur program, you'll learn vocabulary and grammar correctly and easily in conversation without mindless repetition.

Albanian Newspaper Reader, Set. David L. Cox. 2 cass. (Running Time: 1 hr. 30 min. per cass.). (ALB.). 1998. 19.00 (3146) Dunwoody Pr.
Sixty-five selections intended to provide beginning & intermediate students with a collection of authentic materials, in this case contemporary newspaper articles, for the practice in reading & comprehending journalistic prose. Read by a native speaker.

Albert Camus: Reading from His Novel & Essays. unabr. ed. Albert Camus. Read by Albert Camus. 1 cass. Incl. Chute. (SWC 1138); Ete. (SWC 1138); Etranger. (FRE.). (SWC 1138); Peste. (SWC 1138); (FRE.). (J). 1984. 12.95 (978-0-694-50101-4(8), SWC 1138) HarperCollins Pubs.

Albert Einstein. Marie Hammontree & Lloyd James. 3 cass. (Running Time: 5 hrs. 30 mins.). 2002. 23.95 (978-0-7861-2034-5(7), 2798) Blckstn Audio.

Albert Einstein. unabr. ed. Berg, Ivan Association Staff. 1 cass. (Running Time: 1 hr. 6 min.). (History Maker Ser.). 12.95 (C41001) J Norton Pubs.
Einstein changed our understanding of whole areas of science with inspired theories which led the way to the development of much of our technology today. His contributions, which are detailed on this tape, have been formidable.

Albert Einstein: A Photographic Story of a Life. unabr. ed. Ed. by Dorling Kindersley Publishing Staff. 1 cass. (Running Time: 1 hr. 30 mins.). (SmartReader Ser.). 1998. pap. bk. & tchr. ed. 19.95 (978-0-7887-1154-1(7), 794113) Recorded Bks.
Albert Einstein wasn't always a brilliant & famous mathematician & teacher. He once struggled just to keep up in school! Here's his inspirational life story.

Albert Einstein: Creator & Rebel. unabr. ed. Banesh Hoffman. Read by Nadia May. 6 cass. (Running Time: 9 hrs.). 1995. 44.95 (978-0-7861-0910-4(6), 1712) Blckstn Audio.
This remarkable study is the model of what the biography of a scientist should be. Its author, a noted scientist himself, collaborated with & was a friend of Albert Einstein. On these pages we come to know Albert Einstein, the "backward" child, the academic outcast, the reluctant world celebrity, the exile, the pacifist, the philosopher, the humanitarian, the tragically saddened "father" of the atomic bomb, & above all, the unceasing searcher after scientific truth. At the same time, we are given a superb & essential introduction to the creative process & the concepts that shattered an age-old view of the universe & ushered in a revolution whose reverberations continue to touch us all.

Albert Einstein: Physicist, Philosopher, Humanitarian. Instructed by Don Howard. 2008. 129.95 (978-1-59803-472-1(3)); audio compact disk 69.95 (978-1-59803-457-8(X)) Teaching Co.

Albert Einstein: Young Thinker. unabr. ed. Robert Doremus. Read by Lloyd James. 4 cass. (Running Time: 5 hrs. 30 mins.). (Childhood of Famous Americans Ser.). (gr. 1-3). 2001. 35.95 (978-0-7861-2035-2(5), K2798) Blckstn Audio.
Albert Einstein's curiosity & ability to solve problems are evident at a young age. When he receives a compass on his fifth birthday, he questions why the needle always points north. Growing up in a Jewish family in Germany gives a unique perspective on the rise of Hitler prompting Albert's eventual migration to America.

***Albert Einstein: Young Thinker.** unabr. ed. Marie Hammontree. Read by Lloyd James. (Running Time: 5 hrs. 0 mins.). 2010. 29.95 (978-1-4417-5077-8(0)); audio compact disk 55.00 (978-1-4417-5074-7(6)) Blckstn Audio.

Albert Ellis Live at the Learning Annex. 2 cass. (Running Time: 97 min.). 19.95 Set. (C038) Inst Rational-Emotive.
Presents the basics of REBT for a general audience. Includes live demonstrations & audience questions. Lively, outrageous, educational.

Albert Ellis Live at the Learning Annex, Set. 2 cass. (Running Time: 97 min.). 19.95 (C038) A Ellis Institute.
Albert Ellis presenting the basics of REBT for a general audience. Includes two demonstrations & audience questions. Lively, outrageous, educational.

Albert Goldbarth. unabr. ed. Read by Albert Goldbarth & Rebekah Presson. Ed. by James McKinley. 1 cass. (Running Time: 29 min.). (New Letters on the Air Ser.). 1992. 10.00 (090492); 18.00 2-sided cass. New Letters.
Goldbarth is interviewed by Rebekah Presson & reads from his poems.

Albert Gore: Public vs. Private Power see Buckley's Firing Line

Albert Russo: Mixed Blood. Albert Russo. Read by Albert Russo. Interview with Rebekah Presson. 1 cass. (Running Time: 29 min.). 1990. 10.00 (020990) New Letters.
Russo lives in Paris where he writes in both English & French. Here, he reads from his novel, "Mixed Blood", which draws on his personal experience of having been raised in French Colonial Africa.

Albert Schweitzer: Reverence for Life. unabr. ed. Albert Schweitzer. Read by Marvin Miller. Tr. by Reginald H. Fuller. 4 cass. (Running Time: 6 hrs.). 1990. 23.80 (D-205) Audio Bk.
Albert Schweitzer (1875-1965) Alsatian philosopher, theologian, musician, mission doctor & winner of the Nobel Prize in 1952. A world figure in the theological studies, he was an organist of concert calibre & an interpreter of rare & original perception of Bach. This collection of his theological thoughts demonstrates Dr. Schweitzer's own original contribution of "Reverence for Life" as the true & effective basis for a civilized world.

Albert Schweitzer Discusses Goethe. unabr. ed. 1 cass. (Running Time: 90 mins.). (GER.). 14.95 (C23140) J Norton Pubs.
With sentence by sentence translation by Thornton Wilder.

Albert Schweitzer Reading from Reverence for Life. abr. ed. Albert Schweitzer. Perf. by Albert Schweitzer. 1 cass. (Running Time: 60 min.). (GER.). 1984. 12.95 (978-0-694-50215-8(4), SWC 1335) HarperCollins Pubs.
Schweitzer reads about his work in Africa & his many other interests. He describes building the leprosarium at Lambarene & reflects on his childhood & early education.

Albert Schweitzer's Mission: Healing & Peace. unabr. collector's ed. Norman Cousins. Read by Larry McKeever. 8 cass. (Running Time: 12 hrs.). 1988. 64.00 (978-0-7366-1279-1(3), 2188) Books on Tape.
In 1952, Dr. Albert Schweitzer was awarded the Nobel Peace Prize for his work as a medical missionary in Africa. At that point, his career included - as well as medicine - theology, music & philosophy. His final quest was to wake the public to the dangers of nuclear war.

Albert Speer: The End of a Myth. unabr. collector's ed. Matthias Schmidt. Read by Richard Wulf. 8 cass. (Running Time: 8 hrs.). 1987. 48.00 (978-0-7366-1234-0(3), 2152) Books on Tape.
Speer created his own legend as a "good Nazi". This book debunks it.

Albertina Walker: I'm Still Here. 1997. 10.98 (978-0-7601-1722-4(5)); audio compact disk 15.98 (978-0-7601-1723-1(3)) Pub: Brentwood Music. Dist(s): Provident Mus Dist
Collection of tunes on this project are synonymous with what fans consider to be the heartbeat of traditional gospel music, simple songs delivered with overwhelming inspiration & conviction, songs that have become standards in congregations across the country.

Albertine Desaparecido. unabr. ed. Proust Marcel. Read by Santiago Munevar. (SPA.). 2007. audio compact disk 17.00 (978-958-8318-20-2(3)) Pub: Yoyo Music COL. Dist(s): YoYoMusic

Album for the Young - Tchaikovsky. Transcribed by Ken Hummer. 1999. pap. bk. 17.95 (978-0-7866-2857-5(X), 96646BCD) Mel Bay.

Album of Memories: Personal Histories from the Greatest Generation. unabr. ed. Tom Brokaw. 6 cass. (Running Time: 9 hrs.). 2001. 44.95 (978-0-7366-6843-9(8)) Books on Tape.

Album of Negro Spirituals. Created by Alfred Publishing. (ENG.). 2007. audio compact disk 12.95 (978-0-7390-4529-9(6)) Alfred Pub.

Album of Negro Spirituals: Low Voice. Composed by Harry T. Burleigh. (ENG.). 2007. audio compact disk 12.95 (978-0-7390-4531-2(8)) Alfred Pub.

Alcahuete y Otras Historias Eroticas. unabr. ed. Marquis de Sade.Tr. of Procurer & Other Erotic Stories. (SPA.). 2002. audio compact disk 13.00 (978-958-43-0141-3(1)) YoYoMusic.

Alcatraz: The Rock. Jerry Stemach. Ed. by Jerry Stemach. Ed. by Gail Portnuff Venable et al. Illus. by Philip Dizick. Narrated by Ed Smaron. (Start-to-Finish Books). (J). (gr. 2-3). 1999. (978-1-893376-08-3(7), Fo3K2) D Johnston Inc.
In this story, Nick and the kids are on Alcatraz Island in San Francisco Bay. The park ranger there has asked Nick to help complete an environmental impact report. During their stay, Jeff and Mandy witness the attempted murder of a man from China who is attempting to sneak into the United States on a fishing boat. Jeff and Mandy save the man from drowning and learn that the boat is filled with illegal fireworks and drugs.

Alcatraz Cellhouse Tour & Booklet. Antenna Audio Tours Staff. 1 cass. (Running Time: 35 min.). 1993. 9.95 incl. bklet. (978-0-9625206-3-1(2)) Gldn Gate Natl Parks.

Alcatraz, the Rock. Jerry Stemach. (Nick Ford Mysteries Ser.). 1999. audio compact disk 18.95 (978-1-4105-0130-1(2)) D Johnston Inc.

Alcatraz Versus the Evil Librarians. unabr. ed. Brandon Sanderson. Read by Charlie McWade. (Alcatraz Ser.). (J). 2007. 54.99 (978-1-60252-815-4(2)) Find a World.

***Alchemaster's Apprentice: A Culinary Tale from Zamonia by Optimus Yarnspinner.** unabr. ed. Walter Moers. Read by Bronson Pinchot. (Running Time: 13 hrs. NaN mins.). (ENG.). 2011. 29.95 (978-1-4417-5785-2(6)); 79.95 (978-1-4417-5781-4(3)); audio compact disk 32.95 (978-1-4417-5784-5(8)); audio compact disk 109.00 (978-1-4417-5782-1(1)) Blckstn Audio.

Alchemical Consciousness As the Modern Paradigm. Diane Martin. Read by Diane Martin. 3 cass. (Running Time: 3 hrs. 45 min.). 1991. 24.95 set. (978-0-7822-0360-8(4), 459) C G Jung IL.
Jung considered alchemy the most complete & instructive system to represent the individuation process. In recent times there is a revival of interest in this esoteric subject, due to its ability to hold both highly differentiated & highly oppositional sets. Diane Martin leads a seminar which focuses on decoding key alchemical images, processes & envisionings so that the numinous & the everyday can attain their natural reciprocity.

Alchemist see Twentieth-Century Poetry in English, No. 2, Recordings of Poets Reading Their Own Poetry

Alchemist see Alchimiste

***Alchemist.** unabr. ed. Paulo Coelho. Read by Jeremy Irons. (ENG.). 2005. (978-0-06-087906-8(8), Harper Audio); (978-0-06-087907-5(6), Harper Audio) HarperCollins Pubs.

Alchemist. 10th unabr. ed. Paulo Coelho & Paul Coelho. Read by Jeremy Irons. 4 CDs. (Running Time: 5 hrs.). 2001. audio compact disk 29.95 (978-0-694-52444-0(1)) HarperCollins Pubs.

Alchemist: A Fable about Following Your Dream see Alquimista

Alchemist's Son Pt. II: Soul Stealer. unabr. ed. Martin Booth. Narrated by Steven Crossley. 5 cass. (Running Time: 7 hrs. 15 mins.). 2005. 45.75 (978-1-4193-5073-3(0), 98115) Recorded Bks.
In this riveting sequel to Martin Booth's wildly popular Doctor Illuminatus, siblings Pip and Tim once again come to the aid of Sebastian - a 600-year-old alchemist's son. An evil man has hatched a plan to steal the souls of millions. The three children must rely on the mysterious art of alchemy and their own courage in order to save the day. Soul Stealers was shortlisted for the Writers Guild Award.

Alchemy. Instructed by Manly P. Hall. 5 cass. 8.50 ea. o.p. Pt. 1: Adepts of the Alchemical Tradition. (800163-A) Philos Res.

Alchemy, Set. unabr. ed. Jose Arguelles & Miriam Arguelles. 3 cass. (Running Time: 4 hr. 8 min.). 1970. 26.00 (12902) Big Sur Tapes.
These talks provide both broad historical background & intricate detail of the uses of symbols for meditation & spiritual development. Mandalas, a specialty of artist & scholar Jose Arguelles, occur in practically every culture & can also be observed in nature. The specialized symbols of alchemy remain psychologically relevant to seekers, especially those raised Western countries.

Alchemy & Meggy Swann. unabr. ed. Karen Cushman. Read by Katherine Kellgren. (ENG.). (J). (gr. 5). 2010. 28.00 (978-0-307-71022-2(X), Listening Lib) Pub: Random Audio Pubg. Dist(s): Random

Alchemy As a Key to Social Regeneration. Instructed by Manly P. Hall. 8.95 (978-0-89314-003-8(1), C851110) Philos Res.

Alchemy of Awareness: An in-Depth Inquiry with Mukti. 5 Audio CDs. Featuring Mukti. (ENG.). 2008. audio compact disk 40.00 (978-1-933986-41-8(7)) Open Gate Pub.

Alchemy of Gender. Beverley Zabriskie. Read by Beverley Zabriskie. 1 cass. (Running Time: 80 min.). 1993. 10.95 (978-0-7822-0454-4(6), 532) C G Jung IL.

Alchemy of Love & Lust: Discover Our Sex Hormones & Determine Who We Love CST. Theresa L. Crenshaw. 2004. 7.95 (978-0-7435-4094-0(8)) Pub: S&S Audio. Dist(s): S and S Inc

Alchemy of the Analytic Relationship. Read by Nathan Schwartz-Salant. 4 cass. (Running Time: 5 hrs. 30 min.). 1989. 31.95 Set. (978-0-7822-0250-2(0), 372) C G Jung IL.

Alchemy of the Heart. abr. ed. Reshad Feild. Read by Reshad Feild. 2 cass. (Running Time: 3 hrs.). 1995. 15.95 (978-0-944993-57-6(5)) Audio Lit.
Field's message of the acceptance of Love as the only truth shines through this examination of pain, death, consciousness & the divine order.

Alchemy of the Heart: How to Give & Receive More Love. unabr. ed. Elizabeth Clare Prophet & Patricia R. Spadaro. 1 cass. (Running Time: 1 hr. 30 mins.). 2002. 18.95 (978-0-922729-70-8(0), 942-056) Pub: Summit Univ. Dist(s): Natl Bk Netwk

Alchemyst. unabr. ed. Michael Scott. Read by Denis O'Hare. 8 CDs. (Running Time: 10 hrs. 10 mins.). (Secrets of the Immortal Nicholas Flamel Ser.: Bk. 1). (J). (gr. 4-7). 2007. audio compact disk 60.00 (978-0-7393-5104-8(4), Listening Lib) Pub: Random Audio Pubg. Dist(s): Random

Alchemyst. unabr. ed. Michael Scott. Read by Denis O'Hare. (Running Time: 36120 sec.). (Secrets of the Immortal Nicholas Flamel Ser.: Bk. 1). (ENG.). (J). (gr. 5-12). 2007. audio compact disk 40.00 (978-0-7393-5032-4(3), Listening Lib) Pub: Random Audio Pubg. Dist(s): Random

Alchimiste. Annabel Malak. Adapted by Paulo Coelho. Illus. by Marie-Jose Beaudoin. 2 CDs, bklet. (Running Time: 3 hrs.).Tr. of Alchemist. (FRE.). cass. & audio compact disk 19.95 (978-2-921997-33-1(9)) Pub: Coffragants CAN. Dist(s): Penton Overseas
Recorded completely in international French language by well-known actors or speakers.

Alchimiste. Annabel Malak. Adapted by Paulo Coelho. Illus. by Marie-Jose Beaudoin. 1 cass., bklet. (Running Time: 90 mins.).Tr. of Alchemist. (FRE.). (J). cass. & audio compact disk 14.95 (978-2-921997-29-4(0)) Pub: Coffragants CAN. Dist(s): Penton Overseas

Alcohol. unabr. ed. Nancy B. Peacock. 1 cass. (Running Time: 1 hr. 30 min.). (J). 2003. 10.00 (978-1-4025-0139-5(0)) Recorded Bks.
Informs about the effects of alcohol.

Alcohol: Our Biggest Drug Problem. unabr. collector's ed. Joel Fort. Read by Michael Prichard. 6 cass. (Running Time: 6 hrs.). 1985. 36.00 (978-0-7366-1025-4(1), 1955) Books on Tape.
Dr. Fort labels the alcohol industry as the most institutionalized drug culture.

Alcohol & Ketamine. Olga Luchkova. Interview with Elizabeth Gips. 1 cass. 1999. 11.00 (32009) Big Sur Tapes.
1992 Santa Cruz.

Alcohol-Drugs: Overcoming a Dependency. Richard Jafolla & Mary-Alice Jafolla. Read by Richard Jafolla & Mary-Alice Jafolla. (Overcoming Ser.). 1986. 12.95 (130) Stppng Stones.
Motivational tapes that work on the subconscious mind (subliminal) & conscious mind to bring about self-improvement.

Alcoholics Anonymous. 7 cass. 1986. 35.00 (2010) Hazelden.
The basic introduction to AA, how it works & its many personal stories. Braille labelled.

Alcoholics Anonymous: How Many Thousands of Men & Women Have Recovered. Prod. by The Recovery Zone. 5 CDs. (Running Time: 4 hours, 30 mins). 2002. cd-rom 24.95 (978-0-9762328-0-3(4)) Recovery Zone.
Originally written in 1938 by Alcoholics Anonymous World Services, this book has served as the basic text for AA for over 60 years. This is a 4.5 hour audio recording of this book. The Recovery Zone is not affiliated with Alcoholics Anonymous World Services.

Alcoholism. Bruce Goldberg. Read by Bruce Goldberg. 1 cass. (Running Time: 25 min.). (ENG.). 2006. 13.00 (978-1-885577-37-5(0)) Pub: B Goldberg. Dist(s): Baker Taylor
Remove the need to drink, and return to a happy and fuctional life through self-hypnosis.

Alcoholism: Program from the Award Winning Public Radio Show. Interview. Hosted by Fred Goodwin. 1 CD. (Running Time: 1 hr). 2001. audio compact disk 21.95 (978-1-932479-19-5(8), LCM 272) Lichtenstein Creat.
Chances are that you have a close family member who has a drinking problem. But if alcoholism is a disease, why is it that too often we look at the drinker as the problem? In today's program, we explore the latest research on alcohol dependence and alcohol abuse, the largest research study to date on treating alcoholism, and promising new treatments, including a clinical trial to treat alcohol dependence with a medication commonly used to control epilepsy.

Alcoholism & Addiction Cure: A Holistic Approach to Total Recovery. Chris Prentiss. Read by Chris Prentiss. (Running Time: 36000 sec.). 2005. audio compact disk 39.95 (978-0-943015-51-4(0)) Pub: Power Press. Dist(s): SCB Distributors

Alcoholism & Astrology. Albert Gaulden. Read by Albert Gaulden. 1 cass. (Running Time: 90 min.). 1994. 8.95 (1148) Am Fed Astrologers.

Alcoholism & the Family. Janet G. Woititz. 4 cass. 1986. 34.95 (1696) Hazelden.
The author of Adult Children of Alcoholics tape offers revelations & reflections about the effects of alcohol abuse on the family.

Alcoholism in America. 1 cass. (Running Time: 50 min.). 1988. 10.95 (I0440B090, HarperThor) HarpC GBR.

Alcools. Poems. Guillaume Apollinaire. Read by Daniel Gelin. 1 cass. (FRE.). 1991. 22.95 (1403-LQP) Olivia & Hill.
A famous collection of poems.

Aldous Huxley. Aldous Huxley. Interview with Mike Wallace. 1 cass. 1999. 11.00 (01128) Big Sur Tapes.
1958 Radio Interview.

Aldrich Family. Created by Radio Spirits. (Running Time: 10800 sec.). 2004. audio compact disk 9.98 (978-1-57019-706-2(7)) Radio Spirits.

Aldrich Family. collector's ed. Perf. by Ezra Stone. 6 cass. (Running Time: 9 hrs.). 1998. bk. 34.98 (4012) Radio Spirits.
Henry Alrich is the boy who could mess up any situation. 18 episodes of wholesome fun.

Aldrich Family: Debate Team Victory? & Battle for the Last Turkey. unabr. ed. 1 cass. (Running Time: 1 hr.). 2001. 6.98 (2453) Radio Spirits.

Aldrich Family: Girl Trouble with Kathleen & Lead in the School Musical. unabr. ed. 1 cass. (Running Time: 1 hr.). 2001. 6.98 (1733) Radio Spirits.

Aldrich Family: Girlfriend Mixup & Generous Gentleman. unabr. ed. 1 cass. (Running Time: 1 hr.). 2001. 6.98 (2073) Radio Spirits.

Aldrich Family: Henry & Homer Sell War Bonds & Henry Forgot to Mail Letter. unabr. ed. 1 cass. (Running Time: 1 hr.). 2001. 6.98 (1733) Radio Spirits.

Aldrich Family: Toy Repair & Weekly Party. unabr. ed. 1 cass. (Running Time: 1 hr.). 2001. 6.98 (2431) Radio Spirits.

Aldrich Family: Valentine Party Mix-Up & Stolen Bicycles. unabr. ed. 1 cass. (Running Time: 1 hr.). 2001. 6.98 (2112) Radio Spirits.

Alef Bet. Ed. by Randee Friedman & Donna Lander. Arranged by Debbie Friedman. Composed by Debbie Friedman. Executive Producer Randee Friedman. Arranged by Dassi Rosenkrantz-Cabo. (Running Time: 39 mins.). (HEB.). (J). 2001. audio compact disk 15.95 (978-1-890161-45-3(4), 0606261616129) Sounds Write.
Learn the Alef Bet through Debbie?s signature song and get a delicious taste of Hebrew grammar, vocabulary, greetings, the importance of friendship and sharing, and other value lessons.

Alef Bet. Ed. by Randee Friedman & Donna Lander. Arranged by Debbie Friedman. Composed by Debbie Friedman. Executive Producer Randee Friedman. Prod. by Dassi Rosenkrantz-Cabo. Arranged by Dassi Rosenkrantz-Cabo. (Running Time: 39 min.). (HEB.). (J). 2001. 9.95 (978-1-890161-44-6(6), 0606261616143) Sounds Write.

Alegria. 2006. audio compact disk 14.99 (978-0-8297-5056-0(8)) Zondervan.

Alegria de Ser Tu y Yo. 1 cass. (Running Time: 35 min.).Tr. of Bein' with You This Way. (SPA.). (J). 2001. 15.95 (VXS-38C) Kimbo Educ.

Alegria de Ser Tu y Yo. W. Nikola-Lisa. 1 cass. (Running Time: 8 mins.). (SPA., 1999. 9.95 (978-0-87499-552-7(3)) Live Oak Media.
Playground rap that introduces children to how people are the same.

Alegria de Ser Tu y Yo. W. Nikola-Lisa. Illus. by Michael Bryant. 11 vols. (Running Time: 8 mins.). 1999. bk. 28.95 (978-1-59519-126-7(7)); pap. bk. 39.95 (978-1-59519-125-0(9)); audio compact disk 12.95 (978-1-59519-123-6(2)) Live Oak Media.

Alegria de Ser Tu y Yo. W. Nikola-Lisa. Illus. by Michael Bryant. 11 vols. (Running Time: 8 mins.). (SPA.). (J). 1999. pap. bk. 18.95 (978-1-59519-124-3(0)) Pub: Live Oak Media. Dist(s): AudioGO

Alegria de Ser Tu y Yo. unabr. ed. W. Nikola-Lisa. Perf. by Jocelyn Martinez. Tr. by Yanitzia Canetti from ENG. Illus. by Michael Bryant. 11 vols. (Running Time: 8 mins.). (SPA.). (J). (gr. k-3). 1999. pap. bk. 16.95 (978-0-87499-549-7(3)) AudioGO.
How people are different, yet the same.

Alegria de Ser Tu y Yo. unabr. ed. W. Nikola-Lisa. Perf. by Jocelyn Martinez. Tr. by Yanitzia Canetti from ENG. Illus. by Michael Bryant. 11 vols. (Running Time: 8 mins.). (SPA.). (J). (gr. k-3). 1999. bk. 25.95 (978-0-87499-550-3(7)) Live Oak Media.

Alegria de Ser Tu y Yo, Grades K-3. unabr. ed. W. Nikola-Lisa. Perf. by Jocelyn Martinez. Tr. by Yanitzia Canetti from ENG. Illus. by Michael Bryant. 14 vols. (Running Time: 8 mins.).Tr. of Bein' with You This Way. (SPA.). (J). 1999. pap. bk. & tchr. ed. 37.95 Reading Chest. (978-0-87499-551-0(5)) Live Oak Media.

Alejandro's Gift. unabr. ed. Richard E. Albert. 1 cass. (Running Time: 7 min.). (J). (gr. k-4). 1994. pap. bk. 17.90 (978-0-8045-6825-8(1), 6825) Spoken Arts.
This uplifting story and environment lesson will prompt children to look at the world around them in a new way.

Aleksandr Pushkin see Classical Russian Poetry

Aleman de Cada Dia. (SPA.). 2002. bk. 8.90 (978-84-494-2382-6(1), 1402) Oceano Grupo ESP.

Alentejo Blue. abr. unabr. ed. Monica Ali. (Running Time: 540 hrs. NaN mins.). 2006. audio compact disk 29.95 (978-0-7861-7573-4(7)) Blckstn Audio.

Alentejo Blue. abr. unabr. ed. Monica Ali. Read by Anna Fields. 6 cass. (Running Time: 28800 sec.). 2006. 25.95 (978-0-7861-4544-7(7)) Blckstn Audio.

Alentejo Blue. unabr. ed. Monica Ali. Read by Anna Fields. (Running Time: 27000 sec.). 2006. 54.95 (978-0-7861-4634-5(6)); audio compact disk 63.00 (978-0-7861-6830-9(7)) Blckstn Audio.

Alentejo Blue. unabr. ed. Monica Ali. 8 CDs. (Running Time: 28800 sec.). 2006. audio compact disk 27.95 (978-0-7861-7134-7(0)) Blckstn Audio.

Aleph-Bet Story Book: Five Stories-Song. Deborah Pessin. 1 cass. (J). (ps-4). 1988. 9.95 (978-0-944633-00-7(5)) J Chernak.
A story for each of the first 5 letters of the Hebrew alphabet, and the Aleph-Bet song.

Alert Program: Songs for Self-Regulation. unabr. ed. Aubrey Carton & Bob Wiz. Perf. by Therapyworks, Inc. Staff. 1 cass. (Running Time: 1 hr. 14 min.). (Belle Curve Clinical Ser.). (J). (ps-2). 1995. 15.00 (978-1-893601-03-1(X), BCRI-5) Sensory Res.
Car engine speed analogy is used to teach children strategies for self-regulation.

Alert Program with Songs for Self-Regulation. 2 CDs. (Running Time: 1 hr 40 min). 1995. audio compact disk 20.00 (978-0-9643041-2-3(0)) Therapy Wrks.

Alerta Sings: Children's Songs in Spanish & English. Perf. by Suni Paz. 1 cass. (ENG & SPA.). (J). (gr. k-8). 1992. (0-9307-45012-4-5) Smithsonian Folkways.
Helps children learn songs from different cultures. Designed for children of diverse backgrounds as a way for them to develop an appreciation of the cultural diversity of America.

Alerta Sings & Songs for the Playground: Canciones Para el Recreo. Suni Paz. 1 cass. (Running Time: 75 min.). (SPA.). (J). (ps-5). 2000. 8.50 (SFW45055); audio compact disk 14.00 Smithsonian Folkways.
Notes include lyrics in Spanish & English.

Aleutian Sparrow. Karen Hesse. Read by Sarah Jones. (Running Time: 1 hr. 45 mins.). (J). (gr. 5-9). 2004. 15.00 (978-0-8072-1967-6(3), Listening Lib); audio compact disk 24.00 (978-0-8072-2014-6(0), Listening Lib) Random Audio Pubg.

Alex: The Life of Field Marshal Earl Alexander of Tunis. unabr. ed. Nigel Nicolson. Read by Geoffrey Howard. 9 cass. (Running Time: 13 hrs. 30 mins.). 2000. 72.00 (978-0-7366-6012-9(7)) Books on Tape.
Unruffled in defeat, modest in success, Alex was the image of a great commander.The last British soldier to leave Dunkirk, he was also Montgomery's C-in-C at Alamein.Twice in Tunisia & northern Italy, he forced the surrender of an entire German Army Group & he captured Rome.

***Alex & Me.** unabr. ed. Irene Pepperberg. Read by Julia Gibson. (ENG.). 2008. (978-0-06-176934-4(7), Harper Audio); (978-0-06-176936-8(3), Harper Audio) HarperCollins Pubs.

Alex & Me: How a Scientist & a Parrot Discovered a Hidden World of Animal Intelligence - And Formed a Deep Bond in the Process. unabr. ed. Irene Pepperberg. Read by Julia Gibson. 5 CDs. (Running Time: 5 hrs. 30 mins.). 2008. audio compact disk 29.95 (978-0-06-173494-6(2), Harper Audio) HarperCollins Pubs.

Alex & the Ironic Gentleman. unabr. ed. Adrienne Kress. Read by Christopher Lane. 8 CDs. (Running Time: 32400 sec.). (J). 2007. audio compact disk 92.25 (978-1-4233-4753-8(6), 9781423347538, BriAudCD Unabrid) Brilliance Audio.

Alex & the Ironic Gentleman. unabr. ed. Adrienne Kress. Read by Christopher Lane. (Running Time: 9 hrs.). 2007. 39.25 (978-1-4233-4757-6(9), 9781423347576, BADLE); 24.95 (978-1-4233-4756-9(0), 9781423347569, BAD); 74.25 (978-1-4233-4751-4(X), 9781423347514, BrilAudUnabridg) Brilliance Audio.

Alex & the Ironic Gentleman. unabr. ed. Adrienne Kress. Read by Christopher Lane. 1 MP3-CD. (Running Time: 32400 sec.). (J). (gr. 4-7). 2007. audio compact disk 39.25 (978-1-4233-4755-2(2), 9781423347552, Brinc Audio MP3 Lib); audio compact disk 24.95 (978-1-4233-4754-5(4), 9781423347545, Brilliance MP3) Brilliance Audio.

Alex & the Ironic Gentleman. unabr. ed. Adrienne Kress. Read by Christopher Lane. 8 CDs. (Running Time: 9 hrs.). (YA). (gr. 5 up). 2007. audio compact disk 29.95 (978-1-4233-4752-1(8), 9781423347521, Bril Audio CD Unabri) Brilliance Audio.

Alex & the Raynhams. unabr. ed. Iris Bromige. Read by Gwen Cherrell. 6 cass. (Running Time: 7 hrs. 11 mins.). (Isis Ser.). (J). 2004. 54.95 (978-1-85089-689-0(5), 20392) Pub: ISIS Lrg Prnt GBR. Dist(s): Ulverscroft US

Alex & Zig. unabr. ed. Barbara M. Klopp. Read by Leitha Christie. 1 cass. (Running Time: 50 mins.). (J). (ps-4). 1995. 9.95 (978-1-889112-02-2(X)) Earbks.
Four short stories about a boy & his Angel.

Alex Cross's Trial. unabr. ed. James Patterson & Richard DiLallo. Read by Dylan Baker. (Running Time: 9 hrs.). (Alex Cross Ser.: No. 15). (ENG.). 2009. 19.98 (978-1-60024-854-2(3)) Pub: Hachet Audio. Dist(s): HachBkGrp

***Alex Cross's Trial.** unabr. ed. James Patterson & Richard DiLallo. Narrated by Dylan Baker & Shawn Andrews. 1 MP3-CD. (Running Time: 9 hrs.). 2009. 49.99 (978-1-60024-948-8(5)); audio compact disk 79.99 (978-1-60024-943-3(4)) Pub: Hachet Audio. Dist(s): HachBkGrp

Alex Cross's Trial. unabr. ed. James Patterson & Richard DiLallo. Read by Dylan Baker. (Running Time: 9 hrs.). (Alex Cross Ser.: No. 15). (ENG.). 2010. audio compact disk 19.98 (978-1-60788-189-6(6)) Pub: Hachet Audio. Dist(s): HachBkGrp

***Alex et Zoe et Compagnie 1: Chansons et Comptines: Methode de Francais.** Colette Samson. (FRE.). (J). 2005. audio compact disk (978-2-09-032127-2(X)) Cle Intl FRA.

Alex Haley. Interview with Alex Haley. 1 cass. (Running Time: 45 mins.). 12.95 (L031) TFR.
Haley discusses his first published book, "The Autobiography of Malcolm X," & talks about Malcolm's complicated self-hate. In a separate interview on "Roots," he reveals that the only prejudice he experienced in researching the book was on religious rather than racial grounds.

Alex Hawke: Assassin, Pirate, Spy. abr. ed. Ted Bell. Read by John Shea. (Running Time: 18 hrs.). (Hawke Ser.). 2007. audio compact disk 34.95 (978-1-4233-3424-8(8), 9781423334248, BACD) Brilliance Audio.

Alex 2005. unabr. ed. 2005. 9.99 (978-0-8297-4634-1(X)) Zondervan.

Alexander. John Bonaccorsi. Narrated by Larry A. McKeever. (Ancient Greek Mystery Ser.). (J). 2007. 10.95 (978-1-58659-131-1(2)); audio compact disk 14.95 (978-1-58659-365-0(X)) Artesian.

Alexander - Santa's Newest Reindeer. unabr. ed. Poems. Judy Strigel. Read by Judy Strigel. Read by Cliff Erickson. Perf. by Cliff Erickson & Doug Leightenheimer. Illus. by Linda Edwards. 1 cass. (Running Time: 30 min.). Dramatization. (J). (gr. 2-4). 1997. pap. bk. 3.00 (978-1-885527-11-0(X)) Feather Fables.
Poem written by Philip (little elf): Santa talking to boys & girls about his newest reindeer & Grandma riding the reindeer.

Alexander & the Car with the Missing Headlight. (J). 2004. 8.95 (978-1-56008-825-7(7)); cass. & flmstrp 30.00 (978-0-89719-640-6(6)) Weston Woods.

Alexander & the Car with the Missing Headlight; Lion & the Rat, the; Hare & the Tortoise, the; Charley, Charlotte & the Golden Canary; Gilberto & the Wind. (J). 2004. (978-0-89719-823-3(9)); cass. & flmstrp (978-0-89719-731-1(3)) Weston Woods.

Alexander & the Terrible, Horrible, No Good, Very Bad Day see Alexander y el Dia Terrible, Horrible, Espantoso, Horroroso

Alexander & the Terrible, Horrible, No Good, Very Bad Day. Read by Blythe Danner. Ed. by Judith Viorst. 1 cass. (Running Time: 54 mins.). (J). 11.95 (HarperChildAud) HarperCollins Pubs.

Alexander & the Terrible, Horrible, No Good, Very Bad Day. Read by Johnny Heller. Ed. by Judith Viorst. 1 cass. (Running Time: 15 mins.). (Alexander Ser.). (J). (gr. k-3). 1999. pap. bk. 23.24 (978-0-7887-3177-8(7), 40912) Recorded Bks.
When Alexander wakes up with gum in his hair, he thinks that maybe it's going to be a bad day. When he trips on the skateboard by his bed, he knows it's going to be even worse than he thought. Kids will recognize themselves in this story.

Alexander & the Terrible, Horrible, No Good, Very Bad Day. abr. ed. Read by Blythe Danner. Ed. by Judith Viorst. 1 cass. (Running Time: 1 Hr). 2003. 7.99 (978-0-06-058462-7(9)) HarperCollins Pubs.

Alexander & the Terrible, Horrible, No Good, Very Bad Day. unabr. ed. Ed. by Judith Viorst. Narrated by Johnny Heller. 1 cass. (Running Time: 15 mins.). (Alexander Ser.). (gr. k up). 1999. 10.00 (978-0-7887-3158-7(0), 95831E7) Recorded Bks.

Alexander & the Terrible, Horrible, No Good, Very Bad Day. unabr. abr. ed. Read by Blythe Danner. Ed. by Judith Viorst. 1 cass. (Running Time: 54 mins.). Incl. Alexander, Who Used to Be Rich Last Sunday. Judith Viorst. (Alexander Ser.). (J). (gr. k-3). 1989. (CPN 1722); If I Were in Charge of the World. (J). (ps-3). 1989. (CPN 1722); My Mama Says There Aren't Any Zombies, Ghosts, Vampires, Creatures, Demons, Monsters, Fiends, Goblins, or Things. (J). (ps-3). 1989. (CPN 1722); Tenth Good Thing about Barney. (J). (ps-3). 1989. (CPN 1722); (Alexander Ser.). (J). (gr. k-2). 1989. 12.00 (978-0-89845-867-1(6), CPN 1722) HarperCollins Pubs.
The trials & tribulations of growing up are treated in these stories.

Alexander & the Terrible, Horrible, No Good, Very Bad Day. unabr. abr. ed. Judith Viorst. Read by Blythe Danner. 1 CD. (Running Time: 1 hr.). (J). 2004. 13.95 (978-0-06-072331-6(9)) HarperCollins Pubs.

Alexander & the Terrible, Horrible, No Good, Very Bad Day, Class set. Read by Johnny Heller. Ed. by Judith Viorst. 1 cass. (Running Time: 15 mins.). (Alexander Ser.). (J). (gr. k-3). 1999. 80.70 (978-0-7887-3223-2(4), 46879) Recorded Bks.
When Alexander wakes up with gum in his hair, he thinks that maybe it's going to be a bad day. When he trips on the skateboard by his bed, he knows it's going to be even worse than he thought. Kids will recognize themselves in this story.

Alexander & the Wonderful, Marvelous, Excellent, Terrific Ninety Days. unabr. ed. Judith Viorst. Read by Laural Merlington. (Running Time: 3 hrs. 30 mins. 0 sec.). (ENG.). 2007. audio compact disk 19.99 (978-1-4001-0528-1(5)) Pub: Tantor Media. Dist(s): IngramPubServ

Alexander & the Wonderful, Marvelous, Excellent, Terrific Ninety Days: An Almost Completely Honest Account of What Happened to Our Family When Our Youngest Son, His Wife, & Their Baby, Their Toddler, & Their Five-Year-Old Came to Live with Us for Three Months. unabr. ed. Judith Viorst. Read by Laural Merlington. (Running Time: 3 hrs. 30 mins. 0 sec.). (ENG.). 2007. audio compact disk 39.99 (978-1-4001-3528-8(1)) Pub: Tantor Media. Dist(s): IngramPubServ

Alexander & the Wonderful, Marvelous, Excellent, Terrific Ninety Days: An Almost Completely Honest Account of What Happened to Our Family When Our Youngest Son, His Wife, & Their Baby, Their Toddler, & Their Five-Year-Old Came to Live with Us for Three Months. unabr. ed. Judith Viorst. Read by Laural Merlington. (Running Time: 3 hrs. 30 mins. 0 sec.). (ENG.). 2007. audio compact disk 19.99 (978-1-4001-5528-6(2)) Pub: Tantor Media. Dist(s): IngramPubServ

***Alexander Cipher: A Thriller.** unabr. ed. Will Adams. Narrated by David Colacci. (Running Time: 13 hrs. 0 mins. 0 sec.). (Daniel Knox Ser.). (ENG.). 2010. 24.99 (978-1-4001-6699-2(3)); 34.99 (978-1-4001-9699-9(X)); 17.99 (978-1-4001-8699-0(4)); audio compact disk 34.99 (978-1-4001-1699-7(6)); audio compact disk 69.99 (978-1-4001-4699-4(2)) Pub: Tantor Media. Dist(s): IngramPubServ

Alexander Dia Terrible. (Running Time: 9 mins.). 1991. 9.95 (978-1-59112-146-6(9)) Live Oak Media.

Alexander Disease - A Bibliography & Dictionary for Physicians, Patients, & Genome Researchers. Compiled by Icon Group International, Inc. Staff. 2007. ring bd. 28.95 (978-0-497-11320-9(1)) Icon Grp.

Alexander Graham Bell. Cerebellum Academic Team. (Running Time: 30 mins.). (Just the Facts Ser.). 2010. 24.95 (978-1-59163-386-0(9)) Cerebellum.

Alexander Hamilton: An Intimate Portrait. unabr. ed. Noemie Emery. Narrated by Steve Flanagin. 6 cass. (Running Time: 9 hrs.). 1984. 51.00 (978-1-55690-007-5(4), 84150E7) Recorded Bks.
America's first secretary of the treasury began life in humble circumstances & ended it in bizarre ones.

Alexander of Russia. unabr. ed. Henri Troyat. Read by John MacDonald. 10 cass. (Running Time: 15 hrs.). 80.00 (978-0-7366-0655-4(6), 1617) Books on Tape.
Grandson of Catherine the Great, Alexander was the Czar who out-fought Napoleon.

Alexander Pope: The Rape of the Lock see Great English Literature of the 18th Century

Alexander Pope: The Rape of the Lock. abr. ed. Alexander Pope. Read by Robert Speaight & Maxine Audley. 1 cass. 10.95 (SAC 8020X) Spoken Arts.

Alexander Pushkin: Tales of Belkin. unabr. ed. 3 cass. (Running Time: 3 hrs.). (RUS.). bk. 49.50 (SRU260) J Norton Pubs.

Alexander, Que Era Rico el Domingo Pasado. Judith Viorst. Illus. by Ray Cruz. 14 vols. (Running Time: 12 mins.). 1991. pap. bk. 35.95 (978-1-59519-129-8(1)); 9.95 (978-1-59112-001-8(2)); audio compact disk 12.95 (978-1-59519-127-4(5)) Live Oak Media.

Alexander, Que Era Rico el Domingo Pasado. Judith Viorst. Illus. by Ray Cruz. 11 vols. (Running Time: 12 mins.). (SPA.). (J). 1991. pap. bk. 18.95 (978-1-59519-128-1(3)) Pub: Live Oak Media. Dist(s): AudioGO

Alexander, Que Era Rico el Domingo Pasado. unabr. ed. Judith Viorst. Read by Marilyn Sanabria. Illus. by Ray Cruz. 11 vols. (Running Time: 12 mins.). (Alexander Ser.). (SPA.). (J). (gr. k-3). 1991. pap. bk. 16.95 (978-0-87499-222-9(2)) AudioGO.
Readalong of Spanish translation of Alexander Who Used to Be Rich Last Sunday.

Alexander, Que Era Rico el Domingo Pasado. unabr. ed. Judith Viorst. Read by Marilyn Sanabria. Illus. by Ray Cruz. 14 vols. (Running Time: 12 mins.). (Alexander Ser.). (SPA.). (J). 1991. pap. bk. & tchr. ed. 33.95 Reading Chest. (978-0-87499-224-3(9)) Live Oak Media.

Alexander, Que Era Rico el Domingo Pasado. unabr. ed. Judith Viorst. 1 cass. (Running Time: 12 mins.). (SPA.). (J). (gr. 2-5). 1991. 9.95 Live Oak Media.

Alexander Scourby Bible-KJV. Alexander Scourby. Read by Alexander Scourby. 2003. 69.99 (978-1-930034-04-4(0)) Casscomm.

Alexander Scourby Bible-KJV. Read by Alexander Scourby. 2006. 49.99 (978-1-930034-29-7(6)); 39.99 (978-1-930034-27-3(X)) Casscomm.

Alexander Scourby Bible-KJV. Alexander Scourby. 2006. audio compact disk 79.99 (978-1-930034-65-5(2)) Casscomm.

Alexander Scourby New Testament-KJV. Read by Alexander Scourby. 2003. 19.99 (978-1-930034-05-1(9)); audio compact disk 24.99 (978-1-930034-16-7(4)) Casscomm.

Alexander Series. Judith Viorst. 22 vols. (Running Time: 22 mins.). (J). (gr. 1-6). 2000. pap. bk. 30.95 (978-0-87499-478-0(0)) Live Oak Media.

Alexander Solzhenitsyn. unabr. ed. 2 cass. (Running Time: 4 hrs. 10 mins.). (RUS.). 44.50 (SRU101) J Norton Pubs.
The author reads the text of "One Day in the Life of Ivan Denisovich".

Alexander Technique. John Barron. 1 cass. 1999. 11.00 (30002) Big Sur Tapes.
1997 Radio Interview.

Alexander the Breat & His Time. Agnes Savill. Read by Nadia May. 9 CDs. (Running Time: 11 hrs. 30 mins.). 2005. audio compact disk 81.00 (978-0-7861-8228-2(8), 1449) Blckstn Audio.

Alexander the Great. unabr. ed. Paul Cartledge. Read by John Lee. (Running Time: 9.5 hrs. 0 mins.). (ENG.). 2009. 29.95 (978-1-4332-9576-8(8)); 59.95 (978-1-4332-9572-0(5)); audio compact disk 90.00 (978-1-4332-9573-7(3)) Blckstn Audio.

Alexander the Great. unabr. ed. E. E. Rice. Read by Martyn Read. 2 cass. (Running Time: 2 hrs. 20 mins.). 1999. 24.95 (978-0-7531-0571-9(3), 990215) Pub: ISIS Audio GBR. Dist(s): Ulverscroft US
Alexander the Great of Macedonia was one of the greatest military commanders the world has ever known & has been a mythical figure since his own time. This book seeks to dispel some of the myths which have grown up around him, while providing an up-to-date account of his life.

Alexander the Great: A Life of Ambition & Achievement. William Grimshaw & Goldsmith. Narrated by Ross M. Armetta. 3 CDs. (Running Time: Approx. 3 hours.). 2005. audio compact disk 19.95 (978-1-59733-502-7(9), Antecdent Wisdom) InfoFount.
Alexander the Great: A Life of Ambition and Achievement Alexander the Great: A Life of Ambition and Achievement is an informative and entertaining biographical audiobook and historical account about Alexander the Great and the events of his life. Born Alexander III the son a King Philip of Macedon in 356 BC he became known as Alexander The Great. Alexander was one of the most successful military commanders of the ancient world. Alexander's conquests heralded the spread of Greek culture and the fusion of eastern and western cultures. Alexander conquered the Persian Empire, Egypt and other smaller kingdoms. At his death Alexander's empire ranged from Greece to Northern India. Alexander's conquests were legendary and his impact on the civilized world is still evident currently.This audiobook explores Alexander?s life from that of a young prince, to an ambitious king, and feared warrior. It covers in detail all of Alexander?s major expeditions and conquests. It also provides background and an understanding of the environment and context of the world of his influence during his lifetime.

Alexander the Great: Journey to the End of the Earth. unabr. ed. Norman F. Cantor & Bronson Pinchot. (Running Time: 6.5 hrs. NaN mins.). 2008. 29.95 (978-1-4332-2321-1(X)); 44.95 (978-1-4332-2317-4(1)); audio compact disk 60.00 (978-1-4332-2318-1(X)) Blckstn Audio.

Alexander the Great: King, Commander & Statesman. unabr. collector's ed. Nicholas G. Hammond. Read by Michael Prichard. 10 cass. (Running Time: 15 hrs.). 1984. 80.00 (978-0-7366-0821-3(4), 1770) Books on Tape.
Alexander was much more than a general. A distinguished scholar analyzes Alexander's achievements.

Alexander the Great: Lessons from History's Undefeated General. unabr. ed. Bill Yenne. (Running Time: 9 hrs. 30 mins.). (World Generals Ser.). 2010. 29.95 (978-1-4417-2954-5(2)); audio compact disk 29.95 (978-1-4417-2953-8(4)) Blckstn Audio.

***Alexander the Great: Lessons from History's Undefeated General.** unabr. ed. Bill Yenne. (Running Time: 9 hrs. 30 mins.). (World Generals Ser.). 2010. 59.95 (978-1-4417-2950-7(X)); audio compact disk 90.00 (978-1-4417-2951-4(8)) Blckstn Audio.

Alexander the Great & His Time. movie tie-in unabr. ed. Agnes Savill. Read by Nadia May. 13 vols. (Running Time: 11 hrs. 30 mins.). 2004. audio compact disk 24.95 (978-0-7861-8405-7(1), 1449) Blckstn Audio.

Alexander the Great & His Time. movie tie-in unabr. ed. Agnes Savill. Read by Nadia May. 8 cass. (Running Time: 12 hrs. 30 min.). 2004. reel tape 32.95 (978-0-7861-2819-8(4)); audio compact disk 39.95 (978-0-7861-8396-8(9)) Blckstn Audio.

Alexander the Great & His Times. unabr. ed. Agnes Savill. Read by Nadia May. 8 cass. (Running Time: 11 hrs. 30 mins.). 1994. 56.95 (978-0-7861-0498-7(8), 1449) Blckstn Audio.
"To be mystical & intensely practical, to dream greatly & to do greatly, is," says Agnes Savill, "not given to many men; it is this combination which gives Alexander his place in history. Aristotle had taught him that man's highest good lay in right activity of mind & body both. (Alexander)...gives a strangely vivid impression of one whose body was his servant." He was trained by Aristotle in every branch of human learning, conquered much of Asia & was one of the greatest leaders in the history of the world. He was unquestionably one of the most brilliant & commanding generals of all time. He greatly influenced the spread of Hellinism & is responsible for profound changes in the course of world development.

Alexander the Great & the Hellenistic Age, Pts. 1&2. Instructed by Jeremy McInerney. 12 cass. (Running Time: 12 hrs.). 54.95 (978-1-56585-073-6(4), 327) Teaching Co.

Alexander the Great & the Hellenistic Age, Pts. I-II. Instructed by Jeremy McInerney. 12 CDs. (Running Time: 12 hrs.). 2000. bk. 69.95 (978-1-56585-322-5(9), 327) Teaching Co.

Alexander the Great & the Hellenistic Age, Vol. 2. Instructed by Jeremy McInerney. 6 cass. (Running Time: 6 hrs.). 2000. 129.95 (978-1-56585-074-3(2)); audio compact disk 179.95 (978-1-56585-323-2(7)) Teaching Co.

***Alexander the Great & the Macedonian Empire.** Instructed by Kenneth W. Harl. 2010. audio compact disk 269.95 (978-1-59803-652-7(1)) Teaching Co.

Alexander, Who Used to Be Rich Last Sunday see Alexander & the Terrible, Horrible, No Good, Very Bad Day

Alexander, Who Used to Be Rich Last Sunday. Judith Viorst. Read by Johnny Heller. (Alexander Ser.). (J). (gr. k-3). 1999. pap. bk. 24.24 (978-0-7887-3634-6(5), 40999) Recorded Bks.
Alexander's two brothers have money in their pockets. All he has are bus tokens. It isn't fair. He had money last Sunday when his grandparents gave them each a dollar. Now it's all gone.

Alexander, Who Used to Be Rich Last Sunday, unabr. ed. Judith Viorst. Narrated by Johnny Heller. 1 cass. (Running Time: 15 mins.). (Alexander Ser.). (ps up). 2000. 11.00 (978-0-7887-3507-3(1), 95901E7) Recorded Bks.

Alexander, Who Used to Be Rich Last Sunday, unabr. ed. Judith Viorst. Read by Johnny Heller. 1 cass. (Running Time: 15 mins.). (Alexander Ser.). (J). (gr. k-3). 2000. pap. bk. 24.24 (40999X4) Recorded Bks.

Alexander, Who Used to Be Rich Last Sunday, Class set. Judith Viorst. Read by Johnny Heller. 1 cass. (Running Time: 15 mins.). (Alexander Ser.). (J). (gr. k-3). 1999. wbk. ed. 81.70 (978-0-7887-3663-6(9), 46966) Recorded Bks.

Alexander, Who's Not (Do You Hear Me? I Mean It!) Going to Move. Judith Viorst. Read by Johnny Heller. 1 cass. (Running Time: 15 mins.). (Alexander Ser.). (J). (gr. k-3). 1999. pap. bk. 23.24 (978-0-7887-3789-3(9), 41033) Recorded Bks.
Alexander's dad has a new job a thousand miles away, so now his family has to move. Alexander would rather have poison ivy. He's ready to hide until Dad decides that getting a dog might make the move easier.

Alexander, Who's Not (Do You Hear Me? I Mean It!) Going to Move. unabr. ed. Judith Viorst. Narrated by Johnny Heller. 1 cass. (Running Time: 15 mins.). (Alexander Ser.). (J). (gr. k-3). 2000. pap. bk. 23.24 (41033X4) Recorded Bks.

Alexander, Who's Not (Do You Hear Me? I Mean It!) Going to Move. unabr. ed. Judith Viorst. Narrated by Johnny Heller. 1 cass. (Running Time: 15 mins.). (Alexander Ser.). (ps up). 2000. 10.00 (978-0-7887-3810-4(0), 95945E7) Recorded Bks.

Alexander, Who's Not (Do You Hear Me? I Mean It!) Going to Move, Class set. Judith Viorst. Read by Johnny Heller. 1 cass. (Running Time: 15 mins.). (Alexander Ser.). (J). (gr. k-3). 1999. wbk. ed. 80.70 (978-0-7887-3860-9(7), 47025) Recorded Bks.

Alexander y el Dia Terrible, Horrible, Espantoso, Horroroso. 1 cass. (Running Time: 35 min.). (SPA.). (J). 2001. 15.95 (VXS-30C) Kimbo Educ.

Alexander y el Dia Terrible, Horrible, Espantoso, Horroroso. Judith Viorst. Illus. by Ray Cruz. 14 vols. (Running Time: 9 mins.).Tr. of Alexander & the Terrible, Horrible, No Good, Very Bad Day. 1991. bk. 28.95 (978-1-59519-133-5(X)); pap. bk. 35.95 (978-1-59519-132-8(1)); 9.95 (978-1-59112-000-1(4)); audio compact disk 12.95 (978-1-59519-130-4(5)) Live Oak Media.

Alexander y el Dia Terrible, Horrible, Espantoso, Horroroso. Judith Viorst. Illus. by Ray Cruz. 11 vols. (Running Time: 9 mins.).Tr. of Alexander & the Terrible, Horrible, No Good, Very Bad Day. (SPA.). (J). 1991. pap. bk. 18.95 (978-1-59519-131-1(3)) Pub: Live Oak Media. Dist(s): AudioGO

Alexander y el Dia Terrible, Horrible, Espantoso, Horroroso. unabr. ed. Judith Viorst. Read by Marilyn Sanabria. Illus. by Ray Cruz. 11 vols. (Running Time: 9 mins.). (Alexander Ser.).Tr. of Alexander & the Terrible, Horrible, No Good, Very Bad Day. (SPA.). (J). (gr. k-3). 1991. bk. 25.95 (978-0-87499-220-5(6)); pap. bk. 16.95 (978-0-87499-219-9(2)); pap. bk. & tchr. ed. 33.95 Reading Chest. (978-0-87499-221-2(4)) Live Oak Media.
Readalong of the Spanish translation of Alexander & the Terrible, Horrible, No Good, Very Bad Day.

Alexander y el Dia Terrible, Horrible, Espantoso, Horroroso. unabr. ed. Judith Viorst. 1 cass. (Running Time: 9 min.). (Alexander Ser.).Tr. of Alexander & the Terrible, Horrible, No Good, Very Bad Day. (SPA.). (J). (gr. k-3). 1991. 9.95 Live Oak Media.

Alexander's Bridge. Willa Cather. Read by Marguerite Gavin. 2000. 17.95 (978-0-7861-1992-9(6), P2762) Blckstn Audio.
"The sun sank rapidly; the silvery light had faded from the bare boughts and the watery twilight was setting in when Wilson at last walked down the hill, descending into cooler and cooler depths of grayish shadow. The description of a man in mid-life crisis. Bartley Alexander is a master bridge engineer. At forty-three he is at the height of his power, comfortable with success and all it brings. Yet he yearns for the lost vibrancy of his youth. He leads a double life, veering between his beautiful, accomplished wife, and his mistress, an actress he knew as a student in Paris.

***Alexander's Bridge.** unabr. ed. Willa Cather. Read by Marguerite Gavin. (Running Time: 2.5 hrs. NaN mins.). (ENG.). 2011. 19.95 (978-1-4417-8479-7(9)); audio compact disk 28.00 (978-1-4417-8477-3(2)) Blckstn Audio.

Alexander's Bridge, Set. unabr. ed. Willa Cather. Read by Flo Gibson. 2 cass. (Running Time: 3 hrs.). 1993. 14.95 (978-1-55685-287-9(8)) Audio Bk Con.
Willa Cather's first novel is a love story set in sophisticated Boston & London drawing-rooms. A successful bridge builder, Bartley Alexander, is torn between two women, his beloved, charming wife & the beautiful Irish actress who had been his first love & reappears to enchant & disrupt his middle age.

Alexander's Feast see Treasury of John Dryden

Alexander's Feast, or, The Power of Music: An Ode in Honor of St. Cecilia's Day see Poetry of John Dryden

Alexander's Path. unabr. collector's ed. Freya Stark. Read by Donada Peters. 8 cass. (Running Time: 8 hrs.). 1991. 48.00 (978-0-7366-1909-7(7), 2735) Books on Tape.
Tales of travel along the Turkish coastline by one of our finest travel writers. Incomparable linkage of past to present.

Alexander's Read & Sing-A-Long. 1. (Running Time: 40 mins.). (J). 2007. audio compact disk 19.99 (978-0-9742806-7-7(4)) Heart.

Alexandria. unabr. ed. Lindsey Davis. Narrated by Christian Rodska. 1 Playaway. (Running Time: 11 hrs. 16 mins.). (Marcus Didius Falco Ser.). 2009. 89.95 (978-0-7927-6466-3(8)); 54.95 (978-0-7927-6465-6(X)); audio compact disk 89.95 (978-0-7927-5959-1(1)) AudioGO.

***Alexandria.** unabr. ed. Lindsey Davis. Narrated by Christian Rodska. 10 CDs. (Running Time: 10 hrs. 0 mins. 0 sec.). (ENG.). 2010. audio compact disk 34.95 (978-1-4084-2771-2(0)) Pub: AudioGO. Dist(s): Perseus Dist

Alexandria & Alexandria (Arlington) County, Virginia: Minister Returns & Marriage Bonds, 1801-1852. T. Michael Miller. 2002. audio compact disk 9.50 (978-0-7884-2208-9(1)) Heritage Bk.

Alexandria Link. abr. ed. Steve Berry. Read by Eric Singer. (Running Time: 21600 sec.). (Cotton Malone Ser.: Bk. 2). (ENG.). 2007. audio compact disk 14.99 (978-0-7393-6573-1(8), Random AudioBks) Pub: Random Audio Pubg. Dist(s): Random

Alexandria Link. unabr. ed. Steve Berry. Read by Scott Brick. 14 CDs. (Running Time: 17 hrs.). (Cotton Malone Ser.: Bk. 2). (ENG.). 2007. audio compact disk 49.95 (978-0-7393-4230-5(4), Random AudioBks) Pub: Random Audio Pubg. Dist(s): Random

Alexandria Quartet. abr. ed. Lawrence Durrell. Read by Nigel Anthony. 12 CDs. bk. 73.98 (978-962-634-240-4(4), NAX24012) Naxos.

Alexia's Secrets. Una-Mary Parker. 2008. 61.95 (978-0-7531-3193-0(5)); audio compact disk 79.95 (978-0-7531-3194-7(3)) Pub: Isis Pubng Ltd GBR. Dist(s): Ulverscroft US

Alfie. abr. ed. Bill Naughton. Read by Jason Flemyng. 2 cass. 2002. (978-1-901768-40-4(6)) CSA Telltapes GBR.

Alfie Finds the Other Side of the World. (J). 2004. 8.95 (978-1-56008-826-4(5)); cass. & flmstrp 30.00 (978-0-89719-641-3(4)) Weston Woods.

Alfie Finds the Other Side of the World; The North Wind & the Sun; Brian Wildsmith's Birds; What Do You Do Dear?; Let's Be Enemies. (J). 2004. (978-0-89719-825-7(5)); cass. & flmstrp (978-0-89719-733-5(X)) Weston Woods.

Alfombra Roja. Tr. of Red Carpet. (SPA.). 2004. 8.95 (978-0-7882-0255-1(3)) Weston Woods.

Alfred Hitchcock's & Ellery Queen's Mystery Magazines, abr. ed. Lawrence Block & Mary Higgins Clark. Read by Angie Dickinson et al. 4 cass. (Running Time: 6 hrs.). (Great Mysteries - Louis L'Amour Ser.). 2000. 12.99 (978-1-57815-156-1(2), 4405, Media Bks Audio) Media Bks NJ.

Alfred Hitchcock's & Ellery Queen's Mystery Magazines: Mean Streets & a Vacation to Die For. unabr. ed. Lawrence Block & Mary Higgins Clark. Read by Dennis Franz et al. 5 vols. (Great Mystery Ser.). 2001. audio compact disk 14.99 (978-1-57815-538-5(X), Media Bks Audio) Media Bks NJ.

Alfred Kisubi. Alfred Kisubi. 1 cass. (Running Time: 29 min.). Incl. Time Winds. 1987. (13); 1987. 10.00 (13) New Letters.
Kisubi reads from his new books of poems & talks about the unpredictable nature of life in modern day Africa.

Alfred Marshall & Neoclassicism. unabr. ed. Robert Hebert. Ed. by Israel M. Kirzner & Mike Hassell. Narrated by Louis Rukeyser. 2 cass. (Running Time: 80 min. per cass.). Dramatization. (Great Economic Thinkers Ser.). 1988. 17.95 (978-0-938935-34-6(8), 10204) Knowledge Prod.
Alfred Marshall, more than any other person, professionalized economics. He invented many economic concepts that are commonplace today & created "neoclassical" economics. Neoclassicism has heavily influenced today's mainstream thinking that economics is a rigorous science.

Alfred Marshall & Neoclassicism: Economics Becomes a Science. Robert Hirbert. Read by Louis Rukeyser. (Running Time: 7200 sec.). (Great Economic Thinkers Ser.). 2006. audio compact disk 25.95 (978-0-7861-6931-3(1)) Pub: Blckstn Audio. Dist(s): NetLibrary CO

Alfreda's Story Rhyme Festival One. unabr. ed. Alfreda C. Doyle. Read by Alfreda C. Doyle. 1 cass. (Running Time: 30 min.). (J). (gr. 3-9). 1995. 14.95 (978-1-56820-124-5(9)) Story Time.
A collection of educational rhyming stories.

***Alfred's Basic Adult Piano Course CD for Lesson Book: Level 3.** Contrib. by Willard A. Palmer et al. (Alfred's Basic Adult Piano Course Ser.). (ENG.). 2010. audio compact disk 10.99 (978-0-7390-6954-7(3)) Alfred Pub.

Alfred's Basic Adult Piano Course Lesson Book CD: Level 1. Morton Manus et al. (Basic Adult Piano Library). (ENG.). 1995. audio compact disk 10.95 (978-0-7390-1752-4(7), 14039) Alfred Pub.

Alfred's Basic Adult Piano Course, Lesson Book 2, Morton Manus et al. 1 CD. (Running Time: 1 hr.). (Alfred's Basic Piano Library). (ENG.). 1997. audio compact disk 10.95 (978-0-7390-1943-6(0), 18106) Alfred Pub.

Alfred's Basic Adult Play Piano Now! Level 1, Bk. 1. Ruby T. Palmer et al. 1 CD. (Running Time: 1 hr. 30 mins.). (Alfred's Basic Piano Adult Ser.). (ENG.). 2000. audio compact disk 10.95 (978-0-7390-1455-4(2), 19656) Alfred Pub.

Alfred's Basic Bass Method. Ron Manus & L. C. Harnsberger. (ENG.). 2007. audio compact disk 9.95 (978-0-7390-4943-3(7)) Alfred Pub.

Alfred's Basic Bass Method. Ron Manus & L. C. Harnsberger. (Alfred's Basic Bass Guitar Library Ser.). (ENG.). 2008. audio compact disk 9.95 (978-0-7390-5394-2(9)) Alfred Pub.

Alfred's Basic Group Piano Course: Level 1 , 2 CDs, Bk. 1. Gayle Kowalchyk et al. 1CD. (Alfred's Basic Piano Library). (ENG.). 1997. audio compact disk 14.95 (978-0-7390-0221-6(X), 18085) Alfred Pub.

Alfred's Basic Guitar Method. 3rd rev. ed. Morton Manus & Ron Manus. (Alfred's Basic Guitar Library Ser.). (ENG.). 1995. audio compact disk 9.95 (978-0-7390-4939-6(9)) Alfred Pub.

Alfred's Basic Guitar Method. 3rd rev. ed. Morton Manus & Ron Manus. (Alfred's Basic Guitar Library Ser.). (ENG.). 1997. audio compact disk 9.95 (978-0-7390-4940-2(2)) Alfred Pub.

Alfred's Basic Guitar Method 3. 3rd ed. Created by Alfred Publishing. (Alfred's Basic Guitar Library). (ENG.). 1997. audio compact disk 9.95 (978-0-7390-4941-9(0)) Alfred Pub.

Alfred's Basic Piano Course CD for Lesson Book: Level 1B. Willard A. Palmer & Morton Manus. (Alfred's Basic Piano Library Ser.). (ENG.). 1996. audio compact disk 8.95 (978-0-7390-2751-6(4)) Alfred Pub.

Alfred's Basic Piano Course CD for Lesson Book: Level 2. Willard A. Palmer & Morton Manus. (Alfred's Basic Piano Library Ser.). (ENG.). 1996. audio compact disk 8.95 (978-0-7390-2752-3(2)) Alfred Pub.

Alfred's Basic Piano Course CD for Lesson Book: Level 3. Willard A. Palmer & Morton Manus. (Alfred's Basic Piano Library Ser.). (ENG.). 1996. audio compact disk 8.95 (978-0-7390-3177-3(5)) Alfred Pub.

Alfred's Basic Piano Course Top Hits! CD for Solo Book: Level 1B. Ed. by E. L. Lancaster & Morton Manus. (Alfred's Basic Piano Library Ser.). (ENG.). 2001. audio compact disk 10.95 (978-0-7390-1241-3(X)) Alfred Pub.

Alfred's Basic Prep Course, Lesson Book B. Willard A. Palmer et al. (Basic Piano Library). (ENG.). 1999. audio compact disk 8.95 (978-0-7390-0349-7(6), 17160) Alfred Pub.

Alfred's Basic Prep Lesson Book, Level A. Willard A. Palmer et al. (Alfred's Basic Piano Library). (ENG.). 1999. audio compact disk 8.95 (978-0-7390-0348-0(8), 17159) Alfred Pub.

Alfred's Basic Prep Lesson Book, Level C. Willard A. Palmer et al. (Alfred's Basic Piano Library). (ENG.). 1999. audio compact disk 8.95 (978-0-7390-0350-3(X), 17161) Alfred Pub.

Alfred's Basic Prep Lesson Book, Level D. Willard A. Palmer et al. (Alfred's Basic Piano Library). (ENG.). 1999. audio compact disk 8.95 (978-0-7390-0351-0(8), 17162) Alfred Pub.

Alfred's Basic Prep Lesson Book, Level E. Willard A. Palmer et al. (Alfred's Basic Piano Library). (ENG.). 1999. audio compact disk 8.95 (978-0-7390-0352-7(6), 17163) Alfred Pub.

Alfred's Basic Prep Lesson Book, Level F. Willard A. Palmer et al. (Alfred's Basic Piano Library). (ENG.). 1999. audio compact disk 8.95 (978-0-7390-0353-4(4), 17164) Alfred Pub.

Alfred's Drumset Method. David Black & Saul Feldstein Music Staff. (ENG.). 1996. audio compact disk 10.95 (978-0-7390-1769-2(1), 16925) Alfred Pub.

Alfred's Interactive Musician: Network Version. Morton Manus. (ENG.). 2004. audio compact disk 249.95 (978-0-7390-3532-0(0)) Alfred Pub.

Alfred's Piano 101: Level 1 , 6 CDs. E. L. Lancaster et al. (ENG.). 1999. audio compact disk 49.95 (978-0-7390-0256-8(2), 14589) Alfred Pub.

Alfred's Piano 101: Level 2 , 6 CDs, Bk. 2. E. L. Lancaster & Kenon D. Renfrow. 1 CD. (Running Time: 1 hr. 30 mins.). (ENG.). 2000. audio compact disk 49.95 (978-0-7390-0258-2(9), 14592) Alfred Pub.

***Alfred's Play Acoustic Guitar 1: The Ultimate Multimedia Instructor.** Created by Alfred Publishing. (Play (Alfred) Ser.). (ENG., 2010. pap. bk. (978-0-7390-6577-8(7)) Alfred Pub.

***Alfred's Play Acoustic Guitar 2: The Ultimate Multimedia Instructor.** Created by Alfred Publishing. (Play (Alfred) Ser.). (ENG., 2010. pap. bk. (978-0-7390-6579-2(3)) Alfred Pub.

***Alfred's PLAY Beginning Acoustic Guitar: The Ultimate Multimedia Instructor, CD-ROM.** Alfred Publishing Staff. (Alfred's Play Ser.). (ENG.). 2010. audio compact disk 29.99 (978-0-7390-6558-7(0)) Alfred Pub.

***Alfred's PLAY Beginning Electric Bass: The Ultimate Multimedia Instructor, CD-ROM.** Alfred Publishing Staff. (Alfred's Play Ser.). (ENG.). 2010. audio compact disk 29.99 (978-0-7390-6562-4(9)) Alfred Pub.

***Alfred's PLAY Beginning Jazz Guitar: The Ultimate Multimedia Instructor, CD-ROM.** Alfred Publishing Staff. (Alfred's Play Ser.). (ENG.). 2010. audio compact disk 29.99 (978-0-7390-6559-4(9)) Alfred Pub.

***Alfred's Play Blues Guitar 1: The Ultimate Multimedia Instructor.** Created by Alfred Publishing. (Play (Alfred) Ser.). (ENG., 2010. pap. bk. (978-0-7390-6573-0(4)) Alfred Pub.

***Alfred's Play Blues Guitar 2: The Ultimate Multimedia Instructor.** Created by Alfred Publishing. (Play (Alfred) Ser.). (ENG., 2010. pap. bk. (978-0-7390-6575-4(0)) Alfred Pub.

***Alfred's Play Electric Bass Basics: The Ultimate Multimedia Instructor.** Created by Alfred Publishing. (Play (Alfred) Ser.). (ENG., 2010. pap. bk. (978-0-7390-6585-3(8)) Alfred Pub.

***Alfred's Play Jazz Guitar 1: The Ultimate Multimedia Instructor.** Created by Alfred Publishing. (Play (Alfred) Ser.). (ENG., 2010. pap. bk. (978-0-7390-6581-5(5)) Alfred Pub.

***Alfred's Play Jazz Guitar 2: The Ultimate Multimedia Instructor.** Created by Alfred Publishing. (Play (Alfred) Ser.). (ENG., 2010. pap. bk. (978-0-7390-6583-9(1)) Alfred Pub.

***Alfred's Play Rock Guitar 1: The Ultimate Multimedia Instructor.** Created by Alfred Publishing. (Play (Alfred) Ser.). (ENG., 2010. pap. bk. (978-0-7390-6569-3(6)) Alfred Pub.

***Alfred's Play Rock Guitar 2: The Ultimate Multimedia Instructor.** Created by Alfred Publishing. (Play (Alfred) Ser.). (ENG., 2010. pap. bk. (978-0-7390-6571-6(8)) Alfred Pub.

Alfred's Teach Yourself Chords & Progressions at the Keyboard. Ed. by Alfred Publishing. (ENG.). 1998. audio compact disk 9.95 (978-0-7390-2649-6(6)) Alfred Pub.

Alfred's Teach Yourself to Improvise at the Keyboard. Bert Konowitz. (Teach Yourself Ser.). (ENG.). 1996. audio compact disk 9.95 (978-0-7390-2652-6(6)) Alfred Pub.

Alfred's Teach Yourself to Play Bass. Ed. by Alfred Publishing. (ENG.). 2003. audio compact disk 9.95 (978-0-7390-3365-4(4)) Alfred Pub.

Alfred's Teach Yourself to Play Bass. Morton Manus & Ron Manus. (ENG.). 1996. audio compact disk 10.95 (978-0-7390-2175-0(3)) Alfred Pub.

Alfred's Teach Yourself to Play Drums. Patrick Wilson. (ENG.). 1993. audio compact disk 10.95 (978-0-88284-682-8(5)) Alfred Pub.

Alfred's Teach Yourself to Play Guitar. Ed. by Alfred Publishing. (ENG.). 2002. audio compact disk 9.95 (978-0-7390-2972-5(X)) Alfred Pub.

Alfred's Teach Yourself to Play Guitar. Morton Manus & Ron Manus. (ENG.). 1994. audio compact disk 9.95 (978-0-88284-677-4(9)) Alfred Pub.

Alfred's Teach Yourself to Play Guitar: Acoustic Songs. Ed. by Alfred Publishing. (ENG.). 2007. audio compact disk 29.95 (978-0-7390-4671-5(3)) Alfred Pub.

Alfred's Teach Yourself to Play Guitar: Blues Songs. Ed. by Alfred Publishing. (ENG.). 2007. audio compact disk 29.95 (978-0-7390-4673-9(X)) Alfred Pub.

Alfred's Teach Yourself to Play Guitar: Chordxpress. Created by Alfred Publishing. (ENG.). 2007. audio compact disk 29.95 (978-0-7390-5019-4(2)) Alfred Pub.

Alfred's Teach Yourself to Play Guitar: Handy Guide. Morton Manus & Ron Manus. (ENG.). 1995. audio compact disk 9.95 (978-0-88284-695-8(7)) Alfred Pub.

Alfred's Teach Yourself to Play Guitar: Rock Songs. Ed. by Alfred Publishing. (ENG.). 2007. audio compact disk 29.95 (978-0-7390-4672-2(1)) Alfred Pub.

Alfred's Teach Yourself to Play Harmonica. Ed. by Alfred Publishing. (ENG.). 2002. audio compact disk 9.95 (978-0-7390-2974-9(6)) Alfred Pub.

Alfred's Teach Yourself to Play Like a Pro at the Keyboard. Bert Konowitz. (Teach Yourself Ser.). (ENG.). 1998. audio compact disk 9.95 (978-0-7390-2654-0(2)) Alfred Pub.

Alfred's Teach Yourself to Play Piano. Morton Manus & Willard A. Palmer. (ENG.). 2002. audio compact disk 9.95 (978-0-7390-2973-2(8)) Alfred Pub.

Alfred's Teach Yourself to Play Piano: Enhanced CD. Morton Manus et al. (Teach Yourself Ser.). (ENG.). 1994. audio compact disk 9.95 (978-0-88284-672-9(8)) Alfred Pub.

Alfred's Teach Yourself to Play Recorder. Morton Manus. (ENG.). 1996. audio compact disk 10.95 (978-0-88284-667-5(1)) Alfred Pub.

Alfred's Teach Yourself to Sing. Karen Famum Surmani. (ENG.). 1995. audio compact disk 10.95 (978-0-88284-663-7(9)) Alfred Pub.

Algebra: Beginning Syllabus. 2nd ed. Al Gray. (J). 1976. 164.35 (978-0-89420-125-7(5), 367007) Natl Book.

Algebra & Trigonometry with Analytic Geometry. 11th ed. Earl William Swokowski & Jeffery A. Cole. (C). 2004. audio compact disk 16.95 (978-0-534-49458-2(7)) CENGAGE Learn.

Algebra & Trigonometry/Precalculus: With Modeling & Visualization. 3rd ed. Rockswold. (Math XL Ser.). 2005. audio compact disk 26.67 (978-0-321-34823-4(0)) AddisonWesley.

Algebra for College Students. 2nd ed. Allen R. Angel. (CD Lecture Ser.). 2003. audio compact disk 44.00 (978-0-13-141087-9(3)) Pearson Educ CAN CAN.

Algebra 1. Coxford. (gr. 9-12). 1990. stu. ed. 64.00 (978-0-15-353640-3(3)) Harcourt Schl Pubs.

Algebra 1. Created by McDougal Littell. (gr. 6-12). 2006. audio compact disk (978-0-618-43977-5(3), 2-05846) Holt McDoug.

Algebra 1: The Learning Equation. South-Western Educational Publishing Staff. 1998. audio compact disk 117.95 (978-0-538-68448-4(8)) South-West.

Algebra 1 Course 2: Assessment - Item Listing with Answer Key. Holt, Rinehart and Winston Staff. 2001. cd-rom 29.66 (978-0-03-051303-9(0)) Holt McDoug.

Algebraic Thinking Electronic PDF. Compiled by National Training Network. 2007. audio compact disk (978-1-57290-206-0(X)) Natl Trning.

***Algebraic Thinking Foundations - Digital Version of the Teacher & Student Book.** 2010. audio compact disk (978-1-57290-368-5(6)) Natl Trning.

***Algebraic Thinking Part One - Digital Version of the Teacher & Student Book.** 2010. audio compact disk (978-1-57290-418-7(6)) Natl Trning.

***Algebraic Thinking Part Two - Digital Version of the Teacher & Student Book.** 2010. audio compact disk (978-1-57290-403-3(8)) Natl Trning.

Alger Hiss & the Battle for History. unabr. ed. Susan Jacoby. Read by Laural Merlington. (Running Time: 5 hrs. 30 mins. 0 sec.). (ENG.). 2009. audio compact disk 24.99 (978-1-4001-1155-8(2)); audio compact disk 19.99 (978-1-4001-6155-3(X)); audio compact disk 49.99 (978-1-4001-4155-5(9)) Pub: Tantor Media. Dist(s): IngramPubServ

Alger, Mai 1958: La Fin D'Une Republique. 1 cass. (FRE.). 1995. 16.95 (1735-RF) Olivia & Hill.
On 13 May 1958, the "pieds noirs" & the army overthrow the Fourth Republic & bring General de Gaulle back to power.

Alhambra. collector's ed. Washington Irving. Read by Michael Prichard. 10 cass. (Running Time: 15 hrs.). 2000. 80.00 (978-0-7366-5569-9(7), 2165) Books on Tape.
Like the Moorish castle it celebrates, this enchanting book draws the reader in with enticing tales of this spectacular monument. Published in 1851, it sketches the Moors & Spaniards on the plains of Castile & La Mancha & the environs of Granada.

Alhambra. unabr. ed. Washington Irving. Read by Michael Prichard. 13 CDs. (Running Time: 19 hrs. 30 mins.). 2003. audio compact disk 104.00 (978-0-7366-8292-3(9)) Books on Tape.
Published in 1851, it sketches the Moors and Spaniards on the plains of Castile and LaMancha and the environs of Granada. Irving brings life to the stately rooms, labyrinthine hallways, pools, and courtyards with the history, legends, strivings and celebrations of the people he met during his stay in 1829. Mostly though, Irving takes us through the passageways to the Moorish empire that laid upon Spain for centuries and yet found no permanent foothold. We meet the kings, the faithful Moslems, the devout Christians, the exotic courts, and the clever poor. Part ARABIAN NIGHTS, part travel guide these sketches are thoroughly delightful.

Ali: The Greatest. Alan Venable. (Overcoming the Odds Sports Biographies Ser.). 2000. audio compact disk 18.95 (978-1-4105-0145-5(0)) D Johnston Inc.

Ali: The Greatest. Alan Venable. Ed. by Jerry Stemach et al. Illus. by Jeff Ham. Narrated by Bernard Mixon. Contrib. by Ted S. Hasselbring. (Start-to-Finish Books). (J). (gr. 2-3). 2000. 100.00 (978-1-58702-972-1(3)) D Johnston Inc.

Ali Vol. 3: The Greatest. Alan Venable. Ed. by Jerry Stemach et al. Illus. by Jeff Ham. Narrated by Bernard Mixon. Contrib. by Ted S. Hasselbring. (Start-to-Finish Books). (J). (gr. 2-3). 2000. 35.00 (978-1-58702-471-9(3), F18K2) D Johnston Inc.
The world's most famous athlete ever was heavyweight boxer Muhammad Ali. From the moment young Ali wandered into a Louisville, Kentucky youth boxing program, the sport became his life. An Olympic champion at age 18, Ali rose quickly to the top. More than any other man in the 60s, Ali spread the word that "Black is beautiful." Colorful and funny, he spouted crazy poetry to rile and upset opponents and prove that boxers weren't all just tongue-tied gorillas.

Ali Vol. 3: The Greatest. unabr. ed. Alan Venable. Ed. by Jerry Stemach et al. Illus. by Jeff Ham. Narrated by Bernard Mixon. Contrib. by Ted S. Hasselbring. 1 cass. (Running Time: 1 hr.). (Start-to-Finish Books). (J). (gr. 2-3). 2000. (978-1-893376-57-1(5), F18K2) D Johnston Inc.

Ali Baba. 1 cass. (FRE.). (J). (gr. 4). 1991. bk. 14.95 (1AD036) Olivia & Hill.
Ali Baba & the Forty Thieves.

Ali Baba & the Forty Thieves. 1 cass. (J). 3.98 Clamshell. (978-1-55886-109-1(2), BB/PT 436) Smarty Pants.

Alias Grace. unabr. ed. Margaret Atwood. Read by Shelley Thompson. 12 cass. (Running Time: 18 hrs.). 1998. 79.95 (978-0-7540-0061-7(3), CAB 1484) Pub: Chivers Audio Bks GBR. Dist(s): AudioGO
After murdering her employer & his lover 16 years ago, Grace has no recollection of the murders. Dr. Jordan now has the task of examining her mind.

Alias Jimmy Valentine. O. Henry. Ed. by Walter Pauk & Raymond Harris. Illus. by Robert J. Pailthorpe. (Classics Ser.). (YA). (gr. 6-12). 1980. pap. bk. 17.96 (978-0-89061-193-7(9)) Jamestown.

Alias the Saint. unabr. ed. Leslie Charteris. Read by David Case. 5 cass. (Running Time: 5 hrs.). (Saint Ser.). 1991. 30.00 (978-0-7366-1911-0(9), 2737) Books on Tape.
Vacationing in the English country side, Simon Templar treats city thugs to rural justice. Very entertaining & fast paced.

Alibi. Sandra Brown. Read by Dennis Redfield. 1999. 72.00 (978-0-7366-4739-7(2)) Books on Tape.

Alibi. abr. ed. Joseph Kanon. Read by Holter Graham. 2005. 14.95 (978-1-59397-760-3(3)) Pub: Macmill Audio. Dist(s): Macmillan

Alibi. abr. unabr. ed. Teri Woods. Read by Paula Jai Parker-Martin. (Running Time: 6 hrs. 30 mins.). (ENG.). 2009. 18.98 (978-1-60024-644-9(3)); audio compact disk 26.98 (978-1-60024-643-2(5)) Pub: Hachet Audio. Dist(s): HachBkGrp

Alibi. unabr. ed. Sydney Bauer. Read by Bill Ten Eyck. (Running Time: 17 hrs. 8 mins.). 2009. audio compact disk 118.95 (978-1-74214-521-1(3), 9781742145211) Pub: Bolinda Pubng AUS. Dist(s): Bolinda Pub Inc

***Alibi.** unabr. ed. Sydney Bauer. Read by Bill Ten Eyck. (Running Time: 17 hrs. 8 mins.). 2010. 54.95 (978-1-74214-596-9(5), 9781742145969) Pub: Bolinda Pubng AUS. Dist(s): Bolinda Pub Inc

Alibi, Set. abr. ed. Sandra Brown. Read by Dylan Baker. 4 cass. 1999. 25.95 (FS9-50984) Highsmith.

Alibi, Set. abr. ed. Sandra Brown. Read by Dylan Baker. 5 CDs. (Running Time: 6 hrs.). 2000. audio compact disk 29.95 (Random AudioBks) Random Audio Pubg.

Alibi, Set. unabr. ed. Sandra Brown. Read by Dennis Redfield. 9 cass. 1999. 39.95 (FS9-51036) Highsmith.

Alibi Club. unabr. ed. Francine Mathews. Read by Ellen Archer. (YA). 2008. 59.99 (978-1-60514-552-5(1)) Find a World.

Alibi Club. unabr. ed. Francine Mathews. Read by Ellen Archer. 7 CDs. (Running Time: 8 hrs. 30 mins. 0 sec.). (ENG.). 2006. audio compact disk 34.99 (978-1-4001-0313-3(4)); audio compact disk 24.99 (978-1-4001-5313-8(1)); audio compact disk 69.99 (978-1-4001-3313-0(0)) Pub: Tantor Media. Dist(s): IngramPubServ

Alibi for a Corpse. unabr. ed. Elizabeth Lemarchand. Read by Gordon Griffin. 5 cass. (Running Time: 7 hrs. 30 min.). (Sound Ser.). 2004. 49.95 (978-1-85496-664-3(2), 66642) Pub: UlverLrgPrint GBR. Dist(s): Ulverscroft US
When a pair of inquisitive children on holiday discover a skeleton hidden in the trunk of an abandoned car, Detective Superintendent Pollard faces an uncomfortable feeling of frustration, for never before has there been such an uncommunicative corpse - no dental work, no old fractures, & no missing persons corresponding to the skeleton's size & age. Pollard had to find out not only "whodunit", but to whom.

Alibi Ike. Perf. by Joe E. Brown et al. 1 cass. (Running Time: 1 hr.). 1999. 6.98 (978-1-57019-205-0(7), 4166) Radio Spirits.

Alibi Ike. Ring Lardner. 10.00 (LSS1112) Esstee Audios.

Alibi Man. abr. ed. Tami Hoag. Read by Beth McDonald. (Running Time: 21600 sec.). (ENG.). 2008. audio compact disk 14.99 (978-0-7393-6569-4(X), Random AudioBks) Pub: Random Audio Pubg. Dist(s): Random

Alibi Man. unabr. ed. Tami Hoag. Read by Beth McDonald. 8 CDs. (Running Time: 36000 sec.). (ENG.). 2007. audio compact disk 39.95 (978-0-553-50286-2(7)) Pub: Random Audio Pubg. Dist(s): Random

Alice: The Life & Times of Alice Roosevelt Longworth. unabr. collector's ed. Howard Teichmann. Read by Jay Fitts. 7 cass. (Running Time: 7 hrs.). 1984. 42.00 (978-0-7366-0824-4(9), 1774) Books on Tape.
Teichmann illuminates this biography of Theodore Roosevelt's daughter with sources both familiar & arcane, through correspondence & interviews.

***Alice Adams.** Booth Tarkington. Read by Amy von Lecteur. 2009. 27.95 (978-1-60112-964-2(5)) Babblebooks.

Alice Adams. unabr. ed. Booth Tarkington. (Running Time: 11 hrs. 0 mins.). 2008. 29.95 (978-1-4332-4789-7(5)); 65.95 (978-1-4332-4786-6(0)); audio compact disk 90.00 (978-1-4332-4787-3(9)) Blckstn Audio.

Alice Adams, Set. Booth Tarkington. Read by Flo Gibson. 6 cass. (Running Time: 8 hrs. 30 min.). 1999. 24.95 (978-1-55685-398-2(X)) Audio Bk Con.
The plucky & romantic Alice tries to rise above the crudities of her hopelessly shabby background.

Alice Adams: Interview with Alice Adams & Kay Bonetti. (Running Time: 49 min.). 13.95 (978-1-55644-175-2(4), 7012) Am Audio Prose.
An interview with the author.

Alice Alone. Amanda Brookfield. Narrated by Gerri Halligan. 5 cass. (Running Time: 6 hrs.). 52.00 (978-1-84197-313-5(0)); audio compact disk 62.00 (978-1-4025-2087-7(5)) Recorded Bks.

Alice & Greta: A Tale of Two Witches. Steven J. Simmons. Narrated by Kate Forbes. (Running Time: 15 mins.). (gr. k up). 10.00 (978-0-7887-9975-4(4)) Recorded Bks.

Alice au Pays des Merveilles, Set. Lewis Carroll, pseud. Read by Muriel Flory & Philippe Jouaris. 2 cass.Tr. of Alice in Wonderland. (FRE.). (J). 1992. bk. 35.95 (1GA063) Olivia & Hill.
Alice, the Cheshire Cat & all the fascinating characters of Wonderland are gathered here.

Alice Bredin's Employee Training Kit for Successful Telecommuting. Alice Bredin. 1 cass. 1994. 12.00 (5091) Toolkit Media.
Highlights: how to thrive in a home office, coping with isolation, keeping in the office loop, time management, setting up a home/mobile office & tax/legal issues related to telecommuting.

Alice Bredin's Guide to Running a Successful Home-Based Business. Alice Bredin. 2 cass. 1995. 39.00 Set. (5087) Toolkit Media.
Offers insight on both the human & technical issues that arise when starting or running a home-based business.

Alice Bredin's Manager's Guide to Successful Telecommuting. Alice Bredin. 1 cass. 1994. 69.00 (5089) Toolkit Media.
Educates managers & employees about how to succeed with a telecommuting program. Also discusses the pioneering telecommuting programs of Federal Express, IBM & Travelers' Insurance.

Alice Cooper, Golf Monster: A Rock 'n' Roller's 12 Steps to Becoming a Golf Addict. abr. ed. Alice Cooper. Read by Alice Cooper. Told to Kent Zimmerman. (Running Time: 14400 sec.). (ENG.). 2007. audio compact disk 27.95 (978-0-7393-4414-9(5), Random AudioBks) Pub: Random Audio Pubg. Dist(s): Random

Alice Dugdale. Anthony Trollope. Narrated by Sheila Lash. (Running Time: 2 hrs. 30 mins.). 1986. 18.95 (978-1-59912-853-5(5)) Iofy Corp.

Alice Dugdale. Anthony Trollope. Read by Sheila Lash. 3 cass. (Running Time: 4 hrs.). 1989. 18.00 incl. album. (C-158) Jimcin Record.
Delightful short romance.

Alice Dugdale. unabr. collector's ed. Anthony Trollope. Read by Sheila Lash. 3 cass. (Running Time: 3 hrs.). (Jimcin Recording Ser.). 1986. 18.00 (978-0-7366-3917-0(9), 9155) Books on Tape.
Trollope captured the victorian era with great accuracy, thus his novels live.

Alice Dugdale, Set. Anthony Trollope. Read by Flo Gibson. 2 cass. (Running Time: 2 hrs. 30 min.). 1996. 14.95 (978-1-55685-431-6(5)) Audio Bk Con.
Alice suffers in silence while the much sought after Major cavorts with Georgiana Wanless.

Alice Fulton. Poems. Alice Fulton. Read by Alice Fulton. 1 cass. (Running Time: 29 min.). 1986. 10.00 New Letters.
The poet reads from "Dance Script with Electric Ballerina".

***Alice I Have Been.** unabr. ed. Melanie Benjamin. Read by Samantha Eggar. 10 CDs. 2010. audio compact disk 90.00 (978-0-307-71346-9(6), BksonTape) Pub: Random Audio Pubg. Dist(s): Random

Alice I Have Been. unabr. ed. Melanie Benjamin. Read by Samantha Eggar. 6 CDs. (Running Time: 6 hrs.). 2010. audio compact disk 35.00 (978-0-307-71344-5(X), Random AudioBks) Pub: Random Audio Pubg. Dist(s): Random

Alice, I Think. unabr. ed. Susan Juby. Read by Angela Goethals. (J). 2008. 39.99 (978-1-60514-623-2(4)) Find a World.

Alice, I Think. unabr. ed. Susan Juby. 5 cass. (Running Time: 8 hrs.). 2003. 45.00 (978-1-4025-6446-8(5)) Recorded Bks.
After years of home schooling brought on by a traumatic first-grade experience involving over-indulgent parents, underimaginative classmates, and a homemade hobbit suit, 15-yearold Alice has decided to go to high school. She's not actually ready or anything, but her counselor could use a boost in his self-esteem. And attending a real school is not the only life goal Alice is determined to achieve.

Alice, I Think. unabr. abr. ed. Susan Juby. Read by Angela Goethals. 4 cass. (Running Time: 6 hrs.). (J). 2003. 24.00 (978-0-06-054340-2(X)) HarperCollins Pubs.

Alice in Cyberspace. David Demchuk. 2 CDs. (Running Time: 3 hrs.). 2005. audio compact disk 24.95 (978-0-660-18184-4(3)) Pub: Canadian Broadcasting CAN. Dist(s): Georgetown Term
Now you can join Alice in her adventures beyond the computer monitor as she meets the White Rabbit, the Music Master and her PET (Personal Electronics Telecommunicator).

Alice in Jeopardy: A Novel. unabr. ed. Ed McBain. Read by. 7 cass. (Running Time: 10 hrs. 30 min.). 2005. 81.00 (978-1-4159-0831-0(1)) Books on Tape.

Alice in Wonderland see Alice au Pays des Merveilles

Alice in Wonderland see Anya V Stranye Chudes

Alice in Wonderland. Read by Denise Bryer. 1 cass. (J). (ps-2). 2.98 (978-1-55886-031-5(2)) Smarty Pants.
A children's fairy tale about the adventures of a young girl.

Alice in Wonderland. J. Otto Seibold. Illus. by J. Otto Seibold. 1 cass. (Running Time: 1 hr. 30 mins.). 2001. 18.95 (CART002) Lodestone Catalog.

Alice in Wonderland. Prod. by Walt Disney Productions Staff. 1 cass. (J). 1998. 19.95 (978-0-7634-0388-1(1)) W Disney Records.
Music - Popular.

Alice in Wonderland: A Mad Tea-Party see Alice's Adventures in Wonderland

Alice in Wonderland: Advice from a Caterpillar see Alice's Adventures in Wonderland

Alice in Wonderland: Alice's Evidence see Alice's Adventures in Wonderland

Alice in Wonderland: Down the Rabbit Hole see Alice's Adventures in Wonderland

Alice in Wonderland: Pig & Pepper see Alice's Adventures in Wonderland

Alice in Wonderland: The Cheshire-Cat see Alice's Adventures in Wonderland

Alice in Wonderland: The Mock Turtle's Story see Alice's Adventures in Wonderland

Alice in Wonderland: The Pool of Tears see Alice's Adventures in Wonderland

Alice in Wonderland: The Queen's Croquet-Ground see Alice's Adventures in Wonderland

Alice in Wonderland: Who Stole the Tarts see Alice's Adventures in Wonderland

Alice in Wonderland & Through the Looking Glass. Lewis Carroll, pseud. Read by Ralph Cosham. (Running Time: 5 hrs.). (J). 2002. 22.95 (978-1-59912-039-3(9), Audiofy Corp) Iofy Corp.

***Alice in Wonderland & Through the Looking Glass.** unabr. ed. Lewis Carroll. Narrated by Robin Field. (ENG.). 2010. 14.98 (978-1-59644-955-8(1), MissionAud); audio compact disk 21.98 (978-1-59644-954-1(3), MissionAud) christianaud.

Alice in Wonderland & Through the Looking Glass. unabr. ed. Lewis Carroll, pseud. Read by Donada Peters. 6 cass. (Running Time: 6 hrs.). (J). 1993. 20.00 Set. (3182) Books on Tape.
Two of the most beloved classics of childhood.

Alice in Wonderland & Through the Looking Glass. unabr. ed. Lewis Carroll, pseud. Read by Ralph Cosham. (J). 2006. 34.99 (978-1-59895-162-2(9)) Find a World.

Alice in Wonderland & Through the Looking Glass. unabr. ed. Lewis Carroll, pseud. Read by Ralph Cosham. 1 cd. (Running Time: 4 hrs 50 mins). (J). 2002. audio compact disk 18.95 (978-1-58472-379-0(3), In Aud) Pub: Sound Room. Dist(s): Baker Taylor
MP3 format.

Alice in Wonderland & Through the Looking Glass. unabr. ed. Lewis Carroll, pseud. Read by Ralph Cosham. 5 cds. (Running Time: 4 hrs 51 mins). (J). 2002. audio compact disk 29.95 (978-1-58472-202-1(9), 022, In Aud) Pub: Sound Room. Dist(s): Baker Taylor

***Alice in Wonderland & Through the Looking Glass.** unabr. ed. Lewis Carroll, pseud. Narrated by Shelly Frasier & Renée Raudman. (Running Time: 6 hrs. 30 mins. 0 sec.). (ENG.). 2010. audio compact disk 22.99 (978-1-4001-2027-7(6)) Pub: Tantor Media. Dist(s): IngramPubServ

Alice in Wonderland Read Along. 1 cass. (Running Time: 30 mins.). (J). (ps-3). 1999. pap. bk. 6.98 (978-0-7634-0589-2(2)) W Disney Records.

Alice in Wonderland; Through the Looking-Glass; What Alice Found There. unabr. ed. Lewis Carroll, pseud. Perf. by Cybill Shepherd & Lynn Redgrave. 4 cass. (Running Time: 6 hrs.). 2004. 25.00 (978-1-59007-111-3(5)) Pub: New Millenn Enter. Dist(s): PerseuPGW
Enter a magical world with this enchanting adaptation of Lewis Carroll's classic, accompanied by specially composed music. When Alice steps through the looking glass she enters a world of chess pieces and nursery-rhyme characters who behave very oddly.

Alice Munro Interview with Kay Bonetti. Alice Munro. 1 cass. (Running Time: 72 min.). 1987. 13.95 (978-1-55644-187-5(8), 7052) Am Audio Prose.
Munro discusses artists who have influenced her, her complicated relationship with feminist critics, the emergence of Canadian literature, & the particular problems & advantages of women as writers.

***Alice Now!** (J). 1998. 15.00 (978-0-9789155-5-1(0)) Manor of Grace.

Alice Rose & Sam. unabr. ed. Kathryn Lasky. Narrated by Christina Moore. 4 cass. (Running Time: 4 hrs. 45 mins.). (J). 2001. pap. bk. & stu. ed. 52.24 Recorded Bks.
Alice Rose hates her home in Virginia City, only Sam Clemens, a new reporter at her father's paper, keeps things interesting. Sam has a colorful way with words & a habit of saying just what he thinks, especially when he's using his pen name.

Alice Rose & Sam. unabr. ed. Kathryn Lasky. Narrated by Christina Moore. 4 pieces. (Running Time: 4 hrs. 45 mins.). (gr. 4 up). 2001. 37.00 (978-0-7887-4723-6(1), 96397E7) Recorded Bks.

***Alice, the Ballet.** Perf. by R. A. Zuckerman. Composed by R. A. Zuckerman. (ENG.). 2010. 12.95 (978-1-891083-15-0(5)) ConcertHall.

Alice the Brave. unabr. ed. Phyllis Reynolds Naylor. Narrated by Christina Moore. 3 pieces. (Running Time: 3 hrs. 30 mins.). (Alice Ser.). (gr. 5 up). 27.00 (978-0-7887-0532-8(6), 94727E7) Recorded Bks.
Alice is ready for eighth grade, but she isn't ready for this summer. All her friends are spending their days swimming in the neighborhood pool - all of them except Alice. Available to libraries only.

Alice the Fairy. David Shannon. Narrated by Kate Simses. 1 CD. (Running Time: 5 mins.). (ENG.). (J). (ps-k). 2009. audio compact disk 18.95 (978-0-545-11946-7(4)) Scholastic Inc.

Alice the Fairy. David Shannon. Illus. by David Shannon. Narrated by Kate Simses. (ENG.). (J). (ps-ps). 2009. audio compact disk 9.95 (978-0-545-11758-6(5)) Scholastic Inc.

Alice Through the Looking Glass. unabr. ed. Lewis Carroll, pseud. Narrated by Full Cast. (Running Time: 2 hrs. 0 mins. 0 sec.). (ENG.). 2010. audio compact disk 24.95 (978-1-60283-848-2(8)) Pub: AudioGO. Dist(s): Perseus Dist

Alice to Nowhere. unabr. ed. Evan Green. Read by Richard Aspel. 8 cass. (Running Time: 11 hrs.). 2004. 64.00 (978-1-86340-660-4(3), 560915) Pub: Bolinda Pubng AUS. Dist(s): Lndmrk Audiobks
Once a fortnight, Fred Crawford drives his battered truck on the toughest mail run in the world - across the Stony Desert. For the men & women of the remote cattle stations on the way, Fred's visit is a welcome diversion, especially when he brings a new nursing sister for the tiny mission hospital at Birdsville. But trouble arrives. Two vicious men have stowed away, fleeing a brutal murder.

Alice to Nowhere. unabr. ed. Evan Green. Read by Richard Aspel. (Running Time: 11 hrs.). 2007. audio compact disk 98.95 (978-1-74093-842-6(9)) Pub: Bolinda Pubng AUS. Dist(s): Bolinda Pub Inc

Alice to Nowhere. unabr. ed. Evan Green. Read by Richard Aspel. (Running Time: 11 hrs.). 2009. 43.95 (978-1-74214-158-9(7), 9781742141589) Pub: Bolinda Pubng AUS. Dist(s): Bolinda Pub Inc

Alice Walker: Interview with Alice Walker & Kay Bonetti. 1 cass. (Running Time: 45 min.). 1981. 13.95 (978-1-55644-030-4(8), 1162) Am Audio Prose.
A wide ranging interview, from the writer's craft to the state of the world, but concentrating on American attitudes as portrayed in literature and real life.

***Alice's Adventures in Wonderland.** Lewis Carroll. Narrated by Alexis O'Donahue. (ENG.). 2010. 6.95 (978-1-936455-02-7(1)) Open Bk Aud.

Alice's Adventures in Wonderland. Lewis Carroll, pseud. Narrated by Heather Walters & Kelly Ryan. Prod. by Ralph LaBarge. (ENG.). (J). 2006. 12.95 (978-0-9798626-4-9(7)) Alpha DVD.

***Alice's Adventures in Wonderland.** Lewis Carroll, pseud. 2009. (978-1-60136-572-9(1)) Audio Holding.

Alice's Adventures in Wonderland. Lewis Carroll, pseud. 2 CDs. (Running Time: 2 hrs. 30 mins.). 2005. audio compact disk 27.00 (978-0-7861-8133-9(8), 1997) Blckstn Audio.

Alice's Adventures in Wonderland. Lewis Carroll, pseud. Read by Sally Field. 2 CDs. (Running Time: 2 hrs. 24 mins.). 2001. audio compact disk 20.00 Books on Tape.
Takes us on a topsy-turvy adventure through Wonderland. Stunning interpretation brings Alice, the Mad Hatter, the White Rabbit, the Cheshire Cat & all of the characters to life.

Alice's Adventures in Wonderland. Lewis Carroll, pseud. Read by Patricia Routledge. 3 cass. (Running Time: 3 hrs. 10 min.). (J). (gr. 2-4). 19.95 (CC/020) C to C Cassettes.
One 'golden afternoon' in 1862 Charles Dodgson first told the story of Alice sending his heroine, as he later recalled 'straight down a rabbit hole...without the least idea what would happen afterwards'.

Alice's Adventures in Wonderland. Lewis Carroll, pseud. 1 cass. (J). 18.95 (CART002) CA Artists.

Alice's Adventures in Wonderland. Based on a work by Lewis Carroll, pseud. (ENG.). (J). 2007. audio compact disk 13.00 (978-0-9802006-2-1(8)) DARIAN Enter.

Alice's Adventures in Wonderland. Lewis Carroll, pseud. Read by Mary Woods. (Running Time: 3 hrs.). 1997. 17.95 (978-1-59912-406-3(8)) Iofy Corp.

Alice's Adventures in Wonderland. Lewis Carroll, pseud. Read by Adelaida Espinoza. (Running Time: 3 hrs.). 2002. 16.95 (978-1-60083-184-3(2), Audiofy Corp) Iofy Corp.

Alice's Adventures in Wonderland. Lewis Carroll, pseud. Read by Shelly Frasier. (Running Time: 2 hrs. 48 mins.). 2003. 21.95 (978-1-60083-633-6(X), Audiofy Corp) Iofy Corp.

Alice's Adventures in Wonderland. Lewis Carroll, pseud. Narrated by Catherine O'Hara. (Running Time: 1 hr.). 2006. 14.95 (978-1-60083-003-7(X)) Iofy Corp.

Alice's Adventures in Wonderland. Lewis Carroll, pseud. Read by Cindy Hardin. 3 cass. (Running Time: 3 hrs.). (J). (gr. 4 up). 1989. 21.00 incl. album. (C-17) Jimcin Record.
Down the rabbit hole to adventure!.

Alice's Adventures in Wonderland. Lewis Carroll, pseud. 2 CDs. (Running Time: 2 hrs. 30 mins.). (J). 2003. audio compact disk 17.99 (978-1-58926-167-9(4), C05M-0060, Oasis Kids) Oasis Audio.

Alice's Adventures in Wonderland. Lewis Carroll, pseud. 1 cass. (Running Time: 1 hr.). (Radiobook Ser.). (J). 1987. 4.98 (978-0-929541-09-9(X)) Radiola Co.

Alice's Adventures in Wonderland. Lewis Carroll, pseud. Sean Taylor. Directed By David Nevland. 2. Dramatization. 2008. audio compact disk 12.95 (978-1-932226-71-3(0)) Wizard Acdmy.

Alice's Adventures in Wonderland. abr. ed. Lewis Carroll, pseud. Narrated by Marvin Miller & Jane Webb. 2 cass. (Running Time: 2 hrs. 24 min.). (J). 12.95 (978-0-89926-122-5(1), 810) Audio Bk.

Alice's Adventures in Wonderland. abr. ed. Lewis Carroll, pseud. Perf. by St. Charles Players. 2 cass. (Running Time: 1 hr. 26 min.). Dramatization. (Story Theatre for Young Readers Ser.). (J). (gr. 4-7). 1999. 16.95 (978-1-56994-506-3(3), 300524, Monterey SoundWorks) Monterey Media Inc.
My, oh my! Down the rabbit hole, advice from a Caterpillar, a mouse at a Mad party of tea...to dance the Lobster-Quadrille, a Queen, a King, a journey of such wonder that you can't help but see, it's a magical fantastical journey...Tweedledum, Tweedledee.

Alice's Adventures in Wonderland. abr. ed. Lewis Carroll, pseud. Read by Fiona Shaw. 2 CDs. (Running Time: 2 hrs. 23 mins.). (J). 1997. audio compact disk 17.98 (978-962-634-137-7(8), NA213712, Naxos AudioBooks) Naxos.
Alice's fantasy world includes characters as varied and well-known as The White Rabbit, The Mad Hatter, The Queen of Hearts and The Cheshire Cat.

Alice's Adventures in Wonderland. abr. ed. Lewis Carroll, pseud. Read by Fiona Shaw. 2 cass. (Running Time: 2 hrs. 23 mins.). (J). 1997. 13.98 (978-962-634-637-2(X), NA213714, Naxos AudioBooks) Naxos.

Alice's Adventures in Wonderland. unabr. ed. Lewis Carroll. Narrated by Flo Gibson. (Running Time: 2 hrs. 44 mins.). (J). (gr. 2-10). 2004. audio compact disk 16.95 (978-1-55685-770-6(5)) Audio Bk Con.

***Alice's Adventures in Wonderland.** unabr. ed. Lewis Carroll. Read by Shannon Parks. (Running Time: 3 hrs.). (ENG.). 2010. 2.98 (978-1-59659-557-6(4), GildAudio) Pub: Gildan Media. Dist(s): HachBkGrp

Alice's Adventures in Wonderland. unabr. ed. Lewis Carroll, pseud. Read by Jane Webb. 4 cass. (J). 23.80 (E-312) Audio Bk.
Complete adventures of Alice.

Alice's Adventures in Wonderland. unabr. ed. Lewis Carroll, pseud. Read by Flo Gibson. 2 cass. (Running Time: 3 hrs.). (J). 2004. 14.95 (978-1-55685-044-8(1), 1984) Audio Bk Con.
When Alice falls down a rabbit hole she meets with many adventures in a world viewed from the inside out.

Alice's Adventures in Wonderland. unabr. ed. Lewis Carroll, pseud. Read by Patricia Routledge. 2 cass. (Running Time: 3 hrs.). (J). (gr. 1-8). 1999. 18.95 (CTC 020, Chivers Child Audio) AudioGO.

***Alice's Adventures in Wonderland.** unabr. ed. Lewis Carroll, pseud. Perf. by David Bamber. Narrated by Roy Hudd & Sarah-Jane Holm. 2 CDs. (Running Time: 1 hr. 53 mins.). (J). 2007. audio compact disk 29.95 (978-0-7927-4996-7(0)) AudioGO.

Alice's Adventures in Wonderland. unabr. ed. Lewis Carroll, pseud. 2 CDs. (Running Time: 3 hrs. 0 mins. 0 sec.). (ENG.). 2010. audio compact disk 14.95 (978-1-60283-660-0(4)) Pub: AudioGO. Dist(s): Perseus Dist

Alice's Adventures in Wonderland, unabr. ed. Lewis Carroll, pseud. Read by Susan O'Malley. 2 cass. (Running Time: 2 hrs. 30 mins.). (gr. 6-8). 1997. 17.95 (978-0-7861-1214-2(X), 1997) Blckstn Audio.
A fairy tale about the trials & tribulations of growing up - or down, or all turned round - as seen through the expert eyes of a child.

Alice's Adventures in Wonderland. unabr. ed. Lewis Carroll, pseud. 2 cass. (Running Time: 9000 sec.). (J). 2005. 14.95 (978-0-7861-3455-7(0), E1997); audio compact disk 14.95 (978-0-7861-8032-5(3), ZE1997); audio compact disk 24.95 (978-0-7861-8424-8(8), 1997) Blckstn Audio.

Alice's Adventures in Wonderland. unabr. ed. Lewis Carroll, pseud. Read by Michael York. (Running Time: 10800 sec.). 2008. 24.95 (978-1-4332-1362-5(1)) Blckstn Audio.

Alice's Adventures in Wonderland. unabr. ed. Lewis Carroll, pseud. Read by Michael York. (Running Time: 10800 sec.). (J). (gr. 3). 2008. audio compact disk 19.95 (978-1-4332-1364-9(8)); audio compact disk & audio compact disk 40.00 (978-1-4332-1363-2(X)) Blckstn Audio.

Alice's Adventures in Wonderland. unabr. ed. Lewis Carroll, pseud. Read by Michael York. 3 CDs. (J). (gr. 4-7). 2008. audio compact disk & audio compact disk 19.95 (978-1-4332-1365-6(6)) Blckstn Audio.

***Alice's Adventures in Wonderland.** unabr. ed. Lewis Carroll, pseud. Read by Miriam Margolyes. (Running Time: 3 hrs. 23 mins.). (J). 2010. audio compact disk 54.95 (978-1-74214-713-0(5), 9781742147130) Pub: Bolinda Pubng AUS. Dist(s): Bolinda Pub Inc

Alice's Adventures in Wonderland. unabr. ed. Lewis Carroll, pseud. Read by Jean DeBarbieris. 2 cass. (Running Time: 3 hrs.). (J). 16.95 (978-1-55686-118-5(4), 118) Books in Motion.
Alice dreams that she follows an entrancing white rabbit down a rabbit hole to a strange land.

Alice's Adventures in Wonderland. unabr. ed. Lewis Carroll, pseud. Perf. by Joan Greenwood & Stanley Holloway. 1 cass. (Running Time: 90 mins.). Incl. Alice in Wonderland: A Mad Tea-Party. (J). (CPN 1097); Alice in Wonderland: Advice from a Caterpillar. (J). (CPN 1097); Alice in Wonderland: Alice's Evidence. (J). (CPN 1097); Alice in Wonderland: Down the Rabbit Hole. (J). (CPN 1097); Alice in Wonderland: Pig & Pepper. (J). (CPN 1097); Alice in Wonderland: The Cheshire-Cat. (J). (CPN 1097); Alice in Wonderland: The Mock Turtle's Story. (J). (CPN 1097); Alice in Wonderland: The Pool of Tears. (J). (CPN 1097); Alice in Wonderland: The Queen's Croquet-Ground. (J). (CPN 1097); Alice in Wonderland: Who Stole the Tarts. (J). (CPN 1097); (J). 1984. 9.95 (978-0-89845-899-2(4), CPN 1097) HarperCollins Pubs.
Other performers include: Peter Bryant, Timothy Bateson, Carleton Hobbs, Billie Hill, Patricia Somerset, John Hollis, Janet Barrow, & James McKechnie.

Alice's Adventures in Wonderland. unabr. ed. Lewis Carroll, pseud. (Running Time: 4 hrs.). 2001. 24.95 (978-1-60083-672-5(0)) Iofy Corp.

Alice's Adventures in Wonderland. unabr. ed. Lewis Carroll, pseud. Read by David Horovitch et al. 3 CDs. (Running Time: 14276 sec.). (Classic Literature with Classical Music Ser.). (J). 2006. audio compact disk 22.98 (978-962-634-384-5(2), Naxos AudioBooks) Naxos.

Alice's Adventures in Wonderland. unabr. ed. Lewis Carroll, pseud. Read by Jim Dale. 3 CDs. (Running Time: 2 hrs. 57 mins.). (J). (gr. 3). 2008. audio compact disk 30.00 (978-0-7393-6765-0(X), Listening Lib) Pub: Random Audio Pubg. Dist(s): Random

Alice's Adventures in Wonderland. unabr. ed. Lewis Carroll, pseud. Narrated by Flo Gibson. 2 pieces. (Running Time: 2 hrs. 30 mins.). (gr. 5 up). 1999. 19.00 (978-1-55690-002-0(3), 80060E7) Recorded Bks.
Alice follows a white rabbit into a world where magic rules over logic in this fantasy classic.

Alice's Adventures in Wonderland. unabr. ed. Lewis Carroll, pseud. Read by Ralph Cosham. 2 cass. (Running Time: 3 hrs.). (Carroll Ser.). (J). 1994. bk. 16.95 (978-1-883049-40-9(7), 390330, Commuters Library) Sound Room.
The fairy tale that has been part of growing up for generations. Once again follow alice down the rabbit hole. Witty, harming & delightfully magical, it remains a classic.

Alice's Adventures in Wonderland. unabr. ed. Lewis Carroll, pseud. Read by Ralph Cosham. 2 cass. (Running Time: 2 hrs. 40 mins.). 1994. lib. bdg. 18.95 (978-1-883049-46-1(6)) Sound Room.
The fairy tale that has been part of growing up for generations. Once again follow Alice down the rabbit hole. Witty, charming & delightfully magical, Alice's Adventures in Wonderland remains a classic.

Alice's Adventures in Wonderland. unabr. ed. Lewis Carroll, pseud. Narrated by Shelly Frasier. 1 MP3 CD. (Running Time: 2 hrs. 51 mins.). (ENG.). (J). 2003. 17.00 (978-1-4001-5065-6(5)); audio compact disk 52.00 (978-1-4001-3065-8(4)) Pub: Tantor Media. Dist(s): IngramPubServ
Alice is wondering what to do one day, when a talking rabbit steals her attention. She is so intrigued that she follows him into his hole, and tumbles down into Wonderland. Alice soon discovers that reality and logic, as she knows them, do not apply here. In an attempt get out of the hole and into, "the loveliest garden you ever saw", she eats a cake to grow large enough to reach the key to the garden. However, this backfires as she grows way too large to fit through the opening. Alice becomes frustrated and cries a pool of tears, into which fall many curious talking creatures, including a Mouse, a Dodo, a Lory and an Eaglet. Alice is whisked along some of the most bizarre and imaginative adventures in children's literature. Lewis Carroll's Alice's Adventures in Wonderland is a classic that is beloved by listeners of all ages.

Alice's Adventures in Wonderland. unabr. ed. Lewis Carroll, pseud. Narrated by Shelly Frasier. (Running Time: 3 hrs. 0 mins. 0 sec.). (ENG.). (J). (gr. 4-7). 2008. 17.99 (978-1-4001-5858-4(3)); audio compact disk 17.99 (978-1-4001-0858-9(6)) Pub: Tantor Media. Dist(s): IngramPubServ

Alice's Adventures in Wonderland. unabr. ed. Lewis Carroll, pseud. Read by Jim Dale. (Running Time: 10620 sec.). (ENG.). (J). (gr. 3). 2008. audio compact disk 25.00 (978-0-7393-6738-4(2), Listening Lib) Pub: Random Audio Pubg. Dist(s): Random

Alice's Adventures in Wonderland, Set. unabr. ed. Lewis Carroll, pseud. Read by Robert L. Halvorson. 2 cass. (Running Time: 180 min.). (J). 14.95 (94) Halvorson Assocs.

***Alice's Adventures in Wonderland & Through the Looking Glass.** unabr. ed. Lewis Carroll. Read by Christopher Plummer. (ENG.). 2010. (978-0-06-199745-7(5)); (978-0-06-199685-6(8)) HarperCollins Pubs.

Alice's Adventures in Wonderland & Through the Looking-Glass: And What Alice Found There. collector's ed. Lewis Carroll, pseud. Read by Donada Peters. 6 cass. (Running Time: 6 hrs.). (J). (gr. 4-7). 1993. 36.00 (978-0-7366-2415-2(5), 3182) Books on Tape.
These two stories have enchanted adults as well as children of all ages for over one hundred years.

Alice's Adventures in Wonderland & Through the Looking-Glass: And What Alice Found There. unabr. ed. Lewis Carroll, pseud. Read by Michael Page. (Running Time: 6 hrs.). 2005. 39.25 (978-1-59600-981-3(0), 9781596009813, BADLE); 24.95 (978-1-59600-980-6(2), 9781596009806, BAD); audio compact disk 39.25 (978-1-59600-979-0(9), 9781596009790, Brlnc Audio MP3 Lib); audio compact disk 24.95 (978-1-59600-978-3(0), 9781596009783, Brilliance MP3); audio compact disk 74.25 (978-1-59600-977-6(2), 9781596009776, BriAudCD Unabrid); audio compact disk 29.95 (978-1-59600-976-9(4), 9781596009769, Bril Audio CD Unabri) Brilliance Audio.
First published in 1865, these endearing tales of an imaginative child's dream world by Lewis Carroll, pen name for Charles Lutwidge Dodgson, are written with charming simplicity. While delighting children with a heroine who represents their own thoughts and feelings about growing up, the tale is appreciated by adults as a gentle satire on education, politics, literature, and Victorian life in general. All the delightful and bizarre inhabitants of Wonderland are here: the White Rabbit and the Cheshire Cat, the hooka-smoking Caterpillar and the Mad Hatter, the March Hare and the Ugly Duchess . . .and, of course, Alice herself - growing altemately taller and smaller, attending demented tea parties and eccentric croquet games, observing everything with clarity and rational amazement.

Alice's Adventures in Wonderland & Through the Looking-Glass: And What Alice Found There. unabr. ed. Lewis Carroll, pseud. Read by Ralph Cosham. 5 cds. (Running Time: 9 hrs.). 2000. audio compact disk 52.00 (978-1-58472-109-3(X)) Sound Room.

Alice's Adventures in Wonderland & Through the Looking-Glass: And What Alice Found There, Set. unabr. ed. Lewis Carroll, pseud. Read by Ralph Cosham. 6 cass. (Running Time: 9 hrs.). (Timeless Treasures Collection). (J). 1999. 34.95 (978-1-883049-76-8(8), Commuters Library) Sound Room.
Stories to be savored by young & old for their wit, humor & the sheer delight of fantasy.

Alice's Adventures in Wonderland Through the Looking Glass. 2 cass. (Running Time: 2 hrs.). (Stage Ser.). (J). 2004. 18.99 (978-1-894003-11-7(X)) Pub: Scenario Prods CAN. Dist(s): PerseuPGW

Alice's Adventures in Wonderland, with eBook. unabr. ed. Lewis Carroll, pseud. Narrated by Shelly Frasier. (Running Time: 3 hrs. 0 mins. 0 sec.). (ENG.). (J). (gr. 4-7). 2008. audio compact disk 35.99 (978-1-4001-3858-6(2)) Pub: Tantor Media. Dist(s): IngramPubServ

Alice's Adventures Through the Looking-Glass. Lewis Carroll, pseud. (Running Time: 1 hr.). (Radiobook Ser.). 1987. 4.98 (978-0-929541-10-5(3)) Radiola Co.

Alice's Healthy Options DIET FREE All-Day Breakfast Snacks. Alice Melesio. Prod. by Mike Nofsinger. 1 cassette. (Running Time: 22:02 minutes). 2002. 6.50 (978-0-9720062-3-1(0), 0-9720062-3-0CS); audio compact disk 10.00 (978-0-9720062-2-4(2), 0-9720062-2-2CD) Alice's Health.
Healthy and flavorful DIET FREE snack recipes that can be eaten for breakfast or any time of the day. Includes quick and simple instructions and helpful health tips.

Alice's Healthy Options DIET FREE Shake Recipes. Alice Melesio. Prod. by Mike Nofsinger. 1 cassette. (Running Time: 10:02 minutes). 2002. 6.50 (978-0-9720062-1-7(4), 0-9720062-1-4CS); audio compact disk 10.00 (978-0-9720062-0-0(6), 0-9720062-0-6CD) Alice's Health.
Healthy and flavorful DIET FREE shake recipes with quick and simple instructions and helpful health tips.

Alicia. unabr. ed. Read by Cassandra Morris & Stephanie Wolfe. Created by Lisi Harrison. (Running Time: 3 hrs. 30 mins.). (Clique Summer Collection: No. 3). (ENG.). 2009. 9.98 (978-1-60024-698-2(2)) Pub: Hachet Audio. Dist(s): HachBkGrp

Alicia en el País de las Maravillas. unabr. abr. ed. Lewis Carroll, pseud. Read by Adelaida Espinoza. 3 CDs. (Running Time: 3 hrs.). (SPA.). 2002. audio compact disk 17.00 (978-958-9494-65-3(X)) YoYoMusic.
Alicia en el país de las Maravillas es una de esas obras mágicas de la literatura que apela tanto a grandes como a niños, ya que para los primeros está la ironía y el fino humor con que Carroll se burlaba de las convenciones sociales de su tiempo, mientras que los más pequeños pueden seguir, también con una sonrisa, las increíbles aventuras de Alicia en ese lugar donde todo parece suceder al revés. Carroll, que creó esta obra maestra de la literatura universal, como entretenimiento para una amiguita, hija de unos vecinos era en sus momentos serios un catedrático respetado de matemáticas, y nunca imaginó que esa creación le diera la inmortalidad.

Alicia en el País de las Maravillas; La Isla del Tesoro. Lewis Carroll, pseud & Robert Louis Stevenson. (Playaway Young Adult Ser.). (SPA.). (YA). 2009. 60.00 (978-1-60775-576-0(9)) Find a World.

Alicia Keys: The Unauthorized Biography of Alicia Keys. Ben Graham. (Maximum Ser.). (ENG., 2003. audio compact disk 14.95 (978-1-84240-181-1(5)) Pub: Chrome Dreams GBR. Dist(s): IPG Chicago

Alien Abduction Handbook: A Pre-Flight Briefing for Future Abductees. Based on a book by Peggy Lee Johnson. (ENG.). 2008. audio compact disk 12.00 (978-0-9794672-2-6(5)) AudioBookMan.

Alien Affair. abr. ed. L. Ron Hubbard. 2 cass. (Running Time: 3 hrs.). (Mission Earth Ser.: Vol. 4). 2002. 15.95 (978-1-59212-060-4(1)) Gala Pr LLC.

Alien at School. Michelle Brown. (Reading & Training, Elementary Ser.). (J). (gr. 4-7). 2005. pap. bk. 21.95 (978-88-7754-757-6(X)) Cideb ITA.

Alien Encounter. Susannah Brin. Narrated by Larry A. McKeever. (Chillers Ser.). (J). 2001. audio compact disk 14.95 (978-1-58659-295-0(5)) Artesian.

Alien Encounter. unabr. ed. Susannah Brin. Narrated by Larry A. McKeever. 1 cass. (Running Time: 40 mins.). (Take Ten Ser.). (J). (gr. 3-12). 2001. 10.95 (978-1-58659-056-7(1), 54126) Artesian.

***Alien Invasion & Other Inconveniences.** unabr. ed. Philip Yancey. (Running Time: 4 hrs.). 2010. audio compact disk 19.99 (978-1-4418-8996-6(5), 9781441889966, Candlewick Bril) Brilliance Audio.

***Alien Invasion & Other Inconveniences.** unabr. ed. Philip Yancey & Brian Yansky. (Running Time: 4 hrs.). 2010. 39.97 (978-1-4418-8999-7(X), 9781441889997, Candlewick Bril); 19.99 (978-1-4418-8998-0(1), 9781441889980, Candlewick Bril) Brilliance Audio.

***Alien Invasion & Other Inconveniences.** unabr. ed. Philip Yancey & Brian Yansky. Read by Alexander Cendese. (Running Time: 4 hrs.). 2010. audio compact disk 22.99 (978-1-4418-8994-2(9), 9781441889942, Candlewick Bril); audio compact disk 39.97 (978-1-4418-8997-3(3), 9781441889973, Candlewick Bril); audio compact disk 44.97 (978-1-4418-8995-9(7), 9781441889959, Candlewick Bril) Brilliance Audio.

Alien Next Door. (J). 2005. cass. & cd-rom 24.95 (978-0-9771381-8-0(6)) Geoffrey Williams.

Alien Secrets. unabr. ed. Annette Curtis Klause. Narrated by Christina Moore. 5 pieces. (Running Time: 6 hrs. 30 mins.). (gr. 6 up). 1997. 44.00 (978-0-7887-0686-8(1), 94860E7) Recorded Bks.
In this swashbuckling interplanetary adventure Puck, a seventh grade girl, is expelled from a boarding school on earth for bad grades. During her spaceship ride home to her disappointed parents on Shoon, she finds herself making friends with grey-skinned, cone-headed Hush & hiding from an interplanetary hit man.

Alien Voices Presents H. G. Wells' The First Men in the Moon. abr. ed. H. G. Wells. Read by Leroy Nimroy & John De Lance. 2 cass. (Running Time: 2 hrs.). 1998. Rental 20.00 CD.; audio compact disk 28.00 S&S Audio.

Alienated Youth. Gregory Boyle. 1 cass. (Running Time: 1 hr. 19 mins.). 1994. 8.95 (TAH321) Alba Hse Comns.
In this very down-to-earth talk, Fr. Boyle uses his experience in working with gangs at the Dolores Misison, Los Angeles as a springboard to present a gospel centered response to alienated youth. Excellent for youth groups. Entertains while it instructs. A lively discussion starter.

Alienation. unabr. ed. Nathaniel Branden. 1 cass. (Running Time: 51 mins.). 12.95 (AF0552) J Norton Pubs.
Branden discusses the problem of "personal identity," attacks the work of Erich Fromm & others who have attempted to blame "alienation" in modern society on capitalism & shows the relationship between political freedom & psychological well-being.

Alienist. Caleb Carr. Narrated by George Guidall. 14 cass. (Running Time: 20 hrs. 15 mins.). 114.00 (978-1-4025-3396-9(9)) Recorded Bks.

ALIENIST. Caleb Carr & Carr. Read by Edward Herrmann. 2004. 15.95 (978-0-7435-2008-9(4)) Pub: S&S Audio. Dist(s): S and S Inc

Alienist. unabr. ed. Caleb Carr. Read by Jonathan Marosz. 13 cass. (Running Time: 19 hrs. 30 min.). 1995. 104.00 (978-0-7366-2898-3(3), 3598) Books on Tape.
In New York City, 1896, New York Times reporter John Schuyler Moore is summoned to the East River by former Harvard classmate Dr. Laszlo Kreiller, a psychologist, or "alienist." Police Commissioner Theodore Roosevelt enlists the two men to help solve the murder of a prostitute from one of the city's infamous brothels.

Aliens Ate My Homework. Bruce Coville. Read by William Dufris. 2 cass. (Running Time: 3 hrs. 37 mins.). (J). 2000. 18.00 (978-0-7366-9088-1(3)) Books on Tape.
About aliens.

Aliens Ate My Homework. unabr. ed. Bruce Coville. Read by William Dufris. 2 cass. (Running Time: 3 hrs. 30 mins.). (J). (gr. 1-8). 1997. 23.00 (978-0-7451-7391-7(8), LL 0108) AudioGO.
Rod is a boy who has problems telling lies, no matter how silly the truth might sound. When he tells his teacher that aliens ate his homework, nobody believes him & nobody asks where the aliens come from.

Aliens Ate My Homework. unabr. ed. Bruce Coville. Read by William Dufris. 2 cass. (Running Time: 3 hrs. 19 mins.). (I Was a Sixth Grade Alien Ser.). (J). (gr. 3-6). 1997. 23.00 (978-0-8072-7831-4(9), YA928CX, Listening Lib) Random Audio Pubg.

Aliens Ate My Homework. unabr. ed. Read by William Dufris. Ed. by Bruce Coville. 2 vols. (Running Time: 3 hrs. 19 mins.). (I Was a Sixth Grade Alien Ser.). (J). (gr. 3-6). 1997. pap. bk. 29.00 (978-0-8072-7832-1(7), YA928SP, Listening Lib) Random Audio Pubg.

Aliens Ate My Homework, Set. unabr. ed. Bruce Coville. Read by William Dufris. 2 cass. (YA). 1999. 16.98 (FS9-34199) Highsmith.

Aliens in America. unabr. ed. Sandra Tsing-Loh. Read by Sandra Tsing-Loh. 1 cass. (Running Time: 1 hr. 20 mins.). 2000. 19.95 (978-1-58081-169-9(8), TPT145) L A Theatre.

Aliens Rule. Nancy Kress et al. Ed. by Allan Kaster. (ENG.). 2009. audio compact disk 23.99 (978-1-884612-87-9(3), Infinivox) AudioText.

Aliento de Adoración 2. Rudy Rodriguez. (SPA.). 2006. audio compact disk 14.99 (978-0-8297-5062-1(2)) Zondervan.

Aligning IEPs to Academic Standards: For Students with Moderate & Severe Disabilities. 2005. pap. bk. 35.00 (978-1-57861-548-3(8), IEP Res) Attainment.

Aligning Our Lives with His Good Pleasure: The Heavenly Benefits of Godly Stewardship. 4. (Running Time: 4 hrs.). 2000. 20.00 (978-1-57399-112-4(0)) Mac Hammond.
In this down-to-earth series, Mac Hammond leads us through our calling as God's stewards. When we move the center of our life's ambition from ourselves to focus on those things that please Him, it'll produce an experience of life instead of death...it'll manifest the peace of God that passes all understanding in your life...it'll produce the increase of every good thing, including finances. Best of all, we'll position ourselves to fulfill our divine purpose of God.

Aligning with Source: Who Moved My Chi Series. Narrated by Laurie Morse. 2005. audio compact disk Rental 15.99 (978-0-9767262-0-3(3)) L Morse.

Aliki Says. unabr. ed. Irini Savvides. Read by Edwina Wren. (Running Time: 5 hrs. 45 mins.). (YA). 2007. audio compact disk 63.95 (978-1-74093-883-9(6)) Pub: Bolinda Pubng AUS. Dist(s): Bolinda Pub Inc

Aline. Contrib. by Aline. 2005. audio compact disk 14.98 (978-5-558-80668-7(0)) Integrity Music.

***Alington Inheritance.** Patricia Wentworth. 2010. 61.95 (978-0-7531-4215-8(5)); audio compact disk 79.95 (978-0-7531-4216-5(3)) Pub: Isis Pubng Ltd GBR. Dist(s): Ulverscroft US

Alington Inheritance. unabr. ed. Patricia Wentworth. Read by Nadia May. 5 cass. (Running Time: 7 hrs.). 1992. 39.95 (978-0-7861-0318-8(3), 1279) Blckstn Audio.
The pretty, seventeen-year-old orphan Jenny Hill finds it hard to believe when her dying guardian tells her that she is the rightful owner of the Alington estate & that the proof lies in a letter in an old chest. Jenny can't find the papers, & by the time she goes to live at Alington House to act as governess for the two young girls living there she has completely dismissed the idea. But her unscrupulous relatives know the truth & will do anything in an effort to keep control of the property. One night young Jenny overhears them plotting against her, & she feels the house. Her discovery marks her for murder. After the sharp-eyed Miss Silver steps onto the scene to investigate, the tension erupts into a seething climax.

Alison Lurie. Interview. Interview with Alison Lurie & Kay Bonetti. 1 cass. (Running Time: 1 hr.). 13.95 (978-1-55644-114-1(2), 4122) Am Audio Prose.
Includes discussion of Lurie's interest in children's literature & folk & her problems in carving out a writing career while raising a family.

Alistair Maclean's Code Breaker. Alastair MacNeill. Read by Peter Wickham. 12 cass. 2001. (978-1-84283-098-7(8)) Soundings Ltd GBR.
In a sudden, terrifying attack, Sergei Kolchinsky, Deputy Director of UNACO, is shot and his colleague Abe Silverman, along with coded documents of unmeasurable value, is captured. Liaising with the Portuguese Special Forces, the UNACO team of C.W. Whitlock, Mike Graham and Sabrina Carver set about tracking down the vital secrets.Before long, they realise they are dealing with one of the most successful and dangerous military minds of the former Soviet Union and, worse still, they are under threat at home from an investigative journalist determined to blow their cover.A pulsating story that builds to a nail-biting climax, Alistair MacLean?s Code Breaker is a thriller worthy of the master himself.

Alive. unabr. collector's ed. Piers Paul Read. Read by Dick Estell. 8 cass. (Running Time: 12 hrs.). 1987. 64.00 (978-0-7366-1092-6(8), 2016) Books on Tape.
First soccer, then survival. This flight over the Andes ended up in cannibalism.

Alive Again! William D. Banks. 3 cass. (Running Time: 70 mins. per cass.). 1980. 19.95 (978-0-89228-106-0(5)) Impact Christian.
Faith building testimony & scriptural teaching by the once terminally ill author.

Alive & Kickin' The Healing Power of God Brought to Life in You. Jeremy Pearsons. (ENG.). (YA). 2006. audio compact disk 5.00 (978-1-57562-915-5(1)) K Copeland Pubns.

Alive & Transported. Contrib. by Tobymac et al. Prod. by Toby McKeehan & Dave Wyatt. 2008. audio compact disk 18.99 (978-5-557-47785-7(3)) FF Rcds.

Alive Day: A Story of Love & Loyalty. unabr. ed. Tom Sullivan. Narrated by Tom Sullivan. (Running Time: 5 hrs. 40 mins. 17 sec.). (ENG.). 2009. 16.09 (978-1-60814-510-2(7)); audio compact disk 22.99 (978-1-59859-571-0(7)) Oasis Audio.

Alive in Christ Jesus. David Haas. 1 cass., 1 CD. 1998. 10.95 (CS-416); audio compact disk 15.95 (CD-416) GIA Pubns.

Alive in South Africa. Contrib. by Israel & New Breed. Prod. by Aaron W. Lindsey & Israel Houghton. Contrib. by Don Moen. 2005. audio compact disk 17.98 (978-5-558-73810-0(3)) Integrity Music.

Alive on the Andrea Doria! The Greatest Sea Rescue in History. Pierette Domenica Simpson. (ENG.). 2009. audio compact disk 49.95 (978-1-60037-655-9(X)) Pub: Morgan James Pubng. Dist(s): IngramPubServ

Alive to God: Romans 6:1-12. Ed Young. 1996. 4.95 (978-0-7417-2114-3(7), 1114) Win Walk.

Alixandra's Wings. unabr. ed. Freedan Wakoa & Pat MacEnulty. 1 cass. (J). (gr. 1-8). 1998. 23.95 (978-0-9670926-0-7(4), 001) Golden Wings Med.
Alixandra lives on the planet Lumin. Everyone is born with wings but they haven't forgotten how to fly. Alixandra is determined to learn to fly.

Alkaptonuria - A Bibliography & Dictionary for Physicians, Patients, & Genome Researchers. Compiled by Icon Group International, Inc. Staff. 2007. ring bd. 28.95 (978-0-497-11321-6(X)) Icon Grp.

Alkmene see Winter's Tales

All Aboard. Perf. by John Denver. 1 cass. (Family Artist Ser.). (J). (ps up). 1997. 9.98 (Sony Wonder); audio compact disk 13.98 CD. Sony Music Ent.
Collection of 14 of America's most beloved train songs.

All Aboard America. 39 mins. (Running Time: 39 mins.). 2004. pap. bk. 12.98 (978-0-9743549-1-0(0)) Bald Eagle Med.

All Aboard the Learn along Train: Learning Skills for Little Ones. Perf. by Janice Buckner. 1 CD. (Running Time: 1 hr.). (Learn along Song Ser.: Vol. 1). (J). 2001. audio compact disk 15.00 Moonlight Rose.
The three R's for little folks - Rhyming, Repetition & Rhythm! Young passengers learn about animals, numbers, colors, letters & foreign languages. Includes sing-it-yourself side.

All Aboard the Learn along Train: Learning Skills for Little Ones. Janice Buckner. 1 cass. (Running Time: 1 hr.). (Learn along Song Ser.: Vol. 1). (J). 1992. 9.98 (978-1-56479-119-1(X), MR119-4) Moonlight Rose.

All Aboard with Thomas: Special Pop-Up Playset. 1 cass. (Running Time: 1 hr.). (J). 2002. 21.99 (978-0-7379-0172-6(1), 76718); audio compact disk 26.98 (978-0-7379-0171-9(3), 76718) Rhino Enter.

All about Adams Apple. Box Toy Box Productions Staff. 2000. (978-1-887729-27-7(5)) Toy Box Prods.

All about Adam's Apple. unabr. ed. Joe Loesch. Ed. by Cheryl J. Hutchinson. Illus. by Ott Denney. 1 cass. (Bible Stories for Kids Ser.: Vol. 3). (J). (ps-3). 1996. pap. bk. 14.95 (978-1-887729-10-9(0)); pap. bk. 16.95 (978-1-887729-11-6(9)) Toy Box Prods.
Hear Professor Patulli tell the story of Creation & what happened in the Garden where life began.

All about Animals. Perf. by Marcia Lane et al. (J). 1999. audio compact disk 14.95 (978-1-58467-005-6(3)) Gentle Wind.

All about Animals: Songs & Stories For Children (Sampler 6) Perf. by Lisa Atkinson et al. 1 cass. (Running Time: 35 mins.). (J). 1993. 9.95 (978-0-939065-55-4(X), GW1059) Gentle Wind.
Includes songs about animals from a number of Gentle Wind artists.

All about Attention Deficit Disorder: The Information, Tools & Emotional Support You Need. 2nd unabr. ed. Thomas W. Phelan. 4 cass. (Running Time: 4 hrs. 30 min.). (ENG.). 2003. 24.95 (978-1-889140-05-6(8)) Pub: ParentMagic. Dist(s): IPG Chicago
All About ADD provides a thorough description of the symptoms, diagnosis & treatment of ADD. Both professional & personal experience afford Dr. Phelan a unique insight to this often misunderstand condition.

All about Baptism. Perf. by Peace Mtn. Media Works Staff. 1 cass. (Running Time: 45 mins.). Dramatization. (All About Ser.). (J). (ps-3). 1992. 5.95 (978-1-887938-05-1(2)) Snd Concepts.
Teaches children the principle of baptism.

All about Channeling. Ron Scolastico. 2 cass. (Running Time: 2 hrs. 40 mins.). (Wisdom of the Guides Ser.). 1994. 19.95 (978-0-943833-03-3(5), 630) Hay House.
This is a two-tape set from the Guides that will give you a comprehensive understanding of the phenomenon of channeling.

All about Christmas. Frank E. Peretti. 1 cass. (Running Time: 30 min.). (Wild & Wacky Totally True Bible Stories Ser.). (J). (ps-7). 2001. 3.99; audio compact disk 5.99 Nelson.
Four stories in Mr. Henry's unique style that come alive as children meet characters from the Bible.

All about Colors. Steven Traugh. 1 cass. (Sing & Learn Ser.). (J). bk. 8.95 (00330501) H Leonard.
Teaches through the use of movement games, echo chants, fun-filled activities. Nine songs including: "Mixing My Colors," "Colorful Moves," "Rainbows," "Colors in Our World" & more.

All about Computer Charts. Richard Nolle. 1 cass. 8.95 (571) Am Fed Astrologers.
Do Astrology on your home computer.

All about Continents: Early Explorers Fluent Set A Audio CD. Benchmark Education Staff. (J). 2006. audio compact disk 10.00 (978-1-4108-7639-3(X)) Benchmark Educ.

All about Eve. abr. ed. Hollywood. 1 cass. 1999. 13.10 (978-1-900912-67-9(8)) Pub: Mr Punch Prodns GBR. Dist(s): Ulverscroft US
Eve Harrington cleverly manipulates her way into the life of aging Broadway star Margo Channing in this venomous depiction of show business life that has become one of Hollywood's all time masterpieces.

All about Faith. Perf. by Peace Mtn. Media Works Staff. 1 cass. (Running Time: 45 min.). Dramatization. (All About Ser.). (J). (ps-3). 1992. 5.95 (978-1-887938-03-7(6)) Snd Concepts.
Teaches children the principle of faith through music & fun.

All about Family Adventures: Faith, Repentance, Baptism, the Holy Ghost, Sunday & Temples. Created by Roger Hoffman et al. 2 CDs. (J). 2003. audio compact disk 14.95 (978-1-887938-65-5(6)) Snd Concepts.

All about Forgiveness. Read by Frank E. Peretti. 1 cass. (Running Time: 30 mins.). (Wild & Wacky Totally True Bible Stories Ser.). (J). 2000. 3.99 Nelson.

All about God. Featuring Neale Donald Walsch & Deepak Chopra. 1 cass. (Running Time: 1 hr.). (Dialogues at the Chopra Center for Well Being Ser.). 2000. 10.95 (978-1-56170-735-5(X), 4039) Hay House.
Walsch recounts the events leading up to the publication of his book.

All about Hanukkah. unabr. ed. Judyth Saypol Groner & Madeline Wikler. Perf. by Margie Rosenthal & Ilene Safyan. Narrated by Peninnah Schram. 1 CD. (Running Time: 45 mins.). (J). (gr. k-5). 1989. bk. 19.95 CD Set, incl. pap. bk. (978-1-58013-059-2(3), Kar-Ben) Lerner Pub.
The narration of the story of Hanukkah, from the book "All about Hanukkah", plus 30 mins. of favorite holiday songs.

All about Hanukkah in Story & Song. unabr. ed. Judyth Groner & Madeline Wikler. Perf. by Margie Rosenthal & Ilene Safyan. Narrated by Peninnah Schram. 1 cass. (Running Time: 45 mins.). (J). (gr. k-3). 1989. 8.95 (978-0-930494-84-1(9), Kar-Ben); audio compact disk 16.95 (978-1-58013-056-1(9), Kar-Ben) Lerner Pub.
The narration of the story of Hanukkah, from the book "All about Hanukkah", plus 30 mins. of favorite holiday songs.

All about Helping Others. Frank E. Peretti. 1 cass. (Running Time: 30 min.). (J). (ps-7). 2001. 3.99 Nelson.
Four stories in Mr. Henry's unique style that come alive as children meet characters from the Bible.

All about Jealousy. Read by Frank E. Peretti. 1 cass. (Running Time: 30 mins.). (Wild & Wacky Totally True Bible Stories Ser.). (J). 2000. audio compact disk 3.99 Nelson.

All About Jeeves. unabr. ed. P. G. Wodehouse. Read by Edward Duke & Mark Richards. 2 cass. (Running Time: 3 hrs.). 2000. 16.95 (978-1-882071-98-2(0)) B-B Audio.
Edward Duke brilliantly performs an entire cast of characters in these delightful stories by P.G. Wodehouse, the greatest humorous writer of his age. These selections are adapted from Dukes stage show performed worldwide.Includes 4 Jeeves stories: Jeeve.

All about Letters. abr. ed. Nina Mattikow. Perf. by Purple Balloon Players. 1 cass. (Running Time: 60 mins.). (Cassettes for Kids Ser.). (J). 1992. 5.95 (978-1-55569-531-6(0), 20007) Great Am Audio.
Songs, raps, rhymes & stories.

All about Love. 1 cass. (Music Machine Ser.). (J). 9.95 (AMMA) Brdgstn Multimed Grp.
Children will thrill to even more of the wonderful sounds presented in this series with the original "Music Machine II" tape, a Dove Award & Grammy Award nominee.

All about Love. Stephanie Laurens. Narrated by Simon Prebble. 10 cass. (Running Time: 14 hrs. 15 mins.). (Cynster Family Ser.: Bk. 6). 89.00 (978-0-7887-9638-8(0)) Recorded Bks.

All about Love Cass. Bridgestone Staff. 2004. audio compact disk 5.98 (978-0-7378-0170-5(0)) Brntwd HV.

***All about Lulu.** unabr. ed. Jonathan Evison. Read by Michael Mish. (ENG.). 2011. audio compact disk 34.95 (978-1-61573-528-0(3), 1615735283) Pub: HighBridge. Dist(s): Workman Pub

All about Mars. Bob McDonald. 1 CD. (Running Time: 1 hr.). 2005. audio compact disk 15.95 (978-0-660-19297-0(7)) Canadian Broadcasting CAN.

All about Mortgages. 2nd ed. Contrib. by Garton-Good, Julie. 1999. pap. bk. 19.95 (978-0-7931-3231-7(2)) Kaplan Pubng.

All about Numbers. abr. ed. Nina Mattikow. Perf. by Purple Balloon Players. 1 cass. (Running Time: 60 mins.). (Cassettes for Kids Ser.). (J). 1992. 5.95 (978-1-55569-532-3(9), 20008) Great Am Audio.
Songs, raps, rhymes & stories.

All about Obedience. Read by Frank E. Peretti. 1 cass. (Running Time: 30 mins.). (Wild & Wacky Totally True Bible Stories Ser.). (J). 2000. 3.99 Nelson.

All about Prosperity. Howard Caesar. 3 cass,. (Running Time: 4 hrs. 30 mins.). 1999. 17.95 (978-0-87159-813-4(2)) Unity Schl Christ.

All about Repentance. Perf. by Peace Mtn. Media Works Staff. 1 cass. (Running Time: 45 mins.). Dramatization. (All About Ser.). (J). (ps-3). 1992. 5.95 (978-1-887938-04-4(4)) Snd Concepts.
Teaches children the principle of repentance through music & fun.

All about Scales & How to Use Them. Duane Shinn. 1 cass. 19.95 (HAR-6) Duane Shinn.
Teaches how to form various kinds of piano scales: major, minor (3 varieties-harmonic, melodic & natural), chromatic, whole step, pentatonic & all the modes - Dorian, Lydian, Mixolydian, Frigian, etc.

All about... Series. Perf. by Peace Mtn. Media Works Staff. 3 cass. (Running Time: 2 hrs. 45 mins.). Dramatization. (J). (ps-3). 1992. 21.95 (978-1-887938-09-9(5)) Snd Concepts.

All about Sleep. abr. ed. Jeff Warren. Contrib. by Paul Kennedy. Prod. by Alan Guettel. 2 CDs. (Running Time: 7200 sec.). 2007. audio compact disk 19.95 (978-0-660-19677-0(8), CBC Audio) Pub: Canadian Broadcasting CAN. Dist(s): Georgetown Term
Sleep is a biological and psychological mystery. Producer, Jeff Warren takes us on a 2-CD adventure into the world of sleep and dreams. Jeff slept the sleep of our ancestors enjoying the pleasant awakenings between what they called their first and second sleeps of the night. He also learned what it takes to control what happens in our dreams in a lucid dreaming workshop. He me the first ever historian of sleep and the first anthropologist to study sleep in its natural state. And Jeff found out first hand what researchers are learning about what your brain has been up to while you were out.

All about Songs of Joy. Perf. by Peace Mtn. Media Works Staff. 1 cass. (Running Time: 45 mins.). (All About Ser.). (J). (ps-3). 1995. 9.95 (978-1-887938-12-9(5)) Snd Concepts.
Songs from the "All about...Series".

All about Songs of Love & Family. Perf. by Peace Mtn. Media Works Staff. 1 cass. (Running Time: 45 mins.). (All About Ser.). (J). (ps-3). 1995. 9.95 (978-1-887938-11-2(7)) Snd Concepts.

All about Songs of Peace. Perf. by Peace Mtn. Media Works Staff. 1 cass. (Running Time: 45 mins.). (All About Ser.). (J). (ps-3). 1995. 9.95 (978-1-887938-10-5(9)) Snd Concepts.

All about Stacy. unabr. ed. Patricia Reilly Giff. 1 cass. (Running Time: 46 mins.). (New Kids at the Polk Street School Ser.). (J). (gr. 1-2). 1990. 15.98 incl. pap. bk. & guide. (978-0-8072-0187-9(1), FTR 143 SP, Listening Lib) Random Audio Pubg.

All about Sunday. Perf. by Peace Mtn. Media Works Staff. 1 cass. (Running Time: 45 mins.). Dramatization. (All About Ser.). (J). (ps-3). 1992. 5.95 (978-1-887938-07-5(9)) Snd Concepts.
Teaches the children about Sunday through music & fun.

All about Sunday & Temples. Read by Peace Mtn. Media Works Staff. 1 cass. (Running Time: 45 mins.). Dramatization. (All Abouts Ser.). (J). (ps-3). 1992. 7.95 (978-1-887938-16-7(8)) Snd Concepts.
Teaches children about Sunday & Temples.

All about Temples. Perf. by Peace Mtn. Media Works Staff. 1 cass. (Running Time: 45 mins.). Dramatization. (All About Ser.). (J). (ps-3). 1992. 5.95 (978-1-887938-08-2(7)) Snd Concepts.
Teaches children about the importance of temples through music & fun.

All about Temptation. Read by Frank E. Peretti. 1 cass. (Running Time: 30 mins.). (Wild & Wacky Totally True Bible Stories Ser.). (J). 2000. 3.99 Nelson.

All about the Alphabet. 1 CD. (Running Time: 25 mins.). (J). 1999. audio compact disk 14.95 Ed Activities.
Listeners are introduced to the individual letters, their sounds, & the formation of words from these letters.

All about the Alphabet. Steven Traugh. 1 cass. (Sing & Learn Ser.). (J). bk. 8.95 (00330500) H Leonard.
Teaches skills with letters & phonics. Nine songs including: "The Alpha-Zeto Zoo," "Alphabet Soup," "Aerobics A-Z," & more.

All about the Holy Ghost. Mac Hammond. 1 cass. (Running Time: 1 hour). 2005. 5.00 (978-1-57399-199-5(6)); audio compact disk 5.00 (978-1-57399-264-0(X)) Mac Hammond.

All about the Holy Ghost. Perf. by Peace Mtn. Media Works Staff. 1 cass. (Running Time: 45 mins.). Dramatization. (All About Ser.). (J). (ps-3). 1992. 5.95 (978-1-887938-06-8(0)) Snd Concepts.
Teaches children about the Holy Ghost through music & fun.

All about the U. S. Constitution. Compiled by Linda N. Hackett. 2008. audio compact disk 9.95 (978-1-4276-3088-9(7)) AardGP.

All about the Whole You Vol. 4: The Riddle of Me at the Heart-Wood Tree. Ardys Reverman. Read by Andy Reverman. Illus. by Charlotte Lewis. 1 cass. (Running Time: 1 hr. 33 mins.). (Friendly Universe Collection). 1998. pap. bk. 9.95 (978-0-9625385-5-1(8)) Friendly Univ Pr.
A fantasy adventure with four at risk kids about our senses, offering an evolutionary approach to growth, redefining what it means to be smart, because working together really works.

All about Time. Perf. by Ray Heatherton. 1 CD. (Running Time: 25 min.). (J). 1999. 11.95 (978-0-7925-4256-8(8)); audio compact disk 14.95 (978-0-7925-4257-5(6)) Ed Activities.
Explanations are provided from the second all the way up to a full day. The music combined with the narration provides a basic introducton to the topics.

All about Trees: Early Explorers Early Set B Audio CD. Christopher O'Brien. Adapted by Benchmark Education Staff. (J). 2007. audio compact disk 10.00 (978-1-4108-8215-8(2)) Benchmark Educ.

All about Trust. Read by Frank E. Peretti. (Running Time: 30 mins.). (Wild & Wacky Totally True Bible Stories Ser.). (J). (gr. 2 up). 2000. audio compact disk 3.99 Nelson.

All about You. Dahia Shabaka. (Living & Working Together Ser.). (J). (gr. k). 2000. 7.98 (978-1-58120-976-1(2)) Metro Teaching.

All about You & Your Lover. Howard S. Berg. 1 cass. (Running Time: 1 hr. 30 mins.). 8.95 (493) Am Fed Astrologers.
Get it together by the stars.

All about Your Glory. Composed by Tommy Walker. Contrib. by Bradley Knight & Regi Stone. 2007. audio compact disk 24.98 (978-5-557-49191-4(0), Word Music) Word Enter.

All Alone in the Universe. unabr. ed. Lynne Rae Perkins. Read by Hope Davis. 2 vols. (Running Time: 2 hrs. 54 mins.). (J). (gr. 3-5). 2004. pap. bk. 29.00 (978-0-8072-0443-6(9), Listening Lib); 23.00 (978-0-8072-8419-3(X), YA168CX, Listening Lib) Random Audio Pubg.
When her best friend starts acting as though Debbie doesn't exist, Debbie finds out the hard way about loneliness. But at the end of this coming-of-age story, discover that even the hourly tragedies of elementary school can have a silver lining.

All Along the Way. Perf. by Larnelle Harris. 1 cass. 1998. 7.98 HiLo Plus. (978-0-7601-2574-8(0)) Brentwood Music.

All-American Boys (Unabridged) Audio Book. Walter Cunningham. 2007. audio compact disk 49.99 (978-1-4276-1736-1(8)) AardGP.

All-American Girl. Meg Cabot. 5 cass. (Running Time: 7 hrs. 9 mins.). (All American Girl Ser.: Vol. 1). (J). (gr. 7 up). 2004. 36.00 (978-0-8072-0902-8(3), Listening Lib) Random Audio Pubg.

All-American Girl. Meg Cobot. Read by Ariadne Meyers. 5 vols. (Running Time: 7 hrs. 9 mins.). (J). (gr. 7 up). 2004. pap. bk. 44.00 (978-0-8072-2281-2(X), Listening Lib) Random Audio Pubg.

All-American Girl. unabr. ed. Meg Cabot. Read by Ariadne Meyers. 6 CDs. (Running Time: 7 hrs. 9 mins.). (All American Girl Ser.: Vol. 1). (J). (gr. 7 up). 2004. audio compact disk 42.50 (978-0-8072-1597-5(X), S YA 398 CD, Listening Lib) Pub: Random Audio Pubg. Dist(s): NetLibrary CO

All-American Girls: The U. S. Women's National Soccer Team. Marla Miller. Read by Barbara Caruso. 3 cass. (Running Time: 4 hrs. 15 mins.). (YA). 1999. pap. bk. 40.24 (978-0-7887-3653-7(1), 41019) Recorded Bks.
Introduces the 1999 World Cup team who put women's soccer on front pages everywhere. You'll follow the players from their earliest days on the field to their record-breaking careers.

All-American Girls: The U. S. Women's National Soccer Team. unabr. ed. Marla Miller. Narrated by Barbara Caruso. 3 pieces. (Running Time: 4 hrs. 15 mins.). (gr. 7 up). 2000. 27.00 (978-0-7887-3621-6(3), 95944E7) Recorded Bks.

All-American Girls: The U. S. Women's National Soccer Team, unabr. ed. Marla Miller. Read by Barbara Caruso. 3 cass. (Running Time: 4 hrs. 15 mins.). (YA). 2000. pap. bk. 40.24 (41019X4) Recorded Bks.
Introduces the 1999 World Cup team who put women's soccer on front pages everywhere. You'll follow the players from their earliest days on the field to their record-breaking careers. Includes study guide.

All-American Girls Class set: The U. S. Women's National Soccer Team. Marla Miller. Read by Barbara Caruso. 3 cass. (Running Time: 4 hrs. 15 mins.). (YA). 1999. 97.70 (978-0-7887-3682-7(5), 46986) Recorded Bks.
Introduces the 1999 World Cup team who put women's soccer on front pages everywhere. You'll follow the players from their earliest days on the field to their record-breaking careers.

All-American Harp Solos. Charlie McCoy. 1 cass. (Running Time: 90 mins.). (Learn to Play Ser.). 1998. pap. bk. 17.95 (978-0-7119-6680-2(X)) Music Sales.

All-American Heroes: Superman with Batman & Robin on Radio, collector's ed. Contrib. by DC Comics Staff. 20 cass. (Running Time: 30 hrs.). 1999. bk. & pap. bk. 39.98 (4196) Radio Spirits.
The last survivor of the doomed planet Krypton was the ultimate immigrant, the perfect hero for a young nation of immigrants. As all-American as baseball, Superman championed the oppressed and fought a never-ending battle for "truth, justice and the American way" in his long running radio serial. This collection of 119 episodes brings together some of his greatest radio adventures. "The Baby from Krypton," "Clark Kent, Reporter," "The Shark-Part 1," "The Shark-Part 2," 'The Story of Marina Baum," "Drought in Feeville," "The Monkey Burglar," "Knights of the White Carnation," "The Man Without a Face," "Mystery of the Lost Planet," "The Phantom of the Sea," "Superman vs. Kryptonite." Includes booklet.

All Are Welcome. Marty Haugen. 1995. 10.95 (327); audio compact disk 15.95 (327) GIA Pubns.

All Around America: The Time Traveler's Talk Show. Interview. Anne Siebert & Raymond C. Clark. 2 CD's. (Running Time: 2 hrs. 30 mins.). (AFR.). (gr. 6-12). 2004. audio compact disk 20.00 (978-0-86647-185-5(5)) Pro Lingua.

All Around the Town. Mary Higgins Clark. Read by Kate Nelligan. 2004. 10.95 (978-0-7435-4095-7(6)) Pub: S&S Audio. Dist(s): S and S Inc

All Around the Town. unabr. ed. Mary Higgins Clark. Read by Mary Peiffer. 6 cass. (Running Time: 9 hrs.). 1992. 48.00 (978-0-7366-2271-4(3), 3059) Books on Tape.
College coed accused of professor's murder harbors a murderous second personality.

All Around the World. Skip West. 1 cass. (Running Time: 40 mins.). (J). (ps-2). 1993. pap. bk. 9.98 (978-0-9660947-6-3(X), EK5003) Emphasis Ent.
Wide variety of multinational songs with kid-centered themes whose rythms & melodies represent many lands.

All Around the World. Skip West. Perf. by Skip West. 1 CD. (Running Time: 40 mins.). (J). (ps-2). 1999. audio compact disk 14.98 (978-1-893967-01-4(8), EKCD5003) Emphasis Ent.

All Aunt Hagar's Children. unabr. ed. Edward P. Jones. Narrated by Peter Francis James. 11 cass. 2006. 94.95 (978-0-7927-4532-7(9), CSL 1048) AudioGO.

All Aunt Hagar's Children. unabr. ed. Edward P. Jones. Narrated by Peter Francis James. 12 CDs. (Running Time: 15 hrs.). 2006. audio compact disk 112.95 (978-0-7927-4518-1(3), SLD 1048); audio compact disk 69.95 (978-0-7927-4555-6(8), CMP 1048) AudioGO.

All Aunt Hagar's Children. unabr. ed. Edward P. Jones. Read by Peter Francis James. 13 CDs. (Running Time: 55800 sec.). 2006. audio compact disk 44.95 (978-0-06-085290-0(9), Harper Audio) HarperCollins Pubs.

***All Aunt Hagar's Children: Stories.** unabr. ed. Edward P. Jones. Read by Peter Francis James. (ENG.). 2006. (978-0-06-113459-3(7), Harper Audio); (978-0-06-113460-9(0), Harper Audio) HarperCollins Pubs.

All Because of Jesus. Contrib. by Casting Crowns. (Mastertrax Ser.). 2007. audio compact disk 9.98 (978-5-557-60391-1(3)) Beach St.

All Because of You. Perf. by Lori Wilke. 1 cass. (Running Time: 4 min.). 1998. 9.98 Sound track. (978-1-891916-34-2(3)) Spirit To Spirit.

All Blues Soloing for Jazz Guitar: Scales, Licks, Concepts & Choruses. Jim Ferguson. 2001. audio compact disk 24.95 (978-0-7866-4285-4(8)) Mel Bay.

All Bones & Lies. unabr. ed. Anne Fine. Read by Martyn Read. 6 cass. (Running Time: 8 hrs.). 2001. (978-0-7531-1192-5(6)) ISIS Audio GBR.
On the face of it Colin is an ideal citizen. He holds down a responsible job for the council. He visits his aged mother, Norah, shops for her, cooks for her, and listens to her grumbles. He also keeps in touch with his sister Dilys, long estranged from his mother, in a vain attempt to maintain family ties. But neither Dilys, Norah nor Colin?s colleagues know about his other ? much more secret ? life that involves a garden shed, a circus acrobat, a much adored three-year- old charmer, and a certain Mr Haksar?s increasingly disquieting penchant for squabbling with his neighbours.

All Brave Sailors: The Sinking of the Anglo Saxon 1940. J. Revell Carr. Read by George Wilson. 2004. 15.95 (978-0-7435-4096-4(4)) Pub: S&S Audio. Dist(s): S and S Inc

All but My Life. unabr. ed. Gerda Weissmann Klein. Read by Grace Conlin. 7 cass. (Running Time: 10 hrs.). 1997. 49.95 (978-0-7861-1157-2(7), 1927) Blckstn Audio.
A young woman's three frightful years as a slave laborer of the Nazis & her miraculous liberation.

***All but My Life.** unabr. ed. Gerda Weissmann Klein. Read by Grace Conlin. (Running Time: 9 hrs. 30 mins.). 2010. 29.95 (978-1-4417-6725-7(8)); audio compact disk 90.00 (978-1-4417-6723-3(1)) Blckstn Audio.

All but My Life. unabr. ed. Gerda Weissmann Klein. Narrated by Suzanne Toren. 7 cass. (Running Time: 9 hrs. 45 mins.). 1997. 60.00 (978-0-7887-1313-2(2), 95046E7) Recorded Bks.
An unforgettable testament to the power of human courage & love in the midst of the Holocaust. Her remarkable memoirs have been made into the stirring documentary, "One Survivor Remembers.".

All By Myself/Family Fun. Steck-Vaughn Staff. 2002. (978-0-7398-5907-0(2)) SteckVau.

***All Clear.** unabr. ed. Connie Willis. Read by Katherine Kellgren. (Running Time: 19 hrs.). 2010. 44.97 (978-1-4418-7579-2(4), 9781441875792, BADLE); 29.99 (978-1-4418-7577-8(8), 9781441875778, Brilliance MP3); 44.97 (978-1-4418-7578-5(6), 9781441875785, Brlnc Audio MP3 Lib); audio compact disk 39.99 (978-1-4418-7575-4(1), 9781441875754, Bril Audio CD Unabri); audio compact disk 99.97 (978-1-4418-7576-1(X), 9781441875761, BriAudCD Unabrid) Brilliance Audio.

All Clear: Idioms in Context. 2nd ed. Helen K. Fragiadakis & Larry Statan. (J). 1993. stu. ed. 36.00 (978-0-8384-4126-8(2)) Heinle.

All Corvettes Are Red. unabr. ed. James Schefter. Read by Raymond Todd. 10 cass. (Running Time: 14 hrs. 30 mins.). 2000. 69.95 (978-0-7861-1677-5(3), 2503) Blckstn Audio.
Inside story of the people who saved & reinvented the Corvette, from the drawing board to the assembly line.

All Corvettes Are Red. unabr. ed. James Schefter. Read by Raymond Todd. (Running Time: 14 hrs. NaN mins.). 2008. cass. & audio compact disk 110.00 (978-1-4332-3447-7(5)); cass. & audio compact disk 29.95 (978-1-4332-3448-4(3)) Blckstn Audio.

All Creatures Great & Small. 1 cass. 1985. 9.95 (978-0-440-85020-5(7), Random AudioBks) Random Audio Pubg.

All Creatures Great & Small. unabr. ed. James Herriot. Read by Christopher Timothy. 12 CDs. (Running Time: 56160 sec.). (Vet Ser.). 2006. audio compact disk 110.95 (978-0-7927-4506-8(X), SLD1036) AudioGO.

All Creatures Great & Small. unabr. rev. ed. James Herriot. Read by Christopher Timothy. 12 CDs. (Running Time: 16 hrs. 0 mins. 0 sec.). (ENG., 2002. audio compact disk 49.95 (978-1-55927-773-0(4)) Pub: Macmill Audio. Dist(s): Macmillan

All Day Singin' Directed By Dave Streit. Contrib. by Bill & Gloria Gaither and Their Homecoming Friends & Bill Gaither. Prod. by Bill Gaither & Donald Boggs. (Gaither Gospel Ser.). 2005. 19.98 (978-5-558-66380-8(4)) Gaither Music Co.

All Day Singin' at the Dome. Directed By Ben Speer. Contrib. by Bill & Gloria Gaither and Their Homecoming Friends. Prod. by Bill Gaither. (Gaither Gospel Ser.). 1998. audio compact disk 13.98 (978-7-474-05246-9(6)) Spring House Music.

All Fall Down. abr. ed. Lee Gruenfeld. Read by Frank Muller. 2 cass. (Running Time: 3 hrs.). 1995. 16.95 (978-1-879371-90-3(1), 20380) Pub Mills.
A brilliant extortionist nicknamed Captain Marvel has figured out how to make airline navigational systems go haywire at will, holding hostage the entire U.S. air traffic system & in effect, the American public. FBI agent Jack Webster & his former assistant, Dr. Amy Goldberg, head a team of bureaucrats & techno-wizards assigned to stop the mad genius as he engages them in a hightech cross country game of cat-&-mouse. Bo Kinkaid, an ace flying pilot decorated in Vietnam & WWII, is drawn into the web of intrigue as events unite him & Agent Webster in a fateful intersection with the terrorist.

All Fishermen Are Liars: True Tales from the Dry Dock Bar. unabr. ed. Linda Greenlaw. Read by Linda Greenlaw. (Running Time: 6 hrs.). 2004. 39.25 (978-1-59335-834-1(2), 1593358342, Brlnc Audio MP3 Lib); 24.95 (978-1-59335-664-4(1), 1593356641, Brilliance MP3); 27.95 (978-1-59355-101-8(0), 1593551010, BAU); 69.25 (978-1-59355-102-5(9), 1593551029, BrilAudUnabridg); audio compact disk 29.95 (978-1-59355-103-2(7), 1593551037, Bril Audio CD Unabri); audio compact disk 82.25 (978-1-59355-104-9(5), 1593551045, BriAudCD Unabrid) Brilliance Audio.
Just before Christmas, Linda meets up with her best friend and fellow fisherman Alden Leeman for lunch and a drink at the Dry Dock, a well-worn watering hole in Portland, Maine. Alden, the captain of Linda's first fishing expedition, has seen his share of mishaps and adventures at sea. When Linda shares memories of navigating her ship through one of the craziest storms she's ever seen, Alden quickly follows up with his own tales. Then other fishermen, who are sitting on the periphery attentively listening, decide to weigh in with yarns of their own. All Fishermen Are Liars brims with true stories of the most eccentric crew member, the funniest episode, the biggest fish, and the wildest night at sea. Denizens of the Dry Dock drift in and out as the bar begins to swell with rounds of drinks and tales that increase in drama. Here are some of the greatest fishing stories ever - all relayed by Linda Greenlaw in her inimitable style. All Fishermen Are Liars will give listeners what they have come to love and expect from Linda Greenlaw - luminous descriptions and edge-of-the-seat thrills. It's the perfect book for anyone who loves fishing and the sea.

All Fishermen Are Liars: True Tales from the Dry Dock Bar. unabr. ed. Linda Greenlaw. Read by Linda Greenlaw. (Running Time: 6 hrs.). 2004. 39.25 (978-1-59710-008-3(0), 1597100080, BADLE); 24.95 (978-1-59710-009-0(9), 1597100099, BAD) Brilliance Audio.

All for Alex: A Circle of Friends. Barbara Maines & George Robinson. 1998. 55.95 (978-1-873942-42-0(7)) Pub: P Chapman GBR. Dist(s): SAGE

All for Freedom. Perf. by Sweet Honey in the Rock. 1 cass. (J). (gr. k up). 1989. 9.98 incl. Norelco pkg. (978-1-877737-33-6(X), MLP 2230); audio compact disk 12.98 CD. (978-1-877737-34-3(8)) MFLP CA.
Musical celebration of Afro-American roots, history & future with stories.

All for Love. Contrib. by Lenny LeBlanc & Don Moen. 2007. audio compact disk 13.99 (978-5-557-63540-0(8)); audio compact disk 29.98 (978-5-557-63539-4(4)) Integrity Music.

All for the Union: The Civil War Diary & Letters of Elisha Hunt Rhodes. unabr. ed. Robert H. Rhodes. Narrated by Norman Dietz. 8 cass. (Running Time: 11 hrs. 30 mins.). 1991. 70.00 (978-1-55690-008-2(2), 91406E7) Recorded Bks.
Elisha Hunt Rhodes was 19 when he began as a private in the Union Army, so narrow-chested & slope-shouldered the examining physician was tempted to bar him from the service. His fellow recruits elected him first sergeant, although he admitted later that he had little idea just what a first sergeant's duty might be. He left the army four years later at the age of 23, having risen within the ranks to colonel of his 2nd Rhode Island regiment. It is the character of the diarist himself which propels us through four years of diary entries & letters.

All for You (Dedication to Nat King Cole Trio) Perf. by Diana Krall et al. 1 cass., 1 CD. 8.78 (IMP 182); audio compact disk 13.58 CD Jewel box. (IMP 182) NewSound.

***All Frontiers Are Jealous.** unabr. ed. L. Ron Hubbard. Read by Richard Rocco et al. Narrated by R. F. Daley. 2 CDs. (Running Time: 1 hr. 20 mins.). (Stories from the Golden Age Ser.). (YA). (gr. 7 up). 2010. audio compact disk 9.95 (978-1-59212-338-4(4)) Gala Pr LLC.

All Goalies Are Crazy. unabr. ed. Rob Childs. Read by Tom Watt. 1 cass. (Running Time: 1 hrs. 25 mins.). 2002. (978-1-85549-780-1(8)) Cover To Cover GBR.
Luke's enthusiasm and crazy antics make him a surprisingly serious rival to the Swilsby Swifts regular goalie.

All God's Children & Blue Suede Shoes. unabr. ed. Kenneth A. Myers. Read by Jeff Riggenbach. 5 cass. (Running Time: 7 hrs.). 1995. 39.95 (978-0-7861-0854-1(1), 1652) Blckstn Audio.
Where did popular culture come from? Why is it the way it is? How does it influence Americans in general & Christians in particular? Ken Myers provides fascinating answers to these questions. He sees pop culture as a culture of diversion, preventing people from asking questions about their origin & destiny & about the meaning of life.

All God's Children & Blue Suede Shoes: Christians & Popular Culture. unabr. ed. Kenneth A. Myers. Read by Jeff Riggenbach. (Running Time: 7 hrs. 0 mins.). 2010. 29.95 (978-1-4417-2597-4(0)); audio compact disk 69.00 (978-1-4417-2594-3(6)) Blckstn Audio.

All God's Children Need Traveling Shoes. unabr. ed. Maya Angelou. Narrated by Lynne Thigpen. 5 cass. (Running Time: 7 hrs. 15 mins.). 1995. 44.00 (978-0-7887-0111-5(8), 94352E7) Recorded Bks.
Poet, musician & performer Maya Angelou's exploration of what it means to be an African-American in Ghana, where she moved in 1962 to join a community of "Revolutionary Returnees" inspired by the promise of pan-Africanism.

All God's Children Sing. Perf. by Sharon L. Beckstead. 2 cass. (Running Time: 2 hrs.). 1992. 24.95 (978-1-55145-304-0(5)) Pub: Wood Lake CAN. Dist(s): Words Distrib

All God's Dangers, Pt. 1. unabr. collector's ed. Theodore Rosengarten. Read by John MacDonald. 7 cass. (Running Time: 10 hrs. 30 mins.). 1988. 56.00 (978-0-7366-1318-7(8), 2224-A) Books on Tape.
Story of a remarkable man who stood up for his rights in the early 1900's, in black skin, in the south.

All God's Dangers, Pt. 2. collector's ed. Theodore Rosengarten. Read by John MacDonald. 7 cass. (Running Time: 10 hrs. 30 min.). 1988. 56.00 (978-0-7366-1319-4(6), 2224-B) Books on Tape.

All Gone: L-Book. RJ Nolan. Sheri. 2007. 13.95 (978-0-9800846-0-3(1)) Lbook Pub.

All Good Things. Michael Jan Friedman. (Star Trek). 2004. 10.95 (978-0-7435-4625-6(3)) Pub: S&S Audio. Dist(s): S and S Inc

All Grown up & No Place to Go. Rick Reynolds. 1 CD. (Running Time: 1 hr. 30 mins.). 2001. audio compact disk 19.98 (R2 72623) Rhino Enter.

All Hail. Perf. by B. J. Thomas. 2006. audio compact disk 12.95 (978-1-59987-417-3(2)) Braun Media.

All Hallows' Moon. unabr. ed. Thomas E. Fuller. 1 CD. (Running Time: 90 min.). Dramatization. 1997. audio compact disk 15.00 (978-0-929483-30-6(8)) Centauri Express Co.

All Hallows' Moon. unabr. ed. Thomas E. Fuller. 1 cass. (Running Time: 90 min.). Dramatization. 2002. 12.95 (978-0-929483-22-1(7)) Centauri Express Co.
The setting is the Old West: Mother Lode, New Mexico. A handful of people - drovers, saloon girls, barkeep, preacher and sheriff - wait in a saloon on a stormy Hallowe'en night. They wait for the dawn, when they will go their separate ways, and Mother Lode will truly become a ghost town.

All Hands Down: The True Story of the Soviet Attack on the USS Scorpion. unabr. ed. Jerome Preisler & Kenneth Sewell. Read by Malcolm Hillgartner. (Running Time: 27000 sec.). 2008. audio compact disk 29.95 (978-1-4332-4620-3(1)); audio compact disk & audio compact disk 29.95 (978-1-4332-4619-7(8)) Blckstn Audio.

All Hands Down: The True Story of the Soviet Attack on USS Scorpion. unabr. ed. Kenneth Sewell & Jerome Preisler. Read by Malcolm Hillgartner. (Running Time: 8 hrs. 0 mins.). 2008. 54.95 (978-1-4332-4617-3(1)); audio compact disk 60.00 (978-1-4332-4618-0(X)) Blckstn Audio.

All Hands On: An Introduction to West African Percussion Ensembles. Lynne Jessup. Perf. by Isaac Hirt-Manheimer. 2000. pap. bk. 14.95 (978-0-937203-94-1(7)) World Music Pr.

All He Ever Wanted. unabr. ed. Anita Shreve. Read by Dennis Boutsikaris. (ENG.). 2005. 14.98 (978-1-59483-232-1(3)) Pub: Hachet Audio. Dist(s): HachBkGrp

All He Ever Wanted. unabr. ed. Anita Shreve. Read by Dennis Boutsikaris. (Running Time: 9 hrs.). (ENG.). 2009. 64.98 (978-1-60024-958-7(2)) Pub: Hachet Audio. Dist(s): HachBkGrp

All I Ever Wanted Was to Be Loved: Adult Child & Relationships. Earnie Larsen. 1 cass. (Running Time: 1 hr.). 1989. 10.95 (978-1-56047-017-5(8), A121) E Larsen Enterprises.
Discusses common syndromes in an attempt to get love while stuck in co-dependency.

All I Have Is Blue. unabr. ed. James Colbert. Narrated by Mark Hammer. 6 cass. (Running Time: 8 hrs.). 1994. 51.00 (978-0-7887-0033-0(2), 94232E7) Recorded Bks.
When a Louisiana cop saves a young boy from a burning boat, his life is turned upside down.

All I Hold Dear. abr. ed. Jennie L. Hansen. 2 cass. (Running Time: 2 hrs.). 1999. 13.95 (978-1-57734-478-0(2), 07002106) Covenant Comms.

All I Know about Animal Behavior I Learned in Loehmann's Dressing Room. Erma Bombeck. Narrated by Barbara Rosenblat. 4 CDs. (Running Time: 4 hrs. 15 mins.). 2001. audio compact disk 33.00 (978-0-7887-3711-4(2), C1068E7) Recorded Bks.
The behavioral patterns of the creatures in the wild & the couple in the duplex next door.

All I Know about Animal Behavior I Learned in Loehmann's Dressing Room. unabr. ed. Erma Bombeck. Read by Kate Reading. 4 cass. (Running Time: 4 hrs.). 1996. 24.00 (978-0-7366-3245-4(X), 3904) Books on Tape.
Bombeck's wit is brought to life in her ruminations of the strikingly similar behaviors of the animal kingdom & that of the human species.

All I Know about Animal Behavior I Learned in Loehmann's Dressing Room. unabr. ed. Erma Bombeck. Narrated by Barbara Rosenblat. 3 cass. (Running Time: 4 hrs. 15 mins.). 26.00 (978-0-7887-0453-6(2), 94645E7) Recorded Bks.
In this collection of hilarious tidbits, Bombeck turns her talents to the animal kingdom: the behavioral patterns of the creatures in the wild & the couple in the duplex next door. Available to libraries only.

All I Know about Animal Behavior I Learned in Loehmann's Dressing Room. unabr. ed. Erma Bombeck. Narrated by Barbara Rosenblat. 1 CD. 1999. audio compact disk 33.00 (C1068) Recorded Bks.

All I Need Is You. abr. ed. Johanna Lindsey. Read by Sandra Burr. (Running Time: 3 hrs.). (Straton Ser.). 2009. audio compact disk 14.99 (978-1-4233-6617-1(4), 9781423366171, BCD Value Price) Brilliance Audio.

All I Need Is You. unabr. ed. Johanna Lindsey. Read by Sandra Burr. (Running Time: 9 hrs.). (Straton Ser.). 2009. 39.97 (978-1-4233-6614-0(X), 9781423366140, Brlnc Audio MP3 Lib); 39.97 (978-1-4233-6616-4(6), 9781423366164, BADLE); 24.99 (978-1-4233-6613-3(1), 9781423366133, Brilliance MP3); 24.99 (978-1-4233-6615-7(8), 9781423366157, BAD); audio compact disk 87.97 (978-1-4233-6612-6(3), 9781423366126, BriAudCD Unabrid); audio compact disk 29.99 (978-1-4233-6611-9(5), 9781423366119, Bril Audio CD Unabri) Brilliance Audio.

All I Need Is You, Set. unabr. ed. Johanna Lindsey. Read by Sandra Burr. 6 cass. 1999. 57.25 (FS9-34384) Highsmith.

All I Really Need to Know I Learned in Kindergarten: Fifteenth Anniversary Edition Reconsidered, Revised, & Expanded with Twenty-Five New Essays. 15th unabr. ed. Robert Fulghum. Read by Robert Fulghum. 4 CDs. (Running Time: 5 hrs.). (ENG.). 2003. audio compact disk 29.95 (978-0-7393-0810-3(6)) Pub: Random Audio Pubg. Dist(s): Random

All I Want, Level 5. Margaret Johnson. Contrib. by Philip Prowse. (Running Time: 3 hrs. 2 mins.). (Cambridge English Readers Ser.). (ENG.). 2000. 15.00 (978-0-521-79455-8(2)) Cambridge U Pr.

All I Want for Christmas. unabr. ed. Nora Roberts. Read by Patrick G. Lawlor. (Running Time: 3 hrs.). 2009. 14.99 (978-1-4418-2993-1(8), 9781441829931, Brilliance MP3); 39.97 (978-1-4418-2994-8(6), 9781441829948, Brlnc Audio MP3 Lib); 39.97 (978-1-4418-2995-5(4), 9781441829955, BADLE); audio compact disk 14.99 (978-1-4418-2991-7(1), 9781441829917, Bril Audio CD Unabri); audio compact disk 79.97 (978-1-4418-2992-4(X), 9781441829924, BriAudCD Unabrid) Brilliance Audio.

All in One Piece. Cecelia Tishy. Read by Anna Fields. (Running Time: 30600 sec.). 2006. 72.95 (978-0-7861-4516-4(1)); audio compact disk 90.00 (978-0-7861-7188-0(X)) Blckstn Audio.

All in One Piece. unabr. ed. Cecelia Tishy. Read by Anna Fields. (Running Time: 30600 sec.). 2006. audio compact disk 29.95 (978-0-7861-7622-9(9)) Blckstn Audio.

All in the Family: 1 Samuel 25:23-25. Ed Young. 1991. 4.95 (978-0-7417-1860-0(X), 860) Win Walk.

All in the Family Doctor Included. unabr. ed. Vladimir Tsesis. Read by Pat Bottino. 9 cass. (Running Time: 13 hrs. 30 min.). 1999. 62.95 (2435) Blckstn Audio.
Brings poignant moments, cozy chuckles & sage advice from his busy pediatrics practice. Speaks about the importance & the beauty of the American family & its glorious triumphs over the dramatic predicaments facing modern society.

All in the Family, Doctor Included. unabr. ed. Vladimir A. Tsesis. Read by Pat Bottino. 9 cass. (Running Time: 13 hrs.). 2006. 62.95 (978-0-7861-1607-2(2), 2435) Blckstn Audio.

All in the Golden Afternoon see Treasury of Lewis Carroll

All Inclusive. Judy Astley. 7 cass. (Running Time: 7 hrs. 55 mins.). (Isis Cassettes Ser.). (J). 2005. 54.95 (978-0-7531-3407-8(1)) Pub: ISIS Lrg Prnt GBR. Dist(s): Ulverscroft US

All Inclusive. unabr. ed. Judy Astley. Read by Jacqueline King. 7 CDs. (Running Time: 7 hrs. 55 mins.). (Isis (CDs) Ser.). (J). 2005. audio compact disk 71.95 (978-0-7531-2444-4(0)) Pub: ISIS Lrg Prnt GBR. Dist(s): Ulverscroft US

All Inclusive Love & Removing the Mask. Marianne Williamson. Read by Marianne Williamson. 1 cass. (Running Time: 90 mins.). (Lectures on a Course in Miracles). 1999. 10.00 (978-1-56170-548-1(9), M853) Hay House.

***All Is Forgotten, Nothing Is Lost.** unabr. ed. Lan Samantha Chang. 2010. audio compact disk 26.95 (978-1-61573-560-0(7), 1615735607) Pub: HighBridge. Dist(s): Workman Pub

All Is Vanity: A Novel. unabr. ed. Christina Schwarz. Read by Blair Brown. 7 cass. (Running Time: 10 hrs. 30 mins.). 2002. 64.00 (978-0-7366-8817-8(X)) Books on Tape.
Hungry for the world's regard, Margaret struggles against the stagnation in her life and betrays her childhood friend Letty.

All Is Well. Perf. by Myrrh. 1 CD. (Running Time: 1 hr.). 2002. audio compact disk 14.99 (978-0-9725443-4-4(8)); 9.99 (978-0-9725443-5-1(6)) Pub: Myrrh Pub. Dist(s): STL Dist NA
A Christmas recording that features both group vocals and violin. There is incredible diversity on this project, with everything from jazz, to adult contemporary, to sacred violin. Myrrh's approach breaks the stereotype surrounding Christmas songs, by "spicing up" many old favorites.

All It Takes Is Guts. unabr. ed. Walter Williams. Read by Peter Kjenaas. 5 cass. (Running Time: 7 hrs.). 1988. 39.95 (978-0-7861-0020-0(6), 1020) Blckstn Audio.
A collection of Walter Williams' essays, drawn from his syndicated column.

All-Jazz Real Book. Contrib. by Chuck Sher. 2005. pap. bk. 44.00 (978-1-883217-14-3(8), 00242119); pap. bk. 44.00 (978-1-883217-34-1(2), 00242120); pap. bk. 44.00 (978-1-883217-35-8(0), 00242121) Pub: Sher Music. Dist(s): H Leonard

All Kinds of Minds. 5 cass. 1993. 48.90 (978-0-8388-2091-9(3)) Ed Pub Serv.

All Kinds of Weather Audio CD. Adapted by Benchmark Education Company Staff. Based on a work by Francisco Blane. (My First Reader's Theater Ser.). (J). (gr. k-1). 2008. audio compact disk 10.00 (978-1-60634-088-2(3)) Benchmark Educ.

All Mortal Flesh. unabr. ed. Julia Spencer-Fleming. Narrated by Suzanne Toren. 11 CDs. (Running Time: 51180 sec.). (Clare Fergusson/Russ Van Alstyne Mystery Ser.). 2006. audio compact disk 99.95 (978-0-7927-4368-2(7), SLD 992) AudioGO.

All My Children: 11 Sam. 3:2-5, 12-25. Ed Young. 1 cass. (Running Time: 60 min.). 1991. 4.95 (978-0-7417-1862-4(6), 862) Win Walk.

All My Dangerous Friends. unabr. ed. Sonya Hartnett. Read by Kate Hosking. 5 cass. (Running Time: 5 hrs.). (YA). 1999. 40.00 (978-1-74030-051-3(3), 591216) Pub: Bolinda Pubng AUS. Dist(s): Bolinda Pub Inc

All My Fathers: Characters in a Small Texas Town that Gave a Boy His Most Memorable Life Lessons. Short Stories. Tuck Kamin. 2cds. (Running Time: 131 mins.). (ENG.). 2006. audio compact disk 17.95 (978-0-9771231-0-0(3)) T Kamin.

All My Friends Are Going to Be Strangers: A Novel. unabr. ed. Larry McMurtry. Narrated by John Randolph Jones. 6 cass. (Running Time: 8 hrs. 45 mins.). 1990. 51.00 (978-1-55690-009-9(0), 90003E7) Recorded Bks.
Set in the early 60s, this is a very funny (& raunchy) satire of life in Texas & California & a true American portrait of an artist as a young man.

All My Friends Are Going to Be Strangers: A Novel. unabr. collector's ed. Larry McMurtry. Read by Wolfram Kandinsky. 7 cass. (Running Time: 10 hrs. 30 mins.). 1986. 56.00 (978-0-7366-1044-5(8), 1974) Books on Tape.
Danny Deck is a promising young writer whose nearly fatal mistake is to cut himself off from his roots. He drifts from his native Texas to California & back, falls in love & looks for ties that will bind him to people & places.

All My Life. Contrib. by Michael Lawrence. (ENG.). 2008. audio compact disk 24.99 (978-5-557-43539-0(5)) Allegis.

All My Praise. Contrib. by Selah. (Worship Tracks (Word Tracks) Ser.). 2006. audio compact disk 8.98 (978-5-558-26927-7(8), Word Music) Word Enter.

All My Relations. unabr. ed. Grandmother Kitty. Composed by Jason Brown. Featuring David Catlin-Birch. 1 cass. (Running Time: 1 hr. 12 mins.). 1997. 5.00 (978-0-9663401-1-2(6), 101-4) Pub: BMA Studios. Dist(s): Baker Taylor
GRANDMOTHER KITTY, descended from the Nakota people was a captivating storyteller. The cassette is approximately 72 minutes long and is appropriate for all age groups. The humorous short tales appeal to children of all ages. The stories have deeper meanings and teachings appealing to adults including a poignant reminiscence of Grandmother's traditional Nakota Grandparents and the wisdom they imparted to her. The accompanying music designed by Jason Brown is based on traditional songs and instruments. David Catlin-Birch of World Party contributes guitar solos.ALL MY RELATIONS has been heard on Northeast Public Radio and the 28 affiliated stations of AIROS (American Indian Radio On Satellite).

All My Relations. unabr. ed. Grandmother Kitty. Composed by Jason Brown. Featuring David Catlin-Birch. 1 CD. (Running Time: 1 hr. 12 mins.). (ENG.). (YA). 1997. audio compact disk 15.00 (978-0-9663401-0-5(8), 101-2) BMA Studios.

All My Sons. unabr. abr. ed. Arthur Miller. Perf. by James Farentino et al. 2 CDs. (Running Time: 1 hr. 49 mins.). Dramatization. (gr. 9-12). 2001. audio compact disk 25.95 (978-1-58081-110-1(8), CDWTA7) Pub: L A Theatre. Dist(s): NetLibrary CO
World War II is over & peace reigns in American suburbia. Under a tree in the Keller family's placid backyard - planted to commemorate a son missing in action - Chris Keller courts Annie, the charming, forthright young woman his brother left behind. But their growing passion disturbs the surface calm of the Keller household. When a storm blows down the memorial tree, the family secret is uprooted, setting the characters on a terrifying journey toward truth.

All-New Atkins Advantage: 12 Weeks to a New Body, a New You, a New Life. Stuart L. Trager & Colette Heimowitz. 2007. audio compact disk 24.95 (978-1-4272-0287-1(7)) Pub: Macmill Audio. Dist(s): Macmillan

All Night Long. abr. ed. Jayne Ann Krentz. Read by David Colacci & Kathy Garver. 5. (Running Time: 21600 sec.). Orig. Title: Ooru naito rongu 3: Saishuu-shô. 2007. audio compact disk 14.99 (978-1-59737-357-9(5), 9781597373579, BCD Value Price) Brilliance Audio.
Please enter a Synopsis.

All Night Long. unabr. ed. Jayne Ann Krentz. Read by David Colacci & Kathy Garver. 7 cass. (Running Time: 36000 sec.). Orig. Title: Ooru naito rongu 3: Saishuu-shô. 2005. 32.95 (978-1-59600-255-5(7), 9781596002555) Brilliance Audio.
Shy, studious Irene Stenson and wild, privileged Pamela Webb had been the best of friends for one short high school summer. Their friendship ended the night Pamela dropped Irene off at home - and Irene walked in to discover her parents' bodies on the kitchen floor. It was ruled a murder-suicide, and Irene fled the northern California town of Dunsley. But seventeen years later, when Pamela sends a cryptic email asking for help, Irene returns to her hometown to find her old friend has died suddenly, leaving behind a lot of ugly, unanswered questions. Caught up in a firestorm of desperate deceit and long-buried secrets, Irene knows it would probably be smarter to just pack up and leave Dunsley behind again, but her reporter's instinct - and her own hunger to know the truth - compel her to extend her stay at the local lodge. Even more compelling is the man who runs the place - a hazel-eyed ex-Marine who's as used to giving orders as Irene is to ignoring them. Luke Danner can see the terror beneath Irene Stenson's confident exterior - and he is intent on protecting her. But he is also driven by passions of his own, and together they will risk far more than local gossip to sort out what happened to Pamela Webb, and what really happened on that long-ago summer night.

All Night Long. unabr. ed. Jayne Ann Krentz. Read by Kathy Garver and David Colacci. (Running Time: 10 hrs.). Orig. Title: Ooru naito rongu 3: Saishuu-shô. 2006. 39.25 (978-1-59710-889-8(8), 9781597108898, BADLE); 24.95 (978-1-59710-888-1(X), 9781597108881, BAD) Brilliance Audio.

All Night Long. unabr. ed. Jayne Ann Krentz. Read by David Colacci & Kathy Garver. (Running Time: 36000 sec.). Orig. Title: Ooru naito rongu 3: Saishuu-shô. 2006. 82.25 (978-1-59600-256-2(5), 9781596002562, BriAudUnabridg); audio compact disk 92.25 (978-1-59600-259-3(X), 9781596002593, BriAudCD Unabrid); audio compact disk 34.95 (978-1-59600-258-6(1), 9781596002586); audio compact disk 39.25 (978-1-59335-976-8(4), 9781593359768, Brinc Audio MP3 Lib) Brilliance Audio.

All Night Long. unabr. ed. Jayne Ann Krentz. Read by Kathy Garver. 1 MP3-CD. (Running Time: 36000 sec.). Orig. Title: Ooru naito rongu 3: Saishuu-shô. 2006. audio compact disk 24.95 (978-1-59335-975-1(6), 9781593359751, Brilliance MP3) Brilliance Audio.

All-of-a-Kind Family. Sydney Taylor. Read by Suzanne Toren. (Running Time: 4 hrs.). 2005. 21.95 (978-1-60083-555-1(4)) Iofy Corp.

All-of-a-Kind Family. Sydney Taylor. Read by Suzanne Toren. (Running Time: 14400 sec.). (J). (gr. 4-7). 2006. audio compact disk 27.95 (978-1-59316-086-9(0)) Listen & Live.

All-of-a-Kind Family. unabr. ed. Sydney Taylor. Read by Suzanne Toren. 3 cass. (Running Time: 4 hrs.). (Sydney Taylor Ser.). (J). (gr. 3-7). 2000. 21.95 (978-1-885408-53-2(6), LL045) Listen & Live.
Meet the All-of-a-Kind Family: Ella, Henny, Sarah, Charlotte & Gertie. They live with their parents in New York City at the turn of the century.

All-of-A-Kind Family. unabr. ed. Sydney Taylor. Read by Suzanne Toren. (J). 2007. 34.99 (978-1-59895-919-2(0)) Find a World.

All-of-a-Kind Family Downtown. Sydney Taylor. Read by Suzanne Toren. (Running Time: 4 hrs.). 2005. 21.95 (978-1-60083-556-8(2)) Iofy Corp.

All-of-a-Kind Family Downtown. Sydney Taylor. Read by Suzanne Toren. (Running Time: 14400 sec.). (J). (gr. 4-7). 2006. audio compact disk 27.95 (978-1-59316-087-6(9)) Listen & Live.

All-of-a-Kind Family Downtown. unabr. ed. Sydney Taylor. Narrated by Suzanne Toren. 3 cass. (Running Time: 4 hrs.). (Sydney Taylor Ser.). (J). (gr. 3-6). 2001. 21.95 (978-1-885408-62-4(5), LL054) Listen & Live.
This sequel finds talented Ella, mischevious Henny, studious Sarah, dreamy Charlotte, & little Gertie helping Mama with their new baby brother, Charlie.

All-of-A-Kind Family Downtown. unabr. ed. Sydney Taylor. Read by Suzanne Toren. (J). 2007. 34.99 (978-1-59895-976-5(X)) Find a World.

All of Grace. Ed. by Lloyd Hildebrand. (Pure Gold Classics). (ENG., 2007. pap. bk. 11.99 (978-0-88270-335-0(8)) Bridge-Logos.

All of Grace. unabr. ed. Charles H. Spurgeon. 3 CDs. (Running Time: 3 hrs. 30 mins. 0 sec.). (ENG.). 2006. audio compact disk 18.98 (978-1-59644-266-5(2), Hovel Audio) christianaud.

All of Life Is a Holy Festival. abr. ed. Joyce Rupp. (Running Time: 3540 sec.). 2006. audio compact disk 16.95 (978-1-59471-120-6(8)) Ave Maria Pr.

All of Me. Contrib. by Selah. (Sound Performance Soundtracks Ser.). 2005. audio compact disk 5.98 (978-5-559-22555-5(X)) Pt of Grace Ent.

All of Us Will Shine. Perf. by Tickle Tune Typhoon Staff. 1 cass. (J). 8.98 (201) MFLP CA.
Songs include: "Let's Be Friends," "Flower," "East-West," "Pearly White Waltz," "Fine Wind Blowing" & many more.

All of Us Will Shine. Tickle Tune Typhoon Staff. 1 cass. (Running Time: 42 mins.). (J). (gr. k-6). 1987. 9.98 (978-0-945337-05-8(1), TTTCA 003) Tickle Tune Typhoon.
Features a collection of original & traditional songs.

All on a Christmas Day. Told to Dennis and Nan Allen. Created by Custer & Hoose. 2002. audio compact disk 90.00 (978-5-557-69164-2(2)) Allegis.

All on a Christmas Day. Created by Lillenas Publishing Company. 2002. audio compact disk 90.00 (978-5-557-69163-5(4)) Lillenas.

All on Fire Pt. 1: William Lloyd Garrison & the Abolition of American Slavery. collector's ed. Henry Mayer. Read by Michael Kramer. 11 cass. (Running Time: 16 hrs. 30 min.). 2000. 88.00 (978-0-7366-4918-6(2)) Books on Tape.
An absorbing examination of William Lloyd Garrison, who emerges from this text as an American hero on a par with Abraham Lincoln.

All on Fire Pt. 2: William Lloyd Garrison & the Abolition of American Slavery. collector's unabr. ed. Henry Mayer. Read by Michael Kramer. 10 cass. (Running Time: 15 hrs.). 2000. 80.00 (978-0-7366-5221-6(3)) Books on Tape.

All One Earth: Songs for the Generations. Perf. by Michael J. Caduto. 1 CD. (Running Time: 47 mins.). audio compact disk 14.95 (978-1-55591-210-9(9)) Fulcrum Pub.
Features twelve exciting songs for families that add a new dimension to the lessons of the Keepers books. All One Earth includes 10 original compositions & lyrics for every song.

All One Earth: Songs for the Generations. Perf. by Michael J. Caduto. 1 cass. (Running Time: 47 mins.). (J). (ps-3). 1994. 9.95 (978-1-55591-209-3(5)) Fulcrum Pub.

All or Nothing. unabr. ed. Elizabeth A. Adler. Read by Maxine Howe. 9 CDs. (Running Time: 9 hrs. 40 mins.). (Isis Ser.). (J). 2002. audio compact disk 84.95 (978-0-7531-1488-9(7)) Pub: ISIS Lrg Prnt GBR. Dist(s): Ulverscroft US
An open-and-shut case of love and murder turns out to be more deadly for an idealistic young lawyer and her lover. Fast-moving and romantic, this is an enthralling story of love and justice from a mistress of the storyteller's art.

All or Nothing. unabr. ed. Elizabeth A. Adler & Maxine Howe. 8 cass. (Running Time: 9 hrs. 40 mins.). (Isis Ser.). (J). 2002. 69.95 (978-0-7531-1017-1(2)) Pub: ISIS Lrg Prnt GBR. Dist(s): Ulverscroft US

All or Nothing at All - ShowTrax. Arranged by Kirby Shaw. 1 CD. (Running Time: 5 mins.). 2000. audio compact disk 19.95 (08742200) H Leonard.
From the a cappella beginning into the walking bass accompaniment to the full swinging shout chorus, this chart is a straight-ahead vocal jazz feature that will bring life to every performance.

All Other Nights. unabr. ed. Dara Horn. Narrated by William Dufris. (Running Time: 15 hrs. 30 mins. 0 sec.). (ENG.). 2009. audio compact disk 75.99 (978-1-4001-4212-5(1)); audio compact disk 24.99 (978-1-4001-6212-3(2)); audio compact disk 37.99 (978-1-4001-1212-8(5)) Pub: Tantor Media. Dist(s): IngramPubServ

All Our Yesterdays. unabr. ed. Robert B. Parker. Read by Michael Prichard. 10 cass. (Running Time: 15 hrs.). 1994. 80.00 (978-0-7366-2899-0(1), 3599) Books on Tape.
Sprawling family saga spanning the 20th century, from the author of the Spenser novels.

All Our Yesterdays. unabr. ed. Robert B. Parker. Narrated by John Randolph Jones. 8 cass. (Running Time: 11 hrs. 45 mins.). 1994. 70.00 (978-0-7887-0154-2(1), 94376E7) Recorded Bks.
Three generations of Boston cops are both haunted & defined by the violence, obsessions & deceits of their heritage.

All Out. Winans, The. 1 cass., 1 CD. 10.98 (45213-4); audio compact disk 15.98 CD. (45213-2) Warner Christian.

All Out War: Investigating Spiritual Warfare. Doug Fields. (Super-Ser.). 2007. audio compact disk 60.00 (978-5-557-78146-6(3)) Group Pub.

All over but the Shoutin' unabr. ed. Rick Bragg. Narrated by Frank Muller. 10 CDs. (Running Time: 11 hrs. 30 mins.). 1999. audio compact disk 89.00 (978-0-7887-3719-0(8), C1076E7) Recorded Bks.
Rick Bragg, a Pulitzer Prize-winning journalist, tells the story of his mother, a woman who endured years of hardship & deprivation to raise her three sons. Against the backdrop of a dirt-poor South, this is more than just praise for his mother, it is a perceptive examination of the bonds that hold a family together.

All over but the Shoutin' unabr. ed. Rick Bragg. Narrated by Frank Muller. 8 cass. (Running Time: 11 hrs. 30 mins.). 1999. 75.00 (978-0-7887-3095-5(9), 95806E7) Recorded Bks.

All over Creation. Ruth L. Ozeki. Narrated by Anna Fields. (Running Time: 16 hrs.). 2003. 44.95 (978-1-59912-407-0(6)) Iofy Corp.

All over Creation. unabr. ed. Ruth L. Ozeki. Read by Anna Fields. 11 cass. (Running Time: 16 hrs.). 2003. 76.95 (978-0-7861-2442-8(3), 3121) Blckstn Audio.
The emotionally resonant and utterly unique story of an ordinary woman just trying to make sense of it all as the unceasing cycle of all creation continues around her.

All over Creation. unabr. ed. Ruth L. Ozeki. Read by Anna Fields. 13 CDs. (Running Time: 16 hrs.). 2003. audio compact disk 104.00 (978-0-7861-9239-7(9), 3121); audio compact disk 24.95 (978-0-7861-9003-4(5), 3121) Blckstn Audio.

All over Creation. unabr. ed. Ruth L. Ozeki. Read by Anna Fields. 11 cass. 2004. 44.95 (978-0-7861-4404-4(1)); audio compact disk 49.95 (978-0-7861-7432-4(3)) Blckstn Audio.

All over Creation. unabr. ed. Ruth L. Ozeki. Read by Anna Fields. 11 cass. 2004. reel tape 44.95 (978-0-7861-2485-5(7)); audio compact disk 49.95 (978-0-7861-9197-0(X)) Blckstn Audio.
Yumi Fuller is a rebellious daughter who returns to her family's Idaho potato farm to check on her ailing parents only to find herself in the midst of a firestorm involving genetically engineered spuds in this tale of family, food, and corporate greed.

***All over the Map.** unabr. ed. Laura Fraser. Narrated by Kirsten Potter. (Running Time: 8 hrs. 0 mins. 0 sec.). (ENG.). 2010. 19.99 (978-1-4001-6869-4(4)); 29.99 (978-1-4001-9869-6(0)); 15.99 (978-1-4001-8869-7(5)); audio compact disk 71.99 (978-1-4001-4869-1(3)); audio compact disk 29.99 (978-1-4001-1869-4(7)) Pub: Tantor Media. Dist(s): IngramPubServ

All over the Road. Danika Dinsmore & Matthew Burgess. 1 CD. (Running Time: 74 mins.). 2000. audio compact disk 10.00 (978-1-890051-05-1(5)) En Theos Prodns.
Original spokenword selections with music.

All Pets Go to Heaven: The Spiritual Lives of the Animals We Love. Sylvia Browne. Read by Jeanie Hackett. (Playaway Adult Nonfiction Ser.). (ENG.). 2009. 44.99 (978-1-60812-585-2(8)) Find a World.

All Pets Go to Heaven: The Spiritual Lives of the Animals We Love. abr. unabr. ed. Sylvia Browne. Read by Jeanie Hackett. 4 CDs. (Running Time: 5 hrs.). (ENG., 2009. audio compact disk 26.95 (978-1-59887-697-0(X), 159887697X) Pub: HighBridge. Dist(s): Workman Pub

All Pleasures Are Painful to the Wise. Swami Jyotirmayananda. (129) Yoga Res Foun.

All Pleasures Are Painful to the Wise. Swami Jyotirmayananda. 1 cass. (Running Time: 1 hr.). 1990. 12.99 (129) Yoga Res Foun.

All-Pro Diet: Lose Fat, Build Muscle, & Live Like a Champion. unabr. ed. Tony Gonzalez & Mitzi Dulan. Narrated by Chris Gonzalez. (Running Time: 4 hrs. 19 mins. 43 sec.). (ENG.). 2009. 16.09 (978-1-60814-529-4(8), SpringWater); audio compact disk 22.99 (978-1-59859-589-5(X), SpringWater) Oasis Audio.

All Quiet in the Western Front see Sin Novedad en el Frente

All Quiet in the Western Front. Erich-Maria Remarque. Read by Pedro Montoya. (Running Time: 3 hrs.). 2002. 16.95 (978-1-60083-275-8(X), Audiofy Corp) Iofy Corp.

All Quiet on the Western Front. Erich Maria Remarque. Read by Frank Muller. 4 Cass. (Running Time: 7 Hrs.). 19.95 (978-1-4025-1659-7(2)) Recorded Bks.

All Quiet on the Western Front. unabr. ed. Erich Maria Remarque. Read by Simon Calburn. 6 cass. (Running Time: 9 hrs.). 2000. 49.95 (978-0-7451-6230-0(4), CSL 011) Pub: Chivers Audio Bks GBR. Dist(s): AudioGO
In 1914, a group of German teenagers volunteer for action on the Western front in the war between the German and French trenches. In these trenches the horrors of World War I became realized.

All Quiet on the Western Front. unabr. ed. Erich Maria Remarque. Read by Frank Muller. 6 CDs. (Running Time: 7 Hours). audio compact disk 34.95 (978-1-4025-2234-5(7)) Recorded Bks.

All Quiet on the Western Front, unabr. ed. Erich Maria Remarque. Narrated by Frank Muller. 5 cass. (Running Time: 7 hrs.). 1994. 42.00 (978-1-55690-960-3(8), 94103E7) Recorded Bks.
Paul Baumer is just 19 years old when he & his classmates enlist. They are Germany's Iron Youth who enter the war with high ideals & leave it disillusioned or dead. As Paul struggles with the realities of the man he has become & the inscrutable world to which he must return, he is led like a ghost of his former self into the war's final hours. One of the greatest war novels of all time, an eloquent expression of the futility, hopelessness & irreparable losses of war.

All Quiet on the Western Front. unabr. ed. Erich Maria Remarque. Narrated by Frank Muller. 6 CDs. (Running Time: 7 hrs.). 2000. audio compact disk 54.00 (978-0-7887-3441-0(5), C1047E7) Recorded Bks.

All Relationships Must End in Love. Tara Singh. 1 cass. (Exploring a Course in Miracles Ser.). 9.95 (978-1-55531-166-7(0), #A135) Life Action Pr.
Offers keys to come to harmony in all relationships.

All Rivers Flow to the Sea. unabr. ed. Alison McGhee. Read by Carine Montbertrand. 4 cass. (Running Time: 5 hrs.). (YA). 2006. 39.75 (978-1-4193-7148-6(7), 98275) Recorded Bks.
Acclaimed author Alison McGhee poetically addresses the stages of grief and the importance of family and friends in this unforgettable story. After a tragic car accident, Rose Latham's older sister Ivy lies comatose in a convalescent home. Rose is forced to move on with her life, returning to school to face whispers and avoidance. Stuck between grief and hope, she seeks relief through evening trips to the gorge with different boys. But with

the help of her fatherly neighbor William T. and classmate Tom Miller, Rose may find a way to grieve and move on.

All Rivers to the Sea: A Novel. Bodie Thoene & Brock Thoene. (Galway Chronicles: Bk. 4). 2000. 15.99 (978-0-7852-6935-9(5)) Nelson.

All Roads Lead to Rome: Romans 1:1-17. Ed Young. 1983. 4.95 (978-0-7417-1346-9(2), 346) Win Walk.

All Sail Set. unabr. collector's ed. Armstrong Sperry. Read by Michael Prichard. 5 cass. (Running Time: 5 hrs.). (J). 1986. 30.00 (978-0-7366-1027-8(8), 1957) Books on Tape.

A Newberry prize (for younger readers) book. Life story of the sailing ship Flying Cloud.

All Saints: The Unauthorized Biography of the All Saints. Tim Footman. 1 CD. (Running Time: 1 hr.). (Maximum Ser.). (ENG.). 2001. audio compact disk 14.95 (978-1-84240-015-9(0)) Pub: Chrome Dreams GBR. Dist(s): IPG Chicago

A girl group with attitude, appealing to pop, indie, R'n'B and rap fans all over the world. The girls exploded onto the music scene with their first single 'I Know Where It's At' and held the top of the charts with 'Never Ever' for weeks in the U.K. But where did these.

All Shall Be Well. unabr. ed. Deborah Crombie. Read by Michael Deehy. 6 cass. (Duncan Kincaid/Gemma James Novel Ser.). 2005. 54.95 (978-0-7927-3449-9(1), CSL 746); audio compact disk 74.95 (978-0-7927-3450-5(5), SLD 746) AudioGO.

All Shall Be Well - All Shall Be One. Alla R. Bozarth. Read by Alla R. Bozarth. 1 cass. (Running Time: 1 hr. 45 mins.). 1995. 12.95 Wisdom House.

From ancient feminine Eucharistic rites to present day feminism, women's spirituality has a rich tradition of ritual & creativity to enhance wellness for the individual & the community. Illness & death are not opposites of wellness & life, but dynamic components.

All She Ever Wanted. unabr. ed. Lynn Austin. Read by Linda Stephens. 13 CDs. (Running Time: 15 hrs.). 2006. audio compact disk 119.75 (978-1-4193-8174-4(1), CK185); 94.75 (978-1-4193-8172-0(5), K1189) Recorded Bks.

A three-time Christy Award winner, Lynn Austin crafts rousing tales of hope and redemption. All She Ever Wanted stars Kathleen Seymour, a woman who seems to have it all, though she hides a dark family secret. To her horror, everything comes crashing down when she loses her job and her daughter is caught shoplifting. Desperate to regain control over her life, Kathleen returns to her estranged family to mend her severely broken relationships before it is too late.

All Shook Up: Music, Passion, & Politics. Carson Holloway. Read by Nadia May. (Running Time: 23400 sec.). 2006. 44.95 (978-0-7861-4569-0(2)); audio compact disk 55.00 (978-0-7861-7045-6(X)) Blckstn Audio.

All Shook Up: Music, Passion, & Politics. unabr. ed. Carson Holloway. Read by Nadia May. (Running Time: 23400 sec.). 2006. audio compact disk 29.95 (978-0-7861-7558-1(3)) Blckstn Audio.

All Souls: A Family Story from Southie. unabr. ed. Michael Patrick MacDonald. Read by William Dufris. 8 vols. (Running Time: 12 hrs.). 2000. bk. 69.95 (978-0-7927-2376-9(7), CSL 265, Chivers Sound Lib) AudioGO.

The anti-busing riots of 1974 forever changed Southie, Boston's working class Irish community, branding it as a violent, racist enclave. The author grew up in Southie's Old Colony housing project & describes the way this world within a world felt to the troubled yet keenly gifted observer he was evan as a child. But the threats - poverty, drugs, a shadowy gangster world - were real. A heartbreaking testimony to lives lost too early & the story of how a place so filled with pain could still be "the best place in the world".

All Souls' Rising. unabr. ed. Madison Smartt Bell. Read by Michael Kramer. 15 cass. (Running Time: 22 hrs. 30 mins.). 1996. 120.00 (978-0-7366-3273-7(5), 3929) Books on Tape.

When slaves revolted in Haiti, groups chose sides that mirrored politics in the French revolution. Epic historical fiction.

All Spelled Out: Basic Spelling Patterns for Learners of English. H. Elaine Kirn. (YA). (gr. 7 up). 1981. 16.95 (978-0-87789-217-5(2)) ELS Educ Servs.

All Spirits Sing. Perf. by Joanne Shenandoah. 1 cass.; 1 CD. 1998. 9.98 (978-1-56628-129-4(6), 72748); audio compact disk 15.98 CD. (978-1-56628-128-7(8), 72748D) MFLP CA.

All-Star, Bk. 1. Linda Lee et al. 2004. 73.75 (978-0-07-284667-6(4)) McGraw.

All-Star, Bk. 4. Created by McGraw-Hill Staff. 2005. audio compact disk 38.75 (978-0-07-284691-1(7), 9780072846911, ESL/ELT) Pub: McGrw-H Hghr Educ. Dist(s): McGraw

All Star United - Smash Hits. 1 CD. (Running Time: 30 mins.). 2000. audio compact disk (978-0-7601-3509-9(6)) Brentwood Music.

Songs include: "Smash Hit," "Bright Red Carpet," "Beautiful Thing," "Superstar" & more.

All-Star 1: Student Book, CDs 1-5: Pre-Unit, Units 1-10. Created by McGraw-Hill Staff. 5 CDs. (All-Star Ser.). 2004. audio compact disk 73.13 (978-0-07-284668-3(2), 9780072846683, ESL/ELT) Pub: McGrw-H Hghr Educ. Dist(s): McGraw

All-Star 2: Student Book, CDs 1-5: Pre-Unit, Units 1-10. Created by McGraw-Hill Staff. 3 CDs. 2004. audio compact disk 61.88 (978-0-07-284678-2(X), ESL/ELT) Pub: McGrw-H Hghr Educ. Dist(s): McGraw

All Star 2 Audiocassette Program. Linda Lee et al. 4 cass. (All-Star Ser.). 2004. 73.13 (978-0-07-284677-5(1), ESL/ELT) Pub: McGrw-H Hghr Educ. Dist(s): McGraw

All Star 3, Bk. 3. Linda Lee. 4 cass. (C). 2005. 52.50 (978-0-07-284682-9(8), ESL/ELT); audio compact disk 52.50 (978-0-07-284683-6(6), ESL/ELT) Pub: McGrw-H Hghr Educ. Dist(s): McGraw

All Star 4 Audiocassette Program: Pre-Unit, Units 1-8. Created by McGraw-Hill Companies Staff. 4 cass. (All-Star Ser.). 2005. 36.88 (978-0-07-284690-4(9), 9780072846904, ESL/ELT) Pub: McGrw-H Hghr Educ. Dist(s): McGraw

All Stories Are True. unabr. ed. John Edgar Wideman. Read by Clifton Davis. Ed. by Greg Knowles. 4 cass. (Running Time: 6 hrs.). 1993. 24.95 (978-1-882320-01-1(8)) Helion Audio.

These ten short stories depict life in urban black America. Stories dealing with visiting a brother in prison, a youth's initiation to sexual experience, a graduate student putting up with racist hate "signs" & the thoughts & feelings of an infant falling to its death.

All-Terrain Vehicles in Finland: A Strategic Reference 2006. Compiled by Icon Group International, Inc. Staff. 2007. ring bd. 195.00 (978-0-497-35935-5(9)) Icon Grp.

All That God Is. unabr. ed. Read by Gayle D. Erwin. 1 cass. (Running Time: 1 hr.). 1992. 4.95 (978-1-56599-510-9(4), C-10) Yahshua Pub.

Colossians 1, 2.

All That I Can Be. 2003. audio compact disk 22.95 (978-0-9627982-7-6(4)) Arete USA Pubg Co.

All That I Can Be - 15 Unison Songs to Build Character & Integrity in Young People. Jay Althouse. Composed by Sally K. Albrecht. (ENG.). 2002. audio compact disk 29.95 (978-0-7390-2351-8(9)) Alfred Pub.

All That I Can Be - 15 Unison Songs to Build Character & Integrity in Young People: Sing & Learn. Composed by Sally K. Albrecht & Jay Althouse. (ENG.). 2005. audio compact disk 13.99 (978-0-7390-3791-1(9)) Alfred Pub.

All That Is Within Me. Contrib. by MercyMe. 2007. 21.98 (978-5-557-59756-2(5)); audio compact disk 16.98 (978-5-557-59757-9(3)) INO Rec.

All That Lives, from the Earliest Hour see Classical Russian Poetry

All That Remains. abr. ed. Patricia Cornwell. Read by Kate Burton. 2 cass. (Running Time: 3 hrs.). (Kay Scarpetta Ser.: No. 3). 1992. 16.00 (978-1-55994-526-4(5)) HarperCollins Pubs.

Cornwell's slick new thriller puts forensic doctor Kay Scarpetta on the trail of a serial murderer. Scarpetta is investigating the murder of the daughter of a prominent Washington drug enforcement official. This woman's child may have been the target of political assassination, or is she the latest victim in a string of grisly murders? Working in a buddy-buddy relationship with a female investigative reporter for the Washington Post, Scarpetta pieces together heretofore fragmentary & unrelated evidence. Yet there is the creeping sense that somehow her efforts are being blocked by the FBI, the CIA & others. The murders, then, may be tied to a larger, more sinster conspiracy.

All That Remains. unabr. ed. Patricia Cornwell. Narrated by C. J. Critt. 11 CDs. (Running Time: 12 hrs. 30 mins.). (Kay Scarpetta Ser.: No. 3). 2000. audio compact disk 111.00 (978-0-7887-4905-6(6), C1280E7) Recorded Bks.

A serial killer is stalking Virginia's young lovers, taking their lives & taunting police with a single clue: a jack of hearts. For two years, the meaning of this has eluded FBI investigators but as Scarpetta begins searching the victims' remains for microscopic clues, she begins to suspect that someone in the FBI knows more about the murderer.

All That Remains. unabr. ed. Patricia Cornwell. Narrated by C. J. Critt. 9 cass. (Running Time: 12 hrs. 30 mins.). (Kay Scarpetta Ser.: No. 3). 1995. 78.00 (978-0-7887-0168-9(1), 94393E7) Recorded Bks.

Four young couples have been murdered, their bodies left deep in the woods of the Virginia countryside bearing a jack of hearts as the only clue. Kay Scarpetta must find the killer based on the forensic evidence.

All That Remains. unabr. collector's ed. Patricia Cornwell. Read by Donada Peters. 7 cass. (Running Time: 10 hrs. 30 min.). (Kay Scarpetta Ser.: No. 3). 1992. 56.00 (978-0-7366-2239-4(X), 3029) Books on Tape.

A serial killer is loose in Richmond who is skilled at eliminating every clue. Chief Medical Examiner, Dr. Kay Scarpetta, frustrated by her inability to determine the cause of death of the victims found in the woods months later, hires an ace crime reporter & a psychic. Kay's courage, intuition & will to stop the killer before he can strike again are her best resources.

All the Best Answers for the Worst Kid Problems: Anti-Social Youth. Ruth Herman Wells. 2000. 13.00 (978-1-891881-24-4(8)) Youth Change.

All the Best Answers for the Worst Kid Problems: Anti-Social Youth. Read by Ruth Herman Wells. 2000. 39.00 (978-1-891881-23-7(X)) Youth Change.

All the Best Answers for the Worst Kid Problems: Forgotten, Favorite Strategies. Read by Ruth Herman Wells. 2000. 13.00 (978-1-891881-26-8(4)) Youth Change.

All the Best Answers for the Worst Kid Problems: Maximum-Strength Motivation-Makers. Read by Ruth Herman Wells. 2000. 13.00 (978-1-891881-25-1(6)) Youth Change.

All the Best, George Bush: My Life in Letters & Other Writings. George H. W. Bush. 2004. 15.95 (978-0-7435-4097-1(2)) Pub: S&S Audio. Dist(s): S and S Inc

All the Best People. unabr. collector's ed. Sloan Wilson. Read by Dan Lazar. 12 cass. (Running Time: 18 hrs.). 1982. 96.00 (978-0-7366-0425-3(1), 1397) Books on Tape.

Middle-class materialism is a sad substitute for success.

All the Best Songs for Kids: Early Childhood. Compiled by Ken Bible. 1 cass. (Running Time: 1 hr.). (J). (ps-7). 2001. 12.99 (TA-9220S) Lillenas.

Anyone who uses music with kids of any age will want this one-of-a-kind treasury. Two hundred & thirty songs divided into age-group sections: early childhood, early elementary & late elementary. Songs also divided by topic, with a wide variety of general & seasonal themes well-covered. Songbook format, including melody words, piano accompaniment & chord symbols. All 230 songs recorded on cassette in a split-channel format, useful for listening or sing-along. A fantastic resource for teachers, children's church & VBS workers, children's choir directors, parents & grandparents.

All the Best Songs for Kids: Early Elementary. Compiled by Ken Bible. 1 cass. (Running Time: 1 hr.). (J). (ps-7). 2001. 19.99 (TA-9221S) Lillenas.

All the Best Songs for Kids Late Elementary. Compiled by Ken Bible. 1 cass. (Running Time: 1 hr.). (J). (gr. 3-5). 2001. 19.99 (TA-9222S) Lillenas.

All the Best Songs for Youth. Arranged by Tom Fettke. Compiled by Dennis Allen. Arranged by Dennis Allen & Steven Taylor. 3 cass. (Running Time: 4 hrs. 30 min.). (YA). 1997. 34.99 (TA-9214S) Lillenas.

102 of the best songs for youth. This collection contains new songs, choruses, praise songs & favorites from artists & writers including Audio Adrenaline, Newsboys, Al Denson, Steven Curtis Chapman, Clay Crosse, Twila Paris, Michael W. Smith & more. A great all-around resource for group singing youth choirs or solos.

All the Best Songs for Youth. Arranged by Tom Fettke et al. Compiled by Dennis Allen. Arranged by Dennis Allen et al. 1 cass. (Running Time: 1 hr.). (YA). 1997. 12.99 (TA-9214C) Lillenas.

102 of the best songs for youth. This collection contains new songs, choruses, praise songs & favorites from artists & writers including Audio Adrenaline, Newsboys, Al Denson, Steven Curtis Chapman, Clay Crosse, Twila Paris, Michael W. Smith & more. A great all-around resource for group singing youth choirs or solos.

***All the Broken Pieces.** Ann Burg. (ENG.). 2010. audio compact disk 29.99 (978-0-545-24839-6(6)) Scholastic Inc.

***All the Colors of Darkness.** unabr. ed. Peter Robinson. Read by Simon Prebble. (Inspector Banks Mystery Ser.). 2009. (978-0-06-187484-0(1), Harper Audio); (978-0-06-179846-7(0), Harper Audio) HarperCollins Pubs.

All the Colors of the Earth. (J). 2004. pap. bk. 18.95 (978-1-55592-100-2(0)); pap. bk. 38.75 (978-1-55592-627-4(4)); pap. bk. 32.75 (978-1-55592-180-4(9)); pap. bk. 14.95 (978-1-55592-050-0(0)); audio compact disk 12.95 (978-1-55592-957-2(5)) Weston Woods.

All the Colors of the Earth. Sheila Hamanaka. Perf. by Crystal Taliefero. 1 cass. (Running Time: 30 min.). (J). (ps-4). bk. 24.95 Weston Woods.

Soaring text & beautiful art celebrate the glorious diversity of children. Contains both spoken word & sing-along versions.

All the Colors of the Earth, Sheila Hamanaka. Perf. by Crystal Taliefero. 1 cass, 5 bks. (Running Time: 30 min.). (J). (ps-4). pap. bk. 32.75 Weston Woods.

All the Colors of the Earth. Sheila Hamanaka. Perf. by Crystal Taliefero. 1 cass. (Running Time: 30 min.). (J). (ps-4). 2000. pap. bk. 12.95 Weston Woods.

All the Colors of the Earth. unabr. ed. Pe[illegible] Crystal Taliefero. Prod. by Paul Gagne. 1 cass. (Running Time: 7 mins.). (J). 1997. 8.95 (978-1-56008-814-1(1), RAC360) Weston Woods.

All the Cowboys Ain't Gone. unabr. ed. Jacobson, John J Jacobson. (Running Time: 1 hr. 0 mins.). (ENG.). 2009. 29.95 (978-1-4417-0036-0(6)); 44.95 (978-1-4417-0032-2(3)); audio compact disk 55.00 (978-1-4417-0033-9(1)) Blckstn Audio.

All the Dead Lie Down. unabr. ed. Mary Willis Walker. Read by Anna Fields. 8 cass. (Running Time: 12 hrs.). 1998. 64.00 (978-0-7366-4220-0(X), 4718) Books on Tape.

All the Dead Lie Down, unabr. ed. Mary Willis Walker. Narrated by C. J. Critt. 9 cass. (Running Time: 13 hrs.). 1998. 78.00 (978-0-7887-2166-3(6), 95462E7) Recorded Bks.

Texas crime journalist, Molly Cates, must track down & confront demons from her past to thwart present dangers.

***All the Dead Voices.** Declan Hughes. 2010. 69.95 (978-1-4450-0215-6(9)); audio compact disk 84.95 (978-1-4450-0216-3(7)) Pub: Isis Pubng Ltd GBR. Dist(s): Ulverscroft US

All the Dead Were Strangers. unabr. ed. Ethan Black. Read by James Daniels. 8 cass. (Running Time: 12 hrs.). 2001. 32.95 (978-1-58788-735-2(5), 1587887355, BAU); 87.25 (978-1-58788-736-9(3), 1587887363, CD Unabrid Lib Ed) Brilliance Audio.

Conrad Voort, the sexy and charismatic NYC detective, takes on a dangerously invisible killer in the most textured, complex and commercial Ethan Black thriller yet. . . Voort meets his childhood friend Meechum at a downtown bar for a drink and a disturbing conversation. His long-lost friend is paranoid and troubled, and vaguely hints at a military career gone terribly wrong . . . and then he suddenly disappears, and is later found dead under curious circumstances. A devastated Voort is left with only one clue: a list of names on a napkin that Meechum has asked him to investigate. One after another, Voort discovers that the people on the list are dead: victims of seemingly innocent accidents that begin to look more and more suspicious as the next comes to light. As he sifts through more information, Voort begins to uncover a mysterious plot masterminded by a former Army hero who is following a lethal agenda - - a plot involving a covert U.S. military operation targeting Americans suspected of terrorist leanings. Voort quickly learns that he must battle two enemies as they battle each other: one, a champion of valor turned cold blooded killer, and the other an ordinary man about to unleash a massive and deadly attack.

All the Dead Were Strangers. unabr. ed. Ethan Black. Read by James Daniels. (Running Time: 12 hrs.). 2004. 39.25 (978-1-59335-652-1(8), 1593356528, Brlnc Audio MP3 Lib); 24.95 (978-1-59335-291-2(3), 1593352913, Brilliance MP3) Brilliance Audio.

All the Dead Were Strangers. unabr. ed. Ethan Black. Read by James Daniels. (Running Time: 12 hrs.). 2004. 39.25 (978-1-59710-010-6(2), 1597100102, BADLE); 24.95 (978-1-59710-011-3(0), 1597100110, BAD) Brilliance Audio.

All the Drowning Seas. unabr. ed. Alexander Fullerton. Read by Gordon Griffin. 10 cass. (Running Time: 13 hrs. 30 mins.). 2000. 84.95 (978-1-86042-631-5(X), 2631X) Pub: Soundings Ltd GBR. Dist(s): Ulverscroft US

February 1942: as Japanese invaders sweep across the Pacific, a handful of British, American, Australian & Dutch ships prepare for a last-ditch battle in defense of Java. Not only is the Allied force doomed to defeat: any surviving ships will be trapped, since escape routes south & west are blocked. Nick Everard, commanding the cruiser Defiant, is badly wounded & his ship heavily damaged. Back in Surabaya after the battle he also has a surviving US destroyer under his wing. Two ships & their companies face destruction & either death or captivity unless he can find some way out of the trap.

All the Drowning Seas. unabr. ed. Alexander Fullerton. Read by Gordon Griffin. 12 CDs. (Running Time: 13 hrs.). (Sound Ser.). 2002. audio compact disk 99.95 (978-1-84283-109-0(7)) Pub: UlverLrgPrint GBR. Dist(s): Ulverscroft US

All the Finest Girls. unabr. ed. Alexandra Styron. Read by Alexandra Styron. 5 cass. (Running Time: 7 hrs.). 2001. 61.25 (978-1-58788-597-6(2), 1587885972, Unabridge Lib Edns); 27.95 (978-1-58788-596-9(4), 1587885964, BAU) Brilliance Audio.

An elegantly written and unforgettable story about a daughter's love - and where that love lodges when her parents are less than lovable. Addy Abraham was practically a feral child, untamable and wild - until a new babysitter arrived, Louise, who gave her a haven from her parents' pitched battles. News of Louise's death startles Addy out of the trance that has become her adult life. She flies to the Caribbean for the funeral, and amid the chaos and grief of Louise's family, Addy confronts the myths that helped her survive her childhood - the same ones that have made her adult life a barren ground. Celebrating Louise's life, she arrives at a new hope for her own.

All the Finest Girls. unabr. ed. Alexandra Styron. Read by Alexandra Styron. (Running Time: 7 hrs.). 2005. 39.25 (978-1-59600-678-2(1), 9781596006782, BADLE); 24.95 (978-1-59600-677-5(3), 9781596006775, BAD); 39.25 (978-1-59600-676-8(5), 9781596006768, Brlnc Audio MP3 Lib); 24.95 (978-1-59600-675-1(7), 9781596006751, Brilliance MP3) Brilliance Audio.

***All the Flowers are Dying.** abr. ed. Lawrence Block. Read by Lawrence Block. (ENG.). 2005. (978-0-06-083896-6(5), Harper Audio); (978-0-06-083897-3(3), Harper Audio) HarperCollins Pubs.

All the Flowers Are Dying. unabr. ed. Lawrence Block. Read by Alan Sklar. (Matthew Scudder Mystery Ser.: No. 16). 2005. 29.95 (978-0-7927-3515-1(3), CMP 771); 54.95 (978-0-7927-3513-7(7), CSL 771); audio compact disk 74.95 (978-0-7927-3514-4(5), SLD 771) AudioGO.

All the French You'll Need: Complete Learning Guide & Tapescript. Mark Frobose. 8 cass. (Running Time: 8 hrs.). (FRE & ENG.). 1999. 69.00 (978-1-893564-24-4(X)) Macmill Audio.

All the Italian You'll Need: Complete Learning Guide & Tapescript. Mark Frobose. 6 cass. (Running Time: 6 hrs.). (ITA.). 1999. stu. ed. 49.00 (978-1-893564-31-2(2)) Macmill Audio.

All the King's Men. Robert Penn Warren. (Running Time: 75600 sec.). 2005. audio compact disk 39.99 (978-1-4193-4450-3(1)) Recorded Bks.

All the King's Men: Strength in Character Through Friendships. Stu Weber. 1 cass. 1998. 15.98 (Mltnmah) Doubday Relig.

***All the Little Live Things.** unabr. ed. Wallace Stegner. (Running Time: 12 hrs. 30 mins.). 2010. 29.95 (978-1-4417-3642-0(5)); 72.95 (978-1-4417-3638-3(7)); audio compact disk 105.00 (978-1-4417-3639-0(5)) Blckstn Audio.

***All the Living.** unabr. ed. C. E. Morgan. Narrated by Julia Gibson. 1 Playaway. (Running Time: 7 hrs. 30 mins.). 2009. 56.75 (978-1-4407-2174-8(2)); audio compact disk 72.75 (978-1-4361-7854-9(1)) Recorded Bks.

***All the Living.** unabr. collector's ed. C. E. Morgan. Narrated by Julia Gibson. 6 CDs. (Running Time: 7 hrs. 30 mins.). 2009. audio compact disk 34.95 (978-1-4361-7855-6(X)) Recorded Bks.

All the Love You Could Ever Want! Set: Six-Tape Audio Course in Love. unabr. ed. Scott Peck & Shannon Peck. Read by Scott Peck & Shannon Peck. 6 cass. (Running Time: 8 hrs.). 2000. 39.95 (978-0-9659976-6-9(9)) Lifepath Pub.

***All the Lovely Bad Ones.** unabr. ed. Mary Downing Hahn. (Running Time: 5 hrs.). 2011. 39.97 (978-1-61106-950-1(5), 9781611069501, BADLE); 24.99 (978-1-61106-947-1(5), 9781611069471, Brilliance MP3); 39.97 (978-1-61106-948-8(3), 9781611069488, Brinc Audio MP3 Lib); audio compact disk 24.99 (978-1-61106-945-7(9), 9781611069457, Bril Audio CD Unabri); audio compact disk 54.97 (978-1-61106-946-4(7), 9781611069464, BriAudCD Unabrid) Brilliance Audio.

All the Marbles: The Jazz Compositions of les Thimmig. Les Thimmig. (ENG.). 2009. audio compact disk 15.00 (978-1-931569-20-0(7)) Pub: U of Wis Pr. Dist(s): Chicago Distribution Ctr

All the Money in the World: How the Forbes 400 Make - and Spend - Their Fortunes. abr. ed. Read by Rick Adamson. (Running Time: 21600 sec.). (ENG.). 2007. audio compact disk 29.95 (978-0-7393-5751-4(4), Random AudioBks) Pub: Random Audio Pubg. Dist(s): Random

All the Pooh Stories. unabr. ed. A. A. Milne. Read by Bernard Cribbins. 4 cass. (Running Time: 6 hrs.). 2002. (978-1-85549-315-5(2)) Cover To Cover GBR.

All the President's Men. Bob Woodward. Narrated by Carl Bernstein. 11 CDs. (Running Time: 13 hrs.). 2004. audio compact disk 34.99 (978-1-4025-7562-4(9), 01542) Recorded Bks.

All the President's Men. unabr. ed. Carl Bernstein & Bob Woodward. 1 cass. (Running Time: 56 mins.). 12.95 (C40069) J Norton Pubs.

All the President's Men. unabr. ed. Carl Bernstein & Bob Woodward. Read by Richard Poe. 11 CDs. (Running Time: 13 hrs.). 2004. audio compact disk 109.75 (978-1-4025-7970-7(5)) Recorded Bks.
The Watergate scandal that brought down the Nixon administration remains as fascinating as it was 30 years ago. The account by reporters Bernstein and Woodward of how the Washington Post uncovered an intricate web of deception also remains engrossing because of its thriller-like quality. Presenting the story in the third person, the authors become characters as vivid as G. Gordon Liddy, E. Howard Hunt, and the other Watergate figures. The reporters offer an honest view of their professional and personal failings and their frequent tempestuous disagreements. Their saga is also still timely because of the refusal of so many public figures to learn its lessons about the consequences of lies and cover-ups.

***All the Pretty Girls.** unabr. ed. J. T. Ellison. Read by Joyce Bean. (Running Time: 11 hrs.). (Taylor Jackson Ser.). 2010. 24.99 (978-1-4418-3841-4(4), 9781441838414, Brilliance MP3); 24.99 (978-1-4418-3843-8(0), 9781441838438, BAD); 39.97 (978-1-4418-3842-1(2), 9781441838421, Brinc Audio MP3 Lib); 39.97 (978-1-4418-3844-5(9), 9781441838445, BADLE); audio compact disk 29.99 (978-1-4418-3839-1(2), 9781441838391, Bril Audio CD Unabri); audio compact disk 79.97 (978-1-4418-3840-7(6), 9781441838407, BriAudCD Unabrid) Brilliance Audio.

All the Pretty Horses. unabr. ed. Cormac McCarthy. Read by Frank Muller. 6 CDs. (Running Time: 7 hrs.). (Border Trilogy: No. 1). 2000. audio compact disk 50.00 (978-0-694-52344-3(5)) HarperCollins Pubs.

***All the Pretty Horses.** unabr. ed. Cormac McCarthy. Read by Frank Muller. (ENG.). 2004. (978-0-06-081816-6(6), Harper Audio); (978-0-06-081815-9(8), Harper Audio) HarperCollins Pubs.

All the Pretty Horses. unabr. ed. Cormac McCarthy. Narrated by Frank Muller. 7 cass. (Running Time: 10 hrs.). (Border Trilogy: No. 1). 1999. 60.00 (978-1-55690-660-2(9), 92403E7) Recorded Bks.
John Grady Cole, sixteen in 1949, leaves his Texas home to seek his fortune in the wilds of Mexico, a land in which he finds both beauty & violence, poverty & riches, love & death.

All the Pretty Horses. unabr. collector's ed. Cormac McCarthy. Read by Alexander Adams. 6 cass. (Running Time: 9 hrs.). (Border Trilogy: No. 1). 1993. 48.00 (978-0-7366-2416-9(3), 3183) Books on Tape.
It's 1949 & 16 year olds still have dreams. Young John Cole has his - to grow up on his grandfather's Texas ranch & to live the same kind of life, wild 7 free. But when his grandfather dies, John suffers. It's like the life has gone out of him. He takes off fro Mexico, but instead of escape, he finds a blood price to be paid.

All the Queen's Men. unabr. ed. Linda Howard. Read by Kate Forbes. 8 vols. (Running Time: 12 hrs.). 2001. bk. 69.95 (978-0-7927-2467-4(4), CSL 356, Chivers Sound Lib); audio compact disk 94.95 (978-0-7927-9914-6(3), SLD 065, Chivers Sound Lib) AudioGO.
John Medina, the CIA's legendary Black Ops specialist, works in the shadows of the government's deadliest missions & no one knows the dangers of getting close to him better than does communications expert Niema Burdock. Five years ago, Niema & her husband, Dallas, worked with Medina on an explosive mission that trapped Dallas in the crossfire, fatally. Although she has slowly healed from her terrible loss, Niema never planned to see Medina again. But now John Medina needs her.

All the Right Stuff: James 1:19-27, 621. Ed Young. 1987. 4.95 (978-0-7417-1621-7(6), 621) Win Walk.

All the Sad Young Literary Men. unabr. ed. Keith Gessen. Read by Scott Brick. (Running Time: 28800 sec.). 2008. 24.95 (978-1-4332-1241-3(2)); 54.95 (978-1-4332-1239-0(0)); audio compact disk 24.95 (978-1-4332-1242-0(0)); audio compact disk 29.95 (978-1-4332-1243-7(9)); audio compact disk & audio compact disk 60.00 (978-1-4332-1240-6(4)) Blckstn Audio.

All the Seasons of George Winston. 1 cass. 8.78 (WH 11266); audio compact disk 14.38 CD Jewel box. (WH 11266) NewSound.

All the Secrets of Magic - Revealed: Tricks & Illusions of the World's Greatest Magicians. Herbert L. Becker. Read by Billy Nash. 2 cass. 1998. 17.95 (978-1-57949-024-9(7)) Destination Success.

All the Shah's Men: An American Coup & the Roots of Middle East Terror. unabr. ed. Stephen Kinzer. Narrated by Michael Prichard. (Running Time: 10 hrs. 30 mins. 0 sec.). (ENG.). 2003. audio compact disk 79.99 (978-1-4001-3106-8(5)); audio compact disk 39.99 (978-1-4001-0106-1(9)); audio compact disk 22.99 (978-1-4001-5106-6(6)) Pub: Tantor Media. Dist(s): IngramPubServ
Half a century ago, the United States overthrew a Middle Eastern government for the first time. The victim was Mohammad Mossadegh, the democratically elected prime minister of Iran. Although the coup seemed a success at first, today it serves as a chilling lesson about the dangers of foreign intervention. In this book, veteran New York Times correspondent Stephen Kinzer gives the first full account of this fateful operation. His account is centered around an hour-by-hour reconstruction of the events of August 1953, and concludes with an assessment of the coup's "haunting and terrible legacy.".

All the Spanish You'll Need: Complete Learning Guide & Tapescript. Mark Frobose. 8 cass. (Running Time: 8 hrs.). (SPA.). 1999. stu. ed. 59.00 (978-1-893564-23-7(1)) Macmill Audio.

All the Sweet Promises. unabr. ed. Elizabeth Elgin. Read by Anne Dover. 18 cass. (Running Time: 24 hrs.). (Isis Cassettes Ser.). 2000. 109.95 (978-0-7531-0616-7(7), 990804) Pub: UlverLrgPrint GBR. Dist(s): Ulverscroft US
The compelling story of three women entering the WRENS during World War II & the men with whom they find love. Vi's husband is missing in action & the WRENS become her reason for living. For upper-class Lucinda, joining up provides a means of escape. For the lovely Jane, there is a little choice when she gets her call-up papers. Their backgrounds are different, yet together they will share their finest hours.

All the Tea. Perf. by Timberwolf Press. 6 CDs. (Running Time: 8 hrs.). 2001. audio compact disk 34.95 (WOLF004) Lodestone Catalog.
The U. S. & Japan have been working on a top secret nuclear fusion reactor, suddenly the black veil of secrecy is shredded & the Chinese want the prize for themselves.

All the Trouble in the World: The Lighter Side of Overpopulation, Famine, Plague, Ecological Disaster, Ethnic Hatred, & Poverty. unabr. ed. P. J. O'Rourke. Read by Christopher Hurt. 8 cass. (Running Time: 11 hrs. 30 mins.). 1995. 56.95 (978-0-7861-0873-2(8), 1676) Blckstn Audio.
In "All the Trouble in the World," best-selling political humorist P. J. O'Rourke tackles the "fashionable worries" - enormous global problems that are endlessly in the news & constantly on our minds but about which we mostly don't have a clue. O'Rourke crisscrosses the globe asking not just "What's the answer?" but "What the hell's the question?".

All the Way: A Biography of Frank Sinatra 1915-1998. unabr. ed. Michael Freedland. Read by Robert Whitfield. 12 cass. (Running Time: 18 hrs.). 1999. 83.95 (2427) Blckstn Audio.
Fitting tribute to a singer, actor & hell-raiser, one of the legendary figures of entertainment, a man who, in every aspect of his personal & professional life, took it "All the Way".

All the Way: A Biography of Frank Sinatra 1915-1998. unabr. ed. Michael Freedland. Read by Robert Whitfield. 12 cass. (Running Time: 17 hrs. 30 mins.). 2001. 83.95 (978-0-7861-1599-0(8), 2427) Blckstn Audio.

All the Way Home. Ann Tatlock. Narrated by Christina Moore. 12 cass. (Running Time: 16 hrs. 45 mins.). 2002. 98.00 (978-1-4025-4413-2(8)) Recorded Bks.

All the Way to Kingdom Come (4CD Set) Thomas S. Jones et al. 2009. 18.00 (978-1-57782-243-1(9)) Discipleshp.

All the Wealth You Want: How You Can Make & Keep More Money, Eliminate Debt & Live Financially Free. Jim Donovan. 4 CD's & workbook. (Running Time: 4 hours). 2007. audio compact disk 129.00 (978-0-9786891-0-0(0)) Austin Bay.

All the Weyrs of Pern. abr. ed. Scripts. Anne McCaffrey. Read by Mark Rolston. 2 cass. (Running Time: 3 hrs.). (Pern Ser.). 2003. 18.00 (978-1-59007-351-3(7), N Millennium Audio) Pub: New Millenn Enter. Dist(s): PerseuPGW

All the Weyrs of Pern. abr. ed. Anne McCaffrey. Read by Anne McCaffrey. 2 cass. (Running Time: 3 hrs.). (Pern Ser.). 1992. 15.95 (978-1-879371-11-8(1)) Pub Mills.
She has created a self-contained universe whose own hermetic logic has attracted a small legion of hard-core fans. This is the story of the planet Pern, under attack for centuries by something called "thread," a "voracious organism." In order to intercept this matter as it falls from the skies, warriors ride around on flying dragons, whose job it is to eat thread.

All the Weyrs of Pern. unabr. ed. Anne McCaffrey. Read by Mel Foster. (Running Time: 18 hrs.). (Dragonriders of Pern Ser.). 2008. 44.25 (978-1-4233-5738-4(8), 9781423357384, Brinc Audio MP3 Lib); 44.25 (978-1-4233-5740-7(X), 9781423357407, BADLE); 29.95 (978-1-4233-5739-1(6), 9781423357391, BAD); 29.95 (978-1-4233-5737-7(X), 9781423357377, Brilliance MP3); audio compact disk 29.99 (978-1-4233-5735-3(3), 9781423357353, Bril Audio CD Unabri); audio compact disk 127.25 (978-1-4233-5736-0(1), 9781423357360, BriAudCD Unabrid) Brilliance Audio.

All the Weyrs of Pern. unabr. ed. Scripts. Anne McCaffrey. Read by Mark Rolston. 10 cass. (Running Time: 15 hrs.). (Pern Ser.). 2003. 37.95 (978-1-59007-352-0(5), N Millennium Audio) Pub: New Millenn Enter. Dist(s): PerseuPGW

All the Weyrs of Pern. unabr. ed. Anne McCaffrey. Read by Mark Rolston. 10 cass. (Running Time: 15 hrs.). (Pern Ser.). 1996. 39.95 (978-1-879371-92-7(8), 70040) Pub Mills.

All the Winters That Have Been. unabr. ed. Evan Maxwell. Narrated by George Guidall. 4 cass. (Running Time: 5 hrs. 45 mins.). 1997. 35.00 (978-0-7887-0933-3(X), 95073E7) Recorded Bks.
Dan shattered Helen's love 20 years ago with his betrayal - now he's fighting for a second chance at love. But this time Helen has a secret that could drive them apart forever.

All the World. Contrib. by Point of Grace. Prod. by Brown Bannister. (Studio Ser.). 2007. audio compact disk 9.99 (978-5-557-63573-8(4), Word Records) Word Enter.

All the World's a Stage. Neville Goddard. 1 cass. (Running Time: 62 mins.). 1971. 8.00 (93) J & L Pubns.
He taught Imagination Creates Reality. He was a powerfully influential teacher of God as Consciousness.

All These Things Shall Give Thee Experience Book on CD. Neal A. Maxwell. 2007. audio compact disk 15.95 (978-1-59038-820-4(8)) Deseret Bk.

All Things Are Possible When You Believe. unabr. ed. Ed Foreman. Read by Norman Vincent Peale. 2 cass. (Running Time: 2 hrs.). 1998. 29.95 (978-1-893603-07-3(5)) Exec Dev Syst.
Dr. Peale shares two of his great messages, "The Amazing Power of Thought," & "All Things Are Possible When You Believe." Foreman shares his "Positive Self-Talk" for positive follow through with your daily conversations with yourself.

All Things Bright & Beautiful. unabr. ed. James Herriot. Read by Christopher Timothy. 11 CDs. (Running Time: 47880 sec.). (Vet Ser.). 2006. audio compact disk 99.95 (978-0-7927-4507-5(8), SLD1037) AudioGO.

All Things Bright & Beautiful. unabr. rev. ed. James Herriot. Read by Christopher Timothy. 12 CDs. (Running Time: 13 hrs. 0 mins. 0 sec.). (ENG.). 2004. audio compact disk 44.95 (978-1-59397-545-6(7)) Pub: Macmill Audio. Dist(s): Macmillan

All Things Censored, Vol. 1. Mumia Abu-Jamal. (AK Press Audio Ser.). (ENG.). 2003. audio compact disk 14.98 (978-1-902593-06-7(5)) Pub: AK Pr GBR. Dist(s): Consort Bk Sales

All Things Change: Maylene the Mermaid. Trenna Sutphen. Read by Trenna Sutphen. 1 cass. (Running Time: 30 mins.). (One to Grow On! Ser.). (J). (gr. 4 up). 7.95 (12000) Trenna Prods.

All Things Change: Maylene the Mermaid. unabr. ed. Trenna Daniells. Read by Trenna Daniells. 12 cass. (Running Time: 30 mins.). (One to Grow On Ser.). (J). (gr. k-6). 1982. 9.95 (978-0-918519-01-6(2), 12000) Trenna Prods.
Helps children understand that all things do change & enables them to view change in a positive light.

All Things Change - Maylene the Mermaid. Trenna Daniells. Narrated by Trenna Daniells. (ENG.). (J). 2009. (978-0-918519-02-3(0)) Trenna Prods.

All Things Considered. 10th anniv. ed. 1 cass. (Running Time: 30 mins.). 8.00 (J008DB090, HarperThor) HarpC GBR.

All Things New. Bob George. Read by Bob George. 1 cass. (Running Time: 70 mins.). 1997. 6.00 (978-1-57838-084-8(7)) CrossLife Express.
Discussion of the Christians' new life in Christ.

All Things New Music CD. Perf. by Ken Norberg. 2005. audio compact disk 14.99 (978-0-9771318-7-7(4)) Pub: Hope Harvest Pub. Dist(s): Baker Taylor

All Things Wise & Wonderful. James Herriot. Read by Christopher Timothy. 2003. 29.95 (978-1-59397-175-5(3)) Pub: Macmill Audio. Dist(s): Macmillan

All Things Wise & Wonderful. abr. ed. James Herriot. Read by Edmund Stoiber. 2 cass. 12.95 (978-0-89926-121-8(3), 809) Audio Bk.
Selected chapters from the best seller about the life of a veterinarian in Yorkshire, England.

All Things Wise & Wonderful. unabr. ed. James Herriot. Narrated by Edmund Stoiber. 10 cass. 59.50 (A-204) Audio Bk.
An entertaining account of a Yorkshire veterinary surgeon. All those things which should not happen to a vet did in fact happen to Herriot.

All Things Wise & Wonderful. unabr. ed. James Herriot. Read by Christopher Timothy. 12 CDs. (Running Time: 54660 sec.). (Vet Ser.). 2006. audio compact disk 110.95 (978-0-7927-4508-2(6), SLD1038) AudioGO.

All Things Wise & Wonderful. unabr. rev. ed. James Herriot & James Herriot. Read by Christopher Timothy. 11 CDs. (Running Time: 15 hrs. 0 mins. 0 sec.). (ENG.). 2004. audio compact disk 49.95 (978-1-59397-544-9(9)) Pub: Macmill Audio. Dist(s): Macmillan

All Through the Night. Stan Pethel. 1995. 11.98 (978-0-7673-0663-8(5)) LifeWay Christian.

All Through the Night. abr. ed. Mary Higgins Clark & Mary Higgins Clark. Read by Carol Higgins Clark. (Running Time: 3 hrs. 0 mins. 0 sec.). (ENG.). 2009. audio compact disk 9.99 (978-0-7435-8347-3(7)) Pub: S&S Audio. Dist(s): S and S Inc

All Through the Night: A Troubleshooter Christmas. Suzanne Brockmann. Read by Michael Holland. (Troubleshooter Ser.: No. 12). 2008. 64.99 (978-1-60640-583-3(7)) Find a World.

All Through the Night: A Troubleshooter Christmas. unabr. ed. Suzanne Brockmann. (Running Time: 8 hrs.). (Troubleshooter Ser.: No. 12). 2007. 24.95 (978-1-4233-4288-5(7), 9781423342885, BAD) Brilliance Audio.

All Through the Night: A Troubleshooter Christmas. unabr. ed. Suzanne Brockmann. Read by Michael Holland. (Running Time: 8 hrs.). (Troubleshooter Ser.: No. 12). 2007. 39.25 (978-1-4233-4289-2(5), 9781423342892, BADLE); 87.25 (978-1-4233-4283-0(6), 9781423342830, BrilAudUnabridg); audio compact disk 92.25 (978-1-4233-4285-4(2), 9781423342854, BriAudCD Unabrid); audio compact disk 39.25 (978-1-4233-4287-8(9), 9781423342878, Brinc Audio MP3 Lib); audio compact disk 24.95 (978-1-4233-4286-1(0), 9781423342861, Brilliance MP3) Brilliance Audio.

All Through the Night: A Troubleshooter Christmas. unabr. ed. Suzanne Brockmann. Read by Michael Holland. (Running Time: 8 hrs.). (Troubleshooter Ser.: No. 12). 2008. audio compact disk 14.99 (978-1-4233-8062-7(2), 9781423380627, BCD Value Price) Brilliance Audio.

All Through the Night: Lovesongs & Lullabies. Mae Robertson & Don Jackson. 1 cass. (Running Time: 46 mins.). 1994. 10.00 (978-0-9649164-0-1(1)); audio compact disk 15.00 CD. (978-0-9649164-1-8(X)) Lyric Prtnrs.
Collection of lullabies & love songs sure to please both adults & children.

All Through the Night Cassette Kit. Stan Pethel. 1995. 54.95 (978-0-7673-0146-6(3)) LifeWay Christian.

All Through the Night Spanish. Greg Skipper. 1996. 10.98 (978-0-7673-0711-6(9)) LifeWay Christian.

All Through the Night You Can! Series. Stan Pethel. 1995. 40.00 (978-0-7673-0701-7(1)) LifeWay Christian.

All-Time Children's Favorites. 1 cass. (Running Time: 1 hr.). (J). 2001. 10.95 (KUB 4000C); audio compact disk 14.95 (KUB 4000CD) Kimbo Educ.
Favorite medleys that have been sung for generations. Boogie with a camel named Alice, rock 'n' roll with the Itsy Bitsy Spider, Hokey Pokey & more.

All-Time Favorite Children's Games. 1 cass. (Running Time: 1 hr.). (J). 2001. pap. bk. 10.95 (KIM 9068C) Kimbo Educ.
Fun for all. Structured to develop listening skills, attention span & behavioral control. Musical Chairs, Statues, Follow the Leader & more. Includes manual.

All-Time Favorite Children's Games. Georgiana Stewart. 1 CD. (Running Time: 1 hr.). (J). 2001. pap. bk. 14.95 (KIM 9068CD) Kimbo Educ.

All-Time Favorite Dances. Dennis Book. 1 cass. (Running Time: 1 hr.). (J). 2001. pap. bk. 10.95 (KIM 9126C); pap. bk. 11.95 (KIM 9126); pap. bk. 14.95 (KIM 9126CD) Kimbo Educ.
These group-participation dances often require no partner & are great for all ages. Terrific for special party events, recreation programs & school settings. Includes The Chicken, Alley Cat, Hora, Hokey Pokey, Bunny Hop & more! The step by step demonstrations of the more complicated routines makes learning these dances a snap. Includes guide.

All-Time Favorite Songs. Penton Overseas, Inc. Staff. 1 CD. (Running Time: 1 hr.). (Ready-Set-Sing Collection). (ENG.). (J). (ps-7). 2003. audio compact disk 4.99 (978-1-56015-243-9(5)) Penton Overseas.
These four new collections of kids favorite sing-along songs include fun activity songs to get everyone up, moving & having great fun.

All Together: Linda Schrade & Her Musical Friends. Perf. by Linda Schrade et al. (J). 1984. audio compact disk 14.95 (978-0-939065-91-2(6)) Gentle Wind.

All Together: Linda Schrade & Her Musical Friends. Perf. by Linda Schrade et al. 1 cass. (Running Time: 30 min.). (J). (gr. k-7). 1984. 9.95 (978-0-939065-23-3(1), GW 1027) Gentle Wind.
Presents a sing along with dancing vegetables, singing animals, a friendly light-house & a Beatles tune.

All Together Dead. Charlaine Harris. Narrated by Johanna Parker. (Running Time: 36000 sec.). (Sookie Stackhouse Ser.: Bk. 7). 2007. audio compact disk 34.99 (978-1-4281-4780-5(2)) Recorded Bks.

All Together Dead. unabr. ed. Charlaine Harris. Narrated by Johanna Parker. 8 cass. (Running Time: 10 hrs.). (Sookie Stackhouse Ser.: Bk. 7). 2007. 72.75 (978-1-4281-4438-5(2)); audio compact disk 102.75 (978-1-4281-4267-1(3)) Recorded Bks.

All Together in One Place. abr. ed. Jane Kirkpatrick. 4 cass. (Running Time: 7 hrs. 30 min.). 2003. 25.99 (978-1-58926-143-3(7), W68L-0140) Oasis Audio.
This is a story of discovering how to come to terms with disappointment and facing that life, as these women knew it, had ended. It is a story of walking in the wilderness of landscape, relationship and spirit and the power of family, friends and faith can see us through.

All Together in One Place. abr. ed. Jane Kirkpatrick. Narrated by Aimee Lilly. 4 CDs. (Running Time: 7 hrs. 30 min.). (Kinship & Courage Ser.). (ENG.). 2004. audio compact disk 29.99 (978-1-58926-144-0(5), W68L-014D) Oasis Audio.

***All together Now.** Monica McInerney. Read by Catherine Milte. (Running Time: 6 hrs. 20 mins.). 2009. 69.99 (978-1-74214-553-2(1), 9781742145532) Pub: Bolinda Pubng AUS. Dist(s): Bolinda Pub Inc

All together Now. unabr. ed. Monica McInerney. Read by Catherine Milte. (Running Time: 6 hrs. 20 mins.). 2009. audio compact disk 77.95 (978-1-74214-360-6(1), 9781742143606) Pub: Bolinda Pubng AUS. Dist(s): Bolinda Pub Inc

All Too Human: A Political Education. abr. ed. George Stephanopoulos. (Running Time: 3 hrs.). (ENG.). 2006. 14.98 (978-1-59483-660-2(4)) Pub: Hachet Audio. Dist(s): HachBkGrp

All Too Human: A Political Education. unabr. ed. George Stephanopoulos. Narrated by Jeff Woodman. 14 cass. (Running Time: 18 hrs. 30 mins.). 1999. 117.00 (978-0-7887-3462-5(8), 95885E7) Recorded Bks.
George Stephanopoulos was senior advisor during Clinton's first term. Now he shares an insider's view of the Clinton White House and recounts his journey from young idealist to seasoned realist. Captures both political greatness & human frailty.

All-True Travels & Adventures of Lidie Newton: A Novel. unabr. ed. Jane Smiley. Read by Anna Fields. 13 cass. (Running Time: 19 hrs. 30 mins.). 1998. 104.00 (978-0-7366-4142-5(4), 4646) Books on Tape.
In 1855, a young woman searches for the killers of her abolitionist husband in "Bloody Kansas".

All-True Travels & Adventures of Lidie Newton: A Novel, Set. abr. ed. Jane Smiley. Read by Anna Fields. 2 cass. (Running Time: 3 hrs.). 2000. 24.00 (978-0-679-40173-5(3), Random AudioBks) Random Audio Pubg.

***All Unquiet Things.** unabr. ed. Anna Jarzab. Narrated by Mike Chamberlain & Allyson Ryan. 9 CDs. (Running Time: 10 hrs. 38 mins.). (YA). (gr. 9 up). 2010. audio compact disk 60.00 (978-0-307-70633-1(8), Listening Lib) Pub: Random Audio Pubg. Dist(s): Random

All Unquiet Things. unabr. ed. Anna Jarzab. Read by Mike Chamberlain & Allyson Ryan. (ENG.). (J). (gr. 9). 2010. 44.00 (978-0-307-70631-7(1), Listening Lib) Pub: Random Audio Pubg. Dist(s): Random

All Vitality of the Physical Plane & Its Respective Limbs, One Their Existence & Well Being to the Presence of the Energy of the Spirit Current: Volume 12, Vol. 12. Speeches. Bhagat Singh Thind. (Running Time: 60 mins.). (ENG., 2003. audio compact disk 12.00 (978-1-932630-13-8(9)) Pub: Dr Bhagat Sin. Dist(s): Baker Taylor

All Vitality of the Physical Plane & Its Respective Limbs, One Their Existence & Well Beng to the Presence of the Energy of the Spirit Current: Volume 12, Vol. 12. Speeches. As told by Bhagat Singh Thind. (Running Time: 60 mins). (ENG., 2003. 6.50 (978-1-932630-36-7(8)) Pub: Dr Bhagat Sin. Dist(s): Baker Taylor

All We Ever Wanted Was Everything. abr. ed. Janelle Brown. Read by Rebecca Lowman. 5 CDs. (Running Time: 6 hrs.). (ENG.). 2008. audio compact disk 29.95 (978-0-7393-5826-9(X), Random AudioBks) Pub: Random Audio Pubg. Dist(s): Random

All We Know of Heaven. unabr. ed. Anna Tuttle Villegas. Read by Multivoice Production Staff et al. (Running Time: 6 hrs.). 2009. 39.97 (978-1-4233-8571-4(3), 9781423385714, Brinc Audio MP3 Lib); 39.97 (978-1-4233-8573-8(X), 9781423385738, BADLE); 24.99 (978-1-4233-8570-7(5), 9781423385707, Brilliance MP3); 24.99 (978-1-4233-8572-1(1), 9781423385721, BAD) Brilliance Audio.

All Within Reach. Perf. by Wendee et al. 1 cass. (Running Time: 1 hr.). (J). (ps-3). 1997. 11.99 (978-0-9656457-1-3(1)) REACH Fnd.
Beginning with the classic "Rock around the Clock," this collection of 23 songs features a variety of pop & rock styles performed by eleven groups of talented children's artists.

All Wound Up! A Family Music Party. unabr. ed. 1 cass. (Running Time: 44 mins.). 2001. 8.99 (978-1-57940-066-8(3)) Rounder Kids Mus Dist.
Eight original & four traditional pieces are played & sung in a variety of musical styles.

All You Need Is Kids. unabr. ed. Jonathan Hatch et al. Perf. by Missy Goldberg et al. 1 cass. (Running Time: 36 mins.). (J). (gr. k-3). 1991. 9.95 (978-1-881567-02-8(8)) Happy Kids Prods.
10 popular Beatles songs sung by children with a storyline about "Ob-la-di" & "Ob-la'da", coming to life as characters & teaching kids the "magic" of the Beatles.

All You Need to Know about the Music Business. abr. ed. Donald S. Passman. Read by Donald S. Passman. 2 cass. (Running Time: 3 hrs.). 1995. 16.95 (978-1-879371-94-1(4), 20410) Pub Mills.
From one of the music industry's most sought-after lawyers, here is a savvy insider's guide to legal & financial aspects of the business. Whether you want a career as a performer, writer, executive, or professional, or whether you are just curious about the multibillion-dollar music industry, you will benefit from this comprehensive overview of the entire business.

All You Need to Know to Celebrate Kwanzaa. unabr. ed. R. S. Rodgers. Read by LaDonna Mabry et al. 1 cass. (Running Time: 90 mins.). 2000. 16.95 MasterBuy Audio Bks.

All You Want to Know about Giants of Philosophy Cs: All You Want to Know Series. Knowledge Products. 2004. 15.95 (978-0-7435-4098-8(0)) Pub: S&S Audio. Dist(s): S and S Inc

All you want to know about giants of politicl Thou: Common Sense & the Declaration of Independence, the Federalist Papers. Knowledge Products. Read by Craig Deitschmann. 2004. 15.95 (978-0-7435-4099-5(9)) Pub: S&S Audio. Dist(s): S and S Inc

All you want to know about religion scriptures Spi. Knowledge Products. 2004. 18.95 (978-0-7435-4101-5(4)) Pub: S&S Audio. Dist(s): S and S Inc

All you want to know about science & Discovery: Isaac Newton's New Physics; Darwin & Evolution; Einstein's Revolution. Knowledge Products & Knowledge Products. Read by Edwin Newman. 2004. 18.95 (978-0-7435-4115-2(4)) Pub: S&S Audio. Dist(s): S and S Inc

All you want to know about: secrets of the great I: Money Managers & Mutual Funds Taxes, Asset Protection, & Estate Planning. Knowledge Products. 2004. 15.95 (978-0-7435-4116-9(2)) Pub: S&S Audio. Dist(s): S and S Inc

All You Want to Know about United States at War: The Civil War. Knowledge Products. 2004. 15.95 (978-0-7435-4120-6(0)) Pub: S&S Audio. Dist(s): S and S Inc

All You Want to Know about United States Constitution: The Constitution, the Bill of Rights & Additional Amendments. Walter Cronkite. 2004. 15.95 (978-0-7435-4123-7(5)) Pub: S&S Audio. Dist(s): S and S Inc

All You Want to Know: Kosovo, Serbia, Bosnia: The History Behind the Conflict in Central Europe. Knowledge Prdcts. Read by Richard C. Hottelet. 2004. 10.95 (978-0-7435-4100-8(6)) Pub: S&S Audio. Dist(s): S and S Inc

All Your Worth: The Ultimate Lifetime Money Plan. abr. ed. Elizabeth Warren & Amelia Warren Tyagi. 2005. 17.95 (978-0-7435-5110-6(9)) Pub: S&S Audio. Dist(s): S and S Inc

***All 10.** adpt. ed. EDCON Publishing Group Staff. (Bring the Classics to Life Ser.). (ENG.). 2008. audio compact disk 124.00 (978-1-55576-591-0(2)); audio compact disk 124.00 (978-1-55576-595-8(5)) EDCON Pubng.

***All 10 Level 1 Read along Books & Audio CDs: Bring the Classics to Life.** adpt. ed. EDCON Publishing Group Staff. (Bring the Classics to Life Ser.). 2008. pap. bk. 199.00 (978-1-55576-604-7(8)) EDCON Pubng.

***All 10 Level 2 Read along Books & Audio CDs: Bring the Classics to Life.** adpt. ed. EDCON Publishing Group Staff. (Bring the Classics to Life Ser.). 2008. pap. bk. 199.00 (978-1-55576-605-4(6)) EDCON Pubng.

***All 10 Level 3 Read-along Books & Audio CDs: Bring the Classics to Life.** adpt. ed. EDCON Publishing Group Staff. (Bring the Classics to Life Ser.). 2008. pap. bk. 199.00 (978-1-55576-606-1(4)) EDCON Pubng.

***All 10 Level 4 Read-along Books & CDs: Bring the Classics to Life.** adpt. ed. EDCON Publishing Group Staff. (Bring the Classics to Life Ser.). 2008. pap. bk. 199.00 (978-1-55576-607-8(2)) EDCON Pubng.

***All 10 Level 5 Read-Alongs: Bring the Classics to Life.** adpt. ed. EDCON Publishing Group Staff. (Bring the Classics to Life Ser.). 2008. pap. bk. 199.00 (978-1-55576-608-5(0)) EDCON Pubng.

***All 50 Audio Compact Discs: Bring the Classics to Life.** adpt. ed. EDCON Publishing Group Staff. (Bring the Classics to Life Ser.). 2008. audio compact disk 610.00 (978-1-55576-596-5(3)) EDCON Pubng.

***All 50 Read Alongs: Bring the Classics to Life.** adpt. ed. EDCON Publishing Group Staff. (Bring the Classics to Life Ser.). 2008. pap. bk. 995.00 (978-1-55576-609-2(9)) EDCON Pubng.

Allan Quatermain. unabr. ed. H. Rider Haggard. Read by Fred Williams. 8 cass. (Running Time: 11 hrs. 30 mins.). 1997. 56.95 (978-0-7861-1102-2(X), 1866) Blckstn Audio.
Three men & their guide Umslopogaas trek into the remote interior of Africa in search of a lost white race. Through unknown territories their perilous journey finally takes them to Zu-Vendis, a kingdom ruled by the beautiful twin sisters Nyleptha & Sorais. The sequel to "King Solomon's Mines" is filled with the spirit of adventure.

Allan Quatermain. unabr. ed. H. Rider Haggard. Read by Fred Williams. (Running Time: 11 hrs. 30 mins.). 2009. audio compact disk 100.00 (978-1-4417-1591-3(6)) Blckstn Audio.

Allegheny County Court of Common Pleas Civil Practice Manual. 1991. 26.00 (AC-629) PA Bar Inst.

Allegories of One's Own Mind: Melancholy in Victorian Poetry. abr. ed. David G. Riede. 2005. audio compact disk 9.95 (978-0-8142-9085-9(X)) Pub: Ohio St U Pr. Dist(s): Chicago Distribution Ctr

Allegro see Treasury of John Milton

Allegro see Poetry of John Milton

Allegro see Palgrave's Golden Treasury of English Poetry

Allegro, Adagio E Follia: For Violin & Keyboard, with optional Cello. Ed. by Roberto De Caro. 2007. pap. bk. 22.95 (978-1-902455-86-0(X), 190245586X) Pub: Schott Music Corp. Dist(s): H Leonard

Alleluia: Songs of Worship. Contrib. by Bill & Gloria Gaither and Their Homecoming Friends & Bill Gaither. Prod. by Bill Gaither. (Gaither Gospel Ser.). 2007. audio compact disk 13.99 (978-5-557-57266-8(X)) Gaither Music Co.

Alleluia & Hosanna. Tim Lester. Illus. by Maria Lester. 1 cass. 9.95 (978-1-929785-09-4(7)); audio compact disk 12.95 (978-1-929785-08-7(9)) Connexions KY.
Original gospel & contemporary songs.

Allen Dulles: Central Intelligence see Buckley's Firing Line

Allen Ginsberg. Allen Ginsberg. Read by Allen Ginsberg. 1 cass. (Running Time: 29 mins.). 1988. 10.00 (040188) New Letters.
The best-known of the living beat poets reflects on fame & on sacred speech.

***Allen Ginsberg Poetry Collection.** unabr. ed. Allen Ginsberg. Read by Allen Ginsberg. (ENG.). 2004. (978-0-06-082216-3(3), Harper Audio); (978-0-06-082217-0(1), Harper Audio) HarperCollins Pubs.

Allen Ginsberg Poetry Collection. unabr. ed. Allen Ginsberg. Read by Allen Ginsberg. 2 CDs. (Running Time: 3 hrs.). 2004. audio compact disk 22.00 (978-0-06-073415-2(9)) HarperCollins Pubs.

Allen Grossman. Read by Allen Grossman. 1 cass. (Running Time: 29 min.). 1985. 10.00 New Letters.
One of a weekly half-hour radio program with authors talking & presenting their own works.

Allen Jay & the Undergound Railroad. Marlene Targ Brill. Illus. by Janice Lee Porter. 1 cass. (Running Time: 19 mins.). (Readalongs for Beginning Readers Ser.). (J). (gr. 1-3). 2007. pap. bk. 16.95 (978-1-59519-945-4(4)) Live Oak Media.

Allen Jay & the Undergound Railroad, Set. Marlene Targ Brill. Illus. by Janice Lee Porter. 1 cass. (Running Time: 19 mins.). (Readalongs for Beginning Readers Ser.). (J). (gr. 1-3). 2007. pap. bk. 37.95 (978-1-59519-947-8(0)) Live Oak Media.

Allen Jay & the Underground Railroad. Marlene Targ Brill. Illus. by Janice Lee Porter. Narrated by Jay O. Sanders. (J). (gr. k-4). 2007. 9.95 (978-1-59519-944-7(6)) Live Oak Media.

Allen Jay & the Underground Railroad. abr. ed. Marlene Targ Brill. Read by Jay O. Sanders. (J). (gr. k-4). 2007. audio compact disk 12.95 (978-1-59519-948-5(9)) Live Oak Media.

Allergies: Ancient Truths, Natural Remedies & the Latest Findings for Your Health Today. unabr. ed. Don Colbert. Narrated by Steve Hiller. (Running Time: 1 hr. 30 mins.). (Bible Cure Ser.). (ENG.). 2003. audio compact disk 9.99 (978-1-58926-114-3(3)) Oasis Audio.
Bestselling BibleCure series from Dr. Don Colbert.

Allergies & Weight Control, Set. unabr. ed. Gary Null. 2 cass. 1995. 16.95 (978-1-879323-21-6(4)) Sound Horizons AV.
Gary Null, best-selling author, nutritionist, health advocate, radio & television personality lays down the stepping stones to an entirely new lifestyle. Gary informs us that as we age we develop cyclic allergies to the foods that comprise the staples of our diet. He then explains the step by step cleansing process for the rebalancing of the body.

Allergies, Asthma, Arthritis, Back Pain, Pack, Vol. 3. unabr. ed. Don Colbert. (Running Time: 18000 sec.). (Family Guide to Health Ser.). (ENG.). 2007. audio compact disk 19.99 (978-1-59859-307-5(2)) Oasis Audio.

Allergy. Bruce Goldberg. 1 cass. (Running Time: 20 mins.). (ENG.). 2006. 13.00 (978-1-885577-09-2(5)) Pub: B Goldberg. Dist(s): Baker Taylor
This self hypnosis tape trains the listener to overcome allergies.

Alles Gute, Vol. 1. 3rd ed. Jeanine Briggs. 1 cass. (Running Time: 90 min.). (GER.). (C). 1994. stu. ed. 29.06 (978-0-07-911540-9(3), Mc-H Human Soc) Pub: McGrw-H Hghr Educ. Dist(s): McGraw

Alles Gute, Vol. 2. 4th ed. Jeanine Briggs. 1 cass. (Running Time: 90 min.). 1994. stu. ed. 25.00 (978-0-07-911871-4(2), Mc-H Human Soc) Pub: McGrw-H Hghr Educ. Dist(s): McGraw

Alles in Allem: Readings & Activities. Jeanine Briggs. 1 cass. (Running Time: 90 min.). (GER & ENG.). (C). 1994. 65.63 (978-0-07-911435-8(0), 0079114350, Mc-H Human Soc) Pub: McGrw-H Hghr Educ. Dist(s): McGraw

Alleviate Pain. Betty L. Randolph. 1 stereo cass. (Running Time: 45 mins.). (Self-Hypnosis Ser.). 9.98 (101) Randolph Tapes.
Side 1 discusses handling pain. Side 2 ...relaxation & imagery. Music background & spoken word.

Alley Cats. (Sails Literacy Ser.). (gr. 2 up). 10.00 (978-0-7578-2665-8(2)) Rigby Educ.

Allez Viens!, Level 2. 3rd ed. Holt, Rinehart and Winston Staff. 2002. audio compact disk 367.80 (978-0-03-065678-1(8)) Holt McDoug.
With Allez, viens!, everything you need to transport your students to the French-speaking world is at your fingertips. The program?s integrated approach to language-learning develops students? listening, reading, writing, and speaking skills with a variety of print and technology resources. Students learn to communicate effectively and express themselves with confidence.

Allez Viens! Holt French 1. Holt, Rinehart and Winston Staff. 1996. 305.80 (978-0-03-095113-8(5)) Holt McDoug.

Allez Viens! Holt French 2. Holt, Rinehart and Winston Staff. (YA). 1996. 305.80 (978-0-03-095143-5(7)) Holt McDoug.

Allez Viens! Holt French 3. Holt, Rinehart and Winston Staff. 1996. 305.80 (978-0-03-095183-1(6)) Holt McDoug.

Allez Viens! Level 1. Holt, Rinehart and Winston Staff. 1996. audio compact disk 371.33 (978-0-03-008353-2(2)) Holt McDoug.

Allez Viens! Level 1. 3rd ed. Holt, Rinehart and Winston Staff. 2002. audio compact disk 367.80 (978-0-03-065669-9(9)) Holt McDoug.

Allez Viens! Level 2. Holt, Rinehart and Winston Staff. 1996. audio compact disk 371.33 (978-0-03-008358-7(3)) Holt McDoug.

Allez Viens! Level 3. 3rd ed. Holt, Rinehart and Winston Staff. 2002. audio compact disk 367.80 (978-0-03-065684-2(2)) Holt McDoug.

Allies. unabr. ed. Christie Golden. Read by Marc Thompson. (Star Wars Ser.). (ENG.). 2010. audio compact disk 40.00 (978-0-7393-7669-0(1), Random AudioBks) Pub: Random Audio Pubg. Dist(s): Random

Allie's Christmas. 1 cass. (J). 9.98 Long Cass. Blister. (978-1-57132-179-4(9), 9597) Lyrick Studios.
Mix of traditional carols & Christmas favorites, along with a new song or two & with an original Allie Christmas story.

Allies in Educational Reform: How Teachers, Unions & Administrators Can Join Forces for Better Schools. Jerome M. Rosow et al. (Education-Higher Education Ser.). 1988. bk. 36.95 (978-1-55542-158-8(X), Jossey-Bass) Wiley US.

Allies Years. Perf. by Bob Carlisle. 1 cass. audio compact disk 5.98 CD. (978-1-57908-167-6(3), 7045) Platinm Enter.

Alligator Alley. (Sails Literacy Ser.). (gr. 1 up). 10.00 (978-0-7578-2655-9(5)) Rigby Educ.

Alligator in the Elevator. Rick Charette. Read by Rick Charette. 1 cass. (Running Time: 45 mins.). (Snappy Songs for Kids Ser.). (J). (gr. k-5). 1985. 9.98 (978-1-884210-00-6(7), PPC-001); 9.98 (978-1-884210-02-0(3)) Pine Pt Record.
With imaginative songs for children including the title song, "The Pony" the number one hit, "I Love Mud", Rick Charette has become a leading songwriter for children.

Alligator Pie & Other Poems. unabr. ed. Dennis Lee. Perf. by Dennis Lee. 1 cass. (J). 1984. 9.95 (978-0-89845-839-8(0), CPN 1530) HarperCollins Pubs.

Alligators All Around. (J). 2004. bk. 24.95 (978-0-7882-0568-2(4)); pap. bk. 14.95 (978-0-7882-0633-7(8)); 8.95 (978-1-56008-827-1(3)); cass. & flmstrp 30.00 (978-0-89719-642-0(2)) Weston Woods.

Alligators All Around: An Alphabet. Maurice Sendak. 1 cass. (Running Time: 1 hr.). (J). (ps-3). 2000. pap. bk. 12.95 Weston Woods.
In this delightful rhyme, a group of alligators dances & sings its way through the alphabet in style.

Allison & Busby see Above the Bright Blue Sky

***Allligators, Bees, & Surprise, Oh, My! Folktales Revived!** Adapted by Mary Hamilton. Retold by Mary Hamilton. (J). 2009. audio compact disk 15.00 (978-1-885556-09-7(8)) Hidden Sprng.

Allons a Paris! R. De Roussey De Sales. (Uncle Charles Adventure Ser.). (YA). (gr. 8-10). 15.00 (978-0-8442-1027-8(7)) M-H Contemporary.
Presents a collection of dialogues designed for intermediate students.

Allons Y! 5th ed. Jeannette D. Bragger & Rice. stu. ed. 12.50 (978-0-8384-0251-1(8)); 6.50 (978-0-8384-0253-5(4)) Heinle.

Allons Y! 5th ed. Jeannette D. Bragger & Rice. 1 cass. (Running Time: 1 hr.). 2002. tchr. ed. 6.25 (978-0-8384-0252-8(6)) Heinle.
French teaching and learning with its emphasis on communicative competence, allowing students to use language creatively from the outset and function effectively in contexts likely to be encountered in real life.

Allons Y! 5th ed. Jeannette D. Bragger & Rice. 2000. bk. 63.75 (978-0-8384-0242-9(9)) Heinle.
Introductory French teaching and learning with its emphasis on communicative competence, allowing students to use language creatively from the outset and function effectively in contexts likely to be encountered in real life.

Allons Y! 5th ed. Bragger & Rice. (C). bk. 119.95 (978-0-8384-8463-0(8)) Heinle.

Allons-Y! 6th ed. Jeannette D. Bragger & Donald B. Rice. (C). 2003. bk. 94.95 (978-0-8384-6018-4(6)) Pub: Heinle. Dist(s): CENGAGE Learn
Introductory French program with emphasis on French and francophone culture, fine-tuned organization, and the latest technologies.

***Allons Y.** 6th ed. Donald B. Rice & Jeannette D. Bragger. (ENG.). (C). 2003. 60.95 (978-1-4130-0200-3(5)) Pub: Heinle. Dist(s): CENGAGE Learn

Allowance Kit: A Hands-on Money Management System for Kids. abr. ed. Michael J. Searls. Illus. by Todd Clary. Contrib. by Jeff Marlin. 1 cass. (Running Time: 30 mins.). (J). (gr. 2-9). 1996. bk. 29.95 (978-0-9648265-9-5(3)) Summit Finan.
A fun & interactive way for kids to learn about money.

Allowing Consciousness to Rise. Swami Amar Jyoti. 1 cass. 1982. 9.95 (C-33) Truth Consciousness.
Rising, not falling, in Love. Higher consciousness has all the answers for the lower stages.

Allowing Kids to Choose Success. 2004. audio compact disk (978-1-930429-58-1(4)) Love Logic.

All's Well That Ends Well. Prod. by Barbara Worthy. 3 CDs. (Running Time: 3 hrs.). 2005. audio compact disk 24.95 (978-0-660-19035-8(4)) Pub: Canadian Broadcasting CAN. Dist(s): Georgetown Term
The play relates the efforts of Helena, daughter of a renowned physician, to make Bertram, the Count of Rousillon, her husband. When the gravely ill king of France summons Bertram, Helena follows and administers a cure that had been provided by her father. In return, the king invites her to select a husband, her choice being the evasive Bertram.

***All's Well That Ends Well.** abr. ed. William Shakespeare. Read by Claire Bloom. (ENG.). 2003. (978-0-06-074331-4(X), Caedmon) HarperCollins Pubs.

***All's Well That Ends Well.** abr. ed. William Shakespeare. Read by Claire Bloom. (ENG.). 2004. (978-0-06-081462-5(4), Caedmon) HarperCollins Pubs.

All's Well that Ends Well. unabr. ed. William Shakespeare. Read by Emily Woof et al. (Arkangel Shakespeare Ser.). (ENG.). 2005. audio compact disk 24.95 (978-1-932219-02-9(1)) Pub: AudioGO. Dist(s): Perseus Dist
As a reward for her service, the King of France allows Helena to choose a husband from among his court, but Count Bertram heads off to battle rather than marry beneath his station. Helena's daring plan to win the man she loves highlights this dark comedy.

All's Well that Ends Well. unabr. ed. William Shakespeare. 2 vols. (Running Time: 2 hrs.). Dramatization. 2003. audio compact disk 29.95 (978-0-563-49676-2(2)) BBC Worldwide.

All's Well that Ends Well. unabr. ed. William Shakespeare. Perf. by Claire Bloom & Eric Portman. 2 cass. (Running Time: 2 hrs. 47 mins.). Dramatization. 17.95 (H145) Blckstn Audio.
The adaptation from the Boccaccio Decameron is a "dark" comedy which eloquently explores human virtue & gullibility. It is the story of Helena, who cures the king of France & asks for the hand of Bertram in return.

All's Well that Ends Well. unabr. ed. William Shakespeare. Read by Audio Partners Staff. 2 cass. (Running Time: 2 hrs. 37 mins.). (Arkangel Shakespeare Ser.). 2004. 17.95 (978-1-932219-42-5(0), Atlntc Mnthly) Pub: Grove-Atltic. Dist(s): PerseuPGW

All's Well that Ends Well. unabr. ed. William Shakespeare. Perf. by Claire Bloom & Lynn Redgrave. 2 cass. (Running Time: 2 hrs.). Dramatization. HarperCollins Pubs.

All's Well that Ends Well. unabr. ed. William Shakespeare. Perf. by Anton Lesser & Robert Stephens. 2 cass. (Running Time: 2 hrs.). 17.95 (SCN 192) J Norton Pubs.
In Helena, Shakespeare has created one of his most intelligent & forceful heroines, who plots, intrigues & conspires to win the love of her husband, the young, arrogant Count of Rossillion.

All's Well that Ends Well. unabr. ed. William Shakespeare. Perf. by Claire Bloom et al. 2 cass. (Running Time: 3 hrs.). Dramatization. 2000. 22.00 (21514E5); 34.24 (40746E5) Recorded Bks.

All's Well that Ends Well. unabr. ed. William Shakespeare. Narrated by Flo Gibson. 2 cass. (Running Time: 3 hrs.). 2003. 14.95 (978-1-55685-713-3(6)) Audio Bk Con.
By subterfuge Helena regains the ring that finally brings her love to fruition.

Allure of Gnosticism for Jung. Robert Segal. Read by Robert Segal. 1 cass. (Running Time: 88 mins.). 1993. 10.95 (978-0-7822-0426-1(0), 509) C G Jung IL.
Robert Segal, editor of The Gnostic Jung, explores Jung's interest in Gnosticism, his interpretation of Gnosticism as the ancient counterpart to analytical psychology, his possible misinterpretation of the psychological meaning of Gnosticism & the common characterization of Jung himself as a Gnostic.

Ally's World: Angels, Arguments & a Furry, Merry Christmas. unabr. ed. Karen McCombie. Read by Daniela Denby-Ashe. 4 CDs. (Running Time: 3 hrs. 55 mins.). (YA). (gr. 5-8). 2008. audio compact disk 34.95 (978-1-4056-5763-1(4), Chivers Child Audio) AudioGO.
'Tis the season to be jolly... So it's a shame Rowan comes over a bit too festive with her fairy lights and nearly causes a major emergency! What with bickering sisters, a half-eaten angel and troublesome mates, I'm in need of a Christmas miracle. Like a kiss under the mistletoe, maybe.

Ally's World: Boys, Brothers & Jelly-Belly Dancing. Karen McCombie. Read by Daniela Denby-Ashe. (Running Time: 13500 sec.). (J). (gr. 4-7). 2001. audio compact disk 29.95 (978-0-7540-6780-1(7)) AudioGo GBR.

Ally's World: Friends, Freak-Outs & Very Secret Secrets. Karen McCombie. Read by Daniela Denby-Ashe. (Running Time: 11640 sec.). (J). (gr. 4-7). 2001. audio compact disk 29.95 (978-0-7540-6746-7(7)) AudioGo GBR.

Ally's World: Sisters, Super-Creeps & Slushy, Gushy Love Songs. unabr. ed. Karen McCombie. Read by Daniela Denby-Ashe. 3 CDs. (Running Time: 3 hrs. 35 mins.). (YA). (gr. 5-8). 2006. audio compact disk 29.95 (978-1-4056-5512-5(7), Chivers Child Audio) AudioGO.

Alma August & Maud: From Sweden to the Sea. Prod. by Patience Wes. 2008. audio compact disk 28.00 (978-1-4276-3325-5(8)) AardGP.

Almanac of Business & Industrial Financial Ratios on CD. Leo Troy. 2005. audio compact disk (978-0-8080-1411-9(0), 05787400) Toolkit Media.

Almanac of Words at Play. unabr. ed. Read by Heywood Hale Broun & Willard Espy. 1 cass. (Running Time: 56 mins.). (Broun Radio Ser.). 12.95 (C40223) J Norton Pubs.

Almayer's Folly. unabr. ed. Joseph Conrad. Read by Geoffrey Howard. (Running Time: 21600 sec.). 2007. audio compact disk 29.95 (978-0-7861-6213-0(9)); audio compact disk & audio compact disk 45.00 (978-0-7861-6212-3(0)) Blckstn Audio.

Almayer's Folly: A Story of an Eastern River. Joseph Conrad. (1091) Books on Tape.

Almayer's Folly: A Story of an Eastern River, unabr. ed. Joseph Conrad. Read by Geoffrey Howard. 4 cass. (Running Time: 6 hrs.). 1997. 32.95 (978-0-7861-1115-2(1), 1882) Blckstn Audio.
Though married to a bitter & hateful Malayan wife, Almayer refuses to accept the financial ruin which he has precipitated. Instead he dreams of fantastic wealth & a return to the civilization of his youth, accompanied by his loving daughter, Nina. But when Nina turns away from his elusive fantasies to the stark reality of her native lover, Almayer must face his inevitable destruction.

Almighty Bach. 1 cass. (Vox - Turnabout Classical Ser.). 3.98 (CTX 4809) VOX Music Grp.

almohadon que hizo Mama. (SPA.). (gr. k-1). 10.00 (978-0-7635-6261-8(0)) Rigby Educ.

Almost a Backslider. Dan Corner. 1 cass. 3.00 (11) Evang Outreach.

Almost a Crime. unabr. ed. Penny Vincenzi. Read by Laura Brattan. 22 cass. (Running Time: 27 hrs.). 1999. 109.95 (978-0-7531-0658-7(2), 991203) Pub: ISIS Audio GBR. Dist(s): Ulverscroft US
Tom & Octavia Fleming have what is known as a "power marriage", high profile & mutually supportive, both professionally & personally. They are attractive, rich & successful & their lives are a whirlwind of networking opportunities, corporate entertainment & breakfast meetings. They seem to have the perfect package, until, that is, Octavia discovers that Tom has been having an affair & is forced to questions who she really is without the camouflage of her not-so-powerful marriage.

***Almost Astronauts: 13 Women Who Dared to Dream.** Tanya Lee Stone. Contrib. by Susan Ericksen. Frwd. by Margaret A. Weitekamp. (Playaway Young Adult Ser.). (J). 2009. 49.99 (978-1-4418-3277-1(7)) Find a World.

***Almost Astronauts: 13 Women Who Dared to Dream: 13 Women Who Dared to Dream.** unabr. ed. Tanya Lee Stone. Read by Susan Ericksen. (Running Time: 4 hrs.). 2010. 39.97 (978-1-4418-9059-7(9), 9781441890597, Candlewick Bril); 14.99 (978-1-4418-9056-6(4), 9781441890566, Candlewick Bril); audio compact disk 14.99 (978-1-4418-9055-9(6), 9781441890559, Candlewick Bril); audio compact disk 19.99 (978-1-4418-9054-2(8), 9781441890542, Candlewick Bril); audio compact disk 54.97 (978-1-4418-9057-3(2), 9781441890573, Candlewick Bril); audio compact disk 39.97 (978-1-4418-9058-0(0), 9781441890580, Candlewick Bril) Brilliance Audio.

Almost Eden. abr. ed. Dorothy Garlock. Read by Carrie Gordon Lowrey. 1 cass. (Running Time: 90 mins.). 1995. 5.99 (978-1-57096-038-3(0), RAZ 938) Romance Alive Audio.
In the uncharted Missouri territory of the late 19th century, half-French, half-Indian woodsman Baptiste Lightbody & ethereal woodsprite & beauty Maggie travel through the perilous woodlands finding a love that deepens with every step & the mountain-top home of their dreams.

Almost Famous: How to Market Yourself for Success. Nicolette Lemmon. 2 cass. (Running Time: 1 hr. 40 mins.). 1996. 29.95 (978-0-9650880-1-5(4)) Lemmon Pubng Grp.
How to market yourself for success & career management.

Almost Heaven. abr. ed. Becky L. Weyrich. Read by Emelia Baum. 1 cass. (Running Time: 90 mins.). 1995. 5.99 (RAZ 927) Romance Alive Audio.
When Angela Gentry Rhodes' perfect life is cut short by a tragic car accident, she must learn what it is to become a guardian angel. She must untangle the web of her past lives & bring peace to those she has left behind before she can find the glorious happiness that awaits her for all time.

Almost Home. unabr. ed. Debbie Macomber et al. (Running Time: 14 hrs.). 2009. 24.99 (978-1-4418-0075-6(1), 9781441800756, BAD) Brilliance Audio.

Almost Home. unabr. ed. Debbie Macomber et al. Read by Joyce Bean et al. (Running Time: 14 hrs.). 2009. 39.97 (978-1-4418-0074-9(3), 9781441800749, Brlnc Audio MP3 Lib) Brilliance Audio.

Almost Home. unabr. ed. Debbie Macomber et al. Read by Laural Merlington et al. (Running Time: 14 hrs.). 2009. 39.97 (978-1-4418-0076-3(X), 9781441800763, BADLE) Brilliance Audio.

Almost Home. unabr. ed. Debbie Macomber et al. Read by Joyce Bean et al. (Running Time: 14 hrs.). 2009. audio compact disk 34.99 (978-1-4418-0071-8(9), 9781441800718, Bril Audio CD Unabri); audio compact disk 87.97 (978-1-4418-0072-5(7), 9781441800725, BriAudCD Unabrid) Brilliance Audio.

Almost Home. unabr. ed. Laural Merlington et al. Read by Cathy Lamb et al. (Running Time: 14 hrs.). 2009. 24.99 (978-1-4418-0073-2(5), 9781441800732, Brilliance MP3) Brilliance Audio.

Almost Home: Queen of Hearts: A Selection from the Almost Home Anthology. unabr. ed. Judy Duarte. (Running Time: 3 hrs.). 2009. 24.99 (978-1-4418-0083-1(2), 9781441800831, BAD); 39.97 (978-1-4418-0084-8(0), 9781441800848, BADLE) Brilliance Audio.

Almost Home: Whale Island: A Selection from the Almost Home Anthology. unabr. ed. Cathy Lamb. (Running Time: 4 hrs.). 2009. 24.99 (978-1-4418-0081-7(6), 9781441800817, BAD); 39.97 (978-1-4418-0082-4(4), 9781441800824, BADLE) Brilliance Audio.

Almost Like Being in Love. unabr. ed. Christina Dodd. Read by Natalie Ross. (Running Time: 10 hrs.). (Lost Texas Hearts Ser.: No. 1). 2010. 39.97 (978-1-4418-2486-8(3), 9781441824868, BADLE) Brilliance Audio.

Almost Like Being in Love. unabr. ed. Christina Dodd. Read by Natalie Ross. (Running Time: 10 hrs.). (Lost Texas Hearts Ser.: No. 2). 2010. 39.97 (978-1-4418-2484-4(7), 9781441824844, Brlnc Audio MP3 Lib); 24.99 (978-1-4418-2483-7(9), 9781441824837, Brilliance MP3); 24.99 (978-1-4418-2485-1(5), 9781441824851, BAD); audio compact disk 89.97 (978-1-4418-2482-0(0), 9781441824820, BriAudCD Unabrid); audio compact disk 29.99 (978-1-4418-2481-3(2), 9781441824813, Bril Audio CD Unabri) Brilliance Audio.

Almost Moon. unabr. ed. Alice Sebold. Read by Joan Allen. (Running Time: 9 hrs. 30 mins.). (ENG.). 2007. 14.98 (978-1-60024-031-7(3)) Pub: Hachet Audio. Dist(s): HachBkGrp

Almost Moon. unabr. ed. Alice Sebold. Read by Joan Allen. 8 CDs. (Running Time: 9 hrs.). 2007. audio compact disk 90.00 (978-1-4159-4595-7(0), BksonTape) Pub: Random Audio Pubg. Dist(s): Random
Clair and Helen Knightly are a parent and child locked in a relationship so unrelenting that they have become the center of each other's worlds. But as this electrifying novel opens, Helen crosses a boundary she never thought she would approach. And while her act is almost unconscious, it somehow seems like the fulfillment of a lifetime's unspoken wishes. Over the next twenty-four hours, Helen's life rushes in at her as she is forced to confront the choices that have brought her to this one riveting crossroad. As a woman who spent years trying to win the love of someone who had none to spare, she now faces an uncertain and dangerous freedom.

***Almost Our Time: Generation X Takes on America's Challeges.** Rob Stam. (ENG.). (C). 2010. 10.99 (978-0-9830140-0-3(0)) Sozo Media.

***Almost Perfect.** unabr. ed. Susan Mallery. Read by Tanya Eby. (Running Time: 9 hrs.). (Fool's Gold Ser.). 2010. 19.99 (978-1-4418-4233-6(0), 9781441842336, BAD); 19.99 (978-1-4418-4231-2(4), 9781441842312, Brilliance MP3); 39.97 (978-1-4418-4234-3(9), 9781441842343, BADLE); 39.97 (978-1-4418-4232-9(2), 9781441842329, Brlnc Audio MP3 Lib); audio compact disk 19.99 (978-1-4418-4229-9(2), 9781441842299, Bril Audio CD Unabri); audio compact disk 79.97 (978-1-4418-4230-5(6), 9781441842305, BriAudCD Unabrid) Brilliance Audio.

Almost There: The Onward Journey of a Dublin Woman. unabr. ed. Nuala O'Faolain. 2004. 21.95 (978-0-7435-4125-1(1)) Pub: S&S Audio. Dist(s): S and S Inc

***Almost True Story of Ryan Fisher: A Novel.** unabr. ed. Rob Stennett. (Running Time: 9 hrs. 26 mins. 0 sec.). (ENG.). 2009. 12.99 (978-0-310-77210-1(9)) Zondervan.

almuerzo en el jardín Audio CD: Emergent Set A. Benchmark Education Staff. Ed. by Katherine Scraper. (Early Explorers Ser.). (J). 2008. audio compact disk 10.00 (978-1-60437-241-0(9)) Benchmark Educ.

Aloft. unabr. ed. Chang-Rae Lee. Read by Don Leslie. 9 CDs. (Running Time: 12 hrs.). (ENG.). 2004. audio compact disk 34.95 (978-1-56511-889-8(8), 1565118898) Pub: HighBridge. Dist(s): Workman Pub

Aloha Anniversary. (Luau Celebration Ser.). 5.00 (978-1-58513-068-9(0), 1-HE-A) Dance Fantasy.

Alone see Raven & Other Works

Alone. abr. ed. Lisa Gardner. Read by Holter Graham. 4 CDs. (Running Time: 18000 sec.). (ENG.). 2006. audio compact disk 14.99 (978-0-7393-2448-6(9), Random AudioBks) Pub: Random Audio Pubg. Dist(s): Random

Alone. unabr. ed. Lisa Gardner. Read by Anna Fields. 7 cass. (Running Time: 10 hrs.). 2005. 81.00 (978-1-4159-1557-8(1)) Books on Tape.
As a sniper with the elite Massachusetts State Police SWAT Team, Bobby Dakota saved a woman and her young son by shooting her armed husband. But vicious rumors begin to circulate the next morning when Bobby loses his gun and his privileges. It turns out the dead man was the son of a prominent Boston judge and had accused his wife of poisoning their son. Facing awkward stares and a crippling wrongful death lawsuit, Bobby begins his own investigation into the fateful shooting-and a fight to reclaim the life he holds dear. As the trail takes him into a twisted minefield of sordid wealth and family secrets, he is learning that nothing - and no one - is what they seem.

Alone. unabr. collector's ed. Richard E. Byrd. Read by Wolfram Kandinsky. 9 cass. (Running Time: 9 hrs.). 1987. 54.00 (978-0-7366-1108-4(8), 2034) Books on Tape.
The South Pole solo. Admiral Byrd spent six months by himself in a frozen, sub-arctic winter.

***Alone: Orphaned on the Ocean.** unabr. ed. Richard Logan & Tere Dupperault Fassbender. Narrated by Johnny Heller & Jo Anna Perrin. (Running Time: 7 hrs. 0 mins.). 2010. 14.99 (978-1-4001-8857-4(1)); 19.99 (978-1-4001-6857-6(0)); audio compact disk 29.99 (978-1-4001-1857-1(3)); audio compact disk 71.99 (978-1-4001-4857-8(X)) Pub: Tantor Media. Dist(s): IngramPubServ

Alone Across the Atlantic. unabr. collector's ed. Francis Chichester. Read by Peter MacDonald. 7 cass. (Running Time: 7 hrs.). 1987. 42.00 (978-0-7366-1131-2(2), 2054) Books on Tape.
A brave man & his small boat alone on a big sea.

Alone & Together: Personal & Collective Dimensions of Religious Experience. Tesse Donnelly. Read by Tesse Donnelly. 2 cass. (Running Time: 2 hrs. 30 mins.). 1991. 18.95 (978-0-7822-0355-4(8), 451) C G Jung IL.

Alone but Not Alone. Contrib. by Marvin Winans & Michelle S. Duffie. 2007. audio compact disk 13.99 (978-5-557-59353-3(5)) Pure SpringG.

Alone but Not Lonely: I Cor. 7. Ed Young. 1989. 4.95 (978-0-7417-1756-6(5), 756) Win Walk.

Alone in Eden. Stephen R. Pastore. 2006. pap. bk. 14.95 (978-0-9777196-9-3(3)) Cohort Pr.

Alone in Eden. Stephen R. Pastore. Read by Michael G. Stanton. 3 CDs. (Running Time: 3 hrs, 30 mins.). 2006. audio compact disk 39.95 (978-0-9777196-8-6(5)) Cohort Pr.

Alone over the Tasman Sea. unabr. collector's ed. Francis Chichester. Read by Edward Faridany. 7 cass. (Running Time: 10 hr. 30 min.). 1988. 56.00 (978-0-7366-1254-8(8), 2168) Books on Tape.
What this man did on sea, he did first in the air. A 1931 flight from New Zealand to Australia.

Alone with Christ. Edd Anthony. Read by Edd Anthony. 2007. audio compact disk 16.95 (978-1-881586-21-0(9)) Canticle Cass.

Alone with God. Elbert Willis. 1 cass. (Increasing Spiritual Assurance Ser.). 4.00 Fill the Gap.

Alone with God. unabr. ed. Elisabeth Elliot. Read by Elisabeth Elliot. 3 cass. (Running Time: 2 hrs. 44 mins.). 1990. 14.95 (978-0-8474-2018-6(3)) Back to Bible.
A look at how to find encouragement, instruction & light on life's path from God & His Word.

Alone with the Dead. unabr. ed. Robert J. Randisi. Read by Stephen Berger. 8 vols. (Running Time: 8 hrs.). (Joe Keough Mystery Ser.: Bk. 1). 1999. bk. 69.95 (978-0-7927-2267-0(1), CSL 156, Chivers Sound Lib) AudioGO.
When a string of murdered young women are found, the New York City Police Department launches an all-out effort to catch the killer who is dubbed "The Lover," but Detective Joe Keough, branded a liability by the department & dumped at an out-of-the-way Brooklyn precinct, believes that the murders are the work of two men. With nothing to lose, he's willing to challenge the system that scorned him in order to find the truth.

Alone yet Not Alone: The Story of Barbara & Regina Leininger. Tracy Leininger. Narrated by Ladonna Day. 3 cass. (Running Time: 3hrs.). (YA). 2001. 21.00 (978-0-9724287-0-5(4)) His Seasons.
Reading of the book title "Alone Yet Not Alone".

Along Came a Spider. abr. ed. James Patterson. Read by Alton Fitzgerald White & Michael Cumpstey. (Alex Cross Ser.: No. 1). (ENG.). 2005. 14.98 (978-1-59483-270-3(6)) Pub: Hachet Audio. Dist(s): HachBkGrp

Along Came a Spider. abr. ed. James Patterson. 5 CDs. (Running Time: 6 Hours). (Alex Cross Ser.: No. 1). 2004. audio compact disk 29.98 (978-0-694-52449-5(2)) HarperCollins Pubs.

Along Came a Spider. abr. ed. James Patterson. Read by Alton Fitzgerald White & Michael Cumpstey. 4 cass. (Running Time: 6 hrs.). (Alex Cross Ser.: No. 1). 2005. 14.98 (978-1-59483-120-1(3)) Pub: Hachet Audio. Dist(s): HachBkGrp

Along Came a Spider. unabr. ed. James Patterson. Read by Michael Kramer. 10 CDs. (Running Time: 12 hrs.). (Alex Cross Ser.: No. 1). 2001. audio compact disk 80.00 Books on Tape.

Along Came a Spider. unabr. ed. James Patterson. 9 cass. (Running Time: 13 hrs. 30 mins.). (Alex Cross Ser.: No. 1). 2000. 72.00 (978-0-7366-5524-8(7)) Books on Tape.

Along Came a Spider. unabr. ed. James Patterson. Read by Charles Turner. (Alex Cross Ser.: No. 1). (ENG.). 2005. 16.98 (978-1-59483-420-2(2)) Pub: Hachet Audio. Dist(s): HachBkGrp

Along Came a Spider. unabr. ed. James Patterson. (Running Time: 9 hrs.). (Alex Cross Ser.: No. 1). (ENG.). 2009. 59.98 (978-1-60788-075-2(X)) Pub: Hachet Audio. Dist(s): HachBkGrp

***Along came Dylan.** Stephen Foster. Read by Nicholas Bell. (Running Time: 4 hrs. 35 mins.). 2009. 59.99 (978-1-74214-551-8(5), 9781742145518) Pub: Bolinda Pubng AUS. Dist(s): Bolinda Pub Inc

Along Came Dylan. unabr. ed. Stephen Foster. Read by Nicholas Bell. 4 CDs. (Running Time: 4 hrs. 35 mins.). 2009. audio compact disk 57.95 (978-1-74214-079-7(3), 9781742140797) Pub: Bolinda Pubng AUS. Dist(s): Bolinda Pub Inc

Along for the Ride. AIO Team Staff. Created by Focus on the Family Staff. 4 CDs. (Running Time: 5 hrs.). (Adventures in Odyssey Ser.). (ENG.). (J). 2005. audio compact disk 24.99 (978-1-58997-078-6(0)) Pub: Focus Family. Dist(s): Tyndale Hse

Along for the Ride. unabr. ed. Sarah Dessen. 11 CDs. (Running Time: 13 hrs.). (ENG.). (YA). (gr. 7 up). 2009. audio compact disk 34.95 (978-0-14-314466-3(9), PengAudBks) Penguin Grp USA.

***Along for the Ride.** unabr. ed. Sarah Dessen. Narrated by Rachel Botchan. 11 CDs. (Running Time: 12 hrs. 45 mins.). 2009. audio compact disk 108.75 (978-1-4407-3027-6(X)) Recorded Bks.

***Along for the Ride.** unabr. ed. Sarah Dessen. Read by Rachel Botchan. 1 Playaway. (Running Time: 12 hrs. 45 mins.). 2009. 59.75 (978-1-4407-3033-7(4)); 88.75 (978-1-4407-3023-8(7)) Recorded Bks.

***Along for the Ride.** unabr. collector's ed. Sarah Dessen. Read by Rachel Botchan. 11 CDs. (Running Time: 12 hrs. 45 mins.). 2009. audio compact disk 46.95 (978-1-4407-3031-3(8)) Recorded Bks.

Along Greathouse Road. Poems. Read by Anne McCrady. 2 CDs. (Running Time: 94 mins.). 2005. audio compact disk (978-0-9720699-2-2(5)) InSpiritry Pubs.
Along Greathouse Road is an audio book version of the award-winning poetry collection of the same name written by poet & storyteller Anne McCrady, with poems read by the author over a backdrop of varied acoustic musical instrumentation. Like postcards of life outside the city, each track, each tune, each poem offers a story all its own. Many of the poems feature Texas settings, rural characters and family moments.

Along the Luangwa: A Story of an African Floodplain. Schuyler Bull. Read by Randye Kaye. Illus. by Alan Male. 1 cass. (Running Time: 14 mins.). (Nature Conservancy Habitat Ser.: Vol. 13). (ENG.). (J). (gr. 1-4). 1999. 19.95 (978-1-56899-778-0(7), BC7013) Soundprints.
In the silver moonlight fifty Nile Crocodile babies hatch in the Luangwa River Valley of Zambia.

Along the Path of Action Tapes. Read by Jack Schwarz. 3 cass. 35.00 (#100) Aletheia Psycho.

Alonso to Ferdinand see Twentieth-Century Poetry in English, No. 1, Recordings of Poets Reading Their Own Poetry

Alpha. unabr. ed. Catherine Asaro & Hillary Huber. (Running Time: 11 hrs. 5 mins.). 2008. 29.95 (978-1-4332-5270-9(8)); 72.95 (978-1-4332-5268-6(6)); audio compact disk 90.00 (978-1-4332-5269-3(4)) Blckstn Audio.

Alpha, Beta, Gamma, Dead. Betty Rowlands. 2008. 54.95 (978-1-84559-970-6(5)); audio compact disk 71.95 (978-1-84559-971-3(3)) Pub: Soundings Ltd GBR. Dist(s): Ulverscroft US

Alpha-Blocke: Alpha-Blocke.com Learning Forum Animals, Art & the Alphabet Series with Case & Talking CD. Conrad Heiderer. 2004. spiral bd. 39.95 (978-0-9746699-0-8(3)) C Heiderer.

Alpha Capers Audio. Created by ECS Learning Systems. (J). 1998. (978-1-57022-191-0(X)) ECS Lrn Systs.

Alpha Capers Tape & Book. (J). 1998. (978-1-57022-190-3(1)) ECS Lrn Systs.

Alpha Hand ABC Shorthand: Notetaking & Secretarial. Steve Rosen. (Alpha Hand Ser.). 1989. 7.50 (978-0-936862-33-0(5), 98) DDC Pub.

Alpha Kardia Relaxation System: In the Heart. Executive Producer Kelly Rein. Music by Kelly Rein. Voice by Judy Ellison. 1 CD. (Running Time: 57 mins.). 2005. audio compact disk 15.99 (978-0-9767288-0-1(X)) Alapha LLC.

Alpha List, Ted Allbeury. Read by Gordon Griffin. 5 cass. (Running Time: 7 hrs 30 min.). 1999. 39.95 (63279) Pub: Soundings Ltd GBR. Dist(s): Ulverscroft US

Alpha Phonics. (YA). 1992. 20.00 (978-0-941995-19-1(4)) Paradigm ID.

Alpha Relaxation System. Jeffrey Thompson. 2 CDs. (Running Time: 2 hrs.). 1999. audio compact disk 20.00 (978-1-55961-508-2(7), 82-0042) Relaxtn Co.
Studies of Zen meditators have revealed that their minds enter what is known as an alpha state during meditation, the level of deepest healing and relaxation. Now you can easily achieve this altered consciousness. A psychoacoustic 3-D recording containing music layered with hidden pulses to entrain the brainwaves to induce alpha relaxation. Includes instructional booklet.

Alpha Relaxation System. unabr. ed. Jeffrey Thompson. (Running Time: 1:00:00). 2001. audio compact disk 19.98 (978-1-55961-756-7(X)) Sounds True.

***Alpha Song Audio Tape with Flashcards.** Benchmark Education Company Staff. (Phonics Ser.). (J). 2000. reel tape 32.00 (978-1-58344-594-5(3)) Benchmark Educ.

Alpha Strike. Keith Douglass. Read by Edward Lewis. 7 cass. (Running Time: 10 hrs. 30 min.). (Carrier Ser.: No. 8). 1999. 29.95 (978-0-7366-4597-3(7)) Books on Tape.
The stage is set for a second Cold War when the Chinese claim the disputed & oil-rich Spratly Islands in the South China Sea. Carrier Battle Group Fourteen, under the command of Rear Admiral Magruder, is sent to maintain a presence in the area. But America is not welcome in the area & when the Chinese fire missiles on American jets it leaves Magruder with a simple decision: allow the sea to become a Chinese lake or fight.

Alpha Strike. unabr. collector's ed. Keith Douglass. Read by Edward Lewis. 7 cass. (Running Time: 10 hrs. 30 mins.). (Carrier Ser.: No. 8). 1998. 56.00 (978-0-7366-4315-3(X), 4771) Books on Tape.

Alpha Worship. 2002. 8.99 (978-1-931808-41-5(4)); audio compact disk 14.99 (978-1-931808-42-2(2)) Alpha NA.

Alpha Worship: A Comprehensive Training Resource for Those Wishing to Introduce Worship on the Alpha Course. 2002. Rental 31.99 (978-1-931808-38-5(4)) Alpha NA.

Alpha-1 Antitrypsin Deficiency - A Bibliography & Dictionary for Physicians, Patients, & Genome Researchers. Compiled by Icon Group International, Inc. Staff. 2007. ring bd. 28.95 (978-0-497-11322-3(8)) Icon Grp.

Alphabears. Kathleen Hague. Illus. by Michael Hague. (Running Time: 7 mins.). (J). (ps-2). 1985. audio compact disk 12.95 (978-1-59519-240-0(9)) Live Oak Media.

Alphabears. Kathleen Hague. Illus. by Michael Hague. 14 vols. (Running Time: 7 mins.). 1985. pap. bk. 35.95 (978-1-59519-242-4(5)); 9.95 (978-1-59112-002-5(0)) Live Oak Media.

Alphabears. Kathleen Hague. Illus. by Michael Hague. 11 vols. (Running Time: 7 mins.). (J). 1985. pap. bk. 18.95 (978-1-59519-241-7(7)) Pub: Live Oak Media. Dist(s): AudioGO

Alphabears. unabr. ed. Kathleen Hague. Read by Peter Fernandez. Illus. by Michael Hague. 1 cass. (Running Time: 7 mins.). (J). (gr. k-3). 1985. pap. bk. 16.95 (978-0-941078-97-9(3)) Pub: Live Oak Media. Dist(s): AudioGO
Twenty-six bears, each with its own unique characteristics, serve to introduce the twenty-six letters of the alphabet.

Alphabears. unabr. ed. Kathleen Hague. Read by Peter Fernandez. Illus. by Michael Hague. 1 cass. (Running Time: 7 mins.). (J). (gr. k-3). 1985. bk. 24.95 (978-0-941078-99-3(X)) Live Oak Media.

Alphabears, Grades Preschool-3. Kathleen Hague. Read by Peter Fernandez. Illus. by Michael Hague. 14 vols. (Running Time: 7 mins.). 1985. pap. bk. & tchr. ed. 33.95 Reading Chest. (978-0-941078-98-6(1)) Live Oak Media.

AlphaBeat: Songs, Dances, Poems, & Imaginary Journey for Children. Perf. by Kate Kuper & Neal Robinson. Lyrics by Kate Kuper. Prod. by Neal Robinson. (J). 2001. audio compact disk 15.00 (978-0-9706066-0-0(5)) K Kuper.

Alphabet. 1 CD. (Running Time: 1 hr.). (J). (ps-k). 2001. pap. bk. 13.95 (RL 957CD) Kimbo Educ.
Teaches the alphabet, letter recognition & words that begin with each letter. Includes a separate song for each letter. Includes activity book.

Alphabet. 1 cass. (RAP-ability Ser.). (J). (ps-2). 2001. pap. bk. 10.95 (RAP1391C) Kimbo Educ.
Kids learn phonics by singing along with wholesome, fun rap music. It's the easiest teaching aid ever. Includes lyric & teaching guide.

Alphabet. unabr. ed. Rock 'N Learn, Inc. Staff. Illus. by Anthony Guerra & Bart Harlan. 1 cass. (Running Time: 30 mins.). (Rock 'N Learn Ser.). (J). (ps-k). 1995. pap. bk. 12.99 (978-1-878489-57-9(7), RL957) Rock N Learn.
The fun way to learn the alphabet, letter recognition & words that begin with each letter. Songs & musical games on audiocassette with a full-color illustrated book.

Alphabet Affirmations. Bunny Hull. Composed by Bunny Hull. Illus. by Synthia Saint-James. 1 CD. (Running Time: Approximately 20 minutes). (gr. k-5). 2003. pap. bk. & act. bk. ed. 16.95 (978-0-9721478-2-8(9), KCC/AAfCD829) BrassHeart.
Song and story. "Alphabet Affirmations", "Alphabet City", "Adventures in Alphabet City" and special bonus song "Let It Shine"Music is an inspiring setting for activities that not only teach children their ABC?s but combine them with ideas and activities that develop a positive attitude which will go on to serve them well into their adult lives. Learning to view the world as a place rich with possibilities creates a mental and emotional environment that gives a child a sense of well being, of self-acceptance, and that stimulates learning, initiates personal growth and creates positive self image.

Alphabet & Counting Songs. abr. ed. Alphabet. 1 cass. (Running Time: 1 hr. 20 mins.). (J). (978-1-84032-045-9(1), HoddrStoughton) Hodder General GBR.
Lively songs & nursery rhymes.

Alphabet Day. 1 cass. (Running Time: 90 mins.). (Pooh Learning Ser.). (J). (ps-3). 2000. pap. bk. 6.98 (978-0-7634-0472-7(1)) W Disney Records.

Alphabet in Action. Jill Gallina & Michael Gallina. 2 cass. (Running Time: 2 hrs.). (J). 2001. pap. bk. 25.95 (KIM 1210C); pap. bk. 18.95 (KIM 1210XC); pap. bk. & pupil's gde. ed. 27.95 (KIM 1210); pap. bk. & pupil's gde. ed. 20.95 (KIM 1210X) Kimbo Educ.
Come "bounce the ball for B," visit the "haunted house of H" & "island of I." Fun activities teach initial consonants & vowels. Includes 30 spirit masters for reinforcement & activity guide.

Alphabet Juice: The Energies, Gists, & Spirits of Letters, Words, & Combinations Thereof - Their Roots, Bones, Innards, Piths, Pips, & Secret Parts, Tinctures, Tonics, & Essences - With Examples of Their Usage Foul & Savory. abr. unabr. ed. Roy Blount, Jr. 4 CDs. (Running Time: 5 hrs. 0 mins. 0 sec.). (ENG.). 2008. audio compact disk 24.95 (978-1-4272-0493-6(4)) Pub: Macmill Audio. Dist(s): Macmillan

Alphabet of Dreams. unabr. ed. Susan Fletcher. Read by Meera Simhan. 8 CDs. (Running Time: 9 hrs. 20 mins.). (J). 2006. audio compact disk 60.00 (978-0-7393-3614-4(2), Listening Lib); 45.00 (978-0-7393-3613-7(4), Listening Lib) Pub: Random Audio Pubg. Dist(s): Random
Mitra and her little brother, Babak, are beggars in the city of Rhagae, scratching out a living as best as they can with what they can beg for - or steal. But Mitra burns with hope and ambition, for she and Babak are not what they seem. They are of royal blood, but their father's ill-fated plot against the evil tyrant, King Phraates, has resulted in their father's death and their exile. Now disguised as a boy, Mitra has never given up believing they can rejoin what is left of their family and regain their rightful standing in the world. Then they discover that Babak has a strange gift: If he sleeps with an item belonging to someone, he can know that person's dreams. Soon Babak and his abilities come to the attention of a powerful Magus - one who has read portents in the stars of the coming of a new king and the dawn of a new age. Soon Mitra and Babak find themselves on the road to Bethlehem... The acclaimed author of Shadow Spinner returns to ancient Persia in this spellbinding saga - a tale filled with the color of the caravansaries and the heat of the desert, a tale that reimagines the wonder and spirit of a lost age.

Alphabet Operetta. Perf. by Mindy M. Little. 1 cass. (J). (ps-1). 9.98 (271) MFLP CA.
From "An Alligator Ate an Ant" to "Zig-Zag Z," this rollicking romp through the alphabet using a wide variety of musical styles to teach children their letters.

Alphabet Puppets: Paper Sack Puppets & Stories. Jan Sawyer. (J). 2005. ring bd. 20.00 (978-1-930443-87-7(0)) LogosPr.

Alphabet Sisters. Monica McInerney. Read by Catherine Milte. (Running Time: 13 hrs. 30 mins.). 2009. 94.99 (978-1-74214-261-6(3), 9781742142616) Pub: Bolinda Pubng AUS. Dist(s): Bolinda Pub Inc

Alphabet Sisters. unabr. ed. Monica McInerney. Read by Catherine Milte. (Running Time: 13 hrs. 30 mins.). 2008. audio compact disk 113.95 (978-1-921415-63-0(0), 9781921415630) Pub: Bolinda Pubng AUS. Dist(s): Bolinda Pub Inc

Alphabet Sisters. unabr. ed. Monica McInerney. Read by Catherine Milte. (Running Time: 13 hrs. 30 mins.). 2009. 43.95 (978-1-74214-488-7(8), 9781742144887) Pub: Bolinda Pubng AUS. Dist(s): Bolinda Pub Inc

Alphabet Sounds: Rhoades to Reading. Jacqueline Rhoades. 1999. 20.00 (978-1-930006-23-2(3)) Rhoades.

Alphabet Versus the Goddess. unabr. ed. Leonard Shlain. 6 CDs. (Running Time: 9 hrs.). 2005. audio compact disk 38.00 (978-1-57453-571-6(4)) Audio Lit.
Is it sheer coincidence that the European witch hunts quickly followed the invention of the printing press? In his groundbreaking work The Alphabet Versus the Goddess, Leonard Shlain proposes that the invention of writing, particularly alphabetic writing, rewired the human brain, causing profound cultural changes in history, religion, and gender relations. While the advent of literacy brought innumerable benefits to society, the switch to left-brain thinking upset the balance between men and women.

Alphabetcha. unabr. ed. 1 cass. (Running Time: 90 mins.). (Romper Room Sing & Read-Alongs Ser.). (J). 1986. 5.95 incl. bk. & sheet music. (978-0-89845-315-7(1), RRC 3151) HarperCollins Pubs.

Alphabetical Sleepy Sheep. Rory Zuckerman. Illus. by Maryn Roos. 1 CD. (Running Time: 18 mins.). (Sleepy Sheep Ser.). (J). (ps-k). 2007. bds. 7.95 (978-0-9796393-1-9(X)) Little Lion Pr.

Alphabetics. Suse MacDonald. (J). 1987. bk. 49.32 (978-0-676-87034-3(1)) SRA McGraw.
The letters of the alphabet are transformed and incorporated into twenty-six illustrations, so that the hole in "b" becomes a balloon and "y" turns into the head of a yak.

Alphas, No. 1. unabr. ed. Lisi Harrison. Read by Adriana Stimola. (Running Time: 5 hrs.). (Alphas Ser.: Bk. 1). (ENG.). 2010. 15.98 (978-1-60788-304-3(X)) Pub: Hachet Audio. Dist(s): HachBkGrp

***Alphaville: 1988, Crime, Punishment, & the Battle for New York City's Lower East Side.** unabr. ed. Michael Codella. Read by To be Announced. (Running Time: 10 hrs. NaN mins.). (ENG.). 2010. 29.95 (978-1-4417-8743-9(7)); 59.95 (978-1-4417-8740-8(2)); audio compact disk & audio compact disk 90.00 (978-1-4417-8741-5(0)) Blckstn Audio.

Alphie & the Alphabets: A Fun Way to Learn to Read. Alayne Sayles. Illus. by Greg Platt. (J). 2005. spiral bd. 79.95 (978-0-9767506-0-4(0)) Read Studio Pr.

Alpine Stream. 1 CD. (Running Time: 60 mins.). 1994. audio compact disk 15.95 (2364, Creativ Pub) Quayside.
Captures the melody of a mountain creek as it rushes down a rocky streambed.

Alpine Stream. 1 cass. (Running Time: 60 mins.). 1994. 9.95 (2362, NrthWrd Bks) TandN Child.

Alport Syndrome - A Bibliography & Dictionary for Physicians, Patients, & Genome Researchers. Compiled by Icon Group International, Inc. Staff. 2007. ring bd. 28.95 (978-0-497-11323-0(6)) Icon Grp.

Alquimista. Paulo Coelho. 2 cass. (Running Time: 2 hrs.).Tr. of Alchemist: A Fable about Following Your Dream. (SPA., 2001. 19.50 (978-970-05-0799-6(8)) Pub: Grijalbo Edit MEX. Dist(s): Lectorum Pubns
For the millions of Paulo Coelho's fans comes this beautiful, full-color illustrated edition of his international bestseller, featuring the art of Moebius. 35 color illustrations.

Already Dead. unabr. ed. Charlie Huston. Read by Scott Brick. (Running Time: 9 hrs. 0 mins.). (J). 2008. 29.95 (978-1-4332-3582-5(X)); audio compact disk 80.00 (978-1-4332-3579-5(X)) Blckstn Audio.

Already Dead. unabr. ed. Charlie Huston. Read by Scott Brick. (Running Time: 9 hrs. 0 mins.). 2008. 59.95 (978-1-4332-3578-8(1)) Blckstn Audio.

Already Someplace Warm. Bill Harley. 2002. audio compact disk 15.00 (978-1-878126-17-7(2)) Round Riv Prodns.
Original music about today's world for grownups.

Already Someplace Warm. unabr. ed. Bill Harley. Read by Bill Harley. 1 cass. 1995. 10.00 (978-1-878126-14-6(8), RRR202C) Round Riv Prodns.

ALS Healing. Steven Gurgevich. (ENG.). 2005. audio compact disk 19.95 (978-1-932170-31-3(6), HWH) Tranceformation.

ALS Skills Review DVD. American Academy of Orthopaedic Surgeons (AAOS). 2009. 55.95 (978-0-7637-5224-8(X)) Jones Bartlett.

Also Sprach Zarathustra. Friedrich Nietzsche. 3 cass. (Running Time: 3 hrs.). (GER.). 1996. pap. bk. 39.50 (978-1-58085-201-2(7)) Interlingua VA.
Includes introductory chapters, German transcription. The combination of written text & clarity & pace of diction will open the door for intermediate & advanced students to genuine comprehension & the use of literary texts for advancement in rapid understanding of written & oral language materials. The audio text plus written text concept makes foreign languages accessible to a much wider range of students than books alone.

Alsos Mission. unabr. ed. Clive Egleton. Read by Steven Crossley. 8 cass. (Running Time: 12 hrs.). 2001. 69.95 (978-1-86042-520-2(8), 25208) Pub: Soundings Ltd GBR. Dist(s): Ulverscroft US

Alström Syndrome - A Bibliography & Dictionary for Physicians, Patients, & Genome Researchers. Compiled by Icon Group International, Inc. Staff. 2007. ring bd. 28.95 (978-0-497-11324-7(4)) Icon Grp.

Alt Ed. unabr. ed. Catherine Atkins. Narrated by Johanna Parker. 4 cass. (Running Time: 5 hrs.). 2003. 37.00 (978-1-4025-5904-4(6)) Recorded Bks.
Unveils the complex lives of today?s teens in a story told through the raw, uncensored voices of its young characters. Shy, fat Susan Calloway knows she has nothing in common with the five other students in the afterschool group counseling sessions she?s forced to attend to avoid expulsion. But as Susan and the others verbally attack each other and defend their own viewpoints each week, they begin to understand that none of their lives are as simple and straightforward as they appear on the surface.

Altar & the Cross. Rick Joyner. 1 cass. (Running Time: 90 mins.). (Foundation Ser.: Vol. 8). 2000. 5.00 (RJ05-008) Morning NC.
As an overview of God's plan for His church, this series contains essential truths for everyone who wants to see the church become all that she is called to be.

Altar & the Door. Contrib. by Casting Crowns. (Soundtraks Ser.). 2007. audio compact disk 8.99 (978-5-557-52834-4(2)) Christian Wrld.

Altar & the Door. Contrib. by Casting Crowns & Terry Hemmings. Prod. by Mark A. Miller. 2007. audio compact disk 17.98 (978-5-557-70625-4(9)) Beach St.

Altar Boys Set: Gut Level Music - Against the Grain. 2 CDs. 1999. audio compact disk 12.99 (KMGD8649) Provident Mus Dist.

Altar Ego. unabr. ed. Kathy Lette. Read by Shirley Barthelmie. 8 CDs. (Running Time: 8 hrs. 45 mins.). 2006. audio compact disk 87.95 (978-1-74093-695-8(7)) Pub: Bolinda Pubng AUS. Dist(s): Bolinda Pub Inc

***Altar in the World.** unabr. ed. Barbara Brown Taylor. Read by Barbara Brown Taylor. (ENG.). 2010. (978-0-06-198159-3(1), Harper Audio) HarperCollins Pubs.

***Altar in the World: A Geography of Faith.** unabr. ed. Barbara Brown Taylor. Read by Barbara Brown Taylor. (ENG.). 2010. (978-0-06-198158-6(3), Harper Audio) HarperCollins Pubs.

Altar of Eden. unabr. ed. James Rollins. Read by Paula Christensen. 2010. audio compact disk 39.99 (978-0-06-184199-6(4), Harper Audio) HarperCollins Pubs.

***Altar of Eden: A Novel.** unabr. ed. James Rollins. Read by Paula Christensen. (ENG.). 2009. (978-0-06-196745-0(9), Harper Audio); (978-0-06-196746-7(7), Harper Audio) HarperCollins Pubs.

Altar of the Dead see Great American Short Stories, Vol. II, A Collection

Altar of the Dead. unabr. ed. Henry James. Read by Jim Killavey. 1 cass. (Running Time: 87 mins.). Dramatization. 1986. 7.95 (S-71) Jimcin Record.

Alte Siegel. Adalbert Stifter. 3 cass. (Running Time: 3 hrs.).Tr. of Old Seal. (GER.). 1996. pap. bk. 39.50 (978-1-58085-205-0(X)) Interlingua VA.
Includes German transcription. The combination of written text & clarity & pace of diction will open the door for intermediate & advanced students to genuine comprehension & the use of literary texts for advancement in rapid understanding of written & oral language materials. The audio text plus written text concept makes foreign languages accessible to a much wider range of students than books alone.

Alteration. unabr. collector's ed. Kingsley Amis. Read by Richard Green. 8 cass. (Running Time: 8 hrs.). 1978. 48.00 (978-0-7366-0114-6(7), 1121) Books on Tape.
Set in the year 1976 in an all Catholic world. The reformation never took place because Martin Luther made a deal with Rome & became Pope Martin I. The present Pope John XXIV wishes Hubert Anvil, a brilliant 10 year old boy soprano to go through "the alteration" so that his soprano voice can continue to be used to glorify the church, but the boy has doubts.

Altered Carbon. unabr. ed. Richard K. Morgan. Narrated by Todd McLaren. (Running Time: 17 hrs. 30 mins. 0 sec.). (Takeshi Kovacs Novels Ser.). (ENG.). 2005. audio compact disk 25.99 (978-1-4001-5137-0(6)); audio compact disk 89.99 (978-1-4001-3137-2(5)); audio compact disk 44.99 (978-1-4001-0137-5(9)) Pub: Tantor Media. Dist(s): IngramPubServ

Altered Land. unabr. ed. Jules Hardy. Read by Anna Bentinck & Glen McCready. 9 cass. (Running Time: 11 hrs. 22 mins.). (Isis Cassettes Ser.). (J). 2004. 76.95 (978-0-7531-1683-8(9)) Pub: ISIS Lrg Prnt GBR. Dist(s): Ulverscroft US

Altered Land. unabr. ed. Jules Hardy. Read by Anna Bentinck & Glen McCready. 10 CDs. (Running Time: 11 hrs. 22 mins.). (Isis (CDs) Ser.). (J). 2006. audio compact disk 89.95 (978-0-7531-2500-7(5)) Pub: ISIS Lrg Prnt GBR. Dist(s): Ulverscroft US

Altered State Sounds. Dick Sutphen. 1 cass. (Running Time: 1 hr.). (RX17 Ser.). 14.98 (978-0-87554-357-4(X), RX204) Valley Sun.

Altered States. unabr. ed. Anita Brookner. Read by Steven Crossley. 6 cass. (Running Time: 8 hrs.). 1997. 54.95 (970402); 54.95 (970402) Eye Ear.
Focuses on particularly bright, despairingly self-aware members of the British upper-middle class & upper class caught unawares in hapless romances.

Altered States. unabr. ed. Anita Brookner. Read by Steven Crossley. 9 cass. (Running Time: 7 hrs. 45 mins.). (Isis Ser.). (J). 2001. 54.95 (978-0-7531-0177-3(7), 970402) Pub: ISIS Lrg Prnt GBR. Dist(s): Ulverscroft US

Altered States. unabr. ed. Anita Brookner. Read by Steven Crossley. 7 CDs. (Running Time: 10 hrs. 30 min.). (Isis Ser.). (J). 2001. audio compact disk 71.95 (978-0-7531-1130-7(6), 111306) Pub: ISIS Lrg Prnt GBR. Dist(s): Ulverscroft US

Altered States of Consciousness. John Tamiazzo. 1 cass. 8.95 (335) Am Fed Astrologers.
An AFA Convention workshop tape.

Altered States Without Drugs. Andrew Weil. 1 cass. (Running Time: 58 mins.). 1976. 11.00 (02604) Big Sur Tapes.
Modern science has only recently recognized that the two hemispheres of the brain represent two entirely different kinds of consciousness, but humanity has been intuitively aware of the difference for thousands of years & has traditionally symbolized the rational part of the mind by the sun & the intuitive part of the mind by the moon. Weil emphasizes that sun & moon are not just abstract symbols but in some way really influence our perceptions, so that a moonlit landscape evokes entirely different feelings than the same landscape seen by daylight. Our civilization favors the solar mode, tending to dismiss the lunar mode as vague daydreaming. Any altered state of consciousness involves shifting the balance of mental energy toward the lunar mode, freeing the "un-conscious" from the domination of the rational mind.

Alternadad: The True Story of One Family's Struggle to Raise a Cool Kid in America. Neal Pollack. 2007. audio compact disk 39.99 (978-1-4281-2471-4(3)) Recorded Bks.

Alternative Dispute Resolution. 1997. bk. 99.00 (ACS-1290) PA Bar Inst.
Alternative dispute resolution has progressed over the last decade from a mere buzzword to an important tool in every lawyer's arsenal for resolution of their clients' disputes. This book is intended for all practitioners regardless of their years of experience or area of practice. Also provided is background information & practical techniques required to become knowledgeable about ADR.

Alternative Dispute Resolution: How to Prepare the Case & Represent Your Client. Michael Landrum. 1988. 150.00 (978-1-55917-009-3(3)) Natl Prac Inst.

Alternative Dispute Resolution: How to Use It to Your Advantage. 8 cass. (Running Time: 12 hrs.). 1998. 275.00 Incl. course materials. (MC55) Am Law Inst.
Features practical concerns as how & when to initiate ADR; the drafting of pre-dispute ADR clauses & how to avoid the booby traps in arbitration; how to keep employee disputes out of court & maintain or enhance employee morale; how to avoid pitfalls; & useful techniques to follow to help the experienced practitioner use arbitration & mediation more effectively.

Alternative Dispute Resolution Conference: Top Partners on Winning Legal Strategies for ADR, Mediations & Negotiations. ReedLogic Conference Staff. 2005. audio compact disk 499.00 (978-1-59622-378-3(2)) Aspatore Bks.

Alternative Futures. unabr. ed. Willis Harman. 1 cass. (Running Time: 90 mins.). 1980. 11.00 (00902) Big Sur Tapes.
Harman poses the questions: What can I do with my relationship with the world? What can I do with my own life, wanting to put myself in the balance where it counts? He presents some of the broader choices that are required for clarity on these questions.

Alternative Golf. abr. ed. Marty Trachenberg. Read by Marty Trachenberg. 2 cass. (Running Time: 3 hrs.). 1998. 18.00 (978-1-57511-030-1(X)) Pub Mills.
A unique approach to golfing success by the founder of alternative golf.

Alternative History: The Message of the Sphinx, Fingerprints of the Gods & The 12th Planet, 6 cass. (Running Time: 9 hrs.). 1998. bk. 49.95 (978-1-57453-287-6(1)) Audio Lit.
Includes: "The Message of the Spinx," written by Graham Hancock & Robert Bauval, read by Nick Ullett; "Fingerprints of the Gods," written by Graham Hancock, read by Peter Reckell; "The 12th Planet," written by Zecharia Sitchin, read by Bill Jenkins.

Alternative Medicine in Pediatrics. Contrib. by Kathi Kemper et al. 1 cass. (American Academy of Pediatrics UPDATE: Vol. 19, No. 5). 1998. 20.00 Am Acad Pediat.

Alternative Rock Guitar. 1 CD. (Running Time: 1 hr. 30 mins.). (Fast Forward Ser.). 2004. audio compact disk 15.95 (978-0-7119-8211-6(2), AM958530) Pub: Music Sales. Dist(s): H Leonard

Alternatives in Arthritis A to Z. Gary Silverman. 2 cass. (Motivational Medicine Ser.: Vol. 4). 1997. 15.00 (978-1-888202-03-8(3)) Motivat Med.
Motivational Medicine Medutainment Medical education that is entertaining Topic Traditional & alternative approaches to arthritis.

Alternatives to Reaganomics. Read by Robert Krulwich. 1 cass. (Running Time: 45 mins.). 10.00 (L0050B090, HarperThor) HarpC GBR.

Alterwise by Owl Light see Dylan Thomas Reading His Poetry

Altisimo Señor. unabr. ed. Torre Fuerte & Heriberto Hermosillo. (SPA.). 1998. 8.99 (978-0-8297-2697-8(7)) Pub: Vida Pubs. Dist(s): Zondervan

Altman Code. abr. ed. Robert Ludlum & Gayle Lynds. Read by Don Leslie. 5 CDs. (Running Time: 6 hrs. 0 mins. 0 sec.). (Covert-One Ser.). (ENG.). 2005. audio compact disk 14.95 (978-1-59397-886-0(3)) Pub: Macmill Audio. Dist(s): Macmillan

Altman Runaway Heart Audio 12 Copy Mixed Assort. 2003. 311.40 (978-1-55927-972-7(9)) Pub: Macmill Audio. Dist(s): Macmillan

Alto Antics: A Beginning Alto Recorder Ensemble Book. Amchin Robert. Ed. by Brent Holl. Mavin Ambrose. Karen Holl & Michael Nichols. (ENG.). (J). 2008. pap. bk. 19.95 (978-0-9797522-4-7(8)) Beatin Path.

Alto Honor. unabr. ed. Giovanni Rios & Zondervan Publishing Staff. 2002. audio compact disk 9.99 (978-0-8297-4162-9(3)) Zondervan.

Alto Saxophone with Piano Accompaniment: An Exciting Collection of Ten Swing Tunes Expertly Arranged for the Beginning Soloist with Piano Accompaniment. Perf. by David Pearl. Arranged by David Pearl. 1 CD. (Solo Plus Ser.). 1999. pap. bk. 12.95 (978-0-8256-1678-5(6), Amsco Music) Music Sales.

Altogether Lovely. Contrib. by McKameys. (Soundtraks Ser.). 2006. audio compact disk 8.99 (978-5-558-04358-7(X)) Christian Wrld.

Altonberrys of Sandwich Bay. Leo Carpenter. 2 cass. (Running Time: 2 hrs. 40 mins.). 1997. 16.95 (978-0-9653966-7-7(3)) Pub: Karmichael Pr. Dist(s): Baker Taylor
An illustrated story in verse. A humorous & touching look at everyday happenings in a year in the life of an older couple who find love & companionship in their golden years.

Altruism: Program from the Award Winning Public Radio Show. Interview. Hosted by Fred Goodwin. Comment by John Hockenberry. 1 CD. (Running Time: 1 Hour). 2001. audio compact disk 21.99 (978-1-932479-20-1(1), 152) Lichtenstein Creat.
Is everything we do motivated by selfishness? Can a person ever act only in the best interest of another person? And when we do charitable acts - such as giving money to a homeless person - is that a truly selfless act? Guests in this one hour program include Dr. C. Daniel Batson, professor of psychology at the University of Kansas in Lawrence; Stacy Palmer, editor of "The Chronicle of Philanthropy;" Dr. Elliot Sober and Dr. David Sloan Wilson, authors of "Unto Others: The Evolution and Psychology of Unselfish Behavior;" and a panel discussion with four religious leaders. With commentary by John Hockenberry.

Altruism Pays Big Dividends: Matthew 6:1-4. Ed Young. (J). 1979. 4.95 (978-0-7417-1066-6(8), A0066) Win Walk.

Altruist Connection. Peter Schwartz. 1 cass. (Running Time: 90 mins.). 1990. 12.95 (978-1-56114-140-1(2), HS08C) Second Renaissance.

Alturas de Macchu Picchu see Pablo Neruda Reading His Poetry

Aluminium Dagger. Austen Freeman. 1 cass. 1989. 7.95 (S-78) Jimcin Record.
Dr. Thorndyke solves a baffling case.

***Alvin Ho Collection Bks. 1 & 2: Allergic to Girls, School, & Other Scary Things & Allergic to Camping, Hiking, & Other Natural Disasters.** unabr. ed. Lenore Look. Read by Everette Plen. 4 CDs. (Running Time: 4 hrs.). (J). (gr. 2-4). 2009. audio compact disk 38.00 (978-0-7393-7997-4(6), Listening Lib) Pub: Random Audio Pubg. Dist(s): Random

Alvin Ho Collection Bks. 1 & 2: Allergic to Girls, School, & Other Scary Things & Allergic to Camping, Hiking, & Other Natural Disasters. unabr. ed. Lenore Look. Read by Everette Plen. (ENG.). (J). (gr. 1). 2009. audio compact disk 19.95 (978-0-7393-8046-8(X), Listening Lib) Pub: Random Audio Pubg. Dist(s): Random

Alvin Journeyman. unabr. ed. Orson Scott Card. Read by Heather Cogswell et al. (Running Time: 54000 sec.). (Tales of Alvin Maker Ser.). 2007. audio compact disk 99.00 (978-1-4332-0593-4(9)); audio compact disk 29.95 (978-1-4332-0594-1(7)) Blckstn Audio.

Alvin Journeyman. unabr. ed. Orson Scott Card. Read by Orson Scott Card. Read by Heather Cogswell et al. (Running Time: 54000 sec.). 2007. 85.95 (978-1-4332-0592-7(0)) Blckstn Audio.

Alvin Toffler: Future Shock. Read by Alvin Toffler. 1 cass. (Running Time: 27 mins.). 14.95 (24800) MMI Corp.
Discussion about today's increasing pace of scientific & social change.

Always a Body to Trade. unabr. ed. K. C. Constantine. Read by Lloyd James. 6 cass. (Running Time: 9 hrs.). (Mario Balzic Ser.). 1997. 48.00 (978-0-7366-3685-8(4), 4364) Books on Tape.
As the new mayor breaks Balzic's hump over law & order, foul-mouthed Chief Mario Balzic triumphs despite big time crimes in Rocksburg.

Always & Forever. Beverly Jenkins. Narrated by Tony Penny. 8 cass. (Running Time: 11 hrs. 30 mins.). 72.00 (978-1-4025-2032-7(8)) Recorded Bks.

Always & Forever. Perf. by Parachute Band. 1 cass. 1999. 10.98 (978-1-58229-064-5(4), Howard Bks); audio compact disk 16.98 (978-1-58229-063-8(6), Howard Bks) Pub: S and S. Dist(s): S and S Inc
Focused on God's sovereign love & claim on us as his own, this exciting sophomore live praise & worship release from New Zealand features the best new praise & worship songs being sung in Australia which are being embraced by worshipping churches in North America.

Always & Forever: Making Marriage Better from a Christian Perspective. Phil Sanders. (ENG.). 2008. audio compact disk 10.00 (978-0-9796356-7-0(5)) Focus Pr.

Always Be Together: First Light Slide Show Songs. (YA). 2000. audio compact disk 12.00 (978-0-933173-74-3(1)) Chging Church Forum.

Always Being Always Becoming: A Dialogue with Adyashanti & John Astin. Featuring Adyashanti. Interview with John Astin. 3 CDs. (Running Time: 2 hrs., 50 min.). 2005. audio compact disk 29.00 (978-0-9763788-6-0(8), 2ABA) Open Gate Pub.
In this 3-CD dialogue, researcher John Astin draws forth answers from Adyashanti that go straight to the core. Addressing everything from the origin of ego to the alchemy of resting in our being, John leaves no spiritual stone unturned. Adyashanti shares many insights including:? What keeps egos going.? Human relationship: the real teacher.? The types of unconscious denial that occur after awakening.? What life is like when it?s not dominated by the me.? Living from awakeness rather than from conceptual understanding.

***Always Change a Losing Game.** David Posen. 2009. (978-1-60136-574-3(8)) Audio Holding.

Always Leave 'em Dying. unabr. ed. Richard S. Prather. Read by Maynard Villers. 6 cass. (Running Time: 6 hrs. 30 min.). (Shell Scott Ser.). 2001. 39.95 Books in Motion.
P.I. Shell Scott finds himself both literally and figuratively "in a straight jacket," when he tries to find out what happened to a person committed against their will.

***ALWAYS LOOKING UP.** Michael J. Fox. (ENG.). 2009. 14.99 (978-1-4013-9148-5(6)); 14.99 (978-1-4013-9149-2(4)) Pub: Hyperion. Dist(s): HarperCollins Pubs

***Always Looking Up: The Adventures of an Incurable Optimist.** abr. ed. Michael J. Fox. Read by Michael J. Fox. 2010. audio compact disk 14.99 (978-1-4013-9516-2(3), Hyperion Audio) Pub: Hyperion. Dist(s): HarperCollins Pubs

Always on My Mind, Level 2. (Yamaha Clavinova Connection Ser.). 2004. disk 1.04 (978-0-634-09586-3(2)) H Leonard.

Always Outnumbered, Always Outgunned. Walter Mosley. Narrated by Peter Francis James. 6 cass. (Running Time: 7 hrs. 45 mins.). (Socrates Fortlow Ser.). 56.00 (978-1-4025-2136-2(7)) Recorded Bks.

Always Outnumbered, Always Outgunned. unabr. ed. Walter Mosley. Read by Paul Winfield. 4 cass. (Running Time: 6 hrs.). (Socrates Fortlow Ser.). 2001. 25.00 (978-1-59040-072-2(0), Phoenix Audio) Pub: Amer Intl Pub. Dist(s): PerseuPGW

Always Outnumbered, Always Outgunned. unabr. ed. Walter Mosley. Read by Paul Winfield. 4 cass. (Running Time: 6 hrs.). (Socrates Fortlow Ser.). 2004. 25.00 (978-1-59007-202-8(2)) Pub: New Millenn Enter. Dist(s): PerseuPGW
Introduces Walter Mosley's most compelling character since the debut of his immortal detective Easy Rawlins. Socrates Fortlow. After twenty-seven years of hard time for killing a man with his bare hands, Socrates must find life in a world of crime, poverty and racism in a neighborhood called Watts. This exploration of modem day philosophy is a Mosley original.

Always Safe in God's Care. Caryl Krueger. Read by Caryl Krueger. 2 cass. (Running Time: 3 hrs.). 2001. 17.00 Belleridge.

Always There. Pamela Evans. Narrated by Juanita McMahon. 10 cass. (Running Time: 14 hrs. 15 mins.). 2002. 96.00 (978-1-84197-478-1(1)) Recorded Bks.

Always There for You: Contemporary Songs for Youth Choir. Contrib. by Nan Allen. Arranged by Dennis Allen. 1 cass. (Running Time: 1 hr.). (YA). 1989. 12.99 (TA-9113C) Lillenas.
This volume for youth choir includes 14 2-part arrangements & 6 coordinated dramatic sketches. Superb new songs are combined with contemporary favorites by such artists as Petra, Sandi Patty, First Call, Glad & Larnelle Harris. Each selection can be performed either individually or in small packages consisting of songs & skits on the same theme. The sketches add a creative element that enhances both participation & ministry impact.

***Always Time to Die.** abr. ed. Elizabeth Lowell. Read by Maria Tucci. (ENG.). 2005. (978-0-06-088458-1(4), Harper Audio); (978-0-06-088460-4(6), Harper Audio) HarperCollins Pubs.

Always Time to Die. abr. ed. Elizabeth Lowell. Read by Maria Tucci. (Running Time: 21600 sec.). 2006. audio compact disk 14.95 (978-0-06-112655-0(1)) HarperCollins Pubs.

Always Time to Die. unabr. ed. Elizabeth Lowell. Read by Carrington MacDuffie. 2005. 29.95 (978-0-7927-3650-9(8), CMP 806); 69.95 (978-0-7927-3648-6(6), CSL 806); audio compact disk 94.95 (978-0-7927-3649-3(4), SLD 806) AudioGO.

Always True to You in My Fashion. Valerie Wilson Wesley. Narrated by Caroline Clay. 8 cass. (Running Time: 11 hrs. 30 mins.). 2002. 74.00 (978-1-4025-4400-2(6)) Recorded Bks.

Always Your Pal, Gene Autry. Gene Autry. 1 cass. (Family Heritage Ser.). 5.58 (SME 63422); audio compact disk 7.98 Jewel box. (SME 63422) NewSound.
Gene taught audiences all kinds of songs while conveying messages of equality & righteousness.

Always Your Pal, Gene Autry. Gene Autry. 1 cass. (Gene Autry & Family Heritage Ser.). (J). 5.58 (SME 63422); audio compact disk 7.98 NewSound.

Always Your Pal, Gene Autry. Perf. by Gene Autry. 1 cass. (Family Heritage Ser.). 1997. 7.98 Incl. cass. blisterpack. (978-1-57330-818-2(8), Sony Wonder); audio compact disk 11.98 (978-1-57330-819-9(6), Sony Wonder) Sony Music Ent.
As the Singing Cowboy, Autry, along with his famous Cowboy Code, was an icon for generations. Includes: On Top of Old Smoky, Back in the Saddle Again, Smokey the Bear & Rusty the Rocking Horse.

Alysa of the Fields: Book One in the Tellings of Xunar-kun Audio Book. Music by Warren Jeffrey Motter. (ENG.). 2010. audio compact disk 29.95 (978-0-9768585-6-0(8)) T F Howe.

Alyssa, Albert & the Magic Plane. Kaydon A. Stanzione. (J). 1995. 2.75 (978-1-887602-11-2(9)) Praxis Technol Corp.

Alzheimer Disease - A Bibliography & Dictionary for Physicians, Patients, & Genome Researchers. Compiled by Icon Group International, Inc. Staff. 2007. ring bd. 28.95 (978-0-497-11325-4(2)) Icon Grp.

Alzheimer's: Program from the Award Winning Public Radio Series. Hosted by Fred Goodwin. Comment by John Hockenberry. Contrib. by Trey Sunderland et al. 1 cass. (Running Time: 1 hr.). (Infinite Mind Ser.). 1999. audio compact disk 21.95 (978-1-888064-11-7(0), LCM 65) Lichtenstein Creat.
It's called the disease from which people die twice. Only a few generations back, our bodies wore out long before our minds. Today, living longer can also mean losing one's mental capacity to Alzheimer's, a debilitating and terminal disease. However, dramatic inroads in research could lead to the prevention and treatment of this disease within the next decade. This program also looks at geriatric depression. Guests include: Dr. Trey Sunderland from the National Institute of Mental Health, Judy Riggs of the Alzheimer's Association, filmmaker Deborah Hoffmann and Dr. Dan Blazer of Duke University Medical Center.

Alzheimer's Dialogues. Interview. Sherril Bover & Nancy Graham. 2 CDs. (Running Time: 2 hrs.). 2005. audio compact disk 39.95 (978-0-9771625-1-2(6)) SecondWind.
The Alzheimer?s Dialogues are not lectures. They are part talk show, part seminar, part support group. In this interactive and honest presentation, Nancy Graham?s groundbreaking role gives voice to caregivers everywhere. Nancy expresses the feelings and fears family members experience facing a loved one?s descent into dementia. Her brave truth-telling gives the audience permission to feel and process their own emotions and to ask the questions that must be answered. Sherril Bover is there to answer the questions and to bring encouragement and compassion to each caregiver. As the calm, empathetic friend with experience in caregiving, Sherril communicates hope and understanding and lets caregivers know that they were not alone in their Alzheimer?s journey.

Alzheimer's Disease: What You Need to Know. Charles C. Entwistle. Read by Charles C. Entwistle. 1 cass. (Running Time: 1 hr.). 1993. 9.95 (978-0-9617671-0-5(3)) Waterline.
A complete revision of tape published in 1990. The tape describes Alzheimer's disease, medical diagnosis & treatment, problems facing caregivers & legal-financial implications.

Alzheimer's Early Stages: First Steps for Family, Friends & Caregivers. 2nd abr. ed. Daniel Kuhn. Narrated by William Dufris. (Running Time: 10800 sec.). 2003. audio compact disk 22.95 (978-1-933310-02-2(2)) STI Certified.

Alzheimer's Update: Program from the award winning public radio Series. Interview. Hosted by Fred Goodwin. 1 CD. (Running Time: 1hr). (Infinite Mind Ser.). 2002. audio compact disk 21.95 (978-1-888064-77-3(3), LCM 242) Lichtenstein Creat.
In this hour, we explore the latest reseach on Alzheimer's, including advances in treatment, new medications that might eventually prevent the disease, and the hunt for clues to early diagnosis. Guests include Dr. Trey Sunderland, chief of the geriatric psychiatry branch of the National Institute of Mental Health; Dr. David Snowdon, the lead researcher on The Nun Study and professor of neurology at the University of Kentucky; and poet Philip Schultz, who chronicled his mother's slow decline from Alzheimer's.

AM & PM Music for Meditation. audio compact disk (978-1-55961-676-8(8)) Relaxtn Co.

AM Gold: 1971. 1 cass. 1999. 9.99 (G6CTZI); audio compact disk 9.99 (G7B2X7) Time-Life.

Am I Done Yet? Exploring the Tasks of Advanced Healing. David Grudermeyer & Rebecca Grudermeyer. 2 cass. 18.95 incl. handouts. (T-61) Willingness Wrks.

Am I Having Fun Yet? Ed Young. 1994. 4.95 (978-0-7417-1997-3(5), 997) Win Walk.

Am I in Tune? Bernell Christensen. 1 cass. (Running Time: 90 mins.). 2004. 9.95 (978-1-57734-269-4(0), 06005721) Covenant Comms.
Using the spirit as your guide.

Am I My Neighbor's Keeper? see Richard Eberhart Reading His Poetry

Am I Saved? Michael Pearl. 2 CDs. (ENG.). 2006. audio compact disk 10.95 (978-1-892112-68-2(X)) Pub: No Greater Joy. Dist(s): STL Dist NA

Am I Sick for the Glory of God? David T. Demola. 1 cass. 4.00 (2-104) Faith Fellow Min.

Am I Willing to Face Absolute Emptiness? J. Krishnamurti. 1 cass. (Running Time: 75 mins.). (Krishnamurti & Professor David Bohm - 1980 Ser.: No. 10). 8.50 (ABD8010) Krishnamurti.
Krishnamurti & Prof. Bohm offer penetrating, in-depth dialogues which shed light on the fundamental issues of existence.

AM Yoga Mediatations. (Running Time: 1:00:00). 2003. audio compact disk 11.95 (978-1-55961-660-7(1)) Sounds True.

Ama de Verdad, Vive de Verdad. Padre Alberto Cutie. (SPA.). 2007. audio compact disk 24.95 (978-1-933499-35-2(4)) Fonolibro Inc.

AMA de Verdad, Vive de Verdad: 7 Caminos para Lograr una Relacion Solida y Duradera. Alberto Cutié. Read by Alberto Cutié. (Playaway Adult Nonfiction Ser.). (SPA.). 2009. 59.99 (978-1-60847-563-6(8)) Find a World.

***Amada Inmovil.** abr. ed. Amado Nervo. Read by Fabio Camero. (SPA.). 2009. audio compact disk 17.00 (978-958-8318-94-3(7)) Pub: Yoyo Music COL. Dist(s): YoYoMusic

Amadans. unabr. ed. Malachy Doyle. Read by Hugh Lee. 3 CDs. (Running Time: 2 hrs. 49 mins.). (J). 2006. audio compact disk 29.95 (978-0-7540-6785-6(8), Chivers Child Audio) AudioGO.

Amadeus: More Magic of Mozart. 1 cass. (Vox - Turnabout Classical Ser.). 3.98 (CTX 4807); audio compact disk (ACD 8744) VOX Music Grp.

Amadeus & Mr. Mozart. Read by Donia Blumenfeld Clenman. Perf. by Martin Clenman. 1 cass. (Running Time: 44 mins.). (J). 8.95 Flo & Little CAN.
Jonathan is 8 years old and very fond of the music of Wolfgang Amadeus Mozart. His friend, constant companion and music critic - a shiny, green snake with perfect pitch, named Amadeus - shares his affection for Wolfgang. A sudden, mysterious disappearance of Amadeus leaves Jonathan disconsolate and the resulting search sets off a series of dreamlike adventures which are eventually happily resolved on the moon.

Amalgamation Polka. Stephen Wright. Read by Michael Emerson. (Running Time: 42300 sec.). 2006. audio compact disk 39.99 (978-1-4193-7168-4(1)) Recorded Bks.

Amanda Bennett Unit Study, Vol. 2. 2004. audio compact disk 49.95 (978-0-9717494-9-8(3)) A A Bennett.

Amanda Pig & Her Big Brother Oliver. unabr. ed. Jean Van Leeuwen. Read by Suzanne Toren. Illus. by Ann Schweninger. 1 cass. (Running Time: 20 mins.). (Follow the Reader Ser.). (J). (gr. k-3). 1984. pap. bk. 17.00 (978-0-8072-0052-0(2), FTR 81SF, Listening Lib) Random Audio Pubg.
Amanda, the youngest member of the Pig family, wants to share the spotlight with her big brother, Oliver, in these five new tales.

***Amanda Project: Book 1: invisible I.** unabr. ed. Amanda Valentino. Read by Emily Eiden. Illus. by Melissa Kantor. (ENG.). 2009. (978-0-06-196257-8(0)); (978-0-06-195254-8(0)) HarperCollins Pubs.

Amanda Quick: Second Sight, the River Knows, the Third Circle. abr. ed. Amanda Quick, pseud. (Running Time: 14 hrs.). 2009. audio compact disk 34.99 (978-1-4418-0146-3(4), 9781441801463, BACD) Brilliance Audio.

Amanda Quick: The Paid Companion, Wait until Midnight, Lie by Moonlight. abr. ed. Amanda Quick, pseud. Narrated by Michael Page & Anne Flosnik. (Running Time: 16 hrs.). 2007. audio compact disk 34.95 (978-1-4233-3426-2(4), 9781423334262, BACD) Brilliance Audio.

Amanda's Wedding. unabr. ed. Jenny Colgan. Read by Tanya Eby. 6 cass. (Running Time: 8 hrs.). 2001. 29.95 (978-1-58788-230-2(2), 1587882302, BAU); 69.25 (978-1-58788-231-9(0), 1587882310) Brilliance Audio.
A Riotously Funny Story of Love, Life . . . and the Fine Art of Sabotage Meet Melanie and Fran - two charmingly wisecracking young Londoners who simply can't believe it when their old schoolfriend Amanda, Satan's own PR agent, manages to get herself hitched to a laird (Scottish for lord). Who cares that Fraser McConnel has worn the same ratty Converse sneakers for years and that his castle is really a pile of rubble? All the social-climbing queen of preen cares about is the title she'll soon have. She's got Fraser by the nuptials, and she has no intention of letting go. Gentle, decent Fraser is completely innocent to Amanda's wiles, so Mel and Fran, still smarting from Amanda's evil misdeeds years ago in school, join forces with Fraser's adorable younger brother Angus to sabotage the mismatch of the century. Mel's got her hands, and her heart, full between fighting off the attentions of a love-crazed accountant, dealing with her ne'er-do-well rock star wannabe boyfriend, keeping Fran's deadly maneuvers with the opposite sex under control, consuming large quantities of alcohol, and tossing out hysterical barbs that would make Oscar Wilde proud.

Amanda's Wedding. unabr. ed. Jenny Colgan. Read by Tanya Eby Sirois. (Running Time: 8 hrs.). 2008. 39.25 (978-1-4233-3994-6(0), 9781423339946, Brlnc Audio MP3 Lib); 39.25 (978-1-4233-3996-0(7), 9781423339960, BADLE); 24.95 (978-1-4233-3993-9(2), 9781423339939, Brilliance MP3); 24.95 (978-1-4233-3995-3(9), 9781423339953, BAD) Brilliance Audio.

Amant de Lady Chatterley. D. H. Lawrence. Read by C. Deis. 3 cass. (FRE.). 1992. 31.95 (1579-VSL) Olivia & Hill.
Lady Chatterley, married to Sir Clifford, a writer & intellectual confined to his wheelchair through injuries from World War I, has a passionate love relationship with her gamekeeper, Oliver Mellors, son of a miner.

Amante de Lady Chatterley. abr. ed. D. H. Lawrence. Read by Fabio Camero. 3 CDs. (SPA.). 2002. audio compact disk 17.00 (978-958-9494-74-5(9)) YoYoMusic.

***Amante Perfecto: El Tao del Amor y el Sexo.** Mabel Iam. Prod. by FonoLibro Inc. Narrated by C. C. Limardo.Tr. of Perfect Lover. 2010. 19.95 (978-1-933499-90-1(7)) Fonolibro Inc.

***Amante Perfecto (DigVer) El Tao del Amor y el Sexo.** Mabel Iam. Narrated by C. C. Limardo. Prod. by FonoLibro Inc. (Running Time: 222).Tr. of Perfect Lover. (SPA.). 2010. 16.95 (978-1-61154-000-0(3)) Fonolibro Inc.

Amants de Porcelaine. I.t. ed. Georges Coulonges. (French Ser.). (FRE.). 2001. bk. 30.99 (978-2-84011-434-5(8)) Pub: UlverLrgPrint GBR. Dist(s): Ulverscroft US

Amar a Alguien Como Yo. unabr. ed. Luis Mellado & Patty Cabrera. (SPA.). 2003. 9.99 (978-0-8297-3124-8(5)) Pub: Vida Pubs. Dist(s): Zondervan

Amaranth Moon. unabr. ed. Janet Woods. Read by Patience Tomlinson. 8 cass. (Soundings Ser.). 2006. 69.95 (978-1-84559-409-1(6)) Pub: ISIS Lrg Prnt GBR. Dist(s): Ulverscroft US

***Amarcord.** unabr. ed. Marcella Hazan. Read by Concetta Tomei. (ENG.). 2008. (978-0-06-173822-7(0)); (978-0-06-173823-4(9)) HarperCollins Pubs.

Amarcord - Marcella Remembers: The Remarkable Life Story of the Woman Who Started Out Teaching Science in a Small Town in Italy, but Ended up Teaching America How to Cook Italian. unabr. ed. Marcella Hazan. Read by Concetta Tomei. 7 CDs. (Running Time: 8 hrs.). 2008. audio compact disk 34.95 (978-0-06-172073-4(9), Harper Audio) HarperCollins Pubs.

Amaryllis. unabr. collector's ed. Jayne Castle, pseud. Read by Frances Cassidy. 8 cass. (Running Time: 12 hrs.). 1997. 64.00 (978-0-7366-3669-8(2), 4346) Books on Tape.
When psychic detective meets muscular explorer, romance smolders amidst extraterrestrial murder. Jayne Ann Krentz at her spiciest.

Amateur: A Novel of Revenge. unabr. ed. Robert Littell. Read by Scott Brick. 8 CDs. (Running Time: 9 hrs.). 2004. audio compact disk 49.95 (978-1-59007-513-5(7)) Pub: New Millenn Enter. Dist(s): PerseuPGW

Amateur: A Novel of Revenge. unabr. abr. ed. Robert Littell. Read by Scott Brick. 6 cass. (Running Time: 9 hrs.). 2004. 29.95 (978-1-59007-512-8(9)) Pub: New Millenn Enter. Dist(s): PerseuPGW

Amateur Corpse. unabr. ed. Simon Brett. Read by Frederick Davidson. 5 cass. (Running Time: 7 hrs.). 1994. 39.95 (978-0-7861-0483-3(X), 1435) Blckstn Audio.
On the night of the final performance of "The Seagull" in which Charlotte had taken a leading part, her husband Hugo jealously watched her dancing with younger men at the backstage party. He started drinking heavily & continuously. Two days passed in an alcoholic daze, Charlotte disappeared & when her body was found in the coal shed, every sign pointed to Hugo as the murderer. Charles Paris, actor & amateur detective, was an old friend of Hugo's who had been present at the last night of "The Seagull" & the following party. Charles was convinced of Hugo's innocence but to prove it seemed impossible. The only thing to do was to find someone else guilty. It had to be one of the Backstagers, but who & why.

Amateur Corpse. unabr. ed. Simon Brett. Narrated by Simon Prebble. 5 cass. (Running Time: 6 hrs.). (Charles Paris Mystery Ser.: Vol. 4). 2000. 44.00 (978-0-7887-1286-9(1), 95146E7) Recorded Bks.
When a leading lady is murdered, Charles Paris is thrust back into the role of detective.

Amateur Cracksman. E. W. Hornung. Read by Amy von Lecteur. 2009. 27.95 (978-1-60112-979-6(3)) Babblebooks.

Amateur Cracksman. E. W. Hornung. Read by Walter Covell. 6 cass. (Running Time: 8 hrs. 40 mins.). 1989. 26.00 incl. album. (C-199) Jimcin Record.
Short stories about "Ruffles," the most famous rogue in detective fiction.

Amateur Emigrant. unabr. ed. Robert Louis Stevenson. Narrated by Donal Donnelly. 3 cass. (Running Time: 4 hrs. 30 mins.). 1988. 26.00 (978-1-55690-010-5(4), 88460E7) Recorded Bks.
Stevenson traveled to San Francisco from Scotland in 1879 by steerage on an emigrant ship, chronicling the great trek west.

Amateur Emigrant. unabr. collector's ed. Robert Louis Stevenson. Read by David Case. Intro. by Jonathan Raban. 5 cass. (Running Time: 5 hrs.). 1988. 30.00 (978-0-7366-1434-4(6), 2318) Books on Tape.
In 1879 Penny Osbourne telegraphed Robert Louis Stevenson in Edinburgh, begging him to join her in San Francisco. So the penniless young writer boarded an emigrant ship in the Clyde for the long voyage across the Atlantic.

Amateur Marriage. unabr. ed. Anne Tyler. 7 cass. (Running Time: 10 hrs. 30 min.). 2004. 63.00 (978-0-7366-9723-1(3)) Books on Tape.

Amateur Spy. abr. ed. Dan Fesperman. Read by Phil Gigante. (Running Time: 6 hrs.). 2009. audio compact disk 14.99 (978-1-4233-1790-6(4), 9781423317906, BCD Value Price) Brilliance Audio.

Amateur Spy. unabr. ed. Dan Fesperman. Read by Phil Gigante. (Running Time: 14 hrs.). 2008. 39.25 (978-1-4233-1788-3(2), 9781423317883, BADLE); 24.95 (978-1-4233-1787-6(4), 9781423317876, BAD); 107.25 (978-1-4233-1782-1(3), 9781423317821, BrilAudUnabridg); audio compact disk 38.95 (978-1-4233-1783-8(1), 9781423317838, Bril Audio CD Unabri); audio compact disk 24.95 (978-1-4233-1785-2(8), 9781423317852, Brilliance MP3); audio compact disk 112.25 (978-1-4233-1784-5(X), 9781423317845, BriAudCD Unabrid); audio compact disk 39.25 (978-1-4233-1786-9(6), 9781423317869, Brlnc Audio MP3 Lib) Brilliance Audio.

Amateur Telescopes. 1 cass. (Running Time: 29 mins.). 14.95 (23354) MMI Corp.
Discusses telescope building. Covers mirror grinding, telescope principles & more.

Amateurs. unabr. ed. Marcus Sakey. Read by Dan John Miller. (Running Time: 10 hrs.). 2009. 24.99 (978-1-4233-6699-7(9), 9781423366997, Brilliance MP3); 39.97 (978-1-4233-6700-0(6), 9781423367000, Brlnc Audio MP3 Lib); 24.99 (978-1-4233-6701-7(4), 9781423367017, BAD); 39.97 (978-1-4233-6702-4(2), 9781423367024, BADLE); audio compact disk 32.99 (978-1-4233-6697-3(2), 9781423366973); audio compact disk 87.97 (978-1-4233-6698-0(0), 9781423366980, BriAudCD Unabrid) Brilliance Audio.

Amateurs: The Story of Four Young Men & Their Quest for an Olympic Gold Medal. unabr. collector's ed. David Halberstam. Read by Jonathan Marosz. 7 cass. (Running Time: 7 hrs.). 1998. 42.00 (978-0-7366-4017-6(7), 4515) Books on Tape.
A leading journalist explores the world of amateur rowing - its glories & pressures, its extraordinary athletes.

Amazed. Riverview Staff. 1 CD. (Running Time: 45 min.). 2003. audio compact disk 14.95 (978-5-550-29492-5(3)) STL Dist NA.

Amazed - ShowTrax. Arranged by Roger Emerson. 1 CD. (Running Time: 5 mins.). (Pop Choral Ser.). 2000. audio compact disk 19.95 (08201185) H Leonard.
This 1999 #1 country/pop ballad by Lonestar is a natural for your guys' groups, with its heart-felt lyrics & great-sounding harmonies. Also available for mixed voices.

Amazing. 1 cass. 4.98 (978-1-57908-422-6(2)); audio compact disk 5.98 (978-1-57908-416-5(8)) Platinm Enter.

Amazing! Perf. by Robin Goodrow et al. 1 cass. (J). (ps-6). 9.98 (206) MFLP CA.
This recording fills kids with zest & goodwill, promoting self-confidence, peaceful co-existence, multiracial harmony, friendship & good old-fashioned playfulness. Songs include: "The Power," "I'm Cool," "Rainbow of Colors," "Can't Stop Dancin," & "Hello World.".

Amazing Adventures of Kavalier & Clay. abr. ed. Michael Chabon. Read by David Colacci. (Running Time: 9 hrs.). 2005. 39.25 (978-1-59737-162-9(9), 9781597371629, BADLE); 24.95 (978-1-59737-161-2(0), 9781597371612, BAD) Brilliance Audio.

Amazing Adventures of Kavalier & Clay: A Novel. abr. ed. Michael Chabon. Read by David Colacci. 6 cass. (Running Time: 9 hrs.). 2000. 29.95 (978-1-58788-123-7(3), 1587881233, Nova Audio Bks) Brilliance Audio.
It's 1939, in New York City. Joe Kavalier, a young artist who has also been trained in the art of Houdiniesque escape, has just pulled off his greatest feat - smuggling himself out of Hitler's Prague. He's looking to make big money, fast, so that he can bring his family to freedom. His cousin, Brooklyn's own Sammy Clay, is looking for a partner in creating the heroes, stories, and art for the latest novelty to hit the American dreamscape: the comic book. Inspired by their own fantasies, fears, and dreams, Kavalier and Clay create the Escapist, the Monitor, and the otherworldy Mistress of the Night, Luna Moth, inspired by the beautiful Rosa Saks, who will become linked by powerful ties to both men. The golden age of comic books has begun, even as the shadow of Hitler falls across Europe. The Amazing Adventures of Kavalier & Clay is a stunning novel of endless comic invention and unforgettable characters, written in the exhilarating prose that has led critics to compare Michael Chabon to Cheever and Nabokov. In Joe Cavalier, Chabon, writing "like a magical spider, effortlessly spinning out elaborate webs of words that ensnare the reader" (Michiko Kakutani, The New York Times), has created a hero for the century.

Amazing Adventures of Kavalier & Clay: A Novel. abr. ed. Michael Chabon. Read by David Colacci. 7 CDs. (Running Time: 9 hrs.). 2005. audio compact disk 34.95 (978-1-59737-157-5(2), 9781597371575); 39.25 (978-1-59737-160-5(2), 9781597371605, Brlnc Audio MP3 Lib); 24.95 (978-1-59737-159-9(9), 9781597371599, Brilliance MP3); audio compact disk 92.25 (978-1-59737-158-2(0), 9781597371582, BACDLib Ed) Brilliance Audio.

***Amazing American Achievers - Volume 1: Inspirational Stories.** unabr. ed. Charles Margerison. Read by Josh Bergman et al. Frances Corcoran. (Running Time: 1 hr.). (ENG.). 2010. 4.99 (978-1-921629-64-8(9)) Pub: CJMPub AUS. Dist(s): HachBkGrp

***Amazing American Musicians - Volume 1: Inspirational Stories.** unabr. ed. Charles Margerison. Read by Nicolas Bearde & Andrew Chaiken. Frances Corcoran. Emma Braithwaite. (Running Time: 53 mins.). (ENG.). 2010. 4.99 (978-1-921629-57-0(6)) Pub: CJMPub AUS. Dist(s): HachBkGrp

***Amazing American Politicians - Volume 1: Inspirational Stories.** unabr. ed. Charles Margerison. Read by J. S. Gilbert & Markus Hayes. Frances Corcoran. Emma Braithwaite. (Running Time: 45 mins.). (ENG.). 2010. 4.99 (978-1-921629-63-1(0)) Pub: CJMPub AUS. Dist(s): HachBkGrp

***Amazing American Scientists - Volume 1: Inspirational Stories.** unabr. ed. Charles Margerison. Read by Joseph Miller & Mark Smith. Frances Corcoran. Emma Braithwaite. (Running Time: 48 mins.). (ENG.). 2010. 4.99 (978-1-921629-59-4(2)) Pub: CJMPub AUS. Dist(s): HachBkGrp

***Amazing American Women - Volume 1: Inspirational Stories.** unabr. ed. Charles Margerison. Read by Sarah Wintermeyer & Hannah Davis. Frances Corcoran. Emma Braithwaite. (Running Time: 53 mins.). (ENG.). 2010. 4.99 (978-1-921629-67-9(3)) Pub: CJMPub AUS. Dist(s): HachBkGrp

***Amazing Americans: Inspirational Stories.** unabr. ed. Charles Margerison. Read by Markus Hayes et al. Frances Corcoran. Emma Braithwaite. (Running Time: 4 hrs.). (ENG.). 2010. 16.99 (978-1-921629-43-3(6)) Pub: CJMPub AUS. Dist(s): HachBkGrp

Amazing Animal Rescues/Animal Features. Steck-Vaughn Staff. (J). 1999. (978-0-7398-0921-1(0)) SteckVau.

Amazing Auction: Hos 3:1-5. Ed Young. 1988. 4.95 (978-0-7417-1653-8(4), 653) Win Walk.

Amazing Aunt Agatha, Audiocassette. Sheila Samton. (Metro Reading Ser.). (J). (gr. k). 2000. 8.46 (978-1-58120-985-3(1)) Metro Teaching.

Amazing Body Home Connection Kit. Created by Music Movement and Magination. 2009. spiral bd. 19.95 (978-1-935572-12-1(1)) MMnM Bks.

Amazing Body Home Connection Kit - Bilingual. Created by Music Movement and Magination. (ENG.). 2009. spiral bd. 19.95 (978-1-935572-13-8(X)) MMnM Bks.

Amazing Body Supplemental Curriculum Kit. 2nd rev. ed. Created by Music Movement and Magination. (ENG.). 2009. spiral bd. 179.95 (978-1-935572-05-3(9)) MMnM Bks.

Amazing Bone. 2004. bk. 24.95 (978-0-7882-0588-0(9)); pap. bk. 18.95 (978-1-55592-101-9(9)); pap. bk. 38.75 (978-1-55592-628-1(2)); pap. bk. 32.75 (978-1-55592-182-8(5)); pap. bk. 14.95 (978-0-7882-0589-7(7)) Weston Woods.

Amazing Bone. William Steig. (J). 1985. 35.99 (978-0-394-64660-2(6)) SRA McGraw.

Amazing Bone. William Steig. 1 cass. (Running Time: 11 min.). (J). (gr. k-3). bk. 24.95; pap. bk. 32.75 Weston Woods.
From the book by William Steig. A lonely pig named Pearl dawdles along long enough in a field of dandelions to meet a talking bone.

Amazing Bone. William Steig. Narrated by John Lithgow. 1 cass. (Running Time: 11 mins.). (J). (gr. k-3). 1993. pap. bk. 8.95 (978-1-56008-122-7(8), RAC301) Weston Woods.
A lonely pig named Pearl dawdles long enough in a field of dandelions to meet a bone who speaks to her.

Amazing Book. 1 cass. (Amazing Bible Ser.). (J). 9.95 (AAAB) Brdgstn Multimed Grp.
Enjoy the original musical score from the "Amazing Book" video. Catchy, upbeat tunes, including the favorite "Sixty-Six Books," will get kids singing as they learn about the most amazing book ever written.

Amazing Book. 1 cass. (Running Time: 1 hr.). (Amazing Bible Ser.). (J). 2000. 6.99 HARK Ent.
Will fill your home with fun-filled praise of the Lord. Provides wholesome messages that are sure to last a lifetime.

***Amazing Careers - Volume 1: Inspirational Stories.** unabr. ed. Charles Margerison. Read by Markus Hayes et al. Frances Corcoran. Emma Braithwaite. (Running Time: 56 mins.). (ENG.). 2010. 4.99 (978-1-921629-66-2(5)) Pub: CJMPub AUS. Dist(s): HachBkGrp

Amazing Children. 1 cass. (Amazing Bible Ser.). (J). 9.95 (AAAC) Brdgstn Multimed Grp.
This special musical score from "The Amazing Children" video reinforces how truly amazing children are - including the ones from the Bible! Kids will learn about marvelous, miraculous David, Joseph, Daniel, & others.

Amazing Children. 1 cass. (Running Time: 1 hr.). (Amazing Bible Ser.). (J). 2000. 6.99 HARK Ent.
Will fill your home with fun-filled praise of the Lord. Provides wholesome messages that are sure to last a lifetime.

Amazing Children. Bridgestone Staff. 2004. audio compact disk 7.98 (978-1-56371-027-8(7)) Brdgstn Multimed Grp.

***Amazing Classical Musicians - Volume 1: Inspirational Stories.** unabr. ed. Charles Margerison. Read by Charles Margerison. Frances Corcoran. Emma Braithwaite. (Running Time: 1 hr. 5 mins.). (ENG.). 2010. 4.99 (978-1-921629-62-4(2)) Pub: CJMPub AUS. Dist(s): HachBkGrp

Amazing Development of Men. Aliso Armstrong. 2005. audio compact disk 15.00 (978-0-9741435-4-5(5)) Pax Pr Inc.

Amazing Dope Tales: Haight Ashbury Flashbacks. Stephen Gaskin. Read by Stephen Gaskin. 6 cass. 60.00 (A0447-89) Sound Photosyn.
The author dramatically reading his entire classic book of the San Francisco hippy days, affected with sounds & music by Sound Photosynthesis reflecting those adventurous times.

Amazing Dr. Clitterhouse. Perf. by Edward G. Robinson. (DD8865) Natl Recrd Co.

***Amazing Dr. Kyle Powers.** (ENG.). 2010. audio compact disk (978-1-59171-304-3(8)) Falcon Picture.

***Amazing Engineers - Volume 1: Inspirational Stories.** unabr. ed. Charles Margerison. Read by Charles Margerison. Read by Yorvik Kalachinsky-Chenovsky & Mark Smith. Frances Corcoran. Emma Braithwaite. (Running Time: 47 mins.). (ENG.). 2010. 4.99 (978-1-921629-69-3(X)) Pub: CJMPub AUS. Dist(s): HachBkGrp

***Amazing Explorers - Volume 1: Inspirational Stories.** unabr. ed. Charles Margerison. Read by Charles Margerison. Read by Markus Hayes. Frances Corcoran. Emma Braithwaite. (Running Time: 1 hr.). (ENG.). 2010. 4.99 (978-1-921629-61-7(4)) Pub: CJMPub AUS. Dist(s): HachBkGrp

Amazing Fish/Sharks. Steck-Vaughn Staff. 1996. (978-0-8172-6463-5(9)) SteckVau.

Amazing Frecktacle. Ross Venokur. Read by Johnny Heller. 2 cass. (Running Time: 2 hrs.). (YA). 1999. pap. bk. 40.95 (978-0-7887-3182-2(3), 40917) Recorded Bks.
Nicholas Bells has exactly 5,792 freckles. That's why his 5th-grade classmates call him "The Amazing Frecktacle" & he feels like a freak. But his plans to get rid of his freckles & get revenge on his tormentors have unexpected & disastrous results. Includes study guide.

Amazing Frecktacle. unabr. ed. Ross Venokur. Read by Johnny Heller. 2 cass. (Running Time: 2 hrs.). (J). (gr. 4). 1999. pap. bk. 40.95 (40917X4) Recorded Bks.

Amazing Frecktacle. unabr. ed. Ross Venokur. Narrated by Johnny Heller. 2 pieces. (Running Time: 2 hrs.). (gr. 4 up). 2000. 19.00 (978-0-7887-3207-2(2), 95794E7) Recorded Bks.

Amazing Frecktacle, Class set. Ross Venokur. Read by Johnny Heller. 2 cass. (Running Time: 2 hrs.). (YA). 1999. 176.80 (978-0-7887-3228-7(5), 46884) Recorded Bks.

Amazing Grace. 2004. pap. bk. 18.95 (978-1-55592-766-0(1)); pap. bk. 38.75 (978-1-55592-781-3(5)); pap. bk. 32.75 (978-1-55592-184-2(1)); pap. bk. 14.95 (978-1-55592-043-2(8)); 8.95 (978-1-56008-351-1(4)); cass. & flmstrp 30.00 (978-1-56008-803-5(6)); audio compact disk 12.95 (978-1-55592-863-6(3)); audio compact disk 12.95 (978-1-55592-956-5(7)) Weston Woods.

Amazing Grace. Perf. by Mark Barnett & Mountain View Players Staff. 1 cass. 1997. 9.98; audio compact disk 14.98 Pub: Brentwood Music. Dist(s): Provident Mus Dist
Family & faith had added importance in the lives of mountain pioneers & their music told the story of their hardships, hopes & faith. "Amazing Grace" features many of the songs they shared together, at church to bless a newborn child, to join a husband & wife & to comfort those in need.

Amazing Grace. Contrib. by Bill & Gloria Gaither and Their Homecoming Friends. (Gaither Gospel Ser.). 2007. 12.99 (978-5-557-62818-1(5)) Gaither Music Co.

Amazing Grace. Cecilia. 1 CD. (ENG.). 2007. audio compact disk 15.00 (978-1-4019-1860-6(3)) Hay House.

Amazing Grace. Joanna Dessau. Read by Elizabeth Henry. 4 cass. (Running Time: 6 hrs.). 2001. 44.95 (60768) Pub: Soundings Ltd GBR. Dist(s): Ulverscroft US

Amazing Grace. Joanna Dessau. Read by Elizabeth Henry. 4 cass. 1999. 44.95 (60768) Pub: Soundings Ltd GBR. Dist(s): ISIS Pub

Amazing Grace. Bill Gaither & Gloria Gaither. (Gaither Gospel Ser.). 2007. 19.99 (978-5-557-62821-1(5)) Gaither Music Co.

Amazing Grace. Mary Hoffman. Narrated by Andrea Johnson. (Running Time: 15 mins.). (gr. 1 up). audio compact disk 19.00 (978-1-4025-2286-4(X)) Recorded Bks.

Amazing Grace. Mary Hoffman. Read by Andrea Johnson. 1 cass. (Running Time: 15 mins.). (YA). 1999. pap. bk. 32.99 (978-0-7887-4097-8(0), 41103) Recorded Bks.
Grace's class is performing "Peter Pan," but her classmates say she can't play the title role because she's a girl & because she's black. When she dares to try out for the part, wonderful things happen.

Amazing Grace. Mary Hoffman. Illus. by Caroline Binch. Narrated by Alfre Woodard. 1 cass. (Running Time: 8 mins.). (J). (ps-4). pap. bk. 12.95; pap. bk. 32.75 Weston Woods.
Even though her classmates discourage Grace from trying out for Peter Pan, because she is black & a girl, Grace wins the part & proves she can be anything she wants.

Amazing Grace. Created by Provident-Integrity Distribution. (Praise Hymn Traditional Soundtracks Ser.). 2002. audio compact disk 8.98 (978-5-550-12927-2(2)) Pt of Grace Ent.

Amazing Grace. Directed By Ben Speer. Contrib. by Bill & Gloria Gaither and Their Homecoming Friends & Bill Gaither. Prod. by Bill Gaither. (Gaither Gospel Ser.). 2007. audio compact disk 17.99 (978-5-557-62819-8(3)) Gaither Music Co.

Amazing Grace. Danielle Steel. Read by Tom Dheere. (Playaway Adult Fiction Ser.). 2009. 64.99 (978-1-60812-676-7(5)) Find a World.

Amazing Grace. abr. ed. Danielle Steel. Read by Tom Dheere. (Running Time: 5 hrs.). 2009. audio compact disk 9.99 (978-1-4418-0814-1(0), 9781441808141, BCD Value Price) Brilliance Audio.

Amazing Grace. unabr. ed. Mary Hoffman. Narrated by Andrea Johnson. 1 cass. (Running Time: 15 mins.). (gr. 1 up). 2000. 10.00 (978-0-7887-4015-2(6), 96136E7) Recorded Bks.
Grace's class is performing "Peter Pan," but her classmates say she can't play the title role because she's a girl & because she's black. When she dares to try out for the part, wonderful things happen.

Amazing Grace. unabr. ed. Mary Hoffman. 1 cass. (Running Time: 8 mins.). (J). (ps-4). 1994. 8.95 (978-1-56008-415-0(4), RAC354) Weston Woods.
Even though her classmates discourage Grace from trying out for Peter Pan, because she is black & a girl, Grace wins the part & proves she can be anything she wants.

Amazing Grace. unabr. ed. Mary Hoffman. Illus. by Caroline Binch. 1 cass. (Running Time: 8 mins.). (J). (ps-4). 1994. bk. 24.95 (978-0-7882-0656-6(7), PHRA354) Weston Woods.

Amazing Grace. unabr. ed. Eric Metaxes. Read by Johnny Heller. (Running Time: 10 hrs. 0 mins. 0 sec.). (ENG.). 2007. audio compact disk 34.99 (978-1-4001-0427-7(0)) Pub: Tantor Media. Dist(s): IngramPubServ

Amazing Grace. unabr. ed. Danielle Steel. Read by Tom Dheere. (Running Time: 9 hrs.). 2007. 39.25 (978-1-4233-2015-9(8), 9781423320159, BADLE); 24.95 (978-1-4233-2014-2(X), 9781423320142, BAD); 34.95 (978-1-4233-2008-1(5), 9781423320081, BAU); 87.25 (978-1-4233-2009-8(3), 9781423320098, BrilAudUnabridg); audio compact disk 24.95 (978-1-4233-2012-8(3), 9781423320128, Brilliance MP3); audio compact disk 38.95 (978-1-4233-2010-4(7), 9781423320104, Bril Audio CD Unabri); audio compact disk 92.25 (978-1-4233-2011-1(5), 9781423320111, BriAudCD Unabrid); audio compact disk 39.25 (978-1-4233-2013-5(1), 9781423320135, Brinc Audio MP3 Lib) Brilliance Audio.

Amazing Grace, Class set. Mary Hoffman. Read by Andrea Johnson. 1 cass. (Running Time: 15 mins.). (YA). (ps). 1999. wbk. ed. 178.20 (978-0-7887-4098-5(9), 47096) Recorded Bks.
Grace's class is performing "Peter Pan," but her classmates say she can't play the title role because she's a girl & because she's black. When she dares to try out for the part, wonderful things happen.

Amazing Grace: A Vocabulary of Faith. abr. ed. Kathleen Norris. Read by Debra Winger. 2 cass. (Running Time: 3 hrs.). 1998. 17.95 (978-1-57453-258-6(8)) Audio Lit.
Blending history anecdote, memoir & theology, an examination of such terms as judgment, prayer, faith & grace.

Amazing Grace: A Vocabulary of Faith. collector's ed. Kathleen Norris. Read by Kimberly Schraf. 9 cass. (Running Time: 13 hrs. 30 min.). 1998. 72.00 (978-0-7366-4266-8(8), 4765) Books on Tape.
Kathleen Norris struggles with the language of the Christian religion.

Amazing Grace: John 1:43-45. Ed Young. (YA). 1988. 4.95 (978-0-7417-1664-4(X), 664) Win Walk.

Amazing Grace: My Chains Are Gone. 2007. audio compact disk 12.00 (978-5-557-54426-9(7)) Lillenas.

Amazing Grace: Original Score from the Motion Picture. Prod. by David Arnold. Contrib. by Michael Apted. 2007. audio compact disk 17.99 (978-5-557-88996-4(5)) Pt of Grace Ent.

Amazing Grace: The Inspirational Stories of William Wilberforce, John Newton, & Olaudah Equiano. Dave Arnold & Paul McCusker. Created by Focus on the Family Staff. Contrib. by William Wilberforce et al. Prod. by Dave Arnold. (Running Time: 18000 sec.). (Radio Theatre Ser.). (ENG.). 2006. audio compact disk 39.97 (978-1-58997-393-0(3), Tyndale Ent) Tyndale Hse.

***Amazing Grace: The Lives of Children & the Conscience of a Nation.** unabr. ed. Jonathan Kozol. Read by Dick Hill. (Running Time: 9 hrs.). 2010. 24.99 (978-1-4418-4137-7(7), 9781441841377, Brilliance MP3); 39.97 (978-1-4418-4138-4(5), 9781441841384, Brinc Audio MP3 Lib) Brilliance Audio.

Amazing Grace: The Tender Mercies of the Lord. Donald P. Mangum & Brenton G. Yorgason. 1 cass. 1996. 9.95 (978-1-57008-263-4(4), Bkcraft Inc) Deseret Bk.

Amazing Grace: William Wilberforce & the Heroic Campaign to End Slavery. unabr. ed. Eric Metaxas. Read by Johnny Heller. (YA). 2008. 59.99 (978-1-60252-948-9(5)) Find a World.

Amazing Grace: William Wilberforce & the Heroic Campaign to End Slavery. unabr. ed. Eric Metaxes. (Running Time: 10 hrs. 0 mins. 0 sec.). (ENG.). 2007. audio compact disk 24.99 (978-1-4001-5427-2(8)); audio compact disk 69.99 (978-1-4001-3427-4(7)) Pub: Tantor Media. Dist(s): IngramPubServ

Amazing Grace for Those Who Suffer. Jeff Cavins & Matthew Pinto. Read by Chris Knuffke. (Amazing Grace Ser.). 2004. 39.99 (978-1-57058-481-7(8)) St Joseph Communs.

Amazing Grace in the Life of William Wilberforce. John Piper. Read by Wayne Shepherd. Frwd. by Jonathan Aitken. (Running Time: 1 hr. 10 mins.). 2007. audio compact disk 12.99 (978-1-58134-918-4(1)) CrosswayIL.

Amazing Grace (My Chains Are Gone) Contrib. by Chris Tomlin. (Mastertrax Ser.). 2006. audio compact disk 9.98 (978-5-558-02949-9(8)) Pt of Grace Ent.

Amazing Grace (My Chains Are Gone) Contrib. by Chris Tomlin. (Praise Hymn Soundtracks Ser.). 2007. audio compact disk 8.98 (978-5-557-71919-3(9)) Pt of Grace Ent.

Amazing Grace (My Chains Are Gone) Contrib. by Chris Tomlin. (Sound Performance Soundtracks Ser.). 2008. audio compact disk 5.98 (978-5-557-46036-1(5)) Pt of Grace Ent.

Amazing Grace-My Chains Are Gone: An Easter Celebration of Worship for Congregation & Choir. 2007. audio compact disk 90.00 (978-5-557-54419-1(4)) Lillenas.

Amazing Grace-My Chains Are Gone: An Easter Celebration of Worship for Congregation & Choir. Created by Dennis and Nan Allen. 2007. audio compact disk 90.00 (978-5-557-54416-0(X)) Lillenas.

Amazing Gracie. unabr. ed. Sherryl Woods. Read by Janet Metzger. (Running Time: 9 hrs.). 2009. 39.97 (978-1-4418-3557-4(1), 9781441835574, Brinc Audio MP3 Lib); 19.99 (978-1-4418-3556-7(3), 9781441835567, Brilliance MP3); 39.97 (978-1-4418-3559-8(8), 9781441835598, BADLE); 19.99 (978-1-4418-3558-1(X), 9781441835581, BAD); audio compact disk 19.99 (978-1-4418-3554-3(7), 9781441835543, Bril Audio CD Unabri); audio compact disk 79.97 (978-1-4418-3555-0(5), 9781441835550, BriAudCD Unabrid) Brilliance Audio.

Amazing Graze. Perf. by Crystal Gayle. 2006. audio compact disk 12.95 (978-1-59987-413-5(X)) Braun Media.

Amazing Interlude. Mary Roberts Rinehart. Read by Flo Gibson. 5 cass. (Running Time: 7 hrs.). 1995. 20.95 (978-1-55685-372-2(6)) Audio Bk Con.
A deeply moving & glorious wartime love story. Sarah Lee Kennedy goes to the front during World War I to serve soup & bandage the wounded, leaving her disgruntled fiance behind in the U.S. There she meets a brave & dashing Belgian who is a secret agent behind the lines.

Amazing Interlude. Mary Roberts Rinehart. Read by Shelly Frasier. (Running Time: 7 hrs. 15 mins.). 2002. 27.95 (978-1-60083-623-7(2), Audiofy Corp) Iofy Corp.

Amazing Interlude. unabr. ed. Mary Roberts Rinehart. Read by Laurie Klein. 6 cass. (Running Time: 7 hrs. 48 mins.). Dramatization. 1993. 39.95 (978-1-55686-472-8(8), 472) Books in Motion.
Winter 1914. Sara Lee Kennedy reads the newspaper account of the war in Europe. Struggling with compassion, Sara Lee feels compelled to help the suffering Belgian Army. She unexpectedly defies her parents & travels alone to the front lines to help anyway she can.

Amazing Interlude. unabr. ed. Mary Roberts Rinehart. Read by Shelly Frasier. (ENG.). 2002. audio compact disk 72.00 (978-1-4001-3054-2(9)) Pub: Tantor Media. Dist(s): IngramPubServ

Amazing Interlude. unabr. ed. Mary Roberts Rinehart. Narrated by Mary Roberts Rinehart. 6 CDs. (Running Time: 7 hrs. 15 mins.). (ENG.). 2002. audio compact disk 36.00 (978-1-4001-0054-5(2)); audio compact disk 20.00 (978-1-4001-5054-0(X)) Pub: Tantor Media. Dist(s): IngramPubServ
Unabridged Audiobook. 1 MP3 CD - 7 hours, 15 minutes. Narrated by Shelly Frasier.Driven by a sense of duty and a fear of monotony, Sara Lee leaves her comfortable life and fiance in Philadelphia to serve the Red Cross in Belgium during WWI. The spirited heroine finds a niche for herself helping wounded soldiers. She meets a mysterious gentleman and falls into a haunting romance.The Amazing Interlude is a bittersweet journey that draws from Mary Rinehart's own experience as a World War I correspondent. Fusing fiction with fact, she deftly portrays an exhilarating tale of an honorable woman's determination to make a difference in a time of tumultuous war.This audiobook is on one CD, encoded in MP3 format and will only play on computers and CD players that have the ability to play this unique format.

Amazing Interlude, with EBook. unabr. ed. Mary Roberts Rinehart. Narrated by Shelly Frasier. (Running Time: 7 hrs. 0 mins. 0 sec.). (ENG.). 2009. audio compact disk 55.99 (978-1-4001-4115-9(X)); audio compact disk 27.99 (978-1-4001-1115-2(3)); audio compact disk 19.99 (978-1-4001-6115-7(0)) Pub: Tantor Media. Dist(s): IngramPubServ

***Amazing Inventors - Volume 1: Inspirational Stories.** unabr. ed. Charles Margerison. Read by Charles Margerison. Read by Markus Hayes. Frances Corcoran. Emma Braithwaite. (Running Time: 47 mins.). (ENG.). 2010. 4.99 (978-1-921629-68-6(1)) Pub: CJMPub AUS. Dist(s): HachBkGrp

Amazing Jerusalem Makeover. Created by Herb Owens et al. (ENG.). 2005. audio compact disk 59.99 (978-5-558-57757-0(6)) BB Music.

Amazing Journeys: Following in History's Footsteps. Ian Young. (High Five Reading - Green Ser.). (ENG.). (gr. 3-4). 2007. audio compact disk 5.95 (978-1-4296-1439-9(0)) CapstoneDig.

Amazing Journeys 1-3. unabr. ed. (J). 2006. 39.99 (978-1-59895-624-5(8)) Find a World.

Amazing Journeys 3-5. unabr. ed. (J). 2006. 39.99 (978-1-59895-721-1(X)) Find a World.

***Amazing Life of Birds.** unabr. ed. Gary Paulsen. (Running Time: 3 hrs.). 2011. 12.99 (978-1-4558-0180-0(1), 9781455801800, BAD); 39.97 (978-1-4558-0181-7(X), 9781455801817, BADLE); 12.99 (978-1-4558-0178-7(X), 9781455801787, Brilliance MP3); 39.97 (978-1-4558-0179-4(8), 9781455801794, Brinc Audio MP3 Lib); audio compact disk 12.99 (978-1-4558-0176-3(3), 9781455801763, Bril Audio CD Unabri); audio compact disk 39.97 (978-1-4558-0177-0(1), 9781455801770, BriAudCD Unabrid) Brilliance Audio.

Amazing Love. Keith Ferguson. 2000. 75.00 (978-0-633-01330-1(7)); 11.98 (978-0-633-01328-8(5)); audio compact disk 85.00 (978-0-633-01331-8(5)); audio compact disk 16.98 (978-0-633-01329-5(3)) LifeWay Christian.

Amazing Love. Contrib. by Russell Mauldin. 1996. 90.00 (978-0-00-513555-6(9), 75608628); 11.98 (978-0-00-513557-0(5), 75608627); audio compact disk 16.98 (978-0-00-513558-7(3), 75608625) Pub: Brentwood Music. Dist(s): H Leonard

Amazing Love. Albin Whitworth. 1993. 11.98 (978-0-7673-1311-7(9)) LifeWay Christian.

***Amazing Love: True Stories of the Power of Forgiveness.** unabr. ed. Corrie ten Boom. (ENG.). 2010. 9.98 (978-1-61045-094-2(9)) christianaud.

***Amazing Love: True Stories of the Power of Forgiveness.** unabr. ed. Corrie ten Boom. (Running Time: 2 hrs. 45 mins. 0 sec.). (ENG.). 2011. audio compact disk 15.98 (978-1-61045-092-8(2)) christianaud.

Amazing Machine. Jill Eggleton. Illus. by Rob Kieley. (Sails Literacy Ser.). (gr. 3 up). 10.00 (978-0-7578-6991-4(2)) Rigby Educ.

Amazing Marriage. unabr. ed. George Meredith. Narrated by Flo Gibson. 11 cass. (Running Time: 16 hrs.). 2002. 34.95 (978-1-55685-678-5(4),) Audio Bk Con.
Lovely Carinthia is jilted by Lord Fleetwood & seeks her independence.

Amazing Maurice & His Educated Rodents. unabr. ed. Terry Pratchett. Read by Stephen Briggs. 6 CDs. (Running Time: 23880 sec.). (Discworld Ser.). 2002. audio compact disk 64.95 (978-0-7531-1406-3(2)) Pub: ISIS Lrg Prnt GBR. Dist(s): Ulverscroft US

Amazing Maurice & His Educated Rodents. unabr. ed. Terry Pratchett. Read by Stephen Briggs. 6 cass. (Running Time: 22200 sec.). (Discworld Ser.). (J). (gr. 4-7). 2002. 54.95 (978-0-7531-1314-1(7)) Pub: ISIS Lrg Prnt GBR. Dist(s): Ulverscroft US
Rats! They're everywhere: in the breadbins, dancing across tabletops, stealing pies from under the cooks' noses. So what does every town need? A good Piper to lure them away. That's where Maurice comes in. But he's only a cat - albeit one that talks - so although he has the ideas, he needs rats and someone to play the pipe. Who better than the kid to play the pipe? And Dangerous Beans and Peaches. And Hamnpork (who doesn't really like what's been happening since The Change: all a rat leader needs is to be big and stroppy - thinking is just not his thing). Then they arrive in Bad Blintz which is suffering a plague of rats and find there are NO other rats anywhere (though the two resident rat-catchers seem to have plenty of tails to show, at 50 pence each). Someone else has ideas, and Maurice is not pleased.

Amazing Miracles. 1 cass. (Running Time: 1 hr.). (Amazing Bible Ser.). 2000. 6.99 HARK Ent.
Will fill your home with fun-filled praise of the Lord. Provides wholesome messages that are sure to last a lifetime.

Amazing Miracles. 1 cass. (Amazing Bible Ser.). (J). 9.95 (AAAM) Brdgstn Multimed Grp.
Children will be delighted to sing along with these original tunes from "The Amazing Miracles" video. They'll discover through song that God is a God of wonders & miracles! Includes the favorite, "Water, Water".

Amazing Miracles. Bridgestone Staff. 2004. audio compact disk 7.98 (978-1-56371-026-1(9)) Brdgstn Multimed Grp.

Amazing Mrs. Pollifax. Dorothy Gilman. Read by Barbara Rosenblat. 4 Cass. (Running Time: 6.75 Hrs.). (Mrs. Pollifax Mystery Ser.). 19.95 (978-1-4025-2803-3(5)) Recorded Bks.

Amazing Mrs. Pollifax. unabr. ed. Dorothy Gilman. Narrated by Barbara Rosenblat. 5 cass. (Running Time: 6 hrs. 45 mins.). (Mrs. Pollifax Mystery Ser.: Vol. 2). 1989. 44.00 (978-1-55690-011-2(2), 89740E7) Recorded Bks.
Mrs. Emily Pollifax abandons retirement to become a spy for the CIA with amazing consequences.

***Amazing People of London: Inspirational Stories.** unabr. ed. Charles Margerison & Katharine Smith. Ed. by Lisa Moffatt & James Rix. Frances Corcoran. Emily Hamilton & Dennis Bedson. Emma Braithwaite. (Running Time: 1 hr. 7 mins.). (ENG.). 2010. 9.99 (978-1-921629-46-4(0)) Pub: CJMPub AUS. Dist(s): HachBkGrp

***Amazing People of New York: Inspirational Stories.** unabr. ed. Charles Margerison & Katharine Smith. Read by J. S. Gilbert et al. Ed. by Lisa Moffatt. Frances Corcoran. (Running Time: 1 hr. 20 mins.). (ENG.). 2010. 9.99 (978-1-921629-45-7(2)) Pub: CJMPub AUS. Dist(s): HachBkGrp

Amazing Power of Deliberate Intent Pt. 1: Living the Art of Allowing. Esther Hicks & Jerry Hicks. Read by Jerry Hicks. 4 CDs. (Running Time: 14400 sec.). 2006. audio compact disk 23.95 (978-1-4019-1108-9(0)) Hay House.

Amazing Power of Deliberate Intent Pt. 2: Finding the Path to Joy Through Energy Balance. Esther Hicks & Jerry Hicks. Read by Jerry Hicks. 4 CDs. (Running Time: 14400 sec.). 2006. audio compact disk 23.95 (978-1-4019-1109-6(9)) Hay House.

Amazing SAS. unabr. ed. Ian McPhedran. Read by Peter Byrne. (Running Time: 11 hrs. 50 mins.). 2009. audio compact disk 98.95 (978-1-74214-137-4(4), 9781742141374) Pub: Bolinda Pubng AUS. Dist(s): Bolinda Pub Inc

amazing SAS. unabr. ed. Ian McPhedran. Read by Peter Byrne. (Running Time: 11 hrs. 50 mins.). 2009. 43.95 (978-1-74214-501-3(9), 9781742145013) Pub: Bolinda Pubng AUS. Dist(s): Bolinda Pub Inc

***Amazing Science: Ciencia Asombrosa Collection.** Created by Playaway. (Playaway Children Ser.). (ENG & SPA.). (J). 2009. 39.99 (978-1-61587-673-0(1)) Find a World.

***Amazing Scientists - Volume 1: Inspirational Stories.** unabr. ed. Charles Margerison. Read by Charles Margerison. Read by Mark Smith. Frances Corcoran. Emma Braithwaite. (Running Time: 54 mins.). (ENG.). 2010. 4.99 (978-1-921629-65-5(7)) Pub: CJMPub AUS. Dist(s): HachBkGrp

Amazing Secrets of Sun Tzu's the Art of War: An Audio Seminar. Speeches. Gary Gagliardi. 2 CDs. (Running Time: 1 hr. 30 mins.). 2001. audio compact disk 29.95 (978-1-929194-10-0(2)) Clearbridge Pubg.

Amazing Sleepy Time Adventures. Kathleen Caldwell. Perf. by Brooks Caldwell & Genoa Caldwell. 1 cass. (Running Time: 45 mins.). (Live! from Possumtrot, USA Ser.: No. 4). (J). (ps-2). 1996. 10.95 (978-1-888137-03-3(7)) LuvTwoLisn.

"Live! from Possumtrot, USA" audio adventures entertain kids, ages 3-7, in positive, supportive ways, while encouraging imagination, friendship & caring. "The Amazing Sleepy Time Adventures" (for quiet time & bedtime) - Professor Pip & the Possumtrotters take a nighttime adventure to the moon & stars aboard the fabled Snoozemobile.

***Amazing Story of Quantum Mechanics: A Math-Free Exploration of the Science That Made Our World.** unabr. ed. James Kakalios. (Running Time: 12 hrs. 0 mins.). 2010. 34.99 (978-1-4001-9628-9(0)); 17.99 (978-1-4001-8628-0(5)) Tantor Media.

***Amazing Story of Quantum Mechanics: A Math-Free Exploration of the Science That Made Our World.** unabr. ed. James Kakalios. Narrated by Peter Berkrot. (Running Time: 12 hrs. 0 mins. 0 sec.). (ENG.). 2010. 24.99 (978-1-4001-6628-2(4)); audio compact disk 34.99 (978-1-4001-1628-7(7)); audio compact disk 69.99 (978-1-4001-4628-4(3)) Pub: Tantor Media. Dist(s): IngramPubServ

***Amazing Tales for Making Men Out of Boys.** abr. ed. Neil Oliver. Read by Gideon Emery. (ENG.). 2009. (978-0-06-189412-1(5), Harper Audio); (978-0-06-190172-0(5), Harper Audio) HarperCollins Pubs.

Amazing Trains. Contrib. by Raintree Steck-Vaughn Staff. (J). (ps-3). 1997. 9.00 (978-0-8172-7371-2(9)) SteckVau.

Amazing Water. Sundance/Newbridge, LLC Staff. (Early Science Ser.). (gr. k-3). 2007. audio compact disk 12.00 (978-1-4007-6299-6(5)); audio compact disk 12.00 (978-1-4007-6300-9(2)); audio compact disk 12.00 (978-1-4007-6298-9(7)) Sund Newbrdge.

***Amazing Women: Inspirational Stories.** unabr. ed. Charles Margerison. Read by Michelle Plum et al. Frances Corcoran. Emma Braithwaite. (Running Time: 4 hrs.). (ENG.). 2010. 16.99 (978-1-921629-41-9(X)) Pub: CJMPub AUS. Dist(s): HachBkGrp

***Amazing Women in Business - Volume 1: Inspirational Stories.** unabr. ed. Charles Margerison. Read by Michelle Plum et al. Frances Corcoran. Emma Braithwaite. (Running Time: 55 mins.). (ENG.). 2010. 4.99 (978-1-921629-49-5(5)) Pub: CJMPub AUS. Dist(s): HachBkGrp

***Amazing Women in Medicine - Volume 1: Inspirational Stories.** unabr. ed. Charles Margerison. Read by Michelle Plum et al. Frances Corcoran. Emma Braithwaite. (Running Time: 30 mins.). (ENG.). 2010. 4.99 (978-1-921629-51-8(7)) Pub: CJMPub AUS. Dist(s): HachBkGrp

***Amazing Women in War - Volume 1: Inspirational Stories.** unabr. ed. Charles Margerison. Read by Michelle Plum et al. Frances Corcoran. Emma Braithwaite. (Running Time: 37 mins.). (ENG.). 2010. 4.99 (978-1-921629-55-6(X)) Pub: CJMPub AUS. Dist(s): HachBkGrp

***Amazing Women Leaders - Volume 1: Inspirational Stories.** unabr. ed. Charles Margerison. Read by Michelle Plum et al. Frances Corcoran. Emma Braithwaite. (Running Time: 40 mins.). (ENG.). 2010. 4.99 (978-1-921629-47-1(9)) Pub: CJMPub AUS. Dist(s): HachBkGrp

***Amazing Women's Careers - Volume 1: Inspirational Stories.** unabr. ed. Charles Margerison. Read by Michelle Plum et al. Frances Corcoran. Emma Braithwaite. (Running Time: 1 hr. 5 mins.). (ENG.). 2010. 4.99 (978-1-921629-56-3(8)) Pub: CJMPub AUS. Dist(s): HachBkGrp

Amazing Works of John Newton. John Newton. (Pure Gold Classics Ser.). 2009. pap. bk. 14.99 (978-0-88270-809-6(0)) Bridge-Logos.

Amazon Adventure. Created by Saddleback Educational Publishing. (Barclay Family Adventure Ser.). (J). 2003. audio compact disk (978-1-56254-977-0(4)) Saddleback Edu.

Amazon Days - Amazon Nights. Bernie Krause. 1 cass. (Running Time: 60 mins.). (Wild Sanctuary Ser.). 1994. audio compact disk 15.95 (2330, Creativ Pub) Quayside.

Tropical jungle from dawn to dusk, parrots, gentle doves, Howler monkeys, crickets, cicadas, frogs & more.

Amazon Days - Amazon Nights. Bernie Krause. 1 cass. (Running Time: 60 mins.). (Wild Sanctuary Ser.). 1994. 9.95 (2329, NrthWrd Bks) TandN Child.

***Amazon Run.** Mickey Friedman. 2009. (978-1-60136-520-0(9)) Audio Holding.

***Amazonia.** abr. ed. James Rollins. Read by Ruben Santiago-hudson. (ENG.). 2004. (978-0-06-078293-1(5), Harper Audio) HarperCollins Pubs.

***Amazonia.** abr. ed. James Rollins. Read by Ruben Santiago-hudson. (ENG.). 2004. (978-0-06-081442-7(X), Harper Audio) HarperCollins Pubs.

Amazonia. unabr. ed. James Rollins. Narrated by George Guidall. 11 cass. (Running Time: 15 hrs. 45 mins.). 2002. 99.00 (978-1-4025-1816-4(1)) Recorded Bks.

A U.S. Special Forces agent walks out of the Amazon jungle after five years and quickly dies of rampant tumors. What's really bizarre is that this man has twoarms; but when he entered the jungle as part of a biopharmaceutical exploratory expedition, he had only one. The dead agent's body is shipped to the States, hosting a disease that threatens to wipe out the American population.

Amazonia. unabr. ed. James Rollins. Narrated by George Guidall. 11 cass. (Running Time: 15 hrs. 45 mins.). 2002. 49.95 (978-1-4025-1850-8(1), RF920) Recorded Bks.

***Amazonia.** unabr. ed. James Rollins. Read by John Meagher. (ENG.). 2009. (978-0-06-195857-1(3), Harper Audio); (978-0-06-196144-1(2), Harper Audio) HarperCollins Pubs.

Amazonia Foundation's Michael Stuart Ani - Helping the Indigenous People of the Amazon. Hosted by Nancy Pearlman. 1 cass. (Running Time: 30 mins.). 10.00 (1010) Educ Comm CA.

Amazonian Pink River Dolphins & Roxanne Kremer's Research & Ecotour Expeditions in Peru. Hosted by Nancy Pearlman. 1 cass. (Running Time: 28 mins.). 10.00 (1507) Educ Comm CA.

Ambassador. Contrib. by Bobby Jones & James "Jazzy" Jordan. Prod. by Victor Caldwell & Cedric Caldwell. 2007. audio compact disk 17.98 (978-5-557-59910-8(X)) GospoCen.

Ambassador. unabr. ed. Edwina Currie. Read by Simon Shepherd. 12 cass. 1999. 96.95 (978-0-7540-0380-9(9), CAB1803) AudioGO.

In the year 2099, the world is dominated by the European Union. Comprising 42 nations, the EU is more powerful than the United States & while cloning is not mentioned in polite society, it's happening all over. The United States is opposed to the medical advances & when Bill Strether is sent to London by the president, he soon realizes the full extent of the genetic program.

Ambassador. unabr. ed. Morris West. Read by Noel Hodda. 6 cass. (Running Time: 8 hrs. 42 mins.). 2004. 48.00 (978-1-74030-159-6(5), 500845) Pub: Bolinda Pubng AUS. Dist(s): Lndmrk Audiobks

Ambassador in Paris: The Reagan Years. unabr. ed. Evan Galbraith. Read by Matthew Davis. 4 cass. (Running Time: 5 hrs. 30 mins.). 1993. 32.95 (978-0-7861-0009-5(5), 1008) Blckstn Audio.

Evan Galbraith represented America in Paris for four years during Reagan's administration. He paints a vivid picture showing the life of an American ambassador in the grand & glamorous city of Paree.

Ambassadors. Henry James. Narrated by Flo Gibson. (ENG.). 2007. audio compact disk 42.95 (978-1-55685-920-5(1)) Audio Bk Con.

Ambassadors. Derek Prince. 1 cass. (B-4020) Derek Prince.

Ambassadors. unabr. ed. Henry James. Read by Flo Gibson. 11 cass. (Running Time: 16 hrs.). 1992. 34.95 (978-1-55685-232-9(0)) Audio Bk Con.

James considered this book his masterpiece! Various "Ambassadors" are sent to Paris to persuade Chad Newsom to return to his New England town & business interests. Among these envoys, Lambert Strethel is so impressed with Chad's Europeanized suavety & charm that he advises him to remain with Mme. Dr. Vionnet.

***Ambassadors.** unabr. ed. Henry James. Narrated by Stephen Hoye. (Running Time: 18 hrs. 0 mins. 0 sec.). 2010. 29.99 (978-1-4526-5022-7(5)); 22.99 (978-1-4526-7022-5(6)); audio compact disk 39.99 (978-1-4526-0022-2(8)) Pub: Tantor Media. Dist(s): IngramPubServ

Ambassadors. unabr. collector's ed. Henry James. Read by Walter Zimmerman. 13 cass. (Running Time: 19 hrs. 30 mins.). 1998. 104.00 (978-0-7366-3979-8(9), 9527) Books on Tape.

Many critics & James himself, judge this novel of the expatriate American gentleman/Paris sophisticate to be his finest.

Ambassadors for Christ. Featuring Bill Winston. 3 cass. 2005. 15.00 (978-1-59544-111-9(5)); audio compact disk 24.00 (978-1-59544-112-6(3)) Pub: B Winston Min. Dist(s): Anchor Distributors

***Ambassadors (Library Edition)** unabr. ed. Henry James. Narrated by Stephen Hoye. (Running Time: 18 hrs. 0 mins.). 2010. 39.99 (978-1-4526-2022-0(9)); audio compact disk 95.99 (978-1-4526-3022-9(4)) Pub: Tantor Media. Dist(s): IngramPubServ

Ambassadors on Assignment. Featuring Lynne Hammond. 3 cass. 2003. 15.00 (978-1-57399-173-5(2)); audio compact disk 15.00 (978-1-57399-172-8(4)) Mac Hammond.

Ambassador's Wife in Iran. unabr. ed. Cynthia Helms. Narrated by Flo Gibson. 5 cass. (Running Time: 7 hrs.). 1981. 44.00 (978-1-55690-012-9(0), 81010E7) Recorded Bks.

The wife of U. S. Ambassador Richard Helms recounts the events of her husband's posting to pre-revolutionary Iran.

Amber. Ed. by Robert A. Monroe. 1 cass. (Running Time: 30 mins.). (Meta Music Ser.). 1985. 12.95 (978-1-56102-200-7(4)) Inter Indus.

Provides a unique, musical Hemi-Sync vehicle to explore the emotional aspects of your Self - Now, Then & When.

Amber & Amethyst. unabr. ed. Kay Gregory. Read by Lynda Evans. 4 cass. (Running Time: 5 hrs, 36 min.). 2001. 26.95 (978-1-55686-861-0(8)) Books in Motion.

Amber found the ex-university professor a fascinating man, even though Kyle had no intentions of taking her seriously. But Amber found there was more separating them than age difference.

***Amber Beach.** unabr. ed. Elizabeth Lowell. Read by Robin Rowan. (ENG.). 2009. (978-0-06-196695-8(9), Harper Audio); (978-0-06-182976-5(5), Harper Audio) HarperCollins Pubs.

Amber Brown Collection. Paula Danziger. Read by Alicia Witt. 2 cass. (Running Time: 3 hrs.). (J). 2000. 18.00 (978-0-7366-9093-5(X)) Books on Tape.

Includes: "Amber Brown is not a Crayon" "You Can't Eat Your Chicken Pox" "Amber Brown" & "Amber Brown Goes Fourth.".

Amber Brown Collection. unabr. ed. Paula Danziger. Read by Alicia Witt. 2 cass. (Running Time: 3 hrs. 8 mins.). (Amber Brown Ser.). (J). (gr. 2-4). 1997. 23.00 (978-0-8072-7805-5(X), YA923CX, Listening Lib) Random Audio Pubg.

Spunk & good humor help Amber Brown, an unforgettable third grader, survive the joys & sorrows that life delivers.

Amber Brown Collection III. Paula Danziger. Read by Dana Lubotsky. 4 cass. (Running Time: 5 hrs. 37 mins.). (J). (gr. 2-4). 2004. 32.00 (978-0-8072-1795-5(6), Listening Lib); audio compact disk 40.00 (978-0-8072-2016-0(7), Listening Lib) Random Audio Pubg.

Amber Brown Goes Fourth. unabr. ed. Paula Danziger. Read by Alicia Witt. 1 cass. (Running Time: 1 hr. 8 mins.). (Amber Brown Ser.: No. 3). (J). (gr. 2-4). 1997. pap. bk. 17.00 (978-0-8072-0360-6(2), FTR 181 SP, Listening Lib) Random Audio Pubg.

The plucky heroine moves up to the fourth grade where she longs for a new best friend.

Amber Brown Is Feeling Blue. Paula Danziger. Read by Dana Lubotsky. (Running Time: 1 hr. 44 mins.). (Amber Brown Ser.: No. 7). (J). (gr. 2-4). 2004. pap. bk. 17.00 (978-0-8072-2063-4(9), Listening Lib) Random Audio Pubg.

Amber Brown Is Not a Crayon. unabr. ed. Paula Danziger. Read by Alicia Witt. 1 cass. (Running Time: 1 hr. 5 mins.). (Amber Brown Ser.: No. 1). (J). (gr. 2-4). 1997. pap. bk. 17.00 (978-0-8072-0354-5(8), FTR 179 SP, Listening Lib) Random Audio Pubg.

Amber Brown Sees Red. unabr. ed. Paula Danziger. Read by Dana Lubotsky. 1 cass. (Running Time: 1 hr. 18 mins.). (Amber Brown Ser.: No. 6). (J). (gr. 2-4). 1998. pap. bk. 17.00 (978-0-8072-0369-9(6), FTR186SP, Listening Lib) Random Audio Pubg.

How is Amber Brown supposed to like her Mom's new husband when he's keeping her parents apart?.

Amber Brown Series. Paula Danziger. Illus. by Tony Ross. 44 vols. (Running Time: 66 mins.). 2002. pap. bk. 61.95 (978-0-87499-998-3(7)); pap. bk. 68.95 (978-1-59112-856-4(0)) Live Oak Media.

Amber Brown Wants Extra Credit. unabr. ed. Paula Danziger. Read by Dana Lubotsky. 1 cass. (Running Time: 1 hr. 20 mins.). (Amber Brown Ser.: No. 4). (J). (gr. 2-4). 1997. pap. bk. 17.00 (978-0-8072-0363-7(7), FTR 182 SP, Listening Lib) Random Audio Pubg.

The only thing that she wants is for her parents to be together again, but she soon learns that life isn't always fair & you can't always get what you want.

Amber Cat. Hilary McKay. Read by Ron Keith. 3 cass. (Running Time: 4 hrs.). (YA). 1999. pap. bk. & stu. ed. 41.00 (978-0-7887-3635-3(3), 41000) Recorded Bks.

When Robin Brogan & his friend come down with chicken pox, Robin's mother entertains them with tales of her childhood. She tells of a strange girl who mysteriously appeared long ago, then disappeared one day, never to be seen again.

Amber Cat. unabr. ed. Hilary McKay. Narrated by Ron Keith. 3 pieces. (Running Time: 4 hrs.). (gr. 4 up). 2000. 29.00 (978-0-7887-3515-8(2), 95908E7) Recorded Bks.

Amber Cat, Class set. unabr. ed. Hilary McKay. Read by Ron Keith. 3 cass. (Running Time: 4 hrs.). (J). 2000. pap. bk. 41.75 (41000X4) Recorded Bks.

Amber Collector's Series. Roger Zelazny. Read by Roger Zelazny. 6 vols. 2003. (978-1-58807-911-4(2)) Am Pubng Inc.

Amber Collector's Series. Roger Zelazny. Read by Roger Zelazny. 6 vols. No. 2. 2004. (978-1-58807-912-1(0)) Am Pubng Inc.

Amber Collector's Series. Roger Zelazny. Read by Roger Zelazny. 4 vols. No. 3. 2004. (978-1-58807-913-8(9)) Am Pubng Inc.

Amber Collector's Series, Vol. 1. Roger Zelazny. Read by Roger Zelazny. 6 vols. (Amber Collector's Ser.: No. 1). 2003. 35.00 (978-1-58807-458-4(7)) Am Pubng Inc.

Amber Collector's Series, Vol. 2. Roger Zelazny. Read by Roger Zelazny. 6 vols. (Amber Collector's Ser.: No. 2). 2004. 35.00 (978-1-58807-459-1(5)) Am Pubng Inc.

Amber Collector's Series, Vol. 3. Roger Zelazny. Read by Roger Zelazny. 4 vols. (Amber Collector's Ser.: No. 3). 2004. 25.00 (978-1-58807-460-7(9)) Am Pubng Inc.

***Amber Morn.** unabr. ed. Brandilyn Collins. (Running Time: 7 hrs. 36 mins. 2 sec.). (Kanner Lake Ser.). (ENG.). 2009. 13.99 (978-0-310-77204-0(4)) Zondervan.

Amber Room. abr. ed. Steve Berry. Read by Scott Brick. (Running Time: 27000 sec.). (ENG.). 2007. audio compact disk 19.95 (978-0-7393-5407-0(8), Random AudioBks) Pub: Random Audio Pubg. Dist(s): Random

Amber Spyglass. Perf. by Philip Pullman. 12 CDs. (Running Time: 14 hrs. 57 mins.). (His Dark Materials Ser.: Bk. 3). (YA). (gr. 7 up). 2004. audio compact disk 75.00 (978-0-8072-1046-8(3), S YA 169 CD, Listening Lib) Random Audio Pubg.

Amber Spyglass. unabr. ed. Philip Pullman. 14 cass. (Running Time: 15 hrs.). (His Dark Materials Ser.: Bk. 3). (YA). (gr. 7-12). 2001. audio compact disk 70.00 (978-0-8072-8604-3(4), Listening Lib) Random Audio Pubg.

Brings the intrigue of "The Golden Compass" & "The Subtle Knife" to a heart-stopping end. Startling revelations: the painful price Lyra must pay to walk through the land of the dead, the haunting power of Dr. Malone's amber spyglass & the names of who will live & who will die for love. All the while, war rages with the Kingdom of Heaven, a brutal battle that, in its shocking outcome, will uncover the secret of Dust.

Amber Spyglass. unabr. ed. Philip Pullman. Perf. by Philip Pullman. 10 vols. (Running Time: 14 hrs. 54 mins.). (His Dark Materials Ser.: Bk. 3). (YA). (gr. 7 up). 2004. pap. bk. 63.00 (978-0-8072-1593-7(7), S YA 169 SP, Listening Lib) Random Audio Pubg.

Amber Spyglass. unabr. ed. Philip Pullman. Read by Full Cast Production Staff. 12 CDs. (Running Time: 14 hrs. 54 mins.). Dramatization. (His Dark Materials Ser.: Bk. 3). (ENG.). (J). (gr. 7-12). 2004. audio compact disk 54.00 (978-0-8072-6201-6(3), Listening Lib) Pub: Random Audio Pubg. Dist(s): Random

Amber Spyglass, Vol. 3. unabr. ed. Philip Pullman. Read by Philip Pullman. 10 cass. (Running Time: 14 hrs. 54 mins.). (His Dark Materials Ser.: Bk. 3). (J). (gr. 7 up). 2004. 55.00 (978-0-8072-8350-9(9), S YA 169 CX, Listening Lib) Random Audio Pubg.

Amber Was Brave, Essie Was Smart. Read by Barbara Rosenblat et al. 11 vols. (Running Time: 29 mins.). (J). (gr. 4-7). 2003. 16.95 (978-1-59112-185-5(X)) Live Oak Media.

Amber Was Brave, Essie Was Smart. Vera B. Williams. Illus. by Vera B. Williams. 14 vols. (Running Time: 29 mins.). 2003. pap. bk. 37.95 (978-1-59112-187-9(6)); pap. bk. 39.95 (978-1-59112-554-9(5)); 9.95 (978-1-59112-184-8(1)); audio compact disk 12.95 (978-1-59112-337-8(2)) Live Oak Media.

***Amber Was Brave, Essie Was Smart.** unabr. ed. Vera B. Williams. Read by Martha Plimpton. (ENG.). 2009. (978-0-06-180583-7(1), GreenwillowBks); (978-0-06-176240-6(7), GreenwillowBks) HarperCollins Pubs.

Amber Was Brave, Essie was Smart: The Story of Amber & Essie, Told Here in Poems & Pictures. Vera B. Williams. Read by Barbara Rosenblat et al. 11 vols. (Running Time: 29 mins.). (Live Oak Readalong Ser.). (J). 2003. pap. bk. 18.95 (978-1-59112-338-5(0)) Pub: Live Oak Media. Dist(s): AudioGO

Amber Was Brave, Essie Was Smart: The Story of Amber & Essie, Told Here in Poems & Pictures. Vera B. Williams. Illus. by Vera B. Williams. 11 vols. (Running Time: 29 mins.). (J). (gr. k-3). 2003. bk. 25.95 (978-1-59112-186-2(8)) Live Oak Media.

Ambergris & Arrowheads: Growing up on Cape Cod in the 1930's & 1940's. unabr. ed. Anne N. Harmon. Read by Anne N. Harmon. 2 cass. (Running Time: 3 hrs.). 1996. 17.95 (978-1-890564-00-1(1), TCA-1101) Time Capsule.

Sixty stories, legends & adventures from the childhood of author/storyteller Anne N. Harmon, an eighth-generation Cape Codder who grew up in a lively 1930's household that included four of those generations.

Amberwell. D. E. Stevenson. 2009. 69.95 (978-1-4079-0404-7(3)); audio compact disk 84.95 (978-1-4079-0405-4(1)) Pub: Soundings Ltd GBR. Dist(s): Ulverscroft US

Ambience Minimus. Music by Liquid Mind. Composed by Chuck Wild. 1 CD. (Running Time: 65 mins.). 1994. audio compact disk 15.98 (978-0-9742661-0-7(8)) Chuck Wild Recs.

Ambient Music for Sleep. Jeffrey Thompson. (Running Time: 1:01:00). 2003. audio compact disk 11.95 (978-1-55961-670-6(9)) Sounds True.

***Ambition.** unabr. ed. Kate Brian, pseud. Narrated by Cassandra Campbell. (Running Time: 7 hrs. 30 mins. 0 sec.). (Private Ser.). 2010. 19.99 (978-1-4001-6237-6(8)); 14.99 (978-1-4001-8237-4(9)); audio compact disk 29.99 (978-1-4001-1237-1(0)) Pub: Tantor Media. Dist(s): IngramPubServ

Ambition, Vol. 1. Richard Gorham & Orison Swett Marden. Narrated by Richard Gorham. (ENG.). 2006. audio compact disk 14.95 (978-0-9791934-0-8(0)) LshipTools.

Ambition: A Novel. unabr. ed. (ENG.). 2010. audio compact disk 41.99 (978-0-310-32424-9(6)) Zondervan.

***Ambition (Library Edition)** unabr. ed. Kate Brian, pseud. Narrated by Cassandra Campbell. (Running Time: 7 hrs. 30 mins.). (Private Ser.). 2010. 29.99 (978-1-4001-9237-3(4)); audio compact disk 71.99 (978-1-4001-4237-8(7)) Pub: Tantor Media. Dist(s): IngramPubServ

Ambitious Guest see Great American Short Stories

Ambitious Guest. unabr. ed. Nathaniel Hawthorne. Read by Walter Zimmerman. 1 cass. (Running Time: 72 mins.). Dramatization. 1977. 7.95 (N-12) Jimcin Record.

Two stories of tragedy & ambition.

Ambitious Guest, Vol. 9. unabr. ed. Nathaniel Hawthorne. Narrated by Nelita B. Castillo. 1 cass. (Running Time: 41 mins.). (Fantasies Ser.). (J). 1984.

17.95 Incl. holder, scripts, lesson plans, & tchr's. guide. (978-0-86617-050-5(2)) Multi Media TX.
Comprehensive lesson plans that use classic short stories to develop skills in listening, reading, vocabulary, following details, making inferences, visualization, drawing conclusions, critical appreciation & comparison. This module's objective is to retell incidents of plot with identification of foreshadowing.

Ambitious Stepmother. unabr. ed. Fidelis Morgan. Read by Fidelis Morgan. 9 cass. (Running Time: 11 hrs. 51 mins.). (Isis Cassettes Ser.). (J). 2004. 76.95 (978-0-7531-1818-4(1)) Pub: ISIS Lrg Prnt GBR. Dist(s): Ulverscroft US

Ambitious Stepmother. unabr. ed. Fidelis Morgan. Read by Fidelis Morgan. 10 CDs. (Running Time: 11 hrs. 51 mins.). (Isis (CDs) Ser.). (J). 2005. audio compact disk 89.95 (978-0-7531-2467-3(X)) Pub: ISIS Lrg Prnt GBR. Dist(s): Ulverscroft US

Ambler Warning. Robert Ludlum. 2005. 23.95 (978-1-59397-802-0(2)) Pub: Macmill Audio. Dist(s): Macmillan

Ambler Warning. abr. ed. Robert Ludlum. 2005. 17.95 (978-1-59397-801-3(4)) Pub: Macmill Audio. Dist(s): Macmillan

Ambler Warning. abr. ed. Robert Ludlum. Read by Scott Sowers. (Running Time: 7 hrs. 30 mins. 0 sec.). (ENG.). 2009. audio compact disk 14.99 (978-1-4272-0810-1(7)) Pub: Macmill Audio. Dist(s): Macmillan

Ambler Warning. unabr. ed. Robert Ludlum. 10 cass. 2005. 89.95 (978-0-7927-3762-9(8), CSL 847); audio compact disk 115.95 (978-0-7927-3763-6(6), SLD 847); audio compact disk 69.95 (978-0-7927-3836-7(5), CMP 847) AudioGO.

Ambrose Bierce: Alone in Bad Company. unabr. ed. Roy Morris, Jr. Read by Jonathan Reese. 11 cass. (Running Time: 16 hrs. 30 mins.). 1996. 88.00 (978-0-7366-3406-9(1), 4052) Books on Tape.
He made criticism an art form, made a lot of enemies. His disappearance remains a mystery.

Ambrose Bierce Tales of Horror & the Supernatural. unabr. ed. Read by Flo Gibson. 3 cass. (Running Time: 4 hrs.). 1998. 16.95 (978-1-55685-548-1(6)) Audio Bk Con.
A collection of eerie stories explores the shadow side & darkest regions of the mind.

Ambush. Donald Clayton Porter. Read by Lloyd James. Abr. by Odin Westgaard. 4 vols. 2004. 25.00 (978-1-58807-224-5(X)) Am Pubng Inc.

Ambush. Donald Clayton Porter. Read by Lloyd James. Abr. by Odin Westgaard. 5 vols. No. 8. 2004. audio compact disk 30.00 (978-1-58807-408-9(0)) Am Pubng Inc.

Ambush. abr. ed. Donald Clayton Porter. Read by Lloyd James. Abr. by Odin Westgaard. 4 vols. No. 8. 2004. (978-1-58807-755-4(1)); audio compact disk (978-1-58807-847-6(7)) Am Pubng Inc.

Ambush at Fort Bragg. unabr. ed. Tom Wolfe. Read by Edward Norton. 4 cass. (Running Time: 6 hrs..). 1998. 32.95 (D193) Blckstn Audio.
A blistering send-up of one man's drive for fame & glory & the lengths to which the media will go to showcase their version of the truth.

Ambush at Fort Bragg, Set. unabr. ed. Tom Wolfe. Read by Edward Norton. 4 cass. 1999. 21.95 (FS9-34185) Highsmith.

Ambush Creek. unabr. ed. Lewis B. Patten. Read by William Dufris. 4 cass. (Running Time: 4 hrs.). (Sagebrush Western Ser.). (J). 2005. 44.95 (978-1-57490-295-2(4)) Pub: ISIS Lrg Prnt GBR. Dist(s): Ulverscroft US

Ambushers. unabr. ed. Gary McCarthy. Read by Maynard Villers. 4 cass. (Running Time: 5 hrs. 30 mins.). (Horsemen Ser.: Bk. 5). 1994. 26.95 (978-1-55686-539-8(2)) Books in Motion.
On their way to Colorado, Ruff & Dixie Ballou drive their horses through New Mexico where they are arrested as suspects in a robbery.

AMC Presents/Lux Radio Theatre: 1930s Radio Adaptations of Movie Classics. 10 cass. (Running Time: 10 hrs.). 2001. 34.98 (4485); audio compact disk 39.98 (4486) Radio Spirits.
For many years, Cicil B. DeMille, one of Hollywood's legendary movie directors, invited the original box office superstars to recreate their screen roles fro the Lux Radio Theatre. Now American Movie Classics has carefully selected ten all time great performances of silver screen adaptations that originally aired in the 1930s.

Amegroid, New Native American. Des. by ASA Publishing Company. 1999. audio compact disk 29.95 (978-0-9715138-1-5(3), A S A Pub) Natl Assn of Home Based Bus.

Amelia. unabr. ed. Henry Fielding. Read by Flo Gibson. 14 cass. (Running Time: 16 hrs. 30 mins.). (gr. 10 up). 1998. 42.95 (978-1-55685-523-8(0)) Audio Bk Con.
A tale of love & lust in the lives of the beautiful, long-suffering & idealized Amelia & her adoring husband. Laws, prisons & the lack of justice are bitterly examined.

Amelia Bedelia. abr. ed. Peggy Parish. Illus. by Fritz Siebel. (Amelia Bedelia Ser.). (J). (gr. k-3). 2005. 9.99 (978-0-06-078700-4(7), HarperFestival) HarperCollins Pubs.

Amelia Bedelia & the Baby. Peggy Parish. (Amelia Bedelia Ser.). (J). (gr. k-2). 1986. bk. 31.99 (978-0-394-69327-9(2)) SRA McGraw.

Amelia Bedelia & the Baby. unabr. ed. Peggy Parish. Narrated by Barbara Caruso. 1 cass. (Running Time: 18 mins.). (Amelia Bedelia Ser.). (gr. k up). 2001. 10.00 (978-0-7887-0369-0(2), 94561E7) Recorded Bks.

Amelia Bedelia & the Surprise Shower. abr. ed. Peggy Parish & Peggy Parish. Illus. by Barbara Siebel Thomas. (Amelia Bedelia Ser.). (J). (ps-3). 2007. 9.99 (978-0-06-124771-2(5), HarperFestival) HarperCollins Pubs.

Amelia Bedelia & the Surprise Shower. unabr. abr. ed. Peggy Parish. Illus. by Wallace Tripp & Barbara Siebel Thomas. 1 cass. (Amelia Bedelia Ser.). (J). (gr. k-3). 1990. 8.99 (978-1-55994-216-4(9)) HarperCollins Pubs.

***Amelia Bedelia Audio Collection.** unabr. ed. Peggy Parish. Read by Suzanne Toren. (ENG.). 2005. (978-0-06-082430-3(1), GreenwillowBks); (978-0-06-082431-0(X), GreenwillowBks) HarperCollins Pubs.

Amelia Bedelia Audio Collection. unabr. ed. Peggy Parish & Peggy Parish. Read by Suzanne Toren. 2 CDs. (Running Time: 3 hrs.). (J). 2004. 14.99 (978-0-06-074054-2(X), HarperChildAud) HarperCollins Pubs.

Amelia Bedelia Audio Collection, Volume 1. Peggy Parish. Contrib. by Suzanne Toren. (Playaway Top Children's Picks Ser.). (ENG.). (J). 2009. 44.99 (978-1-61574-792-4(3)) Find a World.

Amelia Bedelia Audio Collection, Volume 2. Peggy Parish. (Playaway Top Children's Picks Ser.). (ENG.). (J). 2009. 44.99 (978-1-61574-791-7(5)) Find a World.

Amelia Bedelia 4 Mayor. abr. ed. Herman Parish. Illus. by Lynn Sweat. (Amelia Bedelia Ser.). (J). 2003. 8.99 (978-0-06-009345-7(5)) HarperCollins Pubs.

***Amelia Bedelia's First Day of School.** unabr. ed. Herman Parish. Read by Angela Goethals. (ENG.). 2009. (978-0-06-177605-2(X), GreenwillowBks); (978-0-06-190215-4(2), GreenwillowBks) HarperCollins Pubs.

***Amelia Bedelia's First Valentine.** unabr. ed. Herman Parish. Read by Isabel Keating. (ENG.). 2009. (978-0-06-180844-9(X), GreenwillowBks); (978-0-06-180845-6(8), GreenwillowBks) HarperCollins Pubs.

Amelia Earhart. 10.00 Esstee Audios.
The story of America's great aviatrix.

Amelia Earhart. Prod. by A&E Television Network Staff. 1 cass. 1997. 9.95 (978-0-7670-0475-6(2)) A & E Home.

Amelia Earhart: A Biography. Doris L. Rich. Narrated by Susan Van Dusen. 9 CDs. (Running Time: 11 hours 30 minutes). 2002. audio compact disk 54.95 (978-1-929011-24-7(5)) Scholarly Audio.
This is an engrossing unabridged audiobook version of the biography of Amelia Earhart published by the Smithsonian Institution Press. It details her public and private life as a determined, independent woman who pioneered in aviation and women?s rights.

Amelia Earhart: A Biography. unabr. ed. Doris L. Rich. Read by Susan Van Dusen. 1 CD. (Running Time: 11 hrs. 30 mins.). 2001. audio compact disk 39.99 (978-0-9660180-7-3(9)) Scholarly Audio.
Tells the real story of America's most famous female aviator & outspoken advocate for women's equality with men.

Amelia Earhart: Young Air Pioneer. Jane Moore Howe. Read by Lynne Taccogna. (Running Time: 7200 sec.). (Young Patriots Ser.). (J). 2007. audio compact disk 24.00 (978-1-4332-0144-8(5)) Blckstn Audio.

Amelia Earhart: Young Air Pioneer. Jane Moore Howe. Read by Lynne Taccogna. (Running Time: 7200 sec.). (Young Patriots Ser.). (J). (gr. 4-7). 2007. 22.95 (978-1-4332-0143-1(7)) Blckstn Audio.

Amelia Earhart: Young Air Pioneer. unabr. ed. Jane Moore Howe. Read by Lynne Taccogna. (Young Patriots Ser.). (J). 2007. 34.99 (978-1-60252-635-8(4)) Find a World.

Amelogenesis Imperfecta - A Bibliography & Dictionary for Physicians, Patients, & Genome Researchers. Compiled by Icon Group International, Inc. Staff. 2007. ring bd. 28.95 (978-0-497-11326-1(0)) Icon Grp.

Amen. unabr. ed. Jonathan Settel. (SPA.). 2003. 9.99 (978-0-8297-3674-8(3)) Pub: Vida Pubs. Dist(s): Zondervan

Amen, Amen, Amen: Memoir of a Girl Who Couldn't Stop Praying (Among Other Things) unabr. ed. Abby Sher. Narrated by Abby Sher. (Running Time: 14 hrs. 0 mins. 0 sec.). (ENG.). 2009. 24.99 (978-1-4001-6427-1(3)); audio compact disk 34.99 (978-1-4001-1427-6(6)); audio compact disk 69.99 (978-1-4001-4427-3(2)) Pub: Tantor Media. Dist(s): IngramPubServ

***Amen, Amen, Amen: Memoir of a Girl Who Couldn't Stop Praying (Among Other Things)** unabr. ed. Abby Sher. Narrated by Abby Sher. (Running Time: 14 hrs. 0 mins.). 2009. 19.99 (978-1-4001-8427-9(4)) Tantor Media.

Amen Choral Cassette. Greg Skipper. 2001. 11.98 (978-0-633-02146-7(6)) LifeWay Christian.

Amen Choral Cd. Greg Skipper. 2001. audio compact disk 16.98 (978-0-633-02165-8(2)) LifeWay Christian.

***Amen Solution: 10 Weeks to Boost Your Brain to be Thinner, Smarter, & Happier.** unabr. ed. Daniel G. Amen. Read by Daniel G. Amen. (Running Time: 12 hrs. 30 mins.). (ENG.). 2011. audio compact disk 40.00 (978-0-7393-8493-0(7), Random AudioBks) Pub: Random Audio Pubg. Dist(s): Random

Amendment of Life. Catherine Aird. Read by Bruce Montague. 4 cass. (Running Time: 6 hrs.). 2002. 39.95 (978-0-7540-0892-7(4), CAB 2314) Pub: Chivers Audio Bks GBR. Dist(s): AudioGO

Amendments to the Sewage Facilities Act. 1996. bk. 99.00 (ACS-1058) PA Bar Inst.
The Sewage Facilities Act has had statewide impact on real estate development. Extensive amendments to the Act effective December 15,1995, significantly expand the role of local government in the administration of the Act.

America. abr. ed. Stephen Coonts. Read by John Kenneth. (Running Time: 6 hrs.). (Jake Grafton Novel Ser.: Vol. 9). 2005. audio compact disk 16.99 (978-1-59355-698-3(5), 9781593556983, BCD Value Price) Brilliance Audio.

America. abr. ed. Stephen Coonts. Read by John Kenneth. (Running Time: 6 hrs.). (Jake Grafton Novel Ser.: Vol. 9). 2010. audio compact disk 9.99 (978-1-4418-0836-3(1), 9781441808363, BCD Value Price) Brilliance Audio.

America. rev. unabr. ed. E. R. Frank. Narrated by J. D. Jackson. 4 cass. (Running Time: 6 hrs.). 2002. 40.00 (978-1-4025-2889-7(2)) Recorded Bks.
America, a foulmouthed, yet endearing 16-year-old, attempts suicide and is placed in the care of psychiatrists at Ridgeway mental hospital. There he learns to cope with a past filled with neglect and mistreatment with the help of Dr. B. Alternating between America's present- day stay at the hospital and his past, living in the care of his older brothers, America is a stark exploration of the mind of an inner-city youth.

America. unabr. ed. T. C. Boyle. Read by Sergio Gutierrez. Tr. by Juan Fernando Merino. (Running Time: 55800 sec.). 2007. 85.95 (978-1-4332-1306-9(0)); audio compact disk 29.95 (978-1-4332-1308-3(7)); audio compact disk & audio compact disk 99.00 (978-1-4332-1307-6(9)) Blckstn Audio.

America. unabr. ed. Stephen Coonts. Read by John Kenneth. 9 cass. (Running Time: 13 hrs.). (Jake Grafton Novel Ser.: Vol. 9). 2001. 34.95 (978-1-58788-549-5(2), 1587885492, BAU); 96.25 (978-1-58788-554-9(9), 1587885549, CD Unabrid Lib Ed) Brilliance Audio.
When an experimental nuclear submarine is hijacked in broad daylight, only Admiral Jake Grafton stands between the deadly cargo and its intended target: Washington D.C. Hundreds of people have gathered to watch the launching of the USS America - our newest and most sophisticated nuclear submarine. Then, the unthinkable happens: armed men emerge from the tugboat that is leading her to sea, board the submarine and man her controls. Half of the men onboard are slaughtered and half are put out to sea. Before nearby destroyers can react, the sub disappears. Admiral Jake Grafton is resting at his Delaware beach house when he is asked to find out who has stolen his submarine and why. He learns that a rogue CIA group, originally trained to steal Russian technology during the Cold War, may be behind the operation. And soon it becomes clear that, whatever their purpose, they mean business: within hours a missile launched from the submarine destroys the top floor of the White House and a second missile fells an airliner carrying 283 passengers. Now the race is on to find out where the submarine is, who is behind the nightmare scenario and - most critically - how to stop it.

America. unabr. ed. Stephen Coonts. Read by John Kenneth. (Running Time: 13 hrs.). (Jake Grafton Novel Ser.: Vol. 9). 2004. 39.25 (978-1-59335-346-9(4), 1593353464, Brlnc Audio MP3 Lib) Brilliance Audio.

America. unabr. ed. Stephen Coonts. Read by John Kenneth. (Running Time: 14 hrs.). (Jake Grafton Novel Ser.: Vol. 9). 2004. 39.25 (978-1-59710-013-7(7), 1597100137, BADLE); 24.95 (978-1-59710-012-0(9), 1597100129, BAD) Brilliance Audio.

America. unabr. ed. Stephen Coonts. Read by John Kenneth. (Running Time: 50400 sec.). (Jake Grafton Novel Ser.: Vol. 9). 2007. audio compact disk 107.25 (978-1-4233-3380-7(2), 9781423333807, BriAudCD Unabrid); audio compact disk 38.95 (978-1-4233-3379-1(9), 9781423333791, Bril Audio CD Unabri) Brilliance Audio.

America. unabr. ed. Stephen Coonts. Read by John Kenneth. (Running Time: 13 hrs.). (Jake Grafton Novel Ser.: Vol. 9). 2004. 24.95 (978-1-59335-006-2(6), 1593350066) Soulmate Audio Bks.

America! A Celebration of Freedom from our Nation's Finest. Perf. by U. S. A. F. Band & Singing Sergeants. 1 cass. or 1 CD. Lifedance.

America! A Celebration of Freedom from Our Nation's Finest. Perf. by U. S. A. F. Band & Singing Sergeants. 1 cass. 9.98; audio compact disk 15.98 Lifedance.
Spirited, potent versions of patriotic favorites for the 4th & year-round. Includes "The Air Force Medley," "America Salute," "America the Beautiful," "Armed Forces Medley," "The Battle Hymn of the Republic," "A Cohan Medley," "Give Me Your Tired Your Poor," "Northern Lights," "Revolutionary Etude," "Star Spangled Banner," "The Stars & Stripes Forever," "This Is My Country," & "This Land Is Your Land." Demo CD or cassette available.

America: A Conversation with James Hillman & Ben Sells. unabr. ed. James Hillman & Ben Sells. 1 cass. (Running Time: 1 hrs. 10 mins.). 2004. pap. bk. 10.95 (978-1-879816-19-0(9)) Pub: Spring Pubns. Dist(s): Natl Bk Netwk
Join Hillman and Sells at the crossroads of psychology, philosophy, passion, and politics as they engage these and other topics in a lively and warm spirited conversation about the myth of America.

America: An Outside View. unabr. ed. Alistair Cooke. 1 cass. (Running Time: 56 mins.). 12.95 (978-0-88432-461-4(3), C40036) J Norton Pubs.
Television personality & author Alistair Cooke exchanges views about America with Heywood Hale Broun.

America: Cradle for the Second Coming of the Christ, Vol. 1. abr. ed. Helen M. Wright. Read by Alan Young. 4 cass. (Running Time: 4 hrs. 30 mins.). 1997. pap. bk. 15.50 (978-1-886505-09-4(8)) H M Wright.
Reveals the divine destiny of America as the birthplace for the second coming of Christ as in Christian Science.

America: Lessons from Nehemiah. unabr. ed. David Barton. Read by David Barton. 1 cass. (Running Time: 1 hr.). 1990. 4.95 (978-0-925279-11-8(0), A05) Wallbuilders.
Survey the interesting parallels that exist between the destruction & rebuilding of Jerusalem in the Old Testament & the current moral decline in our nation. Learn how you can apply these principles to the rebuilding of our Godly heritage in America today.

America: Roots of Our Nation, Set. Marshall Jr Peter. 2 cass. 1998. 12.95 (978-1-886463-01-1(8)) Oasis Audio.

America: To Pray or Not to Pray. unabr. ed. David Barton. Read by David Barton. 1 cass. (Running Time: 1 hr.). 1990. 4.95 (978-0-925279-03-3(X), A07) Wallbuilders.
This audio presentation surveys the statistical evidence for what happened to students, families, schools, & the nation when the Court began separating Biblical principles from public affairs.

America Vol. 1: The Last Best Hope: From the Age of Discovery to a World at War. unabr. ed. William J. Bennett. Read by Wayne Shepherd. (Running Time: 70200 sec.). 2007. audio compact disk 130.00 (978-1-4332-0242-1(5)) Blckstn Audio.

America, a Nation of Immigrants: Complete Cambodian Set. unabr. ed. University of Iowa, CEEDE Staff. 1 cass. (CAM.). 1989. tchr.'s training gde. ed. 95.00 (978-0-7836-0744-3(X), 8940) Triumph Learn.

America, a Nation of Immigrants: Complete English Set. unabr. ed. University of Iowa, CEEDE Staff. 1 cass. 1989. 95.00 incl. tchr's. guide, student text, activity masters, CAI disk, ESL grammar activity masters & tchr's. guide for ESL grammar activity masters. (978-0-7836-0745-0(8), 8941) Triumph Learn.

America, a Nation of Immigrants: Complete Hmong Set. unabr. ed. University of Iowa, CEEDE Staff. 1 cass. 1989. tchr.'s training gde. ed. 95.00 (978-0-7836-0746-7(6), 8942) Triumph Learn.
An American history set with readings in Hmong.

America, a Nation of Immigrants: Complete Lao Set. unabr. ed. University of Iowa, CEEDE Staff. 1 cass. (LAO.). 1989. tchr.'s training gde. ed. 95.00 (978-0-7836-0747-4(4), 8943) Triumph Learn.
A complete set of Lao readings of American history.

America, a Nation of Immigrants: Complete Vietnamese Set. unabr. ed. University of Iowa, CEEDE Staff. 1 cass. (VIE.). 1989. tchr.'s training gde. ed. 95.00 (978-0-7836-0748-1(2), 8944) Triumph Learn.
A complete set of Vietnamese readings of American history.

America, a Nation of Immigrants: English. unabr. ed. University of Iowa, CEEDE Staff. 1 cass. 1988. 8.95 (978-0-7836-0650-7(8), 8795) Triumph Learn.
Readings in English promotes the understanding that the United States is a nation made up of immigrants.

America, a Nation of Immigrants: Hmong. unabr. ed. University of Iowa, CEEDE Staff. 1 cass. 1988. 8.95 (978-0-7836-0651-4(6), 8796) Triumph Learn.
Readings in Hmong promotes the understanding that the United States is a nation made up of immigrants.

America, a Nation of Immigrants: Lao. unabr. ed. University of Iowa, CEEDE Staff. 1 cass. (LAO.). 1988. 8.95 (978-0-7836-0652-1(4), 8797) Triumph Learn.
Readings in Lao promotes the understanding that the United States is a nation made up of immigrants.

America, a Nation of Immigrants: Vietnamese. unabr. ed. University of Iowa, CEEDE Staff. 1 cass. (VIE.). 1988. 8.95 (978-0-7836-0653-8(2), 8798) Triumph Learn.
Readings in Vietnamese promote the understanding that the United States is a nation made up of immigrants.

America Alone: The End of the World as We Know It. unabr. ed. Mark Steyn. Read by Brian Emerson. 7 cass. (Running Time: 36000 sec.). 2007. 29.95 (978-0-7861-4972-8(8)); audio compact disk 29.95 (978-0-7861-7074-6(3)); audio compact disk 29.95 (978-0-7861-5793-8(3)) Blckstn Audio.

America Alone: The End of the World As We Know It. unabr. ed. Mark Steyn. Read by Brian Emerson. (Running Time: 36000 sec.). 2006. 65.95 (978-0-7861-4903-2(5)); audio compact disk 81.00 (978-0-7861-5977-2(4)) Blckstn Audio.

America America. unabr. ed. Ethan Canin. Read by Robertson Dean. 12 CDs. (Running Time: 15 hrs.). (ENG.). 2008. audio compact disk 44.95 (978-0-7393-6849-7(4)) Pub: Random Audio Pubg. Dist(s): Random

America, America. unabr. collector's ed. Elia Kazan. Read by Dan Lazar. 4 cass. (Running Time: 4 hrs.). 1986. 24.00 (978-0-7366-0974-6(1), 1916) Books on Tape.
America has always looked grand to the people who immigrated to it.

America & Americans & Selected Nonfiction. John Steinbeck. Narrated by Henry Strozier. 12 cass. (Running Time: 17 hrs. 30 mins.). 112.00 (978-1-4025-2575-9(3)) Recorded Bks.

America & the New Global Economy. Instructed by Timothy Taylor. 2008. 199.95 (978-1-59803-479-0(0)) Teaching Co.

America & the New Global Economy. unabr. ed. Instructed by Timothy Taylor. 18 CDs. (Running Time: 18 hrs.). 2008. audio compact disk 99.95 (978-1-59803-480-6(4)) Teaching Co.

America & the World: A Diplomatic History. Instructed by Mark A. Stoler. (ENG.). 2008. 129.95 (978-1-59803-473-8(1)); audio compact disk 69.95 (978-1-59803-474-5(X)) Teaching Co.

America Anonymous: Eight Addicts in Search of a Life. unabr. ed. Benoit Denizet-Lewis. Narrated by David Drummond. (Running Time: 10 hrs. 0 mins. 0 sec.). (ENG.). 2009. audio compact disk 34.99 (978-1-4001-1135-0(8)); audio compact disk 24.99 (978-1-4001-6135-5(5)); audio compact disk 69.99 (978-1-4001-4135-7(4)) Pub: Tantor Media. Dist(s): IngramPubServ

America at War: Patriotic Broadcasts from World War II. unabr. ed. Norman Corwin et al. Perf. by Bob Hope et al. Contrib. by Franklin D. Roosevelt et al. 20 cass. (Running Time: 20 hrs.). (20 Hour Collections). 2002. 59.98 (978-1-57019-471-9(8), OTR4561) Pub: Radio Spirits. Dist(s): AudioGO

America At War: Patriotic Radio Broadcasts from World War II. Perf. by Bob Hope et al. 1 CD. (Running Time: 20 hours). 2002. audio compact disk 54.98 (804562) Radio Spirits.

America before T. V. A Day in Radio - September 21, 1939. Contrib. by Paul Brennecke. 12 cass. (Running Time: 18 hrs.). 2000. 39.95 (978-1-878481-18-4(5)) Greatapes.

These remarkable tapes present a full day of radio, from Arthur Godfrey's "Sunrise" to the post-midnight concert of the Bob Chester Orchestra, with installments from "The Story of Myrt & Marge", periodic news bulletins, President Roosevelt speaking to Congress, words from French Premier Edouard Daladier, the Indians vs. the Senators, "Amos & Andy, Ask-It-Basket" & More.

***America by Heart: Reflections on Family, Faith, & Flag.** unabr. ed. Sarah Palin. Read by Sarah Palin. (Running Time: 9 hrs. NaN mins.). (ENG.). 2010. 29.95 (978-1-4417-8242-7(7)); 59.95 (978-1-4417-8239-7(7)); audio compact disk & audio compact disk 90.00 (978-1-4417-8240-3(0)) Blckstn Audio.

***America by Heart: Reflections on Family, Faith, & Flag.** unabr. ed. Sarah Palin. (ENG.). 2010. (978-0-06-202692-7(5), Harper Audio); (978-0-06-206452-3(5), Harper Audio) HarperCollins Pubs.

***America by Heart: Reflections on Family, Faith, & Flag.** unabr. ed. Sarah Palin. 2010. audio compact disk 29.99 (978-0-06-202691-0(7), Harper Audio) HarperCollins Pubs.

America, Empire of Liberty: Empire & Evil. unabr. ed. Read by David Reynolds. (Running Time: 6 hrs. 0 mins. 0 sec.). (ENG.). 2010. audio compact disk 49.95 (978-1-60283-804-8(6)) Pub: AudioGO. Dist(s): Perseus Dist

***America, Empire of Liberty: the Complete Radio Series: A New History of the United States.** Read by David Reynolds. (Running Time: 21 hrs. 0 mins. 0 sec.). (ENG.). 2010. audio compact disk 99.95 (978-1-4084-6662-9(7)) Pub: AudioGO. Dist(s): Perseus Dist

America, Empire of Liberty: Volume One: Liberty & Slavery. David Reynolds. (Running Time: 6 hrs. 0 mins. 0 sec.). (ENG.). 2009. audio compact disk 49.95 (978-1-60283-767-6(8)) Pub: AudioGO. Dist(s): Perseus Dist

America, Empire of Liberty: Volume Two: Power & Progress. David Reynolds. (Running Time: 6 hrs. 0 mins. 0 sec.). (ENG.). 2009. audio compact disk 49.95 (978-1-60283-768-3(6)) Pub: AudioGO. Dist(s): Perseus Dist

America Fever. Jocelyn Riley. 1 cass. (Running Time: 15 mins.). (YA). 1994. 8.00 (978-1-877933-51-6(1)) Her Own Words.

Documentary.

America for Sale: Fighting the New World Order, Surviving a Global Depression, & Preserving USA Sovereignty. unabr. abr. ed. Jerome R. Corsi. Read by Jerome R. Corsi. (Running Time: 7 hrs. 0 mins. 0 sec.). (ENG.). 2009. audio compact disk 29.99 (978-0-7435-9826-2(1)) Pub: S&S Audio. Dist(s): S and S Inc

America: History of Our Nation: Spanish Guided Reading Audio CD. James West Davidson & Michael B. Staff. Contrib. by Kate Kinsella & Kevin Feldman. cass. & audio compact disk 54.47 (978-0-13-166833-1(1)) PH School.

America: History of Our Nation: Student Edition on Audio CD. James West Davidson & Michael B. Staff. Contrib. by Kate Kinsella & Kevin Feldman. stu. ed. 207.97 (978-0-13-166850-8(1)) PH School.

America in Gridlock 1985-1995. unabr. ed. Clarence B. Carson. (Running Time: 32400 sec.). (Basic History of the United States Ser.). 2007. audio compact disk 72.00 (978-0-7861-6020-4(9)); audio compact disk 29.95 (978-0-7861-6021-1(7)) Blckstn Audio.

America in Gridlock 1985-1995 Vol. 6: A Basic History of the United States. unabr. ed. Clarence B. Carson. Read by Mary Woods. 7 cass. (Running Time: 1 hr. 30 mins. per cass.). 1998. 49.95 (978-0-7861-1445-0(2), 2307) Blckstn Audio.

Describes the philosophic & religious divide inherent in the issues of materialism & investigates government obstacles to production as well as assaying future trends in work, including self-employment.

America in Prophecy. Jack Van Impe. 1990. 7.00 (978-0-934803-21-2(8)) J Van Impe.

Sermon cassette in which the author presents America's past, present & future in the light of the prophecies of Isaiah, Jeremiah & John.

America in Search of Itself Pt. 1: The Making of the President 1956-1980. unabr. collector's ed. Theodore H. White. Read by Grover Gardner. 8 cass. (Running Time: 12 hrs.). 1986. 64.00 (978-0-7366-0562-5(2), 1534-A) Books on Tape.

White explains the transformation of American politics over the past 25 years.

America in Search of Itself Pt. 2: The Making of the President 1956-1980. unabr. collector's ed. Theodore H. White. Read by Grover Gardner. 7 cass. (Running Time: 10 hrs. 30 mins.). 1986. 56.00 (978-0-7366-0563-2(0), 1534-B) Books on Tape.

America in Song & Story. unabr. ed. Joe Loesch & Readio Theatre Staff. Read by Joe Loesch. (Running Time: 5 hrs. 0 mins. 0 sec.). (ENG.). 2009. audio compact disk 29.99 (978-1-59859-474-4(5), SpringWater) Oasis Audio.

America Is Hard to See see Robert Frost in Recital

America Is in the Heart: A Personal Journey. unabr. ed. Based on a book by Carlos Bulosan. 10 CDs. (Running Time: 12 hrs.). (ENG.). 2004. audio compact disk 39.99 (978-0-9743485-3-7(8)) Pub: Sonic Bks FL. Dist(s): U of Wash Pr

??it was a crime to be a Filipino in California. ?the public streets were not free to my people: we were stopped each time these vigilant patrolman saw us driving a car. We were suspect each time we were seen with a white woman. And perhaps it was this narrowing of our life into an island, into a filthy segment of American society that had driven Filipinos?inward, hating everyone and despising all positive urgencies toward freedom.? - Carlos Bulosan.

America Knits. Melanie Falick. 2007. audio compact disk 29.95 (978-0-9796073-1-8(0)) Knitting Out.

America Knits. abr. ed. Melanie Falick. Read by Christine Marshall. (YA). 2008. 54.99 (978-1-60514-978-3(0)) Find a World.

America, Lost & Found. unabr. collector's ed. Anthony Bailey. Read by Grover Gardner. 5 cass. (Running Time: 5 hrs.). 1987. 30.00 (978-0-7366-1196-1(7), 2114) Books on Tape.

English youngsters were evacuated to USA during WW II. Story continued in ENGLAND, FIRST & LAST.

America, Past & Present. 7th rev. ed. R. Hal Williams et al. 2006. audio compact disk 63.00 (978-0-321-35495-2(8)) Longman.

America Responds: Making Sense in the Aftermath. James C. Dobson. (America Responds Ser.). 8.99 (978-1-58926-053-5(8)) Oasis Audio.

America Rock. Rhino Records Staff. 1 cass. (Schoolhouse Rock Ser.). (J). (ps up). 1998. 11.89 (978-1-56826-774-6(6)) Rhino Enter.

America, September 11th: The Courage to Give, the Triumph of the Human Spirit. abr. ed. Ed. by Jackie Waldman et al. 4 cass. (Running Time: 6 hrs.). 2001. 25.00 (978-1-59040-118-7(2), Phoenix Audio) Pub: Amer Intl Pub. Dist(s): PerseuPGW

America the Beautiful. 9.95 (978-1-59112-950-9(8)) Live Oak Media.

America the Beautiful. Katherine Lee Bates. Read by Wendell Minor. 11 vols. (J). 2005. bk. 25.95 (978-1-59112-952-3(4)); bk. 28.95 (978-1-59112-956-1(7)) Pub: Live Oak Media. Dist(s): AudioGO

America the Beautiful. Prod. by Twin Sisters Productions Staff. 1 CD. (Running Time: 30 mins). (J). 2005. audio compact disk 6.99 (978-1-57583-816-8(8)) Twin Sisters.

Celebrate freedom and all that is good about America with this collection of patriotic songs - songs rich in history and tradition, tributes to those who defend our freedoms, and marches to bring everyone to their feet. Encourage national pride, loyalty and devotion, and a sense of history with time-honored favorites performed by children and adults accompanied by an orchestra. America The Beautiful is ideal for home, classroom, and community celebrations. BONUS! The Enhanced CD includes 71 pages of Sheet Music that can be printed from your home computer.

America the Beautiful. Zig Ziglar. Read by Zig Ziglar. 1 cass. (Zig Ziglar Presents Ser.). 1990. 9.95 (978-1-56207-000-7(2)) Zig Ziglar Corp.

Zig's best speech ever in which he gives moving insights into the advantages of free enterprise & what makes our country great.

America, "The New World" Psychological Consequences of an Historical Image. Read by Phillip Zabriskie. 1 cass. (Running Time: 90 mins.). 1987. 10.95 (978-0-7822-0341-7(8), 281) C G Jung IL.

America Votes 26: 2003-2004, A Handbook of Contemporary American Election Statistics. Richard M. Scammon et al. (gr. 9 up). 2005. audio compact disk 99.00 (978-1-933116-22-8(6), CQ Pr Lib Ref) CQ Pr.

America Without God. Chuck Colson. 1 cass. 2000. 15.95 (978-1-886463-80-6(8)) Oasis Audio.

Why are so many of America's leaders turning their backs on God? Where is the moral foundation on which this country was built? Can it be rebuilt? Vibrant answers make this audiobook a critically important resource for people who care.

Americain sans Peine. 1 cass. (Running Time: 1 hr., 30 min.). (ENG & FRE.). 2000. bk. 75.00 (978-2-7005-1376-9(2)); bk. 95.00 (978-2-7005-1090-4(9)) Pub: Assimil FRA. Dist(s): Distribks Inc

American. abr. ed. Andrew Britton. Read by Christopher Lane. 5. (Running Time: 21600 sec.). (Ryan Kealey Ser.). 2007. audio compact disk 14.99 (978-1-4233-0736-5(4), 9781423307365, BCD Value Price) Brilliance Audio.

American. unabr. ed. Andrew Britton. Read by Christopher Lane. (Running Time: 14 hrs.). (Ryan Kealey Ser.). 2006. 39.25 (978-1-4233-0734-1(8), 9781423307341, BADLE); 97.25 (978-1-4233-0728-0(3), 9781423307280, BrilAudUnabridg); audio compact disk 112.25 (978-1-4233-0730-3(5), 9781423307303, BriAudCD Unabrid); audio compact disk 39.25 (978-1-4233-0732-7(1), 9781423307327, Brinc Audio MP3 Lib); audio compact disk 39.95 (978-1-4233-0729-7(1), 9781423307297, Bril Audio CD Unabri); audio compact disk 24.95 (978-1-4233-0731-0(3), 9781423307310, Brilliance MP3) Brilliance Audio.

At thirty-three, Ryan Kealey has achieved more in his military and CIA career than most men can dream of in a lifetime. He's also seen the worst life has to offer and is lucky to have survived it. But being left alone with his demons is no longer an option. The CIA needs him badly, because the enemy they're facing is former U.S. soldier Jason March. Ryan knows all about March - he trained him. He knows they're dealing with one of the most ruthless assassins in the world, a master of many languages, an explosives expert, a superb sharpshooter who can disappear like a shadow and who is capable of crimes they cannot begin to imagine. And now, March has resurfaced on the global stage, aligning himself with a powerful Middle East terror network whose goal is nothing less than the total destruction of the United States. Teaming up with beautiful and tenacious British-born agent Naomi Kharmai, Ryan intends to break every rule in order to hunt down his former pupil, whatever the cost to himself. As Ryan puts together the pieces of a terrifying puzzle, and as the elusive March taunts him, always staying one step ahead, he discovers the madman's crusade is personal as well as political - and Ryan himself is an unwitting pawn. With the clock ticking down and the fate of the country resting uneasily on his shoulders, Ryan is caught in a desperate game of cat-and-mouse with the most cunning opponent he's ever faced, one who will never stop until he's committed the ultimate act of evil - a man who is all the more deadly for being one of our own.

American. unabr. ed. Andrew Britton. Read by Christopher Lane. (Running Time: 14 hrs.). (Ryan Kealey Ser.). 2006. 24.95 (978-1-4233-0733-4(X), 9781423307334, BAD) Brilliance Audio.

American. unabr. ed. Henry James. Read by Flo Gibson. 10 cass. (Running Time: 14 hrs.). 2003. 44.95 (978-1-55685-308-1(4)) Audio Bk Con.

This international novel places a successful, yet innocent, American business man in Paris, where he is often baffled by the subtleties of European civilization & comes in conflict with the aristocratic family of the woman he chooses to marry.

American. unabr. ed. Henry James. Read by Robin Lawson. 10 cass. (Running Time: 15 hrs.). 1992. 69.95 (978-0-7861-0209-9(8), 1184) Blckstn Audio.

Leon Edel wrote of this novel, "Behind its melodrama & its simple romance is the history of man's dream of better worlds, travel to strange lands & marriage to high & noble ladies. At the same time the book reveals a deep affection for the American innocence & a deep awareness that such innocence carries with it a fund of ignorance. Its novelty lay in its 'international' character & it is spoken of as the first truly international novel".

American. unabr. ed. Henry James. Read by Jim Killavey. 11 cass. (Running Time: 1 hr. 30 min. ea.). 1986. 54.00 incl. album. (C-145) Jimcin Record.

This book reveals a deep affection for American innocence & a deep awareness that such innocence carries with it a fund of ignorance. It is spoken of by critics as the first truly international novel & is also the most popular of James' many novels.

American. unabr. collector's ed. Henry James. Read by Jim Killavey. 11 cass. (Running Time: 16 hrs. 30 mins.). 1986. 88.00 (978-0-7366-3909-5(8), 9145) Books on Tape.

James turned his back on the land of his birth, but wrote this affectionate novel about it.

American: Beyond Our Grandest Notions. Chris Matthews. 2004. 15.95 (978-0-7435-4126-8(X)) Pub: S&S Audio. Dist(s): S and S Inc

***American: Previously Published as A Very Private Gentleman.** unabr. ed. Martin Booth. (Running Time: 9 hrs. 30 mins.). 2010. 59.95 (978-1-4417-7326-5(6)); audio compact disk 90.00 (978-1-4417-7327-2(4)) Blckstn Audio.

***American: Previously Published as A Very Private Gentleman.** unabr. ed. Martin Booth. Read by Ralph Cosham. (Running Time: 9 hrs. 30 mins.). 2010. 29.95 (978-1-4417-7329-6(0)); audio compact disk 29.95 (978-1-4417-7328-9(2)) Blckstn Audio.

American Accent for Success in Business, Disk 1. 2002. audio compact disk (978-0-9741881-1-9(5)) Inte Comm.

American Accent for Success in Business, Disk 2. 2002. audio compact disk (978-0-9741881-2-6(3)) Inte Comm.

American Accent for Success in Business, Disk 3. 2002. audio compact disk (978-0-9741881-3-3(1)) Inte Comm.

American Accent for Success in Business, Disk 4. 2002. audio compact disk (978-0-9741881-4-0(X)) Inte Comm.

American Accent for Success in Business, Disk 5. 2002. audio compact disk (978-0-9741881-5-7(8)) Inte Comm.

American Accent Guide: A Complete & Comprehensive Course on American English Pronunciation for Individuals of All Language Backgrounds. 2nd ed. Beverly A. Lujan. Ed. by C. J. S. Willia. Voice by Mark Cantor & Rebecca Waddoups. 8 cass. (Running Time: 8 hours). 1999. spiral bd. 99.00 (978-0-9634139-8-7(8)) Lingual Arts.

American Accent Guide: A Comprehensive Course on the Sound System of American English/book & MP3 audio (nearly 8 Hours) 2nd ed. Beverly A. Lujan. Ed. by C J S Wallia. 2008. pap. bk. 59.00 (978-0-9634139-0-1(2)) Lingual Arts.

American Accent Guide, 2nd Edition: A Complete & Comprehensive Course on American English Pronunciation for Individuals of All Language Backgrounds. 2nd ed. Prod. by Beverly A. Lujan. 8. (Running Time: 7 hrs. 30 mins.). 2004. audio compact disk 60.00 (978-0-9634139-5-6(3)) Lingual Arts.

Comprehensive instruction on American English pronunciation: intonation, stress, rhythm and phonemes.

American Accent Program. Ford Language Institute Staff. Read by Ford Language Institute Staff. 8 cass. (Running Time: 5 hrs. 20 mins.). 189.00 (978-1-877878-00-8(6)) Ford Lang Inst.

Pronunciation & intonation of American English. Self-instructional audiotext program to improve overall comprehensibility of American English.

American Accent Training: A Guide to Speaking & Pronouncing Colloquial American English. Ann Cook. 3 cass. (Running Time: 1 hr. 30 mins.). 1991. bk. 45.50 (978-0-8120-7763-6(6), BA7636) Pub: Barron. Dist(s): Continental Bk

A special value package for foreign-born students & business people living & traveling in the U.S. Its purpose is to eliminate the speaker's difficult-to-comprehend accent by training in the rhythms & sound-flow of English as it is actually spoken in America. Textbook & cassettes are supplemented with colored markers which facilitate the doing of speech exercises, & with a hand mirror that allows students to watch their lip movement as they learn American speech patterns.

American Addiction: Drugs, Guerillas, & Counterinsurgency in US Intervention in Colombia. Noam Chomsky. 1 CD. (Running Time: 1 hr. 30 min.). (ENG.). 2001. audio compact disk 13.98 (978-1-902593-44-9(8)) Pub: AK Pr GBR. Dist(s): Consort Bk Sales

American Adulterer. unabr. ed. Jed Mercurio. Narrated by Paul Boehmer. (Running Time: 11 hrs. 30 mins. 0 sec.). (ENG.). 2009. 24.99 (978-1-4001-6367-0(6)); audio compact disk 69.99 (978-1-4001-4367-2(5)); audio compact disk 34.99 (978-1-4001-1367-5(9)) Pub: Tantor Media. Dist(s): IngramPubServ

***American Adulterer.** unabr. ed. Jed Mercurio. Narrated by Paul Boehmer. (Running Time: 11 hrs. 30 mins.). 2009. 17.99 (978-1-4001-8367-8(7)) Tantor Media.

American & Canadian Joint Waterfowl Management Plan's 1995 Survey Report. Hosted by Nancy Pearlman. 1 cass. (Running Time: 29 mins.). 10.00 (1311) Educ Comm CA.

American Appetites. unabr. ed. Joyce Carol Oates. Adapted by Nick Olcott. 2 cass. (Running Time: 2 hrs.). 2000. 24.95 L A Theatre.

American Appetites. unabr. ed. Joyce Carol Oates. Perf. by Keith Carradine et al. 1 cass. (Running Time: 1 hr. 28 mins.). 2000. 25.95 (978-1-58081-172-9(8), TPT148) Pub: L A Theatre. Dist(s): NetLibrary CO

American Appetites. unabr. ed. Joyce Carol Oates. Narrated by Barbara Caruso. 10 cass. (Running Time: 14 hrs. 15 mins.). 1996. 85.00 (978-0-7887-0484-0(2), 94677E7) Recorded Bks.

A masterful tale of personal entanglements, fatal decisions & courtroom drama. Ian & Glynnis McCullough, intelligent, professional & successful, are the envy of their affluent friends. But suddenly, an unexpected plea for help & a cancelled check send their tranquility spinning out of control.

American Ascendancy: How the United States Gained & Wielded Global Dominance. Michael H. Hunt. (ENG.). 2007. 34.95 (978-0-8078-8371-6(9)); audio compact disk 39.95 (978-0-8078-8373-0(5)) U of NC Pr.

***American Assassin.** abr. ed. Vince Flynn. Read by Vince Flynn. Read by Armand Schultz. (Running Time: 6 hrs. 0 mins. 0 sec.). (ENG.). 2010. audio compact disk 29.99 (978-1-4423-3520-2(3)) Pub: S&S Audio. Dist(s): S and S Inc

***American Assassin.** unabr. ed. Vince Flynn. Read by George Guidall. (Running Time: 11 hrs. 30 mins. 0 sec.). (ENG.). 2010. audio compact disk 39.99 (978-1-4423-3522-6(X)) Pub: S&S Audio. Dist(s): S and S Inc

American Ballads & Folk Songs. unabr. ed. Perf. by Jim Gold. 1 cass. (Music Ser.). 1987. 10.95 (978-0-8045-1126-1(8), SAC 1126) Spoken Arts.

American Banjo: Three-Finger & Scruggs Style. Contrib. by Mike Seeger & Ralph Rinzler. 1 cass. or CD. (Running Time: 1 hr.). 1990. (0-9307-400370-9307-40037-2-5); audio compact disk (0-9307-40037-2-5) Smithsonian Folkways.

Tunes played by Snuffy Jenkins, Smiley Hobbs & others.

American Bloomsbury: Louisa May Alcott, Ralph Waldo Emerson, Margaret Fuller, Nathaniel Hawthorne, & Henry David Thoreau: Their Lives, Their Loves, Their Work. unabr. ed. Susan Cheever. Narrated by Kate Reading. (Running Time: 7 hrs. 0 mins. 0 sec.). (ENG.). 2007. audio compact disk 19.99 (978-1-4001-5362-6(X)) Pub: Tantor Media. Dist(s): IngramPubServ

American Bloomsbury: Louisa May Alcott, Ralph Waldo Emerson, Margaret Fuller, Nathaninathaniel Hawthorne, & Henry David Thoreau - Their Lives, Theirloves, Their Work. unabr. ed. Susan Cheever. Narrated by Kate Reading. (Running Time: 7 hrs. 0 mins. 0 sec.). (ENG.). 2007. audio compact disk 59.99 (978-1-4001-3362-8(9)) Pub: Tantor Media. Dist(s): IngramPubServ

American Bloomsbury: The Lives of Louisa May Alcott, Ralph Waldo Emerson, Margaret Fuller, Nathaniel Hawthorne, & Henry David Thoreau in Concord, Massachusetts from 1840 To 1868. unabr. ed. Susan Cheever. Narrated by Kate Reading. (Running Time: 7 hrs. 0 mins. 0 sec.). (ENG.). 2007. audio compact disk 29.99 (978-1-4001-0362-1(2)) Pub: Tantor Media. Dist(s): IngramPubServ

American Book of the Dead. E. J. Gold. 2 cass. (Running Time: 2 hrs.). 18.98 set. (TP039) Union Label.

Talk on essence & how it takes rebirth, the mechanism & breakdown of the psyche, death as a form of stress, the corridor of madness & the Bardo Thodol.

American Buffalo: In Search of a Lost Icon. Steven Rinella. Read by Patrick G. Lawlor. (ENG.). 2009. 64.99 (978-1-60812-660-6(9)) Find a World.

American Buffalo: In Search of a Lost Icon. unabr. ed. Steven Rinella. Read by Patrick G. Lawlor. (Running Time: 9 hrs.). 2008. 39.25 (978-1-4233-7417-6(7), 9781423374176, Brlnc Audio MP3 Lib); 39.25 (978-1-4233-7419-0(3), 9781423374190, BADLE); 24.95 (978-1-4233-7418-3(5), 9781423374183, BAD); 24.95 (978-1-4233-7416-9(9), 9781423374169, Brilliance MP3); audio compact disk 87.25 (978-1-4233-7415-2(0), 9781423374152, BriAudCD Unabrid); audio compact disk 32.99 (978-1-4233-7414-5(2), 9781423374145, Bril Audio CD Unabri) Brilliance Audio.

American Business English. Edwin T. Cornelius. (American Business English Satellite Television Program Ser.). 1987. 12.00 (978-0-89209-789-0(2)); 12.00 (978-0-89209-790-6(6)) Pace Grp Intl.

American Business English, No. IA. Edwin T. Cornelius. (American Business English Satellite Television Program Ser.). 1987. 12.00 (978-0-89209-785-2(X)) Pace Grp Intl.

American Business English, No. IB. Edwin T. Cornelius. (American Business English Satellite Television Program Ser.). 1987. 12.00 (978-0-89209-786-9(8)) Pace Grp Intl.

American Business English, No. IIA. Edwin T. Cornelius. (American Business English Satellite Television Program Ser.). 1987. 12.00 (978-0-89209-787-6(6)) Pace Grp Intl.

American Business English, No. IIB. Edwin T. Cornelius. (American Business English Satellite Television Program Ser.). 1987. 12.00 (978-0-89209-788-3(4)) Pace Grp Intl.

American Business English, No. IVA. Edwin T. Cornelius. (American Business English Satellite Television Program Ser.). 1987. 12.00 (978-0-89209-791-3(4)) Pace Grp Intl.

American Business English, No. IVB. Edwin T. Cornelius. (American Business English Satellite Television Program Ser.). 1987. 12.00 (978-0-89209-792-0(2)) Pace Grp Intl.

American Caesar: Douglas MacArthur, 1880-1964, Pt. 2. unabr. ed. William Manchester. Read by Tom Parker. 12 cass. (Running Time: 15 hrs. 30 mins.). 1992. 83.95 (978-0-7861-0244-0(6), 1213A,B) Blckstn Audio.

He was a great thundering paradox of a man, noble & ignoble, inspiring & outrageous, arrogant & shy, the best of men & the worst of men, the most protean, most ridiculous & most sublime. No more baffling, exasperating soldier ever wore a uniform. Flamboyant, imperious & apocalyptic, he carried the plumage of a flamingo, could not acknowledge errors & tried to cover up his mistakes with sly, childish tricks. Yet he was also endowed with great personal charm, a will of iron & a soaring intellect. Unquestionably he was the most gifted man-at-arms this nation has produced.

American Caesar: Douglas MacArthur 1880-1966. unabr. ed. William Manchester. Read by Tom Parker. (Running Time: 32 mins.). 2005. 39.95 (978-0-7861-8956-4(8)) Blckstn Audio.

American Caesar Pt. 1: Douglas MacArthur, 1880-1964. unabr. ed. William Manchester. Read by Tom Parker. 12 cass. (Running Time: 15 hrs. 30 mins.). 1992. 83.95 (978-0-7861-0243-3(8), 1213A,B) Blckstn Audio.

American Caesar Pt. 1: Douglas MacArthur, 1880-1964. unabr. collector's ed. William Manchester. Read by Wolfram Kandinsky. 12 cass. (Running Time: 18 hrs.). 1983. 96.00 (978-0-7366-0723-0(4), 1681-A) Books on Tape.

Biography of the controversial American general who was Supreme Commander for the Allied powers in Japan & United Nations Commander-in-Chief in Korea.

American Caesar Pt. 2: Douglas MacArthur, 1880-1964. collector's ed. William Manchester. Read by Wolfram Kandinsky. 13 cass. (Running Time: 19 hrs. 30 mins.). 1983. 104.00 (978-0-7366-0724-7(2), 1681-B) Books on Tape.

American Caesar (Part A) Douglas MacArthur 1880-1964. William Manchester. Read by Tom Parker. (Running Time: 16 mins.). 2005. audio compact disk 108.00 (978-0-7861-8177-3(X)) Blckstn Audio.

American Caesar (Part B) Douglas MacArthur 1880-1965. William Manchester. Read by Tom Parker. (Running Time: 16 mins.). 2005. audio compact disk 108.00 (978-0-7861-8142-1(7)) Blckstn Audio.

American Catholic Social Teaching. Thomas J. Massaro & Thomas A. Shannon. 2005. pap. bk. 29.95 (978-0-8146-5105-6(4)) Liturgical Pr.

American Chatterbox. J. A. Holderness. 1994. 17.50 (978-0-19-434601-6(3)) OUP.

American Chatterbox. Derek Strange & J. A. Holderness. 1993. 17.50 (978-0-19-434593-4(9)) OUP.

American Chatterbox. Derek Strange & J. A. Holderness. 1993. 17.50 (978-0-19-434597-2(1)) OUP.

American Chatterbox. Derek Strange & J. A. Holderness. 1994. 17.50 (978-0-19-434605-4(6)) OUP.

American Chatterbox: Starter Level. Derek Strange. (Oxford American English Ser.). 1996. 31.95 (978-0-19-434586-6(6)) OUP.

American Chatterbox 5. J. A. Holderness. 1997. 17.50 (978-0-19-434667-2(6)) OUP.

American Childhood. Annie Dillard. Read by Annie Dillard. 1 cass. (Running Time: 29 mins.). 1987. 8.00 (100287) New Letters.

Pulitzer prize-winning author reads from her memoir, "An American Childhood." Includes interview with author.

American Childhood. unabr. ed. Annie Dillard. Narrated by Alexandra O'Karma. 7 cass. (Running Time: 9 hrs. 30 mins.). 1991. 60.00 (978-1-55690-016-7(3), 91113E7) Recorded Bks.

By the age of 10, Annie entered a time brimming over with the fullness of life; the hours & minutes of the years that followed were spent reveling in the delights & the anguishes that accompany being fully alive.

***American Childhood.** unabr. ed. Annie Dillard. Read by Tavia Gilbert. (Running Time: 9 hrs. NaN mins.). (ENG.). 2011. 29.95 (978-1-4417-7392-0(4)); 59.95 (978-1-4417-7389-0(4)); audio compact disk 29.95 (978-1-4417-7391-3(6)); audio compact disk 90.00 (978-1-4417-7390-6(8)) Blckstn Audio.

American Christmas Classics: The Millennia Collection. Ronald M. Clancy. 3 CDs. (Running Time: 2 hrs., 16 mins.). 2001. bk. 59.95 (978-0-615-11507-8(1)) Christ Class.

Traditional Classics. Reflect upon the spiritual heritage of the American Christmas with world renowned carols, including O LITTLE TOWN OF BETHLEHEM, AWAY IN A MANGER, WE THREE KINGS OF ORIENT ARE, and IT CAME UPON A MIDNIGHT CLEAR.Historic Recordings. Enjoy classic recordings with original recording artists, such as WHITE CHRISTMAS (Bing Crosby), THE CHRISTMAS SONG (Nat "King" Cole), RUDOLPH THE REDS-NOSED REINDEER (Gene Autry), and THE LITTLE DRUMMER BOY (The Harry Simeone Chorale), as well as popular carols and songs by traditional American icons like Kate Smith, Mahalia Jackson, Johnny Mathis, Tammy Wynette, and Perry Como.Additional Carol Gems. Delight in the discovery of America's little known jewels, including THE COWBOY CAROL from the Southwest, STAR IN THE EAST from the early frontiers of the South, and THE STAR CAROL and CAROLING, CAROLING from the nation's heartland. Fun for the Children. Sing along with the kids at home to the favorite tunes of JINGLE BELLS, HERE COMES SANTA CLAUS, FROSTY THE SNOW MAN, SANTA CLAUS IS COMIN' TO TOWN, and WINTER WONDERLAND.

***American Church in Crisis: Groundbreaking Research Based on a National Database of over 200,000 Churches.** unabr. ed. David T. Olson. (Running Time: 6 hrs. 50 mins. 0 sec.). (ENG.). 2009. 19.99 (978-0-310-77212-5(5)) Zondervan.

American Citizenship Exam Audio Guide: U. S. Citizenship Procedures & Examination Audio Tape. American Immigration Center Inc. Staff. (Do It Yourself Immigration Ser.). 2001. 12.00 (978-0-9663425-9-8(3)) Amer Immig Ctr.

American Civics. 3rd ed. Holt, Rinehart and Winston Staff. (SPA.). 2003. audio compact disk 208.73 (978-0-03-067706-9(8)) Holt McDoug.

American Civics. 3rd ed. Holt, Rinehart and Winston Staff. 2003. audio compact disk 208.73 (978-0-03-067693-2(2)) Holt McDoug.

American Civics 2003. Holt, Rinehart and Winston Staff. 2003. audio compact disk 73.60 (978-0-03-050943-8(2)) Holt McDoug.

American Civil War. abr. ed. John Keegan. Read by Robin Sachs. (ENG.). 2009. audio compact disk 38.00 (978-0-7393-5463-6(9), Random AudioBks) Pub: Random Audio Pubg. Dist(s): Random

American Civil War. unabr. collector's ed. Winston L. S. Churchill. Read by David Case. 5 cass. (Running Time: 5 hrs.). 1992. 30.00 (978-0-7366-2095-6(8), 2901) Books on Tape.

Churchill's superb account of the American Civil War.

American Civil War, Pts. I-IV. Instructed by Gary W. Gallagher. 24 cass. (Running Time: 24 hrs.). 2000. 99.95 (978-1-56585-264-8(8), 885) Teaching Co.

The author discusses women in conflict, illness and injury, what soldiers ate and wore, the naval theater, African-American troops, political pressures, and life on the homefront during the Civil War. He creates cozy, intriguing biographies of Lee, Lincoln and other principals.

American Civil War, Pts. I-IV. unabr. ed. Instructed by Gary W. Gallagher. 24 CDs. (Running Time: 24 hrs.). 2000. bk. 129.95 (978-1-56585-393-5(8), 885) Teaching Co.

American Civil War, Vol. 2. Instructed by Gary W. Gallagher. 6 cass. (Running Time: 6 hrs.). 2000. 249.95 (978-1-56585-265-5(6)) Teaching Co.

American Civil War, Vol. 3. Instructed by Gary W. Gallagher. 6 cass. (Running Time: 6 hrs.). 2000. 249.95 (978-1-56585-266-2(4)) Teaching Co.

American Civil War, Vol. 4. Instructed by Gary W. Gallagher. 6 cass. (Running Time: 6 hrs.). 2000. 249.95 (978-1-56585-267-9(2)) Teaching Co.

***American Claimant: Narrated by Richard Henzel.** Narrated by Richard Henzel. 2010. audio compact disk 39.99 (978-0-9826688-2-5(1)) R Henzel.

***American Claimant: Narrated by Richard Henzel.** Narrated by Richard Henzel. (ENG.). 2010. 29.99 (978-0-9826688-0-1(5)) R Henzel.

American Collection, Set. unabr. ed. Isaac Asimov et al. 76 cass. 498.38 AudioGO.

Includes: "The Positronic Man" by Isaac Asimov & Robert Silverberg, "Dogs of God" by Pinckney Benedict, "Fahrenheit 451" by Ray Bradbury, "Evidence of Blood" by Thomas H. Cook, "The Liberty Campaign" by Jonathan Dee, "Tender Is the Night" by F. Scott Fitzgerald, "Dead Man" by Joe Gores, "Black Mesa" by Zane Grey, "The Spoils of Pynton" by Henry James, "Double Deuce" by Robert B. Parker.

American Colossus: The Political Genius of Abraham Lincoln. unabr. ed. Doris Kearns Goodwin. 2005. 49.95 (978-0-7435-5017-8(X)) Pub: S&S Audio. Dist(s): S and S Inc

American Colossus: The Political Genius of Abraham Lincoln. unabr. ed. Doris Kearns Goodwin. 2005. audio compact disk 49.95 (978-0-7435-5018-5(8)) Pub: S&S Audio. Dist(s): S and S Inc

***American Colossus: The Triumph of Capitalism, 1865-1900.** unabr. ed. H. W. Brands. Read by Robertson Dean. 2010. audio compact disk 50.00 (978-0-307-73746-5(2), Random AudioBks) Pub: Random Audio Pubg. Dist(s): Random

***American Conspiracies: Lies, Lies, & More Dirty Lies That the Government Tells Us.** unabr. ed. Jesse Ventura & Dick Russell. Narrated by George K. Wilson. 1 MP3-CD. (Running Time: 10 hrs. 30 mins. 0 sec.). 2010. 19.99 (978-1-4001-6666-4(7)); 15.99 (978-1-4001-8666-2(8)); audio compact disk 29.99 (978-1-4001-1666-9(X)); audio compact disk 59.99 (978-1-4001-4666-6(6)) Pub: Tantor Media. Dist(s): IngramPubServ

American Cowboy Songs. 1 cass. (Running Time: 31 mins.). (J). 1998. pap. bk. 9.95 (978-1-887120-04-3(1)) Prodn Assocs.

Collection of all time favorite cowboy songs from the turn of the century. Designed for everyone, young & old alike, who enjoys music from this colorful period in American History.

American Creation: Triumphs & Tragedies at the Founding of the Republic. unabr. ed. Joseph J. Ellis. Read by John H. Mayer. (YA). 2007. 59.99 (978-0-7393-7115-2(0)) Find a World.

American Creation: Triumphs & Tragedies at the Founding of the Republic. unabr. ed. Joseph J. Ellis. Read by John H. Mayer. (ENG.). 2007. audio compact disk 34.95 (978-0-7393-3192-7(2), Random AudioBks); audio compact disk 100.00 (978-1-4159-4275-8(7), BksonTape) Pub: Random Audio Pubg. Dist(s): Random

From the first shots fired at Lexington to the signing of the Declaration of Independence to the negotiations for the Louisiana Purchase, Joseph J. Ellis guides us through the decisive issues of the nation's founding, and illuminates the emerging philosophies, shifting alliances, and personal and political foibles of our now iconic leaders - Washington, Jefferson, Madison, Hamilton, and Adams. He casts an incisive eye on the founders' achievements, arguing that the American Revolution was, paradoxically, an evolution - and that part of what made it so extraordinary was the gradual pace at which it occurred. He explains how the idea of a strong federal government was eventually embraced by the American people and details the emergence of the two-party system, which stands as the founders' most enduring legacy.

American Crisis **see Great American Essays: A Collection**

American Culture, History (& Everything) Workshop. Timothy Leary. 1 cass. 9.00 (A0449-89) Sound Photosyn.

Software casually acted out at Los Angeles Whole Life Expo.

American Culture, History (& Everything) 1960-1999. Timothy Leary. 1 cass. 9.00 (A0391-89) Sound Photosyn.

This densely packed hour at the Whole Earth Expo is still not enough of Tim.

American Culture, 1945-1985. Timothy Leary. 1 cass. (Running Time: 1 hr. 30 min.). 1977. 11.00 (01302) Big Sur Tapes.

American Daughter. Wendy Wasserstein. Read by Full Cast Production Staff. (Playaway Adult Fiction Ser.). 2008. 39.99 (978-1-60640-941-1(7)) Find a World.

American Daughter. unabr. ed. Wendy Wasserstein. Perf. by Mary McDonnell et al. 2 CDs. (Running Time: 2 hrs. 5 mins.). 2001. audio compact disk 25.95 (978-1-58081-186-6(8), CDTPT120) Pub: L A Theatre. Dist(s): NetLibrary CO

American Democrat. unabr. ed. James Fenimore Cooper. Read by Noah Waterman. 4 cass. (Running Time: 5 hrs. 30 mins.). 1994. 32.95 (978-0-7861-0777-3(4), 1505) Blckstn Audio.

Convinced that the American political system was endangered by complacency, demagoguery, party propaganda & the tyranny of public opinion, Cooper felt compelled to write this minor classic of American political theory. Fascinated with deception, he wrote in order to express "the voice of simple, honest & fearless truth" on the peculiarities of the American system of government.

American Democrat, Set. unabr. ed. James Fenimore Cooper. Read by Noah Waterman. 4 cass. 1999. 32.95 (FS9-34229) Highsmith.

American Diction for Singers. Geoffrey G. Forward. (ENG.). 2001. audio compact disk 24.95 (978-0-7390-1920-7(1)) Alfred Pub.

American Dream. abr. ed. Dan Rather. Read by Dan Rather. 4 cass. (Running Time: 6 hrs.). 2001. 25.95 (978-0-694-52552-2(9), Harper Audio) HarperCollins Pubs.

American Dreams. unabr. collector's ed. John Jakes. Read by Michael Kramer. 14 cass. (Running Time: 21 hrs.). 1999. 112.00 (978-0-7366-4355-9(9), 4812) Books on Tape.

The Crown family of Chicago founded a brewing empire that became the source of family wealth. This centers on two of the Crown children, Fritzi & Carl & their cousin Paul. In the decade before WWI, Fritzi wants to be a stage actress but finds herself making silent comedies with D.W. Griffith & Charlie Chaplin. Carl dreams of flying while Paul seeks to capture on film the darker truths behind a dazzling age of industrial advancement.

American Empire: The Center Cannot Hold. unabr. ed. Harry Turtledove. Narrated by George Guidall. (Running Time: 24 hrs. 45 mins.). 2008. 61.75 (978-1-4361-6597-6(0)); audio compact disk 123.75 (978-1-4281-9517-2(3)) Recorded Bks.

***American English File Starter.** Clive Oxenden et al. (ENG.). 2010. audio compact disk 39.95 (978-0-19-477413-0(9)) Pub: OUP-CN CAN. Dist(s): OUP

American English for International Businessmen. National Textbook Company Staff. 6 cass. 90.00 (Natl Textbk Co) M-H Contemporary.

Presents language skills & terminology appropriate to a variety of on-the-job situations. Realistic conversations are accompanied by readings, discussion questions & opportunities to practice written & oral skills.

***American English in Mind.** Herbert Puchta & Jeff Stranks. (Running Time: 2 hrs. 33 mins.). (ENG.). 2010. audio compact disk 42.00 (978-0-521-73341-0(3)) Cambridge U Pr.

***American English in Mind Level 2 Class Audio CDs (3)** Herbert Puchta & Jeff Stranks. (Running Time: 2 hrs. 47 mins. 34 sec.). (ENG.). 2010. audio compact disk 42.00 (978-0-521-73352-6(9)) Cambridge U Pr.

***American English in Mind Starter Class Audio CDs (3)** Herbert Puchta & Jeff Stranks. (Running Time: 2 hrs. 30 mins.). (ENG.). 2010. audio compact disk 42.00 (978-0-521-73331-1(6)) Cambridge U Pr.

American English One, No. 1. Edwin T. Cornelius. (American English One Video Ser.). 1987. 12.00 (978-0-89209-709-8(4)) Pace Grp Intl.

American English One, No. 2. Edwin T. Cornelius. (American English One Video Ser.). 1987. 12.00 (978-0-89209-710-4(8)) Pace Grp Intl.

American English One, No. 3. Edwin T. Cornelius. (American English One Video Ser.). 1987. 12.00 (978-0-89209-711-1(6)) Pace Grp Intl.

American English One, No. 4. Edwin T. Cornelius. (American English One Video Ser.). 1987. 12.00 (978-0-89209-712-8(4)) Pace Grp Intl.

American English One, No. 5. Edwin T. Cornelius. (American English One Video Ser.). 1987. 12.00 (978-0-89209-713-5(2)) Pace Grp Intl.

American English One, No. 6. Edwin T. Cornelius. (American English One Video Ser.). 1987. 12.00 (978-0-89209-714-2(0)) Pace Grp Intl.

American English One, No. 7. Edwin T. Cornelius. (American English One Video Ser.). 1987. 12.00 (978-0-89209-715-9(9)) Pace Grp Intl.

American English One, No. 8. Edwin T. Cornelius. (American English One Video Ser.). 1987. 12.00 (978-0-89209-716-6(7)) Pace Grp Intl.

American English One, No. 9. Edwin T. Cornelius. (American English One Video Ser.). 1987. 12.00 (978-0-89209-717-3(5)) Pace Grp Intl.

American English One, No. 10. Edwin T. Cornelius. (American English One Video Ser.). 1987. 12.00 (978-0-89209-718-0(3)) Pace Grp Intl.

American English One, No. 11. Edwin T. Cornelius. (American English One Video Ser.). 1987. 12.00 (978-0-89209-719-7(1)) Pace Grp Intl.

American English One, No. 12. Edwin T. Cornelius. (American English One Video Ser.). 1987. 12.00 (978-0-89209-720-3(5)) Pace Grp Intl.

American English One, No. 13. Edwin T. Cornelius. (American English One Video Ser.). 1987. 12.00 (978-0-89209-721-0(3)) Pace Grp Intl.

American English One, No. 14. Edwin T. Cornelius. (American English One Video Ser.). 1987. 12.00 (978-0-89209-722-7(1)) Pace Grp Intl.

American English One, No. 15. Edwin T. Cornelius. (American English One Video Ser.). 1987. 12.00 (978-0-89209-723-4(X)) Pace Grp Intl.

American English One, No. 16. Edwin T. Cornelius. (American English One Video Ser.). 1987. 12.00 (978-0-89209-724-1(8)) Pace Grp Intl.

American English Primary Colors 1 Class CD. Diana Hicks & Andrew Littlejohn. (Running Time: 2 hrs.). 2003. audio compact disk 22.00 (978-0-521-53919-7(6)) Cambridge U Pr.

American English Primary Colors 1 Songs CD. Diana Hicks & Andrew Littlejohn. (Running Time: 1 hr. 14 mins.). 2003. audio compact disk 22.00 (978-0-521-53918-0(8)) Cambridge U Pr.

American English Primary Colors 2 Class CD. Diana Hicks & Andrew Littlejohn. (Running Time: 1 hr. 48 mins.). 2003. audio compact disk 23.10 (978-0-521-53923-4(4)) Cambridge U Pr.

Welcome; Unit 1. Hello, Kip!; Unit 2. Hello, Joanne!; Revision; Unit 3. Hello, Tara!; Unit 4. Hello, Tom!; Revision; Unit 5. Hello, Ben!; Unit 6. Goodbye!; Revision.

American English Primary Colors 2 Songs & Stories CD. Diana Hicks & Andrew Littlejohn. (Running Time: 1 hr. 14 mins.). 2003. audio compact disk 23.10 (978-0-521-53922-7(6)) Cambridge U Pr.

American English Primary Colors 3 Class Audio CDs. Diana Hicks & Andrew Littlejohn. (Running Time: 1 hr. 55 mins.). 2002. audio compact disk 23.10 (978-0-521-60802-2(3)) Cambridge U Pr.

American English Primary Colors 3 Songs & Stories. Diana Hicks & Andrew Littlejohn. 2005. audio compact disk 23.10 (978-0-521-60801-5(5)) Cambridge U Pr.

American English Primary Colors 4 Class Audio CDs. Diana Hicks & Andrew Littlejohn. (Running Time: 2 hrs. 8 mins.). 2002. audio compact disk 23.10 (978-0-521-60795-7(7)) Cambridge U Pr.

American English Primary Colors 4 Songs & Stories Audio CD. Diana Hicks & Andrew Littlejohn. (Primary Colours Ser.). 2005. audio compact disk 22.00 (978-0-521-60797-1(3)) Cambridge U Pr.

American English Primary Colors 5 Class Audio CDs. Diana Hicks & Andrew Littlejohn. (Running Time: 2 hrs. 9 mins.). 2008. audio compact disk 43.05 (978-0-521-68264-0(9)) Cambridge U Pr.

American English Primary Colors 6 Class Audio CDs. Diana Hicks & Andrew Littlejohn. (Running Time: 2 hrs. 9 mins.). 2008. audio compact disk 43.05 (978-0-521-68268-8(1)) Cambridge U Pr.

American English Pronunciation: A Guide for International Speakers of English: It's No Good Unless You're Understood. unabr. ed. Scripts. Donna L. Hope. Read by Donna L. Hope. 5 cass. (Running Time: 7 hrs. 30 mins.). 1999. pap. bk. 115.00 (978-1-58631-000-4(3)) Cold Wind.

American English Pronunciation: It's No Good Unless You're Understood. 2nd ed. Scripts. Donna L. Hope. 6 CDs. 2006. pap. bk. 125.00 (978-1-58631-050-9(X)) Cold Wind.

This is the complete course; it contains Books One, Two and Three combined. The course is an accent reduction program for international speakers of English. At the same time, it is rich in both formal and informal American expressions. And it contains exercises and cultural notes prompted, for the most part, by questions from students themselves. The program is now in its second edition. It has been based on and proven successful during years of work with students from many countries.Softcover textbook with 6 audio CDs.

American English Pronunciation Bk. 1: A Guide for International Speakers of English: It's No Good Unless You're Understood. unabr. ed. Donna L. Hope. Read by Donna L. Hope. 2 cass. (Running Time: 2 hrs. 30 mins.). 1999. pap. bk. 42.00 (978-1-58631-002-8(X)) Cold Wind.

An accent reduction program rich in American expressions, exercises & cultural notes.

American English Pronunciation Bk. 1: It's No Good Unless You're Understood. 2nd ed. Scripts. Donna L. Hope. 2CDs. 2006. pap. bk. 45.00 (978-1-58631-052-3(6)) Cold Wind.

American English Pronunciation Bk. 2: A Guide for International Speakers of English: It's No Good Unless You're Understood. unabr. ed. Donna L. Hope. Read by Donna L. Hope. 2 cass. (Running Time: 2 hrs. 30 mins.). 1999. pap. bk. 42.00 (978-1-58631-003-5(8)) Cold Wind.

American English Pronunciation Bk. 2: It's No Good Unless You're Understood. 2nd ed. Donna L. Hope. 2CDs. 2006. pap. bk. 45.00 (978-1-58631-054-7(2)) Cold Wind.

American English Pronunciation Bk. 3: A Guide for International Speakers of English: It's No Good Unless You're Understood. unabr. ed. Donna L. Hope. Read by Donna L. Hope. 2 cass. (Running Time: 3 hrs.). 1999. pap. bk. 42.00 (978-1-58631-004-2(6)) Cold Wind.

American English Pronunciation Bk. 3: It's No Good Unless You're Understood. 2nd ed. Scripts. Donna L. Hope. 2 CDs. 2006. pap. bk. 45.00 (978-1-58631-056-1(9)) Cold Wind.

American English Today! D. H. Howe. 1987. 17.50 (978-0-19-434304-6(9)); 17.50 (978-0-19-434308-4(1)); 31.95 (978-0-19-434312-1(X)) OUP.

American English Today! D. H. Howe. 1992. 31.95 (978-0-19-434316-9(2)); 31.95 (978-0-19-434320-6(0)) OUP.

American English Today! D. H. Howe. 1992. 31.95 (978-0-19-434324-4(3)) OUP.

American Experience: A Collection of Great American Stories. Washington Irving et al. Narrated by Ralph Cosham & Sean Pratt. (Running Time: 47460 sec.). (Unabridged Classics in MP3 Ser.). (ENG.). 2008. audio compact disk 14.95 (978-1-58472-618-0(0), In Aud) Sound Room.

American Experience: A Collection of Great American Stories. abr. ed. Washington Irving et al. (Playaway Young Adult Ser.). 2008. 139.99 (978-1-60640-841-4(0)) Find a World.

American Experience: A Collection of Great American Stories: A Collection of Great American Stories. Edgar Allan Poe et al. Read by Ralph Cosham et al. (Running Time: 13 hrs. 10 mins.). 2003. 36.95 (978-1-59912-040-9(2), Audiofy Corp) Iofy Corp.

American Experiment - What Did Our Founding Fathers Intend? Proceedings of the 45th Annual Convention National Association of Evangelicals Buffalo, New York. Read by Edwin Meese. 1 cass. (Running Time: 60 mins.). 4.00 (302) Nat Assn Evan.

American Fairy Tales: From Rip Van Winkle to the Rootabaga Stories. unabr. ed. Read by Taylor Mali. Compiled by Neil Philip. Pref. by Alison Lurie. 4 cass. (Running Time: 5 hrs.). (YA). (gr. 5 up). 1998. 26.95 (978-1-883332-32-7(X)) Audio Bkshelf.

Twelve tales with indigenous origins by such noted authors as Nathanial Hawthorn, Washington Irving & Louisa May Alcott & by lesser-known writers like Ruth Plumly Thompson. Explains the notion of these stories, which are undoubtedly influenced by their European predecessors but possess their own distinctly American spirit. Musical interludes separate the selections & a brief biography of each author is included.

American Family: Discovering the Values That Make Us Strong. unabr. ed. Dan Quayle & Diane Medved. Read by Jeff Riggenbach. 8 cass. (Running Time: 11 hrs. 30 mins.). 1996. 56.95 (978-0-7861-0982-1(3), 1759) Blckstn Audio.

In this profoundly important, inspirational book, Dan Quayle, America's 44th Vice President, introduces us to five American families who speak bluntly - & often poignantly - about the values that give them strength. Quayle & his collaborator, psychologist Diane Medved, journeyed thousands of miles to meet with & interview a diverse mix of families.

American Family Shakespeare Entertainment, Vol. 1. unabr. ed. Stefan (edited by) Rudnicki. (Running Time: 7 hrs. 0 mins.). (ENG.). 2009. 29.95 (978-1-4332-8762-6(5)); 44.95 (978-1-4332-8758-9(7)); audio compact disk 60.00 (978-1-4332-8759-6(5)) Blckstn Audio.

American Family Shakespeare Entertainment, Vol. 2: Based on Charles & Mary Lamb's Tales from Shakespeare, with scenes, soliloquies & music from Shakespeare's Plays. unabr. ed. Stefan (edited by) Rudnicki & Charles & Mary Lamb. (Running Time: 5 hrs. 0 mins.). (ENG.). 2009. 19.95 (978-1-4332-8943-9(1)); 34.95 (978-1-4332-8939-2(3)); audio compact disk 49.00 (978-1-4332-8940-8(7)) Blckstn Audio.

American Fascists: The Christian Right & the War on America. unabr. ed. Chris Hedges. Read by Chris Hedges. Read by Eunice Wong. (Running Time: 7 hrs. 30 mins. 0 sec.). (ENG.). 2007. audio compact disk 29.99 (978-1-4001-0457-4(2)); audio compact disk 59.99 (978-1-4001-3457-1(9)); audio compact disk 19.99 (978-1-4001-5457-9(X)) Pub: Tantor Media. Dist(s): IngramPubServ

American Fiddle Method, Vol. 1. Brian Wicklund. 2001. bk. 24.95 (978-0-7866-5251-8(9)) Mel Bay.

American Fiddle Method, Vol. 2. Brian Wicklund. 2001. bk. 24.95 (978-0-7866-5252-5(7)) Mel Bay.

American Fiddle Method: Beginning Fiddle Tunes & Techniques. Brian Wicklund. Illus. by Brian Barber. (J). (gr. k-12). 1997. pap. bk. 24.95 (978-1-885701-01-5(2)) Granger Pubns.

American Fiddle Method, Volume 2 - Fiddle: Intermediate Fiddle Tunes & Techniques. Brian Wicklund. 2008. pap. bk. 34.95 (978-0-7866-7802-0(X)) Mel Bay.

American Fiddle Tunes for Mountain Dulcimer. Lois Hornbostel et al. 1997. pap. bk. 26.95 (978-0-7866-3096-7(5), 95527CDP) Mel Bay.

American Folk Dances. 2 cass. 11.95 ea. incl. manual. Kimbo Educ.

Original American folk dances, Polkas, Schottisches & Two-Steps.

American Folk, Game & Activity Songs for Children. Perf. by Pete Seeger. 1 cass. (Running Time: 59 mins.). (J). 2000. 8.50; audio compact disk 14.00 Smithsonian Folkways.

Includes subject index, lyric sheets & recommended activities for each song.

American Folk Songs for Children. Perf. by Mike Seeger & Peggy Seeger. 2 cass. (Running Time: 2 hrs. 20 mins.). (Family Ser.). (J). (ps-5). 1977. 14.98 (978-1-886767-85-0(8), 8001/2); audio compact disk 24.98 (978-1-886767-84-3(X), 11543/4) Rounder Records.

Recordings of material collected by Ruth Crawford Seeger. All of these recordings feature traditional instruments such as the autoharp, concertina, dulcimer, mandolin, panpipes & fiddle.

American Folk Songs for Children. Perf. by Pete Seeger. 1 cass. (J). (ps-5). 9.98 (202) MFLP CA.

The granddaddy of American folk music, Seeger & his banjo or guitar, playing simple versions of all the old favorites that are the backbone of American folk music. Songs include: "Jimmy Crack Corn," "This Old Man," "Train Is A-Coming," "Frog Went A-Courting," "Clap Your Hands" & many more.

American Folk Songs for Children. Perf. by Pete Seeger. 1 cass. (J). (ps-7). 1990. Incl. index for parents & tchrs., lyric sheet & recommended activities for each song. (0-9307-45020-4-4) Smithsonian Folkways.

Includes "Jim Crack Corn," "This Old Man," "Frog Went a-Courting" & many others.

American Folk Songs for Christmas. Perf. by Mike Seeger et al. 2 cass. (Running Time: 1 hr. 51 mins.). (J). 1999. Rounder Records.

Based on the famous Ruth Crawford Seeger book of the same name. Among the 53 songs are "Bright Morning Stars Are Rising," "Look Away to Bethlehem," "Go Tell It on the Mountain," "Sing Hallelu" & "Breaking up Christmas.".

American Folk Songs for Christmas. Perf. by Mike Seeger & Peggy Seeger. 2 CDs. (J). 1999. audio compact disk Rounder Records.

Based on the famous Ruth Crawford Seeger book of the same name. Among the 53 songs are "Bright Morning Stars Are Rising," "Look Away to Bethlehem," "Go Tell It on the Mountain," "Sing Hallelu" & "Breaking up Christmas.".

American Folk Songs for Christmas. Ruth Crawford Seeger. Perf. by Mike Seeger et al. 2 cass. 15.98 (456); audio compact disk 24.98 (D456) MFLP CA.

The ultimate in Christmas folk flavors with 53 acoustic songs by the famous Seeger family.

American Folk Tales. George Gibson. (Green Apple Step One Ser.). (J). (gr. 4-7). 2005. pap. bk. 21.95 (978-88-530-0107-8(0)) Cideb ITA.

***American Freak Show: The Completely Fabricated Stories of Our New National Treasures.** unabr. ed. Willie Geist. Narrated by Johnny Heller & Jo Anna Perrin. (Running Time: 5 hrs. 30 mins.). 2010. 13.99 (978-1-4526-7051-5(X)); 24.99 (978-1-4526-0051-2(1)); 19.99 (978-1-4526-5051-7(9)) Tantor Media.

***American Freak Show (Library Edition) The Completely Fabricated Stories of Our New National Treasures.** unabr. ed. Willie Geist. Narrated by Johnny Heller & Jo Anna Perrin. (Running Time: 5 hrs. 30 mins.). 2010. 59.99 (978-1-4526-3051-9(8)); 24.99 (978-1-4526-2051-0(2)) Tantor Media.

American Front. Harry Turtledove. Narrated by George Guidall. 17 cass. (Running Time: 25 hrs.). (Great War Ser.: Bk. 1). 141.00 (978-1-4025-0623-9(6)) Recorded Bks.

American Front. collector's ed. Harry Turtledove. Narrated by George Guidall. 17 cass. (Great War Ser.: Bk. 1). 2002. 67.95 (978-1-4025-0624-6(4)) Recorded Bks.

Hugo Award winner Harry Turtledove is the master of alternate history. In American Front he envisions World War I as it may have been if fought on American soil. The United States and Germany clash with the Confederacy, France, and Britain as the machines of modern warfare litter the landscape with carnage. Meanwhile, oppressed southern blacks head toward a fateful confrontation.

***American Future.** unabr. ed. Simon Schama. Read by Rupert Degas. (ENG.). 2009. (978-0-06-190186-7(5), Harper Audio); (978-0-06-189427-5(3), Harper Audio) HarperCollins Pubs.

American Game & Activity Songs for Children. Perf. by Pete Seeger. 1 cass. (J). (ps-6). 1990. incl. instructions. (0-9307-45025-4-9) Smithsonian Folkways.

Includes "I Want to Be a Farmer," "Ring-Around-the Rosy," "Shoo Fly" & others.

American Gangster: And Other Tales of New York. unabr. ed. Mark Jacobson. Read by Malcolm Hillgartner. (Running Time: 36000 sec.). 2007. 19.95 (978-1-4332-1171-3(8)); audio compact disk 19.95 (978-1-4332-1172-0(6)); audio compact disk 29.95 (978-1-4332-1173-7(4)) Blckstn Audio.

American Get Ready! Felicity Hopkins. 1990. 17.50 (978-0-19-434436-4(3)); 17.50 (978-0-19-434442-5(8)) OUP.

American Gods. unabr. ed. Neil Gaiman. Read by George Guidall. 2 cass. (Running Time: 3 hrs.). 2001. 44.95 (978-0-694-52549-2(9)) HarperCollins Pubs.

***American Gods.** unabr. ed. Neil Gaiman. Read by George Guidall. (ENG.). 2003. (978-0-06-073558-6(9), Harper Audio) HarperCollins Pubs.

American Gods. unabr. ed. Neil Gaiman. Read by George Guidall. 2005. audio compact disk 34.95 (978-0-06-083625-2(3)) HarperCollins Pubs.

***American Gods.** unabr. ed. Neil Gaiman. Read by George Guidall. 2005. (978-0-06-112291-0(2), Harper Audio) HarperCollins Pubs.

American Gods. unabr. ed. Neil Gaiman. Narrated by George Guidall. 15 cass. (Running Time: 20 hrs. 15 mins.). 2001. 122.00 (978-0-7887-9473-5(6)) Recorded Bks.

Presents a magical blend of fantasy and horror in a delightfully twisted adventure featuring such imaginative creations as seven-foot-tall leprechauns, taxi-driving genies, and a pantheon of unforgettable characters. When Mr. Wednesday offers newly released Shadow a job, the ex-convict figures he's got nothing to lose. But Wednesday is more than he seems; he's one of the thousands of gods brought to America over the centuries by faithful immigrants.

American Gothic: The Story of America's Legendary Theatrical Family - Junius, Edwin, & John Wilkes Booth. unabr. ed. Gene Smith. Narrated by Nelson Runger. 9 cass. (Running Time: 12 hrs. 15 mins.). 2000. 78.00 (978-1-55690-866-8(0), 93308E7) Recorded Bks.

The story of America's great theatrical family, the Booths: Junius Brutus, the patriarch; Edwin, the most famous actor of his day; & John Wilkes, who, on an April evening in 1865, changed the course of history when he assassinated Abraham Lincoln in Ford's Theatre in Washington, D.C.

American Government: People, Institutions & Politics. John Aldrich et al. (C). 1985. 5.00 (978-0-395-40816-2(4)) HM.

American Government: The Political Game. Stephen E. Frantzich & Stephen L. Percy. 1 cass. 1994. (978-0-697-23766-8(4)) Brown & Benchmark.

***American Grace: How Religion Divides & Unites Us.** unabr. ed. Robert D. Putnam & David E. Campbell. (Running Time: 19 hrs. 30 mins.). 2010. 23.99 (978-1-4001-8957-1(8)); 49.99 (978-1-4001-9957-0(3)) Tantor Media.

***American Grace: How Religion Divides & Unites Us.** unabr. ed. Robert D. Putnam & David E. Campbell. Narrated by Dan Miller. (Running Time: 19 hrs. 30 mins. 0 sec.). 2010. 34.99 (978-1-4001-6957-3(7)); audio compact disk 119.99 (978-1-4001-4957-5(6)); audio compact disk 49.99 (978-1-4001-1957-8(X)) Pub: Tantor Media. Dist(s): IngramPubServ

American Greetings Spiritual. 2004. audio compact disk 29.95 (978-0-7630-5130-3(6)) HMHLearTech.

American Greetings Ss Crafts. 2004. audio compact disk 29.95 (978-0-7630-3788-8(5)) HMHLearTech.

American Grit: What It Will Take to Survive & Win in the 21st Century. unabr. ed. Tony Blankley. (Running Time: 8 hrs. NaN mins.). (ENG.). 2009. 29.95 (978-1-4332-1551-3(9)); 26.95 (978-1-4332-1549-0(7)); audio compact disk 26.95 (978-1-4332-1550-6(0)); audio compact disk 70.00 (978-1-4332-1548-3(9)); audio compact disk 54.95 (978-1-4332-1547-6(0)) Blckstn Audio.

American Headway. John Soars & Liz Soars. (American Headway Ser.). 2005. 24.50 (978-0-19-439287-7(2)) OUP.

American Headway. Liz Soars. (American Headway Ser.). 2001. wbk. ed. 24.50 (978-0-19-437931-1(0)) OUP.

American Headway. Liz Soars. 2 CDs. (American Headway Ser.). 2002. stu. ed. 39.95 (978-0-19-437935-9(3)) OUP.

American Headway. Liz Soars & John Soars. 2 CDs. (American Headway Ser.). 2001. stu. ed. 39.95 (978-0-19-437929-8(9)) OUP.

American Headway. Liz Soars & John Soars. 2 cass. (American Headway Ser.). 2001. stu. ed. 39.95 (978-0-19-435378-6(8)) OUP.

American Headway. Liz Soars & John Soars. (American Headway Ser.). 2001. wbk. ed. 24.50 (978-0-19-437936-6(1)); wbk. ed. 24.50 (978-0-19-437937-3(X)) OUP.

American Headway. Liz Soars & John Soars. 2 CDs. (American Headway Ser.). 2003. audio compact disk 39.95 (978-0-19-437941-0(8)) OUP.

American Headway, No. 2. Liz Soars & John Soars. 2 cass. (American Headway Ser.). 2002. stu. ed. 39.95 (978-0-19-435382-3(6)) OUP.

American Headway, No. 3. Liz Soars & John Soars. (American Headway Ser.). 2003. wbk. ed. 24.50 (978-0-19-437942-7(6)) OUP.

American Headway, No. 3. Liz Soars & John Soars. (American Headway Ser.). 2003. wbk. ed. 24.50 (978-0-19-437943-4(4)) OUP.

American Headway, No. 4. John Soars et al. (American Headway Ser.). 2005. wbk. ed. 24.50 (978-0-19-439288-4(0)) OUP.

American Headway, No. 4, Set. John Soars & Liz Soars. 3 vols. (American Headway Ser.). 2005. stu. ed. 39.95 (978-0-19-439285-3(6)); stu. ed. 39.95 (978-0-19-439286-0(4)) OUP.

American Headway Starter. John Soars. 2 CDs. (American Headway Ser.). 2002. stu. ed. 39.95 (978-0-19-437178-0(6)); wbk. ed. 24.50 (978-0-19-437944-1(2)) OUP.

American Headway Starter. John Soars & Liz Soars. (American Headway Ser.). 2002. stu. ed. 39.95 (978-0-19-435390-8(7)); wbk. ed. 24.50 (978-0-19-437945-8(0)) OUP.

American Headway 1: Workbook Cassette. Liz Soars & John Soars. (American Headway Ser.). 2001. wbk. ed. 24.50 (978-0-19-437930-4(2)) OUP.

American Headway 3: Student Book Cassettes. Liz Soars & John Soars. 2 cass. (American Headway Ser.). 2003. 39.95 (978-0-19-435386-1(9)) OUP.

American Hedge Fund: How I Made $2 Million as a Stock Operator & Created a Hedge Fund. unabr. ed. Timothy Sykes. Read by Brett Barry. (YA). 2007. 39.99 (978-1-60252-949-6(3)) Find a World.

American Heiress. unabr. ed. Dorothy Eden. Read by Liza Ross. 7 cass. (Running Time: 10 hrs. 30 mins.). (Sound Ser.). 2004. 61.95 (978-1-85496-551-6(4), 65514) Pub: UlverLrgPrint GBR. Dist(s): Ulverscroft US

American Heritage History of the Civil War. Bruce Catton. Read by Barrett Whitener. 7 CDs. (Running Time: 8 hrs.). 2005. audio compact disk 56.00 (978-0-7861-8592-4(9), 3261) Blckstn Audio.

American Heritage's Great Minds of American History. Read by Stephen E. Ambrose & David McCullough. 2004. 15.95 (978-0-7435-4128-2(6)) Pub: S&S Audio. Dist(s): S and S Inc

***American Heroes.** unabr. ed. Edmund S. Morgan. Narrated by David Chandler. 1 Playaway. (Running Time: 11 hrs. 45 mins.). 2009. 59.75 (978-1-4407-3683-4(9)); 82.75 (978-1-4407-3680-3(4)) Recorded Bks.

***American Heroes.** unabr. ed. Edmund S. Morgan. Read by David Chandler. 10 CDs. (Running Time: 11 hrs. 45 mins.). 2009. audio compact disk 123.75 (978-1-4407-3681-0(2)) Recorded Bks.

***American Heroes.** unabr. collector's ed. Edmund S. Morgan. Narrated by David Chandler. 10 CDs. (Running Time: 11 hrs. 45 mins.). 2009. audio compact disk 51.95 (978-1-4407-3682-7(0)) Recorded Bks.

***American Heroes, No. 3.** Jonathan Sprout. 1 CD. (Running Time: 44 mins.). (J). (gr. 1-5). 2009. audio compact disk 12.99 (978-0-9677954-2-3(7)) Sprout Recordings.

American Heroes: In the Fight Against Radical Islam. Oliver North. Read by Phil Gigante. Ed. by Chuck Holton. (Playaway Adult Nonfiction Ser.). 2009. 65.00 (978-1-60775-519-7(X)) Find a World.

American Heroes: In the Fight Against Radical Islam. Oliver North. 2004. audio compact disk 34.99 (978-1-4193-0296-1(5)) Recorded Bks.

American Heroes: In the Fight Against Radical Islam. abr. ed. Oliver North. Read by Phil Gigante. (Running Time: 6 hrs.). (War Stories Ser.). 2009. audio compact disk 14.99 (978-1-4233-5503-8(2), 9781423355038, BCD Value Price) Brilliance Audio.

American Heroes: In the Fight Against Radical Islam. unabr. ed. Oliver North. Read by Phil Gigante. Ed. by Chuck Holton. (Running Time: 9 hrs.). (War Stories Ser.). 2008. 39.25 (978-1-4233-5501-4(6), 9781423355014, BADLE); audio compact disk 39.25 (978-1-4233-5499-4(0), 9781423354994, Brinc Audio MP3 Lib); audio compact disk 92.25 (978-1-4233-5497-0(4), 9781423354970, BriAudCD Unabrid); audio compact disk 34.95 (978-1-4233-5496-3(6), 9781423354963, Bril Audio CD Unabri); audio compact disk 24.95 (978-1-4233-5498-7(2), 9781423354987, Brilliance MP3) Brilliance Audio.

American Heroes: In the Fight Against Radical Islam. unabr. ed. Oliver North & Chuck Holton. Read by Phil Gigante. (Running Time: 9 hrs.). (War Stories Ser.). 2008. 24.95 (978-1-4233-5500-7(8), 9781423355007, BAD) Brilliance Audio.

American Heroes: Sports Greats of the Nineties. abr. ed. Contrib. by Sports Illustrated Staff. (Running Time: 35 mins.). (ENG.). 2006. 9.99 (978-1-59483-861-3(5)) Pub: Hachet Audio. Dist(s): HachBkGrp

American Heroes: 6 Great Character-Building Stories. (Running Time: 1 hr.). (Your Story Hour Ser.). 2006. audio compact disk 24.99 (978-0-8127-0400-6(2)) Review & Herald.

***American Heroes in Special Operations.** unabr. ed. Oliver North. Read by Phil Gigante. Ed. by Chuck Holton. (Running Time: 7 hrs.). (War Stories Ser.). 2010. 24.99 (978-1-4233-5507-6(5), 9781423355076, Brilliance MP3); 39.97 (978-1-4233-5508-3(3), 9781423355083, Brinc Audio MP3 Lib); audio compact disk 29.99 (978-1-4233-5505-2(9), 9781423355052, Bril Audio CD Unabri) Brilliance Audio.

***American Heroes in Special Operations.** unabr. ed. Oliver North & Chuck Holton. Read by Phil Gigante. (Running Time: 7 hrs.). (War Stories Ser.). 2010. 24.99 (978-1-4233-5509-0(1), 9781423355090, BAD); 39.97 (978-1-4233-5510-6(5), 9781423355106, BADLE); audio compact disk 79.97 (978-1-4233-5506-9(7), 9781423355069, BriAudCD Unabrid) Brilliance Audio.

American History: Dramatized Events. unabr. ed. 1 cass. 165.00 (S19300) J Norton Pubs.

American History on File. (gr. 6-12). 2003. audio compact disk 199.95 (978-0-8160-4970-7(X)) Facts On File.

American History Through Folksong. Keith McNeil & Rusty McNeil. Read by Keith McNeil & Rusty McNeil. (Running Time: 14 hrs. 15 mins.). (American History Through Folksong Ser.). (J). (gr. 4 up). 1994. 99.95 (978-1-878360-07-6(8), 600C) WEM Records.
280 songs with Historical Narration. Volume titles: Colonial & Revolution Songs; Moving West Songs; Civil War Songs; Working & Union Songs; Cowboy Songs; Western Railroad Songs.

American History Through Folksong: With Historical Narration. Keith McNeil & Rusty McNeil. Read by Keith McNeil & Rusty McNeil. (YA). (gr. 4 up). 1996. audio compact disk 124.95 (978-1-878360-15-1(9)) WEM Records.

American Holidays: Exploring Traditions, Customs & Backgrounds. Barbara Klebanow. 1999. 11.00 (978-0-86647-118-3(9)) Pro Lingua.

American Holidays: Exploring Traditions, Customs, & Backgrounds. 2nd ed. Barbara Klebanow & Sara Fischer. 1 CD. (gr. 4-12). 2005. stu. ed. 28.00 (978-0-86647-217-3(7)); audio compact disk 18.00 (978-0-86647-214-2(2)) Pro Lingua.

American Holidays Package: Exploring Traditions, Customs & Backgrounds. Barbara Klebanow. 1999. pap. bk. 19.00 (978-0-86647-119-0(7)) Pro Lingua.

American Home Front: 1941-1942. abr. ed. Alistair Cooke. Read by John Byrne Cooke. (Running Time: 6 hrs.). 2007. audio compact disk 14.99 (978-1-4233-2122-4(7), 9781423321224, BCD Value Price) Brilliance Audio.

American Home Front: 1941-1942. unabr. ed. Alistair Cooke. Read by John Byrne Cooke. (Running Time: 46800 sec.). 2006. audio compact disk 39.95 (978-1-4233-2115-6(4), 9781423321156); audio compact disk 24.95 (978-1-4233-2117-0(0), 9781423321170, Brilliance MP3) Brilliance Audio.
Shortly after the bombing of Pearl Harbor in 1941, Alistair Cooke set out to see America as it was undergoing monumental change. A newly naturalized citizen, Cooke wanted to see what the war had done to people, to the towns he might go through, to some jobs and crops, to stretches of landscape he loved and had seen at peace; and to let significance fall where it might. The result is America at War, a fascinating artifact, a charming travelogue, and a sharp portrait that shows a nation switching from civilian pursuits to military engagement, from the production of consumer goods to materials of war. America at War is also a fascinating record of American life. Cooke travels small highways, with their advertising signs and local topography, in an age before the Interstate highway system. He chronicles the regional glories he encounters, elements of long lost culture such as his beloved soda fountains, and the reactions of citizens, from indifference to grief, from opportunism to resilience under military threat. The manuscript is filled with touching personal stories of the affects of war, from a Japanese family facing internment who try to sell Cooke their car to the unemployed relocating in hopes of jobs in a gunpowder factory. America at War is the work of an experienced, talented journalist; it is intelligent, touchingly fluid and funny.

American Home Front: 1941-1942. unabr. ed. Alistair Cooke. Read by John Byrne Cooke. (Running Time: 13 hrs.). 2006. 39.25 (978-1-4233-2120-0(0), 9781423321200, BADLE); 24.95 (978-1-4233-2119-4(7), 9781423321194, BAD); 92.25 (978-1-4233-2114-9(6), 9781423321149, BrilAudUnabridg); 36.95 (978-1-4233-2113-2(8), 9781423321132); audio compact disk 107.25 (978-1-4233-2116-3(2), 9781423321163, BriAudCD Unabrid); audio compact disk 39.25 (978-1-4233-2118-7(9), 9781423321187, Brinc Audio MP3 Lib) Brilliance Audio.

American Homeplace. unabr. ed. Donald McCaig. Narrated by Nelson Runger. 6 cass. (Running Time: 7 hrs. 45 mins.). 51.00 (978-1-55690-781-4(8), 93103E7) Recorded Bks.
In the early 1960s McCaig left his job at a hot New York advertising agency & his Greenwich Village apartment for a rustic farm in a remote county in Virginia's Shenandoah Valley. This is his story of farming in contemporary America, a timely tribute to a dying way of life. Available to libraries only.

American Hostage. abr. ed. Micah Garen & Marie-Helene Carleton. Read by Micah Garen & Marie-Helene Carleton. 2006. 15.95 (978-0-7435-6742-8(0)) Pub: S&S Audio. Dist(s): S and S Inc

American Hotline: Early Intermediate Level. Tom Hutchinson. 1997. 17.50 (978-0-19-434941-3(1)) OUP.

American Hotline: Intermediate Level. Tom Hutchinson. 1997. 31.95 (978-0-19-434945-1(4)) OUP.

American Hotline: Starter. Tom Hutchinson. 1996. 17.50 (978-0-19-434933-8(0)) OUP.

American Humor & Satire. 6 cass. (Running Time: 5 hrs. 1 min.). 1995. 44.95 (8643Q) Filmic Archives.
This collection contains works by Washington Irving, Artemus Ward, J. S. Robb, Bret Harte, Mark Twain, Frank Stockton, Joel Chandler Harris, Ernest L. Thayer, O Henry, Booth Tarkington, Ring Lardner, Robert Benchley, Ogden Nash, James Thurber & William Saroyan.

American Humor & Satire. unabr. ed. Silhouette Staff. Read by William Saroyan et al. 6 cass. (Running Time: 4 hrs. 55 mins.). (Cassette Library). 1977. 44.98 (978-0-8072-3005-3(7), CXL524CX, Listening Lib) Random Audio Pubg.

American Humor & Satire. unabr. ed. Read by Jack Whitaker & James Thurber. 2 cass. (Running Time: 3 hrs.). Dramatization. 1992. 15.95 (978-0-8072-3494-5(X), CB 129 CXR, Listening Lib) Random Audio Pubg.

American Humorists. abr. ed. Will Rogers et al. 2 cass. (Running Time: 1 hr. 39 mins.). 12.95 (978-0-89926-119-5(1), 807) Audio Bk.

American Humorists. unabr. ed. Washington Irving et al. 6 cass. (C-402) Audio Bk.
A sampling of American humor read by a variety of voices. Includes the works of Washington Irving, Artemus Ward, Bret Harte, Mart Twain, Joel Chandler Harris, Will Rogers, Robert Benchley, Ogden Nash & James Thurber.

American Icon. unabr. ed. Pat Booth. Read by Kate Harper. 10 vols. (Running Time: 13 hrs. 15 mins.). 1999. bk. 84.95 (978-0-7927-2276-2(0), CSL 165, Chivers Sound Lib) AudioGO.
Kate is a bestselling author, a magazine publisher & head of a home-making empire. She & her husband, a successful literary agent move to the Hamptons & have a daughter. Personal & business pressures drive Kate & Peter into the arms of other lovers. But when tragedy befalls their daughter, they come to realize the truth of their commitment to each other & to their family.

American Ideal: Farm Life. 1 cass. (Running Time: 30 mins.). 9.95 (GO-030, HarperThor) HarpC GBR.

American Ideals: Founding a Republic of Virtue. Instructed by Daniel Robinson. 6 cass. (Running Time: 6 hrs.). bk. 29.95 (978-1-56585-894-7(8), 4855) Teaching Co.

American Ideals: Founding a Republic of Virtue. Instructed by Daniel Robinson. 6 CDs. (Running Time: 6 hrs.). 2004. bk. 39.95 (978-1-56585-896-1(4), 4855) Teaching Co.

American Identity, Vol. I-IV. Instructed by Patrick N. Allitt. 24 CDs. (Running Time: 24 hrs.). 2005. bk. 129.95 (978-1-59803-019-8(1), 8540) Teaching Co.

American Identity, Vol. I-IV. Instructed by Patrick N. Allitt. 24 cass. (Running Time: 24 hrs.). 2005. bk. 99.95 (978-1-59803-017-4(5), 8540) Teaching Co.

American Idioms. unabr. ed. 2 cass. 34.50 (SEN305) J Norton Pubs.

American in the French Languedoc. Marques Vickers. (ENG., 2007. cd-rom & audio compact disk 19.95 (978-0-9706530-7-9(7)) Marquis Pubng.

American in the South of France: Escape to the French Languedoc. Marques Vickers. (ENG., 2007. cd-rom & audio compact disk 19.95 (978-0-9706530-3-1(4)) Marquis Pubng.

American Indian & Jungian Orientation. unabr. ed. Joseph Henderson. 1 cass. (Running Time: 1 hr. 21 mins.). 1970. 11.00 (06601) Big Sur Tapes.
Suggests that the internal spiritual orientation of the American Indian contrasts sharply with the predominately external orientation of European Americans. Perhaps through Jungian understanding of archetypal images, we can begin to comprehend the images which the Indian has always cultivated.

American Indian Legends, Vol. 1. Read by Jackalene C. Hiendlmayr. 1 cass. (Running Time: 1 hr.). Dramatization. 1993. bk. 8.00 (978-1-891307-00-3(2)) CAI Record.
Traditional native American stories with background music.

American Indian Legends, Vol. 2. Read by Jackalene C. Hiendlmayr. 1 cass. (Running Time: 1 hr.). 1994. bk. 8.00 (978-1-891307-01-0(0)) CAI Record.

American Indian Legends, Vol. 3. Read by Jackalene C. Hiendlmayr. 1 cass. (Running Time: 1 hr.). 1995. bk. 8.00 (978-1-891307-02-7(9)) CAI Record.

American Indian Legends, Vol. 4. Read by Jackalene C. Hiendlmayr. 1 cass. (Running Time: 1 hr.). (YA). 1997. bk. 8.00 (978-1-891307-03-4(7)) CAI Record.

American Indian Songs & Chants. Perf. by Bala Sinem Choir Staff. 1 cass. (J). 9.98 (203) MFLP CA.
This is a varied repertoire of American Indian songs with an all-Native American group singing traditional songs from many tribes.

American Indian Stories. unabr. ed. Zitkala-Sa. Read by Nancy Lee. (YA). 2007. 34.99 (978-1-60252-874-1(8)) Find a World.

American Industrial Ballads. Perf. by Pete Seeger. Anno. by Irwin Silber. 1 cass. 1992. (0-9307-40058-9307-40058-2-8); audio compact disk (0-9307-40058-2-8) Smithsonian Folkways.
Songs of struggle from coal mines, textile mills & farmfields, that spoke of issues important to the American laborer. Twenty-four songs written about consequences of industrialization, including "Peg & Awl," "The Farmer Is the Man" & "Winnsboro Cotton Mill Blues".

American Inquisition: The Hunt for Japanese American Disloyalty in World War II. Eric L. Muller. (ENG., 2007. 27.50 (978-0-8078-8560-4(6)); audio compact disk 32.95 (978-0-8078-8562-8(2)) U of NC Pr.

***American Insurgents, American Patriots: The Revolution of the People.** unabr. ed. T. H. Breen. Narrated by John Pruden. (Running Time: 13 hrs. 30 mins. 0 sec.). 2010. 29.99 (978-1-4001-6770-8(1)); 19.99 (978-1-4001-8770-6(2)); 39.99 (978-1-4001-9770-5(8)); audio compact disk 39.99 (978-1-4001-1770-3(4)); audio compact disk 95.99 (978-1-4001-4770-0(0)) Pub: Tantor Media. Dist(s): IngramPubServ

American Journey of Barack Obama. Life Magazine Editors. Read by Richard Allen. (Running Time: 4 hrs.). (ENG.). 2009. 16.98 (978-1-60024-873-3(X)); audio compact disk 24.98 (978-1-60024-872-6(1)) Pub: Hachet Audio. Dist(s): HachBkGrp

American Killing. unabr. ed. Mary-Ann Tirone Smith. Read by Susan Ericksen. (Running Time: 12 hrs.). 2008. 24.95 (978-1-4233-5945-6(3), 9781423359456, BAD); 24.95 (978-1-4233-5943-2(7), 9781423359432, Brilliance MP3); 39.25 (978-1-4233-5946-3(1), 9781423359463, BADLE); 39.25 (978-1-4233-5944-9(5), 9781423359449, Brinc Audio MP3 Lib) Brilliance Audio.

American Labor Movement: Student Syllabus. Charlotte A. Butsch. (J). 1976. 25.60 (978-0-89420-206-3(5), 330000) Natl Book.

American Leadership Tradition: Moral Vision from Washington to Clinton. unabr. ed. Marvin Olasky. Read by Jeff Riggenbach. 8 cass. (Running Time: 12 hrs.). 2000. 69.95 (978-0-7861-1763-5(X), 2567) Blckstn Audio.
In the first modern systematic examination of the bond between morals & politics, the author examines the lives & careers of thirteen noted American leaders, including the great, the good & the deeply flawed.

American Legal English, Second Edition: Using Language in Legal Contexts. Debra Suzette Lee et al. (Running Time: 0 hr. 40 mins. 2 sec.). (Michigan Series in English for Academic & Professional Purposes). (ENG.). 2007. audio compact disk 22.00 (978-0-472-00325-9(9)) U of Mich Pr.

American Legend: Frank Sinatra. abr. ed. Nancy Sinatra. Read by Nancy Sinatra. 2 cass. (Running Time: 3 hrs.). 1995. 16.95 B-B Audio.

American Liberalism: An Interpretation for Our Time. John McGowan. (ENG.). 2007. 24.95 (978-0-8078-8523-9(1)); audio compact disk 29.95 (978-0-8078-8525-3(8)) U of NC Pr.

American Liberty. Arranged by Rich Herman. (YA). 2004. audio compact disk 9.95 (978-0-9765630-6-8(1)) Family Bks N CDs.

American Life. abr. ed. Ronald Reagan. 2004. 15.95 (978-0-7435-4153-4(7)) Pub: S&S Audio. Dist(s): S and S Inc

American Lightning: Terror, Mystery, & the Birth of Hollywood. unabr. ed. Howard Blum. Read by John H. Mayer. 9 CDs. (Running Time: 10 hrs. 30 mins.). (ENG.). 2008. audio compact disk 34.95 (978-0-7393-7455-9(9), Random AudioBks) Pub: Random Audio Pubg. Dist(s): Random

American Lion: Andrew Jackson in the White House. abr. ed. Jon Meacham. Read by John H. Mayer. (ENG.). 2008. audio compact disk 39.95 (978-0-7393-3458-4(1), Random AudioBks) Pub: Random Audio Pubg. Dist(s): Random

American Lion: Andrew Jackson in the White House. unabr. ed. Jon Meacham. Narrated by Richard McGonagle. 10 cass. (Running Time: 17 hrs. 15 mins.). 2008. 129.00 (978-1-4159-6100-1(X), BksonTape); audio compact disk 129.00 (978-1-4159-5711-0(8), BksonTape) Pub: Random Audio Pubg. Dist(s): Random

American Listener's Theatre: Telling Tales of Civil Warriors. Adapted by Timothy Patrick Miller. Narrated by Timothy Patrick Miller. 3 CDs. (Running Time: 3 hrs. 6 mins.). (YA). (gr. 7 up). 2008. audio compact disk 9.99 (978-0-9649040-2-6(0)) Am Listeners.

American Literature. (gr. 11 up). 2001. (978-0-395-97163-5(2), 2-80699); audio compact disk (978-0-395-97140-6(3), 2-80687) Holt McDoug.

American Literature. (gr. 11 up). 2004. audio compact disk (978-0-618-28964-6(X), 2-04268); audio compact disk (978-0-618-28972-1(0), 2-04276); audio compact disk (978-0-618-28992-9(5), 2-04284) Holt McDoug.

American Literature. Francis E. Skipp. (Running Time: 16200 sec.). (Barron's EZ-101 Study Keys Ser.). 2005. 34.95 (978-0-7861-3769-5(X)); audio compact disk 36.00 (978-0-7861-7597-0(4)) Blckstn Audio.

American Literature. unabr. ed. Francis E. Skipp. Read by Stuart Langston. 4 cass. (Running Time: 16200 sec.). (Barron's EZ-101 Study Keys Ser.). 2005. 24.95 (978-0-7861-3661-2(8), E3528); audio compact disk 27.95 (978-0-7861-7734-9(9), ZE3528); audio compact disk 29.95 (978-0-7861-7958-9(9), ZM3528) Blckstn Audio.

American Lung Association's 7 Steps to a Smoke-Free Life. unabr. ed. Edward B. Fisher. Read by Richard Beebe. 2 cass. 1998. 17.95 (978-1-55935-303-8(1)) Soundelux.

American-Made: The Enduring Legacy of the WPA: When FDR Put the Nation to Work. Nick Taylor. Read by James Boles. (Playaway Adult Nonfiction Ser.). 2008. 79.99 (978-1-60640-550-5(0)) Find a World.

American-Made: The Enduring Legacy of the WPA: When FDR Put the Nation to Work. unabr. ed. Nick Taylor. (Running Time: 20 hrs. 30 mins. 0 sec.). (ENG.). 2008. audio compact disk 99.99 (978-1-4001-3651-3(2)) Pub: Tantor Media. Dist(s): IngramPubServ

American-Made: The Enduring Legacy of the WPA: When FDR Put the Nation to Work. unabr. ed. Nick Taylor. Read by James Boles. (Running Time: 20 hrs. 30 mins. 0 sec.). (ENG.). 2008. audio compact disk 34.99 (978-1-4001-5651-1(3)); audio compact disk 49.99 (978-1-4001-0651-6(6)) Pub: Tantor Media. Dist(s): IngramPubServ

American Marriage Mores. unabr. ed. Margaret Mead. 1 cass. (Running Time: 1 hr.). 12.95 (35023) J Norton Pubs.
She discusses marriage & marriage mores in America & how changing societal attitudes shape our individual values.

American Martyrs. John A. O'Brien. 6 cass. 24.95 (712) Ignatius Pr.
Isaac Jogues, John de Brebeuf & the first Jesuit missions in North America.

American Melody Sampler. Prod. by Phil Rosenthal. 1 cass. (Running Time: 45 mins.). (J). (gr. k-6). 1995. 9.98 (978-1-879305-20-5(8), AMC501); audio compact disk 14.98 (978-1-879305-22-9(4), CAM-CD5501) Am Melody.
16 folk & bluegrass songs from award winning recordings on the acclaimed American Melody label.

American Mind. Instructed by Allen Guelzo. 18 cass. (Running Time: 18 hrs). 79.95 (978-1-59803-109-6(0)) Teaching Co.

American Mind. Instructed by Allen Guelzo. 12 CDs. (Running Time: 12 hrs). 2005. audio compact disk 99.95 (978-1-59803-111-9(2)) Teaching Co.

American Mobsters - Baby Face Nelson - Bonnie & Clyde - Chicago's Gangland Days. Jimmy Gray & Ron Jordan. Read by Ron Jordan et al. (Running Time: 3 hrs. 12 mins.). (C). 2005. 22.95 (978-1-60083-567-4(8), Audiofy Corp) Iofy Corp.

***American More! Level 1 Class Audio CDs (2)** Herbert Puchta et al. (Running Time: 2 hrs. 38 mins.). (ENG.). 2010. audio compact disk 41.00 (978-0-521-17121-2(0)) Cambridge U Pr.

***American More! Level 2 Class Audio CDs (2)** Herbert Puchta et al. (Running Time: 2 hrs. 17 mins.). (ENG.). 2010. audio compact disk 41.00 (978-0-521-17133-5(4)) Cambridge U Pr.

***American More! Level 3 Class Audio CDs (2)** Herbert Puchta et al. (Running Time: 2 hrs. 38 mins.). (ENG.). 2010. audio compact disk 41.00 (978-0-521-17150-2(4)) Cambridge U Pr.

***American More! Level 4 Class Audio CDs (2)** Herbert Puchta et al. (Running Time: 2 hrs. 10 mins.). (ENG.). 2010. audio compact disk 41.00 (978-0-521-17166-3(0)) Cambridge U Pr.

***American Music.** unabr. ed. Jane Mendelsohn. (Running Time: 8 hrs. 30 mins.). 2010. 29.95 (978-1-4417-5523-0(3)); audio compact disk 29.95 (978-1-4417-5522-3(5)) Blckstn Audio.

American Names see Poetry of Benet

American Nation. Andrew Davidson & Stoff. stu. ed. 207.97 (978-0-13-058828-9(8)) PH School.

American Nation. Holt, Rinehart and Winston Staff. 2000. audio compact disk 208.73 (978-0-03-055724-8(0)) Holt McDoug.

American Nation. 3rd ed. Holt, Rinehart and Winston Staff. 2002. audio compact disk 208.73 (978-0-03-066006-1(8)) Holt McDoug.

American Nation. 3rd unabr. ed. Holt, Rinehart and Winston Staff. (SPA.). 2002. audio compact disk 208.73 (978-0-03-066011-5(4)) Holt McDoug.
Reader-friendly narrative helps students comprehend this engaging, informative text. The focus on skills and assessment prepares your students for standardized testing.

American Nation: Civil War. Holt, Rinehart and Winston Staff. 2000. audio compact disk 208.73 (978-0-03-055788-0(7)); audio compact disk 208.73 (978-0-03-055794-1(1)) Holt McDoug.

American Nation: Student Edition on Audiotapes. Andrew Davidson et al. stu. ed. 207.97 (978-0-13-435803-1(1)) PH School.

American Nation: The Modern Era. 3rd ed. Holt, Rinehart and Winston Staff. 2002. audio compact disk 208.73 (978-0-03-066013-9(0)); audio compact disk 208.73 (978-0-03-066018-4(1)) Holt McDoug.

American Nightmare American Dream. unabr. ed. Suge Knight. Read by Suge Knight. 7 CDs. (Running Time: 8 hrs.). (ENG.). audio compact disk 25.95 (978-0-399-15137-8(0), PutBerkAud) Penguin Grp USA.

American Notes. Charles Dickens. Read by Peter Joyce. 7 cass. 2000. 61.95 (978-1-86015-466-9(2)) Ulverscroft US.

American Notes. unabr. collector's ed. Charles Dickens. Read by Angela Cheyne. 7 cass. (Running Time: 10 hrs. 30 mins.). 1976. 56.00 (978-0-7366-0030-9(2), 1042) Books on Tape.
An account of Dickens' first trip to the United States in 1842.

*American on Purpose. unabr. ed. Craig Ferguson. Read by Craig Ferguson. (ENG.). 2009. (978-0-06-196145-8(0), Harper Audio); (978-0-06-196146-5(9), Harper Audio) HarperCollins Pubs.

American on Purpose: The Improbable Adventures of an Unlikely Patriot. unabr. ed. Craig Ferguson. (Running Time: 5.5 hrs. 0 mins.). 2009. 29.95 (978-1-4332-9502-7(4)); 34.95 (978-1-4332-9498-3(2)); audio compact disk 55.00 (978-1-4332-9499-0(0)) Blckstn Audio.

American on Purpose: The Improbable Adventures of an Unlikely Patriot. unabr. ed. Craig Ferguson. Read by Craig Ferguson. 2009. audio compact disk 39.99 (978-0-06-184193-4(5), Harper Audio) HarperCollins Pubs.

American O'Sheas. Steve Floyd. Narrated by John Randall. (ENG., (YA). 2008. pap. bk. 10.95 (978-0-615-20643-1(3)) Pub: ESOH. Dist(s): R J Comns

American O'Sheas (Audio CD) Steve Floyd. Narrated by John Randall. (ENG.). (YA). 2008. audio compact disk 44.95 (978-0-615-24058-9(5)) ESOH.

American Outrage. abr. ed. Tim Green. Read by Scott Brick. (Running Time: 6 hrs.). (ENG.). 2007. 14.98 (978-1-59483-885-9(2)) Pub: Hachet Audio. Dist(s): HachBkGrp

American Paradise. Marianne Williamson. Read by Marianne Williamson. 1 cass. (Running Time: 90 mins.). (Lectures on a Course in Miracles). 1999. 10.00 (978-1-56170-440-8(7), M823) Hay House.

American Pastoral. unabr. ed. Philip Roth. Read by Ron Silver. (YA). 2008. 64.99 (978-1-60252-946-5(9)) Find a World.

American Patriots: The Story of Blacks in the Military from the Revolution to Desert Storm. Gail Lumet Buckley. 2001. 80.00 (978-0-7366-7050-0(5)); 72.00 (978-0-7366-7145-3(5)) Books on Tape.

African Americans have served heroically in every major American war from the Revolution to Desert Storm.

***American Piano Album.** 2nd ed. Perf. by R. A. Zuckerman. Composed by R. A. Zuckerman. (ENG.). 2010. 9.95 (978-1-891083-10-5(4)) ConcertHall.

American Piano Classics. Perf. by Erich Kunzel & Cincinnati Pops Orchestra. 1 cass., 1 CD. 7.98 (TA 30112); audio compact disk 12.78 CD Jewel box. (TA 80112) NewSound.

American Pioneers Classic. Douglas Back. 1994. 10.98 (978-0-7866-0052-6(7), 95203C) Mel Bay.

American Plague. unabr. ed. 3 cass. (Running Time: 4 hrs.). 2004. 28.75 (978-1-4025-8443-5(1)) Recorded Bks.

Story of the 1793 yellow fever epidemic. Bizarre medical practices of the time are discussed, as well as popular historical figures, such as George Washington and Benjamin Rush, who were involved in finding a cure for this horrific outbreak. Pat Bottino¿s captivating narration adds appeal to this interesting historical tale.

American Portrait: Old Style see Robert Penn Warren Reads Selected Poems

American Presidents. 12 cass. (Running Time: 12 hrs.). 52.50 Alpha Tape.

Presents a study of every American president from Washington through Ford.

***American Presidents: Abraham Lincoln.** Cerebellum Academic Team. (Running Time: 30 mins.). (Just the Facts Ser.). 2010. 24.95 (978-1-59163-271-9(4)) Cerebellum.

***American Presidents: Franklin Delano Roosevelt.** Cerebellum Academic Team. (Running Time: 30 mins.). (Just the Facts Ser.). 2010. 24.95 (978-1-59163-274-0(9)) Cerebellum.

***American Presidents: George Washington.** Cerebellum Academic Team. (Running Time: 30 mins.). (Just the Facts Ser.). 2010. 24.95 (978-1-59163-273-3(0)) Cerebellum.

***American Presidents: John F Kennedy.** Cerebellum Academic Team. (Running Time: 30 mins.). (Just the Facts Ser.). 2010. 24.95 (978-1-59163-275-7(7)) Cerebellum.

***American Presidents: Nixon.** Cerebellum Academic Team. (Running Time: 30 mins.). (Just the Facts Ser.). 2010. 24.95 (978-1-59163-272-6(2)) Cerebellum.

***American Presidents: Ronald Reagan.** Cerebellum Academic Team. (Running Time: 30 mins.). (Just the Facts Ser.). 2010. 24.95 (978-1-59163-276-4(5)) Cerebellum.

***American Presidents: Theodore Roosevelt.** Cerebellum Academic Team. (Running Time: 30 mins.). (Just the Facts Ser.). 2010. 24.95 (978-1-59163-270-2(6)) Cerebellum.

***American Presidents: Thomas Jefferson.** Cerebellum Academic Team. (Running Time: 30 mins.). (Just the Facts Ser.). 2010. 24.95 (978-1-59163-278-8(1)) Cerebellum.

American Presidents Assortment 12 Copies. 2002. 305.40 (978-1-55927-846-1(3)) Pub: Macmill Audio. Dist(s): Macmillan

American Presidents Collection. unabr. ed. 49 CDs. 2006. audio compact disk 495.00 (978-0-7927-4495-5(0), SLD1025) AudioGO.

American Presidents Series: World Events over Time Collection. Eugene Lieber. (ENG.). 2006. audio compact disk 220.00 (978-1-935069-15-7(2)) IAB Inc.

***American Presidents 9 Program Series.** Cerebellum Academic Team. (Running Time: 4 hrs. 30 mins.). (Just the Facts Ser.). 2010. 199.95 (978-1-58565-337-9(3)) Cerebellum.

American Pride: A Collection of Poetry. 2006. 29.95 (978-1-59649-668-2(1)) Whsprng Pine.

A fascinating collection of poetry that will leave you wanting more, American Pride is an outstanding addition to author, Karen Jean Matsko Hood's impressive body of work. Each poem in this collection is drawn from Hood's deep feelings of pride, patriotism, and love for America, as well as her profound sense of the values that define being an American. Written with warmth and candor, the inspirational poetry featured in American Pride is likely to put a spring in your step and will remind you daily of what it means to be American. 224 pp., 6 x 9 inches. Whispering Pine Press, Inc. (c) 2006.

American Pride: A Collection of Poetry. Karen Jean Matsko Hood. 2006. 29.95 (978-1-59210-522-9(X)); audio compact disk 24.95 (978-1-59210-523-6(8)) Whsprng Pine.

American Pride Catholic Edition. Karen Jean Matsko Hood. 2010. audio compact disk 29.95 (978-1-59210-960-9(8)) Whsprng Pine.

American Prince: A Memoir. abr. ed. Peter Golenbock & Tony Curtis. Read by Tony Curtis & Mitchell Greenberg. (Running Time: 6 hrs.). (ENG.). 2008. audio compact disk 29.95 (978-0-7393-6862-6(1), Random AudioBks) Pub: Random Audio Pubg. Dist(s): Random

American Prince: A Memoir. unabr. ed. Tony Curtis & Peter Golenbock. Read by Don Leslie. 9 CDs. (Running Time: 10 hrs. 30 mins.). 2008. audio compact disk 90.00 (978-1-4159-5454-6(2), BksonTape) Pub: Random Audio Pubg. Dist(s): Random

American Prometheus: The Triumph & Tragedy of J. Robert Oppenheimer. Kai Bird & Martin J. Sherwin. Read by Jeff Cummings. (Running Time: 95400 sec.). 2007. audio compact disk 140.00 (978-1-4332-0011-3(2)); audio compact disk 44.95 (978-1-4332-0012-0(0)) Blckstn Audio.

American Prometheus Part 1: The Triumph & Tragedy of J. Robert Oppenheimer. Kai Bird & Martin J. Sherwin. Read by Jeff Cummings. (Running Time: 48600 sec.). 2007. 72.95 (978-1-4332-0010-6(4)) Blckstn Audio.

American Prometheus Part 2: The Triumph & Tragedy of J. Robert Oppenheimer. Kai Bird & Martin J. Sherwin. Read by Jeff Cummings. (Running Time: 46800 sec.). 2007. 72.95 (978-1-4332-0013-7(9)) Blckstn Audio.

American Protestantism Today. John A. Hardon. 9 cass. (Running Time: 90 mins. per cass.). 36.00 (95K) IRL Chicago.

American Psycho. unabr. ed. Bret Easton Ellis. Read by Pablo Schreiber. (Running Time: 17 hrs.). 2010. 24.99 (978-1-4418-0631-4(8), 9781441806314, Brilliance MP3); 39.97 (978-1-4418-0632-1(6), 9781441806321, Brlnc Audio MP3 Lib); 44.97 (978-1-4418-0633-8(4), 9781441806338, BADLE); audio compact disk 29.99 (978-1-4418-0629-1(6), 9781441806291, Bril Audio CD Unabri); audio compact disk 99.97 (978-1-4418-0630-7(X), 9781441806307, BriAudCD Unabrid) Brilliance Audio.

American Rebel: The Life of Clint Eastwood. unabr. ed. Marc Eliot. Narrated by Marc Eliot. 2 MP3-CDs. (Running Time: 13 hrs. 0 mins. 0 sec.). (ENG.). 2009. 29.99 (978-1-4001-6347-2(1)); audio compact disk 79.99 (978-1-4001-4347-4(0)); audio compact disk 39.99 (978-1-4001-1347-7(4)) Pub: Tantor Media. Dist(s): IngramPubServ

***American Rebel: The Life of Clint Eastwood.** unabr. ed. Marc Eliot. Narrated by Marc Eliot. (Running Time: 13 hrs. 0 mins.). 2009. 18.99 (978-1-4001-8347-0(2)) Tantor Media.

American Religious History, Pts. I-II. Instructed by Patrick Allitt. 12 cass. (Running Time: 12 hrs.). 54.95 (978-1-56585-270-9(2), 897) Teaching Co.

American Religious History, Pts. I-II. Instructed by Patrick Allitt. 12 CDs. (Running Time: 12 hrs.). 2001. audio compact disk 69.95 (978-1-56585-395-9(4), 897) Teaching Co.

American Religious History, Vol. 2. Instructed by Patrick Allitt. 6 cass. (Running Time: 6 hrs.). 2001. 129.95 (978-1-56585-271-6(0)) Teaching Co.

American Revolution. Kenneth Bruce. 1 cass. (Running Time: 1 hr.). Dramatization. (Excursions in History Ser.). 12.50 Alpha Tape.

American Revolution. Instructed by Allen C. Guelzo. 2008. 129.95 (978-1-59803-432-5(4)); audio compact disk 69.95 (978-1-59803-433-2(2)) Teaching Co.

American Revolution. unabr. ed. Bruce Lancaster. Narrated by Alan Bergreen. 8 cass. (Running Time: 11 hrs. 30 mins.). 1986. 70.00 (978-1-55690-013-6(9), 86320E7) Recorded Bks.

A panoramic history of America's revolution. Depicts the true history of our country's struggle for independence, from Lexington to Yorktown, the whole story of a hard, cruel & bloody war we came perilously close to losing.

American Revolution. unabr. ed. George H. Smith. Read by George C. Scott. (Running Time: 18000 sec.). (United States at War Ser.). 2007. audio compact disk 19.95 (978-0-7861-6244-4(9)) Blckstn Audio.

American Revolution, Pt. 1. unabr. ed. George H. Smith. Ed. by Wendy McElroy. Narrated by George C. Scott. 2 cass. (Running Time: 1 hr. 15 mins. per cass.). Dramatization. (United States at War Ser.). (YA). (gr. 9 up). 1989. 17.95 (978-0-938935-51-3(8), 10251) Knowledge Prod.

Many founding fathers believed the real American Revolution was not the war with Britain, but the revolution in ideas which preceded & caused the war. This presentation explores the character & the ideas of 18th century Americans & examines what caused them to rebel.

American Revolution, Pt. 2. unabr. ed. George H. Smith. Ed. by Wendy McElroy. Narrated by George C. Scott. 2 cass. (Running Time: 1 hr. 15 mins. per cass.). Dramatization. (United States at War Ser.). 1989. 17.95 (978-0-938935-52-0(6), 10252) Knowledge Prod.

On July 2, 1776, the second Continental Congress proclaimed American independence. But it would take seven years & the loss of many thousands of lives for independence to become a reality. This is the story of America's battle for freedom.

American Revolution: A History. Gordon S. Wood. Narrated by Jack Garrett. 5 cass. (Running Time: 6 hrs. 45 mins.). 2002. 52.00 (978-1-4025-3998-5(3)) Recorded Bks.

American Revolution as Seen by a British Historian. unabr. ed. Edmund Wright. 1 cass. (Running Time: 32 mins.). 12.95 (19005) J Norton Pubs.

This is an analysis of the influence of English heritage on the formation of the colonies. It illustrates historical perspective in light of military leadership & points out that the historian is a child of his own times. The author cautions that we must see history as made up of living men.

American Revolution Audio CD Theme Set: Set of 6 Set A. Adapted by Benchmark Education Staff. (English Explorers Ser.). (J). (gr. 3-6). 2007. audio compact disk 60.00 (978-1-4108-9844-9(X)) Benchmark Educ.

American Rhapsody. abr. ed. Joe Eszterhas. Read by David Dukes et al. 4 cass. (Running Time: 6 hrs.). 2000. 25.00 (978-1-893224-31-5(7), N Millennium Audio) New Millenn Enter.

In your face look at the people running this country, also it is a rollicking good tale filled with humor, tragedy, suspense, high drama & melodrama. And, of course, with plenty of sex.

American Rhapsody. abr. ed. Joe Eszterhas. Read by Edward Asner et al. 5 CDs. (Running Time: 6 hrs.). 2004. audio compact disk 39.95 (978-1-893224-40-7(6), N Millennium Audio) New Millenn Enter.

The author covers the Clintons, Monica Lewinsky & Linda Tripp in Washington, D.C.; Sharon Stone, Farrah Fawcett & David Geffen on the West Coast & everyone involved in politics & entertainment.

American Rhapsody. unabr. ed. Joe Eszterhas. Read by David Dukes et al. 12 cass. (Running Time: 18 hrs.). 2004. 39.95 (978-1-893224-43-8(0), N Millennium Audio) New Millenn Enter.

In your face look at the people running this country, also is a rollicking good tale filled with humor, tragedy, suspense, high drama & melodrama. And, of course, with plenty of sex.

American Rock. Rhino Records Staff. 1 cass., 1 CD. (Schoolhouse Rock Ser.). (J). (ps-3). 1998. 7.89 (978-1-56826-773-9(8)) Rhino Enter.

American Roots. World Music Network Staff & Rough Guides Staff. (Rough Guide World Music Cds Ser.). 2004. audio compact disk 45.00 (978-1-84353-354-2(5)) DK Pub Inc.

***American Rose: A Nation Laid Bare: the Life & Times of Gypsy Rose Lee.** unabr. ed. Karen Abbott. Read by Bernadette Dunne. (ENG.). 2010. audio compact disk 45.00 (978-0-307-87709-3(4), Random AudioBks) Pub: Random Audio Pubg. Dist(s): Random

American Routes: Songs & Stories from the Road. unabr. ed. Nick Spitzer. 2 CDs. (Running Time: 2 hrs. 30 mins.). (ENG., 2008. audio compact disk 22.95 (978-1-59887-625-3(2), 1598876252) Pub: HighBridge. Dist(s): Workman Pub

American Scene. unabr. ed. Henry James. Narrated by Flo Gibson. 12 cass. (Running Time: 17 hrs.). 2003. 39.95 (978-1-55685-703-4(9)) Audio Bk Con.

Sometime's provokingly verbose travelogue there are insights and amusing comments.

American Scene: Comments by Jean Shepherd. Read by Jean Shepherd. 1 cass. (Running Time: 1 hr.). 10.95 (G0150B090, HarperThor) HarpC GBR.

American Scholar see Ralph Waldo Emerson: Poems and Essays

American School: Why Johnny Can't Think. Leonard Peikoff. Read by Leonard Peikoff. 1 cass. (Running Time: 90 mins.). 1984. 12.95 (978-1-56114-054-1(6), LP03C) Second Renaissance.

The systematic attempt in today's classrooms to paralyze the child's conceptual capacity.

***American Scoundrel.** Thomas Keneally. Read by Humphrey Bower. (Running Time: 13 hrs. 45 mins.). 2010. 104.99 (978-1-74214-620-1(1), 9781742146201) Pub: Bolinda Pubng AUS. Dist(s): Bolinda Pub Inc

***American Scoundrel: Murder, Love & Politics in Civil War America.** unabr. ed. Thomas Keneally. Read by Humphrey Bower. (Running Time: 13 hrs. 45 mins.). 2004. audio compact disk 108.95 (978-1-74093-437-4(7)) Pub: Bolinda Pubng AUS. Dist(s): Bolinda Pub Inc

Charming and ambitious, Dan Sickles literally got away with murder. His protector was none other than the President himself, the ageing James Buchanan; his political friends quickly gathered round; and Sickles was acquitted. His trial is described with all Thomas Keneally's powers of dash and drama, against a backdrop of double-dealing, intrigue and 'the slavery question'. Enslaved, in her turn, by the hypocrisy of nineteenth-century society, his wife was shunned and thereafter banned from public life. Sickles, meanwhile, was free to accept favours and patronage. He raised a regiment for the Union, and went on to become a general in the army, rising to the rank of brigadier-general and commanding a flank at the Battle of Gettysburg - at which he lost a leg, which he put into the military museum in Washington where he would take friends to visit it.

American Scoundrel: The Life of the Notorious Civil War General Dan Sickles. unabr. ed. Thomas Keneally. 7 cass. (Running Time: 13 hrs. 45 mins.). 2002. 56.00 (978-1-74030-811-3(5)) Pub: Bolinda Pubng AUS. Dist(s): Bolinda Pub Inc

American Senator, Pt. 2. unabr. ed. Anthony Trollope. 5 cass. (Running Time: 7 hrs. 30 mins.). (Classic Books on Cassette). 1988. 35.95 Audio Bk Con.

An American senator observes with some perplexity country life & all its social echelons during the late 1800s as we follow the romances & intrigues of flirtatious Arabella Trefoil.

American Senator, Pts. 1 & 2. unabr. ed. Anthony Trollope. 13 cass. (Running Time: 19 hrs. 30 mins.). 82.95 Audio Bk Con.

An American senator observes, with some perplexity, English country life in the late 1800;s in all its social echelons & we follow the romances & intrigues of the flirtatious Arabella Trefoil.

American Senator (Part 1), Vol. 1. unabr. ed. Anthony Trollope. Read by Flo Gibson. 8 cass. (Running Time: 13 hrs.). (Classic Books on Cassette). 1988. 26.95 (978-1-55685-107-0(3)) Audio Bk Con.

An American senator observes, with some perplexity, English country life in the late 1800's in all its social echelons & we follow the romances & intrigues of the flirtatious Arabella Trefoil.

American Senator (Part 2), Vol. 2. unabr. ed. Anthony Trollope. Narrated by Flo Gibson. (Running Time: 7 hrs. 15 mins.). 1987. 20.95 (978-1-55685-786-7(1)) Audio Bk Con.

American Senator (Parts 1 And 2) unabr. ed. Anthony Trollope. Narrated by Flo Gibson. (Running Time: 19 hrs. 6 mins.). 1987. 41.95 (978-1-55685-787-4(X)) Audio Bk Con.

American Short Stories. abr. ed. Short Stories. Listening Library Staff. 1 cass. (Running Time: 110 mins.). 1986. 15.95 (978-0-8072-3427-3(3), Listening Lib) Random Audio Pubg.

American Sketches: Great Leaders, Creative Thinkers, & Heroes of a Hurricane. abr. ed. Walter Isaacson. Read by John Slattery & Cotter Smith. (Running Time: 6 hrs. 0 mins. 0 sec.). (ENG.). 2009. audio compact disk 29.99 (978-1-4423-0407-9(3)) Pub: S&S Audio. Dist(s): S and S Inc

American Sketches: Suite for Classical Guitar. Peter Madlem. 2001. bk. 14.95 (978-0-7866-5420-8(1), 98756BCD) Mel Bay.

***American Soldier.** abr. ed. Tommy R. Franks. Read by Tommy R. Franks. (ENG.). 2004. (978-0-06-081366-6(0), Harper Audio); (978-0-06-078426-3(1), Harper Audio) HarperCollins Pubs.

***American Soldier.** unabr. ed. Tommy R. Franks. Read by Eric Conger. (ENG.). 2004. (978-0-06-081491-5(8), Harper Audio); (978-0-06-078428-7(8), Harper Audio) HarperCollins Pubs.

American Soldier. unabr. ed. Tommy R. Franks. Read by Tommy R. Franks. Read by Eric Conger. 2004. audio compact disk 44.95 (978-0-06-077612-1(9)) HarperCollins Pubs.

American Soldier. unabr. abr. ed. Tommy R. Franks. Read by Tommy R. Franks. 6 CDs. (Running Time: 9 hrs.). 2004. audio compact disk 29.95 (978-0-06-075012-1(X)) HarperCollins Pubs.

***American Soldiers: Ground Combat in the World Wars, Korea, & Vietnam.** unabr. ed. Peter S. Kindsvatter. Narrated by Joshua Swanson. (Running Time: 19 hrs. 30 mins. 0 sec.). 2010. 29.99 (978-1-4001-6950-4(X)); 21.99 (978-1-4001-8950-2(0)); audio compact disk 39.99 (978-1-4001-1950-9(2)) Pub: Tantor Media. Dist(s): IngramPubServ

***American Soldiers (Library Edition) Ground Combat in the World Wars, Korea, & Vietnam.** unabr. ed. Peter S. Kindsvatter. Narrated by Joshua Swanson. (Running Time: 17 hrs. 0 mins.). 2010. 39.99 (978-1-4001-9950-1(6)); audio compact disk 95.99 (978-1-4001-4950-6(9)) Pub: Tantor Media. Dist(s): IngramPubServ

American Spartans. 2006. 79.95 (978-0-7861-3032-0(6)); audio compact disk 99.00 (978-0-7861-7596-3(6)) Blckstn Audio.

American Spartans: The U. S. Marines: A Combat History from Iwo Jima to Iraq. unabr. ed. James Warren. Read by Dick Hill. 8 cass. (Running Time: 48600 sec.). 2005. 29.95 (978-0-7861-3048-1(2), E3440); audio compact disk 29.95 (978-0-7861-8025-7(0), ZE3440); audio compact disk 29.95 (978-0-7861-8121-6(4), ZM3440) Blckstn Audio.

American Spartans: The US Marines in Combat, from Iwo Jima to Iraq. unabr. ed. James Warren. Read by Dick Hill. (YA). 2006. 69.99 (978-1-59895-687-0(6)) Find a World.

American Sphinx: The Character of Thomas Jefferson. unabr. ed. Joseph J. Ellis. Read by Susan O'Malley. 11 cass. (Running Time: 16 hrs.). 1999. 76.95 (978-0-7861-1475-7(4), 2327) Blckstn Audio.

Portrait of a man who, at the grass roots, is no longer liberal or conservative, agrarian or industrialist, pro- or anti-slavery, privileged or populist. We understand why we should neither beatify Jefferson nor consign him to the rubbish heap of history.

American Sphinx: The Character of Thomas Jefferson. unabr. ed. Joseph J. Ellis. Read by Susan O'Malley. (Running Time: 15 hrs. 0 mins.). 2010. 29.95 (978-1-4417-1756-6(0)); audio compact disk 118.00 (978-1-4417-1753-5(6)) Blckstn Audio.

***American Spirit.** unabr. ed. Brian Tracy. (Running Time: 6 hrs.). (ENG.). 2011. audio compact disk 29.98 (978-1-59659-529-3(9)) Pub: Hachet Audio. Dist(s): HachBkGrp

***American Spirit.** unabr. ed. Brian Tracy & Ed Feulner. Read by Authors. (Running Time: 6 hrs.). (ENG.). 2011. 27.00 (978-1-59659-646-7(5), GildAudio) Pub: Gildan Media. Dist(s): HachBkGrp

American Standard. Perf. by Every Day Life Staff. Composed by Michael Knott. 1 CD. 1997. audio compact disk 15.99 (D8608) Diamante Music Grp.
The group has been compared with Korn & Rage Against the Machine, but quickly has become known for their own defining sound. The group is known for its outspoken views on politics inside & out of the church.

American Star. Jackie Collins. 2004. 15.95 (978-0-7435-4129-9(4)) Pub: S&S Audio. Dist(s): S and S Inc

American Start with English. 2nd rev. ed. D. H. Howe. (American Start with English, 2nd Edition Ser.). 1996. 24.50 (978-0-19-434024-3(4)) OUP.

American Start with English. 2nd rev. ed. D. H. Howe. (American Start with English, 2nd Edition Ser.). 1997. 24.50 (978-0-19-434032-8(5)) OUP.

American Start with English. 2nd rev. ed. D. H. Howe. (American Start with English, 2nd Edition Ser.). 1997. 39.95 (978-0-19-434037-3(6)) OUP.

American Start with English, No. 2. 2nd rev. ed. D. H. Howe. 2 cass. (Running Time: 3 hrs.). (American Start with English, 2nd Edition Ser.). 1996. 24.50 (978-0-19-434020-5(1)) OUP.

American Start with English, No. 4. 2nd rev. ed. D. H. Howe. (American Start with English, 2nd Edition Ser.). 1996. 24.50 (978-0-19-434028-1(7)) OUP.

American Start with English, Vol. 1. 2nd unabr. rev. ed. D. H. Howe. 1 cass. (Running Time: 90 min.). (American Start with English, 2nd Edition Ser.). 1996. 24.50 (978-0-19-434016-8(3)) OUP.

American Steel: Hot Metal Men & the Resurrection of the Rust Belt, unabr. ed. Richard Preston. Narrated by George Wilson. 10 cass. (Running Time: 14 hrs.). 1991. 85.00 (978-1-55690-014-3(7), 91209K8) Recorded Bks.
The story of the collapse of the American steel industry is an old one, but it's not the story Preston tells. His is a tale of renewal, about a renegade company called Nucor, planted at the heart of the Indiana rust belt.

American Story. Debra J. Dickerson. Narrated by Robin Miles. 10 cass. (Running Time: 13 hrs. 45 mins.). 92.00 (978-1-4025-2128-7(6)) Recorded Bks.

American Story: The Odyssey of Solomon Northrup. abr. ed. Solomon Northrup. Read by Allen Gilmore. 4 cass. (Running Time: 6 hrs.). 2002. 24.95 (978-0-9645593-3-2(1)) MasterBuy Audio Bks.

American Story: The Odyssey of Solomon Northrup. abr. ed. Solomon Northrup. Read by Allen Gilmore. 4 cass. (Running Time: 6 hrs.). 2000. 24.95 MasterBuy Audio Bks.

American Storytellers & Songsters. unabr. ed. Harold Courlander et al. Read by Frank J. Dobie et al. 6 cass. (Running Time: 4 hrs. 54 mins.). 1986. 55.00 (978-0-8045-0070-8(3), PCC 70) Spoken Arts.
This Collection Presents Stories with That Flavor Unique to America & Tunes Which Recall Its Most Colorful Eras. Includes: Tales of the Hopi Indians, California Fairy Tales, Eskimo Stories, Southwest Folk Tales, Some Mountain Tales about Jack & Introduction to American Folk Songs.

***American Subversive.** unabr. ed. David Goodwillie. Narrated by Tavia Gilbert & David Drummond. (Running Time: 12 hrs. 30 mins. 0 sec.). (ENG.). 2010. audio compact disk 90.99 (978-1-4001-4754-0(9)) Pub: Tantor Media. Dist(s): IngramPubServ

***American Subversive: A Novel.** unabr. ed. David Goodwillie. Narrated by Tavia Gilbert & David Drummond. (Running Time: 13 hrs. 0 mins.). 2010. 37.99 (978-1-4001-9754-5(6)); 18.99 (978-1-4001-8754-6(0)) Tantor Media.

***American Subversive: A Novel.** unabr. ed. David Goodwillie. Narrated by Tavia Gilbert & David Drummond. (Running Time: 12 hrs. 30 mins. 0 sec.). (ENG.). 2010. 24.99 (978-1-4001-6754-8(X)); audio compact disk 37.99 (978-1-4001-1754-3(2)) Pub: Tantor Media. Dist(s): IngramPubServ

American Tabloid. unabr. collector's ed. James Ellroy. Read by Michael Prichard. 14 cass. (Running Time: 21 hrs.). (Underworld USA Trilogy: No. 1). 1996. 112.00 (978-0-7366-3279-9(4), 3935) Books on Tape.
Three bent lawmen follow trail of corruption & political intrigue leading to the Kennedy assassination.

***American Taliban: A Novel.** unabr. ed. Pearl Abraham. Read by Jay Snyder. (Running Time: 10 hrs.). 2010. 24.99 (978-1-4418-7843-4(2), 9781441878434, Brilliance MP3); 39.97 (978-1-4418-7844-1(0), 9781441878441, Brlnc Audio MP3 Lib); 39.97 (978-1-4418-7845-8(9), 9781441878458, BADLE); audio compact disk 29.99 (978-1-4418-7841-0(6), 9781441878410, Bril Audio CD Unabri); audio compact disk 79.97 (978-1-4418-7842-7(4), 9781441878427, BriAudCD Unabrid) Brilliance Audio.

American Tall Tales. abr. ed. Adrien Stoutenburg. Read by Ed Begley. 4 cass. (Running Time: 3 hrs.). (J). (gr. 4-6). 1992. 25.00 (978-1-55994-610-0(5)) HarperCollins Pubs.
Eight of the most beloved & true American folk heroes are brought to life. From Davy Crockett to Johnny Appleseed to Pecos Bill to Paul Bunyan, this collection is made up of stories of people who lived to become legends & heroes who became real to us through legend.

American Tall Tales. unabr. ed. Mary Pope Osborne. Narrated by Scott Snively. 2 CDs. (Running Time: 2 hrs. 25 mins.). (J). 2002. audio compact disk 24.95 (978-1-883332-81-5(8), CD3-02) Audio Bkshelf.
The compelling classic of a boy's coming of age during the Civil War is based on stories the author's grandfather told her about his own life.

American Tall Tales. unabr. ed. Mary Pope Osborne. Read by Scott Snively. 2 cass. (Running Time: 2 hrs. 25 mins.). (YA). (gr. 4 up). 2002. 17.95 (978-1-883332-77-8(X), 3-02) Audio Bkshelf.
Scott Snively takes the listener on a wild ride from sea to shining sea in this classic collection of larger than life folk heroes. Includes: Davy Crocket, Sally Ann Thunder, Ann Whirlwind, Johnny Appleseed, Stormalong, Mose, Febold Feboldson, Pecos Bill, John Henry & Paul Bunyan.

American Tall Tales. unabr. ed. Mary Pope Osborne. Read by Scott Snively. (J). 2008. 34.99 (978-1-60514-806-9(7)) Find a World.

American Tall Tales. unabr. ed. Adrien Stoutenburg. Read by Ed Begley. 4 cass. (J). HarperCollins Pubs.

American Tall Tales. unabr. ed. Jim Weiss. 1 CD. (Running Time: 1 hr. 30 mins.). 2003. audio compact disk 14.95 (978-1-882513-81-9(9)) Greathall Prods.

American Tall Tales. unabr. ed. Short Stories. As told by Jim Weiss. 1 cass. (Running Time: 1 hr.). Dramatization. (Storyteller's Version Ser.). (J). 2003. 10.95 (978-1-882513-56-7(8), 1124-32) Greathall Prods.
Tales of Paul Buyan, Johnny Appleseed, Pecos Bill and More.

American Tall Tales, Set. unabr. ed. Adrien Stoutenburg. Read by Ed Begley. 4 cass. (Running Time: 6 hrs.). Incl. Davy Crockett. (J). (SBC 110); Joe Magarac. (J). (SBC 110); John Henry. (J). (SBC 110); Johnny Appleseed. (J). (SBC 110); Mike Fink. (J). (SBC 110); Paul Bunyan. (J). (SBC 110); Pecos Bill. (J). (SBC 110); Stormalong. (J). (SBC 110); (J). 1985. 29.95 (978-0-89845-044-6(6), SBC 110) HarperCollins Pubs.

***American Tempest: The Heroes & Villains of the Boston Tea Party.** unabr. ed. Harlow Giles Unger. (Running Time: 9.5 hrs. NaN mins.). (ENG.). 2011. 29.95 (978-1-4417-7914-4(0)); audio compact disk 29.95 (978-1-4417-7913-7(2)) Blckstn Audio.

***American Tempest: The Heroes & Villains of the Boston Tea Party.** unabr. ed. Harlow Giles Unger. Read by To be Announced. (Running Time: 9.5 hrs. NaN mins.). (ENG.). 2011. 59.95 (978-1-4417-7911-3(6)); audio compact disk 90.00 (978-1-4417-7912-0(4)) Blckstn Audio.

American Theatre. unabr. ed. David Merrick. 1 cass. (Running Time: 1 hr.). 1967. 12.95 (32014) J Norton Pubs.
From William Buckley's "Firing Line" program, this is a debate with David Merrick on the American theatre.

American Theocracy: The Peril & Politics of Radical Religion, Oil, & Borrowed Money in the 21st Century. unabr. ed. Kevin Phillips. Read by Scott Brick. 11 cass. (Running Time: 15 hrs.). 2006. 99.00 (978-1-4159-2800-4(2)); audio compact disk 104.00 (978-1-4159-2801-1(0)) Books on Tape.

American Thighs: The Sweet Potato Queens' Guide to Preserving Your Assets. unabr. ed. Jill Conner Browne. Read by Jill Conner Browne. (Running Time: 9 hrs.). (Sweet Potato Queens Ser.). 2008. 24.99 (978-1-4233-1138-6(8), 9781423311386, Brilliance MP3); 39.97 (978-1-4233-1139-3(6), 9781423311393, Brlnc Audio MP3 Lib); 39.97 (978-1-4233-1141-6(8), 9781423311416, BADLE); 24.99 (978-1-4233-1140-9(X), 9781423311409, BAD); audio compact disk 26.99 (978-1-4233-1136-2(1), 9781423311362); audio compact disk 74.97 (978-1-4233-1137-9(X), 9781423311379, BriAudCD Unabrid) Brilliance Audio.

American Too. unabr. ed. Elisa Bartone. Narrated by Barbara Caruso. 1 cass. (Running Time: 30 mins.). (gr. k up). 1997. 10.00 (978-0-7887-0801-5(5), 94950E7) Recorded Bks.
A nostalgic look at the immigrants who flocked to America in the early part of this century. Rosie doesn't want to be like all her Italian neighbors & family. So when she is chosen as queen of a feast day parade, she determines to prove her point.

***American Tragedy.** Theodore Dreiser. Narrated by Flo Gibson. (ENG.). 2010. audio compact disk 68.95 (978-1-60646-217-1(2)) Audio Bk Con.

American Tragedy. unabr. ed. Theodore Dreiser. Narrated by Flo Gibson. (Running Time: 31 hrs. 2 mins.). 2000. 59.95 (978-1-55685-789-8(6)) Audio Bk Con.

American Tragedy, Part 1. unabr. ed. Theodore Dreiser. Narrated by Flo Gibson. 12 cass. (Running Time: 18 hrs.). 1999. 39.95 (978-1-55685-632-7(6)) Audio Bk Con.
Based on a true story, Clyde Griffiths revolts against the poverty & missionary zeal of his parents & he pursues job advancement, acceptance in the world of society & two women. When his first girl becomes pregnant he decides to kill her. His trial & execution are vividly described in this haunting, sometimes horrific, story.

American Tragedy, Part 2. unabr. ed. Theodore Dreiser. Narrated by Flo Gibson. 9 cass. (Running Time: 13 hrs. 9 mins.). 2000. 28.95 (978-1-55685-788-1(8)) Audio Bk Con.

American Tragedy, Pt. 2. unabr. ed. Theodore Dreiser. 9 cass. (Running Time: 13 hrs. 30 mins.). 1999. 59.95 Audio Bk Con.

American Trash... 14 Songs & a Book. Dan Dubelman. Contrib. by Betty Dylan (Musical group) Staff. (American Trash...14 Songs & a Book). (YA). 2001. mass mkt. 19.95 (978-0-9708363-0-4(9)) Daz Unlimit.

***American Type: A Novel.** unabr. ed. Henry Roth. (Running Time: 11 hrs. 0 mins.). 2010. 29.95 (978-1-4417-4960-4(8)); 65.95 (978-1-4417-4956-7(X)); audio compact disk 100.00 (978-1-4417-4957-4(8)) Blckstn Audio.

American Urological Association Lecture: Medical Education & the Academic Health Center in a Time of Change. 1 cass. (Named Lectures: C85-NL1). 7.50 (8531) Am Coll Surgeons.

American Voices, American Choices. abr. ed. 1 cass. 1999. 10.00 (978-0-9673547-1-2(4)) Voices Across America.
American youth storytelling of history.

American War for Independence-CD: Men & Battles. 10 cass. 2005. 35.00 (978-1-59128-555-7(0)) Canon Pr ID.

American War for Independence-tape. (ENG.). 2005. 35.00 (978-1-59128-556-4(9)) Canon Pr ID.

American Wars Series: World Events over Time Collection. Eugene Lieber. (ENG.). 2006. audio compact disk 180.00 (978-1-935069-12-6(8)) IAB Inc.

American Way of War: Guided Missiles, Misguided Men, & a Republic in Peril. unabr. ed. Eugene Jarecki. (Running Time: 12 hrs. 0 mins. 0 sec.). (ENG.). 2008. audio compact disk 75.99 (978-1-4001-3980-4(5)); audio compact disk 37.99 (978-1-4001-0980-7(9)); audio compact disk 24.99 (978-1-4001-5980-2(6)) Pub: Tantor Media. Dist(s): IngramPubServ

American West. Retold by Gina D. B. Clemen. (Green Apple Step One Ser.). (J). (gr. 4-7). 2005. pap. bk. 21.95 (978-88-7754-969-3(6)) Cideb ITA.

American West. Larry Schweikart. 1 cass. (Running Time: 1 hr.). 10.95 (GO-020, HarperThor) HarpC GBR.

American West. abr. ed. Dee Brown. Read by Mitchell Ryan. 4 cass. (Running Time: 6 hrs.). 1995. 26.95 (978-0-944993-93-4(1)) Audio Lit.
A panorama of the myths & realities of the old West.

American Wife. abr. ed. Curtis Sittenfeld. Read by Kimberly Farr. (ENG.). 2008. audio compact disk 34.95 (978-0-7393-2386-1(5), Random AudioBks) Pub: Random Audio Pubg. Dist(s): Random

American Wife. unabr. ed. Curtis Sittenfeld. Read by Kimberly Farr. 19 CDs. (Running Time: 23 hrs. 30 mins.). 2008. audio compact disk 129.00 (978-1-4159-5697-7(9), BksonTape) Pub: Random Audio Pubg. Dist(s): Random

American Wives & English Husbands. unabr. ed. Gertrude Franklin Horn Atherton. Read by Flo Gibson. 5 cass. (Running Time: 7 hrs. 30 mins.). 1997. 20.95 (978-1-55685-488-0(9), 4889) Audio Bk Con.
An amusing look at the lives of aristocratic Californians & their marriages with British nobles.

American Wow! American Window on the World. Rob Nolasco. 1994. 31.95 (978-0-19-434803-4(2)) OUP.

American Wow! Level 2: American Window on the World. Rob Nolasco. 1994. 31.95 (978-0-19-434808-9(3)) OUP.

American Wow! Level 3: American Window on the World. Rob Nolasco. 1994. 31.95 (978-0-19-434813-3(X)) OUP.

American Writers, Set. British Library Curatorial Staff. 3 CDs. (Running Time: 3 hrs. 51 mins. 0 sec.). (British Library - British Library Sound Archive Ser.). 2008. audio compact disk 35.00 (978-0-7123-0544-0(0)) Pub: Britis Library GBR. Dist(s): Chicago Distribution Ctr

Americana, Vol. 1. abr. ed. Janet Dailey. Perf. by Gabrielle De Cuir et al. 4 cass. (Running Time: 6 hrs.). 2001. 25.00 (978-1-59040-081-4(X), Phoenix Audio) Pub: Amer Intl Pub. Dist(s): PerseuPGW
This is the first volume of romance fifty stories; each novel is set in a different state of the Union. This volume includes: "Dangerous Masquerade" (Alabama), "Northern Magic" (Alaska), "Sonora Sundown" (Arizona) and "Valley of the Vapours" (Arkansas).

Americana: Historical Spotlights in Song. Prod. by Carla Sciaky. 1 cass. 1998. 15.95 (978-0-943327-14-3(8), JP7148) JAG Pubns.
Fourteen favorite folk songs that can be found in the related text book "Americana: Historical Spotlights in Story & Song." This musical group harmonizes & pronounces clearly, so even foreign students may sing along.

Americana Pak: Charles Kuralt's America & More News from Lake Wobegon. abr. ed. Read by Charles Kuralt & Garrison Keillor. 2 cass. (Running Time: 2 hrs. 30 mins.). 2001. 34.95 (978-0-929071-60-2(3)) B-B Audio.
Plugn Play Travelpaks contain everything your customers will need for many hours of audiobook listening. 2 Fantastic Audiobooks with1 Portable Cassette Player plus1 Comfortable Headset plus 2 Batteriers AMERICANA PAK 2.5 HoursCHARLES KURALTS AMER.

Americana Sampler Fall '04. Excerpts. Compiled by Americana Publishing Inc. 1 CD. 2004. audio compact disk (978-1-58943-100-3(6)) Am Pubng Inc.
Americana's audiobook offerings as of Fall, 2004.

Americanism. Gary W. Potter. 1 cass. (Running Time: 1 hr.). 2000. 7.00 (20003) Cath Treas.
With the precision of a seasoned journalist, Potter identifies the nature of the peculiarly U.S. heresy cited by Pope Leo XIII as "Americanism," a serious enough problem 93 years ago to require Papal condemnation & the dismissal of the first rector of Catholic University of America because of his Americanist beliefs. Delivered in California during his 1992 book signing tour, this in-depth talk demonstrates the broad scope of Mr. Potter's research & an analysis of the current crisis in the Church. Encouragingly, he identifies the hope of the future which resides in those who have rejected Americanism & the "American Catholic Church" & tells where to find those groups actively engaged in reversing this heretical trend.

Americanization of Benjamin Franklin. unabr. ed. Gordon S. Wood. Read by Peter Johnson. (Running Time: 10 hrs.). (ENG.). 2004. audio compact disk 34.95 (978-1-56511-886-7(3), 1565118863) Pub: HighBridge. Dist(s): Workman Pub

Americanos. 1 cass. (Running Time: 1 hr. 30 min.). (POR & ENG., 1997. bk. 75.00 (978-2-7005-1023-2(2)) Pub: Assimil FRA. Dist(s): Distribks Inc

Americanos. 1 CD. (Running Time: 1 hr. 30 min.). (ENG & POR.). 2000. bk. 95.00 (978-2-7005-1097-3(6)) Pub: Assimil FRA. Dist(s): Distribks Inc

Americanos. Brigitte Balster et al. 3 cass. (Running Time: 4 hrs. 30 min.). (SPA.). 2000. pap. bk. 75.00 (978-2-7005-1334-9(7)) Pub: Assimil FRA. Dist(s): Distribks Inc

Americans. abr. ed. John Jakes. Read by Bruce Watson. 4 cass. (Running Time: 6 hrs.). (Kent Family Chronicles: No. 8). 2000. 12.99 (978-1-57815-167-7(8), 4416, Media Bks Audio) Media Bks NJ.

Americans, Pt. 1. unabr. collector's ed. John Jakes. Read by Michael Kramer. 9 cass. (Running Time: 13 hrs. 30 mins.). (Kent Family Chronicles: No. 8). 1993. 72.00 (978-0-7366-2506-7(2), 3263A) Books on Tape.
The Kent family reignites its American dream in the face of immigrant hordes.

Americans, Pt. 2. unabr. collector's ed. John Jakes. Read by Michael Kramer. 9 cass. (Running Time: 13 hrs. 30 mins.). (Kent Family Chronicles: No. 8). 1993. 72.00 (978-0-7366-2507-4(0), 3263-B) Books on Tape.
The Kent family reignites its American dream in the face of immigrant hordes.

Americans: Chapter Summary. (ENG & SPA.). (gr. 6-12). 2002. (978-0-395-86991-8(9), 2-80334) Holt McDoug.

Americans: Reading Study Guide. (gr. 6-12). 2005. audio compact disk (978-0-618-42423-8(7), 2-00701); audio compact disk (978-0-618-42424-5(5), 2-00702) Holt McDoug.

Americans: The Colonial Experience. unabr. ed. Daniel J. Boorstin. Read by Michael Prichard. 12 cass. (Running Time: 18 hrs.). 1988. 96.00 (978-0-7366-1280-7(7), 2189) Books on Tape.
A superb panorama of life in America from the first settlements on through the whit-hot days of the Revolution, an amazingly brilliant study of America's past.

Americans: The Democratic Experience. unabr. ed. Daniel J. Boorstin. Read by Michael Prichard. 10 cass. (Running Time: 15 hrs.). 1988. 80.00 (2225-B) Books on Tape.
"Never had a Promised Land looked more unpromising. But within a century & a half - even before the American Revolution - this forbidding scene had become one of the more 'civil' parts of the world. The large outlines of a new nation had been drawn. How did it happen?".

Americans: The National Experience. unabr. ed. Daniel J. Boorstin. Read by Michael Prichard. 8 cass. (Running Time: 12 hrs.). 1999. 128.00 (978-0-7366-1342-2(0)) Books on Tape.
Second in Trilogy. From the American Revolution to the Civil War.

Americans Pt. 1: The Democratic Experience. unabr. ed. Daniel J. Boorstin. Read by Michael Prichard. 11 cass. (Running Time: 16 hrs. 30 mins.). 1988. 88.00 (978-0-7366-1320-0(X), 2225-A) Books on Tape.
Third in trilogy. The United States in the century following the Civil War.

Americans Pt. 2: The National Experience. unabr. ed. Daniel J. Boorstin. Read by Michael Prichard. 8 cass. (Running Time: 12 hrs.). 1988. 64.00 (2245-B) Books on Tape.
The second volume in The Americans trilogy follows the frontier that stretched to the west. Within less than a century, the fringe of colonial settlements became a continental nation.

Americans Pt. 3: The Democratic Experience. unabr. ed. Read by Michael Prichard. 2 pts. on 21 cass. (Running Time: 31 hrs. 30 mins.). 168.00 (2225-A/B) Books on Tape.
The third volume in The Americans trilogy & winner of the Pulitzer Prize, this is an exploration of the United States in the century following the Civil War. Examines the revolutions in economy, technology & social rearrangements.

Americans & the California Dream, 1850-1915, Pt. 1. collector's ed. Kevin Starr. Read by Lloyd James. 9 cass. (Running Time: 13 hrs. 30 mins.). 1999. 72.00 (978-0-7366-4878-3(X), 5102-A) Books on Tape.
The emergence of California as a regional civilization in the late nineteenth century was far more than a dramatic & colorful chapter in American history.

Americans & the California Dream, 1850-1915, Pt. 2. collector's ed. Kevin Starr. Read by Lloyd James. 8 cass. (Running Time: 12 hrs.). 1999. 64.00 (978-0-7366-4879-0(8), 5102-B) Books on Tape.

Americans at War. Stephen E. Ambrose. Read by Barrett Whitener. 1999. audio compact disk 72.00 (978-0-7366-6169-0(7)) Books on Tape.

Americans at War. unabr. ed. Stephen E. Ambrose. Read by Barrett Whitener. 8 cass. (Running Time: 12 hrs.). 1999. 64.00 (978-0-7366-4555-3(1)) Books on Tape.
America's foremost historian depicts the personalities of American military and political leaders during war.

Americans at War. unabr. collector's ed. Stephen E. Ambrose. Read by Barrett Whitener. 9 CDs. (Running Time: 13 hrs. 30 mins.). 2001. audio compact disk 72.00 Books on Tape.

***Americans in Paris: Life & Death under Nazi Occupation.** unabr. ed. Charles Glass. (Running Time: 19 hrs.). 2010. 44.95 (978-1-4417-6628-1(6)); 99.95 (978-1-4417-6625-0(1)); audio compact disk 123.00 (978-1-4417-6626-7(X)); audio compact disk 34.95 (978-1-4417-6627-4(8)) Blckstn Audio.

Americans on Everest, Pt. 1 unabr. collector's ed. James R. Ullman. Read by Larry McKeever. 7 cass. (Running Time: 10 hrs. 30 mins.). 1989. 56.00 (978-0-7366-1472-6(9), 2351A) Books on Tape.
For the first time, in 1963, an American mountain-climbing expedition reached the top of the world's highest peak. They did it after weeks of exposure to the thin & bitterly cold air of Everest . . . & after one of their group was killed by a falling ice wall. Success first came on May 1, when two men gained the summit via the South Col route. This was followed three weeks later with four more men making the peak - two via the West Ridge, which had never before been negotiated.

Americans on Everest, Pt. 2. collector's ed. James R. Ullman. Read by Larry McKeever. 6 cass. (Running Time: 9 hrs.). 1989. 48.00 (978-0-7366-1473-3(7)) Books on Tape.
Story of the first American expedition (1963) to make a successful ascent of Everest.

Americans: Reconstruction Through the 20th Century: Chapter Summary. (ENG & SPA.). (gr. 6-12). 2002. (978-0-395-89100-1(0), 2-80385) Holt McDoug.

Americans: Reconstruction to the 21st Century: Reading Study Guide. (Americans Ser.). (gr. 6-12). 2005. audio compact disk (978-0-618-42598-3(5), 2-00703); audio compact disk (978-0-618-42599-0(3), 2-00704) Holt McDoug.

American's Tale see Tales of the Supernatural

Americans with Disabilities Act. 3 cass. (Running Time: 3 hrs. 30 mins.). 1992. pap. bk. & stu. ed. 150.00 (M938); pap. bk. & stu. ed. 60.00 (U217) Am Law Inst.
Highlights the dramatic changes embodied in Title I, the employment law provisions, which became law for employers with 25 or more employees on July 26, 1992 & for employers with 15 or more employees on July 26, 1994.

Americans with Disabilities Act (ADA) Covers Children Who Are Blind & Visually Impaired Too! unabr. ed. 1 cass. (Running Time: 1 hr. 30 mins.). 14.95 (978-0-89128-235-8(1)) Am Foun Blind.
A plain language, conversational overview of the Americans with Disabilities Act as it relates to services for children who are blind or visually impaired.

Americans with Disabilities Act of Nineteen Ninety: Employment & Access Issues in Private Industry. 1990. 45.00 (AC-599) PA Bar Inst.

America's Black Spartacus Remembered: The Confession of Nat Turner. abr. ed. Perf. by Bernard Addison & Michael Collins. Music by Odetta. 1 cass. (Running Time: 1 hrs. 30 mins.). 1999. 16.95 (978-0-9645593-2-5(3)) MasterBuy Audio Bks.
Provides context for the "confession" of Turner, a slave who led a bloody revolt in South Hampton County, VA., in 1831. On August 21, 1831, Nat Turner led a small band of slaves on a rebellion of terror & devastation near the small village of Jerusalem, Virginia. When the carnage was complete, men, women & even children lay dead, both black & white. As Nat waits his turn with the hangman's noose, he is questioned. These are his answers. Was he a deluded fanatic or just his firm determination to be free?.

America's Disappearing Wetlands. 1 cass. (Running Time: 50 mins.). 10.95 (ME-87-09-07, HarperThor) HarpC GBR.

America's Fallen Forts - the Alamo & Fort Phil Kearney. Jimmy Gray. Read by Donnie Blanz et al. (Running Time: 3 hrs. 30 mins.). 2005. 22.95 (978-1-60083-566-7(X), Audiofy Corp) Iofy Corp.

America's Favorite Pastime: The History of Baseball. unabr. ed. Steven Womack. Read by Ron Jordan. (YA). 2008. 54.99 (978-1-60252-945-8(0)) Find a World.

America's First Dynasty: The Adamses, 1735-1918. unabr. ed. Richard Brookhiser. Read by Dan Cashman. 7 cass. (Running Time: 10 hrs. 30 mins.). 2002. 56.00 (978-0-7366-8554-2(5)) Books on Tape.
the story of America's longest and still-greatest dynasty - the Adamses, the only family in our history to play a leading role in American affairs for nearly two centuries. John Adams was only the first of the Adamses to occupy the highest office in the land; his son, John Quincy Adams, ascended to the presidency as an equal champion of liberty. Following in this great legacy were writers Charles Francis Adams and Henry Adams, the latter of whom proved as able to write on art history as on affairs of state and government; Henry Adams won a Pulitzer Prize for his work.

America's Foundation of Faith: A Collection of Quotations from the Founding Fathers & Other Great Americans. Focus Press Inc. Staff. 2009. audio compact disk 1.00 (978-0-9796356-4-9(0)) Focus Pr.

America's Freedom Founded on Faith. Instructed by Stephen McDowell. 2000. 5.95 (978-1-887456-31-9(7)) Providence Found.

America's Future - An Interview with Ayn Rand. Ayn Rand. 1 cass. (Running Time: 30 mins.). 1997. 14.95 (978-1-56114-330-6(8), AR60C) Second Renaissance.
The outlook for freedom in America.

America's Game: Baseball. Richard Kostelanetz. 1 cass. 1999. pap. bk. 150.00 Archae Edns.
A critical description of a classic electro-acousticcomposition, on audio-only VHS, of & about the sound of baseball as a reflection of the Americas.

America's Godly Heritage. unabr. ed. David Barton. Read by David Barton. 1 cass. (Running Time: 1 hr.). 1995. 4.95 (978-0-925279-48-4(X), A01) Wallbuilders.
This captivating presentation sets forth the beliefs of many of the famous Founding Fathers concerning the proper role of Christian principles in education, government & public affairs of the nation.

America's Godly Heritage, Pt. 2. unabr. ed. 1996. 4.95 (978-0-925279-51-4(X)) Wallbuilders.
Adds additional founding fathers & quotes as well as current court decisions to the original best seller "America's Godly Heritage" concerning the proper role of Christian principles in education, government & public affairs of America.

America's Great Depression. unabr. ed. Murray N. Rothbard. Read by Brian Emerson. (Running Time: 12 hrs. 50 mins.). 2008. 72.95 (978-1-4332-1933-7(6)); 29.95 (978-1-4332-1937-5(9)); cass. & audio compact disk 90.00 (978-1-4332-1934-4(4)) Blckstn Audio.

America's Greatest Need: Micah 3:1-12. Ed Young. (J). 1981. 4.95 (978-0-7417-1186-1(9), A0186) Win Walk.

America's Heart: 11 Chronicles 7:14. Ed Young. 1982. 4.95 (978-0-7417-1264-6(4), 264) Win Walk.

***America's Hidden History: Untold Tales of the First Pilgrims, Fighting Women & Forgotten Founders Who Shaped a Nation.** unabr. ed. Kenneth C. Davis. (ENG.). 2010. audio compact disk 14.99 (978-0-307-75135-5(X), Random AudioBks) Pub: Random Audio Pubg. Dist(s): Random

Americas in the Revolutionary Era, Vol. I-II. Instructed by Marshall Eakin. 12 cass. (Running Time: 12 hrs.). bk. 54.95 (978-1-56585-870-1(0), 8617) Teaching Co.

Americas in the Revolutionary Era, Vol. I-II. Instructed by Marshall Eakin. 12 CDs. (Running Time: 12 hrs.). 2004. bk. 69.95 (978-1-56585-872-5(7), 8617) Teaching Co.

America's March to Socialism: Why We're One Step Closer to Giant Missile Parades. adpt. unabr. ed. Glenn Beck. Read by Glenn Beck. 1 CD. (Running Time: 1 hr. 30 mins. 0 sec.). (ENG.). 2009. audio compact disk 14.99 (978-0-7435-9854-5(7)) Pub: S&S Audio. Dist(s): S and S Inc

America's Musical Landscape. 2nd ed. Jean Ferris. (C). 1993. pap. bk. 39.87 (978-0-697-16946-4(4)); (978-0-697-12518-7(1)) Brown & Benchmark.

America's New Witch Hunt: Examining the Myths & Hysteria Around Sexual Abuse of Children. Foster W. Cline. Read by Foster W. Cline. Read by Bert Gurule Mizke. 2 cass. (Running Time: 1 hr. 56 mins.). 1994. 16.95 (978-0-944634-11-0(7)) Love Logic.
In recent years Americans have become increasingly aware of the problem of childhood sexual abuse. Along with this awareness has come an accompanying hysteria, making it difficult to separate fact from fiction. Internationally-renowned child & adult psychiatrist, Foster W. Cline, M.D., addresses one of today's most disturbing topics & debunks many of the myths spawned by fear & misinformation & often perpetuated by media hype, misguided therapists & those caught in a victim mentality.

America's Newest Praise & Worship Favorites. Prod. by Dave Williamson. Arranged by Dave Williamson. 1 CD. 1999. audio compact disk (978-0-7601-3029-2(9)) Brentwood Music.
These choruses, performed by a contemporary worship choir & praise band, reflect the fresh, new spirit & style of worship sweeping through today's church.

America's Newest Praise & Worship Favorites, Vol. 2. Prod. by Dave Williamson. Arranged by Dave Williamson. 1 CD. (Running Time: 56 mins.). 1999. audio compact disk (978-0-7601-2889-3(8)); (978-0-7601-2890-9(1)); (978-0-7601-3030-8(2)) Brentwood Music.

America's Occult Holidays. Ed. by Alan H. Peterson. As told by Doc Marquis. (American Focus on Satanic Crime Ser.: Vol. 22). 2000. 39.95 (978-1-877858-70-3(6)) Amer Focus Pub.

America's Past & Promise: Chapter Summary. (ENG & SPA.). (gr. 6-12). 1998. (978-0-395-89070-7(5), 2-16762) Holt McDoug.

America's Past Collection. Thomas Paine et al. Read by George Vafiadis & Grover Gardner. (Running Time: 15 hrs.). 2006. 54.60 (978-1-60083-351-9(9), Audiofy Corp) Iofy Corp.

America's Persecuted Minority: Big Business. Ayn Rand. Read by Ayn Rand. 1 cass. (Running Time: 60 min.). 12.95 (978-1-56114-073-2(2), AR13C) Second Renaissance.
This talk focuses on the injustice of the anti-trust laws & the manner in which they penalize success for being success. It is a powerful demonstration of the fact that the result - & the goal - of antitrust law is to sacrifice talented ability to envious mediocrity.

America's Persecuted Minority: Big Business. Comment by Ayn Rand. 1 cass. (Running Time: 60 mins.). (Ford Hall Forum Ser.). 1961. 12.95 (AR13C) Second Renaissance.
Injustice of the antitrust laws & the manner in which they penalize success for being success.

America's Persecuted Minority: Big Business - Q & A. Ayn Rand. 1 cass. (Running Time: 35 mins.). 1993. 12.95 (978-1-56114-287-3(5), AR46C) Second Renaissance.

***America's Prophet.** unabr. ed. Bruce Feiler. Read by Bruce Feiler. (ENG.). 2009. (978-0-06-196697-2(5), Harper Audio); (978-0-06-196696-5(7), Harper Audio) HarperCollins Pubs.

America's Prophet: Moses & the American Story. unabr. ed. Bruce S. Feiler. Read by Bruce S. Feiler. 2009. audio compact disk 39.99 (978-0-06-171260-9(4), Harper Audio) HarperCollins Pubs.

America's Public Experience in Presidential Elections. Read by Frank Bennack. 1 cass. (Running Time: 60 mins.). (National Press Club Ser.). 10.95 (NP-88-01-20, HarperThor) HarpC GBR.

America's Queen: A Life of Jacqueline Kennedy Onassis. abr. ed. Sarah Bradford. Read by Sandra Burr. 8 CDs. (Running Time: 9 hrs.). 2000. audio compact disk 37.95 (978-1-58788-145-9(4), 1587881454, CD); 29.95 (978-1-58788-144-2(6), 1587881446, Nova Audio Bks) Brilliance Audio.
Jacqueline Kennedy Onassis has captivated the American public for more than five decades. From her introduction to the world as "debutante of the year" in 1947 to her untimely death in 1994, she has truly remained America's answer to royalty. In America's Queen, the acclaimed biographer of Queen Elizabeth and Princess Grace reveals the real Jackie in a sympathetic but frank portrait of an amazing woman who has dazzled us for years. Using remarkable new sources - including in-depth interviews with Jackie's sister, Lee Radziwell - Sarah Bradford has written a timely celebration of a life that was more private than commonly supposed. Jackie's privileged upbringing instilled rigid self-control while her expedient marriage into the overwhelming Kennedy clan consolidated her determination. Revealing new testimony from many of the couple's friends shows the profound complexities both of this apparently very public relationship and of her controversial marriage to Aristotle Onassis. Here is the private Jackie - neglected wife, vigilant mother, and working widow - whose contradictory and fascinating nature is illuminated by all that Bradford has discovered.

America's Queen: A Life of Jacqueline Kennedy Onassis. abr. ed. Sarah Bradford. Read by Sarah Bradford. Read by Sandra Burr. 8 CDs. (Running Time: 9 hrs.). 2000. audio compact disk 89.25 (978-1-58788-182-4(9), 1587881829, Unabridge Lib Edns) Brilliance Audio.

America's Queen: The Life of Jacqueline Kennedy Onassis. abr. ed. Sarah Bradford. Read by Sandra Burr. (Running Time: 9 hrs.). 2008. 39.25 (978-1-4233-4004-1(3), 9781423340041, BADLE); 39.25 (978-1-4233-4002-7(7), 9781423340027, Brinc Audio MP3 Lib); 24.95 (978-1-4233-4003-4(5), 9781423340034, BAD); 24.95 (978-1-4233-4001-0(9), 9781423340010, Brilliance MP3) Brilliance Audio.

America's Secret Nuclear Policy. Comment by Daniel Ellsberg. (Running Time: 56 mins.). 1987. Original Face.
Addresses the hidden objectives that underlie America's ongoing quest for nuclear superiority & preemptive first-strike capability.

America's Secret War: Inside the Hidden Worldwide Struggle between America & Its Enemies. George Friedman. Read by Brian Emerson. (Running Time: 13 hrs. 30 mins.). 2004. 41.95 (978-1-59912-408-7(4)) Iofy Corp.

America's Secret War: Inside the Hidden Worldwide Struggle between the United States & Its Enemies. George Friedman. Read by Brian Emerson. 9 cass. (Running Time: 13 hrs.). 2004. 72.95 (978-0-7861-2894-5(1), 3390); audio compact disk 90.00 (978-0-7861-8282-4(2), 3390) Blckstn Audio.

America's Secret War: Inside the Hidden Worldwide Struggle Between the United States & Its Enemies. unabr. ed. George Friedman. Read by Brian Emerson. 20 cass. (Running Time: 13 hrs.). 2005. reel tape 29.95 (978-0-7861-2893-8(3), E3390); audio compact disk 29.95 (978-0-7861-8283-1(0), ZE3390); audio compact disk 29.95 (978-0-7861-8322-7(5), 3390) Blckstn Audio.

America's Tallest Tales. Scripts. 1 cass. or 1 CD. (Running Time: 35 mins.). (J). (gr. 3-7). 2000. pap. bk. & tchr. ed. 29.95 Bad Wolf Pr.
Babe's disappearance is a big mystery - now Paul Bunyan, with the help of Bess Call, the strong-armed, cattle-friendly heroine of the Adirondacks, is crisscrossing America in search of his missing companion. Has Pecos Bill rustled the big ox? Did Annie Christmas, Queen of the Mississippi keelboaters, borrow him to pull her boat up the river? In the course of their adventures Paul & Bess run into John Henry, Alfred Bulltop Stormalong & a host of other stars. Sheet music available.

America's Twenty-Five Favorite Hymns, Vol. 4. Prod. by Don Marsh. 1997. 10.98 Split. (978-0-7601-1501-5(X), C50052); 10.98 Stereo. (978-0-7601-1493-3(5), C50048); audio compact disk 15.98 CD Split. (978-0-7601-1502-2(8), CD50052); audio compact disk 15.98 CD Stereo. (978-0-7601-1494-0(3), CD50048) Pub: Brentwood Music. Dist(s): Provident Mus Dist
Timeless hymns of faith filled with a message of hope & peace that have inspired the hearts of believers for generations. Rich treasury of songs, a collection of twenty-five ageless melodies that will lift your eyes toward heaven.

Americas Twenty-Five Praise & Worship: For Kids. 1 CD. 1999. audio compact disk 13.99 (978-0-7601-2203-7(2)) Provident Music.

Americas Twenty-Five Praise & Worship Kids Two. 1 cass. 1999. 8.99 (978-0-7601-2202-0(4)); audio compact disk 16.98 (978-0-7601-2866-4(9)) Provident Music.

Americas Twenty-Five Praise & Worship Kids Two. 1 cass. (J). 1999. 10.98 (978-0-7601-2867-1(7)) Provident Music.

America's Victory. unabr. ed. David W. Shaw. Read by Patrick Cullen. 7 CDs. (Running Time: 9 hrs.). 2004. audio compact disk 56.00 (978-0-7861-8892-5(8), 3211); 44.95 (978-0-7861-2621-7(3), 3211) Blckstn Audio.
This is an account of the America¿s Cup, but it is also the story of a victory and the American spirit that bravely lives on today.

America's Wars-CD. 1997. 28.00 (978-1-59128-293-8(4)) Canon Pr ID.

America's Wars-tape. 8 cass. 1997. 28.00 (978-1-59128-295-2(0)) Canon Pr ID.

America's Women: Four Hundred Years of Dolls, Drudges, Helpmates, & Heroines. abr. ed. Gail Collins. Read by Jane Alexander. 2003. audio compact disk 29.95 (978-0-06-057256-3(6)) HarperCollins Pubs.

***America's Women: Four Hundred Years of Dolls, Drudges, Helpmates, & Heroines.** abr. ed. Gail Collins. Read by Jane Alexander. (ENG.). 2004. (978-0-06-079970-0(6), Harper Audio); (978-0-06-074636-0(X), Harper Audio) HarperCollins Pubs.

America's #1 College Research Tool For Parents. Gary A. Eberlin. 1 CD. (Running Time: 1 hr. 30 mins.). (YA). (gr. 11-12). 2002. 24.99 (978-0-9723208-0-1(6), 07/2002) Eberlin & Assocs.
Contains current information over 3200 4-year and 2-year college's and universities in America. Information includes tuition and fees, financial aid, links to campus tours and videos, over 1700 college, university and research libraries, admissions offices and college test preparation sites for ACT/SAT, scholarship resources, e-learning colleges as well as a step-by-step guide for parents to follow through the entire college selection/enrollment process in each of the junior and senior high school years.

Amerigo. unabr. ed. Felipe Fernández-Armesto. (Running Time: 9 hrs. 30 mins. 0 sec.). (ENG.). 2007. audio compact disk 34.99 (978-1-4001-0433-8(5)) Pub: Tantor Media. Dist(s): IngramPubServ

Amerigo: The Man Who Gave His Name to America. unabr. ed. Felipe Fernández-Armesto. Narrated by Michael Prichard. (Running Time: 9 hrs. 30 mins. 0 sec.). (ENG.). 2007. audio compact disk 24.99 (978-1-4001-5433-3(2)); audio compact disk 69.99 (978-1-4001-3433-5(1)) Pub: Tantor Media. Dist(s): IngramPubServ

Amerika: the Missing Person: A New Translation by Mark Harman Based on the Restored Text. unabr. ed. Franz Kafka. Read by George Guidall. (Running Time: 9 hrs. 30 mins.). (ENG.). 2009. 34.98 (978-1-59659-362-6(8), GildAudio) Pub: Gildan Media. Dist(s): HachBkGrp

Amerikaner. 1 cass. (Running Time: 1 hr. 30 min.). (ENG & GER.). 2000. bk. 75.00 (978-2-7005-1049-2(6)) Pub: Assimil FRA. Dist(s): Distribks Inc

Amerikids. Kathie Hill. 1996. 75.00 (978-0-7673-0816-8(6)); audio compact disk 85.00 (978-0-7673-0817-5(4)) LifeWay Christian.

Ames du Purgatoire. Prosper Merimee. Read by Marine Mouton. 2 cass. (FRE.). 1995. 26.95 (1760-KFP) Olivia & Hill.
The 19th-century author tells his version of Don Juan's dissolute life of vice & conquests.

Amethyst Dreams. unabr. ed. Phyllis A. Whitney. Read by Anna Fields. 6 cass. (Running Time: 8 hrs. 30 mins.). 1997. 44.95 (978-0-7861-1170-1(4), 1954) Blckstn Audio.
For several years, time & circumstance have managed to separate Hallie Knight & her old friend Susan Trench, but when Susan disappears from her grandfather's seaside home, it is Hallie whom Nicholas Trench calls for help. When she arrives from California, she finds the old man surrounded by an odd collection of friends & relatives, all of whom seem to know a little more than they're willing to tell.

Amethyst Dreams. unabr. ed. Phyllis A. Whitney. Read by Anna Fields. (Running Time: 7 hrs. 30 mins.). 2010. 29.95 (978-1-4417-2612-4(8)); audio compact disk 69.00 (978-1-4417-2609-4(8)) Blckstn Audio.

Amethyst Dreams. unabr. ed. Phyllis A. Whitney. Read by Susan Ericksen. (Running Time: 7 hrs.). 2009. 24.99 (978-1-4418-1857-7(X), 9781441818577, Brilliance MP3); 39.97 (978-1-4418-1860-7(X), 9781441818607, BADLE); 24.99 (978-1-4418-1859-1(6), 9781441818591, BAD); 39.97 (978-1-4418-1858-4(8), 9781441818584, Brinc Audio MP3 Lib) Brilliance Audio.

Amethyst Heart. unabr. ed. Penelope J. Stokes. Narrated by Sally Darling. 10 cass. (Running Time: 14 hrs. 15 mins.). 2000. 93.00 (978-0-7887-4840-0(8), K0002E7) Recorded Bks.
A weave of the past & present into an unforgettable story of one Mississippi family's joy, sorrow & hope. On Amethyst's 93rd birthday, her son announces plans to put her in a retirement facility & sell the family home. Will Amethyst be able to hang onto her home with its rich legacy of stories.

Amethyst Remembrance. Mary M. Slappey. Read by Mary M. Slappey. 1 cass. (Running Time: 30 mins.). 10.00 Interspace Bks.
One act play about the New England Poet Emily Dickinson, her poetry, her loves, her life.

Amethysts & Arson, Set. Lynn Gardner. 2 cass. 19.95 (978-1-57734-509-1(6), 07002130) Covenant Comms.

Amharic. unabr. ed. Foreign Service Institute Staff. 26 cass. (Running Time: 27 hrs.). (AMH & ENG.). (J). (gr. 10-12). pap. bk. 295.00 (978-0-88432-154-5(1), AFAM10) J Norton Pubs.
The official language of Ethiopia, spoken by about 7 million people in a small but populous area of the country which includes the capital, Addis Ababa.

Amharic Basic Course, Level 1 and 2. Sergie Obolensky et al. (Multilingual Books Intensive Cassette Foreign Language Ser.). 1964. spiral bd. 350.00 (978-1-58214-156-5(8)) Language Assocs.

Amharic Basic Course CDs & Text. 21 CDs. (Running Time: 27 hrs.). (Foreign Service Institute Basic Course Ser.). (AMH.). 2005. audio compact disk 295.00 (978-1-57970-161-1(2), AFAM10D) J Norton Pubs.

Amharic Newspaper Reader. Mulugeta Kebede. 1984. 29.00 (978-0-931745-11-9(X)) Dunwoody Pr.

Amharic Newspaper Reader. Mulugeta Kebede & John D. Murphy. 4 cass. (Running Time: 1 hr. 30 mins. per cass.). (AMH.). 1984. 29.00 (3066) Dunwoody Pr.
Fifty selections assist the intermediate student in bridging the gap between the exercises of the standard elementary textbooks & the natural language of newspapers.

Amigo. unabr. ed. Byrd Baylor. Read by Byrd Baylor. 1 cass. (Running Time: 17 mins.). (Byrd Baylor: Storyteller Ser.). (J). (gr. k-6). 1990. 5.95 (978-0-929937-18-2(X)) SW Series.
Amigo is about two young friends: Francisco who wants a pet & Amigo, a puppy prairie dog who wants a pet too!.

Amigo, Vol.1, Bk.1, Cds1-6. (ENG & SPA., 1984. pap. bk. 69.95 (978-0-9647863-3-2(8)) Audio Vis Lang.

Amigo Fritz. abr. ed. Emile Erckmann & Alexandre Chatrian. Read by Yadira Sánchez. 3 CDs.Tr. of My Friend Fritz. (SPA.). 2002. audio compact disk 17.00 (978-958-8161-05-1(3)) YoYoMusic.

***Amigo I: Pronounce in Spanish Reading in English, vol 1and 3 cds.** (SPA & ENG.). 1995. pap. bk. 59.95 (978-0-9647863-9-4(7)) Audio Vis Lang.

***Amigo MP3 I.** 2009. 99.00 (978-0-9647863-2-5(X)) Audio Vis Lang.

***Amigo MP3 II.** 2009. 99.00 (978-0-9826663-0-2(6)) Audio Vis Lang.

***Amigo MP3 III.** 2009. 149.00 (978-0-9826663-1-9(4)) Audio Vis Lang.

Amigos. Alma Flor Ada. Illus. by Viví Escrivá. (Libros Para Contar Ser.).Tr. of Friends. (SPA.). (J). (gr. k-3). 4.95 (978-1-58105-257-2(X)) Santillana.

Amigos! Canciones para Ninos... Escritas por Ninos. unabr. ed. Peter Vaque et al. Perf. by Cenzontles, los. 1 cass. (Running Time: 30 mins.). (SPA.). (J). (ps-9). 1995. 9.95 (978-0-9632276-7-6(X)); audio compact disk 14.95 CD. (978-0-9632276-6-9(1)) Natl Self Esteem.
Amigos! Songs for Kids - by Kids: Spanish version of B.E.S.T. Friends. Ten hot songs from Latin, ballad, best, fusion, New Orleans swing & bolero to Caribbean, Puerto Rican & rock all about friendship, cooperation, self-esteem, non-violence, peer pressure; drug & street gang prevention; taking care of ourselves, others & the earth. Believe in yourself, empower yourself, stand up for yourself, trust yourself - B.E.S.T. by the Esteem Team, NSERDC's nationally acclaimed flagship program. Other performers are: Peter Josneff, Jaime Rosales, David Rotarius, Martha Negrete, Shota Osabe, Lindsey Ferguson, Keith Crossan, Tom Corwin, Jack Jewel & Carlos Barreda.

Amigos de la Granja. (Cuenta y Canta una Historia Ser.). 18.95 (978-88-536-0224-4(4)) EMC-Paradigm.

Amigos Fiasco see Tales of the Supernatural

Amigos Fiasco. 1981. (S-9) Jimcin Record.

Amigos y canciones para Siempre. (SPA.). 2009. audio compact disk 14.99 (978-0-8297-6138-2(1)) Pub: Vida Pubs. Dist(s): Zondervan

Amiri Baraka. Poems. Amiri Baraka, pseud. Read by Amiri Baraka, pseud. 1 cass. (Running Time: 29 mins.). 1988. 10.00 (021288) New Letters.
Poet reads from his book of poems about jazz & talks about his life.

Amish Christmas. unabr. ed. Richard Ammon. Narrated by Johnny Heller. 1 cass. (Running Time: 45 mins.). (gr. 3 up). 1997. 10.00 (978-0-7887-0723-0(X), 94900E7) Recorded Bks.
Share the simple yet special joys of the Amish in a gentle story of one family's holiday season.

***Amish Christmas: A Novel.** unabr. ed. Cynthia Keller. Read by Cassandra Campbell. (ENG.). 2010. audio compact disk 25.00 (978-0-307-75105-8(8), Random AudioBks) Pub: Random Audio Pubg. Dist(s): Random

***Amish Country Crossroads.** abr. ed. Beverly Lewis. Narrated by Aimee Lilly. (Running Time: 9 hrs. 0 mins. 0 sec.). (Amish Country Crossroads Ser.). (ENG.). 2010. audio compact disk 24.98 (978-1-59644-922-0(5), christaudio) christianaud.

Amish Gathering: Life in Lancaster County. unabr. ed. Beth Wiseman. 2010. audio compact disk 29.99 (978-1-4003-1621-2(9)) Nelson.

Amish Grace: How Forgiveness Transcended a Tragedy. unabr. ed. Donald B. Kraybill et al. Read by Paul Michael Garcia. (Running Time: 25200 sec.). 2008. 44.95 (978-1-4332-4462-9(4)); audio compact disk 29.95 (978-1-4332-4466-7(7)); audio compact disk & audio compact disk 60.00 (978-1-4332-4463-6(2)) Blckstn Audio.

Amish Peace: Simple Wisdom for a Complicated World. unabr. ed. Suzanne Woods Fisher. Narrated by Christian Taylor. (Running Time: 4 hrs. 48 mins. 51 sec.). (ENG.). 2009. 13.99 (978-1-60814-601-7(4)); audio compact disk 19.99 (978-1-59859-649-6(7)) Oasis Audio.

***Amish Prayers.** unabr. ed. Compiled by Beverly Lewis. (ENG.). 2010. 9.98 (978-1-61045-028-7(0)) christianaud.

***Amish Prayers.** unabr. ed. Compiled by Beverly Lewis. (Running Time: 2 hrs. 0 mins. 0 sec.). (ENG.). 2011. audio compact disk 14.98 (978-1-61045-029-4(9)) christianaud.

Amish Wedding. unabr. ed. Richard Ammon. Narrated by Christina Moore. 1 cass. (Running Time: 15 mins.). (J). 2001. pap. bk. & stu. ed. 34.00 Recorded Bks.
The author has many Amish friends who helped with the accuracy of the clothing & customs that go along with an Amish wedding.

Amish Wedding. unabr. ed. Richard Ammon. Narrated by Christina Moore. 1 cass. (Running Time: 15 mins.). (gr. 3 up). 2001. 10.00 (978-0-7887-4709-0(6), 96263E7) Recorded Bks.

Amish Year. Richard Ammon. Read by Johnny Heller. 1 cass. (Running Time: 15 mins.). (J). 1999. pap. bk. & stu. ed. 34.95 (978-0-7887-4325-2(2), 41120) Recorded Bks.
For the Amish, each season is filled with hard work. But there is always time for friendship, too. Let young Anna guide you through a year on her family's farm.

Amish Year. unabr. ed. Richard Ammon. Narrated by Johnny Heller & Christian Moore. 1 cass. (Running Time: 15 mins.). (gr. 3 up). 2000. 11.00 (978-0-7887-4231-6(0), 96207E7) Recorded Bks.

Amish Year, Class set. Richard Ammon. Read by Johnny Heller. 1 cass. (Running Time: 15 mins.). (YA). 1999. 188.80 (978-0-7887-4426-6(7), 47117) Recorded Bks.

Amistad. abr. ed. David Pesci. Read by Courtney B. Vance. 4 cass. (Running Time: 6 hrs.). 1997. 24.95 (978-1-57511-041-7(5)) Pub Mills.
Historically accurate retelling of the takeover of slave ship "Amistad" & subsequent trial.

Amistad con Dios: Instrumental. Claudio Freidzon. Contrib. by Claudio Freidzon. Prod. by Gustavo J. Castillo. (SPA.). 2007. audio compact disk 10.99 (978-0-8297-5319-6(2)) Pub: Vida Pubs. Dist(s): Zondervan

Amitabha Buddha's Name. audio compact disk 10.00 (978-0-88139-729-1(6)) Buddhist Text.

Amitabha Recitation. audio compact disk 10.00 (978-0-88139-727-7(X)) Buddhist Text.

Amitok: Legend of the North. unabr. ed. Paul Sullivan. Read by Ric Benson. 4 cass. (Running Time: 4 hrs. 42 min.). (Legends of the North Ser.). 2001. 26.95 (978-1-58116-080-2(1)) Books in Motion.
Wolf pup Amitok fights to survive, and eventually to assert his dominance.

Amityville Horror. unabr. ed. Jay Anson. Read by Ray Porter. (Running Time: 8 hrs. 30 mins.). 2010. 29.95 (978-1-4417-2716-9(7)); 59.95 (978-1-4417-2712-1(4)); audio compact disk 76.00 (978-1-4417-2713-8(2)) Blckstn Audio.

Amityville Horror. unabr. ed. Jay Anson. Read by Ray Porter. (Running Time: 8 hrs. 30 mins.). 2010. audio compact disk 24.95 (978-1-4417-2715-2(9)) Blckstn Audio.

Amjad Ali Khan (Sarod), Vol. 1. Music by Amjad Ali Khan. 1 cass. (Music Today Presents Ser.). 1992. (A92028) Multi-Cultural Bks.

Amjad Ali Khan (Sarod), Vol. 2. Music by Amjad Ali Khan. 1 cass. (Music Today Presents Ser.). 1992. (A92029) Multi-Cultural Bks.

Ammon & Aaron's Excellent Missionary Adventure. Dan Hess. 1 cass. 1998. 9.95 (978-1-57008-427-0(0), Bkcraft Inc) Deseret Bk.

Amnesia: Program from the Award Winning Public Radio Show. Interview. Hosted by Fred Goodwin. Comment by John Hockenberry. 1 CD. (Running Time: 1 hr.r). 2000. audio compact disk 21.95 (978-1-932479-21-8(X), LCM 117) Lichtenstein Creat.
When most of us think of amnesia, we think of soap opera story-lines where a character returns from a long absence with no memory of their old life or as a plot twist in Hollywood films. But amnesia that severe, where someone forgets everything, is very uncommon. Guests include author Jill Robinson; Dr. Neal Cohen, head of the Amnesia Research Laboratory at the Beckman Institute for Advanced Science and Technology; Dr. Brian Richards, who treats amnesia patients at The Baycrest Hospital in Toronto; author Jonathan Lethem, reading from his upcoming book "The Vintage Book of Amnesia;" and Professor Stephen Bertman, author of "Cultural Amnesia: America's Future and the Crisis of Memory." Plus, commentary by John Hockenberry.

Amoeba Hop. Christine Lavin. Illus. by Betsy Franco Feeney. (J). (gr. 2-3). 2003. bk. 19.95 (978-0-9726487-4-5(7)) Puddle Jump.

Among School Children. unabr. ed. Tracy Kidder. Read by Stephen Yankee. (Running Time: 9 hrs.). 2008. 24.95 (978-1-4233-5917-3(8), 9781423359173, BAD); 24.95 (978-1-4233-5915-9(1), 9781423359159, Brilliance MP3); 39.25 (978-1-4233-5918-0(6), 9781423359180, BADLE); 39.25 (978-1-4233-5916-6(X), 9781423359166, Brinc Audio MP3 Lib) Brilliance Audio.

Among School Children. unabr. ed. Tracy Kidder. Narrated by George Guidall. 8 cass. (Running Time: 10 hrs. 45 mins.). (gr. 6). 1999. 70.00 (978-1-55690-015-0(5), 90006E7) Recorded Bks.
Author Kidder spent one year observing a fifth grade class. He presents the problems & leaves the listener to ponder the solutions.

Among the Eagles. G. Clifton Wisler. Read by John Guerassio. 4 cass. (Running Time: 6 hrs.). 1999. 44.95 (69234) Pub: Soundings Ltd GBR. Dist(s): Ulverscroft US

Among the Giant Trees. unabr. ed. 1 cass. (Solitudes Ser.). 9.95 (C11203) J Norton Pubs.
This tape tunes in the sounds & experiences of the natural environment.

Among the Gods. unabr. ed. Lynn Austin. Read by Suzanne Toren. 11 cass. (Running Time: 13 hrs. 30 mins.). (Chronicles of the Kings: Bk. 5). 2007. 92.75 (978-1-4281-2887-3(5)) Recorded Bks.

Among the Hidden. unabr. ed. Margaret Peterson Haddix. Narrated by Jonathan Davis. 3 cass. (Running Time: 4 hrs. 15 mins.). (Shadow Children Ser.: Bk. 1). (YA). 2004. 24.95 (978-1-4025-7617-1(X)) Recorded Bks.
Luke Garner has spent his entire life all 12 years in hiding. The government has outlawed families with more than two children. As the Garners' third child, Luke's very life is in danger. When Luke meets Jen, another shadow child, he begins to question the government's policies.

Among the Mad. unabr. ed. Jacqueline Winspear. Read by Orlagh Cassidy. 8 CDs. (Running Time: 9 hrs. 0 mins. 0 sec.). (Maisie Dobbs Mystery Ser.: Bk. 6). (ENG.). 2009. audio compact disk 39.95 (978-1-4272-0605-3(8)) Pub: Macmill Audio. Dist(s): Macmillan

Among the Porcupines. abr. ed. Carol Matthau. Read by Carol Matthau. 2 cass. (Running Time: 3 hrs.). 1992. 15.95 (978-1-879371-34-7(0), 20240) Pub Mills.
Carol Matthau epitomizes a kind of glamour not known today - a prized original in both New York & Hollywood. In her inimitable voice - sly, unflinching, incisive, hilarious - she tells her stories of: the company she's kept - the husbands she's had - the life she's lived.

Among the Russians: From the Baltic to the Caucasus. unabr. ed. Colin Thubron. Read by Frank Duncan. 8 cass. (Running Time: 11 hrs. 15 mins.). (Isis Ser.). (J). 1989. 69.95 (978-1-85089-706-4(9), 89072) Pub: ISIS Lrg Prnt GBR. Dist(s): Ulverscroft US

Among the Russians: From the Baltic to the Caucasus. unabr. collector's ed. Colin Thubron. Read by David Case. 8 cass. (Running Time: 12 hrs.). 1990. 64.00 (978-0-7366-1672-0(1), 2521) Books on Tape.
A story of the author's 10,000 mile drive between the Baltic & the Caucasus, camping out with his hosts.

Among Thorns. 1 cass. 1999. 10.98; audio compact disk 16.98 Provident Music.

Amor auténtico, amor Constructivo. P. Miguel Carmena. (SPA.). (YA). 2006. audio compact disk 9.95 (978-0-9674222-6-8(4)) Hombre Nuevo.

Amor de Beatriz. (SPA.). 6.95 (978-88-8148-911-4(2)) EMC-Paradigm.

amor en Familia. Lupita Venegas.Tr. of Family Love. (SPA.). 2009. audio compact disk 15.00 (978-1-935405-37-5(3)) Hombre Nuevo.

Amor, Erotismo e Intimidad. Deepak Chopra. 3 cass. (Running Time: 3 hrs.).Tr. of Path of Love. (SPA.). 2002. (978-968-5163-09-5(X)) Taller del Exito.
Describes the seven stages of love, beginning and culminating in ecstasy.

Amor vs Roma: Cathars & the birth of the Inquisition. Hosted by Bob Chelmick. Prod. by Bob Chelmick. 2 CDs. (Running Time: 2 hrs.). 2005. audio compact disk 19.95 (978-0-660-19130-0(X)) Pub: Canadian Broadcasting CAN. Dist(s): Georgetown Term

Amores Que Matan. Rosa Beltrán. 2 cass. (Running Time: 2 hrs.). (SPA.). 19.95 (978-1-4025-8761-0(9)) Recorded Bks.

Amos & Andy. ltd. ed. 5 vols. (Running Time: 5 hrs.). (Limited Edition Chronical Ser.). 2003. bk. 39.95 (978-0-7413-0165-9(2), OTR49510) Pub: Great Am Audio. Dist(s): AudioGO
With 40 million listeners-one third of all Americans-Amos 'n' Andy was the most popular program in the history of broadcasting.

Amos & Andy. ltd. ed. 5 vols. (Running Time: 5 hrs.). (Limited Edition Chronical Ser.). 2002. bk. (978-0-7413-0164-2(4), OTR43510) Radio Spirits.

Amos & Andy, Vol. 1. (Nostalgia Classics Ser.). 24.98 Moonbeam Pubns.
Includes "Andy's New Wife;" "The Maestro;" "Courtroom Catastrophe;" "The Locked Trunk's Secret;" "Matrimonial Mishap;" "Turkey Trouble;" "Man's Best Friend;" "Candy for Caroline;" "Bookends & Babies;" "The Marriage Counselor;" "New Year's Eve, Pt. I & II".

Amos & Andy, Vol. 2. (Nostalgia Classics Ser.). 24.98 Moonbeam Pubns.
Includes "Making Sapphire Proud;" "Orchids & Violets;" "Charles Boyer's Valet;" "Wind Fall;" "Missing Person's Bureau;" "Three Times & You're Out;" "Ruby's Diamond Sunday, Monday or Always;" "Looking for Madam Queen;" "Sign on the Dotted Line;" "Insurance Fraud;" "Hoovering Between Life & Death".

Amos & Andy, Vol. 3. (Nostalgia Classics Ser.). 24.98 Moonbeam Pubns.
Includes "Long Lost Harold;" "Dating Club Disaster;" "The Butler Did It;" "Of Sound Mind & Body;" "The Brother-in-Law;" "The Electric Clock Caper;" "Impersonating an Officer;" "And the Winner is...;" "Andy, the Fugitive;" "Nazi Spy;" "Shirt Tail;" "One Step Ahead of the Law".

Amos & Andy Show, Vol. 1. collector's ed. Perf. by Freeman Gosden & Charles Correll. 6 cass. (Running Time: 5 hrs. 30 mins.). 1998. bk. 24.98 (4221) Radio Spirits.
Comedy favorite with millions of Americans. 11 episodes.

Amos & Andy Show, Vol. 2. collector's ed. Perf. by Freeman Gosden & Charles Correll. 6 cass. (Running Time: 6 hrs.). 1998. bk. 24.98 (4222) Radio Spirits.
12 episodes.

Amos & Andy Show, Vol. 3. collector's ed. 6 cass. (Running Time: 6 hrs.). 1998. bk. 24.98 (4223) Radio Spirits.

Amos Fortune, Free Man. Elizabeth Yates. Read by Ray Childs. (Running Time: 14400 sec.). (YA). (gr. 8-13). 2007. audio compact disk 39.95 (978-0-9761932-7-2(2)) Audio Bkshelf.

Amos Gets Engaged & A Will for John. Perf. by Don Ameche. 1 cass. (Running Time: 60 mins.). Dramatization. (Bickersons Ser.). 1947. 6.00 Once Upon Rad.
Radio broadcasts - humor.

Amos 'n' Andy. 1 cass. (Running Time: 60 mins.). (Old Time Radio Classic Singles Ser.). 4.95 (978-1-57816-086-0(3), AA120) Audio File.
Includes: 1) "The Lovelorn Column" Andy gets in trouble writing an advice column (2/2/45). 2) "The Insulting Valentine" Kingfish tries to find out who sent him a nasty card (2/16/45).

Amos 'n' Andy. 1 cass. (Running Time: 60 min.). Incl. Amos 'N Andy: The Marriage Broker. (CC-5045); Amos 'N Andy: Their Life Story. (CC-5045); 7.95 (CC-5045) Natl Recrd Co.
"Their Life Story", starts with the time they met & goes to the present. "In the Marriage Broker", Sapphire informs the Kingfish that she wants him to find a husband for her widowed 225-pound girlfriend.

Amos n' Andy. 1 cass. (Running Time: 60 mins.). Incl. Amos n' Andy: The Kingfish Gets an Insulting Valentine. (CC-7010); Amos n' Andy: The Lovelorn Column. (CC-7010); 7.95 (CC-7010) Natl Recrd Co.
"In the Lovelorn Column," Andy is writing a lovelorn column under an assumed name & he ends up giving some bad advice. In "The Kingfish Gets An Insulting Valentine," Andy helps Kingfish to find out who sent the valentine.

Amos 'n' Andy. 3 cass. (Running Time: 3 hrs.). (3-Hour Collectors' Editions Ser.). 2002. 9.98 (978-1-57019-572-3(2), 27794) Radio Spirits.

Amos 'N' Andy. 6 CDs. (Running Time: 6 hrs.). 2004. audio compact disk 29.95 (978-1-57816-216-1(5)) Audio File.

Amos 'n' Andy. Perf. by Freeman Gosden & Charles Correll. 6 cass. 24.95 (978-1-57816-035-8(9), 1014AA) Audio File.
A dozen classic comedy broadcasts from one of the most popular shows of the Golden Age of Radio. Complete with commercials for Rinso Detergent. Includes: "The Sure-Fire Investment" (12-8-44); "Mail Order Bride" (12-15-44); "Income Tax Problems" (3-2-45); "More Tax Problems" (3-9-45); "The Antique Desk" (1-12-45); "Andy Gets Adopted" (2-23-45); "Andy Plays Soldier" (2-9-45); "Sapphire's Old Boyfriend" (2-23-45); "Andy Buys a Cabin" (5-18-48); "The Raffle Ticket" (5-25-48); "Fountain Pen Agency" (12-1-44); "The 500 Dollar Reward" (4-4-48).

Amos 'n' Andy. Radio Spirits Staff. Read by Freeman Gosden. 3 CDs. (Running Time: 3 hrs.). (3-Hour Collectors' Editions Ser.). 2005. audio compact disk 9.98 (978-1-57019-573-0(0), 27292) Radio Spirits.

Amos 'n' Andy. unabr. ed. 4 CDs. (Running Time: 6 hrs.). 1998. audio compact disk 26.00 (978-1-928848-12-7(5)) Radio Era.

Amos n' Andy. unabr. ed. 2 cass. (Running Time: 2 hrs.). (Double Pack Ser.). 1990. 9.95 (7101) Great Am Audio.
Four Classic episodes from Radio's most popular show featuring Kingfish, Sapphire & Mama.

Amos 'n' Andy. unabr. ed. Prod. by Freeman Gosden & Charles Correll. 2 cass. (Running Time: 2 hrs.). 10.95 (978-1-57816-039-6(1), AA2401) Audio File.
Four classic comedy radio shows includes: "The Lovelorn Column" (2/2/45); "The Insulting Valentine" (2/16/45); "Their Life Story" (2/24/53); "The Marriage Broker" (1/7/47).

Amos 'n Andy, Vol. 2. collector's ed. Perf. by Freeman Gosden & Charles Correll. 6 cass. (Running Time: 9 hrs.). 1999. bk. 34.98 (4113) Radio Spirits.
18 episodes including The Trial, Trunk Moving Mixup, Andy becomes Refined, Andy's in Love with Eloise Walker, Kingfish and Sapphire Try to Imitate the Happy Harringtons, Andy's Inheritance, Aunt Minerva's Visit, Mistaken Identity, Kingfish Joins the Army and 7 more.

Amos 'n Andy, Vol. 3. collector's ed. Perf. by Freeman Gosden & Charles Correll. 6 cass. (Running Time: 9 hrs.). 1998. bk. 34.98 (4151) Radio Spirits.
18 episodes including Adopting Andy, Kicking Andy Out, Kingfish Runs a Rest Home, Evicted, Old I.O.U. and the Car, Raiding the Piggy Bank, Kingfish's Luggage Stand, Kingfish the Nightclub Spotter, Wedding Invitation Mix-Up, $500 to Break Up Andy and Madame Queen and 8 more.

Amos 'n Andy, Vol. 4. collector's ed. Perf. by Freeman Gosden & Charles Correll. 6 cass. (Running Time: 9 hrs.). 1999. bk. 34.98 (4179) Radio Spirits.
18 classic episodes.

Amos 'n Andy, Vol. 5. collector's ed. Perf. by Freeman Gosden & Charles Correll. 6 cass. (Running Time: 9 hrs.). 2001. bk. 34.98 (4427) Radio Spirits.
Collection of 18 comedy classics including many of the earliest episodes from the sitcom version of the series.

Amos 'n' Andy: A Birthday Gift for Sapphire & Sapphire's a Wanted Criminal. unabr. ed. Perf. by Freeman Gosden & Charles Correll. 1 cass. (Running Time: 1 hr.). 2001. 6.98 (1953) Radio Spirits.

Amos 'n' Andy: Cat Burglar & Kingfish the Detective. unabr. ed. Perf. by Freeman Gosden & Charles Correll. 1 cass. (Running Time: 1 hr.). 2001. 6.98 (1607) Radio Spirits.

Amos n' Andy: Christmas Show. (ENG.). 2008. audio compact disk 12.95 (978-1-57970-514-5(6), Audio-For) J Norton Pubs.

Amos 'n' Andy: Kingfish to Catch a Spy & Kingfish Wrecks a Car. unabr. ed. Perf. by Freeman Gosden & Charles Correll. 1 cass. (Running Time: 1 hr.). 2001. 6.98 (1845) Radio Spirits.

Amos 'n' Andy: Kingfish to Clean Office Typewriters & Kingfish M.D. unabr. ed. Perf. by Freeman Gosden & Charles Correll. 1 cass. (Running Time: 1 hr.). 2001. 6.98 (2003) Radio Spirits.

Amos 'n' Andy: Pancake-Mix Contest & Rich Aunt Matilda Looks for a Husband. unabr. ed. Perf. by Freeman Gosden & Charles Correll. 1 cass. (Running Time: 1 hr.). 2001. 6.98 (1606) Radio Spirits.

Amos 'n Andy: The Kingfish Gets an Insulting Valentine see Amos n' Andy

Amos n' Andy: The Kingfish Sells Andy a Car Without a Motor. 1 cass. (Running Time: 60 mins.). 7.95 (CC-8514) Natl Recrd Co.
The Kingfish needs one hundred dollars to take Sapphire on a trip, so he sells Andy a car; appearances by The Jubilaires & Jeff Alexander's Orchestra. In "Lum & Abner" Lum is upset at the price charged for a valentine so he decides to make one himself & save money.

Amos n' Andy: The Lovelorn Column see Amos n' Andy

Amos 'n' Andy: The Lucky Buck Contest & Tux Rental Business. unabr. ed. Perf. by Freeman Gosden & Charles Correll. 1 cass. (Running Time: 1 hr.). 2001. 6.98 (1884) Radio Spirits.

Amos 'N Andy: The Marriage Broker see Amos 'n' Andy

Amos 'n' Andy: The Meaning of Friendship & Counterfeiters Rent an Office. unabr. ed. Perf. by Freeman Gosden & Charles Correll. 1 cass. (Running Time: 1 hr.). 2001. 6.98 (2492) Radio Spirits.

Amos 'N Andy: Their Life Story see Amos 'n' Andy

Amos 'n' Andy: Uncle Sylvester to Marry & Sapphire's Faith in Kingfish. unabr. ed. Perf. by Freeman Gosden & Charles Correll. 1 cass. (Running Time: 1 hr.). 2001. 6.98 (1863) Radio Spirits.

Amos n' Andy Show: A Phony Antique Desk & Andy Gets Adopted. unabr. ed. 1 cass. (Running Time: 60 mins.). Dramatization. (Amos 'N Andy Special Edition Ser.: No. 3). 1945. 7.95 Norelco box. (CC8563) Natl Recrd Co.
A Phony Antique Desk: The Kingfish buys an antique desk for 6.00 dollars after being told it once belonged to George Washington! Some love letters were put into the desk & signed by George. The Kingfish thinks they were written by George Washington & worth 10,000 dollars. Andy buys half interest in the letters for 12.00 dollars. Rinso. Andy Gets Adopted: An old lady walks into the lodge looking for an orphanage. She wants to adopt a son, now that she is a rich widow with a big house. The Kingfish says the son should be age 40, the age her son would have been if she had one. She agrees & Andy becomes her adopted son. Rinso.

Amos n' Andy Show: Andy Buys a Cabin & The Raffle Ticket. unabr. ed. 1 cass. (Running Time: 60 mins.). Dramatization. (Amos 'N Andy Special Edition Ser.: No. 5). 1948. 7.95 Norelco box. (CC8565) Natl Recrd Co.
Andy Buys a Cabin: The Kingfish has a beat-up cabin in the mountains that cost him 100 dollars. He sells the cabin to Andy for 250 dollars, by telling him it is an historical place..."where George Washington gave his Gettysburg address." It also has a "pan-aroma" view. Then the Kingfisher learns that he can get 500 dollars for the cabin. The plot thickens. Rinso. The Raffle Ticket: Andy wins a Plymouth Roadster with a raffle ticket he bought. The Kingfish plans on getting the ticket from Andy, but the ticket has been lost. They find the ticket, but the presentation is to have much publicity so the Kingfish has to get Andy out of town. Very funny turn of events. Rinso.

Amos n' Andy Show: Andy Plays Soldier & Sapphire's Old Boyfriend. unabr. ed. 1 cass. (Running Time: 60 mins.). Dramatization. (Amos 'N Andy Special Edition Ser.: No. 4). 1945. 7.95 Norelco box. (CC8564) Natl Recrd Co.
Andy Plays Soldier: Once again, Andy is worried about a breach of promise suit. His lawyer, Gabby, tells Andy that a service man cannot be sued. Andy borrows a corporal's uniform & visits the "breach-ee" with the uniform on to show her he is in the army & cannot be sued. Full of complications. Rinso. Sapphire's Old Boyfriend: The Kingfish becomes jealous when he sees Sapphire talking to an old boyfriend. He is upset & is going to do something about it. He decides that the best thing he can do is keep Sapphire busy, so he gets her a job where there are no men. Of course, it doesn't work out the way the Kingfish expected. Rinso.

Amos n' Andy Show: Income Tax Problems & More Income Tax Problems. unabr. ed. 1 cass. (Running Time: 60 mins.). Dramatization. (Amos 'N Andy Special Edition Ser.: No. 2). 1945. 7.95 Norelco box. (CC8562) Natl Recrd Co.
Income Tax Problems: Andy earned only 250 dollars in 1944, but to impress his new girlfriend he tells her that he earned 7,000 dollars. He signs a tax form with the 7,000 dollar declared amount, but plans to change it back to 250 when he gets the form back. However, the tax form is filed & he now owes 1,200 dollars on his taxes for 1944. Rinso. More Income Tax Problems: Andy is afraid that he will have to go to jail because he owes 1,200 dollars on his income tax return...a mix-up. His attorney, Shorty, tells him to flee the state & a collection from his lodge gives him enough money "to take a subway ride." Then the Kingfish takes over & Andy's problems...well, you know the Kingfish's finagling. Rinso.

Amos n' Andy Show: The Fountain Pen Agency & The 500 Dollar Reward. unabr. ed. 1 cass. (Running Time: 60 mins.). Dramatization. (Amos 'N Andy Special Edition Ser.: No. 6). 7.95 Norelco box. (CC8566) Natl Recrd Co.
The Fountain Pen Agency: The Ink Flow Fountain Pen Company is offering an exclusive agency for the most sales made in the area. Andy & the Kingfish get together to sell 3,000 pens. They sell two pens...one to each other...but they haven't collected yet for the 2 pens. They rehire Miss Blue as secretary & then the trouble really starts. Rinso, 1944. The 500 Dollar Reward: Andy saves a man from drowning who turns out to be millionaire & the Kingfish tries to claim a reward. Rinso, 1948.

Amos n' Andy Show: The Sure-Fire Investment & Mail Order Bride. unabr. ed. 1 cass. (Running Time: 60 mins.). Dramatization. (Amos 'N Andy Special Edition Ser.: No. 1). 1944. 7.95 Norelco box. (CC8561) Natl Recrd Co.
The Sure-Fire Investment: Fire destroys Kingfish's furniture & he gets 400 dollars from his insurance company. Sapphire tells him to put the money in the bank, but the Kingfish decides to invest his money with the Frank Morgan Investment Co. He will double his money overnight with Brazilian Brass Mines. Frank Morgan Guest. Rinso. Mail Order Bride: Andy is a member of a lonely hearts club & he proposes to a beautiful girl by mail...No. 66 in the catalog. An error has been made & he has proposed to No. 99, a very homely girl. To get out of the proposal, Andy's lawyer says he must be dead. The Kingfish arranges a fake suicide & then the fun begins. Rinso.

***Amos 'n' Andy, Volume 1.** RadioArchives.com. (Running Time: 600). (ENG.). 2007. audio compact disk 29.98 (978-1-61081-067-8(8)) Radio Arch.

***Amos 'n' Andy, Volume 2.** RadioArchives.com. (Running Time: 600). (ENG.). 2008. audio compact disk 29.98 (978-1-61081-071-5(6)) Radio Arch.

***Amos 'n' Andy, Volume 3.** RadioArchives.com. (Running Time: 600). (ENG.). 2008. audio compact disk 29.98 (978-1-61081-073-9(2)) Radio Arch.

***Amos 'n' Andy, Volume 4.** RadioArchives.com. (Running Time: 600). (ENG.). 2008. audio compact disk 29.98 (978-1-61081-077-7(5)) Radio Arch.

Amos n' Andy 10,000th Broadcast. 1 cass. (Running Time: 60 mins.). 1952. 7.95 (CC-2779) Natl Recrd Co.
Freeman Gosden & Charles Correll reminisce about their radio career, how they met Kingfish, started the Fresh Air Taxi Company & of Andy's famous romance with Madame Queen. Charlie McCarthy's last program includes highlights of Edgar Bergen's & Charlie McCarthy's 11 years with their sponsor; features Ken Carpenter, Ray Noble & The Bickersons.

Amount Due. unabr. ed. Mark Paul Sebar. Perf. by Mark Paul Sebar. Perf. by Toni Attell et al. 1 CD. (Running Time: 74 mins.). 2000. audio compact disk 9.99 (978-1-930246-06-5(4), 1930246064) Sebar Pubng.
When a young Harvard grad joins an L.A. based Mortgage & Loan, he finds a war with the company's crooked V.P.

Amount Due MP3. Mark Paul Sebar. 2001. audio compact disk 9.99 (978-1-930246-23-2(4), 1930246234) Sebar Pubng.

Amour. Jacques Prevert. Read by Jacques Prevert. 1 cass. (FRE.). 1995. 16.95 (1668-RF) Olivia & Hill.
All Prevert's work has to do with love, love from others, love of others, love for a life that could be better.

Amour de Swann. Marcel Proust. Contrib. by Henri Tisot. 1 cass. (FRE.). 1991. 16.95 (1105-RF) Olivia & Hill.

Amour De Swann. Marcel Proust. audio compact disk 12.95 (978-0-8219-3761-7(8)) EMC-Paradigm.

Amour de Swann, Pt. 1. Marcel Proust. Read by Andre Dussollier. 4 cass. (FRE.). 1995. 39.95 (1707-TH) Olivia & Hill.
Noted actor Andre Dussollier's admiration of Proust shines through his reading of Swann's love for the unattainable Odette de Crecy.

Amour de Swann, Pt. 2. Marcel Proust. Read by Andre Dussollier. 4 cass. (FRE.). 1995. 39.95 (1708-TH) Olivia & Hill.
Noted actor Andre Dussollier's admiration of Proust shines through his reading of Swann's love for the unattainable Odette de Crecy.

Amour de Swann, Pts. 1-2. Marcel Proust. Read by Andre Dussollier. 8 cass. (FRE.). 1995. 69.95 (1707/8-TH) Olivia & Hill.
Noted actor Andre Dussollier's admiration of Proust shines through his reading of Swann's love for the unattainable Odette de Crecy.

Amours. Poems. Pierre de Ronsard. Read by G. Bejean & C. Deis. 2 cass. (FRE.). 1991. 26.95 (1424-VSL) Olivia & Hill.
The love poems of this 16th-century poet.

Amours, Delices et Orgues. Alphonse Allais. Read by G. Faraoun. 1 cass. (FRE.). 1991. 21.95 (1004-VSL) Olivia & Hill.
Once again, Allais offers us some quick, humorous & witty recipes for success in areas such as adultery, politics & marriage.

Ampendectomy. Perf. by Resurrection Band. 1 CD. 1997. audio compact disk 15.99 (D3500) Diamante Music Grp.
Resurrection Band is celebrating 25 years of music ministry with a new sound. Thousands have heard them before, but they haven't heard them like this. They pull the plug & bring you their first all acoustic music offering. This collection features their finest songs in their most intimate & personal setting yet.

Amphetamines & Other Uppers. unabr. ed. Linda Bayer. Narrated by Jack Garrett. 1 cass. (Running Time: 1 hr. 30 min.). (J). 2003. 10.00 Recorded Bks.

Amplifying your Money Magnetism. Created by Matthew Ferry. 1 CD. 2005. audio compact disk 25.00 (978-0-9761929-3-0(4)) Spirit Pub CA.

AM/PM Yoga Chants. audio compact disk (978-1-55961-665-2(2)) Relaxtn Co.

AM/PM Yoga Mediatations. G. Chiarella. audio compact disk (978-1-55961-659-1(8)) Relaxtn Co.

AM/PM Yoga Meditations. unabr. ed. Gael Chiarella. (Running Time: 2:00:00). 2003. audio compact disk 19.98 (978-1-55961-752-9(7)) Sounds True.
Our AM/PM Yoga series offers music, Yoga chant and Yoga meditation recordings created by leading Yoga teachers from Yoga Zone, Kripalu and Sivananda Yoga Ashram.

A.M./P.M. Yoga Meditations, Vol. 1 & 2. Gael Chiarella. 2 CDs. (Running Time: 2 hrs.). 2001. audio compact disk 20.00 (93-0202) Relaxtn Co.
Frame your day with healing music and sound. A.M. starts your day with calm, clarity and vitality. Com full circle with P.M. for an evening of relaxation and sleep. Each CD consists of four 15-minute programs. A.M. offers programs for energizing, creativity, chakra balance and physical balance. P.M. address releasing the day's tensions, body scanning, creative dreaming and guided breathing.

AM/PM Yoga Melodies. audio compact disk (978-1-55961-662-1(8)) Relaxtn Co.

Amsterdam. Ian McEwan. Read by Alan Bates. 4 cass. (Running Time: 5 hrs.). 1999. 18.70 (978-0-00-105566-7(6)) Ulvrscrft Audio.
In this contemporary morality tale, as profound as it is witty, two old friends meet to pay their last respects to Molly Lane. Both had been Molly's lovers in the days before they reached their current eminence, one as Britain's most successful modern composer, the other as editor of a quality broadsheet.

Amsterdam. unabr. ed. Ian McEwan. Read by Arthur Addison. 3 cass. (Running Time: 4 hrs. 30 mins.). 1999. 24.00 (978-0-7366-4451-8(2), 4896) Books on Tape.
On a chilly February day, two old friends meet in the throng & pay their last respects to Molly Lane. Both Clive Linley & Vernon Halliday had been Molly's lovers. Clive is Britain's most successful modern composer; Vernon is editor of the quality broadsheet "The Judge." Gorgeous, feisty Molly had other lovers, too, notably Julian Garmony, foreign secretary, a notorious right-winger tapped to be the next prime-minister. In the days that neither has foreseen. Each will make a disastrous moral decision, their friendship will be tested to its limits & Julian Garmony will be fighting for his political life.

Amsterdam. unabr. ed. Ian McEwan. Read by Arthur Addison. 4 CDs. (Running Time: 4 hrs. 48 mins.). 2001. audio compact disk 32.00 Books on Tape.
On a chilly February day, two old friends meet in the throng & pay their last respects to Molly Lane. Both Clive Linley & Vernon Halliday had been Molly's lovers. Clive is Britain's most successful modern composer; Vernon is editor of the quality broadsheet "The Judge." Gorgeous, feisty Molly had other lovers, too, notably Julian Garmony, foreign secretary, a notorious right-winger tapped to be the next prime-minister. In the days that neither has foreseen, each will make a disastrous moral decision, their friendship will be tested to its limits & Julian Garmony will be fighting for his political life.

Amsterdam. unabr. ed. Ian McEwan. Read by Maxwell Caulfield. 4 cass. (Running Time: 6 hrs.). 1999. 24.95 (978-1-57511-060-8(1)) Pub Mills.
In the weeks following the funeral of a former lover, two friends find themselves at odds with much more than friendship at risk.

Amsterdam Connection, Level 4. Sue Leather. Contrib. by Philip Prowse. (Running Time: 2 hrs. 20 mins.). (Cambridge English Readers Ser.). (ENG.). 2001. 15.75 (978-0-521-79503-6(6)) Cambridge U Pr.

Amsterdam Gold Conference, Nineteen Seventy-Four. unabr. ed. Harry Schultz et al. 5 cass. (Running Time: 8 hrs. 30 mins.). 44.00 (266) J Norton Pubs.

Amulet Meditation. 1 cass. (Tara Sutphen Meditation Tapes Ser.). 11.98 (978-0-87554-483-0(5), TS208) Valley Sun.

Amulet of Samarkand. unabr. ed. Jonathan Stroud. Read by Simon Jones. 8 cass. (Running Time: 13 hrs. 32 mins.). (Bartimaeus Trilogy: Bk. 1). (J). (gr. 7 up). 2004. 50.00 (978-0-8072-1954-6(1), Listening Lib) Random Audio Pubg.
Nathaniel is a young magician with only one thing on his mind: revenge. As an apprentice to the great magician Underwood, Nathaniel is gradually being schooled in the traditional art of magic. All is well until he has a life-changing encounter with Simon Lovelace, a rising, star magician. When Simon brutally humiliates Nathaniel in front of everyone he knows, Nathaniel decides to speed up his magical education, teaching himself spells way beyond his years.

Amulet of Samarkand. unabr. ed. Jonathan Stroud. Read by Simon Jones. (Running Time: 48720 sec.). (Bartimaeus Trilogy: Bk. 1). (ENG.). (J). (gr. 5-12). 2007. audio compact disk 50.00 (978-0-7393-5613-5(5), Listening Lib) Pub: Random Audio Pubg. Dist(s): Random

Amusing. Contrib. by Chris Rice. Prod. by Monroe Jones. 2005. audio compact disk 17.98 (978-5-558-93312-3(7)) INO Rec.

Amusing Ourselves to Death: Public Discourse in the Age of Show Business. unabr. ed. Neil Postman. Read by Jeff Riggenbach. 4 cass. (Running Time: 5 hrs. 30 mins.). 1994. 32.95 (978-0-7861-0460-4(0), 1412) Blckstn Audio.
In this eloquent & persuasive book, Neil Postman examines the deep & broad effects of television culture on the manner in which we conduct our public affairs, on how "entertainment values" have corrupted the very way we think. As politics, news, religion, education & commerce are given expression less & less in the form of printed or spoken words, they are rapidly being reshaped & staged to suit the requirements of television. Mr. Postman argues that public discoursse, the advancing of arguments in logical order for the public good - once the hallmark of American cultures - is being converted from exposition & explanation to entertainment.

***Amusing Ourselves to Death: Public Discourse in the Age of Show Business.** unabr. ed. Neil Postman. Read by Jeff Riggenbach. (Running Time: 5 hrs.). 2010. 19.95 (978-1-4417-6738-7(X)); audio compact disk 49.00 (978-1-4417-6736-3(3)) Blckstn Audio.

Amy. unabr. ed. Read by Heywood Hale Broun & Jean Cloud. 1 cass. (Running Time: 56 mins.). (Broun Radio Ser.). 12.95 (40212) J Norton Pubs.
A conversation with the author of "Amy Lowell & the Imagist Poets".

Amy & Isabelle. abr. ed. Elizabeth Strout. Read by Lili Taylor. 4 cass. (Running Time: 4 hrs.). 1999. 24.00 (FS9-43316) Highsmith.

Amy & Isabelle. unabr. ed. Elizabeth Strout. Read by Stephanie Roberts. 10 vols. (Running Time: 15 hrs.). 2000. bk. 84.95 (978-0-7927-2343-1(0), CSL 232, Chivers Sound Lib) AudioGO.
Amy Goodrow, a shy high school student in a small mill town, falls in love with her math teacher & together they cross the line between fantasy & reality. When discovered, this emotional & physical trespass brings disgrace to Amy's mother & intensifies the shame she feels about her own past. Both mother & daughter withdraw completely from one another as their conflict intensifies.

Amy & Isabelle. unabr. ed. Elizabeth Strout. Read by Stephanie Roberts. 12 CDs. (Running Time: 18 hrs.). 2001. audio compact disk 110.95 (978-0-7927-9907-8(0), SLD 058, Chivers Sound Lib) AudioGO.

Amy Gerstler. Amy Gerstler. 1 cass. (Running Time: 29 mins.). (New Letters on the Air Ser.). 1992. 10.00 (122791) New Letters.
Gerstler reads & talks about her book, "Bitter Angel".

Amy Grant: Greatest Hits. Contrib. by Amy Grant. 2007. 18.99 (978-5-557-59290-1(3)); audio compact disk 13.99 (978-5-557-59291-8(1)) Pt of Grace Ent.

Amy Grant: the Collection: Digitally Remastered. Contrib. by Amy Grant. 2007. audio compact disk 13.99 (978-5-557-62605-7(0)) Pt of Grace Ent.

Amy Tan CD Collection: The Opposite of Fate, Saving Fish from Drowning. abr. ed. Amy Tan. Read by Amy Tan. (Running Time: 15 hrs.). 2010. audio compact disk 19.99 (978-1-4418-4985-4(8), 9781441849854, BACD) Brilliance Audio.

Amyotrophic Lateral Sclerosis - A Bibliography & Dictionary for Physicians, Patients, & Genome Researchers. Compiled by Icon Group International, Inc. Staff. 2007. ring bd. 28.95 (978-0-497-11327-8(9)) Icon Grp.

An Trentiesme de mon Eage see Twentieth-Century Poetry in English, No. 29, Recordings of Poets Reading Their Own Poetry

Ana Karenina. Leo Tolstoy. 2 CDs. (Running Time: 2 hrs.). (SPA.). 2006. audio compact disk 16.95 (978-1-933499-24-6(9)) Fonolibro Inc.

Ana Karenina. abr. ed. Leo Tolstoy. 3 CDs. (SPA.). 2002. audio compact disk 17.00 (978-958-43-0189-5(6)) YoYoMusic.

Ana Vidovic: Guitar Virtuoso. Contrib. by Ana Vidovic. (Running Time: 1 hr. 3 mins.). 2006. 24.95 (978-5-558-09180-9(0)) Mel Bay.

Anaheim Partner Conference. 2003. (978-1-59024-117-2(7)) B Hinn Min.

Anais Nin in Recital: Diary Excerpts & Comments. abr. ed. Anais Nin. 1 cass. (Running Time: 90 mins.). 1984. 12.95 (978-0-694-50947-8(7), SWC 1613) HarperCollins Pubs.

Anal Canal & Perianal Malignancies. 2 cass. (Colon & Rectal Surgery Ser.: C84-CR1). 1984. 15.00 (8428) Am Coll Surgeons.

Anal Disease & Painful Anal Afflictions. 2 cass. (Spring Meeting Philadelphia, PA Ser.: S87-GS6). 1987. 19.00 (8706) Am Coll Surgeons.
Includes management, anal fissure, acute hemorrhoidal disease, anal fistuale, abscess, painful sexually related anorectal disorders.

Anal Fistulae: Current Concepts. 2 cass. (Colon & Rectal Surgery Ser.: C85-CR4). 15.00 (8558) Am Coll Surgeons.

Analisis Cognitivo-Perceptivo de la Combinatoria de los Verbos de Transferencia: Se Incluye CD-ROM con Actividades para Estudiantes de Linguistica, Lenguas y Traduccion, Vol. 27. Montaner Montava & Maria Amparo. (Studien Zur Romanischen Sprachwissenschaft und Interkulturellen Kommunikation Ser.). (SPA, GER & FRE., (C). 2005. pap. bk. 57.95 (978-3-631-53328-4(4)) P Lang Pubng.

Analysis & Individuation. Read by John Van Eenwyk. 2 cass. (Running Time: 1 hr. 45 mins.). 1991. 16.95 (978-0-7822-0321-9(3), 445) C G Jung IL.
Part of the "Intensive Overview of Analytical Psychology" set.

Analysis As a Cultural Artifact: Conscious Individuation As Salvation. Read by T. J. Kapacinskas. 1 cass. (Running Time: 2 hrs.). 1987. 12.95 (978-0-7822-0109-3(1), 250) C G Jung IL.

Analysis for Decision Making. Howard Raiffa. 20 cass. (Running Time: 20 hrs.). (C). ring bd. 995.00 incl. 10 bks. (978-1-55678-012-7(5), 1431, Lrn Inc) Oasis Audio.
Harvard professor Howard Raiffa's 1 semester course on decision making. Covers decision making performance, thinking process for structuring complex problems & develops flexible technique for quick or complex decisions.

Analysis of Musical Form. James Mathes. 2007. audio compact disk 26.67 (978-0-13-158468-6(5), P-H) Pearson Educ CAN CAN.

Analysis of Outer Space. Contrib. by Forensic Quarterly Authors Staff. 2 cass. (Running Time: 2 hrs.). (Debate Audio Cassettes Ser.). 1990. 12.00 Natl Fed High Schl Assns.
Designed for use at clinics or for classroom use in preparing debaters.

Analysis of the NEC 1996. unabr. ed. J. Philip Simmons. Read by John Moore. 4 cass. (Running Time: 4 hrs.). 1995. bk. 57.95; 44.95 Intl Assn Elec Inspect.
Discusses the major changes in the 1996 National Electrical Code.

Analysis of the Plumed Serpent. Bruce Hawkins. 1 cass. 7.00 (A0037-86) Sound Photosyn.
An interesting interpretation original to Hawkins, presented at the 1986 International Conference for the Study of Shamanism.

Analysis of Two Satires. unabr. ed. Margaret Duckett. 1 cass. (Running Time: 55 mins.). 12.95 (23036) J Norton Pubs.
A comparison of techniques & possible emotional sources of some wit & humor in two satires, the "Muck-a-muck" of Bret Harte & "Fenimore Cooper's Literary Offenses" by Mark Twain.

Analytical Applications of Enzymes. George G. Guilbalt. 8 cass. (Running Time: 9 hrs. 12 min.). 245.00 incl. manual. (978-0-8412-1034-9(9), 75); 47.00 manual. (978-0-8412-1035-6(7)) Am Chemical.
This course will teach you how to use enzymes for analytical & industrial uses.

Analytical Procedures. William W. Holder. 1 cass. (Running Time: 1 hr.). wbk. ed. 119.00 (751811KQ); wbk. ed. 69.50 (751821KQ) Am Inst CPA.
Provides guidance on the development & use of analytical procedures & evaluating their effectiveness & efficiency in detecting errors & irregularities.

Analytical Psychology & Higher Education. Read by Thayer Greene. 1 cass. (Running Time: 90 mins.). 1984. 10.95 (978-0-7822-0081-2(8), ND7303) C G Jung IL.

Analytical Spanish Made Easier. Jim Hoover. 1 cass. (Running Time: 90 mins.).Tr. of Espanol Analitico Hecho Mas Facil. (ENG & SPA.). 1982. pap. bk. 20.00 (978-0-9703234-0-8(9)) J Ray Co.

Analytical Spanish Made Easier. Jim Hoover. Ed. by Jim Hoover. 2 cass. (Running Time: 3 hrs.).Tr. of Espanol Analitico Hecho Mas Facil. (ENG & SPA.). 1982. bk. 50.00 J Ray Co.
Spanish from basic pronunciation, present tense, preterite, imperfect, present subjunctive clear understanding almost immediately, student led questions & answers. Small book lays the foundation for advanced spanish & professional acquisition.

Analytical Techniques for Short-Term Events. John Van Zandt. 1 cass. 8.95 (596) Am Fed Astrologers.
Minute differences in short time spans.

Analyzing Financial Statements. unabr. ed. Eric Press. Narrated by Jeff Woodman. 2 CDs. (Running Time: 2 hrs. 30 mins.). (New York Times Ser.). 2003. audio compact disk 19.95 (978-1-885408-97-6(8)) Listen & Live.

Analyzing Financial Statements: 25 Keys to Understanding the Numbers. unabr. ed. Eric Press. Read by Jeff Woodman. 2 cass. (Running Time: 3 hrs.). (New York Times Pocket MBA Ser.). 2000. pap. bk. 27.95 Listen & Live.
Learn the 25 keys to unlocking the powerful & useful information buried in corporate financial statements.

Analyzing Financial Statements: 25 Keys to Understanding the Numbers. unabr. ed. Eric Press. Read by Jeff Woodman. 2 cass. (Running Time: 2 hrs. 30 mins.). (New York Times Pocket MBA Ser.). 2000. 16.95 (978-1-885408-38-9(2), LL031) Listen & Live.

Analyzing Health in Natal Charts. Diane Cramer. 1 cass. (Running Time: 90 mins.). 1988. 8.95 (646) Am Fed Astrologers.

Analyzing Libertarianism: A Case-Study in Thinking in Principles. Peter Schwartz. 1 cass. (Running Time: 90 mins.). 1992. 12.95 (978-1-56114-165-4(8), CS04C) Second Renaissance.

Analyzing Medical Records. 1 cass. (Running Time: 1 hr.). 1988. bk. 115.00; 65.00 PA Bar Inst.

Anam Cara. John O'Donohue. 1996. audio compact disk 69.95 (978-1-59179-787-6(X)) Sounds True.

Anamaniacs. Steven Speilberg. (J). 1993. 9.98 (978-1-56826-324-3(4)) Rhino Enter.

Ananda Talks about Marriage, Series. 8 cass. 52.00 incl. vinyl storage album. (DMI-6) Crystal Clarity.
Topics include: Why Marry?; Friendship, Love & Sex; Communication & Support; Magnetizing Your Marriage; Practical Issues - money, decisions, housework & family life & child raising.

Anansi & the Magic Stick. Eric A. Kimmel. Illus. by Janet Stevens. (Running Time: 12 mins.). (J). (gr. k-3). 2003. 9.95 (978-1-59112-480-1(8)); audio compact disk 12.95 (978-1-59112-505-1(7)) Live Oak Media.

Anansi & the Magic Stick. Eric A. Kimmel. Illus. by Janet Stevens. 11 vols. (Running Time: 13 mins.). (J). 2003. bk. 25.95 (978-1-59112-482-5(4)); pap. bk. 37.95 (978-1-59112-483-2(2)); pap. bk. 39.95 (978-1-59112-519-8(7)) Live Oak Media.

Anansi & the Magic Stick. Eric A. Kimmel. Illus. by Janet Stevens. 11 vols. (Running Time: 13 mins.). (J). 2005. pap. bk. 16.95 (978-1-59112-481-8(6)); pap. bk. 18.95 (978-1-59112-506-8(5)) Pub: Live Oak Media. Dist(s): AudioGO

Anansi & the Moss-Covered Rock. Scripts. 1 CD or cass. (Running Time: 25 mins.). (J). (gr. 1-4). 2000. pap. bk. & tchr. ed. 29.95 Bad Wolf Pr.

Anansi & the Moss-Covered Rock. Eric A. Kimmel. Illus. by Janet Stevens. 11 vols. (Running Time: 11 mins.). (J). 1991. pap. bk. 16.95 (978-0-87499-170-3(6)) AudioGO.

Anansi & the Moss-Covered Rock. Eric A. Kimmel. (J). (ps-3). 2001. bk. 15.95 (VX-170C) Kimbo Educ.
Anansi the Spider, a master trickster, uses the powers of a magical rock to dupe his neighbors. Includes book.

Anansi & the Moss-Covered Rock. Eric A. Kimmel. Illus. by Janet Stevens. (Running Time: 11 mins.). 1991. 9.95 (978-1-59112-004-9(7)); audio compact disk 12.95 (978-1-59112-674-6(0)) Live Oak Media.

Anansi & the Moss-Covered Rock. Eric A. Kimmel. Illus. by Janet Stevens. 11 vols. (Running Time: 11 mins.). (J). 1991. pap. bk. 18.95 (978-1-59112-675-1(4)) Pub: Live Oak Media. Dist(s): AudioGO

Anansi & the Moss-Covered Rock. unabr. ed. Eric A. Kimmel. 1 cass. (Running Time: 11 mins.). (J). (gr. k-3). 1991. 9.95 Live Oak Media.
Anansi the spider cleverly uses the powers of a magic rock to dupe his animal neighbors & steal their food hoards until Little Bush Deer turns the tables on him.

Anansi & the Moss-Covered Rock. unabr. ed. Eric A. Kimmel. Read by Jerry Terheyden. Illus. by Janet Stevens. 11 vols. (Running Time: 11 mins.). (J). (gr. k-3). 1991. bk. 25.95 (978-0-87499-171-0(4)); pap. bk. & tchr. ed. 37.95 Reading Chest. (978-0-87499-172-7(2)) Live Oak Media.

Anansi & the Talking Melon. Eric A. Kimmel. Read by Jerry Terheyden. Illus. by Janet Stevens. 11 vols. (Running Time: 11 mins.). (J). (gr. k-3). 1995. pap. bk. 16.95 (978-0-87499-339-4(3)) AudioGO.
Finding himself trapped inside one of Elephant's melons following a ravenous snack, Anansi talks to Elephant who is convinced he has grown a talking melon. Elephant sets off to present this treasure to the King, picking up an entourage of fellow animals on the way. It is only when they reach the King that Anansi stops talking, much to the chagrin to all concerned - all but Anansi.

Anansi & the Talking Melon. Eric A. Kimmel. (J). (ps-3). 2001. bk. 15.95 (VX-339C) Kimbo Educ.
Trapped inside one of Elephant's melons after eating too much, Anansi speaks to Elephant who is convinced he has grown a talking melon. Includes book.

Anansi & the Talking Melon. Eric A. Kimmel. Illus. by Janet Stevens. (Running Time: 11 mins.). (J). (gr. k-3). 1995. audio compact disk 12.95 (978-1-59112-682-9(7)) Live Oak Media.

Anansi & the Talking Melon. Eric A. Kimmel. Illus. by Janet Stevens. 11 vols. (Running Time: 11 mins.). 1995. bk. 28.95 (978-1-59112-684-3(3)); pap. bk. 39.95 (978-1-59112-685-0(1)); 9.95 (978-1-59112-005-6(5)) Live Oak Media.

Anansi & the Talking Melon. Eric A. Kimmel. Illus. by Janet Stevens. 11 vols. (Running Time: 11 mins.). (J). 1995. pap. bk. 18.95 (978-1-59112-683-6(5)) Pub: Live Oak Media. Dist(s): AudioGO

Anansi & the Talking Melon. Eric A. Kimmel. Read by Jerry Terheyden. Illus. by Janet Stevens. 11 vols. (Running Time: 11 mins.). (J). (gr. k-3). 1995. bk. 25.95 (978-0-87499-340-0(7)); pap. bk. & tchr. ed. 37.95 Reading Chest. (978-0-87499-341-7(5)) Live Oak Media.
Finding himself trapped inside one of Elephant's melons following a ravenous snack, Anansi talks to Elephant who is convinced he has grown a talking melon. Elephant sets off to present this treasure to the King, picking up an entourage of fellow animals on the way. It is only when they reach the King that Anansi stops talking, much to the chagrin to all concerned - all but Anansi.

Anansi Boys. 2005. 39.99 (978-1-59895-043-4(6)) Find a World.

Anansi Boys. unabr. ed. Neil Gaiman. 12 cass. 2005. 96.95 (978-0-7927-3782-7(2), CSL 857, Chivers Sound Lib); audio compact disk 117.95 (978-0-7927-3783-4(0), SLD 857, Chivers Sound Lib); audio compact disk 49.95 (978-0-7927-3842-8(X), CMP 857, Chivers Sound Lib) AudioGO.

Anansi Boys. unabr. ed. Neil Gaiman. Read by Lenny Henry. (YA). 2007. 69.99 (978-1-60252-939-7(6)) Find a World.

***Anansi Boys.** unabr. ed. Neil Gaiman. Read by Lenny Henry. (ENG.). 2005. (978-0-06-088982-1(9), Harper Audio); (978-0-06-088981-4(0), Harper Audio) HarperCollins Pubs.

Anansi Boys. unabr. ed. Neil Gaiman. Read by Lenny Henry. 8 CDs. (Running Time: 10 hrs.). (gr. 9 up). 2005. audio compact disk 39.95 (978-0-06-082384-9(4)) HarperCollins Pubs.

Anansi Goes Fishing. Eric A. Kimmel. (J). (ps-3). 2001. bk. 15.95 (VX-188C) Kimbo Educ.
Anansi the Spider's plan to trick his friend, Turtle, into doing all the work while he teaches Anansi to catch fish. Includes book.

Anansi Goes Fishing. Eric A. Kimmel. Read by Jerry Terheyden. Illus. by Janet Stevens. 14 vols. (Running Time: 12 mins.). (J). (gr. k-3). 1993. pap. bk. & tchr. ed. 37.95 Reading Chest . (978-0-87499-190-1(0)) Live Oak Media.
Anansi the spider's plan to trick his friend turtle into doing all the work while he teaches Anansi to catch fish somehow gets turned around. While Anansi doesn't learn his lesson, he does learn how to weave a net, an invaluable skill for a spider.

Anansi Goes Fishing. Eric A. Kimmel. Illus. by Janet Stevens. 11 vols. (Running Time: 12 mins.). 1993. bk. 28.95 (978-1-59112-680-5(0)); pap. bk. 39.95 (978-1-59112-681-2(9)); 9.95 (978-1-59112-003-2(9)); audio compact disk 12.95 (978-1-59112-678-2(9)) Live Oak Media.

Anansi Goes Fishing. unabr. ed. Eric A. Kimmel. Read by Jerry Terheyden. Illus. by Janet Stevens. 11 vols. (Running Time: 12 mins.). (J). (gr. k-3). 1993. pap. bk. 16.95 (978-0-87499-188-8(9)) AudioGO.

Anansi Goes Fishing. unabr. ed. Eric A. Kimmel. Read by Jerry Terheyden. Illus. by Janet Stevens. 11 vols. (Running Time: 12 mins.). (J). (gr. k-3). 1993. bk. 25.95 Incl. cloth bk. & cass. (978-0-87499-189-5(7)) Live Oak Media.

Anansi Moss Rock. Eric A. Kimmel. Illus. by Janet Stevens. 9.95 (978-1-59112-301-9(1)) Live Oak Media.

Anansi Series. Eric A. Kimmel. Illus. by Janet Stevens. 44 vols. (Running Time: 43 mins.). 2003. pap. bk. 68.95 (978-1-59112-840-3(4)) Live Oak Media.

Anansi the Spider. 2004. pap. bk. 38.75 (978-1-55592-629-8(0)); 8.95 (978-1-56008-828-8(1)); 8.95 (978-1-56008-133-3(3)); cass. & flmstrp 30.00 (978-0-89719-627-7(9)) Weston Woods.

Anansi the Spider. (J). 2004. bk. 24.95 (978-0-89719-858-5(1)); pap. bk. 32.75 (978-1-55592-185-9(X)); pap. bk. 32.75 (978-1-55592-186-6(8)); audio compact disk 12.95 (978-1-55592-955-8(9)) Weston Woods.

Anansi the Spider: A Tale from the Ashanti. Gerald McDermott. 1 cass. (Running Time: 10 min.). (J). (ps-4). bk. 24.95; pap. bk. 32.75; 8.95 (RAC151) Weston Woods.
Ashanti is saved from a terrible fate by his six sons, each of whom must share just one reward for their loyalty.

Anansi the Spider: A Tale from the Ashanti. Gerald McDermott. 1 cass. (Running Time: 10 mins.). (J). (ps-4). 2004. pap. bk. 14.95 (978-1-56008-046-6(9), PRA151) Weston Woods.

Anansi the Spider; Beast of Monsieur Racine, the; Sultan's Bath, the; Through the Window. (J). 2004. (978-0-89719-837-0(9)); cass. & flmstrp (978-0-89719-745-8(3)) Weston Woods.

Anansi Time with Bobby Norfolk. Bobby Norfolk. 1999. audio compact disk 14.95 (978-0-87483-748-3(0)) Pub: August Hse. Dist(s): Natl Bk Netwk

Anansi Time with Bobby Norfolk. unabr. ed. Contrib. by Bobby Norfolk. 1 cass. (Running Time: 47 mins.). (YA). 1999. 12.00 (978-0-87483-540-3(2)) Pub: August Hse. Dist(s): Natl Bk Netwk
Visiting a small village in Africa, Bobby Norfolk discovered Anansi Time, an afternoon storytelling break enjoyed by the whole community.

Anansi Time with Bobby Norfolk. unabr. ed. Bobby Norfolk. Read by Bobby Norfolk. (J). 2007. 34.99 (978-1-59895-843-0(7)) Find a World.

***Anansis Hat Shaking Dance.** Anonymous. 2009. (978-1-60136-592-7(6)) Audio Holding.

Anarchists' Convention. Short Stories. Read by John Sayles. 1 cass. (Running Time: 25 mins.). 13.95 (978-1-55644-081-6(2), 3121) Am Audio Prose.
Reading by actor, filmmaker, screenwriter, novelist & author of "Pride of the Bimbos" & "Union Dues".

Anarchy in America: Prophecies of Events Preceeding the Establishment of the New Jerusalem. unabr. ed. Duane S. Crowther. Read by Duane S. Crowther. 1 cass. (Running Time: 90 mins.). 1993. 13.98 (978-0-88290-343-9(8), 1827) Horizon Utah.
Presents in detail the momentous events foretold to occur during the period between two future world wars.

***Ana's Story: A Journey of Hope.** unabr. ed. Jenna Bush Hager. Read by Jenna Bush Hager. (ENG.). 2007. (978-0-06-147460-6(6)); (978-0-06-147461-3(4)) HarperCollins Pubs.

Ana's Story: A Journey of Hope. unabr. ed. Jenna Bush Hager. Read by Jenna Bush Hager. (Running Time: 10800 sec.). (J). (gr. 8-12). 2007. audio compact disk 21.95 (978-0-06-144154-7(6), HarperChildAud) HarperCollins Pubs.

Anastasia. 1 cass., 1 CD. 7.98 (ATL 83053); audio compact disk 14.38 Jewel box. (ATL 83053) NewSound.

Anastasia. Lynn Ahrens & Stephen Flaherty. 1 cass. (J). 7.78 Soundtrack. (ATL 83053); audio compact disk 14.38 CD Jewel box, soundtrack. (ATL 83053) NewSound.
An adventure chronicling the end of Imperial Russia, the chaos of the Revolution & the life-&-death struggle between the evil Rasputin & a girl who may be the last Princess of a lost empire.

Anastasia: Music from the Motion Picture. 1 cass. (J). 1997. pap. bk. 10.98 Blisterpack. (978-1-887688-10-9(2)); 10.98 (978-1-887688-09-3(9)); 10.98 Blisterpack. (978-1-887688-08-6(0)); 17.98 CD Blisterpack. (978-1-887688-06-2(4)); audio compact disk 17.98 (978-1-887688-07-9(2), 830532) WEA.

Anastasia: The Last Grand Duchess. unabr. ed. Carolyn Meyer. Read by Renée Raudman. (J). 2007. 39.99 (978-1-60252-545-0(5)) Find a World.

Anastasia: The Last Grand Duchess - Russia 1914. unabr. ed. Carolyn Meyer. Read by Renée Raudman. 4 CDs. (Running Time: 4 hrs. 0 mins. 0 sec.). (Royal Diaries). (ENG.). (J). (gr. 4-7). 2006. audio compact disk 49.99 (978-1-4001-3244-7(4)) Pub: Tantor Media. Dist(s): IngramPubServ

Anastasia: The Last Grand Duchess - Russia 1914. unabr. ed. Carolyn Meyer. Read by Josephine Bailey. (Running Time: 4 hrs. 0 mins. 0 sec.). (Royal Diaries). (ENG.). (J). (gr. 4-7). 2006. audio compact disk 19.99 (978-1-4001-5244-5(5)) Pub: Tantor Media. Dist(s): IngramPubServ

Anastasia: The Last Grand Duchess - Russia 1914. unabr. ed. Carolyn Meyer. Read by Renée Raudman. 4 CDs. (Running Time: 4 hrs. 0 mins. 0 sec.). (Royal Diaries). (ENG.). (J). (gr. 4-7). 2006. audio compact disk 24.99 (978-1-4001-0244-0(8)) Pub: Tantor Media. Dist(s): IngramPubServ
In this fictionalized journal, Anastasia Romanov lives again. Through her eyes, we witness the day-to-day splendor the czar's family experienced before the onslaught of the Russian Revolution. However, one senses also that crowding the outskirts of Anastasia's ornate diary are hundreds of thousands of teeming serfs, just beginning to percolate.

Anastasia at Your Service. unabr. ed. Lois Lowry. 1 read-along cass. (Running Time: 1 hr. 23 mins.). (Anastasia Krupnik Ser.). (J). (gr. 4-6). 1984. 15.98 incl. bk. & guide. (978-0-8072-1118-2(4), SWR40SP, Listening Lib) Random Audio Pubg.
Anastasia's thoughts of earning money during her summer vacation literally go down the drain when on her first day employed as a maid, she mangles a sterling silver spoon in the Bellingham's garbage disposal.

Anastasia Krupnik. unabr. ed. Lois Lowry. Narrated by C. J. Critt. 2 pieces. (Running Time: 2 hrs. 30 mins.). (Anastasia Krupnik Ser.). (gr. 4 up). 19.00 (978-1-55690-958-0(6), 93441E7) Recorded Bks.
Ten year old Anastasia deals with growing up, boys & the arrival of a baby brother. Available to libraries only.

Anastasia Krupnik. unabr. ed. Lois Lowry. Narrated by C. J. Critt. 3 CDs. (Running Time: 2 hrs. 30 mins.). (Anastasia Krupnik Ser.). (gr. 4 up). 2000. audio compact disk 29.00 (978-0-7887-4962-9(5), C1307E7) Recorded Bks.
Ten year old Anastasia deals with growing up, boys & the arrival of a baby brother.

Anastasia (Sing-Along) Contrib. by Lynn Ahrens & Stephen Flaherty. 1 cass. (J). 8.78 Blisterpack. (ATL 83065) NewSound.
An adventure chronicling the end of Imperial Russia, the chaos of the Revolution & the life-&-death struggle between the evil Rasputin & a girl who may be the last Princess of a lost empire.

Anastasia Syndrome. Mary Higgins Clark. 2004. 9.95 (978-0-7435-4154-1(5)) Pub: S&S Audio. Dist(s): S and S Inc

Anastasia Syndrome & Other Stories. unabr. ed. Mary Higgins Clark. Read by Mary Peiffer. 7 cass. (Running Time: 10 hrs. 30 mins.). 1993. 56.00 (978-0-7366-2325-4(6), 3105) Books on Tape.
A woman confronts the appalling truth about a wave of terrorist bombings plus four miniature masterpieces of suspense.

Anathem. unabr. ed. Neal Stephenson. Read by Neal Stephenson. Read by William Durfris et al. 28 CDs. (Running Time: 34 hrs. 0 mins. 0 sec.). (ENG.). 2008. audio compact disk 69.95 (978-1-4272-0590-2(6)) Pub: Macmill Audio. Dist(s): Macmillan

Anatoly Shcharansky: Human Rights. Narrated by Anatoly Shcharansky. 1 cass. (Running Time: 64 min.). 11.95 (K0270B090, HarperThor) HarpC GBR.

Anatomia del Espiritu. Caroline Myss. 2 cass. (Running Time: 2 hrs.).Tr. of Anatomy of the Spirit: The Seven Stages of Power & Healing. (SPA.). 2002. (978-968-5163-13-2(8)) Taller del Exito.
Discover the links between emotional and spiritual stresses and specific illnesses in the context of the anatomy of the human energy system. Learn the specific emotional, psychological, and physical factors that lie at the root of illness.

Anatomia del Maestro. Ramtha. (SPA.). 2007. audio compact disk 25.00 (978-0-9740337-9-2(0)) Voxrames.

Anatomical Principal of Endoscopic Sinus Surgery. Bradoo. 2005. audio compact disk 75.00 (978-81-8061-346-3(1)) Jaypee Brothers IND.

Anatomy & Medical Jargon for Lawyers. 1997. bk. 99.00 (ACS-1293); bk. 99.00 (ACS-1293) PA Bar Inst.
One of the keys to successfully handling a personal injury or disability claim is a basic understanding of the body system involved & the descriptive medical terminology. This can't make you a physician overnight but it can give a basic road map of anatomy & the medical terminology needed to find your way.

Anatomy & Medical Records. 1990. bk. 99.00 (ACS-576); bk. 99.00 (ACS-576) PA Bar Inst.
Designed for personal injury & disability lawyers.

Anatomy & Physiology of the Visual System Vol. 1: An Occupational Perspective. Sara Pazell. 1 cass. (Running Time: 39 mins.). 1998. bk. 15.00 (978-1-58111-071-5(5)) Contemporary Medical.
Discussion includes common visual disorders.

Anatomy of a Church. 8 cass. 24.95 (2098, HarperThor); 3.95 study guide. (40598, HarperThor) HarpC GBR.

Anatomy of a City: Proceedings of the 45th Annual Convention National Association of Evangelicals Buffalo, New York. Read by Raymond Bakke. 1 cass. (Running Time: 60 mins.). 1987. 4.00 (322) Nat Assn Evan.

Anatomy of a Civil Trial. Robert S. Sigman. Read by Robert S. Sigman. 1 cass. (Running Time: 50 mins.). (Law for the Layman Ser.). 1991. 16.95 (978-1-878135-10-0(4)) Legovac.
What you need to know before you see an attorney!.

Anatomy of a Commercial Trial. (Running Time: 6 hrs.). 1999. bk. 99.00 (ACS-2233) PA Bar Inst.
Expert lawyers help you master the parts of a commercial trial & then tie them together into a winning strategy. Read the "how-to's" brief lectures & then watch as experienced litigators present demonstration openings & closings. From the first pleading, through discovery, trial preparation & the trial itself, learn tactics that can't be found in books or by trial & error. Employing a multitude of learning tools from judges, business economic experts & others, you'll develop the skills & insight that separate succesful commerical litigators from those who finish in the pack.

Anatomy of a Jury. unabr. collector's ed. Seymour Wishman. Read by Dick Estell. 9 cass. (Running Time: 9 hrs.). 1987. 54.00 (978-0-7366-1214-2(9), 2133) Books on Tape.
The author, a criminal lawyer, examines the way in which citizens perform on juries.

Anatomy of a Murder. unabr. collector's ed. Robert Traver. Read by Wolfram Kandinsky. 12 cass. (Running Time: 18 hrs.). 1979. 96.00 (978-0-7366-0156-6(2), 1156) Books on Tape.
Detailed account of a celebrated murder trial. A woman's husband kills the man his wife says assaulted her. Based on a true story.

Anatomy of a Shipwreck: Acts 27:1-42. Ed Young. 2000. 4.95 (978-0-7417-2256-0(9)) Win Walk.

Anatomy of a Star. 1 cass. (Running Time: 23 mins.). 14.95 (8368) MMI Corp.
Discusses stars, age of stars, size, distance & characteristics of stars.

Anatomy of a Successful Salesman. Arthur Mortell. 1 cass. (Running Time: 47 mins.). 11.00 (978-0-89811-258-0(3), 9447) Meyer Res Grp.
Explains the cause, effect & cure for call reluctancy, anxiety, frustration, attitude & self-image problems in salespeople.

Anatomy of a Successful Salesman. Arthur Mortell. 1 cass. 10.00 (SP100062) SMI Intl.
Learn the cause, effect & proper response to call reluctance, anxiety, frustration, attitude & self-image. The twenty-four techniques for developing the sales "self" explained here will prove indispensable to the experienced salespeople as well as the novice.

Anatomy of an Astronaut. 1 cass. (Running Time: 59 mins.). 14.95 (14883) MMI Corp.
Discusses the meaning of the space program in 1969, just before the moon flight.

Anatomy of an Illness. unabr. collector's ed. Norman Cousins. Read by Dan Lazar. 4 cass. (Running Time: 4 hrs.). 1980. 24.00 (978-0-7366-0332-4(8), 1319) Books on Tape.
How the author & a team of physicians whipped a disease that was supposed to be irreversible.

Anatomy of Faith: Hebrews 11:17-20. Ed Young. 1992. 4.95 (978-0-7417-1919-5(3), 919) Win Walk.

***Anatomy of Faith & the Quest for Reason.** Featuring Ravi Zacharias. 2009. audio compact disk 9.00 (978-1-61256-059-5(8)) Ravi Zach.

***Anatomy of Ghosts.** Andrew Taylor. Narrated by John Telfer. (Running Time: 12 hrs. 0 mins. 0 sec.). (ENG.). 2011. audio compact disk 29.95 (978-1-60998-149-5(9)) Pub: AudioGO. Dist(s): Perseus Dist

Anatomy of Greed: The Unshredded Truth from an Enron Insider. unabr. ed. Brian Cruver. Read by Mel Foster. 7 cass, Library ed. (Running Time: 10 hrs.). 2002. 82.25 (978-1-59086-448-7(4), 1590864484, Unabridge Lib Edns); 32.95 (978-1-59086-447-0(6), 1590864476, BAU); audio compact disk 38.95 (978-1-59086-449-4(2), 1590864492, CD Unabridged); audio compact disk 97.25 (978-1-59086-450-0(6), 1590864506, CD Unabrid Lib Ed) Brilliance Audio.
Brian Cruver first entered the "Death Star," Enron's office complex, in March 2001. He was twenty-nine years old, an eager MBA ready to cash in as a new hire with one of America's most highly valued companies. But, from his first day - when his new boss warned him, "there was a mix-up in the hiring process," but that it was "no big deal...just think of it like you're adopted" - to his last, when he and his colleagues were given thirty minutes to leave the building, Cruver found himself enmeshed in a business cult that each day grew only more bizarre. With dark humor and page-turning momentum, Cruver lays out firsthand: the giddy group-think nurtured by Enron's leadership, whose incessant cheerleading for the company's stock price rendered many Enronians unable to believe that they were routinely being spoon-fed lies; the "rank and yank" peer review process that fostered horse-trading among managers over which employees would be given poor evaluations; the traders who made dubious deals to ensure their own lucrative bonuses; and the sinister designs and funding of Enron's fraudulent off-the-books partnerships. As Cruver probes the sleazy escapades that Enron executives milked for personal gain, he introduces us, up close and personal, to such storied figures as Ken Lay, Jeff Skilling, and Andy Fastow, along with other important Enron personalities like Rebecca Mark; Lou Pai; Thomas White, George W. Bush's Secretary of the Army; Joe Sutton; the "Mr. Blue", a disillusioned Enron executive; and Cruver's trading floor neighbor, a machine he christened "Sherman the Shredder" - who was always working overtime. Cruver's day-by-day chronicle, which includes a running stock ticker to show the trajectory of Enron's collapse, is instantly reminiscent of such bestsellers as Liar's Poker and Barbarians at the Gate. Told in a fresh, empathetic voice, Anatomy of Greed is brimming with grist for political pundits and comic relief for victims of corporate collateral damage. It is also the personal story of a young executive, a Houston native, whose dream job and dream company crashed around him in an avalanche of lies and greed. From the wreckage, this newly hardened veteran of the corporate wars has written a cautionary tale that our leaders must heed - or imperil us all to future disasters.

Anatomy of Greed: The Unshredded Truth from an Enron Insider. unabr. ed. Brian Cruver. Read by Mel Foster. (Running Time: 10 hrs.). 2004. 39.25 (978-1-59335-333-9(2), 1593353332, Brinc Audio MP3 Lib) Brilliance Audio.

Anatomy of Greed: The Unshredded Truth from an Enron Insider. unabr. ed. Brian Cruver. Read by Mel Foster. (Running Time: 10 hrs.). 2004. 39.25 (978-1-59710-014-4(5), 1597100145, BADLE); 24.95 (978-1-59710-015-1(3), 1597100153, BAD) Brilliance Audio.

Anatomy of Greed: The Unshredded Truth from an Enron Insider. unabr. ed. Brian Cruver. Read by Mel Foster. (Running Time: 10 hrs.). 2004. 24.95 (978-1-59335-010-9(4), 1593350104) Soulmate Audio Bks.

Anatomy of Insight. unabr. ed. J. Krishnamurti et al. Read by J. Krishnamurti et al. Ed. by Krishnamurti Foundation of America Staff. 1 cass. (Running Time: 1 hr. 30 mins.). 1991. 8.50 (AAI81) Krishnamurti.
Discussion on the nature of computers & the similarities with the human brain & the thing that sets them apart - insight.

Anatomy of Melancholy: Commentary from Part. 1, Sect. 2, Memb. 4, Subs. 1 to the End of the Second Partition see Cambridge Treasy Burton

Anatomy of Mid-Life Crises: Age Thirty-Eight to Forty-Four. Linda Savage. 1 cass. 8.95 (583) Am Fed Astrologers.

Anatomy of Outer Space. Read by Kenneth Franklin. 1 cass. (Running Time: 34 mins.). 14.95 (13605) MMI Corp.
Discusses galaxies, constellations, solar system, red shift & more.

Anatomy of Peace: Resolving the Heart of Conflict. unabr. ed. Arbinger Institute Staff. Narrated by Oliver Wyman. (Running Time: 25980 sec.). (ENG.). 2008. audio compact disk 29.95 (978-1-60283-446-0(6)) Pub: AudioGO. Dist(s): Perseus Dist

Anatomy of Pleasure. Victoria Zdrok. Narrated by Victoria Zdrok. 4 CDs. (Running Time: 4 hrs., 53 mins., 25 secs). 2006. audio compact disk 24.95 (978-1-60031-002-7(8)) Spoken Books.
A head-to-toe guide to understanding human sexuality that explores psychology and techniques aimed at improved love making. Read by the author, a well-known sexologist, psychologist, author and international sex symbol, Dr. Victoria Zdrok, Ph.D. This book is a comprehensive guide to the sexual receptivity of the human body. Each technique that men and women need to know to become true experts in bringing sexual joy to their partners is set forth in detail. This is the one book that every great lover must have - and the one book which will make every listener into a great lover!.

Anatomy of Slang, Pt. II. (23325) J Norton Pubs.

Anatomy of the Spirit. Demonstrated by Melva Martin. 2 CDs. (Running Time: 2 hrs. 30 mins.). 2001. audio compact disk 24.95 (978-1-56455-844-2(4), W502D) Sounds True.

Anatomy of the Spirit: The Seven Stages of Power & Healing see Anatomia del Espiritu

Anayil is Sad see Anayiz Gen Lapenn

Anayiz Al Nan Fet. Maude Heurtelou. Illus. by Louis Louissaint. 1 cass. (Running Time: 1 hr.).Tr. of Anayiz Goes to a Party. (CRP.). (J). (gr. 3-5). 1999. pap. bk. 19.00 (978-1-881839-88-0(5)) Educa Vision.

Anayiz ap Aprann Ijyen. Maude Heurtelou. Illus. by Louis Louissaint. 1 cass. (Running Time: 1 hr. 30 mins.).Tr. of Anayiz Learns about Hygiene. (CRE.). (J). (gr. 3-5). 1999. 19.00 (978-1-881839-86-6(9)) Educa Vision.

Anayiz Gen Lapenn. Maude Heurtelou. Illus. by Louis Louissaint. 1 cass. (Running Time: 1 hr. 30 mins.).Tr. of Anayil is Sad. (CRP.). (J). (gr. 3-5). 1999. pap. bk. 19.00 (978-1-881839-87-3(7)) Educa Vision.

Anayiz Goes to a Party see Anayiz Al Nan Fet

Anayiz Learns about Hygiene see Anayiz ap Aprann Ijyen

Ancestral Journeys. Luisah Teish. 2 cass. 18.00 (A0243-87) Sound Photosyn.
This video is a soulful, musical, effective view of what a priestess can do. You will be tempted to join in with the wonderful singing of the African tradition. There are instructions for setting up an alter & humorous things to try when you are addressing your long lost loved ones.

Anchor for the Soul: Help for the Present, Hope for the Future. abr. ed. Ray Pritchard. Narrated by Rob Lamont. (Running Time: 2 hrs. 0 mins. 0 sec.). (ENG.). 2007. 9.09 (978-1-60814-033-6(4)) Oasis Audio.

Anchor for the Soul: Help for the Present, Hope for the Future. abr. ed. Ray Pritchard. Narrated by Rob Lamont. (Running Time: 2 hrs. 0 mins. 0 sec.). (ENG.). 2007. audio compact disk 12.99 (978-1-59859-281-8(5)) Oasis Audio.

Anchor Man. abr. ed. Steve Farrar. Read by Steve Farrar. 2 cass. (Running Time: 2 hrs. 20 mins.). 1998. 15.99 (978-0-7852-7064-5(7), 70647) Nelson.
Encourages, exhorts & demonstrates with biblical concepts, how to raise a godly family.

Anchored: Reflections from a Reporter's Notebook CD. Drexel Gilbert. (ENG.). 2008. audio compact disk (978-0-9818464-2-2(4)) D Gilbert Enter.

Anchoring: The Oldest Mystery in NLP. John Grinder & Robert Dilts. Read by John Grinder & Robert Dilts. 8 cass. (Running Time: 12 hrs.). (Syntax of Behavior One Ser.: Vol. II). 1988. 99.95 Metamorphous Pr.
Nearly all of the applications of NLP include a judicious use of anchoring, yet little is understood about its internal structure. John & Robert explore in depth the implications, structure & development of the phenomena of anchoring. Questions such as "What is anchored? Is it the behavior, the state, the strategy? Does anchoring respect logical levels?" are discussed.

Anchoring Your Heart Close To. Beckett. 2004. 12.99 (978-0-8474-5310-8(3)) Back to Bible.

Anchoring Your Life in God. Daya Mata. 1984. 6.50 (2120) Self Realization.
Explains how Paramahansa Yogananda's teachings enable one to rise above the dualities of life & perceive God as the supreme Reality. Discussion includes applying the power of meditation techniques; understanding the purpose of tests & trials; the all-protecting power of divine love.

Anchors Away: Hebrews 6:9-12. Ed Young. 1991. 4.95 (978-0-7417-1895-2(2), 895) Win Walk.

Ancient. unabr. ed. R. A. Salvatore. Read by Erik Singer. 13 CDs. (Running Time: 12 hrs. 0 mins. 0 sec.). Bk. 2. 2008. audio compact disk 44.95 (978-1-4272-0278-9(8)) Pub: Macmill Audio. Dist(s): Macmillan

Ancient & Medieval Worlds Series: World Events over Time Collection. Eugene Lieber. (ENG.). 2006. audio compact disk 120.00 (978-1-935069-20-1(9)) IAB Inc.

Ancient & Modern Psychopathology. Michael Mayer. 2 cass. 18.00 (A0694-90) Sound Photosyn.
A discussion of "labeling" in psychopathology compared with the "name-giving" insights of ancient cosmologies & myths, this is an exploration of the imaginative alternatives to understanding pathology through symbolic unfolding.

Ancient & Modern Songs of Ireland for Piano. Gail Smith. 1993. spiral bd. 24.95 (978-0-7866-1165-2(0), 94883P) Mel Bay.

Ancient & Modern Songs of Ireland for Piano. Gail Smith. 1993. 10.98 (978-1-56222-909-2(5), 94883C) Mel Bay.

Ancient & Modern Songs of Scotland for Piano. Gail Smith. 1996. pap. bk. 27.95 (978-0-7866-2337-2(3), 95745CDP); pap. bk. 22.95 (978-0-7866-2517-8(1), 95745P) Mel Bay.

Ancient Asian View of Man. unabr. ed. Sarvepalli Radhakrishnan. 1 cass. (Running Time: 20 mins.). 1963. 12.95 (C25018) J Norton Pubs.
An analysis & summary of the Asian view of man. The fulfillment of man's life is religious experience & the people of Asia may be able to provide a spiritual orientation to the Western world's scientific achievement & technology.

Ancient Chants & Hymns for Guitar. Gerard Garno. 2002. per. 39.95 (978-0-7866-1808-8(6), 98276BCD) Mel Bay.

Ancient Civilizations Audio CD Theme Set: Set of 6 Set A. Adapted by Benchmark Education Staff. (English Explorers Ser.). (J). (gr. 3-6). 2007. audio compact disk 60.00 (978-1-4108-9845-6(8)) Benchmark Educ.

Ancient Echoes. Music by Christopher Moroney. 2003. audio compact disk 17.00 (978-1-58459-164-1(1)) Wrld Lib Pubns.
Music from the time of Jesus and Jerusalem's second temple. Christopher Moroney and SAVAE have reconstructed instruments of the period and recreated music from Hebrew melodic fragments, Babylonian Jewish music, and traditional songs that have passed down throught the ages from the time of Jesus.

Ancient Egypt. unabr. ed. 1 cass. 12.95 (C07347) J Norton Pubs.

Ancient Egyptian Art: The Brooklyn Museum: Jewel Case. Robb Lazarus et al. 1994. audio compact disk 49.95 (978-1-886664-35-7(8)); audio compact disk 49.95 (978-1-886664-36-4(6)) Digital Collect.

Ancient Empires before Alexander. Instructed by Robert L. Dise. 2009. 199.95 (978-1-59803-555-1(X)); audio compact disk 269.95 (978-1-59803-556-8(8)) Teaching Co.

Ancient Evil: The Knight's Tale of Mystery & Murder as He Goes on Pilgrimage from London to Canterbury. unabr. ed. Paul C. Doherty. 6 cass. (Running Time: 6 hrs.). 1998. 69.95 (978-1-85903-149-0(8)) Pub: Magna Story GBR. Dist(s): Ulverscroft US

Ancient Fighting Secrets of the Yin-Yang. Sid Campbell. (Running Time: 4 hrs. 30 mins.). 29.95 Gong Prods.

***Ancient Forces Collection.** Bill Myers. (Running Time: 8 hrs. 11 mins. 46 sec.). (Forbidden Doors Ser.). (ENG.). (YA). 2010. 12.99 (978-0-310-42636-3(7)) Zondervan.

***Ancient Forces Collection: the Ancients.** Bill Myers. (Running Time: 2 hrs. 35 mins. 0 sec.). (Forbidden Doors Ser.). (ENG.). (YA). 2010. 4.99 (978-0-310-77263-7(X)) Zondervan.

***Ancient Forces Collection: the Cards.** Bill Myers. (Running Time: 3 hrs. 2 mins. 0 sec.). (Forbidden Doors Ser.). (ENG.). (YA). 2010. 4.99 (978-0-310-72036-2(2)) Zondervan.

***Ancient Forces Collection: the Wiccan.** Bill Myers. (Running Time: 2 hrs. 36 mins. 0 sec.). (Forbidden Doors Ser.). (ENG.). (YA). 2010. 4.99 (978-0-310-72035-5(4)) Zondervan.

Ancient Greek Civilization, Course No. 323. Instructed by Jeremy McInerney. 2 cass. (Running Time: 12 hrs.). 49.95 incl. course guide. Teaching Co.
Covers the eleven centuries from the end of the Neolithic period to the conquests of Alexander the Great. Contains 24 lectures.

Ancient Greek Civilization, Pt. 1,2. Instructed by Jeremy McInerney. 12 cass. (Running Time: 12 hrs.). 1998. 54.95 (978-1-56585-071-2(8), 323) Teaching Co.

Ancient Greek Civilization, Pts. I-II. Instructed by Jeremy McInerney. 12 CDs. (Running Time: 12 hrs.). 1998. bk. 69.95 (978-1-56585-320-1(2), 323) Teaching Co.

Ancient Greek Civilization, Vol. 2. Instructed by Jeremy McInerney. 6 cass. (Running Time: 6 hrs.). 1998. 129.95 (978-1-56585-072-9(6)); audio compact disk 179.95 (978-1-56585-321-8(0)) Teaching Co.

Ancient Greek Philosophy: An Introduction. Tom Griffith & Hugh Griffith. Read by Crawford Logan et al. 2007. audio compact disk 41.98 (978-962-634-444-6(X), Naxos AudioBooks) Naxos.

Ancient Indian Concepts of Love & Sex. unabr. ed. Ajit Mookerjee. Read by Ajit Mookerjee. 1 cass. (Running Time: 53 mins.). 1979. 11.00 (13102) Big Sur Tapes.
A thorough discussion of attitudes & practices throughout Indian history & mythology, with references to the Kama Sutra & erotic sacred sculpture.

Ancient Magical Prayer: Insights from the Dead Sea Scrolls. abr. ed. Deepak Chopra & Gregg Braden. 1 CD. 2005. audio compact disk 10.95 (978-1-4019-0447-0(5)) Hay House.

Ancient Mediterranean View of Man. Arnold J. Toynbee. 1 CD. (Running Time: 24 MINS.). 2005. audio compact disk 12.95 (978-1-57970-227-4(9), C19015D) J Norton Pubs.

Ancient Mediterranean View of Man. unabr. ed. Arnold J. Toynbee. 1 cass. (Running Time: 24 mins.). 12.95 (19015) J Norton Pubs.
An analysis of man's present knowledge of Greek life, especially the contributions of the city-states to art, poetry, science, philosophy & war.

Ancient Myth of Men & Women. Narrated by Ralph Cissne. Prod. by Mike Wimberly. 1 CD. (Running Time: 45 mins.). 1999. audio compact disk 14.98 (978-0-9701443-0-0(X)) Morgan Rd.
Seventeen thematic spoken word tracks featuring original music by jazz veteran Mike Wimberly.

Ancient Near Eastern Mythology, Parts I-II. Instructed by Shalom Goldman. 12 cass. (Running Time: 12 hrs.). 2003. bk. 54.95 (978-1-56585-771-1(2), 2917); bk. 69.95 (978-1-56585-772-8(0), 2917) Teaching Co.

Ancient Noels. Maggie Sansone. 1994. pap. bk. 17.95 (978-0-7866-1201-7(0), 95079P); pap. bk. 22.95 (978-0-7866-1200-0(2), 95079CDP) Mel Bay.

Ancient Ones. unabr. ed. Kirk Mitchell. Read by Stefan Rudnicki. (Running Time: 12 hrs. 0 mins.). 2010. 29.95 (978-1-4417-1574-6(6)); 72.95 (978-1-4417-1570-8(3)); audio compact disk 105.00 (978-1-4417-1571-5(1)) Blckstn Audio.

Ancient Rhymes, a Dolphin Lullaby: With Audio CD & Score. John Denver. Illus. by Christopher Canyon. (Sharing Nature with Children Book Ser.). (J). (ps-6). 2004. bk. 19.95 (978-1-58469-064-1(X)) Dawn CA.

Ancient Songs of the TAO: Music of the Spheres. Bruce Frantzis. Narrated by Bruce Frantzis. (ENG.). 2008. audio compact disk 69.00 (978-1-55643-758-5(9)) Pub: North Atlantic. Dist(s): Random

Ancient Sun CD: ThunderBeat. Music by ThunderBeat ThunderVision Records. (ENG.). (J). 2009. audio compact disk 18.95 (978-0-9814651-9-7(6), ThundrBeat) Pub: ThunderVision. Dist(s): New Leaf Dist

Ancient Tower. Perf. by Robert Lepley. 1 cass. (Running Time: 1 hr.). 1998. 10.98 (978-1-56628-068-6(0), 42577); audio compact disk 15.98 (978-1-56628-067-9(2), 42577D) MFLP CA.

Ancient Ways, Future Days: A Celtic Season of Songs by Liam Lawton. Liam Lawton. 1 cass. 2000. 10.95 (CS-475); audio compact disk 15.95 (CD-475) GIA Pubns.

Ancient Wisdom. Swami Amar Jyoti. 1 cass. 1982. 9.95 (K-54) Truth Consciousness.
The time-tested, well-seasoned classical science of the physical, psychological & spiritual. Redressing the afflictions of humanity. The fulfillment of all branches of knowledge.

Ancient Wisdom & Modern Science (Bombay) unabr. ed. Stanislav Grof. 1 cass. (Running Time: 42 mins.). 1982. 11.00 (00805) Big Sur Tapes.

Ancient Wisdoms: The Path of the Unknown Sages. Instructed by Stuart Wilde. 1 cass. (Self-Help Tape Ser.). 9.95 (978-0-930603-33-5(8)) White Dove NM.
In this tape Stuart Wilde discusses the evolution of mankind through the great civilizations of Egypt, Lemuria & China & talks of cataclysms that have heralded new evolutions for the earth plane. Side two deals with Taoist philosophy & the esoteric concepts of unknown sages.

Ancient/Modern Witch: The Halloween Lecture. unabr. ed. Marion Weinstein. Read by Marion Weinstein. 1 cass. (Running Time: 52 mins.). 1991. 9.95 (978-0-9604128-3-9(2)) Earth Magic.
Live lecture analysis of positive Witchcraft; history & modern application as a life-affirming revivalist religion in the 90's.

***And: The Gathered & Scattered Church.** unabr. ed. Hugh Halter & Matt Smay. (Running Time: 6 hrs. 55 mins. 36 sec.). (Exponential Ser.). (ENG.). 2010. 18.99 (978-0-310-57632-7(6)) Zondervan.

***And Another Thing.** unabr. ed. Eoin Colfer. Read by Simon Jones. 2010. audio compact disk 14.99 (978-1-4013-9521-6(X)) Pub: Hyperion. Dist(s): HarperCollins Pubs

And Be a Villain. unabr. ed. Rex Stout. Read by Michael Prichard. 6 cass. (Running Time: 8 hrs.). (Nero Wolfe Ser.). 1999. 29.95 (978-1-57270-121-2(8), N61121u) Pub: Audio Partners. Dist(s): PerseuPGW
Madeline Fraser, radio talk show host extraordinaire, has a natural dread of dead air. So when one of her on-air guests keels over at the mike after drinking a glass of the sponsor's beverage, it was a broadcaster's nightmare come true. Archie & Wolfe successfully solve this most oblique case.

And Be a Villain. unabr. ed. Rex Stout. Narrated by Michael Prichard. (Running Time: 25500 sec.). (Nero Wolfe Ser.). (ENG.). 2005. audio compact disk 29.95 (978-1-57270-498-5(5)) Pub: AudioGO. Dist(s): Perseus Dist
Radio talk show host Madeline Fraser's fear of dead air becomes literal when a guest keels over after drinking a glass of her sponsor's beverage. Enter Nero Wolfe and his assistant, Archie. Nero lends his considerable sleuthing skills to the case but soon discovers that everyone connected to the case is lying about it. What's more, the portly private eye soon learns that the secret worth lying about only hides another worth killing for. Michael Prichard's dramatic reading brings this vintage 1948 whodunit to life.

And Be a Villain. unabr. collector's ed. Rex Stout. Read by Michael Prichard. 8 cass. (Running Time: 8 hrs.). (Nero Wolfe Ser.). 1995. 64.00 (978-0-7366-3039-9(2), 3721) Books on Tape.
Nero Wolfe gets mixed signals at a radio station when a live guest drops dead while on the air. Playful & puzzling.

***And Both Were Young.** unabr. ed. Madeleine L'Engle. Read by Ann Marie Lee. (ENG.). 2010. audio compact disk 45.00 (978-0-7393-8095-6(8), Listening Lib) Pub: Random Audio Pubg. Dist(s): Random

And Death Shall Have No Dominion see Dylan Thomas Reading: And Death Shall Have No Dominion and Other Poems

And Death Shall Have No Dominion see Dylan Thomas Reading His Poetry

And Eternity. Piers Anthony. Narrated by Barbara Caruso. 10 cass. (Running Time: 12 hrs. 45 mins.). (Incarnations of Immortality Ser.: Bk. 7). 2002. 82.00 (978-1-4025-1350-3(X), 96476) Recorded Bks.
In the triumphant finale of this series, the Incarnation of Good dominates. Orlene has died and we follow her into the afterlife. Joining forces with two women, Jolie, Satan's consort and Vita, a troubled mortal, together these three women will test the limits of morality.

And Finally... But Not Immediately: Col. 4:3-18. Ed Young. 1982. 4.95 (978-0-7417-1261-5(X), 261) Win Walk.

And Four to Go. unabr. collector's ed. Rex Stout. Read by Michael Prichard. 7 cass. (Running Time: 7 hrs.). (Nero Wolfe Ser.). 1997. 56.00 (978-0-7366-4059-6(2), 4570) Books on Tape.
This foursome contains a fatal fete, a toxic orchid, a speech turned funeral oration, & a murderer dressed to kill. Vintage mystery fare.

***And Furthermore.** unabr. ed. Judi Dench. Read by Samantha Bond. (ENG.). 2011. audio compact disk 29.99 (978-1-4272-1102-6(7)) Pub: Macmill Audio. Dist(s): Macmillan

***And God Thinks Otherwise.** Kenneth Wapnick. 2010. 10.00 (978-1-59142-499-4(2)); audio compact disk 12.00 (978-1-59142-498-7(4)) Foun Miracles.

And Hope to Die. unabr. ed. Read by Humphrey Bower. (Running Time: 38700 sec.). 2007. audio compact disk 93.95 (978-1-74093-992-8(1), 9781740939928) Pub: Bolinda Pubng AUS. Dist(s): Bolinda Pub Inc

And I Mean It, Stanley Book & Tape. abr. ed. Crosby N. Bonsall. Illus. by Crosby N. Bonsall. 1 cass. (I Can Read Bks.). (J). (ps-2). 1990. 8.99 (978-1-55994-265-2(7)) HarperCollins Pubs.

***And If I Die.** unabr. ed. John Aubrey Anderson. Read by G. Valmont Thomas. (Running Time: 12 hrs. 0 mins.). 2010. 29.95 (978-1-4332-2457-7(7)); 72.95 (978-1-4332-2453-9(4)); audio compact disk 105.00 (978-1-4332-2454-6(2)) Blckstn Audio.

And If the Moon Could Talk. Kate Banks. Illus. by Georg Hallensleben. 1 cass. (Running Time: 15 min.). (J). (gr. k-2). 2001. bk. 25.95 (978-0-8045-6867-8(7), 6867) Spoken Arts.
Shows us what the moon might see - and say - if it could talk.

And It Is Still That Way. abr. ed. Byrd Baylor. Read by Joe Hayes. 1 cass. (Running Time: 45 mins.). (J). (gr. 1-6). 1987. 10.95 (978-0-939729-07-4(5)) Trails West Pub.
A Selection of American Indian Tales.

...and It's All Your Fault: How to Overcome Anger & Interpersonal Conflict. David Burns. 11 cass. (Running Time: 13 hours). 2004. 149.00 (978-0-9755159-2-1(6)); audio compact disk 149.00 (978-0-9755159-7-6(7)) IAHB.

And It's Christmas. Kidzup Productions Staff. 1 cass. (Running Time: 90 mins.). (Kidzup Ser.). (J). 2000. 8.99 (978-1-894281-19-5(5)); audio compact disk 12.99 (978-1-894281-20-1(9)) Pub: Kidzup CAN. Dist(s): Penton Overseas

...And June Whitfield: The Autobiography. unabr. ed. June Whitfield. Read by June Whitfield. 8 cass. (Running Time: 12 hrs.). 2001. 69.95 (978-0-7540-0672-5(7), CAB 2094) Pub: Chivers Audio Bks GBR. Dist(s): AudioGO
June Whitfield writes perceptively about the great comics she has known in her long professional life. She views the changing fashions in television with benign detachment, and relishes being in the modern comedy loop.

And Justice for All. 2002. (978-0-7398-5195-1(0)) SteckVau.

And Justice for All. Steck-Vaughn Staff. 2002. pap. bk. 41.60 (978-0-7398-6980-2(9)) SteckVau.

And Justice for All: 11 Peter 2:1-10. Ed Young. 1983. 4.95 (978-0-7417-1313-1(6), 313) Win Walk.

And Justice for All Level 4. (J). 2002. audio compact disk (978-0-7398-5351-1(1)) SteckVau.

And Justice for Some: An Expose of the Lawyers & Judges Who Let Dangerous Criminals Go Free. unabr. ed. Wendy Murphy. Read by Joyce Bean. Frwd. by Bill O'Reilly. (Running Time: 7 hrs. 30 mins. 0 sec.). (ENG.). 2007. audio compact disk 29.99 (978-1-4001-0514-4(5)); audio compact disk 59.99 (978-1-4001-3514-1(1)); audio compact disk 19.99 (978-1-4001-5514-9(2)) Pub: Tantor Media. Dist(s): IngramPubServ

And Justice There Is None. Deborah Crombie. Read by Michael Deehy. 10 CDs. (Running Time: 41820 sec.). (Duncan Kincaid/Gemma James Novel Ser.). 2006. 94.95 (978-0-7927-3558-8(7), SLD 930) AudioGO.

And My Mean Old Mother Will Be Sorry, Blackboard Bear. unabr. ed. Martha Alexander. 1 cass. (Running Time: 6 mins.). (J). (ps-3). 1989. pap. bk. 14.45 (978-0-8045-6508-0(2), 6508) Spoken Arts.

And Never Let Her Go: Thomas Capano: The Deadly Seducer. Ann Rule. Read by Melissa Leo. 2004. 15.95 (978-0-7435-4155-8(3)) Pub: S&S Audio. Dist(s): S and S Inc

And Never Let Her Go Set: Thomas Capano: The Deadly Seducer. abr. ed. Ann Rule. Read by Melissa Leo. 2 cass. 1999. 25.00 (FS9-51075) Highsmith.

And Never Stop Dancing. Gordon Livingston. Read by Bruce Barker. (Running Time: 4 hrs.). (C). 2006. 21.95 (978-1-60083-128-7(1)) Iofy Corp.

And Never Stop Dancing: Thirty More True Things We Need to Know Now. Gordon Livingston. Read by Bruce Barker. (Running Time: 14400 sec.). 2006. audio compact disk 19.95 (978-1-59316-081-4(X)) Listen & Live.

And No Birds Sang. abr. ed. Farley Mowat. Narrated by Farley Mowat. Prod. by CBC Radio Staff. 2 cass. (Running Time: 2 hrs. 30 mins.). (Between the Covers Classics). (ENG.). 2005. 16.95 (978-0-86492-282-3(5)) Pub: BTC Audiobks CAN. Dist(s): U Toronto Pr

And No Birds Sang. unabr. ed. Farley Mowat. Read by David Case. 8 cass. (Running Time: 8 hrs.). 1990. 48.00 (978-0-7366-1815-1(5), 2651) Books on Tape.
Youthful idealism falls victim to the realities of war. Mowat's recollection of growing up in combat in WW II.

... And Now Miguel. Joseph Krumgold. (J). 1985. 21.33 (978-0-394-76936-3(8)) SRA McGraw.

And Now We Are Going to Have a Party: Liner Notes to a Writer's Early Life. Nicola Griffith. Music by Nicola Griffith. (ENG., 2007. pap. bk. 50.00 (978-0-9789114-1-6(5)) Payseur Schmidt.

And One & Two. Ella Jenkins. 1 CD. (Running Time: 1 hr.). (J). 2001. audio compact disk 15.00 Kimbo Educ.

And One & Two. Perf. by Ella Jenkins. 1 cass. (Running Time: 1 hr.). (J). (ps). 1990. (0-9307-450160-9307-45016-2-7); audio compact disk (0-9307-45016-2-7) Smithsonian Folkways.
Simple songs & rhythm exercises for young children, including "I'm Going to School Today," "Rhythms around the Chair" & "Dredle, Dredle, Dredle".

And One for Luck. unabr. ed. Lynda Page. Read by Carolyn Oldershaw. 12 cass. (Running Time: 16 hrs.). 1999. 108.95 (978-1-85903-253-4(2)) Pub: Magna Story GBR. Dist(s): Ulverscroft US
Each day as she takes on another challenge, Grace begins to realise that it is time to break out, to make something of her life, before it is too late.

And One More Thing Before You Go. unabr. ed. Maria Shriver. 2005. 7.95 (978-0-7435-5150-2(8)) Pub: S&S Audio. Dist(s): S and S Inc

***And Party Every Day: The Inside Story of Casablanca Records.** unabr. ed. Larry Harris. Read by To be announced. (Running Time: 10 hrs. NaN mins.). (ENG.). 2011. 29.95 (978-1-4417-7949-6(3)) Blckstn Audio.

***And Party Every Day: The Inside Story of Casablanca Records.** unabr. ed. Larry Harris. Read by To be Announced. (Running Time: 10 hrs. NaN mins.). (ENG.). 2011. 65.95 (978-1-4417-7946-5(9)) Blckstn Audio.

***And Party Every Day: The Inside Story of Casablanca Records.** unabr. ed. Larry Harris. Read by To be announced. (Running Time: 10 hrs. NaN mins.). 2011. audio compact disk 29.95 (978-1-4417-7948-9(5)) Blckstn Audio.

***And Party Every Day: The Inside Story of Casablanca Records.** unabr. ed. Larry Harris. Read by To be Announced. (Running Time: 10 hrs. NaN mins.). (ENG.). 2011. audio compact disk 90.00 (978-1-4417-7947-2(7)) Blckstn Audio.

And Quiet Flows the Don, Pt. A. unabr. collector's ed. Mikhail Sholokhov. Read by Wolfram Kandinsky. 9 cass. (Running Time: 13 hrs. 30 mins.). 1979. 72.00 (978-0-7366-0184-9(8), 1185-A) Books on Tape.
The portrayal of a Cossack village, from the days of the Czar through war & revolution.

And Quiet Flows the Don, Pt. B. collector's ed. Mikhail Sholokhov. Read by Wolfram Kandinsky. 6 cass. (Running Time: 9 hrs.). 1979. 48.00 (978-0-7366-0185-6(6), 1185-B) Books on Tape.
The Nobel prize-winner brings to life a cossack village under the czar before the Russian Revolution.

And She Drinks. 1 cass. (Running Time: 30 mins.). 8.00 (I0210, HarperThor) HarpC GBR.

And Should We Die. Don J. Black. 1 cass. 1999. 9.95 (978-1-57734-431-5(6), 06005942) Covenant Comms.
A comforting look at the hereafter.

And Sometimes Why. unabr. ed. Mame Farrell. Narrated by Scott Shina. 3 pieces. (Running Time: 3 hrs. 30 mins.). (gr. 6 up). 2002. 28.00 (978-1-4025-1721-1(1)) Recorded Bks.
Jack and Christy have been best friends for over seven years. They're almost in high school, and they're growing up fast. Always a tomboy, Chris is suddenly turing into a world class beauty. Now all the boys are falling for her, including Jack. But does he really love her. or is he just afraid of losing her to another boy?.

And Sometimes Why. unabr. ed. Rebecca Johnson. Narrated by Cassandra Campbell. (Running Time: 11 hrs. 30 mins. 0 sec.). (ENG.). 2008. audio compact disk 69.99 (978-1-4001-3591-2(5)) Pub: Tantor Media. Dist(s): IngramPubServ

And Sometimes Why. unabr. ed. Rebecca Johnson. Read by Cassandra Campbell. (Running Time: 11 hrs. 30 mins. 0 sec.). (ENG.). 2008. audio compact disk 34.99 (978-1-4001-0591-5(9)); audio compact disk 24.99 (978-1-4001-5591-0(6)) Pub: Tantor Media. Dist(s): IngramPubServ

And Sometimes Y: Volume 3. abr. ed. Prod. by Nicola Luksic & Andrew Kaufman. (Running Time: 18000 sec.). (And Sometimes Y Ser.). (ENG.). 2007. audio compact disk 39.95 (978-0-660-19741-8(3)) Canadian Broadcasting CAN.

And Sometimes Y, Volume 1. abr. ed. (Running Time: 18000 sec.). (ENG.). 2007. audio compact disk 39.95 (978-0-660-19675-6(1)) Canadian Broadcasting CAN.

And Sometimes Y, Volume 2. Contrib. by Russell Smith. (Running Time: 18000 sec.). (And Sometimes Y Ser.). (ENG.). 2007. audio compact disk 39.95 (978-0-660-19740-1(5)) Canadian Broadcasting CAN.

And Soon I'll Come to Kill You. unabr. ed. Susan Kelly. Read by Pamela Klein. (Running Time: 6 hrs.). 2008. 39.25 (978-1-4233-7186-1(0), 9781423371861, BADLE); 24.95 (978-1-4233-7185-4(2), 9781423371854, BAD); 24.95 (978-1-4233-7183-0(6), 9781423371830, Brilliance MP3); 39.25 (978-1-4233-7184-7(4), 9781423371847, Brinc Audio MP3 Lib) Brilliance Audio.

And Still I Rise: A Selection of Poems Read by the Author. unabr. ed. Maya Angelou. Read by Maya Angelou. 1 CD. (Running Time: 30 mins.). (ENG.). 2001. audio compact disk 12.00 (978-0-375-41949-2(7), RH AudioV) Pub: Random Audio Pubg. Dist(s): Random

And Suddenly Spring. Ed. by Stanley H. Barkan. Tr. by Adam Szyper. (Review Chapbook Ser.: No. 26: Polish Poetry). (ENG & POL.). 1991. 10.00 (978-0-685-26550-5(1)) Cross-Cultrl NY.

And the Desert Blooms. unabr. ed. Iris Johansen. Narrated by Angela Brazil. (Running Time: 18900 sec.). (ENG.). 2008. audio compact disk 19.95 (978-1-60283-550-4(0)) Pub: AudioGO. Dist(s): Perseus Dist

And the Dish Ran Away with the Spoon. As told by Janet Stevens & Susan Stevens Crummel. 1 cass. (Running Time: 1 hr.). (J). (gr. k-3). 2001. bk. (6882) Spoken Arts.
Every night the rhyme gets read. Every night Dish and Spoon run away. And every night they return - until tonight. The rhyme can't go on without them, so Cat, Cow and Dog set out to search for their missing friends.

And the Dish Ran Away with the Spoon. Janet Stevens & Susan Stevens Crummel. 1 cass. (Running Time: 24 mins.). (J). (gr. k-3). 2002. bk. 27.95 (978-0-8045-6882-1(0)) Spoken Arts.

And the Fans Roared & the Crowd Goes Wild. Joe Garner & Bob Costas. 1 CD. (Running Time: 1 hr.). 2000. bk. 94.95 (978-1-57071-659-1(5), MediaFusion) Sourcebks.

And the Hippos Were Boiled in Their Tanks. unabr. ed. William S. Burroughs & Jack Kerouac. (Running Time: 7 hrs. 0 mins.). 2008. 29.95 (978-1-4332-4913-6(8)); 44.95 (978-1-4332-4910-5(3)) Blckstn Audio.

And the Hippos Were Boiled in Their Tanks. unabr. ed. William S. Burroughs & Jack Kerouac. Narrated by Ray Porter. 4 CDs. (Running Time: 4 hrs. 30 mins.). 2008. audio compact disk 60.00 (978-1-4332-4911-2(1)) Blckstn Audio.

And the Hippos Were Boiled in Their Tanks. unabr. ed. Jack Kerouac & William S. Burroughs. Read by Ray Porter. 4 CDs. (Running Time: 4 hrs. 30 mins.). 2008. audio compact disk 19.95 (978-1-4332-4912-9(X)) Blckstn Audio.

... & the Rest Will Follow. Contrib. by Project 86. Prod. by Ben Kaplan. 2005. audio compact disk 13.98 (978-5-558-86601-8(2)) Tooth & Nail.

And the Show Goes On. Dennis Allen & Nan Allen. 1993. 11.98 (978-0-7673-1309-4(7)) LifeWay Christian.

***And the Show Went On: Cultural Life in Nazi-Occupied Paris.** unabr. ed. Alan Riding. (Running Time: 14 hrs. 0 mins.). 2010. 19.99 (978-1-4001-8833-8(4)); 29.99 (978-1-4001-6833-0(3)); audio compact disk 39.99 (978-1-4001-1833-5(6)) Pub: Tantor Media. Dist(s): IngramPubServ

***And the Show Went On: Cultural Life in Nazi-occupied Paris.** unabr. ed. Alan Riding. (Running Time: 14 hrs. 0 mins. 0 sec.). (ENG.). 2010. audio compact disk 95.99 (978-1-4001-4833-2(2)) Pub: Tantor Media. Dist(s): IngramPubServ

***And the Show Went on (Library Edition) Cultural Life in Nazi-Occupied Paris.** unabr. ed. Alan Riding. (Running Time: 14 hrs. 0 mins.). 2010. 39.99 (978-1-4001-9833-7(X)) Tantor Media.

And the Stars Go with You. Perf. by Jonn Serrie. 1 cass. (Running Time: 1 hr.). 9.98 (MPC2001); audio compact disk 14.98 Miramar Images.
A decade of experience composing music for leading planetariums is a heavy influence in his recording. Dedicated to Christa McAuliffe, Teacher in Space Program.

And the Two Become One. 2003. 6.95 (978-1-932631-04-3(6)); audio compact disk 6.95 (978-1-932631-07-4(0)) Ascensn Pr.

And the Walls Came Tumbling down, Part 1: Conquering the Giants in Your Promised Land, 5 of faith series. Mac Hammond. 4 Cds. 2006. audio compact disk 20.00 (978-1-57399-317-3(4)) Mac Hammond.
Something standing in your way? There are five biblical steps you can take to overcome any obstacle. Find out what they are and how to apply them in your life.

And the Walls Came Tumbling down! Part 2: Turning Defeat into Victory, 6 of Faith Series. Mac Hammond. 4 cass. (Running Time: 4 hrs.). 2005. 10.00 (978-1-57399-234-3(8)) Mac Hammond.
There exists a special Promised Land for every believer. A place of blessing, fulfillment, and rest. Hear biblical keys to identifying your Promised Land and find out what it takes to get there.

And the Walls Came Tumbling down, Part 2: Turning Defeat into Victory, 6 of the faith series. Mac Hammond. 4 CDs. 2006. audio compact disk 20.00 (978-1-57399-318-0(2)) Mac Hammond.
There exists a special Promised Land for every believer. A place of blessing, fulfillment, and rest. Hear biblical keys to identifying your Promised Land and find out what it takes to get there.

... And the Walls Came Tumbling down!, the Faith Series Vol. 5: Conguering the Giants in Your Promised Land, Part 1. Mac Hammond. 4 cass. 1995. 20.00 (978-1-57399-146-9(5)) Mac Hammond.
Something standing in your way? There are five biblical steps you can take to overcome any obstacle. Find out what they are and how to apply them in your life.

And the waters turned to blood: the ultimate biological threat Cassette. Rodney Barker. 2004. 10.95 (978-0-7435-4156-5(1)) Pub: S&S Audio. Dist(s): S and S Inc

And the Winner Is. 1 cass. (Running Time: 1 hr.). 1995. 12.98 (978-1-55723-959-4(2)); audio compact disk 19.95 (978-1-55723-960-0(6)) W Disney Records.

And the Winner Is. unabr. ed. 1 cass. (Running Time: 90 min.). (J). 10.99 Norelco. (978-1-55723-723-1(9)); audio compact disk 16.99 Jewel Box. (978-1-55723-725-5(5)) W Disney Records.

And the Word Was Hip Hop. Contrib. by HipHopEMass. 2006. audio compact disk 15.00 (978-0-89869-533-5(3)) Church Pub Inc.

And the World Was God. 1 cass. (Running Time: 60 mins.). (Mother Angelica Live Ser.). 10.00 (978-1-55794-051-3(7), T2) Eternal Wrd TV.

And Then Some. Emmet L. Robinson. Read by Emmet L. Robinson. 1 cass. (Running Time: 17 mins.). 1994. 7.95 King Street.
How to make money by giving things away.

And Then the Darkness: The Disappearance of Peter Falconio & the Trials of Joanne Lees. unabr. ed. Sue Williams. Read by Kate Hood. (Running Time: 38700 sec.). 2006. audio compact disk 98.95 (978-1-74093-839-6(9)) Pub: Bolinda Pubng AUS. Dist(s): Bolinda Pub Inc

And Then the End Shall Come. Derek Prince. 4 cass. (Running Time: 4 hrs.). 1990. 19.95 (I-TEC1) Derek Prince.
The Bible vividly depicts the climax of the present age, showing us how we may complete our task & be ready to meet the Lord at His return.

And Then There Were None. (Paws & Tales Ser.: No. 33). 2002. 3.99 (978-1-57972-484-9(1)); audio compact disk 5.99 (978-1-57972-485-6(X)) Insight Living.

And Then There Were None. unabr. ed. Agatha Christie. Read by Hugh Fraser. 4 cass. (Running Time: 6 hrs.). Orig. Title: Ten Little Indians. 2001. 24.95 (978-1-57270-250-9(8), N41250) Pub: Audio Partners. Dist(s): PerseuPGW
Ten people arrive on Indian Island off England?s southwest coast. They have been drawn there, to a grand mansion, by enticing invitations from a mysterious host. Of them, none will leave alive. They are the prey of a diabolical killer.

And Then There Were None. unabr. ed. Agatha Christie. Read by Hugh Fraser. (Mystery Masters Ser.). Orig. Title: Ten Little Indians. (ENG.). 2004.

audio compact disk 27.95 (978-1-57270-449-7(7)) Pub: AudioGO. Dist(s): Perseus Dist

***And Then There Were None: A BBC Full-Cast Radio Drama.** Agatha Christie. Narrated by Full Cast. (Running Time: 1 hr. 30 mins. 0 sec.). (ENG.). 2011. audio compact disk 24.95 (978-1-4084-6760-2(7)) Pub: AudioGO. Dist(s): Perseus Dist

And Then What Happened, Paul Revere? (J). 2004. bk. 24.95 (978-0-89719-697-0(X)); pap. bk. 14.95 (978-1-56008-157-9(0)); pap. bk. 32.75 (978-1-55592-349-5(6)); 8.95 (978-0-7882-0069-4(0)) Weston Woods.

And Then What Happened, Paul Revere? Jean Fritz. Illus. by Margot Tomes. 1 cass., 5 bks. (Running Time: 1 hr.). pap. bk. 32.75 Weston Woods.
Paul Revere comes to life in this meticulously detailed story of what he did before, between & after his patriotic adventures.

And Then What Happened, Paul Revere? Jean Fritz. Illus. by Margot Tomes. 1 cass. (Running Time: 1 hr.). (J). bk. 24.95; pap. bk. 12.95 Weston Woods.

***And Then What Happened, Paul Revere?** Weston Woods Staff. (YA). audio compact disk 12.95 (978-0-439-72282-7(9)) Weston Woods.

And Then You Die. unabr. ed. Michael Dibdin. Read by Michael Tudor Barnes. 6 cass. (Running Time: 6 hrs. 50 mins.). (Isis Ser.). (J). 2002. 54.95 (978-0-7531-1386-8(4)); audio compact disk 71.95 (978-0-7531-1414-8(3)) Pub: ISIS Lrg Prnt GBR. Dist(s): Ulverscroft US
Aurelio Zen of Rome's elite Criminalpol is back, but nobody's supposed to know it. After months in the hospital recovering from a bomb attack on his car, he is lying low under a false name at a beach resort on the Tuscan coast and waiting to testify in an anti-Mafia trial. Zen has instructions to enjoy the classic Italian beach holiday. But he is getting restless and, an number of people are dropping dead around him. Abruptly, the pleasant monotony of beach life is cut short as Zen finds himself transported to a remote and strange world. But wherever he goes, trouble follows. He must rely on his innate ability to navigate treacherous waters in order to stay alive.

And Then You Die. unabr. ed. Iris Johansen. Narrated by Richard Poe. 6 cass. (Running Time: 9 hrs.). 1998. 56.00 (978-0-7887-1975-2(0), 95362E7) Recorded Bks.
Seasoned photojournalist Bess Grady confronts a chilling scene of destruction on a travel magazine assignment in rural Mexico.

And Then You Die. unabr. ed. Iris Johansen. Narrated by Richard Poe. 8 CDs. (Running Time: 9 hrs.). 2000. audio compact disk 78.00 (978-0-7887-4472-3(0), C1169E7) Recorded Bks.

And There Was Light: Autobiography of Jacques Lusseyran: Blind Hero of the French Resistance. abr. ed. Jacques Lusseyran. Read by Andre Gregory. 3 cass. (Running Time: 4 hrs. 30 mins. 0 sec.). (ENG.). 1998. 19.95 (978-0-930407-27-8(X), 321-010) Pub: Morning Light Pr. Dist(s): PerseuPGW
Blinded at age eight, Lusseyran nevertheless became an important student leader in the French Resistance, was arrested by the Gestapo, and survived imprisonment at Buchenwald. This spellbinding and inspirational memoir reveals to us his unique experience of blindness. For Lusseyran, becoming blind brought an extraordinary gift of "inner sight" reaching far beyond ordinary senses. This audio version illuminates the life, depth of spirit and ultimate triumph of Lusseyran.

***And Thereby Hangs a Tale.** unabr. ed. Jeffrey Archer. Read by Gerard Doyle. (Running Time: 7 hrs. 30 mins. 0 sec.). (ENG.). 2010. audio compact disk 29.99 (978-1-4272-1028-9(4)) Pub: Macmill Audio. Dist(s): Macmillan

And to Think That I Saw It on Mulberry Street see Dr. Seuss Audio Collection

***And When the Sky Was Opened.** (ENG.). 2010. audio compact disk (978-1-59171-273-2(4)) Falcon Picture.

***And You Know You Should Be Glad.** abr. ed. Bob Greene. Read by Bob Greene. (ENG.). 2006. (978-0-06-113505-7(4), Harper Audio); (978-0-06-113504-0(6), Harper Audio) HarperCollins Pubs.

And You Shall Be a Blessing. Debbie Friedman. Ed. by Randee Friedman. Tr. by Randee Friedman. 1 cass. (Running Time: 31 mins.). 1989. 9.95 (978-1-890161-09-5(8)) Sounds Write.
Twelve contemporary original Jewish songs inspired by liturgical & biblical themes.

And You Shall Be a Blessing. Debbie Friedman. Ed. by Randee Friedman. Tr. by Randee Friedman. 1 CD. (Running Time: 31 mins.). 1989. audio compact disk 15.95 (978-1-890161-10-1(1)) Sounds Write.

Andalucian suite, No. 1. Juan Martin. (ENG.). 2008. pap. bk. 19.95 (978-0-7866-8005-4(9)) Mel Bay.

Andamos. Alma Flor Ada. 1 cass. (Running Time: 33 mins.). (SPA.). (J). (gr. k-1). 1987. 3.28 incl. script. (978-0-201-16871-6(5)) Pearson ESL.

Andando Con El Invisible. Rodolfo Garza. 6 cass. 2004. 25.00 Christ for the Nations.

Andando con el Invisible. Rodolfo Garza. (SPA.). 2004. 30.00 (978-0-89985-437-3(0)); audio compact disk 30.00 (978-0-89985-436-6(2)) Christ for the Nations.

Andean Fantasy/Fantasia Andiana. Tribus Futuras. Perf. by Tribus Futuras. 1 CD. (Running Time: 59 mins.). (ENG & SPA.). (J). 1999. audio compact disk 14.98 (978-1-893967-15-1(8), EK5013) Emphasis Ent.
An enchanting children's story comparing the natural elements of the world, with musical accompaniment on Andean instruments.

Andersen-Tawil Syndrome - A Bibliography & Dictionary for Physicians, Patients, & Genome Researchers. Compiled by Icon Group International, Inc. Staff. 2007. ring bd. 28.95 (978-0-497-11328-5(7)) Icon Grp.

Andersen's Fairy Tales. Hans Christian Andersen. Narrated by Flo Gibson. (ENG.). (J). 2007. audio compact disk 19.95 (978-1-55685-949-6(X)) Audio Bk Con.

Andersen's Fairy Tales. Hans Christian Andersen. Read by Erica Johns. (Running Time: 2 hrs. 30 mins.). 1998. 20.95 (978-1-60083-673-2(9)) Iofy Corp.

Andersen's Fairy Tales. Short Stories. Read by Erica Johns. Tr. by Hans Christian Andersen from DAN. 2 CDs. (Running Time: 2 hrs. 35 mins.). (J). (ps-3). 1994. audio compact disk 17.98 (978-962-634-012-7(6), NA201212, Naxos AudioBooks) Naxos.
Includes classic favorites such as The ugly Duckling, The Emperor's New Clothes, Little match Girl, Big Claus and Little Claus and many, many more.

Andersen's Fairy Tales. Read by Erica Johns. Tr. by Hans Christian Andersen from DAN. 2 cass. (Running Time: 2 hrs. 35 mins.). (J). (ps-3). 1995. 14.98 (978-962-634-512-2(8), NA201214, Naxos AudioBooks) Naxos.
Includes classic favorites such as "The Ugly Duckling," " The Emperor's New Clothes," "The Little Match Girl," " Big Claus and Little Claus" and many, many more.

***Andersen's Fairy Tales.** unabr. ed. Hans Christian Andersen. Compiled by James Baldwin. Narrated by Robin Field. (ENG.). 2010. 14.98 (978-1-59644-957-2(8), MissionAud); audio compact disk 21.98 (978-1-59644-956-5(X), MissionAud) christianaud.

Andersen's Fairy Tales, unabr. ed. Read by Flo Gibson. Tr. by Hans Christian Andersen. 3 cass. (Running Time: 4 hrs.). (J). 1992. 16.95 (978-1-55685-227-5(4)) Audio Bk Con.
This collection includes the early translations of "The Snow Queen", "The Princess & the Pea", "Thumbelina", "The Emperor's New Clothes", "The Last Pearl", "The Hardy Tin Soldier", "The Ugly Duckling", "The Little Sea Maid", "The Money Pig", & "The Red Shoes".

Andersen's Tales. Hans Christian Andersen. Read by Yadira Sánchez. (Running Time: 3 hrs.). 2001. 16.95 (978-1-60083-171-3(0), Audiofy Corp) Iofy Corp.

Anderson Tapes. unabr. ed. Lawrence Sanders. Read by Barry Cooper. 7 cass. (Running Time: 9 hrs.). 1986. 41.65 (B-121) Audio Bk.
"John Duke" Anderson was a man with a dream. He wanted to invade a Manhattan luxury apartment building, take it over & systematically loot it. Anderson's plan did not take into account that every person in the building was being secretly tape recorded.

Anderson's Ohio Criminal Practice & Procedure. 10th ed. Thomas Hagel. pap. bk. 310.00 (978-1-59345-231-5(4)) Pub: LexisNexis Matthew Bender. Dist(s): LEXIS Pub

Andersonville Diary. unabr. ed. John L. Ransom. Narrated by Adrian Cronauer. 5 cass. (Running Time: 7 hrs. 30 mins.). 1988. 44.00 (978-1-55690-017-4(1), 88090E7) Recorded Bks.
A true account by a prisoner-of-war in the infamous confederate camp in Georgia.

Andersonville Trial. Saul Levitt. Read by Mark Moorhead et al. Ed. by Kevin Holley. 1 cass. (Running Time: 3 hrs.). Dramatization. 1990. 14.95 (978-1-878080-00-4(8)) Audio Theatre.
Dramatization of the Broadway play: the trial of Captain Henry Wirz, who headed the notorious Confederate prision camp where some 14,000 Union prisoners died during the Civil War.

Andre. Lew Dietz. Read by Rachel Sieben. Afterword by Toni Goodridge. Intro. by Toni Goodridge. (Running Time: 5400 sec.). (J). 2007. audio compact disk 24.95 (978-0-9761932-3-4(X)) Audio Bkshelf.

Andre. unabr. ed. Lew Dietz. Read by Rachel Sieben. Music by Brent Thompson. Intro. by Toni Goodridge. 2 cass. (Running Time: 1 hr. 30 min.). (J). (gr. 2 up). 1994. reel tape 14.95 (978-1-883332-06-8(0)) Audio Bkshelf.
This warm, fuzzy true story about a Maine family's adoption of a harbor seal will capture young imaginations. Sieben's compassion draws listeners into the family's dilemmas & delights with their unusual pet.

Andre Dubus: Interview with Andre Dubus & Kay Bonetti. 1 cass. (Running Time: 1 hr. 15 mins.). 1984. 13.95 (978-1-55644-100-4(2), 4052) Am Audio Prose.
Dubus discusses the possible interpretations of "A Father's Story".

Andrea del Sarto see Poetry of Robert Browning

Andrea's Painless Approach to Using APA Style: CD Version-PC or MAC. Created by eWorld Learning. Des. by Andrea L. Edmundson. (ENG.). 2009. audio compact disk 39.95 (978-0-9820857-0-7(2)) eWorld Lrng.

Andrea's Painless Approach to using APA Style: Downloadable Version-PC Only. Created by eWorld Learning. Des. by Andrea L. Edmundson. (ENG.). 2009. 39.95 (978-0-9820857-1-4(0)) eWorld Lrng.

Andrei Cordrescu. Andrei Codrescu. Read by Andrei Codrescu. Interview with Rebekah Presson. 1 cass. (Running Time: 29 mins.). 1991. 10.00 (010188) New Letters.

Andrei Voznesensky. Tr. by William J. Smith. Interview with Andrei Voznesensky. 1 cass. (Running Time: 25 mins.). 1978. 12.95 (L078) TFR.
The Russian poet explains how he criticizes the Soviet establishment without getting into trouble. He also reads some of his poems, with English translation.

Andrei Voznesensky. Read by Andrei Voznesensky et al. 1 cass. (Running Time: 29 mins.). 1985. 10.00 New Letters.
Russian poet Andrei Voznesensky was recorded at a public reading at Syracuse University.

Andresito Y el Leon. Tr. of Andy & the Lion. (SPA.). 2004. 8.95 (978-0-7882-0258-2(8)) Weston Woods.

Andrew Britton CD Collection: The American, the Assassin, the Invisible. abr. ed. Andrew Britton. (Running Time: 18 hrs.). 2009. audio compact disk 34.99 (978-1-4233-9729-8(0), 9781423397298, BACD) Brilliance Audio.

Andrew Carnegie. unabr. rev. ed. David Nasaw. Read by Grover Gardner. (Running Time: 33 hrs.). (ENG.). 2007. audio compact disk 29.98 (978-1-59659-124-0(2), GildAudio) Pub: Gildan Media. Dist(s): HachBkGrp

Andrew Jackson. Robert Vincent Remini. (Running Time: 25200 sec.). 2005. audio compact disk 24.95 (978-0-7861-9661-6(0), 1434) Blckstn Audio.

Andrew Jackson. Linda R. Wade. (Presidential Read along Ser.). (J). (gr. 4-12). 1993. lib. bdg. 9.99 (978-0-87386-091-8(8)) Jan Prods.

Andrew Jackson. unabr. ed. Tom Parker. 13 vols. (Running Time: 7 hrs.). 2005. audio compact disk 29.95 (978-0-7861-7969-5(4), ZM1434) Blckstn Audio.

Andrew Jackson, unabr. ed. Robert V. Remini. Read by Tom Parker. 5 cass. (Running Time: 7 hrs.). 1994. 39.95 (978-0-7861-0482-6(1), 1434) Blckstn Audio.
Portrays the President as a shrewd & able politician, a pioneer in using the office of the Presidency for both national & narrowly partisan purposes.

Andrew Jackson. unabr. ed. Robert V. Remini. Read by Tom Parker. 6 CDs. (Running Time: 7 hrs.). 2000. audio compact disk 48.00 (978-0-7861-9843-6(5), 1434) Blckstn Audio.

Andrew Jackson. unabr. ed. Robert V. Remini. Read by Tom Parker. 1 CD. (Running Time: 7 hrs.). 2001. audio compact disk 19.95 (zm1434) Blckstn Audio.

Andrew Jackson. unabr. ed. Robert V. Remini. (Running Time: 7.5 hrs. NaN mins.). (Great Generals Ser.). 2008. 29.95 (978-1-4332-4726-2(7)); audio compact disk & audio compact disk 29.95 (978-1-4332-4725-5(9)) Blckstn Audio.

Andrew Jackson. unabr. ed. Robert Vincent Remini. 5 cass. (Running Time: 25200 sec.). 2005. 27.95 (978-0-7861-3654-4(5), E1434) Blckstn Audio.

Andrew Jackson. unabr. ed. Robert Vincent Remini. Read by Tom Parker. 6 CDs. (Running Time: 25200 sec.). 2005. audio compact disk 29.95 (978-0-7861-7743-1(8), ZE1434) Blckstn Audio.

Andrew Jackson: Great Generals Series. unabr. ed. Robert V. Remini. (Running Time: 7.5 hrs. NaN mins.). 2008. 54.95 (978-1-4332-4723-1(2)); audio compact disk 60.00 (978-1-4332-4724-8(0)) Blckstn Audio.

Andrew Jackson: His Life & Times. abr. ed. H. W. Brands. Read by Chuck Montgomery. 8 CDs. (Running Time: 28800 sec.). (ENG.). 2005. audio compact disk 39.95 (978-0-7393-2169-0(2)) Pub: Random Audio Pubg. Dist(s): Random
The extraordinary story of Andrew Jackson—the colorful, dynamic, and forceful president who ushered in the Age of Democracy and set a still young America on its path to greatness—told by the bestselling author of The First American. The most famous American of his time, Andrew Jackson is a seminal figure in American history. The first “common man” to rise to the presidency, Jackson embodied the spirit and the vision of the emerging American nation; the term “Jacksonian democracy” is embedded in our national lexicon. With the sweep, passion, and attention to detail that made The First American a Pulitzer Prize finalist and a national bestseller, historian H.W. Brands shapes a historical narrative that’s as fast-paced and compelling as the best fiction. He follows Andrew Jackson from his days as rebellious youth, risking execution to free the Carolinas of the British during the Revolutionary War, to his years as a young lawyer and congressman from the newly settled frontier state of Tennessee. As general of the Tennessee militia, he put down a massive Indian uprising in the South, securing the safety of American settlers, and his famous rout of the British at the Battle of New Orleans during the War of 1812 made him a national hero. But it is Jackson’s contributions as president, however, that won him a place in the pantheon of America’s greatest leaders. A man of the people, without formal education or the family lineage of the Founding Fathers, he sought as president to make the country a genuine democracy, governed by and for the people. Jackson, although respectful of states’ rights, devoted himself to the preservation of the Union, whose future in that age was still very much in question. When South Carolina, his home state, threatened to secede over the issue of slavery, Jackson promised to march down with 100,000 federal soldiers should it dare. In the bestselling tradition of Founding Brothers and His Excellency by Joseph Ellis and of John Adams by David McCullough, Andrew Jackson is the first single-volume, full-length biography of Jackson in decades. This magisterial portrait of one of our greatest leaders promises to reshape our understanding of both the man and his era and is sure to be greeted with enthusiasm and acclaim.

Andrew Jackson & His Indian Wars. V. Remini Robert. Read by Gardner Grover. 8 cass. (Running Time: 13 hrs.). 2004. 56.95 (978-0-7861-2722-1(8), 3281); audio compact disk 80.00 (978-0-7861-8676-1(3), 3281) Blckstn Audio.

Andrew Jackson the Gunfighter President & Hero of His Country, abr. ed. 3 cass. (Running Time: 4 hrs. 24 min.). (History As It Happens Ser.: Vol. 1). 2000. 19.95 (978-1-889252-04-9(2)) Photosensitive.

Andrew Johnson & The Reconstruction. (Presidency Ser.). 10.00 Esstee Audios.
Illustration of the man who tried to heal the nation's wounds.

Andrew Lloyd Webber: A Vocal Collection Sung by Beth Lawrence. Composed by Andrew Lloyd Webber. Lyrics by Tim Rice et al. 1 CD. 1998. audio compact disk 13.98 (978-0-9656196-4-6(8), JM8038-2) Junie Moon Mus.

Andrew Lloyd Webber: Love Songs. Composed by Andrew Lloyd Webber. 1 cass. 1998. 18.98 Lifedance.
Favorite songs sung by four of the stars from the original London casts.

Andrew Lost: Books 1-4:#1: Andrew Lost on the Dog; #2: Andrew Lost in the Bathroom; #3: Andrew Lost in the Kitchen; #4: Andrew Lost in the Garden. J. C. Greenburg. 2 cass. (Running Time: 3 hrs.). (Andrew Lost Ser.: Bks. 1-4). (J). (gr. 2-4). 2004. 19.55 (978-1-4000-8977-2(8), Listening Lib) Pub: Random Audio Pubg. Dist(s): NetLibrary CO

Andrew Marvell: Ralph Richardson Reads Andrew Marvell. unabr. ed. Narrated by Ralph Richardson. 1 cass. 12.95 (ECN 138) J Norton Pubs.
Reflects in the nature of God & through suffering man recognize grace. Includes Sir Ralph Richardson presenting his favorite Marvell's verse & talks with understanding & affection. Also Odes search for inner truth & the essence of things.

Andrew Weil Audio Collection. Andrew Weil. 4 CDs. (Running Time: 4 hrs. 15 mins.). 2001. stu. ed. 39.95 (978-1-56455-949-4(1), AW00590D) Sounds True.
Includes these two insightful sessions: Breathing: The Master Key to Self Healing and Meditation for Optimum Health.

Andrew Young: We Are Stronger. Andrew Young. Read by Andrew Young. 1 cass. (Running Time: 1 hr.). 10.95 (K0420B090, HarperThor) HarpC GBR.

Androgen Insensitivity Syndrome - A Bibliography & Dictionary for Physicians, Patients, & Genome Researchers. Compiled by Icon Group International, Inc. Staff. 2007. ring bd. 28.95 (978-0-497-11329-2(5)) Icon Grp.

Androgenetic Alopecia - A Bibliography & Dictionary for Physicians, Patients, & Genome Researchers. Compiled by Icon Group International, Inc. Staff. 2007. ring bd. 28.95 (978-0-497-11330-8(9)) Icon Grp.

Androgenic Disorders. Contrib. by Gerson Weiss et al. 1 cass. (American College of Obstetrics & Gynecologists UPDATE: Vol. 21, No. 5). 1998. 20.00 Am Coll Obstetric.

Androgyny: The Next Step in the Evolution of Consciousness. Read by June Singer. 1 cass. (Running Time: 90 mins.). 1976. 10.95 (978-0-7822-0258-8(6), 024B) C G Jung IL.

Androgyny & Transformation. Read by Joan Halifax. 1 cass. (Running Time: 90 mins.). 1976. 10.95 (978-0-7822-0084-3(2), 025) C G Jung IL.

Androgyny As Biological Destiny. Read by Sheldon Hendler. 1 cass. (Running Time: 90 mins.). 1976. 10.95 (978-0-7822-0090-4(7), 024A) C G Jung IL.

Androgyny, Polarity & Sexuality: Re-Membering the Intimate Other. Kenneth James. Read by Kenneth James. 1 cass. (Running Time: 90 mins.). 1993. 10.95 (978-0-7822-0457-5(0), 534) C G Jung IL.

Android Sisters. unabr. ed. Meatball Fulton. Read by Tim Clark et al. 1 cass. (Running Time: 40 mins.). Dramatization. (Songs of Electronic Despair Ser.). 1984. 8.50 (978-1-881137-08-5(2)) ZBS Found.
Featured in several of the Ruby episodes are the song stylings of a high-tech, electrifying duo known as The Android Sisters. Their humorous, satirical music is now available separately.

***Andromeda Klein.** unabr. ed. Frank Portman. Read by Deirdre Lovejoy. 12 CDs. (Running Time: 14 hrs. 25 mins.). (YA). (gr. 10 up). 2009. audio compact disk 70.00 (978-0-7393-6294-5(1), Listening Lib) Pub: Random Audio Pubg. Dist(s): Random

Andromeda Klein. unabr. ed. Frank Portman. Read by Deirdre Lovejoy. (ENG.). (J). (gr. 9). 2009. audio compact disk 54.00 (978-0-7393-6292-1(5), Listening Lib) Pub: Random Audio Pubg. Dist(s): Random

Andy & the Lion see Andresito Y el Leon

Andy & the Lion. 2004. 8.95 (978-1-56008-829-5(X)); cass. & flmstrp 30.00 (978-0-89719-528-7(0)) Weston Woods.

Andy & the Lion. (J). 2004. bk. 24.95 (978-0-89719-698-7(8)) Weston Woods.

Andy & the Lion; Biggest Bear, the; Caps for Sale; Little Toot. 2004. (978-0-89719-803-5(4)) Weston Woods.

Andy & the Lion; Biggest Bear, the; Caps for Sale, Little Toot. 2004. cass. & flmstrp (978-0-89719-712-0(7)) Weston Woods.

Andy Andrews Presents the Guided Traveler Experience: A Personal Journey into the Seven Decisions. (ENG.). 2008. audio compact disk 295.00 (978-0-9629620-6-6(6)) Lightning Crown Pub.

Andy Andrews, the Seven Decisions Audio CD: An Evening with New York Times Bestselling Author Andy Andrews: the Seven Decisions. As told by Andy Andrews. 2005. bk. 19.99 (978-0-9776246-7-6(6)) Lightning Crown Pub.

Andy Catlett: Early Travels. unabr. ed. Wendell Berry. Read by Paul Michael. (Running Time: 4 hrs. 12 mins. 0 sec.). (ENG.). 2008. audio compact disk 23.98 (978-1-59644-531-4(9)) christianaud.

***Andy Catlett: Early Travels: A Novel.** unabr. ed. Wendell Berry. Narrated by Paul Michael. (Yasmin Peace Ser.). (ENG.). 2008. 14.98 (978-1-59644-532-1(7), christaudio) christianaud.

Andy Griffin Show: 11 Kings 4:1-7. Ed Young. 1991. 4.95 (978-0-7417-1853-2(7), 853) Win Walk.

Andy Griffith Show V42. unabr. ed. Thomas B. Costain. 1 cass. 1993. 80.00 Books on Tape.

Andy Kaufman Revealed! Best Friend Tells All. abr. ed. Bob Zmuda & Matthew S. Hanson. Read by Bob Zmuda. Narrated by Jim Carrey. 2 cass. (Running Time: 3 hrs.). 1999. 17.98 (978-1-57042-765-7(8)) Hachet Audio.

Andy Lopez, the Invisible Gardener, Demonstrates Natural Pest Control Techniques; A Report on the Fire Ant Invasion. Hosted by Nancy Pearlman. 1 cass. (Running Time: 29 mins.). 10.00 (1403) Educ Comm CA.

Andy Shane & the Pumpkin Trick. Jennifer Richard Jacobson. Read by Rachel Lillis. Illus. by Abby Carter. (Andy Shane Ser.). (J). 2008. bk. 28.95 (978-1-4301-0316-5(7)) Live Oak Media.

Andy Shane & the Pumpkin Trick. Jennifer Richard Jacobson. Read by Rachel Lillis. Illus. by Abby Carter. 1 CD. (Running Time: 17 mins.). (Andy Shane Ser.). (J). (gr. 1-3). 2008. bk. 18.95 (978-1-4301-0315-8(9)) Live Oak Media.

Andy Shane & the Pumpkin Trick. Jennifer Richard Jacobson. Read by Rachel Lillis. Illus. by Abby Carter. (Andy Shane Ser.). (J). (ps-3). 2008. bk. 25.95 (978-1-4301-0313-4(2)); pap. bk. 16.95 (978-1-4301-0312-7(4)) Live Oak Media.

Andy Shane & the Very Bossy Dolores Starbuckle. Jennifer Richard Jacobson. Read by Rachel Lillis. Illus. by Abby Carter. (Andy Shane Ser.). (J). 2008. bk. 28.95 (978-1-4301-0324-0(8)); pap. bk. 18.95 (978-1-4301-0323-3(X)) Live Oak Media.

Andy Shane & the Very Bossy Dolores Starbuckle. Jennifer Richard Jacobson. Read by Rachel Lillis. Illus. by Abby Carter. (Andy Shane Ser.). (J). (ps-3). 2008. bk. 25.95 (978-1-4301-0321-9(3)); pap. bk. 16.95 (978-1-4301-0320-2(5)) Live Oak Media.

Andy Warhol. Wayne Koestenbaum. Read by Arthur Addison. 5 cass. (Running Time: 7 hrs. 30 mins.). 2001. 40.00 (978-0-7366-7624-3(4)) Books on Tape.
reveals the man behind the blond wig and dark glasses. Nimbly weaving brilliant and witty analysis into an absorbing narrative, a convincing case for Warhol as a serious artist, one whose importance goes beyond the sixties. Focusing on Warhol's provocative, powerful films (many of which have been out of circulation since their initial release), Warhol's oeuvre, in its variety of forms (films, silkscreens, books, "happenings" and so on), maintains a striking consistency of theme: Warhol discovered in classic American images (Brillo boxes, Campbell soup cans, Marilyn's face) a secret history, the eroticism of time and space.

Andy Warhol. unabr. ed. Wayne Koestenbaum. 4 cass. (Running Time: 6 hrs.). 2001. 24.95 (978-0-7366-6811-8(X)) Books on Tape.
With entertaining & playful prose, acclaimed scholar Wayne Koestenbaum delves beneath Andy Warhol's mysterious facade & shows his profound depth as an artist & as a philosopher.

Andy Warhol. unabr. ed. Wayne Koestenbaum. Read by Arthur Addison. 6 CDs. (Running Time: 9 hrs.). 2002. audio compact disk 48.00 (978-0-7366-8543-6(X)) Books on Tape.
Nimbly weaving brilliant and witty analysis into an absorbing narrative, Koestenbaum makes a convincing case for Warhol as a serious artist, one whose importance goes beyond the sixties. Focusing on Warhol's provocative, powerful films (many of which have been out of circulation since their initial release), Koestenbaum shows that Warhol's oeuvre, in its variety of forms (films, silkscreens, books, "happenings" and so on), maintains a striking consistency of theme: Warhol discovered in classic American images (Brillo boxes, Campbell soup cans, Marilyn's face) a secret history, the eroticism of time and space.

Anecdotes of Destiny. unabr. collector's ed. Isak Dinesen. Read by Wanda McCaddon. 8 cass. (Running Time: 8 hrs.). 1984. 48.00 (978-0-7366-0916-6(4), 1859) Books on Tape.
A collection of stories by the author of OUT OF AFRICA.

Anecdotes of the Anglo-Boer War. Rob Milne. 2001. audio compact disk 17.50 (978-0-620-25439-7(4)) Pub: Covos-Day Bks ZAF. Dist(s): CEG

Anemia, Clotting Disorders & Thrombocytopenia. Contrib. by Susan B. Shurin et al. 1 cass. (American Academy of Pediatrics UPDATE: Vol. 16, No. 1). 1998. 20.00 Am Acad Pediat.

Anesthesiology for PDAs & Desktop PCs: 2002-2003 Edition. 2002nd ed. Mark Ezekiel. (Current Clinical Strategies Medical Book Ser.). 2001. 28.95 (978-1-929622-13-9(9)) Pub: Current Clin Strat. Dist(s): Matthews Medical Bk Co

Angel. Terry Oldfield. 1 cass. 10.95 (LA207); audio compact disk 15.95 (LA207D) Lghtwrks Aud & Vid.
Through keyboard, flute & percussion, spirals of angelic choirs & hovering metaphysical strains infuse the senses with reverence, leading them upwards to ever higher realms of light. "Angel" is a mystical & consciousness-expanding experience, & yet one can always enjoy the tranquil effects of the music simply for its intrinsic beauty.

Angel. unabr. ed. Barbara Taylor Bradford. Read by Lorelei King. 8 cass. (Running Time: 8 hrs.). (Isis Ser.). (J). 2001. 69.95 (978-1-85695-720-5(9), 931105) Pub: ISIS Lrg Prnt GBR. Dist(s): Ulverscroft US

Angel. unabr. ed. Barbara Taylor Bradford. Read by Lorelei King. 10 CDs. (Running Time: 10 hrs.). (Isis Ser.). (J). 2001. audio compact disk 89.95 (978-0-7531-0693-8(0), 106930) Pub: ISIS Lrg Prnt GBR. Dist(s): Ulverscroft US

***Angel.** unabr. ed. James Patterson. (Running Time: 6 hrs.). (Maximum Ride Ser.). (ENG.). 2011. 15.98 (978-1-60788-697-6(9)); audio compact disk 22.98 (978-1-60788-696-9(0)) Pub: Hachet Audio. Dist(s): HachBkGrp

***Angel at My Door: Amazing Things That Happen When Angels Show Up!** unabr. ed. Robert Strand. Narrated by Maurice England. (ENG.). 2010. 8.98 (978-1-59644-945-9(4)); audio compact disk 10.98 (978-1-59644-944-2(6)) christianaud.

Angel at the Fence. unabr. ed. Herman Rosenblat. Read by Melisa Foster. (Running Time: 8 hrs.). 2009. 24.99 (978-1-4233-7638-5(2), 9781423376385, BAD) Brilliance Audio.

Angel at the Grave see Selected Short Stories by Edith Wharton

Angel Band. John Horman. (gr. 2-6). 2004. bk. 16.00 (978-0-687-04535-8(5)); bk. 12.00 (978-0-687-04565-5(7)) Abingdon.

Angel Band: A Christmas Musical Based on Luke 2:1-20. John Horman. Contrib. by Nylea Butler-Moore. (gr. 2-6). bk. 60.00 (978-0-687-04555-6(X)) Abingdon.

Angel Band: A Christmas Musical Based on Luke 2:1-20. John Horman. 1 cass. (Running Time: 90 min.). (gr. 2-6). 2004. bk. 12.00 (978-0-687-02871-9(X)); bk. 40.00 (978-0-687-02862-7(0)) Abingdon.

Angel Band Preview Pak: A Christmas Musical Based on Luke 2:1-20. John Horman. (gr. 2-6). 2002. bk. 10.00 (978-0-687-02881-8(7)) Abingdon.

Angel Band Set: A Christmas Musical Based on Luke 2:1-20. John Horman. (gr. 2-6). 2002. bk. 40.00 (978-0-687-04525-9(8)) Abingdon.

Angel Band Value Pak: A Christmas Musical Based on Luke 2:1-20. ldr.'s ed. John Horman. (gr. 2-6). 2004. bk. 26.00 (978-0-687-02852-8(3)) Abingdon.

***Angel Bear Adventure Stories.** Narrated by Mark Eley. (ENG.). 2007. audio compact disk 19.99 (978-0-9789060-4-7(7)) Angel Bear.

Angel Beauty. Erik Berglund. 1 cass. 9.95 (LA202); audio compact disk 15.95 (LA202D) Lghtwrks Aud & Vid.
Immerse yourself deeply into the world of the angels with the fluid harp & synthesizer music of Mount Shasta artist Erik Berglund. Designed to assist in soothing & healing those parts of us that need more love, joy, compassion, faith & trust.

***Angel Connection: Solo Harp for Deep Relaxation, Meditation, & Healing.** Carol J. Spears. (Playaway Adult Nonfiction Ser.). (ENG.). 2010. 39.99 (978-1-61587-631-0(6)) Find a World.

Angel Creek. Linda Howard. Read by Natalie Ross. (Playaway Adult Fiction Ser.). 2009. 64.99 (978-1-60812-661-3(7)) Find a World.

Angel Creek. unabr. ed. Linda Howard. Read by Natalie Ross. (Running Time: 9 hrs.). 2008. 39.25 (978-1-4233-6302-6(7), 9781423363026, Brlnc Audio MP3 Lib) Brilliance Audio.

Angel Creek. unabr. ed. Linda Howard. Read by Natalie Ross-Turski. (Running Time: 9 hrs.). 2008. 24.95 (978-1-4233-6301-9(9), 9781423363019, Brilliance MP3) Brilliance Audio.

Angel Creek. unabr. ed. Linda Howard. Read by Natalie Ross. (Running Time: 9 hrs.). 2008. 24.95 (978-1-4233-6303-3(5), 9781423363033, BAD); audio compact disk 92.25 (978-1-4233-6300-2(0), 9781423363002, BriAudCD Unabrid) Brilliance Audio.

Angel Creek. unabr. ed. Linda Howard. Read by Natalie Ross-Turski. (Running Time: 9 hrs.). 2008. audio compact disk 29.99 (978-1-4233-6299-9(3), 9781423362999, Bril Audio CD Unabri) Brilliance Audio.

Angel Creek. unabr. ed. Linda Howard. Read by Natalie Ross. (Running Time: 9 hrs.). 2009. 39.97 (978-1-4418-5025-6(2), 9781441850256, BADLE) Brilliance Audio.

Angel Doll. unabr. ed. Jerry Bledsoe. Read by J. Charles. (Running Time: 1 hr.). 2009. 39.97 (978-1-4233-8913-2(1), 9781423389132, Brlnc Audio MP3 Lib); 39.97 (978-1-4233-8915-6(8), 9781423389156, BADLE); 24.99 (978-1-4233-8912-5(3), 9781423389125, Brilliance MP3); 24.99 (978-1-4233-8914-9(X), 9781423389149, BAD) Brilliance Audio.

Angel Dust. unabr. ed. Roderic Vickers. Perf. by Roderic Vickers. 1 cass. (Running Time: 1 hr.). 1995. 9.95 (978-1-886956-01-8(4)) Star Concepts.
2 thirty minute pieces for meditation.

Angel Encounters. Bruce Goldberg. (ENG.). 2005. audio compact disk 17.00 (978-1-57968-041-1(0)); audio compact disk 17.00 (978-1-57968-068-8(2)) Pub: B Goldberg. Dist(s): Baker Taylor

Angel Encounters. Bruce Goldberg. Read by Bruce Goldberg. 1 cass. (Running Time: 25 mins.). (ENG.). 2006. 13.00 (978-1-885577-27-6(3)) Pub: B Goldberg. Dist(s): Baker Taylor
Meet a guardian angel through hypnosis. Be prepared to experience much love and understanding concerning karmic purpose.

Angel Eyes. abr. ed. Loren D. Estleman. Read by Alan Zimmerman. 4 vols. (Running Time: 360 min.). (Amos Walker Ser.). 2000. 25.00 (978-1-58807-045-6(X)) Am Pubng Inc.

Angel Eyes. abr. ed. Loren D. Estleman. Read by Alan Zimmerman. 4 vols. (Amos Walker Ser.). 2001. (978-1-58807-602-1(4)) Am Pubng Inc.

***Angel Fall: A Novel.** Coleman Luck. (Running Time: 12 hrs. 41 mins. 0 sec.). (ENG.). 2009. 14.99 (978-0-310-77305-4(9)) Zondervan.

***Angel Falls.** abr. ed. Kristin Hannah. 2011. audio compact disk 9.99 (978-1-4418-6712-4(0)) Brilliance Audio.

Angel Falls. unabr. ed. Kristin Hannah. Read by Bruce Reizen. (Running Time: 8 hrs.). 2004. 49.97 (978-1-59600-454-2(1), 1596004541, BADLE); 24.95 (978-1-59600-453-5(3), 1596004533, BAD); 39.25 (978-1-59600-452-8(5), 1596004525, Brlnc Audio MP3 Lib); 24.95 (978-1-59600-451-1(7), 1596004517, Brilliance MP3) Brilliance Audio.
This richly nuanced novel tells of an ordinary man faced with an incredible dilemma - to save his wife's life he must risk losing her forever. Michaela, beloved wife and mother of two, lies in a coma. Doctors have told her husband Liam not to expect a recovery, but he maintains hope that love can accomplish what medicine cannot. Day after day, he sits by her bedside, holding her hand, sharing the stories of their life together. Then he discovers the evidence of his wife's secret past - a long hidden first marriage to international movie star Julian True. When he sees photos of her glowing happiness with Julian, he knows the actor was more than simply Michaela's first husband. He was the love of her life. Liam senses that Julian is the one person who can bring her back to life, but at what cost? Can Liam love his wife enough to risk losing her to a man no woman could resist?.

Angel Falls. unabr. ed. Kristin Hannah. Read by Bruce Reizen. (Running Time: 8 hrs.). 2010. audio compact disk 29.99 (978-1-4418-3566-6(0), 9781441835666, Bril Audio CD Unabri); audio compact disk 89.97 (978-1-4418-3567-3(9), 9781441835673, BriAudCD Unabrid) Brilliance Audio.

Angel Fire East. unabr. ed. Terry Brooks. Narrated by George Wilson. 9 cass. (Running Time: 13 hrs. 15 mins.). (Word & the Void Ser.: Bk. 3). 1999. 80.00 (978-0-7887-4052-7(0), 96159E7) Recorded Bks.
After 25 years of battling the Void for fate of humanity, John Ross has discovered a newly born gypsy morph. This powerful creature could prove an invaluable tool against evil. But can he solve its mystery before the Void destroys it?.

***Angel from Hell: Real Life on the Front Lines.** unabr. ed. Ryan A. Conklin. (Running Time: 12 hrs. 30 mins. 0 sec.). (ENG.). 2010. 24.99 (978-1-4001-6408-0(7)); 17.99 (978-1-4001-8408-8(8)); audio compact disk 34.99 (978-1-4001-1408-5(X)); audio compact disk 69.99 (978-1-4001-4408-2(6)) Pub: Tantor Media. Dist(s): IngramPubServ

Angel Hour: Music of Healing from the Film a Servant's Heart. 2004. audio compact disk 10.00 (978-0-9747366-6-2(X)) Erie Chapman.

Angel Hunt. Mike Ripley & Jack Paulin. 2008. 61.95 (978-1-84652-213-0(7)); audio compact disk 79.95 (978-1-84652-214-7(5)) Pub: Magna Story GBR. Dist(s): Ulverscroft US

Angel in the Family. Dan Yates. 2 cass. (Running Time: 2 hrs.). (J). 1999. 12.95 (978-1-57734-283-0(6), 07001800) Covenant Comms.
Angelic adventure by the author of "Angels Don't Knock!".

Angel in the Family. Dan Yates. 1998. 9.95 (978-1-57734-302-8(6)) Covenant Comms.

Angel in the House. unabr. ed. Mike Ripley. Read by Dave John. 8 cass. (Running Time: 10 hrs. 35 mins.). (Story Sound Ser.). 2007. 69.95 (978-1-85903-979-3(0)); audio compact disk 89.95 (978-1-84652-098-3(3)) Pub: Mgna Lrg Print GBR. Dist(s): Ulverscroft US

Angel Inside: Michelangelo's Secrets for Following Your Passion & Finding the Work You Love. unabr. ed. Chris Widener. Read by Chris Widener. (Running Time: 7200 sec.). (ENG.). 2007. audio compact disk 19.95 (978-0-7393-4313-5(0), Random AudioBks) Pub: Random Audio Pubg. Dist(s): Random

Angel Island. abr. ed. Dan Yates. 4 CDs. 2004. audio compact disk 15.95 (978-1-59156-718-9(1)) Covenant Comms.

Angel Landing, unabr. ed. Alice Hoffman. Read by Bonnie Hurren. 8 vols. (Running Time: 9 hrs. 30 mins.). 1999. bk. 69.95 (978-0-7927-2315-8(5), CSL 204, Chivers Sound Lib) AudioGO.
Natalie, a therapist, is in love with Carter. However, he is deeply dedicated to his environmental work & the fate of their relationship takes a back-seat to the fate of the planet. Then a new client walks into Natalie's office. He is an intriguing man with an incredible tale to tell. Under his influence, she faces questions about the direction of her own passion, the true meaning of commitment & the possibility of finding the love she seeks.

Angel Meadow. Audrey Howard. Read by Carole Boyd. 12 cass. (Running Time: 18 hrs.). 2002. 96.95 (978-0-7540-0695-4(6), CAB 2117) AudioGO.

Angel Medicine: How to Heal the Body & Mind with the Help of the Angels. Doreen Virtue. 1. 2004. audio compact disk 10.95 (978-1-4019-0364-0(9), 3649) Hay House.

Angel Medicine: How to Heal the Body & Mind with the Help of the Angels. Doreen Virtue. 2 CDs. 2005. audio compact disk 18.95 (978-1-4019-0611-5(7), 6117) Hay House.

Angel, Mine. Deborah Milton. Perf. by High Sierra Players Staff. Narrated by Dave Hamilton. Score by Dave Fabrizio. Directed By Dave Fabrizio. Illus. by Katrina Kirkpatrick. 3 CDs. (Running Time: 3 hrs. 42 mins.). Dramatization. 2004. audio compact disk 19.95 (978-1-58124-021-4(X)) Pub: Fiction Works. Dist(s): Brodart

Angel of Darkness. Caleb Carr. Narrated by George Guidall. 18 cass. (Running Time: 26 hrs.). 1998. 149.00 (978-1-4025-3519-2(8)) Recorded Bks.

ANGEL of DARKNESS. Caleb Carr. 2004. 15.95 (978-0-7435-4157-2(X)) Pub: S&S Audio. Dist(s): S and S Inc

Angel of Darkness. unabr. ed. Caleb Carr. Read by Jonathan Marosz. 9 cass. (Running Time: 13 hrs. 30 mins.). 1998. 72.00 (978-0-7366-4114-2(9), 4619-A); 72.00 (978-0-7366-4115-9(7), 4619-B) Books on Tape.
Caleb Carr revisits turn-of-the-century New York. A year has passed since Dr. Laszlo Kriezler, a pioneer in forensic psychiatry, an "alienist" in the parlance of the times, tracked down a brutal serial killer with the help of his team of trusted companions. now the team reunites to find a Spanish diplomat's daughter kidnapped in Central Park.

Angel of Death. Paul C. Doherty. Narrated by Paul Matthews. 6 CDs. (Running Time: 6 hrs.). 2001. audio compact disk 62.00 (978-1-84197-200-8(2), C1346E7) Recorded Bks.
King Edward I's clerk, Hugh Corbett, is called upon again to solve a mystery or at the very least, repair the damage done to his master, by clearing him of suspicion. War has bled the English coffers dry! Royal pressure convenes the wealthy church's officials for Mass & to discuss money. During the service, Walter de Montfort, the King's enemy, dies shockingly & dramatically. There is clear evidence of murder. One person has a glaring obvious motive for the death & that is King Edward I!.

Angel of Death. Johnny Quarles. Read by Jef Fontana. 4 cass. (Running Time: 6 hrs.). Dramatization. 1997. Rental 24.95 (978-1-890990-10-7(8)) Otis Audio.
Seventeen-year-old Clayton Crist stood in front of a long line of boxcars. He carried two pistols, his rifle & a bowie knife. The enthusiasm was so strong inside him, he remembered. He was on his way to Nashville to join the Third & Eleventh regiments. Clayton served with the First Tennessee regiment throughout the entire Civil War, seeing action from Shiloh to Chickamauga. His fearless conduct during combat made him a legendary figure who some say killed 25 men in one battle.

Angel of Death. unabr. ed. Paul C. Doherty. Narrated by Paul Matthews. 5 cass. (Running Time: 6 hrs.). 2000. 47.00 (978-1-84197-086-8(7), H1087E7) Recorded Bks.
King Edward I's clerk, Hugh Corbett, is called upon again to solve a mystery or at the very least, repair the damage done to his master, by clearing him of suspicion. War has bled the English coffers dry! Royal pressure convenes the wealthy church's officials for Mass & to discuss money. During the service, Walter de Montfort, the King's enemy, dies shockingly & dramatically. There is clear evidence of murder. One person has a glaring obvious motive for the death & that is King Edward I!.

Angel of Death. unabr. ed. Jack Higgins. Read by Michael Page. (Running Time: 8 hrs.). (Sean Dillon Ser.). 2010. audio compact disk 29.99 (978-1-4418-3869-8(4), 9781441838698, Bril Audio CD Unabri) Brilliance Audio.

***Angel of Death.** unabr. ed. Jack Higgins. Read by Michael Page. (Running Time: 8 hrs.). (Sean Dillon Ser.). 2010. 24.99 (978-1-4418-3871-1(6), 9781441838711, Brilliance MP3); 39.97 (978-1-4418-3872-8(4), 9781441838728, Brlnc Audio MP3 Lib); audio compact disk 87.97 (978-1-4418-3870-4(8), 9781441838704, BriAudCD Unabrid) Brilliance Audio.

***Angel of Death.** unabr. ed. Jack Higgins. (Running Time: 8 hrs.). (Sean Dillon Ser.). 2011. audio compact disk 14.99 (978-1-4418-3876-6(7), 9781441838766, BCD Value Price) Brilliance Audio.

Angel of Death. unabr. ed. Roy H. Lewis. Read by Robbie MacNab. 6 cass. (Running Time: 8 hrs.). 1999. 69.95 (978-1-85903-264-0(8)) Ulvrscrft Audio.
A member of the archaeological team is found brutally murdered. Suspicion falls on Professor Westwood, who had been involved in a feud with the dead woman.

Angel of Eleventh Avenue. Roy Bates. Narrated by Cynthia Darlow. 2 cass. (Running Time: 2 hrs. 15 mins.). 21.00 (978-1-4025-4007-3(8)) Recorded Bks.

Angel of Honour. Jennifer Bacia. Read by Jane Badler. 8 cass. (Running Time: 12 hrs.). 2000. (978-1-876584-69-6(6), 591003) Bolinda Pubng AUS.
Her mother was a legendary screen goddess. Her father was the President. Wild, beautiful, passionate, she rebels against her convent upbringing to pursue secret desires & forbidden pleasures. Rejecting the land of her birth for fame & fortune in Europe, she loses herself in the decadent high society of Paris & London.

Angel of Hope. unabr. ed. Lurlene McDaniel. Narrated by Christina Moore. 3 pieces. (Running Time: 4 hrs. 30 mins.). (Mercy Trilogy). (gr. 7 up). 2002. 28.00 (978-0-7887-5288-9(X)) Recorded Bks.

Angel of Light. Scripts. Diana Cooper. 2 CDs. (Running Time: 2 hrs.). (ENG.). 2004. audio compact disk 21.99 (978-1-84409-019-8(1)) Pub: Findhorn Pr GBR. Dist(s): IPG Chicago
CD1Learning about Angels, Angel stories and how they can help us in our daily livesHow Angels can heal and lighten up our lives. How to work safely with angels.CD2Meeting your Angel and getting your Angel?s name. Increase your confidence and heal your heart. Finding your inner child. Singing with the Angels and journeying into the Archangels? retreats. A

visualisation and detachment exercise to release inappropriate ties, and a meditation into visiting the Archangels? chambers.

Angel of Light. Joyce Carol Oates. Read by Joyce Carol Oates. Prod. by Moveable Feast Staff. 1 cass. (Running Time: 30 mins.). 1981. 8.95 (AMF-8) Am Audio Prose.
Joyce Carol Oates reads "Angel of Light" & discusses violence, slavery, revenge, grotesques & the American novel.

Angel of Mercy. unabr. ed. Lurlene McDaniel. Narrated by Christina Moore. 3 pieces. (Running Time: 4 hrs. 15 mins.). (Mercy Trilogy). (gr. 7 up). 2002. 28.00 (978-0-7887-5287-2(1)) Recorded Bks.
After high school, 18-year-old Heather Barlow joins a missionary group on a hospital mercy ship bound for Africa. She will spend several months working in remote medical camps and villages. But arriving in Uganda, she is unprepared for the disease, famine, and misery she sees. Now Heather is struggling to look beyond these horrors and keep focused on ways to help the sick and needy. She draws strength from her friendship with a gentle medical student, Ian. As their feelings grow into love, Heather also learns how fragile the threads of life are.

Angel on My Shoulder: An Autobiography. Natalie Cole & Digby Diehl. 2002. (978-1-58621-087-8(4)) Hachet Audio.

Angel on My Shoulder: An Autobiography. abr. ed. Natalie Cole & Digby Diehl. Read by Natalie Cole. (ENG.). 2005. 14.98 (978-1-59483-449-3(0)) Pub: Hachet Audio. Dist(s): HachBkGrp

Angel on the Inside. Mike Ripley & Dave John. 2009. 76.95 (978-1-84652-461-5(X)); audio compact disk 89.95 (978-1-84652-462-2(8)) Pub: Magna Story GBR. Dist(s): Ulverscroft US

Angel on the Square. Gloria Whelan. 4 cass. (Running Time: 5 hrs. 30 min.). (YA). (gr. 5-9). 2004. 37.00 (978-1-4025-4192-6(9)) Recorded Bks.
Offers an insider's view of tsarist Russia and the Russian Revolution through the eyes of Katya, a playmate of the daughters of Tsar Nicholas II. When unrest sweeps through St. Petersburg the , the friends must come to terms with the fact that life will not remain the sam for the aristocracy Narrator Julie Dretzin gives life to the mobility and the commoners, and listeners will become immersed in the language and feeling of with Hugh Brewster's Anastasia's Album so students can see photos of the actual people and setting.

Angel on the Square. unabr. ed. Gloria Whelan. Narrated by Julie Dretzin. 5 CDs. (Running Time: 5 hrs. 30 min.). 2004. audio compact disk 48.75 (978-1-4025-6594-6(1)) Recorded Bks.

Angel Out of Tune. Glenn I. Latham. 1997. bk. 16.95 (978-0-9725742-4-2(7)); audio compact disk 19.95 (978-0-9725742-5-9(5)) P T ink.

Angel Passing Over. Alexandra Connor. Read by Nicolette McKenzie. 12 cass. (Sound Ser.). (J). 2002. 94.95 (978-1-84283-186-1(0)) Pub: ISIS Lrg Prnt GBR. Dist(s): Ulverscroft US

Angel Protection Guidelines Series, Elbert Willis. 4 cass. (Running Time: 4 hrs.). 13.00 Fill the Gap.

Angel-Seaxisc Grammaticcraeft. Richard L. Groff. 1 cass. (Beginning Anglo-Saxon Wordsmid Ser.). 1992. 15.98 (978-0-9630718-3-5(1)) New Dawn NY.

Angel Seekers Beware: Twenty Warnings. unabr. ed. Lynne Logan. Read by Lynne Logan. 1 cass. (Running Time: 1 hrs.). 1995. 11.00 (978-1-890907-02-0(2), 0003) Heaven Only.
Biblical information on angels.

***Angel Sister: A Novel.** unabr. ed. Ann H. Gabhart. (Running Time: 13 hrs. 0 mins. 0 sec.). (ENG.). 2011. audio compact disk 39.99 (978-1-59859-912-1(7)) Oasis Audio.

Angel Sleep. Med Goodall. 1 cass. (Running Time: 1 hr.). 10.95 (LA008); audio compact disk 15.95 (LA008D) Lghtwrks Aud & Vid.
A collection of delicately restful motifs to gently transport you, on the wings of infinity to the realm of the Angels. Here the soft humming of sleep comes to greet you in tones of ethereal lightness. Med's unique guitar style floats in an aura of relaxing, dreamlike sounds, creating a serene & calming environment for your still moments or for regaining your center at the end of an active day.

Angel Therapy Meditations. Doreen Virtue. 1 CD. 2008. audio compact disk 10.95 (978-1-4019-1832-3(8)) Hay House.

Angel Time. unabr. ed. Anne Rice. Read by Paul Michael. (Songs of the Seraphim Ser.: No. 1). (ENG., 2009. audio compact disk 35.00 (978-0-7393-1608-5(7), Random AudioBks) Pub: Random Audio Pubg. Dist(s): Random

Angel Touch. Mike Ripley & Jack Paulin. 2008. 61.95 (978-1-84652-215-4(3)); audio compact disk 79.95 (978-1-84652-216-1(1)) Pub: Magna Story GBR. Dist(s): Ulverscroft US

Angel Treasury. Belinda Womack. 2 cass. 1998. 22.00 (978-0-9659850-1-7(6)) Pubng Joy.

Angel Trumpet. Ann McMillan. Read by Kimberly Schraf. 1999. 56.00 (978-0-7366-4797-7(X)) Books on Tape.

Angel Trumpet: A Civil War Mystery, Ann McMillan. Read by Kimberly Schraf. 7 cass. (Running Time: 10 hrs. 30 mins.). 2000. 56.00 (5145) Books on Tape.
This sequel to "Dead March" takes place in 1861. A homecoming colonel returns to a plantation outside Richmond & finds his whole family butchered by their servants who, clutching knives, lie dead around them. Narcissa Powers, a well-to-do white widow & Judah Daniel, a free black herbalist, along with their British journalist friend, Brit Wallace, explore this bizarre crime.

Angel Within You. Joan Fericy. 1 cass. (Running Time: 1 hr.). 1991. 10.00 (978-0-9622371-0-2(8)) J Fericy.
Meditation, Self-Help, & Religion.

Angela. unabr. ed. James Moloney. Read by Kate Hosking. 5 cass. (Running Time: 6 hrs. 50 mins.). (YA). 2000. 40.00 (978-1-74030-108-4(0), 500327) Pub: Bolinda Pubng AUS. Dist(s): Bolinda Pub Inc

Angela. unabr. ed. James Moloney. Read by Kate Hosking. 6 CDs. (Running Time: 6 hrs. 50 mins.). (YA). 2001. audio compact disk 77.95 (978-1-74030-600-3(7)) Pub: Bolinda Pubng AUS. Dist(s): Bolinda Pub Inc

Angela & Diabola, unabr. ed. Lynne Reid Banks. Read by Lynne Reid Banks. 3 cass. (Running Time: 3 hrs.). (J). (gr. 1-8). 1999. 23.98 (LL 0113, Chivers Child Audio) AudioGO.

Angela & Diabola, unabr. ed. Lynne Reid Banks. Read by Lynne Reid Banks. 3 cass. (Running Time: 3 hrs.). (YA). 1999. 23.98 (FS9-34627) Highsmith.

Angela & Diabola. unabr. ed. Lynne Reid Banks. 3 cass. (Running Time: 3 hrs.). (J). 19.18 blisterpack. (BYA 948) NewSound.
Twins Angela & Diabola, are as different as can be. One is perfectly good, the other is perfectly evil. It is only Angela who has the power to change her twin for the better, but it will come at a high price for her.

Angela & Diabola. unabr. ed. Lynne Reid Banks. Read by Lynne Reid Banks. 3 cass. (Running Time: 4 hrs. 30 mins.). (J). (gr. 4-6). 1998. 28.98 (978-0-8072-7954-0(4), YA948SP, Listening Lib) Random Audio Pubg.
Angela & Diabola are twin sisters who are completely opposite. Only Angela can save them.

Angela & Diabola. unabr. ed. Lynne Reid Banks. Read by Lynne Reid Banks. 3 cass. (Running Time: 4 hr.). (J). (gr. 4-6). 2001. 30.00 (978-0-8072-7953-3(6), LL 0113, Listening Lib) Random Audio Pubg.
Jill & Jane, also known as Angela & Diabola, are twins who are complete opposites. One is good & one is evil. As the parents struggle to raise a child born of pure evil along with an angel awash in goodness, they discover that it is only the balance of the two extremes that brings any peace to their lives.

Angela Jackson, Pts. I & II. Read by Angela Jackson. 2 cass. (Running Time: 1 hr.). 1985. 10.00 ea. One-sided cass.; 18.00 Two-sided cass. New Letters.
Angela Jackson, author of "Voodoo-Love Magic" & "Solo in the Boxcar Third Floor E," gives a lively reading of her poems.

Angela's Ashes: A Memoir. abr. ed. Frank McCourt. Read by Frank McCourt. 4 cass. 1999. 24.00 (FS9-34493) Highsmith.

Angela's Ashes: A Memoir. abr. ed. Frank McCourt. Read by Frank McCourt. (Running Time: 43 hrs. 0 mins. 0 sec.). (ENG.). 2009. audio compact disk 14.99 (978-0-7435-8149-3(0)) Pub: S&S Audio. Dist(s): S and S Inc

Angela's Ashes: A Memoir. unabr. ed. Frank McCourt. Narrated by Frank McCourt. 13 CDs. (Running Time: 15 hrs.). audio compact disk 124.00 (978-0-7887-4909-4(9), C1290E7) Recorded Bks.
An unflinching vision of life on the dole in Ireland. It is also a powerful testament to the resilience of human spirit. Frank McCourt's early years are a nightmare. His father is a drunk & his mother is often pregnant, social services provides too little, too late but despite this deprivation, McCourt grows up with a passionate love of storytelling & an unerring eye for detail. He survives the squalor, cruelty & insensitive surrounding him by seasoning his memories with strains of music & compassion. McCourt now lives in New York, where he has been a teacher & an actor. Available to libraries only.

Angela's Ashes: A Memoir. unabr. ed. Frank McCourt. Narrated by Frank McCourt. 11 cass. (Running Time: 15 hrs.). 1997. 96.00 (978-0-7887-1172-5(5), 95045E7) Recorded Bks.
In this memoir, filled with poverty & humor, suffering & grace, the author traces his childhood in Limerick, Ireland.

Angela's Ashes: A Memoir. unabr. ed. Frank McCourt. Read by Frank McCourt. 12 CDs. (Running Time: 150 hrs. 0 mins. 0 sec.). (ENG.). 2005. audio compact disk 49.95 (978-0-7435-5092-5(7)) Pub: S&S Audio. Dist(s): S and S Inc

Angela's Ashes: A Memoir of a Childhood. Frank McCourt. 2004. 15.95 (978-0-7435-4158-9(8)); 18.00 (978-0-7435-4159-6(6)) Pub: S&S Audio. Dist(s): S and S Inc

Angela's Ashes: A Memoir of a Childhood. unabr. ed. Frank McCourt. Read by Frank McCourt. 2005. 29.95 (978-0-7435-1890-1(X)) Pub: S&S Audio. Dist(s): S and S Inc

Angeles y Demonios. Dan Brown. Narrated by Raul Amundaray.Tr. of Angels & Demons. (SPA.). 2009. 64.99 (978-1-60775-715-3(X)) Find a World.

Angeles y Demonios. abr. ed. Scripts. Dan Brown. 18 CDs. (Running Time: 22 hrs).Tr. of Angels & Demons. (SPA.). 2005. audio compact disk 34.95 (978-0-9728598-9-9(6)) Fonolibro Inc.

Angeles y Demonios. abr. movie tie-in ed. Dan Brown.Tr. of Angels & Demons. (SPA.). 2009. audio compact disk 28.95 (978-1-933499-83-3(4)) Fonolibro Inc.

Angeles y Demonios. unabr. abr. ed. Dan Brown. Read by Raul Amundaray. 8 CDs. (Running Time: 32400 sec.).Tr. of Angels & Demons. (SPA.). 2006. audio compact disk 28.95 (978-1-933499-27-7(3)) Fonolibro Inc.

***Angelic.** unabr. ed. Kelley Armstrong. Narrated by Laural Merlington. (Running Time: 1 hr. 30 mins. 0 sec.). (ENG.). 2010. 19.99 (978-1-4001-6528-5(8)); 10.99 (978-1-4001-8528-3(9)); audio compact disk 49.99 (978-1-4001-4528-7(7)); audio compact disk 24.99 (978-1-4001-1528-0(0)) Pub: Tantor Media. Dist(s): IngramPubServ

Angelic Avengers. unabr. collector's ed. Isak Dinesen. Read by Donada Peters. 9 cass. (Running Time: 13 hrs. 30 mins.). 1985. 72.00 (978-0-7366-0915-9(6), 1858) Books on Tape.
A young woman, expecting a marriage proposal, is propositioned instead.

***Angelic Devil.** Featuring Ravi Zacharias. 1983. audio compact disk 9.00 (978-1-61256-021-2(0)) Ravi Zach.

Angelic Fire see Fuego Angelical: Magia, Leyendas y Tradiciones

Angelic Healing. Edwards-Ticehur. 2005. audio compact disk 12.95 (978-0-9756878-3-3(2)) Joshua Bks AUS.

Angelic Healing for a Strong Heart. 1997. 29.95 (978-1-893027-11-4(2)) Path of Light.

Angelic Healing for Accidents. 2nd ed. 1997. 29.95 (978-1-893027-08-4(2)) Path of Light.

Angelic Healing for Allergies. 1997. 29.95 (978-1-893027-13-8(9)) Path of Light.

Angelic Healing for Auto-Immune. 2nd ed. 1997. 29.95 (978-1-893027-06-0(6)) Path of Light.

Angelic Healing for Cancer. 2nd ed. 1997. 29.95 (978-1-893027-09-1(0)) Path of Light.

Angelic Healing for Colds, Flus & Viruses. 1997. 29.95 (978-1-893027-12-1(0)) Path of Light.

Angelic Healing for Digestive System. 1997. 29.95 (978-1-893027-10-7(4)) Path of Light.

Angelic Healing for Endocrine. 2nd ed. 1997. 29.95 (978-1-893027-07-7(4)) Path of Light.

Angelic Healing for Environmental Damage. 1997. 29.95 (978-1-893027-17-6(1)) Path of Light.

Angelic Healing for Fears & Anxieties. 1997. 29.95 (978-1-893027-18-3(X)) Path of Light.

Angelic Healing for Headaches. 1997. 29.95 (978-1-893027-29-9(5)) Path of Light.

Angelic Healing for Muscular & Skeletal Systems. 1997. 29.95 (978-1-893027-30-5(9)) Path of Light.

Angelic Healing for Pain. 1997. 29.95 (978-1-893027-14-5(7)) Path of Light.

Angelic Healing for Sleep. 1997. 29.95 (978-1-893027-16-9(3)) Path of Light.

Angelic Healing for Surgery. 1997. 29.95 (978-1-893027-15-2(5)) Path of Light.

Angelic Meditations. Alma Daniel. 1 cass. 1994. 10.98 (978-0-9638186-1-4(9)) Astromusic.

Angelic Meditations. Alma Daniel. Music by Gerald Jay Markoe. 1 cass. 10.95 (LA111) Lghtwrks Aud & Vid.
Guided meditations are designed to bring you into an enhanced awareness of your higher self. Each of the six meditations was angelically inspired & is approximately 10 minutes long. The accompanying background music was chosen to deepen the meditations, which although brief, are profoundly powerful & transformational.

Angelic Morning-Inner Peace Music. 2007. audio compact disk 16.95 (978-1-56136-410-7(X)) Master Your Mind.

Angelic Realm - Poetry. Poems. Thomas Merton. 1 cass. 1995. 8.95 Credence Commun.

Angelica. Arthur Phillips. Narrated by Susan Lyons. (Running Time: 46800 sec.). 2007. audio compact disk 39.99 (978-1-4281-2478-3(0)) Recorded Bks.

Angelica: Rock, Stock & Barrel, 2 CDs. (Running Time: 2 hrs.). 1999. audio compact disk 12.99 (KMGD8663) Provident Mus Dist.

***Angelina: An Unauthorized Biography.** unabr. ed. Andrew Morton. Read by Bronson Pinchot. (Running Time: 12 hrs. 0 mins.). 2010. 29.95 (978-1-4417-5515-5(2)); 72.95 (978-1-4417-5511-7(X)); audio compact disk 34.95 (978-1-4417-5514-8(4)); audio compact disk 105.00 (978-1-4417-5512-4(8)) Blckstn Audio.

Angelina Ballerina & Other Stories. Katharine Holabird. Perf. by Sally Struthers. 1 cass. (Running Time: 1 hr.). (Angelina Ballerina Ser.). (J). (ps-3). 1993. 9.98 (269) MFLP CA.
Angelina, that adorable little mouse, wants nothing more than to be a prima ballerina. When her parents allow her to take ballet lessons, she couldn't be happier. Join Angelina & her mischievous cousin Henry for five stories: "Angelina Ballerina," "Angelina & the Princess," "Angelina at the Fair," "Angelina's Christmas," & "Angelina Onstage.".

Angelman Syndrome - A Bibliography & Dictionary for Physicians, Patients, & Genome Researchers. Compiled by Icon Group International, Inc. Staff. 2007. ring bd. 28.95 (978-0-[illegible]1331-5(7)) Icon Grp.

Angelology. unabr. ed. Danielle Trusson[illegible]b. by Susan Denaker. 17 CDs. (Running Time: 21 hrs.). (ENG.). (gr. 1[illegible] 2010. audio compact disk 39.95 (978-0-14-314526-4(6), PengAudBks) Penguin Grp USA.

***Angelology.** unabr. ed. Danielle Trussoni. Narrated by Susan Denaker. 17 CDs. (Running Time: 21 hrs. 30 mins.). 2010. audio compact disk 100.00 (978-0-307-57749-8(X), BksonTape) Pub: Random Audio Pubg. Dist(s): Random

Angels. (Running Time: 60 mins.). 2002. audio compact disk 15.99 (978-1-904972-31-0(4)) Global Jrny GBR GBR.

Angels. Mother Angelica & Father Michael. 1 cass. (Running Time: 60 mins.). (Mother Angelica Live Ser.). 1989. 10.00 (978-1-55794-115-2(7), T66) Eternal Wrd TV.

Angels. Running Press Staff. 1 CD. audio compact disk 16.98 (978-1-57908-488-2(5), 5354) Platinm Enter.

Angels. Cheryl Salem. 2 cass. (Running Time: 2 hrs.). 2001. 10.00 (TCS-01) Harrison Hse.
Cheryl Salem teaches on angels and gives her own eye-witness testimony of the reality of angels.

Angels. unabr. ed. Billy Graham. Narrated by Jack Garrett. 4 cass. (Running Time: 5 hrs. 30 mins.). 2001. 36.00 (978-0-7887-5210-0(3), K0040E7) Recorded Bks.
Dr. Billy Graham remains one of the most popular evangelists in history. He lifts the veil of mystery between the visible & invisible world, providing astonishing insight into God's behind the scenes secret agents.

Angels. unabr. ed. Marian Keyes. Narrated by Gerri Halligan. 10 cassettes. (Running Time: 13.50 hrs). 2005. 89.75 (978-1-84197-490-3(0)) Recorded Bks.

Angels, unabr. ed. Running Press Staff. 1 cass. (Running Time: 1 hr.). 10.98 (978-1-57908-489-9(3), 5354) Platinm Enter.

Angels. unabr. ed. Myrtle Smith. Prod. by David Keyston. 1 cass. (Running Time: 1 hrs. 32 mins.). (Myrtle Smyth Audiotapes Ser.). 1998. (978-1-893107-13-7(2), M13) Healing Unltd.

Angels: God's Secret Agents. Based on a book by Billy Graham. 1995. (978-0-913367-43-8(5)) Billy Graham Evangelistic Association.

Angels: Messengers from God. Lester Sumrall. 8 cass. (Running Time: 12 hrs.). 1999. 32.00 (978-1-58568-007-8(9)) Sumrall Pubng.

Angels: Messengers of God's Love. Steven A. Cramer. 2004. 9.95 (978-1-57734-735-4(8)); audio compact disk 10.95 (978-1-57734-736-1(6)) Covenant Comms.

Angels: Messengers of the Future. unabr. ed. Stephan Hoeller. 1 cass. (Running Time: 1 hr. 30 mins.). 1996. 11.00 (40022) Big Sur Tapes.
Examines the history & mythology associated with angel visitations, emphasizing how we respond to the experience - what it can mean personally in our lives, whether we can see we are not in charge, how to recognize angels as messengers between the Divine & the human.

Angels - Constant Companions. 1 cass. (Running Time: 60 min.). (Mother Angelica Live Ser.). 10.00 (978-1-55794-069-8(X), T20) Eternal Wrd TV.

Angels, Aliens & Archetypes. 12 cass. (AA & A Symposium Ser.). 108.00 set. (A0300-87) Sound Photosyn.
Contain the complete symposium, an in depth scholarly look at approaches to UFOs & related phenomenon including visual artworks.

Angels, Aliens & Common Sense. Marilyn Ferguson. 1 cass. (AA & A Symposium Ser.). 9.00 (A0301-87) Sound Photosyn.

Angels among Us. Brian Hill & Karen Hill. 1 cass. 9.98 (978-1-57734-213-7(5), 06005691) Covenant Comms.
Inspiring stories from the Sesquicentennial wagon train.

Angels among Us. Interview with Michael Toms. Featuring Doreen Virtue. (New Dimensions Ser.). 2002. 10.95 (978-1-56170-944-1(1)) Hay House.

Angels & Demons see Angeles y Demonios

Angels & Demons. Dan Brown. 2006. cd-rom 49.99 (978-1-59895-477-7(6)) Find a World.

Angels & Demons. abr. ed. Dan Brown. 2005. 49.99 (978-1-59895-018-2(5)) Find a World.

Angels & Demons. abr. ed. Dan Brown. Read by Richard Poe. 6 CDs. (Running Time: 60 hrs. 0 mins. 0 sec.). (ENG.). 2003. audio compact disk 30.00 (978-0-7435-3577-9(4), Audioworks) Pub: S&S Audio. Dist(s): S and S Inc
THE ORIGINAL ROBERT LANGDON THRILLER FROM THE #1 BESTSELLING AUTHOR OF THE DA VINCI CODE An ancient secret brotherhood. A devastating new weapon of destruction. An unthinkable target. World-renowned Harvard symbologist Robert Langdon is summoned to a Swiss research facility to analyze a cryptic symbol seared into the chest of a murdered physicist. What he discovers is unimaginable: a deadly vendetta against the Catholic Church by a centuries-old underground organization - the Illuminati. Desperate to save the Vatican from a powerful time bomb, Langdon joins forces in Rome with the beautiful and mysterious scientist Vittoria Vetra. Together they embark on a frantic hunt through sealed crypts, dangerous catacombs, deserted cathedrals, and the most secretive vault on earth?the long-forgotten Illuminati lair.

Angels & Demons. abr. ed. Dan Brown. Read by Richard Poe. 2004. 15.95 (978-0-7435-5020-8(X)) Pub: S&S Audio. Dist(s): S and S Inc

Angels & Demons. abr. movie tie-in ed. Dan Brown. Read by Richard Poe. (Running Time: 7 hrs. 0 mins. 0 sec.). (ENG.). 2009. audio compact disk 29.99 (978-0-7435-8045-8(1)) Pub: S&S Audio. Dist(s): S and S Inc

Angels & Demons. collector's ed. Dan Brown. Narrated by Richard Poe. 13 cass. (Running Time: 18 hrs. 30 min.). 2003. 44.95 (978-1-4025-6746-9(4)) Recorded Bks.

Angels & Demons. unabr. ed. Dan Brown. Narrated by Richard Poe. 13 cass. Lib. Ed. (Running Time: 17 hrs. 30 min.). 2003. 99.75

(978-1-4025-6745-2(6)); audio compact disk 109.75 (978-1-4025-6788-9(X)) Recorded Bks.

Angels & Demons. unabr. ed. Dan Brown. Read by Richard Poe. 2004. 29.95 (978-0-7435-3976-0(1)) Pub: S&S Audio. Dist(s): S and S Inc

Angels & Demons. unabr. collector's ed. Dan Brown. Narrated by Richard Poe. 15 CDs. (Running Time: 18 hrs. 30 min.). 2003. audio compact disk 49.95 (978-1-4025-7714-7(1), CC011) Recorded Bks.
Harvard symbologist Robert Langdon. Langdon is summoned to Switzerland when the dead body of a physicist turns up bearing the distinguishing mark of the ancient brotherhood of the Illuminati. Soon, Langdon suspects this mysterious cult is determined to destroy Catholicism with an unimaginably powerful new weapon.

Angels & Demons. unabr. movie tie-in ed. Dan Brown. Read by Richard Poe. (Running Time: 19 hrs. 0 mins. 0 sec.). (ENG.). 2009. 29.99 (978-0-7435-9718-0(4)); audio compact disk 49.99 (978-0-7435-8046-5(X)) Pub: S&S Audio. Dist(s): S and S Inc

***Angels & Demons: A Novel.** abr. ed. Dan Brown. Read by Richard Poe. (Running Time: 7 hrs. 0 mins. 0 sec.). (ENG.). 2010. audio compact disk 14.99 (978-1-4423-3811-1(3)) Pub: S&S Audio. Dist(s): S and S Inc

Angels & Donkeys: Tales for Christmas & Other Times. abr. ed. Andre Trocme. Tr. by Nelly Trocme Hewett. 2 cass. (Running Time: 3 hrs.). (ps-3). 2000. 18.00 (978-1-56148-320-4(6)) Pub: Good Bks PA. Dist(s): STL Dist NA

Angels & Guides: Chakra Meditation. Edwards-Ticehur. 2001. audio compact disk 12.95 (978-0-646-19137-9(3)) Joshua Bks AUS.

Angels & Guides Healing Meditations. abr. ed. Sylvia Browne. 2 CDs. 2006. audio compact disk 18.95 (978-1-4019-1715-9(1)) Hay House.

Angels & Insects. unabr. ed. A. S. Byatt. Read by Nadia May. 8 cass. (Running Time: 11 hrs. 30 mins.). 1996. 56.95 (978-0-7861-0950-0(5), 1727) Blckstn Audio.
In these breathtakingly accomplished novellas, A.S. Byatt explores the landscape of Victorian England, where science & spiritualism are both popular manias & domestic decorum coexists with brutality & perversion. The shipwrecked naturalist who is the protagonist of "Morpho Eugenia" is rescued by a family whose clandestine passions come to seem as inscrutable as the behavior of insects. In "The Conjugial Angel," a circle of fictional mediums finds itself haunted by the ghost of a very real historical personage. "Angels & Insects" offers further proof of Byatt's prodigious powers & magical sympathy for characters who might be our great-great-grandparents.

Angels & Insects. unabr. ed. A. S. Byatt. Read by Nadia May. (Running Time: 11 hrs. 50 mins.). (ENG.). 2009. 29.95 (978-1-4417-0323-1(3)); audio compact disk 100.00 (978-1-4417-0320-0(9)) Blckstn Audio.

Angels & Insects, unabr. ed. A. S. Byatt. Read by Nadia May. 8 cass. (Running Time: 8 hrs.). 1999. 56.95 (FS9-51121) Highsmith.

Angels & Spirit Guides: How to Call upon Your Angels & Spirit Guide for Help. Sylvia Browne. 2 cass. (Running Time: 2 hrs.). 1999. 16.95 (978-1-56170-691-4(4), 4008) Hay House.
She addresses the fascinating concepts surrounding angels & spirit guides. Includes a meditation that invokes the presence of our angels & individual spirit guides & invites them to communicate with us.

Angels & Spirit Guides: How to Call upon Your Angels & Spirit Guide for Help. Speeches. Sylvia Browne. 2 CDs. 2003. audio compact disk 18.95 (978-1-4019-0134-9(4), 1344) Hay House.

Angel's Answer-Music. 2007. audio compact disk 16.95 (978-1-56136-436-7(3)) Master Your Mind.

Angels Are Singing: A Women's Bluegrass Gospel Collection. 2002. audio compact disk Provident Mus Dist.

Angels Around Us. Perf. by Robert Kochis & Robin Kochis. 1 cass. (Running Time: 90 mins.). 1999. 10.95 (T8106); audio compact disk 15.95 (K1104) Liguori Pubns.
Songs include: "Angels Around Us," "Into the Rainbow," "Visit to Earth," "Do Angels Cry," "I Believe in Angels" & many more.

Angels at Christmas. unabr. ed. Debbie Macomber. Read by Sandra Burr. (Running Time: 12 hrs.). (Angels Everywhere Ser.). 2009. 24.99 (978-1-4418-0762-5(4), 9781441807625, Brilliance MP3); 39.97 (978-1-4418-0763-2(2), 9781441807632, Brinc Audio MP3 Lib); 24.99 (978-1-4418-0764-9(0), 9781441807649, BAD); 39.97 (978-1-4418-0765-6(9), 9781441807656, BADLE); audio compact disk 26.99 (978-1-4418-0760-1(8), 9781441807601, Bril Audio CD Unabri); audio compact disk 97.97 (978-1-4418-0761-8(6), 9781441807618, BriAudCD Unabrid) Brilliance Audio.

Angels at Your Side. Caryl Krueger. Read by Caryl Krueger. 2 cass. (Running Time: 3 hrs.). 2001. 17.00 Belleridge.

Angels Bar & Grill. Scripts. Richard A. Panzer & Sam Harley. Prod. by Kevin Pickard. 1 cass. 1 CD. (Running Time: 30 mins.). Dramatization. (YA). 1996. cass. & audio compact disk 12.00 (978-1-888933-05-5(4)) Ctr Educ Media.
Two college students, Bill & Sandy, meet Marilyn Monroe, Malcolm X, Jack Kerouac & Sigmund Freud at a mysterious diner. Discuss Sexual Revolution, sexual ethics, sexual abstinence, marriage & life.

***Angels' Blood.** unabr. ed. Nalini Singh. Narrated by Justine Eyre. (Running Time: 10 hrs. 30 mins. 0 sec.). (Guild Hunter Ser.). (ENG.). 2010. audio compact disk 34.99 (978-1-4001-1715-4(1)) Pub: Tantor Media. Dist(s): IngramPubServ

***Angel's Blood.** unabr. ed. Nalini Singh. Narrated by Justine Eyre. (Running Time: 10 hrs. 30 mins. 0 sec.). (Guild Hunter Ser.). (ENG.). 2010. 24.99 (978-1-4001-6715-9(9)); 34.99 (978-1-4001-9715-6(5)); 17.99 (978-1-4001-8715-7(X)); audio compact disk 69.99 (978-1-4001-4715-1(8)) Pub: Tantor Media. Dist(s): IngramPubServ

Angels by My Side: Morning & Evening Guided Meditations for Earth Angels. Joy Yoxall. Contrib. by Bryan Perez. (Running Time: 3840 sec.). (Sacred Light Ser.). 2007. audio compact disk 17.95 (978-1-901923-81-0(9)) Pub: Divinit Pubing GBR. Dist(s): Bookworld

Angel's Command. unabr. ed. Brian Jacques. 8 cass. (Running Time: 11 hrs.). (Castaways of the Flying Dutchman Ser.: No. 2). 2003. 104.99 (978-1-4025-1588-0(X)) Recorded Bks.
The immortal Ben and Ned are high in the Pyrenees Mountains, where they make new allies and fight to save a man from a legendary tribe strong in the black arts.

Angel's Command. unabr. ed. Brian Jacques. Narrated by Brian Jacques. 8 CDs. (Running Time: 11 hrs.). (Castaways of the Flying Dutchman Ser.: No. 2). 2004. audio compact disk 97.75 (978-1-4025-8067-3(3)) Recorded Bks.

Angel's Command. unabr. ed. Brian Jacques & Brian Jacques. 7 cass. (Running Time: 11 hrs.). (Castaways of the Flying Dutchman Ser.: No. 2). 2004. 29.99 (978-1-4025-3684-7(4), 02674) Recorded Bks.

Angels Cry Sometimes. unabr. ed. Josephine Cox. Read by Maggie Ollerenshaw. 10 cass. (Running Time: 10 hrs.). 2000. 84.95 (978-0-7540-0379-3(5), CAB 1802') Pub: Chivers Audio Bks GBR. Dist(s): AudioGO
The marriage of Marcia & Curt Ratheter seemed incredibly happy. But one fateful day in 1931 tore Marcia's world apart & left her two daughters bereft. Barty Bendall had always loved her & the girls needed a father, so Marcia moved to Blackburn with him. However, Barty began tyrannizing the family.

Angels, Demons & Spirit Possession: New Perspectives on the Collective Unconscious & the Daimonic. Robert Moore. Read by Robert Moore. 5 cass. (Running Time: 7 hrs.). 39.95 (978-0-7822-0534-3(8), 600) C G Jung IL.
Presents a survey of current spiritual phenomenology & turns to Jung's psychology to aid understanding of interest in angels, channeling & spirit posession. Prominent consideration is given to Jung's differentation between personal psychological contents which should be integrated & phenomena which should not. The workshop concludes with questions about the dominant paradigms in philosophy & science.

Angels, Devas, Shining Beings. Swami Amar Jyoti. 1 cass. 1987. 9.95 (K-95) Truth Consciousness.
The hierarchy of creation. What are angels, devas & what do they do? Their eagerness to help us. How to regain the contact.

Angels Dining at the Ritz. John E. Gardner. 2007. 69.95 (978-0-7531-3765-9(8)) Pub: ISIS Audio GBR. Dist(s): Ulverscroft US

Angels Dining at the Ritz. John E. Gardner. 2008. audio compact disk 84.95 (978-0-7531-2734-6(2)) Pub: ISIS Audio GBR. Dist(s): Ulverscroft US

Angels Don't Knock, Dan Yates. 2 cass. (Running Time: 2 hrs.). 2004. 11.98 (978-1-55503-723-9(2), 079432) Covenant Comms.
An extra-terrestrial love story.

Angel's Draught. Composed by Carrie Crompton. 1 cass. (Running Time: 1 hr.). 9.98 incl. Norelco pkg. (978-1-877737-32-9(1), EB 2194); audio compact disk 12.98 (978-1-877737-54-1(2)) MFLP CA.
Musical arrangements combining the simplicity of traditional music with the elegance of Baroque performance.

Angel's Dream Garden-Music. (J). 2007. audio compact disk 16.95 (978-1-56136-126-7(7)) Master Your Mind.

Angels Fall. abr. ed. Nora Roberts. Read by Joyce Bean. (Running Time: 21600 sec.). 2007. audio compact disk 14.99 (978-1-4233-0655-9(4), 9781423306559, BCD Value Price) Brilliance Audio.

Angels Fall. unabr. ed. Nora Roberts. Read by Joyce Bean. (Running Time: 15 hrs.). 2006. 39.25 (978-1-59710-930-7(4), 9781597109307, BADLE); 24.95 (978-1-59710-931-4(2), 9781597109314, BAD); 36.95 (978-1-59600-187-9(9), 9781596001879, BAU); 97.25 (978-1-59600-188-6(7), 9781596001886, BrilAudUnabridg); audio compact disk 112.25 (978-1-59600-191-6(7), 9781596001916, BriAudCD Unabrid); audio compact disk 39.95 (978-1-59600-190-9(9), 9781596001909, Bril Audio CD Unabri); audio compact disk 24.95 (978-1-59335-960-7(8), 9781593359607, Brilliance MP3); audio compact disk 39.25 (978-1-59335-961-4(6), 9781593359614, Brinc Audio MP3 Lib) Brilliance Audio.
Please enter a Synopsis.

Angels Flight. Michael Connelly. Read by Dick Hill. (Harry Bosch Ser.: No. 6). 2008. 69.99 (978-1-60640-799-8(6)) Find a World.

Angels Flight. abr. ed. Michael Connelly. (Running Time: 4 hrs.). (Harry Bosch Ser.: No. 6). (ENG.). 2006. 14.98 (978-1-59483-661-9(2)) Pub: Hachet Audio. Dist(s): HachBkGrp

Angels Flight. unabr. ed. Michael Connelly. Read by Dick Hill. 7 cass. (Running Time: 11 hrs.). (Harry Bosch Ser.: No. 6). 1999. 39.95 (978-1-56740-410-4(3), 1567404103, BAU) Brilliance Audio.
The man most hated by the LAPD - a black lawyer who has made his name by bringing lawsuits alleging racism and brutality by police officers - has been found murdered on the eve of a high-profile trial. The list of suspects includes half the police force. And Harry Bosch is the detective chosen to lead the investigation. The political dangers of the case are huge. If it's not investigated fairly, the public outcry could make the Rodney King riots look tame. But a full investigation will take Bosch into the ugliest corners of law enforcement. To make matters worse, Bosch's wife, Eleanor, has disappeared. Bosch fears she has left him - or succumbed to her gambling addiction. He's not sure which would be worse. Angels Flight reads in a white heat. It continues to up the ante of the series that is "raising the hard-boiled detective novel to a new level - adding substance and depth to modern crime fiction." (Boston Globe).

Angels Flight. unabr. ed. Michael Connelly. Read by Dick Hill. (Running Time: 11 hrs.). (Harry Bosch Ser.: No. 6). 2005. 39.25 (978-1-59737-690-7(6), 9781597376907, BADLE); 24.95 (978-1-59737-689-1(2), 9781597376891, BAD); audio compact disk 97.25 (978-1-59737-686-0(8), 9781597376860, BriAudCD Unabrid); audio compact disk 39.25 (978-1-59737-688-4(4), 9781597376884, Brinc Audio MP3 Lib); audio compact disk 36.95 (978-1-59737-685-3(X), 9781597376853, Bril Audio CD Unabri); audio compact disk 24.95 (978-1-59737-687-7(6), 9781597376877, Brilliance MP3) Brilliance Audio.

Angels Flight, unabr. ed. Michael Connelly. Read by Dick Hill. 7 cass. (Running Time: 7 hrs.). (Harry Bosch Ser.: No. 6). 1999. 73.25 (FS9-43363) Highsmith.

Angels from the Realms of Glory. Contrib. by Michael Lawrence. Created by James Montgomery. 2007. audio compact disk 24.98 (978-5-557-77105-4(0), Word Music) Word Enter.

Angel's Game. unabr. ed. Carlos Ruiz Zafón. Illus. by Carlos Ruiz Zafón. Read by Dan Stevens. 14 CDs. (Running Time: 17 hrs.). 2009. audio compact disk 100.00 (978-1-4159-6302-9(9), BksonTape) Pub: Random Audio Pubg. Dist(s): Random

Angel's Game. unabr. ed. Carlos Ruiz Zafón. Illus. by Carlos Ruiz Zafón. Read by Dan Stevens. Tr. by Lucia Graves. 13 CDs. (Running Time: 15 hrs. 30 mins.). (ENG.). 2009. audio compact disk 45.00 (978-0-7393-8192-2(X), Random AudioBks) Pub: Random Audio Pubg. Dist(s): Random

Angel's Gate. unabr. ed. Gary Crew. Read by Stig Wemyss. 5 cass. (Running Time: 7 hrs.). 2002. (978-1-876584-65-8(3)) Bolinda Pubng AUS.
The night the first wild child was captured, I was woken from my sleep by the sound of car doors slamming. I opened my eyes, lights were flashing across the ceiling of my bedroom. I sat up at once & there, holding aside the lace curtain of my window, was my sister Julia. "They've caught one, ' I whispered. 'Haven't they?" She took her hand from the curtains & turned away. 'They get all of us sooner or later,' she said. Then she vanished into the darkness of the hall.

Angels, Good & Bad. Michael Pearl. (ENG.). 2007. audio compact disk (978-1-934794-28-9(7)) No Greater Joy.

Angels, Guides, & Ghosts. Sylvia Browne. 1 CD. 2004. audio compact disk 10.95 (978-1-4019-0423-4(8)) Hay House.

Angels Heal My Body. Jan Yoxall. (Sacred Light Ser.). 2007. audio compact disk 17.95 (978-1-901923-83-4(5)) Divinit Pubing GBR.

Angels in Our Midst. Joan W. Anderson. 1 cass. (Running Time: 60 mins.). 9.95 (AT5018) Lghtwrks Aud & Vid.
Best-selling author Joan Wester Anderson (Where Angels Walk) has gathered dozens of stories of encounters with angels by people from all walks of life. Included in this "Timeless Voyager Audio" interview is her firsthand account of her son's near-fatal evening when saved by an "impossible" set of circumstances.

Angels in the Gloom. abr. ed. Anne Perry. Read by Michael Page. (Running Time: 6 hrs.). (World War One Ser.). 2006. audio compact disk 16.99 (978-1-59600-865-6(2), 9781596008656, BCD Value Price) Brilliance Audio.
Angels in the Gloom is an intense saga of love, hate, obsession, and murder that features an honorable English family - brothers Joseph and Matthew Reavley, and their sisters, Judith and Hannah. In March 1916, Joseph, a chaplain at the front, and Judith, an ambulance driver, are fighting not only the Germans but the bitter cold and the appalling casualties of the Battle of Somme. Scarcely less at risk, Matthew, an officer in England's Secret Intelligence Service, fights the war covertly from London. Only Hannah, living with her young children in the old family home in tranquil Cambridgeshire, seems safe. Appearances, however, are deceiving. By the time Joseph returns home, rumors of spies and traitors are rampant in Cambridgeshire. And when the body of a savagely murdered weapons scientist is discovered in a village byway, the fear that haunts the battlefields settles over the town - along with the shadow of the obsessed ideologue who murdered the four siblings' parents on the eve of the war. Once again, this icy, anonymous powerbroker, the Peacemaker, is plotting to kill. Perry's kaleidoscopic new novel illuminates an entire world, from the hell of the trenches to a London nightclub where a beautiful Irish spy plies her trade; from the sequestered laboratory where a weapon that can end the war is being perfected to the matchless glory of the English countryside in spring. Angels in the Gloom is a masterpiece, steeped in history and radiant with truth. It warms the heart even as it chills the blood.

Angels in the Gloom. unabr. ed. Anne Perry. Read by Michael Page. (Running Time: 12 hrs.). (World War One Ser.). 2005. 39.25 (978-1-59710-017-5(X), 9781597100175, BADLE); 24.95 (978-1-59710-016-8(1), 9781597100168, BAD); audio compact disk 36.95 (978-1-59355-060-8(X), 9781593550608, Bril Audio CD Unabri); audio compact disk 102.25 (978-1-59355-061-5(8), 9781593550615, BriAudCD Unabrid); 34.95 (978-1-59355-057-8(X), 9781593550578, BAU); 87.25 (978-1-59355-058-5(8), 9781593550585, BrilAudUnabridg); audio compact disk 39.25 (978-1-59335-839-6(3), 9781593358396, Brinc Audio MP3 Lib); audio compact disk 24.95 (978-1-59335-705-4(2), 9781593357054, Brilliance MP3) Brilliance Audio.

Angels in the Rain. Randall Leonard. 1 cass. (Running Time: 51 mins.). 1994. 10.95 (611) Hay House.
Original piano solos of heartfelt music to help you access higher realms of awareness.

Angels in the Snow & Other Stories. Aaron Trompeter. Read by Aaron Trompeter. (Running Time: 1 hr. 13 mins.). 2000. audio compact disk 13.95 (978-0-9678993-1-2(1)) Float Rock.
A collection of narratives anchored in the lands of Northern Minnesota. Expertly written, heart-wrenching & beautiful, they tell of friends, courage, dignity & heroes.

Angels Love Me-Childen's. unabr. ed. Mary Richards. Perf. by Joanne Robinson. 1 cass. (Running Time: 60 mins.). (Angels Bedtime Ser.). (J). 2007. audio compact disk 19.95 (978-1-56136-214-1(X)) Master Your Mind.
An imaginative journey on a rainbow to an enchanted place. Feel the love of the angels. Discover how they help you as you drift off to sleep.

Angel's Love Me-Children's Series-00000000000000000000. (J). 2007. audio compact disk 19.95 (978-1-56136-136-6(4)) Master Your Mind.

Angel's Lulaby-Children's Series. (J). 2007. audio compact disk 19.95 (978-1-56136-135-9(6)) Master Your Mind.

***Angels of Destruction.** unabr. ed. Keith Donohue. Narrated by Cassandra Campbell. 12 CDs. (Running Time: 14 hrs. 15 mins.). 2009. audio compact disk 100.00 (978-1-4159-6017-2(8), BksonTape) Pub: Random Audio Pubg. Dist(s): Random

Angels of Destruction. unabr. ed. Keith Donohue. Read by Cassandra Campbell. (ENG.). 2009. audio compact disk 39.95 (978-0-7393-7719-2(1), Random AudioBks) Pub: Random Audio Pubg. Dist(s): Random

Angels of Light. 1 cass. (Tara Sutphen Meditation Tapes Ser.). 11.98 (978-0-87554-591-2(2), TS210) Valley Sun.

Angels of the Blue. Contrib. by Glenn Harrold & Aly Harrold. (Running Time: 3240 sec.). 2007. audio compact disk 17.95 (978-1-901923-82-7(7)) Pub: Divinit Pubing GBR. Dist(s): Bookworld

Angels on Assignment. Featuring Bill Winston. 4. 2004. audio compact disk 32.00 (978-1-59544-041-9(0)); 20.00 (978-1-59544-040-2(2)) Pub: B Winston Min. Dist(s): Anchor Distributors
As a born again Believer, it is our responsibility to manifest Heaven on Earth. God did not leave us in this earth alone. He left us with resources that we can draw upon at anytime to share the Gospel of Jesus Christ with the world, and demonstrate the covenant blessings reserved for citizens of The Kingdom of God.Let Pastor Bill Winston teach you step-by-step, line ?upon-line straight from the Word of God how to:?Manage the earth by cooperating with God?Exercise your authority a mature Believer?Speak the Word of God?Instruct Angels to work on your behalf?Distinguish the divine characteristics of God and the deceptive traps of the enemy, and so much more!As a child of God, you are a witness for the world to see the power and anointing of God working in your life. Stop waiting on God and start giving instructions to your angels so that they can help you create Heaven on Earth!.

Angels on Assignment. unabr. ed. Perry Stone. Narrated by Dean Gallagher. (Running Time: 4 hrs. 27 mins. 16 sec.). (ENG.). 2009. 13.99 (978-1-60814-586-7(7)); audio compact disk 19.99 (978-1-59859-634-2(9)) Oasis Audio.

Angels on Horseback. Perf. by Myrna Loy. 1 cass. 10.00 (MC1010) Esstee Audios.
Radio drama.

Angels on the Roof, Martha A. Moore. Read by Christina Moore. 4 cass. (Running Time: 4 hrs. 45 mins.). 1998. bk. 105.70 Class set. (978-0-7887-3256-0(0), 46075) Recorded Bks.
Shelby wants to know her father's name & why her mother moves so often-no matter whom the answers hurt.

Angels on the Roof, unabr. ed. Martha A. Moore. Narrated by Christina Moore. 4 pieces. (Running Time: 4 hrs. 45 mins.). (gr. 7 up). 1998. 35.00 (978-0-7887-1807-6(X), 95279E7) Recorded Bks.
Fourteen-year-old Shelby is determined to know her father's name & why her mother moves so often. After Mom drags her to a hick town in the Texas panhandle, Shelby is determined to find answers, no matter whom it hurts.

Angels on the Roof, unabr. ed. Martha A. Moore. Read by Christina Moore. 4 cass. (Running Time: 4 hrs. 45 mins.). (YA). 1998. 48.24 (978-0-7887-1962-2(9), 40633) Recorded Bks.
Shelby wants to know her father's name & why her mother moves so often-no matter whom the answers hurt.

Angels Passing. unabr. ed. Graham Hurley. 12 cass. (Isis Ser.). (J). 2003. 94.95 (978-0-7531-1593-0(X)) Pub: ISIS Lrg Prnt GBR. Dist(s): Ulverscroft US

Angels Protect Me-Children's Guided. unabr. ed. Mary Richards. Music by Charles Albert. 1 cass. (Running Time: 50 mins.). (Angels Bedtime Ser.). (J). 2007. audio compact disk 19.95 (978-1-56136-215-8(8)) Master Your Mind.
An imaginative bedtime journey. Imagine the protection of angels all during the surgery. Drift off to sleep & happy dreams.

Angel's Protect Me-Children's Series-0000000000000000. (J). 2007. audio compact disk 19.95 (978-1-56136-134-2(8)) Master Your Mind.

Angel's Share. Mike Ripley & Jack Paulin. 2008. 61.95 (978-1-84652-221-5(8)); audio compact disk 79.95 (978-1-84652-222-2(6)) Pub: Magna Story GBR. Dist(s): Ulverscroft US

Angel's Slumber. unabr. ed. Roderic Vickers. Perf. by Roderic Vickers. 1 cass. (Running Time: 1 hr.). 1995. 9.95 (978-1-886956-05-6(7)) Star Concepts.
2 thirty minute pieces, very peaceful, to help induce sleep.

Angel's Song-Music. 2007. audio compact disk 16.95 (978-1-56136-423-7(1)) Master Your Mind.

Angel's Tip. unabr. ed. Alafair Burke. Read by Eliza Foss. (Running Time: 11 hrs. 15 mins.). 2008. 61.75 (978-1-4407-0005-7(2)); 82.75 (978-1-4361-5099-6(X)); audio compact disk 123.75 (978-1-4361-5101-6(5)) Recorded Bks.

Angel's Tip. unabr. collector's ed. Alafair Burke. Read by Eliza Foss. 10 CDs. (Running Time: 11 hrs. 15 mins.). 2008. audio compact disk 39.95 (978-1-4361-5102-3(3)) Recorded Bks.

Angels to the Rescue, Dan Yates. 2 cass. (Running Time: 2 hrs.). 1999. 11.98 (978-1-57734-211-3(9), 07001606) Covenant Comms.
Sequel to "Angels Don't Knock!" & "Just Call Me an Angel.".

Angels Unaware. Nathaniel Holcomb. 3 cass. (Running Time: 4 hrs. 30 mins.). 1998. (978-1-930918-22-1(4)) Its All About Him.

Angels Unaware. unabr. ed. Priscilla A. Maine. Read by Celeste Lawson. 8 CDs. (Running Time: 10 hrs.). 2004. audio compact disk 64.00 (978-0-7861-8494-1(9), 3327); 44.95 (978-0-7861-2800-6(3), 3327) Blckstn Audio.
It was 1895 and time for a change, or so Rebecca thought. For thirteen years Rebecca Rice had suffocated under the social restraints of widowhood, soaking up the leftovers of other people¿s lives like s sponge. She can¿t remember a time in her life when she didn¿t do exactly what was expected of her¿until now. Armed with a knowledge of nursing and faith healing that she learned from a visiting missionary group, she heads for the hill country of southeastern Oklahoma, Indian Territory, to share her new vocation. The clannish folk of the hill country, reared and groomed in suspicion and superstition, resent Rebecca¿s presence in their midst.

***Angels, Vampires & Douche Bags.** unabr. ed. Carla Collins. (Running Time: 3 hrs.). (ENG.). 2010. 19.98 (978-1-59659-592-7(2), GildAudio) Pub: Gildan Media. Dist(s): HachBkGrp

Angels Watching over Me. Lurlene McDaniel. Read by Kate Forbes. 3 cass. (Running Time: 3 hrs. 30 mins.). (Angels Trilogy: No. 1). (YA). 1999. pap. bk. & stu. ed. 42.24 (978-0-7887-3790-9(2), 41034) Recorded Bks.
Two weeks before Christmas Leah Lewis-Hall is stuck in a hospital room. Alone & afraid, Leah finds unexpected friends in her Amish roommates family & a mysterious "night nurse".

Angels Watching over Me. unabr. ed. Lurlene McDaniel. Narrated by Kate Forbes. 3 pieces. (Running Time: 3 hrs. 30 mins.). (Angels Trilogy: No. 1). (gr. 5 up). 1999. 29.00 (978-0-7887-3832-6(1), 96040E7) Recorded Bks.
Sixteen-year-old Leah is diagnosed with bone cancer two weeks before Christmas while her mother is in Japan on a honeymoon with her most recent husband. Facing her medical trials alone in a hospital, Leah meets Rebekah, a little Amish girl possessing strong religious beliefs & a very supportive family.

Angels Watching over Me, Class set. Lurlene McDaniel. Read by Kate Forbes. 3 cass. (Running Time: 3 hrs. 30 mins.). (Angels Trilogy: No. 1). (YA). 1999. stu. ed. 99.70 (978-0-7887-3861-6(5), 47026) Recorded Bks.
Two weeks before Christmas Leah Lewis-Hall is stuck in a hospital room. Alone & afraid, Leah finds unexpected friends in her Amish roommates family & a mysterious "night nurse".

Angels Watching over Me: Hebrews 1:4-14. Ed Young. 1991. Rental 4.95 (978-0-7417-1875-4(8), 875) Win Walk.

Angels Weep. unabr. ed. Wilbur Smith. Read by Stephen Thorne. 16 cass. (Running Time: 16 hrs.). 1999. 124.95 (978-0-7540-0400-4(7), CAB1823) AudioGO.
At the dawn of a new century, the pioneers of Rhodesia have staked their claims & stocked their farms in the land they have carved as their own. But in the hills, the Matabele indunas are preparing for the bloody rebellion which will forever scar all future generations.

Angels Weep, Pt. 1. unabr. collector's ed. Wilbur Smith. Read by Richard Brown. 8 cass. (Running Time: 12 hrs.). (Ballantyne Novels Ser.). 1988. 64.00 (978-0-7366-1344-6(7), 2246-A) Books on Tape.
How Russia looked in pre-Glasnost days. Written by New York Times Moscow Bureau Chief.

Angels Weep, Pt. 2. collector's ed. Wilbur Smith. Read by Richard Brown. 8 cass. (Running Time: 12 hrs.). (Ballantyne Novels Ser.). 1988. 64.00 (978-0-7366-1345-3(5), 2246-B) Books on Tape.

Angels 101: An Introduction to Connecting, Working, & Healing with the Angels. abr. ed. Doreen Virtue. Read by Doreen Virtue. 1 CD. (Running Time: 7200 sec.).Tr. of ABC de los Angeles: Como Comenzar a Conectarse, Trabajar y Sanarse con los Angeles. 2006. audio compact disk 10.95 (978-1-4019-0761-7(X)) Hay House.

Angelspeake: How to Talk with Your Angels. abr. ed. Barbara Mark & Trudy Griswold. Read by Barbara Mark & Trudy Griswold. 1 cass. (Running Time: 1 hr. 30 min.). 2004. 10.95 (978-1-59007-470-1(X)) Pub: New Millenn Enter. Dist(s): PerseuPGW

Angelspeake: How to Talk with Your Angels. abr. ed. Barbara Mark & Trudy Griswold. Read by Barbara Mark & Trudy Griswold. 1 cass. (Running Time: 90 mins.). 1995. 10.95 (978-1-57511-000-4(8), 10050) Pub Mills.
In clear fashion, "Angelspeake" explains that Angels are God's messengers, providing comfort, healing, guidance & love & that the act of writing to our Angels means that we can take the initiative & actively ask for help, for understanding, for love. We can take control of our lives while we get Angelic support.

Anger. 1 cass. (Running Time: 60 mins.). 10.95 (040) Psych Res Inst.
Gaining control of emotions through positive reactions to adverse situations.

Anger. 1 cass. (Running Time: 1 hr.). 2001. 9.95 (CA602) Pub: VisnQst Vid Aud. Dist(s): TMW Media
Acknowledge and release anger to open yourself up to forgiveness to gain a more peaceful, happier life.

Anger. unabr. ed. Thich Nhat Hanh. Read by Ken McLeod. (Running Time: 6 hrs. 6 cass.). 2003. 24.95 (7669X); audio compact disk 40.00 (76703) Parallax Pr.
Offers a wise and loving way to transform an explosive emotion into peace and bring harmony and healing to all the areas and relationships in our lives that have been affected by anger.

Anger. unabr. ed. Terry Teykl. 6 cass. 1996. 25.00 (978-1-57892-029-7(9)) Prayer Pt Pr.
Sermon/teaching on anger.

Anger: A Precious Part of Ourselves? 4 cass. Incl. Anger: Anger As Gift in Community. Jane Mason & Betsy Poist. 1977.; Anger: Real Anger & the Human Condition. Inge Snipes. 1977.; Anger: The Theology of Anger. Bill Gregory & Steve Stalonas. 1977.; Anger: Using Hidden Anger in Honest & Creative Ways. Robert Leopold. 1977.; 1977. 15.00; 4.50 ea. Pendle Hill.

Anger: Anger As Gift in Community see Anger: A Precious Part of Ourselves?

Anger: Deal with It Before It Deals with You! William G. DeFoore. (ENG.). 2004. audio compact disk 44.99 (978-0-9785244-1-8(1)) Halcyon Life.

Anger: Good or Bad? Speeches. Creflo A. Dollar. 5 cass. (Running Time: 5 hrs. 45 mins.). 2005. audio compact disk 25.00 (978-1-59089-994-6(6)); audio compact disk 34.00 (978-1-59089-995-3(4)) Creflo Dollar.

Anger: Handling a Powerful Emotion in a Healthy Way. unabr. ed. Gary Chapman. Narrated by Gary Chapman. (ENG.). 2007. 15.39 (978-1-60814-034-3(2)); audio compact disk 21.99 (978-1-59859-280-1(7)) Oasis Audio.

Anger: Its Use in Recovery. Carole Riley. 3 cass. (Running Time: 2 hrs. 33 mins.). 1991. 26.95 (TAH247) Alba Hse Comns.
Dr. Riley draws upon her years of teaching & her experience as a counselor & spiritual director to teach & encourage us to use anger properly.

Anger: Program from Award Winning Public Radio Series. Interview. Hosted by Fred Goodwin. Comment by John Hockenberry. 1 CD. (Running Time: 1 hr). (Infinite Mind Ser.). 2002. audio compact disk 21.95 (978-1-888064-85-8(4), LCM 213) Lichtenstein Creat.
Anger can be the most natural emotion in the world... and the most destructive. In "Anger" we explore the differences between constructive and destructive forms of anger, talk with a comedian and Academy Award winning actress about anger on stage, hear about the Tibetan Buddhist perspective on anger, and reflect on the role that this explosive emotion plays in ongoing struggles in the Middle East. Guests include comedian Lewis Black; author and psychiatrist Dr. Norman Rosenthal, professor of clinical psychiatry at Georgetown University; Academy and Tony Award-winning actress Mercedes Ruehl, now playing a spurned wife in Edward Albee's new play, "The Goat: Or who is Sylvia?" and Dr. Robert Thurman, professor of religion at Columbia University and president of New York City's Tibet House. Commentary by John Hockenberry focuses on what may be the world's angriest spot, the Middle East.

Anger: Real Anger & the Human Condition see Anger: A Precious Part of Ourselves?

Anger: The Primitive Emotion. Lois F. Timmins. Read by Lois F. Timmins. 1 cass. (Running Time: 55 mins.). (Our Secret World of Feelings Ser.: Vol. IV). 1986. 12.95 (978-0-931814-07-5(3)) Comn Studies.
For many people anger is the easiest feeling to get in touch with, while others block it out of awareness & insist they never feel anger. If coped with, anger can give a person self-assurance & make them feel brave. It can help a person mobilize their energies and direct them toward constructive activities. Bottled up, misdirected, ignored or acted out, anger can be deadly. Understanding anger gives insight into priorities.

Anger: The Theology of Anger see Anger: A Precious Part of Ourselves?

Anger: Using Hidden Anger in Honest & Creative Ways see Anger: A Precious Part of Ourselves?

Anger: Where From? Where To? A Biblical Study. abr. ed. Sandra Van Drimmelen. 3 cass. (Running Time: 3 hrs.). (From Human to Human Ser.: Vol. 5). 19.95 (978-1-890267-00-1(7), 52995) Restoration Ministries.
Detailed study of bible passages & words plus Hebrew/Jewish concepts.

Anger - The Good & the Bad. Dan Corner. 1 cass. 3.00 (12) Evang Outreach.

Anger & Inner Bonding. Speeches. Margaret Paul. Instructed by Margaret Paul. 1. (Running Time: 1 hr). 1997. 12.00 (978-0-912389-09-7(5)) Evolving Pubns.
Overview of the Six Steps of Inner Bonding, acted out, including a three-step anger process.

Anger Busters: The New ABCs for Angry Men, Newton Hightower. 6 cass. (Running Time: 6 hrs.). 2000. 59.95 (978-1-886298-00-2(9)) Bayou Pubng.
Teaches angry men how to control their rageful tendencies in order to prevent angry & sometimes violent outbursts. A must-have resource for therapists, rageful men & the women who love them.

Anger Control. Bob Griswold. Read by Bob Griswold. 1 CD. (Running Time: 63 mins.). (Love Tapes Ser.). 2005. audio compact disk 15.98 (978-1-55848-157-2(5), Love Tapes) EffectiveMN.
Everyone experiences anger. But if you get angry frequently and it seems uncontrollable, this is the program for you. You'll learn to express your feelings while remaining calm and totally in control of yourself and the situation. It will do wonders for your relationships and your peace of mind.This CD contains 3 programs. The first is a guided meditation with powerful imagery and techniques for achieving your ideal weight. It also includes two excellent subliminal programs, one with the sound of ocean waves and the other with relaxing original music.

Anger Control. Robert E. Griswold. Read by Robert E. Griswold. (Running Time: 58 mins.). (Love Tapes Ser.). 1988. 10.95 (978-1-55848-055-1(2)) EffectiveMN.
Helps in controlling frequent & uncontrollable anger & in expressing thoughts & feelings while remaining calm.

Anger, Depression & Indecision. Earnie Larsen. 6 cass. (Running Time: 6 hrs.). 1990. 45.95 (978-1-56047-040-3(2), A610) E Larsen Enterprises.
How angry have you felt? How much sadness, grief, or depression has that anger caused? What are the problems that keep you from making confident decisions & taking bold action to free yourself from this anchor? Understanding leads to power. Personal freedom leads to freedom. Freedom is recovery.

Anger in Teens: Understanding & Helping Adolescents with Anger Management. William G. DeFoore. (ENG.). 2005. audio compact disk 29.99 (978-0-9814740-0-7(4)) Halcyon Life.

Anger, Its Cause & Cure: Overcoming the Most Useless & Dangerous of Human Emotions. Instructed by Manly P. Hall. 8.95 (978-0-89314-004-5(X), C771118) Philos Res.

Anger Management. 3-CDs. 2004. audio compact disk (978-1-59548-019-4(6)) A Wommack.

Anger Management. 3 cassette tapes. 2004. (978-1-59548-018-7(8)) A Wommack.

Anger Management: Helping Clients Manage Their Anger More Effectively: Complete Kit. Gary Gintner. 6 cass. (Running Time: 9 hrs.). 1995. 124.00 (74221) Am Coun Assn.
This insightful Home-Study takes a look at the real need of today's counselors & other human development specialists to improve their ability to help clients manage anger more effectively. You'll find the secrets that keep your clients cool, calm & in control - enabling them to strengthen relationships, increase productivity & renew enthusiasm.

Anger Management: Helping Clients Manage Their Anger More Effectively: Exam. Gary Gintner. 6 cass. (Running Time: 9 hrs.). 1995. 70.00 exam. (74222) Am Coun Assn.

Anger Management Techniques: Healthy Ways to Control & Express Anger. William G. DeFoore. (ENG.). 2005. audio compact disk 19.99 (978-0-9785244-0-1(3)) Halcyon Life.

Anger of Achilles. unabr. collector's ed. Robert Graves. Read by Bill Kelsey. 10 cass. (Running Time: 15 hrs.). 1989. 80.00 (978-0-7366-1580-8(6), 2446) Books on Tape.
A new interpretation of the Illiad, bright, witty, alive.

Anger Releasing. Louise L. Hay. 1 cass. (Running Time: 33 mins.). 1999. 10.00 (80513) Courage-to-Change.
Visualization exercises for moving past emotional barriers & releasing your anger.

Anger Releasing. Louise L. Hay. Read by Louise L. Hay. 1 cass. (Running Time: 1 hr. 6 mins.). (Personal Power Through Imagery Ser.). 1989. 10.95 (978-0-937611-60-9(3), 220) Hay House.
Guides you through an imagery exercise that helps you to dissolve past anger that is holding you back from achieving your goals.

Anger Releasing. Louise L. Hay. 1 CD. 2004. audio compact disk 10.95 (978-1-4019-0403-6(3)) Hay House.

Angie & Debbie Winans. Perf. by Angie Winans & Debbie Winans. 1 cass. 1999. 10.98 (KMGC9470); audio compact disk 16.98 (KMGD9470) Provident Mus Dist.

Angie, I Says, abr. ed. Avra Wing. Read by Theresa Saldana. 2 cass. (Running Time: 3 hrs.). 1994. 16.95 (978-1-879371-64-4(2)) Pub Mills.
Tina Scacciapensieri, a caustic, sexy & funny half-Italian/half-Jewish Brooklyn woman finds herself pregnant by her plumber boyfriend but infatuated with & possibly falling in love with an uptown lawyer.

Angielski z Deanem Mouscherem 1. Dean Mouscher. 2 CDs and booklet. (POL.). 2003. audio compact disk (978-0-9793821-0-9(6)) English Ctr.

Angielski z Deanem Mouscherem 2. Dean Mouscher. 2 CDs and booklet. (POL.). 2003. audio compact disk (978-0-9793821-1-6(4)) English Ctr.

Angielski z Deanem Mouscherem 3. Dean Mouscher. 2 CDs and booklet. 2003. audio compact disk (978-0-9793821-2-3(2)) English Ctr.

Angielski z Deanem Mouscherem 4. Dean Mouscher. 2 CDs and booklet. (POL.). 2003. audio compact disk (978-0-9793821-3-0(0)) English Ctr.

Angielski z Deanem Mouscherem 5. Dean Mouscher. 2 CDs and booklet. (POL.). 2003. audio compact disk (978-0-9793821-4-7(9)) English Ctr.

Angielski z Deanem Mouscherem 6. Dean Mouscher. 2 CDs and booklet. (POL.). 2003. audio compact disk (978-0-9793821-5-4(7)) English Ctr.

***Angie's Delight.** unabr. ed. Phillip Margolin. Read by Austin Cooper. (ENG.). 2008. (978-0-06-136541-6(6), Harper Audio); (978-0-06-172669-9(9)) HarperCollins Pubs.

Anglais. Anthony Bulger. 2005. audio compact disk & audio compact disk 95.00 (978-2-7005-2052-1(1)) Assimil FRA.

Angle of Attack. abr. ed. Rex Burns. Read by Charlton Griffin. 2 vols. No. 3. 2003. (978-1-58807-667-0(9)) Am Pubng Inc.

Angle of Impact. unabr. ed. Bonnie MacDougal. Read by Sandra Burr. (Running Time: 12 hrs.). 2008. 39.25 (978-1-4233-5306-5(4), 9781423353065, BADLE); 24.95 (978-1-4233-5305-8(6), 9781423353058, BAD); audio compact disk 39.25 (978-1-4233-5304-1(8), 9781423353041, Brlnc Audio MP3 Lib); audio compact disk 24.95 (978-1-4233-5303-4(X), 9781423353034, Brilliance MP3) Brilliance Audio.

Angle of Repose. unabr. ed. Wallace Stegner. Read by Mark Bramhall. (Running Time: 21 hrs. 30 mins.). 2009. 44.95 (978-1-4417-1428-2(6)); 109.95 (978-1-4417-1424-4(3)); audio compact disk 123.00 (978-1-4417-1425-1(1)) Blckstn Audio.

Angle of Repose. unabr. ed. Wallace Stegner. (Running Time: 20 hrs.). 2010. audio compact disk 44.95 (978-1-4417-1427-5(8)) Blckstn Audio.

Angle of Repose, Pt. 1. unabr. collector's ed. Wallace Stegner. Read by Larry McKeever. 9 cass. (Running Time: 13 hrs. 30 mins.). 1996. 72.00 (978-0-7366-3281-2(6), 3937 A) Books on Tape.
A retired historian discovers himself as he researches his grandparents' lives on the Western Frontier.

Angle of Repose, Pt. 2. unabr. collector's ed. Wallace Stegner. Read by Larry McKeever. 10 cass. (Running Time: 15 hrs.). 1996. 80.00 (978-0-7366-3282-9(4), 3937-B) Books on Tape.
A portrait of an American family through four generations.

Angles & Chambers. Arthur Dobrin. (Review Long Island Writers Chapbook Ser.: No. 2). 1991. 10.00 (978-0-89304-259-2(5)) Cross-Cultrl NY.

Anglesey & Lleyn Shipwrecks & Lifeboat VC. unabr. collector's ed. Ian Skidmore. Read by Ralph Cosham. 8 cass. (Running Time: 8 hrs.). 1985. 48.00 (978-0-7366-0760-5(9), 1717) Books on Tape.
From ancient times these coasts have claimed ships & men have sailed out to rescue them.

Anglo-American - Native American, Joe Giordano. Narrated by George Guidall. Contrib. by Mary Ann Broken Nose et al. 6 cass. (Running Time: 3 hrs.). (Growing Up in America Ser.: Vol. 2). 1997. 12.00 (978-1-891207-02-0(4)) Ethnic Prods.

Anglo-American Songs & Ballads. unabr. ed. 1 cass. 1994. 10.95 (978-0-88432-367-9(6), S11235) J Norton Pubs.
Includes 9-page booklet.

Anglo-Catholic Congresses see Sir John Betjeman Reading His Poetry

Anglo Files: A Field Guide to the British. unabr. ed. Sarah Lyall. Narrated by Cassandra Campbell. 8 CDs. (Running Time: 10 hrs. 0 mins. 0 sec.). (ENG.). 2008. audio compact disk 34.99 (978-1-4001-0835-0(7)); audio compact disk 69.99 (978-1-4001-3835-7(3)) Pub: Tantor Media. Dist(s): IngramPubServ

Anglo Files: A Field Guide to the British. unabr. ed. Sarah Lyall. Read by Cassandra Campbell. 1 MP3-CD. (Running Time: 10 hrs. 0 mins. 0 sec.). (ENG.). 2008. audio compact disk 24.99 (978-1-4001-5835-5(4)) Pub: Tantor Media. Dist(s): IngramPubServ

Anglo-Irish Murders. Ruth Dudley Edwards. Read by Bill Wallis. 6 CDs. (Running Time: 9 hrs.). 2001. audio compact disk 64.95 (978-0-7540-5435-1(7), CCD 126) Pub: Chivers Audio Bks GBR. Dist(s): AudioGO
The British and Irish governments have chosen Baroness Troutbeck to chair a conference on Anglo-Irish cultural sensitivities. When a delegate plummets off the battlements, no one can decide whether it was by accident or design.

Anglo-Irish Murders. unabr. ed. Ruth Dudley Edwards. Read by Bill Wallis. 6 cass. (Running Time: 9 hrs.). 2001. 54.95 (978-0-7540-0664-0(6), CAB 2086) Pub: Chivers Audio Bks GBR. Dist(s): AudioGO
Foolishly, the British and Irish governments have chosen the tactless and impatient Baroness Troutbeck to chair a conference on Anglo-Irish cultural sensitivities. She instantly press-gangs her friend Robert Amiss into becoming conference organizer. The interested parties seem intent upon living up to the worst stereotypes, and when a delegate plummets off the battlements, no one can decide whether it was by accident or design.

Angotti Live. Composed by John Angotti. (Running Time: 5400 sec.). 2005. audio compact disk 17.00 (978-1-58459-285-3(0)) Wrld Lib Pubns.

***Angry?** Cerebellum Academic Team. (Running Time: 13 mins.). (Lesson Booster Ser.). 2008. cd-rom 79.95 (978-1-59443-692-5(4)) Cerebellum.

Angry & Oppositional Students. 2002. audio compact disk (978-1-930429-36-9(3)) Love Logic.

Angry & Oppositional Students: Calming Classrooms with Love & Logic. Charles Fay. 2 cass. (Running Time: 3 hrs. 40 min.). 2001. 17.95 (978-1-930429-12-3(6)) Pub: Love Logic. Dist(s): Penton Overseas
Gives long-term solutions rather than temporary bandages for a positive yet powerful approach to preventing school violence.

Angry Heart. unabr. ed. Elizabeth Lord. Read by Patricia Gallimore. 12 cass. (Running Time: 14 hrs. 10 mins.). (Isis Cassettes Ser.). (J). 2004. 94.95 (978-0-7531-1827-6(0)) Pub: ISIS Lrg Prnt GBR. Dist(s): Ulverscroft US

Angry Housewives Eating Bon Bons. unabr. ed. Lorna Landvik. 14 cass. Lib. Ed. (Running Time: 19 hrs. 15 min.). 2004. 99.75 (978-1-4025-6253-2(5), 97538) Recorded Bks.

Angry Housewives Eating Bon Bons. unabr. collector's ed. Lorna Landvik. 11 cass. (Running Time: 16 hrs.). 2004. 39.95 (978-1-4025-6254-9(3), RG793) Recorded Bks.

Angry Interactions: Conflict & Compatability. Bruce A. Baldwin. Read by Bruce A. Baldwin. (Running Time: 60 mins.). (Personal Development Ser.). 1983. 8.95 (978-0-933583-12-2(5), PDC837) Direction Dynamics.
Book on Tape: Chapter from "It's All in Your Head." Teaches how to handle anger with three attitude adjustments & a workable "Code of Ethics" for positive conflict resolution.

***Angry Intruder.** unabr. ed. Catherine Marshall. Adapted by C. Archer. Narrated by Jaimee Draper. (Catherine Marshall's Christy Ser.). (ENG.). 2010. 7.00 (978-1-60814-702-1(9), SpringWater) Oasis Audio.

Angry Island. James Pattinson. Read by Peter Wickham. 4 cass. (Sound Ser.). (J). 2003. 44.95 (978-1-84283-526-5(2)) Pub: ISIS Lrg Prnt GBR. Dist(s): Ulverscroft US

Angry Man: New Life Clinic. Stephen Arterburn et al. 2 cass. (Running Time: 3 hrs.). (Minirth Meier New Life Clinic Ser.). 1995. 12.95 (978-1-886463-04-2(2)) Oasis Audio.
These expert Christian counselors help you come face to face with many different expressions of anger, some of which are quite healthy. They help you understand the difference & to stay in control.

Angry Moon, unabr. ed. Terrill Lankford. Read by Brian Emerson. 7 cass. (Running Time: 10 hrs.). 1998. 49.95 (978-0-7861-1347-7(2), 2250) Blckstn Audio.
Ry Caulder is a burned out hit man who wants to quit the business, but the ties that bind are tight - his one last job is to hunt down & kill his mentor. A deadly game of cat & mouse plays out. With spectacular apparent successes, Caulder finds his prey survives - inexplicably. In the course of the action he discovers the truth behind his mentor's indestructibility & unlocks the door to his own future.

Angry People. Warren W. Wiersbe. Read by Warren W. Wiersbe. 3 cass. (Running Time: 4 hrs. 30 mins.). 1987. 14.95 (978-0-8474-2312-5(3)) Back to Bible.
Looks at the anger of several biblical characters & shows that anger is a force that one must understand & use for God's glory.

Angry Tide. unab. ed. Winston Graham. Read by Tony Britton. 14 cass. (Running Time: 21 hrs.). (Poldark Ser.: Bk. 7). 2000. 89.95 (CAB 1717) Pub: Chivers Audio Bks GBR. Dist(s): AudioGO
Ross Poldark sits for the borough of Truro as an MP, his time divided between London and Cornwall, his heart divided about his wife, Demelza. His old feud with George Warleggan still flares, as does the illicit love between Morwenna and Drake. But before the new century dawns, George and Ross will be drawn together by a loss far greater than their rivalry.

Angry Tide, Set unabr. ed. Winston Graham. Read by Tony Britton. 14 cass. (Poldark Ser.). 1999. 110.95 (CAB 1717) AudioGO.

Angry Tide, Vol. 7. unabr. ed. Winston Graham. Read by Tony Britton. 14 cass. (Running Time: 14 hrs.). (Poldark Ser.: Vol. 7). 1999. 110.95 (978-0-7540-0294-9(2), CAB 1717) AudioGO.

Angrymoon. Terrill Lankford. 1 cass. 1997. 23.00 (978-1-56876-071-1(X), SoundSpectrum) Soundlines Ent.

Anguish see Poetry of Edna St. Vincent Millay

Angular Harmonics - Four Techniques. Charles Hannan. 1 cass. 8.95 (142) Am Fed Astrologers.
Four approaches to angular harmonic charting.

Angus & the Cat see Angus Y el Gato

Angus & the Cat. 2004. 8.95 (978-1-56008-830-1(3)); cass. & flmstrp 30.00 (978-0-89719-643-7(0)) Weston Woods.

Angus & the Cat. (J). 2004. bk. 24.95 (978-0-89719-699-4(6)) Weston Woods.

Angus & the Ducks. 2004. 8.95 (978-1-56008-831-8(1)); audio compact disk 12.95 (978-1-55592-899-5(4)) Weston Woods.

Angus & the Ducks. (J). 2004. pap. bk. 18.95 (978-1-55592-369-3(0)); pap. bk. 38.75 (978-1-55592-370-9(4)); pap. bk. 32.75 (978-1-55592-187-3(6)) Weston Woods.

Angus & the Ducks. Marjorie Flack. 1 cass., 5 bks. (Running Time: 12 min.). (J). (ps-2). pap. bk. 32.75 Weston Woods.
One day the door to Angus' house is left open by mistake & the curious Scottish Terrier goes exploring.

Angus & the Ducks. unabr. ed. Marjorie Flack. 1 cass. (Running Time: 12 mins.). (J). (ps-2). 1998. pap. bk. 14.95 (978-0-7882-0694-8(X), PRA039) Weston Woods.

Angus & the Ducks. unabr. ed. Marjorie Flack. Narrated by Debby Boone. Music by Harry Manfredini. Adapted by Susan Osborn & Gary Templeton. 1 cass. (Running Time: 12 mins.). (J). (ps-2). 1998. 8.95 (978-0-7882-0091-5(7), RAC039) Weston Woods.
One day the door to Angus' house is left open by mistake & the curious Scottish Terrier finally gets his chance to find out what's making the noise on the other side of the tall green hedge.

Angus, Thongs & Full-Frontal Snogging. Louise Rennison. Narrated by Stina Nielsen. 5 CDs. (Running Time: 5 hrs.). (Confessions of Georgia Nicolson Ser.: No. 1). (gr. 7 up). audio compact disk 48.00 (978-1-4025-0465-5(9)) Recorded Bks.

Angus, Thongs & Full-Frontal Snogging. Louise Rennison. Narrated by Stina Nielsen. 4 pieces. (Running Time: 5 hrs.). (Confessions of Georgia Nicolson Ser.: No. 1). (gr. 7 up). 2001. 38.00 (978-0-7887-9416-2(7)) Recorded Bks.

Angus, Thongs & Full-Frontal Snogging. Louise Rennison & Louise Rennison. 3 cass. (Running Time: 5 hrs.). (Confessions of Georgia Nicolson Ser.: No. 1). 2004. 14.99 (978-1-4025-0866-0(2), 70014) Recorded Bks.
The trials of 14-year-old Georgia Nicholson. She's in love with a total sex God who probably doesn't notice her because her nose is too big, her enormous cat enjoys terrorizing Mrs. Next Door's poodle, and her little sister likes using Georgia's bedroom as a bathroom.

Angus, Thongs & Full-Frontal Snogging. unabr. ed. Louise Rennison. Read by Louise Rennison. 3 cass. (Running Time: 3 hrs. 45 mins.). (Confessions of Georgia Nicolson Ser.: No. 1). 2002. (978-1-85549-166-3(4)) Cover To Cover GBR.
It's bad enough being a teenager, but Georgia's problems go way beyond the average! Georgia relates her tale of love, life and full-frontal snogging in her diary, where she records all her dramas and crises.

Angus Wilson. unabr. ed. Interview with John Raleigh & Angus Wilson. 1 cass. (Running Time: 42 mins.). 1967. 12.95 (23077) J Norton Pubs.
John H. Raleigh interviews Angus Wilson who talks about his own novels & British writers, past & present.

Angus Y el Gato. Tr. of Angus & the Cat. (SPA.). (J). 2004. 8.95 (978-0-7882-0288-9(X)) Weston Woods.

Anifeiliaid. 2005. audio compact disk (978-1-85644-884-0(3)) UWACES GBR.

Anifeiliaid Anwes. Fflach. 2005. 4.99 (978-0-00-087272-2(5)) Zondervan.

Anil's Ghost. Michael Ondaatje. (ENG., 2001. (978-0-333-90329-2(3)) Macmillan UK GBR.

Anil's Ghost. unabr. ed. Michael Ondaatje. Read by Alan Cumming. 6 cass. (Running Time: 9 hrs.). 2000. 34.95 (978-0-7366-5074-8(1), 5288) Books on Tape.
Set amidst the sectarian upheaval that ripped Sri Lanka apart in the 1980s and '90s. Anil Tissera, a native Sir Lankan, returns, after 15 years in the United States, as a member of an international human rights fact-finding mission. A forensic anthropologist, she is thrown in with Sarath Diyasena, an archaeologist whose political affiliations, if any, are murky. Together they search for the group behind the organized murders on the island, only to discover evidence of a government sponsored murder. As Anil begins the investigation, she is caught in a web of politics, paranoia, and tragedy.

Anima. Read by Josip Pasic. 2 cass. (Running Time: 2 hrs. 30 mins.). 1986. 18.95 (978-0-7822-0223-6(3), 202) C G Jung IL.

Anima & Animus. Ginger Chalford. 1 cass. 8.95 (639) Am Fed Astrologers.
An AFA Convention Workshop tape.

Anima & Animus. Read by James Wyly. 2 cass. (Running Time: 1 hr. 45 mins.). 1991. 16.95 (978-0-7822-0337-0(X), 442) C G Jung IL.
Part of the "Intensive Overview of Analytical Psychology" set.

Anima & the Art of Vincent van Gogh. Read by John Van Eenwyk. 2 cass. (Running Time: 2 hrs.). 1989. 16.95 (978-0-7822-0319-6(1), 368) C G Jung IL.

Anima As True Feminine. Read by Josip Pasic. 2 cass. (Running Time: 2 hrs.). 1989. 16.95 (978-0-7822-0225-0(X), 367) C G Jung IL.

Anima Christi & the Fundamentum. Read by Thomas P. Lavin. 1 cass. (Running Time: 2 hrs.). (Role of Imaging in the Spiritual Life: Jung's Commentary on the Spiritual Exercises of Ignatius Loyola Ser.: No. 3). 1988. 12.00 (978-0-7822-0140-6(7), 339-3) C G Jung IL.

Anima in Midlife. Read by Murray Stein. 1 cass. (Running Time: 90 mins.). 1989. 10.95 (978-0-7822-0294-6(2), 366) C G Jung IL.

Animal Alphabet see Abecedario de los Animales

Animal Alphabet. 1 cass. Dramatization. (J). pap. bk. 6.95 (978-0-86545-096-7(X)) Spizzirri.

Animal Alphabet. Ed. by Publications International Staff. (J). 2007. audio compact disk 3.98 (978-1-4127-3905-4(5)) Pubns Intl Ltd.

Animal Anatomy on File#153;, CD-ROM. Diagram Staff. (gr. 6-12). 2004. audio compact disk 149.95 (978-0-8160-5403-9(7)) Facts On File.

Animal Antics. Perf. by Hap Palmer. 1 LP. (J). pupil's gde. ed. 11.95 (EA 604); 11.95 (EA 604C) Kimbo Educ.
Hippo Is Heavy - Floppy Dog - Rabbit Moves Fast - Don't Mess with Gorilla - My Kitty Cat, Clip Clip Clop & more.

Animal Ark. Lucy Daniels. 4 cass. (Running Time: 4 hrs.). (J). 1998. (978-1-84032-082-4(6), HoddrStoughton) Hodder General GBR.
Includes "Goat in the Garden," "Goose on the Loose," "Calf in the Cottage," & "Hamster in the Holly".

Animal Ark: Kitten & Sheepdog. abr. ed. Lucy Daniels. Read by Lucy Daniels. 2 cass. (Running Time: 2 hrs.). (J). 1998. 15.00 Ulvrscrft Audio.
Two Animal Ark Christmas adventures.

Animal Classics. Perf. by Jeanette Smith et al. 1 cass. (Running Time: 1 hr.). (J). 1997. 7.98 Incl. blisterpak. (Sony Wonder); audio compact disk 11.98 (Sony Wonder) Sony Music Ent.
"Animal Classics" starts out with well known classical pieces, then adds fun lyrics about animals to make the melodies come alive for small children. As children become exposed to these songs, they start to recognize the melodies & what was unapproachable suddenly becomes familiar & accessible.

Animal Clues: Audiocassette. (gr. k-1). 10.00 (978-0-7635-6283-0(1)) Rigby Educ.

Animal Cognition. Edwin Locke. Read by Edwin Locke. 1 cass. (Running Time: 90 mins.). 1989. 12.95 (978-1-56114-084-8(8), IL04C) Second Renaissance.
Can animals think? It is a commonly held view in psychology & related fields that animals are able to understand language & can engage in human-like thinking. This talk categorically refutes this belief & shows that animals are devoid of a conceptual capacity. It demonstrates that the various experiments with chimpanzees, for example, reveal no ability on their part to comprehend language, even sign language, except on a purely "perceptual" level. Dr. Lock rigorously identifies the scientific & epistemological errors made by researchers in the course of these experiments & defines the fundamental distinctions between human & animal cognition.

Animal Communication. Carol Gurney. 1 cass. (Running Time: 60 mins.). 9.95 (AT5015) Lghtwrks Aud & Vid.
Carol Gurney communicates with animals telepathically. In this "Timeless Voyager Audio" interview, Carol provides information on how we can trace lost pets & be open to thoughts of animals close to us.

Animal Communication Journeys: Heart to Heart; Mind to Mind Guided by Marla Steele. Voice by Marla Steele. (ENG.). (J). 2008. audio compact disk 18.00 (978-0-9815479-0-9(7)) M Steele.

***Animal Communication Mastery Series.** Penelope Smith. (ENG.). 2005. audio compact disk 75.00 (978-0-936552-18-7(2)) Pub: AnimaMundi. Dist(s): Bk Clearing Hse

Animal Communication/Wilderness Talk. Created by Steck-Vaughn Staff. (Running Time: 6232 sec.). (Pair-It Bks.). 2002. (978-0-7398-6218-6(9)) SteckVau.

Animal Companions: Program from the Award Winning Public Radio Series. Interview. Hosted by Fred Goodwin. 1 CD. (Running Time: 1 hr.). (Infinite Mind Ser.). 2002. audio compact disk 21.95 (978-1-888064-67-4(6), LCM 203) Lichtenstein Creat.
In this hour, we explore Animal Companions. Can having a fish help people with Alzheimer's disease? Does having a dog lower your risk of depression? We hear the latest research on the health and mental health benefits of having pets. Guests include Dr. Alan Beck, Director of the Center for the Human-Animal Bond at the School of Veterinary Medicine at Purdue University and co-author of Between Pets and People: The Importance of Animal Companionship; Dr. Susan Cohen, a social worker at the Animal Medical Center in New York City; Dr. Harriet Ritvo, a professor of history at MIT whose books include The Animal Estate: The English and Other Creatures in the Victorian Age; and pet trainer Bash Dibra whose books include DogSpeak and Cat Speak.

ANIMAL COMPANIONS in Our Hearts, Our Lives, & Our World. Read by Diane Pomerance. (ENG.). 2006. audio compact disk 7.95 (978-0-9795218-4-3(X)) Pub: Polaire Pubna. Dist(s): Baker Taylor

ANIMAL COMPANIONS Your Friends, Teachers & Guides. Read by Diane Pomerance. (ENG.). 2006. audio compact disk 7.95 (978-0-9795218-3-6(1)) Pub: Polaire Pubna. Dist(s): Baker Taylor

Animal Consciousness. Daisie Radner & Michael Radner. (Frontiers of Philosophy Ser.). (ENG.). 1996. 23.98 (978-1-57392-114-5(9)) Prometheus Bks.

Animal Crackers. Mary Miche. 1 cass. (J). (ps-6). 1988. 11.50 (978-1-883505-04-2(6)) Song Trek Music.
Selection of 19 educational songs on animals for children.

Animal Crackers. unabr. ed. Hannah Tinti. Read by Laural Merlington & Dan John Miller. 1 MP3-CD. (Running Time: 5 hrs.). 2009. 24.99 (978-1-4233-8526-4(8), 9781423385264, Brilliance MP3); 24.99 (978-1-4233-8528-8(4), 9781423385288, BAD); 39.97 (978-1-4233-8527-1(6), 9781423385271, Brlnc Audio MP3 Lib); 39.97 (978-1-4233-8529-5(2), 9781423385295, BADLE); audio compact disk 24.99 (978-1-4233-8524-0(1), 9781423385240, Bril Audio CD Unabri); audio compact disk 74.97 (978-1-4233-8525-7(X), 9781423385257, BriAudCD Unabrid) Brilliance Audio.

Animal Death: A Spiritual Journey. Penelope Smith. 1 cass. (Running Time: 1 hr. 30 mins.). 14.95 (978-0-936552-09-5(3)) AnimaMundi.
The death of an animal companion is a painful & often confusing experience for those left behind. Explore the subject of animal death from a spiritual perspective. Includes a guided visualization to help you communicate with a departed animal friend.

Animal Dreaming: Encounters in the Natural World. unabr. ed. Short Stories. Perf. by Rafe Martin. 1 cass. (Running Time: 1 hr. 10 mins.). (J). (gr. 5 up). 1992. 9.95 (978-0-938756-41-5(9)) Yellow Moon.
Stories that come from the experience of feeling linked to the natural world. If you believe that we are stewards of the earth, this tape is for you.

Animal Dreams, unabr. ed. Barbara Kingsolver. Narrated by C. J. Critt. 10 cass. (Running Time: 13 hrs. 45 mins.). 1994. 85.00 (978-0-7887-0047-7(2), 94246E7) Recorded Bks.
When Cosima returns to Grace, Arizona, she has come to reconcile memories by confronting her ailing father.

ANIMAL ELDERS Caring about Our Aging Animal Companions. Read by Diane Pomerance. (ENG.). 2006. audio compact disk 7.95 (978-0-9795218-2-9(3)) Pub: Polaire Pubna. Dist(s): Baker Taylor

***Animal Factory: The Looming Threat of Industrial Pig, Dairy, & Poultry Farms to Humans & the Environment.** unabr. ed. David Kirby. (Running Time: 17 hrs. 0 mins.). 2010. 44.95 (978-1-4417-3971-1(8)); 89.95 (978-1-4417-3967-4(X)); audio compact disk 39.95 (978-1-4417-3970-4(X)) Blckstn Audio.

***Animal Factory: The Looming Threat of Industrial Pig, Dairy, & Poultry Farms to Humans & the Environment.** unabr. ed. David Kirby. Read by William Hughes. 17 CDs. (Running Time: 21 hrs.). 2010. audio compact disk 123.00 (978-1-4417-3968-1(8)) Blckstn Audio.

Animal Farm. George Orwell. Read by Ralph Cosham. 4 CDs. (Running Time: 4 hrs.). 2005. audio compact disk 36.00 (978-0-7861-8386-9(1), 1221) Blckstn Audio.

Animal Farm. George Orwell. Read by Richard Matthews. 2002. 24.00 (978-0-7366-8812-3(9)); audio compact disk 28.00 (978-0-7366-8963-2(X)) Books on Tape.

Animal Farm, unabr. ed. George Orwell. Read by Richard Brown. 3 cass. (Running Time: 4 hrs.). (gr. 9-12). 1991. 23.95 (978-0-7861-0253-2(5), 1221) Blckstn Audio.
An account of the bold struggle that transforms Mr. Jones's Manor Farm into Animal Farm - a wholly democratic society built on the credo that All Animals Are Created Equal. Out of their cleverness, the pigs Napoleon, Squealer & Snowball emerge as leaders of the new community in a subtle evolution that bears an insidious familiarity. The climax is the brutal betrayal of the faithful horse Boxer, when totalitarian rule is reestablished with the bloodstained postscript to the founding slogan: But Some Animals Are More Equal Than Others.

Animal Farm. unabr. ed. George Orwell. Read by Richard Brown. 3 cass. (Running Time: 4 hrs.). 2005. reel tape 24.95 (978-0-7861-2796-2(1), E1221); audio compact disk 24.95 (978-0-7861-8462-0(0), 1221); audio compact disk 25.95 (978-0-7861-8477-4(9), ZE1221) Blckstn Audio.
George Orwell's classic satire of the Russian Revolution is an intimate part of our contemporary culture. Orwell's succinct, frightening words have been heard since 1946 as unsparingly descriptive of the fate of those who suffer totalitarian regimes.

Animal Farm. unabr. ed. George Orwell. Read by Ralph Cosham. (Running Time: 3 hrs. 0 mins.). 2008. audio compact disk 14.95 (978-1-4332-1039-6(8)) Blckstn Audio.

Animal Farm. unabr. ed. George Orwell. 2 cass. (Running Time: 3 hrs.). 2002. 24.00 (978-0-7366-9242-7(8)) Books on Tape.

Animal Farm. unabr. ed. George Orwell. Read by Richard Green. 3 cass. (Running Time: 4 hrs.). 2001. 17.95 (978-0-7366-6773-9(3)) Books on Tape.
Animals play the parts of humans in Orwell's deflation of the socialist mystique.

Animal Farm. unabr. ed. George Orwell. Narrated by Patrick Tull. 3 cass. (Running Time: 3 hrs. 15 mins.). 1987. 26.00 (978-1-55690-018-1(X), 87430E7) Recorded Bks.
The animals drive the humans off Mr. Jones' farm but some of them find the temptation to imitate their former human masters too great to resist.

Animal Farm. unabr. ed. George Orwell. Narrated by Patrick Tull. 3 CDs. (Running Time: 3 hrs. 15 mins.). 2000. audio compact disk 29.00 (978-0-7887-4475-4(5), C1172E7) Recorded Bks.

Animal Farm. unabr. collector's ed. George Orwell. Read by Richard Green. 3 cass. (Running Time: 3 hrs.). (J). 1981. 28.00 (978-0-7366-0567-0(3), 1539) Books on Tape.
Animals play the part of humans in Orwell's deflation of the socialist mystique. A great narration.

Animal Farm: The Audio BookNotes Guide. (Audio BookNotes Guide). (C). 2002. audio compact disk 9.95 (978-1-929011-01-8(6)) Scholarly Audio.

Animal Folk Songs for Children: And Other People Too!, Perf. by Mike Seeger et al. 2 cass. (Running Time: 2 hrs. 3 mins.). (Family Ser.). (J). 1992. 14.98 (8023/4); audio compact disk 24.98 (8023/4) Rounder Records.
This recording contains songs sung & played by Ruth Crawford Seeger's four children & six of her grandchildren in tradition-based styles on banjo, guitar, piano, fiddle, tin whistle, ukelele, mandolin, jaw harp, lap dulcimer, quills & other acoustic instruments.

Animal Friends. 1 cass. (Running Time: 20 min.). (Disney Babies Audio Playset Ser.). (J). bk. 9.98 Disney Prod.

Animal Friends: Point & Learn. (Point & Learn Ser.). (J). (ps). 1999. pap. bk. 6.98 (978-0-7634-0586-1(8)) W Disney Records.

Animal Friends for Sale. Tonja Evetts Weimer. Perf. by Tonja Evetts Weimer. 1 cass. (Running Time: 30 min.). (J). (ps-1). 1983. 9.98 (978-0-936823-06-5(2)) Pearce Evetts.
Features children folksongs about animals selected for their rhythm and memorability.

Animal Giants. unabr. ed. Peter M. Spizzirri. Read by Charles Fuller. Ed. by Linda Spizzirri. 1 cass. (Running Time: 15 mins.). Dramatization. (Educational Coloring Book & Cassette Ser.). (J). (gr. 1-8). 1987. pap. bk. 6.95 (978-0-86545-104-9(4)) Spizzirri.
Featuring the largest animals in the world like the Anaconda, Moose, Capybara & more.

Animal Groove. James Coffey. 1 cass. (Running Time: 90 mins.). (J). 1999. 9.95; audio compact disk 14.95 Blue Vision Music.
James friendly voice and inimitable keyboard is designed to get children up & moving.

***Animal Healing Power.** Penelope Smith. (ENG.). 2008. audio compact disk 11.00 (978-0-936552-19-4(0)) Pub: AnimaMundi. Dist(s): Bk Clearing Hse

Animal Husbandry. Laura Zigman. Read by Laura Hicks. 6 CDs. 2004. audio compact disk 54.95 (978-0-7927-3187-0(5), SLD 257, Chivers Sound Lib) AudioGO.

Animal Husbandry. unabr. ed. Laura Zigman. Read by Laura Hicks. 8 vols. (Running Time: 12 hrs.). 2004. 69.95 (978-0-7927-2368-4(6), CSL 257, Chivers Sound Lib) AudioGO.
Ray makes the move. Jane feels the rush. Ray says the L-word. Jane breaks her lease. Then suddenly, inexplicably, he dumps her. Just. Like. That. Now black is the only color in Jane's closet and Kleenex is clinging to her nose. Why did it happen? How could it have happened? Jane is going to get an answer. Not from Ray. Not from her best friends, David and Joan. From an astounding new discovery of her own: The Old-Cow-New-Cow theory. Forced to move into the apartment of a womanizing alpha male named Eddie, Jane is seeing the world of men and women in a brilliant new light. When she takes her theory public, it will change her career and her whole life. Unless, of course, she got it all wrong.

Animal Instincts. unabr. ed. Alan Titchmarsh. Narrated by Alan Titchmarsh. 6 cass. (Running Time: 7 hrs. 30 mins.). 2000. 58.00 (978-1-84197-218-3(5), H1186L8) Recorded Bks.
Rupert Lavery is a well-known conservationist. When he dies, his son Kit returns from ten years in Australia to inherit his nature reserve in the heart of the British countryside. Kit finds the nature reserve more trouble than it is worth. But when he meets Jinty O'Hare, the beautiful niece of the local Master of Foxhounds, he soon discovers there is more charm to the Devonshire coast than he first realized.

Animal Intelligence: Program from the Award Winning Public Radio Series. Hosted by Fred Goodwin. Composed by John Hockenberry. Contrib. by Stan Kuczaj et al. 1 cass. (Running Time: 1 hr.). (Infinite Mind Ser.). 1998. audio compact disk 21.95 (978-1-888064-28-5(5), LCM 34) Lichtenstein Creat.
Dr. Goodwin hosts three top animal researchers. Dr. Sally Boysen is a professor of psychology and director of the Chimpanzee Center at Ohio State University. Her work focuses on animal cognition. Dr. Stan Kuczaj is professor and chair of the Psychology Department at the University of Southern Mississippi. He works with killer whales and dolphins and studies dolphin communication and problem-solving abilities. Dr. Irene Pepperberg is probably the world's best-known researcher into bird intelligence, and she and her African grey parrot, Alex, come to The Infinite Mind from the University of Arizona. Alex is heard throughout the scientists' discussion, sometimes answering questions and sometimes butting in.

Animal Intelligence & Awareness. rev. ed. Penelope Smith. 1 cass. (Running Time: 1 hr.). (Interspecies Telepathic Connection Tape Ser.: No. 2). 1994. 9.95 (978-0-936552-14-9(X)) AnimaMundi.
Find out how other animals' comprehension, reasoning & awareness compare to human ability, based on actual telepathic communication & observable responses from animals. Guaranteed to jog your preconceptions & stimulate your intelligence & awareness.

Animal Life Cycles CD: Growing & Changing. Bobbie Kalman & Rebecca Sjonger. (ENG.). (J). 2008. audio compact disk 10.00 (978-0-7787-7721-2(9)) CrabtreePubCo CAN.

Animal Life of Denmark see Danmarks Dyreliv, 9, De danske graeshopper. (Orthoptera.) (the Danish Grasshoppers.)

Animal Magnetism: My Life with Creatures Great & Small. unabr. ed. Rita Mae Brown. Narrated by Karen White. 1 MP3-CD. (Running Time: 7 hrs. 0 mins. 0 sec.). (ENG.). 2009. 19.99 (978-1-4001-6322-9(6)); audio compact disk 29.99 (978-1-4001-1322-4(9)); audio compact disk 59.99 (978-1-4001-4322-1(5)) Pub: Tantor Media. Dist(s): IngramPubServ

***Animal Magnetism: My Life with Creatures Great & Small.** unabr. ed. Rita Mae Brown. Read by Karen White. (Running Time: 7 hrs. 0 mins.). 2009. 14.99 (978-1-4001-8322-7(7)) Tantor Media.

Animal Moves & Fishy Tales for Tots. Prod. by Angela Russ. Lyrics by Angela Russ. Arranged by Bill Burchell. Composed by Bill Burchell. 1 CD. (Running Time: 30 min). (J). 2002. audio compact disk 13.99 (978-0-9660122-8-6(3)) Russ Invis.
Children sing and dance to easy, instructional, active lyrics that keep them flying, growling, snapping, swimming, hopping, creeping and crawling to kid's favorite songs and lullabies. Some songs are even sung with a bilingual twist.

Animal Nursery Rhyme Time. Kidzup Productions Staff. 1 cass. (Running Time: 90 mins.). (Kidzup Toddler Ser.). (J). 1999. 7.99 (978-1-894281-09-6(8)); audio compact disk 9.99 (978-1-894281-10-2(1)) Pub: Kidzup CAN. Dist(s): Penton Overseas
A classic repertoire of 20 international favorites.

Animal Opposites/Who Has More? Steck-Vaughn Staff. 2002. (978-0-7398-5913-1(7)) SteckVau.

Animal Planet: Sing with the Animals. 1 cass. 1998. 7.98 (978-1-56826-909-2(9)) Rhino Enter.

Animal Planet: Sing with the Animals. 1 CD. (J). 1998. audio compact disk 11.98 (978-1-56826-910-8(2), 75462) Rhino Enter.

Animal Realm: The Dog, Friend or Foe - Primitive Aspects of the Child Archetype. John Giannini. 1 cass. (Running Time: 1 hr. 35 mins.). (Language & Life of Symbols Ser.). 1995. 10.95 (978-0-7822-0491-9(0), 567) C G Jung IL.

***Animal Rescue Team Collection: Gator on the Loose! & Special Delivery.** unabr. ed. Sue Stauffacher. Read by Harlie Vaughn. 6 CDs. (J). 2010. audio compact disk 34.00 (978-0-307-73839-4(6), Listening Lib) Pub: Random Audio Pubg. Dist(s): Random

***Animal Rescue Team Collection: Hide & Seek; Show Time, Vol. 2.** unabr. ed. Sue Stauffacher. (Animal Rescue Team Ser.: Nos. 3-4). (J). 2011. audio compact disk 34.00 (978-0-307-73841-7(8), Listening Lib) Pub: Random Audio Pubg. Dist(s): Random

Animal Research & Experimentation - A Look at Both Sides. Hosted by Nancy Pearlman. 1 cass. (Running Time: 29 mins.). 10.00 (219) Educ Comm CA.

Animal Rights - Religious Perspectives. Hosted by Nancy Pearlman. 1 cass. (Running Time: 29 mins.). 10.00 (409) Educ Comm CA.

Animal Rights & You: A Guide to Sharing the Planet. Ingrid Newkirk. 1 cass. (Running Time: 1 hr.). 10.95 (978-0-945093-26-8(8)) Enhanced Aud Systs.
A fun, upbeat audio program which explains why it is so important for people to give thought to animals & their treatment.

Animal Romp & Stomp for Kids. Speeches. Perf. by Angela Russ et al. Prod. by Angela Russ. Arranged by Bill Burchell. Composed by Bill Burchell. 1 CD. (Running Time: 29 mins.). 2002. audio compact disk 13.99 (978-0-9720234-1-2(0), 0-9720234-1-0) Russ Invis.
KIDS romp and stomp to this captivating, INTERACTIVE music. Each song features easy, instructional lyrics that teach children about a variety of animals. They waddle like penguins, stomp like elephants, wiggle like fish, jump like kangaroos, and rattle like snakes ? all to some of kid?s favorite songs and lullabies. Kids get so excited about expressing their WILD side that they don?t realize how much they?re learning about animals. This CD is the third in the series and takes children romping and stomping through another group of action-style songs.The 3rd in this interactive series, Animal Romp & Stomp, focuses on the characteristics of a variety of animals and wildlife, teaching kids to appreciate nature with all of its subtle and obvious differences. It features 5 of the most popular animal songs in the series, and like it?s sister CDs, challenges kid?s motor skills throughout, ending with a cool down and resting songs. Other CDs in the series: Movin' & Shakin' and Twistin' & Groovin'. Animal Romp & Stomp for Kids will be available on video or DVD mid 2002.

Animal Songs. Perf. by Phil Rosenthal. 1 cass. (Running Time: 40 min.). 1996. 9.98 incl. lyrics. (978-1-879305-23-6(2), AM-C-117); audio compact disk 13.98 incl. lyrics. (978-1-879305-24-3(0), AM-CD-5117) Am Melody.
Original & traditional songs about animals in lively bluegrass & folk musical styles.

Animal Songs Sing-Along: Heaven's Sake Kids. 1 cass. (Disney Ser.). (J). bk. 9.58 Blisterpack. (DISN 60966) NewSound.

Animal-Speak: Understanding Animal Messengers, Totems, & Signs. Ted Andrews. 3 CDs. (Running Time: 10800 sec.). 2007. audio compact disk 24.95 (978-1-59179-586-5(9), AW01155D) Sounds True.

***Animal Spirit Call: Interspecies Communication Power Circle.** Penelope Smith. (ENG.). 2003. audio compact disk 16.00 (978-0-936552-21-7(2)) Pub: AnimaMundi. Dist(s): Bk Clearing Hse

Animal Spirits: How Human Psychology Drives the Economy, & Why It Matters for Global Capitalism. unabr. ed. George A. Akerlof. (Running Time: 10 hrs.). 2009. 39.97 (978-1-4418-1666-5(6), 9781441816665, BADLE) Brilliance Audio.

Animal Spirits: How Human Psychology Drives the Economy, & Why It Matters for Global Capitalism. unabr. ed. George A. Akerlof. Read by Marc Vietor. (Running Time: 8 hrs.). 2009. 24.99 (978-1-4418-1664-1(X), 9781441816641, Brilliance MP3) Brilliance Audio.

Animal Spirits: How Human Psychology Drives the Economy, & Why It Matters for Global Capitalism. unabr. ed. George A. Akerlof & Robert J. Schiller. Read by Marc Vietor. (Running Time: 8 hrs.). 2009. audio compact disk 69.97 (978-1-4418-1663-4(1), 9781441816634, BriAudCD Unabrid) Brilliance Audio.

Animal Spirits: How Human Psychology Drives the Economy, & Why It Matters for Global Capitalism. unabr. ed. George A. Akerlof & Robert J. Shiller. Read by Marc Vietor. (Running Time: 8 hrs.). 2009. 39.97 (978-1-4418-1665-8(8), 9781441816658, Brlnc Audio MP3 Lib); audio compact disk 29.99 (978-1-4418-1662-7(3), 9781441816627, Bril Audio CD Unabri) Brilliance Audio.

Animal Stickers. (Art Rom Create Your Own... Ser.). (J). 2004. pap. bk. 9.99 (978-1-84229-736-0(8)) Top That GBR.

Animal Stories. As told by Mark B. Ropers. Adapted by Mark B. Ropers. (ENG.). (J). 2008. audio compact disk 13.99 (978-0-578-00012-1(1)) Box of Stories.

Animal Stories. abr. rev. unabr. ed. James Herriot & James Herriot. Read by Christopher Timothy. (Running Time: 3 hrs. 0 mins. 0 sec.). (ENG.). 2004. audio compact disk 19.95 (978-1-59397-353-7(5)) Pub: Macmill Audio. Dist(s): Macmillan

Animal Stories. unabr. ed. Read by Nigel Anthony & Nerys Hughes. 1 cass. (Running Time: 1 hr., 30 min.). (J). (gr. 1-8). 1999. 9.95 (CTC 773, Chivers Child Audio) AudioGO.

Animal Stories. unabr. ed. Walter de la Mare. Read by Lynn Redgrave. 1 cass. (Running Time: 90 min.). Incl. Animal Stories: All Gone. (J). (CDL5 1456); Animal Stories: Mrs. Fox. (J). (CDL5 1456); Animal Stories: The Hare & the Hedgehog. (J). (CDL5 1456); Animal Stories: The Mouse, the Bird & the Sausage. (J). (CDL5 1456); Animal Stories: The Wolf & the Fox. (J). (CDL5 1456); (J). 1975. 11.00 (978-0-694-50786-3(5), CDL5 1456) HarperCollins Pubs.

Animal Stories. unabr. ed. Narrated by Gerald Hausman. 1 cass. (Running Time: 1 hr.). 14.95 (C11313) J Norton Pubs.
Stories collected from the Navajo, Cheyenne, Hopi, Kwakiutl, Tlingit & Iroquois tribes.

Animal Stories: All Gone see Animal Stories

Animal Stories: Mrs. Fox see Animal Stories

Animal Stories: The Hare & the Hedgehog see Animal Stories

Animal Stories: The Mouse, the Bird & the Sausage see Animal Stories

Animal Stories: The Wolf & the Fox see Animal Stories

Animal Tails: Traditional Stories & Songs. Short Stories. Perf. by Lee Ellen. 1 cass. (Running Time: 60 mins.). (J). (ps-3). 1989. 9.95 (978-0-938756-24-8(9), 60) Yellow Moon.
Traditional folktales & songs which invites the young listener to come out & play.

Animal Tales. Narrated by Naomi Adler. Illus. by Amanda Hall. (Running Time: 1 hr. 23 mins. 42 sec.). (J). audio compact disk 19.99 (978-1-84148-977-3(8)) BarefootBksMA.

Animal Tales. Read by Joseph Bruchac. 1 cass. (Wonder Ser.). (J). (ps-3). 1995. bk. 9.95 (978-1-57098-054-1(3)) Robs Rinehart.
Stories & folk tales read aloud. Focuses on wild animals threatened by human activities.

Animal Tales. Short Stories. Read by Jim Weiss. 1 cass. (Running Time: 1 hr.). Dramatization. (Storyteller's Version Ser.). (J). (ps up). 1990. 10.95 (978-1-882513-07-9(X), 1124-07); audio compact disk 14.95 (978-1-882513-32-1(0), 1124-007) Greathall Prods.
The perfect tape when a child is ready to move beyond listening to music to spoken word. Features tales by Aesop, Grimm, Chaucer and others. Includes "The Three Billy Goats Gruff," "The Lion and the Mouse," "City Mouse and Country Mouse," "Giggly Biggley and the Invitation," "Goat Gets Away" and others.

Animal Tales. Read by Jim Weiss. 1 cass. (Running Time: 1 hr.). (J). NewSound.

Animal Tales. abr. ed. Bill Shontz. 1 cass. (Running Time: 40 min.). (J). (ps-5). 1993. 8.98 (978-1-879496-42-2(9)); audio compact disk 12.98 compact disc. (978-1-879496-70-5(4)); audio compact disk 12.98 incl. sing-along coloring bk. (978-1-879496-71-2(2)) Lightyear Entrtnmnt.
This album reflects Bill's love of animals & the world we share with them.

Animal Tales. abr. ed. Bill Shontz. 1 cass. (Running Time: 40 mins.). (J). (ps-5). 1993. pap. bk. 8.98 incl. coloring bk. (978-1-879496-43-9(7)) Lightyear Entrtnmnt.

Animal Tales: Raccoon, Bear & Coyote. Melody Warnick. Read by Tavia Gilbert & Steven McLaughlin. (Running Time: 0 hr. 48 mins. 0 sec.). (PlainTales Explorers Ser.). (ENG.). (J). (gr. k-2). 2009. audio compact disk 12.95 (978-0-9820282-4-7(5)) Pub: PlainTales. Dist(s): IPG Chicago

Animal Tales from the Bible. LaNell Seay. 2 cass. (Running Time: 30 mins.). Dramatization. (Lamb's Tales Ser.: Vol. 1). (J). (gr. k-4). 1996. 14.95 (978-1-891797-01-9(8)) Silver Fox TX.
The four Bible stories include: "Ramsey, the Wayward Lamb"; "Hosanna!"; "King Darius' Dilemma"; & "The Merciful Neighbor"; all written from animals p.o.v. & the children are encouraged to "read more about it".

Animal Tales Told in the Gullah Dialect (1) Albert H. Stoddard. 8.95 incl. brochure. (L 44) Lib Congress.
Includes How Buh Houn Got His Long Mouth, How Bun Houn Got E Long Tongue & others.

Animal Tales Told in the Gullah Dialect (2) Read by Albert H. Stoddard. 8.95 incl. brochure. (L45) Lib Congress.
Includes Man Git E Adam Apple, Buh Partridge Outhides Buh Rabbit & others.

Animal Tales Told in the Gullah Dialect (3) Read by Albert H. Stoddard. 8.95 incl. brochure. (L 46) Lib Congress.
Includes Cow Tail Een De Ma-a-ash, Buh Rabbit & Buh Wolf Go Hunting & others.

Animal Teeth/Machines That Work. Steck-Vaughn Staff. (J). 2002. (978-0-7398-5983-4(8)) SteckVau.

Animal, the Vegetable, & John D. Jones. unabr. ed. Betsy Byars. 1 read-along cass. (Running Time: 1 hr. 7 mins.). (Children's Cliffhangers Ser.). (J). (gr. 5-6). 1985. pap. bk. 15.98 incl. bk. & guide. (978-0-8072-1128-1(1), SWR45SP, Listening Lib) Random Audio Pubg.
Clara & Deanie are thrilled about spending time with their father now that the divorce is final until they discover that his girlfriend & her stuck-up son are coming along.

Animal Triste. Monika Maron. (GER.). 2001. 22.00 (978-2-226-10058-0(X)) Pub: Presses Pocket FRA. Dist(s): Distribks Inc

Animal Tunes. Penton Overseas, Inc. Staff. 1 cass. (Running Time: 60 mins.). (Ready-Set-Sing Collection). (ENG.). (J). 2003. 4.49 (978-1-56015-973-5(1)) Penton Overseas.
Includes: "Kookaburra," "B-I-N-G-O," "This Little Pig" and more.

***Animal, Vegetable, Miracle.** unabr. ed. Barbara Kingsolver. Read by Barbara Kingsolver. Read by Camille Kingsolver & Steven L. Hopp. (ENG.). 2007. (978-0-06-144994-9(6), Harper Audio); (978-0-06-144993-2(8), Harper Audio) HarperCollins Pubs.

Animal, Vegetable, Miracle: A Year of Food Life. unabr. ed. Barbara Kingsolver. Read by Barbara Kingsolver. Read by Steven L. Hopp & Camille Kingsolver. Told to Steven L. Hopp & Camille Kingsolver. 12 CDs. (Running Time: 14 hrs. 30 mins.). 2007. audio compact disk 39.95 (978-0-06-085357-0(3), Harper Audio) HarperCollins Pubs.

Animal, Vegetable, Miracle: A Year of Food Life. unabr. ed. Barbara Kingsolver. Read by Barbara Kingsolver et al. (Running Time: 52200 sec.). 2007. 85.95 (978-1-4332-0730-3(3)); audio compact disk 29.95 (978-1-4332-0732-7(X)); audio compact disk 99.00 (978-1-4332-0731-0(1)) Blckstn Audio.

Animal Walks. 1 cass. (Running Time: 1 hr.). (J). 2001. pap. bk. 10.95 (KIM 9107C); pap. bk. & pupil's gde. ed. 11.95 (KIM 9107) Kimbo Educ.
Children have so much fun imitating the unique & special walks of animals, they don't even realize they're exercising! Muscles are strengthened, coordination is improved & imaginations are unleashed as kids leap like a kangaroo, do the penguin shuffle, the giraffe stretch, crocodile creep & more. Includes guide.

Animal Walks. Georgiana Stewart. 1 CD. (Running Time: 1 hr.). (J). 2001. pap. bk. 14.95 (KIM 9107CD) Kimbo Educ.

Animal Wife. unabr. ed. Elizabeth Marshall Thomas. Narrated by Frank Muller. 8 cass. (Running Time: 12 hrs.). 1996. 70.00 (978-0-7887-0361-4(7), 94553E7) Recorded Bks.
When the pale-eyed hunter, Kori, sees a strange woman climbing from an icy pond, he is driven to possess her. But capturing this wild, untamed creature is only the beginning.

Animal Within Us: Lessons about Life from Our Animal Ancestors. unabr. collector's ed. Jay D. Glass. Read by Arthur Addison. 4 cass. (Running Time: 6 hrs.). 1998. 32.00 (978-0-7366-4224-8(2), 4725) Books on Tape.
A provocative understanding of the human mind, The Animal Within Us shows us what we can learn about our lives from our animal kin.

Animalerie en Comptines. Kidzup Productions Staff. 1 CD. (Running Time: 90 mins.). (Kidzup Foreign Language Ser.). (FRE.). (J). 1999. audio compact disk 12.99 (978-1-894281-36-2(5)) Pub: Kidzup CAN. Dist(s): Penton Overseas
A classic repertoire of international favorites.

Animales. 1 cass. (Primeros Pasos en Ciencia Ser.). (SPA.). (J). 12.00 (Natl Textbk Co) M-H Contemporary.
Helps children in grades 1-4 discover the process of scientific investigation. Part of the First Steps in Science Program.

***Animales en Sus HáBitats Audio Cd.** Debra Castor. Adapted by Benchmark Education Company, LLC. (Content Connections Ser.). (SPA.). (J). 2009. audio compact disk 10.00 (978-1-935472-53-7(4)) Benchmark Educ.

Animales No Se Visten. Judi Barrett. Illus. by Ron Barrett. (Running Time: 4 mins.).Tr. of Animals Should Definely Not Wear Clothes. 1991. audio compact disk 12.95 (978-1-59519-134-2(8)) Live Oak Media.

Animales No Se Visten. Judi Barrett. Illus. by Ron Barrett. 14 vols. (Running Time: 4 mins.).Tr. of Animals Should Definely Not Wear Clothes. 1991. pap. bk. 51.95 (978-1-59519-136-6(4)); 9.95 (978-1-59112-006-3(3)) Live Oak Media.

Animales No Se Visten. Judi Barrett. Illus. by Ron Barrett. 11 vols. (Running Time: 4 mins.).Tr. of Animals Should Definely Not Wear Clothes. (SPA.). (J). 1991. pap. bk. 18.95 (978-1-59519-135-9(6)) Pub: Live Oak Media. Dist(s): AudioGO

Animales No Se Visten. unabr. ed. Judi Barrett. Read by Angel Pineda. Illus. by Ron Barrett. 11 vols. (Running Time: 4 mins.).Tr. of Animals Should Definely Not Wear Clothes. (SPA.). (J). (gr. 1-3). 1991. pap. bk. 16.95

(978-0-87499-227-4(3), LK4507); pap. bk. & tchr. ed. 49.95 Reading Chest. (978-0-87499-229-8(X)) Live Oak Media.
Readalong of Spanish translation of Animals Should Definitely Not Wear Clothing.

Animales No Se Visten. unabr. ed. Judi Barrett. 1 cass. (Running Time: 4 mins.).Tr. of Animals Should Definely Not Wear Clothes. (SPA.). (J). (gr. k-3). 1991. 9.95 Live Oak Media.

Animaloopidy. 1 CD. (Running Time: 1 hr.). (J). audio compact disk 11.98 Jewel box. (ANIM 1002) NewSound.

Animals see Twentieth-Century Poetry in English, No. 23, Recordings of Poets Reading Their Own Poetry

Animals. Brad Caudle & Melissa Caudle. Perf. by Brad Caudle et al. Perf. by Alan Bradley et al. Illus. by Anthony Guerra. 1 cass. (Running Time: 50 mins.). (Rock 'N Learn Ser.). (J). (ps-k). 1995. pap. bk. 12.99 (978-1-878489-49-4(6), RL949) Rock N Learn.
A musical program teaching the sounds, habitats & traits of over 60 animals from common pets to farm, forest & zoo animals. Kids interact with characters on tape using a full-color book. Also features the performances of: Erick Leikam, Laina Reinsmith, Robert Witherspoon, Lee Jenkins & Jack Mattingly.

Animals. Kindersley Dorling. 1 cass. (First Steps in Science Ser.). (J). 12.00 (Natl Textbk Co) M-H Contemporary.
Helps children in grades 1-4 discover the process of scientific investigation. Part of the First Steps in Science Program.

Animals, Vol. I. Tonja Evetts Weimer. Perf. by Tonja Evetts Weimer. (Running Time: 18 mins.). (Fingerplays & Action Chants). (J). (ps-1). 1995. 8.95 (978-0-936823-01-0(1)) Pearce Evetts.
Illustrated book/cassette helps children learn counting, story sequence & other pre-reading skills. Winner of seven awards. Contains rhymes & chants about animals with finger games to enrich storyline.

Animals, Vol. 1. 2nd rev. ed. Tonja Evetts Weimer. Perf. by Tonja Evetts Weimer. Illus. by Yvonne Kozlina. (Running Time: 18 mins.). (Fingerplays & Action Chants). (J). (ps-1). 1995. pap. bk. 14.95 (978-0-936823-13-3(5)) Pearce Evetts.

***Animals: CD add-on Set.** Perf. by Millmark Education Staff. (ConceptLinks Ser.). 2009. audio compact disk 50.00 (978-1-61618-345-5(4)) Millmark Educ.

Animals: Unforgettable Encounters in the Wild. unabr. ed. Narrated by Jon Hamilton. (ENG.). 2010. audio compact disk 14.95 (978-1-61573-062-9(1), 161573062l) Pub: HighBridge. Dist(s): Workman Pub

Animals Act Like People. 9.95 (978-1-59112-007-0(1)); audio compact disk 12.95 (978-1-59112-824-3(2)) Live Oak Media.

Animals & Ethics. unabr. ed. Rem B. Edwards. Read by Robert Guillaume. Ed. by John Lachs & Mike Hassell. Prod. by Pat Childs. (Running Time: 10800 sec.). (Morality in Our Age Ser.). 2006. audio compact disk 25.95 (978-0-7861-6631-2(2)) Pub: Blckstn Audio. Dist(s): NetLibrary CO

Animals & Ethics. unabr. ed. Rem B. Edwards. Read by Robert Guillaume. Ed. by John Lachs & Mike Hassell. 2 cass. (Running Time: 3 hrs.). Dramatization. (Morality in Our Age Ser.). 1995. 17.95 (978-1-56823-029-0(X), 10508) Knowledge Prod.
For most of human history, killing animals or plants presented few moral problems; they seemed made for our use. But the rapid growth & increasing dominance of human civilization, along with the view that we are "animals" ourselves, raises many questions about the moral standing & "rights" of other living things. Is it morally wrong to hunt, eat meat, wear fur or leather, eradicate pests, or to conduct medical experiments on animals? Do we have a duty to protect animals & plants?.

Animals & Other Stories. Prod. by Jay Allison. 1 cass. (Running Time: 1 hr.). 11.95 (F0430B090, HarperThor) HarpC GBR.

Animals & the Afterlife. Agnes J. Thomas. 2006. 16.99 (978-0-9770964-3-5(2)) Salty Cove Pr.

Animals & the Seasons Audio CD. Adapted by Benchmark Education Company Staff. Based on a work by Margaret McNamara. (Content Connections Ser.). (J). (gr. k-2). 2008. audio compact disk 10.00 (978-1-60634-898-7(1)) Benchmark Educ.

Animals & Their Babies. Sundance/Newbridge, LLC Staff. (Early Science Ser.). (gr. k-3). 2007. audio compact disk 12.00 (978-1-4007-6217-0(0)); audio compact disk 12.00 (978-1-4007-6218-7(9)); audio compact disk 12.00 (978-1-4007-6219-4(7)) Sund Newbrdge.

Animals As Pets & Companions, Whale Art on Walls, Black Rhino Preservation & Education about Sharks. Hosted by Nancy Pearlman. 1 cass. (Running Time: 30 mins.). 10.00 (919) Educ Comm CA.

Animals as Pets & Therapy. Hosted by Nancy Pearlman. 1 cass. (Running Time: 29 mins.). 10.00 (208) Educ Comm CA.

Animals at the Farm/Animales de la Granja. abr. ed. Created by Mark Wesley & Gladys Rosa-Mendoza. (English Spanish Foundations Ser.). (J). 2008. audio compact disk 9.95 (978-1-931398-61-9(5)) Me Mi Pubng.

***Animals Audio CD.** Perf. by Millmark Education Staff. (ConceptLinks Ser.). 2008. audio compact disk 28.00 (978-1-4334-0145-9(2)) Millmark Educ.

Animals Born Alive & Well. unabr. ed. Ruth Heller. 1 cass. (Running Time: 6 mins.). (J). (gr. 1-4). 1989. pap. bk. 17.95 (978-0-8045-6652-0(6), 6551-B) Spoken Arts.
This program is bright with mammals, large, tiny, prehistoric... they are all here in repeatable rhymes.

Animals Came in One by One. Buster Lloyd-Jones. Read by David Learner. 4 cass. (Running Time: 6 hrs.). 1999. 44.95 (66170) Pub: Soundings Ltd GBR. Dist(s): Ulverscroft US

Animals' Christmas Tree: A Tree-mendous Mini-Musical for Unison & 2-Part Voices (SoundTrax) Composed by Andy Beck et al. (ENG.). 2008. audio compact disk 44.99 (978-0-7390-5070-5(2)) Alfred Pub.

Animals Come First. unabr. ed. Mary Bowring. Read by Patricia Gallimore. 5 cass. (Running Time: 8 hrs.). 2000. 49.95 (978-1-85496-958-3(7), 69587) Pub: Soundings Ltd GBR. Dist(s): Ulverscroft US
As wife of a vet with a country practice, Mary Bowring never has a dull moment. Her days & nights are governed by the unforeseen: a call to help a foaling racehorse, an agonizing decision about a much-loved dog, a rescue operation for an ailing tiger or ostrich. In her role as receptionist & auxiliary nurse, the author has found out much about animals & their owners & these insights form part of her amusing narrative.

Animals Could Talk: Aesop's Fables Retold in Song. Heather Forest. (Running Time: 42 mins.). 1994. audio compact disk 14.95 (978-0-87483-750-6(2)) Pub: August Hse. Dist(s): Natl Bk Netwk

Animals Could Talk: Aesop's Fables Retold in Song. unabr. ed. Heather Forest. Read by Heather Forest. 1 cass. (Running Time: 42 mins.). (American Storytelling Ser.). (J). (ps-3). 1995. bk. 12.95 (978-0-87483-344-7(2)) August Hse.
Norelco box with 32 page illustrated booklet in blister pack. Aesop's fables retold in song with original music.

Animals Have Patterns Audio CD. Adapted by Benchmark Education Company Staff. Based on a work by Francisco Blane. (My First Reader's Theater Ser.). (J). (gr. k-1). 2008. audio compact disk 10.00 (978-1-60634-100-1(6)) Benchmark Educ.

Animals in Hiding. Sundance/Newbridge, LLC Staff. (Early Science Ser.). (gr. k-3). 2007. audio compact disk 12.00 (978-1-4007-6353-5(3)); audio compact disk 12.00 (978-1-4007-6354-2(1)); audio compact disk 12.00 (978-1-4007-6352-8(5)) Sund Newbrdge.

Animals in That Country see Poetry & Voice of Margaret Atwood

Animals in the Human Environment. Hosted by Nancy Pearlman. 1 cass. (Running Time: 28 mins.). 10.00 (228) Educ Comm CA.

Animals in Their Habitats Audio CD. Adapted by Benchmark Education Company Staff. Based on a work by Margaret McNamara. (Content Connections Ser.). (J). (gr. k-2). 2008. audio compact disk 10.00 (978-1-60634-893-2(0)) Benchmark Educ.

Animals in Translation: Using the Mysteries of Autism to Decode Animal Behavior. unabr. ed. Temple Grandin. Narrated by Shelly Frasier. 11 CDs. (Running Time: 12 hrs. 0 mins. 0 sec.). (ENG.). 2005. audio compact disk 37.99 (978-1-4001-0146-7(8)); audio compact disk 75.99 (978-1-4001-3146-4(4)) Pub: Tantor Media. Dist(s): IngramPubServ
How is Animals in Translation different from every other animal book ever published? Animals in Translation is like no other animal book because of Temple Grandin. As an animal scientist and a person with autism, her professional training and personal history have created a perspective like no other thinker in the field, and this is her exciting, groundbreaking view of the intersection of autism and animal. Unlike other well-known writers in the field of animal behavior - When Elephants Weep by psychoanalyst Jeffrey Moussaleff Masson, How Dogs Think by psychologist and dog trainer Stanley Coren, and The Hidden Life of Dogs by anthropologist Elizabeth Marsha Thomas - Temple Grandin is an animal scientist who has devoted the last 30 years of her life to the study of animals. Animals in Translation is the culmination of that life's work - a book whose sweep is huge, including just about anything that gallops, trots, slithers, walks, or flies. Temple Grandin is like no other author on the subject of animals because of her training and because of her autism; understanding animals is in her blood and her bones.

Animals in Translation: Using the Mysteries of Autism to Decode Animal Behavior. unabr. ed. Temple Grandin & Catherine Johnson. Read by Shelly Frasier. 2 MP3 CDs. (Running Time: 12 hrs. 0 mins. 0 sec.). (ENG.). 2005. audio compact disk 22.99 (978-1-4001-5146-2(5)) Pub: Tantor Media. Dist(s): IngramPubServ

Animals Inc: A Business Parable for the 21st Century. abr. ed. Kenneth A. Tucker & Vandana Allman. Read by Jim Ward. (ENG.). 2005. 14.98 (978-1-59483-309-0(5)) Pub: Hachet Audio. Dist(s): HachBkGrp

Animals, Inc: A Business Parable for the 21st Century. abr. ed. Kenneth A. Tucker & Vandana Allman. Read by Jim Ward. (Running Time: 3 hrs.). (ENG.). 2009. 39.98 (978-1-60024-568-8(4)) Pub: Hachet Audio. Dist(s): HachBkGrp

Animals Make Us Human: Creating the Best Life for Animals. unabr. ed. Temple Grandin. Narrated by Andrea Gallo. 10 cass. (Running Time: 11 hrs. 45 mins.). 2009. 82.75 (978-1-4361-6303-3(X)); audio compact disk 123.75 (978-1-4361-6305-7(6)) Recorded Bks.

Animals Make Us Human: Creating the Best Life for Animals. unabr. ed. Temple Grandin. Narrated by Andrea Gallo. (Running Time: 11 hrs. 45 mins.). 2009. 61.75 (978-1-4361-9257-6(9)) Recorded Bks.

Animals on the Loose. unabr. ed. Short Stories. Perf. by Naomi Leithold. 1 cass. (Running Time: 1 hr.). (J). 1997. 10.00 (978-0-9701891-2-7(5)) Simply Storytelling.

Animal's Place in the Universal Plan. Instructed by Manly P. Hall. 8.95 (C820404) Philos Res.

***Animals SB1 Audio CD Traits & Habitats.** Perf. by Millmark Education Staff. (Content Literacy Libraries Ser.). 2008. audio compact disk (978-1-4334-0420-7(6)) Millmark Educ.

***Animals SB2 Audio CD Classification.** Perf. by Millmark Education Staff. (Content Literacy Libraries Ser.). 2008. audio compact disk (978-1-4334-0421-4(4)) Millmark Educ.

***Animals SB3 Audio CD Adaptations.** Perf. by Millmark Education Staff. (Content Literacy Libraries Ser.). 2008. audio compact disk (978-1-4334-0422-1(2)) Millmark Educ.

***Animals SB4 Audio CD Surviving Change.** Perf. by Millmark Education Staff. (Content Literacy Libraries Ser.). 2008. audio compact disk (978-1-4334-0423-8(0)) Millmark Educ.

Animals Should Definely Not Wear Clothes see Animales No Se Visten

Animals Should Definitely Not Act Like People. Judi Barrett. Read by Peter Fernandez. Illus. by Ron Barrett. 1 cass. (Running Time: 30 mins.). (J). 2000. pap. bk. 19.97 (978-0-7366-9222-9(3)) Books on Tape.
In this sequel to the popular "Animals Should Definitely Not Wear Clothing" the consequences of unanimal like behavior are humorously portrayed.

Animals Should Definitely Not Act Like People. Judi Barrett. 1 cass. (Running Time: 35 min.). (J). (ps-4). 2001. pap. bk. 15.95 (VX-82C) Kimbo Educ.
What would happen if a hippopotamus decided to take a bath in a tub? What if a sheep got a permanent wave? Includes book to read along with.

Animals Should Definitely Not Act Like People. Judi Barrett. 1 cass. (J). bk. 9.95; pap. bk. 15.95 Live Oak Media.

Animals Should Definitely Not Act Like People. Judi Barrett. Illus. by Ron Barrett. 14 vols. pap. bk. 35.95 (978-1-59112-827-4(7)) Live Oak Media.

Animals Should Definitely Not Act Like People. Judi Barrett. Read by Linda Terheyden. Illus. by Ron Barrett. 14 vols. (J). (gr. k-3). pap. bk. 33.95 Reading Chest. (978-0-87499-232-8(X)) Live Oak Media.
In this sequel to the popular "Animals Should Definitely Not Wear Clothing," the consequences of unanimal like behavior are humorously portrayed.

Animals Should Definitely Not Act Like People. Judi Barrett. Read by Linda Terheyden. Illus. by Ron Barrett. 1 cass. (J). (gr. k-3). 1991. pap. bk. 15.95 (978-0-87499-230-4(3)) Live Oak Media.

Animals Should Definitely Not Wear Clothing. 1 cass. (Running Time: 35 min.). (J). (ps-4). 2001. pap. bk. 15.95 (VX-76C) Kimbo Educ.
Though animals wear their own built-in clothing, this book speculates on what might happen if animals dressed up the way humans do. Includes read along book.

Animals Should Definitely Not Wear Clothing. Judi Barrett. Read by Peter Fernandez. Illus. by Ron Barrett. 1 cass. (Running Time: 30 mins.). (J). 2000. pap. bk. 19.97 (978-0-7366-9197-0(9)) Books on Tape.

Animals Should Definitely Not Wear Clothing. Judi Barrett. Illus. by Ron Barrett. (Running Time: 4 mins.). (J). (ps-2). 1990. 9.95 (978-1-59112-008-7(X)) Live Oak Media.

Animals Should Definitely Not Wear Clothing. Judi Barrett. Read by Peter Fernandez. Illus. by Ron Barrett. 11 vols. (Running Time: 4 mins.). (J). (gr. k-3). 1990. pap. bk. 16.95 (978-0-87499-146-8(3)) Pub: Live Oak Media. Dist(s): AudioGO

Animals Should Definitely Not Wear Clothing. Judi Barrett. Interview with Ron Barrett. 1 readalong cass. (Running Time: 4 mins.). (J). (ps-4). 1990. pap. bk. 33.95 incl. four books & guide to reading & language arts skills activities. Live Oak Media.
A quirky look at what might happen if animals decided to don additional apparel.

Animals Should Definitely Not Wear Clothing. Judi Barrett. Illus. by Ron Barrett. (Running Time: 4 mins.). 1990. audio compact disk 12.95 (978-1-59112-689-8(4)) Live Oak Media.

Animals Should Definitely Not Wear Clothing. Judi Barrett. Read by Peter Fernandez. 11 vols. (Running Time: 4 mins.). (J). 2005. pap. bk. 18.95 (978-1-59112-690-4(8)) Pub: Live Oak Media. Dist(s): AudioGO

Animals Should Definitely Not Wear Clothing. Judi Barrett. Illus. by Ron Barrett. (J). (gr. k-3). 1990. pap. bk. 15.95 (978-0-87488-146-2(3)) Live Oak Media.

Animals Should Definitely Not Wear Clothing. Judi Barrett. Illus. by Ron Barrett. Interview with Ron Barrett. 14 vols. (Running Time: 4 mins.). (J). (gr. k-3). 1990. pap. bk. & tchr. ed. 33.95 Reading Chest. (978-0-87499-148-2(X)) Live Oak Media.
A quirky look at what might happen if animals decided to don additional apparel.

Animals Should Definitely Not Wear Clothing. Judi Barrett. Read by Peter Fernandez. Illus. by Ron Barrett. Interview with Ron Barrett. 1 cass. (Running Time: 4 mins.). (J). (gr. k-3). 1990. bk. 24.95 (978-0-87499-147-5(1)) Live Oak Media.
A quirky look at what might happen if animals decided to don additional apparel.

Animals Should Definitely Not Wear Clothing: Los Animales No Se Visten. unabr. ed. Judi Barrett. Tr. by J. Davis. Illus. by Ron Barrett. 22 vols. (Running Time: 8 mins.). (ENG & SPA.). (J). (gr. 1-3). 1999. pap. bk. 33.95 (978-0-87499-564-0(7)) Live Oak Media.

Animals Side by Side: Early Explorers Early Set B Audio CD. Jennifer Boudart. Adapted by Benchmark Education Staff. (J). 2007. audio compact disk 10.00 (978-1-4108-8237-0(3)) Benchmark Educ.

Animals Use of Psychedelics. Lou De Bourbon. Interview with Elizabeth Gips. 1 cass. 1999. 11.00 (32010) Big Sur Tapes.
1983 Santa Cruz.

Animals with No Eyes: Cave Adaptation. Kelly Regan Barnhill. Contrib. by Patrick Olson & Charity Jones. (Extreme Life Ser.). (ENG.). (gr. 3-4). 2008. audio compact disk 12.99 (978-1-4296-3202-7(X)) CapstoneDig.

Animals You'll Never Forget. Steck-Vaughn Staff. (J). 2002. (978-0-7398-6213-1(8)) SteckVau.

Animaniac: Christmas. Haynes. 1995. 7.98 (978-1-57042-326-0(1)) GrandCentral.

Animaniacs. Created by Steven Spielberg. 1 CD. (Running Time: 1 hr.). (J). 2002. audio compact disk 16.98 (978-1-56826-728-9(2), 71571) Rhino Enter.
Meet the zany, out-of-control, over-the-top Animaniacs from the hit TV series. Features 17 original songs like "Yakko's World," "I'm Mad," "Wakko's America," and more. Complete lyrics included.

Animaniacs: Variety Pack. Created by Steven Spielberg. 1 CD. (Running Time: 1 hr.). (J). 2002. audio compact disk 16.98 (978-1-56826-601-5(4), 72181) Rhino Enter.
The Animaniacs' third album! This 16-track collection features tunes such as "Variety Speak," "Pinky & the Brain," "Dot's Quiet Time," and many, many more.

Animated CD-ROM for Glenn/Gray's Hodges' Harbrace Handbook. 16th ed. (C). 2006. audio compact disk 50.95 (978-1-4130-1680-2(4)) Pub: Heinle. Dist(s): CENGAGE Learn

Animated CD-ROM for Glenn/Gray's the Writer's Harbrace Handbook, 3rd. 3rd ed. (C). 2006. audio compact disk 28.95 (978-1-4130-1690-1(1)) Pub: Heinle. Dist(s): CENGAGE Learn

Animated CD-ROM for Kirszner/Mandell's the Brief Wadsworth Handbook, 5th. 5th ed. (C). 2006. audio compact disk 45.95 (978-1-4130-2195-0(6)) Pub: Heinle. Dist(s): CENGAGE Learn

Anime X-Plode! 1 CD. 2004. audio compact disk 14.98 (978-1-57813-930-9(9), CD/010, ADV Music) A D Vision.

Ánimo. Isabel Isern Vivancos. (YA). 2010. audio compact disk 300.00 (978-0-19-915432-6(5)) OUP.

Animosity. David Lindsey. Read by Scott Brick. 2001. audio compact disk 72.00 (978-0-7366-8063-9(2)) Books on Tape.

Animosity. David Lindsey. 2001. 56.00 (978-0-7366-6839-2(X)) Books on Tape.

Animosity. abr. ed. David Lindsey. Read by Joe Pantoliano. (ENG.). 2005. 14.98 (978-1-59483-419-6(9)) Pub: Hachet Audio. Dist(s): HachBkGrp

Animus. Read by Anne Avery. 1 cass. (Running Time: 90 mins.). 1986. 10.95 (978-0-7822-0010-2(9), 203) C G Jung IL.

Animus: A Non-Gender Perspective. Read by Cathy Rives. 2 cass. (Running Time: 2 hrs.). 1989. 16.95 (978-0-7822-0229-8(2), 377) C G Jung IL.

Animus As Servant to the Self. Read by Caroline Stevens. 2 cass. (Running Time: 2 hrs.). 1989. 16.95 (978-0-7822-0305-9(1), 376) C G Jung IL.

Animus Images in Dreams, Myths & Fairytales. Read by Lois Khan. 2 cass. (Running Time: 2 hrs.). 1989. 16.95 (978-0-7822-0124-6(5), 375) C G Jung IL.

***Anita Blake Vampire Hunter': Micah, Danse Macabre.** abr. ed. Laurell K. Hamilton. (Running Time: 11 hrs.). (Anita Blake, Vampire Hunter Ser.: Vols. 13 & 14). 2010. audio compact disk 19.99 (978-1-4418-5037-9(6), 9781441850379) Brilliance Audio.

***Anita Blake Vampire Hunter: The Harlequin, Blood Noir.** abr. ed. Laurell K. Hamilton. Read by Cynthia Holloway. (Running Time: 14 hrs.). (Anita Blake, Vampire Hunter Ser.: Vols. 15 & 16). 2010. audio compact disk 19.99 (978-1-4418-5051-5(1), 9781441850515) Brilliance Audio.

Anita's Big Day. Elizabeth Laird. 1 cass. (Running Time: 1 hr.). (978-0-582-27536-2(9), PutnaJuv) Penguin Grp USA.

Anjali. (Running Time: 1 hr. 7 mins.). audio compact disk 14.00 (978-0-87612-503-8(8)) Self Realization.

***Ankylosaurus Fights Back.** Laura Gates Galvin. Illus. by Adrian Chesterman. (Smithsonian's Prehistoric Pals Ser.). (ENG.). (J). 2009. audio compact disk 21.95 (978-1-59249-813-0(2)) Soundprints.

Ankylosing Spondylitis - A Bibliography & Dictionary for Physicians, Patients, & Genome Researchers. Compiled by Icon Group International, Inc. Staff. 2007. ring bd. 28.95 (978-0-497-11332-2(5)) Icon Grp.

Ann Beattie Interview. 20.97 (978-0-13-090473-7(2)) P-H.

Ann Deagon. Read by Ann Deagon. 1 cass. (Running Time: 29 min.). 1987. 10.00 New Letters.
Deagon is a professor in Classics in North Carolina & author of several books of fiction & poetry.

Ann Mayo Muir: So Goes My Heart. Contrib. by Gordon Bok & Joseph A. Trickett. 1 cass. 9.98 (C-99) Folk-Legacy.
Ann leads all the songs here, backed by Bok & Trickett.

Ann Royale Affair. 10.00 Esstee Audios.
The story of how a lady takes on the National Bank, with all of its power & how her newspaper wins with the help of Andrew Jackson.

Ann Stanford Memorial. Ann Stanford. Read by Ann Stanford. 1 cass. (Running Time: 29 mins.). 1987. 10.00 (090487) New Letters.
This program comes from a San Diego reading given by Stanford in 1985 & never before broadcast.

Ann Struthers. Read by Ann Struthers. 1 cass. (Running Time: 29 mins.). Incl. Jim Barnes. Read by Jim Barnes.; 1985. 10.00 New Letters.
Jim Barnes of Missouri & Ann Struthers of Iowa read poems of the Midwest.

Ann Veronica. H. G. Wells. Read by Anais 9000. 2008. 27.95 (978-1-60112-154-7(7)) Babblebooks.

Anna & the King of Siam. Margaret Landon. Read by Kate Reading. 1999. audio compact disk 112.00 (978-0-7366-8045-5(4)) Books on Tape.

Anna & the King of Siam. collector's ed. Margaret Landon. Read by Kate Reading. 12 hrs. (Running Time: 18 hrs.). 1999. 96.00 (978-0-7366-4647-5(7), 5028) Books on Tape.

Anna Banana. Kathleen Gibson. 1 CD. (Running Time: 35 mins.). (J). (ps-4). 1994. audio compact disk 15.00 (978-1-888862-06-5(8), RR2110) Rompin Records.
Parent's Choice Honor Award Winner. Exuberant, danceable music that is filled with the joy of childhood.

Anna Banana & Me. Lenore Blegvad. Read by Rick Adamson. Illus. by Erik Blegvad. 11 vols. (Running Time: 9 mins.). (J). (gr. k-3). 1988. pap. bk. 16.95 (978-0-87499-103-1(X)) AudioGO.
Anna Banana's ability to meet life head-on inspires her young friend to confront & overcome his own imagined fear.

Anna Banana & Me. Lenore Blegvad. Illus. by Erik Blegvad. Narrated by Rick Adamson. (J). (ps-2). 1998. audio compact disk 12.95 (978-1-59519-294-3(8)) Live Oak Media.

Anna Banana & Me. Lenore Blegvad. Illus. by Erik Blegvad. (Running Time: 9 mins.). 1988. 9.95 (978-1-59112-009-4(8)) Live Oak Media.

Anna Banana & Me. Lenore Blegvad. Read by Rick Adamson. Illus. by Erik Blegvad. 14 vols. (Running Time: 9 mins.). (J). (gr. k-3). 1988. pap. bk. & tchr. ed. 33.95 Reading Chest. (978-0-87499-105-5(6)) Live Oak Media.

Anna Banana & Me. Lenore Blegvad. Read by Rick Adamson. (Live Oak Readalong Ser.). (J). 2005. pap. bk. 18.95 (978-1-59519-295-0(6)) Pub: Live Oak Media. Dist(s): AudioGO

Anna Bristlecone. Dennis W. Froberg. Read by Dennis W. Froberg. 1 cass. (Running Time: 20 mins.). (J). 2000. 8.95 Writers Mrktpl.
A delightful & educational story about Anna Bristlecone & how she grew into an adult tree.

Anna Christie. unabr. ed. Eugene O'Neill. Perf. by Dwier Brown et al. 2 CDs. (Running Time: 1 hr. 44 mins.). (L. A. Theatre Works). 2000. audio compact disk 25.95 (978-1-58081-174-3(4), CDTPT127) Pub: L A Theatre. Dist(s): NetLibrary CO

Anna Christie. unabr. ed. Eugene O'Neill. Perf. by Stacy Keach et al. 1 cass. (Running Time: 1 hr. 44 mins.). 2000. 20.95 (978-1-58081-133-0(7), TPT127) L A Theatre.
The passion of a coal barge captain's daughter & a rough-hewn sailor takes a tumultuous turn when her secret past is revealed.

Anna in the Tropics. Nilo Cruz. 2 CDs. (Running Time: 1 hr. 40 mins.). 2005. audio compact disk 25.95 (978-1-58081-334-1(8), LA 075) Pub: L A Theatre. Dist(s): NetLibrary CO

Anna Karenina. Leo Tolstoy. Narrated by Nadia May. (Running Time: 35 hrs.). 1993. 76.95 (978-1-59912-415-5(7)) Iofy Corp.

Anna Karenina. Leo Tolstoy. Read by Laura Paton. (Running Time: 5 hrs.). 2000. 28.95 (978-1-60083-674-9(7)) Iofy Corp.

Anna Karenina. Leo Tolstoy. 3 CDs. (Running Time: 3 Hrs. 45 Mins.). 2004. audio compact disk 9.99 (978-1-57050-036-7(3)) Multilingua.

Anna Karenina. Leo Tolstoy. Read by Laura Paton. 4 cass. (Running Time: 5 hrs.). 1996. 22.98 (978-962-634-581-8(0), NA408114, Naxos AudioBooks) Naxos.

Anna Karenina. Leo Tolstoy. (Running Time: 1 hr.). (Radiobook Ser.). 1987. 4.98 (978-0-929541-28-0(6)) Radiola Co.

Anna Karenina. abr. ed. Leo Tolstoy. Read by Alfred Molina. (Running Time: 3 hrs.). (ENG.). 2006. audio compact disk 19.95 (978-1-59887-080-0(7), 1598870807) Pub: HighBridge. Dist(s): Workman Pub

Anna Karenina. abr. ed. Leo Tolstoy. Read by Saskia Wickham. 2 cass. (Running Time: 3 hrs.). 2000. 13.95 (978-1-84032-481-5(3), HoddrStoughton) Pub: Hodder General GBR. Dist(s): Trafalgar
Anna, miserable in her loveless marriage, does the barely thinkable and succumbs to her desires for the dashing Vronsky.

Anna Karenina. abr. ed. Leo Tolstoy. Read by Jane Seymour. 2 cass. (Running Time: 3 hrs.). 2000. 7.95 (978-1-57815-118-9(X), 1080, Media Bks Audio) Media Bks NJ.

Anna Karenina. abr. ed. Leo Tolstoy. Read by Laura Paton. 4 CDs. (Running Time: 5 hrs.). (J). (gr. 9-12). 1996. audio compact disk 28.98 (978-962-634-081-3(9), NA408112) Naxos.

Anna Karenina. unabr. ed. Leo Tolstoy. Read by Nadia May. 24 cass. 2005. reel tape 75.95 (978-0-7861-2821-1(6)); audio compact disk 79.95 (978-0-7861-8441-5(8)); audio compact disk 39.95 (978-0-7861-8957-1(6), 1397A,B) Blckstn Audio.

Anna Karenina. unabr. ed. Leo Tolstoy. Read by Nadia May. (YA). 2008. 199.99 (978-1-60514-708-6(7)) Find a World.

***Anna Karenina.** unabr. ed. Leo Tolstoy. Read by Kate Lock. 31 CDs. (Running Time: 41 hrs.). 2010. audio compact disk 162.98 (978-962-634-130-8(0)) Naxos.

***Anna Karenina.** unabr. ed. Leo Tolstoy. Narrated by Lorna Raver. (Running Time: 40 hrs. 0 mins. 0 sec.). (ENG.). 2010. 44.99 (978-1-4001-6610-7(1)); 36.99 (978-1-4001-8610-5(2)); audio compact disk 64.99 (978-1-4001-1610-2(4)); audio compact disk 129.99 (978-1-4001-4610-9(0)) Pub: Tantor Media. Dist(s): IngramPubServ

Anna Karenina, Pt. 1. unabr. ed. Leo Tolstoy. Read by Nadia May. 13 cass. (Running Time: 25 hrs.). 2003. 85.95 (978-0-7861-0445-1(7), 1397A,B) Blckstn Audio.
Anna Karenina, the sister of Stepan Oblonsky, comes to Moscow in an attempt to patch up a dispute between her brother & his wife, Dolly. While there, she meets a handsome young officer named Aleksei Vronski, who is rumored to be in love with Dolly's younger sister, Kitty. However, Konstantine Levin is also in love with Kitty & he succeeds in marrying her. The forbidden romance between Anna & Vronsky has tragic consequences, & is masterfully set in counterpoint to Kitty's more enduring marriage with Levin, who is a reflection of Tolstoy himself, often illuminating the author's search for meaning in life, his love of a natural, simple existence & various other views & convictions.

Anna Karenina, Pt. 1. unabr. ed. Leo Tolstoy. Narrated by Davina Porter. 15 cass. (Running Time: 21 hrs. 30 mins.). 1989. 100.00 (978-1-55690-019-8(8), 89840E7) Recorded Bks.
Anna Karenina abandons her marriage to a boorish husband for the dashing Count Vronsky but happiness proves to be elusive.

Anna Karenina, Pt. 2. unabr. ed. Leo Tolstoy. Read by Nadia May. 11 cass. (Running Time: 25 hrs.). 2003. 76.95 (978-0-7861-0646-2(8), 1397A,B) Blckstn Audio.
Anna Karenina, the sister of Stepan Oblonsky, comes to Moscow in an attempt to patch up a dispute between her brother & his wife, Dolly. While there, she meets a handsome young officer named Aleksei Vronski, who is rumored to be in love with Dolly's younger sister, Kitty. However, Konstantine Levin is also in love with Kitty & he succeeds in marrying her. The forbidden romance between Anna & Vronsky has tragic consequences, & is masterfully set in counterpoint to Kitty's more enduring marriage with Levin, who is a reflection of Tolstoy himself, often illuminating the author's search for meaning in life, his love of a natural, simple existence & various other views & convictions.

Anna Karenina, Pt. 2. unabr. ed. Leo Tolstoy. Narrated by Davina Porter. 12 cass. (Running Time: 17 hrs.). 1989. 86.00 (978-1-55690-020-4(1), 89850E7) Recorded Bks.

Anna Karenina, Pt. C. collector's unabr. ed. Leo Tolstoy. Read by Jill Masters. 9 cass. (Running Time: 13 hrs. 30 mins.). 1984. 72.00 (978-0-7366-3986-6(1), 9531-C) Books on Tape.
Tolstoy was born in 1828 to a family of aristocratic landowners & was steeped in the traditions of the Russian nobility. The story of Anna follows her romance with the young Russian soldier Count Alexey Vronsky. Meeting by chance in Moscow, Vronsky returns with Anna to St. Petersburg, where rumors of their relationship soon reach her husband.

Anna Karenina, Pt. A. collector's ed. Leo Tolstoy. Read by Jill Masters. 10 cass. (Running Time: 15 hrs.). 1984. 80.00 (978-0-7366-3984-2(5), 9531-A) Books on Tape.

Anna Karenina, Pt. B. collector's unabr. ed. Leo Tolstoy. Read by Jill Masters. 10 cass. (Running Time: 15 hrs.). 1984. 80.00 (978-0-7366-3985-9(3), 9531-B) Books on Tape.

Anna Karenina: Abridged. (ENG.). 2007. (978-1-60339-003-3(0)) Listenr Digest.

Anna Karenina: Abridged. (ENG.). (C). 2007. cd-rom & audio compact disk (978-1-60339-004-0(9)) Listenr Digest.

Anna Karenina (Part 1) unabr. ed. Leo Tolstoy. Narrated by Flo Gibson. 12 cass. (Running Time: 18 hrs.). 2004. 39.95 (978-1-55685-754-6(3)) Audio Bk Con.
Theadulterous love affair of Anna and her handsome officer, Vronsky, ends in tragedy.

Anna Karenina (Part 2), Vol. 2. unabr. ed. Leo Tolstoy. Narrated by Flo Gibson. (Running Time: 18 hrs. 15 mins.). 2004. 39.95 (978-1-55685-790-4(X)) Audio Bk Con.

Anna Karenina (Parts 1 And 2) unabr. ed. Leo Tolstoy. Narrated by Flo Gibson. (Running Time: 36 hrs. 7 mins.). 2004. 64.95 (978-1-55685-791-1(8)) Audio Bk Con.

Anna Marie's Blanket. unabr. ed. Joanne Barkan. 1 cass. (Running Time: 10 mins.). (J). (gr. k-4). 1994. pap. bk. 15.90 (978-0-8045-6821-0(9), 6821) Spoken Arts.
IRA-CBC Childrens Choice Award.

Anna of the Five Towns. unabr. ed. Arnold Bennett. Read by Flo Gibson. 5 cass. (Running Time: 7 hrs. 30 mins.). (J). (gr. 8 up). 1997. 20.95 (978-1-55685-462-0(5), 462-5) Audio Bk Con.
This forerunner to "The Old Wives' Tale" deals with moral & religious pressures in the Potteries region, which lead to embezzlement & suicide. Anna, loved by two men, discovers that she is rich & is filled with compassion & remorse. There are lyrical descriptions of the countryside & of seeing the ocean for the first time.

Anna of the Five Towns. unabr. ed. Arnold Bennett. Read by Patsy Byrne. 6 cass. (Running Time: 7 hrs. 42 mins.). 1993. 54.95 (978-1-85089-492-6(2), 92043) Pub: ISIS Audio GBR. Dist(s): Ulverscroft US
Anna is a young girl, dominated by a miserly father, who is wooed for her money but falls in love unsuitably & courageously defies her parents.

Anna of the Five Towns. unabr. ed. Arnold Bennett. Read by Peter Joyce. 6 cass. (Running Time: 6 hrs.). 1997. 54.95 (978-1-86015-447-8(6)) Pub: UlverLrgPrint GBR. Dist(s): Ulverscroft US
Anna, a young woman in 19th century England, finds that as her fortune grows, so does her understanding of the poor working class.

Anna Papers. unabr. collector's ed. Ellen Gilchrist. Read by Mary Peiffer. 7 cass. (Running Time: 10 hrs. 30 mins.). 1993. 56.00 (978-0-7366-2370-4(1), 3143) Books on Tape.
Six-day wake for a passionate Southern writer brings together old friends, lovers & family.

Anna, Schmidt und Oskar, Level 1B. Barbara Derkow-Disselbeck et al. 2 cass. (GER.). (J). (gr. 2-6). 1993. 17.50 (978-3-468-96863-1(9)) Langenscheidt.
A German language video course for children.

Anna, Schmidt und Oskar, Level 2A. Barbara Derkow-Disselbeck & Dieter Kirsch. 2 cass. (Running Time: 2 hrs.). (GER.). 2005. 17.50 (978-3-468-96842-6(6)) Langenscheidt.

Anna, Schmidt und Oskar, Level 2B. Barbara Derkow-Disselbeck & Dieter Kirsch. 2 cass. (Running Time: 2 hrs.). (GER.). 2005. 17.50 (978-3-468-96843-3(4)) Langenscheidt.

Anna, Where Are You? Patricia Wentworth. 2009. 54.95 (978-0-7531-4207-3(4)); audio compact disk 79.95 (978-0-7531-4208-0(2)) Pub: Isis Pubng Ltd GBR. Dist(s): Ulverscroft US

Anna, Where Are You?, unabr. ed. Patricia Wentworth. Read by Nadia May. 6 cass. (Running Time: 8 hrs. 30 mins.). 1992. 44.95 (978-0-7861-0317-1(5), 1278) Blckstn Audio.
Patricia Wentworth's Miss Silver - always unruffled & wise - epitomizes the civilized charm of British mystery. It is perhaps fitting that her long-time devotion to Tennyson provides one of the major clues in this perplexing case.

Annabel Lee see Classic American Poetry

Annabel Lee see Raven & Other Works

Annabel Lee see Best of Edgar Allan Poe

Annabel Lee see Famous Story Poems

Annabella. unabr. ed. Aileen Armitage. Read by Charlotte Strevens. 8 cass. (Running Time: 10 hrs. 30 mins.). 2000. 69.95 (978-0-7531-0549-8(7), 991113) Pub: ISIS Audio GBR. Dist(s): Ulverscroft US
Inside the beautiful Anna Braithwaite are two very different women. To the society world she is born into, Anna appears to be the shy daughter of a MP. Engaged to a young aristocrat & living in a Victorian Mansion, she seems a loved innocent. But at night, Anna makes the journey into Bella's world of passion & avarice, centered in the city's most exclusive club for entertaining gentlemen. Each time she is followed by the one man who really loves her, trying desperately to find what has driven her into Bella's world, whilst striving to keep himself from temptation.

Annabelle Swift, Kindergartner. Amy Schwartz. Read by Randye Kaye. 1 cass. (J). 2000. pap. bk. 19.97 (978-0-7366-9198-7(7)) Books on Tape.
She is more than ready for kindergarten, for she has been tutored by her older sister, Lucy. Poor Annabelle embarasses herself but proves her mettle, by becoming the first kindergarten milk monitor.

Annabelle Swift, Kindergartner. Amy Schwartz. (J). (gr. k-4). 2001. bk. 15.95 (VX-99C) Kimbo Educ.
Annabelle is embarrassed when she follows her know-it-all sister's advice on the first day of school. Includes book.

Annabelle Swift, Kindergartner. Amy Schwartz. Illus. by Amy Schwartz. (Running Time: 13 mins.). (J). (ps-2). 1996. audio compact disk 12.95 (978-1-59112-686-7(X)) Live Oak Media.

Annabelle Swift, Kindergartner. Amy Schwartz. Illus. by Amy Schwartz. 14 vols. (Running Time: 13 mins.). 1996. pap. bk. 39.95 (978-1-59112-688-1(6)); 9.95 (978-1-59112-010-0(1)) Live Oak Media.

Annabelle Swift, Kindergartner. Amy Schwartz. Illus. by Amy Schwartz. Read by Randye Kaye. 11 vols. (Running Time: 13 mins.). (Live Oak Readalong Ser.). (J). (gr. k-3). 1996. pap. bk. 16.95 (978-0-87499-355-4(5)); pap. bk. 37.95 Reading Chest . (978-0-87499-357-8(1)) Live Oak Media.
Annabelle Swift is more than ready for kindergarten, for she has been tutored by her older sister, Lucy. Poor Annabelle embarrasses herself, (but) proves her mettle by successfully counting the milk money & becoming the first kindergarten milk monitor.

Annabelle Swift, Kindergartner. Amy Schwartz & Randye Kaye. 11 vols. (Running Time: 13 mins.). (Live Oak Readalong Ser.). (J). 2004. pap. bk. 18.95 (978-1-59112-687-4(8)) Pub: Live Oak Media. Dist(s): AudioGO

Annals of Tacitus - Excerpts. unabr. ed. Excerpts. Cornelius Tacitus. Narrated by George Wilson. 3 cass. (Running Time: 4 hrs. 30 mins.). 1994. 26.00 (978-1-55690-764-7(8), 92409E7) Recorded Bks.
The Annals, the last & greatest achievement of Tacitus, records the history of the Julio-Claudian emperors from the death of Augustus (14 AD.) to the reign of Nero (54-68). They are stories of mutiny & murder, of whole armies disappearing beyond the Rhine, of an unstable & gloomy frontier. Tacitus brings us Nero himself, whose reign saw the burning of Rome & the mass slaughter of Christians, & whose vices still captivate & startle by their imagination & cruelty.

Annals of the Kings & Rulers. unabr. ed. J. R. R. Tolkien. Narrated by Rob Inglis. 3 cass. (Running Time: 3 hrs.). 1990. 26.00 (978-1-55690-021-1(X), 90071E7) Recorded Bks.
Appendix A of Tolkien's fantasy trilogy, The Lord of the Rings. An explanation of the Realms in Exile, a listing of the heirs of Isildur & a listing of the heirs of Anarion of Gondor, part of the tale of Aragorn & Arwen, an essay on the House of Earl & concluding a essay on Durin's Folk.

Annapolis. abr. ed. William Martin. Read by John Rubinstein. 2 cass. 2001. 7.95 (978-1-57815-195-0(3), Media Bks Audio) Media Bks NJ.

Annapolis, Pt. 1. unabr. ed. William Martin, Jr. Read by Jonathan Reese. 8 cass. (Running Time: 12 hrs.). 1997. 64.00 (978-0-7366-3589-9(0), 4243A) Books on Tape.
In this historical epic, the lives of two navy families intertwine through eight generations. Sweeping, romantic adventure.

Annapolis, Pt. II. William Martin. Read by Jonathan Reese. 9 cass. (Running Time: 13 hrs. 30 min.). 1997. 72.00 (4243-B) Books on Tape.

Anna's Book. abr. ed. Barbara Vine, pseud. Read by Wanda McCaddon. 2 cass. (Running Time: 3 hrs.). 1995. 16.95 (978-0-945353-98-0(7), N20398) Pub: Audio Partners. Dist(s): PerseuPGW
A young Danish immigrant in turn-of-the-century London confides her rebellious thoughts in her diary. Decades later, her granddaughter stumbles across missing portions of the diary that may offer a clue to an unsolved murder.

Anna's Book. abr. ed. Barbara Vine, pseud. Read by Wanda McCaddon. 2 cass. (Running Time: 3 hrs.). 2000. 7.95 (978-1-57815-183-7(X), 1123, Media Bks Audio) Media Bks NJ.
Anna & family move from Denmark to England in 1905. She expresses her sincerest beliefs & emotions about her detached existence in a diary as she desperately searches for her individuality. A mysterious murder & a concealed adoption spin a suspicious web around Anna's past.

Annas, Killer of Jesus. Scripts. Glenn Kimball. 1 CD. (Running Time: 00:49:56). 2005. audio compact disk 15.00 (978-1-59772-042-7(9), Your Own Wrld Bks) Your Own Wrld.
Sleuthing the murderer of Jesus is one of the most revealing investigations ever hidden from the public. Nobody wanted to take the blame. The truth reveals a story that extends far beyond Jerusalem, from the courts of Caesar to events in western Europe and trade to the Far East.The murderous motivation of Annas and his High Priest dynasty began before the birth of Jesus, extended during his whole life and ended in the ?Final straw,? when Jesus destroyed his money changing concessions at the temple of Herod two days before the cructhxion. Annas couldn?t kill Jesus directly?Why? Herod couldn?t kill Jesus, though his father had sought the life of Jesus from the time he was born. The ?Scapegoat? had to be Pontius Pilate who didn?t want anything to do with the death of Jesus. The secret was not public pressure from the Jews. Pilate didn?t care about public Jewish opinion. Pilate was being blackmailed by Annas. The greatest historians on the life of Jesus and hidden manuscripts written by Matthew tell us... the rest of the story.

Anna's Old Boot. Short Stories. Mike Anderson. 1 CD. (Running Time: 56 mins). (J). 2004. audio compact disk 15.00 (978-1-929050-12-3(7)) MW Prods.

Anna's Return. abr. ed. Marta Perry. Read by Tanya Eby. (Running Time: 3 hrs.). (Pleasant Valley Ser.: Bk. 3). 2010. audio compact disk 19.99 (978-1-4418-0876-9(0), 9781441808769, BACD) Brilliance Audio.

Anna's Return. abr. ed. Marta Perry. (Running Time: 4 hrs.). (Pleasant Valley Ser.: Bk. 3). 2011. audio compact disk 9.99 (978-1-4418-0877-6(9), 9781441808776, BCD Value Price) Brilliance Audio.

Anna's Return. unabr. ed. Marta Perry. Read by Tanya Eby. (Running Time: 8 hrs.). (Pleasant Valley Ser.: Bk. 3). 2010. 24.99 (978-1-4418-0872-1(8), 9781441808721, Brilliance MP3); 24.99 (978-1-4418-0874-5(4), 9781441808745, BAD); 39.97 (978-1-4418-0873-8(6), 9781441808738, Brlnc Audio MP3 Lib); 39.97 (978-1-4418-0875-2(2), 9781441808752, BADLE); audio compact disk 29.99 (978-1-4418-0870-7(1), 9781441808707, Bril Audio CD Unabri); audio compact disk 79.97 (978-1-4418-0871-4(X), 9781441808714, BriAudCD Unabrid) Brilliance Audio.

Anne Frank: The Diary of a Young Girl. Anne Frank. Narrated by Susan Adams. 8 CDs. (Running Time: 9 hrs.). 2000. audio compact disk 78.00 (978-0-7887-4666-6(9), C1226E7) Recorded Bks.
The first-hand account of a young Jewish girl in hiding from the Germans in occupied Amsterdam.

Anne Frank: The Diary of a Young Girl. Anne Frank & Susan Adams. 5 Cass. (Running Time: 9 Hrs). 24.95 (978-1-4025-2364-9(5)) Recorded Bks.

Anne Frank: The Diary of a Young Girl. Read by Julie Harris. 2 cass. (Running Time: 1 hr. 40 mins.). 19.95 (8010Q) Filmic Archives.
This is a remarkable literary & historical document, beloved by both adults & adolescents. Julie Harris's dramatic reading captures the positive life spirit of the young girl. Now that we are observing the 50th anniversary of WW II, this personal perspective is more relevant than ever.

Anne Frank: The Diary of a Young Girl. abr. ed. Anne Frank. Perf. by Claire Bloom. 1 cass. 1984. 8.98 (CDL5 1522) HarperCollins Pubs.
From July 1942 until August 1944, a young girl named Anne Frank kept a diary. Keeping a diary isn't unusual. Lots of girls do. But Anne's diary was unique. It chronicled the two years she and her family spent hiding from the Germans who were determined to annihilate all the Jews in Europe.

Anne Frank: The Diary of a Young Girl. abr. ed. Anne Frank. Read by Julie Harris. 2 cass. (Running Time: 1 hr. 27 mins.). 10.95 ea. (978-0-8045-3007-1(6), SAC 7201, 7202) Spoken Arts.

Anne Frank: The Diary of a Young Girl. unabr. ed. Anne Frank. 1 read-along cass. (Running Time: 64 min.). (Young Adult Cliffhangers Ser.). (YA). (gr. 4-6). 1984. 15.98 incl. bk. & guide. (978-0-8072-1816-7(2), JRH108SP, Listening Lib) Random Audio Pubg.
A story of hope & courage as revealed through the inner thoughts of a sensitive young Jewish girl living in Nazi-occupied Europe.

Anne Frank: The Diary of a Young Girl. unabr. ed. Anne Frank. (ENG.). (J). 2010. 40.00 (978-0-307-73785-4(3), Listening Lib) Pub: Random Audio Pubg. Dist(s): Random

Anne Frank: The Diary of a Young Girl. unabr. ed. Anne Frank. Narrated by Susan Adams. 6 cass. (Running Time: 9 hrs.). (gr. 7). 1982. 51.00 (978-1-55690-023-5(6), 82017E7) Recorded Bks.
The first-hand account of a young Jewish girl in hiding from the Germans in occupied Amsterdam.

Anne Frank: The Diary of a Young Girl. unabr. ed. Anne Frank. Narrated by Susan Adams. 8 CDs. (Running Time: 9 hrs). 2002. audio compact disk 39.95 (978-1-4025-2377-9(7)) Recorded Bks.

Anne Frank: The Diary of a Young Girl. unabr. ed. Anne Frank. Narrated by Julie Harris. 2 cass. (Running Time: 3 hrs.). (J). (gr. 3-8). 2001. pap. bk. 26.90 (6768) Spoken Arts.
Anne Frank's diary of her experiences during WW II survives as an endearing testament to the human spirit.

Anne Frank Remembered: The Story of the Woman Who Helped to Hide the Frank Family. unabr. ed. Miep Gies & Alison Leslie Gold. Read by Barbara Rosenblat. 7 CDs. (Running Time: 9 hrs. 9 mins. 54 sec.). 2009. audio compact disk 29.99 (978-1-59859-523-9(7)) Oasis Audio.

Anne Frank Remembered: The Story of the Woman Who Helped to Hide the Frank Family. unabr. ed. Miep Gies & Alison Leslie Gold. Read by Barbara Rosenblat. (Running Time: 9 hrs. 9 mins. 54 sec.). 2009. 20.99 (978-1-60814-482-2(8), SpringWater) Oasis Audio.

Anne Frank's Story. unabr. ed. Carol Ann Lee. Read by Barbara Rosenblat. 2 cass. (Running Time: 2 hrs. 30 mins.). 2003. 17.95 (978-0-7861-2444-2(X), 3123); audio compact disk 16.00 (978-0-7861-9233-5(X), 3123) Blckstn Audio.
Follows Anne Frank from her birth in Germany and her happy childhood in Amsterdam through the years she and her family spent in hiding from the Nazis to her imprisonment and eventual death in the concentration camps.

Anne Frank's Tales from the Secret Annex. unabr. ed. Anne Frank. Read by Kathe Mazur. (J). 2010. 30.00 (978-0-307-73781-6(0), Listening Lib) Pub: Random Audio Pubg. Dist(s): Random

Anne Manx & the Empress Blair Project. 2 CD's. (Running Time: 2 hrs). Dramatization. (YA). 2009. audio compact disk 24.95 (978-0-9771342-0-5(2)) Radio Repertory.

Anne Manx & the Trouble on Chromius. unabr. ed. 2 cass. (Running Time: 1 hr 40 mins). Dramatization. 2002. 24.95 (978-0-9660392-8-3(9)) Pub: Radio Repertory. Dist(s): Timberwolf Pr

Anne McCaffrey Pern Collection: Dragonseye; The Masterharper of Pern; The Skies of Pern. abr. ed. Anne McCaffrey. Read by Dick Hill. 8 cass. (Running Time: 12 hrs.). (Dragonriders of Pern Ser.). 2002. bk. 19.95 (978-1-59086-535-4(9), 1590865359, Nova Audio Bks) Brilliance Audio.
Dragonseye: Thread: deadly silver strands that fall from the sky like rain, devouring every organic thing in their path - animals, plants, and people alike. Who could believe that such a horrible thing could exist? After all, it's been two hundred years since Thread supposedly fell on Pern. No one alive remembers that first onslaught. There's no sign of it anywhere in the world. Only the dragons, originally created to be a weapon against Thread, are still around to remind people that once before their population was decimated, their hopes and dreams and livelihoods almost destroyed forever. For two centuries the dragonriders have been practicing and training, passing down from generation to generation the Threadfighting techniques learned on the fly by their besieged ancestors. And most of the Lord Holders are prepared to protect their people, to provide sanctuary, to assemble groundcrews to search out and destroy any Thread that might be missed by the dragons soaring overhead. All but one. Even now the ominous signs are appearing: the violent winter storms and volcanic eruptions that are said to herald the approach of the Red Star and its lethal spawn. Impossibly, one stubborn Lord Holder, Chalkin of Bitra, refuses to believe - and that disbelief could spell disaster for all of Pern. So while the dragonriders desperately train to face an enemy they've never fought before, they and the other Lord Holders must find a way to deal with Chalkin and protect Bitra. The Masterharper of Pern: In a time when no Thread has fallen for centuries - when, indeed, many are beginning to dare to hope that Thread will never fall again - a boy is born to Harper Hall. His name is Robinton, and he is destined to be one of the most famous and beloved leaders Pern has ever known. It is a perilous time for harpers. They sing of Thread, yet more and more people are beginning to doubt the return of that deadly scourge. They teach reading, writing, history, but Fax - who hates the harpers in general - is determined to keep his growing area of influence free of the learning that might sow unrest. And they extol the dragonriders, whom many view increasingly as a drain on the resources of the Holds. Now harpers are being turned away from the holds; and, worse yet, they are being derided, attacked, even beaten. It is the climate of unrest that Robinton will come into his own. For despite the tragedies that beset his own life, he continues to believe in music and in the dragons, and is determined to save his beloved Pern from itself . . .so that the dragonriders can be ready to fly against the dreaded Thread when it at last returns! The Skies of Pern: Now that Pern can look forward to a future without the threat of Threadfall, the people are free to leave their protective stone holds and spread across more of the planet, as well as improve their lives with the newly discovered ancient technology. Not everyone is happy, though. Some resist the change, and consider anything new to be an "abomination." And the dragonriders are uncertain: without Thread, what will their purpose be in Pernese society? Then a new danger - again from the skies - looms. Once again, the people must pull together . . . And turn to the only ones who can solve the crisis: the dragonriders of Pern!.

Anne McLaughlin: A Better American Work Force. 1 cass. (Running Time: 1 hr.). 10.95 (NP-88-04-21, HarperThor) HarpC GBR.

Anne Morrow Lindbergh: Her Life. unabr. ed. Susan Hertog. Read by Marguerite Gavin. 12 cass. (Running Time: 17 hrs. 30 mins.). 2000. 83.95 (978-0-7861-1846-5(6), 2645) Blckstn Audio.
Illuminated by nearly five years of interviews with Anne Morrow Lindbergh & offers insights into her thoughts on her life & writing. It may finally unravel the mystery of Charles Lindbergh's entanglements in the German Reich, which threatened to destroy their marriage. Tells the journey of a young bride who overcame the pressures of fame, personal tragedy & social constrain to find answers that continue to illuminate the lives of women today.

***Anne Morrow Lindbergh: Her Life.** unabr. ed. Susan Hertog. Read by Marguerite Gavin. (Running Time: 17 hrs. 5 mins.). (ENG.). 2011. 44.95 (978-1-4417-8503-9(5)); audio compact disk 123.00 (978-1-4417-8501-5(9)) Blckstn Audio.

Anne Murray - What a Wonderful World. Anne Murray. 2000. bk. (978-1-894454-08-7(1)) Bal2mur Entertain CAN.

Anne of Avonlea. L. M. Montgomery. Narrated by Susan O'Malley. (Running Time: 9 hrs.). (J). 1998. 30.95 (978-1-59912-416-2(5)) Iofy Corp.

Anne of Avonlea. L. M. Montgomery. Read by Liza Ross. (Running Time: 2 hrs. 15 mins.). 2003. 20.95 (978-1-60083-675-6(5)) Iofy Corp.

Anne of Avonlea. L. M. Montgomery. Read by Shelly Frasier. (Running Time: 8 hrs. 36 mins.). 2005. 27.95 (978-1-60083-659-6(3), Audiofy Corp) Iofy Corp.

Anne of Avonlea. L. M. Montgomery. Read by Liza Ross. 2 cass. (Running Time: 2 hrs. 15 mins.). (Avonlea Ser.: No. 2). (YA). (gr. 5-8). 1999. 13.98 (978-962-634-669-3(8), NA216914, Naxos AudioBooks) Naxos.
The second volume in the poignant, yet amusing tale of the perky red-headed tales of Anne of Green Gables.

Anne of Avonlea. L. M. Montgomery. Read by Shelly Frasier. (Running Time: 31140 sec.). (ENG.). (J). (gr. 4-7). 2005. audio compact disk 69.99 (978-1-4001-3093-1(X)) Pub: Tantor Media. Dist(s): IngramPubServ

Anne of Avonlea. abr. ed. L. M. Montgomery. Read by Megan Follows. 2 cass. (Running Time: 3 hrs.). (Avonlea Ser.: No. 2). (YA). (gr. 5-8). 2000. 18.00 (978-0-7366-9044-7(1)) Books on Tape.
For over half a century, Anne Shirley, the charmingly unpredictable heroine of "Anne of Green Gables," has captured the hearts & the imaginations of millions. This sequel has our heroine beginning her new role as a full fledged schoolma'am. Join Anne & her friends as they encounter accidents & adventures, scandal & romance & at last, a wedding.

Anne of Avonlea. abr. ed. L. M. Montgomery. Read by Liza Ross. 2 CDs. (Running Time: 2 hrs. 30 mins.). (Avonlea Ser.: No. 2). (J). (gr. 3-8). 1999. audio compact disk 17.98 (978-962-634-169-8(6), NA216912) Naxos.
The second volume in the poignant , yet amusing tale of the perky red-headed tales of Anne of Green Gables. This classic favorite is one of the best-selling titles in children's literature ever.

Anne of Avonlea. unabr. ed. L. M. Montgomery. Narrated by Flo Gibson. 6 cass. (Running Time: 9 hrs.). (Avonlea Ser.: No. 2). (YA). (gr. 5-8). 1987. 24.95 (978-1-55685-089-9(1)) Audio Bk Con.
Anne's vivid imagination & romanticism lead to many embarrassing & amusing episodes as she begins her career as a teacher.

Anne of Avonlea, unabr. ed. L. M. Montgomery. Read by Kathryn Yarman. 7 cass. (Running Time: 10 hrs. 30 mins.). (Avonlea Ser.: No. 2). (gr. 5-8). 1992. audio compact disk 63.00 (978-0-7861-0314-0(0), 2289) Blckstn Audio.
A sequel to "Anne of Green Gables." Five years have passed since the orphan girl Anne Shirley came to live with Marilla & Matthew Cuthbert. She has returned to Avonlea to teach in the same village school where she herself was taught. Her earlier friends have also become teachers at neighboring village schools.

Anne of Avonlea. unabr. ed. L. M. Montgomery. Read by Susan O'Malley. 7 cass. (Running Time: 10 hrs.). (Avonlea Ser.: No. 2). (gr. 3-8). 1998. 49.95 (978-0-7861-1428-3(2), 2289) Blckstn Audio.
It seemed only yesterday that the skinny, freckled redhead had first come to Prince Edward Island. Now, Anne is sixteen & all grown up. Well, not quite grown up.

Anne of Avonlea. unabr. ed. L. M. Montgomery. Read by Susan O'Malley. 8 CDs. (Running Time: 10 hrs.). (Anne of Green Gables Ser.: Vol. 3). 2000. audio compact disk 64.00 (978-0-7861-9580-0(0), 2289) Blckstn Audio.

Anne of Avonlea. unabr. ed. L. M. Montgomery. 13 vols. (Running Time: 32400 sec.). (J). (ps-7). 2005. DVD & audio compact disk 29.95 (978-0-7861-8156-8(7), ZM2289) Blckstn Audio.

Anne of Avonlea. unabr. ed. L. M. Montgomery. Read by Susan O'Malley. 7 cass. (Running Time: 32400 sec.). (J). (ps-7). 2005. 24.95 (978-0-7861-3453-3(4), E2289); audio compact disk 24.95 (978-0-7861-8030-1(7), ZE2289) Blckstn Audio.

Anne of Avonlea. unabr. ed. L. M. Montgomery. Read by Laurie Klein. 8 cass. (Running Time: 9 hrs. 15 mins.). Dramatization. (Avonlea Ser.: Bk. 2). (YA). (gr. 5-8). 1992. 49.95 (978-1-55686-448-3(5), 448) Books in Motion.
Skinny little red-haired Anne has changed into a pretty sixteen year-old & all grown-up, well, sort of grown-up. This story opens with Anne as a school teacher at Avonlea School.

Anne of Avonlea. unabr. ed. L. M. Montgomery. Read by Shelly Frasier. (YA). 2007. 59.99 (978-1-59895-786-0(4)) Find a World.

Anne of Avonlea. unabr. ed. L. M. Montgomery. Read by Kathryn Yarman. 7 cass. (Running Time: 7 hrs.). (Avonlea Ser.: No. 2). (YA). (gr. 5-8). 1999. 49.95 (FS9-34194) Highsmith.

Anne of Avonlea. unabr. ed. L. M. Montgomery. Narrated by Barbara Caruso. 7 cass. (Running Time: 9 hrs. 15 mins.). (Avonlea Ser.: No. 2). (gr. 5-8). 2001. 62.00 (978-0-7887-0535-9(0), 94730E7) Recorded Bks.
The sequel to Anne of Green Gables follows this charming heroine to the prettiest little town on Prince Edward Island, which is the prettiest island in all of Canada. Years ago, Anne came to Prince Edward Island as an orphan - a mischievous, talkative redhead with a shabby suitcase & a heart full of dreams. Now, however, Anne is the town's schoolteacher & as the school year passes, wonderful adventures await.

Anne of Avonlea. unabr. ed. L. M. Montgomery. Narrated by Shelly Frasier. (Running Time: 8 hrs. 30 mins. 0 sec.). (Anne of Green Gables Ser.). (ENG.). (J). (gr. 4-7). 2008. 19.99 (978-1-4001-5868-3(0)); audio compact disk 27.99 (978-1-4001-0868-8(3)); audio compact disk 55.99 (978-1-4001-3868-5(X)) Pub: Tantor Media. Dist(s): IngramPubServ

Anne of Green Gables. Richard Ganci. L. M. Montgomery. (Classic Adventures Ser.). 2000. audio compact disk 18.95 (978-1-4105-0149-3(3)) D Johnston Inc.

Anne of Green Gables. L. M. Montgomery. Ed. by Jerry Stemach. Illus. by Jeff Ham. Retold by Richard Ganci. Narrated by Wendy Morgan. 2000. audio compact disk 200.00 (978-1-58702-500-6(0)) D Johnston Inc.

Anne of Green Gables. L. M. Montgomery. Read by Kevin Sullivan. (Running Time: 4 hrs. 20 mins. 0 sec.). (ENG.). (J). (gr. 4-7). 2008. audio compact disk 29.95 (978-0-9782552-9-9(1)) Pub: Davenport CAN CAN. Dist(s): IPG Chicago

Anne of Green Gables. L. M. Montgomery. Narrated by Susan O'Malley. (Running Time: 11 hrs. 30 mins.). (J). 1998. 34.95 (978-1-59912-417-9(3)) Iofy Corp.

Anne of Green Gables. L. M. Montgomery. Read by Liza Ross. (Running Time: 2 hrs. 15 mins.). 2001. 20.95 (978-1-60083-676-3(3)) Iofy Corp.

Anne of Green Gables. L. M. Montgomery. Read by Shelly Frasier. (Running Time: 10 hrs. 15 mins.). 2006. 29.95 (978-1-60083-639-8(9), Audiofy Corp) Iofy Corp.

Anne of Green Gables. L. M. Montgomery. Read by Liza Ross. 2 CDs. (Running Time: 2 hrs. 15 mins.). (Avonlea Ser.: No. 1). (J). (gr. 3-8). 1997. audio compact disk 17.98 (978-962-634-123-0(8), NA212312) Naxos.
Eleven-year-old orphan Anne Shirley has red hair and cannot stop talking. Quite a shock for Matthew and Marilla Cuthbert, who wanted a boy to help on their farm. Anne is soon the talk of the town who wins the hearts of everyone around her.

Anne of Green Gables. L. M. Montgomery. Read by Liza Ross. 2 cass. (Running Time: 2 hrs. 15 mins.). (Junior Classics Ser.: No. 1). (YA). (gr. 4-7). 1997. 13.98 (978-962-634-623-5(X), NA212314, Naxos AudioBooks) Naxos.

Anne of Green Gables. L. M. Montgomery. Narrated by Barbara Caruso. 9 CDs. (Running Time: 10 hrs. 15 mins.). audio compact disk 89.00 (978-0-7887-9524-4(4)) Recorded Bks.

Anne of Green Gables. L. M. Montgomery. 2004. audio compact disk 19.99 (978-1-4193-2696-7(1)) Recorded Bks.

Anne of Green Gables. Ed. by Oxford University Press Staff. 2008. audio compact disk 11.95 (978-0-19-478975-2(6)) OUP.

Anne of Green Gables. abr. ed. L. M. Montgomery. Read by Elizabeth Rude & Beth Baxter. 2 cass. (Running Time: 3 hrs.). (Avonlea Ser.: No. 1). (YA). (gr. 5-8). 1986. pap. bk. 12.95 (978-1-882071-07-4(7), 009) B-B Audio.
The orphanage was suppose to send a boy to help with the farm chores. Instead they send the chatty, mischief filled little red-headed Anne.

Anne of Green Gables. abr. ed. L. M. Montgomery. Narrated by Elizabeth Rude. 2 cass. (Running Time: 3 hrs.). 2000. 16.95 (978-0-929071-97-8(2)) B-B Audio.
There has been a mistake.The orphanage was supposed to send a strong, obedient boy to help them with the farm chores. Instead they send the chatty, mischief filled little red-headed Anne. From then on, Green Gables is never the same. Anne wins th.

Anne of Green Gables. adpt. ed. Prod. by Focus on the Family Staff. Adapted by Paul McCusker. L. M. Montgomery. (Running Time: 240 hrs. 0 mins.). (Radio Theatre Ser.). (ENG.). (J). 2007. audio compact disk 14.97 (978-1-58997-502-6(2), Tyndale Ent) Tyndale Hse.

Anne of Green Gables, unabr. ed. L. M. Montgomery. Read by Flo Gibson. 8 cass. (Running Time: 10 hrs. 30 mins.). (Avonlea Ser.: No. 1). (YA). (gr. 5-8). 1986. 26.95 (978-1-55685-045-5(X)) Audio Bk Con.
An elderly spinster & her brother decide to adopt a boy to help with the farm chores. The mischievous, talkative & imaginative Anne arrives instead & the longer she stays the more no one can imagine Green Gables without her.

Anne of Green Gables. unabr. ed. L. M. Montgomery. Read by Barbara Barnes. 2 CDs. (Running Time: 2 hrs. 30 mins.). 2008. audio compact disk 29.95 (978-0-7927-4993-6(6)) AudioGO.

Anne of Green Gables, unabr. ed. L. M. Montgomery. Read by Lois Betterton. 9 cass. (Running Time: 13 hrs. 30 mins.). (Avonlea Ser.: No. 1). (gr. 5-8). 1991. audio compact disk 120.00 (978-0-7861-0247-1(0), 1216) Blckstn Audio.
Anne, the orphan child who brings happiness & love into the lives of her foster parents, is one of the most beloved heroines in all literature. But life was not kind to her at the start of her great adventure. For when Marilla & Matthew Cuthbert, living alone, decided to adopt a child from the local orphanage, they asked for a boy. Their dismay & disappointment were great when a lonely, pathetic little girl was sent by mistake. At first Marilla was determined that Anne must be returned at once to the orphanage, but kindly, warmhearted Matthew urged that she be given a chance to prove herself.

Anne of Green Gables. unabr. ed. L. M. Montgomery. Read by Susan O'Malley. 8 cass. (Running Time: 11 hrs. 30 mins.). (Avonlea Ser.: No. 1). (gr. 3-8). 1998. 56.95 (978-0-7861-1315-6(4), 2240) Blckstn Audio.
Story of an orphan child who brings happiness & love to the lives of her foster parents.

Anne of Green Gables. unabr. ed. L. M. Montgomery. 8 cass. (Running Time: 39600 sec.). (J). (ps-7). 2005. 24.95 (978-0-7861-3452-6(6), E2240); DVD & audio compact disk 29.95 (978-0-7861-8155-1(9), ZM2240) Blckstn Audio.

Anne of Green Gables. unabr. ed. L. M. Montgomery. Read by Susan O'Malley. 9 CDs. (Running Time: 39600 sec.). (J). (ps-7). 2005. audio compact disk 24.95 (978-0-7861-8029-5(3), ZE2240) Blckstn Audio.

Anne of Green Gables. unabr. ed. L. M. Montgomery. Read by Susan O'Malley. 9 CDs. (Running Time: 11 hrs. 30 mins.). (Anne of Green Gables Ser.: Vol. 1). 2006. audio compact disk 72.00 (978-0-7861-9583-1(5), 2240) Blckstn Audio.

Anne of Green Gables. unabr. ed. L. M. Montgomery. Read by Laurie Klein. 8 cass. (Running Time: 10 hrs. 48 mins.). Dramatization. (Avonlea Ser.: Bk. 1). (J). 1992. 49.95 (978-1-55686-447-6(7), 447) Books in Motion.
Matthew & Marilla Cuthbert had no intention of adopting the talkative, mischievous, red-headed girl the orphanage sent by mistake. Still, there was something about the little girl that gave them second thoughts.

Anne of Green Gables. unabr. ed. L. M. Montgomery. Read by Shelly Frasier. (J). 2006. 74.99 (978-1-59895-677-1(9)) Find a World.

Anne of Green Gables. unabr. ed. L. M. Montgomery. Read by Lois Betterton. 9 cass. (Avonlea Ser.: No. 1). (YA). (gr. 5-8). 1999. 56.95 (FS9-34190) Highsmith.

Anne of Green Gables. unabr. ed. L. M. Montgomery. Read by St. Charles Players. 2 cass. (Running Time: 1 hr. 30 min.). (Audio Theatre Ser.). (YA). (gr. 5 up). 2001. 16.95 (978-1-56994-533-9(0), Monterey SoundWorks) Monterey Media Inc.
A willful orphan arrives at the home of an elderly sister and brother, and a wonderful life adventure begins as Anne matures from a skinny girl into an intriguing young woman.

Anne of Green Gables. unabr. ed. L. M. Montgomery. Read by Kate Burton. 8 CDs. (Running Time: 10 hrs. 21 mins.). (YA). (gr. 5-8). 2008. audio compact disk 50.00 (978-0-7393-6721-6(8), Listening Lib) Pub: Random Audio Pubg. Dist(s): Random

Anne of Green Gables. unabr. ed. L. M. Montgomery. Read by Kate Burton. Frwd. by Margaret Atwood. (Running Time: 37320 sec.). (ENG.). (J). (gr. 5). 2008. audio compact disk 19.95 (978-0-7393-6720-9(X), Listening Lib) Pub: Random Audio Pubg. Dist(s): Random

Anne of Green Gables. unabr. ed. L. M. Montgomery. Narrated by Barbara Caruso. 7 cass. (Running Time: 10 hrs. 15 mins.). (Avonlea Ser.: No. 1). (gr. 5-8). 1989. 60.00 (978-1-55690-022-8(8), 89150E7) Recorded Bks.
An eleven-year-old orphan arrives at the home of her adoptive father on the Avonlea Peninsula in the Gulf of St. Lawrence to begin a new life.

Anne of Green Gables. unabr. ed. L. M. Montgomery. Narrated by Shelly Frasier. (Running Time: 10 hrs. 0 mins. 0 sec.). (Anne of Green Gables Ser.). (ENG.). (J). (gr. 4-7). 2008. audio compact disk 65.99 (978-1-4001-3842-5(6)) Pub: Tantor Media. Dist(s): IngramPubServ

Anne of Green Gables. unabr. ed. L. M. Montgomery. Narrated by Shelly Frasier. (Running Time: 10 hrs. 0 mins. 0 sec.). (Anne of Green Gables Ser.). (ENG.). (J). (gr. 5-9). 2008. audio compact disk 32.99 (978-1-4001-0842-8(X)); audio compact disk 22.99 (978-1-4001-5842-3(7)) Pub: Tantor Media. Dist(s): IngramPubServ

Anne of Green Gables. unabr. collector's ed. L. M. Montgomery. Read by Rebecca C. Burns. 7 cass. (Running Time: 10 hrs. 30 mins.). (Avonlea Ser.: No. 1). (YA). (gr. 5-8). 1998. 56.00 (978-0-7366-4150-0(5), 896035) Books on Tape.
Expecting a boy when they adopt an orphan, the Cuthberts are dismayed by the arrival of a girl, Anne Shirley. But Anne soon charms them.

Anne of Green Gables. 100th ed. L. M. Montgomery. Contrib. by Barbara Barnes et al. (Running Time: 9000 sec.). (ENG.). (J). (gr. 4-7). 2008. audio compact disk 14.95 (978-1-60283-362-3(1)) Pub: AudioGO. Dist(s): Perseus Dist

Anne of Green Gables, Vol. 6. L. M. Montgomery. Ed. by Jerry Stemach et al. Retold by Richard Ganci. Illus. by Jeff Ham. Narrated by Wendy Morgan. Contrib. by Ted S. Hasselbring. (Start-to-Finish Books). (J). (gr. 2-3). 2000. 35.00 (978-1-58702-501-3(9)) D Johnston Inc.

Anne of Green Gables, Vol. 6. unabr. ed. L. M. Montgomery. Ed. by Jerry Stemach et al. Retold by Richard Ganci. Illus. by Jeff Ham. Narrated by Wendy Morgan. Contrib. by Ted S. Hasselbring. 1 cass. (Running Time: 1 hr.). (Start-to-Finish Books). (J). (gr. 2-3). 2000. (978-1-893376-99-1(0), F22K2) D Johnston Inc.
Matthew and Marilla Cuthbert are an elderly brother and sister who live on a farm called Green Gables in Canada. Matthew is getting too old to do all the work on the farm, so Marilla decides to adopt a young orphan boy to help out. But when Matthew Cuthbert goes to the train station to pick up the boy, he's in for a surprise! Instead of a little boy, Matthew meets Anne, a red-haired eleven-year-old orphan girl who's gleeful to be going home with him.

Anne of Green Gables Value Collection. L. M. Montgomery. Read by Megan Follows. 6 cass. (Running Time: 8 hrs. 24 min.). (YA). 2001. (Listening Lib) Random Audio Pubg.
"Anne of Green Gables," "Anne of Avonlea" "Anne of the Island".

Anne of the Island. L. M. Montgomery. Read by Susan O'Malley. (Running Time: 8 hrs.). (J). 2000. 30.95 (978-1-59912-418-6(1)) Iofy Corp.

Anne of the Island. abr. ed. L. M. Montgomery. Read by Megan Follows. 2 cass. (Running Time: 3 hrs.). (Avonlea Ser.: No. 4). (YA). (gr. 5-8). 2000. 18.00 (978-0-7366-9045-4(X)) Books on Tape.
There has never been a heroine as enchanting as Anne shirley or a series as well loved as "Anne of Green Gables." In the third book, Anne is heading off for four years of college & the handsome Gilbert Blythe wants to win her heart. Suddenly Anne must decide if she's ready for love & to leave Green Gables forever.

Anne of the Island, unabr. ed. L. M. Montgomery. Read by Flo Gibson. 5 cass. (Running Time: 7 hrs.). (Avonlea Ser.: No. 4). (YA). (gr. 5-8). 1999. 35.95 (978-1-55685-580-1(X)) Audio Bk Con.
Anne leaves Avonlea for college & new adventures. Tears & laughter occur as she discovers a new life & romance.

Anne of the Island. unabr. ed. L. M. Montgomery. 13 vols. (Running Time: 28800 sec.). (Avonlea Ser.: Vol. 3). (J). (ps-7). 1992. DVD & audio compact disk 24.95 (978-0-7861-9419-3(7), 2698) Blckstn Audio.
In this third installment, free-spirited Anne decides to leave her beloved Prince Edward Island for college. Eager for new adventure, she faces hard choices, her secret aspiration to be a writer conflicts with finding a good husband. When she receives surprise marriage proposals from the most unlikely young men, she may shock friends & Islanders alike with her decision. Then, when tragedy strikes, she learns a valuable lesson that prepares her to make the most important choice of all.

Anne of the Island, unabr. ed. L. M. Montgomery. Read by Susan O'Malley. 6 cass. (Running Time: 8 hrs. 30 mins.). (Avonlea Ser.: No. 4). (gr. 6-8). 1999. 44.95 (978-0-7861-1905-9(5), 2698) Blckstn Audio.

Anne of the Island. unabr. ed. L. M. Montgomery. Read by Susan O'Malley. 7 CDs. (Running Time: 8 hrs. 30 mins.). (Avonlea Ser.: No. 4). (gr. 6-8). 2000. audio compact disk 56.00 (978-0-7861-9789-7(7), 2698) Blckstn Audio.

Anne of the Island. unabr. ed. L. M. Montgomery. 6 cass. (Running Time: 28800 sec.). (J). (ps-7). 2005. 24.95 (978-0-7861-3472-4(0), E2698) Blckstn Audio.

Anne of the Island. unabr. ed. L. M. Montgomery. Read by Susan O'Malley. 7 CDs. (Running Time: 8 hrs.). 2005. audio compact disk 24.95 (978-0-7861-8049-3(8), ZE2698) Blckstn Audio.

Anne of the Island. unabr. ed. L. M. Montgomery. Read by Laurie Klein. 6 cass. (Running Time: 8 hrs. 30 mins.). Dramatization. (Avonlea Ser.: Bk. 4). (YA). (gr. 5-8). 1993. 39.95 (978-1-55686-461-2(2), 461) Books in Motion.
Anne heads off for four years of college at Redmond College. She meets a wonderful new friend in Philippa Gordon. Philippa's family ties, combined with her beauty & charms, open the gates of all the social cliques & clubs at Redmond.

Anne of the Island. unabr. ed. L. M. Montgomery. Read by Susan O'Malley. (J). 2008. 49.99 (978-1-60514-709-3(5)) Find a World.

Anne of the Island, unabr. ed. L. M. Montgomery. Read by Kathryn Yarman. 7 cass. (Running Time: 7 hrs.). (Avonlea Ser.: No. 4). (YA). (gr. 5-8). 1999. 49.95 (FS9-34197) Highsmith.

Anne of the Island, unabr. ed. L. M. Montgomery. Narrated by Barbara Caruso. 6 cass. (Running Time: 8 hrs. 30 mins.). (Avonlea Ser.: No. 4). (gr. 5-8). 1996. 53.00 (978-0-7887-0598-4(9), 94776E7) Recorded Bks.
The curious waif who changed Green Gables has grown into a lovely young woman. Leaving the tranquility of her home on Prince Edward Island, she begins a new life as a freshman at Redmond College. As she journeys into a wider world, she faces the tantalizing decisions of young adulthood.

Anne of the Island. unabr. ed. L. M. Montgomery. Read by Renée Raudman. (Running Time: 9 hrs. 0 mins. 0 sec.). (Anne of Green Gables Ser.). 2008. 19.99 (978-1-4001-5637-5(8)); audio compact disk 59.99 (978-1-4001-3637-7(7)); audio compact disk 29.99 (978-1-4001-0637-0(0)) Pub: Tantor Media. Dist(s): IngramPubServ

Anne Rivers Siddons Audio Treasury: Colony & Hill Towns. abr. ed. Anne Rivers Siddons. Read by Judith Ivey & Marcia Gay Harden. (Running Time: 21600 sec.). 2006. audio compact disk 14.95 (978-0-06-115382-2(6)) HarperCollins Pubs.

Anne Sexton: A Self-Portrait in Letters. Interview with Anne Sexton. 1 cass. (Running Time: 30 mins.). 1971. 12.95 (L068) TFR.
Sexton talks about her poetry & sings some of it, accompanied by a "Rock Chamber" orchestra. The result is evaluated by a literary critic & a professor of music, both of whom give it high grades.

Anne Sexton: A Self-Portrait in Letters. unabr. ed. Anne Sexton. 1 cass. (Author Speaks Ser.). 1991. 14.95 J Norton Pubs.
Archival recordings of 20th-century authors.

Anne Waldman. Anne Waldman. Read by Anne Waldman. 1 cass. (Running Time: 29 mins.). 1988. 8.00 (040888) New Letters.
One of the few women to emerge from the beat movement.

Anne's House of Dreams. L. M. Montgomery. Narrated by Susan O'Malley. (Running Time: 8 hrs. 30 mins.). (J). 1997. 27.95 (978-1-59912-419-3(X)) Iofy Corp.

Anne's House of Dreams. unabr. ed. 6 cass. (Running Time: 8 hrs. 45 min.). (YA). 2004. 54.75 (978-1-4025-8433-6(4)) Recorded Bks.

Anne's House of Dreams, unabr. ed. L. M. Montgomery. Read by Flo Gibson. 5 cass. (Running Time: 7 hrs. 30 mins.). (Avonlea Ser.: No. 5). (YA). (gr. 5-8). 1999. 20.95 (978-1-55685-586-3(9)) Audio Bk Con.
The newlyweds, Anne & Gilbert, move into their house of dreams where they share joys & sorrows with special neighbors Captain Jim, Leslie Moore & Cornelia. The births of their first children are a moving part of the story.

Anne's House of Dreams, unabr. ed. L. M. Montgomery. Read by Susan O'Malley. 6 cass. (Running Time: 8 hrs. 30 mins.). (Avonlea Ser.: No. 5). (gr. 5-8). 1997. 44.95 (978-0-7861-1230-2(1), 1976) Blckstn Audio.
Anne is about to leave Green Gables forever & travel with her cherished Gilbert to the misty purple shore of Four Winds Harbor. Can all Anne's dreams come true here? Anne is soon investigating the ghostly tragedy haunting Leslie Moore, the golden-haired beauty next door; & finding a husband for the man-hating Miss Cornelia, as this volume captures our hearts once again.

Anne's House of Dreams. unabr. ed. L. M. Montgomery. Read by Susan O'Malley. 7 CDs. (Running Time: 8 hrs. 30 mins.). (Anne of Green Gables Ser.: Vol. 4). 2006. audio compact disk 63.00 (978-0-7861-8134-6(6), 1976) Blckstn Audio.

Anne's House of Dreams. unabr. ed. L. M. Montgomery. Read by Kelly Faulkner-Beck. 6 cass. (Running Time: 8 hrs.). (Avonlea Ser.: Bk. 4). 2001. 39.95 (978-1-55686-958-7(4)) Books in Motion.
In the sunshine of the old orchard, Anne and Dr. Gilbert Blythe exchange wedding vows. The happy couple begins life together on the shores of Four Winds Harbour, in their own house of dreams, among new friends, and home to their first child.

Anne's House of Dreams. unabr. ed. L. M. Montgomery. Read by Susan O'Malley. (J). 2008. 59.99 (978-1-60514-710-9(9)) Find a World.

Anne's House of Dreams, unabr. ed. L. M. Montgomery. Read by Susan O'Malley. 6 cass. (Running Time: 6 hrs.). (Avonlea Ser.: No. 5). (YA). (gr. 5-8). 1999. 44.95 (FS9-34408) Highsmith.

***Annexed.** unabr. ed. Sharon Dogar. 1 MP3-CD. (Running Time: 9 hrs.). (YA). 2010. 24.99 (978-1-4418-7810-6(6), 9781441878106, Brilliance MP3); 39.97 (978-1-4418-7811-3(4), 9781441878113, Brlnc Audio MP3 Lib); 39.97 (978-1-4418-7812-0(2), 9781441878120, BADLE); audio compact disk 29.99 (978-1-4418-7808-3(4), 9781441878083, Bril Audio CD Unabri); audio compact disk 79.97 (978-1-4418-7809-0(2), 9781441878090, BriAudCD Unabrid) Brilliance Audio.

Annie Bananie: Best Friends to the End. unabr. ed. Leah Komaiko. Narrated by Christina Moore. 1 cass. (Running Time: 1 hr.). (Annie Bananie Ser.: No. 1). (gr. 2 up). 10.00 (978-0-7887-1174-9(1), 95214E7) Recorded Bks.
Whether it's her fun-loving rottweiler, Boris, or the way she makes everything she does just a little more enjoyable, everyone in school wants to be Annie's best friend & you will too. Available to libraries only.

Annie Dillard: Interview with Annie Dillard & Key Bonetti. unabr. ed. 1 cass. 1989. 13.95 (978-1-55644-323-7(4), 9012) Am Audio Prose.

Annie Dillard Interview. 20.97 (978-0-13-090457-7(0)) P-H.

Annie Jennings PR: Be A Hot Radio Guest. 2004. audio compact disk 19.95 (978-1-933139-00-5(5)) A Jennings PR.

Annie John. unabr. ed. Jamaica Kincaid. Read by Jamaica Kincaid. 4 cass. (Running Time: 6 hrs.). 1995. 18.95 (978-1-885608-01-7(2)) Airplay.
Already a classic. Here the author reads her own universally familiar story of the headstrong, brilliant, heroine Annie John & her touching & tumultous passage into adolescence.

Annie John. unabr. ed. Jamaica Kincaid. Read by Jamaica Kincaid. 4 CDs. (Running Time: 4 hrs.). 2001. audio compact disk 30.00 (978-1-885608-29-1(2)) Airplay.

Annie John, Lucy & at the Bottom of the River. Excerpts. Jamaica Kincaid. Read by Jamaica Kincaid. 1 cass. (Running Time: 1 hr. 30 mins.). 1991. 13.95 (978-1-55644-362-6(5), 11021) Am Audio Prose.

Annie May & Friends: We Say Together - Mother Goose Poems. Poems. Read by Anne Costello. 1 cass. (Running Time: 50 mins.). (Annie May & Friends Ser.). (J). (ps-2). 1997. 10.99 (978-1-890719-01-2(3), 71901) Jo-An Pictures.
Learn Mother Goose poems together with all the children listening & joining in. When the children get wiggly, Annie May will give some stretch exercises that they all do in place.

Annie Oakley. As told by Keith Carradine. Music by Los Lobos. Illus. by Fred Warner. 1 cass. (Running Time: 1 hr.). 9.95 Weston Woods.
With two six guns blazin', Annie Oakley was the star fo the Buffalo Bill Cody's famous Wild West Show for almost 20 years. A spirited tale of a talented frontier woman whose sharp shooting exploits brought her international fame.

Annie Oakley: Woman at Arms. unabr. ed. Courtney Ryley Cooper. Narrated by Jonathan Reese. (Running Time: 6 hrs. 0 mins. 0 sec.). (ENG.). 2008. audio compact disk 55.99 (978-1-4001-3802-9(7)); audio compact disk 19.99 (978-1-4001-5802-7(8)) Pub: Tantor Media. Dist(s): IngramPubServ

Annie Oakley: Woman at Arms. unabr. ed. Courtney Ryley Cooper. Read by Jonathan Reese. (Running Time: 6 hrs. 0 mins. 0 sec.). (ENG.). 2008. audio compact disk 27.99 (978-1-4001-0802-2(0)) Pub: Tantor Media. Dist(s): IngramPubServ

Annie Oakley: Woman at Arms, unabr. collector's ed. Courtney Ryley Cooper. Read by Jonathan Reese. 6 cass. (Running Time: 6 hrs.). 1996. 36.00 (978-0-7366-3489-2(4), 694579) Books on Tape.
A charming biography of Annie Oakley a.k.a. "Little Miss Sure-Shot" who was the acknowledged headliner for so many years in Buffalo Bill Show.

Annie Oakley - Woman at Arms. unabr. ed. Courtney Ryley Cooper. Read by Jonathan Reese. (YA). 2008. 39.99 (978-1-60514-870-0(9)) Find a World.

Annie of Albert Mews. Dee Williams. Read by Jacqueline King. 10 cass. (Running Time: 15 hrs.). 1999. 84.95 (68467) Pub: Soundings Ltd GBR. Dist(s): Ulverscroft US

Annie of Albert Mews. unabr. ed. Dee Williams. Read by Jacqueline King. 10 cass. 1993. 84.95 (978-1-85496-846-3(7)) Pub: UlverLrgPrint GBR. Dist(s): Ulverscroft US

Annie on My Mind. unabr. ed. Nancy Garden. Read by Rebecca Lowman. 6 CDs. (Running Time: 7 hrs. 15 mins.). (YA). (gr. 9 up). 2008. audio compact disk 55.00 (978-0-7393-6745-2(5), Listening Lib) Pub: Random Audio Pubg. Dist(s): Random

Annie Sunshine & the White Owl of the Cedars. Annette Martin. Illus. by Pat Tadena. 1 cass. (Running Time: 1 hr.). (J). (ps-3). 1995. pap. bk. 7.95 Incl. coloring bk. & activity pad in hanging container. (978-1-885764-03-4(0)) Artistic Visions Inc.
This is a story about a "magic child" among Native American. The story teaches that it is okay to be different & accept others who are not like you, that being different is actually important & that we all have a special purpose in life. Side A: The story, entertaining & educational. Side B: Sleepy time adventure to relax & prepare your child for sleep.

***Annie's Dream Dance Suite.** Perf. by R. A. Zuckerman. Composed by R. A. Zuckerman. (ENG.). 2010. 12.95 (978-1-891083-22-8(8)) ConcertHall.

Annie's Girl. Audrey Howard. Read by Carole Boyd. 12 cass. (Running Time: 18 hrs.). 2002. 96.95 (978-0-7540-0869-9(X), CAB 2291) Pub: Chivers Audio Bks GBR. Dist(s): AudioGO

Annie's Legacy. Ken McCoy. (Story Sound CD Ser.). (J). 2002. audio compact disk 89.95 (978-1-85903-636-5(8)) Pub: Mgna Lrg Print GBR. Dist(s): Ulverscroft US

Annie's Prize Pet. unabr. ed. Michele Sobel Spirn. 1 cass. (Running Time: 5 mins.). (Read Along ...For Fun Ser.). (J). (gr. k-2). 1984. bk. 16.99 (978-0-934898-71-3(5)); pap. bk. 9.95 (978-0-934898-83-6(9)) Jan Prods.
All the children in school are happy about the pet show; they all have pets but Annie; "Why don't you look outside?" asks her mother; Does Annie find a pet?.

Annie's Rainbow, unabr. ed. Fern Michaels. Read by Valerie Leonard. 8 vols. (Running Time: 12 hrs.). (Chivers Sound Library American Collections). 2000. bk. 69.95 (978-0-7927-2322-6(8), CSL 211, Chivers Sound Lib) AudioGO.
It came out of the blue: a half-million dollars on graduation day. For Anna Daisy Clark, it was the capital she needed to start a business & secure her future. It was also money that didn't belong to her. Vowing to pay it back one day, she kept the bag of cash she'd found & never looked back. Ten years later, Annie's investment has paid off. The owner of a successful chain of elegant coffee bars, she's engaged to coffee plantation owner Parker Grayson. But just as her life seems complete, the dark history of the money returns & Annie's life is plunged into danger.

***annihilation Agenda.** A. J. Butcher. Read by Sean Mangan. (Running Time: 7 hrs. 15 mins.). (Spy High Ser.). (YA). 2009. 69.99 (978-1-74214-561-7(2), 9781742145617) Pub: Bolinda Pubng AUS. Dist(s): Bolinda Pub Inc

annihilation Agenda. unabr. ed. A. J. Butcher. Read by Sean Mangan. (Running Time: 7 hrs. 15 mins.). (Spy High Ser.). (YA). 2009. audio compact disk 77.95 (978-1-74214-086-5(6), 9781742140865) Pub: Bolinda Pubng AUS. Dist(s): Bolinda Pub Inc

Anniversary see Love Poems of John Donne

Anniversary see Asimov's Mysteries

Anniversary see Best of Isaac Asimov

Anniversary. unabr. ed. Amy Gutman. Read by Melanie Ewbank. 7 cass. (Running Time: 10 hrs.). 2003. 32.95 (978-1-59086-618-4(5), 1590866185, BAU); 82.25 (978-1-59086-619-1(3), 1590866193, CD Unabrid Lib Ed) Brilliance Audio.
Laura Seton has put her past behind her. Several years earlier, her former boyfriend was put to death after being linked to the murder of more than 100 women. On the fifth anniversary of his death, a chilling note is left at her door - a note that might have come from her dead lover. Unbeknownst to her, two other women receive identical notes - someone is forcing them all to confront a past they've tried to forget. Steven Gage was a charming and elusive psychopathic serial killer. Five years after his capture and execution, his ex-girlfriend, the lawyer who defended him on Death Row, and the writer who turned his story into a bestselling true crime book reach the edge of terror as they are hunted by a shape-shifting shadow from the past.

Anniversary. unabr. ed. Amy Gutman. Read by Melanie Ewbank. (Running Time: 10 hrs.). 2004. 39.25 (978-1-59335-621-7(8), 1593356218, Brlnc Audio MP3 Lib) Brilliance Audio.

Anniversary. unabr. ed. Amy Gutman. Read by Melanie Ewbank. (Running Time: 10 hrs.). 2004. 39.25 (978-1-59710-018-2(8), 1597100188, BADLE); 24.95 (978-1-59710-019-9(6), 1597100196, BAD) Brilliance Audio.

Anniversary. unabr. ed. Amy Gutman. Read by Melanie Ewbank. (Running Time: 10 hrs.). 2004. 24.95 (978-1-59335-211-0(5), 1593352115) Soulmate Audio Bks.

***Anniversary Man.** unabr. ed. R. J. Ellory. (Running Time: 13 hrs. 30 mins.). 2010. audio compact disk 32.95 (978-1-4417-4251-3(4)) Blckstn Audio.

***Anniversary Man.** unabr. ed. R. J. Ellory. Read by Steven Weber. (Running Time: 13 hrs. 30 mins.). 2010. 29.95 (978-1-4417-4252-0(2)); 79.95 (978-1-4417-4248-3(4)); audio compact disk 109.00 (978-1-4417-4249-0(2)) Blckstn Audio.

Annonaceae: Neotropical Genera & Species. M. E. Bakker & J. Koek-Noorman. (World Biodiversity Database Ser.). 2000. audio compact disk 206.00 (978-3-540-14804-3(3)) Spri.

Annotated Shakespeare. unabr. ed. Heywood Hale Broun. Read by A. L. Rowse. 1 cass. (Running Time: 56 mins.). (Broun Radio Ser.). 12.95 (40358) J Norton Pubs.

Announcement of His Presidential Candidacy. unabr. ed. John M. Ashbrook. 1 cass. (Running Time: 35 mins.). 12.95 (AF0101) J Norton Pubs.

Annual Auto Law Update: Including UM - UIM. 1998. bk. 59.00 (AC-2042) PA Bar Inst.
Become slip-opinion current on the ever-changing law in this important area & learn in practical terms how to get the best results in auto cases. These Philadelphia faculty-prepared two-book set offers both substantive laws & tips & techniques for practitioners of all levels of expertise.

Annual Fall Employee Benefits Law & Practice. rev. ed. 1 cass. (Running Time: 4 hrs.). 1999. 165.00 Incl. study outline. (VA991) Am Law Inst.

Annual Fall Employee Benefits Law & Practice Update: Focusing on APRSC & Other Remedial IRS Programs; Roth IRAs; New Treasury Proposed Regulations & IRS Guidance; New Section 401(k) Rules; Department of Labor Plan Audits; Determination Letter Procedure. 3 cass. (Running Time: 3 hrs. 30 mins.). 1998. 165.00 incl. study guide. (D278) Am Law Inst.
Discusses the most important aspects of employee benefits law & practice for ERISA practitioners, providing current analysis from practitioners who have nationally recognized expertise & key Federal Government officials who are involved in formulating policy & regulations in the topic areas.

Annual Fall Estate Planning Practice Update. 2 cass. (Running Time: 3 hrs.). 1999. 155.00 Set; incl. study guide. (VA995) Am Law Inst.

Annual Harmonics. Louise C. Bromley. 1 cass. 1992. 8.95 (1014) Am Fed Astrologers.

Annual Harmonics. Charles Hannan & L. Hannan. 2 cass. 1992. 8.95 ea. Am Fed Astrologers.

Annual Harmonics - A New Discovery. Charles Hannan. 1 cass. 8.95 (143) Am Fed Astrologers.
Introduction to harmonic progressions.

An Asterisk (*) at the beginning of an entry indicates that the title is appearing for the first time.

Annual Immigration & Naturalization Institute. 22nd unabr. ed. Contrib. by Austin T. Fragomen, Jr. 8 cass. (Running Time: 11 hrs.). 1989. 50.00 course handbk. (T7-9246) PLI.
In this recording of PLI's October 1989 seminar, an expert panel of government administrators & private attorneys addresses the implementation of the Free Trade Agreement with Canada & a number of important federal court decisions interpreting standards for H-1 & L-2 admissions. Other issues include: obtaining benefits under the law for business entrepreneurs, case & policy development of the standards for H & L nonimmigrant admission, policies & procedures governing the Immigration Marriage Fraud Amendments of 1986, including waiver applications under the law, latest developments in asylum practice, enforcement of employer sanctions & INS policies & procedure on employment authorization, guidelines for admission of business persons in the B-1 visitor category & progress report on the status of pending immigration reform legislation in the 101st Congress.

Annual Spring Employee Benefits Law & Practice Update. 3 cass. (Running Time: 3 hrs. 30 mins.). stu. ed. 165.00 (D283) Am Law Inst.
Features the most current & important issues in employee benefit law & practice, including significant regulatory & other legal developments to ERISA practitioners.

Annual Spring Estate Planning Practice Update. 2 cass. (Running Time: 3 hrs.). 1999. 155.00 Set; incl. study guide. (D281) Am Law Inst.
Intermediate level update discusses new tax & non-tax developments & trends & examines various drafting techniques & approaches for estate planning.

Annual Symposium International Council on Systems Engineering, 13th, 2002: Engineering Tomorrow's World Today. 2003. audio compact disk 60.00 (978-0-9720562-1-2(1)) Intl Council Sys Enginer.
Symposium Proceedings: Papers and panels presented at INCOSE 2002.

Annual Tax Update. Dorinda DeScherer. 2 cass. 1994. wbk. ed. 119.00 (740052VC) Am Inst CPA.
This annual tax update course shows you exactly how the IRS & the courts are handling critical new issues - & alerts you to tax-saving opportunities for your clients or employer (as well as tax pitfalls to avoid). It brings you up-to-speed on all the important federal tax developments related to: Individual income taxes, Business taxes, Estates & trusts, Employment taxes, Tax procedures. Covering developments from RRA '93 through June 30, 1994, the course materials include the texts of selected pertinent regulations, rulings & court decisions.

Annual Teleconference on Securities Regulation. Contrib. by Harvey L. Pitt. 3 cass. (Running Time: 3 hrs. 50 mins.). 1990. 75.00 (T7-9298); 50.00 hdbk. (B4-6935) PLI.
This June 1990 recording of the first Teleconference Satellite Program on Securities Regulation discusses the rapidly changing corporate, financial & regulatory climate & the effect of current economic & business trends on corporations & those who advise them. The experienced faculty includes Directors of the Corporation Finance & Enforcement Divisions of the SEC, joined by five leading members of the private bar. Key subjects include: problem areas in securities disclosure, SEC enforcement actions, including related civil & criminal litigation actions, i.e., TROs & preliminary injunctions, financial disclosures & fraudulent activities by financial institutions, changing role of boards of directors & the attorneys who advise corporations on mergers & acquisitions, as well as proxies.

Annual Winter Estate Planning Practice. 2 cass. (Running Time: 3 hrs.). 1999. stu. ed. 155.00 (D280) Am Law Inst.
Intermediate-level program emphasizes end-of-year guidance released from the U.S. Treasury Department in discussing important current practice issues.

Annunciation. unabr. collector's ed. Ellen Gilchrist. Read by Ruth Stokesberry. 7 cass. (Running Time: 10 hrs. 30 mins.). 1989. 56.00 (978-0-7366-1521-1(0), 2392) Books on Tape.
A woman finds herself caught in an affair that is escalating rapidly out of control.

Annunciation of Francesca Dunn. unabr. ed. Janis Hallowell. Read by Tyler Bunch et al. (YA). 2006. 39.99 (978-1-59895-533-0(0)) Find a World.

Annunciations see Poetry of Geoffrey

Anointed. Bobby Hilton. 4 cass. 2000. 22.00 (978-1-930766-19-8(X)) Pub: Bishop Bobby. Dist(s): STL Dist NA

Anointed & His Anointing. Kenneth Copeland. Perf. by Kenneth Copeland. 1 cass. (Anointed & His Anointing Ser.: Tape 5). 1995. cass. & video 5.00 (978-1-57562-032-9(4)) K Copeland Pubns.

Anointed & His Anointing. Perf. by Kenneth Copeland. 8 cass. 1998. cass. & video 40.00 (978-0-88114-979-1(9)) K Copeland Pubns.
Biblical teaching on the anointing.

Anointed for an Appointed Time. George Bloomer. audio compact disk Whitaker Hse.

Anointed for an Appointed Time. George Bloomer. 2003. audio compact disk 14.99 (978-0-88368-967-7(7)) Whitaker Hse.

Anointed for Batttle CD. abr. ed. Reinhard Bonnke. (Running Time: Approx: 50 min.). 2001. audio compact disk 7.00 (978-1-933106-00-7(X)) E-R-Productions.
Reinhard Bonnke relates that he never felt the flow of God's anointing as during this meeting, when a wonderful impartation of spiritual gifts took place. This is a call of action, into Gods army are you ready?.

Anointed for Business: How Christians Can Use Their Influence in the Marketplace to Change the World. 4 Cassettes. (Running Time: 7 hours). 2002. 23.95 (978-0-9723740-1-9(9)); audio compact disk 29.95 (978-0-9723740-0-2(0)) E Silvoso.
Unabriged audiobook read by the author. Audiobook version has added comments and teaching not included in the printed version of the book. The notion that labor for profit and worship of God are now, and always have been, worlds apart, is patently false. The Early Church founders were mostly community leaders and highly successful business people. Today, more than ever, the heart of our cities is the marketplace. Yet the perceived wall between commercial pursuit and service to God continues to be a barrier to advancing His Kingdom. Ed Silvoso invites all Christians in business to knock down that wall and build the foundation for an unparalleled marketplace revival.

Anointed Word. Kenneth Copeland. 6 cass. 2006. 30.00 (978-1-57562-377-1(3)) K Copeland Pubns.

Anointed Word. Kenneth Copeland. 6 cass. (Running Time: 6 hrs.). 1982. bk. & stu. ed. 30.00 (978-0-938458-27-2(2)) K Copeland Pubns.
How the word is annointed.

Anointing. Bill Winston. 6 cass. 1995. 30.00 (978-1-931289-77-1(8)) B Winston Min.

Anointing: God's Yoke Destroying Power. Kenneth Copeland. Perf. by Kenneth Copeland. 1 cass. (Anointed & His Anointing Ser.: Tape 1). 1995. cass. & video 5.00 (978-1-57562-028-2(6)) K Copeland Pubns.

Anointing: 1 John 2:20-23. Ed Young. 1984. 4.95 (978-0-7417-1378-0(0), 378) Win Walk.

Anointing Factor. Kenneth Copeland. 10 cass. (Running Time: 10 hrs.). 1993. 50.00 (978-0-88114-852-7(0)) K Copeland Pubns.
Biblical teaching on the believer's anointing.

Anointing Message. Kenneth Copeland. Perf. by Kenneth Copeland. 1 cass. (Anointed & His Anointing Ser.: Tape 3). 1995. cass. & video 5.00 (978-1-57562-030-5(8)) K Copeland Pubns.

Anointing of Forgetting. Creflo A. Dollar. 15.00 (978-1-59089-025-7(6)) Pub: Creflo Dollar. Dist(s): STL Dist NA

Anointing of Recovery. 2007. audio compact disk (978-0-9789883-6-4(1)) TSEA.

Anointing Series. Mark Hanby. 4 cass. (Running Time: 4 hrs.). 1992. 29.00 (978-0-938612-64-3(6)) Destiny Image Pubs.

Anointing Teaches You. Lynne Hammond. 1 cass. (Running Time: 1 hr.). 2005. 5.00 (978-1-57399-250-3(X)); audio compact disk 5.00 (978-1-57399-272-5(0)) Mac Hammond.

Anointing to Prosper. Creflo A. Dollar. 15.00 (978-1-59089-097-4(3)) Pub: Creflo Dollar. Dist(s): STL Dist NA

Anointing to Prosper. unabr. ed. MiChelle A. Butler. 1 cass. (Running Time: 1 hr. 30 mins.). 2001. 5.00 (A161) Word Faith Pubng.

Anointing to Rule. Kenneth Copeland et al. 3 cass. 2006. 15.00 (978-1-57562-877-6(5)); audio compact disk 15.00 (978-1-57562-879-0(1)) K Copeland Pubns.

Anomalies, Archetypes, Aliens: Steps Toward a New Science of Imagination. Michael Grosso. 2 cass. (Running Time: 2 hrs.). 18.00 (A0250-87) Sound Photosyn.
This talk, at Institute for the Study of Consciousness, is a more in depth expansion of ideas expressed at the AA&A Conference.

Anomaly. unabr. ed. Willie Smith et al. Read by Willie Smith et al. 1 cass. (Running Time: 90 mins.). Dramatization. 1989. 6.00 (978-0-944215-08-1(4)) Ninth St Lab.
Poetry & prose by the writers themselves some with accompaniment, some not.

Anomaly 2. Harry Polkinhorn et al. Read by Harry Polkinhorn et al. Ed. by Jake Berry. 1 cass. (Running Time: 1 hr.). Dramatization. 1990. 6.00 (978-0-944215-10-4(6), EAD 013) Ninth St Lab.
Dramatic performances of the author's poetry & prose.

Anomaly 3. Willie Smith et al. Read by Willie Smith et al. Ed. by Jake Berry. 1 cass. (Running Time: 1 hr.). Dramatization. 1991. 6.00 (978-0-944215-11-1(4), EAD 015) Ninth St Lab.

Anonymous: How Do You Do? see Gathering of Great Poetry for Children

Anonymous: John Henry see Classic American Poetry

Anonymous Lawyer. unabr. ed. Jeremy Blachman. Read by Ray Porter. (Running Time: 25200 sec.). 2006. 54.95 (978-0-7861-4756-4(3)); audio compact disk 55.00 (978-0-7861-6340-3(2)); audio compact disk 29.95 (978-0-7861-7259-7(2)) Blckstn Audio.

Anonymous Rex: A Detective Story. abr. ed. Eric Garcia. Read by Maxwell Caulfield. 4 cass. (Running Time: 6 hrs.). 2001. 24.95 (978-1-57511-066-0(0)) Pub Mills.
What if dinosaurs were not really extinct, but have assumed clever human camouflage & living amongst us? Follow Vincent rubio, L.A.. private investigator & Velociraptor & just one of many of these cunning creatures as he tries to keep his true identity concealed while cracking a case that would have baffled Sam Spade.

Anorganische Chemie. 7th ed. Erwin Riedel & Christoph Janiak. 2007. bk. 98.00 (978-3-11-018903-2(8)) De Gruyter.

Another American Revolution. Carolyn Torkko. Read by Carolyn Torkko. 1 cass. (Running Time: 90 mins.). 1994. 8.95 (1126) Am Fed Astrologers.

***Another Bullshit Night in Suck City: A Memoir.** unabr. ed. Nick Flynn. Read by Scott Brick. (Running Time: 9 hrs. 30 mins.). 2010. 29.95 (978-1-4417-3345-0(0)); 59.95 (978-1-4417-3341-2(8)); audio compact disk 90.00 (978-1-4417-3342-9(6)); audio compact disk 29.95 (978-1-4417-3344-3(2)) Blckstn Audio.

Another Chance. Jack Boland. 1 cass. (Super Ser.). 8.00 (BI10) Master Mind.

Another Chance. Candie Checketts. 3 cass. 2004. 14.95 (978-1-59156-182-8(5)) Covenant Comms.

Another City, Not My Own: A Novel in the Form of a Memoir. abr. ed. Dominick Dunne. 4 cass. (Running Time: 6 hrs.). 2001. 25.00 (978-1-59040-074-6(7), Phoenix Audio) Pub: Amer Intl Pub. Dist(s): PerseuPGW

Another City, Not My Own: A Novel in the Form of a Memoir, unabr. ed. Dominick Dunne. Read by Michael Kramer. 8 cass. (Running Time: 12 hrs.). 1998. 64.00 (978-0-7366-4111-1(4), 106016) Books on Tape.
In this "novel in the form of a memoir," the author examines the O.J. Simpson trial. A thinking person's meditation on guilt & innocence.

Another Country. unabr. ed. James Baldwin. Narrated by Dion Graham. 2 MP3-CDs. (Running Time: 16 hrs. 15 mins.). 2009. 69.95 (978-0-7927-6185-3(5)); audio compact disk 110.95 (978-0-7927-6051-1(4)) AudioGO.

Another Country: The Emotional Terrain of Our Elders. Mary Pipher. 2004. 10.95 (978-0-7435-4160-2(X)) Pub: S&S Audio. Dist(s): S and S Inc

***Another Faust.** unabr. ed. Daniel and Dina Nayeri. Read by Katherine Kellgren. (Running Time: 11 hrs.). 2010. 19.99 (978-1-4418-9062-7(9), 9781441890627, Candlewick Bril); 39.97 (978-1-4418-9065-8(3), 9781441890658, Candlewick Bril); audio compact disk 19.99 (978-1-4418-9061-0(0), 9781441890610, Candlewick Bril); audio compact disk 24.99 (978-1-4418-9060-3(2), 9781441890603, Candlewick Bril); audio compact disk 39.97 (978-1-4418-9064-1(5), 9781441890641, Candlewick Bril); audio compact disk 69.97 (978-1-4418-9063-4(7), 9781441890634, Candlewick Bril) Brilliance Audio.

Another Fine Myth. unabr. ed. Robert Asprin. Narrated by Jeff Woodman. 5 cass. (Running Time: 6 hrs. 15 mins.). 1997. 44.00 (978-0-7887-0924-1(0), 95064E7) Recorded Bks.
When a magician master is murdered, young Skeeve, his apprentice, vows vengeance. Soon demon Aahz joins Skeeve in his search through the universe.

Another Great Achiever Biographies Read-along Series. 4 CDs. Dramatization. (Another Great Achiever Ser.). (J). 2003. lib. bdg. 95.80 (978-1-57537-744-5(6)); lib. bdg. 95.80 (978-1-57537-794-0(2)); audio compact disk 67.80 (978-1-57537-544-1(3)) Advance Pub.

Another Great Achievers Biographies Read-along Series. 4 cass. Dramatization. (Another Great Achiever Ser.). (J). 2003. 67.80 (978-1-57537-594-6(X)) Advance Pub.

Another Homecoming. Janette Oke & T. Davis Bunn. Narrated by Christina Moore. 6 cass. (Running Time: 8 hrs. 15 mins.). 54.00 (978-0-7887-5109-7(3)) Recorded Bks.

Another I, Another You. unabr. ed. Richard Schickel. Read by Emile Jolbert. 4 cass. 23.80 (E-124) Audio Bk.
A contemporary novel about love on the rebound between two middle-aged friends facing the bitterness of divorce.

Another Kind of Cinderella. unabr. ed. Angela Huth. Read by Robert Kee. 5 cass. (Running Time: 6 hrs. 15 mins.). 1997. 49.95 (978-0-7531-0156-8(4), 970202) Pub: ISIS Audio GBR. Dist(s): Ulverscroft US
The ghost of a doomed romance haunts an Oxford undergraduate's idyllic summer affair; a tragedy of hopeless love & murderous frustration is played out against a backdrop of a repertory company; passion & hatred flower side by side in suburban back gardens. This collection of stories features elderly ladies living out extraordinary fantasy lives & betrayed wives wreaking subtle revenge, drawing out their secret disappointments & their dreams of glamour.

Another Kind of Life. Catherine Dunne. Read by Dearbhla Molloy. (Chivers Audio Bks.). 2003. 84.95 (978-0-7540-8397-9(7)) Pub: Chivers Audio Bks GBR. Dist(s): AudioGO

Another Kind of Magic. unabr. ed. Mollie Harris. Read by Patricia Gallimore. 4 cass. (Running Time: 4 hrs.). 1999. 34.95 (978-0-7531-0401-9(6), 980915) Pub: ISIS Audio GBR. Dist(s): Ulverscroft US
In this sequel to "A Kind of Magic," Harris describes her journeys on foot & by bicycle over the hills & through the villages of the Cotswolds & recounts the hilarious country tales she was told by the people she met.

Another Life. unabr. ed. Peter Anghelides. Narrated by John Barrowman. (Running Time: 4 hrs. 0 mins. 0 sec.). (ENG.). 2010. audio compact disk 29.95 (978-1-60283-829-1(1)) Pub: AudioGO. Dist(s): Perseus Dist

Another Life. unabr. ed. Andrew Vachss. Read by Christopher A. Lane. (Running Time: 9 hrs.). (Burke Ser.). 2008. 39.25 (978-1-4233-6754-3(5), 9781423367543, BADLE) Brilliance Audio.

Another Life. unabr. ed. Andrew Vachss. Read by David Joe Wirth & Christopher Lane. (Running Time: 9 hrs.). (Burke Ser.). 2008. 39.25 (978-1-4233-6752-9(9), 9781423367529, Brlnc Audio MP3 Lib); 24.95 (978-1-4233-6753-6(7), 9781423367536, BAD) Brilliance Audio.

Another Life. unabr. ed. Andrew Vachss. Read by David Joe Wirth & Christopher A. Lane. (Running Time: 9 hrs.). (Burke Ser.). 2008. 24.95 (978-1-4233-6751-2(0), 9781423367512, Brilliance MP3) Brilliance Audio.

Another Life. unabr. ed. Andrew Vachss. Read by Christopher Lane. (Running Time: 9 hrs.). (Burke Ser.). 2008. audio compact disk 92.25 (978-1-4233-6750-5(2), 9781423367505, BriAudCD Unabrid) Brilliance Audio.

Another Life. unabr. ed. Andrew Vachss. Read by Christopher A. Lane. (Running Time: 9 hrs.). (Burke Ser.). 2008. audio compact disk 34.95 (978-1-4233-6749-9(9), 9781423367499, Bril Audio CD Unabri) Brilliance Audio.

Another Lone Nut. Richard Belzer. Read by Richard Belzer. 2000. audio compact disk 16.98 (978-1-929243-17-4(0)) Uproar Ent.

Another Look at Faith Series. Kenneth W. Hagin, Jr. 6 cass. 1996. 24.00 (37J) Faith Lib Pubns.

Another Look at Financial Astrology. Edward Helin. 1 cass. (Running Time: 90 mins.). 1988. 8.95 (674) Am Fed Astrologers.

Another Man's Child. June Francis. Read by Margaret Sircom. 9 vols. (Story Sound Ser.). (J). 2001. 76.95 (978-1-85903-414-9(4)) Pub: Mgna Lrg Print GBR. Dist(s): Ulverscroft US

Another Man's Poison. unabr. ed. Ann Cleeves. Read by Alexander John. 6 cass. (Running Time: 9 hrs.). 2003. 54.95 (978-0-7540-0935-1(1), CAB 2357) AudioGO.

Another Op'nin, Another Show (15 Broadway Favorites for Solo Singers) Ed. by Andy Beck & Brian Fisher. (ENG.). 2006. audio compact disk 15.95 (978-0-7390-4086-7(3)) Alfred Pub.

***Another Pan.** unabr. ed. Daniel and Dina Nayeri. Read by Katherine Kellgren. (Running Time: 11 hrs.). (YA). 2010. 39.97 (978-1-4233-9953-7(6), 9781423399537, Brlnc Audio MP3 Lib); 39.97 (978-1-4233-9955-1(2), 9781423399551, BADLE); audio compact disk 69.97 (978-1-4233-9951-3(X), 9781423399513, BriAudCD Unabrid) Brilliance Audio.

***Another Pan.** unabr. ed. Daniel Nayeri & Dina Nayeri. Read by Katherine Kellgren. (Running Time: 11 hrs.). (YA). 2010. 19.99 (978-1-4233-9954-4(4), 9781423399544, BAD) Brilliance Audio.

***Another Pan.** unabr. ed. Dina Nayeri & Daniel Nayeri. Read by Katherine Kellgren. (Running Time: 11 hrs.). (YA). 2010. 19.99 (978-1-4233-9952-0(8), 9781423399520, Brilliance MP3); audio compact disk 24.99 (978-1-4233-9950-6(1), 9781423399506, Bril Audio CD Unabri) Brilliance Audio.

Another Part of the Wood. unabr. ed. Beryl Bainbridge. Read by Michael Tudor Barnes. 6 CDs. (Running Time: 7 hrs.). (Sound Ser.). (J). 2003. audio compact disk 64.95 (978-1-84283-689-7(7)) Pub: ISIS Lrg Prnt GBR. Dist(s): Ulverscroft US

Another Part of the Wood. unabr. ed. Beryl Bainbridge. Narrated by Michael Tudor Barnes. 6 cass. (Running Time: 6 hrs. 50 mins.). (Soundings Ser.). (J). 2004. 54.95 (978-1-84283-565-4(3)) Pub: ISIS Lrg Prnt GBR. Dist(s): Ulverscroft US

Another Realm: The Soaking Presence III. Contrib. by John Belt. 2004. audio compact disk 15.00 (978-0-9748236-3-8(5)) Pub: Live in His Presence. Dist(s): STL Dist NA

Another Shore, unabr. ed. Nancy Bond. Narrated by Barbara Caruso. 10 cass. (Running Time: 14 hrs. 45 mins.). (gr. 9 up). 1992. 87.00 (978-1-55690-592-6(0), 92128E7) Recorded Bks.
Lyn Paget finds herself swept back in time to 18th Century Nova Scotia.

Another Small Town Kid. 2001. (978-1-928843-08-5(5)) Ad Lib Res.

Another Song about the King. Kathryn Glasgow Stern. Read by Karen White. 7 cass. (Running Time: 10 hrs. 30 mins.). 2000. 29.95 (978-0-7366-4950-6(6)) Books on Tape.
A mother's desperate desire for fame, fueled by the memory of a long ago date with Elvis, provokes an intense rivalry with her daughter.

Another Song about the King. collector's ed. Kathryn Glasgow Stern. Read by Karen White. 7 cass. (Running Time: 10 hrs. 30 min.). 2000. 56.00 (978-0-7366-4988-9(3)) Books on Tape.
Silvia Page, determined to escape the control & frustrations of her mother, has started a life of her own in New York. Still, her entangled & competitive relationship with her mother, Mimi, continues to haunt her.

Another Song about the King. unabr. collector's ed. Kathryn Glasgow Stern. Read by Karen White. 9 CDs. (Running Time: 13 hrs. 30 mins.). 2001. audio compact disk 72.00 Books on Tape.
Silvie Page, determined to escape the control and frustrations of her mother, has started a life of her own in New York. Frustrated by her life as a housewife in the sixties, Mimi names her daughter "Silvie", the closest anagram she can find for Elvis. Caught up in a fantasy world of the King and fame, Mimi remains mired in unfulfilled artistic ambitions and the need to dominate her family. As Silvie begins to free herself from Mimi, a family crisis draws her back.

***Another Thing to Fall.** unabr. ed. Laura Lippman. Read by Linda Emond. (ENG.). 2008. (978-0-06-163011-8(X)); (978-0-06-163026-2(8)) HarperCollins Pubs.

Another Thing to Fall. unabr. ed. Laura Lippman. Read by Linda Emond. (Running Time: 32400 sec.). (Tess Monaghan Ser.: No. 10). 2008. audio compact disk 39.95 (978-0-06-145302-1(1), Harper Audio) HarperCollins Pubs.

Another Time. unabr. ed. Ronald Harwood. Perf. by Jeffrey Jones et al. 2 cass. (Running Time: 1 hr. 52 mins.). 2000. 23.95 (978-1-58081-170-5(1), TPT146) L A Theatre.

Another Time, Another Place: Timeless Christian Classics. Contrib. by Avalon. Prod. by Shaun Shankel & Mark Hammond. 2008. audio compact disk 13.99 (978-5-557-62794-8(4)) Pt of Grace Ent.

Another Turn of Zero. Ko Won. Ed. by Stanley H. Barkan. (Review Asian-American Writers Chapbook Ser.: No. 2). (ENG & KOR.). 1992. 10.00 (978-0-89304-984-3(0)) Cross-Cultrl NY.

Another View. unabr. ed. Rosamunde Pilcher. Read by Sian Thomas. 4 cass. (Running Time: 5 hrs. 5 mins.). 2000. 24.95 (978-1-57270-158-8(7), M41158u) Pub: Audio Partners. Dist(s): PerseuPGW
This captivating story reveals that letting go is the first step to keeping love. Emma Litton searches for her past & finds truth about herself.

Another View. unabr. ed. Rosamunde Pilcher. Read by Donada Peters. 5 cass. (Running Time: 5 hrs.). 1992. 40.00 (978-0-7366-2096-3(6), 2902) Books on Tape.
Searching for truth about her father, a young woman learns the bitter truth about herself. Poignant & memorable.

***Another Whole Nother Story.** unabr. ed. Cuthbert Soup. (Running Time: 6 hrs.). 2010. 19.99 (978-1-4418-7561-7(1), 9781441875617, BAD); 39.97 (978-1-4418-7562-4(X), 9781441875624, BADLE); 19.99 (978-1-4418-7559-4(X), 9781441875594, Brilliance MP3) Brilliance Audio.

***Another Whole Nother Story.** unabr. ed. Cuthbert Soup. Read by Dick Hill. (Running Time: 8 hrs.). 2010. 39.97 (978-1-4418-7560-0(3), 9781441875600, Brlnc Audio MP3 Lib); audio compact disk 19.99 (978-1-4418-7557-0(3), 9781441875570, Bril Audio CD Unabri); audio compact disk 54.97 (978-1-4418-7558-7(1), 9781441875587, BriAudCD Unabrid) Brilliance Audio.

Another Woman. unabr. ed. Penny Vincenzi. Read by Laura Brattan. 16 cass. (Running Time: 20 hrs.). (Isis Ser.). (J). 1998. 104.95 (978-1-85695-221-7(5), 951206) Pub: ISIS Lrg Prnt GBR. Dist(s): Ulverscroft US

Another World. Pat Barker. Read by Steven Crossley. 7 CDs. (Running Time: 7 hrs. 30 mins.). 2000. audio compact disk 69.00 (978-0-7887-4751-9(7), C1239E7) Recorded Bks.
As Nick struggles with angry stepchildren & a miserably pregnant wife, his grandfather relives wartime memories on his deathbed.

Another World. Pickens. 2002. 14.95 (978-1-890460-21-1(4)) Pub: Corwin Pr. Dist(s): SAGE

Another World. unabr. ed. Pat Barker. Narrated by Steven Crossley. 6 cass. (Running Time: 7 hrs. 30 mins.). 2000. 51.00 (978-0-7887-4151-7(9), 96181E7) Recorded Bks.

ANPANO: An American Indian Odyssey. Jamake Highwater. (J). 1986. 26.66 (978-0-07-507849-4(X)) Glencoe.

ANPAO: An American Indian Odyssey. unabr. ed. Jamake Highwater. Narrated by George Guidall. 5 pieces. (Running Time: 6 hrs. 45 mins.). (gr. 7 up). 1994. 44.00 (978-0-7887-0070-5(7), 94303E7) Recorded Bks.
Combining the myths & stories from many Native American tribes, Highwater tells the story of the spiritual quest of a young brave.

Ans Crt Int Ocean SCI. 3rd ed. (C). 2005. audio compact disk 16.95 (978-0-534-42226-4(8)) Pub: Brooks-Cole. Dist(s): CENGAGE Learn

Anselm Hollo. Read by Anselm Hollo. 1 cass. (Running Time: 29 min.). 1985. 8.00 New Letters.
A poet of Finnish origin, Anselm Hollo's works include "Maya" & "Sojourner Microcosms.".

Answer: Grow Any Business, Achieve Financial Freedom, & Live an Extraordinary Life. abr. ed. John Assaraf & Murray Smith. Read by John Assaraf & Murray Smith. (Running Time: 6 hrs. 0 mins. 0 sec.). (ENG.). 2008. audio compact disk 29.95 (978-0-7435-7114-2(2)) Pub: S&S Audio. Dist(s): S and S Inc

Answer As a Man. unabr. ed. Taylor Caldwell. Narrated by John McDonough. 16 cass. (Running Time: 23 hrs.). 1980. 99.75 (978-1-4193-2179-5(X), K0020MC) Recorded Bks.

Answer Book. abr. ed. Hank Hanegraaff. 1 cass. 1998. 15.99 Nelson.

Answer Is Not in the Refrigerator. unabr. ed. 1 cass. (Running Time: 75 min.). 1996. 14.95 (978-0-9630939-1-2(6)) Chair Dancing.
A live lecture audio cassette, eating behavior worksheet, and reminder refrigerator magnet, featuring Jodi's sensible approach to eating management, seasoned with her humor and anecdotal teaching style.

Answer Is Yes. Mark Crow. 9 cass. (Running Time: 9 hrs.). 2001. (978-1-931537-22-3(4)) Vision Comm Creat.

***Answer Is You: Waking up to Your True Potential.** Michael Bernard Beckwith. (Running Time: 2:00:00). 2010. audio compact disk 19.95 (978-1-60407-445-1(0)) Sounds True.

Answer Man. unabr. ed. Roy Johansen. Narrated by George Wilson. 7 cass. (Running Time: 9 hrs. 45 mins.). 1999. 66.00 (978-0-7887-3134-1(3), 95826E7) Recorded Bks.
A tale of the power of temptation set in a gritty, contemporary Atlanta. At 30-something, polygraph operator Ken Parker is struggling to make ends meet. Enter Myth Daniels, a drop-dead beautiful lawyer, with an offer of $50,000. All Ken has to do is teach her client how to beat the lie detector. It's a deadly game of greed & deception Ken is drawn into.

Answer Technique. Diane L. Golz. (Running Time: 60 mins). 2002. 12.00 (978-0-9717957-0-9(3)); audio compact disk 16.00 (978-0-9717957-1-6(1)) Abundance Harm Joy.
Through this audio material Diane L. Golz guides the listener through each step of ?The Answer Technique? to become proficient at using intuitive powers to get life enriching ?yes? and ?no? answers.Track 1: Introduction & PracticeTrack 2: Using the TechniqueRecorded in a Professional Sound StudioShrink Wrapped.

Answer to Loneliness: Prov. 15:13. Ed Young. 1993. 4.95 (978-0-7417-1962-1(2), 962) Win Walk.

Answer to the Riddle Of 666. Clinton McDaniels. (ENG.). 2008. (978-0-9802472-2-0(5)) Backwards WA.

Answer To Your #1 Problem: Matthew 5:3. Ed Young. 1999. 4.95 (978-0-7417-2229-4(1), 1229) Win Walk.

Answered Prayer. 2003. (978-1-59024-105-9(3)) B Hinn Min.

Answered Prayer. Contrib. by Lisa Bevill & Bob Carlisle. (Christian World Soundtraks Ser.). 2005. audio compact disk 8.99 (978-5-559-15692-7(2)) Christian Wrld.

Answered Prayer. Kenneth E. Hagin. 4 cass. (Obtainable Goal Ser.). 16.00 (50H) Faith Lib Pubns.

Answered Prayers. Danielle Steel. Read by Ron McLarty. 2002. 64.00 (978-0-7366-8849-9(8)); audio compact disk 88.00 (978-0-7366-8850-5(1)) Books on Tape.

Answering Common Objections. Scott Hahn. 5 cass. 1995. 24.95 (132-C) Ignatius Pr.
The Pope: Holy Father; Purgatory: Holy Fire; Mary: Holy Mother; The Saints: Holy Siblings; The Eucharist: Holy Meal.

Answering His Call. 2000. 54.95 (978-1-888992-39-7(5)) Catholic Answers.

Answering Objections to the Deity of Christ. Dan Corner. 1 cass. 3.00 (13) Evang Outreach.

Answering Our Own Call for Love. unabr. ed. Paul Ferrini. Read by Paul Ferrini. 1 cass. (Running Time: 65 mins.). (Christ Mind Talks & Workshops Ser.). 1997. audio compact disk 10.00 (978-1-879159-33-4(3)) Heartways Pr.
A talk given at Pacific Church of Religious Science in November 1997.

Answering the 8 Cries of Spirited Children: Strong Children Need Confident Parents (Life of Glory) unabr. ed. David Arp & Claudia Arp. (ENG.). 2003. 18.19 (978-1-60814-035-0(0)) Oasis Audio.

Answering the 8 Cries of the Spirited Children: Strong Children Need Confident Parents. unabr. ed. David Arp & Claudia Arp. 4 cass. (Running Time: 5 hrs. 30 min). 2003. 25.99 (978-1-58926-248-5(4), H69M-0020) Oasis Audio.
Find workable answers and practical help in how to turn unpleasant, day-to-day hassles into win-win experiences through well-thought-out strategies for your not-so-compliant child. Help is on the way!.

Answers about Angels. Ben Young. 1997. 4.95 (978-0-7417-6023-4(1), B0023) Win Walk.

Answers Are Within You: Unveiling Life's Greatest Spiritual Secrets in the Shadow of Your Soul. unabr. ed. Debbie Ford. Read by Debbie Ford. (Running Time: 60 hrs. 0 mins. 0 sec.). (ENG.). 2004. audio compact disk 35.00 (978-0-7435-3724-7(6), Nightgale) Pub: S&S Audio. Dist(s): S and S Inc

Answers Rest Within. Ragini E. Michaels. Read by Ragini E. Michaels. Music by Divyam Ambodha. 1 cass. (Running Time: 30 mins.). (Remembrance Ser.). 1988. 14.95 (978-0-9628686-3-4(9), FTAT-101) Facticity Tr.
Provides a beautiful & relaxing way to re-educate the unconscious mind to look within for the answers being sought. Soothing combination of feminine voice & original music.

Answers Through Transit. Elaine Randisi. 1 cass. 8.95 (288) Am Fed Astrologers.
Study effects of transit to learn astrology.

Answers to Distraction. Edward M. Hallowell. 2004. 7.95 (978-0-7435-4162-6(6)) Pub: S&S Audio. Dist(s): S and S Inc

Answers to Distraction. Edward M. Hallowell & John J. Ratey. Narrated by John McDonough. 9 cass. (Running Time: 12 hrs. 30 mins.). 76.00 (978-1-4025-0984-1(7)) Recorded Bks.

Answers to Life's Toughest Questions. Rick Warren. (Running Time: 3 hrs. 36 mins. 19 sec.). (Living with Purpose Ser.). (ENG.). 2006. 12.99 (978-0-310-27552-7(0)) Zondervan.

Answers to Praise. 4 cass. 11.95 Incl. album. (978-0-943026-17-6(2), A3) Carothers.

Answers To Questions About Innerrancy: 1 Peter 3:15. Ed Young. 1987. 4.95 (978-0-7417-1606-4(2), 606) Win Walk.

Answers with Ken Ham. Ken Ham. 2002. DVD 99.99 (978-0-89051-347-7(3)) Master Bks.

Answers You Have Been Seeking. Read by Mother Basilea Schlink. 1 cass. (Running Time: 30 mins.). 1985. (0227) Evang Sisterhood Mary.
Includes: Doesn't God Hear My Prayers? The Power of Obedience, The Command of the Hour.

Ant see Best of Mark Twain

Ant & the Elephant: Leadership for the Self. Vince Poscente. Read by Vince Poscente. 3 CDs. (Running Time: 3 hrs. 7 mins.). 2004. audio compact disk 19.99 (978-1-893430-15-0(4)) Grnlf Bk Grp.
A renowned speaker, business consultant, record-setting speed skier and Olympian, Vince Poscente believes in the enormous potential of the unconscious mind. Poscente likens the dynamic between the conscious and subconscious minds to an ant and an elephant: ?Our minds are separated into two distinct functions ? the conscious and subconscious elements. Our ant is the intentional part of the brain, but our elephant is the instinctual, impulsive part of the brain that houses emotions and memories and even guides the body to perform vital functions. While we tend to know our conscious minds ? our ants ? rather well, we often overlook the power of our elephantine subconscious minds. When we do, unfortunately, we squander a wellspring of human potential.? Having seen too many books focused on what a problem or solution is and too few focused on how to solve the problem, Poscente, with his trademark wit, wisdom and steely resolve, created The Ant and the Elephant ? Leadership for the Self: A Parable and Five-Step Action Plan to Transform Workplace Performance.

Ant, Badger, Locust, & Lizard: Proverbs 3:24-28. Ed Young. 1991. 4.95 (978-0-7417-1892-1(8), 892) Win Walk.

Ant Plays Bear. Betsy Byars. Read by Bonnie Kelly-Young. Illus. by Marc Simont. 1 cass. (Running Time: 30 mins.). (J). 2000. pap. bk. 19.97 (978-0-7366-9213-7(4)) Books on Tape.
Four more stories illuminating the affectionate relationship between Ant & his big brother, Byars has created a memorable pair of complementary personalities. Her stories hinge on the tension between the older brother's greater knowledge of the world & Ant's more naive, creative outlook on life.

Ant Plays Bear. Betsy Byars. Illus. by Marc Simont. 11 vols. (Running Time: 13 mins.). 1996. bk. 28.95 (978-1-59112-631-7(2)); pap. bk. 31.95 (978-1-59112-632-4(0)) Live Oak Media.

Ant Plays Bear. Betsy Byars. Illus. by Marc Simont. (Running Time: 13 mins.). 1999. 9.95 (978-0-87499-544-2(2)); audio compact disk 12.95 (978-1-59112-629-4(0)) Live Oak Media.

Ant Plays Bear. Betsy Byars. Read by Jeff Woodman. 1 cass. (Running Time: 15 mins.). (YA). 1999. pap. bk. & stu. ed. 24.24 (41001) Recorded Bks.
Ant plays lots of games. First he's a bear, then he's a dog. When his older brother joins Ant, the brother is a great, growling bear. But sometimes Ant & his brother play the games too well. Sequel to "My Brother, Ant".

Ant Plays Bear. unabr. ed. Betsy Byars. Read by Bonnie Kelly-Young. Illus. by Marc Simont. 11 vols. (Running Time: 13 mins.). (Ant Ser.). (J). (gr. k-3). 1999. bk. 25.95 (978-0-87499-542-8(6)); pap. bk. 16.95 (978-0-87499-541-1(8)); pap. bk. & tchr. ed. 29.95 Reading Chest. (978-0-87499-543-5(4)) Live Oak Media.
Affectionate relationship between Ant & his big brother.

Ant Plays Bear. unabr. ed. Betsy Byars. Narrated by Jeff Woodman. 1 cass. (Running Time: 15 mins.). (gr. 1 up). 2000. 10.00 (978-0-7887-3510-3(1), 95904E7) Recorded Bks.
Ant plays lots of games. First he's a bear, then he's a dog. When his older brother joins Ant, the brother is a great, growling bear. But sometimes Ant & his brother play the games too well. Sequel to "My Brother, Ant".

Ant Plays Bear, Class set. Betsy Byars. Read by Jeff Woodman. 1 cass. (Running Time: 15 mins.). (J). (gr. 1 up). 1999. stu. ed. 70.70 (978-0-7887-3665-0(5), 46968) Recorded Bks.
Ant loves games & plays many in which he becomes an animal. When his brother joins him, he plays a s a bear. Sometimes, when Ant & his brother play games they play too well.

Ant Series. Betsy Byars. Read by Bonnie Kelly-Young. Illus. by Marc Simont. 2 cass. (Running Time: 24 mins.). (J). (gr. k-3). 2000. pap. bk. 29.95 Live Oak Media.
Includes: "My Brother Ant" & "Ant Plays Bear.".

Ant Series. Betsy Byars. Illus. by Marc Simont. 22 vols. (Running Time: 24 mins.). 1999. pap. bk. 30.95 (978-0-87499-704-0(6)); pap. bk. 34.95 (978-1-59112-857-1(9)) Live Oak Media.

Antagonists. unabr. ed. Ernest K. Gann. Narrated by John Aulicino. 8 cass. (Running Time: 12 hrs.). (gr. 8). 1990. 70.00 (978-1-55690-024-2(4), 90052E7) Recorded Bks.
This novel centers on the heroic defense of Masada by Jewish partisans from the encircling Roman legions.

Antarayami Upasana. Swami Jyotirmayananda. 1 cass. (Running Time: 1 hr.). 1990. 12.99 Yoga Res Foun.

Antarctic Antics. (J). 2004. bk. 24.95 (978-1-55592-058-6(6)); pap. bk. 18.95 (978-1-55592-122-4(1)); pap. bk. 18.95 (978-1-55592-615-1(0)); pap. bk. 38.75 (978-1-55592-616-8(9)); pap. bk. 32.75 (978-1-55592-614-4(2)); pap. bk. 14.95 (978-1-55592-613-7(4)); 8.95 (978-1-55592-987-9(7)) Weston Woods.

Antarctic Antics. 1 CD. (Running Time: 1 hr. 30 mins.). (J). (ps up). 2004. audio compact disk 12.95 (978-1-55592-972-5(9)) Weston Woods.

Antarctic Antics: A Book of Penguin Poems. Judy Sierra. Illus. by Jose Aruego & Ariane Dewey. 1 cass. (Running Time: 30 min.). (J). bk. 24.95 Weston Woods.

Antarctic Antics: A Book of Penguin Poems. Judy Sierra. Illus. by Jose Aruego & Ariane Dewey. Narrated by Mary McDonnell. Music by Randy Scruggs. 1 cass. (Running Time: 18 min.). (J). (ps-3). 2000. bk. 24.95 (QHRA391) Weston Woods.
Imagine growing up in a colony of emperor penguins on the iciest continent on earth. Come visit Antarctica, but you'd better wear your park-tica, to celebrate the slips & slides & swims & glides of these delightful creatures in poetry & song.

Antarctica. 1 cass. (Running Time: 1 hr.). 9.00 (B0040B090, HarperThor) HarpC GBR.

Antarctica. unabr. ed. Stanley Johnson. Read by Gordon Dulieu. 8 cass. (Running Time: 10 hrs.). (Isis Ser.). 1994. 69.95 (978-1-85089-721-7(2), 89061) Eye Ear.
Antarctica is probably the world's last great unexplored wilderness. Its snow covered caverns & inhospitable terrain have long been a magnet for explorers & adventurers.

Antarctica. unabr. ed. Stanley Johnson. Read by Gordon Dulieu. 8 cass. (Running Time: 12 hrs.). 2001. 69.95 (89061) Pub: ISIS Audio GBR. Dist(s): Ulverscroft US

Antarctica, Pt. 1. unabr. collector's ed. Charles Neider. Read by Walter Zimmerman. 7 cass. (Running Time: 10 hrs. 30 mins.). 1989. 56.00 (978-0-7366-1581-5(4), 2447-A) Books on Tape.
A collection of first-hand accounts of pioneering journeys into this remote, desolate continent.

Antarctica, Pt. 2. unabr. collector's ed. Charles Neider. Read by Walter Zimmerman. 7 cass. (Running Time: 10 hrs. 30 mins.). 1989. 56.00 (978-0-7366-1582-2(2), 2447-B) Books on Tape.

Antarctica: The Last Frontier. (J). 2005. cass. & cd-rom 24.95 (978-0-9771381-9-7(4)) Geoffrey Williams.

Ante Has Gone Up: The Conscience of the Post-Modern Artist. Read by John Beebe. 1 cass. (Running Time: 90 mins.). 1987. 10.95 (978-0-7822-0013-3(3), 243) C G Jung IL.
Part of the conference set "Civilization in Transition: Jung's Challenge to Culture in Crisis.".

Ante Mortem see Poetry of Robinson Jeffers

Anteater of Death: A Zoo Mystery. unabr. ed. Betty Webb. Read by Hillary Huber. (Running Time: 8 hrs. NaN mins.). 2008. 29.95 (978-1-4332-5221-1(X)); audio compact disk 70.00 (978-1-4332-5220-4(1)); audio compact disk 54.95 (978-1-4332-5219-8(8)) Blckstn Audio.

Antelope of Canteloupe see Twentieth-Century Poetry in English, No. 28, Recordings of Poets Reading Their Own Poetry

***Antelope Wife.** abr. ed. Louise Erdrich. Read by Louise Erdrich. (ENG.). 2004. (978-0-06-082446-4(8), Harper Audio); (978-0-06-082447-1(6), Harper Audio) HarperCollins Pubs.

Antelope Wife: A Novel. unabr. ed. Louise Erdrich. Read by Anna Fields. 6 cass. (Running Time: 9 hrs.). 1999. 48.00 (978-0-7366-4277-4(3), 4775) Books on Tape.
A soldier deserts the cavalry during a cruel raid on an Indian village & rescues an infant girl. The descendants of the soldier, baby girl & of the bereaved mother are connected by a potent mix of tragedy, farce & mystical revelation.

Antena 1: Curso de Espanol para Extranjeros. Equipo Avance. 1 cass. (Running Time: 1 hr. 30 mins.). (SPA.). (978-84-7143-628-3(0)) Sociedad General ESP.

Antena 2: Curso de Espanol para Extranjeros. Equipo de Expertos 2100 Staff. 1 cass. (Running Time: 1 hr. 30 mins.). (SPA.). (978-84-7143-629-0(9)) Sociedad General ESP.

Anteojos! Tr. of Goggles!. (SPA.). (J). 2004. 8.95 (978-0-7882-0290-2(1)) Weston Woods.

Antepartum Fetal Assessment. Contrib. by Frank A. Manning et al. 1 cass. (American College of Obstetrics & Gynecologists UPDATE: Vol. 23, No. 1). 1998. 20.00 Am Coll Obstetric.

Antes. Carmen Boullosa. Narrated by Carmen Boullosa. 3 cass. (Running Time: 4 hrs.).Tr. of Before. 32.00 (978-1-4025-1266-7(X)) Recorded Bks.

Antes de Ser Libre Before We Were Free. Tr. of Julia Alvarez. (SPA.). (J). (gr. 6-8). audio compact disk 50.00 (978-0-307-20650-3(5), LIS33992) Lectorum Pubns.

Anthem. unabr. ed. Ayn Rand. Read by Christopher Lane. 2 cass. (Running Time: 2 hrs. 30 mins.). 1997. 17.95 (978-0-7861-1152-7(6), 1919) Blckstn Audio.
He lived in the dark ages of the future. In a loveless world he dared to love the woman of his choice. In an age that had lost all trace of science & civilization he had the courage to seek & find knowledge. But these were not the crimes for which he would be hunted.

Anthem. unabr. ed. Ayn Rand. Read by Christopher Lane. 3 CDs. (Running Time: 2 hrs. 30 mins.). 2000. audio compact disk 24.00 (978-0-7861-9929-7(6), 1919) Blckstn Audio.

Anthem. unabr. ed. Ayn Rand. Read by Christopher Lane. 1 CD. (Running Time: 2 hrs. 30 mins.). 2001. audio compact disk 19.95 (1919) Blckstn Audio.

Anthem. unabr. ed. Ayn Rand. Read by Christopher Lane. (Running Time: 2 hrs. 30 mins.). 2004. audio compact disk 24.95 (978-0-7861-9614-2(9), 1919) Blckstn Audio.

Anthem. unabr. ed. Ayn Rand. Read by Christopher Lane. 2 pieces. (Running Time: 3 hrs.). 2004. reel tape 16.95 (978-0-7861-2921-8(2)); audio compact disk 17.95 (978-0-7861-8229-9(6)) Blckstn Audio.

Anthem. unabr. ed. Ayn Rand. Read by Christopher Lane. 2 cass. (Running Time: 3 hrs.). 2004. 19.95 (978-0-7861-2489-3(X)); audio compact disk 24.95 (978-0-7861-9191-8(0)) Blckstn Audio.

Anthem. unabr. abr. ed. Ayn Rand. Read by Paul Meier. 2 CDs. (Running Time: 2 hrs. 30 mins.). (ENG.). 2002. audio compact disk 22.95 (978-1-56511-548-4(1), 1565115481) Pub: HighBridge. Dist(s): Workman Pub

Anthem. 50th unabr. anniv. ed. Ayn Rand. Intro. by Leonard Peikoff. 2 cass. (Running Time: 3 hrs.). 17.95 (AR46W) Second Renaissance.
In a regimented world, where the word "I" no longer exists, one defiant man rediscovers the meaning of individualism.

anthologie Audio. abr. ed. Jacques Attali. Read by Jacques Attali. Read by Nelly Rochas et al. (YA). 2007. 79.99 (978-2-35569-085-3(5)) Find a World.

***Anthologist: A Novel.** unabr. ed. Nicholson Baker. Narrated by Nicholson Baker. (Running Time: 7 hrs. 0 mins. 0 sec.). (ENG.). 2010. 19.99 (978-1-4001-6663-3(2)); 13.99 (978-1-4001-8663-1(3)); 24.99 (978-1-4001-9663-0(9)); audio compact disk 24.99 (978-1-4001-1663-8(5)); audio compact disk 49.99 (978-1-4001-4663-5(1)) Pub: Tantor Media. Dist(s): IngramPubServ

Anthology, Development of Western Music: A History. K. Marie Stolba. 1 cass. (C). 1990. (978-0-697-10724-4(8)) Brown & Benchmark.

Anthology, Development of Western Music: A History. K. Marie Stolba. 1 cass. (C). 1990. (978-0-697-10725-1(6)) Brown & Benchmark.

Anthology, Development of Western Music: A History. K. Marie Stolba. 1 cass. (C). 1993. (978-0-697-12551-4(3)); (978-0-697-12552-1(1)) Brown & Benchmark.

Anthology I: The Best of Marty Haugen, 1980-1984. Marty Haugen. 1997. 10.95 (400); audio compact disk 15.95 (400) GIA Pubns.

Anthology Martiana - Poetry & Prose see Antologia Martiana

Anthology Martiana - Poetry & Prose. Jose Marti. Read by Carlos Muñoz et al. (Running Time: 3 hrs.). 2003. 16.95 (978-1-60083-287-1(3), Audiofy Corp) Iofy Corp.

Anthology of African American Poetry for Young People. Sterling A. Brown et al. Read by Arna Bontemps. 1 cass. (J). (gr. k-6). 1992. (0-9307-45044-4-4) Smithsonian Folkways.

Anthology of American Folk Music, Ed. by Harry Smith. 6 CDs. audio compact disk Smithsonian Folkways.

***Anthology of Contest Fiddle Tunes.** Joe Carr. (ENG.). 2009. pap. bk. 19.99 (978-0-7866-4913-6(5)) Mel Bay.

Anthology of Jewish Art Song: The Lazar Weiner Collection. Ed. by Yehudi Wyner. 2007. pap. bk. 24.95 (978-0-8074-0993-0(6), 993277) URJ Pr.

***Anthology of Kannada Songs Composed by Sri Purandara Dasa: Sung by M. V. Rajalakshmi.** Perf. by M. V. Rajalakshmi. Composed by Sri Purandara Dasa. (KAN.). 2011. audio compact disk 40.00 (978-0-9824491-5-8(1)) Karina Library.

Anthology of Pedal Steel Guitar. Dewitt Scott. 1980. spiral bd. 29.95 (978-0-7866-1622-0(9), 93714CDP) Mel Bay.

Anthology of Pedal Steel Guitar. Dewitt Scott. 1995. audio compact disk 15.98 (978-0-7866-1621-3(0), 93714CD) Mel Bay.

Anthology of Poetry for Children. unabr. ed. Read by Cecil Bellamy et al. 1 cass. Incl. Fly. William Oldys. (J). 1984. (SAC 977); On a Favorite Cat. Thomas Grey. (J). 1984. (SAC 977); Owl & the Pussycat. Edward Lear. (J). 1984. (SAC 977); Tyger. William Blake. (J). 1984. (SAC 977); (J). 1984. 10.95 (978-0-8045-0977-0(8), SAC 977) Spoken Arts.

Anthology of Sacred Carols for Classical Guitar. James Sundquist. 2004. audio compact disk 14.98 (978-5-550-15940-8(6)) Nairi ARM.

Anthology of the Sacred Carol. Perf. by James Sundquist. 1 cass. (Running Time: 1 hr.). 10.95 (C0580B090, HarperThor) HarpC GBR.

Anthology of 19th Century American Poets. abr. ed. Henry Wadsworth Longfellow et al. Read by Donald Hall et al. 1 cass. 1984. 10.95 (978-0-8045-0963-3(8), SAC 7031) Spoken Arts.

***Anthony Ant & Grady Grasshopper: Read-along CD.** 2nd rev. ed. Lindamichelle Baron. Narrated by Wally Amos. (Running Time: 10 mins.). 2004. audio compact disk 10.00 (978-0-940938-30-4(8)) Harlin Jacque.

***Anthony Ant & Grady Grasshopper: Read-along CD Lapbook Edition.** Lindamichelle Baron. Narrated by Wally Amos. (Running Time: 10 mins.). 2004. audio compact disk 10.00 (978-0-940938-45-8(6)) Harlin Jacque.

Anthony Burgess. unabr. ed. Anthony Burgess. (Author Speaks Ser.). 1991. 14.95 J Norton Pubs.
Archival recordings of 20th-century authors.

Anthony Hargis: Individual Secession see James Gallagher: Independence Movement for California's Coastal Islands

Anthony Hecht. Read by Anthony Hecht. 1 cass. (Running Time: 29 mins.). 1985. 8.00 New Letters.
This Pulitzer prize winner was recorded at a public reading of his poetry.

Anthony Hecht Two. unabr. ed. Anthony Hecht. Read by Anthony Hecht. 1 cass. (Running Time: 29 mins.). 1988. 8.00 (030488) New Letters.
Winner of the Pulitzer Prize & the Prix de Rome, Hecht discusses his art with WETA FM Producer Robert Aubrey Davis.

Anthony Robbin's Power Talk: Conquer the Crash. Interview. Anthony Robbins & Robert R. Prechter, Jr. 3 CDs. (Running Time: 3 hrs. 30 mins.). 2002. audio compact disk 27.95 (978-0-9723451-0-1(8)) N American Parenting Inst.
PowerTalk is an audio magazine which provides the listener strategies for lifelong success. With each issue of PowerTalk, Anthony Robbins offers you a wealth of powerful ideas and strategies that you can use immediately to increase your income, influence others, advance you career, enhance your relationships, improve your health, eliminate your fears, and experience more joy and fulfillment everyday in your life!.

Anthony Sobin. unabr. ed. Poems. Anthony Sobin. Read by Anthony Sobin. 1 cass. (Running Time: 29 mins.). 1986. 8.00 New Letters.
The Kansas poet reads from "The Sunday Naturalist," poems about the visual arts & movies.

Anthony Trollope, Pt. 1. unabr. collector's ed. Victoria Glendinning. Read by David Case. 8 cass. (Running Time: 12 hrs.). 1995. 64.00 (978-0-7366-2900-3(9), 3600A) Books on Tape.
The emphasis is on family life, in this sympathetic view of one of England's most beloved & prolific novelists.

Anthony Trollope, Pt. 2. collector's ed. Victoria Glendinning. Read by David Case. 8 cass. (Running Time: 12 hrs.). 1995. 64.00 (978-0-7366-2901-0(7), 3600-B) Books on Tape.

Anthony Trollope: Christmas Day at Kirkby Cottage. abr. ed. Anthony Trollope. Read by Eva Haddon. Contrib. by Ronald Russell. 1 cass. 12.95 (ECN 009) J Norton Pubs.
Trollope depicts a Victorian Christmas in loving detail & chronicles the romance between a young man who finds Christmas a bore & the daughter of the house, who believes she cannot possibly love a person holding such views.

Anthony Trollope Quintet: Lady Anna , Sir Harry Hotspur of Humblethwaite', an Eye for an Eye , Cousin Henry & Linda Tressel. Anthony Trollope. Narrated by Flo Gibson. (ENG.). 2008. 69.95 (978-1-60646-043-6(9)) Audio Bk Con.

Anthony Trollope Selected Short Stories, Read by Flo Gibson. 11 cass. (Running Time: 16 hrs.). 1996. 34.95 (978-1-55685-430-9(7)) Audio Bk Con.
Courtship & marriage are explored in many moods & many lands in this unusual collection.

***Anthropomorphic Dreams Vol. 1: The Furry Fiction Podcast.** Will Sanborn. (C). 2010. audio compact disk 9.95 (978-1-935599-21-0(6), FurPlanetProd) Argyll Product.

Anthroposophy in Everyday Life: Four Lectures by Rudolf Steiner, unabr. ed. Rudolf Steiner. Read by Marie Hubonette. 2 cass. (Running Time: 2 hrs. 30 mins.). 14.95 (978-0-9650869-2-9(5)) Parzival.
Includes: "Practical Training in Thought," "Overcoming Nervousness," "Facing Karma" & "The Four Temperaments.".

***Anti-Aging Miracle They Don't Want You to Know About.** abr. ed. Kevin Trudeau. (Running Time: 5 hrs.). 2010. 14.99 (978-1-4418-9310-9(5), 9781441893109, BAD); audio compact disk 14.99 (978-1-4418-9308-6(3), 9781441893086, BACD) Brilliance Audio.

***Anti-Aging Miracle They Don't Want You to Know About.** unabr. ed. Kevin Trudeau. (Running Time: 11 hrs.). 2010. 24.99 (978-1-4418-9306-2(7), 9781441893062, BAD); 24.99 (978-1-4418-9304-8(0), 9781441893048, Brilliance MP3); 39.97 (978-1-4418-9307-9(5), 9781441893079, BADLE); 39.97 (978-1-4418-9305-5(9), 9781441893055, Brinc Audio MP3 Lib); audio compact disk 29.99 (978-1-4418-9302-4(4), 9781441893024, Bril Audio CD Unabri); audio compact disk 99.97 (978-1-4418-9303-1(2), 9781441893031, BriAudCD Unabrid) Brilliance Audio.

Anti-Aging Secrets. Steven S. Sadleir. 4. (Running Time: 6 hrs.). 2005. 20.00 (978-1-883544-12-6(2)) Self Awareness.
This CD course in all natural techniques for maximizing your biological age includes: (1) Kaya Kalpa cell regeneration techniques, (2) Facial Acupressure massage, (3) Techniques for increasing your HGH ("human growth hormone") levels naturally, (4) Internal cleansing and herbs and (5) Techniques for reducing stress, growing thicker and stronger hair, nails and skin and enhancing sex drive, vitality and strength.

***Anti-Aging Zone.** abr. ed. Barry Sears. Read by Barry Sears. (ENG.). 2005. (978-0-06-085671-7(8), Harper Audio); (978-0-06-085670-0(X), Harper Audio) HarperCollins Pubs.

Anti-Americanism. Jean-Francois Revel. Read by Christopher Lane. (Running Time: 7 hrs. 30 mins.). 2004. 27.95 (978-1-59912-420-9(3)) Iofy Corp.

Anti-Americanism. unabr. ed. Revel Jean-Francois. Read by Christopher Lane. 5 cass. (Running Time: 7 hrs.). 2004. 39.95 (978-0-7861-2769-6(4), 3257); audio compact disk 48.00 (978-0-7861-8599-3(6), 3257); audio compact disk 24.95 (978-0-7861-8558-0(9), 3257) Blckstn Audio.
After the 9/11 attack on the United States, the brief moment of global sympathy for America soon began giving way to blame. In France and other quarters of Europe, and elsewhere in the world, it was said that the Americans had brought this violence upon themselves. The United States was a ¿cowboy¿ nation disinclined to abide by the will of the United Nations and other multilateral institutions and bent on pursuing its objectives at any cost.

Anti-Americanism. unabr. ed. Jean-Francois Revel. Read by Christopher Lane. 8 CDs. (Running Time: 7 hrs.). 2004. audio compact disk 32.95 (978-0-7861-8697-6(6)); reel tape 29.95 (978-0-7861-2678-1(7)) Blckstn Audio.
After the September 11 attack on the United States, the brief moment of global sympathy for America soon gave way to blame. In Europe and elsewhere, it was said that American had brought the violence upon itself, that it was a "cowboy" nation bent on pursuing its objectives at any cost, a "hyperpower" whose riches were acquired at the price of Third World impoverishment. No wonder it had been attacked! Angered by these assaults on a nation he knows and admires, the distinguished French intellectual Jean-Francois Revel has come to America's defense in Anti-Americanism.

Anti-Chomsky Reader. unabr. ed. Peter Collier & David Horowitz. Read by Kirk Jordan. (Running Time: 28800 sec.). 2007. audio compact disk & audio compact disk 99.00 (978-1-4332-1335-9(4)) Blckstn Audio.

Anti-Chomsky Reader. unabr. ed. Read by Kirk Jordan. (Running Time: 28800 sec.). 2007. 85.95 (978-1-4332-1334-2(6)); audio compact disk 29.95 (978-1-4332-1336-6(2)) Blckstn Audio.

Anti-Communist Voices of Yesterday (1951-1952) unabr. ed. Read by Joseph McCarthy et al. 1 cass. (Running Time: 44 mins.). 12.95 (AF0123) J Norton Pubs.
Four programs discuss Truman-Acheson foreign policy, 1952 presidential bid, views on war, the ineffectiveness of Radio Free Europe & suggests alternative propaganda measures.

Anti-Death League. unabr. collector's ed. Kingsley Amis. Read by David Case. 8 cass. (Running Time: 12 hrs.). 1988. 64.00 (978-0-7366-1406-1(0), 2295) Books on Tape.
Humorous treatment of sex, the arms race, psychiatry & fidelity by author of LUCKY JIM.

Anti-Diet Book. Jack L. Groppel. Read by Jack L. Groppel. 1 cass. (Running Time: 2 hrs.). 1997. 14.95 (978-1-890009-05-2(9)) Exec Excell.

Anti-Hero. 1 CD. 1999. audio compact disk 16.98 (978-1-57908-481-3(8), 5358) Platinm Enter.

***Anti-Inflammation Zone.** abr. ed. Barry Sears. Read by Barry Sears. (ENG.). 2005. (978-0-06-085686-1(6), Harper Audio); (978-0-06-085685-4(8), Harper Audio) HarperCollins Pubs.

Anti-Inflammation Zone: Reversing the Silent Epidemic That's Destroying Our Health. abr. ed. Barry Sears. Read by Barry Sears. 2005. audio compact disk 22.00 (978-0-06-072705-5(5)) HarperCollins Pubs.

Anti-Malathion Lawyer Live on Something's Happening! Bill Moore. 1 cass. 9.00 (A0633-90) Sound Photosyn.
Bill describes his 30 years of fighting for medical freedom & the malathion issue.

***Anti-Prom.** unabr. ed. Abby McDonald. (Running Time: 8 hrs.). 2011. 39.97 (978-1-61106-515-2(1), 9781611065152, Candlewick Bril); 14.99 (978-1-61106-511-4(9), 9781611065114, Candlewick Bril); 39.97 (978-1-61106-512-1(7), 9781611065121, Candlewick Bril); audio compact disk 19.99 (978-1-61106-509-1(7), 9781611065091, Candlewick Bril); audio compact disk 44.97 (978-1-61106-510-7(0), 9781611065107, Candlewick Bril) Brilliance Audio.

Antibiotics - A Bridge to the 21st Century. Contrib. by Michael Marcy et al. 1 cass. (American Academy of Pediatrics UPDATE: Vol. 18, No. 5). 1998. 20.00 Am Acad Pediat.

Antibiotics in Obstetrics & Gynecology. Contrib. by Ronald S. Gibbs et al. 1 cass. (American College of Obstetrics & Gynecologists UPDATE: Vol. 22, No. 4). 1998. 20.00 Am Coll Obstetric.

Antibodies. Short Stories. Charles Stross. Narrated by Shondra Marie & Jared Doreck. 1 CD. (Running Time: 54 mins.). (Great Science Fiction Stories Ser.). 2005. audio compact disk 10.99 (978-1-884612-47-3(4)) AudioText.

Antic Hay, unabr. ed. Aldous Huxley. Read by Flo Gibson. 6 cass. (Running Time: 8 hrs. 51 mins.). 1998. 24.95 (978-1-55685-559-7(1)) Audio Bk Con.
The lifestyles, careers, romances & peccadilloes of various British intellectuals, scientists and artists are dealt with, often with hilarity & sometimes with dark comedy & sophisticated banter.

Antic Hay. unabr. ed. Aldous Huxley. 7 cass. (Running Time: 10 hrs. 30 min.). 1999. 49.95 (978-0-7861-1517-4(3), 2367) Blckstn Audio.

***Antic Hay.** unabr. ed. Aldous Huxley. Read by Robert Whitfield. (Running Time: 9 hrs. 30 mins.). 2010. 29.95 (978-1-4417-6700-4(2)); audio compact disk 90.00 (978-1-4417-6698-4(7)) Blckstn Audio.

Anticancer: A New Way of Life. unabr. ed. David Servan-Schreiber. Illus. by Robert Fass. 7 CDs. (ENG.). 2008. audio compact disk 29.95 (978-1-60283-475-0(X)) Pub: AudioGO. Dist(s): Perseus Dist

Anticancer: A New Way of Life. unabr. ed. David Servan-Schreiber. Narrated by Robert Fass. 1 MP3-CD. (Running Time: 8 hrs. 55 mins.). 2008. 49.95 (978-0-7927-5754-2(8)); audio compact disk 79.95 (978-0-7927-5635-4(5)) AudioGO.

Antichrist: The Alternate Ending. Chuck Missler. 2 CD's. (Running Time: 2 hrs.). (Briefing Packages by Chuck Missler). 2002. audio compact disk 19.95 (978-1-57821-195-1(6)) Koinonia Hse.
He may not be who you think! One of the dominant topics among prophecy buffs is the identity of the coming leader, whom we call "the Antichrist." We know from Daniel 9 that he will emerge out of the Roman Empire, which we often presume is Western Europe. However, we may have been subject to myopia by overlooking an important fact. The Roman Empire had an eastern leg that, in fact, survived the western leg by a thousand years!.

Antichrist & False Prophet. Dan Corner. 1 cass. 3.00 (14) Evang Outreach.

Anticlericalisme. Jacques Prevert. 1 cass. (FRE.). 1995. 16.95 (1667-RF) Olivia & Hill.
Through readings & interviews, Prevert shows his dislike & distrust of religious dogmas & other "isms.".

Antidepressant Remission Rates, Safety, & Tolerability: An Interview with Dr. Stephen M. Stahl & Dr. Michael Gitlin, vol. 3. Interview. Interview with Stephen M. Stahl. Featuring Michael Gitlin. 1. 2005. audio compact disk (978-1-4225-0031-6(4)) NEI Pr.

Antidote to Depression. Aaron T. Beck. Read by Aaron T. Beck. 1 cass. (Running Time: 45 mins.). 9.95 (I0050B090, HarperThor) HarpC GBR.

Antietam. James Reasoner. Read by Lloyd James. (Running Time: 11 hrs.). (Civil War Battle Ser.: Bk. 3). 2003. 34.95 (978-1-59912-421-6(1)) Iofy Corp.

Antietam. Contrib. by Time-Life Audiobooks Staff. (Voices of the Civil War Ser.). 1999. (978-1-57042-729-9(1)) Hachet Audio.

Antietam. unabr. ed. James Reasoner. Read by Lloyd James. 8 cass. (Running Time: 11 hrs. 30 mins.). (Civil War Battle Ser.: Bk. 3). 2003. 56.95 (978-0-7861-2524-1(1), 3157); audio compact disk 72.00 (978-0-7861-9129-1(5), 3157) Blckstn Audio.

Antigone. Jean Anouilh. Tr. by Christopher Nixon. Directed By Brendon Fox. 2 CDs. (Running Time: 7320 sec.). 2005. audio compact disk 25.95 (978-1-58081-333-4(X), LA 071) Pub: L A Theatre. Dist(s): NetLibrary CO

Antigone, abr. ed. Sophocles & Dudley Fitts. Perf. by Dorothy Tutin & Max Adrian. Tr. by Robert Fitzgerald. 2 cass. (Running Time: 4 hrs.). Dramatization. 1984. 19.95 (978-0-694-50854-9(3), SWC 320) HarperCollins Pubs.
Cast includes: Jeremy Brett, Eileen Atkins, Geoffrey Dunn, Arthur Hewlitt, June Jago, Willoughby Goddard, Douglas Muir, Richard Goolden, Thomas Kempinski & Stephen Moore.

Antigone. unabr. ed. Richard Woodman. 8 cass. (Soundings Ser.). (J). 2006. 69.95 (978-1-84559-139-7(9)); audio compact disk 84.95 (978-1-84559-152-6(6)) Pub: ISIS Lrg Prnt GBR. Dist(s): Ulverscroft US

Antigua & My Life Before see Antigua Vida Mia

Antigua Vida Mia. unabr. ed. Marcela Serrano. Narrated by Adriana Sananes. 7 cass. (Running Time: 10 hrs.).Tr. of Antigua & My Life Before. (ENG & SPA.). 1995. 69.75 (978-1-4025-9364-2(3), E1075MC, Griot Aud) Recorded Bks.

***Antimacassar City.** Guy Mccrone. 2010. 61.95 (978-1-4079-0816-8(2)); audio compact disk 71.95 (978-1-4079-0817-5(0)) Pub: Soundings Ltd GBR. Dist(s): Ulverscroft US

Antimatter. Hugh Hazelton. 2003. audio compact disk 12.00 (978-1-896647-97-5(9)) Broken Jaw Pr CAN.

Antimicrobial Therapy. Read by Robert C. Moellering, Jr. 1 cass. (Running Time: 9 mins.). 1986. 12.00 (C8623) Amer Coll Phys.

Antimicrobial Therapy: The New & the Best of the Old. Moderated by Harold C. Neu. Contrib. by Donald Kaye et al. 1 cass. (Running Time: 90 mins.). 1985. 12.00 (A8507) Amer Coll Phys.
This topic is discussed by a moderator & experts who offer differing opinions.

Antipodean: The Secret of Mirror Lake. unabr. ed. (YA). 2007. audio compact disk (978-0-9788454-1-4(2)) Voice for Life.

***Antiques: A Basic Guide.** Karen Jean Matsko Hood. (ENG.). 2011. audio compact disk 24.95 (978-1-59434-886-0(3)) Whsprng Pine.

Antitrust. Thomas D. Morgan. 4 cass. (Running Time: 4 hrs.). (Gilbert Law Summaries Ser.). (C). 2002. 39.95 (978-0-15-900341-1(5)) Barbri Grp.

Antitrust. unabr. ed. James R. McCall. 5 cass. (Running Time: 6 hrs. 45 mins.). (Outstanding Professors Ser.). 1995. 50.00 (978-0-940366-73-2(8), 28391) Pub: Sum & Substance. Dist(s): West Pub
Lecture by a prominent American law school professor.

Antitrust - Intellectual Property Claims in High Technology Markets: Litigating & Advising. 9 cass. (Running Time: 13 hrs. 30 mins.). 1999. stu. ed. 345.00 (AD72) Am Law Inst.
Advanced course informs in-house, plaintiffs' & defendants' counsel of the latest trends & developments in antitrust & intellectual property law practice, as well as trial counseling techniques.

Antitrust 2006. Christopher Leslie. 51.95 (978-0-314-16071-3(X), gilbert) West.

Antiviral Therapy. Contrib. by Richard Jacobs et al. 1 cass. (American Academy of Pediatrics UPDATE: Vol. 19, No. 1). 1998. 20.00 Am Acad Pediat.

Antologia. Juan Jose Arreola. Narrated by Francisco Rivela. 2 cass. (Running Time: 3 hrs.). 19.00 (978-1-4025-1662-7(2)) Recorded Bks.

Antologia. unabr. ed. 2004. audio compact disk 16.99 (978-0-8297-4813-0(X)) Zondervan.

Antologia. unabr. ed. Zondervan Publishing Staff. Marcos Witt. 2004. DVD & audio compact disk 16.99 (978-0-8297-4812-3(1)) Zondervan.

Antologia de la coleccion Entre Voces. (ESP.). 2005. audio compact disk 7.95 (978-7-5098-2700-0(0)) Fondo CA.

Antologia Martiana. unabr. ed. Jose Marti. 3 CDs.Tr. of Anthology Martiana - Poetry & Prose. (SPA.). 2003. audio compact disk 17.00 (978-958-8218-24-3(1)) YoYoMusic.

***Antologia Noble de la Poesia Mexicana.** abr. ed. Read by Adeliada Espinosa & Fabio Camero. (SPA.). 2008. audio compact disk 17.00 (978-958-8318-45-5(9)) Pub: Yoyo Music COL. Dist(s): YoYoMusic

***Antología Poética.** Gonzalo Rojas. (Entre Voces Ser.). 2002. audio compact disk 14.99 (978-968-16-7918-7(0)) Pub: Fondo MEX. Dist(s): Fondo CA

Anton Chekhov. unabr. ed. Anton Chekhov. Read by Michael Redgrave. 1 cass. (Running Time: 50 mins.). Incl. First Class Passenger. (SAC 7141); On the Harmfulness of Tobacco. (SAC 7141); Transgression. (SAC 7141); 10.95 (978-0-8045-0828-5(3), SAC 7141) Spoken Arts.

Anton Chekhov: A Life. Donald Rayfield. Read by Fred Williams, Jr. 8 cass. (Running Time: 8 hrs.). 2000. 56.95 (2496-B) Blckstn Audio.
The author spent over three years traveling throughout Russia to uncover thousands of documents & letters from Chekhov's lovers, friends & family.

Anton Chekhov: A Life. unabr. ed. Donald Rayfield. Read by Fred Williams. (Running Time: 102600 sec.). 2008. audio compact disk & audio compact disk 160.00 (978-1-4332-3451-4(3)) Blckstn Audio.

Anton Chekhov: His Life. unabr. ed. Ronald Rayfield. Read by Fred Williams. (Running Time: 102600 sec.). 2008. audio compact disk & audio compact disk 44.95 (978-1-4332-3452-1(1)) Blckstn Audio.

Anton Chekhov: Six Simple Stories. unabr. ed. Short Stories. Anton Chekhov. 1 cass., bklet. (Running Time: 64 mins.). (RUS.). 2001. pap. bk. 19.95 (SRU270) J Norton Pubs.
Includes: "The Orator," "Dachnik, the Tutor" & "The Clever Porter." The stories are as originally written with facing notes & extensive end vocabulary, thus providing greater access to the work of the short story master.

Anton Chekhov Pt. 2: A Life. unabr. ed. Donald Rayfield. Read by Fred Williams, Jr. 9 cass. (Running Time: 32 hrs.). 2000. 62.95 (978-0-7861-1757-4(5), 2560A,B) Blckstn Audio.
Anton Chekhov's life was short, intense & dominated by battles, both with his dependents & with the tuberculosis that killed him at age forty-four. He was one of the greatest playwrights & short-story writers ever born, but he was torn between medicine & literature, solitude & a need for company. Rayfield's biography strips the whitewash from the image of Chekhov & shows us what lay behind his restrained, ironic facade. The result does not denigrate him but shows him in the full heroism of his brief, prodigiously creative life.

Anton Chekhov - Selected Readings see Sound of Classical Drama

***Anton Chekhov Short Story Collection: In A Strange Land & Other Stories, Vol. 1.** Anton Chekhov. Ed. by Max Bollinger. Tr. by Constance Garnett. Illus. by Max Bollinger. Music by Pyotr Tchaikovskiy. (ENG.). 2010. audio compact disk 35.00 (978-1-907832-02-4(5), Sovereig) Max Bollinger GBR.

Anton Chekov Pt. 1: A Life. unabr. ed. Donald Rayfield. Read by Fred Williams, Jr. 11 cass. (Running Time: 32 hrs.). 2000. 76.95 (978-0-7861-1756-7(7), 2560A,B) Blckstn Audio.

Anton Reicha: 36 Fugues for piano, Op. 36. (Running Time: 1 hr. 59 mins.). 43.99 Books on Tape.

Antoni Tapies: Recent Work. Dan Cameron. 1 cass. 2000. (978-1-878283-92-4(8)) PaceGallery.
Published in conjunction with an exhibition at PaceWildenstein.

Antonin Dvorak: Symphony No. 8 in G Major. Dvorak. (ENG.). 2006. pap. bk. 19.99 (978-3-7957-6532-3(3), 3795765323) Pub: Schott Music Corp. Dist(s): H Leonard

Antonio S. & the Mysterious Theodore Guzman. unabr. ed. Odo Hirsch. Read by Catherine Milte. 4 cass. (Running Time: 4 hrs.). 2002. (978-1-876584-17-7(3), BAB990689) Bolinda Pubng AUS.
Antonio S is a boy who knows all sorts of things. Scarrabo the Magnificent is a magician. Professor Kettering is a doctor. They live at the top of a grand old house built long ago for a duke. But who is Theodore Guzman, the secretive old man who lives downstairs? What mysterious things does he know? It takes someone like Antonio S to find out.

Antonio S & the Mystery of Theodore Guzman. unabr. ed. Odo Hirsch. Read by Catherine Milte. (Running Time: 14400 sec.). (J). (gr. 4-7). 2007. audio compact disk 57.95 (978-1-74093-419-0(9)) Pub: Bolinda Pubng AUS. Dist(s): Bolinda Pub Inc

Antonio Skarmeta. unabr. ed. Antonio Skármeta. Read by Antonio Skármeta. 1 cass. (Running Time: 29 mins.). 1988. 8.00 New Letters.
Chilean-in-exile Antonio Skarmeta is interviewed & a portion of his novel Burning Patience is read.

Antonio Vivaldi: Violin Concerto in a Minor, Opus 3 No. 6. Contrib. by Zakhar Bron. (Running Time: 1 hr.). 2005. 36.95 (978-5-558-11328-0(6)) Mel Bay.

Antonio's Quest for Peace - the Friends of Peace. alt. ed. Anthony M. Benjamin, Sr. 2005. audio compact disk 60.00i (978-0-9764590-0-2(0)) A M Benjamin.

Antony & Cleopatra. William Shakespeare. Perf. by Pamela Brown & Anthony Quayle. 1 cass. (J). (ps up). 1977. 14.00 (978-0-694-50136-6(0), SWC 1183) HarperCollins Pubs.
Cast includes: Paul Daneman, David Dodimead, James Hayter, Jack Gwillim, Nigel Davenport, Michael Meacham, Edgar Wreford, John Saunders, James Cairncross, Christopher Guinee, Ronald Ibbs, Peter Bayliss, Thomas Kempinski, Ronnie Stevens, Norman Rossington, Newton Blick, Jeanne Hepple, Caroline John, Sarah Long.

Antony & Cleopatra. William Shakespeare. Narrated by Full Cast Production Staff. (Running Time: 2 hrs.). 2006. 14.95 (978-1-59912-989-1(2)) Iofy Corp.

Antony & Cleopatra. William Shakespeare. Narrated by Kimberly Schraf. 3 cass. (Running Time: 2 hrs. 11 min.). (Classic Books on Cassette). 2005. 16.95 (978-1-55685-856-7(6)) Audio Bk Con.

Antony & Cleopatra. William Shakespeare. Narrated by Kimberly Schraf. 2008. audio compact disk 19.95 (978-1-55685-996-0(1)) Audio Bk Con.

Antony & Cleopatra. abr. ed. William Shakespeare. 3 CDs. (Running Time: 3 hrs). 2005. audio compact disk 19.95 (978-0-660-18966-6(6)) Pub: Canadian Broadcasting CAN. Dist(s): Georgetown Term

Antony & Cleopatra. abr. ed. William Shakespeare. Read by Full Cast Production Staff. (YA). 2007. 34.99 (978-1-60252-598-6(6)) Find a World.

***Antony & Cleopatra.** abr. ed. William Shakespeare. (ENG.). 2003. (978-0-06-074329-1(8), Caedmon) HarperCollins Pubs.

***Antony & Cleopatra.** abr. ed. William Shakespeare. (ENG.). 2004. (978-0-06-081463-2(2), Caedmon) HarperCollins Pubs.

Antony & Cleopatra. unabr. ed. Colleen McCullough. Narrated by Sneha Mathan. 3 MP3-CDs. (Running Time: 25 hrs. 15 mins.). (Masters of Rome Ser.: No. 7). 2008. 84.95 (978-0-7927-5320-9(8)); audio compact disk 139.95 (978-0-7927-5230-1(9)) AudioGO.
Mark Antony, famous warrior and legendary lover, expects that he will be Julius Caesar's successor. But when Caesar is murdered, his eighteen-year-old nephew, Octavian, is named as his heir. No one, least of all Antony, expects Octavian to last; but his youth and slight frame conceal a remarkable determination and a sharp strategic mind. Under Octavian's rule, the empire is divided, with Antony responsible for the fabulously rich East. There he meets Cleopatra, who is still mourning Caesar, her lover and the father of her only son. Despite his marriage to Octavian's sister, Antony is fascinated by the Egyptian queen. Drawn together by grief, ambition, passion and politics, they begin a very public love affair, and the tension between Antony and Octavian, already simmering, soon threatens to erupt into war.

Antony & Cleopatra. unabr. ed. Colleen McCullough. Read by Sneha Mathan. (Masters of Rome Ser.: No. 7). (YA). 2008. 124.99 (978-1-60514-871-7(7)) Find a World.

Antony & Cleopatra. unabr. ed. William Shakespeare. Read by Ciaran Hinds et al. 2 cass. (Running Time: 3 hrs. 23 mins.). 2004. 17.95 (978-1-932219-43-2(9)) Pub: Arkangel Audio. Dist(s): PerseuPGW
Struggling to save her empire, Cleopatra, the Queen of Egypt, becomes entrenched in a deadly romantic triangle with Roman leaders Mark Antony and Julius Caesar. From one of history's great love stories, Shakespeare crafts an epic tragedy of the clash between love and duty.

Antony & Cleopatra. unabr. ed. William Shakespeare. (Running Time: 12180 sec.). (Arkangel Shakespeare Ser.). (ENG.). 2005. audio compact disk 24.95 (978-1-932219-03-6(X)) Pub: AudioGO. Dist(s): Perseus Dist

Antony & Cleopatra. unabr. ed. William Shakespeare. Perf. by Anthony Quale & Pamela Brown. 2 cass. (Running Time: 3 hrs.). Dramatization. 17.95 (H166) Blckstn Audio.
Shows how a man born to rule the world is destroyed by his weaknesses & lusts.

Antony & Cleopatra. unabr. ed. William Shakespeare. Perf. by Anthony Quayle & Pamela Brown. 3 cass. Dramatization. HarperCollins Pubs.
Cast includes: Paul Daneman, Jack Gwillim, David Dodimead, James Hayter, Michael Meacham, Nigel Davenport, Edgar Wreford, John Saunders, James Cairncross, Christopher Guinee, Ronald Ibbs, Peter Bayliss, Thomas Kempinski, Ronald Stevens, Norman Rossington, Newton Blick, Jeanne Hepple, Caroline John, Sarah Long & John Gayford.

Antony & Cleopatra. unabr. ed. William Shakespeare. Perf. by Anthony Quayle & Pamela Brown. 3 cass. (Running Time: 5 hrs.). Dramatization. (J). 1984. 27.95 (978-0-694-50749-8(0), SWC 235) HarperCollins Pubs.

Ants. Joe Scruggs. (Running Time: 36 mins.). (J). (ps-4). 1994. 9.95 (978-0-916123-35-2(9), SPR-350) Ed Graphics Pr.
13 songs with witty lyrics & outstanding music promoting individuality & creativity.

Ants: Music for Kids with Ants in Their Pants. (Joe Scruggs Ser.). (J). (ps-3). 1998. 9.98 (978-1-57064-252-4(4)) Lyrick Studios.

Ants: Music for Kids with Ants in Their Pants. Joe Scruggs. 1 CD. (Joe Scruggs Ser.). (J). 1997. audio compact disk 14.98 (978-1-57064-253-1(2)) Robs Rinehart.

Ants: Music for Kids with Ants in Their Pants. Joe Scruggs. 1 cass. (Joe Scruggs Ser.). (J). (ps-3). 1997. 9.98 (978-1-57064-251-7(6)) Robs Rinehart.

Ants Go Marching. Perf. by Jill Connolly et al. (Running Time: 1 hr.). (J). (ps up). 6.00 Story Stone.
A diverse musical experience for you and your child. Every song has simple words that children already know or can learn quickly, and the arrangements are elegantly filled with musical treasures to delight your ears.

Ants Have a Picnic: Early Explorers Early Set A Audio CD. Benchmark Education Staff. (J). 2006. audio compact disk 10.00 (978-1-4108-7626-3(8)) Benchmark Educ.

Antsy Does Time. unabr. ed. Neal Shusterman. Read by Neal Shusterman. 6 CDs. (Running Time: 6 hrs. 31 mins.). (YA). (gr. 7-10). 2008. audio compact disk 50.00 (978-0-7393-7241-8(6), Listening Lib) Pub: Random Audio Pubg. Dist(s): Random
It was a dumb idea, but one of those dumb ideas that accidentally turns out to be brilliant - which, I've come to realize, is much worse than being dumb. My name's Antsy Bonano - but you probably already know that - and unless you got, like, memory issues, you'll remember the kid named the Schwa, who I told you about last time. Well, now there's this other kid, and his story is a whole lot stranger. It all started when Gunnar Ümlaut and I were watching three airborne bozos struggle with a runaway parade balloon. That's when Gunnar tells me he's only got six months to live. Maybe it was because he said he was living on borrowed time, or maybe it was just because I wanted to do something meaningful for him, but I gave him a month of my life ...And that's when things began to get seriously weird.

Antsy Does Time. unabr. ed. Neal Shusterman. Read by Neal Shusterman. (ENG.). (J). (gr. 7). 2008. audio compact disk 34.00 (978-0-7393-7239-5(4), Listening Lib) Pub: Random Audio Pubg. Dist(s): Random

Anturiaethau Jini Me. Sain. 2005. audio compact disk 16.99 (978-88-88043-74-6(8)) Scuola Istruzione ITA.

***Anubis Gates.** unabr. ed. Tim Powers. (Running Time: 13 hrs. 30 mins.). 2010. 29.95 (978-1-4417-5729-6(5)); audio compact disk 32.95 (978-1-4417-5728-9(7)) Blckstn Audio.

Anver Versi - An African's View of His Environment. Hosted by Nancy Pearlman. 1 cass. (Running Time: 29 mins.). 10.00 (805) Educ Comm CA.

Anxiety. 1 cass. (Running Time: 1 hr.). 2001. 9.95 (CA603) Pub: VisnQst Vid Aud. Dist(s): TMW Media

Anxiety. Bruce Goldberg. (ENG.). 2005. audio compact disk 17.00 (978-1-57968-085-5(2)) Pub: B Goldberg. Dist(s): Baker Taylor

Anxiety. Bruce Goldberg. Read by Bruce Goldberg. 1 cass. (Running Time: 25 mins.). (ENG.). 2006. 13.00 (978-1-885577-50-4(8)) Pub: B Goldberg. Dist(s): Baker Taylor
Through self-hypnosis, regain peace and harmony and increase resistance to stress.

Anxiety. unabr. ed. Marvin R. Goldfried. 1 cass. (Running Time: 1 hr.). 14.95 (C29353) J Norton Pubs.

Anxiety: Friend or Foe? Susan M. Heitler. Perf. by Melissa King & Rob MacMullan. 1 cass. (Running Time: 1 hr. 5 mins.). 1995. 14.95 (978-1-884998-08-9(9)) Listen-to-Lrn.
Psychologist Dr. Susan Heitler teaches easy-to-learn strategies for transforming anxiety into a positive life force. Includes a lively lecture-demonstration, followed by excerpts from therapy treatment sessions (with actors role playing patients).

Anxiety: Program from the Award Winning Public Radio Series. Hosted by Fred Goodwin. Comment by John Hockenberry. Contrib. by Michael Davis et al. 1 cass. (Running Time: 1 hr.). (Infinite Mind Ser.). 1998. audio compact disk 21.95 (978-1-888064-45-2(5), LCM 10) Lichtenstein Creat.
With Dr. Steven Hyman, director of the National Institute of Mental Health, Mary Guardino of the national advocacy group Freedom From Fear and Dr. Michael Davis, a top anxiety researcher at Yale University Medical Center. Includes discussion of anxiety and panic disorders, post-traumatic stress disorder, obsessive-compulsive disorder and phobias, along with listener phone calls. Plus, John Hockenberry reflects on the wonder of new life, and news from the editors of Psychology Today magazine.

Anxiety: Symptoms & Circuits. Interview. Featuring Stephen M. Stahl. Interview with Javaid Sheikh. 2005. audio compact disk (978-1-4225-0005-7(5)) NEI Pr.

Anxiety: The Cool Way. Created by Robert Aveberry. 2001. audio compact disk 29.95 (978-0-914937-16-6(2)) Ind Pubns.

Anxiety: The Cool Way Audiobook. Read by Robert I. Shapiro. Robert I. Shapiro. 2008. cd-rom 69.00 (978-0-914937-21-0(9)) Ind Pubns.

Anxiety Vol. 1: Treatment Issues. Interview. Interview with Stephen Stahl. Featuring Javaid Sheikh. 1 CD. 2004. audio compact disk (978-1-4225-0008-8(X)) NEI Pr.

Anxiety - Agoraphobia Treatment Program. Ann Seagrave & Faison Covington. Read by Ann Seagrave & Faison Covington. 16 cass. 475.00 CHAANGE.
This is a therapeutic process accompanied by books, workbooks & other reading material. Progress is monitored either by the affiliated therapist or through written evaluation forms. Participation is subject to a screening evaluation & information is available by mail.

Anxiety & Conflicts. 1 cass. (Introduction to Chemical Dependency Ser.). 8.95 (1460G) Hazelden.

Anxiety & Panic. Scripts. Steven Gurgevich. Prod. by Steven Gurgevich. 1 CD. (Running Time: 45 min). (ENG.). 2002. audio compact disk 19.95 (978-1-932170-06-1(5), HWH) Tranceformation.

Anxiety & Panic Reactions. unabr. ed. Mercedes Leidlich. Read by Mercedes Leidlich. 1 cass. (Running Time: 1 hr.). 1992. 10.95 in Norelco box. (978-1-882174-05-8(4), MLL-006) UFD Pub.
Anxiety can be debilitating, & can appe[illegible] the form of several disorders, including generalized anxiety disorder, [illegible]as, panic disorder, post-traumatic stress disorder, or obse[illegible] compulsive disorder. This tape teaches the symptoms of anxiety & how to naturally diminish the body's physiological responses to stress. Side B of this tape is a relaxation exercise set to soothing harp music.

Anxiety & Stress. Eldon Taylor. Read by Eldon Taylor. Interview with XProgress Aware Staff. 1 cass. (Running Time: 1 hr. 30 mins.). (Power Imaging Ser.). 16.95 incl. script. (978-1-55978-179-4(3), 8005) Progress Aware Res.
Hypnosis & soundtrack with underlying subliminal affirmations.

Anxiety & Tension: How to Suffer Less & Enjoy More. Richard Wessler. 1 cass. (Running Time: 63 mins.). 9.95 (C001) A Ellis Institute.
Useful techniques for decreasing stressful habits & increasing pleasure & relaxation.

Anxiety & Tension: How to Suffer Less & Enjoy More. Richard Wessler. 1 cass. (Running Time: 63 mins.). 9.95 (C001) Inst Rational-Emotive.

Anxiety-Free. Paul R. Scheele. Read by Paul R. Scheele. 1 cass. (Running Time: 40 mins.). (Paraliminal Tapes Ser.). 1990. 24.95 (978-0-925480-13-2(4)) Learn Strategies.
Helps listener gain freedom from fears & anxieties.

Anxiety Free: Unravel Your Fears Before They Unravel You. Robert L. Leahy & Robert Leahy. 4 CDs. 2009. audio compact disk 23.95 (978-1-4019-2167-5(1), 608) Hay House.

Anxiety into Energy. Ken Dychtwald. 6 cass. (Running Time: 6 hrs.). 1991. 59.95 (1751A) Nightingale-Conant.
Dr. Ken Dychtwald explores society's #1 health hazard - stress - & shows you how to change things so you can live life as well & as long as you're supposed to.

Anxiety Release. Dorothy J. Papin-Griffith. 2005. audio compact disk 14.95 (978-0-9765935-2-2(1)) Gry L Prodns Inc.

Anxiety Relief. Martin Rossman. 1 CD. (Running Time: 1 hr. 15 mins.). (Guided Self-Healing Ser.). 2006. audio compact disk 15.95 (978-1-59179-190-4(1), W825D) Sounds True.
"Human beings have the unique ability to compress a lifetime of stress into every passing moment," says Dr. Martin Rossman. When we worry, he teaches, the body prepares for "fight or flight," putting in motion a chain of physiological effects that can leave us exhausted, depressed, or physically ill. Anxiety Relief shows listeners how to reverse these debilitating effects through relaxing, rejuvenating guided imagery techniques Dr. Rossman has prescribed to thousands challenged by stress. One information-packed CD session includes: deep body-mind relaxation; the inner wisdom dialogue; and the "worry warrior" technique for converting fear and worry into positive energy.

***Anxiety Relief: Relax the Body & Calm the Mind, Manage Fear & Worry, & Cultivate Positive Energy.** Martin L. Rossman. (Running Time: 2:00:00). 2010. audio compact disk 14.95 (978-1-59179-778-4(0)) Sounds True.

Anxiety Resolution, Relaxation & Systematic & Flexible Hierarchy Guides, Set-AH. Russell E. Mason. Read by Russell E. Mason. 6 cass. (Running Time: 5 hrs. 54 mins.). (Train-Ascendance Ser.). 1975. pap. bk. 45.00 (978-0-89533-009-3(1), 58.GT-AR) F I Comm.
Fosters positive feeling states & copes with anxious & depressive states. Also, encourages practical applications of relaxation.

Anxiety, the Economy, & You. Hosted by Peter Lambrou & Kevin Skinner. (ENG.). 2009. audio compact disk 29.95 (978-0-9772208-3-0(4)) GrowthClimate Inc.

***Anxious Souls Will Ask: The Christ Centered Spirituality of Dietrich Bonhoeffer.** unabr. ed. John Matthews. Narrated by Simon Vance. (ENG.). 2005. 9.98 (978-1-59644-225-2(5), Hovel Audio) christianaud.

Anxious Souls Will Ask: The Christ-Centered Spirituality of Dietrich Bonhoeffer. unabr. ed. John W. Matthews. Narrated by Simon Vance. 2 CDs. (Running Time: 2 hrs. 18 mins. 0 sec.). (ENG.). 2005. audio compact disk 15.98 (978-1-59644-224-5(7), Hovel Audio) christianaud.

Any Dream Will Do: Medley ShowTrax. Music by Andrew Lloyd Webber. Arranged by Ed Lojeski. 1 CD. (Running Time: 11 mins.). 2000. audio compact disk 40.00 (08621177) H Leonard.
The music of Andrew Lloyd Webber has moved millions with its passion & spectacle. This medley makes an excellent feature for women's voices. Includes: "Any Dream Will Do," "As If We Never Said Goodbye," "Love Changes Everything" & "Masquerade.".

Any friend of the Movement: Networking for birth Control 1920-1940. Jimmy Elaine Wilkens Meyer. (Women & Health C & S Perspective Ser.). 2004. audio compact disk 9.95 (978-0-8142-9034-7(5)) Pub: Ohio St U Pr. Dist(s): Chicago Distribution Ctr

Any Given Day. abr. ed. Jessie Lee Brown Foveaux. 2 cass. (Running Time: 3 hrs.). 1997. 17.00 Hachet Audio.

Any Given Day: The Life & Times of Jessie Lee Brown Foveaux. abr. ed. Jessie Lee Brown Foveaux. (ENG.). 2006. 14.98 (978-1-59483-842-2(9)) Pub: Hachet Audio. Dist(s): HachBkGrp

Any Idiot Can Make It Through a Good Day, How to Think Positive in Difficult Times. Jay Block. 2005. audio compact disk 29.95 (978-0-9770328-8-4(4)) AardGP.

Any Kind of Dog. Lynn W. Reiser. Read by Peter Fernandez. 1 cass. (Running Time: 5 mins.). (J). (gr. k-3). 1996. bk. 24.95 (978-0-87499-380-6(6)); pap. bk. 15.95 (978-0-87499-379-0(2)); pap. bk. 31.95 Reading Chest. (978-0-87499-381-3(4)) Live Oak Media.
Richard longs for a dog. His mother provides other pets which Richard likens to pictures in books about dogs. The simple repetitive text, finds a most suitable vehicle in this read-along format. A male narrator reads slowly & sprightly music & animal sounds begin & end the presentation.

Any Minute. abr. ed. Joyce Meyer & Deborah Bedford. Read by Ellen Archer. (Running Time: 6 hrs.). (ENG.). 2009. 19.98 (978-1-60024-631-9(1)); audio compact disk 29.98 (978-1-60024-630-2(3)) Pub: Hachet Audio. Dist(s): HachBkGrp

Any Ol' Bush: Exodus 3:1-10. Ed Young. 1984. 4.95 (978-0-7417-1418-3(3), 418) Win Walk.

Any Place I Hang My Hat. unabr. ed. Susan Isaacs. Read by Carol Monda. 14 CDs. (Running Time: 13 hrs.). 2004. audio compact disk 119.75 (978-1-4193-1504-6(8)) Recorded Bks.

Any Place I Hang My Hat. unabr. ed. Susan Isaacs. Narrated by Carol Monda. 9 cass. (Running Time: 13 hrs. 15 mins.). 2004. 99.75 (978-1-4193-1502-2(1), 97899MC) Recorded Bks.

Any Way You Slice It; Quiet on the Set! unabr. ed. Nancy Krulik. Read by Anne Bobby. 2 CDs. (Running Time: 1 hr. 59 mins.). (Katie Kazoo, Switcheroo Ser.: Nos. 9-10). (J). (gr. 2-4). 2007. audio compact disk 24.00 (978-0-7393-5142-0(7), Listening Lib) Pub: Random Audio Pubg. Dist(s): Random

Anya V Stranye Chudes, Set. Lewis Carroll, pseud. Read by Angela Sarkissian. Tr. by Vladimir Nabokov. 4 cass.Tr. of Alice in Wonderland. (RUS.). 1996. pap. bk. 49.50 (978-1-58085-580-8(6)) Interlingua VA.
Includes complete Russian text. The combination of written text & clarity & pace of diction will open the door for intermediate & advanced students to genuine comprehension & the use of literary texts for advancement in rapid understanding of written & oral language materials. The audio text plus written text concept makes foreign languages accessible to a much wider range of students than books alone.

Anybodies & The Nobodies. N. E. Bode. 2005. bk. 34.95 (978-0-06-082644-4(4), HarperChildAud) HarperCollins Pubs.

***Anybodies & the Nobodies.** unabr. ed. N. E. Bode. Read by Oliver Platt. (ENG.). 2005. (978-0-06-088140-5(2)); (978-0-06-088138-2(0)) HarperCollins Pubs.

***Anybody Out There?** unabr. ed. Marian Keyes. Read by Terry Donnelly. (ENG.). 2006. (978-0-06-117443-8(2), Harper Audio); (978-0-06-117442-1(4), Harper Audio) HarperCollins Pubs.

Anyone but Me; Out to Lunch. unabr. ed. Nancy Krulik. Read by Anne Bobby. 2 cass. (Running Time: 2 hrs. 9 mins.). (Katie Kazoo, Switcheroo Ser.: Nos. 1-2). (J). (gr. 4-7). 2005. 23.00 (978-0-307-20690-9(4), BksonTape); audio compact disk 20.40 (978-0-307-20689-3(0), BksonTape) Pub: Random Audio Pubg. Dist(s): NetLibrary CO

Anyone but Me; Out to Lunch. unabr. ed. Nancy Krulik. Read by Anne Bobby. 2 CDs. (Running Time: 2 hrs.). (Katie Kazoo, Switcheroo Ser.: Nos. 1-2). (ENG.). (J). (gr. 3). 2005. audio compact disk 19.99 (978-0-307-20641-1(6), ImaginStudio) Pub: Random Audio Pubg. Dist(s): Random

Anyone but You. unabr. ed. Jennifer Crusie, pseud. Read by Susan Ericksen. (Running Time: 5 hrs.). 2005. 39.25 (978-1-4233-0494-4(2), 9781423304944, BADLE); 24.95 (978-1-4233-0493-7(4), 9781423304937, BAD); 62.25 (978-1-4233-0488-3(8), 9781423304883, BrilAudUnabridg); 24.95 (978-1-4233-0487-6(X), 9781423304876, BAU); audio compact disk 74.25 (978-1-4233-0490-6(X), 9781423304906, BriAudCD Unabrid); audio compact disk 39.25 (978-1-4233-0492-0(6), 9781423304920, Brinc Audio MP3 Lib); audio compact disk 24.95 (978-1-4233-0491-3(8), 9781423304913, Brilliance MP3); audio compact disk 26.95 (978-1-4233-0489-0(6), 9781423304890, Bril Audio CD Unabri) Brilliance Audio.
For Nina Askew, turning forty means freedom - from the ex-husband whose career always came first, from their stuffy suburban home. Freedom to have her own apartment in the city, freedom to focus on what she wants for a change. And what she wants is something her ex always vetoed - a puppy. A bouncy puppy to cheer her up. Instead she gets...Fred. Overweight, smelly and obviously suffering from some kind of doggy depression, Fred is light-years from perky. But for all his faults, he does manage to put Nina face-to-face with Alex Moore, her gorgeous, younger downstairs neighbor. Alex looks great on paper - a sexy, seemingly sane, surprisingly single E.R. doctor who shares Fred's abiding love for Oreos - but a ten-year difference in age, despite his devastating smile, is too wide a gap for Nina to handle. Ignoring her insistent best friend, some interfering do-gooders and the ubiquitous Fred - not to mention her suddenly raging hormones - Nina thinks anyone but Alex would be a better bet for a relationship. But with every silver-haired stiff she dates, the more she suspects it's the young dog-loving doctor she wants to sit and stay!.

Anyone Can Consult! How to Employ What You Already Know. Victor K. Pryles. 2003. audio compact disk 17.00 (978-0-9786162-0-5(0)) V Pryles MA.

Anyone Can Get Rich. 10.00 (HT410) Esstee Audios.

Anyone Can Play Classic Guitar. Created by Mel Bay Publications Inc. (Running Time: 45 mins.). (Anyone Can Play (Mel Bay) Ser.). 2005. 14.95 (978-5-558-09029-1(4)) Mel Bay.

Anyone Can Play C6 Lap Steel Guitar. Demonstrated by Rob Haines. (Anyone Can Play Videos Ser.). 2008. 14.95 Mel Bay.

Anyone Can Play Djembe. Demonstrated by Paulo Mattioli. (Anyone Can Play Videos Ser.). 2008. 14.95 Mel Bay.

Anyone Can Play Dobro. Created by Mel Bay Publications Inc. (Running Time: 50 mins.). (Anyone Can Play (Mel Bay) Ser.). 2005. 14.95 (978-5-558-08987-5(3)) Mel Bay.

Anyone Can Play E9 Pedal Steel Guitar. Demonstrated by Rob Haines. (Anyone Can Play Videos Ser.). 2008. 14.95 Mel Bay.

Anyone Can Play Portable Keyboard. Created by Mel Bay Publications Inc. (Running Time: 30 mins.). (Anyone Can Play (Mel Bay) Ser.). 2005. 14.95 (978-5-558-09061-1(8)) Mel Bay.

Anyone Can Play Saxophone. Created by Mel Bay Publications Inc. (Running Time: 1 hr.). (Anyone Can Play (Mel Bay) Ser.). 2005. 14.95 (978-5-558-08951-6(2)) Mel Bay.

Anyone Can Sing. Created by Mel Bay Publications Inc. (Running Time: 45 mins.). 2005. 14.95 (978-5-558-09016-1(2)) Mel Bay.

Anything but Truth. Graham Roberts. Read by Michael Underwood. 4 cass. (Running Time: 6 hrs.). 2001. 54.95 (23337) Pub: Soundings Ltd GBR. Dist(s): Ulverscroft US

Anything but Typical. unabr. ed. Nora Raleigh Baskin. Read by Tom Parks. (Running Time: 4 hrs.). 2009. 39.97 (978-1-4233-8133-4(5), 9781423381334, BADLE); 39.97 (978-1-4233-8131-0(9), 9781423381310, Brinc Audio MP3 Lib); 24.99 (978-1-4233-8130-3(0), 9781423381303, Brilliance MP3); 24.99 (978-1-4233-8132-7(7), 9781423381327, BAD); audio compact disk 24.99 (978-1-4233-8128-0(9), 9781423381280, Bril Audio CD Unabri) Brilliance Audio.

Anything but Typical. unabr. ed. Nora Raleigh Baskin. Read by Tom Parks. 3 CDs. (Running Time: 4 hrs.). (gr. 4-7). 2009. audio compact disk 48.97 (978-1-4233-8129-7(7), 9781423381297, BriAudCD Unabrid) Brilliance Audio.

Anything Considered. abr. ed. Peter Mayle. Read by Tim Curry. 2003. 9.95 (978-1-59397-180-9(X)) Pub: Macmill Audio. Dist(s): Macmillan

Anything Considered. unabr. ed. Peter Mayle. Read by David Case. 8 cass. (Running Time: 8 hrs.). 1996. 48.00 (978-0-7366-3453-3(3), 4097) Books on Tape.
An Englishman in France flees from a shady business scheme with the boss's ex-girlfriend, sampling food & wine en route. Vintage Mayle.

Anything for a Quiet Life. unabr. ed. Michael Gilbert. Read by Christopher Scott. 7 cass. (Running Time: 8 hrs. 20 mins.). (Isis Ser.). (J). 2004. 61.95 (978-1-85695-422-8(6), 92092) Pub: ISIS Lrg Prnt GBR. Dist(s): Ulverscroft US

Anything for Billy: A Novel. unabr. collector's ed. Larry McMurtry. Read by Wolfram Kandinsky. 8 cass. (Running Time: 12 hrs.). 1989. 64.00 (978-0-7366-1536-5(9), 2406) Books on Tape.
The story of Billy the Kid. Had he lived out his allotted span, he would be forgotten. But his youthful death immortalized him.

Anything for Love: Theme Song from the Blockbuster Romance Novel, the Blue Ribbon. Perf. by Ron Hevener. 1 CD. (Running Time: 4 mins 32 seconds). 2003. audio compact disk 5.00 (978-0-9679514-2-3(9), Anythig For Love) Pennywood Pr.
Classy love theme to the blockbuster romance novel, "The Blue Ribbon.".

Anything Goes! What I've Learned from Pundits, Politicians & Presidents. abr. ed. Larry King. Read by Larry King. 4 cass. (Running Time: 6 hrs.). 2004. 25.00 (978-1-931056-17-5(X), N Millennium Audio) New Millenn Enter.

Anything I Ever Really Needed to Know I Learned from Anime. Sid Narged. Read by Sid Narged. (ENG.). (YA). 2008. 12.95 (978-0-9793080-4-8(6)) S Narged.

Anything Is Possible. Swami Amar Jyoti. 1 cass. 1982. 9.95 (M-25) Truth Consciousness.
All is potential within us, the infinite possibilities of the Creator.

Anything Is Possible. Perf. by Youth Edition Staff. 1 CD. 2000. audio compact disk 17.98 (978-0-7601-3450-4(2), SO33210) Pub: Brentwood Music. Dist(s): Provident Mus Dist
Songs include: "Anything Is Possible," "All Day Long," "Best Friend," "Tell Me" & more.

Anything You Want To: Shakespeare's Lost Comedie. Firesign Theatre Firesign Theatre Staff. 2 cass. (Running Time: 2 hrs.). 1996. 16.95 (978-1-57677-054-2(0)) Lodestone Catalog.
Here is the funniest & most accomplished Shakespeare parody ever attempted, with a powerful appeal for fans of the Bard & the Firesign Theatre alike. This 1975 radio production has never before been available without cuts or modifications. Packed full with layers of topical jokes, ancient puns, multiple entendres, allusions to the Bard's plays - & many devious & delightful references to Firesign's other works.

Anything You Want To: Shakespeare's Lost Comedie. Perf. by Firesign Theatre Firesign Theatre Staff. 1 CD. (Running Time: 1 hr.). 1998. audio compact disk 15.95 (978-1-57677-104-4(0), MSUG009) Lodestone Catalog.

Anything Your Little Heart Desires: An American Family Story, unabr. ed. Patricia Bosworth. Read by Julia Delfino. 8 cass. (Running Time: 12 hrs.). 1999. 64.00 (978-0-7366-4464-8(4), 4909) Books on Tape.
About Roosevelt's New Deal, the triumphant Left, the victory of World War II, & then the fall of liberalism & the dawn of the Cold War. Political turmoil followed; anti-Communist hysteria ruined many lives full of promise. Among them was the author's father, Bartley Cavanaugh Crum, a heroic California lawyer of the thirties & forties, a Truman adviser & a crusader against the Hollywood blacklist until he himself became its victim.

Anythynge You Want To: Shakespeare's Lost Comedie. Perf. by Firesign Theatre. Text by Firesign Theatre. 1 CD. (Running Time: 58 mins). Dramatization. 2005. audio compact disk 15.95 (978-1-59938-024-7(2), FTR) Lode Cat.
Its Firesign Theatre in Shakespearean verse! Densely-packed and smarter than ever, this CD is stuffed full to bursting with multiple layers of jokes, puns, multiple-entendres and references to the Bard's plays. The Firesign's love of language is never more evident than in this production. This is a piece to delve into and revel in, finding new delights at every listening. A must for everyone who loves theatre, Shakespeare, or the English language.

Anytime Anywhere Audio Adventure. 2004. 1.99 (978-1-4003-0355-7(9)) Nelson.

Anytime... for as Long as You Want: A Man's 15-Day Course to Improve Life & Sex: Strength, Genius, Libido, & Erection by Integrative Sex Transmutation. Excerpts. Charles Edward Runels, Jr. 1 CD. (Running Time: 72 mins). 2004. bk. 35.00 (978-0-9765219-0-7(3)) LifeStream Medical.

Anytown USA: The Firesign Theatre LIVE at the Westbury Music Festival. unabr. ed. Firesign Theatre Firesign Theatre Staff. 2 CDs. (Running Time: 2 hrs.). 2000. 24.95 (978-1-57677-146-4(6), MSUG011) Lodestone Catalog.
Performances from the group's classic first period, contains large sections of material from "Don't Crush That Dwarf" and "We're All Bozo On This Bus".

Anyway. Contrib. by Martina McBride. (Soundtraks Ser.). 2007. audio compact disk 8.99 (978-5-557-60858-9(3)) Christian Wrld.

Anyway. Contrib. by Martina McBride. (Mastertrax Ser.). 2007. audio compact disk 8.98 (978-5-557-70336-9(5)) Pt of Grace Ent.

Anyway. Contrib. by Martina McBride. (Praise Hymn Soundtracks Ser.). 2007. audio compact disk 8.98 (978-5-557-63295-9(6)) Pt of Grace Ent.

Anyway. Contrib. by Martina McBride. (Sound Performance Soundtracks Ser.). 2007. audio compact disk 5.98 (978-5-557-58520-0(6)) Pt of Grace Ent.

Anywhere & Everywhere People see Carl Sandburg's Poems for Children

Anywhere but Here. Mona Simpson. Read by Mona Simpson. 1 cass. (Running Time: 90 mins.). 1987. 13.95 (978-1-55644-195-0(9), 7071) Am Audio Prose.
With a variety of family voices, Simpson reads the first chapter & the "Other People's Secrets" section of her first & bestselling novel.

AO Principles of Fracture Management. T. P. Ruedi & W. M. Murphy. 2001. bk. 369.00 (978-0-86577-886-3(8)) Thieme Med Pubs.

AO Principles of Fracture Management. T. P. Ruedi & W. M. Murphy. 2002. DVD & audio compact disk (978-1-58890-108-8(4)) Thieme Med Pubs.

Ao Principles of Fracture Management. Thomas Ruedi & William Murphy, II. 2002. DVD & audio compact disk (978-3-13-131731-5(0)) G Thieme DEU.

AO Principles of Fracture Management. Thomas P. Ruedi & W. M. Murphy. 2001. bk. (978-3-13-117441-3(2)) G Thieme DEU.

'A'ohe Inoa Komo 'Ole O Ka 'Ai. William H. Wilson. Illus. by Brook Parker. 1 cass. (HAW.). (J). (gr. 2-4). 1999. pap. bk. 5.95 (978-1-58191-058-2(4)) Aha Punana Leo.

AP English Language & Composition 2009: Your Audio Guide to Getting a Five. Awdeeo. Narrated by Awdeeo. (YA). 2008. 39.99 (978-0-9818187-7-1(3)) PrepLogic.

AP English Literature & Composition 2009: Your Audio Guide to Getting A 5. Awdeeo. Narrated by Awdeeo. (ENG.). (YA). 2008. 39.99 (978-0-9818187-4-0(9)) PrepLogic.

AP European History 2009: Your Audio Guide to Getting A 5. Awdeeo. Narrated by Awdeeo. (YA). 2009. 39.99 (978-0-9818187-6-4(5)) PrepLogic.

AP French: A Guide for the Language Course, Set. Richard Ladd & Colette Girard. (J). (gr. 10-12). 1992. 39.95 (978-0-8013-0642-6(6), 78582) Longman.

AP Spanish: A Guide for the Language Course, Set. Jose Diaz et al. 1989. 39.95 (978-0-8013-0169-8(6), 78003) Longman.

AP Test Prep: Mastering the Advanced Placement Spanish Language Exam. Jay Duhl & Felipe Mercado. audio compact disk 24.95 (978-0-8219-3495-1(3)); audio compact disk 39.95 (978-0-8219-3872-0(X)) EMC-Paradigm.

AP US History AudioLearn. 2 CDs. (Running Time: 2.2 hrs). 2008. audio compact disk 79.99 (978-1-59262-016-6(7)) AudioLearn.

Apache. Jane Coleman. (Running Time: 0 hr. 24 mins.). 1999. 10.95 (978-1-60083-490-5(6)) Iofy Corp.

***Apache.** Jane Candia Coleman. 2009. (978-1-60136-418-0(0)) Audio Holding.

Apache. Donald Clayton Porter. Read by Lloyd James. 4 vols. No. 14. 2004. 25.00 (978-1-58807-230-6(4)); (978-1-58807-761-5(6)); audio compact disk 30.00 (978-1-58807-414-0(5)) Am Pubng Inc.

Apache. Dana Fuller Ross, pseud. Read by Lloyd James. 5 vols. No. 14. 2004. audio compact disk (978-1-58807-878-0(7)) Am Pubng Inc.

Apache Ambush. unabr. ed. Will Cook. Read by William Dufris. 5 cass. (Running Time: 7 hrs.). (Sagebrush Western Ser.). (J). 1999. 49.95 (978-1-57490-226-6(1)) Pub: ISIS Lrg Prnt GBR. Dist(s): Ulverscroft US

Apache (Jicarilla) CDs & Text. Alan Wilson & Rita V. Martine. 4 CDs. (Running Time: 4 hrs.). (APA.). 2005. audio compact disk 75.00 (978-1-57970-162-8(0), AFAP10D) J Norton Pubs.

Apache Medicine & the Hard Way: Unabridged Stories from the Tonto Woman & Other Western Stories. Elmore Leonard. 2004. 5.95 (978-0-7435-4670-6(9)) Pub: S&S Audio. Dist(s): S and S Inc

Apache Moon. unabr. ed. A. L. McWilliams. Read by Maynard Villers. 6 cass. (Running Time: 6 hrs. 18 mins.). 1996. 39.95 (978-1-55686-683-8(6)) Books in Motion.
New Mexico Territory, 1876, back when the region was erupting with racial tension & violence. Apaches, Mexicans & Anglos were fighting for control of New Mexico. Romance included.

Apache Mountain Justice. unabr. ed. Ray Hogan. Read by William Dufris. 4 cass. (Running Time: 4 hrs.). (Sagebrush Western Ser.). (J). 1999. 44.95 (978-1-57490-294-5(6)) Pub: ISIS Lrg Prnt GBR. Dist(s): Ulverscroft US

***apacible y poderosa voz de Dios: Como escuchar a Dios y tener agallas para Responder.** unabr. ed. Zondervan. (SPA.). 2010. audio compact disk 14.99 (978-0-8297-5839-9(9)) Pub: Vida Pubs. Dist(s): Zondervan

***apacible y poderosa voz de Dios: Hearing God, Having the Guts to Respond.** unabr. ed. Zondervan. (Running Time: 9 hrs. 26 mins. 45 sec.). (ENG & SPA.). 2010. audio compact disk 14.99 (978-0-8297-5840-5(2)) Pub: Vida Pubs. Dist(s): Zondervan

Apathetic Ep. Contrib. by Relient K. Prod. by Mark Lee Townsend & Matthew Thiessen. Contrib. by Toby McKeehan & Joey Elwood. 2005. audio compact disk 13.98 (978-5-558-71334-3(8)) Gotee Records.

Ape House. unabr. ed. Sara Gruen. Read by Paul Boehmer. 9 CDs. (Running Time: 11 hrs.). 2010. audio compact disk 40.00 (978-0-7393-6854-1(0), Random AudioBks) Pub: Random Audio Pubg. Dist(s): Random

Ape Who Guards the Balance, Elizabeth Peters, pseud. Narrated by Barbara Rosenblat. 12 cass. (Running Time: 15 hrs.). (Amelia Peabody Ser.: No. 10). 1998. 96.00 (978-0-7887-2473-2(8), 95548E7) Recorded Bks.
When the youngest members of the Peabody Emerson expedition purchase a papyrus of an ancient magical manuscript, the prospects for the 1907 archaeological season in Egypt turns from dull to deadly. Includes an exclusive author interview.

Ape Who Guards the Balance. abr. ed. Elizabeth Peters, pseud. Read by Samantha Eggar. 4 cass. (Running Time: 6 hrs.). (Amelia Peabody Ser.: No. 10). 2001. 25.00 (978-1-59040-136-1(0), Phoenix Audio) Pub: Amer Intl Pub. Dist(s): PerseuPGW

Apellate Advocacy & Procedure: Pennsylvania & Federal. 1987. bk. 90.00; 45.00 PA Bar Inst.

Apert Syndrome - A Bibliography & Dictionary for Physicians, Patients, & Genome Researchers. Compiled by Icon Group International, Inc. Staff. 2007. ring bd. 28.95 (978-0-497-11333-9(3)) Icon Grp.

Apex Hides the Hurt. unabr. ed. Colson Whitehead. Read by Peter Jay Fernandez. 4 cass. (Running Time: 6 hrs.). 2006. 39.75 (978-1-4193-8710-4(3), 98331) Recorded Bks.
Best-selling author Colson Whitehead has been a finalist for numerous prestigious honors, including the Pulitzer Prize. His works are lauded for their insight into the state of race in America. Here, a small Midwestern town is having an identity crisis - should they have a new techno-savvy name or a name honoring the freedmen who founded the town? Or is the current name just fine? They call in a professional naming consultant, famous for naming Apex bandages - guaranteed to match any skin color. But even he is losing his faith in monikers.

Apex Memory Adventage - The Exam Dyamic. abr. ed. 2 cass. (Running Time: 2 hrs.). 1997. bk. 22.95 (978-0-9670753-0-3(0)) Apex Audio Bks.
In need of retaining information & recalling it back.

Aphasia: Program from the Award-Winning Public Radio Series, 437. Interview. Hosted by Peter Kramer. 1 CD. (Running Time: 59 minutes). 2006. audio compact disk 21.95 (978-1-933644-33-2(8)) Lichtenstein Creat.
This week, The Infinite Mind looks at Aphasia, when words literally fail you.Aphasia is the terrifying loss of language; destruction of speech, reading, writing or comprehension. It occurs when there is damage to the brain from a stroke, head trauma, certain neurological diseases, that has affected the language areas of their brain.To begin, The Infinite Mind?s Nina Mitchell visits with two aphasia patients.Dr. Fred Goodwin talks with Dr. David Caplan, a Harvard neurologist, to understand where the language centers are, and what aphasia has taught scientists about the brain.Next, we chat with, and listen to, renowned mezzo-soprano Jan Curtis, who lost much of her speech from a stroke, but still maintains the capacity to sing as she used to, beautifully.Harvard historian of science Dr. Anne Harrington talks about the way aphasia was discovered in the 1800's, and its resistance from religious figures. If language was localized, in a specific part of the brain, where was the soul?We discuss with Dr. Audrey Holland, a professor of speech pathology at the University of Arizona, how speech therapists treat aphasia, and we talk with Tom Flynn, is a high level patient who just occasionally slips up. He tells us what aphasia has done to his relationship

with his wife.For futuristic treatment options, we speak with neurologist Dr. Steven Small of the University of Chicago, who envisions placing patients in MRIs to see where their brains light up, so that they can have the most useful speech therapy treatment possible.Finally, commentary from John Hockenberry, who himself is rarely silent.

Aphasia "My Life in the Mists" Rosemary K. Collett. Read by Neva Duyndam. 1 cass. (Running Time: 45 mins.). 1991. 9.95 (978-1-878159-17-5(8)) Duvall Media.
The author, a writer & lecturer, tells how she learned to communicate after a stroke. Written with compassion & humor.

APHC Christmas: With Garrison Keillor & Hundreds of Friends & Acquaintances. unabr. abr. ed. Garrison Keillor. 2 CDs. (Running Time: 2 hrs.). (ENG.). 1995. audio compact disk 24.95 (978-1-56511-124-0(9), 1565111249) Pub: HighBridge. Dist(s): Workman Pub

APHC Movie Tie-in 10-Copy Prepack. Garrison Keillor. (Running Time: 16 hrs. 15 mins.). (ENG.). 2006. audio compact disk 199.50 (978-1-59887-061-9(0)) Pub: Penguin-HghBrdg. Dist(s): Penguin Grp USA

Aphrodite. Pierre Louys. Read by C. Deis. 2 cass. (FRE.). 1991. 26.95 (1074-VSL) Olivia & Hill.
The late 19th-century poet & novelist tells the story of the courtesan Chrysis, whose beauty was often compared to that of Aphrodite & her lover Dimitrion whom she has decided to put to a test.

Aphrodite. unabr. ed. Russell Andrews. Read by Buck Schirner. 7 cass. (Running Time: 11 hrs.). 2004. 32.95 (978-1-59086-950-5(8), 1590869508, BAU); 87.25 (978-1-59086-951-2(6), 1590869516, Unabridge Lib Edns) Brilliance Audio.
It looked for all the world like a terrible, tragic accident. Susanna Morgan had gotten up in the middle of the night, tripped, fallen, and broken her neck. Yet when detective Justin Westwood inspects the victim's apartment, he can't help noticing that the details don't quite add up. The glass on the bedside table is knocked over but there are no cuts on her body. The scrape on her knee looks suspiciously fresh. And then a terrified witness comes forward, confirming his worst fear. This is no accident. This is murder. Justin Westwood moved to East End Harbor to escape a dark, disturbing past, and to lead a quiet life. He had retreated from reality by taking a menial post with a small-town Long Island police department, drowning his troubles in mindless traffic duty and lots of booze. Now his dormant professionalism is awakened after Susanna's brutal murder. This is just the kind of reality check that Justin needs, and he will stop at nothing to get to the bottom of this madness - to find the meaning of the mysterious "Aphrodite" - and maybe save himself in the process.

Aphrodite. unabr. ed. Russell Andrews. Read by Buck Schirner. (Running Time: 11 hrs.). 2004. 39.25 (978-1-59335-492-3(4), 1593354924, Brinc Audio MP3 Lib) Brilliance Audio.

Aphrodite. unabr. ed. Russell Andrews. Read by Buck Schirner. (Running Time: 11 hrs.). 2004. 39.25 (978-1-59710-021-2(8), 159710218, BADLE); 24.95 (978-1-59710-020-5(X), 159710020X, BAD) Brilliance Audio.

Aphrodite. unabr. ed. Russell Andrews. Read by Buck Schirner. (Running Time: 11 hrs.). 2004. 24.95 (978-1-59335-261-5(1), 1593352611) Soulmate Audio Bks.

Aphrodite & Eros. Read by James Wyly. 1 cass. (Running Time: 2 hrs.). (Facing the Gods Ser.: No. 7). 1987. 16.95 (978-0-7822-0335-6(3), 291) C G Jung IL.

Apiculteur. l.t. ed. Maxence Fermine. (French Ser.). 2001. bk. 30.99 (978-2-84011-414-7(3)) Pub: UlverLrgPrint GBR. Dist(s): Ulverscroft US

Apocalipsis de San Juan. unabr. ed. San Juan. Read by Pedro Montoya.Tr. of Apocalypse of Saint John. (SPA.). 2002. audio compact disk 13.00 (978-958-43-0140-6(3)) YoYoMusic.

***Apocalipsis Revelando el Fin: Tercer Acto: el Telón Final.** Charles R. Swindoll. 2009. audio compact disk 38.00 (978-1-57972-762-8(X)) Insight Living.

Apocalipsis Revelando el Fin, Primer Acto: El Escenario Celestial. Charles R. Swindoll.Tr. of Revelation Unveiling the End, Act 1: Unveiling the End. 2008. audio compact disk 35.00 (978-1-57972-760-4(3)) Insight Living.

Apocalipsis Revelando el Fin, Segundo Acto: El Drama Terrenal. Charles R. Swindoll.Tr. of Revelation Unveiling the End, Act 2: the Earthly Drama. 2008. audio compact disk 35.00 (978-1-57972-761-1(1)) Insight Living.

Apocalypse: The Book of Revelation within Orthodox Christian Tradition. Speeches. Thomas Hopko. 4. 2006. audio compact disk 29.00 (978-0-88141-305-2(4)) St Vladimirs.
This lecture series on the Book of Revelation links the early Christian liturgy with the symbols in the scripture, and, discrediting futuristic prophecy, concentrates instead on the experience of eternal life in Christ Jesus in the worship of the Christian community.

Apocalypse Burning: Apocalypse Series. Mel Odom. 2004. 38.99 (978-1-4143-0034-4(4)) Tyndale Hse.

Apocalypse Manana: Opera Electrónica for the New Millenium. Guillermo Gomez-Pena & Guillermo Galindo. 1 CD. (Running Time: 90 min.). 2002. audio compact disk 15.00 (978-0-9717035-1-3(5)) Pub: Calaca Pr. Dist(s): SPD-Small Pr Dist
"This is old-fashioned West Coast vision and prophecy time-warped into a future of digital polyculturalism that's already here. Gómez-Peña speaks, shouts, whispers, and gushes in forked and curled tongues... Galindo surrounds him in cut-up sound clouds of opera, speed metal, and urban noise -a jagged electro-ambience that converts the Hotel California into "la mansión de la muerte.".

Apocalypse of Saint John see Apocalipsis de San Juan

Apocalypse of Saint John. San Juan. Read by Pedro Montoya. (Running Time: 1 hr.). 2002. 14.95 (978-1-60083-140-9(0), Audiofy Corp) Iofy Corp.

Apocalypse Watch. unabr. ed. Robert Ludlum. Read by Michael Prichard. 19 cass. (Running Time: 28 hrs. 30 mins.). 1995. 152.00 (978-0-7366-3162-4(3), 3826 A/B) Books on Tape.
CIA agent goes undercover to find out if huge neo-Nazi group has high-ranking U.S. officials on its rolls. Ludlum at his best.

Apocalypse Watch, Pt. 1. unabr. ed. Robert Ludlum. Read by Michael Prichard. 10 cass. (Running Time: 1 hr. 30 min. per cass.). 1995. 80.00 (3833-A) Books on Tape.
Deep in Austria's Hausruck mountains lies the fortress of a huge neo-Nazi organization, the Brotherhood of the Watch. Born just after the Third Reich's defeat, it's cash-rich, heavily armed, well-connected - & planning to take over the world. No one knows that better than Harry Latham, an American undercover agent who's penetrated the Brotherhood's highest ranks. Then Harry's cover is blown & he disappears. The CIA holds its collective breath until Harry emerges with an explosive list of Brotherhood supporters, many of them high U.S. officials. But is the list a fake? To find out, Harry's brother, Drew, also a CIA agent, takes on his brother's identity. Now he's got to dodge assassins who want him & his brother - dead.

Apocalypse Watch, Pt. 2. unabr. ed. Robert Ludlum. Read by Michael Prichard. 9 cass. (Running Time: 13 hrs. 30 mins.). 1995. 72.00 (3833-B) Books on Tape.

Apocalypse wow: a memoir for the end of Time. James Finn Garner. 2004. 7.95 (978-0-7435-4163-3(4)) Pub: S&S Audio. Dist(s): S and S Inc

Apollinaire. Poems. Read by Jean Vilar. 1 cass. (Golden Treasury of Poetry & Prose Ser.). (FRE.). 1992. 16.95 (1054-SA) Olivia & Hill.

Apollinaire, Cocteau, Eluard, Aragon. unabr. ed. 1 cass. (FRE.). 15.95 (CFR400) J Norton Pubs.

Apollo & Dionysius. Ayn Rand. Read by Ayn Rand. 2 cass. (Running Time: 2 hrs.). 24.95 (978-1-56114-008-4(2), AR03D) Second Renaissance.
A probing concretization of the issue of reason versus emotion via an analysis of two contrasting events: the glorious achievement of the Apollo 11 moon flight & the mindless mud-wallowing of the Woodstock festival. An extensive question period covers such issues as: the irrationality of the Vietnam War - & of the student protestors; the motive behind the attacks on saccharine & cyclamates; why Ayn Rand devoted time to writing social commentary.

Apollo Theater: Revival for Black Entertainment. 1 cass. (Running Time: 30 mins.). 8.00 (G0600B090, HarperThor) HarpC GBR.

Apollo Thirteen. abr. ed. Jim Lovell & Jeffrey Kluger. 2 cass. (Running Time: 2 hrs.). 1996. 20.50 (53543) Books on Tape.
True story of the moon flight that nearly ended in catastrophe. Lovell relives the rescue that brought astronauts back to earth despite crippled craft, impossible odds.

Apollo 13: The Real Mission. Ed. by Pent. 1 cass. 1996. 10.95 (978-1-885959-46-1(X), JRCS7031) Jerden Recs.
Actual voices & sound of the Apollo 13 mission during the most critical times in outer space.

Apollo's Gold, Level 2. Antoinette Moses. Contrib. by Philip Prowse. (Running Time: 1 hr. 18 mins.). (Cambridge English Readers Ser.). (ENG.). 2000. 9.45 (978-0-521-77547-2(7)) Cambridge U Pr.

Apollyon: An Experience in Sound & Drama. unabr. ed. Tim LaHaye & Jerry B. Jenkins. Read by Jack Sondericker. 9 CDs. (Running Time: 10 hrs. 48 min.). (Left Behind Ser.: Bk. 5). 2001. audio compact disk 58.50 (978-1-58116-129-8(8)) Books in Motion.
Rayford Steel and the surviving members of the Tribulation Force now face a plague of scorpionlike locusts led by Apollyon, chief demon of the abyss.

Apollyon: The Destroyer Is Unleashed. Tim LaHaye & Jerry B. Jenkins. Narrated by Richard Ferrone. 9 CDs. (Running Time: 10 hrs. 45 mins.). (Left Behind Ser.: Bk. 5). 2000. audio compact disk 89.00 (978-0-7887-4770-0(3), C1236E7) Recorded Bks.
The Tribulation Force is gathering in Jerusalem for the Meeting of the Witnesses. But as judgement prophecies are fulfilled, the sun dims & a plague of anguish is released on earth.

Apollyon: The Destroyer Is Unleashed. Tim LaHaye & Jerry B. Jenkins. Read by Richard Ferrone. 6 cass. (Running Time: 10 hrs. 45 mins.). (Left Behind Ser.: Bk. 5). 2004. 29.95 (978-0-7887-5127-1(1), 00074); audio compact disk 39.95 (978-0-7887-5136-3(0), 00072) Recorded Bks.

Apollyon: The Destroyer Is Unleashed. unabr. ed. Tim LaHaye & Jerry B. Jenkins. Read by Jack Sondericker. 8 cass. (Running Time: 10 hrs. 48 min.). (Left Behind Ser.: Bk. 5). 1999. 49.95 (978-1-55686-934-1(7)) Books in Motion.
Rayford Steel and the surviving members of the Tribulation Force now face a plague of scorpionlike locusts led by Apollyon, chief demon of the abyss.

Apollyon: The Destroyer Is Unleashed. unabr. ed. Tim LaHaye & Jerry B. Jenkins. Narrated by Richard Ferrone. 8 cass. (Running Time: 10 hrs. 45 mins.). (Left Behind Ser.: Bk. 5). 2000. 70.00 (978-0-7887-4050-3(4), 95870E7) Recorded Bks.
The Tribulation Force is gathering in Jerusalem for the Meeting of the Witnesses. But as judgement prophecies are fulfilled, the sun dims & a plague of anguish is released on earth.

Apologetics: Who, What, When, Why, & How? John Robbins. 1 cass. (Blue Banner Lectures Ser.: No. 1). 5.00 Trinity Found.

Apologetics in Evangelism-mp3. Read by Douglas Wilson & Douglas M. Jones. 1999. 9.50 (978-1-59128-341-6(8)) Canon Pr ID.

Apologetics in Evangelism-tape. Read by Douglas Wilson & Douglas M. Jones. 4 cass. 1999. 15.00 (978-1-59128-343-0(4)) Canon Pr ID.

Apologetics of Jesus & Paul. John Robbins. 1 cass. (Blue Banner Lectures Ser.: No. 5). 5.00 Trinity Found.

Apologetics on the High Seas. 2006. audio compact disk 39.95 (978-1-888992-98-4(0)) Catholic Answers.

Apologia Pro Vita Sua & Six Sermons see Cambridge Treasury of English Prose: Dickens to Butler

Apologie for Poetrie see Cambridge Treasy Malory

Apologies. Marianne Williamson. Read by Marianne Williamson. 1 cass. (Running Time: 90 mins.). (Lectures on a Course in Miracles). (ENG.). 1995. 10.00 (978-1-56170-175-9(0), M703) Hay House.

Apologize, Apologize! unabr. ed. Elizabeth Kelly. Read by Jeff Woodman. 9 CDs. (Running Time: 10 hrs. 15 mins.). 2009. audio compact disk 34.95 (978-1-59887-864-6(6), 1598878646) Pub: HighBridge. Dist(s): Workman Pub

Apology: The Importance & Power of Saying I'm Sorry. Sheila Quinn Simpson. 1 CD. 2004. audio compact disk 10.00 (978-0-9755497-1-1(5)) Balcony Pubns.
This CD is an audio version of the printed book, "Apology: The Importance and Power of Saying 'I'm Sorry'". Read by the author...a perfect inspirational gift for those too busy to sit down and read the book.

Apology; Crito & The Republic, Bks. I, II. unabr. ed. Plato. Read by Walter Covell. 4 cass. (Running Time: 4 hrs. 50 mins.). 1989. 35.00 (C-192) Jimcin Record.
Socratic dialogues.

Apology for Bad Dreams see Poetry of Robinson Jeffers

Apology for Raymond Sebond, unabr. ed. Michel de Montaigne. Read by Robert L. Halvorson. 6 cass. (Running Time: 9 hrs.). 42.95 (33) Halvorson Assocs.

Apology for Socrates, unabr. ed. Plato. Read by Robert L. Halvorson. 2 cass. (Running Time: 3 hrs.). Incl. Crito. (1); 14.95 (1) Halvorson Assocs.

Apology for Socrates, Crite & The Republic. collector's ed. Plato. Read by Walter Covell. 5 cass. (Running Time: 5 hrs.). 1988. 30.00 (978-0-7366-3946-0(2), 9192) Books on Tape.
Three books in which Plato carries on the work of Socrates, his master.

Aponitolau & the Star Maiden: From Mga Kuwentong Bayan: Folk Stories from the Philippines. Read by Alex Torres. Perf. by Mahal. Ed. by Alice Lucas. 2 cass. (Running Time: 2 hrs.). (ENG & TAG.). (J). (gr. k-12). 1995. 15.00 SF Study Ctr.
Dramatic reading in English & Tagalog of a folk tale from Mga Kuwentong Bayan, with music played on indigenous instruments.

Apostle. abr. ed. Brad Thor. Read by Armand Schultz. (Running Time: 6 hrs. 0 mins. 0 sec.). (ENG.). 2009. audio compact disk 29.99 (978-0-7435-7931-5(3)) Pub: S&S Audio. Dist(s): S and S Inc

***Apostle.** abr. ed. Brad Thor. Read by Armand Schultz. (Running Time: 6 hrs. 0 mins. 0 sec.). (ENG.). 2011. audio compact disk 14.99 (978-1-4423-4074-9(6)) Pub: S&S Audio. Dist(s): S and S Inc

Apostle. unabr. ed. Brad Thor. Read by Armand Schultz. (Running Time: 10 hrs. 30 mins. 0 sec.). 2009. audio compact disk 39.99 (978-0-7435-7933-9(X)) Pub: S&S Audio. Dist(s): S and S Inc

Apostle Paul. Instructed by Luke Timothy Johnson. 6 CDs. (Running Time: 6 hrs.). (C). bk. 39.95 (978-1-56585-367-6(9), 657) Teaching Co.

Apostle Paul, Vol. 1. Instructed by Luke Timothy Johnson. 6 pieces. (Running Time: 6 hrs.). (C). bk. 29.95 (978-1-56585-183-2(8), 657) Teaching Co.

Apostles & Shepherds. Derek Prince. 4 cass. 19.95 (A-AS1) Derek Prince.

Apostolic Anointing. Francis Frangipane. 1 cass. (Running Time: 90 mins.). (Strategies for our Cities Ser.: Vol. 10). 2000. 5.00 (FF06-010) Morning NC.
This series provides practical, biblical solutions that have been tested & have born fruit for those with a vision for their cities.

Apostolic Calling & Ministry Series. Rick Joyner. 3 cass. (Running Time: 4 hrs. 30 mins.). 2000. 15.00 (RJ07-000) Morning NC.
This series gives a foundational understanding of the true apostolic authority that is being restored to the church.

Apostolic Church to Constantine. Stephen Mansfield. 1 cass. (Running Time: 90 mins.). (Basic Church History Ser.: Vol. 2). 2000. 5.00 (SM01-002) Morning NC.
Stephen does a masterful job of making church history come to life. This is an overview starting from pentecost & continuing through the 20th century.

Apostolic Function. Rick Joyner. 1 cass. (Running Time: 90 mins.). (Apostolic Calling & Ministry Ser.: Vol. 2). 2000. 5.00 (RJ07-002) Morning NC.
This series gives a foundational understanding of the true apostolic authority that is being restored to the church.

Apostolic Succession of Christian Mystics: Some Examples. John Yungblut. 5 cass. (Running Time: 5 hrs.). Incl. Apostolic Succession of Christian Mystics: The Aesthetic Mysticism of Augustine of Hippo. 1 cass. (Running Time: 1 hr.). 1977.; Apostolic Succession of Christian Mystics: The Christ-Centered Mysticism of Paul the Apostle. 1 cass. (Running Time: 1 hr.). 1977.; Apostolic Succession of Christian Mystics: The God-Centered Mysticism of the Fourth Gospel. 1 cass. (Running Time: 1 hr.). 1977.; Apostolic Succession of Christian Mystics: The Material Mysticism of Teilhard de Chardin. 1977.; Apostolic Succession of Christian Mystics: The Philosophical Mysticism of Meister Eckhardt. 1977.; 1977. 17.50; Pendle Hill.

Apostolic Succession of Christian Mystics: The Aesthetic Mysticism of Augustine of Hippo see Apostolic Succession of Christian Mystics: Some Examples

Apostolic Succession of Christian Mystics: The Christ-Centered Mysticism of Paul the Apostle see Apostolic Succession of Christian Mystics: Some Examples

Apostolic Succession of Christian Mystics: The God-Centered Mysticism of the Fourth Gospel see Apostolic Succession of Christian Mystics: Some Examples

Apostolic Succession of Christian Mystics: The Material Mysticism of Teilhard de Chardin see Apostolic Succession of Christian Mystics: Some Examples

Apostolic Succession of Christian Mystics: The Philosophical Mysticism of Meister Eckhardt see Apostolic Succession of Christian Mystics: Some Examples

Apostolic Teams. Derek Prince. 3 cass. 14.95 (I-AT1) Derek Prince.

Apothecary Rose. unabr. ed. Candace Robb. Read by Stephen Thorne. 8 cass. (Running Time: 9 hrs.). (Owen Archer Mystery Ser.: Vol. 1). 1997. 69.95 (961006) Pub: ISIS Audio GBR. Dist(s): Ulverscroft US
In 1363, in the cathedral city of York, people are dying in mysterious circumstances. But there seems to be a common thread - the herbal remedies dispensed by Nicholas Wilton, Master Apothecary. Owen Archer apprentices himself to the apothecary, although it is from Wilton's wife Lucie that he must learn the arcane secrets of the trade. And when the deaths continue, he realizes to his horror he must count Lucie among the suspects.

Apothecary Rose. unabr. ed. Candace Robb. Read by Stephen Thorne. 10 CDs. (Running Time: 10 hrs. 45 mins.). 1999. audio compact disk 99.95 (978-0-7531-0706-5(6), 107066) Pub: ISIS Audio GBR. Dist(s): Ulverscroft US

***Apothecary's Daughter.** abr. ed. Julie Klassen. Narrated by Tavia Gilbert. (ENG.). 2009. 14.98 (978-1-59644-703-5(6), christaudio) christianaud.

Apothecary's Daughter. abr. ed. Julie Klassen. Narrated by Tavia Gilbert. (Running Time: 10 hrs. 45 mins. 0 sec.). (ENG.). (YA). 2009. audio compact disk 24.98 (978-1-59644-702-8(8), christaudio) christianaud.

Apotheosis Saga. Voice by David Ossman et al. 3 cass. (Running Time: 3 hrs.). 2001. 29.95 (CPOD128); audio compact disk 39.95 (CPOD030) Lodestone Catalog.

Apotheosis Saga, Episodes 1-8. Cephalopod Productions Staff. 3 cass. 29.95 (978-1-57677-081-8(8), CPOD128) Lodestone Catalog.

Apotheosis Saga: Division; Many Friends, Episodes 7 - 8. Cephalopod Productions Staff. 1 cass. 12.94 (978-1-57677-079-5(6), CPOD003) Lodestone Catalog.

Appalachian Sketches. Perf. by Gloriae Dei Cantores & Mark O'Connor. 2001. audio compact disk 16.95 (978-1-55725-281-4(5), GDCD031) Paraclete MA.

Appaloosa. unabr. ed. Robert B. Parker. 4 cass. (Running Time: 6 hrs.). 2005. 36.00 (978-1-4159-2019-0(2)); audio compact disk 38.25 (978-1-4159-2136-4(9)) Pub: Books on Tape. Dist(s): NetLibrary CO

Apparition see Love Poems of John Donne

Apparition of Mrs. Veal see Classic Ghost Stories, Vol. 1, A Collection

Apparition of Mrs. Veal. Daniel Defoe. 1980. (N-38) Jimcin Record.

Apparitions in the Ukraine. Father Michael. 1 cass. (Running Time: 60 mins.). (Mother Angelica Live Ser.). 1989. 10.00 (978-1-55794-118-3(1)) Eternal Wrd TV.
Tells about the plight of the persecuted Catholics in the Ukraine & Our Lady's message to them.

Appeal. abr. ed. John Grisham. (ENG.). 2009. audio compact disk 14.99 (978-0-7393-8214-1(4), Random AudioBks) Pub: Random Audio Pubg. Dist(s): Random

Appeal. unabr. ed. John Grisham. 7 cassettes. (Running Time: 1 hr, 48 min). 2008. (978-1-4159-4875-0(5)) Books on Tape.

Appeal. unabr. ed. John Grisham. Read by Michael Beck. 10 CDs. 2008. audio compact disk 100.00 (978-1-4159-4358-8(3), BksonTape) Pub: Random Audio Pubg. Dist(s): Random
In a crowded courtroom in Mississippi, a jury returns a shocking verdict against a chemical company accused of dumping toxic waste into a small town's water supply, causing the worst "cancer cluster" in history. The company appeals to the Mississippi Supreme Court, whose nine justices will one day either approve the verdict or reverse it. Who are the nine? How will they vote? Can one be replaced before the case is ultimately decided? The chemical company is owned by a Wall Street predator named Carl Trudeau,

and Mr. Trudeau is convinced the Court is not friendly enough. With judicial elections looming, he decides to try to purchase himself a seat on the Court. The cost is a few million dollars, a drop in the bucket for a billionaire like Mr. Trudeau. Through an intricate web of conspiracy and deceit, his political operatives recruit a young, unsuspecting candidate. They finance him, manipulate him, market him, and mold him into a potential Supreme Court justice. Their Supreme Court justice.

Appeal. unabr. ed. John Grisham. Read by Michael Beck. 10 CDs. (Running Time: 12 hrs. 30 mins.). (John Grisham Ser.). (ENG.). 2008. audio compact disk 44.95 (978-0-7393-1653-5(2), Random AudioBks) Pub: Random Audio Pubg. Dist(s): Random

Appearance of Evil. unabr. ed. Christopher A. Lane. Read by Juanita Parker. 12 cass. (Running Time: 13 hrs. 30 mins.). 2000. 64.95 (978-1-55686-980-8(0)) Books in Motion.
Was it really Satanic ritual abuse, or something more human & just as deadly?.

Appearances. unabr. ed. Chief Little Summer. Interview with Warm Night Rain. 1 CD. (Appearances). (J). (gr. 6-12). 1999. audio compact disk 14.95 CD. (978-1-880440-11-7(3)) Piqua Pr.
Humor via parapsychology. Historical teaching/educational time travel via teleportation.

Appeasement: A Study in Political Decline. unabr. ed. A. L. Rowse. Read by Stuart Courtney. 5 cass. (Running Time: 5 hrs.). 1984. 30.00 (978-0-7366-0595-3(9), 1562) Books on Tape.
A study of the appeasement of Hitler & its disastrous consequences.

Appel, Pts. 1-3, set. Charles de Gaulle. Read by Francois Cognard. 9 cass. (FRE.). 1995. 94.95 (1762-4) Olivia & Hill.
De Gaulle's memoirs.

Appel Pt. 1: La Pente, la Chute, la France Libre. Charles de Gaulle. Read by Francois Cognard. 3 cass. (Running Time: 3 hrs.). (FRE.). 1995. 34.95 (1762-LV) Olivia & Hill.
The military, political & diplomatic events that lead to World War II, the reasons for France's defeat & the setting up of Free France in London.

Appel Pt. 2: L'Afrique, Londres, l'Orient. Charles de Gaulle. Read by Francois Cognard. 3 cass. (Running Time: 3 hrs.). (FRE.). 1995. 34.95 (1763-LV) Olivia & Hill.
The difficulties in rallying French colonies & the tenuous relationships with the English.

Appel Pt. 3: Les Allies, la France Combattante. Charles de Gaulle. Read by Francois Cognard. 3 cass. (FRE.). 1995. 34.95 (1764-LV) Olivia & Hill.
The entry of the United States in the war, the difficult relationship with the Americans & the governments in exile.

Appel de la Foret, Jack London. Read by Jacques Weber. 2 cass. (Running Time: 2 hrs.).Tr. of Call of the Wild. (FRE.). 1992. bk. 35.95 (1GA070) Olivia & Hill.
The dog Buck has been living peacefully for four years in the garden of Judge Miller when he is stolen & sold. Gold has been discovered in the Yukon & intelligent dogs are needed to pull the sleds. Buck is projected into a life of misery.

Appel de l'Abbe Pierre. Abbe Pierre. 1 cass. (FRE.). 1995. 16.95 (1660-RF) Olivia & Hill.
The radio series "l'Histoire en Direct' brings us l'Abbe Pierre's February 1954 appeal to the French nation on behalf of the homeless. Plus many other documents & interviews of the period from French oral archives.

Appellate Advocacy. Read by Richard B. Wickersham. 1 cass. 1988. 20.00 (AL-42) PA Bar Inst.

Appellate Advocacy & Procedure: Pennsylvania & Federal. 1987. bk. 90.00 incl. book.; 45.00 cass. only.; 45.00 book only. PA Bar Inst.

Appellate Practice: Viewpoints by, Before & Behind the Bench. Contrib. by Melvin P. Antell et al. (Running Time: 4 hrs.). 1985. 85.00 incl. program handbk. NJ Inst CLE.
Includes how to file & appeal, interlocutory appeals, appellate motion practice, resolving problems peculiar to criminal appeal, Appellate Division settlement program & more.

Appetite for Life: Julia Child, unabr. ed. Noel R. Fitch. Read by Nadia May. 16 cass. (Running Time: 24 hrs.). 1998. 99.95 (978-0-7861-1334-7(0), 2231) Blckstn Audio.
Julia Child became a household name when she entered the lives of millions of americans through our hearts & kitchens. Yet few know the richly varied private life that lies behind this icon whose stratuesque height & warmly enthused warble have become synonymous with the art of cooking. We meet the earthy & outrageous Julia, who, at age eighty-five, remains a complex role model.

Appetite for Self-Destruction: The Spectacular Crash of the Record Industry in the Digital Age. unabr. ed. Steve Knopper. Read by Dan John Miller. (Running Time: 11 hrs.). 2009. 39.97 (978-1-4233-7523-4(8), 9781423375234, BADLE); 39.97 (978-1-4233-7521-0(1), 9781423375210, Brlnc Audio MP3 Lib); 24.99 (978-1-4233-7522-7(X), 9781423375227, BAD); 24.99 (978-1-4233-7520-3(3), 9781423375203, Brilliance MP3); audio compact disk 92.97 (978-1-4233-7519-7(X), 9781423375197, BriAudCD Unabrid); audio compact disk 34.99 (978-1-4233-7518-0(1), 9781423375180, Bril Audio CD Unabri) Brilliance Audio.

Appetizers & Ambience: Piano. Prod. by Kevin Rhoads & Chuck Dennie. pap. bk. Spirit Led.

Appetizers & Ambience: Saxophone. 2002. pap. bk. Spirit Led.

Applause! Ed. by Lynn Freeman Olson. Contrib. by Valery Lloyd-Watts. (ENG.). 1992. audio compact disk 10.95 (978-0-7390-2273-3(3)) Alfred Pub.

Applause 1. Carole L. Bigler et al. (ENG.). 1992. audio compact disk 10.95 (978-0-7390-1837-8(X), 4051) Alfred Pub.

Apple a Day. Sundance/Newbridge, LLC Staff. (Early Science Ser.). (gr. k-3). 2007. audio compact disk 12.00 (978-1-4007-6363-4(0)); audio compact disk 12.00 (978-1-4007-6362-7(2)); audio compact disk 12.00 (978-1-4007-6361-0(4)) Sund Newbrdge.

Apple Barrel. unabr. ed. Susan Sallis. Read by Anne Dover. 14 CDs. (Running Time: 14 hrs. 18 mins.). (Sound Ser.). (J). 2002. audio compact disk 104.95 (978-1-86042-933-0(5)) Pub: ISIS Lrg Prnt GBR. Dist(s): Ulverscroft US

Apple Barrel. unabr. ed. Susan Sallis. Read by Anne Dover. 12 cass. (Running Time: 12 hrs.). 2001. 94.95 (978-1-86042-807-4(X)) Pub: Soundings Ltd GBR. Dist(s): Ulverscroft US

***Apple Cart: Interlude.** abr. ed. Noel Coward. Read by Simon Jones. (ENG.). 2006. (978-0-06-125281-5(6), Harper Audio) HarperCollins Pubs.

Apple from Eden. Emma Blair. Read by Eve Karpf. 10 cass. (Running Time: 15 hrs.). 2002. 84.95 (CAB 1688) AudioGO.

Apple from Eden, Set. unabr. ed. Emma Blair. Read by Eve Karpf. 10 cass. 1999. 84.95 (CAB 1688) AudioGO.

Apple of His Eye. Neville Goddard. 1 cass. (Running Time: 62 mins.). 1965. 8.00 (9) J & L Pubns.
He taught Imagination Creates Reality. He was a powerfully influential teacher of God as Consciousness.

Apple Pie Family/Apples & More Apples. Steck-Vaughn Staff. 1 cass. (Running Time: 40 min.). (J). 1996. (978-0-8172-6460-4(4)) SteckVau.

Apple Pie 1A Cassette: Delta's Beginning ESL Program, Vol. 1. rev. ed. Jean Owensby et al. Ed. by Adae Iwataki. Illus. by Jim Ruskowski et al. 1995. audio compact disk 13.50 (978-0-937354-99-5(6), DeltPubng) Delta Systems.

Apple Pie 1B Cassette No. 1B: Delta's Beginning ESL Program. rev. ed. Jean Owensby et al. Ed. by Sadae Iwataki. Illus. by Jim Ruskowski et al. 1995. 13.50 (978-0-937354-50-6(3), DeltPubng) Delta Systems.

Apple Tree. Elvi Rhodes. 10 cass. (Soundings Ser.). (J). 2005. 84.95 (978-1-84283-888-4(1)); audio compact disk 99.95 (978-1-84283-918-8(7)) Pub: ISIS Lrg Prnt GBR. Dist(s): Ulverscroft US

Apple Tree & Other Tales. unabr. ed. John Galsworthy. Narrated by Flo Gibson. 4 cass. (Running Time: 5 hrs. 30 min.). 2003. 19.95 (978-1-55685-704-1(7)) Audio Bk Con.

Apple Tree Cottage: A Heart-Warming Tale of Life in an English Country Village. Rose Boucheron. Read by Patience Tomlinson. 5 cass. (Running Time: 6 hrs. 35 mins.). 2005. 49.95 (978-1-85903-857-4(3)) Pub: UlverLrgPrint GBR. Dist(s): Ulverscroft US

Apple-Tree Table & Other Sketches see Melville: Six Short Novels

***Apple Turnover Murder.** Joanne Fluke. (Hannah Swensen Mystery Ser.: No. 13). 2010. audio compact disk 34.99 (978-1-4407-8826-0(X)) Recorded Bks.

Apple Way: 12 Management Lessons from the World's Most Innovative Company. abr. ed. Jeffrey L. Cruikshank. Narrated by Grover Gardner. (Running Time: 16200 sec.). 2007. audio compact disk 28.00 (978-1-933309-25-5(3)) Pub: A Media Intl. Dist(s): Natl Bk Netwk

Appleby's, Elvi Rhodes. Read by Anne Dover. 8 cass. (Running Time: 8 hrs.). 1999. 69.95 (6805X) Pub: Soundings Ltd GBR. Dist(s): Ulverscroft US

Apples & Oranges. George Bloomer. audio compact disk Whitaker Hse.

Apples in Eden: Seven Deadly Sins. Albert Haase. 2 cass. (Running Time: 2 hrs.). 2001. 16.95 (A6570) St Anthony Mess Pr.

Appleworks Simplified: An Individualized Instruction Program Manual. John De Beck. (J). 1986. 151.50 (978-0-89420-249-0(9), 222030) Natl Book.

Appley Dapply's Nursery Rhymes. (Running Time: 15 mins.). (Beatrix Potter's Tales Ser.). (ps up). 10.00 (978-1-4025-1686-3(X)) Recorded Bks.

Applicant Interview Matching System. Richard G. Hammes. Read by Richard G. Hammes. 1 cass. (Running Time: 1 hr. 10 mins.). 1992. 19.95 (978-1-882561-25-4(2)) Hammes & Assocs.
Interview training program to assist managers to interview more effectively. Covers process, EEO issues, determining "fit" & how to access critical information.

Application of Faith & the Word in Life's Crisis & Challenges Workshop CD: What Will You Do When You Have Lost Your Momentum? 2005. audio compact disk 12.00 (978-0-9742312-9-7(0)) Treasure The Monemt.

Applications in the Afternoon. 2 cass. 1990. 16.00 set. Recorded Res.

Applied Calculus. (C). 2008. audio compact disk 13.95 (978-0-534-42383-4(3)) Pub: Brooks-Cole. Dist(s): CENGAGE Learn

Applied Calculus for the Managerial, Life, & Social Sciences. 6th ed. (C). 2005. audio compact disk 16.95 (978-0-495-01534-5(2)) Pub: Brooks-Cole. Dist(s): CENGAGE Learn

Applied Differentiation-Making it Work in the Classroom - Elementary, Vol. 1502E. (Enabling Teachers & Students to Thrive Ser.: Vol. 1500). (C). 2006. video 645.00 (978-1-58740-153-4(3)) SchImprove.

Applied Differentiation-Making it Work in the Classroom - Secondary, Vol. 1502S. (Enabling Teachers & Students to Thrive Ser.: Vol. 1500). 2006. video 645.00 (978-1-58740-154-1(1)) SchImprove.

Applied Economics: Thinking Beyond Stage One. Thomas Sowell. Read by Brian Emerson. (Running Time: 28800 sec.). 2006. 54.95 (978-0-7861-4503-4(X)); audio compact disk 55.00 (978-0-7861-7226-9(6)) Blckstn Audio.

Applied Economics: Thinking Beyond Stage One. unabr. ed. Thomas Sowell. Read by Brian Emerson. (Running Time: 28800 sec.). 2006. audio compact disk 29.95 (978-0-7861-7660-1(1)) Blckstn Audio.

Applied Economics: Thinking Beyond Stage One: Second Edition. unabr. ed. Thomas Sowell. (Running Time: 13 hrs. 5 mins.). (ENG.). 2009. audio compact disk 32.95 (978-1-4332-9130-2(4)) Blckstn Audio.

Applied Economics: Thinking Beyond Stage One: Second Edition. unabr. ed. Thomas Sowell. Read by Bill Wallace. (Running Time: 13 hrs. 50 mins.). (ENG.). 2009. 29.95 (978-1-4332-9131-9(2)); 79.95 (978-1-4332-9127-2(4)); audio compact disk 109.00 (978-1-4332-9128-9(2)) Blckstn Audio.

Applied Music Theory for Managers, Engineers, Producers & Artists 2nd Edition: What You Should Know & Why You Should Know It. 2nd rev. ed. Rev. by One Omik Music. 2nd. (ENG., 2008. pap. bk. 59.99 (978-0-9711360-0-7(9), lbm2505) One Omk Musc.

Applied Problem Solving Through Creative Thinking. Instructed by J. D. Reid. 6 cass. (Running Time: 5 hrs. 42 mins.). 25.00 manual. (35) Am Chemical.
Emphasizes techniques for the solution of problems requiring creative thinking.

Applied Relaxation Training. Matthew McKay & Patrick Fanning. 2 CDs. (Running Time: 75 mins). (Relaxation Skills CD Ser.). (ENG.). 2008. audio compact disk 13.95 (978-1-57224-637-9(5)) New Harbinger.

Applying for a Job, Level 1. 2 cass. (Running Time: 3 hrs.). (SmartReader Ser.). (J). 1999. pap. bk. & tchr. ed. 19.95 (978-0-7887-1155-8(5), 79416T3) Recorded Bks.
By following several important steps, completing a job application & preparing for an interview can be easier & more successful.

Applying for a Job, Level 2. 1 cass. (Running Time: 1 hr. 30 mins.). (SmartReader Ser.). (YA). 1999. pap. bk. & tchr. ed. 19.95 (978-0-7887-0553-3(9), 79335T3) Recorded Bks.

Applying Godly Wisdom: Ecc. 7:23-29. Ed Young. 1993. 4.95 (978-0-7417-1990-4(8), 990) Win Walk.

Applying Right Values. Swami Amar Jyoti. 1 cass. 1981. 9.95 (K-44) Truth Consciousness.
Wrong values can never satisfy. The way we think, we create. Opening the brain to the cosmic computer. God's mercy.

Applying the Benziger Model to Education. Featuring Katherine Benziger. 1993. audio compact disk 30.00 (978-1-880931-52-3(4)) KBA LLC.

Applying the Blood of Jesus. Lynne Hammond. 1 cass. (Running Time: 1 hr.). 2005. 5.00 (978-1-57399-218-3(6)); audio compact disk 5.00 (978-1-57399-266-4(6)) Mac Hammond.

Applying the Theory of Process to Psychology. unabr. ed. Frank Barr. 2 cass. (Running Time: 2 hrs.). 1985. 18.00 (978-1-56964-666-3(X), A0006-85) Sound Photosyn.
Referring to Arthur Young's theory, Frank is interestingly information dense.

Applying the Workbook Principles to All Gardens. 2 cass. (Running Time: 3 hrs.). 2004. 14.95 (978-0-927978-18-7(0), ST-109) Perelandra Ltd.

Applying the 10 Secrets for Success & Inner Peace. Wayne W. Dyer. 8 CDs. (ENG.). 2005. audio compact disk 69.95 (978-1-4019-0650-4(8)) Hay House.

Applying the 7 Steps to a 720 Credit Score Workbook & CD. Philip X. Tirone. Ed. by Jocelyn Baker. 2006. pap. bk. 79.95 (978-0-9768656-5-0(3)) SevenSteps.

Appoint Elders in Every City. Derek Prince. 1 cass. (I-5043) Derek Prince.

Appointed Time. Reuven Doron. 1 cass. (Running Time: 90 mins.). (Mystery of Israel & the Church Ser.: Vol. 3). 2000. 5.00 (RD01-003) Morning NC.
Reuven offers insight into the proper relationship between Israel & the church.

Appointment. 2004. DVD & audio compact disk 9.99 (978-0-01-222980-4(6)) D Christiano Films.

Appointment for Love. Perf. by Charles Boyer. 1 cass. (Running Time: 1 hr.). 7.95 (CC5065) Natl Recrd Co.

Appointment in Calcutta, unabr. ed. Elliot Tokson. Narrated by Alexander Spencer. 6 cass. (Running Time: 9 hrs.). 1982. 51.00 (978-1-55690-025-9(2), 82043E7) Recorded Bks.
In the early 20th century, India was still a frontier to the Westerner & a struggle for the native. Mix into this stew the Irish revolution & a man named Bull Dog McLaughlin. Add a dash of spice with the then new technologies, the airplane & the machine gun & top it all off with a quest for Alexander the Great's lost scrolls & the result is an irresistibly good yarn.

Appointment with Death: A Hercule Poirot Mystery. unabr. ed. Agatha Christie. Narrated by Hugh Fraser. (Running Time: 21600 sec.). (Hercule Poirot Mystery Ser.). (ENG.). 2006. audio compact disk 27.95 (978-1-57270-523-4(X)) Pub: AudioGO. Dist(s): Perseus Dist

Appointment with Death: A Hercule Poirot Mystery. unabr. ed. Agatha Christie & Hugh Fraser. (Running Time: 21600 sec.). (Hercule Poirot Mystery Ser.). 2006. 27.95 (978-1-57270-524-1(8)) Pub: Audio Partners. Dist(s): PerseuPGW

***Appointment with Fear: Classic BBC Radio Horror.** Compiled by Broadcasting Corp. British. Narrated by Valentine Dyall. (Running Time: 2 hrs. 0 mins. 0 sec.). (ENG.). 2010. audio compact disk 24.95 (978-1-4084-6699-5(6)) Pub: AudioGO. Dist(s): Perseus Dist

Appointment with God. 1 cass. 1990. 9.95 (978-0-00-147102-3(3)) BJUPr.

Appointments & Reservations: American English. unabr. ed. Scripts. Natasha Cooper. Prod. by Phillip Richards. 2 CDs. (Running Time: 2 hrs. 26 mins.). Dramatization. (Speaking Problem-Solvers Ser.). 2000. audio compact disk 44.99 (978-0-9677755-5-5(8)); 35.99 (978-0-9677755-4-8(X)) Cooper Learn Syst.
Conversational American English.

Appointments & Reservations: English That Takes You Where You Want to Go. Scripts. Natasha Cooper. 2 cass. (Running Time: 3 hrs. 15 mins.). Dramatization. (ENG & RUS.). 2000. pap. bk. 49.99 (978-1-932521-19-1(4)); pap. bk. Rental 59.99 (978-1-932521-20-7(8)) Cooper Learn Syst.
450 phrases, 30 real-life dialogues and scenarios for appointments and reservation: making them - confirming - cancelling, etc. Cassettes in soft poly cases.

Appointments & Reservations: English That Takes You Where You Want to Go. Scripts. Natasha Cooper. 2 cass. (Running Time: 3 hrs. 15 mins.). Dramatization. 2003. pap. bk. 49.99 (978-1-932521-13-9(5)); pap. bk. 59.99 (978-1-932521-12-2(7)) Cooper Learn Syst.
Packaged in a multi-media vinyl album.

Appointments at the Ends of the World: Memoirs of a Wildlife Veterinarian. abr. ed. William B. Karesh. 2 cass. (Running Time: 3 hrs.). 1999. 17.98 (978-1-57042-664-3(3)) Hachet Audio.

Appollinaire, Cocteau, Eluard, Aragon. 1 cass. (Golden Treasury of Poetry & Prose Ser.). (FRE.). 1991. 16.95 (1056-SA) Olivia & Hill.

Appomattox. James Reasoner. Narrated by James Lloyd. (Running Time: 37800 sec.). (Civil War Battle Ser.). 2006. audio compact disk 81.00 (978-0-7861-7186-6(3)) Blckstn Audio.

Appomattox. James Reasoner. Read by Lloyd James. (Running Time: 37800 sec.). (Civil War Battle Ser.). 2006. 65.95 (978-0-7861-4518-8(8)) Blckstn Audio.

Appomattox. unabr. ed. James Reasoner. Narrated by James Lloyd. (Running Time: 37800 sec.). (Civil War Battle Ser.). 2006. audio compact disk 29.95 (978-0-7861-7620-5(2)) Blckstn Audio.

Appraisal Key Point. rev. ed. Carr S. Lawson & Kaplan Publishing Staff. 2 vols. (ENG.). 2004. audio compact disk 34.95 (978-1-4195-0368-9(5), Dearbrn Real Est Ed) Pub: Kaplan Pubng. Dist(s): S and S Inc

Appreciating the Trait of High Sensitivity. unabr. ed. Perf. by Elaine N. Aron. 1 cass. (Running Time: 1 hr. 15 mins.). 1998. 12.95 (978-0-9671393-0-2(9)) Aron Pubg.
Characteristics of the Highly Sensitive Person (HSP) trait are discussed as well as coping strategies. Substantial research shows that the trait is inherited by 15 to 20 % of the population.

Appreciative Inquiry. David L. Cooperrider & Diana Whitney. (Tools in Appreciative Inquiry Ser.: Vol. I). 2001. audio compact disk 12.00 (978-1-893435-44-5(X)) Lakeshore Comm.

Appreciative Inquiry Handbook: The First in a Series of AI Workbooks for Leaders of Change. David L. Cooperrider et al. 2003. per. 66.00 (978-1-893403-10-6(1)) Crown Custom.

Apprende en Voiture - Anglais. unabr. ed. 2 cass. (Running Time: 3 hrs.). (FRE & ENG.). 16.95 Incl. guide. Penton Overseas.
For students or foreign residents who wish to learn or improve their English. Teaches key words first, then builds grammar & new vocabulary into sentences, developing the listener's ability to quickly comprehend & converse.

***Apprentice.** abr. ed. Tess Gerritsen. Read by Dennis Boutsikaris. (ENG.). 2011. audio compact disk 14.99 (978-0-307-93310-2(5), Random AudioBks) Pub: Random Audio Pubg. Dist(s): Random

Apprentice. unabr. ed. Tess Gerritsen. 7 cass. (Running Time: 10 hrs. 30 mins.). (Jane Rizzoli & Maura Isles Ser.: Bk. 2). 2002. 72.00 (978-0-7366-8762-1(9)); audio compact disk 68.00 (978-0-7366-8763-8(7)) Pub: Books on Tape. Dist(s): NetLibrary CO
It is a boiling summer in Boston. Adding to the city's woes is a series of shocking crimes that end in abduction and death. The pattern suggests one man: "The Surgeon," serial killer Warren Hoyt, known for his partial dissection of his victims. Police can only assume its a maniac basing his attacks on the twisted medical techniques of the madman he admires. That's what Detective Jane Rizzoli thinks. Forced to confront the killer who scarred her, she is determined to finally end Hoyt's awful influence. But Rizzoli isn't counting on becoming a target herself. Yet once Hoyt is suddenly free, he joins his mysterious blood brother in a vicious vendetta.

***Apprentice: Walking the Way of Christ.** Steve Chalke. (Running Time: 4 hrs. 49 mins. 12 sec.). (ENG.). 2010. 14.99 (978-0-310-58969-3(X)) Zondervan.

Apprentice to Genius: My Years with Frank Lloyd Wright. unabr. ed. Heywood Hale Broun. Read by Edgar Tafel. 1 cass. (Heywood Hale Broun Ser.). 11.95 (40385) J Norton Pubs.

Apprenticeship of Duddy Kravitz. abr. ed. Mordecai Richler. Narrated by Paul Hecht. Prod. by CBC Radio Staff. 4 cass. (Running Time: 4 hrs. 30 mins.). (ENG.). (gr. 9-12). 2005. 24.95 (978-0-86492-245-8(0)) Pub: BTC Audiobks CAN. Dist(s): U Toronto Pr

Apprenticeship of Duddy Kravitz. abr. ed. Mordecai Richler & Rohinton Mistry. Read by Paul Hecht. 4 CDs. (Running Time: 4 hrs. 30 mins.). (ENG.). 2005. audio compact disk 29.95 (978-0-86492-363-9(5)) Pub: BTC Audiobks CAN. Dist(s): U Toronto Pr

Apprenticeship of Lucas Whitaker. unabr. ed. Cynthia C. DeFelice. Narrated by John McDonough. 3 cass. (Running Time: 4 hrs. 30 min.). 2003. 27.00 (978-0-7887-8513-9(3)) Recorded Bks.
Twelve-year-old Lucas heroically attacks a mystery that even the adults can't solve.

Apprenticeship of Lucas Whitaker. unabr. ed. Cynthia C. DeFelice. Narrated by John McDonough. 3 pieces. (Running Time: 4 hrs. 30 mins.). (gr. 6 up). 1997. 27.00 (978-0-7887-0885-5(6), 95023E7) Recorded Bks.
A gripping tale based on a mid-1800s cure for "consumption." After his family members die, 12-year-old Lucas heroically attacks a mystery that even the adults can't solve.

Approach to Diagnosis & Management of Infections to the Central Nervous System. Read by Morton N. Swartz. 1 cass. (Running Time: 90 mins.). 1986. 12.00 (C8626) Amer Coll Phys.

Approach to the Korean Language: Historical, Literary, & Cultural. Alexander Arguelles & Jong-Rok Kim. 2000. pap. bk. 46.50 (978-1-56591-180-2(6)) Hollym Intl.

Approaches to Christian Mysticism. David Steindl-Rast. 6 cass. (Running Time: 7 hrs. 11 mins.). 1987. 56.00 (05103) Big Sur Tapes.

Approaching. Parker Po-fei Huang. Ed. by Stanley H. Barken & Diana Chang. (Review Asian-American Writers Chapbook Ser.: No. 1). 1989. 10.00 (978-0-89304-629-3(9)) Cross-Cultrl NY.

Approaching A Course in Miracles: A Commentary on Workbook Lesson 188: the Peace of God Is Shining in Me Now. Kenneth Wapnick. 1 CD. 2005. audio compact disk 6.00 (978-1-59142-219-8(1), CD71) Foun Miracles.

Approaching Fury: Voices of the Storm, 1820-1861. unabr. ed. Stephen B. Oates. 16 cass. (Running Time: 22 hrs. 45 mins.). 1998. 128.00 (978-0-7887-1996-7(3), 95383E7) Recorded Bks.
Emotion-packed monologues for abolitionist William Lloyd Garrison & others. Account of the years leading to the American Civil War.

***Approaching Storm.** abr. ed. Alan Dean Foster. (Running Time: 6 hrs.). (ENG.). 2007. 14.98 (978-0-553-71466-1(X), Random AudioBks) Pub: Random Audio Pubg. Dist(s): Random

Appropriations Process in a Nutshell (CD) Featuring James Saturno. Prod. by TheCapitol.Net. 2006. 107.00 (978-1-58733-043-8(1)) TheCapitol.

Approval Addiction: Overcoming Your Need to Please Everyone. abr. ed. Joyce Meyer. Read by Pat Lentz. (ENG.). 2005. 14.98 (978-1-59483-163-8(7)); audio compact disk 29.98 (978-1-59483-023-5(1)) Pub: Hachet Audio. Dist(s): HachBkGrp

Approval Addiction: Overcoming Your Need to Please Everyone. abr. ed. Joyce Meyer. Read by Pat Lentz. (Running Time: 6 hrs.). (ENG.). 2009. 44.98 (978-1-60788-036-3(9)) Pub: Hachet Audio. Dist(s): HachBkGrp

Approved in Christ. Derek Prince. 1 cass. (Running Time: 60 mins.). 5.95 (B-4239) Derek Prince.

Aprenda en Su Auto - Ingles: English for Spanish Speakers. abr. ed. 2 cass. (Running Time: 3 hrs.). (SPA & ENG.). 16.95 Penton Overseas.
For students or foreign residents who wish to learn or improve their English. Teaches key words first, then builds grammar & new vocabulary into sentences, developing the listener's ability to quickly comprehend & converse. Includes Listening Guide with complete recorded program text plus important grammar rules.

Aprenda en Su Auto Ingles Nivel Tres, Vol. 3. Henry N. Raymond. 2 cass. (Running Time: 3 hrs.). (Learn in Your Car Ser.).Tr. of Learn in Your Car: English. (SPA & ENG.). 2004. 16.95 (978-1-56015-174-6(9)) Penton Overseas.

Aprenda Guitarra de Rock. Ed Lozano. (SPA.). 2004. pap. bk. 14.95 (978-0-8256-2831-3(8), Schirmer Trade Bks) Pub: Music Sales. Dist(s): H Leonard

Aprenda Japones en 30 Dias (Learn Japanese in 30 Days) Equippo Expertos Staff. (SPA., (978-84-315-1588-1(0)) De Vecchi ESP.

Aprende a Leer a Traves de Musica, Juegos y Ritmos. Ursula O. Ronnholm. Ed. by Osdila O. Deliz. Illus. by Miguel Montero. (SPA.). (J). (gr. k up). 1986. bk. 20.00 (978-0-941911-01-6(2)) Two Way Bilingual.

Aprende a Leer a Traves de Musica, Juegos y Ritmos. rev. ed. Ursula O. Ronnholm. Ed. by Edda Rabell. Tr. by Edda Rabell. Illus. by Miguel Montero. (SPA.). (J). (gr. k-2). 1989. pap. bk. 20.00 (978-0-941911-07-8(1)) Two Way Bilingual.

Aprende a Relajarte. Angel Escudero. 1 cass. (Running Time: 1 hr. 30 mins.).Tr. of Learn to Relax. (SPA.). 2001. Astran.

Aprende Como Hablar Ingles see Learn How to Speak English

Aprende Ya! a Tocar Escalas para Guitarra. Ed Lozano. (SPA.). 2004. pap. bk. 9.95 (978-0-8256-2846-7(6), Schirmer Trade Bks) Pub: Music Sales. Dist(s): H Leonard

Aprende Ya Guitarra Comienza. Ed Lozano. 3 vols. 2005. pap. bk. 29.95 (978-0-8256-2982-2(9), AM980276, Amsco Music) Pub: Music Sales. Dist(s): H Leonard

Aprender a Estudiar. Antonella Esposito.Tr. of Learn to Study. (SPA.). 2001. 19.75 (978-84-315-1727-4(1)) Astran.

Aprendiendo a Andar por Gracia: Romanos 6-11. 2004. audio compact disk 44.00 (978-1-57972-585-3(6)) Insight Living.

Aprendiendo a Leer con Mili y Molo: Learn How to Read in Spanish. Speeches. Mónica Mejías. Illus. by Mónica Mejías. 1 CD. (Running Time: 74min.). Dramatization.Tr. of Lernen Sie Spanish Lesen, Impara a leggere in Spagnolo, Aprenda a ler Espanhol, Apprenez à lire L'espagnol. (J). 2004. audio compact disk 12.00 (978-0-9753799-0-5(9)) Ediciones Alas.
The CD contains two songs: Mili and Molo's song and the ABC. Each lesson is also complemented by its respective recording so learning becomes an audio-visual experience.

Aprendiendo a ser Felices. ANISA, Inc. audio compact disk 14.95 (978-1-56835-525-2(4)) Prodns Anisa.

Apres le Deluge - Vous! unabr. ed. Samuel E. Konkin, III. 1 cass. (Running Time: 51 mins.). 12.95 (AF0401) J Norton Pubs.
Konkin discusses his basic theory of Counter-Economics as a route to achieving a free society, then proceeds to apply this theory to future wars, depressions, or hyperinflations.

April Fool! Karen Gray Ruelle. Narrated by Suzanne Toren. (Running Time: 15 mins.). 2002. 10.00 (978-1-4025-4220-6(8)) Recorded Bks.

April Fool. unabr. ed. Michele Sobel Spirn. 1 cass. (Running Time: 20 min.). (Fun to Read Ser.). (J). (gr. 3-6). 1983. bk. 16.99 (978-0-934898-36-2(7)); pap. bk. 9.95 (978-0-934898-24-9(3)) Jan Prods.
Every year, Bob's older brother plays an April F04231430xe on him. This year Bob is determined to get his brother first - with a trick he'll never forget!.

April Fool Dead. unabr. ed. Carolyn G. Hart. Read by Kate Reading. 6 cass. (Running Time: 9 hrs.). (Death on Demand Mystery Ser.: No. 13). 2002. 48.00 (978-0-7366-8617-4(7)) Books on Tape.
To celebrate an April Fool's Day appearance by the island's most famous mystery author, Death on Demand bookstore owner Annie Darling creates a unique promotion. Offering a free book to anyone who can solve a series of clues about popular whodunits, Annie and husband Max pass out their flyers all over town. But an April Fool prankster is distributing a counterfeit flyer - complete with not-so-vague accusations of murder. Now, Annie is out to find the culprit - a search complicated by a troubled friend and by her own unpredictable mother-in-law, whose latest kick is finding lost pirate booty. But it's no laughing matter when murder is added to the mix, for now Annie and her handsome husband, Max, must unmask a killer before he strikes again.

April fool's Day. Bryce Courtenay. Read by Humphrey Bower. (Running Time: 19 hrs. 20 mins.). 2009. 114.99 (978-1-74214-202-9(8), 9781742142029) Pub: Bolinda Pubng AUS. Dist(s): Bolinda Pub Inc

April Fool's Day. unabr. ed. Bryce Courtenay. Read by Humphrey Bower. (Running Time: 19 hrs. 20 mins.). 2006. 54.95 (978-1-74093-853-2(4)) Pub: Bolinda Pubng AUS. Dist(s): Bolinda Pub Inc

April Fool's Day. unabr. ed. Bryce Courtenay. Read by Humphrey Bower. (Running Time: 69600 sec.). 2007. audio compact disk 123.95 (978-1-74093-852-5(6)) Pub: Bolinda Pubng AUS. Dist(s): Bolinda Pub Inc

April Ghouls' Day. unabr. ed. Tom B. Stone. Narrated by Jeff Woodman. 2 cass. (Running Time: 2 hrs. 15 mins.). (Graveyard School Ser.: No. 11). (gr. 3-7). 2001. 19.00 (978-0-7887-0711-7(6), 94887E7) Recorded Bks.
Adventure of spooky danger & grisly humor centers around a school so weird that its students are dying to go to class.

April in Moscow. Stephen Rabley. 1 cass. (Running Time: 1 hr.). (J). (978-0-582-06253-5(5), PutnaJuv) Penguin Grp USA.

April in New England: 75 Royalty Free Images of New England. Marques Vickers. 2002. cd-rom & audio compact disk 39.95 (978-0-9706530-5-5(0)) Marquis Pubng.

April Inventory see Twentieth-Century Poetry in English, No. 27, Recordings of Poets Reading Their Own Poetry

April Morning. unabr. ed. Howard Fast. Narrated by Jamie Hanes. 4 CDs. (Running Time: 4 hrs. 45 min.). 2003. audio compact disk 50.00 Recorded Bks.

April Morning. unabr. ed. Howard Fast. Narrated by Jamie Hanes. 4 cass. (Running Time: 4 hrs. 45 mins.). (gr. 6). 1988. 35.00 (978-1-55690-026-6(0), 88320E7) Recorded Bks.
The author re-tells the opening events of the American Revolution through the eyes of Adam, a young participant.

April Showers. unabr. ed. Kathleen Dayus. Read by Diana Bishop. 6 cass. (Running Time: 9 hrs.). 2000. 54.95 (978-0-7531-0773-7(2), 000101) Pub: ISIS Audio GBR. Dist(s): Ulverscroft US

April Twilights & More: Plus Poems by Ralph Waldo Emerson. Poems. Willa Cather. Read by Flo Gibson. 2 cass. (Running Time: 2 hrs.). 1997. 14.95 (978-1-55685-481-1(1), 481-1) Audio Bk Con.
Willa Cather's book of poems is joined by works of several great poetesses. Emerson's poetry is featured on the second cassette.

April 1865: The Month That Saved America. Jay Winik. Narrated by Jay Winik. 12 cass. (Running Time: 15 hrs.). 2001. 98.00 (978-0-7887-9952-5(5), 96847) Recorded Bks.
April 1865 was a month that could have unravelled the nation. Instead, it saved it. Provocative, bold, exquisitely rendered and stunningly original, Winik's deeply researched account is the first major reassesment of the war's close.

April 1865: The Month That Saved America. Jay Winik. 10 cass. (Running Time: 17 hrs.). 2004. 39.99 (978-1-4025-0219-4(2), 00644) Recorded Bks.
April 1865 was a month that could have unravelled the nation. Instead, it saved it. Noted historian Jay Winik offers a brilliant new look at the Civil War's end and the nation's new beginning. A gripping narrative, this fresh iconoclastic account is uniquely set within the larger sweep of history and filled with rich profiles of larger-than-life figures.

April 4 1968: Martin Luther King, Jr. 's Death & How It Changed America. unabr. ed. Michael Eric Dyson. Read by Michael Eric Dyson. (Running Time: 23400 sec.). 2008. 44.95 (978-1-4332-4487-2(X)); audio compact disk 29.95 (978-1-4332-4489-6(6)) Blckstn Audio.

April 4, 1968: Martin Luther King, Jr.'s Death & How It Changed America. unabr. ed. Michael Eric Dyson. Read by Michael Eric Dyson. 5 CDs. 2008. audio compact disk & audio compact disk 19.95 (978-1-4332-4616-6(3)); audio compact disk & audio compact disk 50.00 (978-1-4332-4488-9(8)) Blckstn Audio.

April's Kittens. unabr. ed. Clare Turlay Newberry. Narrated by Barbara Caruso. 1 cass. (Running Time: 30 mins.). (gr. 1 up). 10.00 (978-0-7887-1118-3(0), 95112E7) Recorded Bks.
Six-year-old April is very sad. She dearly loves her silky black cat, Sheba & its three newborn kittens. But April & her parents live in a small New York apartment where there is room for only one cat. Listeners of all ages will be delighted by the gentle solution to April's problem. Available to libraries only.

Aprobado. Carthew & Martin Webb. (J). (gr. 1-9). 1986. pap. bk. 22.61 (978-0-582-33177-8(3), 72066) Longman.

Apt Pupil. Stephen King. Read by Frank Muller. (Running Time: 7 hrs.). (ENG.). (gr. 12 up). 2009. audio compact disk 29.95 (978-0-14-314396-3(4), PengAudBks) Penguin Grp USA.

Apt Pupil. unabr. ed. Stephen King. Read by Frank Muller. 4 cass. 1999. 24.95 (FS9-43445) Highsmith.

***Apt Pupil.** unabr. ed. Stephen King. (Running Time: 7 hrs.). (ENG.). 2010. audio compact disk 14.95 (978-0-14-242803-0(5), PengAudBks) Penguin Grp USA.

Apt Pupil. unabr. ed. Stephen King. Narrated by Frank Muller. 5 cass. (Running Time: 7 hrs. 30 mins.). 1984. 44.00 (978-1-55690-027-3(9), 84065E7) Recorded Bks.
Todd Bowdon, a straight-A student, discovers a war criminal living incognito in his neighborhood. Now, Todd wants to learn what it feels like to kill another human being.

Apt 3. (J). 2004. 8.95 (978-1-56008-833-2(8)); 8.95 (978-0-7882-0295-7(2)); cass. & flmstrp 30.00 (978-0-89719-645-1(7)) Weston Woods.

Apt. 3. Ezra Jack Keats. 1 cass. (Running Time: 8 min.). (J). (ps-3). 2000. pap. bk. 12.95 Weston Woods.
The sounds of a harmonica lead to an understanding between a blind man & two boys who live in the same building in the city.

Aptitude Testing. unabr. ed. Jum C. Nunnally. 1 cass. (Running Time: 26 mins.). 1968. 12.95 (C29234) J Norton Pubs.
The value of aptitude tests & aptitude test batteries in contrast to measures of general intelligence.

Aquamarine MOD-3909. 1 cass. (Running Time: 1 hr.). (Interludes Music Ser.). 1989. 9.95 (978-1-55569-296-4(6), MOD-3909) Great Am Audio.

Aquarelles. G. Kaplan. 2006. audio compact disk (978-1-4276-0324-1(3)) AardGP.

Aquarian Age. Philip Sedgwick. 1 cass. (Running Time: 90 min.). 1990. 8.95 (711) Am Fed Astrologers.

Aquarian Gospel of Jesus the Christ. abr. ed. Levi. Read by Michel Corhan. 2 cass. (Running Time: 3 hrs.). 1996. 17.95 (978-1-57453-045-2(3)) Audio Lit.
Offers an almost complete record of the word & works of Jesus, including those years about which the New Testament Gospels are silent. Covers Jesus' 18 years of study & travel in the East, when he is said to have visited the snowbound monasteries of Tibet & the temples of Egypt, India, Persia & Greece.

Aquarium Weight Management Program. Perf. by R. M. Peluso. Created by R. M. Peluso. 2006. audio compact disk 23.95 (978-0-9794674-3-1(8)) R M Peluso.

Aquarius. Narrated by Patricia G. Finlayson. Music by Mike Cantwell. Contrib. by Marie De Seta & TMY Communications Staff. 1 cass. (Running Time: 30 mins.). (Astrologer's Guide to the Personality Ser.: Vol. 11). 1994. 7.99 (978-1-878535-22-1(6)) De Seta-Finlayson.
Astrological description of the sign of Aquarius; individually customized, covering love, money, career, relationships & more.

Aquarius: January Twenty - February Eighteen. Barrie Konicov. 1 cass. 11.98 (978-0-87082-089-2(3), 003) Potentials.
The author explains how each sign of the Zodiac has its positive & negative aspects & that, as individuals, in order to master our own destiny we must enhance our positive traits.

Aquarius: Unleash the Power of Your True Self. 1 cass. (Running Time: 1 hr.). 1999. 9.99 (978-1-928996-10-1(8)) MonAge.

Aquarius: Your Relationship with the Energy of the Universe. Loy Young. 1993. 9.95 (978-1-882888-23-8(5)) Aquarius Hse.

Aquarius Now. Guy Spiro. 1 cass. 8.95 (328) Am Fed Astrologers.
Social & political implications of New Age.

Aquarius Obscured. Robert Stone. Read by Robert Stone. 1 cass. (Running Time: 1 hr.). 13.95 (978-1-55644-059-5(6), 2141) Am Audio Prose.
Reading short story dealing with the more destructive side of the '60s & Father Egan's rum laced sermon.

Aquatic Inservice Manual: Case Studies. Bruce M. Carney. 2000. audio compact disk 245.00 (978-0-7637-1363-8(5), 1363-5) Jones Bartlett.

Aquellos Dias de Dinosaurios, EDL Level 14. (Fonolibros Ser.: Vol. 14). (SPA.). 2003. 11.50 (978-0-7652-1035-7(5)) Modern Curr.

Aqui viene el que se Poncha! see Here Comes the Strikeout

Aquila. unabr. ed. Andrew Norriss. Read by Brian Cant. 3 cass. (Running Time: 3 hrs.). (J). (gr. 1-8). 1999. 24.95 (CCA 3488, Chivers Child Audio) AudioGO.

Aquinas for Armchair Theologians. unabr. ed. Timothy Renick. Narrated by Kate Reading. 3 CDs. (Running Time: 3 hrs. 12 mins. 0 sec.). (ENG.). 2005. audio compact disk 18.98 (978-1-59644-192-7(5), Hovel Audio) christianaud.

***Aquinas for Armchair Theologians.** unabr. ed. Timothy M. Renick. Narrated by Kate Reading. (ENG.). 2005. 10.98 (978-1-59644-193-4(3), Hovel Audio) christianaud.

Aquinas for Armchair Theologians. unabr. ed. Timothy Mark Renick. Read by Kate Reading. (Running Time: 10800 sec.). 2006. audio compact disk 27.00 (978-0-7861-6332-8(1)) Blckstn Audio.

Aquitaine Progression, Pt. 1. unabr. collector's ed. Robert Ludlum. Read by Michael Prichard. 11 cass. (Running Time: 16 hrs. 30 mins.). 1985. 88.00 (978-0-7366-0996-8(2), 1931-A) Books on Tape.
The author imagines the top generals of the largest nations conspire to control the world.

Aquitaine Progression, Pt. 2. collector's ed. Robert Ludlum. Read by Michael Prichard. 9 cass. (Running Time: 13 hrs. 30 mins.). 1985. 72.00 (978-0-7366-0997-5(0), 1931-B) Books on Tape.

Ar Aon Bhuille / Matching Beats. Contrib. by Antoin MacGabhann. (ENG.). 1994. 13.95 (978-0-8023-7105-8(1)); audio compact disk 21.95 (978-0-8023-8105-7(7)) Pub: Clo Iar-Chonnachta IRL. Dist(s): Dufour

***Ar Bord Leis Na Hancairi.** Na Hancairi. (ENG.). 1990. 11.95 (978-0-8023-7046-4(2)) Pub: Clo Iar-Chonnachta IRL. Dist(s): Dufour

Ar Fhoscadh na GCnoc. Contrib. by Gearoidin Bhreathnach. (ENG.). 1997. 12.95 (978-0-8023-7130-0(2)) Pub: Clo Iar-Chonnachta IRL. Dist(s): Dufour

Arab American - African American. Joe Giordano. Narrated by George Guidall. Contrib. by Elaine Pinderhuges & Nuha Abudabbeh. 6 cass. (Running Time: 3 hrs.). (Growing Up in America Ser.: Vol. 4). 1997. 12.00 (978-1-891207-04-4(0)) Ethnic Prods.

Arab-American Economic Relations: Politics & Trends. unabr. ed. Clovis Maksoud & Gerald L. Parsky. 1 cass. (Running Time: 59 mins.). 12.95 (454) J Norton Pubs.

Arab & Jew: Wounded Spirits in a Promised Land. David K. Shipler. Read by Barrett Whitener. 2003. audio compact disk 19.95 (978-0-7861-9216-8(X)) Blckstn Audio.

Arab & Jew: Wounded Spirits in a Promised Land. unabr. ed. David K. Shipler. Read by Robert Blumenfeld. (Running Time: 100800 sec.). 2006. audio compact disk 44.95 (978-0-7861-6085-3(3)) Blckstn Audio.

Arab & Jew: Wounded Spirits in a Promised Land. unabr. ed. David K. Shipler. Read by Robert Blumenfeld. 2 pieces. (Running Time: 100800 sec.). 2007. audio compact disk 39.95 (978-0-7861-9203-8(8), 2957A,B) Blckstn Audio.
The Jew, according to the Arab stereotype, is a brutal, violent coward; the Arab, to the prejudiced Jew, is a primitive creature of animal vengeance and cruel desires. In this monumental work, the author delves into the origins of the prejudices that have been intensified by war, terrorism, and nationalism. Focusing on the diverse cultures that exist side by side in Israel and Israeli-controlled territories, he examines the process of indoctrination that begins in schools.

Arab & Jew: Wounded Spirits in a Promised Land. unabr. ed. David K. Shipler & Robert Blumenfeld. (Running Time: 99000 sec.). 2007. audio compact disk 140.00 (978-0-7861-5796-9(8)) Blckstn Audio.

Arab & Jew Pt. 1: Wounded Spirits in a Promised Land. unabr. ed. David Shipler. Read by Barrett Whitener. 11 cass. (Running Time: 40 hrs. 30 mins.). 2002. 76.95 (978-0-7861-2233-2(1), 2957A,B) Blckstn Audio.
Delves into the origins of the prejudices that have been intensified by war, terrorism, and nationalism.

Arab & Jew Pt. 9: Wounded Spirits in a Promised Land. unabr. ed. David Shipler. Read by Barrett Whitener. 9 cass. (Running Time: 40 hrs. 30 mins.). 2002. 62.95 (978-0-7861-2283-7(8), 2957A,B) Blckstn Audio.
The Jew, according to the Arab stereotype, is a brutal, violent coward; the Arab, to the prejudiced Jew, is a primitive creature of animal vengeance and cruel desires. In this monumental work, the author delves into the origins of the prejudices that have been intensified by war, terrorism, and nationalism. Focusing on the diverse cultures that exist side by side in Israel and Israeli-controlled territories, he examines the process of indoctrination that begins in schools.

Arab Balance of Payments. unabr. ed. Basil Al-Bustany. 1 cass. (Running Time: 44 mins.). 12.95 (AF0456) J Norton Pubs.

Arab Music. unabr. ed. 1 cass. 12.95 (C7198) J Norton Pubs.

Arab Nationalism. 10.00 (RME114) Esstee Audios.

Arab Refugees. 10.00 (RME117) Esstee Audios.

Arabe: La Historia Que Immortalizo a Rodolfo Valentino. abr. ed. Edith M. Hull. Contrib. by Anna Silvetti & Edwin Dorado. (Running Time: 7200 sec.). (SPA.). 2007. audio compact disk 16.95 (978-1-933499-47-5(8)) Fonolibro Inc.

Arabe sans Peine, Level 1. 1 cass. (Running Time: 1 hr., 30 min.). (ARA & FRE., 1997. pap. bk. 75.00 (978-2-7005-1042-3(9)) Pub: Assimil FRA. Dist(s): Distribks Inc

Arabe sans Peine, Vol. 2. 1 cass. (Running Time: 1 hr., 30 min.). (ARA & FRE., 1997. pap. bk. 75.00 (978-2-7005-1043-0(7)) Pub: Assimil FRA. Dist(s): Distribks Inc

Arabe sin Esfuerzo. 1 cass. (Running Time: 1 hr.).Tr. of Arabic with Ease. (ARA & SPA.). 2000. bk. 75.00 (978-2-7005-1304-2(5)) Pub: Assimil FRA. Dist(s): Distribks Inc

Arabe sin Esfuerzo. Tr. by J. J. Schmidt & Fortunato Riloba from FRE. (Sin Esfuerzo Ser.).Tr. of Arabic with Ease. 1982. 49.95 (978-2-7005-1154-3(9)) Pub: Assimil FRA. Dist(s): Distribks Inc

***Arabel's Raven.** Joan Aiken. Read by Sneha Mathan. (Playaway Children Ser.). (ENG.). (J). 2010. 39.99 (978-1-61587-641-9(3)) Find a World.

Arabia: A Journey Through the Labyrinth. unabr. collector's ed. Jonathan Raban. Read by David Case. 10 cass. (Running Time: 15 hrs.). 1990. 80.00 (978-0-7366-1673-7(X), 2522) Books on Tape.
Arabia as seen through the eyes of this best-selling travel writer.

Arabian Dance see Christmas with Ogden Nash

Arabian Investments & Imports. unabr. ed. Phillip Bradley & Farid Abolfathi. 1 cass. (Running Time: 53 mins.). 12.95 (AF0455) J Norton Pubs.

Arabian Nights. Short Stories. As told by Jim Weiss. 1 CD. (Running Time: 1 hr.). Dramatization. (Storyteller's Version Ser.). (J). (gr. k up). 1999. audio compact disk 14.95 (978-1-882513-28-4(2), 1124-003) Greathall Prods.
Scheherazade, who first spun the tales, leads into a selection of stories with a unique fascination. Includes: "Scheherazade," "Ali Baba and the Forty Thieves," "The Fisherman and the Genie" and "The Bird Who Speaks".

Arabian Nights. Short Stories. As told by Jim Weiss. 1 cass. (Running Time: 1 hr.). Dramatization. (Storyteller's Version Ser.). (J). (gr. k up). 1989. 10.95 (978-1-882513-03-1(7), 1124-03) Greathall Prods.

Arabian Nights. Read by Jim Weiss. 1 cass. (Running Time: 1 hr.). (J). 1999. NewSound.

Arabian Nights. collector's ed. Read by Donada Peters. Ed. by Andrew Lang. 2 cass. (Running Time: 3 hrs.). 2000. 24.00 (978-0-7366-5065-6(2)) Books on Tape.
As early as the tenth century, a Persian collection of tales told of a king who was in the habit of killing his wives after their first night together. Finally, he married the Wezir's clever daughter who nightly told him a tale which she left unfinished at dawn so that his curiosity led him to spare her until the tale could be completed.

Arabian Nights. unabr. ed. Perf. by Jennifer Bacon et al. Adapted by Mary Zimmerman. 1 cass. (Running Time: 2 hrs.). 1993. 22.95 (978-1-58081-102-6(7)) L A Theatre.
Brings to life the centuries old collection of Indian, Persian & Arabian stories that open the door to a lost world of wisdom, faith & divine beauty of the heart with the Lookingglass Theatre Ensemble.

Arabian Nights: The Book of a Thousand Nights & a Night. abr. ed. Richard F. Burton. Read by Philip Madoc. 3 CDs. (Running Time: 3 hrs. 45 mins.). 1995. audio compact disk 22.98 (978-962-634-029-5(0), NA302912, Naxos AudioBooks) Naxos.
Though generally known as stories for children, they were originally tales for adults, full of adventure, sexuality, violence and the supernatural.

Arabian Nights: Their Best-Known Tales. unabr. ed. Read by Johanna Ward. Ed. by Kate Douglas Wiggin & Nora A. Smith. 8 cass. (Running Time: 11 hrs. 30 mins.). (gr. 4-7). 2000. 56.95 (978-0-7861-1798-7(2), 2597) Blckstn Audio.
Find golden palaces, gem studded caves & breathtaking gardens, sit by mysterious fountains, hear the crash of gleaming waterfalls, unearth magic lamps, take a long voyage to exotic shores & meet flying men & mythical beasts.

Arabian Nights: Their Best-Known Tales. unabr. ed. Read by Johanna Ward. Ed. by Kate Douglas Wiggin & Nora A. Smith. 10 CDs. (Running Time: 39600 sec.). 2000. audio compact disk 80.00 (978-0-7861-9866-5(4), 2597) Blckstn Audio.
Find golden palaces, gem studded caves & breathtaking gardens; sit by mysterious fountains, hear the crash of gleaming waterfalls, unearth magic lamps, take a long voyage to exotic shores & meet flying men & mythical beasts.

***Arabian Nights Entertainment.** unabr. ed. Jonathan Scott. Narrated by Robin Field. (ENG.). 2010. 14.98 (978-1-59644-959-6(4), MissionAud); audio compact disk 24.98 (978-1-59644-958-9(6), MissionAud) christianaud.

Arabian Nights Tale see Historia de Abu-Dir, el Tintorero y Abu-Sir, el Barbero - Cuento de las Mil y una Noches

Arabian Nights Tale. Read by Laura García. (Running Time: 1 hr.). 2002. 14.95 (978-1-60083-137-9(0), Audiofy Corp) Iofy Corp.

Arabic. 2 cass. (Running Time: 1 hr. 10 mins.). (Language - Thirty Library). bk. 16.95 vinyl album. Moonbeam Pubns.
Using the proven method based on the famous U.S. Military accelerated language learning program, Language/30 courses stress conversationally useful words & phrases.

Arabic. unabr. ed. Ed. by Charles Berlitz. 2 cass. (Running Time: 1 hr. 30 mins.). (Language/30 Brief Course Ser.). pap. bk. 21.95 (AF1032) J Norton Pubs.

Arabic, Set. David F. Dimeo. (For Dummies Ser.). 2008. audio compact disk 19.99 (978-0-470-25154-6(9), For Dummies) Wiley US.

Arabic: Language 30. Educational Services Corporation Staff. 2004. audio compact disk 21.95 (978-1-931850-00-1(3)) Educ Svcs DC.

Arabic: Language 30. rev. ed. Educational Services Corporation Staff. Intro. by Charles Berlitz. 2 cass. (Running Time: 2 hrs.). (ARA.). 1994. pap. bk. 21.95 (978-0-910542-70-8(8)) Educ Svcs DC.
Arabic self-teaching language course.

Arabic: Learn to Speak & Understand Arabic with Pimsleur Language Programs. 2nd unabr. ed. Pimsleur Staff. Created by Simon and Schuster Staff. 5 CDs. (Running Time: 50 hrs. 0 mins. 0 sec.). (Basic Ser.). (ARA & ENG.). 2005. audio compact disk 24.95 (978-0-7435-5074-1(9), Pimsleur) Pub: S&S Audio. Dist(s): S and S Inc

Arabic: Learn to Speak & Understand Eastern Arabic with Pimsleur Language Programs. 2nd unabr. ed. Pimsleur Staff. 8 CDs. (Running Time: 80 hrs. 0 mins. 0 sec.). (Instant Conversation Ser.). (ARA & ENG.). 2005. audio compact disk 49.95 (978-0-7435-5048-2(X), Pimsleur) Pub: S&S Audio. Dist(s): S and S Inc

Arabic Vol. 11: Learn to Speak & Understand Arabic with Pimsleur Language Programs. 2nd ed. Pimsleur Staff. 16 CDs. (Running Time: 160 hrs. 0 mins. 0 sec.). (Comprehensive Ser.). (ARA.). 2007. audio compact disk 345.00 (978-0-7435-4490-0(0), Pimsleur) Pub: S&S Audio. Dist(s): S and S Inc

Arabic - English: Level I. Vocabulearn. 2 cass. (Running Time: 90 mins. per cass.). (VocabuLearn Ser.). (ARA & ENG.). 1989. 15.95 (978-0-939001-76-7(4)) Penton Overseas.

Arabic Adeni Textbook. 1991. 19.00 (978-0-931745-52-2(7)) Dunwoody Pr.

Arabic Adeni Textbook, Habaka J. Feghali & Alan S. Kaye. 2 cass. (Running Time: 3 hrs.). (ARA.). 1991. 19.00 (3055) Dunwoody Pr.
Intended for the student with some grounding in Modern Standard Arabic who wishes to become familiar with the dialect of Yemen, particularly the Aden area. Dialogues reflect the educated urban style of speech.

Arabic Alphabet. Nazih Girgis. Illus. by C. Lowry-Elks. 1 cass. (Running Time: 30 min.). (ARA.). (J). (gr. k-12). 1983. pap. bk. 14.95 (978-0-86685-340-8(5)) Intl Bk Ctr.

Arabic Beat, Set. World Music Network Staff & Rough Guides Staff. (Rough Guide World Music Cds Ser.). 2004. audio compact disk 45.00 (978-1-84353-355-9(3)) DK Pub Inc.

Arabic (Eastern) Paul Pimsleur. 6 cass. (Pimsleur Language Learning Ser.). 1991. 345.00 incl. study guide. (0671-57904-5) SyberVision.

Arabic (Eastern) for Speakers of English, One. unabr. ed. 16 cass. (Running Time: 15 hrs.). (Pimsleur Tapes Ser.). (ARA.). 1991. 345.00 (18250, Pimsleur) S&S Audio.
Spoken foreign-language proficiency training. Thirty, half-hour, intensive, spoken-language lesson units to be completed at the rate of one lesson per day for 30 days. By achieving eighty-percent correct answers to the questions in each unit, the Pimsleur Spoken Language Programmed Instructional Method will enable the learner to achieve the ACTFL Intermediate-Low Spoken Proficiency Level.

Arabic (Eastern) III: Learn to Speak & Understand Arabic unabr. ed. Pimsleur. (Running Time: 16 hrs. 0 mins. 0 sec.). (Comprehensive Ser.). (ENG.). 2009. audio compact disk 345.00 (978-0-7435-6388-8(3), Pimsleur) Pub: S&S Audio. Dist(s): S and S Inc

Arabic (Egyptian) Short Course. Paul Pimsleur. 5 cass. (Running Time: 5 hrs.). (Pimsleur Language Learning Ser.). 1997. pap. bk. & stu. ed. 149.95 (0671-57906-1) SyberVision.

Arabic (Egyptian) World Citizen Edition. unabr. ed. 2003. 95.00 (978-0-7887-9700-2(X)); audio compact disk 115.00 (978-0-7887-9767-5(0)) Recorded Bks.
Think and converse in Arabic (Egyptian) in ten lessons as a beginner.

Arabic (Egyptian) for Speakers of English, One. unabr. ed. 16 cass. (Running Time: 15 hrs.). (Pimsleur Tapes Ser.). 1997. 345.00 (18253, Pimsleur) S&S Audio.
Spoken foreign-language proficiency training. Thirty, half-hour, intensive, spoken-language lesson units to be completed at the rate of one lesson per day for 30 days. By achieving eighty-percent correct answers to the questions in each unit, the Pimsleur Spoken Language Programmed Instructional Method will enable the learner to achieve the ACTFL Intermediate-Low Spoken Proficiency Level.

Arabic Express. Pimsleur Staff. (Running Time: 11 hrs. 50 mins. 0 sec.). (ENG.). 2004. audio compact disk 11.95 (978-0-7435-3707-0(6), Pimsleur) Pub: S&S Audio. Dist(s): S and S Inc

Arabic for the Deploying Service Member. William M. Wininger. 1. (Running Time: 64:27). (ENG & ARA.). 2006. audio compact disk 12.95 (978-0-9791035-0-6(9)) MilitaryMouth.
Translates words and phrases, questions and commands that a US service member deploying to Iraq or an Arabic-speaking country may find useful. Drills important expressions and provides the bare-essential building blocks so that the soldier can improvise immediately rather than labor through difficult grammar lessons and useless vocabulary.Each track in English and in Arabic by native speakers. Lengthy tracks on Arab culture and Islam. Blends Modern Standard, Levantine, and Iraqi dialects of Arabic to allow the soldier to speak comfortably throughout the greater Middle East. Recommend also: Field Manual companion. Has additional material. Same publisher.Ideal for Iraq, Kuwait, Jordan, Saudi Arabia, Lebanon, Syria, and the Palestinian Occupied Territories. Useful for Army soldiers, USMC Marine Corps marines, Navy sailors, USAF Air Force airmen, USCG Coast Guard.

Arabic Guaranteed. Ghazi Abuhakema & Berlitz Publishing Staff. (Berlitz Guaranteed Ser.). (ARA & ENG., 2007. audio compact disk 19.95 (978-981-268-183-6(3)) Pub: APA Pubns Serv SGP. Dist(s): IngramPubServ

Arabic Hijazi Reader. (Arabic Dialect Series, Saudi Arabia). (J). 1991. 24.00 (978-0-931745-87-4(X)) Dunwoody Pr.

Arabic Hijazi Reader, Habaka J. Feghali & John D. Murphy. 3 cass. (Running Time: 4 hrs. 30 mins.). (ARA.). 1991. 24.00 (3079) Dunwoody Pr.
Forty selections familiarize the student with Saudi Arabian Hijazi dialect & culture through a look at modern life.

Arabic in 60 Minutes. Created by Berlitz. (Berlitz in 60 Minutes Ser.). (ARA & ENG., 2007. audio compact disk 9.95 (978-981-268-204-8(X)) Pub: APA Pubns Serv SGP. Dist(s): Langenscheidt

Arabic Iraqi Dialect: Orientation Course. Joe Kallu et al. 4 cass. (Running Time: 6 hrs.). (C). 2000. pap. bk. 85.00 (978-1-57970-082-9(9), AFA550) J Norton Pubs.
Presumes rudimentary knowledge of Arabic. Designed to supplement existing texts. Stresses pronunciation & Iraqi dialect sounds. Vocabulary of common situations.

Arabic Moroccan Reader. 1989. 19.00 (978-0-931745-51-5(9)) Dunwoody Pr.

Arabic Moroccan Reader, Habaka J. Feghali & Alan S. Kaye. 2 cass. (Running Time: 3 hrs.). (ARA.). 1989. 19.00 (3067) Dunwoody Pr.
Provides the student with important terms & vocabulary in the areas of politics, economy, education, military affairs & culture, as well as general information about Morocco.

Arabic New Testament: Van Dyck Version. 2002. 35.00 (978-1-57449-093-0(1), 107705) Pub: Hosanna NM. Dist(s): Am Bible

Arabic New Testament Bible on Cassette: Van Dyke Edition. Narrated by William Jundy. 16 cass. 1994. 39.97 (978-1-58968-064-7(2), 8101A) Chrstn Dup Intl.

Arabic Parts in Relationships. Ann E. Parker. 1 cass. 8.95 (758) Am Fed Astrologers.

Arabic Pick of the Month. unabr. ed. 1 cass. (Running Time: 1 hr.). (ARA.). 13.50 (CARPTM); 98.00 12-month subscript., 1 cass. per mo. (S45010) J Norton Pubs.

Arabic Qaidah - Yassernaa al-Qur'an Pt. 30: Rythmic Methods of Learning Quranic Arabic with Tajweed - Juzu 'Amma. unabr. ed. M. Shamsul Haque. Read by Usama Amar. 1 cass. (Running Time: 1 hr. 30 mins.). (J). (gr. k-4). 1999. pap. bk. 7.50; 3.00 Namuk Intl Inc.
This program is taught in most of the Islamic schools in the United States, Canada, Australia & Europe. Enables readers to read Qur'an within shortest time.

Arabic Qaidah - Yassernaa al-Qur'an Pts. 1-3: Rythmic Methods of Learning Quranic Arabic with Tajweed - Sura Bagarah. unabr. ed. M. Shamsul Haque. Read by Usama Amar. 2 cass. (Running Time: 3 hrs.). (J). (gr. k-4). 1999. Namuk Intl Inc.

Arabic Qaidah with Important Doas: Yasserna Al-Qur'an Rythmic Methods of Learning Qur'anic Arabic. Muhammed S. Haque. 1 cass. (Running Time: 1 hr. 30 mins.). 1998. bk. 4.50; 3.00 (978-0-933057-07-4(5)) Namuk Intl Inc.
Includes each lesson number & page number.

Arabic Religious Rhetoric Set: A Reader. Peter D. Molan. 2 cass. (Running Time: 1 hr. 30 min. per cass.). (ARA.). 1997. 19.00 (3147) Dunwoody Pr.
Texts taken from taped lectures or sermons by radical Saudi Sheiks, are of special interest beyond that of language; & the author's judicious selection from the lectures intensifies that interest.

Arabic Vol 1 Earworms. (EARWORMS Ser.). 2009. audio compact disk 24.95 (978-0-8416-1067-5(3)) Pub: Berlitz Pubng. Dist(s): Langenscheidt

Arabic with Ease see Arabe sin Esfuerzo

Arabic with Ease see Arabisch Ohne Muhe

Arabic with Ease see Arabe sin Esfuerzo

Arabic You Need CDs & Text. Hadia H. Harb. 2 CDs. (Running Time: 2 hrs.). (ARA.). 2006. audio compact disk 49.50 (978-1-57970-372-1(0), SAR300D, Audio-For) J Norton Pubs.
This brief self-study course in spoken Arabic for beginners was developed by Hadia H. Harb, who has specialized in teaching Arabic to foreigners in the Education Division, Beirut University. The recordings by native speakers are in the Lebanese dialect, one of the easiest to learn and spoken primarily in Lebanon, Syria, Jordan,a nd the Gulf area. The programmed text contains 25 lesson unit, each divided into 5 parts: conversational situations and dialogs; listen, read, and say; questions and answers; exercises; and applications. Each unit ends with a glossary of important words along with their grammatical classifications.

Arabic You Need (Lebanese) Hadia H. Harb. 2 cass. (Running Time: 2 hrs.). 1992. pap. bk. 49.50 (978-0-88432-820-9(1), SAR300, Audio-For) J Norton Pubs.
Brief self-study course in spoken Arabic for beginners. The recordings by native speakers are in the Lebanese dialect, one of the easiest to learn & spoken primarily in Lebanon, Syria, Jordan & the Gulf area. Pt. I: conversational situations & dialogs; Pt. II: listen, read & say; Pt. III: questions & answers; Pts. IV & V: exercises & applications. Each unit ends with a glossary of important words along with their grammatical classifications.

Arabisch Ohne Muhe. 1 cass. (Running Time: 1 hr. 30 min.).Tr. of Arabic with Ease. (ARA & GER.). 2000. bk. 75.00 (978-2-7005-1008-9(9)) Pub: Assimil FRA. Dist(s): Distribks Inc

Arabs: Journeys Beyond the Mirage. unabr. ed. David Lamb. Narrated by Nelson Runger. 10 cass. (Running Time: 14 hrs. 15 mins.). 1991. 85.00 (978-1-55690-621-3(8), 91421E7) Recorded Bks.
A survey of the Arab world through portraits of its people, customs & history. This closeup study knocks down the Western stereotypes of Arabs.

Arabs & Jews Historically. 1 cass. (Running Time: 18 mins.). 1978. 8.00 (RME111) Esstee Audios.
Consists primarily of an analysis of Jewish life under Muslim rule & of the very necessary & unique role the Jews have played in Muslim society.

Aradia: Gospel of the Witches. abr. ed. Charles G. Leland. Read by Barbara Marciniak. 1 cass. (Running Time: 1 hr. 30 mins.). 1996. 11.95 (978-1-57453-039-1(9), 330108) Audio Lit.

Araknophobia. Read by Peter Sallis & Gareth Armstrong. 2 cass. (J). 1998. pap. bk. 16.99 (978-1-84032-171-5(7), HoddrStoughton) Pub: Hodder General GBR. Dist(s): Trafalgar
A man & his dog see an invitation to attend an Invention Convention - with a $100 first prize for best new invention.

***Araminta Spookie.** unabr. ed. Angie Sage. Read by Katherine Kellgren. (ENG.). 2006. (978-0-06-122887-2(7), KTegenBooks); (978-0-06-122888-9(5), KTegenBooks) HarperCollins Pubs.

***Araminta Spookie Vol. 2: Frognapped & Vampire Brat.** unabr. ed. Angie Sage. Read by Katherine Kellgren. (ENG.). 2007. (978-0-06-155421-6(9)); (978-0-06-155423-0(5)) HarperCollins Pubs.

Aran Islands, unabr. ed. John Millington Synge. Narrated by Donal Donnelly. 5 cass. (Running Time: 6 hrs. 30 mins.). 1997. 44.00 (978-0-7887-0875-6(9), 95012E7) Recorded Bks.
While living with the island's natives for weeks at a time, he record folklore & anecdotes that immortalize the Aran Island & its people.

Arap Petry Velikovo. Alexander Pushkin. 1 cass. (Running Time: 1 hr.). (RUS.). 1996. pap. bk. 19.50 (978-1-58085-560-0(1)) Interlingua VA.
Includes Russian text. The combination of written text & clarity & pace of diction will open the door for intermediate & advanced students to genuine comprehension & the use of literary texts for advancement in rapid understanding of written & oral language materials. The audio text plus written text concept makes foreign languages accessible to a much wider range of students than books alone.

Arban's Complete Conservatory Method for Trumpet (Cornet) Ed. by Edwin Franko Goldman & Walter M. Smith. Text by Claude Gordon. 1982. pap. bk. 41.95 (978-0-8258-5852-9(6)) Fischer Inc NY.

Arbitration: Alternative Dispute Negotiation - CLE Program. Paul Chait. (Running Time: 2 hrs). 2002. pap. bk. 75.00 (978-0-9728424-0-2(3)) Continuing Legal Educ.

***Arborist.** M. S. Holm. Read by Jamil Gaines. (ENG.). (J). 2010. cd-rom 19.95 (978-0-9796199-6-0(3), Sentry Bks) Great W Pub.

Arca De Noe' Historias Dramatizadas En Casete, Vol. 1. Tr. of Noah's Ark Dramatized Stories on Cassette. 2002. 5.99 (978-0-8254-0965-3(9)) Kregel.

Arca De Noe' Historias Dramatizadas En Casete, Vol. 2. Tr. of Noah's Ark Dramatized Stories on Cassette. 2002. 5099.00 (978-0-8254-0966-0(7)) Kregel.

Arca De Noe' Historias Dramatizadas En Casete, Vol. 3. Tr. of Noah's Ark Dramatized Stories on Cassette. 2002. 5.99 (978-0-8254-0967-7(5)) Kregel.

Arca de Noe Paquete. 3 cass. (Sabio y Prudente Ser.).Tr. of Package Noah's Ark. (SPA.). (J). (ps-2). 2002. bk. 24.99 (978-0-8254-0968-4(3), Edit Portavoz) Kregel.

***Arcadia.** unabr. ed. Tom Stoppard. 3 CDs. (Running Time: 2 hrs. 45 mins.). 2009. audio compact disk 29.95 (978-1-58081-596-3(0)) L A Theatre.

***Arcadia Falls.** Carol Goodman. Narrated by Jen Taylor. (Running Time: 12 hrs. 37 mins. 0 sec.). (ENG.). 2011. audio compact disk 29.95 (978-1-60998-156-3(1)) Pub: AudioGO. Dist(s): Perseus Dist

***Arcadia Falls.** unabr. ed. Carol Goodman. Narrated by Jen Taylor. 1 MP3-CD. (Running Time: 12 hrs. 30 mins.). 2010. 59.95 (978-0-7927-7065-7(X)); audio compact disk 94.95 (978-0-7927-6353-6(X)) AudioGO.

Arcanum: The Extraordinary True Story. abr. ed. Janet Gleeson. (Running Time: 3 hrs. 30 mins.). (ENG.). 2006. 14.98 (978-1-59483-662-6(0)) Pub: Hachet Audio. Dist(s): HachBkGrp

Arch Oboler: Retrospective. Perf. by Arch Oboler et al. 2009. audio compact disk 39.98 (978-1-57019-899-1(3)) Radio Spirits.

Arch Oboler's Plays: Back to the Indians, The Day the Sun Exploded, The Laughing Man & Johnny Got His Gun. unabr. ed. Hosted by Arch Oboler. 1 cass. (Running Time: 1 hr.). 2001. 6.98 (2074) Radio Spirits.

Arch Oboler's Plays: Strange Morning & Night. unabr. ed. Hosted by Arch Oboler. 1 cass. (Running Time: 1 hr.). 2001. 6.98 (2551) Radio Spirits.

Arch Oboler's Plays: The Naked Mountain & The Truth. unabr. ed. Hosted by Arch Oboler. 1 cass. (Running Time: 1 hr.). 2001. 6.98 (2113) Radio Spirits.

Arch Oboler's Plays: The Parade & Mirage. unabr. ed. Hosted by Arch Oboler. 1 cass. (Running Time: 1 hr.). 2001. 6.98 (2053) Radio Spirits.

Arch of Forgiveness. Kenneth Wapnick. 3 CDs. 2004. audio compact disk 16.00 (978-1-59142-166-5(7), CD104) Foun Miracles.

Arch of Triumph. Erich Maria Ramarque. Read by Ralph Cosham. 11 cass. (Running Time: 16 hrs.). 2004. 85.95 (978-0-7861-2878-5(X), 3381); audio compact disk 108.00 (978-0-7861-8292-3(X), 3381) Blckstn Audio.

Arch of Triumph. Erich-Maria Remarque. Read by Ralph Cosham. (Running Time: 15 hrs.). 2004. 44.95 (978-1-59912-422-3(X)) Iofy Corp.

Arch of Triumph. unabr. ed. Erich Maria Ramarque. Read by Ralph Cosham. 13 vols. (Running Time: 16 hrs.). 2005. audio compact disk 24.95 (978-0-7861-8357-9(8), 3381) Blckstn Audio.

Arch of Triumph. unabr. ed. Erich-Maria Remarque. Read by Ralph Cosham. 11 cass. (Running Time: 54000 sec.). 2005. 34.95 (978-0-7861-3467-0(4), E3381); audio compact disk 39.95 (978-0-7861-8044-8(7), ZE3381) Blckstn Audio.

Arch Wizard. unabr. ed. Ed Greenwood. Read by Christopher Lane & Phil Gigante. (Running Time: 13 hrs.). (Falconfar Saga Ser.). 2009. 39.97 (978-1-4233-5120-7(7), 9781423351207, BADLE); 39.97 (978-1-4233-5118-4(5), 9781423351184, Brinc Audio MP3 Lib); 24.99 (978-1-4233-5119-1(3), 9781423351191, BAD) Brilliance Audio.

Arch Wizard. unabr. ed. Ed Greenwood. Read by Christopher A. Lane & Phil Gigante. 1 MP3-CD. (Running Time: 13 hrs.). (Falconfar Saga Ser.). 2009. 24.99 (978-1-4233-5117-7(7), 9781423351177, Brilliance MP3) Brilliance Audio.

Arch Wizard. unabr. ed. Ed Greenwood. Read by Christopher Lane & Phil Gigante. 11 CDs. (Running Time: 13 hrs.). (Falconfar Saga Ser.). 2009. audio compact disk 89.97 (978-1-4233-5116-0(9), 9781423351160, BriAudCD Unabrid) Brilliance Audio.

Arch Wizard. unabr. ed. Ed Greenwood. Read by Christopher A. Lane & Phil Gigante. 11 CDs. (Running Time: 13 hrs.). (Falconfar Saga Ser.). 2009. audio compact disk 32.99 (978-1-4233-5115-3(0), 9781423351153, Bril Audio CD Unabri) Brilliance Audio.

Archaeology at Aksum, Ethiopia, 1993-7. David W. Phillipson. 2001. 237.50 (978-1-872566-13-9(8)) Pub: Brit Inst Estrn Africa GBR. Dist(s): David Brown

Archaeology of the Early Islamic Settlement in Palestine. Jodi Magness. 2004. bk. 49.50 (978-1-57506-070-5(1)) Eisenbrauns.

Archaeology of the Trobriand Islands, Milne Bay Province, Papua New Guinea: Excavation Season 1999. Ed. by Goran Burenhult. (BAR International Ser.: Vol. 1080). 2002. audio compact disk 75.00 (978-1-84171-457-8(7)) Pub: British Arch Reports GBR. Dist(s): David Brown

Archangel. unabr. ed. Robert Harris. Read by Michael Kitchen. 10 CDs. 2000. audio compact disk 94.95 (978-0-7540-5356-9(3), CCD 047) Pub: Chivers Audio Bks GBR. Dist(s): AudioGO
Fluke Kelso is in Moscow to attend a conference on the newly opened Soviet archives. At his hotel, he meets a man who claims to have been with Stalin when he died. Kelso checks out the old man's story. But what begins as idle curiosity soon turns into a murderous chase across Russia.

Archangel: A Novel. unabr. ed. Paul Watkins. Narrated by George Guidall. 8 cass. (Running Time: 11 hrs. 45 mins.). 1999. 70.00 (978-0-7887-0573-1(3), 94750E7) Recorded Bks.
Deep in the woods of Maine, a crippled but powerful businessman & a reclusive environmentalist clash over acres of valuable trees.

Archangel Crusader. (Archangel Ser.: 1). (ENG.). 2006. 39.00 (978-1-930501-06-5(4)) Blue Planet Bks.

Archangel Raphael: Angel Guide of Tobias. 1 CD. (Running Time: 70 min). 2006. audio compact disk 8.95 (978-0-9774914-1-4(2)) Archangel Audio.

***Archangel's Kiss.** unabr. ed. Nalini Singh. Narrated by Justine Eyre. (Running Time: 10 hrs. 0 mins. 0 sec.). (Guild Hunter Ser.). (ENG.). 2010. 24.99 (978-1-4001-6716-6(7)); 16.99 (978-1-4001-8716-4(8)); audio compact disk 69.99 (978-1-4001-4716-8(6)); audio compact disk 34.99 (978-1-4001-1716-1(X)) Pub: Tantor Media. Dist(s): IngramPubServ

Archangels the Saga #5. Eternal Staff. 2004. 4.50 (978-1-887814-51-5(5)) Eternal Stud.

***Archangels 101: How to Connect Closely with Archangels Michael, Raphael, Uriel, Gabriel & Others for Healing, Protection, & Guidance.** Doreen Virtue. (ENG.). 2010. audio compact disk 39.95 (978-1-4019-3072-1(7)) Hay House.

Archbishop Pio Laghi on Papal Visit. Interview with Mother Angelica & Pio Laghi. 1 cass. (Running Time: 60 mins.). (Mother Angelica Live Ser.). 1987. 10.00 (978-1-55794-095-7(9), T46) Eternal Wrd TV.

ArchEnemy. Frank Beddor. Narrated by Gerard Doyle. (Looking Glass Wars Trilogy: Bk. 3). (J). (gr. 7). 2009. audio compact disk 34.95 (978-0-545-10323-7(1)) Scholastic Inc.

ArchEnemy. unabr. ed. Frank Beddor. Narrated by Gerard Doyle. 8 CDs. (Running Time: 9 hrs. 15 mins.). (Looking Glass Wars Trilogy: Bk. 3). (ENG.). (YA). (gr. 7 up). 2009. audio compact disk 74.95 (978-0-545-10324-4(X)) Scholastic Inc.

Archer in the Marrow see Peter Viereck

Archer's Quest. unabr. ed. Linda Sue Park. Read by Feodor Chin. 3 CDs. (Running Time: 3 hrs. 48 mins.). (J). (gr. 4-7). 2007. audio compact disk 24.00 (978-0-7393-4854-3(X)) Books on Tape.

Archer's Story. unabr. ed. Patrice De Cygne. Read by Patrice De Cygne. 1 cass. (Running Time: 40 mins.). 1994. 10.00 (978-0-943907-10-9(1)) Bruce Finson.
This is an original work of fiction, a narrative of the adventures of a timeless Everyman.

***Archer's Tale.** abr. ed. Bernard Cornwell. Read by Tim Pigott-Smith. (ENG.). 2005. (978-0-06-083889-8(2), Harper Audio); (978-0-06-078448-5(2), Harper Audio) HarperCollins Pubs.

Archer's Tale. unabr. ed. Bernard Cornwell. Narrated by Colin McPhillamy. 10 cass. (Running Time: 14 hrs. 15 mins.). (Grail Quest Ser.: No. 1). 2001. 96.00 (978-0-7887-9954-9(1)) Recorded Bks.

Arches National Park Database: Part of the World Arch Database. (World Arch Data Base: Vol. 2). 2001. audio compact disk 16.95 (978-1-891858-34-5(3)) Arch Hunter Bks.

Archetypal Astrology. unabr. ed. Richard Tarnas. 1 cass. (Running Time: 1 hr. 28 mins.). 1980. 11.00 (11403) Big Sur Tapes.

Archetypal Energy Constellations in Analysis. Read by Murray Stein. 1 cass. (Running Time: 90 mins.). 1976. 10.95 (978-0-7822-0263-2(2), 021) C G Jung IL.
Part of the "Energy" conference set.

Archetypal Images of the King & the Warrior. Read by Robert Moore. 1 cass. (Running Time: 2 hrs.). 1988. 12.95 (978-0-7822-0178-9(4), 327) C G Jung IL.

Archetypal Images of the Magician & the Lover. Read by Robert Moore. 1 cass. (Running Time: 2 hrs.). 1988. 12.95 (978-0-7822-0179-6(2), 328) C G Jung IL.

Archetypal Kingdom. unabr. ed. 8 cass. (Running Time: 16 hrs.). 40.00 (978-0-917189-25-8(6)) A R Colton Fnd.
Focuses on the three heavens & their inhabitants of spiritual mediators, who work telepathically with mankind.

Archetypal Realities of Everyday Life. Read by Anthony Stevens. 2 cass. (Running Time: 4 hrs.). 1986. 21.95 (978-0-7822-0299-1(3), 191) C G Jung IL.

Archetypal Self: Hope or Illusion? Read by James Hall. 3 cass. (Running Time: 6 hrs.). 1986. 28.95 (978-0-7822-0085-0(0), 194) C G Jung IL.

Archetypal Shadow in Myth, Folklore & Religion. Read by Robert Moore. 2 cass. (Running Time: 2 hrs.). (Satan Ser.: No. 1). 1989. 14.00 (978-0-7822-0188-8(1), 379-1) C G Jung IL.

Archetype of the Cosmic Shaman. Kenneth Ring. 1 cass. (AA & A Symposium Ser.). 9.00 (A0252-87) Sound Photosyn.
Ken & Alise Agar put the elegant & unusual Angels, Aliens, & Archetypes Symposium together, & this was its opening talk.

Archetype of the Green Man: Men, the Earth & the Growth Spirit. Nancy Dougherty. Read by Nancy Dougherty. 1 cass. (Running Time: 53 mins.). 1993. 9.95 (978-0-7822-0458-2(9), 535) C G Jung IL.

Archetypes. Caroline Myss. (Archetypes). 1997. 55.00 (978-1-893869-56-1(3)) Celbrtng Life.

Archetypes & Sacred Contracts. Caroline Myss. (Archetypes & Sacred Contracts). 1998. 55.00 (978-1-893869-57-8(1)) Celbrtng Life.

Archetypes; Healing Powers. Jonathan Murro & Ann Ree Colton. 1 cass. 7.95 A R Colton Fnd.
Discusses the goal of God Realization.

Archetypes of the Divine. Read by Thomas Newbold. 1 cass. (Running Time: 2 hrs.). 1977. 12.95 (978-0-7822-0220-5(9), 031) C G Jung IL.

Archie Andrews. collector's ed. Perf. by Bob Hastings. 6 cass. (Running Time: 9 hrs.). 2001. bk. 34.98 (4558) Radio Spirits.
The misadventures of Archie Andrews, a high school student in the town of Riverdale, and his pals Jughead Jones, Betty Cooper and Veronica Lodge. 18 episodes.

Archie Andrews: Big Ballgame & Riverdale Formal Dance. unabr. ed. Perf. by Bob Hastings & Harlan Stone, Jr. 1 cass. (Running Time: 1 hr.). 2001. 6.98 (1543) Radio Spirits.

Archie Andrews: Bubble Bath Soap for Veronica & The Double Date. unabr. ed. Perf. by Bob Hastings & Harlan Stone, Jr. 1 cass. (Running Time: 1 hr.). 2001. 6.98 (2392) Radio Spirits.

Archie Andrews: Late for School Dance & Flat Tire Fiasco. unabr. ed. Perf. by Bob Hastings & Harlan Stone, Jr. 1 cass. (Running Time: 1 hr.). 2001. 6.98 (1864) Radio Spirits.

Archie Fisher: The Man with a Rhyme. 1 cass. (Running Time: 1 hr.). 9.98 (C-61); audio compact disk 14.98 (CD-61) Folk-Legacy.
Classic recording of an important Scottish artist.

Architect: A Novel. abr. ed. Keith Ablow. Read by Denis O'Hare. 2005. 17.95 (978-1-59397-718-4(2)) Pub: Macmill Audio. Dist(s): Macmillan

Architectural Design Market in China: A Strategic Reference 2006. Compiled by Icon Group International, Inc. Staff. 2007. ring bd. 195.00 (978-0-497-35861-7(1)) Icon Grp.

Architectural Design Services in China: A Strategic Reference 2006. Compiled by Icon Group International, Inc. Staff. 2007. ring bd. 195.00 (978-0-497-35862-4(X)) Icon Grp.

Architectural Design Services in Japan: A Strategic Reference 2006. Compiled by Icon Group International, Inc. Staff. 2007. ring bd. 195.00 (978-0-497-36045-0(4)) Icon Grp.

Architectural Drafting Using AutoCAD 2005. David A. Madsen & Ron M. Palma. (gr. 9-13). tchr. ed. 35.40 (978-1-59070-380-9(4)) Goodheart.

Architecture of Happiness. unabr. ed. Alain de Botton. (Running Time: 9 hrs. NaN mins.). 2009. 29.95 (978-1-4332-2297-9(3)); audio compact disk 59.95 (978-1-4332-2293-1(0)); audio compact disk 70.00 (978-1-4332-2294-8(9)) Blckstn Audio.

Architecture of Man. Chuck Missler. 2 cass. (Running Time: 2.5 hours +). (Briefing Packages by Chuck Missler). 1993. vinyl bd. 14.95 Incls. notes . (978-1-880532-95-9(6)) Koinonia Hse.
What is the pattern of our internal system design? If God really indwells us, why do we behave the way we do?What does the Bible really mean by "Heart"? "Soul"? "Spirit"? "Mind"?Chuck provides insights on the design of computer systems garnered from his over 30 years in the computer industry. He helps us to understand our own "system design" as the Ultimate System Architect has provided it to us.Seven times the New Testament points us to Solomon's Temple as the key to understanding ourselves.

Architecture of Man. Chuck Missler. 2 CD's. (Running Time: 120 mins.). (Briefing Packages by Chuck Missler). 1993. audio compact disk 19.95 (978-1-57821-305-4(3)) Koinonia Hse.

***Architectures Without Place: 1968/2008.** Ed. by Ramon Faura Coll. 2010. pap. bk. 59.95 (978-84-96842-44-1(4)) Colegio Arquit ESP.

***Archives Masters, Volume 1.** RadioArchives.com. (Running Time: 600). (ENG.). 2005. audio compact disk 29.98 (978-1-61081-038-8(4)) Radio Arch.

Archivist: A Novel, unabr. ed. Martha Cooley. Narrated by George Guidall & Suzanne Toren. 7 cass. (Running Time: 10 hrs.). 1999. 60.00 (978-0-7887-2474-9(6), 95549E7) Recorded Bks.
Matthias Lane, a university archivist, has been asked to open letters sealed in the library - ones written by T. S. Elliot to his close friend, Emily Hale. As he considers the request, Matthias is confronted with parallels between the poet's life & his own.

Archus Legacy. unabr. ed. Rene Smeraglia. Read by Maynard Villers. 6 cass. (Running Time: 7 hrs. 30 mins.). 1996. 39.95 (978-1-55686-643-2(7)) Books in Motion.
Three space adventurers, in search of a missing brother, are stranded on the forbidden planet of Archus, pursued by killers, & thousands of miles away from their only hope of rescue.

Arctic Adventure: Inuit Life in the 1800s. Dana Meachen Rau. Illus. by Peg Magovern. 1 cass. (Running Time: 13 mins.). Dramatization. (Smithsonian Odyssey Ser.). (ENG.). (J). (gr. 2-5). 1997. 7.95 (978-1-56899-422-2(2), C6005) Soundprints.
Standing before the Polar Eskimo exhibit at the National Museum of Natural History, Tomas sees a diorama of a boy who has just caught his first seal. Instantly transported, Tomas finds he has become a young Inuit boy on the eve of his first hunt. Follow him through this adventure.

Arctic Adventure Incl. toy: Inuit Life in the 1800s. Dana Meachen Rau. Illus. by Peg Magovern. (Smithsonian Odyssey Ser.). (J). (gr. 2-5). 1997. pap. bk. 25.95 (978-1-56899-420-8(6)) Soundprints.

Arctic Audio CD. Adapted by Benchmark Education Company Staff. Based on a work by Katherine Scraper. (Early Explorers Set C Ser.). (J). (gr. 1). 2008. audio compact disk 10.00 (978-1-60437-534-3(5)) Benchmark Educ.

Arctic Drift. abr. ed. Clive Cussler & Dirk Cussler. (Running Time: 6 hrs.). No. 20. (ENG.). (gr. 8). 2008. audio compact disk 29.95 (978-0-14-314368-0(9), PengAudBks) Penguin Grp USA.

Arctic Drift. unabr. ed. Clive Cussler & Dirk Cussler. Read by Scott Brick. 11 CDs. (Running Time: 13 hrs.). No. 20. (ENG.). (gr. 8). 2008. audio compact disk 39.95 (978-0-14-314367-3(0), PengAudBks) Penguin Grp USA.

Arctic Drift. unabr. ed. Clive Cussler & Dirk Cussler. Read by Scott Brick. 11 CDs. (Dirk Pitt Ser.: No. 20). 2008. audio compact disk 110.00 (978-1-4159-6255-8(3), BksonTape) Pub: Random Audio Pubg. Dist(s): Random
A potential breakthrough discovery to reverse global warming . . . a series of unexplained sudden deaths in British Columbia . . . a rash of international incidents between the United States and one of its closest allies that threatens to erupt into an actual shooting war . . . NUMA director Dirk Pitt and his children, Dirk. Jr. and Summer, have reason to believe there's a connection here somewhere, but they also know they have very little time to find it before events escalate out of control. Their only real clue might just be a mysterious silvery mineral traced to a long-ago expedition in search of the fabled Northwest Passage. But no one survived from that doomed mission, captain and crew perished to a man - and if Pitt and his colleague Al Giordino aren't careful, the very same fate may await them.

Arctic Event. unabr. ed. Robert Ludlum & James Cobb. Read by Jeff Woodman. 10 CDs. (Running Time: 13 hrs.). (ENG.). 2007. audio compact disk 39.98 (978-1-59483-654-1(X)) Pub: GrandCentral. Dist(s): HachBkGrp

Arctic Event. unabr. ed. Robert Ludlum & James Cobb. Read by Jeff Woodman. (Running Time: 13 hrs.). (Covert-One Ser.). (ENG.). 2007. 26.98 (978-1-59483-796-8(1)) Pub: Hachet Audio. Dist(s): HachBkGrp

Arctic Fire. collector's ed. Keith Douglass. Read by Edward Lewis. 6 cass. (Running Time: 9 hrs.). (Carrier Ser.: No. 9). 2000. 48.00 (978-0-7366-5628-3(6)) Books on Tape.
The Cold War may be over, but in the Bering Sea, it's far from quiet on America's Western front. A Russian splinter group has captured the Aleutian Islands off the coast of Alaska. Rear Admiral "Tombstone" Magruder & Carrier Battle Group Fourteen are sent to the Aleutians on the mission they prayed would never come: repel invaders from American soil.

Arctic Gold. abr. ed. Stephen Coonts & William H. Keith. Read by Phil Gigante. (Running Time: 5 hrs.). (Deep Black Ser.: No. 7). 2010. audio compact disk 14.99 (978-1-4233-4412-4(X), 9781423344124, BCD Value Price) Brilliance Audio.

Arctic Gold. unabr. ed. Stephen Coonts & William H. Keith. Read by Phil Gigante. (Running Time: 12 hrs.). (Deep Black Ser.: No. 7). 2009. 39.97 (978-1-4233-4410-0(3), 9781423344100, BADLE); 39.97 (978-1-4233-4408-7(1), 9781423344087, Brinc Audio MP3 Lib); 24.99 (978-1-4233-4409-4(X), 9781423344094, BAD); 24.99 (978-1-4233-4407-0(3), 9781423344070, Brilliance MP3); audio compact disk 97.97 (978-1-4233-4406-3(5), 9781423344063, BriAudCD Unabrid); audio compact disk 34.99 (978-1-4233-4405-6(7), 9781423344056, Bril Audio CD Unabri) Brilliance Audio.

Arctic Incident. Eoin Colfer. Read by Nathaniel Parker. 4 cass. (Running Time: 6 hrs. 8 mins.). (Artemis Fowl Ser.: Bk. 2). (J). (gr. 6 up). 2004. 32.00 (978-0-8072-0893-9(0), Listening Lib); audio compact disk 40.00 (978-1-4000-8593-4(4), Listening Lib) Random Audio Pubg.

Arctic Incident. unabr. ed. Eoin Colfer. Read by Nathaniel Parker. 5 CDs. (Running Time: 6 hrs. 8 mins.). (Artemis Fowl Ser.: Bk. 2). (ENG.). (J). (gr. 7). 2004. audio compact disk 28.00 (978-1-4000-8592-7(6), Listening Lib) Pub: Random Audio Pubg. Dist(s): Random

Ardent Spirits: The Rise & Fall of Prohibition. unabr. ed. John Kobler & Brenda N. Gill. Read by John Kobler & Brenda N. Gill. Read by Heywood Hale Broon. 1 cass. (Running Time: 56 mins.). 12.95 (40045) J Norton Pubs.
Recalls an era of speakeasies, bathtub gin & the crusade of the Anti-Saloon League & Prohibition Path to bring about a "noble" experiment that had both tragic & comic results.

Are Brains Necessary? unabr. ed. John Lorber et al. 1 cass. 1990. 12.95 (ECN212) J Norton Pubs.

Are Men Necessary? When Sexes Collide. unabr. ed. Maureen Dowd. 10 CDs. (Running Time: 12 hrs.). 2005. audio compact disk 90.00 (978-1-4159-2549-2(6)); 72.00 (978-1-4159-2548-5(8)) Books on Tape.
Four decades after the sexual revolution, nothing has worked out the way it was supposed to. The sexes are circling each other as uneasily and comically as ever, from the bedroom to the boardroom to the Situation Room, and now the New York Times columnist who won a Pulitzer Prize in 1999 for saucy and incisive commentary about the dangerous liaisons of Bill, Monica, Hillary and Ken Starr digs into the Y and X files, exploring the mysteries and muddles of sexual combat in America. In a new book filled with chapters that surprise and amuse, Dowd explains why getting ready for a date went from glossing and gargling to Paxiling and Googling; why men are in an evolutionary and romantic shame spiral; why women have reeled backward in many ways; why men may be biologically unsuited to hold higher office, given their diva fits and catfights, teary confessions and fashion obsessions; why women are fixated on their looks more than ever, freezing their faces and emotions in an orgy of plasticity that makes the Stepford Wives look authentic; why male politicians and male institutions get tripped up in so much monkey business; why many alpha women, from Martha to Hillary, can have a successful second act only after becoming humiliated victims; and why the new definition of Having It All is less about empowerment and equality than about flirting and getting rescued, downshifting from "You go, girl!" to "You go lie down, girl." In addition, Dowd, who has reported on historic moments on the sexual battlefield, from Geraldine Ferraro's vice-presidential run to the Anita Hill-Clarence Thomas hearings to Hillary Rodham Clinton's reign as copresident, explores not only how many of these shining feminist triumphs backfired on women but also

how Hillary, a feminist icon busy plotting her campaign to be the first woman president, delivered the final blow to female solidarity herself.

Are Mormons Christians? Stephen E. Robinson. 3 cass. (Running Time: 3 hrs.). 1998. 19.95 (978-1-57008-434-8(3), Bkcraft Inc) Deseret Bk.

Are the Mentally Ill More Violent? Program from the Award Winning Public Radio Series. Read by Fred Goodwin. Comment by John Hockenberry. Contrib. by John Monahan et al. 1 cass. (Running Time: 1 hr.). (Infinite Mind Ser.). 1998. audio compact disk 21.95 (978-1-888064-34-6(X), LCM 28) Lichtenstein Creat.

Mental illness often appears in the media in connection with violent acts, so that fairly or not, many think the two are linked. Are they? Top mental health experts and advocates disagree on that connection, and on how it affects public policy.

Are the Nukes Already Killing Us? 1 cass. (Running Time: 1 hr.). 9.00 (OP-80-02-07, HarperThor) HarpC GBR.

Are We Almost There? Victor Cockburn & Judith Steinbergh. Perf. by Troubadour Staff. 1 cass. (Running Time: 36 min.). (J). (gr. k-3). 1984. 9.95 (978-0-939065-22-6(3), GW1026) Gentle Wind.

Songs & poems that are drawn from family life.

Are We Almost There? Perf. by Troubadour Staff. (J). 1999. audio compact disk 14.95 (978-0-939065-85-1(1)) Gentle Wind.

***Are We Born Racist?** Hosted by Adam/L Perkins. 2010. cd-rom 11.99 (978-0-9793927-5-7(6), RR&R) Posit Prints.

Are We Morally Responsible for the Advice We Give Other People. Instructed by Manly P. Hall. 8.95 (978-0-89314-006-9(6), C840722) Philos Res.

Are We More Neurotic Today: Fulton J. Sheen, Vol. I. unabr. ed. Fulton J. Sheen. 7 cass. (Running Time: 10 hrs. 30 mins.). (Life Is Worth Living Ser.: 5). 1985. 29.95 F Sheen Comm.

The late Bishop Sheen explains how our gift of love shared with others can give new joy to our lives.

Are We Ready for the Great Leap into a Peaceful World? Manly P. Hall. 8.95 (978-0-89314-007-6(4), C880522) Philos Res.

Explains philosophy & religion.

Are We Really Letting Go? & Is My Well Running Dry? 1 cass. (Recovery Is Forever Ser.). 8.95 (1532G) Hazelden.

Are We There Yet? 1 cass. (Running Time: 64 mins). 1999. Art of Hearing.

An American family on summer vacation traveling across the country while pulling a travel trailer, this family meets the funniest characters imaginable. Every family vacation you ever took will come back to you!.

Are We There Yet? unabr. ed. Martha Gellhorn et al. 3 CDs. (Running Time: 3 hrs. 0 mins. 0 sec.). (Selected Shorts Ser.). (ENG.). 2008. audio compact disk 28.00 (978-1-934033-05-0(7)) Pub: Symphony Space. Dist(s): IPG Chicago

Are We There Yet? - How Much Am I Worth? Charles Lawther. 1 CD. (Running Time: 1 hr. 30 mins.). 2005. audio compact disk 12.95 (978-0-660-18652-8(7)) Pub: Canadian Broadcasting CAN. Dist(s): Georgetown Term

An in-depth look at the struggles and triumphs of immigrants who have come to Canada over the past 20 years.Most of these new Canadians are extremely well educated, yet remain unable to be accredited in Canada.

Are You a Caregiver? Annemarie Demens & Paul Crumby. Read by Annemarie Demens & Paul Crumby. 6 cass. (Running Time: 50 mins. per cass.). 1997. 79.95 incl. script Set. (978-1-891474-07-1(3)) Caregivers.

Provides information for family caregivers of elderly relatives.

Are You a Winner? Lynne Palmer. Read by Lynne Palmer. 1 cass. (Running Time: 90 min.). 1994. 8.95 (1115) Am Fed Astrologers.

Gambling & astrology.

***Are You Afraid of the Dark?** abr. ed. Sidney Sheldon. (ENG.). 2004. (978-0-06-079235-0(3), Harper Audio); (978-0-06-081475-5(6), Harper Audio) HarperCollins Pubs.

Are You Afraid of the Dark? abr. ed. Sidney Sheldon. Read by Marsha Mason. 6 CDs. (Running Time: 9 hrs.). 2004. audio compact disk 29.95 (978-0-06-073830-3(8)) HarperCollins Pubs.

***Are You Afraid of the Dark?** unabr. ed. Sidney Sheldon. Read by Kit Flanagan. (ENG.). 2004. (978-0-06-078657-1(4), Harper Audio); (978-0-06-081455-7(1), Harper Audio) HarperCollins Pubs.

Are You Afraid of the Dark? A Novel. unabr. ed. Sidney Sheldon. Read by Kit Flanagan. 2004. 29.95 (978-0-06-073832-7(4)) HarperCollins Pubs.

Are You Asleep at the Wheel? Ben Young. 1996. 4.95 (978-0-7417-6015-9(0), B0015) Win Walk.

Are You Being Served? Camping In. Created by Broadcasting Corp. British. (Running Time: 2 hrs. 0 mins. 0 sec.). (ENG.). 2009. audio compact disk 24.95 (978-1-60283-744-7(9)) Pub: AudioGO. Dist(s): Perseus Dist

***Are You Being Served? - The Clock: Four Classic Episode Soundtracks.** Created by Broadcasting Corp. British. (Running Time: 2 hrs. 0 mins. 0 sec.). (ENG.). 2010. audio compact disk 24.95 (978-1-4084-1035-6(4)) Pub: AudioGO. Dist(s): Perseus Dist

Are You Born? see Poetry & Voice of Muriel Rukeyser

Are You Coming Back, Phin Montana? Jane Coleman. (Running Time: 0 hr. 48 mins.). 2000. 10.95 (978-1-60083-543-8(0)) Iofy Corp.

***Are You Coming Back, Phinn Montana.** Jane Candia Coleman. 2009. (978-1-60136-419-7(9)) Audio Holding.

Are You Dreaming? Mystical Electronica That Echoes the Tribal Heartbeat. One at Last. (Running Time: 60 mins.). 2006. audio compact disk 17.98 (978-1-59179-526-1(5), M1080D) Sounds True.

***Are You Dying to Have Sex?(c): Student/online/downloadable Version.** Compiled by Human Development Resource Council. (ENG.). (YA). 2010. suppl. ed. (978-0-9777625-4-5(8)) Human Dev Res.

***Are You Dying to Have Sex?(c): Teacher Edition.** ed. Compiled by Human Development Resource Council. (ENG.). 2010. 50.00 (978-0-9777625-7-6(2)) Human Dev Res.

Are You Fit for Life? unabr. ed. Jack Graham. (Running Time: 5 hrs. 15 mins. 0 sec.). (ENG.). 2007. audio compact disk 26.98 (978-1-59644-487-4(8), Hovel Audio) christianaud.

***Are You Fit for Life?** unabr. ed. Jack Graham. Narrated by Raymond Todd. (ENG.). 2007. 16.98 (978-1-59644-488-1(6), Hovel Audio) christianaud.

Are You from Another Planet or What? unabr. ed. Alyce P. Cornyn-Selby. Read by Alyce P. Cornyn-Selby. 1 cass. 1994. bk. 11.95; 11.95 (978-0-941383-21-9(0)) Beynch Pr.

Men & women communicating & not communicating; what's right with the way they communicate now; what can be done to improve it; practical; living one day as a woman; living one day as a man.

Are You Going Through the Motions? Jack Marshall. 1 cass. 2004. 9.98 (978-1-57734-152-9(X), 06005667) Covenant Comms.

Getting out of religious ruts to come unto Christ.

Are You Greater Than Jacob? John 4:12, 710. Ed Young. 1989. 4.95 (978-0-7417-1710-8(7), 710) Win Walk.

Are You Happy? Jeff Cavins. 2004. audio compact disk 7.95 (978-1-932927-38-2(7)) Ascensn Pr.

Are You in Love? Speeches. Creflo A. Dollar. 3 cass. (Running Time: 3 hrs. 15 mins.). 2006. 15.00 (978-1-59944-003-3(2)); audio compact disk 21.00 (978-1-59944-004-0(0)) Creflo Dollar.

Are You Listening? Jesus Teaches Holiness in the Sermon on the Mount - A Layman's View. Charles W. Thornton. 2007. audio compact disk 40.99 (978-1-60247-451-2(6)) Tate Pubng.

Are You Living in the Right Place. Carolyn Dodson. 1 cass. 8.95 (864) Am Fed Astrologers.

Are You Now or Have You Ever Been. Eric Bentley. 2 CDs. (Running Time: 5220 sec.). 1998. audio compact disk 25.95 (978-1-58081-324-2(0)) L A Theatre.

Are You Now or Have You Ever Been? unabr. ed. Eric Bentley. Read by Edward Asner et al. 1 cass. (Running Time: 1 hr. 29 mins.). 1994. 20.95 (978-1-58081-055-5(1), RDP3) L A Theatre.

In the mid-1950's the House Un-American Activities Committee began investigating communist influence in the entertainment industry. Judy Garland, Lillian Helmond, Arthur Miller, Paul Robeson & other deplored the witchhunt. This searing docudrama from actual transcripts of the committee hearings reveals how decent people were persuaded to "name names", & the steep price paid by those who refused.

Are You Ready! To Take Charge, Lose Weight, Get in Shape, & Change Your Life Forever. abr. ed. Bob Harper. Read by Bob Harper. (ENG.). 2008. audio compact disk 19.95 (978-0-7393-5841-2(3), Random AudioBks) Pub: Random Audio Pubg. Dist(s): Random

Are You Ready to Shape-Up? 11 Cor. 1:1-2. Ed Young. 1990. 4.95 (978-0-7417-1774-0(3), 774) Win Walk.

Are You Ready to Succeed? Unconventional Strategies for Achieving Personal Mastery in Business & Life. abr. ed. Srikumar S. Rao. Read by Srikumar S. Rao. 3 CDs. (Running Time: 14400 sec.). 2006. audio compact disk 24.98 (978-1-4013-8333-6(5), Hyperion Audio) Pub: Hyperion. Dist(s): HarperCollins Pubs

Are You Saved? A Mormon's View of Faith, Works, Grace & Salvation. unabr. ed. Duane S. Crowther. Read by Duane S. Crowther. 1 cass. (Running Time: 90 mins.). 1985. 13.98 (978-0-88290-401-6(9), 1814) Horizon Utah.

Features a comparison of the Protestant & Mormon views. Topics discussed are: the fall of Adam, atonement, how the Lord was able to pay for man's sins, faith, works, justification, sanctification & being born again.

Are You Somebody? The Accidental Memoir of a Dublin Woman, unabr. ed. Nuala O'Faolain. Read by Donada Peters. 6 cass. (Running Time: 9 hrs.). 1999. 29.95 (978-0-7366-4475-4(X)) Books on Tape.

Born one of nine children in a penniless North Dublin family, she not only survived but pushed at the boundaries of the confining Catholic Ireland she grew up in.

Are You Somebody? The Accidental Memoir of a Dublin Woman, unabr. collector's ed. Nuala O'Faolain. Read by Donada Peters. 6 cass. (Running Time: 9 hrs.). 1999. 48.00 (978-0-7366-4469-3(5), 4912) Books on Tape.

Born one of nine children in a penniless North Dublin family, the author not only survived but pushed at the boundaries of the confining Catholic Ireland she grew up in. As a little girl, Nuala had a passion for reading. While boarding school was an alien world, Nuala was aware of the quality of education it provided & built on that gift by earning a scholarship to Oxford. From there she made a career in journalism.

Are You the One? unabr. ed. Read by Gayle D. Erwin. 1 cass. (Running Time: 1 hr.). 1992. 4.95 (978-1-56599-505-5(8), C-5) Yahshua Pub.

John 1: 29-34.

Are You the One for Me? Knowing Who's Right & Avoiding Who's Wrong. abr. rev. ed. Barbara De Angelis. Read by Barbara De Angelis. 3 CDs. (Running Time: 3 hrs. 0 mins. 0 sec.). 2004. audio compact disk 19.95 (978-1-59397-355-1(1)) Pub: Macmill Audio. Dist(s): Macmillan

Are You There Alone? The Unspeakable Crime of Andrea Yates. Suzanne O'Malley. Read by Betty Ann Baker. 2004. 15.95 (978-0-7435-3929-6(X)) Pub: S&S Audio. Dist(s): S and S Inc

Are You There God? It's Me, Margaret. Judy Blume. Read by Laura Hamilton. 2 cass. (Running Time: 2 hrs. 10 mins.). (J). 2000. 18.00 (978-0-7366-9157-4(X)) Books on Tape.

Being eleven-going-on-twelve is hard enough, but when Margaret Simon's family moves to New Jersey she knows she needs to talk to someone. Is God listening?.

Are You There God? It's Me, Margaret. Judy Blume. Read by Laura Hamilton. 3 CDs. (Running Time: 3 hrs. 9 mins.). (J). (gr. 5-9). 2004. audio compact disk 30.00 (978-1-4000-8994-9(8), Listening Lib) Random Audio Pubg.

Are You There God? It's Me, Margaret. unabr. ed. Judy Blume. Read by Lorna Hamilton. 2 cass. (Running Time: 1 hr. 50 mins.). (J). 1997. 23.00 (978-0-7540-5026-1(2), LL 3045, Chivers Child Audio) AudioGO.

There doesn't seem to be anyone that Margaret can talk to about the problems of growing up - boys, school & parents. So Margaret decides to chat with God.

Are You There God? It's Me, Margaret, unabr. ed. Judy Blume. Read by Laura Hamilton. 2 cass. (Running Time: 2 hrs.). (YA). 1999. 16.98 (FS9-35699) Highsmith.

Are You There God? It's Me, Margaret. unabr. ed. Judy Blume. 1 read-along cass. (Running Time: 1 hr. 22 mins.). (Children's Cliffhangers Ser.). (J). (gr. 4-6). 1985. 14.98 incl. bk. & guide. (978-0-8072-1138-0(9), SWR52SP, Listening Lib) Random Audio Pubg.

Margaret Simon has a lot to think about making friends in a new school, boys & dances & parties, growing up physically "normal" & choosing a religion.

Are You There God? It's Me, Margaret. unabr. ed. Judy Blume. Read by Laura Hamilton. 2 vols. (Running Time: 3 hrs. 9 mins.). (J). (gr. 5-9). 1997. pap. bk. 29.00 (978-0-8072-7869-7(6), YA937SP, Listening Lib) Random Audio Pubg.

Life isn't easy when you're going on twelve - just ask Margaret who also has to contend with a new school, boys, slow physical development & choosing a religion. This is the book to reassure girls of their normalcy.

***Are You There God? It's Me, Margaret.** unabr. ed. Judy Blume. Read by Laura Hamilton. (ENG.). (J). 2011. audio compact disk 25.00 (978-0-307-74568-2(6), Listening Lib) Pub: Random Audio Pubg. Dist(s): Random

Are You There, Vodka? It's Me, Chelsea. unabr. ed. Chelsea Handler. Read by Chelsea Handler. CDs 5. (Running Time: 6 hrs. 30 mins. 0 sec.). (ENG.). 2008. audio compact disk 29.95 (978-0-7435-7364-1(1)) Pub: S&S Audio. Dist(s): S and S Inc

***Are You Tired & Wired? Your Simple 30-Day Program for Overcoming Adrenal Fatigue & Feeling Fantastic Again.** Marcelle Pick. (ENG.). 2011. audio compact disk 29.95 (978-1-4019-2821-6(8)) Hay House.

Are You Under a Curse. Derek Prince. 1 cass. (Running Time: 1 hr.). (B-4171) Derek Prince.

Are Your Eating Habits Making You Sick? If You Want to Be Tough, You Have to Eat Good Stuff. Illus. by Angela Brown & Wayne Pickering. Voice by Les Lingle. 1 cass. (Running Time: 30 mins.). (Words of Wellness - Your Show for Simple Solutions Ser.: 315). 2000. 12.95 (978-1-930995-07-9(5), LLP315) Life Long Pubg.

Looking for Robust Energy? Clear Complexion? Perfect Weight? Sound Sleep? Toned Muscles? Ageless Looking Skin? Look no further than your eating habits.

Are Your Running A Business or Just Doin' Hair. DeShawn F. Bullard. 1 CD. (Running Time: 1 hr). 2003. audio compact disk 59.95 (978-0-9743698-1-5(0)) Salon Industry.

Audio Presentaion of the Book: "Are You Running A Business Or Just Doin' Hair".

Area at the Park Audio CD: Set B. Benchmark Education Co. (Math Explorers Ser.). (J). (gr. 3-8). 2009. audio compact disk 10.00 (978-1-935441-68-7(X)) Benchmark Educ.

Area in the City Audio CD: Set B. Benchmark Education Co. (Math Explorers Ser.). (J). (gr. 3-8). 2009. audio compact disk 10.00 (978-1-935441-66-3(3)) Benchmark Educ.

Area on the Ranch Audio CD: Set B. Benchmark Education Co. (Math Explorers Ser.). (J). (gr. 3-8). 2009. audio compact disk 10.00 (978-1-935441-67-0(1)) Benchmark Educ.

Area 7. Matthew Reilly. Read by Sean Mangan. (Running Time: 13 hrs. 5 mins.). 2009. 94.99 (978-1-74214-274-6(5), 9781742142746) Pub: Bolinda Pubng AUS. Dist(s): Bolinda Pub Inc

Area 7. unabr. ed. Matthew Reilly. 9 cass. (Running Time: 13 hrs. 6 mins.). 2002. 72.00 (978-1-74030-754-3(2)) Pub: Bolinda Pubng AUS. Dist(s): Bolinda Pub Inc

Area 7. unabr. ed. Matthew Reilly. Read by Sean Mangan. 11 CDs. (Running Time: 13 hrs. 6 mins.). 2003. audio compact disk 103.95 (978-1-74093-099-4(1)) Pub: Bolinda Pubng AUS. Dist(s): Bolinda Pub Inc

Areas of Battle. Francis Frangipane. 1 cass. (Running Time: 90 mins.). (Three Battlegrounds Ser.: Vol. 1). 2000. 5.00 (FF03-001) Morning NC.

This two-tape series is brief, but foundational.

Areas of My Expertise. abr. ed. John Hodgman. Read by John Hodgman. 6 CDs. (Running Time: 7 hrs.). (ENG.). (gr. 8). 2006. audio compact disk 29.95 (978-0-14-305909-7(2), PengAudBks) Penguin Grp USA.

Areas of Protection. Elbert Willis. 1 cass. (Angel Protection Guidelines Ser.). 4.00 Fill the Gap.

Arenas del Alma. unabr. ed. Dante Gebel. (SPA & ENG.). 2009. audio compact disk 14.99 (978-0-8297-5733-0(3)) Pub: Vida Pubs. Dist(s): Zondervan

Areopagitica, unabr. ed. John Milton. Read by Robert L. Halvorson. 2 cass. (Running Time: 2 hrs.). 14.95 (49) Halvorson Assocs.

Arginase Deficiency - A Bibliography & Dictionary for Physicians, Patients, & Genome Researchers. Compiled by Icon Group International, Inc. Staff. 2007. ring bd. 28.95 (978-0-497-11334-6(1)) Icon Grp.

Argininosuccinic Aciduria - A Bibliography & Dictionary for Physicians, Patients, & Genome Researchers. Compiled by Icon Group International, Inc. Staff. 2007. ring bd. 28.95 (978-0-497-11335-3(X)) Icon Grp.

Arguing with Idiots: How to Stop Small Minds & Big Government. abr. ed. Glenn Beck. Read by Glenn Beck. Told to Steve Burguiere & Pat Gray. 7 CDs. (Running Time: 8 hrs.). 2009. audio compact disk 29.99 (978-0-7435-9687-9(0)) Pub: S&S Audio. Dist(s): S and S Inc

Argument Culture: Moving from Debate to Dialogue. Deborah Tannen. 2004. 10.95 (978-0-7435-4165-7(0)) Pub: S&S Audio. Dist(s): S and S Inc

Argumentation. 2nd ed. Instructed by David Zarefsky. 12 cass. (Running Time: 12 hrs). 2005. 129.95 (978-1-59803-114-0(7)); audio compact disk 69.95 (978-1-59803-116-4(3)) Teaching Co.

Argumentation Pts. I-II: The Study of Effective Reasoning. Instructed by David Zarefsky. 12 CDs. (Running Time: 12 hrs.). 2001. bk. 69.95 (978-1-56585-357-7(1), 499) Teaching Co.

Argumentation Vol. 1: The Study of Effective Reasoning, Parts I-II. Instructed by David Zarefsky. 12 cass. (Running Time: 12 hrs.). 2001. 54.95 (978-1-56585-144-3(7), 499) Teaching Co.

Argumentation Vol. 2: The Study of Effective Reasoning. Instructed by David Zarefsky. 6 cass. (Running Time: 6 hrs.). 2001. 129.95 (978-1-56585-149-8(8)) Teaching Co.

Aria: The Opera Album. Perf. by Andrea Bocelli. 1 cass. (Running Time: 1 hr.). 8.78 (PHI 462033); audio compact disk 14.38 Jewel box. (PHI 462033) NewSound.

Ariana: A Glimpse of Eternity, Rachel Nunes. 2 cass. (Running Time: 2 hrs.). 13.95 (978-1-57734-437-7(5), 07002009) Covenant Comms.

Ariana: A New Beginning, Rachel Nunes. 2 cass. (Running Time: 2 hrs.). 1999. 11.95 (978-1-57734-259-5(3), 07001673) Covenant Comms.

Novel about the power of love.

Ariana Set: A Gift Most Precious. Rachel Nunes. 2 cass. 1999. 11.98 (978-1-57734-148-2(1), 07001568) Covenant Comms.

Story of love & forgiveness in life's darkest hours.

Ariana Set: The Making of a Queen. Rachel Nunes. 2 cass. 2004. 11.98 (978-1-57734-026-3(4), 07001436) Covenant Comms.

Novel about love & renewal.

Arianna Kelt & the Renegades of Time: Wizards of Skyhall, Book 2. unabr. ed. J. R. King. Narrated by Ron Knowles. (Running Time: 6 hrs. 52 mins.). (ENG.). (YA). 2009. 19.95 (978-1-57545-314-9(2), RP Audio Pubng) Pub: Reagent Press. Dist(s): OverDrive Inc

Arianna Kelt & the Wizards of Skyhall. unabr. ed. J. R. King. Read by Ron Knowles. (J). 2008. 54.99 (978-1-60514-553-2(X)) Find a World.

Arianna Kelt & the Wizards of Skyhall: Wizards of Skyhall, Book 1. unabr. ed. J. R. King. Narrated by Ron Knowles. (Running Time: 4 hrs. 38 mins.). (ENG.). (J). 2008. 19.95 (978-1-57545-315-6(0), RP Audio Pubng) Pub: Reagent Press. Dist(s): OverDrive Inc

Arias for Acoustic Guitar. James Edwards. 1997. pap. bk. 19.95 (978-0-7866-0655-9(X), 95565BCD) Mel Bay.

Arias for tenor & orchestra from the repertoire of andrea Bocelli. Miroslav Christoff. 1999. pap. bk. 39.98 (978-1-59615-553-4(1), 586-089) Pub: Music Minus. Dist(s): Bookworld

Ariel. unabr. ed. Lawrence Block. Narrated by Alexandra O'Karma. 7 cass. (Running Time: 9 hrs. 45 mins.). 2002. 61.00 (978-1-4025-0196-8(X)) Recorded Bks.

Twelve-year-old Ariel is a strange, solitary girl. Recently, Ariel and her mother have seen a ghostly figure in their house. As a result, they are both having dreams that are becoming stranger, yet more and more real. What is the link between this frightening manifestation and the house?.

Ariel & Mysterious World Above: Read-Alongs. 1 cass. (Running Time: 15 mins.). (J). bk. 5.98 Disney Prod.

Ariel & the Mysterious World Above. unabr. ed. Hans Christian Andersen. 1 cass. (Running Time: 90 mins.). (Disney Read-Alongs Ser.). (J). (ps-3). 1997. bk. 7.99 (978-0-7634-0288-4(5)) Walt Disney.

Ariel & the Secret Grotto. Hans Christian Andersen. 1 cass. (Running Time: 90 mins.). (Read-Along Ser.). (J). bk. 7.99 (978-0-7634-0287-7(7)) W Disney Records.

Ariel & the Secret Grotto Read-Along. 1 cass. (Running Time: 15 min.). (J). bk. 5.98 Disney Prod.

Ariel's Christmas under the Sea Read-Along. 1 cass. (Running Time: 15 min.). (J). bk. 5.98 Disney Prod.

Ariel's Favorite Songs. 1 cass. (Running Time: 90 min.). (J). 11.99 (978-0-7634-0360-7(1)); 11.99 Norelco. (978-0-7634-0359-1(8)); audio compact disk 19.99 Jewel Box. (978-0-7634-0362-1(8)) W Disney Records.

Ariel's Favorite Songs. 1 CD. (Running Time: 1 hr.). (Little Mermaid Ser.). (J). (ps-3). 1998. audio compact disk 19.99 (978-0-7634-0361-4(X)) W Disney Records.

Ariel's Favorites. 1 cass. (Running Time: 1 hr.). (Disney Ser.). (J). 9.58 (DISN 60628); audio compact disk 14.38 Jewel box. (DISN 60628) NewSound.
Includes 15 original songs: "What's it Like to Be a Mermaid," "My Room in the Sea," "Limbo Rock," "Scuttle Strut," "Octopus' Garden" & more.

Aries. Narrated by Patricia G. Finlayson. Music by Mike Cantwell. Contrib. by Marie De Seta & TMY Communications Staff. 1 cass. (Running Time: 30 mins.). (Astrologer's Guide to the Personality Ser.: Vol. 1). 1994. 7.99 (978-1-878535-12-2(9)) De Seta-Finlayson.
Astrological description of the sign of Aries; individually customized, covering love, money, career, relationships & more.

Aries: March Twenty-One - April Twenty. Barrie Konicov. 1 cass. 11.98 (978-0-87082-090-8(7), 004) Potentials.
The author explains how each sign of the Zodiac has its positive & negative aspects & that, as individuals, in order to master our own destiny we must enhance our positive traits.

Aries: Unleash the Power of Your True Self. 1 cass. (Running Time: 1 hr.). 1999. 9.99 (978-1-928996-00-2(0)) MonAge.
Provides valuable insights into personality, relationships & explores attitudes & challenges regarding money, home, health & career.

Aries: Your Relationship with the Energy of the Universe. Loy Young. 1993. 9.95 (978-1-882888-13-9(8)) Aquarius Hse.

Arise. Clancys. 2005. audio compact disk 14.99 (978-0-88368-892-2(1)) Whitaker Hse.

Arise: A New Celebration of Worship. Contrib. by Don Moen. Prod. by Paul Mills. 2006. audio compact disk 24.98 (978-5-558-35325-9(2)) Integrity Music.

Arise - Awake. Swami Amar Jyoti. 1 cass. 1977. 9.95 (K-13) Truth Consciousness.
Freeing the mind. The role of morality & ethics in raising our consciousness. Higher ethics, the perfect foundation for touching the Spirit.

Arise & Walk. Marty Copeland. Perf. by Marty Copeland. 1 cass. (Audio-Video Ser.). 1996. cass. & video 25.00 Incl. video. (978-1-57562-038-1(3), 04-1700) K Copeland Pubns.
Biblical teaching on overcoming.

Arise & Walk. gif. ed. Perf. by Marty Copeland. cass. & video 25.00 (978-1-57562-040-4(5), AVC-040-5) Pub: K Copeland Pubns. Dist(s): Harrison Hse
A brilliant new novel of ultimate feminist revenge from the author of Wild at Heart - whose cult following continues to grow. In this colorful, modern tale of American madness, a group of misfits in New Orleans is bent on improving the world and altering the universe. From churches to TV channels, they hand out hope as they redefine righteousness.

Arise, My Love (Best of) Perf. by NewSong. 1 cass. 1999. 10.98 (978-0-7601-2132-0(X)); audio compact disk 16.98 (978-0-7601-2133-7(8)) Provident Music.

Arise! Shine! Music by Judy Rogers & Becky Morecraft. 1 cass. (Running Time: 1 hr.). 2002. 8.50 (JR00008) Christian Liberty.
Young people and adults will enjoy this praise to our great God. Scripture songs and choruses that glorify our Lord and Savior Jesus Christ.

Aristocats. 1 cass. (Running Time: 90 min.). (Disney Read-Alongs Ser.). (J). bk. 7.99 (978-1-55723-022-5(6)) Walt Disney.

Aristocats - EP. unabr. ed. 1 cass. (Running Time: 90 min.). (J). 7.99 (978-0-7634-0047-7(5)); 7.99 Norelco. (978-0-7634-0046-0(7)); audio compact disk 13.99 (978-0-7634-0048-4(3)); audio compact disk 13.99 Jewel Box. (978-0-7634-0049-1(1)) W Disney Records.

Aristocrats. Stella Tillyard. Read by Serena Gordon. 2 cass. (Running Time: 3 hrs.). 1999. 16.85 Set. (978-0-00-105568-1(2)) Ulvrscrft Audio.
The story of the four Lennox sisters & their turbulent lives, spanning the Georgian period of English & Irish history.

Aristocrats, unabr. ed. John Lane. Read by Flo Gibson. 3 cass. (Running Time: 4 hrs. 30 mins.). 1997. 16.95 (978-1-55685-498-9(6), 498-6) Audio Bk Con.
In these letters to an English Countess from Lady Helen, who has brought her tubercular brother to the Adirondacks for a cure. There are beautiful descriptions of the mountains & lakes. Political, literary & moral discussions are pervaded with a certain British superiority. However, prepare to laugh even if offended.

Aristophanes' Birds. unabr. ed. Aristophanes. 2 cass. J Norton Pubs.

Aristophanes' Birds. unabr. ed. Read by Stephen G. Daitz. Ed. by Stephen G. Daitz. 2 cass. (Running Time: 2 hrs.). (Living Voice of Greek & Latin Ser.). (GRE.). pap. bk. 39.95 (978-0-88432-117-0(7), S23670) J Norton Pubs.

Aristotle, unabr. ed. A. E. Taylor. Read by Frederick Davidson. 3 cass. (Running Time: 4 hrs.). 1993. 23.95 (978-0-7861-0423-9(6), 1375) Blckstn Audio.
Writing to inform the beginner & stimulate the expert, Taylor presents a searching analysis of Aristotle's thought, including classification of the sciences; formal logic; theory of knowledge; matter & form; the four causes; God; physics; biology; sensation; ethics; theory of the state; the fine arts. He also considers Aristotle's provincialism & errors regarding the nervous system.

Aristotle: An Introduction. abr. ed. Hugh Griffith. Read by Hugh Ross & Roy McMillan. (Running Time: 18107 sec.). 2008. audio compact disk 28.98 (978-962-634-854-3(2), Naxos AudioBooks) Naxos.

Aristotle: Father of Romanticism. unabr. ed. Robert Mayhew. 3 cass. (Running Time: 4 hrs. 30 mins.). 1997. 39.95 (978-1-56114-522-5(X), CM51D) Second Renaissance.
An in-depth examination of Aristotle's reply to Plato in his "Poetics".

Aristotle: Greece (384-322 B. C.) abr. ed. Thomas C. Brickhouse. Ed. by George H. Smith & Wendy McElroy. Narrated by Charlton Heston. 2 cass. (Running Time: 3 hrs.). (Giants of Philosophy Ser.). 1990. 17.95 (978-0-938935-18-6(6), 390154) Pub: Knowledge Prod. Dist(s): APG
Aristotle, in revising Plato's ideas, thought human beings are one with the rest of nature yet set apart from it by their ability to reason. Aristotle codified the laws of thought, gave a complete account of nature & of God & developed an attractive view of the good life & the good society.

Aristotle: Greece (384-322 B. C.) abr. ed. Narrated by Charlton Heston. (Running Time: 7955 sec.). (Audio Classics: the Giants of Philosophy Ser.). 2006. audio compact disk 25.95 (978-0-7861-6944-3(3)) Pub: Blckstn Audio. Dist(s): NetLibrary CO

Aristotle: Greece (384-322 B. C.), unabr. ed. Read by Charlton Heston. 2 cass. (Running Time: 2 hrs.). (Giants of Philosophy Ser.). 17.95 (K118) Blckstn Audio.
See how one of the world's most important philosophers created a complete system of thought, including his views on ethics, metaphysics, politics & aesthetics. Learn about his epistemology - how we know what we know.

Aristotle: Greece (384-322 B. C.) unabr. ed. Narrated by Charlton Heston. 2 CDs. (Running Time: 2 hrs. 16 mins.). (Giants of Philosophy Ser.). audio compact disk 16.95 (978-1-56823-068-9(0)) Pub: Knowledge Prod. Dist(s): APG

Aristotle - an Introduction. unabr. ed. Hugh Griffith. Read by Hugh Ross & Roy Mcmillan. (YA). 2008. 54.99 (978-1-60514-700-0(1)) Find a World.

Aristotle & an Aardvark Go to Washington: Understanding Political Doublespeak Through Philosophy & Jokes. Thomas Cathcart & Daniel Klein. Narrated by Johnny Heller. (Running Time: 12600 sec.). (Recorded Books Unabridged Ser.). 2008. audio compact disk 19.99 (978-1-4361-0493-7(9)) Recorded Bks.

Aristotle for Everybody: Difficult Thought Made Easy. unabr. ed. Mortimer J. Adler. Read by Frederick Davidson. 4 cass. (Running Time: 5 hrs. 30 mins.). 1993. 32.95 (978-0-7861-0465-9(1), 1417) Blckstn Audio.
Because Aristotle's wisdom & philosophical insights are grounded in the common experience we all possess, this easy-to-listen-to exposition of his thought about the world of nature, about the actions & productions of man & about the conduct of life, confirms convictions that most of us hold, though we may not always be fully aware of them, proving that his ideas are eternal.

Aristotle in 90 Minutes. Paul Strathern. Narrated by Robert Whitfield. (Running Time: 1 hr. 30 mins.). 2003. 17.95 (978-1-59912-423-0(8)) Iofy Corp.

Aristotle in 90 Minutes. unabr. ed. Paul Strathern. Read by Robert Whitfield. 2 CDs. (Running Time: 1 hr. 30 mins.). 2001. audio compact disk 16.00 (978-0-7861-9091-1(4), 3117) Blckstn Audio.

Aristotle in 90 Minutes. unabr. ed. Paul Strathern. Read by Robert Whitfield. (Running Time: 1 hr. 30 mins.). 2006. 14.95 (978-0-7861-2438-1(5), 3117); reel tape 14.95 (978-0-7861-2534-0(9)); audio compact disk 14.95 (978-0-7861-9041-6(8)) Blckstn Audio.

Aristotle; Today's Intellectual State. Ayn Rand. Read by Ayn Rand. 1 cass. (Running Time: 60 mins.). 12.95 (978-1-56114-020-6(1), AR09C) Second Renaissance.
Two appearances by Ayn Rand on a campus radio program: 1) A reading of her own review of John Randall's book Aristotle, with brief additional comments by her on what constituted Aristotle's greatness. 2) A discussion, just before the 1968 Presidential election, of how "me-too" Republicans were urging the abandonment of all principle - as they did in the pivotal elections of 1940 & 1952 - to appease liberal Democrats.

Aristotle's Nicomachean Ethics Audiobook. Aristotle. Read by Graeme Malcolm. Tr. by Christopher Rowe. 6 cass. 2005. 14.95 (978-1-56585-988-3(X)); audio compact disk 19.95 (978-1-59803-004-4(3)) Teaching Co.

Aristotle's Nostril. Morris Gleitzman. Read by Morris Gleitzman. (Running Time: 2 hrs. 20 mins.). (J). 2009. 44.99 (978-1-74214-380-4(6), 9781742143804) Pub: Bolinda Pubng AUS. Dist(s): Bolinda Pub Inc

Aristotle's Nostril. unabr. ed. Morris Gleitzman. Read by Morris Gleitzman. (Running Time: 8400 sec.). (J). (gr. 3-11). 2006. audio compact disk 43.95 (978-1-74093-766-5(X)) Pub: Bolinda Pubng AUS. Dist(s): Bolinda Pub Inc

Aristotle's Political Philosophy. Robert Mayhew. 6 cass. (Running Time: 5 hrs.). 1996. 39.95 (978-1-56114-405-1(3), CM40D) Second Renaissance.
A critical examination of the essentials of Aristotle's political philosophy.

Arithmetic see Carl Sandburg's Poems for Children

Arithrombotic Therapy: Asking the Right Questions; Getting the Right Answers. Read by Daniel Deykin. 1 cass. (Running Time: 90 min.). 1986. 12.00 (C8644) Amer Coll Phys.

Arizona! Dana Fuller Ross, pseud. Read by Lloyd James. 4 vols. (Wagons West Ser.: No. 21). 2004. 25.00 (978-1-58807-153-8(7)); (978-1-58807-622-9(9)) Am Pubng Inc.

Arizona Ames, unabr. ed. Zane Grey. Read by Brian O'Neill. 6 vols. (Running Time: 9 hrs.). 1998. bk. 54.95 (978-0-7927-2235-9(3), CSL 124, Chivers Sound Lib) AudioGO.
Fast-shooting, big-hearted Arizona Ames carved himself a legend as he rode the untamed West. He was ultimately seeking a place to call home. But when a friend gets caught in a deadly love triangle, Arizona doesn't hesitate to take matters into his own hands.

Arizona Clan. unabr. ed. Zane Grey. Read by Gene Engene. 4 cass. (Running Time: 5 hrs. 30 mins.). 26.95 (978-1-55686-103-1(6), 103) Books in Motion.
Ex-Gunslinger, Dodge Mercer, hungry for the quiet life, drifted west looking for a spread of his own. He settled in the rugged, dangerous Tonto Basin country of Arizona joining up with the Lilley clan. Dodge falls in love with beautiful Nan Lilley & runs up against tough two-fisted Buck Hathaway who claims Nan for his own. A blazing feud takes place - Dodge & the Lilleys against the Hathaways.

Arizona Clan. unabr. ed. Zane Grey. Read by Gene Engene. 5 CDs. (Running Time: 5 hrs. 30 mins.). 2001. audio compact disk 32.50 (978-1-58116-172-4(7)) Books in Motion.
Ex-gunslinger Dodge Mercer drifts west. He joins up with the Lilley clan in the rugged Tonto Basin of Arizona and finds himself involved in a blazing feud.

Arizona Heart Institute Atlas of Cardiovascular CT Imaging DVD-ROM. John A. Sutherland. 2007. 86.95 (978-0-7637-4921-7(4)) Jones Bartlett.

Ark: A Novel. unabr. ed. Boyd Morrison. Read by Boyd Gaines. (Running Time: 15 hrs. 0 mins. 0 sec.). (ENG.). 2010. audio compact disk 39.99 (978-1-4423-0512-0(6)) Pub: S&S Audio. Dist(s): S and S Inc

Ark & America: 1 Samuel 4:21. Ed Young. 1983. 4.95 (978-0-7417-1309-4(8), 309) Win Walk.

Ark Angel. unabr. ed. Anthony Horowitz. Read by Simon Prebble. 6 cass. (Running Time: 8 hrs.). (Alex Rider Ser.: Bk. 6). 2006. 59.75 (978-1-4193-9425-6(8), 98374); audio compact disk 74.75 (978-1-4193-9430-0(4), C3729) Recorded Bks.
Author Anthony Horowitz's multimillion-selling Alex Rider series reaches thrilling new heights with Ark Angel, which is full of the blistering action and slick gadgets young readers love. When MI6 Agent Alex Rider wakes up in a hospital, he is thrilled to be alive. Left for dead by his dreaded nemesis Scorpia, Alex has survived to fight another day. Almost immediately, he locks horns with a super-rich Russian businessman who is building a luxury hotel in space.

Ark Fever. unabr. ed. Robert Cornuke. Narrated by Kevin King. (ENG.). 2005. 18.89 (978-1-60814-036-7(9)) Oasis Audio.

Ark Fever: The True Story of One Man's Search for Noah's Ark. unabr. ed. Robert Cornuke. Narrated by Kevin King. (Running Time: 21600 sec.). (ENG.). 2005. audio compact disk 26.99 (978-1-59859-022-7(7)) Oasis Audio.

Ark of Death. unabr. ed. Howard H. Hilton. Read by Kevin Foley. 8 cass. (Running Time: 9 hrs. 42 mins.). (Howard H. Hilton International Mystery Ser.). 1996. 49.95 (978-1-55686-674-6(7)) Books in Motion.
Struggling to save his failing company, an industrial tycoon secretly produces internationally banned chemicals & ships them by water to an African Third-World country.

Ark of Peace. Kenneth Wapnick. 1 CD. (Running Time: 2 hrs. 39 mins. 15 secs.). 2006. 13.00 (978-1-59142-275-4(2), 3m129); audio compact disk 16.00 (978-1-59142-274-7(4), CD129) Foun Miracles.

Ark of the Liberties: America & the World. unabr. ed. Ted Widmer. Read by Grover Gardner. (Running Time: 14 hrs. 50 mins.). 2008. 29.95 (978-1-4332-4859-7(X)); 85.95 (978-1-4332-4856-6(5)); audio compact disk 110.00 (978-1-4332-4857-3(3)) Blckstn Audio.

Ark of the Liberties: America & the World. unabr. ed. Ted Widmer. Read by William Hughes. 11 CDs. (Running Time: 13 hrs. 30 mins.). 2008. audio compact disk 29.95 (978-1-4332-4858-0(1)) Blckstn Audio.

Ark upon the Number: Latin-American (Cuban) Poetry. Jose Kozer. Ed. by Stanley H. Barkan. Tr. by Ammiel Alcalay. (Review Chapbook Ser.: No. 28). (SPA & ENG.). 1982. 10.00 (978-0-89304-728-3(7)) Cross-Cultrl NY.

Arkadians, unabr. ed. Lloyd Alexander. Read by Full Cast Production Staff. 4 cass. (Running Time: 4 hrs.). (J). (gr. 1-8). 1999. 29.98 (LL 0124, Chivers Child Audio) AudioGO.

Arkadians. unabr. ed. Lloyd Alexander. Read by Words Take Wing Repertory Company Staff. 4 cass. (Running Time: 5 hrs. 51 mins.). (J). (gr. 5 up). 1998. pap. bk. 37.00 (978-0-8072-8022-5(4), YA969SP, Listening Lib) Random Audio Pubg.
Lucien, a young bean counter, is about to be put to death, but he escapes & his adventures lead him to romance & danger.

Arkadians. unabr. ed. Lloyd Alexander. Read by Words Take Wing Repertory Company Staff. 4 cass. (Running Time: 5 hrs. 51 mins.). (Southern Biography Ser.). (YA). (gr. 5 up). 1998. 32.00 (978-0-8072-8021-8(6), YA969CX, Listening Lib) Random Audio Pubg.

Arkansas Mischief. unabr. ed. Jim McDougal & Curtis Wilkie. Read by Lloyd James. 9 cass. (Running Time: 13 hrs.). 1998. 62.95 (978-0-7861-1319-4(7), 2244) Blckstn Audio.
Jim McDougal's vivid self-portrait, completed only days before his death, reveals the hidden intersections of politics & special interests in Arkansas & the betrayals that followed. It is the story of how ambitious men & women climbed out of rural obscurity & "how friendships break down & lives are ruined.".

Arkansas Murders: Why? Hosted by Leonard Peikoff. 1 cass. (Philosophy: Who Needs It? Ser.). 1998. 12.95 (LPXXC51) Second Renaissance.

Arkansas Raiders. unabr. ed. Larry D. Names. Read by Maynard Villers. 6 cass. (Running Time: 7 hrs. 24 min.). (Creed Ser.: Bk. 10). 2001. 39.95 (978-1-55686-824-5(3)) Books in Motion.
The whole town wanted Dick Barth dead. Except for Creed, who needs him breathing and confessing. But freedom for both men is difficult when the wager must be paid in blood.

Arkansas River. unabr. ed. Jory Sherman. Read by Michael Taylor. 8 cass. (Running Time: 9 hrs. 30 min.). (Rivers West Ser.: Bk. 8). 2001. 49.95 (978-1-55686-773-6(5)) Books in Motion.
Three bold men with separate visions forge ahead to blaze the trails and carve different futures in the Arkansas River Valley.

Arkansas Workers' Compensation Laws & Rules Annotated, 2003 Edition with CD-ROM & 2004 Supplement. Ed. by Lexis Editorial Staff. pap. bk. 28.00 (978-0-8205-9072-1(X)) LEXIS Pub.

Arkham Asylum. Heroclix DC. 2008. 11.99 (978-1-59041-672-3(4)) Pub: WizKids. Dist(s): Diamond Book Dists

Arlesienne. Alphonse Daudet. Read by Mary Marquet & Pierre Larquey. 1 cass. (FRE.). 1996. 21.95 (1818-LQP) Olivia & Hill.
Play based on a tale of the same name in "Les Lettres de Mon Moulin." The tragic story of Frederi who loves the unfaithful "arlesienne.".

Arlie the Alligator. Deborah Bel Pfleger & Sandra Warren. 1 cass. (Running Time: 10 mins.). Dramatization. (J). (ps-4). 1992. 5.95 (978-1-880175-12-5(6)) Arlie Enter.
Alligator tries to speak to the children on the beach. Communication theme. Delightful. Fully produced with actors & music.

Arlie the Alligator. Sandra Warren & Deborah Bel Pfleger. Illus. by Deborah Thomas. 1 cass. (Running Time: 12 mins.). Dramatization. (J). (ps-4). 1992. bk. 19.90 (978-1-880175-11-8(8)) Arlie Enter.
Alligator tries to speak to the children on the beach. Communication theme. Delightful. Cassette fully produced with actors & music.

Arlie the Alligator. Sandra Warren & Deborah Bel Pfleger. (J). (ps-4). 2000. audio compact disk 9.95 (978-1-880175-15-6(0)) Arlie Enter.

Arlie the Alligator. Sandra Warren & Deborah Bel Pfleger. Illus. by Deborah Thomas. (J). 2000. bk. 23.90 (978-1-880175-16-3(9)) Arlie Enter.

***ARM & the Woman.** unabr. ed. Laura Lippman. Read by Linda Emond & Francois Battiste. 2008. (978-0-06-176287-1(3), Harper Audio); (978-0-06-176286-4(5), Harper Audio) HarperCollins Pubs.

***Arm Candy.** unabr. ed. Jill Kargman. Read by Joyce Bean. (Running Time: 9 hrs.). 2010. 24.99 (978-1-4418-4221-3(7), 9781441842213, BAD); 39.97 (978-1-4418-4220-6(9), 9781441842206, Brlnc Audio MP3 Lib); 39.97 (978-1-4418-4222-0(5), 9781441842220, BADLE); 24.99 (978-1-4418-4219-0(5), 9781441842190, Brilliance MP3) Brilliance Audio.

***Arm Candy.** unabr. ed. Jill Kargman. Read by Susan Ericksen & Joyce Bean. (Running Time: 9 hrs.). 2010. audio compact disk 87.97 (978-1-4418-4218-3(7), 9781441842183, BriAudCD Unabrid); audio compact disk 29.99 (978-1-4418-4217-6(9), 9781441842176, Bril Audio CD Unabri) Brilliance Audio.

Arm Essntls Rsk Cntrl Ppt Cd. Ed. by Kaplan Publishing Staff. 2005. (978-1-4195-1979-6(4)) Dearborn Financial.

Arm Essntls Rsk Cntrl Terms Cd. Ed. by Kaplan Publishing Staff. 2005. (978-1-4195-1958-1(1)) Dearborn Financial.

Arm Essntls Rsk Mgt Trm Ppt Cd. Ed. by Kaplan Publishing Staff. 2005. (978-1-4195-1952-9(2)) Dearborn Financial.

Arm Risk Financing Ppt Cd. Ed. by Kaplan Publishing Staff. 2005. (978-1-4195-1974-1(3)) Dearborn Financial.

Arm Risk Financing Terms Cd. Ed. by Kaplan Publishing Staff. 2005. (978-1-4195-1975-8(1)) Dearborn Financial.

Arm 54 - Risk Management. Ed. by Kaplan Publishing Staff. 2005. cd-rom 10.00 (978-1-4195-2394-6(5)) Dearborn Financial.

Arm 54 - Risk Mgmt Audio Cd 2E. Ed. by Kaplan Publishing Staff. 2006. cd-rom (978-1-4195-4932-8(4)) Dearborn Financial.

Arm 55 - Risk Control. Ed. by Kaplan Publishing Staff. 2005. cd-rom 10.00 (978-1-4195-2412-7(7)) Dearborn Financial.

Arm 55-Risk Cntrl Audio Cd 2E. Ed. by Kaplan Publishing Staff. 2006. cd-rom (978-1-4195-4927-4(8)) Dearborn Financial.

Arm 56 - Risk Financing. Ed. by Kaplan Publishing Staff. 2005. cd-rom 10.00 (978-1-4195-2416-5(X)) Dearborn Financial.

Armada. unabr. ed. Garrett Mattingly. Read by James Cunningham. 9 cass. (Running Time: 13 hrs. 30 mins.). 1978. 72.00 (978-0-7366-0056-9(6), 1068) Books on Tape.
Definitive study of England's defeat of Spanish Armada in 1588.

Armada of Thirty Whales see Twentieth-Century Poetry in English, No. 28, Recordings of Poets Reading Their Own Poetry

Armadale. Wilkie Collins. Narrated by Flo Gibson. 21 cass. (Running Time: 32 hrs. 14 min). 2006. 59.95 (978-1-55685-886-4(8)) Audio Bk Con.

Armadillo. unabr. ed. William Boyd. Read by David Case. 8 cass. (Running Time: 12 hrs.). 1999. 64.00 (978-0-7366-4648-2(5), 5029) Books on Tape.
Lorimer Black, a London insurance adjuster, calls on a client, only to discover that he has hanged himself.

Armadillo at Riverside Road. Laura Gates Galvin. 1 cass. (Running Time: 35 min.). (J). (gr. k-4). 2001. 19.95 (SP 5011C) Kimbo Educ.
Armadillo emerges from its burrow, ready for a night of insect-hunting. Includes read along book.

Armadillo at Riverside Road. Laura Gates Galvin. Narrated by Alexi Komisar. Illus. by Katy Bratun. 1 cass. (Smithsonian's Backyard Ser.). (J). (ps-2). 1996. 5.00 (978-1-56899-333-1(1), C5011) Soundprints.
As evening falls on Riverside Road, a funny animal emerges from a burrow in the backyard of the white house. Pointy nose & leathery ears, an armored shell & tail - it's Armadillo, ready for a night of insect hunting. She wanders through the yard, looking for a meal. But Armadillo's night is not peaceful. A coyote & the nearby road turn her search into an adventure!.

Armageddon. unabr. ed. Duane S. Crowther. Read by Duane S. Crowther. 1 cass. (Running Time: 90 mins.). 1988. 13.98 (978-0-88290-333-0(0), 1824) Horizon Utah.
Talks of the great battle of Armageddon which is to take place in the last days shortly before the Lord's second coming.

Armageddon: An Experience in Sound & Drama - The Cosmic Battle of the Ages. adpt. ed. Tim LaHaye & Jerry B. Jenkins. 4 CDs. (Left Behind Ser.: Bk. 11). (ENG., 2003. audio compact disk 19.99 (978-0-8423-4348-0(2)) Tyndale Hse.

Armageddon: The Cosmic Battle of the Ages. Tim LaHaye & Jerry B. Jenkins. 10 CDs. (Left Behind Ser.: Bk. 11). 2003. audio compact disk 39.95 (978-1-4025-3600-7(3)) Recorded Bks.

Armageddon: The Cosmic Battle of the Ages. Tim LaHaye & Jerry B. Jenkins. 10 CDs. (Running Time: 11 hrs. 15 mins.). (Left Behind Ser.: Bk. 11). 2004. audio compact disk 39.95 (978-1-4025-4523-8(1), 01072) Recorded Bks.

Armageddon: The Cosmic Battle of the Ages. abr. ed. Tim LaHaye & Jerry B. Jenkins. Read by Steve Sever. 3 CDs. (Running Time: 3 hrs.). (Left Behind Ser.: Bk. 11). (ENG., 2003. audio compact disk 19.99 (978-0-8423-3972-8(8)) Tyndale Hse.

Armageddon: The Cosmic Battle of the Ages. unabr. ed. Tim LaHaye & Jerry B. Jenkins. Read by Richard Ferrone. 7 cass. (Running Time: 11 hrs. 15 mins.). (Left Behind Ser.: Bk. 11). 2004. 29.95 (978-1-4025-3599-4(6), 02524) Recorded Bks.
It is the final year of the Great Tribulation-and no one is safe. The scattered Tribulation Force is drawn toward the Middle East, where all the world's armies are gathered for the battle of the ages. Earth is a ticking time bomb poised to explode as Armageddon approaches, with the promise of the Glorious Appearing for those who survive.

Armageddon in Retrospect. unabr. ed. Kurt Vonnegut. Read by Rip Torn. 1 MP3-CD. 2008. 29.95 (978-1-4332-4350-9(4)) Blckstn Audio.

Armageddon in Retrospect. unabr. ed. Kurt Vonnegut. Read by Rip Torn. Intro. by Mark Vonnegut. 4 cass. 2008. 34.95 (978-1-4332-4348-6(2)); audio compact disk 60.00 (978-1-4332-4349-3(0)) Blckstn Audio.

Armageddon in Retrospect. unabr. ed. Kurt Vonnegut. Read by Rip Torn. (Running Time: 6 hrs.). (ENG.). (gr. 8). 2008. audio compact disk 34.95 (978-0-14-314315-4(8), PengAudBks) Penguin Grp USA.

Armageddon Mode. unabr. ed. Keith Douglass. Read by David Hilder. 8 cass. (Running Time: 12 hrs.). (Carrier Ser.: No. 3). 2001. 29.95 (978-0-7366-6789-0(X)) Books on Tape.
Tombstone Magruder jumps in the middle of a potential nuclear skirmish. Electrifying air & sea battles.

Armageddon Mode. unabr. collector's ed. Keith Douglass. Read by David Hilder. 8 cass. (Running Time: 12 hrs.). (Carrier Ser.: No. 3). 1995. 64.00 (978-0-7366-3129-7(1), 3804) Books on Tape.
It's one of the Pentagon's most dreaded doomsday scenarios: India launches a preemptive strike against Islamic Pakistan & nuclear hostilities may boil over. To avert a global catastrophe, the President dispatches the U.S. Carrier Battle Group Fourteen, led by the supercarrier Thomas Jefferson. When an American battleship goes down & thermonuclear payloads are launched, Lt. Commander Tombstone Magruder & his battle group shift into Armageddon mode - the ultimate battle by land, sea or air.

Armageddon Soon? unabr. ed. William MacDonald. Read by William MacDonald. 1 cass. (Running Time: 42 min.). (Upward Call Ser.: Vol. 4). 1995. 8.95 (978-0-9629152-7-7(0)) Lumen Prodns.
Christ is coming, but are you ready? "Armageddon Soon" explains the biblical chronology of end time events & how you can prepare for Christ's return.

Armageddon Summer. Jane Yolen & Bruce Coville. Read by Kate Forbes & Johnny Heller. 5 cass. (Running Time: 6 hrs. 30 mins.). (YA). (gr. 7 up). 1999. pap. bk. & stu. ed. 60.24 (978-0-7887-3002-3(9), 40884) Recorded Bks.
A realistic exploration of cult dynamics. As the end of the millennium approaches, a religious group moves to a mountain top to await Armageddon. The vigil is chronicled by two teenaged members: Jed & Marina tracing their growing friendship as they try to understand the group's increasingly militant preparations.

Armageddon Summer, unabr. ed. Jane Yolen & Bruce Coville. Narrated by Kate Forbes & Johnny Heller. 5 pieces. (Running Time: 6 hrs. 30 mins.). (gr. 8 up). 1999. 46.00 (978-0-7887-2972-0(1), 95744E7) Recorded Bks.

Armageddon Summer, Class set. Jane Yolen & Bruce Coville. Read by Kate Forbes & Johnny Heller. 5 cass. (Running Time: 6 hrs. 30 mins.). (YA). 1999. 126.70 (978-0-7887-3032-0(0), 46849) Recorded Bks.

Armageddon, the War That Ends in Peace. Instructed by Manly P. Hall. 8.95 (978-0-89314-008-3(2), C810809) Philos Res.

Armageddon's Children. Terry Brooks. Read by Dick Hill. (Playaway Adult Fiction Ser.). (ENG.). 2009. 79.99 (978-1-60775-507-4(6)) Find a World.

Armageddon's Children. abr. ed. Terry Brooks. Read by Dick Hill. (Running Time: 21600 sec.). (Genesis of Shannara Ser.: Bk. 1). 2007. audio compact disk 14.99 (978-1-4233-2263-4(0), 9781423322634, BCD Value Price) Brilliance Audio.

Armageddon's Children. abr. ed. Terry Brooks & #1 Genesis of Shannara. 2010. audio compact disk 9.99 (978-1-4418-4178-0(4)) Brilliance Audio.

Armageddon's Children. unabr. ed. Terry Brooks. Read by Dick Hill. (Running Time: 14 hrs.). (Genesis of Shannara Ser.). 2006. 24.95 (978-1-4233-2260-3(6), 9781423322603, BAD) Brilliance Audio.

Armageddon's Children. unabr. ed. Terry Brooks. Read by Dick Hill. (Running Time: 14 hrs.). (Genesis of Shannara Ser.: Bk. 1). 2006. 39.25 (978-1-4233-2261-0(4), 9781423322610, BADLE); 97.25 (978-1-4233-2255-9(X), 9781423322559, BrilAudUnabridg); audio compact disk 39.25 (978-1-4233-2259-7(2), 9781423322597, Brinc Audio MP3 Lib); audio compact disk 112.25 (978-1-4233-2257-3(6), 9781423322573, BriAudCD Unabrid); audio compact disk 38.95 (978-1-4233-2256-6(8), 9781423322566, Bril Audio CD Unabri); audio compact disk 24.95 (978-1-4233-2258-0(4), 9781423322580, Brilliance MP3) Brilliance Audio.
Fifty years from now, our world is a very different place. Governments have fallen. Pollution has poisoned the skies, water, and soil. Thousands live in highly fortified strongholds; others roam the landscape, as either predator or prey. The demons have taken over. Standing against them are a very few Knights of the Word. Imbued with powerful magic and sworn to destroy the demons and every evil created by them, are men and women like Logan Tom and Angel Perez. Their quest is to rescue a group of young people who hold the hope of the world.

Armance. Stendhal. 8 cass. (Running Time: 8 hrs.). (FRE.). 1996. pap. bk. 89.50 (978-1-58085-360-6(9)) Interlingua VA.
Includes French text with notes. The combination of written text & clarity & pace of diction will open the door for intermediate & advanced students to genuine comprehension & the use of literary texts for advancement in rapid understanding of written & oral language materials. The audio text plus written text concept makes foreign languages accessible to a much wider range of students than books alone.

Armand Hammer: Can Russia & America Be Friends? Armand Hammer. Read by Armand Hammer. 1 cass. (Running Time: 1 hr.). 10.95 (K0330B090, HarperThor) HarpC GBR.

Arme Junge im Grab. Jacob W. Grimm & Wilhelm K. Grimm. 1 cass. (Running Time: 60 mins.). (Bruder Grimm Kinder & Hausmarchen Ser.). (GER.). 1996. pap. bk. 19.50 (978-1-58085-208-1(4), GR-03) Interlingua VA.
Includes German transcription & English translation. Includes title story, Der Ranzen, das Hutlein und das Hornlein, Fundevogel, Das Hirtenbublein, Die Geschenke des kleinen Volkes, Der Riese und der Schneider, Gottes Speise. The combination of written text & clarity & pace of diction will open the door for intermediate & advanced students to genuine comprehension & the use of literary texts for advancement in rapid understanding of written & oral language materials. The audio text plus written text concept makes foreign languages accessible to a much wider range of students than books alone.

Armed for the Conflict, Pt. 1. unabr. ed. Warren W. Wiersbe. Read by Warren W. Wiersbe. 1 cass. (Running Time: 1 hr. 18 mins.). 1989. 4.95 (978-0-8474-2342-2(5)) Back to Bible.
Messages from I Peter 1:1-2:10 on salvation & sanctification.

Armed for the Conflict, Pt. 2. unabr. ed. Warren W. Wiersbe. Read by Warren W. Wiersbe. 1 cass. (Running Time: 1 hr. 16 mins.). 1989. 4.95 (978-0-8474-2345-3(X)) Back to Bible.
Messages from I Peter 2:11-3:22 on having the right attitude about submission & suffering.

Armed Madhouse: Who's Afraid of Osama Wolf? China Floats, Bush Sinks, the Scheme to Steal '08, No Child's Behind Left, & Other Dispatches from the Front Lines of the Class War. abr. ed. Greg Palast. Read by Greg Palast. Told to Edward Asner. Based on a work by Brod Bagert & Medea Benjamin. 2006. 17.95 (978-0-7435-6429-8(4), Audioworks) Pub: S&S Audio. Dist(s): S and S Inc

Armenian, Eastern. 6 cass. (Running Time: 3 hrs.). pap. bk. 125.00 (AFAR10) J Norton Pubs.

Armenian (Eastern) Learn to Speak & Understand Armenian with Pimsleur Language Programs. unabr. ed. Pimsleur Staff. 5 cass. (Running Time: 500 hrs. 0 mins. NaN sec.). (Pimsleur Language Program Ser.). (ARM & ENG.). 1997. 95.00 (978-0-671-57907-4(X), Pimsleur) Pub: S&S Audio. Dist(s): S and S Inc
SPEAK ARMENIAN TO LEARN ARMENIAN The Pimsleur Method will have you speaking Armenian in just a few short, easy-to-use lessons. Learn at your own pace, comfortably and conveniently. No books to study. No memorization drills. LEARN ARMENIAN AS YOU LEARNED ENGLISH You learned English by listening. With Pimsleur, you listen to learn Armenian. This Language Program was developed by renowned memory expert, Dr. Paul Pimsleur. His research led him to the realization that the most important use of memory is in language learning. Based on this, Dr. Pimsleur designed a learning program that works for any language. The Pimsleur Language Program is an integrated system which immerses you in the language, encouraging you to hear, understand and use the language all at the same time. Now you can take advantage of Dr. Pimsleur's research. At the completion of these eight lessons you will comfortably understand and speak at a beginner level.

Armenian (Eastern) Learn to Speak & Understand Eastern Armenian with Pimsleur Language Programs. unabr. ed. Pimsleur Staff. (Running Time: 50 hrs. 0 mins. 0 sec.). (Compact Ser.). (ARM & ENG.). 2006. audio compact disk 49.95 (978-0-7435-5063-5(3), Pimsleur) Pub: S&S Audio. Dist(s): S and S Inc

Armenian (Eastern) Short Course. Paul Pimsleur. 5 cass. (Running Time: 5 hrs.). (Pimsleur Language Learning Ser.). 1996. 149.95 SyberVision.

Armenian (Eastern) World Citizen Edition. unabr. ed. 10 CDs - Library Ed. 2003. audio compact disk 115.00 (978-0-7887-9768-2(9)) Recorded Bks.
Dr. Paul Pimsleur's original and unique method enables you to acquire another language as easily as you learned English-by listening. With the Pimsleur program, you'll learn vocabulary and grammar correctly and easily in conversation without mindless repetition. Pimsleur is the only language program that includes exclusive, copyrighted memory training that ensures you will always remember what you have learned.

Armenian (Eastern) Newspaper Reader & Grammar. Louisa Baghdasarian & R. David Zorc. 1 cass. (Running Time: 60 mins.). (ARM.). 1995. 8.00 (3122) Dunwoody Pr.
Includes thirty readings & translations drawn from several representatives of the Yerevan press between 1991-1993. Explains the Armenian sound system, then details the complexities of word formation & compounding & goes on to treat the derivation & inflection of all parts of speech.

Armenian (Eastern) Programmed Reading Course & Sound Drills. R. David Zorc. Perf. by Hratch'ya Hovanesyan & Thomas Gorguissian. 1 cass. (Running Time: 1 hr. 30 mins.). (ARM.). 1996. 12.00 (3123) Dunwoody Pr.
Examples of Armenian sounds not found in English; each word is read by an Eastern Armenian & then by a Western Armenian to illustrate the differences between these dialects.

Armenian Music Through the Ages. Richard Hagopian. 1 cass. or CD. 1993. (0-9307-404140-9307-40414-2-0); audio compact disk (0-9307-40414-2-0) Smithsonian Folkways.

Armenian New Testament. Narrated by Jacob Jambazian & Knar Jambazion. 16 cass. 2000. (978-7-902031-35-6(6)) Chrstn Dup Intl.

Armenian Sound Drills. R. David Zorc. 1992. 12.00 (978-0-931745-98-0(5)) Dunwoody Pr.

Armenian, Western. 8 cass. (Running Time: 8 hrs.). 225.00 (AFAR15) J Norton Pubs.
Speakers of West Armenian (about two million) live in Lebanon, Syria, Turkey, Egypt & the U.S. The text assumes that you have acquired the ability to read the Armenian alphabet. Text includes English-Armenian & Armenian-English glossaries.

Armenian (Western) Learn to Speak & Understand Armenian with Pimsleur Language Programs. Pimsleur Staff & Pimsleur. (Running Time: 500 hrs. 0 mins. NaN sec.). (Compact Ser.). (ENG.). 2004. audio compact disk 115.00 (978-0-7435-3688-2(6), Pimsleur) Pub: S&S Audio. Dist(s): S and S Inc

Armenian (Western) Learn to Speak & Understand Armenian with Pimsleur Language Programs. unabr. ed. Pimsleur Staff. 5 cass. (Running Time: 500 hrs. 0 mins. NaN sec.). (Pimsleur Language Program Ser.). (ARM & ENG.). 1997. 95.00 (978-0-671-57960-9(6), Pimsleur) Pub: S&S Audio. Dist(s): S and S Inc
With Pimsleur Language Programs you don't just study a language, you learn it - the same way you mastered English! And because the technique relies on interactive spoken language training, the Pimsleur Language Programs are totally audio - no book is needed! The Pimsleur programs provide a method of self-practice with an expert teacher and native speakers in lessons specially designed to work with the way the mind naturally acquires language information. The various components of language - vocabulary, pronunciation and grammar - are all learned together without rote memorization and drills. Using a unique method of memory recall developed by renowned linguist, Dr. Paul Pimsleur, the programs teach listeners to combine words and phrases to express themselves the way native speakers do. By listening and responding to thirty minute recorded lessons, students easily and effectively achieve spoken proficiency. No other language program or school is as quick, convenient, and effective as the Pimsleur Language Programs. The Comprehensive Program is the ultimate in spoken language learning. For those who want to become proficient in the language of their choice, the Comprehensive programs go beyond the Basic Programs to offer spoken-language fluency. Using the same simple method of interactive self-practice with native speakers, these comprehensive programs provide a complete language learning course. The Comprehensive Program is available in a wide variety of languages and runs through three levels (thirty lessons each) in French, German, Italian, Japanese, Russian and Spanish. At the end of a full Comprehensive Program listeners will be conducting complete conversations and be well on their way to mastering the language. The Comprehensive Programs are all available on cassettes and are also on CD in the six languages in which we offer the Basic Program on CD.

Armenian (Western) Learn to Speak & Understand Western Armenian with Pimsleur Language Programs. unabr. ed. Pimsleur Staff & Pimsleur. 5 CDs. (Running Time: 50 hrs. 0 mins. 0 sec.). (Compact Ser.). (ARM & ENG.). 2006. audio compact disk 49.95 (978-0-7435-5065-9(X), Pimsleur) Pub: S&S Audio. Dist(s): S and S Inc

Armenian (Western) Short Course, Set. Paul Pimsleur. 5 cass. (Pimsleur Language Learning Ser.). 1997. 149.95 Set. (0671-57960-6) SyberVision.

Armenian (Western) World Citizen Edition. unabr. ed. 10 Cass. (Running Time: 10 hrs.). 2003. audio compact disk 115.00 (978-0-7887-9769-9(7)) Recorded Bks.

Armenien sans Peine. 1 cass. (Running Time: 1 hr., 30 min.). (ARM & FRE.). 2000. bk. 75.00 (978-2-7005-1377-6(0)) Pub: Assimil FRA. Dist(s): Distribks Inc

Armies of the Raj. unabr. ed. Byron Farwell. Read by Bill Kelsey. 8 cass. (Running Time: 12 hrs.). 1994. 64.00 (978-0-7366-2691-0(3), 3426) Books on Tape.
Panoramic view of Indian army under British rule, 1858-1947.

Arminius: The Scapegoat of Calvinism. Vic Reasoner. 1 cass. 3.00 (VR2) Evang Outreach.

***Armonia: Musica E Imagenes para Estimular y Relajar A Tu Bebe.** Macarena Carmona & Isabel Lunansky. Illus. by Sara Rojo. (SPA.). (J). 2010. bk. 27.95 (978-84-7942-434-3(6)) Heinemann Ib ESP.

Armor. unabr. ed. John Steakley. Read by Christopher Lane. (Running Time: 14 hrs. 0 mins.). (ENG.). 2009. 29.95 (978-1-4332-9486-0(9)); 79.95 (978-1-4332-9482-2(6)); audio compact disk 109.00 (978-1-4332-9483-9(4)) Blckstn Audio.

Armor for the Age of Deceit. Chuck Missler. 2 CD's. (Running Time: 2 hrs.). (Briefing Packages by Chuck Missler). 1996. audio compact disk 19.95 (978-1-57821-291-0(X)) Koinonia Hse.
In this age of deceit and treachery it is vital to be protected from the consequences of the spiritual war raging around us. The Bible tells us to put on the whole armor of God. What is it? And when do you put it on?.

Arms & the Man. 2 CDs. (Running Time: 7200 sec.). Dramatization. (Stratford Festival Ser.). 2006. audio compact disk 19.95 (978-0-660-19546-9(1), CBC Audio) Canadian Broadcasting CAN.

Arms & the Man. unabr. ed. George Bernard Shaw. 1 CD. (Running Time: 5580 sec.). 2006. audio compact disk 25.95 (978-1-58081-353-2(4)) Pub: L A Theatre. Dist(s): NetLibrary CO

Arms & Woman. unabr. ed. Gilbert Highet. 1 cass. (Running Time: 30 mins.). (Gilbert Highet Ser.). 12.95 (C23329) J Norton Pubs.
Ever since "Gone with the Wind" ladies have been writing historical novels in which pretty women play leading parts & many great books have been written by men & women exiled from their native land or imprisoned.

Arms Maker of Berlin. unabr. ed. Dan Fesperman. Read by Dick Hill. (Running Time: 14 hrs.). 2009. 39.97 (978-1-4233-4670-8(X), 9781423346708, BADLE) Brilliance Audio.

Arms Maker of Berlin. unabr. ed. Dan Fesperman. Read by Christopher Lane & Dick Hill. (Running Time: 14 hrs.). 2009. 39.97 (978-1-4233-4668-5(8), 9781423346685, Brinc Audio MP3 Lib); 24.99 (978-1-4233-4669-2(6), 9781423346692, BAD); audio compact disk 99.97 (978-1-4233-4666-1(1), 9781423346661, BriAudCD Unabrid) Brilliance Audio.

***Arms Maker of Berlin: A Novel.** unabr. ed. Dan Fesperman. Read by Dick Hill. (Running Time: 16 hrs.). 2010. 19.99 (978-1-4418-7081-0(4), 9781441870810, Brilliance MP3); audio compact disk 19.99 (978-1-4418-7080-3(6), 9781441870803, BCD Value Price) Brilliance Audio.

Arms of Krupp 1587-1968, Pt. 1. unabr. collector's ed. William Manchester. Read by Peter McDonald. 15 cass. (Running Time: 22 hrs. 30 mins.). 1984. 120.00 (978-0-7366-0716-2(1), 1679A) Books on Tape.
In their dedication to German military supremacy the Krupps moved from traditional industrialism to acquisition, monopoly, finance & politics. At its peak, the Krupp network embraced iron & steel, chemicals, rubber, oil, shipyards, railways, aircraft design & manufacturing cranes, trucks, housing, & even atomic energy. Their influence was ubiquitous in Germany for more than a century. The Krupps not only armed Germany but helped finance three major wars. They misjudged Hitler, believing they could control him, & bankrolled his notorious "Terror Election" of 1933, a mistake in judgement that was to have devastating consequences. For his part in Hitler's rise & Germany's martial aggressions, Alfred Krupp was tried at Nuremburg.

Arms of Krupp 1587-1968, Pt. 2. collector's ed. William Manchester. Read by Peter McDonald. 15 cass. (Running Time: 22 hrs. 30 mins.). 1984. 120.00 (978-0-7366-0717-9(X), 1679-B) Books on Tape.
This great industrial family armed & financed three German wars. Amazingly, none of them went to prison after WW II.

Arms of Nemesis: A Novel of Ancient Rome. Steven Saylor & Scott Harrison. 8 cass. (Running Time: 11 hrs. 30 mins.). 2002. 56.95 (978-0-7861-1129-9(1), 1894) Blckstn Audio.

Arms of Nemesis: A Novel of Ancient Rome, unabr. ed. Steven Saylor. Read by Scott Harrison. 8 cass. (Running Time: 12 hrs.). 1997. 56.95 (1894) Blckstn Audio.
South of Rome on the Gulf of Puteoli stands the villa of Marcus Crassus, Rome's wealthiest citizen. When the estate overseer is murdered, Crassus concludes that the deed was done by two missing slaves. Unless they are found within five days he vows to massacre his remaining ninety-nine slaves. To Gordianus the Finder falls the fateful task of resolving this riddle. As the hour of the massacre approaches, Gordianus realizes that the labyrinthine path he has chosen may lead to his own destruction.

Army at Dawn: The War in North Africa (1942-1943) abr. ed. Rick Atkinson. 2004. 15.95 (978-0-7435-4167-1(7)) Pub: S&S Audio. Dist(s): S and S Inc

Army at Dawn: The War in North Africa 1942-1943. abr. ed. Rick Atkinson. Read by Rick Atkinson. (Running Time: 70 hrs. 0 mins. 0 sec.). (ENG.). 2007. audio compact disk 14.99 (978-0-7435-7099-2(5)) Pub: S&S Audio. Dist(s): S and S Inc

Army Life in a Black Regiment. unabr. ed. Thomas W. Higginson. Read by Jim Roberts. 7 cass. (Running Time: 10 hrs. 30 mins.). 1993. 49.00 set in vinyl album. Jimcin Record.
The story of the first regiment of Black troops enlisted in the Union Army by their proud commanding officer.

Army-McCarthy Hearings. 1 cass. (Running Time: 37 min.). 10.95 (H0190B090, HarperThor) HarpC GBR.

Army of Hell Pt. 1: Rev. 9:1-11. Ed Young. 1986. 4.95 (978-0-7417-1565-4(1), 565) Win Walk.

Army of Love. Perf. by Jake. 2002. audio compact disk 17.98 Reunion Recs.

Army of the Potomac Pt. 1: Mr. Lincoln's Army. unabr. ed. Bruce Catton. Read by James Cunningham. 9 cass. (Running Time: 13 hrs. 30 mins.). 1979. 72.00 (978-0-7366-0133-7(3), 1139-A) Books on Tape.
Accounts gathered from diaries, letters & published reports of ordinary foot soldiers who discovered that their skylarking "picture book" war was grim & deadly, as wars must ever be.

Army of the Potomac Pt. II: Glory Road. unabr. ed. Bruce Catton. Read by James Cunningham. 10 cass. (Running Time: 15 hrs.). 1979. 80.00 (1139-B) Books on Tape.
This book recounts the campaigns of late 1862 & early 1863, highlighting the fierce encounters at Fredericksburg, Chancellorsville & Gettysburg. Excerpts from letters, diaries, recollections & official reports impart an air of reality to the descriptions of battles, camps & the citizen soldiers.

Army of the Potomac Pt. III: A Stillness at Appomattox. unabr. ed. Bruce Catton. Read by James Cunningham. 11 cass. (Running Time: 16 hrs. 30 mins.). 1979. 88.00 (1139-C) Books on Tape.
Describes the last year of the Civil War, after Grant became commander of the armies.

Army Wives: The Unwritten Code of Military Marriage. unabr. ed. Tanya Biank. Read by Laural Merlington. (Running Time: 11 hrs.). 2008. 39.25 (978-1-4233-5733-9(7), 9781423357339, BADLE); 24.95 (978-1-4233-5732-2(9), 9781423357322, BAD); audio compact disk 39.25 (978-1-4233-5731-5(0), 9781423357315, Brlnc Audio MP3 Lib); audio compact disk 36.95 (978-1-4233-5728-5(0), 9781423357285, Bril Audio CD Unabri); audio compact disk 97.25 (978-1-4233-5729-2(9), 9781423357292, BriAudCD Unabrid) Brilliance Audio.

Army Wives: The Unwritten Code of Military Marriage. unabr. ed. Tanya Biank. Read by Laural Merlington. Directed By Colleen Willits. Contrib. by Cory Young. (Running Time: 39600 sec.). 2008. audio compact disk 24.95 (978-1-4233-5730-8(2), 9781423357308, Brilliance MP3) Brilliance Audio.

Arnie DeLuca: Telemarketing. unabr. ed. Arnold A. DeLuca. 3 cass. (Running Time: 3 hrs.). (Telemarketing Ser.). 1985. 65.00 Dynamo Intl.
Telemarketing for newspaper & shopper publications.

Arnie DeLuca's Advertising Salesmanship Seminar. Arnold A. DeLuca. 6 cass. 1985. bk. Dynamo Intl.
The selling of newspaper & shopper display advertising space to merchants for the advertising of their goods & services.

Arnie the Doughnut. Laurie Keller. Illus. by Laurie Keller. Narrated by Michael McKean et al. (J). (gr. k-4). 2005. bk. 24.95 (978-0-439-76639-5(7), WHRA649); bk. 29.95 (978-0-439-76641-8(9), WHCD649) Weston Woods.
Arnie Looks like an average doughnut, made by one of the best bakeries in town. When Mr. Bing buys him and brings him home to his breakfast table, however, Arnie realizes his carefree days are about to end - unless he persuades Mr. Bing that a doughnut can bemore than just a snack.

Arno Karlen. unabr. ed. Poems. Arno Karlen. Read by Arno Karlen. 1 cass. (Running Time: 29 mins.). 1986. 8.00 New Letters.
The New York writer reads dramatic poems about historical & literary figures as well as family & love themes.

Arnold Keith Storm: Take the News to Mother. 1 cass. 9.98 (C-18) Folk-Legacy.
Sentimental songs in the Indiana tradition.

Arnold Lobel. unabr. ed. Arnold Lobel. Read by Mark Linn-Baker. (J). 2009. audio compact disk 13.99 (978-0-06-189969-0(0), HarperChildAud) HarperCollins Pubs.

***Arnold Lobel Audio Collection.** unabr. ed. Arnold Lobel. Read by Mark Linn-baker. (ENG.). 2009. (978-0-06-196699-6(1)); (978-0-06-196698-9(3)) HarperCollins Pubs.

Aromatherapy, Vol. 10. Jonathan Parker. 2 cass. (Running Time: 2 hrs.). 1998. 17.00 (978-1-58400-009-9(0)) QuantumQuests Intl.

Aromatherapy: A Personal Journey Through Your Senses. Patricia Betty. Read by Patricia Betty. Ed. by Amelia Sheldon & Adrian Westnay. 1 cass. (Running Time: 1 hr.). Dramatization. 1995. 29.95 (978-0-9641205-9-4(3)) Escent Yours.
Guided meditation through imagining the plants in nature, plus imaginary scenarios around these plants, with sound effects & music.

Aromatherapy Vol. 2, set: Mini Course. Jonathan Parker. Read by Jonathan Parker. 2 CDs. (Running Time: 2 hrs.). (Natural Health Ser.: Vol. 5). 1999. audio compact disk (978-1-58400-053-2(8)) QuantumQuests Intl.

Aromatic Blend: The Book of Coffee Poems. Don Anawalt. 1 CD. (Running Time: 30 min.). 1999. audio compact disk 11.97 (978-0-9668414-2-8(5)) Abongold.

Around & about New York City & Long Island. Ralph Stern & Dell Wade. Read by Dell Wade. 2 cass. (Running Time: 3 hrs. 30 min.). Dramatization. 1992. 11.95 Set. (978-1-879677-04-3(0)) Spector Audio.
Audio travel guide with lively narrative - background music & interviews. Tells the stories behind the must see sights of New York City & Long Island ranging from unusual to popular. For people of all ages & interests. Tape is packaged in book size reusable case, with travel tips, handy telephone numbers, hotels, tour operators, all the sights to see - even those not narrated, & a "retrieval system" index which makes it possible to re-listen to specific portions.

Around the Campfire. Perf. by Peter, Paul and Mary. 1 cass., 1 CD. (J). 11.18 Double. (WB 46873); audio compact disk 15.98 CD Jewel box, double. (WB 46873) NewSound.
Twenty-five song anthology. Includes: "This Land is Your Land," "Garden Song," "Kisses Sweeter Than Wine," "It's Raining" & more.

Around the Pond. Ann Cooper & Pat Ramsey Beckman. 2001. 9.95 (978-1-57098-222-4(8)) Pub: Robs Rinehart. Dist(s): Rowman

Around the Ward in 80 Days, Set. abr. ed. Joni Hilton. Read by Suzanne Decker. 2 cass. 1993. 13.95 (978-1-55734-464-3(2), 07002041) Covenant Comms.
Fiction.

Around the World. (J). audio compact disk 13.99 (978-1-56229-738-1(4), Christian Livng) Pneuma Life Pub.

Around the World. Perf. by Jessi Colter & Waylon Jennings. 1 cass. (Running Time: 90 mins.). (J). 2000. 7.98; audio compact disk 9.98 Peter Pan.
Takes kids to places around the world as they sing along to "La Cucaracha," "Frere Jacques," "Funiculi Funicula" & other all-time favorites.

Around the World. Perf. by Lou DelBianco. 1 cass. (J). (gr. k-6). 10.00 (978-0-9642659-6-7(6), CL3384); audio compact disk 15.00 CD. (978-0-9642659-5-0(8)) Story Maker.
Stories from around the world.

Around the World: The Elena Duran Collection 2, Volume 3. Ed. by Elena Duranm. Created by Hal Leonard Corporation Staff. 2007. pap. bk. 19.95 (978-1-902455-66-2(5), 1902455665) Pub: Schott Music Corp. Dist(s): H Leonard

Around the World Automobile Race. Kenneth Bruce. 1 cass. (Running Time: 65 min.). Dramatization. (Excursions in History Ser.). 12.50 Alpha Tape.

Around the World for Lunch/Festival of Foods. Steck-Vaughn Staff. (J). 1999. (978-0-7398-2441-2(4)) SteckVau.

Around the World in Eighty Days, Set. unabr. ed. Jules Verne. Read by Flo Gibson. 5 cass. (Running Time: 7 hrs.). (gr. 7 up). 1991. 20.95 (978-1-55685-213-8(4)) Audio Bk Con.
A wager made at London's Reform Club sends the impeturbable Phileas Fogg, his loyal valet Passepartout, & the beautiful Aouda on a journey around a world fraught with obstacles, peril, & humor.

Around the World in Eighty Days: Abridged. (ENG.). 2007. (978-1-60339-049-1(9)); cd-rom & audio compact disk (978-1-60339-050-7(2)) Listenr Digest.

Around the World in Eighty Days, with EBook. unabr. ed. Jules Verne. Narrated by Michael Prichard. (Running Time: 7 hrs. 30 mins. 0 sec.). (ENG.). (J). (gr. 3-6). 2009. audio compact disk 27.99 (978-1-4001-0906-7(X)); audio compact disk 19.99 (978-1-4001-5906-2(7)) Pub: Tantor Media. Dist(s): IngramPubServ

Around the World in Eighty Days, with eBook. unabr. ed. Jules Verne. Narrated by Michael Prichard. (Running Time: 7 hrs. 30 mins. 0 sec.). (ENG.). (J). (gr. 3-6). 2009. audio compact disk 55.99 (978-1-4001-3906-4(6)) Pub: Tantor Media. Dist(s): IngramPubServ

Around the World in 8 1/2 Days. unabr. ed. Megan McDonald. Read by Kate Forbes. 2 cass. (Running Time: 1 hr. 50 mins.). (Judy Moody Ser.: No. 7). (J). (gr. 2-4). 2007. 15.75 (978-1-4281-3377-8(1)); audio compact disk 15.75 (978-1-4281-3382-2(8)) Recorded Bks.

Around the World in 80 Days see Tour du Monde en 80 Jours

Around the World in 80 Days. Michael Palin. 2004. audio compact disk 64.95 (978-0-563-52473-1(1)) AudioGO.

Around the World in 80 Days. Jules Verne. 1993. 33.95 (978-0-7861-0635-6(2)) Blckstn Audio.

Around the World in 80 Days. Jules Verne. Read by Harry Burton. (Running Time: 2 hrs. 30 mins.). 1999. 20.95 (978-1-60083-678-7(X)) Iofy Corp.

Around the World in 80 Days. Jules Verne. Read by Fabio Camero. (Running Time: 3 hrs.). 2001. 16.95 (978-1-60083-159-1(1), Audiofy Corp) Iofy Corp.

Around the World in 80 Days. Jules Verne. Read by Ralph Cosham. (Running Time: 6 hrs.). 2002. 22.95 (978-1-59912-041-6(0), Audiofy Corp) Iofy Corp.

Around the World in 80 Days. Jules Verne. Read by Harry Burton. 2 cass. (Running Time: 2 hrs. 30 mins.). (YA). 1995. 13.98 (978-962-634-533-7(0), NA203314, Naxos AudioBooks) Naxos.
Chronicles the dramatic dash from continent to continent to win a wager by the eccentric Englishman, Phileas Fogg.

Around the World in 80 Days. Jules Verne. (Dominoes Ser.). 2002. 14.25 (978-0-19-424353-7(2)) OUP.

Around the World in 80 Days. Jules Verne. (Dominoes Ser.). 2004. 12.95 (978-0-19-424422-0(9)) OUP.

Around the World in 80 Days. abr. ed. Jules Verne. Read by Harry Burton. 2 CDs. (Running Time: 2 hrs. 30 mins.). (YA). 1995. audio compact disk 17.98 (978-962-634-033-2(9), NA203312, Naxos AudioBooks) Naxos.
Chronicles the dramatic dash from continent to continent to win a wager by the eccentric Englishman, Phileas Fogg.

Around the World in 80 Days. abr. ed. Jules Verne. Perf. by Christopher Casson Company. 1 cass. 1985. 10.95 (978-0-8045-1066-0(0), SAC 1066) Spoken Arts.
The intrepid Englishman who circumnavigates the globe in record time.

Around the World in 80 Days. abr. adpt. ed. Jules Verne. (Bring the Classics to Life: Level 2 Ser.). (gr. 3-6). 2008. audio compact disk 12.95 (978-1-55576-588-0(2)) EDCON Pubng.

Around the World in 80 Days. unabr. ed. Prod. by Listening Library Staff. 5 cass. (Running Time: 7 hrs. 55 mins.). 2005. 40.00 (978-0-307-20628-2(9), Listening Lib); audio compact disk 46.75 (978-0-307-20682-4(3), Listening Lib) Pub: Random Audio Pubg. Dist(s): NetLibrary CO

Around the World in 80 Days. unabr. ed. Jules Verne. Read by Frederick Davidson. 8 cass. (Running Time: 7 hr. 30 min.). 1994. reel tape 25.95 (978-0-7861-2820-4(8), 1451) Blckstn Audio.
Phileas Fogg, a distinguished member of London's Reform Club, takes up a wager to circle the globe in just eighty days. Together with manservant Passepartout and a detective named Fix, Fogg makes a fantastic world tour utilizing every means of transportation available in the 1870s. This is a marvelous travelogue mixed with dazzling suspense, delightful fantasy, and lively comedy.

Around the World in 80 Days. unabr. ed. Jules Verne. Read by Tim Behrens. 6 cass. (Running Time: 7 hrs. 30 mins.). Dramatization. 1990. 39.95 (978-1-55686-331-8(4), 752360) Books in Motion.
On October 1, 1872, Mr. Phileas Fogg makes a wager that he could go around the world in eighty days. With the bet made, the adventure begins.

Around the World in 80 Days. unabr. ed. Jules Verne. Read by David Case. 7 cass. (Running Time: 11 hrs.). 2001. 29.95 (978-0-7366-6818-7(7)) Books on Tape.
Phineas Fogg's famous journey around the world in order to win a wager displays his limitless resourcefulness & his fortitude.

Around the World in 80 Days. unabr. ed. Jules Verne. Read by David Colacci. (Running Time: 6 hrs.). 2005. 39.25 (978-1-59737-042-4(8), 9781597370424, BADLE); 24.95 (978-1-59737-041-7(X), 9781597370417, BAD); audio compact disk 39.25 (978-1-59737-040-0(1), 9781597370400, Brlnc Audio MP3 Lib); audio compact disk 24.95 (978-1-59737-039-4(8), 9781597370394, Brilliance MP3); audio compact disk 74.25 (978-1-59737-038-7(X), 9781597370387, BriAudCD Unabrid); audio compact disk 29.95 (978-1-59737-037-0(1), 9781597370370, Bril Audio CD Unabri) Brilliance Audio.

Around the World in 80 Days. unabr. ed. Jules Verne. Read by Ralph Cosham. (YA). 2006. 59.99 (978-1-59895-163-9(7)) Find a World.

Around the World in 80 Days. unabr. ed. Jules Verne. Read by Walter Covell. 5 cass. (Running Time: 7 hrs. 30 min.). Dramatization. 1989. 29.00 incl. album. (C-60) Jimcin Record.
Incredible journey of Phinias Fogg & his race around the world.

Around the World in 80 Days. unabr. ed. Jules Verne. Read by Jim Dale. 7 CDs. (Running Time: 7 hrs. 53 mins.). (ENG.). (J). (gr. 3). 2005. audio compact disk 30.00 (978-0-307-20642-8(4), Listening Lib) Pub: Random Audio Pubg. Dist(s): Random

Around the World in 80 Days, unabr. ed. Jules Verne. Narrated by Patrick Tull. 5 cass. (Running Time: 7 hrs.). (gr. 10 up). 1986. 44.00 (978-1-55690-028-0(7), 86460E7) Recorded Bks.
Phileas Fogg lays a wager with members of the Reform Club that he can circumnavigate the globe in 80 days.

Around the World in 80 Days. unabr. ed. Jules Verne. Read by Ralph Cosham. 1 CD. (Running Time: 6 hrs 5 mins). (YA). 2002. audio compact disk 18.95 (978-1-58472-380-6(7), In Aud) Pub: Sound Room. Dist(s): Baker Taylor
MP3 format.

Around the World in 80 Days. unabr. ed. Jules Verne. Read by Ralph Cosham. 5 cds. (Running Time: 6 hrs 5 mins). (YA). 2002. audio compact disk 29.95 (978-1-58472-204-5(5), 073, In Aud) Pub: Sound Room. Dist(s): Baker Taylor
Phileas Fogg races against time to win a sizeable wager.

Around the World in 80 Days. unabr. ed. Jules Verne. Narrated by Michael Prichard. (ENG.). 2004. audio compact disk 19.99 (978-1-4001-5131-8(7)) Pub: Tantor Media. Dist(s): IngramPubServ

Around the World in 80 Days. unabr. ed. Jules Verne. Read by Michael Prichard. (ENG.). 2004. audio compact disk 59.99 (978-1-4001-3131-0(6)) Pub: Tantor Media. Dist(s): IngramPubServ

Around the World in 80 Days. unabr. collector's ed. Jules Verne. Read by David Case. 7 cass. (Running Time: 7 hrs.). (J). 1993. 56.00 (978-0-7366-2556-2(9), 3307) Books on Tape.
Phineas Fogg's famous journey around the world in order to win a wager displays this limitless resourcefulness & his fortitude.

Around the World in 80 Days. 4th abr. ed. Jules Verne. Read by Arte Johnson. 4 cass. (Running Time: 6 hrs.). 2004. 25.00 (978-1-59007-027-7(5)) Pub: New Millenn Enter. Dist(s): PerseuPGW
It's hard to imagine what it must have been like travelling around the world one hundred years ago, because the trips abroad were really more like expeditions. To make a trip entirely around the earth's surface was barely even possible. But Phileas Fogg, an English gentleman, dares the impossible on a bet when he sets out to complete such a trip with his French manservant, Passepartout. The voyage is a muddle of railroads, lumbering elephants, steamships, schedules, dangerous encounters & humor which leads us to a once in a lifetime adventure.

***Around the World in 80 Days: Bring the Classics to Life.** adpt. ed. Jules Verne. (Bring the Classics to Life Ser.). 2008. pap. bk. 21.95 (978-1-55576-599-6(8)) EDCON Pubng.

***Around the World in 80 Days: Value-Priced Edition.** Read by Michael Palin. (Running Time: 7 hrs. 40 mins. 0 sec.). (ENG.). 2010. audio compact disk 14.95 (978-1-60998-001-6(8)) Pub: AudioGO. Dist(s): Perseus Dist

Around the World in 80 Days: 2004 Movie Tie-in. Jules Verne. Read by Frederick Davidson. 5 cass. (Running Time: 7 hrs.). 2004. 39.95 (978-0-7861-0636-3(0), 1451) Blckstn Audio.

Around the World in 80 Days: 2004 Movie Tie-in. unabr. ed. Jules Verne. Read by Frederick Davidson. 6 CDs. (Running Time: 7 hrs.). 2005. audio compact disk 29.95 (978-0-7861-8444-6(2)); audio compact disk 24.95 (978-0-7861-8456-9(6), 1451) Blckstn Audio.

Around the World in 80 Rounds: Chasing a Golf Ball from Tierra del Fuego to the Land of the Midnight Sun. unabr. ed. David Wood. Read by David Wood. (Running Time: 11 hrs.). 2008. 39.25 (978-1-4233-5076-7(6), 9781423350767, BADLE); 24.95 (978-1-4233-5075-0(8), 9781423350750, BAD); audio compact disk 97.25 (978-1-4233-5072-9(3), 9781423350729, BriAudCD Unabrid); audio compact disk 39.25 (978-1-4233-5074-3(X), 9781423350743, Brlnc Audio MP3 Lib); audio compact disk 24.95 (978-1-4233-5073-6(1), 9781423350736, Brilliance MP3); audio compact disk 36.95 (978-1-4233-5071-2(5), 9781423350712, Bril Audio CD Unabri) Brilliance Audio.

Around the World on Two Wheels: Annie Londonderry's Extraordinary Ride. unabr. ed. Peter Zheutlin. Read by Barrett Whitener. (Running Time: 7 hrs. 0 mins. 0 sec.). (ENG.). 2007. audio compact disk 29.99 (978-1-4001-0547-2(1)); audio compact disk 59.99 (978-1-4001-3547-9(8)) Pub: Tantor Media. Dist(s): IngramPubServ

Around the World on Two Wheels: Annie Londonderry's Extraordinary Ride. unabr. ed. Peter Zheutlin. Read by Lloyd James et al. (Running Time: 7 hrs. 0 mins. 0 sec.). (ENG.). 2007. audio compact disk 19.99 (978-1-4001-5547-7(9)) Pub: Tantor Media. Dist(s): IngramPubServ

Around the World on Two Wheels: One Woman, One Bicycle, One Unforgettable Journey. Peter Zheutlin. Read by Barrett Whitener. (Playaway Adult Nonfiction Ser.). 2009. 59.99 (978-1-60812-792-4(3)) Find a World.

Around the World with Earth Mama. Joyce J. Rouse. 1 cass. (Running Time: 40 min.). (J). 1997. 14.95 (978-1-887712-03-3(8)) Rouse Hse Prodns.
Thirteen classic Earth Mama songs for fund & sustainable living. Packaged in recycled holder. Used by teachers & environmental educators internationally.

Around the World with Me: Movement & Activity Songs for Kids. John Jacobson & Alan Billingsley. 1998. audio compact disk 19.95 (978-0-7935-9747-5(1)) H Leonard.

Around the World with the U. S. Weightlifting Team. 2006. audio compact disk 4.95 (978-0-9772573-8-6(X)) P Anderson Youth Home.

Around the Year with Jay O'Callahan. Short Stories. Jay O'Callahan. 1 CD. (Running Time: 1 hr. 06 min. per cass.). Dramatization. 1993. audio

compact disk 15.00 (978-1-877954-24-5(1)) Pub: Artana Prodns. Dist(s): Yellow Moon
A collection of tales to celebrate special days of the year. Includes: "Super Bowl Sunday," "Connor & the Leprechaun," "Tulips," "The Bubble," "Brian," Nonsense," "Don't You Dare," "Jonathan," "Woe is Me Bones," "The Red Ball," "Old Man Daniker," "Christmas Candles," "Mary, New Year's Eve".

Arraignment. abr. ed. Steve Martini. Read by Joe Mantegna. (Paul Madriani Ser.: No. 7). 2006. 18.95 (978-0-7435-6172-3(4)) Pub: S&S Audio. Dist(s): S and S Inc

Arrancame la Vida. Angeles Mastretta. 6 cass. (Running Time: 8 hrs.). (SPA.). bk. 59.75 (978-1-4025-6316-4(7)) Recorded Bks.

Arranged Marriage. unabr. ed. Bali Rai. Read by Kish Sharma. 6 cass. (Running Time: 5 hrs. 39 mins.). (Isis Cassettes Ser.). (J). 2004. 54.95 (978-0-7531-1876-4(9)) Pub: ISIS Lrg Prnt GBR. Dist(s): Ulverscroft US
Set partly in the UK and partly in the Punjab region of India, this is a fresh, bitingly perceptive and totally up-to-the minute look at one young man's fight to free himself from family expectations and to be himself, free to dance to his own tune.

Arrangement, Pt. 1. unabr. collector's ed. Elia Kazan. Read by Dan Lazar. 8 cass. (Running Time: 12 hrs.). 1986. 64.00 (978-0-7366-0975-3(X), 1917-A) Books on Tape.
Eddie Anderson is successful, well-off with a nice home & an attentive wife. But he's restless so he has a mistress & now she wants to change that arrangement. How Eddie got into this mess & how he tries to get out is the story of this book.

Arrangement, Pt. 2. collector's ed. Elia Kazan. Read by Dan Lazar. 6 cass. (Running Time: 9 hrs.). 1986. 48.00 (978-0-7366-0976-0(8), 1917-B) Books on Tape.
An upwardly mobile mistress wants to change places with the hero's wife.

Arranging Music for the Real World: Classical & Commercial Aspects. Excerpts. Vince Corozine. 1 CD. (ENG.). 2002. per. 29.95 (978-0-7866-4961-7(5)) Mel Bay.

Arrest of Arsene Lupin see Extraordinary Adventures of Arsene Lupin

Arriba! Communicacion y Cultura. 4th ed. Eduardo Zayas-Bazan & Susan M. Bacon. 2005. bk. 134.00 (978-0-13-173757-0(0)) Pearson Educ CAN CAN.

Arriba! Comunicacion y Cultura. 4th ed. Eduardo Zayas-Bazan & Susan M. Bacon. 2004. bk. & pap. bk. 124.93 (978-0-13-170578-4(4)) Pearson Educ CAN CAN.

Arriba! Comunicacion y Cultura. 5th ed. Zayas-Bazan et al. 2007. audio compact disk 103.33 (978-0-13-158982-7(2)) Pearson Educ CAN CAN.

***Arrival.** 2010. audio compact disk (978-1-59171-211-4(4)) Falcon Picture.

Arrival of the Unexpected. Perf. by Kenneth G. Mills. 1 cass., 1 CD. (Running Time: 1 hrs. 8 min.). 1998. 8.98 (KMOD36-4); audio compact disk 14.98 CD. (KMOD36-2) Ken Mills Found.
Keyboard soliloquies composed & performed in one pass on 4 MIDI keyboards, each representing orchestral instruments. Nine tracks including "Fireflies," "Exotic Fanfare," "Pleading" & "Arrival of the Unexpected".

Arrogance. (712) Yoga Res Foun.

Arrogance. Swami Jyotirmayananda. 1 cass. (Running Time: 1 hr.). 1990. 12.99 Yoga Res Foun.

Arrogance: Rescuing America from the Media Elite. abr. ed. Bernard Goldberg. (ENG.). 2005. 14.98 (978-1-59483-304-5(4)) Pub: Hachet Audio. Dist(s): HachBkGrp

Arrogance: Rescuing America from the Media Elite. abr. ed. Bernard Goldberg. (Running Time: 6 hrs.). (ENG.). 2009. 49.98 (978-1-60024-992-1(2)) Pub: Hachet Audio. Dist(s): HachBkGrp

Arrogant Armies. unabr. collector's ed. James M. Perry. Read by Jonathan Reese. 9 cass. (Running Time: 13 hrs. 30 min.). 1997. 72.00 (978-0-7366-3663-6(3), 4337) Books on Tape.
Drunkenness, arrogance, debauchery & plain stupidity, mix them together & what do you have? The makings of a disastrous military expedition James M. Perry chronicles two hundred years of botched military campaigns, from colonial America to Khartoum, from Mesopotamia to South Africa. Seated high on heaps of rubble & human casualties are the dunced generals, many of whom shared the fate of their men. Some were unlucky, others were inept. Their stories from a fascinating history & trenchant critique of the politics of battle & humanity's deadly preoccupation with war.

Arrorro, Mi Nino: Latino Lullabies & Gentle Games. abr. ed. Contrib. by Cantare. (Running Time: 1647 sec.). (J). (ps-k). 2006. audio compact disk 12.95 (978-1-60060-123-1(5)) Lee n Low Bks.

Arrow & the Song see Best Loved Poems of Longfellow

Arrow of God & Anthills of the Savannah. Chinua Achebe. Read by Chinua Achebe. 1 cass. (Running Time: 88 min.). 1988. 13.95 (978-1-55644-283-4(1), 8011) Am Audio Prose.
Flawless reading performance by the man who is arguably Africa's greatest living writer.

Arrow of Gold: A Story Between Two Notes. unabr. collector's ed. Joseph Conrad. Read by Wolfram Kandinsky. 10 cass. (Running Time: 15 hrs.). 1993. 80.00 (978-0-7366-2371-1(X), 3144) Books on Tape.
English sea captain running Carlist munitions falls in love with Spanish beauty financing the project.

Arrow to the Sun see Flecha al Sol: Un Cuento de los Indios Pueblo

Arrow to the Sun see Flecha Al Sol

Arrow to the Sun see Flecha al Sol: Un Cuento de los Indios Pueblo

Arrow to the Sun. 2004. pap. bk. 32.75 (978-1-55592-189-7(2)) Weston Woods.

Arrow to the Sun. (J). 2004. bk. 24.95 (978-0-89719-859-2(X)); pap. bk. 18.95 (978-1-55592-371-6(2)); pap. bk. 38.75 (978-1-55592-373-0(9)); 8.95 (978-1-56008-834-9(6)); cass. & flmstrp 30.00 (978-0-89719-630-7(9)); audio compact disk 12.95 (978-1-55592-898-8(6)) Weston Woods.

Arrow to the Sun: A Pueblo Indian Tale. Gerald McDermott. 1 cass. (Running Time: 10 min.). (J). (ps-4). bk. 24.95; pap. bk. 32.75; 8.95 (RAC184) Weston Woods.
How the spirit of the sun was brought to the world of men is explained in this pueblo Indian myth.

Arrow to the Sun: A Pueblo Indian Tale. Gerald McDermott. 1 cass. (Running Time: 10 min.). (J). (ps-4). 2004. pap. bk. 14.95 (978-1-56008-047-3(7), PRA184) Weston Woods.

Arrow to the Sun: A Pueblo Indian Tale. Adapted by Gerald McDermott. (J). (gr. 3-5). 2004. 8.95 (978-1-56008-134-0(1)) Weston Woods.

Arrows of Longing. Virginia Moriconi. 10 cass. (Running Time: 12 hrs.). (Soundings Ser.). (J). 2005. 84.95 (978-1-84283-953-9(5)) Pub: ISIS Lrg Prnt GBR. Dist(s): Ulverscroft US

Arrows of the Lord. Stephen Hill. 1 cass. 1996. 14.00 (978-0-7684-0021-2(X)) Destiny Image Pubs.

Arrowsmith. Sinclair Lewis. Narrated by Flo Gibson. (ENG.). 2008. audio compact disk 47.95 (978-1-60646-016-0(1)) Audio Bk Con.

Arrowsmith. Perf. by Tyrone Power. 1 cass. 10.00 (MC1006) Esstee Audios.
Radio drama.

Arrowsmith, unabr. ed. Sinclair Lewis. Narrated by Flo Gibson. 11 cass. (Running Time: 16 hrs.). (gr. 10 up). 2000. 34.95 (978-1-55685-617-4(2)) Audio Bk Con.
A Pulitzer Prize winning novel about a physician & researcher who dedicates himself to pursue scientific truth even in the face of personal tragedy, corruption & greed.

Arrowsmith. unabr. ed. Sinclair Lewis. Narrated by John McDonough. 15 cass. (Running Time: 21 hrs.). 2001. 122.00 (978-0-7887-5986-4(8)) Recorded Bks.
Story of a brilliant young man who dedicates his life to science, yet finds that hypocrisy, not disease, is his greatest foe.

Arroz con Leche. Lulu Delacre. Illus. by Lulu Delacre. 1 cass. (SPA.). (J). (gr. 1-3). 1992. 4.95 (978-0-590-60035-4(4), Schol Pbk) Scholastic Inc.
Poetry & nursery rhymes.

Arroz con Leche CD & Book. 1 CD. (Running Time: 14 mins.). (SPA.). 2005. audio compact disk 17.95 (978-1-57970-107-9(8), SSP310D) J Norton Pubs.

Arrullos. 1. (Running Time: 1 hr. 30 mins.). (J). (ps-3). 12.00 (978-1-57417-019-1(8), AC2922); audio compact disk 16.00 (978-1-57417-008-5(2), AC6875) Arcoiris Recs.

Ars poetica see Twentieth-Century Poetry in English, No. 29, Recordings of Poets Reading Their Own Poetry

Arsenal. unabr. collector's ed. Keith Douglass. Read by Edward Lewis. 7 cass. (Running Time: 10 hrs. 30 min.). (Carrier Ser.: No. 10). 2000. 56.00 (978-0-7366-5916-1(1)) Books on Tape.
A Carrier Battle Group is lead into a reckless attack against a group of insurgents who have taken control of Cuba.

Arsene Lupin et la Barre-y-va, Set. Maurice Leblanc. 4 cass. (FRE.). 1991. 38.95 (1473-LV) Olivia & Hill.

Arsene Lupin, Gentleman Burglar. Maurice LeBlanc. Read by Walter Covell. 4 cass. (Running Time: 6 hrs.). 1989. 28.00 incl. album. (C-97) Jimcin Record.
French thief rivals Sherlock Holmes.

Arsene Lupin in Prison see Extraordinary Adventures of Arsene Lupin

Arsene Lupon et l'Aiguille creuse, Set. Maurice Leblanc. 4 cass. (FRE.). 1991. 38.95 (1418-LV) Olivia & Hill.
An Arsene Lupin adventure.

Arsenic & Old Lace. Perf. by Boris Karloff et al. 1946. (MM-5740) Natl Recrd Co.

Arson. unabr. ed. Sarah Lacey. Read by Tessa Gallagher. 5 cass. (Running Time: 6 hrs. 35 min.). 1998. 63.95 Set. (978-1-85903-172-8(2)) Pub: Magna Story GBR. Dist(s): Ulverscroft US
When a warehouse burns down & Old Rosie dies in the flames, Billy - a teenager with a liking for matches & a thick file with the child psychology service - is charged with arson. When Billy dies in custody & tax inspector Leah Hunter begins to delve into a financial scam, she finds that Billy's death was just a mite too convenient. Suddenly it starts to look as if Billy was innocent after all. Which makes Leah the target for some very dangerous people.

Art. Patrick McDonnell. Narrated by Bobby McFerrin. 1 CD. (Running Time: 5 mins.). (J). (ps-3). 2009. bk. 29.95 (978-0-545-10697-9(4)); audio compact disk 12.95 (978-0-545-10693-1(1)) Weston Woods.

***Art.** Yasmina Reza. Read by Bob Balaban & Jeff Perry. Tr. by Christopher Hampton from FRE. 2 CDs. (Running Time: 2 hrs.). 2009. audio compact disk 25.95 (978-1-58081-583-3(9)) L A Theatre.

Art. unabr. ed. Aldous Huxley. 1 cass. (Running Time: 1 hr.). (Human Situation Ser.). 1959. 11.00 (01118) Big Sur Tapes.
Explains that art is a mysterious thing at its highest level can somehow bypass the essential ineffability of experience & create a kind of experiential equivalent with symbols.

Art: Immoral or Immortal? unabr. ed. Wladimir Eliasberg. Read by W. G Eliasberg. 1 cass. (Running Time: 24 mins.). 1970. 12.95 (C11017) J Norton Pubs.
Eliasberg presents the pornographic criterion - a device to judge morality in art.

Art & A Course in Miracles: Reflections of Holiness. Kenneth Wapnick. 4 CDs. 2005. audio compact disk 23.00 (978-1-59142-190-0(X), CD110) Foun Miracles.
Against a backdrop of James Joyce's distinction between proper and improper art, the workshop discusses the perfect integration of form and content as the core of great art, as well as the essence of what A Course in Miracles calls advanced teachers of God. The true work of art (form) thus emanates from the artist's inner experience (content), as opposed to being the result of external (i.e., special) concerns such as fame, power, or approval. Parallels are drawn between the artist's integrating the content of the Holy Spirit's truth within the forms of specific artistic expression, and students of the Course who strive for the same integration in their personal lives. Thus do both artist and student become reflections of the holiness within, expressed in whatever form that holiness can be communicated without fear.

***Art & A Course in Miracles: Reflections of Holiness.** Kenneth Wapnick. 2009. 19.00 (978-1-59142-468-0(2)) Foun Miracles.

Art & Aesthetics. unabr. ed. Nathaniel Branden. 2 cass. (Running Time: 78 mins.). 19.95 (AFO842-AFO843) J Norton Pubs.
An examination of art as universal to the extent that it addresses itself to basic themes & values that are relevant to the human race; aesthetics as a legitimate branch of philosophy that draws on psychology.

Art & Aesthetics (audio CD Set) Nathaniel Branden. (ENG.). 2007. audio compact disk 19.95 (978-1-57970-464-3(6), Audio-For) J Norton Pubs.

Art & Craft of Conducting Depositions. Contrib. by Melvyn H. Bergstein. (Running Time: 4 hrs.). 1983. 70.00 incl. program handbk. NJ Inst CLE.
Teaches how to probe for information , how to produce testimony in admissible form for use at trial, how to protect your client & witness from an adversary's overreaching questions, how to prepare a witness for a deposition.

Art & Discipline of Strategic Leadership. abr. ed. Mike Freedman. Read by Chris Ryan. Told to Benjamin B. Tregoe. (Running Time: 16200 sec.). 2005. audio compact disk 28.00 (978-1-932378-64-1(2)) Pub: A Media Intl. Dist(s): Natl Bk Netwk

Art & Dynamics of Protest. Derrick Bell. 1 cass. (Running Time: 1 hr. 12 mins.). 2001. 12.95 Smithson Assocs.

Art & Life. Read by Anthony Stevens. 1 cass. (Running Time: 90 mins.). 1986. 10.95 (978-0-7822-0298-4(5), 190) C G Jung IL.

Art & Madness: Program from the Award Winning Public Radio Series. Interview. Hosted by Fred Goodwin. Comment by John Hockenberry. 1CD. (Running Time: 1 hr). (Infinite Mind Ser.). 2001. audio compact disk 21.95 (978-1-888064-98-8(6), LCM 155) Lichtenstein Creat.
Images of the tormented artist, poet, painter and composer are familiar? but is there really a link between madness and art? Guests include: actress Margot Kidder; Dr. Louis Sass, a professor of clinical psychology and comparative literature at Rutgers University; Dr. David Schuldberg, a professor in the Department of Psychology at the University of Montana in Missoula; Dr. Richard Kogan, a psychiatrist and concert pianist; Linda Gray Sexton, writer and daughter of Pulitzer Prize-winning poet Anne Sexton. With commentary by John Hockenberry.

Art & Psychology. unabr. ed. Rudolf Arnheim. 1 cass. (Running Time: 30 mins.). 1959. 12.95 (C11006) J Norton Pubs.
A lecture on the psychological implications of creative art.

Art & Science of Burn Wound Management. Hanumadass. 2004. audio compact disk 50.00 (978-81-8061-219-0(8)) Jaypee Brothers IND.

***Art & Science of Healing.** Cardwell C. Nuckols. Ed. by Charles Hodge. Executive Producer Dennis S. Miller. (ENG.). 2010. audio compact disk 55.00 (978-1-55982-026-4(8)) Grt Lks Training.

Art & Science of Healing Music. Will Seachnasaigh. 4 cass. (Running Time: 4 hrs.). 1998. 29.95 (978-1-55961-498-6(6)); audio compact disk 34.95 (978-1-55961-497-9(8)) Relaxtn Co.

Art & Science of Meditation. 2 cass. (Running Time: 2 hrs.). (Essence of Yoga Ser.). 14.95 (ST-27) Crystal Clarity.
Features: What is meditation; meditation as a stage towards absorption; concentation as essential to spiritual & worldy success; the importance of relaxation; meditation as a means of discovering what is already there; techniques as the science of meditation.

Art & Science of Persuasion: Program from the Award Winning Public Radio Series. Read by Fred Goodwin. Comment by John Hockenberry. Contrib. by Kathy Kellerman et al. 1 cass. (Running Time: 1 hr.). (Infinite Mind Ser.). 1999. audio compact disk 21.95 (978-1-888064-12-4(9), LCM 64) Lichtenstein Creat.
Persuasion is all around us, from advertising to political campaigns to getting the kids dressed in the morning. But how does it work, and in what ways are we persuaded without even knowing it? In this hour, Dr. Goodwin talks to experts on different types of persuasion about what it is, how it works, and what to look out for. His guests are communications professor Dr. Kathy Kellerman, ad executive Ken Krimstein and persuasion researcher Dr. Anthony Pratkanis. Additionally, we sit in on a medical hypnosis session.

Art & Science of Problem Solving. Bill Gibson. 6 cass. (Running Time: 6 hrs.). 59.95 (257A) Nightingale-Conant.

Art & Skill of Conversation. unabr. ed. Edward L. Fritsch & Nathan P. Rosenblatt. 2 cass. (Running Time: 3 hrs.). 2001. 18.00 (978-1-59040-020-3(8), Phoenix Audio) Pub: Amer Intl Pub. Dist(s): PerseuPGW
Two top communications experts provide practical strategies to conduct winning conversations.

Art & the Bible. unabr. ed. Francis A. Schaeffer. Frwd. by Michael Card. 1 CD. (Running Time: 1 hr. 15 mins. 0 sec.). (ENG.). 2007. audio compact disk 12.98 (978-1-59644-475-1(4)) christianaud.

***Art & the Bible: Two Essays.** unabr. ed. Francis A. Schaeffer. Narrated by Nadia May. (ENG.). 2007. 8.98 (978-1-59644-476-8(2), Hovel Audio) christianaud.

Art & the Soul. James Hillman. 1 cass. 9.00 (A0333-88) Sound Photosyn.
At the Embodying the Spiritual in the Art of the Future symposium. With Carolyn Marks.

Art Buchwald. Read by Art Buchwald. 1973. (L006) TFR.

Art, Creativity & Women's Spirituality. Read by Julia Jewett. 1 cass. (Running Time: 90 mins.). 1988. 10.95 (978-0-7822-0103-1(2), 335) C G Jung IL.

Art de la Compassion. Perf. by Dalai Lama XIV. 2 CDs. (Running Time: 2 hrs. 30 mins.). 2003. audio compact disk 18.95 (978-2-89558-117-8(7)) Pub: Coffragants CAN. Dist(s): Penton Overseas

***Art Detective: Fakes, Frauds, & Finds & the Search for Lost Treasures.** unabr. ed. Philip Mould. Narrated by James Langton. (Running Time: 7 hrs. 0 mins. 0 sec.). (ENG.). 2010. 19.99 (978-1-4001-6698-5(5)); 15.99 (978-1-4001-8698-3(6)); audio compact disk 29.99 (978-1-4001-1698-0(8)); audio compact disk 59.99 (978-1-4001-4698-7(4)) Pub: Tantor Media. Dist(s): IngramPubServ

Art d'Etre Grand-Pere, Poems. Victor Hugo. Read by G. Bejean. 3 cass. 1992. 31.95 (1572-VSL) Olivia & Hill.
A collection of the poet's later years celebrating family life & love.

Art Dog. Thacher Hurd. Read by John Beach. 1 cass. (Running Time: 30 mins.). (J). 2000. pap. bk. 19.97 (978-0-7366-9194-9(4)) Books on Tape.
Part mystery, part parody, he will especially tickle kids who know a bit of art history. Funky jazz, realistic sound effects of street scenes & museum openings & the exaggerated strokes of brushes enhance the mystery & the appeal.

Art Dog. Thacher Hurd. 1 cass. (Running Time: 35 min.). (J). 2001. pap. bk. 15.95 (VX-90C) Kimbo Educ.
Who is that masked dog with an eye for justice? Why, Art Dog, of course, a superhero for all times.

Art Dog. Thacher Hurd. Read by John Beach. 1 cass. (Running Time: 9 mins.). (J). (gr. k-3). 1999. bk. 24.95 (978-0-87499-509-1(4)); pap. bk. 16.95 (978-0-87499-508-4(6)); pap. bk. & tchr. ed. 41.95 Reading Chest. (978-0-87499-510-7(8)) Live Oak Media.
Part mystery, part parody, Art Dog will especially tickle kids who know a bit of art history. Funky jazz, realistic sound effects of street scenes & museum openings & the exaggerated strokes of brushes enhance the mystery & the appeal.

Art Dog. Thacher Hurd. Illus. by Thacher Hurd. 14 vols. (Running Time: 9 mins.). 1999. pap. bk. 43.95 (978-1-59112-526-6(X)); 9.95 (978-0-87499-511-4(6)); audio compact disk 12.95 (978-1-59112-307-1(0)) Live Oak Media.

Art Forum. Interview with Terry Barrett et al. 3 cass. (Running Time: 3 hrs.). (Professional Development Ser.). 1995. (978-0-945666-44-8(6)) Crizmac.
Interviews with six leaders in the field of art education.

Art from Many Cultures Theme - Audio CD. ed. (J). 2004. audio compact disk (978-1-4108-1834-8(9)) Benchmark Educ.

Art History Interactive. Created by Pearson/Prentice Hall. 2005. audio compact disk 28.60 (978-0-13-220691-4(9)) Pearson Educ CAN CAN.

Art in Everyday Life. Read by Osel Tendzin. 3 cass. 1985. 34.00 (A114) Vajradhatu.
Three talks. Art means the natural expression of one's being, when it is uninterrupted by self inflicted chaos. In our time we need to be concerned with art because there is so much confusion.

Art in Everyday Life. Vajracarya. Read by Chogyam Trungpa. 3 cass. 1974. 29.50 (A023) Vajradhatu.
Three talks. Direct everday experience is the source of all creativity. Viewed without aggression, the whole world is a work of art.

Art Lesson. unabr. ed. Tomie dePaola. Read by Tomie dePaola. 1 cass. (Running Time: 11 mins.). (Picture Book Read-Along Ser.). (J). (gr. k-3).

1991. pap. bk. 17.00 (978-0-8072-6003-6(7), PRA 809SP, Listening Lib) Random Audio Pubg.
Tommy always knew he would be an artist when he grew up. This perceptive story is about the author's life & keeping one's individuality.

***Art Modles Ultra Becca.** Created by Live Model Books. (ENG.). 2010. audio compact disk 49.95 (978-0-9816249-9-0(5)) Live Model.

Art of Aging: A Doctor's Prescription for Well-Being. abr. ed. Sherwin B. Nuland. Read by Sherwin B. Nuland. (Running Time: 21600 sec.). (ENG.). 2007. audio compact disk 29.95 (978-0-7393-4400-2(5), Random AudioBks) Pub: Random Audio Pubg. Dist(s): Random

Art of Amazement: Transcendental Love, Alexander Seinfeld. 1 CD. (Running Time: 1 hr). 2004. audio compact disk 10.00 (978-0-9717229-2-7(7)) Daas Bks.
The author of the popular "Art of Amazement" book presents a second volume of teachings based on the book.

Art of Arabic Drumming. Perf. by Trevor Salloum. 2007. 19.95 Mel Bay.

Art of Arabic Drumming. Contrib. by Trevor Salloum. 2007. 19.95 (978-5-557-49798-5(6)) Mel Bay.

Art of Autobiography. unabr. ed. Jill Ker Conway. Read by Jill Ker Conway. 1999. 9.95 Smithson Assocs.
Historian and educator, analyzes the public's fascination with autobiography and the circumstances that led her to write her own history.

Art of Aztec Mexico. 1 cass. (Running Time: 30 min.). 8.00 (F0480B090, HarperThor) HarpC GBR.

Art of Balance: Mediations for Power, Passion & Peace. unabr. ed. Tricia Brennan. Read by Tricia Brennan. (Running Time: 17100 sec.). 2006. audio compact disk 63.95 (978-1-74093-740-5(6)) Pub: Bolinda Pubng AUS. Dist(s): Bolinda Pub Inc

Art of Balance: Meditations for Power, Passion & Peace. unabr. ed. Tricia Brennan. Read by Tricia Brennan. 5 x CDs. (Running Time: 17100 sec.). 2006. audio compact disk 34.95 (978-1-74094-931-6(5)) Bolinda Pubng AUS.

Art of Being. Erich Fromm. Read by Raymond Todd. (Running Time: 16200 sec.). 2006. 24.95 (978-0-7861-3512-7(3)); audio compact disk 27.00 (978-0-7861-7839-1(6)) Blckstn Audio.

Art of Being Human: Standalone Audio CD. 8th ed. Richard Janaro & Altshuler. 14.97 (978-0-321-35487-7(7)) Addson-Wesley Educ.

Art of Being Me. Nancy Rockland-Miller. 1 cass. (Running Time: 40 min.). (J). (gr. k-5). 1992. 9.98 (978-0-9649933-1-0(7)) Mud Pie Prods.
Original songs for children ages 3-12.

Art of Being Selfless. (201) Yoga Res Foun.

Art of Being Selfless. Swami Jyotirmayananda. 1 cass. (Running Time: 1 hr.). 1990. 12.99 Yoga Res Foun.

***Art of Being You: How to Live as God's Masterpiece.** Zondervan. (ENG.). 2010. 18.99 (978-0-310-32566-6(8)) Zondervan.

Art of Biology Today CD-ROM Ed3. 3rd rev. ed. Minkoff & Baker. 2004. cd-rom 83.00 (978-0-8153-4159-8(8), Garland Sci) Taylor and Fran.

Art of Body Singing, Vol. 1. Breck Alan. Ed. by Wendy Rubin et al. Illus. by Peggy Pellett. Photos by Wendy Rubin. 1 CD. (YA). 2000. per. 14.95 (978-0-9705382-0-8(0), BAM10000) Pub: B A Music. Dist(s): Music Sales

Art of Breaking. Contrib. by Thousand Foot Krutch. Prod. by Arnold Lanni. Contrib. by Arnold Lanni. 2005. audio compact disk 16.98 (978-5-558-92594-4(9)) Tooth & Nail.

Art of Breath & Relaxation. Perf. by Rodney Yee. 2 cass. (Running Time: 1 hr. 30 mins.). 1997. 19.98 (978-0-945671-41-1(5), LA-3030) Gaiam Intl.
Yoga teacher Rodney Yee guides you in an innovative, two part program of gentle yoga breathing & relaxation exercises.

Art of Breathing & Centering: Discover the Powerful Gifts of the Air You Breathe! unabr. ed. Gay Hendricks. Read by Gay Hendricks. (Running Time: 1 hr. 0 mins. 0 sec.). (ENG.). 2005. audio compact disk 14.95 (978-1-59397-592-0(9)) Pub: Macmill Audio. Dist(s): Macmillan

Art of Cantilation Vol. 2: A Step-by-Step Guide to Chanting Haftarot & Megilot. Marshall Portnoy & Josee Wolff. 2 vols. 2004. pap. bk. 24.95 (978-0-8074-0756-1(9), 383504) URJ Pr.

ART of Caring: Insights into Alzheimer Disease & Patient Care, Vol. 1. As told by Leopold Liss. (ENG.). 2009. audio compact disk 25.00 (978-0-615-31249-1(7)) ArtCaring.

Art of Choosing: The Decisions We Make Everyday - What They Say about Us & How We Can Improve Them. unabr. ed. Sheena Iyengar. Read by Orlagh Cassidy. (Running Time: 10 hrs. 30 mins.). (ENG.). 2010. 24.98 (978-1-60024-811-5(X)); audio compact disk 34.98 (978-1-60024-810-8(1)) Pub: Hachet Audio. Dist(s): HachBkGrp

Art of Closing the Sale. (Listen & Learn USA! Ser.). 1984. 8.95 (978-0-88684-029-7(5)) Listen USA.
Gives the four main reasons why customers do & don't buy & explains how to turn this knowledge power into sales power.

***Art of Closing the Sale: The Key to Making More Money Faster in the World of Professional Selling.** unabr. ed. Brian Tracy. (Running Time: 5 hrs.). (ENG.). 2010. 24.98 (978-1-59659-566-8(3), GildAudio) Pub: Gildan Media. Dist(s): HachBkGrp

Art of Closing the Sale: The Key to Making More Money Faster in the World of Professional Selling. unabr. ed. Brian Tracy. (Running Time: 5 hrs.). (ENG.). 2010. audio compact disk 29.98 (978-1-59659-445-6(4), GildAudio) Pub: Gildan Media. Dist(s): HachBkGrp

Art of Conscious Creation: How You Can Transform the World. Jackie Lapin. 2007. audio compact disk 39.95 (978-1-60194-016-2(5), Elevate) Pub: Ad Media Group. Dist(s): IngramPubServ

Art of Creative Lettering. Featuring Becky Higgins. Prod. by Primedia Staff. 2001. audio compact disk 36.95 (978-1-929180-27-1(6)) Creating Keepsakes.

Art of Creative Listening. 1980. audio compact disk (978-0-89811-290-0(7)) Meyer Res Grp.

Art of Creative Listening. Paul J. Meyer. 1 cass. (Running Time: 35 mins.). 11.00 (978-0-89811-139-2(0), 7180) Meyer Res Grp.
Creative listening is important in business, in social life & in the family.

Art of Creative Listening. Paul J. Meyer. 1 cass. 10.00 (SP100033) SMI Intl.
Listening is the sincerest compliment you can pay another - & the best way to learn what you need to know. Creative listening is important in business, in social life, & in the family.

Art of Creative Risktaking. unabr. ed. David Schiffman. 8 cass. 72.00 (OC109) Sound Horizons AV.

Art of Critical Decision Making. Instructed by Michael A. Roberto. (ENG.). 2009. 129.95 (978-1-59803-537-7(1)); audio compact disk 179.95 (978-1-59803-538-4(X)) Teaching Co.

Art of Cross Examination. Henry B. Rothblatt. 1971. 50.00 (978-1-55917-012-3(3)) Natl Prac Inst.

Art of Cross-Examination. Read by Henry B. Rothblatt. 50.00 incl. 46 page manual. (NO. 881) Natl Prac Inst.
How to handle every conceivable type of witness.

Art of Dancing with Life. unabr. ed. Paul Lowe. 2 cass. 1995. 16.95 (978-1-879323-40-7(0)) Sound Horizons AV.
For most people, living life freely in love & acceptance seems an impossibility. Our life's experience is filtered through the conditioned mind, allowing us only to function at a fraction of our limitless potential. Paul Lowe uses his powerful clarity to confront the "thinking our way through life" method as a means of avoiding direct experience, proposing that true change & intimacy can come only through total presence with the moment.

Art of Deception. abr. ed. Ridley Pearson. Read by Dick Hill. (Running Time: 6 hrs.). (Lou Boldt/Daphne Matthews Ser.). 2007. audio compact disk 14.99 (978-1-4233-1959-7(1), 9781423319597, BCD Value Price) Brilliance Audio.

Art of Deception. unabr. ed. Ridley Pearson. Read by Ridley Pearson. 8 cass. Library Ed. (Running Time: 12 hrs.). (Lou Boldt & Daphne Matthews Mystery Ser.: Vol. 8). 2002. 87.25 (978-1-59086-075-5(6), 1590860756, Unabridge Lib Edns); audio compact disk 102.25 (978-1-59086-227-8(9), 1590862279, CD Unabrid Lib Ed) Brilliance Audio.
A troubled Mary Ann Walker takes a nosedive off a bridge. Seattle's police department macho man John LaMoia takes the call, along with the beauteous cop psychologist Daphne Matthews. They suspect her boyfriend, known to beat Mary Ann. Her seething brother, Ferrell, is convinced the boyfriend did the deed. But the case somehow becomes too slippery to close. Lou Boldt, the supervising officer, is entangled in a conundrum of his own: two women have disappeared and a road crew worker's death may have a connection to the missing women. A peeper who's photographing undressed women at tourist hotels becomes Boldt's best suspect, along with a man who is stalking and terrifying Daphne. As both cases heat up, so does the sexual tension between Matthews and LaMoia leading them both into unknown emotional territory. A hair-raising chase through Seattle's Underground, a little-known network of hundred-year-old streets that were paved over by the city decades ago, brings the story to its white-knuckle climax.

Art of Deception. unabr. ed. Read by Ridley Pearson. 8 cass. (Running Time: 12 hrs.). (Lou Boldt & Daphne Matthews Mystery Ser.: Vol. 8). 2002. 32.95 (978-1-59086-074-8(8), 1590860748, BAU) Brilliance Audio.

Art of Deception. unabr. ed. Ridley Pearson. Read by Ridley Pearson. (Running Time: 12 hrs.). (Lou Boldt/Daphne Matthews Ser.). 2004. 39.25 (978-1-59335-526-5(2), 1593355262, Brinc Audio MP3 Lib) Brilliance Audio.

Art of Deception. unabr. ed. Ridley Pearson. Read by Ridley Pearson. (Running Time: 12 hrs.). (Lou Boldt/Daphne Matthews Ser.). 2004. 39.25 (978-1-59710-022-9(6), 1597100226, BADLE); 24.95 (978-1-59710-023-6(4), 1597100234, BAD) Brilliance Audio.

***Art of Deception.** unabr. ed. Ridley Pearson. Read by Ridley Pearson. (Running Time: 12 hrs.). (Lou Boldt/Daphne Matthews Ser.). 2010. audio compact disk 29.99 (978-1-4418-7223-4(X), 9781441872234, Bril Audio CD Unabri) Brilliance Audio.

Art of Deception. unabr. ed. Ridley Pearson. Read by Ridley Pearson. (Running Time: 12 hrs.). (Lou Boldt/Daphne Matthews Ser.). 2004. 24.95 (978-1-59335-200-4(X), 159335200X) Soulmate Audio Bks.

Art of Deception: An Introduction to Critical Thinking. rev. ed. Nicholas Capaldi. Read by Nicholas Capaldi. 2 pieces. (Running Time: 3 hrs.). (ENG.). 1996. 21.98 (978-1-57392-057-5(6)) Prometheus Bks.

Art of Detection. Laurie R. King. Narrated by Alyssa Bresnahan & Robert Ian MacKenzie. (Running Time: 49500 sec.). (Kate Martinelli Mystery Ser.: No. 5). 2006. audio compact disk 39.99 (978-1-4193-9663-2(3)) Recorded Bks.

Art of Detection. unabr. ed. Laurie R. King. Read by Alyssa Bresnahan & Robert Ian MacKenzie. 12 CDs. (Running Time: 13 hrs.). (Kate Martinelli Mystery Ser.: No. 5). 2006. audio compact disk 119.75 (978-1-4193-8908-5(4), C3688); 94.75 (978-1-4193-0542-9(5), 97853) Recorded Bks.
The Art of Detection is another spellbinding tale starring San Francisco homicide inspector Kate Martinelli. The victim is Sherlock Holmes aficionado Philip Gilbert, whose collection of priceless memorabilia is definitely worth killing for. It's up to Kate and her trusted partner Al Hawkin to follow the clues and bring a rather peculiar murderer to justice.

Art of Discernment. Patrick O'Leary. Read by Patrick O'Leary. 8 cass. (Running Time: 7 hrs.). 1992. 49.95 set. (AA2594) Credence Commun.
An advanced workshop using the enneagram for spiritual development.

Art of Drinking Tea. Shenghuo Cha Yi. (Light on China Ser.). audio compact disk 9.95 (978-7-88363-090-6(3), VCDART-11) China Bks.

Art of Dying. Neville Goddard. 1 cass. (Running Time: 62 mins.). 1965. 8.00 (16) J & L Pubns.
Neville taught Imagination Creates Reality. He was a powerfully influential teacher of God as Consciousness.

Art of Editing. SERCON Panel. 1 cass. 9.00 (A0310-87) Sound Photosyn.
Writers of all genre can benefit from this inside information. Presented at the SF writers convention by David Hartwell, Edwards, Meacham, Schwartz, & Carr.

Art of Exceptional Living. Jim Rohn. 6 cass. (Running Time: 6 hrs.). 59.95 (664AX) Nightingale-Conant.
"The possibilities for life change are unlimited," says world-famous speaker Jim Rohn. And in this uplifting program, he gives you a clear & simple guide for making positive changes in your life right now. You'll learn the four lessons everyone must master for success. The three questions that will evaluate every relationship you have. How to overcome self-imposed restrictions. And you'll discover how self-discipline turns dreams into reality.

Art of Exceptional Living. abr. ed. Jim Rohn. Read by Jim Rohn. (Running Time: 20 hrs. 0 mins. 0 sec.). (ENG.). 2003. audio compact disk 19.95 (978-0-7435-2906-8(5), Nightgale) Pub: S&S Audio. Dist(s): S and S Inc

Art of Extreme Self-Care: Transform Your Life One Month at a Time. Cheryl Richardson. 2 CDs. 2009. audio compact disk 18.95 (978-1-4019-1830-9(1)) Hay House.

Art of Fair Isle Knitting. Ann Feitelson. (ENG.). 2007. audio compact disk 14.95 (978-0-9796073-5-6(3)) Knitting Out.

Art of Falling. Deborah Lawrenson. 2009. 76.95 (978-0-7531-4274-5(0)); audio compact disk 89.95 (978-0-7531-4275-2(9)) Pub: Isis Pubng Ltd GBR. Dist(s): Ulverscroft US

Art of Fearbusting: How to Be Powerful in the Face of Our Fears. Speeches. Based on a book by Susan Jeffers. 1 CD. (Running Time: 60 mins). 2005. audio compact disk 14.00 (978-0-9745776-2-3(6)) Pub: Jeffers Pr. Dist(s): Natl Bk Netwk
The Art of Fearbusting is an original, live talk given by Susan based on her huge best-seller Feel the Fear And Do It Anyway, which has sold over 2 million copies in fully 100 countries and 35 languages. Packed with transformative exercises, this CD recording shows us how to handle fear from a position of self-confidence and love. Susan's delivery is delightful: lively, compassionate and full of insightful stories. It's an exuberant and empowering presentation that listeners will play over and over again.

Art of Fiction. unabr. ed. Ayn Rand. Read by Marguerite Gavin. 6 CDs. (Running Time: 7 hrs.). 2004. audio compact disk 48.00 (978-0-7861-8884-0(7), 3126); 39.95 (978-0-7861-2447-3(4), 3126); audio compact disk 24.95 (978-0-7861-8719-5(0), 3126) Blckstn Audio.
Ayn Rand discusses how a writer combines abstract ideas with concrete action and description to achieve a unity of theme, plot, characterization, and style, the four essential elements of fiction. Here, too, are Rand's illuminating analyses of passages from famous writers, rewrites of scenes from her own works, and fascinating rules for building dramatic plots and characters with depth.

Art of Fiction. unabr. ed. Ayn Rand. Read by Marguerite Gavin. 5 pieces. 2004. reel tape 29.95 (978-0-7861-2496-1(2)); audio compact disk 32.95 (978-0-7861-9031-7(0)) Blckstn Audio.

Art of Flower Arranging. Thich Nhat Hanh & Parallax Press Staff. (Running Time: 1 hr. 15 mins.). (ENG.). 2003. audio compact disk 15.00 (978-1-888375-38-1(8)) Pub: Parallax Pr. Dist(s): PerseuPGW

Art of Foreclosure: The Ultimate Guide for Investors. 2005. audio compact disk (978-0-9743923-6-3(7), GCC Pubs) Lib Soldiers.

Art of Forgiveness & the Return to Peace. Michael Chojnacki. 1 CD. (Running Time: 75 mins). 2006. audio compact disk 16.00 (978-0-9786006-0-0(6)) Infinite Wisdm.

Art of Friendship: 70 Simple Rules for Making Meaningful Connections. unabr. ed. Roger Horchow & Sally Horchow. Read by Roger Horchow et al. Read by Malcolm Gladwell et al. 3 CDs. (Running Time: 3 hrs. 0 mins. 0 sec.). (ENG.). 2006. audio compact disk 19.95 (978-1-4272-0027-3(0)) Pub: Macmill Audio. Dist(s): Macmillan

Art of Getting Along. abr. ed. Leo J. Fishbeck. Read by Leo J. Fishbeck. 3 cass. (Running Time: 3 hrs. 6 mins.). 1993. 30.00 (978-1-883373-01-6(8)) R S Outreach.
Spiritual & mental strategies for creating harmonious relationships in all areas.

Art of Giving & Receiving Criticism. abr. ed. John L. Lund. 4 cass. (Running Time: 5 hrs. 45 mins.). 1997. bk. 24.95 (978-1-891114-27-4(1)) Commun Co.
Includes "Do I Criticize too Much", "The Art of Giving Criticism", "The Art of Receiving Criticism", "Dealing with the Toxic Person".

Art of Going Within. Michael P. Bovines. 2 cass. (Running Time: 1 hr. 30 mins.). (Empowerment Ser.). 1992. pap. bk. 16.98 (978-1-885768-04-9(4)) Circle of Light.
Tape 1 - Discussion: Art of Going Within - How to Meditate. Tape 2 - Morning & Evening Meditation.

Art of Graceful Change: Lessons in the Gremlin Taming Method. Rick Carson. 2003. audio compact disk 79.95 (978-0-9746951-0-5(6)) Gremlin Tmng Prdtns.

Art of Greatness. Art Fettig. 2 cass. (Run[illegible] Time: 2 hrs.). 19.95 (PD-A2) Growth Unltd.
Unlock the "success consciousness" th[illegible] deep within you. This program gives you the golden key.

Art of Handling Adversity. Swami Jyotirmayananda. 1 cass. (Running Time: 45 mins.). 1990. 10.00 Yoga Res Foun.

Art of Happiness: A Handbook for Living. Howard C. Cutler. Illus. by Dalai Lama XIV & Dalai Lama XIV. 2004. 10.95 (978-0-7435-4169-5(3)) Pub: S&S Audio. Dist(s): S and S Inc

Art of Happiness: A Handbook for Living. abr. ed. Howard C. Cutler. Read by Howard C. Cutler. Illus. by Dalai Lama XIV & Dalai Lama XIV. 3 CDs. (Running Time: 3 hrs. 0 mins. 0 sec.). (ENG.). 1998. audio compact disk 25.00 (978-0-7435-0630-4(8), Sound Ideas) Pub: S&S Audio. Dist(s): S and S Inc

Art of Happiness: A Handbook for Living. unabr. ed. Howard C. Cutler. Illus. by Dalai Lama XIV & Dalai Lama XIV. 6 vols. (Running Time: 9 hrs.). 2001. bk. 54.95 (978-0-7927-2475-9(5), CSL 364, Chivers Sound Lib) AudioGO.
The Dalai Lama shows us how to defeat day-to-day anxiety, insecurity, anger & discouragement. Together with Dr. Cutler, he explores many facets of everyday life, including relationships, loss & the pursuit of wealth, to illustrate how to ride through life's obstacles on a deep & abiding source of inner peace. Based on 2,500 years of Buddhist meditations mixed with a healthy dose of common sense, this book crosses the boundaries of traditions to help readers with difficulties common to all human beings.

Art of Happiness: A Handbook for Living. unabr. ed. Read by Grover Gardner. Illus. by Dalai Lama XIV & Dalai Lama XIV. 8 CDs. (Running Time: 12 hrs.). 2001. audio compact disk 79.95 (978-0-7927-9915-3(1), SLD 066, Chivers Sound Lib) AudioGO.

Art of Happiness at Work. Howard C. Cutler. Read by B. D. Wong. Ed. by Dalai Lama XIV. 2004. 18.95 (978-0-7435-4172-5(3)) Pub: S&S Audio. Dist(s): S and S Inc

Art of Happiness at Work. unabr. ed. Howard C. Cutler. Ed. by Dalai Lama XIV. 6 CDs. (Running Time: 53 hrs. 0 mins. 0 sec.). (ENG.). 2003. audio compact disk 29.95 (978-0-7435-3557-1(X), Sound Ideas) Pub: S&S Audio. Dist(s): S and S Inc

Art of Happiness in a Troubled World. abr. unabr. ed. Dalai Lama XIV & Howard C. Cutler. Read by Howard C. Cutler. (ENG.). 2009. audio compact disk 40.00 (978-0-7393-3441-6(7), Random AudioBks) Pub: Random Audio Pubg. Dist(s): Random

Art of Harp. 1 cass. (Running Time: 1 hr.). 1998. 10.98 (978-1-56628-108-9(3), 72496); audio compact disk 15.98 (978-1-56628-107-2(5), 72496D) MFLP CA.

Art of Hawaiian Steel Guitar. Stacy Phillips. 1991. spiral bd. 23.95 (978-0-7866-1022-8(0), 94383P) Mel Bay.

Art of Hawaiian Steel Guitar. Stacy Phillips. 1993. 9.98 (978-1-56222-877-4(3), 94383C) Mel Bay.

Art of Healing. Lewis E. Mehl & Gayle Peterson. bk. (978-0-318-61266-9(6)) Irvington.

Art of Health & Happiness. Ed. by Robert Marion. (ENG.). 2007. audio compact disk (978-0-9768988-1-8(0), Wlake) Westlake Found.

Art of Hiring & Retaining Employees... at Your FingerTip. Jay Eckhaus. Prod. by FingerTip Manuals. (ENG.). 2008. audio compact disk 24.95 (978-0-9799314-6-8(0)) Finger.

Art of Howard Karp: Concert Recordings, 1964-2000. UW Sch of Music Staff. Contrib. by Howard Karp. 2000. audio compact disk 30.00 (978-0-9658834-7-4(7)) Pub: U of Wis Pr. Dist(s): Chicago Distribution Ctr

Art of Influence: Persuading Others Begins with You. unabr. ed. Chris Widener. Read by Chris Widener. 2 CDs. (Running Time: 1 hrs. 45 mins.). 2008. audio compact disk 24.00 (978-1-4159-4905-4(0), BksonTape) Pub: Random Audio Pubg. Dist(s): Random
The Art of Influence will make you think twice about everything you've ever learned about influence. As Chris Widener's inspiring story reveals, it's not something you "do" to other people but rather something that starts with how you shape and transform your own life. Forget about manipulation and slick fast-talking; The Art of Influence teaches that your ability to influence others begins from within.

Art of Influence: Persuading Others Begins with You. unabr. ed. Chris Widener. Read by Chris Widener. (Running Time: 2 hrs.). (ENG.). 2008. 7.50 (978-0-7393-6626-4(2)) Pub: Random Audio Pubg. Dist(s): Random

An Asterisk (*) at the beginning of an entry indicates that the title is appearing for the first time.

Art of Influence: Shaping Your Success Through Relationships. Debra Pestrak. 6 cass. (Running Time: 4 hrs. 30 mins.). 1998. cass. & video 169.00 (978-0-9665932-0-4(0)) Succ Unleashed.
Demonstrates visual skills for "reading another person" & establishing rapport.

Art of Introduction to Protein Structure. Carl Branden & John Tooze. 1999. cd-rom 83.00 (978-0-8153-3328-9(5)) Taylor and Fran.

Art of Invective. unabr. ed. Gilbert Highet. 1 cass. (Running Time: 30 mins.). (Gilbert Highet Ser.). 9.95 (C23328) J Norton Pubs.
How to make a speech or write a newspaper piece which utterly crushes your opponent & how to point out the ridiculous in speeches & poems & novels which are overblown & absurd.

Art of Invective & A Bouquet of Poison Ivy. Gilbert Highet. 1 CD. (Running Time: 30 min.). (Gilbert Highet Ser.). 2006. audio compact disk 12.95 (978-1-57970-367-7(4), C23328D, Audio-For) J Norton Pubs.
Track 1 contains "The Art of Invective": How to make a speech or write a newspaper piece which utterly crushes your foe. Track 2 contains "A Bouquet of Poison Ivy": The art of parody, how to point out the ridiculous in speeches and poems and novels which are overblown and absurd; the needle point deflating the balloon full of gas.

Art of Japanese Management, unabr. ed. Richard Pascale & Anthony Athos. Narrated by James Hamilton. 6 cass. (Running Time: 9 hrs.). 1982. 51.00 (978-1-55690-029-7(5), 82036E7) Recorded Bks.
Japanese managers run their companies quite differently from their American counterparts & their success is now undisputed. They have much to teach American managers at all levels, from the loading dock to the boardroom & this book is a worthy guide.

Art of Jazz Trumpet. John McNeil. 2004. audio compact disk 24.95 (978-0-9628467-6-2(7)) Pub: Gerard Sarzin Pub. Dist(s): H Leonard

Art of Letter Writing. Greville Janner. 1989. 46.95 (978-0-566-02751-2(8), Gower Pubng) Pub: Ashgate Pub GBR. Dist(s): Ashgate Pub

***Art of Letting Go: Living the Wisdom of St. Francis.** Richard Rohr. (Running Time: 6:00:00). 2010. audio compact disk 69.95 (978-1-59179-752-4(7)) Sounds True.

Art of Letting Go of Stuff, Vol. 1. unabr. ed. Darren Johnson. 2 cass. (Running Time: 1 hr. 37 mins.). (Change-N-U Ser.: Vol. 2). 1998. 19.95 (978-0-9652307-3-5(2), Change-N-U Lrning) InsideOut Learning.
Teaches how to manage change & stress; how to focus on what you can control vs focusing on what you cannot control in life & how to consciously choose to stay focused on the "right stuff".

Art of Listening. Ben Bissell. 1 cass. (Running Time: 39 mins.). 15.00 C Bissell.
One of the most powerful ways to influence a person's behavior is to listen to them. Dr. Bissell examines the barriers to listening & roadways to becoming a more effective listener.

Art of Listening. J. Krishnamurti. 1 cass. (Running Time: 1 hr.). (Krishnamurti with Dr. Allan W. Anderson Ser.: No. 10). 8.50 (APA7410) Krishnamurti.
These 1974 dialogues cover the entire spectrum of Krishnamurti's teaching in a series highly regarded for its depth of inquiry into each particular subject.

Art of Listening II. 1 cass. (Running Time: 1 hr.). Bd. with Art of Speaking II. 1987.; 12.99 (165) Yoga Res Foun.

Art of Living see Arte de Vivir

Art of Living. Swami Amar Jyoti. 1 cass. 1978. 9.95 (A-1) Truth Consciousness.
Qualities needed for the art of living. Spirituality teaches the meaning of life.

Art of Living. André Maurois. Read by Daniel Quintero. (Running Time: 3 hrs.). 2005. 16.95 (978-1-60083-296-3(2), Audiofy Corp) Iofy Corp.

Art of Living: Vipassana Meditation: As Taught by S. N. Goenka. unabr. ed. Excerpts. Read by William Hart & S. N. Goenka. 4 cass. (Running Time: 5 hrs. 10 mins.). 1999. 24.95 (978-0-9649484-8-8(6), Pariyatti Audio) Pariyatti Pubng.
Introduction to Vipassana and discourses at ten-day meditation.

Art of Living in the Moment: A Bilingual Adventure in Transformation. Ariel Kane & Shya Kane. Ed. by Eric Pomert. 2 CDs. (Running Time: 2hrs. 14min). (ENG & GER.). 2002. audio compact disk (978-1-888043-12-9(1)) ASK Prodns.
Join the Kanes and German participants as they have a lively, practical and down-to-earth conversation about the Art of Living in the Moment. Learn the keys to living in the Moment and having a magnificent life: The Principles of Transformation and how they can help you reconnect with your creativity, spontaneity and excitement, and more.

Art of Living Volume 2 - the Art of Working & Giving Orders. André Maurois. Read by Daniel Quintero. (Running Time: 3 hrs.). 2006. 16.95 (978-1-60083-297-0(0), Audiofy Corp) Iofy Corp.

Art of Loving, unabr. ed. Erich Fromm. Narrated by James Hamilton. 3 cass. (Running Time: 4 hrs.). 1981. 26.00 (978-1-55690-030-3(9), 81170E7) Recorded Bks.
A philosophical inquiry into the nature & power of this elemental emotion. Reveals daring prescriptions for overcoming the fear of love... using love to conquer anxiety & developing a more exhilarating love life.

Art of Loving: Getting & Staying Together. Henry Niemann. 1 cass. 8.95 (252) Am Fed Astrologers.
Chart shows how one express love & expects from others.

Art of Loving Discipline. 1 cass. (Running Time: 75 mins.). (Spiritual Child-Raising Ser.). 9.95 (DM-7) Crystal Clarity.
Discusses such questions as what is discipline?; why do some people fear it?; why is love essential to effective discipline?.

Art of Loving Leadership. Kriyananda, pseud. 1 cass. 9.95 (ST-74) Crystal Clarity.
Topics include: The "vision" as the essence of any undertaking; the importance of balancing the vision & your followers' needs; the difference between leadership & mere coordination; applying leadership principles in all relationships.

Art of Making Money: The Story of a Master Counterfeiter. unabr. ed. Jason Kersten. Read by Jim Bond. (Running Time: 9 hrs.). 2009. 39.97 (978-1-4233-9916-2(1), 9781423399162, Brlnc Audio MP3 Lib); 39.97 (978-1-4233-9918-6(8), 9781423399186, BADLE); 24.99 (978-1-4233-9917-9(X), 9781423399179, BAD); 24.99 (978-1-4233-9915-5(3), 9781423399155, Brilliance MP3); audio compact disk 87.97 (978-1-4233-9914-8(5), 9781423399148, BriAudCD Unabrid); audio compact disk 29.99 (978-1-4233-9913-1(7), 9781423399131, Bril Audio CD Unabri) Brilliance Audio.

Art of Managing People, unabr. collector's ed. Tony Alessandra. Read by Tony Alessandra. 3 cass. (Running Time: 3 hrs.). 1983. Rental 11.95 (978-0-7366-0848-0(6), 1799) Books on Tape.
Offers techniques for communicating better with others.

Art of Mediation. Advantage Legal Seminars. (ENG.). 2008. 177.00 (978-0-9795737-9-8(3)) Anzman Publg.

Art of Meditation. Osho Oshos. Read by Osho Oshos. 1 cass. (Running Time: 1 hr. 30 min.). 2001. 10.95 (DCM-0007) Oshos.
Answers Questions such as "What is Meditation", "There are many people all over the world who are very interested in meditation, but nothing real is happening to them" & "What is the matter".

Art of Meditation. Stuart Wilde. 2 cass., 2 CDs. 10.00 (384) Hay House.
Reveals the amazing benefits you can derive from generating theta & delta waves during meditation.

Art of Meditation. abr. ed. Patricia W. Carson. Read by Patricia W. Carson. 1 cass. (Running Time: 60 mins.). 1999. 10.00 (978-1-928652-03-8(4)) Motivational OH.
Side A: how to tap into your inner light. Side B: meditation exercise.

Art of Meditation: Four Classic Meditative Techniques Adapted for Modern Life. abr. rev. unabr. ed. Daniel Goleman. Read by Daniel Goleman. 2 CDs. (Running Time: 1 hr. 0 mins. 0 sec.). (ENG.). 2001. audio compact disk 20.00 (978-1-55927-639-9(8)) Pub: Macmill Audio. Dist(s): Macmillan

Art of Mending. Elizabeth Berg. Read by Joyce Bean. (Playaway Adult Fiction Ser.). 2008. 59.99 (978-1-60640-780-6(5)) Find a World.

Art of Mending. unabr. ed. Elizabeth Berg. Read by Joyce Bean. 5 cass. (Running Time: 6 hrs.). 2004. 27.95 (978-1-59355-767-6(1), 1593557671, BAU); 69.25 (978-1-59355-768-3(X), 159355768X, BrilAudUnabridg); audio compact disk 29.95 (978-1-59355-769-0(8), 1593557698, Bril Audio CD Unabri); audio compact disk 82.25 (978-1-59355-770-6(1), 1593557701, BriAudCD Unabrid) Brilliance Audio.
It begins with the sudden revelation of astonishing secrets - secrets that have shaped the personalities and fates of three siblings, and now threaten to tear them apart. In renowned author Elizabeth Berg's moving new novel, unearthed truths force one seemingly ordinary family to reexamine their disparate lives and to ask themselves: Is it too late to mend the hurts of the past? Laura Bartone anticipates her annual family reunion in Minnesota with a mixture of excitement and wariness. Yet this year's gathering will prove to be much more trying than either she or her siblings imagined. As soon as she arrives, Laura realizes that something is not right with her sister. Forever wrapped up in events of long ago, Caroline is the family's restless black sheep. When Caroline confronts Laura and their brother, Steve, with devastating allegations about their mother, the three have a difficult time reconciling their varying experiences in the same house. But a sudden misfortune will lead them all to face the past, their own culpability, and their common need for love and forgiveness.

Art of Mending. unabr. ed. Elizabeth Berg. Read by Joyce Bean. (Running Time: 6 hrs.). 2004. 39.25 (978-1-59335-653-8(6), 1593356536, Brlnc Audio MP3 Lib); 24.95 (978-1-59335-292-9(1), 1593352921, Brilliance MP3) Brilliance Audio.

Art of Mending. unabr. ed. Elizabeth Berg. Read by Joyce Bean. (Running Time: 6 hrs.). 2004. 39.25 (978-1-59710-026-7(9), 1597100269, BADLE); 24.95 (978-1-59710-027-4(7), 1597100277, BAD) Brilliance Audio.

Art of Mentoring & Coyote Teaching. Jon Young. Interview with Ellen Haas. 1 cass. (Running Time: 90 min.). 1997. 12.95 (978-1-57994-004-1(8)) Owlink.
Tells history of native "invisible" schools & draws out principles for mentoring in today's teaching circumstances. Unique techniques inspire student curiosity & encourage self-sufficiency in the field & in the classroom. For parents, educators, & home schoolers.

Art of Mentoring & Coyote Teaching. Jon Young. Ellen Haas. Walker Korby & Justin Boe. Prod. by John Gallagher. (ENG., 2008. audio compact disk 27.95 (978-1-57994-020-1(X)) Owlink.

Art of Midwifery. Ina M. Gaskin. 2 cass. 18.00 set. (A0719-90) Sound Photosyn.
The latest from Ina May, in Berkeley. Active integrity from the beginnings.

Art of Mindful Living. Thich Nhat Hanh. 2 cass. (Running Time: 90 min.). 2003. 19.00 (99020); audio compact disk 24.95 (57987) Parallax Pr.
Offers practical teachings about how to bring love and mindful awareness into our daily experience.

Art of Mindful Living: How to Bring Love, Compassion, & Inner Peace into Your Daily Life. Thich Nhat Hanh. 2 CDs. (Running Time: 2 hrs. 30 min.). 2000. audio compact disk 24.95 (978-1-56455-798-8(7), AE00499) Sounds True.
A workshop about how to bring mindful awareness, or the welcoming of all experience into all aspects of daily life. Topics include the two kinds of consciousness; true love vs. possessive love; handling hurt feelings; & more.

Art of Mingling: Proven Techniques for Mastering Any Room. unabr. ed. Jeanne Martinet. Read by Jeanne Martinet. 3 CDs. (Running Time: 5 hrs. 0 mins. 0 sec.). (ENG.). 2006. audio compact disk 24.95 (978-1-4272-0029-7(7)) Pub: Macmill Audio. Dist(s): Macmillan

Art of Mingling: Proven Techniques for Mastering Any Room. unabr. rev. ed. Jeanne Martinet. Narrated by Jeanne Martinet. 3 CDs. (Running Time: 18240 sec.). 2006. audio compact disk 39.95 (978-0-7927-4375-0(X), SLD 999) AudioGO.

Art of Moderation. Swami Jyotirmayananda. 1 cass. (Running Time: 45 min.). 1990. 10.00 Yoga Res Foun.

Art of Money Getting: The 21 Must Know / Must Use Commandments for Personal & Business Financial Success: Sure & Proven Ways to become Financially Successful. P. T. Barnum. Narrated by Ross M. Armeta. 1 CD. (Running Time: Approx. 60 Mins.). 2005. audio compact disk 11.99 (978-1-59733-008-4(6)) InfoFount.
The Art of Money Getting: Sure and proven ways to become wealthy The 21 must know / must use commandments for personal and business financial success by P. T. Barnum, Barnum, Phineas T. Barnum The full, complete, and unabridged text.The well known and very successful showman explains his principles of wealth in a simple, straightforward, and proven system that anyone can use to become financially successful.Those who really desire to attain independence, have only to settheir minds upon it, and adopt the proper means, as they do in regard toany other object which they wish to accomplish, and the thing is easilydone. The road to wealth is as plain as the road to the store. It is, no doubt, often true, as Shakespeare says:"There is a tide in the affairs of men, Which, taken at the flood, leadson to fortune."Use The Art of Money Getting: Sure and proven ways of becoming wealthy to bring you to a high tide. If you hesitate, some bolder hand will stretch out before you and getthe prize. Remember the proverb of Solomon: "He becometh poor thatdealeth with a slack hand; but the hand of the diligent maketh rich."Opportunity, is staring you in the face - are you going to take it ?This audiobook is narrated in a lively, show-like atmosphere, by a bunch of ?different personalities and characters.? Though entertaining the information is clear and its importance and truth is enhanced by the ?expert? coaches.CONTENTS of The Art of Money Getting: Sure and proven ways of becoming wealthy The 21 must know / must use commandments for personal and business financial success.DON'T MISTAKE YOUR VOCATIONSELECT THE RIGHT LOCATIONAVOID DEBTPERSEVEREWHATEVER YOU DO, DO IT WITH ALL YOUR MIGHTDEPEND UPON YOUR OWN PERSONAL EXERTIONSUSE THE BEST TOOLSDON'T GET ABOVE YOUR BUSINESSLEARN SOMETHING USEFULLET HOPE PREDOMINATE, BUT BE NOT TOO VISIONARYDO NOT SCATTER YOUR POWERSBE SYSTEMATICREAD THE NEWSPAPERSBEWARE OF "OUTSIDE OPERATIONS"DON'T ENDORSE WITHOUT SECURITYADVERTISE YOUR BUSINESS"DON'T READ THE OTHER SIDE"BE POLITE AND KIND TO YOUR CUSTOMERSBE CHARITABLEDON'T BLABPRESERVE YOUR INTEGRITY.

Art of Negotiating. Gerard Nerenberg. Read by Gerard Nerenberg. Read by Richard A. Zeif. 12 cass. (Running Time: 6 hrs. 15 min.). 1978. bk. 95.00 Negotiation Inst.
Covers a two-day seminar on Art of Negotiating.

Art of Negotiating. Gerard I. Nierenberg. 1990. bk. & stu. ed. 69.95 (978-0-924967-00-9(5)) Intl Ctr Creat Think.

***Art of Negotiating.** PUEI. 2009. audio compact disk 199.00 (978-1-935041-76-4(2), CareerTrack) P Univ E Inc.

Art of Negotiating. Richard A. Zeif & Gerard I. Nierenberg. Read by Gerard I. Nierenberg. 12 cass. 295.00 incl. manual. Negotiation Inst.
Teaches the art of negotiating in an aspect of Life. Includes conceptual framework for negotiation as well as its practical applicaton.

Art of Negotiating: How to Become a Skilled Negotiator. abr. ed. Gerard I. Nierenberg. Read by Gerard I. Nierenberg. 4 cass. (Running Time: 6 hrs.). 2004. 25.00 (978-1-931056-41-0(2), N Millennium Audio) New Millenn Enter.
Since the early 1060s, the author has been an outstanding negotiation trainer. The advice and counsel and associates are sought worldwide as they lecture, train and negotiate business, industry and government. It's no wonder he is recognized as the father of contemporary negotiating. You can have no better teacher on the subject.

***Art of Non-Conformity: Set Your Own Rules, Live the Life You Want, & Change the World.** unabr. ed. Chris Guillebeau. Narrated by Dan John Miller. (Running Time: 6 hrs. 30 mins. 0 sec.). 2010. 19.99 (978-1-4001-6999-3(2)); 29.99 (978-1-4001-9999-0(9)); 14.99 (978-1-4001-8999-1(3)); audio compact disk 71.99 (978-1-4001-4999-5(1)); audio compact disk 29.99 (978-1-4001-1999-8(5)) Pub: Tantor Media. Dist(s): IngramPubServ

Art of Nonfiction. unabr. ed. Ayn Rand. Read by Marguerite Gavin. 6 CDs. (Running Time: 7 hrs.). 2004. audio compact disk 48.00 (978-0-7861-8885-7(5), 3127); 39.95 (978-0-7861-2448-0(2), 3127) Blckstn Audio.
Takes listeners step by step through the writing process, providing insightful observations and invaluable techniques along the way.

Art of Nonfiction. unabr. ed. Ayn Rand. Read by Marguerite Gavin. 5 pieces. 2004. reel tape 29.95 (978-0-7861-2497-8(0)); audio compact disk 32.95 (978-0-7861-9030-0(2)) Blckstn Audio.

Art of Nonfiction: A Guide for Writers & Readers. unabr. ed. Robert Mayhew. Ed. by Robert Mayhew. Read by Anna Fields. Intro. by Peter Schwartz. 1 MP3. (Running Time: 25200 sec.). 2004. audio compact disk 24.95 (978-0-7861-8720-1(4), 3127) Blckstn Audio.

Art of Parenting Teens & Other Miracles. abr. ed. John L. Lund. 4 cass. (Running Time: 5 hrs. 10 min.). 1997. bk. 24.95 Set. (978-1-891114-28-1(X)) Commun Co.
Includes "The Art of Parenting Teens", "Understanding the Teenage Mind", "The Goal of Every Parent", & "An Emotionally Healthy Teen".

Art of Persistence: From Building Relationships to Getting Any Job You Desire. unabr. ed. Sanjay Burman & Luke Chao. Read by Sanjay Burman. (Running Time: 1 hr. 30 mins.). (ENG.). 2008. 14.98 (978-1-59659-259-9(1), GildAudio) Pub: Gildan Media. Dist(s): HachBkGrp

Art of Political War: And Other Radical Pursuits. unabr. ed. David Horowitz. Read by Jeff Riggenbach. 1 CD. (Running Time: 7 hrs. 30 min.). 2001. audio compact disk 19.95 Blckstn Audio.
Politics is war, but in America one side is doing all the shooting liberals. Shell-shocked conservatives blame their failures on the media or unscrupulous opponents, but they refuse to name the real culprit: themselves. Shows how Bill Clinton's generation, having mastered the art of political war, has spent the last ten years clobbering the conservatives in and out of government.

Art of Political War: And Other Radical Pursuits. unabr. ed. David Horowitz. Read by Jeff Riggenbach. 5 cass. (Running Time: 7 hrs.). 2001. 39.95 (978-0-7861-2074-1(6), 2835) Blckstn Audio.

Art of Political War & Other Radical Pursuits. unabr. ed. David Horowitz. Read by Jeff Riggenbach. (Running Time: 6.5 hrs. NaN mins.). 2008. 29.95 (978-1-4332-6678-2(4)); audio compact disk 50.00 (978-1-4332-6675-1(X)) Blckstn Audio.

Art of Positive Parenting. Art Fettig. 2 cass. 20.00 Set. (PR-A1) Growth Unltd.
Recorded live at one of Art Fettig's famous seminars on Positive Parenting.

***Art of Possibility.** unabr. ed. Rosamund Stone Zander & Benjamin Zander. (Running Time: 8 hrs. 30 mins. 0 sec.). (ENG.). 2011. audio compact disk 29.99 (978-1-4272-1176-7(0)) Pub: Macmill Audio. Dist(s): Macmillan

Art of Power. unabr. ed. Thich Nhat Hanh. 5 CDs. (Running Time: 6 hrs. 30 mins. 0 sec.). (ENG.). 2007. audio compact disk 29.99 (978-1-4001-0510-6(2)) Pub: Tantor Media. Dist(s): IngramPubServ

Art of Power. unabr. ed. Thich Nhat Hanh. Read by Lloyd James. (Running Time: 6 hrs. 30 mins. 0 sec.). (ENG.). 2007. audio compact disk 19.99 (978-1-4001-5510-1(X)); audio compact disk 59.99 (978-1-4001-3510-3(9)) Pub: Tantor Media. Dist(s): IngramPubServ

Art of Power. unabr. ed. Thich Nhat Hanh. Read by Lloyd James. (YA). 2008. 54.99 (978-1-60514-625-6(0)) Find a World.

Art of Practical Spirituality: How to Bring More Passion, Creativity & Balance into Everyday Life. unabr. ed. Elizabeth Clare Prophet. Told to Patricia R. Spadaro. 2002. 10.95 (978-0-922729-74-6(3), 942-059) Pub: Summit Univ. Dist(s): Natl Bk Netwk

Art of Practice. unabr. ed. Lance Giroux. Interview with Jeanna Gabellini. 1 cass. (Running Time: 1 hr. 5 mins.). 1999. 10.00 (978-0-9710787-0-3(X)) Mstr Pce Coach Train.
A bold instruction about taking the necessary steps to sustain changes for healthy personal & professional results. Created to get & keep you on track, it is your personal coach in your pocket.

Art of Presence. unabr. ed. Eckhart Tolle. 6 CDs. (Running Time: 25200 sec.). 2007. audio compact disk 69.95 (978-1-59179-637-4(7), AF01206D) Sounds True.

Art of Profitability. abr. unabr. ed. Adrian J. Slywotzky. Read by Scott Mosenson & Jack Ong. (ENG.). 2005. 14.98 (978-1-59483-239-0(0)) Pub: Hachet Audio. Dist(s): HachBkGrp

Art of Profitability. unabr. ed. Adrian Slywotzky. Read by Scott Mosenson. (Running Time: 6 hrs.). (ENG.). 2009. 49.98 (978-1-60788-055-4(5)) Pub: Hachet Audio. Dist(s): HachBkGrp

Art of Public Speaking. Millard Bennett. 1 cass. 10.00 (SP100019) SMI Intl.
Everyone admires the person who expresses ideas confidently & persuasively. Become a more effective public speaker. Hold the attention of an audience - a few friends, a crowd, or hundreds. Be more influential & self-confident by expressing your ideas effectively.

__Art of Public Speaking.__ Art Fettig. 4 cass. Dramatization. 1987. 49.95 Set. (PSA-1) Growth Unltd.
Learn to use humor effectively. How to stack the odds in your favor. Recorded live.

__Art of Public Speaking.__ abr. ed. Millard Bennett. 1 cass. (Running Time: 42 min.). 11.00 (978-0-89811-035-7(1), 5181) Meyer Res Grp.
Become a more effective public speaker. Be more influential & self-confident by expressing your ideas effectively.

__Art of Publicity see Great American Essays: A Collection__

*__Art of Racing in the Rain.__ unabr. ed. Garth Stein. Read by Christopher Evan Welch. (ENG.). 2008. (978-0-06-163067-5(5)); (978-0-06-163068-2(3)) HarperCollins Pubs.

__Art of Racing in the Rain.__ unabr. ed. Garth Stein. Read by Christopher Evan Welch. 6 CDs. (Running Time: 7 hrs.). 2009. audio compact disk 14.99 (978-0-06-178030-1(8), Harper Audio) HarperCollins Pubs.

*__Art of Raising a Puppy.__ The Monks of New Skete. (Running Time: 9 hrs.). (ENG.). 2011. 24.98 (978-1-60941-194-7(3)); audio compact disk & audio compact disk 29.98 (978-1-60941-189-3(7)) Pub: Hachet Audio. Dist(s): HachBkGrp

__Art of Raising a Puppy.__ abr. ed. Monks of New Skete. (Running Time: 4 hrs. 15 mins.). (ENG.). 2006. audio compact disk 24.95 (978-1-59887-051-0(3), 1598870513) Pub: HighBridge. Dist(s): Workman Pub

__Art of Raising a Puppy.__ abr. ed. The Monks of New Skete. Read by Michael Wager. (YA). 2007. 49.99 (978-1-60252-739-3(3)) Find a World.

__Art of Reading.__ Instructed by Timothy Spurgin. 2009. 129.95 (978-1-59803-565-0(7)) Teaching Co.

__Art of Reading.__ Instructed by Timothy Spurgin. 12 CDs. (Running Time: 12 hrs.). 2009. audio compact disk 179.95 (978-1-59803-566-7(5)) Teaching Co.

__Art of Reflection.__ 1 cass. (Running Time: 1 hr.). 12.99 (183) Yoga Res Foun.

__Art of Relaxation.__ 6 cass., 6 CD's. 1999. 29.95 Set. (45591); audio compact disk 34.95 CD Set. (45602) Courage-to-Change.
Unwind anywhere with beautiful, relaxing music.

__Art of Relaxation.__ 6 CDs. (Running Time: 6 hrs.). audio compact disk 34.95 (978-1-55961-422-1(6)) Relaxtn Co.

__Art of Relaxation Ten Year Collection.__ 6 cass. (Running Time: 6 hrs.). 1996. 29.95 (978-1-55961-396-5(3)); audio compact disk 34.95 (978-1-55961-395-8(5)) Relaxtn Co.

__Art of Relaxing the Mind.__ Swami Jyotirmayananda. 1 cass. (Running Time: 45 min.). 1990. 10.00 Yoga Res Foun.

__Art of Remembering.__ William D. Hersey. 1 cass. 10.00 (SP100031) SMI Intl.
Use your hidden memory power to store any amount of information you desire. Learn to recall names, faces, lists, information, & plans for action. Your life will be easier & more enjoyable.

__Art of Restful Sleeping Without Drugs.__ Alfred Jones. 1 cass. 10.00 (SP100058) SMI Intl.
No day is complete without a period of sleep & restoration. Restful sleep prepares you for top performance. Insomnia is a common problem. Sleep-inducing drugs often lead to further complications, but Dr. Jones will show you how to relax & get the sleep you need.

__Art of Ruth Draper.__ unabr. ed. Ruth Draper. Read by Ruth Draper. 5 cass. (Running Time: 3 hrs. 56 min.). Dramatization. 1986. 55.00 (978-0-8045-0066-1(5), PCC 66) Spoken Arts.
Ruth Draper performs her own monologues, ranging from farce to tragedy.

__Art of Safety.__ Art Fettig. 6 cass. Dramatization. 1988. 59.95 set. (ASC) Growth Unltd.
Six marvelous programs. Enjoy, become inspired & rededicated to safety.

__Art of Samoan Dance Booklet w/Audio CD.__ Vicki Corona. (Celebrate the Cultures Ser.: II-23-B). 1989. pap. bk. 24.95 (978-1-58513-152-5(0)) Dance Fantasy.

__Art of Seduction.__ abr. ed. Robert Greene et al. Read by Jeff David. 4 CDs. (Running Time: 4 hrs. 45 mins.). (ENG.). 2001. audio compact disk 26.95 (978-1-56511-521-7(X), 156511521X) Pub: HighBridge. Dist(s): Workman Pub

__Art of Self-Acceptance.__ unabr. ed. Nathaniel Branden. 1 cass. (Running Time: 34 min.). 12.95 (855) J Norton Pubs.
Learn to give up being at war with yourself; learn to own, accept & integrate all of your thoughts, feelings & experiences.

__Art of Self-Disclosure Set: How Much of Me Do I Show?__ David Grudermeyer & Rebecca Grudermeyer. 2 cass. 18.95 INCL. HANDOUTS. (T-41) Willingness Wrks.

__Art of Self Relaxation.__ Prod. by Imagine. Created by Sharon Penchina & Stuart Hoffman. 2 CDs. (Running Time: 54 Mins). 2002. audio compact disk 19.95 (978-0-9740684-2-8(X)) Two Imagine.
2 Program set.The Break-through technologies of Neuro-Linguistic Programming and Synchronized Brain Research makes this CD unique and highly effective.Enter the deepest state of relaxation imaginable as you activate your ?Whole-brain? function. *Utilizes DUAL-SYNC technologyThis 2-program set is digitally recorded and mastered on one disc producing a 3-D sound as you are guided by a precise blend of music and the spoken word.

__Art of Sexual Ecstasy.__ Read by Margo Anand & Steven Halpern. 1 cass. (Running Time: 60 min.). 1993. 9.98 (978-1-878625-20-5(9), SRXB 1069) Inner Peace Mus.
Guided instructional tape for adults.

__Art of Sleeping Restfully.__ Nick Kemp & Tina Taylor. 2006. audio compact disk 27.95 (978-0-9551104-0-5(8)) Transforming Pr.

__Art of Social War.__ unabr. ed. Jodi Wing. (Running Time: 10 hrs. 0 mins.). 2008. 29.95 (978-1-4332-5540-3(5)); audio compact disk 80.00 (978-1-4332-5538-0(3)); audio compact disk 59.95 (978-1-4332-5537-3(5)) Blckstn Audio.

__Art of Social War.__ unabr. ed. Jodi Wing. (Running Time: 10 hrs. 0 mins.). 2008. audio compact disk 19.95 (978-1-4332-5539-7(1)) Blckstn Audio.

__Art of Solo Bass, the Chordal Approach.__ Michael Dimin. (ENG.). 2009. lib. bdg. 19.99 (978-0-7866-0653-5(3)) Mel Bay.

__Art of South American Cookery.__ 2nd rev. ed. Myra Waldo. (Hippocrene International Cookbook Ser.). (ENG., 1996. audio compact disk 12.95 (978-0-7818-0485-1(X)) Hippocrene Bks.

__Art of Speaking, No. 3.__ Swami Jyotirmayananda. 1 cass. (Running Time: 1 hr.). 1990. 12.99 Yoga Res Foun.

__Art of Speaking II see Art of Listening II__

__Art of Speedreading People: Harness the Power of Personality Type & Create What You Want in Business & in Life.__ unabr. ed. Paul D. Tieger & Barbara Barron-Tieger. 1 cass. (Running Time: 1 hr. 30 min.). 1998. 12.98 (978-1-57042-582-0(5)) Hachet Audio.
Tieger's unique system of decoding personalities is a powerful advantage in communicating more successfully with coworkers & employees, with friends & family members, & with propective customers & clients.

__Art of Spiritual Dreaming.__ unabr. ed. Harold Klemp & Rich Miller. 6 vols. (Running Time: 8 hrs. 54 mins.). 2004. bk. 28.00 (978-1-57043-183-8(3)) Pub: Eckankar. Dist(s): Hushion Hse

__Art of Spiritual Leadership in Business: How to Lead with Spiritual Purpose, Values, & Creativity.__ abr. ed. William Miller. 2003. audio compact disk 34.95 (978-1-59179-019-8(0)) Sounds True.

__Art of Spooning.__ unabr. ed. Jim Grace & Lisa Goldblatt Grace. Read by Kathy Garver. 1 cass. (Running Time: 1 hr.). 2000. bk. 20.95 (LC017) Listen & Live.
Spooning is a kind of horizontal hug, two bodies curling up so they fit perfectly into each other's nooks & comfy places - like two spoons in a drawer.

__Art of Spooning.__ unabr. ed. Jim Grace & Lisa Goldblatt Grace. Read by Kathy Garver. 1 cass. (Running Time: 1 hr.). (For Both Ser.). 1998. 12.95 (978-1-885408-24-2(2), LL017) Listen & Live.

*__Art of Standing Still: A Novel.__ Zondervan. (Running Time: 10 hrs. 41 mins. 45 sec.). (ENG.). 2010. 9.99 (978-0-310-86938-2(2)) Zondervan.

__Art of Successful Worrying.__ unabr. ed. Larry Losoncy. 1 cass. 10.95 (1905) J Norton Pubs.
Learn how to turn worry into productive worry. Ten practical ways are given for converting "plain old worry" into a positive mental system.

__Art of Supportive Leadership: A Practical Guide for People in Positions of Responsibility.__ 2nd unabr. ed. J. Donald Walters. Read by J. Donald Walters. 1 cass. (Running Time: 1 hr. 30 mins.). 2000. 10.95 (978-1-56589-144-9(9)) Crystal Clarity.
A practical approach, drawn from Eastern wisdom, which views leadership in terms of shared accomplishment rather than personal advancement.

__Art of Surrendering.__ Jack Boland. 1 cass. (Super Ser.). 8.00 (BI01) Master Mind.

__Art of Talking to Anyone: Essential People Skills for Success in Any Situation.__ abr. ed. Rosalie Maggio. Read by Bernadette Dunne. (Running Time: 16200 sec.). 2006. audio compact disk 28.00 (978-1-932378-95-5(2)) Pub: A Media Intl. Dist(s): Natl Bk Netwk

__Art of Talking to Yourself & Others.__ Harry Hazel. 1 cass. (Running Time: 41 mins.). 1988. 11.00 (978-0-89811-269-6(9), SP100074) Meyer Res Grp.
How to build your self-esteem, boost your self-confidence, enhance your ability to remember important facts & names & turn criticism into strengths.

__Art of Talking to Yourself & Others.__ Harry Hazel. 1 cass. 10.00 (SP100074) SMI Intl.
Learn to build self-esteem. Boost self-confidence. Remember important facts & names. Turn criticism into strengths. Win over worry. Motivate others & lead a balanced life.

__Art of Tantra Sex.__ Ormond McGill. 2000. (978-1-933332-23-9(9)) Hypnotherapy Train.

__Art of the Duo.__ Contrib. by John Abercrombie & Andy Laverne. (Running Time: 1 hr. 9 mins.). 2006. 24.95 (978-5-558-09175-5(4)) Mel Bay.

__Art of the Examination: Why Patient Care Goes Beyond Clincial Correctness.__ Barry Polansky. 2002. audio compact disk 99.95 (978-0-9714516-4-3(8)) Word of Mouth Entprs.

__Art of the Novel see Poetry & Voice of Marilyn Hacker__

__Art of the Novel.__ Henry James. 2 cass. (Running Time: 2 hrs. 30 mins.). 1994. 17.95 (978-1-879557-20-8(7)) Audio Scholar.
Written by novelist Henry James to serve as both retrospect of his work & statement on his art. The result is a consciousness-raising journey into the creative mind of a genius.

*__Art of the Solo Clarinet: Orchestral Excerpts.__ Created by Hal Leonard Corp. (ENG.). 2006. pap. bk. 29.98 (978-1-59615-233-5(8), 1596152338) Pub: Music Minus. Dist(s): H Leonard

__Art of the Spirits.__ Perf. by Lucy Lewis's Group. 1 cass. 9.00 (A0384-88) Sound Photosyn.
From ICSS '8.

__Art of the Start: The Time-Tested, Battle-Hardened Guide for Anyone Starting Anything.__ unabr. ed. Guy Kawasaki. Narrated by Paul Boehmer. (Running Time: 7 hrs. 0 mins. 0 sec.). (ENG.). 2009. audio compact disk 59.99 (978-1-4001-4063-3(3)); audio compact disk 19.99 (978-1-4001-6063-1(4)) Pub: Tantor Media. Dist(s): IngramPubServ

__Art of the Start: The Time-Tested, Battle-Hardened Guide for Anyone Starting Anything.__ unabr. ed. Guy Kawasaki. Narrated by Paul Boehmer. (Running Time: 7 hrs. 0 mins. 0 sec.). (ENG.). 2009. audio compact disk 29.99 (978-1-4001-1063-6(7)) Pub: Tantor Media. Dist(s): IngramPubServ

__Art of the Steal.__ unabr. ed. Frank W. Abagnale. Narrated by Barrett Whitener. 6 cass. (Running Time: 8 hrs. 30 mins.). 2002. 44.95 (978-0-7861-2137-3(8), 2888); audio compact disk 56.00 (978-0-7861-9597-8(5), 2888); audio compact disk 24.95 (978-0-7861-9400-1(6), 2888) Blckstn Audio.
The world-famous former con artist now reveals the mind-boggling tricks of the scan trade, with advice that has made him one of America's most sought after fraud-prevention experts. Technology may have made it easier to track down criminals, but cyberspace has spawned a skyrocketing number of ways to commit crime, much of it untraceable.

__Art of the Steal.__ unabr. ed. Frank W. Abagnale. Read by Barrett Whitener. 6 pieces. (Running Time: 9 hrs.). 2004. reel tape 29.95 (978-0-7861-2213-4(7)); audio compact disk 35.95 (978-0-7861-9484-1(7)) Blckstn Audio.

__Art of Theological Reflection Series: Connecting Faith & Life.__ John Shea. 6 cass. (Running Time: 9 hrs.). 1997. 29.95 vinyl binder. (978-0-87946-157-7(8), 330) ACTA Pubns.
Help people discern the presence & power of God in the activities of their daily lives through a process that awakens them to the divine presence in the boardroom, classroom, living room & bedroom.

__Art of Thinking.__ Leonard Peikoff. 15 cass. (Running Time: 15 hrs.). 1994. 175.00 Set. (978-1-56114-257-6(3), LP35D) Second Renaissance.
Course in how to think properly.

__Art of Timelessness: Having Enough Time.__ unabr. ed. Galexis. 2 cass. (Running Time: 3 hrs.). 1995. 19.95 Set. (978-1-56089-041-6(X), G119) Visionary FL.
How to live "off the clock" in a clock-ridden world. Meditation included.

__Art of Torah Cantillation: A Step by Step Guide to Torah Cantillation.__ Josee Wolff & Marshall Portnoy. 2004. pap. bk. 22.95 (978-0-8074-0734-9(8), 386503) URJ Pr.

__Art of Training Astrologers.__ A. C. T. Staff. 1 cass. (Workshop Ser.). 8.95 (013) Am Fed Astrologers.

__Art of Transformation.__ Contrib. by Grits. 2005. audio compact disk 7.99 (978-5-558-62325-3(X)) Gotee Records.

__Art of Transmutation.__ Doris C. Doane. 1 cass. 8.95 (650) Am Fed Astrologers.
An AFA Convention workshop tape.

__Art of Travel.__ Alain de Botton. Read by Alain de Botton. 2 cass. (Running Time: 3 hrs.). (ENG., 2002. (978-0-14-086793-0(7)) Pnguin Bks Ltd GBR.

__Art of Travel.__ unabr. ed. Alain de Botton. Narrated by Steven Crossley. 4 cass. (Running Time: 5 hrs. 30 mins.). 2002. 40.00 (978-1-84197-493-4(5)) Recorded Bks.

__Art of Two Line Improvisation.__ Jimmy Wyble. Ed. by David Oakes. 2001. bk. 19.95 (978-0-7866-4525-1(3)) Mel Bay.

__Art of Victory.__ unabr. ed. Gregory Copley. Read by Lloyd James. (Running Time: 10 hrs. 0 mins. 0 sec.). (ENG.). 2006. audio compact disk 34.99 (978-1-4001-0312-6(6)) Pub: Tantor Media. Dist(s): IngramPubServ

__Art of Victory: Strategies for Success & Survival in a Changing World.__ unabr. ed. Gregory R. Copley. (Running Time: 10 hrs. 0 mins. 0 sec.). (ENG.). 2006. audio compact disk 24.99 (978-1-4001-5312-1(3)); audio compact disk 69.99 (978-1-4001-3312-3(2)) Pub: Tantor Media. Dist(s): IngramPubServ

__Art of War.__ Read by Alexander Adams. Tr. by Samuel B. Griffith. Des. by Sun Tzu. 1994. audio compact disk 40.00 (978-0-7366-8283-1(X)) Books on Tape.

__Art of War.__ Read by Scott Brick. Des. by Sun Tzu. (Running Time: 2 hrs.). (C). 2003. 21.95 (978-1-60083-635-0(6), Audiofy Corp) Iofy Corp.

__Art of War.__ Read by Shelly Frasier & Scott Brick. Des. by Sun Tzu. (ENG.). 2003. audio compact disk 46.00 (978-1-4001-3067-2(0)) Pub: Tantor Media. Dist(s): IngramPubServ

__Art of War.__ Lorna Raver. Tr. by John Minford. Des. by Sun Tzu. 7 cass. (Running Time: 10 hrs.). 2002. 49.95 (978-0-7861-2723-8(6), 3282) Blckstn Audio.

__Art of War.__ Des. by Sun Tzu. Narrated by Joe Mantegna. Intro. by Ralph D. Sawyer. 4 CDs. (Running Time: 5 hrs.). 2004. audio compact disk 19.99 (978-1-4025-6101-6(6), 01182) Recorded Bks.

__Art of War.__ unabr. ed. Read by Alexander Adams. Tr. by Samuel B. Griffin. Des. by Sun Tzu. 6 cass. (Running Time: 9 hrs.). 2002. 29.95 (978-0-7366-6751-7(2)) Books on Tape.
These essays have never been surpassed in comprehensiveness & depth of understanding & might well be termed the concentrated essence of wisdom on the conduct of war. Terse & aphoristic, they contain principles still acted upon by Chinese generals today.

__Art of War.__ unabr. ed. Read by Scott Brick & Shelly Frasier. Des. by Sun Tzu. (YA). 2007. 39.99 (978-1-59895-844-7(5)) Find a World.

__Art of War.__ unabr. ed. Read by Scott Brick & Shelly Frasier. Des. by Sun Tzu. (Running Time: 2 hrs. 0 mins. 0 sec.). (ENG.). 2008. audio compact disk 35.99 (978-1-4001-3841-8(8)); audio compact disk 17.99 (978-1-4001-5841-6(9)) Pub: Tantor Media. Dist(s): IngramPubServ

__Art of War,__ unabr. ed. Stefan Rudnicki. Read by B. D. Wong & Ron Silver. Des. by Sun Tzu. 2 cass. (Running Time: 3 hrs.). 2000. 18.00 (978-1-57453-360-6(6)) Audio Lit.
Offers modern listeners insights into negotiating conflicts & achieving success in life.

__Art of War.__ unabr. ed. Tr. by Ralph D. Sawyer. Des. by Sun Tzu. Narrated by George Guidall & Joe Montegna. 3 cass. (Running Time: 4 hrs. 15 mins.). 2002. 32.00 (978-1-4025-1240-7(6)); audio compact disk 42.00 (978-1-4025-2914-6(7)) Recorded Bks.
In recent years, people from all walks of life have utilized this new translated text to gain a competitive edge. The practical wisdom, strategy, and philosophy prove time and again to be an indispensable guide and resource.

__Art of War.__ unabr. ed. Perf. by Ron Silver & B. D. Wong. Des. by Sun Tzu. Adapted by Stefan Rudnicki. Intro. by Stefan Rudnicki. 2 cass. (Running Time: 3 hrs.). 2001. 18.00 (978-1-59040-019-7(4), Phoenix Audio) Pub: Amer Intl Pub. Dist(s): PerseuPGW
This classic written by a Chinese philosopher-general will help you negotiate conflicts and succeed.

__Art of War.__ unabr. ed. Sun-Tzu. Read by Scott Brick & Shelly Frasier. (Running Time: 2 hrs. 0 mins. 0 sec.). (Tantor Unabridged Classics Ser.). (ENG.). 2008. audio compact disk 17.99 (978-1-4001-0841-1(1)) Pub: Tantor Media. Dist(s): IngramPubServ

__Art of War.__ unabr. ed. SunZi et al. Narrated by Ross M. Armetta & Urara Tsukamoto. 1 CD. (Running Time: 72 Mins. Aprox.). 2005. audio compact disk 12.99 (978-1-59733-201-9(1), Martial Strat) InfoFount.
The Art of War by Sun Tzu complete, unabridged with BonusThe best Art of War for application in competitive situations.How much can one big mistake cost ? Everything ?The Art of War provides strategies and tactics for conventional war / competition. It is useful in developing offensive strategies and a critical guide for defense: learning what not to do and how to avoid competitive / enemy traps. It also explains external and internal psychological strategies. Sun Tzu advises ?know the enemy and yourself." Martial Strategists studied competitive Art of War audiobooks before making its edition to ensure that you get the best, most useful Art of War. It was designed from the ground up to be the most practical version for application in combat - be it war, business, sports, or any other form - winning in competition and avoiding costly mistakes. Its usefulness was achieved by being faithful to the text of the Art of War. The Art of War includes the bonus ?Sun Tzu and the Concubine? story and ?The Biography of Confucius.?Stylistically, the Martial Strategists version is quick paced and driving. You are involved in a critical mission - YOUR VICTORY - and the general is doing everything in his power to aid you. It is designed to interest and engage you. You will retain more and find it more useful when are your involved in the audiobook. That is why Martial Strategists have incorporated sound effects, music, and some levity to keep you interested and involved unlike the competitive versions that read to you slowly, . . . with . . . very . . . tedious . . . useless . . . information . . . . placed . . . out of context, giving you a headache, and putting you to sleep. Martial Strategist""s Art of War is the best available for application in competitive situations. Martial Strategists, a specialty division of Infofount, are strategy specialists and translate, obtain, and rewrite the most useful versions of classic military and strategy texts available. Martial Strategist""s audiobooks are said to be "unequaled for entertainment, practical application,and value." It is a quality production recorded in 2005 with music and sound effects. This audiobook has real actors and is performed in a manner that is easy to understand and entertaining. It is a concise and accurate translation with the actors clearly and comprehensively articulating the text. It is not dry and boring as some other versions are. It has some levity in appropriate places. Also available discounted in InfoFount?s ?Martial Strategy Pack.?More information is available at www.InfoFount.comThe Art of War Deluxe (3 Disks) This version integrates the comments and explanations of 2500 years of China""s most respected experts on Sun Tzu""s text seamlessly into the audiobook. It "fills in the blanks" and clarifies the military vocabulary, concepts, and strategies within the text that taken at face value can easily be misunderstood. If you are serious about fully understanding all the concepts and will take the time and effort to listen to it several times - We suggest the Deluxe 3 disk version. Sun Tzu wrote in a terse, somewhat abstract style, and, of course, wrote of vastly different times and conditions (500 BC China). The integrated commentary and explanations on the 3 disk set can greatly help clarify these aspects of Sun Tzu""s Art of War.The comments and explanations were very carefully integrated to clarify and enhance without disrupting, the

flow and comprehension of Sun Tzu""s text. When you hear Sun Tzu talking about some obscure term or concept you will not be lost. Incredibly there are other versions that never explain some critical and counter intuitive and ambiguous writings - you can only take your chances and guess. Some of The Art of War if taken literally would be an inaccurate interpretation and potentially disastrous. Sun Tzu wrote in a somewhat abstract, poetic style assuming that the reader was familiar with military and cultural matters as it related to 500 BC China. The integrated comments are related to strategy, victory, and crucial historical and cultural background and context. Unlike other versions that focus on teaching Buddhism / Pacifism and Chinese military history the Martial Strategists? version focuses on strategy and victory so as not to confuse the meaning of Sun Tzu""s text and over burden the listener with irrelevant, useless, information - SO YOU ARE PROVIDED IN GREATER DEPTH THE CRUCIAL INFORMATION - HOW TO PROPERLY INTERPRET SUN TZU""S TEXT AND APPLY IT TO WIN, SURVIVE, AND SUCEED IN YOUR EFFORTS !.

Art of War. unabr. ed. Read by Jeffrey Tambor. Tr. by Jessica Steindorff & Michael Viner. Des. by Sun Tzu. 2 cass. (Running Time: 3 hrs.). 2004. 18.00 (978-1-59007-500-5(5)); audio compact disk 25.00 (978-1-59007-501-2(3)) Pub: New Millenn Enter. Dist(s): PerseuPGW

Art of War. unabr. ed. Des. by Sun Tzu. 8 cass. (Running Time: 5 hrs.). 2004. 19.99 (978-1-4025-0862-2(X), 00984) Recorded Bks.

Art of War. unabr. ed. Sun Tzu. Read by David Warrilow. Tr. by Thomas Cleary. (Running Time: 3600 sec.). (ENG.). 2008. audio compact disk 12.95 (978-1-59030-547-8(7)) Pub: Shambhala Pubns. Dist(s): Random

***Art of War.** unabr. ed. Sun Tzu. Narrated by Dave Heath. (ENG.). 2010. 8.98 (978-1-61045-064-5(7), MissionAud); audio compact disk 10.98 (978-1-61045-063-8(9), MissionAud) christianaud.

Art of War. unabr. collector's ed. Read by Alexander Adams. Tr. by Samuel B. Griffith. Des. by Sun Tzu. 6 cass. (Running Time: 6 hrs.). 1994. 48.00 (978-0-7366-2663-7(8), 3400) Books on Tape.
Ancient Chinese manual on planning & conducting of military operations, still relevant to students of strategy & war.

Art of War: Judges 6 & 7. Ed Young. 1999. 4.95 (978-0-7417-2230-0(5), 1230) Win Walk.

Art of War: The Denma Translation. Excerpts. Sun-Tzu. Tr. by Denma Translation Group et al from CHI. Based on a book by Shambhala Publishing Staff. 3 CDs. (Running Time: 3.5 hours). 2003. audio compact disk 29.95 (978-1-59179-041-9(7)) Sounds True.
This new and unusually faithful translation carefully preserves the enigmatic quality of the original - allowing us to discover innumerable insights in its lines millenia after this oral tradition was first set down.

Art of War: The Essential Translation of the Classic Book of Life. unabr. ed. Sun-Tzu. Read by Lorna Raver. Tr. by John Minford. 8 CDs. (Running Time: 10 hrs.). 2000. audio compact disk 64.00 (978-0-7861-8648-8(8), 3282) Blckstn Audio.

Art of War: The Essential Translation of the Classic Book of Life. unabr. ed. Sun-Tzu. Read by Ray Porter. Tr. by John Minford. (Running Time: 34200 sec.). 2008. 19.95 (978-1-4332-1249-9(8)) Blckstn Audio.

Art of War: The Essential Translation of the Classic Book of Life. unabr. ed. Sun-Tzu. Read by Ray Porter & Lorna Raver. Tr. by John Minford. (Running Time: 34200 sec.). 2008. 65.95 (978-1-4332-1491-2(1)) Blckstn Audio.

Art of War: The Essential Translation of the Classic Book of Life. unabr. ed. Sun-Tzu. Read by Ray Porter. Tr. by John Minford. (Running Time: 34200 sec.). 2008. audio compact disk 19.95 (978-1-4332-1250-5(1)) Blckstn Audio.

Art of War: The Essential Translation of the Classic Book of Life. unabr. ed. Sun-Tzu. Read by Lorna Raver. Tr. by John Minford. (Running Time: 34200 sec.). 2008. audio compact disk & audio compact disk 80.00 (978-1-4332-1492-9(X)) Blckstn Audio.

Art of War: The Essential Translation of the Classic Book of Life. unabr. ed. Sun-Tzu. Read by Ray Porter & Lorna Raver. Tr. by John Minford. (Running Time: 9.2 hrs. 5 mins.). 2008. audio compact disk 29.95 (978-1-4332-1493-6(8)) Blckstn Audio.

Art of War: With Commentary, Explanations & Bonus the Sayings of Confucius. unabr. deluxe ed. Sun-Tzu & Sunzi. Tr. by Lionel Giles. Narrated by Ross M. Armetta. 3 CDs. (Running Time: 3 hrs. 30 min.). 2005. audio compact disk 16.99 (978-1-59733-202-6(X), Martial Strat) InfoFount.
The best Art of War for application in competitive situations.How much can one big mistake cost ? Everything ?The Art of War Deluxe provides strategies and tactics for conventional war / competition. It is useful in developing offensive strategies and a critical guide for defense: learning what not to do and how to avoid competitive / enemy traps. It also explains external and internal psychological strategies. The Deluxe (3CD) version seamlessly integrates the comments and explanations of China's most respected experts on Sun Tzu's text since 500 BC. It "fills in the blanks" and clarifies the military vocabulary, concepts, and strategies within the text which taken at face value can easily be misunderstood. It also includes the bonus ?Sun Tzu and the Concubine? story and ?The Sayings of Confucius.?Stylistically, the Martial Strategists version is quick paced and driving. You are involved in a critical mission - YOUR VICTORY - and the general is doing everything in his power to aid you. Sound effects, music, and some levity are used to keep you interested and engaged: helping you retain more and making the information actually useful.Sun Tzu advises ?know the enemy and yourself." Competitive versions were studied before making this edition to ensure that you get the best, most useful Art of War. It was designed to be the most practical version for application in combat - be it war, business, sports, or any other form. Its focus is winning and avoiding costly mistakes. The integrated comments are related to strategy, victory, and crucial historical and cultural background and context. Unlike other versions that focus on teaching Buddhism / Pacifism and Chinese military history this version focuses on strategy and victory as Sun Tzu intended. It provides THE CRUCIAL INFORMATION - HOW TO PROPERLY INTERPRET SUN TZU'S TEXT AND APPLY IT TO WIN, SURVIVE, AND SUCEED IN YOUR EFFORTS! The Art of War Deluxe contents include; The Art of War Background information; Sun Tzu and the Concubine Story; Laying Plans; Waging War; Attack by Stratagem; Tactical Dispositions; Energy; Weak Points and Strong; Maneuvering; Variation in Tactics; The Army on the March; Terrain;The Nine Situations;The Attack by Fire: The Use of Spies.Martial Strategists, a specialty division of Infofount, are strategy specialists and translate, obtain, and rewrite the most useful versions of classic military and strategy texts available. Martial Strategist"s audiobooks are said to be "unequaled for entertainment, practical application, and value." It is a quality production recorded in 2004 with music and sound effects. This audiobook has real actors and is performed in a manner that is easy to understand and entertaining. It is a concise and accurate translation with the actors clearly and comprehensively articulating the text. It is not dry and boring as some other versions are. It has some levity in appropriate places. It is also available discounted in InfoFount?s ?Martial Strategy Pack.?More information is available at www.InfoFount.com.

art of war for Executives. Donald G. Krause. Read by Francis Greenslade. (Running Time: 3 hrs. 30 mins.). 2009. 54.99 (978-1-74214-257-9(5), 9781742142579) Pub: Bolinda Pub AUS. Dist(s): Bolinda Pub Inc

Art of War for Executives. unabr. ed. Donald G. Krause. Read by Francis Greenslad. (Running Time: 12600 sec.). 2008. audio compact disk 54.95 (978-1-921334-50-4(9), 9781921334504) Pub: Bolinda Pubng AUS. Dist(s): Bolinda Pub Inc

Art of War for Women: Sun Tzu's Ancient Strategies & Wisdom for Winning at Work. unabr. ed. Chin-Ning Chu. Read by Marguerite Gavin. (Running Time: 6 hrs.). (ENG.). 2007. audio compact disk 29.98 (978-1-59659-128-8(5), GildAudio) Pub: Gildan Media. Dist(s): HachBkGrp

Art of Weakness: The Recipe for Joy. Clyde A. Bonar. 4 cass. (Running Time: 5 hrs. 8 mins.). 1995. 34.95 (TAH331) Alba Hse Comns.
This fresh examination of the beatitudes provides practical applications of these time-honored declarations of Jesus. With an innovative focus on the core message of these ancient yet timely blessings, we may develop a new sense of the spirit guiding us to be reformed in the image & likeness of Jesus as savior.

Art of Wonder. Osho Oshos. 1 cass. 9.00 (A0655-89) Sound Photosyn.

Art of Woo: Using Strategic Persuasion to Sell Your Ideas. Richard G. Shell & Mario Moussa. Read by Alan Sklar. (Playaway Adult Nonfiction Ser.). 2008. 64.99 (978-1-60640-990-9(5)) Find a World.

Art of Woo: Using Strategic Persuasion to Sell Your Ideas. unabr. ed. G. Richard Shell & Mario Moussa. Narrated by Alan Sklar. (Running Time: 10 hrs. 30 mins. 0 sec.). (ENG.). 2007. audio compact disk 69.99 (978-1-4001-3530-1(3)); audio compact disk 24.99 (978-1-4001-5530-9(4)) Pub: Tantor Media. Dist(s): IngramPubServ

Art of Woo: Using Strategic Persuasion to Sell Your Ideas. unabr. ed. G. Richard Shell & Mario Moussa. Read by Alan Sklar. 8 CDs. (Running Time: 10 hrs. 30 mins. 0 sec.). (ENG.). 2007. audio compact disk 34.99 (978-1-4001-0530-4(7)) Pub: Tantor Media. Dist(s): IngramPubServ

Art of Writing Comedy. 2005. audio compact disk 59.95 (978-0-9769097-0-5(7)) Fade.

Art Riddle Contest: Artists & Art. Steck-Vaughn Staff. 1 cass. (Running Time: 1 hr. 30 min.). (J). 1999. (978-0-7398-0924-2(5)) SteckVau.

Art, Society & the Collective Archetypes. Read by Ian Williamson. 1 cass. (Running Time: 2 hrs.). 1985. 12.95 (978-0-7822-0329-5(9), 175) C G Jung IL.

Art Song in America. John K. Hanks. bk. 29.95 (978-0-8223-2051-7(7)) Duke.

Art That Pays: The Emerging Artist's Guide to Making a Living. 3rd ed. Adele Slaughter & Jeff Kober. Based on a book by Judith Luther. Created by Warren Christensen. Orig. Title: For the Working Artist. 2005. pap. bk. 29.00 (978-0-945941-14-9(5)) NNAP.

Art, the Arts, & the Great Ideas. unabr. ed. Mortimer J. Adler. Read by Nadia May. 2 cass. (Running Time: 2 hrs. 30 mins.). 1995. 17.95 (978-0-7861-0703-2(0), 1580) Blckstn Audio.
Adler challenges us to precision in language, tracing the historical permutations of pivotal words like "art," "idea" & "significance." He ambitiously defines these three words in terms of their everyday meanings & then their (often very different) philosophical meanings. Fundamental to his argument is the question of whether art (such as paintings & sculptures) & the performing arts (such as music & dancing) can elicit the discussion of ideas & basic concepts.

Art Thief. unabr. ed. Noah Charney. Read by Simon Vance. 7 cass. (Running Time: 36000 sec.). 2007. 24.95 (978-1-4332-0372-5(3)); audio compact disk 24.95 (978-1-4332-0373-2(1)) Blckstn Audio.

Art Thief. unabr. ed. Noah Charney. Read by Simon Vance. 7 cass. (Running Time: 36000 sec.). 2007. 44.95 (978-1-4332-0370-1(7)); audio compact disk 55.00 (978-1-4332-0371-8(5)) Blckstn Audio.

Art Thieme: On the River. 1 cass. 9.98 (C-527) Folk-Legacy.
River songs by one of the Midwest's most popular folksingers.

Art Thieme: On the Wilderness Road. 1 cass. 9.98 (C-105) Folk-Legacy.
American folksongs with banjo & guitar.

Art Thieme: That's the Ticket. 1 cass. 9.98 (C-90) Folk-Legacy.
Mostly traditional songs from this popular Midwest folksinger.

***Art to Hear: Botticelli.** Sandro Botticelli. Text by Ursula Vorwerk. (ENG.). 2010. audio compact disk 30.00 (978-3-7757-2483-8(4)) Pub: Hatje Cantz DEU. Dist(s): Dist Art Pubs

Art 20. 2nd rev. ed. Thames and Hudson Staff. (ENG., 2005. audio compact disk 125.00 (978-0-500-10019-6(5)) Pub: Thames Hudson. Dist(s): Norton

Art 20: The Thames & Hudson Multimedia Dictionary of Modern Art. Thames & Hudson. 1999. audio compact disk 125.00 (978-0-500-10015-8(2)) Pub: Thames Hudson. Dist(s): Norton

arte de agradar a los Demas. Cesar Lozano. (SPA.). (YA). 2009. audio compact disk 16.95 (978-1-935405-68-9(3)) Hombre Nuevo.

Arte de Hacer Dinero: Una Nueva Perspectiva para Desarrollar su Inteligencia Financiera. Mario Borghino. (SPA.). 2009. 60.00 (978-1-60775-582-1(3)) Find a World.

***Arte de la Guerra: Estrategias Milenarias para Lideres de Todos los Tiempos.** Sun Tzu. (SPA.). 2010. audio compact disk (978-607-457-071-7(X)) Lectorum MEX.

Arte de Vender Cualquier Cosa. Tom Hopkins. Read by Omar Periu. 8 cass. (Running Time: 6 hrs. 30 min.). (SPA.). 1992. 75.00 (978-0-938636-25-0(1), 1031) T Hopkins Intl.
Spanish translation of million selling book "How to Master the Art of Selling." General selling strategies.

Arte de Vivir. unabr. ed. André Maurois. Read by Daniel Quintero. 3 CDs.Tr. of Art of Living. (SPA.). 2005. audio compact disk 17.00 (978-958-8218-53-3(5)) YoYoMusic.

Arte de Vivir: El Arte de Trabajar y de Mandar. unabr. ed. André Maurois. Read by Daniel Quintero. (SPA.). 2006. audio compact disk 17.00 (978-958-8218-66-3(7)) Pub: Yoyo Music COL. Dist(s): YoYoMusic

Arte Poetica see Pablo Neruda Reading His Poetry

Artemis: A Kydd Novel. unabr. ed. Julian Stockwin. 8 cass. (Running Time: 12 hrs.). 2002. 72.00 (978-0-7366-8757-7(2)) Books on Tape.
valiant seamen at the turn of the nineteenth century, aboard the great ships of the British Navy. Thomas Kydd was impressed into service for the Navy in Stockwin's previous book, KYDD. Now, in ARTEMIS, he has been transferred with his friend Nicholas Renzi from his trying stint aboard his first ship, THE PRINCE WILLIAM, to the crack frigate ARTEMIS. Almost immediately, they are forced into fierce battle with a French frigate, from which they emerge victorious. But ARTEMIS must undertake a second voyage, much grimmer than the first, in which Kydd's and Renzi's friendship is sorely tested, and in which the ship and its crew head into potential devastation.

Artemis & Aphrodite Need Not Apply. Read by Thomas P. Lavin. 3 cass. (Running Time: 3 hrs. 30 mins.). 1990. 22.95 (978-0-7822-0143-7(1), 418) C G Jung IL.

***Artemis Begins: A Story from Guys Read: Funny Business.** unabr. ed. Eoin Colfer. (ENG.). 2010. (978-0-06-206245-1(X)); (978-0-06-202766-5(2)) HarperCollins Pubs.

Artemis Fowl. Eoin Colfer. Read by Nathaniel Parker. 4 cass. (Running Time: 6 hrs. 7 mins.). (Artemis Fowl Ser.: Bk. 1). (J). (gr. 6 up). 2004. 32.00 (978-0-8072-0890-8(6), Listening Lib); audio compact disk 40.00 (978-1-4000-8591-0(8), Listening Lib) Random Audio Pubg.

Artemis Fowl. unabr. ed. Eoin Colfer. Read by Nathaniel Parker. 6 CDs. (Running Time: 6 hrs. 5 mins.). (Artemis Fowl Ser.: Bk. 1). (J). (gr. 3-6). 2002. audio compact disk (978-1-85549-191-5(5)) Cover To Cover GBR.
12 year old Artemis Fowl is a brilliant criminal mastermind. But even Artemis doesn't know what he's taken on when he kidnaps a fairy, Captain Holly Short of the Leprecon Unit. These aren't the fairies of bedtime stories - they are dangerous. . .

Artemis Fowl. unabr. ed. Eoin Colfer. Read by Nathaniel Parker. (Artemis Fowl Ser.: Bk. 1). (J). 2006. 44.99 (978-0-7393-7117-6(7)) Find a World.

Artemis Fowl. unabr. ed. Eoin Colfer. Read by Nathaniel Parker. 5 CDs. (Running Time: 6 hrs. 7 mins.). (Artemis Fowl Ser.: Bk. 1). (ENG.). (YA). (gr. 7). 2004. audio compact disk 19.99 (978-1-4000-8586-6(1), Listening Lib) Pub: Random Audio Pubg. Dist(s): Random

Artes Latinae: Roma - Urbs et Orbis Filmstrip. 1 cass. 60.00 (978-0-86516-391-1(X)) Bolchazy-Carducci.

Artes Latinae: Roma Antiqua Filmstrip. 1 cass. 60.00 (978-0-86516-390-4(1)) Bolchazy-Carducci.

Artes Latinae - Classical Latin, Pt. III. Waldo E. Sweet. 6 cass. (Running Time: 3 hrs.). (LAT., 1969. pap. bk. 145.00 (978-1-57970-033-1(0), S26150) J Norton Pubs.

Artes Latinae - Classical Latin, Pt. IV. Waldo E. Sweet. 8 cass. (Running Time: 4 hrs. 30 mins.). (LAT., 1969. pap. bk. 145.00 (978-1-57970-034-8(9), S26250) J Norton Pubs.

Artes Latinae Level I, Units 1-2. Sweet. 1 cass. 14.00 (978-0-86516-359-1(6)) Bolchazy-Carducci.

Artes Latinae Level I, Units 11-12. Sweet. 1 cass. 14.00 (978-0-86516-364-5(2)) Bolchazy-Carducci.

Artes Latinae Level I, Units 13-14. Sweet. 1 cass. 14.00 (978-0-86516-365-2(0)) Bolchazy-Carducci.

Artes Latinae Level I, Units 15-16. Sweet. 1 cass. 14.00 (978-0-86516-366-9(9)) Bolchazy-Carducci.

Artes Latinae Level I, Units 17-18. Sweet. 1 cass. 14.00 (978-0-86516-367-6(7)) Bolchazy-Carducci.

Artes Latinae Level I, Units 19-20. Sweet. 1 cass. 14.00 (978-0-86516-368-3(5)) Bolchazy-Carducci.

Artes Latinae Level I, Units 21-22. Sweet. 1 cass. 14.00 (978-0-86516-369-0(3)) Bolchazy-Carducci.

Artes Latinae Level I, Units 23-24. Sweet. 1 cass. 14.00 (978-0-86516-370-6(7)) Bolchazy-Carducci.

Artes Latinae Level I, Units 25-26. Sweet. 1 cass. 14.00 (978-0-86516-371-3(5)) Bolchazy-Carducci.

Artes Latinae Level I, Units 27-28. Sweet. 1 cass. 14.00 (978-0-86516-372-0(3)) Bolchazy-Carducci.

Artes Latinae Level I, Units 29-30. Sweet. 1 cass. 14.00 (978-0-86516-373-7(1)) Bolchazy-Carducci.

Artes Latinae Level I, Units 3-4. Sweet. 1 cass. 14.00 (978-0-86516-360-7(X)) Bolchazy-Carducci.

Artes Latinae Level I, Units 5-6. Sweet. 1 cass. 14.00 (978-0-86516-361-4(8)) Bolchazy-Carducci.

Artes Latinae Level I, Units 7-8. Sweet. 1 cass. 14.00 (978-0-86516-362-1(6)) Bolchazy-Carducci.

Artes Latinae Level I, Units 9-10. Sweet. 1 cass. 14.00 (978-0-86516-363-8(4)) Bolchazy-Carducci.

Artes Latinae Level II, Units 1-2. Sweet. 1 cass. 14.00 (978-0-86516-375-1(8)) Bolchazy-Carducci.

Artes Latinae Level II, Units 11-12. Sweet. 1 cass. 14.00 (978-0-86516-380-5(4)) Bolchazy-Carducci.

Artes Latinae Level II, Units 13-14. Sweet. 1 cass. 14.00 (978-0-86516-382-9(0)) Bolchazy-Carducci.

Artes Latinae Level II, Units 15-16. Sweet. 1 cass. 14.00 (978-0-86516-383-6(9)) Bolchazy-Carducci.

Artes Latinae Level II, Units 17-18. Sweet. 1 cass. 14.00 (978-0-86516-384-3(7)) Bolchazy-Carducci.

Artes Latinae Level II, Units 19-20. Sweet. 1 cass. 14.00 (978-0-86516-385-0(5)) Bolchazy-Carducci.

Artes Latinae Level II, Units 21-22. Sweet. 1 cass. 14.00 (978-0-86516-386-7(3)) Bolchazy-Carducci.

Artes Latinae Level II, Units 23-24. Sweet. 1 cass. 14.00 (978-0-86516-387-4(1)) Bolchazy-Carducci.

Artes Latinae Level II, Units 3-4. Sweet. 1 cass. 14.00 (978-0-86516-376-8(6)) Bolchazy-Carducci.

Artes Latinae Level II, Units 5-6. Sweet. 1 cass. 14.00 (978-0-86516-377-5(4)) Bolchazy-Carducci.

Artes Latinae Level II, Units 7-8. Sweet. 1 cass. 14.00 (978-0-86516-378-2(2)) Bolchazy-Carducci.

Artes Latinae Level II, Units 9-10. Sweet. 1 cass. 14.00 (978-0-86516-379-9(0)) Bolchazy-Carducci.

Arthritis. 1 cass. (Running Time: 1 hr.). 2001. 9.95 (CA604) Pub: VisnQst Vid Aud. Dist(s): TMW Media

Arthritis. Read by Robert S. Friedman & Kelly Howell. 1 cass. (Running Time: 60 mins.). (Sound Techniques for Healing Ser.). 1993. 11.95 (978-1-881451-23-5(2)) Brain Sync.
A revitalizing flow of energy through the autonomic nervous system activates the release of the body's natural cortisone to help reduce joint pain & swelling.

Arthritis. Bruce Goldberg. Read by Bruce Goldberg. 1 cass. (Running Time: 25 min.). (ENG.). 2006. 13.00 (978-1-885577-80-1(X)) Pub: B Goldberg. Dist(s): Baker Taylor
Eliminate discomfort and improve circulation through self-hypnosis.

Arthritis: Ancient Truths, Natural Remedies & the Latest Findings for Your Health Today. unabr. ed. Don Colbert. 1 cass. (Running Time: 1 hr. 30 mins.). (Bible Cure Ser.). 2002. 7.99 (978-1-58926-037-5(6)) Oasis Audio.

Arthritis: Ancient Truths, Natural Remedies & the Latest Findings for Your Health Today. unabr. ed. Don Colbert. Narrated by Steve Hiller. (Bible Cure Ser.). (ENG.). 2003. 6.99 (978-1-60814-046-6(6)); audio compact disk 9.99 (978-1-58926-115-0(1)) Oasis Audio.

Arthritis? Relief Through Good Food. Michael Klaper. 1 cass. (Running Time: 30 mins.). (Help Yourself to Health Ser.). 7.00 (978-0-929274-04-1(0)) Gentle World.
One of a series of tapes discussing the relationship between a diet free of animal products & improving one's health or a particular disease.

Arthritis: The Chinese Way of Healing & Prevention. Jwing-Ming Yang. Read by Richard Crittendon. 2 cass. (Running Time: 1 hr. 58 mins.). 1996.

bk. 15.95 (978-1-886969-41-4(8), A004) Pub: YMAA Pubn. Dist(s): Natl Bk Netwk
A description of traditional Chinese Qigong theory & how it is applied to relieve & prevent arthritis.

Arthritis Meditation. 1 cass. (Holistic Support Meditations Ser.). 14.98 (978-0-87554-578-3(5), MH101) Valley Sun.

Arthritis Pain Control: In Control. unabr. ed. 2 cass. (Running Time: 2 hrs.). 1989. bk. 74.95 incl. 60 min. video. (978-1-57970-039-3(X), S02015) J Norton Pubs.
The Arthritis Foundation program of exercises, self-management & problem-solving techniques based on self-help.

Arthritis Pain Relief. 2 CDs. 1980. audio compact disk 27.98 (978-1-56001-954-1(9)) Potentials.
Hypnosis can help relieve the pain of arthritis in any location of your body. If properly motivated, your mind can increase blood flow to the affected area and you'll probably feel better after listening to your program, for the first time.This 2-CD program from our Super Consciousness series is our newest, most powerful format. On the self-hypnosis CD, SC programs have the Subliminal Persuasion soundtrack added under Barrie?s voice. And the 17th Century Baroque music on the Subliminal CD has the same beat as your body's natural rhythm, thereby allowing the suggestions to enter deeply and effortlessly.

Arthritis Pain Relief. Barrie Konicov. 1 cass. 11.98 (978-0-87082-314-5(0), 005) Potentials.
Explores how hypnosis can help relieve the pain of arthritis - regardless of its location in your body, by suggestions of progressive relaxation & increasing the flow of warm blood to the afflicted area. Available at no charge to those over 65 & living on a fixed or limited income.

Arthritisize: Arthritis Exercise Program. Scripts. 1. (Running Time: 69). 2000. 29.95 (978-0-9745352-1-0(4)); cass. & video 29.95 (978-0-9745352-2-7(2)) Arthritisize.
(Note: Arthritisize videotape must be viewed before listening to Arthritisize audiocassette)Arthritisize is a series of gentle exercises that can be done in the comfort of your own bed. Arthritisize was developed by Barbara Curty, who suffered from extremely painful osteo and rheumatoid arthritis, including painful scoliosis of the spine and servere cartilage loss in many joints of her body. Barbara knew that exercise was the key to lessening her pain but found that traditional exercises were just too painful. Arthritisize works to relieve Barbara's back, neck, shoulders, ribs, hips, knees, elbows, legs, fingers, wrists, ankles, toes, joint and muscle pain, with amazing results! Arthritisize is not for arthritics only. Anyone who suffers from chronic pain and stiffness can benefit from this remarkable program. As always, remember to consult with your physician before starting this or any exercise program.

Arthur. unabr. ed. Stephen R. Lawhead. Read by Nadia May & Frederick Davidson. 14 cass. (Running Time: 21 hrs.). (Pendragon Cycle Ser.: Bk. 3). 1995. 89.95 (978-0-7861-0766-7(9), 1615) Blckstn Audio.
They called him unfit to rule - a lowborn, callow boy, Uther's bastard. But his coming had been foretold in the songs of the bard Taliesin. He had learned powerful secrets at the knee of the mystical sage, Merlin. He was Arthur, Pendragon of the Island of the Mighty - who would rise to legendary greatness in a Britain torn by violence, greed & war...who would usher in a glorious reign of peace & prosperity...& who would fall at the treacherous hands of the one he loved more than life.

Arthur: The Pendragon Cycle, Book 3. unabr. ed. Stephen R. Lawhead & Frederick Davidson. (Running Time: 19 hrs. NaN mins.). 2008. 44.95 (978-1-4332-5504-5(9)); audio compact disk 120.00 (978-1-4332-5503-8(0)) Blckstn Audio.

Arthur & Friends: The First Almost Real Not Live. Perf. by Ziggy Marley et al. Characters created by Marc Brown. (Running Time: 43 mins.). (Arthur Ser.). (J). audio compact disk (978-1-57940-040-8(X)) Rounder Records.
Now parents & children have a musical recording that carries on the positive message of the beloved Arthur books & television program, instilling self-esteem & respect for others. With the much-loved theme song (performed by Ziggy Marley) & many other songs associated with this Emmy award-winning program, this recording features all the favorite characters from the program, including Arthur, D.W., Francine & more.

Arthur & Friends: The First Almost Real Not Live. Perf. by Ziggy Marley et al. Characters created by Marc Brown. 1 CD. (Running Time: 1 hr.). (Arthur Ser.). (J). 1999. audio compact disk (978-1-57940-038-5(8)); audio compact disk (978-1-57940-041-5(8)) Rounder Records.

Arthur & Friends Collection: Buster's Dino Dilemma - Who's in Love with Arthur - Arthur Rocks with Binky - Francine, Believe it or Not. unabr. ed. Marc Brown. Read by Mark Linn-Baker. (Running Time: 9300 sec.). (ENG.). (J). (gr. 1-4). 2007. audio compact disk 19.95 (978-0-7393-3875-9(7), Listening Lib) Pub: Random Audio Pubg. Dist(s): Random

Arthur & George. Julian Barnes. Read by Nigel Anthony. 12 cass. (Running Time: 62220 sec.). (Sound Library). 2006. 96.95 (978-0-7927-3862-6(4), CSL 884) AudioGO.

***Arthur & George.** Julian Barnes. Narrated by Nigel Anthony. (Running Time: 5 hrs. 0 mins. 0 sec.). (ENG.). 2010. audio compact disk 34.95 (978-1-84607-166-9(6)) Pub: AudioGO. Dist(s): Perseus Dist

Arthur & George. unabr. ed. Julian Barnes. Read by Nigel Anthony. 14 CDs. (Running Time: 62220 sec.). (Sound Library). 2006. audio compact disk 115.95 (978-0-7927-3863-3(2), SLD 884) AudioGO.

Arthur & the Cootie-Catcher, Vol. 15. unabr. ed. Marc Brown. Read by Mark Linn-Baker. Text by Stephen Krensky. 1 cass. (Running Time: 44 mins.). (Arthur Chapter Bks.: Bk. 15). (J). (gr. 2-4). 2004. pap. bk. 17.00 (978-0-8072-0346-0(7), Listening Lib) Random Audio Pubg.

Arthur & the Crunch Cereal Contest. unabr. ed. Stephen Krensky. Read by Mark Linn-Baker. Characters created by Marc Brown. 2 cass. (Running Time: 41 mins.). (Arthur Chapter Bks.: Bk. 4). (J). (gr. 2-4). 1998. pap. bk. 17.00 (978-0-8072-0382-8(3), FTR190SP, Listening Lib) Random Audio Pubg.
Arthur enters the Crunch Cereal Contest & finds out the meaning of honesty.

Arthur & the Invisibles. movie tie-in abr. ed. Luc Besson. Read by Jim Dale. (Running Time: 34200 sec.). (J). (gr. 3-7). 2006. audio compact disk 27.95 (978-0-06-082103-6(5), HarperChildAud) HarperCollins Pubs.

Arthur & the Lost Diary. unabr. ed. Marc Brown. Read by Mark Linn-Baker. Text by Stephen Krensky. 2 cass. (Running Time: 36 mins.). (Arthur Chapter Bks.: Bk. 9). (J). (gr. 2-4). 1999. pap. bk. 17.00 (978-0-8072-0404-7(8), EFTR200SP, Listening Lib) Random Audio Pubg.

***Arthur & the Minimoys & Arthur & the Forbidden City U.** abr. ed. Luc Besson. Read by Jim Dale. (ENG.). 2006. (978-0-06-128745-9(8), HarperFestival); (978-0-06-128746-6(6), HarperFestival) HarperCollins Pubs.

Arthur & the Popularity Test. unabr. ed. Marc Brown. Read by Mark Linn-Baker. 2 cass. (Running Time: 41 mins.). (Arthur Chapter Bks.: Bk. 12). (J). (gr. 2-4). 2004. pap. bk. 17.00 (978-0-8072-0413-9(7), FTR204SP, Listening Lib) Random Audio Pubg.
When the gang takes a popularity test in a magazine for teenage girls, something strange happens to Fern & Sue Ellen. Fern, usually quiet, suddenly turns aggressive, while Sue Ellen typically so good at everything, starts to falter in all she attempts.

Arthur & the Scare-Your-Pants-off Club. unabr. ed. Stephen Krensky. Read by Mark Linn-Baker. Characters created by Marc Brown. 2 cass. (Running Time: 35 mins.). (Arthur Chapter Bks.: Bk. 2). (J). (gr. 2-4). 1998. pap. bk. 17.00 (978-0-8072-0376-7(9), FTR188SP, Listening Lib) Random Audio Pubg.
Arthur & his friends want to stop their favorite book from being banned.

Arthur & the True Francine. Marc Brown. 1 cass. (Arthur Adventure Ser.). (J). (gr. k-3). bk. 7.98 Blisterpack. (LBC 11946) NewSound.

Arthur Ashe. collector's ed. Caroline Lazo. Read by Ted Daniels. 1 cass. (Running Time: 90 mins.). (Biography Ser.). (YA). (gr. 5-12). 2000. 9.95 (978-0-7366-5034-2(2), 5215) Books on Tape.
He became the first African-American male tennis player to be ranked number one in the world. His contributions both on & off the tennis court continue to inspire people around the world.

Arthur Ashe. collector's ed. Caroline Lazo. Read by Ted Daniels. 2 cass. (Running Time: 3 hrs.). (YA). (gr. 5-12). 2000. 12.95 (978-0-7366-5219-3(1), 5215) Books on Tape.

Arthur Ashe. unabr. ed. Caroline Lazo. Read by Ted Daniels. 1 CD. (Running Time: 1 hr. 30 mins.). 2001. audio compact disk Books on Tape.

Arthur Ashe. unabr. ed. Caroline Lazo. Read by Ted Daniels. 1 cass. (Running Time: 1 hr. 30 min.). (YA). (gr. 5-12). 2000. 9.95 (978-0-7366-4707-6(4), 5215) Books on Tape.
Arthur Ashe became the first African-American male tennis player to be ranked number one in the world. His contributions both on & off the tennis court continue to inspire people around the world.

Arthur Babysits: A Story from Arthur's Audio Favorites, Volume 2. unabr. ed. Marc Brown. Read by Marc Brown. (Running Time: 12 mins.). (ENG.). 2009. 1.98 (978-1-60788-131-5(4)) Pub: Hachet Audio. Dist(s): HachBkGrp

Arthur Blessitt's Street University. Arthur Blessitt. 6 cass. (Running Time: 9 hrs.). 1985. 40.00 (978-0-934461-01-6(5)) Blessitt Pub.
Informal & educational about Christian Evangelism.

Arthur C. Clarke. Interview with Arthur C. Clarke. 1 cass. (Running Time: 45 mins.). 12.95 (L013) TFR.
The master of science fiction talks about the movie "2001: A Space Odyssey," based on his book & recalls his early prediction of the communications satellite; he also calls it a "scandal" that man has failed to domesticate any animal since the dog.

Arthur C. Clarke. unabr. ed. Arthur C. Clarke. 4 cass. (Running Time: 6 hrs.). Incl. Childhood's End. (SBC 121); Fountains of Paradise. Arthur C. Clarke. (SBC 121); Transit of Earth. (SBC 121); 2001: A Space Odyssey. Arthur C. Clarke. Read by Arthur C. Clarke. (SBC 121); 1985. 29.95 bklet. (978-0-89845-023-1(3), SBC 121) HarperCollins Pubs.

Arthur C. Clarke Audio Collection. abr. ed. Arthur C. Clarke. Read by Arthur C. Clarke. 4 cass. (Running Time: 4 hrs.). 1996. 19.95 (978-0-694-51622-3(8), CPN 1038) HarperCollins Pubs.
Author reads selections from his classic science fiction novels. Includes: "2001: A Space Odyssey", "Transit of Earth & Other Stories", "The Fountains of Paradise" & "Childhood's End".

Arthur Chapter Books Series Vol. 1: Arthur's Mystery Envelope; Arthur & the Scare-Your-Pants-Off Club; Arthur Makes the Team. unabr. ed. Marc Brown. Read by Mark Linn-Baker. 2 cass. (Arthur Chapter Bks.: Nos. 1-3). (J). (gr. 3-6). 1999. 16.98 (LL 0118, Chivers Child Audio) AudioGO.

Arthur Chapter Books Series Vol. 2: Arthur & the Crunch Cereal Contest; Arthur Accused!; Locked in the Library. unabr. ed. Marc Brown. Read by Mark Linn-Baker. 2 cass. (Arthur Chapter Bks.: Nos. 4-6). (J). (gr. 3-6). 1999. 16.98 (LL 0119, Chivers Child Audio) AudioGO.

Arthur Chapter Books Series Vol. 3: Buster's Dino Dilemma; The Mystery of the Stolen Bike; Arthur & the Lost Diary. unabr. ed. Marc Brown. Read by Mark Linn-Baker. 2 cass. (Arthur Chapter Bks.: Nos. 7-9). (J). (gr. 3-6). 1999. 16.98 (LL 0138, Chivers Child Audio) AudioGO.

Arthur Chapter Books Series Vol. 4: Who's in Love with Arthur?; Arthur Rocks with Binky; Arthur & the Popularity Test. Marc Brown. Read by Mark Linn-Baker. 2 cass. (Running Time: 60 mins. per cass.). (Arthur Chapter Bks.: Nos. 10-12). (J). (gr. 3-6). 2000. 18.00 (5161) Books on Tape.
Arthur & his gang are back again in a brand new collection of adventures. Includes "Who's in Love with Arthur," "Arthur Rocks with BINKY" & "Arthur & the Popularity Test.".

Arthur Chapter Books Series Vol. 4: Who's in Love with Arthur?; Arthur Rocks with Binky; Arthur & the Popularity Test. unabr. ed. Marc Brown. Read by Mark Linn-Baker. 2 cass. (Arthur Chapter Bks.: Nos. 10-12). (J). (gr. 3-6). 1999. 16.98 (LL 0149, Chivers Child Audio) AudioGO.

Arthur Conan Doyle: A Life. Hesketh Pearson. Read by Tim Pigott-Smith. 2 cass. (Running Time: 2 hrs. 30 min.). (YA). 2001. 13.98 (978-962-634-742-3(2), NA224214, Naxos AudioBooks); audio compact disk 17.98 (978-962-634-242-8(0), NA224212, Naxos AudioBooks) Naxos.
Comprehensive biography includes Doyle's background as a doctor and his enduring (and public) belief in spiritualism.

Arthur Conan Doyle: A Life. abr. ed. Hesketh Pearson. Read by Tim Pigott-Smith. 2 cass. (Running Time: 2 hrs. 30 min.). 2001. 13.98 (Naxos AudioBooks); audio compact disk 15.98 (Naxos AudioBooks) Naxos.

Arthur Conan Doyle Set: Sherlock Holmes Mysteries. unabr. ed. Arthur Conan Doyle. Read by Ralph Cosham. 6 cass. (Running Time: 8 hrs. 30 min.). (Great Authors Ser.). 1997. 34.95 (978-1-883049-74-4(1), Commuters Library) Sound Room.
Includes: "The Hound of the Baskervilles," "The Musgrave Ritual," "The Red-Headed League," "The Adventure of the Speckled Band" & "The Final Problem".

Arthur Conan Doyle: A Life: A Life. Hesketh Pearson. Read by Tim Pigott-Smith. (Running Time: 2 hrs. 30 mins.). (C). 2005. 20.95 (978-1-60083-679-4(8)) Iofy Corp.

Arthur Goes to Camp: A Story from Arthur's Audio Favorites, Volume 2. unabr. ed. Marc Brown. Read by Marc Brown. (Running Time: 12 mins.). (ENG.). 2009. 1.98 (978-1-60788-127-8(6)) Pub: Hachet Audio. Dist(s): HachBkGrp

Arthur Gregor. unabr. ed. Poems. Arthur Gregor. Read by Arthur Gregor. 1 cass. (Running Time: 29 min.). 1986. 8.00 New Letters.
Often ranked with the European symbolist poets, Gregor reads from "Embodiment & Other Poems".

Arthur, High King of Britain. unabr. ed. Michael Morpurgo. Read by Michael Morpurgo. 4 cass. (Running Time: 6 hrs.). (J). (gr. 1-8). 1999. 32.00 (LL 0157, Chivers Child Audio) AudioGO.

Arthur, High King of Britain. unabr. ed. Michael Morpurgo. Read by Michael Morpurgo. 4 cass. (Running Time: 4 hrs.). (YA). 1999. 29.98 (FS9-50955) Highsmith.

Arthur, High King of Britain. unabr. ed. Michael Morpurgo. Read by Michael Morpurgo. 4 cass. (Running Time: 6 hrs. 36 mins.). (J). (gr. 5-9). 2004. 32.00 (978-0-8072-8112-3(3), YA106CX, Listening Lib) Random Audio Pubg.
The timeless legend of King Arthur & the Round Table. This modern retelling begins in our own century, when a half-drowned boy regains consciousness in a strange sea cave & discovers his life has been saved by Arthur Pendragon High King of Britain.

Arthur King & the Curious Case of the Time Train. Dean Wilkinson. 4 CDs. 2006. audio compact disk 34.95 (978-0-7540-6729-0(7), Chivers Child Audio) AudioGO.

Arthur Koestler. unabr. ed. Arthur Koestler. 1 cass. (Author Speaks Ser.). 1991. 14.95 (AS26) J Norton Pubs.
Archival recordings of 20th-century authors.

Arthur Laffer: The Laffer Curve & the Future of Supply & Demand in Our Society. (Running Time: 60 mins.). (Cypress College). 1980. 9.00 (F111) Freeland Pr.
Explores various situations involving current "so-called" solutions to our present economic crisis.

Arthur Levitt: After the Crash, Now What? 1 cass. (Running Time: 1 hr.). 10.95 (NP-88-04-05, HarperThor) HarpC GBR.

Arthur Makes the Team. unabr. ed. Stephen Krensky. Read by Mark Linn-Baker. Characters created by Marc Brown. 1 cass. (Running Time: 37 mins.). (Arthur Chapter Bks.: Bk. 3). (J). (gr. 2-4). 1998. pap. bk. 17.00 (978-0-8072-0379-8(3), FTR189SP, Listening Lib) Random Audio Pubg.
Arthur tries out for a school team & learns what sportsmanship is about.

Arthur Meets the President: A Story from Arthur's Audio Favorites, Volume 2. unabr. ed. Marc Brown. Read by Marc Brown. (Running Time: 13 mins.). (ENG.). 2009. 1.98 (978-1-60788-130-8(6)) Pub: Hachet Audio. Dist(s): HachBkGrp

Arthur Miller Audio Collection. abr. unabr. ed. Arthur Miller & Arthur Miller. Read by Lee J. Cobb & Lincoln Center Theater Staff. Perf. by Mildred Dunnock et al. Directed By John D. Berry et al. 4 CDs. (Running Time: 4 hrs.). (gr. 9-12). 2002. audio compact disk 29.95 (978-0-06-050178-5(2)) HarperCollins Pubs.

Arthur Rocks with Binky, Vol. 11. unabr. ed. Marc Brown. Read by Mark Linn-Baker. Text by Stephen Krensky. 1 cass. (Running Time: 41 mins.). (Arthur Chapter Bks.: Bk. 11). (J). (gr. 2-4). 2004. pap. bk. 17.00 (978-0-8072-0410-8(2), FTR203SP, Listening Lib) Random Audio Pubg.
Arthur & the gang are thrilled to learn that the rock group Binky - not Binky Barnes - is giving a concert in their town. But thanks to D.W.'s indecision over a new pair of shoes, Arthur lands in row ZZZ.

Arthur Schopenhauer: Germany (1788-1860) Mark Stone. Read by Charlton Heston. Ed. by George H. Smith & Wendy McElroy. 2 cass. (Running Time: 3 hrs.). (Giants of Philosophy Ser.). 1995. 17.95 (978-0-938935-25-4(9), 10309) Knowledge Prod.
Schopenhauer was the most articulate & influential pessimist in the history of human thought. He believed the space & time of ordinary life are illusions, & that we can flourish only at each other's expense.

Arthur Schopenhauer: Germany (1788-1860) abr. ed. Narrated by Charlton Heston. (Running Time: 8018 sec.). (Audio Classics: the Giants of Philosophy Ser.). 2006. audio compact disk 25.95 (978-0-7861-6940-5(0)) Pub: Blckstn Audio. Dist(s): NetLibrary CO

Arthur Schopenhauer: Germany (1788-1860). unabr. ed. Read by Charlton Heston. 2 cass. (Giants of Philosophy Ser.). 17.95 (K125) Blckstn Audio.
See how one of the world's most important philosophers created a complete system of thought, including his views on ethics, metaphysics, politics & aesthetics. Learn about his epistemology - how we know what we know.

Arthur Sze. unabr. ed. Read by Arthur Sze. 1 cass. (Running Time: 29 min.). 1987. 8.00 (11) New Letters.
A second generation Chinese-American poet, Sze reads works by T'ao Ch'ien & Wang Wei & discusses his experiences in China.

Arthur Travelpak: Arthur & the Crunch Cereal Contest & Arthur Makes the Team. unabr. ed. Marc Brown. 2 cass. (Running Time: 2 hrs.). (J). 1999. 34.95 (978-0-929071-52-7(2)) B-B Audio.
Plugn Play Travelpaks contain everything your customers will need for many hours of audiobook listening. 2 Fantastic Audiobooks with1 Portable Cassette Player plus1 Comfortable Headset plus 2 Batteriers ARTHUR TRAVELPAK 2 HoursARTHUR AND THE CRU.

Arthur Writes a Story (A Story from Arthur's Audio Favorites, Volume 1) unabr. ed. Marc Brown. Read by Marc Brown. (Running Time: 10 mins.). (ENG.). 2008. 3.98 (978-1-60024-308-0(8)) Pub: Little Brn Bks. Dist(s): HachBkGrp

Arthurian Omen. G. G. Vandagriff. Read by Jane Hughes. (Running Time: 31500 sec.). 2008. audio compact disk 24.95 (978-1-59038-889-1(5), Shadow Mount) Deseret Bk.

Arthur's April Fool. Marc Brown. (Arthur Adventure Ser.). (J). (gr. k-3). 1986. 42.66 (978-0-676-30730-6(2)) SRA McGraw.

Arthur's Audio Favorites, Vol. 1. unabr. ed. Marc Brown. Read by Marc Brown. (Running Time: 1 hr. 15 mins.). (ENG.). 2007. 14.98 (978-1-60024-093-5(3)) Pub: Little Brn Bks. Dist(s): HachBkGrp

Arthur's Audio Favorites, Vol. 2. unabr. ed. Marc Brown. Read by Marc Brown. (Running Time: 1 hr.). (ENG.). 2009. audio compact disk 13.98 (978-1-60024-659-3(1)) Pub: Hachet Audio. Dist(s): HachBkGrp

Arthur's Audio Favorites, Volume 2. unabr. ed. Marc Brown. Read by Marc Brown. (Running Time: 1 hr.). (ENG.). 2009. 9.98 (978-1-60024-660-9(5)) Pub: Hachet Audio. Dist(s): HachBkGrp

Arthur's Baby. Marc Brown. 1 cass. (Running Time: 10 min.). (Arthur Adventure Ser.). (J). (gr. k-3). 1997. bk. 9.95 Pub: Little Brn Bks. Dist(s): Little

Arthur's Baby: A Story from Arthur's Audio Favorites, Volume 2. unabr. ed. Marc Brown. Read by Marc Brown. (Running Time: 10 mins.). (ENG.). 2009. 1.98 (978-1-60788-129-2(2)) Pub: Hachet Audio. Dist(s): HachBkGrp

Arthur's Birthday. Marc Brown. 1 cass. (Running Time: 30 mins.). (Arthur Adventure Ser.). (J). (gr. k-3). 2000. pap. bk. 9.98 (T 4941 SP, Listening Lib) Random Audio Pubg.

Arthur's Birthday (A Story from Arthur's Audio Favorites, Volume 1) unabr. ed. Marc Brown. Read by Marc Brown. (Running Time: 10 mins.). (ENG.). 2008. 3.98 (978-1-60024-307-3(X)) Pub: Little Brn Bks. Dist(s): HachBkGrp

***Arthur's Camp-Out.** unabr. ed. Lillian Hoban. Read by Lillian Hoban. (ENG.). 2007. (978-0-06-145216-1(5)); (978-0-06-146920-6(3)) HarperCollins Pubs.

***Arthur's Christmas Cookies.** unabr. ed. Lillian Hoban. Read by Lillian Hoban. (ENG.). 2007. (978-0-06-146927-5(0)); (978-0-06-145220-8(3)) HarperCollins Pubs.

Arthur's Christmas Cookies. unabr. abr. ed. Lillian Hoban. Illus. by Lillian Hoban. 1 cass. (I Can Read Bks.). (J). (gr. k-3). 1990. 8.99 (978-1-55994-217-1(7)) HarperCollins Pubs.

Arthur's Christmas Cookies, Level 2. Lillian Hoban. 1 read-along cass. (Running Time: 15 mins.). (I Can Read Bks.). (J). (gr. k-3). 1986. bk. 5.98 (978-0-694-00162-0(7), JC-145) HarperCollins Pubs.

Arthur's Family Vacation: A Story from Arthur's Audio Favorites, Volume 2. unabr. ed. Marc Brown. Read by Marc Brown. (Running Time: 12 mins.). (ENG.). 2009. 1.98 (978-1-60788-132-2(2)) Pub: Hachet Audio. Dist(s): HachBkGrp

Arthur's First Sleepover (A Story from Arthur's Audio Favorites, Volume 1) unabr. ed. Marc Brown. Read by Marc Brown. (Running Time: 10 mins.). (ENG.). 2008. 3.98 (978-1-60024-306-6(1)) Pub: Little Brn Bks. Dist(s): HachBkGrp

***Arthur's Funny Money.** unabr. ed. Lillian Hoban. Read by Lillian Hoban. (ENG.). 2007. (978-0-06-145221-5(1)); (978-0-06-146924-4(6)) HarperCollins Pubs.

Arthur's Funny Money. unabr. abr. ed. Lillian Hoban. Illus. by Lillian Hoban. (I Can Read Bks.). (J). (gr. k-3). 1990. 8.99 (978-1-55994-218-8(5)) HarperCollins Pubs.

Arthur's Halloween: A Story from Arthur's Audio Favorites, Volume 2. unabr. ed. Marc Brown. Read by Marc Brown. (Running Time: 11 mins.). (ENG.). 2009. 1.98 (978-1-60788-128-5(4)) Pub: Hachet Audio. Dist(s): HachBkGrp

***Arthur's Honey Bear.** unabr. ed. Lillian Hoban. Read by Lillian Hoban. (ENG.). 2007. (978-0-06-146923-7(8)); (978-0-06-145222-2(X)) HarperCollins Pubs.

Arthur's Honey Bear. unabr. abr. ed. Lillian Hoban. Illus. by Lillian Hoban. 1 cass. (I Can Read Bks.). (J). (gr. k-3). 1990. 8.99 (978-1-55994-219-5(3)) HarperCollins Pubs.

Arthur's Loose Tooth. abr. ed. Lillian Hoban. Illus. by Lillian Hoban. (I Can Read Bks.). (J). (ps-3). 2003. 8.99 (978-0-694-01578-8(4)) HarperCollins Pubs.

Arthur's Mystery Envelope. unabr. ed. Stephen Krensky. Read by Mark Linn-Baker. Characters created by Marc Brown. 1 cass. (Running Time: 34 mins.). (Arthur Chapter Bks.: Bk. 1). (J). (gr. 2-4). 1998. pap. bk. 17.00 (978-0-8072-0372-9(6), FTR187SP, Listening Lib) Random Audio Pubg.
Arthur brings an envelope home from school.

Arthur's New Puppy. Marc Brown. 1 cass. (Arthur Adventure Ser.). (J). (gr. k-3). bk. 7.98 Blisterpack. (LBC 11949) NewSound.
Features the theme song "Say Hello to Arthur" & includes turn-the-page signals on one side & uninterrupted narration on the other.

Arthur's New Puppy (A Story from Arthur's Audio Favorites, Volume 1) unabr. ed. Marc Brown. Read by Marc Brown. (Running Time: 10 mins.). (ENG.). 2008. 3.98 (978-1-60024-304-2(5)) Pub: Little Brn Bks. Dist(s): HachBkGrp

***Arthur's Pen Pal.** unabr. ed. Lillian Hoban. Read by Lillian Hoban. (ENG.). 2007. (978-0-06-145219-2(X)); (978-0-06-146926-8(2)) HarperCollins Pubs.

Arthur's Pen Pal. unabr. abr. ed. Lillian Hoban. Illus. by Lillian Hoban. 1 cass. (I Can Read Bks.). (J). (gr. k-3). 1990. 8.99 (978-1-55994-238-6(X)) HarperCollins Pubs.

Arthur's Pet Business (A Story from Arthur's Audio Favorites, Volume 1) unabr. ed. Marc Brown. Read by Marc Brown. (Running Time: 10 mins.). (ENG.). 2008. 3.98 (978-1-60024-309-7(6)) Pub: Little Brn Bks. Dist(s): HachBkGrp

Arthur's Prize Reader. Lillian Hoban. 1 read-along cass. (Running Time: 15 mins.). (I Can Read Bks.). (J). (gr. 1-3). HarperCollins Pubs.
One side has a turn-the-page beep signal & the other side is uninterrupted narration for more experienced readers.

***Arthur's Prize Reader.** unabr. ed. Lillian Hoban. Read by Lillian Hoban. (ENG.). 2007. (978-0-06-146922-0(X)); (978-0-06-145225-3(4)) HarperCollins Pubs.

Arthur's Really Rockin' Music Mix. 1 CD. (Running Time: 44 mins.). 2001. audio compact disk 13.98 Rhino Enter.

Arthur's Tooth (A Story from Arthur's Audio Favorites, Volume 1) unabr. ed. Marc Brown. Read by Marc Brown. (Running Time: 10 mins.). (ENG.). 2008. 3.98 (978-1-60024-305-9(3)) Pub: Little Brn Bks. Dist(s): HachBkGrp

Arthur's Valentine. Marc Brown. (Arthur Adventure Ser.). (J). (gr. k-3). 1986. bk. 42.52 (978-0-394-69884-7(3)) SRA McGraw.

Artichokes & Brussels Sprouts. Fran Avni. Read by Fran Avni. 1 cass. (Running Time: 1 hr.). (J). (ps-1). 1992. 9.98 (978-1-877737-85-5(2), MLP 275) MFLP CA.
Activity & sing along songs - samples of jazz, march, classical, reggae & others.

Articles from Classic Issues. 1 cass. 1986. 5.50 (3004) Hazelden.
Articles taken from the "AA Grapevine," the monthly international journal of Alcoholics Anonymous.

Articles of Faith. Omni Marketing Staff. 1 cass. bk. 6.95 (978-1-57008-021-0(6), Bkcraft Inc) Deseret Bk.

Articles of Faith. James E. Talmage & John R. Fishbein. Narrated by Rex Campbell. 9 cass. (Running Time: 9 hrs.). 2004. 29.95 (978-1-55503-352-1(0), 030015) Covenant Comms.

Articles of Faith. unabr. ed. James E. Talmage. 11 CDs. 2004. audio compact disk 29.95 (978-1-59156-283-2(X)) Covenant Comms.

Articles of War. unabr. ed. Nick Arvin. Read by J. D. Cullum. (YA). 2007. 44.99 (978-1-60252-816-1(0)) Find a World.

Articulate Executive: Learn to Look, Act, & Sound Like a Leader. Granville N. Toogood. 3 cass. (Running Time: 4 hrs. 30 min.). 2003. 24.00 (978-1-932378-08-5(1)) Pub: A Media Intl. Dist(s): Natl Bk Netwk

Articulate Executive: Learn to Look, Act, & Sound Like a Leader. Granville N. Toogood. 3 cass. (Running Time: 4 hrs. 30 mins.). 2003. audio compact disk 28.00 (978-1-932378-09-2(X)) Pub: A Media Intl. Dist(s): Natl Bk Netwk

Artifact. Patrick Astre. Read by Patrick Cullen. (Running Time: 28800 sec.). 2006. 54.95 (978-0-7861-4591-1(9)); audio compact disk 63.00 (978-0-7861-6997-9(4)) Blckstn Audio.

Artifact. unabr. ed. Patrick Astre. Read by Patrick Cullen. (Running Time: 28800 sec.). 2006. audio compact disk 29.95 (978-0-7861-7513-0(3)) Blckstn Audio.

Artifact Collective Audio. Jack Foley et al. Read by Jack Foley et al. 1 cass. (Running Time: 1 hr.). (Artifact Collective Ser.). 1989. 6.00 (978-0-944215-06-7(8)) Ninth St Lab.
Includes performances of poetry & prose by the poets & authors, some with accompaniment, some not.

Artificial Intelligence: Program from the Award Winning Public Radio Series. Hosted by Fred Goodwin. 1 CD. (Running Time: 1 Hour). 2001. audio compact disk 21.95 (978-1-932479-22-5(8), LCM 166) Lichtenstein Creat.
Here we are in the year 2001, and - despite the movie's predictions - computers have yet to develop minds of their own. How close are we to developing machines that can simulate human thought? This week on the Infinite Mind, we look at the latest research on Artificial Intelligence. Guests include Brian Aldiss, writer of the short-story, "Super Toys Last All Summer Long," which is the inspiration for Steven Spielberg's upcoming movie, AI: Artificial Intelligence; Dr. Peter Norvig, co-author of the standard textbook on AI, Artificial Intelligence: A Modern Approach and Chief of the Computational Sciences Division at NASA's Ames Research Center in California; Dr. Rosalind Picard, founder and director of the Affective Computing Research Group at the MIT Media Lab; and Dr. Marvin Minsky, a pioneer in the field of AI, who's now a professor in the MIT Media Lab and was co-founder and, for many years, director of the MIT Artificial Intelligence Lab.

***Artificial Night.** unabr. ed. Seanan McGuire. Read by Mary Robinette Kowal. (Running Time: 12 hrs.). (October Daye Ser.). 2010. 39.97 (978-1-4418-5813-9(X), 9781441858139, BADLE); 24.99 (978-1-4418-5812-2(1), 9781441858122, BAD); 39.97 (978-1-4418-5811-5(3), 9781441858115, Brinc Audio MP3 Lib); 14.99 (978-1-4418-5810-8(5), 9781441858108, Brilliance MP3); audio compact disk 29.99 (978-1-4418-5808-5(3), 9781441858085, Bril Audio CD Unabri); audio compact disk 89.97 (978-1-4418-5809-2(1), 9781441858092, BriAudCD Unabrid) Brilliance Audio.

ARTineraries Tour: Basilica of St. Francis of Assisi: Assisi. Created by Art&Media Communications. Prod. by Art&Media Communications.Tr. of Basilica di San Francesco. (ENG & ITA.). 2007. 14.95 (978-0-9778932-3-2(5), Artineraries Tours) Art N Media MI.

ARTineraries Tour: Journey to the IIc. A. D.: Ostia Antica. Created by Art&Media Communications. Prod. by Art&Media Communications.Tr. of Viaggio nel IIc. D. c. (ENG & ITA.). 2008. 14.95 (978-0-9778932-6-3(X), Artineraries Tours) Art N Media MI.

ARTineraries Tour: Paris - London - Edinburgh - Milan: in the Footsteps of Da Vinci. Scripts. Created by Art&Media Communications. Prod. by Art&Media Communications. 2 CDs. (Running Time: 90 mins). (ENG.). 2006. 13.50 (978-0-9778932-2-5(7), Artineraries Tours) Art N Media MI.
Join our very own Symbologist, and you?ll soon be following in the footsteps of Leonardo Da Vinci from the Louvre to Milan where he lived and worked, and onto London and Edinburgh in search of the Holy Grail, Newton?s Tomb, and the Knights Templar. In 90 mins. of audio, we?ll reveal the facts behind the fictional players and the fabulous places of the Da Vinci Code.Artineraries Tour 2 Cd set includes mini-guide to Da Vinci?s works, Paris, the Louvre and more!Artineraries...Exceptional Sounds for Extraordinary Sights?.

ARTineraries Tour: Temple of the Gods. Created by Art&Media Communications. Prod. by Art&Media Communications.Tr. of Tempio degli Dei. (ENG & ITA.). 2007. 4.95 (978-0-9778932-5-6(1), Artineraries Tours) Art N Media MI.

ARTineraries Tour Padova: Giotto¿s Scrovegni Family Chapel. Created by Art&Media Communications. Prod. by Art&Media Communications.Tr. of Cappella degli Scrovegni di Giotto. (ENG & ITA.). 2007. 4.95 (978-0-9778932-4-9(3), Artineraries Tours) Art N Media MI.

ARTineraries Tour Torino: Majestic & Magical City. Scripts. Created by Art&Media Communications. Prod. by Art&Media Communications. 1 CD. (Running Time: 70 mins.). Dramatization.Tr. of Maestosa & Magica Città. (ENG & ITA.). 2006. 11.95 (978-0-9778932-0-1(0), Artineraries Tours) Art N Media MI.
Put on your walking shoes and Download the Past? through an informative and entertaining walking tour of Turin, Italy?s first capital city. You?ll discover the Majesty & Magic of Baroque Turin, with Amedeo Castellamonte, Chief Architect to the Dukes of Savoy and their Madame Royale, as your guide.As you explore the city?s fabulous palaces and piazzas, long kept secrets of Italy?s first royal family will be revealed along with Torino?s historical past, its underground secrets and its place as a source of black and white magic, with many enticing tidbits along the way!Artineraries...Exceptional Sounds for Extraordinary Sights?.

ARTineraries Vatican Tour: Sister Wendy's Sistine Chapel. As told by Sister Wendy Beckett. 2 CDs. (Running Time: 95 mins). 2006. 14.95 (978-0-9778932-1-8(9), Artineraries Tours) Art N Media MI.
See the Sistine Chapel and St. Peter's Basilica as you have never seen them before! In an Audio Tour lovingly narrated by Sister Wendy, you'll open your eyes and heart to the magnificent wonders of the Vatican Museums and Sistine Ceiling, and be immersed in the spirituality that permeates St. Peter's Basilica and the entire Vatican City.90 minute Travel Guide for download.

Artist As Seer. Mark Levy. 1 cass. 9.00 (A0436-88) Sound Photosyn.
ICSS '88, Levy explains his thoughts well for a non-viewing audience. With Suzanne Palmer & Hill.

Artist Descending a Staircase. unabr. ed. Tom Stoppard. Perf. by Stephen Murray et al. 1 cass. 12.95 (ECN 043) J Norton Pubs.
In this specially commissioned radio play, Stoppard set out to write a piece that could not be transferred to the stage.

Artist-Entrepreneurs: Saint Gaudens, MacMonnies, Parish. unabr. ed. Dianne Durante. 1 cass. (Running Time: 1 hrs. 30 mins.). 1998. 13.95 (978-1-56114-477-8(0), MD52C) Second Renaissance.
An overview of the lives & works of three American artists at the turn of the century.

Artist of the Floating World. collector's ed. Kazuo Ishiguro. Read by David Case. 7 cass. (Running Time: 7 hrs.). 1999. 56.00 (978-0-7366-4773-1(2), 5117) Books on Tape.
Bohemian artist Masuji Ono envisioned a strong & powerful Japan of the future & put his work in the service of the imperialist movement that led Japan into World War II. Drifting in disgrace in postwar Japan, indicted by society for its defeat & reviled for his past aesthetics, he relives the personal history that makes him both a hero & a coward.

Artistic Creativity. Mary Lee LaBay. 2006. audio compact disk 9.95 (978-1-934705-11-7(X)) Awareness Engin.

Artistic Destruction: The Chinese Cultural Revolution. 1 cass. (Running Time: 30 mins.). 9.95 (B0140B090, HarperThor) HarpC GBR.

Artistic Differences. unabr. ed. Charlie Hauck. Narrated by George Guidall. 6 cass. (Running Time: 8 hrs.). 1993. 51.00 (978-1-55690-895-8(4), 93337E7) Recorded Bks.
Hollywood insider Hauck spoofs Burbank in this raucous comedy about two producer/writers looking to score a syndicated television series. When their leading lady takes charge, look for the action & the laughs to run in overdrive.

Artistry of Artificial Hair. Milady Publishing Company Staff. 1 cass. (Standard Ser.: Chapter 15). 1995. 11.95 (978-1-56253-287-1(1), Milady) Pub: Delmar. Dist(s): CENGAGE Learn

Artistry of Ruth Draper. Ruth Draper. Read by Ruth Draper. 2 cass. (Running Time: 1 hr. 47 mins.). 15.95 (AO-045, HarperThor); 9.95 no. 1, 58 mins. (AO-04A, HarperThor); 9.95 no. 2, 49 mins. (AO-04B, HarperThor) HarpC GBR.

Artists Acappella: The Signature Songs. 1 cass. (Running Time: 1 hr.). 1998. 10.98 (978-1-878990-99-0(3)); audio compact disk 16.98 (978-1-878990-98-3(5)) Provident Mus Dist.
The songs that changed our lives, from the artists that carried the message.

Artist's Blue. Jody Wright. 2 CDs. 2003. audio compact disk 19.95 (978-0-9722299-4-4(9)) WSG Gallery.

Artists in a Time of War. Howard Zinn. (AK Press Audio Ser.). (ENG.). 2002. audio compact disk 14.98 (978-1-902593-65-4(0)) Pub: AK Pr GBR. Dist(s): Consort Bk Sales

Artists in Crime. Ngaio Marsh. 2009. 61.95 (978-0-7531-4452-7(2)); audio compact disk 79.95 (978-0-7531-4453-4(0)) Pub: Isis Pubng Ltd GBR. Dist(s): Ulverscroft US

Artists in Crime. abr. ed. Ngaio Marsh. Read by Benedict Cumberbatch. (Running Time: 3 hrs. 44 mins. 0 sec.). (ENG.). 2008. audio compact disk 29.95 (978-1-4055-0510-9(9)) Pub: Little BrownUK GBR. Dist(s): IPG Chicago

Artists in Crime. unabr. ed. Ngaio Marsh. Read by Nadia May. 7 cass. (Running Time: 10 hrs.). 1994. 49.95 (978-0-7861-0692-9(1), 1477) Blckstn Audio.
When murder upsets the creative tranquility of an artists' colony, Scotland Yard sends in its most famous investigator. And what begins as a routine case turns out to be the most momentous of Roderick Alleyn's career. For before he can corner the killer, his heart is captured by one of the suspects - the flashing-eyed painter Agatha Troy, who has nothing but scorn for the art of detection.

Artists in Crime. unabr. ed. Ngaio Marsh. Read by James Saxon. 8 cass. (Running Time: 12 hrs.). (Inspector Alleyn Mystery Ser.). 2000. 59.95 (978-0-7451-4138-1(2), CAB 821) Pub: Chivers Audio Bks GBR. Dist(s): AudioGO
It began as a student exercise, the knife under the drape, and the model's pose chalked in place. But before Agatha Troy, artist and instructor, returns to the class, the pose has been re-enacted in earnest. It is a difficult case for Inspector Alleyn, who loves Agatha, but nobody is above suspicion.

***Artists in Crime.** unabr. ed. Ngaio Marsh. Read by Nadia May. (Running Time: 10 hrs.). 2010. 29.95 (978-1-4417-4363-3(4)); audio compact disk 90.00 (978-1-4417-4360-2(X)) Blckstn Audio.

Artists of Brown County. Lyn Letsinger-Miller. Prod. by Lyn Letsinger-Miller. Narrated by Clyde Lee. Contrib. by Jon Kay. (Running Time: 1800 sec.). (ENG.). 2007. 14.95 (978-0-253-35044-2(1)) Ind U Pr.

Artist's Proof. unabr. ed. Gordon Cotler. Narrated by Richard Poe. 6 cass. (Running Time: 8 hrs. 30 mins.). 1998. 51.00 (978-0-7887-1307-1(8), 95149E7) Recorded Bks.
Retired policeman, Sid Shale, is living in a shabby beach house as an artist. But his sleepy community is rocked by the murder of a 16-year- old girl.

Artist's Struggle for Integrity. unabr. ed. James Baldwin. Read by James Baldwin. 1 cass. (Running Time: 32 mins.). 1962. 12.95 (23029) J Norton Pubs.
A speech by Baldwin at the Community Church in New York. He points out that his title is really a metaphor.

Artist's Way. Julia Cameron. (ENG.). (gr. 8). 2005. audio compact disk 25.95 (978-0-14-305825-0(8), PengAudBks) Penguin Grp USA.

Artists Way at Work: Riding the Dragon: Twelve Weeks to Creative Freedom. Mark Bryan. Based on a work by Julia Cameron. 2004. 10.95 (978-0-7435-4173-2(1)) Pub: S&S Audio. Dist(s): S and S Inc

Artist's Widow. unabr. ed. Shena Mackay. Read by Rachel Atkins. 4 cass. (Running Time: 6 hrs.). (Isis Ser.). (J). 2000. 44.95 (978-0-7531-0819-2(4), 001115) Pub: ISIS Lrg Prnt GBR. Dist(s): Ulverscroft US

Arts & Culture: Standalone Music CD. 2nd ed. Benton & Di Yanni. audio compact disk 18.97 (978-0-13-192000-2(6)) PH School.

Arts & Culture: Volume 2: an Introduction to the Humanities. 2nd ed. Janetta Rebold Benton & Robert DiYanni. 2004. pap. bk. 100.40 (978-0-13-162185-5(8)) Pearson Educ CAN CAN.

Arts & Letters. unabr. ed. 1 cass. (Berkeley University Weekly Broadcasts Ser.). 12.95 (23701) J Norton Pubs.
"Legacy of Letters" on Mark Twain's correspondence with William Dean Howells; "Catlin's Country" on George Catlin, the first great painter of American Indians; "Secret Life of Samuel Pepys" about the most famous diary in the world; & "Letters of Genius" about Michaelangelo's correspondence with his family.

Arts in Medical Education: A Practical Guide. Elaine Powley & Roger Higson. 2005. pap. bk. 75.00 (978-1-85775-626-5(6)) Pub: Radcliffe Pubng GBR. Dist(s): JAMCO Dist

Art's Prospect. Roger Kimball. Read by Christopher Lane. (Running Time: 7 hrs. 30 mins.). 2003. 27.95 (978-1-59912-424-7(6)) Iofy Corp.

Art's Prospect. Roger Kimball & Christopher Lane. 6 cass. (Running Time: 8 hrs. 30 mins.). 2002. 44.95 (978-0-7861-2587-6(X), 3188) Blckstn Audio.

Art's Prospect: The Challenge of Tradition in an Age of Celebrity. unabr. ed. Roger Kimball. Read by Christopher Lane. 7 CDs. (Running Time: 8 hrs. 30 mins.). 2003. audio compact disk 56.00 (978-0-7861-8979-3(7), 3188) Blckstn Audio.

ArtSource Clip Art Library Version 2.0. unabr. ed. Created by Church Art Works. 1999. audio compact disk 59.95 (978-0-310-22759-5(3)) Youth Spec.

Artsource Clip Art Library 3.0: More Than 1,750 Youth Group-Specific Images for Every Imaginable Ministry Use. unabr. ed. Church Artworks Staff & Art Parts Staff. 2003. audio compact disk 59.99 (978-0-310-24645-9(8)) Zondervan.

Arturo Arias: After the Bombs. unabr. ed. Arturo Arias. Read by Arturo Arias. Interview with Rebekah Presson. 1 cass. (Running Time: 29 min.). 1991. 8.00 (011891) New Letters.
A prominent Central American writer, Arias, helped write the screenplay for the movie "El Norte". Here, he reads from his novel "After the Bombs".

Arty, the Love Angel. rev. ed. Gina Beth Clark. 1 cass. (Running Time: 1 hr. 30 min.). 2001. (978-0-9712681-1-8(8)) G B C Audio Bk.
Story of an angel who has one last task before earning his wings.

Arty, the Love Angel. rev. ed. Gina Beth Clark. 1 CD. (Running Time: 1 hr. 30 mins.). 2002. audio compact disk (978-0-9712681-9-7(3), 043-014) G B C Audio Bk.

***Artza Alinu: (We Are Ascending)** Jill Gallina. (Running Time: 2 mins.). (ENG.). 2010. audio compact disk 26.99 (978-1-4234-8584-1(X), 142348584X) Pub: Shawnee Pr. Dist(s): H Leonard

***Arutiunian - Trumpet Concerto & Goedicke - Concert Etude: For Trumpet.** Composed by Alexander Arutiunian & Alexander Goedicke. Richard Steuart. 2009. pap. bk. 34.98 (978-1-59615-099-7(8), 1596150998) Pub: Music Minus. Dist(s): H Leonard

As a Driven Leaf. abr. ed. Milton Steinberg. Read by George Guidall. 5 cass. (Running Time: 7 hrs. 40 mins.). 2000. 39.95 (978-1-893079-04-5(X), JCCAUDIOBOOKS) Jewish Contempry Classics.
Novel of the clash between Judaism & the pagan world of Rome, in which the fictional & historic characters co-exist & mingle.

As a Man Speaketh, So Is He. Grant Von Harrison. Read by Ted Gibbons. 1 cass. (Personal Enrichment Ser.). 6.95 (978-0-929985-28-2(1)) Jackman Pubng.
Using the New Testament as the basic text. It explores the idea of the way one speaks reflecting what they are.

As a Man Thinketh. James Allen. Read by Billy Nash. 2 cass. (Running Time: 2 hrs.). 1997. 17.95 (978-1-57949-010-2(7)) Destination Success.
You are what you think. You are literally the sum of your thoughts. Action only comes once the seeds of thought have been planted & sowed. You are who you are by the virtue of the thoughts which you choose & pursue.

As a Man Thinketh. James Allen. 2007. audio compact disk 19.99 (978-956-8351-62-5(0)) Edit Benei CHL.

As a Man Thinketh. James Allen. Read by Charlie Tremendous Jones. (Life-Changing Classics Ser.). (ENG.). 2007. audio compact disk 19.95 (978-1-933715-38-4(3)) Executive Bks.

As a Man Thinketh. James Allen. Narrated by Billy Nash. 2 cass. (Running Time: 2 hrs.). 1997. 17.95 Set. F Fell Pubs Inc.
Shows how you are "the master of thought, the molder of character & the maker & shaper of condition, environment & destiny." You are who you are by virtue of the thoughts which you choose & pursue.

As a Man Thinketh. James Allen. (5172) Meyer Res Grp.

As a Man Thinketh. Taylor Clark-Falksen. 1 cass. 8.95 (055) Am Fed Astrologers.

As a Man Thinketh. unabr. ed. James Allen. Read by Robert Young. 1 cass. (Running Time: 60 mins.). 1988. 9.95 (978-0-87516-605-6(9)) DeVorss.
The power of thought.

***As A Man Thinketh.** unabr. ed. James Allen. Narrated by Ray Porter. (Running Time: 0 hr. 56 mins. 0 sec.). (ENG.). 2010. audio compact disk 9.98 (978-1-61045-087-4(6), MissionAud) christianaud.

As a Man Thinketh: Bonus by Woodrow Wilson When a Man Comes to Himself. James Allen. Narrated by Ross M. Armetta. 1 CD. (Running Time: 72 Mins. Aprox.). 2005. audio compact disk 12.99 (978-1-59733-004-6(3), Trans Greats) InfoFount.
As a Man Thinketh by James Allen has been universally recognized for almost 100 years as one of, if not the, most inspiring and powerful books ever written for self transformation. Written in simple, clear, and complete terms it describes how a person?s thinking will directly influence their life. It provides powerful suggestions on how a person may influence and better their life by controlling, their actions and circumstances - by what they think. As a Man Thinketh is not an overwhelming, complex treatise of useless theories. It is a concise, inspiring, and imminently useful audiobook. It will provide the keys for you to change yourself in relation to yourself and external forces.

As a Man Thinketh 2: As You Think So You Are. Ross M. Armetta. Based on a book by James Allen. 1 CD. (Running Time: 72 Mins. Aprox.). 2005. audio compact disk 12.99 (978-1-59733-003-9(5), Trans Greats) InfoFount.
This is a new, modernized, and supplemented audiobook version of James Allen?s classic As a Man Thinketh titled As a Man Thinketh 2: As You Think - So You Are by Ross Armetta. As a Man Thinketh has been universally recognized for almost 100 years as one of the most inspiring and powerful books ever written for self- transformation. It describes how your thinking will directly influence your life. It provides powerful suggestions on how you may influence and better your life by controlling your actions and circumstances - by what they think. The new As a Man Thinketh 2 / As You Think-So You Are Is more accessible and more actable than As a Man Thinketh. You can understand and use it easier and more effectively instead of just sensing the beauty and truth in it.

As a River of Light. Composed by John Foley. 1 cass. (Running Time: 1 hr.). 10.95 (5382); 39.95 instr. pkg. for performance. (5385); 7.95 choral pts. w/piano, single copy.; 19.95 conductor's full score. (5384); audio compact disk 15.95 (5381) OR Catholic.
A musical drama from the Gospel of Luke.

As a Woman Thinketh. C. Daniel Litchford. 2 cass. 7.98 incl. a bonus cass. of jingles. (978-1-55503-060-5(2), 0700584) Covenant Comms.

As Bad As It Gets. unabr. ed. Julian Rathbone. Narrated by Christopher Kay. 7 cass Lib. Ed. (Running Time: 9 hrs. 30 min.). 2004. 69.75 (978-1-84197-938-0(4), R1571) Recorded Bks.

As Bad As It Gets. unabr. collector's ed. Julian Rathbone. Narrated by Christopher Kay. 7 cass. (Running Time: 9 hrs. 30 min.). 2004. 32.95 (978-1-4025-7688-1(9), RH060) Recorded Bks.
Chris Shovelin is a private investigator on the move. He's just finished a job in Mombasa where he has been checking out the unsuspicious death of a millionaire's son in a scuba accident. He's made enough money to treat himself to a safari holiday, but he can't resist the offer of acting as minder to a wealthy woman who is planning the same vacation.

***As Easy as Falling off the Face of the Earth.** unabr. ed. Lynne Rae Perkins. Read by Chris Sorensen. (ENG.). 2010. (978-0-06-199152-3(X), GreenwillowBks); (978-0-06-199297-1(6), GreenwillowBks) HarperCollins Pubs.

As Far as the Curse Is Found: Human Suffering & the Hope of the Gospel. unabr. ed. Joni Eareckson Jada et al. 6 CDs. (Running Time: 5 hrs.). 2003. audio compact disk 35.95 (978-1-930921-25-2(X)) Resources.

As He Is, So Are We (in the Earth) David T. Demola. 1 cass. 4.00 (3-083) Faith Fellow Min.

***As Husbands Go: A Novel.** unabr. ed. Susan Isaacs. Read by Hillary Huber. 1 Playaway. (Running Time: 12 hrs.). 2010. 64.99 (978-1-4417-4818-8(0)) Blckstn Audio.

***As Husbands Go: A Novel.** unabr. ed. Susan Isaacs. (Running Time: 12 hrs. 0 mins.). 2010. audio compact disk 105.00 (978-1-4417-4812-6(1)) Blckstn Audio.

***As Husbands Go: A Novel.** unabr. ed. Susan Isaacs. Read by Hillary Huber. 1 MP3-CD. (Running Time: 12 hrs.). 2010. 29.95 (978-1-4417-4815-7(6)); 72.95 (978-1-4417-4811-9(3)); audio compact disk 32.95 (978-1-4417-4814-0(8)) Blckstn Audio.

As I Have Loved You. Kitty de Ruyter Bons. 2004. 9.95 (978-1-59156-197-2(3)); audio compact disk 11.95 (978-1-59156-198-9(1)) Covenant Comms.

As I Have Loved You. Kitty De Ruyter. 1 cass. 9.95 (978-1-55503-126-8(9), 06008902); audio compact disk 10.98 (978-1-55503-966-0(9), 2500736) Covenant Comms.
Her inspiring wartime & conversion story.

As I Lay Dying. unabr. ed. William Faulkner. Read by Wolfram Kandinsky. 8 cass. (Running Time: 8 hrs.). 1994. 48.00 (978-0-7366-2664-4(6), 3401) Books on Tape.
Grim, sometimes comic novel about a family's bizarre journey to bury their wife & mother.

As I Rode Out. 1 cass. (Running Time: 30 min.). 8.00 (B0260B090, HarperThor) HarpC GBR.

As I See It. William Wait. Ed. by Michele R. Garvin. 1 cass. 7.98 (978-1-55503-855-7(7), 06005136) Covenant Comms.
A potpourri of wit & wisdom.

As I Step over a Puddle see Poetry & Voice of James Wright

As I Walked Out One Evening: Songs, Ballads, Lullabies, Limericks & Other Light Verse see Dylan Thomas Reading

As I Walked Out One Evening: Songs, Ballads, Lullabies, Limericks & Other Light Verse see Evening with Dylan Thomas

As I Walked Out One Midsummer Morning. unabr. ed. Laurie Lee. Read by Laurie Lee. 7 cass. (Running Time: 7 hrs. 50 mins.). 2001. 61.95 (978-1-85695-662-8(8), 88051) Pub: ISIS Audio GBR. Dist(s): Ulverscroft US
In 1934, nineteen-year-old Laurie Lee left home for London. He continued to Spain, travelling on foot, where he became trapped by the outbreak of the Civil War. With stunning accuracy he recaptures the sensations & experiences of his youth & the beauty & violence of Spain.

As I Walked Out One Midsummer Morning. unabr. ed. Laurie Lee. Read by Laurie Lee. 7 CDs. (Running Time: 8 hrs.). 2000. audio compact disk 71.95 (978-0-7531-0728-7(7), 107287) Pub: ISIS Audio GBR. Dist(s): Ulverscroft US
The author has captured the atmosphere of Spain seen with all the freshness & beauty of a young man's vision in the 1930s, creating a lyrical & lucid picture of the beautiful & violent country that was to involve him inextricably.

As I Walked Out One Midsummer Morning. unabr. ed. Laurie Lee. Narrated by John Horton. 5 cass. (Running Time: 7 hrs.). (gr. 10 up). 1990. 44.00 (978-1-55690-031-0(7), 90004E7) Recorded Bks.
Author Laurie Lee left his quiet village to journey to Spain at the outset of the Civil War.

As I Was Saying, Set. Jack C. Richards. 1987. 44.10 (978-0-201-06435-3(9)) AddisonWesley.

As Iron Sharpens Iron. Read by Howard Hendricks. 1 cass. 1995. 14.99 (978-0-8024-5630-4(8)) Moody.

as It Happens Files. abr. ed. Compiled by Mary Lou Finlay & Jeff Warren. (Running Time: 3600 sec.). (As It Happens Ser.). (ENG.). 2008. audio compact disk 15.95 (978-0-660-19861-3(4), CBC Audio) Canadian Broadcasting CAN.

As It Is in Heaven. Niall Williams. (ENG., 2001. (978-0-333-78257-6(7)) Macmillan UK GBR.

As It Is in Heaven. abr. ed. Niall Williams. (Running Time: 3 hrs.). (ENG.). 2006. 14.98 (978-1-59483-663-3(9)) Pub: Hachet Audio. Dist(s): HachBkGrp

As Long as I Breathe. Contrib. by Zemer Levav & Yochanan Ben Yehuda. Prod. by Yochanan Ben Yehuda et al. 2007. audio compact disk 16.98 (978-5-557-58536-1(2)) Pt of Grace Ent.

As Long As I Have You. abr. ed. Dean Hughes. Read by Dean Hughes. 2 cass. (Running Time: 2 hrs.). (Children of the Promise Ser.: Vol. 5). 2003. 19.95 (978-1-57345-882-5(1)) Deseret Bk.
The war is over, and the Thomas family is slowly coming back together at home in Salt Lake City. But that doesn't mean all is well in Zion.

As Long as I Live. abr. ed. Read by Jacob D. Eppinga. 4.00 (978-1-56212-673-5(3), 151335) FaithAliveChr.

***As Long as We Both Shall Live: Experience the Marriage You've Always Wanted.** unabr. ed. Gary Smalley et al. Narrated by Adam Verner. (Running Time: 5 hrs. 30 mins. 0 sec.). (ENG.). 2009. audio compact disk 21.98 (978-1-59644-805-6(9), christianSeed) christianaud.

***As Long as We Both Shall Live: Experience the Marriage You've Always Wanted.** unabr. ed. Greg Smalley & Ted Cunningham. Narrated by Adam Verner. (ENG.). 2009. 12.98 (978-1-59644-806-3(7), christianSeed) christianaud.

As Man Thinketh. unabr. ed. James Allen. (ENG.). 2005. 1.98 (978-1-59659-050-2(5), GildAudio) Pub: Gildan Media. Dist(s): HachBkGrp

As Nature Made Him. unabr. ed. John Colapinto. Read by Adam Henderson. 10 CDs. (Running Time: 15 hrs.). 2002. audio compact disk 94.95 (978-0-7927-9870-5(8), SLD 121, Chivers Sound Lib) AudioGO.
In 1967, after a baby boy suffered a botched circumcision, his family agreed to radical treatment. On the advice of an expert in gender identity and sexual reassignment at John Hopkins Hospital, the boy was surgically altered to live as a girl. But the case was a failure from the outset. With uncommon insight and compassion, John Colapinto tells this extraordinary story for the first time.

As Nature Made Him: The Boy Who Was Raised As a Girl. John Colapinto. Read by Adam Henderson. 8 vols. (Running Time: 12 hrs.). 2001. bk. 69.95 (978-0-7927-2432-2(1), CSL 321, Chivers Sound Lib) AudioGO.
In 1967, after a baby boy suffered a botched circumcision, his family agreed to a radical treatment. With the advice of an expert in gender identity & sexual reassignment at Johns Hopkins Hospital, the boy was surgically altered to live as a girl. This landmark case, initially reported to be a great success, seemed all the more remarkable since the boy had been born an identical twin.

As Nature Made Him: The Boy Who Was Raised As a Girl. John Colapinto. Read by Howard McGillin. 2004. 15.95 (978-0-7435-4174-9(X)) Pub: S&S Audio. Dist(s): S and S Inc

***AS OCR Chemistry.** John Older & Mike Smith. 2008. tchr. ed. & spiral bd. 159.50 (978-1-84489-335-5(9)) Pub: Hodder Edu GBR. Dist(s): Trans-Atl Phila

As Simple As Snow. Gregory Galloway. (Running Time: 9 hrs. 0 mins.). 2005. 59.95 (978-0-7861-2892-1(5)) Blckstn Audio.

As Simple as Snow. Gregory Galloway. Read by Scott Brick. (Running Time: 32400 sec.). 2005. audio compact disk 72.00 (978-0-7861-8284-8(9)) Blckstn Audio.

As Simple as Snow. Gregory Galloway. Read by Scott Brick. (Running Time: 9 hrs.). 2005. 30.95 (978-1-59912-425-4(4)) Iofy Corp.

As Simple As Snow. unabr. ed. Gregory Galloway. Read by Scott Brick. 20 cass. (Running Time: 8 hrs. 30 mins.). 2005. reel tape 29.95 (978-0-7861-2891-4(7), E3389); audio compact disk 29.95 (978-0-7861-8285-5(7), ZE3389); audio compact disk 29.95 (978-0-7861-8323-4(3), ZM3389) Blckstn Audio.

As Strong As Anyone Can Be. Cathy Winter & Betsy Rose. 1 cass. (Running Time: 33 mins.). (J). (gr. 1-7). 1982. 9.95 (978-0-939065-10-3(X), GW1010) Gentle Wind.
Humorous songs, serious songs, pretty songs & silly songs all full of positive self images for girls & boys alike.

As Strong As Anyone Can Be. Perf. by Cathy Winter & Betsy Rose. (J). 1982. audio compact disk 14.95 (978-0-939065-68-4(1)) Gentle Wind.

As Sure As the Dawn. abr. ed. Francine Rivers. Read by Wayne Shepherd. 2 cass. (Running Time: 3 hrs.). (Mark of the Lion Ser.: Vol. 3). 1995. 17.99 (978-1-886463-18-9(2)) Oasis Audio.
Atretes vows to find his son & return to Germania. Only one thing stands in his way: Rizpah, the young widow who adopted his abandoned baby.

As the Crow Flies. Jeffrey Archer. Narrated by Alec McCowen. 2 cass. (Running Time: 3 hrs.). 2000. 16.99 (978-0-00-104653-5(5)) Pub: HarpC GBR. Dist(s): Trafalgar
When Charlie Trumper inherits his grandfather's fruit and vegetable barrow, he also inherits his enterprising spirit, which gives Charlie the drive to lift himself out of the poverty of Whitechapel, in London's East End. Success, however, does not come easily or quickly, particularly when World War 1 sends Charlie into an ongoing struggle with a vengeful enemy who will not rest until Charlie is destroyed.

As the Crow Flies. abr. rev. ed. Jeffrey Archer. Read by Martin Jarvis. 3 CDs. (Running Time: 3 hrs. 45 mins. 0 sec.). 2004. audio compact disk 14.95 (978-1-59397-409-1(4)) Pub: Macmill Audio. Dist(s): Macmillan

As the Crow Flies. unabr. ed. Jeffrey Archer. Narrated by Simon Prebble & Barbara Rosenblat. 16 cass. (Running Time: 23 hrs. 15 mins.). 1995. 128.00 (978-0-7887-0107-8(X), 94348E7) Recorded Bks.
The rise to fame & fortune of a poor English huckster, who builds one of the largest department stores empires in the world.

As the Deer. Michael Joncas. 1 cass. (Running Time: 1 hr.). 1998. 10.95 (CS-421); audio compact disk 15.95 (CD-421) GIA Pubns.

As the Eagle Goes. Anne Schraff. Narrated by Larry A. McKeever. (Standing Tall 2 Mystery Ser.). (J). 2000. audio compact disk 14.95 (978-1-58659-270-7(X)) Artesian.

As the Eagle Goes. unabr. ed. Anne Schraff. Narrated by Larry A. McKeever. 1 cass. (Running Time: 40 mins.). (Standing Tall 2 Mystery Ser.). (J). 2000. 10.95 (978-1-58659-096-3(0), 54136) Artesian.

As the New Year Begins. Swami Jyotirmayananda. Read by Swami Jyotirmayananda. 1 cass. (Running Time: 60 mins.). 12.99 (707) Yoga Res Foun.

As the Oceans Rise: Meeting the Challenges of Global Warming. 2007. 9.95 (978-0-9802200-4-9(1)) Susta Planet.

As the Third Millennium Draws Near: Apostolic Letter of John Paul II. John Paul II, pseud. Read by George Rutler. 3 cass. 19.95 (5515-C) Ignatius Pr.
Document for understanding the Pope's whole vision of the Church in the coming millennium & the significance of the "Great Jubilee Year 2000 Celebration".

As the Twig Is Bent: The Hazards of Growing Up. Instructed by Manly P. Hall. 8.95 (978-0-89314-009-0(0), C860727) Philos Res.

As the Ward Turns. abr. ed. Joni Hilton. Read by Suzanne Decker. 2 cass. (Running Time: 2 hrs.). 1991. 11.98 (978-1-55503-410-8(1), 0700878) Covenant Comms.
Fiction.

As They Were. M. F. K. Fisher. Read by C. M. Herbert. 8 CDs. (Running Time: 8 hrs. 30 mins.). 2001. audio compact disk 64.00 (978-0-7861-9703-3(X), 2810) Blckstn Audio.
Through a series of vignettes, the listener experiences events filled with wonderful details of people, places, foods and thoughts, traveling America and Europe, through decades of M. F. K. Fisher's life.

As They Were. unabr. ed. M. F. K. Fisher. Read by C. M. Herbert. 6 cass. (Running Time: 8 hrs. 30 mins.). 2001. 44.95 (978-0-7861-2050-5(9), 2810) Blckstn Audio.
Through a series of vignettes, M. K. Fisher brings us a sampling of her adventures done in her fine prosaic style. The events are filled with wonderful details of people, places, foods and thoughts, traveling America and Europe, through decades of her life.

As Time Flies. C. Lee. 2002. 41.99 (978-1-929409-14-3(1), 700) Blade Pubg.
Five black women struggle to maintain their friendships, marriages, children and their reputations after the past comes back to haunt them.

As Time Goes By. Michael Walsh. 1999. (978-1-57042-742-8(9)) Hachet Audio.

As Time Goes By. abr. ed. Michael Walsh. (Running Time: 3 hrs.). (ENG.). 2006. 14.98 (978-1-59483-664-0(7)) Pub: Hachet Audio. Dist(s): HachBkGrp

As Time Goes By. unabr. ed. Michael Walsh. Read by Alexander Adams. 7 cass. (Running Time: 10 hrs. 30 mins.). 1998. 56.00 (978-0-7366-4248-4(X), 4747) Books on Tape.
A story filled with wartime adventure & intrigue. Tells what happened after Ilsa & Victor Laszlo left Casablanca, takes a journey into the past as it answers questions about the lives of those in the film.

As We Are Now. May Sarton. Read by May Sarton. 1 cass. (Running Time: 54 mins.). 1982. 13.95 (978-1-55644-055-7(3), 2121) Am Audio Prose.
A beautifully wrought mesh of materials from the work & life of poet-novelist-journalist Sarton.

***As We Forgive: Stories of Reconciliation from Rwanda.** Catherine Claire Larson. (Running Time: 9 hrs. 3 mins. 0 sec.). (ENG.). 2009. 15.99 (978-0-310-77322-1(9)) Zondervan.

As You Like It. William Shakespeare. Directed By Charles Warburton. (Running Time: 1 hr.). 2005. audio compact disk 15.95 (978-0-660-19380-9(9)) Canadian Broadcasting CAN.

As You Like It. abr. ed. William Shakespeare. Perf. by Folio Theatre Players. 1 cass. Dramatization. 10.95 (978-0-8045-0880-3(1), SAC 7010) Spoken Arts.

***As You Like It.** abr. ed. William Shakespeare. Read by Vanessa Redgrave. (ENG.). 2003. (978-0-06-079960-1(9), Caedmon); (978-0-06-074320-8(4), Caedmon) HarperCollins Pubs.

As You Like It. unabr. ed. William Shakespeare. Contrib. by Arkangel Cast et al. (Running Time: 8940 sec.). (Arkangel Shakespeare Ser.). (ENG.). 2005. audio compact disk 19.95 (978-1-932219-04-3(8)) Pub: AudioGO. Dist(s): Perseus Dist

As You Like It. unabr. ed. William Shakespeare. Read by Vanessa Redgrave et al. Directed By Peter Wood. Contrib. by Neville Marriner. 2 cass. (Running Time: 2 hrs. 19 mins.). Dramatization. 17.95 (H139) Blckstn Audio.
A virtuoso performance of Shakespeare's idyllic romance.

As You Like It. unabr. ed. William Shakespeare. 2 cass. (Running Time: 2 hrs.). 1999. 15.95 (FS9-51062) Highsmith.

As You Like It. unabr. ed. William Shakespeare. Perf. by Vanessa Redgrave & Stanley Holloway. 2 cass. (Running Time: 2 hrs. 30 mins.). Dramatization. 2000. pap. bk. 37.20 (40747E5); 22.00 (21516E5) Recorded Bks.

As You Like It. unabr. ed. William Shakespeare. Read by Niamh Cusack et al. 2 cass. (Running Time: 2 hrs. 29 mins.). (Arkangel Shakespeare Ser.). 2004. 17.95 (978-1-932219-44-9(7)) Pub: Audio Partners. Dist(s): PerseuPGW

As You Like It. unabr. ed. William Shakespeare. Read by Kimberly Schraf. 2 cass. (Running Time: 3 hrs.). 1993. 14.95 (978-1-55685-310-4(6)) Audio Bk Con.
Shakespeare transplants the sophisticated denizens of the court to the starkly simple Forest of Arden, then stands back to see what happens. Witty clowns woo country wenches, philosophers wax melancholic & girls will be boys as Rosalind follows her heart & love conquers all.

As You Like It. unabr. ed. William Shakespeare. Read by Vanessa Redgrave. 2 CDs. (Caedmon Shakespeare Ser.: Vol. 2). (gr. 9-12). 1996. audio compact disk 25.00 (978-0-694-51665-0(1), Harper Audio) HarperCollins Pubs.

As You Think. James Allen. Read by Marc Allen. (Running Time: 3960 sec.). (ENG.). 2007. audio compact disk 13.95 (978-1-57731-581-0(2)) Pub: New Wrld Lib. Dist(s): PerseuPGW

As You Thinketh. James Allen & Tag Powell. Read by Judith L. Powell. 1 cass. (Running Time: 1 hr.). 1998. 12.95 (978-1-56087-009-8(5)) Top Mtn Pub.
Book on cassette. The listener can hear the entire age-old classic for year-round inspiration. Entails how to rise above circumstance to accomplish your dreams, goals & ideals.

Asa Baber. unabr. ed. Asa Baber. Read by Asa Baber. 1 cass. (Running Time: 29 mins.). 1986. 10.00 New Letters.
Asa Baber, whose writing appears regularly in "Playboy," reads a short story & an article about Central America.

Asbestos: Handling New Jersey Cases. Contrib. by Andrew T. Berry et al. (Running Time: 5 hrs. 30 min.). 1985. 100.00 incl. program handbk. NJ Inst CLE.
Discusses theories of liability: development of case law, preparing the plaintiff's asbestos action, conducting the defense of an asbestos action.

***Ascendance (part 1 Of 2) The Demon Wars (Book 5)** R. A. Salvatore. 2010. audio compact disk 19.99 (978-1-59950-650-0(5)) GraphicAudio.

***Ascendance (part 2 Of 2) The Demon Wars (Book 5)** R. A. Salvatore. (Demon Wars Ser.: Bk. 5). 2010. audio compact disk 19.99 (978-1-59950-658-6(0)) GraphicAudio.

Ascendant: Key to Early Environment. Diana Stone. 1 cass. 8.95 (589) Am Fed Astrologers.
Analyze 12 signs behavior patterns, conditions.

Ascendant Sun. Catherine Asaro. Read by Anna Fields. (Running Time: 12 hrs.). 2003. 36.95 (978-1-59912-426-1(2)) Iofy Corp.

Ascendant Sun. unabr. ed. Catherine Asaro. Read by Anna Fields. (Running Time: 13 hrs.). 2003. 24.95 (978-0-7861-8905-2(3)); 62.95 (978-0-7861-2517-3(9)); audio compact disk 80.00 (978-0-7861-9140-6(6)) Blckstn Audio.

Ascended Master Instruction (Vol 4-Audio Cass. Tape Album) By the Ascended Master Saint Germain, Vol. 4. unabr. ed. Saint Germain. Read by Gerald A. Craig. Godfre Ray King. 14 cass. (Running Time: 8 hrs. 24 mins.). (Saint Germain Ser.: Vol. 4). (ENG.). 1989. 60.00 (978-1-878891-22-8(7), St Germain Ser) St Germain.
Twenty-eight Discourses by the Ascended Master Saint Germain, presenting Instruction for the true seeker of Light.

Ascending: A Novel. Blaine M. Yorgason. 1996. 14.95 (978-0-9649968-3-0(9)) Gentle Breeze.

Ascension. Swami Amar Jyoti. 1 cass. 1990. 12.95 (K-122) Truth Consciousness.
Transcending, living in higher consciousness is for all. Straightforward advice for seekers.

Ascension. Perf. by Robert Kochis et al. 1 cass. (Running Time: 55 mins.). 1999. 10.95 (T8115); audio compact disk 15.95 (K1115) Liguori Pubns.
Brings the beauty of the Holy Spirit to your home, office or car, capturing a soothing tranquility.

Ascension! An Analysis of the Art of Ascension As Taught by the Ishayas. unabr. ed. MSI Staff. 1 cass. (Running Time: 6 hrs.). 1998. 27.00 (978-0-931783-52-4(6)) SFA Pubns.

Ascension - State of Grace. Bruce Goldberg. (ENG.). 2005. audio compact disk 17.00 (978-1-57968-062-6(3)) Pub: B Goldberg. Dist(s): Baker Taylor

Ascension - State of Grace. Bruce Goldberg. Read by Bruce Goldberg. 1 cass. (Running Time: 25 mins.). (ENG.). 2006. 13.00 (978-1-885577-95-5(8)) Pub: B Goldberg. Dist(s): Baker Taylor
Through self-hypnosis learn to perfect the soul & ascend to the higher planes to rejoin God.

Ascension & the New Age. Kryon. Read by Lee Carroll. 1 cass. (Running Time: 55 mins.). 1996. 10.00 (978-1-888053-00-5(3)) Kryon Writings.
Recording of live event. Channeling of spiritual information.

Ascension Harmonics. Richard Shulman & Samuel Welsh. 1 cass. (Running Time: 72 min.). 10.95 (LA208); audio compact disk 15.95 (LA208D) Lghtwrks Aud & Vid.
Sacred musical attunements to activate one's personal ascension process. Beautiful & harmoniously-designed instrumental keyboard & chorus based on The Divine Template Attunements to help people manifest their soul's essence into physical form.

Ascension through Orbs Meditations. Diana Cooper & Kathy Crosswell. (Running Time: 2 hrs. 0 mins. 0 sec.). (ENG.). 2009. audio compact disk 21.95 (978-1-84409-155-3(4)) Pub: Findhorn Pr GBR. Dist(s): IPG Chicago

Ascension Training CD Album. Bruce Goldberg. (ENG.). 2005. audio compact disk 75.00 (978-1-57968-052-7(6)) Pub: B Goldberg. Dist(s): Baker Taylor

Ascension Training Program Cassette Album. Bruce Goldberg. Read by Bruce Goldberg. 6 cass. (Running Time: 3 hrs.). (ENG.). 2005. 65.00 (978-1-885577-96-2(6)) Pub: B Goldberg. Dist(s): Baker Taylor
Self-hypnosis training to eliminate the need to reincarnate by perfecting the soul.

Ascent. unabr. ed. Jed Mercurio. Narrated by Todd McLaren. (Running Time: 7 hrs. 30 mins. 0 sec.). (ENG.). 2007. audio compact disk 59.99 (978-1-4001-3368-0(8)); audio compact disk 19.99 (978-1-4001-5368-8(9)) Pub: Tantor Media. Dist(s): IngramPubServ

Ascent. unabr. ed. Jed Mercurio. Read by Todd McLaren. (Running Time: 7 hrs. 30 mins. 0 sec.). (ENG.). 2007. audio compact disk 29.99 (978-1-4001-0368-3(1)) Pub: Tantor Media. Dist(s): IngramPubServ

Ascent of George Washington: The Hidden Political Genius of an American Icon. unabr. ed. John Ferling & John E. Ferling. (Running Time: 17 hrs. 0 mins. 0 sec.). (ENG.). 2009. audio compact disk 79.99 (978-1-4001-4199-9(0)); audio compact disk 29.99 (978-1-4001-6199-7(1)); audio compact disk 39.99 (978-1-4001-1199-2(4)) Pub: Tantor Media. Dist(s): IngramPubServ

Ascent of Man. unabr. ed. Interview with Jacob Bronowski & Heywood Hale Broun. 1 cass. (Running Time: 56 min.). 12.95 (40065) J Norton Pubs.
Provides a fascinating summary of the achievements of man that is an affirmation of homosapiens' adaptive nature.

Ascent of Man CD. Interview. Jacob Bronowski. Interview with Heywood Hale Broun. 1 CD. (Running Time: 55 mins.). (Heywood Hale Broun Ser.). 1974. audio compact disk 9.95 (978-1-57970-357-8(7), C40065D, Audio-For) J Norton Pubs.

***Ascent of Money: A Financial History of the World.** unabr. ed. Neil Ferguson. Narrated by Simon Prebble. 1 Playaway. (Running Time: 11 hrs. 30 mins.). 2009. 64.99 (978-1-61545-663-5(5)) Find a World.

Ascent of Money: A Financial History of the World. unabr. ed. Niall Ferguson. Narrated by Simon Prebble. 1 MP3-CD. (Running Time: 11 hrs. 30 mins. 0 sec.). (ENG.). 2008. 24.99 (978-1-4001-6033-4(2)); audio compact disk 34.99 (978-1-4001-1033-9(5)); audio compact disk 69.99 (978-1-4001-4033-6(1)) Pub: Tantor Media. Dist(s): IngramPubServ

Ascent of Mt Carmel. unabr. ed. John of the Cro. (Running Time: 13 hrs. 0 mins. 0 sec.). (ENG.). 2009. audio compact disk 24.98 (978-1-59644-813-1(X), Hovel Audio) christianaud.

***Ascent of Mt Carmel.** unabr. ed. St John of the Cross. Narrated by James Adams. (ENG.). 2009. 14.98 (978-1-59644-814-8(8), Hovel Audio) christianaud.

Ascent of Rum Doodle. unabr. ed. W. E. Bowman. Read by Terry Wale. 4 cass. (Isis Ser.). (J). 2003. 44.95 (978-0-7531-1428-5(3)); audio compact disk 51.95 (978-0-7531-1556-5(5)) Pub: ISIS Lrg Prnt GBR. Dist(s): Ulverscroft US

Asch Recordings, Vols. 1-4. Woody Guthrie et al. 4 CDs. (YA). (gr. 7 up). 1999. 42.00 Smithsonian Folkways.
Includes historical, biographical & song notes, artwork & illustrations.

Asdescent-Anacatabasis. Read by Richard Kostelanetz. 1 cass. (Running Time: 46 mins.). 1978. 8.00 (978-0-932360-36-6(X)) Archae Edns.
Electronically modified readings of texts radically reworked from the King James Version.

ASE Automotive Test Prep Video Set. Delmar Publishers Staff. (C). 2000. audio compact disk 1674.95 (978-0-7668-8042-9(7)) Pub: Delmar. Dist(s): CENGAGE Learn

Asesinato en el Camarote A-13. 1 cass. (Running Time: 1 hr. 30 mins.). (SmartReader Ser.).Tr. of Murder in Cabin A-13. (SPA & ENG.). (J). 1999. pap. bk. & tchr. ed. 19.95 (978-0-7887-0283-9(1), 79323T3) Recorded Bks.

Asesinos: Mision: Jerusalen, Blanco: el Anticristo. unabr. ed. Tim LaHaye & Jerry B. Jenkins. Narrated by Francisco Rivela. 9 cass. (Running Time: 12 hrs.). (Left Behind Ser.: Vol. 6). (ENG & SPA.). 1999. 79.75 (978-1-4025-7171-8(2), E1050MC, Griot Aud) Recorded Bks.

Ash Tree. 1981. (S-19) Jimcin Record.
Strange rites seeking evil forces.

Ash Wednesday. unabr. ed. Ethan Hawke. Read by Ethan Hawke. 5 cass. (Running Time: 7 hrs.). 2004. 29.95 (978-1-59007-250-9(2)) Pub: New Millenn Enter. Dist(s): PerseuPGW
Jimmy has gone AWOL from the Army, but he's about to embark on the biggest commitment of his life. Christy is pregnant with Jimmy's first child, and she's heading home, with or without Jimmy, to confront her past and prepare for her future. Barrelling across America in a souped up Chevy Nova, the road trip transforms Christy and Jimmy from passionate but conflicted lovers into a young family on a magnificent journey.

Ash Wednesday (in five parts) see Twentieth-Century Poetry in English, No. 3, Recordings of Poets Reading Their Own Poetry

Ashamed of the Gospel: When the Church Becomes Like the Rest of the World. unabr. ed. John F. MacArthur, Jr. Read by Jonathon Marosz. 8 CDs. (Running Time: 8 hrs. 45 mins. 0 sec.). (ENG.). 2006. audio compact disk 26.98 (978-1-59644-268-9(9), Hovel Audio) christianaud.

***Ashamed of the Gospel: When the Church Becomes Like the World.** unabr. ed. John MacArthur. Narrated by Jonathan Marosz. (ENG.). 2006. 16.98 (978-1-59644-269-6(7), Hovel Audio) christianaud.

Ashamed or Not Ashamed - God Knows the Heart. Dan Corner. 1 cass. 3.00 (15) Evang Outreach.

Ashanti to Zulu. (J). 2004. pap. bk. 14.95 (978-0-7882-0674-0(5)) Weston Woods.

Ashanti to Zulu: African Traditions. 2004. cass. & flmstrp 30.00 (978-0-89719-646-8(5)) Weston Woods.

Ashanti to Zulu: African Traditions. (J). 2004. bk. 24.95 (978-1-56008-159-3(7)) Weston Woods.

Ashanti to Zulu: African Traditions. Margaret W. Musgrove. Illus. by Leo Dillon & Diane Dillon. 1 cass. (Running Time: 17 min.). (J). (gr. k-4). 2000. pap. bk. 12.95 Weston Woods.
The customs & traditions of twenty-six African tribes are explained & enriched by remarkably accurate & beautiful art.

Ashanti to Zulu: African Traditions; Ote; The Hole in the Dyke; Woodcutter's Duck. 2004. (978-0-89719-843-1(3)) Weston Woods.

Ashanti to Zulu; African Traditions. 2004. 8.95 (978-1-56008-835-6(4)) Weston Woods.

Ashanti to Zulu; African Traditions; Ote; Hole in the Dike, the; Woodcutter's Duck, the; Stay Away. 2004. cass. & flmstrp (978-0-89719-751-9(8)) Weston Woods.

Ashenden: The British Secret Agent. unabr. ed. W. Somerset Maugham. Narrated by Neil Hunt. 6 cass. (Running Time: 9 hrs.). 1988. 51.00 (978-1-55690-032-7(5), 88860E7) Recorded Bks.
Willy Ashenden is dispatched to Vladivostok on a secret mission.

Ashes & Snow Soundtrack (CD) Perf. by Lisa Gerrard et al. Prod. by Gregory Colbert. 1 CD. (Ashes & Snow Media Ser.). (ENG.). 2006. audio compact disk 25.00 (978-0-9766715-7-2(3)) Pub: Flying Elephants. Dist(s): Perseus Dist

Ashes for Gold: A Tale from Mexico. Retold by Katherine Maitland. 1 cass. (Running Time: 30 mins.). (Folktales Ser.). (J). (ps-4). 1999. 7.95 (978-1-57255-180-0(1)) Mondo Pubng.
When Tomaso tricks his friend Pancho into believing he can get rich selling ashes, Pancho looks like a fool. Or does he?.

Ashes for Gold: A Tale from Mexico. Katherine Maitland. Illus. by Elise Mills. (J). 1995. 7.95 (978-1-879531-16-1(X)) Mondo Pubng.

Ashes of Eden. abr. ed. William Shatner. (Star Trek Ser.). 2004. 10.95 (978-0-7435-4679-9(2)) Pub: S&S Audio. Dist(s): S and S Inc

***Ashes of Midnight.** unabr. ed. Lara Adrian. Narrated by Hillary Huber. (Running Time: 10 hrs. 0 mins. 0 sec.). (Midnight Breed Ser.). 2010. 24.99 (978-1-4001-6462-2(1)); 16.99 (978-1-4001-8462-0(2)); audio compact disk 34.99 (978-1-4001-1462-7(4)) Pub: Tantor Media. Dist(s): IngramPubServ

***Ashes of Midnight (Library Edition)** unabr. ed. Lara Adrian. Narrated by Hillary Huber. (Running Time: 10 hrs. 0 mins.). (Midnight Breed Ser.). 2010. 34.99 (978-1-4001-9462-9(8)); audio compact disk 83.99 (978-1-4001-4462-4(0)) Pub: Tantor Media. Dist(s): IngramPubServ

Ashes of Worlds. unabr. ed. Kevin J. Anderson. Read by David Colacci. 2 MP3-CDs. (Running Time: 20 hrs.). (Saga of Seven Suns Ser.: Bk. 7). 2008. 29.95 (978-1-4233-5753-7(1), 9781423357537, Brilliance MP3); 44.25 (978-1-4233-5756-8(6), 9781423357568, BADLE); 44.25 (978-1-4233-5754-4(X), 9781423357544, Brinc Audio MP3 Lib); 29.95 (978-1-4233-5755-1(8), 9781423357551, BAD); audio compact disk 39.95 (978-1-4233-5751-3(5), 9781423357513, Bril Audio CD Unabri); audio compact disk 132.25 (978-1-4233-5752-0(3), 9781423357520, BriAudCD Unabrid) Brilliance Audio.

Ashes to Ashes. Tami Hoag. Read by Melissa Leo. 2004. 15.95 (978-0-7435-4175-6(8)) Pub: S&S Audio. Dist(s): S and S Inc

Ashes to Ashes. Lillian Stewart Carl. 11 CD's. (Running Time: 12.5 Hours). 2003. lib. bdg. 50.00 (978-0-932079-05-3(9), 79059) TimeFare AudioBks.
Historian Rebecca Reid comes to a replica castle in Ohio to catalog a collection of priceless artifacts, and finds ghosts and ghoulies, mystery, and love.A delightful modern gothic!Narrated by: Elly LeavertonMusic By: Elly leaverton and David LandonCover Art by: Amy Madden.

Ashes to Ashes. abr. ed. Tami Hoag. Read by Melissa Leo. 4 cass. 1999. 25.00 (FS9-43370) Highsmith.

Ashes to Ashes. deluxe unabr. ed. Lillian Stewart Carl. 8 cass. (Running Time: 12 hrs. 30 min). 2001. lib. bdg. 50.00 (978-0-932079-07-7(5), 79075) TimeFare AudioBks.

Ashes to Ashes. unabr. ed. Tami Hoag. 12 vols. (Running Time: 55800 sec.). (Sound Library). 2000. 96.95 (978-0-7927-2365-3(1), CSL 254, Chivers Sound Lib) AudioGO.
The newspapers have dubbed him the Cremator. He has already claimed three lives. But this time, Angie DiMarco, a teenage runaway, witnesses the murder. Enter Kate Conlan, a former FBI agent who helps victims & protects witnesses. Although she has the help of John Quinn, the FBI's ace profiler of serial killers, she is confronted with the most difficult role of her career & her life. For she is the one woman who can stop the Cremator & the one woman he wants next.

Ashes to Ashes. unabr. ed. Tami Hoag. Read by Carrington McDuffie. 16 CDs. (Running Time: 24 hrs.). 2001. audio compact disk 119.95 (978-0-7927-9992-4(5), SLD 043, Chivers Sound Lib) AudioGO.

Ashgrove. unabr. ed. Diney Costeloe. 10 cass. (Soundings Ser.). (J). 2005. 84.95 (978-1-84559-121-2(6)) Pub: ISIS Lrg Prnt GBR. Dist(s): Ulverscroft US

Ashland-Eugene. Dan Heller. 1 cass. 1994. 9.95 (978-1-885433-01-5(8)) Takilma East.

Ashley Bryan: Poems & Folktales. Ashley Bryan. (Running Time: 6300 sec.). 2007. audio compact disk 24.95 (978-0-9761932-2-7(1)) Audio Bkshelf.

Ashley Bryan: Poems & Folktales. unabr. ed. Poems. Ashley Bryan. Read by Ashley Bryan. 2 cass. (Running Time: 2 hrs.). (J). (ps up). 1994. reel tape 14.95 (978-1-883332-11-2(7)) Audio Bkshelf.
Bryan reads the folktales with humor, spirit & his own unique voice changes...the performance of the poems are especially delightful & should leave children with the impression that poetry can be visceral & joyous.

Ashley Bryan's Beautiful Blackbird & Other Folktales. unabr. ed. Short Stories. Ashley Bryan. Read by Ashley Bryan. 1 CD. (Running Time: 80 min.). (J). 2004. audio compact disk 21.95 (978-1-883332-99-0(0), 2-04) Audio Bkshelf.
Ashley Bryan performs the following six AfricanFolktales: Beautiful Blackbird, Why Frog and SnakeNever Play Together, Tortoise, Hare, and the SweetPotatoes, Hen and Frog, Frog and His Two Wives,How Animals Got Their Tails.

Ashtanga Yoga. 2 cass. (Running Time: 2 hrs.). (Essence of Yoga Ser.). 14.95 (ST-30) Crystal Clarity.
Includes: a comparison of Eastern & Western approaches to knowing; the relativity of moral & spiritual growth; Patanjali's 8-fold path as inspired doctrine; the practicality of Patanjali's definitions; yoga as a desires increases energy.

Ashtanga Yoga "The Practice" First Series. abr. ed. David Swenson. Perf. by David Swenson. 1 cass. (Running Time: 1 hr. 30 mins.). 10.95 (978-1-891252-04-4(6)) Ashtanga Yoga.

Ashtanga Yoga "The Practice" Second Series. abr. ed. David Swenson. Perf. by David Swenson. 1 cass. (Running Time: 1 hr. 30 mins.). 10.95 (978-1-891252-05-1(4)) Ashtanga Yoga.

Ashtar Command. Yvonne Cole. 1 cass. (Running Time: 60 mins.). 9.95 (AT5021) Lghtwrks Aud & Vid.
Yvonne Cole, a telepathic receiver for Theodora of the "Group Mind", relays important channelled information about those extraterrestrials who wish to assist humanity at this cosmically historic time.

Asi Es. 3rd ed. Jack S. Levy. (C). bk. 106.95 (978-0-8384-7969-8(3)); bk. 113.95 (978-0-8384-8138-7(8)); bk. 128.95 (978-0-8384-8219-3(8)); bk. 233.95 (978-0-8384-8310-7(0)); bk. 133.95 (978-0-8384-8357-2(7)); bk. 123.95 (978-0-8384-8424-1(7)); bk. 119.95 (978-0-8384-8444-9(1)); bk. 168.95 (978-0-8384-8451-7(4)); bk. 273.95 (978-0-8384-8670-2(3)) Heinle.

Asi Es. 3rd ed. Jack S. Levy. 1 CD. (Running Time: 1 hr.). 2002. bk. 117.95 (978-0-8384-8426-5(3)) Heinle.
Beginning Spanish program provides a solid grammatical foundation, strong skill-building tools for communicative success, and broad exposure to Hispanic culture.

Asi Es. 3rd ed. Jack S. Levy. (C). 2002. bk. 111.95 (978-0-8384-8366-4(6)) Heinle.

Asi Es. 3rd ed. Jack S. Levy. (C). 2003. bk. 92.95 (978-0-8384-8223-0(6)) Heinle.
Provides a solid grammatical foundation, strong skill-building tools for communicative success, and broad exposure to Hispanic culture through innovative video and other media supplements.

Asi Es. 3rd ed. Nancy Levy-Konesky & Karen Daggett. (SPA.). 2000. bk. (978-0-03-031116-1(0)); lab manual ed. (978-0-03-025936-4(3)); lab manual ed. (978-0-03-025934-0(7)) Harcourt Coll Pubs.

Asi Es. 3rd ed. Nancy Levy-Konesky & Karen Daggett. (SPA.). 1999. bk. & stu. ed. 86.95 (978-0-03-031111-6(X)) Heinle.
Spanish program provides a solid grammatical foundation, strong skill-building tools for communicative success, and broad exposure to Hispanic culture.

Asi Es: Testing Program. 3rd ed. Nancy Levy-Konesky & Karen Daggett. (SPA.). 2000. (978-0-03-025944-9(4)) Harcourt Coll Pubs.

Así Habló Zarathustra. abr. ed. Friedrich Nietzsche. Read by Pedro Montoya. 3 CDs. (SPA.). 2001. audio compact disk 17.00 (978-958-9494-54-7(4)) YoYoMusic.

Asi Me Gusta. Miguel Llobera et al. (SPA.). 2003. 18.00 (978-84-8323-318-4(5)) Cambridge U Pr.

Asi Me Gusta 1. Miguel Llobera et al. (SPA.). 2003. audio compact disk 18.00 (978-84-8323-319-1(3)) Cambridge U Pr.

Asi Me Gusta 2. Miguel Llobera et al. (Running Time: 1 hr. 12 mins.). (SPA.). 2003. 18.00 (978-84-8323-324-5(X)); audio compact disk 18.00 (978-84-8323-325-2(8)) Cambridge U Pr.

***Asi Que, Quiere Ser Como Cristo?** Charles R. Swindoll.Tr. of So, You Want to Be Like Christ?. 2010. audio compact disk 24.00 (978-1-57972-865-6(0)) Insight Living.

!asi Se Dice! Glencoe Spanish 2. Created by McGraw-Hill-Glencoe Staff. (SPA.). 2009. audio compact disk 158.00 (978-0-07-888637-9(6)) McGraw.

Asi Somos los Espanoles: Spanish Skills for Advanced Students. Michael Truman et al. 2004. 20.95 (978-0-415-16378-1(1)) Pub: Routledge. Dist(s): Taylor and Fran

Asian Beat, Set. World Music Network Staff & Rough Guides Staff. (Rough Guide World Music Cds Ser.). 2004. audio compact disk 45.00 (978-1-84353-356-6(1)) DK Pub Inc.

Asian Wildlife Abuse & African Wildlife Patrols. Hosted by Nancy Pearlman. 1 cass. (Running Time: 28 mins.). 10.00 (902) Educ Comm CA.

Asies. Jack S. Levy. (C). bk. 192.95 (978-0-8384-7308-5(3)) Heinle.

Asies. 3rd ed. Jack S. Levy. (C). bk. 120.95 (978-0-8384-8130-1(2)) Heinle.

Asimov - Science Fiction. unabr. ed. Isaac Asimov. Read by Isaac Asimov. 2 cass. (Running Time: 1 hr. 58 mins.). (Cassette Bookshelf Ser.). 1985. 15.98 (978-0-8072-3418-1(4), CB106CX, Listening Lib) Random Audio Pubg.

Asimov's Mysteries. unabr. ed. Isaac Asimov. Read by Dan Lazar. 8 cass. (Running Time: 8 hrs.). Incl. Anniversary. (1136); Billiard Ball. (1136); Dust of Death. (1136); Dying Night. (1136); I'm in Marsport Without Hilda. (1136); Loint of Paw. (1136); Marooned off Vesta. (1136); Obituary. (1136); Pate de Foie Gras. (1136); Singing Bell. (1136); Starlight. (1136); Talking Stone. (1136); What's in a Name? (1136); 1979. 48.00 (978-0-7366-0130-6(9), 1136) Books on Tape.
Fourteen short stories designed to please mystery fans & science fiction devotees. Including "Anniversary," "Obituary" & "Starlight".

***Ask.** unabr. ed. Sam Lipsyte. Read by Sam Lipsyte. 7 CDs. (Running Time: 8 hrs.). 2010. audio compact disk 89.95 (978-0-7927-7079-4(X)) AudioGO.

***Ask.** unabr. ed. Sam Lipsyte. Read by Sam Lipsyte. 7 CDs. (Running Time: 7 hrs.). 2010. audio compact disk 23.99 (978-1-4272-1005-0(5)) Macmill Audio.

Ask a Mexican. unabr. ed. Gustavo Arellano. Read by William Dufris et al. (Running Time: 9 hrs. 0 mins. 0 sec.). (ENG.). 2007. audio compact disk 34.99 (978-1-4001-0464-2(5)); audio compact disk 69.99 (978-1-4001-3464-9(1)); audio compact disk 24.99 (978-1-4001-5464-7(2)) Pub: Tantor Media. Dist(s): IngramPubServ

Ask a Plumber. Interview. Created by Western Media Products. 3 CDss. (Running Time: 12600 sec.). (AudioTopics Ser.). 2006. audio compact disk 14.95 (978-0-9647401-7-4(6)) Western Media.
AUDIOTOPICS is a listen-and-learn series of audio CD interview programs on a variety of practical and current topics. "Ask a Plumber" is a deatiled consultation with a master plumber on dozens of money saving tips and procedures for the homeowner. Easy and fun to hear while driving to work, etc.

Ask a Security Expert. Interview. Created by Western Media Products. 3 audio CDs. (Running Time: 12600 sec.). (AudioTopics Ser.). 2006. audio compact disk 14.95 (978-0-9647401-8-1(4)) Western Media.
AUDIOTOPICS is a listen-and-learn audio CD series on current and practical topics for a wide audience. "Staying Safe" is an indepth interview with a security expert on many ways a family or individual can avoid confrontations with dangerous people. Covers: how to prtect your family, how to stay safe at home, when out and about, when traveling. Protecting children, protecting the elderly, being a good witness, and much more.

Ask a Ski Instructor. Interview. Created by Western Media Products. 2 CDs. (Running Time: 12600 sec.). (AudioTopics Ser.). 2006. audio compact disk 14.95 (978-0-9779361-0-6(4)) Western Media.
"Ask a Ski Instructor" is a 2-1/2 hour interview with top-rated PSIA ski instructor Bryan Olsen, describing all the elements of contemporary ski instruction. Just like having a private lesson, this program offers techniques for all type of snow and terrain in a friendly conversational manner. This program addresses all levels of skiing ability, but particulalry focuses on the person who has skied for some time and wishes to break old habits and improve his or her technique. This program is well suited for listening in the car while heading for the mountains. Get mentally prepared!.

Ask a Tax Advisor. Interview. Contrib. by Audiotopics. 2 CDs. (Running Time: 9000 sec.). (AudioTopics Ser.). 2006. audio compact disk 14.95 (978-0-9647401-5-0(X)) Western Media.
AUDIOTOPICS is a listen-and-learn way to stay current and get consultation from experts in a variety of fields tahtaffect all of us. "Ask a Tax Advisor" is an easy-to-listen update on tax laws, tax planning, retirement planning, tips for avoding audits, and much more. 2-1/2 hours on 2 audio CDs.

***Ask Again Later.** unabr. ed. Jill A. Davis. Read by Ilyana Kadushin. (ENG.). 2007. (978-0-06-126244-9(7), Harper Audio); (978-0-06-126243-2(9), Harper Audio) HarperCollins Pubs.

Ask Again Later. unabr. ed. Jill A. Davis. Read by Ilyana Kadushin. (Running Time: 21600 sec.). 2007. audio compact disk 29.95 (978-0-06-123632-7(2)) HarperCollins Pubs.

***Ask Amy Green: Boy Trouble: Boy Trouble.** unabr. ed. Sarah Webb. Read by Justine Eyre. (Running Time: 6 hrs.). 2010. 19.99 (978-1-4418-8892-1(6), 9781441888921, Candlewick Bril); 39.97 (978-1-4418-8893-8(4), 9781441888938, Candlewick Bril); 19.99 (978-1-4418-8890-7(X), 9781441888907, Candlewick Bril); 39.97 (978-1-4418-8891-4(8), 9781441888914, Candlewick Bril); audio compact disk 22.99 (978-1-4418-8888-4(8), 9781441888884, Candlewick Bril); audio compact disk 54.97 (978-1-4418-8889-1(6), 9781441888891, Candlewick Bril) Brilliance Audio.

***Ask Amy Green: Summer Secrets: Summer Secrets.** unabr. ed. Sarah Webb. (Running Time: 7 hrs.). (Amy Green Ser.). 2011. 39.97 (978-1-4558-0347-7(2), 9781455803477, Candlewick Bril); 19.99 (978-1-4558-0346-0(4), 9781455803460, Candlewick Bril); 19.99 (978-1-4558-0344-6(8), 9781455803446, Candlewick Bril); 39.97 (978-1-4558-0345-3(6), 9781455803453, Candlewick Bril); audio compact disk 22.99 (978-1-4558-0342-2(1), 9781455803422, Candlewick Bril); audio compact disk 49.97 (978-1-4558-0343-9(X), 9781455803439, Candlewick Bril) Brilliance Audio.

Ask an Acupuncture Doctor. Interview. Contrib. by Audiotopics. 3 audio CDs. (Running Time: 12600 sec.). (AudioTopics Ser.). 2006. audio compact disk 14.95 (978-0-9647401-9-8(2)) Western Media.
AUDIOTOPICS is a listen-and-learn series of audio CDs on a wide range of current and practical topics. Ideal for commuters and anyone who wants to listen and learn. "Ask an Acupuncture Doctor" is a detailed radio-talk-show style interview on the subject of acupuncture and herbal medicine. For anyone who has wondered about the subect, this is the chepaest way to get a profesisonal consulation.

Ask an Angel Live, No. 1. unabr. ed. Stevan Thayer. 2 cass. (Running Time: 2 hrs.). 1998. 15.00 (978-1-887010-08-5(4)) Edin Bks.
Channeled answers to questions from people nationwide.

Ask an Angel Live, No. 2. unabr. ed. Stevan Thayer. 2 cass. (Running Time: 2 hrs.). 1998. 15.00 (978-1-887010-09-2(2)) Edin Bks.
More channeled answers to audience questions.

***Ask & the Answer.** unabr. ed. Patrick Ness. (Running Time: 12 hrs.). (Chaos Walking Ser.). 2010. 39.97 (978-1-4418-8899-0(3), 9781441888990, Candlewick Bril); 14.99 (978-1-4418-8898-3(5), 9781441888983, Candlewick Bril) Brilliance Audio.

***Ask & the Answer.** unabr. ed. Patrick Ness. Read by Nick Podehl & Angela Dawe. 11 CDs. (Running Time: 13 hrs.). (Chaos Walking Ser.). 2010. audio compact disk 19.99 (978-1-4418-8894-5(2), 9781441888945, Candlewick Bril) Brilliance Audio.

***Ask & the Answer.** unabr. ed. Patrick Ness. Read by Angela Dawe & Nick Podehl. 1 MP3-CD. (Running Time: 13 hrs.). (Chaos Walking Ser.). 2010. audio compact disk 14.99 (978-1-4418-8896-9(9), 9781441888969, Candlewick Bril) Brilliance Audio.

***Ask & the Answer.** unabr. ed. Patrick Ness. Read by Nick Podehl & Angela Dawe Podehl. 11 CDs. (Running Time: 13 hrs.). (Chaos Walking Ser.). 2010. audio compact disk 74.97 (978-1-4418-8895-2(0), 9781441888952, Candlewick Bril); audio compact disk 39.97 (978-1-4418-8897-6(7), 9781441888976, Candlewick Bril) Brilliance Audio.

***Ask & You Will Succeed: 1001 Extraordinary Questions to Create Life-Changing Results.** unabr. ed. Ken D. Foster. (Running Time: 6 hrs.). (ENG.). 2009. 27.98 (978-1-59659-486-9(1), GildAudio) Pub: Gildan Media. Dist(s): HachBkGrp

***Ask Ilse: An Advisors Guide to Cosmetic Plastic Surgery, vol.1.** Ilse Wolf. 2010. 6.99 (978-0-9827081-0-1(6)) AuthorsDig.

Ask Me Why Time is Money Vol. II: Joseph F. Dunphy M.B.A. Registered Representative. unabr. ed. Joseph F. Dunphy. Read by Joseph F. Dunphy. Contrib. by Richard Poklemba et al. 1 cass. (Running Time: 15 mins.). 1996. Incl. letters of intro. & business cards. (978-1-892359-01-8(4)) Mint Condtn Grph.
Designed to help prospective clients decide if their investment philosophy is compatible with their goals.

Ask Mr. Bear. Marjorie Flack. 1 cass. (Running Time: 35 min.). (J). (ps-4). 2001. 15.95 (VX-79C) Kimbo Educ.
A small boy seeking a birthday gift for his Mom is directed by barnyard animals to Mr. Bear - who suggests a big, warm hug.

Ask Mr Bear. Marjorie Flack. Illus. by Marjorie Flack. 14 vols. (Running Time: 8 mins.). 1990. pap. bk. 35.95 (978-1-59519-246-2(8)); 9.95 (978-1-59112-011-7(X)); audio compact disk 12.95 (978-1-59519-243-1(3)) Live Oak Media.

Ask Mr. Bear. Marjorie Flack. Illus. by Marjorie Flack. Read by Peter Fernandez. 11 vols. (Running Time: 8 mins.). (J). (gr. k-3). 1990. bk. 25.95 (978-0-87499-044-7(0)); pap. bk. 16.95 (978-0-87499-043-0(2)); pap. bk. & tchr. ed. 33.95 Reading Chest. (978-0-87499-045-4(9)) Live Oak Media.
Danny disregards the suggestions of various animals he questions about a suitable birthday gift for his mother, until he consults with Mr. Bear, who suggest a big hug! This charming book has been delighting young readers for more than half a century!.

Ask Not: The Inauguration of John F. Kennedy & the Speech That Changed America. abr. ed. Thurston Clarke. 2004. 14.95 (978-1-59397-552-4(X)) Pub: Macmill Audio. Dist(s): Macmillan

Ask the Cards a Question. unabr. ed. Marcia Muller. Read by Bernadette Dunne. 6 cass. (Running Time: 6 hrs.). (Sharon McCone Mystery Ser.: No. 2). 1996. 48.00 (978-0-7366-3454-0(1), 4098) Books on Tape.
Sharon McCone uncovers big-time deals & blackmail while she sleuths to clear a friend of murder charges. Complex & well-plotted.

Ask the Parrot. unabr. ed. Richard Stark, pseud. Narrated by William Dufris. 6 cass. (Running Time: 21120 sec.). 2006. 59.95 (978-0-7927-4545-7(0), CSL 990); audio compact disk 79.95 (978-0-7927-4356-9(3), SLD 990); audio compact disk 49.95 (978-0-7927-4575-4(2), CMP 990) AudioGO.

Ask Whatever You Will. Francis Frangipane. 1 cass. (Running Time: 90 mins.). (Abide in Him Ser.: Vol. 2). 2000. 5.00 (FF08-002) Morning NC.
A subject Francis teaches on with great gifting, this series deals with the advantages of walking in the "abiding principle".

Ask Your Guides: How to Connect with Your Spiritual Support System. Sonia Choquette. 6 CDs. (ENG.). 2007. audio compact disk 39.95 (978-1-4019-1767-8(4)); audio compact disk 23.95 (978-1-4019-1766-1(6)) Hay House.

***Asked & Answered.** Featuring Ravi Zacharias. 2006. audio compact disk 9.00 (978-1-61256-067-0(9)) Ravi Zach.

Asking for the Moon. unabr. ed. Reginald Hill. Read by Graham Roberts. 8 cass. (Running Time: 9 hrs. 15 mins.). (Dalziel & Pascoe Ser.). 1997. 69.95 (978-0-7531-0190-2(4), 970504) Pub: ISIS Audio GBR. Dist(s): Ulverscroft US
"Pascoe's Ghost" finds the inspector investigating the fate of a woman who seems to have slipped out of the world & hasn't been seen by a soul for a year - unless you count her brother, who claims her ghost is haunting him. "Dalziel's Ghost" sees the man who normally wouldn't be seen dead in a graveyard, expressing a surprising interest in "the other side." "One Small Step" looks to the future where murder on the moon requires the personal intervention of Commissioner Peter Pascoe.

Asking for the Moon. unabr. ed. Short Stories. Reginald Hill. Read by Graham Roberts. 10 CDs. (Running Time: 10 hrs. 30 min.). (Dalziel & Pascoe Ser.). (J). 2001. audio compact disk 89.95 (978-0-7531-1322-6(8)) Pub: ISIS Lrg Prnt GBR. Dist(s): Ulverscroft US
A collection of short stories. The Last National Service Man - divulges for the first time how Fat Andy and Peter Pascoe met, thus making crime-writing history. Pascoe's Ghost - the inspector investigates the fate of a woman who hasn't been seen for a year - unless you count her brother who claims her ghost is haunting him. Dalziel's Ghost - sees Dalziel expressing a surprising interest in "the other side". One Small Step - looks to the future and murder on the moon.

Asking for Trouble. Ann Granger. Read by Kim Hicks. 6 vols. (Running Time: 9 hrs.). 2003. 54.95 (978-0-7540-8315-3(2)) Pub: Chivers Audio Bks GBR. Dist(s): AudioGO

Asking Price. unabr. ed. Jessica Stirling. Read by Kara Wilson. 8 cass. (Running Time: 9 hrs. 10 mins.). (Nicholson Quartet Ser.). 1991. 69.95 (978-0-7451-6313-0(0), CAB 557) AudioGO.
The compelling sequel to "The Good Provider", "The Asking Price" continues the story of Kirsty & Craig Nicholson who escaped a life of labour in the Ayrshire farmlands to run off to Glasgow. "The Asking Price" explores the value of love & loyalty & the search for happiness among people who have nothing to fall back on but their pride.

Asking Questions. unabr. ed. H. R. F. Keating. Read by Garard Green. 6 cass. (Running Time: 8 hrs.). (Inspector Ghote Mystery Ser.: No. 22). 1997. 54.95 (970511) Pub: ISIS Audio GBR. Dist(s): Ulverscroft US
Inspector Ghote is more than a little surprised to find the Commissioner of Police outside his house early one morning. The Commissioner, on behalf of a famous movie star, would like Ghote to make discreet inquiries into the Mira Behn Institute for Medical Research. It seems someone there is smuggling out a dangerous drug, made from the venom of highly poisonous snakes. Ghote's interviews point him toward one obvious suspect - the snake-handler Chandra Chagoo. But the Reptile Room is locked & Chagoo is nowhere to be found, until, that is, the Reptile Room is unlocked. There lies the body of Chagoo, a deadly Russell's Viper slithering across his back.

Asking the Fathers. unabr. ed. Aelred Squire. Read by Christopher Codol. 9 cass. 36.95 (946) Ignatius Pr.
Drawing from the writings of the early spiritual fathers to the saints of the 16th century, this work initiates a dialogue between the teachings of these masters & those who are prepared to listen.

Asking the Great Questions. Jeffrey Mishlove. 1 cass. 9.00 (A0265-87) Sound Photosyn.
Principal host of Thinking Allowed Productions, Dr. Mishlove has made his mark in the studies of psychic phenomena studies as well as media presentation. During this talk at the Institute for the Study of Consciousness he discusses the perennial questions & offers answers from his long experience interviewing the aware minds of our times.

Asking the Holy Spirit. Kenneth Wapnick. 3 CDs. 2006. audio compact disk 16.00 (978-1-59142-278-5(7), CD130) Foun Miracles.

Asking the Holy Spirit. Kenneth Wapnick. 1 CD. (Running Time: 2 hrs. 41 mins. 12 secs.). 2006. 13.00 (978-1-59142-279-2(5), 3m130) Foun Miracles.

Asklepios. Melissa Fischer. Perf. by Melissa Fischer. (ENG.). 2008. audio compact disk 15.99 (978-0-9802170-0-1(8)) M Fischer.

AskTheInternetTherapist. com Pain Reduction Hypnosis. Jef Gazley. Music by Dean Evenson. 1 Cass. 1996. 19.95 (978-1-933154-18-3(7)); audio compact disk 24.99 (978-1-933154-19-0(5)) Int Therapist.

AskTheInternetTherapist. com Self-Esteem Beach Hypnosis. Jef Gazley. Music by Dean Evenson. 1 Cass. 1996. 19.95 (978-1-933154-14-5(4)); audio compact disk 24.99 (978-1-933154-15-2(2)) Int Therapist.

AskTheInternetTherapist. com Self-Esteem Forest Hypnosis. Jef Gazley. Music by Dean Evenson. 1. 1996. 19.95 (978-1-933154-12-1(8)); audio compact disk 24.99 (978-1-933154-13-8(6)) Int Therapist.

AskTheInternetTherapist. com Sleep-Beach Hypnosis. Jef Gazley. Music by Dean Evenson. 1. 1996. 19.95 (978-1-933154-10-7(1)); audio compact disk 24.99 (978-1-933154-11-4(X)) Int Therapist.

AskTheInternetTherapist. com Sleep-Forest. Jef Gazley. Music by Dean Evenson. 1. 1996. audio compact disk 24.99 (978-1-933154-09-1(8)) Int Therapist.

AskTheInternetTherapist. com Sleep-Forest Hypnosis Tape. Jef Gazley. Music by Dean Evenson. 1. 1996. 19.95 (978-1-933154-08-4(X)) Int Therapist.

AskTheInternetTherapist. com Smoking Cessation Hypnosis. Jef Gazley. Music by Dean Evenson. 1 Cass. 1996. 19.95 (978-1-933154-20-6(9)); audio compact disk 24.99 (978-1-933154-21-3(7)) Int Therapist.

AskTheInternetTherapist. com Weight Reduction Hypnosis. Jef Gazley. Music by Dean Evenson. 1 Cass. 1996. 19.95 (978-1-933154-16-9(0)); audio compact disk 24.99 (978-1-933154-17-6(9)) Int Therapist.

ASL Worship Workshop I. Perf. by Raymond Montoya. 1. (YA). 2003. audio compact disk 12.00 (978-0-9758596-2-9(5)) CommissionBel.

ASL Worship Workshop II: At His Throne. Perf. by Raymond Montoya. (YA). 2004. audio compact disk 12.00 (978-0-9758596-5-0(X)) CommissionBel.

Asleep at the Helm: About Changes in Traditional Sex Roles. Perf. by Peter Alsop. 1 cass. 11.00 Moose Schl Records.

Asmodeus & the Bottler of Djinns: A Story from Nelson Mandela's Favorite African Folktales. Read by Whoopi Goldberg. Compiled by Nelson Mandela. (Running Time: 15 mins.). (ENG.). 2009. 1.99 (978-1-60024-783-5(0)) Pub: Hachet Audio. Dist(s): HachBkGrp

Asombroso Poder de las Emociones: Permita que Sus Sentimientos Sean Su Guia. Esther Hicks & Jerry Hicks. Read by Jerry Hicks. (Playaway Adult Nonfiction Ser.). 2008. 64.99 (978-1-60640-619-9(1)) Find a World.

ASP Programming for the Absolute Beginner. John Gosney. (Absolute Beginner's Guide Ser.). 2001. pap. bk. 29.99 (978-0-7615-3620-8(5), CourTech) Course Tech.

Aspartame Disease: An Ignored Epidemic: A Medical, Public Health & Legal Overview. H. J. Roberts. 3 cass. (Running Time: 4 hrs. 30 min.). 2003. (978-1-884243-20-2(7)) Sunshine Sentinel.
A summary of Aspartame (Nutrasweet) approval and consumption and pharmacology; nature of reactions in database of 1,200 reactors; public health ramifications; legal issues; hazards of supplements; aspartame reactions.

Aspects. Glenda Tomosovich. 1 cass. 8.95 (347) Am Fed Astrologers.

Aspects. unabr. ed. Robert A. Monroe. Read by Robert A. Monroe. (Running Time: 45 mins.). (Explorer Ser.). 1986. 12.95 (978-1-56113-028-3(1), 29) Monroe Institute.
A discussion about the theory of overlaid aspects that contribute to the personality traits.

Aspects: What Orbs to Allow. Greg Konrad. 1 cass. 8.95 (548) Am Fed Astrologers.
Old orbs vs. new ones. Who's right.

Aspects, a Look at Inner Dialogue. Jeanne Avery. 1 cass. 8.95 (025) Am Fed Astrologers.
Misunderstood aspects: A psychological look at inner dialogue.

Aspects & Aspect Patterns. Mary Elness. 1 cass. 8.95 (741) Am Fed Astrologers.

Aspects in Comparison. Clara Darr. 1 cass. (Running Time: 90 min.). 1990. 8.95 (818) Am Fed Astrologers.

Aspects of Geriatrics Ministry. William Wagner. 1986. 10.80 (0108A) Assn Prof Chaplains.

Aspects of God. Swami Amar Jyoti. 1 cass. 1977. 9.95 (N-3) Truth Consciousness.
On personal & impersonal God; belief & unbelief; increasing our capacity to love. Function of awsterities. What are heaven, hell & salvation.

Aspects of One. Sai Maa Lakshmi Devi. 2002. audio compact disk 16.00 (978-0-9766664-7-9(2)) HIU Pr.

Aspects of the Novel. unabr. collector's ed. E. M. Forster. Read by Richard Brown. 6 cass. (Running Time: 6 hrs.). 1994. 36.00 (978-0-7366-2765-8(0), 3486) Books on Tape.
A lively study of elements common to English-language novels: story, people, plot, fantasy, prophecy, pattern & rhythm.

Aspects, Stages in Human Development. Stephanie Clement. 1 cass. 8.95 (754) Am Fed Astrologers.

Aspen & the Stream see Richard Wilbur Readings

Asperger's Syndrome: Program from the Award Winning Public Radio Series. Interview. Hosted by Peter Kramer. 1 CD. (Running Time: 1 Hour). 2005. audio compact disk 21.95 (978-1-932479-24-9(4), LCM 375) Lichtenstein Creat.
In one of our most important programs to date, this second of a two-part special report on Asperger's Syndrome offers a groundbreaking and extraordinary look at Asperger's in children and young adults. We meet Anders, a 17-year-old boy with Asperger's, and his mother Carol, who talks about her surprise when Anders suddenly began speaking like a professor and using four-syllable words. We also speak with film producer Robert Lawrence, about his forthcoming film, Mozart and the Whale, starring Josh Hartnett and co-written by "Rain Man" screenwriter Ron Bass, which tells the tale of Donald and Isabelle, two "Aspies in love." Dr. Stanley Greenspan, founder of the DIR/Floortime approach, explains how children with autistic disorders can significantly build their capacity for emotional understanding and interpersonal connections through intensive play. Dr. Richard Howlin, a psychologist works with teens with Asperger's, talks about the special challenges it poses with family, school, peers and especially dating. Finally, summing up the two-part series is commentator and visionary Howard Bloom, who reaches back to his childhood in Buffalo, and even further back to the dawn of man, to examine the lessons each of us can glean from our own weaknesses.

Asperger's Syndrome: Program from the Award Winning Public Radio Series. Hosted by Peter Kramer. 1 CD. (Running Time: 1 Hour). 2005. audio compact disk 21.30 (978-1-932479-23-2(6), LCM 374) Lichtenstein Creat.

In this, the first in a two-part special report on Asperger?s Syndrome, Dr. Peter Kramer talks with Dr. Simon Baron-Cohen, a researcher at Cambridge University, on recent advances in recognizing the condition. We meet Dr. Michael Fitzgerald of Trinity College, Dublin, Ireland, a child psychiatrist who?s made quite a stir diagnosing Asperger?s Syndrome among the dead. Then, in a panel discussion, three adults ? Liane Holliday Willey, Stephen Shore, and Michael John Carley ? talk about growing up as loners with Asperger?s. Now they celebrate their membership in the community of ?Aspies.? Finally, in a commentary, Dr. Arthur Caplan, head of the Center for Bioethics at the University of Pennsylvania, asks, ?If you could go back in time and stop the birth of the world?s most famous nerd, would you have done so??.

Aspern Papers. Henry James. Narrated by Grover Gardner. (ENG.). 2009. audio compact disk 19.95 (978-1-60646-074-0(9)) Audio Bk Con.

Aspern Papers. Henry James. Read by Jonathan Epstein. 3 CDs. (Running Time: 3 hrs. 30 mins.). 2006. bk. 22.50 (978-0-9663401-7-4(5)) BMA Studios.

The Aspern Papers, one of Henry James best known shorter works, is based on a story he heard about a collector of Shelley's manuscripts who attempted to acquire valuable letters from a mysterious old woman living in Florence. Set in Venice, James's elegant tale of suspense and romance takes the reader down the canals and inner chambers of a bygone era.

Aspern Papers. Henry James. Narrated by Campbell Renton. Prod. by Alcazar AudioWorks. Music by David Thorn. Engineer Scott Weiser. (ENG.). 2009. audio compact disk 24.95 (978-0-9821853-8-4(3)) Alcazar AudioWorks.

Aspern Papers. Henry James. Read by Alfred von Lecteur. 2009. 27.95 (978-1-60112-982-6(3)) Babblebooks.

Aspern Papers. unabr. ed. Henry James. Read by Grover Gardner. 3 cass. (Running Time: 4 hrs.). 1992. 16.95 (978-1-55685-240-4(1)) Audio Bk Con.

In this superb novelette we witness a battle between a strong-willed woman, determined to keep the secrets of a famous poet & an unscrupulous man who is equally determined to uncover them.

Aspern Papers. unabr. ed. Henry James. Narrated by Adrian Cronauer. 3 cass. (Running Time: 3 hrs. 45 mins.). 1986. 26.00 (978-1-55690-033-4(3), 86340E7) Recorded Bks.

A literary editor tries to wrest the personal papers of Jeffrey Aspern from their possessor, Juliana Bordereau.

Aspern Papers. unabr. collector's ed. Henry James. Read by Walter Zimmerman. 5 cass. (Running Time: 5 hrs.). 1983. 30.00 (978-0-7366-3967-5(5), 9509) Books on Tape.

The story of a man with an unnatural passion for the relics of a dead poet & the reclusive spinster who guards them & her romantic past.

Aspho Fields. unabr. ed. Karen Traviss. Narrated by David Colacci. (Running Time: 12 hrs. 0 mins. 0 sec.). (Gears of War Ser.). (ENG.). 2009. audio compact disk 24.99 (978-1-4001-6214-7(9)); audio compact disk 34.99 (978-1-4001-1214-2(1)); audio compact disk 69.99 (978-1-4001-4214-9(8)) Pub: Tantor Media. Dist(s): IngramPubServ

Aspiration for Self Realization. (703) Yoga Res Foun.

***Aspire.** unabr. ed. Kevin Hall. Read by Patrick Lawlor. (ENG.). 2010. (978-0-06-198886-8(3), Harper Audio) HarperCollins Pubs.

***Aspire: Discovering Your Purpose Through the Power of Words.** unabr. ed. Kevin Hall. Read by Patrick Lawlor. (ENG.). 2010. (978-0-06-198885-1(5), Harper Audio) HarperCollins Pubs.

Assassin. abr. ed. Andrew Britton. Read by Christopher Lane. (Running Time: 21600 sec.). (Ryan Kealey Ser.). 2008. audio compact disk 14.99 (978-1-4233-0746-4(1), 9781423307464, BCD Value Price) Brilliance Audio.

Assassin. abr. ed. Stephen Coonts. Narrated by Dennis Boutsikaris. 6 CDs. (Running Time: 7 hrs. 0 mins. 0 sec.). No. 3. (ENG.). 2008. audio compact disk 29.95 (978-1-59397-959-1(2)) Pub: Macmill Audio. Dist(s): Macmillan

***Assassin.** abr. ed. Stephen Coonts. (Running Time: 7 hrs. 0 mins. 0 sec.). (ENG.). 2011. audio compact disk 14.99 (978-1-4272-1188-0(4)) Pub: Macmill Audio. Dist(s): Macmillan

Assassin. abr. ed. David Hagberg. Read by Bruce Watson. 4 vols. (Kirk McGarvey Ser.). 2003. (978-1-58807-680-9(6)) Am Pubng Inc.

Assassin. abr. ed. Barry Sadler. Read by Charlton Griffin. 2 vols. (Casca Ser.: No. 13). 2003. 18.00 (978-1-58807-113-2(8)); (978-1-58807-544-4(3)) Am Pubng Inc.

Assassin. abr. ed. Barry Sadler. Read by Charlton Griffin. 2 vols. (Casca Ser.: No. 13). 2004. audio compact disk 25.00 (978-1-58807-287-0(8)); audio compact disk (978-1-58807-718-9(7)) Am Pubng Inc.

Assassin. unabr. ed. Ted Bell. Read by John Shea. (Running Time: 15 hrs.). (Hawke Ser.). 2005. 39.25 (978-1-59737-370-8(2), 9781597373708, BADLE); 24.95 (978-1-59737-369-2(9), 9781597373692, BAD); 39.25 (978-1-59737-368-5(0), 9781597373685, Brinc Audio MP3 Lib); 97.25 (978-1-59737-362-3(1), 9781597373623, BrilAudUnabridg); 32.95 (978-1-59737-361-6(3), 9781597373616, BAU); DVD & audio compact disk 24.95 (978-1-59737-367-8(2), 9781597373678, Brilliance MP3); audio compact disk 112.25 (978-1-59737-364-7(8), 9781597373647, BriAudCD Unabrid); audio compact disk 36.95 (978-1-59737-363-0(X), 9781597373630, Bril Audio CD Unabri) Brilliance Audio.

In an elegant palazzo on the Grand Canal, an American ambassador's tryst turns deadly. In the seamy underbelly of London, a pub-crawling killer is on the loose. And in a storybook chapel nestled in the Cotswolds, a marriage made in heaven turns to hell on earth. Isolated incidents? Or links in a chain of events hurtling towards catastrophe? So begins Assassin, the tour de force thriller that heralds the return of every terrorist's worst nightmare, Alex Hawke. A shadowy figure known as the Dog is believed to be the ruthless terrorist who is systematically and savagely assassinating American diplomats and their families around the globe. As the deadly toll mounts inexorably, Hawke, along with former NYPD cop and Navy SEAL Stokely Jones, is called upon by the U.S. government to launch a search for the assassin behind the murders. Hawke, who "makes James Bond look like a "slovenly, dull-witted clockpuncher" (Kirkus Reviews), is soon following a trail that leads back to London in the go-go nineties, when Arab oil money fueled lavish, and sometimes fiendish, lifestyles. Other murky clues point to the Florida Keys, where a vicious killer hides behind the gates of a fabled museum. And to a remote Indonesian island where a madman tinkers with strains of a deadly virus and slyly bides his time. Hawke must call upon resources deep within himself. He must enter a race against time to stop a cataclysmic attack on America's most populous cities and avenge the inexplicable and horrific crime that has left him devastated.

Assassin. unabr. ed. Andrew Britton. Read by Christopher Lane. (Running Time: 19 hrs.). (Ryan Kealey Ser.). 2007. 44.25 (978-1-4233-0742-6(9), 9781423307426, Brlnc Audio MP3 Lib); 29.95 (978-1-4233-0741-9(0), 9781423307419, Brilliance MP3); 44.25 (978-1-4233-0744-0(5), 9781423307440, BADLE); 92.25 (978-1-4233-0738-9(0), 9781423307389, BrilAudUnabridg); audio compact disk 107.25 (978-1-4233-0740-2(2), 9781423307402, BriAudCD Unabrid); audio compact disk 39.95 (978-1-4233-0739-6(9), 9781423307396, Bril Audio CD Unabri) Brilliance Audio.

Assassin. unabr. ed. Andrew Britton. Read by Christopher Lane. (Running Time: 19 hrs.). (Ryan Kealey Ser.). 2007. 29.95 (978-1-4233-0743-3(7), 9781423307433, BAD) Brilliance Audio.

Assassin. unabr. ed. Stephen Coonts. Narrated by Dennis Boutsikaris. (Running Time: 11 hrs. 30 mins.). (Tommy Carmellini Ser.: No. 3). 2008. 69.95 (978-0-7927-5590-6(1), Chivers Sound Lib); audio compact disk 99.95 (978-0-7927-4869-4(7), Chivers Sound Lib) AudioGO.

Assassin. unabr. ed. Stephen Coonts. Narrated by Dennis Boutsikaris. 12 CDs. (Running Time: 11 hrs. 30 mins. 0 sec.). No. 3. (ENG.). 2008. audio compact disk 39.95 (978-1-59397-957-7(6)) Pub: Macmill Audio. Dist(s): Macmillan

Assassin. unabr. collector's ed. W. E. B. Griffin. Read by Michael Russotto. 12 cass. (Running Time: 18 hrs.). (Badge of Honor Ser.: Vol. 5). 1994. 96.00 (978-0-7366-2851-8(7), 133263) Books on Tape.

A political assassin gets ready to make his move. The police department hasn't a clue, just a single, perfectly typed bomb threat. In a few short days, the corruption of one cop & the madness of an assassin can blow the whole city sky high!.

Assassin in the Greenwood: A Medieval Mystery Featuring Hugh Corbett. unabr. ed. Paul C. Doherty. 6 cass. (Running Time: 6 hrs.). 1998. 69.95 (978-1-85903-123-0(4)) Pub: Magna Story GBR. Dist(s): Ulverscroft US

***Assassin of Gor.** unabr. ed. John Norman. Read by Ralph Lister. (Running Time: 16 hrs.). 2011. 24.99 (978-1-4418-4918-2(1), 9781441849182, Brilliance MP3); 39.97 (978-1-4418-4919-9(X), 9781441849199, Brlnc Audio MP3 Lib); audio compact disk 29.99 (978-1-4418-4916-8(5), 9781441849168, Bril Audio CD Unabri); audio compact disk 79.97 (978-1-4418-4917-5(3), 9781441849175, BriAudCD Unabrid) Brilliance Audio.

Assassination. unabr. ed. Douglas Hirt. Read by Rusty Nelson. 8 cass. (Running Time: 9 hrs. 12 min.). (Riverboat Ser.: Bk. 3). 2001. 49.95 (978-1-55686-899-3(5)) Books in Motion.

Campaigning for the presidency of the United States, passenger Stephen Douglas is the target of assassins who hope to benefit from a war between the states.

Assassination: The Death of a President. Kenneth Bruce. 1 cass. (Running Time: 1 hr.). Dramatization. (Excursions in History Ser.). 12.50 Alpha Tape.

Assassination in America see James McKinley I

Assassination in America. unabr. ed. James McKinley. Interview with James McKinley. 1 cass. (Running Time: 29 mins.). 1985. 10.00 New Letters.

These passages concern the assassinations of John Kennedy, Martin Luther King & Bobby Kennedy. Author also discusses the theme of this book.

***Assassination of Jesse James by the Coward Robert Ford.** abr. ed. Ron Hansen. Read by Sam Freed. (ENG.). 2007. (978-0-06-122990-9(3), Harper Audio); (978-0-06-122989-3(X), Harper Audio) HarperCollins Pubs.

Assassination of Jesse James by the Coward Robert Ford. abr. ed. Ron Hansen. Read by Sam Freed. (Running Time: 21600 sec.). 2007. audio compact disk 19.95 (978-0-06-112981-0(X)) HarperCollins Pubs.

Assassination of Jesse James by the Coward Robert Ford. unabr. ed. Ron Hansen. 10 cass. (Running Time: 46800 sec.). 2007. 65.95 (978-1-4332-1084-6(3)); audio compact disk 81.00 (978-1-4332-1085-3(1)); audio compact disk 29.95 (978-1-4332-1086-0(X)) Blckstn Audio.

Assassination of Robert F. Kennedy. unabr. ed. 1 cass. (Running Time: 50 min.). 12.95 (19014) J Norton Pubs.

This is a documentary made at the Kennedy headquarters in the Ambassador Hotel, Los Angeles. It covers the entire horrifying incident.

Assassination Vacation. abr. ed. Sarah Vowell. 2005. 15.95 (978-0-7435-5029-1(3)) Pub: S&S Audio. Dist(s): S and S Inc

Assassination Vacation. unabr. abr. ed. Sarah Vowell. Read by Sarah Vowell. 6 Cds. (Running Time: 70 hrs. 0 mins. 0 sec.). (ENG.). 2005. audio compact disk 29.95 (978-0-7435-4005-6(0)) Pub: S&S Audio. Dist(s): S and S Inc

Assassins. abr. ed. Oliver North & Joe Musser. Read by Jon Gauger. 8 CDs. (Running Time: 32400 sec.). 2006. audio compact disk 29.99 (978-0-8054-4090-4(9)) BH Pubng Grp.

Assassins. unabr. collector's ed. Elia Kazan. Read by Dan Lazar. 8 cass. (Running Time: 12 hrs.). 1986. 64.00 (978-0-7366-0977-7(6), 1918) Books on Tape.

A revolutionary daughter confronts her conformist dad in the USA of the 70's.

Assassins: An Experience in Sound & Drama. adpt. ed. Tim LaHaye & Jerry B. Jenkins. 4 CDs. (Running Time: 25 min.). (Left Behind Ser.: Bk. 6). (ENG., 2001. audio compact disk 19.99 (978-0-8423-4338-1(5)) Tyndale Hse.

Assassins: Assignment: Jerusalem, Target: Antichrist. Tim LaHaye & Jerry B. Jenkins. Narrated by Richard Ferrone. 10 CDs. (Running Time: 11 hrs. 15 mins.). (Left Behind Ser.: Bk. 6). 2000. audio compact disk 97.00 (978-0-7887-4900-1(5), C1275E7) Recorded Bks.

It is now 38 months into the Tribulation. As the believers in Christ find sanctuary in safe houses, they continue to receive spiritual strength from their leader. But one of the faithful, desperate to hasten the fulfillment of prophecy, is secretly planning to assassinate the Antichrist, Nicolae Carpathia.

Assassins: Assignment: Jerusalem, Target: Antichrist. abr. ed. Tim LaHaye & Jerry B. Jenkins. Read by Frank Muller. 3 CDs. (Running Time: 2 hrs.). (Left Behind Ser.: Bk. 6). (ENG., 1999. audio compact disk 19.99 (978-0-8423-3682-6(6)) Tyndale Hse.

Assassins: Assignment: Jerusalem, Target: Antichrist. unabr. ed. Tim LaHaye & Jerry B. Jenkins. Read by Jack Sondericker. 8 cass. (Running Time: 11 hrs. 12 min.). (Left Behind Ser.: Bk. 6). 2001. 49.95 (978-1-55686-962-4(2)); audio compact disk 65.00 (978-1-58116-130-4(1)) Books in Motion.

Rayford Steel and Buck Williams plan to dethrone Nicolae Carpathia and expose him as the Antichrist. But will Carpathia survive?.

Assassins: Assignment: Jerusalem, Target: Antichrist. unabr. ed. Tim LaHaye & Jerry B. Jenkins. Read by Frank Muller. 1 CD. (Running Time: 1 hr. 30 mins.). (Left Behind Ser.: Bk. 6). 2001. audio compact disk Books on Tape.

Assassins: Assignment: Jerusalem, Target: Antichrist. unabr. ed. Tim LaHaye & Jerry B. Jenkins. Narrated by Richard Ferrone. 8 cass. (Running Time: 11 hrs. 15 mins.). (Left Behind Ser.: Bk. 6). 2000. 77.00 (978-0-7887-4400-6(3), 95871E7) Recorded Bks.

It is now 38 months into the Tribulation. As the believers in Christ find sanctuary in safe houses, they continue to receive spiritual strength from their leader. But one of the faithful, desperate to hasten the fulfillment of prophecy, is secretly planning to assassinate the Antichrist, Nicolae Carpathia.

Assassins: Assignment: Jerusalem, Target: Antichrist. unabr. ed. Tim LaHaye & Jerry B. Jenkins. Read by Richard Ferrone. 7 cass. (Running Time: 11 hrs. 15 mins.). (Left Behind Ser.: Bk. 6). 2004. 29.95 (978-0-7887-5128-8(X), 00104); audio compact disk 39.95 (978-0-7887-5137-0(9), 00082) Recorded Bks.

As the sixth volume, Assassins, follows the fulfillment of Biblical prophecy, terrifying portents of judgement appear. It is now thirty-eight months into the Tribulation. Giant horsemen ride the earth, scorching thousands with their fiery wrath. The believers in Christ, finding sanctuary in safe houses, continue to receive spiritual strength from their leader. But one of the faithful, desperate to hasten events, is secretly planning to assassinate the Antichrist, Nicolae Carpathia.

Assassin's Accomplice: Mary Surratt & the Plot to Kill Abraham Lincoln. unabr. ed. Kate Clifford Larson. Read by Laural Merlington. (Running Time: 8 hrs.). 2008. 39.25 (978-1-4233-6377-4(9), 9781423363774, BADLE); 24.95 (978-1-4233-6376-7(0), 9781423363767, BAD); audio compact disk 24.95 (978-1-4233-6374-3(4), 9781423363743, Brilliance MP3); audio compact disk 29.95 (978-1-4233-6372-9(8), 9781423363729, Bril Audio CD Unabri); audio compact disk 39.25 (978-1-4233-6375-0(2), 9781423363750, Brlnc Audio MP3 Lib); audio compact disk 87.25 (978-1-4233-6373-6(6), 9781423363736, BriAudCD Unabrid) Brilliance Audio.

***Assassin's Apprentice.** unabr. ed. Robin Hobb. Narrated by Paul Boehmer. (Running Time: 15 hrs. 30 mins.). (Farseer Ser.). 2010. 39.99 (978-1-4001-9434-6(2)); 20.99 (978-1-4001-8434-7(7)) Tantor Media.

***Assassin's Apprentice.** unabr. ed. Robin Hobb. Narrated by Paul Boehmer. (Running Time: 17 hrs. 30 mins. 0 sec.). (Farseer Ser.). (ENG.). 2010. 29.99 (978-1-4001-6434-9(6)); audio compact disk 39.99 (978-1-4001-1434-4(9)); audio compact disk 79.99 (978-1-4001-4434-1(5)) Pub: Tantor Media. Dist(s): IngramPubServ

Assassin's Destiny. unabr. ed. J. M. Shaw. Read by Kevin Foley. 8 cass. (Running Time: 8 hrs 42 mins.). 1996. 49.95 (978-1-55686-692-0(5)) Books in Motion.

Nostradamus predicts the destruction of New York in 1999. Ben Lewis believes if he kills Juda Abbah, a moslem leader, the prediction can be thwarted.

Assassin's Express. Carol Eason. Read by Carol Eason. 3 CDs. (Running Time: 3 hrs.). (Mercenary Ser.: No. 8). 2004. audio compact disk (978-1-58807-898-8(1)); audio compact disk 25.00 (978-1-58807-332-7(7)) Am Pubng Inc.

Hank Frost is the one-eyed mercenary who takes jobs others fear. His assignment is to protect a woman agent back in the U.S. from a deep cover operation. She carries the knowledge of the undercover agents who infiltrated the FBI and CIA. Frost must drive her from Los Angeles to the White House to meet with the president. But someone wants both of them dead. So does the KGB. Even the weather conspires against them. If Frost can keep the woman alive it will take all his skill and cunning to overcome all the trials ahead of them.

Assassin's Express. abr. ed. Axel Kilgore. Read by Carol Eason. Abr. by Odin Westgaard. 2 vols. No. 8. 2003. 18.00 (978-1-58807-164-4(2)); (978-1-58807-655-7(5)) Am Pubng Inc.

Assassins of Athens. unabr. ed. Jeffrey Siger. (Running Time: 13 hrs. 0 mins.). 2010. 29.95 (978-1-4417-1651-4(3)); 79.95 (978-1-4417-1647-7(5)); audio compact disk 109.00 (978-1-4417-1648-4(3)) Blckstn Audio.

Assassins of Rome. unabr. ed. Caroline Lawrence. Read by Justine Eyre. 3 cass. (Running Time: 4 hrs. 24 mins.). (Roman Mysteries Ser.: Bk. 4). (J). 2006. 30.00 (978-0-307-20659-6(9), Listening Lib); audio compact disk 38.00 (978-0-7393-3603-8(7), Listening Lib) Pub: Random Audio Pubg. Dist(s): Random

Assault see Poetry of Edna St. Vincent Millay

Assault from the Ivory Tower. Leonard Peikoff. 1 cass. (Running Time: 90 mins.). 1983. 12.95 (978-1-56114-056-5(2), LP07C) Second Renaissance.

Assault in Norway. unabr. ed. Thomas Gallagher. Read by Dan Lazar. 8 cass. (Running Time: 8 hrs.). 1976. 48.00 (978-0-7366-0033-0(7), 1045) Books on Tape.

True story of allied attack on German heavy water plant in Nazi occupied Norway.

Assault on Lake Casitas. unabr. collector's ed. Brad A. Lewis. Read by Paul Shay. 8 cass. (Running Time: 8 hrs.). 1992. 48.00 (978-0-7366-2166-3(0), 2965) Books on Tape.

More than a quest for an Olympic rowing gold medal, it is about challenging convention, overcoming & working outside the system.

Assault on Reason. unabr. ed. Al Gore. Read by Will Patton. 9 CDs. (Running Time: 10 hrs.). (ENG.). (gr. 12 up). 2007. audio compact disk 39.95 (978-0-14-314215-7(1), PengAudBks) Penguin Grp USA.

Assault on the Empress. Jerry Ahern. Read by Carol Eason. 2 vols. No. 2. 2004. 18.00 (978-1-58807-490-4(0)); (978-1-58807-942-8(2)) Am Pubng Inc.

Assault with Intent. unabr. collector's ed. William X. Kienzle. Read by Edward Holland. 7 cass. (Running Time: 10 hrs. 30 min.). (Father Koesler Mystery Ser.: No. 4). 1997. 56.00 (978-0-7366-3994-1(2), 4459) Books on Tape.

Four gunmen are stalking Detroit's seminaries & every priest is a target. Father Koesler's on the case. A much-praised mystery series.

***Assaulted by Joy: The Redemption of a Cynic.** Stephen W. Simpson. (Running Time: 5 hrs. 38 mins. 0 sec.). (ENG.). 2008. 14.99 (978-0-310-30226-1(9)) Zondervan.

Assegai. unabr. ed. Wilbur Smith. Read by Simon Vance. (Running Time: 16 hrs. 0 mins. 0 sec.). (ENG.). 2009. audio compact disk 49.95 (978-1-4272-0676-3(7)) Pub: Macmill Audio. Dist(s): Macmillan

Assembling California: From Annals of the Former World. unabr. ed. John McPhee. Narrated by Nelson Runger. 7 cass. (Running Time: 10 hrs.). 1993. 60.00 (978-1-55690-889-7(X), 93331E7) Recorded Bks.

Thirty years ago, the theory that continents are comprised of drifting plates evoked more scorn than serious research. Today, this revolutionary theory continues to dazzle & challenge geologists & laymen alike. Explores an area uniquely demonstrative of the plate tectonic theory: California, which according to "tectonicists," is breaking apart at its seams.

Assembly. Norman Finkelstein. (ENG.). 2005. 4.00 (978-1-933675-01-5(2)) Dos Madres Pr.

Assembly of Women: Ecclesiazusae. Aristophanes. Tr. by Robert Mayhew from GEC. Intro. by Robert Mayhew. (Literary Classics Ser.).Tr. of Ecclesiazusae. (ENG.). 1997. 16.98 (978-1-57392-133-6(5)) Prometheus Bks.

***Assertive Communication Skills for Managers.** PUEI. 2009. audio compact disk 199.00 (978-1-935041-79-5(7), CareerTrack) P Univ E Inc.

Assertive Communication Skills for Professionals. PUEI. 1994. audio compact disk 89.95 (978-1-933328-03-4(7), CareerTrack) P Univ E Inc.

Assertive Communication Skills for Professionals: How to Combine Strength with Sensitivity to Get More of What You Want. Carol Price. 4 cass. (Running Time: 3 hrs. 30 mins.). wbk. ed. 59.95 (V10173) CareerTrack Pubns.
Ever notice how assertive people can be honest & forthright - & still respect the feelings of others? Their interpersonal skills & style earn them respect & cooperation at every level. Now, with the all-new Assertive Communication Skills for Professionals program, you & your staff can learn to handle your communication challenges with confidence, openness & competence.

Assertive Communication Skills for Women. abr. ed. Chris Abiera. Read by Chris Abiera. 2 cass. (Running Time: 3 hrs.). 1996. bk. 21.95 (978-1-878542-72-4(9),) SkillPath Pubns.
Teaches both the verbal & nonverbal communication skills spelling the difference between success & stagnation in meeting professional & personal goals.

Assertive Sex: Close Encounters of an Intimate Kind. Arynne Simon. 4 cass. (Running Time: 4 hrs.). 1995. bk. 59.95 (978-1-882389-11-7(5)) Wilarvi Communs.
Sex & sexuality in today's reality.

Assertiveness. 1 cass. 10.00 (978-1-58506-034-4(8), 66) New Life Inst OR.
Learn to assert yourself with self-confidence & self-respect.

Assertiveness. (Running Time: 45 mins.). (Educational Ser.). 9.98 (978-1-55909-119-0(3), 96S) Randolph Tapes.

Assertiveness. Bruce Goldberg. (ENG.). 2005. audio compact disk 17.00 (978-1-57968-096-1(8)); 13.00 (978-1-885577-17-7(6)) Pub: B Goldberg. Dist(s): Baker Taylor
This self hypnosis cassette trains the listeners to become more assertive & take charge of their life.

Assertiveness. Cal LeMon. Read by Cal LeMon. 2 cass. (Running Time: 3 hrs.). (National Seminars Ser.). 1998. 17.95 (978-1-886463-46-2(8)) Oasis Audio.
Learn how to assert yourself in a way that treats others with respect, while achieving your goals.

Assertiveness: Gettin' What You Want. Instructed by Stuart Wilde. 2 cass. (Running Time: 2 hrs.). (Self-Help Tape Ser.). 21.95 (978-0-930603-41-0(9)) White Dove NM.
Learn how to hone your will so that life gives you what you want, with no other excuse, reason or apology other than that you demand it.

Assertiveness: The Right Choice. Cal LeMon. 4 cass. (Running Time: 4 hrs.). wbk. ed. 49.95 (814-C47); 4.95 addtl. wkbk. (814WB) Natl Seminars.
Being assertive often is confused with being aggressive. Learn the difference & how it can be a positive influence in your life. Everyday situations are presented & appropriate assertive responses taught.

Assertiveness for Career & Personal Success. 4 cass. (Running Time: 4 hrs.). wbk. ed. 139.00 (978-0-7612-0466-4(0), 80198) AMACOM.
You'll learn how to: Recognize & avoid seven self-defeating, non-assertive roles; Express your desires, feelings, & ideas fully & completely to others; Free yourself to say & do all the things you truly want; Handle stress; Improve your interpersonal relationships; Manage others without being aggressive or manipulative; Respond to other people's needs without giving up your own & much more.

Assertiveness Power Vol. 19: Strengthen Your Personal Power. Jonathan Parker. 2 cass. (Running Time: 1 hr. 45 mins.). 1992. 17.00 (978-1-58400-018-1(X)) QuantumQuests Intl.

Assertiveness Skills for Managers & Supervisors. PUEI. 2006. audio compact disk 89.95 (978-1-933328-59-1(2), Fred Pryor) P Univ E Inc.

Assertiveness Training. Helga Rhode. 4 cass. (Running Time: 3 hrs. 44 mins.). 49.95 CareerTrack Pubns.
Develop the assertive style of today's most successful professionals. Discusses how to strike a powerful balance between being "too nice" & "coming on strong".

Assertiveness Training. abr. ed. Martha Davis. Read by Jerry Landis. 1 cass. (Running Time: 62 mins.). (Messages Tapes Ser.). (ENG.). 1988. reel tape 11.95 (978-0-934986-36-6(3), 17) New Harbinger.

Assertiveness Training for Professionals. Helga Rhode. 4 cass. (Running Time: 4 hrs.). 64.95 (V10002) CareerTrack Pubns.
You'll learn how self-respect, honesty & self-control build an assertive style. You'll also understand where your responsibility for others begins & ends. Assertiveness helps you get lasting cooperation from all the important people in your life. The result? You & your whole team will be more relaxed, open & productive.

Assertiveness Training for Professionals. Helga Rhode. 4 cass. (Running Time: 4 hrs.). 1995. 19.95 (978-0-943066-14-1(X)) CareerTrack Pubns.

Assertiveness Training for Women. unabr. ed. Janet L. Wolfe. 1 cass. (Running Time: 48 mins.). 12.95 (C29347) J Norton Pubs.
Assertiveness training procedures have been demonstrated to be useful in helping women develop a sense of greater personal effectiveness. Wolfe shows how & when to use assertiveness training & gives behavioral techniques to treat beliefs that impede assertion.

Assertiveness Training Workshop. Aliyah Stein. 4 cass. (Running Time: 4 hrs.). 36.00 (A0372-89) Sound Photosyn.
At the end of the day-long training, you will be able to state your position in the situations that present themselves, or know what is keeping you from doing so.

Assessing & Diagnosing Social Skills Training for Nonverbal Communication. Contrib. by Maria Antoniadas & Kathryn McCarthy. 1 cass. (Running Time: 1 hr. 30 mins.). 20.00 (19-007A) J W Wood.
Discusses treatment models of social skills group, defines social competence, addresses non-verbal communication & specific socio-emotional/adaptational difficulties of NLD, describes general principals of intervention in NLD & group treatment programs utilized.

Assessing & Diagnosing the Individual with Nonverbal Learning Disorders. Contrib. by Duane Kosters. 1 cass. (Running Time: 1 hrs. 30 mins.). 20.00 (19-006A) J W Wood.
Thorough & informative overview of NLD. Discusses the types of deficient performances.

Assessing & Promoting Social Competence in Preschool Children with Communication Disorders. Michael J. Guralnick & Mabel L. Rice. 1 cass. (Running Time: 1 hr.). 2000. pap. bk. 79.00 (978-1-58041-076-2(6), 0112344) Am Speech Lang Hearing.
Reviews ways communication affects the development of social competence in preschool children & examines inclusive classrooms as an example that fosters social interaction & help develop social competence.

Assessing Lab Values. Patricia Hoefler. 1991. (978-1-56533-092-4(7)) MEDS Pubng.

Assessment of the Renal System. unabr. ed. Instructed by Michael Shapiro. 4 cass. (Running Time: 7 hrs.). 1990. bk. 79.00 (HT03) Ctr Hlth Educ.
Play a leading role in assessing this vital system. Staying in balance is the key. This course gives simple explanations of the complex fluid & electrolyte system. It is designed for critical care nurses & is especially beneficial for nurses involved with dialysis.

Asset Allocation Explained: Innovative Strategies for Managing Client Expectations. Instructed by Michael Kresh. (Running Time: 116 mins.). 2004. audio compact disk 19.95 (978-1-59280-133-6(1)) Marketplace Bks.
Rediscover an essential concept to investment success that has long been overlooked: asset allocation. Join leading investment advisor and top wealth manager, Michael Kresh CFP a in his new thought provoking and highly entertaining presentation, ?Asset Allocation Explained: Innovative strategies for managing client expectations?.Gain straightforward insight into the steps essential to involving clients in the asset allocation process. As Kresh acknowledges, it's a dynamic new investment world that requires a new style of diversification to help clients better understand ? and appreciate ? the role that an advisor plays in achieving their investment goals. Kresh goes on to explain the essential strategies and concepts of asset allocation such as:-The role, functions, and goal of asset allocation-The basic concepts of the Modern Portfolio Theory ? alpha, beta, and R-squared-The critical role that Investment Policy Statements play in your role as advisor-Understanding the impact of timing vs. time horizon-Using software to determine correlations and how to interpret the data into a way clients will understand-Utilizing asset allocation within a variable and non-variable product-The risks, traps, and pitfalls related with asset allocation and so much more!You'll benefit by learning the effective means essential to accurately conveying the need for asset allocation to your clients.

Asset-Based Lending Including Commercial Finance & Acquisition Financing. Peter H. Weil. 8 cass. (Running Time: 11 hrs. 15 mins.). 1990. 125.00 (T7-9261) PLI.
Examines both owner (end-user) & dealer financing.

Asset Protection. Ed. by Socrates Media Editors. 2005. audio compact disk 29.95 (978-1-59546-084-4(5)) Pub: Socrates Med LLC. Dist(s): Midpt Trade

Asset Protection: How Far Should You Go? 4 cass. (Running Time: 3 hrs. 20 mins.). 1998. pap. bk. 225.00 (YB80) Am Law Inst.

Asset Protection Strategies. 2005. audio compact disk 289.00 (978-0-8080-8927-8(7)) Toolkit Media.

Assets. unabr. ed. Ted Allbeury. Narrated by Garrick Hagan. 5 cass. (Running Time: 7 hrs. 30 mins.). 2001. 47.00 (978-1-84197-182-7(0), H1166E7) Recorded Bks.
Operation MK Ultra is a CIA top secret project involving hypnotic mind control. In many cases, the subjects are not even aware they have been hypnotized. Unfortunately, keeping it secret is proving difficult, so the powers that be call in Joe Maguire. His unenviable task is to monitor the results of the CIA's illicit & sometimes tragic experiments - to pick up the pieces when it all goes wrong. Picked because of his personal ethics & general decency, Joe soon finds that it's these very qualities that are getting in the way of his job.

Asshole: How I Got Rich & Happy by Not Giving a Damn about Anyone & How You Can, Too. unabr. ed. Martin Kihn. Read by Malcolm Hillgartner. (Running Time: 21600 sec.). 2008. audio compact disk 29.95 (978-1-4332-1247-5(1)) Blckstn Audio.

Assholes Finish First. abr. adpt. ed. Tucker Max. Read by Tucker Max. (Running Time: 8 hrs. 30 mins. 0 sec.). 2010. audio compact disk 29.99 (978-0-7435-7110-4(X)) Pub: S&S Audio. Dist(s): S and S Inc

Assimil Language Learning: Arabic with Ease - Multimedia Pack: Course Book. Assimil Staff & Jacques J. Schmidt. Adapted by Stephen Geist. 3. 2002. cass. & audio compact disk 170.00 (978-2-7005-2069-9(6)) Laurier Bks CAN.

Assistance to the Minister's Family: Proceedings of the 45th Annual Convention National Association of Evangelicals Buffalo, New York. Read by Jack Mottweiler. 1 cass. (Running Time: 60 mins.). 1987. 4.00 (331) Nat Assn Evan.

Assistant. unabr. ed. Bernard Malamud. Read by George Guidall. 6 cass. 1999. 38.50 (978-1-893079-01-4(5), JCCAUDIOBOOKS) Jewish Contempry Classics.
Classic novel of a young man's journey to personal redemption & his life changing relationship with a poor grocer & his family.

Assistive Technology Solutions: For IEP Teams. Sherry L. Purcell & Debbie Grant. (gr. k-3). 2002. spiral bd. 49.00 (978-1-57861-136-2(9), IEP Res) Attainment.

Assize of the Dying. Ellis Peters, pseud. Read by Di Langford. 5 cass. (Running Time: 7 hrs. 30 mins.). (Isis Ser.). 2001. 49.95 (940609) Pub: ISIS Audio GBR. Dist(s): Ulverscroft US

Assize of the Dying. Ellis Peters, pseud. Read by Di Langford. 6 CDs. (Running Time: 9 hrs.). (Isis Ser.). 2001. audio compact disk 64.95 (978-0-7531-1129-1(2)) Pub: ISIS Audio GBR. Dist(s): Ulverscroft US

Assize of the Dying. unabr. ed. Ellis Peters, pseud. Read by Di Langford. 5 cass. (Running Time: 7 hrs.). (Isis Ser.). (J). 1995. 49.95 (978-1-85695-709-0(8), 940609) Pub: ISIS Lrg Prnt GBR. Dist(s): Ulverscroft US

Associate. abr. ed. John Grisham. Read by Erik Singer. (Running Time: 6 hrs.). (ENG.). 2009. 15.00 (978-0-7393-3302-0(X)) Pub: Random Audio Pubg. Dist(s): Random

***Associate.** abr. ed. John Grisham. Read by Erik Singer. (Running Time: 6 hrs.). (ENG.). 2010. audio compact disk 14.99 (978-0-307-75090-7(6), Random AudioBks) Pub: Random Audio Pubg. Dist(s): Random

Associate. abr. ed. Phillip Margolin. Read by Margaret Whitton. 4 cass. (Running Time: 6 hrs.). 2001. 25.95 (978-0-694-52610-9(X)); audio compact disk 29.95 (978-0-694-52611-6(8)) HarperCollins Pubs.

***Associate.** abr. ed. Phillip Margolin. Read by Margaret Whitton. (ENG.). 2004. (978-0-06-079790-4(8), Harper Audio); (978-0-06-081427-4(6), Harper Audio) HarperCollins Pubs.

Associate. abr. ed. Phillip Margolin. Read by Margaret Whitton. 2005. audio compact disk 14.95 (978-0-06-076356-5(6)) HarperCollins Pubs.

Associate. unabr. ed. John Grisham. Read by Erik Singer. 10 CDs. 2008. audio compact disk 100.00 (978-1-4159-5889-6(0), BksonTape) Pub: Random Audio Pubg. Dist(s): Random

Associate. unabr. ed. John Grisham. Read by Erik Singer. (Running Time: 11 hrs.). (ENG.). 2009. 22.50 (978-0-7393-3305-1(4)); audio compact disk 44.95 (978-0-7393-3304-4(6), Random AudioBks) Pub: Random Audio Pubg. Dist(s): Random

***Associate.** unabr. ed. Phillip Margolin. Read by Scott Brick. (ENG.). 2004. (978-0-06-081347-5(4), Harper Audio); (978-0-06-075576-8(8), Harper Audio) HarperCollins Pubs.

Associate. unabr. collector's ed. Phillip Margolin. Read by Scott Brick. 6 cass. (Running Time: 9 hrs.). 2001. 48.00; audio compact disk 64.00 Books on Tape.
A young, ambitious attorney, in the middle of a multi-billion dollar case of fraud, becomes the target of a killer's bullets.

Assorted Prose. unabr. collector's ed. John Updike. Read by Wolfram Kandinsky. 8 cass. (Running Time: 12 hrs.). Incl. Beerbohm & Others. (1276); Dogwood Tree: A Boyhood. (1276); Drinking from a Cup Made Cinchy. (1276); Faith in Search of Understanding. (1276); Lucid Eye in Silver Town. (1276); More Love in the Western. (1276); My Uncle's Death. (1276); On the Sidewalk, Mr. Ex-Resident. (1276); 1982. 64.00 (978-0-7366-0288-4(7), 1276) Books on Tape.
A compendium of this noted author's essays & reviews.

Assume the Feeling of the Wish Fulfilled. Neville Goddard. 1 cass. (Running Time: 62 mins.). 1964. 8.00 (68) J & L Pubns.
Neville taught Imagination Creates Reality. He was a powerfully influential teacher of God as Consciousness.

Assumption. Narrated by William Biersach & Charles A. Coulombe. 2 cass. (Running Time: 2 hrs.). 2000. 14.00 (20142) Cath Treas.
A thought-provoking look at the historical origin, theological meaning & practical implications of this great mystery, as well as its connection to the Doctrine of the Immaculate Conception.

Assurance. unabr. ed. Robert A. Monroe. Read by Roland Simon. 1 cass. (Running Time: 30 mins.). (Human Plus Ser.). (FRE.). 1993. 14.95 (978-1-56102-100-0(8)) Inter Indus.
Address groups or individuals with ease.

Assurance of Victory. 4 cass. (Running Time: 4 hrs.). stu. ed. 15.95 (20133, HarperThor) HarpC GBR.

Assurance When You Suffer. unabr. ed. R. Eugene Sterner. Read by R. Eugene Sterner. 2 cass. (Running Time: 1 hr.). 1998. 16.95 (978-1-891314-02-5(5), 14025, Jordan) Evangel Pub Hse.
Dr. Sterner counsels with a person who is seriously ill, answering the listener's spiritual questions: "Why me? Is God punishing me for something? How can I get throught this? What if I am not healed?".

Assuring Spiritual Well-Being of Patients. Gus Verdery. 1986. 10.80 (0103A) Assn Prof Chaplains.

Assymetric Time in Physics. 1 cass. (Running Time: 56 mins.). 14.95 (CBC1010) MMI Corp.
Physicists look at the problem of irreversibility including classical probability calculus, statistical mechanics, etc. Is time reversible? Discussion of theoretical time.

Assyrian Rejuvinator. unabr. ed. Clifford Ashdown. Read by Walter Covell. 1 cass. (Running Time: 56 min.). Dramatization. 1981. 7.95 (S-56) Jimcin Record.
Flim-flam foiled by Romney Pringle.

Astaire: The Man, the Dancer. abr. ed. Bob Thomas. Perf. by Tommy Tune. Frwd. by Peter Bart. 4 cass. (Running Time: 6 hrs.). (Hollywood Classics Ser.). 2001. 25.00 (978-1-931056-44-1(7), N Millennium Audio) New Millenn Enter.
In January 1933, a young Broadway star Fred Astaire entered the RKO studios for a screen test, "Can't act, Slightly bald. Also dances," was the reaction of one official. Thus began the amazing film career of one of the world's most celebrated dancers. Captures the elegance and mystique of the most recognized and loved figures ever to dance across the silver screen. During nearly eighty years in every major entertainment medium, he persevered and excelled. He never quit, never passed up an opportunity to push himself and to dance to new levels of achievement.

Asteroid Comparison. Bernice P. Grebner. 1 cass. 8.95 (792) Am Fed Astrologers.

Asteroids. Lois Daton. 1 cass. 8.95 (077) Am Fed Astrologers.

Asteroids. Emma B. Donath. 1 cass. 8.95 (094) Am Fed Astrologers.
Four principal asteroids in natal, synastry, directions.

Asteroids: Roman or Greek. Nona G. Press. Read by Nona G. Press. 1 cass. (Running Time: 90 mins.). 1994. 8.95 (1158) Am Fed Astrologers.

Asteroids: The Minor Planets. 1 cass. (Running Time: 28 mins.). 14.95 (23334) MMI Corp.
Discusses location, characteristics, asteroid belt & more.

Asteroids of the Moment. Nona G. Press. 1 cass. 1992. 8.95 (1085) Am Fed Astrologers.

Asthma. Bruce Goldberg. Read by Bruce Goldberg. 1 cass. (Running Time: 25 mins.). (ENG.). 2005. Rental 13.00 (978-1-885577-34-4(6)) B Goldberg.
Use self-hypnosis to restore normal breathing by eliminating this type of allergic response.

Asthma: Ancient Truths, Natural Remedies & the Latest Findings for Your Health Today. unabr. ed. Don Colbert. 1 cass. (Running Time: 1 hr.). (Bible Cure Ser.). 2004. 7.99 (978-1-58926-707-7(9)) Oasis Audio.

Asthma: Ancient Truths, Natural Remedies & the Latest Findings for Your Health Today. unabr. ed. Don Colbert. Narrated by Tim Lundeen. 1 CD. (Running Time: 1 hr.). (Bible Cure Ser.). (ENG.). 2004. audio compact disk 9.99 (978-1-58926-708-4(7)) Oasis Audio.

Asthma & Breathing. Steven Gurgevich. (ENG.). 2002. audio compact disk 19.95 (978-1-932170-19-1(7), HWH) Tranceformation.

Asthma-Breathing. 1 cass. (Running Time: 1 hr.). 2001. 9.95 (CA605) Pub: VisnQst Vid Aud. Dist(s): TMW Media

Asthma Meditation. 1 cass. (Holistic Support Meditations Ser.). 14.98 (978-0-87554-579-0(3), MH102) Valley Sun.

Astonishing Adventures of Fanboy & Goth Girl. unabr. ed. Barry Lyga. Read by Scott Brick. 8 CDs. (Running Time: 9 hrs. 58 mins). (YA). (gr. 9 up). 2007. audio compact disk 60.00 (978-0-7393-4861-1(2), Random AudioBks) Pub: Random Audio Pubg. Dist(s): Random

Astonishing Adventures of Fanboy & Goth Girl. unabr. ed. Barry Lyga. Read by Scott Brick. (Running Time: 35880 sec.). (ENG.). (J). (gr. 9-12). 2007. audio compact disk 50.00 (978-0-7393-3904-6(4), Listening Lib) Pub: Random Audio Pubg. Dist(s): Random

Astonishing Power of Emotions, Set. Esther Hicks & Jerry Hicks. Read by Jerry Hicks. 8 CDs. 2007. audio compact disk 39.95 (978-1-4019-1247-5(8)) Hay House.

Astragale. Albertine Sarrazin. Read by C. Deis et al. 4 cass. (Running Time: 4 hrs.). (FRE.). 1991. 34.95 (1484-VSL) Olivia & Hill.
A young female convict breaks her anklebone, i.e. the astragalus, while escaping over the prison wall. An authentic picture of life on the run.

Astral Dreams. (Running Time: 60 mins.). 2002. audio compact disk 15.99 (978-1-904972-40-2(3)) Global Jrny GBR GBR.

Astral Experience. Robert A. Monroe. Hosted by Bruce Stephen Holmes. 1 cass. (Running Time: 60 mins.). 9.95 (AT5025) Lghtwrks Aud & Vid.
As the most well-known author on out-of-body travel, Robert Monroe shares his years of expertise at the Monroe Institute with host Bruce Stephen Holmes in this exclusive "Timeless Voyager Audio" interview.

Astral Project & Remember. 1 cass. (Tara Sutphen Sleep Programming Tapes Ser.). 11.98 (978-0-87554-552-3(1), 2101) Valley Sun.

Astral Projection. 1 cass. 10.00 (978-1-58506-044-3(5), 86) New Life Inst OR.
You can project your consciousness into dimensions of the past, present, & future.

Astral Projection. Barrie Konicov. 1 cass. (Running Time: 1 hr.). 11.98 (978-0-87082-395-4(7), 006) Potentials.
In this program the author shows how people are able to successfully complete their first astral trip. You can join the increasing number of people who are experiencing out-of-body experiences.

Astral Projection. Barrie Konicov. 1 CD. 2003. audio compact disk 16.98 (978-0-87082-968-0(8)) Potentials.
Join the increasing number of people who are having out-of-body experiences. You will find the self-hypnosis on track 1 and the subliminal on track 2. The easy-listening music of the subliminal, together with the self-hypnosis, is the original format which most people love and with which they are most familiar.

Astral Projection. Dick Sutphen. 2 cass. pap. bk. 24.98 (978-0-911842-55-5(1), C814) Valley Sun.
Explains how to condition yourself to leave your body with hypnosis.

Astral Projection, Vol. 6. Jonathan Parker. Read by Jonathan Parker. 2 CDs. (Running Time: 2 hrs.). (Guided Meditation Ser.: Vol. 6). 1999. audio compact disk (978-1-58400-066-2(X)) QuantumQuests Intl.

Astral Projection: Achieving the Out-of-Body Experience. Melita Denning & Osborne Phillips. Featuring Melita Denning & Osborne Phillips. 1988. 9.95 (978-1-59157-017-2(4)) Assn for Cons.

Astral Projecton: Proyeccion Astral. Barrie Konicov. 1 cass. (Running Time: 1 hr. 30 mins.). (Spanish-Language Audios Ser.). (SPA.). 1995. 11.98 (978-0-87082-770-9(7), 006) Potentials.
Use this tape to prepare for your astral journeys - experience the exhilaration of an out-of-body experience.

Astral Sounds. 1 cass. (Running Time: 60 mins.). 15.00 (978-0-87082-621-4(2), AS486) Potentials.

Astral Voyaging CD Album. Bruce Goldberg. (ENG.). 2005. audio compact disk 75.00 (978-1-57968-050-3(X)) Pub: B Goldberg. Dist(s): Baker Taylor

Astral Voyaging Program Cassette Album. Bruce Goldberg. Read by Bruce Goldberg. 6 cass. (Running Time: 3 hrs.). (ENG.). 2006. 65.00 (978-1-885577-86-3(9)) Pub: B Goldberg. Dist(s): Baker Taylor
Learn how to leave the body and explore other dimensions through self-hypnosis.

Astrid & Veronika. Linda Olsson. 2007. audio compact disk 29.99 (978-1-4281-7052-0(9)) Recorded Bks.

Astro - Genetics. Lawrence A. Williams. 1 cass. 8.95 (787) Am Fed Astrologers.

Astro-Art Chart: An Astrological Art Form. Maryanne Hoffman. 1 cass. 8.95 (161) Am Fed Astrologers.
Mythological and symbolic paintings of charts.

Astro Cartography. Edith Hathaway. 1 cass. 1992. 8.95 (1041) Am Fed Astrologers.

Astro-Diplomacy. Jill Daniels. 1 cass. 8.95 (391); 8.95 (392) Am Fed Astrologers.

Astro-Heredity. Mary Shea. 1 cass. 8.95 (312) Am Fed Astrologers.
Chart characteristics passed along & roles they play.

Astro-Marketing Tips. Charles J. Miller. 1 cass. 1992. 8.95 (1067) Am Fed Astrologers.

Astro-Rhythm: Numerology-Astrology. Maryanne Hoffman. 1 cass. 8.95 (162) Am Fed Astrologers.
Personal year and seven mystical cycles relate to chart.

Astro-Rhythmics. Maryanne Hoffman. 1 cass. 8.95 (676) Am Fed Astrologers.
An AFA Convention workshop tape.

Astro-Theology: How Astrology Has Influenced Mankind. Instructed by Manly P. Hall. 5 cass. 8.50 ea. o.p. Pt 1: Zodiac & the Great Platonic Year. (800115-A) Philos Res.

Astro-Theology: How Astrology Has Influenced Mankind. Instructed by Manly P. Hall. 5 cass. (Running Time: 7 hrs. 30 mins.). 1999. 40.00 incl. album. (978-0-89314-011-3(2), S800115) Philos Res.

Astrodiagnosis. Luis Salvadhor. 1 cass. 8.95 (819) Am Fed Astrologers.

Astroendocrinology. Ingrid Naiman. 8 cass. (Running Time: 12 hrs.). 50.00 (978-1-882834-94-5(1)) Seventh Ray.
The evolution of the Chakras & their effects on the endocrine system.

Astrologer, a Multi-Level Nutritionist. Therese Rossignol. 1 cass. 8.95 (297) Am Fed Astrologers.
Get balance into client's life - physical, emotional, spiritual.

Astrological Aspect of Music. Jerry Markoe. 1 cass. 8.95 (450) Am Fed Astrologers.

Astrological Business & Publishing. ACT Staff. Read by ACT Staff. 1 cass. (Running Time: 90 min.). 1984. 8.95 (001) Am Fed Astrologers.

Astrological Charts in Music of Famous & Infamous People. Jerry Markoe. 1 cass. 8.95 (449) Am Fed Astrologers.

Astrological Counseling. John L. Ahern. 1 cass. 8.95 (485) Am Fed Astrologers.
Astrologer's real purpose.

Astrological Degrees of Life. Harold Hason. 1 cass. 8.95 (414) Am Fed Astrologers.
Use decanates & dwads to unfold inner being.

Astrological Family Tree. Lawrence A. Williams. 1 cass. 8.95 (366) Am Fed Astrologers.
Four generations in a family appear in a chart.

Astrological Health & Healing. Charles Emerson. 1 cass. 8.95 (107) Am Fed Astrologers.
Analyzing for physical, astral, and etheric weakness.

Astrological Houses. Mohan Koparkar. Read by Mohan Koparkar. 1 cass. (Running Time: 90 min.). 1994. 8.95 (1156) Am Fed Astrologers.
Houses of the horoscope.

Astrological Profile of Famous Fashion Designer. John L. Ahern. 1 cass. 8.95 (485) Am Fed Astrologers.
Timed chart & cosmodynes explain success.

Astrological Training: What is Missing. ACT Staff. 1 cass. 8.95 (471) Am Fed Astrologers.
How do students get training.

Astrological Work of Nostradamus. Michael Morin. 1 cass. 8.95 (244) Am Fed Astrologers.
Astrological work on future events (1985-2026).

Astrology: Cosmos & Psyche. Ralph Metzner. 2 cass. (Running Time: 2 hrs.). 18.00 (A0441-89) Sound Photosyn.
Very clear & concise overview of the overview - a good introduction.

Astrology: Fate vs. Free Will. ACT Staff. 1 cass. 8.95 (473) Am Fed Astrologers.
Are our actions predetermined?.

Astrology: Great Counseling Tool. John Soric. 1 cass. 8.95 (584) Am Fed Astrologers.
Helps with all kinds of problems in life.

Astrology - Tarot: Divine Marriage. Margie Herskovitz. 1 cass. 8.95 (159) Am Fed Astrologers.
Correspondence of Tarot cards to astrological symbols.

Astrology & Biorhythm in Everyday Life. John H. Goode. 1 cass. 8.95 (131) Am Fed Astrologers.
Astrology really works. A report of personal experiences.

Astrology & Crystals. Brett Bravo. 1 cass. 1992. 8.95 (1009) Am Fed Astrologers.

Astrology & Dreams. Sara A. Keller. 1 cass. 8.95 (682) Am Fed Astrologers.
An AFA Convention workshop tape.

Astrology & Epidemical Disease. Instructed by Manly P. Hall. 8.95 (978-0-89314-010-6(4), C580302) Philos Res.

Astrology & Gestalt - Integrated Personalities. Ruth Eichler. 1 cass. 8.95 (104) Am Fed Astrologers.

Astrology & Healing. Bradley Clark. 1 cass. 8.95 (052) Am Fed Astrologers.
The natural connection between astrology and the healing arts.

Astrology & Health. Gail A. Guttman. 1 cass. 8.95 (530) Am Fed Astrologers.
An AFA Convention workshop tape.

Astrology & Health. Joan Titsworth. 1 cass. 8.95 (466) Am Fed Astrologers.
Physical & psychological correspondence.

Astrology & Homeopathy. Eileen Nauman. 1 cass. 8.95 (702) Am Fed Astrologers.
An AFA Convention workshop tape.

Astrology & Karma. P. Kay. 1 cass. 1992. 8.95 (1051) Am Fed Astrologers.

Astrology & Numerology. Sandipan Chaudhuri. 1 cass. (Running Time: 60 mins.). 1992. 8.95 (1017) Am Fed Astrologers.

Astrology & Path of Transformation. Greg Bogart. 1 cass. (Running Time: 1 hr. 30 mins.). 8.95 (590) Am Fed Astrologers.

Astrology & Planetary Consciousness. unabr. ed. Dane Rydhyar. 2 cass. (Running Time: 3 hrs.). 1966. 18.00 (10101) Big Sur Tapes.
Rudhyar offers a general overview of astrology, followed by a discussion of three stages along "the path" symbolized by Uranus, Neptune & Pluto.

Astrology & Psychology. Linda Savage. 1 cass. 8.95 (305) Am Fed Astrologers.
Early life influences & psychodynamics - case studies.

Astrology & Reincarnation. Maria K. Simms. 1 cass. (Running Time: 1 hr. 30 min.). 8.95 (426) Am Fed Astrologers.

Astrology & Religion. ACT Staff. 1 cass. 8.95 (004) Am Fed Astrologers.
Is astrology a religion? How close are they.

Astrology & Romance. Joan Titsworth. 1 cass. 1992. 8.95 (1092) Am Fed Astrologers.

Astrology & Spiritual Healing. Helen Garrett. 1 cass. 8.95 (661) Am Fed Astrologers.
An AFA Convention workshop tape.

Astrology & Sports. Rose Cosentino. 1 cass. 8.95 (502) Am Fed Astrologers.
Predict winners astrologically.

Astrology & the Bible. K. Tumson. 1 cass. 1992. 8.95 (1095) Am Fed Astrologers.

Astrology & the Consciousness Movement. unabr. ed. Dane Rudhyar. 1 cass. (Running Time: 1 hr. 56 mins.). 1970. 11.00 (10109) Big Sur Tapes.
An in-depth examination of the place astrology has occupied in the broader human potential & consciousness movements & a look at what the future of these might be.

Astrology & the Kabbalah. unabr. ed. Robert Hand. 2 cass. 1992. 18.00 (OC323-69) Sound Horizons AV.

Astrology & Your Emotions. Lynne Koiner. 1 cass. 8.95 (546) Am Fed Astrologers.
Understand your feelings.

Astrology As a Diagnostic Tool. Capel McCutcheon. 1 cass. 8.95 (227) Am Fed Astrologers.
Use infants' charts for forecasting physical problems.

Astrology Basics. Mary E. Korpan-Roy. Read by Mary E. Korpan-Roy. 1 cass. (Running Time: 1 hr. 30 mins.). 1994. 8.95 (1140) Am Fed Astrologers.

Astrology Can Answer Your Question. Katherine De Jersey. 1 cass. 8.95 (510) Am Fed Astrologers.
An AFA Convention workshop tape.

Astrology Chart - There Are No Accidents. Jan Spiller. 1 cass. 8.95 (326) Am Fed Astrologers.

Astrology Coloring Book. Irene Diamond. 1 cass. 8.95 (396) Am Fed Astrologers.
Know & understand your body.

Astrology, Diet & Health. Susan Zuber. 1 cass. 8.95 (376) Am Fed Astrologers.
Natal clues to good health.

Astrology for Beginners. Constance DeMarco. 1 cass. 8.95 (395) Am Fed Astrologers.
Use of time & time correction.

Astrology for Children & Adolescents. Jeanne Darling. 1 cass. 8.95 (072) Am Fed Astrologers.
Define talents & problem areas - counseling techniques.

Astrology for Health. Laura Des Jardins. 1 cass. 8.95 (084) Am Fed Astrologers.
Stay healthy, maintain healthy balance using natal signatures.

Astrology for Health, 1988. Laura Des Jardins. Read by Laura Des Jardins. 1 cass. (Running Time: 1 hr. 30 mins.). 1988. 8.95 (728) Am Fed Astrologers.
How one's birth time affects health.

Astrology for the Novice. Rose Lineman. 1 cass. (Running Time: 1 hr. 30 mins.). 8.95 (553) Am Fed Astrologers.
Get the real story of Astrology.

Astrology, Karma & More. P. Kay. 1 cass. (Running Time: 1 hr. 30 mins.). 1992. 8.95 (1052) Am Fed Astrologers.

Astrology of Ancient Mexico. Bruce Scofield. 1 cass. (Running Time: 1 hr. 30 mins.). 8.95 (306) Am Fed Astrologers.

Astrology, Psychedelics & the Archetypes. unabr. ed. Richard Tarnas. 1 cass. (Running Time: 1 hr. 25 min.). 1979. 11.00 (11401) Big Sur Tapes.
Tarnas says that astrology seems to be a highly developed form of meditation into archetypal consciousness; a series of "highly subtle, very liberating clues" to help us map experiences that transcend our normal conceptions of ourselves & the external world.

Astrology Then & Now. Robert A. Hughes. 1 cass. (Running Time: 1 hr. 30 mins.). 8.95 (538) Am Fed Astrologers.

Astrology, Women & Eating Disorders. Priscilla Costello. 1 cass. (Running Time: 1 hr. 30 mins.). 8.95 (504) Am Fed Astrologers.
Case studies of anorexia, obesity, bulemia.

Astrology's Roots in Ancient Traditions. ACT Staff. 1 cass. (Running Time: 1 hr. 30 mins.). 8.95 (474) Am Fed Astrologers.
Is Astrology outgrowth of mystery schools.

Astrology's Timeline Through History. Maria K. Simms. 1 cass. (Running Time: 1 hr. 30 mins.). 8.95 (182) Am Fed Astrologers.
An AFA Convention workshop tape.

Astronaut. 1 cass. (Science Ser.). (J). bk. (TWIN 420) NewSound.
Learn about weightlessness, the history of space travel & the possibility of living in space someday.

Astronaut. Kim Mitzo Thompson & Karen Mitzo Hilderbrand. 1 cass. (Running Time: 39 mins.). (I'd Like to Be a Ser.). (J). (ps-4). 1996. pap. bk. & act. bk. ed. 9.98 24p. (978-1-57583-015-5(9), TWIN 420) Twin Sisters.
Twelve upbeat songs teach children that getting along with others, being in good physical shape & studying hard in school are important for becoming an astronaut. Children learn about weightlessness, the history of space travel & the possibility of someday living in space.

Astronaut's Journal. Jeff Hoffman. Read by Jeff Hoffman. 1 cass. (Running Time: 45 min.). 10.95 (B0010B090, HarperThor) HarpC GBR.

Astronomical Dimensions. Read by James Pickering. 1 cass. (Running Time: 33 mins.). 14.95 (13488) MMI Corp.
Covers star distances, spectroscopes, telescopes & more.

Astronomical Distances. 1 cass. (Running Time: 28 mins.). 14.95 (23351) MMI Corp.
Discusses measuring in space, geometries, radio signals, star brightness & more.

Astronomical Explosion. 1 cass. (Running Time: 27 mins.). 14.95 (23567) MMI Corp.
Formulation of a nebula, sun flares, novae, Crab nebula, cosmic explosions & more are discussed.

Astronomical Expression. 1 cass. (Running Time: 20 min.). 14.95 (23567) MMI Corp.

Astronomy: The Heavenly Challenge. unabr. ed. Jack Arnold. Read by Edwin Newman. (Running Time: 10800 sec.). (Audio Classics: Science & Discovery Ser.). 2006. audio compact disk 25.95 (978-0-7861-6436-3(0)) Pub: Blckstn Audio. Dist(s): NetLibrary CO

Astronomy: The Heavenly Challenge. unabr. ed. Jack Arnold. Read by Edwin Newman. Ed. by Jack Sommer & Mike Hassell. 2 cass. (Running Time: 2 hrs. 45 mins.). Dramatization. (Science & Discovery Ser.). (YA). (gr. 11 up). 1993. 17.95 (978-0-938935-69-8(0), 10404) Knowledge Prod.
As optics improved, man began to see the solar system. Tycho Brahe in Denmark, Nicolaus Copernicus of Poland, Johannes Kepler of Germany & Italy's Galileo Galilei all began to see a new relationship between the world & the stars. Their questions & their unholy answers toppled the idea that man & the Church are at the center of the universe.

Astronomy for Astrologers. Michael Munkasey. 1 cass. (Running Time: 1 hr. 30 mins.). 8.95 (248) Am Fed Astrologers.
Intro to basic astronomy behind astrological chart.

***Astronomy Online Laboratory CD-ROM.** 4th rev. ed. Gordon. (ENG.). 2010. audio compact disk 40.70 (978-0-7575-5009-6(6)) Kendall-Hunt.

Astronomy Smarts by Dancing Beetle. Perf. by Eugene Ely. 1 cass. (Running Time: 79 mins.). (J). 1994. 10.00 Erthviibz.
Astronomical facts, history & theories come together when Ms. Starfish & the spunky musical humans read & sing with dancing beetle.

Astronomy Today: Instructor CD with CTB. 5th rev. ed. Chaisson & McMillan. (YA). (gr. 11-12). audio compact disk 49.97 (978-0-13-117609-6(9)) PH School.

Astrophysical Directions: Cosmic Structure. Michael Erlewine. 1 cass. 8.95 (110) Am Fed Astrologers.
Cosmic structure, deep space, black holes, etc.

Astropower at the Racetrack. Emily Faugno. 1 cass. (Running Time: 1 hr. 30 mins.). 8.95 (115) Am Fed Astrologers.

ASVAB Practice Test. Comex Systems Staff. 2007. audio compact disk 50.00 (978-1-56030-225-4(9)) Comex Systs.

Asylum. Jane Coleman. (Running Time: 1 hr. 6 mins.). 1999. 10.95 (978-1-60083-516-2(3)) Iofy Corp.

***Asylum.** Jane Candia Coleman. 2009. (978-1-60136-386-2(9)) Audio Holding.

Asylum. Patrick McGrath. Read by Ian McKellen. 6 cass. 54.95 (978-0-7927-3333-1(9), CSL 699); audio compact disk 74.95 (978-0-7927-3334-8(7), SLD 699); audio compact disk 29.95 (978-0-7927-3335-5(5), CMP 699) AudioGO.

***Asylum: The Renegades Who Stole the World's Oil Market.** unabr. ed. Leah McGrath Goodman. (ENG.). 2011. (978-0-06-204714-4(0), Harper Audio) HarperCollins Pubs.

Asymmetric Time in Physics. 1 cass. (Running Time: 56 min.). 14.95 (CBC 1010) MMI Corp.

At All Costs. 1985. (0225) Evang Sisterhood Mary.

At All Costs. abr. ed. John Gilstrap. Read by Philip Bosco. (ENG.). 2006. 14.98 (978-1-59483-843-9(7)) Pub: Hachet Audio. Dist(s): HachBkGrp

At All Costs. abr. ed. John Gilstrap. Read by Philip Bosco. 2 cass. 2001. 7.95 (978-1-57815-196-7(1), Media Bks Audio) Media Bks NJ.

At All Costs: How a Crippled Ship & Two American Merchant Mariners Turned the Tide of World War II. unabr. ed. Sam Moses. Narrated by Michael Prichard. (Running Time: 11 hrs. 30 mins. 0 sec.). (ENG.). 2006. audio compact disk 69.99 (978-1-4001-3304-8(1)) Pub: Tantor Media. Dist(s): IngramPubServ

At All Costs: How a Crippled Ship & Two American Merchant Mariners Turned the Tide of World War II. unabr. ed. Sam Moses. Read by Michael Prichard. (Running Time: 11 hrs. 30 mins. 0 sec.). (ENG.). 2006. audio compact disk 24.99 (978-1-4001-5304-6(2)) Pub: Tantor Media. Dist(s): IngramPubServ

At All Costs: How a Crippled Ship & Two American Merchant Marines Turned the Tide of World War II. unabr. ed. Sam Moses. Narrated by Michael Prichard. (Running Time: 11 hrs. 30 mins. 0 sec.). (ENG.). 2006. audio compact disk 34.99 (978-1-4001-0304-1(5)) Pub: Tantor Media. Dist(s): IngramPubServ

At Any Cost: Jack Welch, General Electric & the Pursuit of Profit. unabr. ed. Thomas F. O'Boyle. Read by Edward Lewis. 12 cass. (Running Time: 17 hrs. 30 mins.). 1999. 83.95 (978-0-7861-1615-7(3), 2443) Blckstn Audio.
Jack Welch, CEO of General Electric & one of the most renowned figures in today's business world, has been seen by some as the model corporate leader & by others as the quintessential unmitigated pursuer of profit. The man & his methods & the legendary company he runs, are examined.

At Babci's Knee. Ed. by Alicja Padzik. Tr. by Aska Zurawiecka. Compiled by Patricia J. Lehman. Illus. by Barbara W. Knowlton. (Little La Ser.). (ENG & POL.). (J). (ps). 1985. (978-0-935003-00-0(2)) Talent-Ed.

At Babci's Knee. unabr. ed. (Running Time: 1 hr.). (J). (ps up). 1985. pap. bk. 25.00 Talent-Ed.
Collection of Polish language games, rhymes & fingerplays. Designed with young children in mind, it can be used to introduce even an infant to the sounds, rhythms & fun of the Polish language.

At Babci's Knee. unabr. ed. Ed. by Alicja Padzik. Tr. by Aska Zurawiecka. Compiled by Patricia J. Lehman. Illus. by Barbara W. Knowlton. (Running Time: 1 hr.). (Little La Ser.). (ENG & POL.). (J). (ps up). 1985. pap. bk. 25.00 (978-0-935003-01-7(0)) Talent-Ed.

At Belleau Wood. unabr. ed. Robert B. Asprey. 8 cass. (Running Time: 12 hrs.). 2000. 64.00 (978-0-7366-5527-9(1)) Books on Tape.
The dramatic story of America's greatest World War I battle and how it led to the end of the war a few months later.

At Bertram's Hotel. unabr. ed. Agatha Christie. Read by Rosemary Leach. 6 cass. (Running Time: 7 hrs. 35 min.). (Miss Marple Ser.: No. 13). 2002. 29.95 (978-1-57270-280-6(X), Audio Editions) Pub: Audio Partners. Dist(s): PerseuPGW

On holiday at London's chic Bertram's Hotel, Miss Marple finds the place so correct in every detail that she grows suspicious. Soon the police arrive to investigate a tip regarding a gang of criminals based in the hotel. Abduction, train robbery, and murder muddy the waters, but Miss Marple sees clearly who is responsible.

At Bertram's Hotel: A BBC Full-Cast Radio Drama. unabr. ed. Agatha Christie. Narrated by Full Cast. (Running Time: 2 hrs. 0 mins. 0 sec.). (ENG.). 2010. audio compact disk 24.95 (978-1-60283-810-9(0)) Pub: AudioGO. Dist(s): Perseus Dist

At Blackwater Pond: Mary Oliver Reads Mary Oliver. unabr. ed. Read by Mary Oliver. 1 CD. (Running Time: 1 hr). (ENG.). 2006. audio compact disk (978-0-8070-0700-6(5)) Beacon Pr.

At Canaan's Edge: America in the King Years, 1965-68. abr. ed. Taylor Branch. Read by Joe Morton. 2006. 23.95 (978-0-7435-6447-2(2)) Pub: S&S Audio. Dist(s): S and S Inc

At Casterbridge Fair see Poetry of Thomas Hardy

At Castle Boterel see Poetry of Thomas Hardy

At Dawn We Slept Pt. 1: The Untold Story of Pearl Harbor. unabr. collector's ed. Gordon W. Prange. Read by John MacDonald. 10 cass. (Running Time: 15 hrs.). 1985. 80.00 (978-0-7366-1046-9(4), 1976-A) Books on Tape.

The finest account ever written of the Pearl Harbor disaster.

At Dawn We Slept Pt. 2: The Untold Story of Pearl Harbor. collector's ed. Gordon W. Prange. Read by John MacDonald. 8 cass. (Running Time: 12 hrs.). 1985. 64.00 (978-0-7366-1047-6(2), 1976-B) Books on Tape.

Gordon Prange devoted his life to understanding our war with Japan. He saw Pearl Harbor for what it was, a military classic, one of the great surprise attacks in history. He also saw it as a warning to keep us from an even more dreadful opening blow.

At Dawn We Slept Pt. 3: The Untold Story of Pearl Harbor. collector's ed. Gordon W. Prange. Read by John MacDonald. 8 cass. (Running Time: 12 hrs.). 1985. 64.00 (978-0-7366-1048-3(0), 1976-C) Books on Tape.

At Ease. Created by Dharma Moon. 2006. audio compact disk 16.98 (978-1-59179-507-0(9)) Sounds True.

At Fault. Kate Chopin. Narrated by Flo Gibson. (ENG.). 2008. 20.95 (978-1-60646-045-0(5)) Audio Bk Con.

At First I Was Given Centuries see Poetry & Voice of Margaret Atwood

At First Sight. abr. ed. Stephen J. Cannell. Read by Scott Brick. 4 CDs. (Running Time: 5 hrs.). 2008. audio compact disk 24.95 (978-1-4233-6780-2(4), 9781423367802, BACD) Brilliance Audio.

At First Sight. unabr. ed. Stephen J. Cannell. Read by Scott Brick. 1 MP3-CD. (Running Time: 9 hrs.). 2008. 39.25 (978-1-4233-6777-2(4), 9781423367772, Brinc Audio MP3 Lib); 39.25 (978-1-4233-6779-6(0), 9781423367796, BADLE); 24.95 (978-1-4233-6778-9(2), 9781423367789, BAD); 24.95 (978-1-4233-6776-5(6), 9781423367765, Brilliance MP3); audio compact disk 87.25 (978-1-4233-6775-8(8), 9781423367758, BriAudCD Unabrid); audio compact disk 34.95 (978-1-4233-6774-1(X), 9781423367741, Bril Audio CD Unabri) Brilliance Audio.

At First Sight. unabr. ed. Nicholas Sparks. Read by David Aaron Baker. 5 cass. (Running Time: 7 hrs. 30 mins.). 2005. 45.00 (978-1-4159-2513-3(5)); audio compact disk 63.00 (978-1-4159-2514-0(3)) Books on Tape.

At First Sight. unabr. ed. Nicholas Sparks. Read by David Aaron Baker. (YA). 2007. 54.99 (978-1-60252-875-8(6)) Find a World.

At First Sight. unabr. ed. Nicholas Sparks. Read by David Aaron Baker. (ENG.). 2005. 14.98 (978-1-59483-255-0(2)) Pub: Hachet Audio. Dist(s): HachBkGrp

At First Sight. unabr. ed. Nicholas Sparks. Read by David Aaron Baker. (Running Time: 8 hrs. 30 mins.). (ENG.). 2007. audio compact disk 14.98 (978-1-60024-254-0(5)) Pub: Hachet Audio. Dist(s): HachBkGrp

At First Sight. unabr. ed. Nicholas Sparks. Read by David Aaron Baker. (Running Time: 8 hrs.). (ENG.). 2009. 59.98 (978-1-60788-065-3(2)) Pub: Hachet Audio. Dist(s): HachBkGrp

At First Sight-ABR. abr. ed. Stephen J. Cannell. Read by Scott Brick. (Running Time: 5 hrs.). 2009. audio compact disk 14.99 (978-1-4233-6781-9(2), 9781423367819) Brilliance Audio.

At Folk City. Perf. by Jean Ritchie & Doc Watson. Anno. by Joe Wilson. 1 cass. (Running Time: 47 min.). 1990. (0-9307-400050-9307-40005-2-6); audio compact disk (0-9307-40005-2-6) Smithsonian Folkways.

1963 performances of "Amazing Grace," "Storms Are on the Ocean," "Wabash Cannonball" & more.

***At Grave's End: A Night Huntress Novel.** unabr. ed. Jeaniene Frost. Read by Tavia Gilbert. (Running Time: 11 hrs. 30 mins.). (Night Huntress Novels Ser.). 2010. 29.95 (978-1-4417-6899-5(8)); 72.95 (978-1-4417-6896-4(3)); audio compact disk 29.95 (978-1-4417-6898-8(X)); audio compact disk 105.00 (978-1-4417-6897-1(1)) Blckstn Audio.

***At Home: A Short History of Private Life.** abr. unabr. ed. Bill Bryson. Read by Bill Bryson. (Running Time: 16 hrs. 30 mins.). (ENG.). 2010. audio compact disk 45.00 (978-0-7393-1526-2(9), Random AudioBks) Pub: Random Audio Pubg. Dist(s): Random

At Home & Abroad. AIO Team Staff. Prod. by Focus on the Family Staff. Created by Marshal Younger. (Running Time: 5 hrs. 0 mins.). (Adventures in Odyssey Gold Ser.). (ENG.). (J). 2006. audio compact disk 24.99 (978-1-58997-289-6(9)) Pub: Focus Family. Dist(s): Tyndale Hse

At Home, at School Audio CD: Fiction-to-Fact Kindergarten Theme. Orig. Title: Coming to School Audio CD. (J). 2004. audio compact disk 10.00 (978-1-4108-1676-4(1)) Benchmark Educ.

"At Home" Childbirth Education Program: A Complete Course for the Childbearing Years. Paula Doughman & Valerie J. Malott. Photos by Tony Walsh. 1999. bk. 59.95 (978-0-9677660-0-3(1)) Childbirth Inst.

At Home in Mitford. adpt. ed. Jan Karon. Adapted by Paul McCusker. 6 CDs. (Running Time: 6 hrs. 30 min.). Dramatization. (Mitford Ser.: Bk. 1). (ENG.). 2003. audio compact disk 34.97 (978-1-58997-000-7(4)) Pub: Focus Family. Dist(s): Tyndale Hse

At Home in Mitford. unabr. ed. Jan Karon. Read by John McDonough. (Running Time: 20 hrs.). (Mitford Ser.: Bk. 1). (gr. 12 up). 2006. audio compact disk 39.95 (978-0-14-305923-3(8), PengAudBks) Penguin Grp USA.

At Home in Mitford. unabr. ed. Jan Karon. Narrated by John McDonough. 16 CDs. (Running Time: 19 hrs. 15 mins.). (Mitford Ser.: Bk. 1). 2002. audio compact disk 142.00 (978-1-4025-2969-6(4)) Recorded Bks.

At Home in the Coral Reef. unabr. ed. Katy Muzik. 1 cass. (Running Time: 11 mins.). (SPA.). (J). (gr. k-4). 1994. bk. 25.90 (6814S); pap. bk. 17.90 (978-0-8045-6814-2(6), 6814) Spoken Arts.

American Bookseller Pick of the Lists.

At Home in the Universe. unabr. ed. Perf. by Eknath Easwaran. 1 cass. (Running Time: 1 hr.). 1987. 7.95 (978-1-58638-501-9(1)) Nilgiri Pr.

At Home in the Woods. unabr. collector's ed. Vena Angier & Bradford Angier. Read by Dan Lazar. 8 cass. (Running Time: 8 hrs.). 1979. 48.00 (978-0-7366-0197-9(X), 1197) Books on Tape.

A remarkable couple proves that life can still be lived on your terms.

At Home in the World: A Memoir. abr. ed. Joyce Maynard. Read by Joyce Maynard. 2 cass. (Running Time: 3 hrs.). 1998. 17.95 (978-1-55935-289-5(2), 289-2BK) Soundelux.

Joyce Maynard's autobiography of her affair 25 years ago with J.D. Salinger.

At Home in the World: A Memoir. unabr. ed. Joyce Maynard. Read by Bernadette Dunne. 9 cass. (Running Time: 13 hrs. 30 min.). 1999. 72.00 (978-0-7366-4309-2(5), 4799) Books on Tape.

In the spring of 1972, when she was a freshman at Yale, the author published a cover story in the New York Times Magazine about life as a young person in the sixties. Among the letters she received in response was one from the famously reclusive author, J.D. Salinger. They embarked on a correspondence & within months she had dropped out of college & moved in with him, believing that despite the 35 year age difference she had found her life-long soulmate. A short nine months later Salinger sent the author packing, an event so devastating she retreated from the world for two years in a New Hampshire farmhouse. Breaking a 25-year silence about what had taken place with Salinger, the author confronts with honesty, compassion & surprising humor the most painful truths of her experience.

At Home in Thrush Green. unabr. ed. Miss Read. Read by Gwen Watford. 6 cass. (Running Time: 6 hrs. 50 mins.). 2000. 29.95 (978-1-57270-151-9(X), M61151u) Pub: Audio Partners. Dist(s): PerseuPGW

In this new release, the townsfolk struggle with the future of home development in their village. There are plenty of wrinkles to iron out before any newcomers will feel at home in Thrush Green.

At Home with Bev & Frank Herbert. Frank Herbert. 2 cass. (Running Time: 2 hrs.). 18.00 (A0040-83) Sound Photosyn.

In Port Townsend with the well-known author of the "Dune" series, Brian captures Faustin's interview.

At Home with Bob & Arlen Talking Gonzo Sociology. Robert A. Wilson & Arlen R. Wilson. 1 cass. 9.00 (A0460-89) Sound Photosyn.

Listen up 'cause Arlen has a new slant on things that will turn a few heads & stand a few of their wild hairs on end.

At Home with Daddy's Stories. Kathryn Tucker Windham. 1 CD. (Running Time: 1 hr.). 2002. audio compact disk 14.95 (978-0-87483-692-9(1)) Pub: August Hse. Dist(s): Natl Bk Netwk

The author remembers her Daddy for his love of literature, his magnetic good humor, and his prominent eyes, often used to emphasize the punch line of a favorite story.

At Home with the Family Circus. Bil Keane. 1 cass. (Running Time: 30 mins.). (Family Circus Sings! Ser.). (J). 1994. pap. bk. 5.95 Penton Overseas.

Here's a series that brings the whole family together to sing along & enjoy catchy, good-time tunes. Sure to capture the heart & imagination of any child.

At Home with the Family Circus. Bil Keane. 1 CD. (Running Time: 30 mins.). (Family Circus Sings! Ser.). (J). (ps-2). 1994. 8.95 (978-1-56015-414-3(4)) Penton Overseas.

At Home with the Marquis DeSade: A Life. Francine Du Plessix Gray. Read by Donada Peters. 13 cass. (Running Time: 19 hrs. 30 mins.). 1999. 104.00 (5024) Books on Tape.

The two closest & best friends, that were the greatest influence in hs life were his wife & mother-in-law.

At Knit's End: Meditations for Women Who Knit Too Much. unabr. ed. Stephanie Pearl-McPhee. Read by Stephanie Pearl-McPhee. (YA). 2007. 49.99 (978-1-60252-740-9(7)) Find a World.

At Knit's End: Meditations for Women Who Knit Too Much. unabr. ed. Stephanie Pearl-McPhee. Read by Stephanie Pearl-McPhee. 3 CDs. (Running Time: 3 hrs. 30 mins.). (ENG.). 2007. audio compact disk 19.95 (978-1-59887-520-1(5), 1598875205) Pub: HighBridge. Dist(s): Workman Pub

At Last. 2004. audio compact disk 15.00 (978-0-9759263-3-8(0)) iVue Graphics.

At Last Comes Love. unabr. ed. Mary Balogh. Read by Anne Flosnik. 1 MP3-CD. (Running Time: 11 hrs.). (Huxtable Quintet: Bk. 3). 2009. 39.97 (978-1-4233-8903-3(4), 9781423389033, Brinc Audio MP3 Lib); 39.97 (978-1-4233-8905-7(0), 9781423389057, BADLE); 24.99 (978-1-4233-8902-6(6), 9781423389026, Brilliance MP3); 24.99 (978-1-4233-8904-0(2), 9781423389040, BAD); audio compact disk 89.97 (978-1-4233-8901-9(8), 9781423389019, BriAudCD Unabrid); audio compact disk 28.99 (978-1-4233-8900-2(X), 9781423389002) Brilliance Audio.

At My Fathers Wedding. John Lee. 2 cass. 1993. 18.00 (OC329-70) Sound Horizons AV.

At Paradise Gate. Jane Smiley. Read by Suzanne Toren. 7 Cds. (Running Time: 8.5 Hrs). audio compact disk 34.95 (978-1-4025-6296-9(9)) Recorded Bks.

At Paradise Gate. unabr. ed. Jane Smiley. Read by Anna Fields. 5 cass. (Running Time: 7 hrs. 30 min.). 2000. 40.00; 40.00 (978-0-7366-4902-5(6), 5208) Books on Tape.

This novel portrays the domestic drama of the Robinson family. While 77-year-old Ike Robinson is dying in his bedroom upstairs, his wife defends the citadel of their marriage against an ill-considered, albeit loving, invasion by their three middle-aged daughters and their 23-year-old granddaughter. Amply fulfilling the expectations raised by Smiley's other celebrated works.

At Paradise Gate. unabr. ed. Jane Smiley. Read by Suzanne Toren. 5 Cass. (Running Time: 8.5 Hrs). 24.95 (978-1-4025-6295-2(0)) Recorded Bks.

At Paradise Gate. unabr. ed. Jane Smiley. Narrated by Suzanne Toren. 6 cass. (Running Time: 8 hrs. 30 mins.). 1998. 51.00 (978-0-7887-2129-8(1), 95439E7) Recorded Bks.

While her seventy-seven-year-old husband lies upstairs slowly dying, Anna Robinson grapples with her middle-aged daughters' squabbling & ill-considered advice.

At Play in the Fields of the Lord. unabr. ed. Peter Matthiessen. Narrated by George Guidall. 11 cass. (Running Time: 16 hrs.). 1999. 91.00 (978-1-55690-701-2(X), 92414E7) Recorded Bks.

An epic story in the Peruvian rain forests with a diverse cast of characters. Native people, missionaries-Protestants & Catholic, mercenaries, the local sheriff. It is a story about everything & then some.

At Play in the Fields of the Lord. unabr. ed. Peter Matthiessen. (Running Time: 10 hrs. 0 mins.). (ENG.). 2009. 79.95 (978-1-4332-9988-9(7)); audio compact disk 109.00 (978-1-4332-9989-6(5)) Blckstn Audio.

At Play in the Fields of the Lord. unabr. ed. Peter Matthiessen. Read by Anthony Heald. (Running Time: 13 hrs.). (ENG.). 2010. 29.95 (978-1-4332-9992-6(5)); audio compact disk 34.95 (978-1-4332-9991-9(7)) Blckstn Audio.

At Risk. unabr. ed. Patricia Cornwell. Read by Kate Reading. 3 cass. (Running Time: 4 hrs.). (Win Garano Ser.: No. 1). 2006. 54.00 (978-1-4159-3105-9(4)); audio compact disk 72.00 (978-1-4159-3106-6(2)) Books on Tape.

A Massachusetts state investigator is called home from Knoxville, Tennessee, where he is completing a course at the National Forensic Academy. His boss, the district attorney, an attractive but hard-charging woman, is planning to run for governor, and as a showcase she's planning to use a new crime initiative called At Risk, its motto "Any crime, any time." In particular, she's been looking for a way to employ some cutting-edge DNA technology, and she thinks she's found it in a twenty-year-old murder - in Tennessee. If her office solves the case, they'll all end up looking pretty good, right? Her investigator is not so sure but before he can open his mouth, a shocking piece of violence intervenes... and they're about to get much worse. Sparks fly, traps spring, twists abound - this is the master working at the top of her game.

At Risk. unabr. ed. Patricia Cornwell. Read by Kate Reading. (Running Time: 4 hrs.). No. 1. (ENG.). (gr. 8). 2006. audio compact disk 25.95 (978-0-14-305873-1(8), PengAudBks) Penguin Grp USA.

At San Francisco's Kabuki Theatre. William S. Burroughs. 1 cass. 9.00 (A0018-83) Sound Photosyn.

A historical piece. Wry & wild, elegant & eloquent the author of "Naked Lunch".

At School Audio CD. Adapted by Benchmark Education Company Staff. Based on a work by Francisco Blane. (My First Reader's Theater Ser.). (J). (gr. k-1). 2008. audio compact disk 10.00 (978-1-60634-095-0(6)) Benchmark Educ.

At Some Disputed Barricade. abr. ed. Anne Perry. Read by Michael Page. (Running Time: 6 hrs.). (World War One Ser.). 2008. audio compact disk 14.99 (978-1-4233-0650-4(3), 9781423306504, BCD Value Price) Brilliance Audio.

At Some Disputed Barricade. unabr. ed. Anne Perry. Read by Michael Page. (Running Time: 12 hrs.). (World War One Ser.). 2007. 39.25 (978-1-59710-028-1(5), 9781597100281, BADLE); 24.95 (978-1-59710-029-8(3), 9781597100298, BAD); 39.25 (978-1-59335-840-2(7), 9781593358402, Brinc Audio MP3 Lib); 24.95 (978-1-59335-706-1(0), 9781593357061, Brilliance MP3); 92.25 (978-1-59355-064-6(2), 9781593550646, BrilAudUnabridg); audio compact disk 39.95 (978-1-59355-066-0(9), 9781593550660, Bril Audio CD Unabri); audio compact disk 107.25 (978-1-59355-067-7(7), 9781593550677, BriAudCD Unabrid) Brilliance Audio.

Please enter a Synopsis.

At the Altar of Sexual Idolatry. Steve Gallagher. 2003. audio compact disk 16.99 (978-0-9715470-4-9(1)) Pub: Pure Life. Dist(s): STL Dist NA

At the Altar of Speed. Leigh Montville. 2004. 10.95 (978-0-7435-4176-3(6)) Pub: S&S Audio. Dist(s): S and S Inc

At the Altar of Speed: The Fast Life & Tragic Death of Dale Earnhardt Sr. unabr. ed. Leigh Montville. Read by Grover Gardner. 8 vols. (Running Time: 12 hrs.). 2002. bk. 69.95 (978-0-7927-2521-3(2), CSL 410, Chivers Sound Lib); audio compact disk 79.95 (978-0-7927-9850-7(3), SLD 101, Chivers Sound Lib) AudioGO.

Takes readers behind the scenes of Earnhardt's celebrated life, tracing his rags-to-riches journey to the top of America's fastest-growing sport. Examines how a ninth-grade dropout started on the dusty dirt tracks of the South, went through two marriages and [illegible] string of nonfuture jobs before turning twenty-five, then took about a [illegible] left turns to glory. Through the pitfalls and triumphs, Earnhardt would [illegible]ely become a celebrated champion, whose lifetime earnings wou[illegible] forty-one million dollars.

At the Back of the North Wind. George MacDonald. Narrated by Flo Gibson. 6 cass. (Running Time: 9 hrs.). (J). 1987. 24.95 (978-1-55685-085-1(9)) Audio Bk Con.

The mystical travels of Diamond, a coachman's son, through distant lands & strange events while cushioned at the back of the beautiful north wind.

***At the Back of the North Wind.** George MacDonald. Narrated by Flo Gibson. (J). 2010. audio compact disk 29.95 (978-1-60646-146-4(X)) Audio Bk Con.

At the Back of the North Wind. adpt. ed. Read by Juliette Stevenson et al. George MacDonald. Adapted by Murray Watts et al. (Running Time: 240 hrs. 0 mins.). (Radio Theatre Ser.). (ENG.). (J). (gr. 3). 2007. audio compact disk 14.97 (978-1-58997-508-8(1), Tyndale Ent) Tyndale Hse.

At the Beach. Read by Mary Richards. 1 cass. (Running Time: 60 mins.). (Energy Break Ser.). 2007. audio compact disk 19.95 (978-1-56136-159-5(3)) Master Your Mind.

***At the Center of the Storm.** abr. ed. George Tenet. Read by Eric Conger. (ENG.). 2007. (978-0-06-145123-2(1), Harper Audio); (978-0-06-145122-5(3), Harper Audio) HarperCollins Pubs.

***At the Center of the Storm.** unabr. ed. George Tenet. Read by Eric Conger. (ENG.). 2007. (978-0-06-123063-9(4), Harper Audio); (978-0-06-123064-6(2), Harper Audio) HarperCollins Pubs.

At the Center of the Storm: My Years at the CIA. abr. ed. George Tenet. Read by Eric Conger. Told to Bill Harlow. 11 CDs. (Running Time: 46800 sec.). 2007. audio compact disk 39.95 (978-0-06-115086-9(X)) HarperCollins Pubs.

At the Circus: Early Explorers Early Set B Audio CD. Jennifer Boudart. Adapted by Benchmark Education Staff. (J). 2007. audio compact disk 10.00 (978-1-4108-8240-0(3)) Benchmark Educ.

At the City's Edge. unabr. ed. Marcus Sakey. Narrated by Grover Gardner. 8 CDs. (Running Time: 10 hrs. 19 mins.). 2008. audio compact disk 79.95 (978-0-7927-5228-8(7)) AudioGO.

Home from Iraq and still reeling from his discharge, Jason Palmer plans to spend the summer drinking too much and chasing girls. But when his brother is brutally murdered, Jason is all that stands between his eight-year-old nephew and a pair of ruthless killers with a mysterious agenda. As he struggles to protect all that remains of his family, Jason finds himself embroiled in something much larger than a simple quest for justice. Chicago is burning, set ablaze by gang warfare and the passions of wicked men, and the battle for Jason's South Side neighborhood is looking more and more like the war he just left.

At the Close of Day: Audio Version. Excerpts. Lance Davis & Bert Keller. Contrib. by David Brookbank. Frwd. by Jerry Mitchell. 9 CDs. 2004. audio compact disk 49.95 (978-0-9753488-1-9(7)) Streamline Pr.

The authors, a physician and a pastor/ethicist, read their own expert advice on end-of-life planning and care. True to the print version with some additional insights. Serves as a valuable complement to the print version and is ideal to use as a focus for family meetings regarding end-of-life issues.

At the Core. unabr. ed. Marge Piercy. Read by Marge Piercy. 1 cass. (Running Time: 58 mins.). (Watershed Tapes of Contemporary Poetry). 1976. 12.95 (23633) J Norton Pubs.

An overview of the work of a popular American feminist poet.

At the Cross. Composed by Michael Farren & Jason Ingram. Contrib. by Dave Williamson & Scott Williamson. 2007. audio compact disk 24.98 (978-5-557-49190-7(2), Word Music) Word Enter.

At the Cross: Music of the Billy Graham Library. Tommy Coomes & Billy Graham Evangelistic Association. 2008. audio compact disk 16.99 (978-1-59328-226-4(5)) Billy Graham Evangelistic Association.

At the Crossing Places. Kevin C. Holland. 6 cass. (Running Time: 8 hrs.). (Arthur Trilogy). (J). (gr. 6 up). 2004. 40.00 (978-0-8072-0548-8(6), Listening Lib) Random Audio Pubg.

At the Crossroads. Bernell Christensen. 1 cass. 3.95 (978-1-57734-377-6(8), 34441166) Covenant Comms.

At the Crossroads & Book of Mormon Blessings at Home. Bernell Christensen. 1 cass. 5.98 (978-1-55503-116-9(1), 06003606) Covenant Comms.

***At the Devil's Table: The Man Who Brought down the Cali Cartel.** unabr. ed. William Rempel. (Running Time: 10 hrs.). (ENG.). 2011. audio compact disk 35.00 (978-0-307-93235-8(4), Random AudioBks) Pub: Random Audio Pubg. Dist(s): Random

At the Drive In: The Unauthorized Biography of at the Drive In. Michael Sumsion. (Maximum Ser.). (ENG., 2001. audio compact disk 14.95 (978-1-84240-134-7(3)) Pub: Chrome Dreams GBR. Dist(s): IPG Chicago

At the Earth's Core. unabr. ed. Edgar Rice Burroughs. Read by James Slattery. 4 cass. (Running Time: 6 hrs.). 1996. 32.95 (978-0-7861-1024-7(4), 1785) Blckstn Audio.
They found themselves in a prehistoric land - thousands of miles underground. When David Innes & his inventor friend pierced the crust of the Earth in their new burrowing device, they broke out into a strange new inner world of eternal daylight - a world in back of the Stone Age, where prehistoric monsters still lived & cave men & women battled against cruel, inhuman masters.

At the Earth's Core. unabr. ed. Edgar Rice Burroughs. Read by David Sharp. 4 cass. (Running Time: 4 hrs. 54 min.). 1994. 26.95 (978-1-55686-497-1(3)) Books in Motion.
David & inventor Perry are trapped in the control room of a runaway earth-boring machine. It takes them to the earth's core where they encounter a strange subterranean world.

At the Earth's Core. unabr. ed. Edgar Rice Burroughs. Narrated by Patrick G. Lawlor. 5 CDs. (Running Time: 5 hrs. 14 mins.). (Pellucidar Ser.). (ENG.). 2003. audio compact disk 33.00 (978-1-4001-0081-1(X)); audio compact disk 20.00 (978-1-4001-5081-6(7)) Pub: Tantor Media. Dist(s): IngramPubServ
David Innes is a young man who has just inherited a large mining company. An eccentric inventor, Abner Perry, convinces Innes to underwrite a project to build an 'iron mole', claiming it will make them both wealthy. The mechanical beast works well, actually too well. On the maiden voyage, instead of digging for a few minutes and returning, they plunge straight through the earth's crust into the 'inner world' of Pellucidar. This world resembles earth but is a horizon-less, primeval tropical landscape where the sun neither sets nor rises, and is populated by 'Sagoth' gorilla men, wild human slaves, and the ruling hypnotic reptilian 'Mahars'.

Upon arrival at this strange world, the men are immediately captured and enslaved. But soon Perry learns to read the language of the Mahars, and discovers a secret way to turn the tables! True to Burroughs form, this non-stop fantasy thriller weaves together savage islanders, pterodactyls, telepathy, and, of course, romance.

At the Earth's Core. unabr. ed. Edgar Rice Burroughs. Read by Patrick G. Lawlor. (Pellucidar Ser.). (ENG.). 2003. audio compact disk 66.00 (978-1-4001-3081-8(6)) Pub: Tantor Media. Dist(s): IngramPubServ

At the Earth's Core. unabr. ed. Edgar Rice Burroughs. Narrated by Patrick G. Lawlor. (Running Time: 5 hrs. 0 mins. 0 sec.). (Pellucidar Ser.). (ENG.). 2009. audio compact disk 45.99 (978-1-4001-4118-0(4)) Pub: Tantor Media. Dist(s): IngramPubServ

At the Earth's Core, with EBook. unabr. ed. Edgar Rice Burroughs. Narrated by Patrick G. Lawlor. (Running Time: 5 hrs. 0 mins. 0 sec.). (Pellucidar Ser.). (ENG.). 2009. 19.99 (978-1-4001-6118-8(5)); audio compact disk 22.99 (978-1-4001-1118-3(8)) Pub: Tantor Media. Dist(s): IngramPubServ

At the Edge. Perf. by Mickey Hart et al. 1 cass. (Running Time: 1 hr.). 9.95 (978-0-06-250415-9(0)); audio compact disk 13.95 (978-0-06-250416-6(9)) White Dove NM.
A series of compositions that express the wide variety of rhythms, tone & lyric powers of percussion - music that "blends with the sound of nature, resonating & awakening a memory of a far-off time before speech, but not before song".

***At the Edge of the Precipice: Henry Clay & the Compromise That Saved the Union.** unabr. ed. Rober V. Remini. (Running Time: 7 hrs. 0 mins.). 2010. 44.95 (978-1-4417-4021-2(X)); audio compact disk 69.00 (978-1-4417-4022-9(8)) Blckstn Audio.

***At the Edge of the Precipice: Henry Clay & the Compromise that Saved the Union.** unabr. ed. Robert V. Remini. (Running Time: 7 hrs. 0 mins.). 2010. 29.95 (978-1-4417-4025-0(2)); audio compact disk 29.95 (978-1-4417-4024-3(4)) Blckstn Audio.

At the Eleventh Hour: The Biography of Swami Rama. unabr. ed. Pandit Rajmani Tigunait. Read by D. C. Rao. 9 cass. (Running Time: 13 hrs. 30 mins.). 2002. 39.95 (978-0-89389-223-4(8)) Himalayan Inst.

At the End of a Rope, in Mississippi: Poetry & Spoken Word by Jolivette Anderson 'the Poet Warrior' Poems. Perf. by Jolivette Anderson. Executive Producer Jolivette Anderson. 1 CD. (Running Time: 74 mins.). 2001. audio compact disk 12.95 (978-1-893926-05-9(2)) Sisterlove Prodns.

***At the Farm Giant Floor Puzzle.** Created by Twin Sisters. (Giant Floor Puzzles Ser.). (ENG.). (J). 2008. audio compact disk (978-1-59922-348-3(1)) Twin Sisters.

At the Feet of God. Perf. by Jerry Sullivan & Tammy Sullivan. 1 cass. audio compact disk 15.99 CD. (D2029) Diamante Music Grp.
This album expresses the joy of the spiritual journey, while capturing the emotions of an impassioned soul.

At the Feet of the Master. J. Alcyone, pseud & Jiddu Krishnamurti. 2000. 5.95 (978-0-8356-2005-5(0), Quest) Pub: Theos Pub Hse. Dist(s): Natl Bk Netwk

At the Fillmore see Philip Levine

At the Fishhouses see Twentieth-Century Poetry in English, No. 9, Recordings of Poets Reading Their Own Poetry

At the Foot of the Rainbow. unabr. ed. Gene Stratton-Porter. Read by Rusty Nelson. 4 cass. (Running Time: 5 hrs. 30 min.). 2001. 26.95 (978-1-55686-948-8(7)) Books in Motion.
Porter's novel uses fishing as a backdrop to tell the story of Irish-Americans Jimmy Malone and Dannie Micnoun. These longtime friends and partners are hurt by each other in a most unusual way.

***At the Gates of Darkness.** unabr. ed. Raymond E. Feist. Read by Richard Ferrone. (ENG.). 2010. (978-0-06-201593-8(1), Harper Audio) HarperCollins Pubs.

***At the Gates of Darkness: Book Two of the Demonwar Saga.** unabr. ed. Raymond E. Feist. Read by Richard Ferrone. (ENG.). 2010. (978-0-06-201496-2(X), Harper Audio) HarperCollins Pubs.

At the Golden Door. Swami Amar Jyoti. 1 dolby cass. 1983. 8.98 (M-43) Truth Consciousness.
Pujya Swamiji asks what we would do if we suddenly arrived at the Golden Door?.

At the Grave of the Unknown Fisherman. abr. ed. John Gierach. Narrated by Michael Prichard. (Running Time: 16200 sec.). 2005. audio compact disk 28.00 (978-1-932378-72-6(3)) Pub: A Media Intl. Dist(s): Natl Bk Netwk

At the Heart of Power. abr. ed. George Stephanopoulos. Read by George Stephanopoulos. 2 cass. (Running Time: 3 hrs.). 1999. 17.98 Hachet Audio.

At the Keyhole see Dylan Thomas Reads the Poetry of W. B. Yeats & Others

At the Mile End Gate. Sally Worboyes. Read by Carole Boyd. 8 cass. (Sound Ser.). (J). 2002. 69.95 (978-1-84283-196-0(8)) Pub: ISIS Lrg Prnt GBR. Dist(s): Ulverscroft US

At the Mill Valley Book Depot. Riane Eisler. 1 cass. 9.00 (A0405-88) Sound Photosyn.
The author, reading from "The Chalice & the Blade" & offering explanations gives quick understanding to the concepts that may turn this whole dominator aspect of society around.

At the Mountains of Madness. unabr. ed. H. P. Lovecraft. Featuring Jerry Ahern et al. 1 cass. (Running Time: 90 min.). Dramatization. 2002. 12.95 (978-0-929483-09-2(X)) Centauri Express Co.
In that interview a number of terrible truths come out. The truth about an expedition to Antarctica in the 1920's where everyone died horribly. The truth about an attempt to find the expedition's mysterious killers. The truth about a desolate plateau in the heart of a frozen continent. The truth about life and intelligence on the planet Earth. And the truth about the prehistoric horror that still waits lurking.

At the Museum. Jane O'Connor. Illus. by Robin Preiss Glasser. (I Can Read Book 1 Ser.). (J). 2009. 9.99 (978-0-06-170658-5(2), HarperFestival) HarperCollins Pubs.

At the Phoenix Bookstore. Lynn Andrews. 1 cass. (Roy Tuckman Interview Ser.). 9.00 (A0498-89) Sound Photosyn.

At the Phoenix Bookstore with Roy Tuckman & Bruno Bettelheim. Bruno Bettelheim. 1 cass. 9.00 (A0497-89) Sound Photosyn.
Short & sweet & to the point.

At the Plate with... Ken Griffey Jr. unabr. ed. Glenn Stout. Narrated by Ramon de Ocampo. 2 cass. (Running Time: 2 hrs. 30 min.). 2003. 19.00 (978-1-4025-0772-4(0)) Recorded Bks.
The son of a star outfielder, Ken Griffey Jr. grew up around Major League baseball. His earliest dream was to become a big leaguer like his father. This dream came true when he was drafted by the Seattle Mariners. Known for his infectious grin and the fun he brings to playing the game every day, he has become one of baseball's brightest stars. And with each monster home run and every spectacular catch, Junior keeps working closer to his ultimate goal: winning a championship.

***At the Scent of Water.** abr. ed. Linda Nichols. Narrated by Traci Svensgaard. (ENG.). 2009. 14.98 (978-1-59644-709-7(5), christaudio) christianaud.

At the Scent of Water. abr. ed. Linda Nichols. Narrated by Traci Svensgaard. (Running Time: 9 hrs. 12 mins. 0 sec.). (ENG.). (YA). 2009. audio compact disk 24.98 (978-1-59644-708-0(7), christaudio) christianaud.

At the Sign of the Star. Katherine Sturtevant. Narrated by Emily Gray. 3 pieces. (Running Time: 4 hrs.). (gr. 4 up). 2002. 32.00 (978-1-4025-2021-1(2)); audio compact disk 39.00 (978-1-4025-3302-0(0)) Recorded Bks.

At the Sign of the Star. unabr. ed. Katherine Sturtevant. 3 cass. (Running Time: 3 hrs. 30 min.). (YA). (gr. 5-9). 2001. 22.00 (978-0-8072-0481-8(1), Listening Lib) Random Audio Pubg.
Meg Moore is motherless & the only heir to her father's thriving bookstore in 1677 Restoration London. Meg knows that with her anticipated dowry comes an unusual degree of freedom. But everything changes when her father remarries. Not only must she resist the overtures of her stepmother, she must accept the possibility that her inheritance will be lost with the birth of a half brother.

At the Sound of the Beep. Great American Audio. 3 cass. (Running Time: 3 hrs.). 1990. 19.95 (978-1-55569-411-1(X), 7166) Great Am Audio.
Contains 3-60 minute digitally mastered cassettes for your answering machine.

At the Sound of the Beep, Vol. 1. 1 cass. (Telephone Answering Tapes Ser.). 1987. 6.95 (978-1-55569-103-5(X), 6120) Great Am Audio.
Seven pre-recorded announcements for your telephone answering machines. Also includes pre-recorded sound effects for creating your own messages.

At the Sound of the Beep, Vol. II. 1 cass. (Running Time: 60 mins.). (Telephone Answering Tapes Ser.). 1988. 6.95 (978-1-55569-220-9(6), 6130) Great Am Audio.
Features answering machine messages & sound effects.

At the Table of Jesus. Carey Landry & Carol J. Kinghorn. Read by Carey Landry & Carol J. Kinghorn. 1 cass. (J). 10.95 (5525) OR Catholic.
All-new & thoroughly contemporary, this recording features the added benefit of Carey & Carol Jean speaking directly to the children about the liturgy. Teachers, catechists & parents will appreciate this sensitive, gentle way of helping children understand the liturgical prayer experience.

At the Table of the World. 5810th ed. 2001. audio compact disk 16.00 (978-1-58459-035-4(1)) Wrld Lib Pubns.

At the Table of the World. 5811th ed. 2001. 11.00 (978-1-58459-036-1(X)) Wrld Lib Pubns.

At the Tourist Center in Boston see Poetry & Voice of Margaret Atwood

At the Villa of Reduced Circumstances. Alexander McCall Smith. (von Igelfeld Ser.). 2004. audio compact disk 22.99 (978-1-4193-1696-8(6)) Recorded Bks.

At the Villa of Reduced Circumstances. unabr. ed. Alexander McCall Smith. 3 cass. (Running Time: 4 hrs.). (von Igelfeld Ser.). 2004. 22.99 (978-1-4025-9056-6(3)) Recorded Bks.

At the Villa Rose. unabr. ed. A. E. W. Mason. Read by Flo Gibson. 5 cass. (Running Time: 7 hrs.). (gr. 8 up). 1998. 20.95 (978-1-55685-590-0(7)) Audio Bk Con.
The brilliant detective Hanaud unravels two mysterious & gruesome murders.

At Thomas Hardy's Birthplace see Poetry & Voice of James Wright

At Thy Word Lord, I Will: A Call to Men. Bobby Hilton. 4 cass. (Running Time: 6 hrs.). 1999. 18.00 (978-1-930766-07-5(6)) Bishop Bobby.
Religious ministry program.

At Twelve Mr. Byng Was Shot. unabr. ed. Dudley Pope. Read by Bill Kelsey. 9 cass. (Running Time: 13 hrs. 30 mins.). 1995. 72.00 (978-0-7366-3126-6(7), 3801) Books on Tape.
The British botched a naval campaign, then blames Admiral John Byng, who led the fleet. A gross injustice & a heart breaker.

At War at Sea: Sailors & Naval Combat in the Twentieth Century. Ronald H. Spector. Narrated by Robert O'Keefe. 14 cass. (Running Time: 20 hrs. 15 mins.). 117.00 (978-0-7887-9400-1(0)) Recorded Bks.

At War at Sea: Sailors & Naval Warfare in the Twentieth Century. unabr. ed. Ronald H. Spector. Narrated by Robert O'Keefe. 14 cass. (Running Time: 20 hrs. 15 mins.). 2002. 59.95 (978-1-4025-3351-8(9), RG249) Recorded Bks.
Ronald H. Spector is a former Marine who served in Vietnam and now teaches history and international relations at George Washington University. His expertise and vigorous writing style make At War at Sea the definitive history of 20th-century naval combat. Based on more than a hundred personal accounts, this book provides a sailor's-eye view of such conflicts as Jutland, Midway, and even the Persian Gulf War.

At-Will Employment. Contrib. by H. Reed Ellis et al. (Running Time: 4 hrs.). 1985. 85.00 incl. program handbk. NJ Inst CLE.
Analyzes the current status of the at-will doctrine, including the effect of public policy & federal & state legislation, which procedures will result in effective discharge & which will fail, protecting employer's rights of privacy.

At Wit's End. unabr. ed. Erma Bombeck. Read by Nancy Dannevik. 5 cass. (Running Time: 5 hrs.). 1979. 30.00 (978-0-7366-0163-4(5), 1165) Books on Tape.
Humorous reflections on family life by a high-spirited survivor of same.

At Work in the U. S. 2002. audio compact disk 17.00 (978-1-56420-429-5(4)) New Readers.

At Your Service: English for the Travel & Tourist Industry. Trish Stott & Angela Buckingham. 1995. 17.50 (978-0-19-451331-9(9)) OUP.

Atajo 3.0. Noblitt. (C). bk. 112.95 (978-0-8384-8506-4(5)) Heinle.

Atajo 3.0. Noblitt. 2002. bk. 140.85 (978-0-8384-0375-4(1)) Heinle.

Atala, Rene. Francois-Rene de Chateaubriand. 6 cass. (Running Time: 6 hrs.). (FRE.). 1996. pap. bk. 59.50 Incl. plastic box & text. (978-1-58085-359-0(5)) Interlingua VA.

Atando Cabos. 2nd ed. Maria Gonzalez-Aguilar & Marta Rosso O'Laughlin. 2004. audio compact disk 22.60 (978-0-13-184523-7(3)) Pearson Educ CAN CAN.

Ataxia-Telangiectasia - A Bibliography & Dictionary for Physicians, Patients, & Genome Researchers. Compiled by Icon Group International, Inc. Staff. 2007. ring bd. 28.95 (978-0-497-11336-0(8)) Icon Grp.

Athanasian Creed. Narrated by William Biersach & Charles A. Coulombe. 3 cass. (Running Time: 3 hrs.). 2000. pap. bk. 21.00 (20143) Cath Treas.
In the first talk, Mr. Biersach presents the background of St. Athanasius, Bishop of Alexandria, known in his own lifetime as a champion of orthodoxy, even though he was exiled repeatedly & even excommunicated by Pope Liberius. In the second talk, Mr. Biersach is joined by Mr. Coulombe in a discussion of the details &implications of this venerable saint's Creed itself. Includes a copy of the Three Creeds of the Catholic Church & a diagram which helps to illustrate the concept of the Holy Trinity.

Atheism: The Case Against God. unabr. ed. George H. Smith. 1 cass. (Running Time: 57 mins.). 12.95 (AFO450) J Norton Pubs.

Atheism: Where is God in an Ungodly World? Scott Hahn. 4 cass. 1995. 22.95 (5271-C) Ignatius Pr.
In this series, Hahn tackles one of the central issues of contemporary apologetics head-on - Atheism. In a largely pagan world, believers must confront the issues raised by the spectra of Atheism, mainly, "Where is God in an Ungodly world?" A must series for any one wanting to prove the existence of God, & understand the problem of good & evil.

Atheist Universe Audio Book. Interview. David Mills. 1 CD. (Running Time: 1 hour, 13 mins.). 2005. audio compact disk 9.95i (978-0-9770378-0-3(0)) D Mills.

Athena. Read by Anne Avery. 1 cass. (Running Time: 90 min.). (Facing the Gods Ser.: No. 5). 1987. 10.95 (978-0-7822-0011-9(7), 289) C G Jung IL.

***Athena Project.** abr. ed. Brad Thor. Read by Elizabeth Marvel. (Running Time: 6 hrs. 0 mins. 0 sec.). (ENG.). 2010. audio compact disk 29.99 (978-1-4423-3578-3(5)) Pub: S&S Audio. Dist(s): S and S Inc

***Athena Project.** unabr. ed. Brad Thor. Read by Elizabeth Marvel. 8 CDs. (Running Time: 9 hrs. 0 mins. 0 sec.). (ENG.). 2010. audio compact disk 39.99 (978-1-4423-3580-6(7)) Pub: S&S Audio. Dist(s): S and S Inc

Athletic Recruiting & Scholarship Guide for High School Athletes & Parents: Learn the Secrets to Maximizing Exposure to Coaches & Achieving Scholarship Potential. Excerpts. Wayne Mazzoni. 2. (Running Time: 87 mins). (YA). 2002. 19.95 (978-0-9663557-4-1(1)) Mazz Mktg.
Unfortunately, most high school athletes, coaches, and guidance counselors don't understand the college athlete recruiting process. While no one can promise you a scholarship, this cd, based on the book of the same name, will give you the secrets to getting exposure to college coaches - the the crucial ingredient in the process. You will learn how to reduce tuition costs with an athletic scholarship and how to increase lifelong earning power as well by using athletics to gain admission to the best college possible.

Athletic Shorts. Chris Crutcher. Narrated by Frank Muller. 4 CDs. (Running Time: 4 hrs.). (gr. 7 up). audio compact disk 39.00 (978-1-4025-2289-5(4)) Recorded Bks.

Athletic Shorts. unabr. ed. Short Stories. Chris Crutcher. Narrated by Frank Muller. 3 pieces. (Running Time: 4 hrs.). (gr. 7 up). 1995. 27.00 (978-0-7887-0367-6(6), 94559E7) Recorded Bks.
Stories that deal with a variety of issues, including AIDS, prejudice & parent child relations. The first story about Angus Bethune was the basis for the summer movie "Angus".

Atkins Advantage: The 12 Week Low-Card Program to Lose Weight, Shape up & Revitalize Your Life. abr. ed. Stuart Trager & Atkins Nutritionals Inc. Staff. 3 CDs. (Running Time: 3 hrs.). (ENG.). 2006. audio compact disk 24.95 (978-1-59397-605-7(4)) Pub: Macmill Audio. Dist(s): Macmillan

***Atkins Diabetes Revolution: The Groundbreaking Approach to Preventin.** abr. ed. Robert C. Atkins. Read by Sara Krieger. (ENG.). 2004. (978-0-06-082482-2(4), Harper Audio); (978-0-06-082483-9(2), Harper Audio) HarperCollins Pubs.

***Atkins Essentials.** abr. ed. Atkins Health & Medical Information Serv. Read by Eric Conger. (ENG.). 2004. (978-0-06-078331-0(1), Harper Audio) HarperCollins Pubs.

***Atkins Essentials.** abr. ed. Atkins Health & Medical Information Serv. Read by Eric Conger. (ENG.). 2004. (978-0-06-081484-7(5), Harper Audio) HarperCollins Pubs.

Atkins Essentials: A Two-Week Program to Jump-Start Your Low Carb Lifestyle. abr. ed. Robert C. Atkins & Atkins Health and Medical Information Services Staff. Read by Eric Conger. (Running Time: 10800 sec.). 2008. audio compact disk 14.95 (978-0-06-146708-0(1), Harper Audio) HarperCollins Pubs.

Atlanta. Judy Aspes. 1 cass. (Running Time: 36 min.). (FRE.). 1996. 10.00 (978-0-9651021-2-4(2)) Ring Home.
Information on visiting Atlanta. Things to see & do, history, transportation, shopping, etc.

Atlanta. Judy Aspes. Read by Steve McCoy & Vicki Locke. 1 cass. (Running Time: 36 mins.). 1996. 10.00 (978-0-9651021-0-0(6)) Ring Home.

Atlanta. Contrib. by Time-Life Audiobooks Staff. (Voices of the Civil War Ser.). 1999. (978-1-57042-723-7(2)) Hachet Audio.

Atlanta Homecoming. Contrib. by Bill & Gloria Gaither and Their Homecoming Friends. (Gaither Gospel Ser.). 1998. audio compact disk 13.98 (978-7-474-05240-7(7)) Spring House Music.

Atlanta on Tape. Judy Aspes. 1 cass. (Running Time: 36 mins.). (SPA.). 1996. 10.00 (978-0-9651021-1-7(4)); 10.00 (978-0-9651021-3-1(0)) Ring Home.

Atlanta's National Black Arts Festival: Looking to the Future. Rex A. Barnett. (YA). 16.99 (978-0-924198-13-7(3)) Hist Video.

Atlantean Hypothesis. Instructed by Manly P. Hall. 5 cass. (Running Time: 1hr. 50 mins.). 1999. 40.00 incl. album. (978-0-89314-012-0(0), S580528) Philos Res.

Atlantian Heart Chakra Meditation - Atlantis, No. 4. Kathleen Milner. Music by Paul Lincoln. 1 cass. (Running Time: 30 mins.). 11.00 (978-1-886903-52-4(2)) K Milner.
Group meditation using candles & combined consciousness to explore other realities & to bring back healing for the members of the group & for Mother Earth. From a meditation called Synergy that was channeled to William Buehler, a priest in the Church of Antioch.

***Atlantic: Great Sea Battles, Heroic Discoveries, Titanic Storms, & a Vast Ocean of a Million Stories.** unabr. ed. Simon Winchester. Read by Simon Winchester. (ENG.). 2010. (978-0-06-200712-4(2), Harper Audio); (978-0-06-206232-1(8), Harper Audio); audio compact disk 39.99 (978-0-06-186612-8(1), Harper Audio) HarperCollins Pubs.

Atlantic Alliance & U. S. Space Global Strategy. Robert Pfaltzgraff. 1986. 3.00 (149) ISI Books.

Atlantic Campaign: World War II's Great Struggle at Sea. Dan Van der Vat. Read by Richard Brown. 9 cass. (Running Time: 13 hrs. 30 min.). 1990. 72.00 (2523-B) Books on Tape.

Atlantic Campaign Pt. 1: World War II's Great Struggle at Sea. unabr. ed. Dan Van der Vat. Read by Richard Brown. 8 cass. (Running Time: 12 hrs.). 1990. 64.00 (978-0-7366-1674-4(8), 2523-A) Books on Tape.
The battle between Germany & the Allies for control of the Atlantic was prolonged & for years indecisive. Churchill called it "a war of groping & drowning, of ambuscade & statagem, of science & seamanship." Sailors on both sides fought under burdens of fear & hardship & bet their lives on tactical innovation, secret intelligence & embryonic technologies. How the admirals plotted the grand strategy of the campaign is recounted here, as are the dramas played out on & under the Atlantic: the Allie's elusive systems of convoy sailing; the German surface raiders & disguised motherships; the devastating mass attacks by U-Boats at night, when confusion & terror peaked.

Atlantic Fish. unabr. ed. Ed. by Linda Spizzirri. 1 cass. (Running Time: 15 mins.). Dramatization. (Educational Coloring Book & Cassette Package Ser.). (J). (gr. k-8). 1989. pap. bk. 6.95 (978-0-86545-148-3(6)) Spizzirri.
Presents information on Atlantic coast fish such as the 20 foot manta & the 12 inch flying fish.

Atlantic Fury, unabr. ed. Hammond Innes. Narrated by Ian Stuart. 6 cass. (Running Time: 9 hrs.). 1988. 51.00 (978-1-55690-034-1(1), 88110E7) Recorded Bks.
On a mysterious island in the North Sea, two strangers must work together to survive the bitter cold. One is an artist looking for quiet isolation; the other a WWII soldier hiding a desperate secret.

Atlantic Fury. unabr. collector's ed. Hammond Innes. Read by Charles Garst. 7 cass. (Running Time: 10 hrs. 30 mins.). 1984. 56.00 (978-0-7366-0856-5(7), 1807) Books on Tape.
In the wild out-islands of Hebrides, a killer storm nearly does in the crew of a military landing craft.

Atlantis. Charles Frazee. Narrated by Larry A. McKeever. (Ancient Greek Mystery Ser.). (J). 2007. 10.95 (978-1-58659-132-8(0)); audio compact disk 14.95 (978-1-58659-366-7(8)) Artesian.

Atlantis: The Lost Empire Read Along. Narrated by Chuck Riley. 1 CD. (Running Time: 1 hr. 30 mins.). (J). 2001. pap. bk. (978-0-7634-0783-4(6)) W Disney Records.

Atlantis & Lemuria. Nancy A. Clark. Read by Nancy A. Clark. 1 cass. (Running Time: 1 hr.). (Journeys of Remembrance Ser.). 1996. 9.95 (978-0-9648307-9-0(5)) Violet Fire Pubns.
Side A: Travel back to Atlantis to awaken memories of life there & the healing Temple of Dolphins. Side B: Learn about ancient Lemuria & visit the Temple of Wisdom to learn your purpose in this life time.

Atlantis & Lemurya. Nancy A. Clark. 1 cass. (Running Time: 60 mins.). (Journeys of Rememberance Audio Ser.). 9.95 (A5385) Lghtwrks Aud & Vid.
Travel back in time to Atlantis at the height of her glory (on side A). Awaken your memories as you walk through the streets observing the people in their daily lives. Visit the Temple of the Dolphins for a healing session. Then, (on side B) travel further back in time to visit ancient Lemurya. Feel the tremendous difference in the climate, homes & communities. Learn how Lemuryans built their roads, what they ate & what they believed. Then, as the high point of your visit, enter into the Temple of Wisdom where you can seek the answers to your most personal questions including information on the purpose of your Lemuryan lifetimes.

***Atlantis & Other Places: Stories of Alternate History.** unabr. ed. Harry Turtledove. (Running Time: 13 hrs. 30 mins. 0 sec.). (ENG.). 2010. 24.99 (978-1-4001-6814-9(7)); 18.99 (978-1-4001-8814-7(8)); 37.99 (978-1-4001-9814-6(3)); audio compact disk 90.99 (978-1-4001-4814-1(6)); audio compact disk 37.99 (978-1-4001-1814-4(X)) Pub: Tantor Media. Dist(s): IngramPubServ

***Atlantis Complex.** unabr. ed. Eoin Colfer. (Running Time: 9 hrs.). (Artemis Fowl Ser.: Bk. 7). (ENG.). (J). 2010. 20.00 (978-0-307-71160-1(9), Listening Lib) Pub: Random Audio Pubg. Dist(s): Random

***Atlantis Complex.** unabr. ed. Eoin Colfer. Narrated by Nathaniel Parker. 6 CDs. (Artemis Fowl Ser.: No. 7). 2010. audio compact disk 37.00 (978-0-307-71161-8(7), Listening Lib) Pub: Random Audio Pubg. Dist(s): Random

Atlantis Complex. unabr. ed. Eoin Colfer. Read by Nathaniel Parker. (Artemis Fowl Ser.: Bk. 7). (ENG.). (J). 2010. audio compact disk 37.00 (978-0-307-71159-5(5), Listening Lib) Pub: Random Audio Pubg. Dist(s): Random

Atlantis Found. unabr. ed. Clive Cussler. Read by Michael Prichard. 14 CDs. (Running Time: 14 hrs.). 2001. audio compact disk Books on Tape.
A highly advanced civilization is destroyed by a comet. An ancient British ship is found frozen in Antarctica. A Nazi submarine prowls beneath the seas.

Atlantis Found. unabr. ed. Clive Cussler. Read by Michael Prichard. 14 cass. (Running Time: 21 hrs.). (Dirk Pitt Ser.). 2000. 112.00 (978-0-7366-4781-6(3), 5126) Books on Tape.
Dirk Pitt discovers Atlantis, in a breathtaking novel from the grandmaster of adventure fiction.

Atlantis Revelation. unabr. ed. Thomas Greanias. Read by Scott Brick. (Running Time: 7 hrs. 0 mins. 0 sec.). (ENG.). 2009. audio compact disk 29.99 (978-0-7435-8249-0(7)) Pub: S&S Audio. Dist(s): S and S Inc

Atlas, Pt. 2. Act-Two Staff. 12 cass. (Running Time: 18 hrs.). 69.95 (AR82W) Second Renaissance.

Atlas, Pt. 3. Act-Two Staff. 15 cass. (Running Time: 22 hrs. 30 mins.). 87.95 (AR83W) Second Renaissance.

Atlas & Manual Coronary Intrav Ultr. Schoenhagen. 2004. audio compact disk 159.95 (978-1-84214-292-9(5)) Taylor and Fran.

Atlas of Cardiac Nuclear Medicine: Volumes I & II. Diwakar Jain & Archana Gowda. 2007. audio compact disk 260.00 (978-1-84184-597-5(3), Informa Health) Pub: Tay Francis Ltd GBR. Dist(s): Taylor and Fran

Atlas of Chronic Obstructive Pulmonary Disease. Peter J. Barnes & Trevor Hansel. 2004. audio compact disk 139.95 (978-1-84214-270-7(4)) Taylor and Fran.

Atlas of Great Jewish Communities. (gr. 4-6). pap. bk. & tchr. ed. 24.95 (978-0-8074-0802-5(6), 223941) URJ Pr.

Atlas of Human Anatomy. Singh. 2004. audio compact disk 25.00 (978-81-8061-223-7(6)) Jaypee Brothers IND.

Atlas of Prostatic Disease. 3rd ed. R. S. Kirby. 2004. audio compact disk 139.95 (978-1-84214-301-8(8)) Taylor and Fran.

Atlas Shrugged. Ayn Rand. Intro. by Leonard Peikoff. 256.85 (AR84W) Second Renaissance.
About the men of the mind on strike against the creed of self-sacrifice. Total run time is 57 hours.

Atlas Shrugged. abr. ed. Ayn Rand. Read by Edward Herrmann. 10 CDs. (Running Time: 12 hrs.). (ENG.). (gr. 9-12). 2000. audio compact disk 34.95 (978-1-56511-417-3(5), 1565114175) Pub: HighBridge. Dist(s): Workman Pub

Atlas Shrugged. abr. ed. Ayn Rand. Read by Edward Herrmann. 10 CDs. (Running Time: 12 hrs.). 2000. audio compact disk 49.95 HighBridge.
About a man who said he would stop the motor of the world & did is one of the most influential audios of our time.

***Atlas Shrugged.** unabr. ed. Ayn Rand. Read by Scott Brick. (Running Time: 63 hrs. 0 mins.). 2010. audio compact disk 160.00 (978-1-4417-3745-8(6)) Blckstn Audio.

Atlas Shrugged, Pt. 1. Ayn Rand. Read by Christopher Hurt. 14 CDs. (Running Time: 55 hrs. 30 mins.). 2003. audio compact disk 112.00 (978-0-7861-9625-8(4), 1204A,B,C) Blckstn Audio.

Atlas Shrugged, Pt. 1. unabr. ed. Ayn Rand. Read by Christopher Hurt. 11 cass. (Running Time: 55 hrs. 30 mins.). 1991. 76.95 (978-0-7861-0232-7(2), 1204A,B,C) Blckstn Audio.
This is the story of a man who said that he would stop the motor of the world & did. Is he a destroyer or a liberator? Why does he have to fight his battle not against his enemies but against those who need him most? Why does he fight his hardest battle against the woman he loves? The answers are revealed when you discover the reason behind the baffling events that play havoc with the lives of the amazing men & women in this remarkable book.

Atlas Shrugged, Pt. 1. unabr. ed. Ayn Rand. Read by Kate Reading. 11 cass. (Running Time: 16 hrs. 30 mins.). 1995. 88.00 (978-0-7366-3189-1(5), 3857-A) Books on Tape.
Atlas shrugged, and the world took a turn with the publication of this novel. The author incited a philosophical revolution, a revolution about having creativity and independence in a technological society, a revolution of ultimate importance to individuality.

Atlas Shrugged, Pt. 2. Ayn Rand. Read by Christopher Hurt. 15 CDs. (Running Time: 55 hrs. 30 mins.). 2003. audio compact disk 120.00 (978-0-7861-9599-2(1), 1204A,B,C) Blckstn Audio.

Atlas Shrugged, Pt. 2. unabr. ed. Ayn Rand. Read by Christopher Hurt. 12 cass. (Running Time: 55 hrs. 30 mins.). 2003. 83.95 (978-0-7861-0233-4(0), 1204A,B,C) Blckstn Audio.
This is the story of a man who said that he would stop the motor of the world & did. Is he a destroyer or a liberator? Why does he have to fight his battle not against his enemies but against those who need him most? Why does he fight his hardest battle against the woman he loves? The answers are revealed when you discover the reason behind the baffling events that play havoc with the lives of the amazing men & women in this remarkable book.

Atlas Shrugged, Pt. 2. unabr. ed. Ayn Rand. Read by Kate Reading. 12 cass. (Running Time: 18 hrs.). 1995. 96.00 (978-0-7366-3190-7(9), 3857-B) Books on Tape.
Atlas shrugged, and the world took a turn with the publication of this novel. The author incited a philosophical revolution, a revolution about having creativity and independence in a technological society, a revolution of ultimate importance to individuality.

Atlas Shrugged, Pt. 3. Ayn Rand. Read by Christopher Hurt. 2003. audio compact disk 152.00 (978-0-7861-9598-5(3)) Blckstn Audio.

Atlas Shrugged, Pt. 3. unabr. ed. Ayn Rand. Read by Christopher Hurt. 19 CDs. (Running Time: 55 hrs. 30 mins.). 2003. audio compact disk 152.00 (978-0-7861-0234-1(9), 1204A,B,C) Blckstn Audio.
This is the story of a man who said that he would stop the motor of the world & did. Is he a destroyer or a liberator? Why does he have to fight his battle not against his enemies but against those who need him most? Why does he fight his hardest battle against the woman he loves? The answers are revealed when you discover the reason behind the baffling events that play havoc with the lives of the amazing men & women in this remarkable book.

Atlas Shrugged, Pt. 3. unabr. ed. Ayn Rand. Read by Kate Reading. 15 cass. (Running Time: 22 hrs. 30 mins.). 1995. 120.00 (978-0-7366-3191-4(7), 3857-C) Books on Tape.
Atlas shrugged, and the world took a turn with the publication of this novel. The author incited a philosophical revolution, a revolution about having creativity and independence in a technological society, a revolution of ultimate importance to individuality.

Atlas Shrugged: New Edition. unabr. ed. Ayn Rand. Read by Scott Brick. (Running Time: 64 hrs. 0 mins.). 2008. 69.95 (978-1-4332-5619-6(3)); audio compact disk 59.95 (978-1-4332-5618-9(5)) Blckstn Audio.

Atlas Shrugged Part A: New Edition. unabr. ed. Ayn Rand. Read by Scott Brick. (Running Time: 20 hrs. 5 mins.). 2008. audio compact disk 99.95 (978-1-4332-5613-4(4)) Blckstn Audio.

Atlas Shrugged Part B: New Edition. unabr. ed. Ayn Rand. Read by Scott Brick. (Running Time: 20 hrs. 0 mins.). 2008. audio compact disk 99.95 (978-1-4332-5614-1(2)) Blckstn Audio.

Atlas Shrugged Part C: New Edition. unabr. ed. Ayn Rand. Read by Scott Brick. (Running Time: 23 hrs. 5 mins.). 2008. audio compact disk 109.95 (978-1-4332-5615-8(0)) Blckstn Audio.

Atlas 1. David Nunan. 2 cass. (Running Time: 3 hrs.). 2000. bk. & wbk. ed. 47.95 (978-0-8384-9745-6(4)) Heinle.
Atlas is a four-level series for teenagers to adults. Its solid language development and task-based approach helps students successfully learn English.

Atlas 1 & 2. David Nunan et al. 2002. audio compact disk 1.50 (978-0-8384-5699-6(5)) Heinle.
Language development.

Atlas 2. David Nunan. pap. bk. & wbk. ed. 28.95 (978-0-8384-5499-2(2)); pap. bk. & wbk. ed. 47.95 (978-0-8384-9744-9(6)) Heinle.

Atlas 2. David Nunan. (Global ESL/ELT Ser.). (J). 1994. suppl. ed. 28.95 (978-0-8384-4098-8(3)) Heinle.

Atlas 3. David Nunan. (Global ESL/ELT Ser.). (J). 1994. suppl. ed. 28.95 (978-0-8384-4099-5(1)); wbk. ed. 28.95 (978-0-8384-5500-5(X)) Heinle.

Atlas 3 & 4: Learning-Centered Communication. David Nunan et al. 1 CD. (Running Time: 1 hr.). 2002. audio compact disk 1.50 (978-0-8384-5881-5(5)) Heinle.
Solid language development and task-based approach help students successfully learn English.

Atlas 4. David Nunan. (Global ESL/ELT Ser.). (J). 1995. suppl. ed. 28.95 (978-0-8384-4100-8(9)) Heinle.

ATLS Prep: Advanced Trauma Life Support for Nurses. unabr. ed. Instructed by Scott Bourn et al. 8 cass. (Running Time: 12 hrs.). 1990. 99.00 cass. & soft-bound bk. (HT143) Ctr Hlth Educ.
Emergency nurses, this is just for you. ATLS is the basis for treating any trauma patient. Be on the cutting edge of medical technology. This course equips you to assess a multi-trauma victim in only 90 seconds. Make prompt, accurate decisions & treat your patient effectively.

Atman's Ultimate ScriptWriting Course, Vol. 1. unabr. ed. Sally Atman. Read by Sally Atman. 3 cass. (Running Time: 4 hrs. 28 mins.). 1999. 15.00 (978-1-928843-04-7(2)) Ad Lib Res.
Seminar/workshop which teaches the structure of scriptwriting using accelerated learning methods.

***Atmosfera.** (SPA.). 2009. audio compact disk 14.99 (978-0-8297-6148-1(9)) Pub: CanZion. Dist(s): Zondervan

Atmosphere for Healing. collector's ed. 2003. audio compact disk (978-1-59024-114-1(2)) B Hinn Min.

Atmosphere for Healing II. 2001. (978-0-9708141-4-2(3)); (978-0-9708141-5-9(1)); audio compact disk (978-0-9708141-1-1(9)) B Hinn Min.

Atmosphere for Healing II, Vol. 2. 2001. (978-0-9708141-3-5(5)); audio compact disk (978-0-9708141-0-4(0)) B Hinn Min.

Atmosphere for Healing II, Vol. II. 2001. audio compact disk (978-0-9708141-2-8(7)) B Hinn Min.

Atmosphere for Healing 1. 2003. (978-1-59024-107-3(X)); audio compact disk (978-1-59024-106-6(1)) B Hinn Min.

Atmosphere for Healing 2. 2003. (978-1-59024-109-7(6)); audio compact disk (978-1-59024-108-0(8)) B Hinn Min.

Atmosphere for Healing 3. 2003. (978-1-59024-091-5(X)); audio compact disk (978-1-59024-090-8(1)) B Hinn Min.

Atmosphere of a Brief Life, Program 10. Read by Richard Bauer. (F007EB090) Natl Public Radio.

Atmosphere of Greatness. unabr. ed. Read by Bob Richards. 1 cass. (Running Time: 30 mins.). 15.00 B R Motivational.
A recorded live speech by Bob Richards on the importance of motivating people to believe great things can happen to them, surrounding them with a positive atmosphere.

Atmospheric Disturbances. unabr. ed. Rivka Galchen. Read by Malcolm Hillgartner. (Running Time: 27000 sec.). 2008. audio compact disk 24.95 (978-1-4332-1445-5(8)) Blckstn Audio.

Atmospheric Disturbances. unabr. ed. Rivka Galchen. Read by Malcolm Hillgartner. (Running Time: 27000 sec.). 2008. 24.95 (978-1-4332-1443-1(1)); 44.95 (978-1-4332-1441-7(5)); audio compact disk 60.00 (978-1-4332-1442-4(3)); audio compact disk & audio compact disk 24.95 (978-1-4332-1444-8(X)) Blckstn Audio.

Atom in Religion & Philosophy. Instructed by Manly P. Hall. 5 cass. (Running Time: 1hr. 40 mins.). 1999. 40.00 incl. album. (978-0-89314-013-7(9), S610712) Philos Res.

Atomic Bazaar: The Rise of the Nuclear Poor. unabr. ed. William Langewiesche. Read by Tom Weiner. 7 cass. (Running Time: 18000 sec.). 2007. 29.95 (978-0-7861-4978-0(7)); 59.95 (978-0-7861-6809-5(9)); audio compact disk 29.95 (978-0-7861-5786-0(0)); audio compact disk 29.95 (978-0-7861-6959-7(1)); audio compact disk 72.00 (978-0-7861-6808-8(0)) Blckstn Audio.

Atomic Bombers. unabr. ed. Russell Vandenbroucke. Perf. by Larry Cox et al. 1 cass. (Running Time: 1 hr. 32 mins.). Dramatization. 1995. 19.95 (978-1-58081-097-5(7)) L A Theatre.
Set in 1943, something strange is going on in the New Mexican desert. By night, the starkly beautiful canyons of Los Alamos fill with the sound of exploding graphite & by day, the crackle of scientific brainpower. Fifty years after Hiroshima, this takes us into those secretive canyons to meet the cadre of brilliant scientists who worked there. With wisecracking physicist Dr. Richard Feynman as our guide, the race to the atom bomb comes alive as a very human endeavor, filled with humor, playfulness & dread.

***Atomic Lobster.** unabr. ed. Tim Dorsey. Read by Oliver Wyman. (ENG.). 2008. (978-0-06-162877-1(8)); (978-0-06-162878-8(6)) HarperCollins Pubs.

Atomic Lobster. unabr. ed. Tim Dorsey. Read by Oliver Wyman. 9 CDs. (Running Time: 10 hrs.). (Serge Storms Ser.: Bk. 11). 2008. audio compact disk 39.95 (978-0-06-145291-8(2), Harper Audio) HarperCollins Pubs.

Atomic, Molecular, & Optical Physics Handbook. Ed. by Gordon W. Drake. 1996. audio compact disk 160.00 (978-1-56396-596-8(8)) Spri.

Atomic Romance. unabr. ed. Bobbie Ann Mason. 7 cass. (Running Time: 27000 sec.). 2005. 29.95 (978-0-7861-3658-2(8), E3526); audio compact disk 29.95 (978-0-7861-7731-8(4), ZE3526) Blckstn Audio.

Atomic Romance: A Novel. Bobbie Ann Mason. Read by Mark Bramhall. (Running Time: 10 mins.). 2005. 59.95 (978-0-7861-3675-9(8)); audio compact disk 72.00 (978-0-7861-7689-2(X)) Blckstn Audio.

Atomic Romance: A Novel. unabr. ed. Bobbie Ann Mason. 13 vols. (Running Time: 10 mins.). 2005. 29.95 (978-0-7861-7962-6(7), ZM3526) Blckstn Audio.

Atoms, Snowflakes & God: The Convergence of Science & Religion. John Hitchcock. Read by John Hitchcock. 1 cass. (Running Time: 1 hr. 30 mins.). 1992. 10.95 (978-0-7822-0406-3(6), 499) C G Jung IL.
Physicist & author John Hitchcock lectures on the parallels between scientific & religious ways of understanding, seeking to reveal their essential unity.

Atonement. 2002. 25.00 (978-1-59007-294-3(4)) New Millenn Enter.

Atonement. Ian McEwan. 2005. audio compact disk 29.99 (978-1-4193-3691-1(6)) Recorded Bks.

Atonement. George W. Pace. 1 cass. 7.98 (978-1-55503-232-6(X), 06003354) Covenant Comms.
Learning of the power & importance of Christ's atonement.

Atonement. Derek Prince. 1 cass. (Running Time: 1 hr.). (B-2016) Derek Prince.

Atonement. abr. ed. Ian McEwan. Read by Josephine Bailey. (YA). 2008. 54.99 (978-1-60514-669-0(2)) Find a World.

Atonement. abr. ed. Ian McEwan. Read by Ian McEwan. Read by Josephine Bailey. 4 cass. 2004. 24.95 (978-1-59007-453-4(X)); audio compact disk 37.95 (978-1-59007-454-1(8)) Pub: New Millenn Enter. Dist(s): PerseuPGW

Atonement. abr. ed. Ian McEwan. Read by Ian McEwan. 4 cass. (Running Time: 5 hrs.). 2002. audio compact disk 35.00 (978-1-57511-114-8(4)) Pub: Pub Mills. Dist(s): TransVend

On the hottest day of the summer of 1935, 13-year-old Briony Tallis sees her older sister Cecilia strip off her clothes and plung into the fountain in the garden of their country house. Also watching Cecilia is their housekeeper's son Robbie Turner, a childhood friend who, along with Briony's sister, has recently graduated graduated from Cambridge. By the end of the day the lives of all three will be forever changed. Robbie and Cecilias will cross a boundary they never before dared to approach, becoming victims of the younger girl's scheming imagination. And Briony will commit a dreadful crime, with consequences that will color her entire life.

Atonement. abr. ed. Ian McEwan. Read by Ian McEwan. Read by Josephine Bailey. 4 cass. (Running Time: 6 hrs.). 2002. 24.95 (978-1-57511-113-1(6)) Pub Mills.

Atonement. movie tie-in ed. Ian McEwan. 2007. audio compact disk 29.99 (978-1-4281-7772-7(8)) Recorded Bks.

Atonement. movie tie-in unabr. ed. Ian McEwan. Narrated by Jill Tanner. 12 CDs. (Running Time: 14 hrs. 30 mins.). 2007. audio compact disk 29.99 (978-1-4281-7777-2(9)) Recorded Bks.

Atonement. unabr. ed. Ian McEwan. Read by Ian McEwan. Narrated by Jill Tanner. 8 cass. (Running Time: 14 hrs. 15 mins.). 2004. 34.99 (978-1-4025-1178-3(7), 01234) Recorded Bks.

In 1935, 13-year-old Briony Tallis' young cousin is assaulted on the grounds of the Tallis family estate. Briony, letting her hyperactive imagination get the better of her, triggers a devastating chain of events when she blames the atrocity on Robbie Turner, her older sister's new love.

Atonement, Album 1. Derek Prince. 5 cass. (Running Time: 5 hrs.). 1990. 24.95 (A-ATN1) Derek Prince.

By the perfect, all-sufficient sacrifice, Jesus cancelled forever the effects of sin, & provided complete well-being for every believer. These messages unfold main aspects of this sacrifice & steps by which to appropriate its provisions.

Atonement, Album 2. Derek Prince. 5 cass. (Running Time: 5 hrs.). 1990. 24.95 (A-ATN2) Derek Prince.

Atonement & You. Steven A. Cramer. 1 cass. 7.98 (978-1-55503-243-2(5), 06001009) Covenant Comms.

A descriptive meaning of the Atonement & its effects.

Atonement Child. Francine Rivers. 1 cass. (Running Time: 1 hr.). (Living Audio Ser.). 1997. 14.99 (978-0-8423-0283-8(2)) Tyndale Hse.

Chronicles the stories of three women faced with the issue of abortion.

Atonement Child. abr. ed. Francine Rivers. Narrated by Liz Curtis Higgs. (ENG.). 2007. 10.49 (978-1-60814-037-4(7)) Oasis Audio.

Atonement Child. abr. ed. Francine Rivers. Read by Liz Curtis Higgs. (ENG.). 2007. audio compact disk 14.99 (978-1-59859-261-0(0)) Oasis Audio.

Atrevete. Heining. (C). bk. 122.95 (978-0-8384-8563-7(4)) Heinle.

ATSDR'S Toxicological Profiles. 5th rev. ed. Ed. by Cassandra Smith-Simon. 2002. audio compact disk 354.95 (978-0-8493-1649-4(9)) Pub: CRC Pr. Dist(s): Taylor and Fran

Attachment: Program from the Award Winning Public Radio Series. Interview. Hosted by Fred Goodwin. 1CD. (Running Time: 1 hr). (Infinite Mind Ser.). 2001. audio compact disk 21.95 (978-1-888064-93-3(5), LCM 153) Lichtenstein Creat.

It's human to connect. Without the opportunity for consistent relationships early in life, though, development founders. This show explores attachment disorder and attachment problems that affect children who have been abused and neglected.Guests include psychiatrist Dr. Charles Zeanah, clinical psychologist Robert Karen, Thais Tepper, the founder of the Network for the Post-Institutionalized Child, and Joyce Peters, the adoptive mother of a child with attachment disorder.

***Attachments: A Novel.** unabr. ed. Rainbow Rowell. (Running Time: 9 hrs.). 2011. 39.97 (978-1-61106-985-3(8), 9781611069853, BADLE); 24.99 (978-1-61106-982-2(3), 9781611069822, Brilliance MP3); 39.97 (978-1-61106-983-9(1), 9781611069839, Brinc Audio MP3 Lib); audio compact disk 29.99 (978-1-61106-980-8(7), 9781611069808, Bril Audio CD Unabri); audio compact disk 69.97 (978-1-61106-981-5(5), 9781611069815, BriAudCD Unabrid) Brilliance Audio.

Attachments As Stumbling Blocks. unabr. ed. Robert A. Monroe. Read by Robert A. Monroe. 1 cass. (Running Time: 45 mins.). (Explorer Ser.). 1983. 12.95 (978-1-56113-019-1(2), 20) Monroe Institute.

Attachments as major stumbling blocks to spiritual development.

Attack. Mohammed Moulessehoul. Read by Stefan Rudnicki. (Running Time: 25200 sec.). 2006. 59.95 (978-0-7861-4557-7(9)); audio compact disk 72.00 (978-0-7861-7084-5(0)) Blckstn Audio.

Attack. abr. unabr. ed. Mohammed Moulessehoul. Read by Stefan Rudnicki. 5 cass. (Running Time: 25200 sec.). 2006. 25.95 (978-0-7861-4483-9(1)); audio compact disk 25.95 (978-0-7861-7246-7(0)); audio compact disk 29.95 (978-0-7861-7673-1(3)) Blckstn Audio.

Attack of the Clones. unabr. ed. R. A. Salvatore. Read by Jonathan Davis. 6 cass. (Running Time: 9 hrs.). 2002. 64.00 (978-0-7366-8594-8(4)) Books on Tape.

It's ten years after the events of THE PHANTOM MENACE. Now age twenty, Anakin Skywalker is torn between his personal dreams and his Jedi duties. Faced with temptations of love, violence and betrayal, Anakin and his Master, Obi-Wan Kenobi, struggle with the plots and secret deals that are slowly tearing the Republic apart.

Attack of the Clones. unabr. ed. R. A. Salvatore. Read by Jonathan Davis. CDs. (Running Time: 9 hrs.). 2002. audio compact disk 80.00 (978-0-7366-8605-1(3)) Books on Tape.

Attack of the Fiend. unabr. ed. Joseph Delaney. Narrated by Christopher Evan Welch. 8 CDs. (Running Time: 9 hrs.). (Last Apprentice Ser.: Bk. 4). (YA). (gr. 5-8). 2008. audio compact disk 87.75 (978-1-4281-8806-8(1)); 56.75 (978-1-4281-8801-3(0)) Recorded Bks.

Joseph Delaney's popular Last Apprentice series is a favorite of young adult readers who enjoy a dark and creepy edge to their fiction. Picking up where the bonechilling Night of the Soul Stealer left off, Attack of the Fiend reveals what happens when a coven of witches sets out to raise the devil himself. Can monsterhunter Tom Ward and his mentor the Spook stop them before the outbreak of evil?.

Attack of the Groovy Bushman. 1 CD. (Running Time: 1 hr.). 2001. audio compact disk 15.95 Lodestone Catalog.

Things are tough for Petey Jones. The government stole his idea for the Recyclotron, his wife may be canceled for low ratings & his 5 year-old son Sputnik wants a nuclear weapon, like every other kid in Groovy Bush.

Attack of the Mutant. R. L. Stine. 1 cass. (Running Time: 60 mins.). (Goosebumps Ser.: No. 25). (J). (gr. 3-7). 1996. 6.98 (978-0-7634-0087-3(4)) W Disney Records.

Attack of the Mutant Underwear. unabr. ed. 3 cass. (Running Time: 3 hrs. 30 min.). 2004. 28.00 (978-1-4025-7010-0(4)) Recorded Bks.

Attack of the Paper Bats. Michael Dahl. Illus. by Martin Blanco. (Library of Doom Ser.). (gr. 1-3). 2008. audio compact disk 14.60 (978-1-4342-0601-5(7)) CapstoneDig.

Attack of the Tagger. Wendelin Van Draanen. Read by Daniel Young. (Shredderman (Playaway) Ser.). (J). 2008. 34.99 (978-1-60640-648-9(5)) Find a World.

Attack of the Tagger. unabr. ed. Wendelin Van Draanen. Illus. by Wendelin Van Draanen. Narrated by Johnny Heller. 2 CDs. (Running Time: 6900 sec.). (Shredderman Ser.: Bk. 2). (J). (gr. 3-6). 2006. audio compact disk 22.95 (978-1-59519-757-3(5)) Live Oak Media.

Attack of the Tagger. unabr. ed. Wendelin Van Draanen. Read by Daniel Young. Illus. by Brian Biggs. 2 cass. (Running Time: 6900 sec.). (Shredderman Ser.: Bk. 2). (YA). (gr. 7-11). 2006. 18.95 (978-1-59519-756-6(7)) Live Oak Media.

Will the secret identity of cyber-hero Nolan Byrd be revealed before he can uncover the true graffiti bandit? Fast-paced fun continues in this second, satisfying adventure of Shredderman!.

Attack of the Theater People. unabr. ed. Marc Acito. Read by Jeff Woodman. (Running Time: 9 hrs. 45 mins.). 2008. 56.75 (978-1-4361-6522-8(9)); 82.75 (978-1-4361-3796-6(9)); audio compact disk 123.75 (978-1-4361-3798-0(5)) Recorded Bks.

Attack of the Theater People. unabr. collector's ed. Marc Acito. Read by Jeff Woodman. 9 CDs. (Running Time: 9 hrs. 45 mins.). 2008. audio compact disk 51.95 (978-1-4361-3799-7(3)) Recorded Bks.

Attack of the Two-Inch Teacher. unabr. ed. Bruce Coville. Read by William Dufris. 2 cass. (Running Time: 2 hrs. 30 mins.). (I Was a Sixth Grade Alien Ser.: Vol. 2). (J). (gr. 3-5). 2000. pap. bk. 28.00 (978-0-8072-8354-7(1), YA170SP, Listening Lib) Random Audio Pubg.

Pleskit Meenom is tired of constantly being teased by Jordan Lynch. Pleskit & his friend Tim decide to teach Jordan a lesson & borrow a shrinking ray from the desk of Pleskit's Fatherly One. Unfortunately, the plan backfires & it is Tim & their teacher Ms. Weintrab that get shrunk. If this gets out, it could ruin the alien mission. But how can you hide the fact that you've shrunk your teacher?.

Attack of the Two-Inch Teacher. unabr. ed. Bruce Coville. Read by William Dufris. 2 cass. (Running Time: 2 hrs. 30 mins.). (I Was a Sixth Grade Alien Ser.: Vol. 2). (J). (gr. 3-6). 2000. 23.00 (978-0-8072-8353-0(3), YA170CX, Listening Lib) Random Audio Pubg.

Pleskit Meenom is tired of constantly being teased by Jordan Lynch. Pleskit and his friend Tim decide to teach Jordan a lesson and borrow a shrinking ray from the desk of Pleskit's Fatherly One. Unfortunately, the plan backfires and it is Tim and their teacher Ms. Weintrab that get shrunk. If this gets out, it could ruin the alien mission. But how can you hide the fact that you've shrunk your teacher?.

Attack of the Unsinkable Rubber Ducks. Christopher Brookmyre. 2007. 84.95 (978-0-7531-3814-4(X)); audio compact disk 99.95 (978-0-7531-2795-7(4)) Pub: ISIS Audio GBR. Dist(s): Ulverscroft US

Attack on the Queen. unabr. ed. Richard P. Henrick. Read by Michael Prichard. 10 cass. (Running Time: 15 hrs.). 1999. 80.00 (978-0-7366-4354-2(0), 4811) Books on Tape.

Signalling a new era of global cooperation: the leader of the People's Republic of China agrees to join the upcoming G-7 summit aboard the Queen Elizabeth 2. But a group of ultra-nationalist Chinese terrorists hijacks a nuclear submarine & sets a course to intercept the ocean liner in the North Atlantic. Meanwhile another group of terrorists infiltrates the ship & gains possession of the codes to China's neclear arsenal. Only two brothers, Special Agent Vincent Kellogg of the Secret Service & the BATF's Thomas Kellogg, stand between this moment & Armageddon.

Attack on the Redan. Garry Douglas Kilworth. 10 cass. (Running Time: 11 hrs. 30 mins.). (Soundings Ser.). (J). 2004. 84.95 (978-1-84283-745-0(1)); audio compact disk 89.95 (978-1-84283-967-6(5)) Pub: ISIS Lrg Prnt GBR. Dist(s): Ulverscroft US

Attack upon Christendom: From Kierkegaard to Lacan Via Jung. Read by David Miller. 1 cass. (Running Time: 2 hrs.). 1985. 10.95 (978-0-7822-0168-0(7), 165) C G Jung IL.

Part of the conference set "Jung's Challenge to Contemporary Religion.".

Attacker's Advantage. unabr. ed. Garry Kasparov. (ENG.). 2006. audio compact disk 29.95 (978-0-14-305842-7(8), PengAudBks) Penguin Grp USA.

Attain Good Health. 1 cass. (Running Time: 60 mins.). 10.95 (007) Psych Res Inst.

Mental imaging for continued good health through positive thinking.

Attain Mastery. 1 cass. (Running Time: 60 mins.). 1999. 10.00 (978-1-930455-18-4(6)) E P Inc Pubng Co.

This will get everyone in touch with their incredible power.

Attain Money & Prosperity. Lee Pulos. 2 cass. (Running Time: 2 hrs.). (Self Hypnosis & Subliminal Reinforcement Ser.). 14.95 (978-1-55569-234-6(6), SUB-8010) Great Am Audio.

Presents tools for positive self-change.

Attain Your Goals. 2 cass. (Running Time: 2 hrs.). (Self Hypnosis & Subliminal Reinforcement Ser.). 14.95 (978-1-55569-236-0(2), SUB-8012) Great Am Audio.

Attaining Goals. 1998. 24.95 (978-1-58557-020-1(6)) Dynamic Growth.

Attaining Inner Peace. Gerald G. Jampolsky & Diane Cirincione. 6 cass. (Running Time: 6 hrs.). 1993. 59.95 (250A) Nightingale-Conant.

Attaining Personal Greatness. Melanie Brown. 6 cass. (Running Time: 6 hrs.). 1992. 59.95 (267A) Nightingale-Conant.

Attaining Wealth & Power. Norman J. Caldwell. Read by Norman J. Caldwell. Ed. by Achieve Now Institute Staff. 1 cass. (Running Time: 20 mins.). (Success Now Ser.). 1988. 9.97 (978-1-56273-065-9(7)) My Mothers Pub.

Financial success & power right now!.

Attaining Wisdom. Swami Amar Jyoti. 1 cass. 1979. 9.95 (J-26) Truth Consciousness.

How the inner voice is born. "Let go & let God." the egoless state. Fruits of faith.

***Attenbury Emeralds: Lord Peter Wimsey's First Case.** Jill Paton Walsh. Narrated by Edward Petherbridge. (Running Time: 8 hrs. 0 mins. 0 sec.). (ENG.). 2011. audio compact disk 29.95 (978-1-60998-148-8(0)) Pub: AudioGO. Dist(s): Perseus Dist

***Attending: A Physician's Introduction to Mindfulness.** Scott Rogers. Read by Scott Rogers. (Running Time: 61). (ENG.). 2010. audio compact disk 16.95 (978-0-9773455-3-3(X)) Mind Livi Pr.

attentat. unabr. ed. Khadra. Yasmina. Read by Henri Thomas. (YA). 2007. 84.99 (978-2-35569-099-0(5)) Find a World.

Attention. unabr. ed. Robert A. Monroe. Read by Robert A. Monroe. (Running Time: 30 mins.). (Human Plus Ser.). 1989. 10.95 (978-1-56113-000-9(1), 1) Monroe Institute.

Sharply focuses mind & senses on a particular thought, action or event.

Attention All Shipping. Charlie Connelly. Read by Alex Jennings. 4 cass. (Running Time: 3 hrs. 0 mins. 0 sec.). (ENG., 2005. 22.95 (978-1-4055-0111-8(1)) Pub: Little BrownUK GBR. Dist(s): IPG Chicago

Attention All Shipping: A Journey Round the Shipping Forecast. unabr. ed. Charlie Connelly. Read by Alex Jennings. 3 CDs. (Running Time: 3 hrs. 0 mins. 0 sec.). (ENG., 2005. audio compact disk 19.95 (978-1-4055-0110-1(3)) Pub: Little BrownUK GBR. Dist(s): IPG Chicago

Attention Deficit Disorder (CD) Eric Jensen. 2006. 64.95 (978-1-890460-16-7(8)) Pub: Corwin Pr. Dist(s): SAGE

Attention Deficit Hyperactivity Disorder: Diagnosis, Causes & Treatment. Michael Levin. 1 cass. (Running Time: 60 mins.). 1997. bk. 20.00 (978-1-58111-008-1(1)) Contemporary Medical.

Overview of child with ADHD; functioning at home, school & with peers; compares ADHD to bipolar depressive disorders & generalized anxiety disorder; describes types, characteristics of ADHD.

Attention-Deficit Scales for Adults (ADSA) Santo J. Triolo. 1997. audio compact disk 135.00 (978-0-87630-873-8(6), Brunner-Mazel) Taylor and Fran.

Attention Deficits Disorder in Children: Program from the award winning public radio Series. Interview. Hosted by Fred Goodwin. Comment by John Hockenberry. 1CD. (Running Time: 1 hr). (Infinite Mind Ser.). 2002. audio compact disk 21.95 (978-1-888064-88-9(9), LCM 208) Lichtenstein Creat.

Fidgeting, daydreaming, not paying attention to the teacher, a preoccupation with "Gameboy"... are these characteristics of a typical American kid or signs of an underlying neurobiological disorder? In this show, we explore attention deficit hyperactivity disorder (ADHD) in children. Guests include Dr. Peter Jensen, director of the Center for the Advancement of Children's Mental Health at Columbia University; Dr. Stephen Hinshaw, professor of psychology at the University of California, Berkeley; Clarke Ross, chief executive officer of CHADD (Children and Adults with Attention Deficit Disorder); Debbie Zimmett, author of the children's book Eddie Enough. We hear also from parents of children who have been diagnosed with ADHD... some say incorrectly... and a teenager who had to take on the local Board of Education to get the help he needed in school. And commentary by John Hockenberry.

***Attention! This Book Will Make You Money: How to Use Attention-Getting Online Marketing to Increase Your Revenue.** unabr. ed. Jim F. Kukral. Read by Walter Dixon. (Running Time: 8 hrs.). (ENG.). 2010. 29.98 (978-1-59659-681-8(3), GildAudio) Pub: Gildan Media. Dist(s): HachBkGrp

Attention to Prevention. (J). 1990. 9.95 (978-1-887028-57-8(9)) Slim Goodbody.

Attic Ballads: What People Cherish. 1 cass. (Running Time: 1 hr.). 9.00 (OP-79-01-24, HarperThor) HarpC GBR.

Attic of the Wind; in a Spring Garden. 2004. cass. & flmstrp 30.00 (978-0-89719-647-5(3)) Weston Woods.

Atticus. unabr. ed. Ron Hansen. Narrated by Ed Sala. 5 cass. (Running Time: 7 hrs.). 1997. 44.00 (978-0-7887-0943-2(7), 95076E7) Recorded Bks.

A middle-aged father leaves his Colorado ranch & travels to a shabby town to recover the body of his son, who may have commited suicide. As he pieces together information about his sons life, he uncovers deep feelings in his own heart & suspicious evidence about his death.

Attila. abr. unabr. ed. John Man. Read by James Adams. (Running Time: 37800 sec.). 2006. audio compact disk 29.95 (978-0-7861-7604-5(0)) Blckstn Audio.

Attila. abr. unabr. ed. John Man. Read by James Adams. Created by Blackstone Audiobooks. 9 cass. (Running Time: 37800 sec.). 2006. 29.95 (978-0-7861-4537-9(4)) Blckstn Audio.

Attila: The Barbarian King Who Challenged Rome. abr. unabr. ed. John Man. Read by James Adams. 10 CDs. (Running Time: 37800 sec.). 2006. audio compact disk 29.95 (978-0-7861-7141-5(3)) Blckstn Audio.

Attila: The Barbarian King Who Challenged Rome. unabr. ed. John Man. Read by James Adams. (Running Time: 37800 sec.). 2006. 72.95 (978-0-7861-4637-6(0)); audio compact disk 90.00 (978-0-7861-6833-0(1)) Blckstn Audio.

Attitude! Dealing with Stress & Insecurity. rev. ed. Sydney Banks. 2003. audio compact disk (978-1-55105-401-8(9)) Lone Pine Publ CAN.

Attitude: How to stay sane & lighthearted in stressful times: the Healthy Alternative. Sheryl L. Roush. (ENG.). 2003. audio compact disk 15.95 (978-1-880878-09-5(7)) Sparkle Present.

Attitude & Action: Building Winning Teams at Work & at Home. abr. ed. Mike Singletary. Read by Mike Singletary. Ed. by Vera Derr. 1 cass. (Running Time: 1 hr.). 1997. 12.95 (978-0-85013-310-3(6)) Dartnell Corp.

Mike Singletary, former defensive team captain for the Chicago Bears, explains how to create lasting success. He explains what it takes to be an eagle - a strong individual performer & an effective team player.

***Attitude Is Everything.** abr. ed. Keith Harrell. Read by Keith Harrell. (ENG.). 2006. (978-0-06-113056-4(7), Harper Audio); (978-0-06-113055-7(9), Harper Audio) HarperCollins Pubs.

***Attitude Is Everything: For Educators, Administrators.** Keith Harrell. (ENG.). 2010. audio compact disk 60.00 (978-0-9826101-2-1(2)) Wisdom Know.

Attitude Is Everything: 10 Life-Changing Steps to Turning Attitude into Action. abr. ed. Keith Harrell & Harrell. Read by Keith Harrell. 3 CDs. (Running Time: 4 hrs.). 2000. 29.95 (978-0-694-52282-8(1), Harper Audio) HarperCollins Pubs.

Attitude Is Everything for Success. 2006. 19.95 (978-0-9791281-1-0(0)) Harrell.

Attitude of Gratitude. Keith Harrell. (ENG.). 2003. 23.95 (978-1-4019-0199-8(9), 1999) Hay House.

Attitude Plus Self-Confidence: The Cornerstone for Personal & Professional Success. Keith D. Harrell. 4 CDs. 2004. audio compact disk 23.95 (978-1-4019-0294-0(4), 2944) Hay House.

Attitude Towards Others, No. 1. Swami Jyotirmayananda. 1 cass. (Running Time: 1 hr.). 1990. 12.99 Yoga Res Foun.

Attitude Towards Others I. (708) Yoga Res Foun.

Attitude Towards Others Two. 1 cass. (Running Time: 1 hr.). 12.99 (709) Yoga Res Foun.

Attitudes. 1 cass. (Around the Tables Ser.). 1986. 6.95 (978-0-933685-08-6(4), TP-30) A A Grapevine.

Includes articles from AA Grapevine magazine on coping with anger, fear, resentment, & other problems in sobriety. Features descriptive of AA program.

Attitudes: Getting along with Others. Mental Dynamics Staff. 2 cass. (Running Time: 2 hrs.). 1989. 24.95 (978-1-877897-07-8(8)) Mental Dynamics.
Contains Subliminal Affirmations underneath Contempary Music. And Conscious (Audible) Affirmations.

Attitudes: Goals & Priorities. Mental Dynamics Staff. Read by Barbara L. Mitchell, II & Edward Head. 2 cass. (Running Time: 2 hrs.). 1989. 24.95 (978-1-877897-00-9(0)) Mental Dynamics.

Attitudes: I Am Worthy. Mental Dynamics Staff. Read by Barbara L. Mitchell, II & Edward Head. 2 cass. (Running Time: 2 hrs.). 1989. 24.95 (978-1-877897-10-8(8)) Mental Dynamics.

Attitudes: Mental Side of Golf. Mental Dynamics Staff. Read by Barbara L. Mitchell, II & Edward Head. 2 cass. (Running Time: 2 hrs.). 1989. 24.95 (978-1-877897-01-6(9)) Mental Dynamics.

Attitudes: My Healthy Self Image. Mental Dynamics Staff. 2 cass. (Running Time: 2 hrs.). 1989. 24.95 (978-1-877897-06-1(X)) Mental Dynamics.

Attitudes: Pathways to Destiny. Mac Hammond. 6 cass. (Running Time: 1 hr.). 1997. 36.00 (978-1-57399-062-2(0)) Mac Hammond.
Having the attitudes that will make you a success in life.

Attitudes: Stress Management. Mental Dynamics Staff. Read by Barbara L. Mitchell, II & Edward Head. 2 cass. (Running Time: 2 hrs.). 1989. 24.95 (978-1-877897-02-3(7)) Mental Dynamics.
Contains Subliminal Affirmations underneath Contempary Music. And Conscious (Audible) Affirmations.

Attitudes: Success & Prosperity. Mental Dynamics Staff. Read by Barbara L. Mitchell, II & Edward Head. 2 cass. (Running Time: 2 hrs.). 1989. 24.95 (978-1-877897-03-0(5)) Mental Dynamics.

Attitudes: The Power to Say No. Mental Dynamics Staff. Read by Barbara L. Mitchell, II & Edward Head. 2 cass. (Running Time: 2 hrs.). 1989. 24.95 (978-1-877897-05-4(1)) Mental Dynamics.

Attitudes: Weight Loss. Mental Dynamics Staff. Read by Barbara L. Mitchell, II & Edward Head. 2 cass. (Running Time: 2 hrs.). 1989. 24.95 (978-1-877897-04-7(3)) Mental Dynamics.

Attitudes: You Are Champion. Mental Dynamics Staff. Read by Barbara L. Mitchell, II & Edward Head. 2 cass. (Running Time: 2 hrs.). 1989. 24.95 (978-1-877897-09-2(4)) Mental Dynamics.

Attitudes: You Are Something Special. Mental Dynamics Staff. Read by Barbara L. Mitchell, II & Edward Head. 2 cass. (Running Time: 2 hrs.). 1989. 24.95 (978-1-877897-08-5(6)) Mental Dynamics.

Attitudes, Beliefs & Choices: ABC's Aren't Just for Kids. Alexandra Delis-Abrams. 3 cass. (Running Time: 3 hrs. 30 mins.). 1999. 24.95 album. (978-1-879889-25-5(0)) Adage Pubns.
Simple, practical & playful messages about life.

Attitudes for a Healthy Life & Planet. Hosted by Nancy Pearlman. 1 cass. (Running Time: 26 mins.). 10.00 (509) Educ Comm CA.

Attitudes for Growth. Virgil B. Smith. 1 cass. (Running Time: 15 mins.). 1972. 5.95 (978-1-878507-01-3(X), 22C) Human Grwth Services.
Positive self-talk. Some topics are: self-esteem, cooperation with people, recognizing reality & reasonable independence.

Attitudes of a Devotee. (Introduction to the Spiritual Life Ser.). 9.95 (ST-63) Crystal Clarity.
Topics include: why we need an attitude of learning; the difference between humility & self-abasement; the importance of combining willingness with understanding; how to love the things of this world.

Attitudes of Gratitude: How to Give & Receive Joy Every Day of Your Life. unabr. ed. M. J. Ryan. Read by Gabrielle De Cuir. 2 cass. (Running Time: 3 hrs.). 2001. 18.00 (978-1-57453-443-6(2)) Audio Lit.
Helps listeners identify the areas in their everyday lives where they can experience the positive effects of practicing gratitude.

Attitudes of Meekness. Elbert Willis. 1 cass. (Might of Meekness Ser.). 4.00 Fill the Gap.

Attorney-Client Privilege; Choice of Forum; Mass Torts & Class Actions. Contrib. by W. Burlette Carter et al. 1 cass. (Running Time: 1 hrs. 30 mins.). 1998. 35.00 Incl. study outlines. (N612) Am Law Inst.
Features three presentations from "The Audio Litigator." Professor Carter of George Washington University Law School discusses attorney-client privilege & work product issues; Professor Vairo of Loyola University School of Lawspeaks on choice of forum issues; & attorney Elizabeth J. Cabraser of Lieff, Cabraser, Heimann & Bernstein, LLP in San Francisco talks about developments in thearea of mass torts & class actions.

Attorney General Thornburgh: Three Mile Island. (Running Time: 60 mins.). 1989. 11.95 (N0890328, HarperThor) HarpC GBR.

Attorneys' Fees. 1 cass. 1989. bk. 45.00 (AC-514-S) PA Bar Inst.

Attorneys' Fees, Costs & Penalties. 1 cass. 1990. 15.00 (AL-88) PA Bar Inst.

Attorneys for Christ: Proceedings of the Annual Convention, National Association of Evangelicals Buffalo, New York. Read by Robert Angeser. 1 cass. (Running Time: 60 mins.). 1987. 4.00 (328) Nat Assn Evan.

Attract Love. 1 cass. 10.00 (978-1-58506-021-4(6), 51) New Life Inst OR.
Energize your consciousness to attract the love that you want.

Attract Love. Kelly Howell. 1 cass. (Running Time: 1 hr.). (Brain Wave Subliminal Ser.). 1996. 9.95 (978-1-881451-40-2(2)) Brain Sync.
Your heart opens as your subconscious mind absorbs images of profound love and unlimited joy. You generate a powerful magnetic field of radiance - an attracting force that draws to you the love you desire.

Attract Love. Kelly Howell. 2000. audio compact disk 14.95 (978-1-881451-69-3(0)) Brain Sync.

Attract Love: And Create a Successful Relationship. Dick Sutphen. 5 cass. (Self-Change Programming Ser.). cass. & video 59.95 incl. 4 audio cass. & 1 video cass. (978-0-87554-334-5(0), PK107) Valley Sun.
Includes: Attracting Love Video Hypnosis; Instruction - Motivation Tape; 25 Best Ways to Find Love & Make it Work; Attracting Perfect Love; Charisma (Drawing People to You). Attract Love & Create a Successful Relationship 5-tape Power Package is the ultimate approach to finding love & making it work.

Attract Love Now. 1 cass. (Running Time: 45 min.). (Relationship Ser.). 9.98 (978-1-55909-051-3(0), 49); 9.98 90 mins. extended length stereo music. (978-1-55909-052-0(9), 49M) Randolph Tapes.
Designed to help you attract your ideal companion. Subliminal messages are heard 3-5 minutes before becoming ocean sounds or music.

***Attract Money Now.** unabr. ed. Joe Vitale. Read by Don Hagen. (Running Time: 4 hrs. 30 mins.). (ENG.). 2010. 19.98 (978-1-59659-600-9(7), GildAudio) Pub: Gildan Media. Dist(s): HachBkGrp

***Attract Money Now.** unabr. ed. Joe Vitale. (Running Time: 4 hrs. 30 mins.). (ENG.). 2010. audio compact disk 24.98 (978-1-59659-599-6(X), GildAudio) Pub: Gildan Media. Dist(s): HachBkGrp

Attract the Happiness Your Heart Longs For. Guy Finley. (ENG.). 2006. 7.49 (978-1-929320-52-3(3)) Life of Learn.

Attract Wealth. Kelly Howell. (Running Time: 3600 sec.). 2008. audio compact disk 14.95 (978-1-60568-057-6(5)) Brain Sync.

Attract Your Soulmate. unabr. ed. Dick Sutphen. Read by Dick Sutphen. 1 cass. (Running Time: 1 hr.). (Spirit Guide Meditations). 1999. 14.98 (978-0-87554-637-7(4), SG110) Valley Sun.
Focus energy & concentration upon attracting your true love - the person with whom you are destined to share your life.

Attracting a Mate. Rick Brown. Read by Rick Brown. Ed. by John Quatro. 1 cass. (Running Time: 30 mins.). (Easy Listening Ser.). 1993. 10.95 (978-1-57100-009-5(7), E126); 10.95 (978-1-57100-033-0(X), J126); 10.95 (978-1-57100-057-6(7), N126); 10.95 (978-1-57100-105-4(0), W126); 10.95 (978-1-57100-129-0(8), H126) Sublime Sftware.
Releases old barriers & attracts a new a love.

Attracting Abundance - Hypnosis. Created by Laura Rubinstein. 1. (Running Time: 50 min). (LBR Relaxation Ser.: No. 2). 1999. audio compact disk (978-0-9749845-1-3(5)) L Rubinstein.
Hypnosis CD with 2 tracks. First track is to be used as a power nap which will wake you up at the end. The second track is to be used to fall asleep to.

Attracting & Enhancing Romance, Intimacy & Love. Eldon Taylor. 1 CD. (Running Time: 52 mins.). (Whole Brain Innertalk Ser.). 1998. audio compact disk (978-1-55978-858-8(5)) Progress Aware Res.

Attracting & Enhancing Romance, Intimacy & Love. Eldon Taylor. 1 CD. (Running Time:). (Whole Brain Innertalk Ser.). 1999. audio compact disk (978-1-55978-914-1(X)) Progress Aware Res.

Attracting Genuine Love. Gay Hendricks & Kathleen Hendricks. (Running Time: 1 hr. 15 mins.). 2006. bk. 19.95 (978-1-59179-171-3(5), K843D) Sounds True.

Attracting Genuine Love. Gay Hendricks & Kathlyn Hendricks. Read by Gay Hendricks. 2 cass. (Running Time: 1 hr. 30 mins.). 1999. 16.95 (978-1-891323-01-0(6)) Hendricks Inst.
You will Learn: the three secrets of attracting genuine love; the real rules of love.

Attracting Love. Richard Jafolla & Mary-Alice Jafolla. Read by Mary-Alice Jafolla. (Relationships Ser.). 1986. 12.95 (350) Stppng Stones.
Motivational tapes that work on the subconscious mind (subliminal) & conscious mind to bring about self-improvement.

Attracting Love. Barry Tesar. 1 cass. (Running Time: 1 hr.). (Subliminal Inspiration Ser.). 1992. 9.98 (978-1-56470-014-8(3)) Success Cass.
Subliminal program.

Attracting Love: A Step-by-Step Guide on How to Attract Your Ideal Partner. unabr. ed. Tricia Brennan. Read by Tricia Brennan. (Running Time: 1 hr. 15 mins.). 2008. audio compact disk 39.95 (978-1-921415-65-4(7), 9781921415654) Pub: Bolinda Pubng AUS. Dist(s): Bolinda Pub Inc

Attracting Love: Hypnotic & Subliminal Learning. David Illig. 1985. 14.99 (978-0-86580-041-0(3)) Success World.

Attracting Love (Hypnosis), Vol. 23. Jayne Helle. 1 cass. (Running Time: 29 mins.). 1997. 15.00 (978-1-891826-22-1(0)) Introspect.
To be loved, we must love ourselves & become the type of person we want to be loved by.

Attracting Love (the Ultimate Healer Subliminal Series) Easily create positive, loving, lasting Relationships. Kyrah Malan. 1 CD. (Running Time: 29 mins). 2006. audio compact disk 29.95 (978-0-9787324-8-6(0), SR3) K Malan.
The ultimate in subliminal affirmations. Music, messages and binaural beats are specifically designed to work together to help you transform beliefs and experiences in your relationships. Allow and ATTRACT the best possible love in your life.What you hear is beautiful music that puts you in a calm, receptive state quickly and easily.What your subconscious hears are specially designed affirmations and suggestions, designed to rewrite subconscious beliefs and change behavior faster and more effectively than any subliminal program available today.Unlike typical subliminal programs which recommend you listen to them for at least 30 days, Ultimate healer CDs help create positive results in only 17 days; some people report results in as little as 2 or 3 days!You can play them during everyday activities, while driving, reading, or at work, or listen to them with headphones. You have freedom and flexibility with The Ultimate Healer Subliminal Series.

***Attracting More Love + Personal Magnetism.** Bob Griswold. (Running Time: 55). 2010. 14.95 (978-1-55848-105-3(2), Super Strength Series) EffectiveMN.

Attracting My Soul Mate. 2007. audio compact disk 19.95 (978-1-56136-085-7(6)) Master Your Mind.

Attracting Perfect Love. Dick Sutphen. 1 cass. (Running Time: 1 hr.). (RX17 Ser.). 1986. 14.98 (978-0-87554-293-5(X), RX102) Valley Sun.
You now create the space in your life for the perfect love relationship; are ready to meet the perfect lover; project warmth & openness, which attracts others; are ready to give & receive unconditional love; & focus the power of your subconscious mind upon drawing the perfect lover into your life.

Attracting Prosperity & Success, Vol. 1 Jonathan Parker. Read by Jonathan Parker. 1 CD. (Running Time: 1 hr.). (Subliminal Ser.: Vol. 4). 1999. audio compact disk (978-1-58400-042-6(2)) QuantumQuests Intl.
Positive subliminal messages with classical music on compact disc.

Attracting Prosperity & Success with Tropical Ocean, Vol. 11. Jonathan Parker. Read by Jonathan Parker. 1 CD. (Running Time: 1 hr.). (Subliminal Ser.: Vol. 4). 1999. audio compact disk (978-1-58400-065-5(1)) QuantumQuests Intl.
1 compact disc with subliminal affirmations & tropical ocean.

Attracting Prosperity (Hypnosis), Vol. 22. Jayne Helle. 1 cass. (Running Time: 29 mins.). 1997. 15.00 (978-1-891826-21-4(2)) Introspect.
We have abundance in us. Let go of the fear of not having enough & allow prosperity to flow to you.

Attracting Success. Bruce Goldberg. (ENG.). 2005. audio compact disk 17.00 (978-1-57968-091-6(7)) Pub: B Goldberg. Dist(s): Baker Taylor

Attracting Success. Bruce Goldberg. Read by Bruce Goldberg. 1 cass. (Running Time: 25 mins.). (ENG.). 2007. 13.00 (978-1-885577-56-6(7)) Pub: B Goldberg. Dist(s): Baker Taylor
Through self-hypnosis learn how to create abundance & bring various forms of material rewards into one's life.

Attracting Terrific People. abr. rev. ed. Lillian Glass. 3 CDs. (Running Time: 3 hrs. 0 mins. 0 sec.). (ENG.). 2004. audio compact disk 19.95 (978-1-59397-354-4(3)) Pub: Macmill Audio. Dist(s): Macmillan

Attracting the Abundance of Prosperity. 1 CD. (Running Time: 30 minutes). 1999. 14.95 (978-0-9779472-8-7(9)) Health Wealth Inc.
The soothing voice on this recording guides you gently and easily within, to the experience of a positive state of hypnosis. In this state, and by following the given instructions, you will utilize your imagination to attract all good things into your life. And your imagination is what activates your experience. By using this recording, you begin to build on all levels of prosperity: money, good friends, happiness, health, family, peace of mind . . . a simply wonderful life. It all begins with the experience of well-being that is available to you from the very first time you use this recording.

Attracting the Right Love Relationship. Eldon Taylor. 1 cass. (Running Time: 62 mins.). (Inner Talk Ser.). 16.95 incl. script. (978-1-55978-526-6(8), 53811F) Progress Aware Res.
Soundtrack - Babbling Brook with underlying subliminal affirmations.

Attracting the Right Love Relationship: Easy. Eldon Taylor. Read by Eldon Taylor. Ed. by Leslie Brice. 1 cass. (Running Time: 1 hr.). 1992. 16.95 (978-1-56705-289-3(4)) Gateways Inst.
Self improvement.

Attracting the Right Love Relationship: Ocean. Eldon Taylor. Read by Eldon Taylor. Ed. by Leslie Brice. 1 cass. (Running Time: 1 hr.). 1992. 16.95 (978-1-56705-290-9(8)) Gateways Inst.

Attracting Wealth. Michael P. Kelly. 1 cass. 1992. 14.95 (978-1-883700-12-6(4)) ThoughtForms.
Self help.

Attracting Your Ideal Soul Mate. unabr. ed. Johnny Rockit & Catherine Benejet. Read by Johnny Rockit & Catherine Benejet. 1 cass. (Running Time: 50 mins.). (Inner Light Ser.). 1996. 11.99 (978-1-892654-04-5(0), BET050) FutureLife.
Romance advice.

Attracting Your Perfect Partner: Find the Soulmate of your Dreams. Created by Christine Sherborne. (ENG.). 2007. audio compact disk 19.95 (978-0-9804155-2-0(7)) Pub: Colourstory AUS. Dist(s): APG

Attractive Wife: 1 Peter 3:1-6. Ed Young. 1991. Rental 4.95 (978-0-7417-1854-9(5), 854) Win Walk.

Attractor Factor: 5 Easy Steps for Creating Wealth (or Anything Else) from the Inside Out. unabr. ed. Joe Vitale, Jr.. Read by Joe Vitale, Jr. (Running Time: 6 hrs.). (ENG.). 2007. audio compact disk 29.98 (978-1-59659-091-5(2), GildAudio) Pub: Gildan Media. Dist(s): HachBkGrp

Attractor Factor: 5 Easy Steps for Creating Wealth (or Anything Else) from the Inside Out. 2nd unabr. ed. Joe Vitale. Read by Joe Vitale. (Running Time: 6 hrs. 30 mins.). (ENG.). 2008. 24.98 (978-1-59659-291-9(5), GildAudio) Pub: Gildan Media. Dist(s): HachBkGrp

Attractor Factor: 5 Easy Steps for Creating Wealth (or Anything Else) from the Inside Out. 2nd unabr. ed. Joe Vitale. Read by Joe Vitale. (Running Time: 6 hrs.). (ENG.). 2009. audio compact disk 29.98 (978-1-59659-284-1(2), GildAudio) Pub: Gildan Media. Dist(s): HachBkGrp

Attributes of a Godly Woman. 2003. audio compact disk (978-1-931713-73-3(1)) Word For Today.

Attributes of a Godly Woman, Pack. 2003. audio compact disk (978-1-931713-72-6(3)) Word For Today.

Attributes of a Godly Woman, Pack. 2002. (978-1-931713-15-3(4)) Word For Today.

***Attributes of God Vol. 1: A Journey into the Father's Heart.** unabr. ed. A. w. Tozer. Narrated by Michael Kramer. (ENG.). 2006. 14.98 (978-1-59644-408-9(8), Hovel Audio) christianaud.

***Attributes of God Vol. 2: A Journey into the Father's Heart.** unabr. ed. A. w. Tozer. Narrated by Michael Kramer. (ENG.). 2006. 14.98 (978-1-59644-410-2(X), Hovel Audio) christianaud.

Attributes of God, Volume 1: A Journey into the Father's Heart. unabr. ed. A. W. Tozer. Read by Michael Kramer. 8 CDs. (Running Time: 5 hrs. 12 mins. 0 sec.). (ENG.). 2006. audio compact disk 26.98 (978-1-59644-407-2(X)) christianaud.

Attributes of God, Volume 2: Deeper into the Father's Heart. unabr. ed. A. W. Tozer. Read by Michael Kramer. 8 CDs. (Running Time: 5 hrs. 42 mins. 0 sec.). (ENG.). 2006. audio compact disk 26.98 (978-1-59644-409-6(6)) christianaud.

Attunement: For Inner Harmony & Peace. unabr. ed. Lenore Culin & Craig Pruess. Read by Lenore Culin. 1 cass. (Running Time: 60 mins.). 1997. 11.98 (978-1-893653-01-6(3), ATN-712CS) Attune.
Nurturing words & brilliant soundscapes relieve stress while activating inner qualities.

Attunement to Higher Vibrational Living: Heal Your Spirit, Meet Your Guides, Create Your Dreams, Live in the Present. abr. ed. Sonia Choquette & Mark Stanton Welch. 4 CDs. 2005. audio compact disk 23.95 (978-1-4019-0781-5(4)) Hay House.

Attunements for Dawn & Dusk: Music to Enhance Morning & Evening Meditation. Harish Johari. 2 CDs. (Running Time: 3 hrs.). 2000. audio compact disk 24.95 (978-0-89281-853-2(0), Heal Arts VT) Inner Tradit.

Attunements for Dawn & Dusk Set: Music to Enhance Morning & Evening Meditation. Harish Johari. 2 cass. (Running Time: 2 hrs.). 1992. bk. 15.95 (978-0-89281-370-4(9)) Inner Tradit.
Tape one is ideal for meditation before & after sunrise. Tape two incorporates actual bird calls, designed for close of day.

Attunements for Day & Night: Chants to the Sun & Moon. 2nd ed. Harish Johari. (Running Time: 1 hr.). 2005. bk. 12.95 (978-1-59477-073-9(5), Destiny Recs) Inner Tradit.

Atwater: Fixin' to Die. Robert Myers. 1 CD. (Running Time: 4080 sec.). (L. A. Theatre Works Audio Theatre Collections). 2001. audio compact disk 25.95 (978-1-58081-210-8(4), CDTPT150) Pub: L A Theatre. Dist(s): NetLibrary CO
The "dirty tricks" political strategist and self-styled master of negative campaigning, Lee Atwater was a tightly wound country boy who rose to the chairmanship of the Republican Party before dying of a brain tumor in 1991 at the age of 40. Atwater was the most audacious of the architects of George Bush's 1988 presidential campaign.

Au Bord de Lit, L'Enfant, Reveil, La Confession, Le Pere, Le Baiser une Passion, Une Aventure Parisienne. Guy de Maupassant. Read by Madeleine Renaud. 2 cass. (Running Time: 2 hrs.). (FRE.). 1991. 26.95 (1252-RF) Olivia & Hill.

Au Bout Be l'Ete. l.t. ed. Rosamunde Pilcher. (French Ser.). (FRE., 2000. bk. 30.99 (978-2-84011-360-7(0)) Pub: UlverLrgPrint GBR. Dist(s): Ulverscroft US

Au Dela des Trouees Noires. Dan Dastier. Read by Yves Belluardo. 4 cass. (Running Time: 4 hrs.). (FRE.). 1995. 32.95 (1792-CO) Olivia & Hill.
When they land on Syrglia, Kael Talvac, Mig Tausen & Christa Sanders are unaware that their fate is already being decided somewhere beyond the Black Holes.

***AU-Piense y Hagase Rico: Cinco pasos para crear una mentalidad de Riqueza.** Napoleon Hill. Ed. by Taller del Exito Inc.Tr. of Think & Grow Rich. (SPA.). 2009. audio compact disk 24.95 (978-1-60738-002-3(1)) Taller del Exito.

Au Plaisir de Dieu, Vol. 1-4. Jean D'Ormesson. Read by Jean-Claude Rey. 14 cass. 38.95 Vol. 1, "La tradition et la splendeur du passe" 4 cass. (1592-LV); 38.95 Vol. 2, "Les Breches et la doutes" 4 cass. (1593-LV); 34.95 Vol. 3, "L'agonie et l'eclatement" 3 cass. (1594-LV); 34.95 Vol. 4, "Le souvenir et l'espoir" 3 cass. (1595-LV) Olivia & Hill.
The Plessis-Vaudreuil family lives in a castle haunted by the saints, heroes & ne'redowells of their ancestors. Family traditions are assaulted by the modern world: wars, marriages, etc. The story of this family is the story of

our century as seen through the eyes of the "grande famille." Partly autobiographical.

Au Plaisir de Dieu, Vol. 1-4, set. Jean D'Ormesson. Read by Jean-Claude Rey. 14 cass. (FRE.). 1992. 129.95 (1592-95) Olivia & Hill.

Aube. Elie Wiesel. Read by Eric Dufay. 2 cass. (Running Time: 2 hrs.). (FRE.). 1996. 26.95 (1804-LV) Olivia & Hill.
The Nobel Prize writer tells the tale of Elisha, a survivor of the death camps now fighting for the creation of the state of Israel, whose mission is to execute a British soldier at dawn in retaliation for the execution of a Zionist fighter.

Auction see Gathering of Great Poetry for Children

Auctioneer - ShowTrax. Arranged by Kirby Shaw. (Running Time: 5 mins.). 2000. audio compact disk 19.95 (08201195) H Leonard.
A country-styled novelty highlight now available in multiple voicings. This rambunctious story-song is loads of fun!.

Auctioneering, Motivation, Success & the Leroy Van Dyke Story. Leroy Van Dyke. 6 cass. (Running Time: 6 hrs.). 1992. pap. bk. 79.95 (978-0-9674957-0-5(9)) L Van Dyke.

Aud CD Music/Wstrn Civ,Vol 1. SIMMS & Tony Wright. (C). 2005. 23.95 (978-0-495-00632-9(7)) Pub: Wadsworth Pub. Dist(s): CENGAGE Learn

Aud CD Music/Wstrn Civ,Vol 2. SIMMS & Tony Wright. (C). 2005. 40.95 (978-0-495-00633-6(5)) Pub: Wadsworth Pub. Dist(s): CENGAGE Learn

Aud CD Music/Wstrn Civ,Vol 3. SIMMS & Tony Wright. (C). 2005. 40.95 (978-0-495-00634-3(3)) Pub: Wadsworth Pub. Dist(s): CENGAGE Learn

Aud 3 Cds-Music Peoples/Wrld. (C). 2005. audio compact disk 28.95 (978-0-534-60555-1(9)) Pub: Wadsworth Pub. Dist(s): CENGAGE Learn

***Audacia de la Esperanza.** Barack Obama. Prod. by FonoLibro Inc. Narrated by Erwin Dorado. (SPA.). 2010. audio compact disk 19.95 (978-1-61154-004-8(6)) Fonolibro Inc.

Audacia de la Esperanza: Reflexiones Sobre Cómo Restaurar el Sueño Americano. Barack Obama. 2008. audio compact disk 24.95 (978-1-933499-81-9(8)) Fonolibro Inc.

Audacious Audiopuzzles, Bk. 1. unabr. ed. Audiopuzzles.com Staff. 2 CDs. (Running Time: 1 hrs. 49 mins.). (YA). (gr. 5 up). 2007. audio compact disk 14.99 (978-0-9762377-1-6(7)) Leave a Little Room Found.

Audacity of Hope: Thoughts on Reclaiming the American Dream. abr. ed. Barack Obama. Read by Barack Obama. 5 CDs. (Running Time: 6 hrs.). 2006. audio compact disk 40.00 (978-1-4159-3740-2(0)) Books on Tape.

Audacity of Hope: Thoughts on Reclaiming the American Dream. abr. ed. Barack Obama. Read by Barack Obama. (YA). 2008. 44.99 (978-1-60514-852-6(0)) Find a World.

Audacity of Hope: Thoughts on Reclaiming the American Dream. abr. ed. Barack Obama. Read by Barack Obama. 5 CDs. (Running Time: 6 hrs.). (ENG.). 2007. audio compact disk 19.99 (978-0-7393-6641-7(6), Random AudioBks) Pub: Random Audio Pubg. Dist(s): Random

Audacity of Hope: Thoughts on Reclaiming the American Dream. unabr. ed. Barack Obama. 10 CDs. (Running Time: 15 hrs.). 2006. audio compact disk 42.50 (978-1-4159-3301-5(4)) Pub: Books on Tape. Dist(s): NetLibrary CO

Audacity to Win: The Inside Story & Lessons of Barack Obama's Historic Victory. unabr. ed. David Plouffe. Contrib. by Erik Davies. (Running Time: 20 hrs.). (ENG.). (gr. 12 up). 2009. audio compact disk 39.95 (978-0-14-314272-0(0), PengAudBks) Penguin Grp USA.

***Audacity to Win: The Inside Story & Lessons of Barack Obama's Historic Victory.** unabr. ed. David Plouffe. Read by Erik Davies. 15 CDs. (Running Time: 19 hrs.). 2009. audio compact disk 100.00 (978-1-4159-6732-4(6)) Random.

Audiation Assistant. Bruce Dalby. 2000. audio compact disk 49.95 (CD-483) GIA Pubns.

Audience Questions Answered by Frs. Hardon, McCaffrey, & L. Dudley Day after Talks on February 25. 1995, Regional Meeting in Tampa, Florida. 1 cass. 4.00 (95C4) IRL Chicago.

Audio Arcade: Games for Grownups: Episode 1-Feed the Beast. 1 cass. (Running Time: 30 mins.). 9.95 (J010AB090, HarperThor) HarpC GBR.

Audio Arcade: Games for Grownups: Episode 2-Identity - Invasion of the Goose Bump People. 1 cass. (Running Time: 30 mins.). 9.95 (J010BB090, HarperThor) HarpC GBR.

Audio Arcade: Games for Grownups: Episode 3-Survival of the Fittest. 1 cass. (Running Time: 30 mins.). 9.95 (J010CB090, HarperThor) HarpC GBR.

Audio Arcade: Games for Grownups: Episode 4-Inner Space Invaders. 1 cass. (Running Time: 30 mins.). 9.95 (J010DB90, HarperThor) HarpC GBR.

Audio Bible. Contrib. by E. W. Jeffries. 1 cass. 1993. 99.98 (978-7-902031-33-2(X)) Chrstn Dup Intl.
New American Standard Bible.

Audio Bible. Contrib. by E. W. Jeffries. 1 cass. 1994. 99.98 (978-7-902031-40-0(2)) Chrstn Dup Intl.

Audio Bible. Narrated by E. W. Jeffries. 1 cass. 1995. 89.50 (978-7-902030-30-4(9)) Chrstn Dup Intl.

Audio Bible. Contrib. by Paul Mims. 1 cass. 1994. 83.50 (978-7-902030-56-4(2)); 99.98 (978-7-902030-77-9(5)) Chrstn Dup Intl.
King James Bible.

Audio Bible. Contrib. by Paul Mims. 48 cass. (Running Time: 48 hrs.). 1995. 99.98 (978-7-902030-42-7(2)) Chrstn Dup Intl.

Audio Bible. deluxe ed. Contrib. by Paul Mims. 1 cass. 1997. 134.98 (978-7-902030-93-9(7)) Chrstn Dup Intl.

Audio Bible-NKJV. Narrated by Stephen Johnston. 2005. audio compact disk 99.95 (978-1-56563-802-0(6)) Hendrickson MA.

Audio Biblia-NVI. unabr. ed. Created by Vida Publishers. (SPA.). 2005. audio compact disk 79.99 (978-0-8297-4638-9(2)) Pub: Vida Pubs. Dist(s): Zondervan

Audio Cassette: Used with ... Chan-College Oral Communication 1. (YA). 2005. 22.36 (978-0-618-23033-4(5), 326352) CENGAGE Learn.

Audio Cassette: Used with ... Delk-College Oral Communication 3. (YA). 2005. 22.36 (978-0-618-23035-8(1), 326354) CENGAGE Learn.

Audio Cassette: Used with ... Jones-College Oral Communication 4. (YA). 2005. 22.36 (978-0-618-23036-5(X), 326355) CENGAGE Learn.

Audio Cassette: Used with ... Kozyrev-Sound Bites!: Pronunciation Activities. Kozyrev. (YA). 2004. 22.36 (978-0-618-25995-3(3), 330540) CENGAGE Learn.

Audio Cassette: Used with ... Roemer-College Oral Communication 2. (YA). 2005. 22.36 (978-0-618-23034-1(3), 326353) CENGAGE Learn.

Audio Cassette Collection: Includes 30 Audio Cassettes & Storage Box. (Fonolibros Ser.). 2003. 277.95 (978-0-7652-0984-9(5)) Modern Curr.

Audio Cassette Program to Accompany Camino Oral. 2nd ed. Richard V. Teschner. (ENG.). (C). 1999. 17.19 (978-0-07-235190-3(X), 007235190X, Mc-H Human Soc) Pub: McGrw-H Hghr Educ. Dist(s): McGraw

Audio Cassette Program to Accompany Russian Grammar in Literary Contexts. unabr. ed. Benjamin Rifkin. 4 cass. (Running Time: 6 hrs.). 1996. 30.94 (978-0-07-912952-9(8), Mc-H Human Soc) Pub: McGrw-H Hghr Educ. Dist(s): McGraw

Audio Cassette 2 on Location. Thomas Bye. 2005. 36.88 (978-0-07-288679-5(X), 007288679X, ESL/ELT) Pub: McGrw-H Hghr Educ. Dist(s): McGraw

Audio Cassette 3 on Location. Thomas Bye. 2005. 50.63 (978-0-07-288682-5(X), 007288682X, ESL/ELT) Pub: McGrw-H Hghr Educ. Dist(s): McGraw

Audio Cassettes: Level I. 3 cass. (Adventures Ser.). 45.00 (Natl Textbk Co) M-H Contemporary.
Provides listening practices, exercises & songs for the classroom.

Audio Cassettes: Level II. 3 cass. (Adventures Ser.). 45.00 (978-0-8442-1549-5(X), Natl Textbk Co) M-H Contemporary.

Audio CD: Practical English Language Teaching. NUNAN et al. (Practical English Language Teaching Ser.). 2006. audio compact disk 23.44 (978-0-07-326976-4(X), 007326976X, ESL/ELT) Pub: McGrw-H Hghr Educ. Dist(s): McGraw

Audio Cd: Used with ... Chan-College Oral Communication 1. (YA). 2005. audio compact disk 22.36 (978-0-618-23037-2(8), 326356) CENGAGE Learn.

Audio Cd: Used with ... Delk-College Oral Communication 3. (YA). 2004. audio compact disk 22.36 (978-0-618-23039-6(4), 326358) CENGAGE Learn.

Audio Cd: Used with ... Jones-College Oral Communication 4. (YA). 2004. audio compact disk 22.36 (978-0-618-23040-2(8), 326359) CENGAGE Learn.

Audio Cd: Used with ... Kozyrev-Talk It up!: Listening, Speaking, & Pronunciation, 1. 2nd ed. Kozyrev. (YA). 2001. 22.36 (978-0-618-14397-9(1), 330523) CENGAGE Learn.

Audio Cd: Used with ... Roemer-College Oral Communication 2. (YA). 2005. audio compact disk 22.36 (978-0-618-23038-9(6), 326357) CENGAGE Learn.

Audio CD for use with Introducing American Folk Music. 2nd ed. Christopher Lornell. (C). 2001. cd-rom 35.00 (978-0-07-251266-3(0), 9780072512663, Mc-H Human Soc) Pub: McGrw-H Hghr Educ. Dist(s): McGraw

Audio CD Grade 1 Practice Cards 1-48. Benchmark Education Staff. (Fluency Ser.). 2008. audio compact disk (978-1-60437-093-5(9)) Benchmark Educ.

Audio CD Grade 1 Practice Cards 49-56 & Mini-Lessons. Benchmark Education Staff. (Fluency Ser.). 2008. audio compact disk (978-1-60437-094-2(7)) Benchmark Educ.

Audio CD Grade 2 Practice Cards 1-40. Benchmark Education Staff. (Fluency Ser.). 2008. audio compact disk (978-1-60437-101-7(3)) Benchmark Educ.

Audio CD Grade 2 Practice Cards 41-56 & Mini-Lessons. Benchmark Education Staff. (Fluency Ser.). 2008. audio compact disk (978-1-60437-102-4(1)) Benchmark Educ.

Audio CD Grade 3 Practice Cards 1-40. Benchmark Education Staff. (Fluency Ser.). 2008. audio compact disk (978-1-60437-107-9(2)) Benchmark Educ.

Audio CD Grade 3 Practice Cards 41-56 & Mini-Lessons. Benchmark Education Staff. (Fluency Ser.). 2008. audio compact disk (978-1-60437-108-6(0)) Benchmark Educ.

Audio CD Part B t/a Dos Mundos. 7th ed. Tracy D. Terrell et al. (ENG.). (C). 2009. audio compact disk 61.88 (978-0-07-730478-2(0), 0077304780, Mc-H Human Soc) Pub: McGrw-H Hghr Educ. Dist(s): McGraw

Audio CD Program: Used with ... Dietiker-En Bonne Forme. 7th ed. Simone R. Dietiker. (FRE.). (YA). 2001. cass. & cd-rom 35.56 (978-0-618-01245-9(1), 313934) CENGAGE Learn.

Audio CD Program to accompany Deux Mondes: A Communicative Approach. 6th ed. Tracy D. Terrell et al. (ENG.). (C). 2008. audio compact disk 44.38 (978-0-07-332687-0(9), 0073326879, Mc-H Human Soc) Pub: McGrw-H Hghr Educ. Dist(s): McGraw

Audio CD-ROM for Wright/Simms' Music in Western Civilization: Antiquity Through the Baroque, Volume I. (C). 2005. audio compact disk 50.95 (978-0-495-09179-0(0)) Pub: Wadsworth Pub. Dist(s): CENGAGE Learn

Audio CD-ROM for Wright/Simms' Music in Western Civilization: the Enlightenment to the Present, Volume Ii. (C). 2005. audio compact disk 58.95 (978-0-495-09180-6(4)) Pub: Wadsworth Pub. Dist(s): CENGAGE Learn

Audio CD-ROM Set for Lefkowitz's Music Theory. Lefkowitz. (C). 2006. 23.95 (978-0-534-64595-3(X)) Pub: Wadsworth Pub. Dist(s): CENGAGE Learn

***Audio CD set for use with America's Musical Landscape.** 6th ed. Jean Ferris. (ENG.). (C). 2010. audio compact disk 70.00 (978-0-07-724031-8(6), 0077240316, Mc-H Human Soc) Pub: McGrw-H Hghr Educ. Dist(s): McGraw

Audio CD to Accompany Identidades: Exploraciones E Interconexiones. Matilde O. Castells et al. 2004. audio compact disk 15.60 (978-0-13-141695-6(2)) Pearson Educ CAN CAN.

Audio CD Wallet Fluency Kit Levels F-M with CD's. (Fluency Skill Set Ser.). (J). 2008. audio compact disk (978-1-60437-867-2(0)) Benchmark Educ.

Audio CD Wallet Fluency Kit Levels N-U with CD's. (Fluency Skill Set Ser.). (J). 2008. audio compact disk (978-1-60437-868-9(9)) Benchmark Educ.

Audio CD Wallet Grade 1 Practice Cards 1-48 with CD's. (Fluency Skill Set Ser.). (J). 2008. audio compact disk (978-1-60437-861-0(1)) Benchmark Educ.

Audio CD Wallet Grade 1 Practice Cards 49-56 & Mini-Lessons with CD's. (Fluency Skill Set Ser.). (J). 2008. audio compact disk (978-1-60437-862-7(X)) Benchmark Educ.

Audio CD Wallet Grade 2 Practice Cards 41-56 & Mini-Lessons with CD's. (Fluency Skill Set Ser.). (J). 2008. audio compact disk (978-1-60437-864-1(6)) Benchmark Educ.

Audio CD Wallet Grade 3 Practice Cards 1-40 with CD's. (Fluency Skill Set Ser.). (J). 2008. audio compact disk (978-1-60437-865-8(4)) Benchmark Educ.

Audio CD Wallet Grade 3 Practice Cards 41-56 & Mini-Lessons with CD's. (Fluency Skill Set Ser.). (J). 2008. audio compact disk (978-1-60437-866-5(2)) Benchmark Educ.

Audio CD Wallet Spanish Fluency Kit Levels F-M with CD's. (Fluency Skill Set Ser.). (J). 2008. audio compact disk (978-1-60437-871-9(9)) Benchmark Educ.

Audio CD Wallet Spanish Fluency Kit Levels N-U with CD's. (Fluency Skill Set Ser.). (SPA.). (J). 2008. audio compact disk (978-1-60437-872-6(7)) Benchmark Educ.

Audio CDs. NUMRICH. 2007. audio compact disk (978-0-13-199220-7(1)) Longman.

Audio CDs for Modern Real Estate Practice. 16th abr. rev. ed. Dearborn Real Estate Education Firm Staff & Kaplan Publishing Staff. 2 vols. 2002. audio compact disk 29.15 (978-0-7931-6077-8(4), Dearbrn Real Est Ed) Kaplan Pubng.

Audio CDs for use with Music: The Art of Listening. 7th ed. Jean Ferris. (C). 2006. cd-rom 49.06 (978-0-07-312715-6(9), 9780073127156, Mc-H Human Soc) Pub: McGrw-H Hghr Educ. Dist(s): McGraw

Audio CDs Part B to accompany Prego! an Invitation to Italian. 7th ed. Graziana Lazzarino & Andrea Dini. (C). 2007. audio compact disk 59.38 (978-0-07-326664-0(7), 9780073266640, Mc-H Human Soc) Pub: McGrw-H Hghr Educ. Dist(s): McGraw

Audio CDs Part 2 (Component) to accompany Débuts: an Introduction to French. 3rd ed. H. Jay Siskin et al. (ENG.). (C). 2009. audio compact disk 29.69 (978-0-07-730559-8(0), 0077305590, Mc-H Human Soc) Pub: McGrw-H Hghr Educ. Dist(s): McGraw

Audio CDs to Accompany Facile a Dire! Les Sons du Francais. Annie Dumenil. 2002. audio compact disk 19.67 (978-0-13-095030-7(0)) Pearson Educacion ESP.

Audio CDs to accompany Lab Manual. 4th ed. Eduardo F. Zayas-Bazán et al. 2004. 54.80 (978-0-13-146661-6(5), Prentice Hall) P-H.

Audio CDs to accompany Pause-caf_. Nora Megharbi et al. (C). 2008. audio compact disk 32.81 (978-0-07-296487-5(1), 9780072964875, Mc-H Human Soc) Pub: McGrw-H Hghr Educ. Dist(s): McGraw

Audio CDs to accompany Text. 4th ed. Eduardo F. Zayas-Bazán et al. 2004. cd-rom 13.80 (978-0-13-117555-6(6), Prentice Hall) P-H.

Audio CDs to Accompany Trato Hecho! Spanish for Real Life. 3rd ed. Created by Pearson/Prentice Hall. 2005. audio compact disk 15.20 (978-0-13-191423-0(5)) Pearson Educ CAN CAN.

Audio Estate Planner. American Law Institute-American Bar Association, Committee on Continuing Professional Education Staff. 4 cass. (Running Time: 6 hrs.). 85.00 Am Law Inst.
For guidance that goes beyond the printed word on: Business Planning, Estate Planning, Insurance, Professional Practice & Responsibility, Recent Developments, Taxation & Trusts. 4 issues annually.

Audio Estate Planner, Vol. 14, No. 1. 1 cass. (Running Time: 1 hr. 30 mins.). 1997. 25.00 (N453) Am Law Inst.
Includes: Marital Deduction Funding with the Family-Owned Business Exclusion; ACTEC Commentaries on the Model Rules of Professional Conduct (Pt. 1); Tax Considerations in Negotiating the Sale of a Family Business.

Audio Estate Planner, Vol. 14, No. 1-3. unabr. ed. 4 cass. (Running Time: 6 hrs.). 85.00 Am Law Inst.
Issues concerning business planning, estate planning professional practice and responsibility, recent developments, taxation and trusts.

Audio Estate Planner, Vol. 14, No. 2. 1 cass. (Running Time: 1 hr. 30 mins.). 1997. 25.00 (N454) Am Law Inst.
Includes: Alaska & Delaware Trust Act Changes; Charitable Remainder Trust Developments; Electing Small Business Trust (ESBT) Rule Clarifications; QTIP Developments; Qualified Pre-Paid Tuition Plans; ACTEC Commentaries on the Model Rules of Professional Conduct (Pt. II).

Audio Estate Planner, Vol. 14, No. 3. 1 cass. (Running Time: 1 hr. 30 mins.). 1998. 25.00 (N455) Am Law Inst.
Includes: New Regulations on Qualified Disclaimers of Joint Property Interests; Roth IRAs; Qualified Family Owned Business Interests (AFOB); Qualified Personal Residence Trust (QPRT) Regulations; Selected Issues in Planning for the Second Marriage.

Audio Estate Planner, Vol. 14, No. 3. 1 cass. (Running Time: 1 hr. 30 mins.). 1998. 25.00 (N455) Am Law Inst.
Includes: New Regulations on Qualified Disclamers of Joint Property Interests; Roth IRA's; Qualified Family Owned Business Interests (QFOB); Quailfied Personal Residence Trust ((QPRT) Regulations; & Selected Issues in Planning for the Second Marriage.

Audio Estate Planner, Vol. 14, No. 4. 1 cass. (Running Time: 1 hr. 30 mins.). 1997. 25.00 (N452) Am Law Inst.
Estate Planning under the Taxpayer Relief Act of 1997.

Audio Estate Planner Magazine: Summer 1995 Issue. American Law Institute-American Bar Association, Committee on Continuing Professional Education Staff. 1 cass. 20.00 (N444) Am Law Inst.
Generation-Skipping Transfer Tax Primer (Part II - Exclusions, Exemptions, & Tax Calculation) by Richard Z. Kabaker; Estate & Gift Tax Treatment of Joint Tenancies by Stephen S. Case; Using an S-Corporation to Hold Potential Loss Property by John B. Huffaker; Avoiding Conflict-of-Interest Problems When Representing Married Couples by Anne K. Hilker & Jeffrey N. Pennell.

Audio Excerpts - John Pinto's Little Green Book of Ophthalmology. John Pinto. (ENG.). 2008. audio compact disk 30.00 (978-1-929196-11-1(3)) Am Opthlmc Admin.

Audio: Experiencing the Word: Experiencing the Word: New Testament. Read by David Payne. Music by Michael Stanton. 12 cass. (Holman CSB Audio Ser.). bk. 34.99 (978-1-58640-014-9(2)) BH Pubng Grp.

Audio Financial Planning Report. 24 cass. (Running Time: 24 hrs.). 395.00 incl. monthly written transcripts, yearly albums & quizzers. (CPE2320) Bisk Educ.

Audio Financial Planning Report. William L. Raby. 12 cass. (Running Time: 12 hrs.). 225.00 incl. monthly written transcripts, yearly albums & quizzers. (CPE2310) Bisk Educ.
Stay current on latest financial planning trends, techniques. Learn how to expand the scope of services offered by your firm & increase your client base.

Audio Fluency French: Complete Learning Guide & Tapescript. Mark Frobose. 8 cass. (Running Time: 8 hrs.). (FRE.). 1999. stu. ed. 69.00 (978-1-893564-20-6(7)) Macmill Audio.

Audio Fluency German: Complete Learning Guide & Tapescript. Mark Frobose. 6 cass. (Running Time: 6 hrs.). (GER.). 1999. stu. ed. 49.00 (978-1-893564-39-8(8)) Macmill Audio.

Audio Fluency Italian: Complete Learning Guide & Tapescript. Mark Frobose. 6 cass. (Running Time: 6 hrs.). (ITA.). 1999. stu. ed. 49.00 (978-1-893564-38-1(X)) Macmill Audio.

Audio Fluency Spanish: Complete Learning Guide & Tapescript. Mark Frobose. 8 cass. (Running Time: 8 hrs.). 1999. stu. ed. 69.00 (978-1-893564-19-0(3)) Macmill Audio.

Audio Governmental Accounting Report. Lucinda V. Upton & Betty A. King. 12 cass. (Running Time: 12 hrs.). 1993. bk. 225.00 incl. yearly album & quizzers. (CPE4060); bk. 395.00 incl. yearly album & quizzers. (CPE4062) Bisk Educ.
This monthly subscription service discusses what's new & forthcoming from GASB, plus expert guidance on how to apply past GASB statements to current engagements, features on the Yellow Book, state & local governmental developments, relevant SASs & other curretnet develeopments affecting the governmental accounting & auditing industry.

Audio Greek New Testament: Byzantine Textform 2005. Read by Louis Tyler. 2008. 30.00 (978-1-4276-4259-2(1)) AardGP.

Audio Greek New Testament: Westcott & Hort Greek New Testament. 2003. audio compact disk 15.00 (978-1-931848-02-2(5)) Christ Class Ethereal.
Complete narration of Westcott & Hort Greek New Testament by Marilyn Phemster in Koine Greek. Requires MP3-compatible playback device. Also includes full text in HTML format.

Audio Greek New Testament: Westcott-Hort Text. Read by Louis Tyler. 2008. 30.00 (978-1-4276-4258-5(3)) AardGP.

Audio guide Londres. unabr. ed. Olivier Maisonneuve & Marlène Duroux. Read by Marlène Duroux & Julien Dutel. (YA). 2007. 69.99 (978-2-35569-015-0(4)) Find a World.

Audio guide Paris. unabr. ed. Olivier Maisonneuve & Marlène Duroux. Read by Delphine Guillot & Julien Dutel. (YA). 2007. 79.99 (978-2-35569-013-6(8)) Find a World.

Audio guide Venise. unabr. ed. Olivier Maisonneuve & Marlène Duroux. Read by Marlène Duroux. (YA). 2007. 69.99 (978-2-35569-023-5(5)) Find a World.

Audio Hebrew Bible: Tanakh. Read by Louis Tyler. 2008. 45.00 (978-1-4276-4257-8(5)) AardGP.

Audio Keyboard Speed Development Program: S32 Series. rev. ed. 5 cass. 1990. 94.50 Incl. prog. guide. (978-0-937901-02-1(4), 13110-2) Reinforcement Lrn.
Program provides a vehicle for building accurate speeds through a series of tightly controlled audio pacing exercises combining four basic reinforcement techniques: audio letter & numeric dictation, rhythmic keyboarding signals & line-by-line speed control.

Audio Lecture Series for the Customs Broker Exam. Speeches. Compiled by Boskage Commerce Publications. 4 CDs. (Running Time: 4 hrs). 2003. audio compact disk (978-1-893495-32-6(9)) Boskage.
Four 60-minute lectures on the U.S. Customs Regulations, for use with the Broker's License Study Plan.

Audio Library I: Sing-Aloud. (gr. 1-8). 1996. 16.25 (978-0-382-21626-8(1)) Silver.

Audio Mastering. Craig Anderton. 1 cd. (Quick Start Ser.). 2003. pap. bk. 14.95 (978-0-7119-9620-5(2), AM975227, Amsco Music) Music Sales.

Audio Mastery Course for Crucial Conversations. unabr. ed. Kerry Patterson et al. 6 cass. (Running Time: 6 hrs.). 2002. 39.95 (978-0-9711967-4-2(5)) Vital Smarts.
Highlights and examples from crucial conversations. Discussion about handling difficult conversations effectively. Introduced to the concept of dialogue.

Audio Mastery Course for Crucial Conversations. unabr. ed. Kerry Patterson et al. 6 CDs. (Running Time: 6 hrs). 2001. audio compact disk 49.95 (978-0-9711967-3-5(7)) Vital Smarts.

Audio Mental Training CD for Wrestling. (YA). 2005. audio compact disk 24.95 (978-0-9772622-1-2(9)) Mike Clay.

Audio Microcomputer Report. Totaltape Editorial Board. 12 cass. 225.00 incl. 1-Year Subscription, monthly transcripts, yearly album, index & quizzers. (CPE0010) Bisk Educ.
A monthly audio magazine that teaches efficiency & client services with new hardware and software now available.

Audio Microcomputer Report (Two Years) 24 cass. (Running Time: 24 hrs.). 395.00 incl. monthly written transcripts, yearly albums & quizzers. (CPE0011) Bisk Educ.

Audio New Testament - World English Bible. 2003. audio compact disk 15.00 (978-1-931848-05-3(X)) Christ Class Ethereal.
Requires an MP3-compatible playback device. Also includes the full text of the World English Bible (requires an Internet browser).

Audio New Testament-NKJV. Narrated by Stephen Johnston. 2002. audio compact disk 29.95 (978-1-56563-836-5(0)) Hendrickson MA.

***Audio on Community Property.** Gail Bird. (Sum & Substance Ser.). 2010. audio compact disk 68.00 (978-0-314-26712-2(3), West Lglwrks) West.

Audio Phobia. Jay Bonansinga. 1 cass. (Running Time: 1 hr.). 2001. 12.95 (AUDI001) Lodestone Catalog.

Audio Program. 3rd ed. Widmaier & Widmaier. (GER.). 2002. 36.00 (978-0-13-095351-3(2), Prentice Hall) P-H.

Audio Program & in Ascolto Listening Comprehension CD to Accompany Prego! An Invitation to Italian. 7th ed. Andrea Dini & Graziana Lazzarino. (ENG.). (C). 2007. audio compact disk 76.56 (978-0-07-326663-3(9), 0073266639, Mc-H Human Soc) Pub: McGrw-H Hghr Educ. Dist(s): McGraw

Audio Program Cassettes: Used with ... Valette-Contacts: Langue et Culture Frangaises. 7th ed. Jean-Paul Valette. (YA). 2001. 35.56 (978-0-618-08612-2(9), 357117) CENGAGE Learn.

Audio Program Cds: Used with ... Dollenmayer-Neue Horizonte: A Brief Course. David B. Dollenmayer. (YA). 2001. cass. & cd-rom 35.56 (978-0-618-09873-6(9), 314095) CENGAGE Learn.

Audio Program CDs: Used with ... Valette-Contacts: Langue et Culture Françaises. 7th ed. Jean-Paul Valette. (YA). 2001. cass. & cd-rom 35.56 (978-0-618-00757-8(1), 357109) CENGAGE Learn.

***Audio Program for Punto y aparte: Expanded Edition.** Sharon Foerster & Anne Lambright. (ENG.). (C). 2010. audio compact disk 55.00 (978-0-07-739443-1(7), 0077394437, Mc-H Human Soc) Pub: McGrw-H Hghr Educ. Dist(s): McGraw

Audio Program to Accompany Popular Proverbs. Nasser Isleem. (ENG.). 2009. 5.95 (978-0-9821595-2-1(8)) Alucen Learn.

Audio Program to Accompany Sol y Viento en Breve: A Cinematic Journey for Beginning Spanish. Bill VanPatten. (ENG.). (C). 2007. audio compact disk 55.00 (978-0-07-328091-2(7), 0073280917, Mc-H Human Soc) Pub: McGrw-H Hghr Educ. Dist(s): McGraw

Audio Program 2: Used with ... Hatasa-Nakama 2: Japanese Communication, Culture, Context. Yukiko Abe Hatasa. (YA). 1999. cass. & cd-rom 29.96 (978-0-618-02783-5(1), 322676) CENGAGE Learn.

Audio Renaissance Spring 2003 Catalog. Audio Renaissance Staff. (978-1-55927-918-5(4)) Macmill Audio.

Audio Renaissance Spring/Summer Catalog. 2004. (978-1-59397-757-3(3)) Macmill Audio.

Audio Rochester Routes Cassette. Patricia Braus. Narrated by Cindy Boyer. (Running Time: 74 min.). 2001. 9.95 (978-0-9763910-0-5(7)) Landmark Soc.

Audio Salvage. Prod. by Meredith Smith & Jeffrey Smith. 1 cass. (Running Time: 1 hr.). 2001. 10.00 (FCML201) Lodestone Catalog.

Audio Self-Defense. Donna L. Betancourt. 1 cass. 1995. 10.99 (978-0-9639693-1-6(5)) DLB Pubng.
How to self-defense. Side 1: personal protection lecture. Side 2: physical technique instruction for everyone, but especially helpful to the visually impaired.

Audio Tape Program: A Workbook. Anne Lindell. (C). 1983. pap. bk. 165.00 (978-0-472-00212-2(0), 00212) U of Mich Pr.

***Audio Tapes for Best Practice Elementary.** Bill Mascull. (ENG.). (C). 2004. 60.95 (978-1-4130-0905-7(0)) Pub: Heinle. Dist(s): CENGAGE Learn

***Audio Tapes for Intensive Spoken Chinese.** Zhang Pengpeng. (CHI.). 2001. reel tape 14.95 (978-2-02-001000-9(3)) Pub: Sinolingua CHN. Dist(s): China Bks

Audio Tax Report. William L. Raby. 12 cass. (Running Time: 12 hrs.). 225.00 (CPE0001) Bisk Educ.
Features tax developments, new laws, regulations, decisions, rulings & more.

Audio Tax Report (Two Years) William L. Raby. 24 cass. (Running Time: 24 hrs.). 395.00 incl. monthly written transcripts. (CPE0002) Bisk Educ.

Audio Tour of Pikes Peak - America's Mountain. 2001. 8.95 (978-0-9712830-2-2(8)) Seasons Scen.

Audio Tribute to Princess Diana. Ed. by Pent. 1 cass. (Running Time: 1 hr.). 1997. audio compact disk 14.95 (978-1-885959-56-0(7), JRAB9600) Jerden Recs.
An audio tribute to Princess Diana & excerpts of her many speeches given over the years in her own words.

Audio-Visual Broadcasting Equipment & Services in France: A Strategic Reference 2006. Compiled by Icon Group International, Inc. Staff. 2007. ring bd. 195.00 (978-0-497-35943-0(X)) Icon Grp.

Audio-Visual Equipment & Services in Ireland: A Strategic Reference 2007. Compiled by Icon Group International, Inc. Staff. 2007. ring bd. 195.00 (978-0-497-36035-1(7)) Icon Grp.

Audio Vocabulary Builder for the Traveler. 1 cass. (Running Time: 60 mins.). (RUS.). 2001. 14.95 (SRU260) J Norton Pubs.
Provides 101 essential words & phrases for the traveler. Native speakers & pauses for repetition.

Audio Vocabulary Builder in Portuguese. 1 cass. (Running Time: 60 mins.). (POR & ENG.). 2001. 14.95 (SPG010) J Norton Pubs.
This concise recorded dictionary provides words & phrases for the traveler. Native speakers & pauses for repetition.

Audio Voice Coach for DJs & Entertainers. Roy Hanschke. 3 cass. 2003. 39.95 (978-0-9707324-4-6(9)) B C Product.

Audio Writing. Richard Kostelanetz. Read by Richard Kostelanetz. 1 cass. (Running Time: 91 mins.). 1984. pap. bk. 12.00 (978-0-932360-39-7(4)) Archae Edns.
An introductory, comprehensive lecture-demonstration of his "publishing" with audiotape, including examples from over a dozen works.

Audio 4-Cd Set-Music Incultural Contexts. (C). 2005. 37.95 (978-0-534-54523-9(8)) Pub: Wadsworth Pub. Dist(s): CENGAGE Learn

Audio/Bob & Ray: The Lost Episodes 4 Cassettes/4 Hours. 2000. (978-1-892091-58-1(5)); (978-1-892091-57-4(7)) Radio Found.

Audiobook for All Seasons. Liz Curtis Higgs. 1 cass. (Running Time: 60 mins.). (Parable Ser.). (J). (gr. 3 up). 1997. 9.99 (978-0-8499-5812-0(1)) Nelson.

Audiobook to How to Set up a Business: A Step-by-Step Approach. Read by Barbara Cooper. 1 cass. (Running Time: 48 mins.). 2000. 12.99 (978-0-9703081-1-5(6)) GA Transcript & Med Clms.
Information on corporate status versus sole proprietor or partnership, licensure, insurances, taxes, accountant.

Audiocasete David y Goliat: Serie Heroes de la fe. (J). 1999. (978-1-57697-686-9(6)) Untd Bible Amrcas Svce.

Audiocasete Jeremias un Profeta de Dios: Serie Heroes de la fe. (J). 1999. (978-1-57697-687-6(4)) Untd Bible Amrcas Svce.

Audiocasete Pablo o un Llamado Especial: Serie Heroes de la fe. 1999. (978-1-57697-688-3(2)) Untd Bible Amrcas Svce.

Audiocasete Pedro Pescador de Hombres: Serie Heroes de la fe. 1999. (978-1-57697-689-0(0)) Untd Bible Amrcas Svce.

Audiocasete Pedro y la Duda: Serie Heroes de la fe. 1999. (978-1-57697-690-6(4)) Untd Bible Amrcas Svce.

Audiocassette: Used with ... Kozyrev-Talk It Over!: Listening, Speaking, & Pronunciation, 3. 2nd ed. Joann Kozyrev. (YA). 2002. reel tape 22.36 (978-0-618-14403-7(X), 330532) CENGAGE Learn.

Audiocassette: Used with ... Kozyrev-Talk It Through!: Listening, Speaking, & Pronunciation, 2. Kozyrev. (YA). 2000. 22.36 (978-0-395-96074-5(6), 330713) CENGAGE Learn.

Audiocassette: Used with ... Kozyrev-Talk It up!: Listening, Speaking, & Pronunciation, 1. 2nd ed. Kozyrev. (YA). 2001. 20.76 (978-0-618-14021-3(2), 330522) CENGAGE Learn.

Audiocassette Package: 12 Audiocassettes (1 version per Side) 12 cass. (ENG & SPA.). (gr. k-1). 100.00 (978-0-7635-6264-9(5)) Rigby Educ.

AudioDrama 101 Vol. 2: Early American. 6 cass. 1998. 14.95 Lend-A-Hand Soc.

AudioDrama 101 vol. 9: Hidden Treasures-Little Known 20th Century Short Stories. unabr. ed. Mary Orr. Ed. by John Rockwell. 6 cass. (Running Time: 6 hrs.). (AudioDrama 101 Ser.: Vol. 9). 2002. 14.95 (978-1-892077-09-7(4)) Lend-A-Hand Soc.
Stories such as The Wisdom of Eve and More About Eve which inspired the movie All About Eve.

AudioGuide NYC: Four Audiocassette Walking Tours of New York City. abr. ed. Lauren Hertel. Read by Lauren Hertel. 2 cass. (Running Time: 3 hrs.). 1999. 17.95 (978-0-9668639-0-1(9)) Lone Daughter.
Hertel is a professional New York City tour guide.

Audioguides. 3rd ed. 1997. 11.56 (978-0-07-015798-9(7)) McGrw-H Hghr Educ.

Audioguides, Vol. II. 3rd ed. (C). 1997. 15.93 (978-0-07-015801-6(0), Mc-H Human Soc) Pub: McGrw-H Hghr Educ. Dist(s): McGraw

AudioLearn-MCAT (MCAT Audiolearn) Shahrad Yazdani. 4 cass. (Running Time: 3 hrs.). 2002. 124.99 (978-0-9704199-0-3(2)) AudioLearn.
A complete & comprehensive science review for the MCAT. With over 700 pages professionally narrated, covers every fact, formula, rule, theory, law & equation in biology, organic chemistry, inorganic chemistry & physics.

AudioLearn-PCAT (PCAT AudioLearn) Shahrad Yazdani. 3 cass. (Running Time: 4 hrs. 30 mins.). 2000. 99.00 (978-0-9704199-2-7(9)) AudioLearn.
Complete & comprehensive science review, with over 500 pages professionally narrated. Covers every fact, formula, rule, theory, law & equation in biology, organic chemistry & inorganic chemistry.

AudioLearn-PCAT (PCAT Audiolearn) Shahrad Yazdani. 3 cass. (Running Time: 4 hrs. 30 mins.). 2002. 99.00 (978-0-9704199-1-0(0)) AudioLearn.
Complete & comprehensive science review for the DAT, with over 500 pages professionally narrated. Covers every fact, formula, rule, theory, law & equation in biology, organic chemistry & inorganic chemistry.

Audioquarterly. abr. ed. Ed. by Daren Wang. Created by University of Georgia Press Staff. (Running Time: 9000 sec.). (Verb Ser.). 2005. 19.95 (978-0-9765625-1-1(0)) Pub: Verb Prods. Dist(s): U of Ga Pr

Audios #1-31 for Realtime Theory Vol. 1131: Realtime Machine Shorthand. unabr. ed. Beverly L. Ritter. 31 cass. (Running Time: 31 hrs.). 1991. 140.00 (978-0-938643-37-1(1), 103A) Stenotype Educ.
Dictation for Volume I: Theory (Lessons 1-40).

Audioscript to Accompany Deutsch: Na Klar! An Introductory German Course. unabr. ed. Di Donato Staff. 1999. (978-0-07-013712-7(9)) McGrw-H Hghr Educ.
Students using Deutsch: Na Klar! practice all 4 skills, but work more on the receptive skills of listening and reading than in a traditional German text. A classroom listening comprehension program and the very engaging authentic readings provide this additional skill practice.

Audiotape/CD for Accent Activities. Elaine Kirn. 2000. audio compact disk 12.00 (978-1-891077-29-6(5)) Authors Editors.

Audiotapes for Medical Terminology: A Student-Centered Approach. (C). 2003. 99.95 (978-0-7668-1525-4(0)) Pub: Delmar. Dist(s): CENGAGE Learn

Audiotapes for Medical Transcription: Techniques & Procedures. 6th ed. Marcy O. Diehl. (C). 2007. 250.00 (978-1-4160-3654-8(7), SaunElsHlth) Elsevier HthSci.

Audiotapes to Accompany Learning Medical Terminology. 9th ed. Miriam G. Austrin & Harvey R. Austrin. 1 cass. (Running Time: 1 hr. 30 min.). (C). 1998. 15.95 (978-0-323-00280-6(3), MosElsHlth) Elsevier HthSci.

Audioteca: Technology. (McGraw-Hill. Lectura Ser.). (ENG & SPA.). (gr. k up). 2001. (978-0-02-186232-0(X)); audio compact disk (978-0-02-188389-9(0)) Macmillan McGraw-Hill Schl Div.

Audioteca: Technology. (McGraw-Hill. Lectura Ser.). (ENG & SPA.). (gr. 1 up). 2001. (978-0-02-186233-7(8)); audio compact disk (978-0-02-188390-5(4)) Macmillan McGraw-Hill Schl Div.

Audioteca: Technology. (McGraw-Hill. Lectura Ser.). (ENG & SPA.). (gr. 2 up). 2001. (978-0-02-186234-4(6)); audio compact disk (978-0-02-188391-2(2)) Macmillan McGraw-Hill Schl Div.

Audioteca: Technology. (McGraw-Hill. Lectura Ser.). (ENG & SPA.). (gr. 3 up). 2001. audio compact disk (978-0-02-186235-1(4)); audio compact disk (978-0-02-188392-9(0)) Macmillan McGraw-Hill Schl Div.

Audioteca: Technology. (McGraw-Hill. Lectura Ser.). (ENG & SPA.). (gr. 4 up). 2001. audio compact disk (978-0-02-186236-8(2)) Macmillan McGraw-Hill Schl Div.

Audioteca: Technology. (McGraw-Hill. Lectura Ser.). (ENG & SPA.). (gr. 5 up). 2001. (978-0-02-186237-5(0)) Macmillan McGraw-Hill Schl Div.

Audioteca: Technology. (McGraw-Hill. Lectura Ser.). (ENG & SPA.). (gr. 6 up). 2001. (978-0-02-186238-2(9)) Macmillan McGraw-Hill Schl Div.

AudioText. (SPA.). (gr. k up). 2000. 48.99 (978-0-673-59568-3(4)); audio compact disk 89.04 (978-0-673-59578-2(1)) Addson-Wesley Educ.

AudioText. (SPA.). (gr. 1 up). 2000. 48.99 (978-0-673-59569-0(2)); audio compact disk 89.04 (978-0-673-59579-9(X)) Addson-Wesley Educ.

AudioText. (SPA.). (gr. 2 up). 2000. 48.99 (978-0-673-59570-6(6)); audio compact disk 89.04 (978-0-673-59580-5(3)) Addson-Wesley Educ.

AudioText. (SPA.). (gr. 3 up). 2000. 76.10 (978-0-673-59571-3(4)); audio compact disk 110.34 (978-0-673-59581-2(1)) Addson-Wesley Educ.

AudioText. (SPA.). (gr. 4 up). 2000. 76.10 (978-0-673-59572-0(2)); audio compact disk 110.34 (978-0-673-59582-9(X)) Addson-Wesley Educ.

AudioText. (SPA.). (gr. 5 up). 2000. 76.10 (978-0-673-59576-8(5)); audio compact disk 110.34 (978-0-673-59583-6(8)) Addson-Wesley Educ.

AudioText. (SPA.). (gr. 6 up). 2000. 76.10 (978-0-673-59577-5(3)); audio compact disk 110.34 (978-0-673-59584-3(6)) Addson-Wesley Educ.

AudioText. 1 cass. (Running Time: 1 hr.). (Scott Foresman Science Ser.). (gr. k up). 2003. 45.93 (978-0-673-59414-3(9)); audio compact disk 83.48 (978-0-673-59554-6(4)) Addson-Wesley Educ.
AudioText gives students with reading difficulties, limited English proficiency, or auditory learning styles full access to the contents of Scott Foresman Science. Complete narrations of the Pupil Edition, directed reading strategies, and math connections help students learn science more effectively.

AudioText. 1 cass. (Running Time: 1 hr.). (Scott Foresman Science Ser.). (gr. 1 up). 2003. 45.93 (978-0-673-59415-0(7)); audio compact disk 83.48 (978-0-673-59555-3(2)) Addson-Wesley Educ.

AudioText. 1 cass. (Running Time: 1 hr.). (Scott Foresman Science Ser.). (gr. 2 up). 2003. 45.93 (978-0-673-59416-7(5)); audio compact disk 83.48 (978-0-673-59556-0(0)) Addson-Wesley Educ.

AudioText. 1 cass. (Running Time: 1 hr.). (Scott Foresman Science Ser.). (gr. 3 up). 2003. 71.35 (978-0-673-59417-4(3)); audio compact disk 103.45 (978-0-673-59557-7(9)) Addson-Wesley Educ.

AudioText. 1 cass. (Running Time: 1 hr.). (Scott Foresman Science Ser.). (gr. 4 up). 2003. 71.35 (978-0-673-59418-1(1)); audio compact disk 103.45 (978-0-673-59558-4(7)) Addson-Wesley Educ.

AudioText. 1 cass. (Running Time: 1 hr.). (Scott Foresman Science Ser.). (gr. 5 up). 2003. 71.35 (978-0-673-59419-8(X)); audio compact disk 103.45 (978-0-673-59559-1(5)) Addson-Wesley Educ.

AudioText. 1 cass. (Running Time: 1 hr.). (Scott Foresman Science Ser.). (gr. 6 up). 2003. 71.35 (978-0-673-59420-4(3)); audio compact disk 103.45 (978-0-673-59560-7(9)) Addson-Wesley Educ.

Audio/Visual. Contrib. by Bleach & Tyson Paoletti. 2005. 13.99 (978-5-558-78010-9(X)) Tooth & Nail.

Audit Procedures, 2008 (with CD-ROM) 2008th rev. ed. Luis Puncel. 2007. pap. bk. 190.00 (978-0-8080-9123-3(9)) Toolkit Media.

Audit Requirements of OMB Circular A-133. rev. ed. William A. Broadus, Jr. 3 cass. (Running Time: 3 hrs.). 1994. wbk. ed. 129.00 (754101VC); wbk. ed. 69.50 (754111VC) Am Inst CPA.
This course provides guidance to both the auditor of a nonprofit organization receiving federal assistance & the nonprofit officer. The 1994 edition of the course covers: Newly revised OMB Circular A-110, Revisions in OMB Circular A-21, SOP 92-9, Proposals to improve single audits, including A-133 audits. The course also includes the complete texts of OMB Circulars A-133, A-110, A-21 & A-122, plus OMB's Compliance Supplement for Institutions of Higher Learning & Q's & A's on A-133 & AICPA's Audits of Not-for-Profit Organizations Receiving Federal Awards.

Audit Requirements of OMB Circular A-133: (Updated for Late 1991 Developments) William A. Broadus, Jr. 3 cass. wbk. ed. 129.00 (754100KQ); 69.50 (745110KQ) Am Inst CPA.
Thousands of not-for-profit organizations that get funding directly or indirectly from the federal government must undergo an annual or biannual audit. If you audit such nonprofit organizations this in-depth course helps you answer the questions an A-133 audit must cover. The course also includes the complete texts of OMB Circulars A-133, A-110, revised A-21 & A-122, plus OMB's Compliance Supplement for Institutions of Higher Learning & Q's & A's on A-133 a valuable reference source.

Audition: A Memoir. Barbara Walters. Read by Bernadette Dunne. 15 cass. 2008. 129.00 (978-1-4159-5500-0(X), BksonTape) Pub: Random Audio Pubg. Dist(s): Random

Audition: A Memoir. abr. ed. Barbara Walters. Read by Barbara Walters. 5 CDs. (Running Time: 6 hrs.). (ENG.). 2008. audio compact disk 29.95 (978-0-7393-4398-2(X), Random AudioBks) Pub: Random Audio Pubg. Dist(s): Random

Audition: A Memoir. unabr. ed. Barbara Walters. Read by Bernadette Dunne. 21 CDs. (Running Time: 26 hrs. 45 mins.). 2008. audio compact disk 129.00

(978-1-4159-4366-3(4), BksonTape) Pub: Random Audio Pubg. Dist(s): Random

Audition Songs for Female Singers. 2004. pap. bk. 14.95 (978-0-8256-2870-2(9), Schirmer Trade Bks) Pub: Music Sales. Dist(s): H Leonard

Auditory Perception. F. Alton Everest. 4 cass. (Running Time: 2 hrs.). 1986. pap. bk. 160.00 incl. manual. (978-0-9608352-1-8(0)) F A Everest.
(1) Loudness, pitch & timbre; (2) How one sound masks another; (3) How the ear analyzes sound; (4) Non-linearities in the auditory system; (5) Perception of delayed sounds; (6) Why some sounds are more pleasant than others; (7) How we locate sounds; (8) True binaural listening.

Audits of Farmers Home Administration Programs. rev. ed. Max E. Hunt. 2 cass. (Running Time: 2 hrs.). 1994. wbk. ed. 119.00 (741802VC); wbk. ed. 69.50 (741803VC) Am Inst CPA.
This intermediate-level, completely revised course reflects the FmHA's new regulations governing multiple family housing loan & grant recipients, & also contains a brandnew chapter on construction cost audits. Includes a generous array of sample reports, examples of pertinent financial statements, & checklists. The course includes FmHA's audit guide & covers its regulations for the mutli-family programs. In addition, it highlights the findings of recent Department of Agriculture Office of Inspector General reviews of CPA workpapers.

Audits of HUD-Assisted Projects. Max E. Hunt. 2 cass. 1994. wbk. ed. 129.00 (752006VC); wbk. ed. 69.50 (752016VC) Am Inst CPA.
Highlights key changes made by HUD's Consolidated Audit Guide for Audits of HUD Programs, issued in July 1993. Basic in approach, it is the ideal primer for staff that have not previously worked on HUD audits, especially staff that will be concerned with audits under the Section 8 program - the principal rental assistance program for federally-assisted multifamily housing. This course gives you in-depth, hands-on information about HUD - its organizaiton, programs, policies & procedures.

Audits of State & Local Government Units. rev. ed. Gary Giroux & Donald R. Dies. 1 cass. wbk. ed. 129.00 (743877KQ); wbk. ed. 69.50 (743878KQ) Am Inst CPA.
This course reflects the AICPA Guide, Audits of State & Local Governmental Units, the Single Audit Act of 1984, the 1988 revision of the Yellow book, SASs 53-61, SAS 63 on compliance auditing & SOP 89-6. It also includes significant supplementary information to provide additional background on events of the last decade & current GAAP.

Audits of State & Local Governments. Melvin B. Seiden. 3 cass. pap. bk. 99.00 incl. quizzer. (CPE3140) Bisk Educ.
Offers advice to help you comply with current rules on performing audits of state & local governments.

Audre Lorde: The Black Unicorn. unabr. ed. Audre Geraldine Lorde. Read by Audre Geraldine Lorde. 1 cass. (Running Time: 29 min.). 1991. 10.00 (022479) New Letters.
Black poet Lorde reads selections from her book, "The Black Unicorn".

Audrey Handler: Glass Artist. Jocelyn Riley. 1 cass. (Running Time: 15 mins.). (YA). 1995. 12.00 (978-1-877933-61-5(9), 15003) Her Own Words.

Audrey Hepburn. unabr. ed. Barry Paris. Read by Frances Cassidy. 14 cass. (Running Time: 21 hrs.). 1997. 112.00 (978-0-7366-3696-4(X), 4375) Books on Tape.
The definitive biography of Audrey Hepburn, Hollywood's emblem of style & elegance. Richly detailed & revealing.

Audrey Hepburn: A Biography. unabr. ed. Warren G. Harris. Read by Nadia May. 9 cass. (Running Time: 13 hrs.). 1995. 62.95 (978-0-7861-0821-3(5), 1644) Blckstn Audio.
Traces Hepburn's affairs & her unhappy marriages, as well as her later work as goodwill ambassador for UNICEF. He illuminates her special ability to exude grace & style, both on screen & off.

Audrey Hepburn: A Biography. unabr. ed. Warren G. Harris. Read by Nadia May. (Running Time: 11 hrs. 30 mins.). 2010. 29.95 (978-1-4417-1776-4(5)); audio compact disk 105.00 (978-1-4417-1773-3(0)) Blckstn Audio.

Audrey Hepburn: Children of Poverty-Manmade Disgrace. 1989. 11.95 (K0690B090, HarperThor) HarpC GBR.

Audrey Hepburn's Enchanted Tales. abr. ed. Read by Audrey Hepburn. (Running Time: 3600 sec.). 2007. audio compact disk 17.00 (978-1-4332-0561-3(0)) Blckstn Audio.

Audrey Hepburn's Enchanted Tales. unabr. ed. Mary Sheldon. Perf. by Audrey Hepburn. 1 cass. (Running Time: 1 hr.). (J). 2001. (N Millennium Audio) New Millenn Enter.
Stories of unselfish devotion, courage & true love.

Audrey Hepburn's Enchanted Tales. unabr. ed. Mary Sheldon. Perf. by Audrey Hepburn. 1 CD. (Running Time: 1.5 hrs.). 2004. audio compact disk 15.00 (978-1-931056-53-3(6), N Millennium Audio) New Millenn Enter.
Children of all ages will be captivated by these captivating class tales. Includes music from Mother Goose Suite. Stories include "sleeping Beauty," "Tom Thumb," "Beauty and the Beast" and "Laidronette, princess of the Pagodes". Stories of unselfish devotion, courage and true love are narrated with charm and elegance by the late Audrey Hepburn.

Audrey Hepburn's Enchanted Tales. unabr. abr. ed. Perf. by Audrey Hepburn. Adapted by Mary Sheldon. 1 cass. (Running Time: 1.5 hrs.). 2004. 15.00 (978-1-931056-52-6(8), N Millennium Audio) New Millenn Enter.

Audrey Hepburn's Enchanted Tales. unabr. abr. ed. Read by Audrey Hepburn. (Running Time: 3600 sec.). (J). 2007. audio compact disk 14.95 (978-1-4332-0562-0(9)) Blckstn Audio.

Auel, Kidder, King. unabr. ed. Contrib. by Jean M. Auel et al. 3 cass. (Running Time: 4 hrs. 30 mins.). (Author Talks Ser.). 1997. 26.00 (978-1-55690-792-0(3), 92431) Recorded Bks.
Features: Jean Auel - best-selling author of the Plains of Passage series; Tracy Kidder - Pulitzer Prize-winning author of American non-fiction & Stephen King - best-selling author of the macabre.

Auerbach Will. unabr. ed. Stephen Birmingham. Read by multivoice. (Running Time: 13 hrs.). 2009. 24.99 (978-1-4418-0801-1(9), 9781441808011, Brilliance MP3); 39.97 (978-1-4418-0802-8(7), 9781441808028, Brlnc Audio MP3 Lib); 24.99 (978-1-4418-0803-5(5), 9781441808035, BAD); 39.97 (978-1-4418-0804-2(3), 9781441808042, BADLE) Brilliance Audio.

Auf Deutsch! 2003. (978-0-618-02977-8(X)); (978-0-618-02983-9(4)); audio compact disk (978-0-618-02980-8(X)); audio compact disk (978-0-618-02981-5(8)) Holt McDoug.

Auf Deutsch!, Level 2. 2003. (978-0-618-02984-6(2)) Holt McDoug.

Auf Deutsch!, Level 3. 2003. (978-0-618-02979-2(6)); (978-0-618-02985-3(0)); audio compact disk (978-0-618-02982-2(6)) Holt McDoug.

Auf Deutsch, Bitte. Jutta B. Hicks. 10 cass. (Running Time: 10 hrs.). (GER.). 175.00 (978-0-8325-9685-8(X), Natl Textbk Co) M-H Contemporary.
Using immediate classroom situations, along with real life experiences, students quickly learn to converse & acquire the cultural awareness needed to interact with confidence in casual, work & social situations.

August Celebration: A Molecule of Hope for a Changing World. Linda Grover. 1 cass. (Running Time: 5 hrs. 41 mins.). 1994. 24.95 (978-0-9639538-1-0(8)) Gilbert Hoover & Clarke.
Motivational, health, business, biography, self-help, environment, nutrition, social change.

August Folly. unabr. ed. Angela Thirkell. Read by Nadia May. (Running Time: 8 hrs. 0 mins.). (ENG.). 2009. 29.95 (978-1-4332-1641-1(8)); 54.95 (978-1-4332-1637-4(X)); audio compact disk 76.00 (978-1-4332-1638-1(8)) Blckstn Audio.

***August Heat: An Inspector Montalbano Mystery.** unabr. ed. Andrea Camilleri. Read by Grover Gardner. (Running Time: 6 hrs. 30 mins.). 2010. 29.95 (978-1-4417-2172-3(X)); 44.95 (978-1-4417-2169-3(X)); audio compact disk 69.00 (978-1-4417-2170-9(3)) Blckstn Audio.

Augusta: Home of the Masters Tournament. unabr. ed. Steve Eubanks. Read by Tom Parker. 5 cass. (Running Time: 7 hrs.). 1999. 39.95 (978-0-7861-1508-2(4), 2358) Blckstn Audio.
Explores the significant role Roberts played in Augusta member-to-be Dwight Eisenhower's ascension to the presidency; Roberts' suicide & the club's subsequent loss of the pistol he used; the exclusion of African-American Charlie Sifford from the Masters field; Augusta's impetuous relationship with CBS; & the Tiger Woods-Fuzzy Zoeller brouhaha of 1997.

Augusta: Home of the Masters Tournament. unabr. ed. Steve Eubanks. Read by Tom Parker. 5 cass. (Running Time: 7 hrs. 30 mins.). 2000. 27.95 Pub: Blckstn Audio. Dist(s): Penton Overseas
Required reading for any golf fan, this is the behind-the-scenes look at America's exclusive Augusta National Golf Club, recounting some of the glories & controversies of the prestigious Masters Tournament.

Augustine: Philosopher & Saint. Instructed by Phillip Cary. 6 CDs. (Running Time: 6 hrs). audio compact disk 39.95 (978-1-59803-104-1(X)) Teaching Co.

Augustine: Philosopher & Saint. Instructed by Phillip Cary. 6 cass. (Running Time: 6 hrs.). 29.95 (978-1-56585-165-8(X)) Teaching Co.

Augustine: Philosopher & Saint, Course 611. Instructed by Phillip Cary. 6 cass. (Running Time: 6 hrs.). 29.95 Incl. course guide. (611) Teaching Co.
Twelve lectures paint a rich & detailed portrait of this remarkable figure whose own search for God has left an indelible imprint on Christianity.

***Augustine for Armchair Theologians.** unabr. ed. Stephen A. Cooper. Narrated by Simon Vance. (ENG.). 2005. 14.98 (978-1-59644-189-7(5), Hovel Audio) christianaud.

Augustine for Armchair Theologians. unabr. ed. Stephen A. Cooper. Narrated by Simon Vance. 5 CDs. (Running Time: 5 hrs. 18 mins. 0 sec.). (ENG.). 2005. audio compact disk 23.98 (978-1-59644-188-0(7), Hovel Audio) christianaud.

Augustine's Conversion. abr. ed. Saint Augustine. Narrated by Max McLean. 1 CD. (Listener's Collection of Classic Christian Literature Ser.). 2007. audio compact disk 10.95 (978-1-931047-58-6(8)) Fellow Perform Arts.

***Augustus.** unabr. ed. John Williams. (Running Time: 11 hrs. 5 mins.). (ENG.). 2011. 29.95 (978-1-4417-7455-2(6)); 65.95 (978-1-4417-7452-1(1)); audio compact disk 29.95 (978-1-4417-7454-5(8)); audio compact disk 100.00 (978-1-4417-7453-8(X)) Blckstn Audio.

Augustus: The Life of Rome's First Emperor. Anthony Everitt. Narrated by John Curless. (Running Time: 56700 sec.). 2006. audio compact disk 39.99 (978-1-4281-0191-3(8)) Recorded Bks.

Augustus John Pt. 1: The New Biography. unabr. collector's ed. Michael Holroyd. Read by Stuart Langton. 14 cass. (Running Time: 21 hrs.). 1997. 112.00 (978-0-7366-3719-0(2), 4401-A) Books on Tape.
This newly-revised biography treats the rebel artist par excellence, a Welshman who challenged the direction of British art in the 20th century.

Augustus John Pt. 2: The New Biography. unabr. collector's ed. Michael Holroyd. Read by Stuart Langton. 9 cass. (Running Time: 13 hrs. 30 mins.). 1997. 72.00 (978-0-7366-3720-6(6), 4401-B) Books on Tape.
The man who changed the direction of British art in the twentieth century.

Auld Lang Syne see Poetry of Robert Burns & Border Ballads

Aumentando el Fluir del Favor. Tr. of Increasing the Flow of Favor. (SPA.). 2006. audio compact disk 14.00 (978-0-944129-10-4(2)) High Praise.

Aunt Addie & the Cattle Rustler. Jane Coleman. (Running Time: 0 hr. 24 mins.). 1998. 10.95 (978-1-60083-474-5(4)) Iofy Corp.

***Aunt Addie & the Cattle Rustler.** Jane Candia Coleman. 2009. (978-1-60136-420-3(2)) Audio Holding.

Aunt Chip & the Great Triple Creek Dam Affair. Patricia Polacco. Narrated by Patricia Polacco. 1 cass. (Running Time: 1 hr.). (J). (gr. k-3). 1997. bk. 27.95 (978-0-8045-6836-4(7), 6836) Spoken Arts.

Aunt Dimity Beats the Devil. unabr. ed. Nancy Atherton. Narrated by Christina Moore. 6 CDs. (Running Time: 6 hrs. 45 mins.). (Aunt Dimity Ser.: No. 6). 2001. audio compact disk 58.00 (978-1-4025-1007-6(1), C1585) Recorded Bks.
When Lori Shepherd journeys to northern England's Wyrdhurst Hall to evaluate a rare book collection, she falls under the spell of the old building. As she digs through the volumes, Lori unearths a story of forbidden passion during World War I that may explain the not-so-friendly spirit who seemingly haunts Wyrdhurst. But Lori also has a ghost on her side - Aunt Dimity - who is always available for guidance and comfort. With plenty of romance, an abundance of intrigue, and a few good scares, Atherton weaves the sort of delightful tale her fans adore.

Aunt Dimity Beats the Devil. unabr. ed. Nancy Atherton. Narrated by Christina Moore. 5 cass. (Running Time: 6 hrs. 45 mins.). (Aunt Dimity Ser.: No. 6). 2001. 48.00 (978-0-7887-5093-9(3), 96533x7) Recorded Bks.
When Lori Shepherd journeys to Wyrdhurst Hall to evaluate a rare book collection, she falls under the spell of the old building. As she digs, Lori unearths family secrets, a tale of doomed romance & some not-so-friendly spirits. The narrator captures both the spooks & delights of this warm novel.

Aunt Dimity's Death. unabr. ed. Nancy Atherton. Narrated by Christina Moore. 5 cass. (Running Time: 6 hrs. 45 mins.). (Aunt Dimity Ser.: No. 1). 2000. 45.00 (978-0-7887-4414-3(3), 96042E7) Recorded Bks.
Lori Shepherd is shocked to learn that a character from her mother's bedtime stories, Aunt Dimity, was a real person & has recently died. Summoned to an eccentric law office, Lori's bewilderment grows when informed that Dimity has left a task for her & a handsome reward upon its completion.

Aunt Dimity's Death. unabr. ed. Nancy Atherton. Narrated by Christina Moore. 7 CDs. (Running Time: 7 hrs. 30 mins.). (Aunt Dimity Ser.: No. 1). 2001. audio compact disk 69.00 (978-0-7887-5196-7(4), C1353E7) Recorded Bks.

Aunt Laura's Bible Stories - Sing with Jean. Jean Wilson. Read by Jean Wilson. Ed. by Sound Impressions Staff. 2 cass. (Running Time: 1 hr. 30 mins.). 1992. 9.95 (978-0-89265-664-6(6), 28077) Randall Hse.

Aunt Margaret's Lover. unabr. ed. Mavis Cheek. Read by Eve Matheson. 8 cass. (Running Time: 12 hrs.). 2002. 59.95 (978-0-7540-0780-7(4), Chivers Child Audio) AudioGO.

Aunt Morbelia & the Screaming Skulls. unabr. ed. Joan D. Carris. Narrated by George Guidall. 3 cass. (Running Time: 3 hrs. 15 mins.). (gr. 3 up). 1994. 27.00 (978-0-7887-0176-4(2), 94401E7) Recorded Bks.
A young boy is surprised when his creepy old aunt turns out to be the perfect teacher to help him with his learning disability.

Aunt Nina & Her Nephews & Nieces. 2004. 8.95 (978-1-56008-837-0(0)); cass. & fmstrp 30.00 (978-0-89719-648-2(1)) Weston Woods.

Aunt Nina & Her Nephews & Nieces. (J). 2004. bk. 24.95 (978-1-56008-160-9(0)) Weston Woods.

Aunt Ruth's Puppet Scripts, Bk. I. Ruth Bivens. Perf. by Jonathan Thigpen & Patti Bumpus. 3 cass. (Running Time: 1 hr. 30 min.). (J). (gr. 1-8). 1986. pap. bk. 19.95 (978-0-89265-096-5(6)) Randall Hse.
Printed puppet scripts for Christian children.

Aunt Ruth's Puppet Scripts, Bk. II. Ruth Bivens. Perf. by Jonathan Thigpen & Patti Bumpus. 3 cass. (Running Time: 1 hr. 30 mins.). (J). 1986. bk. 19.95 (978-0-89265-114-6(8)) Randall Hse.

Aunt Ruth's Puppet Scripts, Bk. III. Ruth Bivens. Perf. by Jonathan Thigpen & Patti Bumpus. 3 cass. (Running Time: 1 hr. 30 mins.). (J). (gr. 1-6). 1987. bk. 19.95 (978-0-89265-119-1(9)) Randall Hse.

Aunt Ruth's Puppet Scripts, Bk. IV. Ruth Bivens. Perf. by Jonathan Thigpen & Patti Bumpus. 3 cass. (Running Time: 1 hr. 30 mins.). (J). 1987. ring bd. 19.95 (978-0-89265-122-1(9)) Randall Hse.

Aunt Sue's Stories see Poetry of Langston Hughes

Auntie Mame. Patrick Dennis. 7 cass. (Running Time: 7 hrs.). 1991. 56.00 (978-5-553-81858-6(3)) Books on Tape.

Auntie Mame. unabr. collector's ed. Patrick Dennis. Read by Donada Peters. 7 cass. (Running Time: 10 hrs. 30 mins.). 1991. 56.00 (978-0-7366-1968-4(2), 2788) Books on Tape.
Patrick Dennis, still in short pants when his father dies, goes off to live with his maiden aunt, Mame. He just knows that life with her is going to be one big bore. But Auntie Mame lives by her own rules & boredom isn't one.

Aura. Carlos Fuentes. Read by Gregorio Rosenblum. Music by Tim Clark. 1 cass. (Running Time: 60 mins.). 9.95 (AA) ZBS Ind.
Binaural sound.

Aura. Geoffrey Hodson. Read by Geoffrey Hodson. Read by Tim Boyd et al. 2 cass. (Running Time: 2 hrs.). 1988. 14.95 (978-0-8356-2091-8(3), Quest) Pub: Theos Pub Hse. Dist(s): Natl Bk Netwk
This two-hour program is based on the lectures by renowned clairvoyant author Geoffrey Hodson.

Aura. unabr. ed. Carlos Fuentes. Read by Gregorio Rosenblum et al. 1 cass. (Running Time: 60 mins.). Dramatization. (J). 1984. 10.00 (978-1-881137-34-4(1)) ZBS Found.
Carlos Fuentes' dreamy, hypnotic tale of a man drawn to Mexico City by forces he cannot understand. With splendid music by Tim Clark.

***Aura O las Violetas.** abr. ed. Vargas Vila. Read by Daniel Quintero. (SPA.). 2008. audio compact disk 17.00 (978-958-8318-47-9(5)) Pub: Yoyo Music COL. Dist(s): YoYoMusic

Aural Comprehension Tests: Form C. 15.00 (Natl Textbk Co) M-H Contemporary.

Aural Training Practice. Ronald Smith. 1951. bk. 1.60 (978-1-86096-000-0(6), 1860960006) H Leonard.

Aurelia. Gérard de Nerval. 2 cass. (Running Time: 2 hrs.). (FRE.). 1991. 27.95 (1385-LV) Olivia & Hill.
Also called "Le Reve et la vie," it is Nerval's last novel. The author, who was suffering from a fatal mental illness, chronicles his own demise.

Aurora Borealis. Perf. by Dave Kenney. Ed. by Charles Beres & Randy Beres. 1 cass. (Running Time: 37 min.). 1995. 9.95 (978-1-883152-08-6(9)); audio compact disk 15.95 (978-1-883152-09-3(7)) Amirra Pr.
Musical interpretation of the Northern Lights. Orchestral music, whales & wolf sounds complement. Story included in the liner notes.

Aurora County All-Stars. unabr. ed. Deborah Wiles. Read by Kate Jackson. 5 CDs. (Running Time: 5 hrs. 38 mins.). (J). (gr. 5-7). 2007. audio compact disk 45.00 (978-0-7393-5138-3(9), Listening Lib) Pub: Random Audio Pubg. Dist(s): Random
House Jackson, age twelve, star pitcher and team captain of the Aurora County All-Stars, has a secret. For the past year, while sidelined with a broken elbow, he has spent every afternoon at the bedside of a mysterious old man the other kids call Mean-Man Boyd - and he doesn't want anyone to know. Now House is finally ready to play ball again, but his team's biggest (and ONLY) game of the year might be canceled, thanks to the very girl who caused his broken elbow. It's almost too much to bear. But in the standoff that ensues, House finds a courage he didn't know he possessed - and discovers that just about everyone in Aurora County, Mississippi, has a secret.

Aurora County All-Stars. unabr. ed. Deborah Wiles. Read by Kate Jackson. 5 CDs. (Running Time: 20280 sec.). (J). (gr. 3-7). 2007. audio compact disk 30.00 (978-0-7393-4883-3(3), Listening Lib) Pub: Random Audio Pubg. Dist(s): Random

Aurora Floyd. unabr. ed. Mary Elizabeth Braddon. Read by Flo Gibson. 12 cass. (Running Time: 17 hrs. 31 mins.). 2001. vinyl bd. 39.95 (978-1-55685-661-7(X)) Audio Bk Con.
After "Lady Audley's Secret," this is considered to be one of the finest of Braddon's 70 novels. Wild, beautiful, young Aurora elopes with a no-good horse trainer, commits bigamy, is blackmailed & suspected of murder.

Aurora's Diary: A Girl's Memories of the Revolution see Diario de Aurora: Vivencias de una Joven en la Revolucion

Auschwitz. unabr. ed. Miklos Nyiszli. Read by Noah Waterman. 5 cass. (Running Time: 7 hrs.). 1995. 39.95 (978-0-7861-0757-5(X), 1607) Blckstn Audio.
"Auschwitz" was one of the first books to bring the full horror of the Nazi death camps to the American public. Although much has since been written about the Holocaust, this eyewitness account remains, as the New York Review of Books said in 1987, "the best brief account of the Auschwitz experience available".

Auschwitz & the Allies: A Devastating Account of How the Allies Responded to the News of Hitler's Mass Murder. unabr. collector's ed. Martin Gilbert. Read by David Case. 15 cass. (Running Time: 22 hrs. 30 mins.). 1996. 120.00 (978-0-7366-3098-6(8), 3774) Books on Tape.
The reports that reached Washington & London in late 1942 were explicit: Nazis were exterminating Jews. But what could the Allies do? Germany dominated the continent & a military decision was years away.

Auschwitz Lullaby. unabr. ed. James C. Wall. 2 cass. (Running Time: 2 hrs. 14 mins.). 1999. 18.99 (978-1-889889-02-3(4)); audio compact disk 18.99 (978-1-889889-03-0(2)) Plays On Tape.
Inspired by true events documented in the Auschwitz diaries of Dr. Miklos Nyiszli, about a young girl who survived a gas chamber event.

Aussie Bites: Peg Leg Meg; The Water Dragons; Too Much to Ask For; No One. unabr. ed. Nan Bodsworth et al. Read by Stig Wemyss. 2 cass. (Running Time: 2 hrs. 46 mins.). (Aussie Bites Ser.). (J). 2000. lib. bdg.

24.00 (978-1-74030-143-5(9), 500428) Pub: Bolinda Pubng AUS. Dist(s): Bolinda Pub Inc

Aussie Bites: The Hand Knitted Hero; No Place for Grubbs!; The Worst Team Ever; Fort Island. unabr. ed. David Metzenthen et al. Read by Stig Wemyss. 2 cass. (Running Time: 3 hrs. 35 mins.). (Aussie Bites Ser.). (J). 2000. lib. bdg. 24.00 (978-1-74030-148-0(X), 500636) Pub: Bolinda Pubng AUS. Dist(s): Bolinda Pub Inc

Aussie Nibbles. unabr. ed. Meredith Costain et al. Read by Justin D'Ath. 1 cass. (Running Time: 1 hr. 23 mins.). (Aussie Nibbles: Ser.). (J). 2001. 18.00 (978-1-74030-459-7(4)) Pub: Bolinda Pubng AUS. Dist(s): Bolinda Pub Inc

Austenland. unabr. ed. Shannon Hale. Read by Katherine Kellgren. 5 CDs. (Running Time: 6 hrs. 30 mins. 0 sec.). (ENG.). 2008. audio compact disk 14.95 (978-1-4272-0483-7(7)) Pub: Macmill Audio. Dist(s): Macmillan

Austere Academy. collector's unabr. ed. Lemony Snicket, pseud. Narrated by Lemony Snicket, pseud. 3 cass. (Running Time: 3 hrs. 30 min.). (Series of Unfortunate Events Ser.: Bk. 5). (YA). (gr. 5 up). 2004. 24.95 (978-1-4025-3736-3(0)) Recorded Bks.
When Violet, Klaus, and Sunny Baudelaire go to boarding school, they have a jolly good time making new friends and winning gold medals for translating cheerful Latin phrases like Memento Mori. Not really. For like all of the other adventures of these three pitiful orphans, this book is actually filled with hideous things like snapping crabs, dripping fungus, the metric system, and a man who cannot play the violin but insists on doing so anyway.

Austere Academy. unabr. ed. Lemony Snicket, pseud. 3 cass. (Running Time: 3 hrs. 30 min.). (Series of Unfortunate Events Ser.: Bk. 5). (YA). 2004. 30.75 (978-1-4025-3735-6(2)) Recorded Bks.

Austere Academy. unabr. ed. Lemony Snicket, pseud. Narrated by Lemony Snicket, pseud. 4 CDs. (Running Time: 3 hrs. 30 min.). (Series of Unfortunate Events Ser.: Bk. 5). (YA). (gr. 5 up). 2004. audio compact disk 40.75 (978-1-4025-3737-0(9)) Recorded Bks.

Austere Academy. unabr. abr. ed. Lemony Snicket, pseud. Read by Lemony Snicket, pseud. Read by Tim Curry. 3 CDs. (Running Time: 5 hrs.). (Series of Unfortunate Events Ser.: Bk. 5). (J). (gr. 3-8). 2003. audio compact disk 25.95 (978-0-06-056619-7(1)) HarperCollins Pubs.

Austerity. Swami Jyotirmayananda. 1 cass. (Running Time: 1 hr.). 1990. 12.99 Yoga Res Foun.

Austerlitz. unabr. ed. W. G. Sebald. Read by Richard Matthews. 5 cass. (Running Time: 7 hrs. 30 mins.). 2002. 40.00 (978-0-7366-8550-4(2)); audio compact disk 48.00 (978-0-7366-8560-3(X)) Books on Tape.
Jacques Austerlitz is a retired art historian who, until he was fifteen, believed that he was Dafydd Elias, raised from the age of four by a dour Welsh minister. Now, in conversations with the narrator, taking place over thirty years in railway stations, he reveals his search for his identity, finding himself to be the child of Prague Jews, one killed in the Holocaust, the other missing.

Austin City Blue. Jan Grape. Narrated by Margo Skinner. 6 cass. (Running Time: 7 hrs. 30 mins.). 54.00 (978-1-4025-2262-8(2)) Recorded Bks.

Austin City Blues. unabr. ed. Jan Grape. Narrated by Margo Skinner. 6 cass. (Running Time: 7 hrs. 30 mins.). 2002. 34.95 (978-1-4025-2263-5(0), RG070) Recorded Bks.

Australia Smarts by Dancing Beetle. Perf. by Eugene Ely. 1 cass. (Running Time: 88 mins.). (J). 1993. 10.00 Erthviibz.
Australian science, myth, ecology & nature sounds come together when Ms. Kookabura & the spunky musical humans read & sing with Dancing Beetle.

Australia Street. unabr. ed. Ann Whitehead. Read by Julie Nihill. (Running Time: 12 hrs. 45 mins.). 2009. audio compact disk 103.95 (978-1-74214-008-7(4), 9781742140087) Pub: Bolinda Pubng AUS. Dist(s): Bolinda Pub Inc

***Australian Bush Poetry Classics.** Ed. by Jack Drake. Music by Restless Music Staff. 2009. pap. bk. 18.00 (978-0-9578477-6-7(9)) Pub: DrakeJ AUS. Dist(s): Interactive Pubns

Australian English Course 1. David Nunan & Jane Lockwood. (Running Time: 31 mins.). (Australian English Course Ser.). 1992. 24.99 (978-0-521-39596-0(8)) Cambridge U Pr.

Australian Feature Films: One Hundred Years of Australian Film Production. British Film Institute Staff. 1996. audio compact disk 59.95 (978-0-86444-355-7(2)) Ind U Pr.

Australian Psylloidea: Jumping Plantlice & Lerp Insects. D. Hollis. 2004. 44.00 (978-0-642-56836-6(7)) Pub: CSIRO AUS. Dist(s): Stylus Pub VA

Austrian Case for the Free Market Process. unabr. ed. William H. Peterson. Ed. by Israel M. Kirzner & Mike Hassell. Narrated by Louis Rukeyser. 2 cass. (Running Time: 1 hr. 40 mins.). Dramatization. (Great Economic Thinkers Ser.). 1988. 17.95 (978-0-938935-40-7(2), 10210) Knowledge Prod.
Two great thinkers, Mises & Hayek, defended free markets when others favored economic control by governments. Mises developed a concept of economics as human action & Hayek challenged the possibilities for efficient socialism.

Austrian Case for the Free Market Process: Ludwig Von Mises & Friedrich Hayek. William Peterson. Read by Louis Rukeyser. (Running Time: 10800 sec.). (Great Economic Thinkers Ser.). 2006. audio compact disk 25.95 (978-0-7861-6947-4(8)) Pub: Blckstn Audio. Dist(s): NetLibrary CO

Austrian Economics. unabr. ed. Murray Newton Rothbard et al. 1 cass. (Running Time: 1 hr. 8 mins.). 12.95 (AFO746) J Norton Pubs.
An introduction to the Austrian School of economics, including a discussion of its achievements & its uniqueness.

Authentic Christianity: Activating the Flow of the Spirit to You & Through You. Lynne Hammond. 3 CDs. 2006. audio compact disk 15.00 (978-1-57399-357-9(3)) Mac Hammond.

***Authentic Faith: The Power of a Fire-Tested Life.** (ENG.). 2010. 14.99 (978-0-310-41579-4(9)) Zondervan.

Authentic Friendship. Thomas Merton. 1 cass. (Running Time: 60 mins.). (Chastity Ser.). 4.50 (AA2130) Credence Commun.
Discussions on the positive, symbolic dimension of chastity.

Authentic Happiness: Using the new Positive Psychology to Realize Your Potential for Lasting Fulfillment. abr. ed. Martin E. P. Seligman & Martin Seligman. Read by John Dossett. 4 CDs. (Running Time: 43 hrs. 0 mins. 0 sec.). (ENG.). 2002. audio compact disk 30.00 (978-0-7435-2491-9(8), Sound Ideas) Pub: S&S Audio. Dist(s): S and S Inc
Teaches readers that happiness can be cultivated by identifying and using many of the strengths and traits that they already possess - including kindness, originality, humor, optimism, and generosity.

Authentic Indian Dances & Folklore. 1 cass. (Running Time: 1 hr.). (J). (gr. 3-6). 2001. pap. bk. 10.95 (KIM 9070C); pap. bk. 14.95 (KIM 9070CD) Kimbo Educ.
Become acquainted with the history & culture of the Chippewa Indians through an actual interview with chief "Little Elk." Talk through & walk through dance instruction. Includes Corn Dance, War Dance, Rain Dance & Strawberry Dance. Includes guide.

Authentic Life of Billy, the Kid. Pat F. Garrett. Read by Anais 9000. 2008. 27.95 (978-1-60112-173-8(3)) Babblebooks.

Authentic Life of Billy the Kid. unabr. ed. Pat F. Garrett. Read by Daniel Luna. 4 cass. (Running Time: 21600 sec.). 1997. 32.95 (978-0-7861-1185-5(2), 1944) Blckstn Audio.
Pat Garrett was the sheriff of Lincoln county when he cornered & killed Billy the Kid on the night of July 14, 1881. Between that date & April 1882, when Garrett's book appeared, eight lurid "dime novels: had glorified & falsified the kid, making him into a murderous super-outlaw. Garrett's book tells the more genuine story of a young, reckless cowhand who became a cattlerustler in the Texas panhandle & a hired gun. Garrett explains the public sympathy that Southwesterners accorded youths like Bonney & challenges the Kid's boast of killing twenty one men.

Authentic Life of Billy the Kid. unabr. ed. Pat F. Garrett. Read by Daniel Luna. (Running Time: 19800 sec.). 2007. audio compact disk 45.00 (978-0-7861-5855-3(7)); audio compact disk 29.95 (978-0-7861-5856-0(5)) Blckstn Audio.

Authentic Listening & Discussion for Advanced Students, Set. Jayne Gaunt-Leshinsky. 2002. 111.65 (978-0-13-371709-9(7)) Longman.

Authentic Outlaw Ballads. 1 cass. (Running Time: 56 mins.). (NG500); audio compact disk (NG-CD-500) Native Ground.
Songs of the colorful yet deadly outlaws of the 19th Century. Includes: "Sam Bass," "Jesse James," "Boston Burglar," "Wild Bill Jones," "Tom Dula," "Rambling Boy," "Cole Younger," "BadLee Brown," "Billy the Kid," "John Hardy," "Messin' with the Law," "Hangman's Reel," & "Sherman's Barroom".

Authentic Outlaw Ballads. Wayne Erbsen. 14.95 (978-1-883206-17-8(0)) Native Ground.

Authentic Power: Aligning Personality with Soul. Interview with Gary Zukav & Michael Toms. 1 cass. (Running Time: 1 hr. 30 mins.). (New Dimensions Ser.). 1997. reel tape 10.95 (978-1-56170-450-7(4), 996) Hay House.
Explains how we create the events in our lives with our thoughts & intentions & puts us in touch with an ability to transform ourselves & the planet by accepting our own inherent, authentic power.

Authentic Power: Aligning Personality with Soul. abr. ed. Gary Zukav & Michael Toms. 1 CD. 2005. audio compact disk 10.95 (978-1-4019-0439-5(4)) Hay House.

Authentic Reproductions: The Art of Reflecting Christ in Your Life. John MacArthur, Jr. 2 cass. 7.95 (22-21, HarperThor) HarpC GBR.

Authentic Self. Carolyn Marks. 1 cass. 9.00 (A0209-87) Sound Photosyn.
From ICSS '87, O'Connell & Swan contribute to the topic.

Authentic Self-Expression: Develop Confident, Creative Expression of Yourself in the World. Mark Bancroft. Read by Mark Bancroft. 1 cass., 1 bklet. (Running Time: 1 hr.). (Spirituality & Consciousness Ser.). 1999. wbk. ed. 12.95 (978-1-58522-018-2(3), 709) EnSpire Pr.
Two complete sessions plus printed instructionmanual/guidebook. With healing music soundtrack.

Authentic Self Expression: Develop Confident, Creative Expression of Yourself in the World. Mark Bancroft. Read by Mark Bancroft. 1 CD, 1 bklet. (Running Time: 1 hr.). (Spirituality & Consciousness Ser.). 2006. audio compact disk 20.00 (978-1-58522-070-0(1)) EnSpire Pr.

Authentic Worship: Logos June 13, 1999. Ben Young. 1999. 4.95 (978-0-7417-6137-8(8), B0137) Win Walk.

Authenticity of Performance. unabr. ed. Narrated by George Malcolm. 1 cass. 12.95 (ECN 086) J Norton Pubs.
Problems trying to establish performance of composer's work which is true to the style & instrumentation of the period in question; also includes two violinists & a violin restorer who listened to a 19th century instruments made in 1975.

Author & Photographer Evelyn Gallardo & Primatologist Dr. Gary Shapiro: Studying & Protecting Wild Orangutans & Releasing Captives in Southeast Asia. Hosted by Nancy Pearlman. 1 cass. (Running Time: 29 mins.). 10.00 (1405) Educ Comm CA.

***Author & Printer in Victorian England.** Allan C. Dooley. (Victorian Literature & Culture Ser.). (ENG.). 27.50 (978-0-8139-2931-6(8)) U Pr of Va.

Author As Torturer. unabr. ed. Ian Watson. 1 cass. 1987. 9.00 (978-1-56964-819-3(0), A0148-87) Sound Photosyn.
As keynote speaker of the SERCON science fiction writers' convention he addresses the question of the validity of titillating a reading audience with violence & torture. Well done.

Author! Author! Doris Lessing. 1 cass. 9.00 (A0480-89) Sound Photosyn.
Enjoy some time with a charming woman, a spritely reader, her intelligent selections & interesting answers.

Author Bites the Dust. unabr. ed. Arthur W. Upfield. Read by Peter Hosking. 6 cass. (Running Time: 9 hrs.). (Inspector Napoleon Bonaparte Mysteries). 2000. (978-1-876584-98-6(X), 591210) Bolinda Pubng AUS.
A cat, a ping-pong ball & a drunken gardener. With these slight clues to go on, Detective Inspector Bonaparte investigates the mysterious death of famous author, Mervyn Blake, who dies an agonizing death late one night in his writing room.

author bites the Dust. unabr. ed. Arthur W. Upfield. Read by Peter Hosking. (Running Time: 6 hrs. 45 mins.). (Inspector Napoleon Bonaparte Mysteries). 2009. audio compact disk 77.95 (978-1-74214-009-4(2), 9781742140094) Pub: Bolinda Pubng AUS. Dist(s): Bolinda Pub Inc

Author Speaks Series. unabr. ed. 37 cass. 14.95 ea. Set. J Norton Pubs.
Archival recordings of 37 20th-century authors.

Author Talks. unabr. ed. Contrib. by Barbara W. Tuchman et al. 3 cass. (Running Time: 4 hrs. 30 min.). (Author Talks Ser.). 26.00 (978-1-55690-794-4(X), 92433) Recorded Bks.
Here's your chance to find out what your favorite author would say if given the chance to talk. "The Author Talks" series offers you exclusive interviews with some of America's most popular contemporary writers. Features: Barbara Tuchman - Pulitzer - prize historian; David Freeman Hawke-author of outstanding biographies of famous Americans; & Martin Cruz Smith - popular author of suspense fiction. Available to libraries only.

Author Unknown, Author Undaunted. 1999. (978-0-615-12117-8(9)) GG Bks.
Anonymous, a regional author, shares self-publishing memoirsand resourceful information. The author wrote part of this story as a book in progress. Interviews were obtained from the 2001 midwest writer's workshop in Muncie, Indiana. Let anonymous tell you the inside story about a revitalized publishing industry.

Author 101. Contrib. by Rick Frishman & Robyn Freedman Spizman. (ENG.). 2008. audio compact disk 119.95 (978-1-60037-254-4(6)) Pub: Morgan James Pubng. Dist(s): IngramPubServ

Authoritarians - audiobook, Downloadable. Robert Altemeyer. Frwd. by John W. Dean. Prod. by Cherry Hill Publishing. Featuring John Lisanti. (ENG.). 2008. 4.95 (978-0-9723298-2-8(X)) Cherry Hill Pubng.

Authoritarians - CD Audio. Robert Altemeyer. Narrated by Robert Altemeyer. Frwd. by John W. Dean. Featuring John Lisanti. Prod. by Cherry Hill Publishing. (ENG.). 2008. audio compact disk 14.95 (978-0-9723298-8-0(9)) Pub: Cherry Hill Pubng. Dist(s): Baker Taylor

***Authoritarians - MP3.** Bob Altemeyer. Read by Bob Altemeyer. (ENG.). 2009. 9.95 (978-0-9843759-0-5(2)) Pub: Cherry Hill Pubng. Dist(s): Baker Taylor

Authority. Bill Winston. 6 cass. (C). 1994. 30.00 (978-1-931289-60-3(3)) Pub: B Winston Min. Dist(s): Anchor Distributors

Authority & Freedom in the Church. unabr. ed. Cormac Burke. Read by Mark Taheny. 7 cass. (Running Time: 7 hrs.). 28.95 (124) Ignatius Pr.
A remarkably clear presentation by an ecclesial judge concerning the tension between church authority & individual freedom - & how the authority established by Christ is the only path to freedom & Catholic unity.

Authority of the Believer. Kenneth Copeland. 6 cass. (Running Time: 6 hrs.). 1983. stu. ed. 30.00 (978-0-938458-53-1(1)) K Copeland Pubns.
Biblical authority of the believer.

Authority of the Believer. Read by Tim Greenwood. 2 cass. (Running Time: 2 hrs.). 1999. 10.00 (978-0-9666689-3-3(6)) TGMinist.

Authority of the Believer. Kenneth E. Hagin. 4 cass. 16.00 (35H) Faith Lib Pubns.

Authority of the Believer. Speeches. Joel Osteen. 1 Cass. (Running Time: 30 Mins.). (J). 2000. 6.00 (978-1-59349-063-8(1), JA0063) J Osteen.

Authority of the Believer. Speeches. Joel Osteen. 1 Cass. (Running Time: 30 Mins). 2002. 6.00 (978-1-59349-138-3(7), JA0138) J Osteen.

Authority Speaks, Vol. 3. Speeches. Creflo A. Dollar. 4 cass. (Running Time: 4 hrs.). 2005. 20.00 (978-1-59089-918-2(0)); audio compact disk 28.00 (978-1-59089-919-9(9)) Creflo Dollar.

Authority to Dominate, Vol. 2. Speeches. Creflo A. Dollar. 4 cass. (Running Time: 4 hrs.). 2005. 15.00 (978-1-59089-915-1(6)); audio compact disk 21.00 (978-1-59089-916-8(4)) Creflo Dollar.

Authority vs. Authoritarianism: The Willingness to Submit. unabr. ed. Thomas Szasz et al. 1 cass. (Running Time: 1 hr. 30 mins.). 1973. 11.00 (10702) Big Sur Tapes.
The pros & cons of the question: Is there a difference between genuine authority & authoritarianism? One point of agreement is that authority is bestowed upon an individual by the respect of other people for his outstanding expertise in one field, while the authoritarian is one who tries to make other people regard him as an authority, whether or not he merits their respect.

Authorizations & Appropriations in a Nutshell. Ed. by TheCapitol.Net. 2005. audio compact disk 107.00 (978-1-58733-029-2(6)) TheCapitol.

Authorizing Policy. abr. ed. Thad E. Hall. (Parliaments & Legislatures Ser.). 2004. audio compact disk 9.95 (978-0-8142-9042-2(6)) Ohio St U Pr.

Author's Mind in Transformation. unabr. ed. George Leonard. 1 cass. (Running Time: 1 hr. 30 mins.). 1971. 11.00 (03804) Big Sur Tapes.
In the process of writing The Transformation, which deals with alternate systems of perceiving & being that he has personally glimpsed, Leonard takes us on his journey of thought & inspiration in the writing of this book.

Author's Secrets: A Crash Course for Writing, Publishing & Marketing Your Book. Hosted by Robin Jay. Contrib. by John Kremer et al. 2008. 299.00 (978-0-9754581-3-6(2)) TwoBirds Pubng.

Autism. Contrib. by Richard Solomon et al. 1 cass. (American Academy of Pediatrics UPDATE: Vol. 18, No. 9). 1998. 20.00 Am Acad Pediat.

Autism: Program from the Award Winning Public Radio Series. Featuring Edwin Cook. (Infinite Mind Ser.). 1998. audio compact disk 21.95 (978-1-888064-36-0(6), LCM 19) Lichtenstein Creat.
Locked inside the silent world of the autistic child is an unimaginable richness of color, sensation and sound. As if an opera singer was performing a beautiful aria in the forest - with no audience to hear. The brain of the autistic child becomes locked away, unreachable by language. Until recently blamed on bad parenting, autism is now known to be a genetic disorder, with medications and behavioral therapies able to help many children.As reported cases of autism skyrocket, we hear from parents and people living with autistic disorders including Cure Autism Now founder and Hollywood producer Jonathan Shestack and author Temple Grandin, and the latest scientific research. Actor Anthony Edwards from the hit TV show ER shares his own experiences, and Suzanne Vega performs.

Autism: Week of July 13, 1998. Read by Fred Goodwin. Perf. by Suzanne Vega. Comment by John Hockenberry. Contrib. by Edwin Cook et al. 1 cass. (Running Time: 1 hr.). (Infinite Mind Ser.). 15.00 Lichtenstein Creat.
New developments in autism research & therapy, parents of autistic children, a professor who recovered from autism.

Autism Can Be Cured. Created by Barry Neil Kaufman. 1 CD. (Running Time: 69 mins.). 2005. audio compact disk 17.50 (978-1-887254-20-5(X)) Epic Century.
An attitudinal method for loving children back to life.Case studies and effective alternatives.

Autism in Childhood: Sponsored by the Occupational Therapy Association of California. Valerie Adams. 3 cass. (Running Time: 4 hrs. 27 mins.). 1997. bk. 125.08 (978-1-58111-015-9(4)) Contemporary Medical.
Describes autism; occupational therapy assessment & intervention methods; successful treatments.

***Autism in the Classroom: Simple & Effective Strategies to Learn Today & Use Tomorrow.** Instructed by Nicole Beurkens & Erin Roon. (ENG.). 2010. audio compact disk 97.00 (978-0-9794787-6-5(6)) Horizons DRC.

Auto-confianza. Carlos Gonzalez. 1 CD. (Running Time: 32 mins). (SPA.). 2003. audio compact disk 15.00 (978-1-56491-122-3(5)) Imagine Pubs.

Auto-Confianza: (Self Confidence) Carlos González. Read by Carlos González. Ed. by Dina Gonzalez. 1 cass. (Running Time: 32 mins.). (SPA.). 1990. 10.00 (978-1-56491-012-7(1)) Imagine Pubs.
In Spanish. Practical advice to increase self confidence.

Auto Italian, Advanced. 3 cass. (Advanced Auto Language Packages Ser.). (ITA.). 1993. pap. bk. 24.95 (978-0-8120-8109-1(9)) Barron.
Designed for people who already have good general knowledge of the foreign language, but who want to improve their skills in idiomatic, fluent, conversational speaking & comprehending.

Auto Psycho Suggestion: A Program for Self-Management. Steven Lance. 1 cass. 1990. pap. bk. 24.95 (978-0-9629820-0-2(8)) Auto Psycho.

Auto-Realizacion: Mire Dentro de Usted Mismo. unabr. ed. Lilburn S. Barksdale. Read by Juan Francisco Estrada. Tr. by George Teague. 1 cass. (Running Time: 24 mins.). (SPA.). 1994. 9.95 (978-0-918588-41-8(3), 121S) NCADD.
Two exercises are given to confirm the truth about yourself & your relationship to a beneficent universe. This inspiring tape puts you in touch with your inner being, affirms your innate worth & importance & reflects on the meaning & purpose of life.

Auto Russian, Advanced. 3 cass. (Advanced Auto Language Packages Ser.). (RUS.). 1993. pap. bk. 24.95 set. (978-0-8120-8110-7(2)) Barron.
Designed for people who already have good general knowledge of the foreign language, but who want to improve their skills in idiomatic, fluent, conversational speaking & comprehending.

Auto Spanish Two, Advanced. 3 cass. (Advanced Auto Language Packages Ser.). (SPA.). 1993. pap. bk. 24.95 set. (978-0-8120-7983-8(3)) Barron.

Auto Taming. unabr. ed. Gordon Yaswen. 1 cass. (Running Time: 60 mins.). 1986. 9.95 (978-0-9620747-0-7(5)) Yascom Endeavors.
Auto mechanic discusses how the average driver can prevent garage & repair rip-offs.

***Autoanalisis.** L. Ron Hubbard. (Running Time: 5 hrs. 14 mins. 0 sec.). (SPA.). 2010. audio compact disk 25.00 (978-1-4031-9609-5(5)) Bridge Pubns Inc.

Autobahn Guru. unabr. ed. Ole Nydahl & Elizabeth Gips. 1 cass. (Running Time: 1 hr. 30 mins.). 1998. 11.00 (32001) Big Sur Tapes.

Autobiographical Reflections. unabr. ed. Eric Voegelin. Read by Bernard Mayes. 4 cass. (Running Time: 5 hrs. 30 mins.). 1992. 32.95 (978-0-7861-0349-2(3), 1306) Blckstn Audio.
An ideal introduction to the ideas of a man whom many regard as the greatest thinker of our time. Here we encounter the stages of development of his unique philosophy of consciousness, his key intellectual breakthroughs, his theory of history & his diagnosis of the political ills of the modern age. Provides a veritable catalog of the thinkers who created the intellectual foundation of the 20th century. Voegelin's association with & recollection of these men provide fresh insight into their thought as well.

Autobiography. unabr. ed. Peter Cushing. Read by Peter Cushing. 6 cass. (Running Time: 9 hrs.). 2001. 54.95 (89021) Pub: ISIS Audio GBR. Dist(s): Ulverscroft US

Autobiography. unabr. ed. Anthony Trollope. Read by Bernard Mayes. 8 cass. (Running Time: 11 hrs. 30 mins.). 1997. 56.95 (978-0-7861-1153-4(4), 1923) Blckstn Audio.
Trollope was born in 1815. He was the victim of vicious bullying, but he had inherited his mother's determination & managed later to carve out a successful career.

Autobiography: The Best of Scott Krippayne. Contrib. by Scott Krippayne. Prod. by Phil Johnson. 2006. audio compact disk 12.99 (978-5-558-10949-8(1)) Sprg Hill Music Group.

***Autobiography: The Story of My Experiments with Truth.** unabr. ed. Mohandas K. (Mahatma) Gandhi. Read by Bill Wallace. (Running Time: 19 hrs. 30 mins.). 2010. 44.95 (978-1-4417-4992-5(6)); 99.95 (978-1-4417-4988-8(8)); audio compact disk 123.00 (978-1-4417-4989-5(6)) Blckstn Audio.

Autobiography of a Hunted Priest. John Gerard. 9 cass. 36.95 (710) Ignatius Pr.
A Jesuit priest risks his life as a missionary in the late 16th century England.

Autobiography of a Modern Prophet. unabr. ed. Harold Klemp. Read by Rich Miller. 8 cass. (Running Time: 13 hrs. 59 mins.). 2004. 35.00 (978-1-57043-197-5(3)) Pub: Eckankar. Dist(s): Hushion Hse

Autobiography of a Supertramp. W. H. Davies. 2001. pap. bk. 79.95 (978-1-86015-003-6(9)) Ulverscroft US.

Autobiography of a Supertramp. W. H. Davies. Read by Peter Joyce. 6 cass. 2001. 54.95 (978-1-86015-469-0(7)) Ulverscroft US.

Autobiography of a Yogi. Paramhansa Yogananda. Read by Ben Kingsley. 12 cass. (Running Time: 18 hrs.). 1999. 79.95 (83-0036) Explorations.
The history of Yogananda's life, his search for an enlightened teacher, 10 years of training in the hermitage of a revered yoga master & the more than 30 years he lived & taught in America.

Autobiography of a Yogi. abr. ed. J. Donald Walters. Read by Swami Kriyananda. 6 cass. (Running Time: 10 hrs.). 1997. 29.95 (978-1-56589-109-8(0)) Pub: Crystal Clarity. Dist(s): Natl Bk Netwk
Taken from the verbatim original 1946 edition, including key chapters read by a close disciple who lived and studied with Yogananda.

Autobiography of a Yogi. unabr. ed. Paramhansa Yogananda. 15 cass. (Running Time: 18 hrs.). audio compact disk 48.00 (978-0-87612-095-8(8)) Self Realization.

Autobiography of a Yogi: A New Approach to Renunciation. Paramhansa Yogananda. 2008. audio compact disk 48.00 (978-1-56589-233-0(X)) Pub: Crystal Clarity. Dist(s): Natl Bk Netwk

Autobiography of an Ex-Colored Man. James Weldon Johnson. Read by Anais 9000. 2008. 27.95 (978-1-60112-176-9(8)) Babblebooks.

Autobiography of an Ex-Colored Man. abr. ed. James Weldon Johnson. Read by Allen Gilmore. 2 cass. (Running Time: 3 hrs.). 1995. 19.95 (978-0-9645593-7-0(4)) MasterBuy Audio Bks.
Fictional autobiography of an African-American man born to a black mother & white father, whose identity crisis deepens until the horror of a lynching draws him across the color line to the white world. Includes biographical information about the author.

***Autobiography of an Ex-Colored Man.** unabr. ed. James Weldon Johnson. Narrated by Alan Bomar Jones. (Running Time: 6 hrs. 0 mins.). 2010. 54.99 (978-1-4526-3061-8(5)); 19.99 (978-1-4526-5061-6(6)); 22.99 (978-1-4526-0061-1(9)); 13.99 (978-1-4526-7061-4(7)) Tantor Media.

***Autobiography of an Ex-Colored Man (Library Edition)** unabr. ed. James Weldon Johnson. Narrated by Alan Bomar Jones. (Running Time: 6 hrs. 0 mins.). 2010. 22.99 (978-1-4526-2061-9(X)) Tantor Media.

Autobiography of an Execution. unabr. ed. David R. Dow. Read by David R. Dow. (Running Time: 8 hrs.). (ENG.). 2010. 16.98 (978-1-60788-136-0(5)) Pub: Hachet Audio. Dist(s): HachBkGrp

Autobiography of Andrew Carnegie. Andrew Carnegie. Read by Anais 9000. 2009. 27.95 (978-1-60112-212-4(8)) Babblebooks.

Autobiography of Anthony Trollope. Anthony Trollope. Narrated by Flo Gibson. 7 cass. (Running Time: 6 hrs. 12 mins.). 2005. 25.95 (978-1-55685-855-0(8)) Audio Bk Con.

Autobiography of Benjamin Franklin. Benjamin Franklin. Read by Grover Gardner. (Playaway Young Adult Ser.). (ENG.). 2008. 79.99 (978-1-60640-839-1(9)) Find a World.

Autobiography of Benjamin Franklin. Benjamin Franklin. Narrated by Walter Covell. (Running Time: 6 hrs.). 1987. 23.95 (978-1-59912-141-3(7)) Iofy Corp.

Autobiography of Benjamin Franklin. Benjamin Franklin. Read by Grover Gardner. (Running Time: 6 hrs.). (C). 2003. 22.95 (978-1-59912-042-3(9), Audiofy Corp) Iofy Corp.

Autobiography of Benjamin Franklin. Based on a work by Benjamin Franklin. Abr. by Deems Weldon. (ENG.). 2007. 5.00 (978-1-60339-120-7(7)) Listenr Digest.

Autobiography of Benjamin Franklin. Benjamin Franklin. Read by Graeme Malcolm & Jason Culp. 5 cass. 2005. 14.95 (978-1-56585-984-5(7)) Teaching Co.

Autobiography of Benjamin Franklin. Benjamin Franklin. Read by Graeme Malcolm. 7 cds. 2005. audio compact disk 19.95 (978-1-59803-000-6(0)) Teaching Co.

Autobiography of Benjamin Franklin. unabr. ed. Read by Michael Edwards. 5 cass. (Running Time: 7 hrs.). 1989. 39.95 (978-0-7861-0025-5(7), 1024) Blckstn Audio.
Franklin's autobiography captures the essence of his spirit. In it we can see him as a product of 18th century enlightenment, a type of Yankee statesman who could use the language of Addison, Steele, Swift & Defoe.

Autobiography of Benjamin Franklin. unabr. ed. Benjamin Franklin. Read by Fredd Wayne. 4 cass. (Running Time: 6 hrs.). 2004. 22.95 (978-1-57270-043-7(2), E41043u) Pub: Audio Partners. Dist(s): PerseuPGW
An influential biography of this American founding father, Ben Franklin's own lively story of his early years is fascinating. Printer, scientist & statesman, Franklin wrote these memoirs sporadically over a period of 18 years.

Autobiography of Benjamin Franklin. unabr. ed. Benjamin Franklin. Read by Robert L. Halvorson. 4 cass. (Running Time: 4 hrs.). 28.95 (50) Halvorson Assocs.

Autobiography of Benjamin Franklin. unabr. ed. Benjamin Franklin. Read by Walter Covell. 5 cass. (Running Time: 6 hrs.). 1980. 35.00 incl. album. (C-38) Jimcin Record.
Insights into revolutionary America through the eyes of one of its most famous citizens.

Autobiography of Benjamin Franklin. unabr. ed. Benjamin Franklin. Narrated by Adrian Cronauer. 4 cass. (Running Time: 5 hrs. 30 mins.). (gr. 10 up). 1986. 35.00 (978-1-55690-045-7(7), 86110E7) Recorded Bks.
An account of Benjamin Franklin's life from 1706 to 1757 by his own hand.

Autobiography of Benjamin Franklin. unabr. ed. Benjamin Franklin. Read by Grover Gardner. 5 cds. (Running Time: 6 hrs). 2002. pap. bk. (978-1-58472-208-3(8), In Aud) Sound Room.
From printer's apprentice to internationally famous scientist, inventor, statesman, legislator and diplomat, Benjamin Franklin led a most remarkable life.

Autobiography of Benjamin Franklin. unabr. ed. Benjamin Franklin. Read by Grover Gardner. 5 cds. (Running Time: 6 hrs). 2002. audio compact disk 29.95 (978-1-58472-206-9(1), 081, In Aud) Pub: Sound Room. Dist(s): Baker Taylor
The remarkable story of a scientist, inventor, statesman, legislator and diplomat.

Autobiography of Benjamin Franklin. unabr. ed. Benjamin Franklin. Read by Grover Gardner. 1 cd. (Running Time: 6 hrs). 2002. audio compact disk 18.95 (978-1-58472-381-3(5), In Aud) Pub: Sound Room. Dist(s): Baker Taylor
MP3 format.

Autobiography of Benjamin Franklin. unabr. ed. Benjamin Franklin. Read by Walter A. Costello. (Running Time: 6 hrs. 30 mins. 0 sec.). (ENG.). 2008. 19.99 (978-1-4001-5898-0(2)); audio compact disk 27.99 (978-1-4001-0898-5(5)); audio compact disk 55.99 (978-1-4001-3898-2(1)) Pub: Tantor Media. Dist(s): IngramPubServ

Autobiography of Benjamin Franklin. unabr. ed. Benjamin Franklin. Read by William Costello. (YA). 2006. 44.99 (978-1-59895-669-6(8)) Find a World.

Autobiography of Benjamin Franklin. unabr. collector's ed. Benjamin Franklin. Read by Walter A. Costello. 7 cass. (Running Time: 7 hrs.). 1993. 56.00 (978-0-7366-2372-8(8), 3145) Books on Tape.
Printer, inventor, philosopher, champion of liberty, Franklin's influence has been felt by every American generation.

Autobiography of Benjamin Franklin: A Fully Rounded Portrait of the Many-Sided Franklin, Notably the Moralist, Humanitarian, Scientist, & Unconventional Human Being. unabr. ed. Benjamin Franklin. Narrated by Fredd Wayne. (Running Time: 21960 sec.). (Audio Editions Ser.). (ENG.). 2005. audio compact disk 27.95 (978-1-57270-495-4(0)) Pub: AudioGO. Dist(s): Perseus Dist
Benjamin Franklin was not only one of America's Founding Fathers - he was also a fascinating character who lived an exciting life. Whether carousing with prostitutes in Paris, taunting lightning bolts with kites, or founding America's first volunteer fire fighting organization, Franklin was always at the center of activity. The Autobiography of Benjamin Franklin details this American's early years, his career, and his conflicted relationship with his son. Performed by noted actor Fredd Wayne, this recording brings the classic American to life.

Autobiography of Benjamin Franklin: Part I. Based on a work by Benjamin Franklin. Abr. by Deems Weldon. (ENG.). 2007. 5.00 (978-1-60339-115-3(0)); audio compact disk 5.00 (978-1-60339-116-0(9)) Listenr Digest.

Autobiography of Benjamin Franklin: Part II. Based on a work by Benjamin Franklin. Abr. by Deems Weldon. (ENG.). 2007. 5.00 (978-1-60339-117-7(7)); audio compact disk 5.00 (978-1-60339-118-4(5)) Listenr Digest.

Autobiography of Benjamin Franklin: Part III. Based on a work by Benjamin Franklin. Abr. by Deems Weldon. (ENG.). 2007. 5.00 (978-1-60339-119-1(3)) Listenr Digest.

Autobiography of Benjamin Franklin: Part IV. Based on a work by Benjamin Franklin. Abr. by Deems Weldon. (ENG.). 2007. 5.00 (978-1-60339-121-4(5)) Listenr Digest.

Autobiography of Benjamin Franklin: Part IV. Based on a work by Benjamin Franklin. Animated by Deems Weldon. (ENG.). 2007. audio compact disk 5.00 (978-1-60339-122-1(3)) Listenr Digest.

Autobiography of Benjamin Franklin: Part V. Based on a work by Benjamin Franklin. Abr. by Deems Weldon. (ENG.). 2007. 5.00 (978-1-60339-123-8(1)); audio compact disk 5.00 (978-1-60339-124-5(X)) Listenr Digest.

Autobiography of Benvenuto Cellini. unabr. ed. Benvenuto Cellini. Read by Robert Whitfield. 11 cass. (Running Time: 16 hrs.). 1997. 76.95 (978-0-7861-1164-0(X), 1935) Blckstn Audio.
Master Italian sculptor, goldsmith & writer, Benvenuto Cellini is best remembered for his magnificent autobiography. Cellini chronicles his own flamboyant times. Renaissance historians such as Burkhardt were strongly influenced by this work, seeing it as confirmation that the key to the period is the emergence of modern individualism.

Autobiography of Benvenuto Cellini. unabr. ed. Benvenuto Cellini. Read by Robert Whitfield. Tr. by John Addington Symonds. (Running Time: 55800 sec.). 2007. audio compact disk 29.95 (978-0-7861-6073-0(X)) Blckstn Audio.

Autobiography of Benvenuto Cellini. unabr. ed. Read by Robert Whitfield. Tr. by John Addington Symonds. (Running Time: 55800 sec.). 2007. audio compact disk 99.00 (978-0-7861-6072-3(1)) Blckstn Audio.

Autobiography of Benvenuto Cellini. unabr. collector's ed. Benvenuto Cellini. Read by Jonathan Reese. 12 cass. (Running Time: 18 hrs.). 1997. 96.00 (978-0-7366-4058-9(4), 4569) Books on Tape.
An autobiography of a great sculptor; an extraordinary view of life in Renaissance Italy & France.

Autobiography of G. K. Chesterton. unabr. ed. G. K. Chesterton. Read by Thomas Whitworth. 7 cass. (Running Time: 10 hrs.). 1990. 49.95 (978-0-7861-0172-6(5), 1153) Blckstn Audio.
It is no mere book of reminiscences. It is a biography more orderly than he ever wrote of other men. In it he gives us details of his childhood, marriage, family, great alliance with Belloc, his patriotism, the genesis of Father Brown & his conversion.

Autobiography of Henry VIII, Pt. 1. unabr. collector's ed. Margaret George. Read by David Case. 14 cass. (Running Time: 21 hrs.). 1998. 112.00 (978-0-7366-4238-5(2), 4737-A) Books on Tape.
Brings into focus the larger-than-life King Henry VIII, monarch of prodigious appetites for wine, women & song.

Autobiography of Henry VIII, Pt. 2. unabr. collector's ed. Margaret George. Read by David Case. 15 cass. (Running Time: 22 hrs. 30 mins.). 1998. 120.00 (978-0-7366-4239-2(0), 4737-B) Books on Tape.
In her autobiography of Henry VIII, Margaret imagines Henry speaking for himself.

Autobiography of John Stuart Mill. unabr. ed. John Stuart Mill. Read by Robert L. Halvorson. 4 cass. (Running Time: 4 hrs.). 28.95 (10) Halvorson Assocs.

Autobiography of John Stuart Mill. unabr. ed. John Stuart Mill. Read by Noah Waterman. 5 cass. (Running Time: 7 hrs.). 1998. 39.95 (978-0-7861-1257-9(3), 2165) Blckstn Audio.
Deals with but one part of a life, the life of the mind - but a mind that ranks as one of the most remarkable & significant of the nineteenth century.

Autobiography of John Stuart Mill. unabr. ed. John Stuart Mill. Read by Noah Waterman. (Running Time: 7 hrs. 0 mins.). (ENG.). 2009. 29.95 (978-1-4417-0571-6(6)); audio compact disk 69.00 (978-1-4417-0568-6(6)) Blckstn Audio.

Autobiography of Mark Twain. unabr. ed. Read by Michael Russotto. Ed. by Charles Neider. 15 cass. (Running Time: 20 hrs. 30 mins.). 2003. 95.95 (978-0-7861-0888-6(6), 1549) Blckstn Audio.
Nothing ever happened to Mark Twain in a small way. His adventures were invariably fraught with drama. Success & failure for him were equally spectacular. And so he roared down the years, feuding with publishers, being a sucker for inventors, always learning wisdom at the point of ruin & always relishing the absurd spectacle of humankind, whom he regarded with a blend of vitriol & affection.

***Autobiography of Mark Twain.** unabr. ed. Mark Twain. Read by Michael Russotto. (Running Time: 20 hrs. 30 mins.). 2010. 44.95 (978-1-4417-4467-8(3)); audio compact disk 123.00 (978-1-4417-4464-7(9)) Blckstn Audio.

***Autobiography of Mark Twain, Vol. 1: The Complete & Authoritative Edition.** unabr. ed. Mark Twain. Read by Grover Gardner. (Running Time: 25 hrs. NaN mins.). (ENG.). 2010. audio compact disk 140.00 (978-1-4417-7842-0(X)) Blckstn Audio.

***Autobiography of Mark Twain, Vol. 1 (Part 1 Of 2) The Complete & Authoritative Edition.** unabr. ed. Mark Twain. Read by Grover Gardner. (Running Time: 12 hrs. 5 mins.). (ENG.). 2010. 72.95 (978-1-4417-7840-6(3)) Blckstn Audio.

***Autobiography of Mark Twain, Vol. 1 (Part 2 Of 2) The Complete & Authoritative Edition.** unabr. ed. Mark Twain. Read by Grover Gardner. (Running Time: 12 hrs. 5 mins.). 2010. 72.95 (978-1-4417-7841-3(1)) Blckstn Audio.

***Autobiography of Mark Twain, Volume 1: The Complete & Authoritative Edition.** unabr. ed. Mark Twain. Read by Grover Gardner. (Running Time: 25 hrs. NaN mins.). (ENG.). 2010. audio compact disk 39.95 (978-1-4417-7843-7(8)) Blckstn Audio.

***Autobiography of Mark Twain, Volume 1: The Complete & Authoritative Edition.** unabr. ed. Mark Twain. Read by Grover Gardner. (Running Time: 25 hrs. NaN mins.). 2010. 44.95 (978-1-4417-7844-4(6)) Blckstn Audio.

Autobiography of Martin Luther King, Jr. abr. ed. Clayborne Carson. Read by LeVar Burton. (ENG.). 2005. 14.98 (978-1-59483-327-4(3)) Pub: Hachet Audio. Dist(s): HachBkGrp

Autobiography of Martin Luther King, Jr. abr. ed. Clayborne Carson. Read by Clayborne Carson. Read by Martin Luther King & LeVar Burton. (Running Time: 9 hrs.). (ENG.). 2009. 59.98 (978-1-60788-107-0(1)) Pub: Hachet Audio. Dist(s): HachBkGrp

Autobiography of Martin Luther King, JR. abr. ed. Clayborne Carson. Read by Clayborne Carson. Read by LeVar Burton & Martin Luther King, Jr. 8 CDs. (Running Time: 9 hrs.). (ENG., 2005. audio compact disk 39.98 (978-1-59483-101-0(7)) Pub: Hachet Audio. Dist(s): HachBkGrp

Autobiography of Martin Luther King, Jr. abr. ed. Martin Luther King, Jr. Read by LeVar Burton. 6 cass. (Running Time: 6 hrs.). 1999. 29.98 (FS9-43292) Highsmith.

Autobiography of Miss Jane Pittman. Ernest J. Gaines. 2 cass. (Running Time: 2 hrs.). 1999. 19.95 (SF-45031) African Am Imag.

Autobiography of Miss Jane Pittman. unabr. ed. Ernest J. Gaines. Read by Tonya Jordan. 6 cass. (Running Time: 8 hrs. 30 mins.). 1997. 44.95 (978-0-7861-1053-7(8), 1856) Blckstn Audio.
A novel in the guise of the tape-recorded recollections of a black woman who has lived 110 years, who has been both a slave and a witness to the black militancy of the 60's.

Autobiography of Miss Jane Pittman. unabr. ed. Ernest J. Gaines. Narrated by Lynne Thigpen. 7 pieces. (Running Time: 10 hrs.). (gr. 5 up). 1994. 62.00 (978-0-7887-0072-9(3), 94305E7) Recorded Bks.
A woman recounts the events of her long life, beginning with her days as a slave before the Civil War through her participation in the Civil Rights movement in the 1960's.

Autobiography of Miss Jane Pittman. unabr. collector's ed. Ernest J. Gaines. Read by Roses Prichard. 7 cass. (Running Time: 10 hrs. 30 mins.). 1982. 56.00 (978-0-7366-0513-7(4), 1487) Books on Tape.
The recollection of a black woman who has lived 110 years, who has been both a slave & a witness to the black militancy of the 1960s.

***Autobiography of Mrs. Tom Thumb: A Novel.** unabr. ed. Melanie Benjamin. (ENG.). 2011. audio compact disk 35.00 (978-0-307-71348-3(2), Random AudioBks) Pub: Random Audio Pubg. Dist(s): Random

Autobiography of My Dead Brother. unabr. ed. Walter Dean Myers. Read by J. D. Jackson. 4 CDs. (Running Time: 4 hrs. 15 mins.). (YA). 2006. audio compact disk 49.75 (978-1-4193-8476-9(7), C3663); 49.75 (978-1-4193-8475-2(9), 98326) Recorded Bks.
There's been another drive-by in Jesse's Harlem neighborhood. Who will be next? When long-time friend and blood brother Rise asks Jesse to write his biography, the talented artist has no idea his friend's story will be so short. "Eventually you reach manhood, then you got to go through or turn around and go back," Rise once said. Jesse is going through.

Autobiography of My Mother. 1982. (2031) Am Audio Prose.

Autobiography of My Mother. unabr. ed. Jamaica Kincaid. Read by Jamaica Kincaid. 5 cass. (Running Time: 5 hrs.). 1996. 21.95 (978-1-885608-09-3(8)) Airplay.
The acclaimed author reads her new novel, the harrowing, richly metaphorical "autobiography". A brilliant fable by a first-rate literary artist.

Autobiography of Parley P Pratt. Parley P. Pratt. 10 cass. 2004. 29.95 (978-1-59156-237-5(6)); audio compact disk 29.95 (978-1-59156-238-2(4)) Covenant Comms.

Autobiography of Santa Claus. Jeff Guinn. Read by John H. Mayer. (Running Time: 9 hrs.). 2005. 23.95 (978-1-60083-345-8(4)) Iofy Corp.

Autobiography of Santa Claus. Jeff Guinn. 7 CDs. (Running Time: 8 Hrs). 2004. audio compact disk 29.95 (978-1-59316-036-4(4)) Listen & Live.
It started when Jeff Guinn wrote a story about Christmas for his newspaper. Soon, Jeff is whisked off to the North Pole to meet with a "very important" person to discuss the real stories behind Santa Claus.

Autobiography of Santa Claus. unabr. ed. Jeff Guinn. Read by John H. Mayer. (YA). 2006. 39.99 (978-1-59895-202-5(1)) Find a World.

Autobiography of Shakespeare. unabr. ed. Gilbert Highet. Read by Gilbert Highet. 1 cass. (Running Time: 30 mins.). 12.95 (23284-A) J Norton Pubs.

Autobiography of Shakespeare & A Poet in Italy (audio CD) Gilbert Highet. (ENG.). 2006. audio compact disk 9.95 (978-1-57970-436-0(0), Audio-For) J Norton Pubs.

Autobiography of St. Therese of Lisieux: The Story of a Soul. Read by Sherry Kennedy Brownrigg. Tr. by John Beevers. 5 CDs. (Running Time: 21600 sec.). 2006. audio compact disk 33.95 (978-0-86716-809-9(9)) St Anthony Mess Pr.

AutoCAD & Its Applications: Advanced - 2002 Edition. Terence M. Shumaker & David A. Madsen. (gr. 9-13). 2002. tchr. ed. 30.00 (978-1-56637-903-8(2)) Goodheart.

AutoCAD & Its Applications: Basics - 2002 Edition. Terence M. Shumaker & David A. Madsen. (gr. 9-13). 2002. tchr. ed. 36.00 (978-1-56637-901-4(6)) Goodheart.

AutoCAD & Its Applications: Basics 2005. Terence M. Shumaker & David A. Madsen. (gr. 9-13). tchr. ed. 39.00 (978-1-59070-371-7(5)) Goodheart.

AutoCAD & Its Applications: Comprehensive - 2002 Edition. Terence M. Shumaker & David A. Madsen. (gr. 9-13). 2002. tchr. ed. 52.00 (978-1-56637-980-9(6)) Goodheart.

AutoCAD & its Applications 2004: Advanced 2004 Edition. Terence M. Shumaker & David A. Madsen. (gr. 9-13). tchr. ed. 32.00 (978-1-59070-292-5(1)) Goodheart.

AutoCAD & its Applications 2004: Basics 2004 Edition. Terence M. Shumaker & David A. Madsen. (gr. 9-13). tchr. ed. 38.00 (978-1-59070-290-1(5)) Goodheart.

AutoCAD & its Applications 2004: Comprehensive 2004 Edition. Terence M. Shumaker & David A. Madsen. (gr. 9-13). tchr. ed. 53.28 (978-1-59070-294-9(8)) Goodheart.

AutoCAD LT 2004 Fundamentals Drafting & Design Applications. Ted Saufley & Paul B. Schreiner. (gr. 8-13). tchr. ed. 32.00 (978-1-59070-319-9(7)) Goodheart.

Autocad R14 Expert. 2006. audio compact disk 399.95 (978-0-7668-0767-9(3)) Delmar.

Autoclaved Aerated Concrete - Innovation & Development. Limbachiya/MukeshC. & Roberts/JohnJ. 2005. audio compact disk (978-0-415-38367-7(6)) Taylor and Fran.

Autocrat of the Breakfast Table. Oliver Wendell Holmes. Read by Robert L. Halvorson. 7 cass. (Running Time: 10 hrs. 30 mins.). 49.95 (31) Halvorson Assocs.

Autogenic Relaxation. Read by Mary Richards. 12.95 (506) Master Your Mind.
Discusses how to silently talk to the body, describing the feeling of relaxation throughout the body as it gradually relaxes.

Autogenics & Meditation. Matthew McKay & Patrick Fanning. (Running Time: 50 mins). (Relaxation Skills CD Ser.). (ENG.). 2008. audio compact disk 13.95 (978-1-57224-640-9(5)) New Harbinger.

Autograph Man. unabr. ed. Zadie Smith. Narrated by Steven Crossley. 10 cass. (Running Time: 14 hrs.). 2002. 93.00 (978-1-4025-1797-6(1)) Recorded Bks.

Autograph Man. unabr. ed. Zadie Smith. Narrated by Steven Crossley. 8 cass. (Running Time: 14 hrs.). 2004. 34.99 (978-1-4025-0873-8(5), 01094) Recorded Bks.
Alex-Li Tandem peddles autographs. His business is to hunt down the names people want and sell them. He even fakes them if that's what it takes to give autograph seekers a little taste of fame.

***Autographed Collectibles: A Basic Guide.** Karen Jean Matsko Hood. (ENG.). 2011. audio compact disk 24.95 (978-1-59434-893-8(6)) Whspmg Pine.

Autographs in the Rain. unabr. ed. Quintin Jardine. Read by James Bryce. 8 cass. (Running Time: 9 hrs. 28 mins.). (Isis Ser.). (J). 2002. 69.95 (978-0-7531-1174-1(8)); audio compact disk 89.95 (978-0-7531-1340-0(6)) Pub: ISIS Lrg Prnt GBR. Dist(s): Ulverscroft US
As Deputy Chief Constable Bob Skinner takes an evening stroll with Louise Banks, an old flame and now a film star, it seems his biggest worry is that a new colleague is scheming to enlarge his territory at Skinner's expense. But when a frightening shot-gun attack sends him diving for cover, it seems danger has chosen to zero in on him once again.

Autoharp Method - In Four Easy Steps. Evo Bluestein. 2001. bk. 9.95 (978-0-7866-5777-3(4)) Mel Bay.

Autohypnosis "Diet" How to Program Your Mind to Control Your Weight for Life. Matt Oechsli. Read by Matt Oechsli. 6 cass. pap. bk. 69.95 (881AD) Nightingale-Conant.
Matt Oechsli's method is as easy as daydreaming about the person you want to be. If you can daydream, this amazing program will show you how to: Develop a lifestyle of health & fitness; Completely control your eating compulsions; Avoid eating binges; Eliminate junk food; Eat three well-balanced meals a day; Gain control of tension & stress, factors that often stimulate appetite; Become highly motivated to exercise; & Improve every area of your life.

Autoimmune Disorders: Ancient Truths, Natural Remedies & the Latest Findings for Your Health Today. unabr. ed. Don Colbert. (Running Time: 1 hr. 30 mins.). (Bible Cure Ser.). 2004. 7.99 (978-1-58926-684-1(6)) Oasis Audio.

Autoimmune Disorders: Ancient Truths, Natural Remedies & the Latest Findings for Your Health Today. unabr. ed. Don Colbert. Narrated by Greg Wheatley. 1 CD. (Running Time: 1 hr. 30 mins.). (Bible Cure Ser.). (ENG.). 2004. audio compact disk 9.99 (978-1-58926-685-8(4)) Oasis Audio.

Automagic Horse: An Adventure Story with a Touch of Magic. L. Ron Hubbard. 1 cass. (J). 1995. 11.95 (978-0-88404-932-6(9)) Bridge Pubns Inc.
Educational & entertaining, the story brings to life Hollywood of the late 1930s & the greatest movie "special effects" man of the day, Gadget O'Dowd. Gadget is commissioned to build a replica of a famous race horse for a dangerous stunt in a new movie - & he does a spectacular job. But Gadget's secret - his real purpose - is a project that will take him to the stars.

Automagic Horse: An Adventure Story with a Touch of Magic. L. Ron Hubbard. 2001. 10.95 (978-0-88404-998-2(1)) Bridge Pubns Inc.

Automatic Functions of the Mind. unabr. ed. Barbara Branden. 1 cass. (Running Time: 1 hr. 35 mins.). 12.95 (AFO703) J Norton Pubs.
Includes: the nature of the subconscious; the proper use of the subconscious; subconscious integrations & the emotions; creative thinking & the subconscious; the psychology of inspiration.

Automatic, Manual Transmissions, Transaxles & Drive Trains. rev. ed. Bob Leigh et al. Ed. by Roger L. Fennema & Kalton C. Lahue. Illus. by Ralph J. Butterworth. (Automobile Mechanics Refresher Course Ser.: Bk. 5). 1981. pap. bk. 13.90 (978-0-88098-072-2(9), H M Gousha) Prntice Hall Bks.

Automatic Millionaire: A Powerful One-Step Plan to Live & Finish Rich. unabr. ed. David Bach. Read by David Bach. (Running Time: 50 hrs. 0 mins. 0 sec.). (ENG.). 2004. audio compact disk 29.95 (978-0-7435-3841-1(2), Sound Ideas) Pub: S&S Audio. Dist(s): S and S Inc

Automatic Millionaire: A Powerful One-Step Plan to Live & Finish Rich. unabr. ed. David Bach. 2004. 18.95 (978-0-7435-4177-0(4)) Pub: S&S Audio. Dist(s): S and S Inc

Automatic Millionaire Homeowner: A Powerful Plan to Finish Rich in Real Estate. abr. ed. David Bach. 2006. 25.00 (978-0-7393-2425-7(X), Random AudioBks) Random Audio Pubg.
In his breakout 2004 bestseller, The Automatic Millionaire, David Bach showed why owning your own home is not only smart, it¿s the core secret to becoming a millionaire. In his new book, tailored for a Canadian readership, he shows exactly how to make that happen with a simple, automatic plan you can read in an hour and put into place today. Renters will learn how to buy a first home, even with lousy credit and tiny savings. And existing homeowners will find out how to turn the roof over their heads into a powerful investment that doubles, triples, and quadruples in price while you simply enjoy living in it. And while you don¿t have to be a landlord to finish rich, if you¿re willing to be, David teaches you how simple it really is to buy a rental property even while you¿re paying the mortgage on your home.

Automatic Millionaire Homeowner: A Powerful Plan to Finish Rich in Real Estate. abr. ed. David Bach. Read by Oliver Wyman. 4 CDs. (Running Time: 14400 sec.). (ENG.). 2006. audio compact disk 19.95 (978-0-7393-2426-4(8), Random AudioBks) Pub: Random Audio Pubg. Dist(s): Random
From the author of the bestselling Finish Rich series and The Automatic Millionaire, a new book from David Bach that shows readers how real estate is the surest and quickest way to finish rich. In his quest to show people of average incomes how to achieve financial security, David Bach builds on his Finish Rich wisdom and tackles real estate, one of the surest paths to financial success, in Smart Homeowners Finish Rich. Whether they already own or just want to, Bach shows readers how to pave their way to financial freedom by buying their own homes and investment properties. In crisp, clear detail, this book explains the best way to afford, purchase, and pay down a mortgage on a Canadian first home, even on a modest income and even with debt, and then how to go on to purchase additional properties for investment, building wealth, and creating a steady stream of income. Chock full of encouragement, filled with success stories, examples, charts, and graphs, Smart Homeowners Finish Rich is destined to become the standard how-to book for purchasing a home and turning real estate into lasting wealth and security. From the Hardcover edition.

Automatic Millionaire Homeowner: A Powerful Plan to Finish Rich in Real Estate. unabr. ed. David Bach. Read by Gavin Hammon. 5 CDs. (Running Time: 5 hrs. 45 mins.). 2006. audio compact disk 38.25 (978-1-4159-2697-0(2)); 90.00 (978-1-4159-2695-6(6)) Books on Tape.
In his breakout 2004 bestseller, The Automatic Millionaire, David Bach showed why owning your own home is not only smart, it's the core secret to becoming a millionaire. In his new book, tailored for a Canadian readership, he shows exactly how to make that happen with a simple, automatic plan you can read in an hour and put into place today. Renters will learn how to buy a first home, even with lousy credit and tiny savings. And existing homeowners will find out how to turn the roof over their heads into a powerful investment that doubles, triples, and quadruples in price while you simply enjoy living in it. And while you don't have to be a landlord to finish rich, if you're willing to be, David teaches you how simple it really is to buy a rental property even while you're paying the mortgage on your home.

Automatic Pilot. Paul R. Scheele. Read by Paul R. Scheele. 1 cass. (Running Time: 34 mins.). (Paraliminal Tapes Ser.). 1990. 24.95 (978-0-925480-15-6(0)) Learn Strategies.
Helps listener eliminiate self-sabotage & negative self-talk to move toward goals.

Automatic Update Service. 1997. bk. 139.00 (ACS-1397) PA Bar Inst.
PBI will publish supplements & new editions as appropriate, to keep the book up to date. Everyone who purchases the book will receive each update with an invoice & an option to return it with no further obligation.

Automatic Writing. Tara Sutphen. 1 cass. (Tara Sutphen Meditation Tapes Ser.). 11.98 (978-0-87554-539-4(4), TS205) Valley Sun.

Automating CAD - CAM Databases: Human Factor, Global Engineering Document Management. 1 cass. 1990. 8.50 Recorded Res.

Automating the Legal System: Automation for Police, Prosecution Courts & Corrections. unabr. ed. S. Pal Asija. Read by S. Pal Asija. 12 cass. (Running Time: 12 hrs.). 1974. 100.00 (978-1-891325-05-2(1)) Our Pal.

Automation, Process Control, & Measurement Equipment in Germany: A Strategic Reference 2006. Compiled by Icon Group International, Inc. Staff. 2007. ring bd. 195.00 (978-0-497-35963-8(4)) Icon Grp.

Automobile Accidents. Robert S. Sigman. Read by Robert S. Sigman. 1 cass. (Running Time: 60 mins.). (Law for the Layman Ser.). 1990. 16.95 (978-1-878135-02-5(3)) Legovac.
What you need to know before you see a lawyer.

Automobile Sales. Betty L. Randolph. 1 cass. (Specialized Sales Ser.). 1989. bk. 14.98 (978-1-55909-218-0(1), 120PM); Randolph Tapes.
Ocean Format (P) or Music Format (PM).

Automobiles & Highways: Design Defects & Maintenance Liability. 1 cass. (Running Time: 1 hr.). 1988. bk. 115.00 incl. book.; 65.00 PA Bar Inst.

Automobiles in Bulgaria: A Strategic Reference 2007. Compiled by Icon Group International, Inc. Staff. 2007. ring bd. 195.00 (978-0-497-35847-1(6)) Icon Grp.

Automotive Accessories & Specialty Equipment in Belgium: A Strategic Reference 2006. Compiled by Icon Group International, Inc. Staff. 2007. ring bd. 195.00 (978-0-497-35823-5(9)) Icon Grp.

Automotive Aftermarket Products in Japan: A Strategic Reference 2007. Compiled by Icon Group International, Inc. Staff. 2007. ring bd. 195.00 (978-0-497-82319-1(5)) Icon Grp.

Automotive Aftermarket Products in Netherlands: A Strategic Reference 2006. Compiled by Icon Group International, Inc. Staff. 2007. ring bd. 195.00 (978-0-497-82366-5(7)) Icon Grp.

Automotive Aftermarket Products in South Korea: A Strategic Reference 2006. Compiled by Icon Group International, Inc. Staff. 2007. ring bd. 195.00 (978-0-497-35876-1(X)) Icon Grp.

Automotive ASE Test Prep: Advance Engine Performance, Set 2. Delmar Publishers Staff. (C). 2000. audio compact disk 633.95 (978-0-7668-2496-6(9)) Pub: Delmar. Dist(s): CENGAGE Learn

Automotive Parts & Accessories in Mexico: A Strategic Reference 2007. Compiled by Icon Group International, Inc. Staff. 2007. ring bd. 195.00 (978-0-497-82348-1(9)) Icon Grp.

Automotive Parts & Equipment in Germany: A Strategic Reference 2006. Compiled by Icon Group International, Inc. Staff. 2007. ring bd. 195.00 (978-0-497-35964-5(2)) Icon Grp.

Automotive Services, Parts, & Accessories in Germany: A Strategic Reference 2006. Compiled by Icon Group International, Inc. Staff. 2007. ring bd. 195.00 (978-0-497-35965-2(0)) Icon Grp.

Automotive Tuning Products in Greece: A Strategic Reference 2007. Compiled by Icon Group International, Inc. Staff. 2007. ring bd. 195.00 (978-0-497-35989-8(8)) Icon Grp.

***Auton Invasion.** Terrance Dicks. Narrated by Caroline John. (Running Time: 4 hrs. 0 mins. 0 sec.). (Doctor Who Ser.). (ENG.). 2010. audio compact disk 34.95 (978-1-4056-8766-9(5)) Pub: AudioGO. Dist(s): Perseus Dist

Autophagia. John M. Bennett & Mike Hovancsek. 1 cass. (Running Time: 1 hr. 30 mins.). 1993. 7.00 (978-0-935350-50-0(0)) Luna Bisonte.
Poetry & sound art.

Autopsy for an Empire Pt. 1: The Seven Leaders Who Built the Soviet Regime. collector's ed. Dmitri Volkogonov. Read by Geoffrey Howard. 8 cass. (Running Time: 12 hrs.). 1999. 64.00 (978-0-7366-4660-4(4), 5042-A) Books on Tape.
This profile of the seven successive Soviet leaders from Lenin to Gorbachev, depicts in painstaking detail the progressive self-destruction of the Leninst system. As the later leaders, Brezhnev, Andropov, Chernenko, fiddled, believing that nothing in Leninist politics needed altering, merely perfecting, the Soviet empire began to unravel.

Autopsy for an Empire Pt. 2: The Seven Leaders Who Built the Soviet Regime. collector's ed. Dmitri Volkogonov. Read by Geoffrey Howard. 8 cass. (Running Time: 12 hrs.). 1999. 64.00 (978-0-7366-4723-6(6), 5042-B) Books on Tape.

Autopsy Room. Dennis Cotton & Andrew Richard Cross. Ed. by Simon Cross & Roger Start. 2000. cd-rom 839.00 (978-90-5702-164-0(1)) Pub: CRC Pr. Dist(s): Taylor and Fran

Autour de la Litterature. 4th ed. Schofer & Rice. audio compact disk 6.50 (978-0-8384-0227-6(5)) Heinle.

Autour de la Lune, Level 1. Jules Verne. (FRE.). bk. 14.95 (978-2-09-032982-7(3), CL9823E) Pub: Cle Intl FRA. Dist(s): Continental Bk

Autumn see Poetry of Pasternak

Autumn: Classics for all Seasons. 1 cass. (Running Time: 1 hr.). 7.98 (TA 30327); audio compact disk 8.78 Jewel box. (TA 80327) NewSound.

Autumn Air. unabr. ed. Short Stories. Susan Sawyer & Cynthia Sterling. 1 cass. (Running Time: 1 hr. 30 mins.). (Afterglow Romantic Walks Ser.). 1999. pap. bk. 10.99 (978-1-892026-03-3(1)) Afterglow.
Two original romance stories with Autumn themes.

Autumn Begins see Poetry & Voice of James Wright

Autumn Castle. unabr. ed. Kim Wilkins. Read by Richard Aspel. 17 CDs. (Running Time: 19 hrs. 30 mins.). 2005. audio compact disk 123.95 (978-1-74093-653-8(1)) Pub: Bolinda Pubng AUS. Dist(s): Bolinda Pub Inc

Autumn Castle. unabr. ed. Kim Wilkins. Read by Richard Aspel. (Running Time: 19 hrs. 30 mins.). 2009. 43.95 (978-1-74214-531-0(0), 9781742145310) Pub: Bolinda Pubng AUS. Dist(s): Bolinda Pub Inc

Autumn Garden. unabr. ed. Lillian Hellman. Read by David Clennon & Julie Harris. 2 cass. (Running Time: 2 hrs.). Dramatization. 2001. 22.95; audio compact disk 24.95 L A Theatre.

Autumn Leaves, Leve 2. (Yamaha Clavinova Connection Ser.). 2004. disk 1.04 (978-0-634-09587-0(0)) H Leonard.

Autumn Leaves - ShowTrax. Arranged by Paris Rutherford. 1 CD. (Running Time: 5 mins.). 2000. audio compact disk 19.95 (08742290) H Leonard.
Set in a medium up swing, this tasty standard is easily performed by high school jazz groups.

Autumn Lover. Elizabeth Lowell. Read by Laural Merlington. (Playaway Adult Fiction Ser.). 2008. 84.99 (978-1-60640-584-0(5)) Find a World.

Autumn Lover. abr. ed. Elizabeth Lowell. Read by Laural Merlington. (Running Time: 6 hrs.). 2008. audio compact disk 14.99 (978-1-4233-3215-2(6), 9781423332152, BCD Value Price) Brilliance Audio.

Autumn Lover. unabr. ed. Elizabeth Lowell. Read by Laural Merlington. 1 MP3-CD. (Running Time: 11 hrs.). 2007. 24.95 (978-1-4233-3210-7(5), 9781423332107, Brilliance MP3); 39.25 (978-1-4233-3211-4(3), 9781423332114, Brinc Audio MP3 Lib); 39.25 (978-1-4233-3213-8(X), 9781423332138, BADLE); 24.95 (978-1-4233-3212-1(1), 9781423332121, BAD); 92.25 (978-1-4233-3207-7(5), 9781423332077, BrilAudUnabridg); audio compact disk 34.95 (978-1-4233-3208-4(3), 9781423332084, Bril Audio CD Unabri); audio compact disk 97.25 (978-1-4233-3209-1(1), 9781423332091, BriAudCD Unabrid) Brilliance Audio.

Autumn of the Gun. abr. ed. Ralph Compton. Read by Jim Gough. 4 cass. (Running Time: 6 hrs.). 2000. 24.95 (978-1-890990-49-7(3), 99049) Otis Audio.
The final installment of the "Trail of the Gunfighter" trilogy finds the legendary gunslinger, Nathan Stone, on a collision course with the one man as quick-on-the-draw as he, the teenage son he never knew.

Autumn Rivulets see Twentieth-Century Poetry in English, No. 17, Walt Whitman Speaks for Himself

Autumn Road. Brian Swann. (Osu journal award Poetry Ser.). 2005. audio compact disk 9.95 (978-0-8142-9090-3(6)) Pub: Ohio St U Pr. Dist(s): Chicago Distribution Ctr

Autumn Skies. Elizabeth Lord & Ruth Sillers. (Story Sound Ser.). 2007. 54.95 (978-1-84652-052-5(5)); audio compact disk 71.95 (978-1-84652-053-2(3)) Pub: Mgna Lrg Print GBR. Dist(s): Ulverscroft US

Autumn Song see Twentieth-Century Poetry in English, No. 1, Recordings of Poets Reading Their Own Poetry

Autumnal Tints. unabr. ed. Henry David Thoreau. Narrated by Brett Barry. (Running Time: 1 hr. 12 mins.). 2008. 8.95 (978-0-9793115-3-6(5)); audio compact disk 8.95 (978-0-9793115-2-9(7)) Silver Hollow.

***Autumn's Promise.** unabr. ed. Shelley Shepard Gray. (Running Time: 10 hrs. 30 mins.). (Seasons of Sugarcreek Ser.: Bk. 3). 2010. 29.95 (978-1-4417-7081-3(X)); 65.95 (978-1-4417-7078-3(X)); audio compact disk 100.00 (978-1-4417-7079-0(8)) Blckstn Audio.

Aux Quatre Coins du Monde. l.t. ed. Anne Wiazemsky. (French Ser.). (FRE., 2001. bk. 30.99 (978-2-84011-439-0(9)) Pub: UlverLrgPrint GBR. Dist(s): Ulverscroft US

Availability Analysis. Martin V. Sussman. 6 cass. (Running Time: 6 hrs.). 405.00 incl. manual. (978-0-8412-1135-3(3), 73); 25.00 manual. (978-0-8412-1136-0(1)) Am Chemical.
Teaches the fundamental of availability analysis - the technique used for tracking work energy as it flows through a process.

Avalanche. unabr. ed. Gertrude Franklin Horn Atherton. Read by Flo Gibson. 3 cass. (Running Time: 4 hrs. 1 min.). 1997. 16.95 (978-1-55685-495-8(1), 495-1) Audio Bk Con.
An avalanche of mystery & intrigue surrounds the young French wife of a San Francisco businessman.

Avalanche Express. unabr. ed. Colin Forbes. Read by Clifford Norgate. 8 cass. (Running Time: 11 hrs. 10 mins.). 2001. 69.95 (978-1-85089-710-1(7), 88092) Pub: ISIS Audio GBR. Dist(s): Ulverscroft US
The highest-ranking defector ever to come out of the USSR - a man of vital importance to both East & West - is under the protection of a hand-picked

team of British & American agents. He is tracked by the KGB across half a continent, men with orders to stop at nothing in their mission of extermination.

Avalon. unabr. ed. Eric Newby. 1 cass. 1993. 56.00 Books on Tape.

Avalon High. unabr. ed. Meg Cabot. Read by Debra Wiseman. 4 cass. (Running Time: 6 hrs. 50 mins.). (YA). (gr. 7-10). 2005. 35.00 (978-0-307-20664-0(5), Listening Lib) Pub: Random Audio Pubg. Dist(s): Random
Ellie's parents, medievalist college professors, are on sabbatical and have moved the family from Minnesota to Annapolis, MD, for the school year. Ellie is named after a character in Alfred Lord Tennyson's poem, "The Lady of Shalott." The teen accepts the move and when she meets Will Wagner and his friends while running in the park with her father, there is an instant connection that changes their lives forever.

Avalon Is Rising! Perf. by Isaac Bonewits & Real Magic. 1. 2003. audio compact disk 12.95 (978-1-59157-029-5(8)) Assn for Cons.
A performance of Neo-Pagan Music by Isaac Bonewits, a founder of Ar nDriaocht Fein (A Druid Fellowship), and his band Real Magic.

Avance: Curso de Espanol para Nivel Intermedio. Concha Moreno et al. 1 cass. (Running Time: 1 hr. 30 mins.). (SPA., (978-84-7143-630-6(2)) Sociedad General ESP.

Avant-Garde Methods of Stock Market Prediction. Carol S. Mull. 1 cass. 8.95 (631) Am Fed Astrologers.
An AFA Convention workshop tape.

Avanti! R. Brambilla & A. Crotti. Ed. by J. Owen. (C). 1988. 220.00 (978-0-85950-848-3(X)) Pub: NelsonThorne GBR. Dist(s): Trans-Atl Phila

***Avanzando Mas Alla del Confinamento de la Mente.** Tr. of Advancing Beyond the Confinements of Your Mindset. (SPA.). 2009. audio compact disk 18.00 (978-0-944129-37-1(4)) High Praise.

Avare. Molière. pap. bk. 24.95 (978-88-7754-166-6(0)) Pub: Cideb ITA. Dist(s): Distribks Inc

Avare. Molière. Perf. by Michel Aumont & Francoise Seigner. 2 cass. (Running Time: 2 hrs.). (FRE.). 1991. 26.95 (1089-RF) Olivia & Hill.
In this 17th-century comedy, the rich miser Harpagon lets his avarice get in the way of fatherly love. His greed promotes subterfuge, farce & comedy.

Ava's Man. unabr. ed. Rick Bragg. Narrated by Tom Stechschulte. 6 cass. (Running Time: 7 hrs. 45 mins.). 2002. 60.00 (978-0-7887-9583-1(X)); audio compact disk 72.00 (978-1-4025-2072-3(7)) Recorded Bks.
Everybody's heard of John Henry, Paul Bunyan, and Pecos Bill, but nobody's ever heard of Charlie Bundrum. He's not what you'd call a legend: a man who lived the Depression-era hardscrabble life on the Georgia-Alabama border so intensely and so fully that it became the stuff of poetry in the hands of his grandson, Rick Bragg. It's a rough story about rough people and their rough lives. But like Bundrum's bootleg liquor, it goes down sweetly. He is just brimming with stories about his grandfather, and they're all filled with affection for the man.

Ave Caesar see Poetry of Robinson Jeffers

Ave Maria. 2004. disk 7.95 (978-0-634-08654-0(5)) H Leonard.

Avenger. William Shatner. (Star Trek Ser.). 2004. 10.95 (978-0-7435-4680-5(6)) Pub: S&S Audio. Dist(s): S and S Inc

Avenger. abr. ed. Frederick Forsyth. Read by Eric Conger. (Running Time: 6 hrs. 0 mins. 0 sec.). (ENG.). 2007. audio compact disk 14.95 (978-1-4272-0311-3(3)) Pub: Macmill Audio. Dist(s): Macmillan

Avenger. unabr. ed. Frederick Forsyth. Read by Eric Conger. 8 cass. (Running Time: 12 hrs.). 2003. 69.95 (978-0-7927-3014-9(3), CSL 584, Chivers Sound Lib) AudioGO.

Avenger. unabr. rev. ed. Frederick Forsyth. Read by Eric Conger. 8 cass. (Running Time: 12 hrs. 0 mins. 0 sec.). (ENG., 2003. 39.95 (978-1-55927-947-5(8)) Pub: Macmill Audio. Dist(s): Macmillan

Avenger Distant 12 Copy Mixed Assortment. abr. ed. Robert Ludlum. 2003. 310.40 (978-1-59397-404-6(3)) Pub: Macmill Audio. Dist(s): Macmillan

Avengers: A Jewish War Story. abr. ed. Rich Cohen. Read by Larry King. 4 cass. (Running Time: 6 hrs.). 2004. 25.00 (978-1-931056-03-8(X), N Millennium Audio) New Millenn Enter.
In 1944, a band of Jewish guerrillas emerged from the forest to join the Russian army in its attack on Vilna, the capital of Lithuania. Headed by Abba Kovner & Zionist leader with two teenaged girls as chief lieutenants. In the last days of the war they hatched a plan for retaliation, by smuggling enough poison into Nuremberg to kill 10,000 Nazis. "The Avengers" tells what happened to these rebels, how they took revenge & how they moved beyond the violence & made new lives.

Avenging Angel. abr. ed. Rex Burns. Read by Charlton Griffin. 2 vols. 2003. (978-1-58807-668-7(7)) Am Pubng Inc.

Avenidas. Patti J. Marinelli. (C). bk. & stu. ed. 136.95 (978-0-8384-8210-0(4)) Heinle.

Avenidas. Patti J. Marinelli & Oramas. (C). 2002. audio compact disk 26.25 (978-0-8384-2320-2(5)) Heinle.

Avenidas. Patti J. Marinelli & Mirta Oramas. (C). bk. & stu. ed. 98.95 (978-0-8384-7498-3(5)); bk. & stu. ed. 154.95 (978-0-8384-7769-4(0)); bk. & stu. ed. 134.95 (978-0-8384-7903-2(0)); bk. & stu. ed. 165.95 (978-0-8384-7904-9(9)); bk. & stu. ed. 84.95 (978-0-8384-7930-8(8)); bk. & stu. ed. 107.95 (978-0-8384-7931-5(6)) Heinle.

Avenidas. Patti J. Marinelli & Mirta Oramas. 2002. bk. 3.00 (978-0-8384-2318-9(3)) Heinle.

Avent Llamada America. unabr. ed. Abuelo Historias Del. (SPA.). 2007. audio compact disk 13.00 (978-958-8318-06-6(8)) Pub: Yoyo Music COL. Dist(s): YoYoMusic

Aventura de los Lentes de Oro - Aventuras de Sherlock Holmes. unabr. ed. Arthur Conan Doyle.Tr. of Adventure of the Golden Lenses - Adventures of Sherlock Holmes. (SPA.). 2002. audio compact disk 13.00 (978-958-43-0136-9(5)) YoYoMusic.

Aventura! 1. James F. Funston & Alejandro Vargas Bonilla. 185.95 (978-0-8219-4070-9(8)); 12.95 (978-0-8219-3972-7(6)); 140.95 (978-0-8219-4072-3(4)); 188.95 (978-0-8219-4099-0(6)); 151.95 (978-0-8219-4097-6(X)); audio compact disk 285.95 (978-0-8219-3983-3(1)); audio compact disk 140.95 (978-0-8219-3978-9(5)); audio compact disk 129.95 (978-0-8219-4071-6(6)); audio compact disk 150.95 (978-0-8219-3979-6(3)); audio compact disk 198.95 (978-0-8219-4098-3(8)); audio compact disk 161.95 (978-0-8219-4094-5(5)); audio compact disk 19.95 (978-0-8219-4119-5(4)); audio compact disk 61.95 (978-0-8219-4106-5(2)) EMC-Paradigm.

Aventura! 2. James F. Funston & Alejandro Vargas Bonilla. 185.95 (978-0-8219-4073-0(2)); 120.95 (978-0-8219-4074-7(0)); 140.95 (978-0-8219-4075-4(9)); 188.95 (978-0-8219-4111-9(9)); 151.95 (978-0-8219-4109-6(7)); audio compact disk 285.95 (978-0-8219-4006-8(6)); audio compact disk 140.95 (978-0-8219-3999-4(8)); audio compact disk 129.95 (978-0-8219-3994-9(7)); audio compact disk 150.95 (978-0-8219-4001-3(5)); audio compact disk 198.95 (978-0-8219-4110-2(0)); audio compact disk 19.95 (978-0-8219-4123-2(2)) EMC-Paradigm.

Aventura! 3. James F. Funston & Alejandro Vargas Bonilla. 185.95 (978-0-8219-4076-1(7)); 198.95 (978-0-8219-4104-1(6)); 188.95 (978-0-8219-4105-8(4)); 151.95 (978-0-8219-4103-4(8)); audio compact disk 285.95 (978-0-8219-4023-5(6)); audio compact disk 140.95 (978-0-8219-4019-8(8)); audio compact disk 129.95 (978-0-8219-4015-0(5)); audio compact disk 150.95 (978-0-8219-4021-1(X)); audio compact disk 140.95 (978-0-8219-4078-5(3)); audio compact disk 161.95 (978-0-8219-4100-3(3)); audio compact disk 19.95 (978-0-8219-4127-0(5)) EMC-Paradigm.

Aventura! 4. James F. Funston & Alejandro Vargas Bonilla. 90.95 (978-0-8219-3947-5(5)); 60.95 (978-0-8219-3946-8(7)); 34.95 (978-0-8219-3954-3(8)); audio compact disk 140.95 (978-0-8219-3949-9(1)); audio compact disk 70.95 (978-0-8219-3944-4(0)); audio compact disk 129.95 (978-0-8219-4027-3(9)); audio compact disk 39.95 (978-0-8219-3948-2(3)) EMC-Paradigm.

Aventuras de Arturo Gordon PYM. abr. ed. Edgar Allan Poe. Read by Carlos J. Vega. 3 CDs.Tr. of Adventures of Arthur Gordon PYM. (SPA.). 2002. audio compact disk 17.00 (978-958-9494-92-9(7)) YoYoMusic.

Aventuras de Sherlock Holmes. unabr. ed. Arthur Conan Doyle. Read by Carlos Zambrano. 3 CDs.Tr. of Adventures of Sherlock Holmes. (SPA.). 2002. audio compact disk 17.00 (978-958-9494-88-2(9)) YoYoMusic.

Aventuras de Sherlock Holmes & Mas Aventuras de Sherlock Holmes: The Adventures of Sherlock Holmes & More Adventures of Sherlock Holmes. unabr. ed. Arthur Conan Doyle. Read by Carlos Zambrano. (YA). 2007. 39.99 (978-1-59895-980-2(8)) Find a World.

Aventuras de Tom Sawyer. abr. ed. Mark Twain. Read by Yadira Sánchez. 3 CDs.Tr. of Adventures of Tom Sawyer. (SPA.). 2001. audio compact disk 17.00 (978-958-9494-26-4(9)) YoYoMusic.

Aventuras de un Soldadito de Plomo. Hans Christian Andersen. 1 cass. (Running Time: 1 hr.). (SPA.). (J). 1996. pap. bk. 19.50 (978-1-58085-255-5(6)) Interlingua VA.

Aventuras em Alfabetização: Portuguese Language Teaching. (POR.). 2005. audio compact disk (978-0-7428-1523-0(4)) CCLS Pubg Hse.

Aventuras em Comunicação Livro 3 CD: Portuguese Language Teaching. (POR.). 2006. audio compact disk (978-0-7428-1594-0(3)) CCLS Pubg Hse.

Aventuras em Comunicação Livro 4 CD: Portuguese Language Teaching. (POR.). 2006. audio compact disk (978-0-7428-1595-7(1)) CCLS Pubg Hse.

Aventuras em Comunicação Livros 1 e 2 CD: Portuguese Language Teaching. (POR.). 2006. audio compact disk (978-0-7428-1579-7(X)) CCLS Pubg Hse.

Aventuras Literarias. 2003. (978-0-618-22086-1(0)) CENGAGE Learn.

Aventure de Babar. 1 cass. (FRE.). (J). (gr. 3 up). 1991. bk. 19.95 (1AD076) Olivia & Hill.
While on vacation with the Old Lady Babar is kidnapped.

Aventure de la Cuisiniere. Agatha Christie. Read by Madeleine Barbulee. 1 cass.Tr. of Adventure of the Clapham Cook. (FRE.). 1992. 16.95 (1540-RF) Olivia & Hill.
ercule Poirot mystery.

Aventure e Walter Schnaffs. Guy de Maupassant. Ed. by Albin Michel. 1 cass. (Running Time: 60 mins.). (Lesehefte der Sprachkurse der Genossenschaft Migros Ser.: 2). (FRE.). 11.95 incl. French text & dictations. Interlingua VA.

Aventures d'Alice au Pays de Merveilles: Advanced. unabr. ed. 2 cass. (FRE.). bk. 29.95 (SFR375) J Norton Pubs.

Aventures de Sherlock Holmes, Vol. 1. Arthur Conan Doyle. 2 cass. (Running Time: 2 hrs.).Tr. of Adventures of Sherlock Holmes. (FRE.). 1992. 28.95 (1558-LV) Olivia & Hill.
Includes: "Un scandale en Bohemia"; "La ligue des rouquins"; "Une affaire d'identite.".

Aventures de Sherlock Holmes, Vol. 2. Arthur Conan Doyle. 2 cass.Tr. of Adventures of Sherlock Holmes. (FRE.). 1992. 28.95 (1559-LV) Olivia & Hill.
Le Mysteres du Val Boscombe; Les Cinq Pepins d'orange; L'homme a la levre tordue.

Aventures de Sherlock Holmes, Vol. 3. Arthur Conan Doyle. 2 cass. (Running Time: 2 hrs.).Tr. of Adventures of Sherlock Holmes. (FRE.). 1992. 28.95 (1560-LV) Olivia & Hill.
Includes: "L'Escarboucle bleue"; "La Ruban Mouchete"; "Le Pouce de l'ingenieur.".

Aventures de Sherlock Holmes, Vol. 4. Arthur Conan Doyle. 2 cass. (Running Time: 2 hrs.).Tr. of Adventures of Sherlock Holmes. (FRE.). 1995. 26.95 (1657-LV) Olivia & Hill.
Includes: "Un Aristocrate celibataire"; "Le Diademe de Beryls"; "Les Etres rouges." Read by a cast of actors.

Aventures de Telemaque see Treasury of French Prose

Aviary Gate. unabr. ed. Katie Hickman. Narrated by Josephine Bailey. (Running Time: 12 hrs. 30 mins. 0 sec.). (ENG.). 2008. audio compact disk 29.99 (978-1-4001-5779-2(X)); audio compact disk 79.99 (978-1-4001-3779-4(9)) Pub: Tantor Media. Dist(s): IngramPubServ

Aviary Gate. unabr. ed. Katie Hickman. Read by Josephine Bailey. (Running Time: 12 hrs. 30 mins. 0 sec.). (ENG.). 2008. audio compact disk 39.99 (978-1-4001-0779-7(2)) Pub: Tantor Media. Dist(s): IngramPubServ

Aviation Adventure. Knowledge Adventure. (Adventure Ser.). 35.00 (978-1-56997-089-8(0)) Knowldge Adv.

Aviation Equipment & Services in Germany: A Strategic Reference 2006. Compiled by Icon Group International, Inc. Staff. 2007. ring bd. 195.00 (978-0-497-35966-9(9)) Icon Grp.

Aviation Equipment & Services in Russia: A Strategic Reference 2006. Compiled by Icon Group International, Inc. Staff. 2007. ring bd. 195.00 (978-0-497-82398-6(5)) Icon Grp.

Aviators. unabr. collector's ed. W. E. B. Griffin. Read by Michael Russotto. 11 cass. (Running Time: 16 hrs. 30 mins.). (Brotherhood of War Ser.: No. 8). 1995. 88.00 (978-0-7366-3086-3(4), 133384) Books on Tape.
America's dedicated soldiers assemble Air Assault Division, almost overnight, for battles in Vietnam. It's their best chance at success.

Avicenna & Medieval Muslim Philosophy. unabr. ed. Thomas Gaskill. Read by Lynn Redgrave. (Running Time: 10800 sec.). (World of Philosophy Ser.). 2006. audio compact disk 25.95 (978-0-7861-6386-1(0)) Pub: Blckstn Audio. Dist(s): NetLibrary CO

Avoid Every Kind of Evil. Dan Corner. 1 cass. 3.00 (16) Evang Outreach.

Avoid Premature Aging. Ronald Thayer. 1 cass. (Running Time: 40 mins.). 11.00 (9432) Meyer Res Grp.
Dr. Ronald Thayer presents a guide for achieving & retaining peak all-around condition, using the "Health Triangle" of thoughts, exercise & nutrition.

Avoid Premature Aging. Ronald Thayer. 1 cass. 10.00 (SP100053) SMI Intl.
Age is more a matter of attitude & fitness than it is of years. Use the "Health Triangle" of thoughts, exercise & nutrition to feel young, act young & look young. An easy to follow guide for achieving & retaining peak all-around condition.

Avoid the Conflict Trap. unabr. ed. Pat Wagner. Read by Pat Wagner. Read by Alan Dumas. Ed. by Judy Byers. 1 cass. (Running Time: 55 mins.). 1997. 12.95 (978-0-9642678-6-2(1)) Pattern Res.
Avoid the roles of bully, victim & meddler in the workplace.

Avoiding ERISA Icebergs. 4 cass. (Running Time: 4 hrs.). 1999. bk. 99.00 (ACS-2219) PA Bar Inst.
Plan sponsors, administrators & other plan fiduciaries are being held to ever higher standards by Congress, the IRS, the DOL, & the courts. ERISA litigation continues to increase, producing a growing body of law with ever greater financial stakes for businesses & employees. Lawyers who practice in this area need clear, concise guidance on how to avoid or successfully resolve the many ERISA problems in hiding just beneath the surface.

Avoiding Idols: 1 Cor. 10:14-22. Ed Young. 1986. 4.95 (978-0-7417-1503-6(1), 503) Win Walk.

Avoiding Malpractice in California: Guidance for Professional Responsibility. Read by Ronald Stovitz et al. 5 cass. (Running Time: 5 hrs. 15 mins.). 1990. 97.00 Incl. Ethics: 4.30 hrs., Law Practice Management: 15 min. & Elimination of Substance Abuse/Stress Management: 30 min., & 124p. tape materials. (MI-54130) Cont Ed Bar-CA.
Covers conflicts of interest; fees & fee disputes; advertising; client communications & relationships; insufficient legal background; state disciplinary matters; & problems of substance abuse.

Avoiding Option Trading Traps: What to Look for & Strategies for Success. Instructed by Larry McMillan. 1. (Running Time: 90 mins.). (Trade Secrets Audio Ser.). 2002. 19.95 (978-1-931611-66-4(1)) Marketplace Bks.
Renowned author, Larry McMillan, shows you how to avoid the 5 most common - and costly - mistakes option traders make. Master his methods for using put-call ratios, picking the right option, and deciding how much to risk and so much more. McMillan shows you what to do in typical tough spots - and how to avoid them in the future. This video is "must-viewing" for any investor looking to move beyond the realm of options theory - into the world of option profits.

Avoiding Option Trading Traps: What to Look for & Strategies for Success. Instructed by Larry McMillan. 2005. audio compact disk 19.95 (978-1-59280-234-0(6)) Marketplace Bks.

Avoiding Power Struggles with Kids. 1 CD. (Running Time: 60 mins). 2002. audio compact disk 13.95 (978-1-930429-25-3(8)) Pub: Love Logic. Dist(s): Penton Overseas

Avoiding Sexual Harassment Lawsuits. Ed. by Socrates Media Editors. 2005. audio compact disk 29.95 (978-1-59546-168-1(X)) Pub: Socrates Med LLC. Dist(s): Midpt Trade

Avoiding Spiritual Counterfeiters. John MacArthur, Jr. 4 cass. (Running Time: 4 hrs.). (John MacArthur's Bible Studies). 16.25 (HarperThor) HarpC GBR.

Avoiding Tax Traps under the Revised Inheritance Tax Law. Marcia J. Wexberg. 1 cass. (Running Time: 1 hr.). 1985. 15.00 PA Bar Inst.

Avoiding the Quick Fix Trap. Richard G. Hammes. Read by Richard G. Hammes. 2 cass. (Running Time: 2 hrs.). 29.95 (978-1-882561-75-9(9)) Hammes & Assocs.
Provides insight into how to analyze human resource concerns & determine best solutions, rather than instituting the latest fad.

Avon Lady. abr. ed. Ruchira Avatar Adi Da Samraj staff. 1 cass. 1998. 11.95 (978-1-57097-047-4(5), AT-AL) Dawn Horse Pr.

Avventure di Pinocchio see Pinocchio

Awake & Alert. abr. ed. Robert A. Monroe. Read by Robert A. Monroe. (Mind Food Ser.). 1988. 14.95 (978-1-56102-400-1(7)); Inter Indus.
A powerful stimulus for staying awake with Hemi-Sync signals.

Awake in the Cosmic Dream. Paramhansa Yogananda. 1 cass. (Collector's Ser.: No. 2). 1987. 11.50 (2014) Self Realization.
Paramahansa Yogananda touches upon the entire spectrum of spiritual living - all of the vital necessities for creating a dynamic, living relationship with God. He conveys with delightful humor & compassionate understanding why God is the only permanent solution to the enduring problems of human existence.

Awake in the Cosmic Dream: An Informal Talk by Paramahansa Yogananda. abr. ed. Read by Paramhansa Yogananda. (Collector's Ser.: 2). 2007. audio compact disk 14.00 (978-0-87612-524-3(0)) Self Realization.

Awake Oh Sleeper. Neville Goddard. 1 cass. (Running Time: 62 mins.). 1968. 8.00 (43) J & L Pubns.
Neville taught Imagination Creates Reality. He was a powerfully influential teacher of God as Consciousness.

Awake to the Day. Composed by Ed Bolduc. 2004. audio compact disk 17.00 (978-1-58459-190-0(0)) Wrld Lib Pubns.

Awake, Volume One. 2004. audio compact disk 16.99 (978-7-5124-0072-6(1)) Destiny Image Pubs.

Awaken. Contrib. by Natalie Grant. (Praise Hymn Soundtracks Ser.). 2005. audio compact disk 8.98 (978-5-558-93075-7(6)) Pt of Grace Ent.

Awaken Hope, Shout Jubilee: Los Angeles Religious Education Congress Theme Songs. David Haas et al. 1 CD. 2000. audio compact disk 15.95 (CD-487) GIA Pubns.

Awaken My Heart - The Dawn of Day. Lucien Deiss. 2 cass. (Running Time: 2 hrs.). 17.95 (5309) OR Catholic.
A double collection of music drawn from scriptural inspiration. These well-developed selections are useful throughout the year in eucharistic liturgies, morning or evening prayer promotes the role of the choir as well as an engaging dialogue between choir & congregation.

Awaken the Genie Within(tm) Manifesting Your Heart's Desire. 3 CD's. (Running Time: 3 hrs. 35 mins.). 2005. audio compact disk 49.00 (978-0-9662250-1-3(5)) Kystar Pubg.

Awaken the Genius. Eldon Taylor. 2 cass. (Running Time: 62 mins. per cass.). (Omniphonics Ser.). 29.95 incl. script Set. (978-1-55978-800-7(3), 4001) Progress Aware Res.
3-D soundtrack with underlying subliminal affirmations, night & day versions.

Awaken the Genius: Adventures in Self-Discovery. Patrick K. Porter. Ed. by Mark Horowitz. 2 cass. (Running Time: 2 hrs.). 16.00 (978-0-9637611-4-9(5)) Positive Chngs Hypnosis.
Self-help guided imagery.

Awaken the Genius Audio Book. Patrick K. Porter. 2 cass. (978-1-887630-06-1(6)) Renaissnce Pub.
Psychology self-help.

Awaken the Genius Book on Tape. abr. ed. Patrick K. Porter. Ed. by Mark Horowitz. 2 cass. (Running Time: 2 hrs.). 1995. 16.00 (978-0-9637611-3-2(7)) Positive Chngs Hypnosis.
Psychology - self-help.

Awaken the Giant Within: How to Take Immediate Control of Your Mental, Emotional, Physical & Financial Destiny. abr. ed. Anthony Robbins. Read by Anthony Robbins. 1 cass. (Running Time: 13 hrs. 0 mins. 0 sec.). (ENG.).

1991. 13.00 (978-0-671-75018-3(6), Sound Ideas) Pub: S&S Audio. Dist(s): S and S Inc

The self-help superstar's ultimate guide to success through self-mastery. "Awaken the Giant Within" reveals the secret power of core beliefs, quantum questions & life metaphors & tells listeners to take control of those powers to make them work for them.

Awaken the Giant Within: How to Take Immediate Control of Your Mental, Emotional, Physical & Financial Destiny. abr. ed. Anthony Robbins. 2 CDs. (Running Time: 13 hrs. 0 mins. 0 sec.). (ENG.). 2000. audio compact disk 18.00 (978-0-671-58208-1(9), Sound Ideas) Pub: S&S Audio. Dist(s): S and S Inc

Based on his popular Date with Destiny seminars, Robbins unleashes the sleeping giant that lies within all of us, teaching us to harness our untapped abilities, talents & skills.

Awaken the Greatness Within. Guy Finley. (ENG.). 2006. 7.49 (978-1-929320-53-0(1)) Life of Learn.

Awaken the Leader Within. Bill Perkins. Read by Bill Perkins. (ENG.). 2008. audio compact disk 26.99 (978-1-934384-04-6(6)) Pub: Treasure Pub. Dist(s): STL Dist NA

Awaken the Power of Your Supernatural Self. Guy Finley. (ENG.). 2006. 7.49 (978-1-929320-54-7(X)) Life of Learn.

Awaken the Spanish Verbs Within, Disc I. 2004. audio compact disk (978-0-9753143-1-9(9)) Spanish Acad Cu Inst.

Awaken the Spanish Verbs Within, Disc 2. 2004. audio compact disk (978-0-9753143-2-6(7)) Spanish Acad Cu Inst.

Awaken the Spanish Verbs Within, Disc 3. 2004. audio compact disk (978-0-9753143-3-3(5)) Spanish Acad Cu Inst.

Awaken the Spanish Verbs Within, Disc 4. 2004. audio compact disk (978-0-9753143-4-0(3)) Spanish Acad Cu Inst.

Awaken the Spanish Within. 2004. audio compact disk (978-0-9753143-5-7(1)) Spanish Acad Cu Inst.

Awaken the Spanish Within: Medical. 2004. audio compact disk (978-0-9753143-6-4(X)) Spanish Acad Cu Inst.

Awaken to the Eternal: Nisargadatta Maharaj: A Journey of Self-Discovery. Perf. by Alan W. Anderson. Interview with Jack Kornfield. 1 cass. (Running Time: 57 mins.). Dramatization. 1995. (978-1-878019-02-8(3)) Inner Drctns.

The life & teachings of Nisargadatta Maharaj, taken from the video production of the same name.

Awaken your Genius: Adventures in Accelerated Learning. Patrick K. Porter. Ed. by Mark Horowitz. 2 cass. 1995. 16.00 (978-0-9637611-9-4(6)) Positive Chngs Hypnosis.

Self-help.

Awaken Your Heart at Work: Working with Soul for Breakthough Results. Jack L. Canfield. 2004. 11.95 (978-0-7435-4867-0(1)) Pub: S&S Audio. Dist(s): S and S Inc

Awaken Your Inner Genius: Classic. Eldon Taylor. Read by Eldon Taylor. Ed. by Leslie Brice. 1 cass. (Running Time: 1 hr.). 1992. 16.95 (978-1-56705-215-2(0)) Gateways Inst.

Self improvement.

Awaken Your Inner Genius: Harmonies. Eldon Taylor. Read by Eldon Taylor. Ed. by Leslie Brice. 1 cass. (Running Time: 1 hr.). 1992. 16.95 (978-1-56705-216-9(9)) Gateways Inst.

Awaken Your Inner Genius: Ocean. Eldon Taylor. Read by Eldon Taylor. Ed. by Leslie Brice. 1 cass. (Running Time: 1 hr.). 1992. 16.95 (978-1-56705-217-6(7)) Gateways Inst.

Awaken Your Strongest Self: Break Free of Stress, Inner Conflict, & Self-Sabotage. Neil A. Fiore. 2008. audio compact disk 28.00 (978-1-933309-57-6(1)) Pub: A Media Intl. Dist(s): Natl Bk Netwk

***Awakened.** abr. ed. P. C. Cast & Kristin Cast. (Running Time: 5 hrs. 0 mins. 0 sec.). (House of Night Novels Ser.). (YA). 2011. audio compact disk 17.99 (978-1-4272-1073-9(X)) Pub: Macmill Audio. Dist(s): Macmillan

***Awakened.** unabr. ed. P. C. Cast & Kristin Cast. Read by Caitlin Davies. (Running Time: 11 hrs. 0 mins. 0 sec.). (House of Night Novels Ser.). (YA). 2011. audio compact disk 39.99 (978-1-4272-1180-4(9)) Pub: Macmill Audio. Dist(s): Macmillan

Awakened Dreaming. Eldon Taylor. 1 cass. (Running Time: 62 mins.). (Inner Talk Ser.). 16.95 incl. script. (978-1-55978-513-6(6), 53790F) Progress Aware Res.

Soundtrack - Babbling Brook with underlying subliminal affirmations.

Awakened Dreaming. Eldon Taylor. 1 CD. (Running Time: 52 mins.). (Whole Brain Innertalk Ser.). 1998. audio compact disk (978-1-55978-866-3(6)) Progress Aware Res.

Awakened Dreaming. Eldon Taylor. 1 CD. (Running Time: 52 mins.). (Whole Brain Innertalk Ser.). 1999. audio compact disk (978-1-55978-908-0(5)) Progress Aware Res.

Awakened Life. Read by Wayne W. Dyer. 6 cass. (Running Time: 6 hrs.). 1990. 59.95 incl. poster. (978-1-55525-069-0(6), 854AD) Nightingale-Conant.

Beyond traditional ideas of achievement, there is a way of living that offers true freedom from discontent, from sadness, fear, pain & loneliness.

Awakened Life. abr. ed. Wayne W. Dyer. Read by Wayne W. Dyer. 2 CDs. (Running Time: 2 hrs. 0 mins. 0 sec.). (ENG.). 2006. audio compact disk 19.95 (978-0-7435-5196-0(6), Nightgale) Pub: S&S Audio. Dist(s): S and S Inc

Awakened Living. Swami Amar Jyoti. 2 cass. 1980. 12.95 (A-4) Truth Consciousness.

Building a way of life for the 21st century.

***Awakened Mage.** unabr. ed. Karen Miller. Narrated by Kirby Heyborne. (Running Time: 21 hrs. 0 mins. 0 sec.). (Kingmaker, Kingbreaker Ser.). 2010. 34.99 (978-1-4001-6985-6(2)); 24.99 (978-1-4001-8985-4(3)); audio compact disk 49.99 (978-1-4001-1985-1(5)) Pub: Tantor Media. Dist(s): IngramPubServ

***Awakened Mage (Library Edition)** unabr. ed. Karen Miller. Narrated by Kirby Heyborne. (Running Time: 21 hrs. 0 mins.). (Kingmaker, Kingbreaker Ser.). 2010. 49.99 (978-1-4001-9985-3(9)); audio compact disk 119.99 (978-1-4001-4985-8(1)) Pub: Tantor Media. Dist(s): IngramPubServ

Awakened Mind System. abr. ed. Jeffrey Thompson. (Running Time: 1:00:00). 2004. audio compact disk 19.98 (978-1-55961-714-7(4)) Sounds True.

We all seek a state of higher consciousness that awakens and enlivens our whole being. Masters of meditation and yoga, great artists, inventors, and highly accomplished people in many walks of life have learned to develop and live from such a state.

Awakening. Kate Chopin. Narrated by Walter Zimmeman. (Running Time: 5 hrs. 30 mins.). 1980. 26.95 (978-1-59912-840-5(3)) Iofy Corp.

Awakening. Kate Chopin. Read by Liza Ross. (Running Time: 2 hrs. 30 mins.). 2001. 20.95 (978-1-60083-680-0(1)) Iofy Corp.

Awakening. Kate Chopin. Read by Shelly Frasier. (Running Time: 5 hrs. 48 mins.). 2005. 25.95 (978-1-60083-603-9(8), Audiofy Corp) Iofy Corp.

Awakening. Thomas Eno. 2 cass. (Running Time: 3 hrs.). 11.98 (978-1-57734-147-5(3), 07001576) Covenant Comms.

Awakening. Robert Gass. 1 CD. (Running Time: 1 hr. 2 min.). 2003. audio compact disk (978-1-891319-76-1(0)) Spring Hill CO.

Awakening. Swami Amar Jyoti. 1 cass. 1979. 9.95 (K-25) Truth Consciousness.

Rebirth into the Spirit. Why do we fear God? Principle is higher than relationship.

Awakening. Contrib. by Promise Keepers. Prod. by Bernie Herms. Contrib. by Don Moen & Chris Thomason. 2005. audio compact disk 16.98 (978-5-558-97541-3(5)) Integrity Music.

Awakening. Eldon Taylor. Read by Eldon Taylor. Ed. by Leslie Brice. 1 cass. (Running Time: 1 hr.). 1992. 16.95 (978-1-56705-291-6(6)) Gateways Inst.

Self improvement.

Awakening. Eldon Taylor. 1 cass. (Running Time: 62 mins.). (Inner Talk Ser.). 16.95 incl. script. (978-1-55978-009-4(6), 5409C) Progress Aware Res.

Soundtrack - Musical Themes with underlying subliminal affirmations.

Awakening. abr. ed. Kate Chopin. Read by Liza Ross. 2 CDs. (Running Time: 2 hrs. 30 mins.). 1997. audio compact disk 17.98 (978-962-634-108-7(4), NA210812, Naxos AudioBooks) Naxos.

The story of Edna Pontellier, a beautiful young wife and mother who discovers her true feelings and identity through her love for Robert Lebrun. In doing so, she challenges the bourgeois assumptions of her day.

***Awakening.** unabr. ed. Kelley Armstrong. Read by Cassandra Morris. (ENG.). 2009. (978-0-06-177626-7(2)); (978-0-06-180585-1(8)) HarperCollins Pubs.

***Awakening.** unabr. ed. Kelley Armstrong. Narrated by Cassandra Morris. 1 Playaway. (Running Time: 8 hrs.). (Darkest Powers Trilogy: Bk. 2). (YA). (gr. 7-10). 2009. 64.75 (978-1-4407-3108-2(X)); 56.75 (978-1-4407-3098-6(9)); audio compact disk 77.75 (978-1-4407-3102-0(0)) Recorded Bks.

Awakening. unabr. ed. Kate Chopin. Narrated by Flo Gibson. 4 cass. (Running Time: 5 hrs. 30 mins.). 1986. (978-1-55685-000-4(X)) Audio Bk Con.

A married woman seeks love & the fulfillment of her essential nature outside her stuffy, middle class marriage, at the turn of the century.

Awakening. unabr. ed. Kate Chopin. Narrated by Flo Gibson. (Running Time: 4 hrs. 49 mins.). 2004. audio compact disk 24.95 (978-1-55685-773-7(X)) Audio Bk Con.

Awakening. unabr. ed. Kate Chopin. Read by Grace Conlin. 4 cass. (Running Time: 6 hrs.). 1994. 32.95 (978-0-7861-0848-0(7), 1517) Blckstn Audio.

Edna Pontellier could be mistaken for a modern-day liberated woman. In the summer of her twenty-eighth year, as she watched numerous mothers on a beach, she vowed to satisfy the deep yearnings within herself that she sensed were unfulfilled by marriage & motherhood. She abandoned her conventional role in life & made for herself a controversial & ultimately destructive life.

Awakening. unabr. ed. Kate Chopin. Read by Grace Conlin. 5 CDs. (Running Time: 18000 sec.). 2005. audio compact disk 19.95 (978-0-7861-7643-4(1), ZE1517) Blckstn Audio.

Awakening. unabr. ed. Kate Chopin. Read by Grace Conlin. 1 MP3. (Running Time: 5 hrs. 30 mins.). 2005. 29.95 (978-0-7861-7909-1(0), ZM1517); 19.95 (978-0-7861-3752-7(5), E1517) Blckstn Audio.

Although the book was originally published in 1899, its leading character, Edna Pontellier, could be mistaken for a modern-day liberated woman. In the summer of her twenty-eighth year, as she watched numerous mothers on a beach, she vowed to honor the deep yearnings within her that she sensed were unfulfilled by marriage and motherhood. She abandoned her conventional role in life and made for herself a controversial and ultimately destructive life.

Awakening. unabr. ed. Kate Chopin. Narrated by Laurie Klein. 6 cass. (Running Time: 5 hrs. 30 mins.). 1991. 39.95 (978-1-55686-377-6(2), 377) Books in Motion.

Edna Pontellier has everything: her youth, a successful husband, two healthy children & a beautiful home. But is it enough? One sleepy summer, Edna finds love for the first time & discovers that her life is an orderly prison in which her role as wife & mother requires that she submerge herself & her individuality behind the wall of the needs of others. Edna begins her search for herself.

Awakening. unabr. ed. Kate Chopin. Read by Shelly Frasier. (YA). 2008. 44.99 (978-1-60514-555-6(6)) Find a World.

Awakening. unabr. ed. Kate Chopin. Read by Walter Zimmerman. 5 cass. (Running Time: 6 hrs.). Dramatization. 1981. 26.00 incl. album. (C-62) Jimcin Record.

This early feminist novel caused its author to be ostracized from society.

Awakening. unabr. ed. Kate Chopin. Narrated by Alexandra O'Karma. 4 cass. (Running Time: 5 hrs 30 mins.). 1986. 35.00 (978-1-55690-583-4(1), 86850E7) Recorded Bks.

Edna Pontellier longs for fulfillment of her emotional desire & abandons her comfortable life in pursuit of it.

***Awakening.** unabr. collector's ed. Kelley Armstrong. Narrated by Cassandra Morris. 7 CDs. (Running Time: 8 hrs.). (Darkest Powers Trilogy: Bk. 2). (YA). (gr. 7-10). 2009. audio compact disk 44.95 (978-1-4407-3106-8(3)) Recorded Bks.

Awakening. unabr. collector's ed. Kate Chopin. Read by Frances Cassidy. 5 cass. (Running Time: 5 hrs.). 1995. 30.00 (978-0-7366-2968-3(8), 3659) Books on Tape.

The story of Edna Pontellier, a lovely young woman who has married into upper class Creole society, yet within her is a conflicting need for independence. She abandons the decorous & conventional role common to society & makes for herself a controversial & ultimately destructive life.

Awakening, Vol.. I. Jerry Ahern. Read by Charlie O'Dowd. 2 vols. 2004. 18.00 (978-1-58807-318-1(1)) Am Pubng Inc.

Awakening, Vol.. I. Jerry Ahern. Read by Charlie O'Dowd. 2 vols. No. 10. 2004. (978-1-58807-933-6(3)) Am Pubng Inc.

Awakening, Vol.. II. Jerry Ahern. Read by Charlie O'Dowd. 2 vols. No. 10. 2004. 18.00 (978-1-58807-319-8(X)); (978-1-58807-934-3(1)) Am Pubng Inc.

***Awakening: A New Approach to Faith, Fasting, & Spiritual Freedom.** unabr. ed. Stovall Weems. Narrated by Stovall Weems. (Running Time: 6 hrs. 0 mins. 0 sec.). (ENG.). 2010. 16.09 (978-1-60814-793-9(2)); audio compact disk 22.99 (978-1-59859-917-6(8)) Oasis Audio.

Awakening: Environmental Theme. Eldon Taylor. 1 cass. 16.95 (978-1-55978-537-2(3), 5409F) Progress Aware Res.

Awakening: Obsession, Incarnation, Prayer. Stephen R. Schwartz. 3 cass. 28.00 Riverrun Piermont.

***Awakening & Opening Your Heart: A Journey to Becoming Who You Truly Are.** Ed Rubenstein. (Running Time: 410 minutes). (ENG.). 2009. audio compact disk 18.95 (978-0-9668700-1-5(8)) Stillpt NC.

Awakening at the Gate of Joy. Swami Amar Jyoti. 1 cass. 1986. 9.95 (R-81) Truth Consciousness.

The Absolute without attributes. Theism & devotion in Vedanta. The creation of man. Convergence into wholeness, awakening into Divinity.

Awakening Compassion. Pema Chödrön. 2003. audio compact disk 69.95 (978-1-59179-128-7(6)) Sounds True.

Awakening Consciousness. Swami Amar Jyoti. 1 cass. 1988. 9.95 (R-110) Truth Consciousness.

With guidance of One who knows, finding the inner Light, the highest, brightest point of evolution. In the fully awakened state, all suffering ends. Choosing to transcend ego.

***Awakening Course: Discover the Missing Secret for Attracting Health, Wealth, Happiness, & Love!** unabr. abr. ed. Joe Vitale. (Running Time: 3 hrs. 30 mins.). (ENG.). 2010. 19.98 (978-1-59659-598-9(1), GildAudio); audio compact disk 24.98 (978-1-59659-597-2(3), GildAudio) Pub: Gildan Media. Dist(s): HachBkGrp

Awakening from Experiences. Swami Amar Jyoti. 1 cass. 1982. 9.95 (M-31) Truth Consciousness.

Differences between experiences & consciousness. Coming to direct communion with the Lord.

Awakening God's Gifts. Douglas D. Grimes. 2 CDs. (Running Time: 2 hrs.). 2000. audio compact disk 29.95 (978-0-615-11173-5(4)) CG Prodn.

A spiritual & psychic development program.

Awakening Kundalini. 2 cass. (Running Time: 2 hrs.). (Essence of Yoga Ser.). 14.95 (ST-26) Crystal Clarity.

Explains: why most materialists are bored & unhappy; how the law matter manifest the laws of spirit; how to prepare for the rising of kundalini; kundalini & devotion.

Awakening Kundalini: A Meditation Practice to Transform Your Life. Read by Kelly Howell. 2006. audio compact disk 14.95 (978-1-881451-53-2(4)) Brain Sync.

Awakening Kundalini for Health, Energy, & Consciousness. Chris Kilham. (Running Time: 60 mins.). 2004. audio compact disk 12.95 (978-1-59477-004-3(2)) Inner Tradit.

Awakening Osiris: The Egyptian Book of the Dead. unabr. ed. Read by Jean Houston. Tr. by Normandie Ellis. 2 cass. (Running Time: 3 hrs.). 1995. 15.95 (978-0-944993-31-6(1)) Audio Lit.

This highly-acclaimed rendering of "The Egyptian Book of the Dead" is a brilliant literary illumination of a beautiful spiritual masterpiece.

Awakening Second Sight. Judith Orloff. 3 CDs. (Running Time: 3 hrs 15 mins). 2005. audio compact disk 24.95 (978-1-59179-319-9(X), AW00325D) Sounds True.

Judith Orloff, M.D., is a healer in two worlds: the world of traditional medicine and the invisible world ? the psychic realm. On Awakening Second Sight, Dr. Orloff shares the true story of her struggle to uncover her own psychic abilities ? the patients who inspired her ? and teaches how to awaken your own ?gifts of the spirit.? Join Dr. Orloff in this daring, unique session about:? The true reasons you should develop your own psychic abilities? How to protect yourself from negative psychic energy? Daily practices that use prayer and meditation to ignite your psychic self? Ways to use your dreams as direct conduits to sacred knowledge, healing, and much more.Awakening Second Sight is a respected psychiatrist?s compelling personal story, as well as a provocative guide to the psychic self and how to develop it.

Awakening Series CD Album: Creative Visualizations into Self-Empowerment & Spiritual Identity. Stanley Haluska. 6 CDs. (Running Time: 7 hrs. 39 mins.). 2004. audio compact disk 59.95 (978-0-9758866-0-1(6), AP-106) Awakening Pubns Inc.

The Awakening Series(r) A 5 CD, 10 creative visualization program to guide the individual through the steps of spiritual identification, healing and creation. Through the years it has become evident that these recordings assist in creating a quiet place of relaxation and spiritual attunement. Each individual's experience is unique and appropriate for their own desires and intent. Remember as you journey, the power is not in the recordings, but rather in you, as you are assisted to a place where you can master all things.

***Awakening Series 1.** (ENG.). 1992. 15.95 (978-0-9823691-0-4(7)) Pub: Awakening Pubns Inc. Dist(s): New Leaf Dist

***Awakening Series 2.** (ENG.). 1992. 15.9[illegible] [illegible]978-0-9823691-1-1(5)) Pub: Awakening Pubns Inc. Dist(s): New Le[illegible]

***Awakening Series 3.** (ENG.). 1993. 15.[illegible] [illegible]3-0-9823691-2-8(3)) Pub: Awakening Pubns Inc. Dist(s): New Lea[illegible]

***Awakening Series 4.** (ENG.). 1995. 15.95 (978-0-9823691-3-5(1)) Pub: Awakening Pubns Inc. Dist(s): New Leaf Dist

***Awakening Series 5.** (ENG.). 1995. 15.95 (978-0-9823691-4-2(X)) Pub: Awakening Pubns Inc. Dist(s): New Leaf Dist

Awakening Soul. Lauren Archer. Perf. by Lauren Archer. Music by Todd McGuire. (ENG.). 2006. audio compact disk 22.00 (978-0-9786645-3-4(1)) Positive Central.

Awakening Spirit & Mantra Mysticism. unabr. ed. Russill Paul. (Running Time: 2:00:00). 2008. audio compact disk 19.98 (978-1-55961-970-7(8)) Sounds True.

Awakening Storm. Jonathan Lowe. Read by Barrett Whitener. (Running Time: 7 hrs. 30 mins.). 2003. 27.95 (978-1-59912-427-8(0)) Iofy Corp.

Awakening Storm. unabr. ed. Jonathan Lowe. Read by Barrett Whitener. 6 cass. (Running Time: 8 hrs. 30 mins.). 2000. 44.95 (978-0-7861-2578-4(0), 3184); audio compact disk 24.95 (978-0-7861-8800-0(6), 3184) Blckstn Audio.

Awakening Storm. unabr. ed. Jonathan Lowe. Read by Barrett Whitener. 7 CDs. (Running Time: 8 hrs. 30 mins.). 2003. audio compact disk 56.00 (978-0-7861-8899-4(5), 3184) Blckstn Audio.

Awakening Storm. unabr. ed. Jonathan Lowe. Read by Barrett Whitener. 6 pieces. 2004. reel tape 29.95 (978-0-7861-2614-9(0)); audio compact disk 35.95 (978-0-7861-8925-0(8)) Blckstn Audio.

Awakening the Buddhist Within. abr. ed. Surya Das. Read by Surya Das. 4 cass. (Running Time: 6 hrs.). 2000. 25.95 (Random AudioBks) Random Audio Pubg.

Awakening the Cobra. Nicki Scully. Perf. by Roland Barker. 1 CD. 2004. audio compact disk 16.00 (978-0-9623365-9-1(9)) N Scully.

Awakening the Cobra: A Journey of Initiation. unabr. ed. Nicki Scully. Perf. by Roland Barker. 1 cass. 11.00 (978-0-9623365-3-9(X)) N Scully.

A Journey of initiation that opens energy channels in the body & introduces you to the Cobra as totem & ally.

***Awakening the Entrepreneur Within.** unabr. ed. Michael E. Gerber. Read by Michael E. Gerber. (ENG.). 2008. (978-0-06-163022-4(5)); (978-0-06-163024-8(1)) HarperCollins Pubs.

Awakening the Entrepreneur Within: How Ordinary People Can Create Extraordinary Companies. unabr. ed. Michael E. Gerber. Read by Michael E. Gerber. (Running Time: 25200 sec.). 2008. audio compact disk 29.95 (978-0-06-157447-4(3), Harper Audio) HarperCollins Pubs.

Awakening the Global Mind: A New Philosophy for Healing Ourselves & Our World. Ashok Gangadean. 2008. audio compact disk 69.95 (978-1-59179-798-2(5)) Sounds True.

Awakening the Goddess: Freeing the Female Orgasm. Charles Muir & Caroline Muir. Read by Charles Muir & Caroline Muir. 2 cass. (Running

Time: 2 hrs. 10 mins.). (Tantra: The Art of Conscious Loving Ser.). 1992. 29.95 (978-1-882570-03-4(0)) HI Goddess.
Essential information for women & their men on how to heal emotional & energetic scars which prevent a woman's powerful & instant orgasmic potential. Includes illustrated book.

Awakening the Healer Within. 2 cassettes. 1986. 19.45 (978-1-55841-229-3(8)) Emmett E Miller.
Enhance your grasp on the principles of deep healing with this eloquent and informative live presentation by Dr. Miller.

Awakening the Healer Within. 2 CDs. 1986. audio compact disk 25.50 (978-1-55841-137-1(2)) Emmett E Miller.

Awakening the Higher Self: Guided Meditations to the Angelic Realm. Terra Sonora. (Running Time: 1 hr. 44 mins). 2003. audio compact disk 18.00 (978-0-9744729-1-1(3)) Ctr of Oneness.

Awakening the Leader Within. Emmett Miller. (ENG.). 2007. audio compact disk 16.95 (978-1-55841-141-8(0)) Emmett E Miller.

Awakening the Light of the Mind. Tara Singh. 1 cass. (Running Time: 60 mins.). (Exploring a Course in Miracles Ser.). 1990. 9.95 (978-1-55531-250-3(0), A308) Life Action Pr.
Discusses the difference between the brain & the mind & how the mind can dispel the fear & insecurity of the brain.

Awakening the Physician Within. unabr. ed. Emmett E. Miller. 4 cass. 36.00 (OC8W) Sound Horizons AV.

Awakening the Power of a Modern God: Unlock the Mystery & Healing of Your Spiritual DNA. abr. ed. Gregg Braden. 4 CDs. 2005. audio compact disk 23.95 (978-1-4019-0765-2(7)) Hay House.

Awakening Through Sound. Chloe Goodchild. 5 CDs, 1 DVD. (Running Time: 18900 sec.). 2007. audio compact disk 69.95 (978-1-59179-545-2(1), AF01103D) Sounds True.

Awakening to Life Through Truthful Relationship & on Pain, Perfection & the Work to Relieve Suffering. Comment by Ram Dass. (Running Time: 58 mins.). 1987. Original Face.
Defines a process of using daily life events as a vehicle for self-understanding & spiritual awakening.

Awakening to Oneness, (audio Cassette) Teachings for Transformation. Randi L. Jacobs. Narrated by Randi L. Jacobs. 3 cass. (Running Time: 3 hrs.). (ENG.). 2000. 19.95 (978-0-9700252-1-0(1)) Fndt Transf.

Awakening to the Deathless. Bartholomew. Read by Mary Margaret Moore. 1 cass. (Running Time: 1 hr. 38 mins.). 1995. 10.00 High Mesa Pr.
Channeled info describing the state of awareness each of us will inevitably awaken to (side 1) - Questions answered related to this exciting inevitability (side 2).

Awakening to Your True Nature: The Final Teachings. Miller Richard. (ENG.). 2008. 15.00 (978-1-893099-08-1(3)) Anahata Pr.

Awakening, with EBook. unabr. ed. Kate Chopin. Narrated by Shelly Frasier. (Running Time: 5 hrs. 0 mins. 0 sec.). (ENG.). 2009. audio compact disk 19.99 (978-1-4001-0907-4(8)); audio compact disk 19.99 (978-1-4001-5907-9(5)) Pub: Tantor Media. Dist(s): IngramPubServ

Awakening, with eBook. unabr. ed. Kate Chopin. Narrated by Shelly Frasier. (Running Time: 5 hrs. 0 mins. 0 sec.). (ENG.). 2009. audio compact disk 39.99 (978-1-4001-3907-1(4)) Pub: Tantor Media. Dist(s): IngramPubServ

Awakening You Self Esteem. Scripts. 1. (Running Time: 35 minutes). 2001. 14.95 (978-0-9779472-1-8(1)) Health Wealth Inc.

***Awakening Your Intuitive Gifts: A Spiritual Development Course.** Lisa Williams. 2011. audio compact disk 39.95 (978-1-4019-3142-1(1)) Hay House.

Awakening Your Psychic Strengths: A Complete Program for Developing Your Inner Guidance & Spiritual Potential. John Holland. 4 CDs. 2007. audio compact disk 23.95 (978-1-4019-1865-1(4)) Hay House.

Awakening Your Soul, Pt. 1. Thomas Moore & Richard Rohr. 4 cass. (Running Time: 4 hrs.). 29.95 (AA2719) Credence Commun.
Thomas Moore gave this series of talks with Father Richard Rohr at a gathering at the Nevada Desert Experience. After Father Rohr talked the first day, Moore gave two talks, then he & Rohr had a discussion with passionate participation by the audience.

Awakening Your Soul, Pt. 2. Richard Rohr & Thomas Moore. 4 cass. (Running Time: 4 hrs.). 29.95 Credence Commun.
Our individual & collective spirituality seems to be in an imbalance. Rohr describes this imablance (which is usually too rigid & non-experiential). Then he describes how we need to address that imbalance by the cultivation of soul work, or more accurately, soul-allowing. He makes a brilliant critique of much of our piety, but he also makes many positive suggestions. This material touches on many of the themes in his earlier work, Spirit, Soul & Society.

Awakenings. abr. ed. Oliver Sacks. Read by Oliver Sacks. 1 cass. (Running Time: 1 hr. 10 mins.). 1987. 11.95 (978-0-8045-1176-6(4), SAC 1176) Spoken Arts.
Selected chapters that focus on varied reactions of patients who "awoke" after many years of Parkinson's syndrome when given the drug L-DOPA.

Award Quick: U. S. Army Award Preparation Program. Compiled by Steven W. Moore & Mark S. Gerecht. (ENG.). 2007. audio compact disk 39.95 (978-1-886715-37-0(8)) Byrrd Ent Inc.

Award Series. unabr. ed. Annie Dillard et al. 58 cass. (Running Time: 29 mins. per cass.). 1985. 10.00 ea. New Letters.
A collection of weekly half-hour radio programs with National Book Award & Pulitzer Prize Award winning authors talking & presenting their own works.

Award Winning Science Fiction. unabr. ed. Poul Anderson. Read by Tom Teti. 6 cass. (Running Time: 7 hrs. 39 mins.). Incl. Longest Voyage. 1987. (CXL532CX); Man Who Came Early. 1987. (CXL532CX); No Truce With Kings. 1987. (CXL532CX); Queen of Air & Darkness. Poul Anderson. 1987. (CXL532CX); (Cassette Library). 1987. 44.98 (978-0-8072-3061-9(8), CXL532CX, Listening Lib) Random Audio Pubg.

Aware. Contrib. by Salvador & Otto Price. Prod. by Otto Price & Chris Bevins. 2008. audio compact disk 13.99 (978-5-557-44758-4(X), Word Records) Word Enter.

Aware Ego. Hal Stone & Sidra Stone. 4 cass. (Running Time: 5 hrs. 30 mins.). 1998. 36.00 (978-1-56557-061-0(8), T44) Delos Inc.
Builds upon Voice Dialogue Relationship, & the Psychology of Selves. Leads you on a fascinating in-depth exploration of the Aware Ego & its role in the earthly & spiritual aspects of your life.

Awareness. Eileen J. Garrett. Read by Lisette Coly. 2008. audio compact disk 28.50 (978-5-557-40248-4(9)) Parapsych Foun.

Awareness Arising. Ragini E. Michaels. Read by Ragini E. Michaels. Music by Divyam Ambodha. 1 cass. (Running Time: 30 mins.). (Remembrance Ser.). 1988. 14.95 (978-0-9628686-4-1(7), FTAT-102) Facticity Tr.
Supports developing the ability of your unconscious mind to heighten your awareness & allow you to be in the moment here & now. Soothing combination of feminine voice & original music.

Awareness of True Reality. unabr. ed. Robert A. Monroe. Read by Robert A. Monroe. (Running Time: 45 mins.). (Explorer Ser.). 1983. 12.95 (978-1-56113-006-1(0), 7) Monroe Institute.
What is reality?.

Awareness Through Movement. Moshe Feldenkrais. 6 cass. (Running Time: 8 hrs. 10 mins.). 1972. 56.00 (65801) Big Sur Tapes.
Lecture demonstration, followed by ten 45-min. experiential guided lessons in effortless learning. Including: Mobilizing One Side, Flexors Mostly, Differentiating One Shoulder, Extensors of the Back, Integrating Locomotion, Furthering the Learning, Jelly Pudding, Integrating with Entire Self, Foot Above the Head & Exploring Rythmic Coordination.

Away. abr. collector's ed. Jane Urquhart. Narrated by Seana McKenna. 3 cass. (Running Time: 4 hrs.). (BTC Audiobooks). (ENG.). 1998. 19.95 (978-0-86492-211-3(6)) Goose Ln Eds CAN.
"On the northern coast of Ireland, young Mary O'Malley embraces a drowning sailor washed ashore by the tide. So begins Jane Urquhart's mesmerizing family saga, read by Stratford Festival star Seana McKenna. Away won the Trillium Award and was on the best-seller list of The Globe and Mail for three years.".

Away. unabr. ed. Amy Bloom. Read by Barbara Rosenblat. (YA). 2007. 54.99 (978-1-60252-741-6(5)) Find a World.

Away. unabr. ed. Amy Bloom. Read by Barbara Rosenblat. (ENG.). 2009. audio compact disk 14.99 (978-1-61573-042-1(7), 1615730427) Pub: HighBridge. Dist(s): Workman Pub

Away. unabr. ed. Jane Urquhart. Read by Beth Fowler. 10 vols. (Running Time: 15 hrs.). (Chivers Sound Library American Collections). 2000. bk. 84.95 (978-0-7927-2247-2(7), CSL 136, Chivers Sound Lib) AudioGO.
Esther O'Malley Robertson gazes out at Lake Ontario from her home for perhaps the last time. Her house is part of the landscape now being swallowed by industry. The story of her family begins in the 1840's in Northern Ireland.

Away from It All. Judy Astley. Read by Diana Bishop. 7 CDs. (Running Time: 8 hrs. 11 mins.). (Isis (CDs) Ser.). (J). 2004. audio compact disk 71.95 (978-0-7531-2320-1(7)) Pub: ISIS Lrg Prnt GBR. Dist(s): Ulverscroft US

Away from It All. unabr. ed. Judy Astley. Read by Diana Bishop. 7 cass. (Running Time: 8 hrs. 7 min.). (Isis Ser.). (J). 2003. 61.95 (978-0-7531-1795-8(9)) Pub: ISIS Lrg Prnt GBR. Dist(s): Ulverscroft US
Alice has a scrupulously organized, comfortable life in West London with Noel. but when Alice's bohemian mother Jocelyn becomes ill, Alice goes t look after her, taking her daughter and stepson with her. Noel thinks that Jocelyn should be moved to a sensible, sheltered accommodation but the children love the freedom and beauty that they discover in Cornwall, and Alice begins to wonder if the way of life she has chosen is the right one.

Away from It All. unabr. collector's ed. Sloan Wilson. Read by Ron Shoop. 7 cass. (Running Time: 10 hrs. 30 min.). 1987. 56.00 (978-0-7366-1151-0(7), 2075) Books on Tape.
Wilson tells what happens to him when he decides to abandon his career as a successful novelist & to pursue a life-long dream. The dream is a boat. But to live it he has to include his second wife & their 2 year-old daughter. Wilson takes the chance.

Away in a Manger. 1 cass. 1999. 5.99 (978-5-550-09536-2(X), PHC 8017); audio compact disk 7.99 (978-5-550-09562-1(9), PHD 8017) Provident Mus Dist.

Away in a Manger. unabr. ed. Sarah Hayes. Read by Stephen Thorne. 1 cass. (Running Time: 40 mins.). 2002. (978-1-85549-206-6(7)) Cover To Cover GBR.
The story of Christmas and seven well known cards.

Away in a Manger: Carols of Christmas, Evening Prayer of Christmas. Perf. by Schola Cantorum of St. Peter's in the Loop Church & Grace Lutheran School Centennial Choir. Music by Richard Hiller. Contrib. by J. Michael Thompson & John Folkening. 1 cass. (Running Time: 1 hr. 4 mins.). 1997. audio compact disk 16.95 (978-0-8146-7916-6(1)) Liturgical Pr.

Away Laughing on a Fast Camel: Even More Confessions of Georgia Nicolson. unabr. ed. Louise Rennison. 4 cass. (Running Time: 4:30 hrs). (Confessions of Georgia Nicolson Ser.: No. 5). (YA). (gr. 7 up). 2005. 37.75 (978-1-4025-9931-6(5)) Recorded Bks.

Away Laughing on a Fast Camel: Even More Confessions of Georgia Nicolson. unabr. ed. Louise Rennison. Narrated by Louise Rennison. 4 CDs. (Running Time: 4 hrs. 30 mins.). (Confessions of Georgia Nicolson Ser.: No. 5). 2004. audio compact disk 15.99 (978-1-4025-9343-7(0), 01732) Recorded Bks.
. Robbie the Sex God (yummy scrumboes) is Georgia's official boyfriend! Life should be fab and double cool with knobs. One problem, though. The Sex God is moving to Kiwi-a-gogo land to snog sheep. Distraught, Georgia decides to show extreme glaciosity to all boys. But then along comes the gorgey new Italian-American lead singer for the Stiff Dylans. Away Laughing on a Fast Camel is a hilarious entry in Georgia's confessions.

Away With the Birds. unabr. ed. Errol Broome. Read by Peter Houghton. 1 cass. (Running Time: 1 hr. 6 mins.). 2002. (978-1-74030-624-9(4)) Bolinda Pubng AUS.

Away with the Fairies. Kerry Greenwood. Read by Stephanie Daniel. (Running Time: 8 hrs. 40 mins.). (Phryne Fisher Mystery Ser.). 2009. 69.99 (978-1-74214-234-0(6), 9781742142340) Pub: Bolinda Pubng AUS. Dist(s): Bolinda Pub Inc

Away with the Fairies. unabr. ed. Kerry Greenwood. Read by Stephanie Daniel. 6 cass. (Running Time: 8 hrs. 40 mins.). (Phryne Fisher Ser.). 2005. 48.00 (978-1-74030-699-7(6)); audio compact disk 83.95 (978-1-74093-102-1(5)) Pub: Bolinda Pubng AUS. Dist(s): Bolinda Pub Inc

AWBC Holiday Audio Bible Prepack. Zondervan Publishing Staff. 2003. audio compact disk 349.96 (978-0-310-62861-3(X)) Zondervan.

Awesome God. Contrib. by Don Moen. Created by Integrity Music. Prod. by Aaron W. Lindsey & Israel Houghton. (Shout Praises! Kids Ser.). (J). (ps-3). 2006. audio compact disk 9.99 (978-5-558-16556-2(1)) Integrity Music.

Awesome God: A Tribute to Rich Mullins. Perf. by Rich Mullins. 1 cass. (Running Time: 1 hr.). 1998. 10.98; audio compact disk 16.98 CD. Provident Mus Dist.

Awesome God: Songs of Praise & Devotion. 1 CD. (Running Time: 30 mins.). 1999. audio compact disk (978-0-7601-3520-4(7)) Brentwood Music.
Songs include: "God So Loved," "In Christ Alone," "Lord of Eternity," "Glory" & more.

Awesome Golf Now 6 CD Series. Laura King. (ENG.). 2009. cd-rom 137.47 (978-0-9792996-8-1(3)) Summit Dynamics.

Awesome Power of Married Love. Truman G. Madsen. 1 cass. 1991. 7.95 (978-1-57008-022-7(4), Bkcraft Inc) Deseret Bk.

***Awesome Power of Purpose.** Katie Souza. (ENG.). 2011. audio compact disk 10.00 (978-0-7684-0259-9(X)) Pub: Expected End. Dist(s): Destiny Image Pubs

Awful Pawful. unabr. ed. Darrel Odgers & Sally Odgers. Read by Alan King. (Running Time: 3000 sec.). (Jack Russell: Dog Detective Ser.). (J). 2007. audio compact disk 39.95 (978-1-74093-995-9(6), 9781740939959) Pub: Bolinda Pubng AUS. Dist(s): Bolinda Pub Inc

Awfully Big Adventure. unabr. ed. Beryl Bainbridge. Read by Paul McGann. 4 CDs. (Running Time: 6 hrs.). 2003. audio compact disk 49.95 (978-0-7540-5530-3(2), CCD 221) AudioGO.

Awilihimas: Reflections CD. 2002. audio compact disk 22.00 (978-0-89610-931-5(3)) Island Heritage.

Awkward Age. unabr. ed. Henry James. Read by Flo Gibson. 10 cass. (Running Time: 13 hrs. 30 mins.). 1994. 44.95 (978-1-55685-330-2(0)) Audio Bk Con.
The interwoven relationships of a close circle of friends involved in the launching of two young ladies into society & marriage are examined through repartee.

Awkward Commission. David Donachie. 2007. 76.95 (978-1-84559-786-3(9)); audio compact disk 84.95 (978-1-84559-787-0(7)) Pub: Soundings Ltd GBR. Dist(s): Ulverscroft US

Ax. unabr. ed. Ed McBain, pseud. Read by Jonathan Marosz. 5 cass. (Running Time: 5 hrs.). (87th Precinct Ser.: Bk. 18). 1996. 40.00 (978-0-7366-3506-6(8), 4145) Books on Tape.
The boys of the 87th Precinct know that it took a maniac to kill George Lasser, age 87, with an ax. But the only oddballs who could've done it - Lasser's wife & son - have air-tight alibis.

Ax. unabr. collector's ed. Donald E. Westlake. Read by Michael Kramer. 7 cass. (Running Time: 10 hrs. 30 min.). (Dortmunder Ser.). 1997. 56.00 (978-0-7366-3774-9(5), 4447) Books on Tape.
The victim of corporate downsizing, Burke Devore will do anything to get his job back. Burke is gunning for his competition & his blood-soaked footsteps are leading to an inexpressibly violent end. How far is he willing to go to maintain his creature comforts?.

Ax Tongue. Poems. John M. Bennett. Read by John M. Bennett. Illus. by John M. Bennet. Pref. by Al Ackerman. Music by Byron Smith. 1 cass. (Running Time: 45 mins.). 1986. pap. bk. 7.98 (978-0-935350-16-6(0)) Luna Bisonte.
Avant-garde poetry with avant-jazz music.

Axeman's Jazz. Julie Smith. Narrated by Cristine McMurdo-Wallis. 11 CDs. (Running Time: 13 hrs.). (Skip Langdon Mystery Ser.: Bk. 2). audio compact disk 111.00 (978-0-7887-9880-1(4)) Recorded Bks.

Axeman's Jazz. unabr. ed. Julie Smith. Narrated by Cristine McMurdo-Wallis. 9 cass. (Running Time: 13 hrs.). (Skip Langdon Mystery Ser.: Bk. 2). 2001. 84.00 (978-0-7887-4373-3(2), 95776E7) Recorded Bks.
A career police officer, Skip Langon, recently promoted, finds herself chasing a killer who is preying on members of New Orleans various 12-step programs.

Axiom. unabr. ed. Bill Hybels. Illus. by Bill Hybels. (ENG.). 2008. audio compact disk 19.99 (978-0-310-28540-3(2)) Zondervan.

***Axiom: Powerful Leadership Proverbs.** Bill Hybels. (Running Time: 5 hrs. 38 mins. 0 sec.). (ENG.). 2008. 12.99 (978-0-310-28541-0(0)) Zondervan.

Axis of Life Relationships. Larry Pines. Read by Larry Pines. 1 cass. (Running Time: 1 hr. 30 mins.). 8.95 (1173) Am Fed Astrologers.

Axis Story (Side One); The Magnet of Jesus (Side Two) Jonathan Murro. 1 cass. 1991. 7.95 A R Colton Fnd.
Lectures by Jonathan Murro, a Teacher of the Higher Life for nearly 40 years.

Axle Galench in Search of Barnsfoggon. Read by Rooster Morris. Jody Logsdon. (ENG.). (J). 2005. audio compact disk 15.95 (978-0-9755895-5-7(5)) Axle Pubng Co.

Ayahuasca. unabr. ed. Claudio Naranjo. 1 cass. (Running Time: 1 hr. 23 min.). 1975. 11.00 (04203) Big Sur Tapes.
Takes us on his journey in the 1960s from Harvard University to the jungles of the Amazon, to find ayahuasca.

Ayahuasca Icaros (Sacred Music) unabr. ed. Agustin Rivas. 1 cass. (Running Time: 1 hr.). 1989. 11.00 (09601) Big Sur Tapes.
The Icaros are magic songs by which the shaman communicates with the spirits. The healer learns them during ingestion of the plant-teacher, & are sung or played during ayahuasca ceremonies to heal, to defend against evil, to shape the visions, & to call forth helper spirits.

Ayala's Angel. Anthony Trollope. Read by Amy von Lecteur. 2009. 33.95 (978-1-60112-984-0(X)) Babblebooks.

Ayala's Angel. unabr. collector's ed. Anthony Trollope. Read by Donada Peters. 14 cass. (Running Time: 21 hrs.). 1995. 112.00 (978-0-7366-2902-7(5), 3601) Books on Tape.
Orphaned woman's ideal of a marrying man is challenged by reality in this romantic comedy.

Ayala's Angel, Pt. 1. unabr. ed. Anthony Trollope. Read by Flo Gibson. 8 cass. (Running Time: 12 hrs.). 1987. 41.95 Audio Bk Con.
While the beautiful & sentimental Ayala dreams of her "angel of light", she is courted by a variety of suitors.

Ayala's Angel, Pt. 2. unabr. ed. Anthony Trollope. 6 cass. (Running Time: 9 hrs.). 1987. 41.95 Audio Bk Con.

Ayala's Angel - Part 1, Vol. 1. unabr. ed. Anthony Trollope. Read by Flo Gibson. 8 cass. (Running Time: 12 hrs.). 1987. 26.95 (978-1-55685-086-8(7)) Audio Bk Con.
While the beautiful & sentimental Ayala dreams of her "angel of light", she is courted by a variety of suitors.

Ayala's Angel (Part 2), Vol. 2. unabr. ed. Anthony Trollope. Narrated by Flo Gibson. (Running Time: 8 hrs. 25 mins.). 1987. 24.95 (978-1-55685-792-8(6)) Audio Bk Con.

Ayala's Angel (Parts 1 And 2) unabr. ed. Anthony Trollope. Narrated by Flo Gibson. (Running Time: 20 hrs. 16 mins.). 1987. 42.95 (978-1-55685-793-5(4)) Audio Bk Con.

Ayesha: The Return of She. unabr. ed. H. Rider Haggard. Read by Gordon Dulieu. 8 cass. (Running Time: 12 hrs. 20 mins.). 2001. 69.95 (978-1-85695-413-6(7), 92103) Pub: ISIS Audio GBR. Dist(s): Ulverscroft US
"I die not. I shall come again & shall once more be beautiful. I swear it is true." These were the last strange words that Ayesha uttered before her death, thus prompting Leo Vinley & Ludwig Horace Holly to set out to determine if they are true. Ayesha's prophecy is fulfilled in this novel which is a well executed mythical creation.

Ayn Rand: A Q & A on Objectivism. Ayn Rand. 1 cass. (Running Time: 27 mins.). 1962. 12.95 (978-1-56114-117-3(8), AR37C) Second Renaissance.

Ayn Rand & the "Atlas Shrugged Years" Mary A. Sures & Harry Binswanger. 1 cass. (Running Time: 1 hr. 10 mins.). 1997. 14.95 (978-1-56114-390-0(1), AR61C) Second Renaissance.
Warm reminiscences & Ayn Rand's recollections of the writing of "Atlas Shrugged", given by two close associates of Rand.

Ayn Rand & the History of Individual Rights. John Ridpath. 2 cass. (Running Time: 2 hrs.). 1993. bk. 19.95 (978-1-56114-254-5(9), CR09D) Second Renaissance.

Ayn Rand & the World She Made. unabr. ed. Anne Conover Heller. (Running Time: 28 hrs. 50 mins.). 2009. 44.95 (978-1-4332-7137-3(0)); 105.95 (978-1-4332-7133-5(8)); audio compact disk 59.95 (978-1-4332-7136-6(2)); audio compact disk 123.00 (978-1-4332-7134-2(6)) Blckstn Audio.

***Ayn Rand Answers: The Best of Her Q & A.** unabr. ed. Ayn Rand. Read by Bernadette Dunne. (Running Time: 10 hrs. NaN mins.). (ENG.). 2011. audio compact disk 29.95 (978-1-4332-2648-9(0)) Blckstn Audio.

Ayn Rand Answers: The Best of Her Q & A. unabr. ed. Rand Ayn. Read by Bernadette Dunne. (Running Time: 10 hrs. 0 mins.). 2010. 65.95 (978-1-4332-2645-8(6)); audio compact disk 90.00 (978-1-4332-2646-5(4)) Blckstn Audio.

Ayn Rand Answers: The Best of Her Q & A. unabr. ed. Ayn Rand. Read by Bernadette Dunne. (Running Time: 10 hrs. NaN mins.). (ENG.). 2011. 29.95 (978-1-4332-2649-6(9)) Blckstn Audio.

Ayn Rand at Ford Hall Forum, 1961-69, Vol. 1. Ayn Rand. 9 cass. (Running Time: 9 hrs.). 1969. 105.00 (978-1-56114-288-0(3), AR61D) Second Renaissance.

Ayn Rand at Ford Hall Forum, 1971-81, Vol. 2. Ayn Rand. 10 cass. (Running Time: 10 hrs.). 1981. 115.00 (978-1-56114-291-0(3), AR62D) Second Renaissance.

Ayn Rand Journals. David Harriman. 1 cass. (Running Time: 1 hr. 30 mins.). 1997. 12.95 (978-1-56114-409-9(6), AR63C) Second Renaissance.
A preview of "Journals of Ayn Rand" showing the progressive steps by which she arrived at her philosophy & her novels.

Ayn Rand vs. Karl Marx. John Ridpath. 1 cass. (Running Time: 1 hr. 30 mins.). 1996. 12.95 (978-1-56114-255-2(7), CR42C) Second Renaissance.
Contrasting the philosophies of these two thinkers in answering: "What are the objective needs of human life?".

Ayn Rand's Fictional Characters As Philosophic Archetypes. Andrew Bernstein. 4 cass. (Running Time: 6 hrs. 30 mins.). 1996. 49.95 (978-1-56114-397-9(9), MB42D) Second Renaissance.
A perceptive analysis of the philosophic principles that define & dramatize Ayn Rand's characters.

Ayn Rand's Life: Highlights & Sidelights. Harry Binswanger. 2 cass. (Running Time: 3 hrs.). 1994. 29.95 (978-1-56114-299-6(9), AB01D) Second Renaissance.
Biographical notes on the life of a philosophic genius.

Ayn Rand's Seminars on Non-Fiction Writing: A Preview. Ed. by Robert Mayhew. 1 cass. (Running Time: 1 hr. 30 mins.). 12.95 (CM52C) Second Renaissance.
Lecture previews a forthcoming book based on Ayn Rand's non-fiction writing course (in 1969).

Ayudas Practicas para un Iglesia Lastimada. 2006. audio compact disk 42.00 (978-1-57972-710-9(7)) Insight Living.

Ayurveda. unabr. ed. Vasant Ladd. 5 cass. 45.00 (OC40) Sound Horizons AV.

Ayurveda: Natural Health Practices for Your Body Type from the World's Oldest Healing Tradition. Vasant Lad. 6 CDs. (Running Time: 19800 sec.). 2006. audio compact disk 39.95 (978-1-59179-508-7(7), AW00460D) Sounds True.

Ayurveda of Astrology. Jacquie Hilton. 2 cass. 1992. 8.95 ea. Am Fed Astrologers.

Azazel. l.t. ed. Boris Akounine. (French Ser.). 2001. bk. 30.99 (978-2-84011-427-7(5)) Pub: UlverLrgPrint GBR. Dist(s): Ulverscroft US

Azerbaijani - English Parallel Text. Valeriy Volozov. 3 cass. (Running Time: 4 hrs. 30 mins.). (AZE.). 1995. 24.00 (3114) Dunwoody Pr.
Intended for advanced students. The eleven selections are drawn from contemporary prose writers & the Azerbaijani press.

Azerbaijani, Colloquial. unabr. ed. Kurtulus Oztopcu. 3 cass. (Running Time: 3 hrs. 30 mins.). (AZE & ENG.). 1994. pap. bk. & stu. ed. 75.00 (978-0-88432-788-2(4), AFAZ10) J Norton Pubs.
Mini-course features basic vocabulary for travel & day-to-day living. Reference cards included reinforce newly acquired vocabulary.

Azerbaijani Language Course: Companies-Products-Services. 1994. 175.00 (978-0-614-00721-3(6)) Rector Pr.

Azerbaijani Newspaper Reader. John D. Murphy. 1993. 12.00 (978-1-881265-04-7(8)) Dunwoody Pr.

Azerbaijani Newspaper Reader. rev. ed. John D. Murphy. 1 cass. (Running Time: 1 hr. 30 mins.). (AZE.). 1993. 12.00 (3084) Dunwoody Pr.
Most of the twenty-five selections appeared originally in two Baku newspapers. The subject matter deals primarily with national & international affairs, but other themes also have been included.

Azhe' e Bikenidoots' Osii see Father's Boots

Azimuth's "Saving Species" - Papua New Guinea's Crocodiles, Kenya's Elephants & China's Pandas. Hosted by Nancy Pearlman. 1 cass. (Running Time: 28 mins.). 10.00 (1026) Educ Comm CA.

Aztec Autumn. abr. ed. Gary Jennings. Read by David Dukes. 4 cass. (Running Time: 6 hrs.). 2001. 25.00 (978-1-59040-177-4(8), Phoenix Audio) Pub: Amer Intl Pub. Dist(s): PerseuPGW

Aztec World. Compiled by Benchmark Education Staff. 2005. audio compact disk 10.00 (978-1-4108-5495-7(7)) Benchmark Educ.

Aztecs: Rise & Fall of a Great Empire. Roger Smalley. (High Five Reading Ser.). (ENG.). (gr. 4 up). 2003. audio compact disk 5.95 (978-0-7368-2848-2(6)) CapstoneDig.

Aztecs: Rise & Fall of a Great Empire. Roger Smalley. (High Five Reading - Red Ser.). (ENG.). (gr. 2-3). 2007. audio compact disk 5.95 (978-1-4296-1434-4(X)) CapstoneDig.

***Aztlán Kid: Estranged man in a strange Land.** Robert Michael Krakoff. Ed. by Patricia/Margaret Krakoff. Scott/Brian Krakoff. (ENG.). 2010. 3.99 (978-0-9765153-6-4(9)) Customized News.

Azucena Azul, EDL Level 14. (Fonolibros Ser.: Vol. 24). (SPA.). 2003. 11.50 (978-0-7652-1013-5(4)) Modern Curr.

Azur Like It. Wendy Holden. Read by Helen Lederer. 14 CDs. audio compact disk 115.95 (978-0-7927-3165-8(4), CCD 404) AudioGO.

Azur like It. Read by Helen Lederer. 14 cass. 110.95 (978-0-7927-3164-1(6), CAB 2616) AudioGO.

Azure Bowl. unabr. ed. Anita Burgh. Read by Anne Dover. 16 cass. (Running Time: 21 hrs.). (Sound Ser.). (J). 2002. 104.95 (978-1-84283-184-7(4)) Pub: ISIS Lrg Prnt GBR. Dist(s): Ulverscroft US

Azyade. Pierre Loti. 7 cass. (Running Time: 7 hrs.). (FRE.). 1996. pap. bk. 79.50 (978-1-58085-358-3(7)) Interlingua VA.
Includes French text with notes. The combination of written text & clarity & pace of diction will open the door for intermediate & advanced students to genuine comprehension & the use of literary texts for advancement in rapid understanding of written & oral language materials. The audio text plus written text concept makes foreign languages accessible to a much wider range of students than books alone.

***A117. 1-2009 Accessible & Usable Buildings & Facilities.** ICC. 2010. audio compact disk 39.95 (978-1-58001-972-9(2)) Int Code Counc.

A2J. Perf. by According to John Staff. 1 cass. (YA). 1999. 10.99 (978-7-902462-80-8(2), KMGC8681); audio compact disk 16.99 (978-7-902462-77-8(2), KMGD8681) Provident Mus Dist.
From their beginnings as the house band for Big House, a teen-oriented outreach ministry of First Baptist Woodstock outside of Atlanta, to being picked as one of four bands to be featured in the Acquire the Fire youth conventions this Fall & Spring 2000, this group has quickly made a national impact.

B

"B" Book see Roland the Minstrel Pig & Other Stories

B-E-S-T Friends. unabr. ed. Patricia Reilly Giff. 1 cass. (Running Time: 50 mins.). (New Kids at the Polk Street School Ser.). (J). (gr. 1-2). 1990. 15.98 incl. pap. bk. & guide. (978-0-8072-0178-7(2), FTR 140 SP, Listening Lib) Random Audio Pubg.

B. E. S. T. Friends: Songs for Kids...by Kids...about Friendship, Cooperation, & Self-Esteem. Perf. by Judith Feldman & Esteem Team Kids Staff. 1 cass. (Running Time: 23 min.). (J). (ps-5). 1990. 10.95 (978-0-9632276-1-4(0)) Natl Self Esteem.
An up-beat tape for kids, full of songs, raps cheers, poems about friendship, cooperation, self-esteem. Written & performed by youngsters 9-15, it is the most visible part of The Esteem Team - a highly effective, widely acclaimed, Nationl Abuse & Delinquency Prevention Program. Parents Choice Gold Award winner.

B. F. Skinner - Operant Conditioning. Robert Stone. 1 cass. 1983. 10.00 (978-0-938137-03-0(4)) Listen & Learn.
Topics include dependent-independent variables, positive-negative reinforcement, punishment, extinction, stimulus generalization, reinforcement schedules, functional analysis, development of abnormal behavior, token economies, behavior shaping.

B FL-CDI-Russian New Testament -Blu 8002. 1 cass. 1991. 24.98 Chrstn Dup Intl.

B for Buster. unabr. ed. Iain Lawrence. Read by Jeff Woodman. 6 cass. (Running Time: 8 hrs. 30 mins.). (J). 2005. 54.75 (978-1-4193-5474-8(4), 98166) Recorded Bks.
Lawrence again contemplates war in this novel set in 1943 England. Sixteen-year-old Kak escaped his abusive family in Canada to join the Canadian Air Force. Now a crewman aboard a night-flying bomber bound for Germany, Kak learns of the terror and violence of war firsthand.

B. H. Roberts Story. Truman G. Madsen. 1 cass. 1992. 7.95 (978-1-57008-025-8(9), Bkcraft Inc) Deseret Bk.

***B Is for Beer.** unabr. ed. Tom Robbins. Read by Laura Silverman. (ENG.). 2009. (978-0-06-176864-4(2), Harper Audio); (978-0-06-176865-1(0), Harper Audio) HarperCollins Pubs.

B Is for Beer. unabr. ed. Tom Robbins & Tom Robbins. Read by Laura Silverman. 2009. audio compact disk 17.99 (978-0-06-171908-0(0), Harper Audio) HarperCollins Pubs.

B Is for Bethlehem: A Christmas Alphabet. Isabel Wilner. (J). 1992. 18.66 (978-0-383-05148-6(7)) SRA McGraw.

B Is for Betsy. unabr. ed. Carolyn Haywood. Narrated by Stina Nielsen. 2 cass. (Running Time: 2 hrs.). (J). 2005. 19.75 (978-1-4193-2638-7(4), 97956) Recorded Bks.
School can be kind of scary for someone who is just starting, but Betsy is trying very hard to be brave. It turns out that school is not what she thought it would be - school can be fun! She makes lots of new friends, her teacher is really nice and the classroom is bright and sunny. She learns something new all the time and throughout the school year there are many surprising adventures waiting for her.

B Is for Burglar. abr. ed. Sue Grafton. Read by Judy Kaye. (Running Time: 10800 sec.). (Kinsey Millhone Mystery Ser.). 2007. audio compact disk 14.99 (978-0-7393-5735-4(2), Random AudioBks) Pub: Random Audio Pubg. Dist(s): Random

B Is for Burglar. unabr. collector's ed. Sue Grafton. Read by Mary Peiffer. 8 cass. (Running Time: 8 hrs.). (Kinsey Millhone Mystery Ser.). 1993. 64.00 (978-0-7366-2457-2(0), 3221) Books on Tape.
A wealthy woman needs to find her sister to settle a will. It looks routine, boring. But the case becomes complicated when Kinsey is ordered to call it off. The killer is still at large & looking for her.

B. S. Elimination Guide: Removing Negative People, Bad Careers & Poor Relationships from Your Life. Deanna Michaux. (ENG.). 2009. pap. bk. 10.00 (978-0-9712585-4-9(6)) Pub: JuDe Pubng. Dist(s): Bookazine Co Inc

B-Sides. Perf. by Hokus Pick. 1 cass. 1997. audio compact disk 15.99 CD. (D9865) Diamante Music Grp.
The B-Sides is a unique project that brings together 12 tracks recorded throughout their career that have never been released. Hokus Pick's sense of humor is in full force on tracks like "Learn to Laugh", "Super Hero" & everyone's favorite Christmas song, "Felize Navidad". Other highlights include 2 cover tunes "Train in Vain" (The Clash) & "Adonai" (Petra) & a reworking of Nine Worlds Away from their previous album Bookaboom.

Ba Ba Ba Mo Leanabh: Hush, Hush, Little Baby Traditional Celtic Lullabies. Prod. by Talitha Mackenzie & Matthew Kopka. 1 CD. (Running Time: 1 hr.). (J). 1996. bk. 15.95 (978-1-55961-391-0(2), Ellipsis Kids) Relaxtn Co.

Ba-Ba-Boom! Tales for the Telling. unabr. ed. Mary Lloyd Dugan & Margaret Read MacDonald. 1 cass. (Running Time: 56 mins.). Dramatization. (J). (ps-4). 1994. 9.98 (978-0-9709751-0-2(4)) Dancing Pony Prod.

Baa Baa Black Sheep Sells Her Wool Audio CD. Adapted by Benchmark Education Company Staff. Based on a work by Jeffrey B. Fuerst. (Reader's Theater Nursery Rhymes & Songs Ser.). (J). (gr. k-1). 2008. audio compact disk 10.00 (978-1-60437-989-1(8)) Benchmark Educ.

Baal Shem Tov. unabr. ed. 7 cass. 1995. 65.00 Set. (31003) Big Sur Tapes.
Israel ben Eliezer (1700-1761), known as the Baal Shem Tov, founded modern Hasidism, a movement within Judaism intent on bringing the most profound spiritual teachings to ordinary people. Rabbi Schachter, a spiritual heir of this tradition, delves into the life & wisdom of the "Master of the Good Name".

Baba Yaga see Puss in Boots & Other Fairy Tales from Around the World

Baba Yaga, the Witch. unabr. ed. Keith Bilderbeck. Perf. by Penny Wiggins. 1 cass., 1 CD. (Running Time: 1 hr. 20 min.). (J). (gr. k-6). 1999. 5.00 (978-1-893721-01-2(9), BYR-10014); audio compact disk 8.00 CD. (978-1-893721-00-5(0), BYR-00012) Baba Yaga.
Based on a Russian fairy tale, it tells the story of a clever girl who meets Baba Yaga, a sneaky witch.

Babar & Father Christmas see Babar et le Pere Noel

Babar & Father Christmas. unabr. ed. Jean de Brunhoff. Perf. by Louis Jourdan. Tr. by Merle S. Haas. 1 cass. (Running Time: 90 mins.). (Babar Ser.).Tr. of Babar et le Pere Noel. (J). (ps-3). 1984. 9.95 (978-1-55994-067-2(0), CPN 1488) HarperCollins Pubs.

Babar & His Children. Jean de Brunhoff. (Babar Ser.).Tr. of Babar en Famille. (J). (ps-3). (CPN 1488) HarperCollins Pubs.

Babar & the Wizard. abr. ed. Created by Laurent de Brunhoff. 1 cass. (Babar Ser.). (J). (ps-3). 1999. 7.50 (978-1-86117-143-6(9)) Ulvrscrft Audio.
Babar was born in the forest & lived there until his mother was killed. He then fled to the large city. Babar missed the forest, so he returned to become King & marry his sweetheart.

Babar & the Wully-Wully. Jean de Brunhoff & Laurent de Brunhoff. (Babar Ser.). (J). (ps-3). (CPN 1583) HarperCollins Pubs.

Babar & Zephir. Jean de Brunhoff. (Babar Ser.). (J). (ps-3). (CPN 1487) HarperCollins Pubs.

Babar au Cirque. Jean de Brunhoff & Laurent de Brunhoff. 1 cass. (Babar Ser.). (FRE., (J). (ps-3). 1991. bk. 14.95 (1AD040) Olivia & Hill.
After being rescued at sea, Babar & Celeste are forced to perform in a circus.

Babar Audio Collection. unabr. ed. Jean de Brunhoff. Read by Louis Jordan. 4 cass. (Running Time: 2 hrs. 30 min.). (J). (ps-1). 1994. 25.00 Set. (978-1-55994-950-7(3), HarperChildAud) HarperCollins Pubs.
Guaranteed to delight both adults & children, this collection of stories about everyone's favorite elephant is performed with French flair by Louis Jordan. Included: "The Story of Babar," "The Travels of Babar," "Babar the King," "Babar & His Children," "Babar & Father Christmas," "Babar Comes to America" & other favorites.

Babar en Famille see Babar & His Children

Babar et le Pere Noel see Babar & Father Christmas

Babar et le Pere Noel. Jean de Brunhoff. 1 cass. (Babar Ser.).Tr. of Babar & Father Christmas. (FRE.). (J). (ps-3). 1991. bk. 14.95 (1AD074) Olivia & Hill.
Babar sets out for the North Pole to find Santa Claus.

Babar Loses His Crown. Laurent de Brunhoff. (Babar Ser.). (J). (ps-3). 1975. bk. 28.37 (978-0-394-03636-6(0)) SRA McGraw.

Babar Musicien. Laurent de Brunhoff. 1 cass. (Babar Ser.). (FRE., (J). (ps-3). 1991. bk. 14.95 (1AD039) Olivia & Hill.
Babar & his friends prepare a concert for Celesteville.

Babar the Elephant Comes to America. unabr. ed. Jean de Brunhoff. Perf. by Louis Jourdan. Tr. by Jean M. Craig. 1 cass. (Running Time: 90 mins.). (Babar Ser.). (J). (ps-3). 1984. 9.95 (978-0-89845-931-9(1), CPN 1551) HarperCollins Pubs.

Babar the King. unabr. ed. Jean de Brunhoff. Perf. by Louis Jourdan. Tr. by Merle S. Haas. 1 cass. (Babar Ser.).Tr. of Roi Babar. (J). (ps-3). 1994. 9.95 (978-0-89845-930-2(3), CPN 1487) HarperCollins Pubs.

Babar's Birthday Surprise. Laurent de Brunhoff. (Babar Ser.). (J). (ps-3). (CPN 1551) HarperCollins Pubs.

Babar's House see Chateau de Babar

Babbie Mason: The Definitive Gospel Collection. Contrib. by Babbie Mason. (Definitive Gospel Collection). 2008. audio compact disk 7.99 (978-5-557-49742-8(0), Word Records) Word Enter.

Babbitt. Sinclair Lewis. Narrated by Flo Gibson. 2008. audio compact disk 34.95 (978-1-55685-997-7(X)) Audio Bk Con.

Babbitt. Sinclair Lewis. Perf. by Ed Asner et al. (Running Time: 14 hrs. 30 min.). Dramatization. 70.00 (AO-050, HarperThor) HarpC GBR.

Babbitt. Sinclair Lewis. 1989. 79.95 (BA881002, HarperThor) HarpC GBR.

Babbitt. Sinclair Lewis. Read by Fabio Camero. (Running Time: 3 hrs.). 2002. 16.95 (978-1-60083-257-4(1), Audiofy Corp) Iofy Corp.

Babbitt. Sinclair Lewis. 1 cass. (Running Time: 1 hr.). (Radiobook Ser.). 1987. 4.98 (978-0-929541-04-4(9)) Radiola Co.

Babbitt. Narrated by Mike Vendetti. (ENG.). 2009. audio compact disk 9.99 (978-1-934814-09-3(1)) Red Planet Au.

Babbitt. abr. ed. Sinclair Lewis. Read by Fabio Camero. 3 CDs. (SPA.). 2002. audio compact disk 17.00 (978-958-8161-52-5(5)) YoYoMusic.

Babbitt, unabr. ed. Sinclair Lewis. Read by Flo Gibson. 8 cass. (Running Time: 11 hrs. 8 mins.). 1999. 26.95 (978-1-55685-433-0(1)) Audio Bk Con.
This satire portrays Babbitt as an opportunistic, materialistic, self-important & unimaginative middle-aged realtor & general go-getter in Zenith, the "Zip City." His brief spree & attempt at liberalism is curbed by fear of criticism & ostracism & causes him to conform to the wills of fellow citizens & club members.

Babbitt. unabr. ed. Sinclair Lewis. Read by Wolfram Kandinsky. 11 cass. (Running Time: 16 hrs. 30 mins.). 2001. 76.95 (978-0-7861-2018-5(5), R2786); audio compact disk 104.00 (978-0-7861-9717-0(X), ZP2786) Blckstn Audio.
George F. Babbitt is a lonely middle-aged man who doesn't understand his family, who has an unsuccessful fling at an affair, who voices sympathy for some striking workers and is almost financially ruined by his action, who finds his only safety lies deep in the fold of those who play it safe.

Babbitt. unabr. ed. Sinclair Lewis. Read by Edward Asner et al. 10 cass. (Running Time: 14 hrs.). 1993. 80.95 (978-1-58081-054-8(3), RDP1) L A Theatre.
The classic novel about conformity in small-town America in the 1920's.

Babbitt. unabr. ed. Sinclair Lewis. Read by Edward Asner et al. 14 CDs. (Running Time: 14 hrs.). 2008. audio compact disk 90.95 (978-1-58081-321-1(6)) L A Theatre.

Babbitt, unabr. ed. Sinclair Lewis. Narrated by George Guidall. 10 cass. (Running Time: 14 hrs. 30 mins.). 1998. 85.00 (978-0-7887-1877-9(0), 95299E7) Recorded Bks.
Babbitt is a conformist & a social climber. In his dreams, however, he is tormented by the emptiness of his soul.

***Babbitt.** unabr. ed. Sinclair Lewis. Read by Grover Gardner. (Running Time: 10 hrs. 5 mins.). (ENG.). 2011. 29.95 (978-1-4417-7956-4(6)); 65.95 (978-1-4417-7953-3(1)); audio compact disk 29.95 (978-1-4417-7955-7(8)); audio compact disk 100.00 (978-1-4417-7954-0(X)) Blckstn Audio.

***Babbitt.** unabr. ed. Sinclair Lewis. Narrated by David Colacci. (Running Time: 14 hrs. 0 mins. 0 sec.). 2010. 27.99 (978-1-4526-5021-0(7)); 19.99 (978-1-4526-7021-8(8)); audio compact disk 35.99 (978-1-4526-0021-5(X)); audio compact disk 85.99 (978-1-4526-3021-2(6)) Pub: Tantor Media. Dist(s): IngramPubServ

Babbitt & Religion, Pt. 1. Read by George A. Panichas. 1 cass. 3.00 (114) ISI Books.

Babbitt & Religion, Pt. 2. Read by George A. Panichas. 1 cass. 3.00 (115) ISI Books.

Babbitt & Romanticism, Pt. 1. Read by Alfred O. Aldridge. (115) ISI Books.

Babbitt & Romanticism, Pt. 2. Read by Alfred O. Aldridge. 1 cass. 3.00 (116) ISI Books.

Babbitt & the Problem of Reality, Pt. 1. Read by Claes G. Ryn. (116) ISI Books.

Babbitt & the Problem of Reality, Pt. 2. Read by Claes G. Ryn. 1 cass. 3.00 (117) ISI Books.

Babbitt, Burke & Rousseau, Pt. 1. Read by Peter Stanlis. (117) ISI Books.

Babbitt, Burke & Rousseau, Pt. 2. Read by Peter Stanlis. 1 cass. 3.00 (118) ISI Books.

Babbitt, Burke & Rousseau Panel Discussion, Pt. 1. Read by Thomas R. Nevin et al. (118) ISI Books.

Babbitt, Burke & Rousseau Panel Discussion, Pt. 2. Read by T. John Jamieson et al. 1 cass. 3.00 (119) ISI Books.

***Babbitt (Library Edition)** unabr. ed. Sinclair Lewis. Narrated by David Colacci. (Running Time: 14 hrs. 0 mins.). 2010. 35.99 (978-1-4526-2021-3(0)) Tantor Media.

Babbling Brook. 1 cass. (Running Time: 60 min.). 1994. audio compact disk 15.95 CD. (2464, Creativ Pub) Quayside.
Water tumbling over the cobbles of a brook bed. No words, no music.

Babbling Brook. 1 cass. (Running Time: 60 min.). 1994. 9.95 (0246, NrthWrd Bks) TandN Child.

Babbling Brook. Great American Audio. Composed by Steven Gruskin. Contrib. by Vinnie Della-Rocca. 1 cass. (Running Time: 1 hr.). (Interludes Music Ser.). 1991. 9.95 (978-1-55569-466-1(7), 3808) Great Am Audio.
You are in tune with nature, refreshed & rejuvenated. This is your own private interlude, which you may visit in solitude or share with someone special. Soothing sounds of nature & music.

Babe: Pig in the City. Justine Fontes. Read by Mia Dillon. 1 cass. (Running Time: 1 hr.). (J). 2000. 11.00 (978-0-7366-9040-9(9)) Books on Tape.
Babe ends up in the Big City on a mission to save the farm. The City is no place for a pig, but Babe isn't any ordinary pig. He meets other animals with bigger problems than his own & is soon trying to help.

Babe: Pig in the City. George Miller. Read by Max Dillion. 1 cass. (Running Time: 1 hr.). (J). 1999. 11.25 (978-0-00-105561-2(5)) Ulvrscrft Audio.
In order to save the Hoggett's farm, Babe & Mrs. Hoggett journey to a far away storybook city, & in this magical metropolis the singing mice, Ferdinand the Duck & a new assortment of animal friends help out Babe.

Babe: The Gallant Pig. Dick King-Smith. Read by Stephen Thorne. 2 cass. (Running Time: 2 hrs.). (J). 2000. 18.00 (978-0-7366-9173-4(1)) Books on Tape.
Amazing pig who won the hearts of readers.

Babe: The Gallant Pig. unabr. ed. Dick King-Smith. Read by Stephen Thorne. 2 cass. (YA). 1999. 13.98 (FS9-29904) Highsmith.

Babe: The Gallant Pig. unabr. ed. Dick King-Smith. 2 cass. (Running Time: 3 hrs.). (J). 1996. pap. bk. 17.98 (978-0-8072-7803-1(3), t 6264-1SP, Listening Lib) Random Audio Pubg.
Captivating story of the adorable piglet who learns the art of sheep herding.

Babe: The Legend Comes to Life. unabr. ed. Robert W. Creamer. Read by Tom Parker. 10 cass. (Running Time: 14 hrs. 30 mins.). 1996. 69.95 (978-0-7861-0960-9(2), 1737) Blckstn Audio.
In this extraordinary biography, Robert W. Creamer uncovers the complex & captivating man behind the legend. He presents the truth behind famous Ruth stories (the "called shot" homers, the home run for a dying child), analyzes the astounding statistics with detailed information on specific games, & describes Ruth's varied, often volatile, relations with those around him, from fellow players to fans, friends, & reporters. From Babe Ruth's early days in a Baltimore orphanage, to the glory days with the Yankees, to his final years, Robert W. Creamer has drawn an indelible portrait of a true folk hero.

Babe: The Sheep-Pig. unabr. ed. Dick King-Smith. Read by Stephen Thorne. 2 cass. (Running Time: 1 hr. 50 mins.). 2002. (978-1-85549-360-5(8)) Cover To Cover GBR.
Farmer Hoggett wins a piglet at the fair. It should fatten up nicely. However Fly, the sheep-dog trains Babe, the piglet, to herd sheep, making Babe an indispensable sheep-pig.

Babe: The Sheep-Pig. unabr. ed. Dick King-Smith. Read by Stephen Thorne. 2 cass. (Running Time: 3 hrs.). 2001. 23.00 (LL0095, Listening Lib) Random Audio Pubg.

Babe & Me: A Baseball Card Adventure. unabr. ed. Dan Gutman. Narrated by Johnny Heller. 3 cass. (Running Time: 3 hrs.). (Baseball Card Adventures Ser.). (YA). 2001. pap. bk. & stu. ed. 51.00 Recorded Bks.
Something magical happens whenever Joe Stoshack holds a baseball card. His hand starts to tingle. And if the card is old Joe can travel back in time.

Babe & Me: A Baseball Card Adventure. unabr. ed. Dan Gutman. Narrated by Johnny Heller. 3 pieces. (Running Time: 3 hrs.). (Baseball Card Adventures Ser.). (gr. 5 up). 2001. 29.00 (978-0-7887-4935-3(8), 96461E7) Recorded Bks.

Babe Ruth: An American Legend. Contrib. by Babe Ruth. 1 CD. (Running Time: 45 mins.). 2000. audio compact disk 15.95 Soundworks Intl.
Compilation of quotes & interviews.

Babe Ruth: His Life & Legend. unabr. ed. Kal Wagenheim. Narrated by Richard M. Davidson. 9 cass. (Running Time: 12 hrs. 15 mins.). 2000. 78.00 (978-0-7887-0419-2(2), 94611E7) Recorded Bks.

Babe Ruth, an American Legend: Live audio recordings & expert Narrators. unabr. ed. Geoffrey Giuliano. Read by Geoffrey Giuliano. (YA). 2007. 34.99 (978-1-60252-599-3(4)) Find a World.

Babe Ruth Talks. 1 cass. 10.00 Esstee Audios.
A series of talks by the Bambino on radio & the eulogy to him given by Mel Allen.

Babes in the Wood see Goldilocks & the Three Bears & Other Stories

Babes in the Wood. Ruth Rendell. Read by Nigel Anthony. 10 cass. (Running Time: 15 hrs.). (Inspector Wexford Mystery Ser.: Bk. 19). 2003. 84.95 (978-0-7540-8308-5(X), CAB 2430); audio compact disk 94.95 (978-0-7540-8751-9(4), CCD 303) Pub: AudioGO. Dist(s): AudioGO

Babes in the Wood. unabr. ed. Ruth Rendell. Read by Nigel Anthony. 8 cass. (Running Time: 10 hrs. 30 mins.). (Inspector Wexford Mystery Ser.: Bk. 19). 2003. 34.95 (978-1-57270-310-0(5), 890405) Pub: Audio Partners. Dist(s): PerseuPGW

Babes in the Wood. unabr. ed. Ruth Rendell. Narrated by Nigel Anthony. 10 CDs. (Running Time: 10 hrs. 30 mins.). (Inspector Wexford Mystery Ser.: Bk. 19). (ENG.). 2003. audio compact disk 37.95 (978-1-57270-331-5(8), 100225) Pub: AudioGO. Dist(s): Perseus Dist
When the Dades return home from a trip to Paris they find that their two teenagers and the babysitter have vanished. Could they have drowned in the recent flood caused by terrible rains? The Subaqua Task Force can find no trace of the teenagers or the babysitter, and Mrs. Dade is convinced her children are dead.

Babette see Maupassant's Best Known Stories

Babette's Feast & Sorrow-Acre. unabr. ed. Isak Dinesen. Read by Colleen Dewhurst. 2 cass. (Running Time: 2 hrs. 30 mins.). 2000. 15.95 (978-0-945353-15-7(4), M20206u) Pub: Audio Partners. Dist(s): PerseuPGW
Two stories by the author of "Out of Africa".

Babies, Barns & Red-Neck Yarns. Poems. Graham Weathers. Read by Graham Weathers. 1 cass. (Running Time: 40 min.). 1997. Rental 9.95 (978-0-9664466-1-6(5)) Weathered Bronze.
Earthy poetry for the blue-collar, tobacco chewing, red-neck pick-up drivers & their sweet little ladies.

Babies E. Names. Lawrence Conerly. 2004. per. (978-0-9765669-0-8(7)) L Conerly.

Babies Lullaby. 1 cass. (Babies Ser.). (J). (ps-k). 1996. 7.98 (978-1-55723-200-7(8)); 12.98 (978-1-55723-507-7(4)) W Disney Records.

babouches de Bachir. unabr. ed. Jacques Gohier. Read by Béatrice Pasquier & Patrick Hoft. (J). 2007. 69.99 (978-2-35569-043-3(X)) Find a World.

Babushka's Doll. unabr. ed. Patricia Polacco. Narrated by Barbara Caruso. 1 cass. (Running Time: 15 mins.). (gr. 1 up). 1997. 10.00 (978-0-7887-0898-5(8), 95036E7) Recorded Bks.
When Babushka was a girl, she had a special doll that she played with only once. Now it's her grandmother's turn to learn a valuable lesson about consideration for others.

Baby & Me. Perf. by Rachel Buchman. 1 cass. (Running Time: 50 min.). (J). 1991. 9.95 (978-0-939065-51-6(7), GW 1055) Gentle Wind.
Each side begins with a waking up song, & includes games to play, sounds to distract a fussy baby, & soothing lullabyes.

Baby & Me. Rachel Buchman. 1 cass. (J). (GW1055) NewSound.
Activity songs & lullabies for infants.

Baby & Me: Playsongs & Lullabies to Share with Your Baby. Rachel Buchman. (J). 1991. audio compact disk 14.95 (978-0-939065-72-1(X)) Gentle Wind.

Baby Animals at the Zoo. Mark Eskola. Read by Mark Eskola. 1 cass. (Running Time: 40 min.). (J). (gr. 1-6). 1992. 5.99 incl. activity-coloring book & crayons. (978-1-878963-15-4(5)) Northstar Ent.
Music & activity tape about topics of interest to children ages 3 to 8.

Baby Bach. 1 CD. (Running Time: 1 hr.). (J). 2001. audio compact disk 12.98 (978-1-892309-10-5(6)) Pub: Baby Einstn. Dist(s): Penton Overseas
Based on recent research relating brain stimulation with infant development, these carefully created soundtracks provide an excellent opportunity for parents interested in stimulating the minds of their infants & young children.

Baby Bach. Baby Einstein Music Box Orchestra. 1 CD. (Running Time: 54 mins.). 2001. video & audio compact disk 15.98 (978-1-892309-55-6(6)) Pub: Baby Einstn. Dist(s): Penton Overseas
A collection of language & music verses, recitals & vocabulary-building activities in seven language & performed by the Baby Einstein Music Box Orchestra.

Baby Bach. Music by Johann Sebastian Bach. 1 CD. (Running Time: 1 hr.). audio compact disk 12.98 Pub: Baby Einstn. Dist(s): Penton Overseas

Baby Beethoven. Music by Ludwig van Beethoven. 1 CD. (Running Time: 1 hr.). audio compact disk 12.98 Pub: Baby Einstn. Dist(s): Penton Overseas

Baby Beethoven. Music by Ludwig van Beethoven. 1 cass. (Running Time: 1 hr.). (J). 2000. 9.98 (978-1-892309-13-6(0)) Pub: Baby Einstn. Dist(s): Penton Overseas
Based on recent research relating brain stimulation with infant development, these carefully created soundtracks provide an excellent opportunity for parents interested in stimulating the minds of their infants & young children.

Baby Beethoven. unabr. ed. 1 CD. (Running Time: 35 mins.). (J). 1999. audio compact disk 12.98 (978-1-892309-12-9(2)) Baby Einstn.
An all-Beethoven concert for little ears.

Baby Beluga. Perf. by Raffi. 1 LP. (J). lp 10.95 (KSR 8110); audio compact disk 16.95 (KSR 8110CD) Kimbo Educ.
Biscuits in the Oven - Oats & Beans & Barley - Day O - Thanks a Lot - All I Really Need - Over in the Meadow - This Old Man - Joshua Giraffe - Morningtown Ride.

Baby Beluga. Perf. by Raffi. 1 cass, 1 CD. (J). 2001. 10.95 (KSR 8110C) Kimbo Educ.

Baby Beluga. Perf. by Raffi. 1 cass. (J). (ps up). 10.98 (205); audio compact disk 17.98 (D205) MFLP CA.
A classic in children's music offering singable tunes for the whole family.

Baby Beluga. Perf. by Raffi. 1 cass., 1 CD. (J). 7.98 (RDR 8054); audio compact disk 12.78 CD Jewel box. (RDR 8054) NewSound.

Baby Beluga. Perf. by Raffi. (J). 1999. (978-1-886767-37-9(8)); (978-1-886767-63-8(7)); audio compact disk (978-1-886767-36-2(X)); audio compact disk (978-1-886767-62-1(9)) Rounder Records.
The beloved children's anthem "Baby Beluga" joins other fun-filled favorites & memorable Raffi originals in this collection of musical riches for the whole family.

Baby Bonding Book: 50 Ways to Connect with Your Infant. Victoria Loveland-Coen. Read by Barbara Niles. Music by David Powell. 1. (Running Time: 60 mins.). 2002. audio compact disk 14.95 (978-0-9644765-4-7(1), 002) Love Blessings.
50 fun Activities for a new mother to do with her baby. Activities range from humorous to heartfelt. Includes a 10-min guided relaxation session ready by the author.

Baby Brother Jesus Listening Tape. 10.00 (978-0-687-02343-1(2)) Abingdon.

Baby Brother Jesus Production Tape. 50.00 (978-0-687-02344-8(0)) Abingdon.

Baby Brother's Blues. unabr. ed. Pearl Cleage. Read by Pearl Cleage. 5 cass. (Running Time: 37980 sec.). (Sound Library). 2006. 49.95 (978-0-7927-3928-9(0), Chivers Sound Lib); audio compact disk 74.95 (978-0-7927-3929-6(9), Chivers Sound Lib) AudioGO.

Baby Brother's Blues: A Novel. unabr. ed. Pearl Cleage. 1 MP3-CD. (Running Time: 7 hrs.). 2006. 29.95 (978-0-7927-3972-2(8), Chivers Sound Lib) AudioGO.

Baby Dance. unabr. ed. Jane Anderson. Perf. by David Ellenstein & Valerie Landsburg. 1 cass. (Running Time: 1 hr. 11 min.). 1993. 19.95 (978-1-58081-069-2(1), TPT29) L A Theatre.
A desperate L. A. yuppie couple arrange to buy the unborn child of a dirt poor Louisiana pair.

Baby Days & Lullabye Nights Set. (J). 1994. bk. 14.95 (978-1-59093-056-4(8), Eager Minds) Warehse and Fulfillment.

Baby Dolittle Neighborhood Animals. 1 CD. (J). 2001. video & audio compact disk 15.98 (00043) Pub: Artisan Enter. Dist(s): Rounder Kids Mus Dist

Baby Dolittle Neighborhood Animals. 1 CD. (Running Time: 15 min.). (J). 2001. video & audio compact disk 15.98 (978-1-892309-61-7(0)) Pub: Baby Einstn. Dist(s): Penton Overseas
Introduces animals that can be found close to home.

Baby Dolittle World Animal O/P. unabr. ed. 1 CD. (Running Time: 15 min.). (J). 2001. audio compact disk 15.98 (978-1-892309-65-5(3)) Baby Einstn.
Doolittle World Animals features animals from faraway places.

Baby Einstein. Perf. by Baby Einstein Music Box Orchestra. 1 CD. (Running Time: 54 mins.). 2001. video & audio compact disk 15.98 (978-1-892309-53-2(X)) Pub: Baby Einstn. Dist(s): Penton Overseas
A collection of language & music verses, recitals & vocabulary-building activities in seven languages & performed by the Baby Einstein Music Box Orchestra.

Baby Einstein Art Time Classics. Perf. by Baby Einstein Music Box Orchestra. 1 CD. (Running Time: 35 mins.). (J). 2001. audio compact disk 12.98 (978-1-892309-37-2(8)) Pub: Baby Einstn. Dist(s): Penton Overseas
A wonderful collection of masterpieces from the late 19th & early 20th century. Soundtracks of classic cartoons & TV shows.

Baby Einstein Language Nursery. Perf. by Baby Einstein Music Box Orchestra. 1 CD. (Running Time: 54 mins.). (J). 2001. audio compact disk 12.98 (978-1-892309-39-6(4)) Pub: Baby Einstn. Dist(s): Penton Overseas
A collection of language & music verses, recitals & vocabulary-building activities in seven languages.

Baby Face. unabr. ed. Steve Brewer. Read by Gene Engene. 6 cass. (Running Time: 7 hrs. 12 min.). (Bubba Mabry Mystery Ser.: Bk. 2). 2001. 39.95 (978-1-55686-869-6(3)) Books in Motion.
Bubba's career hits a low point from this street assignment. With a doberman and rogue cops on his tail, Bubba must catch a killer - before the killer catches him.

Baby Face: Activities for Infants & Toddlers. 1 cass. (Running Time: 1 hr.). (J). 2001. pap. bk. 10.95 (KIM 7049C); pap. bk. & pupil's gde. ed. 11.95 (KIM 7049); audio compact disk 14.95 (KIM 7049CD) Kimbo Educ.
Here is a delightful way to turn baby's play time into a fun & meaningful learning experience. Familiar baby songs set the mood for introducing simple rhythms & exercises. Baby's Hokey Pokey, "A" You're Adorable, Ring Around the Rosie, Baby Take a Bow, Pretty Baby & more. Includes guide.

Baby Games. 1 CD. (Running Time: 1 hr.). (J). (ps). 2001. pap. bk. 14.95 (KIM 9102CD) Kimbo Educ.
Silly faces & sounds - babies love it, & so do grownups. Lap games, exercise games, rocking & bouncing games for baby & grownups to share & enjoy. By the author of Diaper Gym, this special playtime activity album will help little ones develop important early skills. Nursery music includes: The Muffin Man, Bye Baby Bunting, Playmates, Hey Diddle Diddle & more. Includes guide.

Baby Games (Six Weeks-One Year) 1 cass. (Running Time: 1 hr.). (J). 2001. pap. bk. 10.95 (KIM 9102C) Kimbo Educ.

Baby Goat see Twentieth-Century Poetry in English, No. 12, Recordings of Poets Reading Their Own Poetry

Baby Growlers Vol. 4: Too Hip to Hop. 1 CD. (Running Time: 42 mins.). (J). 2004. audio compact disk 13.00 (978-1-893185-56-2(7)) TNG Earth.
The message from the very top, Is that frogs no longer hop, They jump and leap and flip and flop, But frogs are way too hip to hop... Childrens music created in Growlerville for the very young, featuring kids music that parents love.

Baby G's Cinque Album. George Lawson-Easley. 1cd. (Running Time: 1hr). (YA). 2010. 14.95 (978-0-9785256-1-3(2), Warzone Recs) Prince Zone Pub.

Baby g's crystal reflection Album. George Lawson-Easley. 1. (Running Time: 1hour). (ENG.). (YA). 2010. 14.95 (978-0-9785256-7-5(1), Warzone Recs) Prince Zone Pub.

Baby Hawk Learns to Fly: Stories about Purpose, Patience, Confidence, & Courage. Bobby Norfolk. (Running Time: 46 mins.). 2004. audio compact disk 14.95 (978-0-87483-747-6(2)) Pub: August Hse. Dist(s): Natl Bk Netwk

Baby in Dreamland. MTL Staff. Illus. by Kathleen Francour. (Flitterbyes Relaxation Ser.). (J). 2003. audio compact disk 6.95 (978-1-59125-408-9(6)) Penton Overseas.

Baby in Dreamland. Penton. 1 CD. (Running Time: 1 hr. 30 mins.). (Relaxation Ser.). (ENG.). (J). 2003. audio compact disk 7.95 (978-1-59125-334-1(9)) Penton Overseas.

Baby Is Three. abr. ed. Theodore Sturgeon. 1 cass. (Running Time: 90 mins.). (Complete Stories of Theodore Sturgeon Ser.: Vol. 6). 1984. 12.95 (978-0-694-50276-9(6), SWC 1492) HarperCollins Pubs.

Baby Language School: Spanish Learning Kit. 2 cass. (Running Time: 2 hrs.). (J). (ps). 2001. pap. bk. 29.95 (BS-7S) Kimbo Educ.
This exciting kit helps babies experience the foundations of Spanish with stimulating visuals & engaging Spanish-language songs. Includes songbook.

Baby Leopard: An African Folktale. Linda Goss & Clay Goss. Illus. by Suzanne Bailey-Jones & Michael R. Jones. (J). (ps-3). 1989. pap. bk. 7.95 (978-0-318-41503-1(8)) RandomHse Pub.

Baby Love. Catherine Anderson. Narrated by Suzanne Toren. 10 cass. (Running Time: 13 hrs. 30 mins.). 88.00 (978-0-7887-9956-3(8)) Recorded Bks.

Baby Love. unabr. ed. Catherine Anderson. Narrated by Suzanne Toren. 11 CDs. (Running Time: 13 hrs. 30 mins.). 2002. audio compact disk 111.00 (978-1-4025-2911-5(2)) Recorded Bks.
With her infant son clutched to her breast, Maggie Stanley flees for her life. She has abandoned everything else to escape her abusive family. Ragged and hungover, Rafe Kendricks is also on the run, trying to erase memories of the accident that killed his wife and child. Maggie and Rafe meet in a moment of mutual need, but soon the young woman will find that Rafe is not whom he appears to be.

Baby Loves Country. Compiled by Dean Diehl. 1 CD. (Running Time: 33 mins.). 2000. audio compact disk Brentwood Music.
Soft country melodies with quiet words of love to rock your baby to sleep. Features handcrafted instruments. Songs include: "Hushaby," "Little One," "Raindrops," "When it's Sleepytime" & more.

Baby Mozart. 1 CD. (Running Time: 1 hr.). (J). 1998. bk. 12.95 (978-1-892309-02-0(5)) Pub: Baby Einstn. Dist(s): Penton Overseas
Based on recent research relating brain stimulation with infant development, these carefully created soundtracks provide an excellent opportunity for parents interested in stimulating the minds of their infants & young children.

Baby Mozart. Audio & Video. 1 cass.; 1 CD. (J). 1998. cass. & video 23.95 (978-1-892309-07-5(6)) Baby Einstn.

Baby Mozart. Perf. by Baby Einstein Music Box Orchestra. 1 CD. (Running Time: 54 mins.). 2001. video & audio compact disk 15.98 (978-1-892309-54-9(8)) Pub: Baby Einstn. Dist(s): Penton Overseas
A collection of language & music verses, recitals & vocabulary-building activities in seven languages & performed by the Baby Einstein Music Box Orchestra.

Baby Mozart. Music by Wolfgang Amadeus Mozart. 1 CD. (Running Time: 1 hr.). audio compact disk 12.98 Pub: Baby Einstn. Dist(s): Penton Overseas

Baby Mozart. Wolfgang Amadeus Mozart. 1 cass. (Running Time: 1 hr.). (J). 1998. bk. 9.98 (978-1-892309-03-7(3)) Pub: Baby Einstn. Dist(s): Penton Overseas
Based on recent research relating brain stimulation with infant development, these carefully created soundtracks provide an excellent opportunity for parents interested in stimulating the minds of their infants & young children.

Baby Mozart. unabr. ed. 1 cass.; 1 CD. (Running Time: 35 min.). (J). 1998. cass. & video 21.95 (978-1-892309-06-8(8)) Baby Einstn.

Baby Names on Tape. 2 cass. (Running Time: 2 hrs.). 1997. (978-0-9656704-0-1(6), 1001) JEBS Creations.
List of boy's & girls names intermixed with advice with a short description, history & meaning of each name. One cassette has boy's names & the other cassette has girl's names.

Baby Newton: Shapes in Motion. Composed by Antonio Vivaldi. (J). 2002. video & audio compact disk 15.98 (978-1-892309-67-9(X)) Pub: Baby Einstn. Dist(s): Penton Overseas
An enriching new approach to learning five shapes through the context of toys, nature, kinetic art and beautiful geodesic forms found in the world around us. This video captures the spirit of a child's fascination with the world around them. The video is accented with arrangements of classical music by Vivaldi. CD soundtrack included.

Baby Proof. Emily Giffin. Narrated by Christine Marshall. 9 CDs. (Running Time: 39300 sec.). (Sound Library). 2006. audio compact disk 89.95 (978-0-7927-4060-5(2), SLD 967) AudioGO.

Baby Proof. abr. ed. Emily Giffin. Read by Cynthia Nixon. (Running Time: 5 hrs. 0 mins. 0 sec.). (ENG.). 2007. audio compact disk 14.95 (978-1-4272-0156-0(0)) Pub: Macmill Audio. Dist(s): Macmillan

Baby Road. Floyd Domino. Perf. by Floyd Domino. 1 cass. (Running Time: 45 min.). (J). 1989. bk. 12.95 (978-0-938971-22-1(0)) JTG Nashville.
Features instrumentals of Beatles songs for children of all ages.

Baby Santa's Music Box. Video. (J). 2002. video & audio compact disk 15.98 (978-1-892309-84-6(X)) Pub: Baby Einstn. Dist(s): Penton Overseas

Baby See Baby Do Story CD (Babytown Storybook) Short Stories. Created by Queen Lane. Illus. by Queen Lane. Voice by Jaina Lane. 1 CD. (Running Time: 22 mins). Dramatization. (BABYTOWN Ser.: Bk. 2). (J). 2005. audio compact disk 10.00 (978-0-9772738-4-3(9)) Quebla.
Can you imagine what life would be like if you were born able to talk? Well, Baby can! Considered the town?s most ambitious under-one-nager, Baby is proud to be like-a-girl as she ventures through life dissecting the who, what, and whys of everything in sight. Baby is the littlest prodigy with the biggest imagination, always ready to save the day. Children of all ages will be delighted to see just how silly things can be through the eyes of an infant.In BABY SEE BABY DO, Baby has her first day at school and makes new friends! Jaina meets teen-sensation Sasha Pearl, but not before Baby has to save the day!.

Baby Shakespeare O/P. (J). 2002. video & audio compact disk 15.98 (978-1-892309-57-0(2)) Pub: Baby Einstn. Dist(s): Penton Overseas

Baby Signing Time Songs Vol. 1. Prod. by Two Little Hands Music. (ENG.). (J). 2005. audio compact disk 9.99 (978-1-933543-54-3(X)) Tw Li Ha Pr LLC.

Baby Signing Time Songs Vol. 2. Prod. by Two Little Hands Music. (J). 2005. audio compact disk 9.99 (978-1-933543-55-0(8)) Tw Li Ha Pr LLC.

Baby Signing Time Volume 3 Songs. Prod. by Two LIttle Hands Music. (J). 2008. audio compact disk 9.99 (978-1-933543-60-4(4)) Tw Li Ha Pr LLC.

Baby Signing Time Volume 4 Songs. Prod. by Two LIttle Hands Music. (J). 2008. audio compact disk 9.99 (978-1-933543-61-1(2)) Tw Li Ha Pr LLC.

Baby Sister for Frances. unabr. abr. ed. Russell Hoban. Perf. by Glynis Johns. Illus. by Lillian Hoban. 1 cass. (Running Time: 20 min.). (Tell Me a Story Bks.). (J). (ps-3). 1995. 8.95 (978-0-694-70018-9(5)) HarperCollins Pubs.

Baby-Sitters Club Soundtrack. Perf. by Matthew Sweet et al. 1 cass. (J). 1995. 10.98 (Sony Wonder); audio compact disk 15.98 CD. Sony Music Ent.
The motion picture soundtrack to the new feature film features popular songs from modern rock artists.

Baby-Sitting Ghost. unabr. ed. Allan Zullo. Read by John Ratzenberger. 2008. 1.37 (978-1-4233-8075-7(4), 9781423380757, BAD) Brilliance Audio.

Baby Snooks. Contrib. by Fanny Brice. (Running Time: 10800 sec.). 2004. 9.98 (978-1-57019-621-8(4)); audio compact disk 9.98 (978-1-57019-622-5(2)) Radio Spirits.

Baby Snooks, Set. unabr. ed. 2 cass. (Running Time: 2 hrs.). 10.95 (978-1-57816-001-3(4), BS2501) Audio File.
Four programs from the radio program.

Baby Snooks, Vol. 2. Radio Spirits Publishing Staff. Read by Fanny Brice. 2006. audio compact disk 9.98 (978-1-57019-814-4(4)) Radio Spirits.

Baby Snooks: Two Comedy Shows. Perf. by Fanny Brice & Hanley Stafford. (CC-5720) Natl Recrd Co.

Baby Snooks: Why, Daddy? Perf. by Fanny Brice & Hanely Stafford. 2009. audio compact disk 18.95 (978-1-57019-901-1(9)) Radio Spirits.

Baby Snooks Visits & Herb Steals Tools. Perf. by Penny Singleton & Arthur Lake. 1 cass. (Running Time: 60 min.). Dramatization. (Blondie Ser.). 1944. 6.00 Once Upon Rad.
Radio broadcasts - humor.

Baby Songs. 1 cass. (J). 10.98 (225) MFLP CA.
Includes "My Mommy Comes Back," "Piggy Toes," "Rub-A-Dub," "Today I Took My Diaper Off," "I Sleep 'till Morning" plus 4 more.

Baby Songs. Perf. by Hap Palmer. 1 LP. (J). (ps). pupil's gde. ed. 11.95 (EA 713); 11.95 (EA 713C); audio compact disk 14.95 CD. (EA 713CD) Kimbo Educ.
Share - My Mommy Comes Back - Daddy, Be a Horsey - Today I Took My Diaper Off - Security (Don't Wash My Blanket) & more.

Baby Sounds: Happy Baby Sounds to Delight Your Baby. Created by Kid Kid Rhino Inc. Staff. 1 CD. 1998. audio compact disk 9.98 (978-1-56826-869-9(6)) Rhino Enter.

Baby Sounds: Happy Baby Sounds to Delight Your Baby. Created by Kid Kid Rhino Inc. Staff. 1 cass. (J). 1998. 5.99 (978-1-56826-868-2(8), 72959) Rhino Enter.
Composed of two distinct halves "Awake Time" and "Sleep Time." This album features babies laughing, cooing, playing and sleeping to entertain your baby.

Baby Talk: How to Interpret Children's Charts. Marion D. March. 1 cass. 8.95 (559) Am Fed Astrologers.
Special approach to child's chart.

Baby Tunes: Classical Baby, Mozart-Awake Time. 1 cass. (Running Time: 1 hr.). (J). 2002. 5.99 (978-1-56826-879-8(3), 72947) Rhino Enter.
Early exposure to classical music can increase math and logic skills in children. Give your kids a head start.

Baby Tunes: Classical Baby, Mozart-Sleepy Time. 1 cass. (Running Time: 1 hr.). (J). 2002. 5.99 (978-1-56826-884-2(X), 72950) Rhino Enter.
Develop your infant's mind as they drift off to sleep with the soothing side of Mozart's music.

Baby Tunes: International Baby, a Gentle African Journey. 1 cass. (Running Time: 1 hr.). (J). 2002. 5.99 (978-1-56826-888-0(2), 72953) Rhino Enter.
Introduce your baby to soothing African rhythms, with this intriguing mix of traditional and contemporary music.

Baby Tunes: Nature Baby, Water Baby. 1 cass. (Running Time: 1 hr.). (J). 2002. 5.99 (978-1-56826-885-9(8), 72951) Rhino Enter.
Orchestral melodies are entwined within the sounds of waterfalls, streams, and the ocean, designed to send your baby on a tranquil journey through sounds of living waters.

Baby Van Gogh O/P. (J). 2002. video & audio compact disk 15.98 (978-1-892309-58-7(0)) Pub: Baby Einstn. Dist(s): Penton Overseas

Baby Villon see Philip Levine

Baby Who Didn't Know Love. Manda Brooks. Illus. by Eboni Reavis. (ENG.). (J). 2008. pap. bk. (978-0-9818234-0-9(8)) His Heart Art.

Baby, Would I Lie. unabr. ed. Donald E. Westlake. Read by Nicola Sheara. 6 cass. (Running Time: 8 hrs. 40 mins.). 2000. 29.95 (978-1-57270-139-7(0), N61139u) Pub: Audio Partners. Dist(s): PerseuPGW
Journalist Sara Joslyn travels to Branson, Missouri, to cover the trial of Ray Jones, a country-western singer accused of rape & murder. She is also hoping to scoop her former employer, the sleazy tabloid, The Weekly Galaxy.

Baby, Would I Lie. unabr. ed. Donald E. Westlake. Read by Nicola Sheara. 8 vols. 2000. bk. 69.95 (978-0-7927-2275-5(2), CSL 164, Chivers Sound Lib) AudioGO.
Welcome to Branson, Missouri, home of Country Music USA, big hairdos, and phony snakeskin boots. The most popular show in Branson is the trial of country music crooner Ray Jones. The wily, inscrutable Jones is accused of murdering a one-night stand, and the media cut-throats of the Weekly Galaxy, Sara Joslyn and Jack Ingersoll, are having a field day! So are a whole bunch of lawyers, the IRS, and thousands of gawking fans.

Baby, Would I Lie. unabr. ed. Donald E. Westlake. Read by Donald E. Westlake. (Running Time: 7 hrs.). 2008. 39.25 (978-1-4233-5266-2(1), 9781423352662, BADLE); 24.95 (978-1-4233-5265-5(3), 9781423352655, BAD); audio compact disk 39.25 (978-1-4233-5264-8(5), 9781423352648, Brlnc Audio MP3 Lib); audio compact disk 24.95 (978-1-4233-5263-1(7), 9781423352631, Brilliance MP3) Brilliance Audio.

***Babycakes.** abr. ed. Armistead Maupin. Read by Armistead Maupin. (ENG.). 2009. (978-0-06-197733-6(0), Harper Audio); (978-0-06-197732-9(2), Harper Audio) HarperCollins Pubs.

Babyhood. unabr. ed. Paul Reiser. Read by Paul Reiser. 4 CDs. (Running Time: 4 hrs. 48 mins.). 2001. audio compact disk Books on Tape.
I'm going to be totally honest. It's not a "how-to," a "when-to," or a "what-to-expect." It's not even endorsed by anyone remotely connected to the medical profession. Instead, this is an amusing look at what is good & bad about being a parent.

Babylon Babies. unabr. ed. Maurice G. Dantec. Read by Joe Barrett. 14 CDs. (Running Time: 17 hrs.). 2008. audio compact disk 24.95 (978-1-4332-1192-8(0)) Blckstn Audio.

Babylon Babies. unabr. ed. Maurice G. Dantec. Read by Joe Barrett. Tr. by Noura Wedell. 16 CDs. (Running Time: 20 hrs.). 2008. audio compact disk 120.00 (978-1-4332-1190-4(4)) Blckstn Audio.

Babylon Babies. unabr. ed. Maurice G. Dantec & Joe Barrett. Tr. by Noura Wedell. (Running Time: 20 hrs. NaN mins.). 2008. 89.95 (978-1-4332-1189-8(0)); audio compact disk 44.95 (978-1-4332-1193-5(9)) Blckstn Audio.

Babylon Revisited see Great Gatsby & Other Stories

Babylon Revisited see Fitzgerald Short Stories

Babylon Revisited, unabr. ed. Short Stories. F. Scott Fitzgerald. Narrated by George Guidall. 8 cass. (Running Time: 11 hrs.). 1997. 70.00 (978-0-7887-0872-5(4), 95013E7) Recorded Bks.
Stories of powerful characters from the glittery cities to the rural hamlets of the 20s & 30s.

Babylon Revisited: And Other Stories. unabr. ed. F. Scott Fitzgerald. Read by Alexander Scourby. 2 cass. (Running Time: 1 hr. 50 min.). Incl. Bridal Party. 1977. (CB 101 CX); Three Hours Between Planes. 1977. (CB 101 CX); 1977. 15.98 (978-0-8072-3421-1(4), CB 101 CX, Listening Lib) Random Audio Pubg.
A sensitive reading of four of F. Scott Fitzgerald's poignant short stories reminiscent of the "jazz age" in both Paris & America.

Babylon Rising. unabr. ed. Tim LaHaye & Greg Dinallo. Read by Jason Culp. 6 cass. (Running Time: 9 hrs.). (Babylon Rising Ser.: Bk. 1). 2003. 57.60 (978-0-7366-9431-5(5)); audio compact disk 68.00 (978-0-7366-9529-9(X)) Pub: Books on Tape. Dist(s): NetLibrary CO
In this Christian thriller, an unlikely hero arises to meet the challenges of a terrifying evil.

Babylon Sisters. unabr. ed. Pearl Cleage. Read by Pearl Cleage. (Running Time: 29280 sec.). (Hercule Poirot Mystery Ser.). 2001. audio compact disk 29.95 (978-0-7927-3507-6(2), CMP 768) AudioGO.

Babylon Sisters. unabr. ed. Pearl Cleage. 6 cass. 2005. 54.95 (978-0-7927-3504-5(8), CSL 768); audio compact disk 79.95 (978-0-7927-3505-2(6), SLD 768) AudioGO.

Babylon Sisters: A Novel. unabr. ed. Pearl Cleage. 2005. 31.95 (978-1-57270-464-0(0)) Pub: Audio Partners. Dist(s): PerseuPGW

Babylon Sisters: A Novel. unabr. ed. Pearl Cleage. (ENG.). 2005. audio compact disk 31.95 (978-1-57270-465-7(9)) Pub: AudioGO. Dist(s): Perseus Dist

***Babyproofing Your Marriage.** abr. ed. Stacie Cockrell. Read by Jennifer Van Dyck & Christopher Burns. (ENG.). 2007. (978-0-06-126224-1(2), Harper Audio); (978-0-06-126225-8(0), Harper Audio) HarperCollins Pubs.

Babyproofing Your Marriage: How to Laugh More, Argue Less, & Communicate Better as Your Family Grows. abr. ed. Stacie Cockrell et al. Read by Jennifer Van Dyck & Christopher Burns. (Running Time: 21600 sec.). 2007. audio compact disk 29.95 (978-0-06-123657-0(8)) HarperCollins Pubs.

Baby's Bedtime. Judy Collins. 1 cass. (J). 1993. pap. bk. 9.98 (978-1-879496-07-1(0)) Lightyear Entrtnmnt.

Baby's Bedtime. unabr. ed. Kay Chorao. Perf. by Judy Collins. 1 CD. (Running Time: 42 min.). (Stories to Remember Ser.). (J). (gr. 1). 1990. pap. bk. 13.98 CD incl. coloring bk. (978-1-56896-028-9(X)); 8.98 (978-1-879496-06-4(2)); 8.98 incl. coloring bk. (978-1-56896-008-1(5)) Lightyear Entrtnmnt.
27 spellbinding lullabies from around the world, performed by Judy Collins, based on the best-selling picture book by Kay Chorao.

Baby's Classics Set. MTL Staff. Illus. by Kathleen Francour. (ENG.). (J). 2006. audio compact disk 20.95 (978-1-59125-403-4(5)) Penton Overseas.

Baby's Day. 1 cass. (Running Time: 20 min.). (Disney Babies Audio Playset Ser.). (J). bk. 9.98 Disney Prod.

Baby's Day: Point & Learn. (Point & Learn Ser.). (J). (ps). 1999. pap. bk. 6.98 (978-0-7634-0585-4(X)) W Disney Records.

Baby's First Animal Songs. 1 cass. (Running Time: 90 mins.). (Baby's First Ser.). (J). (ps-k). 1999. 8.95 (978-1-56015-711-3(9)) Penton Overseas.
Includes: "Three Blind Mice," "Baa Baa Black Sheep" & "Never Smile at a Crocodile.".

Baby's First Animal Songs/Fairy Tales. 2 CDs. (Running Time: 3 hrs.). (Baby's First Ser.). (J). (ps-k). 1999. audio compact disk 24.95 (978-1-56015-722-9(4)) Penton Overseas.
Includes "Three Blind Mice," "Baa Baa Black Sheep," "Never Smile at a Crocodile," "Hansel & Gretel," "The Three Little Pigs," "Beauty & the Beast" & "Sleeping Beauty.".

Babys First Birthday Songs. 1 CD. (Running Time: 90 mins.). (Baby's First Ser.). (J). (ps-k). 1999. audio compact disk 12.95 (978-1-56015-708-3(9)) Penton Overseas.
Includes: "Happy Birthday to You," "The Chicken Dance" & "Jack in the Box.".

Baby's First Birthday Songs. 1 cass. (Running Time: 90 mins.). (Baby's First Ser.). (J). (ps-k). 1999. 8.95 (978-1-56015-709-0(7)) Penton Overseas.

Baby's First Book of Signs Vol. I: An ASL Word Book with Video & Audio Clips. (J). 2005. cd-rom & audio compact disk 14.95 (978-0-9760818-2-1(2)) Inst Disblties.

Baby's First Book of Signs Vol. II: An ASL Word Book with Video & Audio Clips. (J). 2005. cd-rom & audio compact disk 14.95 (978-0-9760818-3-8(0)) Inst Disblties.

Baby's First Book of Signs Vol. III: An ASL Word Book with Video & Audio Clips. (J). 2005. cd-rom & audio compact disk 14.95 (978-0-9760818-4-5(9)) Inst Disblties.

Baby's First CD. Narrated by Jessie Ruffenach & Maybelle Little. Instructed by Beverly Blacksheep. (Running Time: 30 mins). (NAV & ENG.). (J). 2005. audio compact disk 10.95 (978-1-893354-70-8(9)) Pub: Salina Bkshelf. Dist(s): Natl Bk Netwk
Audio narration of the first four books in Salina Bookshelf's "baby series." The four books narrated are Baby's First Laugh, Baby Learns to Count, Baby Learns About Colors, and Baby Learns About Animals.

Baby's First Christmas 2 CD Collection. Twin Sisters Productions Staff. (J). 2009. audio compact disk 4.50 (978-1-59922-170-0(5)) Twin Sisters.

Baby's First Classical Masterpieces. Penton. (ENG.). 2003. audio compact disk 6.95 (978-1-59125-395-2(0)) Penton Overseas.

Baby's First Classics: Music for the Developing Mind. 1 CD. (Running Time: 1 hr.). (Baby's First Ser.). (J). 2002. audio compact disk 12.95 (978-1-56015-706-9(2), Penton Kids) Penton Overseas.

Baby's First Fairy Tales. 1 cass. (Running Time: 90 mins.). (Baby's First Ser.). (J). (ps-k). 1999. 8.95 (978-1-56015-717-5(8)) Penton Overseas.
Includes "Hansel & Gretel," "The Three Little Pigs," "Beauty & the Beast" & "Sleeping Beauty.".

Babys First Fairy Tales. Cd. 1 CD. (Running Time: 90 mins.). (Baby's First Ser.). (J). (ps-k). 1999. audio compact disk 12.95 (978-1-56015-716-8(X)) Penton Overseas.

Baby's First Happy Songs. 1 cass. (Running Time: 90 mins.). (Baby's First Ser.). (J). (ps-k). 1999. 8.95 (978-1-56015-713-7(5)) Penton Overseas.
Includes: "Ring a Ring of Roses," "Pat-a-Cake Pat-a-Cake" & "I'm a Little Teapot.".

Babys First Happy Songs. Cd. 1 CD. (Running Time: 90 mins.). (Baby's First Ser.). (J). (ps-k). 1999. audio compact disk 12.95 (978-1-56015-712-0(7)) Penton Overseas.

Babys First Lullabies. 1 CD. (Running Time: 90 mins.). (Baby's First Ser.). (J). (ps-k). 2000. audio compact disk 12.95 (978-1-56015-700-7(3)) Penton Overseas.
Includes: "Hush a Bye Baby," "Twinkle Twinkle Little Star" & Chopin's "Prelude in A Minor.".

Baby's First Lullabies. 1 cass. (Running Time: 90 mins.). (Baby's First Ser.). (J). (ps-k). 2000. 8.95 (978-1-56015-701-4(1)) Penton Overseas.

Baby's First Lullabies. Prod. by Twin Sisters Productions Staff. 1 CD. (Running Time: 45 min). (J). 2005. audio compact disk 6.99 (978-1-57583-815-1(X)) Twin Sisters.
Quiet your child's heart at the close of each day with this soft, soothing collection of classical melodies, traditional lullabies, and songs of faith. The quiet, instrumental arrangements of Brahms' Lullaby, Jesus Loves Me, Now The Day Is Over and other familiar melodies will bring rest to baby's body and spirit. Perfect for relaxing both mom and baby at home or for quieting a noisy nursery.

Babys First Mozart. unabr. ed. 1 cass. (Running Time: 35 min.). (J). 2000. 8.95 (978-1-56015-703-8(8)) Penton Overseas.

Baby's First Mozart: Music for the Developing Mind. Cd. 1 CD. (Running Time: 1 hr.). (J). 2002. audio compact disk 12.95 (978-1-56015-702-1(X), Penton Kids) Penton Overseas.
Features: Allegro; Andante; Presto; Sonata In C Major.

Baby's First Nursery Rhymes. 1 cass. (Running Time: 90 mins.). (Baby's First Ser.). (J). (ps-k). 1999. 8.95 (978-1-56015-719-9(4)) Penton Overseas.
Includes: "Old MacDonald," "Three Blind Mice" & "Mary Had a Little Lamb.".

Baby's First Nursery Rhymes. Penton. 1 CD. (Running Time: 90 mins.). (Baby's First Ser.). (J). (ps-k). 1999. audio compact disk 12.95 (978-1-56015-718-2(6)) Penton Overseas.

Baby's First Nursery Rhymes/lullabies. Penton. 2 CDs. (Running Time: 3 hrs.). (Baby's First Ser.). (J). (ps-k). 1999. audio compact disk 24.95 (978-1-56015-723-6(2)) Penton Overseas.
Contains "Old MacDonald," "Three Blind Mice," "Mary Had a Little Lamb," "Hush a Bye Baby," "Twinkle Twinkle Little Star" & Chopin's "Prelude in a Mirror.".

Babys First Playtime Songs. 1 CD. (Running Time: 90 mins.). (Baby's First Ser.). (J). (ps-k). 2000. audio compact disk 12.95 (978-1-56015-704-5(6)) Penton Overseas.
Includes: "Hokey Pokey," "Pop Goes the Weasel," "Let's Go Fly a Kite" & "Bananas in Pajamas.".

Baby's First Playtime Songs. 1 cass. (Running Time: 30 min.). (Baby's First Ser.). (J). (ps-k). 2000. 8.95 (978-1-56015-705-2(4)) Penton Overseas.
Includes Hokey Pokey, Pop Goes the Weasel, Let's Go Fly a Kite, Bananas in Pajamas.

Baby's First Playtime Songs/Birthday Songs. 2 CDs. (Running Time: 3 hrs.). (Baby's First Ser.). (J). (ps-k). 1999. audio compact disk 24.95 (978-1-56015-721-2(6)) Penton Overseas.
Contains "Hokey Pokey," "Pop Goes the Weasel," "Happy Birthday to You," "Jack in the Box" & more.

Baby's First Sing-along. Penton. 1 cass. (Running Time: 90 mins.). (Baby's First Ser.). (J). (ps-k). 2000. 8.95 (978-1-56015-743-4(7)) Penton Overseas.

Baby's First Sleepytime. Penton. 1 CD. (Running Time: 90 mins.). (Baby's First Ser.). (J). 2000. audio compact disk 12.95 (978-1-56015-767-0(4)) Penton Overseas.

Baby's First Sleepytime: Music for the Developing Mind. 1 cass. (Running Time: 1 hr.). (Baby's First Ser.). (J). 2002. 8.95 (978-1-56015-707-6(0), Penton Kids) Penton Overseas.

***Baby's First Year Journal & Prayer Book. A Mother's Prayers for her Infant.** Patricia Hull. 2010. reel tape 21.95 (978-0-578-05454-4(X)) Wings Eagles.

Baby's Gift of Music & Stories. Perf. by Judy Collins et al. 4 cass. (J). (ps). 27.98 set. Lightyear Entrtnmnt.
Includes 27 lullabies, 26 poems, 57 nursery rhymes & 15 stories.

Baby's Lap Book. Read by Phylicia Rashad. Music by Jason Miles. 1 cass. (Running Time: 25 min.). (J). (gr. k up). bk. 18.95 (Dut) Penguin Grp USA.

Baby's Lullaby Classics. Perf. by Michael Kolmstetter. 1 cass. (Running Time: 30 min.). (J). (ps-1). 2000. 7.99 (978-1-894677-06-6(4)); audio compact disk 9.99 (978-1-894677-05-9(6)) Kidzup Prodns.

Baby's Lullaby Classics. Perf. by Michael Kolmstetter. 1 cass. (Running Time: 35 min.). (J). 2001. 7.99; audio compact disk 9.99 Penton Overseas.
Classical guitar music for children of all ages.

Baby's Lullabyes. Penton. 1 cass. (Running Time: 1 hr. 30 mins.). (Relaxation Ser.). (ENG.). (J). 2003. audio compact disk 7.95 (978-1-59125-331-0(4)) Penton Overseas.

Baby's Morningtime. unabr. ed. Kay Chorao. Perf. by Judy Collins. 1 CD. (Running Time: 37 min.). (Stories to Remember Ser.). (J). (gr. 1). 1990. pap. bk. 13.98 CD incl. coloring bk. (978-1-56896-013-5(1)); 8.98 (978-1-879496-15-6(1)); 8.98 incl. coloring bk. (978-1-56896-012-8(3)); audio compact disk 13.98 CD. (978-1-56896-030-2(1)) Lightyear Entrtnmnt.
This joyous collection of poems from artist Kay Chorao's acclaimed picture book, pays tribute to the first hours of a new day.

Baby's Nursery Rhymes. unabr. ed. Kay Chorao. Read by Phylicia Rashad. 1 CD. (Running Time: 47 min.). (Stories to Remember Ser.). (J). (gr. 1). 1991. pap. bk. 13.98 CD incl. coloring bk. (978-1-56896-015-9(8)); 8.98 (978-1-879496-18-7(6)); 8.98 incl. coloring bk. (978-1-56896-014-2(X)) Lightyear Entrtnmnt.
Phylicia Rashad brings a lively voice & rhythm to this collection of best-loved nursery rhymes based on Kay Chorao's best-selling picture book.

Baby's Second. MTL Staff. Illus. by Kathleen Francour. (Flitterbyes Classical Masterpieces Ser.). (ENG.). (J). 2003. audio compact disk 6.95 (978-1-59125-405-8(1)) Penton Overseas.

Baby's Second Classical Masterpieces. Penton. (ENG.). 2003. audio compact disk 6.95 (978-1-59125-396-9(9)) Penton Overseas.

Baby's Storytime. unabr. ed. Kay Chorao. Read by Arlo Guthrie. 1 CD. (Running Time: 36 min.). (Stories to Remember Ser.). (J). (gr. 1). 1990. pap. bk. 13.98 CD incl. coloring bk. (978-1-56896-011-1(5)); 8.98 (978-1-879496-09-5(7)); audio compact disk 13.98 CD. (978-1-56896-029-6(8)) Lightyear Entrtnmnt.
Arlo Guthrie lends his wry interpretations to this word-for-word audio adaptation of Kay Chorao's best-selling picture book for preschoolers.

Baby's 1st Animal Songs. 1 CD. (Running Time: 90 mins.). (Baby's First Ser.). (J). (ps-k). 1999. audio compact disk 12.95 (978-1-56015-710-6(0)) Penton Overseas.
Includes: "Three Blind Mice," "Baa Baa Black Sheep" & "Never Smile at a Crocodile.".

Babys 1st Songs Around World. 1 CD. (Running Time: 90 mins.). (Baby's First Ser.). (J). 2000. audio compact disk 12.95 (978-1-56015-758-8(5)) Penton Overseas.

Babysitter Lessons & Safety Training (BLAST) 2nd rev. ed. American Academy of Pediatrics Staff. (C). 2006. audio compact disk 40.95 (978-0-7637-3517-3(5)) Jones Bartlett.

***Babysitter's Code.** unabr. ed. Laura Lippman. Read by Linda Emond & Francois Battiste. (ENG.). 2008. (978-0-06-176291-8(1), Harper Audio); (978-0-06-176290-1(3), Harper Audio) HarperCollins Pubs.

Babysong. Hap Palmer & Martha Palmer. (J). 1985. 11.95 Ed Activities.

Baccalaureate. Ed Young. 1994. 4.95 (978-0-7417-2018-4(3), 1018) Win Walk.

Baccalaureate Service. Ed Young. 1996. 4.95 (978-0-7417-2099-3(X), 1099) Win Walk.

Bacchus see Poetry of Ralph Waldo Emerson

Bacchus see Twentieth-Century Poetry in English: Recordings of Poets Reading Their Own Poetry

Bach, Parts 2 & 3. Ed. by Carole L. Bigler et al. 1 CD. (Running Time: 1 hr.). (Alfred Masterwork Edition Ser.). (ENG.). 1993. audio compact edition 10.95 (978-0-7390-1932-0(5), 4056) Alfred Pub.

Bach: An Introduction to Brandenburg Concertos Nos. 4 & 5. Jeremy Siepmann. 2 CDs. (Running Time: 3 hrs.). (Classics Explained Ser.). 2003. pap. bk. (978-1-84379-010-5(6)) NaxMulti GBR.

Bach: His Story & His Music. 1 cass. (Music Masters Ser.). 4.99 (ACS 8500) VOX Music Grp.

Bach: Inventions for Guitar. Jerry Willard. 2 vols. 2005. pap. bk. 19.95 (978-0-8256-2829-0(6), AM978450, Amsco Music) Pub: Music Sales. Dist(s): H Leonard

Bach: The Greatest Hits. 1 cass. audio compact disk 10.98 CD. (978-1-57908-155-3(X), 3601) Platinm Enter.

Bach - Two-Part Inventions. Ed. by Willard A. Palmer. Composed by Johann Sebastian Bach. (Alfred Masterwork Edition Ser.). (ENG.). 2005. audio compact disk 9.95 (978-0-7390-3699-0(8)) Alfred Pub.

Bach - 18 Short Preludes. Ed. by Willard A. Palmer. Composed by Johann Sebastian Bach. (Alfred Masterwork Edition Ser.). (ENG.). 1998. audio compact disk 10.95 (978-0-7390-2901-5(0)) Alfred Pub.

Bach & the High Baroque, Pts. 1-4. Instructed by Robert Greenberg. 32 CDs. (Running Time: 24 hrs.). 1995. bk. 129.95 (978-1-56585-373-7(3), 720); 99.95 (978-1-56585-205-1(2), 720) Teaching Co.

Bach & the High Baroque, Vol. 2. Instructed by Robert Greenberg. 4 cass. (Running Time: 6 hrs.). 1995. 249.95 (978-1-56585-206-8(0)) Teaching Co.

Bach & the High Baroque, Vol. 3. Instructed by Robert Greenberg. 4 cass. (Running Time: 6 hrs.). 1995. 249.95 (978-1-56585-207-5(9)) Teaching Co.

Bach & the High Baroque, Vol. 4. Instructed by Robert Greenberg. 4 cass. (Running Time: 6 hrs.). 1995. 249.95 (978-1-56585-208-2(7)) Teaching Co.

Bach Chorales for Guitar. Adapted by Bill Purse. 1994. spiral bd. 23.95 (978-0-7866-1189-8(8), 95050P) Mel Bay.

Bach Dances for Hammered Dulcimer. Arranged by Carrie Crompton. 1997. pap. bk. 26.92 (978-0-7866-2881-0(2), 96697CDP) Mel Bay.

Bach Flower Remedies, Vol. 2. Jonathan Parker. 2 cass. (Running Time: 2 hrs.). 1998. 17.00 Set. (978-1-58400-005-1(8)) QuantumQuests Intl.

Bach Flower Remedies Vol.1, Set. Mini Course. Jonathan Parker. Read by Jonathan Parker. 2 CDs. (Running Time: 2 hrs.). (Natural Health Ser.: Vol. 5). 1999. audio compact disk (978-1-58400-052-5(X)) QuantumQuests Intl.

Bach for All Seasons. 2004. audio compact disk 16.98 (978-0-8006-5855-7(8)) Augsburg Fortress.
This audio Cd introduces selections from our Bach for All Seasons choral collection and is wonderful for both listening and learning the repertoire. The CD includes mass, oratorio and cantata movements recorded by the Bach Choir of Holy Trinity Lutheran Church in New York City.

Bach for Book Lovers: A Soothing Companion for Reading. Composed by Johann Sebastian Bach. 1 cass., 1 CD. (Set Your Life to Music Ser.). 5.58 (PHI 456497); audio compact disk 10.38 CD Jewel box. (PHI 456497) NewSound.

Bach for Book Lovers Set: A Soothing Companion for Reading. Composed by Johann Sebastian Bach. 1 cass., 1 CD. (Set Your Life to Music Ser.). 5.58 (PHI 456497); audio compact disk 10.38 CD Jewel box. (PHI 456497) NewSound.

Bach Is Best. 1 cass. (Vox - Turnabout Classical Ser.). 3.98 (CTX 4804) VOX Music Grp.

Bach Motets. 2006. audio compact disk 15.00 (978-1-931569-08-8(8)) Pub: U of Wis Pr. Dist(s): Chicago Distribution Ctr

Bach Opus Set: New Piano Transcriptions of Famous Masterworks. 2000. pap. bk. 15.95 (978-0-634-02609-6(7)) H Leonard.

Bach to Rock: An Introduction to Famous Composers & Their Music. Rosemary Kennedy. Interview with Mary S. Roniger. (Running Time: 90 min.). 1997. bk. 16.95 Rosemary Corp.
This audio features thirty-two excerpts from various musical compositions.

Bachelor Brothers' Bed & Breakfast. abr. ed. Bill Richardson. 2 CDs. (Running Time: 2 hrs. 30 mins.). (ENG.). 2001. audio compact disk 16.95 (978-0-86492-253-3(1)) Pub: BTC Audiobks CAN. Dist(s): U Toronto Pr

Bachelor Brothers' Bed & Breakfast. abr. ed. Bill Richardson. Narrated by Bill Richardson. 2 cass. (Running Time: 2 hrs. 30 mins.). (ENG.). 2001. 16.95 (978-0-86492-251-9(5)) Pub: BTC Audiobks CAN. Dist(s): U Toronto Pr

Bachelor Brothers' Bed & Breakfast. abr. collector's ed. Bill Richardson. 2 vols. (Running Time: 2 hrs. 30 mins.). (Between the Covers Collection). 2003. 16.95 (978-0-86492-207-6(8)) Pub: BTC Audiobks CAN. Dist(s): U Toronto Pr
CBC Radio personality Bill Richardson reads with infectious glee his popular bagatelle about a rustic British Columbia bed and breakfast, run by a pair of eccentric middle-aged twins, and its bookish clientele. A recipient of the Leacock Medal, Richardson is the author of several books of humour.

Bachelor Kisses. unabr. ed. Nick Earls. Read by Francis Greenslade. 7 cass. (Running Time: 11 hrs. 32 mins.). 2004. 56.00 (978-1-74030-530-3(2)) Pub: Bolinda Pubng AUS. Dist(s): Lndmrk Audiobks

Bachelors. Muriel Spark. Read by Nadia May. 6 CDs. (Running Time: 7 hrs.). 2000. audio compact disk 48.00 (978-0-7861-9841-2(9), 2634) Blckstn Audio.
The very British bachelors of Muriel Spark's supreme novel of the 1960's come in every stripe, from a detective, a lovelorn Irishman, a handwriting expert, a priest & a heinous spiritual medium. Chatting contentedly in their clubs or shopping at Fortnum's the bachelors are not set to stay cozy for long. They will keep you guessing which way they will go, from blackmail or pressed to attend horrid seances, then plunged all together, into the nastiest of lawsuits.

Bachelors. unabr. ed. Muriel Spark. Read by Nadia May. 5 cass. (Running Time: 7 hrs.). 2000. 39.95 (978-0-7861-1835-9(0), 2634) Blckstn Audio.

Bachelors. unabr. ed. Muriel Spark. Read by Nadia May. 1 CD. (Running Time: 7 hrs.). 2001. audio compact disk 19.95 (zm2634) Blckstn Audio.
First found contentedly chatting in their London clubs & shopping at Fortnum's, the cozy bachelors are not set to stay cozy for long. Soon enough, the men are variously tormented - defrauded or stolen from; blackmailed & then plunged, all together, into the nastiest of lawsuits.

Bachelors of Broken Hill. unabr. ed. Arthur W. Upfield. Read by Peter Hosking. 4 cass. (Running Time: 6 hrs.). (Inspector Napoleon Bonaparte Mysteries). 2001. (978-1-74030-094-0(7), 500220) Bolinda Pubng AUS.

Bachelors of Broken Hill. unabr. ed. Arthur W. Upfield. Read by Peter Hosking. 5 CDs. (Running Time: 23100 sec.). (Inspector Napoleon Bonaparte Mysteries). 2006. audio compact disk 40.00 (978-1-74093-795-5(3)) Bolinda Pubng AUS.

bachelors of Broken Hill. unabr. ed. Arthur W. Upfield. Read by Peter Hosking. (Running Time: 6 hrs. 25 mins.). (Inspector Napoleon Bonaparte Mysteries). 2009. audio compact disk 77.95 (978-1-74214-053-7(X), 9781742140537) Pub: Bolinda Pubng AUS. Dist(s): Bolinda Pub Inc

Bachelor's Puzzle. abr. ed. Judith Pella. Narrated by Christie O. King. (Patchwork Circle Ser.). (ENG.). 2007. 13.99 (978-1-60814-038-1(5)) Oasis Audio.

Bachelor's Puzzle. abr. ed. Judith Pella. Read by Christy King. (Patchwork Circle Ser.: Bk. 1). (ENG.). 2007. audio compact disk 19.99 (978-1-59859-241-2(6)) Oasis Audio.

Bach's Fight for Freedom. Composed by Johann Sebastian Bach. (Composer's Specials Ser.). 1998. audio compact disk 12.95 (978-0-634-00882-5(X), 063400882X) H Leonard.

Bach's Fight for Freedom - ShowTrax. 1 CD. (Running Time: 1 hr.). 2000. audio compact disk 12.95 (00841333) H Leonard.

Bach's Ornaments: A Lecture Performance. Perf. by Carol Lems-Dworkin. 2000. pap. bk. 12.50 (978-0-9637048-3-2(4)) C Lems-Dworkin Pubs.

Back East. unabr. ed. Ellen Pall. Read by Donada Peters. 7 cass. (Running Time: 7 hrs.). 1987. 42.00 (978-0-7366-1106-0(1), 2032) Books on Tape.
Melanie is a songwriter in L. A. who's sick of California. She returns to New York to resume her career & reestablish ties with her family. But life takes an unexpected turn.

Back from Banishment: The Revival & Fate of the Soul (Conference 1995) 7 cass. (Running Time: 10 hrs.). 1995. 64.95 set. (978-0-7822-0507-7(0), SOUL) C G Jung IL.
This conference explores the perplexing questions that necessarily arise with the revival of the soul. Seven speakers grapple with what may be the most important question for the 21st century: What is our human responsibility in tending to the revival & fate of the soul?.

***Back from the Edge: A Study of Hebrews.** Douglas A. Jacoby. (ENG.). 2010. 10.00 (978-0-9844974-2-3(0)) Illumination MA.

Back from the Grave. Anne Schraff. Narrated by Larry A. McKeever. (Standing Tall 3 Mystery Ser.). (J). 2003. 10.95 (978-1-58659-106-9(1)); audio compact disk 14.95 (978-1-58659-345-2(5)) Artesian.

Back Home. Perf. by Caedmon's Call Staff. 2003. audio compact disk Essential Recs.

Back Home Again. unabr. ed. Melody Carlson. Narrated by Sherri Berger. (Running Time: 6 hrs. 50 mins. 53 sec.). (Grace Chapel Inn Ser.). (ENG.). 2009. 18.19 (978-1-60814-504-1(2)) Oasis Audio.

Back Home Again. unabr. ed. Melody Carlson. Read by Brooke Sanford. Narrated by Sherri Berger. (Running Time: 6 hrs. 50 mins. 53 sec.). (Grace Chapel Inn Ser.). (ENG.). 2009. audio compact disk 25.99 (978-1-59859-479-9(6)) Oasis Audio.

Back in Action: An American Soldier's Story of Courage. David Rozelle. Narrated by Patrick G. Lawlor. (Running Time: 6 hrs. 30 mins.). 2005. 25.95 (978-1-59912-428-5(9)) Iofy Corp.

Back in Action: An American Soldier's Story of Courage, Faith, & Fortitude. David Rozelle. (Running Time: 023400 sec.). 2005. cass. & DVD 44.95 (978-0-7861-3479-3(8)); DVD & audio compact disk 55.00 (978-0-7861-7899-5(X)) Blckstn Audio.

Back in Action: An American Soldier's Story of Courage, Faith & Fortitude. unabr. ed. David Rozelle. Read by Patrick G. Lawlor. 6 CDs. (Running Time: 8 hrs.). 2005. audio compact disk 29.95 (978-0-7861-7926-8(0), ZE3460); 29.95 (978-0-7861-3481-6(X), E3460) Blckstn Audio.
Rozelle tells the whole gripping story: from the day he had to tell his pregnant wife that he was going to war (Valentine's Day 2003) and deployed for Operation Iraqi Freedom, to the fateful day four months later when a land mine tore off his right foot and beyond, through months of agonizing rehabilitation to his final triumphant recertification as "Fit for Duty." David Rozelle was willing to die for freedom, and he is still willing to put his life on the line for it, despite the injury he has already suffered. Back in Action is a stirring reminder of the commitment every American should have to the cause of freedom, if we hope to continue to enjoy that freedom. It's an extraordinary and inspiring story of devotion to duty overcoming all obstacles.

Back in Action: An American Soldier's Story of Courage, Faith & Fortitude. unabr. ed. David Rozelle. Read by Patrick G. Lawlor. 1 MP3. (Running Time: 7 hrs. 18 mins.). 2005. audio compact disk 29.95 (978-0-7861-8105-6(2), ZM3460) Blckstn Audio.

Back in Spite of Popular Demand. 8.95 (16) Bert and I Inc.
Tim Sample describes Unc's Store in Eastport, tells a story about Trailer Life & Teddy Roosevelt visiting Greenville.

Back in the Day. 1 cass. 10.98 (978-1-57908-293-2(9), 1365); 12.98 (978-1-57908-428-8(1)); audio compact disk 15.98 CD. (978-1-57908-292-5(0), 1365); audio compact disk 18.98 (978-1-57908-427-1(3)) Platinm Enter.

Back Labor No More! What Every Woman Should Know Before Labor. Based on a book by Janie McCoy King. 2007. audio compact disk (978-0-926218-01-7(8)) Plenary Systs.

Back on Blossom Street. Debbie Macomber. Read by Laural Merlington. (Blossom Street Ser.: No. 3). 2008. 69.99 (978-1-60640-781-3(3)) Find a World.

Back on Blossom Street. abr. ed. Debbie Macomber. Read by Laural Merlington. (Running Time: 14400 sec.). (Blossom Street Ser.: No. 3). 2008. audio compact disk 14.99 (978-1-4233-0518-7(3), 9781423305187, BCD Value Price) Brilliance Audio.

Back on Blossom Street. unabr. ed. Debbie Macomber. Read by Laural Merlington. (Running Time: 11 hrs.). (Blossom Street Ser.: No. 3). 2007. 39.25 (978-1-4233-0516-3(7), 9781423305163, BADLE); 24.95 (978-1-4233-0515-6(9), 9781423305156, BAD); 82.25 (978-1-4233-0538-5(8), 9781423305385, BrilAudUnabridg); audio compact disk 24.95 (978-1-4233-0513-2(2), 9781423305132, Brilliance MP3); audio compact disk 36.95 (978-1-4233-0511-8(6), 9781423305118, Bril Audio CD Unabri); audio compact disk 97.25 (978-1-4233-0512-5(4), 9781423305125, BriAudCD Unabrid); audio compact disk 39.25 (978-1-4233-0514-9(0), 9781423305149, Brinc Audio MP3 Lib) Brilliance Audio.

Back on My Feet Again! Renee Bondi Testimony. unabr. ed. Perf. by Renee Bondi. 1 cass. (Running Time: 1 hr. 10 min.). 1997. 11.00 (978-1-891335-04-4(9), CRCS 302); audio compact disk 16.00 (978-1-891335-05-1(7), CRCD 301) Capo Recording.
Live recording of Renee Bondi sharing the story of her injury & her faith. She tells how the Lord has provided her every need when her life changed overnight. 5 songs are threaded throughout this presentation. A riveting story that reminds each of us of God's presence in our lives.

Back on the Air. Paul McCusker & AIO Team Staff. Prod. by Focus on the Family Staff. 4 CDs. (Running Time: 6 hrs.). (Adventures in Odyssey Ser.: Vol. 26). (ENG.). (J). (gr. 3-7). 1996. audio compact disk 24.99 (978-1-56179-494-2(5)) Pub: Focus Family. Dist(s): Tyndale Hse

Back on Track: Diary of a Street Kid. unabr. ed. Margaret Clark. Read by Suzi Dougherty. 3 cass. (Running Time: 3 hrs. 45 mins.). 2002. (978-1-74030-145-9(5), 500430) Bolinda Pubng AUS.

Back Pain: Ancient Truths, Natural Remedies & the Latest Findings for Your Health Today. unabr. ed. Don Colbert. Narrated by Tim Lundeen. (Bible Cure Ser.). (ENG.). 2004. audio compact disk 9.99 (978-1-58926-802-9(4)) Oasis Audio.

Back Pain: Comfort & Healing. Steven Gurgevich. (ENG.). 2002. audio compact disk 19.95 (978-1-932170-16-0(2), HWH) Tranceformation.

Back Pain in the Female: Gynecologic, Orthopaedic, Urologic, Psychologic? 3 cass. (Gynecology & Obstetrics Ser.: C85-GO1). 22.50 (8559) Am Coll Surgeons.

Back Road to Murder. deluxe unabr. ed. Ben Wolfe. Engineer Mickee Madden. Executive Producer Mickee Madden. Illus. by Amy Madden. Music by Carlos Miranda. Narrated by Tom Powers. 6 cass. (C). 2001. lib. bdg. 35.00 (978-0-932079-08-4(3), 79083) TimeFare AudioBks.

Back Roads. Tawni O'Dell. Read by Daniel Passer. 2000. 56.00 (978-0-7366-5104-2(7)); audio compact disk 72.00 (978-0-7366-5971-0(4)) Books on Tape.

Back Roads. unabr. ed. Tawni O'Dell. Read by Daniel Passer. 7 cass. (Running Time: 10 hrs. 30 min.). 2000. 56.00 Books on Tape.
In the Pennsylvania backwoods, 19-year-old Harley Altmeyer's bumbling heroics redeem his tattered coal mining family.

Back Roads. unabr. ed. Tawni O'Dell. Read by Daniel Passer. 7 CDs. (Running Time: 8 hrs. 12 mins.). 2001. audio compact disk Books on Tape.

Back Roads. unabr. ed. Tawni O'Dell. Narrated by Scott Shina. 7 cass. (Running Time: 10 hrs.). 2000. 61.00 (978-0-7887-4629-1(4), 96340K8) Recorded Bks.
Nineteen-year-old Harley Altmyer's mom is serving a life term for killing his abusive father. Harley's working two dead-end jobs & taking care of his three younger sisters. His only joys in life are beer & his beautiful, but married neighbor. As their affair continues & secrets from within his family come to light, tragic chain of events is unleashed that threatens to destroy what is left of his world.

Back Spin. unabr. ed. Harlan Coben. Read by Jonathan Marosz. 6 cass. (Running Time: 9 hrs.). (Myron Bolitar Ser.: No. 4). 2000. 48.00 (978-0-7366-5533-0(6), 5373) Books on Tape.
The boy, born and raised on the Main Line, vanished on Philadelphia's mean streets, last seen in a downtown cheater's hotel. The boy's mother, Linda Coldren, is a golf superstar, and Myron Bolitar's client. When he goes after the missing boy, presumed kidnapped, he crashes through a crowd of lowlifes, blue bloods and liars on both sides of the social divide. Meanwhile, Linda's husband, trying to stage a comeback at the U.S. Open, is found dead in a sand trap. Suddenly the family's skeletons are coming out of the closet and Myron is about to find out how deadly golf can get.

Back Spin. unabr. ed. Harlan Coben. Read by Jonathan Marosz. 6 cass. (Running Time: 9 hrs.). (Myron Bolitar Ser.: No. 4). 2001. 29.95 (978-0-7366-6795-1(4)) Books on Tape.
As her agent, Myron Bolitar must find out who kidnapped golfer Linda Coldren's son & murdered her husband.

Back Spin. unabr. ed. Harlan Coben. Read by Jonathan Marosz. 7 CDs. (Running Time: 30600 sec.). (Myron Bolitar Ser.: No. 4). (ENG.). 2007. audio compact disk 19.99 (978-0-7393-4100-1(6), Random AudioBks) Pub: Random Audio Pubg. Dist(s): Random

Back Stab. abr. ed. Elaine Viets. 4 cass. (Running Time: 6 hrs.). (Francesca Vierling Mystery Ser.: No. 1). 2000. 25.00 (978-1-58807-054-8(9)) Am Pubng Inc.
The beauty contestant has fabulous clothes, long hair, and great legs. She looks dam good for a woman - and even better for a man. St. Louis' funniest newspaper columnist, Francesca Vierling, is at the transvestite beauty pageant. Nothing is as it seems here. Things have gone haywire in the rest of Francesca's life, too. Someone is killing her friends and sources, and the police claim there's nothing unusual about their deaths. Francesca enters a world where seeing is not believing, to find a killer before he finds her.

Back Story. Robert B. Parker. (Spenser Ser.). 2003. audio compact disk 34.00 (978-0-7366-9279-3(7)) Pub: Books on Tape. Dist(s): NetLibrary CO

Back Talk. Michael Klaper. 1 cass. (Running Time: 30 min.). (Help Yourself to Health Ser.). 7.00 (978-0-929274-03-4(2)) Gentle World.
One of a series of tapes discussing the relationship between a diet free of animal products & improving one's health or a particular disease.

***Back There.** 2010. audio compact disk (978-1-59171-162-9(2)) Falcon Picture.

Back to Back. Winans, The. 1 cass., 1 CD.; audio compact disk 15.98 CD. (4107-2) Warner Christian.

Back to Basics. 2 CASS. 2004. 9.99 (978-1-58602-218-1(0)); audio compact disk 19.99 (978-1-58602-219-8(9)) E L Long.

Back to Basics, Vol. 1. Ed. by Ames Sweet & Ann Warner. 1 cass. (Running Time: 1 hr. 30 min.). Dramatization. 1991. 6.95 (978-0-933685-19-2(X), TP-14) A A Grapevine.
Personal experiences of Alcoholics Anonymous members with the principles of the AA program.

Back to Basics, Vol. 2. Ed. by Ames Sweet & Ann Warner. 1 cass. (Running Time: 1 hr. 30 min.). Dramatization. 1991. 6.50 (978-0-933685-20-8(3), TP-15) A A Grapevine.

Back to Basics: Addition. 1 cass. (Math Ser.). (J). bk. Incl. 24p. bk. (TWIN 402) NewSound.
Memorize facts while learning mathematical concepts.

Back to Basics: Centerings & Guided Imagerys. unabr. ed. Nancy Spence. Read by Nancy Spence. Ed. by Audio Vision Staff. 1 cass. (Running Time: 1 hr. 30 min.). 1995. pap. bk. 19.95 (978-0-9643818-0-3(X)) InnerVis NC.
This cassette accompanies the workbook "Back to Basics: An Awareness Primer." It has 6 centering exercises which accompany every session in the workbook, & 3 guided imagerys which are 3 sessions of the book.

Back to Basics: Core Selling Skills. Scripts. 2 CD's. 2004. audio compact disk 15.00 (978-0-9616416-4-1(9)) L Giblin.

Back to Basics: Division. 1 cass. (Math Ser.). (J). bk. Incl. 24p. bk. (TWIN 404) NewSound.
Memorize facts while learning mathematical concepts.

Back to Basics: Multiplication. 1 cass. (Math Ser.). (J). bk. Incl. 24p. bk. (TWIN 401) NewSound.

Back to Basics: Subtraction. 1 cass. (Math Ser.). (J). bk. Incl. 24p. bk. (TWIN 403) NewSound.

Back to Basics: Winning with People. Scripts. 1 CD. 2004. audio compact disk 12.00 (978-0-9616416-5-8(7)) L Giblin.

Back to Basics in Religion, Philosophy, & Science. Instructed by Manly P. Hall. 8.95 (978-0-89314-014-4(7), C850908) Philos Res.

Back to Basics Management. unabr. ed. Matthew J. Culligan et al. Read by Nadia May. 4 cass. (Running Time: 5 hrs. 30 mins.). 1993. 32.95 (978-0-7861-0427-7(9), 1379) Blckstn Audio.
Explains the difference between business administration & business management, how this distinction has been obscured & the need to revive the craft of leadership in management. Details the tools used in effective management & it offers concise & comprehensive guidelines for developing & refining primary leadership skills.

Back to Basics Management: The Lost Craft of Leadership. Matthew J. Culligan et al. Read by Nadia May. (Running Time: 18000 sec.). 2006. audio compact disk 45.00 (978-0-7861-6885-9(4)) Blckstn Audio.

Back to Basics Management: The Lost Craft of Leadership. unabr. ed. Matthew J. Culligan et al. Read by Nadia May. (Running Time: 18000 sec.). 2006. audio compact disk 29.95 (978-0-7861-7467-6(6)) Blckstn Audio.

Back to Bologna. unabr. ed. Michael Dibdin. Read by Michael Tudor Barnes. 6 CDs. (Running Time: 25500 sec.). (Isis (CDs) Ser.). 2006. audio compact disk 64.95 (978-0-7531-2488-8(2)) Pub: ISIS Lrg Prnt GBR. Dist(s): Ulverscroft US

Back to Bologna. unabr. ed. Michael Dibdin. Read by Michael Tudor Barnes. 5 cass. (Running Time: 24600 sec.). (Isis Cassettes Ser.). 2006. 49.95 (978-0-7531-3475-7(6)) Pub: ISIS Lrg Prnt GBR. Dist(s): Ulverscroft US

Back to Genesis Conference Album. Featuring Douglas W. Phillips & John Morris. 9 cass. (Running Time: 9 hrs.). 2002. 32.00 (978-1-929241-56-9(9)) Vsn Forum.

Back to Jerusalem Leader's CD. Northwestern Publishing House Staff. (Vacation Bible Study Ser.). 2002. audio compact disk (978-0-8100-1390-2(8)) Northwest Pub.

Back to Kohala. 2002. audio compact disk 16.99 (978-0-89610-904-9(6)) Island Heritage.

Back to School. Perf. by Mr. AL & Stephen Fite. 1 cass. 10.95; audio compact disk 13.95 Child Like.

Back to School. unabr. ed. Wanda E. Brunstetter. Read by Ellen Grafton. (Running Time: 3 hrs.). (Rachel Yoder - Always Trouble Somewhere Ser.). 2010. audio compact disk 14.99 (978-1-4418-1164-6(8), 9781441811646, Bril Audio CD Unabri) Brilliance Audio.

***Back to School.** unabr. ed. Wanda E. Brunstetter. Read by Ellen Grafton. (Running Time: 3 hrs.). (Rachel Yoder - Always Trouble Somewhere Ser.). 2010. 14.99 (978-1-4418-1166-0(4), 9781441811660, Brilliance MP3); 39.97 (978-1-4418-1167-7(2), 9781441811677, Brinc Audio MP3 Lib); 14.99 (978-1-4418-1168-4(0), 9781441811684, BAD); 39.97 (978-1-4418-1169-1(9), 9781441811691, BADLE); audio compact disk 44.97 (978-1-4418-1165-3(6), 9781441811653, BriAudCD Unabrid) Brilliance Audio.

Back to School Again. Perf. by Mr. AL & Stephen Fite. 1 cass. 10.95; audio compact disk 13.95 Child Like.

Back to the Basics. Lee Lefebre. 1 cass. (Running Time: 29 min.). 1996. 6.00 (978-1-57838-070-1(7)) CrossLife Express.
Christian living.

Back to the Beat. (Running Time: 42 min.). (J). (gr. k-4). 1997. 9.98 (978-1-888795-07-3(7)); audio compact disk 14.98 CD. (978-1-888795-06-6(9)) Sugar Beats.

Back to the Beat. Perf. by Sugar Beats. 1 cass., 1 CD. (J). 7.98 (SUG 3); audio compact disk 12.78 CD. NewSound.
Includes James Taylor's classic "Shower the People," "Tommy James," "Mony Mony" & the Kinks' "You Really Got Me".

Back to the Bedroom. unabr. ed. Janet Evanovich. 5 CDs. (Running Time: 5.5 Hrs). 2005. audio compact disk 14.95 (978-0-06-073697-2(6)) HarperCollins Pubs.

Back to the Bedroom. unabr. ed. Janet Evanovich. Read by C. J. Critt. 2005. 14.95 (978-0-06-087425-4(2)) HarperCollins Pubs.

***Back to the Bedroom.** unabr. ed. Janet Evanovich. Read by C. J. Critt. (ENG.). 2005. (978-0-06-087681-4(6), Harper Audio); (978-0-06-087680-7(8), Harper Audio) HarperCollins Pubs.

Back to the Drawing Board. Perf. by L. A. Mass Choir. 1 cass., 1 CD. 1998. 9.98; audio compact disk 15.98 CD. Platinum Chrst Dist.
Includes "Worthy Believe in His Promise," "You Don't Need Permission," "Back to the Drawing Board," "Stand Still," "Be Ye Holy," "Give You the Praise," "Thus Will I Bless Thee," "Hallelujah Oh Lord," & "Oh to be Kept".

Back to the Drawing Board. Perf. by LA Mass Choir. 1 cass. 10.98 (978-1-57908-257-4(2), 1320); audio compact disk 15.98 CD. (978-1-57908-256-7(4), 1320) Platinm Enter.

Back to the Forest. unabr. ed. Winifred Foley. Read by Sarah Sherborne. 5 cass. (Running Time: 7 hrs. 30 mins.). 1999. 34.95 (978-0-7531-0155-1(6), 970614) Pub: ISIS Audio GBR. Dist(s): Ulverscroft US
At the age of fourteen, Winifred Foley moved away from the Forest of Dean for a life of service in London. Although she hated leaving her country home, she soon became accustomed to life in the city. But after 26 years, the strain of city life eventually begins to take its toll.

Back to the Future. 1 cass. (Running Time: 1 hr. 30 mins.). 1997. 6.00 (978-1-58602-056-9(0)) E L Long.

Back to the Future. Stephen Mansfield. 1 cass. (Running Time: 90 mins.). (Basic Church History Ser.: Vol. 1). 2000. 5.00 (SM01-001) Morning NC.
Stephen does a masterful job of making church history come to life. This is an overview starting from pentecost & continuing through the 20th century.

Back to the Future. Don Nori. 3 cass. 1992. 18.00 Set. (978-0-938612-42-1(5)) Destiny Image Pubs.

Back to the Garden. Reuven Doron. 1 cass. (Running Time: 90 mins.). (Back to the Garden Ser.: Vol. 2). 2000. 5.00 (RD05-002) Morning NC.
The message presented in this series will woo you back to the intimacy & innocence of the Garden.

Back to the Garden Series. unabr. ed. Reuven Doron. 3 cass. (Running Time: 4 hrs. 30 mins.). 2000. 15.00 (RD05-000) Morning NC.
Includes:"The Emperor's Clothes," "Back to the Garden" & "Liberated from the World," The message presented in this series will woo you back to the intimacy & innocence of the Garden.

Back to the Moon. Homer Hickam. Read by Michael R. LeGault. 2004. 15.95 (978-0-7435-4183-1(9)) Pub: S&S Audio. Dist(s): S and S Inc

Back to the Moundbuilders World. unabr. ed. Fred Hoffmann. Read by Kevin Foley. 4 cass. (Running Time: 5 hrs. 48 min.). (Moundbuilders Ser.: Bk. 3). 1996. 26.95 (978-1-55686-721-7(2)) Books in Motion.
After bringing Singing Bird & Lean Wolf from the ancient Moundbuilders world to the 20th century, Billy Buck realizes they can't adapt.

Back to Utopia. Braun Media. (ENG.). 2008. audio compact disk 49.95 (978-1-59987-643-6(4)) Braun Media.

Back to Wando Passo. abr. unabr. ed. David Payne. Read by Dick Hill. 11 cass. (Running Time: 72000 sec.). 2006. 29.95 (978-0-7861-4487-7(4)); audio compact disk 32.95 (978-0-7861-7240-5(1)); audio compact disk 44.95 (978-0-7861-7668-7(7)) Blckstn Audio.

Back to Wando Passo. unabr. ed. Payne David. Read by Hill Dick. 2006. audio compact disk 120.00 (978-0-7861-6775-3(0)) Blckstn Audio.

Back to Wando Passo. unabr. ed. David Payne. Read by Dick Hill. (Running Time: 72000 sec.). 2006. 99.95 (978-0-7861-4659-8(1)) Blckstn Audio.

***Back Trail.** T. T. Flynn. 2009. (978-1-60136-421-0(0)) Audio Holding.

Back Trail. T. T. Flynn. (Running Time: 0 hr. 36 mins.). 1998. 10.95 (978-1-60083-462-2(0)) Iofy Corp.

Back-Up Banjo. Janet Davis. 1999. spiral bd. 36.95 (978-0-7866-5116-0(4), 93771CDP) Mel Bay.

Back When We Were Grownups. Anne Tyler. 2001. 48.00 (978-0-7366-6837-8(3)) Books on Tape.
When Joe Davitch first saw Rebecca, it was at a party at the Davitch home - a crumbling 19th century row house in Baltimore where giving parties was the family business. Young Rebecca appeared to Joe as the girl having more fun than anyone in the room and he wanted some of that happiness to spill over onto him, a 33-year-old divorcee with three little girls.

Back When We Were Grownups. unabr. ed. Anne Tyler. Read by Blair Brown. (Running Time: 32400 sec.). (ENG.). 2006. audio compact disk 19.99 (978-0-7393-3342-6(9), Random AudioBks) Pub: Random Audio Pubg. Dist(s): Random

Backfire. Clive Egleton. (Soundings (CDs) Ser.). (J). 2005. audio compact disk 79.95 (978-1-84559-007-9(4)) Pub: ISIS Lrg Prnt GBR. Dist(s): Ulverscroft US

Backfire. unabr. ed. Clive Egleton & Christopher Kay. 8 cass. (Running Time: 10 hrs. 45 mins.). 2001. 69.95 (978-1-86042-715-2(4), 27154) Pub: Soundings Ltd GBR. Dist(s): Ulverscroft US

Background-Building see Para Desarollar el Contexto

Background-Building. 1 cass. (Running Time: 1 hr.). (Scott Foresman Reading Ser.). (J). 2001. stu. ed. 39.36 (978-0-673-62118-4(9), S-Foresman); stu. ed. 69.00 (978-0-673-62315-7(7), S-Foresman) AddWesSchl.
Author interviews, songs, narratives and more are keyed to each reading selection to build background and improve listening skills.

Background-Building. 1 cass. (Running Time: 1 hr.). (Scott Foresman Reading Ser.). (J). (gr. 1). 2001. 39.36 (978-0-673-62119-1(7), S-Foresman); audio compact disk 69.00 (978-0-673-62316-4(5), S-Foresman) AddWesSchl.

Background-Building. (Scott Foresman Lectura Ser.). (SPA.). (gr. 1 up). 2000. audio compact disk 77.28 (978-0-673-64849-5(4)) Addson-Wesley Educ.

Background-Building. (Scott Foresman Reading Ser.). (gr. k up). 2004. 39.36 (978-0-328-02530-5(5)); audio compact disk 69.00 (978-0-328-02532-9(1)) Addson-Wesley Educ.

Background-Building. (Scott Foresman Reading Ser.). (gr. 1 up). 2004. 39.36 (978-0-328-02531-2(3)); audio compact disk 69.00 (978-0-328-02533-6(X)) Addson-Wesley Educ.

Background-Building. 1 cass. (Running Time: 1 hr.). (Scott Foresman Reading Ser.). (gr. 2 up). 2004. 39.36 (978-0-673-62120-7(0)); audio compact disk 69.00 (978-0-673-62317-1(3)) Addson-Wesley Educ.
Author interviews, songs, narratives, and more are keyed to each reading selection to build background and improve listening skills.

Background-Building. 1 cass. (Running Time: 1 hr.). (Scott Foresman Reading Ser.). (gr. 3 up). 2004. 39.36 (978-0-673-62121-4(9)); audio compact disk 69.00 (978-0-673-62318-8(1)) Addson-Wesley Educ.

Background-Building. 1 cass. (Running Time: 1 hr.). (Scott Foresman Reading Ser.). (gr. 4 up). 2004. stu. ed. 39.36 (978-0-673-62122-1(7)); stu. ed. 69.00 (978-0-673-62319-5(X)) Addson-Wesley Educ.

Background-Building. 1 cass. (Running Time: 1 hr.). (Scott Foresman Reading Ser.). (gr. 5 up). 2004. stu. ed. 39.36 (978-0-673-62123-8(5)); stu. ed. 69.00 (978-0-673-62320-1(3)) Addson-Wesley Educ.

Background-Building. 1 cass. (Running Time: 1 hr.). (Scott Foresman Reading Ser.). (gr. 6 up). 2004. stu. ed. 39.36 (978-0-673-62124-5(3)); stu. ed. 69.00 (978-0-673-62321-8(1)) Addson-Wesley Educ.

Background to Danger. unabr. collector's ed. Eric Ambler. Read by Richard Brown. 7 cass. (Running Time: 10 hrs. 30 min.). 1988. 56.00 (978-0-7366-1407-8(9), 2296) Books on Tape.
It began with a game of poker-dice that broke Kenton. So when the stranger on the train offered him 600 marks for a small service, he couldn't refuse. He knew the man wasn't to be trusted & his story was a lie. What of it? He needed cash. That small service put Kenton in the middle of a nasty business.

Background to World War II in the Pacific. Kenneth Bruce. 1 cass. (Running Time: 1 hr.). Dramatization. (Excursions in History Ser.). 12.50 Alpha Tape.

Backhand. unabr. ed. Liza Cody. Narrated by Jill Tanner. 7 cass. (Running Time: 10 hrs.). (Anna Lee Mystery Ser.: Vol. 6). 1993. 60.00 (978-1-55690-808-8(3), 93117E7) Recorded Bks.
London private eye Anna Lee pursues a case among the tennis-playing idle rich of Florida's Gold Coast.

Backlash. unabr. ed. Aaron Allston. Read by Marc Thompson. (Star Wars Ser.). 2010. audio compact disk 40.00 (978-0-7393-7667-6(5), Random AudioBks) Pub: Random Audio Pubg. Dist(s): Random

Backlash. unabr. ed. Morris West. 6 cass. (Running Time: 10 hrs.). 2004. 48.00 (978-1-74030-695-9(3)) Pub: Bolinda Pubng AUS. Dist(s): Lndmrk Audiobks

Backlash: The Undeclared War Against American Women, Set. abr. ed. Susan Faludi. Read by Susan Faludi. 4 cass. (Running Time: 6 hrs.). 1992. 24.95 (978-1-879371-24-8(3), 60000) Pub Mills.
This audio adaptation of the phenomenal Crown New York Times bestseller "Backlash" is a strong & moving account of the backlash in the women's movement. The book details exactly how what once gave women their equality has backlashed against them through the media, in politics & in advertising.

Backoffice Survival Kit. Sams Development Staff. 1997. bk. 179.99 (978-0-672-30953-3(X)) Alpha Pearson.

Backpacking & Camping: The All-Season Companion. unabr. ed. Bill Cohen. 1 cass. (Running Time: 81 mins.). 2000. 10.95 (978-0-9678847-0-7(5)) SafeHome.
"How-to" guide to all-season trekking & camping. Proper gear, food, all-season campfire building, prevention/treatment for heat exhaustion/stroke & hypothermia. Environmentally responsible camping.

Backporch: Keep Praying Child One Day You Will Understand. Bertha J. Vaughns. Read by Bertha J. Vaughns. Perf. by Herbert Norman. 1 cass. (Running Time: 34 min.). (YA). (gr. 7-12). 1999. bk. 15.75 (978-0-9676396-1-1(1), TBP3) Ahtreb Inc.
The Backporch was a special place for a little Southern plantation girl who lived with her aging grandparents. It was a place where she dreamt dreams & made plans.

Backporch: Keep Praying Child One Day You Will Understand. unabr. ed. Bertha J. Vaughns. Read by Bertha J. Vaughns. Perf. by Herbert Norman. Ed. by Ceola Taylor. 1 cass. (Running Time: 34 min.). Dramatization. (YA). (gr. 7-12). 1999. pap. bk. 6.99 (978-0-9676396-0-4(3), TBP2) Ahtreb Inc.

Backroom. Ed. by Robert A. Monroe. 1 cass. (Running Time: 30 min.). (Meta Music Ser.). 1985. 12.95 (978-1-56102-201-4(2)) Inter Indus.
Backroom helps you understand & feel - in slow motion - the moods & complex attitudes of the jazz musician whether it be the sophistication of Gershwin & Ellington, the piano man at Louis', or the guy who simply has the blues.

***Backseat Saints.** Joshilyn Jackson. Read by Author. (Running Time: 13 hrs.). (ENG.). 2011. audio compact disk 19.98 (978-1-60941-379-8(2)) Pub: Hachet Audio. Dist(s): HachBkGrp

Backseat Saints. unabr. ed. Joshilyn Jackson. 8 CDs. (Running Time: 8 hrs.). 2010. audio compact disk 34.98 (978-1-60788-222-0(1)) Pub: Hachet Audio. Dist(s): HachBkGrp

Backseat Saints. unabr. ed. Joshilyn Jackson. Read by Joshilyn Jackson. (Running Time: 13 hrs.). 2010. 24.98 (978-1-60788-223-7(X)) Pub: Hachet Audio. Dist(s): HachBkGrp

Backstabber. abr. ed. Timothy Cockey. Read by Patrick G. Lawlor. 6 CDs. (Running Time: 8 hrs.). (What's New Ser.). 2004. audio compact disk 32.95 (978-1-59316-028-9(3), LL120) Listen & Live.
He's suave, he's sexy, he's cool...and he's an undertaker. Hitchcock Sewell is back in one of the funniest and most fast-paced novels yet in Tim Cockey's celebrated award-winning series. A man has been murdered in his kitchen. And the apparent killer wants Hitch to scoop up the body and take it away...before the police have arrived. Meanwhile, across town, Hitch smells a rat - maybe two - in the nursing home where an old friend of his has taken up residence. With his matchless wit and uncommon ability to dig out the truth, Hitch is once again up to his old tricks...and mystery readers couldn't be happier.

Backstage Fright. unabr. ed. Peg Kehret. Narrated by Carine Montbertrand. 2 cass. (Running Time: 3 hrs.). (Frightmares Ser.: No. 8). (gr. 5 up). 1998. 19.00 (978-0-7887-2221-9(2), 95520E7) Recorded Bks.
Rosie & Kayo are helping backstage at the Oakwood Community Theater. But when they find a painting hidden deep in the theater's storeroom, suddenly the two girls are faced with danger.

Backstage Fright, Class Set. unabr. ed. Peg Kehret. Read by Carine Montbertrand. 2 cass., 10 bks. (Running Time: 3 hrs.). (J). (gr. 4). 1998. bk. 79.70 (978-0-7887-2543-2(2), 46713) Recorded Bks.

Backstage Fright, Homework Set. unabr. ed. Peg Kehret. Read by Carine Montbertrand. 2 cass. (Running Time: 3 hrs.). (Frightmares Ser.: Vol. 8). (J). (gr. 4). 1998. bk. 30.24 (978-0-7887-2238-7(7), 40722) Recorded Bks.

Backstage Wife see Great Soap Operas: Selected Episodes

Backstairs Life in a Country House. unabr. ed. Eileen Balderson & Douglas Goodlad. Read by Sarah Newton. 3 cass. (Running Time: 4 hrs.). 1999. 34.95 (978-0-7531-0523-8(3), 990315) Pub: ISIS Audio GBR. Dist(s): Ulverscroft US
Eileen Balderson's mother died when she was just thirteen years of age & she was urged into domestic service by her father so that she would always have a secure home. Her book covers the years from 1931 to the early postwar period when her time in service was spent in a succession of country houses, first as a between-maid & then as a housemaid. Her straight-forward & detailed account of life backstairs show the gentry were not the monsters or buffoons portrayed in certain books & television programs.

Backtalk: 3 Steps to Stop It Before the Tears & Tantrums Start. Audrey Ricker & Carolyn Crowder. 2004. 7.95 (978-0-7435-4184-8(7)) Pub: S&S Audio. Dist(s): S and S Inc

***Backup Plan.** abr. ed. Sherryl Woods. Read by Tanya Eby. (Running Time: 6 hrs.). (Charleston Ser.). 2010. audio compact disk 14.99 (978-1-61106-276-2(4), 9781611062762, BACD) Brilliance Audio.

***Backup Plan.** unabr. ed. Sherryl Woods. (Running Time: 11 hrs.). (Charleston Trilogy). 2010. 19.99 (978-1-4418-6477-2(6), 9781441864772, Brilliance

MP3); 19.99 (978-1-4418-6479-6(2), 9781441864796, BAD); 39.97 (978-1-4418-6480-2(6), 9781441864802, BADLE); audio compact disk 24.99 (978-1-4418-6475-8(X), 9781441864758, Bril Audio CD Unabri) Brilliance Audio.

***Backup Plan.** unabr. ed. Sherryl Woods. Read by Tanya Eby. (Running Time: 11 hrs.). (Charleston Trilogy). 2010. 39.97 (978-1-4418-6478-9(4), 9781441864789, Brlnc Audio MP3 Lib); audio compact disk 69.97 (978-1-4418-6476-5(8), 9781441864765, BriAudCD Unabrid) Brilliance Audio.

Backward Shadow. unabr. ed. Lynne Reid Banks. Read by Harriet Walter. 8 cass. (Running Time: 8 hrs.). 2000. 69.95 (978-0-7540-0505-6(4), CAB1928) AudioGO.
Jane is living in a remote country cottage trying to forget Toby, her lover & build a new life for herself & her baby. The locals gradually accept her & Jane begins to come to terms with her situation. Then Dottie arrives from London with an idea that could change their lives. The scheme attracts the staunch sponsorship of Henry, whose sad secret make Jane see her own problems in a new light.

Backward Step: A Day-Long Inquiry with Adyashanti. August 11, 2007. 4 Audio CDs. Featuring Adyashanti. (ENG.). 2007. audio compact disk 40.00 (978-1-933986-34-0(4)) Open Gate Pub.

Backwards: Returning to Our Source for Answers. Nanci L. Danison. Read by Nanci L. Danison. (ENG.). 2007. audio compact disk 29.95 (978-1-934482-14-8(5)) AP Lee.

Backwards Land. Perf. by Hap Palmer. 1 LP. (J). pupil's gde. ed. 11.95 (EA 634); 11.95 (EA 634C) Kimbo Educ.
If I Had Wings - When Things Don't Go Your Way - Amanda Schlupp - Helping Mommy in the Kitchen - Chomping Gum & more.

Backwards to Oregon: L-Book. Jae. Sheri. (ENG.). 2007. 18.95 (978-0-9800846-6-5(0)) Lbook Pub.

Backyard Bird Walk. Lang Elliott. 1 cass. (Running Time: 60 min.). (Bird Walks by Habitat Ser.: Vol. 1). 1994. audio compact disk 16.95 CD. (2659, Creativ Pub) Quayside.
A unique audio & visual introduction to the sights & sounds of 24 common backyard birds - perfect for the beginning bird-watcher. Features the tufted titmouse, northern oriole, gray catbird, & downy woodpecker, among others. A full-color 30-page booklet includes an illustration & natural history information about each bird.

Backyard Bird Walk. Lang Elliott. 1 cass. (Running Time: 60 min.). (Bird Walks by Habitat Ser.: Vol. 1). 1994. 12.95 (2658, NrthWrd Bks) TandN Child.

Backyard Bug Battle: A Buzz Beaker Brainstorm. unabr. ed. Scott Nickel. 1 CD. (Buzz Beaker Brainstorm Ser.). (J). (gr. 3-5). 2007. audio compact disk 14.60 (978-1-59889-997-9(X)) CapstoneDig.

Backyard Bunch. Contrib. by Janet McMahan-Wilson & Ted Wilson. 1994. 90.00 (978-0-00-505691-2(8), 75608168) Pub: Brentwood Music. Dist(s): H Leonard

Bacon & Shakespeare - What Was Their Connection? Peter Dawkins. 1 cass. 9.00 (A0024-87) Sound Photosyn.
A talk by one of the vanguards of a movement which suggests that Bacon was the actual author of the many Shakespeare plays.

Bacon's Essays. unabr. ed. Francis Bacon. Read by Bernard Mayes. 4 cass. (Running Time: 5 hrs. 30 mins.). 1990. 32.95 set. (978-0-7861-0238-9(1), 1208) Blckstn Audio.
Among Bacon's lofty subjects are truth, death, nobility, travel, marriage, health, riches, beauty, negotiating & ambition. Rather than merely summarizing popular philosophy, Bacon attempted to change the shape of other men's minds & there is little doubt that many minds have been persuaded by these eloquent essays.

Bacteriology. Milady Publishing Company Staff. 1 cass. (Running Time: 1 hr.). (Standard Ser.: Chapter 2). 1995. 6.95 (978-1-56253-274-1(X), Milady) Delmar.

Bacunador Way - Mobile Audio Learning System: English - Cebuano. Melvin C. Bacunador & Darrell D. Simms. 2006. cd-rom 19.95 (978-0-9630776-2-2(7)) Mgmt Aspects.

Bacunador Way - Mobile Audio Learning System: English - Tagalog. Melvin C. Bacunador & Darrell D. Simms. 2006. cd-rom 19.95 (978-0-9630776-3-9(5)) Mgmt Aspects.

BAD: Or the Dumbing of America. unabr. ed. Paul Fussell. Read by Frederick Davidson. 4 cass. (Running Time: 5 hrs. 30 mins.). 1993. 32.95 (978-0-7861-0424-6(4), 1376) Blckstn Audio.
In this amusing & trenchant book, Paul Fussell zeroes in on the death of American sensibility & taste. "We are living in a moment teeming with raucously overvalued emptiness & trash," he writes in this reference work that exposes American BAD, from BAD Advertising & BAD Banks ("Personal Bankers" who are neither) to BAD Restaurants (where waiters establish friendly relations by announcing their first names - "Hi, I'm Brad"), & BAD TV (where news is presented as "stories" by reporters who don't report, but act & read scripts).

Bad Beginning. abr. ed. Lemony Snicket, pseud. Read by Tim Curry. (Running Time: 9000 sec.). (Series of Unfortunate Events Ser.: Bk. 1). (J). 2007. audio compact disk 14.95 (978-0-06-136533-1(5), HarperChildAud) HarperCollins Pubs.

Bad Beginning. unabr. ed. Lemony Snicket, pseud. Read by Tim Curry. 3 CDs. (Running Time: 3 hrs. 11 mins.). (Series of Unfortunate Events Ser.: Bk. 1). (YA). (gr. 5-8). 2003. audio compact disk 14.99 (978-0-8072-1990-4(8), Listening Lib) Pub: Random Audio Pubg. Dist(s): Random

Bad Beginning. unabr. ed. Lemony Snicket, pseud. 3 CDs. (Running Time: 3 hrs. 17 mins.). (Series of Unfortunate Events Ser.: Bk. 1). (J). (gr. 4-7). 2004. audio compact disk 30.00 (978-0-8072-1158-8(3), S YA 274 CD, Listening Lib) Random Audio Pubg.

Bad Beginning. unabr. ed. Lemony Snicket, pseud. Read by Tim Curry. 2 cass. (Running Time: 3 hrs. 17 mins.). (Series of Unfortunate Events Ser.: Bk. 1). (J). (gr. 4-7). 2004. 23.00 (978-0-8072-8847-4(0), LL0217, Listening Lib) Random Audio Pubg.
After the sudden death of their parents, the three Baudelaire children must depend on each other & their wits when it turns out that the distant relative who is appointed their guardian is determined to use any means necessary to get their fortune. Includes a bonus interview with the author.

Bad Beginning. unabr. abr. ed. Lemony Snicket, pseud. Read by Tim Curry. 3 CDs. (Running Time: 2 hrs. 30 mins.). Dramatization. (Series of Unfortunate Events Ser.: Bk. 1). (gr. 5 up). 2004. audio compact disk 22.00 (978-0-06-076579-8(8), HarperChildAud) HarperCollins Pubs.

***Bad Behavior of Belle Cantrell.** abr. ed. Loraine Despres. Read by Zoe Thomas. (ENG.). 2005. (978-0-06-089383-5(4), Harper Audio); (978-0-06-089384-2(2), Harper Audio) HarperCollins Pubs.

***Bad Behaviour.** unabr. ed. Liz Byrski. Read by Heather Bolton. 13 CDs. (Running Time: 15 hrs. 18 mins.). 2010. audio compact disk 113.95 (978-1-74214-490-0(X), 9781742144900) Pub: Bolinda Pubng AUS. Dist(s): Bolinda Pub Inc

***Bad Behaviour.** unabr. ed. Sheila O'Flanagan. Read by Caroline Lennon. 15 CDs. (Running Time: 17 hrs. 15 mins.). 2009. audio compact disk 123.75 (978-1-4361-9235-4(8)); audio compact disk 59.95 (978-1-4361-9236-1(6)) Recorded Bks.

***Bad Bird.** Chris Knopf. (Running Time: 8 hrs. 0 mins. 0 sec.). (ENG.). 2011. audio compact disk 29.95 (978-1-60998-151-8(0)) Pub: AudioGO. Dist(s): Perseus Dist

Bad Birdwatcher's Companion. abr. ed. Simon Barnes. (Running Time: 17230 sec.). 2007. audio compact disk 28.98 (978-962-634-446-0(6), Naxos AudioBooks) Naxos.

***Bad Blood.** John Sandford, pseud. Contrib. by Eric Conger. (Running Time: 6 hrs.). (Virgil Flowers Ser.: Bk. 4). (ENG.). 2010. audio compact disk 29.95 (978-0-14-242882-5(5), PengAudBks) Penguin Grp USA.

***Bad Blood.** John Sandford, pseud. Contrib. by Eric Conger. (Running Time: 10 hrs.). (Virgil Flowers Ser.: No. 4). (ENG.). 2010. audio compact disk 39.95 (978-0-14-242881-8(7), PengAudBks) Penguin Grp USA.

Bad Blood. abr. ed. Linda Fairstein. Read by Blair Brown. (Alexandra Cooper Mysteries Ser.). 2007. 17.95 (978-0-7435-6326-0(3), Audioworks) Pub: S&S Audio. Dist(s): S and S Inc

Bad Blood. abr. ed. Linda Fairstein. Read by Blair Brown. 5 CDs. (Running Time: 6 hrs. 0 mins. 0 sec.). (ENG.). 2009. audio compact disk 14.99 (978-0-7435-8040-3(0)) Pub: S&S Audio. Dist(s): S and S Inc

Bad Blood. unabr. ed. Linda Fairstein. Read by Barbara Rosenblatt. 10 cass. (Running Time: 11 hrs. 15 mins.). (Alexandra Cooper Mysteries Ser.). 2007. 79.75 (978-1-4281-3123-1(X)); audio compact disk 123.75 (978-1-4281-3125-5(6)) Recorded Bks.
During the trial of a young businessman accused of murdering his wife, an explosion occurs in a tunnel deep below New York City. This sets off a quest for answers when a secret connection between the defendant and the tunnel engineers is discovered. Now Alex is on a frantic search for information that could blow the lid off her case - and the city itself.

Bad Blood: Crisis in the American Red Cross. abr. ed. Judith Reitman. Read by Stephen Yankee. (Running Time: 3 hrs.). 2008. 39.25 (978-1-4233-5374-4(9), 9781423353744, BADLE); 24.95 (978-1-4233-5373-7(0), 9781423353737, BAD); audio compact disk 39.25 (978-1-4233-5372-0(2), 9781423353720, Brlnc Audio MP3 Lib); audio compact disk 24.95 (978-1-4233-5371-3(4), 9781423353713, Brilliance MP3) Brilliance Audio.

Bad Boy. unabr. ed. Olivia Goldsmith. Read by Susan Ericksen. 7 cass. (Running Time: 10 hrs.). 2000. 32.95 (978-1-58788-157-2(8), 1587881578, BAU) Brilliance Audio.
Best friends Tracie and Jonny meet for coffee each Sunday night to discuss their forlorn love lives. Tracie loves boys with an affinity for leather jackets and poetry - classic bad boys who seem too good to be true (and usually are); Jonny falls for girls who never like him in that way . . . until Jonny convinces Tracie to teach him some tricks of the trade. After a wardrobe makeover, learning to return from a dinner date with another phone number scrawled on his hand, scope for women at the airport baggage claim, and always carry a motorcycle helmet (even though he doesn't ride a motorcycle), Jonny quickly becomes a successful heartbreaker. And Tracie discovers that she just might be head-over-heels in love with her best friend. But there are more than a few loose ends. Tracie's current bad boy has at last decided he wants to settle down, her girlfriend has the hots for Jonny, and Jonny can't understand why Tracie never liked him for who he was before the leather. With her inimitable wit, Olivia Goldsmith, bestselling author of The First Wives Club, delivers a smart, laugh-out-loud tale of modern romance sure to keep listeners everywhere in stitches.

Bad Boy. unabr. ed. Olivia Goldsmith. Read by Susan Ericksen. (Running Time: 10 hrs.). 2004. 39.25 (978-1-59335-614-9(5), 1593356145, Brlnc Audio MP3 Lib) Brilliance Audio.

Bad Boy. unabr. ed. Olivia Goldsmith. Read by Susan Ericksen. (Running Time: 10 hrs.). 2004. 39.25 (978-1-59710-030-4(7), 1597100307, BADLE); 24.95 (978-1-59710-031-1(5), 1597100315, BAD) Brilliance Audio.

Bad Boy. unabr. ed. Olivia Goldsmith. Read by Susan Ericksen. (Running Time: 10 hrs.). 2004. 24.95 (978-1-59335-228-8(X), 159335228X) Soulmate Audio Bks.

***Bad Boy.** unabr. ed. Walter Dean Myers. Read by Joe Morton. (ENG.). 2005. (978-0-06-083916-1(3)); (978-0-06-083914-7(7)) HarperCollins Pubs.

***Bad Boy.** unabr. ed. Peter Robinson. Read by Simon Prebble. (Inspector Banks Mystery Ser.). (ENG.). 2010. (978-0-06-200697-4(5), Harper Audio); (978-0-06-206209-3(3), Harper Audio) HarperCollins Pubs.

Bad Boy: A Memoir. unabr. ed. Walter Dean Myers. Read by Joe Morton. (YA). 2008. 39.99 (978-1-60514-556-3(4)) Find a World.

Bad Boy Brawly Brown. unabr. ed. Walter Mosley. Read by M. E. Willis. 7 CDs. (Running Time: 9 hrs.). (Easy Rawlins Mystery Ser.). 2002. audio compact disk 63.00 (978-0-7366-8650-1(9)); 54.00 (978-0-7366-8649-5(5)) Books on Tape.
Easy Rawlins is out of the investigation business and as far away from crime as a black man can be in 1960s Los Angeles. But when an old friend gets in enough trouble to ask for Easy's help, he finds he can't refuse. Young Brawly Brown has disappeared, and Brown's mom asks Easy to make sure her baby's okay. Easy takes the job. His first day on the case, Easy comes face-to-face with a corpse; before he knows it, he's a murder suspect and in the middle of a police raid. It takes everything Easy has just to stay alive as he navigates a world like he never imagined.

Bad Boy Jack. Josephine Cox. Read by Carole Boyd. 12 vols. (Running Time: 18 hrs.). 2003. 96.95 (978-0-7540-0993-1(9)); audio compact disk 110.95 (978-0-7540-8748-9(4)) Pub: Chivers Audio Bks GBR. Dist(s): AudioGO

Bad Boys. 1 CD. (Running Time: 13 mins.). (J). (gr. k-3). 2007. bk. 29.95 (978-0-8045-4179-4(5)); bk. 27.95 (978-0-8045-6956-9(8)) Spoken Arts.

Bad Boys. abr. ed. Isiah Thomas & Matt Dobek. Read by Donald V. Allen. Ed. by Steven Alpert & Greg Nielson. 2 cass. (Running Time: 3 hrs.). Dramatization. 1992. bk. 15.95 Set. (978-1-56703-000-6(9)) High-Top Sports.

Bad Boys-Bad Girls. James T. Meeks. (Bad Boys-Bad Girls). 2000. 17.99 (978-1-931500-07-4(X)) J T M Minist.

Bad Boys Get Cookie! Margie Palatini. 1 CD. (Running Time: 10 mins.). (J). (gr. k-3). 2007. bk. 29.95 (978-0-8045-4180-0(9)); bk. 27.95 (978-0-8045-6957-6(6)) Spoken Arts.

Bad Breath Christians: Logos October 31, 1999. Ben Young. 1999. 4.95 (978-0-7417-6154-5(8), B0154) Win Walk.

Bad Business. unabr. ed. Robert B. Parker. Read by Joe Mantegna. 4 cass. (Running Time: 6 hrs.). (Spenser Ser.). 2004. 36.00 (978-0-7366-9762-0(4)) Books on Tape.
Spenser agrees to shadow a husband to gather irrefutable evidence for a divorce case, perhaps because the self-absorption and stupidity of the wife entertains him in some twisted way. She refuses to tell him her name or her husband's name and answers most of his questions with "It's none of your business." From this unpromising beginning, the case mushrooms into murder, sex, and profiteering. The husband is murdered while Spenser is shadowing him, insulting Spenser's professional competence. Experienced at interpreting Parker's Spenser mysteries, Joe Mantegna gives a fine reading, highlighting Spenser's quirky independence and giving credence to his cryptic responses.

Bad Business. unabr. ed. Robert B. Parker. Read by Joe Mantegna. (Spenser Ser.). (YA). 2007. 39.99 (978-0-7393-7119-0(3)) Find a World.

Bad Business. unabr. abr. ed. Robert B. Parker. Read by Joe Mantegna. 5 CDs. (Running Time: 6 hrs.). (Spenser Ser.). (ENG.). 2005. audio compact disk 14.99 (978-0-7393-1816-4(0)) Pub: Random Audio Pubg. Dist(s): Random

***Bad Childhood - -Good Life: How to Blossom & Thrive in Spite of An.** abr. ed. Laura Schlessinger. Read by Laura Schlessinger. (ENG.). 2006. (978-0-06-087857-3(6), Harper Audio); (978-0-06-087859-7(2), Harper Audio) HarperCollins Pubs.

Bad Childhood Good Life: How to Blossom & Thrive in Spite of an Unhappy Childhood. abr. ed. Laura Schlessinger & L. Schlessinger. Read by Laura Schlessinger. (Running Time: 10800 sec.). 2006. audio compact disk 22.95 (978-0-06-085288-7(7)) HarperCollins Pubs.

Bad Chili. unabr. ed. Joe R. Lansdale. Read by Phil Gigante. 1 MP3-CD. (Running Time: 8 hrs.). (Hap & Leonard Ser.). 2009. 39.97 (978-1-4233-8441-0(5), 9781423384410, Brlnc Audio MP3 Lib); 39.97 (978-1-4233-8443-4(1), 9781423384434, BADLE); 24.99 (978-1-4233-8440-3(7), 9781423384403, Brilliance MP3); 24.99 (978-1-4233-8442-7(3), 9781423384427, BAD); audio compact disk 87.97 (978-1-4233-8439-7(3), 9781423384397, BriAudCD Unabrid); audio compact disk 29.99 (978-1-4233-8438-0(5), 9781423384380, Bril Audio CD Unabri) Brilliance Audio.

Bad Circuits. abr. ed. Engle & Barnes. (Running Time: 2 hrs.). (Strange Matter Ser.). 2006. 9.95 (978-1-4233-0828-7(X), 9781423308287, BAD) Brilliance Audio.

Bad Circuits. abr. ed. Engle & Julian Barnes. Read by Multivoice Production Staff. (Running Time: 2 hrs.). (Strange Matter Ser.). 2006. 25.25 (978-1-4233-0829-4(8), 9781423308294, BADLE) Brilliance Audio.

Bad Circuits. abr. ed. Marty M. Engle & Johnny Ray Barnes, Jr. (Running Time: 7200 sec.). (Strange Matter Ser.). (J). (gr. 4-7). 2006. audio compact disk 25.25 (978-1-4233-0827-0(1), 9781423308270, BACDLib Ed); audio compact disk 9.95 (978-1-4233-0826-3(3), 9781423308263, BACD) Brilliance Audio.
Stephanie Meeker has a secret that's getting too dangerous to keep. Her cousin Daniel is determined to win the Fairfield Junior Science Competition, and he has been working on something in his room for days. Now Stephanie has discovered his shocking secret, the greatest science project in the world, but Daniel has sworn her to secrecy. Even as the project becomes more and more terrifying, Stephanie tells no one about the "Electronic Brain," a computer capable of thinking for itself. Daniel promises Stephanie he can keep it under control until he wins his award. The brain has other things on its mind.

Bad Company. unabr. ed. Liza Cody. Read by Juliet Prague. 6 cass. (Running Time: 6 hrs. 30 min.). (Isis Ser.). (J). 2001. 54.95 (978-1-85695-740-3(3), 940506) Pub: ISIS Lrg Prnt GBR. Dist(s): Ulverscroft US
A motorcycle gang abducts Anna Lee as she attempts to stop them from kidnapping a young girl. Imprisoned in a bare cold room with the terrified victim, Anna tries desperately to escape. In the meantime, her colleagues from the security agency are scouring London in search of her. She has shaken the unsteady balance of the London underworld - & things are about to turn very nasty, not to mention bloody.

Bad Company. unabr. ed. Liza Cody. Read by Juliet Prague. 6 CDs. (Running Time: 6 hrs. 30 mins.). (Isis Ser.). (J). 2001. audio compact disk 64.95 (978-0-7531-0906-9(9), 109069) Pub: ISIS Lrg Prnt GBR. Dist(s): Ulverscroft US
A motorcycle gang has abducted Anna Lee as she attempts to stop them from kidnapping a young girl. Now, imprisoned in a bare cold room with the terrified victim, Anna tries desperately to escape. In the meantime, her colleagues from the security agency are scouring London in search of her. Anna has shaken the unsteady balance of the London underworld & things are about to turn very nasty, not to mention bloody.

Bad Company. unabr. ed. Steve Wick. Read by Stephen Yankee. (Running Time: 8 hrs.). 2008. 24.95 (978-1-4233-7205-9(0), 9781423372059, BAD); 24.95 (978-1-4233-7203-5(4), 9781423372035, Brilliance MP3); 39.25 (978-1-4233-7204-2(2), 9781423372042, Brlnc Audio MP3 Lib); 39.25 (978-1-4233-7206-6(9), 9781423372066, BADLE) Brilliance Audio.

Bad Company. unabr. collector's ed. Jack Higgins. Narrated by Patrick Macnee. 5 cass. (Running Time: 7 hrs.). (Sean Dillon Ser.). 2004. 32.95 (978-1-4025-4369-2(7)) Recorded Bks.

Bad Connection. Michael Ledwidge. Narrated by L. J. Ganser. 5 cass. (Running Time: 6 hrs. 30 mins.). 2002. 50.00 (978-1-4025-0631-4(7), 95888) Recorded Bks.
Sean Macklin is a telephone repairman yearning for a better life for himself and his chronically ill wife. On a service call, he eavesdrops on a conversation concerning a corporate takeover. Using this information, he makes a killing on the stock exchange. However, when Sean listens in on a conversation describing a mass-murder coverup, he must make a decision that will ensnare him in a dangerous and deadly web.

Bad Debts. Peter Temple. Read by Marco Chiappi. 8 cass. (Running Time: 12 hrs.). 2000. (978-1-876584-67-2(X), 591001) Bolinda Pubng AUS.
When Jack Irish receives a puzzling message from a jailed ex-client, he's too deep in misery over Fitzroy's latest loss to take much notice. Next thing Jack knows the ex-client's dead & he's been drawn into a life-threatening investigation involving high-level corruption, dark sexual secrets, shady property deals & murder.

***Bad Debts.** unabr. ed. Peter Temple. Read by Marco Chiappi. 2010. audio compact disk 83.95 (978-1-74214-675-1(9), 9781742146751) Pub: Bolinda Pubng AUS. Dist(s): Bolinda Pub Inc

Bad Desire. abr. ed. Gary Devon. Read by Mark Rolston & Jennette Goldstein. 2 cass. (Running Time: 3 hrs.). 1991. 7.95 Set. (978-1-57815-037-3(X), 1012) Media Bks NJ.

Bad Detective. unabr. ed. H. R. F. Keating. Read by Vincent Brimble. 6 cass. (Running Time: 7 hrs.). 1997. 54.95 Set. (960910) Eye Ear.
Detective Sargeant Jack Stallworthy has been accepting pay-offs for most of his career. Lily, the pretty wife he deeply loves, dreams of retirement on the paradise island of Ko Samui. Influential businessman Emslie Warnaby offers Jack Ko Samui on a plate - first class tickets, & ownership of the Calm Seas Hotel. All Jack has to do is steal an incriminating file from police headquarters. Jack plunges deeper & deeper into crime, & soon there is no going back.

Bad Detective. unabr. ed. H. R. F. Keating. Read by Vincent Brimble. 6 cass. (Running Time: 9 hrs.). 1997. 54.95 (978-0-7531-0054-7(1), 960910) Pub: ISIS Audio GBR. Dist(s): Ulverscroft US

Bad Dirt: Wyoming Stories 2. unabr. ed. Annie Proulx. Read by William Dufris. 5 cass. 2005. 49.95 (978-0-7927-3415-4(7), CSL 732); audio compact disk 64.95 (978-0-7927-3416-1(5), SLD 732) AudioGO.

***Bad Dog, Marley!** unabr. ed. John Grogan. Read by Neil Patrick Harris. Illus. by Richard Cowdrey. (ENG.). 2007. (978-0-06-144746-4(3)); (978-0-06-144992-5(X)) HarperCollins Pubs.

Bad Dogs Have More Fun: Selected Writings on Family, Animals, & Life from the Philadelphia Inquirer. unabr. ed. John Grogan. Read by Arte Johnson. (YA). 2008. 54.99 (978-1-60514-698-0(6)) Find a World.

Bad Dreams. unabr. ed. Anne Fine. Read by Susannah Harker. 2 cass. (Running Time: 2 hrs. 25 mins.). 2002. (978-1-85549-879-2(0)) Cover To Cover GBR.
A gripping tale of real life and story-lives - and the importance of being free to be yourself.

Bad Dreams, unabr. ed. R. L. Stine. Narrated by Alyssa Bresnahan. 3 pieces. (Running Time: 4 hrs.). (Fear Street Ser.). (gr. 8 up). 1994. 28.00 (978-0-7887-0074-3(X), 94307E7) Recorded Bks.
In this clever tale of suspense, teenager Maggie Travers has a mysterious recurring nightmare of a murder committed in her new bed.

Bad Dreams. unabr. ed. R. L. Stine. Narrated by Alyssa Bresnahan. 4 CDs. (Running Time: 4 hrs.). (Fear Street Ser.). (gr. 8 up). 2000. audio compact disk 39.00 (978-0-7887-4735-9(5), C1218E7) Recorded Bks.

Bad Eagle, Hot Topics - -Patriotism: The Rantings of a Conservative Comanche. David A. Yeagley. 2007. audio compact disk 12.95 (978-1-4276-2405-5(4)) AardGP.

Bad Faith Litigation & Insurer vs. Insurer Disputes. unabr. ed. Contrib. by Jeffrey N. Haney. 4 cass. (Running Time: 5 hrs.). 1989. 50.00 course handbk. (T7-9212) PLI.
This recording of PLI's May 1989 program examines the changing law of extra-contractual liability of insurers to their insureds & to third parties. The faculty considers: remedies for the breach of the covenant of good faith & fair dealing, first party cases & third party cases, comparative bad faith & other defenses, developments in reinsurance & the effect of extra-contractual damages & punitive damages on reinsurers, insurers' duty to defend, disputes among primary insurers, excess insurers & reinsurers, recent trends & developments in punitive damages & unfair claims practices.

Bad Fire. Campbell Armstrong. Read by James Bryce. 10 cass. (Sound Ser.). (J). 2002. 84.95 (978-1-84283-197-7(6)) Pub: ISIS Lrg Prnt GBR. Dist(s): Ulverscroft US

Bad Girl Magdalene. Jonathan Gash et al. 2008. 84.95 (978-1-84652-299-4(4)); audio compact disk 99.95 (978-1-84652-300-7(1)) Pub: Magna Story GBR. Dist(s): Ulverscroft US

Bad Girls. Radio Spirits Staff. Read by Gregory Peck. 2007. 39.98 (978-1-57019-832-8(2)) Pub: Radio Spirits. Dist(s): AudioGO

Bad Girls. unabr. ed. Jacqueline Wilson. Read by Josie Lawrence. 3 CDs. (Running Time: 4 hrs. 30 mins.). (J). 2002. audio compact disk 29.95 (978-0-7540-6529-6(4), CHCD 029, Chivers Child Audio) AudioGO.

Bad Girls. unabr. ed. Jacqueline Wilson. Read by Josie Lawrence. 3 CDs. (Running Time: 4 hrs. 20 mins.). 2002. audio compact disk (978-1-85549-183-0(4)) Cover To Cover GBR.

Bad Girls, Set. unabr. ed. Ahrgus Juilliard. Read by Adrienne Barbeau. 2 cass. (Running Time: 3 hrs.). 1994. 16.95 (978-1-56876-025-4(6)) Soundlines Ent.
A western tale about four pistol packing cowgirls who find that living in world where women must be strong, it is important to have friends.

Bad Girls of the Bible: And What We Can Learn from Them. Liz Curtis Higgs. 2 cass. (Running Time: 3 hrs.). (ENG.). 1999. 14.99 (978-1-57856-220-6(1), WaterB Pr) Pub: Doubday Relig. Dist(s): Random
Offers a unique & clear-sighted approach to understand those "other women" in scripture, combining a contemporary retelling of their stories with a verse-by-verse study of their mistakes & what lessons we can learn from them.

Bad Ground. unabr. ed. W. Dale Cramer. Narrated by Pete Bradbury. 8 cass. (Running Time: 11 hrs. 30 mins.). 2004. 79.75 (978-1-4193-0995-3(1), K1116MC) Recorded Bks.

Bad Ground: Inside the Beaconsfield Mine Rescue. unabr. ed. Tony Wright. Read by Humphrey Bower. (Running Time: 9 hrs. 30 mins.). 2007. audio compact disk 87.95 (978-1-74093-936-2(0), 9781740939362) Pub: Bolinda Pubng AUS. Dist(s): Bolinda Pub Inc

Bad Hair Day: An Eclaire Mystery. unabr. ed. Sophie Dunbar. Read by Lynda Evans. 6 cass. (Running Time: 7 hrs. 12 min.). (Claire & Dan Claiborne Eclaire Mystery Ser.: Bk. 3). 2001. 39.95 (978-1-55686-853-5(7)) Books in Motion.
Claire is pulled into a network of drug dealing and bizarre New orleans relationships when a night club owner is found dead, poisoned at a friend's salon.

Bad Land: An American Romance. unabr. collector's ed. Jonathan Raban. Read by David Case. 8 cass. (Running Time: 12 hrs.). 1999. 64.00 (978-0-7366-4304-7(4), 4795) Books on Tape.
Seduced by the government's offer of 320 acres per homesteader, Americans & Europeans rushed to Montana & the Dakotas to fulfill their own American dream in the first decade of the century. The author strips away the myth - while preserving the romance - that has shrouded our understanding of our own heartland.

Bad Love. unabr. ed. Jonathan Kellerman. Read by Alexander Adams. 8 cass. (Running Time: 12 hrs.). (Alex Delaware Ser.: No. 8). 1994. 64.00 (3551) Books on Tape.
It came in a plain brown wrapper, no return address, an audiocassette of a soul-lacerating scream, followed by an enigmatic, haunting message delivered in a childlike voice: "Bad love, Bad love, Don't give me the bad love." For psychologist-detective Dr. Alex Delaware, the chant, repeated over & over like a twisted nursery rhyme, is the first intimation that he is about to enter a living nightmare. If Alex fails to decipher the twisted logic of the stalker's mind games, he will be the next to die.

Bad Love. unabr. ed. Jonathan Kellerman. Read by Alexander Adams. 10 CDs. (Running Time: 12 hrs.). (Alex Delaware Ser.: No. 8). 2004. audio compact disk 90.00 (978-1-4159-1623-0(3)) Books on Tape.
It came in a plain brown wrapper, no return address - an audiocassette of a soul-lacerating scream, followed by an enigmatic, haunting message delivered in a childlike voice: "Bad love. Bad love. Don't give me the bad love." For psychologist-detective Dr. Alex Delaware, the chant, repeated over and over like a twisted nursery rhyme, is the first intimation that he is about to enter a living nightmare. If Alex fails to discover the escalating pattern of violence and to decipher the twisted logic of the stalker's mind games, he will be the next to die.

Bad Love: Level 1. Sue Leather. Contrib. by Philip Prowse. (Cambridge English Readers Ser.). (ENG., 2003. 9.45 (978-0-521-53654-7(5)) Cambridge U Pr.

Bad Luck & Trouble. abr. ed. Lee Child. Read by Dick Hill. (Running Time: 21600 sec.). (Jack Reacher Ser.). (ENG.). 2008. audio compact disk 14.99 (978-0-7393-6568-7(1), Random AudioBks) Pub: Random Audio Pubg. Dist(s): Random

Bad Luck & Trouble. unabr. ed. Lee Child. Read by Dick Hill. 12 CDs. (Running Time: 15 hrs.). (Jack Reacher Ser.). 2007. audio compact disk 110.00 (978-1-4159-3646-7(3)); 110.00 (978-1-4159-3865-2(2)) Books on Tape.
From a helicopter high above the empty California desert, a man is sent free-falling into the night... In Chicago, a woman learns that an elite team of ex-army investigators is being hunted down one by one.... And on the streets of Portland, Jack Reacher - soldier, cop, hero - is pulled out of his wandering life by a code that few other people could understand. From the first shocking scenes in Lee Child"s explosive new novel, Jack Reacher is plunged like a knife into the heart of a conspiracy that is killing old friends - and is on its way to something even worse.

Bad Luck & Trouble. unabr. ed. Lee Child. Read by Dick Hill. 10 CDs. (Running Time: 46800 sec.). (Jack Reacher Ser.). (ENG.). 2007. audio compact disk 44.95 (978-0-7393-5726-2(3), Random AudioBks) Pub: Random Audio Pubg. Dist(s): Random

Bad Luck Boy. Susannah Brin. Narrated by Larry A. McKeever. (Romance Ser.). (J). 2003. 10.95 (978-1-58659-113-7(4)); audio compact disk 14.95 (978-1-58659-342-1(0)) Artesian.

Bad Monday. unabr. ed. Annette Roome. Narrated by Judith Boyd. 7 cass. (Running Time: 9 hrs. 30 mins.). 2000. 62.00 (978-1-84197-048-6(4), H1059E7) Recorded Bks.
Ex-housewife Chris Martin is a reporter for her local paper. Finally she gets a break, the chance to interview Rick Monday, singer of the defunct 70s group Bad Monday. He recently returned to the area & is now working with local charities & recording a new album. Only hours after her interview, Rick is killed. The motive given is theft, but Chris isn't so sure. Rick's Rolex wasn't taken & there are several other inconsistencies which make Chris decide to investigate. As she persists, she uncovers family lies, secrets & grisly truths about the underside of Rick's world. The same fate could await anyone trying to uncover the past.

Bad Money: Reckless Finance, Failed Politics, & the Global Crisis of American Capitalism. unabr. ed. Kevin Phillips. Read by Scott Brick. 8 CDs. (Running Time: 9 hrs. 30 mins.). 2008. audio compact disk 80.00 (978-1-4159-4990-0(5), BksonTape) Pub: Random Audio Pubg. Dist(s): Random

Bad Moon Rising. unabr. ed. Sherrilyn Kenyon. Read by Holter Graham. 9 CDs. (Running Time: 11 hrs. 0 mins. 0 sec.). Bk. 14. (ENG.). 2009. audio compact disk 39.95 (978-1-4272-0674-9(0)) Pub: Macmill Audio. Dist(s): Macmillan

Bad Neuenahr 2005: The Work with Byron Katie. 2005. audio compact disk 15.00 (978-1-890246-11-2(5)) B Katie Int Inc.

Bad News. Donald E. Westlake. Read by Michael Kramer. (Dortmunder Ser.). 2001. audio compact disk 64.00 (978-0-7366-8066-0(7)) Books on Tape.

Bad News. Donald E. Westlake. (Dortmunder Ser.). 2001. 56.00 (978-0-7366-6852-1(7)) Books on Tape.

Bad News/Good News. unabr. ed. Annie Bryant. (Beacon Street Girls Ser.: No. 2). (ENG.). (J). (gr. 7). 2008. audio compact disk 19.95 (978-0-7393-7308-8(0), Listening Lib) Pub: Random Audio Pubg. Dist(s): Random

Bad Place. unabr. ed. Dean Koontz. Read by Carol Cowan & Michael Hanson. 13 CDs. (Running Time: 15 hrs.). 2004. 24.95 (978-1-59335-714-6(1), 1593357141, Brilliance MP3); 39.25 (978-1-59335-848-8(2), 1593358482, Brlnc Audio MP3 Lib); 29.95 (978-1-59355-340-1(4), 1593553404, BAU); audio compact disk 42.95 (978-1-59355-342-5(0), 1593553420, Bril Audio CD Unabri) Brilliance Audio.

Bad Place. unabr. ed. Dean Koontz. Read by Michael Hanson & Carol Cowan. (Running Time: 15 hrs.). 2004. audio compact disk 112.25 (978-1-59355-343-2(9), 1593553439, BriAudCD Unabrid) Brilliance Audio.

Bad Place. unabr. ed. Dean Koontz. Read by Carol Cowan & Michael Hanson. (Running Time: 15 hrs.). 2004. 39.25 (978-1-59710-033-5(1), 1597100331, BADLE) Brilliance Audio.

Bad Place. unabr. ed. Dean Koontz. Read by Carol Cowan and Michael Hanson. (Running Time: 15 hrs.). 2004. 24.95 (978-1-59710-032-8(3), 1597100323, BAD) Brilliance Audio.

Bad Place. unabr. ed. Dean Koontz. Read by Carol Cowan & Michael Hanson. 10 cass. (Running Time: 15 hrs. 37 min.). 1992. 60.00 (978-0-9624010-3-9(X), 112749) Readers Chair.
Frank Pollard develops a fear of sleep: each time he wakes he finds strange objects in his hands & pockets. A husband & wife detective team agree to help him solve the mystery. Slowly they are drawn into Pollard's dream world, where an ominous figure stalks Pollard.

Bad Samaritans: The Myth of Free Trade & the Secret History of Capitalism. Ha-Joon Chang. Read by Jim Bond. (Playaway Adult Nonfiction Ser.). 2008. 64.99 (978-1-60640-900-8(X)) Find a World.

Bad Samaritans: The Myth of Free Trade & the Secret History of Capitalism. unabr. ed. Ha-Joon Chang. (Running Time: 9 hrs.). 2007. 39.25 (978-1-4233-4688-3(2), 9781423346883, BADLE); 24.95 (978-1-4233-4687-6(4), 9781423346876, BAD) Brilliance Audio.

Bad Samaritans: The Myth of Free Trade & the Secret History of Capitalism. unabr. ed. Ha-Joon Chang. Read by Jim Bond. 9 cass. (Running Time: 32400 sec.). 2007. 87.25 (978-1-4233-4682-1(3), 9781423346821, BrilAudUnabridg); audio compact disk 92.25 (978-1-4233-4684-5(X), 9781423346845, BriAudCD Unabrid); audio compact disk 39.25 (978-1-4233-4686-9(6), 9781423346869, Brlnc Audio MP3 Lib); audio compact disk 24.95 (978-1-4233-4685-2(8), 9781423346852, Brilliance MP3); audio compact disk 34.95 (978-1-4233-4683-8(1), 9781423346838, Bril Audio CD Unabri) Brilliance Audio.

Bad Sister. Denise Robertson. Read by Penelope Freeman. (Running Time: 43800 sec.). (Isis Cassettes Ser.). 2007. 84.95 (978-0-7531-3676-8(7)) Pub: ISIS Lrg Prnt GBR. Dist(s): Ulverscroft US

Bad Spell for the Worst Witch. Jill Murphy. Read by Miriam Margolyes. 1 cass. (Worst Witch Ser.). (J). (gr. 1-3). (CC/032) C to C Cassettes.
More adventures for Mildred Hubble & her friends at Miss Cackle's Academy for Young Witches.

Bad Things Happen. unabr. ed. Harry Dolan. Read by Abby Erik Davies. 9 CDs. (Running Time: 11 hrs.). (ENG.). (gr. 12 up). 2009. audio compact disk 39.95 (978-0-14-314459-5(6), PengAudBks) Penguin Grp USA.

***Bad Things Happen.** unabr. ed. Harry Dolan. Read by Erik Davies. 9 CDs. (Running Time: 11 hrs.). 2009. audio compact disk 100.00 (978-1-4159-6584-9(6), BksonTape) Pub: Random Audio Pubg. Dist(s): Random

Bad Twin. abr. ed. Gary Troup. Read by Scott Brick. 2006. 24.98 (978-1-4013-8494-4(3)) Pub: Hyperion. Dist(s): HarperCollins Pubs

Bad Wolf School: Primary Grade Musical Pack. Scripts. 9 cass. or CDs. (J). 2000. pap. bk. 180.00 Bad Wolf Pr.
Includes: "Aesop's Fables Deluxe," "Anansi & the Moss-Covered Rock," "Coyote Steals the Summer," "The Garden Show," "Goldilocks & the Three Bears," "Jack & the Beanstalk," "The Rumpus in the Rain Forest," "The Turkeys Go on Strike," "The Weather Show," plus "Earthworms on Parade" Sheet music available.

Bad Wolf School: Upper Grade Musical Pack. Scripts. 9 cass. or CDs. (J). 2000. pap. bk. & tchr. ed. 180.00 Bad Wolf Pr.
Includes: "13 Colonies," "America's Tallest Tales," "The Emperor's New Clothes," "Gold Dust or Bust," "The Incredible Westward Movement," "Little Red Riding Hood," "Macbeth, the Musical Comedy," "Theseus & the Minotaur," "Tide Pool Condos," plus Bad Wolf Teaching Video. Sheet music available.

Badge of the Assassin. unabr. ed. Robert K. Tanenbaum & P. Rosenberg. Read by Connor O'Brien. 9 cass. (Running Time: 13 hrs. 30 min.). 1997. 72.00 (978-0-7366-3656-8(0), 4327) Books on Tape.
Gunmen ambushed two policemen in the Bronx in a1971 horrific murder case.

Badger Boy. Elmer Kelton. Narrated by Jonathan Davis. 7 cass. (Running Time: 9 hrs. 30 mins.). (Texas Rangers Ser.: No. 2). 2002. 66.00 (978-0-7887-9445-2(0)) Recorded Bks.

Badger's Beech & Badger's Moon. unabr. ed. Elleston Trevor. Read by Gary Martin. 8 cass. (Running Time: 1 hr. per cass.). (Woodlander Ser.). (J). 1992. 64.00 (978-0-7366-2843-3(6), 2900) Books on Tape.
A secret tunnel may lead to hidden treasure & a very secret affair finds the Grey Wizard building a machine inside Green Mountain.

Badger's Beech & Badger's Moon. unabr. collector's ed. Elleston Trevor. Read by Gary Martin. 8 cass. (Running Time: 8 hrs.). (Woodlander Ser.). (J). 1992. 48.00 (978-0-7366-2094-9(X), 2900) Books on Tape.
A secret tunnel may lead to hidden treasures & a very secret affair finds Grey Wizard building a machine inside Green Mountain.

Badger's Wood. unabr. collector's ed. Elleston Trevor. Read by Wanda McCaddon. 4 cass. (Running Time: 4 hrs.). (J). 1983. 24.00 (978-0-7366-0732-2(3), 1689) Books on Tape.
Talks about the denizens of Deep Wood - Old Stripe the Badger, Potter Otter, Woo Owl, Little Digger Mole & their neighbors of copse & river & treetop.

Badlands. Peter Bowen & Christopher Lane. 5 cass. (Running Time: 7 hrs.). 2002. 39.95 (978-0-7861-2540-1(3), 3171) Blckstn Audio.

Badlands. unabr. ed. Peter Bowen. Read by Christopher Lane. (Running Time: 7 hrs.). 2000. audio compact disk 24.95 (978-0-7861-8862-8(6), 3171) Blckstn Audio.

Badlands. unabr. ed. Peter Bowen. Read by Christopher Lane. 5 CDs. (Running Time: 7 hrs.). 2001. audio compact disk 40.00 (978-0-7861-9037-9(X), 3171) Blckstn Audio.

Badlands. unabr. ed. Peter Bowen. Read by Christopher Lane. 5 pieces. 2004. reel tape 29.95 (978-0-7861-2574-6(8)); audio compact disk 35.95 (978-0-7861-9079-9(5)) Blckstn Audio.

Badrinath. Music by Alaka D. Marulkar. 1 cass. (Tirth Ser.: Vol. 4). 1996. (D96004) Multi-Cultural Bks.

Baffled about Baby? A Quick & Easy Audio Guide to Baby Care. United Parents Group. Read by Alize Warwick. Prod. by Angela Russ. Directed By Angela Russ. (YA). (gr. 11 up). 2001. audio compact disk 16.99 (978-0-9660122-3-1(2)) Russ Invis.

***Bag Lady Papers: The Priceless Experience of Losing It All.** unabr. ed. Alexandra Penney. Narrated by Marguerite Gavin. (Running Time: 5 hrs. 30 mins.). 2010. 13.99 (978-1-4001-8545-0(9)); 19.99 (978-1-4001-6545-2(8)); audio compact disk 59.99 (978-1-4001-4545-4(7)); audio compact disk 29.99 (978-1-4001-1545-7(0)) Pub: Tantor Media. Dist(s): IngramPubServ

Bag of Bones. Stephen King. Read by Stephen King. 14 cass. (Running Time: 22 hrs.). 1999. (978-1-84032-192-0(X), HoddrStoughton) Hodder General GBR.
When best-selling crime writer Mike Noonan's wife dies, he suffers from writer's block. He is drawn from Derry to his lakeside retreat where he is determined to get custody of his grandchild. But there are others determined to prevent Mike' success.

Bag of Bones. unabr. ed. Stephen King. Read by Stephen King. 16 cass. 1999. 59.95 (FS9-43225) Highsmith.

Bag of Bones. unabr. ed. Stephen King. Read by Stephen King. (Running Time: 220 hrs. 0 mins. 0 sec.). (ENG.). 2005. audio compact disk 49.95 (978-0-7435-5175-5(3), Audioworks) Pub: S&S Audio. Dist(s): S and S Inc

Bag of Bones. unabr. ed. Stephen King. Read by Stephen King. 2006. 29.95 (978-0-7435-6330-7(1), Audioworks) Pub: S&S Audio. Dist(s): S and S Inc

Bag Talk. John M. Bennett. 1 cass. (Running Time: 90 min.). 1992. 7.00 (978-0-935350-36-4(5)) Luna Bisonte.

Baggage Claim: A Novel. unabr. ed. David E. Talbert. Perf. by Kim Fields. 8 CDs. (Running Time: 9 hrs.). 2004. audio compact disk 45.00 (978-1-59007-517-3(X)) Pub: New Millenn Enter. Dist(s): PerseuPGW

Baggage Claim: A Novel. unabr. abr. ed. David E. Talbert. Perf. by Kim Fields. 6 cass. (Running Time: 9 hrs.). 2004. 29.95 (978-1-59007-516-6(1)) Pub: New Millenn Enter. Dist(s): PerseuPGW

Baghdad Sketches. unabr. collector's ed. Freya Stark. Read by Donada Peters. 6 cass. (Running Time: 6 hrs.). 1990. 36.00 (978-0-7366-1846-5(5), 2679) Books on Tape.
In light of today's headlines, Freya Stark's memoirs of her travels in the Middle East are more valuable than ever. With her eye for detail & her ability to become a part of whatever land she is exploring, Stark paints for us pictures of a Baghdad which has vanished. She shares with us the beauty & picturesqueness of the land as few have ever seen it & that no one will ever have the opportunity to see again.

Bagombo Snuff Box: Uncollected Short Fiction. Kurt Vonnegut. Read by Alexander Marshall. (Playaway Adult Fiction Ser.). 2009. 39.99 (978-1-60812-719-1(2)) Find a World.

Bagombo Snuff Box: Uncollected Short Fiction. unabr. abr. ed. Kurt Vonnegut. Read by Alexander Marshall. (Running Time: 20700 sec.). 2007. audio compact disk 24.95 (978-1-59887-554-6(X), 159887554X) Pub: HighBridge. Dist(s): Workman Pub

Bagthorpes: Absolute Zero. unabr. ed. Helen Cresswell. Read by Clive Mantle. 6 CDs. (Running Time: 5 hrs. 30 mins.). (YA). (gr. 9-11). 2007. audio compact disk 59.95 (978-1-4056-5658-0(1), ChiversChildren) AudioGo GBR.

Bahama Heat. unabr. ed. Barry Estabrook. Read by Frank Muller. 8 cass. (Running Time: 10 hrs. 45 min.). 1994. Rental 16.50 Set. (94350) Recorded Bks.
When he discovers a missing shipment of cocaine belonging to a drug cartel, a down & out preacher tries to save the Bahamian orphanage he loves with the booty.

Bahama Heat, unabr. ed. Harry Estabrook. Narrated by Frank Muller. 8 cass. (Running Time: 10 hrs. 45 mins.). 1994. 70.00 (978-0-7887-0146-7(0), 94350E7) Recorded Bks.

Bahamas Pajamas. Joe Scruggs. 1 cass. (Running Time: 35 min.). (J). (ps-4). 1990. 9.95 (978-0-916123-11-6(1), SPR-250) Ed Graphics Pr.
Contains 13 listening & activity songs. Scruggs once again uses his talent for capturing those simple & familiar moments of growing up & makes them special & delightful all over again.

Bahamas Real Estate Seminar, 1979. unabr. ed. Douglas Casey et al. 3 cass. 65.00 (1340-1342) J Norton Pubs.

Bai xue CD. 2009. audio compact disk 20.00 (978-1-934915-28-8(9)) Premier Music.

Baila Conmigo. Contrib. by Solea. 2007. audio compact disk 19.95 (978-5-557-51960-1(2)) Mel Bay.

Bailes Favoritos Todos los Tiempos. 1 cass. (Running Time: 35 min.). (SPA.). (J). 2001. pap. bk. 10.95 (KMS9126C); pap. bk. 11.95 (KMS 9126) Kimbo Educ.

All-time favorite dances. 13 popular dances featured above in Spanish. Includes instructional guide.

Bailes, ritmos y cantos tradicionales de Puerto Rico. ANISA, Inc. audio compact disk 14.95 (978-1-56835-405-7(3)) Prodns Anisa.

Bailey's Café. unabr. ed. Gloria Naylor. Read by multivoice. (Running Time: 8 hrs.). 2010. 39.97 (978-1-4418-3604-5(7), 9781441836045, Brlnc Audio MP3 Lib); 24.99 (978-1-4418-3603-8(9), 9781441836038, Brilliance MP3); 39.97 (978-1-4418-3606-9(3), 9781441836069, BADLE); 24.99 (978-1-4418-3605-2(5), 9781441836052, BAD) Brilliance Audio.

Bailie's Wake. unabr. ed. Pamela Smith Hill. Read by Lesley Mackie. 4 cass. (Running Time: 5 hrs. 14 min). (Isis Ser.). (J). 2001. 44.95 (978-0-7531-0929-8(8)) Pub: ISIS Lrg Prnt GBR. Dist(s): Ulverscroft US

Mid-Victorian Glasgow may have seemed totally respectable on the surface, but there were undercurrents. The Rev. McPhail, married to a mousy bride, finds his Highland blood stirring at the sight of the beautiful young wife of the elderly millionaire who has founded the parish church.

Baiser au Lepreux, Set. Francois Mauriac. Read by Sami Frey. 2 cass. (Les Cahiers Verts Ser.: 8). (FRE.). 1991. 27.95 (1367-BPI) Olivia & Hill.

When the repulsive & sickly Jean Peloueyre marries the beautiful Noemie, he believes that there is a chance for him to escape from his destiny & from his unbearable solitude.

Bait. abr. ed. Karen Robards. Read by Joyce Bean. (Running Time: 21600 sec.). 2007. audio compact disk 14.99 (978-1-4233-3353-1(5), 9781423333531, BCD Value Price) Brilliance Audio.

Bait, unabr. ed. Kenneth Abel. Narrated by Frank Muller. 6 cass. (Running Time: 8 hrs. 15 mins.). 1995. 51.00 (978-0-7887-0355-3(2), 94547E7) Recorded Bks.

A drunken police detective on a downward spiral kills the only son of a powerful Mafia don in a drunk driving accident. The feds step in & set the cop up as bait in order to catch the Mafioso in an incriminating act, such as killing a cop.

Bait. unabr. ed. Karen Robards. Read by Joyce Bean. (Running Time: 13 hrs.). 2004. 24.95 (978-1-59335-761-0(3), 1593357613, Brilliance MP3); 39.25 (978-1-59335-895-2(4), 1593358954, Brlnc Audio MP3 Lib); 36.95 (978-1-59355-857-4(0), 1593558570, BAU); 92.25 (978-1-59355-858-1(9), 1593558589, BACDLib Ed); audio compact disk 36.95 (978-1-59355-860-4(0), 1593558600, Bril Audio CD Unabri); audio compact disk 107.25 (978-1-59355-861-1(9), 1593558619, BACDLib Ed) Brilliance Audio.

It's a business trip that takes attorney Maddie Fitzgerald down to New Orleans, but it's hardly business as usual when a man breaks into her hotel room and tries to kill her. Barely escaping with her life, the sexy, stylish thirty-two-year-old brunette calls the police and finds herself face-to-face with FBI agent Sam McCabe. Unnerved by his questions - and his good looks - Maddie is told she's been targeted by a hired killer, one who has eluded McCabe for years. Apparently, she's been mistaken for another woman, an FBI informant of the same name who was also staying at the hotel that night. McCabe grills her, and then disappears. Shaken, she finishes her business and returns home to St. Louis. But days later, Maddie is attacked a second time, and again McCabe returns to question her. He convinces her that the only way she'll ever be safe again is if the killer is caught, and the quickest way to nab him is to use her as bait. Maddie reluctantly agrees, and sparks fly and then ignite as McCabe shadows her. But their unexpected romance throws McCabe off his stride - and puts Maddie in the hands of a killer.

Bait. unabr. ed. Karen Robards. Read by Joyce Bean. (Running Time: 13 hrs.). 2004. 39.25 (978-1-59710-035-9(8), 1597100358, BADLE); 24.95 (978-1-59710-034-2(X), 159710034X, BAD) Brilliance Audio.

Bait & Switch: The (Futile) Pursuit of the American Dream. Barbara Ehrenreich. Read by Anne Twomey. 6 CDs. 2005. audio compact disk 32.95 (978-0-7927-3747-6(4), SLD 839) AudioGO.

Bait & Switch: The (Futile) Pursuit of the American Dream. Barbara Ehrenreich. Read by Anne Twomey. 2005. 14.95 (978-1-59397-731-3(X)) Pub: Macmill Audio. Dist(s): Macmillan

Bait & Switch: The (Futile) Pursuit of the American Dream. abr. ed. Barbara Ehrenreich. 2005. 14.95 (978-1-59397-791-7(3)) Pub: Macmill Audio. Dist(s): Macmillan

Bait of Satan: Living Free from the Deadly Trap of Offense. unabr. ed. John Bevere. Narrated by John Bevere. (Running Time: 7 hrs. 0 mins. 0 sec.). (ENG.). 2009. 18.19 (978-1-60814-585-0(9)); audio compact disk 25.99 (978-1-59859-631-1(4)) Oasis Audio.

Baje de Peso Sin Sufrir. Carlos González. Read by Carlos González. Ed. by Dina Gonzalez. 1 cass. (Running Time: 32 min.). (SPA.). 1991. 10.00 (978-1-56491-029-5(6)) Imagine Pubs.

In Spanish. Makes the person have a possitive attitude toward losing weight.

***Baje la Guardia.** Charles R. Swindoll.Tr. of Dropping Your Guard. 2010. audio compact disk 34.00 (978-1-57972-879-3(0)) Insight Living.

Bajo Sexto: Vol. 1, Acordes y Progresiones. Rogelio Maya. (ENG., 2001. pap. bk. 14.95 (978-1-928827-33-7(0)) Mayas Music.

Baker Street Bunch Mysteries. Michael W. Paulson. (J). (gr. 4-6). 2001. audio compact disk 14.95 (978-0-9716804-5-6(0)) M Paulson.

The Baker Street Bunch take on their adversaries; Herman and Baron to save a pig, an owl, pumpkins, a prize winning pie, and more. There is no violence. The kids outsmart the dim-witted adult offenders through disguises and smart thinking blended with brain food supplied by mayonnaise cheeseburgers and fries.

Baker Street Dozen: Sir Arthur Conan Doyle's Thirteen Favorite Sherlock Holmes Stories. Arthur Conan Doyle. Read by David Sharp. 8 cass. (Running Time: 11 hrs.). 1995. 44.95 set. (978-1-55686-583-1(X)) Books in Motion.

Includes thirteen short stories, The Adventures Of: The Engineer's Thumb; The Noble Bachelor; The Beryl Coronet; The Cardboard Box; The Stockbroker's Clerk; The "Gloria Scott"; The Raigate Squires; & others.

Baker Street Dozen: Sir Arthur Conan Doyle's Thirteen Favorite Sherlock Holmes Stories. Arthur Conan Doyle. 6 cass. (Running Time: 540 mins.). 1989. 29.95 (978-0-88142-866-7(3)) Soundelux.

Baker Street Letters: A Mystery. unabr. ed. Michael Robertson. (Running Time: 10 hrs. 0 mins.). 2009. 29.95 (978-1-4332-5736-0(X)); 59.95 (978-1-4332-5732-2(7)); audio compact disk 29.95 (978-1-4332-5735-3(1)); audio compact disk 90.00 (978-1-4332-5733-9(5)) Blckstn Audio.

Baker Towers. unabr. ed. Jennifer Haigh. Read by Anna Fields. 29.95 (978-0-7927-3469-7(6), CMP 745); 54.95 (978-0-7927-3447-5(5), CSL 745); audio compact disk 79.95 (978-0-7927-3448-2(3), SLD 745) AudioGO.

Baker Towers. unabr. ed. Jennifer Haigh. Read by Anna Fields. 2005. audio compact disk 34.95 (978-0-06-075950-6(X)) HarperCollins Pubs.

***Baker Towers.** unabr. ed. Jennifer Haigh. Read by Anna Fields. (ENG.). 2005. (978-0-06-082891-2(9), Harper Audio); (978-0-06-082915-5(X), Harper Audio) HarperCollins Pubs.

Baker's Bluejay Yarn see Great American Short Stories

Baker's Bluejay Yarn see Man That Corrupted Hadleyburg & Other Stories

Baker's Bluejay Yarn see Typhoon

Baker's Cat see Necklace of Raindrops & Other Stories

Bakongo! Drumming Music for Dancers. unabr. ed. Instructed by Geoff Johns. 1 CD. (Running Time: 58 mins.). 1992. audio compact disk 16.98 (978-1-56455-455-0(4), MM00335D) Sounds True.

A drumming tape including eight compositions from different parts of the world, including Haiti, Africa & Cuba.

Bal du Comte d'Orgel, Set. Raymond Radiguet. Read by Philippe De Boissy & Anne De Boissy. 3 cass. (FRE.). 1991. 31.95 (1274-VSL) Olivia & Hill.

In the postwar Parisian world of 1920, the Count d'Orgel has married Mahaut Grimoard de la Verberie. Upon discovering that his young wife is in love with another man, the Count insists upon inviting him to a fancy dress ball.

Bal du Gouverneur. Marie-France Pisier. Read by Marie-France Pisier. 1 cass. (FRE.). 1991. 22.95 (1103-EF) Olivia & Hill.

Set in the colony of New Caledonia during the 1950s, a milieu where conformity & intrigue reign, a girl fascinated by the troubled adult world around her, discovers her own sensuality.

Balaam & His Ass. Michael Pearl. 1 CD. 2005. audio compact disk (978-1-892112-70-5(1)) No Greater Joy.

Balance see Balance

Balance. Grover Bravo.Tr. of Balance. (SPA.). 2009. audio compact disk 15.00 (978-1-935405-53-5(5)) Hombre Nuevo.

***Balance.** Created by Uncommon Sensing LLC. (ENG.). 2009. audio compact disk 60.00 (978-0-9826724-9-5(7)) Uncommon Sens.

Balance: In Search of the Lost Sense. abr. ed. Scott McCredie. Read by Scott McCredie. (Running Time: 3 hrs.). (ENG.). 2007. 14.98 (978-1-59483-915-3(8)) Pub: Hachet Audio. Dist(s): HachBkGrp

Balance: Stress-Free & Relaxed in Minutes. 2000. pap. bk. 7.95 (978-3-8290-3310-7(9)) Konemann.

***Balance at Its Best: How to bring order to your hectic Life.** Lori Salierno. Prod. by Celebrate Life International. (Running Time: 255). (ENG.). 2009. audio compact disk 29.95 (978-0-9826157-0-6(1)) CelebrateLifeGA.

Balance Function Assessment & Management. Ed. by Gary P. Jacobson & Neil T. Shepard. 2007. bk. 139.95 (978-1-59756-100-6(2)) Plural Pub Inc.

Balance of Creation. Swami Amar Jyoti. 1 cass. 1987. 9.95 (K-92) Truth Consciousness.

How creation happens, through the three gunas, in incessant beautiful variety. Nitya Lila, the eternal play. Keeping balance & harmony intact. A love affair with our creator.

Balance of Love. Read by Wayne Monbleau. 2 cass. (Running Time: 2 hrs.). 1993. 10.00 Set. (978-0-944648-15-5(0), LGT-1195) Loving Grace Pubns.

Religious.

Balance of Power. James W. Huston. Read by Adams Morgan. 10 cass. (Running Time: 14 hrs. 30 mins.). 2001. 69.95 (978-0-7861-1874-8(1), 2673); audio compact disk 104.00 (978-0-7861-9809-2(5), 2673) Blckstn Audio.

An ambitious young congressional assistant, Jim Dillon, has discovered a time bomb hidden away in America's Constitution - a provision that could be used to wrest power from the Chief Executive. it is a long-forgotten clause that could incite a devastating consitutional crisis...& plunge the country into chaos.

***Balance of Power.** unabr. ed. James W. Huston. Read by Adams Morgan. (Running Time: 14 hrs. 30 mins.). 2010. audio compact disk 29.95 (978-1-4417-3595-9(X)) Blckstn Audio.

Balance of Power. unabr. ed. Richard North Patterson. Read by Patricia Kalember. 12 cass. (Running Time: 18 hrs.). 2003. 86.40 (978-0-7366-9436-0(6)); audio compact disk 100.80 (978-0-7366-9567-1(2)) Books on Tape.

Five months into his term, young President Kilcannon and his fiance, television journalist Lara Costello, decide at last to marry. When the wedding culminates in a tragic shooting, the President embarks upon a high-stakes battle with the gun lobby. When Kilcannon uses his clout to support a class action suit on behalf of gun victims, the gun industry attempts to use every political tactic in the book to bring him and the lawsuit down.

Balance of Within & Without. Swami Amar Jyoti. 1 cass. 1983. 9.95 (K-55) Truth Consciousness.

Keeping the right proportion of within & without for balance & harmony in life. On the four Yugas, ages or cycles.

Balance Within: The Science Connecting Health & Emotions. Esther M. Sternberg. Read by Arte Johnson. 4 cass. (Running Time: 6 hrs.). 2000. 25.00 Audio Lit.

Balance Within: The Science Connecting Health & Emotions, abr. ed. Esther M. Sternberg. Read by Arte Johnson. 4 cass. (Running Time: 6 hrs.). 2000. 25.00 (978-1-57453-354-5(1)) Audio Lit.

Does stress cause illness? Can love heal? This ground-breaking work by physician & researcher offers hard evidence that emotional & physical health influence each other & examines the critical role relationships, faith & emotional well-being play in resisting disease.

Balance Workshop. Jackie Woods. 4 CDs. 2003. audio compact disk 49.95 (978-0-9659665-7-3(7)) Adawehi Pr.

Balance Your Life (Audio Workshop) Wendy Y. Bailey. 1CD. 2004. audio compact disk 19.00 (978-0-9749914-3-6(0)) Brilliance In Action.

Balance Your LifeAre you running your business or is it running you? Are your personal problems affecting your business? Balance is the answer and that means you need it! Listen and learn the five keys for achieving balance: Responsibility, Awareness, Recognition, Appreciation and Respect. This audio workshop is ideal for women entrepreneurs, small business owners and business professionals. Includes detailed TeleClass notes with challenge assignments.

***Balance Yourself Audio CD.** Susan Diane Matz. (ENG.). 2010. 15.95 (978-0-9841054-8-9(4)) Abriev Ent.

Balanced Body Secret. Nancy Appleton. Read by Nancy Appleton. 4 cass. 1993. 29.95 set incl. wkbk. Rudra Pr.

Balanced Life - How to Deal with Temptation. Kriyananda, pseud. (Running Time: 80 min.). 9.95 (SS-88) Crystal Clarity.

Discusses how egotism affects our level of awareness & why love seeks reciprocation; also how God's power frees us from temptation; finding joy in self-discipline; the importance of transmuting, not suppressing, desires.

Balanced Living. Directed By Gerald T. Rogers. Contrib. by Dennis C. Daley. (Living Sober 2 Ser.: Segment N). 1996. pap. bk. 89.00 NTSC. (978-1-56215-072-3(1), Jossey-Bass) Wiley US.

Balanced Living Series. unabr. ed. Judith L. Powell. Read by Judith L. Powell. 8 cass. (Running Time: 12 hrs.). 1988. 79.95 set. (978-0-914295-64-8(0)) Top Mtn Pub.

Expand your true potential in all areas of your life - spiritual, mental, physical, financial, emotional, personal, social, & family. Mental visualization & subliminals.

Balancing Act Vol. III: Create an Inspiring Life Mentally, Physically, & Spiritually. unabr. ed. David Essel. 1 cass. (Running Time: 1 hrs.). (David Essel's Dynamic Living Ser.). 1997. 9.95 (978-1-893074-01-9(3)) D Essel Inc.

Learn to live a balanced life: m1) Balance life through personal attention, 2) The new definition of success, 3) Changing our beliefs about success, 4) Balance through nutrition, exercise & relaxation, 5) Effortlessly reach your goals.

Balancing In Motion (FTAT-202) Ragini E. Michaels. Read by Ragini E. Michaels. Music by Divyam Ambodha. 1 cass. (Running Time: 30 min.). (Facticity Ser.). 1991. 14.95 (978-0-9628686-8-9(X), FTAT-202) Facticity Tr.

Works to strengthen your unconscious mind's awareness that balance is a process, rather than a position to achieve, freeing you to more easily experience that balancing in motion.

Balancing Masculine Feminine. Marianne Williamson. Read by Marianne Williamson. 1 cass. (Running Time: 90 mins.). (Lectures on a Course in Miracles). 1999. 10.00 (978-1-56170-484-2(9), M847) Hay House.

Balancing Our View of the Man from Nazareth. Zalman Schachter. 1 cass. 9.00 (A0618-89) Sound Photosyn.

At the San Francisco Jewish Community Center.

Balancing the Shields: The Impact of Native American Teachings. Read by Mary Loomis. 1 cass. (Running Time: 1 hr.). 1987. 9.95 (978-0-7822-0148-2(2), 278) C G Jung IL.

Balancing Work & Family. Stephen R. Covey. 2 cass. (Running Time: 3 hrs.). 1998. 17.95 Dragonhawk Pub.

Struggle of trying to cope with work & balancing a family.

Balancing Your Energies & Clearing Blockages Tape Set for Centering, Self-Healing & De-Stressing. Scripts. Marjorie Baker Price. Perf. by Marjorie Baker Price. 2 cassettes. (Running Time: 60 minutes). 1990. 16.95 (978-0-9713013-5-1(2)) Centering Pubns.

Use these two very special tapes to relax, release and recharge yourself and your life from a place of balance and spiritual power that comes through heightened energy, upliftment and deep relaxation. Set includes 2 self-hypnosis cassettes, "Clearing Blockages" and "Balancing Your Energies". Regular listening will promote powerful self-healing responses and allow you to clear physical , mental and emotional blocks at an energetic level.

Balcony, Set. abr. ed. Jean Genet. Perf. by Pamela Brown & Patrick MaGee. Tr. by Bernard Frechtman. 3 cass. (Running Time: 5 hrs.). Dramatization. 1984. 26.94 (CDL5 316) HarperCollins Pubs.

Cast includes: Cyril Cusack, Eileen Atkins, Roland Culver, Colin Blakely, Nigel Davenport, & Denholm Elliott.

Balcony People. Joyce Landorf Heatherley. 1 cass. 1988. 7.95 (978-0-929488-06-6(7)) Balcony Pub Inc.

How can we love & support one another, as Jesus asked us to?.

Bald Bandit. unabr. ed. Ron Roy. Illus. by John Steven Gurney. (Running Time: 42 mins.). (A to Z Mysteries Ser.: No. 2). (J). (gr. k-3). 2004. pap. bk. 17.00 (978-0-8072-1704-7(2), S FTR 270 SP, Listening Lib) Random Audio Pubg.

Baldacci 1st Five Box Set. abr. ed. David Baldacci. (ENG.). 2009. 89.98 (978-1-60788-155-1(1)) Pub: Hachet Audio. Dist(s): HachBkGrp

Balfour Twins. Betty Mcinnes. 2009. 69.95 (978-1-4079-0368-2(3)); audio compact disk 79.95 (978-1-4079-0369-9(1)) Pub: Soundings Ltd GBR. Dist(s): Ulverscroft US

Balinese Culture & Shamanism. unabr. ed. Gregory Bateson. 2 cass. (Running Time: 3 hrs.). 1976. 18.00 Set. (02802) Big Sur Tapes.

Drawing from his personal anthropological observations & experiences, Bateson guides us through a fascinating view of the Balinese.

Balkans: A Short History. Mark Mazower. Narrated by Robert O'Keefe. 5 cass. (Running Time: 6 hrs. 30 mins.). 2000. 52.00 (978-1-4025-1354-1(2)) Recorded Bks.

Ball, a Dog, & a Monkey: 1957 - -the Space Race Begins. unabr. ed. Michael D'Antonio. Read by Alan Sklar. (Running Time: 11 hrs. 0 mins. 0 sec.). (ENG.). 2007. audio compact disk 24.99 (978-1-4001-5503-7(7)) Pub: Tantor Media. Dist(s): IngramPubServ

Ball, a Dog, & a Monkey: 1957 - -the Space Race Begins. unabr. ed. Michael D'Antonio. Read by A. Sklar. (Running Time: 11 hrs. 0 mins. 0 sec.). (ENG.). 2007. audio compact disk 69.99 (978-1-4001-3503-5(6)) Pub: Tantor Media. Dist(s): IngramPubServ

Ball, a Dog, & a Monkey: 1957 - -the Space Race Begins. unabr. ed. Read by Alan Sklar. (Running Time: 11 hrs. 0 mins. 0 sec.). (ENG.). 2007. audio compact disk 34.99 (978-1-4001-0503-8(X)) Pub: Tantor Media. Dist(s): IngramPubServ

Ball & the Cross. G. K. Chesterton. Narrated by Flo Gibson. 5 cass. (Running Time: 7 hrs. 30 mins.). (gr. 10 up). 2000. 20.95 (978-1-55685-644-0(X)) Audio Bk Con.

The humorous & sometimes crazy plot is about the adventures of two naive Scotsmen, a Roman Catholic & an atheist, who challenge each other to a duel.

Ball, Hoop & Ribbon Activities for Young Children. Carol Hammett & Elaine Bueffel. 1 CD. (Running Time: 1 hr.). (J). 2001. pap. bk. 14.95 (KIM 8016CD) Kimbo Educ.

Fun, easy routines using balls, hoops & ribbons are set to popular movie themes & familiar classical music. Instructions for homemade equipment are included. Theme from E.T., Chariots of Fire, Tomorrow & more. Includes manual.

Ball, Hoop & Ribbon Activities for Young Children. Carol Hammett & Elaine Bueffel. 1 cass. (Running Time: 1 hr.). (J). (ps-3). 2001. pap. bk. 10.95 (KIM 8016C); pap. bk. & stu. ed. 11.95 (KIM 8016) Kimbo Educ.

Ball Poem see Twentieth-Century Poetry in English, No. 8, Recordings of Poets Reading Their Own Poetry

Ballad Gospel Classics. 1 CD. audio compact disk 5.98 (978-1-57908-473-8(7), 5343) Platinm Enter.

Ballad Gospel Classics, Set. unabr. ed. 1 cass., 1 CD. 4.98 (978-1-57908-474-5(5), 5343) Platinm Enter.

Ballad Hunter, Pts. 1 and 2. John A. Lomax. Incl. Ballad Hunter Pts. 1 & 2: Blues & Hollers: "Being Lonesome" Songs. (L 49); Ballad Hunter Pts. 1 & 2: Cheyenne: Songs from the Range & the Hill Country. (L 49); 8.95 (L 49) Lib Congress.

Lectures on American folk music with musical illustrations, include Cheyenne with excerpts from Dreary Black Hills & Good-Bye, Old Paint, sung by Alan Lomax & others, & Blues & Hollers with excerpts from Red River Blues sung by Frank Evans & others.

Ballad Hunter, Pts. 3 and 4. John A. Lomax. Incl. Ballad Hunter Pts. 3 & 4: Chisholm Trail: Cowboy Songs Along the Famous Old Cattle Trails. (L 50); Ballad Hunter Pts. 3 & 4: Rock Island Line: Woodcutter's Songs & Songs of Prison Life. (L 50); 8.95 (L 50) Lib Congress.
Lectures on American folk music with musical illustrations, includes Chisholm Trail with excerpts from Trail to Mexico, sung by Woodrow Wilson (Woody) Guthrie & others & Rock Island Line with excerpts from The Rock Island Line & Jumpin' Judy sung by Kelly Pace & group.

Ballad Hunter, Pts. 5 and 6. Read by John A. Lomax. Incl. Ballad Hunter Pts. 5 & 6: Boll Weevil: Songs about the Little Bug that Challenged King Cotton. (L 51); Ballad Hunter Pts. 5 & 6: Two Sailors: Sea Shanties & Canal Boat Ballads. (L 51); 8.95 (L 51) Lib Congress.
Lectures on American folk music with musical illustrations, includes Two Sailors with excerpts from Old Woman under the Hill, sung by Captain Pearl R. Nye & others & Boll Weevil with excerpts from seven Boll Weevil songs sung by Woodrow Wilson (Woody) Guthrie & others.

Ballad Hunter, Pts. 7 and 8. John A. Lomax. Incl. Ballad Hunter Pts. 7 & 8: Railroad Songs: Work Songs for Rail Tamping & Track Laying. (L 52); Ballad Hunter Pts. 7 & 8: Spirituals: Religion Through Songs of Southern Negroes. (L 52); 8.95 (L 52) Lib Congress.
Lectures on American folk music with musical illustrations, includes Spirituals with excerpts from the New Buryin' Ground, sung by Willie Williams & group & others & Railroad Songs with excerpts from Can't You Line 'Em? sung by a group of eight men, & others.

Ballad Hunter, Pts. 9 and 10. John A. Lomax. Incl. Ballad Hunter Pts. 9 & 10: Jordan & Jubilee: Songs from Livingston, Alabama. (L 53); Ballad Hunter Pts. 9 & 10: Sugar Land, Texas: Convict Songs from a Texas Prison. (L 53); 8.95 (L 53) Lib Congress.
Lectures on American folk music with musical illustrations, includes Jordan & Jubilee with excerpts from the Blood Done Sign My Name, sung by Enoch Brown & others, & Sugar Land, Texas with excerpts from Pick a Bale of Cotton, sung by James (Iron Head) & others.

Ballad Hunter, Pts. 1 & 2, Blues & Hollers: "Being Lonesome" Songs see Ballad Hunter

Ballad Hunter, Pts. 1 & 2, Cheyenne: Songs from the Range & the Hill Country see Ballad Hunter

Ballad Hunter, Pts. 3 & 4, Chisholm Trail: Cowboy Songs Along the Famous Old Cattle Trails see Ballad Hunter

Ballad Hunter, Pts. 3 & 4, Rock Island Line: Woodcutter's Songs & Songs of Prison Life see Ballad Hunter

Ballad Hunter, Pts. 5 & 6, Boll Weevil: Songs about the Little Bug that Challenged King Cotton see Ballad Hunter

Ballad Hunter, Pts. 5 & 6, Two Sailors: Sea Shanties & Canal Boat Ballads see Ballad Hunter

Ballad Hunter, Pts. 7 & 8, Railroad Songs: Work Songs for Rail Tamping & Track Laying see Ballad Hunter

Ballad Hunter, Pts. 7 & 8, Spirituals: Religion Through Songs of Southern Negroes see Ballad Hunter

Ballad Hunter, Pts. 9 & 10, Jordan & Jubilee: Songs from Livingston, Alabama see Ballad Hunter

Ballad Hunter, Pts. 9 & 10, Sugar Land, Texas: Convict Songs from a Texas Prison see Ballad Hunter

Ballad of a Strange Thing see Twentieth-Century Poetry in English, No. 8, Recordings of Poets Reading Their Own Poetry

Ballad of Bahia, Program 6. Read by Jorge Amado. (F007CB090) Natl Public Radio.

Ballad of Dinosaur Bob. unabr. ed. William Joyce. Read by Mariel Hemingway. 1 cass. (Running Time: 30 mins.). 1999. bk. 11.98 (T 6249 SH, Listening Lib) Random Audio Pubg.
Includes swing renditions of Bob's favorite sing-a-longs, such as "The Hokey Poke," "Take Me Out to the Ballgame" & more.

Ballad of Frankie Silver. abr. ed. Sharyn McCrumb. Read by Sharyn McCrumb. 4 cass. (Running Time: 6 hrs.). (Ballad Ser.: No. 5). 2001. 25.00 (978-1-59040-007-4(0), Phoenix Audio) Pub: Amer Intl Pub. Dist(s): PerseuPGW
In 1833, 18-year-old Frankie Silver became the first woman in North Carolina to be hanged for murdering her husband. But was she guilty? More than one hundred years later, obsessed by the story of Frankie Silver, Sheriff Spencer Arrowood is determined to reveal the truth about a new murder case that has many parallels to the long-ago murder.

Ballad of Frankie Silver, unabr. ed. Sharyn McCrumb. Read by C. M. Herbert. 9 cass. (Running Time: 13 hrs.). (Ballad Ser.: No. 5). 1998. 62.95 (978-0-7861-1443-6(6), 2305) Blckstn Audio.
A story of murder, simple faith, & blind truth told in alternating viewpoints, flawlessly weaving past & present, truth & fiction, folklore & legend, sweeping from the drawing rooms of the early aristocracy to the ruins of a one-room cabin deep in the Appalachian wilderness.

Ballad of Frankie Silver. unabr. ed. Sharyn McCrumb. Narrated by Barbara Rosenblat & Jeff Woodman. 12 CDs. (Running Time: 14 hrs. 15 mins.). (Ballad Ser.: No. 5). 1999. audio compact disk 109.00 (978-0-7887-3437-3(7), C1043E7) Recorded Bks.
As a convicted killer awaits execution in Tennessee, sheriff Spencer Arrowood uncovers shocking parallels with a hanging over a century ago. Suddenly he finds himself in a frantic struggle to stop history from repeating itself.

Ballad of Frankie Silver. unabr. ed. Sharyn McCrumb. Narrated by Barbara Rosenblat & Jeff Woodman. 11 cass. (Running Time: 14 hrs. 15 mins.). (Ballad Ser.: No. 5). 1998. 94.00 (978-0-7887-2475-6(4), 95550E7) Recorded Bks.
As a convicted killer awaits execution in Tennessee, sheriff Spencer Arrowood uncovers shocking parallels with a hanging over a century ago. Suddenly he finds himself in a frantic struggle to stop history from repeating itself.

***Ballad of Les Darcy.** unabr. ed. Peter FitzSimons. Read by Humphrey Bower. (Running Time: 5 hrs. 50 mins.). 2010. 43.95 (978-1-74214-684-3(8), 9781742146843) Pub: Bolinda Pubng AUS. Dist(s): Bolinda Pub Inc

Ballad of Lucy Whipple. unabr. ed. Karen Cushman. Narrated by Christina Moore. 4 pieces. (Running Time: 4 hrs. 45 mins.). (gr. 4 up). 1997. 35.00 (978-0-7887-0892-3(9), 95030E7) Recorded Bks.
In the summer of 1849, Lucy Whipple's mother packs up her household & her two young children & leaves their home in Massachusetts for the gold fields of California. Lucy's firsthand account of her struggles to make a new home in a rough & tumble land.

Ballad of Orange & Grape see Poetry & Voice of Muriel Rukeyser

Ballad of Peckham Rye. Muriel Spark. Read by Nadia May. 3 cass. (Running Time: 4 hrs.). 2000. 23.95 (978-0-7861-1866-3(0), 2665) Blckstn Audio.
A wickedly farcical fable of a blue-collar town turned upside down. When the firm of Meadows, Meade & Grindley hires Dougal Douglas (a.k.a. Douglas Dougal) to do human research into the private lives of its workforce, they are in no way prepared for the mayhem, mutiny & murder he will stir up.

Ballad of Peckham Rye. Muriel Spark. (Isis (CDs) Ser.). (J). 2005. audio compact disk 51.95 (978-0-7531-2402-4(5)) Pub: ISIS Lrg Prnt GBR. Dist(s): Ulverscroft US

Ballad of Peckham Rye. unabr. ed. Muriel Spark. Read by Nadia May. (Running Time: 4 hrs. 0 mins.). 2010. 19.95 (978-1-4417-1382-7(4)); audio compact disk 49.00 (978-1-4417-1379-7(4)) Blckstn Audio.

Ballad of Peckham Rye. unabr. ed. Muriel Spark. Read by Nick Rawlinson. 4 cass. (Isis Cassettes Ser.). (J). 2005. 44.95 (978-0-7531-1518-3(2)) Pub: ISIS Lrg Prnt GBR. Dist(s): Ulverscroft US

Ballad of Pious Pete see Poetry of Robert W. Service

Ballad of Reading Gaol see Famous Story Poems

Ballad of Reading Gaol. abr. ed. Oscar Wilde. Perf. by James Mason. 1 cass. 1984. 12.95 (978-0-694-50270-7(7), SWC 1473) HarperCollins Pubs.

Ballad of Seul Choix Lighthouse. 2002. audio compact disk 15.00 (978-0-9728212-5-4(2)) Old Country Bks.

Ballad of the Civil War. unabr. ed. Mary Stolz. Narrated by Jeff Woodman. 1 cass. (Running Time: 1 hr.). (gr. 4 up). 1999. 10.00 (978-0-7887-3206-5(4), 95800E7) Recorded Bks.
The young Rigby twins live on their father's southern plantation. Their best friend is a young slave given to them as a present. When their friend is banished from the house, the boys realize they have different attitudes on slavery.

Ballad of the Civil War. unabr. ed. Mary Stolz. Read by Jeff Woodman. 1 cass. (Running Time: 1 hr.). (J). (gr. 4). 1999. 73.30 class set. (978-0-7887-3217-1(X), 46873) Recorded Bks.

Ballad of the Civil War. unabr. ed. Mary Stolz. Narrated by Jeff Woodman. 1 cass. (Running Time: 1 hr.). (J). 2000. pap. bk. 22.50 (40906X4) Recorded Bks.
The young Rigby twins, Tom & Jack, live on their father's southern plantation. Their best friend Aaron is a young slave, given to the boys as a christening present. But when Aaron is banished from the house, Tom realizes that he & jack have very different attitudes towards slavery. Includes study guide.

Ballad of the Gypsy see Poetry & Reflections

Ballad of the Landlord see Poetry of Langston Hughes

Ballad of the Long-Legged Bait see Child's Christmas in Wales

Ballad of the Long-Legged Bait see Dylan Thomas Reading His Poetry

Ballad of the Sad Cafe, Set. unabr. ed. Carson McCullers. Read by Rita Moreno. 2 cass. (Running Time: 2 hrs. 33 mins.). 1987. 15.95 (978-0-89845-657-8(6), A 2103) HarperCollins Pubs.
A highly charged triangle that sets a town talking & waiting for the shattering emotional explosion that is sure to come.

Ballad of the Whiskey Robber: A True Story of Bank Heists, Ice Hockey, Transylvanian Pelt Smuggling, Moonlighting Detectives, & Broken Hearts. unabr. rev. ed. Julian Rubinstein. (Running Time: 11 hrs. 30 mins.). (ENG.). 2006. 14.98 (978-1-59483-493-6(8)) Pub: Hachet Audio. Dist(s): HachBkGrp

Ballad of the White Horse. unabr. ed. G. K. Chesterton. Narrated by James M. Courtright. 2 cass. (Running Time: 2 hrs. 10 min.). 1996. bk. 24.95 Set. Sstrs Srvnts.
This is a ballad of the reign of King Alfred, & describes that monarch's noble exploits, his character, his struggle with the Danes, the story of the White Horse & the battle of Ethandune.

Ballad of Wild Jake Hiccup. unabr. ed. John Deltenre. Perf. by Sol M. Davidson et al. 1 cass. (Running Time: 40 min.). (J). (gr. 3-9). 1992. 9.95 (978-1-56412-001-4(5)) Hse Nine Muses.
Original words & music by midwest folk-singer John Deltenre & His Pioneer Band with stanzas detailing the adventures of Wild Jake Hiccup, America's first frontiersman. The song tells the tall story of the gentle giant of a man who slept betwixt two hills on America's first frontier & who rassled with b'ars for his thrills. Selected chapter readings by the author & by the illustrator are intertwined with the original music on Side 1. The entire ballad is performed without interruption on Side 2 & is then followed by additional readings. Used by numerous school systems in many states.

Ballad of William Sycamore see Poetry of Benet

Ballad of William Sycamore see Twentieth-Century Poetry in English, No. 23, Recordings of Poets Reading Their Own Poetry

Ballad of Yachiyo. unabr. ed. Philip K. Gotanda. Perf. by June Angela et al. 1 cass. (Running Time: 1 hr. 28 min.). 1996. 19.95 (978-1-58081-033-3(0)) L A Theatre.
Tale of illicit passion, set among the lush cane fields of Hawaiian islands in 1919, was inspired by a true incident . Beautiful sixteen year old Yachiyo reluctantly leaves her impoverished parents to live with sophisticated relatives. A Yachiyo acquires civilized graces from her hostess, Okusan, she also struggles with a growing passion for Okusan's dissolute husband.

Balladeer Burl Ives see I'm Too Busy to Talk Now

Ballades. Poems. Victor Hugo. Read by C. Truche & A. D. Bouzina. 1 cass. (FRE.). 1991. 22.95 (1460-VSL) Olivia & Hill.
Famous collection of peoms by the leader of French Romanticism.

Ballades, Set. Poems. Francois Villon. Read by Yves Renier. Contrib. by Jean Favier. 2 cass. (FRE.). 1991. 26.95 (1483-RF) Olivia & Hill.
Poems that celebrate the rough & earthy life.

Ballads & Songs of the Civil War. Perf. by Wayne Erbsen. 1 cass. (Running Time: 50 min.). 1994. 9.95 (978-1-883206-05-5(7), NB004); audio compact disk 14.95 CD. (978-1-883206-03-1(0), NG-CD-004) Native Ground.
A stirring collection of Civil War music from both sides of the conflict performed on old-time instruments.

Ballads & Songs of the Civil War. Jerry Silverman. 1993. pap. bk. 29.95 (978-0-7866-1106-5(5), 94734P); pap. bk. 37.95 (978-0-7866-1105-8(7), 94734CDP) Mel Bay.

Ballads of American History. Fred Cooper. Composed by Fred Cooper. (ENG., 1996. pap. bk. 24.95 (978-0-9765793-7-3(5)) Sing N Learn Pub.

Ballads of Sacco & Vanzetti. Perf. by Woody Guthrie. Anno. by Moses Asch et al. 1 cass. 1996. Incl. letter by Guthrie to the judge in the case. (0-9307-400600-9307-40060-2-3); audio compact disk (0-9307-40060-2-3) Smithsonian Folkways.
Includes "The Flood & the Storm," "You Souls of Boston" & "We Welcome to Heaven".

Ballam on Broadway. Michael Ballam. 1 cass. 9.95 (1100475); audio compact disk 14.95 (1100505) Covenant Comms.

Ballet Class for Dancers & Gymnasts. Music by Ira Gershwin. 1 cass, 1 CD. 15.00 incl. manual. (KIM 3005C); lp 18.00 (KIM 3005CD) Kimbo Educ.
Barre & centre technique.

Ballet Class with Scott Joplin Music. Music by Scott Joplin. 1 LP. (J). pupil's gde. ed. 15.00 (KIM 1012); 15.00 Incl. guide. (KIM 1012C); audio compact disk 18.00 CD Incl. guide. Kimbo Educ.
Barre, centre floor technique & variations.

Ballet Folklorico Booklet w/Music CD & DVD Dance Demo. Vicki Corona. (Celebrate the Cultures Ser.: 2-24C). 1989. pap. bk. 32.95 (978-1-58513-157-0(1)) Dance Fantasy.

Ballet on Broadway. Perf. by Dennis Buck. 1 cass. 15.00 (KIM 9086C) Kimbo Educ.
Enjoy tunes from Broadway shows, past & present, especially arranged for twin pianos. Selections from "La Cage Aux Folles," "Jerry's Girls," & "42nd Street.".

Ballet Party! Jan Carr. 1 cass. (Running Time: 50 min.). (You're Invited to Mary-Kate & Ashley's Ser.). (J). (gr. 2-4). 1998. 8.98 (978-1-56896-314-3(9)); audio compact disk 15.98 CD. (978-1-56896-313-6(0)) Lightyear Entrtnmnt.

Ballet Shoes. unabr. ed. Noel Streatfeild. Read by Elizabeth Sastre. 4 cass. (Running Time: 6 hrs.). (J). 2004. 32.00 (978-1-4000-9140-9(3)); audio compact disk 45.00 (978-1-4000-9497-4(6)) Books on Tape.

Ballet Shoes. unabr. ed. Noel Streatfeild. Read by Elizabeth Sastre. (ENG.). (J). (gr. 3). 2008. audio compact disk 35.00 (978-0-7393-6516-8(9), Listening Lib) Pub: Random Audio Pubg. Dist(s): Random

Ballet Stories. David Angus. Read by Jenny Agutter. (Running Time: 2 hrs. 30 mins.). 2005. 20.95 (978-1-60083-681-7(X)) Iofy Corp.

Ballet Stories: Cappelia, Giselle, Sleeping Beauty, the Nutcracker, Swann Lake. abr. ed. Read by Jenny Agutter. Retold by David L. Angus. 2 CDs. (Running Time: 9000 sec.). 2001. audio compact disk 17.98 (978-962-634-231-2(5), NA223112, Naxos AudioBooks) Naxos.
The stories of the most popular ballets are told in refreshing style against the backdrop of the music written by Delibes, Tchaikovsky and Adam. Naxos draws on its own roots in classical music to present the definitive introduction for children in this sympathetic reading by Jenny Agutter.

Ballet Stories: Coppelia - Giselle - Sleeping Beauty - The Nutcracker - Swann Lake. Read by Jenny Agutter. Retold by David Angus. 2 cass. (Running Time: 2 hrs. 30 min.). (J). 2001. 13.98 (978-962-634-731-7(7), NA223114, Naxos AudioBooks) Naxos.

Ballet Tapes. unabr. ed. Victoria Huckenpahler. 3 cass. (Running Time: 3 hr.). 29.95 (S00761) J Norton Pubs.
This series includes a tape on ballet history, one on the art of Nijinsky, & one on the art of Isadora Duncan.

Ballistic Missile Threat Handbook. Jack Spencer. 2000. reel tape 16.95 (978-0-89195-251-0(9)) Heritage Found.

Ballona Wetlands. Hosted by Nancy Pearlman. 1 cass. (Running Time: 28 min.). 10.00 (202) Educ Comm CA.

Balloon Man. Charlotte MacLeod. Read by Mary Peiffer. 2000. 40.00 (978-0-7366-4914-8(X)) Books on Tape.

Balloon That Ran Away. Michele Sobel Spirn. 1 cass. (Running Time: 7 min.). (Read Along ...For Fun Ser.). (J). (gr. 1-3). 1985. bk. 16.99 (978-0-934898-68-3(5)) Jan Prods.
The tale of Ann's blue balloon, it's flight to freedom & it's safe & happy reunion with Ann.

Balloon That Ran Away: Read Along...for Fun Ser. Michele Sobel Spirn. 1 cass. (Running Time: 7 min.). (J). (gr. 1-3). 1985. pap. bk. 9.95 (978-0-934898-80-5(4)); 23.95 incl. 8 paperback bks. & 1 activity card. Jan Prods.

Balloon to the Moon: A Guide to Vibrant Living. Rhegina Sinozich. 2008. audio compact disk 24.95 (978-0-9706297-9-1(6)) Abrezia Pr.

Balloonia & Magic Shoelaces. Audrey Wood. (J). 10.97 (978-0-85953-373-7(5)) Childs Play GBR.

Balloonia & Magic Shoelaces. unabr. ed. Don Wood & Audrey Wood. Read by Andrew Belling. 1 cass. (Running Time: 20 min.). (Theatre Ser.). (ENG., (J). (ps-3). 1989. 4.99 (978-0-85953-370-6(0)) Childs Play GBR.

Balloons. Mario Herrera & Barbara Hojel. (J). (gr. 1 up). 2005. 59.95 (978-0-7652-6299-8(1)); audio compact disk 59.95 (978-0-7652-6329-2(7)) Longman.

Balloons. Mario Herrera & Barbara Hojel. (J). (gr. 2 up). 2005. 59.95 (978-0-7652-6300-1(9)); audio compact disk 59.95 (978-0-7652-6328-5(9)) Longman.

Balloons. Mario Herrera & Barbara Hojel. (J). (gr. 3 up). 2005. 59.95 (978-0-7652-6301-8(7)); audio compact disk 59.95 (978-0-7652-6331-5(9)) Longman.

Balloons: Complete Storybook. Mario Herrera & Barbara Hojel. (J). 2005. 36.95 (978-0-7652-6330-8(0)) Longman.

Balloons: English for Me! Stories. Mario Herrera & Barbara Hojel. (J). 2005. audio compact disk 34.95 (978-0-7652-6286-8(X)) Longman.

Balloons: Songs by Children in Grades K-5. unabr. ed. Victor Cockburn. Read by Victor Cockburn. 1 cass. (Running Time: 1 hr.). (ENG.). (J). (gr. k-6). 1987. 10.00 (978-0-944941-11-9(7)) Talking Stone Pr.
Songs written by children with songwriter, Victor Cockburn about family, school, dreaming social issues & more.

Ballroom on Magnolia Street. Sharon Owens. Read by Caroline Winterson. 8 CDs. (Running Time: 39600 sec.). 2005. audio compact disk 34.95 (978-1-59316-054-8(2), LL146) Listen & Live.
On the heels of her charming debut, The Tea House On Mulberry Street, comes bestselling Irish author Sharon Owens's new novel of passion, romance, and regret - and the winding paths to falling in love.

Ballroom on Magnolia Street. unabr. ed. Sharon Owens. Read by Caroline Winterson. (YA). 2008. 39.99 (978-1-60514-557-0(2)) Find a World.

Ball's Bluff: A Small Battle & Its Long Shadow. unabr. ed. Byron Farwell. Read by Bill Kelsey. 7 cass. (Running Time: 7 hrs.). 1993. 42.00 (978-0-7366-2557-9(7), 3308) Books on Tape.
When South whipped North at Ball's Bluff in first major fracas of the Civil War, both sides drew the wrong conclusions.

Ballyhoo Years. 10.00 (HT412) Esstee Audios.

Ballykissangel: A Sense of Place. Hugh Miller. 6 CDs. (Sound Ser.). (J). 2002. audio compact disk 64.95 (978-1-84283-519-7(X)) Pub: ISIS Lrg Prnt GBR. Dist(s): Ulverscroft US

Ballykissangel: A Sense of Place. Hugh Miller. Read by Gerry O'Brien. 6 cass. (Sound Ser.). (J). 2003. 54.95 (978-1-84283-259-2(X)) Pub: ISIS Lrg Prnt GBR. Dist(s): Ulverscroft US

Ballykissangel: A Sense of Place. unabr. ed. Hugh Miller. 6 cass. (Running Time: 9 hrs.). (Sound Ser.). (J). 2002. 54.95 (978-1-84283-258-5(1)) Pub: ISIS Lrg Prnt GBR. Dist(s): Ulverscroft US

Ballykissangel: A Sense of Place. unabr. ed. Hugh Miller. Read by Gerry O'Brien. 6 CDs. (Running Time: 7 hrs. 30 min.). (Sound Ser.). (J). 2003. audio compact disk 64.95 (978-1-84283-407-7(X)) Pub: ISIS Lrg Prnt GBR. Dist(s): Ulverscroft US

Balsamic Dreams: A Short but Self-Important History of the Baby Boomer Generation. unabr. ed. Joe Queenan. Narrated by Paul Boehmer. 4 cass. (Running Time: 6 hrs.). 2002. 48.00 (978-0-7366-8632-7(0)) Books on Tape.
With unerring wit, Queenan skewers a generation who abandoned their humanitarian ideals for the comforts of Crate & Barrel.

Balthazar. abr. ed. Lawrence Durrell. Read by Nigel Anthony. 3 CDs. (Running Time: 4 hrs.). (Alexandria Quartet Ser.: Vol. II). 1995. audio compact disk 22.98 (978-962-634-046-2(0), NA304612, Naxos AudioBooks) Naxos.
Reopens the story begun in Justine, drawing out new meanings and combinations from the tale. It explores the mystery of the deaths of some of its characters and the elusive strangeness of life itself.

Balthazar. abr. ed. Lawrence Durrell. Read by Nigel Anthony. 3 cass. (Running Time: 4 hrs.). (Alexandria Quartet Ser.: Vol. II). 1996. 17.98 (978-962-634-546-7(2), NA304614, Naxos AudioBooks) Naxos.

Balthazar. unabr. ed. Lawrence Durrell. Read by Richard Brown. 7 cass. (Running Time: 10 hrs. 30 mins.). (Alexandria Ser.). 1994. 56.00 (978-0-7366-2713-9(8), 3443) Books on Tape.
Set in pre-WW II Alexandria, this second volume in The Alexandria Quartet is a story of sexual obsession.

Baltic Run. l.t. ed. Charles Whiting. Read by Michael Wade. 6 cass. (Storysound Ser.). (J). 2003. 54.95 (978-1-85903-509-2(4)) Pub: Mgna Lrg Print GBR. Dist(s): Ulverscroft US

Baltimore Blues. unabr. ed. Laura Lippman. Narrated by Deborah Hazlett. 8 cass. (Running Time: 35880 sec.). (Tess Monaghan Ser.: No. 1). 2006. 74.95 (978-0-7927-4552-5(3), CSL 1018); audio compact disk 94.95 (978-0-7927-4488-7(8), SLD 1018); audio compact disk 59.95 (978-0-7927-4571-6(X), CMP 1018) AudioGO.

***Baltimore Blues: The First Tess Monaghan Novel.** Laura Lippman. Narrated by Deborah Hazlett. (Running Time: 9 hrs. 58 mins. 0 sec.). (ENG.). 2010. audio compact disk 29.95 (978-1-60998-132-7(4)) Pub: AudioGO. Dist(s): Perseus Dist

Baltimore Waltz. unabr. ed. Paula Vogel. Perf. by Jenny Bacon et al. 1 cass. (Running Time: 1 hr. 20 min.). 1994. 19.95 (978-1-58081-079-1(9), CTA34) L A Theatre.
An Obie Award winning play, centers on Anna, a teacher, & her brother Carl, a librarian. When Anna learns that Carl is terminally ill, she sweeps her brother into a fantasy world. Through the force of her imagination she takes Carl on a last wish trip to Europe.

Baltimore Years. Narrated by Erik Sellin. 2007. audio compact disk 14.99 (978-0-9764805-9-4(X)) C CD Bks.

Balzac. unabr. collector's ed. Graham Robb. Read by David Case. 14 cass. (Running Time: 21 hrs.). 1999. 112.00 (978-0-7366-4486-0(5), 4925) Books on Tape.
This is the perfect subject for biography: a relentless seducer whose successes were as spectacular as his catastrophies; a passionate collector, inventor, explorer & political campaigner; a mesmerizing storyteller with the power to make his fantasies come true.

Balzac & the Little Chinese Seamstress. Sijie Dai. Read by B. D. Wong.Tr. of Balzac et la Petite Tailleuse Chinoise. 2002. audio compact disk 48.00 (978-0-7366-8848-2(X)) Books on Tape.

Balzac & the Little Chinese Seamstress. unabr. ed. Sijie Dai. Read by B. D. Wong. 3 cass. (Running Time: 4 hrs. 30 mins.).Tr. of Balzac et la Petite Tailleuse Chinoise. 2002. 40.00 (978-0-7366-8847-5(1)) Books on Tape.
A hidden cache of Western literature sets the minds of two young Chinese victims of Mao's Cultural Revolution ablaze.

Balzac et la Petite Tailleuse Chinoise see Balzac & the Little Chinese Seamstress

Balzac et la Petite Tailleuse Chinoise. l.t. ed. Sijie Dai. (French Ser.). 2000. bk. 30.99 (978-2-84011-366-9(X)) Pub: UlverLrgPrint GBR. Dist(s): Ulverscroft US

Balzac's Shorter Stories, Set. Honoré de Balzac. Read by Flo Gibson. 2 cass. (Running Time: 3 hrs.). 1990. 14.95 (978-1-55685-177-3(4)) Audio Bk Con.
Warning! Horror & terror permeate these tales, which include "Don Juan" or "The Elixir of Life", "Christ in Flanders", "In the Time of the Terror," "Madame Dey's Last Reception".

Bambi. Random House Disney Staff. 1 cass. (J). 3.98 Clamshell. (978-1-55886-111-4(4), BB/PT 438) Smarty Pants.

Bambi. unabr. ed. Random House Disney Staff. 1 cass. (Read-Along Ser.). (J). bk. 7.99 (978-1-55723-008-9(0)) W Disney Records.

Bambi: A Life in the Woods. unabr. ed. Felix Salten. Read by Frank Dolan. Adapted by Janet Shulman. 1 cass. (Running Time: 52 mins.). (YA). (gr. 1 up). 2002. 13.95 (978-1-883332-78-5(8), 5-02); audio compact disk 15.95 (978-1-883332-82-2(6), CD5-02) Audio Bkshelf.
This classic transports listeners of all ages to the magical forest glade world of Bambi.

Bambi: A Little Spring Shower. unabr. ed. 1 cass. (My First Read Along Ser.). (J). Date not set. bk. 7.99 (978-1-55723-749-1(2)) W Disney Records.

Bambi Soundtrack. 1 cass. (Classics Ser.). (J). 1997. 21.98 (978-1-55723-802-3(2)) W Disney Records.

Bambi Soundtrack. Prod. by Walt Disney Productions Staff. 1 cass. (Classics Ser.). (J). 1997. 12.95 (978-0-7634-0223-5(0)) W Disney Records.
Classics.

Bamboo & Butterflies: To Destroy You Is No Loss. unabr. ed. Joan D. Criddle. Narrated by Christina Moore. 6 cass. (Running Time: 8 hrs. 15 mins.). 1994. 51.00 (978-1-55690-978-8(0), 94117E7) Recorded Bks.
The experiences of a Cambodian family, refugees from the killing Fields, newly arrived in America & facing the Challenges of assimilating into an alien world.

Bamboo on the Mountains: Kmhmu Highlanders from Southeast Asia & the U. S. Frank Proschan. 1 CD. (Running Time: 73 min.). (YA). 1999. audio compact disk 14.00 Smithsonian Folkways.

***Bamboo People.** unabr. ed. Mitali Perkins. (Running Time: 9 hrs.). 2011. 39.97 (978-1-4558-0403-0(7), 9781455804030, BADLE); 19.99 (978-1-4558-0401-6(0), 9781455804016, Brilliance MP3); 39.97 (978-1-4558-0402-3(9), 9781455804023, Brinc Audio MP3 Lib); audio compact disk 19.99 (978-1-4558-0399-6(5), 9781455803996, Bril Audio CD Unabri); audio compact disk 59.97 (978-1-4558-0400-9(2), 9781455804009, BriAudCD Unabrid) Brilliance Audio.

Bamboo Valley. 1 cass. (Running Time: 35 min.). (J). (gr. 1-4). 2001. bk. 19.95 (SP 7006C) Kimbo Educ.
A story about a giant panda in a Chinese bamboo forest. Includes book.

Bamboo Valley: A Story of a Chinese Bamboo Forest. Ann Whitehead Nagda. Read by Randye Kaye. Illus. by Jim Effler. Narrated by Randye Kaye. 1 cass. (Running Time: 12 min.). (Habitat Ser.). (ENG.). (J). (gr. 1-4). 1997. 19.95 (978-1-56899-493-2(1), BC7006) Soundprints.
In China's Woolong Preserve, a giant panda searches the forest for bamboo, but most have flowered & died. The panda moves higher up the mountain range through deepening snow, foraging for food. With a long winter ahead will the panda find fresh bamboo to survive?.

Banana Slug String Band: Slugs at Sea; Adventures on the Air Cycle; Dirt Made My Lunch. Perf. by Banana Slug String Band Staff. 3 cass. (J). (gr. k-7). 23.98 Set. (2174) MFLP CA.
This group not only entertains but encourages exploration of science & the environment. These imaginative musical adventures bubble with happy children, friendly animal bands & colorful characters.

Bananaheart & Other Stories. Marie Hara. 1 cass. 1994. pap. bk. selections from paperback.; 8.00 selections from paperback. (978-0-910043-34-2(5)) Bamboo Ridge Pr.

Bananaphone. Perf. by Raffi. 1 cass., 1 CD. (J). 7.98 (RDR 8062); audio compact disk 12.78 CD Jewel box. (RDR 8062) NewSound.

Bananaphone. Perf. by Raffi. (Running Time: 52 mins.). (J). (978-1-886767-79-9(3)) Rounder Records.
A danceable, magical bunch of songs with a-peel!.

Bananaphone. Perf. by Raffi. 1 cass. (Running Time: 52 mins.). (J). 1999. (978-1-886767-53-9(X)); audio compact disk (978-1-886767-52-2(1)) Rounder Records.
A danceable, magical bunch of songs with a-peel!.

Bancroft Strategy. abr. ed. Robert Ludlum. Read by Scott Sowers. 5 CDs. (Running Time: 7 hrs. 0 mins. 0 sec.). (ENG.). 2006. audio compact disk 29.95 (978-1-59397-965-2(7)) Pub: Macmill Audio. Dist(s): Macmillan

***Bancroft Strategy.** abr. ed. Robert Ludlum. (Running Time: 7 hrs. 0 mins. 0 sec.). (ENG.). 2011. audio compact disk 14.99 (978-1-4272-1187-3(6)) Pub: Macmill Audio. Dist(s): Macmillan

Bancroft Strategy. unabr. ed. Robert Ludlum. 10 cass. 2006. 89.95 (978-0-7927-4535-8(3), CSL 998) AudioGO.

Bancroft Strategy. unabr. ed. Robert Ludlum. Narrated by Scott Sowers. 14 CDs. (Running Time: 70260 sec.). 2006. audio compact disk 115.95 (978-0-7927-4374-3(1), SLD 998); audio compact disk 69.95 (978-0-7927-4559-4(0), CMP 998) AudioGO.

Bancroft Strategy. unabr. ed. Robert Ludlum. Read by Scott Sowers. 14 CDs. (Running Time: 20 hrs. 0 mins. 0 sec.). (ENG.). 2006. audio compact disk 49.95 (978-1-59397-964-5(9)) Pub: Macmill Audio. Dist(s): Macmillan

***Band.** 2010. audio compact disk (978-1-59171-161-2(4)) Falcon Picture.

Band in A Book: Bluegrass Instrumentals Book/2-CD Set. Steve Kaufman. 2006. bk. 24.95 (978-0-7866-5693-6(X), 20426BCD) Mel Bay.

Band in A Book: Gospel Vocal Tunes for Bluegrass. Steve Kaufman. 2006. bk. 24.95 (978-0-7866-5692-9(1), 20424BCD) Mel Bay.

Band of Brothers. Alexander Fullerton. 6 CDs. (Running Time: 7 hrs.). (Soundings (CDs) Ser.). (J). 2004. audio compact disk 64.95 (978-1-84283-969-0(1)) Pub: ISIS Lrg Prnt GBR. Dist(s): Ulverscroft US

Band of Brothers. unabr. ed. Alexander Fullerton. Read by Christopher Kay. 6 cass. (Running Time: 7 hrs.). (Sound Ser.). 2002. 54.95 (978-1-84283-022-2(8)) Pub: UlverLrgPrint GBR. Dist(s): Ulverscroft US
Modeled on official reports, the action of this story occupies eight hours of Sunday night/Monday morning, in early autumn of 1943. The German U-boat supply ship, Heilbronne, is sailing, heavily escorted, from Le Havre to the Atlantic, and a mixed force of motor gunboats and motor torpedo boats from Newhaven in Sussex is ordered to intercept and sink her. But this is also a story about people. Such as, Ben Quarry, the Australian navigator of MGB 875, and the CO, Bob Stack.

Band of Brothers: E Company, 506th Regiment, 101st Airborne, from Normandy to Hitler's Eagle's Nest. Stephen E. Ambrose. 2004. 15.95 (978-0-7435-4185-5(5)) Pub: S&S Audio. Dist(s): S and S Inc

Band of Brothers: E Company, 506th Regiment, 101st Airborne from Normandy to Hitler's Eagle's Nest. abr. movie tie-in ed. Stephen E. Ambrose & Stephen E. Ambrose. Read by Cotter Smith. 4 CDs. (Running Time: 50 hrs. 0 mins. 0 sec.). (ENG., 2001. audio compact disk 32.00 (978-0-7435-0498-0(4), Audioworks) Pub: S&S Audio. Dist(s): S and S Inc

Band of Brothers: E Company, 506th Regiment, 101st Airborne from Normandy to Hitler's Eagle's Nest. unabr. ed. Stephen E. Ambrose. Read by Tim Jerome. 12 CDs. (Running Time: 18 hrs.). 2001. audio compact disk 110.95 (978-0-7927-9932-0(1), SLD 083, Chivers Sound Lib); bk. 84.95 (978-0-7927-2499-5(2), CSL 388, Chivers Sound Lib) AudioGO.
Easy Company, 506th Airborne Division, U.S. Army, was as good a rifle company as any in the world. They were responsible for everything from parachuting into France early D-Day morning to the capture of Hitler's Eagle Nest at Berchtesgaden. It was a company that suffered many casualties and considered the Purple Heart a badge of office.

Bandana Republic: A Literary Anthology by Gang Members & Their Affiliates. Ed. by Louis Reyes Rivera & Bruce George. Narrated by Adisa Banjoko et al. Frwd. by Jim Brown. (ENG.). 2009. 69.99 (978-1-60812-848-8(2)) Find a World.

Bande a Bonape, Set. Henri Viard. Read by M. Risch. 3 cass. (FRE.). 1991. 34.95 (1132-KFP) Olivia & Hill.
Leon Bonape is the leader of a Paris mob in this contemporary gangster adventure published as part of Gallimard Editions "Serie Noire.".

Bandera Trail. abr. ed. Ralph Compton. Read by Jim Grough. 4 cass. (Running Time: 6 hrs.). (Trail Drive Ser.: Vol. 4). 1998. 24.95 (978-1-890990-03-9(5)) Otis Audio.
Trying to rescue their friend Clay Duval who is trapped inside war-torn Mexico, brothers Gil & Van Austin are taken prisoner by Santa Anna's soldiers & must make a daring escape.

***Bandit Lawman.** Luke Short. 2009. (978-1-60136-422-7(9)) Audio Holding.

Bandit Lawman. Luke Short. (Running Time: 0 hr. 54 mins.). 2000. 10.95 (978-1-60083-530-8(9)) Iofy Corp.

Bandits. Elmore Leonard. Read by Frank Muller. 5 Cass. (Running Time: 9 Hrs.). 24.95 (978-1-4025-2813-2(2)) Recorded Bks.

***Bandits.** unabr. ed. Elmore Leonard. Read by Frank Muller. (ENG.). 2010. (978-0-06-199377-0(8), Harper Audio); (978-0-06-206266-6(2), Harper Audio) HarperCollins Pubs.

Bandits, unabr. ed. Elmore Leonard. Narrated by Frank Muller. 6 cass. (Running Time: 9 hrs.). 51.00 (978-1-55690-863-7(6), 93305E7) Recorded Bks.
A New Orleans undertaker's assistant & a cast of wacky characters pursue illicit wealth in a scheme to intercept several million dollars on the way to the Nicaraguan Contras. Available to libraries only.

Bandit's Moon. Sid Fleischman. Narrated by Julia Gibson. 3 CDs. (Running Time: 3 hrs.). (gr. 3 up). audio compact disk 30.00 (978-1-4025-2291-8(6)) Recorded Bks.

Bandit's Moon. Sid Fleischman. Narrated by Julia Gibson. 2 pieces. (Running Time: 3 hrs.). (gr. 3 up). 2002. 19.00 (978-1-4025-0736-6(4)) Recorded Bks.
Annyrose travels to find her missing brother in gold digging territory and comes face-to-face with the legendary bandit, Joaquin Murieta. But instead of an enemy, she finds a friend in Joaquin.

Bandole. Perf. by Santoo Govi & Shastro. 1 cass.; 9.98; audio compact disk 17.98 CD. Lifedance.
Zesty Latin rhythms, led by a host of instruments on these original pieces. Demo CD or cassette available.

Banff National Park: Banff to Columbia Icefield. 1 cass. (Running Time: 90 min.). (Guided Auto Tape Tour). 12.95 (P5) Comp Comms Inc.

Bang! unabr. ed. Sharon G. Flake. Read by Dominic M. Hoffman. 4 cass. (Running Time: 6 hrs. 5 mins.). (J). (gr. 4-7). 2006. 35.00 (978-0-7393-3126-2(4), Listening Lib); audio compact disk 45.00 (978-0-7393-3124-8(8), Listening Lib) Pub: Random Audio Pubg. Dist(s): Random

Bang! unabr. ed. Sharon G. Flake. Read by Dominic Hoffman. (Running Time: 21900 sec.). (ENG.). (J). (gr. 5). 2006. audio compact disk 35.00 (978-0-7393-3115-6(9), Listening Lib) Pub: Random Audio Pubg. Dist(s): Random

Bang-a Burning see Poetry & Voice of Ted Hughes

Bang Goes a Troll: An Awfully Beastly Business. unabr. ed. David Sinden et al. Read by Gerard Doyle. (Running Time: 2 hrs. 30 mins. 0 sec.). (Awfully Beastly Business Ser.). (ENG.). (J). 2009. audio compact disk 19.99 (978-0-7435-9969-6(1)) Pub: S&S Audio. Dist(s): S and S Inc

Bang the Drum Slowly. unabr. ed. Mark Harris. Perf. by Ed Begley, Jr. et al. Adapted by Eric Simonson. 1 cass. (Running Time: 1 hr. 21 mins.). 1992. 20.95 (978-1-58081-034-0(9), TPT5) L A Theatre.
A new adaptation for the theatre of one of the great baseball stories of all time. A poignant, touching & often comic story of a baseball team's friendship & loyalty toward a dying teammate.

Bang the Drum Slowly. unabr. ed. Mark Harris. Narrated by John Randolph Jones. 5 cass. (Running Time: 7 hrs. 30 mins.). (gr. 10). 1991. 44.00 (978-1-55690-035-8(X), 91120E7) Recorded Bks.
The bittersweet years of baseball are recreated in this sequel to "The Southpaw." Bruce Pearson was not the ideal best friend. He was dim-witted, he drank too much & he was one of the worst catchers Henry Wiggen had ever pitched to in all his years in the B-leagues. But Pearson had a secret that was going to get the New York Mammoths to the playoffs.

Bang the Drum Slowly. unabr. collector's ed. Mark Harris. Read by Christopher Hurt. 7 cass. (Running Time: 7 hrs.). 1989. 42.00 (978-0-7366-1537-2(7), 2407) Books on Tape.
The story of the friendship between two members of a baseball team as they - & the rest of the team - come to terms with the fact that one of them is dying.

Bangkok Conference. Thomas Merton. 1 cass. 8.95 (AA2461) Credence Commun.

Bangkok Haunts. John Burdett. 2007. audio compact disk 34.99 (978-1-4281-4345-6(9)) Recorded Bks.

Bangladesh's Ambassador Muhammad Zamir's Work in the United Nations & on World Environmental Treaties. Hosted by Nancy Pearlman. 1 cass. (Running Time: 28 min.). 10.00 (1426) Educ Comm CA.

Banglar Mukh Ami Dekhiachi. Voice by Sheema Mohit. 1 cd. 1999. audio compact disk 10.00 (978-0-9647672-4-9(4)) Beacon Hse IN.

Banish Bedwetting, 2001. 24.95 (978-1-58557-039-3(7)) Dynamic Growth.

Banish Pain: Mind Power Pain Relief. Dick Sutphen. 1 cass. (Running Time: 1 hr.). (RX17 Ser.). 1986. 14.98 (978-0-87554-312-3(X), RX121) Valley Sun.
You now relax & release the discomfort. You feel better & better & better. You mentally control your physical reality. Every in breath heals, every out breath releases. You are healing, you are healed. You feel better. You feel good. You feel great.

Banish Stress & Tension. Mel Gilley. Ed. by Steven C. Eggleston. 1 cass. (World of Hypnosis Ser.). 1987. 6.95 SCE Prod & List & Lrn.
Self-hypnosis to reduce stress & tension.

Banishment. Marion Chesney. Narrated by Jill Tanner. 4 cass. (Running Time: 5 hrs. 15 mins.). (Daughters of Mannerling Ser.: Vol. 1). 38.00 (978-1-4025-0401-3(2)); audio compact disk 48.00 (978-1-4025-2082-2(4)) Recorded Bks.

Banjo Chords. Contrib. by Joe Carr. (Running Time: 30 mins.). 2005. 9.95 (978-5-558-08948-6(2)) Mel Bay.

Banjo Chords: For Beginners. Peter Gelling. 2008. pap. bk. 24.95 (978-1-86469-379-9(7)) Kolala Music SGP.

Banjo Chords Made Easy. Contrib. by Joe Carr. 2007. 9.95 (978-5-557-51964-9(5)) Mel Bay.

Banjo Encyclopedia: Bluegrass Banjo from A to Z. Ross Nickerson. (ENG.). 2003. per. 29.95 (978-0-7866-7074-1(6), 99443BCD) Mel Bay.

Banjo for Beginners. Tony Trischka. (ENG.). 2001. audio compact disk 10.00 (978-0-7390-1105-8(7)) Alfred Pub.

Banjo for the Young Beginner. Alan Munde. (ENG.). 2009. pap. bk. 14.99 (978-0-7866-7836-5(4)) Mel Bay.

Banjo Handbook. Janet Davis. 1993. bk. 18.95 (978-0-87166-404-4(6), 94206P) Mel Bay.

Banjo Handbook. Janet Davis. 1988. 9.98 (978-0-87166-403-7(8), 94206C) Mel Bay.

Banjo Handbook. Janet Davis. 1999. pap. bk. 25.95 (978-0-7866-5118-4(0), 94206CDP) Mel Bay.

***Banjo Picking Pattern Chart.** Janet Davis. (ENG.). 2009. pap. bk. 9.99 (978-0-7866-8170-9(5)) Mel Bay.

Banjo Primer Jam. audio compact disk 14.95 (978-1-893907-46-1(5), 256-548) Watch & Learn.

Banjo Tab Book: Great Bay Stomp. Ryan J. Thomson. Music by Ryan J. Thomson. 2000. spiral bd. 19.95 (978-0-931877-30-8(X)) Captain Fiddle Pubns.

Banjola: Instrumentals by Edward Victor Dick. Composed by Edward Dick. (ENG.). 2007. audio compact disk 19.95 (978-0-9764635-3-5(9)) A Pub LLC.

Bank of Fear, unabr. ed. David Ignatius. Narrated by George Guidall. 9 cass. (Running Time: 12 hrs. 45 mins.). 78.00 (978-0-7887-0300-3(5), 94493E7) Recorded Bks.
A twisting tale of the ruthless greed & money laundering behind today's headlines. A London investment firm hides a grisly five billion dollar secret involving the Ruler of Iraq. When British financial investigator Sam Hoffman & Iraqi computer analyst Lina Alway decide to expose the secret, they are caught in a maze of deception & terror. Their only hope for survival is hiding in a global computer network of the Internet, if they can find it. Available to libraries only.

***Bank on Yourself: The Life-Changing Secret to Growing & Protecting Your Financial Future.** unabr. ed. Pamela Yellen. Read by Pamela Yellen. Read by Sean Pratt. (Running Time: 6 hrs.). (ENG.). 2009. 27.98 (978-1-59659-504-0(3), GildAudio) Pub: Gildan Media. Dist(s): HachBkGrp

Bank Shot. unabr. collector's ed. Donald E. Westlake. Read by Michael Kramer. 6 cass. (Running Time: 6 hrs.). (Dortmunder Ser.). 1996. 48.00 (978-0-7366-3455-7(X), 4099) Books on Tape.
when cops close in, Dortmunder must steal an entire bank (on wheels). Where will he hide it? Funny & well-crafted.

Banker. Dick Francis. Read by Martin Jarvis. 1 cass. (Running Time: 1 hr. 30 min.). (ENG., 2001. (978-0-14-180251-0(0), PengAudBks) Penguin Grp USA.

Banker. unabr. ed. Dick Francis. Read by Tony Britton. 8 cass. (Running Time: 12 hrs.). 2000. 59.95 (978-0-7451-6777-0(2), CAB 1393) Pub: Chivers Audio Bks GBR. Dist(s): AudioGO
Tim Ekaterin's bank only invests in sure things. He's about to invest 5 million pounds in a stallion called Sandcastle. Top breeders reckon it's the safest bet in racing. But racing doesn't just attract the money men of the City, it's riddled with all kinds of dealmakers. People who don't think twice about

breaking bones. People to whom no bet is safe until it's paid in blood, Ekaterin's blood.

Banker. unabr. ed. Dick Francis. Read by Simon Prebble. 6 Cass. (Running Time: 10.25 Hrs). 29.95 (978-1-4025-2357-1(2)) Recorded Bks.

Banker. unabr. ed. Dick Francis. Narrated by Simon Prebble. 7 cass. (Running Time: 10 hrs.). 1998. 61.00 (978-0-7887-2476-3(2), 95551E7) Recorded Bks.
It seems a sure thing when a young investment banker underwrites a multimillion dollar loan for a champion stallion. But instead, plunges headlong into the cutthroat world of racing.

Banker Clayton's Interest. Robert Easton. (Running Time: 0 hr. 18 mins.). 1998. 10.95 (978-1-60083-468-4(X)) Iofy Corp.

***Banker Clayton's Interest.** Robert Eston. 2009. (978-1-60136-423-4(7)) Audio Holding.

Banker to the Poor: Micro-Lending & the Battle Against World Poverty. Muhammad Yunus & Ray Porter. (Running Time: 25200 sec.). 2007. 44.95 (978-0-7861-4986-5(8)); audio compact disk 55.00 (978-0-7861-5777-8(1)) Blckstn Audio.

Banker to the Poor: Micro-Lending & the Battle Against World Poverty. unabr. ed. Muhammad Yunus. Read by Ray Porter. 6 cass. (Running Time: 25200 sec.). 2007. 19.95 (978-0-7861-4973-5(6)); audio compact disk 19.95 (978-0-7861-5792-1(5)) Blckstn Audio.

Banker to the Poor: Micro-Lending & the Battle Against World Poverty. unabr. ed. Muhammad Yunus. Read by Ray Porter. (Running Time: 25200 sec.). 2007. audio compact disk 29.95 (978-0-7861-6964-1(8)) Blckstn Audio.

Banking & Commercial Lending Law: Twentieth Annual Advanced ALI-ABA Course of Study. 9 cass. (Running Time: 12 hrs. 50 min.). 1998. 315.00 Incl. course materials. (MC78) Am Law Inst.
Ongoing annual advanced program intended for attorneys who regularly represent banks & other lending institutions & companies that, in the course of their business, regularly extend credit. It also should be of interest to lawyers who represent companies that periodically borrow from banks & other commercial lenders & lawyers involved in the regulation of banks & other lenders.

Banking & Financial Services Conference. 1988. bk. 245.00 incl. book.; 150.00 cass. only.; 95.00 book only. PA Bar Inst.

Banking & the Business Cycle. unabr. ed. Murray Newton Rothbard. 2 cass. (Running Time: 2 hrs. 1 min.). (Introduction to Free Market Economics Ser.). 19.95 (AFO316) J Norton Pubs.
Includes: Gresham's law; bank credit expansion; fractional reserve banking; central banks; the Federal Reserve System; the business cycle.

Banking & the Business Cycle, Set. ed. Murray N. Rothbard. 2 CDs. (Running Time: 88 mins.). (Introduction to Free Market Economics Ser.). 2006. audio compact disk 14.95 (978-1-57970-398-1(4), AF0316D, Audio-For) J Norton Pubs.
Dr. Rothbard lectures on Gresham's Law, bank credit expansion, fractional reserve banking, central banks, the Federal Reserve System, and the business cycle. (From Dr. Rothbard's series "Introduction to Free-Market Economics").

Banking, Gold, Free Markets & High Prices. unabr. ed. Robert LeFevre. 1 cass. (Running Time: 1 hr. 52 min.). 12.95 (AF1006) J Norton Pubs.
Includes origins & functions of banking & history & fears of a free market.

***Banking in the Glory.** Katie Souza. (ENG.). 2011. audio compact disk 25.00 (978-0-7684-0266-7(2)) Pub: Expected End. Dist(s): Destiny Image Pubs

Banking Law Update. 1998. bk. 99.00 (ACS-2017) PA Bar Inst.
Featuring a complete legislative, case law & practice update on the hottest issues facing the industry, the authors collaborate to bring you their experiences & insights into this continually changing area.

Banking 101. (Smartlink for MBAA Ser.). 2003. audio compact disk 150.00 (978-0-324-20300-4(4)) Pub: South-West. Dist(s): CENGAGE Learn

Bankrupt: The Intellectual & Moral Bankruptcy of the Democratic Party. unabr. ed. David Limbaugh. Read by Raymond Todd. (Running Time: 6 mins. 30 sec.). (J). 2006. 44.95 (978-0-7861-4739-7(3)) Blckstn Audio.

Bankrupt: The Intellectual & Moral Bankruptcy of the Democratic Party. unabr. ed. David Limbaugh. Read by Raymond Todd. 8 cass. (Running Time: 39600 sec.). 2006. 29.95 (978-0-7861-4627-7(3)); audio compact disk 29.95 (978-0-7861-7453-9(6)) Blckstn Audio.

Bankrupt: The Intellectual & Moral Bankruptcy of Today's Democratic Party. unabr. ed. David Limbaugh. Read by Raymond Todd. (Running Time: 39600 sec.). 2006. audio compact disk 25.95 (978-0-7861-6689-3(4)); audio compact disk 55.00 (978-0-7861-6425-7(5)) Blckstn Audio.

Bankruptcy. Douglass Boshkoff. 4 cass. (Running Time: 6 hrs. 25 mins.). (Outstanding Professors Ser.). 1995. 55.50 (978-0-940366-60-2(6), 28392) West.
Lecture given by a prominent American law school professor.

Bankruptcy. Elizabeth Warren. 4 cass. (Running Time: 4 hrs.). (Gilbert Law Summaries Ser.). (C). 1997. 45.95 (978-0-15-900273-5(7)) Barbri Grp.

Bankruptcy: Chapter 13. Contrib. by Santo J. Lalomia et al. (Running Time: 6 hrs.). 1983. 70.00 incl. program handbook. NJ Inst CLE.
Explains the Chapter 13 process from the decision whether to proceed under Chapter 13 to the administration of the estate, including the submission of a confirmed plan & its enforcement.

Bankruptcy: The Last Resort. 1 cass. bk. 55.00 (AC-634) PA Bar Inst.

Bankruptcy Developments for Workout Officers & Lenders Counsel. 7 cass. (Running Time: 9 hrs.). 1990. bk. 95.00 incl. 758-page course handbook. (T6-9154) PLI.

Bankruptcy Issues in Divorce. (Running Time: 4 hrs.). 1999. bk. 99.00 (ACS-2228) PA Bar Inst.
The growing burden of consumer debt has resulted in a rising toll of bankruptcy filings & increased strain on marriages. When spouses seek escape from their financial & matrimonial obligations, the laws of bankruptcy & divorce become hopelessly intertwined.

Bankruptcy Law & Litigation for New York Practitioners: Albany. (Running Time: 5 hrs. 30 min.). 1993. 92.00 Incl. 238p. coursebk. (29322); 30.00 238p. coursebk. (19322) NYS Bar.
Highlights the structure of the Bankruptcy Code, the makeup of the court & its personnel & the procedures for commencing a case, with the Albany session structured on a more basic level than the Garden City session. The panelists for each session consider procedures & customs in use in each respective geographic locale.

Bankruptcy Law & Litigation for New York Practitioners: Garden City. (Running Time: 5 hrs. 45 min.). 1993. 92.00 Incl. 238p. coursebk. (29323) NYS Bar.

Bankruptcy Litigation. Moderated by Alan B. Miller & Martin J. Bienenstock. (Running Time: 11 hrs.). 1992. pap. bk. 295.00 incl. course book. NY Law Pub.
Topics include jurisdiction; stay relief; professional fees; fraudulent conveyance; preference litigation; equitable subordination/lender liability; executory contracts; Chapter 11 plans; DIP financing/asset sales.

Bankruptcy Practice: Recent Developments (1992) Read by Steven H. Felderstein et al. (Running Time: 3 hrs.). 1992. 89.00 Incl. 377p. tape materials. (BU-55132) Cont Ed Bar-CA.
Analyzes the latest developments in handling Chapter 7, 9, 11, 12, & 13 bankruptcies. Topics include: jurisdiction; plan confirmation; preferences & fraudulent conveyances; exemptions; automatic stays, family law & bankruptcy issues, debtor in possession financing, administrative claims, fraudulent transfers, proof of claims, standards of conduct for debt, & bankruptcy crimes.

Bankruptcy Practice Update. Contrib. by Hugh M. Leonard. (Running Time: 4 hrs. 30 min.). 1984. 70.00 incl. program handbook. NJ Inst CLE.
Helps attorneys digest these new provisions & incorporate them into everyday practice.

Bankruptcy Reform Act of 1994: Important Changes & Their Practical Impact. 3 cass. (Running Time: 4 hrs.). 1994. 155.00 incl study materials. (M225) Am Law Inst.

Banks o'Doon see Poetry of Robert Burns & Border Ballads

Banksters, Bosses, & Smart Money: A Social History of the Great Toledo Bank Crash of 1931. Timothy Messer-Kruse. 2004. audio compact disk 9.95 (978-0-8142-9054-5(X)) Pub: Ohio St U Pr. Dist(s): Chicago Distribution Ctr

Banned in the Western Suburbs. Judith Black. 2. (YA). 18.00 (978-0-9701073-9-8(0)) J Black Storyteller.

Banner of the Bull. unabr. collector's ed. Rafael Sabatini. Read by David Case. 8 cass. (Running Time: 8 hrs.). (J). 1991. 48.00 (978-0-7366-1912-7(7), 2738) Books on Tape.
Three stirring episodes in the career of Caesar Borgia, the famous Florentine on whose banners blazed the emblem of the bull. Borgia appears not as a monster, but as a master of statecraft, almost infallible in furthering his schemes. Although ruthless to rivals, he was popular with wisdom & liberality.

Bannister Girls. unabr. ed. Jean Saunders. Read by Marie McCarthy. 9 cass. (Running Time: 12 hrs.). (Story Sound Ser.). (J). 2004. 76.95 (978-1-85903-666-2(X)) Pub: Mgna Lrg Print GBR. Dist(s): Ulverscroft US

Banquet Address. John Thompson. 1 cass. (National Meeting of the Institute, 1992 Ser.). 4.00 (92N6) IRL Chicago.

Banquet Address. unabr. ed. Roger Lea MacBride. 1 cass. (Running Time: 51 min.). 12.95 (731) J Norton Pubs.

Banquet Address at the 1974 Conservative Political Action Conference. unabr. ed. James Buckley. 1 cass. (Running Time: 1 hr. 27 min.). 12.95 (AFO240) J Norton Pubs.

Banquet Address at the 1974 Conservative Political Action Conference. unabr. ed. Ronald Reagan. 1 cass. (Running Time: 1 hr. 11 min.). 12.95 (AFO235) J Norton Pubs.

Banquet Tribute: John Hospers. (Running Time: 90 min.). (Cal State Univ., Long Beach). 1981. 10.00 (F117) Freeland Pr.

Banquet Tribute: Nathaniel Branden. 2 cass. (Running Time: 2 hrs.). (Cal State Univ., Long Beach). 1982. 18.00 (F129A & B) Freeland Pr.
Highlight of the speakers' personal contributions, plus the Mencken Awards are presented for the first time here.

Banquet Tribute to Ayn Rand & the Mencken Awards. (Running Time: 3 hrs.). (Cal State Univ., Long Beach). 1984. 19.00 (F165A & B) Freeland Pr.
Various speakers share their personal experiences of the late Ayn Rand.

Banquo's Ghosts. unabr. ed. Richard Lowry & Keith Korman. (Running Time: 13 hrs. 30 mins. 0 sec.). (ENG.). 2009. 24.99 (978-1-4001-6307-6(2)); audio compact disk 75.99 (978-1-4001-4307-8(1)); audio compact disk 37.99 (978-1-4001-1307-1(5)) Pub: Tantor Media. Dist(s): IngramPubServ

Banshee. unabr. ed. Karen Ackerman. 1 cass. (Running Time: 7 min.). (J). (ps-4). 1993. bk. 25.90 (978-0-8045-6584-4(8), 6584) Spoken Arts.

Banshee & Legend of Sleepy Hollow. Eochaid Ollathair & Washington Irving. 1 cass. (J). (ps-10). 1996. 4.95 (978-1-57555-006-0(7)) Cedar Bay Pr.
Two short stories. "The Banshee" is set in Ireland. "The Legend of Sleepy Hollow" is a classic set in early America.

Banyan Tree. abr. ed. Christopher Nolan. Read by Fiona Shaw. (ENG.). 2005. 14.98 (978-1-59483-466-0(0)) Pub: Hachet Audio. Dist(s): HachBkGrp

Banza: A Haitian Story. Read by Diane Wolkstein. Perf. by Shirley Keller. 1 cass. (Running Time: 15 min.). (J). (gr. k-6). 1988. pap. bk. 10.00 (978-1-879846-00-5(4)) Cloudstone NY.
A small goat defends herself against 10 tigers by creating her own song on the banjo. This Haitian story of an unlikely friendship.

Banza: A Haitian Story. unabr. ed. Diane Wolkstein. Read by Diane Wolkstein. 1 cass. (Running Time: 15 mins.). (Follow the Reader Ser.). (J). (gr. k-2). 1986. 17.00 incl. bk., guide. (978-0-8072-0131-2(6), FTR122SP, Listening Lib) Random Audio Pubg.
Haitain tale of the tiger & the goat.

***Baobab Blast Song CD.** Created by Augsburg Fortress Publishers. (Baobab Blast VBS Ser.). (ENG.). 2010. audio compact disk 25.99 (978-0-8066-9661-4(3)) Augsburg Fortress.

Bapteme see Contes de Maupassant

Baptised in Blood. Janie Bolitho. 6 cass. 2007. 54.95 (978-1-84283-896-9(2)) Pub: Soundings Ltd GBR. Dist(s): Ulverscroft US

Baptism in Spirit. Vincent M. Walsh. 1 cass. 1986. 4.00 Key of David.
Personal stories & examples told to promote a full understanding of the basic powers fo the Renewal.

Baptism in the Holy Spirit: A Two-Part Teaching. Speeches. Lisa Comes. 1 Cassette. (Running Time: 90 mins.). 2002. 4.00 (978-1-931877-03-9(3)) J Osteen.
Two-Part Sermon Series.

Baptism of Fire. Todd Bentley. (Running Time: 1 hr. 51 mins.). 2007. 24.99 (978-1-4245-0691-0(3)) Tre Med Inc.

Baptism of Jesus; Saintly Powers at Easter. Ann Ree Colton & Jonathan Murro. 1 cass. 7.95 A R Colton Fnd.

Baptism of Power Series. Steve Thompson. 2 cass. (Running Time: 3 hrs.). 2000. 10.00 (ST02-000) Morning NC.
Includes: "John the Baptist did not Doubt" & Dependence on the Holy Spirit." This discussion of the baptism of power that Jesus referred to will help you discover the spiritual power available to every Christian.

Baptism of the Holy Spirit. Gospel Light Publications Staff. 1 cass. 1997. 6.99 (978-7-5116-0036-3(0)) Gospel Lght.
Protestant theology.

Baptism of the Holy Spirit. John MacArthur, Jr. 2 cass. 7.95 (22-15, HarperThor) HarpC GBR.

Baptisms of Fire. Todd Bentley. 2006. audio compact disk 24.99 (978-1-59933-012-9(1)) Pub: Morning NC. Dist(s): Destiny Image Pubs

Baptist of the Holy Spirit: Logos January 11, 1998. Ben Young. 1997. 4.95 (978-0-7417-6068-5(1), B0068) Win Walk.

Bar-B-Que Soul-a-Bration! Party Pack. Rhino Records Staff. 1 cass., 2 CDs. 1998. bk. 24.98 (978-1-56826-937-5(4)) Rhino Enter.
It's everything one needs & about what one needs to know about throwing the perfect party.

Bar-B-Que Soul-a-Bration! Party Pack: 2 CD's & Three Ring Binder/Personal Party Planner. Rhino Records Staff. 3 CDs. (Running Time: 3 hrs.). 1998. ring bd. 31.98 (978-1-56826-870-5(X)) Rhino Enter.

Bar Sinister see Great American Short Stories, Vol. III, A Collection

Bar Sinister. unabr. ed. Richard Harding Davis. Perf. by Walter Covell. 1 cass. Dramatization. 1986. 7.95 (S-65) Jimcin Record.
A story of rags to riches in the world of show dogs.

Barack & Michelle: Portrait of an American Marriage. unabr. ed. Christopher Andersen. Read by Dion Graham. (Running Time: 11 hrs.). 2009. 24.99 (978-1-4418-2071-6(X), 9781441820716, BAD); 24.99 (978-1-4418-2069-3(8), 9781441820693, Brilliance MP3); 39.97 (978-1-4418-2070-9(1), 9781441820709, Brinc Audio MP3 Lib); 39.97 (978-1-4418-2072-3(8), 9781441820723, BADLE); audio compact disk 29.99 (978-1-4418-2067-9(1), 9781441820679, Bril Audio CD Unabri); audio compact disk 97.97 (978-1-4418-2068-6(X), 9781441820686, BriAudCD Unabrid) Brilliance Audio.

Barack Like Me: The Chocolate-Covered Truth. abr. unabr. ed. David Alan Grier. Read by David Alan Grier. Told to Alan Eisenstock. (Running Time: 6 hrs. 0 mins. 0 sec.). (ENG.). 2009. audio compact disk 29.99 (978-0-7435-9772-2(9)) Pub: S&S Audio. Dist(s): S and S Inc

***Barack Obama: The movement for Change.** Anthony Painter. Read by Nicholas Bell. (Running Time: 5 hrs. 40 mins.). 2009. 64.99 (978-1-74214-547-1(7), 9781742145471) Pub: Bolinda Pubng AUS. Dist(s): Bolinda Pub Inc

Barack Obama: The movement for Change. unabr. ed. Anthony Painter. Read by Nicholas Bell. (Running Time: 5 hrs. 40 mins.). 2009. audio compact disk 63.95 (978-1-74214-371-2(7), 9781742143712) Pub: Bolinda Pubng AUS. Dist(s): Bolinda Pub Inc

***Barack Obama: The movement for Change.** unabr. ed. Anthony Painter. Read by Nicholas Bell. (Running Time: 5 hrs. 40 mins.). 2010. 43.95 (978-1-74214-665-2(1), 9781742146652) Pub: Bolinda Pubng AUS. Dist(s): Bolinda Pub Inc

***Barack Obama: The Movement for Change.** unabr. ed. Anthony Painter. Read by Nicholas Bell. 5 CDs. (Running Time: 5 hrs. 40 mins.). 2009. audio compact disk 63.95 (978-1-74233-207-9(2), Bolinda Audio Bks) Bolinda Pub Inc.

***Barack Obama's Victory Speech.** Created by Di Teng. (CHI., 2009. pap. bk. 14.30 (978-957-710-531-8(9)) DTPC Ltd TWN.

Baranov's Alaskan Legacy: Russia's Advance from Kodiak to New Archangel. Tim Hostiuck. Read by Tim Hostiuck. 1 cass. (Running Time: 40 min.). 1993. 12.00 (978-1-928952-02-2(X)) Misty Peaks.
From 1790 to 1818 enigmatic Governor Alexander Baranov carries the Russian American Company from the brink of disaster to the brink of empire, securing for his Czar an indisputably Russian stretch of North America's coast.

Barbados Heat. Don Bruns. 4 cass. (Running Time: 5 hrs.). 2002. 32.95 (978-0-7861-2825-9(9), 3260) Blckstn Audio.

Barbados Heat. unabr. ed. Don Bruns. Read by Don Bruns. 6 CDs. (Running Time: 7 hrs.). 2004. audio compact disk 32.95 (978-0-7861-8694-5(1)); reel tape 29.95 (978-0-7861-2681-1(7)) Blckstn Audio.
When Congressman Shapply, a leader in the crusade against offensive lyrics in rap songs, is murdered, his stepson Nick is arrested and charged with murder. For veteran music journalist Mick Sever, covering this case is personal. Sever, a childhood friend of the accused killer, believes his friend's claims of innocence. With the help of an old flame, Mick must penetrate the violent world of rap music and the bizarre Shapply family-the icy matriarch Alicia, the disturbed daughter Amber, and the religious brother-in-law-to find the truth.

Barbados Outdoor Club; Youth at Rio's Earth Summit; IMAX's "Fires of Kuwait;" Texas' Dinosaur State Park. Hosted by Nancy Pearlman. 1 cass. (Running Time: 29 min.). 10.00 (1213) Educ Comm CA.

Barbara Branden: Ayn Rand: The Charisma of Reason. (Running Time: 60 min.). (Long Beach City College). 1983. 9.00 (F155) Freeland Pr.
The author touches upon a facet of Ms. Rand's personality that is not generally known.

Barbara Branden: Who Is Ayn Rand? (Running Time: 60 min.). (Cal State Univ., Long Beach Ser.). 1982. 9.00 (F137) Freeland Pr.
Acquaints us with the ramifacations of cultism within Ayn Rand's followers of Objectivism & guides us through some misconceptions & presents some insights.

Barbara bush a Memoir. Barbara Bush. 2004. 15.95 (978-0-7435-4186-2(3)) Pub: S&S Audio. Dist(s): S and S Inc

Barbara Delinsky: Twilight Whispers - Facets. abr. ed. Barbara Delinsky. (Running Time: 12 hrs.). 2010. audio compact disk 19.99 (978-1-4418-4961-8(0), 978144184961[illegible] Bril Audio CD Unabri) Brilliance Audio.

Barbara Frietchie see Classic American [illegible]ry

Barbara of the House of Grebe see Thomas Hardy: Selected Short Stories

Barbara Tuchman, Historian: On a Confident Democracy. Narrated by Barbara W. Tuchman. 1 cass. (Running Time: 1 hr.). 10.95 (K0170B090, HarperThor) HarpC GBR.

Barbarian. abr. ed. Barry Sadler. Read by Charlton Griffin. 2 vols. (Casca Ser.: No. 5). 2003. (978-1-58807-519-2(2)); audio compact disk 25.00 (978-1-58807-279-5(7)); audio compact disk (978-1-58807-710-3(1)) Am Pubng Inc.

Barbarian. abr. ed. Barry Sadler. Read by Bruce Watson. 2 vols. (Running Time: 3 hrs.). (Casca Ser.: No. 5). 2003. 18.00 (978-1-58807-105-7(7)) Am Pubng Inc.
Entangled in his most enduring romantic interest yet, Casca's latest adventure transports him to the Hold at Helsfjord in the icy Viking terrain of Northern Germany. The beautiful Lida swiftly captures Casca's heart, but with the vile intervention of a despicable sorcerer, the flames of their love are soon doused with heartache. By the hand of deception, Casca is left to battle the brutal monarch of Helsfjord; and, while exiled to a murky dungeon, an existence composed of his own decay, he once again faces his greatest enemy: immortality.

Barbarian Way: Unleash the Untamed Faith Within. abr. ed. Erwin Raphael McManus. Read by Erwin Raphael McManus. (Running Time: 12600 sec.). 2006. audio compact disk 24.99 (978-0-7852-1721-3(5)) Nelson.
Using Jesus' words about John the Baptist in Matthew 11, Erwin McManus urges readers to flee "civilized" religion and return to the "barbarian way" of following Christ. Erwin McManus wasn't raised in a Christian home, so when he came to Christ as a college student, he didn't know the rules of the "religious club." He didn't do well in Shakespeare courses, so he didn't really understand the KJV Bible he was given either. But he did understand that prayer was a conversation, and he learned to talk to God and wait for answers. Erwin's way was passionate and rough around the edges-a sincere, barbaric journey to Christ. Barbaric Christians see Jesus differently than civilized Christians. They see disciples differently, and they see Christ's mission differently. The Barbarian Way is a call to escape

"civilized"Christianity and become original, powerful, untamed Christians-just as Christ intended.

Barbarians: Warriors & Wars of the Dark Ages. unabr. ed. Tim Newark. Narrated by Nelson Runger. 4 cass. (Running Time: 5 hrs. 30 mins.). 1988. 35.00 (978-1-55690-036-5(8), 88140E7) Recorded Bks.
An account of the Dark Ages & Barbarian invasions of Europe. From surviving contemporary literature & artifacts now shrouded in myth & legend.

***Barbarians at the Gate.** abr. ed. Bryan Burrough. Read by John Helyar. (ENG.). 2007. (978-0-06-112747-2(7), Harper Audio); (978-0-06-112746-5(9), Harper Audio) HarperCollins Pubs.

Barbarians at the Gate: The Fall of RJR Nabisco. abr. ed. Bryan Burrough & John Helyar. Read by John Helyar. (Running Time: 10800 sec.). 2007. audio compact disk 14.95 (978-0-06-123208-4(4)) HarperCollins Pubs.

Barbarians at the Gate Pt. 1: The Fall of RJR Nabisco. unabr. ed. Bryan Burrough & John Helyar. Read by Walter Zimmerman. 8 cass. (Running Time: 12 hrs.). 1990. 64.00 (978-0-7366-1784-0(1), 2622-A) Books on Tape.
The fight to control RJR Nabisco late in 1988 was more than just the largest takeover in Wall Street history. Marked by brazen displays of ego not seen since the Robber Barons, it gave greed a new benchmark. With $25 billion at stake, it will be remembered as the ultimate financial story of the 80's. Wall Street Journal reporters Bryan Burrough & John Helyar earned their way into this story. They take us inside strategy meetings, society dinners & boardrooms. They report financial operations at the highest levels, which by extension become a richly textured social history of wealth at the twilight of the Reagan era.

Barbarians at the Gate Pt. 2: The Fall of RJR Nabisco. unabr. ed. Bryan Burrough & John Helyar. Read by Walter Zimmerman. 8 cass. (Running Time: 12 hrs.). 1990. 64.00 (2622-B) Books on Tape.

Barbarous Coast. unabr. ed. Ross MacDonald, pseud. Read by Tom Parker. 5 cass. (Running Time: 7 hrs.). (Lew Archer Mystery Ser.). 2003. 39.95 (978-0-7861-1047-6(3), 1819) Blckstn Audio.
Lew Archer's pursuit of a girl who jackknifed too suddenly from high diving to high living, leads him to an ex-fighter with an unexplained movie contract, a bigtime gambler who died by his own knife & finally to an answer he would rather not have known.

Barbarous Coast. unabr. ed. Ross MacDonald, pseud. Read by Tom Parker. 6 CDs. (Running Time: 7 hrs.). (Lew Archer Mystery Ser.). 2000. audio compact disk 48.00 (978-0-7861-9916-7(4), 1819) Blckstn Audio.

Barbary Coast. unabr. ed. Matt Braun. Read by Gene Engene. 6 cass. (Running Time: 6 hrs. 30 min.). (Luke Starbuck Ser.: Bk. 2). 2001. 39.95 (978-1-58116-069-7(0)) Books in Motion.
San Francisco, 1882. The Barbary Coast, Chinatown, and the international waterfront have made the city the toughest and most corrupt in America. Luke Starbuck plans to blow the waterfront sharks clean out of the bay.

***Barbary Pirates.** unabr. ed. William Dietrich. Read by William Dufris. (ENG.). 2010. (978-0-06-198712-0(3), Harper Audio) HarperCollins Pubs.

***Barbary Pirates: An Ethan Gage Adventure.** unabr. ed. William Dietrich. Read by William Dufris. (ENG.). 2010. (978-0-06-195359-0(8), Harper Audio) HarperCollins Pubs.

Barbe Bleu. 1 cass. (FRE.). (J). (gr. 3 up). 1991. bk. 14.95 (1AD028) Olivia & Hill.
Bluebeard.

Barbe Bleue (Blue Beard) see Contes de Perrault

Barbed Coil. J. V. Jones. 1999. (978-1-57042-344-4(X)) Hachet Audio.

Barbed Coil. abr. ed. J. V. Jones. (Running Time: 2 hrs. 30 mins.). (ENG.). 2006. 14.98 (978-1-59483-665-7(5)) Pub: Hachet Audio. Dist(s): HachBkGrp

Barbed Coil. abr. ed. J. V. Jones. Read by Tony Roberts. 2 cass. 2001. 7.95 (978-1-57815-197-4(X), Media Bks Audio) Media Bks NJ.

Barber of Seville: An Introduction to Rossini's Opera. Thomson Smillie. Read by David Timson. 1 CD. (Running Time: 1 hr. 30 min.). (Opera Explained Ser.). 2003. audio compact disk 8.99 (978-1-84379-089-1(0)) NaxMulti GBR.
The barber, Figaro, stage manages a romance between Count Almaviva and Rosina, and puts to flight the old suitor, Dr. Bartolo.

Barbershop Education Vol. 2: What Makes Us Southerners. Kathryn Tucker Windham. 2001. audio compact disk 16.95 (August Hse Audio) August Hse.

Barboza Credentials. unabr. collector's ed. Peter Driscoll. Read by Richard Green. 7 cass. (Running Time: 10 hrs. 30 min.). 1980. 56.00 (978-0-7366-0279-2(8), 1269) Books on Tape.
Joe Hickey, a retired Rhodesian policeman, operates a lucrative but shady business selling mining equipment to blacklisted countries. His office is in Portuguese Mozambique, & when that country gains independence, the new government will no longer turn a blind eye to his activities.

Barbra: The Way She Is. unabr. ed. Christopher Andersen. Read by Ellen Archer. (YA). 2008. 64.99 (978-1-60252-950-2(7)) Find a World.

Barbra: The Way She Is. unabr. ed. Christopher Andersen. Read by Ellen Archer. (Running Time: 15 hrs. 30 mins. 0 sec.). (ENG.). 2006. audio compact disk 79.99 (978-1-4001-3245-4(2)); audio compact disk 29.99 (978-1-4001-5245-2(3)); audio compact disk 39.99 (978-1-4001-0245-7(6)) Pub: Tantor Media. Dist(s): IngramPubServ
She is a one-name legend, a global icon, the ultimate diva. Yet most of what we know about Barbra Joan Streisand is the stuff of caricature: the Brooklyn girl made good, the ugly duckling who blossomed into a modern-day Nefertiti, the political dilettante driving to the barricades in her Rolls-Royce, the Oscar-winning actress and bona fide movie mogul, the greatest female singer who ever lived, a skinflint, a philanthropist, a connoisseur and a barbarian, the woman whose physical characteristics are instantly identifiable around the planet - -the tapered nails, those slightly crossed eyes, that nose, the voice.

Barbs from the Bard: Shakespearean Insults. unabr. abr. ed. Michael Viner & Stefan Rudniki. Read by Roger Rees. 1 cass. (Running Time: 1 hr. 30 min.). 2004. 15.00 (978-1-931056-42-7(0), N Millennium Audio) New Millenn Enter.
Now you can tell someone off with flair and literacy! Barbs from the Barb offers Shakespearean insults with modem translation and notes. Here is a book that you can't put down. It is catharsis at it's best. Whether you're looking for a snappy comeback or an entertaining example of Shakespearean humor, this is a unique reference book of some of the most clever put-downs ever spoken.

Barcarolle see Twentieth-Century Poetry in English, No. 25, Recordings of Poets Reading Their Own Poetry

Barchester Chronicles. unabr. ed. Anthony Trollope. Read by Stephen Thorne. 15 CDs. (Running Time: 22 hrs. 30 mins). 2003. audio compact disk 117.95 (978-0-563-49596-3(0), BBCD022) BBC Worldwide.

***Barchester Towers.** Anthony Trollope. Narrated by Timothy West. (Running Time: 18 hrs. 0 mins. 0 sec.). (Cover to Cover Ser.). (ENG.). 2010. audio compact disk 29.95 (978-1-60283-881-9(X)) Pub: AudioGO. Dist(s): Perseus Dist

Barchester Towers. unabr. ed. Anthony Trollope. Read by Flo Gibson. 14 cass. (Running Time: 19 hrs. 30 min.). 1992. 42.95 (978-1-55685-256-5(8)) Audio Bk Con.
This social comedy of political & ecclesiastical intrigue in the provincial city of Barchester is enlivened by the formidable Mrs. Proudie, the Bishop's domineering wife, the unctuous Mr. Slope, the kindly ex-warden Mr. Harding, his romantic daughter Eleanor & the forceful Archdeacon Grantly.

Barchester Towers. unabr. ed. Anthony Trollope. Read by Timothy West. 14 cass. (Running Time: 19 hrs. 5 mins.). 1999. 49.95 (978-1-57270-114-4(5), F91114u) Pub: Audio Partners. Dist(s): PerseuPGW
Trollope combines humor with social commentary involving the potential predicament of the Church of England in mid-Victorian society.

Barchester Towers. unabr. ed. Anthony Trollope. Read by Stephen Thorne. 16 CDs. (Running Time: 24 hrs.). 2003. audio compact disk 119.95 (978-0-7540-5568-6(X), CCD 259) AudioGO.

Barchester Towers. unabr. ed. Anthony Trollope. Read by Simon Vance. (Running Time: 68400 sec.). 2006. 95.95 (978-0-7861-4754-0(7)); audio compact disk 120.00 (978-0-7861-6338-0(0)); audio compact disk 44.95 (978-0-7861-7257-3(6)) Blckstn Audio.

Barchester Towers, unabr. ed. Anthony Trollope. Narrated by Margaret Hilton. 15 cass. (Running Time: 21 hrs. 30 mins.). 1988. 120.00 (978-1-55690-037-2(6), 88885E7) Recorded Bks.
Barchester Cathedral has a new bishop & Barchester, new cause for gossip.

Barchester Towers. unabr. collector's ed. Anthony Trollope. Read by David Case. 15 cass. (Running Time: 22 hrs. 30 min.). Incl. Pt. 1. Barchester Towers. 8 cass. Anthony Trollope. Read by Walter Zimmerman. 54.00 (9523-A); Pt. 2. Barchester Towers. 9 cass. Anthony Trollope. Read by Walter Zimmerman. 54.00 (9523-B); 1993. 120.00 (978-0-7366-2373-5(6), 3146) Books on Tape.
The appointment of a new bishop in the cathedral city of Barchester has opposing religious factions awash in intrigues & jealousies. Interwoven in this novel is the captivating love story of a young widow who is pursued by a hypocritical priest she despises while ignored by the man she loves.

Barchester Towers, Vols. 1, 2 & 3. Anthony Trollope. Read by Timothy West. Prod. by Betty Davies. 14 cass. (Running Time: 19 hrs. 5 min.). 87.95 C to C Cassettes.
Chronicles the struggle for control of the diocese between the waspishly ruthless Mrs. Proudie, wife of the new Bishop, & Obadiah Slope, the Bishop's oily & hypocritical chaplain.

Barclay Family Adventures Series 1. Created by Saddleback Publishing. (ENG.). (J). 2003. pap. bk. 169.95 (978-1-56254-987-9(1)) Saddleback Edu.

Bard & Muse. Anne Waldman & Allen Ginsberg. 1 cass. 1976. 12.50 Vajradhatu.

Bardo Dreams. E. J. Gold & Menlo Macfarlane. 1 cass. (Running Time: 1 hr.). Dramatization. 1987. 15.00 (MT013) Union Label.
A guided induction journey through the afterlife visions.

Bardo Therapy: Self-Transformation & Liberation Based upon the Tibetan Book of the Dead. unabr. ed. Joseph P. Reel. Read by Joseph P. Reel. 4 cass. (Running Time: 4 hrs.). 1996. 29.95 Set in album case incl. insert. (978-0-938024-01-9(9)) Human Dev Pr.
Clinical Counselor explores underlying psychological principles of the "Bardo Thodol" (Tibetan Book of the Dead), & how they can be utilized to expand choices & awareness in daily life.

Bards see Dylan Thomas Reading

***Bardy Svabody.** Radio Svaboda. (BEL.). 2010. (978-0-929849-32-4(9)) RFE-RL Inc.

Bare Bones. abr. ed. Kathy Reichs. Read by Michele Pawk. 1 CD. (Running Time: 60 hrs. 0 mins. 0 sec.). No. 6. (ENG.). 2003. audio compact disk 30.00 (978-0-7435-2981-5(2), Audioworks) Pub: S&S Audio. Dist(s): S and S Inc

Bare Bones. abr. ed. Kathy Reichs. Read by Michele Pawk. (Temperance Brennan Ser.: No. 6). 2004. 18.95 (978-0-7435-5022-2(6)) Pub: S&S Audio. Dist(s): S and S Inc

Bare Bones. unabr. ed. Kathy Reichs. Narrated by Barbara Rosenblatt. 7 cass. (Running Time: 9 hrs. 15 mins.). (Temperance Brennan Ser.: No. 6). 2006. 69.75 (978-1-4193-1572-5(2)) Recorded Bks.

Bare Bones. unabr. ed. Kathy Reichs. Read by Michele Pawk. (Temperance Brennan Ser.: No. 6). 2004. 21.95 (978-0-7435-4187-9(1)) Pub: S&S Audio. Dist(s): S and S Inc

Bare Knuckles & Back Rooms. unabr. ed. Ed Rollins. 4 cass. 23.95 Set. (47736) Books on Tape.
A brilliant political consultant, tells how Washington really works, famously outspoken, he is a maverick who's won far more campaigns than he's lost. Here he offers a candid & entertaining account of his 30-year career, including stories about run-ins with Nancy Reagan, Barbara Bush, Ross Perot & Christine Todd Whitman.

Bare Naked Bliss: ... loving from Within. Suzanne Toro. (ENG.). 2009. audio compact disk 35.00 (978-1-60031-063-8(X)) Spoken Books.

Bared Fangs. Max Brand. (Running Time: 2 hrs. 24 mins.). 2000. 10.95 (978-1-60083-540-7(6)) Iofy Corp.

***Bared Fangs.** Max Brand. 2009. (978-1-60136-387-9(7)) Audio Holding.

Baree: The Wolf-Dog. James Oliver Curwood. Read by Patrick G. Lawlor. (Running Time: 24300 sec.). (ENG.). 2003. audio compact disk 19.99 (978-1-4001-5091-5(4)); audio compact disk 29.99 (978-1-4001-0091-0(7)) Pub: Tantor Media. Dist(s): IngramPubServ

Baree: The Wolf-Dog. James Oliver Curwood. Read by Patrick G. Lawlor. (ENG.). 2005. audio compact disk 59.99 (978-1-4001-3091-7(3)) Pub: Tantor Media. Dist(s): IngramPubServ

Baree: The Wolf Dog. unabr. ed. James Oliver Curwood. Narrated by Patrick G. Lawlor. (Running Time: 7 hrs. 0 mins. 0 sec.). (ENG.). 2009. audio compact disk 19.99 (978-1-4001-6120-1(7)) Pub: Tantor Media. Dist(s): IngramPubServ

Baree - The Wolf Dog, with eBook. unabr. ed. James Oliver Curwood. Narrated by Patrick G. Lawlor. (Running Time: 7 hrs. 0 mins. 0 sec.). (ENG.). 2009. audio compact disk 27.99 (978-1-4001-1120-6(X)); audio compact disk 55.99 (978-1-4001-4120-3(6)) Pub: Tantor Media. Dist(s): IngramPubServ

Baree the Wolf-Dog. James Oliver Curwood. Read by Patrick G. Lawlor. (Running Time: 6 hrs. 45 mins.). 2003. 27.95 (978-1-60083-657-2(7), Audiofy Corp) Iofy Corp.

Baree the Wolf-Dog. unabr. ed. James Oliver Curwood. Read by Patrick G. Lawlor. (J). 2007. 44.99 (978-1-60252-547-4(1)) Find a World.

Barefoot. (J). (978-1-84148-474-7(1)) BarefootBksMA.

Barefoot. unabr. abr. ed. Elin Hilderbrand. Read by Katie Hale. (Running Time: 8 hrs.). (ENG.). 2008. 14.98 (978-1-60024-235-9(9)); audio compact disk 19.98 (978-1-60024-234-2(0)) Pub: Hachet Audio. Dist(s): HachBkGrp

Barefoot Book of Knights. John Matthews & John Matthews. Illus. by Giovanni Manna. (Running Time: 2 mins. 55 sec.). (ENG.). (J). 2003. audio compact disk 19.99 (978-1-84148-927-8(1)) BarefootBksMA.

Barefoot Boy see Classic American Poetry

Barefoot Boy. unabr. ed. Poems. John Greenleaf Whittier. Read by Ed Begley. 1 cass. (Running Time: 90 mins.). Incl. Skipper Ireson's Ride. (SWC 1308); Snow-Bound. John Greenleaf Whittier. (SWC 1308); Telling the Bees. (SWC 1308); 1970. 14.00 (978-0-694-50207-3(3), SWC 1308) HarperCollins Pubs.

Barefoot in the Park. Neil Simon. Contrib. by Norman Aronovic et al. (Playaway Adult Fiction Ser.). (ENG.). 2009. 40.00 (978-1-60775-569-2(6)) Find a World.

Barefoot in the Park. unabr. ed. Neil Simon. Perf. by Laura Linney et al. 1 cass. (Running Time: 1 hr. 30 mins.). 2002. 20.95 (978-1-58081-230-6(9), WTA15); audio compact disk 25.95 (978-1-58081-234-4(1), CDWTA15) Pub: L A Theatre. Dist(s): NetLibrary CO
A brand-new lawyer and his young bride are moving into their new high-rent apartment. But, the place is bare of furniture, the paint job is all wrong, the skylight leaks and there is room for only one twin bed, plus the wacky neighbors pop up at the worst times.

Barefoot Soldier: A Story of Extreme Valour. unabr. ed. Johnson Beharry & Nick Cook. Read by Johnson Beharry. (Running Time: 6 hrs. 0 mins. 0 sec.). (ENG., 2006. audio compact disk 25.00 (978-1-4055-0153-8(7)) Pub: Little BrownUK GBR. Dist(s): IPG Chicago

Barely a Bride. unabr. ed. Rebecca Hagan Lee. Narrated by Virginia Leishman. 8 cass. (Running Time: 11 hrs. 15 mins.). 2003. 79.75 (978-1-4193-1181-9(6), L1129MC) Recorded Bks.

Bargain for Frances. abr. ed. Russell Hoban. Illus. by Lillian Hoban. 1 cass. (I Can Read Bks.). (J). (gr. k-3). 1993. 8.99 (978-1-55994-224-9(X), TBC 224X) HarperCollins Pubs.

Bargain for Frances. abr. ed. Russell Hoban. Illus. by Lillian Hoban. (I Can Read Bks.). (J). 2008. 9.99 (978-0-06-133611-9(4), HarperFestival) HarperCollins Pubs.

Bargain for Frances & Other Frances Stories. abr. ed. Russell Hoban. Perf. by Glynis Johns. 1 cass. (Running Time: 90 mins.). Incl. Best Friends for Frances. Russell Hoban. (J). (CDL5 1547); (J). 1984. 9.95 (978-0-89845-473-4(5), CDL5 1547) HarperCollins Pubs.

Bargain Hunters, Contrarians, Cycles & Waves. Narrated by Louis Rukeyser. 2 cass. (Running Time: 2 hrs. 30 mins.). (Secrets of the Great Investors Ser.: Vol. 5). 17.95 (978-1-56823-057-3(5)) Pub: Knowledge Prod. Dist(s): APG
Learn about the timeless strategies, tactics, judgments, & principles that have produced great wealth. Hear history's great figures & personalities - in their own words - describe their techniques & achievements in finance & investing. Now you can listen to these great lessons while commuting, traveling, walking...anytime your hands are busy, but your mind is not.

Bargain Hunters, Contrarians, Cycles & Waves: Knowledge Products Production. unabr. ed. Janet Lowe. Read by Ken Fisher & Louis Rukeyser. (Running Time: 4 mins.). (J). 2006. audio compact disk 25.95 (978-0-7861-6531-5(6)) Pub: Blckstn Audio. Dist(s): NetLibrary CO

Bargaining with the Devil: When to Negotiate, When to Fight. abr. ed. Robert Mnookin. Read by Robert Mnookin. (Running Time: 7 hrs. 0 mins. 0 sec.). (ENG.). 2010. audio compact disk 29.99 (978-1-4423-0416-1(2)) Pub: S&S Audio. Dist(s): S and S Inc

Baritone. Robert W. Smith et al. Contrib. by Linda J. Gammon. (Band Expressions Ser.). (ENG., 2004. pap. bk. 8.95 (978-0-7579-4051-4(X)) Alfred Pub.

Baritone & Bass Solos, Bk. 2. Ed. by Joan Frey Boytim. Created by Hal Leonard Corp. (ENG.). 1997. audio compact disk 18.99 (978-0-7935-8650-9(X), 079358650X, G Schirmer) H Leonard.

Baritone Uke Chords. Contrib. by Joe Carr. (Running Time: 30 mins.). 2005. 9.95 (978-5-558-08946-2(6)) Mel Bay.

Bark, George. 2004. 8.95 (978-1-55592-542-0(1)); audio compact disk 12.95 (978-1-55592-549-9(9)) Weston Woods.

Bark, George. (J). 2004. pap. bk. 38.75 (978-1-55592-713-4(0)); pap. bk. 32.75 (978-1-55592-709-7(2)) Weston Woods.

Bark, George. Jules Feiffer. 1 cass. (Running Time: 1 hr. 30 min.). 2004. bk. 24.95 (978-1-55592-690-8(8)); pap. bk. 14.95 (978-1-55592-696-0(7)); pap. bk. 18.95 (978-1-55592-706-6(8)) Weston Woods.

Barking. Tom Holt. 2008. 99.95 (978-0-7531-3817-5(4)); audio compact disk 109.95 (978-0-7531-2798-8(9)) Pub: ISIS Audio GBR. Dist(s): Ulverscroft US

Barley Break. Perf. by Lorraine L. Hammond. 1 cass. (Running Time: 1 hrs.). (gr. 4 up). 1992. 9.95 (978-0-938756-40-8(0), 044) Yellow Moon.
Folk music collection of twenty-four Elizabethan tunes with dulcimer tablature; could be used as tool for learning the music.

Barley Break. Perf. by Lorraine L. Hammond. 1 cass. (Running Time: 1 hrs.). (gr. 4 up). 1992. pap. bk. 18.95 (978-0-938756-39-2(7), 045) Yellow Moon.

Barn, unabr. ed. Avi. Narrated by Richard Woodman & Jeff Woodman. 2 pieces. (Running Time: 2 hrs.). (gr. 5 up). 1995. 19.00 (978-0-7887-0213-6(0), 94438E7) Recorded Bks.
In 1855 Oregon Territory, a boy inspires his brother & sister to build the barn their seriously ill father always dreamed of.

Barn Blind. Jane Smiley. Read by Suzanne Toren. 7 CDs. (Running Time: 7.5 Hrs). audio compact disk (978-1-4025-5593-0(8)) Recorded Bks.

Barn Blind. unabr. ed. Jane Smiley. Read by Suzanne Toren. 5 Cass. (Running Time: 7.5 Hrs). 24.95 (978-1-4025-5068-3(5)) Recorded Bks.

Barn Blind. unabr. ed. Jane Smiley. Narrated by Suzanne Toren. 6 cass. (Running Time: 7 hrs. 30 mins.). 1998. 51.00 (978-0-7887-2211-0(5), 95510E7) Recorded Bks.
A woman obsessed with her horse farm drives a wedge between herself & those who love her most. When her husband & four children dare to thwart her interests, the results bring devastation & tragedy.

Barnaby Grimes: Curse of the Night Wolf. unabr. ed. Paul Stewart & Chris Riddell. Read by Alex Kalajzic. (Running Time: 3 hrs.). 2009. 39.97 (978-1-4233-7547-0(5), 9781423375470, BADLE); 39.97 (978-1-4233-7545-6(9), 9781423375456, Brlnc Audio MP3 Lib); 24.99 (978-1-4233-7544-9(0), 9781423375449, Brilliance MP3); 24.99 (978-1-4233-7546-3(7), 9781423375463, BAD); audio compact disk 44.97 (978-1-4233-7543-2(2), 9781423375432, BriAudCD Unabrid); audio compact disk 19.99 (978-1-4233-7542-5(4), 9781423375425, Bril Audio CD Unabri) Brilliance Audio.

Barnaby Rudge. unabr. ed. Charles Dickens. 3 vols. (Running Time: 4 hrs.). 2003. audio compact disk 39.95 (978-0-563-49684-7(3), BBCD 032) BBC Worldwide.
Despite their implacable enmity, the upright and honest Geoffrey Haredale forges a strange alliance with the duplicitous John Chester to thwart the marriage between his niece and Chester's honorable son Edward. But family concerns are eclipsed when brooding tensions erupt into the Gordon riots.

Barnaby Rudge. unabr. ed. Charles Dickens. Read by Robert Whitfield. (Running Time: 86400 sec.). 2008. audio compact disk 44.95 (978-1-4332-4525-1(6)) Blckstn Audio.

Barnaby Rudge. unabr. ed. Charles Dickens & Robert Whitfield. (Running Time: 86400 sec.). 2008. audio compact disk & audio compact disk 140.00 (978-1-4332-4524-4(8)) Blckstn Audio.

Barnaby Rudge, Pt. 1. unabr. ed. Charles Dickens. Read by Robert Whitefield. 9 cass. (Running Time: 14 hrs. 30 mins.). 1996. 62.95 (978-0-7861-1063-6(5), 1834A,B) Blckstn Audio.
Dickens' first historical novel is set in 1780s England at the time of the Gordon Riots. In a case of mistaken identification, Barnaby Rudge, a pale half-wit with long red hair who dresses all in green & carries a large raven named Grip in a basket on his back, is arrested as a leader of a mob of anti-Catholic rioters. He is condemned to death on the gallows but an upright locksmith named Gabriel Varden comes to his aid.

Barnaby Rudge, Pt. 2. unabr. ed. Charles Dickens. 8 cass. (Running Time: 11 hrs.). 53.95 Audio Bk Con.
Baraby, a kind, half-witted young man, joins the Gordon rioters to proudly carry their banner. He, his murderous father, the hangman Dennis & the mapcap Hugh are arrested & condemned to death. There are vivid & gruesome scenes of pillage, battles & executions, as well as myriad characters who are grim, romantic or humorous.

Barnaby Rudge, Pt. 2. unabr. ed. Charles Dickens. Read by Robert Whitefield. 8 cass. (Running Time: 14 hrs. 30 mins.). 1996. 56.95 (978-0-7861-1088-9(0), 1834A,B) Blckstn Audio.
Dickens' first historical novel is set in 1780s England at the time of the Gordon Riots. In a case of mistaken identification, Barnaby Rudge, a pale half-wit with long red hair who dresses all in green & carries a large raven named Grip in a basket on his back, is arrested as a leader of a mob of anti-Catholic rioters. He is condemned to death on the gallows but an upright locksmith named Gabriel Varden comes to his aid.

Barnaby Rudge, Pt. A. unabr. collector's ed. Charles Dickens. Read by David Case. 9 cass. (Running Time: 13 hrs. 30 min.). 1996. 72.00 (978-0-7366-3246-1(8), 3905-A) Books on Tape.
Through the author's brilliant depiction of three riot leaders, we see the horrors of public violence.

Barnaby Rudge, Pt. B. collector's unabr. ed. Charles Dickens. Read by David Case. 10 cass. (Running Time: 15 hrs.). 1996. 80.00 (978-0-7366-3247-8(6), 3905-B) Books on Tape.

Barnaby Rudge (A) abr. ed. Charles Dickens. (Running Time: 7 hrs. 30 mins.). 2009. audio compact disk 34.98 (978-962-634-908-3(5), Naxos AudioBooks) Naxos.

Barnaby Rudge (Part 1), Vol. 1. unabr. ed. Charles Dickens. Read by Flo Gibson. 10 cass. (Running Time: 15 hrs.). 1993. 29.95 (978-1-55685-283-1(5)) Audio Bk Con.
Barnaby, a kind, half-witted young man, joins the Gordon rioters to proudly carry their banner. He, his murderous father, the hangman Dennis & the mapcap Hugh are arrested & condemned to death. There are vivid & gruesome scenes of pillage, battles & executions, as well as myriad characters who are grim, romantic or humorous.

Barnaby Rudge (Part 2), Vol. 2. unabr. ed. Charles Dickens. Narrated by Flo Gibson. (Running Time: 10 hrs. 28 mins.). 1993. 26.95 (978-1-55685-794-2(2)) Audio Bk Con.

Barnaby Rudge (Parts 1 And 2) unabr. ed. Charles Dickens. Narrated by Flo Gibson. (Running Time: 25 hrs. 13 mins.). 1993. 53.95 (978-1-55685-795-9(0)) Audio Bk Con.

Barney Bush & Joy Harjo. unabr. ed. Read by Barney Bush & Joy Harjo. 1 cass. (Running Time: 29 min.). 1986. 10.00 New Letters.
Two Native American writers read their poetry.

Barney Kessel - Guitar Signature Licks. Barney Kessel. 2008. pap. bk. 22.99 (978-1-4234-3047-6(6), 1423430476) H Leonard.

Barney Malloon's Balloon: Audiocassette. (Sails Literacy Ser.). (gr. 2 up). 10.00 (978-0-7578-2666-5(0)) Rigby Educ.

Barney Read along Color Train. 1 cass. (Running Time: 8 mins.). (J). 2000. 6.95 Lyrick Studios.
Engineer Barney introduces colors & sounds via train songs.

Barney Rocks! unabr. ed. 1 CD. (J). 2000. audio compact disk 14.98 (978-1-57132-522-8(0), 9307) Lyrick Studios.

Barney Says "Play Safely" Read by Hinkler Books Staff. (J). 2004. bk. 9.99 (978-1-86515-998-0(0)) Pub: Hinkler AUS. Dist(s): Penton Overseas

Barney's Big Balloon. Read by Hinkler Books Staff. (J). 2004. bk. 9.99 (978-1-86515-997-3(2)) Pub: Hinkler AUS. Dist(s): Penton Overseas

Barney's Big Surprise. (Barney Ser.). (J). (ps-k). 1997. 9.98 (978-1-57064-215-9(X)) Lyrick Studios.

Barney's Favorites, Vols. 1 & 2. 2 cass. (Barney Ser.). (J). (ps-k). Boxed Set Gift Pack, incl. coloring/activity bk., stickers, & sing-along lyrics. (978-1-57150-008-3(1)) EMI Records.
Includes: Vol. 1 - Barney's debut musical album! The best-selling children's recording of 1993-1994; Vol. 2 - Barney's new musical journey filled with adventure & imagination! Featuring Baby Bop, BJ, & new songs from Imagination Island & Barney...Live! in New York.

Barney's Great Adventure. Perf. by Barney Staff. 1 cass., 1 CD. (Barney Ser.). (J). (ps-k). 7.98 (LY 9416); Jewel box. (LY 9418) NewSound.

Barney's Great Adventure. Perf. by Roberta Flack et al. 1 cass., 1 CD. (Barney Ser.). (J). (ps-k). 7.98 Soundtrack. (LY 9416); 5.58 Blisterpack, soundtrack. (LY97733); audio compact disk 11.98 CD Jewel box, soundtrack. (LY 9418) NewSound.

Barney's Great Day for Learning. 1 CD. (Barney Ser.). (J). (ps-k). 1999. audio compact disk 9.98 long blister. (978-1-57132-309-5(0), 9441) Lyrick Studios.

Barney's Outer Space Adventure. Read by Hinkler Books Staff. (J). 2004. bk. 9.99 (978-1-86515-996-6(4)) Pub: Hinkler AUS. Dist(s): Penton Overseas

Barney's Version. Contrib. by Mordecai Richler. 3 CDs. (Running Time: 3 hrs.). 2005. audio compact disk 29.95 (978-0-660-19044-0(3)) Pub: Canadian Broadcasting CAN. Dist(s): Georgetown Term
Relates the life of Barney panofsky-who smokes too many cigars, drinks too much whiskey; whose trashy TV company, Totally Useless Productions, has made him a small fortune; Whose three wives include a martyred feminist icon, a quintessential JCP (Jewish-Canadian Princess), and the incomparable Miriam, the perfect wife, lover, and mother - alas, now married to another man; who recalls with nostalgia and pain his young manhood in the paris of the early fifties, and his lifelong passion for wine, either did or didn't murder his best friend, Boogie, after discovering him in bed with The Second Mrs. Panofsky; whose satirical eye for the idiocies of today's Quebee separatists (as well as for every other kind of political correctness) manages to offend his entire acquaintanceship (and will soon be offending readers everywhere); and whose memory - though not his bile - is, in his sixty-seventh year, definitely slipping.

Barnum & Bailey Circus. (DD8855) Natl Recrd Co.

Barnyard Banter. (J). 2005. audio compact disk (978-1-933796-19-2(7)) PC Treasures.

Barnyard Boogie. 1999. (978-1-883772-75-8(3)) Flying Rhino.

Barnyard Fun & on the Air. Contrib. by Donut Man. (Running Time: 1 hr.). (Donut Man Ser.). (J). (gr. 3-7). 2004. 9.99 (978-5-559-71755-5(X)) Integrity Music.

Barnyard Pals. Fisher-Price Staff. 1 cass. 1998. bk. 7.99 (978-1-56826-780-7(0)) Rhino Enter.

Baron Munchausen Truly Tall Tales. unabr. ed. Rudolph E. Raspe. Read by Peter Ustinov. Ed. by Doris Orgel. 1 cass. (Running Time: 90 mins.). Incl. Baron Munchausen Truly Tall Tales: Astonishing Aspects of Life upon the Moon. (J). (SWC 1409); Baron Munchausen Truly Tall Tales: Climb to the Moon & Get My Hatchet Down. (J). (SWC 1409); Baron Munchausen Truly Tall Tales: Dangling from a Steeple Early in the Morning. (J). (SWC 1409); Baron Munchausen Truly Tall Tales: Frozen Airs: I Carry a Carriage. (J). (SWC 1409); Baron Munchausen Truly Tall Tales: How I Got My Superb Lithuanian Horse. (J). (SWC 1409); Baron Munchausen Truly Tall Tales: I Am Swallowed by a Vast Sea Monster. (J). (SWC 1409); Baron Munchausen Truly Tall Tales: I Continue My Flight with the Eagles. (J). (SWC 1409); Baron Munchausen Truly Tall Tales: I Drop in on Vulcan & Venus. (J). (SWC 1409); Baron Munchausen Truly Tall Tales: Me & the Cherry-Tree Stag. (J). (SWC 1409); Baron Munchausen Truly Tall Tales: More Facts of Life upon the Moon. (J). (SWC 1409); Baron Munchausen Truly Tall Tales: My Favorite Dog. (J). (SWC 1409); Baron Munchausen Truly Tall Tales: My Poor Fur Cloak Gone Mad. (J). (SWC 1409); Baron Munchausen Truly Tall Tales: My Superb Lithuanian's Laurels. (J). (SWC 1409); Baron Munchausen Truly Tall Tales: On Eagles' Wings Across the World. (J). (SWC 1409); Baron Munchausen Truly Tall Tales: The Airs Unfreeze. (J). (SWC 1409); Baron Munchausen Truly Tall Tales: Throw a Hatchet to the Moon. (J). (SWC 1409); Baron Munchausen Truly Tall Tales: Trees Flying Through the Sky & Other Amazing Results of a Storm. (J). (SWC 1409); Baron Munchausen Truly Tall Tales: What to Do If Caught Between a Lion & a Crocodile. (J). (SWC 1409); (J). 1984. 12.95 (978-0-694-50250-9(2), SWC 1409) HarperCollins Pubs.

Baron Munchausen Truly Tall Tales: Astonishing Aspects of Life upon the Moon see Baron Munchausen Truly Tall Tales

Baron Munchausen Truly Tall Tales: Climb to the Moon & Get My Hatchet Down see Baron Munchausen Truly Tall Tales

Baron Munchausen Truly Tall Tales: Dangling from a Steeple Early in the Morning see Baron Munchausen Truly Tall Tales

Baron Munchausen Truly Tall Tales: Frozen Airs: I Carry a Carriage see Baron Munchausen Truly Tall Tales

Baron Munchausen Truly Tall Tales: How I Got My Superb Lithuanian Horse see Baron Munchausen Truly Tall Tales

Baron Munchausen Truly Tall Tales: I Am Swallowed by a Vast Sea Monster see Baron Munchausen Truly Tall Tales

Baron Munchausen Truly Tall Tales: I Continue My Flight with the Eagles see Baron Munchausen Truly Tall Tales

Baron Munchausen Truly Tall Tales: I Drop in on Vulcan & Venus see Baron Munchausen Truly Tall Tales

Baron Munchausen Truly Tall Tales: Me & the Cherry-Tree Stag see Baron Munchausen Truly Tall Tales

Baron Munchausen Truly Tall Tales: More Facts of Life upon the Moon see Baron Munchausen Truly Tall Tales

Baron Munchausen Truly Tall Tales: My Favorite Dog see Baron Munchausen Truly Tall Tales

Baron Munchausen Truly Tall Tales: My Poor Fur Cloak Gone Mad see Baron Munchausen Truly Tall Tales

Baron Munchausen Truly Tall Tales: My Superb Lithuanian's Laurels see Baron Munchausen Truly Tall Tales

Baron Munchausen Truly Tall Tales: On Eagles' Wings Across the World see Baron Munchausen Truly Tall Tales

Baron Munchausen Truly Tall Tales: The Airs Unfreeze see Baron Munchausen Truly Tall Tales

Baron Munchausen Truly Tall Tales: Throw a Hatchet to the Moon see Baron Munchausen Truly Tall Tales

Baron Munchausen Truly Tall Tales: Trees Flying Through the Sky & Other Amazing Results of a Storm see Baron Munchausen Truly Tall Tales

Baron Munchausen Truly Tall Tales: What to Do If Caught Between a Lion & a Crocodile see Baron Munchausen Truly Tall Tales

***Baron of Coyote River.** unabr. ed. L. Ron Hubbard. Read by Martin Kove et al. Narrated by R. F. Daley. 2 CDs. (Running Time: 2 hrs.). (Stories from the Golden Age Ser.). (YA). (gr. 7 up). 2010. audio compact disk 9.95 (978-1-59212-377-3(5)) Gala Pr LLC.

Baron Son: Vade Mecum 7. unabr. rev. ed. D. Marques Patton et al. (Running Time: 6 hrs.). (ENG.). 2006. audio compact disk 29.98 (978-1-59659-073-1(4), GildAudio) Pub: Gildan Media. Dist(s): HachBkGrp

Baroque: The Greatest Hits. 1 cass. audio compact disk 10.98 CD. (978-1-57908-160-7(6), 3606) Platinm Enter.

Baroque & Classical Era. Abr. by iSummaries Staff. 2007. audio compact disk 79.95 (978-1-934488-27-0(5)) L England.

Baroque Era. Friedman-Fairfax and Sony Music Staff. 1 cass. (Life, Times, & Music Ser.). 1995. pap. bk. 15.98 (978-1-56799-000-3(2), Friedman-Fairfax) M Friedman Pub Grp Inc.

Baroque Music for Learning & Relaxation, Vol. 1. Composed by Ivan Barzakov et al. 1 cass. (Running Time: 60 min.). 9.95 Incl. written instructions. (OLC301) OptimaLearning.
Improves memory & comprehension; facilitates test taking & problem solving; enriches teaching or presentations of any kind; speeds up convalescence; aids stress reduction & therapy.

Baroque Music for Learning & Relaxation, Vol. 2. Composed by Ivan Barzakov et al. 1 cass. (Running Time: 60 min.). 9.95 Incl. written instructions. (OLC302) OptimaLearning.

Baroque Music to Empower Learning & Relaxation. Ivan Barzakov. Music by George Frideric Handel et al. 1 cass. (Running Time: 1 hr.). 1998. 9.95 (OLC303); audio compact disk 17.95 (CD-OL303) OptimaLearning.
The latest & most sophisticated sequences from Baroque composers. Empowers studying, exam preparation, teaching, training, story-telling, stress reduction, convalescing. Especially appropriate for slow movement exercises.

Barra Creek. Di Morrissey. Read by Kate Hood. (Running Time: 13 hrs. 15 mins.). 2009. 94.99 (978-1-74214-265-4(6), 9781742142654) Pub: Bolinda Pubng AUS. Dist(s): Bolinda Pub Inc

Barra Creek. unabr. ed. Di Morrissey. Read by Kate Hood. 11 CDs. (Running Time: 13 hrs. 15 mins.). 2005. audio compact disk 103.95 (978-1-74093-684-2(1)) Pub: Bolinda Pubng AUS. Dist(s): Bolinda Pub Inc

Barra Creek. unabr. ed. Di Morrissey. Read by Kate Hood. (Running Time: 13 hrs. 15 mins.). 2009. 43.95 (978-1-74214-112-1(9), 9781742141121) Pub: Bolinda Pubng AUS. Dist(s): Bolinda Pub Inc

Barrack-Room Ballads & Other Poems. Rudyard Kipling. Read by Christopher Casson et al. 1 cass. (Running Time: 47 min.). 10.95 (978-0-8045-1014-1(8), SAC 7015) Spoken Arts.
Kipling's stirring poetry which evokes the life of the British soldier in the Far East.

***Barracuda 945.** abr. ed. Patrick Robinson. Read by David Mccallum. (ENG.). 2004. (978-0-06-081848-7(4), Harper Audio); (978-0-06-081849-4(2), Harper Audio) HarperCollins Pubs.

Barrayar. unabr. ed. Lois McMaster Bujold. Read by Grover Gardner. (Running Time: 8.5 hrs. 0 mins.). (ENG.). 2009. 29.95 (978-1-4332-3201-5(4)); 54.95 (978-1-4332-3197-1(2)); audio compact disk 76.00 (978-1-4332-3198-8(0)) Blckstn Audio.

Barrayar. unabr. ed. Lois McMaster Bujold. (Vorkosigan Ser.). 1999. audio compact disk 29.95 (978-1-885585-15-8(2)) Readers Chair.
Political revolt endangers the lives of Barrayar's present regent & future emperor.

Barrayar. unabr. ed. Lois McMaster Bujold. Perf. by Carol Cowan & Michael Hanson. 9 cass. (Running Time: 11 hrs. 56 min.). (Vorkosigan Ser.). 1997. 54.00 Set. (978-1-885585-01-1(2)) Readers Chair.
Cordelia Naismith had married a simple retired soldier. She's now pregnant with their first child & her husband, Aral Vorkosigan, has been appointed to rule Barrayar. An attempt is made to kill him & they don't know who they can trust.

Barrel Fever & Other Stories. David Sedaris. 1999. (978-1-57042-746-6(1)) Hachet Audio.

Barrel Fever & Other Stories. abr. unabr. ed. David Sedaris. (Running Time: 3 hrs.). (ENG.). 2006. 14.98 (978-1-59483-668-8(X)) Pub: Hachet Audio. Dist(s): HachBkGrp

Barrel Fever & Other Stories. unabr. abr. ed. David Sedaris. Read by David Sedaris. Read by Amy Sedaris. 3 CDs. (Running Time: 3 hrs.). (ENG.). 2001. audio compact disk 24.98 (978-1-58621-221-6(4)) Pub: Hachet Audio. Dist(s): HachBkGrp

Barrel of Laughs, a Vale of Tears. Jules Feiffer. Narrated by Halley Feiffer. 3 pieces. (Running Time: 4 hrs.). (gr. 4 up). 28.00 (978-0-7887-5344-2(4)); audio compact disk 29.00 (978-1-4025-1961-1(3)) Recorded Bks.

Barrell Fever & Other Stories. unabr. ed. David Sedaris. (Running Time: 3 hrs.). (ENG.). 2009. 19.98 (978-1-60024-944-0(2)) Pub: Hachet Audio. Dist(s): HachBkGrp

Barren Ground. unabr. ed. Ellen Glasgow. Narrated by Flo Gibson. 10 cass. (Running Time: 15 hrs.). (YA). 2003. 44.95 (978-1-55685-672-3(5)) Audio Bk Con.
In southern Virginia, Dorinda, passionate & intelligent, struggles to find herself. After being jilted when pregnant & many tragic blows, she returns to devote her energies to the farm & to finding some meaning in her life.

Barrier. unabr. ed. Rex Ellingwood Beach. Read by David Sharp. 6 cass. (Running Time: 8 hrs. 48 min.). 1994. 39.95 (978-1-55686-492-6(2)) Books in Motion.
Men with shadowy pasts pick the Yukon wilderness as the perfect place to hide & at the same time, seek their fortune. But into this wilderness came Lieutenant Meade & his soldiers, with them came the laws of civilization.

Barrier Island. unabr. ed. John D. MacDonald. Read by Michael Prichard. 7 cass. (Running Time: 10 hrs.). 2001. 29.95 (978-0-7366-6782-1(2)) Books on Tape.
The story of a land scam in which the Federal government is the goat.

Barrier Island. unabr. collector's ed. John D. MacDonald. Read by Michael Prichard. 7 cass. (Running Time: 7 hrs.). 1986. 29.95 (978-0-7366-0954-8(7), 1898) Books on Tape.
A luxury cruiser comfortably offshore, float plane landing close by. What could be more idyllic... or misleading. When the two parties meet they exchange more than greetings - money & threats, for example - but part with the promise of favors. But promises are for breaking if Tucker Loomis changes his mind. Which he may do, given the size of his latest scheme: to get the federal government to buy the island from him at many times its real value.

Barrier Islands: "Atlantic's Last Frontier" Hosted by Nancy Pearlman. 1 cass. (Running Time: 28 min.). 10.00 (212) Educ Comm CA.

Barriers & Bridges. Emmet L. Robinson. Read by Emmet L. Robinson. 1 cass. (Running Time: 1 hr. 23 min.). 1994. 14.95 King Street.
How your attitude can made or break your business.

Barriers & Bridges: How Your Attitude Can Make or Break Your Business. Emmet L. Robinson. Read by Emmet L. Robinson. 1 cass. (Running Time: 1 hr. 23 min.). 1994. 14.95 King Street.

***Barriers to Belief.** Featuring Ravi Zacharias. 2009. audio compact disk 9.00 (978-1-61256-034-2(2)) Ravi Zach.

Barron's EZ-101 Study Keys: American History To 1877. unabr. ed. M. Ed. Robert D. Geise. (Running Time: 5 hrs. 0 mins.). (ENG.). 2009. 19.95 (978-1-4332-2361-7(9)); 34.95 (978-1-4332-2357-0(0)); audio compact disk 40.00 (978-1-4332-2358-7(9)) Blckstn Audio.

Barron's EZ-101 Study Keys: American History, 1877 to the Present. unabr. ed. Mary Jane Capozzoli Ingui. (Running Time: 6.5 hrs. 0 mins.). (ENG.). 2009. 29.95 (978-1-4332-2369-3(4)); 44.95 (978-1-4332-2365-5(1)); audio compact disk 60.00 (978-1-4332-2366-2(X)) Blckstn Audio.

Barron's EZ-101 Study Keys: Biology. unabr. ed. Eli C. Minkoff. (Running Time: 5.5 hrs. 0 mins.). (ENG.). 2009. 29.95 (978-1-4332-2353-2(8)); 34.95 (978-1-4332-2349-5(X)); audio compact disk 55.00 (978-1-4332-2350-1(3)) Blckstn Audio.

Barron's EZ-101 Study Keys: Psychology. unabr. ed. Don Baucum & Stuart Langston. 13 vols. (Running Time: 8 hrs. 30 mins.). 2005. 29.95 (978-0-7861-7959-6(7), ZM3530) Blckstn Audio.

Barron's EZ 101 Sudy Keys: Psychology. unabr. ed. Don Baucum & Stuart Langston. 6 cass. (Running Time: 8 hrs. 30 mins.). 2005. 29.95 (978-0-7861-3663-6(4), E3530); audio compact disk 29.95 (978-0-7861-7736-3(5), ZE3530) Blckstn Audio.

Barron's Regents Exams & Answers: French. 2000. 7.95 (978-0-8120-9244-8(9)) Barron.

Barron's Regents Exams & Answers: Spanish. 2000. 7.95 (978-0-8120-9245-5(7)) Barron.

***Barron's TOEIC Audio CD Pack.** 5th rev. ed. Lin Lougheed. (ENG.). 2010. audio compact disk 19.99 (978-1-4380-7020-9(9)) Barron.

Barrow-on-the-Hill see Sir John Betjeman Reading His Poetry

Barry Bear's Very Best Bedtime Story: Jonah - David & Goliath. 1 cass. (Barry Bear's Bedtime Stories Ser.). (J). bk. 10.98 (DMCSBK1027); 10.98 (978-1-56630-054-4(1), DMC1027) Brentwood Music.
Even if you have to be away, Barry Bear can still be there to tell your child a bedtime bible story & sing him to sleep! Allow Barry Bear to take your child on a make believe journey to a very real bible event.

Barry Bear's Very Best Bedtime Story: Noah - Daniel. 1 cass. (Barry Bear's Bedtime Stories Ser.). (J). bk. 10.98 (DMCSBK1025); 10.98 (978-1-56630-053-7(3), DMC1025) Brentwood Music.

Barry Bear's Very Best Christmas Stories. (J). (978-1-56630-015-5(0), DMC1047) Brentwood Music.
Captures the basic story in brief, easy-to-read phrases your child can learn & understand. You will see their understanding of the Scriptures expand as the stories bring exciting events of Christmas to life.

Barry Craig, Confidential Investigator: The Tough Guy & Murder by Error. unabr. ed. 1 cass. (Running Time: 1 hr.). 2001. 6.98 (2091) Radio Spirits.

Barry Goldwater: Conservatism see Buckley's Firing Line

Barry Lane's Recycled Fairy Tales. Short Stories. Barry Lane. 1 CD. 1999. audio compact disk 15.00 (978-1-931492-03-4(4)) Discover Writing.
Barry's revised fairly tales, lyrics included.Barry's revised fairy tale songs are a big hit with students and teachers. Play them in your class and use them along with literature as models for writing assignments on finding new points of view.

Barry Lopez, Vol. II. unabr. ed. Ed. by Jim McKinley. Prod. by Rebekah Presson. 1 cass. (Running Time: 29 min.). (New Letters on the Air Ser.). 1994. 10.00 (100194) New Letters.
The best-selling author of "Crow & Weasel" reads from his fable about two American Indian youths who go on a physical & spiritual adventure trip & talks about his own changing interests. Lopez has written primarily about landscape & its healing properties. he won the National Book Award for "Arctic Dreams," but now he says, he finds himself writing more & more about interrelationships between people.

Barry Lopez: Coyote Stories. unabr. ed. Barry Lopez. Read by Barry Lopez. 1 cass. (Running Time: 29 min.). 1986. 10.00 New Letters.
These "trickers" or coyote stories are hilarious, revealing the true nature of the coyote. Includes: "Giving Birth to Thunder," & "Sleeping with His Daughters: Coyote Builds North America".

Barry Lopez: Interview with Barry Lopez & Kay Bonetti. Interview. Barry Lopez. Interview with Barry Lopez. Interview with Kay Bonetti. 1 cass. (Running Time: 59 min.). 1985. 13.95 (978-1-55644-125-7(8), 5022) Am Audio Prose.
The difference between fine fiction & fine non-fiction prose are discussed.

Barry Lopez Interview. 20.97 (978-0-13-090432-4(5)) P-H.

Barry Louis Polisar's A Little Different: New Songs for Kids. Perf. by Barry Louis Polisar. 1 cass. (Running Time: 45 min.). (Rainbow Morning Music Picture Books Ser.). (J). 1999. 9.95 (978-0-938663-34-8(8), 5199 CASS) Pub: Rainbow Morn. Dist(s): IPG Chicago

Barry Louis Polisar's a Little Different: New Songs for Kids. Barry Louis Polisar. 1 CD. (Running Time: 0 hr. 45 mins. 0 sec.). (Rainbow Morning Music Picture Books Ser.). (ENG.). (J). 1999. audio compact disk 14.95 (978-0-938663-43-0(7), 5199 CD) Pub: Rainbow Morn. Dist(s): IPG Chicago

Barry Lyndon. William Makepeace Thackeray. 2007. 16.95 (978-1-60112-011-3(7)) Babblebooks.

Barry Lyndon. William Makepeace Thackeray. (Isis (CDs) Ser.). (J). 2005. audio compact disk 99.95 (978-0-7531-2399-7(1)) Pub: ISIS Lrg Prnt GBR. Dist(s): Ulverscroft US

Barry Lyndon. unabr. ed. William Makepeace Thackeray. Read by John Cormack. 12 cass. (Running Time: 13 hrs. 19 min.). (Isis Ser.). (J). 2003. 94.95 (978-0-7531-1618-0(9)) Pub: ISIS Lrg Prnt GBR. Dist(s): Ulverscroft US
The fictional autobiography of an adventurer and a rogue. Born into the petty Irish gentry, and outmaneuvered in his first love affair, a ruined Barry volunteers for the british army. After seeing service in Germany he deserts and pursues the career of a gambler in the dissolute clubs and courts of Europe. In a determined effort to enter fashionable society, he marries a titled heiress but only to find himself easily outwitted.

Barry Lyndon. unabr. collector's ed. William Makepeace Thackeray. Read by Dan Lazar. 8 cass. (Running Time: 12 hrs.). 1976. 64.00 (978-0-7366-0016-3(7), 1026) Books on Tape.
The life & adventures of a moral scoundrel but well-mannered gent.

Barry Reid: Creating Personal Privacy. (Running Time: 60 min.). (Cal State Univ., Long Beach). 1984. 9.00 (F170) Freeland Pr.
A presentation of "how to's" for liberty.

Barry Reid: How to Achieve a New World of Privacy. (Running Time: 60 min.). (Freeland II Ser.). 1984. 9.00 (FL6) Freeland Pr.
Computerized data files are a direct threat today & the author offers tactics to deal with that threat. Credit reports, insurance companies, etc., are all part of the "paper trip." Discusses alternate identities.

Barry Took's Pick of the News Quiz, Vol. 2. Barry Took. 2 cass. (Running Time: 2 hrs.). 1998. 16.85 (978-0-563-55772-2(9)) BBC WrldWd GBR.

Barry Trotter & the Unauthorized Parody. unabr. ed. Michael Gerber. Perf. by Christopher Cazenove. 4 cass. (Running Time: 7 hrs.). 2004. 25.00 (978-1-59007-234-9(0)) New Millenn Enter.
A spoof and tongue-in-cheek parody of the famous Hogwart's student, Harry Potter. How would Harry's story be different if he were a more outspoken boy of 11, instead of his obedient and subservient self. The author's realistic table, of more typical relationships between men and women, of a world turned upside down and upside down again, will delight readers of all ages. This fun and twisted story includes the half-giant, Halfwit, the ghostly Nearly Brainless Bill, and an order from Alpo Bumbelbore to stop the movie.

***Barrymore.** unabr. ed. William Luce. 2010. audio compact disk 9.99 (978-1-4418-9218-8(4)) Brilliance Audio.

Bartender's Guide for Women: How to Meet Men. Bryan Redfield. 1 cass. (Running Time: 90 min.). 1990. 19.95 (978-0-9626455-1-8(6)) Bryan Redfield.
Teaches single women how to approach, meet, & ask out men using class, style, & dignity, without resorting to games.

Bartered Bride. unabr. ed. Mary Jo Putney. Read by Michael Page. 8 cass. (Running Time: 11 hrs.). 2002. 32.95 (978-1-59086-094-6(2), 1590860942, BAU); 82.25 (978-1-59086-095-3(0), 1590860950, Unabridge Lib Edns) Brilliance Audio.
After building a fortune amid the splendor and dangers of the China seas, American adventurer and merchant prince Gavin Elliott is sailing for London, where he intends to establish himself in the society that forced his family to leave in disgrace when Gavin was only a child. But fate intervenes on an infamous island in the East Indies when he tries to save a European woman being sold at a slave auction. By the sultan's decree, the woman can only be freed if Gavin wins her by enduring an ancient tribal challenge that may cost him his life. Yet Gavin cannot refuse to help a woman who touches his heart and soul with her indomitable courage. Alexandra Warren ventured to Australia as a young bride eager for adventure. A dozen years later she is returning home as widow and mother when a pirate attack separates her from her beloved daughter and condemns Alex to a life of servitude. Then a miracle arrives in the form of a steely-eyed Yankee captain willing to risk everything to set her free. A shocking turn of events brings an unexpected alliance with her rescuer, and Gavin and Alex arrive in London as intimate strangers joined by too many painful secrets. Yet attraction and affection soon overcome the trial of their first meeting. Until the past reaches out to change Gavin's life - and threaten the passionate love he has found with his irresistible bartered bride.

Bartered Bride. unabr. ed. Mary Jo Putney. Read by Michael Page. (Running Time: 11 hrs.). 2004. 39.25 (978-1-59335-578-4(5), 1593355785, Brlnc Audio MP3 Lib) Brilliance Audio.

Bartered Bride. unabr. ed. Mary Jo Putney. Read by Michael Page. (Running Time: 11 hrs.). 2004. 39.25 (978-1-59710-036-6(6), 1597100366, BADLE); 24.95 (978-1-59710-037-3(4), 1597100374, BAD) Brilliance Audio.

Bartered Bride. unabr. ed. Mary Jo Putney. Read by Michael Page. (Running Time: 11 hrs.). 2004. 24.95 (978-1-59335-062-8(7), 1593350627) Soulmate Audio Bks.

Bartering - Stories about Bartering. unabr. ed. Alfreda C. Doyle. Read by Alfreda C. Doyle. 1 cass. (Running Time: 30 min.). (J). (gr. 3-6). 1996. ring bd. 14.95 (978-1-56820-155-9(9)) Story Time.
Stories that rhyme about bartering.

Bartering Story Rhymes. unabr. ed. Alfreda C. Doyle. Read by Alfreda C. Doyle. 1 cass. (Running Time: 35 min.). (Alfreda's Radio Ser.: Vol. 5). (J). (gr. 5-9). 1998. 16.95 (978-1-56820-309-6(8)) Story Time.
Stories that educate, entertain, inform & rhyme.

Barth, John. unabr. ed. John Barth. 1 cass. (Author Speaks Ser.). 1991. 14.95 J Norton Pubs.
Archival recordings of 20th-century authors.

Bartleby. unabr. ed. Herman Melville. Read by Denis Wetterwald.Tr. of Bartleby the Scrivener. (YA). 2007. 69.99 (978-2-35569-029-7(4)) Find a World.

Bartleby & Other Stories. Herman Melville. Read by Robert Williams. (Running Time: 2 hrs. 30 mins.). 2006. 20.95 (978-1-60083-682-4(8)) Iofy Corp.

Bartleby & Other Stories. unabr. ed. Herman Melville. Read by William Roberts. 2 CDs. (Running Time: 9540 sec.). 2006. audio compact disk 17.98 (978-962-634-401-9(6), Naxos AudioBooks) Naxos.

Bartleby, the Scrivener see Great American Short Stories

Bartleby, the Scrivener see Melville: Six Short Novels

Bartleby the Scrivener see Bartleby

Bartleby, the Scrivener. unabr. ed. Herman Melville. Read by Walter Covell. 1 cass. (Running Time: 75 min.). Dramatization. 1980. 7.95 (N-46) Jimcin Record.
A sad story about a strange man who would "prefer not to".

Barton, Para & Dyer Vol. 1: Johnny Whistletrigger, Civil War Songs from the Western Border. 1 cass., 1 CD. 9.98 (C-513); audio compact disk 14.98 CD. (CD-513) Folk-Legacy.

Barton, Para & Dyer Vol. 2: Rebel in the Woods, Civil War Songs from the Western Border. 1 cass., 1 CD. 9.98 (C-5130); audio compact disk 14.98 CD. (CD-5130) Folk-Legacy.

Barton, Para, the Patons, Trickett: 'Twas on a Night Like This. 1 cass., 1 CD. 9.98 (C-114); audio compact disk 14.98 CD. (CD-114) Folk-Legacy.
Unusual Christmas material.

Barton, Para, the Patons, Trickett, & Tuft: For All the Good People. 1 cass., 1 CD. 9.98 (C-121); audio compact disk 14.98 CD. (CD-121) Folk-Legacy.
A Golden Ring.

Baruch Spinoza: The Netherlands (1632-1677) Thomas H. Cook. Read by Charlton Heston. Ed. by George H. Smith & Wendy McElroy. 2 cass. (Running Time: 3 hrs.). 1995. 17.95 (978-0-938935-21-6(6), 10305) Knowledge Prod.
Spinoza took the unorthodox view that God, an eternal & infinite being, is identical with the world. We are, therefore ourselves merely parts of the Deity. Human fulfillment is possible, he believed, only by rejecting our finite, flawed selves & identifying with the eternal within us.

Baruch Spinoza: The Netherlands (1632-1677) abr. ed. Narrated by Charlton Heston. (Running Time: 7993 sec.). (Audio Classics: the Giants of Philosophy Ser.). 2006. audio compact disk 25.95 (978-0-7861-6939-9(7)) Pub: Blckstn Audio. Dist(s): NetLibrary CO

Baruch Spinoza: The Netherlands (1632-1677), Set. unabr. ed. Read by Charlton Heston. 2 cass. (Giants of Philosophy Ser.). 17.95 (K121) Blckstn Audio.
See how one of the world's most important philosophers created a complete system of thought, including his views on ethics, metaphysics, politics & aesthetics. Learn about his epistemology - how we know what we know.

Basant Bahar, Vol. 1. Music by Bismillah Khan & Kishori Amonkar. 1 cass. (Music of the Seasons Ser.). 1991. (A91021); audio compact disk (CD A91021) Multi-Cultural Bks.

Basant Bahar, Vol. 2. Music by Bhimsen Joshi & Ravi Shankar. 1 cass. (Music of the Seasons Ser.). 1991. (A91022); audio compact disk (CD A91022) Multi-Cultural Bks.

Basant Bahar, Vol. 3. Music by Shiv Kumar Sharma & Mallikarjun Mansur. 1 cass. (Music of the Seasons Ser.). 1991. (A91023); audio compact disk (CD A91023) Multi-Cultural Bks.

Basant Bahar, Vol. 4. Music by Pandit Jasraj & Hariprasad Chaurasia. 1 cass. (Music of the Seasons Ser.). 1991. (A91024); audio compact disk (CD A91024) Multi-Cultural Bks.

Baseball. 1 cass. (Running Time: 60 min.). 10.95 (SP5) Psych Res Inst.
Mental sports conditioning.

Baseball. Eldon Taylor. Read by Eldon Taylor. 1 cass. (Running Time: 62 min.). (Inner Talk Ser.). 16.95 incl. script. (978-0-940699-63-2(X), 5390C) Progress Aware Res.
Soundtrack - Musical Themes with underlying subliminal affirmations.

Baseball: A Celebration of the Short Story. Roger Angell et al. 3 CDs. (Running Time: 9900 sec.). (Selected Shorts Ser.). (ENG.). 2006. audio compact disk 28.00 (978-0-9719218-4-9(9)) Pub: Symphony Space. Dist(s): IPG Chicago
Acclaimed actors from stage and screen perform tales from the baseball diamond in this new three-CD collection of stories from Selected Shorts. Both classic and contemporary works are featured, including a heartwarming piece on some fan habits during a players' strike, by W.P. Kinsella, and a sidesplitting account from T. Coraghessan Boyle of the longest game ever. Many of the readings were recorded during a historic broadcast of the show hosted by the late, beloved baseball commissioner A. Bartlett Giamatti. From the first pitch to the final out, these short stories are a lively listening experience.

***Baseball: An Illustrated History.** abr. ed. Geoffrey C. Ward & Ken Burns. Read by Ken Burns. (ENG.). 2010. audio compact disk 35.00 (978-0-307-87692-8(6), Random AudioBks) Pub: Random Audio Pubg. Dist(s): Random

Baseball: Babbling Brook. Eldon Taylor. 1 cass. 16.95 (978-1-55978-504-4(7), 5390F) Progress Aware Res.

Baseball: Catching. Barrie Konicov. 1 cass. 11.98 (007) Potentials.
This program is designed to enhance your concentration & improve your fielding & batting ability. Covers catching, fielding, batting & running, & specializes in one area.

Baseball: Hitting. Barrie Konicov. 1 cass. 11.98 (978-0-87082-414-2(7), 008) Potentials.
This program is designed to enhance your concentration & improve your fielding & batting ability. Covers catching, fielding, batting & running, & specializes in one area.

Baseball: Pitching. Barrie Konicov. 1 cass. 11.98 (978-0-87082-415-9(5), 009) Potentials.

Baseball: Rhythms. Eldon Taylor. Read by Eldon Taylor. Ed. by Leslie Brice. 1 cass. (Running Time: 1 hr.). 1992. 16.95 (978-1-56705-242-8(8)) Gateways Inst.
Self improvement.

Baseball: Stream. Eldon Taylor. Read by Eldon Taylor. Ed. by Leslie Brice. 1 cass. (Running Time: 1 hr.). 1992. 16.95 (978-1-56705-243-5(6)) Gateways Inst.

Baseball Set: An Illustrated History. abr. ed. Geoffrey C. Ward & Ken Burns. Read by Ken Burns. 4 cass. (Running Time: 4 hrs.). 1999. (391973, Random AudioBks) Random Audio Pubg.
During eight months of the year, it is played professionally every day; all year round, amateurs play it, watch it & dream about it. The sport of baseball produces remarkable Americans: it seizes hold of ordinary people & shapes them into something we must regard with awe.

Baseball & Billions. abr. ed. Andrew Zimbalist. Read by John Storey. 2 cass. (Running Time: 3 hrs.). Dramatization. bk. 15.95 set. (978-1-56703-024-2(6)) High-Top Sports.

Baseball Anecdotes. Daniel Okrent & Steve Wulf. 2 cass. (Running Time: 90 min. per cass.). 1990. 15.95 HarperCollins Pubs.

***Baseball Codes: Beanballs, Sign Stealing, & Bench-Clearing Brawls: the Unwritten Rules of America's Pastime.** unabr. ed. Jason Turbow. (Running Time: 10 hrs.). 2010. audio compact disk 29.95 (978-1-4417-6301-3(5)) Blckstn Audio.

***Baseball Codes: Beanballs, Sign Stealing, & Bench-Clearing Brawls: the Unwritten Rules of America's Pastime.** unabr. ed. Jason Turbow. Read by Michael Kramer. (Running Time: 10 hrs.). 2010. 29.95 (978-1-4417-6302-0(3)); 59.95 (978-1-4417-6299-3(X)); audio compact disk 90.00 (978-1-4417-6300-6(7)) Blckstn Audio.

***Baseball Great.** unabr. ed. Tim Green. Read by Tim Green. (ENG.). 2009. (978-0-06-180544-8(0)); (978-0-06-180545-5(9)) HarperCollins Pubs.

Baseball Great. unabr. ed. Tim Green. Read by Tim Green. (J). 2009. audio compact disk 22.99 (978-0-06-171452-8(6), HarperChildAud) HarperCollins Pubs.

Baseball in April & Other Stories. Gary Soto. Read by Stephanie Diaz & Miguel Gongora. (Running Time: 9000 sec.). (J). (gr. 4-7). 2007. audio compact disk 29.95 (978-0-9761932-1-0(3)) Audio Bkshelf.

Baseball in April & Other Stories. unabr. ed. Short Stories. Gary Soto. Read by Miguel Gongora & Stephanie Diaz. 2 cass. (Running Time: 2 hrs. 45 min.). (J). (gr. 5 up). 2000. 18.95 (978-1-883332-41-9(9)) Audio Bkshelf.
In this unique collection of stories, featuring Latino teens, daily life reveals big themes.

Baseball in '41. unabr. ed. Robert W. Creamer. Read by Tom Parker. 6 cass. (Running Time: 11 hrs. 30 mins.). 1999. 44.95 (978-0-7861-1161-9(5), 1929) Blckstn Audio.
It was the year that Joe DiMaggio set his 56 game hitting streak, that Ted Williams batted .406, that the Dodgers & the Yankees battled each other in a classic World Series & that America went to war. In this look at what he calls "the best baseball season ever," the author interwines all these epochal baseball happenings with an informal history of a pivotal period in American life, as well as with his own memories of what it was like to be eighteen & a baseball fan when a looming war & the game he loved vied for his attention.

Baseball In 41: A Celebration of the Best Baseball Season Ever - in the Year America Went to War. unabr. ed. Robert W. Creamer. (Running Time: 32400 sec.). 2007. audio compact disk 29.95 (978-0-7861-5974-1(X)); audio compact disk 63.00 (978-0-7861-5973-4(1)) Blckstn Audio.

Baseball Pals. unabr. ed. Matt Christopher. Narrated by Norman Dietz. 2 pieces. (Running Time: 2 hrs.). (gr. 2 up). 1995. 19.00 (978-0-7887-0211-2(4), 94436E7) Recorded Bks.
Jimmie has been elected Captain of the baseball team & wants to make himself the pitcher. Even though his teammates think that maybe he's not the best man for the job.

Baseball Saved Us. Ken Mochizuki. Illus. by Dom Lee. 11 vols. (Picture Book Readalong Ser.). bk. 28.95 (978-1-59112-916-5(8)); pap. bk. 39.95 (978-1-59112-917-2(6)); 9.95 (978-1-59112-454-2(9)); audio compact disk 12.95 (978-1-59112-914-1(1)) Live Oak Media.

Baseball Saved Us. Ken Mochizuki. 11 vols. (Picture Book Readalong Ser.). (J). 2005. pap. bk. 16.95 (978-1-59112-455-9(7)); pap. bk. 18.95 (978-1-59112-915-8(X)) Pub: Live Oak Media. Dist(s): AudioGO

Baseball Saved Us. unabr. ed. Ken Mochizuki. 1 cass. (Running Time: 8 min.). (J). (gr. k-4). 1994. bk. 25.90 (978-0-8045-6763-3(8), 6763) Spoken Arts.
Parents Choice Award.

Baseball with Rod Carew. Rod Carew. 4 cass. 39.95 incl. video, training guide. (1318) SyberVision.

Baseball's Greatest Hits, Vol. 1. 1 cass. (Running Time: 1 hr. 30 mins.). 2001. 7.98 (R4 70710); audio compact disk 11.98 (R2 70710) Rhino Enter.

Based upon Availability. abr. ed. Alix Strauss. Read by Therese Plummer. 2010. audio compact disk 29.99 (978-0-06-191218-4(2), Harper Audio) HarperCollins Pubs.

***Based upon Availability.** abr. ed. Alix Strauss. Read by Therese Plummer. (ENG.). 2010. (978-0-06-199302-2(6), Harper Audio) HarperCollins Pubs.

***Based upon Availability: A Novel.** abr. ed. Alix Strauss. Read by Therese Plummer. (ENG.). 2010. (978-0-06-199301-5(8), Harper Audio) HarperCollins Pubs.

Baseless Fabric of This Vision. 1 cass. (Running Time: 29 min.). 12.00 (L340) MEA A Watts Cass.

Basement. unabr. ed. Bari Wood. Read by Frances Cassidy. 8 cass. (Running Time: 12 hrs.). 1995. 64.00 (978-0-7366-3164-8(X), 3834) Books on Tape.
The ghost of a woman hanged for witchcraft haunts a housewife's basement. Can the housewife gain control of the supernatural?.

Bashkir: An Introduction to the Bashkir Gaited Horse. Karen Jean Matsko Hood. 2003. audio compact disk 29.95 (978-1-59210-164-1(X)) Whsprng Pine.

Basic. Composed by Peter F. Marotto. 1 CD. (Running Time: 11mins.). 2003. audio compact disk 20.00 (978-0-9745663-1-3(4), CD1) Allegory Mediation.

Basic Accounting for Lawyers. Contrib. by Arthur R. Pinto. (Running Time: 4 hrs.). 1983. 70.00 incl. program handbk. NJ Inst CLE.
Designed to give the listener a good working knowledge of accounting principles. Digesting accounting terminology, understanding financial statements & recognizing services that are available from accounting firms are all reviewed.

Basic, Advanced Systematic Substitution Training, Set-AS. Russell E. Mason. 1975. pap. bk. 35.00 (978-0-89533-017-8(2)) F I Comm.

Basic Affirmations for Total, Unconditional Acceptance. unabr. ed. Lilburn S. Barksdale. Read by Mark Denis. 1 cass. (Running Time: 28 min.). 1977. 9.95 (978-0-918588-28-9(6), 122) NCADD.
Accepting yourself & others totally & unconditionally is the key to loving relationships. This cassette shows how aligning your awareness with the truth about the human condition makes this acceptance possible.

Basic Afrikaans. unabr. ed. Conversa-Phone Institute Staff. 1 cass. (Running Time: 52 min.). (Round the World Basic Language Program Ser.). 1991. 9.95 (978-1-56752-030-9(8)) Conversa-phone.
Twenty lessons in basic Afrikaans with instruction manual.

Basic American Government, Pt. 1. unabr. ed. Clarence B. Carson. Read by Mary Woods. 11 cass. (Running Time: 16 hrs.). 1994. 76.95 (978-0-7861-0796-4(0), 1529A) Blckstn Audio.
This book gives an account of the general government as established by the Constitution of the state governments which preceded or came after it & their constitutions. More, it details the ancient & modern foundations, scriptural & secular, on which these constitutions & governments rested. The founders of the United States built on a great foundation & the story of that is told in these tapes. The story is told, too, of how the Constitution of 1787 became venerated & accepted as a Higher Law in the 19th century. The account ends with a sobering description of the massive departures from the Constitution in the 20th century, on the way to constructing a leviathan, a government which is now out of control.

Basic American Government, Pt. 2. unabr. ed. Clarence B. Carson. Read by Mary Woods. 8 cass. (Running Time: 11 hrs. 30 mins.). 1994. 56.95 (978-0-7861-0847-3(9), 1529B) Blckstn Audio.

Basic & Self Hypnosis Course. 10 CDs. 2003. audio compact disk (978-1-932163-40-7(9)) Infinity Inst.

Basic & Self Hypnosis Course on Cassette. 1995. (978-1-932163-27-8(1)) Infinity Inst.

Basic Arabic. unabr. ed. Conversa-Phone Institute Staff. 1 cass. (Running Time: 1 hr. 01 min.). (Round the World Basic Language Program). (ARA.). 1991. 9.95 incl. instruction manual. (978-1-56752-011-8(1)) Conversa-phone.
Twenty lessons in basic Arabic.

Basic Astrology You Can Learn. Gladys M. Hall. 1 cass. 8.95 (531) Am Fed Astrologers.
Live happy & successful - easy to learn.

Basic Astrology 1. Sara A. Keller. 1 cass. 8.95 (619) Am Fed Astrologers.
An AFA Convention workshop tape.

Basic Astrology 2. Sara A. Keller. 1 cass. (Running Time: 90 min.). 1988. 8.95 (620) Am Fed Astrologers.

Basic Astrology 3. Sara A. Keller. 1 cass. (Running Time: 90 min.). 1988. 8.95 (621) Am Fed Astrologers.

Basic Black: The Essential Guide for Getting Ahead at Work (and in Life) abr. ed. Cathie Black. Read by Cathie Black. (Running Time: 18000 sec.). (ENG.). 2007. audio compact disk 27.95 (978-0-7393-5452-0(3), Random AudioBks) Pub: Random Audio Pubg. Dist(s): Random

Basic Blues Guitar Method. Drew Giorgi. (ENG.). 2001. audio compact disk 10.00 (978-0-7390-1137-9(5)) Alfred Pub.

Basic Blues Guitar Method. David Hamburger. (ENG.). 2001. audio compact disk 10.00 (978-0-7390-1140-9(5)) Alfred Pub.

Basic Blues Guitar Method. David Hamburger & M. Smith. (ENG.). 2001. audio compact disk 10.00 (978-0-7390-1143-0(X)) Alfred Pub.

Basic Blues Guitar Method. M. Smith. (ENG.). 2001. audio compact disk 10.00 (978-0-7390-1146-1(4)) Alfred Pub.

Basic Brain: Program from the Award Winning Public Radio Series. Interview. Hosted by Fred Goodwin. 1 CD. (Running Time: 1 Hour). 2000. audio compact disk 21.95 (978-1-932479-25-6(2), LCM 127) Lichtenstein Creat.
If you don't know your brain stem from your cerebellum, this is the show for you. This clear and understandable primer on the structure and workings of the human brain features performances by the Brainiacs improvisational comedy troupe.Other guests include: Dr. Norbert Myslinski, University of Maryland professor and director of the International Brain Bee; Otilia Husu, 2000 Brain Bee winner; Dr. John Byrne of the University of Texas; Dr. Lawrence Katz of Duke University and author of "Keep Your Brain Alive: 83 Neurobic Exercises;" and Dr. Charles Jennings, editor of the scientific journal Nature Neuroscience.

Basic Bulgarian. unabr. ed. Conversa-Phone Institute Staff. 1 cass. (Running Time: 52 min.). (Round the World Basic Language Program Ser.). 1991. 9.95 (978-1-56752-031-6(6)) Conversa-phone.
Twenty lessons in basic Bulgarian with instruction manual.

Basic Bulgarian, Vol. II. Foreign Service Institute Staff. 23 cass. (Running Time: 16 hrs.). 2001. pap. bk. 135.00 (AFL500) J Norton Pubs.
Assumes no previous knowledge of Bulgarian or any other Slavic language. The Cyrillic alphabet is taught through side-by-side presentation of English translations & phonetics.

Basic Business Japanese. Nancy B. Young. 1 cass. 1999. 40.00 (978-4-7700-2326-1(X)) Kodansha.

Basic Cantonese. 185.00 (1976, Lrn Inc) Oasis Audio.
Presents methods in learning a second language.

Basic Cantonese, Vol. I. unabr. ed. Foreign Service Institute Staff. 8 cass. (Running Time: 11 hrs.). (CHI.). pap. bk. 185.00 (978-0-88432-020-3(0), AFC131) J Norton Pubs.
Uses the basic grammatical structures of the language & a vocabulary of approximately 950 words. Learn to speak standard Cantonese fluently & grammatically, with acceptable pronunciation, within the scope of topics of daily life. Texts incorporate a modification of the Huang-Kok Yale romanization for all basic grammar structures & vocabulary. Designed to teach only the spoken language.

Basic Cantonese, Vol. II. unabr. ed. Foreign Service Institute Staff. 15 cass. (Running Time: 11 hrs.). (CHI.). 1970. pap. bk. 265.00 (978-0-88432-033-3(2), AFC140) J Norton Pubs.

Basic Cantonese Chinese. unabr. ed. Conversa-Phone Institute Staff. 2 cass. (Running Time: 1 hr. 20 min.). (Round the World Basic Language Program Ser.). 1991. 15.95 Set. (978-1-56752-065-1(0), COC-5161) Conversa-phone.
20 lessons in basic Cantonese Chinese with instruction manual.

Basic Cantonese Chinese: Learn to Speak & Understand Cantonese with Pimsleur Language Programs. unabr. ed. Pimsleur Staff & Pimsleur. 5 CDs. (Running Time: 50 hrs. 0 mins. 0 sec.). (Basic Ser.). (CHI & ENG.). 2006. audio compact disk 24.95 (978-0-7435-5080-2(3), Pimsleur) Pub: S&S Audio. Dist(s): S and S Inc

Basic Catholic Morality One. Fr. Hardon. 8 cass. 32.00 Set. (92M) IRL Chicago.

Basic Catholic Morality Two. Fr. Hardon. 10 cass. 40.00 Set. (93V) IRL Chicago.

Basic Chemical Kinetics. Edward L. King. 8 cass. (Running Time: 9 hrs.). 620.00 incl. 500 pp. manual. (978-0-8412-1257-2(0), 91); 58.00 manual. (978-0-8412-1258-9(9)) Am Chemical.
Shows you how you can get a deeper understanding of the kinetics of chemical changes in bulk samples from a knowledge of the dynamics of individual molecular acts.

Basic Chemistry: Computerized Test Bank. Timberlake. audio compact disk 49.97 (978-0-8053-3991-8(4)) Addson-Wesley Educ.

Basic Chinese Sentences. Wang Hailong. 2 CDs. (Series of Practical Chinese Ser.). (CHI & ENG.). 2003. audio compact disk 9.95 (978-7-88703-182-2(6), BACHSC) Pub: China Lang Univ CHN. Dist(s): China Bks

*__Basic Christianity.__ unabr. ed. John Stott. Narrated by Grover Gardner. (ENG.). 2006. 12.98 (978-1-59644-261-0(1), Hovel Audio) christianaud.

Basic Christianity. unabr. ed. John R. W. Stott. 4 CDs. (Running Time: 4 hrs. 45 mins. 0 sec.). (ENG.). 2006. audio compact disk 21.98 (978-1-59644-260-3(3), Hovel Audio) christianaud.

Basic Chromatic Harmonica. Phil Duncan. 2000. pap. bk. 5.95 (978-0-7866-5080-4(X), 98586BCD) Mel Bay.

Basic Church History Series. unabr. ed. Stephen Mansfield. 6 cass. (Running Time: 9 hrs.). 2000. 30.00 (SM01-000) Morning NC.
A great storyteller, Stephen does a masterful job of making church history come to life. This is an overview starting from Pentecost & continuing through the 20th century.

Basic Civil Practice: The Trial. (Running Time: 5 hrs. 30 min.). 1994. 92.00 Incl. 167p. coursebk. (20284) NYS Bar.
Focuses on the nuts & bolts of successfully handling a civil case during the actual trial. The panelists use a "hands on" approach in describing step-by-step how to successfully handle your case at trial.

Basic Collection, Set. unabr. ed. Margery Allingham et al. 92 cass. 603.30 AudioGO.
Includes: "The China Governess" by Margery Allingham, "The Relic" by Evelyn Anthony, "N or M?" by Agatha Christie, "The Whip" by Catherine Cookson, "Riddle of the Third Mile" by Colin Dexter, "Risk" by Dick Francis, "Envious Casca" by Georgette Heyer, "Wait for What Will Come" by Barbara Michaels, "Sanctuary Sparrow" by Ellis Peters, "Crescent City" by Belva Plain, "Going Wrong" by Ruth Rendell, "Maigret & the Pickpocket" by Georges Simenon.

Basic College Mathematics: With Early Integers. Elayn Martin-Gay. (Martin-Gay Developmental Math Ser.). 2006. audio compact disk 100.00 (978-0-13-235380-9(6)) Pearson Educ CAN CAN.

Basic College Mathematics with Early Integers. Elayn Martin-Gay. (Math XL Ser.). 2006. audio compact disk 26.67 (978-0-13-199846-9(3)) Pearson Educ CAN CAN.

Basic Concepts for Beginning Actors. George M. Churley. 1 cass. 1977. 9.95 (C76) Meriwether Pub.
Actor, director, producer, George Churley believes that the first basic of acting is learning how to control the body's creative energy. Control must be focused on what the actor shows as well as what he says. He explains & demonstrates the methods of acquiring this control. He touches on timing & movement, beats, intent, thought & listening, focus, selective simplicity & essence of believability. Also included are opportunities for participation in games & exercises with a rehearsal script.

Basic Concepts in the Law of Evidence. abr. ed. 15 cass. (Running Time: 12 hrs. 8 min.). 1975. 110.00 (EYXOS) Natl Inst Trial Ad.

Basic Consciousness Raising Meditation. Scripts. Text by Ralph Genter. Prod. by Pleiadian Connection. Voice by George Harris. 1 CD. (Running Time: 43 minutes). 2003. audio compact disk 12.00 (978-0-9640829-2-2(6)) Pub: Pleiadian Connect. Dist(s): New Leaf Dist
This Basic Consciousness Raising Meditation will assist you in clearing all disharmony from your seven major Astral energy centers, and in raising your consciousness through the Astral Plane, into the spiritual realms.

*__Basic Course: How to Communicate with Animals.__ Penelope Smith. (ENG.). 2004. audio compact disk 55.00 (978-0-936552-20-0(4)) Pub: AnimaMundi. Dist(s): Bk Clearing Hse

Basic Course in Arabic Bks. 1-3: Al-Kitaba Assasi. S. Badawi. 11 cass. (Running Time: 990 min.). (Kitab al Assasi Ser.). (ARA.). 1994. 160.00 (978-0-86685-641-6(2)) Intl Bk Ctr.

Basic Creole (Haitian) unabr. ed. Brewster W. Moseley. 1 cass. (Running Time: 30 min.). 1985. 39.95 incl. manual & Creole - English/English - Creole dictionary. B W Moseley.
Dictionary by A. Valdman.

Basic Creole (Haitian) unabr. ed. Brewster W. Moseley. Read by Ramy Louis. Suppl. by A. Valdman. 1 cass. (Running Time: 30 min.). 1985. 39.95 (978-0-9674247-0-5(4)) Moseley Enter Inc.
Introduction to Haitian Creole language.

Basic Critical Care: A Training Program for the Development of Critical Care Nurses with 75 Continuing Education Contact Credit Hours. Daniel Farb et al. 2004. audio compact disk 89.95 (978-1-59491-119-4(3)) Pub: UnivofHealth. Dist(s): AtlasBooks

Basic Critical Care 10 Users. Daniel Farb et al. 2005. audio compact disk 749.95 (978-1-59491-201-6(7)) Pub: UnivofHealth. Dist(s): AtlasBooks

Basic Critical Care 5 Users. Daniel Farb et al. 2005. audio compact disk 399.95 (978-1-59491-200-9(9)) Pub: UnivofHealth. Dist(s): AtlasBooks

Basic Czech. unabr. ed. Conversa-Phone Institute Staff. 1 cass. (Running Time: 52 min.). (Round the World Basic Language Program). (CZE.). 1991. 9.95 incl. instruction manual. (978-1-56752-017-0(0)) Conversa-phone.
Twenty lessons in basic Czech.

Basic Danish. unabr. ed. Conversa-Phone Institute Staff. 2 cass. (Running Time: 1 hr. 20 min.). (Round the World Basic Language Program Ser.). 1991. 15.95 Set. (978-1-56752-058-3(8), COC-5128) Conversa-phone.
20 lessons in basic Danish with instruction manual.

Basic Dictionary. unabr. ed. 10 cass. (Running Time: 15 hrs.). 2003. 45.95 (OX5); audio compact disk 50.95 (4182) New Readers.
Essential language organized around 12 survival topics. Offers pronunciation and extended vocabulary practice.

Basic Documents & Case Law. International Criminal Tribunal for Rwanda. (ENG & FRE.). 2009. audio compact disk 15.00 (978-92-1-056716-9(1)); audio compact disk 15.00 (978-92-1-056725-1(0)) Untd Nat Pubns.

Basic Dutch. unabr. ed. Conversa-Phone Institute Staff. 2 cass. (Running Time: 1 hr. 20 min.). (Round the World Basic Language Program Ser.). 1991. 15.95 Set. (978-1-56752-062-0(6), COC-5146) Conversa-phone.
20 lessons in basic Dutch with instruction manual.

Basic Economics. unabr. ed. Clarence B. Carson. Read by Christopher Hurt. 12 cass. (Running Time: 17 hrs. 30 mins.). 1989. 83.95 (978-0-7861-0099-6(0), 1092) Blckstn Audio.
Provides all you ever wanted to know but were afraid to ask about money, the market, prices, monopoly, competition, land, labor, capital, entrepreneurs, the federal reserve & the distribution of wealth.

Basic Economics: A Citizen's Guide to the Ecomomy. unabr. ed. Thomas Sowell. Read by Brian Emerson. (Running Time: 66600 sec.). 2006. 95.95 (978-0-7861-4671-0(0)); audio compact disk 44.95 (978-0-7861-7461-4(7)); audio compact disk 120.00 (978-0-7861-6735-7(1)) Blckstn Audio.

*__Basic Economics: A Common Sense Guide to the Economy.__ 4th unabr. ed. Thomas Sowell. (Running Time: 21 hrs. NaN mins.). (ENG.). 2010. audio compact disk 39.95 (978-1-4417-7864-2(0)) Blckstn Audio.

Basic Economics: Thinking Beyond Stage One. unabr. ed. Thomas Sowell. Read by Brian Emerson. 12 cass. (Running Time: 66600 sec.). 2006. 29.95 (978-0-7861-4622-2(2)); audio compact disk 29.95 (978-0-7861-6879-8(X)) Blckstn Audio.

*__Basic Economics, Fourth Edition: A Common Sense Guide to the Economy.__ unabr. ed. Thomas Sowell. (Running Time: 21 hrs. NaN mins.). (ENG.). 2010. 44.95 (978-1-4417-7865-9(9)) Blckstn Audio.

*__Basic Economics, Fourth Edition: A Common Sense Guide to the Economy.__ unabr. ed. Thomas Sowell. Read by To be Announced. (Running Time: 21 hrs. NaN mins.). (ENG.). 2010. 105.95 (978-1-4417-7862-8(4)); audio compact disk 123.00 (978-1-4417-7863-5(2)) Blckstn Audio.

Basic Electronics: Syllabus. Norman H. Crowhurst. (J). 1974. bk. 149.75 (978-0-89420-126-4(3)) Natl Book.

Basic, Elementary Systematic Substitution Training, Set-ES. Russell E. Mason. 1973. pap. bk. 35.00 (978-0-89533-015-4(6)) F I Comm.

Basic Elements of Pruning Audio Book on CD. Read by Nick Federoff. 2005. audio compact disk 19.95 (978-0-9771049-1-8(5)) Environ Med.

Basic Elements of Pruning Audio Book on CD. 2nd ed. 2006. audio compact disk 69.95 (978-0-9771049-4-9(X)) Environ Med.

Basic Employment & Labor Law - In Depth, July 7-11, 1997. 19 cass. (Running Time: 27 hrs. 50 min.). 1997. 247.50 Incl. course materials. (MC29) Am Law Inst.
Designed to provide answers & practical approaches to the questions clients ask. Taught by experienced practitioners, provides practical approaches & solutions to common problems. By the end of the program, even novices can recognize problems that arise in the employment context, suggest solutions & draft the necessary documents.

Basic English for Computing. rev. ed. Eric Glendinning & John McEwan. 2003. 22.75 (978-0-19-457472-3(5)) OUP.

Basic English for French. unabr. ed. Conversa-Phone Institute Staff. 1 cass. (Running Time: 52 min.). (Round the World Basic Language Program Ser.). 1991. 9.95 (978-1-56752-039-2(1)) Conversa-phone.
Twenty lessons in basic English for French with instruction manual.

Basic English for German. unabr. ed. Conversa-Phone Institute Staff. 1 cass. (Running Time: 52 min.). (Round the World Basic Language Program Ser.). 1991. 9.95 (978-1-56752-040-8(5)) Conversa-phone.

Basic English for Spanish. unabr. ed. Conversa-Phone Institute Staff. 1 cass. (Running Time: 52 min.). (Round the World Basic Language Program Ser.). 1991. 9.95 (978-1-56752-038-5(3)) Conversa-phone.
Twenty lessons in basic English for Spanish with instruction manual.

Basic English for Spanish Speakers, Set. unabr. ed. Conversa-Phone Institute Staff. 2 cass. (Running Time: 2 hrs. 30 min.). (Modern Method Language Ser.). 1994. 23.95 (978-1-56752-049-1(9)) Conversa-phone.
Full study language course for Spanish speakers to learn American English. Includes 96 page manual with hundreds of pictures for teaching aid as well as both English & Spanish. Also Collins Gem Ingles Spanish pocket dictionary.

Basic Estate & Gift Taxation & Planning: Twenty-First Annual ALI-ABA Course of Study Includes Effects of 1997 Tax Legislation. 12 cass. (Running Time: 18 hrs.). 1998. 345.00 Incl. course materials. (MC70) Am Law Inst.
Sets forth the law & planning as conceived in the Tax Reform Act of 1976 & modified by subsequent legislation, including the Taxpayer Relief Act of 1997. It is intended for lawyers with minimal background in this subject, as well as for those who feel the need to relearn the law from the ground up.

Basic Estonian. unabr. ed. Felix J. Oinas. 32 cass. (Running Time: 30 hrs.). 1993. pap. bk. 295.00 (978-0-88432-460-7(5), AFET10) J Norton Pubs.
Divided into 30 lesson units which include 5 lessons of review. Each unit includes basic sentences, exercises & conversations. An extensive section on pronunciation is followed by pronunciation exercises. The end-of-text glossary is Estonian-English.

Basic Everyday Spelling Workbook: 2 CDs. Elaine Kirn. 2005. audio compact disk 25.00 (978-1-891077-55-5(4)) Authors Editors.

Basic Exercises for Keeping Fit. unabr. ed. William Orban. 1 cass. 10.95 (AF1539) J Norton Pubs.
Developed by Dr. William Orban & based on his exercise plan for the Royal Canadian Air Force, the program offers four sets of 10-minute graduated exercises. Keep fit & physically alert & keep your youthful figure by regularly performing these exercises.

Basic Exercises for Keeping Fit (audio CD) William Orban. (ENG.). 2007. audio compact disk 12.95 (978-1-57970-482-7(4), Audio-For) J Norton Pubs.

Basic Fiddlers Philharmonic: Old-Time Fiddle Tunes. Andrew H. Dabczynski & Bob Phillips. Ed. by Alfred Publishing. (ENG.). 2007. audio compact disk 10.95 (978-0-7390-4865-8(1)) Alfred Pub.

Basic Fiddlers Philharmonic Celtic Fiddle Tunes. Composed by Bob Phillips & Andrew H. Dabczynski. (ENG.). 2009. audio compact disk 10.95 (978-0-7390-6243-2(3)) Alfred Pub.

Basic Finnish. unabr. ed. Conversa-Phone Institute Staff. 2 cass. (Running Time: 1 hr. 20 min.). (Round the World Basic Language Program Ser.). 1991. 15.95 Set. (978-1-56752-064-4(2), COC-5148) Conversa-phone.
20 lessons in basic Finnish with instruction manual.

Basic French. Kate Beeching. 1988. bk. 23.00 (978-0-582-22482-7(9), 78059) Longman.

Basic French. unabr. ed. Conversa-Phone Institute Staff. 1 cass. (Running Time: 61 min.). (Round the World Basic Language Program Ser.). (ENG & FRE.). 1997. pap. bk. 9.95 incl. instruction manual. (978-1-56752-001-9(4)) Conversa-phone.
Twenty lessons in basic French.

Basic French, Pt. A. 185.00 (1968, Lrn Inc) Oasis Audio.
Presents methods in learning a second language.

Basic French, Pt. B. 215.00 (1969, Lrn Inc) Oasis Audio.
Features methods in learning a second language.

Basic French Advanced Level Part B Units 19-24, Vol. 1924. unabr. ed. Foreign Service Institute Staff. 18 cass. (Running Time: 22 hrs.). (FRE.). 1977. pap. bk. 275.00 (978-0-88432-024-1(3), AFF290) J Norton Pubs.
Increases vocabulary & provides progressively more advanced exercises, drill & practice in complex sentence structures. Increased emphasis on reading & writing in French. In addition, contains narratives designed to develop reading skills & conversation exercises for perfecting grammatical usage.

Basic French for Spanish Speakers. unabr. ed. Conversa-Phone Institute Staff. (Modern Method Language Ser.). (FRE & SPA.). 1994. 23.95 (978-1-56752-083-5(9), COC-6506) Conversa-phone.
Full study language program to teach French to Spanish speakers. 96 page manual complete with pictures, grammar & conversation. Includes French-Spanish dictionary.

Basic Gas Chromatography. 2nd ed. Instructed by Harold M. McNair. 6 cass. (Running Time: 5 hrs.). 220.00 incl. 218pp manual. (18) Am Chemical.
Teaches the basic principles of Gas Chromatography.

Basic German. unabr. ed. Conversa-Phone Institute Staff. 1 cass. (Running Time: 61 min.). (Round the World Basic Language Program Ser.). 1991. 9.95 incl. instruction manual. (978-1-56752-002-6(2)) Conversa-phone.
Twenty lessons in basic German.

Basic German, Vol. 1. 185.00 (1970, Lrn Inc) Oasis Audio.
Features methods in learning a second language.

Basic German, Vol. 2. 185.00 (1971, Lrn Inc) Oasis Audio.

Basic German: Learn to Speak & Understand German with Pimsleur Language Programs. 2nd unabr. ed. Pimsleur Staff & Pimsleur. 5 CDs. (Running Time: 50 hrs. 0 mins. 0 sec.). (Basic Ser.). (GER & ENG.). 2005. audio compact disk 24.95 (978-0-7435-5073-4(0), Pimsleur) Pub: S&S Audio. Dist(s): S and S Inc

Basic German for Spanish Speakers. unabr. ed. Conversa-Phone Institute Staff. (Modern Method Language Ser.). (GER & SPA.). 1994. 23.95 Set. (978-1-56752-084-2(7), COC-6507) Conversa-phone.
Program to teach German to Spanish speakers. 96 page illustrated manual with grammar notes & conversation. Includes German-Spanish dictionary.

Basic Goodness: The Opening Talk of the Shambhala Training Program. Read by Chogyam Trungpa. 1 cass. 1978. 12.50 (A128) Vajradhatu.

Basic Grammar in Action. Barbara Foley & Elizabeth Neblett. 2 cass. (Running Time: 3 hrs.). 26.95 (978-0-8384-1120-9(7)) Heinle.

Basic Guide to Bankruptcy. Nathan M. Bisk & Michael S. Kranitz. 5 cass. 159.00 set, incl. textbk. & quizzer. (CPE3150) Bisk Educ.
Learn the essentials of bankruptcy from an accounting perspective. We cover the structure of liquidations & reorganizations, & issues related to professionals retention & compensation.

Basic Guide to Broadcasting: An Audio Adaptation. Tracy St. John. Frwd. by Michael A. McVay. 1 cass. (Running Time: 52 min.). 1988. 14.95 Reeder Pr.
Gives examples of on air broadcasts, details workings of radio stations, outlines jobs, provides information on interviewing, news formats, contracts, etc.

Basic Haitian Creole. unabr. ed. Albert Valdman. 12 cass. (Running Time: 15 hrs. 30 mins.). 1989. pap. bk. 245.00 (978-0-88432-155-2(X), AFCR10) J Norton Pubs.
This 24 lesson program provides dialogs with build-ups, pronunciation guides & exercises consisting of substitution, question & answer, transformation & translation drills.

Basic Hebrew. unabr. ed. Conversa-Phone Institute Staff. 2 cass. (Running Time: 1 hr. 20 min.). (Round the World Basic Language Program Ser.). 1991. 15.95 Set. (978-1-56752-061-3(8), COC-5140) Conversa-phone.
20 lessons in basic Hebrew with instruction manual.

Basic Hindi. unabr. ed. Conversa-Phone Institute Staff. 1 cass. (Running Time: 52 min.). (Round the World Basic Language Program). (HIN.). 1991. 9.95 incl. instruction manual. (978-1-56752-016-3(2)) Conversa-phone.
Twenty lessons in basic Hindi.

Basic History of the United States: The Growth of America, 1878-1928, Vol. 4. unabr. ed. Clarence B. Carson. Read by Mary Woods. 9 cass. (Running Time: 13 hrs.). 2000. 62.95 (978-0-7861-0435-2(X), 1387) Blckstn Audio.

Basic History of the United States Vol. I: The Colonial Experience, 1607-1774. unabr. ed. Clarence B. Carson. Read by Mary Woods. 6 cass. (Running Time: 8 hrs. 30 mins.). 1993. 44.95 set. (978-0-7861-0411-6(2), 1363) Blckstn Audio.
The first volume of a comprehensive five-volume set, covers our heritage, our links to England, how the colonies grew, the mighty force of religion in early America, & the oppression felt by the colonists.

Basic History of the United States Vol. II: The Beginning of the Republic, 1775-1825. unabr. ed. Clarence B. Carson. Read by Mary Woods. 8 cass. (Running Time: 11 hrs. 30 mins.). 1993. 56.95 (978-0-7861-0415-4(5), 1367) Blckstn Audio.
Covers the move toward independence, the Declaration of Independence, the Revolutionary War, the battle for Canada, the struggle for the middle states, the battle for the South, the Constitutional Convention, the making of the Constitution, & the fruits of independence.

Basic History of the United States Vol. III: The Sections & the Civil War. unabr. ed. Clarence B. Carson. Read by Mary Woods. 7 cass. (Running Time: 10 hrs.). 1993. 49.95 (978-0-7861-0431-4(7), 1383) Blckstn Audio.
Carson begins this third volume by diagnosing the root causes which eventually gave rise to sectionalism: regional differences & changes, the election of 1824, the Adams administration, & the emergence of two parties. From there the book covers a great deal of ground including: the meaning of Jacksonian Democracy; the removal of the Indians; the nullification & bank controversies; the plantation system; the Transcendentalists & the development of American literature; the Public School movement; Westward expansion; the election of Lincoln & finally, The Civil War.

Basic History of the United States Vol. IV: The Growth of America, 1878-1928. unabr. ed. Clarence B. Carson. Read by Mary Woods. 6 cass. (Running Time: 9 hrs.). 62.95 Set. (1387) Blckstn Audio.
Starting with the "filling out" of the West, covers more than just the events & standard historical facts of these formative fifty years. Included are discussions of Darwinism & Socialism, & their effects upon American society; regulation & the courts; civil service reform; silver, bimetallism & inflation; regulation & the courts; the rise of labor unions; Populism & Progressivism; the annexation of Hawaii & acquisition of colonies by the U.S.; the Spanish-American War; the Panama Canal; World War I; Bolshevism & the spread of Totalitarianism; Nazism in Germany; monetarism & prosperity; symptoms of moral decline; & the presidencies of Theodore Roosevelt, Taft, Harding, & Coolidge.

Basic History of the United States Vol. V: The Welfare State, 1929-1985. unabr. ed. Clarence B. Carson. Read by Mary Woods. 10 cass. (Running Time: 14 hrs. 30 mins.). 1994. 69.95 (978-0-7861-0440-6(6), 1392) Blckstn Audio.
Commences with The Great Depression & takes us to the mid-eighties. As the author of "Basic Economics," Clarence B. Carson is well suited to diagnose the causes of the stock market crash & the years of economic depression which followed. Further discussions include: The New Deal; The Pink Decade; The Second New Deal; The National Labor Relations Act; the start of Social Security; World War II; The Cold War; Welfare in the U. S. & abroad; the Warren Court; black activism; The Cultural Revolution; Vietnam; the rise of the Conservative movement; Nixon & Watergate; the Carter presidency; & the start of the Regan years.

Basic History of the United States Vol. VI: America in Gridlock, 1985-1995. Clarence B. Carson. Read by Mary Woods. 7 cass. (Running Time: 10 hrs. 30 min.). 1999. 49.95 Blckstn Audio.
Brings U.S. History abreast with the latest developments in our government & culture. Examines the philosophic & religious divide evidenced in materialism & statism; examines the welfare state & the moral breakdown associated with perpetuation & much more.

Basic Home Schooling Workshop. rev. ed. Gregg Harris. 8 cass. 1992. 39.95 Set. (978-0-923463-81-6(X)) Noble Pub Assocs.
Recording of a live workshop on home schooling.

Basic Human Anatomy: Nomenclature, Systems & Tissues. D. Hastings-Nield. (Anatomy Project). 1997. audio compact disk 199.95 (978-1-85070-840-7(1), Parthenon Pbng) Pub: CRC Pr. Dist(s): Taylor and Fran

Basic Human Genetics Art Images. 1998. audio compact disk (978-0-87893-496-6(0)) Sinauer Assocs.

Basic Hungarian. unabr. ed. Conversa-Phone Institute Staff. 2 cass. (Running Time: 1 hr. 20 min.). (Round the World Basic Language Program Ser.). 1991. 15.95 Set. (978-1-56752-059-0(6), COC-5131) Conversa-phone.
20 lessons in basic Hungarian with instruction manual.

Basic Ideas of Science of Mind. abr. ed. Ernest Holmes. Read by Gene Ross. Ed. by John S. Niendorff. 2 cass. (Running Time: 2 hrs. 45 min.). 1986. 14.95 (978-0-911336-98-6(2), T206) Sci of Mind.
This explanation of the philosophy taught by the authors contains excerpts from the book "How to Change Your Life".

Basic Improvising: How to Make up Music As You Go Along. Duane Shinn. 1 cass. 19.95 (WC-1) Duane Shinn.
Discusses how to improvise - make up music as one goes along.

Basic Indonesian. unabr. ed. Conversa-Phone Institute Staff. 1 cass. (Running Time: 52 min.). (Round the World Basic Language Program). (IND.). 1991. 9.95 incl. instruction manual. (978-1-56752-014-9(6)) Conversa-phone.
Twenty lessons in basic Indonesian.

Basic Instructor Guitar, Bk 1. 3rd ed. Alfred Publishing Staff. (ENG.). 2009. audio compact disk 9.00 (978-0-7390-5850-3(9)) Alfred Pub.

***Basic Instructor Guitar, Bk 2.** 2nd ed. Jerry Snyder. (ENG.). 2010. audio compact disk 9.00 (978-0-7390-5853-4(3)) Alfred Pub.

Basic, Intermediate Systematic Substitution Training, Set-IS. Russell E. Mason. 1973. pap. bk. 35.00 (978-0-89533-016-1(4)) F I Comm.

Basic Irish Gaelic. unabr. ed. Conversa-Phone Institute Staff. 1 cass. (Running Time: 52 min.). (Round the World Basic Language Program Ser.). 1991. 9.95 (978-1-56752-026-2(X)) Conversa-phone.
Twenty lessons in basic Irish Gaelic with instruction manual.

Basic Italian. unabr. ed. Conversa-Phone Institute Staff. 1 cass. (Running Time: 61 min.). (Round the World Basic Language Program Ser.). 1991. 9.95 incl. instruction manual. (978-1-56752-003-3(0)) Conversa-phone.
Twenty lessons in basic Italian.

***Basic Italian.** 7th ed. Charles Speroni et al. (ENG & ITA., (C). 1994. 88.95 (978-0-03-007483-7(5)) Pub: Heinle. Dist(s): CENGAGE Learn

Basic Italian for Spanish Speakers. unabr. ed. Conversa-Phone Institute Staff. (Modern Method Language Ser.). (ITA & SPA.). 1994. 23.95 Set. (978-1-56752-085-9(5), COC-6508) Conversa-phone.
Program to teach Italian to Spanish speakers. 96 page illustrated manual with grammar notes & conversation. Includes Italian-Spanish dictionary.

Basic Japanese. 4 cass. (Running Time: 60 min. per cass.). bk. 48.95 Module 2. (978-1-55536-364-2(4)) Oasis Audio.
Covers the basic language instruction, the equivalent of two years of college conversational instruction. Subject material is travel & business related, with grammar introduced at the end of module 2.

Basic Japanese. unabr. ed. Conversa-Phone Institute Staff. 1 cass. (Running Time: 1 hr. 01 min.). (Round the World Basic Language Program). 1991. 9.95 incl. instruction manual. (978-1-56752-013-2(8)) Conversa-phone.
Twenty lessons in basic Japanese.

Basic Japanese, Module 1. 4 cass. (Running Time: 60 min. per cass.). pap. bk. 48.95 Module 1. (978-1-55536-363-5(6)) Oasis Audio.
Covers the basic language instruction, the equivalent of two years of college conversational instruction. Subject material is travel & business related, with grammar introduced at the end of module 2.

Basic Japanese I. 185.00 (2028, Lrn Inc) Oasis Audio.
Features methods in learning a second language.

Basic Japanese II. 245.00 (2029, Lrn Inc) Oasis Audio.

Basic Keyboarding for Medical Assistant. 2nd ed. Edna Jean Moss. 1. (Running Time: 1 hr. 30 min.). 2000. 39.95 (978-0-7668-0957-4(9)) Delmar.
Practice medical transcription.

Basic Kitchen Preparation - FLS. Prod. by Culinary Institute of America Staff. 2007. DVD & audio compact disk (978-1-58315-338-3(1)) Food & Bev Inst.

Basic Korean. unabr. ed. Conversa-Phone Institute Staff. 1 cass. (Running Time: 52 min.). (Round the World Basic Language Program Ser.). 1991. 9.95 (978-1-56752-025-5(1)) Conversa-phone.
Twenty lessons in basic Korean with instruction manual.

Basic Law for Financial & Estate Planning. Sidney Kess & Barbara Weltman. 1 cass. 1995. 69.00 (0944) Toolkit Media.
Covers non-tax areas of law for the financial planner.

Basic Law of Leadership: Neh. 5:14-19. Ed Young. 1990. 4.95 (978-0-7417-1811-2(1), 811) Win Walk.

Basic Laws of Chemistry. unabr. ed. George Porter. 1 cass. 1990. 12.95 (ECN065) J Norton Pubs.

Basic Lithuanian. unabr. ed. Conversa-Phone Institute Staff. 1 cass. (Running Time: 52 min.). (Round the World Basic Language Program Ser.). 1991. 9.95 (978-1-56752-028-6(6)) Conversa-phone.
Twenty lessons in basic Lithuanian with instruction manual.

Basic Malay. unabr. ed. Conversa-Phone Institute Staff. 1 cass. (Running Time: 52 min.). (Round the World Basic Language Program Ser.). 1991. 9.95 (978-1-56752-023-1(5)) Conversa-phone.
Twenty lessons in basic Malay with instruction manual.

Basic Mandarin Chinese. unabr. ed. Conversa-Phone Institute Staff. 2 cass. (Running Time: 1 hr. 20 min.). (Round the World Basic Language Program Ser.). 1991. 15.95 Set. (978-1-56752-057-6(X), COC-5123) Conversa-phone.
20 lessons in basic Mandarin Chinese with instruction manual.

Basic Materials in Music Theory. 11th ed. Steinke & Harder. audio compact disk 9.97 (978-0-13-193101-5(6)) PH School.

***Basic Math Skills: Teacher's Resource Library.** Created by AGS Publishing. 2006. audio compact disk 199.99 (978-0-7854-2956-2(5)) Am Guidance.

Basic Medical Malpractice. unabr. ed. Contrib. by Stephen H. Mackauf. 8 cass. (Running Time: 10 hrs.). 1989. 50.00 course handbk. (T7-9217) PLI.
This recording of PLI's July 1989 program explains the basic concepts necessary to handle medical malpractice cases. Directed principally to attorneys in their first few years of practice, it is also of special value to risk managers, hospital administrators & claims adjusters.

Basic Medical Navajo. unabr. ed. Alan Wilson. 1 cass. (Running Time: 1 hr.). (NAV.). 1992. pap. bk. 39.95 (978-0-88432-453-9(2), AFNV40) J Norton Pubs.
Foreign Language Instruction. An elementary course for physicians & nurses who treat Navajo speakers.

Basic Medical Navajo CD & Text. Alan Wilson. 1 CD. (Running Time: 1 hr.). (NAV.). 2005. audio compact disk 39.95 (978-1-57970-242-7(2), AFNV40D) J Norton Pubs.

Basic Meditation. Vajracarya. Read by Chogyam Trungpa. 4 cass. 1974. 43.00 Vajradhatu.
A five talk seminar. Meditation is the process of learning to know how the mind works and how it can be used with greater precision. Here instruction is given, together with an overview of the Buddhist path.

Basic Modern Greek. unabr. ed. Conversa-Phone Institute Staff. 1 cass. (Running Time: 1 hr. 01 min.). (Round the World Basic Language Program). (GRE.). 1991. 9.95 incl. instruction manual. (978-1-56752-012-5(X)) Conversa-phone.
Twenty lessons in basic modern Greek.

Basic Modern Hebrew. 2nd unabr. ed. Pimsleur Staff. 5 CDs. (Running Time: 50 hrs. 0 mins. 0 sec.). (Basic Ser.). (HEB & ENG.). 2005. audio compact disk 24.95 (978-0-7435-5079-6(X), Pimsleur) Pub: S&S Audio. Dist(s): S and S Inc

Basic Mongolian: Khalkha Dialect. unabr. ed. John G. Hangin. 8 cass. (Running Time: 6 hrs.). 1992. pap. bk. 275.00 incl. text, 208p. (978-0-88432-713-4(2), AFMN10) J Norton Pubs.

Basic Moroccan Arabic. unabr. ed. Richard S. Harrell & Mohammed Abu-Talib. 16 cass. (Running Time: 18 hrs.). (YA). (gr. 10-12). 1985. pap. bk. 265.00 (978-0-88432-052-4(9), AFA300) J Norton Pubs.
This teaches the Arabic of the educated urban population of northwestern Morocco, which includes the cities of Fez, Rabat & Casablanca. Text uses Roman alphabet transcriptions of Arabic words & phrases & includes a glossary & an index of all grammatical points covered in the lessons.

Basic Norwegian. unabr. ed. Conversa-Phone Institute Staff. 2 cass. (Running Time: 1 hr. 20 min.). (Round the World Basic Language Program Ser.). 1991. 15.95 Set. (978-1-56752-060-6(X), COC-5139) Conversa-phone.
20 lessons in basic Norwegian with instruction manual.

Basic Nurse Aide Content for the Written Exam: Basic Nursing Skills. Patricia Hoefler. (Nursing Aide Ser.). 1989. (978-1-56533-160-0(5)) MEDS Pubng.

Basic Nurse Aide Content for the Written Exam: Basic Restorative Services. Patricia Hoefler. (Nursing Aide Ser.). 1989. (978-1-56533-161-7(3)) MEDS Pubng.

Basic Nurse Aide Content for the Written Exam: Test Taking Strategies. Patricia Hoefler. (Nursing Aide Ser.). 1989. (978-1-56533-162-4(1)) MEDS Pubng.

Basic Obligations of Disciples. Swami Amar Jyoti. 2 cass. 1986. 12.95 (E-31) Truth Consciousness.
Much more is expected of the seekers of Reality; majority have still to understand their obligations.

Basic Ojibwe. 4 cass. (Running Time: 4 hrs.). (OJI.). 1990. pap. bk. 75.00 (978-1-57970-009-6(8), AFOJ10) J Norton Pubs.
Covers pronunciation, commands & common expressions.

Basic Ojibwe: Introductory Course. unabr. ed. 4 cass. (Running Time: 4 hrs.). pap. bk. 46.50 Set, incl. 2 bklts. (AFOJ10) J Norton Pubs.

Basic Oxford Picture Dictionary. 2nd ed. Margot F. Gramer. 3 cass. (Basic Oxford Picture Dictionary Program, Second Ed Ser.). 1994. 54.95 (978-0-19-434470-8(3)) OUP.

Basic Oxford Picture Dictionary. 2nd ed. Norma Shapiro & Fiona Armstrong. Told to Margot F. Gramer. (Basic Oxford Picture Dictionary Program, Second Ed Ser.). 1994. tchr. ed. 39.95 (978-0-19-434582-8(3)) OUP.

Basic Persian. unabr. ed. Conversa-Phone Institute Staff. 1 cass. (Running Time: 52 min.). (Round the World Basic Language Program Ser.). 1991. 9.95 (978-1-56752-022-4(7)) Conversa-phone.
Twenty lessons in basic Persian with instruction manual.

Basic Pilates: The First 15 Matwork Exercises. Instructed by Aliesa George. (ENG.). 2006. 12.00 (978-0-9771576-3-1(6)) Ctr Pilates.

Basic Points of Buddhist Meditation. unabr. ed. Tenshin R. Anderson. 2 cass. (Running Time: 3 hrs.). 1984. 18.00 Set. (02702) Big Sur Tapes.
Describes the origins of his own Buddhist practice & teaches the basics of meditation.

Basic Polish. unabr. ed. Conversa-Phone Institute Staff. 2 cass. (Running Time: 1 hr. 20 min.). (Round the World Basic Language Program Ser.). 1991. 15.95 Set. (978-1-56752-063-7(4), COC-5147) Conversa-phone.
20 lessons in basic Polish with instruction manual.

Basic Portuguese. unabr. ed. Conversa-Phone Institute Staff. 1 cass. (Running Time: 1 hr. 01 min.). (Round the World Basic Language Program). (POR.). 1991. 9.95 incl. instruction manual. (978-1-56752-010-1(3)) Conversa-phone.
Twenty lessons in basic Portuguese.

Basic Principles of a Course in Miracles. Lorraine M. Coburn. 2006. 14.99 (978-0-9786516-5-7(0)); audio compact disk 14.99 (978-0-9786516-0-2(X)) Miracles Media.

Basic Principles of Objectivism. unabr. ed. Nathaniel Branden. 20 cass. (Running Time: 24 hrs.). 180.00 Set. (AFNB02) J Norton Pubs.
This monumental course is Branden's famous exposition of Objectivism. Thousands of people attended these lectures all over the world. Here is your chance to own what has become part of the intellectual history of our time. Complete set of 20 cassettes in vinyl binders, or as individual selections.

Basic, Programmatic Spanish, Vol. I. unabr. ed. Foreign Service Institute Staff. 12 cass. (SPA.). bk. 185.00 Set, incl. manual. J Norton Pubs.

Basic Reading. Ruth J. Colvin et al. 1981. 2.25 (978-0-930713-55-3(9)) Lit Vol Am.
Details phonic technique used in reading instruction.

***Basic Reading Inventory: Pre-Primer Through Grade Twelve & Early Literacy Assessments CD-ROM.** 10th rev. ed. Johns. (ENG.). 2010. audio compact disk 58.46 (978-0-7575-5128-4(9)) Kendall-Hunt.

Basic Real Estate. 6th rev. ed. 2001. audio compact disk 19.95 (978-0-934132-10-7(0)) Mogan & Shaw.

Basic Real Estate Financing. unabr. ed. Contrib. by Alan J. Pomerantz. 4 cass. (Running Time: 5 hrs.). 1989. 50.00 course handbk. (T7-9248) PLI.
This recording of PLI's November 1989 program focuses on the major business & legal issues involved in acquisition financing & refinancing of real estate projects. The program discusses such areas as: commitment letters, loan documents, mortgages-title insurance policies, opinion letters, environmental issues & the closing, tracing the legal & business aspects through each phase of an actual financing.

Basic Refrigeration & Charging Procedures Interactive Training CD. 2004. audio compact disk 29.95 (978-1-930044-21-0(6), CDRCP) ESCO PR.

Basic Relaxation & Ego-Strengthening Program. unabr. ed. Nathaniel Branden. 1 cass. (Running Time: 25 min.). 1990. 12.95 (599) J Norton Pubs.
This unusually effective cassette combines insights which Branden has developed in the field of psychotherapy with the principles of hypnosis. Its aim is to produce deep feelings of relaxation in the listener, to promote feelings of physical & psychological well-being & to strengthen feelings of

self-confidence & self-acceptance. This tape is not a lecture but rather a psychological experience which can have very interesting & beneficial effects after a number of repetitions.

Basic Relaxation & Ego-Strengthening Program (audio CD) Nathaniel Branden. (ENG.). 2007. audio compact disk 12.95 (978-1-57970-475-9(1), Audio-For) J Norton Pubs.

Basic Rock & Blues Guitar Method. William Bay. 1997. bk. 17.95 (978-0-7866-2774-5(3), 95045BCD) Mel Bay.

Basic Romanian. unabr. ed. Conversa-Phone Institute Staff. 1 cass. (Running Time: 52 min.). (Round the World Basic Language Program). (RUM.). 1991. 9.95 incl. instruction manual. (978-1-56752-020-0(0)) Conversa-phone.
Twenty lessons in basic Romanian.

Basic Russian. unabr. ed. Conversa-Phone Institute Staff. 1 cass. (Running Time: 1 hr. 01 min.). (Round the World Basic Language Program). (RUS.). 1991. 9.95 incl. instruction manual. (978-1-56752-008-8(1)) Conversa-phone.
Twenty lessons in basic Russian.

Basic Russian, Vol. 2. Mischa Fayer. 2 cass. (Running Time: 3 hrs.). (RUS.). (J). (gr. 9-12). 1977. 50.00 (978-0-8442-4218-7(7)) Glencoe.
An understanding of grammatical principles accompanies intensive oral practice. Stress is placed on aural comprehension, reading & self-expression.

Basic S Corporation Taxation. Nathan M. Bisk & Stephen T. Galloway. 6 cass. 1994. 65.00 set, incl. textbk. & quizzer. (CPE0540); 65.00 extra textbks. & quizzers. (CPE0541) Bisk Educ.
Discover when you should & should not change from a C Corporation to an S Corporation. Identify opportunities & possible problem areas. The program includes amendments made through all recent Tax Acts.

Basic Saudi Arabic. unabr. ed. Foreign Service Institute Staff. 10 cass. (Running Time: 12 hrs.). (YA). (gr. 10-12). 1972. pap. bk. 225.00 (978-0-88432-037-1(5), AFA234) J Norton Pubs.
Be able to satisfy routine social demands & limited business requirements, carry on general conversations & understand speech at a normal rate of speed. Course provides all the basic grammatical structures of the dialect, plus considerable vocabulary.

Basic Securities Law Concepts for the Business Practitioner. (Running Time: 5 hrs. 30 min.). 1994. 92.00 Incl. 368p. coursebk. (20034) NYS Bar.
Presents an overview of, & the latest developments in, the securities law area & is designed to give a basic understanding of key concepts for the general practitioner who is not a securities law specialist but who must be familiar with the statutes, rules & regulations concerning the securities law area to service the needs & answer the questions of corporate clients.

Basic Serbo Croatian. unabr. ed. Conversa-Phone Institute Staff. 1 cass. (Running Time: 52 min.). (Round the World Basic Language Program). (CRO.). 1991. 9.95 incl. instruction manual. (978-1-56752-015-6(4)) Conversa-phone.
Twenty lessons in basic Serbo Croatian.

Basic Skills for Young Children. William Janiak. 1 cass. (Running Time: 1 hr.). (J). 2001. pap. bk. 10.95 (KIM 9117C); pap. bk. & pupil's gde. ed. 11.95 (KIM 9117) Kimbo Educ.
Children learn basic skills through a medium they love so much, music! Today I'm Happy, Moving, Two By Two, I'm a Helper & others encourage learning, development & active participation. Includes guide.

Basic Skills of Being a Counsellor, Side A. Harvey Jackins. 1 cass. 10.00 Rational Isl.
Side A: Jackins describes the basic skills of being a counsellor. Side B: Jackins outlines the stages in the development of co-counseling.

Basic Spanish. unabr. ed. Conversa-Phone Institute Staff. 1 cass. (Running Time: 61 min.). (Round the World Basic Language Program Ser.). 1991. 9.95 incl. instruction manual. (978-1-56752-000-2(6)) Conversa-phone.
Twenty lessons in basic Spanish.

Basic Spanish, Vol. 1. 185.00 (1965, Lrn Inc) Oasis Audio.
Features methods in learning a 2nd language.

Basic Spanish, Vol. 2. 1966. 165.00 (1965, Lrn Inc) Oasis Audio.
Presents methods to learn a second language.

Basic Spanish Grammar. 3rd ed. Ana C. Jarvis et al. (C). 1988. reel tape 2.66 (978-0-669-12242-8(4)) HM Harcourt.

Basic Spanish Pronunciation. Ralph S. Boggs. (YA). (gr. 9-11). 1969. 60.00 Prentice ESL.

Basic Spelling Workbook. unabr. ed. 3 cass. bk. 55.00 incl. 96-page student text, teacher's guide. (SEN120); 5.95 student wkbk. only. (BEN120) J Norton Pubs.
Teaches basic spelling principles & gives practice in their use.

Basic Spiritual Warfare, Pt. 1. Rick Joyner. 1 cass. (Running Time: 90 mins.). (Spiritual Warfare Ser.: Vol. 1). 2000. 5.00 (RJ15-001) Morning NC.
God has designed spiritual weapons of warfare for Christians to use & the insightful teaching in this five-part series will encourage, strengthen & prepare you to wage war against the enemy.

Basic Structures - French Vol. 1: A Textbook for the Learnables. 4th ed. Scripts. Carmen Waggoner. 3 CDs. (Running Time: 2 hrs.30mins.). (FRE.). (YA). (gr. 7 up). 1991. per. 49.00 (978-0-939990-73-3(2), 250CD) Intl Linguistics.

Basic Structures, Spanish Bk. 1: A Textbook for the Learnables. 4th ed. Scripts. Harris Winitz. Tr. by Blanca Sagarna. Illus. by Sydney M. Baker. 3 CDs. (Running Time: 2 hrs. 20 mins.). (Basic Structures: Bk. 1). (SPA.). (YA). (gr. 7 up). 1999. per. 49.00 (978-1-887371-28-5(1)) Intl Linguistics.

Basic Swahili. unabr. ed. Conversa-Phone Institute Staff. 1 cass. (Running Time: 52 min.). (Round the World Basic Language Program). (SWA.). 1991. 9.95 incl. instruction manual. (978-1-56752-021-7(9)) Conversa-phone.
Twenty lessons in basic Swahili.

Basic Swedish. unabr. ed. Conversa-Phone Institute Staff. 1 cass. (Running Time: 1 hr. 01 min.). (Round the World Basic Language Program). (SWE.). 1991. 9.95 incl. instruction manual. (978-1-56752-009-5(X)) Conversa-phone.
Twenty lessons in basic Swedish.

Basic Tactics for Listening. 2nd rev. ed. Jack C. Richards. 3 CDs. 2003. audio compact disk 54.95 (978-0-19-437528-3(5)) OUP.

Basic Tagalog. unabr. ed. Conversa-Phone Institute Staff. 1 cass. (Running Time: 52 min.). (Round the World Basic Language Program Ser.). 1991. 9.95 (978-1-56752-032-3(4)) Conversa-phone.
Twenty lessons in basic Tagalog with instruction manual.

Basic Telephone Training. Anne Watson-Delestree. 1 cass. (Running Time: 1 hr.). 1999. bk. & stu. ed. (978-0-8092-0598-1(X)) M-H Contemporary.

Basic Thai. unabr. ed. Conversa-Phone Institute Staff. 1 cass. (Running Time: 52 min.). (Round the World Basic Language Program Ser.). 1991. 9.95 (978-1-56752-029-3(4)) Conversa-phone.
Twenty lessons in basic Thai with instruction manual.

Basic Training Vol. 1: Faith. Michael D. Christensen. 1 cass. 1998. 9.95 (978-1-57008-567-3(6), Bkcraft Inc) Deseret Bk.

Basic Training for the Army of God: A Must for Christian Soldiers of All Ages. Lynne Hammond. 2008. audio compact disk 18.00 (978-1-57399-402-6(2)) Mac Hammond.

Basic Training in Jewish Mysticism Vol. 1: The Begetting of the Universe - The Classical Kabbalists. Zalman Schachter & Eve Ilsen. 4 cass. 36.00 set. (A0617-89) Sound Photosyn.
Beyond a naive Genesis & a sophisticated Astrophysics the Kabbalah teaches of Divine self-contradiction & primal emanations. This innerstory of our being on earth has direct influence on how we live our lives. The good-natured depth & dignity of Zalman, & of Eve, makes learning a breeze.

Basic Training in Jewish Mysticism Vol. 2: The Four Worlds. Zalman Schachter & Eve Ilsen. 6 cass. 54.00 set. (A0620-90) Sound Photosyn.
A full weekend retreat.

Basic Training in Jewish Mysticism Vol. 3: The Ten Sephirot - The Tree of Life. Zalman Schachter. 6 cass. 54.00 set. (A0622-90) Sound Photosyn.
An in depth weekend.

Basic Training in Jewish Mysticism Vol. 4: Cosmology Updated. Zalman Schachter & Eve Ilsen. 7 cass. 63.00 set. (A0616-90) Sound Photosyn.
A fine weekend retreat.

Basic Turkish. unabr. ed. Conversa-Phone Institute Staff. 1 cass. (Running Time: 52 min.). (Round the World Basic Language Program). (TUR.). 1991. 9.95 incl. instruction manual. (978-1-56752-019-4(7)) Conversa-phone.
Twenty lessons in basic Turkish.

Basic UCC Skills Week 1990: Article 2. 4 cass. (Running Time: 4 hrs. 30 min.). 1990. bk. 65.00 incl. 315-page course handbook. (T6-9132) PLI.

Basic UCC Skills Week 1990: Article 2A. 3 cass. (Running Time: 3 hrs. 30 min.). bk. 55.00 incl. 272-page course handbook. (T6-9133) PLI.

Basic UCC Skills Week 1990: Articles 3, 4 & 4A. 5 cass. (Running Time: 7 hrs.). 1990. bk. 85.00 incl. 2 course handbooks. (T6-9134) PLI.

Basic UCC Skills Week 1990: Articles 5 & 9. 7 cass. (Running Time: 9 hrs.). 1990. bk. 80.00 incl. 523-page course handbook. (T6-9135) PLI.

Basic Ukrainian. unabr. ed. Conversa-Phone Institute Staff. 1 cass. (Running Time: 50 min.). (Round the World Basic Language Program). (UKR.). 1991. 9.95 incl. instruction manual. (978-1-56752-018-7(9)) Conversa-phone.
Twenty lessons in basic Ukrainian.

Basic Vietnamese. unabr. ed. Conversa-Phone Institute Staff. 1 cass. (Running Time: 52 min.). (Round the World Basic Language Program Ser.). 1991. 9.95 (978-1-56752-024-8(3)) Conversa-phone.
Twenty lessons in basic Vietnamese with instruction manual.

Basic Vietnamese. unabr. ed. Created by Pimsleur Staff. 5 CDs. (Running Time: 50 hrs. 0 mins. 0 sec.). (Basic Ser.). (VIE & ENG.). 2006. audio compact disk 24.95 (978-0-7435-5083-3(8), Pimsleur) Pub: S&S Audio. Dist(s): S and S Inc

Basic Will Drafting. Contrib. by Charles M. Aulino. (Running Time: 4 hrs.). 1984. 70.00 Basic Estate Planning Skills Text. NJ Inst CLE.
Reviews basic will drafting techniques, including how to conduct a client interview, how to draft a simple will, when a complex will becomes necessary, how to prepare an estate plan, applicable tax considerations.

Basic Word Patterns. 2003. ring bd. (978-0-9744783-4-0(2)) Spanish Acad Cu Inst.

Basic Word Patterns A-Z. 2003. ring bd. (978-0-9744783-5-7(0)) Spanish Acad Cu Inst.

Basic Yiddish. unabr. ed. Conversa-Phone Institute Staff. 1 cass. (Running Time: 52 min.). (Round the World Basic Language Program Ser.). 1991. 9.95 (978-1-56752-027-9(8)) Conversa-phone.
Twenty lessons in basic Yiddish with instruction manual.

Basic Yoga Meditation: 3, 7, 11, & 30 Minute Guided Practices. (ENG.). 2008. audio compact disk 24.99 (978-0-9724719-2-3(8)) Tranquil Prods.

Basics. unabr. ed. Walter Kempler. 4 cass. (Healthy Family Is...Ser.). 44.95 Kempler Inst.
Tape 1 - The psychology of man reconsidered (Lecture); Tape 2 - All the diagnosis you'll ever need (Lecture); Tape 3 - A new approach to an old matter (2 interviews with a couple in trouble).

Basics: An Introduction to Study Skills. NVS Academic Resource Corporation Staff. 1 cassette. (Running Time: 60 mins.). 2003. 12.00 (978-0-9707614-8-4(1)) NVS Acad Res.

Basics Bookshelf, Set. 3 CDs. (High Point Ser.). (gr. 4-12). audio compact disk 503.15 (978-0-7362-0931-1(X)) Hampton-Brown.

Basics in Listening: Short Tasks for Listening Development. Michael Rost & Munetsugu Uruno. 2002. audio compact disk 76.00 (978-962-00-1032-3(9)) Pub: Longman Far East HKG. Dist(s): Longman

Basics in Pronunciation: Intermediate Practice for Clear Communication, Set. Linda Lane. 2001. 36.50 (978-0-201-69523-6(5)) AddisonWesley.

Basics in Speaking. Michael Rost. 2002. 23.00 (978-962-00-1427-7(8)) Longman Far East HKG.

Basics of Bankruptcy Practice: (With Coverage of the New Bankruptcy Reform Act of 1994) (Running Time: 5 hrs.). 1994. 92.00 Incl. 450p. coursebk. (20314) NYS Bar.
This package is a basic-level seminar on how to handle the nuts & bolts of a bankruptcy case, whether of an individual or a business. The presentations are given by practitioners, a bankruptcy judge & representatives of the U.S. Trustee's office to provide a well-rounded practical view of handling bankruptcy cases.

Basics of Biblical Greek Vocabulary. William D. Mounce. (Running Time: 1 hr. 0 mins. 0 sec.). (ENG.). (C). 2006. 8.44 (978-0-310-27385-1(4)) Zondervan.

Basics of Biblical Greek Vocabulary. abr. ed. William D. Mounce. Read by William D. Mounce. (Running Time: 1 hr. 0 mins. 0 sec.). (ENG.). (gr. 13). 2006. audio compact disk 12.99 (978-0-310-27076-8(6)) Zondervan.

Basics of Biblical Hebrew Voc. unabr. ed. Zondervan Publishing Staff et al. (Running Time: 1 hr. 0 mins. 0 sec.). (ENG.). 2006. audio compact disk 12.99 (978-0-310-27074-4(X)) Zondervan.

Basics of Biblical Hebrew Vocabulary. unabr. ed. Zondervan Publishing Staff et al. (Running Time: 1 hr. 0 mins. 0 sec.). (ENG.). 2006. 8.44 (978-0-310-27306-6(4)) Zondervan.

Basics of Business Etiquette. Contrib. by Marjorie Brody & Barbara Pachter. 1 cass. (Running Time: 45 mins.). pap. bk. 99.95 (1029AV); cass. & video 99.95 (1029AV) J Wilson & Assocs.

Basics of Compilation & Review Services. Pallais. 3 cass. (Running Time: 5 hrs.). 1993. 119.00 set, incl. wkbk. (743663KQ) Am Inst CPA.
This completely rewritten course provides step-by-step explanations of the provisions & applications of the AICPA's Statements on Standards for Accounting & Review Services (SSARS). These standards cover compilation & review of financial statments ... Reporting on comparative financial statements ... Compilation reports on financial statements included in certain prescribed forms ... Communications between predecessor & successor accountants. This course provides useful reference tools including a financial statement preparation checklist ... inquiry & analysis guidelines ... reporting do's & don'ts & alternatives ... & engagement letter preparation.

Basics of Corporate Governance. Anthony Cook. 1 cass. 1995. 135.00 (5322) Natl Prac Inst.

Basics of Deliverance Pt. 1: How to Identify the Enemy. Derek Prince. 1 cass. (B-4128) Derek Prince.

Basics of Deliverance Pt. 2: How to Expel the Enemy. Derek Prince. 1 cass. (B-4129) Derek Prince.

Basics of Pension & Profit-Sharing Plans. Michael Macris. 7 cass. (Running Time: 10 hrs.). 1995. 129.00 set, incl. wkbk. (752608EZ) Am Inst CPA.
The rules governing qualified retirement plans are numerous & complex. This course explains those rules in jargon-free language, enriched with scores of examples that show you how the rules apply in everyday situations.

Basics of Practical Problem Solving. Arynne Simon. 1 cass. 1995. 9.95 (978-1-882389-13-1(1)) Wilarvi Communs.
Teaches the precise skills to recognize, analyze & deal with problems of any depth.

Basics of Profitable Customer Service. 1 cass. (Running Time: 35 mins.). pap. bk. 99.95 (1024AV); pap. bk. 99.95 (1024AV) J Wilson & Assocs.

Basics of Singing. 4th ed. Jan Schmidt. (ENG.). (C). 1997. 66.95 (978-0-02-864879-8(X)) Pub: Wadsworth Pub. Dist(s): CENGAGE Learn

Basics of Spiritual Warfare Series. Francis Frangipane. 8 cass. (Running Time: 12 hrs.). 2000. 40.00 (FF02-000) Morning NC.
Francis combines years of practical experience with a soundbiblical perspective in this popular & important series.

Basics of Supreme Learning American English & Any Other Subject. unabr. ed. Michael Shestor & Robin Robertson. 1 cass. (Running Time: 1 hr. 30 min.). 1999. 59.95 (978-1-929070-12-1(8)) Wayward Ventures.

Basics of Swaps. 4 cass. (Running Time: 5 hrs. 30 min.). 1991. 125.00 Set. (T7-9338) PLI.

Basics Spiritual Warfare. Francis Frangipane. 8 cass. 1990. 32.00 Set. (978-0-00-147086-6(8)) BJUPr.

Basics Step 1: Guitar. UBS Committee. (POR.). 1997. 9.95 (978-0-7692-9151-2(1), Warner Bro) Alfred Pub.

Basics Step 1: Keyboard. UBS Committee. (POR.). 1997. 9.95 (978-0-7692-9149-9(X), Warner Bro) Alfred Pub.

Basics to Improve Your Memory. Hosted by Madelyn Burley-Allen. 1 cass. (Running Time: 54 mins.). pap. bk. 99.95 (1003AV); pap. bk. 99.95 (1003AV) J Wilson & Assocs.

Basics Vocal. 1996. 21.95 (978-0-7692-4774-8(1), Warner Bro) Alfred Pub.

Basie's Bag: Live from Detroit. Perf. by Count Basie Orchestra. 1 cass., 1 CD. 7.98 (TA 33358); audio compact disk 12.78 CD Jewel box. (TA 83358) NewSound.

***Basil.** Wilkie Collins. Read by Anais 9000. 2010. 27.95 (978-1-60112-241-4(1)) Babblebooks.

Basil Bunting. unabr. ed. Basil Bunting. 1 cass. (Author Speaks Ser.). 1991. 14.95 J Norton Pubs.
Archival recordings of 20th-century authors.

Basil Bunting: The Sound of Poetry. 1 cass. (Running Time: 30 min.). 8.00 (F0410B090, HarperThor) HarpC GBR.

Basil Street Blues: A Family Story. unabr. ed. Michael Holroyd. Read by Michael Holroyd. 8 cass. (Running Time: 12 hrs.). (Isis Ser.). (J). 2001. 69.95 (978-0-7531-0956-4(5), 000908) Pub: ISIS Lrg Prnt GBR. Dist(s): Ulverscroft US

Basil Street Blues & Mosaic. unabr. ed. Michael Holroyd. Read by Michael Holroyd. 9 CDs. (Running Time: 9 hrs. 52 min.). (Isis Ser.). (J). 2001. audio compact disk 84.95 (978-0-7531-1324-0(4)) Pub: ISIS Lrg Prnt GBR. Dist(s): Ulverscroft US
Author tells an extraordinary story of his own family. His Swedish mother was born three months prematurely after a terrible fire that killed her two-year-old brother. His Anglo-Irish father, full of inventiveness, met her on the North Sea, but their marriage soon failed and all four of their subsequent marriages were illegal. Michael was brought up by his grandparents, careering towards bankruptcy in an eccentric house in Maidenhead.

Basilica: The Splendor & the Scandal: Building St. Peter's. R. A. Scotti. Read by Josephine Bailey. (Playaway Adult Nonfiction Ser.). 2008. 59.99 (978-1-60640-974-9(3)) Find a World.

Basilica: The Splendor & the Scandal: Building St. Peter's. unabr. ed. Josephine Bailey. Read by Josephine Bailey. (Running Time: 8 hrs. 30 mins. 0 sec.). (ENG.). 2006. audio compact disk 59.99 (978-1-4001-3234-8(7)) Pub: Tantor Media. Dist(s): IngramPubServ

Basilica: The Splendor & the Scandal: Building St. Peter's. unabr. ed. R. A. Scotti. Narrated by Josephine Bailey. (Running Time: 8 hrs. 30 mins. 0 sec.). (ENG.). 2006. audio compact disk 29.99 (978-1-4001-0234-1(0)); audio compact disk 19.99 (978-1-4001-5234-6(8)) Pub: Tantor Media. Dist(s): IngramPubServ

Basilica di San Francesco see ARTineraries Tour: Basilica of St. Francis of Assisi: Assisi

Basin & Range. unabr. ed. John McPhee. Read by Walter Zimmerman. 6 cass. (Running Time: 6 hrs.). 1991. 36.00 (978-0-7366-1876-2(7), 2707) Books on Tape.
The land described by the author is that part of the United States reaching from Utah to eastern California. It is a silent world of austere beauty, of hundreds of high mountain ranges green with junipers or white with snow, a spectacular topography rich with history & consequence. John McPhee crisscrossed this country, rounding out his story of our planet's surface. He tells a story of the earth as a state on which a vast drama is unfolding. He shares his gifts of illumination with us.

Basin & Range: From Annals of the Former World. unabr. ed. John McPhee. Narrated by Nelson Runger. 5 cass. (Running Time: 7 hrs. 15 mins.). 1999. 44.00 (978-0-7887-3778-7(3), 95995E7) Recorded Bks.
McPhee crosses the spectacular Basin & Range region surrounding Nevada with a geology professor in tow. He will dazzle you with the fascinating history of the landscapes he encounters along the way, providing an accessible introduction to plate tectonics.

Basis for the Traditional Rights & Responsibilities of Parents. Read by Raphael T. Waters. 1 cass. 3.00 (120) ISI Books.

Basis for the Traditional Rights & Responsibilities of Parents: Panel Discussion, Pt. 2. Read by Thomas Neuberger et al. 1 cass. 3.00 (121) ISI Books.

Basis of Addiction. Michael P. Marshall. Read by Michael P. Marshall. Ed. by Jonathan C. Renaud. Music by Ted Crook. 1 cass. (Running Time: 52 min.). 1995. 9.00 (978-0-912403-16-8(0)) Prod Renaud.
What causes us to be addicted to everything from love, to food, sex, drugs, people, work, etc. & how to transform addictions.

Basis of Karma Theory. Swami Amar Jyoti. 1 cass. 1975. 9.95 (F-11) Truth Consciousness.
How karma works, the cause & effect link; the way out & a short cut. Guidelines for diet & exercise.

Basis of Love. Swami Amar Jyoti. 1 cass. 1980. 9.95 (R-30) Truth Consciousness.
The open secret of unconditional love. Looking to the immediate or the ultimate Goal. Finding the basic essential unity.

Basix Guitar Method, Bk. 3. Ron Manus & Morty Manus. 1997. pap. bk. 9.95 (978-0-88284-746-7(5)) Alfred Pub.

Basix Guitar Method, Bk. 4. Ron Manus & Morty Manus. 1997. pap. bk. 9.95 (978-0-88284-748-1(1)) Alfred Pub.

Basket Case. Carl Hiaasen. Narrated by Carl Hiaasen. 9 cass. (Running Time: 13 hrs.). 84.00 (978-1-4025-1815-7(3)) Recorded Bks.

Basket Case. unabr. ed. Carl Hiaasen. Narrated by George Wilson. 9 cass. (Running Time: 13 hrs.). 2002. 42.95 (978-1-4025-1849-2(8)) Recorded Bks.
Jack Tagger, a onetime investigative reporter reduced to writing obituaries, lives by the motto, "Always be halfway prepared." Tagger catches the scent of a real news story in the death notice for Jimmy Stoma, lead singer of the once-notorious Jimmy and the Slut Puppies. Hoping to regain his status in the world of journalism, he follows the trail to the not-so-grieving widow, Cleo Rio, who is attempting to give her own career a jump-start.

Basket Case. unabr. ed. Carl Hiaasen. Narrated by Carl Hiaasen. Narrated by George Wilson. 11 CDs. (Running Time: 13 hrs.). 2002. audio compact disk 111.00 (978-1-4025-2901-6(5)) Recorded Bks.

Basket Case: Phil. 3:4-8. Ed Young. 1987. 4.95 (978-0-7417-1608-8(9), 608) Win Walk.

Basket of Flowers. unabr. ed. Read by Marguerite Gavin. Tr. by J. H. St. A. 4 CDs. (Running Time: 5 hrs. 30 mins.). (J). 2003. audio compact disk 32.00 (978-0-7861-9334-9(4)) Blckstn Audio.

Basket of Flowers. unabr. ed. Read by Marguerite Gavin. 3 cass. (Running Time: 5 hrs. 30 mins.). 2000. 23.95 (978-0-7861-2348-3(6)) Blckstn Audio.
Centers on a gardner and his young daughter. Wrongfully accused of theft, they maintain their innocence throughout their trial, conviction, and sentence. Their constant demeanor and unchanging attitude are a source of substantial encouragement to listeners.

Basket of Plums: Songs for the Practice of Mindfulness. Prod. by Joseph Emet. 1 CD. (Running Time: 58 min.). 2003. audio compact disk 15.00 (77PCD) Parallax Pr.
Provides joyful support for Sangha meetings, tea ceremonies, and other mindful gatherings.

Basketball: Babbling Brook. Eldon Taylor. 1 cass. 16.95 (978-1-55978-505-1(5), 5391F) Progress Aware Res.

Basketball: Music Theme. Eldon Taylor. 1 cass. 16.95 (978-0-940699-47-2(8), 5391C) Progress Aware Res.

Basketball: Rhythms. Eldon Taylor. Read by Eldon Taylor. Ed. by Leslie Brice. 1 cass. (Running Time: 1 hr.). 1992. 16.95 (978-1-56705-240-4(1)) Gateways Inst.
Self improvement.

Basketball: Stream. Eldon Taylor. Read by Eldon Taylor. Ed. by Leslie Brice. 1 cass. (Running Time: 1 hr.). 1992. 16.95 (978-1-56705-241-1(X)) Gateways Inst.

Basketball Diaries. abr. ed. Jim Carroll. Read by Jim Carroll. 2 cass. (Running Time: 3 hrs.). 1995. 16.95 (978-0-944993-87-3(7)) Audio Lit.
The stunning record of the author's adventures as a teenager growing up on the "mean streets" of New York & the creation of a musician & poet.

Basketball Jones. unabr. ed. E. Lynn Harris. Read by Mirron Willis. (ENG.). 2009. audio compact disk 29.95 (978-0-7393-8186-1(5), Random AudioBks) Pub: Random Audio Pubg. Dist(s): Random

Basketful of Snowflakes. unabr. ed. Peter Kerr. Read by James Bryce. 8 cass. (Soundings Ser.). (J). 2006. 69.95 (978-1-84559-336-0(7)); audio compact disk 84.95 (978-1-84559-378-0(2)) Pub: ISIS Lrg Prnt GBR. Dist(s): Ulverscroft US

Baskets of Blessings: Luke 19:28-42. 1993. 4.95 (978-0-7417-1963-8(0), 963) Win Walk.

Basni: Russian Tales from Aesop. I. A. Krylof. Read by Irene Vishnevetsky. 1 cass. (Running Time: 25 min.). (RUS.). (J). bk. Incl. transcript; dual language bk. avail. (978-1-58085-585-3(7)) Interlingua VA.
Children's stories in verse.

Basque History of the World. Mark Kurlansky. Narrated by George Guidall. 11 CDs. (Running Time: 12 hrs.). 2001. audio compact disk 97.00 (978-0-7887-5198-1(0), C1355E7) Recorded Bks.
The author offers a celebration of Europe's oldest surviving culture - as mysterious as it is fascinating. The origin of Basque culture is unknown, yet Basques have made profound contributions to global history.

Basque History of the World. unabr. ed. Mark Kurlansky. Read by George Guidall. 9 cass. (Running Time: 15 hrs.). 2004. 39.95 (978-1-59007-249-3(9)) Pub: New Millenn Enter. Dist(s): PerseuPGW
Story of the Basque region and people of Spain. That they are alive is a mystery alone. These people, who firmly believe they should have their own country, have lived a unique and rugged life in their corner of the world. They speak their own language, fight their own battles, and are unique to every other region. This story is one of courage and grace, rejection and rebellion.

Basque History of the World. unabr. ed. Mark Kurlansky. Narrated by George Guidall. 9 cass. (Running Time: 12 hrs.). 2000. 74.00 (978-0-7887-4404-4(6), 96199E7) Recorded Bks.
The author offers a celebration of Europe's oldest surviving culture - as mysterious as it is fascinating. The origin of Basque culture is unknown, yet Basques have made profound contributions to global history.

Basque Unifie (Initiation) 1 cass. (Running Time: 1 hr., 30 min.). (BAQ & FRE.). 2000. bk. 75.00 (978-2-7005-1368-4(1)) Pub: Assimil FRA. Dist(s): Distribks Inc

***Bass Clarinet.** Robert W. Smith et al. Contrib. by Linda J. Gammon. (Band Expressions Ser.). (ENG., 2005. pap. bk. 7.95 (978-0-7579-4043-9(9)) Alfred Pub.

Bass Drum Essentials, Level 4. David Black & Brian Fullen. 1 CD. (Running Time: 1 hr. 30 mins.). (ENG.). 2002. audio compact disk 10.00 (978-0-7390-1450-9(1), 19578) Alfred Pub.

Bass School. Gary Karr. (Suzuki Method Core Materials Ser.). (ENG.). 1998. audio compact disk 15.95 (978-0-87487-369-6(X), Warner Bro) Alfred Pub.

Bass School, 2. Gary Karr. (Suzuki Method Core Materials Ser.). (ENG.). 1998. audio compact disk 15.95 (978-0-87487-379-5(7), Warner Bro) Alfred Pub.

Bass School, Vol. 3. Gary Karr. (Suzuki Method Core Materials Ser.). (ENG.). 1998. audio compact disk 15.95 (978-0-87487-380-1(0), Warner Bro) Alfred Pub.

Bass Today. Jerry Snyder. 1 cass. 1989. pap. bk. 17.50 (978-0-88284-907-2(7), 354); 8.95 (978-0-7390-1781-4(0), 350) Alfred Pub.

Bass Today. Jerry Synder. 1 CD. (Running Time: 1 hr. 30 mins.). (ENG.). 1996. audio compact disk 10.95 (978-0-7390-1449-3(8), 14085) Alfred Pub.

Bassface: Live at Kuumbwa Jazz Center. Perf. by Ray Brown. 1 cass., 1 CD. 7.98 (TA 33340); audio compact disk 12.78 CD Jewel box. (TA 83340) NewSound.

Bastard. abr. ed. John Jakes. Read by Bruce Watson. 4 cass. (Running Time: 6 hrs.). (Kent Family Chronicles: No. 1). 2000. 12.99 (978-1-57815-160-8(0), 4409, Media Bks Audio) Media Bks NJ.

Bastard. unabr. collector's ed. John Jakes. Read by Michael Kramer. 14 cass. (Running Time: 21 hrs.). (Kent Family Chronicles: No. 1). 1993. 112.00 (978-0-7366-2326-1(4), 3106) Books on Tape.
First volume in Kent Family Chronicles, detailing one family's journey in the early years of the American nation.

Bastard of Istanbul. Elif Shafak. Read by Laural Merlington. (Playaway Adult Fiction Ser.). 2008. 69.99 (978-1-60640-146-0(7)) Find a World.

Bastard of Istanbul. unabr. ed. Elif Shafak. Read by Laural Merlington. (Running Time: 13 hrs. 0 mins. 0 sec.). (ENG.). 2007. audio compact disk 39.99 (978-1-4001-0397-3(5)); audio compact disk 29.99 (978-1-4001-5397-8(2)); audio compact disk 79.99 (978-1-4001-3397-0(1)) Pub: Tantor Media. Dist(s): IngramPubServ

***Bastard on the Couch.** abr. ed. Daniel Jones. Read by Daniel Jones. (ENG.). 2004. (978-0-06-077418-9(5), Harper Audio) HarperCollins Pubs.

***Bastard on the Couch.** abr. ed. Daniel Jones. Read by Daniel Jones. (ENG.). 2004. (978-0-06-081394-9(6), Harper Audio) HarperCollins Pubs.

Bastard on the Couch: 23 Men Try Really Hard to Explain Their Feelings about Love, Lust, Fatherhood, & Freedom. unabr. abr. ed. Daniel Jones. Read by Daniel Jones. 2004. audio compact disk 29.95 (978-0-06-073163-2(X)) HarperCollins Pubs.

***Bastion of Darkness.** unabr. ed. R. A. Salvatore. Narrated by Lloyd James. (Running Time: 10 hrs. 30 mins. 0 sec.). (Chronicles of Ynis Aielle Ser.). (ENG.). 2010. 24.99 (978-1-4001-6640-4(3)); audio compact disk 69.99 (978-1-4001-4640-6(2)); audio compact disk 34.99 (978-1-4001-1640-9(6)) Pub: Tantor Media. Dist(s): IngramPubServ

***Bastion of Darkness.** unabr. ed. R. A. Salvatore. Narrated by Lloyd James. (Running Time: 10 hrs. 30 mins.). (Chronicles of Ynis Aielle Ser.). 2010. 16.99 (978-1-4001-8640-2(4)) Tantor Media.

Bat. Mary Roberts Rinehart. Read by Shelly Frasier. (Running Time: 7 hrs.). 2002. 27.95 (978-1-60083-612-1(7), Audiofy Corp) Iofy Corp.

Bat. Mary Roberts Rinehart. Read by Shelly Frasier. (ENG.). 2005. audio compact disk 72.00 (978-1-4001-3041-2(7)) Pub: Tantor Media. Dist(s): IngramPubServ

Bat. unabr. ed. Mary Roberts Rinehart. Narrated by Flo Gibson. 5 cass. (Running Time: 7 hrs.). (gr. 10 up). 2002. 20.95 (978-1-55685-643-3(1)) Audio Bk Con.
Zesty, elderly & courageous Miss Cornelia Van Gorder helps to solve two murders & uncover the identity of the evil " Bat" in this terrifying tale.

Bat. unabr. ed. Mary Roberts Rinehart. Narrated by Shelly Frasier. 6 CDs. (Running Time: 6 hrs. 52 mins.). (ENG.). 2002. audio compact disk 36.00 (978-1-4001-0041-5(0)); audio compact disk 20.00 (978-1-4001-5041-0(8)) Pub: Tantor Media. Dist(s): IngramPubServ

Bat. unabr. ed. Mary Roberts Rinehart. Narrated by Shelly Frasier. (Running Time: 7 hrs. 0 mins. 0 sec.). (ENG.). 2009. audio compact disk 19.99 (978-1-4001-6106-5(1)); audio compact disk 27.99 (978-1-4001-1106-0(4)); audio compact disk 55.99 (978-1-4001-4106-7(0)) Pub: Tantor Media. Dist(s): IngramPubServ

Bat Chat: An Introduction to Echolocation. unabr. ed. Merlin D. Tuttle & Bat Conservation International Staff. 1 cass. (Running Time: 30 mins.). (ENG.). 1998. 9.95 (978-0-292-70854-9(8)) U of Tex Pr.

Bat 6. collector's ed. Virginia Euwer Wolff. Read by Listening Library Staff. 3 cass. (Running Time: 4 hrs. 30 min.). (J). 2000. 24.00 (978-0-7366-9021-8(2)) Books on Tape.
That's the softball game played every year between the sixth-grade girls of Barlow & Bear Creek Ridge, Oregon. This year there are two newcomers on each team: Aki & Shazam. The two girls find themselves on a collision course that explodes catastrophically on the morning of Bat 6, the day they've been preparing for all their lives.

Bat 6. unabr. ed. Virginia Euwer Wolff. 4 cass. (Running Time: 4 hrs.). 2001. 32.00 (LL0170, Chivers Child Audio) AudioGO.

Bat 6. unabr. ed. Virginia Euwer Wolff. 3 vols. (Running Time: 5 hrs. 18 mins.). (J). (gr. 5-9). 2004. pap. bk. 36.00 (978-0-8072-8222-9(7), YYA144SP, Listening Lib); 30.00 (978-0-8072-8221-2(9), LL0170, Listening Lib) Random Audio Pubg.

Batalla por la Tierra No. 2: Paz de las Galaxias. abr. ed. L. Ron Hubbard. Read by Daniel Quintero. 3 CDs.Tr. of Battlefield Earth 2 / Peace in the Galaxies. (SPA.). 2004. audio compact disk 17.00 (978-958-8218-40-3(3)) YoYoMusic.

Batalla por la Tierra No. 3: El Olvido del Dia Final. abr. ed. L. Ron Hubbard. 3 CDs.Tr. of Battlefield Earth 3 / The Forgotten Final Day. (SPA.). 2004. audio compact disk 17.00 (978-958-8218-41-0(1)) YoYoMusic.

Batalla por la Tierra 1 - La Tierra No Se Rinde. abr. ed. L. Ron Hubbard. 3 CDs.Tr. of Battlefield Earth 1 / Earth Never Gives up. (SPA.). 2004. audio compact disk 17.00 (978-958-8218-39-7(X)) YoYoMusic.

Batboy. Mike Lupica. (Running Time: 6 hrs.). (ENG.). (J). 2010. audio compact disk 29.95 (978-0-14-314569-1(X), PengAudBks) Penguin Grp USA.

Batesonian Model for Investigation. John Grinder & Robert Dilts. Read by John Grinder & Robert Dilts. 8 cass. (Running Time: 12 hrs.). (Syntax of Behavior One Ser.: Vol. IV). 1988. 99.95 set. Metamorphous Pr.
Grinder & Dilts explore the questions: what well-formedness constraints on human decision-making & action in the world are implied by Gregory Bateson's work? How are the epistomological constraints present through the reductionist action of human information processing to be accounted for? These themes are addressed as Dilts & Grinder lead the participants through a developmental process which identifies a cybernetically sound model for investigation.

Bath Heaven. (Running Time: 60 mins.). 2002. audio compact disk 15.99 (978-1-904972-19-8(5)) Global Jrny GBR GBR.

Bath Tangle. unabr. ed. Georgette Heyer. Read by Sian Phillips. 10 cass. (Running Time: 15 hrs.). 2000. 69.95 (978-0-7451-4036-0(X), CAB 733) Pub: Chivers Audio Bks GBR. Dist(s): AudioGO
Volatile Lady Serena and gentle Lady Fanny could not be less alike. Having just jilted the Marquis of Rotherman, Serena decides to take a house in Bath with the widowed Fanny. Soon both are caught in the romantic entanglements of the spa, to the chagrin of the Marquis. He has plans of his own for Fanny and Serena, but particularly for the woman who refuses his hand.

Bathhouse. unabr. ed. Farnoosh Moshiri. Read by Bernadette Dunne. (Running Time: 14400 sec.). (J). 2007. 24.95 (978-1-4332-1105-8(X)); audio compact disk 36.00 (978-1-4332-1106-5(8)) Blckstn Audio.

Bathhouse. unabr. ed. Farnoosh Moshiri. Read by Bernadette Dunne. (Running Time: 14400 sec.). 2007. audio compact disk 19.95 (978-1-4332-1107-2(6)) Blckstn Audio.

Bathtime for Biscuit. abr. ed. Alyssa Satin Capucilli. Illus. by Pat Schories. (My First I Can Read Bks.). (J). (ps up). 2002. 8.99 (978-0-06-444299-2(3)) HarperCollins Pubs.

Bathtime for Biscuit. abr. ed. Alyssa Satin Capucilli. Illus. by Pat Schories. (My First I Can Read Bks.). (J). (ps-k). 2007. 9.99 (978-0-06-133538-9(X), HarperFestival) HarperCollins Pubs.

***Bathtime for Biscuit, Biscuit Finds a Friend, & Biscuit.** abr. ed. Alyssa Satin Capucilli. Read by Andrea Kessler. (ENG.). 2006. (978-0-06-124103-1(2)); (978-0-06-124102-4(4)) HarperCollins Pubs.

Bathtime Fun: The Learning Line. Executive Producer Twin Sisters Productions Staff. 1 CD. (Running Time: 30 mins). (J). 2004. audio compact disk 12.99 (978-1-57583-728-4(5)) Twin Sisters.
Great new songs for every parent and child to enjoy together before, during, and after bathtime! Kids will learn to get ready for bathtime, how to point to hands, nose, knees, hands, feet, eyes, ears; right and left; basic counting and more. Enhanced CD includes activities, coloring pages, a parent guide and more to be printed from any home computer.

Bathtime Magic. Read by Joanie Bartels. 6 cass. (Running Time: 50 min.). (Magic Ser.). (J). (ps). 1989. 9.95 (DM6) Discov Music.
Contemporary & traditional songs.

Bathtime Magic. Read by Joanie Bartels. 1 cass. (Running Time: 30 min.). (Magic Ser.). (J). 1990. pap. bk. 8.95 incl. lyric bk. (978-1-881225-06-5(2)) Discov Music.
New packaging includes full length audio cassette & complete full color lyric book with words to "Waterplay tunes" & photos of Joanie & kids.

Batiste Bête Puante-Clovis Crawfish & Bertile's Bon Voyage. Mary Alice Fontenot. Narrated by Mary Alice Fontenot. (Clovis Crawfish Ser.). (ENG.). (J). 1998. 9.95 (978-1-56554-383-6(1)) Pelican.

Batman: Dead White. John Shirley. 2009. audio compact disk 19.99 (978-1-59950-599-2(1)) GraphicAudio.

Batman: Inferno. Alex Irvine. 2009. audio compact disk 19.99 (978-1-59950-554-1(1)) GraphicAudio.

Batman: The Stone King. unabr. ed. Based on a novel by Alan Grant. Narrated by Richard Rohan. 6 CDs. (Running Time: 6 hrs.). 2008. audio compact disk 19.99 (978-1-59950-458-2(8)) GraphicAudio.

Batman Beyond: Original Television Soundtrack. Prod. by Bruce Timm. (J). 2002. 9.98 (75924) Rhino Enter.
The soundtrack to the popular Saturday-morning Kids WB animated series. Features a dynamic combination of industrial rock and club-influenced dance music.

Batman Beyond: Return of the Joker Soundtrack. Perf. by Mephisto Odyssey et al. 1 CD. (Running Time: 1 hr.). (J). 2002. audio compact disk 17.98 (978-0-7379-0122-1(5), 75857) Rhino Enter.
Soundtrack from the Warner Home Video, as well as original tracks by top-selling artist. Also includes "Crash".

Batman Forever. Alan Grant. 1995. 279.68 (978-1-57042-372-7(5)) GrandCentral.

***Batman: the Lazarus Syndrome: A BBC Full-Cast Radio Drama.** Dirk Maggs. Narrated by Full Cast. (Running Time: 1 hr. 0 mins. 0 sec.). (ENG.). 2010. audio compact disk 14.95 (978-1-60998-044-3(1)) Pub: AudioGO. Dist(s): Perseus Dist

Batter Up! unabr. ed. Sherryl Clark. 1 CD. (Aussie Bites Ser.). (J). 2002. audio compact disk 39.95 (978-1-74030-848-9(4)) Pub: Bolinda Pubng AUS. Dist(s): Bolinda Pub Inc

Battering Rams. unabr. ed. Morris Gleitzman & Paul Jennings. Read by Stig Wemyss & Kate Hosking. (Running Time: 1 hr. 12 mins.). (Wicked! Ser.: Bk. 2). (J). audio compact disk 18.00 (978-1-74093-424-4(5)) Bolinda Pubng AUS.

Battering Rams. unabr. ed. Morris Gleitzman & Paul Jennings. 1 cass. (Running Time: 1 hr. 12 mins.). (Wicked! Ser.: Bk. 2). (J). 2001. 18.00 (978-1-74030-458-0(6)) Pub: Bolinda Pubng AUS. Dist(s): Bolinda Pub Inc

Battersea Girl. Martin Knight. 2008. 61.95 (978-1-84559-828-0(8)); audio compact disk 71.95 (978-1-84559-829-7(6)) Pub: Soundings Ltd GBR. Dist(s): Ulverscroft US

Battle: Defeating the Enemies of Your Soul. Thomas E. Trask & Wayde I. Goodall. (Running Time: 60 min.). 1997. 14.99 (978-0-310-21619-3(2)) Zondervan.
Strips the myths from spiritual warfare & shows its realities so you can fight with wisdom, focus & faith.

Battle at Zero Point. abr. ed. Mack Maloney. Abr. by Odin Westgaard. 4 cass. (Running Time: 6 hrs.). (Starhawk Ser.: No. 4). 2004. 25.00 (978-1-58807-350-1(5)) Am Pubng Inc.
The year is 7200 A.D. The Specials have controlled the galaxy for nearly 2000 years with near-immortal power and savage brutality. At the soul of the empire is the militaristic state of Earth?and one man with the courage to destroy the will of the inhuman oppressors dares to raise the flag of rebellion. That man is Hawk Hunter. In the middle of a fierce battle with the Imperial forces, Hunter suddenly finds himself alone. His badly damaged fleet has vanished?gone through a portal to another dimension. They can lay low, rest, make repairs, and build their strength for the next assault. But the enemy also finds the portal, and it leads them to a different dimension where they discover powerful and deadly new allies. Now Hunter must undertake his own interdimensional search for support, because when the portal re-opens, the battle that follows could destroy not only the rebels and the Empire, but also the entire galaxy.

Battle Begins. abr. unabr. ed. Jerry Ahern. Read by Alan Zimmerman. 4 vols. (Running Time: 6 hrs.). (Defender Ser.: No. 1). 2000. 25.00 (978-1-58807-021-0(2)) Am Pubng Inc.
Someone has organized the inner citys toughest gangs, trained and armed them with sophisticated weaponry, and set them loose on the streets. By the time police and politicos can act, its too late; the ruthless armies have turned America into a war zone. Every home and public place is a potential target. In one brutal instant, Professor David Holden has lost everything a man can lose. Now, the ex-Navy SEAL commando is fighting a war only a desperate man can wage. And once hes begun, no force on earth can stop him - not the military, not the government, and certainly not the enemy!.

Battle Begins. unabr. ed. Jerry Ahern. Read by Alan Zimmerman. 4 vols. No. 1. 2002. (978-1-58807-501-7(X)) Am Pubng Inc.

Battle Begins. unabr. ed. Jerry Ahern. Read by Alan Zimmerman. 4 vols. No. 1. 2003. audio compact disk (978-1-58807-694-6(6)) Am Pubng Inc.

Battle Begins. unabr. ed. Jerry Ahern. Read by Alan Zimmerman. 5 vols. (Running Time: 6 hrs.). (Defender Ser.: No. 1). 2003. audio compact disk 30.00 (978-1-58807-263-4(0)) Am Pubng Inc.

Battle Begins: Acts 13::1-52. Ed Young. 1998. 4.95 (978-0-7417-2179-2(1), A1179) Win Walk.

Battle Born. unabr. ed. Dale Brown. Read by Edward Lewis. 12 cass. (Running Time: 18 hrs.). 2000. 96.00 (978-0-7366-4780-9(5), 5125) Books on Tape.
An aerial techno-thriller about a world on the brink of World War III & a new generation of brash young Korean heroes who refuses to give up the newest nuclear power without a fight.

Battle Creek: A Novel. unabr. ed. Scott Lasser. Read by Ethan Hawke. 5 cass. (Running Time: 7 hrs.). 2000. 24.95 Pub Mills.

Battle Creek: A Novel. unabr. ed. Scott Lasser. Read by Ethan Hawke. 5 cass. (Running Time: 7 hrs. 30 mins.). 2001. 29.95 (978-1-57511-055-4(5)) Pub Mills.
An aging minor league baseball coach attempts to lead his team to a championship win while his players & family struggle with personal crises.

Battle Cry for a Generation: The Fight to Save America's Youth. Ron Luce. Read by Eric Martin. (ENG.). (YA). 2006. audio compact disk 24.99 (978-1-930034-67-9(9)) Casscomm.

Battle Cry of Freedom Pt. 1: The Civil War Era. unabr. collector's ed. James M. McPherson. Read by Wolfram Kandinsky. 10 cass. (Running Time: 15 hrs.). 1989. 80.00 (978-0-7366-1583-9(0), 2448-A) Books on Tape.
Filled with new information & fresh interpretations, Battle Cry of Freedom challenges traditional pictures of the Civil War. Starting with the momentous episodes that preceded the conflict - The Dred Scot Decision, the Lincoln-Douglas Debates, John Brown's raid on Harper's Ferry - McPherson recreates the atmosphere of the time. He makes us appreciate that war was inevitable. The war in Mexico two decades earlier had fueled national passions, but which way was the nation to go? One compromise after another failed, leaving finally the grimmest but only alternative - war.

Battle Cry of Freedom Pt. 2: The Civil War Era. collector's ed. James M. McPherson. Read by Wolfram Kandinsky. 10 cass. (Running Time: 15 hrs.). 1989. 80.00 (978-0-7366-1584-6(9), 2448-B) Books on Tape.

Battle Cry of Freedom Pt. 3: The Civil War Era. collector's ed. James M. McPherson. Read by Wolfram Kandinsky. 10 cass. (Running Time: 15 hrs.). 1989. 80.00 (978-0-7366-1585-3(7), 2448-C) Books on Tape.

Battle Flag. Bernard Cornwell. Read by Tom Parker. (Starbuck Chronicles: Vol. 3). 2000. 36.95 (978-1-59912-429-2(7)) Iofy Corp.

Battle Flag. unabr. ed. Bernard Cornwell. Read by Tom Parker. 11 cass. (Running Time: 16 hrs.). (Starbuck Chronicles: Vol. 3). 2001. 76.95 (978-0-7861-1986-8(1), 2756); audio compact disk 104.00 (978-0-7861-9738-5(2), 2756) Blckstn Audio.
After distinguishing himself at the Battle of Cedar Mountain, Confederate Captain Nate Starbuck's career is jeopardized through the suspicion & hostility of his brigade commander, the grandiose General Washington Faulconer.

Battle Flag. unabr. ed. Bernard Cornwell. Read by Hayward Morse. 14 CDs. (Running Time: 21 hrs.). (Starbuck Chronicles: Vol. 3). 2001. audio compact disk 99.95 (978-0-7531-1049-2(0), 110490) Pub: ISIS Audio GBR. Dist(s): Ulverscroft US

Battle Flag. unabr. ed. Bernard Cornwell. Read by Hayward Morse. 12 cass. (Running Time: 16 hrs.). (Starbuck Chronicles: Vol. 3). (J). 2004. 94.95 (978-1-85695-916-2(3), 951005) Pub: ISIS Lrg Prnt GBR. Dist(s): Ulverscroft US

Battle Flag. unabr. ed. Bernard Cornwell. Narrated by Ed Sala. 11 cass. (Running Time: 15 hrs. 30 mins.). (Starbuck Chronicles: Vol. 3). 2000. 94.00 (978-0-7887-4320-7(1), 95777E7) Recorded Bks.
Civil War drama based on the Campaign of Second Manassas in August, 1862. There, Nate Starbuck, a Northerner fighting for the South, faces opponents on all sides: fierce Union soldiers, an ambitious commanding officer & his zealous Yankee father.

Battle for America 2008: The Story of an Extraordinary Election. Dan Balz & Haynes Johnson. Read by Dick Hill. (Playaway Adult Nonfiction Ser.). 2009. 69.99 (978-1-4418-1025-0(0)) Find a World.

Battle for America 2008: The Story of an Extraordinary Election. unabr. ed. Dan Balz & Haynes Johnson. Read by Dick Hill. (Running Time: 17 hrs.). 2009. 24.99 (978-1-4418-0059-6(X), 9781441800596, Brilliance MP3); 39.97 (978-1-4418-0060-2(3), 9781441800602, Brlnc Audio MP3 Lib); 24.99 (978-1-4418-0061-9(1), 9781441800619, BAD); 39.97 (978-1-4418-0062-6(X), 9781441800626, BADLE); audio compact disk 99.97 (978-1-4418-0058-9(1), 9781441800589, BriAudCD Unabrid) Brilliance Audio.

Battle for America 2008: The Story of an Extraordinary Election. unabr. ed. Dan Balz et al. Read by Dick Hill. 14 CDs. (Running Time: 17 hrs.). 2009. audio compact disk 29.99 (978-1-4418-0057-2(3), 9781441800572) Brilliance Audio.

Battle for Freedom, Set. Andrew Cohen. 2 cass. 2000. bk. 17.95 (978-1-883929-31-2(8)) Moksha Pr.

Battle for Gaul. unabr. collector's ed. Julius Caesar. Read by Bob Erickson. 8 cass. (Running Time: 12 hrs.). 1980. 64.00 (978-0-7366-0466-6(9), 1438) Books on Tape.
Contains seven books of Caesar's "Commentaries" on his campaigns in Gaul from 58 to 50 B.C. in their original narrative sequence. These unparalleled accounts of war in Western Europe in the closing years of the Roman Republic are clear & exciting.

Battle for God. abr. ed. Karen Armstrong. Read by Karen Armstrong. 2004. audio compact disk 29.95 (978-0-06-059187-8(0)) HarperCollins Pubs.

Battle for Morningside Heights. unabr. collector's ed. Roger Kahn. Read by Michael Russotto. 7 cass. (Running Time: 10 hrs. 30 min.). 1990. 56.00 (978-0-7366-1847-2(3), 2680) Books on Tape.
Student unrest, racism & war - these issues dominated the Vietnam era & are explored here by a witness to the events. Roger Kahn tells the story of rebellion on a single American campus. What makes it memorable, apart from the courage & the brutality, is that it fired student uprisings throughout the nation. It is the story of a great university, Columbia, torn apart by rage. Though less obvious now, the symptoms lie just below the surface of events today.

Battle for Okinawa. unabr. collector's ed. Hiromichi Yahara. Read by Dick Estell. 8 cass. (Running Time: 8 hrs.). 1996. 48.00 (978-0-7366-3342-0(1), 3992) Books on Tape.
Col. Yahara was one of the Japanese Imperial Army's best strategists. He had the career officer's classically cool, analytical approach to warfare. The "charge the foe" tactics, typical of the Japanese Army, were not his style. His plan at Okinawa, the last campaign of WWII, was to dig in, inflict as many casualties as possible & buy Japan precious time to prepare for the defense of the mainland. The plan worked - so why was Col. Yahara branded a traitor? His crime was surviving in an army that demanded its leaders go down with their troops.

***Battle for Rondo.** unabr. ed. Emily Rodda. Read by Edwina Wren. 9 CDs. (Running Time: 11 hrs. 5 mins.). (J). 2010. audio compact disk 93.95 (978-1-74214-566-2(3), 9781742145662) Pub: Bolinda Pubng AUS. Dist(s): Bolinda Pub Inc

Battle for the Castle. Elizabeth Winthrop. Read by Elizabeth Winthrop. 3 cass. (Running Time: 4 hrs. 30 mins.). (J). 2000. 24.00 (978-0-7366-9019-5(0)) Books on Tape.
Sequel to "The Castle in the Attic", this is about twelve-year-old William & his return to the mystical world of Sir Simon's castle in the Middle Ages. But this time he must defeat an army of rats to save the kingdom!.

Battle for the Castle. unabr. ed. Elizabeth Winthrop. 3 cass. (Running Time: 3 hrs.). 2001. 30.00 (LL0090, Chivers Child Audio) AudioGO.

Battle for the Castle. unabr. ed. Elizabeth Winthrop. Read by Words Take Wing Repertory Company Staff. 3 cass. (Running Time: 4 hrs. 33 mins.). (Castle in the Attic Ser.). (J). (gr. 4-7). 1997. 30.00 (978-0-8072-7793-5(2), YA919CX, Listening Lib) Random Audio Pubg.
Twelve-year old William returns to the mystical world of Sir Simon's castle in the Middle Ages.

Battle for the Castle. unabr. ed. Read by Words Take Wing Repertory Company Staff. Ed. by Elizabeth Winthrop. 3 vols. (Running Time: 4 hrs. 33 mins.). (J). (gr. 4-7). 1997. pap. bk. 36.00 (978-0-8072-7794-2(0), YA9195P, Listening Lib) Random Audio Pubg.

Battle for the Castle, Set. unabr. ed. Elizabeth Winthrop. 3 cass. (YA). 1999. 23.98 (FS9-31422) Highsmith.

Battle for the Mind. David T. Demola. 6 cass. 24.00 (S-1076) Faith Fellow Min.

Battle for the Rhine: The Battle of the Bulge & the Ardennes Campaign 1944. unabr. ed. Robin Neillands. Read by James Adams. (Running Time: 43200 sec.). 2007. audio compact disk 44.95 (978-0-7861-7017-3(4)); audio compact disk 34.95 (978-0-7861-5886-7(7)) Blckstn Audio.

Battle for the Rhine: The Battle of the Bulge & the Ardennes Campaign 1944. unabr. ed. Robin Neillands. Read by James Adams. (Running Time: 43200 sec.). 2007. 89.95 (978-0-7861-6824-8(2)); audio compact disk 120.00 (978-0-7861-6823-1(4)) Blckstn Audio.

Battle for the Soul of Capitalism: How the Financial System Underminded Social Ideals, Damaged Trust in the Markets, Robbed Investors of Trillions - & What to Do about It. abr. rev. ed. John C. Bogle. Read by Stefan Rudnicki. (Running Time: 9 hrs.). (ENG.). 2007. audio compact disk 39.98 (978-1-59659-098-4(X), GildAudio) Pub: Gildan Media. Dist(s): HachBkGrp

Battle for the Soul of Capitalism: How the Financial System Underminded Social Ideals, Damaged Trust in the Markets, Robbed Investors of Trillions - and What to Do about It. abr. ed. John C. Bogle. Read by Stefan Rudnicki. (Playaway Adult Nonfiction Ser.). (ENG.). 2008. 64.99 (978-1-60640-812-4(7)) Find a World.

Battle for the West - Thermopylae. unabr. collector's ed. Ernle Bradford. Read by Walter Zimmerman. 8 cass. (Running Time: 8 hrs.). 1985. 48.00 (978-0-7366-0776-6(5), 1730) Books on Tape.
By their remarkable stand at Thermopylae, the Greeks saved Western civilization.

Battle Hymn for a Lost Lawman. T. T. Flynn. 2009. (978-1-60136-348-0(6)) Audio Holding.

***Battle Hymn of the Tiger Mother.** Amy Chua. (Running Time: 6 hrs.). (ENG.). 2011. audio compact disk 29.95 (978-0-14-242910-5(4), PengAudBks) Penguin Grp USA.

Battle Lines. AIO Team Staff. Created by Focus on the Family Staff. 4 CDs. (Running Time: 6 hrs.). (Adventures in Odyssey Ser.: Vol. 38). (ENG.). (J). 2005. audio compact disk 24.99 (978-1-58997-030-4(6)) Pub: Focus Family. Dist(s): Tyndale Hse

Battle of Alcatraz: An Original Radio Drama. 2005. audio compact disk 12.99 (978-0-9817573-2-2(4)) Scene Unseen.

Battle of Arnhem. collector's ed. Christopher Hibbert. Read by David Case. 6 cass. (Running Time: 9 hrs.). 1999. 48.00 (978-0-7366-4883-7(6), 5105) Books on Tape.
The nine day battle, fought at Arnhem in September 1944, is one of the great tragedies of the British Army. Had the 1st British Airborne Division succeeded in holding the bridgehead until the arrival of the 2nd Army, Field Marshal Montgomery's plan of a single full blooded thrust across the Rhine & into the heart of Germany might have succeeded & the war ended but based on erroneous intelligence & characterized by a succession of miscalculations, Operation Market Garden ended instead in surrender & retrea.

Battle of Brunan Burg see Beowulf & Other Poetry

Battle of Bubble & Squeak, Set. Contrib. by Philippa Pearce. 2 cass. (J). 1996. 14.95 (978-0-86220-049-7(0)) AudioGO.

Battle of Corrin. unabr. ed. Brian Herbert & Kevin J. Anderson. Read by Scott Brick. 17 cass. (Running Time: 25 hrs.). 2004. 128.00 (978-1-4159-0390-2(5)) Books on Tape.
The sequel to Dune: The Machine Crusade, and the last in the prequel trilogy to Frank Herbert's Dune.

Battle of Corrin. unabr. rev. ed. Brian Herbert et al. Read by Scott Brick & Scott Sowers. 22 CDs. (Running Time: 25 hrs. 0 mins. 0 sec.). (Dune Ser.). (ENG.). 2004. audio compact disk 59.95 (978-1-59397-425-1(6)) Pub: Macmill Audio. Dist(s): Macmillan

Battle of Gettysburg. Compiled by Benchmark Education Staff. 2006. audio compact disk 10.00 (978-1-4108-6637-0(8)) Benchmark Educ.

Battle of Gettysburg. unabr. ed. Frank Haskell. Narrated by Tom West. 3 cass. (Running Time: 3 hrs. 30 mins.). 1982. 26.00 (978-1-55690-038-9(4), 82031E7) Recorded Bks.
On the last day of this fateful battle he found himself at the center of the Union line as Pickett charged. Two weeks later, while his memory was fresh & his adrenaline still high, he wrote this.

Battle of Jericho. 6 cass. (Running Time: 8:15 hrs.). (YA). 2005. 54.75 (978-1-4025-6485-7(6)) Recorded Bks.

Battle of Jericho. Sharon M. Draper. audio compact disk (978-1-4025-8741-2(4)) Recorded Bks.

Battle of Kadesh. unabr. ed. Christian Jacq. Read by Stephen Thorne. 10 cass. (Running Time: 15 hrs.). 2001. 84.95 (991106) Pub: ISIS Audio GBR. Dist(s): Ulverscroft US
To save Egypt from the Hittites, Ramses must face the might of a powerful army whose weapons are vastly superior to Egypt's own. War seems inevitable & it is at the impenetrable fortress of Kadesh that the first major battle is to take place. But the health of his beloved wife, Nefertari, is failing rapidly & a pro-Hittite underground network continues to grow. Ramses needs to travel South in search of the Stone Goddess - the last hope to save his dying Queen - but the imminent battle to save his entire civilization is to the North. Will Ramses' father, now a god, answer his desperate pleas for help & guidance?.

Battle of Kadesh. unabr. ed. Christian Jacq. 10 CDs. (Running Time: 38400 sec.). (Ramses Ser.: No. 3). 1999. audio compact disk 89.95 (978-0-7531-1245-8(0), 1245-0) Pub: ISIS Lrg Prnt GBR. Dist(s): Ulverscroft US

Battle of Leyte Gulf: The Greatest Naval Battle in History. unabr. ed. Thomas J. Cutler. Read by John Edwardson. 9 cass. (Running Time: 13 hrs. 30 min.). 1999. 72.00 (978-0-7366-4284-2(6), 4782) Books on Tape.
Reveals the heroism, the flawed strategies & the brutal reality of the greatest naval battle of all time.

Battle of Life. Charles Dickens. Read by Anais 9000. 2008. 27.95 (978-1-60112-201-8(2)) Babblebooks.

Battle of Lynchburg: Audio Driving Tour. Vanloan Naisawald. Narrated by James I. Robertson, Jr. Executive Producer Historic Sandusky Foundation Staff. Music by Martin E. Liebschner, Jr. Directed By Gregory H. Starbuck. 1 cass. (Running Time: 74 mins.). 2002. 7.99 (978-0-9722124-1-0(8)); audio compact disk 9.99 (978-0-9722124-0-3(X)) Histc Sndsky Fndtn.
Narrated history of the Civil War Battle of Lynchburg, Virginia with authentic music and realistic battle sounds. Fold out battlefield map included. Can be used to take a driving tour of Lynchburg's Civil War sites.

Battle of Mazar-E-Sharif & the Uprising of Qala-I-Jangi Prison. abr. ed. Doug Stanton. 5 CDs. (Running Time: 6 hrs.). 2005. audio compact disk 29.98 (978-1-59483-022-8(3)) Hachet Audio.

Battle of Midway. 1 cass. (Running Time: 30 min.). 8.00 (H0140B090, HarperThor) HarpC GBR.

Battle of New Orleans. Robert V. Remini. Read by Raymond Todd. 2000. audio compact disk 19.95 (2694) Blckstn Audio.
This swashbuckling account of Andrew Jackson & the climactic battle of the War of 1812 is ol' fashioned flag-waving, musket-firing American history, by a grandly ol' fashioned American historian.

Battle of New Orleans: Andrew Jackson & America's First Military Victory. unabr. ed. Robert V. Remini. Read by Raymond Todd. 5 cass. (Running Time: 7 hrs.). 2000. 39.95 (978-0-7861-1901-1(2), 2694); audio compact disk 48.00 (978-0-7861-9793-4(5), 2694) Blckstn Audio.

Battle of New Orleans: Andrew Jackson & America's First Military Victory. unabr. ed. Robert V. Remini. Narrated by Richard M. Davidson. 6 cass. (Running Time: 8 hrs. 15 mins.). 2000. 57.00 (978-0-7887-4421-1(6), 96191E7) Recorded Bks.
In January of 1815, several thousand seasoned British soldiers attacked New Orleans expecting an easy victory. However, Andrew Jackson's ragtag army - including free blacks, Indians & pirates - repelled the invasion, finally establishing America as a lasting democracy.

Battle of Peachtree Creek: An Audio Driving Tour. Marianne L. Gardner. 1 cass. 1996. 12.95 (978-0-9676290-1-8(2)) Ghost Tours.
Takes you back in time to the Civil War in Atlanta. Hear the stories of real people who fought the battle. Includes a map.

Battle of the Labyrinth. unabr. ed. Rick Riordan. Read by Jesse Bernstein. (Percy Jackson & the Olympians Ser.: Bk. 4). (J). 2008. 49.99 (978-1-60514-853-3(9)) Find a World.

Battle of the Labyrinth. unabr. ed. Rick Riordan. Read by Jesse Bernstein. 9 CDs. (Running Time: 10 hrs. 23 mins.). (Percy Jackson & the Olympians Ser.: Bk. 4). (YA). (gr. 5-9). 2008. audio compact disk 55.00 (978-0-7393-6476-5(6), Listening Lib) Pub: Random Audio Pubg. Dist(s): Random

Battle of the Labyrinth. unabr. ed. Rick Riordan. Read by Jesse Bernstein. (Running Time: 37980 sec.). (Percy Jackson & the Olympians Ser.: Bk. 4). (J). (gr. 4). 2008. audio compact disk 37.00 (978-0-7393-6474-1(X), Listening Lib) Pub: Random Audio Pubg. Dist(s): Random

Battle of the Little Bighorn. unabr. collector's ed. Mari Sandoz. Read by Dick Estell. 6 cass. (Running Time: 6 hrs.). 1992. 36.00 (978-0-7366-2134-2(2), 2934) Books on Tape.
What would Custer say about the battle that made him a legend? We will never know of course, but Mari Sandoz, in her beautifully written & deeply felt story of his legendary & much disputed battle, provides a suitable coda to that drama of a century ago.

Battle of the Mad Scientists & Other Tales of Survival. unabr. ed. Bill Harley. Read by Bill Harley. 1 cass., 1 CD. (Running Time: 1 hr. 03 min.). (J). (gr. 3-6). 1999. 10.00 (978-1-878126-31-3(8), RRR114); audio compact disk 15.00 CD. (978-1-878126-32-0(6), RRR114J) Round Riv Prodns.

Battle of the Mountain Man. William W. Johnstone. 4 cass. (Running Time: 6 hrs.). (Mountain Man Ser.: No. 21). 2001. 24.95 (978-1-890990-77-0(9)) Otis Audio.
Smoke Jensen has a good woman by his side & all he needs to have the best cattle ranch in Colorado is a prime steer. But with a cattle war turning all into a battleground & a ruthless gang of rustlers hanging around it won't be easy.

Battle of the Rhine: The Battle of the Bulge & the Ardennes Campaign 1944. unabr. ed. Robin Neillands. Read by James Adams. (Running Time: 43200 sec.). 2007. 32.95 (978-0-7861-4936-0(1)) Blckstn Audio.

Battle of the Villa Fiorita. unabr. ed. Rumer Godden. Read by Sheri Blair. 6 cass. (Running Time: 9 hrs.). 1982. 51.00 (978-1-55690-039-6(2), 82038E7) Recorded Bks.
Fanny abandons the family circle for the wildly attractive Rob, a film director writing his next movie at a villa on Lake Garda in Northern Italy.

Battle over Southern California's Sunshine Canyon - A Dump or an Oak Forest? Hosted by Nancy Pearlman. 1 cass. (Running Time: 29 min.). 10.00 (1014) Educ Comm CA.

Battle Ready. abr. ed. Tom Clancy. Read by Tony Zinni. Based on a work by Tony Zinni. Told to Tony Koltz & Robb Webb. 2004. 15.95 (978-0-7435-4188-6(X)) Pub: S&S Audio. Dist(s): S and S Inc

Battle Ready. unabr. ed. Tom Clancy et al. Narrated by Henry Strozier & Alan Nebelthau. 12 cass. (Running Time: 17 hrs. 45 mins.). 2004. 99.75 (978-1-4193-0464-4(X), 97842MC) Recorded Bks.

Battle Ready: Prepare to Be Used by God. unabr. ed. Steve Farrar. Narrated by Jim Sanders. (Running Time: 7 hrs. 24 mins. 52 sec.). (Bold Men of God Ser.). (ENG.). 2009. 19.59 (978-1-60814-519-5(0)); audio compact disk 27.99 (978-1-59859-580-2(6)) Oasis Audio.

Battle Road. Perf. by Colonial Radio Theatre Staff. 1 cass. (Running Time: 64 mins.). 2001. 12.95 (COLR001) Lodestone Catalog.
Nothing is more American than the beginning of the American Revolution, from Paul Revere's famed midnight ride to the retreat from Concord.

Battle Road. Perf. by Colonial Radio Theatre Staff. 1 cass. (Running Time: 1 hr.). Dramatization. (J). 12.98 (978-1-929244-00-3(2), COLR001) Pub: Colonial Radio. Dist(s): Penton Overseas
The Redcoats are coming - one if by land, two if by sea. If ever one single day has been woven in myth & legend, it is the 19th of April, 1775. From the lanterns of the Old North Church to the famous midnight ride, these events have taken on a storybook mystique.

Battle to Fight -Spiritual Warfare for Men. Featuring John Eldredge. (ENG.). 2009. audio compact disk 12.99 (978-1-933207-37-7(X)) Ransomed Heart.

Battle with Satan to Stay Morally Clean. Don J. Black. 1 cass. 2004. 7.98 (978-1-55503-099-5(8), 06002846) Covenant Comms.
An important talk on chastity.

Battlefield Earth: A Saga of the Year 3000. L. Ron Hubbard. Read by Michael Russotto. 30 cass. (Running Time: 45 hrs.). 2000. 79.95 (978-0-7366-4769-4(4), 3403) Books on Tape.
Huge, sprawling science-fiction novel with fast-paced intergalactic action in the year 3000.

Battlefield Earth: A Saga of the Year 3000. abr. ed. L. Ron Hubbard. Read by Roddy McDowall. 6 cass. (Running Time: 8 hrs.). 1991. 29.95 (978-0-88404-682-0(6)) Bridge Pubns Inc.
In Hubbard's 1982 work of "pure" science fiction, the year 3000 is dominated by a brutal race called the Psychlos, who have conquered Earth to establish a mining operation. Jonnie Goodboy Tyler, the story's hero, along with a band of surviving Scotsmen, ingeniously eliminate the Psychlos from Earth

& then go on to do some technological, financial, & diplomatic fast-thinking to keep other alien races from taking the Psychlos' place.

Battlefield Earth: A Saga of the Year 3000. abr. ed. L. Ron Hubbard. Read by Roddy McDowell. 6 cass. (Running Time: 8 hrs.). 1991. 29.95 (978-1-59212-008-6(3)) Gala Pr LLC.
L. Ron Hubbard's groundbreaking novel Battlefield Earth is given a dynamic and versatile portrayal that captures the epic and compelling action along with the unforgettable characters of a science fiction masterpiece.

Battlefield Earth Pt. 1: A Saga of the Year 3000. unabr. collector's ed. L. Ron Hubbard. Read by Michael Russotto. 15 cass. (Running Time: 22 hrs. 30 min.). 1994. 120.00 (978-0-7366-2665-1(4), 3403-A) Books on Tape.
Huge, sprawling science-fiction novel with fast-paced intergalactic action in the year 3000.

Battlefield Earth Pt. 2: A Saga of the Year 3000. collector's ed. L. Ron Hubbard. Read by Michael Russotto. 15 cass. (Running Time: 22 hrs. 30 min.). 1994. 120.00 (978-0-7366-2666-8(2), 3403-B) Books on Tape.

Battlefield Earth 1 / Earth Never Gives up see Batalla por la Tierra 1 - La Tierra No Se Rinde

Battlefield Earth 1 / Earth Never Gives Up. L. Ron Hubbard. Read by Santiago Munevar. (Running Time: 3 hrs.). 2004. 16.95 (978-1-60083-292-5(X), Audiofy Corp) Iofy Corp.

Battlefield Earth 2 / Peace in the Galaxies see Batalla por la Tierra, No. 2, Paz de las Galaxias

Battlefield Earth 2 / Peace in the Galaxies. L. Ron Hubbard. Read by Daniel Quintero. (Running Time: 3 hrs.). 2004. 16.95 (978-1-60083-293-2(8), Audiofy Corp) Iofy Corp.

Battlefield Earth 3 / The Forgotten Final Day see Batalla por la Tierra, No. 3, El Olvido del Dia Final

Battlefield Earth 3 / the Forgotten Final Day. L. Ron Hubbard. Read by Hernando Iván Cano. (Running Time: 3 hrs.). 2004. 16.95 (978-1-60083-294-9(6), Audiofy Corp) Iofy Corp.

Battlefield of the Mind: Winning the Battle in Your Mind. abr. rev. unabr. ed. Joyce Meyer. Read by Joyce Meyer. Read by Pat Lentz. 4 cass. (Running Time: 7 hrs. 30 mins.). (ENG.). 2006. audio compact disk 29.98 (978-1-58621-534-7(5)) Pub: Hachet Audio. Dist(s): HachBkGrp

Battlefield of the Mind: Winning the Battle in Your Mind. unabr. ed. Joyce Meyer. Read by Pat Lentz. (Running Time: 7 hrs. 30 mins.). (ENG.). 2006. 14.98 (978-1-59483-872-9(0)) Pub: Hachet Audio. Dist(s): HachBkGrp

Battlefield of the Mind: Winning the Battle in Your Mind. unabr. ed. Joyce Meyer. Read by Pat Lentz. (Running Time: 7 hrs. 30 mins.). (ENG.). 2009. 44.98 (978-1-60788-288-6(4)) Pub: Hachet Audio. Dist(s): HachBkGrp

Battlefields & Campfires. unabr. ed. Christopher L. Woods. Read by Mark Luce & Rick Moock. Ed. by Julie Elaine Fleming. 2 cass. (Running Time: 2 hrs.). Dramatization. (Civil War Era Songs Ser.: Vol. 1). 1994. 19.95 set. (978-1-884649-03-5(3)) Nouveau Glass.
Cassette (A) has 15 popular songs of the Civil War Era sung by the 97th Regimental String Band wihtout interruption. Cassette (B) has the history of each of the songs popular in both the North & South with anecdotes, parodies & sidelights on their creation, plus an overview of Civil War Era music.

Battleground. unabr. ed. W. E. B. Griffin. Read by Michael Russotto. 12 cass. (Running Time: 18 hrs.). (Corps Ser.: Bk. 4). 1993. 96.00 (978-0-7366-2240-0(3), 3030) Books on Tape.
Tells of the bloody months spanning Midway & Guadalcanal. A story of courage, loyalty, dedication & honor.

Battlers. unabr. ed. Kylie Tennant. Read by Jacklyn Kelleher. 9 cass. (Running Time: 13 hrs. 30 min.). 1998. (978-1-86340-610-9(7), 560208) Bolinda Pubng AUS.
The story of Snow, a drifter & wanderer, Dancy a hard-bitten young woman, & the motley crowd of battlers that travelled the roads of Australia in the '30s, looking for work or avoiding it.

Battles Lost & Won. unabr. ed. Hanson W. Baldwin. Read by Daniel Grace. 12 cass. (Running Time: 18 hrs.). 1976. 96.00 (978-0-7366-0005-7(1), 1015) Books on Tape.
Reviews the eleven great campaigns of World War II. The battles selected present a cross-section of the world's greatest war - from the Polish campaign, where Blitzkrieg was born, to Okinawa, the last battle, where the Kamikaze portended the coming menace of the missile.

Battles of Dune see Dune Trilogy

Battlestar Galactica: The Miniseries. abr. ed. Jeffrey A. Carver. (Running Time: 9 hrs. 0 mins. 0 sec.). 2006. 11.95 (978-1-59397-868-6(5)) Pub: Macmill Audio. Dist(s): Macmillan

Battlewagon see Twentieth-Century Poetry in English, No. 7, Recordings of Poets Reading Their Own Poetry

Battling Unbelief: Defeating Sin with Superior Pleasure. unabr. ed. John Piper. Narrated by Rob Lamont. (ENG.). 2007. 13.99 (978-1-60814-040-4(7)); audio compact disk 19.99 (978-1-59859-189-7(4)) Oasis Audio.

Baudolini see Baudolino

Baudolino. Umberto Eco. Narrated by George Guidall. 13 cass. (Running Time: 19 hrs.).Tr. of Baudolini. 98.00 (978-1-4025-3199-6(0)) Recorded Bks.

Baudolino. unabr. ed. Umberto Eco. 12 cass. (Running Time: 22 hrs.).Tr. of Baudolini. 2002. 34.99 (978-1-4025-2814-9(0)) Recorded Bks.
As Constantinople is being pillaged and burned in April 1204, a young man, Baudolino, manages to save a historian and a high court official from certain death at the hands of crusading warriors. Born a simple peasant, Baudolino has two gifts: his ability to learn languages and to lie. A young man, he is adopted by a foreign commander who sends him to university in Paris. After he allies with a group of fearless and adventurous fellow students, they go in search of a vast kingdom to the East-a kingdom of strange creatures, eunuchs, unicorns and, of course, lovelymaidens.

Bavarian Sunset. James Pattinson. 2009. 49.95 (978-1-4079-0265-4(2)); audio compact disk 59.95 (978-1-4079-0266-1(0)) Pub: Soundings Ltd GBR. Dist(s): Ulverscroft US

Bawdy Beautiful. abr. ed. Nathaniel Hawthorne. 2 cass. (Running Time: 1 hr. 20 min.). 1991. 21.95 (978-1-55656-050-7(8)) Dercum Audio.

Baxter Black - Cowboy Pride. Poems. Baxter Black. Read by Baxter Black. 1 cass. (Running Time: 1 hr.). 1995. 9.99 (978-0-939343-19-5(3)) Coyote Cowboy.
Cowboy Pride - how do you explain it? Well, you can't come any closer than Baxter has on this new hour long collection of poems. All performed by Baxter, each is introduced by a friend, from Ben Johnson to Bobbie Gentry...Dramatic, wry & poignant, these poems describe the cowboy way from the inside out.

Baxter Black & Friends. Poems. Baxter Black. Perf. by Hoyt Axton et al. 1 cass. 9.99 (978-0-939343-26-3(6)) Coyote Cowboy.
Hear Baxter's poetry performed by some of his celebrity friends. Included are such poems as "Supersalesman," "A Time to Stay," "The Silent Partner" & "The Cowboy & His Dog".

Baxter Black Box Set: Cowboy Pride, Bucks Off, Live Uptown, Live at the Grange. Baxter Black. 4 cass. (Running Time: 6 hrs.). (J). 1996. 24.95 (978-0-939343-24-9(X)) Coyote Cowboy.
Variety of material performed in 4 different settings: Including: "Cowboy Pride," " Baxter Black Bucks Off," "Live Uptown," & "Live at the Grange".

Baxter Black Bucks Off. Baxter Black. Read by Baxter Black. 1 cass. (Running Time: 1 hr.). 1995. 9.99 (978-0-939343-20-1(7)) Coyote Cowboy.
Most cowboy poetry is humorous...This is because of the close relationship between humor & tragedy. You see, when you work in the livestock business you get hurt...a lot...& sometimes the only way to deal with that is to laugh about it. Dr. Black has the cure with the "Cow Attack," "Header or Healer," "The Dog & the Rabbit" & 15 others...an hour's worth. Get well soon.

Baxter Black Live. Baxter Black. 1 cass. (Running Time: 1 hr. 30 min.). 1984. 9.99 (978-0-939343-25-6(8)) Coyote Cowboy.
Rollicking performance recorded live a the National Western Stock Show. Included are "One More Year," "Five Flat," "Take Care of Yer Friends" & "The Vegetarian's Nightmare".

Baxter Black Live: Baxter Black & Friends; Generic Cowboy Poetry; The Buckskin Mare. Poems. Baxter Black. 4 cass. 1989. 24.95 set. (978-0-939343-04-1(5)) Coyote Cowboy.
Baxter Black Live - a 90 minute rollicking performance recorded live at the National Western Stock Show. Included are: One More Year, Five Flat, Take Care of Yer Friends, The Vegetarian's Nightmare. Baxter Black & Friends - Hear Baxter's poetry performed by some of his celebrity friends like Hoyt Axton, Red Steagall, Ed Bruce, The Riders in the Sky, the Mystery Lady & Walt Garrison. Included are such poems as Supersalesman, A Time to Stay, The Silent Partner, The Cowboy & His Dog. Generic Cowboy Poetry.

Baxter Black Live at the Grange. Baxter Black. 1 cass. 1992. 9.99 (978-0-939343-11-9(8)) Coyote Cowboy.
This one is rated PC (Pretty Cowy). Recorded live at the Green Valley Grange in Brighton, Colorado. Perfect for the tractor, the rodeo trail, hunting camp, bunkhouse, parlor, grandpa, teenage equestrian or your best friend. Join us in the corral with the No. 2 Hairball, 20th Century Rustler, The Marker, The Cull, Fetal Eye View, El Gallo Con Espuelas & a herd of others.

Baxter Black Live Uptown. Poems. Baxter Black. 1 cass. 1992. 9.99 (978-0-939343-10-2(X)) Coyote Cowboy.
A real live performance recorded at the Horizon Theatre in Denver. Perfect for the new Baxter Black fan. You don't have to have touched a cow to understand what this is all about. Great stories & poetry in the Baxter tradition. You'll laugh out loud as you go Deep Sea Fishing, meet Junior, join the AARP!, hear all about The Angel on the Christmas Tree & Baxter'll give you goose bumps as he takes you into the midst of the Range Fire.

Baxter Black's. Baxter Black. 2 CDs. (Running Time: 3 hrs.). 1999. audio compact disk 24.95 (978-0-939343-32-4(0)) Coyote Cowboy.

***Bay.** Di Morrissey. Read by Kate Hood. (Running Time: 14 hrs. 25 mins.). 2010. 99.99 (978-1-74214-599-0(X), 9781742145990) Pub: Bolinda Pubng AUS. Dist(s): Bolinda Pub Inc

Bay. unabr. ed. Di Morrissey. Read by Kate Hood. (Running Time: 14 hrs. 25 mins.). 2009. audio compact disk 108.95 (978-1-74214-432-0(2), 9781742144320) Pub: Bolinda Pubng AUS. Dist(s): Bolinda Pub Inc

Bay Area to Sacramento on I-80. unabr. ed. Joy Wake. Read by Elaine West. 1 cass. (Running Time: 60 min.). (TripTape Ser.). 1993. 11.95 (978-1-883605-01-8(6)) Pub: Echo Peak Prods. Dist(s): Bookpeople
This TripTape describes historical sights & other points of interest along Interstate 80 between the San Francisco Bay area & Sacramento. Acoustic guitar, fiddle & sound effects.

Bay Cliff Memories. Based on a book by Fred Rydholm. (ENG.). 2004. audio compact disk 14.95 (978-0-9823000-3-9(4)) TopWater Prod.

Bay in Anglesey see Sir John Betjeman Reading His Poetry

Bay of Angels. unabr. ed. Anita Brookner. Read by Eleanor Bron. 6 CDs. (Running Time: 9 hrs.). 2002. audio compact disk 64.95 (978-0-7540-5447-4(0), CCD 138) AudioGO.
Zoe Cunningham is delighted when her widowed mother remarries, particularly as her new stepfather is amiable, generous, and the owner of a villa in Nice. Enchanted visits come to an abrupt end when an entirely unexpected tragedy ensues. This in its turn is followed by a bewildering decline in which both Zoe and Anne, her mother, are trapped." "Surrounded by strangers, however well-meaning, both yearn for home, although that home appears ever more remote. They are forced to learn how and how not to trust appearances.

Bay of Pigs Fiasco. Kenneth Bruce. 1 cass. (Running Time: 1 hr.). Dramatization. (Excursions in History Ser.). 12.50 Alpha Tape.

Bay Sunset. 2007. audio compact disk 19.95 (978-1-56136-161-8(5)) Master Your Mind.

Bay Sunset. Read by Mary Richards. 1 cass. (Running Time: 45 min.). (Energy Break Ser.). 9.95 (103) Master Your Mind.

Bayonets to Lhasa. unabr. collector's ed. Peter Fleming. Read by David Case. 8 cass. (Running Time: 12 hrs.). 1988. 64.00 (978-0-7366-1346-0(3), 2247) Books on Tape.
An account of the 1904 British invasion of Tibet - one of the strangest events in British imperial history.

Bayou Dogs. unabr. ed. Tony Abbott. Read by Nick Podehl. (Running Time: 3 hrs.). (Haunting of Derek Stone Ser.). 2009. 14.99 (978-1-4233-9489-1(5), 9781423394891, Brilliance MP3); 39.97 (978-1-4233-9490-7(9), 9781423394907, Brlnc Audio MP3 Lib); 14.99 (978-1-4233-9491-4(7), 9781423394914, BAD); 39.97 (978-1-4233-9492-1(5), 9781423394921, BADLE); audio compact disk 14.99 (978-1-4233-9487-7(9), 9781423394877, Bril Audio CD Unabri) Brilliance Audio.

Bayou Dogs. unabr. ed. Tony Abbott. Read by Nick Podehl. 3 CDs. (Running Time: 3 hrs.). (Haunting of Derek Stone Ser.: Bk. 2). (J). (gr. 5-7). 2009. audio compact disk 39.97 (978-1-4233-9488-4(7), 9781423394884, BriAudCD Unabrid) Brilliance Audio.

***Bayou Moon.** unabr. ed. Ilona Andrews. (Running Time: 15 hrs. 0 mins.). (Edge Ser.). 2010. 20.99 (978-1-4001-8845-1(8)) Tantor Media.

***Bayou Moon.** unabr. ed. Ilona Andrews. Narrated by Renée Raudman. (Running Time: 16 hrs. 0 mins. 0 sec.). (Edge Ser.). 2010. 29.99 (978-1-4001-6845-3(7)); audio compact disk 39.99 (978-1-4001-1845-8(X)) Pub: Tantor Media. Dist(s): IngramPubServ

***Bayou Moon (Library Edition)** unabr. ed. Ilona Andrews. (Running Time: 15 hrs. 0 mins.). (Edge Ser.). 2010. 39.99 (978-1-4001-9845-0(3)) Tantor Media.

***Bayou Moon (Library Edition)** unabr. ed. Ilona Andrews. Narrated by Renée Raudman. (Running Time: 16 hrs. 0 mins. 0 sec.). (Edge Ser.). 2010. audio compact disk 95.99 (978-1-4001-4845-5(6)) Pub: Tantor Media. Dist(s): IngramPubServ

Bayou Stories. Kate Chopin. Read by Jacqueline Kinlow. (Playaway Adult Fiction Ser.). 2008. 39.99 (978-1-60640-816-2(X)) Find a World.

Bayou Stories. Short Stories. Kate Chopin. Read by Jacqueline Kinlow. 2 cds. (Running Time: 2 hrs 10 mins). 2002. audio compact disk 18.95 (978-1-58472-209-0(6), 002, In Aud) Pub: Sound Room. Dist(s): Baker Taylor
Nine of Chopin's best stories, rich in the culture of Louisiana. 1) Love on the Bon-Dieu 2) A Lady of Bayou St. John 3) The Unexpected 4) At the 'Cadian Ball 5) Tante Cat'rinette 6) Desiree's Baby 7) The Falling in Love of Fedora 8) Story of an Hour 9) Beyond the Bayou.

BBB Bats Song. (Song Box Ser.). (gr. 1-2). bk. 8.50 (978-0-322-00247-0(8)) Wright Group.

BBB Bats Song, Set. (Song Box Ser.). (gr. 1-2). 68.95 (978-0-322-00273-9(7)) Wright Group.

BBC Mystery Series. abr. ed. 6 cass. (Running Time: 9 hrs.). Dramatization. 1991. 39.95 set.; 14.95 Murder Must Advertise by Dorothy Sayers.; 14.95 The Sittaford Mystery by Agatha Christie.; 14.95 Summer's Lease by John Mortimer. Minds Eye.
Dramatizations & abridgments produced by the BBC.

Bbc Sound Effects. Prod. by Bbc World-Wide Americas. (YA). audio compact disk 479.95 (978-0-7365-1693-8(X)) Films Media Grp.

Bbc Sound Effects Library: Set 1. Prod. by Bbc World-Wide Americas. (YA). audio compact disk 89.95 (978-0-7365-1694-5(8)) Films Media Grp.

Bbc Sound Effects Library: Set 2. Prod. by Bbc World-Wide Americas. (YA). audio compact disk 89.95 (978-0-7365-1695-2(6)) Films Media Grp.

Bbc Sound Effects Library: Set 3. Prod. by Bbc World-Wide Americas. (YA). audio compact disk 89.95 (978-0-7365-1696-9(4)) Films Media Grp.

Bbc Sound Effects Library: Set 4. Prod. by Bbc World-Wide Americas. (YA). audio compact disk 89.95 (978-0-7365-1697-6(2)) Films Media Grp.

Bbc Sound Effects Library: Set 5. Prod. by Bbc World-Wide Americas. (YA). audio compact disk 89.95 (978-0-7365-1698-3(0)) Films Media Grp.

Bbc Sound Effects Library: Set 6. Prod. by Bbc World-Wide Americas. (YA). audio compact disk 89.95 (978-0-7365-1699-0(9)) Films Media Grp.

***BBC War Reports - World War Two: The Home Front - Unique Broadcast Material & Interviews from the BBC Archives.** Compiled by British Broadcasting Corporation Staff. (Running Time: 2 hrs. 0 mins. 0 sec.). (ENG.). 2011. audio compact disk 29.95 (978-1-4084-6807-4(7)) Pub: AudioGO. Dist(s): Perseus Dist

BBC's Italianissimo Kit: A Self-Guided Course for Beginners Learning Italian. Denise De Rome. Contrib. by Denise De Rome. 4 cass. (Running Time: 300 min.). (ITA.). 2003. pap. bk. 49.95 (978-0-8442-8694-5(X), Contemporary) Pub: McGraw-Hill Trade. Dist(s): McGraw

BBC's Suenos, Set. Juan Kattán-Ibarra et al. 4 cass. (Running Time: 240 min.). (SPA.). 1999. pap. bk. 49.95 (978-0-8442-2408-4(1), Contemporary) Pub: McGraw-Hill Trade. Dist(s): McGraw

BBC's Suenos: World Spanish Kit. Mike Gonzalez et al. 4 cass. (Running Time: 300 min.). (SPA.). 2003. pap. bk. 49.95 (978-0-8442-0546-5(X), 0546X, Contemporary) Pub: McGraw-Hill Trade. Dist(s): McGraw

B.C. Salvation: Romans 4:1-12. Ed Young. 1996. 4.95 (978-0-7417-2111-2(2), 1111) Win Walk.

Bca Std Kit-Alg/Trig Geo 11e. 11th ed. (C). 2005. audio compact disk 11.95 (978-0-534-25262-5(1)) Pub: Brooks-Cole. Dist(s): CENGAGE Learn

Bca Stdt Kit-Beg/Int Alg 4e. 4th ed. (C). 2004. audio compact disk 10.95 (978-0-534-28065-9(X)) Pub: Brooks-Cole. Dist(s): CENGAGE Learn

Bca Student Kit - Liberal Arts Mathematics. 5th ed. (C). 2005. audio compact disk 10.95 (978-0-534-27511-2(7)) Pub: Brooks-Cole. Dist(s): CENGAGE Learn

Bca Student Kit for Faires/Defranza's Precalculus, 3rd. 3rd ed. (C). 2005. audio compact disk 10.95 (978-0-534-27503-7(6)) Pub: Brooks-Cole. Dist(s): CENGAGE Learn

Bca Tut Stdt Kit-Beg Alg 7e. 7th ed. (C). 2004. audio compact disk 10.95 (978-0-534-28063-5(3)) Pub: Brooks-Cole. Dist(s): CENGAGE Learn

Bca/Ilrn Stdt Kit-Int Alg 7e. 7th ed. (C). 2004. audio compact disk 10.95 (978-0-534-28064-2(1)) Pub: Brooks-Cole. Dist(s): CENGAGE Learn

Bca/Ilrn Stdt Kit-Trig 5e. 5th ed. Mckeague & Turner. (C). 2004. audio compact disk 10.95 (978-0-534-27535-8(4)) Pub: Brooks-Cole. Dist(s): CENGAGE Learn

Bcd Farworld, BK Two: Land Keep. J. Scott Savage. 2009. audio compact disk 39.95 (978-1-60641-168-1(3), Shadow Mount) Deseret Bk.

Bcd Undaunted. Gerald N. Lund. 2009. audio compact disk 69.95 (978-1-60641-192-6(6)) Deseret Bk.

Be a Better Bowler. Barrie Konicov. 1 cass. 11.98 (978-0-87082-416-6(3), 010) Potentials.
Demonstrates how to relax, concentrate, take a breath & throw a strike & do it again & again. You could find yourself adding 10, 15, even 20, pins to your game.

Be a Friend: The Story of African American Music in Song, Words & Pictures. Leotha A. Stanley. Illus. by Henry Hawkins. (J). (gr. 3 up). 1995. pap. bk. 19.95 (978-1-55933-153-1(4)) Zino Pr.

Be a Friend to Trees. abr. ed. Patricia Lauber. Read by Andrea Kessler. Illus. by Holly Keller. Contrib. by Andrea Kessler. (Let's-Read-and-Find-Out Science Ser.). (J). (gr. k-4). 1996. 8.99 (978-0-694-70047-9(9)) HarperCollins Pubs.

Be a Magnet to Money: Dynamic Psychological Breakthrough in How to Attract Money. 4th rev. ed. Michele Blood & Bob Proctor. Illus. by Van Crosby. 2 cass. (Running Time: 1 hr. 05 min.). 1995. audio compact disk 19.95 (978-1-890679-03-3(8), M082) Micheles.
Motivational program to help improve one's life to the positive & toward success.

Be a Peacemaker. Speeches. Joel Osteen. 1 Cass. (Running Time: 30 Mins.). 2002. 6.00 (978-1-59349-157-4(3), JA0157) J Osteen.

Be a Planet Pleaser. unabr. ed. Cindy the Songlady. Read by Cindy the Songlady. 1 cass. (Running Time: 27 min.). (J). (gr. k-3). 1992. 10.00 (978-0-9628207-2-4(5), KFP-03) Kid-Fun Prods.
Positive environmental children's songs. Songs involve children in helping the planet, learning about recycling, conservation, endangered animals - & more.

Be a Smile Millionaire. Paramhansa Yogananda. (Running Time: 1 hr. 3 mins.). 2007. audio compact disk 14.00 (978-0-87612-437-6(6)) Self Realization.

Be Alert - Stay Safe. Eldon Taylor. 1 cass. (Running Time: 62 min.). (Inner Talk Ser.). 16.95 incl. script. (978-1-55978-079-7(7), 5336C) Progress Aware Res.
Soundtrack - Musical Themes with underlying subliminal affirmations.

Be Alert, Stay Safe: Rhythm. Eldon Taylor. Read by Eldon Taylor. Ed. by Leslie Brice. 1 cass. (Running Time: 1 hr.). 1992. 16.95 (978-1-56705-292-3(4)) Gateways Inst.
Self improvement.

Be All That You Are. Read by Mary Richards. (Subliminal - Self Hypnosis Ser.). 12.95 (803); 12.95 (204) Master Your Mind.
Discusses how to relieve feelings of limitation & doubt.

Be All That You Are. Read by Mary Richards. 1 cass. (Running Time: 60 min.). (Series Two Thousand). 2007. audio compact disk 19.95 (978-1-56136-095-6(3)) Master Your Mind.

Be Anxious for Nothing: The Art of Casting Your Cares & Resting in God. Joyce Meyer. 4 cass. (Running Time: 4 hrs.). 2001. 22.00 (TJM-110) Harrison Hse.
Have you been worried lately? Worry torments a person and is totally useless. In the natural there is usually plenty to worry about, but the good news of the Gospel is that believers do not have to live in the natural realm! As believers in the Lord Jesus Christ, we have the privilege of casting our cares on Him. Refusal to worry shows that we are trusting God. We may speak words that say we are trusting, but actions speak louder than words in most instances.

Be-Attitudes for Fathers. Charles B. Beckert. 1 cass. 7.98 (978-1-55503-697-3(X), 06004938) Covenant Comms.
Want to be a great dad? This will help!.

Be-Attitudes for Fathers. Charles B. Beckert. 1 cass. 2004. 3.95 (978-1-57734-370-7(0), 34441085) Covenant Comms.

Be Blessed. Contrib. by Yolanda Adams. (Soundtraks Ser.). 2005. audio compact disk 8.99 (978-5-559-01263-6(7)) Christian Wrld.

Be-Bop Phrasing for Drums. Dominick Moio. 1998. pap. bk. 17.95 (978-0-7866-2869-8(3), 96681BCD) Mel Bay.

Be Buried in the Rain. unabr. ed. Barbara Michaels, pseud. Narrated by Barbara Rosenblat. 7 cass. (Running Time: 10 hrs. 30 mins.). 1992. 60.00 (978-1-55690-719-7(2), 92106E7) Recorded Bks.
Julie Newcomb has been called back to the birthplace of her worst memories, to be a companion to the one person she fears most. The truth lies somewhere on her grandmother's crumbling plantation, as real & terrifying as the two skeletons lying together in the swampy shadows of Deadman's Hollow.

Be Cool. Elmore Leonard. Read by Alexander Adams. 1999. audio compact disk 48.00 (978-0-7366-4761-8(9)) Books on Tape.

Be Cool. unabr. ed. Elmore Leonard. Read by Alexander Adams. 5 cass. (Running Time: 7 hrs. 30 mins.). 1999. 40.00 (978-0-7366-4449-5(0), 4894) Books on Tape.
Chili Palmer's follow-up to his smash hit film "Get Leo" is a disaster & in Hollywood, you're considered only as hot as your last project. Once again outside the system, Chili is exploring an idea for his third film by lunching with a former "associate" from his loan shark days in Brooklyn who's now a record label executive. When lunch begins with iced tea & ends in a mob hit on his pal, Chili soon finds himself in an unlikely alliance with one of LAPD's finest & the very likely next target of Russian gangsters.

Be Cool. unabr. ed. Elmore Leonard. Read by Alexander Adams. 7 CDs. (Running Time: 7 hrs 20 min.). 2000. audio compact disk (978-0-7366-5552-1(2)) Books on Tape.
Chili Palmer's follow-up to his smash hit film "Get Leo" is a disaster & in Hollywood you're considered only as hot as your last project. Once again outside the system, Chili is exploring an idea for his third film by lunching with a former "associate" from his loan shark days in Brooklyn who's now a record label executive. When lunch begins with iced tea & ends in a mob hit on his pal, Chili soon finds himself in an unlikely alliance with one of LAPD's finest & the very likely next target of Russian gangsters.

***Be Cool.** unabr. ed. Elmore Leonard. Read by Campbell Scott. (ENG.). 2005. (978-0-06-082479-2(4), Harper Audio); (978-0-06-082478-5(6), Harper Audio) HarperCollins Pubs.

Be Cool. unabr. ed. Elmore Leonard. Read by Campbell Scott. 6 CDs. (Running Time: 9 hrs.). 2005. audio compact disk 29.95 (978-0-06-077520-9(3)) HarperCollins Pubs.

Be Cool. unabr. ed. Elmore Leonard. Narrated by Ron McLarty. 6 cass. (Running Time: 8 hrs.). 1999. 51.00 (978-0-7887-2916-4(0), 95708E7) Recorded Bks.
Chili Palmer is a smooth operator. He's made a bundle in films & now he's taking on the recording industry. There's a leggy blonde who could be the net big singing star. But she has a funky manager who may be tied to the mob. All Chili has to do is promote the girl, lose the manager & avoid stray bullets.

Be Cool. unabr. ed. Elmore Leonard. Narrated by Ron McLarty. 7 CDs. (Running Time: 8 hrs.). 2000. audio compact disk 59.00 (978-0-7887-3430-4(X), C1036E7) Recorded Bks.

Be Cooperative: Ocean. Eldon Taylor. Read by Eldon Taylor. Ed. by Leslie Brice. 1 cass. (Running Time: 1 hr.). 1992. 16.95 (978-1-56705-320-3(3)) Gateways Inst.
Self improvement.

Be Decisive! Betty L. Randolph. 1 cass. (Running Time: 60 min.). (Educational Ser.). 1989. 9.98 (978-1-55909-206-7(8), 78S) Randolph Tapes.
Tap into the power of your subconscious to make the right decision. Subliminal messages are heard 3-5 minutes before becoming ocean sounds or music.

***Be Different: Adventures of a Free-Range Aspergian, with Practical Advice for Aspergians, Misfits, & Their Parents.** unabr. ed. John Elder Robison. (ENG.). 2011. audio compact disk 35.00 (978-0-307-88131-1(8), Random AudioBks) Pub: Random Audio Pubg. Dist(s): Random

Be Diligent: Serving Others as You Walk with the Master Servant. Warren W. Wiersbe. Read by Warren W. Wiersbe. 1 cass. (Running Time: 50 min.). 1987. 4.95 (978-0-8474-2295-1(X)) Back to Bible.
Presents an admonition to believers to be diligent in being sure of salvation, being ready for Christ's return & in searching the Scriptures.

Be Encouraged. 1 cass. 10.98 (978-1-57908-273-4(4), 1368); audio compact disk 15.98 CD. (978-1-57908-272-7(6), 1368) Platinm Enter.

Be Exalted. Contrib. by Marvin Sapp et al. 2005. audio compact disk 17.98 (978-5-558-93105-1(1), Verity) Brentwood Music.

Be Fit. Mark Victor Hansen. 3 cass. 45.00 (5) M V Hansen.
Reduce your caloric intake, determine your ideal body weight.

Be Fit for Life Series. Created by Laura Boynton King. 6 CD's. 2002. audio compact disk 109.95 (978-0-9748885-1-4(6)) Summit Dynamics.
A 6-volume series of Self-Hypnosis CD's designed to guide the user through a process to achieve and maintain the ideal weight for their body type.

Be Glad Then America. Gloriae Dei Cantores. 1 CD. 1991. audio compact disk 15.95 (978-1-55725-081-0(2)) Paraclete MA.

***Be Grateful to Everyone: An In-Depth Guide to the Practice of Lojong.** unabr. ed. Pema Chodron. (Running Time: 8 hrs. 45 mins.). (ENG.). 2011. audio compact disk 69.95 (978-1-59030-772-4(0)) Pub: Shambhala Pubns. Dist(s): Random

Be Happy! Release the Power of Happiness in You. Robert Holden. 4 CDs. (ENG.). 2009. audio compact disk 34.95 (978-1-4019-2182-8(5)) Hay House.

Be Happy Now. 1 cass. 10.00 (978-1-58506-014-6(3), 41) New Life Inst OR.
You have within you the power to be happy all the time. End the "blahs" & replace them with joy & happiness.

Be Happy Without Being Perfect: How to Break Free from the Perfection Deception in All Aspects of Your Life. abr. ed. Alice D. Domar & Alice Lesch Kelly. Read by Alice D. Domar. (Running Time: 9000 sec.). (ENG.). 2008. audio compact disk 19.95 (978-0-7393-5821-4(9), Random AudioBks) Pub: Random Audio Pubg. Dist(s): Random

***Be Honest - You're Not That into Him Either.** abr. ed. Ian Kerner. (ENG.). 2005. (978-0-06-083480-7(3), Harper Audio); (978-0-06-083481-4(1), Harper Audio) HarperCollins Pubs.

Be Kind, Be Friendly, Be Thankful: The Adventures of Brisky Bear & Trooper Dog. Orig. Title: Friends for Always. (J). 2007. pap. bk. 7.95 (978-0-9795127-0-4(0)) Glory Be Coll.

Be Kind, for Everyone You Meet Is Fighting a Hard Battle. Kenneth Wapnick. 1 CD. (Running Time: 5 hrs. 10 mins. 40 secs.). 2006. 25.00 (978-1-59142-293-8(0), 3m134); audio compact disk 31.00 (978-1-59142-292-1(2), CD134) Foun Miracles.

Be Lifted High. Contrib. by Michael W. Smith. (Sound Performance Soundtracks Ser.). 2007. audio compact disk 5.98 (978-5-557-71912-4(1)) Pt of Grace Ent.

***Be Love Now: The Path of the Heart.** unabr. ed. Ram Dass & Rameshwar Das. (ENG.). 2010. (978-0-06-200703-2(3), Harper Audio); (978-0-06-206806-4(7), Harper Audio) HarperCollins Pubs.

***Be More Chill.** unabr. ed. Ned Vizzini. Read by Jesse Eisenberg. (ENG.). 2005. (978-0-06-085692-2(0), Harper Audio); (978-0-06-085693-9(9), Harper Audio) HarperCollins Pubs.

Be More Creative. 17.95 (833AK) Nightingale-Conant.
Helps you rid yourself of bad habits you want to lose & develop the positive behavior patterns that will lead to a better, happier & more productive life.

Be More Positive. Lee Pulos. 2 cass. (Running Time: 2 hrs.). (Self Hypnosis & Subliminal Reinforcement Ser.). 14.95 (978-1-55569-231-5(1), SUB-8007) Great Am Audio.
Presents tools for positive self-change.

Be Moved by Me to Infinity: A Gathering Consideration. Adi Da Samraj. 2 cass. 1997. 19.95 (978-1-57097-030-6(0)) Dawn Horse Pr.

Be My Baby. Zoe Barnes. (Isis (CDs) Ser.). (J). 2006. audio compact disk 99.95 (978-0-7531-2564-9(1)) Pub: ISIS Lrg Prnt GBR. Dist(s): Ulverscroft US

Be My Baby. unabr. ed. Zoe Barnes. Read by Trudy Harris. 9 cass. (Running Time: 12 hrs. 10 mins.). (Isis Cassettes Ser.). (J). 2006. 76.95 (978-0-7531-3570-9(1)) Pub: ISIS Lrg Prnt GBR. Dist(s): Ulverscroft US

Be My Baby, Set. abr. ed. Ronnie Spector & Vince Waldron. Read by Ronnie Spector. 2 cass. (Running Time: 3 hrs.). 1990. 15.95 (978-0-9627187-1-7(8), 20010) Pub Mills.
Autobiography of Ronnie Spector, lead singer of the Ronettes, whose hit song, Be My Baby, made her a star. She frankly discusses her prison-like marriage to record producer Phil Spector, her alcoholism, trysts & her eventual return to normalcy.

Be My Guest, Set. Francis O'Hara. 1 CD. (Running Time: 1 hr. 31 mins.). (ENG.). 2002. audio compact disk 45.00 (978-0-521-77686-8(4)) Cambridge U Pr.

Be My Guest Set: English for the Hotel Industry, Set. Francis O'Hara. 1 cass. (Running Time: 1 hr. 30 mins.). (ENG.). 2002. 45.00 (978-0-521-77687-5(2)) Cambridge U Pr.

Be My Mistress Short or Tall (A Poem from the Poets' Corner) The One-and-Only Poetry Book for the Whole Family. unabr. ed. Robert Herrick & John Lithgow. Read by John Lithgow. (Running Time: 10 mins.). (ENG.). 2008. 0.99 (978-1-60024-320-2(7)) Pub: Hachet Audio. Dist(s): HachBkGrp

Be near Me. Andrew O'Hagan. Read by Jerome Pride. (Running Time: 5 hrs. 50 mins.). 2009. 79.99 (978-1-74214-273-9(7), 9781742142739) Pub: Bolinda Pubng AUS. Dist(s): Bolinda Pub Inc

Be near Me. unabr. ed. Andrew O'Hagan. Read by Jerome Pride. (Running Time: 8 hrs. 50 mins.). 2007. audio compact disk 87.95 (978-1-74093-917-1(4), 9781740939171) Pub: Bolinda Pubng AUS. Dist(s): Bolinda Pub Inc

Be near Me. unabr. ed. Andrew O'Hagan. Read by Jerome Pride. (Running Time: 8 hrs 50 mins.). 2008. 43.95 (978-1-74214-036-0(X), 9781742140360) Pub: Bolinda Pubng AUS. Dist(s): Bolinda Pub Inc

Be Not Afraid. Victor Harris & J. Brian Ballard. 1 cass. 9.95 (10001239); audio compact disk 14.95 (2800888) Covenant Comms.
A unique, original blend of contemporary religious music.

Be Not Afraid: A Christmas Musical Proclaiming That Hope Is Here. Contrib. by Richard Kingsmore. Created by Kim Messer. 2007. audio compact disk 90.00 (978-5-557-69988-4(0)); audio compact disk 12.00 (978-5-557-69987-7(2)) Lillenas.

Be Not Afraid: A Christmas Musical Proclaiming That Hope Is Here. Richard & Messer Kingsmore. Contrib. by Richard Kingsmore. Created by Kim Messer. 2007. audio compact disk 90.00 (978-5-557-69989-1(9)) Allegis.

Be Not Afraid: Open Wide Your Hearts. 2005. audio compact disk 9.95 (978-1-932927-31-3(X)) Ascensn Pr.

Be on Time. 1 cass. (Running Time: 60 min.). 10.95 (048) Psych Res Inst.
Focuses on the motivation to be prompt & responsible.

Be Pagan Once Again! Perf. by Isaac Bonewits. 1. 2003. audio compact disk 12.95 (978-1-59157-028-8(X)) Assn for Cons.
A performance of Neo-Pagan music by Isaac Bonewits, a founder of Ar nDriaiocht Fein (A Druid Fellowship), and friends from the musical groups Chameleon (the Association for Consciousness Exploration's house band) and Todd Alan & the Quest.

Be Perfect. Derek Prince. 2 cass. 1991. 5.95 ea. Derek Prince.
Have you reached perfection in your Christian walk? Have you given up? Discover seven steps that will take you upward toward perfection in Christ.

Be Positive. Barrie Konicov. 1 cass. 11.98 (978-0-87082-425-8(2), MS 011) Potentials.
You can learn to be positive & protect your mind with this tape which contains a simple procedure that will effectively shield you from the harmful negativity of people around you.

Be Positive. Barrie Konicov. 1 CD. 2003. audio compact disk 16.98 (978-0-87082-966-6(1)) Potentials.
All successful people are able to retreat within themselves when assaulted by the negativity of others. This program teaches you how to effectively shield yourself from negative assaults by others.You will find the self-hypnosis on track 1 and the subliminal on track 2. The easy-listening music of the subliminal, together with the self-hypnosis, is the original format which most people love and with which they are most familiar.

Be Positive. Barrie Konicov. 2 CDs. 2003. audio compact disk 27.98 (978-1-56001-968-8(9)) Potentials.

Be Positive: Hypnotic & Subliminal Learning. David Illig. 2001. audio compact disk 19.99 (978-0-86580-034-2(0)) Success World.

Be Positive: Mentalidad Positiva. Barrie Konicov. 1 cass. (Running Time: 1 hr. 16 min.). (Potentials Unlimited Spanish-Language Audios Ser.). (SPA.). (YA). 1995. 11.98 (978-0-87082-810-2(X), 011) Potentials.
Acquire a "can do" way of looking at the world, & you'll be empowered to live life optimistically. Stumbling blocks become stepping stones, with a positive attitude.

Be Practical. Swami Jyotirmayananda. 1 cass. (Running Time: 45 min.). 1990. 10.00 Yoga Res Foun.

Be Prepared: Matthew 25:1-3. Ed Young. (J). 1982. 4.95 (978-0-7417-1210-3(5), A0210) Win Walk.

Be Pro-Active: Prov. 6:6-8. Ed Young. 1992. 4.95 (978-0-7417-1903-4(7), 903) Win Walk.

Be Ready. Perf. by New Devine Destiny. 1 CD. (Running Time: 1 hr.). 1999. audio compact disk (978-0-7601-3522-8(3)) Brentwood Music.
Songs include: "For All You've Done," "Because of These Things," "Be Ready," "Came to Me" & more.

Be Ready at Eight. 9.95 (978-1-59112-171-8(X)) Live Oak Media.

Be Ready at Eight. Peggy Parish. Illus. by Cynthia Fisher. 11 vols. (Running Time: 17 mins.). 2000. pap. bk. 18.95 (978-1-59112-654-6(1)); pap. bk. 31.95 (978-1-59112-655-3(X)); 9.95 (978-0-87499-620-3(1)); audio compact disk 12.95 (978-1-59112-653-9(3)) Live Oak Media.

Be Ready at Eight. Peggy Parish. Read by Barbara Caruso. Illus. by Cynthia Fisher. 1 cass. (J). (gr. k-3). 2000. bk. 24.95 (978-0-87499-622-7(8)); pap. bk. 16.95 (978-0-87499-621-0(X)) Live Oak Media.
All day, Miss Molly meets people who tell her to "be ready at eight," but she can't think why. On the stroke of eight o'clock, she realizes why everyone's looking forward to seeing her & she helps throw her own surprise party.

Be Ready at Eight. unabr. ed. Peggy Parish. Read by Barbara Caruso. Illus. by Cynthia Fisher. 14 vols. (Running Time: 17 mins.). (J). 2000. pap. bk. & tchr. ed. 29.95 Reading Chest. (978-0-87499-623-4(6)) Live Oak Media.

Be Relaxed & Stress-Free. 1 cass. (Sleep Programming Tapes Ser.). 12.98 (978-0-87554-548-6(3), 1120) Valley Sun.

Be Rich, Bean Entrepreneur. Friday Burke. (ENG.). 2009. audio compact disk (978-0-9791396-0-4(0)) F Burke.

Be Sober for This Final Hour. Lynne Hammond. 1 cass. (Running Time: 1 hr.). 2005. 5.00 (978-1-57399-219-0(4)) Mac Hammond.

Be Somebody Be Yourself. Poet's Workshop Staff. 1 cass. (Running Time: 40 min.). (YA). (gr. 9-12). 1991. 15.95 (37S.O.R.17) Sell Out Recordings.
Poetry on being yourself. "If inventions come to mind, unique of their kind, Be Somebody, Be Yourself.".

Be Still & Know. 1 CD. (Running Time: 1 hour). 1995. 14.95 (978-0-9779472-9-4(7)) Health Wealth Inc.
Be Still & Know contains a meditation/observation exercise which is designed to give you a tool, that with daily practice and application, will allow you to experience your true identity as Spirit, a child of the Divine. Many spiritual or mental exercises prevalent in the world today require that the participant "space out" or leave their body. This is not the aim of this exercise. This recording is designed to guide you, the Spirit, back IN to your body (the Kingdom is Within), so that you may rise higher and higher in vibration and let go of the effort to let go. You will be guided in this practice.

Be Still & Know. Swami Amar Jyoti. 2 cass. 1979. 12.95 (J-20) Truth Consciousness.
The process for stilling the mind. When our mind stills, Cosmic Mind works through us.

Be Still & Know. John Mergenhagen. 4 cass. (Running Time: 4 hrs. 49 min.). 1995. 34.95 Set. (TAH327) Alba Hse Comns.
The nitty gritty aspects of contemplate prayer & prayer in general are not avoided. What do I do when nothing is happening in my prayer? How do I use contemplative prayer in praying for others? What is the difference between contemplative prayer & transcendental meditation, etc.

Be Still & Know: Find Peace Each Day Through Prayers, Music & Reflections. Pat O'Donoghue & Des Hayden. (ENG.). 2002. 14.95 (978-1-85390-670-1(0)); audio compact disk 22.95 (978-1-85390-665-7(4)) Pub: Veritas Pubns IRL. Dist(s): Dufour

Be Still, My Soul. Mark Geslison. 1 cass. 9.95 (10001409); audio compact disk 14.95 (28001052) Covenant Comms.
A beautiful collection of traditional melodies.

***Be Still My Soul.** Jeff Hansen. 2010. audio compact disk 10.00 (978-0-9767874-6-4(6)) Ambassadors of Rec.

Be Still, My Soul: Comfort for Those Who Suffer. Howard Vanderwell & Norma deWaal Malefyt. 1 cass. (Running Time: 1 hr. 30 mins.). 2001. 9.95 (978-1-56212-816-6(7), 420050); audio compact disk 15.95 (978-1-56212-667-4(9), 420060) FaithAliveChr.

Be Still, My Soul: Embracing God's Purpose & Provision in Suffering. unabr. ed. Compiled by Nancy Guthrie. Narrated by Sharilynn Dunn & Kelly Ryan Dolan. (Running Time: 4 hrs. 42 mins. 8 sec.). (ENG.). 2010. audio compact disk 19.99 (978-1-59859-687-8(X)) Oasis Audio.

Be Still My Soul: Finding Peace in the Midst of Turmoil. Steve Hill. (ENG.). 2007. audio compact disk 25.00 (978-1-892853-81-3(7)) Togthr Hrvest.

Be Still, My Soul Set: Embracing God's Purpose & Provision in Suffering. unabr. ed. Compiled by Nancy Guthrie. Narrated by Sharilynn Dunn & Kelly Ryan Dolan. (Running Time: 4 hrs. 42 mins. 8 sec.). (ENG.). 2010. 13.99 (978-1-60814-630-7(8)) Oasis Audio.

Be Strong. Perf. by Martins. 1 cass. 1998. 7.98 HiLo Plus. (978-0-7601-2576-2(7)) Brentwood Music.

Be the Ball: An Audio Recording for Better Golf. unabr. ed. Sean Ryan. Read by Agnes Herrmann. 1 cass. (Running Time: 1 hr. 15 min.). 2000. 16.95 (978-0-9663619-1-9(1), SE Pubng) Pub: Sophie Ent. Dist(s): Biblio Dist
Audio recording for improvement of golf skills using proven mental techniques.

***Be the Change: Your Guide to Freeing Slaves & Changing the World.** unabr. ed. Zach Hunter. (Running Time: 2 hrs. 30 mins. 16 sec.). (Invert Ser.). (ENG.). (YA). 2010. 9.99 (978-0-310-77220-0(6)) Zondervan.

Be the Masterpiece: Your 21-Day Journey of Self-Expression, Movement Three. Melody Ivory. Ed. by Lynda McDaniel. Des. by Maggie Flynn. Photos by Allum Ross Ndiaye. 2009. pap. bk. 9.95 (978-0-9795504-2-3(4)) Melody Ivory.

Be the Pack Leader: Use Cesar's Way to Transform Your Dog... And Your Life. abr. ed. Cesar Millan & Melissa Jo Peltier. Read by Cesar Millan. 4 CDs. (Running Time: 18000 sec.). (ENG.). 2007. audio compact disk 27.95 (978-0-7393-5423-0(X), Random AudioBks) Pub: Random Audio Pubg. Dist(s): Random

Be the Pack Leader: Use Cesar's Way to Transform Your Dog... And Your Life. unabr. ed. Cesar Millan & Melissa Jo Peltier. Read by John H. Mayer. 9 CDs. 2007. audio compact disk 90.00 (978-1-4159-4263-5(3), BksonTape) Pub: Random Audio Pubg. Dist(s): Random
Filled with practical tips and techniques as well as success stories from his fans, clients, and his popular television show Dog Whisperer with Cesar Millan, Cesar helps you understand and read your dog's energy as well as

your own so that you can take your connection with your dog to the next level. The principles of calm-assertive energy will help you become a better pack leader in every area of your life, improving your relationships with friends, family, and coworkers. In addition, Cesar addresses several important issues for the first time, including what you need to know about the major dog behavior tools available and the difference between "personality" and "instability." Ultimately, what emerges from Be the Pack Leader are both happier dogs and happier, more centered owners.

Be Thou a Masterful Teacher. George D. Durrant. 1 cass. 3.95 (978-1-57734-379-0(4), 34441182); 5.98 (978-1-55503-184-8(6), 06003893) Covenant Comms.
Home-grown humor with positive stories that inspire.

Be Thou near to Me. Contrib. by Selah & Jim Brickman. (Praise Hymn Soundtracks Ser.). 2007. audio compact disk 8.98 (978-5-557-63294-2(8)) Pt of Grace Ent.

Be Thou Now Persuaded: Living in a Shakespearean World. Contrib. by Rhino Records Staff. 6 CDs. (Running Time: 9 hrs.). 1999. bk. 59.98 (R2 75816); bk. 39.98 (978-0-7379-0030-9(X), R4 75816) Rhino Enter.
Collection of excerpts from the Bard's plays & poems. Includes aspects of humanity, experiences of love, violent passions & the supernatural, dreams & morality - along with a complete reading of "Romeo & Juliet.".

Be True to Yourself: "I Don't Want to Be a Lion Anymore!" unabr. ed. Trenna Daniells. 1 cass. (Running Time: 30 min.). (One to Grow On! Ser.). (J). (gr. k-6). 1991. 9.95 (978-0-918519-15-3(2)) Trenna Prods.
Deep in the heart of Samburu Territory, Lionel the lion decides he doesn't want to be the king of beasts anymore. He proclaims that "Forever & Always" he will be a giraffe...& ends up with a mouth full of thorns. Surrounded by the sounds of Africa, children learn the lesson, "be true to yourself.".

Be True to Yourself- I Don't Want to Be A Lion Anymore. Trenna Daniells. Narrated by Trenna Daniells. (ENG.). (J). 2009. (978-0-918519-28-3(4)) Trenna Prods.

***Be-with Factor: Mentoring Students in Everyday Life.** Zondervan. (Running Time: 5 hrs. 40 mins. 0 sec.). (ENG.). 2010. 9.99 (978-0-310-86911-5(0)) Zondervan.

Be with Us Today. Composed by Michael John Poirier. (Running Time: 3600 sec.). 2006. audio compact disk 17.00 (978-1-58459-281-5(8)) Wrld Lib Pubns.

Be Ye Transformed: Understanding God's Truth. Speeches. 8 Audio CDs. (Running Time: 8 hours). (King's High Way Ser.). 2007. audio compact disk 29.95 (978-0-9760994-8-2(9)); audio compact disk & audio compact disk 19.95 (978-0-9760994-5-1(4)) Kings High Way.

Be Ye Transformed: Understanding God's Truth. Nancy Missler & Chuck Missler. 8 cass. (Running Time: 12 hrs.). (King's High Way Ser.). 1996. vinyl bd. 29.95 (978-1-880532-90-4(5)) Koinonia Hse.
Understanding God's Truth.

Be Ye Transformed Audio Series: Understanding God's Truth. 8 cass. (Running Time: 8 hours). 2002. 29.95 (978-0-9752534-1-0(7)) Kings High Way.
Paul declares ?...be not conformed to this world, but be ye transformed [how?] by the renewing of your mind...? (Romans 12:2) This is our Biblical injunction from the Lord. The question is: How do we do it? What is the practical application of taking every thought captive, renewing our minds and putting on the Mind of Christ? In this sequel to The Way of Agape, Nancy shares that, ?without a renewed mind, our lives will remain the same as they?ve always been, no matter what we do or try. No matter how many Bible studies we attend, no matter how many Scriptures we know or how much we pray, without a mind change, our lives will still have the same problems, the same failures and the same defeats as they always have. The battle is truly waged in our minds!? - ?Be Ye Transformed is a must-read for anyone who wants to see a positive change in their Christian walk. It not only teaches us how to ?take every thought captive,? renew our minds and put on the Mind of Christ, it also contains an expansion of Nancy?s original model of the human personality (i.e., the hidden chambers), which she meticulously crafted from the Scriptural pattern of Solomon?s Temple. Practical, field-tested examples from years of ministry make Be Ye Transformed a classic Christian work.?William P. Welty, M. Div.Executive Director of the ISV Foundation Translators of the International Standard Version of the Bible.

Be Your Best Body Vol. 1: The Tone-Up System Workout. Suesan L. Pawlitski. Instructed by Jeff Elliot. 1 cass. (Running Time: 1 hr.). 1999. pap. bk. 22.95 (978-0-9668504-0-6(8)); 12.95 (978-0-9668504-1-3(6)) Tone-Up Pubg.
A ballet-inspired non aerobic, basic strength training workout.

Be Your Own Boss: Everything You Need to Start & Succeed in Your Own Business. Entrepreneur Magazine Editors. 1 cass. bk. 84.95 Set in album. (798PAM) Nightingale-Conant.
If you're planning to start your own business, or if you're running one already, here's a complete program with vital facts & keys to make it a resounding success. A powerful course in entrepreneurship with hundreds of ways to get started, keep going & do it right. Includes 334-page looseleaf master manual in binder, 11-page sourcebook of support services & a 50-page opportunity guide.

Be Your Own Matchmaker: You Can't Get What You Want If You Don't Know What It Is. Creative Life Change Institute Staff. 1 cass. 1997. bk. 19.95 Kendall-Hunt.

Be Your Own Person. Pat Carroll. Read by Pat Carroll. Ed. by Tony Carroll. 1 cass. (Running Time: 30 min.). 10.00 Inner-Mind Concepts.
Discusses how to take responsibility for your own actions by allowing your feelings to surface and make changes in your life one at a time.

Be Your Own Psychotherapist. Instructed by Manly P. Hall. 8.95 (978-0-89314-015-1(5), C840401) Philos Res.

Be Your Perfect Weight: Dynamic Psychological Breakthrough in Weight Control. 3rd rev. ed. Michele Blood & Bob Proctor. Illus. by Van Crosby. 2 cass. (Running Time: 2 hrs.). 1995. 19.95 (978-1-890679-00-2(3), M136) Micheles.
Motivational program to help improve one's life to the positive & towards success.

Be Your Perfect Weight Forever! Freedom from Overeating Through Listening to Inner Guidance. Vikki Hansen-Coit. 1 cass. 1989. 9.95 (978-0-936475-03-5(X)) Las Brisas.
Discusses how to overcome overeating.

***Be YourSelf Audio CD.** Susan Diane Matz. Read by Susan Diane Matz. (ENG.). 2010. 15.95 (978-0-9841054-6-5(8)) Abriev Ent.

Be Yourself, Everyone Else Is Already Taken: Transform Your Life with the Power of Authenticity. unabr. ed. Mike Robbins. Read by Mike Robbins. 1 MP3-CD. (Running Time: 5 hrs.). 2009. 39.97 (978-1-4233-7601-9(3), 9781423376019, Brinc Audio MP3 Lib); 24.99 (978-1-4233-7600-2(5), 9781423376002, Brilliance MP3); 39.97 (978-1-4233-7603-3(X), 9781423376033, BADLE); 24.99 (978-1-4233-7602-6(1), 9781423376026, BAD); audio compact disk 24.99 (978-1-4233-7598-2(X), 9781423375982, Bril Audio CD Unabri); audio compact disk 74.97 (978-1-4233-7599-9(8), 9781423375999, BriAudCD Unabrid) Brilliance Audio.

Beach. unabr. ed. Alex Garland. Read by Michael Page. (Running Time: 12 hrs.). 2009. 24.99 (978-1-4233-9142-5(X), 9781423391425, Brilliance MP3); 24.99 (978-1-4233-9144-9(6), 9781423391449, BAD); 39.97 (978-1-4233-9143-2(8), 9781423391432, Brinc Audio MP3 Lib); 39.97 (978-1-4233-9145-6(4), 9781423391456, BADLE) Brilliance Audio.

Beach. unabr. ed. Lena Lencek & Gideon Bosker. Read by Nadia May. 10 cass. (Running Time: 14 hrs. 30 mins.). 2000. 69.95 (978-0-7861-1600-3(5), 2428) Blckstn Audio.

Beach: The History of Paradise on Earth. unabr. ed. Lena Lencek & Gideon Bosker. Read by Nadia May. 10 cass. (Running Time: 15 hrs.). 1999. 69.95 (2428) Blckstn Audio.
Full story of the seashore - its history (natural & human), customs, spectacles, & scandals. The beach's turquoise surf & sugary sand now provide a favorite retreat, but this wasn't always so. Charts the evolution of the seaside from a wasteland at the margins of civilization - when "exotic" meant remote & terrifying - to its present role as a staging ground for escape & relaxation.

Beach at Falesa see Bottle Imp & Other Stories

Beach House. Jane Green. Contrib. by Cassandra Campbell. (Running Time: 11 hrs.). (ENG.). (gr. 12 up). 2008. audio compact disk 39.95 (978-0-14-314327-7(1), PengAudBks) Penguin Grp USA.

***Beach House.** unabr. ed. Mary Alice Monroe. Read by Mary Alice Monroe. (Running Time: 14 hrs.). 2010. 24.99 (978-1-4418-5270-0(0), 9781441852700, Brilliance MP3); 24.99 (978-1-4418-5272-4(7), 9781441852724, BAD); 39.97 (978-1-4418-5271-7(9), 9781441852717, Brinc Audio MP3 Lib); 39.97 (978-1-4418-5273-1(5), 9781441852731, BADLE); audio compact disk 29.99 (978-1-4418-5268-7(9), 9781441852687, Bril Audio CD Unabri); audio compact disk 79.97 (978-1-4418-5269-4(7), 9781441852694, BriAudCD Unabrid) Brilliance Audio.

Beach House. unabr. ed. James Patterson & Peter de Jonge. 5 cass. (Running Time: 7 hrs. 30 mins.). 2002. 39.98 (978-0-7366-8706-5(8)) Books on Tape.
a murderer comes dangerously close to musher Jessie Arnold. When a body is discovered during the renovation of her home, Jessie learns it may be a victim of Alaska's most notorious serial killer. Soon after, another woman disappears in the same vicinity; Jessie suspects the killer is back at work...and that she may be the next victim. With her long knowledge of Alaska, her familiarity with the details of people and location, and her unerring sense of dramatic action, Sue Henry has made a legion of friends for Jessie Arnold as well as a name for herself as a first-rate novelist...not just a crime writer, but an author who seriously explores life and death in our harshest state.

Beach House. unabr. ed. James Patterson & Peter de Jonge. 2002. audio compact disk 46.98 (978-0-7366-8707-2(6)) Books on Tape.
When New York City law student Jack Mullen hears the shocking news that his brother Peter has drowned in the ocean off East Hampton, he knows it couldn't have been an accident. But as Jack tries to unravel the truth, he confronts a barricade of lawyers, police, and paid protectors who separate the multibillionaire summer residents from local workers like Peter. And he learns that his brother wasn't just parking cars at the summer parties of the rich. He was making serious money satisfying the sexual needs of the richest women and men in town.

Beach House. unabr. ed. James Patterson & Peter de Jonge. Read by Gil Bellows. (ENG.). 2005. 14.98 (978-1-59483-368-7(0)) Pub: Hachet Audio. Dist(s): HachBkGrp

Beach House. unabr. ed. James Patterson & Peter de Jonge. Read by Gil Bellows. (Running Time: 6 hrs. 30 mins.). (ENG.). 2009. 49.98 (978-1-60788-094-3(6)) Pub: Hachet Audio. Dist(s): HachBkGrp

Beach House. unabr. rev. ed. James Patterson & Peter de Jonge. Read by Gil Bellows. 6 CDs. (Running Time: 6 hrs. 30 mins.). (ENG.). 2002. audio compact disk 31.98 (978-1-58621-287-2(7)) Pub: Hachet Audio. Dist(s): HachBkGrp

Beach Music. unabr. ed. Pat Conroy. Read by Jonathan Marosz. 19 cass. (Running Time: 28 hrs. 30 mins.). 1995. 152.00 (978-0-7366-3080-1(5), 3761A/B); 72.00 (3761-A); 80.00 (3761B) Books on Tape.
The search for truth is the only thing that can save Jack McCall after his wife commits suicide. He'll find it looking for a lost friend.

Beach Music. unabr. ed. Pat Conroy. Narrated by Frank Muller. 20 cass. (Running Time: 28 hrs. 45 mins.). 158.00 (978-0-7887-0335-5(8), 94527E7) Recorded Bks.
The story of Jack McCall, a man on the run from his past: the suicide of his wife; the destructive influence of his parents; even his faith in the Catholic Church. Conroy shows one man's journey toward the knowledge that everyone carries a tragic secret equal to his own. Available to libraries only.

Beach Road. James Patterson. 2006. cd-rom 39.99 (978-1-59895-486-9(5)) Find a World.

Beach Road. unabr. ed. James Patterson. Read by Billy Baldwin. (YA). 2006. 49.99 (978-1-59895-153-0(X)) Find a World.

Beach Road. unabr. ed. James Patterson & Peter de Jonge. 4 cass. (Running Time: 6 hrs.). 2006. 36.00 (978-1-4159-3096-0(1)) Books on Tape.

Beach Road. unabr. ed. James Patterson & Peter de Jonge. Read by Billy Baldwin. 6 CDs. (Running Time: 6 hrs.). 2006. 54.00 (978-1-4159-3097-7(X)) Books on Tape.

Beach Road. unabr. ed. James Patterson & Peter de Jonge. Read by Billy Baldwin et al. (Running Time: 7 hrs.). (ENG.). 2006. 14.98 (978-1-59483-510-0(1)) Pub: Hachet Audio. Dist(s): HachBkGrp

Beach Road. unabr. ed. James Patterson & Peter de Jonge. Read by Billy Baldwin et al. (Running Time: 7 hrs.). (ENG.). 2007. audio compact disk 14.98 (978-1-60024-251-9(0)) Pub: Hachet Audio. Dist(s): HachBkGrp

Beach Road. unabr. ed. James Patterson & Peter de Jonge. Read by Billy Baldwin et al. (Running Time: 7 hrs.). (ENG.). 2009. 59.98 (978-1-60788-118-6(7)) Pub: Hachet Audio. Dist(s): HachBkGrp

Beachcomber. Josephine Cox. Read by Carole Boyd. (Chivers Audio Bks.). 2003. 96.95 (978-0-7540-8395-5(0)) Pub: Chivers Audio Bks GBR. Dist(s): AudioGO

Beachcomber. Josephine Cox. Read by Carole Boyd. (Running Time: 46800 sec.). 2003. audio compact disk 110.95 (978-0-7540-8785-4(9)) Pub: Chivers Audio Bks GBR. Dist(s): AudioGO

***Beachcombers: A Novel.** unabr. ed. Nancy Thayer. (Running Time: 12 hrs. 0 mins.). 2010. 17.99 (978-1-4001-8728-7(1)) Tantor Media.

***Beachcombers: A Novel.** unabr. ed. Nancy Thayer. Narrated by Karen White. 2 MP3-CDs. (Running Time: 13 hrs.). 2010. 24.99 (978-1-4001-6728-9(0)); audio compact disk 83.99 (978-1-4001-4728-1(X)); audio compact disk 34.99 (978-1-4001-1728-4(3)) Pub: Tantor Media. Dist(s): IngramPubServ

Beacon Street Girls Special Adventure: Katani's Jamaican Holiday. unabr. ed. Annie Bryant. Read by Pamella D'Pella. 5 CDs. (Running Time: 4 hrs. 58 mins.). (J). (gr. 4-7). 2008. audio compact disk 32.00 (978-0-7393-7898-4(8), Listening Lib) Pub: Random Audio Pubg. Dist(s): Random

Beacon Street Mourning. Dianne Day. Read by Anna Fields. 2000. 48.00 (978-0-7366-5934-5(X)) Books on Tape.

Beacon Street Mourning. unabr. ed. Dianne Day. Read by Anna Fields. 6 cass. (Running Time: 9 hrs.). 2000. 48.00 Books on Tape.
Fremont Jone's investigation into her father's death in Boston leads to suspects in some of the least likely places.

Beady Bear. Don Freeman. Illus. by Don Freeman. 14 vols. (Running Time: 8 mins.). 1982. pap. bk. 35.95 (978-1-59519-015-4(5)); 9.95 (978-1-59112-012-4(8)); audio compact disk 12.95 (978-1-59519-013-0(9)) Live Oak Media.

Beady Bear. Don Freeman. Illus. by Don Freeman. 11 vols. (Running Time: 8 mins.). (J). 1982. pap. bk. 18.95 (978-1-59519-014-7(7)) Pub: Live Oak Media. Dist(s): AudioGO

Beady Bear. unabr. ed. Don Freeman. Read by Barrett Clark. 14 vols. (Running Time: 8 mins.). (J). (gr. k-3). 1974. pap. bk. & tchr. ed. 33.95 (978-0-670-15058-8(4)) Live Oak Media.
Believing that he needs only a cave in which to live in order to be truly happy, a stuffed bear comes to realize that love & companionship are more important.

Beady Bear. unabr. ed. Don Freeman. Read by Barrett Clark. 11 vols. (Running Time: 8 mins.). (J). (gr. k-3). 1982. pap. bk. 16.95 (978-0-670-15064-9(9)) Live Oak Media.

Beak of the Finch: A Story of Evolution in Our Time. unabr. ed. Jonathan Weiner. Narrated by John McDonough. 11 cass. (Running Time: 15 hrs. 15 mins.). 1996. 91.00 (978-0-7887-0478-9(8), 94671E7) Recorded Bks.
Peter & Rosemary Grant set up camp on a rocky island in the Galapagos to study populations of finches & discover that the tiny birds are players in an exciting saga of adaptation, survival & serendipity that rivals any Hollywood epic.

Beak of the Finch: A Story of Evolution in Our Time, Set. unabr. ed. Jonathan Weiner. Narrated by John McDonough. 11 cass. (Running Time: 15 hrs. 25 min.). 1999. 91.00 (94671) Recorded Bks.

Beaks of Eagles see Twentieth-Century Poetry in English, No. 5, Recordings of Poets Reading Their Own Poetry

***Bealach an Tsoipin.** Iorras Aithneach. (ENG.). 11.95 (978-0-8023-7012-9(8)) Pub: Clo Iar-Chonnachta IRL. Dist(s): Dufour

Beam Us up Scotty. Scott Huckabay. Prod. by Leonard G. Horowitz. 1. (Running Time: 60). 2007. audio compact disk 19.25 (978-0-923550-05-9(4)) Pub: Tetrahedron Pub. Dist(s): New Leaf Dist

***Bean an Fhir Ruaidh.** Caitlin Ni Dhomhnaill. (ENG.). 1988. 11.95 (978-0-8023-7009-9(8)) Pub: Clo Iar-Chonnachta IRL. Dist(s): Dufour

Bean Bag Activities. Georgiana Liccione Stewart. Perf. by Jill Gallina. 1 cass. (Running Time: 40 min.). (J). 2001. pap. bk. 14.95 (KIM 7055CD); stu. ed. 11.95 (KIM 7055) Kimbo Educ.
A Kimbo hit that develops coordination through games, dances & controlled activities. Songs increase listening skills. Bean Bag Rock, Pass the Bean Bag, Bean Bag Parade & more. Includes guide.

Bean Bag Activities & Coordination Skills: For Early Childhood & Adaptable for Special Education. Georgiana Liccione Stewart. Perf. by Jill Gallina. 1 cass. (Running Time: 40 min.). (J). 2001. pap. bk. 10.95 (KIM 7055C) Kimbo Educ.
A Kimbo hit that develops coordination through games, dances & controlled activities. Songs increase listening skills. Bean Bag Rock, Pass the Bean Bag, Bean Bag Parade & more. Includes guide & bean bag.

Bean Bag Fun. 1 LP. (Running Time: 40 min.). (J). (ps-3). 2001. pap. bk. & pupil's gde. ed. 11.95 (KIM 2018) Kimbo Educ.
Fun-filled games & activities that develop coordination skills. Tom Tom Bean Bag, On the March, Bean Bag Carousel & more. Guide with lyrics and instructions.

Bean Bag Fun. Laura Johnson. 1 cass. (Running Time: 40 min.). (J). (ps-3). 2001. 10.95 (KIM 2018C); audio compact disk 14.95 (KIM 2018CD) Kimbo Educ.

Bean Bag Rock 'n Roll. 1 cass. (Running Time: 38 mins.). (J). (ps). 2000. 10.95 Kimbo Educ.
Upbeat songs help children learn such things as directionality, body identification & listening skills, while using bean bags.

Bean Bag Rock 'n Roll. Georgiana Stewart. 1 CD. (Running Time: 38 mins.). (J). 2000. pap. bk. 14.95 (KIM 9160CD) Kimbo Educ.
Upbeat songs help children learn such things as directionality, body identification & listening skills, while using bean bags. Includes bean bag & guide book.

Bean Bag that Mom Made. (gr. k-3). 10.00 (978-0-7635-6372-1(2)) Rigby Educ.

***Bean Trees.** unabr. ed. Barbara Kingsolver. Read by C. J. Critt. (ENG.). 2009. (978-0-06-190187-4(3), Harper Audio); (978-0-06-190188-1(1), Harper Audio) HarperCollins Pubs.

Bean Trees. unabr. ed. Barbara Kingsolver. Read by C. J. Critt. 2009. audio compact disk 19.99 (978-0-06-178210-7(6), Harper Audio) HarperCollins Pubs.

Bean Trees. unabr. ed. Barbara Kingsolver. Narrated by C. J. Critt. 7 cass. (Running Time: 9 hrs. 30 mins.). 1999. 60.00 (978-0-7887-0054-5(5), 94253E7) Recorded Bks.
When Taylor Greer hits the road she has no real destination, only to get as far from Kentucky as possible. By the time she ends up in Arizona, she has inherited a three-year-old Cherokee girl from an Indian woman she met in a bar. Available to libraries only.

Bean Trees. unabr. ed. Barbara Kingsolver. Narrated by C. J. Critt. 8 CDs. (Running Time: 9 hrs. 30 mins.). 2000. audio compact disk 69.00 (978-0-7887-3398-7(2), C1004E7) Recorded Bks.

Bean Trees, Set. unabr. ed. Read by Barbara Kingsolver. 7 cass. (Running Time: 9 hrs. 30 min.). 58.00 (978-1-78870-054-2(6), 94253R4) Recorded Bks.
Taylor Greer is a tough young woman determined to maintain her independence & to put as many miles between herself & her Kentucky home. As the result of a bizarre encounter on her drive west, she becomes responsible for Turtle, a three year-old Cherokee girl. Together they begin a new life in Arizona. The abused child clings body & soul to her new guardian while Taylor struggles to meet the demands od parenthood along with the challenge of new friendships & love.

Beans of Egypt, Maine. Carolyn Chute. Read by Julia Delfino. 2000. 40.00 (978-0-7366-4855-4(0)) Books on Tape.

Beans of Egypt, Maine. unabr. ed. Carolyn Chute. Read by Joyce Bean & William Dufris. (Running Time: 7 hrs.). 2008. 24.95 (978-1-4233-7454-1(1), 9781423374541, BAD); 24.95 (978-1-4233-7452-7(5), 9781423374527, Brilliance MP3); audio compact disk 29.99 (978-1-4233-7450-3(9), 9781423374503, Bril Audio CD Unabri) Brilliance Audio.

Beans of Egypt, Maine. unabr. ed. Carolyn Chute et al. (Running Time: 7 hrs.). 2008. 39.25 (978-1-4233-7453-4(3), 9781423374534, Brinc Audio

MP3 Lib); 39.25 (978-1-4233-7455-8(X), 9781423374558, BADLE); audio compact disk 97.25 (978-1-4233-7451-0(7), 9781423374510, BriAudCD Unabrid) Brilliance Audio.

Bear. Thomas Merton. 1 cass. (Running Time: 60 min.). (Faulkner: Disaster in Paradise Ser.). 8.95 (AA2079) Credence Commun.
Merton reads some of Faulkner's works containing contemplative & redemptive themes.

Bear & the Dragon, Pt. 1. unabr. ed. Tom Clancy. Read by Michael Prichard. 11 cass. (Running Time: 16 hrs. 30 mins.). 2000. 88.00 (978-0-7366-5571-2(9), 5385-A) Books on Tape.
Jack Ryan has found that being President is not easy: there's a revolution in Liberia; the Asian economy is going down the tubes; and now, in Moscow, someone may have tried to assassinate the chairman of the SVR, the former KGB. Were the potential assassins political enemies, the Russian Mafia, or disaffected former KGB? Or is something far more dangerous at work here.

Bear & the Dragon, Pt. 2. unabr. ed. Tom Clancy. Read by Michael Prichard. 10 cass. (Running Time: 15 hrs.). 2000. 80.00 (978-0-7366-5938-3(2), 5385-B) Books on Tape.

Bear & the Dragon, Pt. 3. unabr. ed. Tom Clancy. Read by Michael Prichard. 10 cass. (Running Time: 15 hrs.). 2000. 80.00 (978-0-7366-5939-0(0), 5385-C) Books on Tape.

Bear Called Paddington. abr. ed. Michael Bond. 1 cass. (Running Time: 56 min.). (Paddington Ser.). (J). (ps-3). 1992. 11.00 (978-1-55994-653-7(9), HarperChildAud) HarperCollins Pubs.
The world's favorite Teddy, Paddington Bear, is beloved by millions of children - & adults. Here are some of his classic first adventures, including when Mr. & Mrs. Brown first adopt a stray bear into their family.

Bear Called Paddington. unabr. ed. Michael Bond. Read by Stephen Fry. 2 CDs. (Running Time: 2 hrs.). (J). 2005. 17.95 (978-0-06-076071-7(0), HarperChildAud) HarperCollins Pubs.

***Bear Called Paddington.** unabr. ed. Michael Bond. Read by Stephen Fry. (ENG.). 2005. (978-0-06-084065-5(X)); (978-0-06-084064-8(1)) HarperCollins Pubs.

Bear Cub Grows: Early Explorers Emergent Set B Audio CD. Carrie Smith. Adapted by Benchmark Education Staff. (J). 2007. audio compact disk 10.00 (978-1-4108-8207-3(1)) Benchmark Educ.

Bear Detectives: The Case of the Missing Pumpkin see Berenstain Bears' Christmas

Bear Goes over the Mountain Audio CD. Adapted by Benchmark Education Company Staff. Based on a work by Jeffrey B. Fuerst. (Reader's Theater Nursery Rhymes & Songs Ser.). (J). (gr. k-1). 2008. audio compact disk 10.00 (978-1-60437-996-9(0)) Benchmark Educ.

Bear Hunt. 2004. 8.95 (978-1-56008-839-4(7)); cass. & flmstrp 30.00 (978-0-89719-650-5(3)) Weston Woods.

Bear in the Attic. unabr. ed. Patrick F. McManus. Narrated by Norman Dietz. 6 cass. (Running Time: 7 hrs. 30 mins.). 2002. 85.00 (978-1-4025-2383-0(1)) Recorded Bks.
Once again the author invites listeners to peek into his unique perspectives on life and his favorite topic, the great outdoors. Here listeners are treated to amazingly absurd tales of young male hijinks, camping mishaps and neighbor-eating bears!.

Bear in the Attic. unabr. ed. Patrick F. McManus. Narrated by Norman Dietz. 6 cass. (Running Time: 7 hrs. 30 mins.). 2002. 34.95 (978-1-4025-2384-7(X), RG082) Recorded Bks.
Peek into his unique perspectives on life and his favorite topic, the great outdoors. Here listeners are treated to amazingly absurd tales of young male hijinks, camping mishaps and neighbor-eating bears.

Bear in the Big Blue House. Prod. by Walt Disney Records Staff. 1 cass. (J). (ps-3). 1998. 12.98 (978-0-7634-0503-8(5)) W Disney Records.

Bear Scouts see Bears' Picnic & Other Stories

Bear Snores On. Karma Wilson. Read by Karma Wilson. (J). (ps-2). 2005. bk. 24.95 (978-0-439-76660-9(5), WHRA666) Weston Woods.
In a cave in the woods, all winter long, Bear sleeps in his cozy lair. Surprise guests stop by to warm up, brew tea and pop corn while Bear snores on. When the smells and the fun finally disturb his slumber, Bear wakes up to find his den full of celebrating critters. Cheerful rhymes and illustrations will charm children as they wait for Bear's BIG reaction.

Bear Snores On. Karma Wilson. Read by Karma Wilson. Music by John Jennings. (J). (ps-2). 2005. bk. 29.95 (978-0-439-76664-7(8), WHCD666) Weston Woods.

Bear Stories: Threadbear, One Bear at Bedtime, Bear. Mick Inkpen. Read by Joss Ackland et al. (ENG.). (J). (gr. k-2). 2004. audio compact disk 8.99 (978-1-84032-989-6(0), HoddrStoughton) Pub: Hodder General GBR. Dist(s): IPG Chicago

Bear, the Bat, & the Dove: 3 Stories from Aesop. Illus. by Baird Hoffmire. As told by Rob Cleveland. (J). 2007. pap. bk. 42.95 (978-0-87483-841-1(X)) Pub: August Hse. Dist(s): Natl Bk Netwk

Bear Wants More. Karma Wilson. Narrated by John McDonough. (Running Time: 15 mins.). (J). 2003. 10.75 (978-1-4193-2035-4(1)) Recorded Bks.

Bear Wants More. unabr. ed. Narrated by Karma Wilson. Illus. by Jane Chapman. 1 CD. (Running Time: 8 mins.). (J). (ps-2). 2006. bk. 29.95 (978-0-439-90578-7(8)); bk. 24.95 (978-0-439-90572-5(9)) Weston Woods.
When springtime comes, Bear wakes up very hungry! His friends help him find good things to eat, but will his hunger EVER be satisfied?.

Bear Went over the Mountain: A Novel. unabr. collector's ed. William Kotzwinkle. Read by Michael Prichard. 8 cass. (Running Time: 8 hrs.). 1997. 48.00 (978-0-7366-3759-6(1), 4434) Books on Tape.
Once in rural Maine, a big black bear found a briefcase under a tree. He was hoping for food but instead found the manuscript of a novel inside.

Beardance. unabr. ed. William Hobbs. Narrated by George Guidall. 4 pieces. (Running Time: 5 hrs. 30 mins.). (gr. 7 up). 1997. 35.00 (978-0-7887-0730-8(2), 94907E7) Recorded Bks.
In this sequel to "Bearstone," Cloyd must draw on his courage, determination & Ute Indian heritage to teach a pair of orphaned grizzly bear cubs how to live in the wild before winter arrives.

Bearded Oaks see Robert Penn Warren Reads Selected Poems

Bearded Oaks see Twentieth-Century Poetry in English, No. 29, Recordings of Poets Reading Their Own Poetry

Beardstown Ladies' Common-Sense Investment Guide: How We Beat the Stock Market & How You Can Too. abr. ed. Beardstown Ladies Investment Club Staff. 1 cass. 9.99 (54186) Books on Tape.
Since the Beardstown Ladies established their investment club in 1983, they've built a $90,000 portfolio with an impressive average return of 23 percent. These women know how to cook in the kitchen, & the stock market! Here they reveal their secret recipe for investment success in a fun, friendly, homespun manner.

Beardstown Ladies' Common-Sense Investment Guide Set: How We Beat the Stock Market & How You Can Too. abr. ed. Beardstown Ladies Investment Club Staff. Read by Beardstown Ladies Investment Club Staff. 2 cass. (Running Time: 2 hrs.). 1995. 16.00 (978-0-671-54186-6(2), 394370, Sound Ideas) S&S Audio.
Offers a very understandable & wise approach to sound investment principles. Topics include IRAs, mutual funds, budgeting, social security benefits, stocks & bonds, & other issues in financial investing. In addition, the principles of saving, personal discipline, sacrifice, & patience are emphasized.

Beardstown Ladies' Stitch-in-Time Guide to Growing Your Nest Egg: Step-by-Step Planning for a Comfortable Financial Future. abr. ed. Beardstown Ladies Investment Club Staff. 2 cass. (Running Time: 3 hrs.). 1999. 9.98 (978-0-671-04598-2(9), Sound Ideas) S&S Audio.

Beare-Stevenson Cutis Gyrata Syndrome - A Bibliography & Dictionary for Physicians, Patients, & Genome Researchers. Compiled by Icon Group International, Inc. Staff. 2007. ring bd. 28.95 (978-0-497-11371-1(6)) Icon Grp.

***Bearers of the Black Staff.** unabr. ed. Terry Brooks. (Running Time: 14 hrs.). (Legends of Shannara Ser.: Bk. 1). 2010. 39.97 (978-1-4418-0505-8(2), 9781441805058, BADLE); 24.99 (978-1-4418-0504-1(4), 9781441805041, BAD) Brilliance Audio.

***Bearers of the Black Staff.** unabr. ed. Terry Brooks. Read by Phil Gigante. 1 MP3-CD. (Running Time: 13 hrs.). (Legends of Shannara Ser.: Bk. 1). 2010. 39.97 (978-1-4418-0503-4(6), 9781441805034, Brlnc Audio MP3 Lib); 24.99 (978-1-4418-0502-7(8), 9781441805027, Brilliance MP3); audio compact disk 92.97 (978-1-4418-0501-0(X), 9781441805010, BriAudCD Unabrid); audio compact disk 38.99 (978-1-4418-0500-3(1), 9781441805003, Bril Audio CD Unabri) Brilliance Audio.

Bearing an Hourglass. unabr. ed. Piers Anthony. Narrated by George Guidall. 12 CDs. (Running Time: 13 hrs. 45 mins.). (Incarnations of Immortality Ser.: Bk. 2). 2000. audio compact disk 116.00 (978-0-7887-4916-2(1), C1297E7) Recorded Bks.
When life seems pointless to Norton, he accepts the position of Incarnation of Time. With the other incarnations, Death, Fate, War & Nature already distracting him, Satan springs a cunning trap. Thought-providing study of good & evil.

Bearing an Hourglass. unabr. ed. Piers Anthony. Narrated by George Guidall. 10 cass. (Running Time: 13 hrs. 45 mins.). (Incarnations of Immortality Ser.: Bk. 2). 1996. 85.00 (978-0-7887-0571-7(7), 94748E7) Recorded Bks.
When life seems pointless to Norton, he accepts the position of Incarnation of Time in this thougt-providing study of good & evil.

Bearing Fruit. David T. Demola. 6 cass. 24.00 (A-1061) Faith Fellow Min.

Bearing Fruit. Bill Winston. 3 cass. (C). 1994. 15.00 (978-1-931289-48-1(4)) Pub: B Winston Min. Dist(s): Anchor Distributors

Bearing the Cross (Part 1 of 2 part cassette Edition) Martin Luther King, Jr. & the Southern Christian Leadership Conference, Vol. 1. unabr. ed. David J. Garrow. Read by Jeff Riggenbach. 11 cass. (Running Time: 35 hrs.). 2003. 76.95 (978-0-7861-1480-1(0), 2332A, B) Blckstn Audio.
Pulitzer Prize winning biography of Martin Luther King Jr. Based on more than 700 interviews with all King's closest surviving associates & with the Southern law men who worked against him.

Bearing the Cross (Part 2 of 2 part cassette Edition) Matin Luther King, Jr. & the Southern Christian Leadership Conference, Vol. 2. unabr. ed. David J. Garrow. Read by Jeff Riggenbach. 13 cass. (Running Time: 35 hrs.). 1999. 85.95 (978-0-7861-1504-4(1), 2332A, B) Blckstn Audio.
The biography of Martin Luther King based on 700 interviews with all King's closest surviving associates & with the Southern law men who worked against him.

Bears' Almanac see Berenstain Bears' Christmas

Bears & Prayers. Michael Dunn. 2004. audio compact disk 10.95 (978-1-57734-630-2(0)); 9.95 (978-1-57734-350-9(6), 06005918) Covenant Comms.
A remarkable story of survival & faith.

Bears Beat Bowls in the Bathtub. unabr. ed. Kathy Teck. Perf. by Geoffrey Holder & Hit-It Band. Illus. by Roy Doty. Narrated by Geoffrey Holder. Contrib. by Hit-It Band Staff. 1 cass. (Running Time: 60 min.). (J). (ps-4). 1997. pap. bk. 19.95 (978-0-9651960-0-0(3), Hit-It Kits) Teck Enter.
Shows fanciful animals playing percussion instruments made of familiar everyday objects; musicians use these for original soundtrack.

Bear's Bicycle. Emilie W. McLeod. Interview with David M. McPhail. 1 cass. (J). (ps up). pap. bk. 15.95 Live Oak Media.
A young boy & an outrageous bear demonstrate how- & how not-to ride a bicycle safely.

Bear's Bicycle. Emilie W. McLeod. Illus. by David M. McPhail. 11 vols. (Running Time: 5 mins.). 1986. pap. bk. 18.95 (978-1-59519-017-8(1)); pap. bk. 35.95 (978-1-59519-018-5(X)); 9.95 (978-1-59112-013-1(6)); audio compact disk 12.95 (978-1-59519-016-1(3)) Live Oak Media.

Bear's Bicycle. Emilie W. McLeod. Read by Peter Fernandez. Illus. by David M. McPhail. 11 vols. (Running Time: 5 mins.). 1986. pap. bk. 16.95 (978-0-87499-023-2(8)) Live Oak Media.
A young boy & an outrageous bear demonstrate how to ride a bicycle safely.

Bear's Bicycle. Emilie W. McLeod. Read by Peter Fernandez. Illus. by David M. McPhail. 14 vols. (Running Time: 5 mins.). 1991. pap. bk. & tchr. ed. 33.95 Reading Chest. (978-0-87499-024-9(6)) Live Oak Media.

Bears in the Night see Bears' Picnic & Other Stories

Bears' New Baby see Bears' Picnic & Other Stories

Bears on Hemlock Mountain. unabr. ed. Alice Dalgliesh. Read by John McDonough. 1 cass. (Running Time: 45 mins.). (J). (gr. 2). 1999. 80.30 Class set . (978-0-7887-3219-5(6), 46875) Recorded Bks.
Jonathan goes over the mountain, but is afraid of bears. The grown-ups tell there are no bears on Hemlock Mountain & he finds that sometimes grown-ups are wrong!.

Bears on Hemlock Mountain. unabr. ed. Alice Dalgliesh. Narrated by John McDonough. 1 cass. (Running Time: 45 mins.). (J). 2000. pap. bk. 23.20 (978-0-7887-3173-0(4), 40908X4) Recorded Bks.
Jonathan has to go over the mountain to borrow Aunt Emma's big iron pot. He is afraid of bears, but the grown-ups assure him there aren't any on Hemlock Mountain. Well, sometimes grown-ups are wrong! Includes study guide.

Bears on Hemlock Mountain, unabr. ed. Alice Dalgliesh. Narrated by John McDonough. 1 cass. (Running Time: 45 mins.). (gr. 1 up). 1999. 10.00 (978-0-7887-3154-9(8), 95827E7) Recorded Bks.
Jonathan goes over the mountain, but is afraid of bears. The gown-ups assure him there are no bears on Hemlock Mountain & he finds that sometimes grown-ups are wrong!.

Bears on Hemlock Mountain. unabr. ed. Alice Dalgliesh. Read by William Dufris. (Running Time: 0 hr. 30 mins. 0 sec.). (ENG.). (J). 2008. audio compact disk 9.99 (978-0-7435-7248-4(3)) Pub: S&S Audio. Dist(s): S and S Inc

Bears' Picnic. Based on a story by Stan Berenstain & Jan Berenstain. (Berenstain Bears Beginner Bks.). (J). (gr. k-3). 1999. 49.32 (978-0-394-12834-4(6)) McKay.

Bears' Picnic & Other Stories. unabr. ed. Stan Berenstain & Jan Berenstain. Perf. by Stan Berenstain & Jan Berenstain. 1 cass. (Running Time: 90 mins.). Incl. Bear Scouts. Stan Berenstain & Jan Berenstain. (Berenstain Bears Beginner Bks.). (J). (ps-3). (CP 1549); Bears in the Night. Stan Berenstain & Jan Berenstain. (Berenstain Bears Bright & Early Bks.). (J). (ps-3). (CP 1549); Bears' New Baby. (J). (CP 1549); Bears' Vacation. Characters created by Stan Berenstain & Jan Berenstain. (Berenstain Bears Beginner Bks.). (J). (gr. k-3). (CP 1549); Big Honey Hunt. Stan Berenstain & Jan Berenstain. (Berenstain Bears Beginner Bks.). (J). (gr. k-3). (CP 1549); (Berenstain Bears Beginner Bks.). (J). (gr. k-3). 1984. 9.95 (978-0-89845-884-8(6), CP 1549) HarperCollins Pubs.

Bear's Toothache. 1 cass. (Running Time: 35 min.). (J). 2001. pap. bk. 15.95 (VX-47C) Kimbo Educ.
A large bear with a large toothache wakes a small boy from his sleep to ask for help. Includes book.

Bear's Toothache. David M. McPhail. Illus. by David M. McPhail. (Running Time: 5 mins.). (J). (ps-2). 1982. 9.95 (978-1-59112-014-8(4)) Live Oak Media.

Bear's Toothache. David M. McPhail. (Running Time: 5 mins.). (J). 1986. 15.95 (978-0-670-15148-6(3)) Live Oak Media.

Bear's Toothache. David M. McPhail. Illus. by David M. McPhail. 14 vols. (Running Time: 5 mins.). 1986. pap. bk. 35.95 (978-1-59519-021-5(X)); audio compact disk 12.95 (978-1-59519-019-2(8)) Live Oak Media.

Bear's Toothache. David M. McPhail. Illus. by David M. McPhail. 11 vols. (Running Time: 5 mins.). (J). 1986. pap. bk. 18.95 (978-1-59519-020-8(1)) Pub: Live Oak Media. Dist(s): AudioGO

Bear's Toothache. unabr. ed. David M. McPhail. Illus. by David M. McPhail. Read by Larry Robinson. 11 vols. (Running Time: 5 mins.). (J). (gr. k-3). 1986. pap. bk. 16.95 (978-0-87499-080-5(7)) AudioGO.
When a large bear with a large toothache wakes a small boy from a deep sleep the boy does what he can to help.

Bear's Toothache. unabr. ed. David M. McPhail. Illus. by David M. McPhail. 11 vols. (Running Time: 5 mins.). (J). (gr. k-2). 1986. bk. 24.95 incl. cloth bk. in bag. (978-0-87499-081-2(5)) Live Oak Media.

Bear's Toothache. unabr. ed. David M. McPhail. Illus. by David M. McPhail. Read by Larry Robinson. 14 vols. (Running Time: 5 mins.). (J). (gr. k-3). 1986. pap. bk. & tchr. ed. 33.95 Reading Chest. (978-0-87499-082-9(3)) Live Oak Media.

Bears' Vacation see Bears' Picnic & Other Stories

Bearstone, unabr. ed. William Hobbs. Narrated by George Guidall. 3 pieces. (Running Time: 4 hrs. 15 mins.). (gr. 7 up). 1997. 27.00 (978-0-7887-0684-4(5), 94858E7) Recorded Bks.
The story of Cloyd, a fourteen-year-old with a nose for trouble. Sent by his tribe to a group home for Indian boys, his feeling of isolation turns to desperation & even more trouble.

Bearwalker & Other Stories. abr. ed. White Bear Woman staff. Read by White Bear Woman staff. 2 cass. (Running Time: 2 hrs.). Dramatization. (Myth & the Natural World Ser.). 1994. 16.95 (978-0-939643-60-8(X), 3596, NrthWrd Bks) TandN Child.
A collection of myths and tales from many lands about bears and their interactions with people.

Beasley on Jury Persuasion. 1 cass. bk. 95.00 (AC-647) PA Bar Inst.

Beasley, Walter Sound Production for Sax. DVD & audio compact disk 24.95 (978-0-7579-2376-0(3), 908073, Warner Bro) Alfred Pub.

Beast. Judith Ivory. Narrated by Barbara Rosenblat. 9 cass. (Running Time: 12 hrs. 45 mins.). 84.00 (978-0-7887-5979-6(5)); audio compact disk 111.00 (978-1-4025-2098-3(0)) Recorded Bks.

Beast. Ally Kennen. Read by Jerome Pride. (Running Time: 5 hrs. 55 mins.). (YA). 2009. 69.99 (978-1-74214-327-9(X), 9781742143279) Pub: Bolinda Pubng AUS. Dist(s): Bolinda Pub Inc

Beast. Donna Jo Napoli. Narrated by Robert Ramirez. 6 CDs. (Running Time: 6 hrs. 30 mins.). (gr. 9 up). audio compact disk 58.00 (978-1-4025-1968-0(0)) Recorded Bks.

Beast. unabr. ed. Ally Kennen. Read by Jerome Pride. (Running Time: 5 hrs. 55 mins.). (YA). 2007. audio compact disk 77.95 (978-1-74093-903-4(4)) Pub: Bolinda Pubng AUS. Dist(s): Bolinda Pub Inc

Beast. unabr. ed. Donna Jo Napoli. Narrated by Robert Ramirez. 5 pieces. (Running Time: 6 hrs. 30 mins.). (gr. 9 up). 2001. 43.00 (978-0-7887-5227-8(8)) Recorded Bks.
A single wrong decision sets in motion a curse that changes the fate of Persian Prince Orasmyn forever.

Beast: Level 3. Carolyn Walker. Contrib. by Philip Prowse. (Running Time: 1 hr. 54 mins.). (Cambridge English Readers Ser.). (ENG.). 2001. 15.00 (978-0-521-75017-2(2)) Cambridge U Pr.

Beast, Antichrist & the False Prophet, Set. Mac Hammond. 5 cass. (Running Time: 5 hrs.). (Last Millennium Ser.: Vol. 5). 2000. (978-1-57399-095-0(7)) Mac Hammond.
Of the many fantastic & disturbing images found in the pages of Revelation, few have sparked as much interest & speculation as that of "the beast.".

Beast Beneath the Stairs. Michael Dahl. Illus. by Patricia Mofett. (Library of Doom Ser.). (gr. 1-3). 2008. audio compact disk 14.60 (978-1-4342-0602-2(5)) CapstoneDig.

Beast Feast. Douglas Florian. Read by Michael Day. 1 cass. (Running Time: 12 min.). (J). (gr. k-3). 1998. pap. bk. 25.95 Incl. tchr's. guide. (978-0-8045-6850-0(2), 6850) Spoken Arts.
Consists of frolicking rhymes, animal h[illegible] & animated wonder so that it will entice the imagination into worlds [illegible]vity & expressive language of children.

Beast in Ms. Rooney's Room. unabr. ed. Patricia Reilly Giff. Read by Suzanne Toren. 1 cass. (Running Time: 1 hr. 20 mins.). (Follow the Reader Ser.). (J). (gr. 2-4). 1984. pap. bk. 17.00 (978-0-8072-0090-2(5), FTR100SP, Listening Lib) Random Audio Pubg.
Follow the kids in Ms. Rooney's second grade class as they learn & grow through an entire school year filled with fun & surprises. Corresponding month: September.

Beast in the Jungle & Other Stories. unabr. ed. Henry James. Read by Donna Barkman. 8 cass. (Running Time: 1 hr. per cass.). 1984. 39.00 (C-117) Jimcin Record.
"The Beast in the Jungle" is the tale of a man's habitual obsession with himself & his deserved fate. "An International Episode" contains satirical vignettes of upper-class American & English life in the 1870s. "The Pupil" narrates a son's long history of parental betrayals & rejections.

Beast in the Jungle & Other Stories. unabr. collector's ed. Henry James. Read by Donna Barkman. 8 cass. (Running Time: 8 hrs.). 1998. 48.00 (978-0-7366-3888-3(1), 9117) Books on Tape.
Tells of a man who persuades his ladyfriend to wait for his premonition to come true.

Beast Master. unabr. ed. Andre Norton. Read by Richard J. Brewer. (Running Time: 7 hrs.). (Beast Master Chronicles Ser.). 2009. 24.99 (978-1-4233-9987-2(0), 9781423399872, Brilliance MP3); 39.97

(978-1-4233-9988-9(9), 9781423399889, Brilnc Audio MP3 Lib); 24.99 (978-1-4233-9989-6(7), 9781423399896, BAD); 39.97 (978-1-4233-9990-2(0), 9781423399902, BADLE); audio compact disk 24.99 (978-1-4233-9985-8(4), 9781423399858); audio compact disk 82.97 (978-1-4233-9986-5(2), 9781423399865, BriAudCD Unabrid) Brilliance Audio.

Beast Must Die. abr. ed. Nicholas Blake, pseud. 2 cass. (Running Time: 3 hrs.). (J). 1999. 16.85 Set. (978-1-901768-10-7(4)) Pub: CSA Telltapes GBR. Dist(s): Ulverscroft US

Beast Must Die. unabr. ed. Nicholas Blake, pseud. Narrated by Steven Crossley. 6 cass. (Running Time: 8 hrs.). 1999. 53.00 (978-1-84197-033-2(6), H1033E7) Recorded Bks.
Frank Cairnes lost his wife in childbirth. Fewer than seven years later, he has lost his only son. Martin was knocked into a ditch by a speeding driver who did not bother to stop. No witnesses, no suspects & no clues mean that the police are stumped. Frank cannot let it rest. His one reason for living is to find & kill the driver. A writer of crime novels in his spare time, he thinks hard about ways to discover a lead, but with no success - until his own ingenuity & a bit of luck set him on the right track.

Beast of Monsieur Racine. 2004. bk. 24.95 (978-0-7882-0587-3(0)); pap. bk. 14.95 (978-1-56008-161-6(9)); 8.95 (978-1-56008-840-0(0)); 8.95 (978-1-56008-135-7(X)); cass. & flmstrp 30.00 (978-0-89719-651-2(1)) Weston Woods.

Beast of Monsieur Racine. Tomi Ungerer. 1 cass. (Running Time: 30 min.). (J). bk. 24.95; pap. bk. 32.75; pap. bk. 12.95; 8.95 (RAC160) Weston Woods.
A suspicious beast becomes friends with a lonely man who proudly presents him to Academy of Science.

Beast of the Earth: Rev. 13:1-18, 572. Ed Young. 1987. 4.95 (978-0-7417-1572-2(4), 572) Win Walk.

Beast of the Sea: Rev. 13:1-10, 570. Ed Young. 1986. 4.95 (978-0-7417-1570-8(8), 570) Win Walk.

Beastie Boys: The Unauthorized Biography of the Beastie Boys. Tim Footman. 1 CD. (Running Time: 1 hr.). (Maximum Ser.). (ENG.). 2001. audio compact disk 14.95 (978-1-84240-030-2(4)) Pub: Chrome Dreams GBR. Dist(s): IPG Chicago

***Beastly.** unabr. ed. Alex Flinn. (Running Time: 7 hrs.). 2010. 24.99 (978-1-4418-4970-0(X), 9781441849700, BAD); 39.97 (978-1-4418-4971-7(8), 9781441849717, BADLE) Brilliance Audio.

***Beastly.** unabr. ed. Alex Flinn. Read by Chris Patton. 1 MP3-CD. (Running Time: 7 hrs.). 2010. 24.99 (978-1-4418-4968-7(8), 9781441849687, Brilliance MP3); 39.97 (978-1-4418-4969-4(6), 9781441849694, Brinc Audio MP3 Lib); audio compact disk 69.97 (978-1-4418-4967-0(X), 9781441849670, BriAudCD Unabrid) Brilliance Audio.

***Beastly.** unabr. ed. Alex Flinn. Read by Chris Patton. 6 CDs. (Running Time: 7 hrs.). (YA). 2010. audio compact disk 24.99 (978-1-4418-4966-3(1), 9781441849663, Bril Audio CD Unabri) Brilliance Audio.

Beasts & Super-Beasts. unabr. ed. Saki. Read by Laurie Klein. 2 cass. (Running Time: 2 hrs. 30 min.). Dramatization. 1991. 16.95 (978-1-55686-373-8(X), 373) Books in Motion.
A compilation of delightful Saki stories, each displaying a member of the animal kingdom. Included: The Open Window, The Lull, Dusk, Fur, The Hen, The Story-Teller, The Boar-Pig, Down Pens, The Romancers, Clovis on Parental Responsibility, & The Stalled Ox.

Beasts by the Bunches. unabr. ed. A. Mifflin Lowe. 1 cass. (Running Time: 27 min.). (J). (ps-3). 1987. 9.95 (978-0-89845-748-3(3), CPN1817) HarperCollins Pubs.

Beasts of Clawstone Castle. unabr. ed. Eva Ibbotson. Read by Jenny Sterlin. 5 CDs. (Running Time: 6 hrs.). (YA). (gr. 5-8). 2006. audio compact disk 49.75 (978-1-4281-2183-6(8)); 39.75 (978-1-4281-2178-2(1)) Recorded Bks.
Madlyn and Rollo's parents have left for the summer. Now the two children are staying with their Great-Aunt Emily and Great-Uncle George at Clawstone Castle, famous for its mysterious herd of wild white cattle. When the children arrive at their new home, they're surprised to see that it's in terrible shape. It seems that the fancy castle down the road is getting all the attention from tourists, and now Clawstone may not survive. So to save the day, Madlyn and Rollo invite some gruesome ghosts to liven up the castle tours. Things are great - until someone kidnaps the entire herd!.

Beasts of Tarzan. Edgar Rice Burroughs. Read by Shelly Frasier. (Running Time: 6 hrs. 15 mins.). 2001. 27.95 (978-1-60083-577-3(5), Audiofy Corp) Iofy Corp.

Beasts of Tarzan. Edgar Rice Burroughs. Read by Shelly Frasier. (Tarzan Ser.). (ENG.). 2001. audio compact disk 72.00 (978-1-4001-3004-7(2)) Pub: Tantor Media. Dist(s): IngramPubServ

Beasts of Tarzan. unabr. ed. Edgar Rice Burroughs. Read by Shelly Frazier. 1 CD. (Running Time: 6 hrs. 30 mins.). 2001. audio compact disk 25.00; audio compact disk 51.00 Books on Tape.
After renouncing his savage life in the jungle for the sake of his wife Jane and newborn son, Tarzan finds his trust in civilization has again been betrayed. Tarzan, now the rich Lord Greystoke, becomes the target of sinister criminals. When he and Jane try to save their abducted son, Jane is kidnapped and Tarzan is stranded on a deserted island. But as the lord of his realm, he calls the beasts of the jungle to his service.

Beasts of Tarzan. unabr. ed. Edgar Rice Burroughs. Narrated by Shelly Frasier. 6 CDs. (Running Time: 6 hrs. 14 mins.). (Tarzan Ser.: Vol. 3). (ENG.). 2001. audio compact disk 36.00 (978-1-4001-0004-0(6)) Pub: Tantor Media. Dist(s): IngramPubServ
After renouncing his savage life in the jungle for the sake of his wife and newborn son, Tarzan finds his trust in civilization has again been betrayed. Tarzan, now the rich Lord Greystoke, becomes the target of sinister criminals. Their son is abducted, Jane is kidnapped and Tarzan is stranded on a deserted island. But the Lord of the Jungle calls his beasts Sheeta and Akut, and the giant warrior Mugambi to his aid in saving his family... if they are still alive!.

Beasts of Tarzan. unabr. ed. Edgar Rice Burroughs. Narrated by Shelly Frasier. (Running Time: 6 hrs. 0 mins. 0 sec.). (Tarzan Ser.). (ENG.). 2009. 19.99 (978-1-4001-5937-6(7)); audio compact disk 27.99 (978-1-4001-0937-1(X)); audio compact disk 55.99 (978-1-4001-3937-8(6)) Pub: Tantor Media. Dist(s): IngramPubServ

Beasts of Tarzan, Bk. 3. unabr. ed. Edgar Rice Burroughs. Read by David Sharp. 6 cass. (Running Time: 6 hrs. 12 min.). Dramatization. 1993. 39.95 (978-1-55686-480-3(9), 480) Books in Motion.
Tarzan's wife & son are kidnapped by Rokoff & his rat like lieutenant. Tarzan assembles an awesome rescue squad: Mugambi, a giant native of the jungle, Sheeta, a sleek & powerful black panther, & the entire tribe of Akut - the great apes.

***Beat.** unabr. ed. Stephen Jay Schwartz. Read by Ray Porter. (Running Time: 11 hrs.). (Hayden Glass Novels Ser.). 2010. 29.95 (978-1-4417-6871-1(8)); 65.95 (978-1-4417-6868-1(8)); audio compact disk 29.95 (978-1-4417-6870-4(X)); audio compact disk 100.00 (978-1-4417-6869-8(6)) Blckstn Audio.

Beat Generation. 3 CDs. (Running Time: 4 hrs. 30 mins.). 2001. bk. 39.98 (R2 70281) Rhino Enter.

Beat Not the Bones. unabr. l.t. ed. Charlotte Jay. Read by Paula Gardner. 6 cass. (Running Time: 8 hrs.). 1997. 48.00 (978-1-86340-726-7(X), 570725) Pub: Bolinda Pubng AUS. Dist(s): Lndmrk Audiobks
A young girl travels to Papua, New Guinea from Australia, determined to discover the truth about her late husband's death.

Beat of a Spoon. 1 CD. (Running Time: 34 mins.). (Baby Growlers Ser.: No. 1). (J). 2004. audio compact disk 13.00 (978-1-893185-51-7(6)) TNG Earth.

***Beat the Band.** unabr. ed. Don Calame. Read by Nick Podehl. (Running Time: 9 hrs.). 2010. 24.99 (978-1-4418-1497-5(3), 9781441814975, BAD); 39.97 (978-1-4418-1498-2(1), 9781441814982, BADLE); 24.99 (978-1-4418-1495-1(7), 9781441814951, Brilliance MP3); 39.97 (978-1-4418-1496-8(5), 9781441814968, Brinc Audio MP3 Lib) Brilliance Audio.

***Beat the Band.** unabr. ed. Don Calame. Read by Nick Podehl. (Running Time: 8 hrs.). (YA). 2010. audio compact disk 24.99 (978-1-4418-1493-7(0), 9781441814937, Bril Audio CD Unabri); audio compact disk 69.97 (978-1-4418-1494-4(9), 9781441814944, BriAudCD Unabrid) Brilliance Audio.

Beat the Reaper. unabr. ed. Josh Bazell. Read by Robert Petkoff. (Running Time: 7 hrs.). 2009. 14.98 (978-1-60024-433-9(5)) Pub: Hachet Audio. Dist(s): HachBkGrp

Beat the Reaper. unabr. ed. Josh Bazell. Read by Robert Petkoff. (Running Time: 7 hrs.). (ENG.). 2009. audio compact disk 14.98 (978-1-60024-819-1(5)) Pub: Hachet Audio. Dist(s): HachBkGrp

Beat the Turtle Drum. unabr. ed. Constance C. Greene. 1 read-along cass. (Running Time: 1 hr. 17 min.). (Children's Cliffhangers Ser.). (J). (gr. 4-6). 1985. 15.98 incl. bk. & guide. (978-0-8072-1122-9(2), SWR42SP, Listening Lib) Random Audio Pubg.
In this story, the author examines one family's handling of what may well be the ultimate family crisis - the death of one of the children.

Beat to Quarters. C. S. Forester. Read by Geoffrey Howard. 2002. audio compact disk 56.00 (978-0-7366-9128-4(6)) Books on Tape.

Beat to Quarters. unabr. ed. C. S. Forester. 6 cass. (Running Time: 6 hrs.). 2002. 48.00 (978-0-7366-8898-7(6)) Books on Tape.

Beat to Quarters. unabr. ed. C. S. Forester. Read by David Case. 8 cass. (Running Time: 12 hrs.). (Hornblower Ser.). 2001. 29.95 (978-0-7366-6755-5(5)) Books on Tape.
Hornblower cuts Napoleon's line on a cruise to Spain & Nicaragua.

Beat to Quarters. unabr. collector's ed. C. S. Forester. Read by David Case. 8 cass. (Running Time: 8 hrs.). (Hornblower Ser.: No. 5). 1984. 64.00 (978-0-7366-0654-7(8), 1615) Books on Tape.
Hornblower, a well known hero of Forester, appears in "Beat the Quarters" as a young captain. On his 36 gun frigate he sets out for Spain & ongoing quest to cut Napoleon's lines wherever he crosses them.

Beat Writing Series. unabr. ed. 9 cass. (Running Time: 29 min. per cass.). 1989. 10.00 ea. New Letters.
Programs with Beat writers Lawrence Ferlinghetti, Allen Ginsberg, Andrei Codrescu, Robert Creeley, john Giorno & Anne Waldman.

Beat Zen - Beat Hasidism. unabr. ed. Alan Watts. 1 cass. (Running Time: 1 hr. 16 min.). 1967. 11.00 (02510) Big Sur Tapes.
An informal exchange of questions & anecdotes, remarking on the Hasidic "serving God with the 'evil' urge" & Watts' notion of "the element of fundamental rascality".

***Beating a Dead Horse: The Life & Times of Jay Marshall.** Narrated by Alexander Marshall. (Running Time: 840). (C). 2010. audio compact disk 39.95 (978-0-9825068-4-4(8)) JuntoPubIng.

Beating Back the Devil. unabr. ed. Maryn McKenna. Read by Ellen Archer. 12 CDs. (Running Time: 11 hrs. 0 mins. 0 sec.). (ENG.). 2004. audio compact disk 34.99 (978-1-4001-0140-5(9)) Pub: Tantor Media. Dist(s): IngramPubServ

Beating Back the Devil: On the Front Lines with the Disease Detectives of the Epidemic Intelligence. unabr. ed. Maryn McKenna. Read by Ellen Archer. (Running Time: 11 hrs. 0 mins. 0 sec.). (ENG.). 2004. audio compact disk 22.99 (978-1-4001-5140-0(6)) Pub: Tantor Media. Dist(s): IngramPubServ

Beating Back the Devil: On the Front Lines with the Disease Detectives of the Epidemic Intelligence Service. unabr. ed. Maryn McKenna. Read by Ellen Archer. (Running Time: 11 hrs. 0 mins. 0 sec.). (ENG.). 2004. audio compact disk 69.99 (978-1-4001-3140-2(5)) Pub: Tantor Media. Dist(s): IngramPubServ

Beating Cancer with Nutrition: Optimal Nutrition Can Improve the Outcome in Medically-Treated Cancer Patients. 4th ed. Patrick Quillin. 2005. pap. bk. 24.95 (978-0-9638372-9-5(X), 291-010) Pub: Nutrit Times. Dist(s): Bookworld

Beating Depression Before It Beats You. Mark Crow. 2 cass. (Running Time: 2 hrs.). 2001. (978-1-931537-13-1(5)) Vision Comm Creat.

Beating Job Burnout: How to Get More Job Satisfaction & Be More Productive. Beverly A. Potter. 1 cass. (Running Time: 60 min.). 1992. 9.95 (978-0-914171-41-6(0)) Ronin Pub.

Beating the ACT 2009 Edition: An Audio Guide to Getting the Score You Need. Awdeeo. Narrated by Awdeeo. (YA). 2009. 39.99 (978-0-9818187-5-7(7)) PrepLogic.

Beating the Bear: Short-Term Trading Tactics for Difficult Markets. Instructed by Jea Yu. 1 cassette. (Running Time: 90 mins.). (Trade Secrets Audio Ser.). 2001. 19.95 (978-1-931611-39-8(4)) Marketplace Bks.
Learn to Prosper - EVEN in today's difficult Markets ...Changing market climates require revised trading tactics. Decimalization, low volatility - they've all diminished profit opportunities for traders. But profits CAN STILL be made - if you're armed with the right tools and techniques. Jea Yu's fast-paced presentation comes with an Online COMPANION MANUAL, and provides straight-on strategies for adapting quickly to the new trading realities.

Beating the Devil: The Incendiary Rants of Alexander Cockburn. Alexander Cockburn. (Running Time: 1 hr. 12 mins.). (AK Press Audio Ser.). (ENG.). 2002. audio compact disk 14.98 (978-1-902593-49-4(9)) Pub: AK Pr GBR. Dist(s): Consort Bk Sales

Beating the Feargators: Critter County Scripture Memory. Christine Wyrtzen & Paula Bussard. 1 cass. (50-Day Spiritual Adventure Ser.). (J). (gr. k-2). 1994. 4.99 (978-1-879050-58-7(7)) Chapel of Air.
1995 50-Day Spiritual Adventure children's scripture memory verses put to music.

Beating the GMAT 2009: An Audio Guide to Getting the Score You Need. Awdeeo. Narrated by Awdeeo. 2009. 39.99 (978-0-9818187-8-8(1)) PrepLogic.

Beating the GRE 2009: An Audio Guide to Getting the Score You Need. Awdeeo. 2009. 39.99 (978-0-9818187-9-5(X)) PrepLogic.

Beating the Holiday Blues. 2002. 24.95 (978-1-58557-054-6(0)) Dynamic Growth.

Beating the PSAT 2009 Edition: An Audio Guide to Getting the Score You Need. Awdeeo. Narrated by Awdeeo. (YA). 2009. 39.99 (978-0-9818187-3-3(0)) PrepLogic.

Beating the SAT 2009: An Audio Guide to Getting the Score You Need. Awdeeo. Narrated by Awdeeo. (YA). 2008. 39.99 (978-0-9818187-2-6(2)) PrepLogic.

Beating the Street: How to Use What You Already Know to Make Money in the Market. Peter Lynch. 2004. 10.95 (978-0-7435-4189-3(8)) Pub: S&S Audio. Dist(s): S and S Inc

Beatitude Attitude. Created by Gospel Gospel Vision Staff. (J). 2002. (978-0-910683-82-1(4)); audio compact disk 13.95 (978-0-910683-83-8(2)) Townsnd-Pr.

Beatitudes. Contrib. by Jay Rouse. Composed by Jay Rouse et al. 2007. audio compact disk 24.98 (978-5-557-48979-9(7)) H Leonard.

Beatitudes: Living the Christian Challenge. Edd Anthony. Read by Edd Anthony. 2007. audio compact disk 16.95 (978-1-881586-18-0(9)) Canticle Cass.

Beatles. unabr. ed. Hunter Davies. Read by Edward Lewis. 12 cass. (Running Time: 17 hrs. 30 mins.). 2001. 83.95 (978-0-7861-1500-6(9), 2350) Blckstn Audio.

Beatles. 2nd rev. ed. Hunter Davies. Read by Edward Lewis. 12 cass. (Running Time: 18 hrs.). 1999. 83.95 (2350) Blckstn Audio.
Behind-the-scenes look at the most famous musical group in history. Follows them during the peak of their popularity, their breakup, & the continuing story of their solo careers.

Beatles: A Biography. abr. ed. Robert Spitz. 2005. 39.95 (978-0-7435-5140-3(0), Audioworks) Pub: S&S Audio. Dist(s): S and S Inc

Beatles: As It Happened. Chrome Dreams Staff. Compiled by John Donegan. 4 cass. (ENG., 2000. audio compact disk 32.50 (978-1-84240-096-8(7)) Pub: Chrome Dreams GBR. Dist(s): IPG Chicago

Beatles: The Biography. abr. ed. Bob Spitz. Read by Alfred Molina. 2005. 23.95 (978-0-7435-5245-5(8)) Pub: S&S Audio. Dist(s): S and S Inc

Beatles Tapes V: The 1965 Help Tour. 1 CD. (Running Time: 1 hr.). 2000. audio compact disk 15.95 Soundworks Intl.
Compilation of quotes & interviews.

***Beatrice & Virgil.** unabr. ed. Yann Martel. Read by Mark Bramhall. (ENG.). 2010. audio compact disk 30.00 (978-0-307-71515-9(9), Random AudioBks) Pub: Random Audio Pubg. Dist(s): Random

Beatrice's Goast. unabr. ed. Page McBrier. (J). (ps-3). 2005. bk. 27.95 (978-0-8045-6938-5(X)) Spoken Arts.
Based on the true account of one family who received aid from Heifer Project International, a charitable organization that donates livestock to poor communities around the world, this moving story is eloquently and gracefully recounted. Vividly evoking the lush tropical landscape of central Africa, Lohstoeter's rich, deeply-hued illustrations perfectly complement the text and make Beatrice and her world affectingly real. Although she may live far removed from the comfortable middle-class lives of many young readers, it is clear that Beatrice is a girl of unusual heart and, like any child, filled with hopes and dreams.

Beatrice's Goat. unabr. ed. Page McBrier. (J). (ps-3). 2005. bk. 29.95 (978-0-8045-4137-4(X)) Spoken Arts.

Beatrix Potter: Artist, Storyteller & Countrywoman (Audiocassette Version) 2004. 8.95 (978-1-56008-435-8(9)) Weston Woods.

Beatrix Potter Audio Gift Pack: More Tales from Beatrix Potter, Vol. 2. Beatrix Potter. Illus. by Beatrix Potter. (Audio Gift Pack Ser.). (J). (ps-2). 1992. bk. 19.98 (978-1-55886-067-4(3), AGP 4-203) Smarty Pants.

Beatrix Potter Audio Gift Pack Vol. 1: Magic of Beatrix Potter. Beatrix Potter. Illus. by Beatrix Potter. (Audio Gift Pack Ser.). (J). (ps-2). 1991. bk. 19.98 (978-1-55886-063-6(0), AGP 4-202) Smarty Pants.

Beatrix Potter Story Hour. Beatrix Potter. (Running Time: 089 mins.). (J). (ps-4). 2001. 9.95 (978-0-89084-905-7(6), 054023) BJUPr.

Beatrix Potter Treasury of Animal Stories, Vol. 2. unabr. ed. Beatrix Potter. Read by Frances Sternhagen. (J). 1988. 10.95 (978-0-8045-1139-1(X), SAC 1139) Spoken Arts.
The Tailor of Gloucester, Two Bad Mice, & Mrs Tiggy-Winkle.

Beats: Conversations in Rhythm for ESL, Speech, LD. Joan R. Keyes. 2 cass. 49.95 set, incl. 78 masters, illus., 10 worksheets, vocabulary list & guide. (978-0-89525-694-2(0), AC 234) Ed Activities.
Choral conversation in rhythm which helps learn vocabulary in area dealing with school, home, family, community & personal relationships; lock into intonations, accents & rhythms of everyday American English; become proficient in all verb tenses & variety of other structures & idiomatic language; develop spontaneity in conversation.

Beau Geste. Percival Wren. Read by David Case. (Running Time: 54000 sec.). (Unabridged Classics in Audio Ser.). (ENG.). 2006. audio compact disk 39.99 (978-1-4001-0213-6(8)); audio compact disk 29.99 (978-1-4001-5213-1(5)); audio compact disk 79.99 (978-1-4001-3213-3(4)) Pub: Tantor Media. Dist(s): IngramPubServ

Beau Geste. unabr. ed. Percival Wren. Narrated by David Case. (Running Time: 15 hrs. 0 mins. 0 sec.). (ENG.). 2009. audio compact disk 35.99 (978-1-4001-1133-6(1)); audio compact disk 72.99 (978-1-4001-4133-3(8)); audio compact disk 27.99 (978-1-4001-6133-1(9)) Pub: Tantor Media. Dist(s): IngramPubServ

Beau Geste. unabr. ed. Percival C. Wren. Read by Geoffrey Howard. 10 cass. (Running Time: 14 hrs. 30 mins.). 1998. 69.95 (978-0-7861-1290-6(5), 2191) Blckstn Audio.
World-famous novel of suspense & adventure...love & glory...courage & treachery. It is the thrilling story of three men who brave the hellish brutality & ruthless savagery of the French Foreign Legion to protect the honor of a woman they love more than their lives.

Beau Geste. unabr. collector's ed. Percival C. Wren. Read by David Case. 11 cass. (Running Time: 16 hrs. 30 mins.). 1993. 88.00 (978-0-7366-2508-1(9), 3264) Books on Tape.
Three English brothers, fleeing criminal past, enlist in French Foreign Legion & encounter a tyrannical sergeant.

Beaufort. unabr. ed. Ron Leshem. Narrated by Dick Hill. (Running Time: 14 hrs. 0 mins. 0 sec.). (ENG.). 2008. audio compact disk 24.99 (978-1-4001-5661-0(0)); audio compact disk 75.99 (978-1-4001-3661-2(X)); audio compact disk 37.99 (978-1-4001-0661-5(3)) Pub: Tantor Media. Dist(s): IngramPubServ

Beautiful. Contrib. by Bethany Dillon. (Mastertrax Ser.). 2006. audio compact disk 9.98 (978-5-558-01854-7(2)) Pt of Grace Ent.

Beautiful & Damned. F. Scott Fitzgerald. Read by William Dufris. 10 cass. (Running Time: 14 hrs. 30 mins.). 2000. 69.95 (978-0-7861-1867-0(9), 2666); audio compact disk 88.00 (978-0-7861-9815-3(X), 2666) Blckstn Audio.
Published in 1922, it chronicles the relationship of Anthony Patch, Harvard-educated, aspiring aesthete & his beautiful wife, Gloria, as they

await to inherit his grandfather's fortune. A devastating satire of the nouveaux rich & New York's nightlife, of reckless ambition & squandered talent.

***Beautiful & Damned.** unabr. ed. F. Scott Fitzgerald. Narrated by Kirby Heyborne. (Running Time: 15 hrs. 30 mins. 0 sec.). 2010. 27.99 (978-1-4001-6961-0(5)); 19.99 (978-1-4001-8961-8(6)); audio compact disk 35.99 (978-1-4001-1961-5(8)); audio compact disk 85.99 (978-1-4001-4961-2(4)) Pub: Tantor Media. Dist(s): IngramPubServ

Beautiful & Damned, Set. unabr. ed. F. Scott Fitzgerald. Read by Flo Gibson. 9 cass. (Running Time: 12 hrs. 30 min.). 1997. 28.95 (978-1-55685-467-5(6), 407.6) Audio Bk Con.
From a life full of beauty & promise Anthony & Gloria's marriage starts on a steady decline due to drunkenness & debauchery.

***Beautiful & the Damned.** unabr. ed. F. Scott Fitzgerald. Read by Don Hagen. (Running Time: 14 hrs. 30 mins.). (ENG.). 2010. 17.98 (978-1-59659-670-2(8), GildAudio) Pub: Gildan Media. Dist(s): HachBkGrp

***Beautiful Assassin: A Novel.** unabr. ed. Michael White. (Running Time: 18 hrs. 0 mins. 0 sec.). (ENG.). 2010. audio compact disk 79.99 (978-1-4001-4430-3(2)) Pub: Tantor Media. Dist(s): IngramPubServ

***Beautiful Assassin: A Novel.** unabr. ed. Michael White. Narrated by Anne Flosnik. (Running Time: 17 hrs. 30 mins.). 2010. 39.99 (978-1-4001-9430-8(X)); 29.99 (978-1-4001-6430-1(3)); 21.99 (978-1-4001-8430-9(4)); audio compact disk 39.99 (978-1-4001-1430-6(6)) Pub: Tantor Media. Dist(s): IngramPubServ

Beautiful Bad Girl: The Vicki Morgan Story. unabr. collector's ed. Gordon Basichis. Read by Barrett Whitener. 8 cass. (Running Time: 12 hrs.). 1995. 64.00 (978-0-7366-3165-5(8), 3835) Books on Tape.
When the police found Vicki Morgan murdered, it opened a can of worms. she was the longtime mistress of Alfred Bloomingdale, the department store heir famous for his love of the good life. Basichis knew her better than anyone, perhaps. He talked with her almost daily during the last nine months of her life. He found an intelligent tomboy who had twice married other men to escape her mistress role & a caring soul who disguised herself to visit a dying Bloomingdale in the hospital. How did her dreams go sour.

***Beautiful Bird Songs from Around the World.** The British Library. (ENG.). 2010. audio compact disk 25.00 (978-0-7123-0543-3(2)) Pub: Britis Library GBR. Dist(s): Chicago Distribution Ctr

***Beautiful Birdsong of Britain: The Music of Nature.** The British Library. (British Library - British Library Sound Archive Ser.). 2011. audio compact disk 15.00 (978-0-7123-5112-6(4)) Pub: Britis Library GBR. Dist(s): Chicago Distribution Ctr

Beautiful Boy: A Father's Journey Through His Son's Addiction. unabr. ed. David Sheff. Read by Anthony Heald. 8 cass. (Running Time: 41400 sec.). 2008. 29.95 (978-1-4332-0467-8(3)); 72.95 (978-1-4332-0465-4(7)); audio compact disk 29.95 (978-1-4332-0468-5(1)); audio compact disk 29.95 (978-1-4332-0469-2(X)); audio compact disk 90.00 (978-1-4332-0466-1(5)) Blckstn Audio.

Beautiful Boy: A Father's Journey Through His Son's Addiction. unabr. ed. David Sheff. Read by Anthony Heald. (YA). 2008. 74.99 (978-1-60252-929-8(9)) Find a World.

Beautiful Bride: Eph. 5:22-33. Ed Young. 1994. 4.95 (978-0-7417-2001-6(9), 1001) Win Walk.

***Beautiful Chaos.** abr. ed. Gary Russell. Narrated by Bernard Cribbins. (Running Time: 2 hrs. 30 mins. 0 sec.). (Doctor Who Ser.). (ENG.). 2010. audio compact disk 24.95 (978-1-4084-2652-4(8)) Pub: AudioGO. Dist(s): Perseus Dist

Beautiful Children. unabr. ed. Charles Bock. Read by Mark Deakins. 12 CDs. (Running Time: 15 hrs.). 2008. audio compact disk 129.00 (978-1-4159-4672-5(8)) Random.

Beautiful Cigar Girl: Mary Rogers, Edgar Allan Poe, & the Invention of Murder. unabr. ed. Daniel Stashower. (ENG.). 2006. audio compact disk 39.95 (978-0-14-305900-4(9), PengAudBks) Penguin Grp USA.

Beautiful City. Contrib. by John Michael Talbot. 2006. audio compact disk 16.99 (978-5-558-24606-3(5)) TroubadorPub GBR.

Beautiful Creatures. unabr. ed. Kami Garcia & Margaret Stohl. Read by Kevin T. Collins. (Running Time: 17 hrs.). (ENG.). 2009. 24.98 (978-1-60024-847-4(0)); 29.98 (978-1-60024-846-7(2)) Pub: Hachet Audio. Dist(s): HachBkGrp

***Beautiful Darkness.** unabr. ed. Kami Garcia & Margaret Stohl. Read by Kevin T. Collins. 2 MP3-CDs. (Running Time: 17 hrs.). (YA). 2010. 29.98 (978-1-60788-721-8(5)); 24.98 (978-1-60788-722-5(3)) Pub: Hachet Audio. Dist(s): HachBkGrp

Beautiful Disaster. unabr. ed. Kate Brian, pseud. Narrated by Justine Eyre. 6 CDs. (Running Time: 7 hrs. 30 mins. 0 sec.). (Privilege Ser.: No. 2). (ENG.). (J). (gr. 8). 2009. audio compact disk 59.99 (978-1-4001-4243-9(1)); audio compact disk 19.99 (978-1-4001-6243-7(2)) Pub: Tantor Media. Dist(s): IngramPubServ

Beautiful Disaster. unabr. ed. Kate Brian, pseud. Narrated by Justine Eyre. 6 CDs. (Running Time: 7 hrs. 30 mins. 0 sec.). (Privilege Ser.: No. 2). (ENG.). (J). (gr. 9-12). 2009. audio compact disk 29.99 (978-1-4001-1243-2(5)) Pub: Tantor Media. Dist(s): IngramPubServ

Beautiful Dreamer. abr. ed. Elizabeth Lowell. Read by Laural Merlington. (Running Time: 3 hrs.). 2008. audio compact disk 14.99 (978-1-4233-3871-0(5), 9781423338710, BCD Value Price) Brilliance Audio.

Beautiful Dreamer. unabr. ed. Elizabeth Lowell. Read by Laural Merlington. (Running Time: 9 hrs.). 2005. 49.97 (978-1-59600-642-3(0), 9781596006423, BADLE); 24.95 (978-1-59600-641-6(2), 9781596006416, BAD); audio compact disk 24.95 (978-1-59600-639-3(0), 9781596006393, Brilliance MP3); audio compact disk 39.25 (978-1-59600-640-9(4), 9781596006409, Brlnc Audio MP3 Lib) Brilliance Audio.
Rio is a man with a reputation for finding water in the desert. What he can't find is a dream in his own heart. He is Brother-to-the-Wind, a man whose only love is traveling with the wind over the empty land. Hope Gardener is a woman whose Nevada ranch is dying for lack of water. Her heart is full of dreams, and they're all of water. She loves her ranch as she has never loved a man. The last thing either Hope or Rio expected to find is love. She isn't prepared for it. He can't accept it. Yet neither can live without it.

***Beautiful Dreamer.** unabr. ed. Elizabeth Lowell. Read by Laural Merlington. (Running Time: 9 hrs.). 2010. audio compact disk 29.99 (978-1-4418-4095-0(8), 9781441840950, Bril Audio CD Unabri); audio compact disk 89.97 (978-1-4418-4096-7(6), 9781441840967, BriAudCD Unabrid) Brilliance Audio.

Beautiful Dreamer, Level 3. (Yamaha Clavinova Connection Ser.). 2004. disk 0.82 (978-0-634-09596-2(X)) H Leonard.

Beautiful Ending: Genesis 45:27. Ed Young. (J). 1982. 4.95 (978-0-7417-1214-1(8), A0214) Win Walk.

Beautiful Energy: By the 12 Girls Band. (Light on China Ser.). audio compact disk 9.95 (978-7-88057-454-8(9), CD-62) China Bks.

Beautiful Hammond Girls. unabr. ed. Sue Sully. Read by June Barrie. 14 cass. (Running Time: 14 hrs.). 1999. 110.95 Set. (978-0-7540-0219-2(5), CAB1642) AudioGO.
Four girls, the daughters of a pre-Raphaelite painter, are united by their love of music. When two of them are drawn to the same man, the family is torn apart. Eventually scandal breaks, forcing the sisters to separate.

Beautiful Hollywood. Perf. by Erich Kunzel & Cincinnati Pops Orchestra. 1 cass., 1 CD. 7.98 (TA 30440); audio compact disk 12.78 CD Jewel box. (TA 80440) NewSound.

Beautiful Lady see Monsieur Beaucaire & Other Stories

Beautiful Lord. Contrib. by Leeland. (Mastertrax Ser.). 2006. audio compact disk 9.98 (978-5-558-20097-3(9)) Pt of Grace Ent.

***Beautiful Malice.** unabr. ed. Rebecca James. (Running Time: 8 hrs. 0 mins.). 2010. 29.99 (978-1-4001-9815-3(1)) Tantor Media.

***Beautiful Malice.** unabr. ed. Rebecca James. Narrated by Justine Eyre. (Running Time: 7 hrs. 30 mins. 0 sec.). (ENG.). 2010. audio compact disk 71.99 (978-1-4001-4815-8(4)) Pub: Tantor Media. Dist(s): IngramPubServ

***Beautiful Malice: A Novel.** unabr. ed. Rebecca James. (Running Time: 8 hrs. 0 mins.). 2010. 15.99 (978-1-4001-8815-4(6)) Tantor Media.

***Beautiful Malice: A Novel.** unabr. ed. Rebecca James. Narrated by Justine Eyre. (Running Time: 7 hrs. 30 mins. 0 sec.). (ENG.). 2010. 19.99 (978-1-4001-6815-6(5)); audio compact disk 29.99 (978-1-4001-1815-1(8)) Pub: Tantor Media. Dist(s): IngramPubServ

***Beautiful Maria of My Soul.** unabr. ed. Oscar Hijuelos. 1 MP3-CD. (Running Time: 11 hrs. 30 mins.). 2010. 29.95 (978-1-4417-4033-5(3)); audio compact disk 105.00 (978-1-4417-4030-4(9)) Blckstn Audio.

***Beautiful Maria of My Soul.** unabr. ed. Oscar Hijuelos. Read by Armando Duran. 1 Playaway. (Running Time: 11 hrs. 30 mins.). 2010. 59.99 (978-1-4417-4036-6(8)); 72.95 (978-1-4417-4029-8(5)); audio compact disk 34.95 (978-1-4417-4032-8(5)) Blckstn Audio.

Beautiful Mind. Sylvia Nasar. Read by Anna Fields. 16 CDs. (Running Time: 19 hrs.). 2003. audio compact disk 128.00 (978-0-7861-9581-7(9), 2548) Blckstn Audio.

Beautiful Mind. unabr. ed. Sylvia Nasar. Read by Anna Fields. 2 CDs. (Running Time: 19 hrs.). 2003. audio compact disk 39.95 (978-0-7861-9351-6(4), 2548) Blckstn Audio.

Beautiful Mind. unabr. ed. Sylvia Nasar. Read by Anna Fields. 13 pieces. (Running Time: 16 hrs.). 2004. reel tape 49.95 (978-0-7861-2215-8(3)) Blckstn Audio.
Sylvia Nasar vividly re-creates the life of a mathematical genius whose career was cut short by schizophrenia and who, after three decades of devastating mental illness, miraculously recovered and was honored with a Nobel Prize. A Beautiful Mind traces the meteoric rise of John Forbes Nash, Jr., a prodigy and legend by the age of thirty, who dazzled the mathematical world by solving a series of deep problems deemed "impossible" by other mathematicians.

Beautiful Mind: A Biography of John Forbes Nash, Jr., Winner of the Nobel Prize for Economics, 1994. unabr. ed. Sylvia Nasar. Read by Anna Fields. 13 cass. (Running Time: 19 hrs.). 2000. 85.95 (978-0-7861-1744-4(3), 2548) Blckstn Audio.
This dramatic biography vividly re-creates the life of a mathematical genius whose career was cut short by schizophrenia & who, after three decades of devastating mental illness, miraculously recovered & was honored with a Nobel Prize. Traces the meteoric rise of John Forbes Nash, Jr., a prodigy & legend by the age of thirty, who dazzled the mathematical world by solving a series of deep problems deemed "impossible" by other mathematicians. A fascinating look at the extraordinary & fragile nature of genius.

Beautiful Mind: The Life of Mathematical Genius & Nobel Laureate John Nash. abr. ed. Sylvia Nasar. 2004. 15.95 (978-0-7435-4075-9(1)) Pub: S&S Audio. Dist(s): S and S Inc

Beautiful Miscellaneous. unabr. ed. Dominic Smith. Read by Michael Garcia. 7 cass. (Running Time: 34200 sec.). 2007. 29.95 (978-0-7861-4979-7(5)) Blckstn Audio.

Beautiful Miscellaneous. unabr. ed. Dominic Smith. Read by Paul Michael Garcia. (Running Time: 34200 sec.). 2007. 59.95 (978-0-7861-6807-1(2)) Blckstn Audio.

Beautiful Miscellaneous. unabr. ed. Dominic Smith. Read by Michael Garcia. 9 CDs. (Running Time: 34200 sec.). 2007. audio compact disk 32.95 (978-0-7861-5785-3(2)) Blckstn Audio.

Beautiful Miscellaneous. unabr. ed. Dominic Smith. Read by Paul Michael Garcia. 1 MP3-CD. (Running Time: 34200 sec.). 2007. audio compact disk 29.95 (978-0-7861-6958-0(3)); audio compact disk 81.00 (978-0-7861-6806-4(4)) Blckstn Audio.

***Beautiful Operatic Melodies for Violin.** Contrib. by William Starr. (ENG.). 2010. audio compact disk (978-0-7390-7066-6(5)) Alfred Pub.

Beautiful Savior. Perf. by New Covenant Orchestra. 1 cass. (Running Time: 45 min.). (New Covenant Ser.). 1988. 5.98 (978-0-570-09665-8(0), 79-7901) Family Films.
The dramatic, vibrant use of stringed instruments lends a unique touch to contemporary renditions of some favorite hymns.

Beautiful Savior. Greg Skipper. 1990. 40.00 (978-0-7673-1845-7(5)) LifeWay Christian.

Beautiful Savior Cassette Kit. Greg Skipper. 1990. 54.95 (978-0-7673-1456-5(5)) LifeWay Christian.

Beautiful Savior Choir. Greg Skipper. 1990. 11.98 (978-0-7673-1844-0(7)) LifeWay Christian.

***Beautiful Stories of Life: Six Greek Myths, Retold.** unabr. ed. Cynthia Rylant. Narrated by Alyssa Bresnahan. 1 CD. (Running Time: 1 hr. 15 mins.). (YA). (gr. 5 up). 2009. 25.75 (978-1-4407-2143-4(2)); audio compact disk 25.75 (978-1-4407-2147-2(5)) Recorded Bks.

Beautiful Symbol: Matthew 3:13-17. Ed Young. (J). 1979. 4.95 (978-0-7417-1054-3(4), A0055) Win Walk.

Beautiful Thing. Perf. by Johann Lai. 1 cass. (Running Time: 90 mins.). (CHI.). (C). 2000. 5.00 (978-1-930490-12-3(7), 10B-205) CCM Pubs.
Everyone has a different aesthetic standard. However, it is truly a beautiful thing when Jesus recognized Mary's act of anointing Him with an expensive perfume as an act of selfless & Christ-centered love. This beautiful act is characterized by doing her best, seeing the unseen & asking for nothing in return.

Beautiful Things Happen When a Woman Trusts God: Audio Book on CD. unabr. ed. Sheila Walsh. 2010. audio compact disk 24.99 (978-1-4003-1624-3(3)) Nelson.

Beautiful Weddings: Audio Book. abr. ed. Abr. by Judith Rivers-Moore. (ENG.). 2006. 21.95 (978-1-890083-54-0(2)) J R Pub.

Beautitudes. 1 cass. (Running Time: 60 min.). (Mother Angelica Live). 10.00 (978-1-55794-067-4(3), T 18) Eternal Wrd TV.

Beauty. Sharon Vargo. 1 CD. (Running Time: 3900 sec.). 2005. audio compact disk 16.98 (978-1-59179-381-6(5), M970D) Sounds True.
Regular favorites on the internationally loved Café del Mar series (over 9 million CDs sold worldwide), Vargo has appeared on over 50 compilations around the globe, including Germany's Space Night and France's Buddha Bar. Now, with Beauty, these frontrunners in the ambient revolution share a story that "begins in the infinite vastness of space and resolves into the discovery and comprehension of beauty in the small and smallest." Says the group's mastermind Ansgar Ueffink, "My aim is to create an atmosphere of comfort and well-being for the listener, an invitation to chill, to unwind, to let go completely." With its soothing electronic soundscapes, mesmerizing philosophical vocals inspired by the words of William Blake and others, and fl amenco guitar and gentle percussion, Beauty makes an excellent choice for yoga, bodywork, dance-and the perfect antidote for the stress and commotion of daily routine. Thirteen evocative tracks include "Get Back to Serenity," "Pure Consciousness," "The Flow," "Infinity," and more.

Beauty: The Invisible Embrace. John O'Donohue. 2 CDs. 2004. audio compact disk 29.95 (978-1-59179-137-9(5), AW00770D) Sounds True.

***Beauty: The Value of Values.** Frederick Turner. (ENG.). 19.50 (978-0-8139-3069-5(3)) U Pr of Va.

Beauty & the Beast see Stories Children Love to Hear

Beauty & the Beast see Belle et la Bete

Beauty & the Beast. 2004. 8.95 (978-1-56008-392-4(1)); cass. & flmstrp 30.00 (978-0-89719-574-4(4)) Weston Woods.

***Beauty & the Beast.** Anonymous. 2009. (978-1-60136-537-8(3)) Audio Holding.

Beauty & the Beast. Narrated by Mia Farrow. 1 cass. (J). 1991. 9.98 BMG Distribution.

Beauty & the Beast. Perf. by Mia Farrow. 1 cass. (J). 1991. 9.98 (978-5-553-25937-2(1)) BMG Distribution.

Beauty & the Beast. Narrated by Mia Farrow. (What's a Good Story? Ser.). (YA). 1989. pap. bk. & stu. ed. 99.00 (60795) Phoenix Films.
Provides the framework for a lively discussion of what components are essential to a good story.

Beauty & the Beast. Anne Waldman & Allen Ginsberg. 1 cass. 1975. 12.50 Vajradhatu.

Beauty & the Beast. unabr. ed. 1 cass. (Running Time: 20 min.). Dramatization. (Magic Looking Glass Ser.). (J). (gr. 2-6). 1989. 9.95 (978-0-7810-0031-4(9), NIM-CW-128-3-C) NIMCO.
A French folk tale.

Beauty & the Beast. unabr. ed. 1 cass. (Read-Along Ser.). (J). bk. 7.99 (978-1-55723-252-6(0)); bk. 11.99 (978-1-55723-720-0(4)) W Disney Records.

Beauty & the Beast. unabr. ed. Mordicai Gerstein. Narrated by Mia Farrow. 1 cass. (Running Time: 1 hr.). (Stories to Remember Ser.). (J). (gr. 1-5). 1990. 8.98 (978-1-879496-00-2(3)); audio compact disk 13.98 CD. (978-1-56896-032-6(8)) Lightyear Entrtnmnt.

Beauty & the Beast. unabr. ed. Ed McBain, pseud. Read by Michael Prichard. 7 cass. (Running Time: 7 hrs.). (Matthew Hope Mystery Ser.: No. 3). 1985. 42.00 (978-0-7366-1034-6(0), 1964) Books on Tape.
Matthew Hope sees Michelle Harper on North Sabal Beach & she's so spectacular he can't help staring. She comes to him as a client claiming her husband beats her. When Michelle turns up murdered, burned to death with her hands & legs bound with wire hangers, the police arrest her husband. He says he's innocent & somehow Hope believes him.

Beauty & the Beast a New Musical. unabr. ed. 1 cass. (J). 14.99 (978-1-55723-614-2(3)); 14.99 Norelco. (978-1-55723-615-9(1)); audio compact disk 24.99 (978-1-55723-617-3(8)) W Disney Records.

Beauty & the Beast a New Musical. unabr. ed. 1 cass. (J). (ps-3). 1994. audio compact disk 24.99 CD. (978-1-55723-616-6(X)) W Disney Records.

Beauty & the Beast & Other Children's Favorites. (J). 2005. audio compact disk (978-1-933796-34-5(0)) PC Treasures.

Beauty & the Beast Audio Playtime Theatre. 1 cass. (Running Time: 30 min.). (J). bk. 19.98 incl. pop-ups. Disney Prod.

Beauty & the Beast Deluxe Hardcover Read-Along with Pop-Ups. 1 cass. (Running Time: 15 min.). (J). bk. 14.98 Disney Prod.

Beauty & the Beast: Enchanted Christmas. Prod. by Walt Disney Productions Staff. 1 cass., 1 CD. (J). 1997. audio compact disk 10.98 CD. (978-0-7634-0345-4(8)) W Disney Records.
Music - Popular.

BEAUTY & the BEAST (English to Hebrew - Level 3) Learn HEBREW Through Fairy Tales. David Burke. (ENG & HEB.). (J). 2007. per. 14.95 (978-1-891888-94-6(3)) Slangman Pubng.

Beauty & the Beast (English to Italian - Level 3) Learn ITALIAN Through Fairy Tales. David Burke. (Learn Italian Through Fairy Tales Ser.). (ENG & ITA., (J). 2007. per. 14.95 (978-1-891888-89-2(7)) Slangman Pubng.

BEAUTY & the BEAST (English to Japanese - Level 3) Learn JAPANESE Through Fairy Tales. David Burke. (ENG & JPN.). (J). 2007. per. 14.95 (978-1-891888-90-8(0)) Slangman Pubng.

BEAUTY & the BEAST (Japanese to English - Level 3) Learn ENGLISH Through Fairy Tales. David Burke. (JPN & ENG.). (J). 2007. per. 14.95 (978-1-891888-05-2(6)) Slangman Pubng.

Beauty & the Beast Read-Along Collection. 1 cass. (Running Time: 15 min.). (J). bk. 14.98 incl. hologram watch. Disney Prod.

Beauty & the Beast, Robin Hood, Hansel & Gretel & Many More Tales see Bella y la Bestia y Muchos Cuentos Mas

Beauty & the Beast, Robin Hood, Hansel & Gretel & Many More Tales. (Running Time: 1 hr.). 2001. 14.95 (978-1-60083-134-8(6), Audiofy Corp) Iofy Corp.

Beauty & the Beast Soundtrack. 1 cass. (J). (ps-3). 1991. 12.98 (978-1-55723-262-5(8)) W Disney Records.

***Beauty Book.** Zondervan. (Lily Ser.). (ENG.). (J). 2009. 12.99 (978-0-310-77311-5(3)) Pub: Zondkidz. Dist(s): Zondervan

Beauty Fades, Dumb Is Forever: The Making of a Happy Woman. unabr. ed. Judy Scheindlin. Read by Anna Fields. 3 cass. (Running Time: 4 hrs. 30 min.). 1999. 24.00 (978-0-7366-4510-2(1), 4918) Books on Tape.
In the course of her career as a family court judge & a presiding judge on the popular courtroom show that bears her name, the author has seen, over & over again, the devastating fallout for women who have made stupid choices on marriage, parenting, & their future. She gives women the "heads up" on feeling unshakably good about themselves. With the help of provocative & hilarious examples from her own life, she instills in women the urgency of building a solid foundation from within. She tells women to get on with it & never forget that "smart is forever," too.

Beauty for Ashes. Perf. by Crystal Lewis. 1 CD. 1999. audio compact disk 8.98 (978-7-5132-6281-1(0), 751-326-2810) Brentwood Music.

Beauty for Inspector West. unabr. ed. John Creasey. Read by Steve Hodson. 6 cass. (Running Time: 9 hrs.). 2003. 54.95 (978-0-7540-0948-1(3), CAB 2370) AudioGO.

Beauty Is from God. Thomas Merton. 1 cass. (Running Time: 60 min.). (Art & Beauty Ser.). 8.95 (AA2075) Credence Commun.
Merton relishes in art relating it to contemplation & God.

Beauty Is the Quiet of the Self Forgotten. J. Krishnamurti. 1 cass. (Running Time: 75 min.). (Saanen, Switzerland Talks - 1985 Ser.: No. 4). 8.50 (AST854) Krishnamurti.
Where there is conscious endeavor is there beauty or is there beauty only when the self is not? Psychologically, is it necessary to have any kind of self-interest?.

Beauty of Boundaries Set: The Path to True Intimacy & Personal Success. David Grudermeyer & Rebecca Grudermeyer. 2 cass. 18.95 Incl. handouts. (T-25) Willingness Wrks.

Beauty of Grace. Contrib. by Krystal Meyers. (Mastertrax Ser.). 2006. audio compact disk 9.98 (978-5-558-02937-6(4)) Essential Recs.

Beauty of Holiness. Derek Prince. 4 cass. 19.95 (I-BH1) Derek Prince.

Beauty of Things see Poetry of Robinson Jeffers

Beauty of Unfoldment. Swami Amar Jyoti. 1 dolby cass. 1984. 9.95 (R-62) Truth Consciousness.
Removing the "importance" from our illusory shifting sands; facing the challenge & coming to conscious living. Our projections interfere with God's working, create ignorance & give no real value.

Beauty of Utah's National Parks & Recreational Areas. Hosted by Nancy Pearlman. 1 cass. (Running Time: 29 min.). 10.00 (817) Educ Comm CA.

Beauty, Pleasure, Sorrow & Love. J. Krishnamurti. 1 cass. (Running Time: 60 min.). (Ojai Talks Ser.). 1989. 9.95 HarperCollins Pubs.

***Beauty Queens - Audio.** Libba Bray. (ENG.). 2011. audio compact disk 39.99 (978-0-545-31523-4(9)) Scholastic Inc.

***Beauty Queens - Audio Library Edition.** Libba Bray. (ENG.). 2011. audio compact disk 74.99 (978-0-545-31538-8(7)) Scholastic Inc.

Beauty Rest Sleep. Read by Mary Richards. 12.95 (305) Master Your Mind.
Presents suggestions for the body to be revitalized & renewed.

Beauty Unfoldment. Kenneth G. Mills. 1977. pap. bk. 10.95 (978-0-919842-50-2(X), KGOM3) Ken Mills Found.
The author states in this spontaneous lecture recorded in 1977, that "beauty is not in the object perceived, but is a quality of the consciousness of the perceiver." Includes transcription booklet.

Beauty Without Nature: Refounding the City. unabr. ed. James Hillman. 2 cass. 1995. 17.95 set. (978-1-879323-38-4(9)) Sound Horizons AV.
Internationally-recognized Jungian theorist & author James Hillman proposes the 21st century's new urbanism, one that integrates city & nature into a harmonious whole. Hillman opens us to a new level of appreciation of the natural beauty lacking in our polluted cities.

***Beauty's Punishment.** abr. ed. Anne Rice. Read by Genvieve Bevier. (ENG.). 2004. (978-0-06-078292-4(7), Harper Audio) HarperCollins Pubs.

***Beauty's Punishment.** abr. ed. Anne Rice. Read by Genvieve Bevier. (ENG.). 2004. (978-0-06-081503-5(5), Harper Audio) HarperCollins Pubs.

Beauty's Punishment. abr. ed. A. N. Roquelaure, pseud & Anne Rice. Read by Genvieve Bevier. 2004. 19.95 (978-0-06-057009-5(1)) HarperCollins Pubs.

***Beauty's Release.** abr. ed. Anne Rice. Read by Genvieve Bevier. (ENG.). 2004. (978-0-06-077907-8(1), Harper Audio); (978-0-06-081381-9(4), Harper Audio) HarperCollins Pubs.

Beauvallet. Georgette Heyer. Read by Cornelius Garrett. 8 cass. (Running Time: 12 hrs.). 2002. 69.95 (978-0-7540-0884-2(3), CAB 2306) Pub: Chivers Audio Bks GBR. Dist(s): AudioGO

Beaux Poemes. Poems. Alfred Vigny. Read by Bernard Merle. 1 cass. (FRE.). 1995. 19.95 (1773-KFP) Olivia & Hill.
"La Mort du loup"; "La Maison du berger"; Dolorida; "La Prison.".

Beaver Island House Party. Laurie K. Sommers. 1996. bk. 19.95 (978-0-87013-453-1(1)) Mich St U Pr.

Beaver Towers. unabr. ed. Nigel Hinton. Read by Nigel Lambert. 2 cass. (Running Time: 2 hrs.). (Beaver Towers Adventures Ser.). (J). (gr. 1-8). 1993. 18.95 (978-0-7451-4455-9(1), CCA3221, Chivers Child Audio) AudioGO.
A magic spell whisks Philip away on his new kite to a far-off island. Guided by a robin, he meets two beavers, Mr. Edgar & his grandson, Baby B. They warn Philip about the wicked witch, Oyin, who has imprisoned most of the island's inhabitants.

Bebe Moore Campbell. unabr. ed. Ed. by Jim McKinley. Prod. by Rebekah Presson. 1 cass. (Running Time: 29 min.). (New Letters on the Air Ser.). 1994. 10.00 (112993) New Letters.
In her first novel, Campbell draws inspiration from the true story of Emmet Till, a black teenager who was lynched in Mississippi in the 1950s for allegedly flirting with a white woman. "Your Blues Ain't Like Mine" sets a fictional story against the historical backdrop of school integration & other milestones in black history. NPR listeners will recognize Campbell as a regular commentator on "Morning Edition".

Bebe's by Golly Wow. Yolanda Joe. 7 CDs. (Running Time: 8 hrs.). audio compact disk 69.00 (978-0-7887-9886-3(3)) Recorded Bks.

Bebe's by Golly Wow! unabr. ed. Yolanda Joe. 6 cass. (Running Time: 8 hrs.). 2001. 52.00 (978-0-7887-5214-8(6), F00225E7) Recorded Bks.
Bebe Thomas is looking for love. Her first date with Isaac seems like the start of something big, until she catches him on the phone with another woman. But this "woman" just happens to be Isaac's 13-year-old daughter, Dash.

BEC Higher: Practice Tests from the University of Cambridge Local Examinations Syndicate. University of Cambridge, Local Examinations Syndicate Staff. (Running Time: hrs. mins.). (BEC Practice Tests Ser.). (ENG.). 2002. 15.75 (978-0-521-75290-9(6)) Cambridge U Pr.

BEC Preliminary: Practice Tests from the University of Cambridge Local Examinations Syndicate. University of Cambridge, Local Examinations Syndicate Staff. (Running Time: hrs. mins.). (BEC Practice Tests Ser.). (ENG.). 2002. 15.00 (978-0-521-75302-9(3)) Cambridge U Pr.

BEC Vantage: Practice Tests from the University of Cambridge Local Examinations Syndicate. University of Cambridge, Local Examinations Syndicate Staff. (Running Time: hrs. mins.). (BEC Practice Tests Ser.). (ENG.). 2002. 15.00 (978-0-521-75305-0(8)) Cambridge U Pr.

BEC Vantage Masterclass. Nina O'Driscoll & Fiona Scott-Barrett. 2009. audio compact disk 39.95 (978-0-19-453204-4(6)) OUP.

Becasse see Treasury of French Prose

Because He Lives. Contrib. by Bill Gaither Trio. Prod. by Bob MacKenzie. (Encore (Provident) Ser.). 2005. audio compact disk 9.99 (978-5-559-07891-5(3)) Pt of Grace Ent.

Because He Lives: Contemporary Songs of Christ's Sacrifice. 1 cass.; audio compact disk Provident Mus Dist.
A collection of songs celebrating & worshipping the One who sacrificed for us.

Because I Could Not Stop for Death see Poems & Letters of Emily Dickinson

Because I Said So: Stories about Mothers & Kids. (Running Time: 3660 sec.). 2005. audio compact disk 14.95 (978-0-87483-792-6(8)) Pub: August Hse. Dist(s): Natl Bk Netwk

Because I Want to. (BI01) Master Mind.

Because It Is Bitter & Because It Is My Heart. Joyce Carol Oates. (Running Time: 30 min.). 1990. 8.95 (AMF-228) Am Audio Prose.
Talks about photography as metaphor, race relations, & creating a Black teen-aged hero.

Because It's Christmas. Richard Kingsmore. 1995. 75.00 (978-0-7673-0697-3(X)); audio compact disk 85.00 (978-0-7673-0722-2(4)); audio compact disk 16.98 (978-0-7673-0681-2(3)) LifeWay Christian.

Because Its Christmas. Richard Kingsmore. 1995. 11.98 (978-0-7673-0661-4(9)) LifeWay Christian.

Because of Bethlehem. Bruce Greer. 1999. 75.00 (978-0-7673-9719-3(3)); 11.98 (978-0-7673-9711-7(8)); audio compact disk 16.98 (978-0-7673-9702-5(9)); audio compact disk 85.00 (978-0-7673-9699-8(5)); audio compact disk 12.00 (978-0-7673-9653-0(7)) LifeWay Christian.

Because of Calvary Series, Set. Elbert Willis. 4 cass. 13.00 Fill the Gap.

Because of Jesus. Kenneth W. Hagin, Jr. 3 cass.Tr. of Debido a Jesus. 12.00 set. (20J) Faith Lib Pubns.

***Because of the Baby.** unabr. ed. Debbie Macomber. Read by Dan John Miller. (Running Time: 5 hrs.). 2010. 14.99 (978-1-4418-5334-9(0), 9781441853349, Brilliance MP3); 14.99 (978-1-4418-5335-6(9), 9781441853356, BAD) Brilliance Audio.

***Because of the Baby.** unabr. ed. Debbie Macomber. Read by Dan John Miller. (Running Time: 5 hrs.). (Midnight Sons Ser.: Bk. 4). 2010. audio compact disk 14.99 (978-1-4418-5333-2(2), 9781441853332, Bril Audio CD Unabri) Brilliance Audio.

Because of Who You Are. Contrib. by Vicki Yohe. (Mastertrax Ser.). 2006. audio compact disk 9.98 (978-5-558-01852-3(6)) Pure SpringG.

Because of Winn-Dixie. unabr. ed. Kate DiCamillo. Read by Cherry Jones. 2 vols. (Running Time: 2 hrs. 28 mins.). (J). (gr. 4-7). 2004. pap. bk. 29.00 (978-0-8072-0707-9(1), Listening Lib); audio compact disk 20.40 (978-0-8072-1162-5(1), S YA 278 CD, Listening Lib); 23.00 (978-0-8072-8856-6(X), LL0219, Listening Lib) Random Audio Pubg.
When 10-year old India Opal Buloni moved to Florida with her preacher father, she didn't expect that she'd adopt Winn-Dixie, a dog she names after the supermarket where they met. Opal is lonely at first, but with such an unusually friendly dog at her side, she makes some unusual friends & finds she has a lot to be thankful for.

Because of Winn-Dixie. unabr. ed. Kate DiCamillo. Read by Cherry Jones. 2 CDs. (Running Time: 2 hrs. 28 mins.). (ENG.). (J). (gr. 3). 2004. audio compact disk 19.99 (978-1-4000-9149-2(7), Listening Lib) Pub: Random Audio Pubg. Dist(s): Random

Because of You. Perf. by Preservation Hall Jazz Band et al. Contrib. by Earl Hines et al. 1 cass., 1 CD. 8.78 (CBS 60327); audio compact disk 13.58 CD Jewel box. (CBS 60327) NewSound.

Because of You. Ed Young. 1990. 4.95 (978-0-7417-1787-0(5), 787) Win Walk.

Because She Can. abr. ed. Bridie Clark. (Running Time: 6 hrs.). (ENG.). 2007. 14.98 (978-1-59483-870-5(4)) Pub: Hachet Audio. Dist(s): HachBkGrp

Because the Horn Is There. unabr. ed. Miles Smeeton. Read by Bill Kelsey. 6 cass. (Running Time: 6 hrs.). 1990. 36.00 (978-0-7366-1757-4(4), 2596) Books on Tape.
Miles & Beryl Smeeton twice capsized while trying to round Cape Horn. For their third attempt they decided to go the hard way, from east to west. Their goal was to "double the horn" from 50 South latitude in the Atlantic to 50 South latitude in the Pacific. Prior to the Smeetons, only two yachts had ever achieved this. One was lost soon afterward, the other was twice their size. The Smeetons beat both their times, one by a full day, sailing their old Tzu Hang.

Because the Night. James Ellroy. Read by L. J. Ganser. 6 cass. 54.95 (978-0-7927-3796-4(2), CSL 864); audio compact disk 79.95 (978-0-7927-3797-1(0), SLD 864); audio compact disk 29.95 (978-0-7927-3852-7(7), CMP 864) AudioGO.

Because They Hate: A Survivor of Islamic Terror Warns America. unabr. rev. ed. Brigitte Gabriel. Read by Brigitte Gabriel. (Running Time: 36000 sec.). (ENG.). 2007. audio compact disk 29.95 (978-1-4272-0168-3(4)) Pub: Macmill Audio. Dist(s): Macmillan

Because You Are. Composed by Scott Phillips. Contrib. by Phillip Keveren. 2007. audio compact disk 24.98 (978-5-557-49189-1(9), Word Music) Word Enter.

Because You Are. Contrib. by Point of Grace. Prod. by Brown Bannister. (Studio Ser.). 2007. audio compact disk 9.99 (978-5-557-63575-2(0), Word Records) Word Enter.

Because You Loved Me. Contrib. by Celine Dion. 2005. audio compact disk 8.99 (978-5-559-15687-3(6)) Christian Wrld.

Because You Loved Me. abr. ed. M. William Phelps. Read by J. Charles. (Running Time: 6 hrs.). 2008. audio compact disk 14.99 (978-1-4233-4913-6(X), 9781423349136, BCD Value Price) Brilliance Audio.

Because You Loved Me. unabr. ed. M. William Phelps. (Running Time: 11 hrs.). 2007. 39.25 (978-1-4233-4911-2(3), 9781423349112, BADLE) Brilliance Audio.

Because You Loved Me. unabr. ed. M. William Phelps. Read by J. Charles. (Running Time: 11 hrs.). 2007. 24.95 (978-1-4233-4910-5(5), 9781423349105, BAD); 92.25 (978-1-4233-4905-1(9), 9781423349051, BrilAudUnabridg); audio compact disk 39.25 (978-1-4233-4909-9(1), 9781423349099, Brinc Audio MP3 Lib); audio compact disk 97.25 (978-1-4233-4907-5(5), 9781423349075, BriAudCD Unabrid); audio compact disk 36.95 (978-1-4233-4906-8(7), 9781423349068, Bril Audio CD Unabri); audio compact disk 24.95 (978-1-4233-4908-2(3), 9781423349082, Brilliance MP3) Brilliance Audio.

***Because You're Mine.** unabr. ed. Lisa Kleypas. (Running Time: 11 hrs.). 2011. 39.97 (978-1-4418-5224-3(7), 9781441852243, BADLE); 24.99 (978-1-4418-5223-6(9), 9781441852236, BAD) Brilliance Audio.

***Because You're Mine.** unabr. ed. Lisa Kleypas. Read by Rosalyn Landor. (Running Time: 11 hrs.). 2011. 39.97 (978-1-4418-5222-9(0), 9781441852229, Brinc Audio MP3 Lib); 24.99 (978-1-4418-5221-2(2), 9781441852212, Brilliance MP3); audio compact disk 79.97 (978-1-4418-5220-5(4), 9781441852205, BriAudCD Unabrid); audio compact disk 29.99 (978-1-4418-5219-9(0), 9781441852199, Bril Audio CD Unabri) Brilliance Audio.

***Becca by the Book.** Laura Jensen Walker. (Running Time: 8 hrs. 20 mins. 0 sec.). (ENG.). 2010. 14.99 (978-0-310-77293-4(1)) Zondervan.

Bech: A Book. unabr. collector's ed. John Updike. Read by Wolfram Kandinsky. 6 cass. (Running Time: 9 hrs.). 1981. 48.00 (978-0-7366-0289-1(5), 1277) Books on Tape.
John Updike debunks the myth of the famous writer who, at young middle-age, has already published his best work & now watches helplessly as "his reputation grows while his powers decline".

Beck Beyond the Sea: Tink, North of Never Land. unabr. ed. Kiki Thorpe & Kimberly Morris. Read by Quincy Tyler Bernstine & Cassandra Morris. (Running Time: 8580 sec.). (Disney Fairies Ser.). (ENG.). (J). (gr. 1-4). 2007. audio compact disk 19.95 (978-0-7393-5617-3(8), Listening Lib) Pub: Random Audio Pubg. Dist(s): Random

Beck Diet Solution: Train Your Brain to Think Like a Thin Person. abr. ed. Judith S. Beck. Read by Eliza Foss. (Running Time: 16200 sec.). (ENG.). 2007. audio compact disk 24.95 (978-1-4272-0260-4(5)) Pub: Macmill Audio. Dist(s): Macmillan

Becker. Martin Kinch. 2005. audio compact disk 19.95 (978-0-660-18923-9(2)) Canadian Broadcasting CAN.

Becket, or the Honor of God. Jean Anouilh. Contrib. by Denis O'Hare et al. (Playaway Adult Fiction Ser.). (ENG.). 2009. 40.00 (978-1-60775-570-8(X)) Find a World.

Beckett Festival of Radio Plays. 1989. 70.00 Set. (A001SB090, HarperThor); 23.90 (A001AB090, HarperThor); 11.95 ea. (A001BB090, HarperThor) HarpC GBR.

Beckett Festival of Radio Plays. Samuel Beckett. 6 cass. (Running Time: 6 hrs.). 70.00 set. (AO-015, HarperThor) HarpC GBR.

Beckett in 90 Minutes. unabr. ed. Paul Strathern. Read by Robert Whitfield. (Running Time: 2 hrs. NaN mins.). 2009. audio compact disk 27.00 (978-1-4332-1766-1(X)); audio compact disk 22.95 (978-1-4332-1765-4(1)) Blckstn Audio.

Beckett or the Honor of God. Jean Anouilh. Contrib. by Simon Templeman & John Vickery. 2 CDs. (Running Time: 7080 sec.). 2005. audio compact disk 25.95 (978-1-58081-329-7(1), LA 067) Pub: L A Theatre. Dist(s): NetLibrary CO

***Beckoners.** Carrie Mac. Read by Edwina Wren. (Running Time: 6 hrs. 55 mins.). (YA). 2009. 49.99 (978-1-74214-330-9(X), 9781742143309) Pub: Bolinda Pubng AUS. Dist(s): Bolinda Pub Inc

Beckoners. unabr. ed. Carrie Mac. Read by Edwina Wren. (Running Time: 6 hrs. 55 mins.). (YA). 2008. audio compact disk 77.95 (978-1-921334-15-3(0), 9781921334153) Pub: Bolinda Pubng AUS. Dist(s): Bolinda Pub Inc

Beckoning Experience with the Divine: Religious Practices & Structures. Diane Martin. Read by Diane Martin. 4 cass. (Running Time: 4 hrs. 15 min.). 1991. 28.95 set. (978-0-7822-0345-5(0), 452) C G Jung IL.
This course examines the correspondence between Jung's theories & the human experience of the divine, helping to provide greater understanding & appreciation of the mysterious workings of the religious function of the psyche. Diane Martin, Ph.D., is a clinical psychologist & Jungian analyst in private practice in Milwaukee & Evanston. She has studied Buddhism in general, & Zen in particular, for 25 years. She facilitates meditation groups in Evanston & Milwaukee.

Beckoning Fair One see Widdershins: The First Book of Ghost Stories

Beckoning Song of Your Soul: A Guidebook for Developing Your Intuition. Nancy Marie. 1 cass. (Running Time: 1 hr. 2 min.). 1998. 10.00 (978-0-9660418-1-1(X)) Inner Eye.
Guides listener through exercises creating an experience similar to working with her privately.

Becky. unabr. ed. E. V. Thompson. Read by Gordon Griffin. 11 cass. (Running Time: 16 hrs. 30 min.). 1997. 89.95 (978-1-86042-143-3(1), 21431) Pub: Soundings Ltd GBR. Dist(s): Ulverscroft US
When an accident brought artist Fergus Vincent's naval career to an end, he headed for the slums of Bristol to join his lifelong friend & mentor, Henry Gordon. Finding his friend killed by drink, Fergus vows to continue his work & use his talents to record the lives of those who did not share in the glories of Victorian England. Here Fergus meets Becky, a ragamuffin orphan who captivates his heart.

Becky: Audio Book. Sara Yoder. Narrated by Fern Ebersole. Prod. by I. G. Publishers. Engineer Good Sound Co. (ENG.). (J). 2007. audio compact disk 19.95 (978-0-9801244-9-1(2)) IG Publish.

Becky Higgins Creative Clips & Fonts. Compiled by Becky Higgins. Des. by Becky Higgins. Prod. by Primedia Staff. 2003. audio compact disk 29.95 (978-1-929180-39-4(X)) Creating Keepsakes.

Becky's Eventful Summer: Audio Book. Sara Yoder. Narrated by Fern Ebersole. Prod. by I. G. Publishers. Engineer Good Sound Co. (ENG.). (J). 2007. audio compact disk 19.95 (978-0-9801244-8-4(4)) IG Publish.

Become a Better Buyer. 10.00 Esstee Audios.
Discusses how to get the most for your money.

Become a Better You: 7 Keys to Improving Your Life Every Day. Joel Osteen. 2007. audio compact disk 34.99 (978-1-60252-223-7(5)) Find a World.

Become a Better You: 7 Keys to Improving Your Life Every Day. abr. ed. Joel Osteen. Read by Joel Osteen. 5 CDs. (Running Time: 6 hrs. 0 mins. 0 sec.). (ENG.). 2007. audio compact disk 29.95 (978-0-7435-6942-2(3)) Pub: S&S Audio. Dist(s): S and S Inc

Become A Great Communicator: Learn the art of intelligent listening, & be confident in all Situations. Created by Christine Sherborne. (ENG.). 2007. audio compact disk 19.95 (978-0-9804155-1-3(9)) Pub: Colourstory AUS. Dist(s): APG

Become A Magnet to Money Through the Sea of Unlimited Consciousness: Through the Sea of Unlimited Consciousness. Bob Proctor & M A Blood. Read by Bob Proctor & M A Blood. (ENG.). 2008. audio compact disk 49.95 (978-1-890679-29-3(1)) Micheles.

Become a Martial Arts Champion. 1 cass. (Martial Arts Programming Ser.). 12.50 (978-0-87554-198-3(4), K108) Valley Sun.
You are totally confident in your martial arts skill. You enjoy the challenge of mastering a difficult art. You are a talented & dedicated martial artist. You know that effort & time will bring you success. Nothing can prevent you from realizing your goal. You are already on your way to bring a martial arts champion.

Become a Millionaire in Three Years. 1 cass. 14.98 (978-0-87554-581-3(5), XP501) Valley Sun.

Become a Money Magnet: The Law of Co-Creation. unabr. ed. Inna Segal. Read by Inna Segal. (Running Time: 1 hr.). (ENG.). 2008. 12.98 (978-1-59659-264-3(8), GildAudio) Pub: Gildan Media. Dist(s): HachBkGrp

Become a New Person. Dick Sutphen. 1 cass. (Running Time: 1 hr.). (RX17 Ser.). 1986. 14.98 (978-0-87554-305-5(7), RX114) Valley Sun.
You now let go of all fears; are self-assured & confident about your future; create the life you want to live; draw joyous experiences into your life; feel peaceful, balanced & harmonious; are independent & responsible; & accept others without expectation or judgment.

Become Calm & Peaceful with Mind Power. Jonathan Parker. Read by Jonathan Parker. 2 CDs. (Running Time: 2 hrs.). (Success Ser.: Vol. 3). 1999. audio compact disk (978-1-58400-039-6(2)) QuantumQuests Intl.
Disc 1 contains several guided visualizations. Disc 2 contains both audible & subliminal positive affirmations with music.

Become Free from Panic & Anxiety. Scott Sulak. 1998. 15.00 (978-1-932659-05-4(6)) Change For Gd.

Become More Sensitive to the Holy Spirit. Kenneth E. Hagin. (Developing the Human Spirit Ser.). 20.00 Faith Lib Pubns.

Become Self-Actualized. unabr. ed. Dick Sutphen. Read by Dick Sutphen. 1 cass. (Running Time: 1 hr.). (Spirit Guide Meditations). 1999. 14.98 (978-0-87554-629-2(3), SG102) Valley Sun.
Your guide helps you to let go of expectations & attachments. Seek awareness of your true self, allowing negativity to flow through you without affecting you.

Become Successful. unabr. ed. Dick Sutphen. Read by Dick Sutphen. 1 cass. (Running Time: 1 hr.). (Spirit Guide Meditations). 1999. 14.98 (978-0-87554-634-6(X), SG107) Valley Sun.
A guide helps to establish clarity of intent & a success mindset.

***Become Super Self-Confident... Auto-matically.** Bob Griswold & Deirdre Griswold. (Running Time: 45). 2010. 15.98 (978-1-55848-713-0(1), While-u-drive) EffectiveMN.

Become the Media. Jello Biafra. Read by Jello Biafra. 3 CDs. (Running Time: 3 hrs.). (ENG.). 2000. audio compact disk 19.98 (978-1-902593-37-1(5)) Pub: AK Pr GBR. Dist(s): Consort Bk Sales

Become Totally Debt-Free in Five Years or Less: Pay off Your Mortgage, Car, Credit Cards. abr. ed. Gwendolyn D. Gabriel. 1 cass. (Running Time: 1 hr.). 2000. 9.95 (978-0-9703022-1-2(5)) Brown Bag Pr.
This self-help book about personal finance & money-management provides hundreds of motivational & inspirational money-saving techniques to help readers become totally debt-free. The book's practical, common-sense & creative money-saving ideas will be easy for any reader to implement. Gabriel uses her expertise as an attorney, a real-estate broker & a cheapskate to provide readers the ideas & techniques she used to get out of debt.

Become Totally Fire. George Maloney. 4 cass. (Running Time: 5 hrs.). 1991. 33.95 set. (TAH242) Alba Hse Comns.
Fr. Maloney moves us to live in the core of our being, become alive enflamed with love of the Spirit & eagerly seek out an intimate relationship with God. He stresses the need to move out of the head, intellect, & move down into our heart, the point of our existence & seek out the God of Fire.

Become Totally Positive Auto-Matically. Bob Griswold & Deirdre Griswold. (Running Time: 3300 sec.). (While-U-Drive Ser.). 2004. audio compact disk 15.98 (978-1-55848-709-3(3)) EffectiveMN.

Become Totally Positive Auto-Matically. Robert E. Griswold & Deirdre Griswold. Read by Robert E. Griswold & Deirdre Griswold. 1 cass. (While-U-Drive Ser.). 1996. 11.98 (978-1-55848-903-5(7)) EffectiveMN.
This program can fill one with positive energy & help to have a much more optimistic outlook on life.

Become What You Believe. Contrib. by Last Tuesday. Prod. by Ethan Luck & Dan Spencer. Contrib. by Mark Lee Townsend. 2006. audio compact disk 13.99 (978-5-558-24605-6(7)) Mono Vs Ster.

Become What You Eat Vol. 3: The Eucharist as Mystagogy. Text by Ed Foley. 2001. audio compact disk (978-1-58459-085-9(8)) Wrld Lib Pubns.

Become What You Pray Vol. 2: The Eucharist As Mystagogy. Text by Ed Foley. 2001. audio compact disk (978-1-58459-084-2(X)) Wrld Lib Pubns.

Become What Your Believe. Short Stories. Joel Osteen. 1 Cass. (Running Time: 30 Mins.). 2002. 6.00 (978-1-59349-161-1(1), JA0161) J Osteen.

Become Who You Are. Contrib. by Mainstay. Prod. by Luke Fredrickson. 2007. audio compact disk 13.99 (978-5-557-59357-1(8)) BEC Recordings.

Becoming. Blaine Yorgason & Brenton Yorgason. 2 cass. 9.98 (978-1-55503-097-1(1), 0400343) Covenant Comms.
A dramatized version of the popular book.

Becoming. unabr. collector's ed. Catherine Lanigan. Read by Anna Fields. 8 cass. (Running Time: 12 hrs.). 1998. 64.00 (978-0-7366-4024-4(X), 4523) Books on Tape.
Tale of a feisty woman who leaves an abusive marriage to find real love.

Becoming a Catholic Even if You Happen to Be One. Peter Kreeft et al. 8 cass. 1995. 39.95 Set. (147-C) Ignatius Pr.
Thomas Howard & Peter Krefft join Scott & Kimberly Hahn on how you can become not just a Catholic but a "convinced," contagious Catholic!.

Becoming a Contagious Christian. abr. ed. Bill Hybels & Mark Mittelberg. (Running Time: 2 hrs. 0 mins. 0 sec.). (ENG.). 2003. 10.99 (978-0-310-25998-5(3)) Zondervan.

***Becoming a Contagious Christian.** unabr. ed. Bill Hybels & Mark Mittelberg. (Running Time: 7 hrs. 28 mins. 0 sec.). (ENG.). 2009. 12.99 (978-0-310-77133-3(1)) Zondervan.

Becoming a Contagious Christian. 2nd rev. abr. unabr. ed. Bill Hybels & Mark Mittelberg. 2 cass. (Running Time: 60 min. per cass.). 1994. 17.99 (978-0-310-48508-7(8)) Zondervan.
The long-awaited book on personal evangelism from the senior pastor of the successful, seeker-friendly Willow Creek Church.

Becoming a Difference Maker. Jeff Conley. 6 cass. (Running Time: 6 hrs.). 1993. 59.95 Set. (10520PA) Nightingale-Conant.

Becoming a Disciplined Trader: Techniques for Achieving Peak Trading Performances. Instructed by Ari Kiev. 2005. audio compact disk 19.95 (978-1-59280-230-2(3)) Marketplace Bks.

Becoming A Man. Michael Pearl. 1 CD. (Running Time: 36 mins). 2006. audio compact disk (978-1-892112-91-0(4)) No Greater Joy.

***Becoming a Man of Unwavering Faith.** unabr. ed. John Osteen. Comment by Joel Osteen. Frwd. by Joel Osteen. (Running Time: 6 hrs. 30 mins.). (ENG.). 2011. 19.98 (978-1-61113-810-8(8)); audio compact disk 24.98 (978-1-61113-809-2(4)) Pub: Hachet Audio. Dist(s): HachBkGrp

Becoming a Parent: Create & Establish a Conscious Foundation for Parenting. Mark Bancroft. Read by Mark Bancroft. 1 cass., bklet. (Running Time: 1 hr.). (Pregnancy & Childbirth Ser.). 1999. 12.95 (978-1-58522-024-3(8), 504) EnSpire Pr.
Two complete sessions plus printed instructionmanual/guidebook. With healing music soundtrack.

Becoming a Parent: Create & Establish a Conscious Foundation for Parenting. Mark Bancroft. Read by Mark Bancroft. 1 CD, 1 bklet. (Running Time: 1 hr.). (Pregnancy & Childbirth Ser.). 2006. audio compact disk 20.00 (978-1-58522-061-8(2)) EnSpire Pr.

Becoming a People of Grace. Charles R. Swindoll. 2009. audio compact disk 70.00 (978-1-57972-846-5(4)) Insight Living.

Becoming a People of Grace: An Exposition of Ephesians. 2003. audio compact disk 83.00 (978-1-57972-528-0(7)) Insight Living.

Becoming a People of Grace: An Exposition of Ephesians. 2001. 62.95 (978-1-57972-367-5(5)) Insight Living.

***Becoming A Prayer Warrior: A Guide to Effective & Powerful Prayer.** unabr. ed. Elizabeth Alves. Narrated by Tavia Gilbert. (Running Time: 6 hrs. 6 mins. 0 sec.). (ENG.). 2010. audio compact disk 21.98 (978-1-59644-247-4(6)) christianaud.

***Becoming A Prayer Warrior: A Guide to Effective & Powerful Prayer.** unabr. ed. Elizabeth Alves. Narrated by Tavia Gilbert. (ENG.). 2010. 12.98 (978-1-59644-248-1(4)) christianaud.

Becoming a Promotable Woman. abr. ed. Sally B. Jenkins. 2 cass. (Running Time: 150 mins.). 2002. 17.99 (978-1-55678-091-2(5), Lm Inc) Oasis Audio.

Becoming a Promotable Woman. abr. ed. Sally B. Jenkins. (Smart Tapes Ser.). 2003. 19.99 (978-1-58926-204-1(2)) Oasis Audio.

Becoming a Promotable Woman. unabr. ed. Sally B. Jenkins. 2 CDs. (Running Time: 3 hrs.). 2003. audio compact disk 19.99 (978-1-58926-205-8(0), N23A-070D); 19.99 (N23A-0700) Oasis Audio.
Combines the basic leadership principles and skills needed for a career woman. Using the latest research on how women move up the career ladder, she can be your guide to help you solve your unique problems as a career woman.

Becoming a Resonant Leader: Develop Your Emotional Intelligence, Renew Your Relationships, Sustain Your Effectiveness. unabr. ed. Annie McKee et al. Read by Jonathan Marosz. (Running Time: 5 hrs. 30 mins.). (ENG.). 2008. 24.98 (978-1-59659-225-4(7), GildAudio) Pub: Gildan Media. Dist(s): HachBkGrp

Becoming a Resonant Leader: Develop Your Emotional Intelligence, Renew Your Relationships, Sustain Your Effectiveness. unabr. ed. Annie McKee et al. Read by Jonathan Marosz. 6 CDs. (Running Time: 5 hrs. 30 mins.). (ENG.). 2008. audio compact disk 29.98 (978-1-59659-165-3(X), GildAudio) Pub: Gildan Media. Dist(s): HachBkGrp

***Becoming a Sales Pro: The Best of Tom Hopkins.** unabr. ed. Tom Hopkins. Read by Tom Hopkins. (Running Time: 5 hrs.). (Made for Success Ser.). 2010. audio compact disk 29.95 (978-1-4417-5290-1(0)) Blckstn Audio.

***Becoming a Sales Pro (Library Edition) The Best of Tom Hopkins.** unabr. ed. Made for Success. Read by Tom Hopkins. (Running Time: 5 hrs. 0 mins.). (Made for Success Ser.). 2010. audio compact disk 105.00 (978-1-4417-5288-8(9)) Blckstn Audio.

Becoming a Super Listener. Shad Helmstetter. 1 cass. (Self-Talk Cassettes Ser.). 10.95 (978-0-937065-38-9(2)) Grindle Pr.

Becoming a Teacher: Recognize & Manifest Your Potential as a Teacher. Mark Bancroft. Read by Mark Bancroft. 1 cass., bklet. (Running Time: 1 hr.). (Business & Career Ser.). 1998. 12.95 (978-1-58522-002-1(7), 319) EnSpire Pr.
Two complete sessions plus printed instructionmanual/guidebook. With healing music soundtrack.

Becoming a Teacher: Recognize & Manifest Your Potential as a Teacher. Mark Bancroft. Read by Mark Bancroft. 1 cass., bklet. (Running Time: 1 hr.). (Business & Career Ser.). 2006. audio compact disk 20.00 CD & bklet. (978-1-58522-003-8(5)) EnSpire Pr.

Becoming a Total Person. unabr. ed. Paul J. Meyer. 1 cass. (Running Time: 37 min.). 1993. 11.00 (978-0-89811-274-0(5), SP100078) Meyer Res Grp.
Focuses on setting & achieving goals in all six areas of life: Family & Home, Financial & Career, Physical & Health, Spiritual & Ethical, Mental & Educational, & Social & Cultural.

Becoming a Transformer see Futureshaping

Becoming a Verbal Visionary. Perf. by James E. Lukaszewski. (ENG.). 2007. audio compact disk 10.00 (978-1-883291-46-4(1)) Lukaszewski.

Becoming a Winner in the Classroom. unabr. ed. Robert J. Rotella & Richard Coop. 3 cass. (Running Time: 90 min.). Dramatization. (YA). (gr. 10-12). 1985. 39.95 Creative Mgmt.
A motivational study progam developed to help student-athletes achieve greater success in the classroom & thus remain eligible for participation in collegiate athletics.

Becoming an Entrepreneur in Your Own Setting. rev. ed. Kathy King Helm & Kathy K. Helm. Read by Kathy King Helm. 2 cass. (Running Time: 2 hrs.). (Study Kit Ser.). 1990. pap. bk. & spiral bd. 70.65 Set. (978-0-88091-084-2(4), 1303-SK3) Am Dietetic Assn.
Discusses the process of turning nutrition services & products into profit-making ventures. Identifying market trends, writing a proposal, setting fees, & actual case studies are among the topics treated in this program.

Becoming an Explorer. unabr. ed. Robert A. Monroe. Read by Robert A. Monroe. (Running Time: 45 min.). (Explorer Ser.). 1985. 12.95 (978-1-56113-025-2(7), 26) Monroe Institute.
An account of one person's efforts to become an Explorer at the Institute.

Becoming an Immuner. 1 CD. (Running Time: 75 mins.). 2004. audio compact disk 15.00 (978-0-9752803-0-0(9)) Wrld Hamon Unif.

Becoming an Imperfectionist. Joni Hilton. 2004. 9.95 (978-1-57734-625-8(4)) Covenant Comms.

Becoming an Oracle: Connecting to the Divine Source for Information & Healing. unabr. ed. Nicki Scully. (Running Time: 6:49:50). 2009. audio compact disk 69.95 (978-1-59179-699-2(7)) Sounds True.

***Becoming Conversant with the Emerging Church: Understanding a Movement & Its Implications.** D. A. Carson. (Running Time: 8 hrs. 47 mins. 0 sec.). (ENG.). 2008. 14.99 (978-0-310-30424-1(5)) Zondervan.

Becoming Enlightened. unabr. ed. Dalai Lama XIV. Narrated by Jeffrey Hopkins. (Running Time: 9 hrs. 45 mins.). 2009. 56.75 (978-1-4407-1319-4(7)); audio compact disk 92.75 (978-1-4407-1317-0(0)) Recorded Bks.

Becoming Enlightened. unabr. ed. Dalai Lama XIV. Read by Jeffrey Hopkins. Jeffrey Hopkins. 6 CDs. (Running Time: 10 hrs. 0 mins. 0 sec.). (ENG.). 2009. audio compact disk 39.99 (978-0-7435-7969-8(0)) Pub: S&S Audio. Dist(s): S and S Inc

Becoming Enlightened. unabr. collector's ed. Dalai Lama XIV. Narrated by Jeffrey Hopkins. 8 CDs. (Running Time: 9 hrs. 45 mins.). 2009. audio compact disk 39.95 (978-1-4407-1318-7(9)) Recorded Bks.

Becoming Free. Swami Amar Jyoti. 1 cass. 1986. 9.95 (K-150) Truth Consciousness.
Destiny & spontaneity. Spiritual power: victory for all. The Master-disciple link. Gradual or instant Realization. Freeing the mind, giving up "me".

Becoming God: The Divinization of Our Humanity. John Welch. 1 cass. (Running Time: 32 min.). 1991. 7.95 (TAH255) Alba Hse Comns.
An introduction to the wonderful tradition of Carmelite Spirituality.

Becoming Human. Speeches. Jean Vanier. 5 CDs. (Running Time: 18000 sec.). (Massey Lectures). (ENG.). 2006. audio compact disk 39.95 (978-0-660-19541-4(0), CBC Audio) Pub: Canadian Broadcasting CAN. Dist(s): Georgetown Term

Becoming Light-Hearted: Managing Stress Through Humor. Perf. by Izzy Gesell. 1 cass. (Running Time: 50 min.). 1997. 10.95 (978-0-9652460-0-2(0), WA2) Wide Angle Humor.
Explains how humor works & how anyone can increase their skill level with humor to find more laughter & joy in life, become a more humorous person & how to turn stressful situations into manageable events.

Becoming Like Little Children: Recovering Your Innocence. John Bradshaw. (Running Time: 21600 sec.). 2008. audio compact disk 130.00 (978-1-57388-189-0(9)) J B Media.

Becoming Miracle Minded & What to Do Now? Marianne Williamson. Read by Marianne Williamson. 1 cass. (Running Time: 90 mins.). (Lectures on a Course in Miracles). 1999. 10.00 (978-1-56170-177-3(7), M705) Hay House.

Becoming More Than a Good Bible Study Girl. unabr. ed. Lysa TerKeurst. (Running Time: 7 hrs. 4 mins. 0 sec.). (ENG.). 2009. audio compact disk 22.99 (978-0-310-59179-5(1)) Zondervan.

***Becoming More Than a Good Bible Study Girl: Living the Faith after Bible Class Is Over.** Lysa TerKeurst. (Running Time: 7 hrs. 4 mins. 0 sec.). (ENG.). 2009. 13.99 (978-0-310-39550-8(X)) Zondervan.

Becoming Naomi Leon. Pam Muñoz Ryan. Read by Annie Kozuch. 3 cass. (J). 2004. 30.00 (978-1-4000-9088-4(1), Listening Lib); audio compact disk 32.30 (978-1-4000-9492-9(5), Listening Lib) Pub: Random Audio Pubg. Dist(s): NetLibrary CO

Becoming Naturally Therapeutic: A Return to the True Essence of Helping. Jacquelyn Small & J. Small. 1 cass. (Running Time: 60 min.). 1993. 10.00 (978-0-89486-916-7(7)) Hazelden.
For anyone who wants to reach out to others - identifies the ten characteristics of responsive & effective caring.

Becoming One with Christ. James B. Cox. 1990. 41.95 (978-0-9646887-2-8(7)) Natl Mrkting.

Becoming One with the Guru. Swami Amar Jyoti. 1 cass. 1975. 9.95 (E-29) Truth Consciousness.
Living for Guru alone. What is a perfect disciple?.

Becoming Process. Swami Amar Jyoti. 1 cass. 1988. 9.95 (M-95) Truth Consciousness.
On thinking, rationality, intellect; where they lead us & what is beyond them. Leaving the domain of darkness. The Om Mani Padme Hum Mantra.

Becoming Remarkable: For Songwriters & Those Who Love Songs. 2nd ed. Harriet Schock. 1998. pap. bk. 19.95 (978-1-57733-034-9(X)) B Dolphin Pub.

Becoming Rich: Without Cutting up Your Credit Cards. abr. ed. Robert T. Kiyosaki & Sharon L. Lechter. Read by Jim Ward. (ENG.). 2005. 14.98 (978-1-59483-303-8(6)) Pub: Hachet Audio. Dist(s): HachBkGrp

Becoming Rich: Without Cutting up Your Credit Cards. abr. ed. Robert T. Kiyosaki & Sharon L. Lechter. (Running Time: 3 hrs.). (ENG.). 2009. 29.98 (978-1-60024-556-5(0)) Pub: Hachet Audio. Dist(s): HachBkGrp

Becoming Rosemary. unabr. ed. Frances M. Wood. Narrated by Barbara Caruso. 4 cass. (Running Time: 4 hrs. 30 mins.). (gr. 5 up). 1997. 35.00 (978-0-7887-1336-1(1), 95185E7) Recorded Bks.
Evokes the rich details of village life in early North Carolina in 1790. During the summer of her 16th year, Rosemary watches the security & tranquility of her life fall apart. Her new friend, Mrs. DiAngeli, has artistic gifts that arouse fear & suspicion in the small village. Soon this distrust is focused on Rosemary's family as well & the young girl begins to fear for the safety of those she loves.

Becoming Smoke Free with Hypnotherapy: Overcoming Nicotine Addiction Naturally. Paul Del Rio. Read by Paul Del Rio. 2001. 14.95 (978-0-9709244-0-7(2)) Perform Res Grp.

Becoming Subject to the Authority of Jesus. Kenneth Copeland. 5 cass. 1995. 25.00 Set. (978-0-88114-972-2(1)) K Copeland Pubns.
Biblical teaching on the authority of Jesus.

Becoming Super Self-Confident Auto-Matically. Robert E. Griswold & Deirdre Griswold. Read by Robert E. Griswold & Deirdre Griswold. 1 cass. (Running Time: 60 min.). (While-U-Drive Ser.). 1997. 11.98 (978-1-55848-907-3(X)) EffectiveMN.
How to discover & develop one's potential leading to happiness, success, & fulfillment.

Becoming the Answer to Our Prayers: Prayer for Ordinary Radicals. unabr. ed. Shane Claiborne & Jonathan Wilson-Hartgrove. (Running Time: 3 hrs. 30 mins. 0 sec.). (ENG.). 2008. audio compact disk 18.98 (978-1-59644-662-5(5)) christianaud.

***Becoming the Answer to our Prayers: Prayer for Ordinary Radicals.** unabr. ed. Shane Claiborne & Jonathan Wilson-Hartgrove. Narrated by Paul Garcia. (ENG.). 2008. 10.98 (978-1-59644-663-2(3), Hovel Audio) christianaud.

Becoming the Goddess. unabr. ed. Perf. by Janet I. Decker. Created by Janet I. Decker. 1 CD. (Running Time: 48 min.). 2001. audio compact disk 16.95 (978-0-9709726-8-2(7)) Pub: Hypno Services. Dist(s): Baker Taylor

Becoming the Thirteenth Juror. Charles J. Ogletree. 1 cass. 1990. 135.00 (0322) Natl Prac Inst.

Becoming the Thirteenth Juror: Successful Trial Techniques. Charles J. Ogletree. 6 cass. 1990. 135.00 Set. (0322) Natl Prac Inst.
The Director of Harvard Law School's Trial Advocacy Workshop discusses all facets of trial advocacy in a dramatic & engaging presentation.

Becoming the Total Person. Shad Helmstetter. 1 cass. (Self-Talk Cassettes Ser.). 10.95 (978-0-937065-40-2(4)) Grindle Pr.

Becoming Unlimited: The Process. unabr. ed. Dianthus. 1 cass. (Running Time: 1 hr. 2 min.). (ENG.). 1996. 11.00 (978-1-890372-01-9(3)) Dianthus.
Completed work that describes the process, the insights into its worth & where this process leads.

Becoming What You Want to See in the World: The Art of Joyful Living. unabr. ed. (Running Time: 6840 sec.). 2007. audio compact disk 19.95 (978-0-9772566-1-7(8)) Pub: River Birch Pub. Dist(s): AtlasBooks

Becoming Your Natural Self. abr. ed. Susan Lipshutz. 1 cass. (Running Time: 36 min.). 1996. 11.00 (978-1-929118-00-7(7)) S Lipshutz.
Guided meditation journeys into the universe within.

Bed by the Window see Poetry of Robinson Jeffers

Bed for the Night see Necklace of Raindrops & Other Stories

Bed in Summer see Child's Garden of Verses

***Bed of Roses.** Nora Roberts. Contrib. by Angela Dawe. (Bride Quartet Ser.: Bk. 2). 2009. 69.99 (978-1-4418-2285-7(2)) Find a World.

Bed of Roses. abr. ed. Nora Roberts. Read by Emily Durante & Angela Dawe. 5 CDs. (Running Time: 5 hrs.). (Bride Quartet Ser.: Bk. 2). 2009. audio compact disk 14.99 (978-1-4233-6884-7(3), 9781423368847, BACD) Brilliance Audio.

Bed of Roses. abr. ed. Nora Roberts. Read by Emily Durante & Angela Dawe. (Running Time: 6 hrs.). (Bride Quartet Ser.: Bk. 2). 2012. audio compact disk 9.99 (978-1-4233-6885-4(1), 9781423368854, BCD Value Price) Brilliance Audio.

Bed of Roses. unabr. ed. Margaret Graham. Read by Judith Porter. 12 cass. (Running Time: 18 hrs.). 2001. 94.95 (978-1-86042-881-4(9), 2-881-9) Pub: Soundings Ltd GBR. Dist(s): Ulverscroft US
Everyone, including her grown-up daughter, expects Fran to marry Michael, a kind, supportive solicitor, her friend for years. But on the morning of her wedding Fran hesitates. Should she say "I do" & fade into the fabric of a life which is safe, sensible & familiar? Or should she say, "Actually, no, thank you" & bolt with a man she hardly knows: Josh, an artist who is wholly different from her, but who makes her heart sing. A man who promises her a bed of roses. A man who says it is time for her to live for herself. But can anyone ever really live for themselves? Can they leave behind their obligations, their past?.

Bed of Roses. unabr. ed. Nora Roberts. Read by Emily Durante & Angela Dawe. 1 MP3-CD. (Running Time: 9 hrs.). (Bride Quartet Ser.: Bk. 2). 2009. 39.97 (978-1-4233-6881-6(9), 9781423368816, Brinc Audio MP3 Lib) Brilliance Audio.

Bed of Roses. unabr. ed. Nora Roberts. Read by Emily Durante. (Running Time: 11 hrs.). (Bride Quartet Ser.: Bk. 2). 2009. 39.97 (978-1-4233-6883-0(5), 9781423368830, BADLE) Brilliance Audio.

Bed of Roses. unabr. ed. Nora Roberts. Read by Emily Durante & Angela Dawe. 1 MP3-CD. (Running Time: 9 hrs.). (Bride Quartet Ser.: Bk. 2). 2009. 24.99 (978-1-4233-6880-9(0), 9781423368809, Brilliance MP3); 24.99 (978-1-4233-6882-3(7), 9781423368823, BAD); audio compact disk 92.97 (978-1-4233-6879-3(7), 9781423368793, BriAudCD Unabrid); audio compact disk 34.99 (978-1-4233-6878-6(9), 9781423368786, Bril Audio CD Unabri) Brilliance Audio.

Bed of Roses. unabr. ed. Katherine Stone. Read by Alysia Reiner. 10 vols. (Running Time: 15 hrs.). 2000. bk. 84.95 (978-0-7927-2231-1(0), CSL 120, Chivers Sound Lib) AudioGO.
Actress Cassandra Winter lies in intensive care, following a merciless attack by an unknown assailant. Now a man appears demanding to see the ravaged actress, claiming that she is his wife. Today Cassandra is famous and celebrated. Eight years ago she had simply been a woman in love with Chase Tessier, a successful wine merchant. But she left their love and vanished with a dark secret. Now the secrets of the past will not be silent, and the assailant who left Cassandra for dead, lusts for her death.

***Bed Rest.** unabr. ed. Sarah Bilston. Read by Elizabeth Sastre. (ENG.). 2006. (978-0-06-117149-9(2), Harper Audio); (978-0-06-117148-2(4), Harper Audio) HarperCollins Pubs.

Bed Wetting. John M. Bennett. 1 cass. (Running Time: 60 min.). 1991. 6.00 (978-0-935350-37-1(3)) Luna Bisonte.

Bedford Boys: One American Town's Ultimate D-Day Sacrifice. Alex Kershaw. Read by William Dufris. 6 vols. 2004. pap. bk. 54.95 (978-0-7927-3206-8(5), CSL 643, Chivers Sound Lib); pap. bk. 74.95 (978-0-7927-3207-5(3), SLD 643, Chivers Sound Lib) AudioGO.

Bedford Row. Claire Rayner. Read by Anne Cater. 10 cass. (Running Time: 12 hrs.). (Performers Ser.: Vol. 5). (J). 2004. 84.95 (978-1-84283-488-6(6)) Pub: ISIS Lrg Prnt GBR. Dist(s): Ulverscroft US

Bedford Square. abr. ed. Anne Perry. Read by David McCallum. 2 cass. (Thomas Pitt Ser.). 1999. 18.00 (FS9-43401) Highsmith.

Bedford Square. unabr. ed. Anne Perry. Read by Terrence Hardiman. 12 vols. (Running Time: 18 hrs.). (Thomas Pitt Ser.). 2001. bk. 96.95 (978-0-7927-2447-6(X), CSL 336, Chivers Sound Lib) AudioGO.
General Balantyne denies all knowledge of the dead body sprawled on his Bedford Square doorstep. But Superintendent Thomas Pitt did not believe him, for in the dead man's pocket was a rare snuffbox that graced the general's study.

Bednaya Liza (Poor Liza) Nicolai Karamzin. 1 cass. (Running Time: 80 min.). (RUS.). 1997. pap. bk. 24.50 (978-1-58085-579-2(2)) Interlingua VA.
Includes Russian text. The combination of written text & clarity & pace of diction will open the door for intermediate & advanced students to genuine comprehension & the use of literary texts for advancement in rapid understanding of written & oral language materials. The audio text plus written text concept makes foreign languages accessible to a much wider range of students than books alone.

Bedroom Talk: Marriage Secrets from a Couple Who Had Six Kinds in Eight Years of Marriage. James Bronner & Stephanie Bronner. 4 CDs. (Running Time: 5 hrs). 2005. audio compact disk 19.95 (978-0-9725818-6-8(3)) MountainWings.

Bedtime. 1 cass., 1 CD. (Mister Rogers' Neighborhood Ser.). (J). 8.98 Lyrics incl. (MRN9201); audio compact disk 13.98 CD. Family Comns.
Mister Rogers weaves music & dialogue together in this audiocassette to help young children get ready for sleep. Includes "There Are Many Ways to Say I Love You," "I Like to Be Told," "Then Your Heart is Full of Love," & many more.

Bedtime! 2004. 8.95 (978-1-56008-841-7(9)); cass. & flmstrp 30.00 (978-0-89719-652-9(X)) Weston Woods.

Bedtime. Perf. by Mister Rogers. 1 cass. (Mister Rogers' Neighborhood Ser.). (J). pap. bk. 8.98 (00815015) H Leonard.
Provides comfort & caring with music & dialogue. Includes "Won't You be My Neighbor," "Good Feeling," "There Are Many Ways to Say I Love You," "I Like to Be Told," "Just for Once," "Tree, Tree, Tree," "Sometimes Isn't Always" & "Then Your Heart Is Full of Love".

Bedtime. Perf. by Mister Rogers. 1 cass. (J). 10.98 (978-0-945267-41-6(X), YM052-CN); audio compact disk 13.98 (978-0-945267-70-6(3), YM052-CD) Youngheart Mus.
Songs include: "Won't You Be My Neighbor?"; "I'm Taking Care of You"; "Just for Once"; "Sometimes Isn't Always"; "I Like to Be Told"; "Then Your Heart Is Full of Love"; "When the Day Turns into Night" & more.

Bedtime Meditations for Kids. Christiane Kerr. 1 CD. (J). 2005. audio compact disk 17.95 (978-1-901923-90-2(8), 247-045) Pub: Divinit Pubing GBR. Dist(s): Bookworld

BEDTIME SH'MA, Book & CD Set. Adapted by Sarah Gershman. Illus. by Kristina Swarner. (ENG & HEB.). (J). 2007. bk. 24.95 (978-0-939144-58-7(1)) EKS Pub Co.

Bedtime Stories. 1 cass. (Running Time: 30 min.). 9.95 (F0460B090, HarperThor) HarpC GBR.

Bedtime Stories. 1 cass. (Running Time: 40 min.). (Picture Book Parade Ser.). (J). (ps-4). 1981. 8.95 (978-0-89719-945-2(6), WW716C) Weston Woods.
Stories include "Hush Little Baby," "Wynken, Blynken & Nod," "The Owl & the Pussy-Cat," "David & Dog," "A Picture for Harold's Room," "The Snowy Day," "Charlotte & the White Horse," "Henry the Explorer," & "Fourteen Rats & a Rat-Catcher".

Bedtime Stories. Clarissa Pinkola Estes. 2003. audio compact disk 15.95 (978-1-56455-961-6(0)) Sounds True.

Bedtime Stories. Great American Audio. 1 cass. (Running Time: 1 hr.). Dramatization. (Children's Audio Ser.). (J). (gr. 1-6). 1990. 9.95 (978-1-55569-383-1(0), CSP-7094) Great Am Audio.
One full hour of bedtime stories ranging from fables, fairy tales, folktales & fantasies.

Bedtime Stories. abr. ed. Nina Mattikow. Perf. by Purple Balloon Players. 3 cass. (Running Time: 3 hrs.). Dramatization. (Triple Packs Ser.). (J). 1992. 11.95 Set. (978-1-55569-536-1(1), 23002) Great Am Audio.
Children will love these delightful folktales, fantasies & fables. Full dramatic presentations with musical accompaniment.

Bedtime Stories. unabr. ed. Read by Nerys Hughes & Stephen Thorne. 1 cass. (Running Time: 1 hr., 30 min.). (J). (gr. 1-8). 1999. 9.95 (CTC 772, Chivers Child Audio) AudioGO.

Bedtime Stories for Adults. 1 cass. (Running Time: 30 min.). 9.95 (HO-84-10-31, HarperThor) HarpC GBR.

Bedtime Stories of the Legendary Ingleside Inn Palm Springs. unabr. ed. Mel Haber. Read by Mel Haber. 1 cass. (Running Time: 6 hrs.). 1996. bk. 24.95 (978-0-9651345-1-4(2)) Ingleside Pr.
Humorous anecdotes about the hotel & restaurant business.

Bedtime Tunes. Penton Overseas, Inc. Staff. 1 cass. (Running Time: 60 mins.). (Ready-Set-Sing Collection). (ENG.). (J). 2003. 4.99 (978-1-56015-974-2(X)) Penton Overseas.
Includes: "Rock-A-By Baby," "Twinkle Twinkle," "Brahms Lullaby" and more.

***Bedwetter.** unabr. ed. Sarah Silverman. Read by Sarah Silverman. (ENG.). 2010. (978-0-06-198714-4(X), Harper Audio) HarperCollins Pubs.

***Bedwetter: Stories of Courage, Redemption, & Pee.** unabr. ed. Sarah Silverman. Read by Sarah Silverman. (ENG.). 2010. (978-0-06-198713-7(1), Harper Audio) HarperCollins Pubs.

Bedwetter: Stories of Courage, Redemption, & Pee. unabr. ed. Sarah Silverman. Read by Sarah Silverman. 5 CDs. (Running Time: 6 hrs.). 2010. audio compact disk 29.99 (978-0-06-195327-9(X), Harper Audio) HarperCollins Pubs.

Bedwetting. 1 cass. (Running Time: 60 min.). 10.95 (049) Psych Res Inst.
Elimination of bedwetting by emphasizing self-confidence & reassurance.

Bedwetting. Bruce Goldberg. Read by Bruce Goldberg. 1 cass. (Running Time: 25 min.). (ENG.). 2006. 13.00 (978-1-885577-54-2(0)) Pub: B Goldberg. Dist(s): Baker Taylor
Through self-hypnosis remove this uncomfortable habit & awaken to a dry bed every morning.

Bee-Attitudes see Bee-Attitudes Teaching Unit

Bee-Attitudes Teaching Unit. 2nd rev. ed. Liz VonSeggen. Prod. by One Way Street Staff. Illus. by LeAnn Kalvada. 2 CDs. Orig. Title: Bee-Attitudes. (J). 2002. audio compact disk 50.00 (978-1-58302-212-2(0)) One Way St.
These two CD albulms provide thematic music and puppet plays and are included in the Bee-Atitude Teaching Unit. Disk one has 6 songs and then the soundtracks of each song. Disk two has 10 Rap Songs for the No Sweat Bee Character then the soundtracks are after.

Bee Double Bopp Cassette. Stephen Cosgrove. 2004. 5.00 (978-1-58804-362-7(2)) PCI Educ.

Bee Farming & Beef Ranching - Howard Lyman & Bob Mearns Discuss Pure Food & Agriculture. Hosted by Nancy Pearlman. 1 cass. (Running Time: 28 min.). 10.00 (1219) Educ Comm CA.

Bee My Valentine. Miriam Cohen. (Miriam Cohen Ser.). (J). (ps-6). 1988. bk. 13.90 (978-0-8045-6648-3(8), SAC 6515-B) Spoken Arts.

Bee My Valentine. unabr. ed. Miriam Cohen. Illus. by Lillian Hoban. 1 cass. (Running Time: 15 min.). (J). (gr. k-3). 2001. pap. bk. 16.95 (6552-B) Spoken Arts.
All the other kids in first grade get lots of valentines, but little George gets hardly any at all. He hides in the coatroom to cover his embarrassment.

Bee Puzzle: Early Explorers Fluent Set A Audio CD. Benchmark Education Staff. (J). 2006. audio compact disk 10.00 (978-1-4108-7634-8(9)) Benchmark Educ.

Bee Season. Myla Goldberg. 7 cass. (Running Time: 12 hrs. 45 mins.). 2004. 29.99 (978-1-4025-0217-0(6), 00624) Recorded Bks.

Bee Season. Myla Goldberg. 2005. audio compact disk 29.99 (978-1-4193-5828-9(6)) Recorded Bks.

Bee Season. unabr. ed. Myla Goldberg. Narrated by Myla Goldberg. 9 cass. (Running Time: 12 hrs.). 2002. 81.00 (978-1-4025-0690-1(2), 96924); audio compact disk 97.00 (978-1-4025-1563-7(4)) Recorded Bks.
Nine-year-old Eliza Naumann is considered an unspectacular child-until she surprises everyone by winning her school spelling bee. But just as Eliza begins to shine, her family starts falling apart. Her deeply spiritual father focuses all his attention on Eliza, encouraging her to seek a higher level of mysticism than he has achieved. Her brother abandons his Jewish faith and fills the void with Hare Krishna. And her mother fills the void in her life by stealing from other people's homes. Goldberg skillfully constructs the unique members of a troubled family as they strive to find their places in life and relate with one anothe.

Bee, the Harp, the Mouse & the Bumclock. 1 cass. (J). (gr. k-6). 1986. 10.00 (978-0-9617007-0-6(X)) G LedBetter.
Folktales winner of Notable Award from American Library Association.

Bee, the Mouse, & the Bumclock. unabr. ed. 1 cass. (Running Time: 20 min.). Dramatization. (Magic Looking Glass Ser.). (J). (gr. 2-6). 1989. 9.95 (978-0-7810-0020-8(3), NIM-CW-126-6-C) NIMCO.
A folk story of Irish descent.

Beef Country. unabr. ed. Gail Taylor. Read by Gail Taylor. Ed. by James B. Kirgan. 1 cass. (Running Time: 1 hr. 30 min.). (Essence of Nature Ser.: Vol. 12). (J). 1989. 12.99 stereo. (978-1-878362-12-4(7)) Emerald Ent.
On this tape Thumper, the adventure dog, travels westward across Texas. This tape includes actual recordings from events held in this state.

Beejum Book. Alice O. Howell. Read by Alice O. Howell. Music by Jason Brown. 6 CDs. (Running Time: 7 hrs. 30 min.). (J). 2005. audio compact disk 25.00 (978-0-9663401-6-7(7)) BMA Studios.

Beejum Book. unabr. ed. Alice O. Howell. Read by Alice O. Howell. Music by Jason Brown. 6 cass. (Running Time: 8 hrs.). 2002. 7.00 (978-0-9663401-3-6(2)) Pub: BMA Studios. Dist(s): SteinerBooks Inc
The author's unabridged audio production.

Beekeeper's Apprentice. Laurie R. King. Narrated by Jenny Sterlin. 12 CDs. (Running Time: 13 hrs. 45 mins.). (Mary Russell Mystery Ser.: Vol. 1). audio compact disk 118.00 (978-0-7887-9878-8(2)) Recorded Bks.

Beekeeper's Apprentice. unabr. ed. Laurie R. King. Narrated by Jenny Sterlin. 10 cass. (Running Time: 13 hrs. 45 mins.). (Mary Russell Mystery Ser.: Vol. 1). 1995. 85.00 (978-0-7887-0319-5(6), 94511E7) Recorded Bks.
A spirited American girl meets a retired Sherlock Holmes & the detective emerges from retirement to join her as she tracks down a fiendish assassin.

Beekeeper's Apprentice. unabr. ed. Laurie R. King. Narrated by Jenny Sterlin. 10 CDs. (Running Time: 13 hrs. 45 min.). (Mary Russell Mystery Ser.: Vol. 1). 2001. audio compact disk 124.00 (C1431) Recorded Bks.
In 1914, a spirited American girl named Mary Russell meets a retired Sherlock Holmes in the English countryside. Instantly realizing that Mary is gifted with astonishing deductive powers, the Great Detective emerges from retirement to join her as she tracks down a fiendish assassin.

Been in the Storm So Long: Spirituals, Folk Tales & Children's Games from Johns Island, South Carolina. 1 cass. 1990. (0-9307-400310-9307-40031-2-1) Smithsonian Folkways.
Sound portrait of one of the oldest African American communities in the western world.

Been in the Storm So Long: Spirituals, Folk Tales & Children's Games from Johns Island, South Carolina. Anno. by Guy Carawan. Selected by Guy Carawan & Candie Carawan. Selected by Candie Carawan. 1 CD. (Running Time: 1 hr.10 mins.). 1990. audio compact disk Smithsonian Folkways.

Been There, Done That. abr. ed. Eddie Fisher. 4 cass. (Running Time: 6 hrs.). 2001. 25.00 (978-1-59040-113-2(1), Phoenix Audio) Pub: Amer Intl Pub. Dist(s): PerseuPGW

Been There, Done That Cancer Thing. . . & So Can You. Steve de C. Cook. 2 CDs. (Running Time: 1 hr. 34 min.). 2003. audio compact disk 19.95 (978-0-9745018-0-2(8)) life hope.
Audio version of book of the same name, read by the author.

Been There...Done That! The Teenage Years Made Simple. John Rosemond. Contrib. by Mary Cox et al. 1 cass. 1997. 19.95 (978-0-9663173-1-2(9)) MC Mktging.
Helps parents communicate with their teenagers.

Beep Beep & Splish Splash. Read by Joanie Bartels. 2 cass. (Running Time: 74 min.). (Magic Series Gift Collection). (J). 1993. 15.98 (978-1-881225-18-8(6)) Discov Music.
The Beep Beep & Splish Splash gift set turns anytime into musical magic. Bathtime Magic is full of waterplay tunes with a bubbly beat while Travelin' Magic turns any trip into a sing-along party! It's the perfect gift for sharing music anytime.

Beer Blast: The Inside Story of the Brewing Industry's Bizarre Battles for Your Money. unabr. ed. Philip Van Munching. Read by Philip Van Munching. 4 cass. (Running Time: 6 hrs.). 1999. 25.00 (978-0-9668567-2-9(4)) MediaBay Audio.
Former beer executive takes a look back & delivers an inside account of the "Great Beer Wars" of the past few decades.

Beerbohm & Others see Assorted Prose

Bee's Kiss. unabr. ed. Barbara Cleverly. Read by Terry Wale. 8 cass. (Detective Joe Sandilands Ser.). (J). 2006. 69.95 (978-1-84559-350-6(2)) Pub: ISIS Lrg Prnt GBR. Dist(s): Ulverscroft US

Bee's Kiss. unabr. ed. Barbara Cleverly. Read by Terry Wale. 8 CDs. (Running Time: 32400 sec.). (Detective Joe Sandilands Ser.). 2006. audio compact disk 79.95 (978-1-84559-361-2(8)) Pub: ISIS Lrg Prnt GBR. Dist(s): Ulverscroft US

Bee's Knees: What's the Buzz?! Composed by Andie Duncan et al. (ENG.). (J). 2007. audio compact disk 16.98 (978-1-897166-49-9(4)) Child Group CAN.

***Bee's Wing.** Johnny Og O. Conghaile. (ENG.). 1990. 11.95 (978-0-8023-7026-6(8)) Pub: Clo Iar-Chonnachta IRL. Dist(s): Dufour

Beet Queen. Louise Erdrich. 1986. (6021) Am Audio Prose.

Beet Queen. abr. ed. Louise Erdrich. Read by Louise Erdrich. Read by Michael Dorris. 2 cass. (Running Time: 4 hrs.). 1991. 15.95 (978-1-55994-211-9(8), CPN 2170) HarperCollins Pubs.

Beethove Musico Sordo. unabr. ed. Abuelo Historias Del. (SPA.). 2007. audio compact disk 13.00 (978-958-8318-09-7(2)) Pub: Yoyo Music COL. Dist(s): YoYoMusic

Beethoven. Contrib. by Ludwig van Beethoven. 1 CD. (Running Time: 1 hr. 30 mins.). (Baby's First Ser.). (ENG.). (J). 2003. audio compact disk 7.95 (978-1-59125-327-3(6)) Penton Overseas.

Beethoven. unabr. ed. Anne P. Baker. Read by Anita Wright. 2 cass. (Running Time: 2 hrs.). (Pocket Biography Ser.). 1998. 24.95 (978-0-7531-0415-6(6), 980815) Pub: ISIS Audio GBR. Dist(s): Ulverscroft US
Considered by many the world's greatest composer, Beethoven achieved his ambitions against almost insurmountable difficulties; the effects of a bullying & drunken father & growing deafness & mounting ill-health, despite which he composed some of his most brilliant works, including the Eroica symphony & the Missa Solemnis. This describes his early employment as a court musician, his studies with Haydn in Vienna & his work during the French Revolution, rise of Napoleon & the French occupation of Vienna. More financially successful after Napoleon's defeat, his emotional life remained tumultuous with several unhappy love affairs & continuous worry over his suicidal nephew, Karl.

Beethoven. unabr. ed. Heywood Hale Broun. Read by Maynard Solomon. 1 cass. (Heywood Hale Broun Ser.). 12.95 (40322) J Norton Pubs.
A discussion with a biographer & Beethoven scholar.

Beethoven: An Introduction to the Pastoral Symphony. Jeremy Siepmann. 2 CDs. (Running Time: 3 hrs.). (Classics Explained Ser.). 2003. pap. bk. (978-1-84379-006-8(8)) NaxMulti GBR.

Beethoven: Revolutionary Artist. unabr. ed. Narrated by John Jones & Antony Hopkins. 1 cass. 12.95 (ECN 204) J Norton Pubs.
Beethoven's philosophy & outlook is explored through the medium of his music. His love of freedom shapes both his political attitude & his forms of musical expression. Side 1 presents "The Artist as Hero," Side 2 presents "How I See Beethoven".

Beethoven: The Greatest Hits. 1 cass. 10.98 CD. (978-1-57908-156-0(8), 3602) Platinm Enter.

Beethoven - Concerto No. 2 in B Flat Major, Op. 19: Piano Book/2-CD Play-along Pack. Composed by Ludwig van Beethoven. Neill Eisenstein. 2008. pap. bk. 39.98 (978-1-4234-6874-5(0), 1423468740) Pub: Music Minus. Dist(s): H Leonard

Beethoven - Violin Concerto in D Major, Op. 61: 2-CD Set. Composed by Ludwig van Beethoven. 2006. pap. bk. 34.98 (978-1-59615-146-8(3), 1596151463) Pub: Music Minus. Dist(s): H Leonard

Beethoven Blockbusters. 1 cass. (VOX-Turnabout Classical Ser.). 3.98 (CTX 4812); audio compact disk (ACD 8716) VOX Music Grp.

Beethoven I: His Life. Jeff Cox. 1 cass. 8.95 (064) Am Fed Astrologers.
Analysis and rectification of his chart using major events.

Beethoven II: His Music. Jeff Cox. 1 cass. 8.95 (065) Am Fed Astrologers.
Astrological overview of his music - emphasis on major works.

Beethoven in Paradise, unabr. ed. Barbara O'Connor. Narrated by Jeff Woodman. 3 pieces. (Running Time: 4 hrs.). (gr. 7 up). 27.00 (978-0-7887-1803-8(7), 95275E7) Recorded Bks.
Martin longs to be a musician, but his father wants him to play baseball & forget about all that "sissy" music stuff. Will Martin's love of music go forever unrequited? Available to libraries only.

Beethoven in Paradise, Class Set. Barbara O'Connor. Read by Jeff Woodman. 3 cass., 10 bks. (Running Time: 4 hrs.). (YA). 1997. bk. 97.30 (978-0-7887-2777-1(X), 46097) Recorded Bks.

Beethoven in Paradise, Homework Set. Barbara O'Connor. Read by Jeff Woodman. 3 cass. (Running Time: 4 hrs.). (YA). (gr. 7). 1997. bk. 40.20 (978-0-7887-1845-8(2), 40625) Recorded Bks.

Beethoven Lives Upstairs. 1 cass. (J). (gr. 1 up). 9.98 (2213); audio compact disk 16.98 (D2213) MFLP CA.
When Mr. Beethoven moves into the upstairs room, young Christoph begins an exchange of letters with his musician-uncle about the deaf genius composer. Christoph soon comes to understand the Master's eccentric ways & is won over by the sheer beauty of the music.

Beethoven Lives Upstairs. Susan Hammond. 1 cass. (J). 1993. 10.98; 18.98 CD. Consort Bk Sales.

Beethoven Lives Upstairs: A Tale of Childhood & Genius. C. Hammond. (J). 1993. audio compact disk (978-1-895404-06-7(1)) CBSD CAN.

Beethoven Naturally. 1 cass. (Running Time: 60 min.). 1994. audio compact disk 15.95 CD. (2624, Creativ Pub) Quayside.
Beethoven's greatest works mixed with a collection of authentic nature sounds.

Beethoven Naturally. 1 cass. (Running Time: 60 min.). 1994. 9.95 (2623, NrthWrd Bks) TandN Child.

Beethoven or Bust. Perf. by Ludwig van Beethoven. 1 cass., 1 CD. 7.98 (TA 30153); audio compact disk 12.78 CD Jewel box. (TA 80153) NewSound.

Beethoven, Schubert & More - Volume 1: Full Scores on DVD-ROM. Franz Schubert. Composed by Ludwig van Beethoven. (ENG.). 2009. audio compact disk 39.95 (978-1-4234-8136-2(4), 1423481364) H Leonard.

Beethoven Was One-Sixteenth Black: And Other Stories. unabr. ed. Nadine Gordimer. Narrated by David Colacci & Susan Ericksen. 1 MP3-CD. (Running Time: 5 hrs.). 2007. 49.95 (978-0-7927-5085-7(3)); audio compact disk 49.95 (978-0-7927-5055-0(1)) AudioGO.

Beethoven Was One-Sixteenth Black: And Other Stories. unabr. ed. Nadine Gordimer. Narrated by David Colacci & Susan Ericksen. 4 CDs. (Running Time: 5 hrs.). 2007. 59.99 (978-1-60514-626-3(9)) Find a World.

Beethoven's Piano Concerto, No. 5. unabr. ed. Robert Greenberg. Read by Robert Greenberg. Ed. by Teaching Company Staff. 2 cass. (Running Time: 3 hrs.). (Concert Masterworks Ser.). 1995. 19.95 set. (978-1-56585-114-6(5)) Teaching Co.
Dr. Greenberg seeks to make the contemporary audience members as informed, & excited, as the audience members of Beethoven's time.

***Beethoven's Piano Music - A Listener's Guide: Unlocking the Masters Series, No. 23.** Victor Lederer. (ENG.). 2011. pap. bk. 22.99 (978-1-57467-194-0(4), 1574671944, AmadeusPress) H Leonard.

Beethoven's Piano Sonatas, Vol. I-III. Instructed by Robert Greenberg. 24 CDs. (Running Time: 18 hrs.). 2005. bk. 99.95 (978-1-59803-014-3(0), 7250) Teaching Co.

Beethoven's Piano Sonatas, Vol. I-III. Instructed by Robert Greenberg. 12 cass. (Running Time: 18 hrs.). 2005. bk. 79.95 (978-1-59803-012-9(4), 7250) Teaching Co.

Beethoven's Wig: Sing along Symphonies. Perf. by Richard Perlmutter. 1 CD. (Running Time: 35 min.). (J). 2002. audio compact disk 12.98 Rounder Kids Mus Dist.

Beethoven's Wig 2: With Lyrics/Activity Booklet. 1 CD. (Running Time: 40 min.). (J). 2004. audio compact disk 12.98 (978-1-57940-100-9(7)) Rounder Records.

Beethoven's Wig 3: Many More Sing along Symphonies. unabr. ed. Richard Pearlmutter. 1 CD. (Running Time: 40 mins.). (J). (gr. k-5). 2006. audio compact disk 12.98 (978-1-57940-114-6(7)) Rounder Records.
With more zany lyrics set to the greatest hits of classical music, these Sing along symphonies feature a variety of different instruments from the familiar to the fascinating.

Beethoven's Wig 4: Dance along Symphonies. Richard Perlmutter. 1 CD. (Running Time: 43 mins.). (J). (ps-5). 2008. audio compact disk 11.99 (978-1-57940-170-2(8)) Rounder Records.

Beetle & Me: A Love Story. Karen Romano Young. Narrated by Alyssa Bresnahan. 4 pieces. (Running Time: 5 hrs. 45 mins.). (gr. 7 up). 2001. 36.00 (978-0-7887-5017-5(8), 96522E7) Recorded Bks.
When 15-year-old Daisy Pandolfi asks her father if she can repair his abandoned 1957 purple Volkswagon Beetle, he tells her "It's got an oil leak that's older than you are!" But with the help of the rest of her car-crazy family, she finally convinces him to let her try.

Beezus & Ramona. Beverly Cleary. Read by Stockard Channing. 2 cass. (Running Time: 3 hrs. 38 mins.). (Ramona Quimby Ser.). (J). (gr. 3-5). 2000. 54.00 (978-0-7366-9142-0(1)) Books on Tape.

Beezus & Ramona. Beverly Cleary. (Ramona Quimby Ser.). (J). (gr. 3-5). 1995. 21.33 (978-0-394-64514-8(6)) SRA McGraw.

Beezus & Ramona. unabr. ed. Beverly Cleary. Read by Stockard Channing. 2 cass. (Running Time: 3 hrs.). (Ramona Quimby Ser.). (J). (gr. 3-5). 1999. 23.00 (LL 3142, Chivers Child Audio) AudioGO.

Beezus & Ramona. unabr. ed. Beverly Cleary. Read by Stockard Channing. 2 cass. (Running Time: 3 hrs.). (Ramona Quimby Ser.). (J). (gr. 3-5). 1996. 17.95 (L179) Blckstn Audio.
Beezus Quimby's four-year-old sister, Ramona, is exasperating. Ramona never seems to understand what she is not supposed to do, & always manages to get her way. Poor Beezus must be the only ten-year-old in the world with a pest for a sister. How can she learn to love her?.

***Beezus & Ramona.** unabr. ed. Beverly Cleary. Read by Stockard Channing. (J). 2010. audio compact disk 14.99 (978-0-06-177405-8(7), HarperChildAud) HarperCollins Pubs.

***Beezus & Ramona.** unabr. ed. Beverly Cleary. Read by Stockard Channing. (ENG.). 2010. (978-0-06-204195-1(9)); (978-0-06-206016-7(3)) HarperCollins Pubs.

Beezus & Ramona. unabr. ed. Beverly Cleary. Read by Stockard Channing. 2 vols. (Running Time: 2 hrs. 21 mins.). (Ramona Quimby Ser.). (J). (gr. 3-7). 1990. pap. bk. 29.00 (978-0-8072-7317-3(1), YA 822 SP, Listening Lib) Random Audio Pubg.
Beezus Quimby's four-year-old sister, Ramona, is exasperating & always manages to get her way. Poor Beezus, she must be the only ten-year-old in the world with such a pest for a sister. How can she learn to love & accept this four-year-old terror?.

Beezus & Ramona/Ramona & Her Father. unabr. ed. Beverly Cleary. Read by Stockard Channing. (Running Time: 16200 sec.). (Ramona Quimby Ser.). (ENG.). (J). (gr. 2-7). 2007. audio compact disk 19.95 (978-0-7393-3889-6(7), Listening Lib) Pub: Random Audio Pubg. Dist(s): Random

Beezy's Big Boy. l.t. ed. Lin Oliver. Illus. by Bill Dodge. (J). 2000. pap. bk. 14.99 (978-1-890647-61-2(6)) Lrning Curve.

Before see Antes

Before a Cashier's Window see Poetry & Voice of James Wright

Before & After. Sam Brown. 2004. 15.95 (978-0-7435-4190-9(1)) Pub: S&S Audio. Dist(s): S and S Inc

Before & After. unabr. ed. Rosellen Brown. Narrated by C. J. Critt et al. 11 cass. (Running Time: 15 hrs. 30 mins.). 2000. 91.00 (978-1-55690-827-9(X), 93127E7) Recorded Bks.
When a teenage boy is accused, & later convicted, of murder, his mother & father come to terms with the shocking reality in different ways.

***Before Another Dies.** Zondervan. (Running Time: 10 hrs. 18 mins. 27 sec.). (Madison Glenn Ser.). (ENG.). 2010. 9.99 (978-0-310-86923-8(4)) Zondervan.

Before Book One Set: Listening Activities for Pre-Beginning Students of English. 2nd ed. John R. Boyd & Mary Ann Boyd. 2002. 86.85 (978-0-13-068313-7(2)) Longman.

Before Brass Tacks: Integrated Skills in English. Lynne Gaetz. 2002. tchr. ed. 21.85 (978-0-13-083849-0(7)) Longman.

Before Death Meditation. Bruce Goldberg. (ENG.). 2005. audio compact disk 17.00 (978-1-57968-038-1(0)) Pub: B Goldberg. Dist(s): Baker Taylor

Before Death Meditation. Bruce Goldberg. Read by Bruce Goldberg. 1 cass. (Running Time: 25 min.). (ENG.). 2006. 13.00 (978-1-885577-24-5(9)) Pub: B Goldberg. Dist(s): Baker Taylor
Instructions on conscious dying techniques.

Before Green Gables. unabr. ed. Budge Wilson. Read by Renée Raudman. 2 MP3-CDs. (Running Time: 14 hrs. 0 mins. 0 sec.). (ENG.). 2008. 24.99 (978-1-4001-5627-6(0)); audio compact disk 34.99 (978-1-4001-0627-1(3)); audio compact disk 69.99 (978-1-4001-3627-8(X)) Pub: Tantor Media. Dist(s): IngramPubServ

Before I Die. unabr. ed. Jenny Downham. Read by Charlotte Parry. 6 CDs. (Running Time: 25740 sec.). (ENG.). (J). (gr. 7-12). 2007. audio compact disk 34.00 (978-0-7393-6288-4(7), Listening Lib) Pub: Random Audio Pubg. Dist(s): Random

Before I Die. unabr. ed. Jenny Downham. Read by Charlotte Parry. 6 CDs. (Running Time: 7 hrs. 10 mins.). (YA). (gr. 9 up). 2007. audio compact disk 50.00 (978-0-7393-6290-7(9), Listening Lib) Pub: Random Audio Pubg. Dist(s): Random

***Before I Fall.** unabr. ed. Lauren Oliver. Read by Sarah Drew. (ENG.). 2010. (978-0-06-197745-9(4)); (978-0-06-193831-3(9)) HarperCollins Pubs.

Before I Got My Eye Put Out see Poems & Letters of Emily Dickinson

Before I Say Good-Bye. abr. ed. Mary Higgins Clark. Read by Jan Maxwell. 4 CDs. (Running Time: 43 hrs. 0 mins. 0 sec.). (ENG.). 2000. audio compact disk 30.00 (978-0-671-04788-7(4), Audioworks) Pub: S&S Audio. Dist(s): S and S Inc

Before I Say Good-Bye. abr. ed. Mary Higgins Clark. Read by Jan Maxwell. 2004. 15.95 (978-0-7435-4191-6(X)) Pub: S&S Audio. Dist(s): S and S Inc

Before I Say Good-Bye. unabr. ed. Mary Higgins Clark. Read by Valerie Leonard. 8 vols. (Running Time: 12 hrs.). 2000. bk. 69.95 (978-0-7927-2387-5(2), CSL 276, Chivers Sound Lib) AudioGO.
When Adam Cauliff's new cabin cruiser, the Cornelia II, blows up in a New York Harbor with him & several close business associates aboard, his wife, Nell McDermott is distraught at the loss & wracked with guilt because she & Adam had quarreled & she told him not to come home. The official confirmations say it was not an accident but foul play. As Nell comes closer to learning the truth, the nearer she is to being the next victim.

Before I Say Good-Bye. unabr. ed. Mary Higgins Clark. Read by Jan Maxwell. 2004. 21.95 (978-0-7435-2001-0(7)) Pub: S&S Audio. Dist(s): S and S Inc

Before I Wake. Perf. by Dee Henderson. (Justice Ser.). 2003. 19.99 (978-1-59052-206-6(0), Mltnmah) Doubday Relig.

Before I Wake: Christian Poetry by Samuel A. Wright. Poems. Samuel Wright Wright. Narrated by Samuel Wright Wright. Music by UniqueTracks.com Staff. 1. (Running Time: 30 mins.). Dramatization. (YA). 2002. audio compact disk Rental 11.95 (978-0-9722998-1-7(5)) wordofmouthpoetry.
Before i Wake is a collection of original Christian and Inspirational Poetry accompanied by light solo piano ballads; an ageless treasure that will inspire and encourage your heart for years to come.

Before Lunch. unabr. ed. Angela Thirkell. Read by Nadia May. 7 CDs. (Running Time: 8 hrs. 30 mins.). 2002. audio compact disk 56.00 (978-0-7861-9386-8(7), 3025); 44.95 (978-0-7861-2366-7(4), 3025) Blckstn Audio.
Lady Bond and Lord Pomfret are compelled to unite with the Middletons and the Stoners to stop the erection of a tea shop and garage on unspoiled Pooker's Piece. The young and the not-so-young all fall in love, not always with the right person, and sort out their affairs in a hilarious welter of cross-purposes.

Before Midnight. unabr. ed. Rex Stout. Read by Michael Prichard. 4 cass. (Running Time: 6 hrs.). (Nero Wolfe Ser.). 2004. 24.95 (978-1-57270-411-4(X)) Pub: Audio Partners. Dist(s): PerseuPGW

Before Midnight. unabr. ed. Rex Stout. Narrated by Michael Prichard. 5 CDs. (Running Time: 7 hrs.). (Nero Wolfe Ser.). (ENG.). 2004. audio compact disk 27.95 (978-1-57270-412-1(8)) Pub: AudioGO. Dist(s): Perseus Dist
In this ingenious whodunit, a perfume company offers a million dollars for correctly identifying certain women in history who used cosmetics. When the advertising genius behind the campaign is murdered and the answers stolen, Nero Wolfe is called in to find both. Archie Goodwin tries bravely to keep Wolfe away from the irritating women involved and focused on the case. But with puzzling phone calls and conflicting instructions from the ad company, it's anybody's guess when - or even if - Wolfe will find the killer.

Before Midnight. unabr. collector's ed. Rex Stout. Read by Michael Prichard. 6 cass. (Running Time: 6 hrs.). (Nero Wolfe Ser.). 1995. 48.00 (978-0-7366-3166-2(6), 3836) Books on Tape.
At the Pour Amour perfume riddle contest, someone murders the contest founder & steals the answers to the riddles. Now Wolfe has to sniff down a trail of clues that leads disturbingly close to home.

***Before My Heart Stops: A Memoir.** Paul Cardall. 2010. 21.99 (978-1-60641-928-1(5)) Deseret Bk.

Before the Beginning Is a Thought. abr. ed. Phil Murray. Read by Phil Murray. 1 cass. (Running Time: 1 hr.). (ENG., 1999. 13.99 (978-1-84032-147-0(4), HoddrStoughton) Pub: Hodder General GBR. Dist(s): IPG Chicago
Understanding your natural mind tools will enable you to accomplish whatever it is you wish for in life. This is not just a pleasant theory, it is fact.

Before the Blood Tribunal see Three Against Hitler

Before the Dawn. Beverly Jenkins. Narrated by Thomas Penny. 8 cass. (Running Time: 11 hrs. 30 mins.). 74.00 (978-1-4025-2036-5(0)) Recorded Bks.

Before the Dawn. Carol Warburton. 3 cass. 2004. 14.95 (978-1-59156-174-3(4)) Covenant Comms.

Before the Dawn: Recovering the Lost History of Our Ancestors. Nicholas Wade. Read by Alan Sklar. (Playaway Adult Nonfiction Ser.). 2008. 64.99 (978-1-60640-866-7(6)) Find a World.

Before the Dawn: Recovering the Lost History of Our Ancestors. unabr. ed. Nicholas Wade. Narrated by Alan Sklar. 11 CDs. (Running Time: 13 hrs. 0 mins. 0 sec.). (ENG.). 2006. audio compact disk 37.99 (978-1-4001-0232-7(4)) Pub: Tantor Media. Dist(s): IngramPubServ

Before the Dawn: Recovering the Lost History of Our Ancestors. unabr. ed. Nicholas Wade. Read by Alan Sklar. 11 CDs. (Running Time: 13 hrs. 0 mins. 0 sec.). (ENG.). 2006. audio compact disk 75.99 (978-1-4001-3232-4(0)) Pub: Tantor Media. Dist(s): IngramPubServ

Before the Dawn: Recovering the Lost History of Our Ancestors. unabr. ed. Nicholas Wade. Read by Michael Prichard. (Running Time: 13 hrs. 0 mins. 0 sec.). (ENG.). 2006. audio compact disk 24.99 (978-1-4001-5232-2(1)) Pub: Tantor Media. Dist(s): IngramPubServ

Before the Fact, Set. unabr. ed. Francis Iles. Read by Bruce Montague. 8 cass. (Running Time: 36180 sec.). (Church of England Ser.). 2000. 69.95 (978-0-7540-0428-8(7), CAB 1851) Pub: Chivers Audio Bks GBR. Dist(s): AudioGO
Despite the warnings of her family, Lina McLaidlaw marries the feckless Johnnie Aysgarth. After the honeymoon, Lina gradually perceives that her husband has a highly irregular attitude to other people's money & disinclination for hard work. And Johnnie seems to exert the most unhappy influence on the health & well-being of his nearest & dearest.

Before the Frost. unabr. ed. Henning Mankell. Read by Cassandra Campbell. (Running Time: 13 hrs. 50 mins.). (ENG.). 2009. 29.95 (978-1-4332-2593-2(X)); 79.95 (978-1-4332-2589-5(1)); audio compact disk 109.00 (978-1-4332-2590-1(5)) Blckstn Audio.

Before the River Came. 1 cass. 1999. 7.98 (978-0-7601-2803-9(0)) Brentwood Music.

Before the Throne of Grace. Contrib. by Johnathan Crumpton & Bradley Knight. Prod. by Ed Kee. (ENG.). 2008. audio compact disk 24.99 (978-5-557-48404-6(3), Brentwood-Benson Music) Brentwood Music.

Before the War see Poetry & Voice of Marilyn Hacker

Before Their Time Vol. 1: Memorial Songs & Music. 1 CD. (Running Time: 1 hr). 2000. audio compact disk 15.00 (978-0-9708386-0-5(3)) Hospice V N H.
A music resource for bereavement support.

Before Their Time Vol. 1: Memorial Songs & Music. unabr. ed. 1 cass. (Running Time: 1 hr). 10.00 Hospice V N H.

Before We Met: An Unabridged Selection from with Ossie & Ruby. unabr. ed. Ruby Dee & Ossie Davis. Read by Ruby Dee & Ossie Davis. (Running Time: 6 hrs.). (ENG.). 2006. 14.98 (978-1-59483-490-5(3)) Pub: Hachet Audio. Dist(s): HachBkGrp

Before We Were Free. Julia Alvarez. 4 vols. (Running Time: 6 hrs.). (J). (gr. 7 up). 2004. pap. bk. 38.00 (978-1-4000-9017-4(2), Listening Lib); 32.00 (978-1-4000-8529-3(2), Listening Lib); audio compact disk 32.30 (978-1-4000-8995-6(6), Listening Lib) Pub: Random Audio Pubg. Dist(s): NetLibrary CO

Before Women Had Wings, abr. ed. Connie May Fowler. Read by Connie May Fowler. 2 cass. (Running Time: 3 hrs.). 1997. 17.95 (978-1-57453-205-0(7)) Audio Lit.
Nine-year-old Bird Jackson's journey of self-discovery leads through myth & hard-core reality to a new vision of herself as she soars to meet the challenge of her name.

Before You Do: Making Great Decisions That You Won't Regret. unabr. ed. T. D. Jakes. Read by T. D. Jakes. (Running Time: 9 hrs. 30 mins. 0 sec.). (ENG.). 2008. audio compact disk 39.99 (978-0-7435-7042-8(1)) Pub: S&S Audio. Dist(s): S and S Inc

Before You Hire A Life Coach: Heal Your Issues Through Pyramid Problem Solving. abr. ed. 2006. audio compact disk 15.95 (978-1-928843-25-2(5)) Ad Lib Res.

Before You Know Kindness. unabr. ed. Chris Bohjalian. Read by Susan Denaker. 13 CDs. (Running Time: 17 hrs.). 2004. audio compact disk 104.00 (978-1-4159-1312-3(9)); 99.00 (978-1-4159-1311-6(0)) Books on Tape.
For ten summers, the extended Seton family met at their country home in New Hampshire, but during the eleventh summer everything changed.

Before You Quit Your Job: 10 Real-Life Lessons Every Entrepreneur Should Know about Building a Multimillion-Dollar Business. abr. ed. Robert T. Kiyosaki & Sharon L. Lechter. Read by Jim Ward & Deanna Hurst. (ENG.). 2005. 14.98 (978-1-59483-250-5(1)) Pub: Hachet Audio. Dist(s): HachBkGrp

Before You Were Mine. Maribeth Boelts. Illus. by David Walker. 1 cass. (Running Time: 7 mins.). (J). (ps-3). 2008. bk. 27.95 (978-0-8045-6961-3(4)); bk. 29.95 (978-0-8045-4184-8(1)) Spoken Arts.

Before You Write That Nonfiction Book. unabr. ed. Gordon Burgett. Read by Gordon Burgett. 3 cass. (Running Time: 3 hrs.). 1994. 44.95 set incl. wkbk. (978-0-910167-06-2(0)) Comm Unltd CA.
Discusses how writers can increase the marketability of a book while reducing the writing time to half by taking steps at the outset.

Before Your Dog Can Eat Your Homework, First You Have to Do It. unabr. ed. John O'Hurley. Read by John O'Hurley. (YA). 2008. 54.99 (978-1-60252-951-9(5)) Find a World.

Before Your Dog Can Eat Your Homework, First You Have to Do It: Life Lessons from a Wise Old Dog to a Young Boy. unabr. ed. John O'Hurley. Read by John O'Hurley. (ENG.). 2007. audio compact disk 26.95 (978-1-59887-534-8(5), 1598875345) Pub: HighBridge. Dist(s): Workman Pub

***Before 1776: Life in the American Colonies.** Instructed by Robert J. Allison. 2009. 199.95 (978-1-59803-613-8(0)) Teaching Co.

***Before 1776: Life in the American Colonies.** Instructed by Robert J. Allison. 2010. audio compact disk 269.95 (978-1-59803-614-5(9)) Teaching Co.

Befriend the Darkness, Welcome the Light. Joyce Rupp. 2 CDs. (Running Time: 7860 sec.). 2006. audio compact disk 24.95 (978-1-59471-118-3(6)) Ave Maria Pr.

Befriending the Beast. Read by Anita Greene. 1 cass. (Running Time: 90 min.). 1986. 10.95 (978-0-7822-0080-5(X), 180) C G Jung IL.

Beggar in Jerusalem. unabr. ed. Elie Wiesel. Read by Frederick Davidson. 5 cass. (Running Time: 7 hrs.). 1996. 39.95 (978-0-7861-1007-0(4), 1784) Blckstn Audio.
In the days following the Six-Day War, a survivor of the Holocaust vists the reunited city of Jerusalem. At the Western Wall in the Old City, he encounters the beggars & madmen who congregate there every evening & who force him to confront the ghosts of his past & his ties to the present. In this novel, Wiesel bids the reader to join him on a spiritual journey back & forth in time, always returning to Jerusalem.

Beggar King & the Secret of Happiness. unabr. ed. Joel Ben Izzy. Read by Joel Ben Izzy. (YA). 2007. 39.99 (978-1-60252-711-9(3)) Find a World.

Beggar King & the Secret of Happiness: A True Story. unabr. ed. Joel Ben Izzy. Read by Joel Ben Izzy. Read by Joel ben Izzy. 4 CDs. (Running Time: 16200 sec.). (ENG.). 2007. audio compact disk 26.95 (978-1-59887-514-0(0), 1598875140) Pub: HighBridge. Dist(s): Workman Pub

Beggar Maid: Stories of Flo & Rose. unabr. collector's ed. Alice Munro. Read by Jeanne Hopson. 9 cass. (Running Time: 9 hrs.). 1983. 54.00 (978-0-7366-0510-6(X), 1484) Books on Tape.
A young woman from the wrong side of a small town. Shaped in her ambition & drive by her stepmother Flo, Rose climbs the ladder of success...a university degree, love, marriage & an acting career.

Beggar of Volubilis. Caroline Lawrence. (Running Time: 3 hrs. 30 mins. 0 sec.). (Roman Mysteries Ser.). (ENG., (J). (gr. 7-9). 2007. audio compact disk 24.99 (978-0-7528-9067-8(0)) Pub: OrnChdms Bks GBR. Dist(s): IPG Chicago

Beggars' Bible. Vernon Louise. Narrated by Fern Ebersole. (ENG.). (YA). 2009. audio compact disk 15.95 (978-0-9801244-1-5(7)) IG Publish.

Beggars in Spain. Short Stories. Nancy Kress. Narrated by Theo Moffett. 3 CDs. (Running Time: 3 hrs. 5 mins.). (Great Science Fiction Stories Ser.). 2005. audio compact disk 19.99 (978-1-884612-42-8(3)) AudioText.

Beggars Would Ride. Mary Minton. (Story Sound CD Ser.). (J). 2002. audio compact disk 99.95 (978-1-85903-569-6(8)) Pub: Mgna Lrg Print GBR. Dist(s): Ulverscroft US

Begin a Newsletter for Astrology Sake. Fayette Cometti. 1 cass. 8.95 (390) Am Fed Astrologers.
An AFA Convention workshop tape.

***Begin Again, Believe Again: Embracing the Courage to Love with Abandon.** Zondervan. (Running Time: 7 hrs. 16 mins. 2 sec.). (ENG.). 2010. 14.99 (978-0-310-41182-6(3)) Zondervan.

Begin at the Beginning. John R. Boyd & Mary Ann Boyd. 1988. 29.95 (978-0-933759-13-8(4)) Abaca Bks.

Begin with the Basics, Pt. I. 2 cass. 1990. 16.00 set. Recorded Res.

Begin with the Basics, Pt. II. 2 cass. 1990. 16.00 set. Recorded Res.

***Beginner Basics Guitar.** Gary Turner. 2010. bk. 34.95 (978-982-9118-14-1(2)) Kolala Music SGP.

***Beginner Basics Guitar Bible.** Gary Turner et al. 2010. bk. 49.95 (978-982-9118-15-8(0)) Kolala Music SGP.

***Beginner Basics Guitar for Kids.** Gary Turner & Andrew Scott. 2010. bk. 29.95 (978-982-9118-17-2(7)) Kolala Music SGP.

***Beginner Basics Music Bible for Kids.** Gary Turner & Andrew Scott. 2010. bk. 39.95 (978-982-9118-16-5(9)) Kolala Music SGP.

Beginner Bass. Gary Turner. (Progressive Ser.). 2004. pap. bk. 19.95 (978-1-86469-164-1(6), 256-131) Kolala Music SGP.

Beginner Blues Guitar: For Beginners. Peter Gelling. 2008. pap. bk. 19.95 (978-1-86469-380-5(0)) Kolala Music SGP.

Beginner Blues Harmonica. Peter Gelling. (Progressive Ser.). 2004. pap. bk. 19.95 (978-1-86469-162-7(X), 256-132) Kolala Music SGP.

Beginner Clarinet. Peter Gelling. (Progressive Ser.). 2004. pap. bk. 19.95 (978-1-86469-177-1(8), 256-133) Kolala Music SGP.

Beginner Classical Guitar. Brett Duncan. (Progressive Ser.). 2004. pap. bk. 19.95 (978-1-86469-201-3(4), 256-134) Kolala Music SGP.

Beginner Drums, Vol. 2. Peter Gelling. (Progressive Ser.). 2004. pap. bk. 19.95 (978-1-86469-165-8(4), 256-135) Kolala Music SGP.

Beginner Fingerpicking Guitar: For Beginners. Peter Gelling. 2008. pap. bk. 19.95 (978-1-86469-378-2(9)) Kolala Music SGP.

Beginner Flute. Gary Turner. (Progressive Ser.). 2004. pap. bk. 19.95 (978-1-86469-126-9(3), 256-136) Kolala Music SGP.

Beginner Guitar. Gary Turner. (Progressive Ser.). 2004. pap. bk. 14.95 (978-1-86469-163-4(8), 256-137) Kolala Music SGP.

Beginner Harmonica. Peter Gelling. (Progressive Ser.). 2004. pap. bk. 19.95 (978-1-86469-171-9(9), 256-138) Kolala Music SGP.

Beginner-Intermediate Pilates: Pilates Matwork with Flow: 23 Exercises. Instructed by Aliesa George. (ENG.). 2006. 12.00 (978-0-9771576-4-8(4)) Ctr Pilates.

Beginner Keyboard. Gary Turner. (Progressive Ser.). 2004. pap. bk. 19.95 (978-1-86469-166-5(2), 256-139) Kolala Music SGP.

Beginner Lead Guitar: For Beginners. Peter Gelling. 2008. pap. bk. 19.95 (978-1-86469-381-2(9)) Kolala Music SGP.

Beginner Music Theory. Peter Gelling. (Progressive Ser.). 2004. pap. bk. 19.95 (978-1-86469-168-9(9), 256-144) Kolala Music SGP.

Beginner Piano. Gary Turner. (Progressive Ser.). 2004. pap. bk. 19.95 (978-1-86469-167-2(0), 256-140) Kolala Music SGP.

Beginner Resources: Spring 1999. 1 cass. (J). (ps-k). 1999. 10.99 Incl. tchr's. visuals. (978-1-57405-480-4(5)) CharismaLife Pub.

Beginner Resources: Summer 1999. 1 cass. (J). (ps-k). 1999. 10.99 Incl. tchr's. visuals. (978-1-57405-532-0(1)) CharismaLife Pub.

Beginner Rhythm Guitar: For Beginners. Peter Gelling. 2008. pap. bk. 19.95 (978-1-86469-382-9(7)) Kolala Music SGP.

Beginner Rock Guitar: For Beginners. Peter Gelling. 2008. pap. bk. 19.95 (978-1-86469-383-6(5)) Kolala Music SGP.

Beginner Rock Singing: For Beginners. Peter Gelling. 2008. pap. bk. 19.95 (978-1-86469-384-3(3)) Kolala Music SGP.

Beginner Saxophone. Peter Gelling. (Progressive Ser.). 2004. pap. bk. 19.95 (978-1-86469-120-7(4), 256-143) Kolala Music SGP.

Beginner Singing. Peter Gelling. (Progressive Ser.). 2004. pap. bk. 19.95 (978-1-86469-132-0(8), 256-142) Kolala Music SGP.

Beginner Trumpet. Peter Gelling. (Progressive Ser.). (SPA.). 2004. pap. bk. 19.95 (978-1-86469-122-1(0), 256-145) Kolala Music SGP.

Beginners Bible: New Testament. 1 cass. (J). 1992. 12.95 Sparrow TN.
Religious.

Beginners Bible: Old Testament. 1 cass. (J). 1992. 12.95 (978-0-917143-12-0(4)) Sparrow TN.

Beginner's Bible - Creation. 1 cass. 1997. bk. 6.98 (978-1-57330-785-7(8)) Sony Music Ent.

Beginner's Bible - Easter. 1 cass. (J). (ps-3). 1997. bk. 6.98 (978-1-57330-783-3(1)) Sony Music Ent.

Beginner's Bible - Moses. 1 cass. (J). 1997. bk. 6.98 (978-1-57330-784-0(X)) Sony Music Ent.

Beginner's Bible Songs. 1 cass., 1 CD. (Beginner's Bible Ser.). (J). 7.98 (SME 67826); audio compact disk 11.18 CD Jewel box. (SME 67826) NewSound.

Beginners' Chart Delineation. Doris C. Doane. Read by Doris C. Doane. 1 cass. (Running Time: 90 min.). 1994. 8.95 (1110) Am Fed Astrologers.
Learning to read the horoscope.

Beginner's Chinese. Yong Ho. 1 cass. (Running Time: 1 hr. 30 mins.). (CHI & ENG.). 12.95 (978-0-7818-0912-2(6)) Hippocrene Bks.

Beginner's Finnish. Agi Risko. (ENG & FIN.). 2007. 26.95 (978-0-7818-1228-3(3)) Hippocrene Bks.

***Beginner's Grace: Bringing Prayer to Life.** unabr. ed. Kate Braestrup. (Running Time: 8 hrs. 0 mins.). 2010. 15.99 (978-1-4001-8983-0(7)); 19.99 (978-1-4001-6983-2(6)); audio compact disk 29.99 (978-1-4001-1983-7(9)) Pub: Tantor Media. Dist(s): IngramPubServ

***Beginner's Grace (Library Edition) Bringing Prayer to Life.** unabr. ed. Kate Braestrup. (Running Time: 8 hrs. 0 mins.). 2010. 29.99 (978-1-4001-9983-9(2)); audio compact disk 71.99 (978-1-4001-4983-4(5)) Pub: Tantor Media. Dist(s): IngramPubServ

Beginner's Greek: A Novel. abr. ed. James Collins. Read by Jerry O'Connell. (Running Time: 6 hrs.). (ENG.). 2008. 24.98 (978-1-60024-075-1(5)) Pub: Hachet Audio. Dist(s): HachBkGrp

Beginner's Guide to Animal Communication. Carol Gurney. (Running Time: 1 hr. 15 mins.). (Beginner's Ser.). 2003. audio compact disk 15.95 (978-1-59179-109-6(X), W743D) Sounds True.

Beginner's Guide to Buddhism. unabr. ed. Jack Kornfield. 1 CD. (Running Time: 1 hr. 15 mins.). (Beginners Ser.). 2002. audio compact disk 15.95 (978-1-56455-886-2(X), W534D) Sounds True.
Author and teacher immerses you in this time-honored approach to living fully and compassionately in the present moment. Join him as he illuminates Buddhism?s most essential teachings, and how they make it possible to overcome the mental states that challenge us every day, such as fear, selfishness, confusion, and anger. Complete with authentic meditations to get you started.

Beginner's Guide to Dream Interpretation. Clarissa Pinkola Estes. (Running Time: 1 hr. 15 mins.). (Beginner's Guide Ser.). 2003. audio compact disk 15.95 (978-1-59179-048-8(4), W680D) Sounds True.

***Beginner¿s Guide to Guitar.** Travis Andrews & Ruth Parry. (ENG.). (YA). 2010. pap. bk. 19.99 (978-1-890490-69-0(5)) Pub: String Letter. Dist(s): H Leonard

Beginner's Guide to Healthy Eating. Andrew Weil. (Running Time: 1 hr. 15 mins.). (Beginner's Guide Ser.). 2003. audio compact disk 15.95 (978-1-59179-050-1(6), W682D) Sounds True.

Beginner's Guide to Mantras: How to Use Sacred Sound to Create Abundance, Health, & Spiritual Insight in Your Life. abr. ed. Thomas Ashley-Farrand. (Running Time: 1 hr. 15 mins.). (Beginners Ser.). 2002. audio compact disk 15.95 (978-1-56455-941-8(6), W582D) Sounds True.

Beginner's Guide to Meditation. Joan Borysenko. 2 cass. (Running Time: 2 hrs.). 1998. 16.95 (978-1-56170-546-7(2), 451) Hay House.
How to meditate.

Beginner's Guide to Meditation. Joan Borysenko. 2 CDs. (Running Time: 7200 sec.). 2006. audio compact disk 18.95 (978-1-4019-0664-1(8)) Hay House.

Beginner's Guide to Meditation. abr. ed. Joan Z. Borysenko. Read by Joan Z. Borysenko. (YA). 2008. 34.99 (978-1-60514-514-3(9)) Find a World.

Beginner's Guide to Meditation. unabr. ed. Shinzen Young. 1 CD. (Running Time: 1 hr. 15 mins.). (Beginners Ser.). 2002. audio compact disk 15.95 (978-1-56455-847-3(9), W505D) Sounds True.
Learn how to start using simple yet effective techniques proven at medical centers and clinics worldwide to promote physical and emotional health.

Beginner's Guide to Misery & Depression. Charles B. Beckert. 1 cass. 7.98 (978-1-55503-729-1(1), 069408) Covenant Comms.
Helpful tips for losers.

Beginner's Guide to Short Selling. Instructed by Toni Turner. 2005. audio compact disk 19.95 (978-1-59280-232-6(X)) Marketplace Bks.

Beginners Guide to Short Selling. Instructed by Toni Turner. (Running Time: 90 mins.). 2002. 19.95 (978-1-931611-81-7(5)) Marketplace Bks.
Fear short selling no more. Toni Turner will take you step by step through the process of selling short. Her systematic top down approach shows you how to pick the right stocks for selling short and it will prove to you that selling short is not as difficult or as scary as you may think.Additional topics covered include; how to use candlesticks to identify short selling candidates, how the convergence of signals can shift the odds in your favor, why it is important to look at different time periods and what it takes to "Make your shorts fall".In today's volatile market you need techniques to trade both the long and the short side of the market.

Beginner's Guide to the Chakras. unabr. ed. Judith Anodea. 2 CDs. (Running Time: 1 hr. 15 mins.). (Beginners Ser.). 2002. audio compact disk 15.95 (978-1-56455-920-3(3), W552D) Sounds True.
Learn how to balance and energize your body?s chakras the seven spinning centers of energy that regulate your physical, mental, and spiritual well-being.

Beginner's Guide to Yoga. Shiva Rea. (Running Time: 1 hr. 15 mins.). (Beginner's Guide Ser.). 2003. audio compact disk 15.95 (978-1-59179-112-6(X), W746D) Sounds True.

Beginner's Luck. Laura Pedersen. Narrated by Katie Hale. (ENG.). 2008. audio compact disk 42.95 (978-1-60031-040-9(0)) Spoken Books.

Beginner's Mind: Buddhism for the Beginner. Akira Endo. Read by Michiko Endo. 2003. 49.99 (978-0-9760980-3-4(2)) PaddHse Pr.

Beginning: The Cove / The Maze. abr. ed. Catherine Coulter. Read by Sandra Burr & Susan Ericksen. (Running Time: 43200 sec.). (FBI Thriller Ser.). 2005. audio compact disk 29.95 (978-1-4233-0947-5(2), 9781423309475, BACD) Brilliance Audio.
"Catherine Coulter can always be counted on to write an exciting thriller" (BookBrowser), and now here are the first two thrillers in the FBI series - The Cove and The Maze - in one volume for the first time ever. The Cove - In this "fast-paced" (Publishers Weekly) page-turner, the daughter of a murdered high-powered lawyer seeks sanctuary in a quaint little town, only to learn that she can't escape her past or the FBI agent hunting her. The Maze - "full of twists and turns" (Rocky Mountain News), this cliffhanger teams Savich and Sherlock for the first time in a case that leads them back to the murder of Sherlock's sister seven years ago - and puts both their lives on the line. "Coulter is a one-of-a-kind author who knows how to hook her readers and keep them coming back for more." - The Best Reviews.

Beginning a Professional Practice. John L. Ahern. 1 cass. (Running Time: 90 min.). 1988. 8.95 (635) Am Fed Astrologers.

Beginning Acoustic Guitar. Greg Horne. 1 CD. (Running Time: 1 hr. 30 mins.). (ENG.). 2000. audio compact disk 11.00 (978-0-7390-0425-8(5), 19336) Alfred Pub.

Beginning Again (Unabridged Audio) Benedictine Wisdom for Living with Illness. Mary C. Earle. Read by Mary C. Earle. (ENG.). 2007. 29.00 (978-0-9798958-4-5(7)) Mat Media.

Beginning Again (Unabridged Audio) Benedictine Wisdom for Living with Illness. Mary C. Earle. Read by Mary C. Earle. (ENG.). 2008. audio compact disk 29.00 (978-0-9798958-2-1(0), NewBeg) Mat Media.

Beginning Algebra. 7th ed. R. David Gustafson & Peter D. Frisk. (C). 2004. audio compact disk 16.95 (978-0-534-46334-2(7)) Pub: Brooks-Cole. Dist(s): CENGAGE Learn

Beginning Algebra. 9th ed. Lial et al. (Math XL Ser.). 2004. audio compact disk 26.67 (978-0-321-29368-8(1)) AddisonWesley.

***Beginning Algebra Student Solutions Manual CD-ROM.** 5th rev. ed. Munem-West. (ENG.). 2010. audio compact disk 89.73 (978-0-7575-0735-9(2)) Kendall-Hunt.

Beginning Algebra with Applications & Visualization. Created by Pearson/Addison Wesley. (Math XL Ser.). 2005. audio compact disk 26.67 (978-0-321-20805-7(6)) AddisonWesley.

Beginning & Intermediate Algebra. 2nd ed. Created by Pearson/Prentice Hall. (Math XL Ser.). 2005. audio compact disk 26.67 (978-0-13-149209-7(8)) Pearson Educ CAN CAN.

Beginning & Intermediate Algebra. 3rd ed. Created by Pearson/Prentice Hall. (Math XL Ser.). 2004. audio compact disk 26.67 (978-0-321-29377-0(0)) Pearson Educ CAN CAN.

Beginning & Intermediate Algebra: The Language & Symbolism of Mathematics. Brian Mercer & James Hall. 2003. audio compact disk 48.44 (978-0-07-286505-9(9), 9780072865059, McG-H Sci Eng) Pub: McGrw-H Hghr Educ. Dist(s): McGraw

Beginning Astrodynes. Lee V. Johnson. 1 cass. 8.95 (180) Am Fed Astrologers.
Church of Light method of calculation for natal, event, etc.

Beginning Bass for Adults. Ed. by Alfred Publishing. (ENG.). 2004. audio compact disk 10.95 (978-1-929395-69-9(8)) Pub: Workshop Arts. Dist(s): Alfred Pub

Beginning Bengali. 2 cass. (Running Time: 2 hrs.). (BEN & ENG.). pap. bk. 39.95 (AFBE10) J Norton Pubs.
Beginning-level course in reading, writing & speaking. "Teach Yourself" includes the written script & sound system & provides dialogs & reading passages, grammar & notes on Indian culture & society.

Beginning Blues Bass. 1997. audio compact disk 19.95 (978-0-8256-1608-2(5)) Music Sales.

Beginning Cherokee. Ruth B. Holmes & Betty S. Smith. 2 cass. (Running Time: 3 hrs.). (J). (gr. 10-12). 1992. pap. bk. 59.95 (978-0-88432-726-4(4), AFCK10) J Norton Pubs.
27 lessons with accompanying exercises, teaching the basics of Cherokee in the dialect of Oklahoma.

Beginning Cherokee, Vol. I. unabr. ed. Ruth B. Holmes et al. 2 cass. (Running Time: 3 hrs.). 1980. bk. 59.95 (978-0-88432-736-3(1), AFV990) J Norton Pubs.
Includes 332-page text.

Beginning Cherokee CD. Holmes/Smith. 1976. audio compact disk 59.95 (978-1-57970-493-3(X), Audio-For) J Norton Pubs.

Beginning Electric Bass. David Overthrow. 1 CD. (ENG.). 2000. audio compact disk 10.00 (978-0-7390-0690-0(8), 19363) Alfred Pub.

Beginning Fingerstyle Blues Guitar. Arnie Berle & Mark Galbo. (ENG., 1993. pap. bk. 21.95 (978-0-8256-2556-5(4), 0825625564, Schirmer Trade Bks) Pub: Music Sales. Dist(s): H Leonard

Beginning flute solos, vol. I. Murray Panitz. 1995. pap. bk. 34.98 (978-1-59615-297-7(4), 586-011) Pub: Music Minus. Dist(s): Bookworld

Beginning French Horn Solos - Volume 1. Mason Jones. 2008. pap. bk. 24.98 (978-1-59615-226-7(5), 1596152265) Pub: Music Minus. Dist(s): H Leonard

Beginning Guitar for Adults: The Grown-Up Approach to Playing Guitar. Nick Vecchio. 1 CD. (ENG.). 1999. audio compact disk 10.95 (978-1-929395-06-4(X)) Pub: Workshop Arts. Dist(s): Alfred Pub

Beginning Guitar Superbook. Hal Leonard Corporation Staff & Will Schmid. (Hal Leonard Guitar Method Ser.). 1996. pap. bk. 32.95 (978-0-7935-6253-4(8), 0793562538) H Leonard.

Beginning Hindi. unabr. ed. 2 cass. (Running Time: 2 hrs.). pap. bk. 39.95 (AFH150) J Norton Pubs.

Beginning Independence for Rock & Alternative Drum. Todd J. Vinciguerra. 1998. pap. bk. 9.95 (978-0-7866-3269-5(0), 96975BCD) Mel Bay.

Beginning Japanese, Pt. 1. Eleanor H. Jorden. 8 cass. (Running Time: 11 hrs. 30 mins.). pap. bk. 185.00 (978-0-614-10697-8(4), AFJ401) J Norton Pubs.
Contains 20 lessons having a basic pattern of dialogs, grammatical notes, drills, comprehensive materials & exercises. There are 5 kinds of drills designed to develop fluency: substitution, grammar, response, formal & informal levels & expansion.

Beginning Japanese, Pt. 1. Eleanor H. Jorden & Hamako Ito Chaplin. 17 CD's. (JPN.). (C). 2004. per. 229.00 (978-1-58214-368-2(4)) Language Assocs.

Beginning Japanese, Pt. 2. Eleanor H. Jorden. 16 cass. (Running Time: 19 hrs.). (YA). pap. bk. 245.00 (978-0-614-10698-5(2), AFJ409) J Norton Pubs.
Incorporates the same format & content organization & provides additional as well as more advanced vocabulary drills & dialogs.

Beginning Japanese Pt. 1: Yale Language Series. Eleanor H. Jorden & Hamako Chaplin. 16 Cass. (JPN.). (C). 2004. per. 199.00 (978-1-58214-366-8(8)) Language Assocs.

Beginning Japanese Part 2. Elizabeth Harz Jorden & Hamako Ito Chaplin. 15 Cass. (JPN.). (C). 2004. per. 225.00 (978-1-58214-367-5(6)) Language Assocs.

Beginning Japanese Vol. 1 CDs & Text. Eleanor Harz Jorden. 16 CDs. (Running Time: 11 hrs. 30 mins.). (JPN.). 2005. audio compact disk 225.00 (978-1-57970-261-8(9), AFJ401D, Audio-For) J Norton Pubs.
This course is concerned only with spoken Japanese in the standard dialect of educated inhabitants of Tokyo. Japanese sounds are transliterated in the text, and method for sound production is explained and demonstrated in the audio portion. Part 1 contains 20 lessons, all havnig a basic pattern of dialogs, grammar notes, drills, comprehension materials, and exercises. The glossary in the book lists 900 stem structures used in the course.

Beginning Jazz Guitar. Jody Fischer. 1 CD. (FRE.). Date not set. pap. bk. (978-0-7390-0831-7(5), 19379) Alfred Pub.

Beginning Jazz Guitar. National Guitar Workshop Arts Staff. 1 CD. (ENG.). 1995. audio compact disk 10.95 (978-0-7390-0109-7(4), 14121) Alfred Pub.

Beginning Listening Cycles. John R. Boyd & Mary Ann Boyd. 1986. 39.95 (978-0-933759-07-7(X)) Abaca Bks.

Beginning Mandarin Chinese, Set. Galal Walker et al. (Foreign Language Publications: No. 127B, Units 1-9). (CHI.). 1995. 160.00 (978-0-87415-318-7(2), 127B) Foreign Lang.

***Beginning Meditation: Enjoying Your Own Deepest Experience.** Sally Kempton. (Running Time: 2:00:00). 2011. audio compact disk 19.95 (978-1-60407-097-2(8)) Sounds True.

Beginning Meditation: Introductory Meditation to Expand Awareness & Create Positive Life Change. Mark Bancroft. Read by Mark Bancroft. 1 cass., bklet. (Running Time: 1 hrs.). (Spirituality & Consciousness Ser.). 1999. 12.95 (978-1-58522-030-4(2), 721, EnSpire Aud) EnSpire Pr.
Two complete sessions plus printed instruction manual/guidebook. With healing music soundtrack.

Beginning Meditation: Introductory Meditation to Expand Awareness & Create Positive Life Change. Mark Bancroft. Read by Mark Bancroft. 1 CD, bklet. (Running Time: 1 hr.). (Spirituality & Consciousness Ser.). 2006. audio compact disk 20.00 (978-1-58522-068-7(X)) EnSpire Pr.
Two complete sessions plus printed instructionmanual/guidebook. With healing music soundtrack.

Beginning Norwegian Through Fairy Tales: The Daisy. Hans Christian Andersen. 1 cass. (Running Time: 18 mins.). (NOR & ENG., (J). 2001. pap. bk. 15.95 (SNW001) J Norton Pubs.

Beginning Norwegian Through Fairy Tales: The Emperor's New Clothes. Hans Christian Andersen. 1 cass. (Running Time: 18 mins.). (NOR & ENG., (J). 2001. pap. bk. 15.95 (SNW002) J Norton Pubs.

Beginning Norwegian Through Fairy Tales: The Nightingale. Hans Christian Andersen. 1 cass. (Running Time: 18 mins.). (NOR & ENG., 2001. pap. bk. 15.95 (SNW003) J Norton Pubs.

Beginning of Increase. Creflo A. Dollar. 5 cass. (Running Time: 7 hrs. 30 mins.). 2001. 25.00 (978-1-931172-88-2(9), TS88, Kidz Faith) Pub: Creflo Dollar. Dist(s): STL Dist NA

Beginning of Our Nation, Set. unabr. ed. 2 cass. (American History for ESL Learners Ser.). 1994. 24.50 (978-0-88432-630-4(6), S19201) J Norton Pubs.
Includes booklet.

Beginning of Sorrows: Enmeshed by Evil... How Long Before America Is No More? unabr. ed. Lynn Gilbert & Alan Morris. Narrated by Paul Hecht. 10 cass. (Running Time: 11 hrs. 45 mins.). 2001. 88.00 (978-0-7887-5143-1(3), K0030G7) Recorded Bks.
The government has ruled that humanity is nature's worst enemy & has herded all of its citizens into a few overcrowded cities. An electricity-eating virus has plunged the nation into blackness.

Beginning of the Armadillos see Favorite Children's Stories: A Collection

Beginning of the Armadillos see Favorite Just So Stories

Beginning of the End: Rev. 15:1-8. Ed Young. 1987. 4.95 (978-0-7417-1575-3(9), 575) Win Walk.

Beginning of the Republic 1775-1825. unabr. ed. Clarence B. Carson. (Running Time: 41400 sec.). (Basic History of the United States Ser.). 2007. audio compact disk 29.95 (978-0-7861-6015-0(2)); audio compact disk 90.00 (978-0-7861-6014-3(4)) Blckstn Audio.

Beginning of Wisdom. Megan McKenna. Read by Megan McKenna. 7 cass. (Running Time: 8 hrs.). 1996. pap. bk. (AA2965) Credence Commun.
Explanation of the parables with stories around the world so that, as she puts it, "all the stories serve the story".

Beginning Passamaquoddy. unabr. ed. 5 cass. (Running Time: 3 hrs. 30 mins.). (YA). (gr. 10-12). 1988. pap. bk. 79.95 (978-0-88432-459-1(1), AFPS10) J Norton Pubs.
Provides basic phrases, structures & vocabulary needed for everyday conversations. Also includes 50p. phrasebook.

Beginning Piano for Adults. Karl Mueller. (ENG.). 2004. audio compact disk 10.95 (978-1-929395-65-1(5)) Pub: Workshop Arts. Dist(s): Alfred Pub

Beginning Piano Techniques. Richard P. Anderson. (C). 2006. spiral bd. 43.95 (978-1-57766-485-7(X)) Waveland Pr.

Beginning Place. unabr. ed. Ursula K. Le Guin. Narrated by Rob Inglis. 5 cass. (Running Time: 7 hrs. 15 mins.). 1999. 44.00 (978-1-55690-040-2(6), 91230E7) Recorded Bks.
Hugh & Irena enter Tembreabrezi, a beginng place like Eden & discover that a threat hangs over it. If they accept the challenge, they may lose everything, their new-found paradie, possibly their lives.

Beginning Practical Magic. Featuring Ian Corrigan. 1987. 9.95 (978-1-59157-019-6(0)) Assn for Cons.

Beginning Slovak, Sylvia Galova-Lorinc & Oscar E. Swan. 8 cass. (Running Time: 8 hrs.). 1992. pap. bk. 225.00 (978-0-88432-521-5(0), AFSL10) J Norton Pubs.
Each lesson focuses on specific, everyday topics & consists of dialogs, vocabulary, exercises, sentences for translation & a reading.

Beginning Slovak CDs & Text. Oscar E. Swan & Sylvia Galova-Lorinc. 9 CDs. (Running Time: 8 hrs.). (SLO.). 2005. audio compact disk 245.00 (978-1-57970-208-3(2), AFSL10D) J Norton Pubs.

Beginning Soprano Solos. Kate Hurney. 2007. pap. bk. 24.98 (978-1-59615-525-1(6), 1596155256) Pub: Music Minus. Dist(s): H Leonard

Beginning Swedish Through Fairy Tales: The Daisy. Hans Christian Andersen. 1 cass. (Running Time: 18 mins.). (SWE & ENG., (J). 2001. pap. bk. 15.95 (SSW001) J Norton Pubs.

Beginning Swedish Through Fairy Tales: The Emperor's New Clothes. Hans Christian Andersen. 1 cass. (Running Time: 18 mins.). (SWE & ENG., (J). 2001. pap. bk. 15.95 (SSW002) J Norton Pubs.

Beginning Swedish Through Fairy Tales: The Nightingale. Hans Christian Andersen. 1 cass. (Running Time: 18 mins.). (SWE & ENG., (J). 2001. pap. bk. 15.95 (SSW003) J Norton Pubs.

Beginning Tagalog, Set. unabr. ed. Neonetta C. Cabrera et al. Tr. by J. Donald Bowen. Illus. by Felipe D. Vale. 24 cass. (Running Time: 33 hrs.). (J). (gr. 10-12). 1968. pap. bk. 295.00 (978-0-88432-103-3(7), AFTG10) J Norton Pubs.
Includes 526-page text & 399-page reader.

Beginning Tagalog CDs, text & Reader. J. Donald Bowen. Ed. by J. Donald Bowen. 40 CDs. (Running Time: 33 hrs.). (TAG.). 2005. audio compact disk 325.00 (978-1-57970-271-7(6), AFTG10D, Audio-For) J Norton Pubs.

Beginning Tarot. unabr. ed. Angeles Arrien. 9 cass. (Running Time: 1 hr. 51 min. per cass.). 1985. 90.00 Set. (AR003) Big Sur Tapes.
Explores tarot symbols from psychological, mythological, & cross-cultural perspectives.

Beginning Tlingit. unabr. ed. 2 cass. (Running Time: 2 hrs.). bk. 55.00 Set. (AFTL50) J Norton Pubs.

Beginning Worship Guitar & CD: Instruction for the Worship Musician. Sandy Hoffman. (ENG., 2000. spiral bd. 17.99 (978-1-883002-72-5(9)) Pub: Emerald WA. Dist(s): YWAM Pub

Beginning Worship Keyboard & CD: Instruction for the Worship Musician. Sandy Hoffman. (ENG., 2002. spiral bd. 18.99 (978-1-883002-92-3(3)) Pub: Emerald WA. Dist(s): YWAM Pub

Beginning Yoga. unabr. ed. Indra Devi. 1 cass. (Running Time: 47 min.). 12.95 (31021) J Norton Pubs.
Devi explains basic asanas with step-by-step directions, breathing instruction & directions for all basic exercises.

Beginnings. (Dovetales Ser.: Tape 1). pap. bk. 6.95; 4.95 DonWise Prodns.

Beginnings. Robert Coover. Read by Robert Coover. 1 cass. (Running Time: 57 min.). 13.95 (978-1-55644-008-3(1), 1051) Am Audio Prose.

Beginnings, Vol. 3. Read by George W. Sarris. 1 cass. (World's Greatest Stories Ser.). 1995. 10.98 (978-1-57919-098-9(7)); audio compact disk 10.98 CD. (978-1-57919-094-1(4)) Randolf Prod.
Dramatic word-for-word readings of excerpts from the New International Version of the Bible. Includes In the Beginning, A Lame Man in Lystra, A Jailer in Philippi, Story of Ruth, & Raising of Lazarus.

Beginnings & Endings - Relaxing with Change. Ragini E. Michaels. Read by Ragini E. Michaels. Music by Divyam Ambodha. 1 cass. (Running Time: 30 min.). (Facticity Ser.). 1991. 14.95 (978-0-9628686-7-2(1), FTAT-201) Facticity Tr.
Relaxing & soothing reminder that change is natural & you can relax in this flow of change & its hidden pattern of movement from one extreme toward its seeming opposite & back again. Soothing combination of feminine voice & original music.

Beginnings KJV. Perf. by George W. Sarris. 5 CD's. (Running Time: about 1 hour each). (World's Greatest Stories Ser.: Volume 3). (J). 1993. audio compact disk 7.95 (978-0-9767744-7-1(X)) GWSPubs.
Bible stories read dramatically by George W. Sarris. The texts for all the stories are taken directly, word for word, from the King James Version Bible, with the addition of carefully selected music and sound effects. Vol 3 contains In the Beginning, The Book of Ruth, The Raising of Lazarus, A Lame Man in Lystra, The Philippian Jailer.

Beginnings K5 Phonics Songs CD. audio compact disk 15.50 (978-1-57924-851-2(9)) BJUPr.

Beginnings NIV. Perf. by George W. Sarris. 5 CD's. (Running Time: about 1 hour). (World's Greatest Stories Ser.: Volume 3). (J). 1993. audio compact disk 7.95 (978-0-9767744-2-6(9)) GWSPubs.
Bible stories read dramatically by George W. Sarris. The texts for all the stories are taken directly, word for word, from the New International Version Bible, with the addition of carefully selected music and sound effects. Vol 3 contains In the Beginning, The Book of Ruth, The Raising of Lazarus, A Lame Man in Lystra, The Philippian Jailer.

Beginnings of Judaism. Instructed by Isaiah M. Gafni. 2008. 129.95 (978-1-59803-396-0(4)); audio compact disk 69.95 (978-1-59803-397-7(2)) Teaching Co.

Beginnings of Our Nation. unabr. ed. Kenneth Bruce. 2 cass. (History Alive! Ser.). (J). (gr. 3 up). 14.95 (S19080) J Norton Pubs.
Allows children today to relive yesterday's events through dramatic recreations by a storyteller & historian.

Beginnings of the Church. Raymond E. Brown. (Running Time: 4 hrs. 20 min.). 2004. 39.00 (978-1-904756-00-2(X)) STL Dist NA.

Beguilement. unabr. ed. Lois McMaster Bujold. Read by Bernadette Dunne. (Running Time: 43200 sec.). (Sharing Knife Ser.). 2007. 72.95 (978-1-4332-0622-1(6)); audio compact disk 29.95 (978-1-4332-0624-5(2)); audio compact disk 90.00 (978-1-4332-0623-8(4)) Blckstn Audio.

Behavioral Response to Intervention: Creating a Continuum of Problem-Solving & Support. Randy Sprick et al. (Randy Sprick's Safe & Civil School Ser.). 2009. pap. bk. (978-1-59909-028-3(7)) Pac North Pub.

Behavioral Science in Dentistry. Leonard G. Horowitz. Read by Leonard G. Horowitz. 1 cass. (Running Time: 60 min.). 1990. 12.95 (978-0-9609386-9-8(9)) Tetrahedron Pub.
What dental professionals need to know about their patients, practice & themselves to achieve excellence.

Behaviorism at Fifty. unabr. ed. B. F. Skinner. Read by B. F. Skinner. 1 cass. (Running Time: 1 hr.). 12.95 (29044) J Norton Pubs.
Skinner discusses behaviorism as a philosophy of science concerned with the subject & methods of psychology.

***Behemoth.** unabr. ed. Scott Westerfeld. Read by Alan Cumming. (Running Time: 9 hrs. 30 mins. 0 sec.). Bk. 2. (ENG.). (YA). 2010. audio compact disk 34.99 (978-1-4423-3410-6(X)) Pub: S&S Audio. Dist(s): S and S Inc

Behind Closed Doors. 2004. 9.99 (978-1-58602-204-4(0)) E L Long.

Behind closed Doors. 2004. audio compact disk 19.99 (978-1-58602-205-1(9)) E L Long.

Behind Closed Doors. abr. ed. Francis A. Quinn. Read by Charlie O'Dowd. 2001. (978-1-58807-083-8(2)) Am Pubng Inc.

Behind Eclaire's Doors. unabr. ed. Sophie Dunbar. Read by Lynda Evans. 6 cass. (Running Time: 7 hrs. 12 min.). (Claire & Dan Claiborne Eclaire Mystery Ser.: Bk. 1). 1998. 39.95 (978-1-55686-804-7(9)) Books in Motion.
On a summer night in New Orleans, Claire finds her ex-husband with another woman. She was shocked upon discovering that the woman with her ex was dead & everything points to his guilt. Clair is determined to find the truth.

Behind Every Great Man: Hebrews 11:32. Ed Young. 1992. 4.95 (978-0-7417-1929-4(0), 929) Win Walk.

Behind Russian Lines. unabr. collector's ed. Sandy Gall. Read by John MacDonald. 8 cass. (Running Time: 8 hrs.). 1986. 48.00 (978-0-7366-0888-6(5), 1832) Books on Tape.
In the summer of 1942, Sandy Gall set off for Afghanistan on the hardest assignment of his life. During his career as a reporter, he had covered wars & revolutions, but he had never been required to walk all the way to an assignment & back again, dodging bombs.

Behind the Armor - Being with Pain. Stephen R. Schwartz. 1 cass. 10.00 Riverrun Piermont.

***Behind the Curtain: An Empire Falls Mystery.** unabr. ed. Peter Abrahams. Read by Colleen Delany. (ENG.). 2006. (978-0-06-113514-9(3), Harper Audio); (978-0-06-113515-6(1), Harper Audio) HarperCollins Pubs.

Behind the Horizon see Mas Alla Del Horizonte: Visiones del Nuevo Milenio

Behind the Lines. abr. ed. W. E. B. Griffin. Read by Dick Hill. 3 CDs. (Running Time: 3 hrs.). (Corps Ser.: Bk. 7). 2002. audio compact disk 14.99 (978-1-59086-457-9(3), 1590864573, CD Value Edn); audio compact disk 62.25 (978-1-59086-458-6(1), 1590864581, CD Lib Edit) Brilliance Audio.
World War II. On the island of Mindanao, the Philippines, a man calling himself "General" Fertig has set himself up as a guerrilla leader to harass the Japanese. Army records show that the only officer named Fertig in the Philippines is a reserve lieutenant colonel of the Corps of Engineers, reported MIA on Luzon. Still, the reports filtering out are interesting, and it's Marine lieutenant Ken McCoy's mission to sneak behind the lines and find out if he's for real. With him is a motley group put together as a compromise between the warring factions of Douglas MacArthur and the OSS chief Bill Donovan. Together, these men will steal into the heart of enemy territory and there, amid firefights and jungle camps, encounter more than they had bargained for. Before they're done, each will undergo a test of his own personal mettle - with results that will surprise even the most hardened of them.

Behind the Lines. unabr. ed. W. E. B. Griffin. Read by Michael Russotto. 13 cass. (Running Time: 19 hrs. 30 mins.). (Corps Ser.: No. 7). 1996. 104.00 (978-0-7366-3307-9(3), 3961) Books on Tape.
On a Philippine island, reports say that an MIA army officer has resurfaced as a self-named leader of guerrillas against the Japanese. Ken McCoy, Marine lieutenant, must sneak behind the lines to take him out. But he's got to take with him a motley team of veterans, assembled as a compromise between General MacArthur, who doesn't believe the reports, & O.S.S. Chief Bill Donovan, who wants control of the operation.

Behind the Lines, unabr. ed. W. E. B. Griffin. Read by Dick Hill. 12 cass. (Running Time: 18 hrs.). (Corps Ser.: No. 7). 1996. 105.25 (978-1-56100-308-2(5), 1561003085, Unabridge Lib Edns) Brilliance Audio.
World War II. On the island of Mindanao, the Philippines, a man calling himself "General" Fertig has set himself up as a guerrilla leader to harass the Japanese. Army records show that the only officer named Fertig in the Philippines is a reserve lieutenant colonel of the Corps of Engineers, reported MIA on Luzon. Still, the reports filtering out are interesting, and it's Marine lieutenant Ken McCoy's mission to sneak behind the lines and find out if he's for real. With him is a motley group put together as a compromise between the warring factions of Douglas MacArthur and the OSS chief Bill Donovan. Together, these men will steal into the heart of enemy territory and there, amid firefights and jungle camps, encounter more than they had bargained for. Before they're done, each will undergo a test of his own personal mettle - with results that will surprise even the most hardened of them.

Behind the Lines. unabr. ed. W. E. B. Griffin. Read by Dick Hill. (Running Time: 18 hrs.). (Corps Ser.: Bk. 7). 2005. 29.95 (978-1-59737-943-4(3), 9781597379434, BAD); audio compact disk 44.25 (978-1-59737-942-7(5), 9781597379427, Brlnc Audio MP3 Lib) Brilliance Audio.

Behind the Lines. unabr. ed. Dick Hill. Read by Dick Hill. (Running Time: 18 hrs.). (Corps Ser.). 2005. 44.25 (978-1-59737-944-1(1), 9781597379441, BADLE); audio compact disk 127.25 (978-1-59737-946-5(8), 9781597379465, BriAudCD Unabrid); audio compact disk 42.95 (978-1-59737-945-8(X), 9781597379458, Bril Audio CD Unabri); audio compact disk 29.95 (978-1-59737-725-6(2), 9781597377256, Brilliance MP3) Brilliance Audio.

Behind the Lines: Powerful & Revealing American & Foreign War Letters & One Man's Search to Find Them. abr. ed. Andrew Carroll. Read by Dion Graham et al. 2005. 15.95 (978-0-7435-5198-4(2)) Pub: S&S Audio. Dist(s): S and S Inc

Behind the Lines, Honor Bound, the Murderers. abr. ed. W. E. B. Griffin. Read by Dick Hill. 6 cass. (Running Time: 9 hrs.). 2001. 19.95 (978-1-58788-745-1(2), 1587887452, Nova Audio Bks) Brilliance Audio.
Behind the Lines World War II. On the island of Mindanao, the Philippines, a man calling himself "General" Fertig has set himself up as a guerrilla leader to harass the Japanese. Army records show that the only officer named Fertig in the Philippines is a reserve lieutenant colonel of the Corps of Engineers, reported MIA on Luzon. Still, the reports filtering out are interesting, and it's Marine lieutenant Ken McCoy's mission to sneak behind the lines and find out if he's for real. Honor Bound It's 1942. First Lieutenant Cletus Frade is fresh from Guadalcanal. He teams up with Second Lieutenant Anthony Pelosi and Sergeant David Ettinger for the most critical OSS operation of the war. Under the direction of the mysterious Colonel Loman, they venture into a simmering stew of German and Allied agents, collaborators, and government security thugs, of men and women hiding their pasts and plotting their futures - all in supposedly neutral city of Buenos Aires. The Murderers A cop is found shot dead in his home - is it connected to corruption in the narcotics division? A bar owner and his partner's wife are in the wrong place at the wrong time and are gunned down together - was it a mob hit? A beautiful, well-connected young woman dies an ugly death in her parents mansion - was it accidental? It's up to Special Operations Division detectives Washington, Payne, and their crew to piece it together and do it quickly.

Behind the Musik (a Boy Name Jonah) Contrib. by KJ-52. Prod. by Aaron Sprinkle et al. 2005. audio compact disk 16.98 (978-5-558-69460-4(2)) BEC Recordings.

Behind the Scenes. Jeni Grossman. 3 cass. 2004. 14.95 (978-1-59156-046-3(2)) Covenant Comms.

Behind the Scenes. Elizabeth Keckley. Read by Anais 9000. 2009. 27.95 (978-1-60112-217-9(9)) Babblebooks.

Behind the Scenes: Or, Thirty Years a Slave, & Four Years in the White House. abr. ed. Elizabeth H. Keckley. Read by Ameria Jones. 2 cass. (Running Time: 3 hrs.). 1996. 16.95 (978-0-9645593-8-7(2)) MasterBuy Audio Bks.
Fictional account of an African-American woman who spent the first 30 years of her life as a slave & later became dressmaker & "best" friend to Mary Todd Lincoln, wife of the President Abraham Lincoln. Her memoir gives an insider's view of the Lincoln White House & America during the Civil War period.

Behind the Scenes at the Museum: A Novel. unabr. ed. Kate Atkinson. Read by Susan Jameson. 10 cass. (Running Time: 10 hrs.). 1997. 84.95 (978-0-7451-6749-7(7), CAB 1365) AudioGO.
Ruby Lennox was born by her mother Bunty while her father, George, was off in a Doncaster pub. Bunty had never wanted to marry George, but he was all that was left. She had wanted to be swept off to America by a romantic hero. But here she was, stuck in a flat beneath York Minster, with sensible Patricia aged five, greedy Gillian who refuses to be ignored, & Ruby, who tells the memorable & eventful story of The Family.

Behind the Scenes: Views of Shakespeare: Shakespeare & His Theater. Read by Daniel Seltzer. 1 cass. (Running Time: 1 hr.). 11.95 (A108CB090, HarperThor) HarpC GBR.

Behind the Scenes: Views of Shakespeare: Shakespeare in Our Time. Read by Maynard Mack. 1 cass. (Running Time: 1 hr.). 11.95 (A108AB090, HarperThor) HarpC GBR.

Behind the Scenes: Views of Shakespeare: Shakespeare the Man. Read by Samuel Schoenbaum. 1 cass. (Running Time: 1 hr.). 11.95 (A108BB090, HarperThor) HarpC GBR.

Behind the Veil. unabr. ed. Lydia Laube. Read by Deidre Rubenstein. 5 cass. (Running Time: 7 hrs. 30 mins.). 1998. (978-1-86340-647-5(6), 560511) Bolinda Pubng AUS.
Lydia, an Australian nurse, worked in Saudi Arabia, in a society that does not allow women to drive, vote, or speak to a man alone. Wearing head-to-toe coverings in stifling heat, & battling administrative apathy, she kept her sanity & got her passport back.

Behind the Wall: A Journey Though China. unabr. collector's ed. Colin Thubron. Read by Richard Brown. 10 cass. (Running Time: 15 hrs.). 1990. 80.00 (978-0-7366-1701-7(9), 2546) Books on Tape.
Behind the Wall is a book as monumental as its subject: "the land of a billion uncomprehended people." Having learned Mandarin, & traveling alone by foot, bicycle & train, Colin Thubron set off on a 10,000 mile journey from Bejing to Tibet, from a tropical paradise near the Burmese border to the windswept wastes of the Gobi desert & the far end of the Great Wall. What he reveals is an astonishing diversity, a land whose still unmeasured resources strain to meet an awesome demand, & an ancient people still reeling from the devastation of the Cultural Revolution.

Behind the Wall: A Journey Through China. unabr. ed. Colin Thubron. Read by Garard Green. 12 cass. (Running Time: 18 hrs.). 1994. 94.95 (978-1-85089-467-4(1), 92021) Pub: ISIS Audio GBR. Dist(s): Ulverscroft US
Ranging from the Burmese frontier to the Gobi desert, from the Yellow Sea to the edge of Tibet, this is a mosaic of scenes & encounters, written in a lyrical, almost poetic, style.

Behind the Wheel - Arabic 1. unabr. ed. Behind the Wheel. (Running Time: 8 hrs. 0 mins. 0 sec.). (ENG.). 2009. audio compact disk 49.95 (978-1-4272-0647-3(3)) Pub: Macmill Audio. Dist(s): Macmillan

Behind the Wheel - French 1. unabr. ed. Behind the Wheel. (Running Time: 8 hrs. 0 mins. 0 sec.). (ENG.). 2008. audio compact disk 49.95 (978-1-4272-0557-5(4)) Pub: Macmill Audio. Dist(s): Macmillan

Behind the Wheel - French 2. unabr. ed. Behind the Wheel. (Running Time: 8 hrs. 0 mins. 0 sec.). (ENG.). 2009. audio compact disk 49.95 (978-1-4272-0718-0(6)) Pub: Macmill Audio. Dist(s): Macmillan

Behind the Wheel - German 1. unabr. ed. Behind the Wheel. (Running Time: 8 hrs. 0 mins. 0 sec.). (ENG.). 2009. audio compact disk 49.95 (978-1-4272-0716-6(X)) Pub: Macmill Audio. Dist(s): Macmillan

Behind the Wheel - German 2. unabr. ed. Created by Mark Frobose. (Running Time: 8 hrs. 0 mins. 0 sec.). (ENG.). 2009. audio compact disk 49.99 (978-1-4272-0824-8(7)) Pub: Macmill Audio. Dist(s): Macmillan

Behind the Wheel - Italian 1. unabr. ed. Behind the Wheel. (Running Time: 8 hrs. 0 mins. 0 sec.). (ENG.). 2008. audio compact disk 49.95 (978-1-4272-0558-2(2)) Pub: Macmill Audio. Dist(s): Macmillan

Behind the Wheel - Italian 2. unabr. ed. Behind the Wheel. (Running Time: 8 hrs. 0 mins. 0 sec.). (ENG.). 2009. audio compact disk 49.99 (978-1-4272-0761-6(5)) Pub: Macmill Audio. Dist(s): Macmillan

Behind the Wheel - Japanese 1. unabr. ed. Behind the Wheel. Created by Mark Frobose. (Running Time: 8 hrs. 0 mins. 0 sec.). (ENG.). 2009. audio compact disk 49.99 (978-1-4272-0722-7(4)) Pub: Macmill Audio. Dist(s): Macmillan

Behind the Wheel - Portuguese 1. unabr. ed. Behind the Wheel. (Running Time: 8 hrs. 0 mins. 0 sec.). (ENG.). 2009. audio compact disk 49.95 (978-1-4272-0645-9(7)) Pub: Macmill Audio. Dist(s): Macmillan

Behind the Wheel - Russian 1. unabr. ed. Behind the Wheel. Created by Mark Frobose. (Running Time: 8 hrs. 0 mins. 0 sec.). (ENG.). 2009. audio compact disk 49.99 (978-1-4272-0720-3(8)) Pub: Macmill Audio. Dist(s): Macmillan

Behind the Wheel - Spanish 1. unabr. ed. Behind the Wheel. Created by Mark Frobose. (Running Time: 8 hrs. 0 mins. 0 sec.). (ENG.). 2008. audio compact disk 49.95 (978-1-4272-0555-1(8)) Pub: Macmill Audio. Dist(s): Macmillan

Behind the Wheel - Spanish 2. unabr. ed. Created by Mark Frobose. (Running Time: 8 hrs. 0 mins. 0 sec.). (ENG.). 2008. audio compact disk 49.95 (978-1-4272-0556-8(6)) Pub: Macmill Audio. Dist(s): Macmillan

Behind the Wheel Arabic: Learn at Home or in Your Car! Mark A. Frobose. 8 CDs. (Running Time: 28800 sec.). 2004. pap. bk. 69.00 (978-1-893564-97-8(5)) Macmill Audio.

Behind the Wheel Chinese. Mark A. Frobose. 8 CDs. (Running Time: 14400 sec.). 2004. audio compact disk 69.00 (978-1-893564-45-9(2)) Macmill Audio.

Behind the Wheel Chinese (Mandarin) / Cassette Version Vol. 2: 8 One Hour Cassettes. Mark Frobose. 8 CDs. 2004. audio compact disk 69.00 (978-1-893564-60-2(6)) Macmill Audio.

Behind the Wheel Express - French 1. unabr. ed. Behind the Wheel Staff. Created by Mark Frobose. 3 CDs. (Running Time: 3 hrs.). 2010. audio compact disk 19.99 (978-1-4272-0927-6(8)) Pub: Macmill Audio. Dist(s): Macmillan

Behind the Wheel Express - Italian 1. unabr. ed. Behind the Wheel. Created by Mark Frobose. 3 CDs. (Running Time: 3 hrs.). 2010. audio compact disk 19.99 (978-1-4272-0929-0(4)) Pub: Macmill Audio. Dist(s): Macmillan

Behind the Wheel Express - Spanish 1. unabr. ed. Behind the Wheel. Created by Mark Frobose. 3 CDs. (Running Time: 3 hrs.). 2010. audio compact disk 19.99 (978-1-4272-0925-2(1)) Pub: Macmill Audio. Dist(s): Macmillan

Behind the Wheel French. Mark Frobose. 8 CDs. (Running Time: 8 hrs.). 2003. audio compact disk 59.00 (978-1-893564-78-7(9)) Macmill Audio.

Behind the Wheel French for Your Car: Complete Learning Guide & Tapescript. Mark Frobose. 8 cass. (Running Time: 8 hrs.). (FRE.). 2006. 59.00 (978-1-893564-68-8(1)) Macmill Audio.

Behind the Wheel German: 6 One Hour CDs. Mark Frobose. 2003. audio compact disk 49.00 (978-1-893564-99-2(1)) Macmill Audio.

Behind the Wheel Italian. Mark Frobose. 6 CDs. (Running Time: 6 hrs.). 2003. audio compact disk 49.00 (978-1-893564-53-4(3)) Macmill Audio.

Behind the Wheel Italian for Your Car: Complete Learning Guide & Tapescript. Mark Frobose. 6 cass. (Running Time: 6 hrs.). (ITA.). 1999. stu. ed. 49.00 (978-1-893564-69-5(X)) Macmill Audio.

Behind the Wheel Portuguese. Mark A. Frobose. 8 CDs. (Running Time: 8 hrs.). 2004. audio compact disk 29.00 (978-1-893564-92-3(4)) Macmill Audio.

Behind the Wheel Spanish. Mark Frobose. 8 CDs. (SPA.). 2002. pap. bk. & stu. ed. 69.00 (978-1-893564-42-8(8)) Macmill Audio.

Behind the Wheel Spanish for Your Car: Complete Learning Guide & Tapescript. Mark Frobose. 8 cass. (Running Time: 8 hrs.). (SPA.). 1999. st. ed. 59.00 (978-1-893564-67-1(3)) Macmill Audio.

Behind the Wheel Spanish Learn at Home or in Your Car. Mark Frobose. (SPA.). 2002. per. & wbk. ed. 24.99 (978-1-893564-32-9(0)) Macmill Audio.

Behind the Wheel Spanish 2 - Level 2. unabr. ed. Mark A. Frobose. 8 CDs. (Running Time: 8 hrs.). 2004. audio compact disk 69.00 (978-1-893564-33-6(9)) Macmill Audio.

Behold. abr. ed. Word Among Us Press Staff. 2005. audio compact disk 16.95 (978-0-932085-71-9(7)) Word Among Us.

Behold, Bless Ye the Lord. Created by Maranatha! Music. (Praise Ser.). 1999. audio compact disk 6.98 (978-7-01-610284-3(X)) Maranatha Music.

Behold, Here's Poison. unabr. ed. Georgette Heyer. Read by Hugh Dickson. 6 cass. (Running Time: 9 hrs). 2002. 29.95 (978-1-57270-202-8(8), Audio Editions) Pub: Audio Partners. Dist(s): PerseuPGW
Inspector Hannasyde faces the deadliest test of his career when members of the wealthy Matthews clan begin to die, one by one. With motives everywhere, it is no easy case for the inspector to solve.

Behold, Here's Poison. unabr. ed. Georgette Heyer. Read by Hugh Dickson. 6 cass. (Running Time: 8 hrs. 15 min.). (Inspector Hannasyide Mysteries Ser.). 1992. 54.95 set. (978-0-7451-6007-8(7), CAB 687) AudioGO.
Take one rambling country house whose owner is found dead - supposedly poisoned. Add one ill-assorted family circle of very odd people - all excellent motives for murder. Introduce the one & only Superintendent Hannasyde facing the deadliest test of his career. Stir well. It adds up to another classic of detection from the incomparable Georgette Heyer.

Behold, I Give You Power. Joyce Meyer. 8 cass. (Running Time: 8 hrs.). 2001. 40.00 (TJM-122) Harrison Hse.
Far too many believers are fainthearted, weak in determination and diseased with an "I can't" attitude - they are lacking in power! Do you desire to be a powerful believer? You don't have to beg God to give you power. You just need to start noticing that you have been given power and then walk in what is already yours!.

Behold that Star. Skipper. 1997. 8.00 (978-0-7673-3294-1(6)) LifeWay Christian.

Behold That Star. Greg Skipper. 1997. 11.98 (978-0-7673-3292-7(X)); 40.00 (978-0-7673-3291-0(1)) LifeWay Christian.

Behold That Star! Preview Pack. Composed by Sally K. Albrecht & Jay Althouse. (ENG.). 2002. audio compact disk 12.95 (978-0-7390-2373-0(X)) Alfred Pub.

Behold That Star Cassette Kit. Greg Skipper. 1997. 54.95 (978-0-7673-3295-8(4)) LifeWay Christian.

***Behold the Bold Umbrellaphant.** abr. ed. Jack Prelutsky. Read by Jack Prelutsky. (ENG.). 2006. (978-0-06-135100-6(8), GreenwillowBks) HarperCollins Pubs.

***Behold the Bold Umbrellaphant: And Other Poems.** unabr. ed. Jack Prelutsky. Read by Jack Prelutsky. (ENG.). 2006. (978-0-06-134823-5(6), GreenwillowBks); (978-0-06-134824-2(4), GreenwillowBks) HarperCollins Pubs.

***Behold the Bold Umbrellaphant: And Other Poems.** unabr. ed. Jack Prelutsky. Read by Jack Prelutsky. (ENG.). 2007. (978-0-06-153698-4(9), GreenwillowBks) HarperCollins Pubs.

Behold the Bold Umbrellaphant CD: And Other Poems. unabr. ed. Poems. Jack Prelutsky. Read by Jack Prelutsky. 1 CD. (Running Time: 3600 sec.). (J). (ps-6). 2006. 13.95 (978-0-06-114046-4(5), HarperChildAud) HarperCollins Pubs.

Behold the Lamb: Young People's Music & Readings for Lent & Easter. Mark Friedman & Janet Vogt. Read by Mark Friedman & Janet Vogt. 1 cass. (J). (gr. k-12). 1997. 12.95 (10375) OR Catholic.
Scripture readings & songs for use in religious education classes and liturgies with children.

Behold the Lamb Set: Young People's Music & Readings for Lent & Easter. Mark Friedman & Janet Vogt. Read by Mark Friedman & Janet Vogt. 2 CDs. (J). (gr. k-12). 1997. audio compact disk 19.95 (10376) OR Catholic.
Scripture readings & songs for us in religious education classes and liturgies with children.

Behold the Man. Gerald N. Lund. Read by Larry A. McKeever. (Running Time: 81900 sec.). (Kingdom & the Crown Ser.). 2008. audio compact disk 49.95 (978-1-59038-941-6(7), Shadow Mount) Deseret Bk.

***Behold the Man: Exalting the Christ of Easter.** Created by Lillenas Publishing Company. (ENG.). 2008. audio compact disk 12.00 (978-5-557-37025-7(0)) Lillenas.

***Behold the Man: Exalting the Christ of Easter.** Contrib. by Joseph Linn. (ENG.). 2008. audio compact disk 90.00 (978-5-557-37026-4(9)) Lillenas.

Behold the Messiah; After-Death Wills. Ann Ree Colton & Jonathan Murro. 1 cass. 7.95 A R Colton Fnd.

Behold Your God: The Sovereignty of God. Ben Young. 1997. 4.95 (978-0-7417-6045-6(2), B0045) Win Walk.

Behold Your Life: 28 Guided Meditations. Macrina Wiederkehr. Composed by Jose Tharakan. 2 CDs. (Running Time: 2 hrs. 23 mins.). 2001. audio compact disk 24.95 (978-0-87793-961-0(6)) Ave Maria Pr.

Behold Your Little Ones. 2004. audio compact disk 14.95 (978-1-59156-326-6(7)) Covenant Comms.

Behold Your Little Ones. Richard Smith & Susan Evans McCloud. 1 cass. 9.95 (10001131); audio compact disk 14.95 (2800780) Covenant Comms.
A choral/symphonic masterpiece.

Beholding Christ, the Son of God. 2003. audio compact disk 42.00 (978-1-57972-529-7(5)) Insight Living.

Beholding Christ... the Son of God. unabr. ed. Charles R. Swindoll. 8 cass. (Running Time: 6 hrs. 30 mins.). 2000. 39.95 (978-1-57972-331-6(4)) Insight Living.

Beholding the One in All. Paramhansa Yogananda. 9.50 (978-0-87612-431-4(7)) Self Realization.

Beholding the One in All. Paramhansa Yogananda. 1985. 9.50 (2012) Self Realization.
With illustrations from the Indian scriptures, humorous & instructive incidents from his own life, & insights flowing from his direct perception of Truth, the author shows that there is one great theme of creation & a single purpose behind all that happens to us: to coax us to look beyond the illusions of this transitory life & discover the glory & the love of God.

Beholding the One in All. Paramhansa Yogananda. (Running Time: 33 mins.). 2007. audio compact disk 14.00 (978-0-87612-444-4(9)) Self Realization.

Beholding the Priesthood. Eugene LaVerdiere. 3 cass. (Running Time: 2 hrs. 27 min.). 1995. 27.95 Set. (TAH346) Alba Hse Comns.
In this three part audio cassette series delivered as a conference for priests, Fr. Laverdiere examines the priesthood from the perspective of scripture, & brings to light several engaging realities that will help to enliven the ministerial efforts of today's priests.

Beijing Conspiracy. Adrian d'Hagé. Read by Jim Daly. (Running Time: 14 hrs. 10 mins.). 2009. 99.99 (978-1-74214-223-4(0), 9781742142234) Pub: Bolinda Pubng AUS. Dist(s): Bolinda Pub Inc

Beijing Conspiracy. unabr. ed. Adrian d'Hagé. Read by Jim Daly. (Running Time: 14 hrs. 10 mins.). 2009. 43.95 (978-1-74214-148-0(X), 9781742141480) Pub: Bolinda Pubng AUS. Dist(s): Bolinda Pub Inc

Beijing Conspiracy: Terror Has a New Weapon. unabr. ed. Adrian D'Hage. Read by Jim Daly. (Running Time: 51000 sec.). 2008. audio compact disk 108.95 (978-1-921334-85-6(1), 9781921334856) Pub: Bolinda Pubng AUS. Dist(s): Bolinda Pub Inc

Bein' a Grandparent Ain't for Wimps: Loving, Spoiling, & Sending Your Grandkids Home. unabr. ed. Karen O'Connor. Narrated by Karen O'Connor. (Running Time: 3 hrs. 14 mins. 52 sec.). (ENG.). 2009. 13.99 (978-1-60814-496-9(8)) Oasis Audio.

Bein' a Grandparent Ain't for Wimps: Loving, Spoiling, & Sending Your Grandkids Home. unabr. ed. Karen O'Connor & Karen O'Connor. Read by Karen O'Connor. Narrated by Karen O'Connor. (Running Time: 3 hrs. 14 mins. 52 sec.). (ENG.). 2009. audio compact disk 19.99 (978-1-59859-482-9(6)) Oasis Audio.

Bein' with You This Way see Alegria de Ser Tu y Yo

Bein' with You This Way see Alegria de Ser Tu y Yo, Grades K-3

Bein' with You This Way. W. Nikola-Lisa. (Running Time: 7 mins.). 1999. 9.95 (978-0-87499-548-0(5)) Pub: Live Oak Media. Dist(s): Lectorum Pubns

Bein' with You This Way. W. Nikola-Lisa. Illus. by Michael Bryant. 11 vols. (Running Time: 7 mins.). 2001. bk. 28.95 (978-1-59112-427-6(1)) Live Oak Media.

Bein' with You This Way. W. Nikola-Lisa. Perf. by Shayla Narvaez et al. 11 vols. (Running Time: 7 mins.). (Live Oak Readalong Ser.). (J). 2001. pap. bk. 18.95 (978-1-59112-400-9(X)) Pub: Live Oak Media. Dist(s): AudioGO

Bein' with You This Way. W Nikola-Lisa. Perf. by Shayla Narvaez et al. Illus. by Michael Bryant. 11 vols. (Running Time: 7 mins.). (SPA.). (J). (gr. k-3). 1999. bk. 25.95 (978-0-87499-546-6(9)); pap. bk. 16.95 (978-0-87499-545-9(0)) Pub: Live Oak Media. Dist(s): AudioGO
An exuberant story. The cheerful faces & colorful outdoor scenes, harmonize so well with the bouncy rapping that children will clamor for an immediate reread.

Bein with You this Way. W. Nikola-Lisa. Illus. by Michael Bryant. (Running Time: 7 mins.). 1999. audio compact disk 12.95 (978-1-59112-399-6(2)) Live Oak Media.

Bein' with You This Way. Cynthia Rylant. 1 cass. (Running Time: 35 min.). (J). (ps-3). 2001. pap. bk. 15.95 Kimbo Educ.
An exuberant playground rap that introduces children to how people are different, yet the same. Includes readalong book.

Bein' with You This Way - La Alegria de Ser Tu y Yo. unabr. ed. W. Nikola-Lisa. Tr. by Yanitzia Ganetti. Illus. by Michael Bryant. 22 vols. (Running Time: 14 mins.). (SPA & ENG.). (J). (gr. k-3). 1999. pap. bk. 33.95 (978-0-87499-561-9(2)) Live Oak Media.

Bein with You this Way cassette LC-751CS. W. Nikola-Lisa. Illus. by Michael Bryant. 9.95 (978-1-59112-498-6(0)) Live Oak Media.

Bein' with You This Way, Grades K-3. W Nikola-Lisa. Perf. by Shayla Narvaez et al. Illus. by Michael Bryant. 14 vols. (Running Time: 7 mins.). (SPA.). (J). 1999. pap. bk. & tchr. ed. 37.95 Reading Chest. (978-0-87499-547-3(7)) Live Oak Media.
An exuberant story. The cheerful faces & colorful outdoor scenes, harmonize so well with the bouncy rapping that children will clamor for an immediate reread.

Being. Paul R. Scheele. Read by Paul R. Scheele. 1 cass. (Running Time: 34 min.). (Personal Celebration Tapes Ser.). 1991. 9.95 (978-0-925480-75-0(4)) Learn Strategies.
A tape to celebrate being all that you are & all that you can become.

Being: A 30 Day Guide to Being Who God Made You to Be. Corey / Donnell Tabor. Read by Corey / Donnell Tabor. Engineer Kevin/Marlon Scott. (ENG.). 2008. 20.00 (978-0-9819377-2-4(1)) III Coaching.

Being: Without Projections. Swami Amar Jyoti. 1 dolby cass. 1984. 9.95 (R-60) Truth Consciousness.
Doing, but not as "the doer." Without the entrapment of projections, everything happens as it should. Earth as a creature. The wisdom of regeneration.

Being a Boy. unabr. collector's ed. Paxton Davis. Read by Wolfram Kandinsky. 6 cass. (Running Time: 9 hrs.). 1991. 48.00 (978-0-7366-2035-2(4), 2849) Books on Tape.
In the days before television & supervised athletics, boys had to create their own amusements. In the Great Depression, when Paxton Davis grew up, this was doubly so. Times & circumstances change, but there is always something to be celebrated in a boyhood fondly remembered, always something to be moumed in its passing.

Being a Celestial Partner. Neal A. Maxwell. 1 CD. audio compact disk 10.98 (978-1-57734-117-8(1), 2500779) Covenant Comms.
Excellent talk on family & fathers' blessings.

Being a Celestial Partner. Neal A. Maxwell. 1 cass. 2004. 7.98 (978-1-55503-093-3(9), 06002316) Covenant Comms.
Excellent talk on family & father's blessings. Collector's Edition.

Being a Child of God. Read by Wayne Monbleau. 2 cass. (Running Time: 3 hrs.). 1994. 10.00 Set. (978-0-944648-33-9(9), LGT-1232) Loving Grace Pubns.
Religious.

Being a Good Disciple. Swami Amar Jyoti. Read by Swami Amar Jyoti. 2 cass. 1978. 12.95 (E-13) Truth Consciousness.
Being a true Master comes only after Awakening, not before. How to be a good disciple first.

Being a Good Governor. Ronald Reagan. Interview with William F. Buckley, Jr. 1 CD. (Running Time: 50 mins.). 2005. audio compact disk 12.95 (978-1-57970-236-6(8), C32063D) J Norton Pubs.

Being a Green Mother. Piers Anthony. Narrated by Barbara Caruso. 11 CDs. (Running Time: 12 hrs. 45 mins.). (Incarnations of Immortality Ser.: Bk. 5). 2001. audio compact disk 111.00 (978-0-7887-5172-1(7), C1334E7) Recorded Bks.
Follows the adventures of Orb, a young girl with a magical gift for music. But when she sets off in search of the land of Llano to find the mystic music that controls all things, she finds herself waylaid by news from her mother, Fate: Orb has been chosen as the new Incarnation of Nature, the Green Mother.

Being a Green Mother. unabr. ed. Piers Anthony. Narrated by Barbara Caruso. 9 cass. (Running Time: 12 hrs. 45 mins.). (Incarnations of Immortality Ser.: Bk. 5). 1987. 81.00 (978-0-7887-4377-1(5), 96003E7) Recorded Bks.

Being a Man of God in Today's World: Proceedings of the 45th Annual Convention National Association of Evangelicals Buffalo, New York. Read by Ted DeMoss. 1 cass. (Running Time: 60 min.). 1987. 4.00 (343) Nat Assn Evan.

Being a Missionary, Set. Ed Pinegar. 6 cass. 1997. 19.95 Set. (978-1-57734-038-6(8), 3444686) Covenant Comms.
The missionary set guaranteed to enhance your mission experience.

Being a Real Woman. Elisabeth Elliot. Read by Elisabeth Elliot. 4 cass. (Running Time: 4 hrs.). 1988. 18.95 (978-0-8474-2001-8(9)) Back to Bible.
Answers four issues: Whose am I? Being masters of ourselves; defining a real woman; & understanding God's assignment.

Being a Sales Rep: Winning Secrets to a Successful & Profitable Career. abr. ed. Ruth Klein. Narrated by Rick Plastina. (Everything Bks.). (ENG.). 2007. 13.99 (978-1-60814-184-5(5)) Oasis Audio.

Being & Doing: The Complete Guide to a Successful Psychotherapy Practice. Bill Kerley. 2000. 39.95 (978-1-886298-07-1(6)) Bayou Pubng.

Being Assertive & Owning Your Life. 1 CD. (Running Time: 25 minutes). 2000. 14.95 (978-0-9779472-5-6(4)) Health Wealth Inc.
This is the kind of recording that will benefit everyone, especially the shy and quiet types. Whatever you see and believe as a person has validity. This recording gives the permission needed so you can stand up and express your perspective in a positive light. It suggests that we all have the power to be our own person, and it is our individuality which is the sacred thing in life. Learning to be assertive, rather than repressing our emotions or thoughts, opens doors and new opportunities. You will discover how much better you feel about yourself when able to come out of the closet so to speak, and just own who you really are.

Being at Peace with Yourself. Speeches. Joel Osteen. 1 cass. (Running Time: 30 Mins.). 2002. 6.00 (978-1-59349-159-8(X), JA0159) J Osteen.

Being Awkward Can Be a Prophylactic Against Dry Humping (an Essay from Things I've Learned from Women Who've Dumped Me) abr. ed. Matt Goodman. Read by Matt Goodman. Ed. by Ben Karlin. (Running Time: 15 mins.). (ENG.). 2008. 1.98 (978-1-60024-348-6(7)) Pub: Hachet Audio. Dist(s): HachBkGrp

Being Cause: And not Effect. Gary Arnold. (ENG.). 2009. audio compact disk 24.95 (978-1-57867-024-6(1)) Windhorse Corp.

Being Connected to the Supernatural. Kenneth Copeland. 10 cass. 1995. 50.00 Set. (978-0-88114-973-9(X)) K Copeland Pubns.
Biblical teaching on the supernatural.

Being Conscious, Being Real. Swami Amar Jyoti. 1 dolby cass. 1986. 9.95 (M-68) Truth Consciousness.
Surrender of ego, ignorance & illusion in order to be what we really are.

Being Dead. unabr. ed. Jim Crace. Narrated by Virginia Leishman. 6 CDs. (Running Time: 7 hrs.). 2002. audio compact disk 58.00 (978-1-4025-1537-8(5)) Recorded Bks.
A middle-aged couple, Joseph and Celice, are murdered on a remote East Coast sand dune. They are not discovered for six days. Both doctors of zoology, Joseph and Celice would recognize what is happening to their decomposing bodies if they could have watched. They are dead, but they remain part of the living for a while as they become food, shelter, icons, and sources of emotional catharsis.

Being Dead. unabr. ed. Jim Crace. Narrated by Virginia Leishman. 5 cass. (Running Time: 7 hrs.). 2001. 64.00 (978-0-7887-9474-2(4)) Recorded Bks.
Six days after their death, the murdered bodies of a middle-aged couple are found in a remote sand dune.

Being Digital. unabr. ed. Nicholas Negroponte. 1 CD. 1999. audio compact disk 12.95 (44145) Books on Tape.
Wired magazine's popular columnist discusses the coming revolution in information technology that will liberate computers from the confines of keyboards & into objects that we talk to, drive with, touch, or even wear. These changes will transform how we learn, work, & entertain ourselves.

Being Elizabeth. abr. ed. Barbara Taylor Bradford. Read by Katherine Kellgren. 5 CDs. (Running Time: 6 hrs. 0 mins. 0 sec.). Bk. 3. (ENG.). 2008. audio compact disk 29.95 (978-1-4272-0530-8(2)) Pub: Macmill Audio. Dist(s): Macmillan

Being Elizabeth. unabr. ed. Barbara Taylor Bradford. Read by Katherine Kellgren. 11 CDs. (Running Time: 13 hrs. 30 mins. 0 sec.). Bk. 3. (ENG.). 2008. audio compact disk 44.95 (978-1-4272-0497-4(7)) Pub: Macmill Audio. Dist(s): Macmillan

Being Emily. Anne Donovan. 2009. 61.95 (978-0-7531-3872-4(7)); audio compact disk 79.95 (978-0-7531-3873-1(5)) Pub: Isis Pubng Ltd GBR. Dist(s): Ulverscroft US

Being Faithful in a Faithless World. Chuck Missler. 2 CDs. (Running Time: 120 mins.). (Briefing Packages by Chuck Missler). 1996. audio compact disk 19.95 (978-1-57821-290-3(1)) Koinonia Hse.
In a world of compromises, the Word of God gives us specific instruction on Godly stewardship.What does it mean to be faithful? What is a fiduciary? And who is the ultimate fiduciary? With a view from the corporate board room, Chuck Missler explores the Biblical requirements of both our personal and professional faithfulness. Many of our current social problems can be traced back to misunderstanding or ignorance of these basic Christian concepts.Chuck Missler has spent most of his career as a multi-national, corporate executive in the high-technology, defense industry specializing in corporate acquisition and rescue.

Being Fearless & Free: The Essential Laws of Peace, Power & Perfect Living. Guy Finley. (ENG.). 2009. 79.00 (978-1-929320-48-6(5)); audio compact disk 95.00 (978-1-929320-35-6(3)) Life of Learn.

Being God Conscious. Swami Amar Jyoti. 1 cass. 1978. 9.95 (G-8) Truth Consciousness.
Being conscious of God while living the life, then sitting in meditation. Applying the Karma Yoga spirit.

Being Human. Sundance/Newbridge, LLC Staff. (Early Science Ser.). (gr. k-3). 2007. audio compact disk 12.00 (978-1-4007-6515-7(3)); audio compact disk 12.00 (978-1-4007-6517-1(X)); audio compact disk 12.00 (978-1-4007-6516-4(1)) Sund Newbrdge.

Being in Balance: 9 Principles for Creating Habits to Match Your Desires. Doreen Virtue & Wayne W. Dyer. 2 CDs. 2006. audio compact disk 18.95 (978-1-4019-1071-6(8)) Hay House.

Being in Balance: 9 Principles for Creating Habits to Match Your Desires. unabr. ed. Wayne W. Dyer. Read by Wayne W. Dyer. (YA). 2007. 34.99 (978-1-60252-742-3(3)) Find a World.

Being in Light. Marianne Williamson. 4 CDs. 2003. audio compact disk 23.95 (978-1-4019-0141-7(7), 1417) Hay House.

Being in Light. abr. ed. Marianne Williamson. 4 cass. (Running Time: 4 hrs.). (ENG.). 1997. 30.00 (978-1-56170-271-8(4), M774) Hay House.
Lectures based on "A Course in Miracles" include: Self-Forgiveness/Meeting Yourself (Tape 1); Self-Esteem & Vulnerability/Being Authentic (Tape 2); Taking Yourself Seriously/Becoming Deep (Tape 3) & The Real You Enlightenment (Tape 4).

Being in the Success Zone. unabr. ed. Marcia Reynolds. 2 cass. (Running Time: 6 hrs.). (Smart Audio Ser.). 2003. 19.99 (978-1-58926-176-1(3), R22J-3280) Oasis Audio.
A three-dimensional state: physical, mental, and magical. It's that state of being where excellence simply happens and success seems effortless and natural.

Being in the Success Zone. unabr. ed. Marcia Reynolds. 2 CDs. (Running Time: 6 hrs.). (Smart Audio Ser.). 2004. audio compact disk 19.99 (978-1-58926-177-8(1), R22J-328D) Oasis Audio.

***Being Jesus in Nashville: Walking on Water at the Corner of 2nd & Broadway.** unabr. ed. Jim Palmer. (ENG.). 2011. 14.99 (978-0-310-77364-1(4)) Zondervan.

Being Martha. Lloyd Allen. Read by Patrick G. Lawlor. (Running Time: 19800 sec.). 2006. audio compact disk 45.00 (978-0-7861-7335-8(1)) Blckstn Audio.

Being Martha: The Inside Story of Martha Stewart & Her Amazing Life. Lloyd Allen. Read by Patrick G. Lawlor. (Running Time: 19800 sec.). 2006. 34.95 (978-0-7861-4448-8(3)) Blckstn Audio.

Being Martha: The Inside Story of Martha Stewart & Her Amazing Life. unabr. ed. Lloyd Allen. Read by Patrick G. Lawlor. 4 CDs. (Running Time: 19800 sec.). 2006. audio compact disk 29.95 (978-0-7861-7476-8(5)) Blckstn Audio.

Being Moldable, Pliable & Willing to Change. Speeches. Joel Osteen. 1 Cass. (Running Time: 30 Mins.). 2002. 6.00 (978-1-59349-142-0(5), JAO142) J Osteen.

***Being Nikki.** collector's unabr. ed. Meg Cabot. Narrated by Stina Nielsen. 7 CDs. (Running Time: 8 hrs. 15 mins.). (YA). (gr. 8 up). 2009. audio compact disk 44.95 (978-1-4407-2561-6(6)) Recorded Bks.

***Being Nikki.** unabr. ed. Meg Cabot. Narrated by Stina Nielsen. 1 Playaway. (Running Time: 8 hrs. 15 mins.). (YA). (gr. 8 up). 2009. 56.75 (978-1-4407-2090-1(8)); 61.75 (978-1-4407-2081-9(9)); audio compact disk 87.75 (978-1-4407-2085-7(1)) Recorded Bks.

Being of Service. John Tschohl. 1 cass. (Running Time: 44 min.). 11.00 (978-0-89811-228-3(1), 9451) Meyer Res Grp.
Discusses methods for keeping customers & increasing sales.

Being of Service. John Tschohl. 1 cass. 10.00 (SP100066) SMI Intl.
Service is a key to success in business. This tape outlines & teaches the characteristics of good service, the performance of good service, & the rewards of good serving.

***Being of the Field.** unabr. ed. Traci Harding. Read by Nicky Talacko. (Running Time: 16 hrs. 54 mins.). (Triad of Being Ser.). 2010. audio compact disk 118.95 (978-1-74214-717-8(8), 9781742147178) Pub: Bolinda Pubng AUS. Dist(s): Bolinda Pub Inc

Being Open. Swami Amar Jyoti. 1 dolby cass. 1983. 9.95 (D-10) Truth Consciousness.
Opening faith & devotion, working on the biggest block first. The cosmic inheritance of those who are open.

Being Patriotic Audio CD. Adapted by Benchmark Education Company Staff. Based on a work by Vickey Herold. (Early Explorers Set C Ser.). (J). (gr. 2). 2008. audio compact disk 10.00 (978-1-60437-545-9(0)) Benchmark Educ.

Being Peace. Parallax Press Staff. Voice by Thich Nhat Hanh. 1 CD. (Running Time: 73 Mins.). (ENG.). 2002. audio compact disk 15.00 (978-1-888375-28-2(0), 75280) Pub: Parallax Pr. Dist(s): PerseuPGW
MERGE WITH LOOKINGDEEPLY - 464 First in the series of Classic Dharma talks by Thich Nhat Hanh.Thich Nhat Hanh delivered the words on this CD to 700 rapt listeners at Green Gulch Zen Center, in Muir Beach, California, on November 3, 1985, inspiring the.

Being Perfect & A Short Guide to a Happy Life. unabr. ed. Anna Quindlen. Read by Anna Quindlen. (Running Time: 1 hr.). (ENG.). 2005. audio compact disk 12.95 (978-0-7393-1792-1(X), Random AudioBks) Pub: Random Audio Pubg. Dist(s): Random
At the heart of this beautiful and insightful audiobook lies "the perfection trap" - what it is, how to avoid falling into it, and how to instead shape a life that is uniquely yours. In BEING PERFECT, Ann Quindlen gives a name to, and invites us to laugh at, a lifestyle that is all too familiar to many people, one that emphasizes the pursuit of trying to be perfect in the eyes of others, and to win the world's good opinion, rather than focusing on the most important goal of all: "Giving up on being perfect and beginning the work of becoming yourself." With wit and wisdom, Quindlen offers a keen understanding of how to create a life that is rich in meaning for you, by living on your own terms and by listening to your own deepest instincts, rather than to the demands and values of the world outside. This audiobook is an inspiring guide to living a rewarding and happy life, a life fulfilling in all its flaws, a life that is truly yours. In A SHORT GUIDE TO A HAPPY LIFE, Quindlen reflects on what it takes to "get a life" - to live deeply every day and form your own unique self, rather than merely to exist through your days. "Knowledge of our own mortality is the greatest gift God ever gives us," Quindlen states, "because unless you know the clock is ticking, it is so easy to waste our days, our lives." Her mother died when Quindlen was nineteen: "It was the dividing line between seeing the world in black and white, and in Technicolor. The lights came on for the darkest possible reason I learned something about enduring, in a very short period of time, about life. And that was that it was glorious, and that you had no business taking it for granted." In A SHORT GUIDE TO A HAPPY LIFE, Quindlen guides us with an understanding that comes from knowing how to see the view, the richness in living.

Being Present in the Darkness: Using Depression As a Tool for Self Discovery. unabr. ed. Cheri Huber. 2 cass. (Running Time: 3 hrs.). 1997. 16.95 (978-1-882071-79-1(4)) B-B Audio.
Being Present in the Darkness suggests that hating and resisting depressionor anything else we dont wantactually maintains it, and that compassionate acceptance of our feelings and ourselves leads you to freedom. Through simple exercises and meditatio.

Being Ready for God. Gloria Copeland. 1 cass. 1986. 5.00 (978-0-88114-799-5(0)) K Copeland Pubns.
Biblical teaching on meditation & prayer.

Being Single. unabr. ed. Jennifer James. Read by Jennifer James. 1 cass. (Running Time: 1 hr.). 9.95 (978-0-915423-18-7(9)) Jennifer J.

Being Somebody: Spring the Mind-Traps That Keep You Fat & Frustrated With Your Life. Patricia Chamberlain. Ed. by Barbara Kyper. Illus. by Ashleigh Brilliant. 1991. 9.99 (978-1-880011-02-7(6)) Dundas-Devonhills Assoc.

Being Strengthened in Adversity. Speeches. Joel Osteen. 1 Cass. (Running Time: 30 Mins.). 2002. 6.00 (978-1-59349-163-5(8), JA0163) J Osteen.

Being the Ball: The Cart Path Toward Golf-Awareness. Bill Muster. 1 cass. 1999. 12.95 (978-0-9670877-7-1(5)) BTB Ent.
Self-help for golfers.

Being the Best. Denis Waitley. Read by Denis Waitley. 6 cass. 59.95 Set. (712AD) Nightingale-Conant.
You can be the best.

Being the Body. abr. ed. Charles Colson. 4 cass. (Running Time: 6 hrs.). 2004. 24.99 (978-1-58926-692-6(7), 6692); audio compact disk 27.99 (978-1-58926-693-3(5), 6693) Oasis Audio.
Ten years ago in The Body, Colson turned his prophetic attention to the church and how it might break out of its cultural captivity and reassert its biblical identity. Today the book's classic truths have not changed. But the world we live in has. Christians in America have had their complacency shattered and their beliefs challenged. Around the world, the clash of world views has never been more strident.

Being the Body. abr. ed. Charles Colson & Ellen Vaughn. (ENG.). 2004. 19.59 (978-1-60814-041-1(5)) Oasis Audio.

Being with Dying. Joan Halifax. 1997. audio compact disk 69.95 (978-1-59179-961-0(9)) Sounds True.

***Being Wrong.** unabr. ed. Kathryn Schulz. Read by Mia Barron. (ENG.). 2010. (978-0-06-201594-5(X), Harper Audio) HarperCollins Pubs.

***Being Wrong: Adventures in the Margin of Error.** unabr. ed. Kathryn Schulz. Read by Mia Barron. (ENG.). 2010. (978-0-06-201240-1(1), Harper Audio) HarperCollins Pubs.

Being Yourself. unabr. ed. Carl Ransom Rogers. 4 cass. 1989. 39.50 (978-0-88432-251-1(3), S05903) J Norton Pubs.
Discusses ways to choose the life one wants instead of letting others plan it.

Beisbol. abr. ed. Michael Oleksak & Mary Oleksak. Read by Del Zamora. Ed. by Steven Albert. 2 cass. (Running Time: 3 hrs.). Dramatization. 1992. bk. 15.95 set. (978-1-56703-003-7(3), 004) High-Top Sports.
The history of hispanics in the grand old game of "Beisbol." This book traces the history since the game was invented.

Bel-Ami see Bel Ami

Bel Ami, Pts. 1-4, set. Read by Jacques Roland. Told to Henri Rene Guy De Maupassant. Gérard Delaisement. 7 cass. (Running Time: 10 hrs.). (Classiques Garnier Ser.).Tr. of Bel-Ami. (FRE.). 1995. 74.95 (1724/25) Olivia & Hill.
Georges Durois, a son of Norman innkeepers, will become Baron Du Roy de Cantel. He owes his meteoric rise in society to the women who are seduced by his youth & beauty.

Bel Ami, Pts. 1 & 2, set. Read by Jacques Roland. Told to Henri Rene Guy De Maupassant. 4 cass. (Running Time: 6 hrs.).Tr. of Bel-Ami. (FRE.). 1995. 48.95 (1724-LQP) Olivia & Hill.

Bel Ami, Pts. 3 & 4, set. Read by Jacques Roland. Told to Henri Rene Guy De Maupassant. Gérard Delaisement. 3 cass. (Running Time: 5 hrs.). (Classiques Garnier Ser.).Tr. of Bel-Ami. (FRE., 1995. 38.95 (1725-LQP) Olivia & Hill.

Bel Canto. unabr. ed. Ann Patchett. Read by Anna Fields. 8 cass. (Running Time: 11 hrs. 30 mins.). 2001. 56.95 (978-0-7861-2056-7(8), 2817); audio compact disk 80.00 (978-0-7861-9731-6(5), 2817) Blckstn Audio.
Somewhere in South America at the home of the country's vice president, a lavish birthday party is being held in honor of a powerful Japanese businessman. A famous American opera diva entertains the international guests. It is a night out of a fairy tale, until a band of gun-wielding terrorists breaks in through the air-conditioning vents & takes the entire party hostage.

Bel Canto. unabr. ed. Ann Patchett. Read by Anna Fields. 8 cass. (Running Time: 12 hrs.). 2001. 39.95 (978-0-694-52533-1(2)) HarperCollins Pubs.

***Bel Canto.** unabr. ed. Ann Patchett. Read by Anna Fields. (ENG.). 2004. (978-0-06-081501-1(9), Harper Audio); (978-0-06-078328-0(1), Harper Audio) HarperCollins Pubs.

Bel Canto. unabr. ed. Ann Patchett. Read by Anna Fields. (Running Time: 41400 sec.). 2007. audio compact disk 19.95 (978-0-06-142949-1(X), Harper Audio) HarperCollins Pubs.

Bel Ria. unabr. ed. Sheila Burnford. Narrated by Flo Gibson. 4 cass. (Running Time: 6 hrs.). (gr. 6). 1981. 36.00 (978-1-55690-041-9(4), 81020E7) Recorded Bks.
A gypsy dog leads its master through war-torn France in the retreat to Dunkirk.

Belgrave Square. unabr. ed. Anne Perry. Read by Kenneth Shanley. 11 cass. (Running Time: 14 hrs. 35 min.). (Thomas Pitt Ser.). 1998. 103.95 (978-1-85903-218-3(4)) Pub: Magna Story GBR. Dist(s): Ulverscroft US
A Victorian Whodunnit. Money lender William Weems is murdered & Inspector Pitts discovers he was a vicious blackmailer.

Belgrave Square. unabr. ed. Anne Perry. Read by Davina Porter. 13 CDs. (Running Time: 14 hrs.). (Thomas Pitt Ser.). 2006. audio compact disk 119.75 (978-1-4193-8970-2(X), C3704); 109.75 (978-1-4193-8968-9(8), 96094) Recorded Bks.
The 12th mystery in the beloved Inspector and Charlotte Pitt Victorian mystery series, now a hardcover success. When a moneylender named William Weems is murdered, there is discreet rejoicing among those whose meager earnings he devoured. But the plot thickens when Inspector Pitt finds a list of London's distinguished gentlemen in Weems' office.

Belief. Paul R. Scheele. 1 cass. (Running Time: 40 min.). (Paraliminal Tapes Ser.). 1992. 24.95 (978-0-925480-18-7(5)) Learn Strategies.
Helps you direct self-fulfilling prophecies by changing limiting beliefs.

Belief Safety Factor. Elbert Willis. 1 cass. (Secret to Believing Prayer Ser.). 4.00 Fill the Gap.

Belief Systems: Methods for Change. John Grinder & Robert Dilts. Read by John Grinder & Robert Dilts. 8 cass. (Running Time: 12 hrs.). (Syntax of Behavior One Ser.: Vol. III). 1988. 99.95 set. Metamorphous Pr.
This volume addresses: What precisely are beliefs & how do they affect our selection of filters that affect our attention & information processing? What are the conditions required to change them? How can stability be sustained in the process of changing beliefs.

Beliefology: Raise your conciousness towealith Health&happiness. Kenneth L. Routson. 2006. audio compact disk 19.95 (978-1-891067-03-7(6)) Tulip Press.

Believe. Contrib. by Jason Breland et al. Prod. by Chris Springer. 2003. audio compact disk 13.99 (978-5-550-28371-4(9)) Integrity Music.

Believe. Tommye Young West. 1 cass. (Running Time: 1 hr.). 2000. 11.99 (978-0-9706112-2-2(6), Serious Records); audio compact disk 17.99 (978-0-9706112-3-9(4), Serious Records) Pt of Grace Ent.

Believe & Achieve. abr. ed. Samuel A. Cypert et al. Read by Stanley Ralph Ross. (Running Time: 2 hrs. 0 mins. 0 sec.). (ENG.). 2003. audio compact disk 22.95 (978-1-932429-18-3(2)) Pub: Highroads Media. Dist(s): Macmillan

Believe & Achieve: Our Future Field of Dreams. Victor Harris. 1 cass. (Running Time: 90 min.). 7.98 (978-1-55503-668-3(6), 06004857) Covenant Comms.
Helping youth achieve potential.

Believe & Receive. Gloria Copeland. 1 cass. (How to Live in God's Best Ser.: No. 4). 1983. 5.00 (978-0-88114-256-3(5)) K Copeland Pubns.
Biblical study on living God's best.

Believe God for the Greater Works. Speeches. Joel Osteen. 1 Cass. (Running Time: 30 Mins.). (J). 2000. 6.00 (978-1-59349-053-9(4), JA0053) J Osteen.

Believe in Him. Neville Goddard. 1 cass. (Running Time: 62 min.). 1965. 8.00 (66) J & L Pubns.
Neville taught Imagination Creates Reality. He was a powerfully influential teacher of God as Consciousness.

Believe in Yourself Audio Story in Spanish. Short Stories. Joy Frost. 1 CD. (Running Time: 20 Min.). Orig. Title: Cree en ti Mismo. (SPA.). (J). 2004. audio compact disk 14.00 (978-0-9745977-5-1(9)) Joy Stories.
Exciting new audio stories by Joy B. Frost are original, metaphorical audio bedtime stories that are aimed at raising self-esteem. These stories are filled with positive messages with that are based on the principles of confidence building. These stories have won 7 awards in the past two years. "Believe In Yourself" is a story of a sea turtle that struggles to overcome obstacles to reach the ocean from its sandy nest. This story models the skills children can use to overcome obstacles in their own lives. Children use the turtle's affirming example of, "I believe in myself." to develop a strong belief in their own abilities. Suggested age 3-9 years old.

Believe in Yourself Audio Story with Finger Puppet. Short Stories. Joy Frost. 1 Compact Disk. (Running Time: 20 min). (J). 2002. 20.00 (978-0-9716991-4-4(3)) Pub: Joy Stories. Dist(s): Baker Taylor
Children's bedtime story for raising self-esteem and a peaceful nights sleep. This comes packaged in its own viny bag with a finger puppet of the stories character.

Believe in Yourself Audio Story with Finger Puppet in Spanish. Short Stories. Joy Frost. 1 CD with finger pup. (Running Time: 20 min.).Tr. of Cree en ti Mismo. (SPA.). (J). 2004. audio compact disk 20.00 (978-0-9745977-7-5(5)) Pub: Joy Stories. Dist(s): Baker Taylor
Exciting new audio stories by Joy B. Frost are original, metaphorical audio bedtime stories that are aimed at raising self-esteem. These stories are filled with positive messages with that are based on the principles of confidence building. These stories have won 7 awards in the past two years. "Believe In Yourself" is a story of a sea turtle that struggles to overcome obstacles to reach the ocean from its sandy nest. This story models the skills children can use to overcome obstacles in their own lives. Children use the turtle's affirming example of, "I believe in myself." to develop a strong belief in their own abilities. Suggested age 3-9 years old.

Believe Me. unabr. ed. Poems. John R. Alden. Read by Christopher Hurt. 5 cass. (Running Time: 7 hrs.). 1992. 39.95 (978-0-7861-0292-1(6), 1256) Blckstn Audio.
It's not often that an acclaimed historian is revealed to be the author of light verse, but Alden here presents us with 1,707 couplets, quatrains & other terse verse in the tradition of Ogden Nash. His subject matter ranges from dinosaurs to computers, from Confucius to Darwin, from Jonah to George Bush. His wit, wisdom & powers of observation are sure to amuse & delight.

***Believe That You Can: Moving with tenacity toward the dream God has Given You.** unabr. ed. Jentezen Franklin. Narrated by Lloyd James. (ENG.). 2009. 12.98 (978-1-59644-746-2(X), christianSeed) christianaud.

Believe That You Can: Moving with tenacity toward the dream God has Given You. unabr. ed. Jentezen Franklin. Read by Lloyd James. (Running Time: 6 hrs. 15 mins. 0 sec.). (ENG.). 2009. audio compact disk 21.98 (978-1-59644-745-5(1), christianSeed) christianaud.

Believer. abr. ed. Stephanie Black. 4 CDs. (Running Time: 5 Hours). 2005. audio compact disk 16.95 (978-1-59156-701-1(7)) Covenant Comms.

Believer. unabr. ed. Ann Gabhart. Narrated by Renee Ertl. (Running Time: 12 hrs. 24 mins. 42 sec.). (ENG.). 2009. 25.89 (978-1-60814-514-0(X)); audio compact disk 36.99 (978-1-59859-575-8(X)) Oasis Audio.

Believer as Prophet, Priest & King: Our Baptismal Role. Jim Nisbet. 8 cass. (Running Time: 8 hrs.). 2001. vinyl bd. 64.95 (A5970) St Anthony Mess Pr.
When we are baptized, each of us is anointed to fulfill the role of prophet, priest and king.

Believers. unabr. ed. Zoë Heller. Read by Andrea Martin. 2009. audio compact disk 39.99 (978-0-06-162993-8(6), Harper Audio) HarperCollins Pubs.

***Believers.** unabr. ed. Zoë Heller. Read by Andrea Martin. (ENG.). 2009. (978-0-06-180524-0(6), Harper Audio); (978-0-06-180522-6(X), Harper Audio) HarperCollins Pubs.

***Believers.** unabr. ed. Zoë Heller. Read by Andrea Martin. 9 CDs. (Running Time: 10 hrs. 30 mins.). 2009. audio compact disk 100.00 (978-1-4159-6406-4(8), BksonTape) Pub: Random Audio Pubg. Dist(s): Random

Believer's Advantage over the World. Speeches. Creflo A. Dollar. 3 cass. (Running Time: 4 hrs.). 2000. 15.00 (978-1-59089-176-6(7)) Creflo Dollar.

Believer's Armor. 12 cass. 35.95 (2064, HarperThor); 4.95 study guide. (40564, HarperThor) HarpC GBR.

Believer's Authority. 6 Cassette Tapes. 2004. (978-1-59548-025-5(0)); audio compact disk (978-1-59548-026-2(9)) A Wommack.

Believer's Authority. Kenneth E. Hagin. 4 cass. 1997. 16.00 (C7139) Faith Lib Pubns.
Titles include: What is Authority?, Exercising Our Authority, Our Place of Authority, & Authority Over Fear.

Believer's Authority. Steve Thompson. 1 cass. (Running Time: 90 mins.). (Understanding Spiritual Authority Ser.: Vol. 1). 2000. 5.00 (ST03-001) Morning NC.
This series reveals the key scriptural foundations & practical applications for moving in true spiritual authority.

Believer's Authority: Compact disc new Release. Created by Awmi. (ENG.). 2009. audio compact disk 35.00 (978-1-59548-172-6(9)) A Wommack.

Believer's Conditional Security: A Study on Perseverance & Falling Away. Daniel D. Corner. 12 cass. 1997. 24.95 Set. (BCS-V) Evang Outreach.
This fully-documented, 761 page volume will take the listener from the origin of once saved, always saved (OSAS) to the present time, as the contemporary OSAS teachers of our day are quoted hundreds of times & their teachings are examined under the light of God's truth. The teaching of OSAS is sometimes equated to grace & the gospel.

Believer's Covenant. Creflo A. Dollar. 2008. audio compact disk 28.00 (978-1-59944-701-8(0)) Creflo Dollar.

Believer's Identity. Read by Lee Lefebre. 1 cass. (Running Time: 1 hr. 25 min.). (GraceLife Conference Ser.: Vol. 6). 1993. 6.00 (978-1-57838-111-1(8)); 6.00 (978-1-57838-010-7(3)) CrossLife Express.
Christian living.

Believer's Security: Radio Debate. Dan Corner. 1 cass. (Running Time: 1 hr.). 5.00 (RF) Evang Outreach.
Live radio debate on the believer's security between Dan Corner & a teaching elder & author from a Reformed Church. Includes call-in questions.

Believers' Spiritual IRA in Financial Management. James W. Parrott, Jr. (C). 2007. audio compact disk 12.00 (978-0-9742312-0-4(7)) Treasure The Monemt.

Believer's Victory. 1 cass. (Running Time: 1 hr. 20 min.). (GraceLife Conference Ser.: Vol. 7). 1993. 6.00 (978-1-57838-112-8(6)) CrossLife Express.
Christian living.

Believer's Victory. Read by Lee Lefebre. 1 cass. (Running Time: 1 hr. 20 min.). (Exchanged Life Conference Ser.: Vol. 7). 1993. 6.00 (978-1-57838-011-4(1)) CrossLife Express.

Believing & Healing: Implications for Pastoral Care. 1 cass. (Care Cassettes Ser.: Vol. 18, No. 4). 1993. 10.80 Assn Prof Chaplains.

Believing Cassandra. Alan Atkisson. (Helen & Scott Nearing Titles Ser.). 2000. audio compact disk 12.95 (978-1-890132-70-5(5)) Chelsea Green Pub.

Believing Catholic. unabr. ed. Daniel E. Pilarczyk. Read by Daniel E. Pilarczyk. 2 cass. (Running Time: 3 hrs.). Orig. Title: We Believe. 2000. 14.95 (978-0-86716-397-1(6), A3976) St Anthony Mess Pr.
Step-by-step guide to the basic story of God's plan for humankind through creation, redemption & salvation. The chapters are the foundational truths that hold all Catholic practice & belief together.

Believing for the Supernatural. As told by Frank Damazio. 6 cass. (Running Time: 5 hrs). 2003. 59.99 (978-0-914936-46-6(8)) CityChristian.

Believing God. Beth Moore. (YA). 2003. audio compact disk 39.95 (978-0-633-19376-8(3)) LifeWay Christian.

Believing God. unabr. ed. Beth Moore. Read by Sandra Burr. (Running Time: 6 hrs.). 2004. 24.95 (978-1-59335-654-5(4), 1593356544, Brilliance MP3); 39.25 (978-1-59710-039-7(0), 1597100390, BADLE); 24.95 (978-1-59710-038-0(2), 1597100382, BAD); audio compact disk 26.95 (978-1-59600-112-1(7), 1596001127); audio compact disk 39.25 (978-1-59335-655-2(2), 1593356552, Brinc Audio MP3 Lib); 24.95 (978-1-59600-110-7(0), 1596001100); audio compact disk 74.25 (978-1-59600-113-8(5), 1596001135, BriAudCD Unabrid) Brilliance Audio.
Do you take God at His word, believing what He has told us, or do you just believe in His existence and the salvation He offers? Beth Moore has believed in God all of her life. She has been dedicated to teaching others to believe in Him as well. But as an adult she came face to face with the single most important question as she meditated on a passage from Isaiah: "You are my witnesses," declares the Lord, "and my servant whom I have chosen, so that you may know and believe me and understand that I am he." - Isaiah 43:10 Come Experience a Fresh Explosion of Faith. What does it mean to believe God? Abraham and Moses believed God. This planted in them a seed of faith that grew into towering oaks of steadfast trust and belief. Hebrews 11 is full of other examples of bold belief. Beth Moore brings these characters to life in a way that will spring forth in you a fresh explosion of faith!.

***Believing God for His Best.** Bill Thrasher. (ENG.). 2010. 14.99 (978-0-9830140-6-5(X)) Sozo Media.

***Believing in Hope.** unabr. ed. Stephanie Perry Moore. Narrated by Robin Miles. (Yasmin Peace Ser.). (ENG.). 2010. 12.98 (978-1-61045-012-6(4), christaudio); audio compact disk 18.98 (978-1-61045-078-2(7), christaudio) christianaud.

Believing in Incredible You. Shad Helmstetter. 1 cass. (Self-Talk Cassettes Ser.). 10.95 (978-0-937065-01-3(3)) Grindle Pr.

Believing in the Unseen. Rick Joyner. 1 cass. (Running Time: 90 mins.). (Growing in Faith Ser.: Vol. 3). 2000. 5.00 (RJ14-003) Morning NC.
With fresh & practical messages centering on faith, this tape series will enable you to better understand essential principles of the Christian walk.

Believing It All. unabr. ed. Marc Parent. (ENG.). 2005. 14.98 (978-1-59483-415-8(6)) Pub: Hachet Audio. Dist(s): HachBkGrp

Believing That You Receive. Kenneth Copeland. 8 cass. 1986. 40.00 Set incl. study guide. (978-0-88114-745-2(1)); 5.00 (978-0-88114-817-6(2)) K Copeland Pubns.
Biblical teaching on receiving from God.

Believing what you can't See see Power of Faith Audio CD (MP3 Disk): Change Defeat to Victory Using the Ingredients of Faith

Believing what you can't See see Power of Faith Paperback book & MP3 Audio CD: Change Defeat to Victory Using the Ingredients of Faith

Believing with the Heart. Kenneth Copeland. 1 cass. 1982. 5.00 (978-0-938458-78-4(7)) K Copeland Pubns.
Indepth biblical study on faith.

Believing Your Knowingness. Black Bear. 1 cass. (Running Time: 1 hr. 30 mins.). 1998. 15.00 (978-0-9700042-2-2(2), DI007) Divine Ideas.
Clear & fascinating teaching on the difference between original, pure thought & the belief systems of the mind which are created from societal teaching.

Belinda & the Swab see Spirits & Spooks for Halloween

Bell. unabr. ed. Iris Murdoch. Read by Miriam Margolyes. 12 cass. (Running Time: 45600 sec.). (Rumpole Crime Ser.). 2000. 96.95 (978-0-7540-0487-5(2), CAB1910) AudioGO.
Outside Imber Abbey, home of an enclosed order of nuns, a new bell is being installed & then the old bell legendary symbol of religion & magic is rediscovered. Dora Greenfield, erring wife, returns to her husband. Michael Meade, leader of the community, is confronted by a man with whom he had a disastrous homosexual relationship, while the wise old Abbess watches & prays. And everyone, or almost everyone, hopes to be saved.

Bell, Book, & Scandal. Jill Churchill. Read by Susan Ericksen. 3 cass. (Jane Jeffry Mystery Ser.). 29.95 (978-0-7927-3384-3(3), CSL 720); audio compact disk 49.95 (978-0-7927-3385-0(1), SLD 720) AudioGO.

Bell for Adano. unabr. ed. John Hersey. Narrated by David Green. 6 cass. (Running Time: 8 hrs. 45 mins.). 1999. 51.00 (978-1-55690-042-6(2), 89550E7) Recorded Bks.
A young American soldier restores a piece of an ancient town in Sicily 1942 & gives the town back its heart.

Bell for Adano. unabr. collector's ed. John Hersey. Read by Dan Lazar. 8 cass. (Running Time: 8 hrs.). 1981. 48.00 (978-0-7366-0316-4(6), 1304) Books on Tape.
Pulitzer Prize novel of reconciliation in Italy between American troops & opposing forces.

Bell Jar. unabr. ed. Sylvia Plath. Read by Maggie Gyllenhaal. 6 cass. (Running Time: 9 hrs.). 2003. 34.95 (978-0-06-056945-7(X)) HarperCollins Pubs.

Bell Jar. unabr. ed. Sylvia Plath. Read by Maggie Gyllenhaal. (Running Time: 25200 sec.). 2006. audio compact disk 19.95 (978-0-06-087877-1(0)) HarperCollins Pubs.

Bell Jar. unabr. ed. Sylvia Plath. Narrated by Christina Moore. 6 cass. (Running Time: 8 hrs. 15 mins.). 51.00 (978-1-55690-656-5(0), 92401E7) Recorded Bks.
American poet Sylvia Plath's semi-autobiographical account of Esther Greenwood, a talented writer who struggles against a society that refuses to take a sensitive female artist seriously. Available to libraries only.

Bell Labs: Life in the Crown Jewel. abr. ed. Narain Gehani. Prod. by Narain Gehani. Read by Stow Lovejoy. Engineer William D. Roome. 2 CDs. 2003. audio compact disk 34.95 (978-0-929306-29-2(5)); audio compact disk (978-0-929306-31-5(7)) Silicon Pr.
Bell Labs, the greatest research lab of the twen-tieth century, has been called America's national treasure and the crown jewel of AT&T. Forced by the marketplace, competition, and economic conditions, the world's most prestigious research lab is in the midst of radical cultural change. Bell Labs: Life in the Crown Jewel tells the fascinating story of this change. The boom years of basic research started to end when AT&T shed its monopoly status. The change, slow at first, sped up in the 1990s with the next breakup of AT&T, which created Lucent, Bell Labs' new parent. After a few good years, Lucent found it-self in financial difficulty in a very tough tele-communications market. Lucent responded by breaking up into smaller companies, which led to a smaller Bell Labs. In addition, Lucent's worsening financial condition forced Bell Labs to downsize. Bell Labs researchers, once free to focus on innovation and research excellence now have to worry about business relevance. The culture of lifetime employment is gone and the pendulum has swung from basic to applied research. Narain Gehani worked at Bell Labs for twenty-three years. He was there when AT&T changed from a monopoly to a competitive com-pany. He was there when AT&T split up again and handed Bell Labs to Lucent. He was there during the rise and fall of Lucent. He was a witness to and participant in the changes in Bell Labs as its parent morphed from a million em-ployee company to a much smaller company which has now less than fifty thousand employ-ees. Narain Gehani shares his insights about Bell Labs and its culture and tells its glorious history. He describes the cultural differences between Research and the business units, the different re-search models; and the challenges facing Bell Labs. Bell Labs: Life in the Crown Jewel is full of interesting and amusing anecdotes that will keep you riveted to reading about a way of life possibly gone forever.

Bell Labs: Life in the Crown Jewel. unabr. ed. Narain Gehani. Prod. by Narain Gehani. Read by Stow Lovejoy. Engineer William D. Roome. 6 CDs. 2003. audio compact disk 49.95 (978-0-929306-28-5(7)) Silicon Pr.
Forced by the marketplace, competition, and economic conditions, the world's most prestigious research lab is in the midst of radical cultural change. The boom years of basic research started to end when AT&T shed its monopoly status. The change, slow at first, sped up in the 1990s with the next breakup of AT&T, which created Lucent, Bell Labs' new parent. After a few good years, Lucent found it-self in financial difficulty in a very tough tele-communications market. Lucent responded by breaking up into smaller companies, which led to a smaller Bell Lab.

Bell Labs: Life in the Crown Jewel. unabr. ed. Narain Gehani. Prod. by Narain Gehani. Read by Stow Lovejoy. Engineer William D. Roome. 6 CDs (Library Editi. 2003. audio compact disk 79.95 (978-0-929306-30-8(9)) Silicon Pr.
Bell Labs, the greatest research lab of the twen-tieth century, has been called America's national treasure and the crown jewel of AT&T. Forced by the marketplace, competition, and economic conditions, the world's most prestigious research lab is in the midst of radical cultural change. Bell Labs: Life in the Crown Jewel tells the fascinating story of this change. The boom years of basic research started to end when AT&T shed its monopoly status. The change, slow at first, sped up in the 1990s with the next breakup of AT&T, which created Lucent, Bell Labs' new parent. After a few good years, Lucent found it-self in financial difficulty in a very tough tele-communications market. Lucent responded by breaking up into smaller companies, which led to a smaller Bell Labs. In addition, Lucent's worsening financial condition forced Bell Labs to downsize. Bell Labs researchers, once free to focus on innovation and research excellence now have to worry about business relevance. The culture of lifetime employment is gone and the pendulum has swung from basic to applied research. Narain Gehani worked at Bell Labs for twenty-three years. He was there when AT&T changed from a monopoly to a competitive com-pany. He was there when AT&T split up again and handed Bell Labs to Lucent. He was there during the rise and fall of Lucent. He was a witness to and participant in the changes in Bell Labs as its parent morphed from a million em-ployee company to a much smaller company which has now less than fifty thousand employ-ees. Narain Gehani shares his insights about Bell Labs and its culture and tells its glorious history. He describes the cultural differences between Research and the business units, the different re-search models; and the challenges facing Bell Labs. Bell Labs: Life in the Crown Jewel is full of interesting and amusing anecdotes that will keep you riveted to reading about a way of life possibly gone forever.

***Bell Ringers: A Novel.** unabr. ed. Henry Porter. Narrated by John Lee. (Running Time: 16 hrs. 30 mins.). 2010. 21.99 (978-1-4001-8658-7(7)); 39.99 (978-1-4001-9658-6(2)); 29.99 (978-1-4001-6658-9(6)); audio compact disk 79.99 (978-1-4001-4658-1(5)); audio compact disk 39.99 (978-1-4001-1658-4(9)) Pub: Tantor Media. Dist(s): IngramPubServ

Bell, the Clapper, & the Cord: Wit & Witticism. 1 cass. (Running Time: 1 hr.). 2003. 3.00 Natl Fed Blind.

Bell, the Clapper, & the Second Cord: Wit & Witticism, Vol. II. 1 cass. (Running Time: 1 hr.). 2003. 3.00 Natl Fed Blind.

Bella. unabr. ed. Dorothy Eden. Read by Jane Jermyn. 6 cass. (Running Time: 9 hrs.). 1999. 54.95 (60849) Pub: Soundings Ltd GBR. Dist(s): Ulverscroft US

Bella Durmiente. 1 cass. (Running Time: 1 hr. 30 min.).Tr. of Sleeping Beauty. (SPA., (J). 2000. bk. 12.95 (978-84-207-6728-4(X)) Pub: Grupo Anaya ESP. Dist(s): Distribks Inc

Bella Durmiente: Cuento Ballet de Pjotr Ilijch Tchaikovsky. Susa Hämmerle. Illus. by Anette Bley. (J). 2007. bk. 30.99 (978-84-96646-06-3(8)) Loguez Ediciones ESP.

Bella Durmiente del Bosque. I.t. ed. Short Stories. Illus. by Graham Percy. 1 cass. (Running Time: 10 mins.). Dramatization. (SPA.). (J). (ps-3). 2001. 8.99 (978-84-87650-14-7(7)) Pub: Peralt Mont ESP. Dist(s): imaJen

Bella of Bow Street. Carol Rivers & Annie Aldington. 2008. 76.95 (978-1-84652-293-2(5)); audio compact disk 89.95 (978-1-84652-294-9(3)) Pub: Magna Story GBR. Dist(s): Ulverscroft US

Bella Poldark. Winston Graham. 3 cass. (Running Time: 4 hrs. 5 mins.). (Poldark Saga Ser.). (ENG., 2003. 18.00 (978-1-4050-0598-2(X)) Pub: Macmillan UK GBR. Dist(s): IPG Chicago

Bella Tuscany: The Sweet Life in Italy. abr. ed. Frances Mayes. Read by Frances Mayes. 4 cass. 1999. 25.00 (FS9-43393) Highsmith.

Bella Tuscany: The Sweet Life in Italy. unabr. ed. Frances Mayes. Read by Frances Mayes. 6 cass. (Running Time: 9 hrs.). 2000. 34.95 (D210) Blckstn Audio.
This passionate & lyrical account of Francis Mayes's enjoyment & connection with the land, art, food, wine & the local people describes the challenges of learning the language, touring, restoring her villa & transitions in her family life.

Bella y la Bestia y Muchos Cuentos Mas, Vol. 5. abr. ed.Tr. of Beauty & the Beast, Robin Hood, Hansel & Gretel & Many More Tales. (SPA.). 2001. audio compact disk 13.00 (978-958-9494-32-5(3)) YoYoMusic.

Bellas Hijas de Mufaro. John L. Steptoe. Illus. by John L. Steptoe. Read by Susan Rybin. Tr. by Clarita Kohen. 14 vols. (Running Time: 20 mins.).Tr. of Mufaro's Beautiful Daughters: An African Tale. (SPA.). 1998. pap. bk. & tchr. ed. 41.95 Reading chest. (978-0-87499-463-6(2)) Live Oak Media.
In this magical journey to Zimbabwe, the King will choose a bride from among the "Most Worthy & Beautiful Daughters in the Land." Mufaro has two beautiful daughters - Nyasha, who is kind & considerate, & Manyara, who is selfish, but determined to be chosen.

Bellas Hijas de Mufaro. unabr. ed. John L. Steptoe. Illus. by John L. Steptoe. Read by Susan Rybin. Tr. by Clarita Kohen. 11 vols. (Running Time: 20 mins.).Tr. of Mufaro's Beautiful Daughters: An African Tale. (SPA.). (J). (gr. k-3). 1998. pap. bk. 16.95 (978-0-87499-461-2(6)) AudioGO.

Bellas Hijas de Mufaro. unabr. ed. John L. Steptoe. Illus. by John L. Steptoe. Read by Susan Rybin. Tr. by Clarita Kohen. 1 cass. (Running Time: 20 mins.).Tr. of Mufaro's Beautiful Daughters: An African Tale. (SPA.). (J). (gr. k-3). 1998. bk. 24.95 (978-0-87499-462-9(4)) Live Oak Media.

Belle au Bois Dormant. (FRE.). pap. bk. 12.95 (978-2-89558-067-6(7)) Pub: Coffragants CAN. Dist(s): Penton Overseas

Belle au Bois Dormant. 1 cass. (FRE.). (J). (gr. 4 up). 1991. bk. 14.95 (1AD022) Olivia & Hill.
Sleeping Beauty.

Belle Case la Follette: 1859-1931. Jocelyn Riley. 1 cass. (Running Time: 15 min.). (YA). 1987. 8.00 (978-1-877933-33-2(3)) Her Own Words.
Documentary.

Belle Dame sans Merci see Treasury of John Keats

Belle Dame sans Merci see Poetry of Keats

Belle Dame sans Merci see Famous Story Poems

Belle Dame Sans Merci (A Poem from the Poets' Corner) The One-and-Only Poetry Book for the Whole Family. unabr. ed. John Keats & John Lithgow. Read by John Lithgow. (Running Time: 10 mins.). (ENG.). 2008. 0.99 (978-1-60024-322-6(3)) Pub: Hachet Audio. Dist(s): HachBkGrp

Belle et la Bete. Madame Le Prince de Beaumont. 1 cass.Tr. of Beauty & the Beast. (FRE.). 1991. 21.95 (1419-VSL) Olivia & Hill.
The story of "la belle" who because of her love for her father goes to live with "la bete". This touching fairytale was filmed by Jean Cocteau.

Belle of Nauvoo, Set. abr. ed. Becky Paget. 2 cass. 11.98 (978-1-55503-701-7(1), 07001010) Covenant Comms.

Belle Prater's Boy. Ruth White. Read by Alison Elliott. 4 cass. (Running Time: 4 hrs.). (YA). 2000. 30.00 (978-0-7366-9067-6(0)) Books on Tape.
Gypsy Lemaster, the town beauty & her cross-eyed cousin Woodrow trade secrets in this tale "that transcends age with its timeless story of loss, love & friendship".

Belle Prater's Boy. unabr. ed. Ruth White. Read by Alison Elliot. 4 vols. (Running Time: 3 hrs. 38 mins.). (J). (gr. 5-9). 2004. pap. bk. 38.00 (978-0-8072-8682-1(6), YA234SP, Listening Lib); 32.00 (978-0-8072-8681-4(8), YA234CX, Listening Lib) Random Audio Pubg.

Belle Prater's Boy. unabr. ed. Ruth White. Read by Alison Elliot. 3 CDs. (Running Time: 3 hrs. 38 mins.). (ENG.). (J). (gr. 5). 2005. audio compact disk 14.99 (978-0-307-20655-8(6), Listening Lib) Pub: Random Audio Pubg. Dist(s): Random

Belle Ruin. unabr. ed. Martha Grimes. Read by Kim Mai Guest. 8 cass. (Running Time: 11 hrs.). (Emma Graham Mysteries Ser.). 2005. 81.00 (978-1-4159-2304-7(3)); audio compact disk 99.00 (978-1-4159-2305-4(1)) Books on Tape.

Belle Ruin. unabr. ed. Martha Grimes. Read by Kim Mai Guest. (Running Time: 12 hrs.). (ENG.). (gr. 12 up). 2005. audio compact disk 39.95 (978-0-14-305830-4(4)) Penguin Grp USA.

Belle Starr. Speer Morgan. Read by Speer Morgan. 1 cass. (Running Time: 35 min.). 13.95 (978-1-55644-021-2(9), 1121) Am Audio Prose.
Portrait of a female character, with dialogue.

Belle Starr's Race Mare. Jane Coleman. (Running Time: 0 hr. 24 mins.). 2000. 10.95 (978-1-60083-532-2(5)) Iofy Corp.

***Belle Star's Race Mare.** Jane Candia Coleman. 2009. (978-1-60136-424-1(5)) Audio Holding.

Belle Teale. unabr. ed. Ann M. Martin. Narrated by Julia Gibson. 4 pieces. (Running Time: 4 hrs. 30 mins.). (gr. 5 up). 2002. 42.00 (978-1-4025-1952-9(4)) Recorded Bks.

Belle Weather: Mostly Sunny with a Chance of Scattered Hissy Fits. unabr. ed. Celia Rivenbark. Read by Celia Rivenbark. (Running Time: 5 hrs.). 2008. 39.95 (978-0-7927-5911-9(7)); audio compact disk 64.95 (978-0-7927-5641-5(X)) AudioGO.

Belle Weather: Mostly Sunny with a Chance of Scattered Hissy Fits. unabr. ed. Celia Rivenbark. Read by Celia Rivenbark. 4 CDs. (Running Time: 5 hrs.). (ENG.). 2008. audio compact disk 24.95 (978-1-4272-0505-6(1)) Pub: Macmill Audio. Dist(s): Macmillan

Belling the Cat. 1 cass. (Bilingual Fables). 12.00 (Natl Textbk Co) M-H Contemporary.
Presents a story in Spanish & English.

Bellini Card. unabr. ed. Jason Goodwin. Narrated by Stephen Hoye. 8 CDs. (Running Time: 10 hrs. 30 mins. 0 sec.). (Yashim the Eunuch Ser.). (ENG.).

2009. audio compact disk 69.99 (978-1-4001-4012-1(9)); audio compact disk 24.99 (978-1-4001-6012-9(X)) Pub: Tantor Media. Dist(s): IngramPubServ

Bellini Card. unabr. ed. Jason Goodwin. Read by Stephen Hoye. 8 CDs. (Running Time: 10 hrs. 30 mins. 0 sec.). (Yashim the Eunuch Ser.). (ENG.). 2009. audio compact disk 34.99 (978-1-4001-1012-4(2)) Pub: Tantor Media. Dist(s): IngramPubServ

Bells see Fall of the House of Usher & Other Works

Bells see Best of Edgar Allan Poe

Bells see Edgar Allan Poe, Set, Short Stories and Poems

Bells. Jo Verity. 2009. 84.95 (978-1-4079-0401-6(9)); audio compact disk 99.95 (978-1-4079-0402-3(7)) Pub: Soundings Ltd GBR. Dist(s): Ulverscroft US

***Bells.** unabr. ed. Richard Harvell. (Running Time: 13 hrs.). 2010. 29.95 (978-1-4417-6323-5(6)); audio compact disk 32.95 (978-1-4417-6322-8(8)) Blckstn Audio.

***Bells: A Novel.** unabr. ed. Richard Harvell. (Running Time: 13 hrs.). 2010. 79.95 (978-1-4417-6320-4(1)); audio compact disk 109.00 (978-1-4417-6321-1(X)) Blckstn Audio.

Bells & Other Poems. (J). (SAC 1023) Spoken Arts.

Bells for John Whiteside's Daughter see Twentieth-Century Poetry in English, No. 5, Recordings of Poets Reading Their Own Poetry

Bells of Bicêtre. unabr. collector's ed. Georges Simenon. Read by Michael Prichard. 8 cass. (Running Time: 8 hrs.). 1984. 48.00 (978-0-7366-0539-7(8), 1513) Books on Tape.
Rene Maugras has risen from obscurity to publisher of a highly influential Paris newspaper. He is a relentless worker, but he enjoys the good things of life as well. Then suddenly he finds himself in a Paris hospital, speechless & paralyzed, yet surprisingly clear of mind. For the first time in his life he is forced to reflect.

Bells of Burracombe. Lilian Harry. (Soundings Ser.). (J). 2006. 94.95 (978-1-84559-331-5(6)); audio compact disk 99.95 (978-1-84559-377-3(4)) Pub: ISIS Lrg Prnt GBR. Dist(s): Ulverscroft US

Bells of Christmas. Perf. by Gloriae Dei Ringers. (Running Time: 57 mins.). Orig. Title: Hear Them Ring: the Bells of Christmas. 2004. audio compact disk 16.95 (978-1-55725-413-9(3), GDCD110) Paraclete MA.

Bells of Christmas. Virginia Hamilton. (J). (CP 1384) HarperCollins Pubs.

Bells of Glocken: Accompaniment/Performance. Anna Laura Page & Jean Anne Shafferman. (ENG.). 2003. audio compact disk 59.95 (978-0-7390-3199-5(6)) Alfred Pub.

Bells of Glocken: Listening. Anna Laura Page & Jean Anne Shafferman. (ENG.). 2003. audio compact disk 14.95 (978-0-7390-3198-8(8)) Alfred Pub.

Bells of San Carlos. Max Brand. (Running Time: 0 hr. 42 mins.). 1998. 10.95 (978-1-60083-466-0(3)) Iofy Corp.

Bells of San Filipo. unabr. ed. Max Brand. Read by Jim Bond. (Running Time: 7 hrs.). 2007. 39.25 (978-1-4233-3518-4(X), 9781423335184, BADLE); 24.95 (978-1-4233-3517-7(1), 9781423335177, BAD) Brilliance Audio.

Bells of San Filipo. unabr. ed. Max Brand. Read by Jim Bond. (Running Time: 8 hrs.). 2007. audio compact disk 24.95 (978-1-4233-3515-3(5), 9781423335153, Brilliance MP3); audio compact disk 39.25 (978-1-4233-3516-0(3), 9781423335160, Brlnc Audio MP3 Lib) Brilliance Audio.

Bells of San Filipo. unabr. ed. Max Brand. Read by Jim Bond. (Running Time: 8 hrs.). 2009. audio compact disk 19.99 (978-1-4418-0453-2(6), 9781441804532, Bril Audio CD Unabri); audio compact disk 59.97 (978-1-4418-0454-9(4), 9781441804549, BriAudCD Unabrid) Brilliance Audio.

Bells of St. Mary's. Perf. by Bing Crosby. 1 cass. (Running Time: 60 min.). 1947. 7.95 (DD-5085) Natl Recrd Co.
In the story "The Bells of St. Marys", Father O'Malley & Sister Benedict do not always agree on how to solve school problems, but they have great respect for each other. In the story "Holiday Inn", Jim turns a farm into a nightclub open only on holidays. Linda gets a job at the Inn & Jim's "Dreaming of a White Christmas" includes her. Jim's ex-partner shows up & complicates things, but true love wins.

Bell's Theorem: Experimental Consequences & Implications. John Clauser. 1 cass. 9.00 (A0022-87) Sound Photosyn.

Bellwether. unabr. ed. Connie Willis. Read by Kate Reading. (Running Time: 6.5 hrs. NaN mins.). 2009. 29.95 (978-1-4332-4626-5(0)); audio compact disk 44.95 (978-1-4332-4623-4(6)); audio compact disk 60.00 (978-1-4332-4624-1(4)) Blckstn Audio.

Belly Button. Perf. by Odds Bodkin. Created by Odds Bodkin. Contrib. by Perkins School for the Blind. 1 cass. (Running Time: 21 mins.). (J). 2002. (978-0-9743510-2-5(4)) Perkins Schl Blind.
This tape builds on the book also titled "Belly Button." Perkins Panda introduces himself and sings an up-tempo song titled "Belly Button" (about the parts of his body) and a lullaby titled "Someone Loves You." This tape is also designed to accompany the Belly Button Activity Guide that provides activities that parents and other caregivers can do with children with visual impairments.

Belly Flop. unabr. ed. Morris Gleitzman. Read by Morris Gleitzman. 2 cass. (Running Time: 2 hrs. 40 mins.). (J). 2003. 24.00 (978-1-74093-011-6(8)) Pub: Bolinda Pubng AUS. Dist(s): Bolinda Pub Inc

Belly Flop. unabr. ed. Morris Gleitzman. Read by Mary-Anne Fahey. 2 CDs. (Running Time: 2 hrs. 40 mins.). (J). 2003. audio compact disk 43.95 (978-1-74093-134-2(3)) Pub: Bolinda Pubng AUS. Dist(s): Bolinda Pub Inc

Belly of Paris. Emile Zola & Frederick Davidson. 9 cass. (Running Time: 13 hrs.). 2002. 62.95 (978-0-7861-1628-7(5), 2456) Blckstn Audio.

Belly of Paris. unabr. ed. Emile Zola. Read by Frederick Davidson. 9 cass. (Running Time: 13 hrs. 30 min.). 1999. 62.95 (2456) Blckstn Audio.
The author chooses as his locale the newly-built food markets of Paris. Into this extravagance of food he places his young hero, the half-starved Florent, who has just escaped imprisonment in Cayenne.

Bellybugs. 1 CD. (Running Time: 20 min.). (Good to Grow Ser.). (J). (ps-3). 2001. pap. bk. & act. bk. ed. 8.95 (978-1-929962-01-3(0)) Write BIG.
Bellybugs teaches about the sanctity of life and the value of compassion for other living things.

BellyliciousRaks. Executive Producer Aleya Pena. 2007. audio compact disk 20.00 (978-1-4276-1640-1(X)) AardGP.

Belong to Me. unabr. ed. Marisa de los Santos. Read by Julia Gibson. 2009. audio compact disk 19.99 (978-0-06-178022-6(7), Harper Audio) HarperCollins Pubs.

***Belong to Me: A Novel.** unabr. ed. Marisa De Los Santos. Read by Julia Gibson. (ENG.). 2008. (978-0-06-163246-4(5)); (978-0-06-163247-1(3)) HarperCollins Pubs.

Belonging to God. Thomas Merton. 1 cass. 1995. 8.95 (AA2805) Credence Commun.
The art of the cross is overcoming evil with the goodness of love. This is only possible if you have been overcome first by love, by belonging to God.

Beloved. Toni Morrison. Read by Lynn Whitfield. Perf. by Oprah Winfrey. 2 cass. (Running Time: 3 hrs.). 1999. 16.85 (978-1-85686-751-1(X)) Ulvrscrft Audio.
It is the mid-1800's. At Sweet Home in Kentucky, an era is ending as slavery comes under attack from the abolitionists. The worlds of Halle & Paul D. are to be destroyed in a cataclysm of torment & agony.

Beloved. unabr. ed. Toni Morrison. Read by Toni Morrison. 8 cass. (Running Time: 12 hrs.). 2000. 39.95 (N140) Blckstn Audio.
Brings the unimaginable experience of slavery into our comprehension. The story of Sethe, an escaped slave who has risked her life, lost a husband & buried a child.

Beloved. unabr. ed. Toni Morrison. 10 CDs. (Running Time: 12 hrs.). 2006. audio compact disk 84.15 (978-1-4159-3535-4(1)) Pub: Books on Tape. Dist(s): NetLibrary CO

Beloved. unabr. ed. Toni Morrison. Read by Toni Morrison. 10 CDs. (Running Time: 43200 sec.). (ENG.). 2007. audio compact disk 29.95 (978-0-7393-4227-5(4), Random AudioBks) Pub: Random Audio Pubg. Dist(s): Random

Beloved: Songs in Praise & Worship of Sri Da Avaghasa (The "Bright") unabr. ed. Perf. by Free Daist Sacred Music Guild. 1 cass. 1992. 11.95 (M-AB) Dawn Horse Pr.
Devotional chants based on traditional religious music, east & west.

Beloved Arias. Michael Ballam. 1 cass. 9.95 (978-1-55503-299-9(0), 1100386); 9.95 (1100386) Covenant Comms.
Classical masterpieces from famous operas.

Beloved Bible Stories: The Creation, Noah & the Ark. unabr. abr. ed. Listening Library Staff & Rabbit Ears Books Staff. Read by Amy Grant & Kelly McGillis. (Running Time: 3600 sec.). (Rabbit Ears Ser.). (ENG.). (J). (gr. 1-4). 2006. audio compact disk 11.95 (978-0-7393-3709-7(2), Listening Lib) Pub: Random Audio Pubg. Dist(s): Random

Beloved Christmas Songs. Perf. by Daryl Coley & Beloved Staff. 1 cass. 1999. (978-0-7601-3076-6(0)); audio compact disk (978-0-7601-3075-9(2)) Brentwood Music.
Songs include: "Carol of the Bells/Silver Bells" medley; "Glory to God"; "Jesus Christ the Reason"; "God's Only Son"; "Oh Come Emmanuel/God Rest Ye Merry Gentlemen" medley; "It Came upon a Midnight Clear/Angels We Have Heard on High" medley; "Emmanuel"; "While Shepherds Watched Their Flocks"; "Christmas Is Here.".

Beloved Dearly. unabr. ed. Doug Cooney. Read by Full Cast Production Staff. (J). 2007. 34.99 (978-1-60252-493-4(9)) Find a World.

Beloved Dearly. unabr. ed. Doug Cooney. Read by Doug Cooney. Read by Full Cast Production Staff. 2 cass. (Running Time: 3 hrs.). (YA). 2002. lib. bdg. 20.00 (978-1-932076-00-4(X)) Full Cast Audio.

Beloved Dearly. unabr. ed. Doug Cooney. Featuring Doug Cooney. Read by Full Cast Production Staff. 2 cass. (Running Time: 3 hrs.). 2002. (978-0-9717540-8-9(X), 02005) Full Cast Audio.

Beloved Disciple. Beth Moore. 2009. audio compact disk 9.99 (978-1-4418-3080-7(4)) Brilliance Audio.

Beloved Disciple: Following John to the Heart of Jesus. abr. ed. Beth Moore. Read by Sandra Burr. 3 CDs. (Running Time: 3 hrs.). 2004. audio compact disk 62.25 (978-1-59355-644-0(6), 1593556446); 17.95 (978-1-59355-641-9(1), 1593556411); 44.25 (978-1-59355-642-6(X), 159355642X); audio compact disk 19.95 (978-1-59355-643-3(8), 1593556438) Brilliance Audio.
John the apostle must have thought he had seen everything. Having been with Jesus all the years of his ministry, John witnessed more miracles than he could count, saw more displays of power than he could comprehend, and experienced more love than he could fathom. And one unforgettable morning young John outran Peter to his Savior's empty tomb. Just as Christ took John on a lifelong journey into the depths of His love, He will do the same for you. The bridegroom's love is unmatched and inexhaustible, and He is waiting to lavish it on you, His beloved. You will not be the same.

Beloved Disciple: Following John to the Heart of Jesus. abr. ed. Beth Moore. Read by Sandra Burr. (Running Time: 3 hrs.). 2006. 39.25 (978-1-4233-0328-2(8), 9781423303282, BADLE); 24.95 (978-1-4233-0327-5(X), 9781423303275, BAD); 39.25 (978-1-4233-0326-8(1), 9781423303268, Brlnc Audio MP3 Lib); 24.95 (978-1-4233-0325-1(3), 9781423303251, Brilliance MP3) Brilliance Audio.

Beloved Disciple: Following John to the Heart of Jesus. unabr. ed. Beth Moore. Read by Sandra Burr. (Running Time: 12 hrs.). 2009. 39.97 (978-1-4418-2527-8(4), 9781441825278, Brlnc Audio MP3 Lib); 39.97 (978-1-4418-2529-2(0), 9781441825292, BADLE); 19.99 (978-1-4418-2526-1(6), 9781441825261, Brilliance MP3); 19.99 (978-1-4418-2528-5(2), 9781441825285, BAD); audio compact disk 19.99 (978-1-4418-2524-7(X), 9781441825247, Bril Audio CD Unabri); audio compact disk 97.97 (978-1-4418-2525-4(8), 9781441825254, BriAudCD Unabrid) Brilliance Audio.

Beloved Disciple the Life & Ministry of John. Beth Moore. (YA). 2003. audio compact disk 39.95 (978-0-633-01854-2(6)) LifeWay Christian.

Beloved Land. Janette Oke & T. Davis Bunn. Read by Marguerite Gavin. (Running Time: 28800 sec.). (Song of Acadia Ser.). 2006. audio compact disk 63.00 (978-0-7861-5994-9(4)) Blckstn Audio.

Beloved Land. Janette Oke & T. Davis Bunn. Narrated by Suzanne Toren. 6 cass. (Running Time: 8 hrs. 45 mins.). (Song of Acadia Ser.: Vol. 5). 2002. 58.00 (978-1-4025-4404-0(9)) Recorded Bks.

Beloved Land. unabr. ed. Janette Oke & T. Davis Bunn. Read by Marguerite Gavin. (Running Time: 28800 sec.). (Song of Acadia Ser.: Vol. 5). 2006. 54.95 (978-0-7861-4886-8(1)); audio compact disk 29.95 (978-0-7861-7114-9(6)) Blckstn Audio.

Beloved Leah. unabr. ed. Cynthia Davis. Read by M. J. Wilde. 4 cass. (Running Time: 6 hrs.). (Footprints from the Bible Ser.: No. 1). 2001. 27.00 (978-1-58807-075-3(1), 691178) Am Pubng Inc.
Leah's life-long journey in the shadow of her sister, Rachel, has consumed her with jealousy and bitterness. It is rumored that she will never marry; but, by the clever deception of her father, Leah is finally wed to her cousin, Jacob bar Isaac. To her distress, the man her father has chosen as her husband is the man who is deeply in love with Rachel. One week after Leah's marriage, the father's agreement reaches fruition, and Rachel is wed to Leah's husband. Leah finds comfort in her ability to please Jacob by bearing many sons in order to carry on his legacy; however, when Rachel is blessed with her first son, Joseph, whom Jacob deems the "special son", jealousy ensues throughout the family. Ultimately, Leah's faith in God is put to the test as she spends a lifetime competing with her sister for the love and affection of Jacob. Can she come to an understanding of the love of her husband and his God before it is too late?.

Beloved Sings of Love: Songs of Meher Baba. Poems. Tr. by Naosherwan Anzar. Music by Jai Uttal. 1 CD. 2003. audio compact disk 14.95 (978-0-9702396-3-1(7)) Beloved Arch.
Reading in Hindustani by Naosherwan AnzarReading in English by Cecilia Kirtland.

Beloved Son. Gloriae Dei Cantores Schola. audio compact disk 16.95 (978-1-55725-296-8(3), GDCD032) Paraclete MA.

Beloved Songs of Faith. Michael Ballam. 1 cass. 9.95 (10001034); audio compact disk 14.95 (2800632) Covenant Comms.

Beloved Vagabond. William J. Locke. Read by Peter Joyce. 2002. pap. bk. 69.95 (978-1-86015-473-7(5)) Ulverscroft US.

Beloved Vagabond. unabr. ed. William J. Locke. Read by Peter Joyce. 10 CDs. 2002. audio compact disk 89.95 (978-1-86015-010-4(1)) Pub: Mgna Lrg Print GBR. Dist(s): Ulverscroft US

Beloved Was Bahamas: A Steer to Remember. unabr. collector's ed. Harriet E. Weaver. Read by Roses Prichard. 6 cass. (Running Time: 6 hrs.). (J). (gr. 4-7). 1981. 36.00 (978-0-7366-0471-0(5), 1446) Books on Tape.
In 1964, the magnificent redwood country of northern California was ravaged by a spectacular flood. "Beloved Was Bahamas" is based on a true incident from that storm: The amazing rescue of a 900 pound steer & its return to its owner by a 15-year old boy.

Beloved Woman. unabr. ed. Kathleen Thompson Norris. Narrated by Flo Gibson. 7 cass. (Running Time: 10 hrs.). 2003. 25.95 (978-1-55685-680-8(6),) Audio Bk Con.
The mystery of her parenthood & the pain in loving two men are part of what Norma has to deal with. There is a sweetness in this novel that is enchanting.

Belt: Ephesians 6:10-13, 642. Ed Young. 1987. Rental 4.95 (978-0-7417-1642-2(9), 642) Win Walk.

Belton Estate. Anthony Trollope. Narrated by Flo Gibson. (ENG.). 2008. audio compact disk 39.95 (978-1-55685-990-8(2)) Audio Bk Con.

Belton Estate. unabr. ed. Anthony Trollope. Narrated by Flo Gibson. 10 cass. (Running Time: 15 hrs.). 2003. 29.95 (978-1-55685-702-7(0)) Audio Bk Con.
Charming, loving Clara Zmedroz is involved with two suitors. How she deals with this dilemma is full of humor and very moving.

Beluga Passage. Linda Lingemann. 1 cass. (Running Time: 35 min.). (J). (ps-2). 2001. bk. 19.95 (SP 4012C) Kimbo Educ.
Beluga Calf's pod is making a passage to the warm waters of the Bering Sea. Includes book.

Beluga Passage. Linda Lingemann. Narrated by Peter Thomas. Illus. by Jon Weiman. 1 cass. (Smithsonian Oceanic Collection). (J). (ps-2). 1996. 5.00 (978-1-56899-312-6(9), C4012) Soundprints.
It is September in the Arctic & Beluga Calf's pod is making a passage to the warm waters of the Bering Sea. On the way, the whales face many dangers; polar bears & orcas are constantly on the prowl. One day, after a surprise encounter with an orca pod, the exhausted belugas fall asleep beneath broken ice. As they sleep, the ice closes in above them & freezes solid. To breathe, the belugas must break through to the surface.

Belva Plain. Interview with Belva Plain. 1 cass. (Running Time: 35 min.). 1980. 12.95 (L064) TFR.
On her best sellers, "Evergreen" & "Random Winds," Plain says one theme characterizes both - a great love that threatens but does not destroy a marriage. She reveals how a chance of observation of a couple, a beautiful young girl & a crippled elderly man, started the thought process that resulted in "Random Winds".

Belvedere Tower. Elizabeth Hawksley. Read by Gordon Griffin. 8 cass. (Running Time: 10 hrs.). (Soundings Ser.). (J). 2004. 69.95 (978-1-84283-573-9(4)) Pub: ISIS Lrg Prnt GBR. Dist(s): Ulverscroft US

Belwin 21s. Jack Bullock & Anthony Maiello. (Belwin 21st Century Band Method Ser.). (ENG.). 1996. audio compact disk 10.95 (978-0-7579-2527-6(8), B21100CD1, Warner Bro) Alfred Pub.

Belwin 21st Band Book CD Accompaniment: Level 2, Vol. 2. Jack Bullock. (Belwin 21st Century Band Method Ser.). (ENG.). 1997. audio compact disk 10.95 (978-0-7692-1747-5(8), Warner Bro) Alfred Pub.

Belwin 21st Century Band Method, Vol. 3. Composed by Jack Bullock & Anthony Maiello. (ENG.). (gr. 3). 1999. audio compact disk 10.95 (978-0-7692-9349-3(2), Warner Bro) Alfred Pub.

BEN & JERRY's DOUBLE-DIP CAPITALISM: LEAD W/YOUR VALUES & MAKE MONEY TOO CST: Lead with Your Values & Make Money Too. Ben Cohen & Jerry Greenfield. 2004. 10.95 (978-0-7435-4192-3(8)) Pub: S&S Audio. Dist(s): S and S Inc

Ben & Me: An Astonishing Life of Benjamin Franklin. Robert Lawson. Narrated by George Guidall. 2 CDs. (Running Time: 1 hr. 45 mins.). (gr. 3 up). audio compact disk 22.00 (978-0-7887-9517-6(1)) Recorded Bks.

Ben & Me: An Astonishing Life of Benjamin Franklin. unabr. ed. Robert Lawson. Narrated by George Guidall. 2 pieces. (Running Time: 1 hr. 45 mins.). (gr. 3 up). 1995. 19.00 (978-0-7887-0180-1(0), 94405E7) Recorded Bks.
The life of Ben Franklin as recounted by his lifelong friend, Amos the mouse.

Ben-Hur. Lew Wallace. Read by Lloyd James. 16 cass. (Running Time: 23 hrs. 30 mins.). 2000. 99.95 (978-0-7861-1886-1(5), 2685) Blckstn Audio.
Born the son of a nobleman, Ben-Hur is condemned to the galleys for life after he accidentally dislodges a piece of tile which falls on the Roman procurator. He is betrayed by his best friend, manages to escape his imprisonment, & gains revenge & glory before the cheering multitudes in the chariot races at the Roman Circus in Antioch. Later he fulfills his true destiny at the foot of the cross on a hill in Jerusalem.

Ben-hur. Lewis Wallace. Read by Yadira Sánchez. (Running Time: 3 hrs.). 2002. 16.95 (978-1-60083-233-8(4), Audiofy Corp) Iofy Corp.

Ben Hur. abr. ed. Lew Wallace. Read by Jeff Harding. 2 cass. (Running Time: 2 hrs. 30 mins.). (Classic Literature with Classical Music Ser.). 1996. 54.98 (978-962-634-507-8(1), NA200714, Naxos AudioBooks) Naxos.
Combines the best elements of popular classic, epic and action story against a background of authoritive historical detail.

Ben Hur. abr. ed. Lew Wallace. Read by Jeff Harding. 2 CDs. (Classic Literature with Classical Music Ser.). 2006. audio compact disk 17.98 (978-962-634-375-3(3), Naxos AudioBooks) Naxos.

Ben-Hur. abr. ed. Lewis Wallace. Read by Yadira Sánchez. 3 CDs. (SPA.). 2002. audio compact disk 17.00 (978-958-8161-22-8(3)) YoYoMusic.

Ben Hur. adpt. ed. Prod. by Focus on the Family Staff. Adapted by Paul McCusker. Lew Wallace. (Running Time: 2 hrs. 10 mins.). (Radio Theatre Ser.). (ENG.). 2007. audio compact dis[illegible]97 (978-1-58997-396-1(8), Tyndale Ent) Tyndale Hse.

Ben Hur. unabr. ed. (Running Time: 23 hrs. [illegible] mins.). (J). 2006. audio compact disk 120.00 (978-0-7861-6288-8(0)) Blckstn Audio.

Ben Hur. unabr. ed. Lew Wallace. Read by Lloyd James. 2. (Running Time: 82800 sec.). 2006. audio compact disk 44.95 (978-0-7861-7215-3(0)) Blckstn Audio.

Ben-Hur. unabr. ed. Lew Wallace. Read by Lloyd James. (YA). 2008. 114.99 (978-1-60514-872-4(5)) Find a World.

Ben-Hur, Pt. 1. unabr. collector's ed. Lew Wallace. Read by Jim Killavey. 8 cass. (Running Time: 12 hrs.). 1991. 64.00 (978-0-7366-3961-3(6), 9217-A) Books on Tape.
Judah Ben-Hur, a wealthy young Jew, makes an ememy of a powerful Roman, Messala, who hungers to topple him. An "accident" sends Ben-Hur

to the galleys. Stripped of his fortune, he works as a slave. He learns the skills of a Roman warrior & the faith of a Christian.

Ben-Hur, Pt. 2. unabr. collector's ed. Lew Wallace. Read by Jim Killavey. 8 cass. (Running Time: 12 hrs.). 1991. 64.00 (978-0-7366-3962-0(4), 9217-B) Books on Tape.

Ben-Hur: A Tale of the Christ. unabr. ed. Lew Wallace. Read by Jim Killavey. 16 cass. (Running Time: 24 hrs.). 1991. 89.00 set. (C-217) Jimcin Record.
Epic story of early Christianity.

Ben, in the World. unabr. ed. Doris Lessing. Read by Martyn Read. 6 CDs. (Running Time: 24300 sec.). (Isis Ser.). 2003. audio compact disk 64.95 (978-0-7531-2226-6(X)) Pub: ISIS Lrg Prnt GBR. Dist(s): Ulverscroft US
Ben Lovatt can never fit in. He seems awkward too big, too strong, inhumanly made. Those who do not understand him want him locked up, including his own mother. Now he has come of age and finds himself alone in the south of France, in Brazil and in the mountains of the Andes, where at last he finds out where he has come from and who are his people.

Ben, in the World: The Sequel to the Fifth Child. unabr. ed. Doris Lessing & Martyn Read. 6 cass. (Isis Ser.). (J). 2003. 54.95 (978-0-7531-1000-3(8)) Pub: ISIS Lrg Prnt GBR. Dist(s): Ulverscroft US

Ben Okri. unabr. ed. Ed. by Jim McKinley. Prod. by Rebekah Presson. 1 cass. (Running Time: 29 min.). (New Letters on the Air Ser.). 1994. 10.00 (022194) New Letters.
The young (34) Nigerian writer has already won Britain's top literary award, the Booker Prize. He received it for "The Famished Road," a novel narrated by an African "spirit child" or "abiku." In his new novel, "Songs of Enchantment," the abiku, Azaro, who would prefer to return to the spirit world, again narrates, this time telling a story of a country coming out from under colonial rule.

Ben Sasway: The Draft: Why I Did Not Register. (Running Time: 60 min.). (Long Beach City College). 1983. 9.00 (F154) Freeland Pr.
Talks about his position on the draft & the consequences.

Ben Tankard: Git Yo Prayze On. 1997. 10.98 (978-0-7601-1724-8(1)); audio compact disk 15.98 CD. (978-0-7601-1725-5(X)) Brentwood Music.
Contemporary gospel & gospel jazz with vocal ensemble showcased on "Git Yo Prayze On," "Sing for the Children," & "Spend Some Time with Me".

Ben Weatherstaff see Secret Garden: A Young Reader's Edition of the Classic Story

Ben Zakkai's Coffin. unabr. ed. Perf. by Harley L. Sachs. 7 cass. (Running Time: 7 hrs.). 2001. 35.00 (978-0-9705390-7-6(X)) I D E V C O.
Born of a Jewish father and a Catholic mother, Herman Bachrach has no religion but is drawn by circumstances into a holocaust vendetta over gold stolen from Jewish depositors by a Swissbank. Herman is seduced by a woman who calls herself "Diana" (no last name) and is suspected by detective sheehan to be her murderer. His Jewish boss provides him with a lawyer, but sends him to Switzerland to finish the job Diana started.

Benchley's Best. unabr. ed. Robert Benchley. Read by Henry Morgan. Intro. by Nathaniel Benchley. 2 cass. (Running Time: 98 min.). (Cassette Bookshelf Ser.). 1987. 15.98 (978-0-8072-3463-1(X), CB121CX, Listening Lib) Random Audio Pubg.
Selections include: "The Treasurer's Report"; "Inter-Office Memo"; "Mystery of Bridge Building;"; "Cleaning Out the Desk"; "Easy Tests"; "Edith's Christmas Burglar"; "Stranger Within Our Gates"; "Paul Revere's Ride"; "Carnival Weel in Sunny Las Los"; "Ladies Wild" & "First-Catch Criminal".

Bend & the Cascades. Dan Heller. 1 cass. 1995. 9.95; 9.95 (978-1-885433-05-3(0)) Takilma East.

Bend in the River. V. S. Naipaul & Simon Vance. 9 CDs. (Running Time: 11 hrs.). 2002. audio compact disk 72.00 (978-0-7861-8448-4(5), 3341) Blckstn Audio.

Bend in the River. unabr. ed. V. S. Naipaul. Read by Simon Vance. 9 cass. (Running Time: 11 hrs.). 2004. 56.95 (978-0-7861-2817-4(8), 3341) Blckstn Audio.

Bend in the Road. Nicholas Sparks. Narrated by L. J. Ganser. 7 cass. (Running Time: 10 hrs. 15 mins.). 2001. 61.00 (978-0-7887-9790-3(5), 96836) Recorded Bks.
The moving tale of a man, a woman and the devastating secret that threatens to keep them apart. When Miles Ryan's beloved wife is killed in a hit-and-run accident, he vows to bring the unknown driver to justice at all costs. He begins to question his oath, however, after he meets his son's school teacher, Sarah Andrews.

Bend in the Road. abr. ed. Nicholas Sparks. Read by John Bedford Lloyd. (ENG.). 2005. 14.98 (978-1-59483-403-5(2)) Pub: Hachet Audio. Dist(s): HachBkGrp

Bend in the Road. unabr. ed. Nicholas Sparks. Read by L. J. Ganser. (ENG.). 2005. 14.98 (978-1-59483-404-2(0)) Pub: Hachet Audio. Dist(s): HachBkGrp

Bend in the Road. unabr. ed. Nicholas Sparks. Read by L. J. Ganser. (Running Time: 10 hrs.). (ENG.). 2009. 70.98 (978-1-60788-073-8(3)) Pub: Hachet Audio. Dist(s): HachBkGrp

Bend in the Road. unabr. ed. Nicholas Sparks. Narrated by L. J. Ganser. 9 CDs. (Running Time: 10 hrs. 15 mins.). 2001. audio compact disk 89.00 (978-0-7887-9850-4(2), C1469) Recorded Bks.
Miles Ryan's life was changed forever the day his beloved wife and first love was killed in a hit-and-run accident. Now two years later, deputy sherrif Miles awaits the day when he will bring the unknown driver to justice. When he meets Sarah Andrews, his son's second grade teacher, he begins to feel things he hasn't felt in years. Sarah has settled in New Bern, North Carolina after a difficult divorce to start afresh. Miles and Sarah connect immediately, and soon find themselves falling deeply in love - but a dark and terrible secret threatens to keep them apart forever.

Bend of the Snake. unabr. ed. Bill Gulick. Read by Jack Sondericker. 6 cass. (Running Time: 7 hrs. 36 min.). 2001. 39.95 (978-1-58116-018-5(6)) Books in Motion.
While trying to run a stage line into Snake River county, Scott Burton & his business partner face powerful & diabolical forces.

***Bend Sinister.** unabr. ed. Vladimir Nabokov. 2010. audio compact disk 29.99 (978-1-4418-7287-6(6)) Brilliance Audio.

Bend the Church & Bow the World. Derek Prince. 6 cass. 29.95 Set. (BCWI) Derek Prince.
The theme of the revival that shook the little nation of Wales in 1904, it is still true today - if the Church will bend, the World will bow.

Bendiceme, Ultima. Rudolfo A. Anaya. 7 cass. (Running Time: 10 hrs.).Tr. of Bless Me, Ultima. (SPA.). 69.75 (978-1-4025-7663-8(3)) Recorded Bks.

Bendicion de vivir bajo Autoridad. Victor Richards. (SPA.). 2003. 11.99 (978-1-885630-74-2(3)) Jayah Producc.

Bendicion de vivir bajo Autoridad. Victor Richards. (SPA.). 2004. audio compact disk 11.99 (978-1-885630-87-2(5)) Jayah Producc.

Beneath a Cross Accompaniment. Deborah Craig-Claar. 1996. audio compact disk 35.00 (978-0-7673-0728-4(3)) LifeWay Christian.

Beneath a Harvest Sky. abr. ed. Tracie Peterson. Read by Sandra Burr. 2 cass. (Running Time: 3 hrs.). (Desert Roses Ser.: Vol. 3). 2003. 17.95 (978-1-59355-157-5(6), 1593551576); 44.25 (978-1-59355-156-8(8), 1593551568); audio compact disk 19.95 (978-1-59355-158-2(4), 1593551584); audio compact disk 62.25 (978-1-59355-159-9(2), 1593551592) Brilliance Audio.
Sharing the unique beauty and history of the Southwest has always delighted Rainy Gordon, and now as a tour guide for the Harvey House Detours, she's given ample opportunity. When the colorful array of well-to-do guests includes a famous movie actor, she is surprised to find his attentions are drawn her way. She is equally intrigued when Duncan Hartford accompanies her trips as a driver trainee. But the past she's left behind threatens to haunt her again when she becomes a suspect in an investigation of stolen Indian artifacts. As evidence continues to mount against her, Rainy fears for her job - and her heart, as well.

Beneath a Harvest Sky. abr. ed. Tracie Peterson. Read by Sandra Burr. (Running Time: 3 hrs.). (Desert Roses Ser.: Vol. 3). 2006. 39.25 (978-1-4233-0372-5(5), 9781423303725, BADLE); 24.95 (978-1-4233-0371-8(7), 9781423303718, BAD); 39.25 (978-1-4233-0370-1(9), 9781423303701, Brlnc Audio MP3 Lib); audio compact disk 24.95 (978-1-4233-0369-5(5), 9781423303695, Brilliance MP3) Brilliance Audio.

Beneath the Ashes. Sue Henry. (Jessie Arnold Mystery Ser.). audio compact disk 56.00 (978-0-7366-6174-4(3)); audio compact disk 17.99 (978-0-7366-7674-8(0)) Books on Tape.

Beneath the Ashes. unabr. ed. Sue Henry. Read by Mary Peiffer. 6 cass. (Running Time: 9 hrs.). (Jessie Arnold Mystery Ser.). 2000. 48.00 (978-0-7366-5590-3(5)) Books on Tape.
Jessie Arnold must stop an arson outbreak, even if doing so means discovering that a friend is a maniacal killer.

Beneath the Ashes. unabr. ed. Sue Henry. Read by Mary Peiffer. 6 cass. (Running Time: 9 hrs.). (Jessie Arnold Mystery Ser.). 2001. 29.95 (978-0-7366-5669-6(3)); audio compact disk Books on Tape.

Beneath the Aurora. unabr. ed. Richard Woodman. Read by Geoffrey Annis. 7 cass. (Running Time: 9 hrs. 15 mins.). (Nathaniel Drinkwater Ser.: Bk. 12). (J). 2004. 61.95 (978-1-85903-650-1(3)) Pub: Mgna Lrg Print GBR. Dist(s): Ulverscroft US

Beneath the Cover: 7 Publishing Secrets Exposed to Help You Sell Your Book. Michael Drew. 1 CD. (Running Time: 50 mins). 2009. audio compact disk 12.95 (978-1-932226-73-7(7)) Wizard Acdmy.

Beneath the Ghost Moon. Jane Yolen. 1 cass. (Running Time: 15 min.). (J). 2001. pap. bk. 16.90 (978-0-8045-6833-3(2), 6833) Spoken Arts.
The farmyard mice are prepared for the Ghost Eve Ball. But the creepy-crawlies destroy their costumes and the mice have to learn how to forgive.

***Beneath the Lion's Gaze.** unabr. ed. Maaza Mengiste. Narrated by Steven Crossley. (Running Time: 11 hrs. 30 mins.). 2010. 34.99 (978-1-4001-9494-0(6)); 24.99 (978-1-4001-6494-3(X)); 17.99 (978-1-4001-8494-1(0)); audio compact disk 34.99 (978-1-4001-1494-8(2)); audio compact disk 69.99 (978-1-4001-4494-5(9)) Pub: Tantor Media. Dist(s): IngramPubServ

Beneath the Mask, Program 7. Read by Carlos Fuentes. (F007DB090) Natl Public Radio.

Beneath the Necessity of Talking. unabr. ed. Ntozake Shange. Read by Ntozake Shange. 1 cass. 1989. 13.95 (978-1-55644-334-3(X), 9051) Am Audio Prose.
Features a dramatic reading performance with musical elements.

Beneath the Skin. Nicci French. Read by Sian Thomas & Chris Pavlo. 1 cass. (Running Time: 1 hr. 30 min.). 2001. (978-0-14-180261-9(8), PengAudBks) Penguin Grp USA.
Zoe is a young schoolteacher, newly arrived in the big city. Jennifer is the prosperous, unhappy mother of three boys. Nadia is a chaotic children's entertainer, wondering what to do with her life. They are three women with nothing in common except the man who wants to kill them.

Beneath the Sky. unabr. collector's ed. Paul Block. Read by Geoffrey Howard. 8 cass. (Running Time: 12 hrs.). 1995. 64.00 (978-0-7366-2931-7(9), 3627) Books on Tape.
A betrayal pits one family against another in this mid-nineteenth century world of fierce trade battles between China & England. An exotic adventure.

Beneath the Southern Cross. unabr. ed. Judy Nunn. 14 cass. (Running Time: 20 hrs. 45 mins.). 2004. 112.00 (978-1-74030-707-9(0)) Pub: Bolinda Pubng AUS. Dist(s): Lndmrk Audiobks

Beneath the Surface. Jeni Grossman. 6 cass. 2004. 24.95 (978-1-57734-829-0(X)); audio compact disk 29.95 (978-1-57734-843-6(5)) Covenant Comms.

Beneath the Surface: Psychic Structure, Gender & Wholeness. Robert Moore. Read by Robert Moore. 1 cass. (Running Time: 74 min.). 1993. 10.95 (978-0-7822-0453-7(8), 531) C G Jung IL.

Beneath the Tree of Life: A Communion Service for All the Churches. Marty Haugen. 1 cass. 1999. 10.95 (CS-463); audio compact disk 15.95 (CD-463) GIA Pubns.

Beneath the Waves. 1 cass. (Running Time: 60 min.). 1994. audio compact disk 15.95 CD. (0265, Creativ Pub) Quayside.
Humpback whales & music. Original music by Stefan Schramm & Jonas Kvarnstrom.

Beneath the Waves. 1 cass. (Running Time: 60 min.). 1994. 9.95 (0264, NrthWrd Bks) TandN Child.

Beneath These Stones. unabr. ed. Ann Granger. Read by Bill Wallis. 8 cass. (Running Time: 12 hrs.). 2000. 69.95 (978-0-7540-0453-0(8), CAB 1876) Pub: Chivers Audio Bks GBR. Dist(s): AudioGO
First, Tammy Franklin lost her mother to illness, then her new stepmother's body was found in a railway embankment near the Franklin farm. This time the death is murder. As Superintendent Marby knows only too well, Tammy stands to have her father taken away from her. For Hugh Franklin is the main suspect.

Benedetto Players & the Guild Jazzmasters in Concert. (Running Time: 1 hr. 11 mins.). 2005. 24.95 (978-5-558-09185-4(1)) Mel Bay.

Benedict Arnold Pt. 1: Patriot & Traitor, unabr. collector's ed. Willard S. Randall. Read by Wolfram Kandinsky. 12 cass. (Running Time: 18 hrs.). 1992. 96.00 (978-0-7366-2135-9(0), 2935A) Books on Tape.
Why did Benedict Arnold betray his country? The author's attempt to answer this disturbing question.

Benedict Arnold Pt. 2: Patriot & Traitor, unabr. collector's ed. Willard S. Randall. Read by Wolfram Kandinsky. 11 cass. (Running Time: 16 hrs. 30 mins.). 1992. 88.00 (978-0-7366-2136-6(9), 2935B) Books on Tape.

Benedict Arnold Pt. A: Revolutionary Hero. unabr. collector's ed. James Kirby Martin. Read by John Edwardson. 8 cass. (Running Time: 12 hrs.). 2001. 64.00 (978-0-7366-6098-3(4)) Books on Tape.
Stories of Benedict Arnold's treason have come to define him, yet Arnold was one of the most heroic & remarkable individuals in all of American history. A brilliant military leader of uncommon bravery, Arnold poured his all into the revolutionary cause, sacrificing his family life, health & financial well-being for a conflict that left him crippled, sullied by false accusations & profoundly alienated from the American cause of liberty.

Benedict Arnold Pt. B: Revolutionary Hero. collector's unabr. ed. James Kirby Martin. Read by John Edwardson. 8 cass. (Running Time: 12 hrs.). 2001. 64.00 (978-0-7366-6099-0(2)) Books on Tape.
Stories of Benedict Arnold's treason have come to define him, yet Arnold was one of the most heroic & remarkable individuals in all of American history. A brilliant military leader of uncommon bravery, Arnold poured his all into the revolutionary cause, sacrificing his family life, health & financial well-being for a conflict that left him crippled, sullied by false accusations & profoundly alienated from the American cause of liberty.

Benedict Canyon. unabr. ed. Laura Van Wormer. Read by Jean Reed Bahle. (Running Time: 12 hrs.). 2008. 24.95 (978-1-4233-5963-0(1), 9781423359630, Brilliance MP3); 39.25 (978-1-4233-5964-7(X), 9781423359647, Brlnc Audio MP3 Lib); 39.25 (978-1-4233-5966-1(6), 9781423359661, BADLE); 24.95 (978-1-4233-5965-4(8), 9781423359654, BAD) Brilliance Audio.

Benediction, 1976 Libertarian Party National Convention. unabr. ed. Murray Newton Rothbard. 1 cass. (Running Time: 33 min.). 12.95 (749) J Norton Pubs.

Benedictus: A Eucharistic Healing Album. Contrib. by Vinny Flynn & Still Waters. 2005. audio compact disk 16.00 (978-1-884479-29-8(4)) Spirit Song.

Benefits for Older Employees, 1989. unabr. ed. Ed. by James P. Klein. 1 cass. (Running Time: 25 min.). (Quarterly Employee Benefits Audio Reports). 1989. 55.00 series of 4. (T7-9265) PLI.
The Employee Benefits Reports, a quarterly series of audiocassettes, is designed to keep practitioners & their clients informed of key litigation, legislation & regulatory actions. This audio series annually provides four twenty to thirty minute reports by experts on the most recent developments affecting employee benefits.

Benefits of Meditation. unabr. ed. Perf. by Eknath Easwaran. 1 cass. (Running Time: 1 hr.). 1987. 7.95 (978-1-58638-502-6(X)) Nilgiri Pr.

Benefitting from Life's Trials. John MacArthur, Jr. 6 cass. 19.75 (HarperThor) HarpC GBR.

Benevent Treasure. Patricia Wentworth. 2008. 61.95 (978-0-7531-3805-2(0)); audio compact disk 84.95 (978-0-7531-2786-5(5)) Pub: ISIS Audio GBR. Dist(s): Ulverscroft US

Benevolence of the Divine Mother. Swami Amar Jyoti. 1 dolby cass. 1985. 9.95 (C-42) Truth Consciousness.
Divine Mother, the Primordial Energy, works & heals in endless benevolence. Rama Rajya, the divine kingdom.

Benevolent Sense of Life. unabr. ed. Nathaniel Branden. 1 cass. (Running Time: 59 min.). (Basic Principles of Objectivism Ser.). 10.95 (580) J Norton Pubs.
Explains why many human beings repress & drive underground, not the worst within them, but the best; a benevolent vs. malevolent sense of life.

Bengal, Vol. 1. 1 cass. 1995. (F95036) Multi-Cultural Bks.

Bengal, Vol. 2. 1 cass. 1995. (F95037) Multi-Cultural Bks.

Bengali Devotional Songs. Perf. by Tapash Ghosh. 1 cass. (Running Time: 40). 1985. 8.95 (978-0-87481-056-1(6)) Vedanta Pr.

Beniamino Gigli. Graeme Kay. 4 CDs. audio compact disk 35.99 (978-1-84379-074-7(2), 8.558148-51) NaxMulti GBR.

Benign Breast Lumps: Possible Causes, Testing & Therapies. unabr. ed. Gary S. Ross. Interview with Kathleen S. Ross. 1 cass. (Running Time: 47 min.). (Natural Treatment Ser.). 1994. 15.00 (978-1-891875-02-1(7), NTS003) Creat Hlth Wrks.
Explains possible related causes of breast lumps & ovarian cysts, & effective natural treatments.

Benign Reality. Harvey Jackins. 16 cass. 10.00 ea. (978-1-885357-77-9(X)) Rational Isl.
Writings on the empowerment of the individual against oppression, discouragement & powerlessness.

Benito Cereno. Herman Melville. Read by Santiago Munévar. (Running Time: 3 hrs.). 2002. 16.95 (978-1-60083-236-9(9), Audiofy Corp) Iofy Corp.

Benito Cereno. Herman Melville. Read by John Chatty. 3 cass. (Running Time: 3 hrs. 30 min.). 1989. 21.00 incl. album. (C-35) Jimcin Record.
Strange mystery of the sea.

Benito Cereno. unabr. ed. Herman Melville. Read by John Chatty. 3 cass. (Running Time: 4 hrs.). 1980. 23.95 (978-0-7861-0542-7(9), 2037) Blckstn Audio.
The balance of forces is complete, the atmosphere one of epic significance, the light cast upon the hero intense to the highest degree, the realization of the human soul profound & the telling of the story orchestrated like a great symphony.

Benito Cereno. unabr. ed. Herman Melville. Read by Santiago Munevar. 3 CDs. (Yoyo Libros Ser.). (SPA.). 2002. audio compact disk 17.00 (978-958-8161-21-1(5)) YoYoMusic.

Benjamin & Tulip. 2004. 8.95 (978-1-56008-842-4(7)); cass. & flmstrp 30.00 (978-0-89719-653-6(8)) Weston Woods.

Benjamin & Tulip. (J). 2004. bk. 24.95 (978-1-56008-037-4(X)); pap. bk. 14.95 (978-1-56008-038-1(8)) Weston Woods.

Benjamin Banneker. 10.00 Esstee Audios.

Benjamin Britten: The Early Years. unabr. ed. Narrated by Donald Mitchell. 2 cass. 15.95 (SCN 201) J Norton Pubs.
This documentary deals with Britten's life up to 1945 & includes unpublished diaries & letters, as well as unknown early compositions & this rich mixture enables the listener to gain deeper insight into his music.

Benjamin Franklin. abr. ed. Benjamin Franklin. Narrated by Michael Rye. 2 cass. (Running Time: 2 hrs. 34 min.). 12.95 (978-0-89926-124-9(8), 812) Audio Bk.
Highlights from the life of America's first great patriot, writer & wit.

Benjamin Franklin. unabr. ed. Carl Van Doren & Patrick Cullen. (Running Time: 33 hrs. NaN mins.). 2008. 59.95 (978-1-4332-5423-9(9)); audio compact disk 110.00 (978-1-4332-5422-2(0)); audio compact disk 110.00 (978-1-4332-5421-5(2)) Blckstn Audio.

Benjamin Franklin. unabr. ed. Ingri Parin D'Aulaire & Edgar Parin D'Aulaire. 1 cass. (Running Time: 6 min.). (J). (gr. 3-5). 1989. pap. bk. 10.00 (6512-F); pap. bk. 20.00 (978-0-8045-6718-3(2), 6512F/6) Spoken Arts.
This versatile statesman had many ups and downs in his life. Includes 6 books.

Benjamin Franklin, Pt. 1. unabr. ed. Carl Van Doren. Read by Patrick Cullen. 13 cass. (Running Time: 35 hrs.). 1996. 85.95 (978-0-7861-0939-5(4), 1690A, B) Blckstn Audio.
From Benjamin Franklin's beginnings as a journalist at age 16 to his retirement from public affairs at 82, there was no break in his activity & accomplishments. As a writer, inventor, & statesman, he was - & still is - unsurpassed by anyone in the range of his natural gifts & the important uses to which he put them. In this monumental biography, which won the Pulitzer Prize when first published in 1939, Carl Van Doren incorporates materials

from Franklin's letters, manuscripts, journals, & published works to give the most accurate & comprehensive portrait ever written of this Great American.

Benjamin Franklin, Pt. 2. unabr. ed. Carl Van Doren. Read by Patrick Cullen. 11 cass. (Running Time: 35 hrs.). 1996. 76.95 (978-0-7861-0940-1(8), 1690A, B) Blckstn Audio.

Benjamin Franklin: An American Life. abr. ed. Walter Isaacson. Read by Boyd Gaines. 6 CDs. (Running Time: 70 hrs. 0 mins. 0 sec.). (ENG.). 2003. audio compact disk 30.00 (978-0-7435-3365-2(8), Audioworks) Pub: S&S Audio. Dist(s): S and S Inc

Benjamin Franklin: An American Life. abr. ed. Walter Isaacson. Read by Boyd Gaines. 2006. 17.95 (978-0-7435-6185-3(6)) Pub: S&S Audio. Dist(s): S and S Inc

Benjamin Franklin: An American Life. unabr. ed. Walter Isaacson. 17 cass. (Running Time: 24 hrs. 45 min.). 2004. 99.75 (978-1-4025-9293-5(0)) Recorded Bks.

Benjamin Franklin: Diplomat. unabr. ed. Benjamin Franklin. Narrated by Adrian Cronauer. 3 cass. (Running Time: 4 hrs. 45 mins.). (gr. 10 up). 1987. 26.00 (978-1-55690-044-0(9), 87910E7) Recorded Bks.
Original letters, papers & documents relating to Franklin's public office. He was a publisher, printer, scientist & inventor, but Ben Franklin's greatest success lay in his work as a diplomat.

Benjamin Franklin: On Love, Marriage & Other Matters. unabr. ed. Benjamin Franklin. Narrated by Adrian Cronauer. 3 cass. (Running Time: 3 hrs. 30 mins.). (Collection of Essays & Letters). 1989. 26.00 (978-1-55690-043-3(0), 88996E7) Recorded Bks.
Selected essays & letters from America's shrewdest observer of mankind & its ways.

Benjamin Franklin: You Know What to Say. Loyd Uglow. Illus. by Greg Budwine. 1cass. Dramatization. (J). 2003. lib. bdg. 23.95 (978-1-57537-791-9(8)); 16.95 (978-1-57537-591-5(5)) Advance Pub.

Benjamin Franklin: Young Printer. unabr. ed. Augusta Stevenson. Read by Lloyd James. 4 cass. (Running Time: 5 hrs. 30 mins.). (Childhood of Famous Americans Ser.). (gr. 1-3). 2001. 35.95 (978-0-7861-2065-9(7), K2826) Blckstn Audio.
Children will enjoy listening to young Benjamin Franklin's thoughts on learning arithmetic and his original approach to subtractions. They will be able to follow the logic of the thinking that led to his first experiment, paddles to help him swim faster, and the excitement of the first trial run.

Benjamin Franklin Autobiography. Benjamin Franklin. Read by Walter A. Costello. (Running Time: 23400 sec.). (Unabridged Classics in Audio Ser.). (ENG.). 2005. audio compact disk 59.99 (978-1-4001-3168-6(5)) Pub: Tantor Media. Dist(s): IngramPubServ

***Benjamin Franklin: Autobiography.** unabr. ed. Benjamin Franklin. Narrated by Robin Field. (ENG.). 2010. 14.98 (978-1-59644-262-7(X), MissionAud); audio compact disk 24.98 (978-1-59644-910-7(1), MissionAud) christianaud.

Benjamin Franklin, Citizen. abr. ed. Fredd Wayne. Read by Fredd Wayne. 1 cass. (Running Time: 1 hr. 10 mins.). Dramatization. (Self-Help Law Kit Ser.). 2004. 12.95 (978-1-57270-002-4(5), D10002a) Pub: Audio Partners. Dist(s): PerseuPGW

Benjamin Franklin Project. unabr. ed. Joe Loesch. Ed. by Cheryl J. Hutchinson. Illus. by Brian T. Cox. 1 CD. (Running Time: 1 hr. 30 mins.). (Backyard Adventure Ser.). (J). 2002. pap. bk. 16.95 (978-1-887729-86-4(0)) Toy Box Prods.
Farley's Raiders journey through time to meet Benjamin Franklin. Ben is best known for his experiments with electricity, but he was also a printer, inventor, writer and philosopher. Join Biff, Pete and Ruby for an electrifying adventure and learn all about America's greatest citizen.

Benjamin Franklin Project. unabr. ed. Joe Loesch. Ed. by Cheryl J. Hutchinson. Illus. by Brian T. Cox. 1 cass. (Running Time: 1 hr. 30 mins.). (Backyard Adventure Ser.). (J). (gr. k-5). 2002. pap. bk. 14.95 (978-1-887729-85-7(2)) Toy Box Prods.

Benjamin Saenz. unabr. ed. Ed. by Jim McKinley. Prod. by Rebekah Presson. 1 cass. (Running Time: 29 min.). (New Letters on the Air Ser.). 1994. 10.00 (032693) New Letters.
The Chicano writer & former Catholic priest reads from his book of poems, "Calendar of Dust" & talks about writing personal poems that draw from historical events. Saenz is a native of New Mexico & grew up poor, an experience he mingles with the history of poverty & cruelty toward outsiders in America in his work.

Benjamin Sweny. unabr. ed. Poems. Benjamin Sweny. Ed. by James McKinley. Prod. by Rebeah Presson. 1 cass. (Running Time: 29 min.). (On the Air Ser.). 1993. 10.00 New Letters.
Chicano writer reads poetry, interview.

Benjie: Audio Book. Sara Yoder. Narrated by Fern Ebersole. Engineer Good Sound Co. Prod. by I.G. Publishers. (ENG.). (J). 2007. audio compact disk 15.95 (978-0-9801244-7-7(6)) IG Publish.

Benjie Goes to School. Narrated by Fern Ebersole. (ENG.). (J). 2009. audio compact disk 19.95 (978-0-9842097-9-8(4)) IG Publish.

***Benjiman: S. K. R. I. P. T.** 2009. audio compact disk 13.98 (978-0-9822699-1-6(9)) Rain On Me.

Benlian see Widdershins: The First Book of Ghost Stories

Bennett-Wiese Live at ACME. John M. Bennett. Read by John M. Bennett. Perf. by Jim Wiese. 1 cass. 1996. 7.00 (978-0-935350-65-4(9)) Luna Bisonte.

Benny: An Adventure Story. Bob Graham. 1 CD. (Running Time: 8 mins.). (J). (gr. k-3). 2006. pap. bk. 19.95 (978-0-8045-4138-1(8)); pap. bk. 17.95 (978-0-8045-6939-2(8)) Spoken Arts.
Benny is one talented dog. As a magician's assistant, he does magic tricks and plays the harmonica. But when Benny upstages his magician master, he's in the doghouse. Now, he's alone in the world with a serious case of the blues. Is there anyone, anywhere, who will give Benny the simple love he seeks?.

Benny & Babe. Eoin Colfer. Narrated by Euan Morton. (Running Time: 26520 sec.). (ENG.). (J). (gr. 4-7). 2007. audio compact disk 34.95 (978-0-545-00513-5(2)) Scholastic Inc.

Benny & Babe. unabr. ed. Eoin Colfer. Read by Euan Morton. (J). 2007. 49.99 (978-1-60252-600-6(1)) Find a World.

Benny & Babe. unabr. ed. Eoin Colfer. 6 CDs. (Running Time: 26520 sec.). (ENG.). (J). (gr. 4-7). 2007. audio compact disk 64.95 (978-0-545-00522-7(1)) Scholastic Inc.

Benny & Omar. Eoin Colfer. Read by Euan Morton. (Running Time: 22800 sec.). (ENG.). (J). (gr. 4-7). 2007. audio compact disk 54.95 (978-0-439-02341-2(6)) Scholastic Inc.

Benny & Omar. unabr. ed. Eoin Colfer. Read by Euan Morton. (J). 2007. 49.99 (978-1-60252-639-6(7)) Find a World.

Benny & Omar. unabr. ed. Eoin Colfer. Read by Euan Morton. 5 CDs. (Running Time: 21600 sec.). (ENG.). (J). (gr. 4-7). 2007. audio compact disk 29.95 (978-0-439-92502-0(9)) Scholastic Inc.

Benny's School Trip/Schools. Steck-Vaughn Staff. 1996. (978-0-8172-6467-3(1)) SteckVau.

Ben's Trumpet. 1 cass. (Running Time: 35 min.). (J). (gr. k-3). 2001. bk. 15.95 (VX-433C) Kimbo Educ.
A trumpet solo of light jazz introduces this story of Ben, a black youngster enamored of the music he hears coming from the Zig Zag Jazz Club in the 1920's. Includes book.

Ben's Trumpet. Rachel Isadora. Read by Charles Turner. 1 cass. (Running Time: 90 mins.). (J). 2000. pap. bk. 19.97 (978-0-7366-9219-9(3)) Books on Tape.
Ben, a black youngster enamored of the music he hears coming form the Zig Zag Jazz Club in the 1920s. Different instrumental solos ably introduce the band members & a distant trumpet effectively portrays Ben's imaginary trumpet.

Ben's Trumpet. Rachel Isadora. Illus. by Rachel Isadora. 14 vols. (Running Time: 7 mins.). 1998. pap. bk. 39.95 (978-1-59112-600-3(2)); audio compact disk 12.95 (978-1-59112-401-6(8)) Live Oak Media.

Ben's Trumpet. Rachel Isadora. Illus. by Rachel Isadora. 11 vols. (Running Time: 7 mins.). (Live Oak Readalong Ser.). (J). 1998. pap. bk. 18.95 (978-1-59112-402-3(6)) Pub: Live Oak Media. Dist(s): AudioGO

Ben's Trumpet. Rachel Isadora. Illus. by Rachel Isadora. 1 CD. (Running Time: 7 mins.). (J). (ps-3). 1998. bk. 28.95 (978-1-59112-423-8(9)) Live Oak Media.

Ben's Trumpet. Rachel Isadora. Illus. by Rachel Isadora. Read by Charles Turner. 14 vols. (Running Time: 7 mins.). (J). (gr. k-3). 1998. pap. bk. & tchr. ed. 37.95 Reading Chest. (978-0-87499-435-3(7)) Live Oak Media.
A trumpet solo of light jazz introduces this story of Ben, a black youngster enamored of the music he hears coming from the Zig Zag Jazz Club in the 1920s. Different instrumental solos ably introduce the band members & a distant trumpet effectively portrays Ben's imaginary trumpet The ambiance aptly conveyed. This is a nice recording for follow-along reading.

Ben's Trumpet. unabr. ed. Rachel Isadora. Read by Charles Turner. 1 cass. (Running Time: 7 mins.). (J). (gr. k-3). 1998. 9.95 (978-0-87499-436-0(5)) Live Oak Media.
Ben stoop-sits, playing a dream horn until the Zig-Zag Club's trumpeter takes him in.

Ben's Trumpet. unabr. ed. Rachel Isadora. Illus. by Rachel Isadora. Read by Charles Turner. 1 cass. (Running Time: 7 mins.). (J). (gr. k-3). 1998. bk. 25.95 (978-0-87499-434-6(9)); pap. bk. 16.95 (978-0-87499-433-9(0)) Pub: Live Oak Media. Dist(s): AudioGO
A trumpet solo of light jazz introduces this story of Ben, a black youngster enamored of the music he hears coming from the Zig Zag Jazz Club in the 1920s. Different instrumental solos ably introduce the band members & a distant trumpet effectively portrays Ben's imaginary trumpet The ambiance aptly conveyed. This is a nice recording for follow-along reading.

Bent & Broken: Luke 13:10-17. Ed Young. (J). 1980. 4.95 (978-0-7417-1131-1(1), A0131) Win Walk.

***Bent Road.** unabr. ed. Lori Roy. (Running Time: 12 hrs. NaN mins.). (ENG.). 2011. 29.95 (978-1-4417-8061-4(0)); audio compact disk 32.95 (978-1-4417-8060-7(2)) Blckstn Audio.

***Bent Road.** unabr. ed. Lori Roy. Read by To be Announced. (Running Time: 12 hrs. NaN mins.). (ENG.). 2011. 72.95 (978-1-4417-8058-4(0)); audio compact disk 105.00 (978-1-4417-8059-1(9)) Blckstn Audio.

Bentley & Blueberry. Randy Houk. Illus. by Randy Houk. Read by Tom Chapin. Narrated by Tom Chapin. 1 cass. (Running Time: 10 min.). (Humane Society of the United States Animal Tales Ser.). (J). (gr. 1-5). 1993. pap. bk. 19.95 (978-1-882728-36-7(X)); pap. bk. 9.95 (978-1-882728-46-6(7)) Benefactory.
Have you ever brought a dog home from the shelter? Bentley & Ms. Moody did! Teaches how to train a new pet with patience & kindness.

Bentley & Blueberry. Randy Houk. Illus. by Randy Houk. Read by Tom Chapin. Narrated by Tom Chapin. 1 cass. (Running Time: 10 min.). (Humane Society of the United States Animal Tales Ser.). (J). (gr. 1-5). 1993. bk. 34.95 (978-1-882728-15-2(7)) Benefactory.

Bent's Fort. unabr. collector's ed. David Lavender. Read by Michael Prichard. 12 cass. (Running Time: 18 hrs.). 1985. 96.00 (978-0-7366-0744-5(7), 1700) Books on Tape.
In 1833 the Bent brothers, men of will & courage, built a symbol of American expansion - Bent's Fort. This great adobe castle on the banks of the Arkansas spearheaded America's drive into the Southwest. Kit Carson & Blackfoot Smith, Old Bill Williams & John Freemont man the fort. From it they open New Mexico, Arizona & California.

Beo's Bedroom. Ned Dickens. 1 CD. (Running Time: 1 hr. 30 mins.). 2005. audio compact disk 12.95 (978-0-660-18969-7(0)) Pub: Canadian Broadcasting CAN. Dist(s): Georgetown Term

Beowulf. Read by Crawford Logan. Tr. by Benedict Flynn from ANG. (Running Time: 8649 sec.). (Complete Classics Ser.). 2006. audio compact disk 17.98 (978-962-634-425-5(3), Naxos AudioBooks) Naxos.

Beowulf. Tr. by Diedrich Wackerbarth. Narrated by Flo Gibson. (ENG.). 2007. audio compact disk 16.95 (978-1-55685-936-6(8)) Audio Bk Con.

***Beowulf.** abr. ed. Read by J. B Bessinger. 2007. (978-0-06-113598-9(4), Harper Audio); (978-0-06-113597-2(6), Harper Audio) HarperCollins Pubs.

Beowulf. abr. ed. Read by J. B Bessinger. (Running Time: 3000 sec.). 2007. audio compact disk 12.95 (978-0-06-137469-2(5), Caedmon) HarperCollins Pubs.

Beowulf. abr. ed. Tr. by Seamus Heaney. (YA). 2007. 39.99 (978-1-60252-494-1(7)) Find a World.

***Beowulf.** unabr. ed. null Anonymous. Narrated by Rosalyn Landor. (Running Time: 3 hrs. 0 mins. 0 sec.). (ENG.). 2010. 17.99 (978-1-4001-6599-5(7)); 11.99 (978-1-4001-8599-3(8)); audio compact disk 17.99 (978-1-4001-1599-0(X)); audio compact disk 35.99 (978-1-4001-4599-7(6)) Pub: Tantor Media. Dist(s): IngramPubServ

Beowulf. unabr. ed. Read by Robertson Dean. Tr. by Robert K. Gordon. 3 CDs. (Running Time: 10800 sec.). 2007. audio compact disk 14.95 (978-1-4332-0014-4(7)) Blckstn Audio.

Beowulf. unabr. ed. R. K. Gordon. Read by Robertson Dean. 2 cass. (Running Time: 2 hrs. 30 mins.). 2004. 17.95 (978-0-7861-2640-8(X), 3246); audio compact disk 24.00 (978-0-7861-8737-9(9), 3246) Blckstn Audio.
One of the most universally studied of the English classics, Beowulf is considered the finest heroic poem in Old English. Written ten centuries ago, it celebrates the character and exploits of Beowulf, a young nobleman of the Geats, a people of southern Sweden. Beowulf first rescues the royal house of Denmark from two marauding monsters, then returns to rule his people for 50 years, ultimately losing his life in a battle to defend the Geats from a dragon?s rampage.

Beowulf. unabr. ed. Tr. by Francis B. Gummere. Narrated by George Guidall. 5 cass. (Running Time: 3 hrs. 15 mins.). 2000. 44.00 (978-0-7887-1169-5(5), 95122E7) Recorded Bks.
Beowulf, a young warrior, achieves glory by fighting & killing three monsters: Grendel in Denmark, Grendel's mother in her underwater cave & a fire-dragon rampaging through Beowulf's Swedish kingdom.

Beowulf, Set. unabr. ed. Poems. Read by Flo Gibson. 2 cass. (Running Time: 3 hrs.). 1998. bk. 14.95 (978-1-55685-556-6(7)) Audio Bk Con.
Early translation from the Anglo-Saxon 7th Century epic poem is based on Norse legends of war & monsters & tells of the heroic deeds of the warrior Beowulf.

Beowulf, Set. unabr. ed. Tr. by Francis B. Gummere. 3 cas. (Running Time: 3 hrs. 40 min.). 1991. 26.00 (978-1-55690-046-4(5), 90053) Recorded Bks.
Written a thousand years ago, this long poem is the very first surviving piece of English literature. The primary story tells of Beowulf, a young warrior, who achieves glory by fighting & killing three monters: Grendel in Denmark, Grendel's mother in her underwater cave & then a fire-dragon rampaging through Beowulf's Swedish kingdom.

Beowulf: A New Verse Translation. unabr. ed. Seamus Heaney. Read by Seamus Heaney. 2 CDs. (Running Time: 2 hrs. 15 mn.). 2001. audio compact disk 24.95 Parabola Bks.
Timeless tale of quest, adventure and fantasy. The poem is about encountering the monstrous (in the form of the grotesque Grendel and his beastly mother,) and having to live in the exhausted aftermath of its defeat.

Beowulf: A New Verse Translation. unabr. abr. ed. Read by Seamus Heaney. Tr. by Seamus Heaney. 2 CDs. (Running Time: 2 hrs. 15 mins.). (ENG.). (gr. 9-12). 2000. audio compact disk 24.95 (978-1-56511-427-2(2), 1565114272) Pub: HighBridge. Dist(s): Workman Pub

Beowulf: Read in Old English. abr. ed. Read by Nevill Coghill & Norman Davis. 1 cass. (Running Time: 36 min.). 11.95 (978-0-8045-0918-3(2), SAC 918) Spoken Arts.
Key excerpts from this great classic with an introduction to its pronunciation & meter.

Beowulf & Other Poetry. unabr. ed. Perf. by J. B. Bessinger, Jr. 5 cass. Incl. Battle of Brunan Burg; Caedmon's Hymn; Dream of the Rood; Wanderer; (ENM.). 1984. 12.95 (SWC 1161) HarperCollins Pubs.

Beowulf: the Complete Story: A Drama. unabr. ed. Tr. by Richard N. Ringler. 3 CDs. 2006. audio compact disk 29.95 (978-0-9715093-2-0(8)) Pub: U of Wis Pr. Dist(s): Chicago Distribution Ctr

Berdache: The Zuni Man-Woman. unabr. ed. Will Roscoe & Elizabeth Gips. 1 cass. (Running Time: 90 min.). 1997. 11.00 (32007) Big Sur Tapes.
The tradition of a third gender that combines the traits & roles of men & women is common to a number of Native American tribes. These individuals are revered as mediators between men, women & the supernatural. They act as healers, artists, & messengers with the spirit world, who have a unique capacity to bring opposites together.

Bereavement: Healing Your Heart. Joyce Alexander. Music by Shawna Selline. Photos by Steve Janowski. Steve Janowski. (ENG.). 2007. (978-0-9709025-0-4(6)) Alex Prodns.

Bereavement & Wellness. 1 cass. (Care Cassettes Ser.: Vol. 14, No. 4). 1987. 10.80 Assn Prof Chaplains.

Bereavement Care Giving: Strategies & Challenges for Chaplains. 1 cass. (Care Cassettes Ser.: Vol. 17, No. 3). 1990. 10.80 Assn Prof Chaplains.

***Berenstain Bears & the Prize Pumpkin.** abr. ed. Jan Berenstain. Read by Jan Berenstain. (ENG.). 2006. (978-0-06-123252-7(1), HarperFestival) HarperCollins Pubs.

Berenstain Bears & the Sitter. Stan Berenstain & Jan Berenstain. (Berenstain Bears First Time Bks.). (J). (gr. k-2). 1989. 21.26 (978-0-676-31506-6(2)) SRA McGraw.

Berenstain Bears & the Spooky Old Tree. Stan Berenstain & Jan Berenstain. (Berenstain Bears Bright & Early Bks.). (J). (ps-3). 1978. 18.66 (978-0-394-00940-7(1)) Random.

Berenstain Bears & the Spooky Old Tree. Stan Berenstain & Jan Berenstain. (Berenstain Bears Bright & Early Bks.). (J). (ps-3). 1978. 18.66 (978-0-07-507095-5(2)) SRA McGraw.

Berenstain Bears CD Holiday Audio Collection. abr. ed. Stan Berenstain & Jan Berenstain. Read by Stan Berenstain & Jan Berenstain. (J). 2005. audio compact disk 13.95 (978-0-06-082129-6(9), HarperChildAud) HarperCollins Pubs.

Berenstain Bears' Christmas. abr. ed. Stan Berenstain & Jan Berenstain. 1 cass. (Running Time: 90 mins.). Incl. Bear Detectives: The Case of the Missing Pumpkin. Characters created by Stan Berenstain & Jan Berenstain. (Berenstain Bears Beginner Bks.). (J). (ps-3). (CPN 1573); Bears' Almanac. (J). (CPN 1573); Bike Lesson. Stan Berenstain & Jan Berenstain. (Berenstain Bears Beginner Bks.). (J). (ps-3). (CPN 1573); He Bear, She Bear. Stan Berenstain & Jan Berenstain. (Berenstain Bears Bright & Early Bks.). (J). (ps-3). (CPN 1573); (I Can Read Bks.). (J). (ps-3). 1989. 9.95 (978-0-89845-901-2(X), CPN 1573) HarperCollins Pubs.

Berenstain Bears Get the Gimmies. Stan Berenstain & Jan Berenstain. Illus. by Stan Berenstain & Jan Berenstain. (Berenstain Bears First Time Bks.). (J). (gr. k-2). 1990. bk. (978-0-318-66803-1(3), RHBYR) RH Chldrns.

***Berenstain Bears Holiday Audio Collection.** abr. ed. Jan Berenstain. Read by Jan Berenstain. (ENG.). 2005. (978-0-06-083174-5(X), HarperFestival); (978-0-06-083173-8(1), HarperFestival) HarperCollins Pubs.

Berenstain Bears Learn about Strangers. Stan Berenstain & Jan Berenstain. (Berenstain Bears First Time Bks.). (J). (gr. k-2). 1989. 26.66 (978-0-676-31929-3(7)) SRA McGraw.

***Berenstain Bears Meet Santa Bear.** abr. ed. Jan Berenstain. Read by Jan Berenstain. (ENG.). 2006. (978-0-06-123254-1(8), HarperFestival) HarperCollins Pubs.

***Berenstain Bears Save Christmas.** abr. ed. Jan Berenstain. Read by Jan Berenstain. (ENG.). 2006. (978-0-06-123255-8(6), HarperFestival) HarperCollins Pubs.

***Berenstain Bears' Stories.** abr. ed. Stan Berenstain. Read by Stan Berenstain. Read by Jan Berenstain. Illus. by Jan Berenstain. (ENG.). 2005. (978-0-06-084629-9(1), HarperFestival); (978-0-06-084630-5(5), HarperFestival) HarperCollins Pubs.

Berenstain Bears' Stories. unabr. ed. Stan Berenstain & Jan Berenstain. Read by Stan Berenstain & Jan Berenstain. 2 CDs. (Running Time: 2 hrs.). (J). 2005. audio compact disk 17.95 (978-0-06-075837-0(6), HarperChildAud) HarperCollins Pubs.

***Berenstain Bears' Thanksgiving.** abr. ed. Jan Berenstain. Read by Jan Berenstain. (ENG.). 2006. (978-0-06-123256-5(4), HarperFestival) HarperCollins Pubs.

Berets. unabr. ed. W. E. B. Griffin. Read by Michael Russotto. 11 cass. (Running Time: 16 hrs. 30 min.). (Brotherhood of War Ser.: No. 5). 1995. 88.00 (3732) Books on Tape.
The Berets, the army's best, meet their greatest challenge in a land unknown to most Americans: Vietnam.

Berets. unabr. collector's ed. W. E. B. Griffin. Read by Michael Russotto. 11 cass. (Running Time: 16 hrs. 30 mins.). (Brotherhood of War Ser.: No. 5). 1995. 88.00 (978-0-7366-3050-4(3), 3732) Books on Tape.
The Berets, the army's finest human fighting machines, meet their greatest challenge in a land unknown to most Americans Vietnam.

Bergdorf Blondes. abr. ed. Plum Sykes. Read by Sonya Walger. 5 CDs. (Running Time: 21600 sec.). 2006. audio compact disk 14.98

(978-1-4013-8420-3(X), Hyperion Audio) Pub: Hyperion. Dist(s): HarperCollins Pubs

Bergen Evans Vocabulary Program. 5 cass. (C). 59.95 incl. student study guide. Communacad.
Five hundred words & over 2000 derivatives in fifty seperate lessons are reviewed. The 40-page Student Study Guide contains pretests & post tests. This program is primarily for the college-bound student & is intended to help students score higher on College Board Examinations.

Bergen Evans Vocabulary Program. Bergen Evans. 2 cass. 10.00 ea. SMI Intl.
A good vocabulary can help you gain respect, express your ideas & communicate more effectively in personal & business relationships. This series, developed by well-known grammarian Bergen Evans, is just what you've been looking for.

Bergen Evans Vocabulary Program. unabr. ed. Bergen Evans. Read by Robert S. Breen. 5 cass. (Running Time: 3 hrs. 50 min.). (YA). (gr. 9 up). 1965. pap. bk. 65.00 (0226) Vocab Inc.
Each of the 500 study words is presented in an example sentence. The sentence is then repeated with short definitions substituted for the study word.

Beric the Briton. Short Stories. Adapted by Jim Weiss. 8 CDs. (Running Time: 9 hrs.). Dramatization. (YA). 2005. 32.95 (978-1-882513-93-2(2)) Greathall Prods.

Berkeley, CA - Neighborhood Services Initiative & Change. unabr. ed. Innovation Groups Staff. 1 cass. (Running Time: 1 hrs. 15 min.). (Transforming Local Government Ser.: Vol. 13). 1999. 10.00 (978-1-882403-69-1(X), IG9913) Alliance Innov.

Berklee Practice Method: Vibraphone. Ed Saindon & Berklee Faculty Staff. 2004. audio compact disk 14.95 (978-0-634-00794-1(7), 50449436, Berklee Pr) H Leonard.

Berklee Practice Method: Violin. Berklee Faculty Staff et al. 2004. audio compact disk 14.95 (978-0-634-00792-7(0), 50449434, Berklee Pr) H Leonard.

Berkshire Stories: Nature. Read by Morgan Bulkeley, Jr. & Madeleine Tramm. Based on a book by Morgan Bulkeley, Sr. Music by Anson Olds & John Humphrey. 2007. audio compact disk 14.00 (978-0-9663401-8-1(3)) BMA Studios.

Berlin: The Downfall 1945. unabr. ed. Antony Beevor. Read by Sean Barrett. 16 CDs. (Running Time: 17 hrs. 34 mins.). (Isis (CDs) Ser.). (J). 2005. audio compact disk 109.95 (978-0-7531-1547-3(6)) Pub: ISIS Lrg Prnt GBR. Dist(s): Ulverscroft US

Berlin: The Downfall 1945. unabr. ed. Antony Beevor. Read by Sean Barrett. 14 cass. (Running Time: 17 hrs. 34 mins.). (Isis Cassettes Ser.). (J). 2005. 99.95 (978-0-7531-1523-7(9)) Pub: ISIS Lrg Prnt GBR. Dist(s): Ulverscroft US

Berlin Diaries: 1940-1945. unabr. ed. Marie Vassiltchikov. Narrated by Alexandra O'Karma. 10 cass. (Running Time: 13 hrs. 30 mins.). 1989. 85.00 (978-1-55690-047-1(3), 89100E7) Recorded Bks.
The personal diaries of a young woman working in Berlin during the Second World War. The author, a princess of White Russian descent, was 23 years old when she was trapped in Berlin by the outbreak of World War II.

Berlin Diary, Pt. 1. unabr. collector's ed. William L. Shirer. Read by Larry McKeever. 8 cass. (Running Time: 12 hrs.). 1988. 64.00 (978-0-7366-1310-1(2), 2217-A) Books on Tape.
Journalistic, eye-witness account of Berlin in the 1930's, & the rise of Nazism. Part 1 of 2.

Berlin Diary, Pt. 2. unabr. collector's ed. William L. Shirer. Read by Larry McKeever. 7 cass. (Running Time: 10 hrs. 30 min.). 1988. 56.00 (978-0-7366-1311-8(0), 2217-B) Books on Tape.

Berlin Encounter. unabr. ed. T. Davis Bunn. 4 cass. (Running Time: 4 hrs. 12 min.). (Destiny Ser.: Bk. 4). 2001. 26.95 (978-1-55686-987-7(8)) Books in Motion.
As Stalin's strangehold on Berlin tightens, Colonel Jake Burnes is assigned to arrange safe passage for two of Germany's top rocket scientists, unaware that Russian spies have secretly infiltrated his group.

Berlin Game. unabr. ed. Len Deighton. Read by Robert Whitfield. 7 cass. (Running Time: 10 hrs.). 1999. 49.95 (978-0-7861-1243-2(3), 2151) Blckstn Audio.
Britain's most reliable agents behind the Iron Curtain is urgently demanding safe passage to the West. Sends a ripple of panic through the highest levels of the British Secret Service. Bernard Samson undertakes the crucial rescue. He is confronted with inescapable evidence that there is a traitor among his colleagues. Samson must sift through layers of lies & follow a web of treachery from London to Berlin until hero & traitor collide.

Berlin Game. unabr. ed. Len Deighton. Read by Paul Daneman. 8 cass. (Running Time: 12 hrs.). (Game, Set, & Match Ser.: Bk. 1). 2000. 59.95 (978-0-7451-4085-8(8), CAB 553) Pub: Chivers Audio Bks GBR. Dist(s): AudioGO
"Brahms Forur" was the best agent the department ever had, but now he desperately wanted to come over the Wall. Sensing danger, there was only one person he trusted: Bernie Samson. Samson goes back into the field after five years behind a desk, with the game in Berlin as treacherous as ever.

***Berlin Game.** unabr. ed. Len Deighton. Read by Robert Whitfield. (Running Time: 9 hrs.). 2010. audio compact disk 19.95 (978-1-4417-3539-3(9)) Blckstn Audio.

***Berlin Game.** unabr. ed. Len Deighton. Read by Robert Whitfield. (Running Time: 9 hrs.). 2010. 29.95 (978-1-4417-3540-9(2)); audio compact disk 90.00 (978-1-4417-3537-9(2)) Blckstn Audio.

Berlin Quartet; Coming of Age: September 3, 1939. unabr. ed. Julian C. Hollick. 2 cass. (Running Time: 60 min. per cass.). 1985. 30.00 Set. (978-1-56709-033-8(8), 1067) Indep Broadcast.
"The Berlin Quartet." The Fall of Berlin, 1945; Berlin & the Cold War; Living on Borrowed Time; Living with the Wall. "Coming of Age: September 3, 1939." A remembrance of the first days of World War II by four who were teenagers in France, Germany & England at the time.

Berlin Song. unabr. ed. Alan Gold. 16 cass. (Running Time: 20 hrs. 30 mins.). 2001. 128.00 (978-1-74030-455-9(1)) Pub: Bolinda Pubng AUS. Dist(s): Bolinda Pub Inc

Berlin Stories. abr. ed. Scripts. Christopher Isherwood. Perf. by Michael York. 2 cass. (Running Time: 3 hrs.). 2004. 15.00 (978-1-59007-198-4(0)) Pub: New Millenn Enter. Dist(s): PerseuPGW

Berlin to North America. unabr. ed. Read by William Joyce. 1 cass. (Running Time: 30 min.). 12.95 (19026) J Norton Pubs.
William Joyce (Lord Haw Haw) propaganda broadcasts to Great Britain from the records of the U.S. Foreign Broadcast Intelligence Service.

Berliner Platz: 1 Textbook/Workbook with CD. 2005. audio compact disk 36.95 (978-3-468-47830-7(5)) Langenscheidt.

Berliner Platz: 2 1 Audio CD for use W/Workbook. (Running Time: 1 hr. 14 mins.). 2005. pap. bk. 15.95 (978-3-468-47856-7(9)) Langenscheidt.

Berliner Platz: 2 2 Audio CDs for use W/Textbook. 2 CDs. (Running Time: 2 hrs.). 2005. pap. bk. 25.00 (978-3-468-47854-3(2)) Langenscheidt.

Berliner Platz: 3 Audio Cassettes (use with Workbook) (Running Time: 1 hr. 14 mins.). 2005. pap. bk. 15.95 (978-3-468-47875-8(5)) Langenscheidt.

Berliner Platz: 3 CD (use with Workbook) (Running Time: 1 hr. 14 mins.). 2005. pap. bk. 15.95 (978-3-468-47876-5(3)) Langenscheidt.

Berliner Platz: 3 2 Audio Cassettes (use with Text) 2 cass. (Running Time: 2 hrs.). 2005. pap. bk. 24.95 (978-3-468-47873-4(9)) Langenscheidt.

Berliner Platz: 3 2 CDs (use with Textbook) 2 CDs. (Running Time: 2 hrs.). 2005. pap. bk. 24.95 (978-3-468-47874-1(7)) Langenscheidt.

Berlitz Arabic Phrase Book & CD. Created by Berlitz. (Berlitz Phrase Book & CD Ser.). (ARA & ENG.). 2007. 12.95 (978-981-268-186-7(8)) Pub: APA Pubns Serv SGP. Dist(s): IngramPubServ

Berlitz Basic Arabic. Kathrin Fietz et al. (Berlitz Basic Ser.). (ARA & ENG., 2009. pap. bk. 29.99 (978-981-268-660-2(6)) Pub: APA Pubns Serv SGP. Dist(s): Langenscheidt

Berlitz Basic French. 3rd rev. ed. Created by Berlitz Publishing Staff. 6 CDs. (Berlitz Basic Ser.). (FRE & ENG., 2007. audio compact disk 29.95 (978-981-268-226-0(0)) Pub: APA Pubns Serv SGP. Dist(s): Langenscheidt

Berlitz Basic German. 3rd rev. ed. Created by Berlitz Publishing Staff. 6 CDs. (Berlitz Basic Ser.). (GER & ENG., 2007. audio compact disk 29.95 (978-981-268-227-7(9)) Pub: APA Pubns Serv SGP. Dist(s): Langenscheidt

Berlitz English Pronunciation Program. 2nd ed. Paulette Dale. Created by Berlitz Guides Staff. 1. (Berlitz Pronunciation Program Ser.). 2005. audio compact disk 13.95 (978-981-246-709-6(2), 467092) Pub: Berlitz Pubng. Dist(s): Langenscheidt

Berlitz French CD Pack. Created by Berlitz Guides. (Berlitz Phrase Book & CD Ser.). (FRE & ENG., 2007. 12.95 (978-981-268-188-1(4)) Pub: APA Pubns Serv SGP. Dist(s): IngramPubServ

Berlitz German Phrase Book. Created by Berlitz Guides. (Berlitz Phrase Book & CD Ser.). (GER & ENG., 2007. 12.95 (978-981-268-189-8(2)) Pub: APA Pubns Serv SGP. Dist(s): IngramPubServ

Berlitz Greek Phrase Book & CD. abr. ed. Created by Berlitz. (Berlitz Phrase Book & CD Ser.). (GRE & ENG., 2008. audio compact disk 14.95 (978-981-268-190-4(6)) Pub: Berlitz Pubng. Dist(s): Langenscheidt

Berlitz Inglis de Frases. pap. bk. & suppl. ed. 9.95 cass., tape script. (978-2-8315-1620-2(X)) Globe Pequot.

Berlitz Intermediate French. 2nd rev. ed. Created by Berlitz Guides Staff. (Running Time: 360 mins.). (Berlitz Intermediate Ser.). (ENG & FRE., 2006. audio compact disk 29.95 (978-981-246-768-3(8), 467688) Pub: Berlitz Pubng. Dist(s): Langenscheidt

Berlitz Intermediate German. 2nd rev. ed. Created by Berlitz Guides Staff. (Berlitz Intermediate Ser.). (ENG & GER., 2006. audio compact disk 29.95 (978-981-246-769-0(6)) Pub: Berlitz Pubng. Dist(s): Langenscheidt

Berlitz Intermediate Italian. 2nd rev. ed. Created by Berlitz Guides Staff. (Running Time: 660 mins.). (Berlitz Intermediate Ser.). (ENG & ITA., 2006. audio compact disk 29.95 (978-981-246-771-3(8), 467718) Pub: Berlitz Pubng. Dist(s): Langenscheidt

Berlitz Intermediate Spanish. 2nd rev. ed. Created by Berlitz Guides Staff. (Running Time: 660 mins.). (Berlitz Intermediate Ser.). (ENG & SPA., 2005. audio compact disk 29.95 (978-981-246-772-0(6), 467726) Pub: Berlitz Pubng. Dist(s): Langenscheidt

Berlitz Intermedio Ingles. 2nd rev. ed. Created by Berlitz Guides Staff. 3 CDs. (Berlitz Intermediate Ser.). 2006. audio compact disk 29.95 (978-981-246-770-6(X), 46770X) Pub: Berlitz Pubng. Dist(s): Langenscheidt

Berlitz Italian Phrase Book. Created by Berlitz Guides. (Berlitz Phrase Book & CD Ser.). (ITA & ENG., 2007. 12.95 (978-981-268-191-1(4)) Pub: APA Pubns Serv SGP. Dist(s): IngramPubServ

Berlitz Japanese Phrase Book & CD. abr. ed. Created by Berlitz. (Berlitz Phrase Books & CD Ser.). (JPN & ENG., 2008. audio compact disk 14.95 (978-981-268-192-8(2)) Pub: Berlitz Pubng. Dist(s): Langenscheidt

Berlitz Junior No. 2: Spanish. (ENG & SPA.). (J). 1994. (978-0-318-72275-7(5), AlaChild) SandS Childrens.

Berlitz Portuguese Phrase Book & CD. abr. ed. Created by Berlitz. (Berlitz Phrase Book & CD Ser.). (POR & ENG., 2008. audio compact disk 14.95 (978-981-268-194-2(9)) Pub: Berlitz Pubng. Dist(s): Langenscheidt

Berlitz Spanish Phrase Book. Created by Berlitz Guides. (Berlitz Phrase Book & CD Ser.). (SPA & ENG.). 2007. 12.95 (978-981-268-195-9(7)) Pub: APA Pubns Serv SGP. Dist(s): IngramPubServ

Berlitz Swedish Phrase Book & CD. abr. ed. Created by Berlitz. (Berlitz Phrase Books & CD Ser.). (SWE & ENG., 2008. audio compact disk 14.95 (978-981-268-196-6(5)) Pub: Berlitz Pubng. Dist(s): Langenscheidt

Berlitz Think & Talk: English for Spanish Speakers. 7 cass. 185.00 Set, incl. 2 wkbks., pocket-sized dictionary. (944-C47) Natl Seminars.
This method of quality language learning, imitated but never duplicated, allows anyone to start talking in another language easily & quickly or your money back.

Berlitz Think & Talk: French. 7 cass. 185.00 Set, incl. 2 wkbks., pocket-sized dictionary. (943-C47) Natl Seminars.

Berlitz Think & Talk: German. 7 cass. 185.00 Set, incl. 2 wkbks., pocket-sized dictionary. (942-C47) Natl Seminars.

Berlitz Think & Talk: Spanish. 7 cass. 185.00 Set, incl. 2 wkbks., pocket-sized dictionary. (940-C47) Natl Seminars.

Berman's Commentary on the Book of Romans: A Verse by Verse Study. David M. Berman. 2007. audio compact disk 34.99 (978-1-60247-604-2(7)) Tate Pubng.

Bermuda Investors Workshop Lecture, 1975. unabr. ed. Harry Schultz. 1 cass. (Running Time: 46 min.). 12.95 (394) J Norton Pubs.

Bermuda Quadrangle: A Beautiful Life. 1 cass. 9.98 (C-606) Folk-Legacy.
Some dandy songs by four men with strong voices.

Bernadette & the Lady. Hertha Paul. 5 cass. (J). 22.95 (507) Ignatius Pr.
The appearances of Mary to Bernadette Soubirous at Lourdes.

Bernard of Clairvaux. Henri Daniel-Rops. 7 cass. 28.95 (742) Ignatius Pr.
Life of St. Bernard by the great French author.

Bernstein Favorites: Ballet Dances. Perf. by New York Philharmonic. 1 cass. (Running Time: 73 min.). (J). 7.98 (2280); audio compact disk 13.98 (D2280) MFLP CA.
Varied selection of ballet music with 16 dances from ten different ballets including "The Firebird," "Billy the Kid," "Swan Lake", & more.

Bernstein Favorites: Children's Classics. Perf. by New York Philharmonic. 1 cass. (Running Time: 1 hr. 41 mins.). (J). 7.98 (2283); audio compact disk 13.98 (D2283) MFLP CA.
Introduction for young ones to classical pieces, includes "Peter & the Wolf," "Young Person's Guide to the Orchestra" & "Carnival of the Animals.".

Berrigan Raps. unabr. ed. Daniel Berrigan. Perf. by Daniel Berrigan. 1 cass. Incl. False Gods, Real Men. (SWC 1402); Interview with Marc N. Weiss at Cornell, 1970. (SWC 1402); Sermon from the Underground. (SWC 1402); Trial Poems I. (SWC 1402); Trial Poems II. (SWC 1402); 1977. 12.95 (978-0-694-50245-5(6), SWC 1402) HarperCollins Pubs.
Berrigan reads his poetry & talks about the Vietnam War, the System, the Church, the future & his arrest.

Berring on Legal Research: Deep Principles for Researching & Understanding the Law. Bob Berring. 2006. 255.00 (978-0-314-17604-2(7), West Lglwrks) West.

Berrings Legal Research for the 21st Century, Vol. 1. Robert C. Berring. 2000. 125.00 (978-0-314-24780-3(7), West Lglwrks) West.

Berrings Legal Research for the 21st Century, Vol. 1-5. Robert C. Berring. 5 cass. 2000. 838.00 (978-0-314-25123-7(5)) West.

Berry, Me & Motown, Set. abr. ed. Raynoma G. Singleton. Read by Raynoma G. Singleton. 2 cass. (Running Time: 3 hrs.). 1990. 15.95 (978-0-9627187-2-4(6), 20020) Pub Mills.
The memoir by the former wife of Berry Gordy, who co-founded Motown Records with him, only to be persuaded to remove her name from the partnership. An inside look at the creation of the Motown Sound & its legendary cast of characters, including Jackie Wilson, Smokey Robinson, Marvin Gaye & Diana Ross.

Berry Vest of Swirling Eddies. 1 CD. 1999. audio compact disk 16.98 (KMGD9534) Provident Mus Dist.

Berryfields of Blair. Anne Forsyth. 2008. 44.95 (978-1-84559-989-8(6)); audio compact disk 51.95 (978-1-84559-990-4(X)) Pub: Soundings Ltd GBR. Dist(s): Ulverscroft US

Bersama-Sama. Heather Hardie & Sue Clark. 4 CDs. (Running Time: 6 hrs.). 2000. audio compact disk 175.00 (978-0-17-010175-2(4)) Pub: CengageAUS AUS. Dist(s): Cheng Tsui

Bersama-Sama, Vol. 2. Heather Hardie & Sue Clark. 4 CDs. (Running Time: 6 hrs.). 2000. audio compact disk 195.00 (978-0-17-010250-6(5)) Pub: CengageAUS AUS. Dist(s): Cheng Tsui

Berserk. Ally Kennen. Read by Jerome Pride. (Running Time: 7 hrs. 20 mins.). (YA). 2009. 69.99 (978-1-74214-328-6(8), 9781742143286) Pub: Bolinda Pubng AUS. Dist(s): Bolinda Pub Inc

Berserk. Tim Lebbon. 2008. audio compact disk 37.95 (978-1-897304-53-2(6)) Pub: AudioRealms CN CAN. Dist(s): Natl Bk Netwk

Berserk. unabr. ed. Ally Kennen. Read by Jerome Pride. (Running Time: 26400 sec.). 2008. audio compact disk 77.95 (978-1-921334-96-2(7), 9781921334962) Pub: Bolinda Pubng AUS. Dist(s): Bolinda Pub Inc

Berserker Fury. unabr. ed. Fred Saberhagen. Read by Paul Michael Garcia. (Running Time: 45000 sec.). (Berserker Ser.). 2007. 85.95 (978-1-4332-0751-8(6)); audio compact disk 29.95 (978-1-4332-0374-9(X)); audio compact disk 99.00 (978-1-4332-0752-5(4)) Blckstn Audio.

Berserker Fury. unabr. ed. Fred Saberhagen & Paul M. Garcia. (Berserker Ser.). 2007. audio compact disk 29.95 (978-1-4332-0753-2(2)) Blckstn Audio.

Berserker Man. unabr. ed. Fred Saberhagen. Read by Barrett Whitener. 5 cass. (Running Time: 7 hrs.). (Berserker Ser.). 2001. 39.95 (978-0-7861-1954-7(3), 2725); audio compact disk 56.00 (978-0-7861-9767-5(6), 2725) Blckstn Audio.
To defeat the ultimate weapon you must become one! Once mankind feared the berserkers, killer machines determined to eradicate all life in the universe. But the Berserker Wars are over & the threat of the sentient doomsday devices is over. Or is it? The berserkers are back, stronger & more unstoppable than before. One strange child, half human & half machine, may be humanity's only hope - or its final destroyer.

***Berserker Man.** unabr. ed. Fred Saberhagen. Read by Barrett Whitener. (Running Time: 7 hrs. 0 mins.). 2010. 29.95 (978-1-4417-5083-9(5)) Blckstn Audio.

Berserker Throne. unabr. ed. Fred Saberhagen. Read by Barrett Whitener. 6 cass. (Running Time: 8 hrs. 30 mins.). (Berserker Ser.). 2001. 44.95 (978-0-7861-1970-7(5), 2740); audio compact disk 56.00 (978-0-7861-9755-2(2), 2740) Blckstn Audio.

Berserkers: The Beginning. Fred Saberhagen. (Running Time: 55800 sec.). (Berserker Ser.). 2005. audio compact disk 99.00 (978-0-7861-7790-5(X)); audio compact disk 29.95 (978-0-7861-7955-8(4)) Blckstn Audio.

Berserkers: The Beginning. unabr. ed. Fred Saberhagen. Read by Barrett Whitener. 11 cass. (Running Time: 16 hrs.). (Berserker Ser.). 1999. 76.95 (978-0-7861-1491-7(6), 2342) Blckstn Audio.
The berserker had met some terrible opponent in battle & been wounded, but soon after its repair machines had sealed the wound. Hemphill & Maria have come through weightless vacuum inside the great machine. He realizes that it has survived a level of attempted destruction that not only had hardly weakened it, but rendered the bomb he carried only a pathetic toy.

Berserker's Planet. unabr. ed. Fred Saberhagen. Narrated by Barrett Whitener. 6 CDs. (Running Time: 7 hrs.). (Berserker Ser.). 2002. audio compact disk 48.00 (978-0-7861-9577-0(0), 2912) Blckstn Audio.
Five hundred years after humanity broke the berserker armada at Stone Place, one of the killer machines hiding in a secret sanctuary on Hunter's World has founded a new cult dedicated to death, for Hunter's World has become Berserker's Planet.

Berserker's Planet. unabr. ed. Fred Saberhagen. Narrated by Barrett Whitener. 5 cass. (Running Time: 7 hrs.). (Berserker Ser.). 2002. 39.95 (978-0-7861-2162-5(9), 2912) Blckstn Audio.

Bert & Ernie's Greatest Hits. 1 cass. (J). 9.98 (Sony Wonder); audio compact disk 13.98 CD. Sony Music Ent.
A new compilation featuring best pals Bert & Ernie singing along to songs such as "Rubber Duckie," "Imagination" & "Doin' the Pigeon".

Bert & I. Narrated by Marshall Dodge & Robert Bryan. (Running Time: 30 min.). 8.95 (978-0-9607546-3-2(6), 1) Bert and I Inc.
DownEast humor. Fun for the whole family. Continues to be company's best selling recording. An all time favorite.

Bert & I: And Other Stories from down East. Perf. by Marshall Dodge & Robert Bryan. 2009. audio compact disk 12.95 (978-1-934031-26-1(7)) Islandport Pr.

Bert & I & More Bert & I. Marshall Dodge & Bob Bryan. audio compact disk 13.95 CD. (978-0-9607546-1-8(X)) Bert and I Inc.
Ever-popular, old favorites such as: the classic Bert & I, Which Way to East Vassalboro, The Body in the Kelp, Albert's Moose, Government Fly.

Bert & I on Stage. Read by Marshall Dodge. (Running Time: 50 min.). 8.95 (978-0-9607546-7-0(9), 12) Bert and I Inc.
Collection of stories from the Bert & I series performed before audience at University of Maine in Orono.

Bert & I Stem Inflation. Narrated by Marshall Dodge & Robert Bryan. (Running Time: 36 min.). 8.95 (978-0-9607546-6-3(0), 11) Bert and I Inc.
Comic tales from DownEast.

Bert Breen's Barn. Walter D. Edmonds. (J). 1986. 9.90 (978-0-394-78000-9(0)) McGraw.

Bertha & the Beeman. Jill Eggleton. (Sails Literacy Ser.). (gr. 1 up). 10.00 (978-0-7578-4041-8(8)) Rigby Educ.

Bertha Bantam. (J). 2003. audio compact disk 17.99 (978-0-9740847-8-7(6)) GiGi Bks.
Is biggest always best? Bertha learned the answer! Cluck along with Bertha as she becomes frustrated with her place in the hen house and decides to strike out on her own. A wonderful story that appeals to the younger siblings as they learn that big or small, young or old, we are all important. This audio production comes complete with an easy to read picture book containing "tickle your tummy" illustrations and a song that will pull your children into doing the chicken dance!.

Berthold Brecht: Leben des Galilei. 1 cass. (Running Time: 1 hr.). (German Literary Criticism Ser.). 2001. 12.95 (G07616) J Norton Pubs.
Recorded at the University of Exeter in England.

Bertrams. Anthony Trollope. Narrated by Flo Gibson. (ENG.). 2008. audio compact disk 48.95 (978-1-60646-030-6(7)) Audio Bk Con.

Bertrams, unabr. ed. Anthony Trollope. Narrated by Flo Gibson. 14 cass. (Running Time: 19 hrs). 1999. 59.95 (978-1-55685-627-3(X)) Audio Bk Con.
We follow the mid-Eastern travels, careers, loves & marriages as three Oxford graduates explore the spirit of competition & mid-Victorian money culture. Full of psychological insight, satire & social comedy.

Bertrand Russel & A. N. Whitehead. unabr. ed. Paul Kuntz. Read by Lynn Redgrave. (Running Time: 10800 sec.). (World of Philosophy Ser.). 2006. audio compact disk 25.95 (978-0-7861-6391-5(7)) Pub: Blckstn Audio. Dist(s): NetLibrary CO

Beryl Coronet see Adventures of Sherlock Holmes

Besetting Sins: Hebrews 12:1. Ed Young. 1982. 4.95 (978-0-7417-1243-1(1), 243) Win Walk.

***Beside a Narrow Stream.** Faith Martin. 2010. 54.95 (978-1-4079-0827-4(8)); audio compact disk 71.95 (978-1-4079-0828-1(6)) Pub: Soundings Ltd GBR. Dist(s): Ulverscroft US

Beside Still Waters. 1 cass. 10.98 (978-1-57908-275-8(0), 1369); audio compact disk 15.98 CD. (978-1-57908-274-1(2), 1369) Platinm Enter.

Beside Still Waters, Vol. 1. 1 CD. audio compact disk 9.99 (978-1-55897-504-0(7), V5033) Pub: Brentwood Music. Dist(s): Provident Mus Dist
Features: When Morning Gilds the Sky, This is My Father's World, Rock of Ages, My Jesus I Love Thee & others.

Beside Still Waters, Vol. 2. 1 cass. audio compact disk 9.99 (978-1-55897-434-0(2), V5070) Pub: Brentwood Music. Dist(s): Provident Mus Dist
Features: What a Friend We Have in Jesus Medley, Blessed Assurance Medley, How Firm a Foundation Medley & other medleys.

Beside Still Waters: Prayer to Restore Your Soul. Mary-Alice Jafolla. Read by Richard Jafolla. 1999. 10.95 (978-0-87159-840-0(X)) Unity Schl Christ.

Beside Still Waters Vol. 1: 22 Golden Hymns of Faith. Perf. by Don Marsh Orchestra. 1 CD. 2000. audio compact disk 13.99 (978-0-7601-3265-4(8)) Pub: Brentwood Music. Dist(s): Provident Mus Dist
Songs include: "When Morning Guilds the Skies," "This Is My Father's World," "Fairest Lord Jesus," "Rock of Ages," "Jesus Loves Me" & more.

Beside Still Waters Vol. 2: 22 Golden Hymns of Faith. Perf. by Don Marsh Orchestra. 1 CD. 2000. audio compact disk 13.99 (978-0-7601-3267-8(4)) Pub: Brentwood Music. Dist(s): Provident Mus Dist
Songs include: "How Great Thou Art," "What a Friend We Have in Jesus," "Sweet Hour of Prayer," "I Must Tell Jesus" & more.

Beside the Still Waters. Voice by Margaret MacArthur. Prod. by Healing Unlimited Staff. (Running Time: 47 min.). 2000. 10.95 (978-1-893107-34-2(5)); audio compact disk 15.95 (978-1-893107-33-5(7)) Pub: Healing Unltd. Dist(s): Bookmark CA
Contemporary Christian and Inspirational Healing Music.

Beside Themselves: Music for Two Harpsichords. Perf. by Phebe Craig & Katherine Westine. 1993. audio compact disk 14.95 (978-0-9769698-5-3(8), Florio Press) KATastroPHE.

Beside Yourself with Comfort: An Audio Program to Help Relieve Pain. 1 CD. (Running Time: 30 mins.). 2004. audio compact disk 15.00 (978-0-9764498-0-5(3)) O'H O'H Inc.
Life can be a pain in the neck sometimes, but if you have unremitting acute or chronic physical pain that hasn't been helped by standard medical intervention, this 30 minute hypnotic program can help. Even though this program may provide immediate relief, please refrain from driving or operating bulldozers, cranes or other heavy machinery while enjoying your audio program lest you create even more pain by having an accident.

Beside Yourself with Comfort: Hypnotic Help for Chronic or Acute Pain Relief CD. Short Stories. Bill O'Hanlon. Narrated by Bill O'Hanlon. 1 CD. (Running Time: 30 mins.). 2009. audio compact disk 16.95 (978-0-9823573-3-0(8)) Crown Hse GBR.

Besides the Autumn Poets Sing see Poems & Letters of Emily Dickinson

Bess W. Truman. Margaret Truman. Read by Betsy Hershberg. 11 cass. (Running Time: 17 hrs.). 1993. 74.80 Set. (978-1-56544-024-1(2), 150003); Rental 11.00 30 day rental Set. (150003) Literate Ear.
After Bess Truman died, over 1,000 love letters from her to Harry, & several hundred from him to her, were found. Their daughter adds her own personal memories to her parents' candid & uninhibited correspondence.

Best American Mystery Stories 2002. unabr. ed. Read by Otto Penzler et al. Ed. by Otto Penzler. James Ellroy. (Running Time: 5 hrs. 30 mins.). (Best American Ser.). (ENG.). 2002. audio compact disk 35.00 (978-0-618-25806-2(X)) HM Harcourt.

Best American Science Writing 2000. unabr. ed. Read by Oliver Sacks. Ed. by James Gleick. 4 cass. (Running Time: 6 hrs.). 2000. 25.95 HarperCollins Pubs.

Best & the Second Best of Car Talk: With Click & Clack. abr. ed. Tom Magliozzi & Ray Magliozzi. 2 CDs. (Running Time: 2 hrs.). (ENG.). 2002. audio compact disk 22.95 (978-1-56511-664-1(X), 156511664X) Pub: HighBridge. Dist(s): Workman Pub

Best Awful: A Novel. abr. ed. Carrie Fisher. 2004. 15.95 (978-0-7435-3918-0(4)) Pub: S&S Audio. Dist(s): S and S Inc

Best Bad Luck I Ever Had. unabr. ed. Kristin Levine. Read by Kirby Heyborne. (ENG.). (J). (gr. 5). 2010. audio compact disk 34.00 (978-0-307-71056-7(4), Listening Lib) Pub: Random Audio Pubg. Dist(s): Random

Best Bandit & the Three Crosses. abr. ed. Max Brand. Read by Barry Corbin. 2 cass. (Running Time: 3 hrs.). 2000. 7.95 (978-1-57815-088-5(4), 1056, Media Bks Audio) Media Bks NJ.
Captures the old West.

Best Barbara Robinson CD Audio Collection Ever. abr. ed. Barbara Robinson. Read by Elaine Stritch. (J). 2005. 25.95 (978-0-06-082121-0(3), HarperChildAud) HarperCollins Pubs.

***Best Candy in the Whole World.** Bill Harley. Perf. by Bill Harley. (ENG.). (J). 2010. audio compact disk 15.00 (978-1-878126-55-9(5)) Round Riv Prodns.

Best Christmas Pageant Ever. unabr. ed. Barbara Robinson. Read by Elaine Stritch. (J). 2008. 34.99 (978-1-60514-712-3(5)) Find a World.

Best Christmas Pageant Ever. unabr. ed. Barbara Robinson. 1 cass. (Running Time: 1 hr. 30 mins.). 2003. 7.99 (978-0-06-058455-9(6)) HarperCollins Pubs.

***Best Christmas Pageant Ever.** unabr. ed. Barbara Robinson. Read by Elaine Stritch. (ENG.). 2005. (978-0-06-087354-7(X)); (978-0-06-087353-0(1)) HarperCollins Pubs.

Best Christmas Pageant Ever. unabr. ed. Barbara Robinson. Read by Elaine Stritch. 1 CD. (Running Time: 5183 sec.). (J). (gr. 4-7). 2006. 17.95 (978-0-06-121522-3(8), HarperChildAud) HarperCollins Pubs.

Best Christmas Pageant Ever, unabr. ed. Barbara Robinson. Narrated by C. J. Critt. 2 pieces. (Running Time: 2 hrs.). (gr. 3 up). 1997. 19.00 (978-0-7887-1792-5(8), 95264E7) Recorded Bks.
The six Herdman children are absolutely the worst kids in the history of the world! No one knows what to expect when they muscle their way into the Christmas play.

Best Christmas Pageant Ever. unabr. ed. Barbara Robinson. Narrated by C. J. Critt. 2 CDs. (Running Time: 2 hrs.). (gr. 3 up). 2000. audio compact disk 19.00 (978-0-7887-3736-7(8), C1107E7) Recorded Bks.

Best Christmas Pageant Ever, Class Set. unabr. ed. Barbara Robinson. Read by C. J. Critt. 2 cass., 10 bks. (Running Time: 2 hrs.). (J). (gr. 5). 1997. bk. & pap. bk. 89.30 (978-0-7887-2258-5(1), 46104) Recorded Bks.

Best Christmas Pageant Ever, Set. unabr. ed. Barbara Robinson. Read by C. J. Critt. 2 cass. (Running Time: 2 hrs.). (J). (gr. 5). 1997. bk. & pap. bk. 32.20 Homework. (978-0-7887-1839-7(8), 40619) Recorded Bks.

Best Cigarette. Billy Collins. Read by Billy Collins. 1 cass. (C). 1997. 10.00 (978-0-9658873-1-1(6)) Antonow Pr.
Selected poems of Billy Collins. Features studio & live tracks of the author reading.

Best Cigarette. unabr. ed. Billy Collins. Read by Billy Collins. 1 cass. (Running Time: 90 mins.). (C). 1997. audio compact disk 12.00 CD. (978-0-9658873-0-4(8)) Antonow Pr.

Best Days see Poetry & Voice of James Wright

Best Defense. Kate Wilhelm. Narrated by Anna Fields. (Running Time: 11 hrs.). 2002. 34.95 (978-1-59912-622-7(2)) Iofy Corp.

Best Defense. unabr. ed. Kate Wilhelm. Read by Anna Fields. 9 CDs. (Running Time: 11 hrs. 30 mins.). 2003. audio compact disk 72.00 (978-0-7861-9293-9(3), 3058); 56.95 (978-0-7861-2381-0(8), 3058) Blckstn Audio.
When the sister of "Baby Killer" Kennerman asks for help, attorney Barbara Holloway reluctantly looks into matters and finds that incompetent lawyers and a smear campaign from the local right-wing press are going to allow a killer to go free.

Best Defense for Women. Sandy Strong. 1 cass. (Running Time: 48 min.). 1986. 8.95 (978-0-88684-097-6(X)) Listen USA.

Best Dog in the World. Sylvia Green. (Running Time: 5280 sec.). (J). (gr. 4-7). 2006. audio compact disk 21.95 (978-1-4056-5577-4(1)) AudioGo GBR.

Best Dog-Walker/World of Dogs. Steck-Vaughn Staff. (J). 1999. (978-0-7398-0927-3(X)) SteckVau.

Best Enemies. unabr. ed. Michele Sobel Spirn. 1 cass. (Running Time: 20 min.). (Fun to Read Ser.). (J). (gr. 3-6). 1983. bk. 16.99 (978-0-934898-37-9(5)); pap. bk. 9.95 (978-0-934898-25-6(1)) Jan Prods.
Amy & Doria are caught up in a feud that's not even their own. Their families have never gotten along, & now they are forcing the girls to compete against each other all the time!.

Best Father Ever Invented, Bang the Drum Slowly, It Looked Like Forever, Something about a Soldier, & Lying in Bed. Mark Harris. Read by Mark Harris. 2 cass. (Running Time: 1 hr. 51 min.). 1987. 13.95 set. (978-1-55644-180-6(0), 7031) Am Audio Prose.
Harris brings the widely various voices of his first-person narrators vividly to life in readings from these five novels.

Best Foot Forward. unabr. ed. Joan Bauer. Read by Kathe Mazur. 3 cass. (Running Time: 4 hrs. 35 mins.). (J). (gr. 4-7). 2005. 30.00 (978-0-307-24612-7(4)); audio compact disk 38.00 (978-0-307-24629-5(9)) Books on Tape.

Best Foot Forward - A Novel. unabr. ed. Don Wall. Read by Pam Kingsley. 3 cass. (Running Time: 4 hrs.). Dramatization. (YA). (gr. 7-9). 1987. 21.95 Set. (978-1-55686-130-7(3), 130) Books in Motion.
Marvelous story about a teenage boy struggling to find his place among his peer group. The accidental loss of one arm makes the struggle all the more difficult.

Best Friends. unabr. ed. Samantha Glen. Read by Juliette Parker. 8 CDs. (Running Time: 12 hrs.). 2001. audio compact disk 64.00 Books on Tape.
Discover a place where every animal is safe, loved and allowed to live out its natural life. Here is the inspiring true story of Best Friends, an animal sanctuary a few dedicated people made happen & thousands of furry & feathered friends have called home.

Best Friends. unabr. ed. Samantha Glen. 7 cass. (Running Time: 10 hrs. 30 mins.). 2001. 56.00 (978-0-7366-6212-3(X)) Books on Tape.

Best Friends. unabr. ed. Ann M. Martin. Read by Ariadne Meyers. (Main Street Ser.). (J). 2008. 54.99 (978-1-60514-684-3(6)) Find a World.

Best Friends. unabr. ed. Martha Moody. Read by Renée Raudman. (Running Time: 17 hrs. 0 mins. 0 sec.). (ENG.). 2007. audio compact disk 39.99 (978-1-4001-0581-6(1)); audio compact disk 79.99 (978-1-4001-3581-3(8)); audio compact disk 29.99 (978-1-4001-5581-1(9)) Pub: Tantor Media. Dist(s): IngramPubServ

Best Friends, Set. unabr. ed. Nora Kay. 12 cass. (Storysound Ser.). (J). 1995. 99.95 (978-1-85903-089-9(0)) Pub: Mgna Lrg Print GBR. Dist(s): Ulverscroft US

Best Friends: The True Story of the World's Most Beloved Animal Sanctuary. Samantha Glen. Read by Juliette Parker. 2001. audio compact disk 64.00 (978-0-7366-7080-7(7)) Books on Tape.

Best Friends - ShowTrax. Mary Donnelly & George L. Strid. 1 CD. 2000. audio compact disk 19.95 H Leonard.
All kids need a special friend! This happy original is a perfect feature for elementary & middle school singers.

Best Friends & Drama Queens. Meg Cabot. Narrated by Tara Sands. (Running Time: 5 hrs.). (Allie Finkle's Rules for Girls Ser.: Bk. 3). (J). (gr. 4-7). 2009. 49.99 (978-1-60775-989-8(6)) Find a World.

Best Friends & Drama Queens. Meg Cabot. Narrated by Tara Sands. (Allie Finkle's Rules for Girls Ser.: Bk. 3). (J). (gr. 4-7). 2009. audio compact disk 19.95 (978-0-545-03950-5(9)) Scholastic Inc.

Best Friends & Drama Queens. unabr. ed. Meg Cabot. Narrated by Tara Sands. 4 CDs. (Running Time: 5 hrs.). (Allie Finkle's Rules for Girls Ser.: Bk. 3). (ENG.). (J). (gr. 4-7). 2009. audio compact disk 49.95 (978-0-545-03968-0(1)) Scholastic Inc.

Best Friends for Frances see Bargain for Frances & Other Frances Stories

Best Friends Forever. abr. ed. Jennifer Weiner. Read by Kate Baldwin & Rick Holmes. 5 CDs. (Running Time: 6 hrs. 0 mins. 0 sec.). (ENG.). 2009. audio compact disk 29.99 (978-0-7435-8231-5(4)) Pub: S&S Audio. Dist(s): S and S Inc

***Best Friends Forever.** abr. ed. Jennifer Weiner. Read by Kate Baldwin & Rick Holmes. (Running Time: 6 hrs. 0 mins. 0 sec.). (ENG.). 2011. audio compact disk 14.99 (978-1-4423-3817-3(2)) Pub: S&S Audio. Dist(s): S and S Inc

Best Friends/Hello, Friend. Created by Steck-Vaughn Staff. (Running Time: 300 sec.). (Primary Take-Me-Home Books Level K Ser.). 1998. 9.80 (978-0-8172-8654-5(3)) SteckVau.

Best Game Ever: Giants vs. Colts, 1958, & the Birth of the Modern NFL. unabr. ed. Mark Bowden. Read by Phil Gigante. (Running Time: 6 hrs.). 2008. 39.25 (978-1-4233-6797-0(9), 9781423367970, BADLE); 24.95 (978-1-4233-6796-3(0), 9781423367963, BAD); audio compact disk 39.25 (978-1-4233-6795-6(2), 9781423367956, Brlnc Audio MP3 Lib); audio compact disk 24.95 (978-1-4233-6794-9(4), 9781423367949, Brilliance MP3) Brilliance Audio.

Best Game Ever: Giants vs. Colts, 1958, & the Birth of the Modern NFL. unabr. ed. Mark Bowden. Read by Phil Gigante. Directed By Matthew Christilaw. 5 CDs. (Running Time: 21600 sec.). 2008. audio compact disk 82.25 (978-1-4233-6793-2(6), 9781423367932, BriAudCD Unabrid); audio compact disk 29.95 (978-1-4233-6792-5(8), 9781423367925, Bril Audio CD Unabri) Brilliance Audio.

Best Guide to Motivation. abr. rev. ed. Jean Marie Stine & Jean Stine. 2 cass. (Running Time: 3 hrs.). (ENG.). 2000. 17.95 (978-1-55927-590-3(1)) Pub: Macmill Audio. Dist(s): Macmillan

Best Halloween Ever. unabr. ed. Barbara Robinson. Read by Elaine Stritch. (J). 2007. 34.99 (978-1-60252-743-0(1)) Find a World.

***Best Halloween Ever.** unabr. ed. Barbara Robinson. Read by Elaine Stritch. (ENG.). 2005. (978-0-06-087356-1(6)); (978-0-06-087355-4(8)) HarperCollins Pubs.

Best Homeschooling Ideas. Debi Pearl. 1 CD. 2003. audio compact disk (978-1-892112-59-0(0)) No Greater Joy.

Best Horror Stories of the Year 1988: Premier Edition. Ed. by Orson Scott Card & Martin Greenberg. 4 cass. (Running Time: 6 hrs.). 21.95 Set, library case. (978-1-55656-130-6(X)) Dercum Audio.
Includes: One-Trick Dog by Bruce Boston, Daemon by James P. Kelly, The Colonization of Edwin Beal by Lisa Tuttle, He-We-Await by Howard Waldrop & Salvage Rites by Ian Watson & Cage 37 by Wayne Wightman.

Best Horror Value Collection. unabr. ed. Lisa Tuttle & Howard Waldrop. Ed. by Orson Scott Card & Martin Greenberg. 4 cass. (Running Time: 6 hrs.). (Dercum Value Collections). 1997. pap. bk. 19.95 Set. (978-1-55656-209-9(8)) Dercum Audio.

Best in Show for Rotten Ralph. Jack Gantos. Read by Jack Gantos. Illus. by Nicole Rubel. (Rotten Ralph Rotten Readers Ser.). (J). 2008. bk. 25.95 (978-1-4301-0448-3(1)); bk. 28.95 (978-1-4301-0451-3(1)) Live Oak Media.

Best in the Game. abr. ed. Dave Molinari. Read by Kevin McNally. 2 cass. (Running Time: 3 hrs.). Dramatization. bk. 15.95 set. (978-1-56703-012-9(2)) High-Top Sports.

Best Investment Advice I Ever Received: Priceless Wisdom from Warren Buffett, Jim Cramer, Suze Orman, Steve Forbes, & Dozens of Other Top Financial Experts. abr. ed. Liz Claman. Read by Jason Singer & Staci Snell. (Running Time: 3 hrs.). (ENG.). 2006. 14.98 (978-1-59483-802-6(X)) Pub: Hachet Audio. Dist(s): HachBkGrp

Best Investment Advice I Ever Received: Priceless Wisdom from Warren Buffett, Jim Cramer, Suze Orman, Steve Forbes, & Dozens of Other Top Financial Experts. unabr. ed. Liz Claman. Read by Jason Singer & Staci Snell. (Running Time: 3 hrs.). (ENG.). 2009. 39.98 (978-1-60788-286-2(8)) Pub: Hachet Audio. Dist(s): HachBkGrp

Best Investments for Franchises Conference: The World's Top Franchise Owners on Best Practices for Success. Speeches. ReedLogic Conference Staff. (Running Time: 4 hrs). 2006. audio compact disk 499.00 (978-1-59701-056-6(1)) Aspatore Bks.
*The Best Investments for Franchises Conference features ten speeches totaling approximately four hours of authoritative, insider?s perspectives on the best practices of the world?s top franchise owners. Featuring executives representing some of the world?s most successful franchises, this conference provides a broad yet comprehensive overview of implementing dynamic strategies to ensure successful franchise operations. Each speaker shares their insight for successful strategies and industry expertise in a format similar to a radio address, with graphics displayed in the background. Simply insert the CD-ROM into your computer, sit back, and watch and learn from the top professionals in the field as they discuss their specific processes for working with clients and best practices for ensuring success. The breadth of perspectives presented enable attendees to get inside some of the great minds of the franchise world without leaving the office. The Conference has been produced on CD-ROM and can be viewed in PowerPoint by any PC-based computer.Conference Features Speeches by:1. Laurie Baggio, VP of Franchise Development: 1-800-GOT-JUNK - ?Know Yourself?2. Daren Carter, CEO: Contours Express - ?Follow The System?3. Eddie Flores, CEO: L&L Franchise Inc. - ?Make a Profit & Like Your Business?4. Jim Fox, President: Fox?s Pizza Den - ?Knowledge is Everything?5. Gordon Logan, President: Sport Clips - ?Be Comfortable?6. Bill Phelps, CEO: Wetzel?s Pretzels - ?Do Your Homework?7. Steve Romainello, CEO: Carvel - ?Love What You Do?8. Dan Steward, President: Pillar To Post -?It?s About Possibilities?9. Ray Titus: President: Sign-A-Rama - ?Good Companies Grow?10. Ken Walker, CEO: Meineke Car Care Centers - ?Be Part of Every Opportunity.?In This CD You Will Learn:*How to evaluate a franchise opportunity financially and calculate risk*The three golden rules of franchising and what constitutes success in terms of profit and revenue*Determining financial goals and the amount of time it should take to reach them*How to establish the perfect location for your franchise*How to protect your business from the affect of competition in a similar location.*

Best Is Yet to Be. unabr. ed. Read by Bob Richards. 1 cass. (Running Time: 30 min.). 15.00 B R Motivational.
A recorded live speech by Bob Richards on the Olympic Games & the attitudes of the Olympic Champions that compete. He tells stories of five Olympic Champions to illustrate this theme.

Best Is yet to Come: 60 Devotions. Fran Fernandez. (Running Time: 4 hrs. 13 mins. 0 sec.). (ENG.). 2009. 16.99 (978-0-310-77323-8(7)) Zondervan.

Best Jazz Age Stories. unabr. ed. F. Scott Fitzgerald. Read by Alexander Scourby. 2 cass. (Running Time: 1 hr. 51 mins.). (gr. 9-12). 2002. 17.95 (978-1-57270-259-2(1)) Pub: Audio Partners. Dist(s): PerseuPGW
In "The Bridal Party," a man is invited to the wedding of his former lover. In "Three Hours Between Planes" childhood sweethearts relive their youth. "Babylon Revisited" explores the repercussions of a man's wild past. In "The Lost Decade," a man ha mysteriously "missed" the last ten years of his life.

Best-Kept Secret. Mary De Laszlo. 7 cass. (Running Time: 9 hrs. 15 mins.). (Story Sound Ser.). (J). 2004. 61.95 (978-1-85903-710-2(0)) Pub: Mgna Lrg Print GBR. Dist(s): Ulverscroft US

Best-Kept Secret. abr. ed. Les Roberts. 4 cass. (Running Time: 6 hrs.). (Milan Jacovich Mystery Ser.). 2000. 25.00 (978-1-58807-043-2(3)) Am Pubng Inc.
A debt to an old friend puts Cleveland P.I. Milan Jacovich in the middle of a sensitive case that's hurting his bank account and his love life. Jason

Crowell, a college freshman, is accused of date rape by a mysterious group called Women Warriors. But who exactly is the alleged victim? Who are Women Warriors? And why is Jason being skewered without evidence? The case turns into a giant dead end, especially when Milan's only lead, a college sexual harassment counselor, is brutally murdered. Then Milan discovers Jason has a secret, one he'd rather do jail time for than reveal. But he's not the only one willing to go to desperate lengths to keep ugly truths from seeing the light of day. Because sometimes the best-kept secrets are the most deadly.

Best-Kept Secret. unabr. ed. Kimberla Lawson Roby. Read by Tracey Leigh. (Reverend Curtis Black Ser.: Bk. 3). 2005. 29.95 (978-0-7927-3458-1(0), CMP 751); 49.95 (978-0-7927-3456-7(4), CSL 751); audio compact disk 64.95 (978-0-7927-3457-4(2), SLD 751) AudioGO.

Best Kept Secret - Philanthro-Nomics? ldr.'s ed. Charles Moore. 1-Audio CD. (Running Time: 80 M). 2003. audio compact disk 29.99 (978-0-914391-74-6(7)) Comm People Pr.

***Best Kept Secret of Christian Mission: Promoting the Gospel with More Than Our Lips.** John Dickson. (Running Time: 5 hrs. 55 mins. 13 sec.). (ENG.). 2010. 22.99 (978-0-310-57201-5(0)) Zondervan.

Best Kept Secrets. abr. ed. Sandra Brown. Read by Dick Hill. (Running Time: 21600 sec.). 2008. audio compact disk 14.99 (978-1-4233-2490-4(0), 9781423324904, BCD Value Price) Brilliance Audio.

Best Kept Secrets. unabr. ed. Sandra Brown. Read by Dick Hill. (Running Time: 13 hrs.). 2007. 39.25 (978-1-4233-2488-1(9), 9781423324881, BADLE); 24.95 (978-1-4233-2487-4(0), 9781423324874, BAD); 92.25 (978-1-4233-2482-9(X), 9781423324829, BrilAudUnabridg); audio compact disk 38.95 (978-1-4233-2483-6(8), 9781423324836, Bril Audio CD Unabri); audio compact disk 24.95 (978-1-4233-2485-0(4), 9781423324850, Brilliance MP3); audio compact disk 107.25 (978-1-4233-2484-3(6), 9781423324843, BriAudCD Unabrid); audio compact disk 39.25 (978-1-4233-2486-7(2), 9781423324867, Brinc Audio MP3 Lib) Brilliance Audio.

Best Kept Secrets of Great Communicators: Nine Secret Weapons to Shine Socially, Uncover Opportunities, & Be Perceived as Smarter, Sharper, & Savvier. unabr. ed. Peter Thomson. Read by Peter Thomson. (Running Time: 60 hrs. 0 mins. 0 sec.). (ENG.). 2003. audio compact disk 35.00 (978-0-7435-3014-9(4), Nightgale) Pub: S&S Audio. Dist(s): S and S Inc

Best Laid Plans. Leta N. Childers. Read by Leta N. Childers. 1 cass. (Running Time: 1 hr. 50 min.). 1999. bk. 6.50 (978-1-58495-025-7(0)) DiskUs Publishing.
Romantic comedy.

Best Laid Plans. Mary A. Larkin. Read by Marie McCarthy. 10 cass. (Running Time: 12 hrs. 30 mins.). (Soundings Ser.). (J). 2004. 84.95 (978-1-84283-776-4(1)) Pub: ISIS Lrg Prnt GBR. Dist(s): Ulverscroft US

***Best Laid Plans.** unabr. ed. Nora Roberts. Read by Christopher Lane. (Running Time: 7 hrs.). (Loving Jack Ser.). 2010. 39.97 (978-1-4418-5419-3(3), 9781441854193, BADLE); 24.99 (978-1-4418-5417-9(7), 9781441854179, Brilliance MP3); 39.97 (978-1-4418-5418-6(5), 9781441854186, Brinc Audio MP3 Lib); audio compact disk 24.99 (978-1-4418-5415-5(0), 9781441854155, Bril Audio CD Unabri); audio compact disk 79.97 (978-1-4418-5416-2(9), 9781441854162, BriAudCD Unabrid) Brilliance Audio.

Best Live Worship Album... Ever! 2007. audio compact disk & audio compact disk 19.99 (978-5-557-67463-8(2)) Pt of Grace Ent.

Best Looking Suit in Town: 1 Peter 5:5. Ed Young. 1988. 4.95 (978-0-7417-1696-5(8), 696) Win Walk.

Best Loved Nursery Rhymes. Perf. by Sound Stage Orchestra. (J). 2000. audio compact disk 4.95 (978-1-878427-77-9(6)) Pub: Cimino Pub Grp. Dist(s): CPG Pub Inc

Best-Loved Poems. Ed. by Richard G. Smith. 1 cass. (Running Time: 1 hr.). 1996. pap. bk. 5.95 Boxed set. (29302-5) Dover.

Best Loved Poems of Longfellow. abr. ed. Henry Wadsworth Longfellow. Perf. by Hal Holbrook. 1 cass. Incl. Arrow & the Song. (SWC 1107); Building of the Ship. (SWC 1107); Children's Hour. (SWC 1107); Jewish Cemetery at Newport. (SWC 1107); Landlord's Tale: Paul Revere's Ride. (SWC 1107); Mezzo Cammin. (SWC 1107); Psalm of Life. (SWC 1107); Skeleton in Armor. (SWC 1107); Village Blacksmith. (SWC 1107); Wreck of the Hesperus. (SWC 1107); Pt. III. Courtship of Miles Standish: The Lover's Errand. (SWC 1107); Pt. III. Song of Hiawatha: Hiawatha's Childhood. (SWC 1107); (J). 1984. 12.95 (978-0-694-50082-6(8), SWC 1107) HarperCollins Pubs.

Best Loved Stories. Ed. by Publications International Staff. (J). 2007. audio compact disk 3.98 (978-1-4127-3792-0(3)) Pubns Intl Ltd.

Best Loved Stories in Song & Dance. Short Stories. As told by Jim Weiss. 1 cass. (Running Time: 1 hr.). Dramatization. (Storyteller's Version Ser.). (J). (gr. k up). 1997. 10.95 (978-1-882513-19-2(3), 1124-19); audio compact disk 14.95 (978-1-882513-44-4(4)) Greathall Prods.
Three of the best-loved classics of all time: " The Twelve Dancing Princesses" (Grimm), "Snow White and Rose Red" (Grimm) and "The Sleeping Beauty" (Perrault).

Best Loved Stories in Song & Dance. Read by Jim Weiss. 1 cass., 1 CD. (Running Time: 1 hr.). (J). 1999. (GHP19) NewSound.

Best Loved Stories of Mark Twain. Mark Twain. 4 cass. 1993. 16.95 Set. (978-0-929541-79-2(0)) Radiola Co.

Best-Loved Stories Told at the National Storytelling Festival. 2 cass. (Running Time: 1 hr. 46 min.). (J). 17.95 Set. (978-1-879991-22-4(5)) Natl Storyling Network.
Recorded live at the National Storytelling Festival, from the companion book by the same name. Includes: "Flowers & Freckle Cream" (Elizabeth Ellis); "Orange Cheeks" (Jay O'Callahan); "A Friend of My Father" (Maggi Kerr Peirce); "Could This Be Paradise?" (Steve Sanfield); "C-R-A-Z-Y" (Donald Davis); "Cindy Ellie" (Mary Carter Smith); "One Day, One Night" (Joe Hayes); "The Innkeeper's Wise Daughter" (Peninnah Schram); "A Bell for Shorty" (Jim May); "Marie Jolie" (J. J. Reneaux).

Best-Loved Stories Told at the National Storytelling Festival. Short Stories. Perf. by Elizabeth Ellis et al. Prod. by National Storytelling Press Staff. 2 CDs. (Running Time: 1 hr. 48 mins.). 1991. audio compact disk 19.95 (978-1-879991-26-2(8), Natl Storytel) Natl Storyting Network.
This sampler, drawn from the hundreds of tales told at the National Storytelling Festival, features some of the best the art has to offer. You'll enjoy timeless traditional folk tales, stories of city life and country life, family and friends - flavored with Cajun spice, Jewish wisdom, and a triumphant zest for life. These tales and 27 more appear in the book Best-Loved Stories Told at the National Storytelling Festival.

Best Man. Gore Vidal. Contrib. by Marsha Mason & Fred Dalton Thompson. (Playaway Adult Fiction Ser.). (ENG.). 2009. 40.00 (978-1-60775-571-5(8)) Find a World.

Best Man to Die, unabr. ed. Ruth Rendell. Narrated by Davina Porter. 5 cass. (Running Time: 7 hrs. 30 mins.). (Inspector Wexford Mystery Ser.: Bk. 4). 1991. 44.00 (978-1-55690-050-1(3), 91124K8) Recorded Bks.
A philandering husband, an unscrupulous dentist & a missing nurse set a mystery for Inspector Wexford.

Best Mystery Value Collection. unabr. ed. Loren D. Estleman & Brendan DuBois. Ed. by Josh Pachter & Martin Greenberg. 4 cass. (Running Time: 6 hrs.). (Dercum Value Collections: Vol. 1). 1997. pap. bk. 19.95 (978-1-55656-212-9(8)) Pub: Dercum Audio. Dist(s): APG

Best Mystery Value Collection, Vol. 2. unabr. ed. Clark Howard & Edward D. Hoch. Ed. by Josh Pachter & Martin Greenberg. 4 cass. (Running Time: 6 hrs.). (Mystery Library: Vol. 2). 1997. pap. bk. 19.95 (978-1-55656-213-6(6)) Pub: Dercum Audio. Dist(s): APG

Best Nest. P. D. Eastman. (J). 1987. bk. 19.95 (978-0-394-01723-5(4)) SRA McGraw.

***Best New Horror.** unabr. ed. Joe Hill. (ENG.). 2007. (978-0-06-155213-7(5)); (978-0-06-155214-4(3)) HarperCollins Pubs.

Best New Paranormal Romance. Paula (Ed) Guran. 2006. audio compact disk 19.95 (978-0-8095-6225-1(1)) Diamond Book Dists.

Best New Paranormal Romance. Paula (Ed) Guran. 2006. audio compact disk 49.95 (978-0-8095-6226-8(X)) Diamond Book Dists.

Best Of. Contrib. by Amy Grant. (Mastertrax Premium Collection). 2007. audio compact disk 14.98 (978-5-557-58518-7(4)) Pt of Grace Ent.

Best of Abbott & Costello. (Running Time: 2 hrs.). 2004. audio compact disk 12.95 (978-1-57816-194-2(0)) Audio File.

Best of Abbott & Costello, Set. 2 cass. (Running Time: 2 hrs.). (Best of Old Time Radio Ser.). 12.95 in bookstyle album. (978-1-57816-016-7(2), BAC201) Audio File.
A collection of hilarious comedy routines & situations featuring those two top funnymen of all time, Bud Abbott & Lou Costello. Includes: "Their Great Comedy Routines"; "Abbott & Costello Show" (10-5-44); "Hertz U-Dirve"; "New Abbott & Costello Show" (10-1-47); "Abbott & Costello Show" (5-5-48); "Bakery/Loafing".

Best of Acoustic Guitar Solos: 1999 Edition. Compiled by William Bay. 1999. pap. bk. 24.95 (978-0-7866-4727-9(2), 98363BCD) Mel Bay.

Best of "All Things Considered" Pt. 5: The First 14 Years 1971-1985. Read by Perla Meyers et al. 1 cass. (Running Time: 30 min.). 9.95 (J008CB090, HarperThor) HarpC GBR.

Best of "All Things Considered" Pts. 1- 2: The First 14 Years, 1971-1985. Hosted by Susan Stamberg et al. 1 cass. (Running Time: 1 hr.). 10.95 (J008AB090, HarperThor) HarpC GBR.

Best of "All Things Considered" Pts. 1-5: The First 14 Years 1971-1985. Hosted by Susan Stamberg et al. 3 cass. (Running Time: 2 hr. 30 min.). 29.95 Set. (HarperThor) HarpC GBR.

Best of "All Things Considered" Pts. 3-4: The First 14 Years 1971-1985. Read by Susan Stamberg et al. 1 cass. (Running Time: 1 hr.). 10.95 (J008BB090, HarperThor) HarpC GBR.

Best of Amos 'n Andy. 2002. 29.95 (978-0-7413-0251-9(9)) Radio Spirits.

Best of Andrew Murray on Prayer: Updated in Today's Language. Andrew Murray. 1998. 4.97 (978-1-57748-210-9(7)) Barbour Pub.

Best of Anime. 1 cass. 1998. 16.98 (978-1-56826-803-3(3)) Rhino Enter.

Best of Anthony Burger. Contrib. by Anthony Burger. (Gaither Gospel Ser.). 2006. 12.99 (978-5-558-46363-7(5)) Gaither Music Co.

Best of Baby Songs. Perf. by Hap Palmer. 1 cass. (Running Time: 1 hr.). (J). 2001. 9.95 (HP2250); audio compact disk 14.95 (HP2250CD) Hap-Pal Music.
Attractive Baby Songs that are used from Hap's original recordings: Peek-a-Boo, We're on Our Way, Turn on the Music & A Child's World of Lullabies.

***Best of Bachata for Lead Guitar.** Juan Pablo Perez A. (ENG.). 2010. pap. bk. 14.99 (978-1-4234-9772-1(4), 1423497724) H Leonard.

Best of Bamboo Ridge: Poetry Selections. Poems. Ed. by Eric Chock et al. 1 cass. (YA). 1991. 8.00 (978-0-910043-27-4(2)) Bamboo Ridge Pr.

Best of Bamboo Ridge: Poetry Selections. Ed. by Eric Chock & Darrell H. Lum. 1 cass. (YA). 1991. pap. bk. Bamboo Ridge Pr.

Best of Bamboo Ridge: Prose Selections. Poems. Ed. by Eric Chock et al. 1 cass. (YA). 1991. 8.00 (978-0-910043-26-7(4)) Bamboo Ridge Pr.

Best of Bamboo Ridge: Prose Selections. Ed. by Eric Chock & Darrell H. Lum. 1 cass. (YA). 1991. pap. bk. Bamboo Ridge Pr.

Best of Beethoven. Perf. by Ludwig van Beethoven. 1 cass., 1 CD. 7.98 (TA 30240); audio compact disk 12.78 CD Jewel box. (TA 80240) NewSound.

Best of Beethoven. Created by Playaway. (YA). 2008. 59.99 (978-1-60640-539-0(X)) Find a World.

***Best of Beethoven: Alto Sax.** Composed by Ludwig van Beethoven. (ENG.). 2010. pap. bk. 10.99 (978-1-60378-268-5(0), 1603782680) Pub: Cherry Lane. Dist(s): H Leonard

***Best of Beethoven: Cello.** Composed by Ludwig van Beethoven. (ENG.). 2010. pap. bk. 10.99 (978-1-60378-274-6(5), 1603782745) Pub: Cherry Lane. Dist(s): H Leonard

***Best of Beethoven: Clarinet.** Composed by Ludwig van Beethoven. (ENG.). 2010. pap. bk. 10.99 (978-1-60378-266-1(4), 1603782664) Pub: Cherry Lane. Dist(s): H Leonard

***Best of Beethoven: Flute.** Composed by Ludwig van Beethoven. (ENG.). 2010. pap. bk. 10.99 (978-1-60378-252-4(4), 1603782524) Pub: Cherry Lane. Dist(s): H Leonard

***Best of Beethoven: Tenor Sax.** Composed by Ludwig van Beethoven. (ENG.). 2010. pap. bk. 10.99 (978-1-60378-269-2(9), 1603782699) Pub: Cherry Lane. Dist(s): H Leonard

***Best of Beethoven: Trombone.** Composed by Ludwig van Beethoven. (ENG.). 2010. pap. bk. 10.99 (978-1-60378-271-5(0), 1603782710) Pub: Cherry Lane. Dist(s): H Leonard

***Best of Beethoven: Trumpet.** Composed by Ludwig van Beethoven. (ENG.). 2010. pap. bk. 10.99 (978-1-60378-267-8(2), 1603782672) Pub: Cherry Lane. Dist(s): H Leonard

***Best of Beethoven: Viola.** Composed by Ludwig van Beethoven. (ENG.). 2010. pap. bk. 10.99 (978-1-60378-273-9(7), 1603782737) Pub: Cherry Lane. Dist(s): H Leonard

***Best of Beethoven: Violin.** Composed by Ludwig van Beethoven. (ENG.). 2010. pap. bk. 10.99 (978-1-60378-272-2(9), 1603782729) Pub: Cherry Lane. Dist(s): H Leonard

Best of Benchley. abr. ed. Robert Benchley. Perf. by Robert J. Elliott. 1 cass. Incl. Good Old-Fashioned Christmas. (CP 1731); Social Life of the Newt. (CP 1731); Treasurer's Report. (CP 1731); Uncle Edith's Ghost Story. (CP 1731); Woolen Mitten Situation. (CP 1731); (J). 1990. 9.95 (978-1-55994-005-4(0), CP 1731) HarperCollins Pubs.

Best of Benny. unabr. ed. Perf. by Jack Benny. 2 CDs. (Running Time: 2 hrs.). audio compact disk 15.95 (978-1-57816-154-6(1), DJB902) Audio File.
Best of Jack Benny from the Golden Age of Radio.

Best of Bergen. 2 CDs. (Running Time: 2 hrs.). 2004. audio compact disk 14.95 (978-1-57816-217-8(3)) Audio File.

Best of Bergen & McCarthy, Set. 2 cass. (Running Time: 2 hrs.). (Best of Old Time Radio Ser.). 12.95 in bookstyle album. (978-1-57816-017-4(0), BBM201) Audio File.
Here is the most unlikely radio Comedy Team, (a ventriloquist & his dummy) that became a legend, in some of their most memorable skits. Features all the Bergen characters: Charlie, Mortimer Snerd & Effie Klinker along with guests Fred Allen, Don Ameche, W. C. Fields, Jack Benny, Marilyn Monroe & more.

Best of Blues Guitar. Fred Sokolow. 1996. bk. 17.95 (978-0-7866-2603-8(8), 94138BCD) Mel Bay.

Best of Bob & Ray. 4 cass. 29.95 Set. (A0120B090, HarperThor) HarpC GBR.

Best of Bob & Ray, Vol. 1. 4 cass. (Running Time: 4 hrs.). 2000. 29.95 (978-1-892091-59-8(3), RadioArt) Radio Found.

Best of Bob & Ray, Vol. 1. 4 cass. (Running Time: 60 min. per cass.). 1998. 19.98 Boxed set. (4321) Radio Spirits.
Laugh inducing segments from "The Bob & Ray Radio Show" of 1982-1986.

Best of Bob & Ray, Vol. 2. 4 cass. (Running Time: 4 hrs.). 29.95 (A0130B090, HarperThor) HarpC GBR.

Best of Bob & Ray, Vol. 2. (Running Time: 4 hrs.). 1989. 29.95 Set. (A0140B090, HarperThor) HarpC GBR.

Best of Bob & Ray, Vol. 2. 4 cass. (Running Time: 4 hrs.). 2000. 29.95 (978-1-892091-60-4(7), RadioArt) Radio Found.

Best of Bob & Ray, Vol. 2. 4 cass. (Running Time: 60 min. per cass.). 1998. 19.98 Boxed set. (4322) Radio Spirits.

Best of Bob & Ray, Vol. 3. 4 cass. (Running Time: 4 hrs.). 2000. 29.95 (978-1-892091-61-1(5), RadioArt) Radio Found.

Best of Bob & Ray, Vol. 3. 4 cass. (Running Time: 60 min. per cass.). 1998. 19.98 Boxed set. (4323) Radio Spirits.

Best of Bob & Ray, Vol. 4. 4 cass. (Running Time: 4 hrs.). 2000. 29.95 (978-1-892091-62-8(3), RadioArt) Radio Found.

Best of Bob & Ray, Vol. 4. 4 cass. (Running Time: 60 min. per cass.). 1998. 19.98 Boxed set. (4324) Radio Spirits.

Best of Bob & Ray Vol. 1: Bob & Ray Public Radio Show. 4 cass. (Running Time: 4 hrs.). 29.95 set. (RA 2001) Radio Found.
Includes "Mr. I Know Where They Are," Hard Luck Stories; Anxiety: Warren Hughie & Weldon Glimbiter; Wing Po, Travelling Philosopher & others. No duplication of contents with any other Bob & Ray title.

Best of Bob & Ray Vol. 1: Excerpts from The Bob & Ray Public Radio Show. Featuring Ray Goulding & Bob Elliot. 4 CDs. 1982. audio compact disk 36.95 (978-1-892091-25-3(9), RadioArt) Radio Found.

Best of Bob & Ray Vol. 1: Excerpts from the Bob & Ray Public Radio Show. Radioart. Featuring Wally Ballou et al. 4 cass. (Running Time: 4 hrs.). 1999. 29.95 (978-1-892091-06-2(2), RadioArt) Radio Found.
64 selections.

Best of Bob & Ray Vol. 2: Bob & Ray Public Radio Show. 4 cass. (Running Time: 4 hrs.). 29.95 set. (RA 2002) Radio Found.
Includes Tippy the Wonder Dog; Army Amateur Hour; Bob & Ray Was There; & others. No duplication of contents with other Bob & Ray title.

Best of Bob & Ray Vol. 2: Excerpts from the Bob & Ray Public Radio Show. Featuring Wally Ballou et al. 4 cass. (Running Time: 4 hrs.). 1999. 29.95 (978-1-892091-07-9(0), RadioArt) Radio Found.
Man of the Street interview, in the Sports Room, Dining Out with Bob & Ray.

Best of Bob & Ray Vol. 3: Bob & Ray Public Radio Show. 4 cass. (Running Time: 4 hrs.). 29.95 set. (RA 2003) Radio Found.
Includes General Pharmacy; VCR Children; Biff Burns with the inventor of the huddle; & others. No duplication of contents with any other Bob & Ray title.

Best of Bob & Ray Vol. 3: Excerpts from the Bob & Ray Public Radio Show. Featuring Wally Ballou et al. 4 cass. (Running Time: 4 hrs.). 1999. 29.95 (978-1-892091-08-6(9), RadioArt) Radio Found.
on the Street interview, in the Sports Room, Dining Out.

Best of Bob & Ray Vol. 4: Bob & Ray Public Radio Show Plus Classic Bob & Ray: Selections from a Career, 1946-1986. 4 cass. (Running Time: 4 hrs.). 29.95 set. (RA 2004) Radio Found.
Includes "Mule Train" & I'd Like to Be a Cow in Switzerland" both sung by Mary McGoon (Ray Goulding); Piel's Beer Commercials; Arthur Sturdley's Talent Scouts & others. No duplication of contents with any other Bob & Ray title.

Best of Bob & Ray Vol. 4: Excerpts from The Bob & Public Radio Show. Featuring Ray Goulding & Bob Elliot. 1982. audio compact disk (978-1-892091-28-4(3)) Radio Found.

Best of Bob & Ray Vol. 4: Excerpts from the Bob & Ray Public Radio Show. Perf. by Bob and Ray Staff. Featuring Wally Ballou et al. 4 cass. (Running Time: 4 hrs.). 1999. 29.95 (978-1-892091-09-3(7), RadioArt) Radio Found.
on the Street interview, in the Sports Room, Dining Out wth Bob & Ray & many more.

Best of Bob & Ray, Volume 2: Excerpts from the Bob & Ray Public Radio Show. Featuring Ray Goulding & Bob Elliot. 1982. audio compact disk 36.95 (978-1-892091-26-0(7)) Radio Found.

Best of Bob & Ray, Volume 3: Excerpts from the Bob & Ray Public Radio Show. Featuring Ray Goulding & Bob Elliot. 1982. audio compact disk (978-1-892091-27-7(5)) Radio Found.

Best of Bob Crisp: 30 Years of Success in Network Marketing. Read by Bob Crisp. (ENG.). 1998. audio compact disk 29.95 (978-1-892018-05-2(5)) R Crisp Ent.

Best of Bogart, 1998th collector's ed. Perf. by Humphrey Bogart. 6 cass. 1998. bk. 17.49 (978-1-57019-072-8(0), 4000) Radio Spirits.

Best of Bogart, Set. unabr. ed. Perf. by Humphrey Bogart. 6 cass. (Running Time: 9 hrs.). 1999. 34.98 (Q101) Blckstn Audio.
Humphrey Bogart began on stage in Shakespearean roles, created characters for radio plays & became Hollywood's unlikely leading man. In this collection of radio shorts from the '40s & '50s, he appears in character & out, with favorite leading ladies & fellow tough-guys.

Best of Bogie. Perf. by Humphrey Bogart. 6 cass. (Running Time: 9 hrs.). 2002. 34.98 (4000) Radio Spirits.
In addition to his brilliant film career, Humphrey Bogart was a regular on the radio. This collection presents some of Bogie's most memorable broadcast appearances, alongside some incredible costars, in 15 classic performances from radio's golden age.

Best of Boris Karloff. Radio Spirits Staff. Read by Boris Karloff. 2005. audio compact disk 39.98 (978-1-57019-646-1(X)) Radio Spirits.

Best of Brahms. Created by Playaway. (Playaway Young Adult Ser.). (YA). 2008. 44.99 (978-1-60640-540-6(3)) Find a World.

Best of Brentwood Jazz Quartet. Perf. by Brentwood Jazz Quartet. 1 cass. 1999. 10.98 (978-0-7601-2687-5(9)); audio compact disk 16.98 (978-0-7601-2688-2(7)) Provident Music.

Best of Broadside 1962-1988: Anthems of the American Underground from the Pages of Broadside Magazine. Ed. by American Broadside Magazine Staff. 5 CDs. (Running Time: 5 hrs.). 2000. bk. 69.99 (978-0-9704942-0-7(3), 40130) Smithsonian Folkways.
Book includes essays by noted historians, lyrics, stories behind the songs & artist interviews.

***Best of Bryson City Tales: Stories of a Doctor's First Years of Practice in the Smoky Mountains.** unabr. ed. Walt, Walt Larimore,. (Running Time: 5 hrs. 20 mins. 0 sec.). (ENG.). 2004. 14.99 (978-0-310-26140-7(6)) Zondervan.

Best of Burl's for Boys & Girls. Perf. by Burl Ives. 1 cass. (J). (ps up). 7.98 (2289) MFLP CA.
This great granddaddy of folk music sets the style & spirit that inspired a whole generation. Songs include: "I Know an Old Lady," "Polly Wolldy Doodle," "Aunt Rhody," "The Man on the Flying Trapeze," "Big Rock Candy Mountain" & more.

Best of C. S. Lewis. unabr. rev. ed. C. S. Lewis. Read by Geoffrey Howard. 10 cass. (Running Time: 15 hrs.). (ENG.). 2001. 39.95 (978-1-56015-996-4(0)) Penton Overseas.
Includes: "Mere Christianity" - brings together what Lewis sees as the fundamental truths of the religion. Rejecting the boundaries that divide Christianity's many denominations, finds a common ground on which all those who have Christian faith can stand together. "Surprised by Joy" - Lewis tells of his search for joy, a spiritual journey that led him from the Christianity of his early youth into atheism and then back to Christianity.

Best of Candi Staton. Perf. by Candi Staton. 1 cass. 10.98 (978-1-57908-339-7(0), 14064); audio compact disk 15.98 CD. (978-1-57908-338-0(2)) Platinm Enter.

Best of Car Talk. unabr. ed. Tom Magliozzi & Ray Magliozzi. Read by Tom Magliozzi & Ray Magliozzi. 1 cass. (Running Time: 57 min.). 1995. 11.95 (978-1-55935-178-2(0)); audio compact disk 14.95 CD. (978-7-5454-0300-8(2)) Soundelux.
"Car Talk" is a grassroots radio phenomenon. The "Tappet" brothers (aka Tom & Ray Magliozzi), "Click" & "Clack," have won over National Public Radio listeners for years with their call-in show. On it, callers detail their car problems. Like sage country doctors, the two mechanics question, analyze, then prescribe. No dummies, the MIT-trained pair act like regular wise guys.

Best of CareerTrack. 2 cass. (Running Time: 2 hrs. 56 min.). 29.95 CareerTrack Pubns.
Various speakers discuss excerpts from Achieving Excellence by Lou Heckler, Stress Management for Professionals by Roger Mellott, Power Communication Skills by Susan Baile & others.

Best of Cary Grant. Created by Radio Spirits. (Running Time: 21600 sec.). (Smithsonian Legendary Performers Ser.). 2006. bk. 34.98 (978-1-57019-776-5(8)) Radio Spirits.

Best of Charles Dickens MP3 Boxed Set. unabr. ed. Charles Dickens. Narrated by Simon Vance. (Running Time: 48 hrs. 30 mins. 0 sec.). (ENG.). 2009. audio compact disk 29.95 (978-1-4001-2030-7(6)) Pub: Tantor Media. Dist(s): IngramPubServ

Best of Chicken Soup for the Soul. abr. ed. Jack L. Canfield & Mark Victor Hansen. 1 cass. (Running Time: 90 min.). (Chicken Soup for the Soul Ser.). 1995. 9.95 (978-1-55874-372-4(3), 3723); audio compact disk 11.95 (978-1-55874-433-2(9), 4339) Health Comm.
A collection of the best stories from the Number 1 New York Times Bestseller, Chicken Soup for the Soul.

Best of Comic Relief 2. Hosted by Robin Williams et al. 1 CD. (Running Time: 1 hr. 30 mins.). 2001. audio compact disk 9.98 (R2 70702) Rhino Enter.

Best of Comic Relief 3. Hosted by Robin Williams et al. 1 CD. (Running Time: 1 hr. 30 mins.). 2001. audio compact disk 9.98 (R2 70893) Rhino Enter.

Best of Comic Relief '90. Hosted by Robin Williams et al. 1 CD. (Running Time: 1 hr. 30 mins.). 2001. audio compact disk 9.98 (R2 71010) Rhino Enter.

Best of Contemporary Christian: Celebrate New Life. Penton. 1 cass. (Running Time: 90 mins.). (Best of Contemporary Christian Ser.). 1999. 9.95 (978-1-56015-726-7(7)) Penton Overseas.
Contemporary Christian music including "For the Sake of the Call," "Go There with You," "Lay It Down" & "Oh How the Years Go By.".

Best of Contemporary Christian: Seasons Change. 1 cass. (Running Time: 90 mins.). (Best of Contemporary Christian Ser.). 1999. 9.95 (978-1-56015-730-4(5)) Penton Overseas.
Contemporary Christian music including "Like I Love You," Marie Evans; "Radically Saved," Joseph Forrester; "Seasons Change," Shirley Church; "Butterfly Kisses," Carl W. Wright.

Best of Contemporary Christian: What Kind of Joy. 1 cass. (Running Time: 90 mins.). (Best of Contemporary Christian Ser.). 1999. 9.95 (978-1-56015-732-8(1)) Penton Overseas.
Contemporary Christian music including "What Kind of Joy," Christian B. Jackson; "Helping Hand," Marie Evans; "Lord of All," Joseph Forrester; "Lost Without You," The Spyres.

Best of Country Sing the Best of Disney. unabr. ed. 1 cass. (J). 13.99 Norelco. (978-0-7634-0034-7(3)); audio compact disk 22.99 (978-0-7634-0037-8(8)) W Disney Records.

Best of Country Sing the Best of Disney. unabr. ed. 1 cass. (J). (ps-3). 1996. 13.99 (978-0-7634-0035-4(1)); audio compact disk 22.99 CD. (978-0-7634-0036-1(X)) W Disney Records.

Best of Darwin Hobbs. Contrib. by Darwin Hobbs. 2007. audio compact disk 13.99 (978-5-557-59358-8(6)) Pt of Grace Ent.

Best of Daryl Coley. Perf. by Daryl Coley. 2002. audio compact disk Provident Mus Dist.

Best of David Glen Hatch: Sacred Selections. David Glen Hatch. 1 cass. 9.95 (109403); audio compact disk 14.95 (289403) Covenant Comms.

Best of Def Leppard: Signature Licks. 1994. pap. bk. 17.95 (978-0-7935-2314-6(1), 00696515) H Leonard.

Best of Dolores Keane. Perf. by Dolores Keane. 1 cass., 1 CD. 10.38 (GH 10038); audio compact disk 13.58 CD Jewel box. (GH 10038) NewSound.

Best of Doreen Virtue: Manifesting with the Angels/Past-Life Regression with the Angels/Karma Releasing/Healing with the Angels. Doreen Virtue. Read by Doreen Virtue. 4 CDs. 2006. audio compact disk 23.95 (978-1-4019-0713-6(X)) Hay House.

Best of Early Horowitz & Friends. Speeches. Based on a work by Leonard G. Horowitz. Concept by Dave Emory. 12 CDs. (Running Time: 14+ hours). 2007. audio compact disk 79.20 (978-0-923550-11-0(9)) Pub: Tetrahedron Pub. Dist(s): Baker Taylor

Best of Early Horowitz & Friends. Created by Leonard G. Horowitz. (ENG.). 2007. audio compact disk 49.40 (978-0-923550-65-3(8)) Pub: Tetrahedron Pub. Dist(s): Baker Taylor

Best of Ed Zern: Fifty Years of Fishing & Hunting from One of America's Best-Loved Outdoor Humorists. Ed Zern. 2007. audio compact disk 28.00 (978-1-933309-47-7(4)) Pub: A Media Intl. Dist(s): Natl Bk Netwk

Best of Edgar Allan Poe. unabr. ed. Edgar Allan Poe. Read by Edward Blake. 6 cass. (Running Time: 5 hrs. 10 mins.). Incl. Annabel Lee. 1980. (CXL514CX); Bells. 1980. (CXL514CX); Black Cat. 1980. (CXL514CX); Cask of Amontillado. 1980. (CXL514CX); Facts in the Case of M. Valdemar. 1980. (CXL514CX); Gold Bug. 1980. (CXL514CX); Masque of the Red Death. 1980. (CXL514CX); Pit & the Pendulum. Edgar Allan Poe. 1980. (CXL514CX); Purloined Letter. Edgar Allan Poe. 1980. (CXL514CX); Raven. 1980. (CXL514CX); Tell-Tale Heart. 1980. (CXL514CX); Ulalume. 1980. (CXL514CX); (Cassette Library). (J). (gr. 7 up). 1980. 40.00 (978-0-8072-2963-7(6), CXL514CX, Listening Lib) Random Audio Pubg.

Best of Edgar Allan Poe, Set. unabr. ed. Edgar Allan Poe. Read by Edward Blake. 6 cass. (YA). 1999. 44.98 (FS9-29893) Highsmith.

Best of Edgar Allan Poe, Set unabr. ed. Edgar Allan Poe. Read by Edward Blake. 6 cass. (J). 1999. 44.98 (LL 0019) AudioGO.

Best of Ellipsis Arts. Ellipsis Arts Staff. 4 CDs. (Running Time: 6 hrs.). 1997. audio compact disk 44.95 (978-1-55961-459-7(5), Ellipsis Arts) Relaxtn Co.

Best of Elmo. 1997. 13.98 (Sony Wonder) Sony Music Ent.
Elmo lets loose with "Drive My Car," "Elmo's Rap Alphabet" & other songs.

Best of Ernie. Western Publishing Co., Inc. Staff. 1 cass. (Golden Music Ser.). (J). 5.99 (Gold Bks) RH Chldrns.

Best of Especially for Mormons. Toby Miller & Fugal. 5 cass. 2004. 19.95 (978-1-57734-772-9(2)) Covenant Comms.

Best of Everything (China-Taiwan, the Crucifixion, "Richard Cory") 1 cass. (Leonard Peikoff Show Ser.). 1996. 12.95 (LPXXC5) Second Renaissance.

Best of Feminist Theology. Elizabeth Johnson. 5 cass. (Running Time: 40 min. per cass.). 7.95 ea. Paulist Pr.
Elizabeth Johnson, one of the most creative theologians of our day, examines key dimensions of the Christian life & thought from a feminist perspective.

Best of Field & Stream: 100 Years of Great Writing from America's Premier Sporting Magazine. abr. ed. Ed. by J. I. Merritt. Narrated by Alan Sklar. Told to Margaret G. Nichols & Field and Stream Editors. (Running Time: 14400 sec.). 2005. audio compact disk 28.00 (978-1-932378-79-5(0)) Pub: A Media Intl. Dist(s): Natl Bk Netwk

Best of Fifth Portion of Chicken Soup for the Soul. abr. ed. Jack L. Canfield & Mark Victor Hansen. 1 cass. (Running Time: 90 min.). (Chicken Soup for the Soul Ser.: Vol. 5). 1998. bk. 9.95 (978-1-55874-546-9(7)) Health Comm.
Selections of the best from the NY Times Bestseller, "A 5th portion of Chicken Soup for the Soul".

Best of Fifth Portion of Chicken Soup for the Soul. abr. ed. Jack L. Canfield & Mark Victor Hansen. 1 cass. (Running Time: 90 min.). (Chicken Soup for the Soul Ser.: Vol. 5). 1998. bk. 11.95 CD. (978-1-55874-545-2(9)) Health Comm.

Best of Fourth Course of Chicken Soup for the Soul. abr. ed. Jack L. Canfield et al. 1 cass. (Running Time: 90 min.). (Chicken Soup for the Soul Ser.: Vol. 4). 1997. audio compact disk 11.95 CD. (978-1-55874-472-1(X)) Health Comm.
Selections of the best from the NY Times Bestseller, "A 4th Course of Chicken Soup for the Soul".

Best of Fourth Course of Chicken Soup for the Soul. abr. ed. Jack L. Canfield et al. 1 cass. (Running Time: 90 min.). (Chicken Soup for the Soul Ser.: Vol. 4). 1997. 9.95 (978-1-55874-471-4(1)) Health Comm.

Best of Fred Allen. 2 CDs. (Running Time: 2 hrs.). 2004. audio compact disk 14.95 (978-1-57816-218-5(1)) Audio File.

Best of Fred Allen, Set. 2 cass. (Running Time: 2 hrs.). (Best of Old Time Radio Ser.). 12.95 in bookstyle album. (978-1-57816-018-1(9), BFA201) Audio File.
Includes: "Allen's Alley No. 1" (4-18-48); "The Big Show No. 1" (1950s); "Fred's Life Story" (10-26-47); " Allen's Alley No. 2" (5-9-48); "Unfinished Script" (5-2-48); "Good Old Days" (1940s); "Allen's Alley No. 3" (4-11-48); "The Big Show No. 2" (4-8-51); "One Long Pan" (4-11-48); "Mrs. Allen" (1-30-49); "Mighty Allen Art Players" (3-20-40); "Studio Tour" (5-26-46).

***Best of Friends.** unabr. ed. Susan Mallery. Read by Renée Raudman. (Running Time: 9 hrs.). 2010. 24.99 (978-1-4418-3484-3(2), 9781441834843, Brilliance MP3); 24.99 (978-1-4418-3486-7(9), 9781441834867, BAD) Brilliance Audio.

***Best of Friends.** unabr. ed. Susan Mallery. Read by Renee Raudman. (Running Time: 9 hrs.). 2010. 39.97 (978-1-4418-3485-0(0), 9781441834850, Brlnc Audio MP3 Lib) Brilliance Audio.

***Best of Friends.** unabr. ed. Susan Mallery. Read by Renée Raudman. (Running Time: 9 hrs.). 2010. 39.97 (978-1-4418-3487-4(7), 9781441834874, BADLE); audio compact disk 19.99 (978-1-4418-3482-9(6), 9781441834829, Bril Audio CD Unabri) Brilliance Audio.

***Best of Friends.** unabr. ed. Mariana Pasternak. Read by Karen Saltus. (ENG.). 2010. (978-0-06-198539-3(2), Harper Audio); (978-0-06-198540-9(6), Harper Audio) HarperCollins Pubs.

***Best of Friends.** unabr. ed. Read by Renee Raudman. (Running Time: 9 hrs.). 2010. audio compact disk 79.97 (978-1-4418-3483-6(4), 9781441834836, BriAudCD Unabrid) Brilliance Audio.

Best of Friends. unabr. ed. Joanna Trollope. Read by Clare Higgins. 8 cass. (Running Time: 12 hrs.). 2000. 59.95 (978-0-7451-6565-3(6), CAB 1181) Pub: Chivers Audio Bks GBR. Dist(s): AudioGO
In the old town of Wittingbourne, a network of deep friendship connects two families. Laurence and Hilary run The Bee House, a small hotel. Meanwhile, Gina and Fergus occupy High Place, a decorator's showcase. as Hilary takes stock of her life, she realizes it isn't how she had hoped it would be.

Best of Friends. unabr. ed. Joanna Trollope. Narrated by Virginia Leishman. 7 cass. (Running Time: 10 hrs. 15 mins.). 1998. 66.00 (978-0-7887-2162-5(3), 95458E7) Recorded Bks.
Gina and Laurence have always been the best of friends. Each has married & raised children. But when Gina's husband abandons her, she turns to Laurence for comfort & sets off a series of devastating events.

***Best of Friends: A Story from Guys Read: Funny Business.** unabr. ed. Mac Barnett. (ENG.). 2010. (978-0-06-202767-2(0)); (978-0-06-204202-6(5)) HarperCollins Pubs.

Best of Friends: Martha & Me. unabr. ed. Mariana Pasternak. Read by Maia Morgenstern & Karen Saltus. 2010. audio compact disk 39.99 (978-0-06-176814-9(6), Harper Audio) HarperCollins Pubs.

Best of Gary North. 2001. 99.95i (978-0-9717326-1-2(2)) Duneroller Pubng.

Best of Gregorian Chant: From the Abbey of St. Michael's. 1 cass. (Running Time: 35 mins.). 1999. 9.95 (T8160); audio compact disk 15.95 (K1240) Liguori Pubns.
Songs include: "Jesus, Redemptor Omnium," "Sanctus," "Kyriale" & more.

Best of Gunsmoke on Radio. unabr. collector's ed. Perf. by William Conrad et al. 20 cass. (Running Time: 30 hrs.). 2000. bk. & pap. bk. 59.98 (4413) Radio Spirits.
Sixty episodes of the violence that moved west with young America and the story of a man who moved with it. 60 episodes including Bum's Rush, Home Surgery, Drop Dead, Spring Term, Lochinvar, Square Triangle, Paid Killer, Yorky, Cyclone, Pussy Cats, Jayhawkers, Gonif, The Soldier, Tacetta, The Buffalo Hunter, Cain, Print Asper, Sundown, Wild West, Hickock, Gone Straight, The Sutler, Prairie Happy, Gunsmuggler plus 36 more and a 64 page booklet.

Best of Heat with John Hockenberry. John Hockenberry. Read by John Hockenberry. 1 cass. (Running Time: 1 hr.). 14.95 (AO-510, HarperThor) HarpC GBR.

Best of Henry James: The Portrait of a Lady, the Bostonians & the Turn of the Screw. abr. ed. Henry James. Read by Carole Boyd et al. (Running Time: 7 hrs. 24 mins. 0 sec.). (ENG.). 2008. audio compact disk 31.95 (978-1-934997-10-9(2)) Pub: CSAWord. Dist(s): PerseuPGW

Best of Homecoming, Volume One. Directed By Ben Speer. Contrib. by Bill & Gloria Gaither and Their Homecoming Friends & Bill Gaither. (Gaither Gospel Ser.). 1997. audio compact disk 13.98 (978-7-474-05187-5(7)) Sprg Hill Music Group.

Best of How to Manage Your Money. abr. ed. Larry Burkett. (ENG.). 2000. 1.50 (978-0-8024-3391-6(X)) Moody.

Best of Isaac Asimov. unabr. ed. Isaac Asimov. Read by Dan Lazar. 8 cass. (Running Time: 12 hrs.). Incl. Anniversary. (1231); Billiard Ball. (1231); C-Chute. (1231); Dead Past. (1231); Deep. (1231); Dying Night. (1231); Fun They Had. (1231); Last Question. (1231); Marooned off Vesta. (1231); Martian Way. (1231); Mirror Images. 12 cass. (Running Time: 12 hrs.). (1231); Nightfall. (1231); 1998. 64.00 (978-0-7366-0235-8(6), 1231) Books on Tape.
Rare collection of the twelve best stories written by Asimov over the past 35 years. Includes "Marooned Off Vesta" & "The Martial Way".

Best of J. S. Bach. Conducted by Oliver Dohnanyi et al. (Playaway Young Adult Ser.). (ENG.). (YA). 2008. 44.99 (978-1-60640-541-3(1)) Find a World.

Best of Jack Benny. Created by Radio Spirits. (Running Time: 36000 sec.). (Legends of Radio Ser.). 2006. audio compact disk 39.98 (978-1-57019-795-6(4)) Radio Spirits.

Best of Jack Benny, Set. Perf. by Jack Benny. 2 cass. (Running Time: 2 hrs.). (Best of Old Time Radio Ser.). 12.95 in bookstyle album. (978-1-57816-015-0(4), BB1002) Audio File.
Jack Benny along with many of the regulars on the show created some of the most memorable characters & situations. Included are 21 specially selected routines: Tape One: "Drugstore Lunch," "Do Wah Ditty I," "Si, Sy I," "Doctor's Office I," "Railroad Station I," "Violin Lesson I," "Sportsmen LS/MFT," "Do Wah Ditty II," "Beverly Hills Beavers." Tape Two: "Cimmaron Rolls I," "Dennis & the Doc," "Si, Sy II," "Railroad Station II," "Violin Lesson II," "At the Races," "Cimmaron Rolls II," "Ronald Colman's Dream," "Chief Radio Engineer," "Doctor's Office II," "Railroad Station III," "Benny's Birthday".

Best of Jack Benny: Old Time Radio. Perf. by Jack Benny. 1 cass. 1985. 3.98 (R260) Radio Spirits.
Includes Jack Benny shows & other classic Old-Time Radio Shows that he starred in including Fred Allen, Burns & Allen, Suspense & The Lux Radio Theatre.

Best of Jack Falvey on Management. unabr. collector's ed. Jack Falvey. Read by Larry McKeever. 10 cass. (Running Time: 15 hrs.). 1992. 80.00 (978-0-7366-2205-9(5), 3000) Books on Tape.
Jack Falvey is a dynamic consultant who runs his own company, trains some of the best sales forces in the world & writes feature columns in "The Wall Street Journal" & other top publications. Each year he collects his "absolutely very best" thoughts & articles &, to our great benefit, publishes them.

Best of Jack London: To Build a Fire. Short Stories. Perf. by Jim Gallant. Engineer Bob E. Flick. Music by Bob E. Flick. Des. by Adam Mayefsky. 1 CD. (Running Time: 46 mins.). Dramatization. (Best of Jack London Ser.: Vol. 1). 2001. audio compact disk 15.00 (978-1-884214-14-1(2)) Ziggurat Prods.
Experience first-hand the dramatic ebb and flow of emotion as classic literature is transformed into the world of your imagination like never before. In TO BUILD A FIRE, the listener journeys alongsidea hungry man and his loyal dog through the vast,bleak tundra of Alaska's Yukon Trail...a landscapeso cold, time itself appears to have frozen in place.

Best of Jack London Vol. 2: Lost Face. Short Stories. Jack London. Engineer Bob E. Flick. Music by Bob E. Flick. Des. by Adam Mayefsky. 1 CD. (Running Time: 32 mins.). Dramatization. (Best of Jack London Ser.: Vol. 2). 2001. audio compact disk 15.00 (978-1-884214-21-9(5)) Ziggurat Prods.
Experience first-hand the dramatic ebb and flow of emotion as classic literature is transformed into the world of your imagination like never before.In LOST FACE, the listener sits right beside a tribal prisoner as he plots to avoid the painful torturethat awaits him next.

Best of Jack London Vol. 3: Love of Life. Short Stories. Jack London. Read by Reg Green. Engineer Bob E. Flick. Music by Bob E. Flick. Des. by Adam Mayefsky. 1 CD. (Running Time: 1 hr. 2 mins.). Dramatization. (Best of Jack London Ser.: Vol. 3). 2002. audio compact disk 15.00 (978-1-884214-25-7(8)) Ziggurat Prods.
Experience first-hand as classic literature dramatically transforms into the world of your imagination like never before. In LOVE OF LIFE, one man struggles to survive an unforgettable journey through time, hunger, & insanity after being deserted by his partner in the lonely Canadian tundra. Only the strongestdesire to survive could sustain him through the bleak, treacherous wasteland against the fearful loom of oncoming winter...only the indestructable love of life!.

***Best of Jack Pine Style.** Andresen Guitar Group. (ENG.). 2010. audio compact disk 16.00 (978-0-924119-08-8(X)) Pub: U of Wis Pr. Dist(s): Chicago Distribution Ctr

Best of Jeff & Sheri Easter. Contrib. by Jeff & Sheri Easter et al. Prod. by Bill Gaither. (Running Time: 1 hr. 35 mins.). 2006. 19.99 (978-5-558-24611-7(1)) Gaither Music Co.

Best of Joe Wise: Music for Kids. Joe Wise. 1987. audio compact disk 15.95 (FH-19-CD) GIA Pubns.

***Best of Jonathan Edwards Sermons.** unabr. ed. Jonathan Edwards. Narrated by David Cochran Heath. (ENG.). 2007. 10.98 (978-1-59644-467-6(3), Hovel Audio) christianaud.

Best of Jonathan Edwards Sermons. unabr. ed. Jonathan Edwards. Read by David C. Heath. (Running Time: 3 hrs. 30 mins. 0 sec.). (ENG.). 2007. audio compact disk 18.98 (978-1-59644-465-2(7)) christianaud.

Best of Kevin Davidson & the Voices. Contrib. by Kevin Davidson & the Voices Staff. 2008. audio compact disk 13.99 (978-5-557-43327-3(9)) Pt of Grace Ent.

Best of Kid Komedy. 1 CD. (YA). 2003. audio compact disk 16.95 (978-1-929243-51-8(0)) Uproar Ent.
For adults and kids - clean and funny entertainment for every generation! Talented "kid comedians" (ages 8-12) LIVE ON STAGE deliver original and sophisticated stand-up comedy with the deftness of a pro!.

Best of Latino Comedy. Perf. by Willie Barcena et al. 4 cass. (Running Time: 4 hrs.). (Spoken Word Humor Ser.). 1999. 29.95 Set, clamshell. (978-1-929243-02-0(2), UPR1003) Uproar Ent.
"The Best of Latino Humor" featuring the top contemporary Latino comics in the U.S. PABLO FRANCISCO (aka "Concession Man"), WILLIE BARCENA (the Tonight Show 4 times), THE HOT & SPICY MAMITAS (the five funniest Latinos ever) & RUDY MORENO, Latino comic par excellence.

Best of Lewis Grizzard. Lewis Grizzard. Read by Lewis Grizzard. Ed. by Bill Anderson. 1 cass. 1991. 9.98 (978-0-945258-23-0(2), STC-0025); 9.98 (978-0-945258-21-6(6), STCD-0025) Sthrn Tracks.

Best of Living Proof Live. Travis Cottrell. 2003. audio compact disk 16.98 (978-0-633-19384-3(4)) LifeWay Christian.

Best of Lori Wick: A Gathering of Hearts. unabr. ed. Lori Wick. Narrated by Laural Merlington. (Running Time: 3 hrs. 45 mins. 55 sec.). (ENG.). 2009. 16.09 (978-1-60814-597-3(2)); audio compact disk 22.99 (978-1-59859-645-8(4)) Oasis Audio.

Best of Marcos see Lo Mejor de Marcos

Best of Mark Hayes. Contrib. by Mark Hayes. 2007. audio compact disk 15.99 (978-5-557-56681-0(3), Glory Snd) Shawnee Pr.

Best of Mark Twain. Mark Twain. Read by Marvin Miller. 4 cass. 23.80 (E-423) Audio Bk.
17 stories.

Best of Mark Twain. abr. ed. Mark Twain & Marvin Miller. 2 cass. (Running Time: 2 hrs. 4 min.). Incl. Ant. (805); Encounter with an Interviewer. (805); Facts in the Case of the Great Beef Contract. (805); Guying the Guides. (805); How I Edited an Agricultural Paper. (805); I Ride a Bucking Horse. (805); Jim Baker's Blue-Jay Yarn. (805); Jim Blaine's Ram. (805); Journalism in Tennessee. (805); Markiss, King of the Liars. (805); Niagara. (805); Notorious Jumping Frog of Calaveras County. (805); Punch, Brothers, Punch. (805); Speech on the Weather. (805); 12.95 (978-0-89926-117-1(5), 805) Audio Bk.

Best of Mark Twain. unabr. ed. Mark Twain. Read by Jack Whitaker. 6 cass. (Running Time: 5 hrs. 46 min.). Incl. Celebrated Jumping Frog of Calaveras County. 1975. (CXL515CX); Guying the Guides. 1975. (CXL515CX); Invalid's Story. 1975. (CXL515CX); Punch, Brothers, Punch. 1975. (CXL515CX); Speech on the Weather. 1975. (CXL515CX); Story of Bad Little Boy. 1975. (CXL515CX); Story of Old Ram. 1975. (CXL515CX); What Stumped the Bluejays. 1975. (CXL515CX); (Cassette Library). 1975. 44.98 (978-0-8072-2970-5(9), CXL515CX, Listening Lib) Random Audio Pubg.
This collection features two of Twain's most popular works, "The Adventures of Huckleberry Finn" & "The Adventures of Tom Sawyer" as well as other Twain favorites. All are sparkling examples of Twain's humor & of his incisive revelations about the human character.

Best of Mark Twain, Set unabr. ed. Mark Twain. Read by Jack Whitaker. 6 cass. (J). (gr. 1-8). 1999. 44.98 (LL 0017, Chivers Child Audio) AudioGO.

Best of Mark Twain in Person, Volume 1: Selections from Richard Henzel's Portrayal of Mark Twain. abr. ed. Speeches. 1 CD. (Running Time: 1 hr. 5 mins.). 2002. audio compact disk 9.99 (978-0-9747237-1-6(1)) R Henzel.
Studio recorded excerpts from Richard Henzel's acclaimed one man theatre show of Mark Twain material.

Best of Mark Twain in Person, Volume 2: Studio recordings of selections from Richard Henzel's long-running Play. Narrated by Richard Henzel. (ENG.). 2007. audio compact disk 9.99 (978-0-9747237-3-0(8)) R Henzel.

Best of Marty Haugen, 1985-1989, Anthology II. Marty Haugen. 1997. 10.95 (401); audio compact disk 15.95 (401) GIA Pubns.

Best of Mary Lu Walker. Mary Lu Walker. (Running Time: 56 mins.). 1996. 11.95 (978-0-8091-8209-1(2), 8209-2) Paulist Pr.

Best of Mary Lu Walker. unabr. ed. Mary Lu Walker. 2 CDs. (Running Time: 56 mins.). 1996. audio compact disk 14.95 (978-0-8091-8208-4(4), 8208-4) Paulist Pr.
Twenty-three of her most loved songs for young children, ideal for classroom or home,.

Best of Master. Nick Jones. 1997. 99.00 (978-1-56253-431-8(9), Milady) Pub: Delmar. Dist(s): CENGAGE Learn

Best of Michael Ballam. Michael Ballam. 1 cass. 9.95 (1100661); audio compact disk 14.95 (1100653) Covenant Comms.
A collection of vintage Michael Ballam renditions.

Best of Michael Rosen: Poetry for Kids. unabr. ed. Michael Rosen. Read by Michael Rosen. 1 cass. (Running Time: 90 min.). (J). (gr. 1-6). 1996. 11.95 (978-1-57143-058-8(X)) RDR Bks.
Poems for kids of all ages on family, school, friends, pets & teachers. Humorous.

Best of Money Matters Cassette Tape. Larry Burkett. (ENG.). 2000. 1.50 (978-0-8024-3390-9(1)) Moody.

Best of Money Minutes Cassette Tape. Larry Burkett. (ENG.). 2000. 1.50 (978-0-8024-3389-3(8)) Moody.

Best of Mozart. 1 cass. 7.98 (TA 30222); 7.98 (TA 30222); audio compact disk 12.78 Jewel box. (TA 80222); audio compact disk 12.78 CD Jewel box. (TA 80222) NewSound.

Best of Mozart. Created by Playaway. (Playaway Young Adult Ser.). (YA). 2008. 59.99 (978-1-60640-542-0(X)) Find a World.

Best of National Public Radio: Eyewitness to History. 1 cass. (Running Time: 1 hr. 30 min.). 1999. 12.98 Hachet Audio.
Featuring: "The Berlin Olympics," "Concentration Camps Liberation," "Electrification," "Marian Anderson," "See It Now," "The Kennedy Assassination," "EgyptAir Flight 648," "Return to Romania," & "Goodbye Saigon.".

Best of National Public Radio: On Creativity. Perf. by Jimmy Landry et al. 1 cass. (Running Time: 1 hr. 30 min.). 1999. 12.98 Hachet Audio.

Best of Nicktoons. 1 cass., 1 CD. (J). 7.98 (KID 75238); audio compact disk 12.78 CD Jewel box. (KID 75238) NewSound.

Best of Nicktoons. 1 cass. (Running Time: 40 min.). (J). (ps-3). 1998. 9.98 (978-1-56826-891-0(2)); 13.98 (978-1-56826-892-7(0)) Rhino Enter.
Compiles the music from breakthrough animation shows such as "Rugrats," "The Ren & Stimpy Show," "AAAHH!!! Real Monsters," " KABLAM!," " Hey Arnold!," " Rocko's Modern Life," & "Angry Beavers".

Best of Nicktoons. unabr. ed. 1 CD. (Running Time: 40 mins.). (J). (gr. k-3). 2001. audio compact disk 13.98 (978-0-7379-0212-9(4), 74356); 10.98 (978-0-7379-0121-4(7), R4 75237) Rhino Enter.
Favorite songs from Nickelodeon's TV programming.

Best of Nineteen Ninety Seven. 12 cass. 49.00 Set. (S01-058) Morning NC.

Best of Nineteen Ninety Six. 12 cass. 49.00 Set. (S01-011) Morning NC.

Best of Noel Coward. unabr. ed. Noel Coward. Narrated by Michael Cochrane. 1999. 29.95 (978-1-85998-267-9(0), HoddrStoughton) Pub: Hodder General GBR. Dist(s): Trafalgar

Best of NPR: A Life in the Arts. unabr. ed. National Public Radio. Read by Janet Fonteyn & Janet Baker. (ENG.). 2006. 9.99 (978-1-59483-534-6(9)) Pub: Hachet Audio. Dist(s): HachBkGrp

Best of NPR: Biography & Autobiography. unabr. ed. National Public Radio. (ENG.). 2006. 9.99 (978-1-59483-535-3(7)) Pub: Hachet Audio. Dist(s): HachBkGrp

Best of NPR: Eyewitness to History. unabr. ed. National Public Radio. (ENG.). 2006. 9.99 (978-1-59483-537-7(3)) Pub: Hachet Audio. Dist(s): HachBkGrp

Best of NPR: On Creativity. unabr. ed. National Public Radio. (ENG.). 2006. 9.99 (978-1-59483-536-0(5)) Pub: Hachet Audio. Dist(s): HachBkGrp

Best of NPR: Public Laughter. unabr. ed. National Public Radio. (ENG.). 2006. 9.99 (978-1-59483-539-1(X)) Pub: Hachet Audio. Dist(s): HachBkGrp

Best of NPR: Writers on Writing. unabr. ed. National Public Radio. (ENG.). 2006. 9.99 (978-1-59483-538-4(1)) Pub: Hachet Audio. Dist(s): HachBkGrp

Best of O. Henry. O. Henry. Read by Michael Hanson. (Running Time: 2 hrs.). 2002. 19.95 (978-1-59912-043-0(7), Audiofy Corp) Iofy Corp.

Best of O. Henry. Short Stories. O. Henry. Read by Michael Hanson. 2 cds. (Running Time: 2 hrs 8 mins). (YA). 2002. audio compact disk 18.95 (978-1-58472-213-7(4), 060, In Aud) Pub: Sound Room. Dist(s): Baker Taylor
Seven time-honored classics by O. Henry 1) Voice of the City 2) The Gift of the Magi 3) The Cop and the Anthem 4) The Romance of a Busy Broker 5) The Green Door 6) The Ransom of Red Chief 7) The Hiding of Black Bill.

Best of O. Henry. O. Henry. Narrated by Michael Hanson. (Running Time: 7680 sec.). (ENG.). 2008. audio compact disk 24.00 (978-1-58472-637-1(7), In Aud) Sound Room.

Best of O. Henry. abr. ed. O. Henry. Narrated by Marvin Miller. 2 cass. (Running Time: 2 hrs. 4 min.). Incl. After Twenty Years. (856); Cop & the Anthem. (856); From the Cabbie's Seat. (856); Gift of the Magi. (856); Innocents of Broadway. (856); Last Leaf. (856); Retrieved Reformation. (856); 12.95 (978-0-89926-163-8(9), 856) Audio Bk.
A collection of O. Henry's best short stories....7 in all.

Best of O. Henry. unabr. ed. O. Henry. 2 CDs. (Running Time: 2 hrs.). 2001. audio compact disk 25.00 (978-1-58472-146-8(4), Commuters Library) Sound Room.

Best of O. Henry: Gift of the Magi, Cop & the Anthem, Twenty Years After. O. Henry. 10.00 (LSS1125) Esstee Audios.

Best of Og Mandino see Lo Mejor de Og Mandino

Best of O'Henry. O. Henry & William Sydney Porter. Read by Michael Hanson. (Playaway Adult Fiction Ser.). 2008. 39.99 (978-1-60640-817-9(8)) Find a World.

Best of Old Time Radio: Burns & Allen. Perf. by Gracie Allen et al. 4 cass. (Running Time: 6 hrs.). 2002. pap. bk. 24.98 Radio Spirits.
For almost 20 years, George Burns and Gracie Allen were radio's best-loved husband and wife comedy team. Listeners across America couldn't wait to hear about the latest misadventures of their favorite scatterbrain and her long-suffering husband. In addition to headlining their own show, Burns and Allen often dropped in on their friends, like Jack Benny, Eddie Cantor Al Jolson. Now, the Smithsonian Institution and Radio Spirits are proud to bring you the finest assortment of these appearances ever assembled.

Best of Old Time Radio: Burns & Allen. Perf. by George Burns et al. 6 CDs. (Running Time: 6 hrs.). 2002. audio compact disk 34.98 (40002) Radio Spirits.

Best of Old-Time Radio - Alfred Hitchcock. Smithsonian Institution Staff. 4 vols. (Running Time: 6 hrs.). (Smithsonian Collection). 2002. bk. 24.98 (978-1-57019-283-8(9), OTR6036) Pub: Radio Spirits. Dist(s): AudioGO

Best of Old Time Radio Alfred Hitchcock. collector's ed. Perf. by Tallulah Bankhead et al. Frwd. by Leonard Maltin. 4 cass., (Running Time: 6 hrs.). 2000. bk. & pap. bk. 24.98 (6036); bk. & pap. bk. 39.98 (6037) Radio Spirits.
Centennial collection of the master of mayhem's classic radio broadcasts, including "The Lodger," the 1940 audio broadcast that introduced audiences to "Suspense." Also includes adaptations of Hitchcock's classic films, "Lifeboat," "Foreign Correspondent," "The 39 Steps," "Rebecca," "Shadow of a Doubt" and "Strangers on a Train." Historical booklet. 8 episodes.

Best of Old-Time Radio Starring Humphrey Bogart, Set. Read by Humphrey Bogart. 4 vols. (Running Time: 6 hrs.). 2002. bk. 24.98 (978-1-57019-415-3(7), OTR5032) Pub: Radio Spirits. Dist(s): AudioGO
One of Hollywood's true legends teams up with talented stars such as Ingrid Bergman and Greer Garson to re-create his greatest film roles on radio. Hear Bogart as Sam Spade in The Maltese Falcon, Rick Blaine in Casablanca and in his Oscarwinning performance as Charlie Allnut in The African Queen. Bogart also displays his comedic talent on The Jack Benny Program and The Eddie Cantor Show. Includes five more classic Bogie radio appearances!.

Best of Old-Time Radio Starring Jack Benny. collector's ed. Frwd. by Irving Fein. 4 vols. (Running Time: 6 hrs.). (Smithsonian Collection). 1999. bk. 24.98 (978-1-57019-157-2(3), OTR5026) Pub: Radio Spirits. Dist(s): AudioGO

Best of Old-Time Radio Starring Jimmy Stewart. Perf. by Cary Grant et al. 6 vols. (Running Time: 6 hrs.). 2002. bk. 34.98 (978-1-57019-484-9(X), OTR5035) Pub: Radio Spirits. Dist(s): AudioGO
This collection features 10 of the best radio performances by one of America's most beloved stars. Stewart re-creates his unforgettable film roles in radio adaptations of It's a Wonderful Life (directed by Frank Capra), The Philadelphia Story and Winchester '73 just to name a few. Joining Stewart are some of Hollywood's biggest names, including Cary Grant, Katherine Hepburn and Carole Lombard. Also includes Stewart's audition broadcast for the classic western series The Six Shooter, which would become his favorite radio role.

Best of Old-Time Radio Starring Jimmy Stewart. Perf. by Cary Grant et al. 4 vols. (Running Time: 6 hrs.). (Smithsonian Legendary Performers Ser.). 2002. bk. 24.98 (978-1-57019-483-2(1), OTR5034) Pub: Radio Spirits. Dist(s): AudioGO

Best of Old-Time Radio Starring Lucille Ball. collector's ed. Perf. by Bob Hope et al. Frwd. by Madelyn Pugh Davis & Bob Carroll, Jr. 4 vols. (Running Time: 6 hrs.). (Smithsonian Collection). 2002. bk. 24.98 (978-1-57019-267-8(7), OTR5028) Pub: Radio Spirits. Dist(s): AudioGO
America loved Lucy years before she became the most beloved star on television. Listen to this collection of 10 Lucy favorites and you'll know why. In addition to her typically hysterical performances on four episodes of My Favorite Husband, Lucy shows her versatility with dramatic roles on Suspense and The Lux Radio Theatre. The 60-page booklet of Lucy-related facts features a foreword by Madelyn Pugh Davis and Bob Carroll, Jr., writers for My Favorite Husband and I Love Lucy.

Best of Old-Time Radio Starring Orson Welles. collector's ed. Perf. by Orson Welles et al. Frwd. by Arthur Anderson. Hosted by Charles Shaw. 4 cass. (Running Time: 6 hrs.). 2001. bk. & pap. bk. 24.98 (5030); bk. & pap. bk. 39.98 (5031) Radio Spirits.
Collection of 8 episodes, includes historical book.

Best of "On the Buses" abr. ed. 2 cass. 1998. 15.00 Set. (978-1-86117-072-9(6)) Ulvrscrft Audio.
The best jokes played on the much-maligned Blakey.

Best of Our Island Story: From the Romans in Britain to Queen Victoria. abr. ed. Read by Anna Bentinck & Daniel Philpott. (Running Time: 18000 sec.). (J). (gr. 4-7). 2006. audio compact disk 28.98 (978-962-634-438-5(5), Naxos AudioBooks) Naxos.

Best of Passion. Contrib. by Passion Band et al. 2006. audio compact disk 17.99 (978-5-558-10135-5(0)) Pt of Grace Ent.

Best of Personal Excellence Vol. 1: The Magazine of Life Enrichment. Read by Richard Blair & Darby Blair. Ed. by Ken Shelton. 2 cass. (Running Time: 2 hrs.). 1997. 14.95 (978-1-890009-00-7(8)) Exec Excell.

Best of Personal Excellence Vol. 1: The Magazine of Life Enrichment, abr. ed. Ed. by Ken Shelton. 2 cass. (Running Time: 2 hrs.). (Personal Excellence Ser.: Vol. 3). 1998. 16.95 Set. (978-1-890009-36-6(9)) Exec Excell.
Compilation of articles from "Personal Excellence" Magazine.

Best of Personal Excellence Vol. 2: The Magazine of Life Enrichment. abr. ed. Ed. by Ken Shelton. 2 cass. (Running Time: 2 hrs.). 1998. 16.95 (978-1-890009-28-1(8)) Exec Excell.

Best of Peter, Paul & Mary. Perf. by Peter, Paul and Mary. 1 cass. (J). (ps up). 9.98 (2507) MFLP CA.
This classic recording includes all the songs that make these soulful singers so well-loved. Songs include: "Lemon Tree," "Blowin' in the Wind," "Early Morning Rain," "500 Miles," "Leaving on a Jet Plane" & many more.

Best of Poe Read Along. Prod. by Saddleback Educational Publishing. (Saddleback's Illustrated Classics Ser.). (YA). 2006. audio compact disk 24.95 (978-1-56254-885-8(9)) Saddleback Edu.

Best of Ray Lynch. 1 cass., 1 CD. 8.78 (WH 11245); audio compact disk 13.58 CD Jewel box. (WH 11245) NewSound.

Best of Reggie White. 2006. audio compact disk 35.00 (978-1-59933-000-6(8)) Morning NC.

Best of Reggie White. Reggie White. 2006. audio compact disk 39.99 (978-1-59933-001-3(6)) Pub: Morning NC. Dist(s): Destiny Image Pubs

Best of Reggie White. Reggie White. (Running Time: 4 hrs. 44 mins.). 2007. 39.99 (978-1-4245-0690-3(5)) Tre Med Inc.

Best of Richardson's Roundup. Contrib. by Bill Richardson. 1 CD. (Running Time: 1 hr.). 2005. audio compact disk 15.95 (978-0-660-19038-9(9)) Pub: Canadian Broadcasting CAN. Dist(s): Georgetown Term

Best of Rio Carnaval. 1 cass. (Running Time: 1 hr.). 1991. 9.98 (978-1-877737-62-6(3), EB 2224); audio compact disk 12.98 CD. (978-1-877737-61-9(5), EB D2224) MFLP CA.
Authentic Brazilian samba enreda. Samba schools competing in Rio de Janero's Carnaval celebration.

Best of Robert & Robin Kochis. Perf. by Robert Kochis & Robin Kochis. 1 cass. (Running Time: 90 mins.). 1999. 10.95 (T8162); audio compact disk 15.95 (K1118) Liguori Pubns.
Songs include: "Sing of Mary," "On Eagles Wings," "Be Not Afraid," "Panis Angelicus" & more.

Best of 'Round the Horne: Featuring Kenneth Horne, with Kenneth Williams, Hugh Paddick, Betty Marsden, & Bill Pertwee. unabr. ed. Created by Barry Took & Marty Feldman. Narrated by Kenneth Horne. (Running Time: 2 hrs. 0 mins. 0 sec.). (ENG.). 2010. audio compact disk 24.95 (978-1-60283-840-6(2)) Pub: AudioGO. Dist(s): Perseus Dist

Best of Russ Taff. Contrib. by Russ Taff et al. Prod. by Bill Gaither. (Running Time: 1 hr. 35 mins.). (Gaither Gospel Ser.). 2007. 19.99 (978-5-557-94927-9(5)) Gaither Music Co.

Best of S. J. Perelman. unabr. collector's ed. S. J. Perelman. Read by Jonathan Reese. 7 cass. (Running Time: 10 hrs. 30 min.). 1993. 56.00 (978-0-7366-2558-6(5), 3309) Books on Tape.
Collection of 50 pieces from comic genius, best known for scripts of Marx Brothers films.

Best of Saratoga Springs. unabr. ed. Thomas M. Lopez. 2 cass. (Running Time: 2 hrs., 5 min.). 1999. 15.95 Set. (978-1-881137-61-0(9), BSAR) ZBS Found.
Shortened version of the original "Saratoga Springs." A parody of small town life based in the real town in upstate New York.

Best of Saratoga Springs. unabr. ed. Thomas M. Lopez. 2 CDs. (Running Time: 2 hrs., 5 min.). (YA). 1999. audio compact disk 22.50 CD Set. (978-1-881137-60-3(0), BSARCD) ZBS Found.

Best of Schoolhouse Rock! (J). 2002. 10.98 (978-1-56826-928-3(5), 75314) Rhino Enter.

Best of Schoolhouse Rock! 1 cass. 1998. 10.98 (978-1-56826-926-9(9), 75315) Rhino Enter.
All the best-loved songs from the Schoolhouse Rock series. Also includes four previously unreleased cuts form Money Rock.

Best of Schoolhouse Rock! 1 CD. (J). 1998. audio compact disk 17.98 (978-1-56826-927-6(7), 75315) Rhino Enter.
All the best loved songs from the Schoolhouse Rock series. Also includes four previously unreleased cuts from Money Rock.

Best of Second City. Contrib. by Edward Asner et al. 4 CDs. (Running Time: 17040 sec.). (L. A. Theatre Works Audio Theatre Collections). 2001. audio compact disk 35.95 (978-1-58081-299-3(6), CDTPT206) Pub: L A Theatre. Dist(s): NetLibrary CO

Best of Second City. unabr. ed. Edward Asner. Perf. by Edward Asner. Perf. by Arye Gross et al. 3 cass. (Running Time: 4 hrs. 44 min.). 1993. 31.95 (978-1-58081-020-3(9), CTA62) L A Theatre.
A ride through decades of hilarity, packed with classic sketches that helped make this America's foremost comedy troupe.

Best of Second City L. A. unabr. ed. Read by L. A. Theatre Works Cast. 4 cass. (Running Time: 6 hr.). Dramatization. 1996. 24.95 Set, retail box. (978-0-8072-3559-1(8), CB139CXR, Listening Lib) Random Audio Pubg.
Chicago's renowned topical & improv comedy ensemble serves up a hilarious retrospective of vintage scenes & song in the tradition of wit & satire that has established the "Second City" as the finest comedy theatre.

Best of Second Helping of Chicken Soup for the Soul. abr. ed. Jack L. Canfield & Mark Victor Hansen. Read by Jack L. Canfield. 2 cass. (Running Time: 90 min.). 1995. 14.95 set. (978-1-55874-376-2(6)); audio compact disk 11.95 CD. (978-1-55874-434-9(7)) Health Comm.
Selections of the best from the NY Times bestseller, "A Second Helping of Chicken Soup for the Soul".

Best of Sherlock Holmes II. unabr. ed. Arthur Conan Doyle. 4 cass. (Running Time: 4 hrs.). 1998. 16.95 (978-1-55569-292-6(3), 5770-11) Great Am Audio.
Features "The Adventure of the Beryl Coronet" "Silver Blaze" "The Five Orange Pips" "The Boscomb Valley Mystery".

Best of Singing News: Choral Collection: Alto. Contrib. by Ed Kee. Prod. by Ed Kee & Richard Kingsmore. Prod. by Richard Kingsmore. (ENG.). 2008. audio compact disk 5.00 (978-5-557-42401-1(6), Brentwood-Benson Music) Brentwood Music.

Best of Singing News: Choral Collection: Bass. Contrib. by Ed Kee. Prod. by Ed Kee & Richard Kingsmore. Prod. by Richard Kingsmore. (ENG.).

2008. audio compact disk 5.00 (978-5-557-42398-4(2), Brentwood-Benson Music) Brentwood Music.

Best of Singing News: Choral Collection: Soprano. Contrib. by Ed Kee. Prod. by Ed Kee & Richard Kingsmore. Prod. by Richard Kingsmore. (ENG.). 2008. audio compact disk 5.00 (978-5-557-42402-8(4), Brentwood-Benson Music) Brentwood Music.

Best of Singing News Choral Collection. Contrib. by Richard Kingsmore. (ENG.). 2008. audio compact disk 10.00 (978-5-557-42403-5(2), Brentwood-Benson Music) Brentwood Music.

Best of Singing News: Choral Collection: Southern Gospel. Contrib. by Johnathan Crumpton & Richard Kingsmore. Prod. by Richard Kingsmore. (ENG.). 2008. audio compact disk 90.00 (978-5-557-42404-2(0), Brentwood-Benson Music) Brentwood Music.

Best of Singing News Choral Collection: Southern Gospel. Contrib. by Richard Kingsmore. (ENG.). 2008. audio compact disk 16.99 (978-5-557-42532-2(2), Brentwood-Benson Music) Brentwood Music.

Best of Singing News: Choral Collection: Tenor. Contrib. by Ed Kee. Prod. by Ed Kee & Richard Kingsmore. Prod. by Richard Kingsmore. (ENG.). 2008. audio compact disk 5.00 (978-5-557-42399-1(0), Brentwood-Benson Music) Brentwood Music.

Best of Sunny Side Up. Lucile Johnson. 4 cass. 16.98 Set. (978-1-55503-635-5(X), 0900109) Covenant Comms.
Favorite talks used in producing her book.

Best of Suspense. 2002. 29.95 (978-0-7413-0250-2(0)) Radio Spirits.

Best of Talks, Set. 4 cass. 16.98 (978-1-55503-169-5(2), 090026) Covenant Comms.
Sixteen classic talks by 14 favorite speakers discussing a variety of subjects.

Best of Texas Folklore: Spoken Word Performances by Elmer Kelton & Other Texas Folklore Society Members, Vol. 2. unabr. ed. Perf. by Texas Folklore Society members. Hosted by Elmer Kelton. 2 cass. (Running Time: 3 hrs.). 2001. 18.95 (978-1-880717-45-5(X)) Writers AudioShop.
More wise and witty talks on Texas folk and lore from members of the legendary Texas Folklore Society. Topics include House Husbands, E-lore, Potted Pork Parts, Pepe's Panaderia (bread), Hell and Heroes and the Horny Toad.

Best of Texas Folklore: Spoken Word Performances by Elmer Kelton & Other Texas Folklore Society Members, Vols. 1 & 2. Perf. by Texas Folklore Society members. Hosted by Elmer Kelton. 6 CDs. 2003. audio compact disk 69.95 (978-1-880717-49-3(2), 829-039) Writers AudioShop.

Best of Texas Folklore, 1999. Read by Texas Folklore Society members. Hosted by Michael Martin Murphey. 2 cass. (Running Time: 3 hrs.). 1999. 17.95 (978-1-880717-40-0(9), 31) Writers AudioShop.
Recorded for the first time ever, 10 of the wise & witty papers presented at the 90th annual meeting of the legendary Texas Folklore Society. Hear members "talk fancy" about Texas peddlers, funeral homes, possums, babies, grandmothers, cow chips & more.

Best of the Best Songs for Youth. 1 CD. (Running Time: 1 hr.). (YA). 1996. audio compact disk 49.99 (DC-9214S) Lillenas.

Best of the Bickersons. Perf. by Don Ameche et al. 2 cass., 2 CDs. (Running Time: 2 hrs.). (Best of Old Time Radio Ser.). audio compact disk 15.95 (978-1-57816-155-3(X), DTB903) Audio File.
The honeymoon is over. Don Ameche & Frances Langford star as John & Blanche Bickerson with Danny Thomas as Blanche's brother Amos in a dozen classic comedy sketches originally broadcast on NBC's "Old Gold Show" & "Drene Time".

Best of the Bickersons, Set. Perf. by Don Ameche et al. 2 cass. (Running Time: 2 hrs.). (Best of Old Time Radio Ser.). 12.95 in bookstyle album. (978-1-57816-019-8(7), BTB201) Audio File.

Best of the Big Band Remotes. unabr. ed. 2 CDs. (Running Time: 2 hrs.). bk. 15.95 (978-1-57816-156-0(8), DBR904) Audio File.
A collection of remote broadcasts of Big Bands on the air coast-coast during the Golden Years of radio now on C.D.

Best of the Big Band Remotes, Set. Contrib. by Karl Pearson. 2 cass. (Running Time: 2 hrs.). (Best of Old Time Radio Ser.). 12.95 in bookstyle album. (978-1-57816-014-3(6), BBR201) Audio File.
A collection of remote broadcasts featuring big bands on the air coast-to-coast during the golden years of radio. Includes: Harry James, Tommy Dorsey, Jan Garber, Andy Kirk, Artie Shaw, Ted Weems, Benny Goodman, Glenn Miller, Larry Clinton, Dick Jurgens, Roy Eldridge, Will Osborne, Chick Webb, Eddy Howard, Jan Savitt, Duke Ellington, Gus Arnheim, Bunny Berigan, Bob Chester, Ray McKinley, Bob Crosby, Stan Kenton, Desi Arnaz, Glen Gray, Jack Teagarden, Orrin Tucker, Bobby Sherwood.

Best of the Big Bands. 1 cass. 1991. 16.95 (978-1-55569-452-4(7)) Great Am Audio.

Best of the Big Bands. unabr. ed. 2 cass. (Running Time: 2 hrs.). (Double Value Pack Ser.). 1990. 9.95 (978-1-55569-375-6(X), 7108) Great Am Audio.
Thirty superstars of the Big Band Era. Goodman, Herman, Dorsey, Basie, Ella & many many more!.

***Best of the Big Bands, Volume 1.** RadioArchives.com. (Running Time: 600). (ENG.). 2003. audio compact disk 29.98 (978-1-61081-012-8(0)) Radio Arch.

***Best of the Big Bands, Volume 2.** RadioArchives.com. (Running Time: 600). (ENG.). 2005. audio compact disk 29.98 (978-1-61081-042-5(2)) Radio Arch.

Best of the Bob Hope Show. unabr. ed. Perf. by Bob Hope et al. Frwd. by Bob Hope. 20 vols. (Running Time: 20 hrs.). (20 Hour Collections). 2002. bk. 59.98 (978-1-57019-506-8(4), OTR40044) Pub: Radio Spirits. Dist(s): AudioGO
One of America's best-loved entertainers, Bob Hope starred on the stage, in movies and on TV-but he achieved his earliest and greatest fame on radio. Hope's Pepsodent Show was radio's top-rated series during the War Years, and his remote broadcasts from military bases helped boost American morale during some of our darkest days. Radio Spirits presents 40 of Bob Hope's all-time greatest broadcasts, available now for the first time since they aired more than 50 years ago. This landmark collection also includes a 32-page behind-the-scenes booklet with a special foreword by Bob Hope himself. Celebrate the glorious career of the beloved comedian who has entertained America for more than 70 years, leaving generations of loyal fans proclaiming "Thanks for the memories.".

Best of the Celebrate Series. 2 vols. pap. bk. 39.95 (978-0-8074-0970-1(7), 93286) URJ Pr.

Best of the Clancy Brothers. Perf. by Clancy Brothers. 1 cass., 1 CD. 3.18 (VAN 507); audio compact disk 7.98 CD Jewel box. (VAN 507) NewSound.

Best of the Comic Strip. abr. ed. 2 cass. 1998. 15.00 Set. (978-1-86117-172-6(2)) Ulvrscrft Audio.

Best of the Dameans, Vol. 1. Gary Daigle et al. 1 cass., 1 CD. 1998. 10.95 (CS-408); audio compact disk 15.95 (CD-408) GIA Pubns.

Best of the Dameans, Vol. 2. Gary Daigle et al. 1 cass., 1 CD. 1998. 10.95 (CS-409); audio compact disk 15.95 (CD-409) GIA Pubns.

Best of the Girl Groups (Medley) - ShowTrax. Arranged by Ed Lojeski. 1 CD. (Running Time: 6 mins.). 2000. audio compact disk 35.00 (08201110) H Leonard.
Showcase your SSA choirs with these classic fun favorites in a medley. Easy to learn, highly entertaining! Includes: "Dancing in the Street" (Martha & the Vandellas, 1964), "My Guy" (Mary Wells, 1964), The Shoop Shoop Song - "It's in His Kiss" (Betty Everett, 1964).

Best of the IQ Builder. abr. ed. BabyGenius. 2000. audio compact disk 9.99 (978-1-928610-24-3(2)) Genius Prod Inc.

Best of the Kingdom of God. Featuring Bill Winston. 2. 2004. 30.00 (978-1-59544-080-8(1)); audio compact disk 48.00 (978-1-59544-081-5(X)) B Winston Min.

Best of the Late Frank Hatch. Perf. by Frank Hatch. 1 cass. 1990. 8.95 (18) Bert and I Inc.
Songs combining humor, nostalgia & love for Maine & old Boston. "Why Doesn't a Clam Get Claustrophobia", "Vote Early & Often for Curley"... All royalties go to THE MAINE COAST HERITAGE TRUST.

Best of the Lost Dogs. Perf. by Lost Dogs. 1 cass. 1999. (978-5-554-33563-1(2)); audio compact disk (978-5-554-32476-5(2)) Brentwood Music.
In the early 90's four of Christian music's most pioneering artists converged & formed this group & recorded three albums. Songs about life, love & the pursuit of God with relentless creative fervor.

Best of the Mormon Youth Chorus & Symphony. Mormon Youth Chorus and Symphony. 1 cass. 9.95 (10001301); audio compact disk 14.95 (2800934) Covenant Comms.

Best of the Muppets. Prod. by Jim Henson Company Staff. 1 CD. (Running Time: 1 hr.). 2002. audio compact disk 17.98 Rhino Enter.
This release will feature favorite musical offerings from both the Muppet TV show and movies. This release will be part of a major brand push for the Muppets across several product categories.

Best of the National Lampoon Radio Hour. 3 CDs. (Running Time: 4 hrs. 30 mins). 2001. bk. 49.98 (R2 72263) Rhino Enter.

Best of the Nylons. Perf. by Nylons, The. 1 cass.; 9.98; audio compact disk 16.98 CD. Lifedance.
Includes "The Lion Sleeps Tonight," "Bop till You Drop," "Chain Gang," "Drift Away," "Happy Together," "Kiss Him Goodbye," "Please," "Poison Ivy," "Prince of Darkness," "Up on the Roof," "Up the Ladder to the Roof," & more. Demo CD or cassette available.

Best of the Omnivore. Jane Farrow. Prod. by Jane Farrow. (Running Time: 1 hr.). 2005. audio compact disk 15.95 (978-0-660-19386-1(8)) Canadian Broadcasting CAN.

Best of the Pleiades. Perf. by Gerald J. Markoe. 1 cass., 1 CD. 7.98 (ASTRO 27); audio compact disk 12.78 CD Jewel box. (ASTRO 27) NewSound.

Best of the Third Serving of Chicken Soup for the Soul. abr. ed. Jack L. Canfield & Mark Victor Hansen. 1 cass. (Running Time: 90 min.). 1996. audio compact disk 11.95 CD. (978-1-55874-435-6(5)) Health Comm.
Selections of the best from the NY Times bestseller, "A 3rd Serving of Chicken Soup for the Soul".

Best of the Wall Street Journal: On Management. unabr. ed. David Asman & Adam Meyerson. Narrated by Nelson Runger & Adrian Cronauer. 5 cass. (Running Time: 7 hrs. 15 mins.). 1988. 44.00 (978-1-55690-049-5(X), 88470E7) Recorded Bks.
The editors of the "Journal's" management column, along with help from top international managers, shed light on subjects as diverse as being fired & office dating.

Best of the Wall Street Journal, 1974. unabr. collector's ed. Wall Street Journal Staff. Read by Daniel Grace. 9 cass. (Running Time: 13 hrs. 30 min.). 1977. 72.00 (978-0-7366-0046-0(9), 1058) Books on Tape.
Fifty-four stories of modern life from the pages of the "Wall Street Journal".

Best of the Wall Street Journal, 1981. unabr. collector's ed. Wall Street Journal Staff. Read by Wolfram Kandinsky. 10 cass. (Running Time: 15 hrs.). 1982. 80.00 (978-0-7366-0765-0(X), 1722) Books on Tape.
A series of short stories that entertain & inform.

Best of the West: Classic Stories from the American Frontier. unabr. ed. Scripts. Cash Gayle Morri McCarthy. 4 cass. (Running Time: 6 hrs.). 2004. 25.00 (978-1-59007-320-9(7)); 25.00 (978-1-59007-365-0(7)); 25.00 (978-1-59007-319-3(3)) Pub: New Millenn Enter. Dist(s): PerseuPGW

Best of the Winner's Minute: Leadership Principles to Help You Win in Every Area of Life. 3. (Running Time: 170 mins.). 2003. audio compact disk 15.00 (978-1-57399-171-1(6)) Mac Hammond.
The Bible is not an archaic, outdated Book to be relegated to an obscure place in society. Rather, it is both relevant and practical for today's modern workplace. This three-CD volume is full of nuggets on leadership principles that work!.

Best of the Witherspoon School of Law & Public Policy. Speeches. Featuring Douglas W. Phillips et al. 16 cass. (Running Time: 21 hrs.). 2002. 95.00 (978-1-929241-51-4(8)) Vsn Forum.

Best of Thomas Perry MP3 Boxed Set. unabr. ed. Thomas Perry. Narrated by Michael Kramer. (Running Time: 31 hrs. 0 mins. 0 sec.). (ENG.). 2009. audio compact disk 29.95 (978-1-4001-2028-4(4)) Pub: Tantor Media. Dist(s): IngramPubServ

Best of Tom Hopkins. Tom Hopkins. Read by Tom Hopkins. 6 cass. (Running Time: 5 hrs. 30 min.). 1996. 95.00 Set. (978-0-938636-35-9(9)) T Hopkins Intl.

Best of Ukrainian Cuisine: A Hippocrene Original Cookbook. Bohdan Zahny. (ENG.). 1996. audio compact disk 12.95 (978-0-7818-0494-3(9)) Hippocrene Bks.

Best of Vanishing Point, Set unabr. ed. 6 cass. (Suspenseful Radio Dramas Ser.). 1999. 44.98 (LL 0034) AudioGO.

Best of Vanishing Point Set: 12 Radio Dramas from the Canadian Broadcasting Corporation. unabr. ed. Listening Library Staff. 6 cass. (Running Time: 5 hrs. 45 min.). (Suspenseful Radio Dramas Ser.). 1990. 44.98 (978-0-8072-3091-6(X), CXL 539CX, Listening Lib) Random Audio Pubg.
Expect the unexpected! These 12 uncanny dramas from the acclaimed radio series aired on CBC & on Public Radio are windows into the world of mystery, fantasy, & illusion. Contains: Death & the Compass, by Jorge Luis Borges; The Playground, by Ray Bradbury; Split Second, by Daphne DuMaurier; The Nine Billion Names of God, by Arthur C. Clarke; A Small Good Thing, by Raymond Carver, & others.

***Best of Vintage Archers.** Compiled by B. B. C. BBC. (Running Time: 2 hrs. 0 mins. 0 sec.). (ENG.). 2011. audio compact disk 24.95 (978-1-4084-6659-9(7)) Pub: AudioGO. Dist(s): Perseus Dist

Best of Wah! The First Major Release from a Rising Star in Kirtan. Wah. (Running Time: 1 hr. 10 mins.). 2006. audio compact disk 17.98 (978-1-59179-525-4(7), M1079D) Sounds True.

Best of Wait Wait... Don't Tell Me! Contrib. by Peter Sagal & Carl Kasell. (ENG., 2008. audio compact disk 22.95 (978-1-59887-729-8(1), 1598877291) Pub: HighBridge. Dist(s): Workman Pub

Best of Weekend Edition. Hosted by Scott Simon. 1 cass. (Running Time: 80 min.). 11.95 (J006AB090, HarperThor) HarpC GBR.

Best of Weekend Edition, Vol. 2. Hosted by Scott Simon. 1 cass. (Running Time: 90 min.). 11.95 (J006BB090, HarperThor) HarpC GBR.

Best of Weekend Edition with Susan Stamberg. Hosted by Susan Stamberg. 1 cass. (Running Time: 90 min.). 11.95 (WE-88-01-17, HarperThor) HarpC GBR.

Best of West. Radio Spirits Publishing Staff. Read by Alan Ladd. 2006. audio compact disk 9.98 (978-1-57019-818-2(7)) Radio Spirits.

Best of William Wait. William Wait. 1 cass. 9.95 (978-1-57734-351-6(4), 06005896) Covenant Comms.
A collection of wise & witty stories.

Best of Witness. 1 CD. audio compact disk 16.98 (978-1-57908-471-4(0), 5348) Platinm Enter.

Best of Witness, Set. unabr. ed. 1 cass., 1 CD. 10.98 (978-1-57908-472-1(9), 5348) Platinm Enter.

Best of Women's Short Stories. unabr. ed. William J. Locke et al. Read by Harriet Walter. 4 CDs. (Running Time: 4 hrs. 44 mins. 29 sec.). (Best of Women's Short Stories Ser.). (ENG.). 2008. audio compact disk 26.95 (978-1-934997-11-6(0)) Pub: CSAWord. Dist(s): PerseuPGW

Best of Women's Short Stories, Volume 3. Read by Rosalind Ayres et al. (Playaway Adult Fiction Ser.). (ENG.). 2009. 60.00 (978-1-60775-552-4(1)) Find a World.

Best of Women's Stories, Volume 1. Read by Harriet Walter. (Playaway Adult Fiction Ser.). (ENG.). 2009. 60.00 (978-1-60775-550-0(5)) Find a World.

Best of Word Jazz, Vol. 1. Ken Nordine. 1 CD. (Running Time: 1 hr. 30 mins.). 2001. audio compact disk 15.98 (R2 70773) Rhino Enter.

Best of Yolanda Adams. Perf. by Yolanda Adams. 1 cass. (New Gospel Legends Ser.). 1999. (978-0-7601-3146-6(5)); audio compact disk (978-0-7601-3145-9(7)) Provident Music.
Collection of the most notable songs performed by the legendary "diva" who had such a profound impact on gospel music. This collection is comprised of songs that spanned two decades of music pioneering.

Best of 2003. 2003. audio compact disk 18.00 (978-1-57972-568-6(6)) Insight Living.

Best of 2004: The Most Requested Messages from Insight for Living. 2005. audio compact disk 14.00 (978-1-57972-665-2(8)) Insight Living.

Best of 2005: The Most Requested Messages from Insight for Living. 2005. audio compact disk 24.00 (978-1-57972-695-9(X)) Insight Living.

***Best Of 2009.** Charles R. Swindoll. 2009. audio compact disk 12.00 (978-1-57972-871-7(5)) Insight Living.

Best Ones. Perf. by For Him Staff. 1 CD. 1999. 17.98 (978-0-7601-2816-9(2)) Pub: Brentwood Music. Dist(s): Provident Mus Dist

Best Ones. Perf. by For Him Staff. 1 cass. 1999. (978-0-7601-2817-6(0)) Brentwood Music.

***Best Practice Pre-Intermediate.** Bill Mascull. (ENG.). (C). 2004. 60.95 (978-1-4130-0909-5(3)) Pub: Heinle. Dist(s): CENGAGE Learn

Best Practices: Building Your Business with Arthur Andersen's Global Best Practices. abr. ed. Robert Hiebeler et al. Read by Cotter Smith. 2 cass. (Running Time: 3 hrs.). (Star Trek). 1997. 18.00 (978-0-671-57716-2(6), 394664, Sound Ideas) S&S Audio.
What makes the world's top companies so adept at providing stellar customer service? How do they meet the needs of every customer & still turn healthy profits? Most important; how can you adapt their practices to fit your business?.

Best Practices for Building Impregnable Networks. 2004. audio compact disk 189.00 (978-1-58205-154-3(2)) Element K Journals.

Best Practices of Successful Women Managers. Connie B. Glaser. 4 cass. (Running Time: 153 min.). 1998. 21.95 (978-1-55977-665-3(X)) CareerTrack Pubns.

Best Prayer. Swami Amar Jyoti. 1 cass. 1975. 9.95 (M-60) Truth Consciousness.
The best prayer of body & mind. Mind is a livable abode if we keep it clean. Uninterrupted remembrance.

Best Revenge. unabr. ed. Stephen White. Read by Dick Hill. 7 cass. (Running Time: 10 hrs.). (Dr. Alan Gregory Ser.). 2003. 82.25 (978-1-59086-394-7(1), 1590863941); 32.95 (978-1-59086-393-0(3), 1590863933) Brilliance Audio.
Psychologist Alan Gregory is living through a season of discontent. With a new daughter, a wonderful wife, and a prospering career, he has little to complain about and lots of regrets: past cases that won't let him go, patients who don't get better, and a growing unease with keeping secrets. But Gregory has two new patients who will drag him out of his introspection - and dare him to enter a storm of injustice and revenge. FBI special agent Kelda James is a hero, a woman who as a rookie agent made a choice, drew her gun, and saved a life, taking another. Now Kelda is hiding from the world a secret pain that is gradually crippling her body - and she has turned to Alan Gregory to help her free from the prison of her pain. Then Kelda refers a patient to Gregory, who is terrifyingly dangerous to them both. Tom Clone served thirteen years on Colorado's death row for a crime he claimed he didn't commit - until an FBI agent dug up evidence that set him free. The agent's name: Kelda Jones. With both Kelda and Clone telling him their innermost secrets, Alan Gregory becomes the one person who can piece together an extraordinary puzzle - of two unsolved violent deaths of vulnerable women, of a man who may be innocent or may be very lucky, and of the strange, fatal attraction between two people trapped in a horrific plot to get revenge - at any price.

Best Revenge. unabr. ed. Stephen White. Read by Dick Hill. (Running Time: 10 hrs.). (Dr. Alan Gregory Ser.). 2004. 39.25 (978-1-59335-406-0(1), 1593354061, Brlnc Audio MP3 Lib) Brilliance Audio.

Best Revenge. unabr. ed. Stephen White. Read by Dick Hill. (Running Time: 10 hrs.). (Dr. Alan Gregory Ser.). 2004. 39.25 (978-1-59710-040-3(4), 1597100404, BADLE); 24.95 (978-1-59710-041-0(2), 1597100412, BAD) Brilliance Audio.

Best Revenge. unabr. ed. Stephen White. Read by Dick Hill. (Running Time: 11 hrs.). (Dr. Alan Gregory Ser.). 2010. audio compact disk 89.97 (978-1-4418-3581-9(4), 9781441835819, BriAudCD Unabrid); audio compact disk 29.99 (978-1-4418-3580-2(6), 9781441835802, Bril Audio CD Unabri) Brilliance Audio.

Best Revenge. unabr. ed. Stephen White. Read by Dick Hill. (Running Time: 10 hrs.). (Dr. Alan Gregory Ser.). 2004. 24.95 (978-1-59335-065-9(1), 1593350651) Soulmate Audio Bks.

Best Revenge: A Novel of Broadway. unabr. ed. Sol Stein. Read by Christopher Lane. (Running Time: 25200 sec.). 2006. 54.95 (978-0-7861-4900-1(0)) Blckstn Audio.

Best Revenge: A Novel of Broadway. unabr. ed. Sol Stein. Read by Geoffrey Howard. (Running Time: 25200 sec.). 2006. audio compact disk 63.00 (978-0-7861-5980-2(4)) Blckstn Audio.

Best Revenge: A Novel of Broadway. unabr. ed. Sol Stein. Read by Christopher Lane. (Running Time: 25200 sec.). 2006. audio compact disk 29.95 (978-0-7861-7102-6(2)) Blckstn Audio.

Best School Year Ever. unabr. ed. Barbara Robinson. Read by Elaine Stritch. (J). 2008. 34.99 (978-1-60514-713-0(3)) Find a World.

***Best School Year Ever.** unabr. ed. Barbara Robinson. Read by Elaine Stritch. (ENG.). 2005. (978-0-06-087358-5(2)); (978-0-06-087357-8(4)) HarperCollins Pubs.

Best School Year Ever. unabr. ed. Barbara Robinson. Narrated by C. J. Critt. 3 pieces. (Running Time: 3 hrs.). (gr. 3 up). 1997. 27.00 (978-0-7887-0826-8(0), 95004E7) Recorded Bks.
There's one horrible Herdman child in each grade at Woodrow Wilson Elementary School. They smoke, steal, blow things up & terrorize the other kids. So when Beth's assignment in fourth grade is to write compliments for each student in the class, she knows it will be hard to find something good to say about Imogene Herdman. When Beth finally does see Imogene do something worthy of a compliment, she is surprised by the kindness & gentleness of this dirty, ragged girl.

Best School Year Ever. unabr. ed. Barbara Robinson. Narrated by C. J. Critt. 3 CDs. (Running Time: 3 hrs.). (gr. 5 up). 2000. audio compact disk 27.00 (978-0-7887-3455-7(5), C1061E5) Recorded Bks.

Best Science Fiction Stories of the Year, Set. 2nd unabr. ed. Short Stories. Prod. by Orson Scott Card & Martin Greenberg. 4 cass. (Running Time: 6 hr.). 21.95 library case. (978-1-55656-147-4(4)) Dercum Audio.
Includes Chump Change by Ray Aldridge; Science Fiction Reader's & Writers Guide to the Unknown by Larry Titten; Etoundi's Monkey by Judith DuBois; The Tall Grass by Steven Utley; Dori Bangs by Bruce Sterling; People Like Us by Nancy Kress; Zelle's Thursday by Tanith Lee; All the Beer in Mars by Gregory Benford.

Best Science Fiction Value Collection, Vol. 1, set. unabr. ed. Walter Jon Williams & Ian Watson. Ed. by Orson Scott Card & Martin Greenberg. 4 cass. (Running Time: 6 hrs.). (Dercum Value Collections: Vol. 1). 1997. pap. bk. 19.95 (978-1-55656-215-0(2)) Dercum Audio.

Best Science Fiction: 2002. unabr. ed. Ed. by Robert A. Silverberg & Karen Haber. 6 cass. (Running Time: 9 hrs.). 2004. 32.00 (978-1-57453-553-2(6), Fantastic Audio) Audio Lit.

Best Served Cold. unabr. ed. Joe Abercrombie. Narrated by Mark Honan & Michael Page. (Running Time: 27 hrs. 30 mins. 0 sec.). (ENG.). 2010. 44.99 (978-1-4001-6327-4(7)); audio compact disk 119.99 (978-1-4001-4327-6(6)); audio compact disk 59.99 (978-1-4001-1327-9(X)) Pub: Tantor Media. Dist(s): IngramPubServ

***Best Served Cold.** unabr. ed. Joe Abercrombie. Narrated by Michael Page. (Running Time: 27 hrs. 30 mins.). 2009. 59.99 (978-1-4001-9327-1(3)); 28.99 (978-1-4001-8327-2(8)) Tantor Media.

Best Service Is No Service: How to Liberate Your Customers from Customer Service, Keep Them Happy, & Control Costs. abr. ed. Bill Price & David Jaffe. Read by Jim Bond. 1 MP3-CD. (Running Time: 10 hrs.). 2008. 39.25 (978-1-4233-6011-7(7), 9781423360117, Brinc Audio MP3 Lib); 24.95 (978-1-4233-6010-0(9), 9781423360100, Brilliance MP3); audio compact disk 97.25 (978-1-4233-6009-4(5), 9781423360094, BriAudCD Unabrid) Brilliance Audio.

Best Service Is No Service: How to Liberate Your Customers from Customer Service, Keep Them Happy, & Control Costs. abr. ed. Bill Price & David Jaffe. Read by Jim Bond. 9 CDs. (Running Time: 36000 sec.). 2008. audio compact disk 36.95 (978-1-4233-6008-7(7), 9781423360087, Bril Audio CD Unabri) Brilliance Audio.

Best Service Is No Service: How to Liberate Your Customers from Customer Service, Keep Them Happy, & Control Costs. unabr. ed. Bill Price & David Jaffe. Read by Jim Bond. (Running Time: 10 hrs.). 2008. 39.25 (978-1-4233-6013-1(3), 9781423360131, BADLE); 24.95 (978-1-4233-6012-4(5), 9781423360124, BAD) Brilliance Audio.

Best Sex Ever: How to Have Great Sex. Doug Fields. (Super-Ser.). 2007. audio compact disk 40.00 (978-5-557-78148-0(X)) Group Pub.

***Best Short Stories of Mark Twain.** unabr. ed. Mark Twain. Read by Robin Field. (Running Time: 10 hrs. 0 mins.). 2010. 29.95 (978-1-4417-2325-3(0)); 59.95 (978-1-4417-2321-5(8)); audio compact disk 90.00 (978-1-4417-2322-2(6)) Blckstn Audio.

Best Small Town. Marshall Younger & Dave Arnold. Created by Focus on the Family Staff. (Running Time: 4 hrs. 0 mins.). (Adventures in Odyssey Audio Ser.). (ENG.). (J). 2008. audio compact disk 24.99 (978-1-58997-487-6(5), Tyndale Ent) Tyndale Hse.

Best Soap Operas, Vol. 1, set. 2 cass. (Running Time: 2 hrs.). 10.95 in vinyl album. (978-1-57816-074-7(X), SO2801) Audio File.
Includes: "Big Sister" (9/21/39); "Aunt Jenny's True Life Stories" (9/21/39); "Lorenzo Jones" (9/1/48); "Just Plain Bill" (8/10/45); "Stella Dallas" (2/22/49); "David Harum" (1/19/45); "Road of Life" (6/7/44); "Romance of Helen Trent" (9/21/39).

Best Soap Operas, Vol. 2, set. 2 cass. (Running Time: 2 hrs.). 10.95 in vinyl album. (978-1-57816-075-4(8), SO2802) Audio File.
Includes: "Front Page Farrell" (8/10/45); "Guiding Light" (7/15/40); "Life Can Be Beautiful" (9/21/39); "Ma Perkins" (6/7/44); "Right to Happiness" (8/10/45); "Wendy Warren & the News" (1950); "Joyce Jordna, M. D." (1940s); "When a Girl Marries" (7/16/48).

Best Soap Operas, Vol. 3, set. 2 cass. (Running Time: 2 hrs.). 10.95 in vinyl album. (978-1-57816-076-1(6), SO2803) Audio File.
Includes: "Portia Faces Life" (11/2/48); "Our Gal Sunday" (9/21/39); "The Goldbergs" (9/21/39); "Woman in White" (6/7/44); "Backstage Wife" (8/10/45); "Young Widder Brown" (1955); "Strange Romance of Evelyn Winters" (2/28/45); "Pepper Young's Family" (8/10/45).

Best Stories of Edgar Allan Poe. Edgar Allan Poe. (Running Time: 8 hrs.). 2006. 24.95 (978-1-59912-145-1(X)) Iofy Corp.

Best Stories of Edgar Allan Poe. unabr. ed. Edgar Allan Poe. Read by John Chatty et al. 6 cass. (Running Time: 9 hrs.). 1989. 36.00 incl. album. (C-56) Jimcin Record.
Eighteen of Poe's best spine-tingling tales, consists of: "The Facts in the Case of M. Valdimar," "William Wilson," "Hop-Frog," "Shadow: A Parable," "Ms: Found in a Bottle," "The Black Cat," "Dr. Tarr & Professor Feather," "Ligeia," "The Murders in the Rue Morgue," "The Purloined Letter," "The Cask of Amontillado," "The Conversation of Eiros & Charmion," "The Fall of the House of Usher," "The Tell-Tale Heart," "The Masque of the Red Death," "The Pit & the Pendulum," etc.

***Best Story.** Eileen Spinelli. 1 CD. (Running Time: 9 mins.). (J). (gr. 1-3). 2009. bk. 29.95 (978-0-8045-4205-0(8)); bk. 27.95 (978-0-8045-6980-4(0)) Spoken Arts.

Best Strategies to Teach Young Writers: Using Wordwalls, Interactive Writing & Guided Writing in a Six Trait Model. abr. ed. Contrib. by Katny Rogers. 6 cass. (Running Time: 6 hrs. 7 mins.). (gr. 1-2). 2004. 89.00 (978-1-886397-60-6(0)) Bureau of Educ.
Live audio program including 6 cassettes and a comprehensive resource handbook.

Best Tape a Parent Could Listen To. unabr. ed. Christina Clement. Read by Thomas Amshay. 1 cass. (Running Time: 1 hr.). 1986. 5.00 (978-0-939401-08-6(8)) RFTS Prod.
How one becomes what one grows up around: How it affects one & how it's passed on to the next generation.

Best Test Preparation for the U. S. Postal Exams: Entrance Test Battery 470 & Rural Carrier Test 460. M. Fogiel. Contrib. by Research and Education Association Staff. 2 CDs. 2004. bk. (978-0-87891-112-7(X)); bk. (978-0-87891-115-8(4)) Res Educ.

Best Toddler Songbook. Audio & Kidzup Productions Staff. 1 cass., 1 CD. (Running Time: 1 hr.). (Toddler Ser.). (J). 2003. pap. bk. 12.99 (978-1-894281-76-8(4)) Pub: Kidzup Prodns. Dist(s): Penton Overseas
The collection of our best Toddler songs compiled for children's sing-alongs & playtime activities.

Best Toddler Tunes. 1 CD. (Running Time: 90 mins.). (Toddler Ser.). (J). 2003. audio compact disk 9.99 (978-1-894281-06-5(3)) Kidzup Prodns.
A terrific variety of toddler favorites that will capture the hearts of your children.

Best Toddler Tunes. Perf. by Wendy Wiseman & Sari Dajani. 1 CD. (Running Time: 48 mins.). (J). 1999. audio compact disk 15.00 (K39926) Pub: Kidzup CAN. Dist(s): Penton Overseas
This mix of traditional & original songs is performed with upbeat cheerfulness & is heavy on synthesized sounds. Includes: "Wheels on the Bus," "Eensy Weensy Spider," "Oh Susanna," "Jungle Fever" & "Mr. Clean" & more.

Best Toddler Tunes. Perf. by Wendy Wiseman & Sari Dajani. 1 cass. (Running Time: 48 mins.). (J). (ps). 1999. 10.00 (K39926) Pub: Kidzup CAN. Dist(s): Penton Overseas

Best Toddler Tunes: A Collection of the Best Toddler Hits. Kidzup Productions Staff. 1 cass. (Running Time: 90 mins.). (Toddler Ser.). (J). 2003. 7.99 (978-1-894281-05-8(5)) Kidzup Prodns.
A terrific variety of toddler favorites that will capture the hearts of your children.

Best Toddler Tunes Blister Pk. Kidzup Productions Staff. 1 cass. (Running Time: 90 mins.). (Kidzup Toddler Ser.). (J). 2000. 8.99 (978-1-894281-61-4(6)); audio compact disk 12.99 (978-1-894281-60-7(8)) Pub: Kidzup CAN. Dist(s): Penton Overseas

Best TOEFL Test Book. Nancy Stanley. (C). 1984. bk. 21.00 (978-0-201-16470-1(1)) AddisonWesley.

Best Town in the World. unabr. ed. Byrd Baylor. Read by Byrd Baylor. 1 cass. (Running Time: 11 min.). (Byrd Baylor: Storyteller Ser.). (J). (gr. k-6). 1990. 5.95 (978-0-929937-19-9(8)) SW Series.
This tape is about the very special place where her father just happened to be born.

Best Transportation System in the World: Railroads, Trucks, Airlines, & American Public Policy in the 20th Century. Rose et al. (Running Time: 19080 sec.). (Historical persp bus Enterpris Ser.). 2006. audio compact disk 9.95 (978-0-8142-9113-9(9)) Pub: Ohio St U Pr. Dist(s): Chicago Distribution Ctr

Best Valentine in the World. unabr. ed. Marjorie Weinman Sharmat. 1 cass. (Running Time: 11 min.). (J). (gr. k-4). 1992. bk. 25.90 (978-0-8045-6664-3(X), 6664) Spoken Arts.
Ferdinand Fox wants to make his sweetheart, Florette, a special valentine and starts to work on it three months ahead of time. When Valentine's Day comes, things don't turn out the way he expects.

Best Worship Songs of the 70s. 2003. audio compact disk Provident Mus Dist.

Best Worship Songs of the 80s. 2003. audio compact disk Provident Mus Dist.

Best Worship Songs of the 90s. 2003. audio compact disk Provident Mus Dist.

Best Years of Our Lives. Perf. by Fredric March & Myrna Loy. Based on a novel by MacKinlay Kantor. 1 cass. (Running Time: 1 hr.). Dramatization. 7.95 (DD8845) Natl Recrd Co.

Best 101 Children's Songs, Set. (J). audio compact disk 17.95 (978-1-878427-71-7(7)) Pub: Cimino Pub Grp. Dist(s): CPG Pub Inc

Bestiary: An Anthology of Poems about Animals. unabr. ed. Poems. Read by Stephen Mitchell. Ed. by Stephen Mitchell. 1 cass. (Running Time: 1 hr. 30 min.). 1997. 11.95 (978-1-57453-201-2(4)) Audio Lit.
Collection of poems about animals from many ages and cultures from ancient Egypt and Japan to great modern poets such as Neruda, Rilke and Wright.

Bestman, the Bride & the Wedding. Narrated by Michael McCoy. 1. (Running Time: 11 hrs. 20 mins.). 2003. audio compact disk 5.00 (978-0-9745431-1-6(X)) scholia.

Bestseller. unabr. ed. Olivia Goldsmith. Read by Frances Cassidy. 16 cass. (Running Time: 24 hrs.). 1997. 83.20 (978-0-7366-3591-2(2), 4244A/B) Books on Tape.
In this irreverent look at how bestsellers are born, inside Davis & Dash, the Manhattan publishing giant, things are heating up for the do-or-die fall season. Whose literary fortune will be made & whose will be unmade?.

Bet. unabr. ed. Anton Chekhov. Read by Walter Zimmerman. 1 cass. (Running Time: 57 min.). Dramatization. Incl. Lament. 1979. (N-30); Slanderer. 1979. (N-30); Work of Art. 1979. (N-30); 1979. 7.95 (N-30) Jimcin Record.
Four gems from the master of the Russian short story.

Bet Me. unabr. ed. Jennifer Crusie, pseud. Read by Deanna Hurst. 10 CDs. (Running Time: 11 hrs.). 2004. audio compact disk 36.95 (978-1-59355-392-0(7), 1593553927, Bril Audio CD Unabri); 32.95 (978-1-59086-030-4(6), 1590860306, BAU); 87.25 (978-1-59086-031-1(4), 1590860314, BAudLibEd); audio compact disk 102.25 (978-1-59355-397-5(8), 1593553978, BriAudCD Unabrid) Brilliance Audio.
Min Dobbs knows that happily-ever-after is a fairy tale, especially with a man who asked her to dinner to win a bet. Cal Morrisey knows commitment is impossible, especially with a woman as cranky as Min Dobbs. When they say good-bye at the end of their evening, they cut their losses and agree never to see each other again. But Fate has other plans, and it's not long before Min and Cal are dealing with a jealous ex-boyfriend, Krispy Kremes, a determined psychologist, chaos theory, a mutant cat, Chicken Marsala, and more risky propositions than either of them ever dreamed of including the biggest gamble of all - real love.

Bet Me. unabr. ed. Jennifer Crusie, pseud. Read by Deanna Hurst. (Running Time: 11 hrs.). 2004. 39.25 (978-1-59335-549-4(1), 1593355491, Brinc Audio MP3 Lib); 24.95 (978-1-59335-275-2(1), 1593352751, Brilliance MP3) Brilliance Audio.

Bet Me. unabr. ed. Jennifer Crusie, pseud. Read by Deanna Hurst. (Running Time: 11 hrs.). 2004. 39.25 (978-1-59710-043-4(9), 1597100439, BADLE); 24.95 (978-1-59710-042-7(0), 1597100420, BAD) Brilliance Audio.

Bet Your Bottom Dollar. Karin Gillespie. (Running Time: 28800 sec.). (Bottom Dollar Girls Ser.: Bk. 1). 2005. 59.95 (978-0-7861-3790-9(8)) Blckstn Audio.

Bet Your Bottom Dollar. Karin Gillespie. Read by Carrington MacDuffie. (Running Time: 28800 sec.). (Bottom Dollar Girls Ser.: Bk. 1). 2005. audio compact disk 72.00 (978-0-7861-7549-9(4)) Blckstn Audio.

Bet Your Bottom Dollar. abr. unabr. ed. Karin Gillespie. Read by Carrington MacDuffie. (Running Time: 28800 sec.). (Bottom Dollar Girls Ser.: Bk. 1). 2005. audio compact disk 29.95 (978-0-7861-7824-7(8)) Blckstn Audio.

Bet Your Bottom Dollar. abr. unabr. ed. Karin Gillespie. Read by Carrington MacDuffie. 7 cass. (Running Time: 28800 sec.). (Bottom Dollar Girls Ser.: Bk. 1). 2006. 19.95 (978-0-7861-4539-3(0)) Blckstn Audio.

Bet Your Bottom Dollar. abr. unabr. ed. Karin Gillespie. Read by Carrington MacDuffie. 8 CDs. (Running Time: 28800 sec.). (Bottom Dollar Girls Ser.: Bk. 1). 2006. audio compact disk 19.95 (978-0-7861-7139-2(1)) Blckstn Audio.

Beta-Globin Type Methemoglobinemia - A Bibliography & Dictionary for Physicians, Patients, & Genome Researchers. Compiled by Icon Group International, Inc. Staff. 2007. ring bd. 28.95 (978-0-497-11257-8(4)) Icon Grp.

Beta-Ketothiolase Deficiency - A Bibliography & Dictionary for Physicians, Patients, & Genome Researchers. Compiled by Icon Group International, Inc. Staff. 2007. ring bd. 28.95 (978-0-497-11338-4(4)) Icon Grp.

Beta Thalassemia - A Bibliography & Dictionary for Physicians, Patients, & Genome Researchers. Compiled by Icon Group International, Inc. Staff. 2007. ring bd. 28.95 (978-0-497-11337-7(6)) Icon Grp.

Betawi & Sundanese Music of the North Coast of Java. Anno. by Philip Yampolsky. 1 cass. (Running Time: 73 min.). (Music of Indonesia Ser.: Vol. 5). 1994. (0-9307-404210-9307-40421-2-0); audio compact disk (0-9307-40421-2-0) Smithsonian Folkways.
Includes village "gamelan" music & a Sundanese repertoire played on brass instruments, gongs & drums.

Bete Humaine see **Gathering of Great Poetry for Children**

Beth Manners' Fun French for Kids. unabr. ed. 1 cass. (Running Time: 28 min.). (J). 1996. 9.98 (978-0-9662876-0-8(6)) Future Boomers.
Stories, games, & songs teach French to 2-6 year old children. Uses music & sound effects throughout.

Beth Manners' Fun Spanish for Kids. Beth Manners. 1 cass. (Running Time: 28 min.). (J). (gr. 2-6). 1998. 9.98 (978-0-9662876-1-5(4)) Future Boomers.
Stories, games & songs teach spanish to 2-6 year old children.

Beth Moore CD Collection: Praying God's Word, Jesus, the One & Only, the Beloved Disciple. abr. ed. Beth Moore. (Running Time: 9 hrs.). 2009. audio compact disk 29.99 (978-1-4233-7734-4(6), 9781423377344, BACD) Brilliance Audio.

Bethany Live: Let the Church Rise. Told to Jonathon Stockstill. Prod. by Jonathon Stockstill. Contrib. by Don Moen & Craig Dunnagan. Prod. by Brent Milligan. 2006. audio compact disk 16.98 (978-5-558-20289-2(0)) Integrity Music.

Bethie's "Really Silly Songs about Animals" Perf. by Bethie Staff. 1 cass. (Running Time: 34 min.). (Bethie's Really Silly Ser.). (J). 1993. bk. 8.95 (978-1-881225-17-1(8)) Discov Music.
Bethie & a goofy cast of critters bring you a tuneful extravaganza of silly songs about favorite animals.

Bethie's Really Silly Stories & Activities. 1 cass. (J). 1994. 6.99 incl. activity bk. with crayons. (978-1-881225-27-0(5)); 6.99 incl. activity bk. with crayons. (978-1-881225-30-0(5)) Discov Music.
Activity book filled with dot-to-dots, mazes, coloring; includes audio cassette featuring the songs "Little Miss Mousie" & "The Four Froggie Brothers".

Bethlehem after Dark. Perf. by Brian Thompson & Laura Sewell. 2002. audio compact disk Provident Mus Dist.

Bethlehem Christmas. Charles R. Swindoll. 2007. audio compact disk 24.00 (978-1-57972-794-9(8)) Insight Living.

Bethlehem Christmas Radio Theater. Charles R. Swindoll. 2008. audio compact disk 12.99 (978-1-57972-830-4(8)) Insight Living.

Bethlehem Road. unabr. ed. Anne Perry. 8 cass. (Running Time: 11.5 hrs.). (Thomas Pitt Ser.). 2005. 69.75 (978-1-4193-4372-8(6)) Recorded Bks.

Bethlehem's Best: A Children's Musical Based on the Story from Luke 2:1-20; Matthew 2:1-2, 8-11. Mark A. Miller & Laurie Zelman. Contrib. by Debi Tyree. 10 CDs. 2004. bk. 60.00 (978-0-687-06310-9(8)); bk. 10.00 (978-0-687-06350-5(7)) Abingdon.

Bethlehem's Best: A Christmas Musical Story Based on Luke 2:1-20, Matthew 2:1-2, 8-11. Mark A. Miller & Laurie Zelman. Prod. by Debi Tyree. 2004. bk. 50.00 (978-0-687-06330-7(2)) Abingdon.

Bethlehem's Child. Greg Skipper. 2000. 11.98 (978-0-633-02962-3(9)); 54.95 (978-0-633-02932-6(7)); 40.00 (978-0-633-00785-0(4)); audio compact disk 16.98 (978-0-633-02957-9(2)); audio compact disk 59.95 (978-0-633-02931-9(9)); audio compact disk 50.00 (978-0-633-00799-7(4)) LifeWay Christian.

Bethlehem's Light: A Christmas Musical for Two-Part Choir. Contrib. by Marty Parks. (ENG.). 1995. audio compact disk 90.00 (978-0-00-509168-5(3)) Lillenas.

Bethoven's Wig. 1 CD. (Running Time: 42 mins.). (J). (ps-6). 2002. audio compact disk 12.98 (978-1-57940-078-1(7)) Rounder Records.
Filled with fact and fancy about the world's most notable composers and their masterpieces, each Sing Along Symphony opens the door to "serious music" in a way that's fun. The orchestral performance of each piece in included.

Betjeman: Poets for Pleasure. John Betjeman. 1999. 18.99 (978-1-85998-369-0(3), HoddrStoughton) Pub: Hodder General GBR. Dist(s): Trafalgar

Betrayal. abr. ed. Aaron Allston. Read by Marc Thompson. (Running Time: 21600 sec.). (Star Wars Ser.). (ENG.). 2006. audio compact disk 29.95 (978-0-7393-2395-3(4), Random AudioBks) Pub: Random Audio Pubg. Dist(s): Random

Betrayal. abr. ed. John Lescroart. Read by David Colacci. (Running Time: 6 hrs.). (Dismas Hardy Ser.: No. 12). 2008. audio compact disk 14.99 (978-1-4233-3975-5(4), 9781423339755, BCD Value Price) Brilliance Audio.

Betrayal. abr. ed. Fern Michaels. (Running Time: 6 hrs.). 2011. audio compact disk 14.99 (978-1-4233-4528-2(2), 9781423345282, BACD) Brilliance Audio.

Betrayal. abr. ed. Fern Michaels. (Running Time: 6 hrs.). 2012. audio compact disk 9.99 (978-1-4233-4529-9(0), 9781423345299, BCD Value Price) Brilliance Audio.

Betrayal. unabr. ed. Clare Francis. Read by Simon Russell Beale. 10 cass. (Running Time: 10 hrs.). 1996. 84.95 Set. (978-0-7451-6668-1(7), CAB 1284) AudioGO.
After the loss of his family business in a bitter takeover, Hugh Wellesley suffers a crisis that threatens his marriage with his wife Ginny. Risking everything, Hugh is on the brink of success when the body of Sylvie Mathieson is found in a Devon river. Years before, Sylvie had been the love of Hugh's life, & as Hugh falls under suspicion, he protests his innocence. Yet he is not telling the truth, & as Ginny & his brother lie for him, damning forensic evidence begins to surface.

Betrayal. unabr. ed. John Lescroart. Read by David Colacci. 1 MP3-CD. (Running Time: 15 hrs.). (Dismas Hardy Ser.: No. 12). 2008. 39.25 (978-1-4233-3971-7(1), 9781423339717, Brlnc Audio MP3 Lib); 39.25 (978-1-4233-3973-1(8), 9781423339731, BADLE); 24.95 (978-1-4233-3972-4(X), 9781423339724, BAD); 107.25 (978-1-4233-3967-0(3), 9781423339670, BrilAudUnabridg); audio compact disk 112.25 (978-1-4233-3969-4(X), 9781423339694, BriAudCD Unabrid); audio compact disk 24.95 (978-1-4233-3970-0(3), 9781423339700, Brilliance MP3); audio compact disk 38.95 (978-1-4233-3968-7(1), 9781423339687, Bril Audio CD Unabri) Brilliance Audio.

Betrayal. unabr. ed. Fern Michaels. (Running Time: 10 hrs.). 2011. 24.99 (978-1-4233-4524-4(X), 9781423345244, Brilliance MP3); 24.99 (978-1-4233-4526-8(6), 9781423345268, BAD); 39.97 (978-1-4233-4525-1(8), 9781423345251, Brlnc Audio MP3 Lib); 39.97 (978-1-4233-4527-5(4), 9781423345275, BADLE); audio compact disk 36.99 (978-1-4233-4522-0(3), 9781423345220, Bril Audio CD Unabri); audio compact disk 97.97 (978-1-4233-4523-7(1), 9781423345237, BriAudCD Unabrid) Brilliance Audio.

***Betrayal.** unabr. ed. Gillian Shields. Read by Emily Durante. (ENG.). 2010. (978-0-06-204334-4(X)) HarperCollins Pubs.

Betrayal: The Crisis in the Catholic Church. Read by Paul Boehmer. 2002. 56.00 (978-0-7366-8931-1(1)) Books on Tape.

Betrayal: The Way of the Snake. Read by Beverley Zabriskie. 1 cass. (Running Time: 90 min.). 1986. 10.95 (978-0-7822-0339-4(6), 181) C G Jung IL.

Betrayal at Cross Creek. unabr. ed. Kathleen Ernst. Narrated by Davina Porter. 3 cass. (Running Time: 4 hrs. 30 mins.). (American Girl History Mysteries Ser.). (J). 2005. 28.75 (978-1-4193-5079-5(X), 98116) Recorded Bks.
Having fled the turmoil of Scotland, Elspeth Monro is learning to love her life in 1775 North Carolina. She likes her new friend and her weaving apprenticeship. But as Loyalists and Patriots strive to recruit her neighbors, a shadowy figure threatens her family. Davina Porter's nuanced narration highlights the polished prose of Kathleen Ernst, nominee for Agatha and Edgar Allen Poe awards.

Betrayal in Death. abr. ed. J. D. Robb, pseud. Read by Susan Ericksen. 4 cass. (Running Time: 6 hrs.). (In Death Ser.). 2001. 53.25 (978-1-58788-196-1(9), 1587881969) Brilliance Audio.
At the luxurious Roarke Palace Hotel, a maid walks into suite 4602 for the nightly turndown - and steps into her worst nightmare. A killer leaves her dead, strangled by a thin silver wire. He's Sly Yost, a virtuoso of music and murder. A hit man for the elite. Lieutenant Eve Dallas knows him well. But in this twisted case, knowing the killer doesn't help solve the crime. Because there's someone else involved. Someone with a more personal motive. And Eve must face a terrifying possibility - that the real target may, in fact, be her husband Roarke.

Betrayal in Death. abr. ed. J. D. Robb, pseud. Read by Susan Ericksen. (Running Time: 21600 sec.). (In Death Ser.). 2007. audio compact disk 14.99 (978-1-4233-1740-1(8), 9781423317401, BCD Value Price) Brilliance Audio.

Betrayal in Death. abr. unabr. ed. J. D. Robb, pseud. Read by Susan Ericksen. (Running Time: 39600 sec.). (In Death Ser.). 2007. audio compact disk 39.25 (978-1-4233-0006-9(8), 9781423300069, Brlnc Audio MP3 Lib); audio compact disk 24.95 (978-1-4233-0005-2(X), 9781423300052, Brilliance MP3) Brilliance Audio.

Betrayal in Death. unabr. ed. J. D. Robb, pseud. Read by Susan Ericksen. (Running Time: 39600 sec.). (In Death Ser.). 2007. 87.25 (978-1-4233-3715-7(8), 9781423337157, BrilAudUnabridg); audio compact disk 36.95 (978-1-4233-1737-1(8), 9781423317371, Bril Audio CD Unabri); audio compact disk 102.25 (978-1-4233-1738-8(6), 9781423317388, BriAudCD Unabrid) Brilliance Audio.

Betrayal in Death. unabr. ed. J. D. Robb, pseud. Read by Susan Ericksen. (Running Time: 11 hrs.). (In Death Ser.). 2007. 39.25 (978-1-4233-0008-3(4), 9781423300083, BADLE); 24.95 (978-1-4233-0007-6(6), 9781423300076, BAD) Brilliance Audio.

***Betrayal of American Prosperity: Free Market Delusions, America's Decline, & How We Must Compete in the Post-Dollar Era.** unabr. ed. Clyde Prestowitz. Narrated by Erik Synnestvedt. (Running Time: 13 hrs. 30 mins. 0 sec.). (ENG.). 2010. 24.99 (978-1-4001-6744-9(2)); audio compact disk 34.99 (978-1-4001-1744-4(5)); audio compact disk 83.99 (978-1-4001-4744-1(1)) Pub: Tantor Media. Dist(s): IngramPubServ

***Betrayal of American Prosperity: Free Market Delusions, America's Decline, & How We Must Compete in the Post-Dollar Era.** unabr. ed. Clyde Prestowitz. (Running Time: 12 hrs. 0 mins.). 2010. 17.99 (978-1-4001-8744-7(3)) Tantor Media.

Betrayal of the Blood Lily. unabr. ed. Lauren Willig. Read by Kate Reading. 12 CDs. (Running Time: 15 hrs.). Bk. 6. (ENG.). (gr. 12 up). 2010. audio compact disk 39.95 (978-0-14-314533-2(9), PenAudBks) Pub: Pnguin Bks Ltd GBR. Dist(s): Penguin Grp USA

***Betrayal of the Blood Lily.** unabr. ed. Lauren Willig. Narrated by Kate Reading. 12 CDs. (Running Time: 15 hrs.). 2010. audio compact disk 100.00 (978-0-307-71276-9(1), BksonTape) Pub: Random Audio Pubg. Dist(s): Random

Betrayal of the Chosen. Chuck Missler. 2 CD's. (Running Time: 120 mins.). (Briefing Packages by Chuck Missler). 1997. audio compact disk 19.95 (978-1-57821-308-5(8)) Koinonia Hse.
History of Modern Israel.Will the current "Peace Process" lead to peace? Why or Why not? Have the victims of the Holocaust now become the villains of the Middle East? Is the plight of the Palestinians fact or fable? From both public and private sources, this Briefing Package summarizes the bizarre, and largely unknown, history behind the State of Israel from the fall of Jerusalem in 70A.D. to the present.Most diligent Bible students understand Israel's history up to the Crucifixion, but few really understand how Israel's present predicament came about and thus fail to fully appreciate the prophetic perspective.

Betrayal of Trust: The Collapse of Global Public Health. abr. ed. Laurie Garrett. 2 cass. (Running Time: 3 hrs.). 2000. 18.00 (978-1-55935-341-0(4)) Soundelux.
The best-selling author of "The Coming of the Plagues," takes listeners around the world to reveal how a series of potential & present health catastrophes mark the death of public health.

***Betrayals.** unabr. ed. Lili St. Crow. Narrated by Alyssa Bresnahan. 1 Playaway. (Running Time: 12 hrs.). (Strange Angels Ser.: Bk. 2). (YA). (gr. 9 up). 2010. 64.75 (978-1-4407-7163-7(4)); 51.75 (978-1-4407-7153-8(7)); audio compact disk 108.75 (978-1-4407-7157-6(X)); audio compact disk 51.95 (978-1-4407-7161-3(8)) Recorded Bks.

***Betrayed.** 2010. 14.99 (978-1-61581-978-2(9)) Dreamspinner.

Betrayed. Lyndsey Harris. 2007. 61.95 (978-0-7531-3728-4(3)); audio compact disk 79.95 (978-0-7531-2695-0(8)) Pub: ISIS Audio GBR. Dist(s): Ulverscroft US

Betrayed. David Hosp. Read by Richard Ferrone. (Running Time: 43200 sec.). 2006. audio compact disk 39.99 (978-1-4281-0002-2(4)) Recorded Bks.

Betrayed. P. C. Cast & Kristin Cast. Read by Edwina Wren. (Running Time: 9 hrs. 55 mins.). (House of Night Ser.). (YA). 2009. 79.99 (978-1-74214-187-9(0), 9781742141879) Pub: Bolinda Pubng AUS. Dist(s): Bolinda Pub Inc

Betrayed. unabr. ed. P. C. Cast & Kristin Cast. Read by Edwina Wren. (Running Time: 9 hrs. 55 mins.). (House of Night Ser.: No. 2). (YA). 2008. audio compact disk 87.95 (978-1-74214-074-2(2), 9781742140742) Pub: Bolinda Pubng AUS. Dist(s): Bolinda Pub Inc

Betrayed. unabr. ed. Read by Elizabeth Henry. Perf. by Judy Chard. 3 cass. (Running Time: 4 hrs. 30 min.). 1999. 34.95 (65484) Pub: Soundings Ltd GBR. Dist(s): Ulverscroft US

***Betrayed.** unabr. ed. P. C. Cast & Kristin Cast. Read by Edwina Wren. (Running Time: 9 hrs. 55 mins.). (House of Night Ser.). (YA). 2010. 43.95 (978-1-74214-668-3(6), 9781742146683) Pub: Bolinda Pubng AUS. Dist(s): Bolinda Pub Inc

Betrayed. unabr. ed. Danielle Steel. (Running Time: 10 hrs.). 2012. audio compact disk 92.97 (978-1-4233-8841-8(0), 9781423388418, BriAudCD Unabrid) Brilliance Audio.

***Betrayed.** unabr. ed. Robert K. Tanenbaum. (Running Time: 13 hrs.). (Butch Karp/Marlene Ciampi Ser.). 2010. 39.97 (978-1-4418-6876-3(3), 9781441868763, BADLE); 24.99 (978-1-4418-6875-6(5), 9781441868756, BAD) Brilliance Audio.

***Betrayed.** unabr. ed. Robert K. Tanenbaum. Read by Mel Foster. (Running Time: 13 hrs.). (Butch Karp/Marlene Ciampi Ser.). 2010. 24.99 (978-1-4418-6873-2(9), 9781441868732, Brilliance MP3); 39.97 (978-1-4418-6874-9(7), 9781441868749, Brlnc Audio MP3 Lib); audio compact disk 29.99 (978-1-4418-6871-8(2), 9781441868718, Bril Audio CD Unabri); audio compact disk 79.97 (978-1-4418-6872-5(0), 9781441868725, BriAudCD Unabrid) Brilliance Audio.

Betrayed by Holy Hands. Robert A. Stovall. 2009. audio compact disk 18.99 (978-1-60696-559-7(X)) Tate Pubng.

***Betrayer of Worlds.** unabr. ed. Larry Niven. Read by Tom Weiner. (Running Time: 11 hrs.). (Fleet of Worlds Ser.). 2010. 29.95 (978-1-4417-6141-5(1)); 65.95 (978-1-4417-6138-5(1)); audio compact disk 29.95 (978-1-4417-6140-8(3)); audio compact disk 100.00 (978-1-4417-6139-2(X)) Blckstn Audio.

***Betrayers: A Nameless Detective Novel.** Bill Pronzini. Narrated by Nick Sullivan. (Running Time: 7 hrs. 2 mins. 0 sec.). (ENG.). 2011. audio compact disk 29.95 (978-1-60998-139-6(1)) Pub: AudioGO. Dist(s): Perseus Dist

Betrothed see Los Novios

Betrothed. Alejandro Manzoni. Read by Laura García. (Running Time: 3 hrs.). 2002. 16.95 (978-1-60083-234-5(2), Audiofy Corp) Iofy Corp.

Betrothed. unabr. ed. Shmuel Yosef Agnon. 3 cass. 1999. 29.95 (978-1-893079-03-8(1), JCCAUDIOBOOKS) Jewish Contempry Classics.
Surreal novella of romance & the return of the lovers to the shores of their origin. By the Israeli Nobel Laureate.

Betsy Ross. unabr. ed. Robert Hogrogian. 1 cass. (Running Time: 16 min.). (People to Remember Ser.: Set I). (J). (gr. 4-7). 1979. bk. 16.99 (978-0-934898-45-4(6)); pap. bk. 9.95 (978-0-934898-03-4(0)) Jan Prods.
A U. S. woman who is remembered wherever the flag is flown.

Betsy Ross: Designer of Our Flag. unabr. ed. Ann Weil. Read by Marguerite Gavin. 3 cass. (Running Time: 4 hrs.). (Childhood of Famous Americans Ser.). (gr. 1-3). 2001. pap. bk. 35.95 (978-0-7861-2069-7(X), K2830) Blckstn Audio.
Ann Weil recreates the childhood of Betsy Ross, maker of the first American flag, which is secretly presented to General George Washington in Philadelphia in 1776.

Betsy Ross: The American Flag & Life in a Young America. unabr. ed. Ryan P. Randolph. Read by Suzy Myers. 1 MP3-CD. (Running Time: 1 hr.). (Library of American Lives & Times Ser.). 2009. 39.97 (978-1-4233-8191-4(2), 9781423381914, Brlnc Audio MP3 Lib); 39.97 (978-1-4233-8192-1(0), 9781423381921, BADLE); 19.99 (978-1-4233-8190-7(4), 9781423381907, Brilliance MP3); audio compact disk 39.97 (978-1-4233-8189-1(0), 9781423381891, BriAudCD Unabrid); audio compact disk 19.99 (978-1-4233-8188-4(2), 9781423381884, Bril Audio CD Unabri) Brilliance Audio.

Betsy-Tacy. unabr. ed. Maud Hart Lovelace. Read by Sutton Foster. (J). 2008. 34.99 (978-1-60252-952-6(3)) Find a World.

***Betsy-Tacy.** unabr. ed. Maud Hart Lovelace. Read by Sutton Foster. (ENG.). 2007. (978-0-06-162427-8(6)); (978-0-06-162428-5(4)) HarperCollins Pubs.

***Betsy's Return.** unabr. ed. Wanda E. Brunstetter. Narrated by Jaimee Draper. (Running Time: 4 hrs. 36 mins. 42 sec.). (Brides of Lehigh Canal Ser.). (ENG.). 2010. 16.09 (978-1-60814-672-7(3)); audio compact disk 22.99 (978-1-59859-721-9(3)) Oasis Audio.

Bette. 2005. 54.95 (978-0-7861-4360-3(6)); audio compact disk 63.00 (978-0-7861-7499-7(4)) Blckstn Audio.

Bette, Vol. 2. unabr. ed. Lyn Cote. 8 cass. (Running Time: 28800 sec.). (Women of Ivy Manor Ser.). 2005. 29.95 (978-0-7861-3665-0(0), E3531) Blckstn Audio.

Bette, Vol. 2. unabr. ed. Lyn Cote. Read by Anna Fields. 9 CDs. (Running Time: 30600 sec.). (Women of Ivy Manor Ser.). 2005. audio compact disk 29.95 (978-0-7861-7729-5(2), ZE3531); audio compact disk 29.95 (978-0-7861-7957-2(0), ZM3531) Blckstn Audio.

Bette Davis. unabr. ed. Barbara Leaming. Read by Grace Conlin. 9 cass. (Running Time: 13 hrs.). 1995. 62.95 (978-0-7861-0702-5(2), 1579) Blckstn Audio.
Off-camera Bette Davis fought endless contractual battles with studios & survived four disastrous marriages, earning a larger-than-life reputation as an actress to be reckoned with. In this extraordinary biography, fans & film historians will discover a different, darker side of Bette Davis. A legend, a star, a remarkable woman, Bette Davis lived her life as if it were a coveted role she was desperately afraid she might not win.

Better: A Surgeon's Notes on Performance. unabr. ed. Atul Gawande. Read by John Bedford Lloyd. 6 CDs. (Running Time: 7 hrs. 30 mins. 0 sec.). (ENG.). 2007. audio compact disk 29.95 (978-1-4272-0098-3(X)) Pub: Macmill Audio. Dist(s): Macmillan

Better & Better Ways of Helping Yourself Emotionally, Set. Albert Ellis. 2 cass. (Running Time: 69 min.). 1999. 9.95 A Ellis Institute.
Dozens of techniques are critiqued in terms of helpfulness vs. palliativeness, followed by REBT techniques for producing long-lasting changes.

Better Boundaries (Audio Workshop) Created by Wendy Y. Bailey. 1 CD. (Running Time: 60 mins.). 2004. audio compact disk 19.00 (978-0-9749914-2-9(2)) Brilliance In Action.
Better BoundariesBoundaries are a life-enhancing system of "yes's" and "no's." They are the stop signs and borders you install to protect yourself so that it is clear that you own your life, make good choices, and pursue the authentic expression of who you are in the way you live, love, give and relate. Join this audio of a TeleClass favorite so you can learn how to strengthen your boundaries and treasure your life! This is an ideal TeleClass for women who have difficulty saying no. Includes detailed TeleClass notes with challenge assignments.

Better Breathing: The Tibetan Caffeine. unabr. ed. Michael G. White. Read by Michael G. White. 1 cass. (Running Time: 50 min.). Dramatization. (Balanced Breathing Ser.). 1997. 12.00 (978-1-883417-15-4(5)) Balance Breath.
Simple guided steps to better breathing.

Better Breathing Exercise Number One: Letting Go of Tension & Negativity. unabr. ed. Michael G. White. 1 cass. (Running Time: 1 hrs.). Dramatization. 1997. (978-1-883417-14-7(7)) Balance Breath.
Access the healing state, strengthen relaxation response.

Better Brown Stories. unabr. ed. Allan Ahlberg. Read by Richard Mitchley. 2 cass. (Running Time: 3 hrs.). (J). (gr. 1-8). 1999. 18.95 (CCA 3489, Chivers Child Audio) AudioGO.

Better Dads, Stronger Sons: How Fathers Can Guide Boys to Become Men of Character. Rick Johnson. Read by Rick Johnson. (Running Time: 18000 sec.). (ENG.). 2008. audio compact disk 26.99 (978-1-934384-08-4(9)) Pub: Treasure Pub. Dist(s): STL Dist NA

Better Days. Contrib. by Robbie Seay Band. Prod. by Jay Joyce & Will Hunt. 2005. audio compact disk 16.98 (978-5-558-96609-1(2)) Pt of Grace Ent.

Better Driving. 1 cass. (Running Time: 60 min.). (Intelligent Body Ser.). 1991. 15.00 (978-1-889618-54-8(3)) Feldenkrais Move.
Movement education - 1 Feldenkrais awareness through movement lessons.

Better English Pronunciation. J. D. O'Connor. 2 cass. (Running Time: 2 hrs. 36 mins.). (ENG.). 1984. 43.00 (978-0-521-26349-8(2)) Cambridge U Pr.

***Better English Pronunciation Audio CDs (2)** J. D. O'Connor. (Running Time: 2 hrs. 12 mins.). (ENG.). 2010. audio compact disk 41.00 (978-0-521-17550-0(X)) Cambridge U Pr.

Better Freedom: Finding Life As Slaves of Christ. Michael Card. (ENG.). 2009. 16.00 (978-0-8308-5569-8(6)) InterVarsity.

Better Homes & Husbands. unabr. ed. Valerie Ann Leff. Read by Carrington MacDuffie. (Running Time: 27000 sec.). 2006. 59.95 (978-0-7861-4674-1(5)); audio compact disk 72.00 (978-0-7861-6785-2(8)); audio compact disk 29.95 (978-0-7861-7417-1(X)) Blckstn Audio.

Better Life. unabr. ed. Elizabeth Lord. Read by Tracey Lloyd. 10 cass. (Running Time: 15 hrs.). 1999. 84.95 (978-0-7531-0512-2(8), 990310) Pub: ISIS Audio GBR. Dist(s): Ulverscroft US
Six years after the Great War, the Farmer family considers itself lucky to have come through intact. The debonair & sophisticated Langley Makepeace sweeps Cissy Farmer off her feet & into the brittle world of which she dreams. And how will Eddie Bennet, the gentle loving boy everyone assumed she would marry, take such a rejection? Only when some of the glamour begins to fade does Cissy question whether she has achieved her dream of a better life.

Better Living Through Chemistry? Program from the Award Winning Public Radio Series. Interview. Hosted by Fred Goodwin. 1 CD. (Running Time: 1 hr.). (Infinite Mind Ser.). 1998. audio compact disk 21.95 (978-1-888064-44-5(7), LCM 11) Lichtenstein Creat.
Should doctors prescribe pharmaceuticals for life enhancement? From Rogaine for nicer hair to Prozac for personality to the new anti-impotency drug Viagra, it?s a question increasingly debated.

Better Match. Contrib. by Parson's Hat. (ENG.). 1992. audio compact disk 21.95 (978-0-8023-8062-3(X)) Pub: Clo Iar-Chonnachta IRL. Dist(s): Dufour

***Better Match.** Parson's Hat. (ENG.). 1991. 11.95 (978-0-8023-7062-4(4)) Pub: Clo Iar-Chonnachta IRL. Dist(s): Dufour

Better Memory. Shad Helmstetter. 1 cass. (Self-Talk Cassettes Ser.). 10.95 (978-0-937065-12-9(9)) Grindle Pr.

Better Memory. Michael P. Kelly. 1 cass. 1992. 14.95 (978-1-883700-16-4(7)) ThoughtForms.
Self help.

Better Not Get Wet, Jessie Bear. unabr. ed. Nancy White Carlstrom. Narrated by John McDonough. 1 cass. (Running Time: 15 mins.). (ps up). 1998. 10.00 (978-0-7887-2056-7(2), 95409E7) Recorded Bks.
How can Mama & Papa Bear expect a little bear to not get wet, when he waters the roses, skips pebbles on the pond, or helps a blackbird with his bath?.

Better off with the Blues. Perf. by Junior Wells & Buddy Guy. 1 cass., 1 CD. 7.98 (TA 33354); audio compact disk 12.78 CD Jewel box. (TA 83354) NewSound.

Better on A Rising Tide-5 CD audio Book. Thomas Henry Kelly. 2004. audio compact disk 35.00 (978-1-56142-192-3(8)) T Kelly Inc.

Better Parents, Better Spouses, Better People. Daniel Goleman & Daniel Siegel. Executive Producer Hanuman Goleman. (ENG.). 2007. audio compact disk 13.95 (978-1-934441-00-8(7)) More Than Snd.

Better Part of Valor. unabr. ed. Tanya Huff. Narrated by Marguerite Gavin. (Running Time: 10 hrs. 0 mins. 0 sec.). (Confederation Ser.). (ENG.). 2009. audio compact disk 24.99 (978-1-4001-5991-8(1)); audio compact disk 69.99 (978-1-4001-3991-0(0)) Pub: Tantor Media. Dist(s): IngramPubServ

Better Part of Valor. unabr. ed. Tanya Huff. Narrated by Marguerite Gavin. (Running Time: 10 hrs. 0 mins. 0 sec.). (Confederation Ser.). (ENG.). 2009. audio compact disk 34.99 (978-1-4001-0991-3(4)) Pub: Tantor Media. Dist(s): IngramPubServ

Better Place. Contrib. by Overflow et al. Prod. by Scotty Wilbanks. 2004. audio compact disk 9.99 (978-5-559-56143-1(6)) Essential Recs.

Better Possession: Heb. 10:26-31. Ed Young. 1992. 4.95 (978-0-7417-1911-9(8), 911) Win Walk.

Better Possession: Hebrews 10:26-31. Ed Young. 1992. 4.95 (978-0-7417-1912-6(6), 912) Win Walk.

Better Principle: Hebrews 11:1-3. Ed Young. 1992. 4.95 (978-0-7417-1913-3(4), 913) Win Walk.

Better Relationships. 1 cass. (Self-Hypnosis Ser.). 9.98 (814) Randolph Tapes.

***Better Safe than Sued: Keeping Your Students & Ministry Alive.** Jack Crabtree. (Running Time: 9 hrs. 12 mins. 0 sec.). (ENG.). 2009. 16.99 (978-0-310-77232-3(X)) Zondervan.

Better Sleeping. Pat Carroll. Read by Pat Carroll. Ed. by Tony Carroll. 1 cass. (Running Time: 30 min.). 10.00 Inner-Mind Concepts.
Presents a new sleep technique.

Better Study Habits. 1 cass. 10.00 (978-1-58506-004-7(6), 05) New Life Inst OR.
When you free your total learning power, you soak up ideas & information fast & easily. Release your total power to learn.

Better Study Habits. Norman J. Caldwell. Read by Norman J. Caldwell. Ed. by Achieve Now Institute Staff. 1 cass. (Running Time: 20 min.). (Academic Achievement Ser.). 1988. 9.97 (978-1-56273-081-9(9)) My Mothers Pub.
Study becomes easier as you relax.

Better Study Habits. Mel Gilley. Ed. by Steven C. Eggleston. 1 cass. (World of Hypnosis Ser.). 1987. 6.95 SCE Prod & List & Lrn.
Self Hypnosis to help improve study habit skills.

Better Table Tennis. Barrie Konicov. 1 cass. 11.98 (978-0-87082-417-3(1), 012) Potentials.
Reveals how to be a competitor & competitive at table tennis.

Better Tennis. Barrie Konicov. 1 cass. 11.98 (978-0-87082-418-0(X), 013) Potentials.
Improve your game of tennis significantly by working with this program at bedtime.

Better Than Good: Get Motivated! unabr. ed. Zig Ziglar. Narrated by Zig Ziglar. (ENG.). 2007. 16.09 (978-1-60814-042-8(3)); audio compact disk 22.99 (978-1-59859-129-3(0)) Oasis Audio.

***Better Than Home.** unabr. ed. Joe Hill. (ENG.). 2007. (978-0-06-155215-1(1)); (978-0-06-155216-8(X)) HarperCollins Pubs.

Better Than I Know Myself. Virginia DeBerry & Donna Grant. 16 CDs. (Running Time: 19 hrs. 30 mins.). 2004. audio compact disk 96.00 (978-0-7861-8537-5(6), 3294) Blckstn Audio.

Better Than I Know Myself. Virginia DeBerry & Donna Grant. Read by Lisa Pitts. (Running Time: 19 hrs. 30 mins.). 2004. 50.95 (978-1-59912-431-5(9)) Iofy Corp.

Better Than I Know Myself. unabr. ed. Virginia DeBerry & Donna Grant. 14 cass. (Running Time: 19 hrs. 30 mins.). 2004. 76.95 (978-0-7861-2747-4(3), 3294) Blckstn Audio.

Better Than I Know Myself. unabr. ed. Virginia DeBerry & Donna Grant. Read by Lisa Reneé Pitts. 11 cass. (Running Time: 15 hrs. 30 mins.). 2005. reel tape 34.95 (978-0-7861-2725-2(2), E3294); audio compact disk 39.95 (978-0-7861-8551-1(1), 3294); audio compact disk 44.95 (978-0-7861-8590-0(2), ZE3294) Blckstn Audio.

Better Than Moses: Hebrews 3:1-6. Ed Young. 1991. 4.95 (978-0-7417-1881-5(2), 881) Win Walk.

Better Than That. Contrib. by Singletons et al. 2006. audio compact disk 17.98 (978-5-558-47740-5(7), Verity) Brentwood Music.

Better Than the Best: Matthew 5:17-20. Ed Young. (J). 1979. 4.95 (978-0-7417-1048-2(X), A0049) Win Walk.

Better to Rest. Dana Stabenow. Read by Marguerite Gavin. (Liam Campbell Mystery Ser.). 2002. 56.00 (978-0-7366-8861-1(7)) Books on Tape.

Better Vision. Richard Jafolla & Mary-Alice Jafolla. Read by Richard Jafolla & Mary-Alice Jafolla. (Health & Healing Ser.). 1986. 12.95 (310) Stppng Stones.
Motivational tapes that work on the subconscious mind (subliminal) & conscious mind to bring about self-improvement.

Better Vision: Do It Yourself. unabr. ed. Cambridge Institute for Better Vision Staff. 3 cass. 49.50 (S1865) J Norton Pubs.
A simple & methodical way to teach your eyes how to focus & relax.

Better Way to Pray. 2003. 30.00 (978-1-881541-86-8(X)); audio compact disk 35.00 (978-1-881541-91-2(6)) A Wommack.

Better Way to Pray: Updated Album. Created by Awmi. (ENG.). 2003. audio compact disk 30.00 (978-1-59548-075-0(7)) A Wommack.

***Betti on the High Wire.** unabr. ed. Lisa Railsback. Read by Rachel Gray. (ENG.). (J). 2010. audio compact disk 34.00 (978-0-307-73826-4(4), Listening Lib) Pub: Random Audio Pubg. Dist(s): Random

Betty Friedan. unabr. ed. Ed. by Jim McKinley. Prod. by Rebekah Presson. 1 cass. (Running Time: 29 min.). (New Letters on the Air Ser.). 1994. 10.00 (091793) New Letters.
The author of "The Feminine Mystique" publishes her first book in ten years this month. In "The Fountain of Age," Friedan tries to debunk the myths of aging, much as she did those of womanhood 30 years ago. She reads from the book & talks about events in her own life that led her to her new subject.

Betty Fussell. unabr. ed. Betty Fussell. Read by Bob Stewart. Ed. by James McKinley. 1 cass. (Running Time: 29 min.). (New Letters on the Air Ser.). 1992. 10.00 (112792); 18.00 2-sided cass. New Letters.
Fussell is interviewed by Robert Stewart & reads from her book, The Story of Corn.

Betty Smith: Songs Traditionally Sung in North Carolina. 1 cass. 9.98 (C-53) Folk-Legacy.
An excellent program by a lovely singer.

Betty Zane. Zane Grey. Read by Michael Prichard. (Playaway Adult Fiction Ser.). (ENG.). 2009. 64.99 (978-1-60775-770-2(2)) Find a World.

Betty Zane. Zane Grey. Narrated by Ed Sala. 8 cass. (Running Time: 11 hrs.). 54.00 (978-1-4025-2065-5(4)) Recorded Bks.

Betty Zane. unabr. ed. Zane Grey. Read by Robert Morris. 7 cass. (Running Time: 10 hrs.). 1994. 49.95 (978-0-7861-0741-4(3), 1497) Blckstn Audio.
Set in the dangerous West Virginia frontier, this is a story which tells of the bravery & heroism of Betty, the beautiful young sister of old Colonel Isaac Zane, one of the most courageous pioneers. Balanced against the grim incidents of the Indian War is the love story of Betty & Alfred Clarke, a handsome young soldier. Their romance, however, is plagued by troubles & endless interruptions before it reaches its stirring climax.

Betty Zane. unabr. ed. Zane Grey. Narrated by Michael Prichard. (Ohio River Trilogy). (ENG.). 2004. audio compact disk 22.99 (978-1-4001-5132-5(5)) Pub: Tantor Media. Dist(s): IngramPubServ

Betty Zane. unabr. ed. Zane Grey. Read by Michael Prichard. (Ohio River Trilogy). (ENG.). 2004. audio compact disk 69.99 (978-1-4001-3132-7(4)) Pub: Tantor Media. Dist(s): IngramPubServ

Betty Zane. unabr. ed. Zane Grey. Narrated by Michael Prichard. (Running Time: 11 hrs. 30 mins. 0 sec.). (Ohio River Ser.). (ENG.). 2009. 22.99 (978-1-4001-5946-8(6)); audio compact disk 65.99 (978-1-4001-3946-0(5)); audio compact disk 32.99 (978-1-4001-0946-3(9)) Pub: Tantor Media. Dist(s): IngramPubServ

Betty Zane, Set. unabr. ed. Zane Grey. Read by Robert Morris. 7 cass. 1999. 49.95 (FS9-34271) Highsmith.

***Between a Rock & a Grace Place: Divine Surprises in the Tight Spots of Life.** Carol Kent. (Running Time: 7 hrs. 11 mins. 13 sec.). (ENG.). 2010. 22.99 (978-0-310-42167-2(5)) Zondervan.

Between a Rock & a Hard Place. abr. ed. Aron Ralston. 2004. 15.95 (978-0-7435-4302-6(5)) Pub: S&S Audio. Dist(s): S and S Inc

Between Cross & Crescent: Jewish Civilization from Mohammed to Spinoza. Instructed by David B. Ruderman. 12 cass. (Running Time: 12 hrs). 54.95 (978-1-59803-119-5(8)) Teaching Co.

Between Cross & Crescent: Jewish Civilization from Mohammed to Spinoza. Instructed by David B. Ruderman. 12 CDs. (Running Time: 12 hrs). 2005. audio compact disk 69.95 (978-1-59803-121-8(X)) Teaching Co.

Between Earth & Sky. Perf. by Robin Bullock. 1 cass., 1 CD. 7.98 (MMS 221); audio compact disk 11.98 CD Jewel box. (MMS 221) NewSound.

Between Friends. unabr. ed. Kathleen Rowntree. Read by Patricia Gallimore. 8 cass. (Running Time: 12 hrs. 19 mins.). (Isis Ser.). (J). 2001. 69.95 (978-0-7531-1081-2(4)) Pub: ISIS Lrg Prnt GBR. Dist(s): Ulverscroft US
Past experience leads Tessa Brierley to suspect that her husband Nick is, once again, having an affair. Her first instinct is to confide in her best friend Maddy, but a chance remark forestalls her as a new and more shocking suspicion dawns. Set in the small English village of Wychwood, this is an astutely witty novel of loyalties and betrayals.

Between, Georgia. unabr. ed. Joshilyn Jackson. Read by Joshilyn Jackson. 7 cass. (Running Time: 9 hrs.). 2006. 63.00 (978-1-4159-3223-0(9)); audio compact disk 81.00 (978-1-4159-3224-7(7)) Books on Tape.
Nonny Frett understands the meanings of "rock" and "hard place" better than any woman ever born. She's got two mothers, "one deaf-blind and the other four baby steps from flat crazy." She's got two men: her husband, who's easing out the back door; and her best friend, who's laying siege to her heart in her front yard. She has a job that holds her in the city, and she's addicted to a little girl who's stuck deep in the country. To top it off, she has two families: the Fretts, who stole her and raised her right; and the Crabtrees, who lost her and can't forget that they've been done wrong. In Between, Georgia, population 90, a feud that began the night Bonny was born is escalating, and a random act of violence will set the torch to a thirty-year-old stash of highly flammable secrets. This might be just what the town needs, if only Nonny wasn't sitting in the middle of it.

Between, Georgia. unabr. ed. Joshilyn Jackson. (Running Time: 9 hrs.). (ENG.). 2006. 14.98 (978-1-59483-525-4(X)) Pub: Hachet Audio. Dist(s): HachBkGrp

Between, Georgia. unabr. ed. Joshilyn Jackson. Read by Joshilyn Jackson. (Running Time: 9 hrs.). (Replay Edition Ser.). (ENG.). 2008. audio compact disk 14.98 (978-1-60024-108-6(5)) Pub: Hachet Audio. Dist(s): HachBkGrp

Between, Georgia. unabr. ed. Joshilyn Jackson. (Running Time: 9 hrs.). (ENG.). 2009. 49.98 (978-1-60788-162-9(4)) Pub: Hachet Audio. Dist(s): HachBkGrp

Between Good & Evil: A Master Profiler's Hunt for Society's Most Violent Predators. abr. ed. Roger L. Depue & Susan Schindehette. Read by David Povall. (ENG.). 2005. 14.98 (978-1-59483-131-7(9)) Pub: Hachet Audio. Dist(s): HachBkGrp

Between Good & Evil: A Master Profiler's Hunt for Society's Most Violent Predators. abr. ed. Roger L. Depue & Susan Schindehette. Read by David Povall. (Running Time: 6 hrs.). (ENG.). 2009. 44.98 (978-1-60788-025-7(3)) Pub: Hachet Audio. Dist(s): HachBkGrp

Between Husband & Wife. Lamb & Brinley. 5 cass. 2004. 19.95 (978-1-57734-616-6(5)); audio compact disk 24.95 (978-1-57734-746-0(3)) Covenant Comms.

Between Life Journey. Read by Mary Richards. 1 cass. (Running Time: 93 min.). (Series Two Thousand). 2007. audio compact disk 19.95 (978-1-56136-109-0(7)) Master Your Mind.

Between Love & Hate. 2000. 12.95 (978-0-9666484-7-8(1)) Dimby Co Inc.

Between Lovers. unabr. ed. Eric Jerome Dickey. Narrated by Dion Graham. 8 CDs. (Running Time: 9 hrs. 45 mins.). 2001. audio compact disk 78.00 (978-1-4025-0915-5(4), C1578) Recorded Bks.
Dickey centers the story on an L.A.-based writer who is obsessed with gorgeous, nubile Nicole - the very same woman who left him at the altar just three years before. Nicole is torn between her ongoing love for him and her passion for the beautiful, and white, Ayanna. It's time for Nicole to make a decision - keep the writer and lose Ayanna, or try to accommodate both and risk losing everything in a conflagration of uninhibited sexuality.

Between Lovers. unabr. ed. Eric Jerome Dickey. Narrated by Dion Graham. 7 cass. (Running Time: 9 hrs 45 mins.). 2001. 68.00 (978-0-7887-9469-8(8)) Recorded Bks.
L.A.-based writer, obsessed with gorgeous, nubile Nicole, the very same woman who left him at the altar just three years before. Nicole is torn between her ongoing love for him and her passion for the beautiful, and white, Ayanna. It's time for Nicole to make a decision - keep the writer and lose Ayanna, or try to accommodate both and risk losing everything in a conflagration of uninhibited sexuality.

Between Me & the River. unabr. ed. Carrie Host. Narrated by Renée Raudman. (Running Time: 10 hrs. 0 mins. 0 sec.). (ENG.). 2009. audio compact disk 59.99 (978-1-4001-4323-8(3)); audio compact disk 19.99 (978-1-4001-6323-6(4)) Pub: Tantor Media. Dist(s): IngramPubServ

Between Me & the River: Living Beyond Cancer - A Memoir. unabr. ed. Carrie Host. Narrated by Renée Raudman. (Running Time: 10 hrs. 0 mins. 0 sec.). (ENG.). 2009. audio compact disk 29.99 (978-1-4001-1323-1(7)) Pub: Tantor Media. Dist(s): IngramPubServ

Between Meals. unabr. ed. A. J. Liebling. Read by Walter Zimmerman. 6 cass. (Running Time: 6 hrs.). 1988. 36.00 (978-0-7366-1347-7(1), 2248) Books on Tape.
Presents an eulogy to the great restaurants in the golden age of Paris dining.

Between Niger & Nile. unabr. collector's ed. Arnold J. Toynbee. Read by David Case. 4 cass. (Running Time: 4 hrs.). 1991. 24.00 (978-0-7366-2036-9(2), 2850) Books on Tape.
Toynbee records his impressions of these lands in an acute, persuasive & knowledgeable manner.

Between One & Three. Max Brand. (Running Time: 0 hr. 42 mins.). 1998. 10.95 (978-1-60083-481-3(7)) Iofy Corp.

***Between One & Three.** Max Brand. 2009. (978-1-60136-388-6(5)) Audio Holding.

Between Oxus & Jumna. unabr. collector's ed. Arnold J. Toynbee. Read by David Case. 6 cass. (Running Time: 9 hrs.). 1991. 48.00 (978-0-7366-1940-0(2), 2762) Books on Tape.
Between the rivers Oxus & Jumna (that is from Iran through Afghanistan, Pakistan & Northern India) there existed 2000 years ago an area nearly blank on contemporary maps. For 500 years it remained virtually terra incognito. While the maps have long since been filled in, the history has not. Now the author, during his lifetime a prodigious digger for facts, tells the story of those lost centuries.

Between Parent & Child. Gloria Star. 1 cass. 8.95 (329) Am Fed Astrologers.
Analysis of relationship as seen in child's chart.

Between Rounds see Favorite Stories by O. Henry

Between Rounds: A Collection of Stories. unabr. ed. O. Henry. Read by Peter Joyce. 4 cass. 1997. 44.95 (978-1-86015-448-5(4)) Pub: UlverLrgPrint GBR. Dist(s): Ulverscroft US
Collection includes: "A Service of Love," "Dry Valley's Indian Summer," "Makes the Whole World Kind," "The Unknown Quantity," "Buried Treasure," "Let Me Feel Your Pulse".

***Between Shades of Gray.** Ruta Sepetys. (Running Time: 8 hrs.). (ENG.). 2011. audio compact disk 25.95 (978-0-14-242897-9(3), PengAudBks) Penguin Grp USA.

***Between Sisters.** abr. ed. Kristin Hannah. Read by Laural Merlington. (Running Time: 6 hrs.). 2010. audio compact disk 9.99 (978-1-4418-6699-8(X), 9781441866998, BCD Value Price) Brilliance Audio.

Between Sisters. abr. ed. Nina Vida. Read by Tia Carrere. 2 cass. (Running Time: 3 hrs.). 2001. 18.00 (978-1-59040-171-2(9), Phoenix Audio) Pub: Amer Intl Pub. Dist(s): PerseuPGW

Between Sisters. unabr. ed. Kristin Hannah. Read by Laural Merlington. 7 cass. (Running Time: 10 hrs.). 2003. 32.95 (978-1-58788-948-6(X), 158788948X, BAU); 82.25 (978-1-58788-949-3(8), 1587889498, CD Unabrid Lib Ed) Brilliance Audio.
Meghann Dontess is a woman haunted by heartbreak. Twenty-seven years ago she was forced to make a terrible choice, one that cost her everything, including the love of her sister, Claire. Now, Meghann is a hotshot divorce attorney who doesn't believe in intimacy - until she meets the one man who can change her mind. Claire Cavenaugh has fallen in love for the first time in her life. As her wedding day approaches, she prepares to face her harsh, judgmental older sister. It is the first time they have been together in more than two decades. Over the course of a hot Pacific Northwest summer, these two women who believe they have nothing in common will try to become what they never were: a family. Tender, funny, bittersweet, and wonderfully moving, Between Sisters celebrates the joys and heartaches that can be shared only by sisters, the mistakes made in the name of love, and the healing power of new beginnings - all beautifully told by acclaimed author Kristin Hannah.

Between Sisters. unabr. ed. Kristin Hannah. Read by Laural Merlington. (Running Time: 10 hrs.). 2004. 39.25 (978-1-59335-410-7(X), 159335410X, Brlnc Audio MP3 Lib) Brilliance Audio.

Between Sisters. unabr. ed. Kristin Hannah. Read by Laural Merlington. (Running Time: 10 hrs.). 2004. 39.25 (978-1-59710-044-1(7), 1597100447, BADLE); 24.95 (978-1-59710-045-8(5), 1597100455, BAD) Brilliance Audio.

***Between Sisters.** unabr. ed. Kristin Hannah. Read by Laural Merlington. (Running Time: 12 hrs.). 2010. audio compact disk 29.99 (978-1-4418-4081-3(8), 9781441840813, Bril Audio CD Unabri); audio compact disk 89.97 (978-1-4418-4082-0(6), 9781441840820, BriAudCD Unabrid) Brilliance Audio.

Between Sisters. unabr. ed. Kristin Hannah. Read by Laural Merlington. (Running Time: 10 hrs.). 2004. 24.95 (978-1-59335-066-6(X), 159335066X) Soulmate Audio Bks.

Between Sundays. unabr. ed. Karen Kingsbury. Read by Kathy Garver. Frwd. by Alex T. Smith. (Running Time: 13 hrs. 0 mins. 0 sec.). (ENG.). 2007. audio compact disk 29.99 (978-0-310-26260-2(7)) Zondervan.

Between Teacher & Parent - Creating the Partnership & Giving the 'Message' Beverly Gross. 1 cass. (Running Time: 90 mins.). 1999. 6.00 (P60FE) Torah Umesorah.

Between the Acts, Set. unabr. ed. Virginia Woolf. Read by Irene Worth. 6 cass. (Running Time: 5 hrs. 23 min.). 1991. 44.98 (978-0-8072-3148-7(7), CXL546CX, Listening Lib) Random Audio Pubg.

***Between the Assassinations.** unabr. ed. Aravind Adiga. Narrated by Harsh Nayyar. 1 Playaway. (Running Time: 10 hrs.). 2009. 59.75 (978-1-4407-3805-0(X)); 67.75 (978-1-4407-3802-9(5)); audio compact disk 92.75 (978-1-4407-3803-6(3)) Recorded Bks.

Between the Assassinations. unabr. ed. Aravind Adiga. Read by Harsh Nayyar. 9 CDs. (Running Time: 10 hrs. 0 mins. 0 sec.). (ENG.). 2009. audio compact disk 39.99 (978-0-7435-9720-3(6)) Pub: S&S Audio. Dist(s): S and S Inc

***Between the Assassinations.** unabr. collector's ed. Aravind Adiga. Narrated by Harsh Nayyar. 9 CDs. (Running Time: 10 hrs.). 2009. audio compact disk 51.95 (978-1-4407-3804-3(1)) Recorded Bks.

Between the Desire & the Dream. Executive Producer Geoffrey Williams. Composed by Stephen O'Connor. Narrated by Dennis Regan. 2007. cd-rom (978-0-9801671-0-8(8)) Geoffrey Williams.

Between the Lines. abr. ed. Steve Howe. Read by Michael Choate. Ed. by Mike Choate et al. 2 cass. (Running Time: 3 hrs. 10 min.). Dramatization. 1992. bk. 15.95 Set. (978-1-56703-004-4(1), 005) High-Top Sports.
The story of drug addiction of one of baseball's premier pitchers.

Between the Lines: Nine Things Baseball Taught Me about Life. unabr. ed. Orel Hershiser & Robert Wolgemuth. (ENG.). 2005. 14.98 (978-1-59483-405-9(9)) Pub: Hachet Audio. Dist(s): HachBkGrp

Between the Plums. Janet Evanovich. (Between-the-Numbers Novel Ser.). pap. bk. (978-1-55927-790-7(4)); pap. bk. (978-1-55927-791-4(2)) Macmill Audio.

Between the Plums. unabr. ed. Janet Evanovich. (ENG.). 2009. audio compact disk 39.99 (978-1-4272-0779-1(8)) Pub: Macmill Audio. Dist(s): Macmillan

Between the Porch & the Altar: I. Mother & Son; II. Adam & Eve; III. Katherine's Dream; IV. At the Altar see Twentieth-Century Poetry in English: Recordings of Poets Reading Their Own Poetry

Between the Rivers: The History of Ancient Mesopotamia. Instructed by Alexis Q. Castor. 18 cass. (Running Time: 18 hrs.). 2006. 199.95 (978-1-59803-258-1(5)); audio compact disk 99.95 (978-1-59803-259-8(3)) Teaching Co.

Between the Sheets. Ava Cadell. Interview with Conley Falk. 2 cass. (Running Time: 2 hrs.). 1997. 19.99 (978-0-9662623-4-6(4)) Peters Publishing.
Discussion on the health aspects of a good sexual relationship.

Between the Sheets: A Collection of Erotic Bedtime Stories. unabr. ed. Read by Eliza Foss et al. Created by Penthouse Magazine Staff. (Running Time: 32400 sec.). (ENG.). 2006. audio compact disk 24.95 (978-0-7393-4089-9(1), Random AudioBks) Pub: Random Audio Pubg. Dist(s): Random

Between Two Worlds: Escape from Tyranny - Growing up in the Shadow of Saddam. Zainab Salbi & Laurie Becklund. Read by Josephine Bailey. (Playaway Adult Nonfiction Ser.). 2008. 64.99 (978-1-60640-992-3(1)) Find a World.

Between Two Worlds: Escape from Tyranny - Growing up in the Shadow of Saddam. unabr. ed. Zainab Salbi & Laurie Becklund. Narrated by Josephine Bailey. (Running Time: 10 hrs. 30 mins. 0 sec.). (ENG.). 2005. audio compact disk 34.99 (978-1-4001-0180-1(8)); audio compact disk 22.99 (978-1-4001-5180-6(5)) Pub: Tantor Media. Dist(s): IngramPubServ

Between Two Worlds: From Tyranny to Freedom My Escape from the Inner Circle of Saddam. unabr. ed. Zainab Salbi & Laurie Becklund. Narrated by Josephine Bailey. (Running Time: 10 hrs. 30 mins. 0 sec.). (ENG.). 2005. audio compact disk 69.99 (978-1-4001-3180-8(4)) Pub: Tantor Media. Dist(s): IngramPubServ

***Between Two Worlds: My Life & Captivity in Iran.** unabr. ed. Roxana Saberi. Narrated by Roxana Saberi. (Running Time: 13 hrs. 0 mins.). 2010. 18.99 (978-1-4001-8695-2(1)); 24.99 (978-1-4001-6695-4(0)); audio compact disk 37.99 (978-1-4001-1695-9(3)); audio compact disk 75.99 (978-1-4001-4695-6(X)) Pub: Tantor Media. Dist(s): IngramPubServ

Between Us. Perf. by Jules Shear et al. 1 cass., 1 CD. 8.78 (HIST 10352); audio compact disk 13.58 CD. (HIST 10352) NewSound.
Features duets with some of today's most respected singers.

Between Walls see William Carlos Williams Reads His Poetry

Between You & Me. Lorraine Kelly. (Running Time: 2 hrs. 24 mins. 0 sec.). (ENG.). 2008. audio compact disk 19.95 (978-1-4055-0543-7(5)) Pub: Little BrownUK GBR. Dist(s): IPG Chicago

Between You & Me: A Memoir. abr. ed. Mike Wallace. Read by Mike Wallace. Told to Gary Paul Gates. 4 cass. (Running Time: 18000 sec.). 2005. 26.98 (978-1-4013-9740-1(9)) Pub: Hyperion. Dist(s): HarperCollins Pubs

Between You & Me: A Memoir. abr. ed. Mike Wallace & Gary Paul Gates. (Running Time: 6 hrs.). 2007. 14.98 (978-1-4013-8738-9(1)) Pub: Hyperion. Dist(s): HarperCollins Pubs

Between You & Me: A Memoir. abr. ed. Mike Wallace & Mike Wallace. Read by Mike Wallace. (Running Time: 6 hrs.). 2007. audio compact disk 14.98 (978-1-4013-8739-6(X)) Pub: Hyperion. Dist(s): HarperCollins Pubs

Between Your Ears: Managing Stress from Within. Bruce A. Baldwin. Read by Bruce A. Baldwin. (Running Time: 60 min.). 1983. 8.95 (978-0-933583-11-5(7), PDC832) Direction Dynamics.
Book on Tape: Chapter from "It's All in Your Head." Techniques for eliminating stress that is generated within one's person.

Beulah Quintet. Mary Lee Settle. Read by Mary Lee Settle. 2 cass. (Running Time: 1 hr 45 min.). 1982. 13.95 (978-1-55644-057-1(X), 2131) Am Audio Prose.
Performance by one of America's finest & deeply intelligent contemporary writers.

Beverly Hillbillies: Exodus 3:7-10. Ed Young. 1991. 4.95 (978-0-7417-1847-1(2), 847) Win Walk.

Beverly Hills Dead. Stuart Woods. Read by Tony Roberts. (Running Time: 9 hrs.). No. 2. (ENG.). (gr. 8). 2008. audio compact disk 29.95 (978-0-14-314289-8(5), PengAudBks) Penguin Grp USA.

Beverly Sills: Combatting Birth Defects. Read by Beverly Sills. 1 cass. (Running Time: 60 min.). 10.95 (NP-87-11-18, HarperThor) HarpC GBR.

***Beware a Scot's Revenge.** unabr. ed. Sabrina Jeffries. Read by Justine Eyre. (Running Time: 9 hrs.). (School for Heiresses Ser.). 2010. 24.99 (978-1-4418-4715-7(4), 9781441847157, Brilliance MP3); 39.97 (978-1-4418-4719-5(7), 9781441847195, Brlnc Audio MP3 Lib); 24.99 (978-1-4418-4717-1(0), 9781441847171, BAD); 39.97 (978-1-4418-4718-8(9), 9781441847188, BADLE); audio compact disk 79.97 (978-1-4418-4716-4(2), 9781441847164, BriAudCD Unabrid); audio compact disk 19.99 (978-1-4418-4714-0(6), 9781441847140, Bril Audio CD Unabri) Brilliance Audio.

Beware of Math Tutors Who Ride Motorcycles (an Essay from Things I've Learned from Women Who've Dumped Me) abr. ed. Read by Will Forte. Will Forte. Ed. by Ben Karlin. (Running Time: 15 mins.). (ENG.). 2008. 1.98 (978-1-60024-331-8(2)) Pub: Hachet Audio. Dist(s): HachBkGrp

Beware of the Boss: Sexual Harassment on the Job. 1 cass. (Running Time: 30 min.). 9.95 (L0100B090, HarperThor) HarpC GBR.

Beware of the Cat! (Sails Literacy Ser.). (gr. 1 up). 10.00 (978-0-7578-2656-6(3)) Rigby Educ.

Beware of the Credit Monster: Win the War for Your Dollars. unabr. ed. Carole M. Wallace. Read by Sara N. Harrell et al. Prod. by Venture Forward, Inc. Staff. 2 cass. (Running Time: 1 hr.). 1994. 14.95 set, incl. molded plastic case. (978-0-9641587-0-2(1)); 18.95 Set, Library ed., incl. vinyl case. (978-0-9641587-1-9(X)) Venture Forward.
Offers financial information to the young adult, age 16 & up. Teaches them the importance of being "smart" with their money, whether spending or investing. Describes how to avoid the credit trap, how to take advantage of their greatest assets - youth & time, & how to enlist the mighty ally of compound interest.

Beware of the Dog. unabr. ed. Peter Corris. Read by Peter Hosking. 3 cass. (Running Time: 5 hrs.). 2001. (978-1-74030-161-9(7), 500847) Bolinda Pubng AUS.

Beware the Laughing Gull. unabr. ed. Lydia Adamson. Read by Norman Dietz. 4 vols. (Running Time: 6 hr.). 1999. bk. 39.95 (978-0-7927-2299-1(X), CSL 188, Chivers Sound Lib) AudioGO.
Lucy Wayles is a retired librarian & hawk-eyed leader of the Olmstead Irregulars, New York City's oddest bird-watchers. A longtime Irregular decides to get married in Central Park & the ceremony ends up in foul play when a roller-blading gunman swoops down & shoots the bride. With the groom in a daze, the cops in a tizzy & a killer in flight, Lucy wastes no time, & gathers up her flock to solve the case. But an investigation into the bride's hot past & a secret lover's cold heart, could target Lucy as the next dead duck.

Beware the Laughing Gull, Set. Lydia Adamson. Read by Norman Dietz. 4 cass. 1999. 39.95 (978-0-7451-2299-1(X), CSL188) AudioGO.

Beware the naked man who offers you his shirt Cassette. Harvey Mackay. 2004. 7.95 (978-0-7435-4193-0(6)) Pub: S&S Audio. Dist(s): S and S Inc

Beware the Pretenders. John MacArthur, Jr. 6 cass. 19.75 (HarperThor) HarpC GBR.

Beware the Ravens, Aunt Morbelia, unabr. ed. Joan D. Carris. Narrated by George Guidall. 3 cass. (Running Time: 3 hrs. 15 mins.). (gr. 3 up). 1997. 27.00 (978-0-7887-1110-7(5), 95103E7) Recorded Bks.
Tale of a spooky summer vacation. Todd Fearing, struggling with dyslexia, usually spends his summers studying in school. But this year he's flying to London with his great-aunt Morbelia to look over the old Fearing estate she has inherited. The only problem is, the ancient stone mansion is haunted.

Beware the Ravens, Aunt Morbelia. unabr. ed. Joan D. Carris. Read by George Guidall. 3 cass. (Running Time: 3 hrs. 15 min.). (J). (gr. 2). 1997. bk. 47.70 (978-0-7887-1268-5(3), 40514); Rental 9.50 Recorded Bks.

Bewitched Court see Coven of Witches' Tales

Bewitched Tree. Compiled by Pony. (YA). 2007. audio compact disk (978-1-933343-65-5(6)) Staben Inc.

***Bewitchin.** 2010. audio compact disk (978-1-59171-299-2(8)) Falcon Picture.

Bewitching. abr. ed. Jill Barnett. Read by Carrie Gordon Lowrey. 1 cass. (Running Time: 90 min.). 1995. 5.99 (978-1-57096-026-0(7), RAZ 926) Romance Alive Audio.
Joyous MacQuarrie is aptly named as an enchanting witch with uncontrollable powers. When she marries handsome but conventional Alec, Duke of Belmore, she must use her fledgling white magic to win his passion & hold their two hearts spellbound.

Beyond, Set. unabr. ed. John Galsworthy. Read by Flo Gibson. 7 cass. (Running Time: 10 hrs. 30 min.). 1992. 25.95 (978-1-55685-226-8(6)) Audio Bk Con.
Beautiful Gypsy's precipitous marriage to a philandering musician leads her to wonder if she has the ability to fall in love. When Bryan Summerhay appears, she learns the depth of her love & passionate nature.

Beyond a Mechanical Science. unabr. ed. Joseph Needham et al. 2 cass. (Running Time: 2 hrs. 30 min.). 19.95 (29370-29371) J Norton Pubs.

Beyond a Wicked Kiss. unabr. ed. Jo Goodman. Narrated by Jenny Sterlin. 12 cass. (Running Time: 17 hrs.). 2004. 99.75 (978-1-4025-4261-9(5), L1096MC, Griot Aud) Recorded Bks.

Beyond All Frontiers. unabr. ed. Perf. by Eknath Easwaran. 1 cass. (Running Time: 1 hr.). 1985. 7.95 (978-1-58638-503-3(8)) Nilgiri Pr.

Beyond Anger: A Guide for Men: How to Free Yourself from the Grip of Anger & Get More Out of Life. unabr. ed. Thomas J. Harbin. Read by Erik Synnesvetd. (Running Time: 7 hrs. 30 mins.). (ENG.). 2009. 24.98 (978-1-59659-331-2(8), GildAudio) Pub: Gildan Media. Dist(s): HachBkGrp

Beyond Anger Management: Guided Spiritual Meditations. unabr. ed. John D. Lentz. 1 CD. (Running Time: 32 min.). 2005. audio compact disk 14.95 (978-0-9740978-3-1(7)) Pub: Healing Words. Dist(s): STL Dist NA

Beyond Anima: The Female Self in the Image of God. Read by Joan Chamberlain Engelsman. 1 cass. (Running Time: 90 min.). 1985. 10.95 (978-0-7822-0062-1(1), 168) C G Jung IL.
Part of the conference set "Jung's Challenge to Contemporary Religion.".

Beyond Bad. unabr. ed. Sandra Lee. Read by Kate Hood. 8 cass. (Running Time: 11 hrs.). 2004. 64.00 (978-1-74093-176-2(9)); audio compact disk 98.95 (978-1-74093-507-4(1)) Pub: Bolinda Pubng AUS. Dist(s): Bolinda Pub Inc

Beyond Band of Brothers: The War Memoirs of Major Dick Winters. Dick Winters. Read by Tom Weiner. (Running Time: 36000 sec.). 2006. 65.95 (978-0-7861-4609-3(5)); audio compact disk 72.00 (978-0-7861-6889-7(7)) Blckstn Audio.

Beyond Band of Brothers: The War Memoirs of Major Dick Winters. unabr. ed. Dick Winters. Read by Tom Weiner. Told to Cole C. Kingseed. 10 CDs. (Running Time: 36000 sec.). 2006. audio compact disk 24.95 (978-0-7861-7029-6(8), ZE3769); audio compact disk 29.95 (978-0-7861-7520-8(6), ZM3769); 24.95 (978-0-7861-4584-3(6), E3769) Blckstn Audio.
Beyond Band of Brothers is Winters's memoir, based on his wartime diary, but it also includes his comrades' untold stories. Virtually all this material is being released for the first time. Only Winters was present from the activation of Easy Company until the war's end. He explains the cohesion behind the Band of Brothers and the comradeship that is war's only redeeming quality, the debilitating effect of combat, the horror of seeing friends killed and wounded, and the key qualities that have made him a role model of cool-headed leadership under fire and a recipient of the Distinguished Service Cross. Neither a protest against war nor a glamorization of combat, this is a moving tribute to the human spirit by a man who earned the love and respect of the men of Easy Company and the adulation of new generations worldwide.

Beyond Basketball: Coach K's Keywords for Success. unabr. ed. Mike Krzyzewski & Jamie K. Spatola. (Running Time: 3 hrs.). (ENG.). 2006. 14.98 (978-1-59483-800-2(3)) Pub: Hachet Audio. Dist(s): HachBkGrp

Beyond Basketball: Coach K's Keywords for Success. unabr. ed. Mike Krzyzewski & Jamie K. Spatola. (Running Time: 3 hrs. 30 mins.). (Replay Edition Ser.). (ENG.). 2009. 19.98 (978-1-60788-272-5(8)) Pub: Hachet Audio. Dist(s): HachBkGrp

Beyond Belief. Roy Johansen. Narrated by Richard Ferrone. 9 CDs. (Running Time: 10 hrs.). audio compact disk 89.00 (978-1-4025-2080-8(8)) Recorded Bks.

Beyond Belief. Roy Johansen. Narrated by Richard Ferrone. 7 cass. (Running Time: 10 hrs.). 2001. 65.00 (978-1-4025-0841-7(7), 96690) Recorded Bks.
Dr. Nelson, chair of a university's parapsychology program, is studying someone with extraordinary telekinetic powers when he is murdered. The police call in Detective Joe Bailey, nicknamed the Spirit Basher, to investigate. But when Joe meets the doctor's subject, a shy, eight-year-old boy, he feels his objectivity begin to waver.

Beyond Belief: The Incredible Impact of a Fully Devoted Follower. Joseph M. Stowell. 2 cass. (Running Time: 60 min. per cass.). 1996. 14.99 Set. (978-0-310-20980-5(3)) Zondervan.
Addresses the liberating reality that God is first & foremost interested in using & empowering followers.

Beyond Belief: The Secret Gospel of Thomas. unabr. ed. Elaine Pagels. Read by Cassandra Campbell. 5 cass. (Running Time: 7 hrs. 30 mins.). 2004. 54.00 (978-1-4159-0072-7(8)) Books on Tape.
A noted scholar of religion takes an alternative look at the early history of Christianity.

Beyond Blessings. unabr. ed. Rama Berch. 1 CD. (Chants of Awakening Ser.: Vol. 2). 1999. audio compact disk (978-1-930559-12-7(7)) STC Inc.
Sanskrit chants for during meditation, relaxation, or yoga.

Beyond Blessings, Vol. 1. unabr. ed. Rama Berch. 1 cass. (Chants of Awakening Ser.: Vol. 2). 1999. (978-1-930559-10-3(0)) STC Inc.
Sanskrit chants for use during meditation, relaxation, or yoga.

Beyond Blessings, Vol. 2. unabr. ed. Rama Berch. 1 cass. (Chants of Awakening Ser.: Vol. 2). 1999. (978-1-930559-11-0(9)) STC Inc.

Beyond Booked Solid: Your Business, Your Life, Your Way - It's All Inside. unabr. ed. Michael Port. Read by Michael Port. (Running Time: 6 hrs. 30 mins.). (ENG.). 2008. 24.98 (978-1-59659-239-1(7), GildAudio) Pub: Gildan Media. Dist(s): HachBkGrp

Beyond Booked Solid: Your Business, Your Life, Your Way - It's All Inside. unabr. ed. Michael Port. Read by Michael Port. 7 CDs. (Running Time: 6 hrs. 30 mins.). (ENG.). 2009. audio compact disk 29.98 (978-1-59659-213-1(3), GildAudio) Pub: Gildan Media. Dist(s): HachBkGrp

Beyond Boundaries: EarthBeat! Sampler. 1 cass. (Running Time: 1 hr.). 1991. 6.98 (978-1-877737-72-5(0), EB 2552); audio compact disk 9.98 (978-1-877737-73-2(9), EB D2552) MFLP CA.
Selections from all EarthBeat! titles. Rhythms, melodies & traditions of a dozen cultures.

Beyond Cape Horn. unabr. ed. Charles Neider. Read by Walter Zimmerman. 11 cass. (Running Time: 16 hrs. 30 mins.). 1988. 88.00 (978-0-7366-1322-4(6), 2226) Books on Tape.
The author went to Antarctica in 1977. Ostensibly an observer, he found he had embarked on a journey of self-discover & with a sure sense of what he is about. He also shares with us the trials of ship-board life in frozen seas, the psychological rigors of surviving the deepest of winters, the excitement of expeditions into an awesome landscape.

Beyond Codependency. Melody Beattie. 1 cass. (Running Time: 60 min.). (Discovery Ser.). 1989. 10.00 (978-0-89486-632-6(X), 5609G) Hazelden.

Beyond Codependency: And Getting Better All the Time. abr. ed. Melody Beattie. Read by Gabrielle De Cuir. 1 cass. (Running Time: 1 hr.). 1998. 11.95 (978-1-57453-268-5(5)) Audio Lit.
Includes: learning to accept and deal with the recycling of old behavior patterns, incorporating positive affirmations into thinking, finding and nurturing healthy relationships, unleashing the healing power of gratitude, overcoming feelings of guilt and shame, improving relationships with children.

Beyond Codependency: And Getting Better All the Time, unabr. ed. Melody Beattie. Read by Gabrielle De Cuir. 6 cass. (Running Time: 9 hrs.). 1999. 34.95 (978-1-57453-339-2(8)) Audio Lit.

Beyond Coincidence. Chuck Missler. 2 cass. (Running Time: 2.5 hours +). (Briefing Packages by Chuck Missler). 1994. vinyl bd. 14.95 Inclds. notes. (978-1-880532-67-6(0)) Koinonia Hse.
Is our universe some kind of cosmic accident, or is it the result of careful and skillful design?What do scientists mean by "The Anthropic Principal"?The precision found in our world has long been considered miraculous - as though the earth were purposely created to support life. Coincidence or Design? The rabbis claim that "coincidence is not a kosher word!", and as one studies the hidden structure of the Biblical text itself, there are hints and evidences of skillful design.If designed, then a Designer; If a Designer, then a Purpose.Purpose communicated by a message, and a destiny therein.

Beyond Coincidence. Chuck Missler. 2 CD's. (Running Time: 120 mins.). (Briefing Packages by Chuck Missler). 1996. audio compact disk 19.95 (978-1-57821-294-1(4)) Koinonia Hse.

Beyond Conception. Swami Amar Jyoti. 1 cass. 1979. 9.95 (R-21) Truth Consciousness.
Touching the Source beyond all formulas & conceptions of relativity. Total extinction of ego equals omnipotence. The proof of spirituality.

Beyond Connecticut, Beyond the Sea see Twentieth-Century Poetry in English, No. 24, Recordings of Poets Reading Their Own Poetry

Beyond Consciousness: Ordinary Spirituality. Speeches. Told to Steven Harrison. 2 pieces. (Running Time: 5 hrs.). 2004. 14.95 (978-1-59181-013-1(2)) Pub: Sentient Pubns. Dist(s): Natl Bk Netwk
A two tape set of dialogues that explore living from an integral perspective.

Beyond Counterfeit Leadership: How to Become a More Authentic Leader. Ken Shelton. 1 cass. 1997. 14.95 (978-1-890009-21-2(0)) Exec Excell.

Beyond Creative Blocks. Thomas R. Condon. 1 cass. (Creativity Unlimited Training Ser.). 12.95 (978-1-884305-80-1(6)) Changeworks.
Hypnotic exercises & discussion to deal with limiting beliefs you may have about how creative you can be. This tape will help you overcome inhibiting blocks & see yourself in a new way.

Beyond Culture. unabr. collector's ed. Edward Hall. Read by Donada Peters. 7 cass. (Running Time: 10 hrs. 30 min.). 1987. 56.00 (978-0-7366-1110-7(X), 2036) Books on Tape.
Argues that there are two related crises in today's world. The first & most visible is the population-environmental crisis. The second, more subtle but equally lethal, is humankind's relationships to its extensions, institutions, ideas, as well as the relationships among the many individuals & groups that inhabit the globe.

Beyond Dailiness: Wordsworth. unabr. ed. Benjamin DeMott. 1 cass. (Running Time: 45 min.). 1968. 12.95 (23253) J Norton Pubs.
Demott discusses Wordworth's poetic individuality & romaticism.

Beyond Desire. Gwynne Forster. Narrated by Kim Staunton. 6 cass. (Running Time: 8 hrs.). 71.00 (978-1-4025-1785-3(8)) Recorded Bks.

Beyond Disability. Narrated by Nancie M. Barwick. 1 CD. (Running Time: 50 mins). 2003. audio compact disk 10.00 (978-0-9663488-4-2(2)) Hypnotherapy Wrks.

Beyond Disability: Toward Self-Acceptance & Peace. Nancie M. Barwick. Read by Nancie M. Barwick. 1 cass. 1997. 15.00 (978-0-9663488-1-1(8)) Hypnotherapy Wrks.
Contains sessions entitled "Remembering The Dreams" & "Making Friends" both FULL LENGTH HYPNOTHERAPY SESSIONS.

Beyond Disability: Toward Self-Acceptance & Peace. unabr. ed. Nancie M. Barwick. Read by Nancie M. Barwick. 1 cass. 1997. 15.00 (978-0-9663488-2-8(6)) Hypnotherapy Wrks.
Contains sessions entitled "Moving Forward" and "Self-Improvement" both full length Hypnotherapy Sessions.

Beyond Duck River. unabr. ed. Angela Martin. Read by Beverley Dunn. 8 cass. (Running Time: 10 hrs. 35 mins.). 2005. 64.00 (978-1-74093-547-0(0)) Pub: Bolinda Pubng AUS. Dist(s): Bolinda Pub Inc

Beyond Education: A New Perspective on Society's Management of Learning. Alan M. Thomas. (Higher & Adult Education Ser.). 1991. bk. 36.45 (978-1-55542-311-7(6), Jossey-Bass) Wiley US.

Beyond Entrepreneurship. unabr. collector's ed. James C. Collins & William C. Lazier. Read by Jonathan Reese. 6 cass. (Running Time: 9 hrs.). 1993. 48.00 (978-0-7366-2458-9(9), 3222) Books on Tape.
Blueprint for turning a business into a great company & an enduring one.

Beyond Euphrates. unabr. collector's ed. Freya Stark. Read by Donada Peters. 10 cass. (Running Time: 15 hrs.). 1989. 80.00 (978-0-7366-1615-7(2), 2475) Books on Tape.
Freya Stark fascinates the world with stories of her intrepid travels to the Middle East & lively accounts of her early life. In her first journey, a trip through the Alps in a basket at the age of two. Euphrates takes up the tale at the start of her Eastern travels in 1928 through 1933, undeterred by an illness which threatened her life. Through letters & snatches of her diary, she describes Baghdad, life in a harem in Damascus, journeys in Persia & a treasure hunt in Luristan.

***Beyond Exile: Day by Day Armageddon.** unabr. ed. J. L. Bourne. Read by Jay Snyder. (Running Time: 7 hrs.). (Day by Day Armageddon Ser.). 2010. 39.97 (978-1-4418-7490-0(9), 9781441874900, BADLE); 24.99 (978-1-4418-7488-7(7), 9781441874887, Brilliance MP3); 39.97 (978-1-4418-7489-4(5), 9781441874894, Brlnc Audio MP3 Lib); audio compact disk 24.99 (978-1-4418-7486-3(0), 9781441874863, Bril Audio CD Unabri); audio compact disk 74.97 (978-1-4418-7487-0(9), 9781441874870, BriAudCD Unabrid) Brilliance Audio.

Beyond Expectations: A Parent's Guide to Your Child's Success. Fred Stewart. 2 cass. (Running Time: 2hours.12mins.). 2000. 24.95 (978-0-9728959-0-3(6)) MasteryZone.

Beyond Expectations: Cunning Capers, Exciting Escapades. AIO Team Staff. Prod. by Focus on the Family Staff. Created by Marshal Younger. 4 CDs. (Adventures in Odyssey Gold Ser.). (ENG.). (J). 2005. audio compact disk 24.99 (978-1-58997-075-5(6)) Pub: Focus Family. Dist(s): Tyndale Hse

Beyond Fate. Margaret Visser. 4 CDs. (Running Time: 6 hrs.). 2005. audio compact disk 29.95 (978-0-660-18785-3(X)) Pub: Canadian Broadcasting CAN. Dist(s): Georgetown Term

Beyond Fear & Addictions: Loving Actions for Inner Worth. Speeches. Margaret Paul. Instructed by Margaret Paul. 2 Cass. (Running Time: 2 hrs). 1997. 20.00 (978-0-912389-10-3(9)) Evolving Pubns.
Overview of the Six-Steps of Inner Bonding, visualization to contact personal spiritual guidance, and demonstration working with a person with the Inner Bonding process.

Beyond Glory. Anne Schraff. Narrated by Larry A. McKeever. (Standing Tall 2 Mystery Ser.). (J). 2000. audio compact disk 14.95 (978-1-58659-271-4(8)) Artesian.

Beyond Glory. unabr. ed. Anne Schraff. Narrated by Larry A. McKeever. 1 cass. (Running Time: 40 min.). (Standing Tall 2 Mystery Ser.). (J). 2000. 10.95 (978-1-58659-097-0(9), 54137) Artesian.

Beyond Goals: The Advance Course in Personal Achievement. Roger Dawson. 6 cass. (Running Time: 6 hrs.). 1992. 59.95 set. (274A) Nightingale-Conant.

Beyond Good & Evil. 1947. (MM-8875) Nat'l Recrd Co.

Beyond Good & Evil. Friedrich Nietzsch[illegible]d by Alex Jennings. Told to Roy McMillan. (Complete Classics (Playaw[illegible]). 2008. 54.99 (978-1-60640-529-1(2)) Find a World.

Beyond Grave. Radio Spirits Publishing Staff. 2005. 29.98 (978-1-57019-809-0(8)) Radio Spirits.

Beyond Grief. Richard Jafolla & Mary-Alice Jafolla. Read by Richard Jafolla & Mary-Alice Jafolla. (Overcoming Ser.). 1986. 12.95 (180) Stppng Stones.
Motivational tapes that work on the subconscious mind (subliminal) & conscious mind to bring about self-improvement.

Beyond Humanity. Donald Keyes. 2 cass. 18.00 set. (A0428-89) Sound Photosyn.
When Mr. Keyes, once a speechwriter for U Thant, speaks, he says something very intriguing about extraterrestrials & us.

***Beyond Integrity: A Judeo-Christian Approach to Business Ethics.** ed. Zondervan. (Running Time: 23 hrs. 59 mins. 27 sec.). (ENG.). 2010. 9.99 (978-0-310-86903-0(X)) Zondervan.

Beyond Jabez: Expanding Your Borders. unabr. ed. Bruce Wilkinson. Read by Bruce Wilkinson. 3 pieces. 22.99 (978-1-58926-915-6(2)) Oasis Audio.

Beyond Jabez: Expanding Your Borders. unabr. ed. Bruce Wilkinson. Narrated by Brian Smith. 2005. audio compact disk 25.99 (978-1-58926-914-9(4)) Oasis Audio.

Beyond Jabez: Expanding Your Borders. unabr. ed. Bruce Wilkinson. Narrated by Bruce Wilkinson. (ENG.). 2005. 18.19 (978-1-60814-043-5(1)) Oasis Audio.

Beyond Mars & Venus: An Enlightened Vision of the Man & Woman Thing. 1 cass. 1996. 12.95 (978-0-88050-011-1(5), SA-310) Oshos.

***Beyond Me: Finding Your Way to Life's Next Level.** Zondervan. (Running Time: 4 hrs. 3 mins. 40 sec.). (ENG.). 2010. 18.99 (978-0-310-42762-9(2)) Zondervan.

Beyond 'Me' & Self Image. Swami Amar Jyoti. 2 cass. 1981. 12.95 (C-25) Truth Consciousness.
The nature of selfishness; giving it up. Self image & His Image.

Beyond Medicare: Achieving Long-Term Care Security. Malvin Schechter. (Health Management Ser.). 1993. bk. 44.00 (978-1-55542-583-8(6), Jossey-Bass) Wiley US.

Beyond Mind Games: The Marketing Power of Psychographics. abr. ed. Rebecca Piirto. (Maro Business Reviews Ser.). 1993. 19.95 (978-0-9627362-2-3(8)) Maro Comns.

Beyond Motivation. unabr. ed. Debra Whiddon. 6 cass. (Running Time: 9 hrs.). (Coaching Ser.). 1995. 59.95 Set. (978-1-886112-03-2(7)) Global Dharma Ctr.
These cassettes contain coaching sessions that were recorded live. The first cassette begins with an interview with Debra Whiddon titled - What Is a Coach?.

Beyond Motivation: Waking up the Knowing Within. abr. ed. Debra Whiddon. Read by Debra Whiddon. Read by Doug Bailey. Ed. by Wendy Lackritz et al. 2 cass. (Running Time: 3 hrs.). 1994. 18.95 Set. (978-1-886112-01-8(0)) Global Dharma Ctr.
The cassette is a direct reading of the book by the same title.

Beyond Nab End. William Woodruff. Read by Sam Kelly. (Chivers Audio Bks.). 2003. audio compact disk 79.95 (978-0-7540-8781-6(6)) Pub: Chivers Audio Bks GBR. Dist(s): AudioGO

Beyond Nab End. William Woodruff. Read by Sam Kelly. 2003. 69.95 (978-0-7540-8389-4(6)) Pub: Chivers Audio Bks GBR. Dist(s): AudioGO

Beyond Peptalks & Handouts. 1 cass. 11.95 (978-1-57025-007-1(3)) Whole Person.
Helps you move beyond lectures to design & teach creative learning experiences that involve & motivate participants.

Beyond Perception. Chuck Missler. 2 CD's. (Running Time: 120 mins.). (Briefing Packages by Chuck Missler). 1994. audio compact disk 19.95 (978-1-57821-296-5(0)) Koinonia Hse.
Why do scientists now believe we live in a 10-dimensional universe?Has physics finally reached the very boundaries of reality? This study explores some discoveries in the strange world of quantum physics, superstrings, and the current quest for a "Theory of Everything."Would you take a course in physics using a 1950's textbook? The Bible hasn't changed. It didn't need to.By studying Genesis Chapter 1, Hebrew Cabalists theorized 800 years ago that God established the universe with 10 dimensions.

Beyond Perception. Chuck Missler. 2 cass. (Running Time: 2.5 hours +). (Briefing Packages by Chuck Missler). 1994. vinyl bd. 14.95 Incls. notes. (978-1-880532-68-3(9)) Koinonia Hse.
Why do scientists now believe we live in a 10-dimensional universe?Has physics finally reached the very boundaries of reality?This study explores some discoveries in the strange world of quantum physics, superstrings, and the current quest for a "Theory of Everything."Would you take a course in physics using a 1950's textbook? The Bible hasn't changed. It didn't need to.By studying Genesis Chapter 1, Hebrew Cabalists theorized 800 years ago that God established the universe with 10 dimensions.

Beyond Performance: How Professional Image & Working Style Shape Your Success on the Job. unabr. ed. Roland D. Nolen. 3 cass. (Running Time: 2 hrs. 46 min.). 1996. 49.95 Set. (978-0-9647697-2-4(7)) New Persp IL.
Business motivational seminar that gives a manager's perspective on what it takes to succeed in the workplace. Provides a new twist to the definition of "working smart".

Beyond Positive Thinking: The Advanced Formula for Total Success Revealing a Guaranteed Path to Getting the Results You Want. Robert Anthony. Read by Joe Vitale, Jr. 6 Disc. (Running Time: 25200 sec.). 2006. audio compact disk 119.95 (978-0-9768491-3-1(5), 0976849135) Pub: Morgan James Pubng. Dist(s): IngramPubServ
A No-Nonsense Formula For Getting The Results You Want by Dr Robert AnthonyA common-sense approach to achieving success in one's life offers workable, step-by-step methods and positive visualization techniques to help readers personalize goals, trust creativity, transcend old beliefs and limitations, and transform positive thinking into positive action. Originally published in 1988 Berkley Publishing under the title of "The Advanced Formula For Total Success". For 13 years it continued to sell under that title. In 2002 Berkley Publishing discontinued publishing "The Advanced Formula For Total Success". As soon as it went out of print, it became a collector's item with copies selling for up to $100 per copy on the Amazon.com used books marketplace. In 2003 Dr. Anthony decided to update the book and republish it under the original name of Beyond Positive Thinking with an introduction by Joe Vitale.

Beyond Psychology. unabr. ed. Terence McKenna. 1 cass. 1983. 10.00 (978-1-56964-708-0(9), A0084-83) Sound Photosyn.
Alexander Shulgin is also on this tape, recorded at the Psychedelic Conference '83.

***Beyond Psychotherapy.** Ira Progoff. 2010. 15.00 (978-1-935859-14-7(5)) Dialogue Assoc.

***Beyond Reach.** Graham Hurley. 2010. 89.95 (978-1-4450-0375-7(9)); audio compact disk 99.95 (978-1-4450-0376-4(7)) Pub: Isis Pubng Ltd GBR. Dist(s): Ulverscroft US

Beyond Reach. Karin Slaughter. Read by Joyce Bean. (Grant County Ser.: Bk. 6). 2009. 80.00 (978-1-60775-532-6(7)) Find a World.

Beyond Reach. abr. ed. Karin Slaughter. Read by Joyce Bean. (Running Time: 6 hrs.). (Grant County Ser.: Bk. 6). 2008. audio compact disk 14.99 (978-1-4233-3329-6(2), 9781423333296, BCD Value Price) Brilliance Audio.

Beyond Reach. unabr. ed. Karin Slaughter. Read by Joyce Bean. (Running Time: 14 hrs.). (Grant County Ser.: Bk. 6). 2007. 39.25 (978-1-4233-3327-2(6), 9781423333272, BADLE); 24.95 (978-1-4233-3326-5(8), 9781423333265, BAD); audio compact disk 24.95 (978-1-4233-3324-1(1), 9781423333241, Brilliance MP3); audio compact disk 38.95 (978-1-4233-3322-7(5), 9781423333227, Bril Audio CD Unabri) Brilliance Audio.

Beyond Reach. unabr. ed. Karin Slaughter. Read by Joyce Bean. 10 cass. (Running Time: 50400 sec.). (Grant County Ser.: Bk. 6). 2007. 97.25 (978-1-4233-3321-0(7), 9781423333210, BrilAudUnabridg); audio compact disk 112.25 (978-1-4233-3323-4(3), 9781423333234, BriAudCD Unabrid); audio compact disk 39.25 (978-1-4233-3325-8(X), 9781423333258, Brinc Audio MP3 Lib) Brilliance Audio.

Beyond Recall. unabr. ed. Robert Goddard. Read by Michael Kitchen. 10 cass. (Running Time: 10 hrs.). 1998. 84.95 Set. (978-0-7540-0088-4(5), CAB1511) AudioGO.
Summer, 1981. At a wedding party being given by the Napier family in Cornwall, Chris Napier, the bride's uncle, recognizes a drunken intruder. It is his childhood friend, Nicky Lanyon. Chris hasn't seen him since Nicky's father was hanged for the 1947 murder of Chris' great uncle, Joshua. But when Nicky hangs himself, Chris realizes that there's a lot more to the murder of his great Uncle Joshua.

Beyond Recall. unabr. ed. Robert Goddard. Read by Michael Kitchen. 10 cass. (Running Time: 15 hrs.). 2000. 69.95 (CAB 1511) Pub: Chivers Audio Bks GBR. Dist(s): AudioGO
Summer, 1981. At a wedding party being given by the Napier family in Cornwell, Chris Napier, the bride's uncle, recognizes a drunken intruder. It is his childhood friend, Nicky Lanyon. Chris hasn't seen him since Nicky's father was hanged for the 1947 murder of Chris's great-uncle, Joshua. But when Nicky hangs himself, Chris realizes that there's alot more to the murder of his great-uncle Joshua.

***Beyond Recognition.** abr. ed. Ridley Pearson. Read by Dale Hull. (Running Time: 3 hrs.). (Lou Boldt/Daphne Matthews Ser.). 2010. audio compact disk 9.99 (978-1-4418-6693-6(0), 9781441866936, BCD Value Price) Brilliance Audio.

Beyond Recognition. unabr. ed. Ridley Pearson. Read by Michael Mitchell. 12 cass. (Running Time: 18 hrs.). 1998. 96.00 (978-0-7366-4092-3(4), 4599) Books on Tape.
A homicidal arsonist is loose in Seattle. Single mothers are being killed in fires that burn hotter than experts have ever seen. The children, however, are spared. Why? For Seattle Police Sergeant Lou Boldt & the department's psychologist, Daphne Matthew, the fuel used in these deadly fires is as much a mystery as the identity of the arsonist who sets them. A twelve-year-old boy, caught in an ugly battle at home, unintentionally witnesses a transaction involving the alleged arsonist.

Beyond Recognition. unabr. ed. Ridley Pearson. Read by Dale Hull. (Running Time: 16 hrs.). (Lou Boldt/Daphne Matthews Ser.). 2005. 49.97 (978-1-59710-046-5(3), 9781597100465, BADLE); 24.95 (978-1-59710-047-2(1), 9781597100472, BAD); 24.95 (978-1-59335-801-3(6), 9781593358013, Brilliance MP3); 39.25 (978-1-59335-935-5(7), 9781593359355, Brinc Audio MP3 Lib) Brilliance Audio.
A strange series of fires is raging in Seattle - white-hot fires that burn so cleanly even the ash is consumed, along with all traces of the fires' victims. Brilliant forensic investigator Police Sergeant Lou Boldt is back, battling the mysterious arsonist. He is also keeping his eye on the Fire Warden, who seems to be a little too close to the heat. But police psychologist Daphne Matthews is more concerned about the victims of the blazes, especially the smart and wily ten-year-old boy who had a terrifying encounter with a disfigured, badly burned man. Beyond Recognition is the story of a deadly, taunting game of cat and mouse, where the stakes are raised to a burning poing that might spell disaster for Boldt - and the city of Seattle.

***Beyond Recognition.** unabr. ed. Ridley Pearson. Read by Dale Hull. (Running Time: 15 hrs.). (Lou Boldt/Daphne Matthews Ser.). 2010. audio compact disk 29.99 (978-1-4418-4043-1(5), 9781441840431, Bril Audio CD Unabri); audio compact disk 89.97 (978-1-4418-4044-8(3), 9781441840448, BriAudCD Unabrid) Brilliance Audio.

Beyond Religion: Spirituality Outside the Churches. John Shea. 1 cass. 1996. 8.95 (978-0-87946-150-8(0), 329) ACTA Pubns.

Beyond Secretary: How to Establish Credibility, Earn Respect & Get Ahead. Debra Sutch. 4 cass. (Running Time: 3 hrs. 24 min.). 49.95 Set incl. 24p. wkbk. (V10151) CareerTrack Pubns.
Think of this program as an investment in your future. It's ideal training for you - & all the secretaries/administrative assistants in your organization.

Beyond Shyness: How to Conquer Social & Performance Anxieties. Scripts. Jonathan Berent. 12 CDs. (Running Time: 10 hrs.). 2003. ring bd. 299.00 (978-0-9669862-1-0(0)) J Berent.
Self-Therapy Audio Program comprised of treatment methodology, self-help technique, and interviews accompanied by a workbook.

Beyond Sing-Along. Brilliant Beginnings, LLC Staff. 1 cass. 1999. audio compact disk (978-0-9665815-8-4(X)) Brllnt Begnngs.

Beyond Solar & Lunar Returns. Barbara J. Junceau. 1 cass. 1992. 8.95 (1050) Am Fed Astrologers.

Beyond Spirit Tailings: Montana's Mysteries, Ghosts, & Haunted Places. abr. ed. Ellen Baumler. Read by Ellen Baumler. (ENG.). 2007. audio compact disk 25.95 (978-0-9721522-9-7(6)) Pub: MT Hist Soc. Dist(s): Globe Pequot

Beyond Spiritual Gifts: Ben Young August 15, 1999. Ben Young. 1999. 4.95 (978-0-7417-6144-6(0), B0144) Win Walk.

Beyond Squirt Gun Christianity Tape #4: Room for Doubt Series. Ben Young. 2000. 4.95 (978-0-7417-6205-4(6), B0205) Win Walk.

Beyond Success. David L. Cook. (ENG.). 2003. audio compact disk 34.95 (978-0-9742650-1-8(2)) Sacred Story.

Beyond Success: The Fifteen Secrets of a Winning Life! Brian D. Biro. 8 cass. (Running Time: 7 hrs. 40 min.). 4.50 Set. (978-0-9647453-9-1(9)) Pygmalion Pr.

Beyond Success: Where Will I Find Life's Meaning, When Ambition Is No Longer Enough? Layne A. Longfellow. Read by Layne A. Longfellow. 1 cass. (Running Time: 70 min.). 1986. 12.00 Lect Theatre.
Topics discussed include: High School Hero Confronts Midlife Reality; Women Seek Competence While Men Seek Intimacy; Going Beyond the Expectations of Others & of Our Own Youth.

Beyond Suffering, Set. Black Bear. 2 cass. (Running Time: 1 hr. 45 mins.). 2000. 30.00 (978-0-9700042-5-3(7), DI014) Divine Ideas.
A message for the year 2000, designed to create understanding of our personal attitudes towards suffering & bliss.

Beyond Summer Dreams. Jennie L. Hansen. 6 cass. 2004. 19.95 (978-1-57734-890-0(7)) Covenant Comms.

Beyond Survival. unabr. ed. Gerry W. Gotro. Read by Rusty Nelson. 8 cass. (Running Time: 10 hrs.). 2001. 49.95 (978-1-55686-751-4(4)) Books in Motion.
A Cessna float plane on a scientific venture into the wilderness of northern Canada crashes and three people are injured and stranded in bitter cold. Now they must combine their skills and prepare for a life and death struggle against natures worst condition.

Beyond Survival: Recovery for Children of Alcoholics. Cathleen Brooks. 1 cass. 1986. 7.95 (6905) Hazelden.
An uplifting talk by the author of "The Secret Everyone Knows".

Beyond Survival Workshop: 90-Minute Convention Workshop. unabr. ed. Diana Waring. Read by Diana Waring. 1 cass. (Running Time: 1 hr. 30 mins.). 1997. 8.95 (978-1-930514-03-4(4)) Diana Waring.

Beyond Survivorship. unabr. ed. Gary Arnold. 1 cass. (Running Time: 1 hr. 03 min.). 1997. pap. bk. 12.95 (978-1-57867-308-7(9)) Windhorse Corp.
Self help on how to handle pain & pleasure, handle problems, honor your potential.

***Beyond Suspicion.** abr. ed. James Grippando. Read by Tom Wopat. (ENG.). 2004. (978-0-06-082403-7(4), Harper Audio); (978-0-06-082404-4(2), Harper Audio) HarperCollins Pubs.

Beyond Suspicion. abr. ed. James Grippando. Read by Tom Wopat. (Running Time: 19800 sec.). 2006. audio compact disk 14.95 (978-0-06-087728-6(6)) HarperCollins Pubs.

Beyond Suspicion. unabr. ed. James Grippando. Narrated by L. J. Ganser. 7 cass. (Running Time: 10 hrs. 15 mins.). 2002. 67.00 (978-1-4025-2685-5(7)) Recorded Bks.

Beyond Suspicion. unabr. ed. James Grippando. Narrated by L. J. Ganser. 7 cass. (Running Time: 10 hrs. 15 mins.). 2002. 49.95 (978-1-4025-2686-2(5), RG143) Recorded Bks.
When Jack?s gorgeous ex-girlfriend Jessie Merrill learns she doesn?t have long to live, she arranges a viatical settlement with her life insurance company. Problems arise when it is discovered she was misdiagnosed. Now that she?s not going to die anytime soon, the investors who paid the 1.5 million against her life-insurance policy want their money back. Jack agrees to help her out pro-bono and amazingly pulls off a brilliant victory on court. However, two days later he finds himself on a collision course with his past and a killer who is "beyond suspicion".

Beyond Territory. Read by Osel Tendzin. 4 cass. 1977. 40.50 (A051) Vajradhatu.
Four talks: 1) Territory & the Three Poisons; 2) Motivation & Attitude; 3) The Process of Ego; 4) The Three Yanas Approach to Territory.

Beyond the Aquila Rift. Alastair Reynolds. Read by Tom Dheere. (ENG.). 2008. audio compact disk 10.99 (978-1-884612-77-0(6)) AudioText.

Beyond the Baby Blues: Program from the Award Winning Public Radio Series. Interview. Hosted by Fred Goodwin. 1 CD. (Running Time: 1 hr). (Infinite Mind Ser.). 2001. audio compact disk 21.95 (978-1-888064-87-2(0), LCM 180) Lichtenstein Creat.
Texas mother Andrea Yates drowned her five children; her family says she was suffering from postpartum depression and psychosis. This week, we look beyond the headlines to explore these potentially devastating illnesses. Guests include psychiatrist Dr. Deborah Sichel, who co-founded the Hestia Institute, a mental health center for women and families; law expert Michelle Oberman, who has written about mothers who kill their children; and Dr. Joseph Hibbeln, a psychiatrist, lipid biologist and Chief of the Outpatient Clinic at the National Institute on Alcohol Abuse and Alcoholism, part of the National Institutes of Health; and women who have suffered from these illnesses.

Beyond the Basics: Communicative Chinese for Intermediate-Advanced Learners. Jianhua Bai et al. 2 cass. (Running Time: 30 mins.). (CHI & ENG.). (gr. k up). 1995. 34.95 (978-0-88727-250-9(9)) Cheng Tsui.

Beyond the Bedroom Wall. Larry Woiwode. Read by Larry Woiwode. 1 cass. (Running Time: 41 min.). 1984. 13.95 (978-1-55644-117-2(7), 4141) Am Audio Prose.
Woiwode gives a performance of "The Street" taken from "Beyond the Bedroom Wall".

Beyond the Black Stump. unabr. ed. Nevil Shute. Read by Robin Bailey. 8 cass. (Running Time: 12 hrs.). 2000. 59.95 (978-0-7451-4080-3(7), CAB 777) Pub: Chivers Audio Bks GBR. Dist(s): AudioGO
Now a successful and well-traveled geologist, Stanton Laird's past wrong's and heritage stay with him still. As a teenager in Oregon, he was involved in a car accident with consequences that continue to haunt him when he travels to Australia on a drilling expedition. When he meets Mollie Regan in this vast and arid land, a new chapter in his life begins. But when they visit America together, cultural and personal differences create trouble. On two vast continents, they must both learn to cross new frontiers and reach new understandings.

Beyond the Black Stump. unabr. ed. Nevil Shute. Narrated by Davina Porter. 7 cass. (Running Time: 9 hrs. 30 mins.). 1988. 60.00 (978-1-55690-051-8(1), 88480E7) Recorded Bks.
When Stanton Laird, American geologist, goes prospecting for the Topeka Exploration Company in the savage Australian outback, he finds something a good deal more precious than oil.

Beyond the Blonde. abr. ed. Kathleen Flynn-Hui. Read by Susan Ericksen. (Running Time: 14400 sec.). 2006. audio compact disk 14.99 (978-1-59737-748-5(1), 9781597377485, BCD Value Price) Brilliance Audio.
Welcome to Jean-Luc, New York's hottest salon du jour, where high above Madison Avenue, Georgia Watkins - star colorist - tends the hair of socialites, actresses, models, and moguls. Georgia wasn't born to the Manhattan elite, but she was born to color hair; back in tiny Weepeekeemie, New Hampshire, her single mother struggled to pay rent on her own small-town beauty parlor to keep the family afloat. Yet Georgia wants more from life. And so, after a stint at Wilfred Academy, she lands a job at Jean-Luc and moves to New York City. Thrust into a glitzy, glittering, over-the-top world, she finds herself highlighting dogs' hair to match that of their owners', making house calls to the Hamptons, and barely batting a well-groomed eyelash at a thousand-dollar tip. A rising star in the salon, Georgia is far too busy for romance or even a day off...until she finds that her quiet, handsome colleague Massimo has more to offer than styling pointers. With a loving boyfriend, a calendar brimming with devoted clients, and unexpected career opportunities at her fingertips, Georgia's life feels as golden as her customers' favorite hair color. But when she is betrayed in an unthinkable turn of events, Georgia Watkins from New Hampshire finds her loyalty and love put to the test - and she must depend on the most unlikely people to help her navigate the ugly side of beauty.

Beyond the Blonde. unabr. ed. Kathleen Flynn-Hui. Read by Susan Ericksen. (Running Time: 8 hrs.). 2005. 39.25 (978-1-59737-746-1(5), 9781597377461, BADLE); 24.95 (978-1-59737-745-4(7), 9781597377454, BAD); 74.25 (978-1-59737-740-9(6), 9781597377409, BrilAudUnabridg); audio compact disk 24.95 (978-1-59737-743-0(0), 9781597377430,

Brilliance MP3); audio compact disk 32.95 (978-1-59737-741-6(4), 9781597377416, Bril Audio CD Unabri); audio compact disk 87.25 (978-1-59737-742-3(2), 9781597377423, BriAudCD Unabrid); audio compact disk 39.25 (978-1-59737-744-7(9), 9781597377447, Brinc Audio MP3 Lib) Brilliance Audio.

Beyond the Blue Hills. Katie Flynn. 2007. 89.95 (978-1-84559-707-8(9)); audio compact disk 99.95 (978-1-84559-708-5(7)) Pub: Soundings Ltd GBR. Dist(s): Ulverscroft US

Beyond the Blush: Facing the Inner Invalid. 1 cass. (Care Cassettes Ser.: Vol. 15, No. 5). 1988. 10.80 Assn Prof Chaplains.

***Beyond the Body Farm.** abr. ed. Bill Bass & Jon Jefferson. Read by Tom Mckeon. (ENG.). 2007. (978-0-06-155433-9(2)); (978-0-06-155435-3(9)) HarperCollins Pubs.

Beyond the Body Farm: A Legendary Bone Detective Explores Murders, Mysteries, & the Revolution in Forensic Science. abr. ed. Bill Bass & Jon Jefferson. Read by Tom McKeon. (Running Time: 21600 sec.). 2007. audio compact disk 29.95 (978-0-06-136358-0(8), Harper Audio) HarperCollins Pubs.

***Beyond the Box: Expand Your Blues/Rock Guitar Soloing.** Buzz Feiten. (ENG.). 2010. pap. bk. 12.99 (978-1-60378-175-6(7), 1603781757) Pub: Cherry Lane. Dist(s): H Leonard

Beyond the Brain: Birth, Death, & Transcendence. unabr. ed. Stanislov Grof. 2 cass. 1987. 18.00 set. (978-1-56964-815-5(8), A0032-87) Sound Photosyn.

Beyond the Chocolate War. unabr. ed. Robert Cormier. Narrated by George Guidall. 6 pieces. (Running Time: 8 hrs. 15 mins.). (gr. 8 up). 1994. 51.00 (978-0-7887-0012-5(X), 94211E7) Recorded Bks.
In this sequel to "The Chocolate War," several months have passed since Jerry Renault took his stand against the Vigils & almost paid for it with his life. Now, the Vigils are up to their old tricks again. But a mood of defiance is growing in the boys at Trinity School & it looks as if even Archie's days as school bully are numbered.

Beyond the City. Arthur Conan Doyle. Contrib. by Shelly Frasier. (Unabridged Classics (Playaway) Ser.). (ENG.). 2009. 59.99 (978-1-60775-764-1(8)) Find a World.

Beyond the City. Arthur Conan Doyle. Read by Shelly Frasier. (ENG.). 2001. audio compact disk 58.00 (978-1-4001-3016-0(6)) Pub: Tantor Media. Dist(s): IngramPubServ

Beyond the City. unabr. ed. Arthur Conan Doyle. Narrated by Shelly Frasier. 4 CDs. (Running Time: 3 hrs. 49 mins.). (ENG.). 2001. audio compact disk 29.00 (978-1-4001-0016-3(X)); audio compact disk 20.00 (978-1-4001-5016-8(7)) Pub: Tantor Media. Dist(s): IngramPubServ

Beyond the City. unabr. ed. Arthur Conan Doyle. Narrated by Shelly Frasier. (Running Time: 3 hrs. 30 mins. 0 sec.). (ENG.). 2009. lab manual ed. 35.99 (978-1-4001-4097-8(8)); audio compact disk 17.99 (978-1-4001-1097-1(1)); audio compact disk 17.99 (978-1-4001-6097-6(9)) Pub: Tantor Media. Dist(s): IngramPubServ

Beyond the Cornucopia Kids (Live) Back to Basics Strategies for Parents. Bruce A. Baldwin. 2 cass. (Running Time: 90 min. per cass.). 1991. 18.95 set, vinyl case. (978-0-933583-19-1(2), PDC 202); 49.95 video, 90 mins. (978-0-933583-17-7(6), VCR 102) Direction Dynamics.
In this program, Dr. Baldwin provides, in one of his popular talks, an overview of the characteristics of Cornucopia Kids & specific strategies for parents to effectively prevent or reverse this pattern so destructive to personal maturity & achievement motivation.

Beyond the Deepwoods. unabr. ed. Paul Stewart & Chris Riddell. Read by Clive Mantle. 5 CDs. (Running Time: 6 hrs. 17 mins.). (Edge Chronicles Ser.: Bk. 1). (J). 2005. audio compact disk 38.25 (978-0-307-24603-5(5), Listening Lib); 35.00 (978-0-307-24602-8(7), Listening Lib) Random Audio Pubg.
Thirteen-year-old Twig, having always looked and felt different from his woodtroll family, learns that he is adopted and travels out of his Deepwoods home to find the place where he belongs.

Beyond the Earth - Two. 1 cass. (Running Time: 28 min.). 14.95 (23349) MMI Corp.
Life on other planets - Can we visit them? Will they be like us? Someday we will have to face other life forms - is the conclusion.

Beyond the Feminine Principle: A Post-Jungian View. Read by Andrew Samuels. 1 cass. (Running Time: 2 hrs.). 1987. 12.95 (978-0-7822-0240-3(3), 261) C G Jung IL.

Beyond the Formula. Brenda Wilbee. 1 cass. (Running Time: 45 min.). (How to Write Best-Selling Romance Ser.: Tape 3). 1988. 7.95 (978-0-943777-10-8(0)) byBrenda.

Beyond the Gap. unabr. ed. Harry Turtledove. Narrated by William Dufris. (Running Time: 15 hrs. 0 mins. 0 sec.). (Opening of the World Ser.). (ENG.). 2007. audio compact disk 39.99 (978-1-4001-0382-9(7)); audio compact disk 29.99 (978-1-4001-5382-4(4)); audio compact disk 79.99 (978-1-4001-3382-6(3)) Pub: Tantor Media. Dist(s): IngramPubServ

Beyond the Gathering Storm. Janette Oke. Narrated by Barbara Caruso. 6 CDs. (Running Time: 7 hrs. 15 mins.). (Canadian West Ser.: Vol. 5). audio compact disk 59.00 (978-0-7887-9877-1(4)) Recorded Bks.

Beyond the Gathering Storm. unabr. ed. Janette Oke. Read by Marguerite Gavin. 5 CDs. (Running Time: 7 hrs.). (Canadian West Ser.: Vol. 5). 2002. audio compact disk 40.00 (978-0-7861-9487-2(1), 2974) Blckstn Audio.
As a youth, Henry was rescued from terrible circumstances by the Delaneys. Their love and care for him helped to heal those painful memories, and he now has grown into a young man of character and deep faith. Henry follows his father into the Royal Canadian Mounted Police, and as representative of the law, he faces some duties that leave him with haunting memories, particularly of the young widow and baby boy whom he longs to help. But her tragic loss and deep grief have left her frightened and emotionally vulnerable.

Beyond the Gathering Storm. unabr. ed. Janette Oke. Read by Marguerite Gavin. 5 cass. (Running Time: 7 hrs.). (Canadian West Ser.: Vol. 5). 2003. 39.95 (978-0-7861-2276-9(5), 2974) Blckstn Audio.

Beyond the Gathering Storm. unabr. ed. Janette Oke. Narrated by Barbara Caruso. 5 cass. (Running Time: 7 hrs. 15 mins.). (Canadian West Ser.: Vol. 5). 2001. 48.00 (978-0-7887-5142-4(5), K0029E7) Recorded Bks.
A close knit family facing separation & change. Years ago, Wynn & Elizabeth Delancy adopted Henry & Christine. Now Christine has moved to a job in the city & Henry has joined the Canadian Mounties.

Beyond the Goal. Eliyahu M. Goldratt. Read by Eliyahu M. Goldratt. (Running Time: 5 hrs. 45 mins.). 2005. 42.95 (978-1-59912-167-3(0)) Iofy Corp.

Beyond the Goal: Eliyahu M. Goldratt Speaks on the Theory of Constraints. unabr. ed. Eliyahu M. Goldratt. 8 CDs. (Running Time: 6 hrs.). (ENG.). 2005. audio compact disk 29.98 (978-1-59659-023-6(8)) Pub: Gildan Media. Dist(s): HachBkGrp

Beyond the Gold. Thomas F. Crum. 1 cass. 1988. 10.00 (978-1-877803-00-0(6)) Aiki Works.
Relationships, self-fulfillment in life & work.

Beyond the Grave. Jude Watson. Read by David Pittu. 4 CDs. (Running Time: 4 hrs. 37 mins.). (39 Clues Ser.: Bk. 4). (J). (gr. 4-7). 2009. audio compact disk 49.95 (978-0-545-13880-2(9)) Scholastic Inc.

Beyond the Grave, Bk. 4. Jude Watson & David Pittu. (ENG.). (J). (gr. 4-7). 2009. audio compact disk 19.95 (978-0-545-13865-9(5)) Scholastic Inc.

Beyond the Great Snow Mountains. unabr. ed. Louis L'Amour. Read by Terrence Mann. 4 cass. 1999. 25.00 (FS9-50891) Highsmith.

Beyond the Green Hills. unabr. ed. Anne Doughty. 10 CDs. (Soundings (CDs) Ser.). 2007. audio compact disk 89.95 (978-1-84559-509-8(2)) Pub: ISIS Lrg Prnt GBR. Dist(s): Ulverscroft US

Beyond the Green Hills. unabr. ed. Anne Doughty. Read by Caroline Lennon. 10 cass. (Soundings Ser.). 2007. 84.95 (978-1-84559-424-4(X)) Pub: ISIS Lrg Prnt GBR. Dist(s): Ulverscroft US

Beyond the Hedge. Roby James. 2006. audio compact disk 19.95 (978-0-8095-6231-2(6)) Diamond Book Dists.

Beyond the Hedge. Roby James. 2006. audio compact disk 29.95 (978-0-8095-6232-9(4)) Diamond Book Dists.

Beyond the Hero. Allan B. Chinen. Read by Dan Keding. 1 cass. (Running Time: 65 min.). (American Storytelling Ser.). 1997. 12.00 (978-0-87483-428-4(7)) August Hse.
These tales from around the world portray fathers & sons battling for power, facing their shadows, meeting the trickster & learning playfulness, camaraderie & wisdom. Finally, they introduce male archetypes that are healers rather than heroes.

Beyond the Highland Mist. unabr. ed. Karen Marie Moning. Read by Phil Gigante. (Running Time: 10 hrs.). (Highlander Ser.). 2007. 39.25 (978-1-4233-4131-4(7), 9781423341314, BADLE); 24.95 (978-1-4233-4130-7(9), 9781423341307, BAD); 82.25 (978-1-4233-4125-3(2), 9781423341253, BrilAudUnabridg); audio compact disk 39.25 (978-1-4233-4129-1(5), 9781423341291, Brinc Audio MP3 Lib); audio compact disk 97.25 (978-1-4233-4127-7(9), 9781423341277, BriAudCD Unabrid); audio compact disk 29.95 (978-1-4233-4126-0(0), 9781423341260, Bril Audio CD Unabri); audio compact disk 24.95 (978-1-4233-4128-4(7), 9781423341284, Brilliance MP3) Brilliance Audio.

***Beyond the Hundredth Meridian: John Wesley Powell & the Second Opening of the West.** unabr. ed. Wallace Stegner. (Running Time: 17 hrs. 30 mins.). 2010. 44.95 (978-1-4417-3601-7(8)); 95.95 (978-1-4417-3597-3(6)); audio compact disk 34.95 (978-1-4417-3600-0(X)); audio compact disk 123.00 (978-1-4417-3598-0(4)) Blckstn Audio.

Beyond the Hundredth Meridian: John Wesley Powell & the Second Opening of the West. unabr. collector's ed. Wallace Stegner. Read by Larry McKeever. 13 cass. (Running Time: 19 hrs. 30 mins.). 1996. 104.00 (978-0-7366-3248-5(4), 3906) Books on Tape.
John Wesley Powell fought in the Civil War & it cost him an arm. But it didn't stop him from exploring the American West.

Beyond the Khyber Pass. unabr. ed. John H. Waller. Read by Grover Gardner. 9 cass. (Running Time: 13 hrs. 30 min.). 1991. 72.00 (978-0-7366-2037-6(0), 2851) Books on Tape.
Chronicles wars & intrigue in India & Afghanistan during the 19th century - the "Great Game" that culminated in the siege of Kabul & the deaths of 16,000 British soldiers, their families & camp followers. Only a handful escaped to tell the story.

Beyond the Koan. Da Avabhasa. 1 cass. 1992. 11.95 (978-0-918801-71-5(0)) Dawn Horse Pr.

Beyond the Last Lamp see Poetry of Thomas Hardy

***Beyond the Law Frontier.** Ray Nafziger. 2009. (978-1-60136-389-3(3)) Audio Holding.

Beyond the Law Frontier. Ray Nafziger. (Running Time: 1 hr.). 2000. 10.95 (978-1-60083-545-2(7)) Iofy Corp.

Beyond the Locket: Surviving Parental Separation. Alan Saunders. 2 CDs. 2004. audio compact disk 22.95 (978-1-881917-13-7(4)) Acovianbooks.

Beyond the Man-Made Mind. J. Krishnamurti. 1 cass. (Running Time: 75 min.). (Krishnamurti & Professor David Bohm - 1980 Ser.: No. 12). 8.50 (ABD8012) Krishnamurti.
Krishnamurti & Prof. Bohm offer penetrating, in-depth dialogues which shed light on the fundamental issues of existence.

Beyond the Map's Boundary: A Timely Sort of an Adventure, Vol. 1. Nibi Soto. Chris Humpherys. Music by Jack Waldenmaier. (Running Time: 407). 1. (ENG., (YA). 2009. audio compact disk 24.95 (978-0-9629060-0-8(X)) Thornock Intl.

Beyond the Mechanical Mind. unabr. ed. Australian Broadcasting Corporation Staff. 12 cass. (Running Time: 15 hrs.). 96.00 (S29372) J Norton Pubs.
Psychologists are interviewed about new science approaches constituting an intellectual & social movement in Western cultures.

Beyond the Mirror: Reflections on Death & Life. 1 cass. (Care Cassettes Ser.: Vol. 18, No. 7). 1991. 10.80 Assn Prof Chaplains.

Beyond the Mirror: Reflections on Death & Life. unabr. ed. Henri J. M. Nouwen. Read by Paul Smith. 1 CD. (Running Time: 3600 sec.). 2006. audio compact disk 16.95 (978-0-86716-813-6(7)) St Anthony Mess Pr.

Beyond the Night Sky. Perf. by Alex De Grassi. 1 cass.; 1 CD. 1998. 10.98 (978-1-56628-101-0(6), 72537); audio compact disk 15.98 CD. (978-1-56628-100-3(8), 72537D) MFLP CA.

Beyond the Outposts. Max Brand & Kristoffer Tabori. 6 cass. (Running Time: 8 hrs.). 2002. 44.95 (978-0-7861-2620-0(5), 3210) Blckstn Audio.

Beyond the Outposts. unabr. ed. Max Brand. Read by Kristoffer Tabori. 7 CDs. (Running Time: 8 hrs.). 2001. audio compact disk 56.00 (978-0-7861-8893-2(6), 3210) Blckstn Audio.

Beyond the Outposts. unabr. ed. Max Brand. Read by Kristoffer Tabori. 7 CDs. (Running Time: 9 hrs.). 2004. audio compact disk 35.95 (978-0-7861-8880-2(4)); reel tape 29.95 (978-0-7861-2656-9(6)) Blckstn Audio.
As Lew Dorset journeys west in search of his father, he meets Chuck Morris and together they fight the Cheyenne. Befriending the Sioux, they absorb the native culture. When Chuck falls into trouble, Lew's attempts to help him culminate in near fatal danger.

Beyond the Outposts. unabr. ed. Max Brand. Read by Kristoffer Tabori. (Running Time: 8 hrs.). 2006. audio compact disk 24.95 (978-0-7861-8755-3(7), 3210) Blckstn Audio.

Beyond the Outsider. unabr. ed. Colin Wilson. 2 cass. 18.00 (OC92) Sound Horizons AV.

Beyond the Pale. unabr. ed. John Hooker. Read by Stanley McGeagh. 14 cass. (Running Time: 21 hrs.). 1999. (978-1-86442-362-4(5), 590167) Bolinda Pubng AUS.
In 1839 John Harrington voyages 12,000 miles from Ireland into the unknown to take up a a sheep-run in the southern regions of Australia. From a distinguished family of Anglo-Irish aristocrats who have fallen on hard times, the youngest son has been sent to the remotest part of the world to make his fortune. For twenty years Harrington prospers but he is plagued by a sense of dislocation & loneliness in a hostile place. When he is joined by his drunken brother & married sister, tragedy & violence ensue. A story of displacement, racial brutality & treachery in an unforgiving & misunderstood landscape.

Beyond the Passion - Audio Book. 3 CDs. (Running Time: 4 hrs. 24 mins.). 2005. audio compact disk 19.99 (978-0-9770146-0-6(6)) Br Bu.

Beyond the Past. Ragini E. Michaels. Read by Ragini E. Michaels. Music by Divyam Ambodha. 1 cass. (Running Time: 30 min.). (Remembrance Ser.). 1988. 14.95 (978-0-9628686-5-8(5), FTAT-103) Facticity Tr.
Guides your unconscious mind how to let go of what is no longer needed, keeping the learnings & freeing you to move beyond those conditionings of long ago. Soothing combination of feminine voice & original music.

Beyond the Reef. unabr. ed. Alexander Kent, pseud. Read by Michael Jayston. 8 cass. (Running Time: 12 hrs.). (Richard Bolitho Ser.: Bk. 19). 2000. 59.95 (978-0-7451-4146-6(3), CAB 829) Pub: Chivers Audio Bks GBR. Dist(s): AudioGO
It is 1808, and war is spreading in Europe as Napoleon holds portugal and threatens Spain. Vice-Admiral Richard Bolitho is ordered to the Cape of Good Hope to establish a permanent naval force. When the ship is capsized, a hundred-mile reef off the Coast of Africa becomes a symbol of survival.

***Beyond the Reflection's Edge.** Bryan Davis. (Running Time: 10 hrs. 16 mins. 31 sec.). (Echoes from the Edge Ser.). (ENG.). (YA). 2009. 12.99 (978-0-310-29425-2(8)) Zondervan.

Beyond the Secret: Spiritual Power & the Law of Attraction. unabr. ed. Lisa Love. Read by Lisa Love. (Running Time: 5 hrs. 20 mins.). (ENG.). 2009. 24.98 (978-1-59659-334-3(2), GildAudio) Pub: Gildan Media. Dist(s): HachBkGrp

Beyond the Shadows. unabr. ed. Robin Lee Hatcher. 5 cass. (Running Time: 7 hrs. 15 mins.). 2004. 59.75 (978-1-4193-1023-2(2), K1123MC) Recorded Bks.

Beyond the Shadows. unabr. ed. Brent Weeks. Narrated by Paul Boehmer. (Running Time: 23 hrs. 30 mins. 0 sec.). (Night Angel Trilogy). (ENG.). 2009. audio compact disk 49.99 (978-1-4001-1288-3(5)) Pub: Tantor Media. Dist(s): IngramPubServ

Beyond the Shadows. unabr. ed. Brent Weeks. Narrated by Paul Boehmer. (Running Time: 23 hrs. 30 mins. 0 sec.). (Night Angel Trilogy: Bk. 3). (ENG.). 2009. 34.99 (978-1-4001-6288-8(2)); audio compact disk 99.99 (978-1-4001-4288-0(1)) Pub: Tantor Media. Dist(s): IngramPubServ

***Beyond the Shadows.** unabr. ed. Brent Weeks. Narrated by Paul Boehmer. (Running Time: 23 hrs. 30 mins.). (Night Angel Trilogy: Bk. 3). 2009. 25.99 (978-1-4001-8288-6(3)); 49.99 (978-1-4001-9288-5(9)) Tantor Media.

***Beyond the Shadows, Pt. 1 of 2** Brent Weeks. (Night Angel Trilogy: Bk. 3). 2010. audio compact disk 19.99 (978-1-59950-681-4(5)) GraphicAudio.

***Beyond the Shadows (2 Of 2) The Night Angel Trilogy.** Brent Week. 2010. audio compact disk 19.99 (978-1-59950-682-1(3)) GraphicAudio.

Beyond the Shining Water. unabr. ed. Audrey Howard. Read by Carole Boyd. 12 cass. (Running Time: 18 hrs.). 2001. 96.95 (978-0-7540-0653-4(0), CAB 2075) AudioGO.
In 19th century Liverpool, Lily Elliott is not so much spoiled as loved, petted and indulged by her adored Ma and Pa, dreaming of the day when she will be captain of Pa's ship, the Lily-Jane of Liverpool. Until the day comes, however, when news arrived that Richard Elliott is dead. As her mother sinks into a dream world and the money that had always seemed sufficient turns out to have been mostly debts, Lily watches bewildered as her safe, happy world falls apart.

Beyond the Spirit World. Gordon T. Allred. 2 cass. 1994. 11.95 Set. (978-1-57008-090-6(9), Bkcraft Inc) Deseret Bk.

Beyond the Subconscious: The Ultimate Mind Game. Chuck Francis. Read by Chuck Francis. 2 cass. (Running Time: 2 hrs. 30 min.). 1989. 15.95 (978-0-9620761-1-4(2)) Imagin Store.
Rendition of the book plus added notes by the author pertaining to The Last Resort section.

Beyond the Summit: The Next Steps in Arms Control. 1 cass. (Running Time: 1 hr.). 10.95 (NP-87-12-15, HarperThor) HarpC GBR.

Beyond the Sunset: 25 Hymn Stories Celebrating the Hope of Heaven. Kenneth W. Osbeck. 1 cass. (Running Time: 1 hr. 30 mins.). 2001. 6.99 (978-0-8254-3444-0(0)) Kregel.

Beyond the Sunset: 25 Hymn Stories Celebrating the Hope of Heaven. Kenneth W. Osbeck. 2001. audio compact disk 11.99 (978-0-8254-3443-3(2)) Kregel.

Beyond the Typewriter. unabr. ed. 6 cass. (Running Time: 6 hrs.). (Seminars on Tape Ser.). 1980. pap. bk. 49.95 Prof Train TX.
Explores changing roles of the office professional, how to work with different management styles, applying assertiveness principles & managing stress for increased effectiveness.

Beyond the Valley of the Gift Police. abr. ed. Jello Biafra. 3 cass. (Running Time: 3 hrs.). 2000. 14.98 (978-1-902593-12-8(X), AK Pr San Fran) AK Pr Dist.

Beyond the Valley of the Gift Police. abr. ed. Jello Biafra. 3 CDs. (Running Time: 3 hrs.). (AK Press Audio Ser.). (ENG.). 1999. audio compact disk 19.98 (978-1-902593-11-1(1)) Pub: AK Pr GBR. Dist(s): Consort Bk Sales

Beyond the Valley of Thorns. Patrick Carman. Read by Aasne Vigesaa. (Land of Elyon Ser.: Bk. 2). (J). 2009. 54.99 (978-1-60775-673-6(0)) Find a World.

Beyond the Valley of Thorns. unabr. ed. Patrick Carman. Read by Aasne Vigesaa. (Running Time: 5 hrs.). (Land of Elyon Ser.: Bk. 2). 2005. 39.25 (978-1-59737-406-4(7), 9781597374064, BADLE); 24.95 (978-1-59737-405-7(9), 9781597374057, BAD) Brilliance Audio.

Beyond the Valley of Thorns. unabr. ed. Patrick Carman. Read by Aasne Vigesaa. (Running Time: 18000 sec.). (Land of Elyon Ser.: Bk. 2). (J). (ps-7). 2005. 62.25 (978-1-59737-400-2(8), 9781597374002, BrilAudUnabridg); audio compact disk 39.25 (978-1-59737-404-0(0), 9781597374040, Brinc Audio MP3 Lib); audio compact disk 24.95 (978-1-59737-403-3(2), 9781597374033, Brilliance MP3); audio compact disk 74.25 (978-1-59737-402-6(4), 9781597374026, BriAudCD Unabrid); audio compact disk 26.95 (978-1-59737-401-9(6), 9781597374019, Bril Audio CD Unabri) Brilliance Audio.
Please enter a Synopsis.

Beyond the Vision. unabr. ed. Kay L. McDonald. Read by Rusty Nelson. 8 cass. (Running Time: 11 hrs. 6 min.). (Vision of the Eagle Ser.: Bk. 4). 2001. 49.95 (978-1-55686-907-5(X)) Books in Motion.
Ross Chestnut leaves his Oregon Cascade Mountain retreat to find the band of Yanktonai Indians who raised him.

Beyond the Wall see Great American Short Stories, Vol. III, A Collection

Beyond the Wall: Essays from the Outside. unabr. collector's ed. Edward Abbey. Read by Paul Shay. 8 cass. (Running Time: 8 hrs.). 1988. 48.00 (978-0-7366-1390-3(0), 2280) Books on Tape.
The author takes us to special pockets of wilderness that stretch from Alaska to Mexico.

Beyond the White House: Waging Peace, Fighting Disease, Building Hope. unabr. ed. Jimmy Carter. Narrated by Tom Stechschulte & Barbara Caruso. 7 cass. (Running Time: 7 hrs. 45 mins.). 2008. 61.75 (978-1-4281-9507-3(6)); audio compact disk 77.75 (978-1-4281-9509-7(2)) Recorded Bks.
Pulitzer Prize winner and former President Jimmy Carter is also the #1 New York Times best-selling author of Our Endangered Values and other thought-provoking works. This retrospective surveys Carter's 25 tireless years of humanitarian efforts as an emissary of the Carter Center - waging peace in troubled lands, fighting diseases among the neglected, and building hope among the hopeless.

Beyond the Winning Streak: Using Conscious Creation to Consistently Win at Life. Lynda Madden Dahl. 2 cass. 1997. 16.95 (978-1-889964-04-1(2)) Pub: Moment Pt Pr. Dist(s): Words Distrib

***Beyond the World of Pooh, Part 1: The Enchanted Places.** unabr. ed. Christopher Milne. Read by Peter Dennis. (Running Time: 10 hrs.). 2010. 29.95 (978-1-4417-6211-5(6)); audio compact disk 24.95 (978-1-4417-6210-8(8)) Blckstn Audio.

***Beyond the World of Pooh, Part 1 (Library Edition) The Enchanted Places.** unabr. ed. Christopher Milne. Read by Peter Dennis. (Running Time: 10 hrs.). 2010. 34.95 (978-1-4417-6208-5(6)); audio compact disk 55.00 (978-1-4417-6209-2(4)) Blckstn Audio.

Beyond the Yellow Brick Road: Our Children & Drugs Audio Book. Perf. by Clint Stonebraker. Bob Meehan. (ENG.). 2007. 40.00 (978-0-9702327-2-4(1)) Meek Pubng.

Beyond the Yellow Star to America, unabr. ed. Inge Auerbacher. Narrated by Christina Moore. 3 cass. (Running Time: 4 hrs. 30 mins.). (gr. 5 up). 1997. 27.00 (978-0-7887-0891-6(0), 95029E7) Recorded Bks.
In this first hand account, we follow the author's journey through childhood as she survives a Nazi concentration camp, fights a debilitating disease & achieves remarkable success in America.

Beyond the 7 Habits. abr. ed. Stephen R. Covey. 2006. 17.95 (978-1-933976-10-5(1)) Pub: Franklin Covey. Dist(s): S and S Inc

Beyond Theism: The God of A Course in Miracles. Kenneth Wapnick. 2008. 10.00 (978-1-59142-348-5(1)); audio compact disk 13.00 (978-1-59142-347-8(3)) Foun Miracles.

Beyond This Moment. abr. ed. Tamera Alexander. (Running Time: 10 hrs. 58 mins. 0 sec.). (Timber Ridge Reflections Ser.: Bk. 2). (ENG.). 2009. audio compact disk 24.98 (978-1-59644-704-2(4), christaudio) christianaud.

***Beyond this Moment.** abr. ed. Tamera Alexander. Narrated by Bernadette Dunne. (ENG.). 2009. 14.98 (978-1-59644-705-9(2), christaudio) christianaud.

Beyond Time & Space. Swami Amar Jyoti. 2 cass. 1979. 12.95 (O-17) Truth Consciousness.
Fourth, fifth & sixth dimensions. On light & space, speed & dimension. Where Spirituality & science merge. Knowing the Truth.

Beyond Time & Space. Chuck Missler. 2 CD's. (Running Time: 120 mins.). (Briefing Packages by Chuck Missler). 1994. audio compact disk 19.95 (978-1-57821-292-7(8)) Koinonia Hse.
Are there more than four dimensions to physical reality?Is it possible to traverse time as well as space? Is there a reality beyond our traditional concepts of time and space?This provocative study explores the impact of the Theory of Relativity and other recent discoveries on the Biblical views of our origin, existence, and destiny.We are all guilty of making linear assumptions in a non-linear world. Time and space are not linear. Why is this important? Find out in this study.Paradoxes: Fate vs. free will Choice vs. predestinationAuthenticating God's WordThe Geometry of Eternity Time: Linear and absolute? Recent discoveries have proven that assumptions from our everyday life are now obsolete.

Beyond Time & Space. Chuck Missler. 2 cass. (Running Time: 2.5 hours plus). (Briefing Packages by Chuck Missler). 1994. 14.95 (978-1-880532-66-9(2)) Koinonia Hse.
** Are there more than four dimensions to physical reality? * Is it possible to traverse time as well as space?* Is there a reality beyond our traditional concepts of time and space?This provocative study explores the impact of the Theory of Relativity and other recent discoveries on the Biblical views of our origin, existence, and destiny.We are all guilty of making linear assumptions in a non-linear world. Time and space are not linear. Why is this important? Find out in this study.Paradoxes: * Fate vs. free will * Choice vs. predestination* Authenticating God's Word * The Geometry of Eternity * Time: Linear and absolute?* Recent discoveries have proven that assumptions from our everyday life are now obsolete.*

Beyond Time & Space. unabr. ed. Fritjof Capra & Christina Grof. 2 cass. (Running Time: 2 hr. 34 min.). 1977. 18.00 (03001) Big Sur Tapes.

Beyond Tomorrow. unabr. ed. Interview with Donna Lander. 1 cass. (Running Time: 38 min.). (ENG & HEB.). (YA). 1998. 9.95 (978-1-890161-32-3(2), SWP104C); audio compact disk 15.95 (978-1-890161-33-0(0), SWP104CD) Sounds Write.
Ten original ballads & liturgical-based songs in Hebrew & English.

Beyond Tomorrow: Incident at Switchpath & The Outer Limit. unabr. ed. 1 cass. (Running Time: 1 hr.). 2001. 6.98 (2171) Radio Spirits.

Beyond Traditional Job Development: The Art of Creating Opportunity. Denise Bissonnette. Read by Denise Bissonnette. 6 cass. (Running Time: 7 hrs. 45 min.). (C). 1995. pap. bk. 74.95 (978-0-942071-29-0(8), 250BC) M Wright & Assocs.
Job developers can benefit from the goldmine of ideas offered: Creating jobs with employment proposals, capitalizing on business & social trends, developing partnerships with employers, targeting new employers, initiating contact with employers, understanding employer needs, communicating with employers - language as art, resolving employer concerns, & providing quality service to employers.

Beyond Traditional Job Development: The Art of Creating Opportunity. Denise Bissonnette. Read by Denise Bissonnette. 6 cass. (Running Time: 7 hrs. 45 min.). 1996. 59.95 (978-0-942071-32-0(8), 251C) M Wright & Assocs.

Beyond Tuesday Morning. unabr. ed. Karen Kingsbury. (Running Time: 10 hrs. 53 mins. 0 sec.). (9/11 Ser.). (ENG.). 2005. 14.99 (978-0-310-26964-9(4)) Zondervan.

Beyond Ups & Downs. Swami Amar Jyoti. 1 cass. 1978. 9.95 (J-13) Truth Consciousness.
Being present, practicing awareness, finding our right level. Transcending illusion, arriving at unconditional joy.

Beyond Wheelchair Jockeys: Preparing Quality Volunteers. 1 cass. (Care Cassettes Ser.: Vol. 13, No. 2). 1986. 10.80 Assn Prof Chaplains.

***Beyond Where All Paths End.** Featuring Adyashanti. (ENG.). 2009. audio compact disk 65.00 (978-1-933986-69-2(7)) Open Gate Pub.

Beyond Wisemen: Matthew 2. Speeches. Instructed by Dan Hayden. 5 CDs. (Running Time: 3 hrs. 49 min.). 2004. audio compact disk 21.95 (978-1-932691-00-9(6)) Pub: Sola Scriptura. Dist(s): STL Dist NA
Matthew's account is an intriguing part of the Christmas story. This study delves into the meaning of the wisemen's gifts and their association with three incredible prophecies.

Beyond Words. Todd Liebenow et al. Music by Mark Bradford. 1 cass. (Running Time: 90 min.). 2001. pap. bk. 15.00 (978-1-58302-192-7(2)) One Way St.

Beyond Zero Point. Gregg Braden. 2 CDs. (Running Time: 009000 sec.). 2005. audio compact disk 19.95 (978-1-59179-305-2(X), AW00407D) Sounds True.

Beyond 2020: The Shape of Things to Come. 1 cass. (Running Time: 1 hr. 30 mins.). 2000. 15.00 (978-0-929656-03-8(2)); audio compact disk 18.00 (978-0-929656-07-6(5)) Positive Prod.

***BFG.** unabr. ed. Roald Dahl. Read by Natasha Richardson. (ENG.). 2006. (978-0-06-087844-3(4)); (978-0-06-087843-6(6)) HarperCollins Pubs.

BFG. unabr. ed. Roald Dahl. Read by Natasha Richardson. (Running Time: 14400 sec.). (J). (gr. 4-7). 2006. audio compact disk 25.99 (978-0-06-085273-3(9), HarperChildAud) HarperCollins Pubs.

Bhagavad Gita. Paul Meier. 1 cass. (Running Time: 1 hr.). 2000. 10.95 (978-0-8356-2010-9(7), Quest) Pub: Theos Pub Hse. Dist(s): Natl Bk Netwk

Bhagavad-Gita. unabr. ed. Read by Jacob Needleman. Tr. by Barbara Stoler-Miller. 2 cass. (Running Time: 2 hrs. 30 min.). (Spiritual Classics on Cassette Ser.). 1995. 15.95 set. Audio Lit.
The Bhagavad-Gita is India's most precious gift to seekers of spiritual truth.

Bhagavad-Gita. unabr. ed. Read by Jacob Needleman. Tr. by Barbara Stoler-Miller. 2 cass. (Running Time: 2 hrs.). 1988. 16.95 (978-0-944993-01-9(X)) Audio Lit.
The "Bhagavad-Gita" has been called the quintessence of the spirituality of India. It has a message for all of us about how the search for higher truth must be conducted in the midst of the forces of life, with all its demands & seductions.

Bhagavad Gita, Vol. 1. Composed by Vanraj Bhatia. 1 cass. 1996. (D96010A); audio compact disk (CD96010A&B) Multi-Cultural Bks.
The Field of Battle, Arjuna's Anguish, The Immortal Soul, Work Without Attachment to Reward, The Delusion of the Senses, Life Is Work; The Path of Action, The Causes of Sin, The Lord of Dharma, The Purity of Wisdom, Renunciation.

Bhagavad Gita, Vol. 2. Composed by Vanraj Bhatia. 1 cass. 1996. (D96010B); audio compact disk (CD96010A&B) Multi-Cultural Bks.
Make Thy Soul Thy Friend, The Unity of Being, The Unsteady Mind, Ever Remember Me, God Is Love, The Wondrous Forms of the Lord, Arjuna's Adoration, Bhaktiyoga, the Path of Devotion, Light, Passion & Darkness, The Tree of Life, The Supreme Being (English), The Path to Salvation.

Bhagavad Gita: Canta Dal Besto Signore. Ed. by Maurizio Falyhera & Cristiana Grocometti. (Visions of the World Ser.). (ITA.). 1999. bk. 29.95 (978-1-58214-126-8(6)) Language Assocs.

Bhagavad Gita: Lessons in Life. Read by Damon D'Oliveira. Contrib. by Piali Roy. 1 CD. (Running Time: 2 hrs.). 2005. audio compact disk 19.95 (978-0-660-19039-6(7)) Pub: Canadian Broadcasting CAN. Dist(s): Georgetown Term
first entered the imagination of the west when the British began to rule India. The British were Looking for something that would help them understand the spiritual life in India. They found the Gita and in 1785 it was translated into English for the first time. Before long, intellectuals, philosophers and the curious were fascinated by this little book. The Bhagavad Gita offered people in the west an entirely different way of looking at spirituality and religion. In 1845, American writer, Henry David Thoreau praised the ideas in the Gita. The Bhagavad Gita is one of the world's classic religious texts. Revered by Hindus and an inspiration for thinkers from Gandhi to Thoreau, it is a meditation on how we should live our lives; how and when to act; for what purpose, and how to let go. At its heart, the Gita guides us to embrace our worldly responsibilities as one of many paths to the Divine.

Bhagavad Gita: The Illumined Man. Eknath Easwaran. Read by Eknath Easwaran. 1 cass. (Running Time: 60 min.). 1988. 7.95 (978-1-58638-505-7(4)) Nilgiri Pr.

Bhagavad-Gita: The Song of God. Read by Christopher Isherwood. Tr. by Christopher Isherwood. Tr. by Swami Prabhavananda. 1 cass. (Running Time: 60 min.). 1988. bk. 9.95 (978-0-06-250403-6(7)) HarperCollins Pubs.
Originally recorded twenty years ago for the Vedanta Society, this luminous translation brings the poetry of the Hindu spiritual calssic to a new generation.

Bhagavad-Gita as It Is. Tr. by Srila Prabhupada. 3 cass. 15.00 Set, incl. 1 vinyl album. Bhaktivedanta.
Universally renowned as the jewel of India's spiritual wisdom, there is no work even comparable in its revelations of man's essential nature, his environment &, ultimately, his relationship with God. The definitive guide to the science of self-realization. The complete book: 18 chapters, 700 verses, & the elaborate Bhaktivedanta purports. The beginning & end of the spiritual quest.

***Bhagavad Gita CD # 12: With Derek O'Neill, vol. 12.** Derek O'Neill. (Running Time: 60). (ENG.). 2009. 9.95 (978-1-936470-11-2(X)) SQWrldwide.

***Bhagavad Gita CD # 13: With Derek O'Neill, vol. 13.** Derek O'Neill. (Running Time: 60). (ENG.). 2009. audio compact disk 9.95 (978-1-936470-12-9(8)) SQWrldwide.

***Bhagavad Gita CD # 14: With Derek O'Neill, vol. 14.** Derek O'Neill. (Running Time: 60). (ENG.). 2009. audio compact disk 9.95 (978-1-936470-13-6(6)) SQWrldwide.

***Bhagavad Gita CD # 4: With Derek O'Neill, vol. 4.** Derek O'Neill. (Running Time: 60). (ENG.). 2009. audio compact disk 9.95 (978-1-936470-03-7(9)) SQWrldwide.

***Bhagavad Gita CD # 5: With Derek O'Neill, vol. 5.** Derek O'Neill. (Running Time: 60). (ENG.). 2009. audio compact disk 9.95 (978-1-936470-04-4(7)) SQWrldwide.

***Bhagavad Gita CD # 6: With Derek O'Neill, vol. 6.** Derek O'Neill. (Running Time: 60). (ENG.). 2009. audio compact disk 9.95 (978-1-936470-05-1(5)) SQWrldwide.

***Bhagavad Gita CD # 7: With Derek O'Neill, vol. 7.** Derek O'Neill. (Running Time: 60). (ENG.). 2009. audio compact disk 9.95 (978-1-936470-06-8(3)) SQWrldwide.

***Bhagavad Gita CD # 8: With Derek O'Neill, vol. 8.** Derek O'Neill. (Running Time: 60). (ENG.). 2009. audio compact disk 9.95 (978-1-936470-07-5(1)) SQWrldwide.

***Bhagavad Gita CD # 9: With Derek O'Neill, vol. 9.** Derek O'Neill. (Running Time: 60). (ENG.). 2009. audio compact disk 9.95 (978-1-936470-08-2(X)) SQWrldwide.

***Bhagavad Gita CD Set: With Derek O'Neill, vol. 1-14.** Derek O'Neill. (Running Time: 60). (ENG.). 2009. audio compact disk 120.00 (978-1-936470-14-3(4)) SQWrldwide.

***Bhagavad Gita CD #10: With Derek O'Neill, vol. 10.** Derek O'Neill. (Running Time: 60). (ENG.). 2009. audio compact disk 9.95 (978-1-936470-09-9(8)) SQWrldwide.

***Bhagavad Gita CD #11: With Derek O'Neill, vol. 11.** Derek O'Neill. (Running Time: 60). (ENG.). 2009. 9.95 (978-1-936470-10-5(1)) SQWrldwide.

***Bhagavad Gita CD #3: With Derek O'Neill, vol. 3.** Derek O'Neill. (Running Time: 60). (ENG.). 2009. audio compact disk 9.95 (978-1-936470-02-0(0)) SQWrldwide.

Bhagavad Gita MP3 - CD: The Song of God. Speeches. Swami Prabhavananda. 1 cd. (Running Time: 54 hrs). 2007. 69.95 (978-0-87481-976-2(8)) Vedanta Pr.

Bhagavad Gita Recitation. unabr. ed. Perf. by Eknath Easwaran. 1 cass. (Running Time: 1 hr.). 1982. 7.95 (978-1-58638-504-0(6)) Nilgiri Pr.

***Bhagavad Gita Series #1: With Derek O'Neill, No.1.** Derek O'Neill SQ Worldwide. (ENG.). 2009. audio compact disk 9.95 (978-1-936470-00-6(4)) SQWrldwide.

Bhaguad Gita: Canta Del Besto Signore. Ed. by Maurizio Falyhera & Cristiana Grocometti. (Visions of the World Ser.). (ITA.). 1999. bk. 19.95 (978-1-58214-125-1(8)) Language Assocs.

Bhajan, Vol. 1. Music by Bhimsen Joshi. 1 cass. 1995. (D95027); audio compact disk (CD D95027) Multi-Cultural Bks.

Bhajan, Vol. 2. Music by Pandit Jasraj. 1 cass. 1995. (D95028); audio compact disk (CD D95028) Multi-Cultural Bks.

Bhajan 1. Yogi Hari. 1 cass. (Running Time: 45 min.). 9.95 (BH1) Nada Prodns.
A collection of bhajans that are highly philosophical in nature: Namo Bhutanata; Sumirana Karalay; Chalo Mana; Narayana Ka Nama Nirala; Paiyogee Mainay; Narayana Ko Bhajan Karo; Laga Lay Prema Ishwar Say; Yamuna Teera Viharee; Kaisay Kaisay Jahon.

Bhajan 2. Yogi Hari. 1 cass. (Running Time: 45 min.). 9.95 (BH2) Nada Prodns.
Devotional songs beautifully arranged to inspire devotion: Sri Ram Chandra; Prabhu Data Ray; May Ray Toe Giridhar Gopal; Shankar Tayre; Racha Prabhu; Sadho Man Ka; Sangata; Thumaka Chalata Rama Chandra.

Bhakti: The Tree of Knowledge. Ann Ree Colton & Jonathan Murro. 1 cass. 7.95 A R Colton Fnd.

Bhakti or Devotion. unabr. ed. Vivekananda. Read by Bruce Robertson. 1 cass. (Running Time: 47 min.). 1987. 7.95 (978-1-882915-02-6(X)) Vedanta Ctr Atlanta.
Practice of devotion in religion, method, goal, meaning of bhakti.

Bhakti Yoga. 1 cass. (Running Time: 1 hr.). 12.99 (198) Yoga Res Foun.

Bhavana, No. 1. Swami Jyotirmayananda. Read by Swami Jyotirmayananda. 1 cass. (Running Time: 60 min.). 12.99 (731) Yoga Res Foun.

Bhavana, No. 2. Swami Jyotirmayananda. 1 cass. (Running Time: 1 hr.). 1990. 12.99 Yoga Res Foun.

Bhavana, No. 3. Swami Jyotirmayananda. 1 cass. (Running Time: 1 hr.). 1990. 12.99 Yoga Res Foun.

Bhavana, No. 4. Swami Jyotirmayananda. 1 cass. (Running Time: 1 hr.). 1990. 12.99 Yoga Res Foun.

Bhavana, No. 6. Swami Jyotirmayananda. 1 cass. (Running Time: 1 hr.). 1990. 12.99 Yoga Res Foun.

Bhavana, No. 7. Swami Jyotirmayananda. 1 cass. (Running Time: 1 hr.). 1990. 12.99 Yoga Res Foun.

Bhavana, No. 8. Swami Jyotirmayananda. 1 cass. (Running Time: 1 hr.). 1990. 12.99 Yoga Res Foun.

Bhavana One. Swami Jyotirmayananda. Read by Swami Jyotirmayananda. 1 cass. (Running Time: 60 min.). 12.99 (730) Yoga Res Foun.

Bhimsen Joshi, Vol. 1. 1 cass. 1997. (A97005); audio compact disk (CD A97005) Multi-Cultural Bks.

Bhimsen Joshi, Vol. 2. 1 cass. 1997. (A97006); audio compact disk (CD A97006) Multi-Cultural Bks.

Bhimsen Joshi, Vol. 3. 1 cass. 1997. (A97007); audio compact disk (CD A97007) Multi-Cultural Bks.

Bhimsen Joshi, Vol. 4. 1 cass. 1997. (A97008); audio compact disk (CD A97008) Multi-Cultural Bks.

Bhimsen Joshi, Vol. 5. 1 cass. 1997. (A97009); audio compact disk (CD A97009) Multi-Cultural Bks.

Bhimsen Joshi, Vol. 6. 1 cass. 1997. (A97010); audio compact disk (CD A97010) Multi-Cultural Bks.

Bhowani Junction. unabr. ed. John Masters. Narrated by Patrick Tull et al. 12 cass. (Running Time: 17 hrs.). 1988. 97.00 (978-1-55690-052-5(X), 88884E7) Recorded Bks.
World War II has finally played itself out & the British are leaving India. Through this vortex is spun a fictional plot of terror & politics that illustrates all-too-well the curse that still plagues India today.

Bhuma Upasana. Swami Jyotirmayananda. 1 cass. (Running Time: 1 hr.). 1990. 12.99 Yoga Res Foun.

Bianca Ryan. Contrib. by Bianca Ryan et al. Prod. by David Foster et al. 2006. audio compact disk 18.98 (978-5-558-08888-5(5)) Columba GBR GBR.

Bias: A CBS Insider Exposes How the Media Distort the News. Bernard Goldberg. Narrated by Bernard Goldberg. 6 cass. (Running Time: 8 hrs. 30 mins.). 52.00 (978-1-4025-1824-9(2)) Recorded Bks.

Bias: A CBS Insider Exposes How the Media Distort the News. unabr. ed. Bernard Goldberg. 5 cass. (Running Time: 8 hrs.). 2004. 24.99 (978-1-4025-1759-4(9), 01374) Recorded Bks.
Shows that the biases, leanings and political affiliations of those who control the media directly affect the way the American public sees and learns about current events - shaping public opinion by distorting the truth.

Biber: Froberger & Richter: Harpsichord Toccatas. Perf. by Michael Sand et al. 1996. audio compact disk 14.95 (978-0-9769698-6-0(6)) KATastroPHE.

Bible. Stephen Johnston. 48 cass. 2004. 79.95 (978-1-56563-768-9(2)); 79.95 (978-1-56563-772-6(0)); 79.95 (978-1-56563-784-9(4)); audio compact disk 99.95 (978-1-56563-748-1(8)); audio compact disk 99.95 (978-1-56563-758-0(5)); audio compact disk 99.95 (978-1-56563-750-4(X)) Hendrickson MA.

Bible. Read by Max E. McLean. 48 cass. (Running Time: 77 hrs.). (47014); audio compact disk (47006) Fellow Perform Arts.

***Bible.** Chuck Missler & Mark Eastman. (ENG.). 2009. audio compact disk 19.95 (978-1-57821-442-6(4)) Koinonia Hse.

Bible. Ed. by Publications International Staff. (J). 2007. audio compact disk 22.98 (978-1-4127-6697-5(4)) Pubns Intl Ltd.

Bible. Read by Alexander Scourby. 48 cass. 2004. 79.95 (978-1-56563-774-0(7)); audio compact disk 99.95 (978-1-56563-759-7(3)); audio compact disk 99.95 (978-1-56563-756-6(9)) Hendrickson MA.

Bible. abr. ed. James Bell. 2004. 25.99 (978-1-58926-818-0(0), 6818) Pub: Oasis Audio. Dist(s): TNT Media Grp

Bible. abr. ed. James Bell & Stan Campbell. (Complete Idiot's Guides). (ENG.). 2004. audio compact disk 27.99 (978-1-58926-819-7(9), 6819) Oasis Audio.

Bible. unabr. ed. Read by George Vafiadis. 2 MP3 discs. (Running Time: 84 hrs). 2002. bk. 24.95 (978-1-58472-362-2(9), In Aud) Sound Room.

Bible: A Biography. unabr. ed. Karen Armstrong. Narrated by Josephine Bailey. 5 CDs. (Running Time: 6 hrs. 0 mins. 0 sec.). (Books That Changed the World Ser.). (ENG.). 2007. audio compact disk 29.99 (978-1-4001-0394-2(0)); audio compact disk 19.99 (978-1-4001-5394-7(8)); audio compact disk 59.99 (978-1-4001-3394-9(7)) Pub: Tantor Media. Dist(s): IngramPubServ

Bible: Adam, Noe. Comment by Elie Wiesel. 1 cass. (FRE.). 1991. 18.95 (1156-RF) Olivia & Hill.

Bible: An Extraterrestrial Message. Chuck Missler & Mark Eastman. 2 cass. (Running Time: 3 hrs). (Creator Ser.). 1996. vinyl bd. 14.95 Set, incl. study notes. (978-1-880532-39-3(5)) Koinonia Hse.
In the 20th century we have witnessed one of the most remarkable discoveries in recorded history: the discovery that the universe is finite. The implications of this discovery are indeed staggering.Beginning with Albert Einstein in 1903, twentieth-century physicists have demonstrated that space-time and matter had a finite, simultaneous beginning!Prior to this discovery, atheistic scientists and philosophers rested comfortably on the notion that the universe was eternal. Consequently, a universe without a beginning needed no cause - it just was.However, a universe that has a beginning either created itself (a logical and scientific absurdity) or it was caused to exist by a Being who preceded it.By definition, that means a transcendent Creator - One who exists outside time and space!Because a transcendent Creator possesses the sufficient means to act in our space-time domain, He also has the capability to get a message to us. The Bible claims to be that message.Based on scientific accuracy, scientific foreknowledge, design of the text, and the predictive prophecy of the Bible, Chuck Missler and Dr. Mark Eastman explore the absolute uniqueness of the Biblical message in light of recent discoveries.

Bible: Isaac, Esau, Jacob. Comment by Elie Wiesel. 1 cass. (FRE.). 1991. 18.95 (1158-RF) Olivia & Hill.

Bible: Jeremie. Comment by Elie Wiesel. 1 cass. (FRE.). 1991. 18.95 (1163-RF) Olivia & Hill.

Bible: Joseph, Moise. Comment by Elie Wiesel. 1 cass. (FRE.). 1991. 18.95 (1159-RF) Olivia & Hill.

Bible: Josue. Comment by Elie Wiesel. 1 cass. (FRE.). 1991. 18.95 (1161-RF) Olivia & Hill.

Bible: Moise. Comment by Elie Wiesel. 1 cass. (FRE.). 1991. 18.95 (1160-RF) Olivia & Hill.

Bible: Old Testament. 67 CDs. (Running Time: 72 hrs.). 2003. audio compact disk (978-1-59007-412-1(2), N Millennium Audio) New Millenn Enter.

Bible: Old Testament, King James Version. unabr. ed. Scripts. 52 cass. (Running Time: 78 hrs.). 2003. 99.95 (978-1-59007-310-0(X), N Millennium Audio) Pub: New Millenn Enter. Dist(s): PerseuPGW

Bible: Samuel, Saul, David. Comment by Elie Wiesel. 1 cass. (FRE.). 1991. 18.95 (1162-RF) Olivia & Hill.

Bible: The Complete Word of God. abr. ed. Perf. by Reduced Shakespeare Co. Staff. 1 CD. (Running Time: 1 HOUR). (YA). 2003. audio compact disk 16.98 (978-1-929243-46-4(4)) Uproar Ent.
THE REDUCED SHAKESPEARE COMPANY is a unique theatre experience. Their fast, funny and slightly off-kilter approach to such traditional subjects as world history, William Shakespeare, and the world's greatest literature have won them international acclaim. With "THE BIBLE" they have taken their irreverance to a new "higher" level. "The Bible" ran for 12 sold out weeks at The Kennedy Center and received a Helen Hayes Award nomination for Outstanding New Play.

Bible: The New Testament. 16 cass. (Running Time: 24 hrs.). 2001. 104.95 (940911) Pub: ISIS Audio GBR. Dist(s): Ulverscroft US

Bible: The New Testament. unabr. ed. Read by Gregory Peck. 12 cass. (Running Time: 18 hrs.). 2001. 53.00 (978-1-57453-445-0(9)) Audio Lit.
A biblical translation of sublime poetic beauty.

Bible: The New Testament Edition. Read by Stephen Johnston. 11 cass. 49.95 Hendrickson MA.

Bible - "L'exode", Set. 3 cass. (FRE.). 1991. 31.95 (1406-VSL) Olivia & Hill.
A group of actors read the ecumenical translation in modern French.

Bible- New Testament NIV- English. 12 cass. (Running Time: 19 hrs. 40 mins.). Dramatization. 2001. 60.00 (978-1-58807-071-5(9)) Am Pubng Inc.
This NIV version of the Bible is beautifully performed in audio theater style with a cast of talented actors. Inspiring music accentuates the drama. This NEW TESTAMENT will be appealing and convenient for frequent listening.

Bible Activities Book #9 see Walking with Jesus

Bible Alive! unabr. ed. Narrated by Stephen Johnston. 61 vols. (Running Time: 70 hrs.). (ENG.). 2003. audio compact disk 79.97 (978-0-8423-7557-3(0)) Tyndale Hse.

Bible Alive!TM Dramatized. Narrated by Stephen Johnston. 15 CDs. (Running Time: 17 hrs. 0 mins.). (ENG.). 2003. audio compact disk 29.97 (978-0-8423-7559-7(7)) Tyndale Hse.

Bible & Astrology. Elizabeth Gaureke. 1 cass. 8.95 (128) Am Fed Astrologers.
References supportive of astrology as it is practiced today.

Bible & Fundamentalism. Carroll Stuhlmueller. 1 cass. 1990. 7.95 (TAH225) Alba Hse Comns.
Fr. Stuhlmueller explains the theological, social & educational presuppositions of fundamentalism. He demonstrates that it is a reality that cuts across denominational lines & is found in Catholicism. The challenge of fundamentalism is real & ongoing.

Bible & Liturgy. Carroll Stuhlmueller. 1 cass. 1990. 7.95 (TAH226) Alba Hse Comns.
In this extraordinary tape, Fr. Stuhlmueller clearly demonstrates the origin, meaning & dynamics of the liturgy. Through a depth understanding of the liturgy we come to know who we are & what we are called to become.

Bible & Prayer. Carroll Stuhlmueller. 1 cass. 1990. 7.95 (TAH224) Alba Hse Comns.
By listening to this tape you will feel confident in your ability to interpret accurately the Word of God for yourself & others. You do not have to be a biblical scholar to understand Fr. Stuhlmueller's refreshing, simple & clear method for approaching the scriptures.

***Bible & Sword: England & Palestine from the Bronze Age to Balfour.** Barbara Wertheim Tuchman. Read by Wanda McCaddon. (Playaway Adult Nonfiction Ser.). (ENG.). 2010. 69.99 (978-1-4417-0222-7(9)) Find a World.

Bible & Sword: England & Palestine from the Bronze Age to Balfour. unabr. ed. Barbara W. Tuchman. Read by Wanda McCaddon. (Running Time: 15 hrs. 0 mins.). (ENG.). 2009. 29.95 (978-1-4417-0219-7(9)); 85.95 (978-1-4417-0215-9(6)); audio compact disk 118.00 (978-1-4417-0216-6(4)) Blckstn Audio.

Bible & Sword: England & Palestine from the Bronze Age to Balfour. unabr. ed. Barbara W. Tuchman. Read by John MacDonald. 8 cass. (Running Time: 12 hrs.). 1990. 64.00 (978-0-7366-1848-9(1), 2681) Books on Tape.
From early times, the British have always been drawn to the Holy Land through two major influences: the translation of the Bible into English & the need to control India & access Middle East oil. With the vividness that characterizes all of her work, Barbara Tuchman explores the complex relationship of Britain & Palestine that led to the founding of the modern Jewish state - & to many of the problems that plague the Middle East today.

Bible & the Bhagavad Gita Tape 1: Original Christianity & Original Yoga. Kriyananda, pseud. 1 cass. (Running Time: 55 min.). 9.95 (ST-128) Crystal Clarity.
A compilation of several short talks comparing exerpts from The New Testament & the Bhagavad Gita.

Bible & the Bhagavad Gita Tape 2: Original Christianity & Original Yoga. Kriyananda, pseud. 1 cass. (Running Time: 85 min.). 1986. 9.95 (BB-2) Crystal Clarity.
This is the second part of a compilation of several short talks comparing exerpts from The New Testament & the Bhagavad Gita.

Bible & the Poor Pt. 1: James 2:14-18, 633. Ed Young. 1987. 4.95 (978-0-7417-1633-0(X), 633) Win Walk.

Bible & the Poor Pt. 2: Cor. 13:1-3, 634. Ed Young. 1987. Rental 4.95 (978-0-7417-1634-7(8), 634) Win Walk.

Bible & the Roman State-Church Doctrine of Authority. Robert Zins. 1 cass. (Conference on Christianity & Roman Catholicism Ser.: No. 4). 5.00 Trinity Found.

Bible & Western Culture, Course 637. Instructed by Michael Sugrue et al. 12 cass. (Running Time: 18 hrs.). 2000. 129.95 (637) Teaching Co.
Series of 24 lectures from the religion curriculum. Scholarly, respectful treatment of the Bible as literature - not a spiritual examination of faith.

Bible & Western Culture, Pts. I-III. Instructed by Michael Sugrue et al. 24 CDs. (Running Time: 18 hrs.). (C). 1996. bk. 99.95 (978-1-56585-362-1(8), 637) Teaching Co.

Bible & Western Culture, Vol. 1. Instructed by Michael Sugrue & Andrew Ford. 4 cass. (Running Time: 6 hrs.). 1996. 129.95 (978-1-56585-173-3(0)) Teaching Co.

Bible & Western Culture, Vol. 2. Instructed by Michael Sugrue et al. 4 cass. (Running Time: 6 hrs.). 1996. 129.95 (978-1-56585-174-0(9)) Teaching Co.

Bible & Western Culture, Vol. 3. Instructed by Michael Sugrue et al. 12 pieces. (Running Time: 18 hrs.). (C). 1996. bk. 79.95 (978-1-56585-172-6(2), 637) Teaching Co.

Bible Answer Book: From the Bible Answer Man. unabr. ed. Hank Hanegraaff. 4 CDs. (Running Time: 4 hrs. 18 mins.). 2004. audio compact disk 19.99 (978-1-4041-0162-3(4)) Nelson.

Bible Answer Man Debate. 1997. 24.95 (978-1-888992-45-8(X)) Catholic Answers.

Bible Answer Man Debate. 2003. audio compact disk 27.95 (978-1-888992-49-6(2)) Catholic Answers.

Bible Answers to Fundamentalist Questions. 2005. audio compact disk 27.95 (978-1-888992-71-7(9)) Catholic Answers.

***Bible as Improv.** Ron Martoia. (Running Time: 7 hrs. 19 mins. 28 sec.). (ENG.). 2010. 14.99 (978-0-310-77325-2(3)) Zondervan.

Bible Audio en français la Sainte Bible, version Louis Segond. Speeches. Engineer Moses/Victor Mahuvi. 58 CDs. (Running Time: 74 hrs). 2007. audio compact disk 130.00 (978-0-9773672-1-4(5)) Fount of Truths.

Bible Boot Camp. (K. I. D. S. Church Ser.: Vol. 2).Tr. of Preparandonos para la victoria. (J). (gr. 1-6). 1998. ring bd. 119.99 (978-1-57405-036-3(2)) CharismaLife Pub.

Bible Break. 1 cass. (J). bk. 5.99 incl. certificate of completion, books of the Bible bookmark & clam-shell pack. (978-0-7601-0067-7(5), CSBK5539) Pub: Brentwood Music. Dist(s): Provident Mus Dist
Teaches children the books of the Bible using catchy rhymes, repetition & a really cool beat making learning fun.

Bible Break. Perf. by Brentwood Kids Staff. 1 cass. (J). cass. & video 7.99 (978-0-7601-0349-4(6), V-5539) Brentwood Music.

Bible Break. Contrib. by Genie Nilson & Troy Nilson. 1996. 25.00 (978-0-7601-0652-5(5), 75606283) Pub: Brentwood Music. Dist(s): H Leonard

Bible Buddies. (J). (gr. 1-3). 2001. audio compact disk 5.95 (978-0-633-01175-8(4)) LifeWay Christian.

Bible Builder. Bridgestone Staff. 2004. cd-rom & audio compact disk 12.95 (978-1-56371-232-6(6)) Brdgstn Multimed Grp.

Bible Code: Discovering the Hidden Truth. abr. ed. Kenneth Hanson. 1 CD. (Running Time: 1542 sec.). 2003. audio compact disk 10.95 (978-0-9707422-6-1(6)) Reel Prodns.
Hebrew sholar and professor Dr. Ken Hanson examines the matrix of the bible codes and reveals in convincing detail the hidden truth behind their amazing mathematical formulations and the ancient texts they were based on.

Bible Collection. Hosted by Charlton Heston. 2 cass. (Running Time: 2 hrs.). pap. bk. 29.99 (99383) Vision Vid PA.

Bible Comes Alive. 5 CDs. (Running Time: 5 hrs.). (J). 2000. audio compact disk 29.99 (978-1-57764-095-0(0)) Bible in Lvng Sound.
Experience the Bible as never before in these dramatized re-enactments of your favorite stories: " the Good Samaritan, "David & Goliath," "Queen Esther," "Noah's Ark," & "Zacchaeus,".

Bible Comes Alive! Dramatized Bible Stories, Set. 5 CDs. 1999. audio compact disk 29.99 HARK Ent.

Bible Comes Alive Series Album 1: 12 Cassette Dramatized Audio Stories. 2006. 45.00 (978-1-60079-000-3(3)) YourStory.

Bible Comes Alive Series Album 1: 12 CD Dramatized Audio Stories. 2006. 45.00 (978-1-60079-023-2(2)) YourStory.

Bible Comes Alive Series Album 2: 12 Cassette Dramatized Audio Stories. 2006. 45.00 (978-1-60079-001-0(1)) YourStory.

Bible Comes Alive Series Album 2: 12 CD Dramatized Audio Stories. 2006. 45.00 (978-1-60079-024-9(0)) YourStory.

Bible Comes Alive Series Album 3: 12 Cassette Dramatized Audio Stories. 2006. 45.00 (978-1-60079-002-7(X)) YourStory.

Bible Comes Alive Series Album 3: 12 CD Dramatized Audio Stories. 2006. 45.00 (978-1-60079-025-6(9)) YourStory.

Bible Comes Alive Series Album 4: 12 Cassette Dramatized Audio Stories. 2006. 45.00 (978-1-60079-003-4(8)) YourStory.

Bible Comes Alive Series Album 4: 12 CD Dramatized Audio Stories. 2006. 45.00 (978-1-60079-026-3(7)) YourStory.

Bible Comes Alive Series Album 5: 12 Cassette Dramatized Audio Stories. 2006. 45.00 (978-1-60079-004-1(6)) YourStory.

Bible Cure for ADD & Hyperactivity: Ancient Truths, Natural Remedies & the Latest Findings for Your Health Today. unabr. ed. Don Colbert. 1 cass. (Running Time: 1 hr. 30 mins.). (Bible Cure Ser.).Tr. of Cura biblica para el DDA y la hiperactividad, La. 2003. 7.99 (978-1-58926-196-9(8), S56L-0210) Oasis Audio.

Bible Cure for ADD & Hyperactivity: Ancient Truths, Natural Remedies & the Latest Findings for Your Health Today. unabr. ed. Don Colbert. Narrated by Greg Wheatley. (Bible Cure Ser.).Tr. of Cura biblica para el DDA y la hiperactividad, La. (ENG.). 2003. 6.99 (978-1-60814-044-2(X)); audio compact disk 9.99 (978-1-58926-197-6(6), S56L-021D) Oasis Audio.

Bible Cure for Allergies: Ancient Truths, Natural Remedies & the Latest Findings for Your Health Today. unabr. ed. Don Colbert. 1 cass. (Running Time: 1 hr. 30 mins.). (Bible Cure Ser.). 2002. 7.99 (978-1-58926-036-8(8)) Oasis Audio.

Bible Cure for Allergies: Ancient Truths, Natural Remedies & the Latest Findings for Your Health Today. unabr. ed. Don Colbert. Narrated by Steve Hiller. (Bible Cure Ser.). (ENG.). 2003. 6.99 (978-1-60814-045-9(8)) Oasis Audio.

Bible Cure for Asthma: Ancient Truths, Natural Remedies & the Latest Findings for Your Health Today. unabr. ed. Don Colbert. Narrated by Tim Lundeen. (Bible Cure Ser.). (ENG.). 2004. 6.99 (978-1-60814-047-3(4)) Oasis Audio.

Bible Cure for Autoimmune Diseases: Ancient Truths, Natural Remedies & the Latest Findings for Your Health Today. unabr. ed. Don Colbert. Narrated by Greg Wheatley. (Bible Cure Ser.). (ENG.). 2004. 6.99 (978-1-60814-048-0(2)) Oasis Audio.

Bible Cure for Back Pain: Ancient Truths, Natural Remedies & the Latest Findings for Your Health Today. unabr. ed. Don Colbert. Narrated by Tim Lundeen. (Bible Cure Ser.). (ENG.). 2004. 6.99 (978-1-60814-049-7(0)) Oasis Audio.

Bible Cure for Cancer: Ancient Truths, Natural Remedies & the Latest Findings for Your Health Today. unabr. ed. Don Colbert. Narrated by Steve Hiller. (Bible Cure Ser.). (ENG.). 2003. 6.99 (978-1-60814-050-3(4)) Oasis Audio.

Bible Cure for Colds, Flu, & Sinus Infections: Ancient Truths, Natural Remedies & the Latest Findings for Your Health Today. unabr. ed. Don Colbert. Narrated by Tim Lundeen. (Bible Cure Ser.). (ENG.). 2004. 6.99 (978-1-60814-052-7(0)) Oasis Audio.

Bible Cure for Depression & Anxiety: Ancient Truths, Natural Remedies & the Latest Findings for Your Health Today. unabr. ed. Don Colbert. Narrated by Steve Hiller. (Bible Cure Ser.). (ENG.). 2002. 6.99 (978-1-60814-053-4(9)) Oasis Audio.

Bible Cure for Diabetes: Ancient Truths, Natural Remedies & the Latest Findings for Your Health Today. unabr. ed. Don Colbert. Narrated by Steve Hiller. (Bible Cure Ser.). (ENG.). 2003. 6.99 (978-1-60814-054-1(7)) Oasis Audio.

Bible Cure for Headaches: Ancient Truths, Natural Remedies & the Latest Findings for Your Health Today. unabr. ed. Don Colbert. 1 cass. (Running Time: 1 hr. 30 mins.). (Bible Cure Ser.). 2003. 7.99 (978-1-58926-194-5(1), S56L-0190) Oasis Audio.

Bible Cure for Headaches: Ancient Truths, Natural Remedies & the Latest Findings for Your Health Today. unabr. ed. Don Colbert. Narrated by Greg Wheatley. (Bible Cure Ser.). (ENG.). 2003. 6.99 (978-1-60814-055-8(5)); audio compact disk 9.99 (978-1-58926-195-2(X), S56L-019D) Oasis Audio.

Bible Cure for Heart Disease. unabr. ed. Don Colbert. 1 cass. (Running Time: 1 hr. 30 mins.). (Bible Cure Ser.). 2003. 7.99 (978-1-58926-190-7(9), S65L-022D) Oasis Audio.

Bible Cure for Heart Disease: Ancient Truths, Natural Remedies & the Latest Findings for Your Health Today. unabr. ed. Don Colbert. Narrated by Greg Wheatley. (Bible Cure Ser.). (ENG.). 2003. 6.99 (978-1-60814-056-5(3)) Oasis Audio.

Bible Cure for High Blood Pressure: Ancient Truths, Natural Remedies & the Latest Findings for Your Health Today. unabr. ed. Don Colbert. Narrated by Tim Lundeen. (Bible Cure Ser.). (ENG.). 2004. 6.99 (978-1-60814-057-2(1)) Oasis Audio.

Bible Cure for High Cholesterol: Ancient Truths, Natural Remedies & the Latest Findings for Your Health Today. unabr. ed. Don Colbert. Narrated by Greg Wheatley. (Bible Cure Ser.). (ENG.). 2004. 6.99 (978-1-60814-058-9(X)) Oasis Audio.

Bible Cure for PMS & Mood Swings: Ancient Truths, Natural Remedies & the Latest Findings for Your Health Today. unabr. ed. Don Colbert. 1 cass. (Running Time: 1 hr. 30 mins.). (Bible Cure Ser.). 2003. 7.99 (978-1-58926-198-3(4), S56L-0170) Oasis Audio.

Bible Cure for PMS & Mood Swings: Ancient Truths, Natural Remedies & the Latest Findings for Your Health Today. unabr. ed. Don Colbert. Narrated by Anita Lustrea. (Bible Cure Ser.). (ENG.). 2003. 6.99 (978-1-60814-059-6(8)); audio compact disk 9.99 (978-1-58926-199-0(2), S56L-017D) Oasis Audio.

Bible Cure for Stress: Ancient Truths, Natural Remedies & the Latest Findings for Your Health Today. unabr. ed. Don Colbert. Narrated by Greg Wheatley. (Bible Cure Ser.). (ENG.). 2003. 6.99 (978-1-60814-060-2(1)) Oasis Audio.

Bible Cure for Weight Loss & Muscle Gain: Ancient Truths, Natural Remedies & the Latest Findings for Your Health Today. unabr. ed. Don Colbert. Narrated by Steve Hiller. (Bible Cure Ser.). (ENG.). 2003. 6.99 (978-1-60814-061-9(X)) Oasis Audio.

Bible Deuteronomy. unabr. ed. Read by Stephen Collins. 2 cass. 2004. 18.00 (978-1-59007-478-7(5)); audio compact disk 25.00 (978-1-59007-479-4(3)) Pub: New Millenn Enter. Dist(s): PerseuPGW

Bible Discovery Library. 2004. cd-rom & audio compact disk 49.95 (978-1-932213-07-2(4)) WORDsearch.

Bible Discovery Museum. Kremer Publications. (ENG.). 2007. audio compact disk 99.00 (978-0-9745631-8-3(8)) Kremer Pubns.

Bible Experience: The Complete Bible. unabr. ed. Media Group Productions Staff. Contrib. by Zondervan Publishing Staff. 79 CDs. (Running Time: 89 hrs. 0 mins. 0 sec.). (ENG.). 2007. audio compact disk 124.99 (978-0-310-92630-6(0)) Zondervan.

Bible Experience: The Complete Bible: Now Including the Complete TNIV Bible Text to Read Along. Zondervan Publishing Staff. (Running Time: 87 hrs. 57 mins. 0 sec.). (ENG.). 2008. 69.99 (978-0-310-94155-2(5)) Zondervan.

Bible Experience NT In-Store Floor Display. Contrib. by Zondervan Publishing Staff. 2006. audio compact disk 449.91 (978-0-310-93778-4(7)) Zondervan.

Bible Explorer Deluxe 30. Epiphany. 2004. audio compact disk 99.97 (978-1-892144-18-8(2)) Epiphany Sftware.

Bible Explorer Discovery 30. Epiphany. 2004. audio compact disk 14.95 (978-1-892144-16-4(6)) Epiphany Sftware.

Bible Explorer Premium 30. Epiphany. 2004. audio compact disk 99.97 (978-1-892144-19-5(0)) Epiphany Sftware.

Bible Explorer Standard 30. 2004. audio compact disk 19.97 (978-1-892144-17-1(4)) Epiphany Sftware.

Bible Explorer Trial Ed 30. 2004. audio compact disk 2.95 (978-1-892144-15-7(8)) Epiphany Sftware.

Bible Eyewitness, Set. collector's ed. AIO Team Staff. Created by Focus on the Family Staff. (Running Time: 15 hrs. 0 mins.). (Adventures in Odyssey Ser.). (ENG.). (J). 2006. audio compact disk 39.97 (978-1-58997-400-5(X), Tyndale Ent) Tyndale Hse.

Bible Eyewitness: New Testament. Prod. by Focus on the Family Staff. 2 episodes, 1 cass. (Running Time: 6 hrs.). (Adventures in Odyssey Classics

Ser.: Vol. 4). (gr. 2-13). 1999. 24.99 (978-1-56179-821-6(5)) Pub: Focus Family. Dist(s): Nelson
Imagine begin there when Jesus is born or when He raises Lazarus from the dead! Picture yourself actually witnessing Jesus turn an enemy named Saul into the apostle Paul in a blinding flash of light! If you've ever dreamed you could watch Jesus perform miracles and see Him change the lives of everyone He meets, here's your opportunity! Plus, you'll enjoy listening to modern-day retelling of Jesus' greatest parables - like the prodigal son, the unmerciful servant, the marriage feast and more.

Bible Eyewitness: Old Testament. Prod. by Focus on the Family Staff. 2 episodes, 1 cass. (Running Time: 6 hrs.). (Adventures in Odyssey Classics Ser.: Vol. 3). (gr. 2-5). 1999. 24.99 (978-1-56179-819-3(3)) Pub: Focus Family. Dist(s): Nelson
Step inside the Imagination Station and become an eyewitness to the most exciting Old Testament adventures of all time! Imagine being there as 10 terrible plagues from God sweep through Egypt, and Moses parts the Red Sea with the Egyptians in hot pursuit! You'll witness fire from heaven in a duel between the false prophets of Baal and the one true God of Elijah! As each story of faith comes to life in a new way, you'll understand the Bible better than ever! In each of these previously released Adventures in Odyssey (r): episodes, you won't just hear stories from the Bible - you'll experience all the thrills as a Bible Eyewitness!.

Bible from the Perspective of A Course in Miracles. Kenneth Wapnick. 2008. audio compact disk 48.00 (978-1-59142-351-5(1)) Foun Miracles.

Bible from the Perspective of A Course in Miracles. Kenneth Wapnick. 2008. 38.00 (978-1-59142-352-2(X)) Foun Miracles.

Bible "Genese", Set. 3 cass. (FRE.). 1991. 31.95 (1405-VSL) Olivia & Hill.

Bible in an Hour: The Heroic Struggle over the Inhabited Universe. 2003. 24.95 (978-0-9723092-0-2(9)) Ballast Pr.
Bible in an Hour is a thematic overview of the Bible as it describes the heroic struggle between God and His arch-creation Lucifer for the possession of the inhabited universe. Using the fruit of a tree, Lucifer tricked Eve into opening the gate of death. God promised to restore the Creation by deceiving Lucifer into forever closing the gate of death, using the fruit of the woman on another tree that Lucifer could not resist.

Bible in Living Sound: Challenged, unabr. ed. 10 CDs. (Running Time: 15 hrs.). 2000. audio compact disk 59.99 (978-1-57764-082-0(9)) Bible in Lvng Sound.
The most inspirational re-enacted Bible stories ever produced. Complete with music & full sound effects, leaves impressions of lasting beauty & wonder. Stunning dramatizations. For kids of all ages.

Bible in Living Sound: Delivered, unabr. ed. 10 CDs. (Running Time: 15 hrs.). 2000. audio compact disk 59.99 (978-1-57764-087-5(X)) Bible in Lvng Sound.

Bible in Living Sound: Freed. unabr. ed. 10 CDs. (Running Time: 15 hrs.). (J). 2000. audio compact disk 59.99 (978-1-57764-081-3(0)) Bible in Lvng Sound.
The most inspirational re-enacted Bible stories ever produced. Complete with music & full sound effects, leaves impressions of lasting beauty & wonder. For kids of all ages.

Bible in Living Sound: Life & Times of the Old Testament; Life & Times of Jesus; Life & Times of Paul, Vols. 1-8, set. Prod. by Leal V. Grunke. Music by Capitol Records Staff. 75 cass. (Running Time: 45 min. per cass.). Incl. Freed. 10 cass. (Running Time: 9 hrs.). 1997. 49.99 (978-1-57764-601-3(0)); Vol. 2 . Challenged. 10 cass. (Running Time: 9 hrs.). (J). 2000. 49.99 (978-1-57764-602-0(9)); Vol. 3 . Tested. 10 cass. (Running Time: 9 hrs.). 2000. 49.99 (978-1-57764-603-7(7)); Vol. 4. Rescued. 10 cass. (Running Time: 9 hrs.). 2000. 49.99 (978-1-57764-604-4(5)); Vol. 5 . Saved. 10 cass. (Running Time: 9 hrs.). 1997. 49.99 (978-1-57764-605-1(3)); Vol. 6. Reclaimed. 10 cass. (Running Time: 9 hrs.). 2000. 49.99 (978-1-57764-606-8(1)); Vol. 7. Delivered. 10 cass. (Running Time: 9 hrs.). 2000. 49.99 (978-1-57764-607-5(X)); Vol. 8. Victorious. 5 cass. (Running Time: 9 hrs.). 2000. 24.99 (978-1-57764-608-2(8)); 1997. 374.92 (978-1-57764-600-6(2)) Bible in Lvng Sound.
The most inspirational re-enacted Bible stories ever produced. Complete with music & full sound effects, leaves impressions of lasting beauty & wonder. Stunning dramatizations. For kids of all ages.

Bible in Living Sound: Reclaimed, unabr. ed. 10 CDs. (Running Time: 15 hrs.). 2000. audio compact disk 59.99 (978-1-57764-086-8(1)) Bible in Lvng Sound.
The most inspirational re-enacted Bible stories ever produced. Complete with music & full sound effects, leaves impressions of lasting beauty & wonder. Stunning dramatizations. For kids of all ages.

Bible in Living Sound: Rescued, unabr. ed. 10 CDs. (Running Time: 15 hrs.). 2000. audio compact disk 59.99 (978-1-57764-084-4(5)) Bible in Lvng Sound.

Bible in Living Sound: Saved, unabr. ed. 10 CDs. (Running Time: 15 hrs.). 2000. audio compact disk 59.99 (978-1-57764-085-1(3)) Bible in Lvng Sound.

Bible in Living Sound: Tested, unabr. ed. 10 CDs. (Running Time: 15 hrs.). 2000. audio compact disk 59.99 (978-1-57764-083-7(7)) Bible in Lvng Sound.

Bible in Living Sound: Victorious, unabr. ed. 10 CDs. (Running Time: 15 hrs.). 2000. audio compact disk 29.99 (978-1-57764-088-2(8)) Bible in Lvng Sound.

***Bible in 90 Days: Week 1: Genesis 1:1 - Exodus 40:38.** unabr. ed. Ed. by Ted Cooper Jr. (Running Time: 6 hrs. 22 mins. 0 sec.). (ENG.). 2007. 2.99 (978-0-310-93931-3(3)) Zondervan.

***Bible in 90 Days: Week 10: Daniel 9:1 - Matthew 26:75.** unabr. ed. Ted Cooper Jr. (Running Time: 5 hrs. 43 mins. 0 sec.). (ENG.). 2007. 2.99 (978-0-310-93940-5(2)) Zondervan.

***Bible in 90 Days: Week 11: Matthew 27:1 - Acts 6:15.** unabr. ed. Ted Cooper Jr. (Running Time: 6 hrs. 37 mins. 0 sec.). (ENG.). 2007. 2.99 (978-0-310-93941-2(0)) Zondervan.

***Bible in 90 Days: Week 12: Acts 7:1 - Colossians 4:18.** unabr. ed. Ted Cooper Jr. (Running Time: 5 hrs. 52 mins. 0 sec.). (ENG.). 2007. 2.99 (978-0-310-93942-9(9)) Zondervan.

***Bible in 90 Days: Week 13: 1 Thessalonians 1:1 - Revelation 22:21.** unabr. ed. Ted Cooper Jr. (Running Time: 4 hrs. 21 mins. 0 sec.). (ENG.). 2007. 2.99 (978-0-310-93943-6(7)) Zondervan.

***Bible in 90 Days: Week 2: Leviticus 1:1 - Deuteronomy 22:30.** unabr. ed. Ted Cooper Jr. (Running Time: 6 hrs. 39 mins. 0 sec.). (ENG.). 2007. 2.99 (978-0-310-93932-0(1)) Zondervan.

***Bible in 90 Days: Week 3: Deuteronomy 23:1 - 1 Samuel 28:25.** unabr. ed. Ted Cooper Jr. (Running Time: 6 hrs. 26 mins. 0 sec.). (ENG.). 2007. 2.99 (978-0-310-93933-7(X)) Zondervan.

***Bible in 90 Days: Week 4: 1 Samuel 29:1 - 2 Kings 25:30.** unabr. ed. Ed. by Ted Cooper Jr. (Running Time: 6 hrs. 6 mins. 0 sec.). (ENG.). 2007. 2.99 (978-0-310-93934-4(8)) Zondervan.

***Bible in 90 Days: Week 5: 1 Chronicles 1:1 - Nehemiah 13:31.** unabr. ed. Ted Cooper Jr. (Running Time: 6 hrs. 18 mins. 0 sec.). (ENG.). 2007. 2.99 (978-0-310-93935-1(6)) Zondervan.

***Bible in 90 Days: Week 6: Esther 1:1 - Psalm 89:52.** unabr. ed. Ted Cooper Jr. (Running Time: 5 hrs. 9 mins. 0 sec.). (ENG.). 2007. 2.99 (978-0-310-93936-8(4)) Zondervan.

***Bible in 90 Days: Week 7: Psalm 90:1 - Isaiah 13:22.** unabr. ed. Ted Cooper Jr. (Running Time: 4 hrs. 50 mins. 0 sec.). (ENG.). 2007. 2.99 (978-0-310-93937-5(2)) Zondervan.

***Bible in 90 Days: Week 8: Isaiah 14:1 - Jeremiah 33:26.** unabr. ed. Ted Cooper Jr. (Running Time: 5 hrs. 23 mins. 0 sec.). (ENG.). 2007. 2.99 (978-0-310-93938-2(0)) Zondervan.

***Bible in 90 Days: Week 9: Jeremiah 34:1 - Daniel 8:27.** unabr. ed. Ted Cooper Jr. (Running Time: 6 hrs. 15 mins. 0 sec.). (ENG.). 2007. 2.99 (978-0-310-93939-9(9)) Zondervan.

Bible Interpretation. Manly P. Hall. 5 cass. 40.00 set incl. album. (978-0-89314-016-8(3), S550714) Philos Res.

Bible Jesus Read. Zondervan Publishing Staff. (Running Time: 3 hrs. 0 mins. 0 sec.). (ENG.). 2006. audio compact disk 29.99 (978-0-310-27357-8(9)) Zondervan.

Bible Jesus Read. abr. ed. Philip Yancey. (Running Time: 3 hrs. 0 mins. 0 sec.). (ENG.). 2003. 10.99 (978-0-310-25999-2(1)) Zondervan.

Bible Jesus Read. abr. unabr. ed. Philip Yancey. 2 cass/. (Running Time: 2 hrs.). 1999. 17.99 (978-0-310-22982-7(0)) Zondervan.

Bible Memory Toolbox Sing-Along Tape. Christine Wyrtzen & Paula Bussard. Read by Christine Wyrtzen. 1 cass. (50-Day Spiritual Adventure Ser.). (J). (gr. k-2). 1996. 6.00 (978-1-57849-017-2(0)) Chapel of Air.

Bible Music K4 Cassette. 1985. 13.00 (978-1-57924-112-4(3)) BJUPr.

Bible of Unspeakable Truths. unabr. ed. Greg Gutfeld. Frwd. by Penn Jillette. (Running Time: 9 hrs.). (ENG.). 2010. 29.98 (978-1-60788-212-1(4)) Pub: Hachet Audio. Dist(s): HachBkGrp

Bible, Old & New Testament see Biblia, Antiguo y Nuevo Testamento

***Bible on the Go.** unabr. ed. Zondervan. (Running Time: 0 hr. 16 mins. 11 sec.). (Best-Loved Stories of the Bible, NIrV Ser.). (ENG.). (J). 2010. 1.99 (978-0-310-86518-6(2)) Pub: Zondkidz. Dist(s): Zondervan

***Bible on the Go, Vol. 27.** unabr. ed. Zondervan. (Running Time: 0 hr. 15 mins. 57 sec.). (Best-Loved Stories of the Bible, NIrV Ser.). (ENG.). (J). 2010. 1.99 (978-0-310-86519-3(0)) Pub: Zondkidz. Dist(s): Zondervan

***Bible on the Go: The Story of Samuel.** unabr. ed. Zondervan. (Running Time: 0 hr. 19 mins. 55 sec.). (Best-Loved Stories of the Bible, NIrV Ser.). (ENG.). (J). 2010. 1.99 (978-0-310-86507-0(7)) Pub: Zondkidz. Dist(s): Zondervan

***Bible on the Go Vol. 16: David & Goliath - David & Jonathan - David & Saul (1 Samuel 17-18, 20, 24, 31)** unabr. ed. Zondervan Publishing Staff. (Best-Loved Stories of the Bible, NIrV Ser.). (ENG.). (J). 2010. 1.99 (978-0-310-86508-7(5)) Pub: Zondkidz. Dist(s): Zondervan

***Bible on the Go Vol. 01: Creation & the Fall (Genesis 1-4)** unabr. ed. Zondervan. (Running Time: 0 hr. 13 mins. 55 sec.). (Best-Loved Stories of the Bible, NIrV Ser.). (ENG.). (J). 2010. 1.99 (978-0-310-86493-6(3)) Pub: Zondkidz. Dist(s): Zondervan

***Bible on the Go Vol. 02: the Flood & the Tower of Babel (Genesis 6-9, 11)** unabr. ed. Zondervan. (Running Time: 0 hr. 10 mins. 54 sec.). (Best-Loved Stories of the Bible, NIrV Ser.). (ENG.). (J). 2010. 1.99 (978-0-310-86494-3(1)) Pub: Zondkidz. Dist(s): Zondervan

***Bible on the Go Vol. 03: the Story of Abraham & Isaac (Genesis 12, 15, 18-19, 21-22)** unabr. ed. Zondervan. (Running Time: 0 hr. 12 mins. 28 sec.). (Best-Loved Stories of the Bible, NIrV Ser.). (ENG.). (J). 2010. 1.99 (978-0-310-86495-0(X)) Pub: Zondkidz. Dist(s): Zondervan

***Bible on the Go Vol. 04: the Story of Isaac & Rebecca; the Story of Jacob (Genesis 24-25, 27-29)** unabr. ed. Zondervan. (Running Time: 0 hr. 15 mins. 28 sec.). (Best-Loved Stories of the Bible, NIrV Ser.). (ENG.). (J). 2010. 1.99 (978-0-310-86496-7(8)) Pub: Zondkidz. Dist(s): Zondervan

***Bible on the Go Vol. 06: Slavery in Egypt & the Story of Moses (Exodus 1-6)** unabr. ed. Zondervan. (Running Time: 0 hr. 11 mins. 18 sec.). (Best-Loved Stories of the Bible, NIrV Ser.). (ENG.). (J). 2010. 1.99 (978-0-310-86498-1(4)) Pub: Zondkidz. Dist(s): Zondervan

***Bible on the Go Vol. 07: the Ten Plagues on Egypt; the First Passover; & the Exodus (Exodus 7-12)** unabr. ed. Zondervan. (Running Time: 0 hr. 17 mins. 11 sec.). (Best-Loved Stories of the Bible, NIrV Ser.). (ENG.). (J). 2010. 1.99 (978-0-310-86499-8(2)) Pub: Zondkidz. Dist(s): Zondervan

***Bible on the Go Vol. 08: the Desert Journey & the Ten Commandments (Exodus 13-16, 19-20, 24, 26)** unabr. ed. Zondervan. (Running Time: 0 hr. 17 mins. 59 sec.). (Best-Loved Stories of the Bible, NIrV Ser.). (ENG.). (J). 2010. 1.99 (978-0-310-86500-1(X)) Pub: Zondkidz. Dist(s): Zondervan

***Bible on the Go Vol. 09: the Holy Tent & the Golden Calf (Exodus 26, 32, 40)** unabr. ed. Zondervan. (Running Time: 0 hr. 13 mins. 9 sec.). (Best-Loved Stories of the Bible, NIrV Ser.). (ENG.). (J). 2010. 1.99 (978-0-310-86501-8(8)) Pub: Zondkidz. Dist(s): Zondervan

***Bible on the Go Vol. 10: Report on the Promised Land; the Bronze Snake; & Baalam's Donkey (Numbers 13-14, 21-22)** unabr. ed. Zondervan. (Running Time: 0 hr. 12 mins. 0 sec.). (Best-Loved Stories of the Bible, NIrV Ser.). (ENG.). (J). 2010. 1.99 (978-0-310-86502-5(6)) Pub: Zondkidz. Dist(s): Zondervan

***Bible on the Go Vol. 13: the Stories of Gideon & Samson (Judges 6-8, 13, 16)** unabr. ed. Zondervan. (Best-Loved Stories of the Bible, NIrV Ser.). (ENG.). (J). 2010. 1.99 (978-0-310-86505-6(0)) Pub: Zondkidz. Dist(s): Zondervan

***Bible on the Go Vol. 14: the Story of Ruth (Ruth 1-4)** unabr. ed. Zondervan. (Running Time: 0 hr. 8 mins. 51 sec.). (Best-Loved Stories of the Bible, NIrV Ser.). (ENG.). (J). 2010. 1.99 (978-0-310-86506-3(9)) Pub: Zondkidz. Dist(s): Zondervan

***Bible on the Go Vol. 17: David Anointed King; David & Bathsheba; David Plans to Build the Temple (2 Samuel 2, 5, 9, 11; 1 Chronicles 22)** unabr. ed. Zondervan. (Running Time: 0 hr. 16 mins. 57 sec.). (Best-Loved Stories of the Bible, NIrV Ser.). (ENG.). (J). 2010. 1.99 (978-0-310-86509-4(3)) Pub: Zondkidz. Dist(s): Zondervan

***Bible on the Go Vol. 18: the Story of King Solomon (1 Kings 2-4, 6-8)** unabr. ed. Zondervan. (Running Time: 0 hr. 15 mins. 19 sec.). (Best-Loved Stories of the Bible, NIrV Ser.). (ENG.). (J). 2010. 1.99 (978-0-310-86510-0(7)) Pub: Zondkidz. Dist(s): Zondervan

***Bible on the Go Vol. 19: the Bad Kings of Israel; the Story of Elijah (1 Kings 14-19, 21; 2 Kings 2)** unabr. ed. Zondervan. (Running Time: 0 hr. 20 mins. 35 sec.). (Best-Loved Stories of the Bible, NIrV Ser.). (ENG.). (J). 2010. 1.99 (978-0-310-86511-7(5)) Pub: Zondkidz. Dist(s): Zondervan

***Bible on the Go Vol. 20: the Story of Elisha (2 Kings 4-5, 17; 2 Chronicles 24)** unabr. ed. Zondervan. (Best-Loved Stories of the Bible, NIrV Ser.). (ENG.). (J). 2010. 1.99 (978-0-310-86512-4(3)) Pub: Zondkidz. Dist(s): Zondervan

***Bible on the Go Vol. 21: Good King Hezekiah (2 Kings 18, 20; 2 Chronicles 29-31)** unabr. ed. Zondervan. (Running Time: 0 hr. 13 mins. 22 sec.). (Best-Loved Stories of the Bible, NIrV Ser.). (ENG.). (J). 2010. 1.99 (978-0-310-86513-1(1)) Pub: Zondkidz. Dist(s): Zondervan

***Bible on the Go Vol. 22: Judah Destroyed; Nebuchadnezzar; King Darius & Rebuilding the Temple (2 Chronicles 36; Ezra 1-6; Nehemiah 7-8)** unabr. ed. Zondervan. (Running Time: 0 hr. 16 mins. 12 sec.). (Best-Loved Stories of the Bible, NIrV Ser.). (ENG.). (J). 2010. 1.99 (978-0-310-86514-8(X)) Pub: Zondkidz. Dist(s): Zondervan

***Bible on the Go Vol. 24: the Story of Queen Esther (Esther 1-5, 7-9)** unabr. ed. Zondervan. (Running Time: 0 hr. 19 mins. 10 sec.). (Best-Loved Stories of the Bible, NIrV Ser.). (ENG.). (J). 2010. 1.99 (978-0-310-86516-2(6)) Pub: Zondkidz. Dist(s): Zondervan

***Bible on the Go Vol. 25: the Story of Job (Job 1-5, 8, 11, 27, 38, 40, 42)** unabr. ed. Zondervan. (Running Time: 0 hr. 14 mins. 26 sec.). (Best-Loved Stories of the Bible, NIrV Ser.). (ENG.). (J). 2010. 1.99 (978-0-310-86517-9(4)) Pub: Zondkidz. Dist(s): Zondervan

***Bible on the Go Vol. 28: Psalm 128, 145, 51, 55, 67, 95, 121, 139.** unabr. ed. Zondervan. (Running Time: 0 hr. 16 mins. 9 sec.). (Best-Loved Stories of the Bible, NIrV Ser.). (ENG.). (J). 2010. 1.99 (978-0-310-86520-9(4)) Pub: Zondkidz. Dist(s): Zondervan

***Bible on the Go Vol. 31: Words from the Prophet Isaiah, Part 2; the Lord Chooses Jeremiah (Isaiah 52, 60, 63; Jeremiah 1, 24; Ezekiel 30)** unabr. ed. Zondervan. (Running Time: 0 hr. 16 mins. 3 sec.). (Best-Loved Stories of the Bible, NIrV Ser.). (ENG.). (J). 2010. 1.99 (978-0-310-86523-0(9)) Pub: Zondkidz. Dist(s): Zondervan

***Bible on the Go Vol. 32: Daniel & the Fiery Furnance, Writing on the Wall, & the Lion's Den (Daniel 3, 5, 6)** unabr. ed. Zondervan. (Running Time: 0 hr. 17 mins. 30 sec.). (Best-Loved Stories of the Bible, NIrV Ser.). (ENG.). (J). 2010. 1.99 (978-0-310-86524-7(7)) Pub: Zondkidz. Dist(s): Zondervan

***Bible on the Go Vol. 33: Prophets' Warnings; Jonah (Hosea 14; Amos 1, 8-9; Jonah 1-3; Micah 6; Nahum 1; Habakkuk 3; Zephaniah 1-2)** unabr. ed. Zondervan. (Running Time: 0 hr. 16 mins. 13 sec.). (Best-Loved Stories of the Bible, NIrV Ser.). (ENG.). (J). 2010. 1.99 (978-0-310-86525-4(5)) Pub: Zondkidz. Dist(s): Zondervan

***Bible on the Go Vol. 34: the Early Life of Jesus (Luke 1-2; Matthew 2)** unabr. ed. Zondervan. (Running Time: 0 hr. 16 mins. 42 sec.). (Best-Loved Stories of the Bible, NIrV Ser.). (ENG.). (J). 2010. 1.99 (978-0-310-86526-1(3)) Pub: Zondkidz. Dist(s): Zondervan

***Bible on the Go Vol. 35: Baptism, Temptation, Disciples, & Miracles of Jesus (Matthew 3-4; Mark 1-2; John 1, 3; Luke 5-6)** unabr. ed. Zondervan. (Running Time: 0 hr. 13 mins. 15 sec.). (Best-Loved Stories of the Bible, NIrV Ser.). (ENG.). (J). 2010. 1.99 (978-0-310-86527-8(1)) Pub: Zondkidz. Dist(s): Zondervan

***Bible on the Go Vol. 38: Parables & Miracles of Jesus, Part 2 (John 6, 9; Matthew 14, 18; Luke 9-10)** unabr. ed. Zondervan. (Running Time: 0 hr. 14 mins. 28 sec.). (Best-Loved Stories of the Bible, NIrV Ser.). (ENG.). (J). 2010. 1.99 (978-0-310-86530-8(1)) Pub: Zondkidz. Dist(s): Zondervan

***Bible on the Go Vol. 39: Parables & Miracles of Jesus, Part 3 (Luke 15, 17, 19; John 11; Matthew 18)** unabr. ed. Zondervan. (Running Time: 0 hr. 14 mins. 31 sec.). (Best-Loved Stories of the Bible, NIrV Ser.). (ENG.). (J). 2010. 1.99 (978-0-310-86531-5(X)) Pub: Zondkidz. Dist(s): Zondervan

***Bible on the Go Vol. 40: the Rich Man; Zacchaeus; Mary's Perfume; Jesus Enters Jerusalem (Mark 10-12; Luke 18-19; John 12; Matthew 21, 24-25)** unabr. ed. Zondervan. (Best-Loved Stories of the Bible, NIrV Ser.). (ENG.). (J). 2010. 1.99 (978-0-310-86532-2(8)) Pub: Zondkidz. Dist(s): Zondervan

***Bible on the Go Vol. 43: Pentecost & the Acts of the Apostles; the Early Believers (Acts 2-8)** unabr. ed. Zondervan. (Running Time: 0 hr. 15 mins. 14 sec.). (Best-Loved Stories of the Bible, NIrV Ser.). (ENG.). (J). 2010. 1.99 (978-0-310-86535-3(2)) Pub: Zondkidz. Dist(s): Zondervan

***Bible on the Go Vol. 44: the Story of Saul; Peter & Cornelius; Peter in Prison (Acts 9-12)** unabr. ed. Zondervan. (Running Time: 0 hr. 13 mins. 49 sec.). (Best-Loved Stories of the Bible, NIrV Ser.). (ENG.). (J). 2010. 1.99 (978-0-310-86536-0(0)) Pub: Zondkidz. Dist(s): Zondervan

***Bible on the Go Vol. 45: Paul & Silas; Priscilla & Aquila; Paul's Letter to the Romans (Acts 16, 18, 20; Romans 1, 5, 8, 12)** unabr. ed. Zondervan. (Running Time: 0 hr. 15 mins. 39 sec.). (Best-Loved Stories of the Bible, NIrV Ser.). (ENG.). (J). 2010. 1.99 (978-0-310-86537-7(9)) Pub: Zondkidz. Dist(s): Zondervan

***Bible on the Go Vol. 46: Paul's Letters to the Corinthians & Galatians (1 Corinthians 12, 13; 2 Corinthians 2, 4, 5; Galatians 5)** unabr. ed. Zondervan. (Running Time: 0 hr. 12 mins. 46 sec.). (Best-Loved Stories of the Bible, NIrV Ser.). (ENG.). (J). 2010. 1.99 (978-0-310-86538-4(7)) Pub: Zondkidz. Dist(s): Zondervan

***Bible on the Go Vol. 47: More of Paul's Letters (Ephesians 1-2, 6; Philippians 2-3; Colossians 3; 2 Thessalonians 1)** unabr. ed. Zondervan. (Running Time: 0 hr. 10 mins. 54 sec.). (Best-Loved Stories of the Bible, NIrV Ser.). (ENG.). (J). 2010. 1.99 (978-0-310-86539-1(5)) Pub: Zondkidz. Dist(s): Zondervan

***Bible on the Go Vol. 49: Letters of John; Jude; Revelation (1 John 3; 3 John; Jude; Revelation 1-2, 4, 19)** unabr. ed. Zondervan. (Running Time: 0 hr. 15 mins. 20 sec.). (Best-Loved Stories of the Bible, NIrV Ser.). (ENG.). (J). 2010. 1.99 (978-0-310-86541-4(7)) Pub: Zondkidz. Dist(s): Zondervan

***Bible on the Go Vol. 50: Revelation 20-22.** unabr. ed. Zondervan. (Running Time: 0 hr. 9 mins. 2 sec.). (Best-Loved Stories of the Bible, NIrV Ser.). (ENG.). (J). 2010. 1.99 (978-0-310-86542-1(5)) Pub: Zondkidz. Dist(s): Zondervan

***Bible on the Go Volumes 1-50 from the Old & New Testaments.** unabr. ed. Zondervan. (Running Time: 12 hrs. 25 mins. 3 sec.). (Best-Loved Stories of the Bible, NIrV Ser.). (ENG.). (J). 2010. 24.99 (978-0-310-72063-8(X)) Pub: Zondkidz. Dist(s): Zondervan

Bible Passages: A Cd Treasury of Audio Scripture. adpt. ed. Ed. by Simon and Schuster Staff. 2006. 17.95 (978-0-7435-6196-9(1)) Pub: S&S Audio. Dist(s): S and S Inc

Bible Passages: A CD Treasury of Audio Scripture. adpt. abr. ed. Created by Simon and Schuster Audio Staff. 4 CDs. (Running Time: 4 hrs. 0 mins. 0 sec.). (ENG.). 2006. audio compact disk 29.95 (978-0-7435-6465-6(0)) Pub: S&S Audio. Dist(s): S and S Inc

Bible Prophecy & Antichrist Revelation, Vol. 4. Speeches. Ronald G. Fanter. 16 cass. (Running Time: 90 mins.). 2003. 80.00 (978-1-931215-42-8(1)) Cut Edge Min.
Tapes Included In This VolumeBabylon The GreatSon of SatanMark of The Beast70th Week of DanielThe Seven TrumpetsSeven Vials of WrathClosing of This DispensationThe Millennial KingdomThe New CreationWhat In The World Is Happening?Lions, Leopards, and BearsThe Islamic ConnectionThe Beast, His Mark, and The GolemThe Mark Of Antichrist's CovenantSet A Cross Upon The ForeheadsThe Two Witnesses.

Bible Prophecy Revelation & Daniel, Vol. 3. Speeches. Ronald G. Fanter. 16 cass. (Running Time: 90 mins.). 2003. 80.00 (978-1-931215-41-1(3)) Cut Edge Min.
Tapes Included In This VolumeThe Rise of IslamThe ReformationThe Five HorsemenThe Great MultitudeChurch of The First Born144,000 First FruitsThe Seventh KingdomThe French RevolutionThe Ten ToesNapoleon and AntichristThe Abrahamic CovenantEphraim And ManassehHitler and AntichristU.N. and AntichristProphetic Trumpet ParallelsThe Turkish Invasion.

Bible Psalms by Dancing Beetle. Perf. by Eugene Ely. 1 cass. (Running Time: 84 min.). (J). 1990. 10.00 Erthviibz.
Bible Psalms & nature sounds come together when Ms. Angelfish & the folk musicians read & sing with Dancing Beetle.

Bible Psychology: Spirit & Soul Album 1: What God's Mirror Reveals. Derek Prince. 4 cass. 19.95 (I-BP1) Derek Prince.

Bible Psychology: Spirit & Soul Album 2: Achieving Inner Harmony. Derek Prince. 4 cass. 19.95 (I-BP2) Derek Prince.

Bible Questions & Answers Four. Finis J. Dake, Sr. (J). (gr. k up). 5.95 (978-1-55829-042-6(7)) Dake Publishing.

Bible Questions & Answers One. Finis J. Dake, Sr. (J). (gr. k up). 5.95 (978-1-55829-039-6(7)) Dake Publishing.
Bible study.

Bible Questions & Answers Three. Finis J. Dake, Sr. (J). (gr. k up). 5.95 (978-1-55829-041-9(9)) Dake Publishing.

Bible Questions & Answers Two, Finis J. Dake, Sr. (J). (gr. k up). 5.95 (978-1-55829-040-2(0)) Dake Publishing.

Bible Skills, Drills, & Thrills. (J). (gr. 1-3). 2004. cd-rom & audio compact disk 24.95 (978-0-633-19427-7(1)) LifeWay Christian.

Bible Skills, Drills, & Thrills. (J). (gr. 4-6). 2004. cd-rom & audio compact disk 24.95 (978-0-633-19428-4(X)) LifeWay Christian.

Bible Smuggler. Louise Vernon. Narrated by Fern Ebersole. (ENG.). (J). 2009. audio compact disk 15.95 (978-0-9801244-0-8(9)) IG Publish.

Bible Songs. 1 cass. (Running Time: 1 hr.). 2001. pap. bk. & tchr. ed. 9.95 (7) Audio Memory.
Eleven original songs based on the "New International Children's Bible," as well as memory verses from "The Sermon on the Mount." Accompaniment tracks on second side.

Bible Songs. 2004. audio compact disk 12.95 (978-1-883028-17-6(5)) Audio Memory.

Bible Songs. 1 cass. (Running Time: 45 mins). 2002. 4.99 (978-1-57583-538-9(X), 3006); audio compact disk 6.99 (978-1-57583-539-6(8), 3007CD) Twin Sisters.
This is one of the first collections of Bible songs you'll want for your children! Watch as they learn simple Biblical principles and truths with these cheerful, upbeat songs! Energetic kids share their joy in the Lord by singing well-known Bible favorites.

Bible Songs. Perf. by Cedarmont Kids. 1 cass. 1999. 3.99 (978-0-00-546328-4(9)) Provident Music.

Bible Songs. Perf. by Cedarmont Kids. 1 CD. (J). 1999. audio compact disk 5.99 (978-0-00-507228-8(X)) Provident Music.

Bible Songs. l.t. ed. Kathy Troxel. Illus. by Ron Wheeler. 1 CD. (Running Time: 1 hr.). (J). (gr. 1-8). 1997. pap. bk. & tchr. ed. 12.95 (978-1-883028-06-0(X), 7CD) Audio Memory.
Eleven original songs based on the "New International Children's Bible," as well as memory verses from the Sermon on the Mount. Accompaniment tracks on second side.

***Bible Songs: Sing-A-Long Bible Songs CD.** unabr. ed. Integrity Music. 2001. audio compact disk 6.98 (978-7-472-02296-9(9)) Nelson.

Bible Stories. Logan Marshall. Narrated by Michael Stevens. Prod. by Ralph LaBarge. (ENG.). (J). 2006. 12.95 (978-0-9798626-8-7(X)) Alpha DVD.

Bible Stories. Ed. by Publications International Staff. (J). 2007. audio compact disk 15.98 (978-1-4127-8479-5(4)) Pubns Intl Ltd.

Bible Stories. Douglas Wilson. 12 CDs. (ENG.). 2003. audio compact disk 40.00 (978-1-59128-459-8(7)) Canon Pr ID.

Bible Stories: In the Beginning. unabr. ed. Read by Paul Newman. 4 cass. (Running Time: 4 hrs.). 1999. 22.00 Set. (978-1-885608-17-8(9)) Airplay.
A clear & captivating telling of the stories which are the core of the Judeo-Christian tradition. Drawn directly from the first five books of the Bible & told in a contemporary voice & clear imagery that will engage listeners of all ages.

Bible Stories - Volume 1. Short Stories. Arranged by Rich Herman. (J). 2004. audio compact disk 9.95 (978-0-9765630-2-0(9)) Family Bks N CDs.
Bible Stories Volume 1 - Contains six fun and exciting stories about: God, David and Goliath, Daniel, Jesus, Moses, and King Solomon. Stories include: In The Beginning, David and Goliath, Daniel and the Lion's Den, Jesus Calms the Storm, How Moses Was Saved, and The King and the Bees. Your children will love these story CDs. Great music and voice talent make these stories come to life!http://www.FamilyBooksandCDs.com.

Bible Stories- Tape. Read by Douglas Wilson. 12 cass. (YA). 2003. 40.00 (978-1-59128-460-4(0)) Canon Pr ID.

Bible Stories for Children. unabr. ed. 2 cass. (J). 10.95 (TC-909) Audio Bk.

Bible Stories for Children, Dramatized, Vol. 1. unabr. ed. 4 cass. (Running Time: 14 min. per cass.). Dramatization. (J). (gr. 3 up). 19.95 (S50081) J Norton Pubs.

Bible Stories for Children, Dramatized, Vol. 2. unabr. ed. 4 cass. (Running Time: 14 min. per cass.). Dramatization. (J). 19.95 (S50082) J Norton Pubs.

Bible Stories for Children from the Old Testament. abr. ed. 2 cass. (J). 10.95 (978-0-89926-213-0(9)) Audio Bk.
Includes "Noah & the Ark," "The Tower of Babel," "Jacob's Ladder," "David & Goliath," & more.

Bible Stories for Growing Kids. unabr. ed. Francine Rivers & Shannon Rivers Coibion. Narrated by Jill Tweeten. (Running Time: 3 hrs. 28 mins. 2 sec.). (ENG.). (J). 2007. audio compact disk 17.99 (978-1-59859-300-6(5)) Oasis Audio.

Bible Stories for Growing Kids. unabr. ed. Francine Rivers & Shannon Rivers Coibion. Narrated by Jill Tweeten. (ENG.). (J). 2007. 12.59 (978-1-60814-062-6(8)) Oasis Audio.

Bible Stories from the New Testament. Read by Martin Jarvis & Rosalind Ayres. 2 cass. (Running Time: 3 hrs.). (J). 1999. 16.85 (978-1-901768-33-6(3)) Pub: CSA Telltapes GBR. Dist(s): Ulverscroft US
Concentrating mainly on the four Gospels, this carefully chosen compilation gives a broad yet coherent view of the New Testament.

Bible Stories from the New Testament. abr. ed. Ed. by Jane Webb. 2 cass. (Running Time: 1 hr. 44 min.). (J). 12.95 (978-0-89926-161-4(2), 849) Audio Bk.

Bible Stories from the Old Testament, Set. Read by Martin Jarvis & Rosalind Ayres. 2 cass. (Running Time: 3 hrs.). (J). 1999. 16.85 (978-1-901768-32-9(5)) Pub: CSA Telltapes GBR. Dist(s): Ulverscroft US
Anthology presenting the Old Testament as a continuous record, the written "history" of a people.

Bible Stories-mp3. Read by Douglas Wilson. 12. 2003. 32.00 (978-1-59128-458-1(9)) Canon Pr ID.

Bible Studies No. 102: National Association of Evangelicals 47th Annual Convention, Columbus Ohio, March 7-9, 1989, (Wednesday) David R. Mains. 1 cass. 1989. 4.24 ea 1-8 tapes.; 4.00 ea. 9 tapes or more. Nat Assn Evan.

Bible Studies No. 103: National Association of Evangelicals, 47th Annual Convention, Columbus, Ohio, March 7-9, 1989 (Thursday) David R. Mains. 1 cass. 1989. 4.25 ea. 1-8 tapes. Nat Assn Evan.

Bible Studies No. 103: National Association of Evangelicals, 47th Annual Convention, Columbus, Ohio, March 7-9, 1989 (Thursday), David R. Mains. 1 cass. 1989. 4.00 ea. 9 tapes or more. Nat Assn Evan.

Bible Studies Pts. 1 & 2: Proceedings of the 45th Annual Convention National Association of Evangelicals Buffalo, New York. Read by William McRae. 1 cass. (Running Time: 60 min.). 1987. 4.00 Pt. 1. (306); 4.00 Pt. 2. (333) Nat Assn Evan.

Bible Study Guide for All Ages: Children's Song Tape. Donald Baker & Brian Baker. 1 cass. (J). (gr. 2-8). 1982. 6.00 (978-1-879614-06-2(5)) Bible Study Gu.
Children's songs listed in the Bible Study Guide for All Ages.

Bible Teasers, Vol. 1. 1 cass. (Running Time: 1 hr.). bk. 12.95 (978-0-89051-183-1(7)) Master Bks.

Bible Teasers Junior, Vol. 1. 1 cass. (Running Time: 1 hr.). (J). bk. 12.95 (978-0-89051-184-8(5)) Master Bks.

Bible Truths for Children. Contrib. by Filling Station Staff. 12 cass. (J). 1995. 19.98 Set. (978-7-902030-09-0(0)) Chrstn Dup Intl.

Bible Truths K5 CD. audio compact disk 15.50 (978-1-59166-241-9(9)) BJUPr.

Bible Truths 2: A Servant's Heart Cassette. 13.00 (978-1-59166-126-9(9)) BJUPr.

BibleQuizMania: Genesis. Steven Sanders. 3 cass. (Running Time: 2 hrs. 10 min.). 19.95 Set. (978-0-929536-06-4(1)) Emb Cassettes.
Educational series incorporating a "quiz" format with Bible studies as the subject matter.

BibleQuizMania: The Easter Story. Steven Sanders. 2 cass. (Running Time: 2 hrs. 5 min.). 14.95 Set. (978-0-929536-07-1(X)) Emb Cassettes.

Biblesoft Best of Larry Burket. Larry Burkett. 2004. audio compact disk 59.95 (978-1-56514-267-1(5)) Biblesoft.

Biblesoft Spiritual Growth Ser. Stanley Charles. 2004. audio compact disk 59.95 (978-1-56514-266-4(7)) Biblesoft.

BibleZone Live! All Ages at Jesus' Feet. bk. (978-0-687-04240-1(2)) Abingdon.

BibleZone Live! All Ages by the Waters. bk. (978-0-687-04231-9(3)) Abingdon.

BibleZone Live! All Ages in a Foreign Land. bk. (978-0-687-04243-2(7)) Abingdon.

BibleZone Live! All Ages in God's House. bk. (978-0-687-04236-4(4)) Abingdon.

BibleZone Live! All Ages in Jerusalem. bk. (978-0-687-04238-8(0)) Abingdon.

BibleZone Live! All Ages in the City of David. bk. (978-0-687-04237-1(2)) Abingdon.

BibleZone Live! All Ages in the Garden. bk. (978-0-687-04233-3(X)) Abingdon.

BibleZone Live! All Ages in the Land of the Messiah. bk. (978-0-687-04241-8(0)) Abingdon.

BibleZone Live! All Ages in the Peaceful Kingdom. bk. (978-0-687-04232-6(1)) Abingdon.

BibleZone Live! All Ages in the Wilderness. bk. (978-0-687-04234-0(8)) Abingdon.

BibleZone Live! All Ages Inside Mud & Stone. bk. (978-0-687-04239-5(9)) Abingdon.

BibleZone Live! All Ages on the Road. bk. (978-0-687-04242-5(9)) Abingdon.

BibleZone Live! Older Elementary Wrap in the Land of the Messiah. Abingdon Press Staff. 2005. 79.99 (978-0-687-04280-7(1)) Abingdon.

Biblia, Antiguo y Nuevo Testamento. Tr. of Bible, Old & New Testament. (SPA.). 2001. (978-84-305-5007-4(0)) Lectorum Pubns.

Biblia de las Americas. Narrated by Samuel Montoya. (SPA.). 2007. audio compact disk 39.99 (978-1-930034-12-9(1)) Casscomm.

Biblia en Canciones No. 1: Twenty-Five Nuevas Canciones para Ninos de 4 a 12 Anos. 1 cass. (Running Time: 36 min.). (J). (ps-6). 1995. 9.95 Liguori Pubns.
Twenty-five songs for 4 to 12 year old Spanish speaking children present characters form the Old & New Testament.

Biblia en Canciones No. 2: Twenty-One Nuevas Canciones para Ninos de 4 a 12 Anos. 1 cass. (Running Time: 42 min.). (J). (ps-6). 1995. 9.95 Liguori Pubns.
Twenty-one new songs for 4 to 12 year old Spanish speaking children present characters from the Old & New Testament.

Biblical Apologetics: Jesus & Logic. John Robbins. 1 cass. (Introduction to Apologetics Ser.: No. 8). 5.00 Trinity Found.

Biblical Apologetics: Jesus & Scripture. John Robbins. 1 cass. (Introduction to Apologetics Ser.: No. 7). 5.00 Trinity Found.

Biblical Apologetics: Paul & Scripture; Paul & Logic. John Robbins. 1 cass. (Introduction to Apologetics Ser.: No. 9). 5.00 Trinity Found.

Biblical Apologetics: Summary & Conclusion. John Robbins. 1 cass. (Introduction to Apologetics Ser.: No. 10). 5.00 Trinity Found.

Biblical Approach to Spanking. abr. ed. Dennis Rainey & Barbara Rainey. Ed. by Keith Lynch. 5 cass. (Running Time: 2 hrs. 30 min.). 1993. 24.95 Set. (978-1-57229-036-5(6)) FamilyLife.

Biblical Basis for Spiritual Conflict. 2000. 22.00 (978-0-9702183-2-2(X)) Aslans Pl.

Biblical Childrearing-mp3. Douglas Wilson. 1996. 9.50 (978-1-59128-215-0(2)) Canon Pr ID.

Biblical Childrearing-tape. Douglas Wilson. 4 cass. 1996. 12.00 (978-1-59128-217-4(9)) Canon Pr ID.

Biblical Courtship-mp3-Vol. 1: Vol. 1, Vol. 1. Read by Douglas Wilson. 1994. 9.50 (978-1-59128-239-6(X)) Canon Pr ID.

Biblical Courtship-mp3-Vol. 2: Walking in Holiness & Wisdom: Vol. 2, Vol. 2. Read by Douglas Wilson & Chris Schlect. 4. 2003. 9.50 (978-1-59128-440-6(6)) Canon Pr ID.

Biblical Courtship-tape-Vol. 1: Vol. 1, Vol. 1. Read by Douglas Wilson. 4 cass. 1994. 12.00 (978-1-59128-241-9(1)) Canon Pr ID.

Biblical Courtship-tape-Vol. 2: Walking in Holiness & Wisdom: Vol. 2, Vol. 2. Read by Douglas Wilson & Chris Schlect. 4 cass. 2003. 12.00 (978-1-59128-442-0(2)) Canon Pr ID.

Biblical Economics. Instructed by Stephen McDowell. 2000. 5.95 (978-1-887456-27-2(9)) Providence Found.

Biblical Evangelism-tape. Read by Douglas Wilson. 4 cass. 1990. 12.00 (978-1-59128-220-4(9)) Canon Pr ID.

Biblical Foundation for Faith. Bill Winston. 6 cass. (Running Time: 8hr.05min.). (C). 1995. 49.00 (978-1-931289-51-1(4)); 49.00 (978-1-931289-53-5(0)) Pub: B Winston Min. Dist(s): Anchor Distributors

Biblical Foundations for Peacemaking: National Association of Evangelicals, 47th Annual Convention, Columbus, Ohio, March 7-9, 1989. John M. Perkins. 1 cass. (Luncheons Ser.: No. 115-Thursd). 1989. 4.00 ea. 1-8.; 4.25 ea. 9 tapes or more. Nat Assn Evan.

Biblical Guidelines: 1 Cor 14:1-15. Ed Younger. 1986. 4.95 (978-0-7417-1516-6(3), 516) Win Walk.

Biblical Guidelines: 1 Cor. 14:17-40. Ed Young. 1986. 4.95 (978-0-7417-1517-3(1), 517) Win Walk.

Biblical Hebrew. 2nd rev. ed. Bonnie Pedrotti Kittel et al. (Yale Language Ser.). (ENG & HEB.). 2004. audio compact disk 36.00 (978-0-300-09864-8(2)) Yale U Pr.

Biblical Home-mp3-Vol. 1: Life in the Front Rooms. Read by Douglas Wilson. 2002. 16.00 (978-1-59128-389-8(2)) Canon Pr ID.

Biblical Home-mp3-Vol. 2: Life in the Back Rooms. Read by Douglas Wilson. 10. 2003. 27.00 (978-1-59128-443-7(0)) Canon Pr ID.

Biblical Home-tape-Vol. 1: Life in the Front Rooms. Read by Douglas Wilson. 6 cass. 2002. 20.00 (978-1-59128-391-1(4)) Canon Pr ID.

Biblical Home-tape-Vol. 2: Life in the Back Rooms. Read by Douglas Wilson. 10 cass. 2003. 34.00 (978-1-59128-445-1(7)) Canon Pr ID.

Biblical Humor: 11 Cor. 12:11; 13:4. Ed Young. 1990. 4.95 (978-0-7417-1800-6(6), 800) Win Walk.

Biblical Illustrator Plus CD-ROM Master. 2004. audio compact disk 7.95 (978-0-633-09915-2(5)); audio compact disk 7.95 (978-0-633-17928-1(0)) LifeWay Christian.

Biblical Illustrator Plus CD-ROM Master. 2004. audio compact disk 7.95 (978-0-633-17929-8(9)) LifeWay Christian.

Biblical Illustrator Plus CD-ROM Master. 2004. audio compact disk 7.95 (978-0-633-17930-4(2)) LifeWay Christian.

Biblical Illustrator Plus CD-ROM Master. 2004. audio compact disk 7.95 (978-0-633-17931-1(0)) LifeWay Christian.

Biblical Illustrator Plus CD-ROM Master. 2005. audio compact disk 7.95 (978-0-633-17932-8(9)) LifeWay Christian.

Biblical Illustrator Plus CD-ROM Master. 2005. audio compact disk 7.95 (978-0-633-17933-5(7)) LifeWay Christian.

Biblical Interpretation Program Series: Truth, in Messiah Yeshua. Speeches. Tim Cohen. Featuring Tim Cohen. 6 CDs. (Running Time: 5 hrs. 31 mins.). 2005. audio compact disk 114.95 (978-1-933689-29-6(3), CDPack02) Prophecy Hse.
Here are twelve fascinating teachings on interpretation of scripture with Tim Cohen. Available on six DVDs (DVDPack02) or six CDs (CDPack02), these programs serve to expose false beliefs, while also offering some powerful new evidence - unrecognized by the Church until now - to effectively share Yeshua with unbelieving Israelites: Sound Doctrine and the Last Days, and Modern Versus God's Principles of Interpretation • Examples of Interpretation: Jesus' Hebrew Name and Messianic Title • Jesus' Hebrew Name and Messianic Title in the Context of the Protoevangelium • The Word of Y'hoveh (yod-hay-vav-hay), Testing and Proving All Things, and According to the Torah or Teaching • Similitudes, and Messiah The Son of Joseph Versus Messiah The Son of David • Similitudes Recap, The Psalms, and Fulfilling the Law of Moses • Fulfilling the Law of Moses: The Weekly Sabbath, and Clean Versus Unclean Foods • Fulfilling the Law of Moses: Peter's Vision and Foods, and Hebrew Christianity • Hebrew Christianity's History; Jacob Versus Esau; and Israel and the Church • The Messiah, David, Solomon, and the AntiChrist • Psalm 22, and "Savior" Versus "Messiah"; and The Length of a Generation • Example of a Super-Similitude: Jericho's Collapse and the Apocalypse (Revelation).

Biblical Numerics, Vol. 2. Narrated by N. Cindy Trimm. 2 CDs. (Running Time: 1 hr. 30 mins). 2002. audio compact disk 20.00 (978-1-931635-06-6(4)) Kingdom Life.

Biblical Picture of Life Without God: Romans 1:24-32. Ed Young. 1983. 4.95 (978-0-7417-1349-0(7), 349) Win Walk.

Biblical Portrait of Marriage Audio Album. Instructed by Bruce Wilkinson. 1998. 29.95 (978-1-885447-92-0(2)) Walk Thru the Bible.
Perhaps no crisis in the church is more urgent than the breakdown of the family. That's why no video series is more timely than A Biblical Portrait of Marriage. From sex to spirituality, from in-laws to God's laws, Dr. Bruce Wilkinson addresses couples at every level of maturity and happiness.

Biblical Principles for the Ballot Box: Voting Your Conscience. Douglas W. Phillips. 3 CDs. (Running Time: 3 hrs.). 2004. audio compact disk 21.00 (978-1-929241-99-6(2)) Pub: Vsn Forum. Dist(s): STL Dist NA

Biblical Proofs of the Book of Mormon. Duane S. Crowther. 2005. audio compact disk 12.99 (978-0-88290-826-7(X), HorPubs) CFI Dist.

Biblical Proofs of the Book of Mormon. unabr. ed. Duane S. Crowther. Read by Duane S. Crowther. 1 cass. (Running Time: 60 min.). 1983. 13.98 (978-0-88290-405-4(1), 1803) Horizon Utah.
Cites and explains Biblical passages warning of the apostacy that began in New Testament times, and indentifies essential characteristics of Christ's church which were lost as that apostacy took place.

Biblical Proofs of the Book of Mormon: The Gospel Scholarship Series. Duane S. Crowther. 2005. audio compact disk 12.99 (978-0-88290-843-4(X), HorPubs) CFI Dist.

Biblical Proofs of the Restored Church. unabr. ed. Duane S. Crowther. Read by Duane S. Crowther. 1 cass. (Running Time: 60 min.). 1979. 13.98 (978-0-88290-138-1(9), 1808) Horizon Utah.
Verse-by-verse explanations are made illustrating the strong Biblical evidence that Old Testament prophets & the Savior Himself knew that the Book of Mormon would some day come forth as another testament of Jesus Christ.

Biblical Reflections. 7 cass. Incl. Biblical Reflections: A Search for the Quaker Jesus. Anne Thomas. 1986.; Biblical Reflections: Coming Home: Reflections on the Gospel of John. Rebecca Mays & Peter Crysdale. 1986.; Biblical Reflections: Discerning the Way. Mary Morrison. 1986.; Biblical Reflections: Provenance: A Context of the New Testament for Friends. Anne Thomas. 1986.; Biblical Reflections: Reading the Bible by the Inner Light. Dorothy Reichart. 1986.; Biblical Reflections: Scriptural Vision of Community. Thomas Jeavons. 1986.; Biblical Reflections: Wrestling with Liberation Theology: A Quaker View. Shirley Dodson. 1986.; 1986. 24.50 Set.; 4.50 ea. Pendle Hill.

Biblical Reflections: A Search for the Quaker Jesus see Biblical Reflections

Biblical Reflections: Coming Home: Reflections on the Gospel of John see Biblical Reflections

Biblical Reflections: Discerning the Way see Biblical Reflections

Biblical Reflections: Provenance: A Context of the New Testament for Friends see Biblical Reflections

Biblical Reflections: Reading the Bible by the Inner Light see Biblical Reflections

Biblical Reflections: Scriptural Vision of Community see Biblical Reflections

Biblical Reflections: Wrestling with Liberation Theology: A Quaker View see Biblical Reflections

Biblical Road to Blessing. abr. ed. Benny Hinn. 1 cass. (Running Time: 140 min.). 1996. pap. bk. 15.99 (978-0-7852-7213-7(5)) Nelson.

Biblical Theology of Covenant Priesthood. Scott Hahn. Read by Scott Hahn. 4 cass. 22.95 Set. (5264-C) Ignatius Pr.
Explains how the essential meaning & responsibilities of the priesthood reflect man's natural role in the family - as father, son, bridegroom & brother. Shows how Christ fulfills this fourfold function through His own sacrificial self-offering, which all baptized people are called to share, especially ordained Priests.

Biblical Understanding of Mary. Scott Hahn. 4 cass. 1995. 22.95 Set. (134-C) Ignatius Pr.
Titles include: "Mary, Mother of Mercy:" Scripture illuminates Christ's mother as the fountain of mercy. "Mary, Queen of the Angels:" God makes Mary the Queen of Heaven, above even the angels. "The Immaculate Conception:" Scott tackles the toughest Marian doctrine for Protestants. "Mary, Ark of the Covenant:" Mary carried in her womb Jesus, the New Covenant of salvation.

Biblical View of Illicit Sex: 1 Cor. 5:1-13. Ed Young. 1986. 4.95 (978-0-7417-1492-3(2), 492) Win Walk.

Biblical View of Money 630: James 5:7-12. Ed Young. 1987. 4.95 (978-0-7417-1629-3(1), 630) Win Walk.

Biblical Wisdom Literature. Instructed by Joseph Koterski. 2009. 199.95 (978-1-59803-523-0(1)); audio compact disk 269.95 (978-1-59803-524-7(X)) Teaching Co.

Biblioteca de Estudio Biblico. 2004. audio compact disk 29.95 (978-1-57799-078-9(1)) Logos Res Sys.

Biblioteca de los Ninos, Set. Océano Staff. Illus. by Maria Pascual. 6 cass. (Running Time: 6 hrs.).Tr. of Children's Library. (SPA.). 2000. 80.00 (978-84-494-1143-4(2), GML07104-176457) Pub: Oceano Grupo ESP. Dist(s): Gale

Biblioteca Multimedia Santillana. Equipo de Expertos 2100 Staff. (SPA.). (J). (gr. k-12). audio compact disk 59.95 (978-84-294-6345-3(3)) Santillana.

Biblioteca Saltamontes Spanish Chapter Books Coleccion Cuentos de Familia: Classroom Set contains 10 copies each of 6 Chapter Books (60 books total), Activity Masters, & Teacher's Guide. (SPA.). (gr. 2-3). reel tape 472.34 (978-0-7362-1609-8(X)); audio compact disk 468.90 (978-0-7362-1610-4(3)) Hampton-Brown.

Biblioteca Saltamontes Spanish Chapter Books Coleccion Viva Chivito! Classroom Set & Manipulatives. (SPA.). (gr. 1-2). bk. 517.82 (978-0-7362-1591-6(3)); bk. 521.25 (978-0-7362-1589-3(1)) Hampton-Brown.

Biblioteca Saltamontes Spanish Chapter Books Coleccion Viva Chivito! Classroom Set with CDs. (SPA.). (gr. 1-2). audio compact disk 433.38 (978-0-7362-1590-9(5)) Hampton-Brown.

Biblioteca Saltamontes Spanish Chapter Books Coleccion Viva Chivito! Classroom Set with Tapes. (SPA.). (gr. 1-2). reel tape 436.82 (978-0-7362-1588-6(3)) Hampton-Brown.

Bicentennial: The African Methodist Episcopal Church. 1 cass. (Running Time: 30 min.). 9.95 (HO-87-07-74, HarperThor) HarpC GBR.

Bicentennial Bliss. Cathleen Elmer. 2007. 14.95 (978-0-9793766-2-7(9)) Burning Brdge.

Bicentennial Buddhism. Vajracarya. 1 cass. 1976. 10.00 Vajradhatu.
A seminar by the scholar & meditation master trained in the philosophical & meditative traditions of Buddhism in Tibet.

Bicentennial of Buddhism. Read by Chogyam Trungpa. 1 cass. 1976. 10.00 (A084) Vajradhatu.

Bichon Frise: A Basic Guide to this Canine Breed. Karen Jean Matsko Hood. 2009. audio compact disk 29.95 (978-1-59808-919-6(6)) Whsprng Pine.

Bichon Frise: A Basic Guide to This Canine Breed. Karen Jean Matsko Hood. 2006. 29.95 (978-1-59808-918-9(8)) Whsprng Pine.

Bickersons. Perf. by Don Ameche et al. 1 cass. (Running Time: 60 min.). 1947. 7.95 (CC-6040) Natl Recrd Co.
Includes one complete half-hour program, a Danny Thomas comedy skit & two sketches on "the-honey-moon-is-over" theme.

Bickersons, No. 2. Perf. by Don Ameche et al. 1 cass. (Running Time: 60 min.). 1947. 7.95 (CC-5025) Natl Recrd Co.

Bickersons: Fun with the Bickersons & More "Fighting" Fun. unabr. ed. Perf. by Don Ameche & Frances Langford. 1 cass. (Running Time: 1 hr.). 2001. 6.98 (2191) Radio Spirits.

***Bickersons: Put Out the Lights.** Perf. by Don Ameche & Frances Langford. 2010. audio compact disk Rental 18.95 (978-1-57019-948-6(5)) Radio Spirits.

Bickersons: Three Comedy Sketches. Perf. by Don Ameche & Danny Thomas. 1 cass. (Running Time: 60 min.). 7.95 (CC-5720) Natl Recrd Co.
"The Bickersons" features three "pre-dawn" ten-minute sketches of the arguing Bickersons & brother-in-law, Amos. In the "Baby Snooks" episodes Snooks donates two of Daddy's best suits to a charity auction, & Daddy has to bid on his clothes to get them back, & Daddy helps Snooks with her homework.

Bickersons: Volume 1, Vol. 1. Created by Radio Spirits. (Running Time: 10800 sec.). 2005. audio compact disk 9.98 (978-1-57019-800-7(4)) Radio Spirits.

Bicycle Days. John Burnham Schwartz. Read by John Burnham Schwartz. (Running Time: 30 min.). 8.95 (AMF-231) Am Audio Prose.
Talks on being American in Japan.

Bicycle Diaries. unabr. ed. David Byrne. Read by David Byrne. (Running Time: 9 hrs.). (gr. 12 up). 2009. audio compact disk 29.95 (978-0-14-314494-6(4), PengAudBks) Penguin Grp USA.

Bicycles & Accessories in Netherlands: A Strategic Reference 2007. Compiled by Icon Group International, Inc. Staff. 2007. ring bd. 195.00 (978-0-497-82367-2(5)) Icon Grp.

Bid for Fortune. unabr. ed. Guy Boothby. Narrated by Flo Gibson. 6 cass. (Running Time: 8 hrs. 39 mins.). 2003. 24.95 (978-1-55685-668-6(7)) Audio Bk Con.
We travel from London to Egypt, Australia & the South Seas, while Hatteras pursues the love of his life who has been kidnapped by the sinister Dr. Nikola.

Bidden or Not Bidden, God Is Present. Speeches. Featuring Gregory F. Augustine Pierce. 2 CDs. 2004. audio compact disk 12.95 (978-0-87946-256-7(6), 415) ACTA Pubns.
This double CD contains two separate talks by Gregory F. Augustine Pierce, author of the award-winning Spirituality @ Work: 10 Ways to Balance Your Life On-the-Job and the President and Co-Publisher of ACTA Publications. The first, "Spirituality of Work: An Oxymoron?" contains an exploration of the true definition and criteria for spirituality and whether or not spirituality can be practiced in the midst of the hustle and bustle of most workplaces. The second, "If We Get the Dismissal Right, We'll Get the Mission Right," uses the Dismissal from Mass as a lens through which to look at the mission of every Christian to "go forth" and work to transform the world. Both talks were recorded live.

Bidii. Marjorie W. Thomas. Narrated by Marjorie W. Thomas. Illus. by Patrick S. Begay. 1 CD. (Running Time: 40 mins.). (NAV & ENG.). (J). 2000. audio compact disk 10.95 (978-1-893354-25-8(3)) Pub: Salina Bkshelf. Dist(s): Natl Bk Netwk
Audio narration of Marjorie Thomas's story Bidii. Read in both Navajo and English by the author.Bidii is the story of a young boy named ?Bidii? or ?Greedy,? who loves showing off in front of his friends. While his family works to get their sheep to the annual sheep dip, however, he learns that he should not be so greedy and that he should refrain from shamelessly showing off in front of others. A humorous story with a valuable lesson, Bidii remains a favorite in the classroom.

Bien l'Bonjour d'Alphonse. Alphonse Allais. Perf. by Compagnie Petits Poids. 1 cass. Dramatization. (FRE.). 1996. 21.95 (1813-LQP) Olivia & Hill.
This play is typical of Allais' ability to mix humor & the absurd.

Bienenkonigin. Jacob W. Grimm & Wilhelm K. Grimm. 1 cass. (Running Time: 60 min.). (Bruder Grimm Kinder & Hausmarchen Ser.). (GER.). 1996. pap. bk. 19.50 (978-1-58085-218-0(1), GR-13) Interlingua VA.
Includes German transcription. Includes title story, Der Barenhauter, Der Arme und der Reiche, Das Meerhaschen, Die Goldene Gans. The combination of written text & clarity & pace of diction will open the door for intermediate & advanced students to genuine comprehension & the use of literary texts for advancement in rapid understanding of written & oral language materials. The audio text plus written text concept makes foreign languages accessible to a much wider range of students than books alone.

Bienveillantes see Kindly Ones

Bienvenido Santos, 1 and 2. unabr. ed. Bienvenido Santos. Read by Bienvenido Santos. 1 cass. (Running Time: 29 min.). Incl. House That I Built. 1984.; Visit to Sulucan. 1984.; 1984. 18.00 New Letters.
This once exiled Filipino author reads two of his short stories & various poems, all set in the Phillipines.

Bienvenidos, Level 3. Dade County Public Schools Staff. 8 cass. (Spanish for Young Americans Ser.). (SPA.). 195.00 (978-0-8442-7183-5(7), Natl Textbk Co) M-H Contemporary.
Third-level program. Model for oral-aural practice.

Big Al & Shrimpy. unabr. ed. Andrew Clements. 1 cass. (Running Time: 15 min.). (J). 2003. 10.00 (978-1-4025-5546-6(6)) Recorded Bks.
In the whole wide blue sea, there's not a fish as clever as Shrimpy. But poor Shrimpy is so small that no one wants to be his friend. Then one day Shrimpy becomes best friends with Big Al, the most popular fish of all. With Big Al beside him, Shrimpy always has plenty to eat, and he gets to swim to wonderful new places. But when Big Al swims too close to the edge of the Big Deep, it's up to clever Shrimpy to save the day.

Big Annie: An American Tall Tale. unabr. ed. Sandra Robbins. Read by Jeff Olmsted & Natalie Robinson. 1 cass. (Running Time: 32 min.). Dramatization. (See-More Ser.). (J). (gr. k-3). 1991. 5.50 (978-1-882601-12-7(2)) See-Mores Wrkshop.
Based on Shadow Box Theatre's Production. Big Annie is a larger-than-life heroine - a Creole flatboat captain who uses her amazing strength & the help of some animal friends, to pull a boatload of toys through a terrible storm one Christmas Eve long ago.

Big Annie: An American Tall Tale (Christmas) Sandra Robbins. Read by Jeff Olmsted. 1 CD. (Running Time: 32 mins). (See-More's Stories Ser.). (J). 1998. pap. bk. 16.95 (978-1-882601-37-0(8)) See-Mores Wrkshop.

Big Backyard: Nature's Musical Verse for Children. Phyllis Rhodes. Perf. by J. C. Horton. Illus. by David Moffett. 1 cass. (Running Time: 25 min.). (J). (ps-1). 1998. bk. 30.00 (978-0-9661359-0-9(3)) Curio Pr.
Celebrates a joyful participation with nature in word & music. A story line & 24 musical verses about different creatures.

Big Bad City. abr. ed. Read by Ed McBain, pseud. 4 cass. (Running Time: 6 hrs.). (87th Precinct Ser.: Bk. 49). 2000. 12.99 (978-1-57815-180-6(5), 4418, Media Bks Audio) Media Bks NJ.
The first thing you need to know about this city is that it is big& the next thing you need to know is that it's dangerous.This week's city tabloids depict the face of a pretty, dead girl who lay sprawled near a park bench not seven blocks from the 87th precinct house, while the late night news reports on the latest exploits of the Cookie Boy, a professional thief who leaves a box of chocolate chip cookies behind after a score.

Big Bad City. abr. ed. Ed McBain, pseud. Read by Ed McBain, pseud. 5 vols. (Running Time: 6 hrs.). (87th Precinct Ser.: Bk. 49). 2001. audio compact disk 14.99 (978-1-57815-534-7(7), Media Bks Audio) Media Bks NJ.

Big Bad City. unabr. ed. Ed McBain, pseud. Read by Jonathan Marosz. 5 cass. (Running Time: 7 hrs. 30 mins.). (87th Precinct Ser.: Bk. 49). 1999. 40.00 (978-0-7366-4460-0(1), 4905) Books on Tape.
Detectives Brown & Carella, out investigating the homicide of a young woman found strangled in the park, run into complications. The victim turns out to be a nun & the nun had breast implants. As they piece together her secrets the detectives search for items stolen by the Cookie Boy, a professional thief who leaves a box of chocolate chip cookies behind after a score. Carella is so distracted by the cases, he doesn't even notice that he's being stalked by the psycho who killed his father.

Big Bad City. unabr. ed. Ed McBain, pseud. Read by Jonathan Marosz. 5 CDs. (Running Time: 6 hrs.). (87th Precinct Ser.: Bk. 49). 2001. audio compact disk Books on Tape.

Big Bad Wolf. unabr. ed. James Patterson. Read by Peter Jay Fernandez & Denis O'Hare. 7 CDs. (Running Time: 8 hrs.). (Alex Cross Ser.: No. 9). (ENG.). 2003. audio compact disk 39.98 (978-1-58621-580-4(9)) Pub: Hachet Audio. Dist(s): HachBkGrp

Big Bad Wolf. unabr. ed. James Patterson. Read by Peter Jay Fernandez & Denis O'Hare. (Alex Cross Ser.: No. 9). (ENG.). 2005. 14.98 (978-1-59483-302-1(8)) Pub: Hachet Audio. Dist(s): HachBkGrp

Big Bad Wolf. unabr. ed. James Patterson. Read by Peter Jay Fernandez & Denis O'Hare. (Running Time: 8 hrs.). (Alex Cross Ser.: No. 9). (ENG.). 2009. 59.98 (978-1-60024-551-0(X)) Pub: Hachet Audio. Dist(s): HachBkGrp

Big Bad Wolves at School. Stephen Krensky. Narrated by Jim Brownold. 1 cass. (Running Time: 9 mins.). (J). (gr. k-3). 2008. bk. 27.95 (978-0-8045-6966-8(5)); bk. 29.95 (978-0-8045-4189-3(2)) Spoken Arts.
Rufus doesn't like school at first. He loves being a wolf and doing wolf stuff-like howling at the moon and running through the woods. But Rufus, like all wolves, must go to school to learn real wolf "work", like wearing clever disguises and speaking sheep. While Rufus learns, he also teaches: Sometimes you have to cut loose and learn to be yourself!.

Big Balloon Race. Eleanor Coerr. 1 read-along cass. (Running Time: 15 min.). (I Can Read Bks.). (J). (gr. 2-4). pap. bk. 5.98 (JC-146) HarperCollins Pubs.

Big Balloon Race Book & Tape. abr. ed. Eleanor Coerr. Illus. by Carolyn Croll. 1 cass. (I Can Read Bks.). (J). (gr. k-3). 1990. 8.99 (978-1-55994-221-8(5), TBC 2215) HarperCollins Pubs.

Big Bam: The Life & Times of Babe Ruth. abr. ed. Leigh Montville. Read by Adam Grupper. 5 CDs. (Running Time: 21600 sec.). (ENG.). 2006. audio compact disk 29.95 (978-0-7393-3273-3(2), Random AudioBks) Pub: Random Audio Pubg. Dist(s): Random

Big Bam: The Life & Times of Babe Ruth. unabr. ed. Leigh Montville. Read by Scott Brick. 10 cass. (Running Time: 15 hrs. 30 mins.). 2006. 90.00 (978-1-4159-3027-4(9)); audio compact disk 96.00 (978-1-4159-3028-1(7)) Books on Tape.

Big Band Christmas. Perf. by Ralph Carmichael. 1 cd. audio compact disk 15.98 (978-1-57908-412-7(5), 1808) Platinm Enter.

Big Band Chronicles: The Lively Story of Swing Music in the Forties. unabr. ed. Interview with John Gilliland. 4 cass. (Running Time: 6 hrs.). (J). (gr. 4-12). 1998. 19.95 Set. (978-1-55935-269-7(8), 269-8BK) Soundelux.
Excerpts fromradio& narration covering the music.

Big Band Gold. 4 cass. 1994. 16.95 Set. (978-1-55569-682-5(1)) Great Am Audio.

Big Band Gospel Hymns. Perf. by Ralph Carmichael. 1 cd. audio compact disk 16.98 (978-1-57908-475-2(3), 5351) Platinm Enter.

Big Band Gospel Hymns, Set. unabr. ed. Perf. by Ralph Carmichael. 1 cass., 1 CD. 10.98 (978-1-57908-476-9(1), 5351) Platinm Enter.

Big Band Hit Parade. Perf. by Erich Kunzel & Cincinnati Pops Orchestra. 1 cass., 1 CD. 7.98 (TA 30177); audio compact disk 12.78 CD Jewel box. (TA 80177) NewSound.

Big Band Swing Classics, Vol. 1. Perf. by Ralph Carmichael. 1 cass. 10.98 (978-1-57908-458-5(3)); audio compact disk 16.98 (978-1-57908-457-8(5)) Platinm Enter.

Big Band Walking: Advanced. 1 cass. (Running Time: 1 hr.). 1991. 9.95 (978-1-55569-462-3(4), 7256) Great Am Audio.
Follow the Big Band beat & walk your way to fitness, fun & increase energy.

Big Band Walking: Beginner. 1 cass. (Running Time: 1 hr.). 1991. 9.95 (978-1-55569-460-9(8), 7254) Great Am Audio.

Big Band Walking: Expert. 1 cass. (Running Time: 1 hr.). 1991. 9.95 (978-1-55569-463-0(2), 7257) Great Am Audio.
Follow the Big Band beat & walk your way to fitness, fun & increased energy.

Big Band Walking: Intermediate. 1 cass. (Running Time: 1 hr.). 1991. 9.95 (978-1-55569-461-6(6), 7255) Great Am Audio.

Big Bands. Friedman-Fairfax and Sony Music Staff. 1 cass. (Life, Times, & Music Ser.). 1995. pap. bk. 15.98 (978-1-56799-003-4(7), Friedman-Fairfax) M Friedman Pub Grp Inc.

Big Bands. Perf. by Benny Goodman. 1 cass. (Running Time: 1 hr. 30 min.). 1999. 9.99 (TADSB9); audio compact disk 9.99 (TBDSG7) Time-Life.

Big Bands Fitness Walking. abr. ed. Nina Mattikow. Perf. by Glenn Miller et al. 3 cass. (Running Time: 3 hrs.). (Three Cassette Pack Ser.). 1992. 19.95 Set. (978-1-55569-499-9(3), 43102) Great Am Audio.
Now you can enjoy the original Big Band sound as you walk with Glenn Miller, Tommy Dorsey, Count Basie & many more.

Big Bands from Chicago. unabr. ed. 6 CDs. (Running Time: 6 hrs.). bk. 39.95 (978-1-57816-153-9(3), BBCD601) Audio File.
Fourteen complete broadcasts of the 1930's, '40's and '50's from Chicago Ballrooms- including Dick Jurgens (1950), Earl "Fatha" Hines (8/3/38), Benny Goodman (8/10/41), Duke Ellington (6/24/53).

Big Bands from Chicago, Set. unabr. ed. 6 cass. (Running Time: 6 hrs.). 34.95 (978-1-57816-009-9(X), BBC601) Audio File.
Fourteen complete remote radio broadcasts of the Big Bands from various Chicago ballrooms, hotels & restaurants, plus a sixteen page booklet with detailed information.

***Big Bands on One Night Stand, Volume 1.** RadioArchives.com. (Running Time: 600). (ENG.). 2008. audio compact disk 29.98 (978-1-61081-079-1(1)) Radio Arch.

***Big Bands on One Night Stand, Volume 2.** RadioArchives.com. (ENG.). 2008. audio compact disk 29.98 (978-1-61081-082-1(1)) Radio Arch.

***Big Bands on One Night Stand, Volume 3.** RadioArchives.com. (Running Time: 600). (ENG.). 2009. audio compact disk 29.98 (978-1-61081-163-7(1)) Radio Arch.

***Big Bang: The Lost Mike Hammer Sixties Novel.** unabr. ed. Mickey Spillane. Read by Stacy Keach. (Running Time: 8 hrs. 0 mins.). 2010. 29.95 (978-1-4417-3517-1(8)); 54.95 (978-1-4417-3513-3(5)); audio compact disk 29.95 (978-1-4417-3516-4(X)); audio compact disk 76.00 (978-1-4417-3514-0(3)) Blckstn Audio.

Big Beanie & the Lost Fish. Miwa Nakaya. (J). 1913. bk. 12.95 (978-1-74126-027-4(2)) Pub: RICPub AUS. Dist(s): SCB Distributors

Big Bears. Sundance/Newbridge, LLC Staff. (Early Science Ser.). (gr. k-3). 2007. audio compact disk 12.00 (978-1-4007-6281-1(2)); audio compact disk 12.00 (978-1-4007-6282-8(0)); audio compact disk 12.00 (978-1-4007-6280-4(4)) Sund Newbrdge.

Big Ben Helps the Town: Early Explorers Early Set A Audio CD. Benchmark Education Staff. (J). 2006. audio compact disk 10.00 (978-1-4108-7630-0(6)) Benchmark Educ.

Big Ben Is Dead. Jerry Stemach. (Nick Ford Mysteries Ser.). 2000. audio compact disk 18.95 (978-1-4105-0141-7(8)) D Johnston Inc.

Big Ben Is Dead. Jerry Stemach. Ed. by Jerry Stemach. Ed. by Gail Portnuff Venable & Dorothy Tyack. Illus. by Jeff Ham. Based on a novel by Ed Smaron. Contrib. by Ted S. Hasselbring. (Start-to-Finish Books). (J). (gr. 2-3). 2002. 100.00 (978-1-58702-983-7(9)) D Johnston Inc.

Big Ben Is Dead, Vol. 5. Jerry Stemach. Ed. by Jerry Stemach. Ed. by Gail Portnuff Venable & Dorothy Tyack. Illus. by Jeff Ham. Narrated by Ed Smaron. Contrib. by Ted S. Hasselbring. (Start-to-Finish Books). (J). (gr. 2-3). 2000. 35.00 (978-1-58702-459-7(4)) D Johnston Inc.

Big Ben Is Dead, Vol. 5. unabr. ed. Jerry Stemach. Ed. by Jerry Stemach. Ed. by Gail Portnuff Venable. Illus. by Jeff Ham. Narrated by Ed Smaron & Dorothy Tyack. Contrib. by Ted S. Hasselbring. 1 cass. (Running Time: 1 hr.). (Start-to-Finish Books). (J). (gr. 2-3). 2000. (978-1-893376-53-3(2), F14K2) D Johnston Inc.
In this story, the British Museum in London has asked Nick to consult on a mummy that the museum has acquired for Egypt. Upon opening the mummy, the scientists have found plant seeds and they wish to learn whether or not the seeds can be terminated. When Nick and the kids arrive in London, they learn that someone has been stealing and vandalizing national treasures including Big Ben, the famous London clock tower, a Van Gogh painting at the National Gallery, and a rare Fountain sculpture of a cat.

Big Bétail - Clovis Crawfish & the Orpan Zo-Zo. Narrated by Mary Alice Fontenot. (Clovis Crawfish Ser.). (ENG.). (J). 1998. 9.95 (978-1-56554-382-9(3)) Pelican.

Big Betail-Clovis Crawfish & the Orphan Zo-Zo. Mary Alice Fontenot. Narrated by Mary Alice Fontenot. (Running Time: 48 mins.). (Clovis

Crawfish Ser.). (FRE & ENG.). (J). 2009. audio compact disk 19.95 (978-1-58980-732-7(4)) Pelican.

Big Big World. unabr. ed. Bill Harley. 1 cass. (Running Time: 51 min.). 1993. 9.95 (978-1-878126-21-4(0), RRR111C) Round Riv Prodns.
Every song is a celebration. Insightful, humorous lyrics backed with bouncy reggae, hand-clapping cajun & rip roaring honky tonk. A family recording with a decidedly world beat! Big Big World; I Don't Wanna Wait; Pirate Song; Pizza Shake; Tommy Says; So Long; Sittin' down to Eat; Listen to Me; Who Made This Mess?; Keep It Green; Do It Together; Walk a Mile; & Turn the World Around.

Big Big World. unabr. ed. Bill Harley. 1 cass. (Running Time: 51 min.). (J). 1993. audio compact disk 15.00 CD. (978-1-878126-22-1(9), RRR111J) Round Riv Prodns.

Big Bill Broonzy Sings Folk Songs. Perf. by Bill Broonzy. Anno. by Charles E. Smith. Contrib. by Moses Asch. 1 cass. (Running Time: 34 min.). 1989. (0-9307-40023-9307-40023-2-2); audio compact disk (0-9307-40023-2-2) Smithsonian Folkways.
Includes traditional blues, gospel & folk songs.

Big Bill Sublette: The Oregon Trail & Beyond (1827-1833), abr. ed. 3 cass. (Running Time: 4 hrs. 20 min.). (History As It Happens Ser.: Vol. 2). 2001. 19.95 (978-1-889252-10-0(7)) Photosensitive.

***Big Bing.** abr. ed. Stanley Bing. Read by Stanley Bing. (ENG.). 2004. (978-0-06-074780-0(3), Harper Audio); (978-0-06-079993-9(5), Harper Audio) HarperCollins Pubs.

Big Bite. unabr. collector's ed. Charles Williams. Read by Michael Russotto. 7 cass. (Running Time: 7 hrs.). 1993. 42.00 (978-0-7366-2459-6(7), 3223) Books on Tape.
Ex-pro football player finds that at blackmail he's strictly an amateur.

Big Blue Soldier. abr. ed. Grace Livingston Hill. Read by Aimee Lilly. 2 cass. (Running Time: 1 hr. 30 mins. per cass.). (Grace Livingston Hill Romances Ser.). 1996. 8.99 (978-1-886463-52-3(2)) Oasis Audio.
A homeless young soldier's involvement in a brief masquerade entangles him in the lives of two unpredictable women. One cassette Over 1-1/2 hours Abridged.

Big Blues. (Running Time: 46 min.). 9.98; audio compact disk 15.98 CD. MFLP CA.
Children learn the ABCs singing along to Fabulous Thunderbirds, "Zip a Dee Doo Dah" & other favorite songs.

Big Blues: The Unmaking of IBM. unabr. collector's ed. Paul Carroll. Read by Alexander Adams. 10 cass. (Running Time: 15 hrs.). 1994. 80.00 (978-0-7366-2714-6(6), 3444) Books on Tape.
Rare is the business book that makes the transition to unabridged audio & rarer still is an account that is able to deliver such an immersive listening experience.

Big Book: First Grade. (On Our Way to English Ser.). (gr. 1 up). audio compact disk 9.95 (978-0-7578-1517-1(0)) Rigby Educ.

Big Book: Kindergarten. (On Our Way to English Ser.). (gr. k up). audio compact disk 9.95 (978-0-7578-1630-7(4)) Rigby Educ.

Big Book: Second Grade. (On Our Way to English Ser.). (gr. 2 up). audio compact disk 9.95 (978-0-7578-1429-7(8)) Rigby Educ.

Big Book: Third Grade. (On Our Way to English Ser.). (gr. 3 up). audio compact disk 9.95 (978-0-7578-4238-2(0)) Rigby Educ.

Big Book Unit 8: Energy & You. 2 pieces. (MacMillan/McGraw-Hill Science Ser.). (gr. 2 up). 1995. reel tape (978-0-02-276607-8(3)) Macmillan McGraw-Hill Schl Div.

Big Book for Our Planet. unabr. ed. Read by Ed Begley, Jr. et al. Ed. by Ann Durell et al. 1 cass. (Running Time: 90 min.). (J). (gr. 4-7). 1993. 10.95 (978-1-879371-61-3(8)) Pub Mills.
The best-loved authors of children's books have pooled their talents in a single volume, honoring one very special planet, the Earth.

Big Book for Peace. Read by Jane Alexander & Milton Berle. Ed. by Ann Duren & Marilyn Sachs. 1 cass. (Running Time: 90 min.). (J). (ps-3). 1991. 10.95 (978-1-879371-10-1(3), 50000) Pub Mills.
Filled with stories, poems, & even a song, it is a book about many kinds of peace. Peace among people living in different lands - but also among next door neighbors. Harmony among people of different races - & among sisters & brothers. Understanding among those separated by their beliefs - & those separated by generations. It is a book for young people to enjoy, to think about, & to share. Some of its contents are funny & fanciful. Others are serious & moving. All celebrate peace & the hope that there will be a peaceful world for every child to inherit.

Big Book for Peace & the Big Book for Our Planet, abr. ed. Read by Media Books Staff. 2 cass. (Running Time: 3 hrs.). (J). (ps-3). 2000. 7.95 (978-1-57815-147-9(3), 1106, Media Bks Audio) Media Bks NJ.
The first part promotes the cause of peace. The second part consists of stories & poems, essays & limericks, all sharing a belief that humans must live in harmony with their environment.

Big Book of Peace & the Big Book for Our Planet: Two Volumes of Stories & Poems by the Best Loved Authors of Children¿s Books. Ed. by Ann Durrell. (ENG.). 2008. 20.00 (978-1-4379-5818-8(4)) DIANE Pub.

Big Book of Showbiz Bloopers & Blunders: Hundreds of Gaffes from Your Favorite TV Shows, Radio, Movies & More. abr. ed. Compiled by Michael Viner & Jessica Steindorff. 7 cass. (Running Time: 10 hrs. 30 mins.). 2004. 32.95 (978-1-59007-565-4(X)); audio compact disk 55.00 (978-1-59007-566-1(8)) Pub: New Millenn Enter. Dist(s): PerseuPGW

Big Book Selection Package. (Scott Foresman Reading Ser.). (gr. k up). 2004. 45.95 (978-0-328-02514-5(3)); audio compact disk 83.50 (978-0-328-02521-3(6)) Addson-Wesley Educ.

Big Book Selection Package. (Scott Foresman Reading Ser.). (gr. 1 up). 2004. 45.95 (978-0-328-02515-2(1)); audio compact disk 83.50 (978-0-328-02522-0(4)) Addson-Wesley Educ.

Big Book Selection Package. (Scott Foresman Reading Ser.). (gr. 2 up). 2004. audio compact disk 83.50 (978-0-328-02523-7(2)) Addson-Wesley Educ.

Big Book Selection Package. (Scott Foresman Reading Ser.). (gr. 3 up). 2004. 71.35 (978-0-328-02517-6(8)); audio compact disk 103.45 (978-0-328-02524-4(0)) Addson-Wesley Educ.

Big Book Selection Package. (Scott Foresman Reading Ser.). (gr. 4 up). 2004. stu. ed. 71.35 (978-0-328-02518-3(6)); stu. ed. 103.45 (978-0-328-02525-1(9)) Addson-Wesley Educ.

Big Book Selection Package. (Scott Foresman Reading Ser.). (gr. 5 up). 2004. stu. ed. 71.35 (978-0-328-02519-0(4)); stu. ed. 103.45 (978-0-328-02526-8(7)) Addson-Wesley Educ.

Big Book Selection Package. (Scott Foresman Reading Ser.). (gr. 6 up). 2004. stu. ed. 71.35 (978-0-328-02520-6(8)); stu. ed. 103.45 (978-0-328-02527-5(5)) Addson-Wesley Educ.

Big Bounce. unabr. ed. Elmore Leonard. Read by Campbell Scott. 2004. 34.95 (978-0-06-057253-2(1)) HarperCollins Pubs.

***Big Bounce.** unabr. ed. Elmore Leonard. Read by Campbell Scott. (ENG.). 2004. (978-0-06-078322-8(2), Harper Audio) HarperCollins Pubs.

***Big Bounce.** unabr. ed. Elmore Leonard. Read by Campbell Scott. (ENG.). 2004. (978-0-06-081485-4(3), Harper Audio) HarperCollins Pubs.

Big Bounce, unabr. ed. Elmore Leonard. Narrated by Mark Hammer. 6 cass. (Running Time: 8 hrs. 15 mins.). 1997. 51.00 (978-0-7887-0402-4(8), 94594E7) Recorded Bks.
Jack Ryan, bored & hard up, is harvesting cucumbers when he meets sultry Nancy Hayes.Together they embark on a risky adventure of thrills & crime, leaving their bleak life behind forever.

Big Bounce. unabr. collector's ed. Elmore Leonard. Read by Alexander Adams. 6 cass. (Running Time: 6 hrs.). 1995. 36.00 (978-0-7366-3115-0(1), 3791) Books on Tape.
Jack Ryan jobbed as a handyman - not much of a life. Then he met Nancy Hayes, a neat seductress who got her kicks breaking the hearts of married men. His was next.

Big Bow Mystery. Israel Zangwill. Read by Alfred von Lecteur. 2009. 27.95 (978-1-60112-985-7(8)) Babblebooks.

Big Bow Mystery. unabr. ed. Israel Zangwill. Read by Walter Covell. 3 cass. (Running Time: 4 hrs.). 1982. 23.95 (978-0-7861-0591-5(7), 2080) Blckstn Audio.
A huge cast of characters knocks against each other trying to solve the mystery behind the strange death of Oliver Constance, one of the most prolific orators of his day.

Big Bow Mystery. unabr. ed. Israel Zangwill. Read by Walter Covell. 3 cass. (Running Time: 4 hrs. 30 min.). 1980. 21.00 incl. album. (C-48) Jimcin Record.
This is the first & one of the most famous "locked room" mysteries. Oliver Constance, a famous orator, is found murdered in his room - with the doors & windows locked from the inside!.

Big Boy Out Loud. Michael Perry. Read by Michael Perry. 1 cass. (Running Time: 30 min.). 1998. 9.95 (978-0-9631695-5-6(6)) Whist & Jugg.
Taken from the book "Why They Killed Big Boy" - essays & humor.

Big Boy Rules: America's Mercenaries Fighting in Iraq. unabr. ed. Steve Fainaru. Narrated by Patrick G. Lawlor. (Running Time: 9 hrs. 0 mins. 0 sec.). (ENG.). 2008. audio compact disk 19.99 (978-1-4001-5782-2(X)) Pub: Tantor Media. Dist(s): IngramPubServ

Big Boy Rules: America's Mercenaries Fighting in Iraq. unabr. ed. Steve Fainaru. Read by Patrick G. Lawlor. (Running Time: 9 hrs. 0 mins. 0 sec.). (ENG.). 2008. audio compact disk 29.99 (978-1-4001-0782-7(2)); audio compact disk 59.99 (978-1-4001-3782-4(9)) Pub: Tantor Media. Dist(s): IngramPubServ

Big Boys, Pt. 1. unabr. collector's ed. Ralph Nader & William Taylor. Read by Larry McKeever. 10 cass. (Running Time: 15 hrs.). 1988. 80.00 (978-0-7366-1391-0(9), 2281-A) Books on Tape.
These snapshots of America's top business leaders draw a fascinating picture of the corporate establishment. More than 650 people contributed to these stories of nine corporate leaders.

Big Boys, Pt. 2. collector's ed. Ralph Nader & William Taylor. Read by Larry McKeever. 10 cass. (Running Time: 15 hrs.). 1988. 80.00 (978-0-7366-1392-7(7), 2281-B) Books on Tape.

Big Brag see Dr. Seuss Audio Collection

Big Bubba Bugg Cassette. Stephen Cosgrove. 2004. 5.00 (978-1-58804-365-8(7)) PCI Educ.

Big Bucks! How to Make Serious Money for Both You & Your Company. unabr. abr. ed. Ken Blanchard & Sheldon Bowles. Read by Sheldon Bowles. 3 cass. (Running Time: 4 hrs.). 2000. 20.00 (978-0-694-52366-5(6)) HarperCollins Pubs.

***Big Buddy Biographies CD.** (Big Buddy Biographies CD Ser.). 2010. cd-rom 162.42 (978-1-61613-069-5(5)) ABDO Pub Co.

***Big Buddy Biographies Site CD.** (Big Buddy Biographies Site CD Ser.). 2010. cd-rom 342.42 (978-1-61613-249-1(3)) ABDO Pub Co.

Big Bug Book. Margery Facklam. Read by Nelson Runger. 1 cass. (Running Time: 45 mins.). (YA). 1999. pap. bk. & stu. ed. 24.20 (978-0-7887-2989-8(6), 40871) Recorded Bks.
Listeners will shiver in delicious horror as they learn about 13 of the world's largest insects. Listeners can look at the huge insects as they hear about them.

Big Bug Book. unabr. ed. Margery Facklam. Narrated by Nelson Runger. 1 cass. (Running Time: 45 mins.). (gr. k up). 1999. 10.00 (978-0-7887-2959-1(4), 95733E7) Recorded Bks.
Listeners will shiver in delicious horror as they learn about 13 of the world's largest insects. With the illustrations in the print book, which is included in the ReadAlong pack, listeners can look at the huge insects as they hear about them.

Big Bug Book, Class set. Margery Facklam. Read by Nelson Runger. 1 cass. (Running Time: 45 mins.). (YA). 1999. pap. bk. 90.30 (978-0-7887-3019-1(3), 46836) Recorded Bks.
Listeners will shiver in delicious horror as they learn about 13 of the world's largest insects. Listeners can look at the huge insects as they hear about them.

Big Burn. unabr. ed. Jeannette Ingold. Read by Boyd Gaines. 4 cass. (Running Time: 5 hrs. 56 mins.). (J). (gr. 7 up). 2004. 32.00 (978-0-8072-0815-1(9), Listening Lib) Random Audio Pubg.
A drama ripped from one of the biggest wildfires of the century.

***Big Burn: Teddy Roosevelt & the Fire That Saved America.** Timothy Egan. Contrib. by Robertson Dean. (Playaway Adult Nonfiction Ser.). 2009. 64.99 (978-1-4418-2982-5(2)) Find a World.

Big Burn: Teddy Roosevelt & the Fire That Saved America. unabr. ed. Timothy Egan. Read by Robertson Dean. (Running Time: 10 hrs.). 2009. 24.99 (978-1-4418-0696-3(2), 9781441806963, Brilliance MP3); 39.97 (978-1-4418-0697-0(0), 9781441806970, Brlnc Audio MP3 Lib); 24.99 (978-1-4418-0698-7(9), 9781441806987, BAD); 39.97 (978-1-4418-0699-4(7), 9781441806994, BADLE); audio compact disk 29.99 (978-1-4418-0694-9(6), 9781441806949, Bril Audio CD Unabri); audio compact disk 89.97 (978-1-4418-0695-6(4), 9781441806956, BriAudCD Unabrid) Brilliance Audio.

***Big Catch: A Robot & Rico Story.** Anastasia Suen. Illus. by Mike Laughead. (Robot & Rico Ser.). (ENG.). 2010. audio compact disk 14.60 (978-1-4342-2587-0(9)) CapstoneDig.

Big Change: America Transforms Itself, 1900-1950. unabr. ed. Frederick L. Allen. Read by Joe Vincent. 7 cass. (Running Time: 10 hrs.). 1989. 49.95 Set. (978-0-7861-0101-6(6), 1094) Blckstn Audio.
This book describes the transformation which took place during the first fifty years of this century in the American way of life & what caused it.

Big Cherry Holler. unabr. ed. Adriana Trigiani. Read by Grace Bennett. 6 vols. (Running Time: 9 hrs.). (Big Stone Gap Ser.: Bk. 2). 2001. bk. 54.95 (978-0-7927-2509-1(3), CSL 398, Chivers Sound Lib) AudioGO.
It's been eight years since town pharmacist and longtime spinster Ave Maria Mulligan married coal miner Jack Mac Chesney. With her newfound belief in love and its possibilities, Ave Maria has made a life for herself and her growing family, hoping her fearless leap into commitment will make happiness stay. What she hasn't counted on is that fate and the ghosts of the past will come to haunt her, and, eventually, test the love she has for her husband.

Big Chief Elizabeth. unabr. ed. Giles Milton. Read by Richard Heffer. 10 CDs. (Running Time: 13 hrs. 15 mins.). (Isis Ser.). (J). 2002. audio compact disk 89.95 (978-0-7531-1484-1(4)) Pub: ISIS Lrg Prnt GBR. Dist(s): Ulverscroft US
In April 1586, a tribe of Native Americans made Queen Elizabeth I their Big chief. Sir Walter Raleigh's first American expedition had brought back a captive, Manteo, who was eventually returned to his homeland. But Raleigh's gamble would lead to a riddle whose solution for many years lay hidden in the forests of Virginia.

Big Chief Elizabeth: How England's Adventurers Gambled & Won the New World. unabr. ed. Giles Milton & Richard Heffer. 8 cass. (Running Time: 10 hrs. 55 mins.). (Isis Ser.). (J). 2002. 69.95 (978-0-7531-1188-8(8)) Pub: ISIS Lrg Prnt GBR. Dist(s): Ulverscroft US

Big Chill: SoundTrax. Jay Althouse. Composed by Sally K. Albrecht. (ENG.). 2004. audio compact disk 44.99 (978-0-7390-3412-5(X)) Alfred Pub.

Big City Eyes. unabr. ed. Delia Ephron. Narrated by C. J. Critt. 6 cass. (Running Time: 8 hrs. 45 mins.). 2000. 59.00 (978-0-7887-4855-4(6), 96201E7) Recorded Bks.
Lilly Davis is a successful freelance writer & single mother who loves her life in Manhattan. Her teenaged son, Sam, is sneaking out to clubs, but when she finds a knife in his room, she decides to move to rural Long Island. It is not the life she imagined, the locals are in a war over what to do about deer population & Sam shaves his head & dates a girl who only speaks Klingon. Lily's job on the local paper draws her into a murder investigation & an affair.Through it all, she writes about the daily tales of small town life through her "Big City Eyes".

Big City Eyes. unabr. ed. Delia Ephron. Narrated by C. J. Critt. 8 CDs. (Running Time: 8 hrs. 45 mins.). 2001. audio compact disk 78.00 (978-0-7887-6179-9(X)) Recorded Bks.
Lily Davis is a successful freelance writer & single mother who loves her life in Manhattan. She knows her teenaged son, Sam, is sneaking out to clubs, but when she finds a knife in his room, she impulsively decides to move to rural Long Island. It is not the picturesque life she imagined. The locals are in a war over what to do about the deer population. Sam shaves his head & starts dating a girl who only speaks Klingon. Lily's job on the local paper draws her into a murder investigation & an affair. Through it all, she writes about the daily trials of small town life as seen through her Big City Eyes.

Big City Race. Matt Oppenheimer. 1 cass. (Running Time: 1 hr.). (Wonder Tales Ser.). (J). (gr. k-5). 2000. 11.98 (978-1-930037-01-4(5), WT0002C) Inter Media Grp.
The listener drives through town to win the race.

Big Con: The True Story of How Washington Got Hoodwinked & Hijacked by Crackpot Economics. unabr. ed. Jonathan Chait. Read by David Drummond. (YA). 2008. 59.99 (978-1-60514-627-0(7)) Find a World.

Big Con: The True Story of How Washington Got Hoodwinked & Hijacked by Crackpot Economics. unabr. ed. Jonathan Chait. Read by David Drummond. (Running Time: 9 hrs. 0 mins. 0 sec.). (ENG.). 2007. audio compact disk 34.99 (978-1-4001-0550-2(1)); audio compact disk 69.99 (978-1-4001-3550-9(8)); audio compact disk 24.99 (978-1-4001-5550-7(9)) Pub: Tantor Media. Dist(s): IngramPubServ

Big Country. 1 cass.; 1 CD. 1998. 9.98 (978-1-56628-065-5(6), 42574); audio compact disk 15.98 CD. (978-1-56628-064-8(8), 42574D) MFLP CA.

Big Country: Ride, You Tonto Raiders & War Party, Vol. 1. unabr. ed. Read by Stefan Rudnicki. 2 CDs. (Running Time: 9000 sec.). 2007. audio compact disk 14.95 (978-1-4332-0208-7(5)) Blckstn Audio.

Big Country Vol. 2: West of the Tularosa; Home of the Valley; West Is Where the Heart Is. unabr. ed. Louis L'Amour. (Running Time: 3 hrs.). 2010. audio compact disk 19.95 (978-1-4417-1541-8(X)) Blckstn Audio.

Big Country Vol. 2: West of the Tularosa; Home of the Valley; West Is Where the Heart Is. unabr. ed. Louis L'Amour. Read by Lloyd James. (Running Time: 3 hrs. 0 mins.). 2010. 19.95 (978-1-4417-1542-5(8)); 24.95 (978-1-4417-1538-8(X)); audio compact disk 30.00 (978-1-4417-1539-5(8)) Blckstn Audio.

***Big Country Vol. 3: Stories of Louis L'Amour.** unabr. ed. Louis L'Amour. (Running Time: 3 hrs. 0 mins.). 2010. 19.95 (978-1-4417-3493-8(7)); 24.95 (978-1-4417-3489-1(9)); audio compact disk 29.95 (978-1-4417-3492-1(9)); audio compact disk 30.00 (978-1-4417-3490-7(2)) Blckstn Audio.

***Big Country, Vol. 4: Stories of Louis L'Amour.** unabr. ed. Louis L'Amour. Read by Mark Bramhall. (Running Time: 3 hrs. 30 mins.). 2010. 19.95 (978-1-4417-6614-4(6)); 24.95 (978-1-4417-6611-3(1)); audio compact disk 30.00 (978-1-4417-6612-0(X)); audio compact disk 19.95 (978-1-4417-6613-7(8)) Blckstn Audio.

Big Country Volume One: Ride, You Tonto Raiders & War Party. unabr. ed. Read by Stefan Rudnicki. (Running Time: 9000 sec.). 2007. 14.95 (978-1-4332-0207-0(7)) Blckstn Audio.

Big Country, Volume 1: Ride, You Tonto Raiders & War Party. unabr. ed. (Running Time: 9000 sec.). 2007. 22.95 (978-1-4332-0308-4(1)); audio compact disk 19.95 (978-1-4332-0209-4(3)); audio compact disk 24.00 (978-1-4332-0309-1(X)) Blckstn Audio.

Big Crash. 10.00 (HT411) Esstee Audios.

Big Decision: 11 Corinthians 6:14-18. Ben Young. 1999. 4.95 (978-0-7417-6124-8(6), B0124) Win Walk.

Big Dig. unabr. ed. Linda Barnes. Read by Bernadette Quigley. 5 cass. (Running Time: 7 hrs.). (Carlotta Carlyle Mystery Ser.). 2002. 27.95 (978-1-59086-503-3(0), 1590865030, BAU); 69.25 (978-1-59086-504-0(9), 1590865049, Unabridge Lib Edns) Brilliance Audio.
Carlotta Carlyle, the six-foot-tall redhead private investigator, thought that working undercover searching out fraud on Boston's Big Dig would be a challenging assignment. After all, the Big Dig, the creation of a central artery highway through downtown Boston, is a 14 billion dollar boondoggle, the largest urban construction project in modern history. But playing a mild-mannered secretary working out of a construction trailer is not quite the thrill ride she had in mind, so Carlotta starts moonlighting, taking on a missing persons case. The search for the missing Veronica James turns up one dead end after another, as do her fraud investigations, and it looks like Carlotta has dug herself one big hole. But the mysterious death of a construction worker stirs up a storm of events, and soon enough Carlotta is really in over her head, grasping at the edges of a vast conspiracy that threatens to make this investigation her last.

Big Dig. unabr. ed. Linda Barnes. Read by Bernadette Quigley. (Running Time: 7 hrs.). (Carlotta Carlyle Mystery Ser.). 2004. 39.25 (978-1-59335-364-3(2), 1593353642, Brlnc Audio MP3 Lib) Brilliance Audio.

Big Dig. unabr. ed. Linda Barnes. Read by Bernadette Quigley. (Running Time: 7 hrs.). (Carlotta Carlyle Mystery Ser.). 2004. 39.25 (978-1-59710-049-6(8), 1597100498, BADLE); 24.95 (978-1-59710-048-9(X), 159710048X, BAD) Brilliance Audio.

Big Dig. unabr. ed. Linda Barnes. Read by Bernadette Quigley. (Running Time: 7 hrs.). (Carlotta Carlyle Mystery Ser.). 2004. 24.95 (978-1-59335-061-1(9), 1593350619) Soulmate Audio Bks.

Big Domino in the Sky: And Other Atheistic Tales. Michael Martin. (ENG.). 1996. 26.98 (978-1-57392-111-4(4)) Prometheus Bks.

Big Dream & Dream Series. Read by Murray Stein. 2 cass. (Running Time: 4 hrs.). 1986. 21.95 Set. (978-0-7822-0268-7(3), 210) C G Jung IL.

Big Enchilada. unabr. ed. Stuart Stevens. Read by Edward Holland. 7 cass. (Running Time: 10 hrs. 30 mins.). 2001. 56.00 (978-0-7366-8094-3(2)) Books on Tape.
behind-the-scenes tour of the Bush presidential campaign. He shows us the hidden moments in the small towns of Texas which added up to success for the former major league baseball owner: the humble Bush practicing his speeches in a small Methodist church in Crawford, Texas; the blue-jeaned Bush, hoping for a chance to "bond" with his strategists; the innocent Bush, convinced he would win despite overwhelming odds and an opponent who was counting on them. With humor, Stevens relays hair-raising tales of the campaign trail.

Big-Enough. collector's ed. Will James. Read by Barrett Whitener. 6 cass. (Running Time: 9 hrs.). 2000. 48.00 (978-0-7366-5946-8(3)) Books on Tape.
A delightful tale for adults & children alike. It's a story of a cowboy & a cow horse, born on the same day, who together grow big enough for most anything. Young Billy was a born cowboy, unfortunately, his parents have other aspirations for him & send him off to be educated & turned into something else. But one day Billy takes his horse, Big Enough, & departs to pursue his true destiny, finding adventure, adversity & ultimately, manhood.

Big Fat Love. unabr. ed. Peter Sheridan. 8 cass. (Isis Cassettes Ser.). (J). 2005. 69.95 (978-0-7531-2003-3(8)) Pub: ISIS Lrg Prnt GBR. Dist(s): Ulverscroft US

Big Fat Yes to Life. Christopher Love. Read by Christopher Love. 1 cass. (Running Time: 30 min.). 1997. 10.95 (978-1-891820-13-7(3)) World Sangha Pubg.
Self-hypnosis meditation for healing, self-improvement & realizing our full & powerful potential as spiritual beings.

***Big Field.** unabr. ed. Mike Lupica. Narrated by Christopher Evan Welch. 1 Playaway. (Running Time: 5 hrs. 30 mins.). (YA). (gr. 5-8). 2009. 54.75 (978-1-4407-3862-3(9)); 51.75 (978-1-4407-3852-4(1)); audio compact disk 66.75 (978-1-4407-3856-2(4)) Recorded Bks.

***Big Field.** unabr. collector's ed. Mike Lupica. Narrated by Christopher Evan Welch. 6 CDs. (Running Time: 5 hrs. 30 mins.). (YA). (gr. 5-8). 2009. audio compact disk 41.95 (978-1-4407-3860-9(2)) Recorded Bks.

Big Fifty. unabr. ed. Johnny D. Boggs. Ed. by Lloyd James. 5 cass. (Running Time: 6 hrs. 30 mins.). 2004. 39.95 (978-0-7861-2778-8(3), 3300) Blckstn Audio.
The reality of frontier life in Kansas in 1872 becomes brutally clear to twelve-year-old Coady McIlvain when his father is scalped by hostile Indians and Coady is taken prisoner. Coady is determined to escape and does so, falling in with a buffalo sharpshooter named Dylan Griffith, whom he sees as the embodiment of his hero, Buffalo Bill Cody, a role in which the circumspect Griffith feels himself totally inadequate.

Big Fifty. unabr. ed. Johnny D. Boggs. Read by Lloyd James. 5 cass. (Running Time: 8 hrs. 30 mins.). 2005. reel tape 35.95 (978-0-7861-2731-3(7), E3300); audio compact disk 24.95 (978-0-7861-8519-1(8), 3300); audio compact disk 39.95 (978-0-7861-8584-9(8), ZE3300) Blckstn Audio.

Big Fifty -Lib. Johnny D. Boggs. Ed. by Lloyd James. 6 CDs. (Running Time: 6 hrs. 30 mins.). 2004. audio compact disk 48.00 (978-0-7861-8542-9(2), 3300) Blckstn Audio.

Big Fish: A Novel of Mythic Proportions. unabr. ed. Daniel Wallace. Narrated by Tom Stechschulte. 5 cass. Library ed. (Running Time: 5 hrs. 30 mins.). 1998. 49.75 (978-0-7887-3761-9(9), 95932E7) Recorded Bks.
As a grown son cares for his dying father, he tries to focus on what he knows about his parent's life. With each memory, the son constructs visions of a mythic man, capable of superhuman feats.

Big Fish: A Novel of Mythic Proportions. unabr. collector's ed. Daniel Wallace. Narrated by Tom Stechschulte. 4 cass. (Running Time: 5 hrs. 30 min.). 2003. 29.95 (978-0-7887-7076-0(4)) Recorded Bks.
Filled with imagination, homespun humor, and hyperbole. Edward Bloom, an aging salesman, is dying. As his grown son, William, cares for him, the young man tries to focus on what he knows about his father's life. Story after story surfaces in William's memory, and he shares mythic visions of a fantastic father who was loved by all, a man who was the best runner, fisherman, businessman, and adventurer in the world.

Big Fix. Kim Klaver. 4 cass. Set. Max Out Prodns.
Includes cassettes: "So...You Want to Be a Networker?," "How to Build a Giant Heap with or without Your Friends, Family or Neighbors" & "How to Be an Awesome Sponsor & Keep Your Heap".

Big Foot. Edgar Wallace. Read by Peter Joyce. 5 cass. 1997. 49.95 (978-1-86015-442-3(5)) Ulverscroft US.

Big Footprints. unabr. collector's ed. Hammond Innes. Read by John MacDonald. 7 cass. (Running Time: 10 hrs. 30 min.). 1984. 56.00 (978-0-7366-0860-2(5), 1811) Books on Tape.
In the story, Innes follows the trail of Africa's surviving elephants.

Big Four. unabr. ed. Agatha Christie. Read by Hugh Fraser. 2004. 25.95 (978-1-57270-431-2(4)) Pub: Audio Partners. Dist(s): PerseuPGW
When a man collapses at Poirot's door, he implicates a vicious international organization called the Big Four. Left in the care of Poirot's landlady, the man dies, and the dapper sleuth realizes this crime may be a deadly diversion. Poirot and his pal Captain Hastings are soon plunged into a complex case full of deception as they themselves dodge death. But do they really avoid the Grim Reaper? Hastings isn't sure when he's invited to Poirot's funeral. Reader Hugh Fraser captures Christie's "cozy mystery" world with his usual panache.This is the 24th title in the Agatha Christie Mystery Masters series, deemed the Best Mystery Series of the 20th Century at Bouchercon, the world's largest mystery convention (held annually). Eccentric and fastidious, egocentric and precise, the little Belgian detective with his sparkling eyes and carefully waxed moustache looks, to the uninitiated, ridiculous. Yet he is one of the most popular characters in all of literature Plump, barely over five feet, four inches tall, the vain Poirot is nevertheless eternally dignified, and always wears formal clothes, down to gleaming white spats and up to his jaunty bowler. He solves murders using, as he insists, nothing but his little grey cells.

Big Four. unabr. ed. Agatha Christie. Narrated by Hugh Fraser. (Mystery Masters Ser.). (ENG.). 2004. audio compact disk 27.95 (978-1-57270-432-9(2)) Pub: AudioGO. Dist(s): Perseus Dist

Big Fun. Greg Scelsa. 1 cass. (Running Time: 1 hr.). (J). 2001. 10.95 (YM 016C); audio compact disk 14.95 (YM 016CD) Kimbo Educ.
10 songs guaranteed to get everyone moving! Silly Willies, In My Backyard, Chicken Dance, The Magic of a Smile, Party Line '98 & more.

Big Fun. Perf. by Greg Scelsa. Music by Steve Millang. 1 cass., 1 CD. (J). 8.78 (YR 16); audio compact disk 11.18 CD Jewel box. (YR 16) NewSound.
A collection of 10 traditional & new songs. Kids get to create their own moves to the new songs. Includes: "Silly Willies," "The Mack Chicken Dance," "The Movement Medley" & more.

Big Gamble. unabr. ed. Michael McGarrity. Read by Dick Hill. 5 cass. (Running Time: 7 hrs.). (Kevin Kerney Ser.: Bk. 7). 2002. 27.95 (978-1-59086-213-1(9), 1590862139, BAU); 69.25 (978-1-59086-214-8(7), 1590862147, Unabridge Lib Edns) Brilliance Audio.

Big Gamble. unabr. ed. Michael McGarrity. Read by Dick Hill. (Running Time: 7 hrs.). (Kevin Kerney Ser.: Bk. 7). 2004. 39.25 (978-1-59335-632-3(3), 1593356323, Brlnc Audio MP3 Lib) Brilliance Audio.
When a fire in an abandoned fruit stand in rural Lincoln County reveals the murdered body of a woman gone missing from Sante Fe years ago, Police Chief Kevin Kerney finds himself cooperating with his estranged son, a man he hardly knows, Deputy Sheriff Clayton Istee. While Kerney digs into the woman's past, hoping to find clues that will lead to a credible suspect, Clayton must unravel two more homicides that seem on the surface totally unrelated. As Kerney chases down clues that raise questions about the legitimacy of a highly regarded modeling and talent agency, Clayton works to discover the identity of a murder suspect alleged to have ties to prostitution and illegal gambling. Set against the backdrop of the high mountains of southern New Mexico, where gambling is big business and private sexual encounters for VIPs can be discreetly arranged, Kerney and Clayton must go up against the rich and politically powerful opponents who are willing to protect their reputations at all costs.

Big Gamble. unabr. ed. Michael McGarrity. Read by Dick Hill. (Running Time: 7 hrs.). (Kevin Kerney Ser.). 2004. 24.95 (978-1-59710-050-2(1), 1597100501, BAD) Brilliance Audio.

Big Gamble. unabr. ed. Michael McGarrity. Read by Dick Hill. (Running Time: 7 hrs.). (Kevin Kerney Ser.: Bk. 7). 2004. 39.25 (978-1-59710-051-9(X), 159710051X, BADLE) Brilliance Audio.

Big Gamble. unabr. ed. Michael McGarrity. Read by Dick Hill. (Running Time: 7 hrs.). (Kevin Kerney Ser.: Bk. 7). 2004. 24.95 (978-1-59335-199-1(2), 1593351992) Soulmate Audio Bks.

Big Game. unabr. ed. Wendy Jenkins. Read by Peter Hardy. 2 cass. (Running Time: 3 hrs. 30 mins.). 2002. (978-1-74030-342-2(3)) Bolinda Pubng AUS.

Big Girl. abr. ed. Danielle Steel. Read by Kathleen McInerney. 5 CDs. (Running Time: 6 hrs.). 2010. audio compact disk 19.99 (978-1-4233-8830-2(5), 9781423388302, BACD) Brilliance Audio.

Big Girl. abr. ed. Danielle Steel. (Running Time: 6 hrs.). 2011. audio compact disk 14.99 (978-1-4233-8831-9(3), 9781423388319, BCD Value Price) Brilliance Audio.

Big Girl. unabr. ed. Danielle Steel. Read by Kathleen McInerney. 1 MP3-CD. (Running Time: 10 hrs.). 2010. 39.97 (978-1-4233-8827-2(5), 9781423388272, Brlnc Audio MP3 Lib); 39.97 (978-1-4233-8829-6(1), 9781423388296, BADLE); 24.99 (978-1-4233-8826-5(7), 9781423388265, Brilliance MP3); 24.99 (978-1-4233-8828-9(3), 9781423388289, BAD); audio compact disk 92.97 (978-1-4233-8825-8(9), 9781423388258, BriAudCD Unabrid); audio compact disk 38.99 (978-1-4233-8824-1(0), 9781423388241, Bril Audio CD Unabri) Brilliance Audio.

Big Girls. unabr. ed. Susanna Moore. Narrated by Robin Miles et al. 6 CDs. (Running Time: 6 hrs. 45 mins.). 2007. audio compact disk 64.95 (978-0-7927-4892-2(1), Chivers Sound Lib) AudioGO.
A crime of unfathomable horror has a ripple-like effect on four profoundly different souls. Helen, a troubled inmate at Sloatsburg women's prison, is serving a life sentence for the murder of her children. Dr. Louise Forrest, the recently divorced mother of an eight-year-old boy, has foresworn the Park Avenue practice for which she trained in favor of the chief of psychiatry job at Sloatsburg. Former New York City narcotics detective Ike Bradshaw is a sardonic corrections officer at the prison. And Angie, an ambitious Hollywood starlet, is intent on nothing but achieving fame. As the alternating narratives unfold, mysteries are revealed and the surprising connection between them is uncovered.

Big Girls Don't Cry. unabr. ed. Connie Briscoe. Narrated by Robin Miles. 9 cass. (Running Time: 13 hrs. 30 mins.). 1996. 84.00 (978-0-7887-5335-0(5), F0034L8) Recorded Bks.
As a teenager growing up in a comfortable Washington, D.C. suburb in the 1960s, Naomi Jefferson is much more concerned with losing her virginity than with the racial tension sweeping across America. But when her older brother is killed on the way to a civil rights demonstration, Naomi dedicates her life to honoring his legacy.

Big Girls Don't Cry, Set. abr. ed. Connie Briscoe. Read by Marilyn McCoo. 2 cass. (Running Time: 3 hrs.). 1999. 18.00 (978-0-694-51686-5(4), 394093) HarperCollins Pubs.
From the author of "Sisters & Lovers," this is the story of Naomi Jefferson, a woman who grows up in the midst of the civil rights movement only to find her largest battles in life lie ahead. A story of love, ambition, & sacrifices made for both, this is a dramatic, sensitive & authentic portrayal of one woman's search for love & purpose.

***Big Girls Don't Cry: The Election That Changed Everything for American Women.** unabr. ed. Rebecca Traister. (Running Time: 12 hrs. 30 mins. 0 sec.). 2010. 24.99 (978-1-4001-6800-2(7)); 16.99 (978-1-4001-8800-0(8)); audio compact disk 83.99 (978-1-4001-4800-4(6)); audio compact disk 34.99 (978-1-4001-1800-7(X)) Pub: Tantor Media. Dist(s): IngramPubServ

***BIG Goals System: The Masters of Goal Setting on Achieving Success.** Made for Success. Read by Zig Ziglar et al. (Running Time: 8.5 hrs. NaN mins.). (Made for Success Ser.). (ENG.). 2011. audio compact disk 32.95 (978-1-4417-7252-7(9)); audio compact disk 118.00 (978-1-4417-7251-0(0)) Blckstn Audio.

Big Green Soundtrack. 1 cass., 1 CD. 1995. 13.98 (978-1-55723-926-6(6)) W Disney Records.

Big Green Soundtrack. 1 cass., 1 CD. (J). 1995. audio compact disk 21.50 CD. (978-1-55723-927-3(4)) W Disney Records.

Big Hairy Spider: Spooky Songs & Stories. unabr. ed. Perf. by Mike Anderson. 1 cass. (Running Time: 48 min.). (J). (gr. 2-12). 1992. 10.00 (978-1-929050-04-8(6)) MW Prods.
A collection of ghost stories & spooky songs.

Big Heat. William P. McGivern. Read by Christopher Lane. (Running Time: 7 hrs.). 2003. 25.95 (978-1-59912-623-4(0)) Iofy Corp.

Big Heat. unabr. ed. William P. Mcgiven. Read by Christopher Lane. 5 cass. (Running Time: 7 hrs.). 2004. 39.95 (978-0-7861-2619-4(1), 3209); audio compact disk 40.00 (978-0-7861-8894-9(4), 3209); audio compact disk 24.95 (978-0-7861-8756-0(5), 3209) Blckstn Audio.

Big Heat. unabr. ed. William P. McGivern. Read by Christopher Lane. 5 pieces. (Running Time: 8 hrs.). 2004. reel tape 29.95 (978-0-7861-2684-2(1)) Blckstn Audio.
It started almost innocently when a cop committed suicide. It was worry over ill health, said his wife. Detective Dave Bannion wasn't so sure, but when he started digging, he was told to lay off-fast! Instead, he turned in his badge and started stalking the city streets and bars in search of the truth where he uncovers a red-hot story of murder and corruption that would blow Philadelphia's underworld sky high. Bannion was big, strong, and angry enough to kill, but he was only one honest man in a city full of mobsters and crooked cops. The big heat was on.

Big Heat. unabr. ed. William P. McGivern. Read by Christopher Lane. (Running Time: 8 hrs.). 2004. audio compact disk 29.95 (978-0-7861-8691-4(7)) Blckstn Audio.

Big Heavy World. Perf. by Chris Lizotte & Lonnie Tubbs. Prod. by Shawn Tubbs. 1 cass. 1997. audio compact disk 15.99 CD. (D0167) Diamante Music Grp.
Showcases Lizotte's straight-ahead style of Rock. Features: Far & Wide, Gold, You Know My Name, The Breath of God, The Sleep Song & more.

Big History: The Big Bang, Life on Earth, & the Rise of Humanity. Instructed by David Christian. (ENG.). 2008. 249.95 (978-1-59803-408-0(1)); audio compact disk 129.95 (978-1-59803-409-7(X)) Teaching Co.

Big Honey Hunt see Bears' Picnic & Other Stories

Big Hugs in the Morning. Prod. by Phillip Sandifer. 1 cass. (Family Sing-a-Long Ser.). 1997. audio compact disk 8.99 CD. (D9735) Diamante Music Grp.
Features songs to start the day, about such everyday activities as tying shoes & making beds.

***Big Hype.** unabr. ed. Avery Corman. Read by David Colacci. (Running Time: 7 hrs.). 2010. 29.99 (978-1-4418-4141-4(5), 9781441841414, Brilliance MP3); 39.97 (978-1-4418-4142-1(3), 9781441841421, Brlnc Audio MP3 Lib); 39.97 (978-1-4418-4144-5(X), 9781441841445, BADLE); 29.99 (978-1-4418-4143-8(1), 9781441841438, BAD) Brilliance Audio.

Big Idea. abr. unabr. ed. Donny Deutsch & Catherine Whitney. Read by Donny Deutsch. 2009. audio compact disk 29.99 (978-1-4013-9252-9(0), Hyperion Audio) Pub: Hyperion. Dist(s): HarperCollins Pubs

***Big Idea: Focus the Messageâ€"Multiply the Impact.** unabr. ed. Dave Ferguson et al. (Running Time: 5 hrs. 0 mins. 0 sec.). (Leadership Network Innovation Ser.). (ENG.). 2009. 16.99 (978-0-310-77184-5(6)) Zondervan.

Big Ideas! Perf. by Patricia Shih. 1 cass. (Running Time: 48 min.). (J). (ps-4). 1990. 9.00 (GR0010) Shih Ents.
Original songs about important social issues: gender roles, multiculturalism, cooperation, hunger, nonviolence, etc. Teaches positive social values, & more about the big world around them.

***Big in China.** unabr. ed. Alan Paul. (ENG.). 2011. (978-0-06-206160-7(7)); (978-0-06-206273-4(5)) HarperCollins Pubs.

Big Island Beaches. Eil Harrington. 2004. audio compact disk 4.95 (978-1-57306-175-9(1)) Bess Pr.

Big Island of Hawaii Real Estate Deluxe Book / 3 CD Set: Living & Investing in the Land of Aloha - the Hawaiian Islands. Ross M. Armetta. Narrated by Ross M. Armetta. Narrated by Ronald Newberry. 3 CDs. (Running Time: 140 Mins. Approx.). 2005. audio compact disk 47.99 (978-1-59733-801-1(X)) InfoFount.
Big Island Of Hawaii Real Estate Deluxe Set is a guide to Big Island of Hawaii, its secrets, and why it is the fastest appreciating market with the best long term prospects for growth in the United States. The Big Island of Hawaii is probably the best place to invest in real estate in the United States. Why ? The appreciation of the land and homes has been dramatic, the island is spectacular, and its future appears bright. The deluxe set is a combination 80 page booklet with dozens of color photos, charts, and 3 audio CDs. The CDs consist of 1 CD (35 minutes approx.) which is a read aloud version of most of the book and a 2 CD set that interviews Ronald Newberry (Realtor / Investor) these two CDs are approximately 105 minutes long.Since 2002 real estate prices on the island have risen over 300%. More importantly the increase is probably just the leading edge of an upward trend due to a wave of baby-boom retirees that should continue to drive prices skyward for years to come.This reason for this boom and the continuing trend are obvious: where would you like to retire? Does Paradise sound like a good choice? An unending flood of affluent baby-boomers are arriving in Hawaii daily with the desire and means to invest, live, and retire here in Hawaii.This set can help you to make a lot of money in this very lucrative market. It can also save you many thousands of dollars by avoiding some of the mistakes that are commonly made.The information is mostly specific to the Big Island of Hawaii although about 80% of the information will be useful for the other islands of Hawaii also.Ross Armetta the author has lived in Hawaii on Oahu (Honolulu) and the Big Island for over 7 years.The audiobook CDs are with Ronald Newberry who has lived in Hawaii for over 25 years. Ron is a real estate broker and has been intimately involved with Real Estate in Hawaii since the early 80?s.Ross and Ron?s knowledge and perspective of Hawaii, its real estate, real estate cycles, it?s little known secrets of making real estate a good investment (hint its not in the purchase and selling price) and many other tips will provide useable information to those interested in making money in Hawaii. The CDs also touch upon Real Estate Paper.The set does not try to sell you anything or over hype Hawaii.It is well balanced providing information on the negatives and gotchas as well as the many positives of Hawaii. Over 5 man weeks are invested in the information to ensure that you have good information, photos, and expertise at your fingertips. You are buying very useful information.The booklet you receive is not professionally manufactured (meaning the booklet is not perfect bound and trimmed) but it is quite functional. It has over 50 full color photographs, charts, graphs, and tables.You are buying information timely, money saving information - not a decoration for your bookshelf.CD CONTENTSDisk 1 ? audio version of the book / overview of Hawaii and its real estate.Disk 2-3 is a 100 minute plus interview with real estate broker Ron Newberry. Ron reviews, all types of properties and investments in real estate, the local market, local market history, market cycles and timing, financing secrets and advantages, the little known, but important, nuances of Hawaiian real estate law, escrow, financing, title clearance, differences in regions / demographics, etc.There are many more topics not listed that are covered. This information is very useful for anyone (in all 50 states, but even more so in Hawaii) interested in real estate either as a first time buyer or an experienced investor.CONTENTSINTRODUCTION6WHY HAWAIIAN REAL ESTATE IS BOOMING6FORTUNES ARE BEING MADE WITH HAWAIIAN REAL ESTATE7HISTORY AND OVERVIEW OF HAWAII8THE FACTS11MAJOR CITIES11DRIVING TIMES15HAWAIIAN WEATHER15ENVIRONMENTAL QUALITY19VOG19GOVERNMENT22POLITICS AND GOVERNMENT22HAWAIIAN LAW25CRIME AND SAFETY26ECONOMY28RACIAL DEMOGRAPHICS31HAWAIIAN LIFESTYLE32TRANSPORTATION32CAR RENTALS34SHOPPING IN HAWAII34FOOD IN HAWAII36SERVICE AND PROFESSIONALISM38RECREATION39EDUCATION43CHURCHES AND RELIGION45MEDICAL46MEDIA46HAWAIIAN REAL ESTATE48LAND48VOLCANIC ACTIVITY AND REAL ESTATE49EARTHQUAKES52FLOODING52BUYING REAL ESTATE53COUNTY FIRE SERVICES53OCEANFRONT LAND IS SPECIAL !56BUILDING A HOUSE59OWNER BUILDERS61 UTILITIES62ELECTRICITY62PHONE AND CELL PHONE

SERVICE63MAIL DELIVERY64WATER64SEWER67GARBAGE AND WASTE67TELEVISION68HIGH-SPEED INTERNET68ROADS69PESTS, NUISANCES, AND POTENTIAL DANGERS70TERMITES70COQUI FROGS71DANGER ? DANGER ? DANGER- NOISE - NOISE - NOISE.72MARIJUANA, DRUGS, AND WAR ZONES75ICE (CRYSTAL METHAMPHETAMINE)76SUMMARY77LINKS AND FURTHER REFERENCE78.

Big Jack. unabr. ed. J. D. Robb, pseud. Read by Susan Ericksen. (Running Time: 8 hrs.). 2010. audio compact disk 14.99 (978-1-4418-4273-2(X), 9781441842732, Bril Audio CD Unabri) Brilliance Audio.

***Big Jack.** unabr. ed. J. D. Robb, pseud. Read by Susan Ericksen. (Running Time: 8 hrs.). 2010. 14.99 (978-1-4418-4275-6(6), 9781441842756, Brilliance MP3); 14.99 (978-1-4418-4277-0(2), 9781441842770, BAD); 39.97 (978-1-4418-4276-3(4), 9781441842763, Brlnc Audio MP3 Lib); 39.97 (978-1-4418-4278-7(0), 9781441842787, BADLE); audio compact disk 49.97 (978-1-4418-4274-9(8), 9781441842749, BriAudCD Unabrid) Brilliance Audio.

***Big Jewish Book for Jews: Everything You Need to Know to Be a Really Jewish Jew.** unabr. ed. Ellis Weiner. (Running Time: 8 hrs. 30 mins.). 2010. audio compact disk 29.95 (978-1-4417-6046-3(6)) Blckstn Audio.

***Big Jewish Book for Jews: Everything You Need to Know to Be a Really Jewish Jew.** unabr. ed. Ellis Weiner. Read by Barbara Davilman. (Running Time: 8 hrs. 30 mins.). 2010. 29.95 (978-1-4417-6047-0(4)) Blckstn Audio.

***Big Jewish Book for Jews: Everything You Need to Know to Be a Really Jewish Jew.** unabr. ed. Ellis Weiner. Read by Barbara, Ellis and Davilman Weiner. (Running Time: 8 hrs. 30 mins.). 2010. 54.95 (978-1-4417-6043-2(1)); audio compact disk 76.00 (978-1-4417-6044-9(X)) Blckstn Audio.

Big Kill. abr. ed. Spillane. 2006. 8.95 (978-0-7435-6252-2(6)) Pub: S&S Audio. Dist(s): S and S Inc

Big Kill. unabr. ed. Mickey Spillane. Read by Larry McKeever. 8 cass. (Running Time: 8 hrs.). (Mike Hammer Ser.). 1992. 48.00 (978-0-7366-2137-3(7), 2936) Books on Tape.

An unknown man deposits a baby in Hammer's arms. The next minute the man is dead. Gritty & exciting.

Big Land. unabr. collector's ed. D. B. Newton. Read by Michael Russotto. 6 cass. (Running Time: 6 hrs.). 1994. 36.00 (978-0-7366-2852-5(5), 3560) Books on Tape.

Oregon ought to be a place of freedom & endless horizons, but its violence brings Chad Osbom reminders of the Civil War.

Big Law. unabr. ed. Chuck Logan. Narrated by Richard Ferrone. 10 cass. (Running Time: 14 hrs.). 1998. 87.00 (978-0-7887-3244-7(7), 95848E7) Recorded Bks.

The Witness Protection Program is designed to shield those who provide vital testimony. But what happens when the informant is lying? Logan's tightly-plotted novel twists around a double-dealing witness & a suitcase full of cash.

***Big Leap.** unabr. ed. Gay Hendricks. Read by Gay Hendricks. (ENG.). 2009. (978-0-06-178016-5(2), Harper Audio); (978-0-06-189648-4(9), Harper Audio) HarperCollins Pubs.

Big Lie: Exodus 20:16. Ed Young. 1999. 4.95 (978-0-7417-2226-3(7), 1226) Win Walk.

Big Lonely. unabr. ed. Sam Brown. Read by Bernard Bridges. Ed. by Richard Haywood. 2 cass. (Running Time: 3 hrs.). 1996. 17.00 (978-1-883268-35-0(4), 394644) Spellbinders.

Casey Wills loved being a cowboy...but hated taking orders from men who cared only about making a profit. Tatum Stagg offered Casey a lot of money...if Casey would turn his back on everything he believed in...but Casey was smart enough not to take integrity for granted...especially his own.

Big Lonesome. unabr. ed. Will Bryant. Read by Cameron Beierle. 12 cass. (Running Time: 12 hrs. 48 min.). 2001. 64.95 (978-1-55686-984-6(3)) Books in Motion.

A young boy and his father come to the Rocky Mountains in search of gold, guided by an old trapper's memories of a gold-rich stream. They find their lives changed not by the elusive gold, but by the grizzlies that roam the mountain valleys.

Big Love. unabr. ed. Sarah Dunn. Read by Eliza Foss. (YA). 2006. 44.99 (978-1-59895-542-2(X)) Find a World.

Big Mama, Linda Izzo's Feel Good Now Plan: Life Change Is a Managed Miracle. Linda Izzo. 1 cass.; 1 CD. (Running Time: 1 hr. 45 min.). 1997. 29.99 Incl. CD, wkbk. & accessories. (978-0-9670993-0-9(7)); 29.99 Set, incl. wkbk & accessories. (978-0-9670993-1-6(5)) Im Okay Ent.

Linda struts & sings her stuff offering the tools to promote self-esteem, confidence & body-acceptance.

Big Match. unabr. ed. Rob Childs. Read by Sean Bean. 1 cass. (Running Time: 1 hrs.). 2002. (978-1-85549-544-9(9)) Cover To Cover GBR.

Andrew and his younger brother Chris are going to play in a vital cup game against Shenby School. Will they win?.

Big Max Book & Tape. unabr. abr. ed. Kin Platt. Illus. by Robert Lopshire. 1 cass. (Running Time: 15 min.). (I Can Read Bks.). (J). (gr. k-3). 1991. 8.99 (978-1-55994-496-0(X), TBC 496X) HarperCollins Pubs.

Big Metronome: Time Development Studies with 3 Audio CDs. Bruce E. Arnold. 3 cds. (ENG.). (C). 1999. spiral bd. 39.99 (978-1-890944-37-7(8)) Muse Eek.

Big Money. unabr. ed. John Dos Passos. Read by Michael Prichard. 13 cass. (Running Time: 1 hr. 30 min. per cass.). (U. S. A. Trilogy: Vol. 3). 104.00 (1344); audio compact disk 19.50 Books on Tape.

America in the boom years of the 20's. Hog-wild material prosperity rules the land & cripples the national life.

***Big Money.** unabr. ed. John Dos Passos. Narrated by David Drummond. (Running Time: 19 hrs. 0 mins. 0 sec.). (U. S. A. Ser.). 2010. 34.99 (978-1-4001-6912-2(7)); 22.99 (978-1-4001-8912-0(8)); audio compact disk 49.99 (978-1-4001-1912-7(X)) Pub: Tantor Media. Dist(s): IngramPubServ

Big Money. unabr. collector's ed. John Dos Passos. Read by Michael Prichard. 13 cass. (Running Time: 19 hrs. 30 min.). (U. S. A. Trilogy). 1984. 104.00 (978-0-7366-0358-4(1), 1344) Books on Tape.

America in the boom years of the 20's. Hog-wild material prosperity rules the land & cripples the national life. "Dos Passos' subject is indeed democracy, but his belief - especially as he goes into the final volume of his trilogy - is that the force of circumstances that is 20th century life is too strong for the average man, who will probably never rise above mass culture, mass superstition, mass slogans".

***Big Money (Library Edition)** unabr. ed. John Dos Passos. Narrated by David Drummond. (Running Time: 19 hrs. 0 mins.). (U. S. A. Ser.). 2010. 49.99 (978-1-4001-9912-9(3)); audio compact disk 119.99 (978-1-4001-4912-4(6)) Pub: Tantor Media. Dist(s): IngramPubServ

Big Moo: Stop Trying to Be Perfect & Start Being Remarkable. unabr. ed. Seth Godin. Read by Seth Godin. (Running Time: 4 hrs. 0 mins. 0 sec.). (ENG.). 2005. audio compact disk 24.99 (978-1-4001-0201-3(4)) Pub: Tantor Media. Dist(s): IngramPubServ

Big Moo: Stop Trying to Be Perfect & Start Being Remarkable. unabr. ed. Ed. by Seth Godin. (Running Time: 4 hrs. 0 mins. 0 sec.). (ENG.). 2005. audio compact disk 49.99 (978-1-4001-3201-0(0)); audio compact disk 19.99 (978-1-4001-5201-8(1)) Pub: Tantor Media. Dist(s): IngramPubServ

***Big Mouth & Ugly Girl.** abr. ed. Joyce Carol Oates. Read by Hilary Swank & Chad Lowe. 2004. (978-0-06-078654-0(X)) HarperCollins Pubs.

***Big Mouth & Ugly Girl.** abr. ed. Joyce Carol Oates. Read by Hilary Swank & Chad Lowe. (ENG.). 2004. (978-0-06-081410-6(1)) HarperCollins Pubs.

Big Mouth & Ugly Girl. unabr. ed. Joyce Carol Oates. Read by Hilary Swank & Chad Lowe. (J). 2008. 54.99 (978-1-60252-953-3(1)) Find a World.

Big Nap. unabr. ed. Bruce Hale. Read by Jon Cryer. (Running Time: 1 hr. 30 mins.). (Chet Gecko Mystery Ser.: No. 4). (J). (gr. 3-6). 2004. pap. bk. 17.00 (978-0-8072-1707-8(7), S FTR 272 SP, Listening Lib) Random Audio Pubg.

Big Nap; Farewell, My Lunchbag. unabr. ed. Bruce Hale. Prod. by Listening Library Staff. 2 cass. (Running Time: 3 hrs. 8 mins.). (Chet Gecko Mystery Ser.: Nos. 3-4). (J). (gr. 3-6). 2003. 23.00 (978-0-8072-1582-1(1), Listening Lib) Pub: Random Audio Pubg. Dist(s): Random

***Big Nate.** unabr. ed. Lincoln Peirce. Read by Fred Berman. (ENG.). 2010. (978-0-06-201207-4(X)) HarperCollins Pubs.

***Big Nate: In a Class by Himself.** unabr. ed. Lincoln Peirce. Read by Fred Berman. (ENG.). 2010. (978-0-06-200261-7(9)) HarperCollins Pubs.

***Big Nate Strikes Again.** unabr. ed. Lincoln Peirce. (ENG.). 2010. (978-0-06-201253-1(3)); (978-0-06-206807-1(5)) HarperCollins Pubs.

Big Nowhere. unabr. collector's ed. James Ellroy. Read by Bill Whitaker. 12 cass. (Running Time: 18 hrs.). (L. A. Quartet). 1990. 96.00 (978-0-7366-1849-6(X), 2682) Books on Tape.

Los Angeles, 1950. Red crosscurrents & a string of brutal killings. Three men caught up in a massive web of ambition, perversion & deceit.

Big on Plans. unabr. collector's ed. Katy Kelly. Read by Tara Sands. 2 cass. (Running Time: 2 hrs. 40 mins.). (J). 2005. 23.00 (978-0-307-20718-0(8), BksonTape); audio compact disk 25.50 (978-0-307-24627-1(2), BksonTape) Pub: Random Audio Pubg. Dist(s): NetLibrary CO

Big One-Oh. unabr. ed. Dean Pitchford. Read by Dean Pitchford. 4 CDs. (Running Time: 4 hrs. 37 mins.). (J). (gr. 3-7). 2007. audio compact disk 30.00 (978-0-7393-6239-6(9), Listening Lib) Pub: Random Audio Pubg. Dist(s): Random

Charley Maplewood has never been one for parties - that would require friends, which he doesn't have. But now that he's turning ten - the big one-oh - he decides to throw a birthday party for himself, complete with a "House of Horrors" theme and a big birthday cake. Of course things don't work out as Charley plans. In trying to make friends, he ends up inviting the class bully Cougar to come, and that's before he ruins the cake and burns down the garage. By the time of the big day, Charley's home really is a house of horrors. Will Charley be able to pull it together before the big one-oh becomes the big OH-NO!? From start to finish, The Big One-Oh is a laugh-out-loud riot, and any listener will relate to the pressures Charley faces both at school and at home in planning his special day. So put on your party hat and celebrate The Big One-Oh today!.

Big One-Oh. unabr. ed. Dean Pitchford. Read by Dean Pitchford. (Running Time: 16620 sec.). (ENG.). (J). (gr. 5-7). 2008. audio compact disk 28.00 (978-0-7393-6237-2(2), Listening Lib) Pub: Random Audio Pubg. Dist(s): Random

Big or Little? Audio CD. Adapted by Benchmark Education Company Staff. Based on a work by Francisco Blane. (My First Reader's Theater Ser.). (J). (gr. k-1). 2008. audio compact disk 10.00 (978-1-60634-102-5(2)) Benchmark Educ.

Big over Easy. unabr. ed. Jasper Fforde. (Nursery Crime Ser.: No. 1). 2005. 29.95 (978-0-7927-3702-5(4), CMP 783); 54.95 (978-0-7927-3542-7(0), CSL 783); audio compact disk 74.95 (978-0-7927-3701-8(6), SLD 783) AudioGO.

Big over Easy. unabr. ed. Jasper Fforde. 10 CDs. (Running Time: 11 hrs.). No. 1. (ENG.). (gr. 12 up). 2005. audio compact disk 29.95 (978-0-14-305770-3(7), PengAudBks) Penguin Grp USA.

Big Oyster: History on the Half Shell. unabr. ed. Mark Kurlansky. 6 cass. (Running Time: 10 hrs.). 2006. 57.60 (978-1-4159-2690-1(5)); audio compact disk 76.50 (978-1-4159-2691-8(3)) Pub: Books on Tape. Dist(s): NetLibrary CO

Big Party: Early Explorers Fluent Set A Audio CD. Benchmark Education Staff. (J). 2006. audio compact disk 10.00 (978-1-4108-7644-7(6)) Benchmark Educ.

Big Pick-Up. unabr. collector's ed. Elleston Trevor. Read by Robert Mundy. 7 cass. (Running Time: 10 hrs. 30 min.). 1982. 56.00 (978-0-7366-0453-6(7), 1426) Books on Tape.

Dunkirk, how the soldiers got there & what happened when they arrived.

Big Picture. AIO Team Staff. Prod. by Focus on the Family Staff. 4 CDs. (Running Time: 6 hrs.). (Adventures in Odyssey Ser.: No. 35). (ENG.). (J). (gr. 2-6). 2004. audio compact disk 24.99 (978-1-56179-909-1(2)) Pub: Focus Family. Dist(s): Tyndale Hse

Big Picture. Douglas Kennedy. 2004. 15.95 (978-0-7435-4194-7(4)) Pub: S&S Audio. Dist(s): S and S Inc

Big Picture. Huston Smith. 2 CDs. (Running Time: 2 hrs. 15 min.). 2002. audio compact disk 24.95 (978-1-56455-963-0(7)) Sounds True.

Big Picture. Perf. by Michael W. Smith. 1 cass. 1986. audio compact disk Brentwood Music.

This now certified gold record features the classics, Rocketown & Old Enough to Know.

Big Picture. unabr. ed. Douglas Kennedy. 10 cass. (Running Time: 11 hrs. 50 mins.). (Isis Cassettes Ser.). (J). 2005. 84.95 (978-0-7531-1454-4(2)) Pub: ISIS Lrg Prnt GBR. Dist(s): Ulverscroft US

Big Picture. unabr. collector's ed. Douglas Kennedy. Read by John Edwardson. 9 cass. (Running Time: 13 hrs. 30 mins.). 1998. 72.00 (978-0-7366-4078-7(9), 4587) Books on Tape.

A lawyer becomes trapped in a web of jealousy & violence when he meets his wife's lover.

Big Picture, Level 1. Sue Leather. Contrib. by Philip Prowse. 1 cass. (Running Time: hrs. mins.). (Cambridge English Readers Ser.). (ENG., 2001. 9.00 (978-0-521-79847-1(7)) Cambridge U Pr.

***Big Picture: Getting Perspective on What's Really Important in Life.** Zondervan. (Running Time: 9 hrs. 2 mins. 14 sec.). (ENG.). 2010. 14.99 (978-0-310-86975-7(7)) Zondervan.

Big Picture: Getting Perspective on What's Really Important in Life. abr. ed. Carson,M.D., Ben. (Running Time: 2 hrs. 0 mins. 0 sec.). (ENG.). 2003. 10.99 (978-0-310-26000-4(0)) Zondervan.

Big Picture: Getting Perspective on What's Really Important in Life. unabr. ed. Ben Carson & Gregg Lewis. 2 cass. (Running Time: 2 hrs.). 1999. 17.99 (978-0-310-22668-0(6)) Zondervan.

Known as the originator of groundbreaking surgical procedures, a doctor who turns impossible hopes into joyous realities. He is known as well as a compassionate humanitarian who reaches beyond corporate boardrooms to touch the lives of inner-city kids. What drives him? The Big Picture. A vision of something truly worth living for, something that calls forth the best of his amazing talents, energy, and focus. In The Big Picture, Dr. Carson shares with you the over-arching philosophy that has shaped his life, causing him to rise form failure to far-reaching influence.

Big Pumpkin. Erica Silverman. Narrated by John McDonough. (Running Time: 15 mins.). (J). 1992. audio compact disk 12.75 (978-1-4193-1769-9(5)) Recorded Bks.

Big Pumpkin. unabr. ed. Erica Silverman. Narrated by John McDonough. 1 cass. (Running Time: 15 mins.). (ps up). 1998. 10.00 (978-0-7887-2523-4(8), 95595E7) Recorded Bks.

The old witch has grown the biggest pumpkin ever for her Halloween pie. But first she must pull it off the vine. A gentle lesson in friendship.

Big Red Barn. abr. ed. Margaret Wise Brown & Brown. Illus. by Felicia Bond. (Share a Story Ser.). (J). (ps up). 1998. 9.99 (978-0-694-70097-4(5)) HarperCollins Pubs.

Big Red Road to the Rose Bowl: The University of Wisconsin 1993-94 Rose Bowl Winning Football Season. unabr. ed. Read by Brian Manthey. 1 cass. (Running Time: 1 hr.). 1994. 9.95 (978-1-885408-01-3(3), CC002) Listen & Live.

Join Brian Manthey, voice of the Badgers, as he narrates the 1993-94 University of Wisconsin football season through the radio broadcast highlights of each exciting game during their most successful season in 31 years.

Big Red Son. abr. ed. David Foster Wallace. Read by David Foster Wallace. (Running Time: 1 hr.). (ENG.). 2008. 2.98 (978-1-60024-312-7(6)) Pub: Hachet Audio. Dist(s): HachBkGrp

Big Red Tequila. Rick Riordan. Narrated by Tom Stechschulte. 8 cass. (Running Time: 11 hrs. 30 mins.). (Tres Navarre Ser.: No. 1). 71.00 (978-1-4025-0600-0(7)) Recorded Bks.

Big Red Train Ride. unabr. collector's ed. Eric Newby. Read by David Case. 8 cass. (Running Time: 12 hrs.). 1994. 64.00 (978-0-7366-2715-3(4), 3445) Books on Tape.

From Moscow to the Pacific on the Trans-Siberian Railway ("the big red train ride") is an eight-day journey of nearly 6,000 miles. Eric Newby made this trip with his wife, an official guide & a photographer. Harrassed by the Soviet conductor, hindered at every stage by bureaucratic officials, off his feed from bad food & worse drinks, Newby still managed to gather a wealth of detail about life in the U.S.S.R. & most importantly, his sense of humor never deserted him.

***Big Rock Candy Mountain.** Wallace Stegner. (ENG.). 2010. 40.00 (978-1-4417-2475-5(3)) Blckstn Audio.

Big Rock Candy Mountain. unabr. ed. Wallace Stegner. (Running Time: 19 hrs. 30 mins.). 2010. 44.95 (978-1-4417-1723-8(4)); 59.95 (978-1-4417-1719-1(6)); audio compact disk 123.00 (978-1-4417-1720-7(X)) Blckstn Audio.

Big Russ & Me: Father & Son - Lessons of Life. Tim Russert. 7 vols. 2004. bk. 59.95 (978-0-7927-3218-1(9), CSL 655, Chivers Sound Lib); bk. 79.95 (978-0-7927-3219-8(7), SLD 655, Chivers Sound Lib) AudioGO.

Big Russ & Me: Father & Son - Lessons of Life. abr. ed. Tim Russert. Read by Tim Russert. 5 CDs. (Running Time: 5 hrs.). 2006. audio compact disk 14.98 (978-1-4013-8496-8(X), Hyperion Audio) Pub: Hyperion. Dist(s): HarperCollins Pubs

Big Sample Chip. Paul Pimsleur et al. Read by Catherine O'Hara & Christopher Reeve. (Running Time: 50 hrs.). 2006. 29.95 (978-1-60083-342-7(X)) Iofy Corp.

Big Scandal: A Christmas Message. Ben Young. 2000. 4.95 (978-0-7417-6212-2(9), B0212) Win Walk.

Big-Screen Drive in Theater. abr. ed. Donald Davis. Contrib. by Donald Davis. (Running Time: 3240 sec.). 1996. audio compact disk 14.95 (978-0-87483-773-5(1)) Pub: August Hse. Dist(s): Natl Bk Netwk

Big-Screen Drive-In Theater. unabr. ed. Donald Davis. 1 cass. (Running Time: 51 mins.). Dramatization. (American Storytelling Ser.). (gr. 5-12). 1996. 12.00 (978-0-87483-535-9(6)) Pub: August Hse. Dist(s): Natl Bk Netwk

Davis relates his hilarious experiences working at a drive-in movie theater for three summers. Davis relates the little quirks that make summer jobs so great.

Big-Screen Drive-in Theater. unabr. ed. Donald Davis. Read by Donald Davis. (J). 2007. 34.99 (978-1-60252-548-1(X)) Find a World.

Big Short: Inside the Doomsday Machine. unabr. ed. Michael Lewis. Read by Jesse Boggs. 8 CDs. (Running Time: 9 hrs. 30 mins. 0 sec.). 2010. audio compact disk 39.99 (978-1-4423-0005-7(1)) Pub: S&S Audio. Dist(s): S and S Inc

Big Show: Inside ESPN's Sportscenter. Keith Olbermann & Dan Patrick. 2004. 10.95 (978-0-7435-4195-4(2)) Pub: S&S Audio. Dist(s): S and S Inc

Big Show: The Greatest Pilot's Story of World War II. unabr. collector's ed. Pierre Clostermann. Read by Gary Martin. 7 cass. (Running Time: 10 hrs. 30 min.). 1987. 56.00 (978-0-7366-1240-1(8), 2157) Books on Tape.

French pilot's account of his World War II flying experiences with the RAF.

***Big Show, Volume 2.** RadioArchives.com. (Running Time: 450). (ENG.). 2006. audio compact disk 29.98 (978-1-61081-043-2(0)) Radio Arch.

***Big Show, Volume 3.** RadioArchives.com. (Running Time: 450). (ENG.). 2006. audio compact disk 29.98 (978-1-61081-049-4(X)) Radio Arch.

***Big Show, Volume 4.** RadioArchives.com. (Running Time: 450). (ENG.). 2007. audio compact disk 29.98 (978-1-61081-061-6(9)) Radio Arch.

***Big Show, Volume 5.** RadioArchives.com. (Running Time: 450). (ENG.). 2008. audio compact disk 29.98 (978-1-61081-072-2(4)) Radio Arch.

Big Shuffle. Laura Pedersen. Narrated by Katie Hale. 2009. audio compact disk 33.95 (978-1-60031-049-2(4)) Spoken Books.

Big Silence. unabr. ed. Stuart M. Kaminsky. Read by Adam Henderson. 8 vols. (Running Time: 12 hrs.). (Abe Lieberman Mystery Ser.: Vol. 6). 2001. bk. 69.95 (978-0-7927-2442-1(9), CSL 331, Chivers Sound Lib) AudioGO.

Abe Lieberman & his Irish partner, Bill Hanrahan, are taken on a journey that will test their consciences to the limit. When the young son of an informant in the government's witness protection program is kidnapped & a grisly death occurs, they will have to make some hard choices to set things right & Lieberman may have to bend the rules to help his partner, whose time has come to face the demons that have been dogging his steps for too many years.

Big Sister, Little Sister: American Indian Women's Stories. Jocelyn Riley. (YA). 1995. 12.00 (978-1-877933-58-5(9), 16003) Her Own Words.

Big Sleep. unabr. ed. Raymond Chandler. Narrated by Elliott Gould. 5 cass. (Running Time: 7 hrs. 30 mins.). 2004. 29.95 (978-1-59007-089-5(5)) Pub: New Millenn Enter. Dist(s): PerseuPGW

This classic case of blackmail and murder involves the strange Sternwood family - a paralyzed California millionaire and his two psychotic daughters.

Big Sleep. unabr. ed. Raymond Chandler. Read by Elliott Gould. 6 CDs. (Running Time: 7.5 hrs.). 2004. audio compact disk 39.95 (978-1-59007-090-1(9)) Pub: New Millenn Enter. Dist(s): PerseuPGW

Big Sleep & The High Window. abr. ed. Raymond Chandler. Read by Ed Bishop et al. 2 cass. (Running Time: 3 hrs.). 1999. 16.85 (978-0-563-55892-7(X)) BBC WrldWd GBR.
In "The Big Sleep" Marlowe finds himself mixed up with a blonde, a brunette, four million dollars & some serious blackmail. Right up his alley. In "The High Window" the search for the missing Linda Conquest leads Marlowe right down into the underworld, where he finds himself knee deep in dead men.

Big Snow. 2004. bk. 24.95 (978-1-56008-162-3(7)); pap. bk. 14.95 (978-1-56008-163-0(5)); 8.95 (978-1-56008-843-1(5)); cass. & flmstrp 30.00 (978-0-89719-654-3(6)) Weston Woods.

Big Snow. Berta H. Hader & Elmer Hader. Read by John McDonough. 1 cass. (Running Time: 15 mins.). (J). (ps-1). 1999. pap. bk. & stu. ed. 25.20 (978-0-7887-2985-0(3), 40867) Recorded Bks.
All through the woods, creatures of every size are storing food for the winter. Soon the big snow is coming. The attractive illustrations will captivate beginning readers while they follow along with the print book included in the ReadAlong Pack.

Big Snow. Berta H. Hader & Elmer Hader. 1 cass. (Running Time: 11 min.). (J). (ps-1). 2000. pap. bk. 12.95 Weston Woods.
Woodland birds & animals busily prepare for the long, cold winter.

Big Snow. unabr. ed. Elmer Hader & Berta H. Hader. Narrated by John McDonough. 1 cass. (Running Time: 15 mins.). (gr. k up). 1999. 10.00 (978-0-7887-2955-3(1), 95730E7) Recorded Bks.
All through the woods, creatures of every size are storing food for the winter. Soon the big snow is coming. The attractive illustrations will captivate beginning readers while they follow along with the print book included in the ReadAlong Pack.

Big Snow, Class Set. Berta H. Hader & Elmer Hader. Read by John McDonough. 1 cass. (Running Time: 15 mins.). (J). (ps-1). 1999. pap. bk. 100.30 (978-0-7887-3015-3(0), 46832) Recorded Bks.
All through the woods, creatures of every size are storing food for the winter. Soon the big snow is coming.

Big Snow, the; Frog Went A-Courtin'; Little Island, the; Madeline's Rescue. 2004. (978-0-89719-807-3(7)); cass. & flmstrp (978-0-89719-716-8(X)) Weston Woods.

Big Splash. Jack D. Ferraiolo. Read by Sean Schemmel. (Playaway Children Ser.). (J). 2008. 59.99 (978-1-60640-681-6(7)) Find a World.

Big Splash. Jack D. Ferraiolo. Narrated by Sean Schemmel. (ENG.). (J). (gr. 4-7). 2008. audio compact disk 29.95 (978-0-545-09101-5(2)) Scholastic Inc.

Big Splash. unabr. ed. Jack D. Ferraiolo. 4 CDs. (Running Time: 4 hrs. 52 mins.). (ENG.). (J). (gr. 4-7). 2008. audio compact disk 49.95 (978-0-545-09107-7(1)) Scholastic Inc.

Big Steps for Little Feet. Mary Hopkins. audio compact disk 14.95 (978-0-8198-1159-2(9), 332-023) Pauline Bks.

Big Stone Gap. abr. ed. Adriana Trigiani. Read by Adriana Trigiani. 3 CDs. (Running Time: 5 hrs.). (Big Stone Gap Ser.: Bk. 1). 2000. audio compact disk 29.95 (978-0-375-41006-2(6), Random AudioBks) Random Audio Pubg.
It's 1978 & 35-year-old Ave Maria Mulligan is the self-proclaimed spinster of Big Stone Gap, Virginia, a sleepy hamlet in the Blue Ridge Mountains. As the local pharmacist, she's been keeping the townfolks' secrets for years, but she's about to discover a skeleton in her own family's tidy closet that will blow the lid right off her quiet, uneventful life.

Big Stone Gap. abr. ed. Adriana Trigiani. Read by Adriana Trigiani. (Running Time: 18000 sec.). (Big Stone Gap Ser.: Bk. 1). (ENG.). 2006. audio compact disk 14.99 (978-0-7393-4035-6(2), Random AudioBks) Pub: Random Audio Pubg. Dist(s): Random

Big Stone Gap. unabr. ed. Adriana Trigiani. Read by Grace Bennett. 8 vols. (Running Time: 12 hrs.). (Big Stone Gap Ser.: Bk. 1). 2000. bk. 69.95 (978-0-7927-2406-3(2), CSL 295, Chivers Sound Lib) AudioGO.
It's 1978 & Ave Maria Mulligan is the thirty-five-year-old self-proclaimed spinster of Big Stone Gap, a sleepy Hamlet in the Blue Ridge Mountains of Virginia. She is content with her life, untill she discovers a skeleton in her family's tidy closet that completely unravels her quiet, conventional life.

Big Stone Gap. unabr. ed. Adriana Trigiani. Read by Grace Bennett. 10 CDs. (Running Time: 15 Hrs.). (Big Stone Gap Ser.: Bk. 1). 2001. audio compact disk 94.95 (978-0-7927-9957-3(7), SLD 008, Chivers Sound Lib) AudioGO.
Ave Maria is content with her life of doing errands & negotiating small details, until she discovers a skeleton in her family's formerly tidy closet that completely unravels her quiet, conventional life.

Big Story: Case of the Counterfeit Coins & a Manhunt in Manhattan. unabr. ed. 1 cass. (Running Time: 1 hr.). 2001. 6.98 (1971) Radio Spirits.

Big Sundae. Randy Horton. Narrated by Larry A. McKeever. (Sport Ser.). (J). 2000. audio compact disk 14.95 (978-1-58659-293-6(9)) Artesian.

Big Sundae. abr. ed. Randy Horton. Narrated by Larry A. McKeever. 1 cass. (Running Time: 40 min.). (Sport Ser.). (J). 2000. 10.95 (978-1-58659-039-0(1), 54119) Artesian.

Big Sur. Jack Kerouac. Read by Tom Parker. 5 CDs. (Running Time: 5 hrs. 30 mins.). 2000. audio compact disk 40.00 (978-0-7861-9887-0(7), 2386) Blckstn Audio.
A humane, precise account of the extraordinary ravages of alcohol delirium tremens on Kerouac, a superior novelist who had the strength to complete his poetic narrative, a task few scribes so afflicted have accomplished - others crack up. Here we meet San Francisco's poets & recognize hero Dean Moriarty ten years after "On the Road".

Big Sur. Jack Kerouac. 4 cass. (Running Time: 5 hrs. 30 mins.). 2000. 24.95 (978-0-7861-1701-7(X)) Pub: Blckstn Audio. Dist(s): Penton Overseas

Big Sur. Jack Kerouac. Narrated by Tom Parker. (Running Time: 5 hrs. 30 mins.). 1998. 24.95 (978-1-59912-432-2(7)) Iofy Corp.

Big Sur. unabr. ed. Jack Kerouac. Read by Grover Gardner. (Running Time: 6 hrs.). 2009. audio compact disk 29.95 (978-1-4417-1151-9(1)) Blckstn Audio.

Big Sur, unabr. ed. Jack Kerouac et al. Read by Tom Parker. 4 cass. (Running Time: 5 hrs. 30 mins.). 1999. 32.95 (978-0-7861-1556-3(4), 2386) Blckstn Audio.

Big Sur - NorthBound Edition: A Driver's Guide to the Hidden Treasures of the Big Sur Coast. Allan J. Frankel. Read by Allan J. Frankel. 1 cass. (Running Time: 1 hr. 30 min.). (Tours on Tape Ser.). 1998. 10.95 Illustrated card. (978-1-891364-01-3(4)) Frankel Pub.
Audio Cassette guided tour of California's Big Sur Coast.

Big Sur- Southbound Edition: A Driver's Guide to the Hidden Treasures of the Big Sur Coast, Vol. 1. Allan J. Frankel. Read by Allan J. Frankel. 1 cass. (Running Time: 1 hrs. 40 min.). (Tours on Tape Ser.). 1997. 10.95 Incl. illustrated J-card. (978-1-891364-00-6(6)) Frankel Pub.
Guided tour of California's Big Sur coast.

Big Sword Swinging: A Weekend Intensive with Adyashanti - Recorded in Santa Monica - January 2005. Featuring Adyashanti. 6 CDs. (Running Time: 5 hrs., 45 min.). 2006. audio compact disk 58.00 (978-1-933986-06-7(9), 2BSS) Open Gate Pub.
This delightful 6-CD set presents satsang at its finest. Exceptionally fresh talks and honest dialogues will cut through the concepts of both new and seasoned listeners, going deeply into the innocent, simple presence of being. Topics include: Where intentions come from, Consciousness as the transformative agent, The wisdom of the void, Children and the unspoken power of love, The transparency of the heart, and Choice and free will."This is like spiritual triage. You're being exposed to an awful lot in two days. I've got the big sword swinging.

***Big Tall Wish.** 2010. audio compact disk (978-1-59171-191-9(6)) Falcon Picture.

Big Things Come in Small Packages: Matthew 13:31-32. Ed Young. 1993. 4.95 (978-0-7417-1966-9(5), 966) Win Walk.

Big Things Come in Small Packages: Matthew 13:31-33. Ed Young. (J). 1981. 4.95 (978-0-7417-1193-9(1), A0193) Win Walk.

Big Think Strategy: How to Leverage Bold Ideas & Leave Small Thinking Behind. unabr. ed. Bernd H. Schmitt. Read by Lloyd James & Sean Pratt. (Running Time: 4 hrs. 30 mins.). (ENG.). 2008. 24.98 (978-1-59659-193-6(5), GildAudio) Pub: Gildan Media. Dist(s): HachBkGrp

Big Think Strategy: How to Leverage Bold Ideas & Leave Small Thinking Behind. unabr. ed. Bernd H. Schmitt. Read by Sean Pratt. 6 CDs. (Running Time: 4 hrs. 30 mins.). (ENG.). 2008. audio compact disk 29.98 (978-1-59659-162-2(5), GildAudio) Pub: Gildan Media. Dist(s): HachBkGrp

Big Three in Economics: John Maynard Keynes, Karl Marx, Adam Smith. Mark Skousen. Read by Jeff Riggenbach. (Running Time: 32400 sec.). 2007. 59.95 (978-1-4332-0091-5(0)); audio compact disk 29.95 (978-1-4332-0093-9(7)); audio compact disk 72.00 (978-1-4332-0092-2(9)) Blckstn Audio.

***Big Time.** unabr. ed. Fritz Leiber. Read by Suzanne Toren. (Running Time: 5 hrs.). 2010. 39.97 (978-1-4418-7515-0(8), 9781441875150, BADLE); 19.99 (978-1-4418-7513-6(1), 9781441875136, Brilliance MP3); 39.97 (978-1-4418-7514-3(X), 9781441875143, Brinc Audio MP3 Lib); audio compact disk 19.99 (978-1-4418-7511-2(5), 9781441875112, Bril Audio CD Unabri); audio compact disk 64.97 (978-1-4418-7512-9(3), 9781441875129, BriAudCD Unabrid) Brilliance Audio.

Big Town. Contrib. by Edward Pawley. (Running Time: 10800 sec.). 2004. 9.98 (978-1-57019-574-7(9)); audio compact disk 9.98 (978-1-57019-575-4(7)) Radio Spirits.

Big Town: Deadly Summons & Chill of Death. unabr. ed. Perf. by Edward Pawley. 1 cass. (Running Time: 1 hr.). 2001. 6.98 (1575) Radio Spirits.

Big Town: Death Rides the Highway. Poems. Perf. by Edward G. Robinson. (CM-4105) Natl Recrd Co.

Big Town: Fatal Alibi & the Confession. unabr. ed. Perf. by Edward Pawley. 1 cass. (Running Time: 1 hr.). 2001. 6.98 (1578) Radio Spirits.

Big Town: Iron Fist & the Hunter. unabr. ed. Perf. by Edward Pawley. 1 cass. (Running Time: 1 hr.). 2001. 6.98 (1577) Radio Spirits.

Big Town: Lost & Found & Deadline at Dawn. unabr. ed. Perf. by Edward Pawley. 1 cass. (Running Time: 1 hr.). 2001. 6.98 (1569) Radio Spirits.

Big Town: The Lost & Found & Prelude to Christmas. unabr. ed. Perf. by Edward Pawley. 1 cass. (Running Time: 1 hr.). 2001. 6.98 (2211) Radio Spirits.

Big Town: The Squeaking Rat & The Lonely Heart. unabr. ed. Perf. by Edward Pawley. 1 cass. (Running Time: 1 hr.). 2001. 6.98 (1576) Radio Spirits.

Big Trouble. unabr. ed. Dave Barry. Read by Dick Hill. 3 CDs. 2002. audio compact disk 62.25 (978-1-59086-547-7(2)) Brilliance Audio.
In the city of Coconut Grove, Florida, these things happen: A struggling adman named Eliot Arnold drives home from a meeting with the Client from Hell. His teenage son, Matt, fills his Squirtmaster 9000 for his turn at a high school game called Killer. Matt's intended victim, Jenny Herk, sits down in front of the TV with her mom for what she hopes will be a peaceful evening - for once. Jenny's alcoholic and secretly embezzling stepfather, Arthur, emerges from the maid's room, angry at being rebuffed - again.

Big Trouble. unabr. ed. Dave Barry. Read by Dick Hill. (Running Time: 7 hrs.). 2008. 49.97 (978-1-4233-3841-3(3), 9781423338413, BADLE); 39.25 (978-1-4233-3839-0(1), 9781423338390, Brinc Audio MP3 Lib); 24.95 (978-1-4233-3838-3(3), 9781423338383, Brilliance MP3); 24.95 (978-1-4233-3840-6(5), 9781423338406, BAD) Brilliance Audio.

Big Trouble, Set. abr. ed. Dave Barry. Read by Dick Hill. 2 cass. 1999. 17.95 (FS9-51021) Highsmith.

Big Two-Hearted River & Other Stories. Ernest Hemingway. Read by Roger Steffens. 1 cass. (Running Time: 90 min.). 1995. 10.95 (978-0-939643-67-7(7)) Audio Pr.
A trilogy of vintage Hemingway Nick Adams stories. The first two tales describe Adams's experiences in Italy as a World War I serviceman. This serves as a preamble for "Big Two-Hearted River," where Adams returns to his native northern Michigan. Here, he digests his wartime experience by removing himself to the wilderness, embarking on a solo flyfishing expedition. He discovers a "burned-over land" mirroring his own psyche, where even the grasshoppers have turned black.

Big Walter Horton with Carey Bell: Intermediate Level. Walter Horton & Carey Bell. Tr. by David Barrett. 1998. pap. bk. 29.95 (978-0-7866-2332-7(2), 95764CDP) Mel Bay.

Big Wander, unabr. ed. William Hobbs. Narrated by Ed Sala. 4 pieces. (Running Time: 5 hrs. 45 mins.). (gr. 6 up). 35.00 (978-0-7887-1806-9(1), 95278E7) Recorded Bks.
It's Clay Lancaster's dream to find his ex-rodeo star uncle. He & his brother plan a trip to find the missing pages of their family history. Available to libraries only.

Big Wander, Class Set. unabr. ed. William Hobbs. Read by Ed Sala. 5 cass., 10 bks. (Running Time: 5 hrs. 45 min.). (J). (gr. 5). 1997. bk. & pap. bk. 100.80 (978-0-7887-3498-4(9), 46110) Recorded Bks.

Big Wander, Homework Set. unabr. ed. William Hobbs. Read by Ed Sala. 4 cass. (Running Time: 5 hrs. 45 min.). (J). 1997. bk. 47.75 (978-0-7887-1848-9(7), 40628) Recorded Bks.

***Big Wheat.** unabr. ed. Richard A. Thompson. (Running Time: 8 hrs. 30 mins.). 2011. 29.95 (978-1-4417-7032-5(1)); 54.95 (978-1-4417-7029-5(1)); audio compact disk 76.00 (978-1-4417-7030-1(5)) Blckstn Audio.

Big Wide Grin. unabr. ed. Keb' Mo'. 1 CD. (Running Time: 48 mins.). 2001. audio compact disk 16.98 (978-0-7389-2189-1(0), Sony Wonder); 9.98 (978-0-7389-2190-7(4), Sony Wonder) Sony Music Ent.
Grammy-winning blues artist Mo' brings his broad talent to a fine album celebrating family in all its guises.

***Big Words for Little People.** unabr. ed. Jamie Lee Curtis. Read by Jamie Lee Curtis. (ENG.). 2008. (978-0-06-165823-5(5)); (978-0-06-170252-5(8)) HarperCollins Pubs.

Big Yellow School Bus plus 19 Splendiferous Songs for Autumn & Winter. Composed by Sally K. Albrecht & Lois Brownsey. (ENG.). 1999. audio compact disk 29.95 (978-0-7390-2132-3(X)) Alfred Pub.

Bigelow-Evans Essential Business Tools: Everything you need to Start & Raise Capital for Your Business. Lynette Bigelow & Mervin Evans. 4 Audio CD. (Running Time: 4 Hours). 2004. audio compact disk 99.99 (978-0-914391-90-6(9)) Comm People Pr.

Bigelow Funding Workshop: Finding Capital Made Easy. Lynette Bigelow. 6 CDs. (Running Time: 6 hrs.). 2004. audio compact disk 149.99 (978-0-914391-91-3(7)) Comm People Pr.

Bigg Family Cassette. Stephen Cosgrove. 2004. 5.00 (978-1-58804-366-5(5)) PCI Educ.

Bigger Than Life. Contrib. by Christ Fellowship Choir. 2008. audio compact disk 16.98 (978-5-557-44803-1(9)) Integrity Music.

Bigger Than Life. Contrib. by Christ Fellowship Choir. Told to Michael Neale. Prod. by Jay Rouse. 2005. audio compact disk 16.98 (978-5-559-11367-8(0)) Pt of Grace Ent.

Bigger Than Life: The Best of Lakewood Live. Contrib. by Lakewood Live & Don Moen. 2008. audio compact disk 13.99 (978-5-557-51561-0(5)) Integrity Music.

Bigger Than Yourself. Perf. by John McCutcheon. 1 CD. (Running Time: 50 mins.). 1997. audio compact disk 14.98 (978-1-57940-008-6(8)) Rounder Records.
Country-rock style with Nashville-level musical accompaniment and back-up chorus. The album's unifying theme is community working together, but the songs are distinct.

Bigger Than Yourself. Perf. by John McCutcheon. 1 cass. (Running Time: 50 mins.). (J). 1997. 9.98 (978-1-57940-009-5(4)) Rounder Records.

Biggest Bear. 2004. pap. bk. 18.95 (978-0-7882-0312-1(6)); pap. bk. 32.75 (978-1-55592-191-0(4)); pap. bk. 14.95 (978-1-56008-094-7(9)); 8.95 (978-1-56008-844-8(3)); cass. & flmstrp 30.00 (978-0-89719-655-0(4)); audio compact disk 12.95 (978-0-7882-0315-2(0)) Weston Woods.

Biggest Bear. Lynd Ward. 1 cass. (Running Time: 7 min.). (J). (ps-3). 12.95 Weston Woods.
Johnny hunts for the biggest bear in the forest, but comes home with a little bear that grows & grows & grows.

Biggest Bear. Lynd Ward. 1 cass. (Running Time: 7 min.). (J). (ps-3). 1993. 8.95 (978-1-56008-115-9(5), RAC010) Weston Woods.
The story of a young boy & his friendship with a bear.

Biggest Bear. Lynd Ward. 1 cass. (Running Time: 7 min.). (J). (ps-3). bk. 24.95 Weston Woods.

Biggest Bear. Lynd Ward. 1 cass. (Running Time: 7 min.). (J). (ps-3). 1993. bk. 24.95 (978-1-56008-095-4(7), PRA010) Weston Woods.

Biggest, Best Snowman. Margery Cuyler. 1 CD. (Running Time: 8 mins.). (J). (ps-2). 2007. pap. bk. 9.95 (978-0-545-01772-5(6)) Scholastic Inc.

***Biggest Liar in Los Angeles.** unabr. ed. Ken Kuhlken. (Running Time: 8 hrs. 0 mins.). 2010. 29.95 (978-1-4417-3925-4(4)); 54.95 (978-1-4417-3921-6(1)); audio compact disk 76.00 (978-1-4417-3922-3(X)) Blckstn Audio.

Biggest Secret of All: Industrial-Strength Self-Responsibility, Set. David Grudermeyer & Rebecca Grudermeyer. 2 cass. 18.95 Incl. handouts. (T-48) Willingness Wrks.

Biggest Snowman Ever. Steven Kroll. (ENG.). (J). (ps-k). 2009. audio compact disk 18.95 (978-0-545-16281-4(5)) Scholastic Inc.

Biggest Time Traps & How to Avoid Them. Julie Morgenstern. 1 CD. 2008. audio compact disk 10.95 (978-1-4019-1061-7(0)) Hay House.

Biggoon & the Little Duck see Puss in Boots & Other Fairy Tales from Around the World

Bigmama's. Donald Crews. 1 cass. (Running Time: 15 min.). (J). (gr. k-3). 2001. pap. bk. 16.90 (978-0-8045-6840-1(5), 6840) Spoken Arts.
Childhood memories of a summer at Bigmama's house in rural Florida.

Bike Lesson see Berenstain Bears' Christmas

Bikeman. unabr. ed. Thomas F. Flynn. Read by Jim Dale. (Running Time: 1 hr.). 2008. 39.25 (978-1-4233-6356-9(6), 9781423363569, BADLE); 14.95 (978-1-4233-6355-2(8), 9781423363552, BAD); audio compact disk 39.25 (978-1-4233-6352-1(3), 9781423363521, BriAudCD Unabrid) Brilliance Audio.

Bikeman: An Epic Poem. unabr. ed. Thomas F. Flynn. Read by Jim Dale. 1 MP3-CD. (Running Time: 1 hr.). 2008. 39.25 (978-1-4233-6354-5(X), 9781423363545, Brinc Audio MP3 Lib); 14.95 (978-1-4233-6353-8(1), 9781423363538, Brilliance MP3); audio compact disk 14.95 (978-1-4233-6351-4(5), 9781423363514, Bril Audio CD Unabri) Brilliance Audio.

Bikol Newspaper Reader. (Philippine Language Ser.). 1992. 19.00 (978-0-931745-88-1(8)) Dunwoody Pr.

Bikol Newspaper Reader, Set. Chito A. Belchez & Pamela J. Moguet. 2 cass. (Running Time: 1 hr. 30 min. per cass.). (MIS.). 1992. 19.00 (3068) Dunwoody Pr.
Forty-nine selections provide a wide range of topics together with all necessary lexical & grammatical information to make the link between spoken language & various genres of published media.

Bilbao Looking Glass. Charlotte MacLeod. Read by Mary Peiffer. 2000. 40.00 (978-0-7366-5930-7(7)) Books on Tape.

***Bilbury Village.** Vernon Coleman. 2010. 69.95 (978-1-4079-0630-0(5)); audio compact disk 84.95 (978-1-4079-0631-7(3)) Pub: Soundings Ltd GBR. Dist(s): Ulverscroft US

Bilingual Edition of the Love Songs of Bernart de Ventadorn in Occitan & English: Sugar & Salt. Ronnie Apter. Tr. by Mark Herman from PRO. Frwd. by Nathaniel Smith. Pref. by Burton Raffel. (Studies in Medieval Literature: Vol. 17). 1999. bk. 119.95 (978-0-7734-8009-4(9)) E Mellen.

***Bilingual Sommer-Time Stories, Set.** ed. Carl Sommer. (Another Sommer-Time Story Bilingual Ser.). (ENG & SPA.). (J). 2009. bk. 646.80 (978-1-57537-199-3(5)) Advance Pub.

Bilingual Songs: English-French. Tracy Irwin-Ayotte. 1 cass. (Running Time: 65 min. 30 secs.). (J). 2003. pap. bk. 14.95 (978-1-894262-77-4(8), JMP F24K) Jordan Music.
The perfect way to have fun while acquiring a second language. Volume 2 teachers counting to 30, counting by 10s to 100, shapes and sizes, emotions, places in the community and countryside, measurment and opposites.

Bilingual Songs Vol. 1: English-French. Tracy Irwin-Ayotte. 1 cass. (Running Time: 52 min. 8 secs.). (J). 2003. pap. bk. 14.95 (978-1-894262-72-9(7), JMP F23K) Jordan Music.
The perfect way to have fun while acquiring a second language. Volume 1 teachers the basic alphabet, counting to 10, days of the week, months of the year, colors, food, animals, parts of the body, clothing and family members.

Bilingual Songs Vol. 1: English-French. Tracy Irwin-Ayotte & Tracy Ayotte-Irwin. 1 CD. (Running Time: 52 mins. 8 secs.). (Songs That Teach French Ser.). (ENG & FRE.). (J). 2003. audio compact disk 13.95

(978-1-894262-74-3(3), JMP F23CDK) Pub: S Jordan Publ. Dist(s): CrabtreePubCo
The perfect way to have fun while aquiring a second language. Volume 1 teaches the basic alphabet, counting to 10, days of the week, months of the year, colors, food, animals, parts of the body, clothing and family members.

Bilingual Songs Vol. 1: English-Spanish. Agustina Tocalli-Beller. Lyrics by Agustina Tocalli-Beller. Ed. by Gloria Ramirez & Joan Howard. Prod. by Sara Jordan. Composed by Sara Jordan. Arranged by Mark Shannon. Engineer Mark Shannon. 1 cass. (Running Time: 51 min. 8 secs.). (SPA & ENG.). (J). 2002. pap. bk. 14.95 (978-1-894262-66-8(2), JMP S23K) Jordan Music.

Bilingual Songs Vol. 2: English-French. Tracy Irwin-Ayotte & Tracy Ayotte-Irwin. 1 CD. (Running Time: 65 min. 30 secs.). (Songs That Teach French Ser.). (ENG & FRE.). (J). 2003. audio compact disk 13.95 (978-1-894262-79-8(4), JMP F24CDK) Pub: S Jordan Publ. Dist(s): CrabtreePubCo
The perfect way to have fun while acquiring a second language. Volume 2 teachers counting to 30, counting by 10s to 100, shapes and sizes, emotions, places in the community and the countryside, measurment and opposites.

Bilingual Songs Vol. 2: English-Spanish. Agustina Tocalli-Beller. Lyrics by Agustina Tocalli-Beller. Ed. by Gloria Ranirez & Joan Howard. Prod. by Sara Jordan. Composed by Sara Jordan. Arranged by Mark Shannon. Engineer Mark Shannon. 1 cass. (Running Time: 66 min. 50 secs). (ENG & SPA.). (J). 2002. pap. bk. 14.95 (978-1-894262-71-2(9), JMP S24K) Jordan Music.

Bilingue Arabe. 1 cass. (Running Time: 1 hr., 30 min.). (ARA & FRE.). 2000. bk. 75.00 (978-2-7005-0141-4(1)) Pub: Assimil FRA. Dist(s): Distribks Inc

Bilingue Chinois. 1 cass. (Running Time: 1 hr., 30 min.). (CHI & FRE.). 2000. bk. 75.00 (978-2-7005-0143-8(8)) Pub: Assimil FRA. Dist(s): Distribks Inc

Bill & Hillary: The Marriage. abr. ed. Christopher Andersen. 2 cass. (Running Time: 3 hrs.). 1999. 17.95 Set. (978-1-55935-322-9(8)) Soundelux.
Draws on important sources - many speaking here for the first time about the President & First Lady's marriage.

Bill Bailey. unabr. ed. Catherine Marchant, pseud. Read by Susan Jameson. 6 cass. (Running Time: 6 hr.). 1993. 54.95 (978-0-7451-5846-4(3), CAB 241) AudioGO.

Bill Bailey's Daughter. unabr. ed. Catherine Marchant, pseud. Read by Susan Jameson. 6 cass. (Running Time: 6 hrs. 15 min.). 1989. 54.95 set. (978-0-7451-5847-1(1), CAB 377) AudioGO.
Fiona Bailey's baby is due at any moment, and all the Baileys - Fiona, Bill, and Fiona's three children from a previous marriage - wonder how the family will change and adjust with the new arrival.

Bill Bailey's Lot. unabr. ed. Catherine Marchant, pseud. Read by Susan Jameson. 8 cass. (Running Time: 8 hrs.). 1993. 69.95 (978-0-7451-5848-8(X), CAB 273) AudioGO.

Bill Barich. unabr. ed. Ed. by Jim McKinley. Prod. by Rebekah Presson. 1 cass. (Running Time: 29 min.). (New Letters on the Air Ser.). 1994. 10.00 (051594) New Letters.
Barich is a staff writer for "The New Yorker" & a widely-published essayist. He reads from a new book, "Big Dreams: Into the Heart of California," which looks at the state & its history by region, starting with the north & moving south to earthquake-ridden Los Angeles.

Bill Bradley on Perestroika: What's in It for the Russians & Americans? 1 cass. (Running Time: 1 hr.). 10.95 (NP-88-05-26, HarperThor) HarpC GBR.

Bill Bryson Collector's Edition: Notes from a Small Island; Neither Here Nor There; I'm a Stranger Here Myself. abr. collector's ed. Bill Bryson. Read by Bill Bryson. 2006. audio compact disk 50.00 (978-0-7393-4262-6(2), Random AudioBks) Pub: Random Audio Pubg. Dist(s): Random

***Bill Carey Rides West; The Town No Guns Could Tame; Bowdrie Rides a Coyote Trail.** unabr. ed. Louis L'Amour. (ENG.). 2010. 14.99 (978-0-307-74872-0(3), Random AudioBks) Pub: Random Audio Pubg. Dist(s): Random

Bill Clinton: Mastering the Presidency. unabr. ed. Nigel Hamilton. (Running Time: 84600 sec.). 2007. 85.95 (978-1-4332-0491-3(6)); audio compact disk 99.00 (978-1-4332-0492-0(4)); audio compact disk 29.95 (978-1-4332-0878-2(4)) Blckstn Audio.

Bill Clinton: Mastering the Presidency. unabr. abr. ed. Nigel Hamilton. Read by James Adams. (Running Time: 45000 sec.). 2007. 34.95 (978-1-4332-0493-7(2)); audio compact disk 34.95 (978-1-4332-0494-4(0)) Blckstn Audio.

Bill Clinton: Mastering the Presidency. unabr. abr. ed. Nigel Hamilton. Read by James Adams. (Running Time: 45000 sec.). 2007. audio compact disk 29.95 (978-1-4332-0495-1(9)) Blckstn Audio.

Bill for Short. abr. ed. Barry Morrow. 1 cass. (Running Time: 1 hr. 12 min.). 1999. 11.95 (978-1-57453-144-2(1)) Audio Lit.
"A man needs three things in life," Bill told Barry. "A good job, a good home & a buddy." Morrow tells the story of Bill, a mentally retarded man blessed with a never-ending reserve of optimism for life.

Bill Gaither. Contrib. by Bill Gaither. Prod. by Michael Sykes. (Gaither Gospel Ser.). 2005. audio compact disk 17.98 (978-5-558-77745-1(1)) Gaither Music Co.

Bill Gaither Remembers Homecoming Heroes. Contrib. by Bill & Gloria Gaither and Their Homecoming Friends. (Gaither Gospel Ser.). 2006. 12.99 (978-5-558-33263-6(8)) Gaither Music Co.

Bill Gaither Remembers Old Friends. Contrib. by Bill & Gloria Gaither and Their Homecoming Friends. (Gaither Gospel Ser.). 2006. 12.99 (978-5-558-33259-9(X)) Gaither Music Co.

Bill Gaither's Favorite Homecoming Songs & Performances. Contrib. by Bill & Gloria Gaither and Their Homecoming Friends. (Gaither Homecoming Classics Ser.). 2005. 14.98 (978-5-559-05746-0(0)) Gaither Music Co.

Bill Gates Speaks: Insights from the World's Greatest Entrepreneur. abr. ed. Janet C. Lowe. 2 cass. (Running Time: 3 hrs.). 1998. 17.95 Set. (978-1-55935-287-1(6), 287-6BK) Soundelux.
Biography compiled from speeches, writings & seminars, by the author of "Warren Buffet Speaks".

Bill Graham Presents. abr. ed. Bill Graham & Robert Greenfield. Read by Robert Greenfield & Peter Wolf. 2 cass. (Running Time: 3 hrs.). 1995. 15.95 (978-0-944993-73-6(7)) Audio Lit.
The inside story, told in his own words, of the man who created the business of rock music as it exists today. Born in Berlin, Graham escaped the holocaust, came to America and spawned a pop-culture revolution.

Bill Guest Anthology of Fiddle Tunes. Bill Guest. 1985. 9.98 (978-1-56222-619-0(3), 94039C) Mel Bay.

Bill Harley Presents... I'm Gonna Let It Shine: A Gathering of Voices for Freedom. unabr. ed. 1 cass. (Running Time: 54 min.). (J). (gr. 4-12). 1990. 10.00 (978-1-878126-06-1(7), RRR401); audio compact disk 15.00 CD. (978-1-878126-07-8(5), RRR401J) Round Riv Prodns.
Traditional & new freedom songs. Get on Board, Children; Hold On (Keep Your Eyes on the Prize); Everybody Says Freedom; Oh Freedom; I'm Gonna Sit at the Welcome Table; Woke up This Morning with My Mind on Freedom; Come by Here; Up over My Head; Sing Mandela Free; Tsenzenina; This Little Light; If You Miss Me from the Back of the Bus, & much more.

Bill Holm: Coming Home Crazy. unabr. ed. Bill Holm. Read by Bill Holm. Interview with Rebekah Presson. 1 cass. (Running Time: 29 min.). 1991. 10.00 (012591) New Letters.
Bill Holm spent a year in China as a professor of English. Holm writes about his experiences in a book of essays titled "Coming Home Crazy".

Bill M. Williams: The Practical "Fractal" - the New Map for Traders. Read by Bill M. Williams. 1 cass. 30.00 Dow Jones Telerate.
Learn the latest that physics & psychology have to offer today's trader; not only why the science of Chaos Theory draws a more accurate picture of market action & intention than other approaches, but how you can apply this theory to your trading & daily life. This rare opportunity will allow you to gain the benefit of years of experience in two hours while learning Profitunity's unique "10 second analysis".

Bill Mack's Memories from the Trenches of Broadcasting. As told by Bill Mack. 2005. audio compact disk 30.00 (978-0-9752630-1-3(3)) UNIT.

Bill Meek of Killinchy, County Down. 1 cass. 9.98 (C-21) Folk-Legacy.
Traditional & original songs by a young Irish singer.

Bill Moyers: The Arab World. adpt. ed. Interview with Bill Moyers et al. 2 cass. (Running Time: 2 hrs. 20 min.). 1991. 16.95 set. (978-1-56176-906-3(1)) Mystic Fire.
In a series of conversations with noted scholars & writers, Bill Moyers seeks to clarify the many misconceptions that mar our understanding of the region stretching from Morocco to Oman.

Bill Moyers' World of Ideas Anthology Collection. Bill Moyers. Read by Bill Moyers. 3 cass. (Running Time: 4 hrs. 21 min.). (World of Ideas Anthology Ser.). 1990. 24.95 set. (978-1-56176-901-8(0)) Mystic Fire.
Bill Moyers talks with writers, philosophers, historians & scientists. They share what is on their minds & in their hearts about issues that concern us all.

Bill of Goods. unabr. ed. John Hospers. 1 cass. (Running Time: 1 hr. 32 min.). 12.95 (419) J Norton Pubs.

Bill of Rights. Compiled by Benchmark Education Staff. 2006. audio compact disk 10.00 (978-1-4108-6644-8(0)) Benchmark Educ.

Bill of Rights & Additional Amendments. Jeffrey Rogers Hummel. Read by Walter Cronkite. (Running Time: 9000 sec.). (U. S. Constitution & Bill of Rights Ser.). 2006. audio compact disk 25.95 (978-0-7861-7328-0(9)) Pub: Blckstn Audio. Dist(s): NetLibrary CO

Bill of Rights & Additional Amendments, Set. unabr. ed. Jeffrey Rogers Hummel. Perf. by Pat Childs et al. Ed. by Wendy McElroy & George H. Smith. Narrated by Walter Cronkite. 2 cass. (Running Time: 75 min.). Dramatization. (U. S. Constitution Ser.). (YA). (gr. 10 up). 1987. 17.95 (978-0-938935-84-1(4), 390265) Knowledge Prod.
Performers also include Hugh Sinclair, Michael Montgomery, Jon Lutz, Don Jones, Travis Hardison, David Ford & Michael Edwards. The Constitution of the United States created a nation with a strong centralized government. The Bill of Rights (the first ten amendments to the Constitution) gave guarantees that individual rights would not be trampled underfoot. Some historians believe that there is a natural tension between the two documents. Certainly, during periods of crisis, additional amendments have been made to modify the Constitution. Through the country's history, the U. S. Constitution has remained a living document.

Bill of Rights in Translation: What It Really Means. Amie J. Leavitt. Contrib. by Scott Combs & Amy Stockhaus. (Kids' Translations Ser.). (ENG.). (gr. 3-4). 2008. audio compact disk 17.32 (978-1-4296-3220-1(8)) CapstoneDig.

Bill of Wrongs: The Executive Branch's Assault on America's Fundamental Rights. abr. unabr. ed. Lou DuBose & Molly Ivins. Read by Liz Smith. (Running Time: 25200 sec.). (ENG.). 2007. audio compact disk 29.95 (978-0-7393-1387-9(8)) Pub: Random Audio Pubg. Dist(s): Random

Bill Oliver & Glen Waldick - Earth's Troubadours. Hosted by Nancy Pearlman. 1 cass. (Running Time: 29 min.). 10.00 (708) Educ Comm CA.

Bill Sharman: Basketball. Read by Bill Sharman. 1 cass. (Running Time: 30 min.). 9.95 (978-0-89811-087-6(4), 7138) Lets Talk Assocs.
Bill Sharman talks about the people & events which influenced his career, & his own approach to shooting the basketball (question-answer format).

Bill Staines: Going to the West. 1 cass., 1 CD. 9.98 (C-5281); audio compact disk 14.98 CD. (CD-5281) Folk-Legacy.
A recent recording, witn some fine new songs.

Bill Staines: Happy Wanderer. 1 cass., 1 CD. (J). 9.98 (C-5285); audio compact disk 14.98 CD. (CD-5285) Folk-Legacy.
A special program of songs "for kids, cars & campfires".

Bill Staines: Just Play One Tune More. 1 cass. 9.98 (C-66) Folk-Legacy.
Bill's first Folk-Legacy recording, with a live audience.

Bill Staines: Looking for the Wind. 1 cass., 1 CD. 9.98 (C-5284); audio compact disk 14.98 CD. (CD-5284) Folk-Legacy.
Bill's 1995 Red House release, & a good one.

Bill Staines: Redbird's Wing. 1 cass. 9.98 (C-5289) Folk-Legacy.

Bill Staines: The Whistle of the Jay. 1 cass. 9.98 (C-70) Folk-Legacy.
One of Bill's finest recordings, a perennial favorite.

Bill Staines: Tracks & Trails. 1 cass., 1 CD. 9.98 (C-5282); audio compact disk 14.98 CD. (CD-5282) Folk-Legacy.

Bill Stern Sports Newsreel: Frankie Carle, Marie McDonald, Don Stanley & Horace Heidt. unabr. ed. Perf. by Frankie Carle et al. 1 cass. (Running Time: 1 hr.). 2001. 6.98 (2432) Radio Spirits.

Bill Stern Sports Newsreel: Jerry Colonna, Rudy Vallee, Zachary Scott & Susan Hayward. unabr. ed. Perf. by Jerry Colonna et al. 1 cass. (Running Time: 1 hr.). 2001. 6.98 (2592) Radio Spirits.

Bill Stern Sports Newsreel: World Series/Jack Benny/Guy Lombardo/Jack Scott. unabr. ed. Perf. by Jack Benny et al. 1 cass. (Running Time: 1 hr.). 2001. 6.98 (1885) Radio Spirits.

Bill Walton. Ed. by Bill Walton. 1 cass. (Running Time: 31 min.). (Reading With Winners: Ser. 1). 1984. 32.95 (978-0-89811-125-5(0), 8804C); Lets Talk Assocs.
This is a "read along" program with the athlete's own voice serving as the reader's tutor/guide.

Bill Walton: Basketball. Read by Bill Walton. 1 cass. (Running Time: 30 min.). 9.95 (978-0-89811-110-1(2), 7161) Lets Talk Assocs.
Bill Walton talks about the people & events which influenced his career, & his own approach to his speciality.

***Bill Warrington's Last Chance.** unabr. ed. James King. (Running Time: 10 hrs. 0 mins.). 2010. 29.95 (978-1-4417-5115-7(7)); 65.95 (978-1-4417-5111-9(4)); audio compact disk 29.95 (978-1-4417-5114-0(9)); audio compact disk 90.00 (978-1-4417-5112-6(2)) Blckstn Audio.

Billabong Songs. 1 cass. (J). 9.95 (ABTI) Brdgstn Multimed Grp.
From the best-selling "Billabong Tales" Video Series by Colin Pearce.

Billboard Presents: Family Christmas Classics. 1 cass. (Running Time: 1 hr.). 2002. 6.98 (978-1-56826-617-6(0), 72171) Rhino Enter.
This compilation features music from the greatest holiday films and television specials including How the Grinch Stole Christmas, Charlie Brown Christmas and Rudolph the Red-Nosed Reindeer.

Billboard Presents: Family Christmas Classics. 1 CD. (Running Time: 1 hr.). (J). 2002. audio compact disk 9.99 (978-1-56826-616-9(2), 72171) Rhino Enter.

Billiard Ball see Asimov's Mysteries

Billiard Ball see Best of Isaac Asimov

Billie & the Parent Plan. unabr. ed. Ann Bryant. Read by Gillian Walton. 3 CDs. (Running Time: 13080 sec.). (J). (gr. 2-5). 2007. audio compact disk 29.95 (978-1-4056-5634-4(4), Chivers Child Audio) AudioGO.

Billie Holiday Story. Keith Rodway. 4 vols. (ENG.). 2001. audio compact disk 24.95 (978-1-84240-086-9(X)) Pub: Chrome Dreams GBR. Dist(s): IPG Chicago

Billie Moore: Talking Basketball. Read by Billie Moore. 4 cass. (Running Time: 2 hrs.). (Exceptional Teachers in Sports Ser.). 39.95 Lets Talk Assocs.
She coached the U.S. olympic team & her first season at UCLA brought a National Championnhip. Billie Moore directs her talk to both players & coaches.

Billingsgate Shoal. Rick Boyer & Christopher Lane. 8 cass. (Running Time: 11 hrs. 30 mins.). 2002. 56.95 (978-0-7861-1202-9(6), 1966) Blckstn Audio.

Billingsgate Shoal. unabr. ed. Rick Boyer. Read by Christopher Lane. 8 cass. (Running Time: 12 hrs.). 1997. 56.95 (1966) Blckstn Audio.
Doc Adams investigates the murder of a friend in the waters off Massachusetts' Cape Cod. There he uncovers a hidden treasure in illegal arms & barely survives a near-fatal confrontation with a gun. The killers he's hunting assume that he is dead. Now Doc can watch for the first wrong move they make.

Billion Dollar Lessons: What You Can Learn from the Most Inexcusable Business Failures of the Last Twenty-five Years. unabr. ed. Paul Carroll & Chunka Mui. Read by Jim Bond. 1 MP3-CD. (Running Time: 11 hrs.). 2008. 39.25 (978-1-4233-7081-9(3), 9781423370819, Brlnc Audio MP3 Lib); 24.95 (978-1-4233-7082-6(1), 9781423370826, BAD); 39.25 (978-1-4233-7083-3(X), 9781423370833, BADLE); 24.95 (978-1-4233-7080-2(5), 9781423370802, Brilliance MP3); audio compact disk 97.25 (978-1-4233-7079-6(1), 9781423370796, BriAudCD Unabrid); audio compact disk 34.95 (978-1-4233-7078-9(3), 9781423370789, Bril Audio CD Unabri) Brilliance Audio.

Billion Dollar Sure Thing. unabr. collector's ed. Paul E. Erdman. Read by Dan Lazar. 8 cass. (Running Time: 8 hrs.). 1980. 48.00 (978-0-7366-0300-3(X), 1288) Books on Tape.
Written when the first Arab oil embargo sent shock waves through our carefully balanced & delicately tuned economic system, this novel describes a plot to control the world's monetary assets.

Billion for Boris. unabr. ed. Mary Rodgers. 1 read-along cass. (Running Time: 37 min.). (Children's Cliffhangers Ser.). (J). (gr. 4-6). 1980. 15.98 incl. bk. & guide. (978-0-8072-1078-9(1), SWR 18SP, Listening Lib) Random Audio Pubg.
Annabel & her friends manage misadvantures of mindboggling proportions. The sequel to "Freaky Friday".

Billionaire Who Wasn't: How Chuck Feeney Secretly Made & Gave Away a Fortune. Conor O'Clery. Read by Erik Synnestvedt. (Playaway Adult Nonfiction Ser.). 2008. 54.99 (978-1-60640-503-1(9)) Find a World.

Billionaire Who Wasn't: How Chuck Feeney Secretly Made & Gave Away a Fortune. unabr. ed. Conor O'Clery. Read by Erik Synnestvedt. (Running Time: 13 hrs. 5 mins.). (ENG.). 2008. 24.98 (978-1-59659-229-2(X), GildAudio) Pub: Gildan Media. Dist(s): HachBkGrp

***Billionaire's Curse.** unabr. ed. Richard Newsome. Read by James Clamp. (ENG.). 2010. (978-0-06-199527-9(4)); (978-0-06-201595-2(8)) HarperCollins Pubs.

Billionairess. unabr. ed. Gigi Levangie Grazer. Read by Phil Gigante & Tanya Eby. 1. (Running Time: 11 hrs.). 2009. 24.99 (978-1-4233-2723-3(3), 9781423327233, Brilliance MP3); audio compact disk 34.99 (978-1-4233-2721-9(7), 9781423327219, Bril Audio CD Unabri) Brilliance Audio.

Bill's Balloon Ride. 2004. 8.95 (978-1-56008-845-5(1)); cass. & flmstrp 30.00 (978-0-89719-656-7(2)) Weston Woods.

Bill's First Day: Early Explorers Emergent Set A Audio CD. Benchmark Education Staff. (J). 2006. audio compact disk 10.00 (978-1-4108-7598-3(9)) Benchmark Educ.

Billy: The Untold Story of a Young Billy Graham & the Test of Faith That Almost Changed Everything. William Paul McKay & Ken Abraham. Read by Bob Souer. (Playaway Adult Nonfiction Ser.). (ENG.). 2009. 59.99 (978-1-60812-765-8(6)) Find a World.

Billy: The Untold Story of a Young Billy Graham & the Test of Faith That Almost Changed Everything. unabr. ed. Bill McKay & Ken Abraham. Narrated by Bob Souer. (Running Time: 6 hrs. 30 mins. 20 sec.). (ENG.). 2008. 18.19 (978-1-60814-063-3(6)); audio compact disk 25.99 (978-1-59859-518-5(0)) Oasis Audio.

Billy Barnstorm, the Birch Lake Bomber. Joel M. Vance. 2 cass. (Running Time: 3 hrs.). (YA). 1995. 14.95 Set. Cedar Glade Pr.

Billy Barnstorm, The Birch Lake Bomber: And Other Tales of Youthful Disaster. unabr. ed. Joel Vance. Read by Joel Vance. 2 cass. (Running Time: 3 hrs.). Dramatization. 1994. 12.95 Set. (978-1-882467-08-2(6)) Wildstone Media.
Collection of humorous stories dealing with growing up in rural Wisconsin.

Billy Boy. 2004. 8.95 (978-1-56008-846-2(X)); cass. & flmstrp 30.00 (978-0-89719-657-4(0)) Weston Woods.

Billy Boy: A Novel. Bud Shrake. Narrated by Pete Bradbury. 5 cass. (Running Time: 6 hrs. 30 mins.). 48.00 (978-1-4025-1597-2(9)) Recorded Bks.

Billy Boy: A Novel. unabr. ed. Bud Shrake. Narrated by Pete Bradbury. 6 CDs. (Running Time: 6 hrs. 30 mins.). 2002. audio compact disk 62.00 (978-1-4025-2932-0(5)) Recorded Bks.
Sixteen-year-old Billy still feels the pain of his mother's death when his hard-drinking father abandons him in Forth Worth, Texas. Desperate, Billy looks for work as a caddie at Colonial Country Club, home course of his hero, Ben Hogan. Help comes unexpectedly with the appearance of Texas legend John Bredemus, designer of Colonial and scores of other golf courses in the region. With Bredemus' guidance and Hogan's support, Billy has a fighting chance to make something of his life.

Billy Budd. Herman Melville. Narrated by Flo Gibson. (ENG.). 2007. audio compact disk 19.95 (978-1-55685-985-4(6)) Audio Bk Con.

Billy Budd. unabr. ed. Herman Melville. Narrated by Flo Gibson. 3 cass. (Running Time: 3 hrs. 30 min.). 2003. 16.95 (978-1-55685-706-5(3)) Audio Bk Con.
The collision of good and evil in this magnificent novella is brilliantly shown when an honorable young sailor is hung for unwittingly killing his cruel master-at arms by striking him in a rage over false accusations.

Billy Budd. unabr. ed. Herman Melville. Read by William Roberts. (YA). 2008. 54.99 (978-1-60514-873-1(3)) Find a World.

Billy Budd, Sailor see Melville: Six Short Novels

Billy Budd, Sailor. Herman Melville. Read by Peter Joyce. 4 CDs. (Running Time: 4 hrs 20 mins). 2006. audio compact disk 17.99 (978-1-86015-015-9(2)) Assembled Stori GBR.
On one level Melville?s tale is an historical adventure story telling of life aboard ship shortly after the mutiny at Spithead in 1797.Billy is taken from a homeward bound merchantman to serve on the Seventy Four? HMS Indomitable. He falls foul of Claggart , the ?Master at Arms? and the final confrontation results in death.However below the surface lie some of Melville?s thematic obsessions-the aristocratic savage pitted against inhumanity born of service and the institutions of war, innocence overtaken by fate and the law, the worthy encompassed by the inevitable. Billy becomes an unwilling martyr - what passes for justice must be implemented because of the rebellious climate of the time.The natures of evil and conscience are explored and Billy Budd is the authors ?last word upon the strange mystery of himself and human destiny?Melville is regarded by many as the finest author America has produced.

Billy Budd, Sailor. Herman Melville. Read by William Roberts. (Running Time: 3 hrs. 30 mins.). 2007. 24.95 (978-1-60083-685-5(2)) Iofy Corp.

Billy Budd, Sailor. Herman Melville. Read by William Roberts. 3 CDs. (Running Time: 3 hrs. 30 min.). 2003. audio compact disk 22.98 (978-962-634-300-5(1)) Naxos.
A moving tale of good versus evil.

Billy Budd, Sailor. abr. ed. Herman Melville. Read by George Rose. 1 cass. 1984. 12.95 (978-0-694-50341-4(X), SWC 1653) HarperCollins Pubs.

Billy Budd, Sailor, unabr. ed. Herman Melville. Narrated by Frank Muller. 3 cass. (Running Time: 3 hrs.). (gr. 8 up). 1981. 26.00 (978-1-55690-053-2(8), 81030E7) Recorded Bks.
Aboard H. M. S. Indomitable in 1791 there is only one punishment for mutiny - death. Billy Budd, a young innocent, finds himself an unlikely suspect of the worst of crimes.

Billy Budd, Sailor. unabr. ed. Herman Melville. Read by Peter Joyce. 3 cass. 1996. 34.95 (978-1-86015-439-3(5)) Pub: UlverLrgPrint GBR. Dist(s): Ulverscroft US
A young man serving aboard the HMS Indomitable has a deadly confrontation with the Master at Arms.

Billy Budd, Sailor: A Classic Tale of Innocence Betrayed on the High Seas. adpt. ed. Read by Scott Neal et al. Adapted by Philip Glassborow & Paul McCusker. Herman Melville. (Running Time: 240 hrs. 0 mins.). (Radio Theatre Ser.). (ENG.). (J). (gr. 3). 2007. audio compact disk 14.97 (978-1-58997-507-1(3)) Pub: Focus Family. Dist(s): Tyndale Hse

Billy Collins Live: A Performance at the Peter Norton Symphony Space April 20 2005. unabr. ed. Billy Collins. Read by Billy Collins. Intro. by Bill Murray. 2 CDs. (Running Time: 4500 sec.). (ENG.). 2005. audio compact disk 19.95 (978-0-7393-2011-2(4)) Pub: Random Audio Pubg. Dist(s): Random

Billy Creekmore. unabr. ed. Tracey Porter. Narrated by Steven Boyer. 6 CDs. (Running Time: 6 hrs. 30 mins.). (YA). (gr. 5-8). 2008. audio compact disk 77.75 (978-1-4361-1596-4(5)); 56.75 (978-1-4361-1591-9(4)) Recorded Bks.
Tracey Porter has been praised for this Dickensian tale, which some critics compare to Huck Finn both in style and substance. Billy Creekmore longs to escape the Guardian Angels Home for Boys, where his smarts cause him more trouble than anything. So when a long-lost uncle shows up to whisk Billy away to the West Virginia coal mines, he jumps at the chance. But his journey is just beginning - before long, Billy hitches a ride with a traveling circus.

Billy Goat Hill. Mark Stanleigh Morris. Narrated by Kevin King. 2005. audio compact disk 27.99 (978-1-58926-932-3(2)) Oasis Audio.

Billy Goat Hill. unabr. ed. Mark Stanleigh Morris. Narrated by Kevin King. (ENG.). 2005. 19.59 (978-1-60814-064-0(4)) Oasis Audio.

Billy Goats Gruff see Las Tres Cabras Gruff

Billy Graham. Terry W. Whalin. Read by Lloyd James. (Running Time: 14400 sec.). 2006. audio compact disk 36.00 (978-0-7861-8382-1(9)) Blckstn Audio.

Billy Graham. abr. ed. Sam Wellman. 1 cass. (Running Time: 1 hrs. 30 min.). (Heroes of the Faith Ser.). (C). 1997. 4.97 (978-1-57748-088-4(0)) Barbour Pub.

Billy Graham. unabr. ed. Terry W. Whalin. Read by Lloyd James. (Running Time: 14400 sec.). 2006. audio compact disk 19.95 (978-0-7861-7516-1(8)) Blckstn Audio.

Billy Graham: His Life & Influence. unabr. ed. David Aikman. Narrated by Bob Souer. (Running Time: 8 hrs. 59 mins. 2 sec.). (ENG.). 2008. 19.59 (978-1-60814-083-1(0)); audio compact disk 27.99 (978-1-59859-363-1(3)) Oasis Audio.

Billy Graham: Men of Faith. Terry W. Whalin. Read by Lloyd James. (Running Time: 14400 sec.). 2006. 24.95 (978-0-7861-2480-0(6)) Blckstn Audio.

Billy Graham Speaks Set: Insights from the World's Greatest Preacher. abr. ed. Janet C. Lowe. Read by Ralph J. Votrian. 2 cass. (Running Time: 3 hrs.). 1999. 17.95 (978-1-55935-305-2(8)) Soundelux.
Unique portrait of the Reverend, drawn from his own words - culled from sermons, newscasts, printed articles, & in-depth interviews.

Billy Graham 50 Years Sermon & Song. Billy Graham. 6.99 (978-1-930800-01-4(0), Prop Voice); audio compact disk 9.99 (978-1-930800-00-7(2), Prop Voice) Iliad TN.

Billy Graham/Eternal Praise, 2 cass. (Running Time: 2 hrs.). 2000. 11.98 (978-1-930800-07-6(X), Prop Voice); audio compact disk 15.98 (978-1-930800-06-9(1), Prop Voice) Iliad TN.

Billy Joel - Classics: Keyboard Play-along Volume 8. Billy Joel. 2008. pap. bk. 14.99 (978-1-4234-4962-1(2), 1423449622) H Leonard.

Billy Joel - Hits: Keyboard Play-along Volume 13. Billy Joel. 2008. pap. bk. 14.99 (978-1-4234-4963-8(0), 1423449630) H Leonard.

Billy London's Girls, Set. unabr. ed. Ruth Hamilton. Read by Marlene Sidaway. 16 cass. (Running Time: 24 hrs.). 1999. 104.95 (978-0-7531-0516-0(0), 990104) Pub: ISIS Audio GBR. Dist(s): Ulverscroft US
Billy was a mean, dark, secretive man who was interested only in lining his pockets at the expense of those around him - most especially his wife & daughters. His wife Ellen was prepared to protect the four girls & fight to give them a chance to escape from the evil & oppressive legacy of Billy London. As the sirens of 1939 herald the advent of war, so the girls begin their own battle for new, triumphant, & fulfilling lives.

Billy Mcbrown. Jill Eggleton. Illus. by Trevor Pye. (Sails Literacy Ser.). (gr. 1 up). 10.00 (978-0-7578-4042-5(6)) Rigby Educ.

Billy Phelan's Greatest Game see Ink Truck

Billy Phelan's Greatest Game, abr. ed. William Kennedy. Read by Jason Robards. 2 cass. (Running Time: 3 hrs.). (Albany Cycle Ser.). 1999. 9.95 (978-0-945353-16-4(2), M20140) Pub: Audio Partners. Dist(s): PerseuPGW
Part of the "Ironweed" trilogy, the story captures the mood of Depression era Albany, a combination of small-time crime, caring & self-searching.

Billy Phelan's Greatest Game. abr. ed. William Kennedy. Read by Jason Robards. 2 cass. (Running Time: 3 hrs.). (Albany Cycle Ser.). 2000. 7.95 (978-1-57815-187-5(2), 1127, Media Bks Audio) Media Bks NJ.
Billy Phelan, a slightly tarnished poker player, pool hustler & small-time bookie, moves through the lurid nightime glare of a tough Depression-era town.

Billy Phelan's Greatest Game. unabr. collector's ed. William Kennedy. Read by Wolfram Kandinsky. 6 cass. (Running Time: 9 hrs.). (Albany Cycle Ser.). 1987. 48.00 (978-0-7366-1101-5(0), 2027) Books on Tape.
Billy Phelan, a slightly tarnished poker player, pool hustler, & small time bookie, moves through the nighttime glare of a tough Depression-era town. Billy works the fringes of Albany sporting life with his own particular style & private code of honor until he finds himself in the dangerous position of potential go-between in the kidnapping of a political boss's son.

Billy Ray & the Good News. unabr. ed. Frank Roderus. Read by Cameron Beierle. 6 cass. (Running Time: 6 hrs.). 2001. 39.95 (978-1-58116-109-0(3)) Books in Motion.
Billy Ray works hard all week to play even harder on payday Saturday night. Whiskey, women, gambling and a good fistfight are all Billy thinks a man needs. That is until a keen-eyed little man faces him down with something greater than his fists or guns. In that moment Billy's life is changed forever.

Billy Ray's Forty Days. unabr. ed. Frank Roderus. Read by Cameron Beierle. 4 cass. (Running Time: 5 hrs.). 2001. 26.95 (978-1-58116-134-2(4)) Books in Motion.
Preacher Billy Ray must win his place in a community that "doesn't want any preacher changing things." A beautiful mysterious young woman crosses Billy's path, and stirs up feelings he's not sure he should have. There's a fight brewing, and Billy may have to pick up his guns or use his fists to save himself, his church and his town.

Billy Straight. Jonathan Kellerman. Read by Alexander Adams. 1998. audio compact disk 104.00 (978-0-7366-6063-1(1)) Books on Tape.

Billy Straight. unabr. ed. Jonathan Kellerman. Read by Alexander Adams. 11 cass. (Running Time: 16 hrs. 30 mins.). 1999. 88.00 (978-0-7366-4302-3(8), 4793) Books on Tape.
It's a fight to survive on L.A.'s meanest streets. But for twenty-year-old Billy Straight, it still beats the life that he faced at home. Late one night, from his hiding place, Billy watches as a man butchers a woman with a knife. The victim turns out to be the ex-wife of a TV star. Billy, struggling to maintain a code of ethics, becomes the center of terrifying attention from the media, from violent bounty hunters & from the murderer himself.

Billy Straight. unabr. ed. Jonathan Kellerman. Read by Alexander Adams. 11 CDs. (Running Time: 13 hrs. 12 mins.). 2001. audio compact disk Books on Tape.

Billy Sunday. Barbour Books Staff. 1998. pap. bk. 4.97 (978-1-57748-399-1(5)) Barbour Pub.

Billy Sunday Story. Narrated by Homer Rodeheaver. 1989. cass. & video 29.97 (BV8951) Chrstn Dup Intl.
The life story of Billy Sunday, "the greatest gospel preacher since the Apostle Paul.".

Billy the Bird: And All Because of Jackson. unabr. ed. Dick King-Smith. Read by Sophie Thompson. 2 cass. (Running Time: 1 hr. 16 mins.). 2002. (978-1-85549-154-0(0)) Cover To Cover GBR.
Every time the full moon rises, Billy the Bird flies. Nobody in the family has ever flown before! Jackson is an unusual rabbit who dreams of going to sea. One day he stows away on a ship in search of a new life.

Billy the Kid. Perf. by Sara Ransom. Music by Sara Ransom. Music by Steve Walters et al. 1 cass. (Running Time: 59 min.). Dramatization. 1994. 12.00 (978-0-9658262-0-4(1)) S Ransom.
Told in story & song, a dramatic recounting of the life of Billy the Kid, based on historically accountable events - the story of a talented, intelligent young man gone bad. Parent's Choice Award 1994, Suitable for middle-school to adult.

Billy the Kid. unabr. ed. Jimmy Gray. Narrated by Donnie Blanz. Prod. by Joe Loesch. 1 cass. (Running Time: 61 mins.). (Wild West Ser.). (YA). 1999. lib. bdg. 12.95 (978-1-887729-73-4(9)) Toy Box Prods.
In the late 1870's, out in the sparsely settled territory of New Mexico, life was cheap. Rustlers, thieves & hired gunmen were drawn to a no-man's land where they were above the law. And into this maelstrom of the fire came a skinny young boy who was to burn his brand across a violent & rugged countryside.

Billy the Kid: A Short & Violent Life. unabr. ed. Robert Marshall Utley. Narrated by Nelson Runger. 6 cass. (Running Time: 8 hrs.). 1990. 51.00 (978-1-55690-054-9(6), 90079E7) Recorded Bks.
An account of the life & times of Henry Antrim, alias Billy the Kid.

Billy the Kid: The Endless Ride. Michael Wallis. Read by Todd McLaren. (Playaway Adult Nonfiction Ser.). 2008. 64.99 (978-1-60640-993-0(X)) Find a World.

Billy the Kid: The Endless Ride. unabr. ed. Michael Wallis. Narrated by Todd McLaren. (Running Time: 9 hrs. 0 mins. 0 sec.). (ENG.). 2007. audio compact disk 34.99 (978-1-4001-0416-1(5)); audio compact disk 24.99 (978-1-4001-5416-6(2)); audio compact disk 69.99 (978-1-4001-3416-8(1)) Pub: Tantor Media. Dist(s): IngramPubServ

Billy the Kid & the Lincoln County War. Dave Southworth. 2 cass/. (Running Time: 1 hr. 25 min.). (Library of Concise Audio Histories). 13.95 Set. (978-1-890778-07-1(9)) Wld Horse Pub.

Billy the Squid. Tom Chapin. Perf. by Tom Chapin. 1 cass. (Running Time: 30 min.). (J). 1992. 8.98 (978-1-56406-545-2(6)); 8.98 Incl. sleeve pack. (978-1-56406-577-3(4)); audio compact disk 13.98 CD. (978-1-56406-564-3(2)) Sony Music Ent.
Thirteen songs for children & parents.

Billy Thunder & the Night Gate. unabr. ed. Isobelle Carmody. 7 cass. (Running Time: 9 hrs.). 2002. (978-1-74030-739-0(9)) Bolinda Pubng AUS.

Billy Thunder & the Night Gate. unabr. ed. Isobelle Carmody. Read by Rebecca Macauley. (Running Time: 32400 sec.). (YA). (gr. 7-16). 2006. audio compact disk 87.95 (978-1-74093-397-1(4)) Pub: Bolinda Pubng AUS. Dist(s): Bolinda Pub Inc

Biloxi Blues. abr. ed. Neil Simon. Directed By Nataki Garrett. (Running Time: 6593 sec.). (L. A. Theatre Works Audio Theatre Collections). 2007. audio compact disk 25.95 (978-1-58081-377-8(1)) L A Theatre.

Biloxi Blues. unabr. ed. Neil Simon. Read by Justine Bateman. (YA). 2008. 34.99 (978-1-60514-981-3(0)) Find a World.

Bimbos of the Death Sun. unabr. ed. Sharyn McCrumb. Narrated by Ruth Ann Phimister. 4 cass. (Running Time: 6 hrs.). 1988. 35.00 (978-0-7887-3758-9(9), 95942E7) Recorded Bks.
Spoof of the bizarre culture surrounding sci-fi/fantasy fandom. Join the merriment as medieval fantasy characters, techno geeks & roleplaying gamers take over an innocent hotel. Just when you think things can't get any wilder, the guest of honor is murdered.

Bin Laden: The Man Who Declared War on America. Yossef Bodansky. Read by Nadia May. 16 cass. (Running Time: 23 hrs. 30 mins.). 2002. 99.95 (978-0-7861-2230-1(7), 2954) Blckstn Audio.
Who is Osama bin Laden, the only terrorist leader ever to have declared a holy war? What drives him and those he leads to hate a West that helped enrich and arm them? Bin Laden's name has been linked to a number of incidents that have cost Americans their lives, including the bombing of the USS Cole in 2000 and the destruction of the American embassies in Kenya and Tanzania in 1998. Now he is linked to the recent catastrophic assaults on the World Trade Center and the Pentagon. Here is a comprehensive account of the rise of bin Laden.

Bin Laden: The Man Who Declared War on America. unabr. ed. Yossef Bodansky. Read by Nadia May. 18 CDs. (Running Time: 23 hrs. 30 mins.). 2002. audio compact disk 144.00 (978-0-7861-9536-7(3), 2954); audio compact disk 39.95 (978-0-7861-9219-9(4), 2954) Blckstn Audio.
Uncovers the events in bin Laden's life that turned the once-promising engineering student into a cold-blooded leader of radical Islam.

Bin Laden: The Man Who Declared War on America. unabr. ed. Yossef Bodansky. Read by Nadia May. 13 pieces. (Running Time: 16 hrs.). 2004. reel tape 49.95 (978-0-7861-2207-3(2)) Blckstn Audio.

Bin Laden: The Man Who Declared War on America. unabr. ed. Yossef Bodansky. Read by Nadia May. (Running Time: 23 hrs. 30 mins.). (J). 2006. audio compact disk 39.95 (978-0-7861-6086-0(1)) Blckstn Audio.

Bin Ramke. unabr. ed. Bin Ramke. Read by Bin Ramke. 1 cass. (Running Time: 29 min.). 1990. 10.00 (032390) New Letters.
Poet reads from his new book, "The Erotic Light of Gardens." Includes interview.

Bindi Babes. Narinder Dhami. 3 cass. (Running Time: 4 hrs. 21 mins.). (J). (gr. 3 up). 2004. 30.00 (978-1-4000-8539-2(X), Listening Lib) Random Audio Pubg.

Binding & Loosing. Neville Goddard. 1 cass. (Running Time: 62 min.). 1964. 8.00 (96) J & L Pubns.
Neville taught Imagination Creates Reality. He was a powerfully influential teacher of God as Consciousness.

Binding the Lord. Blaine Yorgason & Brenton Yorgason. Read by Marvin Payne. 1 cass. (Gospel Power Ser.). 6.95 (978-0-929985-41-1(9)) Jackman Pubng.
A father's letter to his son regarding obedience to God.

Bing Crosby, Set. Perf. by Marilyn Maxwell et al. 2 cass. (Running Time: 2 hrs.). vinyl bd. 10.95 (978-1-57816-043-3(X), BC2401) Audio File.
Includes: "Kraft Music Hall" (2-24-44); "Philco Radio Time (10-16-46); "Bing Crosby Chesterfield Show" (2-13-52); "Bing Crosby General Electric Show" (2-12-53).

Bing Crosby: The Early Years. Gary Giddins. Narrated by Edward Lewis. (Running Time: 23 hrs. 30 mins.). 2000. 57.95 (978-1-59912-433-9(5)) Iofy Corp.

Bing Crosby: The Early Years. unabr. ed. Gary Giddins. Read by Edward Lewis. 16 cass. (Running Time: 24 hrs.). 2001. 99.95 (978-0-7861-2084-0(3), 2845) Blckstn Audio.
In his commanding biography, the eminent cultural critic Gary Giddins takes us on the remarkable journey that brought a provincial young law student from Spokane, Washington, to the pinnacle of the entertainment world. Giddins chronicles Crosby's rise from college minstrel shows through vaudeville; from Paul Whiteman's orchestra to matchless success in Hollywood; from his courtship of the beautiful and tragic Dixie Lee to his triumphs as the sportsman who created the first celebrity pro-am golf tournament and helped build the Del Mar racetrack.

Bing Crosby Show. Perf. by Dean Martin et al. 1 cass. (Running Time: 60 min.). 1951. 7.95 (CC-5055) Natl Recrd Co.
Two separate shows with Bing at his best.

Bing Crosby Show: Bob Hope & Monica Lewis. unabr. ed. Perf. by Bob Hope & Monica Lewis. 1 cass. (Running Time: 1 hr.). 2001. 6.98 (2004) Radio Spirits.

Bing Crosby Show: Ella Fitzgerald & Christmas Show. unabr. ed. Perf. by Ella Fitzgerald. 1 cass. (Running Time: 1 hr.). 2001. 6.98 (2552) Radio Spirits.

Binkey Kok Sampler: Singing Bowls, Didgeridoo, Asian Gongs & Temple Bells for Meditation. 2000. audio compact disk 7.95 (978-1-57863-067-7(3), Red) Red Wheel Weiser.

Binky Brothers, Detectives. James Lawrence. 1 read-along cass. (Running Time: 15 min.). (I Can Read Bks.). (J). (ps-3). HarperCollins Pubs.
One side has a turn-the-page beep signal & the other side is uninterrupted narration for more experienced readers.

Bio-Body. unabr. ed. Robert A. Monroe. Read by Robert A. Monroe. (Running Time: 45 min.). (Gateway Experience - Prospecting Ser.). 1984. 14.95 (978-1-56113-287-4(X)) Monroe Institute.

Bio-Ethics: Who's in Charge Here? 1 cass. (Running Time: 1 hr.). 10.95 (OP-78-08-22, HarperThor) HarpC GBR.

Bio-identical Hormone Workshop: Common Sense Answers! Elizabeth Plourde. 2010. 39.95 (978-0-9661735-6-7(2)) New Voice.

Biochemistry & Behavior. unabr. ed. James V. McConnell. 1 cass. (Running Time: 53 min.). 12.95 (29049) J Norton Pubs.
Discusses research on the chemical basis of memory & the behavioral approaches to psychotherapy which lead to a revolution within the fields of psychology, education & psychiatry.

Biochemistry of Psychedelics Set: An Informal Talk. Alexander Shulgin. 2 cass. (Running Time: 135 Min.). 1999. 18.00 (13701) Big Sur Tapes.
1975 Esalen Institute.

Bioenergetic Analysis: Lecture-Demonstration. unabr. ed. Alexander Lowen & John Pierrakos. 2 cass. (Running Time: 3 hrs.). 1968. 16.00 Set. (07102) Big Sur Tapes.
A talk about how bioenergetics reveals & deals with the bodily obstacles that keep one from knowing, feeling, & expressing oneself fully. Life's experiences create physical blocks in the body, choke off the natural flow of energy, & cripple us emotionally. Bioenergetics finds & frees these blocks.

Bioethical Advisory Committees: Another Day of Hope. 1 cass. (Care Cassettes Ser.: Vol. 11, No. 4). 1984. 10.80 Assn Prof Chaplains.

Bioethical Principles Applied to Cultural Concerns. 1 cass. (Care Cassettes Ser.: Vol. 21, No .). 1994. 10.80 Assn Prof Chaplains.

Bioethical Problems in Practice. Contrib. by Lainie F. Ross et al. 1 cass. (American Academy of Pediatrics UPDATE: Vol. 19, No. 8). 1998. 20.00 Am Acad Pediat.

Biofeedback: The Control of Physiological States. unabr. ed. Joseph Kamiya & Robert Ornstein. 1 cass. (Running Time: 41 min.). 12.95 (33023) J Norton Pubs.
Results of research of the alternatives in our brain waves are examined. The possibilities of the voluntary control of heart activity, muscle tension & the rate of blood-flow is discussed.

Biofeedback & Psychophysiological Training. unabr. ed. Alyce Green & Elmer Green. 2 cass. (Running Time: 3 hrs.). 1972. 16.00 Set. (06401) Big Sur Tapes.
The Greens discuss their research with biofeedback, which is a method of voluntarily controlling involuntary bodily processes. They also describe their work with Swami Rama, a yogi who can voluntarily stop his heartbeat, & the implications for us all of this ability.

Biofuel Equipment & Services in Greece: A Strategic Reference 2007. Compiled by Icon Group International, Inc. Staff. 2007. ring bd. 195.00 (978-0-497-35990-4(1)) Icon Grp.

Biofuel Equipment & Services in Turkey: A Strategic Reference 2007. Compiled by Icon Group International, Inc. Staff. 2007. ring bd. 195.00 (978-0-497-82443-3(4)) Icon Grp.

Biografía del Poder: Caudillos de la Revolución Mexicana, 1910-1940. Enrique Krauze. (SPA., 24.90 (978-968-7723-21-1(1), 6020) Tusquests Ed MEX.

Biographer. unabr. ed. Virginia Duigan. Read by Julie Nihill. (Running Time: 13 hrs.). 2009. audio compact disk 98.95 (978-1-74214-093-3(9), 9781742140933) Pub: Bolinda Pubng AUS. Dist(s): Bolinda Pub Inc

Biographer's Moustache. unabr. collector's ed. Kingsley Amis. Read by Richard Green. 7 cass. (Running Time: 10 hrs. 30 min.). 1997. 56.00 (978-0-7366-3670-4(6), 4347) Books on Tape.
Struggling hack Gordon Scott-Thompson is commissioned to write the biography of veteran novelist & inveterate snob, Jimmie Fane.

Biographer's Tale. unabr. ed. A. S. Byatt. Narrated by Simon Prebble. 7 cass. (Running Time: 9 hrs. 30 mins.). 2001. 63.00 (978-1-84197-207-7(X)) Recorded Bks.

Biographia Literaria: Biographical Sketches of My Literary Life & Opinions see Cambridge Treasury of English Prose: Austen to Bronte

Biographical Sketches of Nobel Laureates. unabr. ed. 3 cass. bk. 44.50 Set, incl. 136p. bk. J Norton Pubs.

Biographies of Great American Saints-mp3. 2000. 22.00 (978-1-59128-347-8(7)) Canon Pr ID.

Biographies of Great American Saints-tape. 8 cass. 2000. 28.00 (978-1-59128-349-2(3)) Canon Pr ID.

Biography of Lawrence of Arabia. abr. ed. Ed. by Barry Cooper. 2 cass. (Running Time: 1 hr. 44 min.). 12.95 (978-0-89926-170-6(1), 852) Audio Bk.

Biography of Libby A. Miller. Fudgie Fufu. Illus. by Fudgie Fufu. Afterword by Ray Psychobay. Photos by Scott Fredette & David Garza. 1 CD. (Running Time: 72 min.,36 sec.). 2002. audio compact disk 10.00 (978-0-9718095-1-2(8)) Chapultepec Pr.
4 Versions Of "Surfin' Dracula" & Other Popular Fudgie & Fufu Remixes.

Biography of the Classics. unabr. ed. Gilbert Highet. Read by Gilbert Highet. 1 cass. (Running Time: 30 min.). 9.95 (23318-A,B) J Norton Pubs.
Explains the hazzards through which the great books of the past had to make their way until they reached us.

Biography Series Take Home Books: CD Rom. Compiled by Benchmark Education Staff. (J). 2007. audio compact disk 10.00 (978-1-4108-8830-3(4)) Benchmark Educ.

Biological Anthropology Parts I-II: An Evolutionary Perspective. Instructed by Barbara King. 12 cass. (Running Time: 12 hrs.). 2002. bk. 54.95 (978-1-56585-547-2(7), 1573); bk. 69.95 (978-1-56585-549-6(3), 1573) Teaching Co.

Biological Foundations of the Nervotron. Marco A. V. Bitetto. Read by Marco A. V. Bitetto. 1 cass. 1999. 37.00 (978-1-58578-001-3(4)) Inst of Cybernetics.

Biological Science: Instructor's Resource CD. 2nd rev. ed. Tom Freeman. audio compact disk 18.97 (978-0-13-141053-4(9)) PH School.

Biology. Eva M. Bushman. (J). 1980. bk. 242.20 (978-0-89420-203-2(0), 238000) Natl Book.

Biology: Guided Reading Program. 4th ed. Holt, Rinehart and Winston Staff. 2003. audio compact disk 228.80 (978-0-03-069921-4(5)) Holt McDoug.

Biology: Guided Reading Program. 4th ed. Holt, Rinehart and Winston Staff. (SPA.). 2003. audio compact disk 228.80 (978-0-03-069989-4(4)) Holt McDoug.

Biology: Problems & Experiments, Set. Steve Johnson. 2004. audio compact disk 598.33 (978-0-03-038078-5(2)) Holt McDoug.

Biology: The Science of Life, Vol. I-VI. Instructed by Stephen Nowicki. 36 cass. (Running Time: 36 hrs.). 2004. bk. 134.95 (978-1-56585-927-2(8), 1500) Teaching Co.

Biology: The Unity & Diversity of Life. 9th ed. Cecie Starr & Ralph Taggart. 2000. bk. 101.95 (978-0-534-37795-3(5)) Brooks-Cole.

Biology: Understanding Life. 3rd ed. Sandra M. Alters. (C). 2000. audio compact disk 161.95 (978-0-7637-1240-2(X), 1240-X) Jones Bartlett.

Biology Vols. 1-6: The Science of Life. Instructed by Stephen Nowicki. 36 CDs. (Running Time: 36 hrs.). 2004. bk. 179.95 (978-1-56585-929-6(4), 1500) Teaching Co.

Biology & Human Behavior: The Neurological Origins of Individuality. 4 cass. (Running Time: 6 hrs.). 1996. 39.95 (978-1-56585-011-8(4)) Teaching Co.

Biology & Human Behavior: The Neurological Origins of Individuality, Course 179. Instructed by Robert M. Sapolsky. 6 cass. (Running Time: 6 hrs.). 2000. 19.95 Teaching Co.
Eight lectures take us on an exciting adventure into our own brain & that mysterious area between biological matter & thought & asks some probing questions.

Biology & Human Behavior: The Neurological Origins of Individuality, I-II. 2nd ed. Instructed by Robert M. Sapolsky. 12 cass. (Running Time: 12 hrs.). 2005. 129.95 (978-1-59803-077-8(9)); audio compact disk 69.95 (978-1-59803-079-2(5)) Teaching Co.

Biology Experiments on File. Diagram Group. (gr. 6-12). 2004. audio compact disk 149.95 (978-0-8160-5612-5(9)) Facts On File.

Biology I. Worldwise Education Staff. 1 cass. (Running Time: 1 hr. 10 min.). (Rap Notes Ser.). (YA). (gr. 7-12). 1993. 9.98 (978-0-9643439-0-0(8)) Wrld Wise Educ.
Biology curriculum set to rap music.

***Biology Independent Study Lab Manual Cd.** 3rd rev. ed. Warwick. (ENG.). 2010. audio compact disk 67.08 (978-0-7575-3786-8(3)) Kendall-Hunt.

Biology Life on Earth: IRCD W/Tests. 7th rev. ed. Audesirk & Byers. audio compact disk 49.97 (978-0-13-100569-3(3)) PH School.

Biology of Belief: Unleashing the Power of Consciousness, Matter & Miracles. Bruce H. Lipton. (Running Time: 11700 sec.). 2006. audio compact disk 24.95 (978-1-59179-523-0(0), AW01077D) Sounds True.

Biology of HTLV, III. Karl Johnson. (AIDS: The National Conference for Practitioners). 1986. 9.00 (978-0-932491-45-9(6)) Res Appl Inc.

Biology of Prayer: Learning to See Yourself As Wondrously Made. Caroline Myss & Ron Roth. (Biology of Prayer Ser.). 1999. 55.00 (978-1-893869-53-0(9)) Celbrtng Life.

Biology of Success. Robert Arnot. 2001. (978-1-58621-012-0(2)) Hachet Audio.

Biology of Success: Set Your Mental Thermostat to High with Dr. Bob Arnot's Prescription for Achieving Your Goals! abr. ed. Robert Arnot. (ENG.). 2005. 14.98 (978-1-59483-475-2(X)) Pub: Hachet Audio. Dist(s): HachBkGrp

Biology One: An Interactive Biology Tutorial Volume 2. 2. 2nd rev. ed. Paul Ramp & Cary Staples. (ENG.). 2010. audio compact disk 31.83 (978-0-7575-4667-9(6)) Kendall-Hunt.

Biology Reprints. Ed. by Marco A. V. Bitetto. 1 cass. 2000. (978-1-58578-029-7(4)) Inst of Cybernetics.

Biomedical Applications of Nano Technologies. Ed. by P. Vincenzini & R. Barbucci. (Advances in Science & Technology Ser.: Vol. 53). audio compact disk 113.00 (978-3-908158-09-7(5)) Trans T Pub CHE.

Biometrics in Japan: A Strategic Reference 2006. Compiled by Icon Group International, Inc. Staff. 2007. ring bd. 195.00 (978-0-497-82320-7(9)) Icon Grp.

Bionda & Other Short Stories. Short Stories. Ugo Betti. 1 cass. (Running Time: 1 hr.).Tr. of Blond. (ITA.). 2000. bk. 19.50 INCL. TRANSCRIPT. (978-1-58085-468-9(0)) Interlingua VA.

Biopoetics: The Energies of Language & Image. Read by Leland Roloff. 2 cass. (Running Time: 2 hrs.). 1976. 16.95 Set. (978-0-7822-0232-8(2), 015) C G Jung IL.

Biosphere, Two. Hosted by Nancy Pearlman. 1 cass. (Running Time: 28 min.). 10.00 (1043) Educ Comm CA.

Biotech: The Sorcerer's New Apprentice. Chuck Missler. 1 CD. (Running Time: 10 hrs.). (Briefing Packages by Chuck Missler). 2001. audio compact disk 14.95 (978-1-57821-133-3(6)) Koinonia Hse.
The astonishing advances in the field of microbiology now offer new remedies for many of mankind's most illusive and devastating diseases and even many genetic defects. New companies are being formed all over the world in their intense pursuit of the incredible opportunities offered in this exploding arena. However, these promises are not without a potential dark side. Dr. Chuck Missler surveys some of the most promising prospects, reviews the types of ventures emerging, and also explores the astonishing discoveries within the living cell. He also reveals some of the concerns emerging among the informed, including some of the provocative Biblical implications.

Biotech '96. 8 cass. (Running Time: 11 hrs. 50 min.). 1996. 275.00 Incl. course materials. (MB44) Am Law Inst.
Presents a detailed analysis & discussion of significant legal & business issues. The need for strong patent protection, the ongoing requirement for capital to support product development, FDA compliance, the need to obtain reimbursement for new products, & the complexities associated with technology transfer & strategic alliances.

Biotechnology: Science for the New Millennium. Ellyn Daugherty. 2007. audio compact disk 51.95 (978-0-7638-2282-8(5)) Paradigm MN.

Biotechnology in Brazil: A Strategic Reference 2006. Compiled by Icon Group International, Inc. Staff. 2007. ring bd. 195.00 (978-0-497-35832-7(8)) Icon Grp.

Biotechnology in Japan: A Strategic Reference 2006. Compiled by Icon Group International, Inc. Staff. 2007. ring bd. 195.00 (978-0-497-82321-4(7)) Icon Grp.

Biotechnology Laboratory Manual. audio compact disk 36.95 (978-0-7638-2902-5(1)) EMC-Paradigm.

Bioterrorism Anthrax: For Healthcare Workers & Public Officers (Allied Health, Nurses, Doctors, Public Health Workers, EMS Workers, Other Emergency, Safety, Fire, Police, & Disaster Planning & Response Personnel) & the Public, Detailed Introduction. Daniel Farb. 2004. audio compact disk 49.95 (978-1-932634-05-1(3)) Pub: UnivofHealth. Dist(s): AtlasBooks

Bioterrorism Anthrax 10 Users. Daniel Farb. 2005. audio compact disk 149.95 (978-1-59491-185-9(1)) Pub: UnivofHealth. Dist(s): AtlasBooks

Bioterrorism Anthrax 100 Users. Daniel Farb. 2005. audio compact disk 899.95 (978-1-59491-229-0(7)) Pub: UnivofHealth. Dist(s): AtlasBooks

Bioterrorism Anthrax 25 Users. Daniel Farb. 2005. audio compact disk 299.95 (978-1-59491-227-6(0)) Pub: UnivofHealth. Dist(s): AtlasBooks

Bioterrorism Anthrax 5 Users. Daniel Farb. 2005. audio compact disk 99.95 (978-1-59491-155-2(X)) Pub: UnivofHealth. Dist(s): AtlasBooks

Bioterrorism Anthrax 50 Users. Daniel Farb. 2005. audio compact disk 499.95 (978-1-59491-228-3(9)) Pub: UnivofHealth. Dist(s): AtlasBooks

Bioterrorism Botulinum: For Healthcare Workers & Public Officers (Allied Health, Nurses, Doctors, Public Health Workers, EMS Workers, Other Emergency, Safety, Fire, Police, & Disaster Planning & Response Personnel) & the Public, Detailed Introduction. Daniel Farb. 2004. audio compact disk 49.95 (978-1-932634-06-8(1)) Pub: UnivofHealth. Dist(s): AtlasBooks

Bioterrorism Botulinum 10 Users. Daniel Farb. 2005. audio compact disk 149.95 (978-1-59491-252-8(1)) Pub: UnivofHealth. Dist(s): AtlasBooks

Bioterrorism Botulinum 5 Users. Daniel Farb. 2005. audio compact disk 99.95 (978-1-59491-247-4(5)) Pub: UnivofHealth. Dist(s): AtlasBooks

Bioterrorism Certificate Program: For Healthcare Workers & Public Officers (Allied Health, Nurses, Doctors, Public Health Workers, EMS Workers, Other Emergency, Safety, Fire, Police, & Disaster Planning & Response Personnel) & the Public, Detailed Introduction to the Most Dangerous Forms of Bioterrorism, Including Anthrax, Botulinum, Hemorrhagic Viruses, Plague, Radiation, Smallpox, & Tularemia. Daniel Farb & Bruce Gordon. 2004. audio compact disk 299.95 (978-0-9743674-1-5(9)) Pub: UnivofHealth. Dist(s): AtlasBooks

Bioterrorism Hemorrhagic Viruses: For Healthcare Workers & Public Officers (Allied Health, Nurses, Doctors, Public Health Workers, EMS Workers, Other Emergency, Safety, Fire, Police, & Disaster Planning & Response Personnel) & the Public, Detailed Introduction & Infection Control. Daniel Farb. 2004. audio compact disk 49.95 (978-1-932634-07-5(X)) Pub: UnivofHealth. Dist(s): AtlasBooks

Bioterrorism Hemorrhagic Viruses 10 Users. Daniel Farb. 2005. audio compact disk 149.95 (978-1-59491-253-5(X)) Pub: UnivofHealth. Dist(s): AtlasBooks

Bioterrorism Hemorrhagic Viruses 5 Users. Daniel Farb. 2005. audio compact disk 99.95 (978-1-59491-248-1(3)) Pub: UnivofHealth. Dist(s): AtlasBooks

Bioterrorism Plague: For Healthcare Workers & Public Officers (Allied Health, Nurses, Doctors, Public Health Workers, EMS Workers, Other Emergency, Safety, Fire, Police, & Disaster Planning & Response Personnel) & the Public, Detailed Introduction & Infection Control with Disease Information. Daniel Farb. 2004. audio compact disk 49.95 (978-1-932634-08-2(8)) Pub: UnivofHealth. Dist(s): AtlasBooks

Bioterrorism Plague 10 Users. Daniel Farb. 2005. audio compact disk 149.95 (978-1-59491-254-2(8)) Pub: UnivofHealth. Dist(s): AtlasBooks

Bioterrorism Plague 5 Users. Daniel Farb. 2005. audio compact disk 99.95 (978-1-59491-249-8(1)) Pub: UnivofHealth. Dist(s): AtlasBooks

Bioterrorism Radiation: For Healthcare Workers & Public Officers (Allied Health, Nurses, Doctors, Public Health Workers, EMS Workers, Other Emergency, Safety, Fire, Police, & Disaster Planning & Response Personnel) & the Public, Detailed Introduction with Disease Information. Daniel Farb & Bruce Gordon. 2004. audio compact disk 49.95 (978-1-932634-09-9(6)) Pub: UnivofHealth. Dist(s): AtlasBooks

Bioterrorism Radiation 10 Users. Daniel Farb & Bruce Gordon. 2005. audio compact disk 149.95 (978-1-59491-255-9(6)) Pub: UnivofHealth. Dist(s): AtlasBooks

Bioterrorism Radiation 5 Users. Daniel Farb & Bruce Gordon. 2005. audio compact disk 99.95 (978-1-59491-250-4(5)) Pub: UnivofHealth. Dist(s): AtlasBooks

Bioterrorism Smallpox: For Healthcare Workers & Public Officers (Allied Health, Nurses, Doctors, Public Health Workers, EMS Workers, Other Emergency, Safety, Fire, Police, & Disaster Planning & Response Personnel) & the Public, Detailed Introduction & Infection Control with Disease Information. Daniel Farb. 2004. audio compact disk 49.95 (978-1-932634-10-5(X)) Pub: UnivofHealth. Dist(s): AtlasBooks

Bioterrorism Smallpox 10 Users. Daniel Farb. 2005. audio compact disk 149.95 (978-1-59491-186-6(X)) Pub: UnivofHealth. Dist(s): AtlasBooks

Bioterrorism Smallpox 5 Users. Daniel Farb. 2005. audio compact disk 99.95 (978-1-59491-156-9(8)) Pub: UnivofHealth. Dist(s): AtlasBooks

Bioterrorism Tularemia: For Healthcare Workers & Public Officers (Allied Health, Nurses, Doctors, Public Health Workers, EMS Workers, Other Emergency, Safety, Fire, Police, & Disaster Planning & Response Personnel) & the Public, Detailed Introduction & Infection Control with Disease Information. Daniel Farb. 2004. audio compact disk 49.95 (978-1-932634-11-2(8)) Pub: UnivofHealth. Dist(s): AtlasBooks

Bioterrorism Tularemia 10 Users. Daniel Farb. 2005. audio compact disk 149.95 (978-1-59491-256-6(4)) Pub: UnivofHealth. Dist(s): AtlasBooks

Bioterrorism Tularemia 5 Users. Daniel Farb. 2005. audio compact disk 99.95 (978-1-59491-251-1(3)) Pub: UnivofHealth. Dist(s): AtlasBooks

Biotinidase Deficiency - A Bibliography & Dictionary for Physicians, Patients, & Genome Researchers. Compiled by Icon Group International, Inc. Staff. 2007. ring bd. 28.95 (978-0-497-11339-1(2)) Icon Grp.

Biowar. abr. ed. Stephen Coonts & Jim DeFelice. Read by J. Charles. (Running Time: 4 hrs.). (Deep Black Ser.: No. 2). 2004. audio compact disk 69.25 (978-1-59355-401-9(X), 159355401X, BACDLib Ed) Brilliance Audio.

Biowar. abr. ed. Stephen Coonts & Jim DeFelice. Read by J. Charles. (Running Time: 4 hrs.). (Deep Black Ser.: No. 2). 2005. audio compact disk 14.99 (978-1-59600-395-8(2), 9781596003958, BCD Value Price) Brilliance Audio.
Dr. James Kegan, a world-renowned scientist specializing in germ warfare, has vanished from his upstate New York home. But this is no ordinary missing-persons case. Kegan has left behind an unidentified dead man with a .22 caliber hole in his skull - and a contact trail that leads to an alleged terrorist cell. Unraveling the mystery is a job for Kegan's best friend, NSA operative Charlie Dean. His mission is to infiltrate the scientist's circle of associates and decipher Kegan's confidential research. Dispatched to cover Charlie is Delta Force trooper Lia Francesca. The trail leads them to the core of a widespread killer fever that's been dormant for centuries - and its link to a virus that's quickly spreading victim by victim. With time running out Charlie and Lia must find Kegan, uncover his secrets, cut a terrorist threat to the quick, and stop the unimaginable outbreak of a new biological nightmare.

Biowar. unabr. ed. Stephen Coonts & Jim DeFelice. Read by J. Charles. 7 cass. (Running Time: 10 hrs.). (Deep Black Ser.: No. 2). 2004. 29.95 (978-1-59086-699-3(1), 1590866991, BAU); 82.25 (978-1-59086-700-6(9), 1590867009, BAudLibEd) Brilliance Audio.

Biowar. unabr. ed. Stephen Coonts & Jim DeFelice. Read by J. Charles. (Running Time: 10 hrs.). (Deep Black Ser.: No. 2). 2004. 24.95 (978-1-59335-314-8(6), 1593353146, Brilliance MP3); 39.25 (978-1-59335-471-8(1), 1593354711, Brinc Audio MP3 Lib) Brilliance Audio.

Biowar. unabr. ed. Stephen Coonts & Jim DeFelice. Read by J. Charles. (Running Time: 10 hrs.). (Deep Black Ser.: No. 2). 2004. 39.25 (978-1-59710-197-4(4), 1597101974, BADLE); 24.95 (978-1-59710-196-7(6), 1597101966, BAD) Brilliance Audio.

Bipolar Child: Program from the Award Winning Public Radio Series. Interview. Hosted by Fred Goodwin. 1 CD. (Running Time: 1 Hour). 2000. audio compact disk 21.95 (978-1-932479-27-0(9), LCM 105) Lichtenstein Creat.
As many as a third of the children diagnosed with ADD - Attention Deficit Disorder - are tragically misdiagnosed. Their tantrums, fidgetiness, self-abuse and inability to pay attention are signs of a major mental illness - bipolar disorder, or manic depression. Worse yet, the standard treatments for ADD - stimulants like Ritalin and anti-depressants like Prozac - can provoke violence, psychosis and even suicidal mania in bipolar children. Guests in this special program include Janice and Dr. Demitri Papolos, best-selling authors of a new and ground-breaking book on bipolar children, and Martha Hellander, director of the Child and Adolescent Bipolar Foundation. The Infinite Mind's host, Dr. Fred Goodwin, one of the world's leading authorities on bipolar disorder, leads the discussion.

Bipolar Disorder Vol. 2: Defining Treatment Options. Interview. Interview with Stephen M. Stahl. Featuring Michael Gitlin. 1 CD. 2004. audio compact disk (978-1-4225-0007-1(1)) NEI Pr.

Bipolar Disorders & Their Treatment. unabr. ed. Mercedes Leidlich. Read by Mercedes Leidlich. 1 cass. (Running Time: 1 hr.). 1992. 10.95 in Norelco box. (978-1-882174-04-1(6), MLL-005) UFD Pub.
This tape teaches symptoms of hypomania, mania, & depression, the three syndromes associated with Bipolar Disorder. There is no relaxation exercise on this tape - it is all lecture. Many people function in a hyperalert state of hypomania without even knowing why they can't slow down. Workaholics, shopaholics, party people, etc., may have Hypomanic Personality Type or Bipolar Disorder. This tape is a valuable tool for clients of psychologists, psychiatrists, treatment centers, & their care givers.

***Bippolo Seed & Other Lost Stories.** unabr. ed. Dr. Seuss. (ENG.). (J). 2011. audio compact disk 10.00 (978-0-307-74605-4(4), Listening Lib) Pub: Random Audio Pubg. Dist(s): Random

Birch Common. unabr. ed. Rose Boucheron. Read by Maggie Mash. 5 cass. (Running Time: 6 hrs. 35 mins.). (Story Sound Ser.). (J). 2004. 49.95 (978-1-85903-643-3(0)) Pub: Mgna Lrg Print GBR. Dist(s): Ulverscroft US

Birches see Classic American Poetry

Birches see Robert Frost Reads

Birches see Caedmon Treasury of Modern Poets Reading Their Own Poetry

Birches (A Poem from the Poets' Corner) The One-and-Only Poetry Book for the Whole Family. unabr. ed. Robert Frost & John Lithgow. Read by John Lithgow. (Running Time: 10 mins.). (ENG.). 2008. 0.99 (978-1-60024-317-2(7)) Pub: Hachet Audio. Dist(s): HachBkGrp

Bird. Angela Johnson. 2 cass. (J). 2004. (978-1-4000-9925-2(0), Listening Lib); audio compact disk (978-1-4000-9926-9(9), Listening Lib) Random Audio Pubg.

Bird & I. Fazil Husnu Daglarca. Ed. by Stanley H. Barkan. Tr. by Talat S. Halman. (Cross-Cultural Review Chapbook Ser.: No. 4: Turkish Poetry 1). (ENG & TUR.). 1980. 10.00 (978-0-89304-828-0(3)) Cross-Cultrl NY.

Bird & the Beetle. Robert Cutler & Jeffrey L. Terrell. Read by R. J. Lupo & Ashley Lupo. Prod. by SSI Records Staff. 1 CD. (Running Time: 30 min.). (J). 2002. audio compact disk 10.99 (978-0-9725163-2-7(8)) SSI Pubng.
An intriguing story for children centered on the importance of keeping a promise. In this story, one made between a bird and a beetle. Both must endure hardships during their two day journey to ensure the promise is kept.

Bird by Bird: Some Instructions on Writing & Life. abr. ed. Anne Lamott. Read by Anne Lamott. 2 cass. (Running Time: 2 hrs. 40 mins.). 2004. 17.95 (978-1-57270-016-1(5), E21016) Pub: Audio Partners. Dist(s): PerseuPGW
Based on her own experience, the author wryly assists & motivates the listener on the subject of writing & life.

Bird Calls & Song. unabr. ed. David Attenborough. 1 cass. (Running Time: 54 min.). (Animal Language Ser.). 12.95 J Norton Pubs.

Bird Came Down the Walk see Gathering of Great Poetry for Children

Bird Came down the Walk see Poems & Letters of Emily Dickinson

***Bird Cloud: A Memoir.** unabr. ed. Annie Proulx. (Running Time: 7 hrs. 30 mins. 0 sec.). (ENG.). 2011. audio compact disk 29.99 (978-0-7435-9724-1(9)) Pub: S&S Audio. Dist(s): S and S Inc

Bird Flu Interview with Carl Wilson. 2004. audio compact disk 9.95 (978-0-9743448-8-1(5)) NMA Media Pr.

Bird in the Tree. unabr. collector's ed. Elizabeth Goudge. Read by Wanda McCaddon. 8 cass. (Running Time: 12 hrs.). 1983. 64.00 (978-0-7366-0483-3(9), 1458) Books on Tape.
In this book we learn the strange history of the family home, so central to the story that it almost becomes a character in its own right & inspires its inhabitants with the traditions of its builder steadfastness & loyalty.

Bird Is the Word: Big Bird's Favorite Songs. 1 cass. (Sesame Street Ser.). (J). 1995. bk. 9.98 (Sony Wonder); audio compact disk 13.98 CD. Sony Music Ent.
Sing along with the biggest bird on the block to favorites such as "ABC-DEF-GHI," "Y'all Fall Down," "Good Morning Mister Sun" & "Tall Enough." Includes lyric book.

Bird Lake Moon. unabr. ed. Kevin Henkes. Narrated by Oliver Wyman. 3 CDs. (Running Time: 3 hrs. 30 mins.). (J). (gr. 4-7). 2008. audio compact disk 30.75 (978-1-4361-1436-3(5)); 30.75 (978-1-4361-1431-8(4)) Recorded Bks.
Caldecott Medal-winning, New York Times bestselling author Kevin Henkes has delighted children with numerous books. With this tale for young teens, he brings readers to a place called Bird Lake where two boys, Spencer and Mitch, are about to jump into a summer of adventure, mystery, and friendship.

***Bird Mimicry: A Remarkable Collection of Imitations by Birds.** Richard Ranft et al. (ENG.). 2010. audio compact disk 15.00 (978-0-7123-0529-7(7)) Pub: Britis Library GBR. Dist(s): Chicago Distribution Ctr

Bird of Happiness. Sally A. Stewart. Read by Anne Dover. 12 CDs. (Running Time: 15 hrs.). (Sound Ser.). (J). 2003. audio compact disk 99.95 (978-1-84283-584-5(X)) Pub: ISIS Lrg Prnt GBR. Dist(s): Ulverscroft US

Bird of Happiness. unabr. ed. Sally A. Stewart. Read by Anne Dover. 10 cass. (Running Time: 15 hrs.). 2000. 84.95 (978-1-85496-783-1(5), 67835) Pub: Soundings Ltd GBR. Dist(s): Ulverscroft US
It was Gertrude Wyndham's third child, Lucy who was to save their home; although she did not love Frank Thornley, son of a wealthy Birmingham factory owner, she married him & hoped that, in time, Providence would make everything come right for all of them.

Bird of Hope Is Singing. unabr. ed. Myrtle Smith. Prod. by David Keyston. 1 cass. (Running Time: 1 hrs.). (Myrtle Smyth Audiotapes Ser.). 1998. , CD. (978-1-893107-19-9(1), M19, Cross & Crown) Healing Unltd.

Bird of Passage. Nicola Thorne. Read by Liz Holliss. 9 cass. (Running Time: 11 hrs. 45 mins.). (Isis Cassettes Ser.). (J). 2006. 76.95 (978-0-7531-3482-5(9)) Pub: ISIS Lrg Prnt GBR. Dist(s): Ulverscroft US

Bird of Time. Kriyananda, pseud. 2003. audio compact disk 10.95 (978-1-56589-173-9(2)) Pub: Crystal Clarity. Dist(s): Natl Bk Netwk

Bird of Truth. unabr. ed. 1 cass. (Running Time: 20 min.). Dramatization. (Magic Looking Glass Ser.). (J). (gr. 2-6). 1989. 9.95 (978-0-7810-0044-4(0), NIM-CW-130-2-C) NIMCO.
A Spanish folk tale.

Bird Song Ear Training Guide: Learn How to Recognize Birdsongs from the Midwest & Northeast States. Prod. by John Feith. 1 CD. (Running Time: 60 minutes). Orig. Title: Bird Song Ear Training Guide: Who Cooks for Poor Sam Peabody?. 2003. audio compact disk 14.95 (978-0-9754434-0-8(2), 0975443402) Caculo.
Audio CD bird song guide designed to help bird-watchers memorize the songs of 189 birds from the Midwest and Northeast United States. It contains a short narrated mnemonic device following each song. It can be used as a field guide or quiz listening game to test and refresh one's knowledge of birdsongs.

Bird Song Ear Training Guide: Who Cooks for Poor Sam Peabody? see Bird Song Ear Training Guide: Learn How to Recognize Birdsongs from the Midwest & Northeast States

Bird Songs: Eastern Region. unabr. abr. ed. Donald Stokes et al. Read by Lang Elliot. 3 CDs. (Running Time: 4 hrs.). (ENG.). 1997. audio compact disk 29.98 (978-1-57042-483-0(7)) Pub: Hachet Audio. Dist(s): HachBkGrp

Bird Songs in Literature: Bird Songs & the Poems They Have Inspired. unabr. ed. Read by Frederick G. Marcham. Ed. by Joseph Wood Krutch & Peter Kellogg. (Running Time: 1800 sec.). 2008. audio compact disk & audio compact disk 19.95 (978-1-4332-3388-3(6)) Blckstn Audio.

Bird Songs in Literature: Bird Songs & the Poems They Have Inspired. unabr. ed. Read by Frederick G. Marcham. Ed. by Joseph Wood Krutch & Peter Kellogg. (Running Time: 1800 sec.). 2008. 15.95 (978-1-4332-3384-5(3)) Blckstn Audio.

Bird Songs in Literature: Bird Songs & the Poems They Have Inspired. unabr. abr. ed. Read by Frederick G. Marcham. Ed. by Joseph Wood Krutch. (Running Time: 1800 sec.). 2008. audio compact disk & audio compact disk 20.00 (978-1-4332-3385-2(1)) Blckstn Audio.

Bird Songs of Belize, Guatemala & Mexico. unabr. ed. Dale Delaney. Read by Dale Delaney. 1 cass. (Running Time: 53 min.). 1992. 9.95 (978-0-938027-08-9(5)) Crows Nest Bird.
A recording of 70 species of birds from Belize, Guatemala, & Mexico.

Bird Songs of the Northwoods. Contrib. by Stan Tekiela. (Soothing Sounds of Nature Ser.). 2005. audio compact disk 12.95 (978-1-59193-119-5(3)) Adventure Pubns.

Bird Songs of the Pacific States. Thomas Sander. 2 cass. (Running Time: 2 hrs. 14 min.). 1996. 14.95 Set. (978-0-938027-23-2(9)); 21.95 2 CDs. (978-0-938027-24-9(7)) Crows Nest Bird.
Recordings of primary songs of 130 species of birds found in the Pacific States.

***Bird Sounds of Madagascar: An Audio Guide to the Island's Unique Birds.** British Library Staff & Vrej Nersessian. (ENG.). 2010. audio compact disk 15.00 (978-0-7123-0534-1(3)) Pub: Britis Library GBR. Dist(s): Chicago Distribution Ctr

Bird Sounds of Trinidad & Tobago. William L. Murphy. 1 cass. (Running Time: 30 min.). 1997. 9.95 Peregrine Enter.

Bird Table. Jonathan Davies. Narrated by Gerri Halligan. 6 cass. (Running Time: 8 hrs. 45 mins.). 56.00 (978-1-84197-438-5(2)) Recorded Bks.

Bird Watching: On Playing & Coaching the Game I Love. abr. ed. Larry Bird & Jackie MacMullan. (Running Time: 2 hrs. 30 mins.). (ENG.). 2006. 14.98 (978-1-59483-666-4(3)) Pub: Hachet Audio. Dist(s): HachBkGrp

Bird Watching: On Playing & Coaching the Game I Love. unabr. ed. Larry Bird & Jackie MacMullan. Narrated by Tom Stechschulte. 7 cass. (Running Time: 9 hrs. 30 mins.). 2000. 66.00 (978-0-7887-4076-3(8), 96167E7) Recorded Bks.
The basketball legend speaks with amazing candor, offering a personal & honest look at his career with the Celtics, his experience with the 92 Olympics Dream Team & his transition from superstar player to respected coach.

Birdcage. unabr. ed. Marcia Willett. Read by June Barrie. 9 cass. (Running Time: 46980 sec.). 2005. 79.95 (978-0-7927-3716-2(4), CSL 830); audio compact disk 99.95 (978-0-7927-3717-9(2), SLD 830) AudioGO.

Birder's Diary: World Edition. 3rd ed. Thayer Birding Staff. 2004. audio compact disk 124.95 (978-1-887148-18-4(3)) Thayer Birding.

Birding by Ear: Eastern & Central North America. unabr. ed. Richard K. Walton et al. Ed. by Roger Tory Peterson. 3 CDs. (Running Time: 3 hrs.). (Peterson Field Guides). (ENG., 2002. audio compact disk 30.00 (978-0-618-22590-3(0)) HM Harcourt.

Birding by Ear Set: Western North America. Richard K. Walton & Robert W. Lawson. Ed. by Roger Tory Peterson. Illus. by John Sill. Contrib. by Roger Tory Peterson. 3 cass. (Peterson Field Guides). (ENG.). 1999. audio compact disk 30.00 (978-0-395-97525-1(5)) HM Harcourt.

Birding for Fun & Science. Hosted by Nancy Pearlman. 1 cass. (Running Time: 28 min.). 10.00 (222) Educ Comm CA.

Birdland. unabr. ed. Tracy Mack. Read by Dion Graham. (Running Time: 4 hrs.). audio compact disk 36.00 (978-0-7861-7680-9(6)) Blckstn Audio.

Birdland. unabr. ed. Tracy Mack. Read by Dion Graham. (Running Time: 4 hrs.). (YA). 2005. 29.95 (978-0-7861-7918-3(X)); 24.95 (978-0-7861-3693-3(6)) Blckstn Audio.

Birdland. unabr. ed. Tracy Mack. Read by Dion Graham. (YA). 2007. 34.99 (978-1-60252-495-8(5)) Find a World.

Birdman. unabr. ed. Mo Hayder. 9 CDs. (Running Time: 11 hrs. 24 mins.). (Isis (CDs) Ser.). (J). 2004. audio compact disk 84.95 (978-0-7531-2357-7(6)) Pub: ISIS Lrg Prnt GBR. Dist(s): Ulverscroft US

Birdman. unabr. ed. Mo Hayder. Read by Damien Goodwin. 8 cass. (Running Time: 11 hrs. 24 mins.). (Isis Cassettes Ser.). (J). 2004. 69.95 (978-0-7531-1765-1(7)) Pub: ISIS Lrg Prnt GBR. Dist(s): Ulverscroft US

Birdman of Alcatraz: The Story of Robert Stroud. unabr. collector's ed. Thomas E. Gaddis. Read by Larry McKeever. 7 cass. (Running Time: 10 hrs. 30 mins.). 1991. 56.00 (978-0-7366-2038-3(9), 2852) Books on Tape.
It was "The Rock." Thirteen acres in the middle of San Francisco Bay, home to the most dangerous men of their time. There was no gas chamber, no gallows, no quick way out. Sealed off & separate, it brooded over its inmates. Robert Stroud, grandson of a judge, was one. Sentenced to life in solitary confinement, he found solace in the birds that landed outside his cell window.

Birds. Daphne Du Maurier. 1 CD. (Running Time: 1 hr. 30 mins.). 2005. audio compact disk 12.95 (978-0-660-18810-2(4)) Pub: Canadian Broadcasting CAN. Dist(s): Georgetown Term

Birds. unabr. ed. Ed. by Linda Spizzirri. 48 cass. (Running Time: 15 min.). Dramatization. (Educational Coloring Book & Cassette Package Ser.). (J). (gr. k-8). 1989. pap. bk. 6.95 (978-0-86545-159-9(1)) Spizzirri.
Some of the lesser known exotic birds are covered, including complete coloring instructions to aid in authentic renderings.

Birds: Repertoire, Duet & Mime. unabr. ed. David Attenborough. 1 cass. (Running Time: 54 min.). (Animal Language Ser.). 12.95 J Norton Pubs.

Birds: Spellbinding Tales of Flight, Feather, & Song. unabr. ed. Narrated by Jon Hamilton. 1 CD. (Running Time: 1 hr.). (ENG.). 2010. audio compact disk 14.95 (978-1-61573-060-5(5), 1615730605) Pub: HighBridge. Dist(s): Workman Pub

Birds & the Bees. Milly Johnson. 2008. 84.95 (978-0-7531-3176-3(5)); audio compact disk 99.95 (978-0-7531-3177-0(3)) Pub: ISIS Audio GBR. Dist(s): Ulverscroft US

Birds, Beasts, & Fishes (Little & Big) Pete Seeger. 1 cass. or CD. (Running Time: 35 min.). (J). (gr. 4-12). 1991. (0-9307-450390-9307-45039-2-8); audio compact disk (0-9307-45039-2-8) Smithsonian Folkways.
Songs to sing along with, to draw pictures about, & to play hand games to.

Birds, Beasts, Bugs & Bigger Fishes. Perf. by Pete Seeger. 1 cass. (Running Time: 35 min.). (J). (ps-6). 1991. Incl. lyrics. (0-9307-45022-4-2) Smithsonian Folkways.
Songs which focus on larger animals. Performed with banjo accompaniments.

Birds, Beasts, Bugs & Fishes (Little & Big) Pete Seeger. 1 cass., 1 CD. (J). 8.78 Double. (FW 45039); audio compact disk 13.58 CD Jewel box, double. (FW 45039) NewSound.
Two classics: "Birds, Beasts, Bugs & Little Fish," & "Birds, Beasts & Bigger Fishes." Songs included: Teency Weency Spider, Frog Went a-Countin', Leatherwing Bat & the Elephant.

Birds, Beasts, Bugs & Little Fishes. Perf. by Pete Seeger. 1 cass. (Running Time: 31 min.). (J). (ps-1). 1991. (0-9307-45021-4-3) Smithsonian Folkways.
Songs about little creatures, including "Frog Went A-Courting," "Teency Weency Spider" & "Skip to My Lou." Ideal for singing along, drawing pictures, or playing hand games.

***Birds Eye Open House, Starring Dinah Shore.** RadioArchives.com. (Running Time: 600). (ENG.). 2004. audio compact disk 29.98 (978-1-61081-027-2(9)) Radio Arch.

Bird's-Eye View. J. F. Freedman. Narrated by Richard Ferrone. 10 cass. (Running Time: 14 hrs. 30 mins.). 94.00 (978-0-7887-9793-4(X)) Recorded Bks.

Bird's-Eye View. abr. ed. J. F. Freedman. Read by Gregory Harrison. (ENG.). 2005. 14.98 (978-1-59483-409-7(1)) Pub: Hachet Audio. Dist(s): HachBkGrp

Bird's-Eye View. collector's unabr. ed. J. F. Freedman. Narrated by Richard Ferrone. 10 cass. (Running Time: 15 hrs.). 2002. 44.95 (978-0-7887-9805-4(7), 96839) Recorded Bks.
Meet Fritz Tullis, lovable failure. After making some bad moves, this former History professor and amateur photographer retreats to his family's estate in southern Maryland. While appreciating nature and watching birds, he witnesses a murder ... and he captures it on film. The body of the dead man turns up in a dumpster in Baltimore and is identified as that of a Russian diplomat. Tullis starts rummaging through something bigger than he ever imagined.

Bird's Eye View of a Neighborhood Audio CD. Adapted by Benchmark Education Company Staff. Based on a work by Margaret McNamara. (Content Connections Ser.). (J). (gr. k-2). 2008. audio compact disk 10.00 (978-1-60634-911-3(2)) Benchmark Educ.

Bird's-Eye View of the Bible: From Genesis to Revelation. unabr. ed. Betty S. Herold. Narrated by Anna Bedford. 3 cass. (Running Time: 5 hrs. 3 min.). 1996. cass. & video 19.95 (978-1-57895-001-0(5), 095515) Bridge Resources.
Observations on familiar passages from Genesis through Revelations.

Birds of a Feather. unabr. ed. Jacqueline Winspear. Read by Kim Hicks. 7 cass. (Maisie Dobbs Mystery Ser.: Bk. 2). 2005. 59.95 (978-0-7927-3664-6(8), CSL 812); audio compact disk 89.95 (978-0-7927-3665-3(6), SLD 812) AudioGO.

Birds of Alabama Audio CDs: Companion to Birds of Alabama Field Guide. Stan Tekiela. 2006. audio compact disk 14.95 (978-1-59193-150-8(9)) Adventure Pubns.

Birds of Alaska. Thayer Birding Staff. 2003. audio compact disk 24.95 (978-1-887148-22-1(1)) Thayer Birding.

Birds of Arizona. Thayer Birding Staff. 2003. audio compact disk 24.95 (978-1-887148-23-8(X)) Thayer Birding.

Birds of Colorado. Thayer Birding Staff. 2003. audio compact disk 24.95 (978-1-887148-26-9(4)) Thayer Birding.

Birds of Delaware. Thayer Birding Staff. 2003. audio compact disk 24.95 (978-1-887148-28-3(0)) Thayer Birding.

Birds of Eastern Ecuador. unabr. ed. Peter H. English & Theodore A. Parker, III. Read by Frances L. Houck. 1 cass. (Running Time: 45 min.). 1992. 12.00 (978-0-938027-06-5(9)) Crows Nest Bird.
Recordings of 99 species of Amazonian birds in a field guide presentation.

Birds of Europe. Ed. by Expert-Center for Taxonomic Identification Staff. 1995. audio compact disk 100.00 (978-3-540-14189-1(8)) Spri.

Birds of Florida Audio CDs: Companion to Birds of Florida Field Guide. Stan Tekiela. 2 CDs. (Running Time: 2 hrs. 6 min). 2005. audio compact disk 14.95 (978-1-59193-106-5(1)) Adventure Pubns.

Birds of Florida Field Guide & Audio CDs Leather Set. Stan Tekiela. 2005. mass mkt. 31.95 (978-1-59193-107-2(X)) Adventure Pubns.

Birds of Georgia. Thayer Birding Staff. 2003. audio compact disk 24.95 (978-1-887148-31-3(0)) Thayer Birding.

Birds of Idaho. Thayer Birding Staff. 2003. audio compact disk 24.95 (978-1-887148-32-0(9)) Thayer Birding.

Birds of Kansas. Thayer Birding Staff. 2003. audio compact disk 24.95 (978-1-887148-36-8(1)) Thayer Birding.

Birds of Maryland. Thayer Birding Staff. 2003. audio compact disk 24.95 (978-1-887148-40-5(X)) Thayer Birding.

Birds of Maryland & Delaware Audio CDs: Includes Washington DC & Chesapeake Bay. Stan Tekiela. 2 CDs. (Running Time: 2 hrs. 14 mins.). 2005. audio compact disk 14.95 (978-1-59193-121-8(5)) Adventure Pubns.

Birds of Massachusetts. Thayer Birding Staff. 2003. audio compact disk 24.95 (978-1-887148-41-2(8)) Thayer Birding.

Birds of Michigan Audio CDs: Companion to Birds of Michigan Field Guide. Stan Tekiela. 2004. audio compact disk 14.95 (978-1-59193-042-6(1)) Adventure Pubns.

Birds of Minnesota Audio CDs: Companion to Birds of Minnesota Field Guide. Stan Tekiela. (Running Time: 60 mins.). 2004. audio compact disk 14.95 (978-1-59193-036-5(7)) Adventure Pubns.

Birds of Minnesota Field Guide, 2nd Edition: Companion to Birds of Minnesota. 2nd ed. Stan Tekiela. (ENG.). 2004. per. 12.95 (978-1-59193-037-2(5)) Adventure Pubns.

Birds of Missouri. Thayer Birding Staff. 2003. audio compact disk 24.95 (978-1-887148-45-0(0)) Thayer Birding.

Birds of Montana. Thayer Birding Staff. 2003. audio compact disk 24.95 (978-1-887148-46-7(9)) Thayer Birding.

Birds of My Region. Thayer Birding Staff. 2004. audio compact disk 29.95 (978-1-887148-88-7(4)) Thayer Birding.

Birds of Nebraska. Thayer Birding Staff. 2003. audio compact disk 24.95 (978-1-887148-47-4(7)) Thayer Birding.

Birds of New Mexico. Thayer Birding Staff. 2003. audio compact disk 24.95 (978-1-887148-51-1(5)) Thayer Birding.

Birds of New York Audio CDs: Companion to Birds of New York Field Guide. Stan Tekiela. 2 CDs. (Running Time: 2 hrs. 5 min). 2005. audio compact disk 14.95 (978-1-59193-109-6(6)) Adventure Pubns.

Birds of New York Field Guide & Audio CDs Leather Set. Stan Tekiela. 2005. mass mkt. 30.95 (978-1-59193-110-2(X)) Adventure Pubns.

Birds of Ohio. Thayer Birding Staff. 2003. audio compact disk 24.95 (978-1-887148-55-9(8)) Thayer Birding.

Birds of Ohio Audio CDs: Companion to Birds of Ohio Field Guide. Stan Tekiela. (Running Time: 60 mins.). 2004. audio compact disk 14.95 (978-1-59193-059-4(6)) Adventure Pubns.

Birds of Ontario. Thayer Birding Staff. 2003. audio compact disk 24.95 (978-1-887148-79-5(5)) Thayer Birding.

Birds of Pennsylvania. Thayer Birding Staff. 2003. audio compact disk 24.95 (978-1-887148-58-0(2)) Thayer Birding.

Birds of Pennsylvania Audio CDs: Companion to Birds of Pennsylvania Field Guide. Stan Tekiela. 2004. audio compact disk 14.95 (978-1-59193-086-0(3)) Adventure Pubns.

Birds of Pennsylvania Field Guide & Audio CD Leather Set. 2nd ed. Stan Tekiela. 2004. per. 29.95 (978-1-59193-088-4(X)) Adventure Pubns.

Birds of Prey. Linda Allison. Read by Jerry Kay. Illus. by Bill Wells. (Running Time: 20 min.). (Science in Action Learning Ser.). (J). (ps-6). 1988. bk. 9.95 Kay Productions.

Birds of Prey. J. A. Jance. Narrated by Ron McLarty. 8 cass. (Running Time: 10 hrs. 30 mins.). (J. P. Beaumont Mystery Ser.). 76.00 (978-0-7887-9032-4(3)) Recorded Bks.

Birds of Prey. Wilbur Smith. Read by Martin Shaw. 2 cass. (Running Time: 3 hrs.). (ENG.). 2001. 16.99 (978-0-333-69866-2(5)) Pub: Macmillan UK GBR. Dist(s): Trafalgar

Birds of Prey. abr. ed. J. A. Jance. Read by Cotter Smith. (J. P. Beaumont Mystery Ser.). 2004. audio compact disk 14.95 (978-0-06-059440-4(3)) HarperCollins Pubs.

Birds of Prey. unabr. ed. J. A. Jance. Read by Gene Engene. 12 cass. (Running Time: 12 hrs.). (J. P. Beaumont Mystery Ser.). 2001. 64.95

(978-1-58116-149-6(2)); audio compact disk 71.50 (978-1-58116-150-2(6)) Books in Motion.
Pulling the pin on 20 hard years with the Seattle police force, Beaumont's semi-retirement takes him on a cruise, when he agrees to chaperon his newly wed grandmother on her honeymoon. But the idyllic setting is shaken when one of Beau's new admirers disappears. What Beau finds aboard is a conspiracy that could have disastrous results for all.

Birds of Prey. unabr. ed. J. A. Jance. Narrated by Ron McLarry. 7 cass. (Running Time: 10 hrs. 30 mins.). (J. P. Beaumont Mystery Ser.). 37.95 (978-0-7887-9033-1(1), RF326) Recorded Bks.
Jonas Beaumont has suffered through two marriages, a thankless career, and now is being forced into retirement. Hoping for rest, Jonas agrees to accompany his grandmother on a cruise, but there is no escaping the terror that lurks on deck. Jonas confronts ghosts from the past, waiting for the perfect opportunity to capture-and kill-their prey. Available to libraries only.

Birds of Prey. unabr. ed. Wilbur Smith. Read by David Case. 9 cass. (Running Time: 13 hrs. 30 mins.). 1997. 72.00 (978-0-7366-3741-1(9), 4417-B) Books on Tape.
In this swashbuckling adventure the Courteneys seek riches and supremacy on the high sea off Africa in the 1660s.

Birds of Prey. unabr. ed. Wilbur Smith. Read by Bernadette Dunne. 11 cass. (Running Time: 16 hrs. 30 mins.). 2000. 88.00 (978-0-7366-5067-0(9), 5281) Books on Tape.
The classic has touched hearts and minds since its first publication over 50 years ago. This is the coming of age story of Francie, a girl in the slums of turn-of-the-century Brooklyn. Francie grows up with a sweet, tragic father, a severly realistic mother and a favored younger brother. She learns early the meaning of hunger and the value of a penny. She faces the disappointments life brings, including not being allowed the luxury of a high school diploma. With poignant honesty and humor, the book cuts to the heart of family life and the American dream.

Birds of Prey, Pt. 1. unabr. ed. Wilbur Smith. Read by David Case. 9 cass. (Running Time: 13 hrs. 30 min.). (Courtney Novels). 1997. 72.00 (978-0-7366-3740-4(0), 4417-A) Books on Tape.
Sir Francis Courteney & his son Hal are aboard their fighting caravel off South Africa, lying in wait for one of the treasure-laden galleons of the Dutch East India Company.

Birds of Prey & Monsoon. abr. ed. Wilbur Smith. Read by Christopher Cazenove. 8 cass. (Running Time: 12 hrs.). 2002. 40.00 (978-1-59040-238-2(3), Phoenix Audio) Pub: Amer Intl Pub. Dist(s): PerseuPGW
Sets the scene for 1667, when Sir Frances Courteney and his son Hal are on patrol in their fighting caravel off the Agulhas Cape of South Africa and continues with Hal, now grown and in command of his own ship.

***Birds of Prey Low Price.** abr. ed. J. A. Jance. Read by Cotter Smith. (ENG.). 2005. (978-0-06-089503-7(9), Harper Audio); (978-0-06-089505-1(5), Harper Audio) HarperCollins Pubs.

Birds of Prince Edward Island. Thayer Birding Staff. 2003. audio compact disk 24.95 (978-1-887148-80-1(9)) Thayer Birding.

Birds of Rhode Island. Thayer Birding Staff. 2003. audio compact disk 24.95 (978-1-887148-59-7(0)) Thayer Birding.

Birds of South Carolina. Thayer Birding Staff. 2003. audio compact disk 24.95 (978-1-887148-60-3(4)) Thayer Birding.

Birds of South Dakota. Thayer Birding Staff. 2003. audio compact disk 24.95 (978-1-887148-61-0(2)) Thayer Birding.

Birds of Texas. Thayer Birding Staff. 2003. audio compact disk 29.95 (978-1-887148-63-4(9)) Thayer Birding.

Birds of the Carolinas Audio CDs: Companion to Birds of the Carolinas Field Guide. Stan Tekiela. 2004. audio compact disk 14.95 (978-1-59193-065-5(0)) Adventure Pubns.

Birds of the Carolinas Field Guide & Audio CD Leather Set, Set. Stan Tekiela. 2004. per. 31.95 (978-1-59193-067-9(7)) Adventure Pubns.

Birds of the District of Columbia. Thayer Birding Staff. 2003. audio compact disk 24.95 (978-1-887148-29-0(9)) Thayer Birding.

Birds of Utah. Thayer Birding Staff. 2003. audio compact disk 24.95 (978-1-887148-64-1(7)) Thayer Birding.

Birds of Vermont. Thayer Birding Staff. 2003. audio compact disk 24.95 (978-1-887148-65-8(5)) Thayer Birding.

Birds of West Virginia. Stan Tekiela. 2008. audio compact disk 14.95 (978-1-59193-071-6(5)) Adventure Pubns.

Birds of West Virginia. Thayer Birding Staff. 2003. audio compact disk 24.95 (978-1-887148-68-9(X)) Thayer Birding.

Birds of Wisconsin Audio CDs: Companion to Birds of Wisconsin Field Guide. Stan Tekiela. 2004. audio compact disk 14.95 (978-1-59193-039-6(1)) Adventure Pubns.

Birds of Wisconsin Field Guide, 2nd Edition: Companion to Birds of Wisconsin. 2nd ed. Stan Tekiela. 2004. per. 12.95 (978-1-59193-040-2(5)) Adventure Pubns.

Birds of Wyoming. Thayer Birding Staff. 2003. audio compact disk 24.95 (978-1-887148-70-2(1)) Thayer Birding.

Birds Without Wings. Reina Murray & Sylvester I. Okoro. 2007. audio compact disk 27.99 (978-1-60247-621-9(7)) Tate Pubng.

Birdsong. unabr. ed. Sebastian Faulks. Read by Peter Firth. 14 CDs. 2000. audio compact disk 115.95 (978-0-7540-5352-1(0), CCD 043) Pub: Chivers Audio Bks GBR. Dist(s): AudioGO
It is 1910 & Stephen Wraysford is in France studying the textile trade. But nearly five years later, Stephen is in the British Army & France has become World War I's bloodiest battlefield. In 1978, a woman finds Wraysford's diary & begins to relive the horrors of the war.

Birdsong for a Murderer see Inner Sanctum: Three Classic Stories

Birdsongs of Nepal. unabr. ed. Scott Connop. Read by Scott Connop. Ed. by Greg Budney & Robert Grotke. 1 cass. (Running Time: 60 min.). 1993. 10.95 (978-0-938027-09-6(3)) Crows Nest Bird.
Songs & calls of 66 important species of birds of Nepal.

Birdsongs of the Himalayas. Scott Connop. 1 cass. (Running Time: 60 min.). 11.95 (978-0-938027-16-4(6)) Crows Nest Bird.
Field guide of 70 species of birds found in the Himalayas. Recorded in Bhutan.

Birmingham, Alabama. Richard H. Magee & Mary Magee. Read by Grover Gardner. 1 cass. (Running Time: 90 min.). (Ride with Me Ser.). 1997. bk. 10.95 (978-0-942649-39-0(7)) RWM Assocs.
Narrative of people, places & events of Birmingham, Alabama.

Birmingham Friends. unabr. ed. Annie Murray. Read by Annie Aldington. 14 CDs. (Running Time: 17 hrs.). (Soundings (CDs) Ser.). (J). 2006. audio compact disk 104.95 (978-1-84559-296-7(4)) Pub: ISIS Lrg Prnt GBR. Dist(s): Ulverscroft US

Birmingham Friends. unabr. ed. Annie Murray. Read by Annie Aldington. 14 cass. (Soundings Ser.). (J). 2006. 99.95 (978-1-84559-285-1(9)) Pub: ISIS Lrg Prnt GBR. Dist(s): Ulverscroft US

Birmingham Rose. Annie Murray. Read by Annie Aldington. 12 cass. (Running Time: 18 hrs.). 2001. 94.95 (978-1-86042-698-8(0), 26980) Pub: Soundings Ltd GBR. Dist(s): Ulverscroft US

Birth - Dues see Poetry of Robinson Jeffers

Birth, Brains, & Beings. John Lilly. 1 cass. 10.00 (A0181-81) Sound Photosyn.

Birth-Chart As Mandala of Personality. unabr. ed. Dane Rudhyar. 1 cass. (Running Time: 1 hr. 16 min.). 1978. 11.00 (10108) Big Sur Tapes.
Looks at the evolution of astrology &, at the astrological birth-chart as a mandala for personal meditation & transformation.

Birth Control & Sex Predetermination. H. Douglas Miller. 1 cass. 8.95 (231) Am Fed Astrologers.
Transits & progressions determine & gender.

Birth Day: A Pediatrician Explores the Science, the History, & the Wonder of Childbirth. abr. ed. Mark Sloan. Narrated by Mark Sloan. (Running Time: 9 hrs. 59 mins. 26 sec.). (ENG.). 2009. 24.49 (978-1-60814-508-9(5), SpringWater) Oasis Audio.

Birth Day: A Pediatrician Explores the Science, the History, & the Wonder of Childbirth. abr. ed. Mark Sloan. Narrated by Mark Sloan. (Running Time: 9 hrs. 59 mins. 26 sec.). (ENG.). 2009. audio compact disk 34.99 (978-1-59859-494-2(X), SpringWater) Oasis Audio.

Birth Defects & Pastoral Care (Pre-Natal Diagnosis) Pastoral Counseling for Genetic Concerns. Kenneth Reed et al. 1986. 10.80 (0310) Assn Prof Chaplains.

Birth of a Book, Pts. I & II. unabr. ed. Gilbert Highet. 1 cass. (Running Time: 30 min.). (Gilbert Highet Ser.). 9.95 (23331) J Norton Pubs.
How an author brings a book into being, from the first conception to the final delivery.

Birth of a New Nation: An Unabridged selection from A Call to Conscience - the Landmark Speeches of Dr. Martin Luther King, Jr. unabr. ed. Read by Leon Sullivan & Martin Luther King, Jr. (Running Time: 30 mins.). (ENG.). 2006. 1.98 (978-1-59483-485-1(7)) Pub: Hachet Audio. Dist(s): HachBkGrp

Birth of A Promise: How to Conceive, Expect & Deliver the Promises of God. Mac Hammond. 3 CDs. 2006. audio compact disk 15.00 (978-1-57399-319-7(0)) Mac Hammond.
In Birth of a Promise, Mac Hammond takes you to the life of Mary, the mother of Jesus, and shows how she became the first person to have a promise from God come to life within her.

Birth of a Promise Set: How to Conceive, Expect & Deliver the Promises of God. Mac Hammond. 3 cass. (Running Time: 3 hrs.). 1999. (978-1-57399-084-4(1)) Mac Hammond.
Mac takes you to the life of Mary, the mother of Jesus & shows you how she became the very first person to have a promise from God come to life.

Birth of an Age. James BeauSeigneur. Narrated by Pete Bradbury. 6 cass. (Running Time: 8 hrs. 30 mins.). (Christ Clone Trilogy: Bk. 2). 2004. 54.00 (978-1-4025-1820-1(X)) Recorded Bks.

Birth of an Exciting Vision see Nacimiento de una Vision Emocionante

Birth of Lord Jagannatha (A); Birth o Lord Krsna (B) 1 cass. (Spiritual Stories Ser.). 5.00 Bhaktivedanta.

Birth of Plenty: How the Modern World of Prosperity was Launched. abr. ed. William Berstein. 3 cass. (Running Time: 4 hrs. 30 mins.). 2004. 24.00 (978-1-932378-56-6(1)) Pub: A Media Intl. Dist(s): Natl Bk Netwk

Birth of Plenty: How the Prosperity of the Modern World Was Created. abr. ed. William Berstein. 4 CDs. (Running Time: 016200 sec.). 2005. audio compact disk 28.00 (978-1-932378-57-3(X)) Pub: A Media Intl. Dist(s): Natl Bk Netwk

Birth of the Blues. Perf. by Bing Crosby et al. 1 cass. (Running Time: 60 min.). (Old Time Radio Classic Singles Ser.). 4.95 (978-1-57816-087-7(1), BC103) Audio File.
Radio version of the film musical (1/18/51) Buick.

Birth of the Blues. Perf. by Bing Crosby et al. 1 cass. (Running Time: 60 min.). 1951. 7.95 (DD-6010) Natl Recrd Co.
Toe-tapping music & fun loving entertainment. The story of a hot trumpet player, an easy-going band leader & his female singer; set in the 1950's.

Birth of the Chaordic Age, abr. ed. Dee Hock. 4 cass. (Running Time: 6 hrs.). 1999. 24.95 (978-1-57453-346-0(0)) Audio Lit.
The author argues that traditional organization forms can no longer work because organizations have become too complex. Hock advocates a new organizational form that he calls "chaordic", simultaneously chaotic & orderly. He credits the worldwide success of VISA to its chaordic structure: It is owned by its member banks, which both compete with each other for customers & cooperate by honoring one another's transactions across borders & currencies. The book shows how these same chaordic concepts are now being put into practice in a broad range of business, social, community & government organizations.

Birth of the Cool of Miles Davis & His Associates. Frank Tirro. Ed. by Michael J. Budds. (ENG.). 2008. pap. bk. 45.00 (978-1-57647-128-9(4)) Pendragon NY.

Birth of the Modern. unabr. ed. Paul Johnson. Read by Bill Kelsey. 13 cass. (Running Time: 19 hrs. 30 min.). 1995. 104.00 (978-0-7366-3087-0(2), 3767-A) Books on Tape.
The world's growth spurted from 1815 to 1830, says the author. Technology & the arts led the way.

Birth of the Modern, Pt. 2. unabr. ed. Paul Johnson. Read by Bill Kelsey. 13 cass. (Running Time: 19 hrs. 30 min.). 1995. 104.00 (3767-B) Books on Tape.
The world's growth spurted from 1815 to 1830, says author Paul Johnson. Technology & the arts led the way.

Birth of the Modern, Pt. 3. unabr. ed. Paul Johnson. Read by Bill Kelsey. 13 cass. (Running Time: 19 hrs. 30 min.). 1995. 104.00 (3878-C) Books on Tape.

Birth of the Modern Pt. 1: World Society, 1815-1830. unabr. ed. Paul Johnson. Read by Nadia May. 13 cass. (Running Time: 38 hrs.). 1991. 85.95 (978-0-7861-0305-8(1), 1269A,B) Blckstn Audio.
This extraordinary chronicle of the period that laid the foundations of the modern world is the history of people, ideas, politics, manners & morals, economics, art, science & technology, diplomacy, business & commerce, literature & revolution.

Birth of the Modern Pt. 2: World Society, 1815-1830. unabr. ed. Paul Johnson. Read by Nadia May. 12 cass. (Running Time: 38 hrs.). 1991. 83.95 (978-0-7861-0306-5(X), 1269A,B) Blckstn Audio.

Birth of the Modern Pt. 3: World Society, 1815-1830. unabr. ed. Paul Johnson. Read by Nadia May. 10 cass. (Running Time: 15 hrs.). 1991. 69.95 (978-0-7861-0307-2(8), 1269-C) Blckstn Audio.

Birth of the Modern Mind: An Intellectual History of the 17th & 18th Centuries. Instructed by Alan Kors. 6 cass. (Running Time: 6 hrs.). 1998. 129.95 (978-1-56585-110-8(2)) Teaching Co.

Birth of the Modern Mind: An Intellectual History of the 17th & 18th Centuries. Alan Charles Kors. 12 cass. (Running Time: 12 hrs.). 49.95 Set; 24 lectures in 2 pts.; incl. course guide. (447) Teaching Co.
Studies the revolution of the intellect that seized Europe between 1600 & 1800 - a revolution whose lights & shadows are all around us still. It challenged previous ways of understanding reality & sparked what Professor Kors calls "perhaps the most profound transformation (ever) of European, if not human, life".

Birth of the Modern Mind Parts I-II, Vol. 1: An Intellectual History of the 17th & 18th Centuries. Instructed by Alan Kors. 12 cass. (Running Time: 12 hrs.). 1998. 129.95 (978-1-56585-107-8(2)) Teaching Co.

Birth of the Modern Mind Pts. I-II: An Intellectual History of the 17th & 18th Centuries. Instructed by Alan Charles Kors. 12 CDs. (Running Time: 12 hrs.). 1998. audio compact disk 69.95 (978-1-56585-350-8(4)) Teaching Co.

Birth of the New Man. Swami Amar Jyoti. 1 cass. 1982. 9.95 (A-21) Truth Consciousness.
The key to the flourishing of our potential & the answer for harmonious living.

Birth of Venus. Sarah Dunant. Read by Kathe Mazur. 2004. audio compact disk 96.00 (978-0-7366-9928-0(7)) Books on Tape.

Birth of Venus. abr. ed. Sarah Dunant. Read by Jenny Sterlin. 5 CDs. (Running Time: 6 hrs.). (ENG.). 2004. audio compact disk 14.99 (978-0-7393-1053-3(4)) Pub: Random Audio Pubg. Dist(s): Random
Alessandra Cecchi is not quite fifteen when her father, a prosperous cloth merchant, brings a young painter back from northern Europe to decorate the chapel walls in the family’s Florentine palazzo. A child of the Renaissance, with a precocious mind and a talent for drawing, Alessandra is intoxicated by the painter’s abilities. But their burgeoning relationship is interrupted when Alessandra’s parents arrange her marriage to a wealthy, much older man. Meanwhile, Florence is changing, increasingly subject to the growing suppression imposed by the fundamentalist monk Savonarola, who is seizing religious and political control. Alessandra and her native city are caught between the Medici state, with its love of luxury, learning, and dazzling art, and the hellfire preaching and increasing violence of Savonarola’s reactionary followers. Played out against this turbulent backdrop, Alessandra’s married life is a misery, except for the surprising freedom it allows her to pursue her powerful attraction to the young painter and his art. The Birth of Venus is a tour de force, the first historical novel from one of Britain’s most innovative writers of literary suspense. It brings alive the history of Florence at its most dramatic period, telling a compulsively absorbing story of love, art, religion, and power through the passionate voice of Alessandra, a heroine with the same vibrancy of spirit as her beloved city. From the Hardcover edition.

Birth Order & You. unabr. ed. Ronald Richardson & Lois Richardson. 1 cass. 2000. 14.95 (978-1-55180-060-8(8)) Self-Counsel Pr CAN.
Adapted from the best-selling book by Dr. Ronald Richardson & Lois Richardson, M.A., this entertaining & enlightening audio program explains how birth order affects the way you think & act as an adult - the type of person you are, the type of spouse you choose, & the type of employer or employee you make. Your position in the family has a far-reaching effect on the way you experience life - it's the cornerstone of your personality.

Birth Order Book: Why You Are the Way You Are. unabr. ed. Kevin Leman. Narrated by Wayne Shepherd. (Running Time: 9 hrs. 22 mins. 40 sec.). (ENG.). 2009. 20.99 (978-1-60814-587-4(5)); audio compact disk 29.99 (978-1-59859-635-9(7)) Oasis Audio.

Birth-Separation. Barrie Konicov. 1 cass. (Emotional Health Ser.). 11.98 (978-0-87082-397-8(3), 015) Potentials.
Discusses the birth experience, how it could be the source of asthma, headaches, depression & body aches & then shows how to release the negative feelings that surrounded your birth.

Birth Survival Decisions & Personality. Jeanne Avery. Read by Jeanne Avery. 1 cass. (Running Time: 90 min.). 1994. 8.95 (1112) Am Fed Astrologers.
Past lives & the natal horoscope.

Birth Trauma. unabr. ed. Stanislav Grof. 2 cass. (Running Time: 1 hr. 55 min.). 1981. 18.00 (00807) Big Sur Tapes.

Birthday. Margaret Yorke. Read by Anne Cater. 4 cass. (Sound Ser.). (J). 2002. 44.95 (978-1-84283-212-7(3)) Pub: ISIS Lrg Prnt GBR. Dist(s): Ulverscroft US

***Birthday Ball.** unabr. ed. Lois Lowry. Read by Elissa Steele. (ENG.). (J). 2010. audio compact disk 25.00 (978-0-307-74620-7(8), Listening Lib) Pub: Random Audio Pubg. Dist(s): Random

Birthday Basket for Tia. unabr. ed. Pat Mora. Illus. by Cecily Lang. 1 cass. (Running Time: 15 min.). (J). (gr. k-3). 2001. pap. bk. 15.95 (978-0-8045-6841-8(3), 6841) Spoken Arts.
Portrays a loving Mexican-American household.

Birthday Box of Tapes. Barbara Davoll & Dennis Hockerman. 3 cass. (Christopher Churchmouse Ser.). (J). (ps-2). 1993. 11.99 Set. (3-3202) David C Cook.

Birthday Boys. unabr. ed. Beryl Bainbridge. Read by Gordon Griffin. 6 CDs. (Running Time: 6 hrs. 19 mins.). (Sound Ser.). (J). 2002. audio compact disk 64.95 (978-1-86042-910-1(6)) Pub: ISIS Lrg Prnt GBR. Dist(s): Ulverscroft US

Birthday Boys. unabr. ed. Beryl Bainbridge. Read by Gordon Griffin. 6 cass. (Running Time: 6 hrs. 19 mins.). (Soundings Ser.). (J). 2004. 54.95 (978-1-86042-812-8(6)) Pub: ISIS Lrg Prnt GBR. Dist(s): Ulverscroft US

Birthday Flowers: Early Explorers Emergent Set A Audio CD. Benchmark Education Staff. (J). 2006. audio compact disk 10.00 (978-1-4108-7590-7(3)) Benchmark Educ.

Birthday Girl. Stephen Leather. 2007. 94.95 (978-0-7531-3591-4(4)); audio compact disk 104.95 (978-0-7531-2651-6(6)) Pub: ISIS Audio GBR. Dist(s): Ulverscroft US

Birthday Hula. 5.00 (978-1-58513-069-6(9), 1-HE-B) Dance Fantasy.

Birthday of a King. Bob Hartman & Michael McGuire. 1 cass. (J). (ps-3). 1994. bk. 11.99 (978-7-900882-48-6(0), 3-1215) David C Cook.
Children's Bible story.

Birthday of a King. Stan Pethel & Kenny Gannon. 1990. 75.00 (978-0-7673-1350-6(X)) LifeWay Christian.

Birthday of the King. Stan Pethel & Kenny Gannon. 1990. 11.98 (978-0-7673-1328-5(3)) LifeWay Christian.

Birthday Parties Audio CD. Adapted by Benchmark Education Company Staff. Based on a work by Francisco Blane. (My First Reader's Theater Ser.). (J). (gr. k-1). 2008. audio compact disk 10.00 (978-1-60634-098-1(0)) Benchmark Educ.

Birthday Party. 1 cass. (J). 9.95 (AABP) Brdgstn Multimed Grp.
A musical celebration for the greatest birthday of all time!.

Birthday Party. 1 cass. (Running Time: 1 hr.). (J). 2000. 6.99 HARK Ent.
Will fill your home with fun-filled praise of the Lord. Provides wholesome messages that are sure to last a lifetime.

Birthday Party. Bridgestone Staff. 2004. audio compact disk 7.98 (978-1-56371-028-5(5)) Brdgstn Multimed Grp.

Birthday Party. Effin Older. Perf. by Mary-Kate Olsen & Ashley Olsen. 1 cass., 1 CD. (You're Invited to Mary-Kate & Ashley's Ser.). (J). (gr. 2-4). 7.18 (LIGHT 54260); audio compact disk 12.78 CD Jewel box. (LIGHT 54260) NewSound.

Birthday Party. Mary-Kate Olsen & Ashley Olsen. 1 cass. (Running Time: 1 hr.). (J). 2002. 15.98 (978-1-56896-274-0(6), 54260-2) Lightyear Entrtnmnt.
America has watched the Olsen twins grow up from their TV series "Full House" to their current series "So Little Time". The whole family can enjoy this series titles. Featuring Moon Bounce Madness, Pool Party, Makeover Machine, The Bare Necessities.

Birthday Party. Perf. by Mary-Kate Olsen & Ashley Olsen. 1 CD. (Running Time: 1 hr.). (You're Invited To Mary-Kate & Ashley's Ser.). (J). 2002. audio compact disk 15.98 (978-1-56896-273-3(8), 54260-2) Lightyear Entrtnmnt.

Birthday Party. unabr. ed. Elvi Rhodes. Read by Anne Dover. 10 CDs. (Running Time: 10.5 hrs.). (Sound Ser.). (J). 2002. audio compact disk 89.95 (978-1-86042-932-3(7)) Pub: ISIS Lrg Prnt GBR. Dist(s): Ulverscroft US

Birthday Party. unabr. ed. Elvi Rhodes. Read by Anne Dover. 10 cass. (Running Time: 15 hrs.). (Sound Ser.). 2002. 84.95 (978-1-86042-854-8(1), 28541) Pub: UlverLrgPrint GBR. Dist(s): Ulverscroft US
A landmark birthday for Poppy brings back memories - not all of them happy ones.

Birthday Party: A Memoir of Survival. unabr. ed. Stanley N. Alpert. Read by Paul Michael Garcia. (Running Time: 8 hrs. 30 mins.). 2009. 29.95 (978-1-4417-1436-7(7)); 54.95 (978-1-4417-1432-9(4)); audio compact disk 76.00 (978-1-4417-1433-6(2)) Blckstn Audio.

Birthday Party! Singalong. 1 cass. (Running Time: 1 hr.). (J). 2002. 3.98 (R4 74261); audio compact disk 6.98 (R2 74261) MFLP CA.
No birthday party is complete without these classic and original tunes, guaranteed to keep a party going or make children look forward to their next big bash! It's a party from start to finish with 13 delicious songs including Come to My Party, The Balloon Game, Pin the Tail Tingalayo, If It's Your Birthday and You Know It, Pinata, Let's Make a Cake, Thank You Song and of course Happy Birthday.

Birthday Party Songs. (Twin Sisters Ser.). (J). bk. 7.98 Blisterpack. (TWIN 432); 7.18 (TWIN 132); bk. Incl. 24p. bk., poster. (TWIN 432) NewSound.
A game set to ensure a smooth-running fun party.

Birthday Party Songs. 1 CD. (Running Time: 1 hr.). (J). 2000. audio compact disk 12.99 (978-1-57583-238-8(0), TWIN132CD) Twin Sisters.
To ensure a smooth-running fun party! Children will march to our original "Musical Chairs" listen for the sound of Bessy the cow in "Pass the Hot Potato", dance to the "Birthday Bee Bop" & learn how to do the "Birthday Limbo". Children will also enjoy the traditional games like "Duck, Duck Goose" & "Simon Says".

Birthday Party Songs. Kim Mitzo Thompson & Karen Mitzo Hilderbrand. Arranged by Hal Wright. (J). 1997. pap. bk. 13.99 (978-1-57583-364-4(6), Twin 432CD) Twin Sisters.

Birthday Room. unabr. ed. Kevin Henkes. Read by Terrence Mann. 2 vols. (Running Time: 3 hrs. 13 mins.). (J). (gr. 3-7). 2004. pap. bk. 29.00 (978-0-8072-0444-3(7), Listening Lib); 23.00 (978-0-8072-8420-9(3), YA171CX, Listening Lib) Random Audio Pubg.

Birthday Songs. unabr. ed. 1 cass. (J). 7.99 (978-0-7634-0207-5(9)); 7.99 Norelco. (978-0-7634-0206-8(0)); audio compact disk 13.99 CD. (978-0-7634-0208-2(7)); audio compact disk 13.99 (978-0-7634-0209-9(5)) W Disney Records.

Birthday Thoughts IV see Twentieth-Century Poetry in English, No. 26, Recordings of Poets Reading Their Own Poetry

Birthdays. unabr. ed. Poems. Sri Chinmoy Centre Staff. Read by Sri Chinmoy Centre Staff. 1 cass. (Running Time: 17 min.). 1998. bk.; 9.95 (978-0-9664613-4-3(7)) Jharna Kala.

Birthing House. unabr. ed. Christopher Ransom. (Running Time: 10 hrs. 0 mins.). (ENG.). 2009. 29.95 (978-1-4332-8925-5(3)); 59.95 (978-1-4332-8921-7(0)); audio compact disk 29.95 (978-1-4332-8924-8(5)) Blckstn Audio.

Birthing House. unabr. ed. Christopher Ransom. Read by Edward Herrmann. 9 CDs. (Running Time: 10 hrs. 30 mins.). 2009. audio compact disk 90.00 (978-1-4332-8922-4(9)) Blckstn Audio.

Birthing the Lamaze Way. unabr. ed. 1 cass. 10.95 (AF1621) J Norton Pubs.

Birthing the Self & Isis & Mary. Marianne Williamson. Read by Marianne Williamson. 1 cass. (Running Time: 90 mins.). (Lectures on a Course in Miracles). 1999. 10.00 (978-1-56170-492-7(X), M848) Hay House.

Birthmark see Great American Short Stories, Vol. III, A Collection

Birthmark. (S-63) Jimcin Record.

Birthmarks: 1 John 3:11-17. Ed Young. 1984. 4.95 (978-0-7417-1387-2(X), 387) Win Walk.

Birthquake Pt. 1: Journey to Wholeness. abr. ed. Tammie Fowles. Read by Tammie Fowles. Read by Kevin Fowles. 1 cass. 1998. 9.95 (978-0-9666900-1-9(X)) SagePlace.

Birthquake Pt. 4: Journey to Wholeness. abr. ed. Tammie Fowles. Read by Tammie Fowles. Read by Kevin Fowles. 1 cass. 1998. 9.95 (978-0-9666900-4-0(4)) SagePlace.

Birthright. Janette Oke & T. Davis Bunn. Narrated by Suzanne Toren. 6 cass. (Running Time: 8 hrs. 15 mins.). (Song of Acadia Ser.: Vol. 3). 54.00 (978-1-4025-2266-6(5)) Recorded Bks.

Birthright. abr. ed. Nora Roberts. Read by Bernadette Quigley. (Running Time: 21600 sec.). 2006. audio compact disk 16.99 (978-1-4233-1941-2(9), 9781423319412, BCD Value Price) Brilliance Audio.
On a hot July afternoon, a worker at an Antietam Creek construction site drives the blade of his backhoe into a layer of soil - and strikes a 5,000-year-old human skull. The discovery draws plenty of attention and a lot of controversy. It also changes the life of one woman in ways she never expected... As an archaeologist, Callie Dunbrook knows a lot about the past. But her own past is about to be called into question. Recruited for her expertise on the Antietam Creek dig, she encounters danger - as a cloud of death and misfortune hangs over the project, and rumors fly that the site is cursed. She finds a passion that feels equally dangerous, as she joins forces in her work with her irritating, but irresistible, ex-husband, Jake. And when a strange woman approaches her, claiming to know a secret about Callie's privileged Boston childhood, some startling and unsettling questions are raised about her very identity. Searching for answers, trying to rebuild, Callie finds that there are deceptions and sorrows that refuse to stay buried. And as she struggles to put the pieces back together, she discovers that the healing process comes with consequences - and that there are people who will do anything to make sure the truth is never revealed.

Birthright. abr. ed. Nora Roberts. Read by Bernadette Quigley. (Running Time: 6 hrs.). 2009. audio compact disk 9.99 (978-1-4418-2645-9(9), 9781441826459, BCD Value Price) Brilliance Audio.

Birthright. unabr. ed. Nora Roberts. Read by Bernadette Quigley. 12 CDs. (Running Time: 16 hrs.). 2003. audio compact disk 42.95 (978-1-59086-339-8(9), 1590863399, CD); 36.95 (978-1-59086-337-4(2), 1590863372, BAU); 97.25 (978-1-59086-338-1(0), 1590863380, CD Unabrid Lib Ed); audio compact disk 112.25 (978-1-59086-340-4(2), 1590863402, CD Unabrid Lib Ed) Brilliance Audio.
On a hot July afternoon, a worker at an Antietam Creek construction site drives the blade of his backhoe into a layer of soil - and strikes a 5,000-year-old human skull. The discovery draws plenty of attention and a lot of controversy. It also changes the life of one woman in ways she never expected... As an archaeologist, Callie Dunbrook knows a lot about the past. But her own past is about to be called into question. Recruited for her expertise on the Antietam Creek dig, she encounters danger - as a cloud of death and misfortune hangs over the project, and rumors fly that the site is cursed. She finds a passion that feels equally dangerous, as she joins forces in her work with her irritating, but irresistible, ex-husband, Jake. And when a strange woman approaches her, claiming to know a secret about Callie's privileged Boston childhood, some startling and unsettling questions are raised about her very identity. Searching for answers, trying to rebuild, Callie finds that there are deceptions and sorrows that refuse to stay buried. And as she struggles to put the pieces back together, she discovers that the healing process comes with consequences - and that there are people who will do anything to make sure the truth is never revealed.

Birthright. unabr. ed. Nora Roberts. Read by Bernadette Quigley. (Running Time: 16 hrs.). 2004. 39.25 (978-1-59335-407-7(X), 159335407X, Brlnc Audio MP3 Lib) Brilliance Audio.

Birthright. unabr. ed. Nora Roberts. Read by Bernadette Quigley. (Running Time: 16 hrs.). 2004. 39.25 (978-1-59710-052-6(8), 1597100528, BADLE); 24.95 (978-1-59710-053-3(6), 1597100536, BAD) Brilliance Audio.

Birthright. unabr. ed. Nora Roberts. Read by Bernadette Quigley. (YA). 2008. 99.99 (978-1-60514-810-6(5)) Find a World.

Birthright. unabr. ed. Nora Roberts. Read by Bernadette Quigley. (Running Time: 16 hrs.). 2004. 24.95 (978-1-59335-067-3(8), 1593350678) Soulmate Audio Bks.

***Birthright: Out of the Servant's Quarters into the Father's House.** Zondervan. (Running Time: 3 hrs. 39 mins. 31 sec.). (ENG.). 2010. 16.99 (978-0-310-42700-1(2)) Zondervan.

Birthright: The Book of Man. unabr. ed. Mike Resnick. Read by Adams Morgan. 11 CDs. (Running Time: 13 hrs.). 2003. audio compact disk 88.00 (978-0-7861-9294-6(1), 3063); 62.95 (978-0-7861-2386-5(9), 3063) Blckstn Audio.
A brilliant novel of science fiction that carefully constructs a blueprint of mankind's history, social, political, economic, scientific, and religious, for the next 18,000 years.

Biryani & Plum Pudding. unabr. ed. Julian C. Hollick. 1 cass. (Running Time: 60 min.). (Passages to India Ser.). 1991. 15.00 (978-1-56709-009-3(5), 1009) Indep Broadcast.
India is a civilization with a unique ability to absorb, incorporate & synthesize other cultures into something new & typically Indian. This program focues on the Muslim & British impacts on India & the manner in which they in turn have been Indianized.

Biscuit. abr. ed. Peggy Parish & Alyssa Satin Capucilli. Illus. by Pat Schories. (I Can Read Bks.). (J). (ps-2). 2005. 9.99 (978-0-06-074105-1(8), HarperFestival) HarperCollins Pubs.

Biscuit Book & Tape. abr. ed. Alyssa Satin Capucilli. Illus. by Pat Schories. 1 cass. (Running Time: 030 min.). (My First I Can Read Bks.). (J). (ps-k). 1999. 8.99 (978-0-694-70101-8(7), HarperFestival) HarperCollins Pubs.

Biscuit Finds a Friend. abr. ed. Alyssa Satin Capucilli. Illus. by Pat Schories. (My First I Can Read Bks.). (J). (ps-k). 2007. 9.99 (978-0-06-124772-9(3), HarperFestival) HarperCollins Pubs.

Biscuit Finds a Friend. unabr. abr. ed. Alyssa Satin Capucilli. Illus. by Pat Schories. 1 cass. (Running Time: 30 mins.). (My First I Can Read Bks.). (J). (ps-k). 2001. 8.99 (978-0-06-029324-6(1)) HarperCollins Pubs.

Biscuit Goes to School. abr. ed. Alyssa Satin Capucilli. Illus. by Pat Schories. (My First I Can Read Bks.). (J). (ps-2). 2005. cass., cass., cass. 9.99 (978-0-06-078686-1(8), HarperFestival) HarperCollins Pubs.

Biscuit Goes to School Book & Tape. abr. ed. Alyssa Satin Capucilli. Illus. by Pat Schories. (Biscuit Ser.). (J). (ps-k). 2003. cass. & cass. 8.99 (978-0-06-009426-3(5)) HarperCollins Pubs.

Biscuit Shooter. Alan LeMay. 2009. (978-1-60136-363-3(X)) Audio Holding.

Biscuits, Fleas, & Pump Handles see See You at the Top

Biscuits, Fleas & Pump Handles. Zig Ziglar. Read by Zig Ziglar. 1 cass. (Zig Ziglar Classics Ser.). 1990. 9.95 (978-1-56207-007-6(X)) Zig Ziglar Corp.
Zig at his all-time best - telling the original stories that made him famous. Zig explains his moving, humorous & exciting approach to life while giving you specific ways to live a happier & more rewarding life.

Biscuits, Fleas & Pump Handles. unabr. ed. Zig Ziglar. Narrated by Zig Ziglar. (Running Time: 1 hr. 9 mins. 59 sec.). (ENG.). 2009. 9.09 (978-1-60814-648-2(0)); audio compact disk 12.99 (978-1-59859-705-9(1)) Oasis Audio.

***Biscuit's New Trick.** Alyssa Satin Capucilli. Illus. by Pat Schories. (My First I Can Read Ser.). (J). 2010. 9.99 (978-0-06-176500-1(7), HarperFestival) HarperCollins Pubs.

***Biscuit's New Trick & Biscuit Goes to School.** abr. ed. Alyssa Satin Capucilli. Read by Andrea Kessler. (ENG.). 2006. (978-0-06-124107-9(5)); (978-0-06-124106-2(7)) HarperCollins Pubs.

Biscuit's New Trick Book & Tape. abr. ed. Alyssa Satin Capucilli. Illus. by Pat Schories. (My First I Can Read Bks.). (J). (ps-k). 2003. 8.99 (978-0-06-444300-5(0)) HarperCollins Pubs.

Bishop & the Beggar Girl of St. Germain. unabr. ed. Andrew M. Greeley. Narrated by George Guidall. 6 CDs. (Running Time: 7 hrs. 30 mins.). (Blackie Ryan Ser.). 2001. audio compact disk 58.00 (978-1-4025-0918-6(9), C1581) Recorded Bks.
Bishop Blackie has no desire to leave the friendly confines of his Chicago neighborhood to traipse around Paris searching for Jean-Claude, a popular priest who has inexplicably vanished while filming a television show. But when his Archbishop boss says, "See to it," Blackie can hardly refuse. As he sifts through a pile of suspects that includes everyone from church leaders to television executives, Blackie begins to wonder whether the reason no one can find Jean-Claude is because Jean-Claude doesn't want to be found.

Bishop & the Beggar Girl of St. Germain. unabr. ed. Andrew M. Greeley. Narrated by George Guidall. 5 cass. (Running Time: 7 hrs. 30 mins.). (Blackie Ryan Ser.). 2001. 52.00 (978-0-7887-9659-3(3)) Recorded Bks.

Bishop & the Missing L Train. Andrew M. Greeley. 6 cass. (Running Time: 7 hrs. 30 mins.). (Blackie Ryan Ser.). 59.00 (978-1-4025-3390-7(X)) Recorded Bks.

Bishop As Pawn. unabr. collector's ed. William X. Kienzle. Read by Edward Holland. 7 cass. (Running Time: 10 hrs. 30 mins.). (Father Koesler Mystery Ser.: No. 16). 2001. 56.00 (978-0-7366-6107-2(7)) Books on Tape.
Father Koesler must discover who killed an unpopular bishop. But what if it's a fellow priest?.

Bishop Clarence Haddon & Cathedral Mass Choir. 1 cass., 1 CD. 10.98 (978-1-57908-408-0(7), 1438); audio compact disk 15.98 CD. (978-1-57908-407-3(9), 1438) Platinm Enter.

Bishop Michael V. Kelsey & the New Samaritan Mass Choir: I'll Sing to You - Live in Washington, Dc. 2002. 9.98 (978-0-9727862-0-1(1)) New Samaritan Bapt Church.

Bishop Michael V. Kelsey & the New Samaritan Mass Choir: I'll Sing to You - Live in Washington, DC. 2002. audio compact disk 14.98 (978-0-9727862-1-8(X)) New Samaritan Bapt Church.

Bishop Michael V. Kelsey & the New Samaritan Mass Choir: Masterpeace. 1. 2004. 10.98 (978-0-9727862-3-2(6)); audio compact disk 16.98 (978-0-9727862-4-9(4)) New Samaritan Bapt Church.

Bishop Orders His Tomb see Poetry of Robert Browning

Bishop Spong Speaks Out! Prod. by Linda Shorten. Contrib. by John Shelby Spong. 1 CD. (Running Time: 1 hr.). 2005. audio compact disk 15.95 (978-0-660-19040-2(0)) Pub: Canadian Broadcasting CAN. Dist(s): Georgetown Term
Bishop Spong believes that September 11th was abundant proof - if proof were needed at all - that our traditional notion of "a God who watches over us" is nothing but an illusion. Bishop Spong suggests we replace that exhausted notion of God with a celebration of the "God experience." He calls for Christians everywhere to mature into a new Christianity, one that recognizes that "WE are solely responsible for our lives, and for the lives of those around us. Bishop John Shelby Spong appears to deny the most basic tenets of Christian faith. In this interview, Spong explains why he thinks Christianity must change or die.

Bishop Tutu: A Tribute to Martin Luther King Jr. 1 cass. (Running Time: 30 min.). 9.95 (F0560B090, HarperThor) HarpC GBR.

Bishop's Apron. unabr. collector's ed. W. Somerset Maugham. Read by Gary Martin. 6 cass. (Running Time: 6 hrs.). 1987. 36.00 (978-0-7366-1197-8(5), 2115) Books on Tape.
Adaptation of Maugham's play of greed & hypocrisy in the upper ranks of the English clergy.

Bishop's Secret. unabr. ed. Fergus W. Hume. Read by Flo Gibson. 7 cass. (Running Time: 10 hrs. 30 min.). 1998. 25.95 (978-1-55685-611-2(3)) Audio Bk Con.
The Bishop lives with a terrible secret & to top it off, he is suspected of murder. There are many appealing & a few poisonous people in this gripping plot.

Bisk GAAP Guide. Nathan M. Bisk & Robert L. Monette. 12 cass. 199.00 Set, incl. 250p. textbk. & quizzer. (CPE0030) Bisk Educ.
Presents theoretical foundations assets & liabilities, intangibles & R & D; taxes leases, pensions, stockholders' equity, equity method, business combinations & foreign operations.

Bisk GAAS Guide. Nathan M. Bisk. 12 cass. 159.00 set, incl. textbk. & quizzer. (CPE0040) Bisk Educ.
Designed to provide an overview of auditing standards, professional ethics & standards applicable to other professional services such as complications-reviews tax & MAS work.

Bismarck. 10.00 (HE800) Esstee Audios.
Explores the life & times of the shaper of the New Realpolitik.

B'Ismillah (in the Name of God) Fes Festival of World Sacred Music. unabr. ed. World Sacred Music Festival. 2 CDs. (Running Time: 2 hrs. 19 min.). 1997. audio compact disk 21.98 (978-1-56455-484-0(8), MM00339D) Sounds True.
The very best of this celebrated festival's second year: Pakistani qawwali chants, Egyptian madih odes, Christian flamenco saeta & much more.

Bison Crossing Near Mt. Rushmore see May Swenson

Bisschen Panik. Angelika Raths. 1 cass. (Running Time: 1 hr.). (GER.). (YA). 2000. 29.00 (978-3-468-49819-0(5)); audio compact disk 29.00 (978-3-468-49820-6(9)) Langenscheidt.

Bistro: Swinging French Jazz, Favorite Parisian Bistro Recipes. Sharon O'Connor. Photos by Paul Moore. (Sharon O'Connor's Menus & Music Ser.: Vol. XIV). 1999. pap. bk. 24.95 (978-1-883914-28-8(0)) Menus & Music.

Bit of a Blur: The Autobiography. abr. ed. Alex James. Read by Alex James. (Running Time: 3 hrs. 1 mins. 0 sec.). (ENG., 2007. audio compact disk 25.00 (978-1-4055-0237-5(1)) Pub: Little BrownUK GBR. Dist(s): IPG Chicago

Bit on the Side. unabr. ed. William Trevor. Narrated by Josephine Bailey & Simon Vance. 5 CDs. (Running Time: 6 hrs. 0 mins. 0 sec.). (ENG.). 2004. audio compact disk 24.99 (978-1-4001-0143-6(3)) Pub: Tantor Media. Dist(s): IngramPubServ

Bit on the Side. unabr. ed. William Trevor. Narrated by Josephine Bailey & Simon Vance. 1 cd. (Running Time: 6 hrs. 0 mins. 0 sec.). (ENG.). 2004. 19.99 (978-1-4001-5143-1(0)); audio compact disk 49.99 (978-1-4001-3143-3(X)) Pub: Tantor Media. Dist(s): IngramPubServ

***Bitch in the House.** unabr. ed. Cathi Hanauer. Read by Cathi Hanauer. (ENG.). 2004. (978-0-06-078264-1(1), Harper Audio); (978-0-06-081395-6(4), Harper Audio) HarperCollins Pubs.

Bitch in the House: Women Tell the Truth about Sex, Solitude, Work, Motherhood, & Marriage. abr. ed. Cathi Hanauer. Read by Cathi Hanauer. 5 CDs. (Running Time: 6 hrs.). 2003. audio compact disk 29.95 (978-0-06-057239-6(6)) HarperCollins Pubs.

Bitch in the House Sampler. Cathi Hanauer. 1 CD. (Running Time: 1 hr. 30 mins.). Date not set. audio compact disk (978-0-06-057448-2(8)) HarperCollins Pubs.

***Bitch Is the New Black.** unabr. ed. Helena Andrews. Read by Karen Murray. (ENG.). 2010. (978-0-06-199746-4(3), Harper Audio) HarperCollins Pubs.

***Bitch Is the New Black: A Memoir.** unabr. ed. Helena Andrews. Read by Karen Murray. 2010. (978-0-06-198883-7(9), Harper Audio) HarperCollins Pubs.

Bite by Bite. Geneen Roth. 2 CDs. (Running Time: 8100 sec.). 2006. audio compact disk 19.95 (978-1-59179-463-9(3), AW01042D) Sounds True.
For more than seventeen years, Geneen Roth, best-selling author of Feeding the Hungry Heart, was either on a diet or on a binge every single day, and in the end there was one thing she completely understood: diets do not work. Today she leads workshops around the world for sold-out audiences, and her books have sold over a million copies. Now, she offers listeners Bite by Bite, her essential step-by-step program to help you determine what you are truly hungry for, and create a healthier relationship with food. Through guided meditations, practical techniques, and Geneen Roth's personal trial-by-error lessons, Bite by Bite will change the way you relate to food, allow you to give up diets permanently, and accept yourself at any weight.

***Bite Me.** unabr. ed. Christopher Moore. Read by Susan Bennett. (ENG.). 2010. (978-0-06-198628-4(3), Harper Audio) HarperCollins Pubs.

***Bite Me: A Love Story.** unabr. ed. Christopher Moore. Read by Susan Bennett. (ENG.). 2010. (978-0-06-195366-8(0), Harper Audio) HarperCollins Pubs.

***Bite Me If You Can.** unabr. ed. Lynsay Sands. Read by Rick Robertson. (ENG.). 2009. (978-0-06-196147-2(7), Harper Audio); (978-0-06-195864-9(6), Harper Audio) HarperCollins Pubs.

***Bite to Remember.** unabr. ed. Lynsay Sands. (ENG.). 2009. (978-0-06-196148-9(5), Harper Audio); (978-0-06-195865-6(4), Harper Audio) HarperCollins Pubs.

Biters & Stingers. Linda Allison. Read by Jerry Kay. Illus. by Bill Wells. (Running Time: 20 min.). (Science in Action Learning Ser.). (J). (ps-6). 1988. bk. 9.95 Kay Productions.

Biter's Fighting Poems. Mark Paul Sebar. 1 CD. (Running Time: 39 min.). 1999. audio compact disk 8.99 (978-1-930246-04-1(8), BIT) Sebar Pubng.
An animated poetic program with 9 bouts by this crazy fighter.

Bites. unabr. ed. Archimede Fusillo et al. Read by Stig Wemyss. 2 cass. (Aussie Bites Ser.). (J). 2003. lib. bdg. 24.00 (978-1-74030-983-7(9)) Pub: Bolinda Pubng AUS. Dist(s): Bolinda Pub Inc

Biting the Moon. Martha Grimes. Read by Bernadette Dunne. 1999. audio compact disk 80.00 (978-0-7366-5182-0(9)) Books on Tape.

Biting the Moon. unabr. ed. Martha Grimes. Read by Bernadette Dunne. 8 cass. (Running Time: 12 hrs.). 1999. 64.00 (978-0-7366-4567-6(5), 4974) Books on Tape.
What would you do if you woke up one morning in a bed & breakfast with no memory of how you got there or anything else about yourself, only the promise of the B&B owner that "Daddy" would be back in a couple of hours. Another tour de force for Grimes & a cause of celebration for her many fans.

Biting the Moon. unabr. ed. Martha Grimes. Read by Bernadette Dunne. 1 CD. (Running Time: 1 hr. 12 mins.). 2001. audio compact disk Books on Tape.

Bitten. unabr. ed. Kelley Armstrong. Read by Aasne Vigesaa. 9 cass. (Running Time: 13 hrs.). (Women of the Otherworld Ser.: Bk. 1). 2001. 96.25 (978-1-56740-987-1(3), 1567409873, Unabridge Lib Edns) Brilliance Audio.
I've got to get out of here - I don't have a lot of time left. Philip doesn't stir when I slip from the bed. There's a pile of clothing tucked underneath my dresser so I won't have to risk the squeaks and groans of opening drawers and closets. I pick up my keys, clasping my fist around them so they don't jangle, ease open the door and creep into the hallway. My legs now itch as well as hurt and I curl my toes to see if the itching stops. It doesn't. It's too late to drive to a safe place now-the itching has crystallized into a sharp burn. I stride out onto the streets, looking for a quiet place to Change. Young, beautiful, and successful, Elena Michaels seems to have it all. Her happy, organized life follows a predictable pattern: filing stories for her job as a journalist, working out at the gym, living with her architect boyfriend, and lunching with her girlfriends from the office. And once a week, in the dead of night, she streaks through a downtown ravine, naked and furred, tearing at the throats of her animal prey. Elena Michaels is a werewolf. The man who made her one has been left behind, but his dark legacy has not. And though Elena struggles to maintain the normal life she's worked so hard to create, she cannot resist the call of the elite pack of werewolves from her past. Her feral instincts will lead her back to them and into a desperate war for survival that will test her own understanding of who, and what, she is.

Bitten. unabr. ed. Kelley Armstrong. Read by Aasne Vigesaa. (Running Time: 13 hrs.). (Women of the Otherworld Ser.: Bk. 1). 2004. 39.25 (978-1-59335-363-6(4), 1593353634, Brlnc Audio MP3 Lib) Brilliance Audio.

Bitten. unabr. ed. Kelley Armstrong. Read by Aasne Vigesaa. (Running Time: 13 hrs.). (Women of the Otherworld Ser.: Bk. 1). 2004. 39.25 (978-1-59710-054-0(4), 1597100544, BADLE); 19.99 (978-1-59710-055-7(2), 1597100552, BAD) Brilliance Audio.

***Bitten.** unabr. ed. Kelley Armstrong. Read by Aasne Vigesaa. (Running Time: 13 hrs.). (Women of the Otherworld Ser.: Bk. 1). 2010. audio compact disk 19.99 (978-1-4418-8808-2(X), 9781441888082, Bril Audio CD Unabri); audio compact disk 59.97 (978-1-4418-8820-4(9), 9781441888204, BriAudCD Unabrid) Brilliance Audio.

Bitten. unabr. ed. Kelley Armstrong. Read by Aasne Vigesaa. (Running Time: 13 hrs.). (Women of the Otherworld Ser.: Bk. 1). 2004. 19.99 (978-1-59335-060-4(0), 1593350600) Soulmate Audio Bks.

Bitter Creek. abr. ed. 4 cass. (Running Time: 6 hrs.). 2000. 25.00 (978-1-58807-035-7(2)) Am Pubng Inc.
Haunted drifter Jim Sutter rides into heavy trouble his first night in Bitter Creek, a Dakota Territory cow town. Caught up in the epic 1886 drought, the town is the focal point for an escalating blood feud between stockmen and homesteaders. Tensions run high, cattle are dying and the stockmen are desperate, for the sodbusters control the river. As the feud grows more deadly, as fists give way to guns, it is clear that only one man is skilled enough and brave enough to step in and save the town from itself. But Jim Sutter, paralyzed by remorse, has given up the gun!.

Bitter Creek. abr. ed. Carter Swart. Read by Alan Zimmerman. 4 vols. 2000. (978-1-58807-603-8(2)) Am Pubng Inc.

Bitter Feast: A Bill Smith-Lydia Chin Mystery. unabr. ed. S. J. Rozan. Read by Agnes Herrmann. 8 vols. (Running Time: 8 hrs.). 1999. bk. 69.95 (978-0-7927-2280-9(9), CSL 169, Chivers Sound Lib) AudioGO.
Lydia & her partner Bill find themselves in the middle of a mysterious conflict between two powerful Chinatown rivals, the New York City police, a struggling union & a shadowy pair of federal agents.

Bitter Harvest. Jeannie Johnson. 2009. 76.95 (978-1-4079-0641-6(0)); audio compact disk 84.95 (978-1-4079-0642-3(9)) Pub: Soundings Ltd GBR. Dist(s): Ulverscroft US

Bitter Harvest: A Woman's Fury, a Mother's Sacrifice. Ann Rule. Read by Kate Reading. 1999. 88.00 (978-0-7366-4627-7(2)); audio compact disk 104.00 (978-0-7366-6065-5(8)) Books on Tape.

Bitter Harvest: A Woman's Fury, a Mother's Sacrifice. Ann Rule. 2004. 15.95 (978-0-7435-4196-1(0)) Pub: S&S Audio. Dist(s): S and S Inc

Bitter Harvest: A Woman's Fury, a Mother's Sacrifice. unabr. ed. Ann Rule. Read by Kate Reading. 11 cass. (Running Time: 16 hr. 30 min.). 1999. 88.00 (5012) Books on Tape.
The case of Debora Green, a doctor & a loving mother who seemed to epitomize the dreams of the American heartland. A small-town girl, she achieved an enviable life: her own medical practice, a handsome physician husband, three perfect children & an opulent home in an exclusive Kansas City suburb. But when a raging fire destroyed that home & took the lives of two of her children, the trail of clues led investigators to a stunning conclusion.

Bitter Harvest: A Woman's Fury, a Mother's Sacrifice. unabr. ed. Ann Rule. Read by Kate Reading. 1 CD. (Running Time: 1 hr. 12 mins.). 2001. audio compact disk Books on Tape.

Bitter Honey, Vol. 1-11. 10th rev. ed. Ed Young. 1986. 4.95 (978-0-7417-1567-8(8), 567) Win Walk.

Bitter Is the New Black: Confessions of a Condescending, Egomaniacal, Self-Centered Smartass, or, Why You Should Never Carry a Prada Bag to the Unemployment Office. unabr. ed. Jen Lancaster. 2009. audio compact disk 39.95 (978-1-4406-4107-7(2), PengAudBks) Penguin Grp USA.

Bitter Lemons of Cyprus. Lawrence Durrell. Read by Andrew Sachs. (Running Time: 3 hrs. 0 mins. 0 sec.). (ENG.). 2009. audio compact disk 22.95 (978-1-934997-50-5(1)) Pub: CSAWord. Dist(s): PerseuPGW

Bitter Medicine. Sara Paretsky. Read by Donada Peters. (V. I. Warshawski Novel Ser.). 1993. audio compact disk 56.00 (978-0-7366-7125-5(0)) Books on Tape.

Bitter Medicine. abr. ed. Sara Paretsky. Read by Sandra Burr. (Running Time: 6 hrs.). (V. I. Warshawski Ser.). 2006. 24.95 (978-1-4233-0011-3(4), 9781423300113, BAD) Brilliance Audio.

Bitter Medicine. abr. ed. Sara Paretsky. Read by Susan Ericksen & Sandra Burr. (Running Time: 6 hrs.). (V. I. Warshawski Ser.). 2010. audio compact disk 14.99 (978-1-4418-3826-1(0), 9781441838261, BCD Value Price) Brilliance Audio.

Bitter Medicine. unabr. ed. Sara Paretsky. (Running Time: 14 hrs.). (V. I. Warshawski Ser.). 2010. 39.97 (978-1-4418-3565-9(2), 9781441835659, BADLE); 24.99 (978-1-4418-3564-2(4), 9781441835642, BAD) Brilliance Audio.

Bitter Medicine. unabr. ed. Sara Paretsky. Read by Susan Ericksen. (Running Time: 10 hrs.). (V. I. Warshawski Ser.). 2010. 24.99 (978-1-4418-3562-8(8), 9781441835628, Brilliance MP3); 39.97 (978-1-4418-3563-5(6), 9781441835635, Brlnc Audio MP3 Lib); audio compact disk 89.97 (978-1-4418-3561-1(X), 9781441835611, BriAudCD Unabrid); audio compact disk 29.99 (978-1-4418-3560-4(1), 9781441835604, Bril Audio CD Unabri) Brilliance Audio.

Bitter Medicine. unabr. ed. Sara Paretsky. Read by Barbara Rosenblat. 7 cass. (Running Time: 9 hrs. 15 mins.). (V. I. Warshawski Novel Ser.). 2000. 58.00 (978-1-55690-695-4(1), 92428) Recorded Bks.
Private Eye V.I. Warshawski investigates the suspicious death of a young mother & her infant in the delivery room of a big Chicago hospital.

Bitter Medicine. unabr. collector's ed. Sara Paretsky. Read by Donada Peters. 6 cass. (Running Time: 9 hrs.). (V. I. Warshawski Novel Ser.). 1993. 48.00 (978-0-7366-2417-6(1), 3184) Books on Tape.
Mother & child's death in childbirth becomes a very personal investigation for V. I. Warshawski.

***Bitter Melon.** unabr. ed. Cara Chow. (Running Time: 8 hrs.). 2010. 19.99 (978-1-61106-070-6(2), 9781611060706, Brilliance MP3); 39.97 (978-1-61106-072-0(9), 9781611060720, BADLE); 39.97 (978-1-61106-071-3(0), 9781611060713, Brlnc Audio MP3 Lib); audio compact disk 19.99 (978-1-61106-068-3(0), 9781611060683, Bril Audio CD Unabri); audio compact disk 59.97 (978-1-61106-069-0(9), 9781611060690, BriAudCD Unabrid) Brilliance Audio.

Bitter Pleasure. 2nd ed. Excerpts. Lyrics by Sen Mett Obi. Music by Sen Mett Obi. Based on a novel by N. K. Ra. 1 CD. 2005. audio compact disk 10.00 (978-0-9765818-1-9(7)) Kheperaungkh Pr.
The CD contains dramatized excerpts of the stories in the book, Pain, Peace, & Pleasure, by Nefer Kheper Ra. It also contains song and spoken word.

Bitter Road to Freedom: The Human Cost of Allied Victory in World War II Europe. unabr. ed. William I. Hitchcock. Read by Mel Foster. (Running Time: 18 hrs. 0 mins. 0 sec.). (ENG.). 2008. audio compact disk 39.99 (978-1-4001-1047-6(5)); audio compact disk 29.99 (978-1-4001-6047-1(2)); audio compact disk 79.99 (978-1-4001-4047-3(1)) Pub: Tantor Media. Dist(s): IngramPubServ

Bitterness. Henry W. Wright. (ENG.). 2007. audio compact disk 34.95 (978-0-9786255-8-0(7)) Be in Hlth.

Bitterroot. James Lee Burke. Narrated by Tom Stechschulte. 11 CDs. (Running Time: 11 hrs. 45 mins.). (Billy Bob Holland Ser.). audio compact disk 97.00 (978-1-4025-2075-4(1)) Recorded Bks.

Bitterroot. James Lee Burke. (Billy Bob Holland Ser.). 2004. 15.95 (978-0-7435-4198-5(7)) Pub: S&S Audio. Dist(s): S and S Inc

Bitterroot. abr. ed. James Lee Burke. Read by Will Patton. (Running Time: 6 hrs. 0 mins. 0 sec.). (Billy Bob Holland Ser.). 2006. audio compact disk 14.95 (978-0-7435-5519-7(8), S&S Encore) Pub: S&S Audio. Dist(s): S and S Inc

Bitterroot. unabr. ed. James Lee Burke. Narrated by Tom Stechschulte. 9 cass. (Running Time: 11 hrs. 45 mins.). (Billy Bob Holland Ser.). 2001. 76.00 (978-0-7887-9471-1(X)) Recorded Bks.
Texas lawyer Billy Bob Holland is in Montana visiting an old friend when he is pulled into an investigation of a string of murders. At first, he seeks to protect his friend. But as the body count rises, Billy Bob begins to see evidence of a grisly vendetta - one that may be as explosive as the one that rocked Oklahoma City.

Bitterroot. unabr. ed. Richard F. Norquist. Read by Rusty Nelson. 8 cass. (Running Time: 9 hrs. 30 min.). 2001. 49.95 (978-1-55686-849-8(9)) Books in Motion.
The virus developed as a defensive weapon by the U.S. Disease Center has been released and is fatal at elevations under 4,000 ft. U.S. citizens attempt to reach the mountains before infection.

Bittersweet. Freddie Lee Johnson, III. 10 cass. (Running Time: 14 hrs. 15 mins.). 88.00 (978-1-4025-3399-0(3)) Recorded Bks.

Bittersweet. Perf. by Michael O'Brien. 1 cass. 1999. 7.98 (978-0-7601-2941-8(X)) Provident Music.

Bittersweet. unabr. ed. Nevada Barr. Narrated by Linda Stephens. 15 CDs. (Running Time: 16 hrs. 30 mins.). 2001. audio compact disk 142.00 (978-1-4025-0504-1(3), C1560) Recorded Bks.
When strong-willed schoolteacher Imogene Grelznik is forced from Philadelphia by scandal, the only position she can find is in rural Pennsylvania. There she meets Sarah, a beautiful young student whose bright light of potential is on the verge of being extinguished by her father's arrangement to marry her off to an abusive, unfeeling man. Branded as lovers, Imogene and Sarah must flee to Nevada amidst suspicion and accusation. In a place of utter desolation, the two women struggle to love and care for each other as they seek freedom from prejudice and intolerance.

Bittersweet. unabr. ed. Nevada Barr. Narrated by Linda Stephens. 12 cass. (Running Time: 16 hrs. 30 mins.). 2001. 98.00 (978-0-7887-5286-5(3), 96553x7) Recorded Bks.
Banded as lovers, strong-willed schoolteacher Imogene Grelznik & Sarah, her bright, beautiful student, must flee to Nevada amidst suspicion & accusation. In a place of utter desolation, the two women struggle to love & care for each other as they seek freedom from prejudice & intolerance.

Bittersweet. unabr. ed. Leslie Li. Narrated by Linda Stephens. 12 cass. (Running Time: 18 hrs. 45 mins.). 1999. 102.00 (978-0-7887-0326-3(9), 94518E7) Recorded Bks.
The 100-year odyssey of a headstrong peasant woman who rises from poverty & endures abandonment, patriarchy & revolution as the wife of the second most powerful man in China.

Bittersweet. unabr. ed. Danielle Steel. Read by Rob Webb. 8 cass. 1999. 39.95 (FS9-43353) Highsmith.

***Bittersweet: Thoughts on Change, Grace, & Learning the Hard Way.** Shauna Niequist. (Running Time: 5 hrs. 35 mins. 8 sec.). (ENG.). 2010. 16.99 (978-0-310-59886-2(9)) Zondervan.

Bittersweet Rain. Erin St. Claire, pseud. Read by Joyce Bean. (Playaway Adult Fiction Ser.). 2009. 60.00 (978-1-60775-514-2(9)) Find a World.

Bittersweet Rain. unabr. ed. Erin St. Claire, pseud. Read by Joyce Bean. (Running Time: 7 hrs.). 2004. 24.95 (978-1-59335-763-4(X), 159335763X, Brilliance MP3); 39.25 (978-1-59335-897-6(0), 1593358970, Brlnc Audio MP3 Lib); 29.95 (978-1-59355-896-3(1), 1593558961, BAU); 69.25 (978-1-59355-897-0(X), 159355897X, BrilAudUnabridg); audio compact disk 82.25 (978-1-59355-899-4(6), 1593558996, BriAudCD Unabrid) Brilliance Audio.
Caroline Dawson survived the town gossips who whispered behind her back. She survived the slow death of her husband, Roscoe Lancaster, the richest man in the county and her senior by three decades. But she feared she might not survive Rink Lancaster, her husband's son. Years before she married, when she and Rink were teens, he had introduced Caroline to her first tremulous taste of love - and then broke her heart. Now Rink is back. He says he wants to settle his father's estate. But driven by a storm of emotions as undeniable as before and more dangerous than ever, what he really wants is to settle the score with Caroline.

Bittersweet Rain. unabr. ed. Erin St. Claire, pseud. Read by Joyce Bean. (Running Time: 7 hrs.). 2004. 39.25 (978-1-59710-057-1(9), 1597100579, BADLE); 24.95 (978-1-59710-056-4(0), 1597100560, BAD) Brilliance Audio.

Bittersweet Rain. unabr. ed. Erin St. Claire, pseud. Read by Joyce Bean. (Running Time: 7 hrs.). 2007. audio compact disk 14.99 (978-1-4233-3349-4(7), 9781423333494, BCD Value Price) Brilliance Audio.

Bitty Fish. Created by Kane Press. (Let's Read Together Ser.). (J). 2005. audio compact disk 4.25 (978-1-57565-172-9(6)) Pub: Kane Pr. Dist(s): Lerner Pub

Biyur Hatefillah; Making Davening a Meaningful Communication. Moshe S. Juravel. 1 cass. (Running Time: 90 mins.). 1999. 6.00 (V60FK) Torah Umesorah.

Biz Plans Made Easy: A Capital Seeker's Step by Step Guide. Mervin L. Evans. 2 cass. (Running Time: 3 hr.). 2002. 29.99 (978-0-914391-49-4(6)) Comm People Pr.

Biz Talk One see Slangman Guide to Biz Speak 1: Slang, Idioms, & Jargon Used in Business English

Biz Talk Two see Slangman Guide to Biz Speak 2: Slang, Idioms, & Jargon Used in Business English

Bizarre Beliefs. Simon Hoggart & Mike Hutchinson. (ENG., 1995. 29.98 (978-1-57392-156-5(4)) Prometheus Bks.

Bizet's Dream - ShowTrax. 1 CD. (Running Time: 1 hr.). 2000. audio compact disk 12.95 (00841338) H Leonard.

Bktrax-Disc-Divine Revelation of Hell. Mary K. Baxter. 2 CDs. 2005. audio compact disk 17.99 (978-0-88368-949-3(9)) Whitaker Hse.

Bktrax-Disc-Divine Revelation of Hell. abr. ed. Mary K. Baxter. 2005. audio compact disk 12.99 (978-0-88368-948-6(0)) Whitaker Hse.

Blabber Mouth. unabr. ed. Read by Mary-Anne Fahey. 2 cass. (Running Time: 2 hrs. 10 mins.). (YA). 2003. 24.00 (978-1-74093-003-1(7)) Pub: Bolinda Pubng AUS. Dist(s): Bolinda Pub Inc

Blabber Mouth. unabr. ed. Read by Mary-Anne Fahey. 2 CDs. (Running Time: 2 hrs. 10 mins.). (YA). 2003. audio compact disk 43.95 (978-1-74093-113-7(0)) Pub: Bolinda Pubng AUS. Dist(s): Bolinda Pub Inc

***Black.** unabr. ed. D. J. MacHale. (Running Time: 11 hrs.). (Morpheus Road Ser.). 2011. 39.97 (978-1-4233-9783-0(5), 9781423397830, Brlnc Audio MP3 Lib); 39.97 (978-1-4233-9785-4(1), 9781423397854, BADLE); 24.99 (978-1-4233-9782-3(7), 9781423397823, Brilliance MP3); 24.99 (978-1-4233-9784-7(3), 9781423397847, BAD); audio compact disk 69.97 (978-1-4233-9781-6(9), 9781423397816, BriAudCD Unabrid); audio compact disk 29.99 (978-1-4233-9780-9(0), 9781423397809, Bril Audio CD Unabri) Brilliance Audio.

Black. unabr. ed. Christopher Whitcomb. Narrated by L. J. Ganser. 12 CDs. (Running Time: 13 hrs. 45 mins.). 2004. audio compact disk 34.99 (978-1-4025-8039-0(8), 01582) Recorded Bks.
Special Agent Jeremy Waller has been chosen for the FBI's elite Hostage Rescue Team. The assignment is a thrill, but Agent Waller's own sense of right and wrong soon clashes with the world of danger and corruption surrounding him. Mixing with wealthy tycoons, ambitious politicians, ruthless killers, and Wall Street wizards, Waller is headed straight into the darkness-where secrets must be kept at all costs, and not everybody survives.

Black: The Birth of Evil. Ted Dekker. Read by Rob Lamont. 8 cass. (Running Time: 12 hrs.). (Books of History Chronicles: Bk. 1). 2004. 32.99 (978-1-58926-568-4(8)) Oasis Audio.

Black: The Birth of Evil. unabr. ed. Ted Dekker. Read by Lamont Rob. 8 cass. (Running Time: 14 hrs.). (Books of History Chronicles: Bk. 1). 2004. 56.95 (978-0-7861-2755-9(4), 3288); audio compact disk 96.00 (978-0-7861-8634-1(8), 3288) Blckstn Audio.
Fleeing assailants through alleyways in Denver late one night, Thomas Hunter narrowly escapes to the roof of an industrial building. Then a silent bullet from the night clips his head and his world goes black. Now Thomas wakes from a deep sleep, remembering the vivid dream he just had of being chased. It was incredibly real. His head is even bleeding, but he?s fallen on a rock. He?s in a green forest, waiting to meet Rachelle, the woman he?s falling madly in love with.

Black: The Birth of Evil. unabr. ed. Ted Dekker. Narrated by Rob Lamont. 12 CDs. (Running Time: 12 hrs. 54 mins. 0 sec.). (Books of History Chronicles: Bk. 1). (ENG.). (YA). 2004. audio compact disk 35.99 (978-1-58926-570-7(X), Oasis Kids) Oasis Audio.

Black: The Birth of Evil. unabr. ed. Ted Dekker. Narrated by Rob Lamont. (Books of History Chronicles: Bk. 1). (ENG.). (YA). 2004. 17.49 (978-1-60814-084-8(9)) Oasis Audio.

Black Abolitionists. unabr. collector's ed. Benjamin Quarles. Read by Jonathan Reese. 7 cass. (Running Time: 10 hrs. 30 min.). 1996. 56.00 (978-0-7366-3313-0(8), 3965) Books on Tape.
Scores of blacks worked boldly to abolish slavery, many of them pioneers in the movement.

Black Adder. Created by Broadcasting Corp. British. (Running Time: 3 hrs. 0 mins. 0 sec.). (ENG.). 2009. audio compact disk 29.95 (978-1-60283-745-4(7)) Pub: AudioGO. Dist(s): Perseus Dist

Black Ajax. unabr. ed. George MacDonald Fraser. Read by David Case. 7 cass. (Running Time: 10 hrs. 30 mins.). 56.00 (978-0-7366-4546-1(2), 4950) Books on Tape.
Story of a black man from the United States who nearly became England's champion boxer during the early 19th century. Based on the true story of Tom Molineaux, a former slave who won his freedom in a boxing match, then traveled to England & refined his skills & almost became the first black champ. The story is told by over a dozen witnesses to Molineaux's bouts with the reigning champion, Tom Cribb. Molineaux's trainer recalls the fighter's awe-inspiring strength & speed. A butler who asks to remain

anonymous divulges information about the fighter's love affair with an English noblewoman.

Black Ajax. unabr. ed. George MacDonald Fraser. Read by Stephen Thorne. 8 cass. (Running Time: 9 hrs. 30 min.). (Isis Cassettes Ser.). 1998. 69.95 (978-0-7531-0344-9(3), 980407) Pub: ISIS Audio GBR. Dist(s): Ulverscroft US
When Captain Buck Flashman sees the black boxer catch a fly in mid-flight, he realizes that he if in the presence of speed such as the prize ring has never seen. Tom Molineaux may be crude & untutored, but "Mad Buck" who, like his son Harry Flashman, has an unerring eye for the main chance, sees this ex-slave from America as a champion in the making. Under his patronage, "Black Ajax" is shaped into the wonder of the Fancy & toast of the town, hailed by the Prince of Wales, dressed by Beau Brummell, & pursued by the ladies. As a natural celebrity, simple Tom Molineaux if carried towards his great dream; to fight the invincible, undefeated Champion of England, the great Tom Cribb.

Black Ajax. unabr. ed. George MacDonald Fraser. Read by Stephen Thorne. 9 CDs. (Running Time: 13 hrs. 30 min.). (Isis (CDs) Ser.). 2001. audio compact disk 89.95 (978-0-7531-1240-3(X), 1240-X) Pub: ISIS Audio GBR. Dist(s): Ulverscroft US
When Captain Buck Flashman sees the black boxer catch a fly in mid-flight, he realizes that he is in the presence of speed such as the prize ring has never seen. Tom Molineaux may be crude & untutored, but "Mad Buck" who, like his son Harry Flashman has an unerring eye for the main chance, sees this ex-slave from America as a champion in the making. Under his patronage, "Black Ajax" is shaped into the wonder of the Fancy & toast of the town, hailed by the Prince of Wales, dressed by Beau Brummell, & pursued by the ladies. As a natural celebrity, simple Tom Molineaux is carried towards his great dream; to fight the invincible, undefeated Champion of England, the great Tom Cribb.

Black Alley, unabr. ed. Mickey Spillane. Narrated by Richard Ferrone. 6 cass. (Running Time: 8 hrs.). (Mike Hammer Ser.). 1996. 51.00 (978-0-7887-0729-2(9), 94906E7) Recorded Bks.
Mike Hammer, the legendary tough-as-mails private detective, is walking a tightrope between crime & justice in this gritty romp through New York's underworld.

Black America Speaks. unabr. ed. Vinnie Burrows et al. Perf. by Langston Hughes et al. 6 cass. (Running Time: 9 hrs.). 1986. 55.00 set. (978-0-8045-0023-4(1), PCC 23) Spoken Arts.
Includes "Walk Together Children," a dramatic performance by Burrows describing the Black experience from plantation days to modern Harlem; "The Dream Awake," the epic poem by Dodson; Martin Luther King's "I Have a Dream" speech.

Black American History Rap & Rhyme. Read by Frieda Carrol. 1 cass. (Running Time: 8 min.). (J). (gr. 4-12). 1989. 11.95 (37 SOR 600CT) Sell Out Recordings.
Presents a poetry reading with a beat on black history. Music, arts, sports, inventors, political and other contributors are covered.

Black American Inventors - A Rhyme. Poet's Workshop Staff. Read by Poet's Workshop Staff. 1 cass. (Running Time: 21 min.). (J). (gr. 4-12). 8.95 Sell Out Recordings.
An overview of some of the many black inventors.

Black American Inventors - A Rhyme. Poet's Workshop Staff. 1 cass. (Running Time: 40 min.). 1992. 11.95 (37SOR303CT) Sell Out Recordings.
A poem that is an overview of Black American inventors.

Black & Blue. unabr. ed. Ian Rankin. Read by Stuart Langton. 10 cass. (Running Time: 15 hrs.). 1998. 80.00 (978-0-7366-4176-0(9), 4675) Books on Tape.
Scotland's Inspector John Rebus is back, investigating the murder of an offshore oilman & the savagery of two serial killers, decades apart.

Black & Blue: A Novel. Anna Quindlen. Read by Kimberly Schraf. 7 cass. (Running Time: 10 hrs. 30 min.). 1999. 29.95 (978-0-7366-4685-7(X)) Books on Tape.
At 19, Fran Benedetto fell in love with Bobby. Their passionate marriage became a nightmare. Although she stayed too long, she finally ran away with her son & started a new life under a new name, always fearing that Bobby would find her. An Oprah Book Club selection.

Black & Blue: A Novel. Anna Quindlen. Read by Kimberly Schraf. 8 cass. (Running Time: 600 min.). 2000. audio compact disk (978-0-7366-4759-5(7)) Books on Tape.

Black & Blue: A Novel. abr. ed. Anna Quindlen. Read by Lili Taylor. 4 cass. 1999. 24.00 (FS9-34516) Highsmith.

Black & Blue: A Novel. collector's ed. Anna Quindlen. Read by Kimberly Scharf. 8 cass. (Running Time: 8 hrs.). 2000. 64.00 (978-0-7366-5140-0(3)) Books on Tape.

Black & Blue: A Novel. unabr. ed. Anna Quindlen. Narrated by Ruth Ann Phimister. 9 CDs. (Running Time: 9 hrs. 45 mins.). 1999. audio compact disk 75.00 (978-0-7887-3713-8(9), C1070E7) Recorded Bks.
Fran Benedetto is running for her life with her ten-year-old son in tow. Living in Florida under an assumed name, she is bravely shaping a new life & trying to escape her painful past.

Black & Blue: A Novel. unabr. ed. Anna Quindlen. Narrated by Ruth Ann Phimister. 7 cass. (Running Time: 9 hrs. 45 mins.). 1998. 60.00 (978-0-7887-2130-4(5), 95440E7) Recorded Bks.

Black & Blue: A Novel. unabr. collector's ed. Anna Quindlen. Read by Kimberly Schraf. 7 cass. (Running Time: 10 hrs. 30 min.). 1998. 56.00 (978-0-7366-4159-3(9), 4662) Books on Tape.
At 19, Fran Benedetto fell in love with Bobby. Their passionate marriage became a nightmare. Although she stayed too long, she finally ran away with her son & started a new life under a new name, always fearing that Bobby would find her. An Oprah Book Club selection.

Black & Tan AudioBook: Essays & Excursions on Slavery, Culture War, & Scripture in America. Douglas Wilson. Read by Aaron Wells. (ENG.). 2007. audio compact disk 20.00 (978-1-59128-357-7(4)) Canon Pr ID.

Black & White. Dan Mahoney. Read by Adams Morgan. 11 cass. (Running Time: 16 hrs.). 2000. 76.95 (978-0-7861-1806-9(7), 2605) Blckstn Audio.
When two NYPD officers find the mutilated body of a woman & the corpse of her male companion, they have no idea that their discovery will provoke a media frenzy. The woman is the daughter of a powerful New York politician & the man is not her husband.

Black & White. unabr. ed. Dani Shapiro. Read by Marguerite Gavin. (Running Time: 8 hrs. 30 mins. 0 sec.). (ENG.). 2007. audio compact disk 34.99 (978-1-4001-0440-6(8)); audio compact disk 69.99 (978-1-4001-3440-3(4)); audio compact disk 24.99 (978-1-4001-5440-1(5)) Pub: Tantor Media. Dist(s): IngramPubServ

***Black & White: A Detective Brian Mckenna Novel.** unabr. ed. Dan Mahoney. Read by Adams Morgan. (Running Time: 16 hrs.). 2010. 29.95 (978-1-4417-4108-0(9)); audio compact disk 118.00 (978-1-4417-4105-9(4)) Blckstn Audio.

Black & White & Dead All Over. unabr. ed. John Darnton. Read by Phil Gigante. (Running Time: 12 hrs.). 2008. 39.25 (978-1-4233-6289-0(6), 9781423362890, Brinc Audio MP3 Lib); 24.95 (978-1-4233-6288-3(8), 9781423362883, Brilliance MP3); 39.25 (978-1-4233-6291-3(8), 9781423362913, BADLE); 24.95 (978-1-4233-6290-6(X), 9781423362906, BAD); audio compact disk 38.95 (978-1-4233-6286-9(1), 9781423362869, Bril Audio CD Unabri); audio compact disk 102.25 (978-1-4233-6287-6(X), 9781423362876, BriAudCD Unabrid) Brilliance Audio.

Black & White VII. Perf. by Danny Wright. 1 cass., 1 CD. 7.98 (NIW 984); audio compact disk 12.78 CD Jewel box. (NIW 984) NewSound.

Black Angels. unabr. ed. Rita Murphy. Narrated by Julia Gibson. 3 pieces. (Running Time: 4 hrs.). (gr. 4 up). 2001. 28.00 (978-0-7887-8972-4(4)) Recorded Bks.
Eleven-year-old Celli lives on the white side of Mystic Georgia. In the summer of 1961, she's wishing the civil rights movement would just go away. Then the Freedom Riders arrive, and Celli meets someone who will change her life forever. The comforting presence of angels adds a gentle touch to this tale set in one of American history's most difficult times.

Black Arrow. Robert Louis Stevenson. Narrated by Flo Gibson. (YA). 2004. 24.95 (978-1-55685-752-2(7)) Audio Bk Con.

Black Arrow. Robert Louis Stevenson. Read by Shelly Frasier. (Running Time: 6 hrs.). 2001. 25.95 (978-1-60083-576-6(7), Audiofy Corp) Iofy Corp.

Black Arrow. Robert Louis Stevenson. Read by Shelly Frasier. (ENG.). 2005. audio compact disk 78.00 (978-1-4001-3003-0(4)) Pub: Tantor Media. Dist(s): IngramPubServ

Black Arrow. Robert Louis Stevenson. Narrated by Flo Gibson. 2008. audio compact disk 29.95 (978-1-60646-038-2(2)) Audio Bk Con.

Black Arrow. unabr. ed. Robert Louis Stevenson. Narrated by Ron Keith. 7 cass. (Running Time: 9 hrs.). (YA). (gr. 7 up). 2003. 61.00 (978-1-4025-6353-9(1)) Recorded Bks.
In a time of shifting loyalties and trecherous alliances, young Dick Shelton is betrayed by his brutal guardian. Intent on rescuing the woman he loves, Dick joins forces with a mysterious fellowship intent on dispensing their own brand of justice.

Black Arrow. unabr. ed. Robert Louis Stevenson. Narrated by Shelly Frasier. 7 CDs. (Running Time: 8 hrs. 3 mins.). (ENG.). 2001. audio compact disk 39.00 (978-1-4001-0003-3(8)) Pub: Tantor Media. Dist(s): IngramPubServ

Black Arrow. unabr. ed. Robert Louis Stevenson. Read by Shelly Frasier. (Running Time: 8 hrs. 0 mins. 0 sec.). (ENG.). 2008. 19.99 (978-1-4001-5914-7(8)); audio compact disk 55.99 (978-1-4001-3914-9(7)) Pub: Tantor Media. Dist(s): IngramPubServ

Black Arrow. unabr. ed. Robert Louis Stevenson. Read by Shelly Frasier. (Running Time: 8 hrs. 0 mins. 0 sec.). (ENG.). 2008. audio compact disk 27.99 (978-1-4001-0914-2(0)) Pub: Tantor Media. Dist(s): IngramPubServ

Black Art see Inner Sanctum

Black As He's Painted. Ngaio Marsh. Narrated by Nadia May. (Running Time: 8 hrs. 30 mins.). 2000. 27.95 (978-1-59912-434-6(3)) Iofy Corp.

Black As He's Painted. unabr. ed. Ngaio Marsh. Read by Nadia May. 6 cass. (Running Time: 8 hrs. 30 mins.). 2001. 44.95 (978-0-7861-2048-2(7), 2808); audio compact disk 56.00 (978-0-7861-9704-0(8), 2808) Blckstn Audio.
When the President of Ng'ombwana proposes to dispense with the usual security arrangements on an official visit to London, his old school mate, Chief Superintendent Alleyn, is called in to try to persuade him otherwise.

Black Attitude. 10.00 Esstee Audios.

Black Banjo Songsters of North Carolina & Virginia. Anno. by Cece Conway. Prod. by Cece Conway & Scott O'Dell. Prod. by Scott O'Dell. 1 CD. (Running Time: 1 hr. 4 mins.). 1998. audio compact disk Smithsonian Folkways.
The sounds & social history of African American banjo playing - 32 instrumentals & vocals, recorded between 1974 & 1997. Extensively annotated with performers' life histories, tunings, lyrics, bibliography, discography.

Black Bear Cub. Alan Lind. 1 cass. (Running Time: 35 min.). (J). (gr. k-4). 2001. 16.95 (SP 3020C) Kimbo Educ.
Black Bear & his sister rise from their winter slumber to thrive & grow. Includes read along book.

Black Beauty. Anna Sewell. Narrated by Flo Gibson. (ENG.). (J). 2007. audio compact disk 24.95 (978-1-55685-906-9(6)) Audio Bk Con.

Black Beauty. Anna Sewell. Narrated by Kate Redding. (Running Time: 18720 sec.). (Unabridged Classics in MP3 Ser.). (ENG.). (J). 2008. audio compact disk 24.00 (978-1-58472-506-0(0), In Aud) Sound Room.

Black Beauty. Retold by Noe Venable. Anna Sewell. (Classic Adventures Ser.). 2000. audio compact disk 18.95 (978-1-4105-0151-6(5)) D Johnston Inc.

Black Beauty. adpt. ed. Anna Sewell. (Bring the Classics to Life: Level 2 Ser.). (gr. 4-7). 2008. audio compact disk 12.95 (978-1-55576-455-5(X)) EDCON Pubng.

Black Beauty. unabr. ed. Anna Sewell. Read by Kate Redding. (J). 2006. 49.99 (978-1-59895-164-6(5)) Find a World.

Black Beauty. unabr. ed. Anna Sewell. Narrated by Simon Vance. (Running Time: 6 hrs. 0 mins. 0 sec.). (ENG.). (J). (gr. 4-7). 2008. audio compact disk 22.99 (978-1-4001-0861-9(6)); audio compact disk 19.99 (978-1-4001-5861-4(3)); audio compact disk 45.99 (978-1-4001-3861-6(2)) Pub: Tantor Media. Dist(s): IngramPubServ

Black Beauty, Set. unabr. ed. Anna Sewell. Read by Flo Gibson. 4 cass. (Running Time: 6 hrs.). (J). 1984. 19.95 (978-1-55685-046-2(8)) Audio Bk Con.
Black Beauty, a spirited thoroughbred horse, tells of his adventures under a series of different masters from a fine gentleman to a drunken groom. His life is filled with a succession of cruel misfortunes until the day his luck suddenly changes.

***Black Beauty: Bring the Classics to Life.** adpt. ed. Anna Sewell. (Bring the Classics to Life Ser.). 2008. pap. bk. 21.95 (978-1-55576-492-0(4)) EDCON Pubng.

Black Beauty: The Autobiography of a Horse. Anna Sewell. Ed. by Jerry Sewell. Retold by Noe Venable. Narrated by Wendy Morgan. 2000. audio compact disk 200.00 (978-1-58702-506-8(X)) D Johnston Inc.

Black Beauty: The Autobiography of a Horse. Anna Sewell. Read by Nigel Lambert. 4 cass. (Running Time: 6 hrs.). (YA). 2001. 44.95 (93052) Pub: ISIS Audio GBR. Dist(s): Ulverscroft US

Black Beauty: The Autobiography of a Horse. Anna Sewell. Read by Kate Redding. (Running Time: 5 hrs. 15 mins.). 2002. 20.95 (978-1-59912-044-7(5), Audiofy Corp) Iofy Corp.

Black Beauty: The Autobiography of a Horse. Anna Sewell. Read by Jonathan Keeble. (Running Time: 2 hrs. 15 mins.). 2002. 20.95 (978-1-60083-686-2(0)) Iofy Corp.

Black Beauty: The Autobiography of a Horse. Anna Sewell. Read by Ben Fogle. (Running Time: 2 hrs. 30 mins.). (J). 2004. 25.95 (978-1-59912-951-8(5)) Iofy Corp.

Black Beauty: The Autobiography of a Horse. Anna Sewell. Read by Simon Vance. (Running Time: 6 hrs.). 2005. 25.95 (978-1-60083-585-8(6), Audiofy Corp) Iofy Corp.

Black Beauty: The Autobiography of a Horse. Anna Sewell. Narrated by Frances Sternhagen. (Running Time: 2 hrs.). 2006. 14.95 (978-1-59912-978-5(7)) Iofy Corp.

Black Beauty: The Autobiography of a Horse. Anna Sewell. Read by John Chatty. 4 cass. (Running Time: 5 hrs. 30 min.). (J). 1989. 28.00 incl. album. (C-64) Jimcin Record.
Autobiography of a horse.

Black Beauty: The Autobiography of a Horse. Anna Sewell. 2 CDs. (Running Time: 2 hrs. 30 mins.). (J). 2004. audio compact disk 17.99 (978-1-58926-640-7(4), Oasis Kids) Oasis Audio.

Black Beauty: The Autobiography of a Horse. Anna Sewell. Narrated by Simon Vance. (Running Time: 21600 sec.). (Unabridged Classics in Audio Ser.). (ENG.). (J). (gr. 4-7). 2005. audio compact disk 49.99 (978-1-4001-3012-2(3)) Pub: Tantor Media. Dist(s): IngramPubServ

Black Beauty: (the Autobiography of a Horse) Anna Sewell. Abr. by Crawford Wesson. (ENG.). 2007. 5.99 (978-1-60339-173-3(8)); audio compact disk 5.99 (978-1-60339-174-0(6)) Listenr Digest.

Black Beauty: The Autobiography of a Horse. abr. ed. Anna Sewell. Read by Jonathan Keeble. 2 CDs. (Running Time: 2 hrs. 15 mins.). (J). 1998. audio compact disk 17.98 (978-962-634-165-0(3), NA216512, Naxos AudioBooks) Naxos.
A thoroughbred horse's adventures of life, cruel misfortunes and ultimate triumph.

Black Beauty: The Autobiography of a Horse. abr. ed. Anna Sewell. Read by Jonathan Keeble. 2 cass. (Running Time: 2 hrs. 15 mins.). (J). 1998. 13.98 (978-962-634-665-5(5), NA216514, Naxos AudioBooks) Naxos.
Black Beauty learns to accept the saddle and bridle and the rule of her masters. But a succession of misfortunes shows that the life of a horse can be harsh and painful.

Black Beauty: The Autobiography of a Horse. unabr. ed. Anna Sewell. Read by Jean DeBarbieris. 5 CDs. (Running Time: 5 hrs. 30 min.). 2001. audio compact disk 32.50 (978-1-58116-160-1(3)) Books in Motion.
A beautiful black horse becomes part of the ever-changing circumstances of its various owners, sometimes tragically, sometimes happily.

Black Beauty: The Autobiography of a Horse. unabr. ed. Anna Sewell. Read by Jean DeBarbieris. 4 cass. (Running Time: 5 hrs. 30 mins.). (J). 1982. 26.95 (978-1-55686-134-5(6), 592122) Books in Motion.
After a careless accident scars him, a colt is sold again & again, enduring many hardships in his search for a happy home. At the last moment he is saved from the knacker by the intervention to two kindly ladies who purchase him.

Black Beauty: The Autobiography of a Horse. unabr. ed. Anna Sewell. Read by Nigel Lambert. 4 cass. (Running Time: 6 hrs.). (Isis Ser.). (J). (gr. 4 up). 1993. 44.95 (978-1-85695-584-3(2), 93052) Pub: ISIS Lrg Prnt GBR. Dist(s): Ulverscroft US

Black Beauty: The Autobiography of a Horse. unabr. ed. Anna Sewell. Read by Hayley Mills. 2 cass. (Read-Along Ser.). (J). 34.95 Incl. read-along bk., learner's guide & exercises. (S23920) J Norton Pubs.

Black Beauty: The Autobiography of a Horse, unabr. ed. Anna Sewell. Narrated by Flo Gibson. 4 cass. (Running Time: 6 hrs.). (gr. 5). 1999. 36.00 (978-1-55690-055-6(4), 82014E7) Recorded Bks.
The story of a great-hearted horse & the travails it endures to find a happy home.

Black Beauty: The Autobiography of a Horse. unabr. ed. Anna Sewell. Read by Eric Synnestvedt. 5 cds. (Running Time: 5 hrs 14 mins). (J). 2002. audio compact disk 29.95 (978-1-58472-215-1(0), 069, In Aud) Pub: Sound Room. Dist(s): Baker Taylor
A sentimental story of a beautiful thoroughbred horse abused by its owners is also a story of courage and love. One of the great children's classics.

Black Beauty: The Autobiography of a Horse. unabr. ed. Anna Sewell. Read by Eric Synnestvedt. 1 cd. (Running Time: 5 hrs 14 mins). (J). 2002. audio compact disk 18.95 (978-1-58472-382-0(3), In Aud) Pub: Sound Room. Dist(s): Baker Taylor
MP3 format.

Black Beauty: The Autobiography of a Horse. unabr. ed. Anna Sewell. Read by John Chatty. 4 cass. (Running Time: 5 hrs. 30 mins.). (gr. 6-8). 1982. 32.95 (978-0-7861-0595-3(X), 2084) Blckstn Audio.
The noble & gallant colt Black Beauty tells his own heartwarming tale of unyielding courage. He is scarred in a careless accident by his owner, a young squire, & is exiled to the life of a London cab horse until two kindly ladies purchase him & ease his misery.

Black Beauty: The Autobiography of a Horse. unabr. collector's ed. Anna Sewell. Read by Donada Peters. 6 cass. (Running Time: 6 hrs.). (Jimcin Recording Ser.). (J). 1993. 36.00 (978-0-7366-2559-3(3), 3310) Books on Tape.
The classic story of the life of a horse, from which many movies have been made.

Black Beauty: The Autobiography of a Horse, Pt. I. abr. ed. Anna Sewell. Composed by Christopher Casson Company. (Running Time: 48 min.). Dramatization. (J). 10.95 (978-0-8045-1111-7(X), SAC 1111) Spoken Arts.

Black Beauty: The Autobiography of a Horse, Vol. 4. Anna Sewell. Ed. by Jerry Stemach et al. Retold by Noe Venable. Illus. by Jeff Ham. Narrated by Wendy Morgan. Contrib. by Ted S. Hasselbring. (Start-to-Finish Books). (J). (gr. 2-3). 2000. 35.00 (978-1-58702-507-5(8)) D Johnston Inc.

Black Beauty: The Autobiography of a Horse, Vol. 4. unabr. ed. Anna Sewell. Ed. by Jerry Stemach et al. Retold by Noe Venable. Illus. by Jeff Ham. Narrated by Wendy Morgan. Contrib. by Ted S. Hasselbring. 1 cass. (Running Time: 1 hr.). (Start-to-Finish Books). (J). (gr. 2-3). 2000. (978-1-58702-300-2(8), F24K2) D Johnston Inc.
Told from the perspective of a horse, illustrates the many ways horses were mistreated in nineteenth century England. Handsome and well-bred, Black Beauty's first position is pulling a carriage at a fancy estate. This means having to wear a bearing rein, a fashionable contraption that holds the horses heads up so unnaturally high that many horses are only good for a few years of work before their backs give out. Black Beauty is ultimately ruined by a drunk driver which condemns Beauty to forms of work father and father.

Black Beauty Read Along: The Autobiography of a Horse. Prod. by Saddleback Educational Publishing. (Saddleback's Illustrated Classics Ser.). (YA). 2005. audio compact disk Rental 24.95 (978-1-56254-887-2(5)) Saddleback Edu.

Black Belt Patriotism: How to Reawaken America. unabr. ed. Chuck Norris. Narrated by Alan Sklar. (Running Time: 6 hrs. 30 mins. 0 sec.). (ENG.). 2008. audio compact disk 29.99 (978-1-4001-0840-4(3)); audio compact disk 59.99 (978-1-4001-3840-1(X)); audio compact disk 19.99 (978-1-4001-5840-9(0)) Pub: Tantor Media. Dist(s): IngramPubServ

Black Betty. unabr. ed. Walter Mosley. Read by Stanley Bennett Clay. 7 cass. (Running Time: 10 hrs. 30 min.). (Easy Rawlins Mystery Ser.). 1994. 56.00 (978-0-7366-2853-2(3), 3561) Books on Tape.
Easy Rawlins follows a trail of chaos & mayhem left by a Beverly Hills beauty known as Black Betty.

Black Book: An Inspector Rebus Novel. unabr. ed. Ian Rankin. Read by Bill Paterson. 8 cass. (Running Time: 12 hrs.). 1995. 59.95 (978-0-7451-6514-1(1), CAB 1130) Pub: Chivers Audio Bks GBR. Dist(s): AudioGO
When a close colleague is brutally attacked, Inspector Rebus is drawn into a case involving a hotel fire, an unidentified body & a long forgotten murder. Rebus must piece together a bizarre puzzle even if it means stepping so far outside the law that there may be no way back.

***Black Book of Secrets.** unabr. ed. F. E. Higgins. Narrated by James Daniel Wilson. 1 Playaway. (Running Time: 6 hrs. 45 mins.). (YA). (gr. 5-8). 2009. 59.75 (978-1-4407-3120-4(9)); 51.75 (978-1-4407-3110-5(1)); audio compact disk 66.75 (978-1-4407-3114-3(4)) Recorded Bks.

***Black Book of Secrets.** unabr. collector's ed. F. E. Higgins. Narrated by James Daniel Wilson. 6 CDs. (Running Time: 6 hrs. 45 mins.). (YA). (gr. 5-8). 2009. audio compact disk 41.95 (978-1-4407-3118-1(7)) Recorded Bks.

***Black Box.** unabr. ed. Julie Schumacher. Read by Lynde Houck. 4 CDs. (Running Time: 3 hrs. 54 mins.). (YA). (gr. 7 up). 2009. audio compact disk 38.00 (978-0-7393-8595-1(X), Listening Lib) Pub: Random Audio Pubg. Dist(s): Random

Black Box. unabr. ed. Julie Schumacher. Read by Lynde Houck. (ENG.). (J). (gr. 7). 2009. audio compact disk 28.00 (978-0-7393-8593-7(3), Listening Lib) Pub: Random Audio Pubg. Dist(s): Random

Black Box: All-New Cockpit Voice Recorder Accounts of In-Flight Accidents. Malcolm MacPherson. Read by Michael Prichard. 2000. audio compact disk 56.00 (978-0-7366-8054-7(3)) Books on Tape.

Black Box: All-New Cockpit Voice Recorder Accounts of In-Flight Accidents. collector's ed. Malcolm MacPherson. Read by Michael Prichard. 6 cass. (Running Time: 9 hrs.). 2000. 48.00 (978-0-7366-5469-2(0), 5340) Books on Tape.
Recording the final moments of any in-flight accident, the "black box" often provides the only explanation of a crash. Inevitably, it provides a heart-breaking, second by second account of intense fear tempered on occasion by remarkable professionalism.

Black Boy. unabr. ed. Richard Wright. Read by Peter Francis James. 8 CDs. (Running Time: 12 hrs.). 2005. audio compact disk 39.95 (978-0-06-076352-7(3)) HarperCollins Pubs.

Black Boy. unabr. ed. Richard Wright. Narrated by Peter Francis James. 15 CDs. (Running Time: 15 hrs. 30 mins.). 1999. audio compact disk 119.00 (978-0-7887-3709-1(0), C1065E7) Recorded Bks.
Richard Wright tells of his coming-of-age in the Jim Crow South & he creates unforgettable pictures of what it meant to be young & black in America.

Black Boy. unabr. ed. Richard Wright. Narrated by Peter Francis James. 11 cass. (Running Time: 15 hrs. 30 mins.). 1998. 96.00 (978-0-7887-2164-9(X), 95460E7) Recorded Bks.
Tells of his coming-of-age in the Jim Crow South & he creates unforgettable pictures of what it meant to be young & black in America.

Black British Literature: Novels of Transformation. Mark Stein. 2004. audio compact disk 9.95 (978-0-8142-9058-3(2)) Pub: Ohio St U Pr. Dist(s): Chicago Distribution Ctr

Black Bull of Norroway see Childe Rowland & Other British Fairy Tales

Black Cabs. unabr. ed. John McLaren. Narrated by Gordon Griffin. 11 cass. (Running Time: 15 hrs.). 2000. 98.00 (978-1-84197-123-0(5), H1120E7) Recorded Bks.
For merchant bankers, success means secrecy; passwords & code names ensure conversations stay private. However, they reckoned without London cabbies Terry, Len & "Einstein," who know the rewards of keeping their ears pricked & their noses in The FT.

Black Cameo. unabr. ed. Donna Baker. Read by Nicolette McKenzie. 12 cass. (Running Time: 18 hrs.). 2001. 94.95 (978-1-84283-092-5(9)) Pub: Soundings Ltd GBR. Dist(s): Ulverscroft US
The people of Stourbridge have long since grown accustomed to the ways of Christina Compson, the beautiful woman who has been so successful in her running of Henzel's glassworks. But the mistakes of her past life come to overshadow the lives of Christina's and Joe's children. The two eldest, Emily and Paul, raised as brother and sister, were drawn together by the stigma that illegitimacy could bring and, as adults, only Paul's love of glass could have parted them.

Black Cat see Invisible Man & Selected Short Stories of Edgar Allan Poe

Black Cat see Tales of Terror

Black Cat see Selected American Short Stories

Black Cat see Raven & Other Works

Black Cat see Best of Edgar Allan Poe

Black Cat see Edgar Allan Poe, Set, Short Stories and Poems

Black Cat see Tales of Horror & Suspense

Black Cat see Masque of the Red Death

Black Cat see Mind of Poe

Black Cat. Christopher Myers. Narrated by Avery Brooks. 1 cass. (Running Time: 15 min.). (J). 2001. bk. (978-0-8045-6863-0(4), 6863) Spoken Arts.
Through pulsating city streets, "black cat" dances to the banging beats and ultimately shows readers what it means to find a place of their own.

Black Cat. unabr. ed. Martha Grimes. Contrib. by John Lee. 7 CDs. (Running Time: 9 hrs.). (ENG.). 2010. audio compact disk 29.95 (978-0-14-242796-5(9), PengAudBks) Penguin Grp USA.

***Black Cat.** unabr. ed. Martha Grimes. Read by John Lee. 7 CDs. 2010. audio compact disk 80.00 (978-0-307-71565-4(5), BksonTape) Pub: Random Audio Pubg. Dist(s): Random

Black Cat: A Mystery in the Air Radio Presentation. Edgar Allan Poe. Perf. by Peter Lorre. 1943. (MM-5760) Natl Recrd Co.

Black Cat & Other Stories. unabr. ed. Short Stories. Edgar Allan Poe. Read by Gene Engene. 4 cass. (Running Time: 5 hrs. 30 mins.). Dramatization. 1990. 26.95 (978-1-55686-094-2(3), 592073) Books in Motion.
This collection of favorite stories from the master of suspense & horror includes: "The Pit & the Pendulum," "The Cask of Amontillado," "The Purloined Letter," "The Tell-Tale Heart," "The Murders in the Rue Morgue," "The Fall of the House of Usher" & more.

Black Cat & the Pit & the Pendulum. unabr. ed. Edgar Allan Poe. 1 cass. (Running Time: 1 hr.). 1993. 7.95 (978-1-882071-01-2(8), 002) B-B Audio.
A double dose of dark in these two stories of horror deep and black. Terror, murder, vengeance and more from the masters bloody hand.

Black Cat Black Dog. John Creed. Read by Sean Barrett. 7 cass. (Running Time: 8 hrs. 50 mins.). (Isis Cassettes Ser.). 2006. 61.95 (978-0-7531-3636-2(8)) Pub: ISIS Lrg Prnt GBR. Dist(s): Ulverscroft US

Black Cat Black Dog. John Creed. Read by Sean Barrett. (Running Time: 31800 sec.). (Isis (CDs) Ser.). 2006. audio compact disk 79.95 (978-0-7531-2614-1(1)) Pub: ISIS Lrg Prnt GBR. Dist(s): Ulverscroft US

Black Cauldron. Lloyd Alexander. Read by James Langton. 4 vols. (Running Time: 5 hrs. 30 mins.). (Chronicles of Prydain Ser.: Bk. 2). (J). (gr. 4-7). 2004. pap. bk. 38.00 (978-1-4000-8636-8(1), Listening Lib); 29.75 (978-0-8072-2317-8(4), Listening Lib) Pub: Random Audio Pubg. Dist(s): NetLibrary CO

Black Cauldron. unabr. ed. Lloyd Alexander. Read by James Langton. (Running Time: 19560 sec.). (Chronicles of Prydain Ser.). (ENG.). (J). (gr. 5-7). 2008. audio compact disk 30.00 (978-0-7393-6354-6(9), Listening Lib) Pub: Random Audio Pubg. Dist(s): Random

Black Cherry Blues. James Lee Burke. (Dave Robicheaux Ser.). 2004. 10.95 (978-0-7435-4199-2(5)) Pub: S&S Audio. Dist(s): S and S Inc

Black Cherry Blues. unabr. ed. James Lee Burke. Narrated by Mark Hammer. 9 cass. (Running Time: 12 hrs. 30 mins.). (Dave Robicheaux Ser.). 2000. 78.00 (978-1-55690-791-3(5), 93106E7) Recorded Bks.
Cajun private eye David Robicheaux tackles a case for his old friend, singer Dixie Lee Pugh, that takes him from bayou honkytonks all the way to Wyoming on the trail of a pair of vicious murderers.

Black Cherry Blues, Set. abr. ed. James Lee Burke. Read by Will Patton. 2 cass. (Running Time: 3 hrs.). (Dave Robicheaux Ser.). 1998. 9.98 (978-0-671-58255-5(0), 390401, Audioworks) S&S Audio.
Haunted by the memory of his wife's murder & his father's death, ex-cop Dave Robicheaux spends his days in a fish-&-tackle business. When an old friend makes a surprise appearance however, Dave's life is thrust back into the violent world.

Black Christ see Poetry of Countee Cullen

Black Circle. unabr. ed. Patrick Carman. Narrated by David Pittu. 4 CDs. (Running Time: 4 hrs.). (39 Clues Ser.). (ENG.). (J). (gr. 3-7). 2009. audio compact disk 49.95 (978-0-545-16086-5(3)) Scholastic Inc.

Black Circle, No. 5. Patrick Carman. Narrated by David Pittu. (39 Clues Ser.: Bk. 5). (ENG.). (J). (gr. 3-7). 2009. audio compact disk 19.95 (978-0-545-16024-7(3)) Scholastic Inc.

Black Coffee. Agatha Christie. Read by David Suchet. Adapted by Charles Osborne. 4 cass. (Running Time: 6 hrs.). 1998. 24.35 Set. (978-0-00-105536-0(4)) Ulvrscrft Audio.
Sir Claude Amory has discovered the formula for a new powerful explosive, which is stolen by one of the large household of relatives and friends.

Black Coffee. unabr. ed. Agatha Christie. Read by Alexandra Thomas. Adapted by Charles Osborne. 4 cass. (Running Time: 6 hrs.). (Hercule Poirot Mystery Ser.). 1998. 24.95 (978-1-55935-281-9(7), 696051) Soundelux.
In the spring of 1934, Poirot is summoned by England's prominent physicist, Sir Claude Amory, who fears that someone in his household is attempting to steal his latest formula. Poirot & Hastings arrive to find that Amory has died, the formula is missing & the house is full of relatives & guests, all suspects.

Black Creek. unabr. ed. Johnny Quarles. Read by Michael Waugh. 4 cass. (Running Time: 6 hrs.). 1998. Rental 24.95 (978-1-890990-15-2(9)) Otis Audio.
An unforgettable story of James Corbin, a World War II Congressional Medal of Honor soldier suffering from post-traumatic stress disorder due to a night in hell in North Africa & his family's struggles in the West Virginia coal mines.

Black Creek Crossing. unabr. ed. John Saul. Read by Dick Hill. 6 cass. (Running Time: 10 hrs.). 2004. 82.25 (978-1-59086-917-8(6), 1590869176, BrilAudUnabridg); 32.95 (978-1-59086-916-1(8), 1590869168, BAU); audio compact disk 36.95 (978-1-59086-918-5(4), 1590869184, Bril Audio CD Unabri); audio compact disk 97.25 (978-1-59086-919-2(2), 1590869192, BriAudCD Unabrid) Brilliance Audio.
Thirteen-year-old Angel Sullivan falls in love with her family's new home - the house that stands at Black Creek Crossing in the small town of Roundtree, Massachusetts. But the idyll is soon shattered as Angel learns a shocking secret about the house. It seems that a double murder took place there, and no one has lived at Black Creek Crossing since. As Angel and her family begin to confront the mounting perils in their new dwelling, increasingly bizarre events occur in Roundtree: terrible storms strike; seemingly inexplicable "accidents" transpire; and rumors of witchcraft, a phenomenon that figured in the town's history hundreds of years earlier, begin to resurface.

Black Creek Crossing. unabr. ed. John Saul. Read by Dick Hill. (Running Time: 10 hrs.). 2004. 39.25 (978-1-59335-541-8(6), 1593355416, Brinc Audio MP3 Lib); 24.95 (978-1-59335-280-6(8), 1593352808, Brilliance MP3) Brilliance Audio.

Black Creek Crossing. unabr. ed. John Saul. Read by Dick Hill. (Running Time: 10 hrs.). 2004. 39.25 (978-1-59710-058-8(7), 1597100587, BADLE); 24.95 (978-1-59710-059-5(5), 1597100595, BAD) Brilliance Audio.

Black Cross. abr. ed. Greg Iles. Narrated by Jay O. Sanders. 4 cass. Library ed. (Running Time: 6 hrs.). 2002. 62.25 (978-1-59086-122-6(1), 1590861221, Lib Edit) Brilliance Audio.
It is January 1944. The whole world awaits the Allied invasion of Europe. But in England, Winston Churchill has learned that Nazi scientists have developed Sarin - a horrifying new weapon that could turn the tide for Hitler. Only a desperate gamble can avert disaster. Two men - a pacifist American doctor and a fanatical Jewish assassin - must embark on a murderous mission into the heart of Germany. Their target: a human hell where Jews fuel Hitler's last hope for victory. Their only allies: a young Jewish widow fighting to save her children and a German nurse who is the image of Aryan perfection. Their orders: destroy the threat no matter how many lives are lost, including their own.

Black Cross. abr. ed. Greg Iles. Read by Jay O. Sanders. (Running Time: 6 hrs.). 2007. audio compact disk 14.99 (978-1-4233-3182-7(6), 9781423331827, BCD Value Price) Brilliance Audio.

Black Cross. unabr. ed. Greg Iles. Read by Dick Hill. (Running Time: 19 hrs.). 2009. 24.99 (978-1-4418-1142-4(7), 9781441811424, Brilliance MP3); 24.99 (978-1-4418-1144-8(3), 9781441811448, BAD); 39.97 (978-1-4418-1143-1(5), 9781441811431, Brinc Audio MP3 Lib); 39.97 (978-1-4418-1145-5(1), 9781441811455, BADLE); audio compact disk 29.99 (978-1-4418-1140-0(0), 9781441811400, Bril Audio CD Unabri); audio compact disk 69.97 (978-1-4418-1141-7(9), 9781441811417, BriAudCD Unabrid) Brilliance Audio.

Black Dahlia. unabr. collector's ed. James Ellroy. Read by Wolfram Kandinsky. 11 cass. (Running Time: 16 hrs. 30 min.). (L. A. Quartet). 1990. 88.00 (978-0-7366-1816-8(3), 2652) Books on Tape.
On January 15, 1947, the tortured body of a beautiful young woman was found in a vacant lot in Hollywood. Elizabeth Short, the Black Dahlia, a young Hollywood hopeful, had been brutally murdered. Her murder sparked one of the greatest manhunts in California history. In this fictionalized treatment of a real case, Bucky Bleichert & Lee Blanchard, both LA cops obsessed with the Black Dahlia, journey through the steamy underside of Hollywood to the core of the dead girl's twisted life.

Black Dawn. unabr. ed. L. J. Smith. Read by Teri Clark Linden. (Running Time: 7 hrs.). (Night World Ser.: Vol. 8). 2010. 39.97 (978-1-4418-2076-1(0), 9781441820761, Brinc Audio MP3 Lib); 19.99 (978-1-4418-2075-4(2), 9781441820754, Brilliance MP3); 39.97 (978-1-4418-2078-5(7), 9781441820785, BADLE); 19.99 (978-1-4418-2077-8(9), 9781441820778, BAD); audio compact disk 59.97 (978-1-4418-2074-7(4), 9781441820747, BriAudCD Unabrid); audio compact disk 19.99 (978-1-4418-2073-0(6), 9781441820730, Bril Audio CD Unabri) Brilliance Audio.

Black Death: A Story of the Plague. Alan Venable. (Step into History Ser.). 2006. pap. bk. 69.00 (978-1-4105-0723-5(8)); audio compact disk 18.95 (978-1-4105-0721-1(1)) D Johnston Inc.

Black Diamonds. rev. abr. ed. John B. Holway. Ed. by Donald V. Allen. 1 cass. 1992. bk. 15.95 (978-1-56703-009-9(2), 0010) High-Top Sports.
Sports.

Black Diamonds: An Oral History of Negro Baseball. Stephen Banker. Interview with Satchel Paige et al. 3 cass. (Running Time: 2 hrs. 30 min.). 1992. 49.95 set. (BD) TFR.
"Black Diamonds" is a series of interviews with some of the best players from the Negro Leagues - before baseball was integrated. The players describe the fun, the excitement & the frustration of those times, on & off the field.

Black Dog Opera Library, Set. Composed by Wolfgang Amadeus Mozart et al. 2005. audio compact disk 99.75 (978-1-57912-514-1(X), 157912514X) Pub: Blck Dog & Leventhal. Dist(s): Workman Pub

Black Dove. Steve Hockensmith. Read by William Dufris. (Playaway Adult Fiction Ser.). (ENG.). 2009. 65.00 (978-1-60775-619-4(6)) Find a World.

Black Dove. unabr. ed. Steve Hockensmith. Read by William Dufris. 9 CDs. (Running Time: 10 hrs. 30 mins. 0 sec.). (Holmes on the Range Ser.). (ENG.). 2008. audio compact disk 34.99 (978-1-4001-0605-9(2)); audio compact disk 24.99 (978-1-4001-5605-4(X)); audio compact disk 69.99 (978-1-4001-3605-6(9)) Pub: Tantor Media. Dist(s): IngramPubServ

Black Duck. unabr. ed. Janet Taylor Lisle. Read by David Ackroyd. 5 CDs. (Running Time: 5 hrs. 30 mins.). (YA). (gr. 7-10). 2007. audio compact disk 45.00 (978-0-7393-4875-8(2), Random AudioBks) Pub: Random Audio Pubg. Dist(s): Random

Black Duck. unabr. ed. Janet Taylor Lisle. Read by David Ackroyd. (Running Time: 19800 sec.). (ENG.). (J). (gr. 5-7). 2007. audio compact disk 35.00 (978-0-7393-4882-6(5), Listening Lib) Pub: Random Audio Pubg. Dist(s): Random

Black Eagles. unabr. collector's ed. Larry Collins. Read by Michael Kramer. 11 cass. (Running Time: 16 hrs. 30 min.). 1996. 88.00 (978-0-7366-3314-7(6), 3966) Books on Tape.
Kevin Grady, DEA agent, & Jack Lind, CIA officer, both work for the United States government. But their efforts are anything but united in this political thriller that's a step from reality.

Black Echo. abr. ed. Michael Connelly. Read by Dick Hill. (Running Time: 6 hrs.). (Harry Bosch Ser.: No. 1). 2005. audio compact disk 16.99 (978-1-59600-096-4(1), 9781596000964, BCD Value Price); audio compact disk 74.25 (978-1-59600-097-1(X), 9781596000971, BACDLib Ed) Brilliance Audio.
For LAPD homicide cop Harry Bosch - hero, maverick, nighthawk - the body in the drainpipe at Mulholland Dam is more than another anonymous statistic. This one is personal. The dead man, Billy Meadows, was a fellow Vietnam "tunnel rat" who fought side by side with him in a nightmare underground war that brought them to the depths of hell. Now, Bosch is about to relive the horror of Nam. From a dangerous maze of blind alleys to a daring criminal heist beneath the city to the torturous link that must be uncovered, his survival instincts will once again be tested to their limit. Joining with an enigmatic and seductive female FBI agent, pitted against enemies inside his own department, Bosch must make the agonizing choice between justice and vengeance, as he tracks down a killer whose true face will shock him.

Black Echo. unabr. ed. Michael Connelly. Read by Dick Hill. (Running Time: 14 hrs.). (Harry Bosch Ser.: No. 1). 2003. 29.95 (978-1-59355-417-0(6), 1593554176, Bkcassette) Brilliance Audio.

Black Echo. unabr. ed. Michael Connelly. Read by Dick Hill. 12 CDs. (Running Time: 14 hrs.). (Harry Bosch Ser.: No. 1). 2004. 39.25 (978-1-59335-630-9(7), 1593356307, Brinc Audio MP3 Lib) Brilliance Audio.

Black Echo. unabr. ed. Michael Connelly. Read by Dick Hill. (Running Time: 14 hrs.). (Harry Bosch Ser.: No. 1). 2004. 39.25 (978-1-59710-061-8(7), 1597100617, BADLE); 24.95 (978-1-59710-060-1(9), 1597100609, BAD) Brilliance Audio.

Black Echo. unabr. ed. Michael Connelly. Read by Dick Hill. (Running Time: 50400 sec.). (Harry Bosch Ser.: No. 1). 2006. audio compact disk 112.25 (978-1-4233-2326-6(2), 9781423323266, BriAudCD Unabrid); audio compact disk 38.95 (978-1-4233-2325-9(4), 9781423323259, Bril Audio CD Unabri) Brilliance Audio.

Black Echo. unabr. ed. Michael Connelly. Read by Lloyd Battista. 12 cass. (Running Time: 18 hrs.). (Harry Bosch Ser.: No. 1). 2000. Rental 13.50 (GKT 046) Chivers Audio Bks GBR.
LAPD homicide detective Hieronymous Bosch has been shaped by hard choices, solitude, and time in Vietnam. A routine drug overdose takes him to Mulholland Dam where he finds Billy Meadows, a fellow "tunnel rat," dead. But when the trail of evidence links Meadows' death to a major theft via a tunnel beneath the bank, Bosch faces a tide of betrayal and must make a decision: justice or vengeance.

Black Echo. unabr. ed. Michael Connelly. Read by Dick Hill. (Running Time: 14 hrs.). (Harry Bosch Ser.: No. 1). 2004. 24.95 (978-1-59335-254-7(9), 1593352549) Soulmate Audio Bks.
For LAPD homicide cop Harry Bosch - hero, maverick, nighthawk - the body in the drainpipe at Mulholland Dam is more than another anonymous statistic. This one is personal. The dead man, Billy Meadows, was a fellow Vietnam "tunnel rat" who fought side by side with him in a nightmare underground war that brought them to the depths of hell. Now, Bosch is about to relive the horror of Nam. From a dangerous maze of blind alleys to a daring criminal heist beneath the city to the torturous link that must be uncovered, his survival instincts will once again be tested to their limit. Joining with an enigmatic and seductive female FBI agent, pitted against enemies inside his own department, Bosch must make the agonizing choice between justice and vengeance, as he tracks down a killer whose true face will shock him.

Black Economics: Solutions for Economic & Community Empowerment. Jawanza Kunjufu. 1 cass. (Running Time: 60 mins.). 1999. 5.95 (AT21) African Am Imag.
How can we keep more of our 500 billion dollars in the Black community? Why do African Americans prefer to maintain a "good job" over operating their own businesses? Why are foreigners "getting over" in the African American community? Why is it important to build an economic base before building a political base?.

Black Elderly. 1 cass. (Running Time: 30 min.). 9.95 (I0750B090, HarperThor) HarpC GBR.

Black Elk: The Gift of the Sacred Pipe. abr. ed. Joseph E. Brown. Read by Fred Contreras. 2 cass. (Running Time: 2 hrs.). (Native America Ser.). 1993. 15.95 (978-0-944993-66-8(4)) Audio Lit.
Oglala Sioux religious ceremonies, told in the words of the great Indian visionary Black Elk.

Black Elk: The Sacred Pipe. abr. ed. Joseph E. Brown. Read by Fred Contreras. Music by Chemo Candelaria. 2 cass. (Running Time: 3 hrs.). (Provincetown Poets Ser.). 1995. 16.95 (978-0-944993-13-2(3)) Audio Lit.
Black Elk, a famous warrior & medicine man of the Oglala Sioux, describes the sacred rites that lie at the heart of Native American religious life.

Black Elk Speaks. abr. ed. John G. Neihardt. Read by Fred Contreras. 2 cass. (Running Time: 3 hrs.). 1999. reel tape 16.95 (978-0-944993-36-1(2)) Audio Lit.
Black Elk, Oglala visionary & medicine man, is recognized as on of the most authentic religous leaders of the American Indian spiritual tradition. This account of his life is now more vital than ever to our understanding of mankind's sacred role in nature.

Black English, Chocolate Grammar: English Too? Sell Out Recordings Staff. 1 cass. 1988. 9.95 Prosperity & Profits.

Black English, Chocolate Grammar or English Too?!! Poet's Workshop Staff. (J). (gr. 8-12). 1991. 12.95 (37SOR510) Sell Out Recordings.
Poetry on black slang.

Black Expatriates. Interview with James Baldwin et al. 1 cass. (Running Time: 30 min.). 9.95 (G0590B090, HarperThor) HarpC GBR.

***Black-Eyed Susan.** unabr. ed. Laura Lippman. Read by Linda Emond & Francois Battiste. (ENG.). 2008. (978-0-06-176324-3(1), Harper Audio); (978-0-06-176292-5(X), Harper Audio) HarperCollins Pubs.

Black-Eyed Susan: A Story of Hope for Children & Families. Demetra Bakas. Illus. by Cheryl Powell. 1 cass. (Running Time: 90 min.). (J). (gr. 1-8). 2000. 3.95 (978-1-929208-00-5(6), Happy Tales) Creation of Celeb.

Black-Eyed Susan Set: A Story of Hope for Children & Families. Demetra Bakas. Illus. by Cheryl Powell. (J). (gr. 1-8). 2000. pap. bk. 9.95 (978-1-929208-04-3(9), Happy Tales) Creation of Celeb.

Black Fairy Tales. abr. ed. Perf. by Claudia McNeil. Ed. by Terry Berger. 1 cass. Incl. Fairy Frog. (J). (CDL5 1425); Moss-Green Princess. (J). (CDL5 1425); Serpent's Bride. (J). (CDL5 1425); (J). 1984. 9.95 (978-0-89845-533-5(2), CDL5 1425) HarperCollins Pubs.
These tales were gathered from the Bantu-speaking tribes of South Africa before white settlers came. They are tales of the Swazis & Shangani, resplendent with customs & lore.

Black Falcon. unabr. collector's ed. Armstrong Sperry. Read by Paul Shay. 6 cass. (Running Time: 6 hrs.). (J). 1988. 36.00 (978-0-7366-1393-4(5), 2282) Books on Tape.
British warships & pirates made the waters off New Orleans a dangerous proposition during the War of 1812. Yet for 16-year-old Thayer & his father, running the blockade of Cuba had to be done.

Black Flower. Howard Bahr & Brian Emerson. 8 cass. (Running Time: 11 hrs. 30 mins.). 2002. 56.95 (978-0-7861-1497-9(5), 2348) Blckstn Audio.

Black Flower. unabr. ed. Howard Bahr. Read by Brian Emerson. 8 cass. (Running Time: 12 hrs.). 1999. 56.95 (2348) Blckstn Audio.
Story not only of war, but of men & women seeking redemption, who are stripped of all that anchors them, & who at last turn to honor & courage & love.

Black Flower. unabr. ed. Howard Bahr. (Running Time: 37800 sec.). 2007. audio compact disk 29.95 (978-0-7861-5968-0(5)); audio compact disk 72.00 (978-0-7861-5967-3(7)) Blckstn Audio.

Black Flower Bus Leaves at Dawn: Sects, Drugs & Rock 'N' Roll. Keith Rodway & Chrome Dreams Staff. Read by Robert Reina. (ENG.). 2000. audio compact disk 15.95 (978-1-84240-077-7(0)) Pub: Chrome Dreams GBR. Dist(s): IPG Chicago

Black Friday. abr. ed. Alex Kava. Read by Tanya Eby. (Running Time: 5 hrs.). (Maggie O'Dell Ser.: Bk. 7). 2009. audio compact disk 24.99 (978-1-59600-912-7(8), 9781596009127, BACD) Brilliance Audio.

Black Friday. abr. ed. Alex Kava. Read by Tanya Eby. (Running Time: 5 hrs.). (Maggie O'Dell Ser.: Bk. 7). 2010. audio compact disk 14.99 (978-1-59600-914-1(4), 9781596009141, BCD Value Price) Brilliance Audio.

Black Friday. abr. ed. James Patterson. Read by Stephen Lang. (ENG.). 2005. 14.98 (978-1-59483-468-4(7)) Pub: Hachet Audio. Dist(s): HachBkGrp

Black Friday. unabr. ed. Alex Kava. Read by Tanya Eby. (Running Time: 8 hrs.). (Maggie O'Dell Ser.: Bk. 7). 2009. audio compact disk 97.97 (978-1-59600-913-4(6), 9781596009134, BACDLib Ed) Brilliance Audio.
Please enter a Synopsis.

Black Friday. unabr. ed. Alex Kava. Read by Tanya Eby. (Running Time: 8 hrs.). (Maggie O'Dell Ser.: Bk. 7). 2009. 39.97 (978-1-59600-916-5(0), 9781596009165, Brinc Audio MP3 Lib); 24.99 (978-1-59600-915-8(2), 9781596009158, Brilliance MP3); 39.97 (978-1-59600-918-9(7), 9781596009189, BADLE); 24.99 (978-1-59600-917-2(9), 9781596009172, BAD); audio compact disk 29.99 (978-1-4233-4446-9(4), 9781423344469, Bril Audio CD Unabri) Brilliance Audio.

Black Friday. unabr. ed. James Patterson. Read by Peter Jay Fernandez. (ENG.). 2005. 16.98 (978-1-59483-467-7(9)) Pub: Hachet Audio. Dist(s): HachBkGrp

Black Friday: The Great Crash. 1 cass. 10.00 Esstee Audios.
The horrible day in 1929 when the nation trembled.

Black Genesis. abr. ed. L. Ron Hubbard. 2 cass. (Running Time: 3 hrs). (Mission Earth Ser.: Vol. 2). 2002. 15.95 (978-1-59212-058-1(X)) Gala Pr LLC.
Jettero Heller (the Royal Officer of the Fleet selected to carry out Mission Earth) and Soltan Gris (the agent sent on a deadly countermission) both travel 22 1/2 light-years to a secret Earth base, where they embark on their powerfully conflicting mission assignments (unbeknownst to Heller).

Black Genesis: Fortress of Evil. L. Ron Hubbard. 2 cass. (Running Time: 3 hrs.). (Mission Earth Ser.: No. 2). 2001. 19.95 (LRON002) Lodestone Catalog.

Black Genesis Set: Fortress of Evil. L. Ron Hubbard. 2 cass. (Running Time: 3 hrs.). Dramatization. (Mission Earth Dekalogy Ser.: Vol. 2). 1994. 19.95 (978-0-88404-686-8(9), LRON002) Bridge Pubns Inc.

Black Girl in Paris. unabr. ed. Shay Youngblood. Narrated by Robin Miles. 5 cass. (Running Time: 7 hrs. 30 mins.). 2001. 43.00 (978-0-7887-5123-3(9), F0010E7) Recorded Bks.
Eden decides that to become a writer she must live a writer's life. Arriving in Paris with $140, she sets out to follow in the footsteps of all the great artists who have come before her.

Black Girl, White Girl. unabr. ed. Patricia Moyes. Read by Donada Peters. 6 cass. (Running Time: 6 hrs.). (Henry Tibbett Mystery Ser.). 1993. 36.00 (978-0-7366-2327-8(2), 3107) Books on Tape.
Amid the deceptive calm of a lush tropic resort Henry & Emmy Tibbett find cocaine trafficking & danger.

Black Girl/White Girl: A Novel. unabr. ed. Joyce Carol Oates. Narrated by Anna Fields. 6 cass. (Running Time: 32040 sec.). 2006. 59.95 (978-0-7927-4539-6(6), CSL 1043); audio compact disk 79.95 (978-0-7927-4513-6(2), SLD 1043) AudioGO.

Black Girl/White Girl: A Novel. unabr. ed. Joyce Carol Oates. Read by Anna Fields. (YA). 2007. 69.99 (978-1-60252-876-5(4)) Find a World.

Black Gospel Explosion, Vol. 2. Perf. by Thomas Whitfield et al. 1 cass. audio compact disk 15.99 CD. (D2027) Diamante Music Grp.

Black Gospel Explosion, Vol. 3. Perf. by Clay Evans et al. 1 CD. 1997. audio compact disk 14.99 (D2042) Diamante Music Grp.

Black Hand: The Bloody Rise & Redemption of Boxer Enriquez, a Mexican Mob Killer. unabr. ed. Chris Blatchford. Narrated by Paul Boehmer. (Running Time: 14 hrs. 0 mins. 0 sec.). (ENG.). 2008. audio compact disk 39.99 (978-1-4001-1048-3(3)); audio compact disk 29.99 (978-1-4001-6048-8(0)) Pub: Tantor Media. Dist(s): IngramPubServ

Black Hand: The Bloody Rise & Redemption of Boxer Enriquez, a Mexican Mob Killer. unabr. ed. Chris Blatchford. Read by Paul Boehmer. Narrated by Paul Boehmer. (Running Time: 14 hrs. 0 mins. 0 sec.). (ENG.). 2008. audio compact disk 79.99 (978-1-4001-4048-0(X)) Pub: Tantor Media. Dist(s): IngramPubServ

Black Hawk Down. Mark Bowden. Read by Joe Morton. 2004. 15.95 (978-0-7435-4203-6(7)) Pub: S&S Audio. Dist(s): S and S Inc

Black Hawk Down: A Story of Modern War. unabr. ed. Mark Bowden. Read by Alan Sklar. 2 CDs. (Running Time: 10 hrs.). 2002. audio compact disk 49.95 (978-0-7927-2661-6(8), CMP 434, Chivers Sound Lib) AudioGO.

Black Heat. Norman Kelley. Narrated by Myra Lucretia Taylor. 9 CDs. (Running Time: 9 hrs. 45 mins.). 2004. audio compact disk 89.00 (978-1-4025-2095-2(6)) Recorded Bks.
explores the seamy side of post-civil rights power politics among America¿s black elite. Civil rights leader Malik Martin stood the middle ground between Dr. Martin Luther King, Jr. and Malcolm X. In 1971, as his organization was set to launch a new program offering unity and economic empowerment, he was assassinated. Twenty years later, when private eye Nina Halligan is hired to search for Martin¿s missing daughter, she suddenly finds herself shadowed by thugs and the NYPD.

Black Heat. unabr. ed. Norman Kelley. Narrated by Myra Lucretia Taylor. 7 cass. (Running Time: 9 hrs. 45 mins.). 1997. 64.00 (978-0-7887-5258-2(8), F0028L8) Recorded Bks.
Civil rights leader Malik Martin stood the middle ground between Dr. Martin Luther King Jr. & Malcolm X. As he prepared to launch a new program offering unity & economic empowerment, he was assassinated.

Black Hills. abr. ed. Nora Roberts. Read by Nick Podehl. (Running Time: 6 hrs.). 2009. audio compact disk 24.99 (978-1-4233-9949-0(8), 9781423399490, BACD) Brilliance Audio.

Black Hills. abr. ed. Nora Roberts. Read by Nick Podehl. (Running Time: 6 hrs.). 2010. audio compact disk 14.99 (978-1-4233-8344-4(3), 9781423383444, BCD Value Price) Brilliance Audio.

Black Hills. unabr. ed. Nora Roberts. (Running Time: 14 hrs.). 2009. 39.97 (978-1-4233-8343-7(5), 9781423383437, BADLE) Brilliance Audio.

Black Hills. unabr. ed. Nora Roberts. Read by Nick Podehl. (Running Time: 14 hrs.). 2009. 39.97 (978-1-4233-8341-3(9), 9781423383413, Brinc Audio MP3 Lib); 24.99 (978-1-4233-8340-6(0), 9781423383406, Brilliance MP3); 24.99 (978-1-4233-8342-0(7), 9781423383420, BAD); audio compact disk 38.99 (978-1-4233-8338-3(9), 9781423383383, Bril Audio CD Unabri); audio compact disk 99.97 (978-1-4233-8339-0(7), 9781423383390, BriAudCD Unabrid) Brilliance Audio.

***Black Hills.** unabr. ed. Dan Simmons. Narrated by Erik Davies & Michael McConnohie. 2 MP3-CDs. (Running Time: 21 hrs. 40 mins.). 2010. 79.99 (978-1-60788-452-1(6)); audio compact disk 129.99 (978-1-60788-346-3(5)) Pub: Hachet Audio. Dist(s): HachBkGrp

Black Hills. unabr. ed. Dan Simmons. Read by Erik Davies & Michael McConnohie. (Running Time: 21 hrs.). (ENG.). 2010. 26.98 (978-1-60024-787-3(3)); audio compact disk 39.98 (978-1-60024-786-6(5)) Pub: Hachet Audio. Dist(s): HachBkGrp

***Black Hills: A Novel.** unabr. ed. Dan Simmons. Read by Erik Davies & Michael McConnohie. (Running Time: 21 hrs.). (ENG.). 2011. audio compact disk 19.98 (978-1-60788-691-4(X)) Pub: Hachet Audio. Dist(s): HachBkGrp

Black History. Read by Eldridge Cleaver. 1 cass. (Running Time: 1 hr.). 10.95 (VW-79-02-04, HarperThor) HarpC GBR.

Black History from God's Perspective. Luther Blackwell. 8 cass. 1992. 65.00 Set. (978-1-56043-999-8(8)) Destiny Image Pubs.

Black History Heroes, Vols. 1 & 2. P. Hilton Taylor & Prince Zaire. Read by P. Hilton Taylor & Prince Zaire. 2 cass. (Running Time: 60 min.). 1991. pap. bk. 15.99 Set. (978-0-9638528-5-4(X)); 7.99 (978-0-9638528-1-6(7)) Brainpower Pubng.
For the time period of 1619 through 1974, these audiocassettes provide highlights of important events & dates related to African-American history, as well as brief biographical profiles of black history heroes.

Black Hole in the Memory. Instructed by Manly P. Hall. 8.95 (978-0-89314-017-5(1), C840318) Philos Res.

Black Hole of Silence. Swami Amar Jyoti. 2 cass. 1982. 12.95 (O-21) Truth Consciousness.
Inherent, latent & full joy in Silence. The seeker as scientist; getting behind the hologram of creation.

Black Hole War: My Battle with Stephen Hawking to Make the World Safe for Quantum Mechanics. unabr. ed. Leonard Susskind. Read by Ray Porter. (Running Time: 13 hrs.). 2008. cass. & cass. 19.95 (978-1-4332-4367-7(9)); cass. & audio compact disk 29.95 (978-1-4332-4368-4(7)) Blckstn Audio.

Black Hole War: My Battle with Stephen Hawking to Make the World Safe for Quantum Mechanics. unabr. ed. Leonard Susskind & Ray Porter. (Running Time: 13 hrs.). 2008. 29.95 (978-1-4332-4369-1(5)); 79.95 (978-1-4332-4365-3(2)); audio compact disk 99.00 (978-1-4332-4366-0(0)) Blckstn Audio.

Black Holes & Baby Universes & Other Essays. unabr. ed. Stephen W. Hawking. Read by Connor O'Brien. 6 cass. (Running Time: 6 hrs.). 1996. 36.00 (978-0-7366-3456-4(8), 4100) Books on Tape.
In this follow-up to a Brief History of Time, this presents 13 essays which reveal more amazing possibilities about the universe. Free from jargon & full of humor, Hawking discusses imaginary time, how black holes spawn baby universes & how scientists continue searching for a complete, unified theory that would predict everything in the cosmos. He also reflects on life & death, how science fiction stacks up to science & how ALS (Lou Gehrig's disease) has affected, but not constrained, he personal 7 intellectual life.

Black Hornet: A Lew Griffin Mystery. unabr. ed. James Sallis. Read by G. Valmont Thomas. (Running Time: 5 hrs. NaN mins.). 2008. 29.95 (978-1-4332-3009-7(7)); audio compact disk 50.00 (978-1-4332-3006-6(2)); audio compact disk 34.95 (978-1-4332-3005-9(4)) Blckstn Audio.

Black Horse Odyssey: Search for the Lost City of Rome in China. unabr. ed. David Harris. Read by Peter Hosking. 6 cass. (Running Time: 9 hrs.). 2004. 48.00 (978-1-74030-549-5(3)) Pub: Bolinda Pubng AUS. Dist(s): Lndmrk Audiobks

Black House. unabr. ed. Stephen King & Peter Straub. 21 CDs. (Running Time: 22 hrs. 30mins.). 2003. audio compact disk 168.00 (978-0-7366-9399-8(8)) Books on Tape.
Jack Sawyer, the 13-year-old hero of The Talisman, has grown up, worked as a police detective in Los Angeles, and retired at age 35 to French Landing, WI. There he gets caught up in a series of bizarre events that reawaken his memories and initiate new experiences in a parallel universe called the "Territories." Part murder mystery and part mythic end-of-the-world struggle.

Black House. unabr. ed. Stephen King & Peter Straub. Read by Frank Muller. 15 cass. (Running Time: 23 hrs.). 2001. 54.98 (Random AudioBks) Random Audio Pubg.
Twenty years ago, Jack Sawyer traveled to a parallel universe called the Territories to save his mother & her Territories "twinner" from an agonizing death that would have brought cataclysm to the other world. Jack, now a retired Los Angeles homicide detective living in Tamarack, Wisconsin, has no recollection of his adventures in the Territories. When a series of gruesome murders occur in western Wisconsin, the killer is dubbed "The Fisherman" & the local chief of police begs Jack to help his inexperienced force find him.

Black House. unabr. ed. Paul Theroux. Read by Michael Prichard. 6 cass. (Running Time: 9 hrs.). 1985. 48.00 (978-0-7366-0923-4(7), 1866) Books on Tape.
The Mundays have taken their failing marriage to the solace of a quaint old country house to try & restore themselves. Then a strange, beautiful apparition enters their life. A deliciously cruel reign of terror begins, a fatal triangle with more than natural consequences.

Black Ice. Robin Brown. 2001. 15.95 (978-0-660-18324-4(2)) Pub: Canadian Broadcasting CAN. Dist(s): Georgetown Term

***Black Ice.** Michael Connelly. 2010. audio compact disk 9.99 (978-1-4418-5696-8(X)) Brilliance Audio.

Black Ice. abr. ed. Michael Connelly. Read by Dick Hill. (Running Time: 6 hrs.). (Harry Bosch Ser.: No. 2). 2005. audio compact disk 74.25 (978-1-59600-099-5(6), 9781596000995, BACDLib Ed); audio compact disk 16.99 (978-1-59600-098-8(8), 9781596000988, BCD Value Price) Brilliance Audio.
Narcotics officer Cal Moore's orders were to look into the city's latest drug killing. Instead, he ends up in a motel room with his head in several pieces and a suicide note stuffed in his back pocket. Years ago, Harry Bosch learned the first rule of the good cop: don't look for the facts, but the glue that holds them together. Now, Harry's making some very dangerous connections, starting with one dead cop and leading to a bloody string of murders that winds from Hollywood Boulevard's drug bazaar to the dusty back alleys south of the border and into the center of a complex and lethal game - one in which Harry is the next and likeliest victim.

Black Ice. unabr. ed. Michael Connelly. Read by Dick Hill. (Running Time: 11 hrs.). (Harry Bosch Ser.: No. 2). 2003. 29.95 (978-1-59355-416-3(8), 1593554168, BAU) Brilliance Audio.

Black Ice. unabr. ed. Michael Connelly. Read by Dick Hill. (Running Time: 39600 sec.). (Harry Bosch Ser.: No. 2). 2004. audio compact disk 39.25 (978-1-59335-639-2(0), 1593356390, Brinc Audio MP3 Lib) Brilliance Audio.

Black Ice. unabr. ed. Michael Connelly. Read by Dick Hill. (Running Time: 11 hrs.). (Harry Bosch Ser.: No. 2). 2004. 39.25 (978-1-59710-062-5(5), 1597100625, BADLE); 24.95 (978-1-59710-063-2(3), 1597100633, BAD) Brilliance Audio.

Black Ice. unabr. ed. Michael Connelly. Read by Dick Hill. (Running Time: 39600 sec.). (Harry Bosch Ser.: No. 2). 2006. audio compact disk 102.25 (978-1-4233-2328-0(9), 9781423323280, BriAudCD Unabrid); audio compact disk 38.95 (978-1-4233-2327-3(0), 9781423323273, Bril Audio CD Unabri) Brilliance Audio.

Black Ice. unabr. ed. Michael Connelly. Read by Lloyd Battista. 12 cass. (Running Time: 18 hrs.). (Harry Bosch Ser.: No. 2). 2000. Rental 13.50 (GKT 031) Chivers Audio Bks GBR.
The corpse in the hotel room is that of a narcotics agent who's been missing for days. Rumor has it that he crossed over, fronting a new drug called Black Ice from Mexico. The police hastily declare the death a suicide. But Detective Harry Bosch isn't so sure. Without authorization, he starts his own investigation. From L.A. to Mexicali, Harry plunges into a game far more lethal than drug smuggling.

Black Ice. unabr. ed. Michael Connelly. Read by Dick Hill. (Running Time: 11 hrs.). (Harry Bosch Ser.: No. 2). 2004. 24.95 (978-1-59335-259-2(X), 159335259X) Soulmate Audio Bks.

Black Ice Score. unabr. ed. Richard Stark, pseud. Read by Michael Kramer. 3 cass. (Running Time: 4 hrs. 30 mins.). 2001. 28.00 (978-0-7366-6202-4(2)) Books on Tape.
Parker's not sure which side to side with when the object is a very large quantity of diamonds.

Black Ink Story. Hassaun Ali Jones-Bey. 1 CD. (Running Time: 55 min.). 2001. audio compact disk 12.00 (978-0-9654248-1-3(2)) Ibn Musa.
Retells the story of the transatlantic slave trade as a mythological heroic quest.

Black Is the Colour of My True-Love's Heart. unabr. ed. Ellis Peters, pseud. Narrated by Simon Prebble. 5 cass. (Running Time: 7 hrs. 30 mins.). (Inspector George Felse Mystery Ser.: Vol. 6). 1993. 44.00 (978-1-55690-894-1(6), 93336E7) Recorded Bks.
Sparks fly when two famous folksingers & former lovers encounter each other at a folk music seminar. When one of them disappears, Dominic Felse & his girlfriend Tossa struggle to find an explanation. Although he doesn't know it, Dominic holds one of the most important clues to solving the mystery.

Black Jack. unabr. ed. Max Brand. Read by Leonard Zola. 6 cass. 1995. 54.95 set. (CAB 253) AudioGO.
They called him Black Jack. Terry Holl's father had earned the name through a career of crime. And although the same blood ran in his veins, Terry was not Black Jack. But his uncle had gone as far as predicting that Terry would kill a man before he was 25. Must Terry now become a killer like his father & break laws because everyone calls him Black Jack?.

Black Jack. unabr. ed. Max Brand. 6 cass. (Running Time: 8 hrs. 30 mins.). 2001. 44.95 (978-0-7861-1959-2(4), 2730) Blckstn Audio.
Black Jack Hollis had been killed as Elizabeth Cornish watched. Recklessly, joyously, his black hair flying, Jack had ridden into town to see his infant son. Then a shotgun, fired from a window, had blasted him from his horse & flung him to his death in the street.

Black Jack. unabr. ed. Max Brand. Read by Patrick Cullen. 8 CDs. (Running Time: 8 hrs. 30 mins.). 2001. audio compact disk 64.00 (978-0-7861-9763-7(3), 2730) Blckstn Audio.

Black Jack. unabr. ed. Leon Garfield. Narrated by Ron Keith. 5 pieces. (Running Time: 6 hrs. 45 mins.). (gr. 10 up). 2001. 43.00 (978-0-7887-5251-3(0), 96539E7) Recorded Bks.
In this darkly humorous tale the fearsome Black Jack fakes his hanging death by lodging a silver tube in his throat. Forcing young Bartholomew

"Tolly" Dorking into his service, Black Jack resumes his mysterious ways, while Tolly falls in love with Belle, a girl who may be crazy. Tolly's honest nature rubs off on Black Jack just in time. Belle is locked up in a madhouse & only the big thug's strength can save her.

Black-Jack Money Management. Thomas B. Gallagher. Read by Thomas B. Gallagher. 1 cass. (Running Time: 40 min.). 1984. 10.95 Thomas Compny.
Instructions on how to use an easy & effective money management when playing Blackjack.

Black Jack Point. Jeff Abbott. Narrated by L. J. Ganser. 7 cass. (Running Time: 10 hrs. 30 mins.). 2002. 66.00 (978-1-4025-1894-2(3)) Recorded Bks.

Black Jacobin: A Biography of C. L. R. James. abr. ed. Jane Lewis. Contrib. by Paul Kennedy. 3 CDs. (Running Time: 10800 sec.). 2006. audio compact disk 24.95 (978-0-660-19620-6(4), CBC Audio) Canadian Broadcasting CAN.

Black Knight in Red Square. unabr. ed. Stuart M. Kaminsky. Narrated by Mark Hammer. 6 cass. (Running Time: 8 hrs. 15 mins.). (Inspector Porfiry Rostnikov Mystery Ser.: No. 2). 1993. 51.00 (978-1-55690-943-6(8), 93439E7) Recorded Bks.
Inspector Rostnikov tries to prevent a terrorist group from blowing up Lenin's tomb. With an American & his drinking buddies lying dead, hundreds of foreigners in town for the Moscow Film Festival & members of an international terrorist organization spotted in the crowd, Rostnikov can feel disaster in the wind.

Black Knight of the Soul. 1 CD. Dramatization. (YA). 2004. audio compact disk 12.95 (978-0-9728150-1-7(5)) Ahquabi Hse.

Black Lamb & Grey Falcon: A Journey Through Yugoslavia, Pt. 1. collector's ed. Rebecca West. Read by Donada Peters. 14 cass. (Running Time: 21 hrs.). 2000. 112.00 (978-0-7366-5066-3(0)) Books on Tape.

Black Lamb & Grey Falcon: A Journey Through Yugoslavia, Pt. 2. collector's ed. Rebecca West. Read by Donada Peters. 12 cass. (Running Time: 18 hrs.). 2000. 96.00 (978-0-7366-5097-7(0)) Books on Tape.

Black Lamb & Grey Falcon: A Journey Through Yugoslavia, Pt. 3. collector's ed. Rebecca West. Read by Donada Peters. 10 cass. (Running Time: 15 hrs.). 2000. 80.00 (978-0-7366-5098-4(9)) Books on Tape.

***Black Leather Jackets.** 2010. audio compact disk (978-1-59171-245-9(9)) Falcon Picture.

Black Lightning. unabr. ed. John Saul. Read by Phil Gigante. (Running Time: 13 hrs.). 2008. 24.95 (978-1-4233-5583-0(0), 9781423355830, Brilliance MP3); 24.95 (978-1-4233-5585-4(7), 9781423355854, BAD); 39.25 (978-1-4233-5586-1(5), 9781423355861, BADLE); audio compact disk 36.95 (978-1-4233-5581-6(4), 9781423355816, Bril Audio CD Unabri); audio compact disk 39.25 (978-1-4233-5584-7(9), 9781423355847, Brlnc Audio MP3 Lib); audio compact disk 107.25 (978-1-4233-5582-3(2), 9781423355823, BriAudCD Unabrid) Brilliance Audio.

Black Lightning. unabr. ed. John Saul. Narrated by Richard Ferrone. 9 cass. (Running Time: 13 hrs. 30 mins.). 1998. 79.00 (978-0-7887-2477-0(0), 95552E7) Recorded Bks.
Journalist Ann Jeffers believes her five-year crusade for justice has finally ended. The sadistic killer, whose heinous crimes she has documented, is finally getting the electric chair. Unfortunately for her, the nightmare is just beginning.

Black Like Me. unabr. ed. John Howard Griffin. 4 cass. (Running Time: 7 hrs.). (YA). 2004. 39.95 (978-0-9741711-0-4(7)) Audio Bkshelf.
An experiment in 1959 to determine the source ofracism changes the author's life and America.

Black Like Me. unabr. ed. John Howard Griffin. Read by Ray Childs. 6 CDs. (Running Time: 7 hrs.). (YA). 2004. audio compact disk 49.95 (978-0-9741711-1-1(5)) Audio Bkshelf.
An experiment in 1959 to discover the source of racism changes the author and America.

Black Like Me. unabr. ed. John Howard Griffin. Read by Ray Childs. (YA). 2008. 69.99 (978-1-60514-558-7(0)) Find a World.

Black Look Back, Set. Gene Simpson. Read by Gene Simpson. 3 cass. (Running Time: 2 hrs. 15 min.). 1995. 20.00 G Simpson.
Audio Actuality/ Narration of Vietnam-Civil Rights Era of the 1960's. Sound at the Assassination of Malcolm X. Martin Luther King Jr. Interview & Funeral.

Black Madonna of Einsiedeln. Read by Fred Gustafson. 1 cass. (Running Time: 1 hr.). 1976. 9.95 (978-0-7822-0083-6(4), 029) C G Jung IL.

Black Magic & Stolen Timber. Yvonne M. Madden. Ed. by Christine W. Madden. 10 cass. (Running Time: 14 hrs. 26 min.). 50.00 Set. (978-0-9619080-2-7(5)) Vonnie Pubng.
A historical novel from 1828-1929 during the logging era. Truth, hearsay, historical happenings, & Indian folklore are combined to make an exciting story. A Canadian Frenchman comes to Wisconsin territory & marries a Chippewa Indian woman. The reader rides the thread of storyteller Yvonne M. Madden as she spins her yarn tracing her family through one hundred years of time.

Black Magic Sanction. unabr. ed. Kim Harrison. Read by Marguerite Gavin. (Running Time: 14 hrs. 30 mins.). (Hollows Ser.: Bk. 8). 2010. 29.95 (978-1-4417-2295-9(5)); 85.95 (978-1-4417-2291-1(2)); audio compact disk 118.00 (978-1-4417-2292-8(0)) Blckstn Audio.

***Black Magic Sanction.** unabr. ed. Kim Harrison. Read by Marguerite Gavin. (ENG.). 2010. (978-0-06-197747-3(0), Harper Audio); (978-0-06-195371-2(7), Harper Audio) HarperCollins Pubs.

Black Male Heroes. Walter Mosley. 1 cass. (Running Time: 44 mins.). 2001. 12.95 Smithson Assocs.

***Black Mamba Boy: A Novel.** unabr. ed. Nadifa Mohamed. (Running Time: 10 hrs. 0 mins.). 2010. 29.95 (978-1-4417-5491-2(1)); 65.95 (978-1-4417-5487-5(3)); audio compact disk 29.95 (978-1-4417-5490-5(3)); audio compact disk 90.00 (978-1-4417-5488-2(1)) Blckstn Audio.

Black Man's Little Book of Success Secrets: 7 Spiritual Secrets for Breaking the Curse of Poverty. abr. ed. L E Coleman. 2 CDs. (Running Time: 1 hr 50 mins). (ENG.). 2007. audio compact disk 19.95 (978-0-9790644-0-1(6)) C Coleman Pub.

Black Maps. abr. ed. Peter Spiegelman. Read by Davide Aaron Baker. 5 CDs. (Running Time: 5 hrs. 30 mins.). (ENG.). 2003. 14.95 (978-0-7393-0704-5(5), Random AudioBks) Pub: Random Audio Pubg. Dist(s): Random
John March, who walked away from his family's venerable merchant bank for the life of a rural deputy sheriff a life that would explode in personal tragedy and professional disaster. Three years later, he's back in Manhattan, working as a PI and running from his grief and the expectations of his wealthy family. March takes the case of Rick Pierro, a self-made man who has everything and who's in danger of losing it all. An anonymous, poisonous threat has implicated him in a vast money-laundering scheme already under investigation by the feds.

Black Mask Audio Magazine, Vol. 1: Classic Hard-Boiled Tales from the Original Black Mask. unabr. ed. Read by Full Cast Production Staff. (Running Time: 5 hrs. 0 mins.). (ENG.). (J). 2008. 34.95 (978-1-4332-4849-8(2)) Blckstn Audio.

Black Mask Audio Magazine, Vol. 1: Classic Hard-Boiled Tales from the Original Black Mask. unabr. ed. Read by Full Cast Production Staff. (Running Time: 5 hrs. 0 mins.). (ENG.). 2008. 19.95 (978-1-4332-4852-8(2)) Blckstn Audio.

Black Mask Audio Magazine, Vol. 1: Classic Hard-Boiled Tales from the Original Black Mask, Vol. 1. unabr. ed. Read by Full Cast Production Staff. (Running Time: 5 hrs. 0 mins.). 2008. audio compact disk 40.00 (978-1-4332-4850-4(6)) Blckstn Audio.

Black Mesa. unabr. ed. Zane Grey. Read by Dave Webber. 6 cass. (Running Time: 6 hrs.). 1995. 54.95 Set. (978-0-7862-9977-5(0), CSL 081) AudioGO.
Two young men come to the forbidding desert at the foot of Black Mesa. Paul Manning, a writer from Kansas City, is running from memories that haunt him. Wess Kintell, a tall, grey-eyed Texan, is hiding from his shady past. Together, they start a cattle ranch at Black Mesa, but a ruthless trader & some wild women enter their lives & threaten their plans. Before it's over, everyone will learn a hard lesson about living, loving, & dying at Black Mesa.

Black Mischief. unabr. collector's ed. Evelyn Waugh. Read by David Case. 7 cass. (Running Time: 7 hrs.). 1991. 42.00 (978-0-7366-1969-1(0), 2789) Books on Tape.
The island of Azania, east of Italian Somaliland & west of the Gulf of Aden, straddles the equator. It is a hot, humid, bug-infested backwater inhabited by degenerate Arabs, cannibal blacks & unctuous Indians. A layer of European floats uneasily on top - venal Armenians, paranoid French, fatuous English. Azania & its people are of course wholly fictitious, which gives the author enormous room for fun. It's a refreshing book to read, because it lampoons all parties equally.

Black Monday. R. Scott Reiss. Read by Dick Hill. (Running Time: 43200 sec.). 2007. 72.95 (978-0-7861-4845-5(4)); audio compact disk 90.00 (978-0-7861-6093-8(4)) Blckstn Audio.

Black Monday. unabr. ed. R. Scott Reiss. Read by Dick Hill. (Running Time: 43200 sec.). 2007. 29.95 (978-0-7861-4844-8(6)); audio compact disk 29.95 (978-0-7861-6094-5(2)) Blckstn Audio.

Black Monday. unabr. ed. R. Scott Reiss & Dick Hill. (Running Time: 43200 sec.). 2007. audio compact disk 29.95 (978-0-7861-7162-0(6)) Blckstn Audio.

Black Money. unabr. ed. Ross Macdonald. (Running Time: 8 hrs. 0 mins.). (ENG.). 2009. 29.95 (978-1-4332-7844-0(8)); 54.95 (978-1-4332-7840-2(5)); audio compact disk 76.00 (978-1-4332-7841-9(3)) Blckstn Audio.

Black Monk. unabr. ed. Short Stories. Anton Chekhov. Read by Ralph Cosham. 2 cds. (Running Time: 2 hrs 16 mins). 2002. audio compact disk 18.95 (978-1-58472-217-5(7), 001, In Aud) Pub: Sound Room. Dist(s): Baker Taylor
Four of Chekhov's best stories. 1) The Black Monk 2) The Kiss 3) The Helpmate 4) Expensive Lessons.

Black Monk. unabr. ed. Short Stories. Anton Chekhov. Read by Richard Setlok. 2 cass. Library ed. (Running Time: 2 hrs. 25 min.). 1993. lib. bdg. 18.95 set incl. vinyl case, notes, author's picture & biography. (978-1-883049-22-5(9)) Sound Room.
Three timeless works: " The Black Monk," " Mire," & "An Artist's Story.".

Black Monk, Set. unabr. ed. Short Stories. Anton Chekhov. Read by Richard Setlok. Ed. by Richard Setlok. 2 cass. (Running Time: 2 hrs. 30 mins.). (Commuter's Library). 1993. bk. 16.95 (978-1-883049-03-4(2), 390222, Commuters Library) Sound Room.
Three timeless stories. "The Black Monk," a profound story of a scholar & his spirituality. "Mire," a young officer & his older cousin must deal with a local temptress. "An Artist's Story," a story of love that also examines the nature of society.

Black Monk & Other Stories. unabr. ed. Short Stories. Anton Chekhov. Narrated by George Guidall. 3 cass. (Running Time: 4 hrs. 30 mins.). 1994. 26.00 (978-0-7887-0038-5(3), 94237E7) Recorded Bks.
Includes the title story plus "The House with the Mezzanine," "The Peasants" & "Gooseberries".

Black Moon. unabr. ed. Winston Graham. Read by Stephen Thorne. 12 cass. (Running Time: 18 hrs.). (Poldark Ser.: Bk. 5). 2000. 79.95 (CAB 1369) Pub: Chivers Audio Bks GBR. Dist(s): AudioGO
It is Cornwell 1794, and the birth of a son to Elizabeth and George Warleggan only accentuates the rift between the Poldark and Warleggan families. And when Morwenna Chynoweth, now governess to Elizabeth's eldest son, falls in love with Drake Carne, Demelza's brother, the enduring rivalry between the Warleggan's and Poldark's finds a new focus for bitter enmity and conflict.

Black Moth. unabr. ed. Georgette Heyer. Read by Maggie Jones. 8 cass. (Running Time: 11 hrs. 30 min.). 1993. 69.95 (978-1-85089-768-2(9), 9011X) Pub: ISIS Audio GBR. Dist(s): Ulverscroft US
Jack Carstares, now rightful Earl of Wyncham, returns to the England he left in disgrace seven years ago. He is determined not to claim his title, & turns highway-man.

Black Mountain. unabr. ed. Les Standiford. Narrated by Richard Ferrone. 7 cass. (Running Time: 9 hrs. 45 mins.). 2001. 65.00 (978-0-7887-5005-2(4), 96248E7) Recorded Bks.
A New York cop Richard Corrigan has traveled to the mountains bordering Yellowstone with a governor's vacation entourage. He is an unofficial part of the security team. When one by one the members of the camping trip meet fatal accidents, it's up to Corrigan to outsmart the unseen silent killers.

Black Mountain. unabr. ed. Rex Stout. Narrated by Michael Prichard. (Running Time: 23400 sec.). (Nero Wolfe Ser.). (ENG.). 2006. audio compact disk 29.95 (978-1-57270-545-6(0)) Pub: AudioGO. Dist(s): Perseus Dist

Black Mountain. unabr. collector's ed. Rex Stout. Read by Michael Prichard. 7 cass. (Running Time: 7 hrs.). (Nero Wolfe Ser.). 1995. 56.00 (978-0-7366-3167-9(4), 3837) Books on Tape.
Nero Wolfe ignores reason, becomes obsessed with chasing his friend's killer around the world. Now he's a target.

Black Mountain Breakdown. unabr. ed. Lee Smith. Narrated by Linda Stephens. 7 cass. (Running Time: 10 hrs.). 1998. 62.00 (978-0-7887-2182-3(8), 95478E7) Recorded Bks.
When Crystal Spangler leaves Appalachia to attend college, she faces a dazzling future. But something in the shadow of Black Mountain keeps calling her back, something that will change her life forever.

Black Museum. Ed. by Orson Welles. 1 cass. (Running Time: 60 min.). Incl. Brass Button. (MM-5140); Sash Cord. (MM-5140); 7.95 (MM-5140) Natl Recrd Co.
In the story "The Brass Button," Jean Morgan known locally as the Swamp Girl, is murdered. The town people, the vicar, the army & the inspector all help solve the mystery. In the story "The Sash Cord," a stagehand is shot through the heart after he is dead! Why? A private & special play gets the murderer.

Black Museum, Vol. 1. collector's ed. Hosted by Orson Welles. 6 cass. (Running Time: 9 hrs.). 1999. bk. 34.98 (4173) Radio Spirits.
Take a walk through Scotland Yard's Black Museum, an entirety of artifacts associated with puzzling murder cases from the past. Each of the 18 shows dramatizes a baffling murder case including They Key, Brick Bat, Spotted Sheet, Little Blue 22, Four Small Bottles, The Hammer, Twin 45s, Walking Stick, Jack Handle and 9 more.

Black Museum, Vol. 2. collector's ed. Perf. by Orson Welles. 6 cass. (Running Time: 9 hrs.). 2001. bk. 34.98 (4432) Radio Spirits.
Each show begins with Orson Welles walking through Scotland Yard's Black Museum, where some ordinary object, a straight razor or an old trunk, prompts him to tell a tale of how the object was used in a puzzling, celebrated murder case from the past. 18 episodes including, The Bathtub, Blood Stained Shoe, The Champagne Glass, Doctor's Prescription, The Glass Shards, The Receipt, The Sash Cord, Sheath Knife, The Shoe, Silencer, The Telegram and 7 more.

Black Museum: Khaki Handkerchief & Service Card. unabr. ed. Perf. by Orson Welles. 1 cass. (Running Time: 1 hr.). 2001. 6.98 (2251) Radio Spirits.

Black Museum: The Gladstone Bag & The Center Fire. unabr. ed. Perf. by Orson Welles. 1 cass. (Running Time: 1 hr.). 2001. 6.98 (2172) Radio Spirits.

Black Museum: The Jacket & The Pike. unabr. ed. Perf. by Orson Welles. 1 cass. (Running Time: 1 hr.). 2001. 6.98 (2232) Radio Spirits.

Black Narcissus. unabr. ed. Rumer Godden. Narrated by Sheri Blair. 5 cass. (Running Time: 9 hrs.). 1982. 44.00 (978-1-55690-056-3(2), 82015E7) Recorded Bks.
A band of nuns takes up residence in the Himalayas, but the peace of their community is soon upset by life outside its walls. Godden deftly employs the clash of local culture with Western civilization in a romantic suspense story.

Black Night, White Snow, Pt. 1. unabr. ed. Harrison E. Salisbury. Read by Wolfram Kandinsky. 10 cass. (Running Time: 15 hrs.). 1981. 80.00 (978-0-7366-0286-0(0), 1275-A) Books on Tape.
The fall of the Romanov dynasty & the triumph of Lenin's revolution catapulted Russia into the 20th century. Calling on documents, letters, reports, diaries, memoirs, novels & newspapers of that time, Salisbury gives us fresh facts about the Revolution.

Black Night, White Snow, Pt. II. Harrison E. Salisbury. Read by Wolfram Kandinsky. 10 cass. (Running Time: 15 hrs.). 1981. 80.00 (1275-B) Books on Tape.

***Black Nile: One Man's Amazing Journey Through Peace & War on the World's Longest River.** unabr. ed. Dan Morrison. (Running Time: 11 hrs. 0 mins. 0 sec.). 2010. 24.99 (978-1-4001-6589-6(X)); 16.99 (978-1-4001-8589-4(0)); 34.99 (978-1-4001-9589-3(6)); audio compact disk 69.99 (978-1-4001-4589-8(9)); audio compact disk 34.99 (978-1-4001-1589-1(2)) Pub: Tantor Media. Dist(s): IngramPubServ

Black Notice. Patricia Cornwell. Read by Kate Reading. (Kay Scarpetta Ser.: No. 10). 1999. audio compact disk 88.00 (978-0-7366-5187-5(X)) Books on Tape.

Black Notice. unabr. ed. Patricia Cornwell. Read by Kate Reading. 9 cass. (Running Time: 13 hrs. 30 min.). (Kay Scarpetta Ser.: No. 10). 1999. 72.00 (978-0-7366-4581-2(0), 4988) Books on Tape.
A cargo ship arriving at Richmond's Deep Water Terminal from Belgium is discovered to be transporting a locked, sealed container holding the decomposed remains of a stowaway. The autopsy performed by Chief Medical Examiner Dr. Kay Scarpetta initially reveals neither a cause of death nor identification. But the victim's personal effects & an odd tattoo take Scarpetta on a hunt for information that leads to INTERPOL's headquarters in Lyons, France, where she receives critical instructions: go to the Paris morgue to receive forbidden, secret evidence & then return to Virginia to carry out a mission. It is a mission that could ruin her career.

Black Notice. unabr. ed. Patricia Cornwell. Read by Kate Reading. 1 CD. (Running Time: 1 hr. 12 mins.). (Kay Scarpetta Ser.: No. 10). 2001. audio compact disk Books on Tape.
A story that careens across international borders, puts Dr. Kay Scarpetta directly in harm's way & places her & those she holds dear at mortal risk.

Black Notice. unabr. ed. Patricia Cornwell. Narrated by C. J. Critt. 10 cass. (Running Time: 14 hrs. 30 mins.). (Kay Scarpetta Ser.: No. 10). 1999. 85.00 (978-0-7887-3458-8(X), 95881E7) Recorded Bks.
When a badly decomposed body is discovered at the Richmond docks, Chief Medical Examiner Scarpetta is puzzled by the evidence. Her search for his identity will lead Scarpetta to a confrontation with the most monstrous villain of her career.

Black Notice. unabr. ed. Patricia Cornwell. Narrated by C. J. Critt. 12 CDs. (Running Time: 14 hrs. 30 mins.). (Kay Scarpetta Ser.: No. 10). 2000. audio compact disk 112.00 (978-0-7887-3975-0(1), C1094E7) Recorded Bks.
When a badly-decomposed body is discovered at the Richmond docks, Chief Medical Examiner Scarpetta is puzzled by the evidence. Her search for his identity will lead Scarpetta to a confrontation with her most monstrous villain of her career.

Black Notice. unabr. ed. Patricia Cornwell. Narrated by C. J. Critt. (Running Time: 14 hrs. 30 mins.). (Kay Scarpetta Ser.: No. 10). 2009. 61.75 (978-1-4361-6787-1(6)) Recorded Bks.

Black Notice. unabr. ed. Patricia Cornwell. Narrated by C. J. Critt. 1 CD. (Kay Scarpetta Ser.: No. 10). 1999. audio compact disk 112.00 (C1094) Recorded Bks.
When a badly decomposed body is discovered at the Richmond docks, Chief Medical Examiner Scarpetta is puzzled by the evidence. Her search for his identity will lead Scarpetta to a confrontation with the most monstrous villain of her career.

Black Notice, Set. abr. ed. Patricia Cornwell. Read by Kate Reading. 4 cass. (Kay Scarpetta Ser.: No. 10). 1999. 24.95 (FS9-50924) Highsmith.

Black Notice, Set. unabr. ed. Patricia Cornwell. Read by Kate Reading. 8 cass. (Kay Scarpetta Ser.: No. 10). 1999. 39.95 (FS9-43433) Highsmith.

Black Opal. unabr. collector's ed. Victoria Holt. Read by Donada Peters. 7 cass. (Running Time: 10 hrs. 30 min.). 1995. 56.00 (978-0-7366-2903-4(3), 3602) Books on Tape.
If Carmel March unlocks her mysterious past, will a man sentenced for murder go free? A story of uncovering childhood secrets.

Black Ops. unabr. ed. W. E. B. Griffin. Read by Dick Hill. 16 CDs. (Running Time: 20 hrs.). Bk. 5. (ENG.). (gr. 8). 2008. audio compact disk 44.95 (978-0-14-314366-6(2), PengAudBks) Penguin Grp USA.

Black or White: The Work with Byron Katie. 2005. audio compact disk 24.00 (978-1-890246-27-3(1)) B Katie Int Inc.

Black Orchids. unabr. collector's ed. Rex Stout. Read by Michael Prichard. 7 cass. (Running Time: 7 hrs.). (Nero Wolfe Ser.). 1994. 56.00 (978-0-7366-2797-9(9), 3512) Books on Tape.
Nero Wolfe finds himself faced with a daring double murder & a twisted case of poison-pen letters.

Black Order. James Rollins. Narrated by Grover Gardner. 13 CDs. (Running Time: 53280 sec.). (Sigma Force Ser.: BK. 3). 2006. audio compact disk 112.95 (978-0-7927-4069-8(6), SLD 976) AudioGO.

Black Order. James Rollins. Narrated by Grover Gardner. 10 cass. (Running Time: 53280 sec.). (Sigma Force Ser.: Bk. 3). 2006. 84.95 (978-0-7927-4234-0(6), CSL 976); audio compact disk & audio compact disk 49.95 (978-0-7927-4235-7(4), CMP 976) AudioGO.

Black Order. unabr. ed. James Rollins. Read by Grover Gardner. (Running Time: 54000 sec.). (Sigma Force Ser.: Bk. 3). 2006. audio compact disk 44.95 (978-0-06-112072-5(3)) HarperCollins Pubs.

***Black Order.** unabr. ed. James Rollins. Read by Grover Gardner. (ENG.). 2006. (978-0-06-122890-2(7), Harper Audio); (978-0-06-122889-6(3), Harper Audio) HarperCollins Pubs.

Black Out. unabr. ed. John Lawton. Read by Nigel Graham. 12 cass. (Running Time: 18 hrs.). (Isis Ser.). (J). 1999. 94.95 (978-1-85695-248-4(7), 970509) Pub: ISIS Lrg Prnt GBR. Dist(s): Ulverscroft US

Black Out. unabr. ed. John Lawton. Read by Nigel Graham. 13 CDs. (Running Time: 14 hrs.). (Isis Ser.). (J). 2002. audio compact disk 99.95 (978-0-7531-1570-1(0)) Pub: ISIS Lrg Prnt GBR. Dist(s): Ulverscroft US
London 1944: during the Blitz, as the Luftwaffe make their last desperate assault on the city, Londoners take to the shelters once again, hoping for the end to the bombardment. In the East End, children lead police to a charred, dismembered corpse buried in a bombsite. It soon becomes clear that this is no ordinary death. The victim is German and for Detective-Sergeant Frederick Troy it is the start of a manhunt. One will lead him into the shadowy world of stateless refugees, military intelligence and corruption in high places: a manhunt in which Troy is both the hunter and the hunted.

Black Pearl see Extraordinary Adventures of Arsene Lupin

Black Pearl. Scott O'Dell. Narrated by Johnny Heller. 2 CDs. (Running Time: 2 hrs. 30 mins.). (gr. 4 up). audio compact disk 22.00 (978-0-7887-4655-0(3)) Recorded Bks.

Black Pearl, unabr. ed. Scott O'Dell. Narrated by Johnny Heller. 2 pieces. (Running Time: 2 hrs. 30 mins.). (gr. 4 up). 1997. 19.00 (978-0-7887-0235-8(1), 94460E7) Recorded Bks.
Ramon Salazar swims into an underwater cave in a lagoon & steals the rarest pearl in the world. But the pearl belongs to a terrifying & monstrous devilfish who will do anything to get his treasure back.

Black Pearl. unabr. ed. Scott O'Dell. Narrated by Johnny Heller & Christina Moore. 4 CDs. (Running Time: 4 hrs. 30 mins.). (gr. 5 up). 2000. audio compact disk 39.00 (978-0-7887-3448-9(2), C1054E7) Recorded Bks.

Black Pearls: The Poetry of Maya Angelou. Poems. Maya Angelou. 1 cass., 1 CD. 8.78 Blisterpack. (RHINO 72987); audio compact disk 13.58 CD Jewel box. (RHINO 72987) NewSound.

Black Pearls: The Poetry of Maya Angelou. Maya Angelou. Read by Maya Angelou. Music by Ed Blank. Intro. by James Baldwin. 1CD. (Running Time: 1 hr. 30 mins.). 1969. audio compact disk 16.98 (978-1-56826-877-4(7), R2 72987) Rhino Enter.

Black Phalanx. unabr. collector's ed. Joseph T. Wilson. Read by Jonathan Reese. 13 cass. (Running Time: 19 hrs. 30 min.). 1996. 104.00 (978-0-7366-3343-7(X), 3993) Books on Tape.
You would think that African Americans proved their loyalty to America after the Revolution & the War of 1812, spilling their blood for a freedom they could not enjoy. But during the Civil War, the Union thought long & hard about arming them for service, even though this time blacks especially would enjoy the fruits of victory. What was the problem? Through anecdotes & eyewitness accounts, Mr. Wilson examines the battles blacks fought, how the Confederacy treated captured black soldiers, & the South's own unbelievable efforts to raise black troops. This is the record of those soldiers whose valor was denied until it was proven in carnage.

Black Pharaoh. Lin Carter. 2007. audio compact disk 29.95 (978-0-8095-7216-8(8)) Diamond Book Dists.

***Black Phone.** unabr. ed. Joe Hill. (ENG.). 2007. (978-0-06-155217-5(8)); (978-0-06-155218-2(6)) HarperCollins Pubs.

Black Pioneers in American History Vol. 1: 19th Century. abr. ed. Perf. by Eartha Kitt & Moses Gunn. Ed. by Jonathan Katz. 1 cass. Incl. Journal of Charlotte L. Forten, a Free Negro in the Slave Era. Charlotte L. Forten. (SWC 1252); Life & Adventures of Nat Love, Better Known in the Cattle Country as "Deadwood Dick" Nat Love. (SWC 1252); Life & Times of Frederick Douglass: His Early Life as a Slave, His Escape from Bondage, & His Complete History to the Present Time. Frederick Douglass. (SWC 1252); Reminiscences of My Life in Camp. Susan K. Taylor. (SWC 1252); 1985. 12.95 (978-0-694-50179-3(4), SWC 1252) HarperCollins Pubs.

Black Pioneers in American History Vol. 2: 19th - 20th Centuries. abr. ed. Perf. by Diana Sands & Moses Gunn. 1 cass. Incl. Colored Woman in a White World. Mary C. Terrell. (SWC 1299); Dusk of Dawn: An Essay Toward an Autobiography of a Race Concept. W. E. B. Du Bois. (SWC 1299); Father Henson's Story of His Own Life. Josiah Henson. (SWC 1299); Freedman's Story. William Parker. (SWC 1299); 1985. 12.95 (978-0-694-50203-5(0), SWC 1299) HarperCollins Pubs.

Black Plumes. unabr. ed. Margery Allingham. Read by Francis Matthews. 6 cass. (Running Time: 9 hrs.). 2002. 54.95 (978-0-7540-0746-3(4), CAB2168) AudioGO.
A cupboard, a corpse, and a cache of family skeletons. The Ivory's lived in sate, in London. All very respectable. But when Francis warned her grandmother that "something was going on," it was the understatement of the decade. Upstairs in a cupboard there was soon to be a corpse, and when that came to light, out fell the whole file of well-suppressed family secrets and hatreds.

Black Plumes. unabr. ed. Margery Allingham. Read by Francis Matthews. 6 CDs. (Running Time: 9 hrs.). 2002. audio compact disk 64.95 (978-0-7540-5475-7(6), CCD 166) AudioGO.
A cupboard, a corpse, and a cache of family skeletons. The Ivorys lived in state, in London. All respectable. But when Frances warned her grandmother that "something was going on," it was the understatement of the decade. Upstairs, in a cupboard, there was soon to be a corpse, and when that came to light, out fell the whole file of well-suppressed family secrets and hatreds.

Black Prince. unabr. ed. Peter Corris. Read by Peter Hosking. 6 cass. (Running Time: 5 hrs.). 2001. (978-1-86442-363-1(3), 590269) Bolinda Pubng AUS.
Sex, sports & steroids, an explosive mix. They called him the Black Prince. Southwestern Uni's top athlete, Clinton seemed to have it all, he was destined for sporting stardom & lucky in love, then it all went horribly wrong. Now Clinton won't rest until he's avenged his girlfriend's death. He's after the dealer who sold Angie bad steroids & nothing's going to get in his way. Can Cliff Hardy find him before he ends up on a murder charge or dead? The trail leads the Sydney P.I. all the way to an Aboriginal community in Far North Queensland & back to the shadowy world of illegal boxing.

Black Prism. unabr. ed. Brent Weeks. Read by Cristofer Jean. (Running Time: 12 hrs.). (Black Prism Ser.). (ENG.). 2010. 29.98 (978-1-60788-252-7(3)) Pub: Hachet Audio. Dist(s): HachBkGrp

Black Profile in Nursing. 1 cass. (Running Time: 40 min.). (Black Achievers Video Ser.). 1999. 16.99 (33-1) Hist Video.
A veteran black woman nurse with more than 30 years of professional experience is interviewed about her successful career. She offers great advice, & direction; & provides razor sharp information about this fast growing profession.

Black Rabbit Bar. Barbara O'Donnell. 2001. audio compact disk 15.00 (978-0-89914-505-1(1)) Third Party Pub.

Black Radicals. 1 cass. (Running Time: 36 min. per cass.). 1979. 10.00 (HB257) Esstee Audios.
Presents an introduction - review of the black leaders & their beliefs in the 1955-65 decade that witnessed the rise of the black pride & black power movement.

Black Rainbow, unabr. ed. Barbara Michaels, pseud. Narrated by Barbara Rosenblat. 7 cass. (Running Time: 10 hrs. 15 mins.). 1991. 60.00 (978-1-55690-057-0(0), 91306E7) Recorded Bks.
A troubled Byronic hero, a young governess blinded by her romantic obsession, a beautiful but forbidding manor & a secret as ominous as the black rainbow that frames the huddled towers of the manor in the moonlight are the romantic elements of this Gothic mystery.

Black Re-Emergence, No. 1. 2 cass. 10.00 ea. (978-1-885357-78-6(8)) Rational Isl.
Shared experiences of Black people about being Black & about Blacks using re-evaluation counseling.

Black Re-Emergence, No. 3. 3 cass. 10.00 ea. (978-1-885357-79-3(6)) Rational Isl.

Black Rednecks & White Liberals. Thomas Sowell. (Running Time: 10 mins. 30 sec.). 2005. 65.95 (978-0-7861-3697-1(9)); audio compact disk 81.00 (978-0-7861-7684-7(9)) Blckstn Audio.

Black Rednecks & White Liberals. unabr. ed. Thomas Sowell. Read by Hugh Mann. 8 cass. (Running Time: 39600 sec.). 2006. 24.95 (978-0-7861-4621-5(4)); audio compact disk 24.95 (978-0-7861-6878-1(1)) Blckstn Audio.

Black Revolutionaries. 10.00 Esstee Audios.

Black Robes, White Justice, abr. ed. Bruce Wright. Narrated by Stan Winiarski. 2 cass. (Running Time: 3 hrs.). 1996. 16.95 (978-1-882071-49-4(2)) B-B Audio.
This prophetic book has ignited national controversy and debate. The author, a former New York State Supreme Court justice and a black man, argues that our legal system is fundamentally unfair toward African-Americans. He documents this assertion with m.

Black Rock Coffin Makers. Louis L'Amour. 1 cass. 1993. 6.95; (978-1-877883-03-3(4)) Cimino Pub Grp.

Black Rock Coffin Makers. unabr. ed. 1 CD. (Running Time: 3600 sec.). 2007. audio compact disk 9.95 (978-1-4332-0008-3(2)) Blckstn Audio.

Black Rock Coffin Makers. unabr. ed. Louis L'Amour. Read by Stan Winiarski. 1 cass. (Running Time: 1 hr.). Dramatization. 1993. 7.95 (978-1-882071-25-8(5), 027) B-B Audio.
Two men in the isolated town of Tucker want the XY ranch-Jim Walker and the ruthless Wing Cary-and one of them wants it badly enough to kill for it. The Black Rock Coffin Makers is a tale of suspense and danger: chases, shootouts, double-crosses and poss.

Black Rock Coffin Makers. unabr. ed. Louis L'Amour. Read by Stefan Rudnicki. (Running Time: 3600 sec.). 2007. 15.95 (978-1-4332-0005-2(8)); audio compact disk 17.00 (978-1-4332-0006-9(6)) Blckstn Audio.

Black Rock Coffin Makers. unabr. ed. Read by Stefan Rudnicki. (Running Time: 3600 sec.). 2007. 9.95 (978-1-4332-0007-6(4)) Blckstn Audio.

***Black Rock Coffin Makers: A Mule for Santa Fe/Case Closed - No Prisoners.** unabr. ed. Louis L'Amour. (ENG.). 2010. audio compact disk 14.99 (978-0-307-74876-8(6), Random AudioBks) Pub: Random Audio Pubg. Dist(s): Random

Black Rock Coffin Makers; Trail to Pie Town; Mistakes Can Kill You. abr. ed. Louis L'Amour. 2 cass. (Running Time: 3 hrs.). (Louis L'Amour Collector Ser.:). 2000. 7.95 (978-1-57815-097-7(3), 1068, Media Bks Audio) Media Bks NJ.
Captures the old west.

Black Rock Coffin Makers; Trail to Pie Town; Mistakes Can Kill You; Lit a Shuck for Texas; The Nest. abr. ed. Louis L'Amour. 3 vols. (Great Mysteries - Louis L'Amour Ser.). 2001. audio compact disk 11.99 (978-1-57815-527-9(4), Media Bks Audio) Media Bks NJ.

Black Room. Gillian Cross. Read by Steven Pacey. (Running Time: 23820 sec.). (YA). (gr. 7-12). 2001. audio compact disk 59.95 (978-0-7540-6776-4(9)) AudioGo GBR.

Black Rose. Nora Roberts. Read by Susie Breck. (In the Garden Trilogy: Bk. 2). 2009. 70.00 (978-1-60775-523-4(8)) Find a World.

Black Rose. abr. ed. Nora Roberts. Read by Susie Breck. (Running Time: 21600 sec.). (In the Garden Trilogy: Bk. 2). 2005. audio compact disk 16.99 (978-1-59737-344-9(3), 9781597373449, BCD Value Price) Brilliance Audio.
A Harper has always lived at Harper House, the centuries-old mansion just outside of Memphis. And for as long as anyone alive remembers, the ghostly Harper Bride has walked the halls, singing lullabies at night... At forty-five, Rosalind Harper is a woman whose experiences have made her strong enough to bend without breaking - and weather any storm. A widow with three grown sons, she survived a disastrous second marriage, and built her In the Garden nursery from the ground up. Through the years, In the Garden has become more than just a thriving business - it is a symbol of hope and independence to Roz, and to the two women she shares it with. Newlywed Stella and new mother Hayley are the sisters of her heart, and together, the three of them are the future of In the Garden. But now that future is under attack, and Roz knows they can't fight this battle alone. Hired to investigate Roz's Harper ancestors, Dr. Mitchell Carnegie finds himself just as intrigued with Roz herself. And as they begin to unravel the puzzle of the Harper Bride's identity, Roz is shocked to find herself falling for the fascinating genealogist. Now it is a desperate race to discover the truth before the unpredictable apparition lashes out at the one woman who can help her rest in peace.

***Black Rose.** abr. ed. Nora Roberts & #2 In The Garden Series. (In the Garden Trilogy: Bk. 2). 2010. audio compact disk 9.99 (978-1-4418-5640-1(4)) Brilliance Audio.

Black Rose. abr. unabr. ed. Nora Roberts. Read by Susie Breck. (Running Time: 39600 sec.). (In the Garden Trilogy: Bk. 2). 2005. audio compact disk 97.25 (978-1-59355-617-4(9), 9781593556174, BACDLib Ed) Brilliance Audio.
Please enter a Synopsis.

Black Rose. unabr. ed. Nora Roberts. Read by Susie Breck. (Running Time: 11 hrs.). (In the Garden Trilogy: Bk. 2). 2005. 39.25 (978-1-59710-065-6(X), 9781597100656, BADLE); 24.95 (978-1-59710-064-9(1), 9781597100649, BAD); audio compact disk 36.95 (978-1-59600-824-3(5), 9781596008243, Bril Audio CD Unabri); 87.25 (978-1-59355-614-3(4), 9781593556143, BrilAudUnabridg); DVD & audio compact disk 39.25 (978-1-59335-879-2(2), 9781593358792, Brlnc Audio MP3 Lib); audio compact disk 24.95 (978-1-59335-745-0(1), 9781593357450, Brilliance MP3) Brilliance Audio.

Black Rose. unabr. collector's ed. Thomas B. Costain. Read by David Case. 13 cass. (Running Time: 19 hrs. 30 min.). 1993. 104.00 (978-0-7366-2418-3(X), 3185) Books on Tape.
Thirteenth-century Englishman finds fame in Mongol Empire then must choose between first love & exotic Eastern flower.

Black Rose Diaries Audio Book. Short Stories. 2. 2005. audio compact disk 15.00 (978-0-9774333-1-5(5)) W McKiver.

***Black Sea Affair.** unabr. ed. Don Brown. (Running Time: 11 hrs. 30 mins. 0 sec.). (ENG.). 2009. 14.99 (978-0-310-30057-1(6)) Zondervan.

Black Ships Before Troy. unabr. ed. Rosemary Sutcliff. Read by Robert Glenister. 2 cass. (Running Time: 3 hrs.). (J). (gr. 1-8). 1999. 18.95 (CTC 787, Chivers Child Audio) AudioGO.

***Black Spartacus.** Gibson Joseph, Jr. 2005. audio compact disk 8.99 (978-0-9764683-2-5(8)) KITABU Pubng.

Black Sphinx to the Wise Wound. Peter Redgrove. 1 cass. 9.00 (A0627-90) Sound Photosyn.
Faustin interviews Redgrove who energetically discusses his Jungian, poetic, mythological approach to pragmatic issues & the phenomena of nature. Peter, & his partner & wife Penelope, have researched & defined a field relating to the menstrual cycle of the female in partnership that should have a significant impact on the psychology of relationships.

Black Sports before Jackie Robinson. 10.00 Esstee Audios.
A black sports figure tells his story.

Black Stallion. Walter Farley. Narrated by Frank Muller. 5 CDs. (Running Time: 5 hrs. 15 mins.). (gr. 4 up). audio compact disk 48.00 (978-1-4025-2292-5(4)) Recorded Bks.

Black Stallion. unabr. ed. Walter Farley. Narrated by Frank Muller. 4 pieces. (Running Time: 5 hrs. 15 mins.). (Black Stallion Ser.). (gr. 4 up). 1995. 34.00 (978-0-7887-0332-4(3), 94524E7) Recorded Bks.
Survival, courage & friendship are some of the themes in this heartwarming story of a wild Arabian stallion & the American boy who love him.

***Black Star, Bright Dawn.** unabr. ed. Scott O'Dell. Read by Jessica Almasy. (Running Time: 3 hrs.). 2010. 39.97 (978-1-4418-7148-0(9), 9781441871480, BADLE); 14.99 (978-1-4418-7146-6(2), 9781441871466, Brilliance MP3); 39.97 (978-1-4418-7147-3(0), 9781441871473, Brlnc Audio MP3 Lib); audio compact disk 14.99 (978-1-4418-7144-2(6), 9781441871442, Bril Audio CD Unabri); audio compact disk 39.97 (978-1-4418-7145-9(4), 9781441871459, BriAudCD Unabrid) Brilliance Audio.

Black Sun. abr. ed. Terry C. Johnston. Read by Dick Wilkinson. 4 cass. (Running Time: 6 hrs.). (Plainsman Ser.). 2002. 24.95 (978-1-890990-95-4(7), 99095) Otis Audio.
Western with sound effects.

Black Sun: A Novel. unabr. collector's ed. Edward Abbey. Read by Paul Shay. 6 cass. (Running Time: 6 hrs.). 1989. 36.00 (978-0-7366-1586-0(5), 2449) Books on Tape.
Black Sun, a bittersweet love story, is about a forest ranger, loner, iconoclast, lover of the rugged life who falls for an utterly beguiling freckle-faced "American princess" half his age. Like Lady Chatterley's lover, he initiates her into the rites of sex & the stark, hidden harmonies of his wild wooded kingdom & canyons. She, in turn, awakens in him the pleasures of loving & being loved. Then she disappears, plunging him into a gloom he can barely support.

Black Sunday. Thomas Harris. Read by Stuart Milligan. 8 cass. (Running Time: 9 hrs. 54 min.). 2001. 36.95 (978-0-7540-0608-4(5)) AudioGO.
An observation balloon above the biggest football game of the season contains an enormous fragmentation bomb. The FBI & Mossad know that something is planned but not where or when & time is running out.

Black Sunday. Thomas Harris. Narrated by Frank Muller. 7 cass. (Running Time: 10 hrs.). 2001. 70.00 (978-0-7887-4357-3(0), 96309E7); audio compact disk 89.00 (978-0-7887-5162-2(X), C1325E7) Recorded Bks.
Though few would suspect it by looking at him, Michael Lander is the most dangerous man in America. A disgruntled veteran with a fascination for explosives, he pilots television blimps over packed sports stadiums each weekend. When a beautiful terrorist operative hands him the explosive firepower he needs, Lander sets in motion a plan that could turn Super Bowl Sunday into the darkest day in American history.

Black Sunday. abr. ed. Thomas Harris. Read by Ron McLarty. 4 CDs. (Running Time: 18000 sec.). (ENG.). 2006. audio compact disk 14.99 (978-0-7393-4342-5(4), Random AudioBks) Pub: Random Audio Pubg. Dist(s): Random

Black Swan: The Impact of the Highly Improbable. Nassim Nicholas Taleb. Narrated by David Chandler. (Running Time: 52200 sec.). 2007. audio compact disk 39.99 (978-1-4281-6654-6(6)) Recorded Bks.

Black Swan Green. unabr. ed. David Mitchell. Read by Kirby Heyborne. 11 CDs. (Running Time: 13 hrs.). 2006. audio compact disk 99.00 (978-1-4159-2850-9(9)); 81.00 (978-1-4159-2849-3(5)) Books on Tape.
Black Swan Green inverts the telescopic vision of Cloud Atlas to track a single year in what is, for 13-year-old Jason Taylor, the sleepiest village in muddiest Worcestershire in a dying Cold War England, 1982. But the 13 chapters create an exquisitely observed world that is anything but sleepy. Pointed, funny, profound, left field, elegiac, and painted with the stuff of life, Black Swan Green is David Mitchell's subtlest yet most accessible achievement to date.

Black Tatoo. unabr. ed. Sam Enthoven. Read by John Lee. 11 CDs. (Running Time: 13 hrs. 57 mins.). (YA). (gr. 6 up). 2006. audio compact disk 75.00 (978-0-7393-3781-3(5), Listening Lib) Pub: Random Audio Pubg. Dist(s): Random

Black Thunder & Battle's End. abr. ed. Max Brand. Read by Barry Corbin. 2 cass. (Running Time: 3 hrs.). 2000. 7.95 (978-1-57815-089-2(2), 1057, Media Bks Audio) Media Bks NJ.
Captures the old West.

Black Tickets & Machine Dreams. Jayne Anne Phillips. Read by Jayne Anne Phillips. 1 cass. (Running Time: 1 hr. 30 min.). 1991. 13.95 Am Audio Prose.
Read "Souvenir" & MACHINE DREAMS (Excerpts).

Black Tide. unabr. ed. Hammond Innes. Read by Stephen Thorne. 10 cass. (Running Time: 15 hrs.). 2000. 69.95 (978-0-7451-6794-7(2), CAB 1410) Pub: Chivers Audio Bks GBR. Dist(s): AudioGO
The tanker Petros Jupiter is lying off the coast of Land's End, spewing a filthy black tide, and it's only a week before the first oil-sodden bodies come ashore. Trevor Rodin's wife is angry at the effect of the oil spill on the environment and the lack of action taken by authorities. She sends Trevor to sea in search of the truth about the wreck.

Black Tide. unabr. ed. Peter Temple. Read by Marco Chiappi. 6 cass. (Running Time: 9 hrs.). 2004. 48.00 (978-1-74030-087-2(4), 500115) Pub: Bolinda Pubng AUS. Dist(s): Lndmrk Audiobks
Jack Irish - lawyer, gambler, part-time cabinetmaker, finder of missing people is recovering from a foray into the criminal underworld when he agrees to look for the son of an old workmate of his father's.

***Black Tide.** unabr. ed. Peter Temple. Read by Marco Chiappi. 8 CDs. (Running Time: 9 hrs.). 2010. audio compact disk 87.95 (978-1-921415-74-6(6), 9781921415746) Pub: Bolinda Pubng AUS. Dist(s): Bolinda Pub Inc

Black Tower. unabr. ed. Louis Bayard. (Running Time: 12 hrs. NaN mins.). 2008. 29.95 (978-1-4332-4660-9(0)); 72.95 (978-1-4332-4657-9(0)); audio compact disk 90.00 (978-1-4332-4658-6(9)) Blckstn Audio.

Black Tower. unabr. ed. Louis Bayard. Read by Simon Vance. 8 CDs. (Running Time: 10 hrs.). 2008. audio compact disk & audio compact disk 32.95 (978-1-4332-4659-3(7)) Blckstn Audio.

Black Tower. unabr. ed. P. D. James. Read by Penelope Dellaporta. 9 cass. (Running Time: 13 hrs. 30 min.). (Adam Dalgliesh Mystery Ser.). 1993. 72.00 (978-0-7366-2509-8(7), 3265) Books on Tape.
Adam Dalgliesh looks for the common thread in a series of baffling murders.

Black Tower. unabr. ed. P. D. James. Read by Michael Jayston. 8 cass. (Running Time: 12 hrs.). (Adam Dalgliesh Mystery Ser.). 2000. 59.95 (978-0-7451-6070-2(0), CAB 445) Pub: Chivers Audio Bks GBR. Dist(s): AudioGO
Adam Dalgliesh, newly promoted to the rank of commander, is facing a crisis with his career. Dissatisfied with his work, he thinks of resigning from the Force. However, an invitation to visit an old family friend in Dorser appeals to him. But when he arrives at Toynton Grange, a private home for the disabled, he discovers his host has died suddenly. Other mysterious deaths soon follow, and Dalgliesh finds that the problem is an enclosed world seething with malice, hatred and murder.

Black Tulip. Alexandre Dumas. Read by John Bolen. (Running Time: 7 hrs. 30 mins.). 2001. 27.95 (978-1-60083-581-0(3), Audiofy Corp) Iofy Corp.

Black Tulip. Alexandre Dumas. Read by John Bolen. (ENG.). 2001. audio compact disk 78.00 (978-1-4001-3008-5(5)) Pub: Tantor Media. Dist(s): IngramPubServ

Black Tulip. unabr. ed. Alexandre Dumas. Narrated by John Bolen. 1 CD (MP3). (Running Time: 7 hrs. 27 mins.). (ENG.). 2001. audio compact disk 20.00 (978-1-4001-5008-3(6)); audio compact disk 39.00 (978-1-4001-0008-8(9)) Pub: Tantor Media. Dist(s): IngramPubServ
The tulip craze of 17th century Holland has a dark side! Cornelius van Baerle, a wealthy but naïve tulip grower, finds himself entangled in the deadly politics of his time. Cornelius' one desire is to grow the perfect black tulip. But, after his godfather is murdered, he finds himself in prison, facing a death sentence. His jailer's lovely daughter holds the key to his survival, and his chance to produce the precious black blossom. Yet he has one more enemy to contend with!.

Black Tulip. unabr. ed. Alexandre Dumas. Narrated by John Bolen. (Running Time: 7 hrs. 30 mins. 0 sec.). (ENG.). 2009. audio compact disk 19.99 (978-1-4001-5938-3(5)); audio compact disk 27.99 (978-1-4001-0938-8(8)); audio compact disk 55.99 (978-1-4001-3938-5(4)) Pub: Tantor Media. Dist(s): IngramPubServ

Black Unicorn. abr. ed. Terry Brooks. Read by Dick Hill. (Running Time: 6 hrs.). (Magic Kingdom of Landover Ser.: No. 2). 2006. 24.95 (978-1-4233-0019-9(X), 9781423300199, BAD) Brilliance Audio.

Black Unicorn. abr. ed. Terry Brooks. Read by Dick Hill. (Running Time: 21600 sec.). (Magic Kingdom of Landover Ser.: No. 2). 2008. audio compact disk 14.99 (978-1-4233-5028-6(6), 9781423350286, BCD Value Price) Brilliance Audio.

Black Unicorn. unabr. ed. Terry Brooks. Read by Dick Hill. (Running Time: 11 hrs.). (Magic Kingdom of Landover Ser.: No. 2). 2008. 39.25 (978-1-4233-5026-2(X), 9781423350262, BADLE); 24.95 (978-1-4233-5025-5(1), 9781423350255, BAD); 92.25 (978-1-4233-5020-0(0), 9781423350200, BrilAudUnabridg); audio compact disk 39.25 (978-1-4233-5024-8(3), 9781423350248, Brinc Audio MP3 Lib); audio compact disk 97.25 (978-1-4233-5022-4(7), 9781423350224, BriAudCD Unabrid); audio compact disk 29.95 (978-1-4233-5021-7(9), 9781423350217, Bril Audio CD Unabri); audio compact disk 24.95 (978-1-4233-5023-1(5), 9781423350231, Brilliance MP3) Brilliance Audio.

Black Velvet Gown. unabr. ed. Catherine Cookson. Read by Elizabeth Henry. 12 cass. (Running Time: 18 hrs.). (Sound Ser.). 2004. 94.95 (978-1-85496-332-1(5), 63325) Pub: UlverLrgPrint GBR. Dist(s): Ulverscroft US

Black Vietnam Veterans. 1 cass. (Running Time: 30 min.). 9.95 (H0240B090, HarperThor) HarpC GBR.

Black Virgin & the Underground Stream. unabr. ed. Ean Begg. 2 cass. 18.00 (OC151) Sound Horizons AV.

Black Virgin, Black Goddess & Gnosis, Set. Stephan Hoeller. 3 cass. 1999. 26.00 (40033) Big Sur Tapes.
1988 Los Angeles.

Black Watch. Ed. by Marco A. V. Bitetto. 2000. (978-1-58578-071-6(5)) Inst of Cybernetics.

Black Water. Composed by John Duffy. Contrib. by Karen Burlingame & Patrick Mason. Joyce Carol Oates. (Playaway Adult Fiction Ser.). 2009. 39.99 (978-1-60775-734-4(6)) Find a World.

Black Water. unabr. ed. John Duffy & Joyce Carol Oates. Perf. by David L. Brewer et al. 2 CDs. (Running Time: 1 hr. 31 mins.). 1998. audio compact disk 25.95 (978-1-58081-118-7(3), TPT118) Pub: L A Theatre. Dist(s): NetLibrary CO
Based on the Chappaquiddick scandal, this is the dark & enthralling tale of an ambitious young woman & the distinguished U.S. Senator who singles her out for attention. LATW's first opera production.

Black Water. unabr. ed. D. J. MacHale. Read by William Dufris. (Running Time: 12 hrs.). (Pendragon Ser.: Bk. 5). 2005. 39.25 (978-1-59737-274-9(9), 9781597372749, BADLE); 24.95 (978-1-59737-273-2(0), 9781597372732, BAD); 29.95 (978-1-59737-267-1(6), 9781597372671, BAU) Brilliance Audio.
Just when fifteen-year-old Bobby Pendragon thinks he understands his purpose as a Traveler - to protect the territories of Halla from the evil Saint Dane - he is faced with an impossible choice. The inhabitants of Eelong are in danger of being wiped out by a mysterious plague. Only Bobby knows how to stop it, but it means bringing the antidote from another territory - Cloral. Since moving items between territories is forbidden by the Traveler rules, if Bobby chooses to save Eelong he could endanger himself, his friends, and the future of every other being in Halla.

Black Water. unabr. ed. D. J. MacHale. Read by William Dufris. (Running Time: 43200 sec.). (Pendragon Ser.: Bk. 5). (J). (ps-7). 2005. DVD & audio compact disk 24.95 (978-1-59737-271-8(4), 9781597372718, Brilliance MP3); 82.25 (978-1-59737-268-8(4), 9781597372688, BrilAudUnabridg); DVD & audio compact disk 39.25 (978-1-59737-272-5(2), 9781597372725, Brinc Audio MP3 Lib) Brilliance Audio.

Black Water. unabr. ed. D. J. MacHale. Read by William Dufris. (Running Time: 12 hrs.). (Pendragon Ser.: Bk. 5). 2009. audio compact disk 19.99 (978-1-4233-9903-2(X), 9781423399032); audio compact disk 49.97 (978-1-4233-9904-9(8), 9781423399049, BriAudCD Unabrid) Brilliance Audio.

Black Water. unabr. ed. T. Jefferson Parker. Read by Aasne Vigesaa. 7 cass. (Running Time: 10 hrs.). (Merci Rayborn Ser.). 2002. 32.95 (978-1-59086-133-2(7), 1590861337, BAU); 78.25 (978-1-59086-134-9(5), 1590861345, Unabridge Lib Edns) Brilliance Audio.
A beautiful young woman is dead in the bathroom of her home. Her husband - a promising young cop named Archie Wildcraft - is shot in the head but still alive. It looks like an attempted murder/suicide, but something tells Detective Merci Rayborn that there's more to the story. When the suspect vanishes from his hospital bed, he draws Merci into a manhunt that leaves the entire department questioning her abilities and her judgment. Is Archie's flight the act of a ruined mind, or a faithful heart? Is his account of the night his wife was murdered half-formed memory, or careful manipulation? Merci and Wildcraft head for a collision in a dizzying succession of cryptic clues, terrifying secrets, and painful truths.

Black Water. unabr. ed. T. Jefferson Parker. Read by Aasne Vigesaa. (Running Time: 10 hrs.). (Merci Rayborn Ser.). 2004. 39.25 (978-1-59335-350-6(2), 1593353502, Brinc Audio MP3 Lib) Brilliance Audio.

Black Water. unabr. ed. T. Jefferson Parker. Read by Aasne Vigesaa. (Running Time: 10 hrs.). (Merci Rayborn Ser.). 2004. 39.25 (978-1-59710-067-0(6), 1597100676, BADLE); 24.95 (978-1-59710-066-3(8), 1597100668, BAD) Brilliance Audio.

Black Water. unabr. ed. T. Jefferson Parker. Read by Aasne Vigesaa. (Running Time: 10 hrs.). (Merci Rayborn Ser.). 2010. audio compact disk 89.97 (978-1-4418-3592-5(X), 9781441835925, BriAudCD Unabrid); audio compact disk 29.99 (978-1-4418-3591-8(1), 9781441835918, Bril Audio CD Unabri) Brilliance Audio.

Black Water. unabr. ed. T. Jefferson Parker. Read by Aasne Vigesaa. (Running Time: 10 hrs.). (Merci Rayborn Ser.). 2004. 24.95 (978-1-59335-009-3(0), 1593350090) Soulmate Audio Bks.

Black Water Rising. unabr. ed. Attica Locke. Read by Dion Graham. 11 CDs. (Running Time: 13 hrs. 30 mins.). 2009. audio compact disk 39.99 (978-0-06-177209-2(7), Harper Audio) HarperCollins Pubs.

***Black Water Rising.** unabr. ed. Attica Locke. Read by Dion Graham. (ENG.). 2009. (978-0-06-190190-4(3), Harper Audio); (978-0-06-190189-8(X), Harper Audio) HarperCollins Pubs.

Black Water Transit. unabr. ed. Carsten Stroud. Read by Bruce Reizen. 8 cass. Library ed. (Running Time: 12 hrs.). 2001. 78.25 (978-1-58788-717-8(7), 1587887177, Unabridge Lib Edns); 32.95 (978-1-58788-716-1(9), 1587887169, BAU) Brilliance Audio.
Jack Vermillion is a businessman with a problem: a son with a criminal record who is in trouble again. This time, Jack's kid is looking at twenty-five to life in maximum security. And there's nothing Jack can do . . .or is there? Black Water Transit is Jack's container ship company, and when Jack is approached by a man wanting to ship his gun collection to Mexico - very simple, very illegal - he sees an opportunity. So Jack cuts a deal with the ATF to trade one illegal gun dealer for one slightly imperfect kid. The deal is set, the weapons on board, the cops and feds in place. Everything should come off without a hitch. . .until the shooting starts and people start dying. As the body count rises, Jack must go on the lam, in a race for his life, and there isn't a law enforcement agency in the world that can help him now.

Black Water Transit. unabr. ed. Carsten Stroud. Read by Bruce Reizen. (Running Time: 12 hrs.). 2005. 39.25 (978-1-59600-684-3(6), 9781596006843, Brinc Audio MP3 Lib); 39.25 (978-1-59600-686-7(2), 9781596006867, BADLE); 24.95 (978-1-59600-685-0(4), 9781596006850, BAD); 24.95 (978-1-59600-683-6(8), 9781596006836, Brilliance MP3) Brilliance Audio.

Black Wave: A Family's Adventure at Sea & the Disaster That Saved Them. unabr. ed. John Silverwood & Jean Silverwood. Read by Carrington MacDuffie & Joe Barrett. 6 CDs. (Running Time: 7 hrs. 30 mins.). 2009. audio compact disk 24.95 (978-1-4332-4966-2(9)) Blckstn Audio.

Black Wave: A Family's Adventure at Sea & the Disaster That Saved Them. unabr. ed. John Silverwood et al. Read by Carrington MacDuffie & Joe Barrett. (Running Time: 7 hrs. 0 mins.). 2008. 29.95 (978-1-4332-4967-9(7)); 44.95 (978-1-4332-4964-8(2)); audio compact disk 60.00 (978-1-4332-4965-5(0)) Blckstn Audio.

Black Wedding see Isaac Bashevis Singer Reader

Black Widow. Randy Wayne White. Read by George Guidall. (Running Time: 11 hrs.). No. 15. (ENG.). (gr. 8). 2008. audio compact disk 39.95 (978-0-14-314288-1(7), PengAudBks) Penguin Grp USA.

Black Widow. unabr. ed. Randy Wayne White. Read by George Guidall. 9 cass. (Running Time: 11 hrs.). (Doc Ford Ser.: No. 15). 2008. 61.75 (978-1-4281-8082-6(6)) Recorded Bks.

Black Widow. unabr. ed. Randy Wayne White. Read by George Guidall. 9 CDs. (Running Time: 11 hrs.). (Doc Ford Ser.: No. 15). 2008. audio compact disk 77.75 (978-1-4281-8084-0(2)) Recorded Bks.
Randy Wayne White's 14 previous Doc Ford novels shot onto the New York Times best-seller lists. In Black Widow, Ford's goddaughter pleads with him to help her out of a jam. An extortionist with a lurid videotape of her bachelorette party is threatening to ruin her imminent marriage. Despite getting paid, the blackmailer releases the tape anyway - and that's only the beginning of Doc's troubles.

Black Widower. unabr. ed. Patricia Moyes. Read by Donada Peters. 7 cass. (Running Time: 7 hrs.). (Henry Tibbett Mystery Ser.). 1992. 42.00 (978-0-7366-2272-1(1), 3060) Books on Tape.
Sir Edward Ironmonger, ambassador to the U. S. from the island republic of Tampica, & his temperamental wife, Mavis, give a party for the Washington diplomatic corp. Despite her promise to behave, Mavis manages to insult the Israeli ambassador & is removed to her room - where her corpse is later discovered. To avoid publicity, Chief Superintendent Henry Tibbett is brought in to investigate.

Black Wind. unabr. ed. Clive Cussler & Dirk Cussler. Read by Scott Brick. 10 cass. (Running Time: 15 hrs.). (Dirk Pitt Ser.). 2004. 99.00 (978-1-4159-0803-7(6)); audio compact disk 104.00 (978-1-4159-0804-4(4)) Books on Tape.
During the last days of World War II, the Japanese tried a kamikaze mission with two submarines headed for the west coast of the U.S. and carrying a cargo of a biological virus. The subs didn't make it to their designated targets.

Black Wind. unabr. ed. Clive Cussler & Dirk Cussler. Read by Scott Brick. 13 CDs. (Running Time: 16 hours). (ENG.). (gr. k-8). 2004. audio compact disk 39.95 (978-0-14-305740-6(5), PengAudBks) Penguin Grp USA.

Black Wings Has My Angel. unabr. ed. Elliott Chaze. Read by Malcolm Hillgartner. (Running Time: 5 hrs. 0 mins.). 2010. 29.95 (978-1-4332-4733-0(X)); 34.95 (978-1-4332-4729-3(1)); audio compact disk 55.00 (978-1-4332-4730-9(5)) Blckstn Audio.

Black Writer Series: Complete Series. 333.95 (978-1-55644-309-1(9), SS-13) Am Audio Prose.
Includes sixteen readings & sixteen interviews. Reader/interviewees include Chinua Achebe, James Baldwin, Toni Morrison, Gloria Naylor, Ntozake Shange, Michael Thelwell, Alice Walker, John Edgar Wideman, John A. Williams, Al Young, Toni Cade Bambara, Ernest Gaines, David Bradley, Jamaica Kincaid, Margaret Walker, & Paul Marshall.

Black Writer Series: Interview Series. unabr. ed. Chinua Achebe et al. Interview with Chinua Achebe et al. 1991. 127.95 (978-1-55644-308-4(0), SS-12) New Letters.
Includes all thirteen author interviews. Other author/interviewees include Toni Morrison, Gloria Naylor, Ntozake Shange, Michael Thelwell, Alice Walker, John Edgar Wideman, John A. Williams, & Al Young.

Black Writers: The James Baldwin Legacy. Rex A. Barnett. (Running Time: 15 min.). (J). 1990. 16.99 (978-0-924198-09-0(5)) Hist Video.
Contributions of black writers & the impact of prolific author James Baldwin is reviewed.

Black Writing Series. unabr. ed. Rita Dove et al. 32 cass. (Running Time: 29 min. per cass.). 1985. 10.00 ea. New Letters.
A collection of weekly half-hour radio programs with black writers talking & presenting their own works.

Blackadder Collection: Radio Dramatization. Richard Curtis & Ben Elton. 9 CDs. (Running Time: 13 hrs. 30 mins.). 2002. audio compact disk 89.95 (978-0-563-53081-7(2), BBCD 009) BBC Worldwide.

Blackadder II. unabr. ed. Richard Curtis. Created by Richard Curtis. Created by Ben Elton. Narrated by Full Cast Production Staff. (Running Time: 4 hrs. 0 mins. 0 sec.). (ENG.). 2010. audio compact disk 29.95 (978-1-60283-838-3(0)) Pub: AudioGO. Dist(s): Perseus Dist

Blackadder Series. Richard Curtis & Ben Elton. 6 cass. (Running Time: 8 hrs. 50 mins.). 1998. 37.45 Boxed set. (978-0-563-55811-8(3)) BBC WrldWd GBR.
Contains 3 volumes of Blackadder's various incarnations: Blackadder II - England 1558 - 1603, Blackadder the Third & Blackadder Goes Forth.

***Blackadder the Third.** Created by Richard Curtis & Ben Elton. Narrated by Rowan Atkinson. 3 CDs. (Running Time: 1 hr. 0 mins. 0 sec.). (ENG.). 2010. audio compact disk 24.95 (978-0-563-49454-6(9)) Pub: AudioGO. Dist(s): Perseus Dist

Blackberry Wine. Joanne Harris. Read by Alex Jennings. (Running Time: 37380 sec.). 2002. 89.95 (978-0-7540-0553-7(4)) Chivers Audio Bks GBR.

Blackberry Wine. unabr. ed. Joanne Harris. Read by Alex Jennings. 10 CDs. (Running Time: 15 hrs.). 2002. audio compact disk 94.95 (978-0-7540-5500-6(0), CCD 191) AudioGO.

Blackbird. unabr. collector's ed. Richard Stark, pseud. Read by Michael Kramer. 4 cass. (Running Time: 6 hrs.). (Alan Grofield Ser.: Bk. 3). 2001. 32.00 Books on Tape.
Grofield lands in the Canadian wilderness where Third World delegates are secretly meeting in what may be a lethal situation.

Blackbird: A Childhood Lost & Found. Jennifer Lauck. 2004. 15.95 (978-0-7435-4205-0(3)) Pub: S&S Audio. Dist(s): S and S Inc

Blackbird: A Childhood Lost & Found. unabr. ed. Jennifer Lauck. Read by Stephanie Roberts. 10 vols. (Running Time: 15 hrs.). 2001. bk. 84.95 (978-0-7927-2454-4(2), CSL 343, Chivers Sound Lib) AudioGO.
The house on Mary Street was home to Jennifer; her older brother, B.J.; their hardworking father, who smelled like aftershave & read her Snow White; & their mother, who called her little daughter Sunshine & embraced Jackie Kennedy's sense of style. Through a child's eyes, the skies of Carson City were forever blue & life was perfect. Even her mother's mysterious illness could be hidden away, but soon everything that Jennifer has come to love begins to crumble, sending her on a roller coaster of loss & loneliness.

Blackbird Papers: A Novel. unabr. ed. Ian Smith. 8 cass. (Running Time: 12 hrs.). 2004. 99.00 (978-1-4159-0125-0(2)); 81.00 (978-1-4159-0088-8(4)) Books on Tape.
When Professor Wilson Bledsoe is brutally murdered, two loathsome white supremacists seem like the obvious culprits. But Bledsoe's younger brother Sterling, an FBI agent in New York, has other ideas. A look around Wilson's lab and interviews with his students, his fellow professors, and the college's president pique Sterling's curiosity about Wilson's nearly-completed project on the mysterious death of hundreds of local blackbirds. But when a tape supposedly incriminating Sterling is sent to the FBI, Sterling becomes a man on the run.

Blackbird Pie & Other Stories. unabr. ed. Short Stories. Raymond Carver. Read by Tim Behrens. 2 cass. (Running Time: 2 hrs.). Dramatization. 1992. 16.95 (978-1-55686-425-4(6), 425) Books in Motion.
These are some of Carver's last & best stories: Blackbird Pie, Intimacy, Boxes, & Whoever Was Using This Bed.

Blackbirder. James L. Nelson. Read by Terry Wale. 10 cass. (Sound Ser.). (J). 2003. 84.95 (978-1-84283-256-1(5)) Pub: ISIS Lrg Prnt GBR. Dist(s): Ulverscroft US

Blackboard Bear. unabr. ed. Martha Alexander. 1 cass. (Running Time: 6 min.). (J). (ps-3). 1989. pap. bk. 14.45 (978-0-8045-6507-3(4), 6507) Spoken Arts.

Blackbringer. unabr. ed. Laini Taylor. Narrated by Davina Porter. 10 cass. (Running Time: 11 hrs. 30 mins.). (Faeries of Dreamdark Ser.: No. 1). (J). 2008. 46.95 (978-1-4361-0660-3(5)); audio compact disk 51.95 (978-1-4361-2941-1(9)) Recorded Bks.

Blackbringer. unabr. ed. Laini Taylor. Narrated by Davina Porter. 10 cass. (Running Time: 11 hrs. 30 mins.). (Faeries of Dreamdark Ser.: No. 1). (YA). (gr. 5-8). 2008. 78.75 (978-1-4361-0659-7(1)); audio compact disk 108.75 (978-1-4361-0664-1(8)) Recorded Bks.

Blackfish Sound. 1 cass. (Running Time: 30 min.). 1994. audio compact disk 15.95 CD. (2230, Creativ Pub) Quayside.
Diverse sounds of orcas (killer whales) as they travel through the coastal waterways of British Columbia.

Blackfish Sound. 1 cass. (Running Time: 30 min.). 1994. 9.95 (2228, NrthWrd Bks) TandN Child.

Blackfoot Returns. 1 cass. (Running Time: 1 hr.). 9.00 (H0310B090, HarperThor) HarpC GBR.

Blackground. unabr. ed. Joan Aiken. Read by Rosemary Davis. 8 cass. (Running Time: 11 hrs.). 1997. 69.95 (978-1-85089-680-7(1), 9102Y) Pub: ISIS Audio GBR. Dist(s): Ulverscroft US
A novel of cunning & intrigue by a mistress of the genre.

Blackie & Red. unabr. ed. Max Brand. Read by Buck Schirner. (Running Time: 7 hrs.). 2007. 39.25 (978-1-4233-3486-6(8), 9781423334866, BADLE); 24.95 (978-1-4233-3485-9(X), 9781423334859, BAD) Brilliance Audio.

Blackie & Red. unabr. ed. Max Brand. Read by Buck Schirner. (Running Time: 7 hrs.). 2007. 39.25 (978-1-4233-3484-2(1), 9781423334842, Brinc Audio MP3 Lib); 24.95 (978-1-4233-3483-5(3), 9781423334835, Brilliance MP3) Brilliance Audio.

Blackie & Red. unabr. ed. Max Brand. Read by Buck Schirner. (Running Time: 7 hrs.). 2009. audio compact disk 19.99 (978-1-4418-0459-4(5), 9781441804594, Bril Audio CD Unabri); audio compact disk 59.97 (978-1-4418-0460-0(9), 9781441804600, BriAudCD Unabrid) Brilliance Audio.

Blackjack Bargainer see O. Henry Favorites

Blacklight Blue. unabr. ed. Peter May. (Running Time: 7 hrs. NaN mins.). 2008. 29.95 (978-1-4332-5211-2(2)); 54.95 (978-1-4332-5209-9(0)); audio compact disk 60.00 (978-1-4332-5210-5(4)) Blckstn Audio.

Blacklist. Sara Paretsky. Read by Sandra Burr. (Playaway Adult Fiction Ser.). (ENG.). 2009. 84.99 (978-1-60775-699-6(4)) Find a World.

Blacklist. abr. ed. Sara Paretsky. Read by Sandra Burr. (Running Time: 6 hrs.). (V. I. Warshawski Ser.). 2009. audio compact disk 14.99 (978-1-4418-0032-9(8), 9781441800329, BCD Value Price) Brilliance Audio.

Blacklist. unabr. ed. Sara Paretsky. Read by Sandra Burr. 10 cass. Library ed. (Running Time: 16 hrs.). (V. I. Warshawski Ser.). 2003. 97.25 (978-1-58788-867-0(X), 158788867X, BriAudUnabridg); 34.95 (978-1-58788-866-3(1), 1587888661, BAU); audio compact disk 40.95 (978-1-58788-869-4(6), 1587888696, Bril Audio CD Unabri); audio compact disk 117.25 (978-1-58788-870-0(X), 158788870X, BriAudCD Unabrid) Brilliance Audio.

Every new Sara Paretsky novel is an event, the chance to reencounter her beloved heroine, V. I. Warshawski - "a private eye with the sharpest tongue and hardest head in Chicago" (The New York Times Book Review) - a cause for rejoicing. But Blacklist is something special. This is a story of secrets and betrayals that stretch across four generations - secrets political, social, sexual, financial: all of them with the power to kill. Eager for something physical to do in the spirit-exhausting wake of 9/11, V.I. accepts a request from an old client to check up on an empty family mansion; subsequently surprises an intruder in the dark; and, giving chase, topples into a pond. Grasping for something to hold on to, her fingers close around a lifeless human hand. It is the body of a reporter who had been investigating events of forty-five years earlier, during the McCarthy era, and V. I.'s discovery quickly sucks her into the history of two great Chicago families - their fortunes intertwined by blood, sex, money, and the scandals that may or may not have resulted in murder all these years later. At the same time, she inadvertently becomes involved in the story of a missing Egyptian boy whose possible terrorist connections make him very much sought after by the government. As the two cases drive her forward-and then shockingly tumble together, pushing her into situations more perilous than she could have imagined-she finds that wealth and privilege, too, bear a terrible price; and the past has no monopoly on patriotic scoundrels. Before everything is over, at least two more people will lie dead...and V.I. might even be one of them.

Blacklist. unabr. ed. Sara Paretsky. Read by Sandra Burr. (Running Time: 16 hrs.). (V. I. Warshawski Ser.). 2004. 39.25 (978-1-59335-629-3(3), 1593356293, Brlnc Audio MP3 Lib) Brilliance Audio.

Blacklist. unabr. ed. Sara Paretsky. Read by Sandra Burr. (Running Time: 16 hrs.). (V. I. Warshawski Ser.). 2004. 39.25 (978-1-59710-068-7(4), 1597100684, BADLE); 24.95 (978-1-59710-069-4(2), 1597100692, BAD) Brilliance Audio.

Blacklist. unabr. ed. Sara Paretsky. Read by Sandra Burr. (Running Time: 16 hrs.). (V. I. Warshawski Novel Ser.). 2004. 24.95 (978-1-59335-237-0(9), 1593352379) Soulmate Audio Bks.

Blacklisted. Tony Kahn. 3 cass. (Running Time: 4 hrs. 30 mins.). Dramatization. 39.95 (978-1-57677-102-0(4), KAHN001) Lodestone Catalog.

***Blacklisted by History: The Untold Story of Senator Joe Mccarthy & His Fight against America's Enemies.** unabr. ed. M. Stanton Evans. (Running Time: 23 hrs.). 2010. 44.95 (978-1-4417-7304-3(5)); audio compact disk 44.95 (978-1-4417-7303-6(7)) Blckstn Audio.

***Blacklisted by History: The Untold Story of Senator Joe Mccarthy & His Fight against America's Enemies.** unabr. ed. M. Stanton Evans. (Running Time: 23 hrs.). 2010. audio compact disk 123.00 (978-1-4417-7302-9(9)) Blckstn Audio.

***Blacklisted by History (Part 1 Of 2) The Untold Story of Senator Joe Mccarthy & His Fight Against America's Enemies.** unabr. ed. M. Stanton Evans. (Running Time: 23 hrs.). 2010. 59.95 (978-1-4417-7301-2(0)) Blckstn Audio.

Blackman's Coffin: A Sam Blackman Mystery. unabr. ed. Mark De Castrique. Read by William Dufris. (Running Time: 7.5 hrs. 0 mins.). 2008. 29.95 (978-1-4332-3522-1(6)); 54.95 (978-1-4332-3518-4(8)); audio compact disk 60.00 (978-1-4332-3519-1(6)) Blckstn Audio.

Blacknock Woman. unabr. ed. Brian Cooper. Read by Christopher Kay. 10 cass. (Running Time: 13 hrs. 30 mins.). 2000. 84.95 (978-1-86042-612-4(3), 26123) Pub: Soundings Ltd GBR. Dist(s): Ulverscroft US

Blackout. abr. ed. John J. Nance. Read by John J. Nance. 4 cass. Library ed. (Running Time: 6 hrs.). 2003. 62.25 (978-1-59086-670-2(3), 1590866703, CD Lib Edit); audio compact disk 74.25 (978-1-59086-883-6(8), 1590868838, BACDLib Ed) Brilliance Audio.

Minutes after a Boeing 747 rises majestically into a Hong Kong sunset, a flash splits the darkening sky. The pilot - suddenly blinded and doubled over in pain - fumbles in the dark in a frantic effort to gain control as the huge jet shudders through its descent. Kat Bronsky, FBI agent and terrorism specialist, is assigned the hunt for a Challenger-class business jet seen nearby just before the incident. The case poses countless questions: Was the flash a pilot error, a missile attack, or a malfunction? Or was it some new kind of weapon? And why are several government agencies interested in what Kat uncovers?.

Blackout. abr. ed. John J. Nance. Read by John J. Nance. (Running Time: 6 hrs.). 2006. 39.25 (978-1-4233-0024-3(6), 9781423300243, BADLE); audio compact disk 39.25 (978-1-4233-0022-9(X), 9781423300229, Brlnc Audio MP3 Lib); audio compact disk 24.95 (978-1-4233-0021-2(1), 9781423300212, Brilliance MP3) Brilliance Audio.

Blackout. abr. ed. John J. Nance. Read by John J. Nance. (Running Time: 6 hrs.). 2006. 24.95 (978-1-4233-0023-6(8), 9781423300236, BAD) Brilliance Audio.

***Blackout.** unabr. ed. Connie Willis. Read by Kellgren Katherine. (Running Time: 19 hrs.). 2010. 44.97 (978-1-4418-7520-4(4), 9781441875204, BADLE) Brilliance Audio.

***Blackout.** unabr. ed. Connie Willis. Read by Katherine Kellgren. (Running Time: 19 hrs.). 2010. 44.97 (978-1-4418-7519-8(0), 9781441875198, Brlnc Audio MP3 Lib) Brilliance Audio.

***Blackout.** unabr. ed. Connie Willis. Read by Kellgren Katherine. (Running Time: 19 hrs.). 2010. audio compact disk 39.99 (978-1-4418-7516-7(6), 9781441875167, Bril Audio CD Unabri) Brilliance Audio.

***Blackout.** unabr. ed. Connie Willis. Read by Katherine Kellgren. (Running Time: 19 hrs.). 2010. audio compact disk 89.97 (978-1-4418-7517-4(4), 9781441875174, BriAudCD Unabrid) Brilliance Audio.

***Blackout.** unabr. ed. Connie Willis & Kellgren Katherine. (Running Time: 19 hrs.). 2010. 29.99 (978-1-4418-7518-1(2), 9781441875181, Brilliance MP3) Brilliance Audio.

Blacks & Politics. 1 cass. (Running Time: 30 min.). 8.00 (K0770B090, HarperThor) HarpC GBR.

Blacksmith's Serenade see Poetry of Vachel Lindsay

Blackstone's Pursuits. unabr. ed. Quintin Jardine. Read by Joe Dunlop. 6 cass. (Running Time: 7 hrs.). (Sound Ser.). (J). 2002. 54.95 (978-1-84283-316-2(2)); audio compact disk 64.95 (978-1-84283-372-8(3)) Pub: ISIS Lrg Prnt GBR. Dist(s): Ulverscroft US

Blackthorn Asylum. Nox Arcana. (ENG.). 2009. audio compact disk 13.99 (978-0-9788857-8-6(3)) Monolith.

Blackthorn Cottage. Rowena Summers & Jilly Bond. 2008. 54.95 (978-1-84652-295-6(1)) Pub: Magna Story GBR. Dist(s): Ulverscroft US

Blackthorn Cottage. Rowena Summers & Jully Bond. 2008. audio compact disk 71.95 (978-1-84652-296-3(X)) Pub: Magna Story GBR. Dist(s): Ulverscroft US

Blackwater. Eve Bunting. Narrated by Jeff Woodman. 3 CDs. (Running Time: 3 hrs.). (gr. 5 up). audio compact disk 29.00 (978-0-7887-9521-3(X)) Recorded Bks.

Blackwater. unabr. ed. Eve Bunting. Narrated by Jeff Woodman. 2 cass. (Running Time: 3 hrs.). (YA). 2001. pap. bk. & stu. ed. 36.20 Recorded Bks.

When his cousin visits, Brodie takes him to the swimming hole alongside Blackwater River. But a harmless prank goes too far.

Blackwater. unabr. ed. Eve Bunting. Narrated by Jeff Woodman. 2 pieces. (Running Time: 3 hrs.). (gr. 5 up). 2001. 22.00 (978-0-7887-4730-4(4), 96404E7) Recorded Bks.

Blackwater: The Rise of the World's Most Powerful Mercenary Army. unabr. ed. Jeremy Scahill. Read by Tom Weiner. 11. (Running Time: 52200 sec.). 2007. cass. & cass. 32.95 (978-1-4332-1186-7(6)); audio compact disk & audio compact disk 32.95 (978-1-4332-1187-4(4)); audio compact disk & audio compact disk 29.95 (978-1-4332-1188-1(2)) Blckstn Audio.

Blackwater: The Rise of the World's Most Powerful Mercenary Army. unabr. ed. Jeremy Scahill. Read by Tom Weiner. (Running Time: 52200 sec.). 2007. 85.95 (978-1-4332-1184-3(X)); audio compact disk & audio compact disk 99.00 (978-1-4332-1185-0(8)) Blckstn Audio.

Blackwater: Mercenary Army. Jeremy Scahill. (Running Time: 1 hr. 0 mins. 0 sec.). (PM Audio Ser.). (ENG.). 2010. audio compact disk 14.95 (978-1-60486-101-3(0)) Pub: Pm Pre. Dist(s): IPG Chicago

Blackwater, Rising. Robert Edwards. 1 cass. (Running Time: 60 min.). 1996. 7.00 (978-1-890193-01-0(1)) Red Dragonfly.

Robert Edwards reads 28 of his poems.

Blackwater Sound. unabr. ed. James W. Hall. Read by Dick Hill. 7 cass. (Running Time: 10 hrs.). (Thorn Ser.). 2002. 32.95 (978-1-58788-892-2(0), 1587888920, BAU); 78.25 (978-1-58788-893-9(9), 1587888939, Unabridge Lib Edns) Brilliance Audio.

The Braswell family had everything people would kill for: money, looks, power. But their eldest son, the family's shining light, died in a bizarre fishing accident. And when he disappeared - hauled into the depths by the giant marlin he had been fighting - he took with him a secret so corrupt that it could destroy the Braswells. Ten years later, a huge airliner crashes in the steamy shallows off the Florida coast, killing all aboard. Helping pull bodies from the water, Thorn finds himself drawn into a bizarre conspiracy: someone has developed a high tech weapon capable of destroying electrical systems in a powerful flash. The terrorist potential is huge. How are the secretive Braswells and their family-owned company, MicroDyne, involved? And what does it have to do with the family's obsessive hunt for the great marlin that killed their golden boy? With the Braswells, James W. Hall introduces one of the most evil and dysfunctional families in the history of fiction. And, along with Thorn, he brings back favorite characters from his earlier books, including Alexandra Rafferty and her father, Lawton Collins, a retired and increasingly dotty former police investigator whose methods of investigation result in his kidnapping. A story that bristles with all the heat and tension of a tropical Florida summer, BLACKWATER SOUND is destined to rank among the greatest suspense thrillers of the new decade.

Blackwater Sound. unabr. ed. James W. Hall. Read by Dick Hill. (Running Time: 10 hrs.). (Thorn Ser.). 2004. 39.25 (978-1-59335-527-2(0), 1593355270, Brlnc Audio MP3 Lib) Brilliance Audio.

Blackwater Sound. unabr. ed. James W. Hall. Read by Dick Hill. (Running Time: 10 hrs.). (Thorn Ser.). 2004. 39.25 (978-1-59710-071-7(4), 1597100714, BADLE); 24.95 (978-1-59710-070-0(6), 1597100706, BAD) Brilliance Audio.

Blackwater Sound. unabr. ed. James W. Hall. Read by Dick Hill. (Running Time: 10 hrs.). (Thorn Ser.). 2004. 24.95 (978-1-59335-180-9(1), 1593351801) Soulmate Audio Bks.

Blackwood Farm. unabr. ed. Anne Rice. 12 cass. (Running Time: 18 hrs.). (Vampire Chronicles: Bk. 9). 2002. 96.00 (978-0-7366-8865-9(X)) Books on Tape.

Bladder Cancer - A Bibliography & Dictionary for Physicians, Patients, & Genome Researchers. Compiled by Icon Group International, Inc. Staff. 2007. ring bd. 28.95 (978-0-497-11372-8(4)) Icon Grp.

Blade Runner. 25th unabr. movie tie-in ed. Philip K. Dick. Read by Scott Brick. 8 CDs. (Running Time: 9 hrs. 30 mins.). Orig. Title: Do Androids Dream of Electric Sheep?. (ENG.). 2007. audio compact disk 34.95 (978-0-7393-4275-6(4), Random AudioBks) Pub: Random Audio Pubg. Dist(s): Random

***Blades of Grass & Pure White Ston.** Steve Amerson. (ENG.). 2007. audio compact disk 15.00 (978-5-558-37405-6(5)) Pub: Amerson Mus Min. Dist(s): STL Dist NA

Blades of Grass (audio, text, illustrations, & cover with player Included) Judy Litman. Perf. by Judy Litman. (ENG., 2009. 2.99 (978-0-9672800-8-0(7)) J Litman Pubn.

Blah, Blah, Blah: More Stories by Bill Harley. (J). 2005. audio compact disk 15.00 (978-1-878126-47-4(4)) Round Riv Prodns.

Blaiseadh: A Collection of Poems, Folktales & Stories. 1995. audio compact disk 19.95 (978-0-8023-0028-7(6)) Pub: Clo Iar-Chonnachta IRL. Dist(s): Dufour

Blake. unabr. collector's ed. Peter Ackroyd. Read by Ian Whitcomb. 13 cass. (Running Time: 19 hrs. 30 mins.). 1997. 104.00 (978-0-7366-3593-6(9), 4245) Books on Tape.

As poet & painter, William Blake ranks among the most brilliant lights of English cultural history & among the strangest.

Blake & Manchild. unabr. ed. Benjamin DeMott. 1 cass. (Running Time: 36 min.). 1968. 12.95 (23254) J Norton Pubs.

Demott discusses the poetry of William Blake, & recommends anthologies & collections containing Blake's work.

Blake by Dancing Beetle. Perf. by Eugene Ely. 1 cass. (Running Time: 78 min.). (J). 1991. 10.00 Erthviibz.

William Blake, parody & nature sounds come together when Ms. Zebra & the spunky musical humans read & sing with Dancing Beetle.

Blake on Religion. Neville Goddard. 1 cass. (Running Time: 62 min.). 1963. 8.00 (51) J & L Pubns.

Neville taught Imagination Creates Reality. He was a powerfully influential teacher of God as Consciousness.

Blake's 7 - Liberator, Episode 3. Based on a story by Terry Nation. Prod. by Andrew Mark Sewell. 2008. audio compact disk 27.98 (978-1-906577-03-2(X)) Pub: BSeven Media GBR. Dist(s): Mikes Comics

Blake's 7 - Rebel, Episode 1. exp. ed. Adapted by Terry Nation. Based on a story by Terry Nation. Prod. by Andrew Mark Sewell. Adapted by Ben Aaronovitch. (ENG., 2008. audio compact disk 15.98 (978-1-906577-01-8(3)) Pub: BSeven Media GBR. Dist(s): Mikes Comics

Blake's 7 - Traitor, Episode 2. exp. ed. Based on a work by Terry Nation. Prod. by Andrew Mark Sewell. (ENG., 2008. audio compact disk 15.98 (978-1-906577-02-5(1)) Pub: BSeven Media GBR. Dist(s): Mikes Comics

Blake's 7: Cygnus Alpha: Based on the BBC TV Series by Terry Nation. Created by Terry Nation. Adapted by Trevor Hoyle. (Running Time: 3 hrs. 0 mins. 0 sec.). (ENG.). 2009. audio compact disk 29.95 (978-1-60283-776-8(7)) Pub: AudioGO. Dist(s): Perseus Dist

Blake's 7 Season One Set with Slilpcase, Season 1. gif. ed. Based on a story by Terry Nation. Prod. by Andrew Mark Sewell. (ENG.). 2008. audio compact disk 59.98 (978-1-906577-04-9(8)) Pub: BSeven Media GBR. Dist(s): Mikes Comics

Blake's 7; the Early Years - Blake. Prod. by Andrew Mark Sewell. (ENG.). 2010. audio compact disk 15.98 (978-1-906577-11-7(0)) Pub: BSeven Media GBR. Dist(s): Mikes Comics

Blake's 7; the Early Years - Cally: Blood & Earth / Flag & Flame. Marc Platt & Ben Aaronovitch. Prod. by Andrew Mark Sewell. Directed By Dominic Devine. (ENG.). 2009. audio compact disk 15.98 (978-1-906577-07-0(2)) Pub: BSeven Media GBR. Dist(s): Mikes Comics

Blake's 7; the Early Years - Jenna: The Dust Run / the Trial. Simon Guerrier. (ENG.). 2009. audio compact disk 15.98 (978-1-906577-08-7(0)) Pub: BSeven Media GBR. Dist(s): Mikes Comics

Blake's 7; the Early Years - Point of No Return / Eye of the Machine: Travis & Avon, Vol. 1213. Ben Aaronovitch & James Swallow. Based on a story by Terry Nation. Prod. by Andrew Mark Sewell. (ENG., 2008. audio compact disk 27.98 (978-1-906577-06-3(4)) Pub: BSeven Media GBR. Dist(s): Mikes Comics

Blake's 7; the Early Years - Servalan. Prod. by Andrew Mark Sewell. (ENG.). 2010. audio compact disk 15.98 (978-1-906577-10-0(2)) Pub: BSeven Media GBR. Dist(s): Mikes Comics

Blake's 7; the Early Years - When Vila Met Gan, Vol. 11. Ben Aaronovitch. Based on a story by Terry Nation. Prod. by Andrew Mark Sewell. (ENG., 2008. audio compact disk 15.98 (978-1-906577-05-6(6)) Pub: BSeven Media GBR. Dist(s): Mikes Comics

Blake's 7; the Early Years - Zen: Escape Velocity. James Swallow. Directed By Andrew Mark Sewell. (ENG.). 2009. audio compact disk 15.98 (978-1-906577-09-4(9)) Pub: BSeven Media GBR. Dist(s): Mikes Comics

Blake's 7: the Way Back: Based on the BBC TV Series by Terry Nation. Created by Terry Nation. Adapted by Trevor Hoyle. (Running Time: 3 hrs. 0 mins. 0 sec.). (ENG.). 2009. audio compact disk 29.95 (978-1-60283-777-5(5)) Pub: AudioGO. Dist(s): Perseus Dist

Blame. unabr. ed. Michelle Huneven. (Running Time: 10 hrs. 30 mins.). 2009. 29.95 (978-1-4332-9336-8(6)); 65.95 (978-1-4332-9332-0(3)); audio compact disk 29.95 (978-1-4332-9335-1(8)); audio compact disk 100.00 (978-1-4332-9333-7(1)) Blckstn Audio.

***Blame it on Barbara.** Cb Lilley. 2009. audio compact disk (978-1-61658-310-1(X)) Indep Pub IL.

Blameless. unabr. ed. Lisa Reardon. Read by Carrington McDuffie. 6 vols. (Running Time: 9 hrs.). 2000. bk. 54.95 (978-0-7927-2391-2(0), CSL 280, Chivers Sound Lib) AudioGO.

Mary Culpepper is a strong woman, fearless & independent to a fault. But when she discovers the body of a child in her small northern Michigan town, she suffers a breakdown that has her family & friends treating her like "sulfuric acid about to spatter". Mary does all she can to keep her mind off the upcoming trial, where she will have to tell what she did & did not witness. As the trial looms closer, Mary's past catches up to her & nothing can fend off the presence of the Night Visitor, a monster of stone & silence who destroys her sleep.

Blanca Nieves y Muchos Cuentos Mas, Vol. 3. abr. ed.Tr. of Snow White, Simbad the Sailor, Alice's Adventures in Wonderland & Many More Tales. (SPA.). 2001. audio compact disk 13.00 (978-958-9494-30-1(7)) YoYoMusic.

Blancanieves y los Siete Enanitos. l.t. ed. Short Stories. Illus. by Graham Percy. 1 cass. (Running Time: 10 mins.). Dramatization. (SPA.). (J). (ps-3). 2001. 9.95 (978-84-86154-53-0(7)) Peralt Mont ESP.

Blanche McCrary Boyd. unabr. ed. Blanche M. Boyd. Read by Blanche M. Boyd. 1 cass. (Running Time: 29 min.). 1987. 10.00 (121187) New Letters.

Author of "The Redneck Way of Knowledge" reads from a story, "My Town." Boyd talks about the effect drugs had on her writing & life.

Blanche Neige et les Sept Nains. 1 CD. (Running Time: 1 hr.).Tr. of Snow White & the Seven Dwarfs. (FRE.). 2002. pap. bk. 12.95 (978-2-89558-064-5(2)) Pub: Coffragants CAN. Dist(s): Penton Overseas

Blanche Neige et les Sept Nains. 1 cass.Tr. of Snow White & the Seven Dwarfs. (FRE.). (J). (gr. 4 up). 1991. bk. 14.95 (1AD019) Olivia & Hill.

Blanco River Tour. Created by Carol King. 2 CDs. 2005. audio compact disk 24.95 (978-0-9668839-2-3(6)) TX Daytripper.

Blandings Castle. unabr. ed. P. G. Wodehouse. Read by James Saxon. 8 cass. (Running Time: 12 hrs.). 2001. 69.95 (978-0-7540-0586-5(0), CAB2009) Pub: Chivers Audio Bks GBR. Dist(s): AudioGO

Attempting to captivate the affections of the Rev. Rupert Bingham's fiancee; Lord Emsworth is striving to remove a pumpkin-shaped blot on the family escutcheon; the Hon. Freddie Threepwood is making a last attempt to convert Lady Alcester to the beneficial quality of Donaldson's Dog-Joy & in the bar-parlor of the Angler's Rest, Mr. Mulliner fascinates everyone with the secret history of old Hollywood.

Blandings Castle. unabr. ed. P. G. Wodehouse. Read by James Saxon. 8 CDs. (Running Time: 12 hrs.). 2001. audio compact disk 79.95 (978-0-7540-5406-1(3), CCD097) Pub: Chivers Audio Bks GBR. Dist(s): AudioGO

Attempting to captivate the affections of the Rev. Rupert Bingham's fiancee, Lord Emsworth is striving to remove a pumpkin-shaped blot on the family escutcheon. The Hon. Freddie Threepwood is making a last-ditch attempt to convert Lady Alcester to the beneficial quality of Donaldson's Dog-Joy & in the bar-parlor of the Angler's Rest, Mr. Mulliner fascinates everyone with the secret history of old Hollywood.

Blanket Bay Lullabies. Perf. by Jennifer Lind & Kelly Kunz. Illus. by Kevin Kinz. 1 cass. (Running Time: 1 hr. 04 min.). (Dreamland Ser.: Vol. 1). (J). 1995. 10.95 (978-0-9651805-0-4(6), Dreamland Mus) Pepper Jelly.

Twelve original & traditional lullabies.

Blanket Full of Dreams. Perf. by Cathy Fink & Marcy Marxer. 1 CD. (Running Time: 41 mins.). (J). audio compact disk (978-1-886767-18-8(1)) Rounder Records.

A collection of songs for nighttime, nap time, or any quiet, reflective time with a child. Lullabies are meant to help children rest peacefully with a sense of love & security - the love of a parent or guardian & the security of knowing that they can sleep all night in a "Blanket of Dreams". This album began as a series of gifts - songs for special children in our lives to give them each a sense of well being before drifting off to sleep. We hope that you'll not only play this music, but sing along with it until the songs become yours. You'll find that your children will also sing them back to you.

Blanket Full of Dreams. Cathy Fink & Marcy Marxer. (Running Time: 42 min.). 1997. 9.98; audio compact disk 14.98 Rounder Records.

This recording combines guitar, banjo & vocals which create a diverse collection of lullabies.

Blanket Full of Dreams. Perf. by Cathy Fink & Marcy Marxer. 1 cass. (Running Time: 41 mins.). (J). 2000. (978-1-886767-19-5(X)) Rounder Records.
A collection of songs for nighttime, nap time, or any quiet, reflective time with a child. Lullabies are meant to help children rest peacefully with a sense of love & security - the love of a parent or guardian & the security of knowing that they can sleep all night in a "Blanket of Dreams". This album began as a series of gifts - songs for special children in our lives to give them each a sense of well being before drifting off to sleep. We hope that you'll not only play this music, but sing along with it until the songs become yours. You'll find that your children will also sing them back to you.

Blanksmanship. Poems. John M. Bennett. Read by John M. Bennett. Music by James Wiese. 1 cass. 1994. pap. bk. 10.00 (978-0-935350-49-4(7)); pap. bk. 6.00 (978-0-935350-48-7(9)) Luna Bisonte.
A long surrealist poetry sequence, accompanied by an audio tape of performances of same.

Blarney Pilgrim - Celtic Fingerstyle Guitar Solos. Compiled by Stefan Grossman. 1999. pap. bk. 19.95 (978-0-7866-4495-7(8), 97242BCD) Mel Bay.

Blasad Gaidhlig. Donald MacLennan. Read by Donald MacLennan. 1 cass., bklet. (Running Time: 56 mins.). (GAE & ENG.). pap. bk. 21.95 J Norton Pubs.
This program, which translates to "A Taste of Gaelic," offers essential words & phrases of everyday conversations, first pronounced slowly by a native speaker with a pause of equal length for repetition by the learner, then spoken in normal conversation with equal pauses & English translations.

***Blasphemer.** unabr. ed. Nigel Farndale. (Running Time: 13 hrs.). 2010. 29.95 (978-1-4417-6509-3(3)); 79.95 (978-1-4417-6506-2(9)); audio compact disk 109.00 (978-1-4417-6507-9(7)); audio compact disk 32.95 (978-1-4417-6508-6(5)) Blckstn Audio.

Blasphemy. unabr. ed. Douglas Preston. Narrated by Scott Sowers. 1 MP3-CD. (Running Time: 14 hrs.). 2008. 59.95 (978-0-7927-5299-8(6)); audio compact disk 99.95 (978-0-7927-5227-1(9)) AudioGO.
The world's biggest supercollider, locked in an Arizona mountain, was built to unlock the secrets of the very moment of creation: the Big Bang itself. Twelve scientists under the leadership of a famed Nobel Laureate are sent to the remote mountain to turn it on...And what they discover must be hidden from the world at all costs. Wyman Ford, ex-monk and CIA operative, is tapped to wrest from the team their secret, a secret that will either destroy the world - or save it.

Blasphemy. unabr. ed. Douglas Preston. Read by Scott Sowers. 11 CDs. (Running Time: 14 hrs. 0 mins. 0 sec.). (ENG.). 2008. audio compact disk 39.95 (978-1-4272-0274-1(5)) Pub: Macmill Audio. Dist(s): Macmillan

***Blast from the Past.** Meg Cabot. (Allie Finkle's Rules for Girls Ser.). (ENG.). 2010. audio compact disk 49.99 (978-0-545-23346-0(1)) Scholastic Inc.

***Blast from the Past.** Meg Cabot. Narrated by Tara Sands. (Allie Finkle's Rules for Girls Ser.). (ENG.). 2010. audio compact disk 19.99 (978-0-545-20963-2(3)) Scholastic Inc.

Blast from the Past. abr. ed. Kinky Friedman. Read by Kinky Friedman. 2 cass. 1998. 17.95 Set. (978-1-55935-282-6(5), 282-5BK) Soundelux.
The prequel to "Roadkill" answers the burning question: "Where did those weird characters come from anyway?".

Blast from the Past, Set. unabr. ed. Ben Elton. Read by Michael Maloney. 8 cass. (Running Time: 12 hrs.). 1999. 69.95 (978-0-7540-0323-6(X), CAB1746) Pub: Chivers Audio Bks GBR. Dist(s): AudioGO
It's 2:15 a.m., you're alone in bed & the phone wakes you. Only someone bad would ring you at such an hour, or someone with bad news. You wait for the answering machine to come on. You listen. And then you hear the one voice in the world you would least expect..your very own Blast from the Past!.

Blast Off: Activity Fun Pack. Sally A. Bonkrude. Ed. by Karla Lange & Steve Bonkrude. Illus. by Terri Bahn. 1 cass. Dramatization. (J). (ps-3). 1988. bk. 12.95 (978-0-924829-03-1(6)); 5.95 (978-0-924829-11-6(7)) Musical Imag.
Tape Covering Gravity, the Sun, Planets & Space Shuttle.

Blast Off: Level One. Victoria Gross et al. Illus. by Jacqueline Thompson. 1 cass. (Running Time: 1 hr. 30 min.). (Lado Kids Ser.). (J). 11.99 (978-1-879580-66-4(7)) Lado Intl Pr.

Blast Off Boy & Blorp the Big Science Fair. Dan Yaccarino. Narrated by L. J. Ganser. (Running Time: 15 mins.). (gr. k up). 10.00 (978-1-4025-3514-7(7)) Recorded Bks.

Blast off with Ellen Ochoa! Audiocassette. (Greetings Ser.: Vol. 3). (gr. 2-3). 10.00 (978-0-7635-5875-8(3)) Rigby Educ.

Blast Past Road Rage. Richard Driscoll & Helen Smith. 1 cass. (Running Time: 1 hr.). 2001. 9.00 (978-0-9634126-3-8(9)) Westside Pubng.
Informaton on road rage & stress reduction training to brush off highway hostility.

Blast to the Past. Scott Nickel. Illus. by Steve Harpster. (Time Blasters Ser.). (J). (gr. 2-5). 2007. 14.60 (978-1-59889-996-2(1)) CapstoneDig.

Blasting from Heaven see Philip Levine

Blath Gach Geag da DTig. Contrib. by Lillis O. Laoire. (ENG.). 1992. audio compact disk 21.95 (978-0-8023-8075-3(1)) Pub: Clo Iar-Chonnachta IRL. Dist(s): Dufour

***Blath Gach Geag Da Dtig.** Lillis O. Laoire. (ENG.). 1992. 11.95 (978-0-8023-7075-4(6)) Pub: Clo Iar-Chonnachta IRL. Dist(s): Dufour

Blath na HOige. Contrib. by Mairtin Tom Sheainin. (ENG.). 1997. 13.95 (978-0-8023-7128-7(0)); audio compact disk 21.95 (978-0-8023-8128-6(6)) Pub: Clo Iar-Chonnachta IRL. Dist(s): Dufour

Blaze. abr. ed. Susan Johnson. Read by Alana Windsor. 1 cass. (Running Time: 90 min.). 1994. 5.99 (978-1-57096-006-2(2), RAZ 907) Romance Alive Audio.
To beautiful Blaze Braddock, the American gold rush was a chance to flee the stifling codes of Boston society. But when Jon Hazard Black, a proud Absarokee chief challenged her father's land claim, Blaze was swept up in a storm of passion she had never before even imagined.

Blaze. unabr. ed. Di Morrissey. Read by Kate Hood. (Running Time: 21 hrs.). 2007. 54.95 (978-1-74093-999-7(9), 9781740939997); audio compact disk 123.95 (978-1-74093-914-0(X), 9781740939140) Pub: Bolinda Pubng AUS. Dist(s): Bolinda Pub Inc

Blaze. unabr. ed. JoAnn Ross. 10 cass. (Running Time: 15 hrs.). 2005. 90.00 (978-1-4159-2370-2(1)); audio compact disk 84.15 (978-1-4159-2371-9(X)) Pub: Books on Tape. Dist(s): NetLibrary CO

Blaze. unabr. ed. Richard Bachman, pseud. Read by Ron McLarty. (Running Time: 7 hrs. 30 mins. 0 sec.). (ENG.). 2008. audio compact disk 24.95 (978-0-7435-7270-5(X)) Pub: S&S Audio. Dist(s): S and S Inc

Ble en Herbe, Set. Sidonie-Gabrielle Colette. Read by C. Deis & D. Blot. 2 cass. (FRE.). 1991. 26.95 (1437-VSL) Olivia & Hill.
Philippe & Vinca have summered on the Brittany coast since their infancy. This summer, they are 16 & 15 respectively & their awkward age has brought them to the brink of a crisis as they face their growing sexuality.

Bleachers. unabr. ed. John Grisham. Read by John Grisham. 3 cass. (Running Time: 4 hrs. 30 min.). 2003. 25.20 (978-0-7366-9658-6(X)); audio compact disk 28.80 (978-0-7366-9659-3(8)) Books on Tape.

Bleachers. unabr. ed. John Grisham. Read by John Grisham. Read by Jack Cristil. 4 CDs. (Running Time: 4 hrs. 30 mins.). (John Grisham Ser.). (ENG.). 2003. audio compact disk 24.95 (978-0-7393-1016-8(X)) Pub: Random Audio Pubg. Dist(s): Random

***Bleak Expectations.** Johnny Vegas & British Broadcasting Corporation Staff. Created by Mark Evans. (Running Time: 3 hrs. 0 mins. 0 sec.). (ENG.). 2010. audio compact disk 29.95 (978-1-4056-8942-7(0)) Pub: AudioGO. Dist(s): Perseus Dist

Bleak Expectations. unabr. ed. British Broadcasting Corporation Staff. Created by Mark Evans. Narrated by Full Cast. (Running Time: 3 hrs. 0 mins. 0 sec.). (ENG.). 2010. audio compact disk 29.95 (978-1-60283-839-0(9)) Pub: AudioGO. Dist(s): Perseus Dist

***Bleak Expectations 3: The Complete Third Series.** Mark Evans. Narrated by Full Cast. (Running Time: 3 hrs. 0 mins. 0 sec.). (ENG.). 2010. audio compact disk 29.95 (978-1-4084-2718-7(4)) Pub: AudioGO. Dist(s): Perseus Dist

Bleak House. Charles Dickens. 4 cass. 1999. 24.35 Set. (978-0-563-55836-1(9)) BBC WrldWd GBR.
A scathing satire on the corruption & imcompetence of the law & a vividly drawn portrait of life in Victorian London.

Bleak House. Charles Dickens. Read by Hugh Dickson. 30 cass. 220.00 (CC/038) C to C Cassettes.

Bleak House. Charles Dickens. Narrated by Jim Killavey. (Running Time: 29 hrs.). 1987. 21.95 (978-1-59912-821-4(7)) Iofy Corp.

Bleak House. Charles Dickens. Read by Jim Killavey. 29 cass. (Running Time: 90 min. per cass.). 1987. 140.00 incl. albums. (C-178) Jimcin Record.
Dickens turns his biting satire on the courts, the slums, the aristocracy & many other targets.

Bleak House. Charles Dickens. Read by David Case. (Running Time: 142200 sec.). (ENG.). 2006. audio compact disk 149.99 (978-1-4001-3264-5(9)); audio compact disk 74.99 (978-1-4001-0264-8(2)); audio compact disk 49.99 (978-1-4001-5264-3(X)) Pub: Tantor Media. Dist(s): IngramPubServ

Bleak House. abr. ed. Charles Dickens. Read by Paul Scofield. (Running Time: 10800 sec.). 2007. audio compact disk 19.95 (978-1-4332-0699-3(4)); audio compact disk & audio compact disk 27.00 (978-1-4332-1347-2(8)) Blckstn Audio.

Bleak House. abr. ed. Charles Dickens. Read by Sean Barrett & Teresa Gallagher. (Running Time: 40548 sec.). 2007. audio compact disk 59.98 (978-962-634-443-9(1), Naxos AudioBooks) Naxos.

Bleak House. abr. ed. Charles Dickens. Read by Paul Scofield. 3 CDs. (Running Time: 3 hrs.). 2004. audio compact disk 24.95 (978-1-59007-569-2(2)); 18.00 (978-1-931056-56-4(0), N Millennium Audio) New Millenn Enter.
A compelling mystery, aromatic tangle of trails followed by three vivid sleuths: the opportunistic guppy, the sinister talking horn & the benevolent bucket.

Bleak House. unabr. ed. Charles Dickens. Narrated by Flo Gibson. (Running Time: 32 hrs. 43 mins.). 1997. 61.95 (978-1-55685-797-3(7)) Audio Bk Con.

Bleak House. unabr. ed. Charles Dickens. Read by Robert Whitfield. (Running Time: 118800 sec.). 2007. audio compact disk 39.95 (978-0-7861-6143-0(4)) Blckstn Audio.

Bleak House. unabr. ed. Charles Dickens. Read by Robert Whitfield. (Running Time: 118800 sec.). 2007. audio compact disk 59.95 (978-0-7861-5874-4(3)) Blckstn Audio.

Bleak House. unabr. ed. Charles Dickens. Read by David Case. (YA). 2007. 99.99 (978-1-59895-787-7(2)) Find a World.

Bleak House. unabr. ed. Charles Dickens. Read by Sean Barrett & Teresa Gallagher. 28 CDs. (Running Time: 126931 sec.). 2006. audio compact disk 152.98 (978-962-634-431-6(8), NAX43112, Naxos AudioBooks) Naxos.

Bleak House. unabr. ed. Charles Dickens. Narrated by David Case. (Running Time: 39 hrs. 30 mins. 0 sec.). (ENG.). 2009. audio compact disk 129.99 (978-1-4001-3908-8(2)) Pub: Tantor Media. Dist(s): IngramPubServ

Bleak House. unabr. ed. Charles Dickens. Read by David Case. (Running Time: 39 hrs. 30 mins. 0 sec.). (ENG.). 2009. 44.99 (978-1-4001-5908-6(3)) Pub: Tantor Media. Dist(s): IngramPubServ

Bleak House, Pt. 1. unabr. ed. Charles Dickens. Read by Flo Gibson. 12 cass. (Running Time: 1 hr. 30 min. per cass.). 1997. 65.95 Part 2 only, set. Audio Bk Con.
Dickens attacks the interminable delays, absurdities, & dissipated funds in litigation that drags on from generation to generation. Illegitimacy, murder & two love stories are also part of this great epic.

Bleak House, Pt. 1. unabr. ed. Charles Dickens. Read by Robert Whitfield. 14 cass. (Running Time: 35 hrs.). 1999. 89.95 (978-0-7861-1478-8(9), 2330A,B) Blckstn Audio.
Embodies Dickens' merciless indictment of the Court of Chancery & its bungling, morally corrupt handling of the endless case of "Jarndyce v. Jarndyce," giving the novel its scope & meaning.

Bleak House, Pt. 2. unabr. ed. Charles Dickens. Read by Robert Whitfield. 10 cass. (Running Time: 35 hrs.). 1999. 69.95 (978-0-7861-1487-0(8), 2330A,B) Blckstn Audio.

Bleak House, Pt. 2, set. unabr. ed. Charles Dickens. 10 cass. (Running Time: 1 hr. 30 min. per cass.). 1997. 65.95 Audio Bk Con.

Bleak House, Pt. 2, set. unabr. ed. Charles Dickens. 10 cass. (Running Time: 15 hrs.). 1999. 65.95 Audio Bk Con.
Dickens attacks the interminable delays, absurdities & dissipated funds in litigation that drags on from generation to generation. Illegitimacy, murder & two love stories are also part of this great epic.

Bleak House, Pt. A. unabr. collector's ed. Charles Dickens. Read by David Case. 14 cass. (Running Time: 21 hrs.). (J). 1992. 112.00 (978-0-7366-2127-4(X), 2929-A) Books on Tape.
The futility of law, the hardships of children, mystery & romance all combined by a master.

Bleak House, Pt. B. unabr. collector's ed. Charles Dickens. Read by David Case. 14 cass. (Running Time: 21 hrs.). (J). 1992. 112.00 (978-0-7366-2128-1(8), 2929-B) Books on Tape.

Bleak House, Set, Pt. 1. unabr. ed. Charles Dickens. Read by Robert Whitfield. 14 cass. 1999. 89.95 (FS9-51109) Highsmith.

Bleak House, Set, Pt. 2. unabr. ed. Charles Dickens. 10 cass. 1999. 69.95 (FS9-51137) Highsmith.

Bleak House Part 1. unabr. ed. Charles Dickens. Read by Robert Whitfield. (Running Time: 64800 sec.). 2007. audio compact disk 120.00 (978-0-7861-5872-0(7)) Blckstn Audio.

Bleak House (Part 1), Vol. 11. unabr. ed. [illegible]es Dickens. Read by Flo Gibson. 12 cass. (Running Time: 1 hr. [illegible]. per cass.). 1997. 39.95 (978-1-55685-448-4(X), 448-X) Audio Bk Con.
Dickens attacks the interminable delays, absurdities, & dissipated funds in litigation that drags on from generation to generation. Illegitimacy, murder & two love stories are also part of this great epic.

Bleak House Part 2. unabr. ed. Charles Dickens. Read by Robert Whitfield. (Running Time: 59400 sec.). 2007. audio compact disk 120.00 (978-0-7861-5873-7(5)) Blckstn Audio.

Bleak House (Part 2), Vol. 2. unabr. ed. Charles Dickens. Narrated by Flo Gibson. (Running Time: 14 hrs. 50 mins.). 1997. 29.95 (978-1-55685-796-6(9)) Audio Bk Con.

Bleak House, with EBook. unabr. ed. Charles Dickens. Narrated by David Case. (Running Time: 39 hrs. 30 mins. 0 sec.). (ENG.). 2009. audio compact disk 64.99 (978-1-4001-0908-1(6)) Pub: Tantor Media. Dist(s): IngramPubServ

Bleak Spring. unabr. ed. Jon Cleary. Read by Christian Rodska. 8 cass. (Running Time: 12 hrs.). 2003. 69.95 (978-0-7540-0921-4(1), CAB 2343) AudioGO.

Bleating Wolves: The Meaning of Evangelical & Catholics Together. John Robbins. 1 cass. (Conference on Christianity & Roman Catholicism Ser.; No. 1). 5.00 Trinity Found.

Blechtrommel see Tin Drum

***Bleed a River Deep.** Brian McGilloway. Read by John Cormack. 2010. 54.95 (978-1-84652-621-3(3)); audio compact disk 71.95 (978-1-84652-622-0(1)) Pub: Magna Story GBR. Dist(s): Ulverscroft US

Bleeders. unabr. ed. Bill Pronzini. Read by Gregory Gorton. 8 CDs. (Running Time: 12 hrs.). (Nameless Detective Mystery Ser.). 2002. audio compact disk 79.95 (978-0-7927-2751-4(7), SLD 511, Chivers Sound Lib) AudioGO.
A blackmail case gets lethally complicated when "Nameless" exposes a nasty scam that involves junior accounts executive Jay Cohalan, his unhappy wife, and a mistress with a serious drug problem. For "Nameless," bleeders - the blackmailers, extortionists, small-time grifters, and other opportunists who prey on the weak and gullible - sit near the top of his most-worthless-human-beings list. But soon his client is dead, and he barely escapes a similar fate. In San Francisco's shadowy underworld, he encounters bleeders of every ilk, and, in a climax as powerful as it is unexpected, finally confronts his own demons.

Bleedership: Biblical First-Aid for Leaders. Jim Lange. 2006. audio compact disk 12.99 (978-1-59886-243-0(X)) Tate Pubng.

Bleeding see May Swenson

Bleeding Hearts. unabr. ed. Ian Rankin. Narrated by Steven Pacey. 9 cass. (Running Time: 45000 sec.). 2006. 84.95 (978-0-7927-4551-8(5), CSL 1005); audio compact disk 94.95 (978-0-7927-4378-1(4), SLD 1005); audio compact disk 59.95 (978-0-7927-4574-7(4), CMP 1005) AudioGO.

Bleeding Hearts. unabr. ed. Ian Rankin. Read by Steven Pacey. (YA). 2007. 79.99 (978-1-60252-817-8(9)) Find a World.

Bleeding Kansas. Sara Paretsky. Read by Susan Ericksen. (Playaway Adult Fiction Ser.). 2008. 89.99 (978-1-60640-586-4(1)) Find a World.

Bleeding Kansas. abr. ed. Sara Paretsky. Read by Susan Ericksen. (Running Time: 6 hrs.). 2008. audio compact disk 14.99 (978-1-4233-1988-7(5), 9781423319887, BCD Value Price) Brilliance Audio.

Bleeding Kansas. unabr. ed. Sara Paretsky. (Running Time: 17 hrs.). (V. I. Warshawski Ser.). 2008. 39.25 (978-1-4233-1986-3(9), 9781423319863, BADLE) Brilliance Audio.

Bleeding Kansas. unabr. ed. Sara Paretsky. Read by Susan Ericksen. 1 MP3-CD. (Running Time: 17 hrs.). (V. I. Warshawski Ser.). 2008. 39.25 (978-1-4233-1984-9(2), 9781423319849, Brinc Audio MP3 Lib); 24.95 (978-1-4233-1983-2(4), 9781423319832, Brilliance MP3); 24.95 (978-1-4233-1985-6(0), 9781423319856, BAD); 117.25 (978-1-4233-1980-1(X), 9781423319801, BrilAudUnabridg); audio compact disk 122.25 (978-1-4233-1982-5(6), 9781423319825, BriAudCD Unabrid); audio compact disk 40.95 (978-1-4233-1981-8(8), 9781423319818, Bril Audio CD Unabri) Brilliance Audio.

Bleeding of Innocents. unabr. ed. Jo Bannister. 6 cass. 1998. 69.95 Set. (978-1-872672-97-7(3)) Pub: Magna Story GBR. Dist(s): Ulverscroft US

Blended Worship 2. Contrib. by Richard Kingsmore & Camp Kirkland. (Easy to Excel Ser.). 2007. audio compact disk 12.00 (978-5-557-54400-9(3)); audio compact disk 90.00 (978-5-557-54397-2(X)); audio compact disk 90.00 (978-5-557-54396-5(1)) Lillenas.

Blended Worship 2: 12 Praise & Worship Songs with 12 Praise & Worship Hymns Arranged in 12 Medleys. Contrib. by Richard Kingsmore & Camp Kirkland. 2007. audio compact disk 16.99 (978-5-557-54399-6(6)) Lillenas.

Blends & Digraphs. Steck-Vaughn Staff. 1 cass. (Running Time: 90 mins.). (J). 2001. (978-0-7398-4658-2(2)) SteckVau.

Blends & Digraphs. Steven Traugh & Susan Traugh. Ed. by Rozanne Lanczak Williams. Illus. by Diane Valko. (Fun Phonics Ser.: Vol. 8028). 1999. pap. bk. & tchr. ed. 13.99 (978-1-57471-642-9(5), 8028) Creat Teach Pr.

Blends & Digraphs Set: Level D. (Sing-along Songs Ser.). (ps-2). bk. 48.46 (978-0-7362-0422-4(9)) Hampton-Brown.

Blenheim. unabr. ed. David Green. Read by Stuart Courtney. 6 cass. (Running Time: 9 hrs.). 1984. 48.00 (978-0-7366-0420-8(0), 1392) Books on Tape.
In August, 1704, during the war of the Spanish succession, an army of British & Austrians under Marlborough & Prince Eugene defeated an army of French & Bavarian soldiers near the village of Blenheim in West Germany. In consideration of his military services, a princely mansion was erected by Parliament for the Duke of Marlborough in Oxfordshire, England, & was named Blenheim Palace.

Blenheim Lectures. Douglas Wilson. (ENG.). 2008. audio compact disk 20.00 (978-1-59128-203-7(9)) Canon Pr ID.

Bless Me Father. unabr. ed. Neil Boyd. Read by Peter Wheeler. 4 cass. (Running Time: 6 hrs.). 2001. 44.95 (60261) Pub: Soundings Ltd GBR. Dist(s): Ulverscroft US

Bless Me, Ultima see Bendiceme, Ultima

Bless Me, Ultima. Rudolfo A. Anaya. Read by Rudolfo A. Anaya. 1 cass. (Running Time: 51 min.). 1984. 13.95 (978-1-55644-034-2(0), 2011) Am Audio Prose.
Anaya reads from the works "Bless Me Ultima" & "La Tortuga".

Bless Me, Ultima. Rudolfo A. Anaya. Contrib. by Robert Ramirez. 2004. audio compact disk 29.99 Recorded Bks.

Bless Me, Ultima. Rudolfo A. Anaya. Contrib. by Robert Ramirez. 10 CDs. (Running Time: 11 hrs. 15 mins.). 2004. audio compact disk 29.99 (978-1-4025-8365-0(6), 02472) Recorded Bks.

Bless That Wonderful Name Choir Cassette. Greg Skipper & Gail Skipper. 1994. 10.98 (978-0-7673-0691-1(0)) LifeWay Christian.

Bless the Broken Road. Contrib. by Selah. (Praise Hymn Soundtracks Ser.). 2006. audio compact disk 8.98 (978-5-558-02970-3(6)) Pt of Grace Ent.

Bless the Broken Road. Contrib. by Selah & Melodie Crittenden. (Sound Performance Soundtracks Ser.). 2006. audio compact disk 5.98 (978-5-558-25633-8(8)) Pt of Grace Ent.

Bless the Children. Robert C. Guenzel, Jr. Read by Kevin Foley. 6 cass. (Running Time: 7 hrs. 48 min.). 1994. 36.95 Set. (978-1-55686-519-0(8)) Books in Motion.
When middle school teacher Stan Lane discovers a students body stuffed in a school locker, his quest for answers leads him down a trail of intrigue & suspense to teen-age gangs.

Bless the Lord: Taize Chants with English Verses. 1 cass. (Running Time: 60 mins.). 1999. 9.95 (T8170) Liguori Pubns.
Songs include: "Bless the Lord," "Kyrie," "My Soul Is at Rest," "Jesus Your Light" & more.

Bless the Lord: Taize Chants with English Verses. Perf. by Reading Phoenix Choir. 1 cass. (Running Time: 65 min.). 10.95 (AA2707); audio compact disk 14.95 CD. (AA2858) Credence Commun.
These prayerful Taize chants were recorded by the Reading Phoenix Choir in London. Some are old favorites like Veni Sancte Spiritus & Watch & Pray but a number of the songs have never been recorded before.

Bless This House. Norah Lofts. 2008. 94.95 (978-1-4079-0045-2(5)); audio compact disk 99.95 (978-1-4079-0046-9(3)) Pub: Soundings Ltd GBR. Dist(s): Ulverscroft US

***Bless This Mouse.** unabr. ed. Lois Lowry. (Running Time: 2 hrs.). (ENG.). (J). 2011. audio compact disk 22.00 (978-0-307-91627-3(8), Listening Lib) Pub: Random Audio Pubg. Dist(s): Random

Blessed & Highly Favored. Contrib. by Clark Sisters. (Soundtraks Ser.). 2007. audio compact disk 8.99 (978-5-557-60865-7(6)) Christian Wrld.

Blessed Angela of Foligno. 2000. audio compact disk 8.00 (978-1-58002-600-0(1)) Journeys Faith.

Blessed Anna Maria Taigi. 2000. audio compact disk 8.00 (978-1-58002-603-1(6)) Journeys Faith.

***Blessed Are the Bored in Spirit: A Young Catholic's Search for Meaning.** unabr. ed. Mark Hart. 2010. audio compact disk 19.95 (978-0-86716-966-9(4)) St Anthony Mess Pr.

Blessed Are the Cheesemakers. unabr. ed. Sarah-Kate Lynch. Read by Heather O'Neill. (YA). 2006. 49.99 (978-1-59895-530-9(6)) Find a World.

Blessed are the Cheesemakers. unabr. ed. Sarah-Kate Lynch. Read by Heather O'Neill. (Running Time: 8 hrs. 30 mins.). (ENG.). 2003. audio compact disk 34.95 (978-1-56511-753-2(0), 1565117530) Pub: HighBridge. Dist(s): Workman Pub

Blessed Are the Meek. Francis Frangipane. 1 cass. (Running Time: 90 mins.). (Seeing the Multitudes Ser.: Vol. 3). 2000. 5.00 (FF07-003) Morning NC.
From the beatitudes, Francis draws applications for ministry to those who need Jesus.

Blessed Are the Merciful. Francis Frangipane. 1 cass. (Running Time: 90 mins.). (Seeing the Multitudes Ser.: Vol. 5). 2000. 5.00 (FF07-005) Morning NC.

Blessed Are the Poor. 1985. (0284) Evang Sisterhood Mary.

Blessed Are They. 1 cass. 1985. 7.95 (978-1-58638-506-4(2)) Nilgiri Pr.
A recitation & commentary on the Beatitudes of Jesus.

Blessed Are They Who Mourn. Francis Frangipane. 1 cass. (Running Time: 90 mins.). (Seeing the Multitudes Ser.: Vol. 2). 2000. 5.00 (FF07-002) Morning NC.
From the beatitudes, Francis draws applications for ministry to those who need Jesus.

Blessed Are You: The Beatitudes in Full. Dick Rice. Read by Dick Rice. 7 cass. (Running Time: 7 hrs. 30 min.). 1991. 49.95 Set. (978-7-900783-12-7(1), AA2450) Credence Commun.
Father Rice presents the Beatitudes & invites you to experience the power of the Beatitudes now.

***Blessed Assurance.** Contrib. by Chris Barron. (ENG.). 2008. audio compact disk 24.99 (978-5-557-43527-7(1)) Lillenas.

Blessed Assurance. Contrib. by Sandi Patty. (Inoriginal Performance Trax Ser.). 2004. audio compact disk 9.98 (978-5-559-38076-6(8)) INO Rec.

Blessed Assurance. Perf. by Les Stahl. 2004. audio compact disk 17.00 (978-1-58459-173-3(0)) Wrld Lib Pubns.

Blessed Assurance: Hebrews 6:13-20. Ed Young. 1991. 4.95 (978-0-7417-1896-9(0), 896) Win Walk.

Blessed Be Your Name. Contrib. by Tree 63. (Mastertrax Ser.). 2006. audio compact disk 9.98 (978-5-558-01850-9(X)) Pt of Grace Ent.

Blessed Be Your Name: Worshiping God on the Road Marked with Suffering. unabr. ed. Matt Redman & Beth Redman. (ENG.). 2005. audio compact disk 14.99 (978-1-59859-079-1(0)) Oasis Audio.

Blessed Be Your Name, Volume 1: Songs of Matt Redman. Contrib. by Matt Redman et al. 2005. audio compact disk 16.98 (978-5-558-96709-8(9)) Pt of Grace Ent.

Blessed by Association. Perf. by John P. Kee & New Life. 2002. audio compact disk Verity Records.

Blessed by Light. Ana Hernndez. Composed by Ruth Cunningham & Ana Hernández. 2008. audio compact disk 18.00 (978-0-89869-632-5(1)) Church Pub Inc.

Blessed Is She Who Believed! Read by Basilea Schlink. 1 cass. (Running Time: 30 min.). 1985. (0231) Evang Sisterhood Mary.
Discusses hope & the encouragement along dark paths of faith & a Christmas message for a world without peace.

Blessed Is the Man, Vol 1: Keys to Embracing God's Principles of Blessing. Mac Hammond. 2009. audio compact disk 30.00 (978-1-57399-408-8(1)) Mac Hammond.

Blessed Is the Man, Vol 2: The Power Source for Change: How to Live in the Holy Spirit's Power for Your Life. Mac Hammond. 2009. audio compact disk 30.00 (978-1-57399-410-1(3)) Mac Hammond.

Blessed Is the Man, Vol 3: Blessings from the Beatitudes: Unlocking Truths in Jesus¿ Sermon on the Mount. Mac Hammond. 2009. audio compact disk 42.00 (978-1-57399-412-5(X)) Mac Hammond.

Blessed Is the Man, Vol 4: God¿s Final Commentary on Blessing:Revealing the Blessings in the Book of Revelation. Mac Hammond. 2009. audio compact disk 24.00 (978-1-57399-413-2(8)) Mac Hammond.

Blessed Jolt: Isiah 6:1. Ed Young. (J). 1980. 4.95 (978-0-7417-1150-2(8), A0150) Win Walk.

Blessed Junipero Serra. 2000. audio compact disk 8.00 (978-1-58002-659-8(1)) Journeys Faith.

Blessed Kateri Tekakwitha. 2000. audio compact disk 8.00 (978-1-58002-601-7(X)) Journeys Faith.

Blessed Margaret of Castello. 2000. audio compact disk 8.00 (978-1-58002-663-5(X)) Journeys Faith.

Blessed Marriage. Douglas W. Phillips. 1 cass. (Running Time: 59 mins.). 2000. 7.00 (978-1-929241-11-8(9)) Pub: Vsn Forum. Dist(s): STL Dist NA

Blessed Marriage. Douglas W. Phillips. 1 CD. (Running Time: 1 hr. 9 mins.). 2000. audio compact disk 10.00 (978-1-929241-73-6(9)) Pub: Vsn Forum. Dist(s): STL Dist NA
It breaks my heart to hear Christians belittle or minimize the significance of the precious gift called marriage. The Bible teaches that parents are to actively prepare their children for it, that couples are to rejoice in it, and that the Church it to reinforce it.

Blessed Miguel Pro. 2000. audio compact disk 8.00 (978-1-58002-667-3(2)) Journeys Faith.

Blessed Unrest: How the Largest Movement in the World Came into Being, & Why No One Saw It Coming. unabr. ed. Paul Hawken. Read by Paul Michael Garcia. (Running Time: 30600 sec.). 2007. 44.95 (978-1-4332-0320-6(0)); audio compact disk 55.00 (978-1-4332-0321-3(9)) Blckstn Audio.

Blessed Unrest: How the Largest Movement in the World Came into Being & Why No One Saw It Coming. unabr. ed. Paul Hawken. Read by Paul Michael Garcia. (Running Time: 30600 sec.). 2007. 25.95 (978-1-4332-0322-0(7)); audio compact disk 25.95 (978-1-4332-0323-7(5)); audio compact disk 29.95 (978-1-4332-0324-4(3)) Blckstn Audio.

Blessedness of Believing: A Devotional Journey of Life's Lessons & God's Promises. Linda Mose Meadows. 2007. audio compact disk 27.99 (978-1-60247-647-9(0)) Tate Pubng.

Blessing see Poetry & Voice of James Wright

Blessing. Jude Deveraux. Read by Boyd Gaines. 2004. 10.95 (978-0-7435-4204-3(5)) Pub: S&S Audio. Dist(s): S and S Inc

Blessing. Gary Smalley & John T. Trent. Read by Gary Smalley & John T. Trent. 2 cass. (Running Time: 2 hrs.). 1990. 14.99 (978-0-8499-1283-2(0)) Nelson.

Blessing. unabr. ed. Jude Deveraux. Read by Don Jellerson. 6 vols. (Running Time: 9 hrs.). 2001. bk. 54.95 (978-0-7927-2478-0(X), CSL 367, Chivers Sound Lib) AudioGO.
When Jason Wilding takes a break from his business for a Christmas visit to his hometown in Kentucky, he has no idea what his brother, David, has in store for him. It seems that Amy Thompkins, a whimsical young widow, has captured David's heart, but courting her with a demanding baby in tow has been difficult. He persuades Jason to move into her home and take care of her son, Max, for a week. Amy's joy for life, her love for her son, and her sparkling humor are irresistible, and soon Jason starts to thaw - the tender feelings and longings he has buried for years are begging to be heard.

Blessing. unabr. ed. Jude Deveraux. Read by Don Jellerson. 8 CDs. (Running Time: 12 hrs.). 2002. audio compact disk 79.95 (978-0-7927-2744-6(4), SLD 367, Chivers Sound Lib) AudioGO.
Jason Wilding, a wealthy, hard-driving corporate genius, returns to his hometown in Kentucky for a Christmas visit with his brother, David. David's heart has been captured by Amy Thompkins, and he persuades Jason to move into her home for a week to take care of her spoiled but adorable son, Max. Soon Jason starts to thaw. Could romance be far behind?.

Blessing: The Root to the Fruit. Creflo A. Dollar. 4 cass. (Running Time: 6 hrs.). (ENG.). 1999. reel tape 20.00 (978-1-931172-74-5(9), TS285, Kidz Faith) Pub: Creflo Dollar. Dist(s): STL Dist NA

Blessing & Honor. Perf. by Larnelle Harris. 1 cass. 1998. 8.98 (978-0-7601-2697-4(6)) Brentwood Music.

Blessing & It's Meaning. Myron Madden. 1986. 10.80 (0102) Assn Prof Chaplains.

Blessing & the Curse: Joshua 8:30-35. Ed Young. 1985. 4.95 (978-0-7417-1453-4(1), 453) Win Walk.

Blessing in Disguise. Elvi Rhodes. Read by Nicolette McKenzie. 14 cass. (Running Time: 16 hrs.). (Soundings Ser.). (J). 2004. 99.95 (978-1-84283-558-6(0)); audio compact disk 104.95 (978-1-84283-646-0(3)) Pub: ISIS Lrg Prnt GBR. Dist(s): Ulverscroft US

Blessing in Disguise. abr. ed. Eileen Goudge. Read by Sheila Hart. 2 cass., notes. (Running Time: 3 hrs.). 2000. 7.95 (978-1-57815-003-8(5), 1001, Media Bks Audio) Media Bks NJ.
A daughter holds clues to her fathers shocking secrets. Only one person knows what really happened, but she is guarding her own dark secret.

Blessing in Disguise. unabr. ed. Eileen Goudge. Read by Donada Peters. 12 cass. (Running Time: 18 hrs.). 1994. 96.00 (978-0-7366-2804-4(5), 133099) Books on Tape.
A daughter holds clues to her father's shocking secrets & her mother would risk anything to protect those secrets. Was Grace Truscott's own father, a senator, guilty of killing his secretary's husband?.

Blessing in Disguise. unabr. ed. Eileen Goudge. Read by Sheila Hart. (Running Time: 18 hrs.). 2008. 29.95 (978-1-4233-5925-8(9), 9781423359258, BAD); 29.95 (978-1-4233-5923-4(2), 9781423359234, Brilliance MP3); 44.25 (978-1-4233-5926-5(7), 9781423359265, BADLE); 44.25 (978-1-4233-5924-1(0), 9781423359241, Brlnc Audio MP3 Lib) Brilliance Audio.

Blessing Is Yours. unabr. ed. Keith A. Butler. 3 cass. (Running Time: 4 hrs. 30 mins.). 2001. 15.00 (A137) Word Faith Pubng.

Blessing of a Skinned Knee: Using Jewish Teachings to Raise Self-Reliant Children. unabr. ed. Wendy Mogel. Read by Carrington MacDuffie. (Running Time: 30600 sec.). 2007. 54.95 (978-0-7861-4994-0(9)); 19.95 (978-0-7861-4951-3(5)); audio compact disk 63.00 (978-0-7861-4995-7(7)); audio compact disk 29.95 (978-0-7861-7004-3(2)) Blckstn Audio.

Blessing of a Still Mind. unabr. ed. Perf. by Eknath Easwaran. 1 cass. (Running Time: 1 hr.). 1987. 7.95 (978-1-58638-507-1(0)) Nilgiri Pr.

Blessing of Abraham: Reality Red. Featuring Bill Winston. 4 CDs. 2005. audio compact disk 32.00 (978-1-59544-157-7(3)) Pub: B Winston Min. Dist(s): Anchor Distributors

Blessing of Abraham: The Reality of Redemption. Bill Williams & Bill Winston. 4 cass. 2005. 20.00 (978-1-59544-156-0(5)) Pub: B Winston Min. Dist(s): Anchor Distributors

Blessing of the Lord, It Maketh Rich. Kenneth Copeland. (ENG.). 2008. audio compact disk 25.00 (978-1-57562-972-8(0)) K Copeland Pubns.

Blessing of Thorns. Nancy Leigh DeMoss. (ENG.). 2005. audio compact disk 12.00 (978-0-940110-70-0(9)) Life Action Publishing.

***Blessing on the Moon.** unabr. ed. Joseph Skibell. Read by Allen Lewis Rickman. (ENG.). 2010. audio compact disk 29.95 (978-1-61573-532-7(1), 1615735321) Pub: HighBridge. Dist(s): Workman Pub

Blessing or Curse: The Choice Is Yours. Mike Atkins. 8. 2005. audio compact disk 56.00 (978-0-9759218-8-3(6)) M Atkins Min.

Blessing Way. Tony Hillerman. Read by Walter Hawn. 4 cass. (Running Time: 5 hrs. 30 min.). (Joe Leaphorn & Jim Chee Novel Ser.). 1993. 39.80 (978-1-56544-006-7(4), 250020); Rental 7.30 30 day rental Set. (250020) Literate Ear.
Lieutenant Joe Leaphorn of the Navajo Tribal Police knows homicides & knows his people. Fearing the role of the supernatural in a murder with no trace of human presence at the scene, he tracks the Wolf-Witch. Leaphorn balances high-tech with the mysticism of the Navajos.

Blessing Way. Tony Hillerman. Read by George Guidall. 4 Cass. (Running Time: 6.5 Hrs). (Joe Leaphorn & Jim Chee Novel Ser.). 19.95 (978-1-4025-2486-8(2)); audio compact disk 29.95 (978-1-4025-2491-2(9)) Recorded Bks.

Blessing Way. abr. ed. Tony Hillerman. Read by Tony Hillerman. 2 cass. (Running Time: 3 hrs.). (Joe Leaphorn & Jim Chee Novel Ser.). 1995. 18.00 (978-1-55994-160-0(X), 394151) HarperCollins Pubs.

Blessing Way. abr. ed. Tony Hillerman. Read by Tony Hillerman. 1 CD. (Running Time: 1 hr. 30 min.). (Joe Leaphorn & Jim Chee Novel Ser.). 2005. audio compact disk 14.95 (978-0-06-081514-1(0)) HarperCollins Pubs.

Blessing Way. unabr. ed. Tony Hillerman. Read by Jonathan Marosz. 6 cass. (Running Time: 6 hrs.). (Joe Leaphorn & Jim Chee Novel Ser.). 1993. 48.00 (978-0-7366-2510-4(0), 3266) Books on Tape.
Navajo Tribal police Lt. Joe Leaphorn & anthropologist Bergen McKee stumble on a series of grisly murders.

Blessing Way. unabr. ed. Tony Hillerman. Narrated by George Guidall. 5 cass. (Running Time: 6 hrs. 30 mins.). (Joe Leaphorn & Jim Chee Novel Ser.). 1990. 44.00 (978-1-55690-058-7(9), 90080E7) Recorded Bks.
A young Navajo dies mysteriously in the canyons of Lukachukai country.

Blessings. Julia Cameron. 2001. (978-0-333-78254-5(2)) Macmillan UK GBR.

Blessings. Anna Quindlen. Read by Joan Allen. 2002. audio compact disk 72.00 (978-0-7366-8781-2(5)) Books on Tape.

Blessings. unabr. ed. Belva Plain. Read by Bonnie Hurren. 8 cass. (Running Time: 8 hrs.). 1996. 69.95 Set. (978-0-7451-6857-9(4), CAB 495) AudioGO.
It has been an outstanding year for lawyer Jennie Rakowsky: she's engaged to wealthy corporate lawyer Jay Wolfe, her own legal work is a huge success, & she is helping an environmental group save a thousand acres of land from developers. But a knock at the door turns her life upside down. Long-forgotten memories are awakened, & as Jennie tries to hide the secrets of her past, she finds her life threatened.

Blessings. unabr. ed. Belva Plain. Read by Pamela Klein. (Running Time: 9 hrs.). 2009. 24.99 (978-1-4418-0004-6(2), 9781441800046, Brilliance MP3); 39.97 (978-1-4418-0005-3(0), 9781441800053, Brlnc Audio MP3 Lib); 24.99 (978-1-4418-0006-0(9), 9781441800060, BAD); 39.97 (978-1-4418-0007-7(7), 9781441800077, BADLE) Brilliance Audio.

Blessings. unabr. ed. Anna Quindlen. Read by Joan Allen. 5 cass. (Running Time: 7 hrs. 30 mins.). 2002. 54.00 (978-0-7366-8780-5(7)) Books on Tape.

Blessings: A Novel. Sheneska Jackson. Narrated by Robin Miles. 12 cass. (Running Time: 16 hrs. 45 mins.). 98.00 (978-1-4025-1262-9(7)) Recorded Bks.

Blessings & Brahms. 1 cass. 6.98 (978-1-57908-453-0(2)); audio compact disk 9.98 (978-1-57908-452-3(4)) Platinm Enter.

Blessings & Miracles: New Updated Audio Cass. Created by Awmi. (ENG.). 2006. 25.00 (978-1-59548-071-2(4)) A Wommack.

Blessings & Miracles: New Updated Compact Disk. Created by Awmi. (ENG.). 2006. audio compact disk 25.00 (978-1-59548-070-5(6)) A Wommack.

Blessings from the Other Side: Wisdom & Comfort from the Afterlife for This Life. Sylvia Browne. 2004. 15.95 (978-0-7435-4206-7(1)) Pub: S&S Audio. Dist(s): S and S Inc

Blessings Given. Rafael Giraldo. 2008. pap. bk. 14.99 (978-0-615-18988-8(1)) RAGA Media.

Blessings of a Skinned Knee: Using Jewish Traditions to Raise Self-Reliant Children. unabr. ed. Wendy Mogel. Read by Carrington MacDuffie. 7 CDs. (Running Time: 30600 sec.). 2007. audio compact disk 19.95 (978-0-7861-5842-3(5)) Blckstn Audio.

Blessings of Abundance, Vol. 11. Jonathan Parker. Read by Jonathan Parker. 2 CDs. (Running Time: 2 hrs.). (Guided Meditation Ser.: Vol. 6). 1999. audio compact disk (978-1-58400-067-9(8)) QuantumQuests Intl.

Blessings of Abundance Vol. 29: Spiritual Attunement for Prosperity. Jonathan Parker. 2 cass. (Running Time: 1 hr. 45 min.). 1992. 17.00 (978-1-58400-028-0(7)) QuantumQuests Intl.

Blessings of Brokenness. abr. ed. Charles F. Stanley. 2 cass. (Running Time: 60 min.). 1997. 14.99 (978-0-310-20421-3(6)) Zondervan.
Helps those who are hurting make sense of why God allows us to be broken.

Blessings of Christmas. 2007. audio compact disk 32.98 (978-5-557-58510-1(9)) Madacy Ent Grp CAN.

Blessings of Daniel. Kenneth Copeland. 4 cass. 1983. bk. & stu. ed. 20.00 (978-0-938458-32-6(9)) K Copeland Pubns.
A picture of the blessed life of Daniel.

Blessings of Prosperity. Read by Marcia Greenwood. 3 cass. (Running Time: 3 hrs.). 1999. 15.00 (978-0-9666689-1-9(X), 6891) TGMinist.

Blessings of the Temple. Herschel Pedersen. 2004. 9.95 (978-1-59156-047-0(0)) Covenant Comms.

Blessings of the Temple. abr. ed. Herschel N. Pedersen. 2002. audio compact disk 11.95 (978-1-59156-048-7(9)) Covenant Comms.

Blest Are They Vol. 1: The Best of David Haas. David Haas. 1 cass. 1995. 10.95 (CS-340) GIA Pubns.

Blest Are They Vol. 1: The Best of David Haas. David Haas. Perf. by David Haas. 1995. audio compact disk 15.95 (CS-340) GIA Pubns.

***Blight of Mages.** unabr. ed. Karen Miller. (Running Time: 13 hrs.). (ENG.). 2011. 26.98 (978-1-61113-811-5(6)) Pub: Hachet Audio. Dist(s): HachBkGrp

Blight Way: A Sheriff Bo Tully Mystery. unabr. ed. Patrick F. McManus. 2006. 27.95 (978-1-57270-538-8(8)) Pub: Audio Partners. Dist(s): PerseuPGW

Blight Way: A Sheriff Bo Tully Mystery. unabr. ed. Patrick F. McManus. Narrated by Charles Leggett. (Mystery Masters Ser.). (ENG.). 2006. audio compact disk 27.95 (978-1-57270-537-1(X)) Pub: AudioGO. Dist(s): Perseus Dist

***Blimpo: The Third Circle of Heck.** unabr. ed. Dale E. Basye. Read by Bronson Pinchot. (Running Time: 10 hrs. NaN mins.). (Circles of Heck Ser.). (ENG.). 2011. 29.95 (978-1-4417-7399-9(1)); 59.95 (978-1-4417-7396-8(7)); audio compact disk 29.95 (978-1-4417-7398-2(3)); audio compact disk 90.00 (978-1-4417-7397-5(5)) Blckstn Audio.

Blind Alley. Iris Johansen. (Eve Duncan Ser.). 2004. 54.00 (978-1-4159-0298-1(4)); audio compact disk 61.20 (978-1-4159-0299-8(2)) Pub: Books on Tape. Dist(s): NetLibrary CO

Blind Ambition. unabr. collector's ed. John W. Dean. Read by Edward Holland. 11 cass. (Running Time: 16 hrs. 30 min.). 1999. 88.00 (978-0-7366-4419-8(9), 4880) Books on Tape.
An insider's account of the fall of Richard Nixon & has remained an indispensable source into Nixon's presidency. This is an autobiographical account of a young lawyer who accelerated to the top of the Federal power structure to become Counsel to the President at thirty years of age, only to discover that when reaching the top he had touched the bottom.

Blind Assassin. abr. ed. Margaret Atwood & Michael O'Brien. 3 CDs. (Running Time: 10800 sec.). Dramatization. (ENG.). 2005. audio compact disk 24.95 (978-0-86492-401-8(1)) Pub: BTC Audiobks CAN. Dist(s): U Toronto Pr

Blind Beauty. unabr. ed. K. M. Peyton. Read by Nicki Paull. 6 cass. (Running Time: 9 hrs.). (YA). 2004. 48.00 (978-1-74030-619-5(8)); 64.00 (978-1-74094-250-8(7)) Bolinda Pubng AUS.

Blind Beauty. unabr. ed. K. M. Peyton. 8 CDs. (Running Time: 9 hrs.). (YA). 2004. audio compact disk 87.95 (978-1-74093-392-6(3)) Pub: Bolinda Pubng AUS. Dist(s): Bolinda Pub Inc

Blind Bloodhound Justice: A Jo Beth Sidden Mystery. unabr. ed. Virginia Lanier. Read by Kate Forbes. 8 vols. (Running Time: 12 hrs.). (Bloodhound Ser.). 2000. bk. 69.95 (978-0-7927-2261-8(2), CSL 150, Chivers Sound Lib) AudioGO.
Jo Beth Sidden trains bloodhounds. She also tracks down missing children, drugs and escaped convicts. Her latest case is thirty years old: two baby girls were kidnapped from an estate and their nanny murdered. The estate owner's daughter was found safe nearby, while the other, the gardener's child, was never found. The man convicted of the crimes, who still swears his innocence, has been paroled. The sheriff is concerned about it's affect on the community, so he turns to Jo Beth to help dig out the long buried secrets of the past.

Blind But Now I See: I Cor. 1:29-31; II Cor. 8:9; Eph. 1:6-7. Ed Young. 1988. 4.95 (978-0-7417-1667-5(4), 667) Win Walk.

***Blind Contessa's New Machine: A Novel.** unabr. ed. Carey Wallace. Read by Aasne Vigesaa. (Running Time: 6 hrs.). 2010. 24.99 (978-1-4418-8134-2(4), 9781441881342, Brilliance MP3); 39.97 (978-1-4418-8135-9(2), 9781441881359, Brlnc Audio MP3 Lib); 24.99 (978-1-4418-8136-6(0), 9781441881366, BAD); 39.97 (978-1-4418-8137-3(9), 9781441881373, BADLE); audio compact disk 29.99 (978-1-4418-8132-8(8), 9781441881328, Bril Audio CD Unabri); audio compact disk 69.97 (978-1-4418-8133-5(6), 9781441881335, BriAudCD Unabrid) Brilliance Audio.

Blind Courage. Bill Irwin & David McCasland. Frwd. by Robert H. Schuller. 1995. 14.95 (978-1-56796-093-8(6)) WRS Group.

Blind Date. Frances Fyfield. Read by Rula Lenska. 8 vols. (Running Time: 12 hrs.). 2003. audio compact disk 79.95 (978-0-7540-5558-7(2)) Pub: Chivers Audio Bks GBR. Dist(s): AudioGO

Blind Date. unabr. ed. Frances Fyfield. Read by Rula Lenska. 8 cass. (Running Time: 8 hrs.). 1998. 69.95 (978-0-7540-0210-9(1), CAB 1633) AudioGO.
Elizabeth Kennedy is haunted by her sister's murder & her own humiliating attempts to lure the killer into a confession. She herself is the victim of a senseless attack, & decides to flee to London, but does not remain there safe for long.

Blind Date & A Case of Nerves. Perf. by Charles Laughton & Edward G. Robinson. 1 cass. (Running Time: 60 min.). Dramatization. (Suspense Ser.). 6.00 Once Upon Rad.
Mystery & suspense radio broadcasts.

Blind Descent. Nevada Barr. Narrated by Barbara Rosenblat. 1 CD. (Anna Pigeon Ser.: No. 6). 1999. audio compact disk 99.00 (C1014) Recorded Bks.
In Anna Pigeon's latest case she reluctantly visits the Carlsbad Caverns National Park to help a friend injured on an expedition. She must overcome her own fears of caves as well as sort out the murders that follow.

Blind Descent. unabr. ed. Nevada Barr. Narrated by Barbara Rosenblat. 9 cass. (Running Time: 12 hrs. 15 mins.). (Anna Pigeon Ser.: No. 6). 1998. 83.00 (978-0-7887-2038-3(4), 95402E7) Recorded Bks.

Blind Descent. unabr. ed. Nevada Barr. Narrated by Barbara Rosenblat. 11 CDs. (Running Time: 12 hrs. 15 mins.). (Anna Pigeon Ser.: No. 6). 2000. audio compact disk 99.00 (978-0-7887-3408-3(3), C1014E7) Recorded Bks.
When park ranger Anna Pigeon embarks on a thrilling subterranean rescue mission, she confronts personal demons & a multitude of life-threatening dangers, not all of them from the hostile terrain.

Blind Descent: The Quest to Discover the Deepest Place on Earth. unabr. ed. James M. Tabor. Read by Don Leslie. (ENG.). 2010. audio compact disk 40.00 (978-0-307-73678-9(4), Random AudioBks) Pub: Random Audio Pubg. Dist(s): Random

Blind Doctor: The Jacob Bolotin Story. Rosalind Perlman. Read by Ed Giron. (ENG.). 2008. audio compact disk 29.95 (978-1-883423-15-5(5)) Blue Pt Bks.

Blind Eye: The Terrifying Story of a Doctor Who Got Away with Murder. unabr. ed. James B. Stewart. Narrated by Richard Poe. 11 CDs. (Running Time: 12 hrs. 15 mins.). 2001. audio compact disk 99.00 (978-0-7887-6172-0(2)) Recorded Bks.
The shocking story of Michael Swango, a physician who may be the most prolific serial killer in American history. From the moment he began medical school, people thought Swango was peculiar. He seemed woefully incompetent in classwork, showed no empathy for patients & was obsessed with violent death. When he interned at Ohio State, patients started dying mysteriously. Then, Swango was convicted of poisoning several co-workers. Incredibly, after his release from prison, he secured hospital positions in South Dakota & New York & the body count continued to rise.

Blind Eye: The Terrifying Story of a Doctor Who Got Away with Murder. unabr. ed. James B. Stewart. Narrated by Richard Poe. 9 cass. (Running Time: 12 hrs. 15 mins.). 2001. 84.00 (978-0-7887-5448-7(3)) Recorded Bks.
Shocking story of Michael Swango, who has never been convicted of any crime worse than fraud, but who may be the most prolific serial killer in American history.

Blind Faith. Ben Elton. 2008. 61.95 (978-0-7531-3061-2(0)); audio compact disk 79.95 (978-0-7531-3062-9(9)) Pub: ISIS Audio GBR. Dist(s): Ulverscroft US

Blind Faith. Ben Elton. Read by Michael Maloney. (Running Time: 4 hrs. 23 mins. 0 sec.). (ENG., 2007. audio compact disk 26.95 (978-1-84657-140-4(5), Audiobks) Pub: Random GBR. Dist(s): IPG Chicago

Blind Faith: The Miraculous Journey of Lula Hardaway, Stevie Wonder's Mother. Dennis Love & Stacy Brown. Read by Viola Davis. 2004. 15.95 (978-0-7435-4207-4(X)) Pub: S&S Audio. Dist(s): S and S Inc

Blind Justice. unabr. ed. Bruce Alexander. Read by Stuart Langton. 7 cass. (Running Time: 10 hrs. 30 min.). (Sir John Fielding Mystery Ser.: Vol. 1). 1998. 56.00 (978-0-7366-4081-7(9), 4590) Books on Tape.
The blind judge & master detective of eighteenth-century London. In 1768, thirteen-year-old Jeremy Proctor arrives in London. The city streets are no place for a boy on his own & trouble rapidly finds him. He is charged with theft & is saved only by Sir John's intelligence & intuition. After clearing Jeremy of the charges, Sir John & his new helper turn to finding answers to crimes that have baffled London's top investigators.

Blind Justice. unabr. ed. William Bernhardt. Read by Jonathan Marosz. 6 cass. (Running Time: 9 hrs.). (Ben Kincaid Ser.: No. 2). 1998. 48.00 (978-0-7366-4106-7(8), 4611) Books on Tape.
Lawyer Ben Kincaid defends a friend against murder. But can he defend himself against a judge who hates him?.

Blind Justice. unabr. ed. William Bernhardt. Read by Larry Block. 10 cass. (Running Time: 15 hrs.). (Ben Kincaid Ser.: No. 2). 2001. (GKT 028) Chivers Audio Bks GBR.
Lawyer Ben Kincaid faces a judge who despises him in a trial he is almost guaranteed to lose. But Ben takes on the odds as he sets out to defend a friend framed for murder.

Blind Justice. unabr. ed. Robin Bowles. Read by Victoria Howell. 15 cass. (Running Time: 22 hrs. 30 min.). 2001. (978-1-86442-347-1(1), 581054) Bolinda Pubng AUS.
The true story of the death of Jennifer Tanner in November 1984. Her death was viewed as a suicide. In 1996 Robin Bowles, hears that a special taskforce has been set up to re-investigate the death after the discovery of human remains in a mineshaft near the property where Jenny died. What unfolds is a true-life detective story, a bizarre tangle of police bungles, cover-ups & family intrigue.

Blind Love. unabr. ed. Wilkie Collins. Narrated by Flo Gibson. 9 cass. (Running Time: 12 hrs. 30 min.). 2003. 28.95 (978-1-55685-745-4(4)) Audio Bk Con.
This suspenseful and romantic drama based on a real criminal case, takes place in Ireland, London and Belgium and is full of unforgettable characters. Iris Henley's blind love is sorely tested.

Blind Man Can See How Much I Love You: Stories. unabr. ed. Amy Bloom. 4 cass. (Running Time: 4 hrs. 15 mins.). 2002. 40.00 (978-1-4025-0236-1(2)) Recorded Bks.
This collection of short stories takes listeners on an emotional ride of pain and perseverance.

Blind Man of Seville. unabr. ed. Robert Wilson. Read by Sean Barrett. 12 cass. (Running Time: 18 hrs.). (Isis Ser.). (J). 2003. 94.95 (978-0-7531-1771-2(1)); audio compact disk 99.95 (978-0-7531-2210-5(3)) Pub: ISIS Lrg Prnt GBR. Dist(s): Ulverscroft US
A leading restaurateur has been found dead in his apartment, bound and gagged before a TV screen. With each new victim, the killer demonstrates an uncanny ability to delve into the secrets of his prey.

***Blind Man's Bluff: The Untold True Story of American Submar.** abr. ed. Sherry Sontag et al. Read by Tony Roberts. (ENG.). 2007. (978-0-06-122928-2(8), Harper Audio); (978-0-06-122929-9(6), Harper Audio) HarperCollins Pubs.

Blind Man's Bluff Set: The Untold Story of American Submarine Espionage, unabr. ed. Sherry Sontag et al. Narrated by George R. Wilson. 11 cass. (Running Time: 15 hrs. 45 mins.). 1998. 96.00 (978-0-7887-3461-8(X), 95884E7) Recorded Bks.
During the tense Cold War, men on board submarines constantly risked death in their secret battle for information. Tells the enthralling, real-life story of American submarines & their perilous missions.

Blind Mercy. Phil Quinton. 2007. 17.99 (978-1-60247-395-9(1)) Tate Pubng.

Blind Miller. unabr. ed. Catherine Cookson. Read by Susan Jameson. 8 cass. (Running Time: 8 hrs.). 1994. 69.95 Set. (978-0-7451-4295-1(8), CAB 978) AudioGO.
Although the social gap between their families was wide, it did not stop Sarah from loving David. Marrying into his family meant getting a new home in the nicest part of town, but also a bullying father-in-law & a domineering mother-in-law. Sarah soon found these people had secrets they were determined to hide.

Blind Miller. unabr. collector's ed. Catherine Cookson. Read by Penelope Dellaporta. 9 cass. (Running Time: 13 hrs. 30 min.). 1988. 72.00 (978-0-7366-1394-1(3), 2283) Books on Tape.
Mary Hetherington ruled the men of her family with authority. When David brought home a girl from the wrong end of the Fifteen Streets, she was gracious for a while. Then she discovered that Sarah was loved not only by David, but by all her menfolk. For Sarah, who was poor, uneducated & badly-dressed, had brought warmth & gaiety in a house devoid of love. Mary realized that Sarah, if allowed to go unchecked, would become a challenge to her authority, the one thing that she could not accept.

Blind Pursuit. unabr. ed. Matthew F. Jones. Read by Michael Mitchell. 8 cass. (Running Time: 8 hrs.). 1997. 48.00 (978-0-7366-3801-2(6), 4472) Books on Tape.
When eight-year-old Jennifer Follett doesn't return home from school one day, the rigidly ordered lives of her parents, Edmund & Caroline, are suddenly upended.

Blind Run. abr. ed. Patricia Lewin. Read by Dick Hill. (Running Time: 4 hrs.). 2004. audio compact disk 69.25 (978-1-59355-802-4(3), 1593558023, BACDLib Ed) Brilliance Audio.
In Blind Run, Patricia Lewin has written a breathless novel of unrelenting suspense and nerve-cracking tension that is also a gripping story of lost love, lost innocence, and a last chance at revenge. Ethan Decker is a specialized "Hunter" for the most secretive agency in the U.S. government, working deep undercover to track down and capture ruthless international mercenaries and fugitives. But when a daring mission takes a lethal turn, a renegade assassin kills Decker's son in retribution. Forced to leave his devastated, unsuspecting wife, Sydney, to save her from the madman's threats, Decker exiles himself in the New Mexican desert to live in a jail of his own guilt and grief. The day starts like any other in the desert: scorching, cloudless. But then, like a mirage, a car appears on the horizon. Inside is Anna Kelsey, a former member of Decker's covert team, a woman Decker presumed dead in the hell following that ill-fated mission three years ago. But she survived - and now she shepherds two children, entrusting them to Decker's protection. Before he can protest, Anna is screeching away in a cloud of dust. Now Decker is reeling from the sudden turn of events - and the shocking sight of Anna's body not far down the road from where she left his trailer and the kids. The Spanish coin under her tongue is a mark Decker hoped to never see again... the signature of the assassin Ramirez. Suddenly the race is on: to reach his ex-wife before Ramirez finds her, and to unlock the mystery behind these two children and why Anna died to give them refuge. But for Decker, Sydney's trust is not his to have any longer, and the children are pawns in a dark conspiracy so vast and so evil that even this former spy could not imagine the peril and terror that lies directly in his path.

Blind Run. unabr. ed. Patricia Lewin. Read by Dick Hill. 6 cass. (Running Time: 9 hrs.). 2003. 74.25 (978-1-59086-544-6(8), 1590865448, Unabridge Lib Edns); 29.95 (978-1-59086-543-9(X), 159086543X, BAU) Brilliance Audio.

Blind Run. unabr. ed. Patricia Lewin. Read by Dick Hill. (Running Time: 9 hrs.). 2004. 39.25 (978-1-59335-575-3(0), 1593355750, Brlnc Audio MP3 Lib) Brilliance Audio.

Blind Run. unabr. ed. Patricia Lewin. Read by Dick Hill. (Running Time: 9 hrs.). 2004. 39.25 (978-1-59710-072-4(2), 1597100722, BADLE); 24.95 (978-1-59710-073-1(0), 1597100730, BAD) Brilliance Audio.

Blind Run. unabr. ed. Patricia Lewin. Read by Dick Hill. (Running Time: 9 hrs.). 2004. 24.95 (978-1-59335-068-0(6), 1593350686) Soulmate Audio Bks.

Blind Side: Evolution of a Game. abr. ed. Michael Lewis. Read by Grover Gardner. 2009. audio compact disk 20.00 (978-0-307-71506-7(X), Random AudioBks) Pub: Random Audio Pubg. Dist(s): Random

Blind Side: Evolution of a Game. unabr. ed. Michael Lewis. Read by Stephen Hoye. 10 CDs. (Running Time: 11 hrs. 45 mins.). 2006. audio compact disk 68.85 (978-1-4159-3304-6(9)) Pub: Books on Tape. Dist(s): NetLibrary CO
In football, as in life, the value we place on people changes with the rules of the games they play. When we first meet the young man at the center of this extraordinary and moving story, he is one of thirteen children by a mother addicted to crack; he does not know his real name, his father, his birthday, or any of the things a child might learn in school. And he has no serious experience playing organized football. What changes? He takes up football, and school, after a rich, Evangelical, Republican family plucks him from the mean streets. Their love is the first great force that alters the world's perception of the boy, whom they adopt. The second force is the evolution of professional football itself. In THE BLIND SIDE, Lewis shows us a largely unanalyzed but inexorable trend in football working its way down from the pros to the high school game, where it collides with the life of a single young man to produce a narrative of great and surprising power.

Blind Spots. unabr. ed. Barbara Francis. Read by Angela Kelley. 6 cass. (Running Time: 9 hrs.). Dramatization. 1991. 39.95 (978-1-55686-401-8(9), 401) Books in Motion.
Bryton Forrester, a young Chicago fashion photographer, finds herself trapped in a terrifying encounter at a backroad farmhouse in southeastern Minnesota.

***Blind Trust.** Terri Blackstock. (Running Time: 7 hrs. 1 mins. 0 sec.). (Second Chances Ser.). (ENG.). 2009. 14.99 (978-0-310-30511-8(X)) Zondervan.

***Blind Visionary: Practical Lessons for Meeting Challenges on the Way to a More Fulfilling Life & Career.** Doug Eadie & Virginia Jacko. (Running Time: 320). (ENG.). 2010. audio compact disk 28.00 (978-0-9798894-6-2(4), Gov Edge) GovEdge.

Blind Willow, Sleeping Woman. unabr. ed. Haruki Murakami. Read by Ellen Archer & Patrick G. Lawlor. (YA). 2008. 59.99 (978-1-60514-666-9(8)) Find a World.

Blind Willow, Sleeping Woman. unabr. ed. Haruki Murakami. (Running Time: 13 hrs. 0 mins. 0 sec.). (ENG.). 2006. audio compact disk 75.99 (978-1-4001-3295-9(9)) Pub: Tantor Media. Dist(s): IngramPubServ

Blind Willow, Sleeping Woman. unabr. ed. Haruki Murakami. Read by Patrick G. Lawlor. (Running Time: 13 hrs. 0 mins. 0 sec.). (ENG.). 2006. audio compact disk 37.99 (978-1-4001-0295-2(2)) Pub: Tantor Media. Dist(s): IngramPubServ

Blind Willow, Sleeping Woman. unabr. ed. Haruki Murakami. Read by Ellen Archer. Ed. by Patrick G. Lawlor. (Running Time: 13 hrs. 0 mins. 0 sec.). (ENG.). 2006. audio compact disk 24.99 (978-1-4001-5295-7(X)) Pub: Tantor Media. Dist(s): IngramPubServ

Blind Years, Set. unabr. ed. Catherine Cookson. Read by Susan Jameson. 4 cass. 1999. 39.95 (978-0-7540-0360-1(4), CAB1783) AudioGO.
Bridget Gether's parents were killed in the wartime Blitz & she had lived with the Overmeers at Balderstone, their sprawling property in the Northumbrian countryside, since she was a child. Unaware that she had been manipulated into agreeing to marry their son Laurence, only an encounter with the son of a neighboring farmer opened her eyes to the possibility that she was making a mistake.

Blind Years, Set. unabr. ed. Catherine Cookson. Read by Susan Jameson. 6 CDs. 1999. audio compact disk 69.95 (978-0-7540-5314-9(8), CCD005) Pub: Chivers Audio Bks GBR. Dist(s): AudioGO

Blinded. abr. ed. Stephen White. Read by Dick Hill. (Running Time: 6 hrs.). (Dr. Alan Gregory Ser.). 2004. audio compact disk 74.25 (978-1-59355-398-2(6), 1593553986, BACDLib Ed) Brilliance Audio.
Relentlessly probing the very edge of the human psyche as only he can, psychologist and New York Times bestselling author Stephen White ratchets up the thrills in BLINDED, a new novel of psychological suspense - his most compelling and powerful yet. Gibbs Storey is a woman no man can resist. When her comfortable life is shattered by the man she thought it was safe to give her heart to, the nightmare has only just begun. Psychologist Alan Gregory is used to dealing with nightmares. But a brutal, shocking confession locks him into darkness - and forces him to choose between saving himself and saving those who will otherwise end their days pleading for mercy at the hands of a vicious serial killer. What Alan can't see is that either choice might cost him his life... In riveting, explosive scenes that have become his hallmark, Stephen White delivers an unsettling and gripping story that penetrates to the heart of terror and transfixes readers like no one else can.

Blinded. abr. ed. Stephen White. Read by Dick Hill. (Running Time: 6 hrs.). (Dr. Alan Gregory Ser.). 2005. audio compact disk 16.99 (978-1-59600-687-4(0), 9781596006874, BCD Value Price) Brilliance Audio.

Blinded. unabr. ed. Stephen White. Read by Dick Hill. 6 cass. (Running Time: 12 hrs.). (Dr. Alan Gregory Ser.). 2004. 87.25 (978-1-59086-398-5(4), 1590863984, BrilAudUnabridg); 34.95 (978-1-59086-397-8(6), 1590863976, BAU) Brilliance Audio.

Blinded. unabr. ed. Stephen White. Read by Dick Hill. (Running Time: 12 hrs.). (Dr. Alan Gregory Ser.). 2004. 39.25 (978-1-59335-537-1(8), 1593355378, Brlnc Audio MP3 Lib); 24.95 (978-1-59335-274-5(3), 1593352743, Brilliance MP3) Brilliance Audio.

Blinded. unabr. ed. Stephen White. Read by Dick Hill. (Running Time: 12 hrs.). (Dr. Alan Gregory Ser.). 2004. 39.25 (978-1-59710-075-5(7), 1597100757, BADLE); 24.95 (978-1-59710-074-8(9), 1597100749, BAD) Brilliance Audio.

***Blinded.** unabr. ed. Stephen White. Read by Dick Hill. (Running Time: 12 hrs.). (Dr. Alan Gregory Ser.). 2010. audio compact disk 29.99 (978-1-4418-4085-1(0), 9781441840851, Bril Audio CD Unabri); audio compact disk 89.97 (978-1-4418-4086-8(9), 9781441840868, BriAudCD Unabrid) Brilliance Audio.

Blinded by the Sight. (Paws & Tales Ser.: Vol. 20). (J). 2002. 3.99 (978-1-57972-424-5(8)); audio compact disk 5.99 (978-1-57972-425-2(6)) Insight Living.

Blinded to New Sight - A Poetry Reading in Honor of Steve Biko, No. 50. Carl Faber. 1 cass. (Running Time: 45 min.). 1986. 9.50 (SR 73-807) Perseus Pr.
An eve.

Blindfold. unabr. ed. Kevin J. Anderson. Read by Larry McKeever. 13 cass. (Running Time: 19 hrs. 30 min.). 1996. 104.00 (978-0-7366-3283-6(2), 3938) Books on Tape.
On Atlas, a struggling colony on a rugged planet, the Truthsayers rule. Only the Truthsayers can use Veritas, a telepathy virus that allows them to read souls & determine guilt. They're never wrong. Their judgements are beyond appeal. So when Troy Boren gets falsely accused of a murder, he figures Kalliana, a young Truthsayer, will straighten it out. But she convicts him. How could it be?.

Blindman's Bluff. unabr. ed. Faye Kellerman. Read by Mitchell Greenberg. 10 CDs . (Running Time: 12 hrs.). 2009. audio compact disk 39.99 (978-0-06-176817-0(0), Harper Audio) HarperCollins Pubs.

***Blindman's Bluff.** unabr. ed. Faye Kellerman. Read by Mitchell Greenberg. (ENG.). 2009. (978-0-06-190248-2(9), Harper Audio); (978-0-06-190249-9(7), Harper Audio) HarperCollins Pubs.

***Blindman's Bluff.** unabr. ed. Faye Kellerman. Read by Mitchell Greenberg. 10 CDs. (Running Time: 12 hrs.). 2009. audio compact disk 100.00 (978-1-4159-6515-3(3), BksonTape) Pub: Random Audio Pubg. Dist(s): Random

Blindness. unabr. ed. José Saramago. Read by Jonathan Davis. 11 CDs. (Running Time: 12 hrs. 30 mins.). 2008. audio compact disk 104.95 (978-0-7927-5501-2(4), Chivers Sound Lib) AudioGO.

Blindness. unabr. ed. José Saramago. Narrated by Jonathan Davis. 11 CDs. (Running Time: 12 hrs. 30 mins.). (ENG.). 2008. audio compact disk 29.95 (978-1-60283-444-6(X)) Pub: AudioGO. Dist(s): Perseus Dist

Blindness. unabr. ed. José Saramago. Read by Jonathan Davis. 11 CDs. (Running Time: 12 hrs. 32 mins.). 2008. audio compact disk 104.95 (978-0-7927-5500-5(6)) AudioGO.
A city is hit by an epidemic of "white blindness" which spares no one. Authorities confine the blind to an empty mental hospital, but there the criminal element holds everyone captive, stealing food rations and raping women. There is one eyewitness to this nightmare who guides seven strangers-among them a boy with no mother, a girl with dark glasses, a dog of tears-through the barren streets, and the procession becomes as uncanny as the surroundings are harrowing. A magnificent parable of loss and disorientation and a vivid evocation of the horrors of the twentieth century, Blindness has swept the reading public with its powerful portrayal of man's worst appetites and weaknesses-and man's ultimately exhilarating spirit.

Blindness in the Eighties. 1 cass. (Running Time: 30 min.). 9.95 (I0590B090, HarperThor) HarpC GBR.

Blindside. abr. ed. Catherine Coulter. Read by Sandra Burr. (Running Time: 21600 sec.). (FBI Thriller Ser.: No. 8). 2003. audio compact disk 16.99 (978-1-4233-1937-5(0), 9781423319375) Brilliance Audio.
Catherine Coulter's fast-paced FBI novels featuring married agents Lacey Sherlock and Dillon Savich have rocketed up the New York Times bestseller lists and garnered millions of fans. Coulter's heady blend of action and intrigue, her "complex plotting and likable characters" (Publishers Weekly), grow more intoxicating with each book - and reach new heights in Blindside. When six-year-old Sam Kettering is kidnapped and then manages to save himself, Savich and Sherlock join his father-former FBI agent Miles Kettering -to determine why Sam would be abducted and brought to eastern Tennessee. Though the local sheriff, Katie Benedict, catches up with Sam before the kidnappers do, the case isn't over -not by a long shot. The unanswered question is: Why do the kidnappers want this little boy so badly? The investigation leads Savich and Sherlock to a charismatic, intense evangelist, Reverend Sooner McCamy, and his enigmatic wife. As if the kidnapping case weren't enough, Savich and Sherlock are at the same time desperate to locate the killer of three teachers in Washington, D.C.

Blindside. abr. ed. Catherine Coulter. Read by Sandra Burr. (Running Time: 6 hrs.). (FBI Thriller Ser.). 2009. audio compact disk 9.99 (978-1-4418-0810-3(8), 9781441808103, BCD Value Price) Brilliance Audio.

Blindside. abr. ed. Catherine Coulter & Daniel Silva. Read by Sandra Burr & Guerin Barry. (Running Time: 6 hrs.). (FBI Thriller Ser.). 2010. audio compact disk 9.99 (978-1-4418-0813-4(2), 9781441808134, BCD Value Price) Brilliance Audio.

Blindside. unabr. ed. Catherine Coulter. Read by Sandra Burr. 7 cass. (Running Time: 10 hrs.). (FBI Thriller Ser.: No. 8). 2003. 32.95 (978-1-58788-850-2(5), 1587888505, BAU); 82.25 (978-1-58788-851-9(3), 1587888513, Unabridge Lib Edns); audio compact disk 36.95 (978-1-58788-853-3(X), 158788853X, BriAudCD Unabrid); audio compact disk 97.25 (978-1-58788-854-0(8), 1587888548, CD Unabrid Lib Ed) Brilliance Audio.
Catherine Coulter's fast-paced FBI novels featuring married agents Lacey Sherlock and Dillon Savich have rocketed up the New York Times bestseller lists and garnered millions of fans. Coulter's heady blend of action and intrigue, her "complex plotting and likable characters" (Publishers Weekly), grow more intoxicating with each book - and reach new heights in Blindside. When six-year-old Sam Kettering is kidnapped and then manages to save himself, Savich and Sherlock join his father-former FBI agent Miles Kettering -to determine why Sam would be abducted and brought to eastern Tennessee. Though the local sheriff, Katie Benedict, catches up with Sam before the kidnappers do, the case isn't over -not by a long shot. The unanswered question is: Why do the kidnappers want this little boy so badly? The investigation leads Savich and Sherlock to a charismatic, intense evangelist, Reverend Sooner McCamy, and his enigmatic wife. As if the kidnapping case weren't enough, Savich and Sherlock are at the same time desperate to locate the killer of three teachers in Washington, D.C.

Blindside. unabr. ed. Catherine Coulter. Read by Sandra Burr. (Running Time: 10 hrs.). (FBI Thriller Ser.: No. 8). 2004. 39.25 (978-1-59335-624-8(2), 1593356242, Brinc Audio MP3 Lib) Brilliance Audio.

Blindside. unabr. ed. Catherine Coulter. Read by Sandra Burr. (Running Time: 10 hrs.). (FBI Thriller Ser.: No. 8). 2004. 39.25 (978-1-59710-076-2(5), 1597100765, BADLE); 24.95 (978-1-59710-077-9(3), 1597100773, BAD) Brilliance Audio.

Blindside. unabr. ed. Catherine Coulter. Read by Sandra Burr. (Running Time: 10 hrs.). (FBI Thriller Ser.: No. 8). 2004. 24.95 (978-1-59335-217-2(4), 1593352174) Soulmate Audio Bks.

Blindsided. unabr. ed. Richard M. Cohen. Read by Richard M. Cohen. Read by Richard Ferrone. 4 CDs. (Running Time: 6 hrs.). 2004. audio compact disk 29.95 (978-0-06-072418-4(8)) HarperCollins Pubs.

***Blindsided.** unabr. ed. Richard M. Cohen. Read by Richard M. Cohen. Read by Richard Ferrone. (ENG.). 2004. (978-0-06-075235-4(1), Harper Audio) HarperCollins Pubs.

***Blindsided.** unabr. ed. Richard M. Cohen. Read by Richard M. Cohen. Read by Richard Ferrone. (ENG.). 2004. (978-0-06-081337-6(7), Harper Audio) HarperCollins Pubs.

Blindsided. unabr. ed. Jay Giles. Narrated by Ron Knowles. (Running Time: 8 hrs. 52 mins.). (ENG.). 2006. 29.95 (978-1-57545-316-3(9), RP Audio Pubng) Pub: Reagent Press. Dist(s): OverDrive Inc

Blindsight. Ricardo Sternberg. (Running Time: 1 hr. 13 mins.). 2004. audio compact disk 12.95 (978-1-894177-03-0(7)) Pub: Cyclops Pr CAN. Dist(s): Literary Pr Gp

Blindsight. unabr. ed. Robin Cook. Read by Donada Peters. 8 cass. (Running Time: 12 hrs.). (Jack Stapleton Ser.: No. 1). 1992. 64.00 (978-0-7366-2167-0(9), 2966) Books on Tape.
Laurie Montgomery, MD & medical examiner, is confronted with string of deaths. Facing a wall of resistance she conducts her own investigation.

Blindsighted. Karin Slaughter. Read by Judith Ivey. (Grant County Ser.: Bk. 1). 1975. 9.99 (978-0-06-074399-4(9)) HarperCollins Pubs.

Blindsighted. abr. ed. Karin Slaughter. Read by Judith Ivey. (Grant County Ser.: Bk. 1). 2005. audio compact disk 14.95 (978-0-06-079107-0(1)) HarperCollins Pubs.

***Blindsighted.** abr. ed. Karin Slaughter. Read by Judith Ivey. (ENG.). 2004. (978-0-06-078296-2(X), Harper Audio) HarperCollins Pubs.

***Blindsighted.** abr. ed. Karin Slaughter. Read by Judith Ivey. (ENG.). 2004. (978-0-06-081418-2(7), Harper Audio) HarperCollins Pubs.

Blindsighted. unabr. ed. Karin Slaughter. 8 cass. (Running Time: 12 hrs.). (Grant County Ser.: Bk. 1). 2002. 64.00 (978-0-7366-8803-1(X)) Books on Tape.
A killer, who cuts lethal crosses into the stomach of his victims, terrorizes Heartsdale, Georgia.

Blindspot: By a Gentleman in Exile & a Lady in Disguise. unabr. ed. Jane Kamensky & Jill Lepore. (Running Time: 19 hrs. 5 mins.). 2008. 44.95 (978-1-4332-5764-3(5)); audio compact disk 44.95 (978-1-4332-5763-6(7)); audio compact disk 120.00 (978-1-4332-5761-2(0)); audio compact disk 99.95 (978-1-4332-5760-5(2)) Blckstn Audio.

Blink, Set. abr. ed. Tom Philbin. Read by James Remar. 2 cass. (Running Time: 3 hrs.). 1994. 16.95 (978-1-56876-010-0(8)) Soundlines Ent.
In the tradition of Hitchcock comes an erotic thriller. A serial killer is on the loose & Emma Brody is the only one to have seen him. Except, she has just had a corneal transplant, & is having random flashbacks. But the killer is stalking Emma, & only one detective believes her, & only he can save her.

Blink: Inteligencia Intuitiva. abr. ed. Malcolm Gladwell. 4 cds. (Running Time: 18000 sec.). (SPA.). 2007. audio compact disk 24.95 (978-1-933499-16-1(8)) Fonolibro Inc.

Blink: The Power of Thinking Without Thinking. unabr. ed. Malcolm Gladwell. Read by Malcolm Gladwell. 7 CDs. (Running Time: 8 hrs.). (ENG.). 2005. audio compact disk 39.98 (978-1-58621-719-8(4)) Pub: Hachet Audio. Dist(s): HachBkGrp

Blink: The Power of Thinking Without Thinking. unabr. ed. Malcolm Gladwell. (Running Time: 7 hrs. 45 mins.). (ENG.). 2006. 14.98 (978-1-59483-170-6(X)) Pub: Hachet Audio. Dist(s): HachBkGrp

Blink: The Power of Thinking Without Thinking. unabr. ed. Malcolm Gladwell. (Running Time: 8 hrs.). (ENG.). 2009. 59.98 (978-1-60024-930-3(2)) Pub: Hachet Audio. Dist(s): HachBkGrp

Blink: The Unauthorized Biography of Blink 182. Martin Harper. (Maximum Ser.). (ENG.). 2001. audio compact disk 14.95 (978-1-84240-075-3(4)) Pub: Chrome Dreams GBR. Dist(s): IPG Chicago

***Blink & Caution.** unabr. ed. Tim Wynne-Jones. (Running Time: 9 hrs.). 2011. 19.99 (978-1-4558-0368-2(5), 9781455803682, Candlewick Bril); 39.97 (978-1-4558-0369-9(3), 9781455803699, Candlewick Bril); 19.99 (978-1-4558-0365-1(0), 9781455803651, Candlewick Bril); 39.97 (978-1-4558-0366-8(9), 9781455803668, Candlewick Bril); audio compact disk 24.99 (978-1-4558-0363-7(4), 9781455803637, Candlewick Bril); audio compact disk 59.97 (978-1-4558-0364-4(2), 9781455803644, Candlewick Bril) Brilliance Audio.

Blink of an Eye. unabr. ed. Ted Dekker. Narrated by Tim Gregory. (Running Time: 11 hrs. 0 mins. 0 sec.). (ENG.). 2009. 24.49 (978-1-60814-602-4(2)); audio compact disk 34.99 (978-1-59859-651-9(9)) Oasis Audio.

Blink 182 Collector's Box. Ben Graham. 3 CDs. 2005. audio compact disk (978-1-84240-319-8(2)) Chrome Dreams GBR.
New-School punk trio Blink-182, formed back in the early 90?s, are at a critical point in their career. Having announced recently a lengthy hiatus that many feel could mean the demise of the band, their future is at best uncertain. However, over the past decade they have released eight albums, numerous singles, the majority of which reached Top Ten status in the UK, and have played sold out shows all across the world. More importantly though, they have built up, without doubt, one of the most dedicated fan bases of any band through the same period. Publicity surrounding Blink and this announcement is therefore feverish, as the world waits to see what will happen next!This Box Set is the perfect collector?s item for all Blink? fans. It includes a set of 3CDs of interviews, audio-biography and reviews as well as posters, booklets, postcards and more?.

Blink 182 X-Posed: The Interview. Chrome Dreams. 1 CD. (ENG., 2002. audio compact disk 14.95 (978-1-84240-167-5(X)) Pub: Chrome Dreams GBR. Dist(s): IPG Chicago

Bliss. 1 CD. (Running Time: 90 min.). 1999. audio compact disk 14.95 (978-1-893792-33-3(1)) Terra Entmnt.

Bliss. unabr. ed. Read by Anna Fields. Tr. by Cigdem Aksoy Fromm. 8 cass. (Running Time: 37800 sec.). 2006. 27.95 (978-0-7861-4625-3(7)); audio compact disk 27.95 (978-0-7861-6846-0(3)); audio compact disk 29.95 (978-0-7861-7464-5(1)) Blckstn Audio.

Bliss. unabr. ed. O. Z. Livaneli. Read by Anna Fields. Tr. by Cigdem Aksoy Fromm. (Running Time: 37800 sec.). 2006. 72.95 (978-0-7861-4835-6(7)); audio compact disk 90.00 (978-0-7861-6135-5(3)) Blckstn Audio.

Bliss & Ecstasy: The Attentiveness Power of the Soul. Jonathan Murro & Ann Ree Colton. 1 cass. 7.95 A R Colton Fnd.

Bliss & Knowing of Being. Swami Amar Jyoti. 1 cass. 1991. 9.95 (R-107) Truth Consciousness.
Real knowing is being, without attributes inexpressible, fully satisfying. The objective is subjective; we perceive only what we are.

Bliss & Other Stories. Katherine Mansfield. Read by Juliet Stevenson. (Playaway Adult Fiction Ser.). (ENG.). 2009. 40.00 (978-1-60775-584-5(X)) Find a World.

Bliss & the Preservation Principle; Virtue & Grace. Ann Ree Colton & Jonathan Murro. 1 cass. 7.95 A R Colton Fnd.

Bliss of Consciousness. unabr. ed. Rama Berch. 1 cass. (Chants of Awakening Ser.: Vol. 1). 1992. (978-1-930559-08-0(9)); audio compact disk (978-1-930559-09-7(7)) STC Inc.
Sanskrit chants for use during meditation, relaxation, or yoga.

***Bliss, Remembered.** unabr. ed. Frank Deford. Read by To be announced. (Running Time: 11 hrs. 5 mins.). (ENG.). 2011. 29.95 (978-1-4417-7963-2(9)) Blckstn Audio.

***Bliss, Remembered.** unabr. ed. Frank Deford. Read by To be Announced. (Running Time: 11 hrs. 5 mins.). (ENG.). 2011. 72.95 (978-1-4417-7960-1(4)) Blckstn Audio.

***Bliss, Remembered.** unabr. ed. Frank Deford. Read by To be announced. (Running Time: 11 hrs. 5 mins.). 2011. audio compact disk 32.95 (978-1-4417-7962-5(0)) Blckstn Audio.

***Bliss, Remembered.** unabr. ed. Frank Deford. Read by To be Announced. (Running Time: 11 hrs. 5 mins.). (ENG.). 2011. audio compact disk 105.00 (978-1-4417-7961-8(2)) Blckstn Audio.

Bliss to You: Trixie's Guide to a Happy Life. Trixie Koontz. Read by Teryn McKewin. Told to Dean Koontz. (Playaway Adult Nonfiction Ser.). (ENG.). 2009. 34.99 (978-1-60775-856-3(3)) Find a World.

Bliss to You: Trixie's Guide to a Happy Life. unabr. ed. Trixie Koontz. Read by Teryn McKewin. Told to Dean Koontz. 1 MP3-CD. (Running Time: 1 hr.). 2008. 39.25 (978-1-4233-7509-8(2), 9781423375098, Brinc Audio MP3 Lib); 39.25 (978-1-4233-7511-1(4), 9781423375111, BADLE); 14.95 (978-1-4233-7508-1(4), 9781423375081, Brilliance MP3); 14.95 (978-1-4233-7510-4(6), 9781423375104, BAD); audio compact disk 39.25 (978-1-4233-7507-4(6), 9781423375074, BriAudCD Unabrid); audio compact disk 14.95 (978-1-4233-7506-7(8), 9781423375067, Bril Audio CD Unabri) Brilliance Audio.

Blissful Eyes of Awakening. Swami Amar Jyoti. 1 dolby cass. 1983. 9.95 (R-51) Truth Consciousness.
Where merging becomes a reality, the light-full eyes of Consciousness open. What happens when the ego truly humbles down? "Be what you truly are".

Blissful Spirit. Joseph Michael Levry. (Healing Beyond Medicine Ser.). 2000. 19.00 (978-1-885562-04-3(7)) Root Light.

Blissmaker. deluxe ed. Royce Richardson. 2001. bk. 36.00 (978-0-9677200-2-9(8)) Ancient River Pubng.

***Blister.** John Taintor Foote. 2009. (978-1-60136-527-9(6)) Audio Holding.

***Blithe Images.** unabr. ed. Nora Roberts. (Running Time: 7 hrs.). 2010. audio compact disk 24.99 (978-1-4418-5420-9(7), 9781441854209, Bril Audio CD Unabri) Brilliance Audio.

Blithe Spirit see Theatre Highlights

Blithe Spirit. Noel Coward. Contrib. by Rosalind Ayres et al. (Playaway Adult Fiction Ser.). (ENG.). 2009. 39.99 (978-1-60775-735-1(4)) Find a World.

Blithe Spirit. unabr. ed. Noel Coward. Perf. by Rosalind Ayres et al. 2 CDs. (Running Time: 1 hr. 45 mins.). Dramatization. 2000. audio compact disk 25.95 (978-1-58081-180-4(9), CDTPT119); 20.95 (978-1-58081-126-2(4), TPT119) L A Theatre.
In the home of Charles Condomine, a remarried widower, a casual, witty evening among friends is transformed by a seance. The ghost of Charles' first wife, Elvira, is conjured from beyond & delights in wreaking havoc & hilarity among the living.

Blithe Spirit: An Improbable Farce. Noel Coward. Perf. by Corin Redgrave et al. 2 cass. (Running Time: 2 hrs. 30 mins.). 2002. 13.98 (978-962-634-763-8(5), NA226314, Naxos AudioBooks); audio compact disk 17.98 (978-962-634-263-3(3), NA226312, Naxos AudioBooks) Naxos.

***Blithe Spirit: Act II, Scene I.** abr. ed. Noel Coward. Read by Simon Jones. (ENG.). 2006. (978-0-06-125280-8(8), Harper Audio) HarperCollins Pubs.

Blithedale Romance. Nathaniel Hawthorne. Narrated by Flo Gibson. 5 cass. (Running Time: 7 hrs. 30 mins.). (gr. 10 up). 2000. 20.95 (978-1-55685-650-1(4)) Audio Bk Con.
A communal experiment in living a utopian pastoral life is shared by lively, beautiful Zenobia, lovely, gentle Priscilla, their demanding leader Hollingsworth & Miles Coverdale, but their dreams are destroyed by the realities of human imperfections.

Blithedale Romance. Nathaniel Hawthorne. Narrated by Flo Gibson. (ENG.). 2008. audio compact disk 27.95 (978-1-55685-956-4(2)) Audio Bk Con.

Blitzcat. unabr. ed. Robert Westall. Read by Alistair Maydon. 6 cass. (Running Time: 6 hrs. 41 min.). (Isis Ser.). (J). 1993. 54.95 (978-1-85089-647-0(X), 20591) Pub: ISIS Lrg Prnt GBR. Dist(s): Ulverscroft US

Blizzard. (YA). 2000. 26.96 (978-1-935430-00-1(9)) Audio Bkshelf.

Blizzard! The Storm That Changed America. abr. ed. Jim Murphy. Read by Taylor Mali. 2 cass. (Running Time: 2 hrs. 30 min.). (YA). 2003. 19.95 (978-1-883332-85-3(0)); audio compact disk 26.95 (978-1-883332-91-4(5)) Audio Bkshelf.

Blizzard of the Blue Moon. unabr. ed. Mary Pope Osborne. Read by Mary Pope Osborne. (Running Time: 4620 sec.). (Magic Tree House Ser.: No. 36). (ENG.). (J). (gr. 1-5). 2006. audio compact disk 14.95 (978-0-7393-3681-6(9), ImaginStudio) Pub: Random Audio Pubg. Dist(s): Random

Blizzard of the Blue Moon; Dragon of the Red Dawn. unabr. ed. Mary Pope Osborne. Read by Mary Pope Osborne. 2 CDs. (Running Time: 2 hrs. 24 mins.). (Magic Tree House Ser.: Nos. 36-37). (J). (gr. 1-3). 2007. audio compact disk 24.00 (978-0-7393-5108-6(7), Listening Lib) Pub: Random Audio Pubg. Dist(s): Random

Blizzard on Blue Mountain. unabr. ed. Kristiana Gregory. (Running Time: 1 hr. 45 mins. 0 sec.). (Cabin Creek Mysteries Ser.). (ENG.). 2009. 10.49 (978-1-60814-098-5(9), SpringWater) Oasis Audio.

Blizzard on Blue Mountain. unabr. ed. Kristiana Gregory. 2 CDs. (Running Time: 1 hr. 45 mins. 0 sec.). (Cabin Creek Mysteries Ser.). (ENG.). (J). (gr. 6). 2009. audio compact disk 14.99 (978-1-59859-510-9(5), SpringWater) Oasis Audio.

Blizzards. Anne Schraff. Narrated by Larry A. McKeever. (Natural Disaster Ser.). (J). 2004. 10.95 (978-1-58659-116-8(9)); audio compact disk 14.95 (978-1-58659-350-6(1)) Artesian.

Blobheads. Paul Stewart & Chris Riddell. Read by Nigel Lambert. 3 CDs. (Running Time: 9720 sec.). (J). 2005. DVD, audio compact disk, audio compact disk 29.95 (978-0-7540-6672-9(X), Chivers Child Audio) AudioGO.

***Block K Rides Tonight!** Walt Coburn. 2009. (978-1-60136-404-3(0)) Audio Holding.

Block K Rides Tonight! Walt Coburn. (Running Time: 1 hr. 30 mins.). 1999. 10.95 (978-1-60083-495-0(7)) Iofy Corp.

***Blockade Billy.** unabr. ed. Stephen King. Read by Craig Wasson & Mare Winningham. (Running Time: 2 hrs. 30 mins. 0 sec.). 2010. audio compact disk 19.99 (978-1-4423-3658-2(7)) Pub: S&S Audio. Dist(s): S and S Inc

Blockbusters. Perf. by W. C. Fields. 9 cass. (Running Time: 9 hrs.). 53.82 Set. Moonbeam Pubns.

Blocks in Our Mind. Swami Amar Jyoti. 1 cass. 1976. 9.95 (P-4) Truth Consciousness.
The steps in removing our blocks. Self-interest vs. the Goal. The dry road of spiritual practices. Going deeper, the world within.

Blocks to Intuition. Thomas R. Condon. 1 cass. (Expanded Intuition Training Tape Ser.). 12.95 (978-1-884305-73-3(3)) Changeworks.
Hypnotic exercises & discussion to help you deal with questions you may have about the nature of intuition. Using this tape will help your conscious mind & unconscious mind work together as a powerful team.

Blocks to Pure Existence. Swami Amar Jyoti. 1 dolby cass. 1983. 9.95 (M-44) Truth Consciousness.
A fresh exposition on the blocks to enlightenment. The overcoming process.

Blog: Understanding the Information Reformation. unabr. ed. Hugh Hewitt. 2005. audio compact disk 27.99 (978-1-58926-850-0(4), 6850) Pub: Oasis Audio. Dist(s): TNT Media Grp

Blog: Understanding the Information Reformation. unabr. ed. Hugh Hewitt. Narrated by Hugh Hewitt. (ENG.). 2005. 13.99 (978-1-60814-085-5(7)) Oasis Audio.

Blond see Bionda & Other Short Stories

***Blonde.** abr. ed. Joyce Carol Oates. 2004. (978-0-06-079400-2(3), Harper Audio); (978-0-06-081441-0(1), Harper Audio) HarperCollins Pubs.

Blonde & Blue: Classic Private Eyes. unabr. ed. Read by Jamie Farr et al. Ed. by Martin Greenberg. 4 cass. (Running Time: 6 hrs.). 2001. 25.00 (978-1-59040-079-1(8), Phoenix Audio) Pub: Amer Intl Pub. Dist(s): PerseuPGW
From the rain-slick streets of the urban jungle to the serene landscape of a major university, modern day private detectives are called upon to solve cases anywhere at anytime. This is fabulous new anthology of private eye stories that will delight the discerning mystery aficionados.

Blonde Eckbert. Archim Seiffarth. pap. bk. 20.95 (978-88-7754-958-7(0)) Pub: Cideb ITA. Dist(s): Distribks Inc

Blonde Faith. unabr. ed. Walter Mosley. Read by Michael Boatman. (Running Time: 7 hrs.). (Easy Rawlins Mystery Ser.). (ENG.). 2007. 24.98 (978-1-60024-043-0(7)); audio compact disk 31.98 (978-1-60024-042-3(9)) Pub: Hachet Audio. Dist(s): HachBkGrp

Blood see Isaac Bashevis Singer Reader

Blood: Heb. 10:19-25. Ed Young. 1992. 4.95 (978-0-7417-1909-6(6), 909) Win Walk.

Blood: Stories of Life & Death from the Civil War. 2009. audio compact disk 24.95 (978-1-59316-449-2(1)) Listen & Live.

Blood: Stories of Life & Death from the Civil War. unabr. ed. Ulysses S. Grant et al. Ed. by Peter Kadzis. 4 cass. (Running Time: 6 hrs.). (Adrenaline Ser.). (gr. 11). 2001. 24.95 (978-1-885408-65-5(X), LL057) Listen & Live.
The Civil War, the most dramatic moment in this nation's history, also produced some of our greatest literature. From tragic charges to prison escapes to the desolation wrought on those who stayed behind, this is an extraordinary collection of reminiscences, fiction, & excerpts from diaries & letters by an array of soldiers, writers, & observers.

Blood & Chocolate. unabr. ed. Annette Curtis Klause. Narrated by Alyssa Bresnahan. 6 pieces. (Running Time: 7 hrs. 45 mins.). (gr. 9 up). 1998. 51.00 (978-0-7887-1102-2(4), 95095E7) Recorded Bks.
Vivian Gandalon, a teen-aged werewolf, tried for years to escape her legacy of violence & forbidden appetites. All she wants is to fit in at school.

Blood & Chocolate: Class Set. unabr. ed. Annette Curtis Klause. Read by Alyssa Bresnahan. 6 cass., 10 bks. (Running Time: 7 hrs. 45 min.). (J). 1997. bk. 228.80 (978-0-7887-2758-0(3), 46113) Recorded Bks.
Vivian Gandalon, a teen-aged werewolf, tried for years to escape her legacy of violence & forbidden appetites. All she wants is to fit in at school.

Blood & Chocolate: Homework Set. unabr. ed. Annette Curtis Klause. Read by Alyssa Bresnahan. 6 cass. (Running Time: 7 hrs. 45 min.). (J). (gr. 5). 1997. bk. 74.95 (978-0-7887-1717-8(0), 12/1997) Recorded Bks.

Blood & Gold. Anne Rice. Read by Roger Rees. (Vampire Chronicles: Bk. 8). 2001. 88.00 (978-0-7366-8075-2(6)) Books on Tape.

Blood & Gold. abr. ed. Anne Rice. 2 cass. (Running Time: 6 hrs.). (Vampire Chronicles: Bk. 8). (ENG.). 2001. 12.95 (978-0-375-41946-1(2), Random AudioBks) Pub: Random Audio Pubg. Dist(s): Random
Out of the pages of the Vampire Chronicles steps the golden-haired Marius, true Child of the Millenia, once mentor to the Vampire Lestat, always and forever the conscientious slayer of the evildoer, and now ready to reveal the secrets of his two-thousand-year-long existence.

Blood & Gold. unabr. ed. Anne Rice. Read by Roger Rees. 11 cass. (Running Time: 11 hrs.). (Vampire Chronicles: Bk. 8). 2001. 35.96 Books on Tape.
Marius, a two-thousand-year-old vampire, describes his origins and his haunting passage through history.

Blood & Gold. unabr. abr. ed. Ralph Compton. (Running Time: 4 hrs. 45 mins.). (ENG.). 2004. audio compact disk 22.95 (978-1-56511-915-4(0), 1565119150) Pub: HighBridge. Dist(s): Workman Pub

Blood & Guts. Richard Wirick. (Running Time: 0 hr. 15 mins.). 2005. 13.95 (978-1-59912-920-4(5)) Iofy Corp.

Blood & Guts in High School. Kathy Acker. Interview with Kathy Acker. 1 cass. (Running Time: 30 min.). 8.95 (AMF-16) Am Audio Prose.
A post-punk novelist from New York's lower East Side, Acker reads from her early novel "Blood & Guts in High School" & talks about nihilism, plagiarism, & rock & roll.

Blood & Honey. unabr. ed. Graham Hurley. Read by Tim Pepper. 12 cass. (Running Time: 15 hrs. 30 mins.). (Isis Cassettes Ser.). 2006. 94.95 (978-0-7531-3539-6(6)) Pub: ISIS Lrg Prnt GBR. Dist(s): Ulverscroft US

Blood & Honor, Pt. 1. unabr. ed. W. E. B. Griffin. Read by Michael Russotto. 10 cass. (Running Time: 15 hrs.). (Honor Bound Ser.: No. 2). 1996. 80.00 (978-0-7366-3594-3(7), 4246A) Books on Tape.
Threading his way between Axis & Allied sympathizers & even between rival OSS & FBI factions, Frade strives his utmost to fulfill his mission, punish his father's assassins & stay alive.

Blood & Honor, Pt. 2. unabr. ed. W. E. B. Griffin. Read by Michael Rossotto. 9 cass. (Running Time: 13 hrs. 30 mins.). (Honor Bound Ser.: Bk. 2). 1997. 72.00 (978-0-7366-3595-0(5), 4246-B) Books on Tape.
In 1942 Buenos Aires, a three-man team of Americans sabotages German ships & submarines.

***Blood & Honor (1 Of 2) The Forest Kingdom Saga (Book 2), Vol. 1.** Simon R. Green. 2010. audio compact disk 19.99 (978-1-59950-659-3(9)) GraphicAudio.

***Blood & Honor (2 Of 2) The Forest Kingdom Saga (Book 2)** Simon R. Green. 2010. audio compact disk 19.99 (978-1-59950-667-8(X)) GraphicAudio.

Blood & Ice. unabr. ed. Robert Masello. Read by Phil Gigante. 1 MP3-CD. (Running Time: 17 hrs.). 2009. 39.97 (978-1-4233-7691-0(9), 9781423376910, Brlnc Audio MP3 Lib); 39.97 (978-1-4233-7693-4(5), 9781423376934, BADLE); 24.99 (978-1-4233-7692-7(7), 9781423376927, BAD); 24.99 (978-1-4233-7690-3(0), 9781423376903, Brilliance MP3); audio compact disk 97.97 (978-1-4233-7689-7(7), 9781423376897, BriAudCD Unabrid); audio compact disk 38.99 (978-1-4233-7688-0(9), 9781423376880, Bril Audio CD Unabri) Brilliance Audio.

Blood & Judgment. unabr. ed. Michael Gilbert. Read by Bruce Montague. 8 cass. (Running Time: 7 hrs. 12 min.). (Isis Ser.). (J). 2004. 69.95 (978-1-85089-645-6(3), 91116) Pub: ISIS Lrg Prnt GBR. Dist(s): Ulverscroft US

Blood & Rubles. unabr. ed. Stuart M. Kaminsky. Read by John Edwardson. 6 cass. (Running Time: 9 hrs.). (Inspector Porfiry Rostnikov Mystery Ser.: No. 10). 1997. 48.00 (978-0-7366-3704-6(4), 4388) Books on Tape.
Murderous thieves terrorize an impoverished neighborhood.

Blood & Rubles. unabr. ed. Stuart M. Kaminsky. Narrated by Mark Hammer. 7 cass. (Running Time: 9 hrs. 45 mins.). (Inspector Porfiry Rostnikov Mystery Ser.: No. 10). 2000. 60.00 (978-0-7887-0511-3(3), 94704E7) Recorded Bks.
In one week, Porfiry Rostnikov and his policemust deal with three cases of violence and greed that are shocking even for the chaos of post-communist Russia. Trying to uphold the law, Rostnikov and his team struggle to maintain their belief in a shaky system of justice and their unpredictable fellow citizens.

Blood & Smoke. abr. ed. Stephen King. Read by Stephen King. 2006. 16.95 (978-0-7435-6367-3(0), Audioworks) Pub: S&S Audio. Dist(s): S and S Inc

***Blood & Smoke.** abr. ed. Stephen King. Read by Stephen King. (Running Time: 4 hrs. 0 mins. 0 sec.). (ENG.). 2010. audio compact disk 14.99 (978-1-4423-3621-6(8)) Pub: S&S Audio. Dist(s): S and S Inc

Blood & the Human Body. unabr. ed. Michael Day. 1 cass. 1990. 12.95 (ECN064) J Norton Pubs.

Blood & Thunder. abr. ed. Max Allan Collins. Read by Max Allan Collins. Ed. by Fran Landt. 2 cass. (Running Time: 3 hrs.). 1999. 16.95 (978-1-882071-57-9(3)) B-B Audio.
Collins fictional hero Nathan Heller returns to investigate the brutal assassination of one of the most charismatic and controversial political figures of our time. The place is Louisiana. The time is 1935 and Huey Long is the current U.S. Senator.

Blood & Thunder. unabr. ed. Max Allan Collins. Read by Alan Sklar. 8 cass. (Running Time: 12 hrs.). 2000. 59.95 (CSL 100) Pub: Chivers Audio Bks GBR. Dist(s): AudioGO
It is Louisiana, 1935. Huey Long, former governor and current senator, is the most potent challenger to the Presidency, and F. D. R. has good reason to fear the next election. Long's quest for power has made him many enemies, and rumors of his assassination are flowing; so Nathan Heller of the A-1 Detective Agency in Chicago is hired to uncover the truth. But after a sudden burst of gunfire, Heller realizes that nothing can keep Long from his destiny.

Blood & Thunder: An Epic of the American West. abr. ed. Hampton Sides. Read by Don Leslie. 10. (Running Time: 23400 sec.). (ENG.). 2006. audio compact disk 29.95 (978-0-553-75681-4(8)) Pub: Random Audio Pubg. Dist(s): Random

Blood at the Bookies. Simon Brett. 2008. 54.95 (978-0-7531-3150-3(1)); audio compact disk 79.95 (978-0-7531-3151-0(X)) Pub: Isis Pubng Ltd GBR. Dist(s): Ulverscroft US

Blood Bond 1. William W. Johnstone. (Running Time: 25200 sec.). (Blood Bond Ser.: No. 2). 2007. audio compact disk 19.99 (978-1-59950-333-2(6)) GraphicAudio.

Blood Bond 10: The Hanging Road. Based on a novel by William W. Johnstone. (Blood Bond Ser.: No. 10). 2008. audio compact disk 19.99 (978-1-59950-442-1(1)) GraphicAudio.

Blood Bond 11: Texas Gundown. Based on a novel by William W. Johnstone. (Blood Bond Ser.: No. 11). 2008. audio compact disk 19.99 (978-1-59950-448-3(0)) GraphicAudio.

Blood Bond 12: Ride for Vengeance. Based on a novel by William W. Johnstone. (Blood Bond Ser.: No. 12). 2008. audio compact disk 19.99 (978-1-59950-456-8(1)) GraphicAudio.

Blood Bond 13: Deadly Road to Yuma. William W. Johnstone & J. A. Johnstone. (Blood Bond Ser.: No. 13). 2009. audio compact disk 19.99 (978-1-59950-589-3(4)) GraphicAudio.

***Blood Bond 14: Moonshine Massacre.** William W. Johnstone. (Blood Bond Ser.: No. 14). 2010. audio compact disk 19.99 (978-1-59950-665-4(3)) GraphicAudio.

Blood Bond 2: Brotherhood of the Gun. William W. Johnstone. Directed By Nanette Savard. Contrib. by Thomas Penny et al. (Running Time: 21600 sec.). (Blood Bond Ser.: No. 1). 2007. audio compact disk 19.99 (978-1-59950-352-3(2)) GraphicAudio.

Blood Bond 3: Gunsight Crossing. William W. Johnstone. (Blood Bond Ser.). 2007. audio compact disk 19.99 (978-1-59950-378-3(6)) GraphicAudio.

Blood Bond 4: Gunsmoke & Gold. William W. Johnstone. Directed By Nanette Savard. Contrib. by Thomas Penny et al. (Running Time: 18000 sec.). (Blood Bond Ser.: No. 5). 2007. audio compact disk 19.99 (978-1-59950-387-5(5)) GraphicAudio.

Blood Bond 5: Devil Creek Crossfire. William W. Johnstone. (Running Time: 18000 sec.). (Blood Bond Ser.). 2007. audio compact disk 19.99 (978-1-59950-397-4(2)) GraphicAudio.

Blood Bond 6: Slaughter Trail. Directed By Nanette Savard. Contrib. by Thomas Penny et al. (Running Time: 18000 sec.). (Blood Bond Ser.). 2007. audio compact disk 19.99 (978-1-59950-402-5(2)) GraphicAudio.

Blood Bond 7: Shootout at Gold Creek. Directed By Ken Jackson. Contrib. by Thomas Penny et al. (Running Time: 18000 sec.). (Blood Bond Ser.). 2007. audio compact disk 19.99 (978-1-59950-414-8(6)) GraphicAudio.

Blood Bond 8: San Angelo Showdown. Directed By Nanette Savard. Contrib. by Thomas Penny et al. (Running Time: 18000 sec.). (Blood Bond Ser.). 2007. audio compact disk 19.99 (978-1-59950-422-3(7)) GraphicAudio.

Blood Bond 9: Death in Snake Creek. Based on a book by William W. Johnstone. (Blood Bond Ser.: No. 8). 2008. audio compact disk 19.99 (978-1-59950-434-6(0)) GraphicAudio.

Blood, Bones, & Butter: The Inadvertent Education of a Reluctant Chef. abr. unabr. ed. Gabrielle Hamilton. Read by Gabrielle Hamilton. (ENG.). 2011. audio compact disk 30.00 (978-0-7393-3244-3(9), Random AudioBks) Pub: Random Audio Pubg. Dist(s): Random

Blood Born. unabr. ed. Linda Howard & Linda Jones. Read by Vanessa Hart. 2010. 35.00 (978-0-307-73624-6(5), Random AudioBks) Pub: Random Audio Pubg. Dist(s): Random

Blood Bought Promises. Gary V. Whetstone. 4 cass. (Running Time: 6 hrs.). (Freedom Ser.). 1993. pap. bk. 35.00 (978-1-58866-209-5(8), VROO2A) Gary Whet Pub.
The awesome covenant God has with you through the Blood of Jesus. A complete understanding of the terms, provisions, & power of the covenant.

Blood Bounty. abr. ed. Dalton Walker. Read by Dick Wilkinson. 2 cass. (Running Time: 3 hrs.). (Shiloh: Vol. 8). 2000. 16.95 (978-1-890990-36-7(1), 99036) Otis Audio.
Western with sound effects & music.

Blood Brothers. abr. ed. Nora Roberts. Read by Phil Gigante. (Running Time: 6 hrs.). (Sign of Seven Trilogy: Bk. 1). 2008. audio compact disk 14.99 (978-1-4233-3773-7(5), 9781423337737, BCD Value Price) Brilliance Audio.

Blood Brothers. unabr. ed. Gary McCarthy. Read by Michael Taylor. 4 cass. (Running Time: 5 hrs. 30 min.). 2001. 26.95 (978-1-55686-774-3(3)) Books in Motion.
The paths from boy to manhood cross as Deputy Ben Pope finds old friend Rick Kilbane on the wrong side of the law as the blood brothers head toward an ultimate showdown.

Blood Brothers. unabr. ed. Nora Roberts. (Running Time: 10 hrs.). (Sign of Seven Trilogy: Bk. 1). 2007. 39.25 (978-1-4233-3771-3(9), 9781423337713, BADLE); 24.95 (978-1-4233-3770-6(0), 9781423337706, BAD) Brilliance Audio.

Blood Brothers. unabr. ed. Nora Roberts. Read by Phil Gigante. 1 MP3-CD. (Running Time: 10 hrs.). (Sign of Seven Trilogy: Bk. 1). 2007. audio compact disk 39.25 (978-1-4233-3769-0(7), 9781423337690, Brlnc Audio MP3 Lib); audio compact disk 97.25 (978-1-4233-3767-6(0), 9781423337676, BriAudCD Unabrid); audio compact disk 92.25 (978-1-4233-3765-2(4), 9781423337652, BrilAudUnabridg); audio compact disk 36.95 (978-1-4233-3766-9(2), 9781423337669, Bril Audio CD Unabri); audio compact disk 24.95 (978-1-4233-3768-3(9), 9781423337683, Brilliance MP3) Brilliance Audio.

Blood Brothers. unabr. ed. Sol Wachtler & David Gould. 11 cass. (Running Time: 16 hrs. 30 min.). 2004. 38.95 (978-1-59007-435-0(1)); audio compact disk 79.95 (978-1-59007-421-3(1)) Pub: New Millenn Enter. Dist(s): PerseuPGW

Blood Canticle. unabr. ed. Anne Rice. Read by David Pittu. 8 cass. (Running Time: 12 hrs.). (Vampire Chronicles: Bk. 10). 2003. 57.60 (978-0-7366-9446-9(3)); audio compact disk 72.00 (978-0-7366-9595-4(8)) Books on Tape.
On the stage set by Blackwood Farm, a cast of vampires and witches convenes to showcase the peregrinations of the Vampire Lestat and his beloved Rowan Mayfair. Once the epitome of evil, Lestat now pursues transformation. Struggling with his vampirism, he yearns for goodness, purity, and love. In turn, the brilliant neurosurgeon and witch Rowan Mayfair finds herself dangerously drawn to him - but she is married, and her husband, Michael Curry, seeks Lestat's help with her temporary madness.

Blood Covenant. 2003. (978-1-59024-095-3(2)); audio compact disk (978-1-59024-094-6(4)) B Hinn Min.

Blood Covenant. Kenneth Copeland. 10 CDs. 2006. audio compact disk 30.00 (978-1-57562-851-6(1)) K Copeland Pubns.

Blood Covenant. Kenneth Copeland. 6 cass. 1983. 30.00 Set incl. study guide. (978-0-88114-266-2(2)) K Copeland Pubns.
Biblical teaching of blood covenant.

Blood Covenant. Gary V. Whetstone. Instructed by June Austin. 7 cass. (Running Time: 10 hrs. 30 mins.). (Theology Ser.: TH105). 1996. 80.00 (978-1-58866-099-2(0), BT 105 A00) Gary Whet Pub.
The application of covenant principles in our daily life & an understanding of the Father & the Holy Spirit through the blood of the Lord Jesus Christ.

Blood Covenant. Bill Winston. 2 cass. (Running Time: 0hr.55min.). (C). 2000. 10.00 (978-1-931289-61-0(1)) Pub: B Winston Min. Dist(s): Anchor Distributors

***Blood Covenant.** Zondervan. (Mission Hope Ser.). (ENG.). 2011. 14.99 (978-0-310-42662-2(6)) Zondervan.

Blood Covenant. unabr. ed. E. W. Kenyon. Read by Stephen Sobozenski. 1 cass. (Running Time: 1 hr. 20 min.). 1997. 6.00 (978-1-57770-021-0(X)) Kenyons Gospel.
A revelation of what the Lord's Table really means - the message the world needs.

Blood Covenant, Pt. 1. Speeches. Ronald G. Fanter. 16 cass. (Running Time: 16 hrs.). 2001. 80.00 (978-1-931215-36-7(7)) Cut Edge Min.
List of messages:Intro. Blood Covenant 1Intro. Blood Covenant 2Covenant TheologyMosaic Covenant of GraceUnderstanding The Spirit WorldCovenant With LuciferCovenant With HeavensCovenant With Morning StarsAncient Covenant PracticesCovenant With The EarthPrimitive Family ReligionOrigin of Threshold CovenantMystery of BloodMystery of MarriageCrossing The ThresholdCovenant of AdoptionComes in a vinyl case.

***Blood Covenant: The Michael Franzese Story.** abr. ed. Michael Franzese. Orig. Title: Quitting the Mob. (ENG.). 2009. 12.98 (978-1-59644-404-1(5), Hovel Audio) christianaud.

Blood Covenant: The Michael Franzese Story. abr. ed. Michael Franzese. Read by Michael Franzese. (Running Time: 6 hrs. 15 mins. 0 sec.). Orig. Title: Quitting the Mob. (ENG.). 2009. audio compact disk 21.98 (978-1-59644-623-6(4), Hovel Audio) christianaud.

Blood Covenant Pt. I: Psalm 25. Ed Young. 1979. 4.95 (978-0-7417-1033-8(1), A0033) Win Walk.

Blood Covenant Pt. II: Genesis 15:1-5. Ed Young. 1980. 4.95 (978-0-7417-1141-0(9), A0141) Win Walk.

Blood Dancing. Jonathan Gash & Jonathan Gash. Read by Graham Padden. 14. 2007. audio compact disk 99.95 (978-1-84652-116-4(5)) Pub: ISIS Audio GBR. Dist(s): Ulverscroft US

Blood Dancing. Jonathan Gash & Jonathan Gash. Read by Graham Padden. 11. 2007. 89.95 (978-1-84652-115-7(7)) Pub: Magna Story GBR. Dist(s): Ulverscroft US

Blood Diamonds. unabr. ed. Greg Campbell. (Running Time: 7 hrs. 30 mins.). (YA). 2006. 24.95 (978-0-7861-4954-4(X)) Blckstn Audio.

Blood Diamonds. unabr. ed. Greg Campbell. Read by Tom Weiner. (Running Time: 25200 sec.). 2006. 44.95 (978-0-7861-4964-3(7)); audio compact disk 55.00 (978-0-7861-5832-4(8)) Blckstn Audio.

Blood Diamonds. unabr. ed. Greg Campbell. Read by Tom Weiner. 6 CDs. (Running Time: 7 hrs. 30 mins.). (YA). 2006. audio compact disk 24.95 (978-0-7861-5839-3(5)) Blckstn Audio.

Blood Diamonds, Level 1. Richard MacAndrew. Contrib. by Philip Prowse. (Running Time: 50 mins.). (Cambridge English Readers Ser.). (ENG.). 2005. 9.45 (978-0-521-53658-5(8)) Cambridge U Pr.

Blood Doctor. unabr. ed. Barbara Vine, pseud. Read by Robert Powell. 12 cass. (Running Time: 18 hrs.). 2003. 96.95 (978-0-7540-0941-2(6)) AudioGO.

Blood Dreams. Kay Hooper. Read by Joyce Bean. 2008. 74.99 (978-1-60640-587-1(X)) Find a World.

Blood Dreams. abr. ed. Kay Hooper. Read by Joyce Bean. (Running Time: 5 hrs.). (Blood Ser.). 2008. audio compact disk 14.99 (978-1-4233-3302-9(0), 9781423333029, BCD Value Price) Brilliance Audio.

Blood Dreams. unabr. ed. Kay Hooper. (Running Time: 8 hrs.). (Blood Ser.). 2007. 39.25 (978-1-4233-3300-5(4), 9781423333005, BADLE); 24.95 (978-1-4233-3299-2(7), 9781423332992, BAD) Brilliance Audio.

Blood Dreams. unabr. ed. Kay Hooper. Read by Joyce Bean. 7 cass. (Running Time: 28800 sec.). (Blood Ser.). 2007. 82.25 (978-1-4233-3294-7(6), 9781423332947, BrilAudUnabridg); audio compact disk 34.95 (978-1-4233-3295-4(4), 9781423332954, Bril Audio CD Unabri); audio compact disk 24.95 (978-1-4233-3297-8(0), 9781423332978, Brilliance MP3); audio compact disk 87.25 (978-1-4233-3296-1(2), 9781423332961, BriAudCD Unabrid) Brilliance Audio.

Blood Dreams. unabr. ed. Kay Hooper. Read by Joyce Bean. Directed By Stephen Helderman. 1 MP3-CD. (Running Time: 28800 sec.). (Blood Ser.). 2007. audio compact disk 39.25 (978-1-4233-3298-5(9), 9781423332985, Brlnc Audio MP3 Lib) Brilliance Audio.

Blood Evidence. abr. ed. Mel Odom. Narrated by Kevin King. (Running Time: 27300 sec.). (NCIS Ser.). (ENG.). 2007. audio compact disk 22.99 (978-1-59859-205-4(X)) Oasis Audio.

Blood Evidence: Ncis. abr. ed. Mel Odom. Narrated by Kevin King. (NCIS Ser.). (ENG.). 2007. 16.09 (978-1-60814-086-2(5)) Oasis Audio.

Blood Fever. unabr. ed. Charlie Higson. Read by Nathaniel Parker. 7 CDs. (Running Time: 8 hrs. 43 mins.). (Young Bond Ser.). (YA). (gr. 5-8). 2007. audio compact disk 55.00 (978-0-7393-4870-3(1), BksonTape) Pub: Random Audio Pubg. Dist(s): Random

Blood Fever. unabr. ed. Charlie Higson. Read by Nathaniel Parker. (Running Time: 31380 sec.). (Young Bond Ser.). (ENG.). (J). (gr. 5). 2007. audio compact disk 37.00 (978-0-7393-3893-3(5), Listening Lib) Pub: Random Audio Pubg. Dist(s): Random

Blood Flies Upwards. unabr. ed. E. X. Ferrars. Read by Julian Franklyn. 5 cass. (Running Time: 7 hrs. 30 min.). 1999. 49.95 (978-1-86042-212-6(8), 22128) Pub: Soundings Ltd GBR. Dist(s): Ulverscroft US
The young woman who took the post of cook-housekeeper at wealthy Eckersall's weekend retreat was not all that she appeared to be. Alison Goodrich was not separated from her husband, as she had claimed. She was the sister of the previous cook-housekeeper, Sally. The more she probed, the more Alison became convinced that there was something sinister about Sally's disappearance.

Blood from a Stone. unabr. ed. Donna Leon. Narrated by David Colacci. (Commissario Guido Brunetti Mystery Ser.: Bk. 14). (ENG.). 2005. audio

compact disk 31.95 (978-1-57270-468-8(3)) Pub: AudioGO. Dist(s): Perseus Dist
On a cold Venetian night just before Christmas, an African street vendor is killed in a scuffle. The only witnesses are tourists who had been browsing the man's wares before his death. Arriving on the scene, Commissario Brunetti wonders why anyone would kill a "vu cumpra," an African purveying goods past normal shop hours and without a work permit. When Brunetti digs deeper into the investigation, he discovers that matters of great value are at stake within the immigrant society. Warned by his superior to resist further involvement in the case, Brunetti becomes even more determined to unearth the truth behind this mysterious killing. How far will he penetrate the murky subculture of the Venetian underworld? Read by David Colacci.

Blood from a Stone. unabr. ed. Donna Leon. Read by David Colacci. (Commissario Guido Brunetti Mystery Ser.: Bk. 14). 2005. 29.95 (978-0-7927-3623-3(0), CMP 786); 54.95 (978-0-7927-3545-8(5), CSL 786); DVD, audio compact disk, audio compact disk 74.95 (978-0-7927-3546-5(3), SLD 786) AudioGO.

Blood Game. abr. ed. Ed Gorman. Read by Alan Zimmerman. 2000. 22.00 (978-1-58807-048-7(4)) Am Pubng Inc.
Leo Guild, sometime bounty hunter, has spent the previous three weeks riding shotgun for one of the last stage lines remaining in the Midwest. But jobs were few and far between and Guild was nearly broke. So it was foolish for Guild to contemplate refusing the simple job he's asked to take - finding a missing prizefighter. Now he finds himself taking an even more intense dislike to the boxing promoter who wants to hire him. Still, the money is good for a few hours work, and Guild decides to take the job.

Blood Game. abr. ed. Iris Johansen. Read by Jennifer Van Dyck. 5 CDs. (Running Time: 6 hrs.). (Eve Duncan Ser.). 2009. audio compact disk 26.99 (978-1-4233-2939-8(2), 9781423329398, BACD) Brilliance Audio.

Blood Game. abr. ed. Iris Johansen. Read by Jennifer Van Dyck. (Running Time: 6 hrs.). (Eve Duncan Ser.). 2010. audio compact disk 14.99 (978-1-4233-2940-4(6), 9781423329404, BCD Value Price) Brilliance Audio.

Blood Game. unabr. ed. Ed Gorman. Read by Alan Zimmerman. 3 vols. 2000. (978-1-58807-575-8(3)) Am Pubng Inc.

Blood Game. unabr. ed. Iris Johansen. Read by Jennifer Van Dyck. 1 MP3-CD. (Running Time: 9 hrs.). (Eve Duncan Ser.). 2009. 24.99 (978-1-4233-2935-0(X), 9781423329350, Brilliance MP3); 24.99 (978-1-4233-2937-4(6), 9781423329374, BAD); 39.97 (978-1-4233-2936-7(8), 9781423329367, Brlnc Audio MP3 Lib); 39.97 (978-1-4233-2938-1(4), 9781423329381, BADLE); audio compact disk 36.99 (978-1-4233-2933-6(3), 9781423329336, Bril Audio CD Unabri); audio compact disk 97.97 (978-1-4233-2934-3(1), 9781423329343, BriAudCD Unabrid) Brilliance Audio.

Blood Groove. unabr. ed. Alex Bledsoe. Read by Stefan Rudnicki. (Running Time: 9 hrs. 0 mins.). (ENG.). 2009. 29.95 (978-1-4332-6391-0(2)); 59.95 (978-1-4332-6387-3(4)); audio compact disk 70.00 (978-1-4332-6388-0(2)) Blckstn Audio.

Blood Hunt. Ian Rankin. Read by Christian Rodska. 8 cass. 2006. 69.95 (978-0-7927-3557-1(9), CSL 930) AudioGO.

Blood Hunt. Ian Rankin. Narrated by Christian Rodska. (Running Time: 47400 sec.). (Sound Library). 2006. audio compact disk 99.95 (978-0-7927-4003-2(3)) AudioGo GBR.

Blood Hunt. Ian Rankin. Narrated by Christian Rodska. (Running Time: 47400 sec.). (Sound Library). 2006. 84.95 (978-0-7927-4002-5(5)) Sound Room.

Blood Hunt. unabr. ed. Will C. Knott. Read by Maynard Villers. 4 cass. (Running Time: 4 hrs.). (Golden Hawk Ser.: Bk. 2). 1995. 26.95 (978-1-55686-639-5(9)) Books in Motion.
Jed Thompson, known as Golden Hawk, is told that his beautiful, white sister, Annabelle, is the captive of a brutal Blackfoot chief.

Blood Hunt. unabr. ed. Ian Rankin. Read by Christian Rodska. (YA). 2007. 84.99 (978-1-60252-877-2(2)) Find a World.

Blood in the Cage: Mixed Martial Arts, Pat Miletich, & the Furious Rise of the UFC. unabr. ed. L. Jon Wertheim. Read by Phil Gigante. (Running Time: 10 hrs.). 2009. 39.97 (978-1-4233-7477-0(0), 9781423374770, Brlnc Audio MP3 Lib); 39.97 (978-1-4233-7479-4(7), 9781423374794, BADLE); 24.99 (978-1-4233-7476-3(2), 9781423374763, Brilliance MP3); 24.99 (978-1-4233-7478-7(9), 9781423374787, BAD); audio compact disk 92.97 (978-1-4233-7475-6(4), 9781423374756, BriAudCD Unabrid); audio compact disk 32.99 (978-1-4233-7474-9(6), 9781423374749, Bril Audio CD Unabri) Brilliance Audio.

***Blood in the Cotswolds.** Rebecca Tope. 2010. 69.95 (978-1-4079-0697-3(6)); audio compact disk 79.95 (978-1-4079-0698-0(4)) Pub: Soundings Ltd GBR. Dist(s): Ulverscroft US

Blood in the Water. Gillian Galbraith. 2008. 54.95 (978-1-4079-0019-3(6)); audio compact disk 64.95 (978-1-4079-0020-9(X)) Pub: Soundings Ltd GBR. Dist(s): Ulverscroft US

Blood Is the Sky. abr. ed. Steve Hamilton. Read by Jim Bond. (Running Time: 4 hrs.). (Alex McKnight Ser.). 2004. audio compact disk 69.25 (978-1-59355-803-1(1), 1593558031, BACDLib Ed) Brilliance Audio.
When a fire is done, what's left is only half-destroyed. It is charred and brittle. It is obscene. There is nothing so ugly in all the world as what a fire leaves behind, covered in ashes and smoke and a smell you'll think about every day for the rest of your life. Reluctant investigator Alex McKnight finds himself drawn by friendship into a long drive north. The brother of Alex's longtime Ojibwa friend Vinnie LeBlanc works as a hunting guide, serving the rich clients from downstate. It seems that Vinnie's brother and his most recent group of hunters have vanished in northern Ontario, and Vinnie is scared enough to ask Alex to help him find them. Their arrival sets in motion a heart-pounding string of events that leaves Alex and his friend miles from civilization, stranded in the heart of the Canadian wilderness with no food, no weapons -and no way out. And there's someone out there who definitely does not want them to make it back alive. At once elegant and enormously suspenseful, Steve Hamilton's Blood Is the Sky heralds his arrival as one of the premier crime writers working today.

Blood Is the Sky. unabr. ed. Steve Hamilton. Read by Jim Bond. 6 cass. Library ed. (Running Time: 9 hrs.). (Alex Mcknight Ser.). 2003. 69.25 (978-1-59086-994-9(X), 159086994X, BAU) Brilliance Audio.
When a fire is done, what's left is only half-destroyed. It is charred and brittle. It is obscene. There is nothing so ugly in all the world as what a fire leaves behind, covered in ashes and smoke and a smell you'll think about every day for the rest of your life. Reluctant investigator Alex McKnight finds himself drawn by friendship into a long drive north. The brother of Alex's longtime Ojibwa friend Vinnie LeBlanc works as a hunting guide, serving the rich clients from downstate. It seems that Vinnie's brother and his most recent group of hunters have vanished in northern Ontario, and Vinnie is scared enough to ask Alex to help him find them. Their arrival sets in motion a heart-pounding string of events that leaves Alex and his friend miles from civilization, stranded in the heart of the Canadian wilderness with no food, no weapons -and no way out. And there's someone out there who definitely does not want them to make it back alive. At once elegant and enormously suspenseful, Steve Hamilton's Blood Is the Sky heralds his arrival as one of the premier crime writers working today.

Blood Is the Sky. unabr. ed. Steve Hamilton. Read by Jim Bond. 6 cass. (Running Time: 9 hrs.). (Alex Mcknight Ser.: Vol. 5). 2003. 29.95 (978-1-59086-993-2(1), 1590869931, BAU) Brilliance Audio.
When a fire is done, what's left is only half-destroyed. It is charred and brittle. It is obscene. There is nothing so ugly in all the world as what a fire leaves behind, covered in ashes and smoke and a smell you'll think about every day for the rest of your life. Reluctant investigator Alex McKnight finds himself drawn by friendship into a long drive north. The brother of Alex's longtime Ojibwa friend Vinnie LeBlanc works as a hunting guide, serving the rich clients from downstate. It seems that Vinnie's brother and his most recent group of hunters have vanished in northern Ontario, and Vinnie is scared enough to ask Alex to help him find them. Their arrival sets in motion a heart-pounding string of events that leaves Alex and his friend miles from civilization, stranded in the heart of the Canadian wilderness with no food, no weapons -and no way out. And there's someone out there who definitely does not want them to make it back alive. At once elegant and enormously suspenseful, Steve Hamilton's Blood Is the Sky heralds his arrival as one of the premier crime writers working today.

Blood Is the Sky. unabr. ed. Steve Hamilton. Read by Jim Bond. (Running Time: 9 hrs.). (Alex Mcknight Ser.). 2004. 39.25 (978-1-59335-583-8(1), 1593355831, Brlnc Audio MP3 Lib) Brilliance Audio.
When a fire is done, what's left is only half-destroyed. It is charred and brittle. It is obscene. There is nothing so ugly in all the world as what a fire leaves behind, covered in ashes and smoke and a smell you'll think about every day for the rest of your life. Reluctant investigator Alex McKnight finds himself drawn by friendship into a long drive north. The brother of Alex's longtime Ojibwa friend Vinnie LeBlanc works as a hunting guide, serving the rich clients from downstate. It seems that Vinnie's brother and his most recent group of hunters have vanished in northern Ontario, and Vinnie is scared enough to ask Alex to help him find them. Their arrival sets in motion a heart-pounding string of events that leaves Alex and his friend miles from civilization, stranded in the heart of the Canadian wilderness with no food, no weapons -and no way out. And there's someone out there who definitely does not want them to make it back alive. At once elegant and enormously suspenseful, Steve Hamilton's Blood Is the Sky heralds his arrival as one of the premier crime writers working today.

Blood Is the Sky. unabr. ed. Steve Hamilton. Read by Jim Bond. (Running Time: 9 hrs.). (Alex Mcknight Ser.). 2004. 39.25 (978-1-59710-079-3(X), 159710079X, BADLE); 24.95 (978-1-59710-078-6(1), 1597100781, BAD) Brilliance Audio.

Blood Is the Sky. unabr. ed. Steve Hamilton. Read by Jim Bond. (Running Time: 9 hrs.). (Alex McKnight Ser.). 2004. 24.95 (978-1-59335-064-2(3), 1593350643) Soulmate Audio Bks.

Blood Legacy: Blood of Kerensky Trilogy. abr. ed. Michael A. Stackpole. 2 cass. (Running Time: 3 hrs.). (Battletech: Vol. 2). 2002. 9.95 (978-1-931953-31-3(7)) Listen & Live.

Blood Lies. unabr. ed. Daniel Kalla. Read by Anthony Heald. (Running Time: 34200 sec.). 2007. 29.95 (978-0-7861-4937-7(X)); audio compact disk 29.95 (978-0-7861-5885-0(9)) Blckstn Audio.

Blood Lies. unabr. ed. Daniel Kalla. Read by Anthony Heald. (Running Time: 34200 sec.). 2007. 65.95 (978-0-7861-6822-4(6)); audio compact disk 29.95 (978-0-7861-7016-6(6)); audio compact disk 81.00 (978-0-7861-6821-7(8)) Blckstn Audio.

Blood Line. abr. ed. Rex Burns. Read by Charlton Griffin. Abr. by Odin Westgaard. 2 vols. No. 9. 2003. (978-1-58807-673-1(3)) Am Pubng Inc.

Blood Lines. abr. ed. Mel Odom. Narrated by Kevin King. (NCIS Ser.). (ENG.). 2008. audio compact disk 22.99 (978-1-59859-351-8(X)) Oasis Audio.

Blood Lines. abr. ed. Ruth Rendell. 2 cass. (Running Time: 3 hrs.). 2000. 7.95 (978-1-57815-168-4(6), 1111, Media Bks Audio) Media Bks NJ.
A collection of long & short stories about, what's behind the patterns of everyday life to pinpoint the desires, deceptions & secrets of human beings.

Blood Lines. abr. ed. Ruth Rendell. 3 CDs. (Running Time: 3 hrs.). (YA). 2000. audio compact disk 11.99 (978-1-57815-503-3(7), 1111 CD3, Media Bks Audio) Media Bks NJ.
A collection of long & short stories that probe behind the patterns of everyday life to pinpoint the desires, deceptions & secrets of human beings.

Blood Lines. unabr. ed. Cynthia Harrod-Eagles. Read by Terry Wale. 9 cass. (Running Time: 12 hrs.). (Bill Slider Mystery Ser.: No. 5). 2004. 76.95 (978-1-86042-490-8(2), 24902) Pub: UlverLrgPrint GBR. Dist(s): Ulverscroft US
Detective Inspector Bill Slider almost welcomes a call out to the ABC IV Centre at White City, where Roger Greatrex, celebrated music critic & opera aficionado, appears to have topped himself - only minutes before due to appear live on a question show. But there are signs that the body has been interfered with & Slider suspects murder. One fellow panelist is known to have quarreled violently with Greatrex just before his death, but won't say what about. Trouble is, two members of the production team also have motives for the murder & nobody in the building has a proper alibi. Then a surprise new witness turns up to add to the confusion, by casting suspicion on one of Slider's own, a personal friend to boot. Slider is under pressure to make an arrest & all his instincts are at odds with the evidence. BETA a dangerous killer is on the loose & could kill again.

Blood Lines. unabr. ed. Ruth Rendell. Read by Nigel Anthony. 6 cass. (Running Time: 6 hrs.). 1996. 54.95 (978-0-7451-6672-8(5), CAB 1288) AudioGO.
"I think you know who killed your stepfather," said Wexford. So begins this scintillating collection of long & short stories. It was clear to both Wexford & Burden that Tom Peterlec was not killed for money, but various people would like to think he was...With unerring insight & style, Ruth Rendell probes behind the patterns of everyday life to pinpoint the guilty secrets of human beings.

Blood Lines. unabr. ed. Ruth Rendell. Read by Donada Peters. 6 cass. (Running Time: 6 hrs.). 1996. 36.00 (978-0-7366-3507-3(6), 4146) Books on Tape.
These vignettes of mystery & wrongdoing put us into familiar Rendell territory - not just the English villages that Chief Constable Wexford calls home, but also the dark places of the human mind.

Blood Lines. unabr. ed. Ruth Rendell. Read by Nigel Anthony. 6 cass. (Running Time: 9 hrs.). 2000. 49.95 (CAB 1288) Pub: Chivers Audio Bks GBR. Dist(s): AudioGO
"I think you know who killed your stepfather," said Wexford. So begins this collection of long and short stories. It was clear to both Wexford and Burden that Tom Peterlec was not killed for money, but various people would like to think he was.

Blood Lines. unabr. ed. Loren Robinson. Read by Ron Varela. 6 cass. (Running Time: 6 hrs. 30 min.). (American Blend Ser.: Bk. 2). 2001. 39.95 (978-1-55686-787-3(5)) Books in Motion.
After escaping a lynching for being a Redcoat during the Revolutionary War, ex-soldier Henry Roberts travels west to start a new life.

Blood Lure. abr. ed. Nevada Barr. Read by Joyce Bean. 5 cass. (Running Time: 6 hrs.). (Anna Pigeon Ser.: No. 9). 2001. audio compact disk 57.25 (978-1-58788-189-3(6), 1587881896) Brilliance Audio.
The laws of nature take a terrifyingly murderous turn in this spellbinding addition to the New York Times bestselling series featuring Park Ranger Anna Pigeon. In Blood Lure, Anna returns to the West, where she is sent on a training assignment to study grizzly bears in Waterton/Glacier National Peace Park, straddling the border between Montana ad Canada. But back in her beloved mountains, where the air is pure and cool, Anna fails to find the spiritual renewal she expected. Instead, nature seems to have become twisted, carrying a malevolence almost human in its focus. Along with Bear researcher Joan Rand and a volatile and unpredictable teenaged boy, Anna hikes the backcountry, seeking signs of the bears. On their second night out, the tables are turned: one of the beasts comes looking for her. Daybreak finds the boy missing and a camper dead, her neck snapped by a single blow, the flesh of her face cut away with a knife. Feeling betrayed by both nature and humanity, Anna must find the beast stalking the trails - leading her readers deep into a gripping wilderness life-or-death mystery.

Blood Lure. abr. ed. Nevada Barr. Read by Joyce Bean. (Running Time: 6 hrs.). (Anna Pigeon Ser.). 2006. 24.95 (978-1-4233-0027-4(0), 9781423300274, BAD) Brilliance Audio.

Blood Lure. abr. ed. Nevada Barr. Read by Joyce Bean. (Running Time: 6 hrs.). (Anna Pigeon Ser.: No. 9). 2006. 39.25 (978-1-4233-0028-1(9), 9781423300281, BADLE); audio compact disk 39.25 (978-1-4233-0026-7(2), 9781423300267, Brlnc Audio MP3 Lib); audio compact disk 24.95 (978-1-4233-0025-0(4), 9781423300250, Brilliance MP3) Brilliance Audio.

Blood Lure. unabr. ed. Nevada Barr. Narrated by Barbara Rosenblat. 10 CDs. (Running Time: 11 hrs. 30 mins.). (Anna Pigeon Ser.: No. 9). 2001. audio compact disk 97.00 (978-0-7887-7193-4(0)) Recorded Bks.
Takes Park Ranger Anna Pigeon high into Glacier Park & deep into a grisly murder case. Anna has joined a bear research team in the vast park that spreads from Montana into Canada. They hope to gather enough information to form a picture of its Grizzly bear population. Instead, one terrifying night, a bear finds them. By morning, their camp is in ruins & the youngest member of the team is missing. A few hours later, the body of a camper is discovered: the neck broken & face mutilated. As Anna sets out to find what, or who, is responsible for the carnage, her search will stretch all her resources - physical, mental & moral - to new limits.

Blood Lure. unabr. ed. Nevada Barr. Narrated by Barbara Rosenblat. 8 cass. (Running Time: 11 hrs. 30 mins.). (Anna Pigeon Ser.: No. 9). 2001. 78.00 (978-0-7887-5206-3(5), 96471E7) Recorded Bks.

Blood Lure. unabr. ed. Nevada Barr. Read by Barbara Rosenblat. 7 cass. (Running Time: 11 hrs. 30 mins.). (Anna Pigeon Ser.: No. 9). 2004. 29.95 (978-0-7887-4974-2(9), 00024) Recorded Bks.

Blood Memories. Barb Hendee. Read by Meg Heimstead & Peter French. 8 CDs. (Running Time: 10 hrs.). 2003. audio compact disk AudioRealms CN CAN.
The Undead walk among us, separated from our perception by a thin veil of ignorance and disbelief. They have hidden, fed and bred their kind in the darkness for thousand of years, keeping low and widely scattered. Things for a young vampire named Eleisha, hidden since the 19th Century, are about to change.

Blood Memory. abr. ed. Greg Iles. Read by Joyce Bean. (Running Time: 21600 sec.). 2005. audio compact disk 16.99 (978-1-59737-334-0(6), 9781597373340, BCD Value Price) Brilliance Audio.
Catherine "Cat" Ferry is a forensic odontologist, a specialist in bite marks and the clues they provide. But while Cat's colleagues know her as a world-class scientist, she secretly attempts to manage her fragile psyche with alcohol, delving into the minds of rapists and murderers yet never allowing her own frightening past to creep into the foreground. Cat's latest case involves a disturbing murder in New Orleans. Banishing her personal demons, she focuses on the potential killer, until one morning she's paralyzed by a panic attack at a grisly murder scene. Praying the attack is a onetime event, she continues her job as a consultant to the New Orleans Police Department, but when another victim dies in the same shocking way - raising fears that a serial killer is at large - Cat blacks out over the victim's mutilated corpse. Suspended from the FBI task force, plagued by nightmares, and at odds with her married lover - a homicide detective - Cat finally reaches her breaking point. In a desperate effort to regain control over a life spiraling out of control, Cat retreats to her hometown of Natchez, Mississippi. But her family's secluded antebellum estate provides no sanctuary. When some of Cat's forensic chemicals are spilled in her childhood bedroom, two bloody footprints are revealed. This sight shocks her more than any corpse she has seen in her career. Cat's father was murdered when she was eight years old, but she always believed the crime occurred in the garden outside their home. The bloody footprints suggest otherwise. Driven by this fragment of her past, Cat attempts a forensic reconstruction of the decades-old crime, even as developments with the New Orleans task force pull her back into the case she left behind. Plagued by troubling nightmares, Cat pieces together the horrifying events she has been shielded from all her life. Soon, both she and the FBI realize that the murders occurring now in New Orleans are intimately bound up with Cat's family and her past. Can Cat trust her own memories? Or has the truth been so distorted that she can never know her family's real history? Finding a solution to these intertwined murders means more than stopping a remorseless killer - it may be the only way to save Cat Ferry's sanity . . . and her life. Greg Iles is a masterful storyteller. In this dramatic novel of suspense he deftly probes the relationship between good and evil, and the unique power of human memory to reconstruct - or completely reinvent - the past.

Blood Memory. abr. ed. Greg Iles. Read by Joyce Bean. (Running Time: 6 hrs.). 2009. audio compact disk 9.99 (978-1-4418-0818-9(3), 9781441808189, BCD Value Price) Brilliance Audio.

Blood Memory. unabr. ed. Greg Iles. Read by Joyce Bean. (Running Time: 20 hrs.). 2005. 44.25 (978-1-59710-081-6(1), 9781597100816, BADLE); 29.95 (978-1-59710-080-9(3), 9781597100809, BAD); 29.95 (978-1-59335-689-7(7), 9781593356897, Brilliance MP3); 44.25 (978-1-59335-823-5(7), 9781593358235, Brlnc Audio MP3 Lib); 39.95 (978-1-59086-598-9(7), 9781590865989, BAU); 107.25 (978-1-59086-599-6(5), 9781590865996, BAudLibEd); audio compact disk 39.95 (978-1-59086-600-9(2), 9781590866009, Bril Audio CD Unabri); audio compact disk 127.25 (978-1-59086-601-6(0), 9781590866016, BriAudCD Unabrid) Brilliance Audio.
Please enter a Synopsis.

Blood Meridian. unabr. ed. Cormac McCarthy. Read by Richard Poe. 12 cass. (Running Time: 13 hrs. 25 mins.). 2006. 92.75 (978-1-4281-1592-7(7)); audio compact disk 123.75 (978-1-4281-1594-1(3)) Recorded Bks.

Blood Money. unabr. ed. Clive Egleton. Read by Christopher Kay. 12 cass. (Running Time: 16 hrs.). 1998. 94.95 (978-1-86042-383-3(3), 23833) Pub: Soundings Ltd GBR. Dist(s): Ulverscroft US
The master of the action-packed thriller is at the top of his form in his new novel, set in the murky twilight world where crime, fanaticism & politics combine in an enthralling story of suspense & terror. The carnage of the Yorkshire safe house shocks even the jaded intelligence operatives who have to put the local police off the scent. Three men - one in a wheelchair - have been butchered & another operative has disappeared, along with the man they were guarding. The first shock for Peter Ashton is that his wife is the one who found the bodies & could have been the next victim - but there is worse to come. Ashton's former lover, the ruthlessly ambitious Jill Sheridan is covering up something about the man who has disappeared & the woman who made it possible. And Jill's secrets have always been lethally dangerous for Ashton.

Blood Money. unabr. ed. Thomas Perry. Narrated by Joyce Bean. (Running Time: 14 hrs. 30 mins. 0 sec.). (Jane Whitefield Ser.). (ENG.). 2010. 24.99 (978-1-4001-6020-4(0)); 19.99 (978-1-4001-8020-2(1)); 37.99 (978-1-4001-9020-1(7)); audio compact disk 75.99 (978-1-4001-4020-6(X)); audio compact disk 37.99 (978-1-4001-1020-9(3)) Pub: Tantor Media. Dist(s): IngramPubServ

Blood, Money & Power: How L. B. J. Killed J. F. K. unabr. ed. Barr McClellan. Read by Barr McClellan. 11 cass. (Running Time: 15 hrs.). (Tarzan Ser.). (ENG.). 2001. audio compact disk 84.00 (978-1-4001-3000-9(X)) Pub: Tantor Media. Dist(s): IngramPubServ

Blood, Money & Power: How L. B. J. Killed J. F. K. unabr. ed. Barr McClellan. Read by Barr McClellan. 12 CDs. (Running Time: 15 hrs. 40 mins. 12 sec.). (ENG.). 2003. audio compact disk 39.99 (978-1-4001-0105-4(0)); audio compact disk 25.99 (978-1-4001-5105-9(8)); audio compact disk 79.99 (978-1-4001-3105-1(7)) Pub: Tantor Media. Dist(s): IngramPubServ

Blood Music. unabr. ed. Greg Bear. Narrated by George Guidall. 8 cass. (Running Time: 11 hrs.). 1999. 70.00 (978-1-55690-622-0(6), 91423E7) Recorded Bks.
Vergil I. Ulam creates cellular units of intelligence, tiny biological computers that he injects into his own bloodstream.

Blood Noir. Laurell K. Hamilton. Read by Cynthia Holloway. (Anita Blake, Vampire Hunter Ser.: No. 16). 2008. 114.99 (978-1-60640-923-7(9)) Find a World.

Blood Noir. abr. ed. Laurell K. Hamilton. Read by Cynthia Holloway. (Running Time: 7 hrs.). (Anita Blake, Vampire Hunter Ser.: No. 16). 2009. audio compact disk 19.99 (978-1-59737-902-1(6), 9781597379021, BCD Value Price) Brilliance Audio.

Blood Noir. unabr. ed. Laurell K. Hamilton. Read by Cynthia Holloway. (Running Time: 13 hrs.). (Anita Blake, Vampire Hunter Ser.: No. 16). 2008. 39.25 (978-1-59737-900-7(X), 9781597379007, BADLE); 24.95 (978-1-59737-899-4(2), 9781597378994, BAD); audio compact disk 24.95 (978-1-59737-897-0(6), 9781597378970, Brilliance MP3); audio compact disk 46.95 (978-1-59737-895-6(X), 9781597378956, Bril Audio CD Unabri); audio compact disk 39.25 (978-1-59737-898-7(4), 9781597378987, Brinc Audio MP3 Lib); audio compact disk 122.25 (978-1-59737-896-3(8), 9781597378963, BriAudCD Unabrid) Brilliance Audio.

Blood Oath. unabr. ed. Christopher Farnsworth. Contrib. by Bronson Pinchot. (Running Time: 10 hrs.). (ENG.). 2010. audio compact disk 39.95 (978-0-14-242774-3(8), PengAudBks) Penguin Grp USA.

***Blood Oath: The President's Vampire.** unabr. ed. Christopher Farnsworth. (Running Time: 13 hrs. 30 mins.). 2010. 29.95 (978-1-4417-3955-1(6)); 79.95 (978-1-4417-3951-3(3)); audio compact disk 109.00 (978-1-4417-3952-0(1)) Blckstn Audio.

Blood of Amber. Roger Zelazny. Read by Roger Zelazny. 2 vols. (Chronicles of Amber: Bk. 7). (978-1-58807-526-0(5)); audio compact disk (978-1-58807-690-8(3)) Am Pubng Inc.

Blood of Amber. Roger Zelazny. Read by Roger Zelazny. (Chronicles of Amber: Bk. 7). 2003. 25.00 (978-1-58807-259-7(2)) Am Pubng Inc.

Blood of Amber. abr. ed. Roger Zelazny. Read by Roger Zelazny. 2 vols. (Running Time: 3 hrs.). (Chronicles of Amber: Bk. 7). 2003. 18.00 (978-1-58807-132-3(4)) Am Pubng Inc.
Pursued by a fiendish enemy, Merle Corey, the vanished Prince of Amber, must battle an intricate web of vengence and murder that threatens the San Francisco Bay area and beyond. The forces seeking to destroy the Royal House have unleashed mad sorceries that can strike anywhere...even at the heart of Amber.

Blood of Angels. Music by Joseph Vargo & William Piotrowski. Nox Arcana. Lyrics by Michelle Belanger. 1 CD. (ENG.). 2006. audio compact disk 13.99 (978-0-9788857-0-0(8)) Monolith.

***Blood of Angels.** abr. ed. Reed Arvin. Read by Michael Tucker. (ENG.). 2005. (978-0-06-088782-7(6), Harper Audio); (978-0-06-088783-4(4), Harper Audio) HarperCollins Pubs.

Blood of Flowers: A Novel. unabr. ed. Anita Amirrezvani. Read by Shohreh Aghdashloo. (Running Time: 13 hrs. 30 mins.). (ENG.). 2007. 14.98 (978-1-59483-913-9(1)) Pub: Hachet Audio. Dist(s): HachBkGrp

Blood of Heaven. Bill Myers. Narrated by Richard Ferrone. 8 cass. (Running Time: 10 hrs. 30 mins.). 71.00 (978-1-4025-0615-4(5)) Recorded Bks.

Blood of Heaven. abr. ed. Bill Myers. (Running Time: 3 hrs. 0 mins. 0 sec.). (ENG.). 2003. 10.99 (978-0-310-26003-5(5)) Zondervan.

Blood of Jesus. abr. ed. Reinhard Bonnke. (Running Time: Approx: 1hr. 5 min.). 2001. audio compact disk 7.00 (978-1-933106-05-2(0)) E-R-Productions.
The consequences of accepting or rejecting the blood sacrifice of Jesus is made so clear that rejection of the Savior becomes an unthinkable option. Get this CD and share it with every un-saved friend or love one.

Blood of Jesus Christ. Dan Corner. 1 cass. 3.00 (19) Evang Outreach.

Blood of the Dragon. Nox Arcana. Composed by Joseph Vargo & William Piotrowski. 1 CD. 2006. audio compact disk 13.99 (978-0-9788857-1-7(6)) Monolith.

Blood of the Fold. abr. ed. Terry Goodkind. Read by Denis De Boisblanc. 2 cass. (Sword of Truth Ser.: Bk. 3). 1998. 16.95 Set. (978-1-55935-238-3(8)) Soundelux.
Sequel to the best-selling epic "Stone of Tears." War & conquest engulf the world of Richard Cypher & Kahlan, breaching the magical forces which have sealed the Old World for three thousand years.

Blood of the Fold. unabr. ed. Terry Goodkind. Read by Buck Schirner. 16 cass. (Running Time: 22 hrs.). (Sword of Truth Ser.: Vol. 3). 2002. 39.95 (978-1-59086-294-0(5), 1590862945, BAU) Brilliance Audio.
In a fantasy world as rich and real as our own, Richard Rahl and Kahlan Amnell stand against the ancient forces which besiege the New World - forces so terrible that when last they threatened, they could only be withstood by sealing off the Old World from whence they came. Now the barrier has been breached, and the New World is again beset by their evil power. War, monsters, and treachery plague the world, and only Richard and Kahlan can save it from an armageddon of unimaginable savagery and destruction. Terry Goodkind, author of the brilliant fantasy bestsellers of the Sword of Truth series, has created his most masterful epic yet, a sumptuous feast of magic and excitement replete with the wonders of his unique fantasy vision.

Blood of the Fold. unabr. ed. Terry Goodkind. Read by Buck Schirner. (Running Time: 22 hrs.). (Sword of Truth Ser.). 2004. 44.25 (978-1-59335-456-5(8), 1593354568, Brinc Audio MP3 Lib) Brilliance Audio.

Blood of the Fold. unabr. ed. Terry Goodkind. Read by Buck Schirner. (Running Time: 22 hrs.). (Sword of Truth Ser.). 2004. 44.25 (978-1-59710-082-3(X), 159710082X, BADLE); 29.95 (978-1-59710-083-0(8), 1597100838, BAD) Brilliance Audio.

Blood of the Fold. unabr. ed. Terry Goodkind. Read by Buck Schirner. (Running Time: 79200 sec.). (Sword of Truth Ser.). 2006. audio compact disk 150.25 (978-1-4233-1396-0(8), 9781423313960, BriAudCD Unabrid); audio compact disk 39.95 (978-1-4233-1395-3(X), 9781423313953, Bril Audio CD Unabri) Brilliance Audio.

Blood of the Fold. unabr. ed. Terry Goodkind. Read by Buck Schirner. (Running Time: 22 hrs.). (Sword of Truth Ser.). 2004. 29.95 (978-1-59335-110-6(0), 1593351100) Soulmate Audio Bks.

Blood of the Innocents. unabr. ed. Chris Collett. Read by Graham Padden. 8 cass. (Running Time: 10 hrs. 35 mins.). (Story Sound Ser.). 2007. 69.95 (978-1-85903-982-3(0)); audio compact disk 84.95 (978-1-84652-099-0(1)) Pub: Mgna Lrg Print GBR. Dist(s): Ulverscroft US

Blood of the Martyrs Is Seed: The Apology of Tertullian. Excerpts. Tertullian. 1 CD. (Running Time: 70 min.). 2003. audio compact disk 8.95 (978-0-924722-16-5(9)) Scroll Pub.
Abridged audio edition of Tertullian's Apology. In it, Tertullian describes what Christianity was like in his day (c. 195) and what they believed.

***Blood on My Hands.** unabr. ed. Todd Strasser. Read by Emily Bauer. (Running Time: 7 hrs.). 2010. 39.97 (978-1-4418-7190-9(X), 9781441871909, BADLE) Brilliance Audio.

***Blood on My Hands.** unabr. ed. Todd Strasser. Read by Emily Bauer. (Running Time: 8 hrs.). (YA). 2010. 19.99 (978-1-4418-7188-6(8), 9781441871886, Brilliance MP3); 39.97 (978-1-4418-7189-3(6), 9781441871893, Brinc Audio MP3 Lib); audio compact disk 59.97 (978-1-4418-7187-9(X), 9781441871879, BriAudCD Unabrid); audio compact disk 19.99 (978-1-4418-7186-2(1), 9781441871862, Bril Audio CD Unabri) Brilliance Audio.

Blood on the Eighteen Wheeler. unabr. ed. M. Lehman. Read by Gene Engene. 6 cass. (Running Time: 6 hrs. 12 min.). Dramatization. 1993. 39.95 (978-1-55686-483-4(3), 483) Books in Motion.
Slick-talking Ben Goring hitches a ride with an unsuspecting truck driver. Later, the driver is found dead off the side of the road with bullets drilled into his body.

Blood on the Moon. James Ellroy. 6 cass. (Running Time: 31560 sec.). 2006. 54.95 (978-0-7927-3896-1(9), CSL 900); audio compact disk 74.95 (978-0-7927-3897-8(7), SLD 900) AudioGO.

Blood Promise. unabr. ed. Richelle Mead. (Running Time: 14 hrs.). (Vampire Academy Ser.: Bk. 4). (ENG.). (YA). 2010. audio compact disk 39.95 (978-0-14-314559-2(2), PengAudBks) Penguin Grp USA.

Blood Proof. unabr. ed. Bill Knox. Read by James Bryce. 8 CDs. (Running Time: 12 hr.). 2001. audio compact disk 79.95 (978-0-7531-1178-9(0), 111780) Pub: ISIS Audio GBR. Dist(s): Ulverscroft US

Blood Proof. unabr. ed. Bill Knox. Read by James Brycel. 6 cass. (Running Time: 7 hrs. 30 min.). (Isis Ser.). (J). 2001. 54.95 (978-0-7531-0232-9(3), 971209) Pub: ISIS Lrg Prnt GBR. Dist(s): Ulverscroft US
Colin Thane, now second in command of the elite Scottish Crime Squad, is sent north to the lonely Scottish Highlands & the heart of the malt whiskey industry to answer a plea for help. A vicious arson attack on the whiskey warehouse has left three men dead & eight million pounds worth of prime stock destroyed.

Blood Rain. unabr. ed. Michael Dibdin. Read by Michael Kitchen. 8 cass. (Running Time: 12 hrs.). (Aurelio Zen Mystery Ser.). 2000. 69.95 (978-0-7540-0463-9(5), CAB 1886) AudioGO.
Inspector Zen receives the order he has been dreading all his professional life: a posting to Sicily. There, he will need all his cunning & skill to survive in a world where unwritten rules are enforced with ruthless violence. The discovery of a decomposed corpse in a railway wagon marks the beginning of Zen's most difficult & dangerous case.

Blood Rain. unabr. ed. Michael Dibdin. Read by Michael Kitchen. 8 CDs. (Running Time: 12 hrs.). (Aurelio Zen Mystery Ser.). 2002. audio compact disk 79.95 (978-0-7540-5543-3(4), CCD 234) Pub: Chivers Audio Bks GBR. Dist(s): AudioGO

***Blood Rain: An Aurelio Zen Mystery.** Michael Dibdin. Narrated by Michael Kitchen. (Running Time: 8 hrs. 20 mins. 0 sec.). (ENG.). 2012. audio compact disk 34.95 (978-1-4084-6758-9(5)) Pub: AudioGO. Dist(s): Perseus Dist

***Blood Ransom.** unabr. ed. Lisa Harris. (Running Time: 8 hrs. 38 mins. 0 sec.). (Mission Hope Ser.). (ENG.). 2010. 15.99 (978-0-310-39559-1(3)) Zondervan.

Blood Red Cross see Classic Detective Stories, Vol. II, A Collection

Blood Red Horse. unabr. ed. K. M. Grant. Narrated by Maggie Mash. 9 CDs. (Running Time: 9 hrs. 45 mins.). (De Granville Trilogy: Bk. 1). (YA). (gr. 5-9). 2005. audio compact disk 89.75 (978-1-4193-5606-3(2), C3415); 65.85 (978-1-4193-5115-0(X), 98122) Recorded Bks.
K.M. Grant pens an exciting tale of historical fiction set in the 12th century. Will is permitted to chose his own warhorse now that he has turned 13. Much to everyone's amusement, he selects a rather small chestnut. But Will sees something magical in this horse. As they accompany King Richard on a crusade to the Holy Land, the noble stallion galvanizes young Will with his displays of strength, courage and loyalty.

Blood Relatives. unabr. ed. Ed McBain, pseud. Read by Michael Prichard. 6 cass. (Running Time: 6 hrs.). (87th Precinct Ser.: Bk. 30). 1987. 36.00 (978-0-7366-1147-3(9), 2071) Books on Tape.
It was exactly the sort of case Detective Carella despised. One girl had been raped & murdered. Another savagely ripped by a psycho's knife. Patricia Lowery survived the slashing attack & could identify her cousin's killer. All Carella needed was the girl's eyewitness testimony & a little luck.

Blood Rites. unabr. ed. Jim Butcher. Read by James Marsters. 11 CDs. (Running Time: 13 hrs.). Bk. 6. (ENG.). 2010. audio compact disk 49.95 (978-0-14-242806-1(X), PengAudBks) Penguin Grp USA.

Blood Rival, abr. ed. Dalton Walker. Read by Dick Wilkinson. 2 cass. (Running Time: 3 hrs.). (Shiloh: Bk. 3). 1999. Rental 16.95 (978-1-890990-28-2(0)) Otis Audio.
As Shiloh hunts for a tycoon's missing daughter, he is sniffed out by a fearsome rival, a man of his own breed - a bounty hunter. Now the hunter is hunted & only one can survive.

Blood Run East, Set. unabr. ed. Philip McCutchan. 6 cass. 1998. 69.95 (978-1-872672-21-2(3)) Pub: Magna Story GBR. Dist(s): Ulverscroft US

***Blood Safari.** unabr. ed. Deon Meyer. Read by Simon Vance. (ENG.). 2010. audio compact disk 34.95 (978-1-61573-544-0(5), 1615735445) Pub: HighBridge. Dist(s): Workman Pub

Blood Shot. unabr. ed. Sara Paretsky. Read by Donada Peters. 7 cass. (Running Time: 10 hrs. 30 min.). (V. I. Warshawski Novel Ser.). 1993. 56.00 (978-0-7366-2328-5(0), 3108) Books on Tape.
V. I. Warshawski attends a basketball team reunion & becomes embroiled in a teammate's search for her father.

Blood Shot. unabr. ed. Sara Paretsky. Narrated by Barbara Rosenblat. 8 cass. (Running Time: 12 hrs.). (V. I. Warshawski Novel Ser.). 1993. 70.00 (978-1-55690-899-6(7), 93341E7) Recorded Bks.
V. I. Warshawski accidently stumbles upon a corporate coverup at a Chicago chemical plant while searching for the identity of a friend's unknown father.

Blood Sinister. unabr. ed. Celia Rees. Read by Shirley Barthelmie. 5 CDs. (Running Time: 18600 sec.). (gr. 9 up). 2007. audio compact disk 63.95 (978-1-74093-869-3(0), 9781740938693) Pub: Bolinda Pubng AUS. Dist(s): Bolinda Pub Inc

Blood Sins. abr. ed. Kay Hooper. Read by Joyce Bean. (Running Time: 5 hrs.). (Blood Ser.). 2009. audio compact disk 14.99 (978-1-4233-3311-1(X), 9781423333111, BCD Value Price) Brilliance Audio.

Blood Sins. unabr. ed. Kay Hooper. Read by Joyce Bean. (Running Time: 9 hrs.). (Blood Ser.). 2008. 24.95 (978-1-4233-3306-7(3), 9781423333067, Brilliance MP3); 39.25 (978-1-4233-3309-8(8), 9781423333098, BADLE); 39.25 (978-1-4233-3307-4(1), 9781423333074, Brinc Audio MP3 Lib); 24.95 (978-1-4233-3308-1(X), 9781423333081, BAD); audio compact disk 32.99 (978-1-4233-3304-3(7), 9781423333043, Bril Audio CD Unabri); audio compact disk 87.25 (978-1-4233-3305-0(5), 9781423333050, BriAudCD Unabrid) Brilliance Audio.

Blood Sisters. Short Stories. Greg Egan. Narrated by Amy Bruce. 1 CD. (Running Time: 52 mins.). (Great Science Fiction Stories Ser.). 2005. audio compact disk 10.99 (978-1-884612-33-6(4)) AudioText.

Blood Sisters. unabr. ed. Greg Egan. Read by Amy Bruce. Ed. by Allan Kaster. 1 cass. (Running Time: 53 min.). (Great Science Fiction Stories Ser.). 1996. 10.99 (978-1-884612-14-5(8)) AudioText.
A biological system designed for warfare escapes from a laboratory. Twin sisters that are exposed to the biological agents are treated similarly but mysteriously different consequences result.

Blood Spilt. Asa Larsson. Read by Hillary Huber. Tr. by Marlaine Delargy. (Running Time: 41400 sec.). 2007. 72.95 (978-0-7861-4820-2(9)); audio compact disk 99.00 (978-0-7861-6182-9(5)) Blckstn Audio.

Blood Spilt. unabr. ed. Read by Hillary Huber. Tr. by Marlaine Delargy. (Running Time: 41400 sec.). 2007. 29.95 (978-0-7861-4819-6(5)) Blckstn Audio.

Blood Spilt. unabr. ed. Read by Hillary Huber. Tr. by Marlaine Delargy. (Running Time: 41400 sec.). 2007. audio compact disk 29.95 (978-0-7861-7168-2(5)) Blckstn Audio.

Blood Spilt. unabr. ed. Asa Larsson. Read by Hillary Huber. Tr. by Marlaine Delargy. 9 CDs. (Running Time: 41400 sec.). 2007. audio compact disk 29.95 (978-0-7861-6181-2(7)) Blckstn Audio.

Blood Sport. Dick Francis. Read by Simon Prebble. 7 CDs. (Running Time: 7.75 Hrs). audio compact disk 34.95 (978-1-4025-3718-9(2)) Recorded Bks.

Blood Sport, unabr. ed. Dick Francis. Read by Geoffrey Howard. 5 cass. (Running Time: 7 hrs.). 1996. 39.95 (978-0-7861-0941-8(6), 1694) Blckstn Audio.
When English agent Gene Hawkins told his boss he'd forego his vacation to search for millionaire Dave Teller's prized missing stallion, he didn't know his retainer would include the attention of his boss's beautiful teenage daughter, or Teller's seldom sober wife. He also didn't know that a trail from London to New York to Las Vegas to California would lead eventually to murder.

Blood Sport. unabr. ed. Dick Francis. Read by Geoffrey Howard. 6 CDs. (Running Time: 7 hrs.). 2006. audio compact disk 48.00 (978-0-7861-8784-3(0), 1694) Blckstn Audio.

Blood Sport. unabr. ed. Dick Francis. Read by Tony Britton. 6 cass. (Running Time: 9 hrs.). 2000. 49.95 (978-0-7451-5947-8(8), CAB 087) Pub: Chivers Audio Bks GBR. Dist(s): AudioGO
Gene Hawkins is an expert at arranging events so they appear as accidents. And when he becomes a witness to an "accident," his curiosity is sparked. A Derby-winning Stallion has vanished into the Blue Grass of Kentucky, while a young man and woman spend a dangerous afternoon in a boat on the River Thames. From these far-apart but related beginnings, Gene Hawkins finds himself trailing lost blood-horses across the United States.

Blood Sport. unabr. ed. Dick Francis. Narrated by Simon Prebble. 6 cass. (Running Time: 7 hrs. 30 mins.). 1991. 51.00 (978-1-55690-059-4(7), 91116E7) Recorded Bks.
Gene Hawkins goes looking for a missing stallion & runs into some very unsporting business.

Blood Sport: The President & His Adversaries. abr. ed. James B. Stewart. 4 cass. 21.95 Set. (56261) Books on Tape.
Stewart investigates mysteries surrounding the Clinton White House. Why did Vincent Foster commit suicide? What really happened in the Whitewater land deal? What transpired between Clinton & Paula Jones in the hotel room? This is also the story of how these scandals have affected the principal characters & national policy.

Blood-Stained Bridal Gown Pt. 3: Mysteries of Winterthurn. unabr. ed. Joyce Carol Oates. Narrated by John McDonough. 6 cass. (Running Time: 7 hrs. 30 mins.). 2000. 51.00 (978-0-7887-0564-9(4), 94763E7) Recorded Bks.
Xavier Kilgarvan receives an urgent plea for help. The bloodied bodies of a young minister and a woman from his parish are found entwined together in his home. Upstairs, the minister's wife is discovered trussed in her bed, clad in gore-spattered wedding dress.

Blood Stock. unabr. ed. John Francome & James MacGregor. Read by John Cormack. 6 cass. (Running Time: 8 hrs.). 1998. 54.95 (978-0-7531-0280-0(3), 980502) Pub: ISIS Audio GBR. Dist(s): Ulverscroft US
As a racehorse, Moondancer had been a champion, but as a stallion he was a total failure. So when he is found dead in his box at the Drumgarrick stud one morning, his owners felt more relived than sorry, & promptly make a massive five million pound insurance claim. But then Drumgarrick's owner disappears & his son Fergus is left facing financial ruin - & a corpse. Fergus has a vested interest in seeing the insurance claim is met in full, but Jack Hendred, the insurance investigator, is sure that it is fraudulent & determined to prove it.

Blood Sympathy, Set. unabr. ed. Reginald Hill. 6 cass. (Joe Sixsmith Ser.). 1998. 69.95 (978-1-85903-203-9(6)) Pub: Magna Story GBR. Dist(s): Ulverscroft US

Blood Test. Jonathan Kellerman. Read by Alexander Adams. (Alex Delaware Ser.: No. 2). 2000. audio compact disk 64.00 (978-0-7366-8058-5(6)) Books on Tape.

Blood Test. abr. ed. Jonathan Kellerman. Read by John Rubinstein. 3 CDs. (Running Time: 10800 sec.). (Alex Delaware Ser.: No. 2). (ENG.). 2005. audio compact disk 14.99 (978-0-7393-2124-9(2), Random AudioBks) Pub: Random Audio Pubg. Dist(s): Random

Blood Test. collector's ed. Jonathan Kellerman. Read by Alexander Adams. 7 cass. (Running Time: 10 hrs. 30 min.). (Alex Delaware Ser.: No. 2). 2000. 56.00 (978-0-7366-5642-9(1)) Books on Tape.
Five year old Woody Swope is ill but his parents refuse to agree to the one treatment that could save his life. Dr. Alex Delaware sets out to convince them only to find that they've left the hospital & taken their son with them. Worse, the sleazy motel room where they had been staying is empty, except for an ominous bloodstain. Now Alex & his friend, homicide detective Millo Sturgis, have no choice but to push the law to the breaking point. They've entered an amoral underworld where drugs, dreams & sex are all for sale, where fantasies are fulfilled at any place, even at the cost of a young boy's life.

Blood Test. unabr. ed. Jonathan Kellerman. Read by Alexander Adams. 7 cass. (Running Time: 10 hrs. 30 min.). (Alex Delaware Ser.: No. 2). 2001. 29.95 (978-0-7366-5718-1(5)) Books on Tape.
Five- year-old Woody Swope is ill, but his parents refuse to agree to the one treatment that could save his life. Dr. Alex Delaware sets out to convince them only to find that they've left the hospital & taken their son with them. Worse, the sleazy motel room where they had been staying is empty, except for an ominous bloodstain. Now Alex & his friend, homicide detective Millo Sturgis, have no choice but to push the law to the breaking point. They've entered an amoral underworld where drugs, dreams & sex are all for sale, where fantasies are fulfilled at any place, even at the cost of a young boy's life.

Blood Tide: A Never Land Book. Dave Barry & Ridley Pearson. Contrib. by Jim Dale. (Never Land Ser.). (J). 2008. 34.99 (978-1-60640-777-6(5)) Find a World.

***Blood Tide: A Never Land Book.** unabr. ed. Dave Barry and Ridley Pearson. Read by Jim Dale. (Running Time: 2 hrs.). (Never Land Adventure Ser.). 2010. audio compact disk 9.99 (978-1-4418-7123-7(3), 9781441871237, Bril Audio CD Unabri) Brilliance Audio.

Blood Tide: A Never Land Book. unabr. ed. Dave Barry & Ridley Pearson. Read by Jim Dale. 1 MP3-CD. (Running Time: 2 hrs.). (Never Land Ser.). 2008. 9.95 (978-1-4233-0968-0(5), 9781423309680, Brilliance MP3); 31.97 (978-1-4233-0971-0(5), 9781423309710, BADLE); 31.97 (978-1-4233-0969-7(3), 9781423309697, Brlnc Audio MP3 Lib); 9.95 (978-1-4233-0970-3(7), 9781423309703, BAD); audio compact disk 37.97 (978-1-4233-0967-3(7), 9781423309673, BriAudCD Unabrid) Brilliance Audio.

Blood Ties. abr. ed. Kay Hooper. Read by Joyce Bean. (Running Time: 5 hrs.). (Blood Ser.). 2010. audio compact disk 24.99 (978-1-4233-3319-7(5), 9781423333197, BACD) Brilliance Audio.

Blood Ties. abr. ed. Kay Hooper. Read by Joyce Bean. (Running Time: 5 hrs.). (Blood Ser.). 2010. audio compact disk 14.99 (978-1-4233-3320-3(9), 9781423333203, BCD Value Price) Brilliance Audio.

Blood Ties. unabr. ed. Pauline Bell. Narrated by Christopher Kay. 5 cass. (Running Time: 7 hrs.). (Benny Mitchell Mystery Ser.). 2000. 47.00 (978-1-84197-040-0(9), H1041E7) Recorded Bks.
Unaware of any tragic consequences, a midwife is forced to make a frantic decision during an air raid on a Yorkshire town in the 1940's. Fifty years later, it's time for the town's occupants to pay the price.

Blood Ties. unabr. ed. Kay Hooper. Read by Joyce Bean. (Running Time: 10 hrs.). (Blood Ser.). 2010. 24.99 (978-1-4233-3315-9(2), 9781423333159, Brilliance MP3); 24.99 (978-1-4233-3317-3(9), 9781423333173, BAD); 39.97 (978-1-4233-3316-6(0), 9781423333166, Brlnc Audio MP3 Lib); 39.97 (978-1-4233-3318-0(7), 9781423333180, BADLE); audio compact disk 34.99 (978-1-4233-3313-5(6), 9781423333135, Bril Audio CD Unabri); audio compact disk 87.97 (978-1-4233-3314-2(4), 9781423333142, BriAudCD Unabrid) Brilliance Audio.

Blood Ties. unabr. ed. C. C. Humphreys. Read by C. C. Humphreys. 14 cass. (Running Time: 16 hrs. 55 mins.). (Isis Cassettes Ser.). (J). 2004. 99.95 (978-0-7531-1939-6(0)) Pub: ISIS Lrg Prnt GBR. Dist(s): Ulverscroft US

Blood, Toil, Tears & Sweat: The Dire Warning: Churchill's First Speech as Prime Minister. John Lukacs. Narrated by John Lee. (Running Time: 10500 sec.). (ENG.). 2008. audio compact disk 19.95 (978-1-60283-442-2(3)) Pub: AudioGO. Dist(s): Perseus Dist

Blood Trail. C. J. Box. Narrated by David Chandler. (Running Time: 33900 sec.). (Joe Pickett Ser.: No. 8). 2008. audio compact disk 34.99 (978-1-4361-0509-5(9)) Recorded Bks.

Blood Trail. unabr. ed. 3 cass. (Running Time: 4 hrs. 30 min.). 2004. 28.75 (978-1-4025-8220-2(X)) Recorded Bks.

Blood Transfusion Therapy: An Audiovisual Program. rev. ed. Patricia Pisciotto & Edward L. Snyder. 250.00 incl. bklt. & 78 slides. (978-1-56395-008-7(1)) Am Assn Blood.
Designed to provide medical & paramedical professionals with the principles of blood component therapy, it includes information on blood component preparation & selection for patient's needs; appropriate use of blood derivatives; blood transfusion practices & recognition & treatment of immediate & delayed transfusion reactions. The program is usable for individual instruction or large group presentation.

***Blood Trinity.** abr. ed. Sherrilyn Kenyon & Dianna Love. (Running Time: 6 hrs.). (Belador Code Ser.). 2010. 14.99 (978-1-4418-8086-4(0), 9781441880864, BAD) Brilliance Audio.

***Blood Trinity.** abr. ed. Sherrilyn Kenyon & Dianna Love. Read by Christina Traister. (Running Time: 6 hrs.). (Belador Code Ser.). 2010. audio compact disk 14.99 (978-1-4418-6357-7(5), 9781441863577, BACD) Brilliance Audio.

***Blood Trinity.** unabr. ed. Sherrilyn Kenyon & Dianna Love. (Running Time: 12 hrs.). (Belador Code Ser.). 2010. 24.99 (978-1-4418-6355-3(9), 9781441863553, BAD); 39.97 (978-1-4418-6356-0(7), 9781441863560, BADLE) Brilliance Audio.

***Blood Trinity.** unabr. ed. Sherrilyn Kenyon & Dianna Love. Read by Christina Traister. 1 MP3-CD. (Running Time: 13 hrs.). (Belador Code Ser.). 2010. 24.99 (978-1-4418-6353-9(2), 9781441863539, Brilliance MP3); 39.97 (978-1-4418-6354-6(0), 9781441863546, Brlnc Audio MP3 Lib); audio compact disk 29.99 (978-1-4418-6351-5(6), 9781441863515, Bril Audio CD Unabri); audio compact disk 89.97 (978-1-4418-6352-2(4), 9781441863522, BriAudCD Unabrid) Brilliance Audio.

Blood Vines. unabr. ed. Erica Spindler. Read by Marguerite Gavin & Orlagh Cassidy. 10 CDs. (Running Time: 10 hrs. 30 mins. 0 sec.). 2010. audio compact disk 39.99 (978-1-4272-0866-8(2)) Pub: Macmill Audio. Dist(s): Macmillan

Blood Wager. unabr. ed. Walt Denver. Read by Maynard Villers. 6 cass. (Running Time: 9 hrs.). 1996. 39.95 (978-1-55686-716-3(6)) Books in Motion.
Dan Brant's brother & top hands are brutally murdered; his ranch & cattle under siege; now he must battle across the harsh Montana Territory against a deadly bunch of bush-whackers.

Blood Will Tell. collector's ed. Dana Stabenow. Read by Marguerite Gavin. 6 cass. (Running Time: 9 hrs.). (Kate Shugak Ser.). 2000. 48.00 (978-0-7366-4913-1(1)) Books on Tape.
Kate Shugak's grandmother, Ekaterina, an Aleut tribal elder, fears a tract of Aleut land will fall into the hands of developers. But she is rapidly losing her allies on the tribal council, two of whom have died in suspicious accidents just before a crucial meeting. She gets Kate to join her in Anchorage to help fight those intent on exploiting Alaska's vast natural resources. Thrown into the thick of tribal politics, Kate discovers how deeply she is tied to the land - & to what lengths she will go to protect it.

Blood Work. abr. ed. Michael Connelly. Read by Dick Hill. 3 CDs. (Running Time: 3 hrs.). 2002. audio compact disk 14.99 (978-1-59086-451-7(4), 1590864514, CD) Brilliance Audio.
Thanks to a heart transplant, former FBI agent Terril McCaleb is enjoying a quiet retirement, renovating the fishing boat he lives on in Los Angeles Harbor. But McCaleb's calm seas turn choppy when a story in the "What Happened To?" column of the LA Times brings him face-to-face with the sister of the woman whose heart now beats in his chest. From her, McCaleb learns a terrible truth: that the donor of his heart was not killed in an accident, as he'd been told, but was murdered. Wracked with guilt over the fact that he's alive because another human being was killed, McCaleb embarks on a private investigation of his donor's murder - a crime as horrific as anything he ever encountered as a serial killer investigator for the FBI.

Blood Work. abr. ed. Michael Connelly. Read by Dick Hill. (Running Time: 3 hrs.). 2009. audio compact disk 9.99 (978-1-4418-0830-1(2), 9781441808301, BCD Value Price) Brilliance Audio.

Blood Work. unabr. ed. Michael Connelly. Read by Dick Hill. 10 cass. (Running Time: 15 hrs.). 1998. 89.25 (978-1-56100-838-4(9), 1561008389, Unabridge Lib Edns) Brilliance Audio.

Blood Work. unabr. ed. Michael Connelly. Read by Dick Hill. (Running Time: 15 hrs.). 2004. 39.25 (978-1-59335-341-4(3), 1593353413, Brlnc Audio MP3 Lib) Brilliance Audio.

Blood Work. unabr. ed. Michael Connelly. Read by Dick Hill. (Running Time: 13 hrs.). 2004. 39.25 (978-1-59710-086-1(2), 1597100862, BADLE); 24.95 (978-1-59710-087-8(0), 1597100870, BAD) Brilliance Audio.

Blood Work. unabr. ed. Michael Connelly. Read by Dick Hill. (Running Time: 46800 sec.). 2007. audio compact disk 107.25 (978-1-4233-3412-5(4), 9781423334125, BriAudCD Unabrid); audio compact disk 38.95 (978-1-4233-3411-8(6), 9781423334118, Bril Audio CD Unabri) Brilliance Audio.

Blood Work. unabr. ed. Michael Connelly. Read by Dick Hill. (YA). 2008. 94.99 (978-1-60514-811-3(3)) Find a World.

Blood Work. unabr. ed. Michael Connelly. Read by Dick Hill. (Running Time: 15 hrs.). 2004. 24.95 (978-1-59335-013-0(9), 1593350139) Soulmate Audio Bks.

Blood Work. unabr. movie tie-in ed. Michael Connelly. Read by Dick Hill. 10 cass. (Running Time: 15 hrs.). 2002. 29.95 (978-1-59086-428-9(X), 159086428X, BAU) Brilliance Audio.

Blood Work, Set. unabr. ed. Michael Connelly. Read by Dick Hill. 10 cass. 1999. 89.25 (FS9-43177) Highsmith.

***Blood Wyne.** unabr. ed. Yasmine Galenorn. (Running Time: 10 hrs. 0 mins.). (Sisters of the Moon Ser.). 2011. 24.99 (978-1-4001-6996-2(8)); 16.99 (978-1-4001-8996-0(9)); 34.99 (978-1-4001-1996-7(0)) Tantor Media.

***Blood Wyne (Library Edition)** unabr. ed. Yasmine Galenorn. (Running Time: 10 hrs. 0 mins.). (Sisters of the Moon Ser.). 2011. 83.99 (978-1-4001-4996-4(7)); 34.99 (978-1-4001-9996-9(4)) Tantor Media.

Bloodfever. Karen Marie Moning. Read by Joyce Bean. (Fever Ser.: No. 2). 2009. 65.00 (978-1-60775-520-3(3)) Find a World.

Bloodfever. unabr. ed. Karen Marie Moning. Read by Joyce Bean. (Running Time: 9 hrs.). (Fever Ser.: No. 2). 2007. 39.25 (978-1-4233-4198-7(8), 9781423341987, BADLE); 24.95 (978-1-4233-4197-0(X), 9781423341970, BAD); 87.25 (978-1-4233-4192-5(9), 9781423341925, BrilAudUnabridg); audio compact disk 92.25 (978-1-4233-4194-9(5), 9781423341949, BriAudCD Unabrid); audio compact disk 39.25 (978-1-4233-4196-3(1), 9781423341963, Brlnc Audio MP3 Lib); audio compact disk 34.95 (978-1-4233-4193-2(7), 9781423341932, Bril Audio CD Unabri); audio compact disk 24.95 (978-1-4233-4195-6(3), 9781423341956, Brilliance MP3) Brilliance Audio.

Bloodgood Set: Detonation. 2 CDs. 1999. audio compact disk 12.99 (KMGD8648) Provident Mus Dist.

Bloodgood Set: Rock in a Hard Place - Out of the Darkness. 2 CDs. 1999. audio compact disk 12.99 (KMGD8677) Provident Mus Dist.

***Bloodhound.** Tamora Pierce. Read by Susan Denaker. 15 CDs. (Running Time: 18 hrs. 7 mins.). (Beka Cooper Ser.: Bk. 2). (YA). (gr. 7 up). 2009. audio compact disk 80.00 (978-0-7393-6420-8(0), Listening Lib) Pub: Random Audio Pubg. Dist(s): Random

Bloodhound. unabr. ed. Tamora Pierce. Read by Susan Denaker. (Beka Cooper Ser.: Bk. 2). (ENG.). (J). (gr. 7). 2009. audio compact disk 63.00 (978-0-7393-5631-9(3), Listening Lib) Pub: Random Audio Pubg. Dist(s): Random

Bloodhounds. unabr. ed. Peter Lovesey. Read by Christopher Kay. 10 cass. (Running Time: 13 hrs. 30 mins.). (Peter Diamond Mystery Ser.). 1999. 84.95 (978-1-86042-283-6(7), 22837) Pub: Soundings Ltd GBR. Dist(s): Ulverscroft US
According to chic, amoral Jessica Shaw the "Bloodhounds of Bath" may be a group of potential murderers but, to new recruit Shirley-Ann Miller they are just a gaggle of misfits. When one of them reveals that he has one of the world's most valuable stamps, stolen from the Postal museum, theft is rapidly overtaken by murder. When one of the "Bloodhounds" is found dead, a classic crime-puzzle begins.

Blooding at Great Meadows: Young George Washington & the Battle That Shaped the Man. unabr. ed. Alan Axelrod. Read by David Drummond. (Running Time: 32400 sec.). 2007. audio compact disk 27.95 (978-0-7861-5897-3(2)) Blckstn Audio.

Blooding at Great Meadows: Young George Washington & the Battle That Shaped the Man. unabr. ed. Alan Axelrod. Read by David Drummond. (Running Time: 32400 sec.). 2007. 59.95 (978-0-7861-6867-5(6)); audio compact disk 29.95 (978-0-7861-7023-4(9)); audio compact disk 72.00 (978-0-7861-6866-8(8)) Blckstn Audio.

Blooding at Great Meadows: Young George Washington & the Battle That Shaped the Man. unabr. ed. Alan Axelrod. Read by David Drummond. (Running Time: 32400 sec.). 2007. 27.95 (978-0-7861-4924-7(8)) Blckstn Audio.

***Bloodlands: Europe Between Hitler & Stalin.** unabr. ed. Timothy Snyder. (Running Time: 15 hrs.). 2010. 29.95 (978-1-4417-6148-4(9)); 85.95 (978-1-4417-6145-3(4)); audio compact disk 32.95 (978-1-4417-6147-7(0)); audio compact disk 118.00 (978-1-4417-6146-0(2)) Blckstn Audio.

Bloodless Shadow. unabr. ed. Victoria Blake. Contrib. by Trudy Harris. 8 cass. (Story Sound Ser.). (J). 2006. 69.95 (978-1-85903-964-9(2)) Pub: Mgna Lrg Print GBR. Dist(s): Ulverscroft US

Bloodless Shadow. unabr. ed. Victoria Blake & Trudy Harris. Contrib. by Trudy Harris. 10 vols. (Story Sound CD Ser.). (J). 2006. audio compact disk 89.95 (978-1-85903-953-3(7)) Pub: Mgna Lrg Print GBR. Dist(s): Ulverscroft US

Bloodletting & Miraculous Cures: Stories. abr. ed. Vincent Lam. Read by Christopher Lane. (Running Time: 6 hrs.). 2008. audio compact disk 14.99 (978-1-4233-4601-2(7), 9781423346012, BCD Value Price) Brilliance Audio.

Bloodletting & Miraculous Cures: Stories. unabr. ed. Vincent Lam. Read by Christopher Lane. (Running Time: 9 hrs.). 2007. 39.25 (978-1-4233-4599-2(1), 9781423345992, BADLE); 24.95 (978-1-4233-4598-5(3), 9781423345985, BAD); 74.25 (978-1-4233-4593-0(2), 9781423345930, BrilAudUnabridg); audio compact disk 39.25 (978-1-4233-4597-8(5), 9781423345978, Brlnc Audio MP3 Lib); audio compact disk 92.25 (978-1-4233-4595-4(9), 9781423345954, BriAudCD Unabrid); audio compact disk 34.95 (978-1-4233-4594-7(0), 9781423345947, Bril Audio CD Unabri); audio compact disk 24.95 (978-1-4233-4596-1(7), 9781423345961, Brilliance MP3) Brilliance Audio.

Bloodline. abr. ed. F. Paul Wilson. Read by Dick Hill. (Running Time: 6 hrs.). (Repairman Jack Ser.: Bk. 10). 2008. audio compact disk 14.99 (978-1-4233-4610-4(6), 9781423346104, BCD Value Price) Brilliance Audio.

Bloodline. unabr. ed. F. Paul Wilson. Read by Dick Hill. (Running Time: 15 hrs.). (Repairman Jack Ser.: Bk. 10). 2007. 39.25 (978-1-4233-4608-1(4), 9781423346081, BADLE); 24.95 (978-1-4233-4607-4(6), 9781423346074, BAD); 112.25 (978-1-4233-4602-9(5), 9781423346029, BrilAudUnabridg); audio compact disk 39.25 (978-1-4233-4606-7(8), 9781423346067, Brlnc Audio MP3 Lib); audio compact disk 97.25 (978-1-4233-4604-3(1), 9781423346043, BriAudCD Unabrid); audio compact disk 24.95 (978-1-4233-4605-0(X), 9781423346050, Brilliance MP3); audio compact disk 36.95 (978-1-4233-4603-6(3), 9781423346036, Bril Audio CD Unabri) Brilliance Audio.

Bloodline. unabr. collector's ed. Ernest J. Gaines. Read by Dan Lazar. 7 cass. (Running Time: 7 hrs.). Incl. Just Like a Tree. (1489); Long Day in November. (1489); Sky in Gray. (1489); Three Men. (1489); 1982. 42.00 (978-0-7366-0515-1(0), 1489) Books on Tape.
Fine short story set in the black south.

Bloodlines. abr. ed. James Axler. 2 cass. (Running Time: 180 min.). (Deathlands Ser.: No. 29). 2000. 7.99 (978-1-55204-455-1(6)) DC Comics.

Bloodlines. abr. ed. Karen Traviss. Read by Marc Thompson. (Running Time: 21600 sec.). (Star Wars Ser.). (ENG.). 2006. audio compact disk 29.95 (978-0-7393-2396-0(2), Random AudioBks) Pub: Random Audio Pubg. Dist(s): Random

Bloodlist. P. N. Elrod. Read by Barrett Whitener. (Running Time: 8 hrs. 18 mins.). 2005. 29.95 (978-0-7861-8070-7(6)); reel tape 54.95 (978-0-7861-3493-9(3)); audio compact disk 63.00 (978-0-7861-7887-2(6)) Blckstn Audio.

Bloodlust: L-Book. Fran Heckrotte. (ENG.). 2008. 14.95 (978-1-934889-02-2(4)) Lbook Pub.

Bloodroot. unabr. ed. Amy Greene. 11 CDs. (Running Time: 13 hrs. 30 mins.). 2010. audio compact disk 40.00 (978-0-307-71323-0(7), Random AudioBks) Pub: Random Audio Pubg. Dist(s): Random

Blood's a Rover. unabr. ed. James Ellroy. Read by Craig Wasson. (Underworld USA Trilogy: No. 3). (ENG.). 2009. audio compact disk 50.00 (978-0-307-57667-5(1), Random AudioBks) Pub: Random Audio Pubg. Dist(s): Random

Bloodscripts: Writing the Violent Subject. Elana Gomel. (Theory & Interpretation of Narrative Ser.). 2003. audio compact disk 9.95 (978-0-8142-9017-0(5)) Pub: Ohio St U Pr. Dist(s): Chicago Distribution Ctr

***Bloodshot.** unabr. ed. Cherie Priest. (Running Time: 13 hrs.). 2011. audio compact disk 29.99 (978-1-4418-9085-6(8), 9781441890856) Brilliance Audio.

***Bloodshot.** unabr. ed. Cherie Priest. Read by Natalie Ross. (Running Time: 13 hrs.). 2011. 39.97 (978-1-4418-9088-7(2), 9781441890887, Brlnc Audio MP3 Lib); 24.99 (978-1-4418-9087-0(4), 9781441890870, Brilliance MP3); audio compact disk 79.97 (978-1-4418-9086-3(6), 9781441890863, BriAudCD Unabrid) Brilliance Audio.

Bloodsmoor Romance. Joyce Carol Oates. Read by Joyce Carol Oates. Prod. by Moveable Feast Staff. 1 cass. (Running Time: 30 min.). 1984. 8.95 (AMF-9) Am Audio Prose.
Joyce Carol Oates reads "A Bloodsmoor Romance" & talks about feminism, the 19th century romance & why she writes so much.

Bloodstone Chronicles: A Journey of Faith. unabr. ed. Bill Myers. (Running Time: 12 hrs. 0 mins. 0 sec.). (ENG.). 2003. 20.99 (978-0-310-26135-3(X)) Zondervan.

Bloodstorm. unabr. ed. Matt Braun. Read by Gene Eugene. 8 cass. (Running Time: 8 hrs. 30 mins.). 1999. 49.95 (978-1-55686-954-9(1)) Books in Motion.
Cole Braddock is a manhunter with a difference. He has an office in Denver with a secretary & a stock portfolio! In fact, his reputation is so widespread that he has to resort to disguises when he conducts his investigations. With Lise Hammond, a top-flight hoofer at one of Denver's swankiest saloons, Cole is recruited to break up the corrupt Santa Fe Ring which is threatening to destroy the town of Cimarron.

Bloodstream. unabr. ed. Tess Gerritsen. Narrated by Richard Poe. 8 cass. (Running Time: 11 hrs. 45 mins.). 1999. 75.00 (978-0-7887-2515-9(7), 95588E7) Recorded Bks.
Takes you to a idyllic town in Maine, where teenagers are beginning to exhibit mysteriously violent behavior. As a young doctor tries to protect her son from the increasing mayhem, she begins to suspect that dark forces are at work.

Bloodsuckers: Bats, Bugs, & Other Bloodthirsty Creatures. Sarah Houghton. (High Five Reading Ser.). (ENG.). (gr. 4 up). 2003. audio compact disk 5.95 (978-0-7368-2854-3(0)) CapstoneDig.

Bloodsuckers: Bats, Bugs, & Other Bloodthirsty Creatures. Sarah Houghton. (High Five Reading - Green Ser.). (ENG.). (gr. 3-4). 2007. audio compact disk 5.95 (978-1-4296-1440-5(4)) CapstoneDig.

Bloodtide. Melvin Burgess. Read by Colin Moody. (Running Time: 11 hrs. 55 mins.). (YA). 2009. 89.99 (978-1-74214-300-2(8), 9781742143002) Pub: Bolinda Pubng AUS. Dist(s): Bolinda Pub Inc

Bloodtide. unabr. ed. Melvin Burgess. Read by Colin Moody. 10 CDs. (Running Time: 42900 sec.). 2006. audio compact disk 98.95 (978-1-74093-718-4(X)) Pub: Bolinda Pubng AUS. Dist(s): Bolinda Pub Inc

Bloody Aachen. unabr. collector's ed. Charles Whiting. Read by Justin Hecht. 5 cass. (Running Time: 5 hrs.). 1986. 30.00 (978-0-7366-0696-7(3), 1659) Books on Tape.
Aachen's citizens, fierce in defense of their city, held off the attacking Americans for six weeks, giving Hitler the time he desperately needed to

mobilize his forces for the battle of the Bulge - an operation that extended the Allied campaign in Europe by six months & cost 80,000 American lives.

Bloody Bones. abr. ed. Laurell K. Hamilton. (Running Time: 6 hrs.). (Anita Blake, Vampire Hunter Ser.: No. 5). (ENG.). 2010. audio compact disk 29.95 (978-0-14-314426-7(X), PenAudBks) Pub: Pnguin Bks Ltd GBR. Dist(s): Penguin Grp USA

Bloody Bones. unabr. ed. Laurell K. Hamilton. (Running Time: 13 hrs.). (Anita Blake, Vampire Hunter Ser.: No. 5). (ENG.). 2010. audio compact disk 39.95 (978-0-14-314405-2(7), PenAudBks) Pub: Pnguin Bks Ltd GBR. Dist(s): Penguin Grp USA

***Bloody Crimes: The Chase for Jefferson Davis & the Death Pageant for Lincoln's Corpse.** unabr. ed. James L. Swanson. Read by Richard Thomas. 2010. (978-0-06-198860-8(X), Harper Audio); (978-0-06-198861-5(8), Harper Audio) HarperCollins Pubs.

Bloody Crimes: The Chase for Jefferson Davis & the Death Pageant for Lincoln's Corpse. unabr. ed. James L. Swanson. Read by Richard Thomas. 2010. audio compact disk 39.99 (978-0-06-198847-9(2), Harper Audio) HarperCollins Pubs.

Bloody Crossroads: Where Literature & Politics Meet. unabr. ed. Norman Podhoretz. Read by Phillip J. Sawtelle. 5 cass. (Running Time: 7 hrs.). 1989. 39.95 (978-0-7861-0029-3(X), 1028) Blckstn Audio.
Examines the literary & cultural sweep of the conflict between totalitarianism & the democratic West.

Bloody Crossroads: Where Literature & Politics Meet. unabr. ed. Norman Podhoretz & Phillip J. Sawtelle. (Running Time: 7 hrs. NaN mins.). 2008. 29.95 (978-1-4332-5478-9(6)); audio compact disk 60.00 (978-1-4332-5477-2(8)) Blckstn Audio.

Bloody Crown of Conan. unabr. ed. Robert E. Howard. Narrated by Todd McLaren. (Running Time: 18 hrs. 30 mins. 0 sec.). (Conan of Cimmeria Ser.). (ENG.). 2009. 29.99 (978-1-4001-6224-6(6)); audio compact disk 79.99 (978-1-4001-4224-8(5)); audio compact disk 39.99 (978-1-4001-1224-1(9)) Pub: Tantor Media. Dist(s): IngramPubServ

Bloody English Women of the Maison Puce. Jill Laurimore. Narrated by Helen Lederer. 7 cass. (Running Time: 9 hrs. 30 mins.). 2002. 67.00 (978-1-84197-484-2(6)) Recorded Bks.

Bloody Field by Shrewsbury. unabr. ed. Edith Pargeter. 10 cass. (Isis Ser.). (J). 2002. 84.95 (978-0-7531-1384-4(8)) Pub: ISIS Lrg Prnt GBR. Dist(s): Ulverscroft US

Bloody Ground. Bernard Cornwell. (Starbuck Chronicles: Vol. 4). 2001. 72.00 (978-0-7366-6831-6(4)) Books on Tape.

Bloody Ground. Bernard Cornwell. Narrated by Tom Parker. (Running Time: 13 hrs.). (Starbuck Chronicles: Vol. 4). 2000. 41.95 (978-1-59912-624-1(9)) Iofy Corp.

Bloody Ground. unabr. ed. Bernard Cornwell. Read by Tom Parker. 9 cass. (Running Time: 13 hrs.). (Starbuck Chronicles: Vol. 4). 2001. 62.95 (978-0-7861-2013-0(4), 2782); audio compact disk 96.00 (978-0-7861-9719-4(6), 2782) Blckstn Audio.

Bloody Ground. unabr. ed. Bernard Cornwell. Read by Hayward Morse. 12 CDs. (Running Time: 18 hrs.). (Starbuck Chronicles: Vol. 4). 2000. audio compact disk 99.95 (978-0-7531-1058-4(X), 11058x); 84.95 (978-0-7531-0049-3(5), 960704) Pub: ISIS Audio GBR. Dist(s): Ulverscroft US
The Bloody Ground is so compelling that it overcomes the competent but often grating reading of British actor Hayward Morse. Recommended for public libraries.

Bloody Jack. unabr. ed. L. A. Meyer. Read by Katherine Kellgren. (Bloody Jack Adventures Ser.). (J). 2007. 44.99 (978-1-60252-818-5(7)) Find a World.

Bloody Jack: Being an Account of the Curious Adventures of Mary "Jacky" Faber, Ship's Boy. unabr. ed. L. A. Meyer. Read by Katherine Kellgren. 6 CDs. (Running Time: 8 hrs.). (Bloody Jack Adventures Ser.: Bk. 1). (J). (gr. 5-13). 2007. audio compact disk 29.95 (978-1-59316-094-4(1)) Listen & Live.

Bloody Knife: Custer's Favorite Scout. abr. ed. Ben Innis. Ed. by Richard E. Collin. 2 cass. (Running Time: 3 hrs.). 1995. 16.98 Set. (978-0-9644389-1-0(7), SC01184) Smoky Water Pr.
Chronicles friction between tribes on the Northern Plains in the 1800's, cultural conflicts, & the ensuing disagreements that culminated in the legendary Battle of the Little Bighorn.

Bloody Mary. J. A. Konrath. Read by Dick Hill. (Playaway Adult Fiction Ser.). 2008. 59.99 (978-1-60640-782-0(1)) Find a World.

Bloody Mary. unabr. ed. J. A. Konrath. Read by Dick Hill & Susie Breck. (Running Time: 7 hrs.). (Jacqueline "Jack" Daniels Mystery Ser.). 2005. 39.25 (978-1-59710-088-5(9), 9781597100885, BADLE); 24.95 (978-1-59710-089-2(7), 9781597100892, BAD) Brilliance Audio.

Bloody Mary. unabr. ed. J. A. Konrath. Read by Dick Hill. (Running Time: 25200 sec.). (Jacqueline "Jack" Daniels Mystery Ser.). 2005. 29.95 (978-1-59355-490-3(7), 9781593554903, BAU); 69.25 (978-1-59355-491-0(5), 9781593554910, BrilAudUnabridg); DVD & audio compact disk 24.95 (978-1-59335-732-0(X), 9781593357320, Brilliance MP3); audio compact disk 82.25 (978-1-59355-493-4(1), 9781593554934, BriAudCD Unabrid); audio compact disk 29.95 (978-1-59355-492-7(3), 9781593554927, Bril Audio CD Unabri); audio compact disk 39.25 (978-1-59335-866-2(0), 9781593358662, Brlnc Audio MP3 Lib) Brilliance Audio.
In Bloody Mary, J. A. Konrath's second mystery, Lieutenant Jacqueline (Jack) Daniels deals with a serial killer who is dismembering women in Chicago, her mother who has shown up to live with her, and her ex-husband who has reappeared.

Bloody Season, Set. unabr. ed. Loren D. Estleman. Read by Norman Dietz. 6 vols. (Running Time: 8 hrs.). 1999. bk. 54.95 (978-0-7927-2304-2(X), CSL 193, Chivers Sound Lib) AudioGO.
On October 26, 1881, nine men met in a street in Tombstone, Arizona Territory. Within fifteen blistering seconds, three spilled their lives out into the alkali dust. The remaining six including Wyatt Earp & Doc Holliday, lived to face trial, and to kill again. An American saga of the gunfighters who have captured the imagination of a nation for over a century.

Bloody Shirt: Terror after the Civil War. unabr. ed. Stephen Budiansky. (Running Time: 10 hrs.). 2008. 24.95 (978-1-4233-5167-2(3), 9781423351672, BAD) Brilliance Audio.

Bloody Shirt: Terror after the Civil War. unabr. ed. Stephen Budiansky. Read by Phil Gigante. (Running Time: 10 hrs.). 2008. 39.25 (978-1-4233-5168-9(1), 9781423351689, BADLE); 87.25 (978-1-4233-5162-7(2), 9781423351627, BrilAudUnabridg); audio compact disk 92.25 (978-1-4233-5164-1(9), 9781423351641, BriAudCD Unabrid); audio compact disk 39.25 (978-1-4233-5166-5(5), 9781423351665, Brlnc Audio MP3 Lib); audio compact disk 24.95 (978-1-4233-5165-8(7), 9781423351658, Brilliance MP3); audio compact disk 34.95 (978-1-4233-5163-4(0), 9781423351634, Bril Audio CD Unabri) Brilliance Audio.

***Bloody Souvenir: A Story from Guys Read: Funny Business.** unabr. ed. Jack Gantos. (ENG.). 2010. (978-0-06-206246-8(8)); (978-0-06-202768-9(9)) HarperCollins Pubs.

Bloody Sunset. Alexander Fullerton. Read by Michael Maloney. 8 cass. (Running Time: 12 hrs.). 2000. bk. 59.95 (CAB 1649) Pub: Chivers Audio Bks GBR. Dist(s): AudioGO
It is the summer of 1918. The aftermath of the Russian Revolution has the Royal Navy holding the Caspian Sea against a Turkish army that is driving eastward. But when Lieutenant Bob Cowan is asked to rescue two of the Tsar's daughters from their refuge near a Bolshevik stronghold, he must decide whether the Navy can afford to help.

Bloody Sunset. unabr. ed. Alexander Fullerton. Read by Michael Maloney. 8 cass. (Running Time: 8 hrs.). 1998. 69.95 (978-0-7540-0226-0(8), CAB 1649) AudioGO.
Lieutenant Bob Cowan is asked to rescue two of the Tsar's daughters from their refuge near a Bolshevik stronghold, he must decide whether the Navy can afford to help him.

Bloom of Autumn Gold. Karen Jean Matsko Hood. 2009. audio compact disk 24.95 (978-1-59210-806-0(7)) Whsprng Pine.

Bloom of Autumn Gold: A Collection of Poetry. Karen Jean Matsko Hood. 2006. audio compact disk 13.95 (978-1-59434-686-6(0)) Whsprng Pine.

Bloom of Autumn Gold: A Collection of Poetry, Seasons of Poetry Series, Book 3. 2005. 29.95 (978-1-59649-678-1(9)) Whsprng Pine.

Bloom Syndrome - A Bibliography & Dictionary for Physicians, Patients, & Genome Researchers. Compiled by Icon Group International, Inc. Staff. 2007. ring bd. 28.95 (978-0-497-11340-7(6)) Icon Grp.

Bloom Where You Are Planted: 1 Cor. 7:17-38. Ed Young. 1986. 4.95 (978-0-7417-1497-8(3), 497) Win Walk.

Bloomability. unabr. ed. Sharon Creech. 3 cass. (Running Time: 4 hrs.). (J). 2000. 25.00 (Random AudioBks) Random Audio Pubg.
Thirteen year old Domenica Santolina Doone, better known as Dinnie, is accustomed to change. Her family is constantly moving from town to town as her father searches for opportunity but when her aunt & uncle whisk her far away to an international school in Switzerland, she's not sure she's ready to face this opportunity alone.

Bloomability. unabr. ed. Sharon Creech. Read by Bonnie Hurren. 4 cass. (Running Time: 5 hrs. 2 mins.). (J). (gr. 4-7). 2004. 32.00 (978-0-8072-8753-8(9), YA257CX, Listening Lib); pap. bk. 38.00 (978-0-8072-8754-5(7), YA257SP, Listening Lib) Random Audio Pubg.
Thirteen-year-old Domenica Santolina Doone, better known as Dinnie, is accustomed to change. Her family is constantly moving from town to town as her father searches for "opportunity." But when her aunt & uncle whisk her far away to an international school in Switzerland, she's not sure she's ready to face this "opportunity" alone.

***Bloomability.** unabr. ed. Sharon Creech. Read by Mandy Siegfried. (ENG.). 2009. (978-0-06-176866-8(9)); (978-0-06-176232-1(6)) HarperCollins Pubs.

Bloomer Family Christmas. George Bloomer. 2004. audio compact disk 14.99 (978-0-88368-819-9(0)) Whitaker Hse.

Blooming: Stories for Girls to Grow On. Narrated by Judith Black. 1 CD. (Running Time: 69 mins.). (J). (gr. 5-9). 2000. audio compact disk 13.00 (978-0-9701073-0-5(7)) J Black Storyteller.
Three adolescent girls who are experiencing self-esteem problems seek out an old friend who shares four stories that encourage the girls to look inward to find their true worth. The four stories are: "Yen Lee's Feet," "Lucy Stone", "The Three Strong Women of Japan" & "Katorah".

Blooming: Stories for Girls to Grow On. Narrated by Judith Black. 1 cass. (Running Time: 1 hr. 9 mins.). (J). (gr. 5-8). 2001. 10.00 (978-0-9701073-1-2(5)) J Black Storyteller.

Bloomsbury Group. 2nd ed. Vrej Nersessian & British Library Staff. (British Library - British Library Sound Archive Ser.). (ENG.). 2009. audio compact disk 25.00 (978-0-7123-0593-8(9)) Pub: Britis Library GBR. Dist(s): Chicago Distribution Ctr

Bloomsday Dead. Adrian McKinty. Read by Gerard Doyle. (Running Time: 39600 sec.). (Dead Trilogy). 2007. 65.95 (978-0-7861-4985-8(X)); audio compact disk 81.00 (978-0-7861-5778-5(X)) Blckstn Audio.

Bloomsday Dead. unabr. ed. Adrian McKinty. Read by Gerard Doyle. (Running Time: 39600 sec.). 2007. 26.95 (978-0-7861-4866-0(7)); audio compact disk 26.95 (978-0-7861-6078-5(0)); audio compact disk 29.95 (978-0-7861-7156-9(1)) Blckstn Audio.

Bloomsday on Broadway XXIV. Hosted by Isaiah Sheffer. Directed By Caraid O'Brien. Based on a book by James Joyce. 4 CDs. (Running Time: Approx. 5hrs.). (ENG & YID.). 2005. audio compact disk 29.00 (978-0-9719218-5-6(7)) Symphony Space.
Bloomsday on Broadway XXIVLove! Literature!Language! Lust!Leopold?s Women BloomAs broadcast live on WBAI and the Pacifica Radio NetworkHosted by Isaiah ShefferDirected by Caraid O?BrienHighlights Include:A Whirlwind Tour of Women in UlyssesThe Chorus of 34 MollysMr. Bloom speaks YiddishBarbara Feldon as Madame Bella CohenBernadette Quigley as GertieStephen Colbert as BloomIsaiah Sheffer narrates the complete Calypso and Lotus Eaters episodesMarian Seldes reads from Finnegans WakeFritz Weaver and Rochelle Oliver read from The DeadTerry Donnelly as MollyPlus several sopranos singing from Molly?s repertoire.

Bloopers. unabr. ed. 2 cass. (Running Time: 2 hrs.). (Double Value Pack Ser.). 1990. 9.95 (978-1-55569-367-1(9), 7100) Great Am Audio.
Sampling of famous slips of the tongue that became a comedy of errors.

Blossom. unabr. ed. Andrew Vachss. Read by Phil Gigante. (Running Time: 8 hrs.). (Burke Ser.). 2010. audio compact disk 29.99 (978-1-4418-2109-6(0), 9781441821096, Bril Audio CD Unabri) Brilliance Audio.

***Blossom.** unabr. ed. Andrew Vachss. Read by Phil Gigante. (Running Time: 8 hrs.). (Burke Ser.). 2010. 24.99 (978-1-4418-2111-9(2), 9781441821119, Brilliance MP3); 24.99 (978-1-4418-2113-3(9), 9781441821133, BAD); 39.97 (978-1-4418-2112-6(0), 9781441821126, Brlnc Audio MP3 Lib); 39.97 (978-1-4418-2114-0(7), 9781441821140, BADLE); audio compact disk 79.97 (978-1-4418-2110-2(4), 9781441821102, BriAudCD Unabrid) Brilliance Audio.

Blossom Like the Rose. unabr. ed. Norah Lofts. Read by Peter Joyce. 7 cass. 1999. 61.95 Set. (978-1-86015-426-3(3)) T T Beeler.
With the help of workers from his father's estate, Philip Ollenshaw rescues Linda, the love of his life, from the squire's clutches. They leave their unbearable existence & join a group of people travelling in the wake of the Pilgrim Fathers to the new world, with the dream of finding their paradise.

Blossom Promise. unabr. ed. Betsy Byars. Read by Blain Fairman. 3 cass. (Running Time: 4 hrs., 30 min.). (Blossom Family Ser.: 4). (J). (gr. 1-8). 1999. 30.00 (LL 3069, Chivers Child Audio) AudioGO.

Blossom Promise. unabr. ed. Betsy Byars. Read by Blain Fairman. Narrated by Blain Fairman. 3 cass. (Running Time: 3 hrs. 28 mins.). (Blossom Family Ser.: Bk. 4). (J). (gr. 4-6). 1990. pap. bk. 24.00 (978-0-8072-7292-3(2), YA826CX, Listening Lib) Random Audio Pubg.

Blossom Promise, Set. unabr. ed. Betsy Byars. Read by Blain Fairman. 3 cass. (Blossom Family Ser.: Bk. 4). 1999. 23.98 (FS9-34169) Highsmith.

Blossom Promise, Set. unabr. ed. Betsy Byars. Narrated by Blain Fairman. 3 cass. (Running Time: 3 hrs. 28 mins.). (Blossom Family Ser.: Bk. 4). (J). (gr. 4-6). 2000. pap. bk. 29.00 Guide. (978-0-8072-7322-7(8), YA826SP, Listening Lib) Random Audio Pubg.

Blossoms & the Green Phantom. unabr. ed. Betsy Byars. Read by Blain Fairman. 3 cass. (Running Time: 4 hrs., 30 min.). (Blossom Family Ser.: 3). (J). (gr. 1-8). 1999. 30.00 (LL 3070, Chivers Child Audio) AudioGO.

Blossoms & the Green Phantom. unabr. ed. Betsy Byars. Narrated by Blain Fairman. 3 cass. (Running Time: 3 hrs. 26 mins.). (Blossom Family Ser.: Bk. 3). (YA). (gr. 4-6). 1990. pap. bk. 29.00 (978-0-8072-7321-0(X), YA825SP, Listening Lib); 24.00 (978-0-8072-7289-3(2), YA825CX, Listening Lib) Random Audio Pubg.
The incredible Blossom family rallies around Junior's Green Phantom invention. But with Pap missing & Mom so worried, will all turn out well for the Blossom clan.

Blossoms & the Green Phantom, Set. unabr. ed. Betsy Byars. Read by Blain Fairman. 3 cass. (Blossom Family Ser.: Bk. 3). (YA). 1999. 23.98 (FS9-34163) Highsmith.

Blossoms Meet the Vulture Lady. unabr. ed. Betsy Byars. Read by Fairman Blain. 3 CDs. (Running Time: 2 hrs. 55 mins.). (J). (gr. 3-6). 2008. audio compact disk 30.00 (978-0-7393-7394-1(3), Listening Lib) Pub: Random Audio Pubg. Dist(s): Random

Blossoms Meet the Vulture Lady. unabr. ed. Betsy Byars. Read by Blain Fairman. 2 cass. (Running Time: 2 hrs 56 mins.). (Blossom Family Ser.: Bk. 2). (J). (gr. 4-6). 1995. bk. 18.00 Incl. Guide. (978-0-8072-7286-2(8), YA824CX, Listening Lib) Random Audio Pubg.
Junior Blossom's inventions always seem to be doomed for failure. But now he's determined to startle the world with the best coyote trap ever, which could prove more disastrous than anything he's ever come up with, especially when he gets caught in his own trap! But Mad Mary, the crazy old vulture lady, rescues him & brings him back to her dark cave & feeds him some varmint stew.

Blossoms Meet the Vulture Lady. unabr. ed. Betsy Byars. Narrated by Blain Fairman. 2 cass. (Running Time: 2 hrs 56 mins.). (Blossom Family Ser.: Bk. 2). (J). (gr. 4-6). 2000. pap. bk. 23.00 Guide. (978-0-8072-7323-4(6), YA824SP, Listening Lib) Random Audio Pubg.

Blossoms Meet the Vulture Lady, Set. unabr. ed. Betsy Byars. Read by Blain Fairman. 2 cass. (Blossom Family Ser.: Bk. 2). (YA). 1999. 16.98 (FS9-34170) Highsmith.

Blott on the Landscape. unabr. ed. Tom Sharpe. Read by David Case. 6 cass. (Running Time: 9 hrs.). 1992. 48.00 (978-0-7366-2241-7(1), 3031) Books on Tape.
Blott plots to block a motorway through rural England. His weapons: chili powder & spiked beer.

Blotto, Twinks & the Ex-King's Daughter. Simon Brett. 2009. 49.95 (978-0-7531-4364-3(X)); audio compact disk 64.95 (978-0-7531-4365-0(8)) Pub: Isis Pubng Ltd GBR. Dist(s): Ulverscroft US

Blount County, Tennessee, Deeds, 1819-1833. Jane K. Thomas. 2002. audio compact disk 11.00 (978-0-7884-2192-1(1)) Heritage Bk.

Blow Fly. abr. ed. Patricia Cornwell. Illus. by Patricia Cornwell. 5. (Running Time: 5 hrs.). No. 12. (ENG.). (gr. k-8). 2004. audio compact disk 12.95 (978-0-14-305744-4(8), PengAudBks) Penguin Grp USA.
In Blow Fly, Kay Scarpetta stands at the threshold of a new life after her work as Virginia's Chief Medical Examiner has come to a jarring end. At the close of The Last Precinct, she knew she would have to leave Richmond if she were to find any peace. She feared that she was about to be fired by the governor. More alarming, she was hounded in the media and in the courtroom, for what some claimed was her involvement in the murder of a deputy police chief. So Scarpetta packed up her belongings and set out for the warmth and solace of the Florida sun. She is settling into a new life as a private forensic consultant and is deep into a case that has left colleagues in Louisiana profoundly disturbed. A woman is found dead in a seedy hotel, dressed to go out, keys in her hand. Her history of blackouts, and her violent outbursts while under their spell, offer more questions than clues about the cause of her death. Then Scarpetta receives news that chills her to the core: Jean-Baptiste Chandonne - the vicious and unrepentant Wolfman, who pursued her to her very doorstep - asks to see her. From his cell on death row, he demands an audience with the legendary Dr. Scarpetta. Only to her will he tell the secrets he knows the authorities desire: the evidence that will bring a global investigation to a swift conclusion. Scarpetta, her niece Lucy, and her colleague Detective Pete Marino are left to wonder: After all the death and destruction, what sort of endgame could this violent psychopath have in mind? And could this request be somehow related to the Louisiana case? Her friends and family by her side, Scarpetta must unravel a twisting conspiracy with an international reach and confront theshock of her life - a blow that will force her to question the loyalty and trust of all she holds dear.

Blow Fly. unabr. ed. Patricia Cornwell. Illus. by Patricia Cornwell. Read by Kate Reading. 10 CDs. (Running Time: 12 hrs.). (Kay Scarpetta Ser.: No. 12). 2003. audio compact disk 86.40 (978-0-7366-9577-0(X)); 80.00 (978-0-7366-9553-4(2)) Books on Tape.
Forensic pathologist Dr. Kay Scarpetta leaves Virginia in the wake of career upheaval. But as she settles into her new life in Florida as a private forensic consultant, she confronts a baffling and horrific murder. Then she receives chilling news: the vicious and unrepentant killer summons her from his cell on death row.

Blow the Shofar in Zion. Perf. by House of Yahweh Choir. 1 cass. (Running Time: 56 min.). 1996. 8.00 (978-1-890967-34-5(3)) Hse of Yahweh.
These inspirational Psalms bless Yahweh & His name for peace & unity among the people of His House.

Blow, Ye Winds, in the Morning. 1 cass. (Running Time: 48 min.). 1984. 7.95 (CA 1084); audio compact disk 14.95 (CD 1084) Revels Recs.
Presents a tapestry of sea songs, chanteys, ballads, street cries, children's games, dance and ritual from England, Scotland, Ireland, Canada, the U. S. and Afro-American sources.

Blow your Horn: How to Market Yourself & Your Career. Jeffrey P. Davidson. 2004. 7.95 (978-0-7435-4208-1(8)) Pub: S&S Audio. Dist(s): S and S Inc

Blow Your Own Horn. Jeff Davidson. 1988. audio compact disk 10.95 (978-1-60729-122-0(3)) Breath Space Inst.

Blow Your Own Horn. jeff davidson. 1988. 9.95 (978-1-60729-339-2(0)) Breath Space Inst.

Blowback. Eric James Fullilove. Narrated by Marc Johnson. 8 cass. (Running Time: 11 hrs.). 74.00 (978-0-7887-9611-1(9)) Recorded Bks.

***Blowback.** unabr. ed. Peter May. Read by To be Announced. (Running Time: 8 hrs. NaN mins.). (Enzo Files Ser.). (ENG.). 2011. 29.95 (978-1-4417-7787-4(3)); 54.95 (978-1-4417-7784-3(9)); audio compact disk 76.00 (978-1-4417-7785-0(7)) Blckstn Audio.

Blowback: The Costs & Consequences of American Empire. unabr. ed. Chalmers Johnson. Read by Tom Weiner. (Running Time: 32400 sec.). 2007. audio compact disk 19.95 (978-1-4332-0478-4(9)) Blckstn Audio.

Blowback: The Costs & Consequences of American Empire. 2nd unabr. ed. Chalmers Johnson. Read by Tom Weiner. (Running Time: 32400 sec.). 2007. 59.95 (978-1-4332-0475-3(4)); audio compact disk 29.95 (978-1-4332-0479-1(7)); audio compact disk 63.00 (978-1-4332-0476-0(2)) Blckstn Audio.

Blowback: The Costs & Consequences of American Empire. 2nd unabr. ed. Chalmers Johnson. Read by Tom Weiner. (Running Time: 32400 sec.). 2007. 19.95 (978-1-4332-0477-7(0)) Blckstn Audio.

Blowin the Blues Book. Sandy Feldstein. 1996. bk. 9.95 (978-0-7692-2599-9(3), Warner Bro) Alfred Pub.

Blowing It. Judy Astley. (Isis (CDs) Ser.). 2007. audio compact disk 71.95 (978-0-7531-2613-4(3)) Pub: ISIS Lrg Prnt GBR. Dist(s): Ulverscroft US

Blowing It. Judy Astley. Read by Polly March. 6 cass. (Running Time: 7 hrs.). (Isis Cassettes Ser.). 2007. 54.95 (978-0-7531-3559-4(0)) Pub: ISIS Lrg Prnt GBR. Dist(s): Ulverscroft US

Blown Away, Set. abr. ed. Kirk Mitchell. Read by Joe Batteer. 2 cass. (Running Time: 3 hrs.). 1994. 16.95 (978-1-56876-021-6(3)) Soundlines Ent.
An explosive action-thriller about the Boston Bomb squad being targeted by an escaped IRA member, who uses his expertise in explosives to take revenge.

Blown Away: A John Becker Thriller. abr. ed. David Wiltse. Perf. by Bruce McGill. 2 cass. (Running Time: 3 hrs.). 1997. 17.00 Set. (978-1-56876-063-6(9)) Soundlines Ent.
FBI agents John Becker & Pegeen Haddad are on the trail of a highly sophisticated bomber whose target is New York City.

Blowout. abr. ed. Catherine Coulter. Read by Sandra Burr. (Running Time: 21600 sec.). (FBI Thriller Ser.: No. 9). 2006. audio compact disk 16.99 (978-1-4233-1938-2(9), 9781423319382) Brilliance Audio.
A long weekend in the Poconos is cut short when Sherlock and Savich are helicoptered back to Washington to lead the investigation into the brutal murder of a Supreme Court Justice. Savich allows Callie Markham, an investigative reporter for The Washington Post, to partner with local Metro Police liaison Ben Raven, since she's got the inside track - she's the stepdaughter of the murdered justice. Despite Detective Raven's unwillingness to have a civilian along, Callie Markham ends up riding shotgun to help look for her stepfather's murderer. Within the next twenty-four hours, a Supreme Court law clerk is found murdered, the M.O. the same. Savich learns he must also solve a thirty-year-old crime after a psychic encounter with the murder victim, Samantha Barrister, who suddenly appears in front of his car and hysterically pleads for his help. Savich and Sherlock discover that at the time of her death Samantha had a six-year-old son, who disappeared as a teenager. Savich is convinced the missing boy is the key. In Blowout, Sherlock and Savich are faced with two of the most baffling and shocking cases of their careers.

Blowout. unabr. ed. Catherine Coulter. Read by Sandra Burr. 7 cass. (Running Time: 11 hrs.). (FBI Thriller Ser.: No. 9). 2004. 32.95 (978-1-58788-856-4(4), 1587888564, BAU); 24.95 (978-1-59335-669-9(2), 1593356692, Brilliance MP3); 39.25 (978-1-59335-803-7(2), 1593358032, Brlnc Audio MP3 Lib); 82.25 (978-1-58788-857-1(2), 1587888572, BrilAudUnabridg); audio compact disk 36.95 (978-1-58788-859-5(9), 1587888599, Bril Audio CD Unabri); audio compact disk 97.25 (978-1-58788-860-1(2), 1587888602, BriAudCD Unabrid) Brilliance Audio.

Blowout. unabr. ed. Catherine Coulter. Read by Sandra Burr. (Running Time: 11 hrs.). (FBI Thriller Ser.: No. 9). 2004. 39.25 (978-1-59710-091-5(9), 1597100919, BADLE); 24.95 (978-1-59710-090-8(0), 1597100900, BAD) Brilliance Audio.

***Blowout-ABR.** Catherine Coulter & #9 Fbi Thriller Series. 2010. audio compact disk 9.99 (978-1-4418-5647-0(1)) Brilliance Audio.

Blowout Center: The Supportive Environment. unabr. ed. R. D. Laing. 2 cass. (Running Time: 2 hrs.). 1967. 18.00 Set. (07003) Big Sur Tapes.

BLS Skills Review DVD. American Academy of Orthopaedic Surgeons (AAOS). 2008. 45.95 (978-0-7637-5223-1(1)) Jones Bartlett.

Blubber. Read by Halley Feiffer. 3 CDs. (Running Time: 2 hrs. 54 mins.). (J). (gr. 3-7). 2004. audio compact disk 30.00 (978-0-8072-1781-8(6), Listening Lib) Random Audio Pubg.

Blubber. unabr. ed. Judy Blume. 1 read-along cass. (Running Time: 49 min.). (Soundways to Reading Ser.). (J). (gr. 4-6). 1983. pap. bk. 15.98 (978-0-8072-1102-1(8), SWR32SP, Listening Lib) Random Audio Pubg.
When the class starts calling Linda "Blubber," Jill can't imagine being in Linda's unpopular place...until she has to.

Blubber. unabr. ed. Judy Blume. 2 vols. (Running Time: 2 hrs. 54 mins.). (J). (gr. 3-7). 2004. pap. bk. 29.00 (978-0-8072-1709-2(3), S YA 1016 SP, Listening Lib) Random Audio Pubg.

Blubber. unabr. ed. Judy Blume. Read by Halley Feiffer. (Running Time: 10440 sec.). (ENG.). (J). (gr. 3). 2007. audio compact disk 14.99 (978-0-7393-4888-8(4), Listening Lib) Pub: Random Audio Pubg. Dist(s): Random

Blue. Ed. by Robert A. Monroe. 1 cass. (Running Time: 30 min.). (Meta Music Ser.). 1989. 12.95 (978-1-56102-202-1(0)) Inter Indus.
Use this Meta Music tape for free-form meditation or for creating patterns in your mind.

Blue Afternoon. unabr. ed. William Boyd. Read by Donada Peters. 8 cass. (Running Time: 12 hrs.). 1997. 64.00 (978-0-7366-3722-0(2), 4403) Books on Tape.
Set in 1930's Hollywood, where the narrator, a young woman, meets an elderly man who claims to be her father.

Blue & Distant Hills. unabr. ed. Judith Saxton. Read by Rowena Cooper. 16 cass. (Running Time: 16 hrs.). 1998. 124.95 Set, Dolby Sound. (978-0-7540-0159-1(8), CAB 1582) AudioGO.
Questa Adamson is stranded in Italy for the duration of World War II. When she returns home to England, she finds that the childhood world she remembers has disappeared. Upon inheriting a run-down manor house, Questa decides to restore the estate to its former glory. And when she meets Marcus, her mysterious neighbor, things begin to turn around.

Blue & Gray Christmas. unabr. ed. Joan Medlicott. Narrated by Marguerite Gavin. (Running Time: 6 hrs. 30 mins.). 2009. 14.99 (978-1-4001-8522-1(X)); 19.99 (978-1-4001-6522-3(9)); audio compact disk 29.99 (978-1-4001-1522-8(1)); audio compact disk 59.99 (978-1-4001-4522-5(8)) Pub: Tantor Media. Dist(s): IngramPubServ

Blue Angel: The Life of Marlene Dietrich. unabr. collector's ed. Donald Spoto. Read by Mary Peiffer. 9 cass. (Running Time: 13 hrs. 30 mins.). 1993. 72.00 (978-0-7366-2460-2(0)) Books on Tape.
Captures well the high kitsch of the twilight of the German aristocracy into which Maria Madgelene Dietrich (1901-92) was born. Her mother drilled the spontaneously honest child never to show her feelings, the birth of the actress's famous mask of alluring remoteness. Ten years of violin lessons trained her for the musical side of her career (her violin teacher deflowered her, she told Billy Wilder) & for some of her funniest & even moving scenes under the direction of Josef von Sternberg, the Svengali who, in The Blue Angel, turned Dietrich into a goddess.

Blue Apple. Nina Cassian. Ed. by Stanley H. Barkan. Tr. by Eva Feiler. (Cross-Cultural Review Chapbook Ser.: No. 13: Romanian Poetry 1). (ENG & RUM.). 1981. 10.00 (978-0-89304-837-2(2)) Cross-Cultrl NY.

Blue at the Mizzen. Patrick O'Brian. Read by David Case. (Aubrey-Maturin Ser.). 1999. audio compact disk 64.00 (978-0-7366-5201-8(9)) Books on Tape.

Blue at the Mizzen. unabr. ed. Patrick O'Brian. (Running Time: 30600 sec.). (Aubrey-Maturin Ser.). 2007. 59.95 (978-1-4332-0254-4(9)) Blckstn Audio.

Blue at the Mizzen. unabr. ed. Patrick O'Brian. Read by Simon Vance. (Running Time: 30600 sec.). (Aubrey-Maturin Ser.). 2007. audio compact disk 63.00 (978-1-4332-0255-1(7)) Blckstn Audio.

Blue at the Mizzen. unabr. ed. Patrick O'Brian. (Running Time: 30600 sec.). (Aubrey-Maturin Ser.). 2008. audio compact disk 29.95 (978-1-4332-0256-8(5)) Blckstn Audio.

Blue at the Mizzen. unabr. ed. Patrick O'Brian. Read by Simon Vance. (Running Time: 30600 sec.). (Aubrey-Maturin Ser.). 2008. audio compact disk 29.95 (978-1-4332-0895-9(4)) Blckstn Audio.

Blue at the Mizzen. unabr. ed. Patrick O'Brian. 6 cass. (Running Time: 9 hrs.). (Aubrey-Maturin Ser.). 1999. 48.00 (978-0-7366-4737-3(6), 5075) Books on Tape.
Twentieth in the series about Captain Jack Aubrey & ship's doctor Stephen Maturin, takes place after the Napoleonic wars. They experience a disastrous night collision at sea, desertion of nearly half the crew, a rounding of Cape Horn & a naval action off the infant republic of Chile.

Blue at the Mizzen. unabr. ed. Patrick O'Brian. Read by David Case. 6 cass. (Running Time: 9 hrs.). (Aubrey-Maturin Ser.). 2000. 29.95 (978-0-7366-4686-4(8)); audio compact disk 34.95 (978-0-7366-4760-1(0)) Books on Tape.

Blue at the Mizzen. unabr. ed. Patrick O'Brian. Narrated by Patrick Tull. 7 cass. (Running Time: 10 hrs.). (Aubrey-Maturin Ser.). 1999. 60.00 (978-0-7887-3769-5(4), 95986E7) Recorded Bks.
Daring frigate commander Jack Aubrey stakes everything on a desperate night raid against the might of the Spanish viceroy in Peru. And ship's surgeon Stephen Maturin is ready to give his heart to a beautiful naturalist, if only she will have him. A vivid picture of the high seas during the Napoleonic era.

Blue at the Mizzen. unabr. ed. Patrick O'Brian. Narrated by Patrick Tull. 9 CDs. (Running Time: 10 hrs.). (Aubrey-Maturin Ser.). 2000. audio compact disk 81.00 (978-0-7887-4204-0(3), C1133E7) Recorded Bks.

Blue at the Mizzen. unabr. ed. Patrick O'Brian. Read by Simon Vance. (Running Time: 30600 sec.). (Aubrey-Maturin Ser.). 2008. 29.95 (978-1-4332-0894-2(6)) Blckstn Audio.

Blue Avenger Cracks the Code. unabr. ed. Norma Howe. Read by John Beach. 4 cass. (Running Time: 6 hrs. 54 mins.). (Blue Avenger Ser.). (J). (gr. 6 up). 2004. 32.00 (978-0-8072-8712-5(1), YA244CX, Listening Lib) Random Audio Pubg.

Blue Banner Lectures Series. John Robbins. 6 cass. 30.00 Set. Trinity Found.

Blue Bedroom. unabr. ed. Rosamunde Pilcher. Read by June Whitfield. 6 cass. (Running Time: 6 hrs.). 1996. 54.95 Set. (978-0-7451-4385-9(7), CAB1069) AudioGO.
An extraordinary blend of love & heartbreak, the plots include a middle-aged mother confronting her empty life, a child's first knowledge of death & a newly-married husband's first faltering moments with his stepchildren.

Blue Bedroom. unabr. ed. Short Stories. Rosamunde Pilcher. Read by Donada Peters. 7 cass. (Running Time: 7 hrs.). 1992. 42.00 (978-0-7366-2273-8(X), 3061) Books on Tape.
Collection of short stories exploring full spectrum of life's mood & emotions with Pilcher's warmth & honesty.

Blue Belle. unabr. ed. Andrew Vachss. Read by Christopher Lane & Phil Gigante. (Running Time: 11 hrs.). (Burke Ser.). 2010. 24.99 (978-1-4418-2093-8(0), 9781441820938, Brilliance MP3); 24.99 (978-1-4418-2095-2(7), 9781441820952, BAD); 39.97 (978-1-4418-2094-5(9), 9781441820945, Brlnc Audio MP3 Lib); 39.97 (978-1-4418-2096-9(5), 9781441820969, BADLE); audio compact disk 29.99 (978-1-4418-2091-4(4), 9781441820914, Bril Audio CD Unabri); audio compact disk 79.97 (978-1-4418-2092-1(2), 9781441820921, BriAudCD Unabrid) Brilliance Audio.

Blue Bird see Istwa Ti Zwazo Ble a

Blue Blood. unabr. ed. Edward Conlon. Narrated by Tom Stechschulte. 19 cass. (Running Time: 28 hrs.). 2004. 109.75 (978-1-4193-0288-6(4)); audio compact disk 119.75 (978-1-4193-0290-9(6)) Recorded Bks.

Blue Blood. unabr. ed. Edward Conlon. 23 CDs. (Running Time: 28 hrs.). 2004. audio compact disk 49.99 (978-1-4193-0286-2(8), 01902) Recorded Bks.
Destined to be a classic, Blue Blood is a New York Times best-seller that acclaimed author Joseph Wambaugh calls "the most stunning memoir ever written about the cop world." Author Edward Conlon is a NYPD detective. Through his eyes, we view the city as never before.

Blue Book of Acoustic Guitars. 3rd ed. S. P. Fjestad. Ed. by S. P. Fjestad. (Blue Book Ser.). (ENG., 1999. audio compact disk 19.95 (978-1-886768-81-9(1)) Pub: Blue Bk Pubns. Dist(s): Alfred Pub

Blue Book of Acoustic Guitars: CD-ROM. Zachary R. Fjestad. (Blue Book Ser.). (ENG.). 2009. audio compact disk 49.95 (978-1-886768-95-6(1)) Pub: Blue Bk Pubns. Dist(s): Alfred Pub

Blue Book of Guitars. 7th ed. S. P. Fjestad. 1 CD. (Running Time: 1 hr. 30 mins.). 2001. audio compact disk 19.95 (978-1-886768-27-7(7)) Blue Bk Pubns.

Blue Book of Guitars: Contains the 11th Edition of Blue Book of Acoustic Guitars & Blue Book of Electric Guitars. 11th rev. ed. Zachary R. Fjestad. Ed. by S. P. Fjestad. (Blue Bk Ser.). (ENG.). 2008. audio compact disk 29.95 (978-1-886768-78-9(1)) Alfred Pub.

Blue Bottle see May Swenson

Blue Bottle Club. unabr. ed. Penelope J. Stokes. Narrated by Alyssa Bresnahan. 10 cass. (Running Time: 14 hrs. 15 mins.). 1999. 85.00 (978-0-7887-3899-9(2), 96080E7) Recorded Bks.
Reporter Brendan delaney discovers a bottle filled with slips of papers recording the dreams of four young girls. As she searches for the now elderly women, she uncovers a common thread running through their lives - one that soon intermingles with her own.

Blue Bullet. unabr. ed. Gary McCarthy. Read by Maynard Villers. 6 cass. (Running Time: 5 hrs. 48 min.). (Horsemen Ser.: No. 4). 1994. 39.95 (978-1-55686-518-3(X)) Books in Motion.
In New Mexico, Ruff & Dixie Ballou take up a money-making challenge to capture Blue Bullet, the legendary stallion no man has tamed.

Blue Carbuncle & Other Stories, Set. unabr. ed. Arthur Conan Doyle. Read by William Barker. 2 cass. (Running Time: 3 hrs.). 1996. lib. bdg. 21.95 (978-1-55656-065-1(6), DAB040) Pub: Dercum Audio. Dist(s): APG

Blue Christmas. Billy Hayes. 1993. audio compact disk 22.95 (978-0-634-09194-0(8)) H Leonard.

***Blue Christmas.** abr. ed. Mary Kay Andrews. Read by Isabel Keating. (ENG.). 2006. (978-0-06-123060-8(X), Harper Audio); (978-0-06-123059-2(6), Harper Audio) HarperCollins Pubs.

Blue Christmas: Now with More Holiday Cheer. unabr. ed. Mary Kay Andrews. Narrated by Isabel Keating. 3 cass. (Running Time: 18120 sec.). 2006. 34.95 (978-0-7927-4549-5(3), CMP 1052); audio compact disk 49.95 (978-0-7927-4522-8(1), SLD 1052) AudioGO.

Blue Christmas: Now with More Holiday Cheer. unabr. ed. Mary Kay Andrews. Read by Isabel Keating. 4 CDs. (Running Time: 18000 sec.). 2006. audio compact disk 29.95 (978-0-06-114265-9(4), Harper Audio) HarperCollins Pubs.

Blue Corn Murders. unabr. ed. Nancy Pickard & Virginia Rich. Read by Agnes Herrmann. 6 vols. (Running Time: 9 hrs.). (Eugenia Potter Mysteries Ser.). 2000. bk. 54.95 (978-0-7927-2286-1(8), CSL 175, Chivers Sound Lib) AudioGO.
Eugenia Potter is visiting the Medicine Wheel Archaeological Camp in Colorado. But trouble looms when a busload of youngsters disappears without a trace, drawing an eerie connection with the lost Anasazi tribe of so many years before. Then two women at Medicine Wheel end up dead. Are their deaths connected? Eugenia Potter must take matters into her own hands as she investigates, hoping to avert another murder before it's too late.

Blue Cornflower. unabr. ed. Joan Eadith. Read by Julia Sands. 7 cass. (Running Time: 9 hrs. 15 min.). 1999. 76.95 (978-1-85903-263-3(X)) Pub: Magna Story GBR. Dist(s): Ulverscroft US
Millicent Dawnay knew she was destined for better things than a life of drudgery & conformity. Her talent for art & design would be her passport out of her grey Lancashire village, she dreams of studying art in Manchester. When she arrives there she finds Hewy Edmundson, once a childhood sweetheart, now a young blade about town. As the country enters the Great War, Milly begins her own adventure. It is the start of her life as an artist & a chance to let her true love come to fruition.

Blue Cross - A Father Brown Mystery. G. K. Chesterton. Narrated by James Arthur. (Running Time: 3 hrs.). 2006. 14.95 (978-1-59912-998-3(1)) Iofy Corp.

Blue Dahlia. Nora Roberts. Read by Susie Breck. (In the Garden Trilogy: Bk. 1). 2008. 89.99 (978-1-60640-904-6(2)) Find a World.

Blue Dahlia. abr. ed. Nora Roberts & #1 IN THE GARDEN. (In the Garden Trilogy: Bk. 1). 2010. audio compact disk 9.99 (978-1-4418-4188-9(1)) Brilliance Audio.

Blue Dahlia. abr. unabr. ed. Nora Roberts. Read by Susie Breck. (Running Time: 11 hrs.). (In the Garden Trilogy: Bk. 1). 2004. audio compact disk 97.25 (978-1-59355-611-2(X), 159355611X, BACDLib Ed) Brilliance Audio.
A Harper has always lived at Harper House, the centuries-old mansion just outside of Memphis. And for as long as anyone alive remembers, the ghostly Harper Bride has walked the halls, singing lullabies at night... Trying to escape the ghosts of the past, young widow Stella Rothchild, along with her two energetic little boys, has moved back to her roots in southern Tennessee - and into her new life at Harper House and In the Garden nursery. She isn't intimidated by the house - nor its mistress, local legend Roz Harper. Despite a reputation for being difficult, Roz has been nothing but kind to Stella, offering her a comfortable new place to live and a challenging new job as manager of the flourishing nursery. As Stella settles comfortably into her new life, she finds a nurturing friendship with Roz and with expectant mother Hayley. And she discovers a fierce attraction with ruggedly handsome landscaper Logan Kitridge. But someone isn't happy about the budding romance...the Harper Bride. As the women dig into the history of Harper House, they discover that grief and rage have kept the Bride's spirit alive long past her death. And now, she will do anything to destroy the passion that Logan and Stella share.

Blue Dahlia. unabr. ed. Nora Roberts. Read by Susie Breck. (Running Time: 11 hrs.). (In the Garden Trilogy: Bk. 1). 2004. 39.25 (978-1-59710-093-9(5), 1597100935, BADLE); 24.95 (978-1-59710-092-2(7), 1597100927, BAD); 24.95 (978-1-59335-743-6(5), 1593357435, Brilliance MP3); 39.25 (978-1-59335-877-8(6), 1593358776, Brlnc Audio MP3 Lib); 87.25 (978-1-59355-608-2(X), 159355608X, BrilAudUnabridg); audio compact disk 36.95 (978-1-59600-822-9(9), 1596008229, Bril Audio CD Unabri) Brilliance Audio.

Blue Danube, Level 3. (Yamaha Clavinova Connection Ser.). 2004. disk 0.82 (978-0-634-09595-5(1)) H Leonard.

Blue Death. Fred Saberhagen. Read by Patrick Cullen. 8 CDs. (Running Time: 36000 sec.). (Berserker Ser.). 2003. audio compact disk 64.00 (978-0-7861-9341-7(7), 3045) Blckstn Audio.

Blue Death. unabr. ed. Fred Saberhagen. Read by Patrick Cullen. 7 cass. (Running Time: 10 hrs.). (Berserker Ser.). 2003. 49.95 (978-0-7861-2343-8(5), 3045) Blckstn Audio.

Blue Death. unabr. ed. Fred Saberhagen. Narrated by Aaron Lustig & Henry Strozier. 5 cass. (Running Time: 6 hrs. 30 mins.). (Berserker Ser.). (gr. 10 up). 1983. 44.00 (978-1-55690-048-8(1), 83059E7) Recorded Bks.
They were vast machines sent out by their long-dead creators for one purpose only - to destroy.

Blue Deer & Other River Tales, Vol. 3. Stephen DiLauro. 1 CD. (Running Time: 1 hr.). 2000. audio compact disk 12.00 (978-0-9651287-6-6(8)) Riv Tales Prod.
This collections tell of characters, animals & others who live near the Delaware River. The tales include: "Blue Deer," "The Cat Stew Widow," "Scarecrow & Boogerberry Man" & others.

Blue Diamond. Arthur Conan Doyle. 2002. 12.95 (978-0-19-424356-8(7)) OUP.

Blue Diamond. Arthur Conan Doyle & Bill Bowler. (Dominoes Ser.). 2004. 14.25 (978-0-19-424425-1(3)) OUP.

Blue Diary. abr. ed. Alice Hoffman. Read by Joyce Bean. (Running Time: 6 hrs.). 2009. audio compact disk 14.99 (978-1-4418-1254-4(7), 9781441812544, BCD Value Price) Brilliance Audio.

Blue Diary. unabr. ed. Alice Hoffman. Read by Joyce Bean. 7 cass. (Running Time: 10 hrs.). 2001. 32.95 (978-1-58788-254-8(X), 158788254X, BAU) Brilliance Audio.
The courage to face the unthinkable is at the core of this magnificent new novel. How do we manage to confront the truths in our lives and find forgiveness in the most unforgiving of circumstances? How do we love truly and deeply in a world that is as brutal as it is beautiful? When Ethan Ford fails to show up for work on a brilliant summer morning, none of his neighbors would guess that for more than thirteen years, he has been running from his past. His true nature has been locked away, as hidden as his real identity. But sometimes locks spring open, and the devastating truths of Ethan Ford's history shatter the small-town peace of Monroe, affecting family and friends alike. This deeply felt and compelling novel makes clear why Alice Hoffman has been called "one of the best writers we have today" (Cleveland Plain Dealer). Honest, shattering, seductive, and ultimately healing, Blue Diary is an unforgettable novel by a writer who tells "truths powerful enough to break a reader's heart" (Time magazine).

Blue Diary. unabr. ed. Alice Hoffman. Read by Joyce Bean. (Running Time: 10 hrs.). 2004. 24.95 (978-1-59335-303-2(0), 1593353030, Brilliance MP3); 39.25 (978-1-59335-462-6(2), 1593354622, Brlnc Audio MP3 Lib) Brilliance Audio.

Blue Diary. unabr. ed. Alice Hoffman. Read by Joyce Bean. (Running Time: 10 hrs.). 2004. 39.25 (978-1-59710-094-6(3), 1597100943, BADLE); 24.95 (978-1-59710-095-3(1), 1597100951, BAD) Brilliance Audio.

Blue Diary. unabr. ed. Alice Hoffman. Read by Joyce Bean. 8 CDs. (Running Time: 10 hrs.). 2009. audio compact disk 29.99 (978-1-4418-1252-0(0), 9781441812520, Bril Audio CD Unabri); audio compact disk 87.97 (978-1-4418-1253-7(9), 9781441812537, BriAudCD Unabrid) Brilliance Audio.

Blue Djinn of Babylon. Philip Kerr. Narrated by Ron Keith. (Running Time: 38700 sec.). (Children of the Lamp Ser.). (J). (gr. 4-7). 2006. audio compact disk 34.99 (978-1-4193-7001-4(4)) Recorded Bks.

Blue Djinn of Babylon. unabr. ed. P. B. Kerr. Read by Ron Keith. 9 CDs. (Running Time: 10 hrs. 45 mins.). (Children of the Lamp Ser.: Vol. 2). (J). 2006. audio compact disk 94.75 (978-1-4193-7093-9(6), C3544); 75.75 (978-1-4193-7088-5(X), 98269) Recorded Bks.

The Solomon Grimoire - a powerful book of magic - has gone missing. When John and Philippa are chosen to retrieve it, their quest sends them trotting across the globe. But what they don¿t know is they are being lured into a trap by the Blue Djinn. When Philippa falls right into the trap, John must embark on a perilous adventure to save his sister. With this second effort, Kerr has established the Children of the Lamp series as a masterful saga that deserves consideration alongside the classics of fantasy fiction. Narrator Ron Keith brings Kerr¿s wondrous world to full and glorious life with his dynamic performance.

Blue Earth. unabr. ed. Jodi Compton. Read by Bernadette Quigley. (Running Time: 8 hrs.). 2003. 74.25 (978-1-59355-117-9(7), 1593551177, BrilAudUnabridg) Brilliance Audio.

On a chilling Minnesota morning, Sarah Pribek comes home to the house she shares with her husband and fellow cop, Michael Shiloh. Shiloh is supposed to be in Virginia, starting his training with the FBI. A seasoned missing-persons investigator, Sarah is used to anxious calls from wives and parents. She's used to innocent explanations that resolve so many of her cases. But from the moment she learns that he never arrived at Quantico, she feels a terrible foreboding. Now, beneath the bed in which they make love, Sarah finds Shiloh's neatly packed bag. And in that instant the cop in her knows: Her husband has disappeared. Suddenly Sarah finds herself at the beginning of the kind of investigation she has made so often. The kind that she and her ex-partner, Genevieve, solved routinely - until a brutal crime stole Genevieve's daughter and ended her career. The kind that pries open family secrets and hidden lives. For Sarah this investigation will mean going back to the beginning, to Shiloh's religion-steeped childhood in Utah, the rift that separated him from his family - and the one horrifying case that struck them both too close to home. As Sarah turns over more and more unknown ground in her husband's past, she sees her lover and friend change into a stranger before her eyes. And as she moves further down a trail of shocking surprises and bitter revelations, Sarah is about to discover that her worst fear - that Shiloh is dead - may be less painful than what she will learn next.

Blue-Eyed Devil. abr. ed. Lisa Kleypas. (Running Time: 6 hrs.). 2009. audio compact disk 14.99 (978-1-59737-868-0(2), 9781597378680, BCD Value Price) Brilliance Audio.

Blue-Eyed Devil. unabr. ed. Lisa Kleypas. Read by Renée Raudman. (Running Time: 10 hrs.). 2008. 39.25 (978-1-59737-866-6(6), 9781597378666, BADLE); 24.95 (978-1-59737-865-9(8), 9781597378659, BAD); audio compact disk 36.95 (978-1-59737-861-1(5), 9781597378611, Bril Audio CD Unabri); audio compact disk 24.95 (978-1-59737-863-5(1), 9781597378635, Brilliance MP3); audio compact disk 97.25 (978-1-59737-862-8(3), 9781597378628, BriAudCD Unabrid); audio compact disk 39.25 (978-1-59737-864-2(X), 9781597378642, Brlnc Audio MP3 Lib) Brilliance Audio.

***Blue-Eyed Devil.** unabr. ed. Robert B. Parker. Narrated by Titus Welliver. 4 CDs. (Running Time: 3 hrs. 45 mins.). 2010. audio compact disk 32.00 (978-0-307-73549-2(4), BksonTape) Pub: Random Audio Pubg. Dist(s): Random

Blue-Eyed Devil. unabr. ed. Robert B. Parker. Read by Titus Welliver. (ENG.). 2010. audio compact disk 32.00 (978-0-307-73547-8(8), Random AudioBks) Pub: Random Audio Pubg. Dist(s): Random

***Blue Feather & Other Classic Westerns: The Wolf Tracker/Quaking-Asp Cabin/Blue Feather.** Zane Grey. Read by Eli Davis et al. (Playaway Young Adult Ser.). (ENG.). (J). 2010. 44.99 (978-1-61637-566-9(3)) Find a World.

Blue Fire. unabr. ed. Phyllis A. Whitney. Read by Kim Hicks. 10 cass. (Running Time: 15 hrs.). 2000. 84.95 (978-0-7540-0472-1(4), CAB 1895) Pub: Chivers Audio Bks GBR. Dist(s): AudioGO

When Susan returns to South Africa as the wife of Dirk Hohenfield, she is apprehensive. Perhaps by seeing her estranged father, she can discover the answers to questions that have haunted her for years. At the center of it lies a magnificent blue diamond that disappeared, a diamond that Dirk thinks she knows something about.

Blue Fire, Pt. 1. James Hillman. Read by James Hillman. 2 cass. (Running Time: 2 hrs.). 1991. pap. bk. 17.95 (978-1-879816-01-5(6)) Pub: Spring Audio. Dist(s): Daimon Verlag

Recorded during a seminar weekend in Rowe, Massachusetts, this cassette is a conflagration of ideas. Hillman revisions himself, his work and archetypal psychology as he finds it today.

Blue Fire, Vol. 2. James Hillman. 2 cass. (Running Time: 2 hrs.). 2004. pap. bk. 17.95 (978-1-879816-02-2(4)) Pub: Spring Audio. Dist(s): Daimon Verlag

Blue Flower. unabr. ed. Penelope Fitzgerald. Read by Edmund Dehn. 5 cass. (Running Time: 7 hrs. 30 mins.). (Isis Ser.). (J). 1999. 49.95 (978-0-7531-0009-7(6), 960203) Pub: ISIS Lrg Prnt GBR. Dist(s): Ulverscroft US

Set at the end of the eighteenth century it tells the story of the young & brilliant Fritz von Hardenberg, a graduate of the Universities of Jena, Leipzig & Wittenberg. The passionate & idealistic Fritz needs his father's permission to announce his engagement to his "heart's heart", the embodiment of all his yearnings, twelve-year-old sophie von Kuhn. It is a betrothal which amuses, astounds & disturbs his family & friends.

Blue-Fly see Robert Graves Reads from His Poetry & the White Goddess

Blue Genes: A Kate Brannigan Mystery. unabr. ed. Val McDermid. Read by Laura Brattan. 6 cass. (Running Time: 8 hrs.). (Isis Ser.). (J). 2000. 54.95 (978-0-7531-0620-4(5), 990703) Pub: ISIS Lrg Prnt GBR. Dist(s): Ulverscroft US

Kate Brannigan is having a bad week. Her boyfriend's death notice is in the newspaper, her plans to capture a team of heartless fraudsters are in disarray & a Celtic neo-punk band wants her to rescue them from saboteurs. As if that isn't enough, Kate's business partner wants her to buy him out so he can emigrate to Australia & private eyes with principles never have that kind of cash. Kate can't even cry on her best friend's shoulder, for Alexis has worries of her own. Confronting betrayal & greed, Kate fights to save her livelihood & her life.

Blue Genes: A Kate Brannigan Mystery. unabr. ed. Val McDermid. Read by Laura Brattan. 8 CDs. (Running Time: 8 hrs.). (Isis Ser.). (J). 2000. audio compact disk 79.95 (978-0-7531-0899-4(2), 108992) Pub: ISIS Lrg Prnt GBR. Dist(s): Ulverscroft US

Blue Giants, White Dwarfs, Black Holes. Read by J. Percy & T. Bolton. 1 cass. (Running Time: 1 hr.). 14.95 (CBC856) MMI Corp.

Discusses life cycle of stars explained for layman.

Blue Gold. Clive Cussler & Paul Kemprecos. 10 cass. (Running Time: 15 hrs.). (NUMA Files Ser.: No. 2). 2001. 80.00 (978-0-7366-6835-4(7)) Books on Tape.

Blue Hammer, unabr. ed. Ross MacDonald, pseud. Read by Tom Parker. 6 cass. (Running Time: 8 hrs. 30 mins.). (Lew Archer Mystery Ser.). 1999. 44.95 (978-0-7861-1031-5(7), 1806) Blckstn Audio.

Lew Archer has been hired to retrieve a stolen canvas reputed to be the work of the celebrated Richard Chantry, who vanished in 1950 from his home in Santa Teresa. The painting, a portrait of an unknown beautiful woman, leads him into a web of family complications & masked brutalities stretching back fifty years.

Blue Hand. unabr. ed. Edgar Wallace. Read by Flo Gibson. 5 cass. (Running Time: 7 hrs. 30 min.). 1998. 20.95 (978-1-55685-612-9(1)) Audio Bk Con.

The mystery surrounding the mark of the blue hand & Eunice's birth, the schemes & plots of the evil Digby Great, murder & the courage & courtship of Jim Stelle make this an exciting novel.

Blue Heaven. unabr. ed. C. J. Box. Narrated by John Bedford Lloyd. 10 CDs. (Running Time: 11 hrs. 30 mins.). 2008. audio compact disk 94.95 (978-0-7927-5229-5(5)) AudioGO.

A twelve-year-old girl and her younger brother go on the run in the woods of northern Idaho, pursued by four men they have just watched commit murder - four men who know exactly who the children are, and where their desperate mother is waiting patiently by the phone for news of her children's fate. In a ranching community increasingly populated by L.A. transplants living in gaudy McMansions, the kids soon find they don't know whom they can trust among the hundreds of retired Southern California cops who've given the area its nickname: Blue Heaven.

Blue Heaven. unabr. ed. C. J. Box. Read by John Bedford Lloyd. 10 CDs. (Running Time: 12 hrs. 0 mins. 0 sec.). (ENG.). 2008. audio compact disk 39.95 (978-1-4272-0268-0(0)) Pub: Macmill Audio. Dist(s): Macmillan

Blue Heron, unabr. ed. Avi. Narrated by Christina Moore. 3 pieces. (Running Time: 4 hrs. 30 mins.). (gr. 5 up). 1994. 27.00 (978-0-7887-0008-8(1), 94207E7) Recorded Bks.

When Maggie sees a great blue heron on the lake near her father's summer cottage, she cannot believe anybody would want to kill such a beautiful bird. As she explores the mystery, she learns more about the strange world of grown-ups & her own confusing place in it.

Blue Highways. William Least Heat-Moon. Read by William Least Heat-Moon. 1 cass. (Running Time: 42 min.). 13.95 (978-1-55644-083-0(9), 3101) Am Audio Prose.

William Least Heat Moon reads from his novel about travel through rural America.

Blue Highways, unabr. ed. William Least Heat-Moon. Narrated by Frank Muller. 11 cass. (Running Time: 16 hrs. 30 mins.). 1984. 91.00 (978-1-55690-060-0(0), 84190E7) Recorded Bks.

The real life of this book lies in the amazing variety of American originals the lonely & curious author meets along his journey: Kentuckians rebuilding log-cabins, a Brooklyn cop turned Trappist monk in Georgia, Cajun musicians on Bayou Teche & the boys in the barbershop in Dime Box, Texas.

Blue Highways: A Journey into America. William Least Heat-Moon. Read by Frank Muller. 10 Cass. (Running Time: 16.5 Hours). 39.95 (978-1-4025-3360-0(8)) Recorded Bks.

Blue Highways: A Journey into America. abr. ed. William Least Heat-Moon. Read by Karl Schmidt. 5 cass. (Running Time: 5 hrs.). 1986. 30.00 (978-0-7366-0964-7(4), 1906) Books on Tape.

When Least Heat Moon (the translation of the tribal name in his mixed blood) lost his job, he got a half-ton Ford van, packed a few neccessities, & set out to follow the track of various ancestors & write a book about America.

Blue Hills. unabr. collector's ed. Elizabeth Goudge. Read by Donada Peters. 7 cass. (Running Time: 7 hrs.). 1986. 42.00 (978-0-7366-0486-4(3), 1461) Books on Tape.

Whatever the reason, each vehicle gets mysteriously lost on its way to the Blue Hills & by the time the travellers meet again over tea & iced birthday cake, they have had such adventures. Adventures with underground streams & robber citadels, live rabbits & carved imps, caves & fairy bowers. None of them is the same person, they are wiser, nicer & much happier.

Blue Horizon. abr. ed. Wilbur Smith. Read by Tim Pigott-Smith. (Running Time: 7 hrs. 0 mins. 0 sec.). (Courtney Family Adventures Ser.). (ENG., 2003. audio compact disk 37.95 (978-1-55927-871-3(4)) Pub: Macmill Audio. Dist(s): Macmillan

The New York Times bestselling author and one of the greatest adventure writers of our time once again creates a lost era and a truly exciting tale of danger, courage, and suspense At the close of Wilbur Smith’s Monsoon, Tom Courtney and his brother Dorian battled on the high seas. In this spellbinding new novel, the next generation of Courtneys are out to stake their claim in southern Africa, travelling along the infamous "Robber’s Road." It is a journey both exciting and hazardous, which takes them through the untouched wilderness of a beautiful land filled with warring tribes and wild animals.

Blue Hotel see Great American Short Stories

Blue Hotel see Red Badge of Courage & Other Stories

Blue Hotel. unabr. ed. Stephen Crane. Read by Jack Benson. 1 cass. (Running Time: 74 min.). Dramatization. 1977. 7.95 (N-15) Jimcin Record.

A Swede finds danger in the American West.

Blue Hour. T. Jefferson Parker. Read by Kevin Patrick. 1999. audio compact disk 72.00 (978-0-7366-5180-6(2)) Books on Tape.

Blue Hour. abr. ed. T. Jefferson Parker. Read by Tavia Gilbert. (Running Time: 5 hrs.). (Merci Rayborn Ser.). 2009. audio compact disk 24.99 (978-1-4418-0723-6(3), 9781441807236, BACD) Brilliance Audio.

Blue Hour. abr. ed. T. Jefferson Parker. Read by Tavia Gilbert. (Running Time: 5 hrs.). (Merci Rayborn Ser.). 2010. audio compact disk 14.99 (978-1-4418-2630-5(0), 9781441826305, BCD Value Price) Brilliance Audio.

Blue Hour. unabr. ed. T. Jefferson Parker. Read by Kevin Patrick. 8 cass. (Running Time: 12 hrs.). 1999. 64.00 (978-0-7366-4563-8(2), 4970) Books on Tape.

Tim Hess is semi-retired veteran cop staring at a death sentence, his own. In the throes of a losing battle against cancer, his time is literally running out. The classic loner cop, three times divorced & childless, Hess i happy to accept a job tracking down a killer who's been abducting beautiful young women from Orange County. Brash, ambitious & impatient, Merci Rayborn has a reputation for causing trouble. She hasn't devoted any time to her personal life & she's not particularly popular with her peers or her superiors. Hess isn't thrilled about taking orders from this difficult but smart woman. and he certainly isn't planning to fall in love with her.

Blue Hour. unabr. ed. T. Jefferson Parker. Read by Kevin Patrick. 1 CD. (Running Time: 1 hr. 12 mins.). 2001. audio compact disk Books on Tape.

Pits an unlikely team of detectives - who become an even more unlikely pair of lovers - against a ruthless serial killer.

Blue Hour. unabr. ed. T. Jefferson Parker. (Running Time: 13 hrs.). (Merci Rayborn Ser.). 2009. 39.97 (978-1-4233-5570-0(9), 9781423355700, Brlnc Audio MP3 Lib); 24.99 (978-1-4233-5571-7(7), 9781423355717, BAD); 39.97 (978-1-4233-5572-4(5), 9781423355724, BADLE); audio compact disk 97.97 (978-1-4233-5568-7(7), 9781423355687, BriAudCD Unabrid) Brilliance Audio.

Blue Hour. unabr. ed. T. Jefferson Parker. Read by Tavia Gilbert. (Running Time: 13 hrs.). (Merci Rayborn Ser.). 2009. 24.99 (978-1-4233-5569-4(5), 9781423355694, Brilliance MP3); audio compact disk 29.99 (978-1-4233-5567-0(9), 9781423355670, Bril Audio CD Unabri) Brilliance Audio.

Blue Hour, Set. abr. ed. T. Jefferson Parker. Read by Richard McGonagle. 4 cass. 1999. 25.00 (FS9-43423) Highsmith.

Blue Ice, unabr. ed. Hammond Innes. Narrated by Jerry Farden. 7 cass. (Running Time: 9 hrs. 30 mins.). 1989. 60.00 (978-1-55690-061-7(9), 89340E7) Recorded Bks.

A secret fortune lies cached among the desolate mountains & cruel glaciers of Norway. Two men pit wills against the landscape & each other in a spectacular chase over the snow-clad wastes.

Blue Jackal - The Foolish Lion. Naseeruddin Shah. 1 cass. (Running Time: 048 min.). (Karadi Tales Ser.). (YA). (gr. 1 up). 1998. bk. 15.99 (978-81-86838-00-6(7)) APG.

Asian fairy tales & folklore.

Blue Jay, Blue Jay. Paul Strausman. 1 cass. (J). 1999. (GW1060) NewSound.

Blue Jay Blue Jay: Play Along Activity Songs for the Younger Years. Paul Strausman. (J). 1997. audio compact disk 14.95 (978-0-939065-66-0(5)) Gentle Wind.

Blue Jay Blue Jay: Play Along Activity Songs for the Younger Years. unabr. ed. Paul Strausman. Perf. by Paul Strausman. 1 cass. (Running Time: 47 min.). (J). (ps). 1997. 9.95 (978-0-939065-59-2(2), GW1060) Gentle Wind.

Participation songs with learning activities; musical version of "The Three Little Pigs".

Blue Jelly, Set. unabr. ed. Debby Bull. Read by Debby Bull. 2 cass. (Running Time: 3 hrs.). 1997. 16.95 (978-1-57511-024-0(5)) Pub Mills.

The author, a former writer for Rolling Stone magazine, searches the world for a cure to the depression she finds herself in after the break up of her relationship & finds it in canning. A hysterically funny look at modern romance & the new cultural landscape.

Blue Lagoon: A Romance. abr. ed. Henry DeVere Stacpoole. 2 cass. (Running Time: 1 hr. 49 min.). 12.95 (978-0-89926-164-5(7), 857) Audio Bk.

The charming story of two children marooned on a South Seas Island.

Blue Last. unabr. ed. Martha Grimes. 9 cass. (Running Time: 13 hrs. 30 min.). (Richard Jury Novel Ser.). 2001. 72.00 (978-0-7366-7641-0(4)) Books on Tape.

Was a brewing magnate's granddaughter killed in the London Blitz and replaced by an imposter?.

Blue Last. unabr. ed. Martha Grimes. 11 CDs. (Running Time: 13 hrs. 30 min..). (Richard Jury Novel Ser.). 2001. audio compact disk 88.00 (978-0-7366-8010-3(1)) Books on Tape.

Blue Level Audiocassettes. (Individual Components Ser.). 155.00 (978-0-8092-9461-9(3)) M-H Contemporary.

Blue Light. Walter Mosley. 2002. (978-1-57042-961-3(8)) Hachet Audio.

Blue Light imagines a world in which human potential is suddenly, amazingly fulfilled a change that calls into question the meaning of human differences and the ultimate purpose and fate of the human race.

Blue Light. abr. ed. Walter Mosley. (Running Time: 3 hrs.). (ENG.). 2006. 14.98 (978-1-59483-669-5(8)) Pub: Hachet Audio. Dist(s): HachBkGrp

Blue Light. unabr. ed. Walter Mosley. Narrated by Richard Ferrone. 8 cass. (Running Time: 10 hrs. 45 mins.). 1999. 75.00 (978-0-7887-2911-9(X), 95540E7) Recorded Bks.

Offers the mind-expanding concepts of the best science fiction & the satisfying elements of serious literature. Hypnotic prophets, messenger coyotes, & blood rituals are among the imaginative elements.

Blue Like Jazz: Non-Religious Thoughts on Christian Spirituality. unabr. ed. Donald Miller. (Running Time: 7 hrs. 48 mins. 0 sec.). (ENG.). 2007. audio compact disk 19.98 (978-1-59644-543-7(2), Hovel Audio) christianaud.

Blue Like Jazz: Nonreligious Thoughts on Christian Spirituality. abr. ed. Donald Miller. Read by Donald Miller. (Running Time: 18000 sec.). 2007. audio compact disk 24.99 (978-0-7852-1626-1(X)) Nelson.

***Blue Like Jazz: Nonreligious Thoughts on Christian Spirituality.** unabr. ed. Donald Miller. Narrated by Scott Brick. (ENG.). 2007. 14.98 (978-1-59644-544-4(0), Hovel Audio) christianaud.

Blue Mars, Vol. 3. collector's ed. Kim Stanley Robinson. Narrated by Richard Ferrone. 22 cass. (Running Time: 32 hrs.). 2002. 79.95 (978-1-4025-1519-4(7), 96113) Recorded Bks.

The once red and barren terrain of Mars is now green and rich with life - plant, animal, and human. But idyllic Mars is in a state of political upheaval, plagued by violent conflict between those who would keep the planet green and those who want to return it to a desert world. Meanwhile, across the void of space, old, tired Earth spins on its decaying axis. A natural disaster threatens to drown the already far too polluted and overcrowded planet. The people of Earth are getting desperate. Maybe desperate enough to wage interplanetary war for the chance to begin again.

Blue Mars, Vol. 3. unabr. ed. Kim Stanley Robinson. Narrated by Richard Ferrone. 22 cass. (Running Time: 32 hrs.). 2002. 171.00 (978-1-4025-1512-5(X)) Recorded Bks.

Blue Max. unabr. ed. Jack D. Hunter. Read by Tom Parker. 7 cass. (Running Time: 10 hrs.). 1995. 49.95 (978-0-7861-0664-6(6), 1565) Blckstn Audio.

Most coveted decoration in all of Germany, the Blue Max was the symbol of power, fame & prestige beyond ordinary mortals. This is the story of the men who killed for it - & died for it. Stachel - murderer & alcoholic. His meteoric rise to glory alienated him from his fellow pilots - & ultimately from human decency. Kettering - collector of pornography. He became the victim of Stachel's ruthless ambition. Von Klugermann - the haughty aristocrat. He delved too deeply into Stachel's torment, only to discover a cobra. Kaeti - the woman who knew them all. Stachel's beautiful mistress, she was an arrogant noblewoman - & a blackmailing nymphomaniac.

Blue Mirror. unabr. ed. 3 cassettes. (Running Time: 3:45 hrs). (J). 2004. 28.75 (978-1-4025-9933-0(1)) Recorded Bks.

Blue Moon. Luanne Rice. Narrated by Tom Stechschulte. 8 cass. (Running Time: 11 hrs. 30 mins.). 72.00 (978-1-4025-3429-4(9)) Recorded Bks.

Blue Moon. abr. ed. Laurell K. Hamilton. (Running Time: 9 hrs.). (Anita Blake, Vampire Hunter Ser.: No. 8). (ENG.). 2010. audio compact disk 29.95 (978-0-14-314431-1(6), PengAudBks) Penguin Grp USA.

Blue Moon. unabr. ed. Laurell K. Hamilton. (Running Time: 15 hrs.). (Anita Blake, Vampire Hunter Ser.: No. 8). (ENG.). 2010. audio compact disk 39.95 (978-0-14-314408-3(1), PengAudBks) Penguin Grp USA.

***Blue Moon.** unabr. ed. Alyson Noël. (Immortals Ser.: Bk. 2). (YA). 2009. 8.99 (978-1-4272-0843-9(3)) Pub: Macmill Audio. Dist(s): Macmillan

Blue Moon. unabr. ed. Alyson Noël. Read by Katie Schorr. 7 CDs. (Running Time: 8 hrs. 0 mins. 0 sec.). (Immortals Ser.: Bk. 2). (YA). (gr. 7-12). 2009. audio compact disk 17.99 (978-1-4272-0842-2(5)) Pub: Macmill Audio. Dist(s): Macmillan

Blue Moon Rising: Part 1 Of 3, Vol. 1. Simon R. Green. 2009. audio compact disk 19.99 (978-1-59950-576-3(2)) GraphicAudio.

Blue Moon Rising: Part 2 Of 3, Vol. 2. Simon R. Green. 2009. audio compact disk 19.99 (978-1-59950-587-9(8)) GraphicAudio.

Blue Moon Rising: Part 3 Of 3, Vol. 3. Based on a novel by Simon R. Green. 2009. audio compact disk 19.99 (978-1-59950-606-7(8)) GraphicAudio.

Blue Moon Valley. Stephen Rabley. 1 cass. (Running Time: 1 hr. 30 mins.). (978-0-582-05860-6(0), PutnaJuv) Penguin Grp USA.

Blue Moose. unabr. ed. Daniel M. Pinkwater. Read by Marshall Dodge. 1 cass. (Running Time: 27 mins.). (Follow the Reader Ser.). (J). (gr. 1-3). 1981. pap. bk. 17.00 incl. bk., guide. (978-0-8072-0000-1(X), FTR50SP, Listening Lib) Random Audio Pubg.
Even though Mr. Breton runs a fine restaurant on the edge of the woods, he's very lonely. Then a moose, with a connoisseur's palate & a diplomats way with the customers wanders in to lend the place a touch of class.

Blue Moose & Wizard Crystal. Daniel M. Pinkwater. 1 cass. (Running Time: 46 min.). (J). 10.95 (AO-160, HarperThor) HarpC GBR.

Blue Mountain. unabr. ed. Meir Shalev. Narrated by George Guidall. 11 cass. (Running Time: 16 hrs. 15 mins.). 1992. 91.00 (978-1-55690-750-0(8), 92116E7) Recorded Bks.
Mirkin, Liberson, Tsirkin & Feyge are four pioneers who emigrate to Israel in the early years of the century. Their story is the story of a nation's beginnings.

Blue Murder. unabr. ed. Graham Ison. Read by Nigel Graham. 6 cass. (Running Time: 9 hrs.). 2001. 54.95 (978-0-7531-0538-2(1), 990204) Pub: ISIS Audio GBR. Dist(s): Ulverscroft US

Blue Nile. unabr. ed. Alan Moorehead. Read by Ian Whitcomb. 8 cass. (Running Time: 12 hrs.). 1976. 64.00 (978-0-7366-0011-8(6), 1021) Books on Tape.
"The Blue Nile" is Moorehead's study of the history of the Nile in the 19th century. The river is used as a framework to recount four thrilling expeditions: James Bruce, the Scotsman who fixed the source of the Nile in 1770; Napoleon's invasion of Egypt in 1798; Mohammed Ali's campaigns in the Sudan in the early 1820's & Napier's thrust against the Ethiopian emperor Theodore at Magadala in 1868.

Blue Nile. unabr. ed. Alan Moorehead. Narrated by Patrick Tull. 8 cass. (Running Time: 12 hrs.). 1988. 70.00 (978-1-55690-062-4(7), 88620E7) Recorded Bks.
A history of the Nile & the events along its banks from 1798 to 1869.

Blue Note. Charlotte Bingham. Read by Judy Bennett. 12 CDs. (Running Time: 15 hrs.). 2001. audio compact disk 110.95 (978-0-7540-5433-7(0), CCD 124) Pub: Chivers Audio Bks GBR. Dist(s): AudioGO
During wartime three orphans are sent to live with sisters. But when the Committee for Evacuation objects to the spinsters' attempt to adopt them, all three children are parted - seemingly forever.

Blue Note. unabr. ed. Charlotte Bingham. Read by Judy Bennett. 12 cass. (Running Time: 18 hrs.). 2001. 96.95 (978-0-7540-0660-2(3), CAB 2082) Pub: Chivers Audio Bks GBR. Dist(s): AudioGO
It is wartime and Miranda, little Cockney orphan Ted and Bobbie have been evacuated to an old-fashioned household in the country. Despite the war, the children's time spent with two unmarried sisters at their rectory is idyllic. But when the local committee for evacuation objects to the spinsters' attempt to adopt all three children, it is Bobbie who is reluctantly sent away.

Blue Notebook. unabr. ed. James A. Levine. Read by Meera Simhan. (ENG.). 2009. audio compact disk 34.95 (978-0-7393-8279-0(9), Random AudioBks) Pub: Random Audio Pubg. Dist(s): Random

Blue Nowhere. Jeffery Deaver. Read by Dennis Boutsikaris. 2004. 15.95 (978-0-7435-4209-8(6)) Pub: S&S Audio. Dist(s): S and S Inc

Blue Nowhere. unabr. ed. Jeffery Deaver. Read by William Dufris. 10 vols. (Running Time: 15 hrs.). 2001. bk. 84.95 (978-0-7927-2477-3(1), CSL 366, Chivers Sound Lib); audio compact disk 110.95 (978-0-7927-9921-4(6), SLD 072, Chivers Sound Lib) AudioGO.
When a sadistic hacker, code-named Phate, sets his sights on Silicon Valley, his victims never know what hit them. He infiltrates their computers, invades their lives, and - with chilling precision - lures them to their deaths. Now Phate is challenging himself anew - by taking his methodology to a new level, with bigger targets.

Blue Ocean Strategy: How to Create Uncontested Market Space & Make the Competition Irrelevant. unabr. ed. W. Chan Kim & Renee Mauborgne. Read by Grover Gardner. (Running Time: 6 hrs. 30 mins.). (ENG.). 2007. 24.98 (978-1-59659-179-0(X), GildAudio) Pub: Gildan Media. Dist(s): HachBkGrp

Blue Ocean Strategy: How to Create Uncontested Market Space & Make the Competition Irrelevant. unabr. rev. ed. W. Chan Kim & Renee Mauborgne. (Running Time: 6 hrs.). (ENG.). 2006. audio compact disk 29.98 (978-1-59659-068-7(8), GildAudio) Pub: Gildan Media. Dist(s): HachBkGrp

Blue Religion: New Stories about Cops, Criminals, & the Chase. unabr. ed. Michael Connelly. Narrated by John Lee et al. (Running Time: 12 hrs. 0 mins. 0 sec.). (ENG.). 2008. audio compact disk 69.99 (978-1-4001-3719-0(5)); audio compact disk 24.99 (978-1-4001-5719-8(6)) Pub: Tantor Media. Dist(s): IngramPubServ

Blue Religion: New Stories about Cops, Criminals, & the Chase. unabr. ed. Read by Alan Sklar et al. Ed. by Michael Connelly. (Running Time: 12 hrs. 0 mins. 0 sec.). (ENG.). 2008. audio compact disk 34.99 (978-1-4001-0719-3(9)) Pub: Tantor Media. Dist(s): IngramPubServ

Blue Road to Atlantis. unabr. ed. Jay Nussbaum. 3 cass. (Running Time: 4 hrs. 30 mins.). 2002. 28.00 (978-0-7366-8719-5(X)); audio compact disk 32.00 (978-0-7366-8720-1(3)) Books on Tape.
A lighthearted yet moving allegory about leading a more fulfilling life. By setting forth the idea that the quest for a higher vision and the acceptance of life's currents brings true peace and happiness, this contemporary tale becomes a profound meditation that is as entertaining as it is transformational. Jay Nussbaum is a lifelong martial artist, most recently teaching a course at Cornell University that explored the connection between martial arts and the soul.

Blue Rose. Anthony Eglin. 8 cass. (Running Time: 11 hrs.). (Soundings Ser.). (J). 2005. 69.95 (978-1-84559-030-7(9)) Pub: ISIS Lrg Prnt GBR. Dist(s): Ulverscroft US

Blue Sapphire. unabr. ed. D. E. Stevenson. Read by Hilary Neville. 10 cass. (Running Time: 43200 sec.). (Soundings Ser.). 2006. 84.95 (978-1-84559-111-3(9)) Pub: ISIS Lrg Prnt GBR. Dist(s): Ulverscroft US

Blue Screen. abr. unabr. ed. Robert B. Parker. Read by Kate Burton. 5 CDs. (Running Time: 21600 sec.). (Sunny Randall Ser.: No. 5). (ENG.). 2006. audio compact disk 29.95 (978-0-7393-2460-8(8), Random AudioBks) Pub: Random Audio Pubg. Dist(s): Random

Blue Screen. unabr. ed. Robert B. Parker. 4 cass. (Running Time: 6 hrs.). (Sunny Randall Ser.: No. 5). 2006. 36.00 (978-1-4159-3057-1(0)); audio compact disk 45.00 (978-1-4159-3058-8(9)) Books on Tape.

Blue Seed. 2002. audio compact disk 14.98 (978-1-57813-394-9(7)) A D Vision.

Blue Sequin see Classic Detective Stories, Vol. III, A Collection

Blue Shoe. unabr. ed. Anne Lamott. Read by Laural Merlington. 7 cass. (Running Time: 10 hrs.). 2002. 32.95 (978-1-59086-351-0(8), 1590863518, BAU); 82.25 (978-1-59086-352-7(6), 1590863526, Unabridge Lib Edns); audio compact disk 38.95 (978-1-59086-354-1(2), 1590863542, CD Unabridged); audio compact disk 97.25 (978-1-59086-355-8(0), 1590863550, CD Unabrid Lib Ed) Brilliance Audio.
Mattie Ryder is a marvelously funny, well-intentioned, religious, sarcastic, tender, angry, and broke recently divorced mother of two young children. Then she finds a small rubber blue shoe - the kind you might get from a gumball machine - and a few other trifles that were left years ago in her father's car. They seem to hold the secrets to her messy upbringing, and as she and her brother follow these clues to uncover the mystery of their past, she begins to open her heart to her difficult, brittle mother and the father she thought she knew. And with that acceptance comes an opening up to the possibilities of romantic love. In a disarming blend of everyday life and the sublime, of reverence and irreverence, and of humor and grace, Anne Lamott speaks directly to our most closely held concerns, bringing comfort to anyone - all of us - whose family life can feel overwhelming and uncontainable.

Blue Shoe. unabr. ed. Anne Lamott. Read by Laural Merlington. 8 CDs. (Running Time: 10 hrs.). 2004. 39.25 (978-1-59335-570-8(X), 159335570X, Brlnc Audio MP3 Lib) Brilliance Audio.

Blue Shoe. unabr. ed. Anne Lamott. Read by Laural Merlington. (Running Time: 10 hrs.). 2004. 39.25 (978-1-59710-097-7(8), 1597100978, BADLE); 24.95 (978-1-59710-096-0(X), 159710096X, BAD) Brilliance Audio.

Blue Shoe. unabr. ed. Anne Lamott. Read by Laural Merlington. (Running Time: 10 hrs.). 2004. 24.95 (978-1-59335-057-4(0), 1593350570) Soulmate Audio Bks.

Blue Shoes & Happiness. Narrated by Lisette Lecat. (Running Time: 29700 sec.). (No. 1 Ladies' Detective Agency Ser.: Bk. 7). 2006. 24.99 (978-1-4193-7567-5(9)) Recorded Bks.

Blue Shoes & Happiness. unabr. ed. Read by Lisette Lecat. 7 CDs. (Running Time: 29700 sec.). (No. 1 Ladies' Detective Agency Ser.: Bk. 7). 2006. audio compact disk 29.99 (978-1-4193-7536-1(9)) Recorded Bks.

Blue Skies, French Fries. unabr. ed. Judy Delton. Narrated by Christina Moore. 1 cass. (Running Time: 1 hr.). (Pee Wee Scouts Ser.: No. 4). (gr. 2-5). 1998. 10.00 (978-0-7887-0750-6(7), 94927E7) Recorded Bks.
Molly & the other scouts get a big surprise. They are going to play a football game against another Pee Wee Scount troop! They practice every day, but can they win the big game?.

Blue Skin of the Sea, unabr. ed. Graham Salisbury. Narrated by Jeff Woodman. 5 pieces. (Running Time: 7 hrs. 30 mins.). (gr. 5 up). 1994. 44.00 (978-0-7887-0131-3(2), 94356E7) Recorded Bks.
A portrait of what it was like to grow up in 1960s Hawaii. Captures the humor & drama of one boy's story of shark hunts, first kisses & unpredictable family adventures.

Blue Sky City. Skip West. 1 cass. (Running Time: 40 min.). (J). (ps-2). 1992. pap. bk. 9.98 (978-0-9660947-5-6(1), EK5002); audio compact disk 14.98 (978-1-893967-00-7(X)) Emphasis Ent.
Wide variety of musical styles with kid-centered themes.

Blue Smoke. abr. ed. Nora Roberts. Read by Joyce Bean. (Running Time: 21600 sec.). 2006. audio compact disk 16.99 (978-1-59600-870-0(9), 9781596008700) Brilliance Audio.
Please enter a Synopsis.

Blue Smoke. unabr. ed. Nora Roberts. Read by Joyce Bean. (Running Time: 14 hrs.). 2005. 39.25 (978-1-59710-928-4(2), 9781597109284, BADLE); 24.95 (978-1-59710-929-1(0), 9781597109291, BAD); 97.25 (978-1-59600-182-4(8), 9781596001824, BriIAudUnabridg); audio compact disk 39.95 (978-1-59600-184-8(4), 9781596001848, Bril Audio CD Unabri); audio compact disk 112.25 (978-1-59600-185-5(2), 9781596001855, BriAudCD Unabrid); audio compact disk 39.25 (978-1-59335-959-1(4), 9781593359591, Brlnc Audio MP3 Lib); audio compact disk 24.95 (978-1-59335-958-4(6), 9781593359584, Brilliance MP3) Brilliance Audio.
In the newest novel by #1 New York Times bestselling author Nora Roberts, arson investigator Catarina Hale is called in on a series of suspicious fires that seem to be connected - not just to each other, but to her.

***Blue Smoke & Murder.** unabr. ed. Elizabeth Lowell. Read by Carol Monda. (ENG.). 2008. (978-0-06-163065-1(9)); (978-0-06-163066-8(7)) HarperCollins Pubs.

Blue Smoke & Murder. unabr. ed. Elizabeth Lowell. Read by Carol Monda. (Running Time: 36000 sec.). 2008. audio compact disk 39.95 (978-0-06-155749-1(8), Harper Audio) HarperCollins Pubs.

Blue Smoke & Murder. unabr. ed. Elizabeth Lowell. Read by Carol Monda. 2009. audio compact disk 19.99 (978-0-06-172755-9(5), Harper Audio) HarperCollins Pubs.

Blue Star. unabr. ed. Tony Earley. Narrated by Kirby Heyborne. 6 CDs. (Running Time: 7 hrs.). 2008. audio compact disk 80.00 (978-1-4159-4943-6(3), BksonTape) Pub: Random Audio Pubg. Dist(s): Random
Eight years ago, readers everywhere fell in love with Jim Glass, the precocious ten-year-old at the heart of Jim the Boy. Now a teenager, Jim returns in a tender and wise story of young love on the brink of World War Two. Jim Glass has fallen in love, as only a teenage boy can fall in love, with his classmate Chrissie Steppe. Unfortunately, Chrissie is Bucky Bucklaw's girlfriend, and Bucky has joined the navy on the eve of war. Jim vows to win Chrissie's heart in Bucky's absence, but the war makes high school less than a safe haven and gives a young man's emotions a grown man's gravity. When Bucky returns to Aliceville a fallen hero, Jim finds himself adrift in a once-familiar town where everything, including Chrissie, seems to be changing.

Blue Streak. unabr. ed. Heather McHugh. Read by Heather McHugh. 1 cass. (Running Time: 59 min.). (Watershed Tapes of Contemporary Poetry). 1980. 12.95 (23646) J Norton Pubs.
A performance from the recent winner of the Yale Younger Poets award.

Blue Suede Shoes: Elvis Songs for Kids. 1 cass. (Running Time: 90 mins.). (J). 2000. 9.98; audio compact disk 15.98 MFLP CA.
Child singers perform some of the King's biggest hits.

Blue Suede Sneakers: Elvis Songs (Not Just) for Kids! Perf. by Shari Lewis et al. 1 cass. (Running Time: 32 min.). (J). (ps-4). 1995. 7.99 (978-1-56896-108-8(1)); audio compact disk 11.99 CD. (978-1-56896-109-5(X)) Lightyear Entrtnmnt.
Several celebrities present Elvis hits with the purpose of introducing "Elvis' music to a new generation".

Blue Sword. Robin McKinley. (J). 1950. 34.66 (978-0-676-30662-0(4)) SRA McGraw.

Blue Sword, unabr. ed. Robin McKinley. Narrated by Diane Warren. 8 cass. (Running Time: 12 hrs.). (YA). (gr. 8). 72.00 (978-1-55690-616-9(1), 92309) Recorded Bks.
An orphan girl, finds her destiny among the descendants of Lady Aerin, she who wielded the blue sword. Available to libraries only.

Blue Turtle Moon Queen. unabr. ed. Pere Butter. Read by Plum Butter. 2 CDs. (Running Time: 2 hrs. 20 mins.). (Water Children Ser.: Vol. W-1). (J). (gr. 1-5). 2002. audio compact disk 11.00 (978-0-915090-92-1(9)) Firefall.
A San Francisco story of brothers and sisters, during the drought, told by a ten year old girl, who finds herself, in her new home.

Blue Water. A. Manette Ansay. (Isis (CDs) Ser.). 2006. audio compact disk 79.95 (978-0-7531-2611-0(7)) Pub: ISIS Lrg Prnt GBR. Dist(s): Ulverscroft US

Blue Water. Manette Ansay. Read by Laurel Lefkow. 7 cass. (Running Time: 8 hrs. 25 mins.). (Isis Cassettes Ser.). 2006. 61.95 (978-0-7531-3630-0(9)) Pub: ISIS Lrg Prnt GBR. Dist(s): Ulverscroft US

Blue Water Coaster. unabr. collector's ed. Francis E. Bowker. Read by Jonathan Reese. 8 cass. (Running Time: 8 hrs.). 1976. 48.00 (978-0-7366-0035-4(3), 1047) Books on Tape.
Captain "Biff" Bowker's book is the true story of two voyages undertaken in sailing schooners during the late 1930's. How it was 50 years ago in the closing days of sail is vividly recalled by Bowker in this year of a youth's adventures at sea. Blue Water Coaster is a shining testimony to man's ability to accomplish so much with so very little.

Blue Willow. abr. ed. Doris Gates. 1 cass. (Running Time: 51 mins.). Dramatization. (J). (gr. 4-7). 1972. 9.95 (978-0-670-17560-4(9)) Live Oak Media.
An account of migrant farm life in the fields of California as experienced by ten-year-old Janey Larkin.

Blue Willow, Set. abr. ed. Doris Gates. 11 vols. (Running Time: 51 mins.). Dramatization. (J). 1972. pap. bk. 15.95 (978-0-670-17562-8(5)) Live Oak Media.

Blue Yodel, Blue Heron. Jack Collom et al. 1 cass. (Running Time: 90 min.). 2002. audio compact disk 10.00 (978-1-887997-53-9(9)) Pub: Baksun Bks. Dist(s): SPD-Small Pr Dist

***Blue Zone.** abr. ed. Andrew Gross. Read by Ilyana Kadushin. (ENG.). 2007. (978-0-06-128744-2(X), Harper Audio); (978-0-06-128743-5(1), Harper Audio) HarperCollins Pubs.

Blue Zone. abr. ed. Andrew Gross. Read by Ilyana Kadushin. (Running Time: 21600 sec.). 2007. audio compact disk 29.95 (978-0-06-128561-5(7), Harper Audio) HarperCollins Pubs.

***Blue Zone.** unabr. ed. Andrew Gross. Read by Ilyana Kadushin. (ENG.). 2007. (978-0-06-128742-8(3), Harper Audio); (978-0-06-128741-1(5), Harper Audio) HarperCollins Pubs.

Blue Zone. unabr. ed. Andrew Gross. Read by Ilyana Kadushin. (Running Time: 32400 sec.). 2007. audio compact disk 39.95 (978-0-06-125658-5(7), Harper Audio) HarperCollins Pubs.

***Blue Zones: Lessons for Living Longer from the People Who've Lived the Longest.** Dan Buettner. (ENG.). 2010. audio compact disk 39.99 (978-1-61120-002-7(4)) Dreamscap OH.

***Blueback.** Tim Winton. Read by Stig Wemyss. (Running Time: 1 hr. 30 mins.). (J). 2009. 44.99 (978-1-74214-556-3(6), 9781742145563) Pub: Bolinda Pubng AUS. Dist(s): Bolinda Pub Inc

Blueback. unabr. ed. Tim Winton. Read by Stig Wemyss. 2 cass. (Running Time: 1 hr. 30 mins.). 2002. 24.00 (978-1-86340-795-3(2), 580234) Pub: Bolinda Pubng AUS. Dist(s): Lndmrk Audiobks
People learning from nature. A wise exploration of the difference between the acquisition of information & the quest for knowledge.

Blueback. unabr. ed. Tim Winton. Read by Stig Wemyss. 2 CDs. (Running Time: 1 hr. 30 mins.). (YA). (gr. 7 up). 2009. audio compact disk 43.95 (978-1-74214-359-0(8), 9781742143590) Pub: Bolinda Pubng AUS. Dist(s): Bolinda Pub Inc

Blueback. unabr. ed. Tim Winton. Read by Stig Wemyss. 2009. audio compact disk 43.95 (978-1-74214-543-3(4), 9781742145433) Pub: Bolinda Pubng AUS. Dist(s): Bolinda Pub Inc

Blueback, Set. unabr. ed. Bill Knox. 5 cass. (Storysound Ser.). (J). 1997. 49.95 (978-1-85903-156-8(0)) Pub: Mgna Lrg Print GBR. Dist(s): Ulverscroft US

Bluebeard see Cinderella & Other Fairy Tales

Bluebeard's Castle. unabr. ed. Gene Kemp. Read by Dominic Taylor. 3 CDs. (Running Time: 4 hrs. 30 mins.). (J). 2002. audio compact disk 29.95 (978-0-7540-6540-1(5), CHCD 040) AudioGO.

Bluebeard's Egg. unabr. ed. Margaret Atwood. Read by Bonnie Hurren. 8 cass. (Running Time: 12 hrs.). 2000. 69.95 (978-0-7540-0545-2(3), CAB 1968) AudioGO.
Funny & honest stories, as we discover a man who finds himself surrounded by women who are becoming paler, more silent & literally smaller; a woman's intimate life which is strangely dominated by the fear of nuclear warfare; a melancholy love that is swept away; as well as a tired, middle-aged affection which is rekindled by an unusual source.

Bluebells in the Windows. Susan Sallis. Read by Jacqueline King. 9 cass. (Running Time: 13 hrs. 30 min.). 2001. 79.95 (28874) Pub: Soundings Ltd GBR. Dist(s): Ulverscroft US

Blueberries for Sal. 2004. pap. bk. 32.75 (978-1-55592-193-4(0)); pap. bk. 32.75 (978-1-55592-194-1(9)); pap. bk. 14.95 (978-1-55592-718-9(1)); 8.95 (978-1-56008-847-9(8)); 8.95 (978-1-56008-136-4(8)); cass. & flmstrp 30.00 (978-0-89719-529-4(9)); audio compact disk 12.95 (978-1-55592-864-3(1)) Weston Woods.

Blueberries for Sal. (J). 2004. bk. 24.95 (978-0-89719-860-8(3)); pap. bk. 18.95 (978-1-55592-799-8(8)); pap. bk. 18.95 (978-1-55592-767-7(X)); pap. bk. 38.75 (978-1-55592-816-2(1)); pap. bk. 38.75 (978-1-55592-782-0(3)) Weston Woods.

Blueberries for Sal. Robert McCloskey. Read by Frank Scardino. 1 cass. (Running Time: 30 mins.). (J). 2000. pap. bk. 19.97 (978-0-7366-9193-2(6)) Books on Tape.

Blueberries for Sal. Robert McCloskey. Illus. by Robert McCloskey. 14 vols. (Running Time: 10 mins.). 1983. pap. bk. 39.95 (978-1-59112-695-9(9)); 9.95 (978-1-59112-015-5(2)); audio compact disk 12.95 (978-1-59112-692-8(4)) Live Oak Media.

Blueberries for Sal. Robert McCloskey. Read by Frank Scardino. 11 vols. (Running Time: 10 mins.). (Live Oak Readalong Ser.). (J). 2004. pap. bk. 18.95 (978-1-59112-693-5(2)) Pub: Live Oak Media. Dist(s): AudioGO

Blueberries for Sal. Robert McCloskey. 1 cass. (Running Time: 9 min.). (J). bk. 24.95; pap. bk. 32.75 Weston Woods.

Blueberries for Sal. Robert McCloskey. 1 cass. (Running Time: 9 min.). (J). (ps-k). pap. bk. 12.95 (RAC041) Weston Woods.
A little girl & a little bear on a blueberry picking trip get all mixed up with each other's mothers on a lovely hillside in Maine.

Blueberries for Sal. Robert McCloskey. 1 read-along cass. (Running Time: 9 min.). (J). 2004. pap. bk. 14.95 (978-1-56008-048-0(5), PRA041) Weston Woods.

Blueberries for Sal. unabr. ed. Robert McCloskey. Read by Frank Scardino. 11 vols. (Running Time: 10 mins.). (J). (gr. k-3). 1978. bk. 25.95 (978-0-670-17594-9(3)); pap. bk. 16.95 (978-0-670-17598-7(6)); pap. bk. & tchr. ed. 37.95 Reading Chest. (978-0-670-17593-2(5)) Live Oak Media.

Blueberries for Sal. unabr. ed. Robert McCloskey. Narrated by Christina Moore. 1 cass. (Running Time: 15 mins.). (J). 2001. pap. bk. & stu. ed. 30.24 Recorded Bks.
One summer day, Sal & her mother climb Blueberry Hill to pick berries for winter. So do a mother bear & her cub.

Blueberries for Sal. unabr. ed. Robert McCloskey. Narrated by Christina Moore. 1 cass. (Running Time: 15 mins.). (gr. 1 up). 2001. 15.00 (978-0-7887-4672-7(3), 96382E7) Recorded Bks.

Blueberries for Sal; Don't Count Your Chicks; Harold & the Purple Crayon; Play with Me. 2004. (978-0-89719-811-0(5)); cass. & flmstrp (978-0-89719-720-5(8)) Weston Woods.

Bluebird & the Sparrow. unabr. ed. Janette Oke. Narrated by Cheryl Haas. 6 cass. (Running Time: 8 hrs.). 1997. 51.00 (978-0-7887-0479-6(6), 94672E7) Recorded Bks.
Glenna is beautiful, charming & outgoing. Her older sister Berta is none of these things. Berta has spent much of her life making herself into the opposite of her adorable sister. But soon, Berta will need to examine her heart for the true reason she tries so desperately to be different from Glenna.

***Bluebirds in Your Backyard: A Basic Guide.** Karen Jean Matsko Hood. (ENG.). 2011. audio compact disk 24.95 (978-1-59434-900-3(2)) Whsprng Pine.

Bluebirds the Music: Beautiful Love Songs. David Frasure. Perf. by Karen Kelly & Ken Hamilton. 1 cass. 1990. 12.95 (978-1-56087-068-5(0)) Top Mtn Pub.
Program 1: Once Again, Who Am I, Bluebirds, Today over the Hill, Look Ma...I Am Flying! Program 2: Marjorie, Time for One Another, Learning What Love Is All About.

Bluebonnet: Bluebonnet of the Hill Country, Bluebonnet at the Alamo, Bluebonnet at the State Fair of Texas. Mary Brooke Casad. (ENG.). (J). 2007. 5.00 (978-1-60339-125-2(8)); audio compact disk 5.00 (978-1-60339-126-9(6)) Listenr Digest.

Bluebonnet Girl. unabr. ed. Michael Lind. Narrated by Richard Poe. 1 cass. (Running Time: 15 min.). 2003. 10.00 (978-1-4025-6206-8(3)) Recorded Bks.
When the rains do not return to the prairie one spring, and the buffalo wander away from the brown grasses, the People grow thin and weak. Spirit Talker tells them that they are being punished for their greed, but they refuse to give up the possessions they treasure most. Can one small girl and her doll with its bonnet of blue jay feathers save her people?.

Bluebook of Cleaning, Reconstruction & Repair Costs: The Bottom Line in Estimating, Cleaning, Repairs & Remodeling. Daniel E. Josipovich. 1999. pap. bk. 64.95 (978-0-918767-03-5(2)) Bluebk Intl.

Bluebottle: A Lew Griffin Mystery. unabr. ed. James Sallis. (Running Time: 5 hrs. 0 mins.). (ENG.). 2009. 19.95 (978-1-4332-3017-2(8)); 34.95 (978-1-4332-3013-4(5)); audio compact disk 40.00 (978-1-4332-3014-1(3)) Blckstn Audio.

Bluegate Fields. unabr. ed. Anne Perry. Narrated by Davina Porter. 8 cass. (Running Time: 10 hrs. 45 mins.). (Thomas Pitt Ser.). 2002. 72.00 (978-1-4025-3604-5(6)) Recorded Bks.

Bluegrass. Friedman. (CD Ser.). 2001. bk. 16.98 (978-1-56799-356-1(7), Friedman-Fairfax) M Friedman Pub Grp Inc.

Bluegrass Band Method, Bk. 1. 5th rev. ed. Jack Hatfield. (Running Time: 74 min.). 1998. pap. bk. 8.00 (978-1-892531-02-5(X), BBM-1 TAPE) Hatfield Mus.
Demonstration, slow & fast, of accompanying instruction book. Rhythm & Banjo on separate channels.

Bluegrass Banjo. Peter Wernick. 2004. audio compact disk 29.95 (978-0-8256-0148-4(7), OK62778) Pub: Music Sales. Dist(s): H Leonard

Bluegrass Banjo for the Complete Ignoramus! Wayne Erbsen. (For the Complete Ignoramus! Ser.). (ENG., 2004. pap. bk. 17.95 (978-1-883206-44-4(8)) Native Ground.

Bluegrass Banjo Method, Bk. 1. Jack Hatfield. 1 cass. (Running Time: 1 hr. 32 min.). 1998. 8.00 (978-0-9651623-1-9(1)); audio compact disk 15.00 CD. (978-1-892531-01-8(1), BBM1-CD) Hatfield Mus.

Bluegrass Banjo Method, Bk. 1. 5th l.t. rev. ed. Jack Hatfield. 1 CD. (Running Time: 90 mins.). 1998. pap. bk. 28.00 (978-1-892531-03-2(8), BBM-1 BCD) Hatfield Mus.

Bluegrass Banjo Method, Bk. 2. Jack Hatfield. 1 cass. (Running Time: 1 hr. 32 min.). 1994. 8.00 (978-0-9651623-4-0(6)) Hatfield Mus.
Slow-fast demonstration of all musical examples in Bluegrass Band Method, Bk. 2. Banjo on one channel. Rhythm instruments on the other.

Bluegrass Banjo Method, Bk. 2. Jack Hatfield. 1 cass. (Running Time: 60 mins.). 1994. pap. bk. 22.00 (978-0-9651623-5-7(4)) Hatfield Mus.

Bluegrass Classics 1946-1948. 1 cass. (Sandy Hook Release Ser.: No. 113). 1989. 7.98 (CSH-2113) Radiola Co.
Featuring Bill Monroe & the Bluegrass Boys, Birch Monroe, Lester Flatt, Earl Scruggs, Chubby Wise, Cedric Rainwater.

Bluegrass Essentials. 1 cass., 1 CD. 8.78 (HIPO 40102); audio compact disk 13.58 CD. (HIPO 40102) NewSound.

***Bluegrass Fiddle & Beyond: Etudes & Ideas for the Modern Fiddler.** Matt Glaser. (ENG.). 2010. pap. bk. 19.99 (978-0-87639-108-2(0), 0876391080, Berklee Pr); pap. bk. 19.99 (978-1-4234-9707-3(4), 1423497074, Berklee Pr) H Leonard.

Bluegrass Spirit: Twelve Songs of Faith. 2002. audio compact disk Rounder Records.

Blue/Orange. Joe Penhall. Contrib. by Daniel Davis et al. (Running Time: 6720 sec.). 2005. audio compact disk 25.95 (978-1-58081-338-9(0)) L A Theatre.

***Blueprint: A Plan for Living above Life's Storms.** unabr. ed. Kirk Franklin. Read by Dion Graham. (Running Time: 8 hrs.). 2010. 24.99 (978-1-4418-5791-0(5), 9781441857910, Brilliance MP3); 14.99 (978-1-4418-5793-4(1), 9781441857934, BAD); 39.97 (978-1-4418-5792-7(3), 9781441857927, Brlnc Audio MP3 Lib); 39.99 (978-1-4418-5794-1(X), 9781441857941, BADLE); audio compact disk 29.99 (978-1-4418-5789-7(3), 9781441857897, Bril Audio CD Unabri); audio compact disk 79.97 (978-1-4418-5790-3(7), 9781441857903, BriAudCD Unabrid) Brilliance Audio.

***Blueprint: Obama's Plan to Subvert the Constitution & Build an Imperial Presidency.** unabr. ed. Ken Blackwell & Ken Klukowski. Narrated by Kevin Foley. (Running Time: 10 hrs. 0 mins. 0 sec.). (ENG.). 2010. 24.99 (978-1-4001-6831-6(7)); 16.99 (978-1-4001-8831-4(8)); audio compact disk 34.99 (978-1-4001-1831-1(X)); audio compact disk 83.99 (978-1-4001-4831-8(6)) Pub: Tantor Media. Dist(s): IngramPubServ

Blueprint for Hot Guitar: Licks, Tricks & Techniques: A Crash Course in Professional Guitar Playing! Karl Aranjo. 2008. pap. bk. 19.95 (978-1-933657-64-6(2)) Pro Music In.

Blues. Nigel Williamson. 2008. audio compact disk 14.95 (978-1-906063-01-6(X)) Pub: Rough Guides GBR. Dist(s): PerseuPGW

Blues, unabr. ed. John Hersey. Narrated by Norman Dietz. 4 cass. (Running Time: 6 hrs. 30 mins.). 1989. 35.00 (978-1-55690-063-1(5), 89520E7) Recorded Bks.
"Bluefish," writes the author, are "animated chopping machines. They will eat anything alive. They have stripped the toes from surfers in Florida. They can't not eat." Hersey weaves fact & legend around his subject, engaging the listener with juicy details of ocean life, philosophy, natural history & the crises into which man has let his environment slide.

Blues: A Living Legend. 1 cass. (Running Time: 30 min.). 9.95 (HO-82-05-12, HarperThor) HarpC GBR.

Blues Acoustic Guitar Method. Brett Duncan. (Progressive Ser.). 1998. pap. bk. (978-1-875690-76-3(X)) Kolala Music SGP.

Blues Acoustic Guitar Method. Brett Duncan. (Progressive Ser.). 2004. pap. bk. 19.95 (978-1-86469-076-7(3), 256-027) Kolala Music SGP.

Blues & Jazz Complete. Bert Konowitz. (ENG.). 1999. audio compact disk 20.00 (978-0-7390-2515-4(5)) Alfred Pub.

Blues & Rock Solos for Guitar. Roger Filliberto, Jr. & Austin Sicard. 1996. bk. 9.95 (978-0-7866-2686-1(0), 96540BCD) Mel Bay.

Blue's Bastards: A True Story of Valor under Fire. unabr. ed. Randy Herrod. Read by Michael Wells. 5 cass. (Running Time: 7 hrs.). 1990. 39.95 (978-0-7861-0086-6(9), 1079) Blckstn Audio.
As a seventeen year old soldier in Vietnam, Randy Herrod fought in a platoon known as "Blue's Bastards," named after combat leader "Blue", Marine Lieutenant oliver North. During a fierce firefight, North, who was know for his conspicuous bravery & who always led from the front, was wounded. herrod dragged him back to safety, saving his life. Later, North performed a similar heroic deem, thus repaying Herrod's favor.

Blues, Beginning Guitar. Workshop Arts Staff. 1994. pap. bk. 18.90 (978-0-7390-1782-1(9), 4485) Alfred Pub.

Blue's Big Treasure Hunt. Rhino Records Staff. Based on a book by Angela C. Santomero. 1 cass. (Blue's Clues Ser.). (J). (ps-k). 1999. 6.98 (978-1-56826-929-0(3), 75625) Rhino Enter.
What is Blue's Favorite Treasure? A your preschooler listens to "Blue's Big Treasure" they'll help Steve play Blue's Clues and find out. They'll sing along with Steve, Blue, and all their friends Tickety Tock, Slippery Soap, Mailbox, Pail, and Shovel.

Blues, Boogie & Rock Guitar. Larry McCabe. 1997. spiral bd. 19.95 (978-0-7866-2769-1(7), 93996BCD) Mel Bay.

Blues Brothers - Trumpet. 2000. bk. 13.95 (978-1-85909-729-8(4), Warner Bro) Alfred Pub.

Blues Brothers Alto Sax. Blues Brothers. 2000. bk. 13.95 (978-1-85909-727-4(8), Warner Bro) Alfred Pub.

Blues Chops for Guitar. Ed. by Alfred Publishing. (ENG.). 2001. audio compact disk 10.95 (978-1-929395-42-2(6)) Pub: Workshop Arts. Dist(s): Alfred Pub

Blues City: A Walk in Oakland. unabr. ed. Ishmael Reed. 4 cass. (Running Time: 6 hrs.). 2003. 32.00 (978-0-7366-9417-9(X)) Books on Tape.
Welcome to one of America's most vibrant cities, what Ishmael Reed calls "planet city." He takes us behind the scenes of Oakland's Japanese jazz clubs and black cowboy parades, through its beautiful hills and waterfronts, and into its fascinating history. Although Oakland is often overshadowed by San Francisco, its neighbor across the Bay, it is an American wonder. The city is surrounded by natural beauty; its architecture mirrors its history as a Spanish mission, Gold Rush outpost, and early twentieth century home of the West's biggest robber barons.

Blues Classics for Acoustic Guitar. Steven Zdenek Eckels. 1997. pap. bk. 17.95 (978-0-7866-2878-0(2), 95273BCD) Mel Bay.

Blue's Clues: A Playdate with Blue. 1 cass. (Running Time: 44 mins.). (J). 2001. audio compact disk 13.98 (978-0-7379-0108-5(X), 79765) Rhino Enter.
Magenta's coming over! Blue and Magenta play a game of Blue's Clues to tell Steve what they want to do on their playdate. Preschoolers learn about friendship[p in a Blue's Clues musical way.

Blue's Clues: A Playdate with Blue. (J). 2002. 9.98 (978-0-7379-0107-8(1), 79764) Rhino Enter.

Blue's Clues: Blue's Big Musical Movie Soundtrack. Steve Burns. 1 CD. (Running Time: 1 hr. 30 mins.). (J). (ps). 2000. audio compact disk 16.98 (R2 79771) Rhino Enter.

Blue's Clues: Blue's Big Musical Movie Soundtrack. Steve Burns. 1 CD. (Running Time: 1 hr. 30 mins.). (J). (ps). 2001. 10.98 (R4 79770) Rhino Enter.

Blue's Clues: Blue's Big Musical Movie Soundtrack. deluxe ltd. ed. Steve Burns. 1 cass. (Running Time: 1 hr. 30 mins.). 2001. 14.98 (R4 79846) Rhino Enter.

Blue's Clues: Blue's Big Musical Movie Soundtrack. deluxe ltd. ed. Steve Burns. 1 CD. (Running Time: 1 hr. 30 mins.). (J). (ps). 2001. audio compact disk 19.98 (R2 79846) Rhino Enter.

Blue's Clues: Blue's Big Musical Playset. (J). 2002. pap. bk. 19.98 (978-0-7379-0144-3(6), 79846); 14.98 (978-0-7379-0145-0(4), 79846) Rhino Enter.
Includes Blue's Big Musicla movie sountrack and a special pop-up book with two interactive Blue's Big Musical stage settings and cut-out characters of Blue, Steve, and seven of their friends. Preschoolers can re-create a musical show of their own while listening to the soundtrack.

Blue's Clues: Blue's Big Musical Soundtrack. Perf. by Ray Charles & Persuasions, The. (J). 2002. 9.98 (978-0-7379-0137-5(3), 79770); audio compact disk 13.98 (978-0-7379-0128-3(4), 79771) Rhino Enter.
Preschoolers will sing, dance, and play with Steve, Blue and friends as they learn they can be anything they want to be. The music from Blue's first full-length feature movie will entertain kids and parents alike with a wide variety of musical styles.

Blue's Clues: Blue's Big Treasure. (J). 2002. audio compact disk 9.98 (978-1-56826-930-6(7), 75626) Rhino Enter.
What is Blue's Favorite Treasure? A your preschooler listens to "Blue's Big Treasure" they'll help Steve play Blue's Clues and find out. They'll sing along with Steve, Blue, and all their friends Tickety Tock, Slippery Soap, Mailbox, Pail, and Shovel.

Blue's Clues: Goodnight Blue. (J). 2002. pap. bk. 9.98 (978-0-7379-0055-2(5), 75840); pap. bk. 6.98 (978-0-7379-0054-5(7), 75840) Rhino Enter.
A nighttime adventure that musically captures a preschooler's bedtime routine. Also features the voices of Steve Burns, Blue, and all their friends and includes original music. Includes Goodnight Blue Mini-Activity Book.

Blue's Clues: What to Do, Blue? 1 cass. (Running Time: 1 hr.). (J). 2002. pap. bk. 7.98 (978-0-7379-0053-8(9), 75694) Rhino Enter.
Blue doesn't know what to do. All of he[illegible]nds are busy. But watching her friends gives Blue an idea, and she so[illegible]es up with something to do, all by herself! Includes a brand-new song, [illegible]ething to Do Stew," which is only available with this book and tape.

Blue's Clues: What to Do, Blue? Steve Burns. 1 cass. (Running Time: 1 hr. 30 mins.). (J). (ps). 2001. bk. 7.98 (R4 75694) Rhino Enter.

Blue's Clues - A Playdate with Blue. Steve Burns. 1 CD. (Running Time: 1 hr. 30 mins.). (J). (ps). 2001. 9.98 (R4 79764); audio compact disk 13.98 (R2 79765) Rhino Enter.

Blue's Clues - Blue's Big Treasure: A Musical Adventure. Steve Burns. 1 cass. (Running Time: 1 hr. 30 mins.). (J). (ps). 2001. 9.98 (R4 75625); audio compact disk 13.98 (R2 75626) Rhino Enter.

Blue's Clues - Goodnight Blue: A Nighttime Musical Adventure. Steve Burns. 1 cass. (Running Time: 1 hr. 30 mins.). (J). (ps). 2001. 9.98 (R4 75839); audio compact disk 13.98 (R2 75840) Rhino Enter.

Blues Dancing. unabr. ed. Diane McKinney-Whetstone. Narrated by Myra Lucretia Taylor. 9 cass. (Running Time: 11 hrs. 45 mins.). 1999. 81.00 (978-0-7887-5115-8(8), F0017L8) Recorded Bks.
Tells the steamy story of Verdi, whose 1970s relationship with street-smart Johnson leads her to the brink of destruction. Rescued by a conservative professor who gives up everything for her, Verdi lives a quiet, comfortable life for 20 years - until Johnson returns to re-ignite old passions.

Blues Drumming. Craig Lauritsen. (Progressive Ser.). 2004. pap. bk. 19.95 (978-1-86469-085-9(2), 256-030) Kolala Music SGP.

Blues Fiddle. Julie L. Lieberman. 1997. audio compact disk 19.95 (978-0-8256-0308-2(0), OK64162) Music Sales.

Blues from the Beginning: A Blues Method for the Absolute Beginner. Kimberly K. Allison. Rick Amaya. 2008. spiral bd. 30.00 (978-0-615-21724-6(9)) Starliner Mus.

Blues Guitar. Peter Gelling. (Progressive Ser.). 2004. pap. bk. 19.95 (978-1-86469-160-3(3), 256-031) Kolala Music SGP.

Blues Guitar Ear Training Course, Set. Brad Davis. 2 CDs. 2002. audio compact disk (99897CD) Mel Bay.

Blues Guitar for Adults: The Grown-Up Approach to Playing Guitar. Wayne Riker. 1 CD. (ENG.). 1999. audio compact disk 10.95 (978-1-929395-07-1(8)) Pub: Workshop Arts. Dist(s): Alfred Pub

Blues Guitar for Beginners. Drew Giorgi. (ENG.). 1997. audio compact disk 9.95 (978-0-7390-1787-6(X)) Alfred Pub.

Blues Guitar Lessons Vol. 1: Over 50 Great Lessons for the Beginning Blues Guitarist. Shea Welsh. 1 CD. (Running Time: 90 min.). 2000. per. 19.95 (978-1-929395-16-3(7)); audio compact disk 10.95 (978-1-929395-17-0(5)) Pub: Workshop Arts. Dist(s): Alfred Pub

Blues Guitar Lessons Vol. 2: Over 50 Great Lessons for the Intermediate Blues Guitarist. Shea Welsh. (ENG.). 2000. audio compact disk 10.95 (978-1-929395-20-0(5)) Pub: Workshop Arts. Dist(s): Alfred Pub

Blues Guitar Lessons Vol. 3: Over 50 Great Lessons for the Advanced Blues Guitarist. Tim Kobza. (ENG.). 2000. audio compact disk 10.95 (978-1-929395-23-1(X)) Pub: Workshop Arts. Dist(s): Alfred Pub

Blues Guitar Licks. Peter Gelling. (Progressive Ser.). 1998. pap. bk. 19.95 (978-1-875690-57-2(3)) Kolala Music SGP.

Blues Guitar Method, Level 2. David Barrett & John Garcia. 2008. pap. bk. 14.95 (978-0-7866-7638-5(8)) Mel Bay.

Blues Guitar Rules. Peter Fischer. audio compact disk 29.95 (978-3-927190-64-1(0), 701203) AMA Verlag DEU.

Blues Guitar Solos. Peter Gelling. (Progressive Ser.). 2004. pap. bk. 19.95 (978-1-875690-86-2(7), 256-033) Pub: Kolala Music SGP. Dist(s): Bookworld

Blues Harmonica Accompaniment Playing. David Barrett. (ENG.). 2009. pap. bk. 14.99 (978-0-7866-7637-8(X)) Mel Bay.

Blues Harmonica for Beginners. J. Fletcher. (ENG.). 1998. audio compact disk 10.00 (978-0-7390-2522-2(8)) Alfred Pub.

***Blues Harmonica Jam Tracks & Soloing Concepts #3 Book/CD Set: Level 3: Complete Blues Harmonica Lesson Series.** David Barrett. 2010. pap. bk. 14.99 (978-0-7866-5666-0(2)) Mel Bay.

Blues Harp. Phil Duncan. 1982. pap. bk. 17.95 (978-0-7866-0939-0(7), 93814P) Mel Bay.

Blues Harp. Phil Duncan. 1985. 9.98 (978-1-56222-355-7(0), 93814C) Mel Bay.

Blues Harp from Scratch. Mick Kinsella. 1 cass. (Running Time: 90 min.). (Learn to Play Ser.). 1998. audio compact disk 19.95 (978-0-7119-4706-1(6)) Pub: Music Sales. Dist(s): H Leonard

Blues Harp Greats. Transcribed by David Barrett. 2002. bk. 29.95 (978-0-7866-6626-3(9), 97324BCD) Mel Bay.

Blues Harp Songbook. Dieter Kropp. 2007. pap. bk. 19.95 (978-3-8024-0621-8(4)) Voggenreiter Pubs DEU.

Blues Harping. Composed by Dieter Kropp et al. (ENG.). 1999. pap. bk. 20.95 (978-3-920468-26-6(0), 3920468260) Pub: Schott Music Corp. Dist(s): H Leonard

Blues Improvising Techniques. Robert Laughlin. 1 cass. 1986. 12.00 (978-0-929983-12-7(2)) New Schl Am Music.
Seven ways that the beginner can start to improvise on the piano. Requires knowledge of basic blues form.

Blues in the Night. unabr. ed. Rochelle Krich. Read by Deanna Hurst. (Running Time: 9 hrs.). (Molly Blume Ser.). 2004. 39.25 (978-1-59710-098-4(6), 1597100986, BADLE); 24.95 (978-1-59710-099-1(4), 1597100994, BAD) Brilliance Audio.

Blues in the Night. unabr. ed. Rochelle Majer Krich. Read by Deanna Hurst. 6 cass. (Running Time: 9 hrs.). (Molly Blume Ser.: No. 1). 2002. 29.95 (978-1-59086-424-1(7), 1590864247, BAU); 74.25 (978-1-59086-425-8(5), 1590864255, Unabridge Lib Edns) Brilliance Audio.
An unidentified woman in a nightgown is the victim of a hit-and-run accident on Mulholland Drive that leaves her unconscious and seriously injured. The image of the young woman stumbling along a dark, winding road is one true-crime writer Molly Blume cannot shake. It draws her to a bedside in intensive care, where, before dying, the victim whispers three names: Robbie, Max, and Nina. It's not a smoking gun, but it is sufficient enough to reinforce Molly's gut instinct that there are sinister circumstances behind the assault on Lenore Saunders. With fearless conviction, Molly asks questions that nobody - including Lenore's mom, her ex-husband, her shrink, or even Molly's LAPD buddy, Detective Connors - wants to answer. Nevertheless,

the astute Molly discovers Lenore lived a fractured life, so different from Molly's own secure and loving Orthodox Jewish background. And as a chilling picture of the unfortunate woman begins to take shape, the menace of murders past and present stirs and quickens.

Blues in the Night. unabr. ed. Rochelle Majer Krich. Read by Deanna Hurst. (Running Time: 9 hrs.). (Molly Blume Ser.: No. 1). 2004. 39.25 (978-1-59335-577-7(7), 1593355777, Brlnc Audio MP3 Lib) Brilliance Audio.

Blues in the Night. unabr. ed. Rochelle Majer Krich. Read by Deanna Hurst. (Running Time: 9 hrs.). (Molly Blume Ser.: No. 1). 2004. 24.95 (978-1-59335-058-1(9), 1593350589) Soulmate Audio Bks.

Blues, Intermediate Guitar. Ed. by Workshop Arts Staff. 1994. pap. bk. 18.90 (978-0-7390-1810-1(8), 4486) Alfred Pub.

Blues Journey. Walter Dean Myers & Christopher Myers. (J). 2005. bk. 25.95 (978-1-59519-429-9(0)) Pub: Live Oak Media. Dist(s): AudioGO

Blues Keyboard Method. Peter Gelling. (Progressive Ser.). 1998. pap. bk. 19.95 (978-1-875690-61-9(1), 256-036) Kolala Music SGP.

Blues Legends. Charles K. Cowdery. 1995. bk. 19.95 (978-0-87905-688-9(6)) GibbsSmith Pub.

Blues Master Guitar. Workshop Arts Staff. 1994. pap. bk. 25.90 (978-0-7390-1821-7(3), 4487) Alfred Pub.

Blues... Naturally. 1 cass. (Running Time: 60 min.). 1994. audio compact disk 15.95 CD. (2344, Creativ Pub) Quayside.
Sounds of woods, water, & wildlife complement moody blues selections.

Blues... Naturally. 1 cass. (Running Time: 60 min.). 1994. 9.95 (2342, NrthWrd Bks) TandN Child.

Blues of Flats Brown. Walter Dean Myers. Illus. by Nina Laden. 11 vols. (Running Time: 21 mins.). 2002. bk. 28.95 (978-1-59112-424-5(7)); pap. bk. 39.95 (978-1-59112-601-0(0)); 9.95 (978-0-87499-939-6(1)); audio compact disk 12.95 (978-1-59112-403-0(4)) Live Oak Media.

Blues of Flats Brown. Walter Dean Myers. Illus. by Nina Laden. 11 vols. (Running Time: 21 mins.). (J). (ps-4). 2002. bk. 25.95 (978-0-87499-941-9(3)); pap. bk. & tchr.'s planning gde. ed. 37.95 (978-0-87499-942-6(1)) Live Oak Media.
Flats and Caleb, blues-pickin' junkyard dogs, play street corners and small clubs, from Memphis to New York City but can't seem to get away from their mean owner who keeps trying to drag them back home. Includes paperback book and teachers guide.

Blues of Flats Brown. Walter Dean Myers. Perf. by Charles Turner. 11 vols. (Running Time: 21 mins.). (Live Oak Readalong Ser.). (J). 2002. pap. bk. 18.95 (978-1-59112-404-7(2)) Pub: Live Oak Media. Dist(s): AudioGO

Blues of Flats Brown. Walter Dean Myers. Perf. by Charles Turner. 11 vols. (Running Time: 21 mins.). (Live Oak Readalong Ser.). (J). (ps-3). 2002. pap. bk. 16.95 (978-0-87499-940-2(5)) Pub: Live Oak Media. Dist(s): AudioGO

Blues of Ruby Matrix see Conrad Aiken Reading

Blues Piano Method. Peter Gelling. (Progressive Ser.). 2004. pap. bk. 19.95 (978-1-86469-207-5(3), 256-040) Kolala Music SGP.

Blues Rhythm Guitar Method. Peter Gelling. (Progressive Ser.). 1998. pap. bk. 23.95 (978-1-875690-59-6(X), 256-041) Kolala Music SGP.

Blues Riffs for Piano. 1 cass., 1 CD. (Great Riffs Ser.). bk. 14.95 (02503614); audio compact disk 17.95 CD & bk. (02503615) H Leonard.
Features performance notes for & accompanying audio examples of fills & embellishments, turnarounds, tags & licks in the style of Ray Charles, Dr. John, Professor Longhair & Johnny Johnson.

Blues-Rock Guitar Handbook: Rock Lines. Mark Lonergan. 1997. bk. 9.95 (978-0-7866-2704-2(2), 94172BCD) Mel Bay.

Blues Routes: Blues & Jazz, Heroes & Tricksters, Work Songs & Street Music. Perf. by Georgia Sea Island Singers et al. 1 CD. (Running Time: 68 min.). (YA). (gr. 9 up). 1999. 14.00 Smithsonian Folkways.
Includes historical analysis of blues, artist biographies & song notes.

Blues Scales: Essential Tools for Jazz Improvising. Dan Greenblatt. 2005. pap. bk. 22.00 (978-1-883217-38-9(5), 00242137); pap. bk. 22.00 (978-1-883217-39-6(3), 00242138); pap. bk. 22.00 (978-1-883217-40-2(7), 00242139) Pub: Sher Music. Dist(s): H Leonard

Blues Scatitudes. Bob Stoloff. 2004. bk. 24.95 (978-1-930080-01-0(8)) Pub: Gerard Sarzin Pub. Dist(s): H Leonard

Blues Sonata & Jazz Standards for Guitar. Charlie Byrd & John Griggs. 2002. bk. 17.95 (978-0-7866-4969-3(0), 98380bcd) Mel Bay.

Blues Summit, Set. 3 cass. 1998. 35.94 (978-1-56826-971-9(4)) Rhino Enter.

Blues/Boogie Solos for Piano. Paul T. Smith. 2000. bk. 19.95 (978-0-7866-5108-5(3)) Mel Bay.

Blueskin the Pirate. abr. ed. Howard Pyle. Perf. by Douglas Fairbanks, Jr. 1 cass. (J). 1984. 8.98 (CDL5 1438) HarperCollins Pubs.
This is the swashbuckling tale of a young man, handicapped from birth & scorned by almost everyone, who outwits & captures a brigand in his own family.

Bluest Blood, unabr. ed. Gillian Roberts. Narrated by Christina Moore. 6 cass. (Running Time: 8 hrs. 30 mins.). (Amanda Pepper Mystery Ser.). 1998. 51.00 (978-0-7887-2518-0(1), 95591E7) Recorded Bks.
When Amanda arrives at a posh fundraiser for the school library, she is horrified to find a burning effigy of the wealthy host swinging from a tree. It seems no one is safe from the book-burning moral ecologists. Unfortunately, Amanda is about to find herself hot on the trail of more serious crimes, including embezzlement & murder. In fact, she's on the list of potential murder victims.

Bluest Eye. Toni Morrison. Narrated by Lynne Thigpen. 6 CDs. (Running Time: 6 hrs. 30 mins.). 2001. audio compact disk 58.00 (978-0-7887-5158-5(1), C1321E7) Recorded Bks.

Bluest Eye. abr. ed. Toni Morrison. Read by Toni Morrison. Read by Ruby Dee. (Running Time: 10800 sec.). (ENG.). 2007. audio compact disk 24.95 (978-0-7393-4373-9(4), Random AudioBks) Pub: Random Audio Pubg. Dist(s): Random

Bluest Eye. unabr. ed. Toni Morrison. Narrated by Peter Francis James & Lynne Thigpen. 5 cass. (Running Time: 6 hrs. 30 mins.). 1970. 53.00 (978-0-7887-4354-2(6), 96306K8) Recorded Bks.

Bluestem Horizon. Evelyn Lee. 1 cass. (Running Time: 35 min.). (J). (gr. k-4). 2001. pap. bk. 19.95 (SP 7010C) Kimbo Educ.
A story of bison on Oklahoma's tallgrass prairie. Includes read along book.

Bluish. unabr. ed. Virginia Hamilton. Read by Lisa Reneé Pitts. 2 cass. (Running Time: 7200 sec.). (J). (gr. 4-7). 2006. 22.95 (978-0-7861-4495-2(5)); audio compact disk 24.00 (978-0-7861-7235-1(5)); audio compact disk 19.95 (978-0-7861-7667-0(9)) Blckstn Audio.

Bluish. unabr. ed. Virginia Hamilton. Read by Lisa Reneé Pitts. (J). 2007. 34.99 (978-1-59895-920-8(4)) Find a World.

Blunder: A Second Look at the New World Order. G Edward Griffin. 1 cass. (Running Time: 90 min.). 1991. 10.00 Am Media.
Mr. Griffin shows conclusively that the present movement to convert the U.N. into a world government would be the biggest blunder of the ages, by temporarily setting aside current evidence of the historical growth of New World Order.

Blunt Instrument. unabr. ed. Georgette Heyer. Read by Hugh Dickson. 6 cass. (Running Time: 9 hrs.). (Inspector Hannayside Mysteries Ser.). 2000. 49.95 (978-0-7451-6006-1(9), CAB 370) Pub: Chivers Audio Bks GBR. Dist(s): AudioGO
Ernest Fletcher was found dead in his study, and it was a mystery, for he was universally liked. However Superintendent Hannayside soon discovers that Fletcher's affairs had recently become very complex, and then another murder occurs.

Blur: The Unauthorized Biography of Blur. Tim Footman. (Maximum Ser.). (ENG.). 2001. audio compact disk 14.95 (978-1-84240-016-6(9)) Pub: Chrome Dreams GBR. Dist(s): IPG Chicago

Blush. unabr. collector's ed. Suzanne Forster. Read by Mary Peiffer. 9 cass. (Running Time: 12 hrs.). 1996. 72.00 (978-0-7366-3443-4(6), 4087) Books on Tape.
Augusta Featherstone arranges her own abduction to escape her parents, but the wrong kidnapper shows up. Will she stay or run.

Blushing. Bruce Goldberg. Read by Bruce Goldberg. 1 cass. (Running Time: 25 min.). (ENG.). 2005. 13.00 (978-1-885577-33-7(8)) Pub: B Goldberg. Dist(s): Baker Taylor
Use self-hypnosis to regain control of the circulatory system and overcome this unwanted tendency.

Bluw Wolf & Friends Music CD, Units 1-4. Prod. by Progressive Language. 1 CD. (Running Time: 25 mins.). 2004. audio compact disk (978-0-9758759-4-0(9)) Prog Lang.
Original childrens songs/music for the Blue Wolf & Friends English Language program learning kit and also found on the Internet at www.bwfriends.com.

***Bmf: The Rise & Fall of Big Meech & the Black Mafia Family.** unabr. ed. Mara Shalhoup & Mara Shalhoup. Read by Hassan Johnson & Hassan Johnson. (Running Time: 10 hrs. 0 mins.). 2010. 59.95 (978-1-4417-3457-0(0)); audio compact disk 90.00 (978-1-4417-3458-7(9)) Blckstn Audio.

***BMF: The Rise & Fall of Big Meech & the Black Mafia Family.** unabr. ed. Mara Shalhoup. (Running Time: 10 hrs. 15 mins.). 2010. audio compact disk 29.95 (978-1-4417-3460-0(0)) Blckstn Audio.

***BMF: The Rise & Fall of Big Meech & the Black Mafia Family.** unabr. ed. Mara Shalhoup. Read by Hassan Johnson. (Running Time: 10 hrs. 0 mins.). 2010. 29.95 (978-1-4417-3461-7(9)) Blckstn Audio.

Bo & Mzzz Mad. unabr. ed. Sid Fleischman. Narrated by Johnny Heller. 2 pieces. (Running Time: 2 hrs.). (YA). 2001. 19.00 (978-1-4025-0740-3(2)) Recorded Bks.

Bo Sebastian's Vocal-Ease. unabr. ed. Bo Sebastian. Read by Bo Sebastian. 2 cass. (Running Time: 92 min.). (Studies for the Singer). 1995. pap. bk. 29.95 Set. (978-0-9646712-0-1(4)) B Sebastian.
Vocal instruction geared to focus on vocal technique for the recording artist.

Boann's Clan: Dance of the Water Gods. Jordan Peters. (Running Time: 1 hr.). 2002. audio compact disk 15.99 (978-1-904972-29-7(2)) Global Jmy GBR GBR.

Board of Claims. 1 cass. (Running Time: 1 hr.). (Advocacy Before Administrative Agencies Ser.). 1985. 20.00 PA Bar Inst.

Board of Director Trends & Best Practices For 2010: What Every Private Company CEO & Board Member Needs to Know. Stella Tsai et al. 2009. 250.00 (978-1-59701-510-3(5)) ReedLogic.

Board of Directors: 25 Keys to Corporate Governance. unabr. ed. Marianne M. Jennings. Read by Eric Conger. 2 cass. (Running Time: 3 hrs.). (New York Times Pocket MBA Ser.). 2000. pap. bk. 27.95 Listen & Live.
Learn the 25 keys to the role of the Board of Directors & the important points in helping to guide the board's policy & strategy.

Board of Directors: 25 Keys to Corporate Governance. unabr. ed. Marianne M. Jennings. Read by Eric Conger. 2 cass. (Running Time: 2 hrs. 30 mins.). (New York Times Pocket MBA Ser.). 2001. 16.95 (978-1-885408-49-5(8), LL042) Listen & Live.

Boarded Window see Tales of Terror & the Supernatural: A Collection

Boarded Window. unabr. ed. Ambrose Bierce. Read by Jim Killavey. 1 cass. (Running Time: 46 min.). Dramatization. Incl. Stranger. 1981. (S-5); Ways of Ghosts. 1981. (S-5); 1981. 7.95 (S-5) Jimcin Record.
Three masterpieces of the macabre.

Boarded Window; The Stranger; The Ways of Ghosts. Ambrose Bierce. 1 cass. 1989. 7.95 (S-5) Jimcin Record.
Masterpieces of the macabre.

Boarding Party: Fair Winds & a Following Sea. 1 cass. 9.98 (C-109) Folk-Legacy.
Another collection of rare shanties.

Boarding Party: 'Tis Our Sailing Time. 1 cass. 9.98 (C-97) Folk-Legacy.
Unusual shanties from an outstanding group.

***Boardwalk Empire: The Birth, High Times, & Corruption of Atlantic City.** unabr. ed. Nelson Johnson. Read by Joe Mantegna & Terrence Winter. (Running Time: 12 hrs.). 2010. 24.99 (978-1-4418-6611-0(6), 9781441866110, Brilliance MP3) Brilliance Audio.

***Boardwalk Empire: The Birth, High Times, & Corruption of Atlantic City.** unabr. ed. Nelson Johnson. Read by Joe Mantegna. (Running Time: 12 hrs.). 2010. 39.97 (978-1-4418-6612-7(4), 9781441866127, Brlnc Audio MP3 Lib) Brilliance Audio.

***Boardwalk Empire: The Birth, High Times, & Corruption of Atlantic City.** unabr. ed. Nelson Johnson. Read by Joe Mantegna & Terrence Winter. (Running Time: 11 hrs.). 2010. 39.97 (978-1-4418-6613-4(2), 9781441866134, BADLE); audio compact disk 29.99 (978-1-4418-6609-7(4), 9781441866097, Bril Audio CD Unabri); audio compact disk 99.97 (978-1-4418-6610-3(8), 9781441866103, BriAudCD Unabrid) Brilliance Audio.

Boat Days/Tropic Nights. 2002. audio compact disk 16.99 (978-0-89610-935-3(6)) Island Heritage.

Boat of Quiet Hours see Jane Kenyon

Boat-4 CD audio Book. Thomas Henry Kelly. 2005. audio compact disk 35.00 (978-1-56142-194-7(4)) T Kelly Inc.

Boats in a Fog see Poetry of Robinson Jeffers

Bob & Ray: A Night of Two Stars. 2 cass. (Running Time: 2 hrs.). 21.95 (A0150B090, HarperThor) HarpC GBR.

Bob & Ray: A Night of Two Stars. Perf. by Bob Elliott & Ray Goulding. 2 cass. (Running Time: 2 hrs.). 2001. 19.95 (RAF0001); audio compact disk 29.95 Lodestone Catalog.
Recorded live at Carnegie Hall, this delightful collection will bring you back, or perhaps introduce you to, the world-famous ultra dry humor of two great artists. Features such classics asSalesman of the Year; House of Toast; Lucy Luscious Nut Fudge; Mr. I Know Where They Are; Reuniting the Whirleys; Tippy the Wonder Dog; Elmer W. Litzinger, Spy; Slow Talkers of America.

Bob & Ray: Featuring Mary Backstayge, Noble Wife: the Soap Operas, Volume 1. Featuring Ray Goulding & Bob Elliot. 1995. audio compact disk 36.95 (978-1-892091-37-6(2)) Radio Found.

Bob & Ray: Featuring Mary Backstayge, Noble Wife: the Soap Operas, Volume 3. Featuring Ray Goulding & Bob Elliot. 1996. audio compact disk 36.95 (978-1-892091-39-0(9)) Radio Found.

Bob & Ray: Featuring Mary Backstayge, Noble Wife: the Soap Operas, Volume 4. Featuring Ray Goulding & Bob Elliot. 1996. audio compact disk 36.95 (978-1-892091-40-6(2)) Radio Found.

Bob & Ray: Featuring Mary Backstayge, Noble Wife: the Soap Operas, Volume 5. Featuring Ray Goulding & Bob Elliot. 2006. audio compact disk 36.95 (978-1-892091-41-3(0)) Radio Found.

Bob & Ray: From Approximately Coast-to-Coast. 1 cass. (Running Time: 1 hr.). 7.95 (CM8497) Natl Recrd Co.

Bob & Ray: Mary Backstayge, Noble Wife Lost in Africa: the Lost Episodes, Volume 3. Featuring Ray Goulding & Bob Elliot. 2002. audio compact disk 36.95 (978-1-892091-42-0(9)) Radio Found.

Bob & Ray: Mary Backstayge, Noble Wife: the Lost Episodes, Volume 4. Featuring Ray Goulding & Bob Elliot. 2002. audio compact disk 36.95 (978-1-892091-43-7(7)) Radio Found.

Bob & Ray: More CBS Years, the Found LPs: the Lost Episodes, Volume 5. Featuring Ray Goulding & Bob Elliot. 2002. audio compact disk 36.95 (978-1-892091-44-4(5)) Radio Found.

Bob & Ray: The Lost Episodes. 4 cass. (Running Time: 4 hrs.). 1999. 29.95 7" ALBUM. (978-1-892091-55-0(0), RadioArt) Radio Found.
Includes: "Mary Backstayge, Noble Wife," "Wally Ballou on the Trophy Train," "The Gathering Dusk," "Wing Po," "Elmer W. Litzinger," "Spy" & much more.

Bob & Ray: The Lost Episodes: Featuring Mary Backstayge, Noble Wife. Featuring Mary Backstayge et al. 4 cass. (Running Time: 4 hrs.). 1999. 29.95 (978-1-892091-24-6(0), RadioArt) Radio Found.

Bob & Ray: The Soap Operas. 4 cass. (Running Time: 4 hrs.). 2000. 29.95 (978-1-892091-71-0(2), RadioArt) Radio Found.

Bob & Ray: The Soap Operas, Volume 2: the Soap Operas, Volume 2. Featuring Ray Goulding & Bob Elliot. 1996. audio compact disk 36.95 (978-1-892091-38-3(0)) Radio Found.

Bob & Ray Vol. 1: The Lost Episodes: Featuring Mary Backstayge, Noble Wife. Featuring Skunkhaven et al. 4 CDs. (Running Time: 4 hrs.). 1999. audio compact disk 34.95 (978-1-892091-53-6(4), RadioArt) Radio Found.

Bob & Ray Vol. 1: The Soap Operas - Mary Backstayge, Noble Wife. 4 cass. (Running Time: 4 hrs.). 1998. 29.98 Boxed set. (4381) Radio Spirits.
Laugh along with this comedy collection.

Bob & Ray Vol. 2: The Lost Episodes. 4 cass. (Running Time: 4 hrs.). 1999. 29.95 7" ALBUM. (978-1-892091-56-7(9), RadioArt) Radio Found.
Includes "Wally Ballou for Transistor Radios," "Bob & Ray for Grime," the ready-made shortening that spreads just like lard; "Mushies," the cereal that gets soggy even without milk; & much more.

Bob & Ray Vol. 2: The Lost Episodes: The Commercials. Featuring Wally Ballou et al. 4 CDs. (Running Time: 4 hrs.). 1999. audio compact disk 36.95 (978-1-892091-54-3(2)) Radio Found.

Bob & Ray Vol. 2: The Lost Episodes: The Commercials. Featuring Wally Ballou & Arthur Godfrey. 4 cass. (Running Time: 4 hrs.). 1999. (978-1-892091-50-5(X), RadioArt) Radio Found.

Bob & Ray Vol. 2: The Soap Operas. 4 cass. (Running Time: 4 hrs.). 2000. 29.95 (978-1-892091-72-7(0), RadioArt) Radio Found.

Bob & Ray Vol. 2: The Soap Operas - Mary Backstayge & Linda Lovely. 4 cass. (Running Time: 4 hrs.). 1998. 29.98 Boxed set. (4382) Radio Spirits.

Bob & Ray Vol. 2: The Soap Operas: Featuring Mary Backstayge, Noble Wife & the Lives & Loves of Linda Lovely. Featuring Mary Backstayge & Linda Lovely. 4 cass. (Running Time: 4 hrs.). 1999. 29.95 (978-1-892091-19-2(4), RadioArt) Radio Found.
These entertaining cassettes feature Mary & Harry Backstayge & all the gang as they travel to Casablanca, Marrakesh & back to Skunkhaven, Long Island, in a series of increasingly improbably adventures.

Bob & Ray Vol. 3: The Lost Episodes: Mary Backstayge Noble Wife Lost in Africa. 4 cass. (Running Time: 4 hrs.). 1999. 29.95 (978-1-892091-51-2(8), RadioArt) Radio Found.
A treasure trove of lost recordings, many of them not heard since their original broadcast over 50 years ago!.

Bob & Ray Vol. 3: The Soap Operas. 4 cass. (Running Time: 4 hrs.). 2000. 29.95 (978-1-892091-73-4(9), RadioArt) Radio Found.

Bob & Ray Vol. 3: The Soap Operas - Mary Backstayge, Noble Wife. 4 cass. (Running Time: 4 hrs.). 1998. 29.98 Boxed set. (4383) Radio Spirits.

Bob & Ray Vol. 3: The Soap Operas: Featuring Mary Backstayge, Noble Wife. Featuring Mary Backstayge & Noble Wife. 4 cass. (Running Time: 4 hrs.). 1999. 29.95 (978-1-892091-20-8(8), RadioArt) Radio Found.
These entertaining cassettes feature Mary & Harry Backstayge & all the gang as they travel to Casablanca, Marrakesh & back to Skunkhaven, Long Island, in a series of increasingly improbably adventures.

Bob & Ray Vol. 4: The Lost Episodes: The New York Years, Part 3. 4 cass. (Running Time: 4 hrs.). 1999. 29.95 (978-1-892091-52-9(6), RadioArt) Radio Found.
A treasure trove of lost recordings, many of them not heard since their original broadcast over 50 years ago!.

Bob & Ray Vol. 4: The Soap Operas. 4 cass. (Running Time: 4 hrs.). 2000. 29.95 (978-1-892091-74-1(7), RadioArt) Radio Found.

Bob & Ray Vol. 4: The Soap Operas - Mary Backstayge, Noble Wife. 4 cass. (Running Time: 4 hrs.). 1998. 29.98 Boxed set. (4384) Radio Spirits.

Bob & Ray Vol. 4: The Soap Operas: Featuring Marybackstayge, Noble Wife. Featuring Mary Backstayge & Noble Wife. 4 cass. (Running Time: 4 hrs.). 1999. 29.95 (978-1-892091-21-5(6), RadioArt) Radio Found.
These entertaining cassettes feature Mary & Harry Backstayge & all the gang as they travel to Casablanca, Marrakesh & back to Skunkhaven, Long Island, in a series of increasingly improbably adventures.

Bob & Ray on a Platter. 1 cass. (Running Time: 1 hr.). 2001. 14.95; audio compact disk 17.95 Lodestone Catalog.
This collection showcases favorites including Charles the Poet; Ladies Grab Your Seats; Non Sequitur; People to People; Wally Ballou, Roving Reporter & more, plus a salute to Shoddy Showmanship Awards.

Bob & Ray on a Platter. Featuring Wally Ballou. 1 cass. (Running Time: 1 hr. 30 min.). 1999. (978-1-892091-05-5(4), RAFO003, RadioArt) Radio Found.
Includes: "Charles the Poet," "Ladies Grab Your Seats," "Late Weather & Sports" (including a hilarious commercial for Rudolph & Irma's Dance Studio), "People to People," "Wally Ballou, Roving Reporter," "Saturday Afternoon TV Football," "Salute to Shoddy Showmanship Awards," & more.

Bob & Ray on a Platter CD RACD 8000. Featuring Wally Ballou. 1 CD. (Running Time: 1 hr. 30 min.). 1999. audio compact disk (978-1-892091-04-8(6), RAFO004, RadioArt) Radio Found.

Bob & Ray the Two & Only: The Broadway Show. Featuring Wally Ballou et al. 1 cass. (Running Time: 1 hr. 30 min.). 1999. (978-1-892091-23-9(2), RadioArt) Radio Found.
Original cast album of their sold-out show that ran for six months on Broadway featuring: "Wally Ballou," "Biff Burns," "Stuffy Hodgson," "Barry

Campbell," "The McBeeBee Twins," "Larry Lovebreath," "Hap Walney," & many others.

Bob & Ray Throw a Stereo Spectacular. Featuring Bob and Ray Staff. Music by Lena Horne et al. 1 CD. (Running Time: 1 hr. 30 min.). 2000. audio compact disk (978-1-892091-22-2(4), RadioArt) Radio Found.
The first RCA LP Stereo demo disk has 15 tracks, including narration with sound effects by Bob & Ray, who wander through this historic recording meeting up with Dr. Ahkbar in his castle & "The Thing".

Bob & Ron Copper: English Shepherd & Farming Songs. 1 cass. 9.98 (C-19) Folk-Legacy.
Classic recording of a family tradition.

Bob Carlisle: Butterfly Kisses. 1 cass. 1997. 10.98 CD single Incl. designer case, sing-along Trax, CD Rom Video, & bonus love song. Pub: Brentwood Music. Dist(s): Provident Mus Dist
A Christian classic song celebrating the relationship between parent & child. Includes "You Must Have Been An Angel".

Bob Carlisle: Butterfly Kisses - Shades of Grace. Perf. by Bob Carlisle. 1 cass., 1 CD. 8.98; audio compact disk 13.98 CD. Provident Mus Dist.

Bob Dyer: River of the Big Canoes. 1 cass. 9.98 (C-514) Folk-Legacy.
A program of fine original songs by a Missouri songmaker.

Bob Dyer: Treasure in the River. 1 cass. 9.98 (C-515) Folk-Legacy.
Central Missouri songmaker presents another collection.

***Bob Dylan in America.** unabr. ed. Sean Wilentz. Read by Sean Wilentz. (ENG.). 2010. audio compact disk 40.00 (978-0-307-71497-8(7), Random AudioBks) Pub: Random Audio Pubg. Dist(s): Random

Bob Hope. Radio Spirits Staff. Read by Bob Hope. 12 CDs. (Running Time: 12 hrs.). 2005. audio compact disk 39.98 (978-1-57019-533-4(1), 4484) Radio Spirits.

Bob Hope. unabr. ed. Read by Bob Hope. 8 cass. (Running Time: 12 hrs.). 2002. 39.98 (978-1-57019-534-1(X), 4483) Radio Spirits.
Commemorates Bob's very special place in the hearts of all Americans.

Bob Hope & Frank Sinatra see Great Christmas Comedy: Selected Sketches

Bob Hope in Show Biz. Featuring Hope/Durante/Crosby/Sinatra. 1953. audio compact disk 12.95 (978-1-57970-503-9(0), Audio-For) J Norton Pubs.

Bob Hope in Show Biz. unabr. ed. Perf. by Bob Hope. 1 cass. (Running Time: 55 min.). 12.95 (493) J Norton Pubs.
Bob talks about his show business career with emphasis on his radio shows. Excerpts from over the years are played with such guests as Jimmy Durante, Bing Crosby & Frank Sinatra.

Bob Hope Show. unabr. ed. Bob Hope. Perf. by Lucille Ball et al. 20 vols. (Running Time: 20 hrs.). (20 Hour Collections). 2002. bk. 69.98 (978-1-57019-507-5(2), OTR40042) Pub: Radio Spirits. Dist(s): AudioGO
One of America's best-loved entertainers, Bob Hope starred on the stage, in movies and on TV-but he achieved his earliest and greatest fame on radio. Hope's Pepsodent Show was radio's top-rated series during the War Years, and his remote broadcasts from military bases helped boost American morale during some of our darkest days. Radio Spirits presents 40 of Bob Hope's all-time greatest broadcasts, available now for the first time since they aired more than 50 years ago. This landmark collection also includes a 32-page behind-the-scenes booklet with a special foreword by Bob Hope himself. Celebrate the glorious career of the beloved comedian who has entertained America for more than 70 years, leaving generations of loyal fans proclaiming "Thanks for the memories.".

Bob Hope Show. unabr. ed. Perf. by Bob Hope et al. 20 cass. (Running Time: 20 hrs.). 2002. 59.98 (40044) Radio Spirits.

Bob Hope Show: Aboard the South Dakota U.S. Naval Ship & Wayne Morris. unabr. ed. Perf. by Bob Hope & Wayne Morris. 1 cass. (Running Time: 1 hr.). 2001. 6.98 (2173) Radio Spirits.

Bob Hope Show: At Naval Training Center & Bing Crosby & Doris Day. unabr. ed. Perf. by Bob Hope et al. 1 cass. (Running Time: 1 hr.). 2001. 6.98 (2153) Radio Spirits.

Bob Hope Show: Peggy Ryan & Herbert Marshall. unabr. ed. Perf. by Bob Hope et al. 1 cass. (Running Time: 1 hr.). 2001. 6.98 (2114) Radio Spirits.

Bob Koppel: The Innergame of Trading. Read by Bob Koppel & Howard Abell. 1 cass. 30.00 Dow Jones Telerate.
Bob will demonstrate how to master the psychological skills essential to successful trading. Bob & Howard, in their joint presentation, will provide a blueprint for you to model the beliefs, mental strategies & internal dialogue of the best traders in the world. Through detailed exercises & illuminating examples they will provide you with the tools to change your beliefs, sharpen your focus & bolster your confidence. They will also show how the skills learned in The Innergame of Trading relate to development of trading systems & the application of technical analysis.

***Bob Marley - Drum Play-along Volume 25 (book/cd)** Bob Marley. (ENG.). 2011. pap. bk. 14.99 (978-1-4234-9536-9(5), 1423495365) H Leonard.

***Bob Prince.** Prod. by Vergil Patrick Hughes. 2010. audio compact disk 15.00 (978-0-9818365-8-4(5)) Baseball Voice.

Bob Rotella Golf, set. gif. ed. Bob Rotella. Read by Bob Rotella. 3 cass. (Running Time: 4 hrs.). 1999. 29.95 (978-0-671-75755-7(5), Audioworks) S&S Audio.

Bob Schneider: When You Dream a Dream. Bob Schneider. Perf. by Bob Schneider. Perf. by Rainbow Kids. 1 cass. (Running Time: 40 min.). (J). (gr. k up). 1989. 9.95 Peter Pan.

Bob Shacochis: Hunger. unabr. ed. Bob Shacochis. Read by Bob Shacochis. Interview with Rebekah Presson. 1 cass. (Running Time: 29 min.). 1991. 10.00 (040486) New Letters.
The 1985 American Book Award winner reads a story, "Hunger," from his collection "Easy in the Islands".

Bob Shacochis Interview with Kay Bonetti. Interview. Interview with Bob Shacochis & Kay Bonetti. 1 cass. (Running Time: 54 min.). 1985. 13.95 (978-1-55644-133-2(9), 5062) Am Audio Prose.
Details the emotions of an "emerging writer" & reads from "Easy in the Islands".

Bob Shacochis Reads "Easy in the Islands" Bob Shacochis. Read by Bob Shacochis. 1 cass. (Running Time: 66 min.). 1985. 13.95 (978-1-55644-132-5(0), 5061) Am Audio Prose.
Author reads excerpts from his book.

Bob Smiley: Bob Out of Mind. Perf. by Bob Smiley. 1 cass. 1999. 10.98 (KMGC8691); audio compact disk 16.98 (KMGD8694) Provident Mus Dist.

Bob the Gambler. unabr. ed. Frederick Barthelme. Read by Adams Morgan. 5 cass. (Running Time: 7 hrs.). 1998. 39.95 (978-0-7861-1295-1(6), 2198) Blckstn Audio.
Ray & Jewel Kaiser try out the Paradise casino in Biloxi, Mississippi, & their luck as novice gamblers. Curious things happen to them involving, among others, their fourteen-year-old daughter, the casino & its personnel, Ray's dead father, & a mother convinced that a sitcom star is visiting across the street make up the fabric of this novel about wising up better late than never.

Bob Uecker: Mr. Baseball. Janell Hughes. (ENG.). 2007. audio compact disk 16.00 (978-0-9818365-3-9(4)) Baseball Voice.

Bob Zentz: Beaucatcher Farewell. 1 cass. 9.98 (C-67) Folk-Legacy.
A fine program with excellent instrumentation & harmonies.

Bob Zentz: It's about Time. 1 cass. 9.98 (C-535) Folk-Legacy.
Songs addressing the topic of time, from a fine Virginia songmaker.

Bob Zentz: Mirrors & Changes. 1 cass. 9.98 (C-51) Folk-Legacy.
Bob's first album, includes "The Ramblin' Conrad Story".

Bobbed Hair & Bathtub Gin: Writers Running Wild in the Twenties. Marion Meade. Read by Lorna Raver. 8 cass. (Running Time: 11 hrs. 30 mins.). 2004. 65.95 (978-0-7861-2877-8(1), 3378); audio compact disk 81.00 (978-0-7861-8298-5(9), 3378) Blckstn Audio.

Bobbie Ann Mason. Interview. Interview with Bobbie Ann Mason & Kay Bonetti. 1 cass. (Running Time: 49 min.). 1985. 13.95 (978-1-55644-129-5(0), 5042) Am Audio Prose.
The author discusses her use of popular culture.

Bobbsey Twins on the Deep Blue Sea. unabr. ed. Laura Lee Hope. Read by Flo Gibson. 3 cass. (Running Time: 4 hrs. 30 min.). (Bobbsey Twins Ser.). (J). (gr. 3-5). 1993. 16.95 (978-1-55685-277-0(0)) Audio Bk Con.
Two sets of twins, Freddie & Flossie & Nan & Bert Bobbsey, embark on a series of adventures at sea.

Bobby & Jackie: A Love Story. unabr. ed. C. David Heymann. Narrated by Dick Hill. 1 MP3-CD. (Running Time: 7 hrs. 30 mins. 0 sec.). (ENG.). 2009. 19.99 (978-1-4001-6422-6(2)); audio compact disk 59.99 (978-1-4001-4422-8(1)); audio compact disk 29.99 (978-1-4001-1422-1(5)) Pub: Tantor Media. Dist(s): IngramPubServ

Bobby Bear & the Bees. M. O. Helmrath & J. L. Bartlett. (Bobby Bear Ser.). (J). (ps-1). 1968. pap. bk. 7.94 (978-0-87783-177-8(7)) Oddo.

Bobby Bear Finds Maple Sugar. M. O. Helmrath & J. L. Bartlett. (Bobby Bear Ser.). (J). (ps-1). 1968. pap. bk. 7.94 (978-0-87783-178-5(5)) Oddo.

Bobby Bear Goes Fishing. M. O. Helmrath & J. L. Bartlett. (Bobby Bear Ser.). (J). (ps-1). 1968. pap. bk. 7.94 (978-0-87783-179-2(3)) Oddo.

Bobby Bear in the Spring. M. O. Helmrath & J. L. Bartlett. (Bobby Bear Ser.). (J). (ps-1). 1968. pap. bk. 7.94 (978-0-87783-180-8(7)) Oddo.

Bobby Bear's Halloween. M. O. Helmrath & J. L. Bartlett. (Bobby Bear Ser.). (J). (ps-1). 1968. pap. bk. 7.94 (978-0-87783-183-9(1)) Oddo.

Bobby Bear's New Home. Marilue. (Bobby Bear Ser.). (J). (ps-1). 1973. pap. bk. 7.94 (978-0-87783-184-6(X)) Oddo.

Bobby Bear's Red Raft. Marilue. (Bobby Bear Ser.). (J). (ps-1). 1973. pap. bk. 7.94 (978-0-87783-185-3(8)) Oddo.

Bobby Bear's Rocket Ride. M. O. Helmrath & J. L. Bartlett. (Bobby Bear Ser.). (J). (ps-1). 1968. pap. bk. 7.94 (978-0-87783-186-0(6)) Oddo.

***Bobby Conroy Comes Back from the Dead.** unabr. ed. Joe Hill. (ENG.). 2007. (978-0-06-155219-9(4)); (978-0-06-155220-5(8)) HarperCollins Pubs.

***Bobby Fischer Goes to War: The True Story of How the Soviets Lost T.** abr. ed. David Edmonds & John Eidinow. Read by Sam Tsoutsouvas. (ENG.). 2004. (978-0-06-075490-7(7), Harper Audio) HarperCollins Pubs.

***Bobby Fischer Goes to War: The True Story of How the Soviets Lost T.** abr. ed. David Edmonds & John Eidinow. Read by Sam Tsoutsouvas. (ENG.). 2004. (978-0-06-081461-8(6), Harper Audio) HarperCollins Pubs.

Bobby Jack Smith You Dirty Coward. unabr. ed. Max Evans. Read by Bernard Bridges. 4 cass. (Running Time: 6 hrs.). 1995. 25.00 Set. (978-1-883268-20-6(6)) Spellbinders.
Bobby Jack Smith is the bawdy, wildly funny story of a half-smart cowboy who rises to success & leadership in Hi Lo; using the tactical war guide of Napoleon as his inspiration.

Bobby Norfolk Spins Timeless Tales. Bobby Norfolk. 1999. audio compact disk 14.95 (978-0-87483-749-0(9)) Pub: August Hse. Dist(s): Natl Bk Netwk

Bobby Norfolk Spins Timeless Tales. Bobby Norfolk. 1 cass. (Running Time: 56 mins.). (World Storytelling from August House Ser.). (gr. 1-4). 2002. 12.00 (978-0-87483-539-7(9)) Pub: August Hse. Dist(s): Natl Bk Netwk
Story teller & stand-up comic performs six selections with setup-to-punch-line zing. With awesome sound effects.

Bobby Norfolk Spins Timeless Tales. unabr. ed. Bobby Norfolk. Read by Bobby Norfolk. (J). 2007. 34.99 (978-1-60252-549-8(8)) Find a World.

Bobby Short. Read by Bobby Short. 1 cass. (Running Time: 60 min.). (Marian McPartland's Piano Jazz Ser.). 13.95 (MM-87-01-01, HarperThor) HarpC GBR.

Bobby Short: Singer. Interview. Interview with Bobby Short. 1 cass. (Running Time: 30 min.). 8.00 (A0620B090, HarperThor) HarpC GBR.

Bob's Favorite Street Songs. Perf. by Bob McGrath. 1 cass. (J). (ps-1). 9.98 (209) MFLP CA.
Selecting a dozen of his favorite Sesame Street tunes, Bob has recorded these classics in fresh, new arrangements in Jazz, Pop, Latin & Motown styles.

Boccherini - Guitar Quintet No. 4 in D, Fandango. Composed by Luigi Boccherini. 2006. pap. bk. 24.98 (978-1-59615-367-7(9), 1596153679) Pub: Music Minus. Dist(s): H Leonard

Bodacious Kid, Set. unabr. ed. Stan Lynde. Read by Stan Lynde. 4 pieces. (Running Time: 6 hrs. 8 mins.). 24.95 (978-1-886370-16-6(8), 1418) Cttnwd Pub.

Bodas de Sangre: Act Three, Part One, Last Scene see Poesia y Drama de Garcia Lorca

Bodega Dreams. Ernesto Quinonez. Narrated by Robert Ramirez. 6 cass. (Running Time: 8 hrs.). 2001. 54.00 (978-0-7887-4671-0(5), 96367E7) Recorded Bks.
Illuminates an underworld of sacred favors & turncoat morals, finding dark humor & surprising honor in the experiences of the street.

Bodhi: The Faculty of Intelligence. Swami Amar Jyoti. 1 dolby cass. 1986. 9.95 (J-53) Truth Consciousness.
The reflections of consciousness into the vessel of mind; opening this faculty. On instinct, reason & intellect. The "realism" of equality & individual freedom.

Bodhicaryavatara. Read by Chogyam Trungpa & Osel Tendzin. 10 cass. 1980. 99.00 (A074) Vajradhatu.
Nine talks. This seminar presents a summary of the classic Buddhist text, the "Bodhicaryavatara," by the Indian poet, Shantideva. It covers such topics as the bodhisattva vow & Mahayana practices.

Bodhisattva Mind: Teachings to Cultivate Courage & Awareness in the Midst of Suffering. Pema Chödrön. 7 CDs. (Running Time: 28800 sec.). 2006. audio compact disk 69.95 (978-1-59179-535-3(4), AF01091D) Sounds True.

Bodhisattva Path. T'ai Situ. 2 cass. 1982. 22.50 Vajradhatu.
A workshop at the 1982 Conference on Christian & Buddhist Meditation.

Bodhisattva Vow: A Practical Guide to Helping Others. Geshe Kelsang Gyatso. Narrated by Michael Sington. (Running Time: 2 hrs. 26 mins. 0 sec.). (ENG., 2003. audio compact disk 19.95 (978-0-948006-92-0(7)) Pub: Tharpa Pubns GBR. Dist(s): IPG Chicago

Bodhran: The Basics. Bill Woods. (ENG.). 2009. pap. bk. 14.99 (978-0-7866-8004-7(0)) Mel Bay.

Bodhran, Bones & Spoons. Contrib. by Tommy Hayes. (Running Time: 1 hr. 45 mins.). (ENG.). 2006. 32.95 (978-5-558-08934-9(2)) Waltons Manu IRL.

Bodhran Book. Steafan Hannigan. 2004. bk. 14.95 (978-0-946005-40-6(0)) Pub: Ossian IRL. Dist(s): H Leonard

Bodies in Bedlam. unabr. ed. Richard S. Prather. Read by Maynard Villers. 6 cass. (Running Time: 6 hrs. 30 min.). (Shell Scott Ser.: Bk. 2). 2001. 39.95 (978-1-55686-894-8(4)) Books in Motion.
Constanza Carmocha was a woman men fell all over themselves to be around. But when two men are found murdered, suspicion points to Constanza's bodyguard, and a more deadly game.

Bodies in Motion. Zane Kotker. Read by Zane Kotker. 1 cass. (Running Time: 58 min.). Incl. Certain Man. (4101); White Rising. (4101); 13.95 (978-1-55644-109-7(6), 4101) Am Audio Prose.
Kotker reads excerpts from three of her novels.

***Bodies Left Behind.** abr. ed. Jeffery Deaver. Read by Holter Graham. (Running Time: 6 hrs. 0 mins. 0 sec.). (ENG.). 2010. audio compact disk 14.99 (978-1-4423-3553-0(X)) Pub: S&S Audio. Dist(s): S and S Inc

Bodies Left Behind. unabr. ed. Jeffery Deaver. Read by Holter Graham. (Running Time: 13 hrs. 0 mins. 0 sec.). (ENG.). 2008. audio compact disk 39.99 (978-0-7435-7994-0(1)) Pub: S&S Audio. Dist(s): S and S Inc

Bodies Out Back. Joseph E. Wright. 2003. audio compact disk 3.95 (978-1-59201-014-1(8)) Bks Unbound Pubng Co.

Bodily Harm. Margaret Atwood. Read by Margaret Atwood. Prod. by Moveable Feast Staff. 1 cass. (Running Time: 30 min.). 1984. 8.95 (AMF-1) Am Audio Prose.
Atwood reads from her novel "Bodily Harm" & talks about politics & the writer & why she writes.

Bodily Harm. Margaret Atwood. Read by Bonnie Hurren. 8 cass. (Running Time: 12 hrs.). 2002. 69.95 (978-0-7540-0865-1(7), CAB 2287) Pub: Chivers Audio Bks GBR. Dist(s): AudioGO

Bodily Harm. Margaret Atwood. Read by Bonnie Hurren. (Running Time: 36480 sec.). (Chivers Audio Bks.). 2003. audio compact disk 79.95 (978-0-7540-8792-2(1)) Pub: Chivers Audio Bks GBR. Dist(s): AudioGO

Bodily Harm. unabr. ed. Robert Dugoni. Read by Dan John Miller. (Running Time: 11 hrs.). (David Sloane Ser.: Bk. 3). 2010. 39.97 (978-1-4233-8739-8(2), 9781423387398, Brinc Audio MP3 Lib); 24.99 (978-1-4233-8738-1(4), 9781423387381, Brilliance MP3); 39.97 (978-1-4233-8741-1(4), 9781423387411, BADLE); 24.99 (978-1-4233-8740-4(6), 9781423387404, BAD); audio compact disk 82.97 (978-1-4233-8737-4(6), 9781423387374, BriAudCD Unabrid); audio compact disk 29.99 (978-1-4233-8736-7(8), 9781423387367, Bril Audio CD Unabri) Brilliance Audio.

Body. Colson. 1 cass. 1992. 14.99 (978-0-8499-6065-9(7), 6051) Nelson.

Body. Stephen King. Read by Frank Muller. (Running Time: 6 hrs.). (ENG.). (gr. 12 up). 2009. audio compact disk 29.95 (978-0-14-314392-5(1), PengAudBks) Penguin Grp USA.

Body. unabr. ed. Milton Diamond. 1 cass. (Running Time: 1 hr.). (Human Sexuality Ser.). 12.95 (34003) J Norton Pubs.

***Body.** unabr. ed. Stephen King. (Running Time: 6 hrs.). (ENG.). 2010. audio compact disk 14.95 (978-0-14-242804-7(3), PengAudBks) Penguin Grp USA.

Body, unabr. ed. Stephen King. Narrated by Frank Muller. 4 cass. (Running Time: 6 hrs.). (gr. 8 up). 1984. 35.00 (978-1-55690-066-2(X), 84064E7) Recorded Bks.
LaChance & three friends set out on a macabre quest that becomes a trial of courage & a rite of passage. Made into the movie "Stand By Me".

Body: An Engine of Destruction. Kenneth Wapnick. 2008. 13.00 (978-1-59142-346-1(5)); audio compact disk 16.00 (978-1-59142-345-4(7)) Foun Miracles.

Body: Controlling Your Destiny by Controlling Your Body. 4. (Running Time: 4 hrs.). (LAWS That Govern Prosperity Ser.: 1). 2002. 20.00 (978-1-57399-106-3(6)); audio compact disk 20.00 (978-1-57399-159-9(7)) Mac Hammond.
Whoever controls your soul controls your destiny. Contending for control of your soul are two opposing forces: your spirit and your body. In this series, Mac Hammond explains the power and destruction of being ruled by the body and how to put the spirit in charge.

Body: Sensuousness & Spirituality. unabr. ed. David Steindl-Rast. 1 cass. (Running Time: 1 hr. 28 min.). 1990. 11.00 (05104) Big Sur Tapes.
Explored are the misunderstandings & confusions created in religious traditions by the words "body," "sensuousness," & "spirituality." When the power of what is real flows into you - "when your body is ablaze in the glow of spirit" - these moments give you the standard from which everything else is measured.

Body - Spirit. unabr. ed. David Steindl-Rast. 1 cass. (Running Time: 59 min.). 1993. 11.00 (05108) Big Sur Tapes.
According to Br. David, "flesh," the traditional opposite of spirit, has often been misinterpreted as "body," when in fact the true meaning of "flesh" is "deadness," decay, the corpse after the life-breath has gone out. When we are truly alive, we can experience spiritual bliss in "our bodies".

Body Adventure. 1 cass. (Running Time: 1 hr.). (J). 2000. 8.99 Kidzup Prodns.

Body Adventure. Kidzup Productions Staff. 1 cass. (Running Time: 90 mins.). (Interactive Learning Kits Ser.). (J). (gr. k-2). 2000. audio compact disk 8.99 (978-1-894281-47-8(0)) Pub: Kidzup CAN. Dist(s): Penton Overseas
Join along with Melody & friends as you explore the human body. Through fun & interactive games & activities, you will learn all about your organs, bones, body parts & more.

Body & Soul: Love Serenade, Set. 2 cass. (Running Time: 1 hr. 30 min.). 1999. 14.99 (3UAFW9) Time-Life.

Body & Soul Set: Love Serenade. 2 CDs. (Running Time: 1 hr. 30 min.). 1999. audio compact disk 16.99 (3VAFW8) Time-Life.

Body & the Self: Selections from the MIT Press. Jonathan Cole et al. 2 cass. (Running Time: 2 hrs. 30 min.). 1996. 17.95 (978-1-879557-44-4(4)) Audio Scholar.
A collection of recently published essays that provide the latest thinking on bodily awareness and self-consciousness. Along with examples come discussions about body image, boundary sensations and the ecology of self.

Body Artist: A Novel. unabr. ed. Read by Don DeLillo. Narrated by Laurie Anderson. 2 cass. (Running Time: 3 hrs.). 2002. 25.00 (978-1-4025-1277-3(5)) Recorded Bks.
Lauren Hartke is a performance artist who manipulates her body to escape the confines of reality. Following the suicide of her film director husband, she returns to their isolated bay-front rental home. While dealing with her grief, she practices her art with an unbridled intensity. One day, Lauren finds a half-naked man sitting on her bed. As Lauren develops an uneasy relationship with this fantastic stranger, she quickly discovers he may have an uncanny connection to her dead husband. She wonders, though - is this man her husband reincarnate or something else entirely?.

Body As a Mirror: Psychosomatics in Childhood & Adolescence. Read by Kaspar Kiepenheuer. 1 cass. (Running Time: 90 min.). 1990. 10.95 (978-0-7822-0126-0(1), 411) C G Jung IL.

Body at Eucharist: Gesture & Posture. J. Michael Sparough et al. 3 cass. (Running Time: 3 hrs.). 2001. vinyl bd. 27.95 (A5700) St Anthony Mess Pr.
Through guided imagery meditation, the authors draw us into the Liturgy of the Word and Liturgy of the Eucharist in new ways.

Body at Eucharist: Senses & Symbols. J. Michael Sparough et al. 2 cass. (Running Time: 2 hrs.). 2001. vinyl bd. 19.95 (A5800) St Anthony Mess Pr.
Appreciate the role of assembly in worship and draw new life from the Eucharist by meditating on the rich spirituality of the symbols and senses of Eucharist.

Body at Prayer, Vol. I. J. Michael Sparough & Bobby Fisher. 2 cass. (Running Time: 2 hrs.). 2001. vinyl bd. 18.95 (A3800) St Anthony Mess Pr.
Guided meditations using gesture, posture and breath, with original music for prayer.

Body at Prayer, Vol. II. J. Michael Sparough & Bobby Fisher. 2 cass. (Running Time: 2 hrs.). 2001. vinyl bd. 19.95 (A4350) St Anthony Mess Pr.
More guided meditations using gesture, posture and breath, with original music for prayer. Includes the very popular "Lord's Prayer" exercise.

Body Awareness & Imagination. Matthew McKay & Patrick Fanning. (Running Time: 50 mins). (Relaxation Skills Ser.). (ENG.). 2008. audio compact disk 13.95 (978-1-57224-638-6(3)) New Harbinger.

Body Awareness-Guided. 2007. audio compact disk 19.95 (978-1-56136-045-1(7)) Master Your Mind.

Body Bags: A Body of Evidence Thriller. Christopher Golden. Narrated by Julie Dretzin. 6 CDs. (Running Time: 6 hrs. 45 mins.). (gr. 9 up). audio compact disk 58.00 (978-1-4025-0463-1(2)) Recorded Bks.

Body Bags: A Body of Evidence Thriller. unabr. ed. Jenna Blake & Christopher Golden. Narrated by Julie Dretzin. 5 pieces. (Running Time: 6 hrs. 45 mins.). (gr. 9 up). 2001. 43.00 (978-0-7887-5368-8(1)) Recorded Bks.

Body Building. 1 cass. (Running Time: 60 min.). 10.95 (SP1) Psych Res Inst.
Mental sports conditioning.

Body Building. Barrie Konicov. 1 cass. 11.98 (978-0-87082-419-7(8), 016) Potentials.
Start seeing the perfect body reflected in your mirror, not just in your mind. It could be yours if you have the determination to make it so.

Body Building. Barrie Konicov. 2 CDs. 2003. audio compact disk 27.98 (978-1-56001-969-5(7)) Potentials.
Close your eyes and imagine the perfect body. Your perfect body. With your determination and this program, you can have the physique of which you dream.This 2-CD program from our Super Consciousness series is our newest, most powerful format. On the self-hypnosis CD, SC programs have the Subliminal Persuasion soundtrack added under Barrie?s voice. And the 17th Century Baroque music on the Subliminal CD has the same beat as your body's natural rhythm, thereby allowing the suggestions to enter deeply and effortlessly.

Body Building. Barrie Konicov. 1 CD. 2004. audio compact disk 27.98 (978-1-56001-664-9(7)) Potentials.
Close your eyes and imagine the perfect body. Your perfect body! With your determination and this program, you can have the physique of which you dream. You will find the self-hypnosis on track 1 and the subliminal on track 2. The easy-listening music of the subliminal, together with the self-hypnosis, is the original format which most people love and with which they are most familiar.

Body Building. Eldon Taylor. 1 cass. (Running Time: 62 min.). (Inner Talk Ser.). 16.95 incl. script. (978-0-940699-22-9(2), 5397C) Progress Aware Res.
Soundtrack - Musical Themes with underlying subliminal affirmations.

Body Building: Babbling Brook. Eldon Taylor. 1 cass. 16.95 (978-1-55978-508-2(X), 5397F) Progress Aware Res.

Body Building: Rhythm. Eldon Taylor. Read by Eldon Taylor. Ed. by Leslie Brice. 1 cass. (Running Time: 1 hr.). 1992. 16.95 (978-1-56705-250-3(9)) Gateways Inst.
Self improvement.

Body Building: Stream. Eldon Taylor. Read by Eldon Taylor. Ed. by Leslie Brice. 1 cass. (Running Time: 1 hr.). 1992. 16.95 (978-1-56705-251-0(7)) Gateways Inst.

Body Building (Subliminal), Vol. 26. Jayne Helle. 1 cass. (Running Time: 26 min.). 1995. 15.00 (978-1-891826-25-2(5)) Introspect.
Helps to increase one's personal best, feel better, & take control of one's body. A "can-do" program.

Body Centered Hypnosis for Pregnancy, Bonding, & Childbirth. 1 cass. 1990. 12.95 (978-0-9625231-3-7(5)) Shadow & Light.
Relaxation for pregnancy & childbirth.

Body Clocks: Program from the Award Winning Public Radio Series. Hosted by Fred Goodwin. Comment by John Hockenberry. Contrib. by Michael Smolensky & Thomas Wehr. 1 cass. (Running Time: 1 hr.). (Infinite Mind Ser.). 1998. audio compact disk 21.95 (978-1-888064-46-9(3), LCM 9) Lichtenstein Creat.
We now know that the body is not at all constant during the 24 hours, but, rather, it's highly cyclic with large variability in a number of biological functions.We'll hear from leading experts who tell us how circadian rhythms and other body clocks can affect everything from jet lag to mood to shift work to your physical health.

Body Count. collector's ed. William X. Kienzle. Read by Edward Holland. 7 cass. (Running Time: 10 hrs. 30 min.). (Father Koesler Mystery Ser.: No. 14). 2000. 56.00 (978-0-7366-5530-9(1)) Books on Tape.
Father John Keating is murdered & the man who did it reveals all to Father Koesler under the sacred seal of the confessional. Ever the traditionalist, Koesler knows he is bound to tell no one. Fortunately, the new priest in residence, Father Nick Dunn, has overheard the killer's case & when the cops call Koesler for help, the sleuthing father discovers that there is only one thing more annoying than an overeager amateur detective priest nipping at his heels, it's another murder.

Body Double. abr. ed. Tess Gerritsen. Read by Anne Heche. (Running Time: 19800 sec.). (Jane Rizzoli & Maura Isles Ser.: Bk. 4). (ENG.). 2006. audio compact disk 14.99 (978-0-7393-3345-7(3), Random AudioBks) Pub: Random Audio Pubg. Dist(s): Random

Body Empowerment. Power of Movement et al. audio compact disk 17.95 (978-0-910261-31-9(8)) Lotus Pr.

Body Farm. Patricia Cornwell. Narrated by C. J. Critt. 8 cass. (Running Time: 11 hrs. 45 mins.). (Kay Scarpetta Ser.: No. 5). 76.00 (978-1-4025-2410-3(2)) Recorded Bks.

Body Farm. Patricia Cornwell. Read by Jill Eikenberry. (Kay Scarpetta Ser.: No. 5). 2004. 10.95 (978-0-7435-4210-4(X)) Pub: S&S Audio. Dist(s): S and S Inc

Body Farm. abr. ed. Patricia Cornwell. Read by Jill Eikenberry. (Running Time: 30 hrs. 0 mins. 0 sec.). No. 5. (ENG.). 2004. audio compact disk 9.95 (978-0-7435-3749-0(1), S&S Encore) Pub: S&S Audio. Dist(s): S and S Inc

Body Farm. unabr. ed. Patricia Cornwell. Read by Kate Reading. 8 cass. (Running Time: 12 hrs.). (Kay Scarpetta Ser.: No. 5). 1995. 64.00 (978-0-7366-3040-5(6), 3722) Books on Tape.
In a remote North Carolina town, an 11-year-old girl turns up dead. The case puzzles the FBI staffers; medical reports baffle them & the photographs of the scene make no sense. No one can nail down the time of death, either, so the feds call in Kay Scarpetta, forensics whiz. She must work her grisly magic on the girl's body at a little-known Tennessee research facility, the Body Farm, that's designed to track precisely a corpse's decay. Only she can interpret the forensic Greek that reveals a horrifying answer.

Body Farm. unabr. ed. Patricia Cornwell. Narrated by C. J. Critt. 8 cass. (Running Time: 11 hrs. 45 mins.). (Kay Scarpetta Ser.: No. 5). 2002. 39.95 (978-1-4025-2411-0(0), RG096) Recorded Bks.
A small town in North Carolina is shaken when an 11-year-old girl is brutally murdered. In this crime, Forensic pathologist Kay Scarpetta sees eerie and disturbing echoes of a serial killer's work. Her investigation will lead her to a macabre research facility and into a truly horrifying world.

Body Fat Solution: Five Principles for Burning Fat, Building Lean Muscle, Ending Emotional Eating, & Maintaining Your Perfect Weight. unabr. ed. Tom Venuto. Read by L. J. Ganser. 9 CDs. (ENG.). 2009. audio compact disk 29.95 (978-1-60283-624-2(8)) Pub: AudioGO. Dist(s): Perseus Dist

***Body for Life.** abr. ed. Bill Phillips & Michael D'orso. Read by Bill Phillips. (ENG.). 2006. (978-0-06-115439-3(3), Harper Audio); (978-0-06-115440-9(7), Harper Audio) HarperCollins Pubs.

Body for Life: 12 Weeks to Mental & Physical Strength. abr. ed. Bill Phillips & Michael D'Orso. Read by Bill Phillips. (Running Time: 7200 sec.). 2008. audio compact disk 14.95 (978-0-06-146769-1(3), Harper Audio) HarperCollins Pubs.

Body for Life for Women: A Woman's Plan for Physical & Mental Transformation. abr. ed. Pamela Peeke. Frwd. by Cindy Crawford. (Running Time: 3 hrs. 30 mins. 0 sec.). (ENG.). 2009. audio compact disk 14.95 (978-1-4272-0710-4(0)) Pub: Macmill Audio. Dist(s): Macmillan

Body-for-Life for Women: 12 Weeks to a Firm, Fit, Fabulous Body at Any Age. abr. ed. Pamela Peeke. Frwd. by Cindy Crawford. 3 CDs. (Running Time: 3 hrs. 30 mins. 0 sec.). (ENG.). 2005. audio compact disk 24.95 (978-1-59397-643-9(7)) Pub: Macmill Audio. Dist(s): Macmillan

Body Garden & Reflections on Water. Sivananda Radha. 1 cass. (Running Time: 30 min.). 1994. 7.95 (978-0-931454-49-3(2)) Timeless Bks.
Swami Radha takes you through a complete visualization of your body as a garden of paradise while encouraging reflection on the element water as it appears in the Kundalini system. Through both these reflections the listener is directed toward deeper levels of awareness.

Body Gathers Vol. One: The Eucharist As Mystogogy. 2696th ed. Text by Ed Foley. 2001. audio compact disk (978-1-58459-078-1(5)) Wrld Lib Pubns.

Body Has a Mind of Its Own: How Body Maps in Your Brain Help You Do (Almost) Everything Better. unabr. ed. Sandra Blakeslee & Matthew Blakeslee. Narrated by Kate Reading. (Running Time: 9 hrs. 0 mins. 0 sec.). (ENG.). 2007. audio compact disk 34.99 (978-1-4001-0497-0(1)); audio compact disk 24.99 (978-1-4001-5497-5(9)); audio compact disk 69.99 (978-1-4001-3497-7(8)) Pub: Tantor Media. Dist(s): IngramPubServ

Body Image: Affirming Meditations for People of All Sizes. Martha Hutchinson. Read by Martha Hutchinson. Music by Synchestra. 1 cass. (Running Time: 1 hrs. 4 min.). 1996. 11.95 (978-1-57025-109-2(6)) Whole Person.
Learn to love & accept the body you have. Listen, respect & trust its messages. Five relaxing & affirming visualizations promote positive self-image, size-acceptance & personal empowerment - no matter what your size or shape.

Body Image: Program from the Award Winning Public Radio Series. Hosted by Fred Goodwin. Comment by John Hockenberry. Contrib. by Katherine Phillips et al. 1 cass. (Running Time: 1 hr.). (Infinite Mind Ser.). 1999. audio compact disk 21.95 (978-1-888064-16-2(1), LCM 55) Lichtenstein Creat.
As Americans spend billions of dollars to look good, what happens when somebody becomes so severely critical of their own appearance that it takes over their life, when they can't bear to even look into the mirror, mirror on the wall?We will talk with those who are affected by body dismorphic disorder, as well as therapists who treat it.

Body Image & Acceptance: Develop Acceptance, Respect & Appreciation for Your Body. Mark Bancroft. Read by Mark Bancroft. 1 cass., bklet. (Running Time: 1 hr.). (Health & Fitness Ser.). 1999. 12.95 (978-1-58522-019-9(1), 405) EnSpire Pr.
Two complete sessions plus printed instructionmanual/guidebook. With healing music soundtrack.

Body Image & Acceptance: Develop Acceptance, Respect, & Appreciation for Your Body. Mark Bancroft. Read by Mark Bancroft. 1 CD, 1 bklet. (Running Time: 1 hr.). (Health & Fitness Ser.). 2006. audio compact disk 20.00 (978-1-58522-054-0(X)) EnSpire Pr.

Body in the Bath House. unabr. ed. Lindsey Davis. Read by Christian Rodska. 9 cass. (Marcus Didius Falco Ser.). 2005. 79.95 (978-0-7927-3461-1(0), CSL 753); audio compact disk 99.95 (978-0-7927-3462-8(9), SLD 753) AudioGO.

Body in the Billiard Room. unabr. ed. H. R. F. Keating. Read by Sam Dastor. 6 cass. (Running Time: 8 hrs.). (Inspector Ghote Mystery Ser.: No. 16). 1988. 49.00 set. (978-1-55690-064-8(3), 88990) Recorded Bks.
A man is murdered in the famous Ooty Club. Inspector Ghote investigates.

Body in the Closet & Plumbing for Willy. unabr. ed. Mary Higgins Clark. Read by Frances Sternhagen. 2 cass. 1999. 18.00 (FS9-43289) Highsmith.

Body in the Closet & Plumbing for Willy: More Stories from the Lottery Winner. Mary Higgins Clark. 2004. 10.95 (978-0-7435-4211-1(8)) Pub: S&S Audio. Dist(s): S and S Inc

***Body in the Library.** Agatha Christie. Narrated by Full Cast Production Staff & June Whitfield. 2 CDs. (Running Time: 1 hr. 30 mins. 0 sec.). (ENG., 2010. audio compact disk 24.95 (978-0-563-51070-3(6)) Pub: AudioGO. Dist(s): Perseus Dist

Body in the Library. unabr. ed. Agatha Christie. Read by Stephanie Cole. 4 cass. (Running Time: 5 hrs. 23 mins.). (Miss Marple Ser.: No. 3). 2003. 25.95 (978-1-57270-324-7(5)) Pub: Audio Partners. Dist(s): PerseuPGW
One morning, Colonel and Dolly Bantry are awakened by their maid and informed that there is a body in the library! They immediately call the authorities and their dear old friend Miss Jane Marple. The dead young woman is soon identified as Ruby Keene, a dance hostess at a hotel. Can Miss Marple's sharp p eyes find the motive, the truth, and the killer.

Body in the Library. unabr. ed. Agatha Christie. Narrated by Stephanie Cole. 5 CDs. (Running Time: 5 hrs. 23 mins.). (Miss Marple Ser.: No. 3). (ENG.). 2003. audio compact disk 27.95 (978-1-57270-325-4(3)) Pub: AudioGO. Dist(s): Perseus Dist

Body in the Transept. unabr. collector's ed. Jeanne M. Dams. Read by Kate Reading. 7 cass. (Running Time: 7 hrs.). (Dorothy Martin Mystery Ser.: Bk. 1). 1996. 56.00 (978-0-913369-23-4(3), 4174) Books on Tape.
Introducing Dorothy Martin, a charming amateur sleuth & lover of outrageous hats. For Dorothy, widowed American removed to England, the christmas service is painful enough; it's her first holiday without Frank. Stumbling over the body of Canon Billings does nothing to improve her mood. A good mystery on a chilly English night does have some appeal. Though the Canon may be dead, Dorothy Martin is very much alive & sleuthing.

Body Language. Suzanne Brockmann. 2008. audio compact disk 14.95 (978-1-60283-410-1(5)) AudioGO.

Body Language. unabr. ed. James W. Hall. Read by Laural Merlington. (Running Time: 10 hrs.). 2009. 39.97 (978-1-4233-8615-5(9), 9781423386155, Brlnc Audio MP3 Lib); 24.99 (978-1-4233-8614-8(0), 9781423386148, Brilliance MP3); 39.97 (978-1-4233-8617-9(5), 9781423386179, BADLE); 24.99 (978-1-4233-8616-2(7), 9781423386162, BAD) Brilliance Audio.

Body, Mind, & Spirit. abr. ed. Louis Hughes. Read by Louis Hughes. 2 cass. (Running Time: 2 hrs. 48 min.). 1992. 16.95 set. (978-0-89622-755-2(3)) Twenty-Third.
Meditative, relaxation techniques with a spiritual trend. Do not attempt to practice or listen to these tapes while driving or operating machinery.

Body, Mind & Spirit of Depression: Medical & Psychoanalytical Perspectives on Depressive Disorders. Kenneth James & Michael Rockwell. Read by Kenneth James & Michael Rockwell. 4 cass. (Running Time: 6 hrs.). 1997. 31.95 Set. (978-0-7822-0532-9(1), 599) C G Jung IL.
The authors consider medical & psychoanalytical viewpoints on depressive disorders, a leading cause for seeking psychotherapy. The workshop also examines the history & physiology of depression, diagnostic procedures from psychiatric & psychoanalytic perspectives, & analytic techniques for working with the dreams of depressed patients.

Body Mind Mastery: Creating Success in Sport & Life. abr. ed. Dan Millman. Read by Dan Millman. 2 cass. (Running Time: 3 hrs.). 1999. 17.95 (978-1-57731-096-9(9)) Pub: New Wrld Lib. Dist(s): PerseuPGW
Reveals a path to success not only in sports but in any life endeavor that requires training & the integration of the body & mind. Includes overview chapters on developing mental, emotional, physical talent, training, competition & the evolution of athletics.

Body Modification. Anne Schraff. Narrated by Larry A. McKeever. (Extreme Customs Ser.). (J). 2006. 10.95 (978-1-58659-127-4(4)); audio compact disk 14.95 (978-1-58659-361-2(7)) Artesian.

Body of Christ: Paul's Message to the City Churches. 5 cass. (Running Time: 7 hrs. 50 min.). 1993. 40.95 Set. (TAH288) Alba Hse Comns.
A thought-provoking & insightful study on St. Paul, Corinth & its people packed with useful & practical information.

Body of Christopher Creed. Carol Plum-Ucci. Narrated by Scott Shina. 6 pieces. (Running Time: 8 hrs.). (gr. 10 up). 54.00 (978-1-4025-0956-8(1)) Recorded Bks.

Body of David Hayes. abr. ed. Ridley Pearson. Read by Dick Hill. 5. (Running Time: 21600 sec.). (Lou Boldt/Daphne Matthews Ser.). 2007. audio compact disk 14.99 (978-1-4233-1960-3(5), 9781423319603, BCD Value Price) Brilliance Audio.

Body of David Hayes. unabr. ed. Ridley Pearson. Read by Dick Hill. 7 cass. (Running Time: 10 hrs.). (Lou Boldt/Daphne Matthews Ser.: Vol. 9). 2004. 32.95 (978-1-59086-744-0(0), 1590867440) Brilliance Audio.
Years ago, Lou's wife Liz had an extramarital affair with David Hayes, a young computer specialist at the bank where she is an executive. Drained by the overwhelming demands of marriage to a high-profile cop, Liz fell into the temptation of an office fling, which she soon regretted. When Liz ended the relationship after reconciling with Lou, Hayes reacted by engaging in a daring embezzlement scheme that left millions missing. The money was never found. Now, years later, David Hayes is released from prison, only to be cornered and pressured by people who will torture and kill to get the missing money. Hayes contacts Liz and tries to coerce her into helping him gain access to the bank's mainframe. But for Liz, the past is only that. Torn between wanting to protect herself, her marriage, and also the bank, she is manipulated into playing double-agent by a former colleague of Boldt's - without her husband's knowledge. Boldt, sworn to uphold the law, but with his wife caught in the middle, must skate a delicate line between duty-bound detective and jealous husband if he is to find the bank's money and keep his family from shattering. Then when Hayes goes missing, and no body is found, Boldt must combine ruse with violent action to sort out lie from fact.

Body of David Hayes. unabr. ed. Ridley Pearson. Read by Dick Hill & Susie Breck. 8 cass. (Running Time: 10 hrs.). (Lou Boldt/Daphne Matthews Ser.: Vol. 9). 2004. 82.25 (978-1-59086-748-8(3), 1590867483) Brilliance Audio.
Years ago, Lou's wife Liz had an extramarital affair with David Hayes, a young computer specialist at the bank where she is an executive. Drained by the overwhelming demands of marriage to a high-profile cop, Liz fell into the temptation of an office fling, which she soon regretted. When Liz ended the relationship after reconciling with Lou, Hayes reacted by engaging in a daring embezzlement scheme that left millions missing. The money was never found. Now, years later, David Hayes is released from prison, only to be cornered and pressured by people who will torture and kill to get the missing money. Hayes contacts Liz and tries to coerce her into helping him gain access to the bank's mainframe. But for Liz, the past is only that. Torn between wanting to protect herself, her marriage, and also the bank, she is manipulated into playing double-agent by a former colleague of Boldt's - without her husband's knowledge. Boldt, sworn to uphold the law, but with his wife caught in the middle, must skate a delicate line between duty-bound detective and jealous husband if he is to find the bank's money and keep his family from shattering. Then when Hayes goes missing, and no body is found, Boldt must combine ruse with violent action to sort out lie from fact.

Body of David Hayes. unabr. ed. Ridley Pearson. Read by Dick Hill. 10 CDs. (Running Time: 10 hrs.). (Lou Boldt/Daphne Matthews Ser.: Vol. 9). 2004. audio compact disk 33.95 (978-1-59086-745-7(9), 1590867459, BAU); audio compact disk 92.25 (978-1-59086-747-1(5), 1590867475) Brilliance Audio.

Body of David Hayes. unabr. ed. Ridley Pearson. Read by Dick Hill. (Running Time: 10 hrs.). (Lou Boldt/Daphne Matthews Ser.). 2004. 39.25 (978-1-59335-551-7(3), 1593355513, Brlnc Audio MP3 Lib); 24.95 (978-1-59335-282-0(4), 1593352824, Brilliance MP3) Brilliance Audio.

Body of David Hayes. unabr. ed. Ridley Pearson. Read by Dick Hill. (Running Time: 10 hrs.). (Lou Boldt/Daphne Matthews Ser.). 2004. 39.25 (978-1-59710-101-1(X), 159710101X, BADLE); 24.95 (978-1-59710-100-4(1), 1597101001, BAD) Brilliance Audio.

Body of Evidence. 1992. 16.00 (978-1-55994-527-1(3)) HarperCollins Pubs.

Body of Evidence. Jeremy Brown. Read by Fred Berman. (Crime Files Ser.). (ENG.). (J). (gr. 4-7). 2006. audio compact disk 19.95 (978-0-439-89554-5(5)) Scholastic Inc.

Body of Evidence. unabr. ed. Patricia Cornwell. Read by Lorelei King. 8 cass. (Running Time: 8 hrs.). (Kay Scarpetta Ser.: No. 2). 1996. 69.95 set. (978-0-7451-6580-6(X), CAB1196) AudioGO.
Someone is stalking reclusive writer Beryl Madison. Terrified, Beryl flees to Key West. Eventually she returns to her Richmond home, & the very night she arrives, Beryl inexplicably invites her killer in...Adding to the intrigue is Beryl's relationship with a prize-winning author & the disappearance of Beryl's own manuscript. Chief Medical Examiner Dr. Kay Scarpetta must retrace Beryl's footsteps. An investigation that begins in the laboratory now leads Scarpetta deep into a nightmare that soon becomes her own.

Body of Evidence. unabr. ed. Patricia Cornwell. Read by Donada Peters. 8 CDs. (Running Time: 9 hrs. 36 mins.). (Kay Scarpetta Ser.: No. 2). 2000. audio compact disk 64.00 (978-0-7366-6051-8(8)) Books on Tape.
Someone is after Beryl Madison - spying on her, making threatening phone calls. Terrified, she flees to Key West. When she comes back home, it's not harassment that's waiting...it's murder. Police work begins with Dr. Kay Scarpetta, Chief Medical Examiner.

Body of Evidence. unabr. ed. Patricia Cornwell. Narrated by C. J. Critt. 11 CDs. (Running Time: 12 hrs. 45 mins.). (Kay Scarpetta Ser.: No. 2). 2000. audio compact disk 98.00 (978-0-7887-3397-0(4), C1003E7) Recorded Bks.
Late one night Beryl Madison turns off her burglar alarm, puts down her gun & opens her door to the man who has stalked & terrorized her for months. Hours later, her brutally mutilated body lies in the city morgue. As Scarpetta begins searching for the microscopic clues to the killer's identity, one question keeps nagging her: why did Beryl let him in?.

Body of Evidence. unabr. ed. Patricia Cornwell. Narrated by C. J. Critt. 9 cass. (Running Time: 12 hrs. 45 mins.). (Kay Scarpetta Ser.: No. 2). 1994. 78.00 (978-0-7887-0048-4(0), 94247E7) Recorded Bks.
A successful romance writer is brutally murdered by a killer it appears she must have known; Kay Scarpetta investigates.

Body of Evidence. unabr. collector's ed. Patricia Cornwell. Read by Donada Peters. 7 cass. (Running Time: 10 hrs. 30 min.). (Kay Scarpetta Ser.: No. 2). 1991. 56.00 (978-0-7366-2001-7(X), 2818) Books on Tape.
Someone is after Beryl Madison - spying on her, making threatening phone calls. Terrified, she flees to Key West. When she comes back home, it's not harassment that's waiting...it's murder. Police work begins with Dr. Kay Scarpetta, Chief Medical Examiner.

Body of Lies. Iris Johansen. Narrated by Cristine McMurdo-Wallis. 7 cass. (Running Time: 10 hrs. 15 mins.). (Eve Duncan Ser.). 68.00 (978-1-4025-1814-0(5)) Recorded Bks.

Body of Lies. unabr. ed. David Ignatius. Read by Dick Hill. (YA). 2007. 59.99 (978-1-60252-819-2(5)) Find a World.

Body of Lies. unabr. ed. David Ignatius. (Running Time: 12 hrs. 30 mins. 0 sec.). (ENG.). 2007. audio compact disk 69.99 (978-1-4001-3443-4(9)); audio compact disk 24.99 (978-1-4001-5443-2(X)) Pub: Tantor Media. Dist(s): IngramPubServ

Body of Lies. unabr. ed. David Ignatius. Read by Dick Hill. (Running Time: 12 hrs. 30 mins. 0 sec.). (ENG.). 2007. audio compact disk 34.99 (978-1-4001-0443-7(2)) Pub: Tantor Media. Dist(s): IngramPubServ

Body of Lies. unabr. ed. David Ignatius. Narrated by Dick Hill. (Running Time: 12 hrs. 30 mins. 0 sec.). (ENG.). 2008. audio compact disk 34.99 (978-1-4001-0993-7(0)); audio compact disk 69.99 (978-1-4001-3993-4(7)); audio compact disk 24.99 (978-1-4001-5993-2(8)) Pub: Tantor Media. Dist(s): IngramPubServ

Body of Lies. unabr. ed. Iris Johansen. Narrated by Cristine McMurdo-Wallis. 9 CDs. (Running Time: 10 hrs. 15 mins.). (Eve Duncan Ser.). 2002. audio compact disk 89.00 (978-1-4025-2899-6(X)) Recorded Bks.
Eve Duncan became a forensic sculptor after the disappearance of her daughter Bonnie, whose remains were discovered ... yet unrecognizable. Driven by a need to liberate innocence from the shroud of death, she obsesses over recreating the likenesses of faceless, decomposed murder victims, using only their bare skulls as a guide.

Body of Work: Meditations on Mortality from the Human Anatomy Lab. unabr. ed. Christine Montross. Read by Renée Raudman. (YA). 2008. 59.99 (978-1-60514-667-6(6)) Find a World.

Body of Work: Meditations on Mortality from the Human Anatomy Lab. unabr. ed. Christine Montross. Read by Renée Raudman. (Running Time: 9 hrs. 30 mins. 0 sec.). (ENG.). 2007. audio compact disk 34.99 (978-1-4001-0487-1(4)); audio compact disk 24.99 (978-1-4001-5487-6(1)); audio compact disk 69.99 (978-1-4001-3487-8(0)) Pub: Tantor Media. Dist(s): IngramPubServ

Body on the Beach. unabr. ed. Simon Brett. Read by Geoffrey Howard. 5 cass. (Running Time: 7 hrs.). 2000. 39.95 (978-0-7861-1839-7(3), 2638) Blckstn Audio.
Carole Seddon is recently retired from the Home Office & living in the overdeveloped residential hamlet of Fethering. Residing in the cottage she purchased with her ex-husband, she maintains a quiet & sensible life with her dog, Gulliver. Then Carole & Gulliver find a corpse on the beach, with two wounds on its neck. But the body mysteriously disappears & the police dismiss Carole as a befuddled middle-aged woman. She almost believes it, until a stranger threatens her to be quiet or else.

Body on the Beach. unabr. ed. Simon Brett. Read by Geoffrey Howard. 6 CDs. (Running Time: 7 hrs.). 2000. audio compact disk 48.00 (978-0-7861-9820-7(6), 2638) Blckstn Audio.

Body on the Beach. unabr. ed. Simon Brett. Read by Simon Brett. Read by Geoffrey Howard. 6 cass. (Running Time: 9 hrs.). 2000. 54.95 (978-0-7531-0836-9(4), 000607) Pub: ISIS Audio GBR. Dist(s): Ulverscroft US
Very little disturbs the orderly calm in Fethering. So the last thing Carole expects to encounter is a new neighbor with an obviously colorful past. "Jude" is not really Fethering, but neither is the body Carole finds on the beach, a body that disappears by the time the police arrive.

Body on the Beach. unabr. ed. Simon Brett. Read by Simon Brett. 7 CDs. (Running Time: 10 hrs. 30 min.). (Fethering Mystery Ser.). 2001. audio compact disk 71.95 (978-0-7531-1127-7(6), 1127-6) Pub: ISIS Audio GBR. Dist(s): Ulverscroft US
Little disturbs the ordered calm of Fethering, a self-contained retirement complex on England's south coast. So the last thing Carole expects is a new neighbor with an obviously colorful past. "Jude" is not really Fethering... but neither is the body Carole finds on the beach - a body that disappears by the time the police arrive. Only Jude is ready to believe what her neighbor says she saw & from that moment on the two women resolve to turn detectives.

Body Parts. unabr. ed. William C. Knott. Read by Maynard Villers. 4 cass. (Running Time: 5 hrs. 24 min.). (Repo-Man Ser.: Bk. 1). 1995. 26.95 (978-1-55686-625-8(9)) Books in Motion.
Lake Placid, NY - Skip Tracewski takes on mad-dog mobsters who killed his friend while in the act of repossessing their Lamborghini.

Body Relationship & Awareness: Enhance Your Relationship with Your Body. Mark Bancroft. Read by Mark Bancroft. 1 cass., bklet. (Running Time: 1 hr.). (Health & Fitness Ser.). 1999. 12.95 (978-1-58522-038-0(8), 407) EnSpire Pr.
Two complete sessions plus printed instructionmanual/guidebook. With healing music soundtrack.

Body Relationship & Awareness: Enhance Your Relationship with Your Body. Mark Bancroft. Read by Mark Bancroft. 1 CD, 1 bklet. (Running Time: 1 hr.). (Health & Fitness Ser.). 2006. audio compact disk 20.00 (978-1-58522-055-7(8)) EnSpire Pr.

Body Snatcher see Bottle Imp & Other Stories

Body Snatcher. Robert Louis Stevenson. Ed. by Raymond Harris. (Classics Ser.). (YA). (gr. 6-12). 1982. pap. bk. 13.00 (978-0-89061-258-3(7), 460) Jamestown.

Body-Snatcher & Other Stories. unabr. ed. Short Stories. Robert Louis Stevenson. Narrated by Alexander Spencer. 2 cass. (Running Time: 3 hrs.). (gr. 8 up). 1981. 18.00 (978-1-55690-065-5(1), 81280E7) Recorded Bks.
Short stories of the macabre & supernatural.

Body Snatcher & Thrawn Janet. unabr. ed. Read by John Chatty. 1 cass. (Running Time: 86 min.). Dramatization. 1986. 7.95 (S-72) Jimcin Record.
Ghost Story.

Body Snatchers. Edgar Allan Poe. 1 cass. 1989. 7.95 (S-72) Jimcin Record.
Ghostly revenge!.

Body, Soul, Spirit. Michael Pearl. 3 CDs. (Running Time: 215 mins). 2005. audio compact disk (978-1-892112-64-4(7)) No Greater Joy.

Body Surfing. unabr. ed. Anita Shreve. Read by Lolita Davidovich. (Running Time: 8 hrs.). (ENG.). 2007. 14.98 (978-1-59483-875-0(5)) Pub: Hachet Audio. Dist(s): HachBkGrp

Body Symbology (Lecture) unabr. ed. Rosalyn Bruyere. 2 cass. 18.00 (OC55L) Sound Horizons AV.

Body Symbology (Workshop) unabr. ed. Rosalyn Bruyere. 8 cass. 72.00 (OC55W) Sound Horizons AV.

Body Talk. Created by Victoria Wizell. Voice by Victoria Wizell. 1 CD. 2001. audio compact disk 39.00 (978-0-9679176-2-7(X)) Hyptalk.
A unique meditation CD that is divided into 4 approximately 15-minute sections. Each section can be played on it's own or combined with another section.

Body Talk: No-Nonsense, Common-Sense, Sixth-Sense Solutions to Create Health & Healing. Christiane Northrup & Mona Lisa Schulz. 6 cass. (Running Time: 6 hrs.). (ENG.). 2001. 59.95 (978-1-56170-852-9(6)) Hay House.
This six-tape audio program teaches you how to identify, work with & transform your thoughts, emotions & behaviors along health-enhancing lines & shows you how to use your body's unique intuitive language to help you heal your body, mind & soul.

Body Talk Set: Forever Yours. 2 cass. (Running Time: 1 hr. 30 min.). 1999. 14.99 (T4BTJ1) Time-Life.

Body Talk Set: Forever Yours. 2 CDs. (Running Time: 1 hr. 30 min.). 1999. audio compact disk 16.99 (T5BTJ0) Time-Life.

Body Temple. unabr. ed. Philip K. Burley. Read by Philip K. Burley. Contrib. by Hilary Stagg. 1 cass. (Running Time: 22 min.). (Stress Management Meditation Ser.). (YA). 1998. 10.00 (978-1-883389-09-3(7)) Adv In Mastery.
Guided visualization for complete physical relaxation & stress management, with harp music in the background.

Body That Will Make You Healthier & Younger. abr. ed. Michael F. Roizen & Mehmet C. Oz. Read by Michael F. Roizen. 2008. audio compact disk 14.95 (978-0-06-146774-5(X), Harper Audio) HarperCollins Pubs.

Body That Will Make You Healthier & Younger. abr. rev. exp. ed. Michael F. Roizen & Mehmet C. Oz. Read by Michael F. Roizen & Mehmet C. Oz. (Running Time: 28800 sec.). 2008. audio compact disk 19.95 (978-0-06-167316-0(1), Harper Audio) HarperCollins Pubs.

Body to Die For. abr. ed. Kate White. Read by Kate Walsh. (ENG.). 2005. 14.98 (978-1-59483-176-8(9)) Pub: Hachet Audio. Dist(s): HachBkGrp

Body to Die For. abr. ed. Kate White. Read by Kate Walsh. (Running Time: 6 hrs.). (ENG.). 2009. 49.98 (978-1-60788-031-8(8)) Pub: Hachet Audio. Dist(s): HachBkGrp

Body Transformation: Inside-Out. unabr. ed. Tricia Brennan. Read by Tricia Brennan. (Running Time: 3600 sec.). 2006. audio compact disk 39.95 (978-1-74093-717-7(1)) Pub: Bolinda Pubng AUS. Dist(s): Bolinda Pub Inc

Body Transformation Inside-Out. unabr. abr. ed. Tricia Brennan. Read by Tricia Brennan. 1 x CD. (Running Time: 3600 sec.). 2006. audio compact disk 16.95 (978-1-74094-921-7(8)) Bolinda Pubng AUS.

Body Vital/ Stress-Free Living. Created by Barry Neil Kaufman. 2 Cds. (Running Time: 50 mins., 71 mins.). 2005. audio compact disk 35.00 (978-1-887254-17-5(X)) Epic Century.
This series is a must for anyone wanting to say "no more" to tension, burnout, stress and fatigue and wanting to say "yes" to a more vital living experience.Barry Neil Kaufman digs through the confusion of recent research and synthesizes the inspiring notion of creating within ourselves The Body Vital (an energetic, vitally alive mind-body experience). In Stress-Free Living, Bears tackles the phenomenon of stress and comes to a most unexpected conclusion. He gives guidance on implementing a stress-free living strategy.

***Body Work.** abr. ed. Sara Paretsky. Read by Susan Ericksen. (Running Time: 7 hrs.). (V. I. Warshawski Ser.). 2010. 9.99 (978-1-4418-9391-8(1), 9781441893918, BAD); audio compact disk 26.99 (978-1-4418-6889-3(5), 9781441868893, BACD) Brilliance Audio.

***Body Work.** unabr. ed. Sara Paretsky. Read by Susan Ericksen. (Running Time: 15 hrs.). (V. I. Warshawski Ser.). 2010. 24.99 (978-1-4418-6887-9(9), 9781441868879, BAD); 24.99 (978-1-4418-6885-5(2), 9781441868855, Brilliance MP3); 39.97 (978-1-4418-6886-2(0), 9781441868862, Brlnc Audio MP3 Lib); 39.97 (978-1-4418-6888-6(7), 9781441868886, BADLE); audio compact disk 36.99 (978-1-4418-6883-1(6), 9781441868831, Bril Audio CD Unabri); audio compact disk 99.97 (978-1-4418-6884-8(4), 9781441868848, BriAudCD Unabrid) Brilliance Audio.

Bodyguard. Suzanne Brockmann. Read by Carrington MacDuffie. 7 vols. 2004. 59.95 (978-0-7927-3107-8(7), CSL 619, Chivers Sound Lib) AudioGO.

Bodyguard. unabr. ed. Suzanne Brockmann. Read by Carrington MacDuffie. 8 CDs. (Running Time: 12 hrs.). 2004. audio compact disk 79.95 (978-0-7927-3108-5(5), SLD 619, Chivers Sound Lib) AudioGO.

Bodyguard of Lies. Anthony Cave Brown. Read by David Case. 2001. 120.00 (978-0-7366-6018-1(6)); 120.00 (978-0-7366-6103-4(4)) Books on Tape.

Bodyguard's Story: Diana, the Crash, & the Sole Survivor. unabr. ed. Trevor Rees-Jones. Read by Peter Wickham. 10 cass. (Running Time: 12 hrs.). (Sound Ser.). (J). 2002. 84.95 (978-1-84283-194-6(1)) Pub: ISIS Lrg Prnt GBR. Dist(s): Ulverscroft US

Bodyguard's Story: Diana, the Crash, & the Sole Survivor. unabr. ed. Trevor Rees-Jones. Read by Peter Wickham. 10 CDs. (Running Time: 12 hrs.). (Sound Ser.). (J). 2003. audio compact disk 89.95 (978-1-84283-581-4(5)) Pub: ISIS Lrg Prnt GBR. Dist(s): Ulverscroft US

Bodywise. Perf. by Kidzup Productions Staff. 1 cass. (J). 1997. 8.99 (K7 019602); audio compact disk 12.99 (KCD 019602) Kidzup Prodns.
Encourages children to exercise while having fun.

***Bog Child.** unabr. ed. Siobhan Dowd. Read by Sile Bermingham. 7 CDs. (Running Time: 8 hrs. 43 mins.). (YA). (gr. 8 up). 2009. audio compact disk 45.00 (978-0-7393-8540-1(2), Listening Lib) Pub: Random Audio Pubg. Dist(s): Random

Bog Child. unabr. ed. Siobhan Dowd. Read by Sile Bermingham. (ENG.). (J). (gr. 7). 2009. audio compact disk 39.00 (978-0-7393-8538-8(0), Listening Lib) Pub: Random Audio Pubg. Dist(s): Random

Bogaazan! unabr. ed. Akira Hayasaka. Perf. by June Angela et al. 1 cass. (Running Time: 54 min.). 1995. 19.95 (978-1-58081-049-4(7)) L A Theatre.
As the Japanese battleship "Yamato" steams toward the island of Okinawa in the closing months of World War II, a naval officer on board makes an unexpected discovery among the stores of rice, leeks & pickled radishes. A child has stowed away there, hoping to return to her mother on Okinawa. The officer's reluctant decision to protect her prompts a voyage of inner discovery & stirs emotions as deep as the seas that threaten to swallow his "unsinkable" ship.

Bogart, Pt. 1 unabr. ed. Eric Lax & A. M. Sperber. Read by Michael Mitchell. 10 cass. (Running Time: 15 hrs.). 1999. 80.00 (978-0-7366-4311-5(7), 4769A) Books on Tape.
Biography of a Hollywood giant whose full story has never been revealed until now.

Bogart, Pt. 2. unabr. ed. Ann M. Sperber & Eric Lax. Read by Michael Mitchell. Illus. by Ann M. Sperber. 9 cass. (Running Time: 13 hrs. 30 mins.). 1999. 72.00 (4769B) Books on Tape.

Bogart: In Search of My Father. unabr. ed. Stephen Humphrey Bogart. Read by Barrett Whitener. 6 cass. (Running Time: 8 hrs. 30 mins.). 1996. 44.95 (978-0-7861-0971-5(8), 1748) Blckstn Audio.
Writing with the encouragement of his famous mother, Lauren Bacall, Stephen calls on his memories & takes full advantage of the extraordinary access he has had to friends & colleagues of his father. The result is an intimate & personal profile of an enigmatic man whose tough image contrasted with very human ambitions & vulnerabilities.Filled with fascinating stories involving Frank Sinatra, Katherine Hepburn, "Swifty" Lazar, John Huston, Stephen Bogart's stepfather, Jason Robards & many others.

Bogart: In Search of My Father. unabr. ed. Stephen Humphrey Bogart. Read by Barrett Whitener. (Running Time: 9 hrs. 0 mins.). (ENG.). 2009. 29.95 (978-1-4417-0564-8(3)); audio compact disk 76.00 (978-1-4417-0561-7(9)) Blckstn Audio.

Boggart. Susan Cooper. Read by David Rintoul. 4 cass. (Running Time: 5 hrs. 50 mins.). (J). 2000. 30.00 (978-0-7366-4966-7(2)) Books on Tape.

Boggart. unabr. ed. Susan Cooper. Read by David Rintoul. 7 cass. (Running Time: 90 min. per cass.). (Boggart Ser.). (J). 1997. 45.00 Set. (4845) Books on Tape.
Boggart, an invisible spirit who resides invisibly & prankishly over a remote Scottish castle, plays pranks on humans, her resourceful sibling protagonists.

Boggart. unabr. ed. Susan Cooper. Read by David Rintoul. 4 cass. (YA). 1999. 29.98 (FS9-25222) Highsmith.

Boggart. unabr. ed. Susan Cooper. Read by David Rintoul. 4 cass. (Running Time: 4 hrs. 47 mins.). (J). (gr. 3-7). 1994. 32.00 (978-0-8072-7431-6(3), YA863CX, Listening Lib) Random Audio Pubg.
A mystical story of an invisible, mischievous, magical spirit that has dwelled for centuries in a tumbledown Scottish castle - until the visiting Volnik family visits. Their lives are changed after they unknowingly bring the Boggart home with them.

Boggart. unabr. ed. Listening Library Staff & Susan Cooper. Read by David Rintoul. 4 vols. (Running Time: 4 hrs. 47 mins.). (J). (gr. 3-7). 1994. pap. bk. 38.00 (978-0-8072-7432-3(1), YA863SP, Listening Lib) Random Audio Pubg.

Boggart & the Monster. Susan Cooper. Read by David Rintoul. 3 cass. (Running Time: 4 hrs. 45 mins.). (J). 2000. 24.00 (978-0-7366-9136-9(7)) Books on Tape.

Boggart & the Monster. unabr. ed. Susan Cooper. Read by David Rintoul. 7 cass. (Running Time: 90 min. per cass.). (Boggart Ser.). (J). 1997. 45.00 Set. (4845) Books on Tape.
The Boggart accompanies Emily Volnik & her brother, Jessup, on an exciting expedition in search of the Loch Ness Monster.

Boggart & the Monster. unabr. ed. Susan Cooper. Read by David Rintoul. 7 cass. (Running Time: 1 hr. 30 min. per cass.). (Boggart Ser.). (J). 1999. 45.00 (4845) Books on Tape.
In the first story, an invisible spirit plays pranks on humans in a remote Scottish castle. In the second story, "the Boggart" accompanies Emily Volnik & her brother, Jessup, on an exciting expedition in search of the Loch Ness monster.

Boggart & the Monster. unabr. ed. Susan Cooper. Read by David Rintoul. 3 cass. (YA). 1999. 23.98 (FS9-31423) Highsmith.

Boggart & the Monster. unabr. ed. Susan Cooper. Read by David Rintoul & Peter Thomas. 3 cass. (Running Time: 4 hrs. 43 mins.). (Boggart Ser.). (J). (gr. 4-7). 1997. 30.00 (978-0-8072-7820-8(3), YA925CX, Listening Lib) Random Audio Pubg.
Pertains to a mischievous shape-sifting spirit.

Boggart & the Monster. unabr. ed. Susan Cooper. Read by David Rintoul. 3 cass. (Running Time: 4 hrs. 43 mins.). (YA). (gr. 5 up). 1997. pap. bk. 35.00 (978-0-8072-7821-5(1), YA925SP, Listening Lib) Random Audio Pubg.

Boggart Series. unabr. ed. Susan Cooper. Read by David Rintoul. 7 cass. (Running Time: 10 hrs. 30 mins.). (J). 1999. 45.00 (978-0-7366-4381-8(8), 4845) Books on Tape.
The Boggart accompanies Emil Volnik & her brother, Jessup, on an exciting expedition in search of the Loch Ness Monster.

Bogie: Golf... as It Was. Charles S. Hellman. 2003. audio compact disk 29.95 (978-0-935938-02-9(8)) LuckySports.

Boheme. rev. ed. Giacomo Puccini. Composed by Georges Bizet. Comment by William Berger. Text by David Foil. 2 vols. (ENG., 2005. audio compact disk 19.95 (978-1-57912-509-7(3), 1579125093) Pub: Blck Dog & Leventhal. Dist(s): Workman Pub

Boheme, Set. Perf. by Licia Albanese et al. Composed by Puccini. Contrib. by Renato Cellini. 2 CDs. 1959. audio compact disk 33.95 Stereo. (VAIA 1188-2) VAI Audio.
From the New Orleans Opera.

Boheme: An Introduction to Puccini's Opera. Thomson Smillie. Read by David Timson. 1 CD. (Running Time: 1 hr. 30 min.). (Opera Explained Ser.). 2003. audio compact disk 8.99 (978-1-84379-037-2(8)) NaxMulti GBR.
The poignant story of Mimi and Rodolfo told in music of tender beauty, allied, as always, to Puccini's intuition of what works in the theatre.

Bohemian Murders. Dianne Day. Read by Anna Fields. 1999. 48.00 (978-0-7366-4620-8(5)) Books on Tape.

Bohemian Murders: A Fremont Jones Mystery. Dianne Day. Read by Anna Fields. 6 cass. (Running Time: 9 hrs.). 1999. 48.00 (5006) Books on Tape.
Nursing a broken heart, Fremont Jones accepts a position as keeper of a lighthouse, only to have a body wash ashore.

Boithrini an Lochain: Sean-Nos Songs from Connemara. Contrib. by Meaiti Jo Sheamuis O. Fatharta. (ENG.). 2003. 13.95 (978-0-8023-7154-6(X)); audio compact disk 22.95 (978-0-8023-8154-5(5)) Pub: Clo Iar-Chonnachta IRL. Dist(s): Dufour

Bok, Muir & Trickett: A Water over Stone. 1 cass. 9.98 (C-80) Folk-Legacy.
Another moving program from the noted trio.

Bok, Muir & Trickett: All Shall Be Well Again. 1 cass. 9.98 (C-96) Folk-Legacy.
Another excellent program of great songs.

Bok, Muir & Trickett: And So Will We Yet. 1 cass., 1 CD. 9.98 (C-116); audio compact disk 14.98 CD. (CD-116) Folk-Legacy.
Splendid performances of some great songs.

Bok, Muir, & Trickett: Fashioned in the Clay. 1 cass. 9.98 (C-104) Folk-Legacy.
More good stuff from the popular trio.

Bok, Muir & Trickett: Language of the Heart. 1 cass., 1 CD. 9.98 (C-5030); audio compact disk 14.98 CD. (CD-5030) Folk-Legacy.
The trio's latest recording on Timberhead.

Bok, Muir & Trickett: Minneapolis Concert. 1 cass. 9.98 (C-110) Folk-Legacy.
A "live" recording of a Midwest concert.

Bok, Muir & Trickett: The Ways of Man. 1 cass. 9.98 (C-68) Folk-Legacy.
A powerful collection from this popular trio.

Bok, Muir & Trickett: Turning Toward the Morning. 1 cass. 9.98 (C-56) Folk-Legacy.
The first recording of the trio; truly a classic.

Bola de Sebo y Otras Narraciones. unabr. ed. Guy de Maupassant. Read by Laura Garcia. 3 CDs.Tr. of Butter-Ball & Other Stories. (SPA.). 2002. audio compact disk 17.00 (978-958-8161-31-0(2)) YoYoMusic.

Bold Benture: Robbery & Haven's Venezuelan Isle. unabr. ed. Perf. by Humphrey Bogart et al. 1 cass. (Running Time: 1 hr.). 2001. 6.98 (1609) Radio Spirits.

Bold Dragoon: The Life of J. E. B. Stuart. unabr. ed. Emory M. Thomas. Narrated by Larry McKeever. 9 cass. (Running Time: 13 hrs.). 1988. 78.00 (978-1-55690-067-9(8), 88670E7) Recorded Bks.
The life of J. E. B. Stuart. Professor of history at the University of Georgia, takes a fresh look at a much-examined hero, the Confederacy's famous cavalry chief. From his childhood in Virginia to his astonishing exploits on the battlefields of the Civil War, from his controversial role in the Battle of Gettysburg to his untimely death at Appomatox.

Bold Fresh Piece of Humanity. unabr. ed. Bill O'Reilly. Read by Bill O'Reilly. 6 CDs. (Running Time: 7 hrs.). 2008. audio compact disk 31.95 (978-0-7393-6946-3(6), Random AudioBks) Pub: Random Audio Pubg. Dist(s): Random

Bold Venture. 6 cass. 24.98 Set. Moonbeam Pubns.

Bold Venture. collector's ed. Perf. by Humphrey Bogart & Lauren Bacall. 6 cass. (Running Time: 9 hrs.). 2000. bk. 34.98 (4511) Radio Spirits.
Slate Shannon is the owner of a small tolerable Cuban hotel always occupied by an assorted cast of characters. Sailor Duval is his articulate and smoldering sidekick. Slate's boat, "Bold Venture," is "ever ready to roar to the rescue of a friend or the search of an enemy." 18 high-adventure stories.

Bold Venture: Alice Ramsey's Husband & Paul Brewer Story. unabr. ed. Perf. by Humphrey Bogart & Lauren Bacall. 1 cass. (Running Time: 1 hr.). 2001. 6.99 (1608) Radio Spirits.

Bold Venture: Matt Jeffrey Poisoned & George Carson Killed. unabr. ed. Perf. by Humphrey Bogart & Lauren Bacall. 1 cass. (Running Time: 1 hr.). 2001. 6.98 (2174) Radio Spirits.

Bold Venture: Robbery & Haven's Venezuelan Isle 1951. unabr. ed. Perf. by Humphrey Bogart et al. 1 cass. (Running Time: 1 hr.). 2001. 6.98 (1609) Radio Spirits.

Boldness & Right Valuation. Swami Amar Jyoti. 1 cass. 1982. 9.95 (K-50) Truth Consciousness.
Boldness of mind. Changing our wrong valuations & rising in consciousness. Joyful unfoldment in evolution. Invoking higher help.

Boldness of Free Thinking. Swami Amar Jyoti. 2 cass. 1982. 12.95 (K-45) Truth Consciousness.
What is boldness? Dispassion to our mental patterns. Purpose of a Retreat. Responsibility of liberal souls towards orthodoxy.

Bolero - Rapsodie Espagnole - La Valse. Perf. by Ravel. 1 cass., 1 CD. (SPA.). 7.98 (TA 30171); audio compact disk 12.78 CD Jewel box. (TA 80171) NewSound.

Bolero for Saying "I Love You" see Para Decir "Te Quiero"

Boleyn Inheritance. abr. ed. Philippa Gregory. Read by Bianca Amato et al. 2006. 17.95 (978-0-7435-6354-3(9), Audioworks) Pub: S&S Audio. Dist(s): S and S Inc

Boleyn Inheritance. abr. ed. Philippa Gregory. Read by Bianca Amato et al. (Running Time: 6 hrs. 0 mins. 0 sec.). (ENG.). 2008. audio compact disk 14.99 (978-0-7435-7092-3(8)) Pub: S&S Audio. Dist(s): S and S Inc

***Bolivian Diary.** abr. ed. Ernesto Che Guevara. Read by Bruno Gerardo. (ENG.). 2009. (978-0-06-188257-9(7), Harper Audio); (978-0-06-180747-3(8), Harper Audio) HarperCollins Pubs.

Bolsillo para Corduroy. Don Freeman. Illus. by Don Freeman. 14 vols. (Running Time: 13 mins.). 1992. pap. bk. 39.95 (978-1-59519-142-7(9)); 9.95 (978-1-59112-016-2(0)); audio compact disk 12.95 (978-1-59519-140-3(2)) Live Oak Media.

Bolsillo para Corduroy. Don Freeman. Illus. by Don Freeman. 11 vols. (Running Time: 13 mins.). (SPA.). (J). 1992. pap. bk. 18.95 (978-1-59519-141-0(0)) Pub: Live Oak Media. Dist(s): AudioGO

Bolsillo para Corduroy. Don Freeman. Illus. by Don Freeman. (Corduroy Ser.). (SPA.). (J). (gr. k-1). 1992. bk. 22.95 (978-0-87499-294-6(X)) Live Oak Media.

Bolsillo para Corduroy. unabr. ed. Don Freeman. Illus. by Don Freeman. Read by Susan Rybin. 14 vols. (Running Time: 13 mins.). (Corduroy Ser.). (SPA.). (J). 1992. pap. bk. & tchr. ed. 37.95 Reading Chest. (978-0-87499-295-3(8)) Live Oak Media.
Read-a-long of Spanish translation of "A Pocket for Corduroy".

Bolsillo para Corduroy. unabr. ed. Don Freeman. Illus. by Don Freeman. Read by Susan Rybin. 11 vols. (Running Time: 13 mins.). (Corduroy Ser.). (SPA.). (J). (gr. k-1). 1992. pap. bk. 16.95 (978-0-87499-293-9(1), LK5313) Pub: Live Oak Media. Dist(s): AudioGO
Having gotten a button for his overalls-and a home for himself as well-Corduroy now yearns for a pocket.

Bolsillo para Corduroy. unabr. ed. Don Freeman. Illus. by Don Freeman. 1 cass. (Running Time: 13 min.). (Corduroy Ser.). (SPA.). (J). (gr. k-1). 1992. 9.95 Live Oak Media.
Read-a-long of Spanish translation of "A Pocket for Corduroy".

Bolsillo para Corduroy & A Pocket for Corduroy. unabr. ed. Don Freeman. Illus. by Don Freeman. 22 vols. (Running Time: 13 mins.). (Corduroy Ser.). (SPA & ENG.). (J). (gr. k-3). 1999. pap. bk. 33.95 (978-0-87499-565-7(5)) Live Oak Media.

Bolt. unabr. ed. Dick Francis. Read by Tony Britton. 6 cass. (Running Time: 9 hrs.). (Kit Fielding Adventure Ser.: Bk. 2). 1993. 49.95 (978-0-7451-4169-5(2), CAB 852) Pub: Chivers Audio Bks GBR. Dist(s): AudioGO
Kit Fielding's patron, Princess Casilia, is in trouble. Her invalid husband is being threatened by a business partner. And to enforce the threat, all of Casilia's best runners are being destroyed...shot by a bolt. Casilia turns to Kit for help. But everywhere he goes, the champion jockey seems to attract bloodshed.

Bolt. unabr. ed. Dick Francis. Narrated by Simon Prebble. 8 CDs. (Running Time: 8 hrs. 30 mins.). (Kit Fielding Adventure Ser.: Bk. 2). 1999. audio compact disk 66.00 (978-0-7887-3435-9(0), C1041E7) Recorded Bks.
Someone is killing racehorses with a "bolt" gun, shooting them silently, leaving no clues. Before one of the noblest families in horse racing is torn apart, jockey Kit Fielding must find the assassin.

Bolt. unabr. ed. Dick Francis. Narrated by Simon Prebble. 6 cass. (Running Time: 8 hrs. 30 mins.). (Kit Fielding Adventure Ser.: Bk. 2). 1999. 51.00 (978-0-7887-2937-9(3), 95719E7) Recorded Bks.

Bomb. Frank Harris. Read by Anais 9000. 2008. 27.95 (978-1-60112-177-6(6)) Babblebooks.

Bomb, unabr. ed. Theodore Taylor. Narrated by George Guidall. 3 pieces. (Running Time: 4 hrs. 30 mins.). (gr. 8 up). 1996. 27.00 (978-0-7887-0537-3(7), 94732E7) Recorded Bks.
In 1946, 16-year-old Sorry Rinamu watches as U.S. Navy warships appear off the coast of Bikini Island. The U.S. Government wants to test the deadly power of the atomic bomb & Sorry's island has been chosen as the test site. He knows he must stop the Americans from dropping the bomb, even if it means defying orders from the U.S. Government & risking his own life.

Bomb Power: The Modern Presidency & the National Security State. unabr. ed. Garry Wills. Narrated by Stephen Hoye. (Running Time: 7 hrs. 30 mins.). 2010. 29.99 (978-1-4001-9508-4(X)); 14.99 (978-1-4001-8508-5(4)); 19.99 (978-1-4001-6508-7(3)); audio compact disk 59.99 (978-1-4001-4508-9(2)); audio compact disk 29.99 (978-1-4001-1508-2(6)) Pub: Tantor Media. Dist(s): IngramPubServ

Bomb Vessel, Set. unabr. ed. Richard Woodman. Narrated by Jeremy Sinden. 5 cass. (Running Time: 7 hrs. 15 min.). (Nathaniel Drinkwater Ser.: Bk. 4). 1994. 42.00 (978-0-7887-0002-6(2), 94141) Recorded Bks.
Lieutenant Nathaniel Drinkwater has been given the command of the Virago, a bomb vessel class ship that has been reduced to a stores tender, with a crew more unscrupulous than fit for battle. Applying a firm hand, the stalwart commander manages to get the Virago commissioned & prepared to join Sir Hyde Park's near disastrous approach to the Danish Coast in the spring of 1801. Richard Woodman, author of The Corvette, & 1805, has created a series with characters as rich as Patrick O'Brian's & as timeless as Forester's Homblower.

Bombay Ice. abr. ed. Leslie Forbes. Read by Lisanne Cole. 2 cass. (Running Time: 3 hrs.). 1998. 17.95 (978-1-55935-277-2(9)) Soundelux.
Journalist Rosalind Bengal travels to Bombay, India in search of her half-sister's killer. Her brother-in-law has been rumored to be the suspect, as he needs financially backing for his film.

Bombay Ice. unabr. ed. Leslie Forbes. Read by Susan O'Malley. 11 cass. (Running Time: 16 hrs.). 1998. 76.95 (978-0-7861-1430-6(4), 2316) Blckstn Audio.
After twenty years in London, Rosalind Bengal still wakes with the cinnamon taste of cassia leaves in her mouth, a dream of her childhood in India, where she learned about meteorology & the history of storms. She receives a letter from her sister, whose husband, a celebrated Bombay film director is suspected of having murdered his first wife & returns to India just before the monsoon. When the two sisters' lives are threatened by the brutal murder of a transvestite, Roz finds her best weapon is not a gun but her knowledge of science.

Bomber. Liza Marklund. Read by Frances Barber. 10 vols. (Running Time: 15 hrs.). 2003. audio compact disk 94.95 (978-0-7540-5592-1(2)) Pub: Chivers Audio Bks GBR. Dist(s): AudioGO

Bomber. unabr. ed. Len Deighton. Read by James Faulkner. 14 cass. (Running Time: 14 hrs.). 1997. 110.95 Set. (978-0-7451-6716-9(0), CAB 1332) AudioGO.
"Bomber" follows the progress of an Allied air raid through a period of 24 hours in the summer of 1943. All the characters are portrayed with vivid imagery, in the air & on the ground, in England & in Germany. In its documentary style & emotional power, it is overwhelming. Len Deighton has combined his talents as both a novelist & as a historian to produce this fictional masterpiece.

Bomber. unabr. ed. Liza Marklund. Read by Frances Barber. 10 cass. (Running Time: 15 hrs.). 2003. 84.95 (978-0-7540-0980-1(7), CAB 2402) AudioGO.

***Bomber: A BBC Full-Cast Radio Drama.** Len Deighton. Narrated by Tom Baker. 3 CDs. (Running Time: 3 hrs. 30 mins. 0 sec.). (ENG.). 2010. audio compact disk 29.95 (978-0-563-52355-0(7)) Pub: AudioGO. Dist(s): Perseus Dist

Bomber's Law. unabr. ed. George V. Higgins. Read by Michael Kramer. 9 cass. (Running Time: 13 hrs. 30 min.). 1994. 72.00 (978-0-7366-2805-1(3), 3519) Books on Tape.
When a known hit man can stay on the loose, something's bent. In this case, it looks like a cop.

Bomber's Law. unabr. ed. George V. Higgins. Narrated by Mark Hammer. 10 cass. (Running Time: 14 hrs.). 1997. 85.00 (978-0-7887-0668-4(3), 94845E7) Recorded Bks.
When Brian Dennison becomes head detective in the Massachusetts State Police Department, he soon realizes Boston's best mobsters won't let him hang around until retirement age.

Bombgrade. unabr. ed. Brian Freemantle. Read by Frederick Davidson. 11 cass. (Running Time: 16 hrs.). 1998. 76.95 (978-0-7861-1426-9(6), 2302) Blckstn Audio.
The Cold War is over & Charlie Muffin is sent to Moscow again, only this time it's to help the old enemy. The Russian Mafia controls the streets, & as the Families battle for supremacy, the embattled boss of bosses plans a job to keep himself in power forever: the ultimate nuclear robbery. The risk is Armageddon & Charlie has been sent to prevent it.

Bombingham: A Novel. Anthony Grooms. Narrated by Dion Graham. 7 cass. (Running Time: 9 hrs. 30 mins.). 61.00 (978-1-4025-2480-6(3)) Recorded Bks.

Bombmaker. unabr. ed. Stephen Leather. Read by Sean Barrett. 10 cass. (Running Time: 15 hrs.). 2001. 84.95 (978-0-7531-0924-3(7), 000707) Pub: ISIS Audio GBR. Dist(s): Ulverscroft US

Bombmaker. unabr. ed. Stephen Leather. Read by Sean Barrett. 11 CDs. (Running Time: 12 hrs. 4 min.). (Isis Ser.). (J). 2003. audio compact disk 99.95 (978-0-7531-2234-1(0)) Pub: ISIS Lrg Prnt GBR. Dist(s): Ulverscroft US
Ten years ago, Andrea Hayes was the best master bombmaker in the business. Then it all went wrong. Five children were killed, when disruption was all that was intended. Now, a new Andrea Hayes lives a safe surburban life, with her loving husband and young daughter. But then her daughter is kidnapped and the past has come knocking.

Bomi Lim: Beethoven Debussy Rachmaninoff. Perf. by Bomi Lim. 2007. audio compact disk 14.95 (978-1-4276-2369-0(4)) AardGP.

Bon Anniversaire. Lone Morton & Mary Risk. 1 cass. (Running Time: 20 min.). (I Can Read Bks.).Tr. of Happy Birthday. (ENG & FRE.). (J). (ps up). 1998. bk. 9.95 (978-0-7641-7187-1(9)) Barron.
Repeats every word of the bilingual text in both languages so that children can hear exactly how the words sound.

Bon Appetit! 1 CD. (Running Time: 0.48:43). 2003. audio compact disk 15.98 (978-1-57940-087-3(6)) Rounder Records.

Bon Appetit: My Life in France with Paul. unabr. ed. Julia Child & Alex Prud'homme. Read by Kimberly Farr. 8 cass. (Running Time: 12 hrs.). 2006. 72.00 (978-1-4159-2723-6(5)); audio compact disk 76.50 (978-1-4159-2724-3(3)) Pub: Books on Tape. Dist(s): NetLibrary CO

Bonac see Twentieth-Century Poetry in English, No. 25, Recordings of Poets Reading Their Own Poetry

Bonaparte's Sons. Richard Howard. (Isis Cassettes Ser.). 1998. 54.95 (978-0-7531-0356-2(7)) Pub: ISIS Lrg Prnt GBR. Dist(s): Ulverscroft US

Bond: Three Young Men Learn to Forgive & Reconnect with Their Fathers. unabr. ed. Sampson Davis et al. Narrated by Richard Allen. 8 CDs. (Running Time: 9 hrs. 30 mins. 0 sec.). (ENG.). 2007. audio compact disk 34.99 (978-1-4001-0568-7(4)) Pub: Tantor Media. Dist(s): IngramPubServ

Bond: Three Young Men Learn to Forgive & Reconnect with Their Fathers. unabr. ed. Sampson Davis et al. Read by Richard Allen. (Running Time: 9 hrs. 30 mins. 0 sec.). (ENG.). 2007. audio compact disk 69.99 (978-1-4001-3568-4(0)) Pub: Tantor Media. Dist(s): IngramPubServ

Bond: Three Young Men Learn to Forgive & Reconnect with Their Fathers. unabr. ed. Sampson Davis et al. Read by Richard Allen. Told to Margaret Bernstein. 1 MP3-CD. (Running Time: 9 hrs. 30 mins. 0 sec.). (ENG.). 2007. 24.99 (978-1-4001-5568-2(1)) Pub: Tantor Media. Dist(s): IngramPubServ

Bond & Beyond. Perf. by Erich Kunzel & Cincinnati Pops Orchestra. 1 cass., 1 CD. 7.98 (TA 30251); audio compact disk 12.78 CD Jewel box. (TA 80251) NewSound.

Bond & Fixed Income Investing for Everyone. unabr. ed. David K. Luhman. Read by David K. Luhman. 1 cass. (Running Time: 1 hr. 30 min.). (Personal Finance for Everyone Ser.: Vol. 5). 1996. 9.00 (978-1-889297-15-6(1)) Numen Lumen.
Why invest in bonds, money market mutual funds, insurers as providers of fixed income investments, the wild world of bond investing, inflation & bonds, the right bond for any purpose, bond maturity & duration, credit risk, junk bonds, other fixed income investments, other risks facing bond investors, the yield curve, municipal bonds, indexed bonds.

***Bond of Brothers: Connecting with Other Men Beyond Work, Weather & Sports.** Zondervan. (Running Time: 6 hrs. 17 mins. 4 sec.). (ENG.). 2010. 16.99 (978-0-310-41229-8(3)) Zondervan.

Bond of Reunion see Graveyard of Ghost Tales

Bond with Your Unborn Child: Develop Closeness with Your Child During Pregnancy. Mark Bancroft. Read by Mark Bancroft. 1 cass., bklet. (Running Time: 1 hr.). (Pregnancy & Childbirth Ser.). 1999. 12.95 (978-1-58522-023-6(X), 503) EnSpire Pr.
Two complete sessions plus printed instructionmanual/guidebook. With healing music soundtrack.

Bond with Your Unborn Child: Develop Closeness with Your Child During Pregnancy. Mark Bancroft. Read by Mark Bancroft. 1 CD, 1 bklet. (Running Time: 1 hr.). (Pregnancy & Childbirth Ser.). 2006. audio compact disk 20.00 (978-1-58522-060-1(4)) EnSpire Pr.

Bondage Breaker. Neil T. Anderson. (Running Time: 10800 sec.). 2006. audio compact disk 18.99 (978-0-7369-2058-2(7)) Harvest Hse.

Bondage Breaker. 2nd abr. ed. Neil T. Anderson. 2 cass. (Running Time: 3 hrs.). 2000. 16.99 (978-0-7369-0369-1(0)) Harvest Hse.

Bondage of the Will. unabr. ed. Martin Luther. (Running Time: 12 hrs. 30 mins. 0 sec.). (ENG.). 2009. audio compact disk 26.98 (978-1-59644-718-9(4), Hovel Audio) christianaud.

***Bondage of the Will.** unabr. ed. Martin Luther. Narrated by Nadia May. (ENG.). 2009. 16.98 (978-1-59644-719-6(2), Hovel Audio) christianaud.

Bonded Together: Contemporary Songs of Love. 1 cass. (Running Time: 1 hrs. 10 min.). 1997. audio compact disk 7.99 CD. (D8006) Diamante Music Grp.

Bonding Before Birth. John W. Harris. Ed. by Robert Brown. Illus. by Robyn D. Harris. 1986. 8.95 (978-0-9618411-1-9(7)) Prsnl Grwth ID.

Bonding Faith & Life. Elizabeth A. Dreyer. 2 cass. (Running Time: 2 hrs.). 2001. 17.95 (A6920) St Anthony Mess Pr.
Reviews historical attitudes toward the sacred and the secular and invites the listener to recognize new patterns of spirituality.

Bondwoman's Narrative. unabr. ed. Hannah Crafts. Read by Anna Deavere Smith. (ENG.). 2005. 14.98 (978-1-59483-391-5(5)) Pub: Hachet Audio. Dist(s): HachBkGrp

Bone-A-Fide. Contrib. by T-Bone et al. 2005. audio compact disk 16.98 (978-5-558-96703-6(X)) Flicker.

Bone & Joint Infections - Pediatric Sudden Death. Robert Felter & Susan Woolsey. (Pediatric Emergency: The National Conference for Practitioner Ser.). 1986. 9.00 (978-0-932491-70-1(7)) Res Appl Inc.

Bone-Appetit: Servin' up Tha Hits. Contrib. by T-Bone & Rene F. Sotomayor. 2007. audio compact disk 13.99 (978-5-557-60940-1(7)) Flicker.

Bone Breath & the Vandals, unabr. ed. Peg Kehret. Narrated by Carine Montbertrand. 2 pieces. (Running Time: 2 hrs. 45 mins.). (Frightmares Ser.: No. 2). (gr. 5 up). 19.00 (978-0-7887-0590-8(3), 94767E7) Recorded Bks.
When sixth grader Kayo Benton is nabbed by vandals, Rosie, her best friend, races against the clock to find her. Available to libraries only.

Bone by Bone. unabr. ed. Peter Matthiessen. Read by George Guidall. 13 Cass. (Running Time: 22.5 Hrs.). bk. 44.95 (978-1-4025-3710-3(7)) Recorded Bks.

Bone by Bone. unabr. ed. Peter Matthiessen. Narrated by George Guidall. 16 cass. (Running Time: 22 hrs. 30 mins.). 1999. 130.00 (978-0-7887-3468-7(7), 95872E7) Recorded Bks.
Prequel to "Killing Mister Watson" & "Lost Man's River." Using an old local tale about a man who was killed by his neighbors, Matthiessen creates a moving story with a powerful, tragic character.

Bone Collector. unabr. ed. Jeffery Deaver. Read by Connor O'Brien. 8 cass. (Running Time: 12 hrs.). (Lincoln Rhyme Ser.: No. 1). 1999. 64.00 (978-0-7366-4133-3(5), 4638) Books on Tape.
Lincoln Rhyme, ex-head of NYPD forensics, was the nation's foremost criminalist until an accident left him a bitter quadriplegic. After reading a crime scene report on a corpse found buried near the railroad tracks, his search leads him to the bone collector.

Bone Dancing. unabr. ed. Jonathan Gash. Read by Francis Middleditch. 8 CDs. (Running Time: 9 hrs. 15 min.). (Story Sound CD Ser.). (J). 2003. audio compact disk 79.95 (978-1-85903-686-0(4)) Pub: Mgna Lrg Print GBR. Dist(s): Ulverscroft US

Bone Dancing. unabr. ed. Jonathan Gash. Read by Francis Middleditch. 7 cass. (Running Time: 33300 sec.). (Storysound Ser.). 2003. 61.95 (978-1-85903-657-0(0)) Pub: Mgna Lrg Print GBR. Dist(s): Ulverscroft US

Bone Deep. abr. ed. David Wiltse. Perf. by Bruce McGill. 2 cass. (Running Time: 3 hrs.). 1996. 17.00 Set. (978-1-56876-052-0(3)) Soundlines Ent.
A tense thriller featuring a cat & mouse struggle between FBI agent John Becker & a diabolical killer who seduces his victims & murders them in the throes of passion.

Bone-Flag. John M. Bennett & Dick Metcalf. 1 cass. (Running Time: 60 min.). 1994. 5.00 (978-0-935350-54-8(3)) Luna Bisonte.
Poetry & sound art.

Bone Garden. abr. ed. Tess Gerritsen. (Running Time: 5 hrs.). (ENG.). 2007. 14.95 (978-0-7393-4325-8(4), Random AudioBks) Pub: Random Audio Pubg. Dist(s): Random

Bone Garden. abr. ed. Tess Gerritsen. Read by Carolyn McCormick. (ENG.). 2008. audio compact disk 14.99 (978-0-7393-7084-1(7), Random AudioBks) Pub: Random Audio Pubg. Dist(s): Random

Bone Garden. unabr. ed. Tess Gerritsen. 11 CDs. 2007. audio compact disk 110.00 (978-1-4159-4309-0(5), BksonTape) Pub: Random Audio Pubg. Dist(s): Random
Present day: Julia Hamill has made a horrifying discovery on the grounds of her new home in rural Massachusetts: a skull buried in the rocky soil - human, female, and, according to the trained eye of Boston medical examiner Maura Isles, scarred with the unmistakable marks of murder. Boston, 1830: In order to pay for his education, medical student Norris Marshall has joined the ranks of local "resurrectionists" - those who plunder graveyards and harvest the dead for sale on the black market. But when a distinguished doctor is found murdered and mutilated on university grounds, Norris finds that trafficking in the illicit cadaver trade has made him a prime suspect. With unflagging suspense and pitch-perfect period detail, THE BONE GARDEN deftly traces the dark mystery at its heart across time and place to a finale as ingeniously conceived as it is shocking.

Bone Garden. unabr. ed. Tess Gerritsen. Read by Susan Denaker. (Running Time: 46800 sec.). (ENG.). 2007. audio compact disk 44.95 (978-0-7393-4324-1(6), Random AudioBks) Pub: Random Audio Pubg. Dist(s): Random

Bone Harvest. unabr. ed. Mary Logue. (Running Time: 7 hrs.). (Claire Watkins Ser.: Bk. 4). 2004. 24.95 (978-1-59335-662-0(5), 1593356625, Brilliance MP3) Brilliance Audio.
The unsolved murders at a remote Wisconsin farmhouse half a century ago have receded into time. But one deranged man will do anything to make sure that all of Pepin County remembers that bloody day. When a quantity of dangerous pesticides is stolen from the local co-op, Deputy Sheriff Claire Watkins is called in to investigate. The thief has left one bizarre clue: the finger bone of a child long dead. The pesticides soon reappear with devastating effect - in flowerbeds, in animal feed, and in a fatal concoction at a Fourth of July picnic. Each time, a tiny human bone is left at the scene. With the help of Harold Peabody, the quirky, aging editor of the Durand Daily, Claire unravels the secrets of the past, leading her to a pair of young lovers, a man enraged over his mother's death, an obsessive recluse, and the deputy who first discovered the corpses of the Schuler family. Claire desperately races against time to find the madman before he uses the lethal pesticide again. But he won't be stopped. Not until he gets what he wants.

Bone Harvest. unabr. ed. Mary Logue. Read by Joyce Bean. (Running Time: 7 hrs.). (Claire Watkins Ser.: Bk. 4). 2004. 39.25 (978-1-59335-854-9(7), 1593358547, Brlnc Audio MP3 Lib); 27.95 (978-1-59355-430-9(3), 1593554303, BAU); 69.25 (978-1-59355-431-6(1), 1593554311, BrilAudUnabridg) Brilliance Audio.

Bone Harvest. unabr. ed. Mary Logue. Read by Joyce Bean. (Running Time: 7 hrs.). (Claire Watkins Ser.). 2004. 24.95 (978-1-59710-102-8(8), 1597101028, BAD) Brilliance Audio.

Bone Harvest. unabr. ed. Mary Logue. Read by Joyce Bean. (Running Time: 7 hrs.). (Claire Watkins Ser.: Bk. 4). 2004. 39.25 (978-1-59710-103-5(6), 1597101036, BADLE) Brilliance Audio.

Bone Harvest. unabr. abr. ed. Mary Logue. Read by Joyce Bean. 6 CDs. (Running Time: 7 hrs.). (Claire Watkins Ser.: Bk. 4). 2004. audio compact disk 29.95 (978-1-59355-936-6(4), 1593559364); audio compact disk 82.25 (978-1-59355-937-3(2), 1593559372) Brilliance Audio.

***Bone House.** unabr. ed. Brian Freeman. Read by To be announced. (Running Time: 11 hrs. 5 mins.). (ENG.). 2011. 29.95 (978-1-4417-8047-8(5)) Blckstn Audio.

***Bone House.** unabr. ed. Brian Freeman. Read by To be Announced. (Running Time: 11 hrs. 5 mins.). (ENG.). 2011. 72.95 (978-1-4417-8044-7(0)) Blckstn Audio.

***Bone House.** unabr. ed. Brian Freeman. Read by To be announced. (Running Time: 11 hrs. 5 mins.). 2011. audio compact disk 32.95 (978-1-4417-8046-1(7)) Blckstn Audio.

***Bone House.** unabr. ed. Brian Freeman. Read by To be Announced. (Running Time: 11 hrs. 5 mins.). (ENG.). 2011. audio compact disk 105.00 (978-1-4417-8045-4(9)) Blckstn Audio.

***Bone Is Pointed.** unabr. ed. Arthur W. Upfield. Read by Peter Hosking. (Running Time: 8 hrs. 11 mins.). (Inspector Napoleon Bonaparte Mysteries). 2010. audio compact disk 83.95 (978-1-74214-680-5(5), 9781742146805) Pub: Bolinda Pubng AUS. Dist(s): Bolinda Pub Inc

Bone Is Pointed. unabr. ed. Arthur W. Upfield. Read by Nigel Graham. 7 cass. (Running Time: 10 hrs.). (Inspector Napoleon Bonaparte Mystery Ser.). 1994. 58.00 (978-0-7887-0030-9(8), 94229) Recorded Bks.
Half-caste detective Napoleon Bonaparte struggles to reconcile his white university education with the acute power of his aboriginal senses as he tackles a case of murder far in the Australian bush.

Bone Machine. Martyn Waites. 2007. 89.95 (978-1-84652-085-3(1)); audio compact disk 99.95 (978-1-84652-086-0(X)) Pub: Magna Story GBR. Dist(s): Ulverscroft US

***Bone Magic.** unabr. ed. Yasmine Galenorn. Narrated by Cassandra Campbell. (Running Time: 10 hrs. 30 mins.). (Sisters of the Moon Ser.). 2010. 16.99 (978-1-4001-8447-7(9)) Tantor Media.

***Bone Magic.** unabr. ed. Yasmine Galenorn. Narrated by Cassandra Campbell. (Running Time: 11 hrs. 30 mins. 0 sec.). (Sisters of the Moon Ser.). (ENG.). 2010. 24.99 (978-1-4001-6447-9(8)); audio compact disk 69.99 (978-1-4001-4447-1(7)); audio compact disk 34.99 (978-1-4001-1447-4(0)) Pub: Tantor Media. Dist(s): IngramPubServ

Bone of Contention. Roberta Gellis. Read by Nadia May. (Running Time: 11 hrs. 30 mins.). 2003. 36.95 (978-1-59912-435-3(1)) Iofy Corp.

Bone of Contention. unabr. ed. Roberta Gellis. Read by Nadia May. 9 cass. (Running Time: 13 hrs.). 2000. 62.92 (978-0-7861-2601-9(9), 3197); audio compact disk 80.00 (978-0-7861-8937-3(1), 3197) Blckstn Audio.

Bone of My Bone Flesh of My Flesh/NSM. George Bloomer. 2004. audio compact disk 14.99 (978-0-88368-451-1(9)) Whitaker Hse.

***Bone Thief.** unabr. ed. Jefferson Bass. Read by Dan Woren. (Body Farm Ser.). (ENG.). 2010. (978-0-06-195370-5(9), Harper Audio); (978-0-06-197748-0(9), Harper Audio) HarperCollins Pubs.

Bone Vault. Linda Fairstein. Read by Blair Brown. (Alexandra Cooper Mysteries Ser.). 2004. 15.95 (978-0-7435-4212-8(6)) Pub: S&S Audio. Dist(s): S and S Inc

Bone Vault. unabr. ed. Linda Fairstein. Narrated by Barbara Rosenblat. 9 cass. (Running Time: 12 hrs. 45 mins.). (Alexandra Cooper Mysteries Ser.). 2003. 85.00 (978-1-4025-4018-9(3)) Recorded Bks.

Bone Walker. unabr. ed. Kathleen O'Neal Gear & W. Michael Gear. Read by Bernadette Dunne. 15 cass. (Running Time: 22 hrs. 30 mins.). 2001. 120.00 (978-0-7366-8486-6(7)) Books on Tape.
In the thirteenth and twentieth centuries, Anasazi warriors and American anthropologists are both on the trail of the Wolf Witch.

***Bone Yard: A Body Farm Novel.** unabr. ed. Jefferson Bass. (ENG.). 2011. (978-0-06-202731-3(X), Harper Audio) HarperCollins Pubs.

Bonecrack. unabr. ed. Dick Francis. Read by David Case. 7 cass. (Running Time: 7 hrs.). 1991. 56.00 (978-0-7366-2039-0(7), 2853) Books on Tape.
When an accident disables Neil Grifton's father, Neil takes charge of his father's racing stable. Its finances are sicker than the owner, whose accident is but one of many. Late one night two goons catch Neil alone. They beat him up for their boss, who wants one of Neil's horses. And not just any horse, but Archangel - the best & a sure winner at the upcoming derby. At least she had better win or the next accident will have Neil's name on it!.

BoneMan's Daughters. unabr. ed. Ted Dekker. Read by Robert Petkoff. (Running Time: 10 hrs. 30 mins.). (ENG.). 2009. 19.98 (978-1-60024-605-0(2)) Pub: Center St. Dist(s): HachBkGrp

BoneMan's Daughters. unabr. ed. Ted Dekker. Read by Robert Petkoff. (Running Time: 10 hrs. 30 mins.). (ENG.). 2010. audio compact disk 19.98 (978-1-60788-322-7(8)) Pub: Center St. Dist(s): HachBkGrp

***Bones.** abr. ed. Jonathan Kellerman. Read by John Rubinstein. 2010. audio compact disk 14.99 (978-0-307-75088-4(4), Random AudioBks) Pub: Random Audio Pubg. Dist(s): Random

Bones. unabr. ed. Jonathan Kellerman. Read by John Rubinstein. 10 CDs. (Alex Delaware Ser.: No. 23). 2008. audio compact disk 100.00 (978-1-4159-5669-4(3), BksonTape); 100.00 (978-1-4159-6087-5(9), BksonTape) Pub: Random Audio Pubg. Dist(s): Random
The anonymous caller has an ominous tone and an unnerving message about something "real dead... buried in your marsh." The eco-volunteer on the other end of the phone thinks it's a prank, but when a young woman's body turns up in L.A.¿s Bird Marsh preserve no one's laughing. And when the bones of more victims surface, homicide detective Milo Sturgis realizes the city's under siege to an insidious killer. Milo's first move: calling in psychologist Alex Delaware. The murdered women are prostitutes - except the most recent victim; a brilliant young musician from the East Coast, employed by a wealthy family to tutor a musical prodigy, Selena Bass seems out of place in the marsh's grim tableau. Conveniently - perhaps ominously==Selena's blueblood employers are nowhere to be found, and their estate's jittery caretaker raises hackles. But Milo's instincts and Alex's insight are too well-honed to settle for easy answers, even given the dark secrets in this troubled man's past. Their investigation unearths disturbing layers - about victims, potential victims, and suspects alike - plunging even deeper into the murky marsh's enigmatic depths. Bizarre details of the crimes suggest a devilish serial killer prowling L.A.¿s gritty streets. But when a new murder deviates from the pattern, derailing a possible profile, Alex and Milo must look beyond the suspicion of madness and consider an even more sinister mind at work. Answers don't come easy, but the darkest of drives and desires may fuel the most devious of foes.

Bones. unabr. ed. Jonathan Kellerman. Read by John Rubinstein. 10 CDs. (Running Time: 12 hrs.). (Alex Delaware Ser.: No. 23). (ENG.). 2008. audio compact disk 44.95 (978-0-7393-6891-6(5), Random AudioBks) Pub: Random Audio Pubg. Dist(s): Random

Bones. unabr. ed. Gabrielle Lord. Read by David Tredinnick. 9 cass. (Running Time: 13 hrs.). 2000. (978-1-74030-064-3(5), 500113) Bolinda Pubng AUS.

Bones & Silence. unabr. ed. Reginald Hill. Read by Brian Glover. 10 cass. (Running Time: 15 hrs.). (Dalziel & Pascoe Ser.). 2000. 69.95 (978-0-7451-6468-7(4), CAB 1085) Pub: Chivers Audio Bks GBR. Dist(s): AudioGO
Andy Dalziel witnessed a murder, but it was on a dark and stormy night, and he was ill at the time. With the case shrouded in uncertainty, anonymous letters arrive with threats of suicide. Meanwhile, Dalziel's colleague, Peter Pascoe, returns with questions about his job and marriage. In the background and sometimes in the foreground are the York Mystery Plays, where Eileen Chung uses and abuses her talents to get the parts she wants. But the mysteries for all three of these people linger long after the performances are over.

Bones!, Listening. Janet Gardner. 1 CD. (Running Time: 1 hr. 30 mins.). (ENG.). 2000. audio compact disk 16.95 (978-0-7390-0453-1(0), 19234) Alfred Pub.

***Bones of Contention: A Dinah Pelerin Mystery.** unabr. ed. Jeanne Matthews. (Running Time: 8 hrs. 30 mins.). 2010. 29.95 (978-1-4417-4292-6(1)); 54.95 (978-1-4417-4288-9(3)); audio compact disk 76.00 (978-1-4417-4289-6(1)) Blckstn Audio.

Bones of Coral. unabr. ed. James W. Hall. Narrated by Richard Ferrone. 10 cass. (Running Time: 13 hrs. 45 mins.). 85.00 (978-1-55690-668-8(4), 92316E7) Recorded Bks.
A paramedic is drawn into the search for a sadistic killer in Key West. Available to libraries only.

Bones of Makaidos. unabr. ed. Bryan Davis. Narrated by Peter Sandon. (Running Time: 20 hrs. 54 mins. 23 sec.). (Oracles of Fire Ser.). (ENG.). (J). 2009. 10.49 (978-1-60814-558-4(1)) Oasis Audio.

Bones of Makaidos. unabr. ed. Bryan Davis. Narrated by Peter Sandon. (Running Time: 20 hrs. 54 mins. 23 sec.). (Oracles of Fire Ser.). (ENG.). (J). 2009. audio compact disk 49.99 (978-1-59859-633-5(0)) Oasis Audio.

Bones of the Barbary Coast. abr. unabr. ed. Daniel Hecht. Read by Anna Fields. 10 cass. (Running Time: 52200 sec.). (Cree Black Thriller Ser.: No. 3). 2006. 32.95 (978-0-7861-4467-9(X)); audio compact disk 32.95 (978-0-7861-7285-6(1)) Blckstn Audio.

Bones of the Barbary Coast. unabr. ed. Daniel Hecht. Read by Anna Fields. (Running Time: 52200 sec.). (Cree Black Thriller Ser.). 2006. 79.95 (978-0-7861-4704-5(0)); audio compact disk 99.00 (978-0-7861-6589-6(8)) Blckstn Audio.

Bones of the Barbary Coast: A Cree Black Novel. unabr. ed. Daniel Hecht. (Running Time: 14 mins. 30 sec.). (Cree Black Thriller Ser.: No. 3). (J). 2006. 29.95 (978-0-7861-7707-3(1)) Blckstn Audio.

Bones of the Dragon see Shadow

Bones of the Dragon. unabr. ed. Margaret Weis & Tracy Hickman. Narrated by Stefan Rudnicki. 16 CDs. (Running Time: 18 hrs.). 2009. audio compact disk 119.95 (978-0-7927-5474-9(3), Chivers Sound Lib) AudioGO.

Bones of the Dragon. unabr. ed. Margaret Weis et al. Read by Stefan Rudnicki. 16 CDs. (Running Time: 18 hrs. 0 mins. 0 sec.). (Dragonships of Vindras Ser.). (ENG.). 2009. audio compact disk 59.95 (978-1-4272-0431-8(4)) Pub: Macmill Audio. Dist(s): Macmillan

Bones!, SoundTrax. Janet Gardner. 1 CD. (Running Time: 1 hr. 30 mins.). (ENG.). 2000. audio compact disk 59.95 (978-0-7390-0452-4(2), 19233) Alfred Pub.

Bones to Ashes. abr. ed. Kathy Reichs. Read by Linda Emond. (Running Time: 5 hrs. 30 mins. 0 sec.). No. 10. (ENG.). 2007. audio compact disk 29.95 (978-0-7435-6615-5(7)) Pub: S&S Audio. Dist(s): S and S Inc

Bones to Ashes. unabr. ed. Kathy Reichs. Read by Linda Emond. 10 CDs. (Running Time: 10 hrs. 30 mins. 0 sec.). No. 10. (ENG.). 2007. audio compact disk 39.95 (978-0-7435-6616-2(5)) Pub: S&S Audio. Dist(s): S and S Inc

Bonesetter's Daughter. abr. unabr. ed. Amy Tan. 6 CDs. (Running Time: 8 hrs.). 2004. audio compact disk 39.95 (978-1-931056-35-9(8), N Millennium Audio) New Millenn Enter.
Conjures the pain of broken dreams, the power of myths, & the strength of love that enables us to recover in memory what we have lost in grief.

Bonesetter's Daughter. abr. unabr. ed. Amy Tan. Read by Joan Chen. 4 cass. (Running Time: 6 hrs.). 2004. 27.00 (978-1-931056-32-8(3), N Millennium Audio) New Millenn Enter.

Bonesetter's Daughter. unabr. ed. Amy Tan. Read by Joan Chen. 8 cass. (Running Time: 4 hrs. 30 min.). 2004. 39.95 (978-1-931056-33-5(1), N Millennium Audio) New Millenn Enter.

Bonesetter's Daughter. unabr. ed. Amy Tan. Narrated by Joan Chen. 10 CDs. (Running Time: 12 hrs.). 2001. audio compact disk 111.00 (978-1-4025-0916-2(2), C1579) Recorded Bks.
Set in contemporary San Francisco and in a Chinese village where Peking Man is being unearthed. The Bonesetter's Daughter is an excavation of the human spirit - the past, its deepest wounds, its most profound hopes. The story conjures the pain of broken dreams, the power of myths, and the strength of love that enable us to recover in memory what we have lost in grief. Over the course of one fog-shrouded year, between one season of falling stars and the next, mother and daughter find what they share in their bones through heredity, history, and inexpressible qualities of love.

Bonesetter's Daughter. unabr. ed. Amy Tan. Narrated by Joan Chen. 8 cass. (Running Time: 12 hrs.). 2002. 75.00 (978-1-4025-0790-8(9)) Recorded Bks.

Boneyard. Janet Lorimer. (Running Time: 3997 sec.). (Pageturners Ser.). (J). 2004. 10.95 (978-1-56254-709-7(7)) Saddleback Edu.

Bonfire: The Siege & Burning of Atlanta. unabr. ed. Marc Wortman. (Running Time: 10 hrs. 50 mins.). 2009. 29.95 (978-1-4332-7978-2(9)); 65.95 (978-1-4332-7974-4(6)); audio compact disk 100.00 (978-1-4332-7975-1(4)); audio compact disk 29.95 (978-1-4332-7977-5(0)) Blckstn Audio.

Bonfire of the Vanities. Tom Wolfe. Read by Tom Wolfe. Prod. by Moveable Feast Staff. 1 cass. (Running Time: 30 min.). 8.95 (AMF-100) Am Audio Prose.
Wolfe reads from "The Bonfire of the Vanities" & talks about racism, ambition & venality in New York City.

Bonfire of the Vanities, Pt. 1. unabr. ed. Tom Wolfe. Read by John MacDonald. 9 cass. (Running Time: 26 hrs.). 1990. 62.95 (978-0-7861-0202-0(0), 1178A,B) Blckstn Audio.
Sherman McCoy is a young investment banker with a fourteen-room apartment in Manhattan. When he is involved in a freak accident in the Bronx, prosecutors, politicians, the press, police, the clergy & assorted hustlers close in on him, licking their chops & giving us a gargantuan helping of the human comedy of New York in the last years of the twentieth century, a city boiling over with racial & ethnic hostilities & burning with the itch to grab it now.

Bonfire of the Vanities, Pt. 1. unabr. collector's ed. Tom Wolfe. Read by Michael Prichard. 9 cass. (Running Time: 13 hrs. 30 min.). 1988. 72.00 (978-0-7366-1369-9(2), 2266-A) Books on Tape.
Sherman McCoy is on the way to having it made. A red-hot young investment banker with a 14-room apartment in Manhattan, he splits in panic from a freak accident in the Bronx but circumstances conspire against him, not to mention police, press, politicians & prosecutors.

Bonfire of the Vanities, Pt. 2. collector's ed. Tom Wolfe. Read by Michael Prichard. 9 cass. (Running Time: 13 hrs. 30 min.). 1988. 72.00 (978-0-7366-1370-5(6), 2266-B) Books on Tape.

Bonfire of the Vanities, Pt. 2. unabr. ed. Tom Wolfe. Read by John MacDonald. 9 cass. (Running Time: 26 hrs.). 1990. 62.95 (978-0-7861-0203-7(9), 1178A,B) Blckstn Audio.
Sherman McCoy is a young investment banker with a fourteen-room apartment in Manhattan. When he is involved in a freak accident in the Bronx, prosecutors, politicians, the press, police, the clergy & assorted hustlers close in on him, licking their chops & giving us a gargantuan helping of the human comedy of New York in the last years of the twentieth century, a city boiling over with racial & ethnic hostilities & burning with the itch to grab it now.

Bonfire of the Vanities, Set, Pt. 1. unabr. ed. Tom Wolfe. Read by John MacDonald. 9 cass. 1999. 62.95 (FS9-51113) Highsmith.

Bonfire of the Vanities, Set, Pt. 2. unabr. ed. Tom Wolfe. Read by John MacDonald. 9 cass. 1999. 62.95 (FS9-51119) Highsmith.

Bonfire of the Vanities: A Novel. unabr. ed. Tom Wolfe. Read by Joe Barrett. (Running Time: 27 hrs. 50 mins.). (ENG.). 2009. 44.95 (978-1-4332-8844-9(3)); 65.95 (978-1-4332-9081-7(2)); 89.95 (978-1-4332-8840-1(0)); audio compact disk 140.00 (978-1-4332-8841-8(9)) Blckstn Audio.

Bonheur du Manchot. l.t. ed. Jean-Pierre Chabrol. (French Ser.). (FRE., 1995. bk. 30.99 (978-2-84011-109-2(8)) Pub: UlverLrgPrint GBR. Dist(s): Ulverscroft US

***Bonhoeffer: Pastor, Martyr, Prophet, Spy.** unabr. ed. Eric Metaxas. (Running Time: 20 hrs. 30 mins.). 2010. 44.95 (978-1-4417-6607-6(3)); 105.95 (978-1-4417-6604-5(9)); audio compact disk 39.95 (978-1-4417-6606-9(5)); audio compact disk 123.00 (978-1-4417-6605-2(7)) Blckstn Audio.

Bonhoeffer: The Cost of Freedom. abr. adpt. ed. Prod. by Focus on the Family Staff. Adapted by Paul McCusker. (Running Time: 240 hrs. 0 mins.). (Radio Theatre Ser.). (ENG.). (J). 2007. audio compact disk 14.97 (978-1-58997-515-6(4), Tyndale Ent) Tyndale Hse.

Bonjour, Ça va? An Introductory Course. 3rd ed. Judith A. Muyskens et al. Ed. by Myrna Bell Rochester. 1991. (978-0-07-053401-8(2)) McGraw.

Bonjour, Mes Amis - Hello, My Friends. Irene Bowers & Linda Weller. 2 cass. (Running Time: 3 hrs.). (FRE & ENG., (J). (ps-3). 1994. pap. bk. 16.95 (978-0-8120-8150-3(1)) Barron.

Bonjour Tristesse, Set. Francoise Sagan. Read by Catherine Deneuve. 2 cass.Tr. of Hello Sadness. (FRE.). 1991. 34.95 (1116-RC) Olivia & Hill.
Sagan was eighteen in the spring of 1954 when she wrote this novel which won the Prix des Critiques & labeled Sagan as "l'enfant terrible" of the sixties. It is the story of young Cecile, who sets out to destroy her father's mistress.

Bonk: The Curious Coupling of Science & Sex. unabr. ed. Mary Roach. Read by Sandra Burr. (Running Time: 10 hrs.). 2008. 24.95 (978-1-4233-1672-5(X), 9781423316725, BAD); 39.25 (978-1-4233-1673-2(8), 9781423316732, BADLE); audio compact disk 34.95 (978-1-4233-1668-8(1), 9781423316688, Bril Audio CD Unabri); audio compact disk 24.95 (978-1-4233-1670-1(3), 9781423316701, Brilliance MP3); audio compact disk 87.25 (978-1-4233-1669-5(X), 9781423316695, BriAudCD Unabrid); audio compact disk 39.25 (978-1-4233-1671-8(1), 9781423316718, Brlnc Audio MP3 Lib) Brilliance Audio.

Bonne Nuit a Tous see Goodnight Everyone

Bonnie & Clyde. unabr. ed. Wyman Windsor. Narrated by Chris Ruleman. Prod. by Joe Loesch. 1 cass. (Running Time: 1 hr.). (Americana Ser.). (YA). 1999. lib. bdg. 12.95 (978-1-887729-72-7(0)) Toy Box Prods.
For twenty-two months, Clyde Barrow & Bonnie Parker blazed a trail of murder & terror across the southwest. And when it was over, they died in a hail of gunfire on a Louisiana back road, betrayed by a friend.

Bonnie & Clyde: The Lives Behind the Legend. unabr. ed. Paul Schneider. Read by Patrick G. Lawlor. (Running Time: 16 hrs. 0 mins. 0 sec.). (ENG.). 2009. audio compact disk 79.99 (978-1-4001-4143-2(5)); audio compact disk 29.99 (978-1-4001-6143-0(6)); audio compact disk 39.99 (978-1-4001-1143-5(9)) Pub: Tantor Media. Dist(s): IngramPubServ

***Bonnie & Sam: The Shadow Brumby.** unabr. ed. Alison Lester. Read by Miranda Nation. (Running Time: 1 hr. 55 mins.). (J). 2008. audio compact disk 24.00 (978-1-921415-38-8(X), 9781921415388) Pub: Bolinda Pubng AUS. Dist(s): Bolinda Pub Inc

Bonnie & Sam 1-4 Bind-up. Alison Lester. Read by Miranda Nation. (Running Time: 2 hrs. 40 mins.). (J). 2009. 54.99 (978-1-74214-166-4(8), 9781742141664) Pub: Bolinda Pubng AUS. Dist(s): Bolinda Pub Inc

Bonnie & Sam 1-4 Bind-up. unabr. ed. Alison Lester. Read by Miranda Nation. (Running Time: 2 hrs. 40 mins.). (J). 2008. audio compact disk 54.95 (978-1-74214-065-0(3), 9781742140650) Pub: Bolinda Pubng AUS. Dist(s): Bolinda Pub Inc

Bonnie Prince Charlie: A Biography. unabr. ed. Carolly Erickson. Narrated by Steven Crossley. 8 cass. (Running Time: 11 hrs. 15 mins.). 1998. 70.00 (978-0-7887-1923-3(8), 95344E7) Recorded Bks.
Twenty-four year old Charles Stuart, the Young Pretender to the British throne, thrilled 1400's Europe when he challenged King George III with a band of Highland Rebels.

Bonnie Raitt: Just in the Nick of Time. abr. ed. Mark Bego. Read by Mark Bego. 2 cass. (Running Time: 3 hrs.). 1997. 16.95 Set. (978-1-882071-65-4(4)) B-B Audio.
This is the first tell-all biography of the formerly hard-drinking, blues-rock mama who had it all, lost it all, and then got it back again. This audiobook reveals the whole story of Bonnie Raitts crash and burn lifestyle which nearly took her down with.

Bonnie-Sue: A Marine Corps Helicopter Squadron in Vietnam. unabr. ed. Marion F. Sturkey. Read by Dennis McKee. 14 cass. (Running Time: 20 hrs. 30 mins.). 2000. 89.95 (978-0-7861-1695-9(1), 2517) Blckstn Audio.
Sturkey, a former Marine "Bonnie-Sue" HMM-265 helicopter pilot in Vietnam, uses After-Action-Reports, Unit Diaries & hundreds of records from the Marine Corps Archives to build the outline for this riveting chronology.

Bonny Dawn. unabr. ed. Catherine Cookson. Read by Susan Jameson. 4 cass. 1997. 39.95 Set. (978-0-7451-6796-1(9), CAB 1412) AudioGO.
Seventeen-year old Brid Stevens has a date with Joe Lloyd, whom she met at the weekly dance. They meet to watch the sunrise. The dawn seems so beautiful to Brid it's almost painful. But the real pain will come when she returns home. Set in Northumbria in the 1960s, this is a story about the loss of innocence.

***Bonobo Handshake: A Memoir of Love & Adventure in the Congo.** unabr. ed. Vanessa Woods. (Running Time: 8 hrs. 0 mins.). 2010. 15.99 (978-1-4001-8745-4(1)) Tantor Media.

***Bonobo Handshake: A Memoir of Love & Adventure in the Congo.** unabr. ed. Vanessa Woods. Narrated by Justine Eyre. (Running Time: 8 hrs. 30 mins. 0 sec.). (ENG.). 2010. 19.99 (978-1-4001-6745-6(0)); audio compact disk 71.99 (978-1-4001-4745-8(X)); audio compact disk 29.99 (978-1-4001-1745-1(3)) Pub: Tantor Media. Dist(s): IngramPubServ

***Bony & the black Virgin.** unabr. ed. Arthur W. Upfield. Read by Peter Hosking. (Running Time: 5 hrs. 36 mins.). (Inspector Napoleon Bonaparte Mysteries). 2010. audio compact disk 63.95 (978-1-74214-661-4(9), 9781742146614) Pub: Bolinda Pubng AUS. Dist(s): Bolinda Pub Inc

Bony & White Savage. unabr. ed. Arthur W. Upfield. Read by Peter Hosking. (Running Time: 6 hrs. 15 mins.). (Inspector Napoleon Bonaparte Mysteries). 2009. audio compact disk 63.95 (978-1-74214-122-0(6), 9781742141220) Pub: Bolinda Pubng AUS. Dist(s): Bolinda Pub Inc

Booby Trapped: Men Beware! The Dirty Seven Sisters: A Dating Guide for the 21st Century. June Marshall. Ed. by Steven Kingsley. 2003. 9.95 (978-1-893798-29-8(1)) AIL New.

Boobytrap. unabr. ed. Bill Pronzini. Read by Nick Sullivan. 6 vols. (Running Time: 8 hrs.). (Nameless Detective Mystery Ser.). 1999. bk. 54.95 (978-0-7927-2269-4(8), CSL 158, Chivers Sound Lib) AudioGO.
Exhausted from the events surrounding his partner's suicide, Nameless welcomes a quiet vacation. It comes when San Francisco D.A. Patrick Dixon proposes that Nameless drive Dixon's wife & son to their summer cottage on Deep Mountain Lake. In exchange, Nameless will have a week's free use of a neighboring cabin. Donald Michael Latimer, an explosives expert, is paroled & decides it's time for revenge against the men who put him away: Dixon & Nameless.

Boogaloo on 2nd Avenue: A Novel of Pastry, Guilt, & Music. Mark Kurlansky. 2005. audio compact disk 39.99 (978-1-4193-2680-6(5)) Recorded Bks.

Boogaloo on 2nd Avenue: A Novel of Pastry, Guilt, & Music. unabr. ed. Mark Kurlansky. Read by George Guidall. 10 CDs. (Running Time: 12 hrs. 30 mins.). 2005. audio compact disk 119.75 (978-1-4193-3922-6(2)); 89.75 (978-1-4193-3920-2(6)) Recorded Bks.
Boogaloo is a musical stew of rhythm and blues, rock'n'roll, soul, and mambo. It provides the metaphor for the human stew of Second Avenue on New York City's Lower East Side in the 1980s, where African American, Dominican, German, Jewish and Puerto Rican neighbors, cuisine, and customs spice the lives of Nathan Seltzer and his family. Nathan struggles with guilt about a marital infidelity and battles a bout of claustrophobia while mulling a purchase offer on his photocopy store, the possibility that his lover's German father has Nazi ties, and a sidewalk murder that has the whole neighborhood jittery.

Boogers Are My Beat: More Lies, but Some Actual Journalism! unabr. ed. Dave Barry. Read by Dick Hill. 4 cass. Library ed. (Running Time: 6 hrs.). 2003. 62.25 (978-1-59086-931-4(1), 1590869311, Unabridge Lib Edns); audio compact disk 26.95 (978-1-59086-932-1(X), 159086932X, BACD); audio compact disk 74.25 (978-1-59086-933-8(8), 1590869338, BACDLib Ed) Brilliance Audio.
The New York Times calls him "the funniest man in America," and his legions of fans agree, laughing and snorting as they put his books on bestseller lists nationwide. In Boogers Are My Beat, Dave gives us the real scoop on: • The scientific search for the world's funniest joke (you can bet it includes the word "weasel") • RV camping in the Wal-Mart parking lot • Outwitting "smart" kitchen appliances and service contracts • Elections in Florida ("You can't spell Florida without 'duh'") • The Olympics, where people from all over the world come together to accuse each other of cheating • The truth about the Dakotas, the Lone Ranger, and feng shui • The choice between death and taxes And much, much more - including some truths about journalism and serious thoughts about 9/11.

Boogers Are My Beat: More Lies, but Some Actual Journalism! unabr. ed. Dave Barry. Read by Dick Hill. (Running Time: 6 hrs.). 2004. 24.95 (978-1-59335-224-0(7), 1593352247) Soulmate Audio Bks.

Boogers Are My Beat: More Lies, but Some Actual Journalism from Dave Barry. unabr. ed. Dave Barry. Read by Dick Hill. (Running Time: 6 hrs.). 2004. 39.25 (978-1-59335-495-4(9), 1593354959, Brlnc Audio MP3 Lib) Brilliance Audio.

Boogers Are My Beat: More Lies, but Some Actual Journalism from Dave Barry. unabr. ed. Dave Barry. Read by Dick Hill. (Running Time: 6 hrs.). 2004. 39.25 (978-1-59710-104-2(4), 1597101044, BADLE); 24.95 (978-1-59710-105-9(2), 1597101052, BAD) Brilliance Audio.

Boogie Nights: The Disco Age. Friedman-Fairfax and Sony Music Staff. 1 cass. (CD Ser.). 1994. pap. bk. 15.98 (978-1-56799-122-2(X), Friedman-Fairfax) M Friedman Pub Grp Inc.

Boogie Patterns: Two-Dozen Boogies You Can Lay Down with Your Left Hand. Duane Shinn. 1 cass. bk. 19.95 (CP-17) Duane Shinn.
Includes each pattern in printed form & demonstrated.

Boogie Woogie Piano, Learn see Learn Boogie Woogie Piano: The Artistry of Albert Ammons, Pete Johnson & Meade Lux Lewis

Boogie Woogie Santa Claus - ShowTrax. Music by Kirby Shaw. 1 CD. (Running Time: 5 mins.). 2000. audio compact disk 19.95 (08742302) H Leonard.
Jump back Jack! Santa's into swing dancin' & he's takin' it 8-to-the-bar!.

Boogiroot. Contrib. by DJ et al. 2005. audio compact disk 13.98 (978-5-558-96647-3(5)) Gotee Records.

Book about Tony Chestnut. Laurie Monopoli. Perf. by Don Monopoli. Illus. by Wendy Sefcik. Lyrics by Don Monopoli. As told by Jeanne Bowyer. The Learning Station. (ENG.). 2010. bk. 19.95 (978-0-615-31139-5(3)) Hug-A-Chug.

Book & the Seven Seals, Set. Mac Hammond. 6 cass. (Running Time: 6 hrs.). (Last Millennium Ser.: Vol. 5). 2000. (978-1-57399-091-2(4)) Mac Hammond.
"Who is worthy to open the book & to loose the seals thereof?" That's the question asked by a strong angel in the opening verses of Revelation, chapter 5.

***Book Club.** unabr. ed. Mary Alice Monroe. Read by Deanna Hurst. (Running Time: 15 hrs.). 2010. 24.99 (978-1-4418-5292-2(1), 9781441852922, Brilliance MP3); 24.99 (978-1-4418-5294-6(8), 9781441852946, BAD); 39.97 (978-1-4418-5293-9(X), 9781441852939, Brlnc Audio MP3 Lib); 39.97 (978-1-4418-5295-3(6), 9781441852953, BADLE); audio compact disk 29.99 (978-1-4418-5290-8(5), 9781441852908, Bril Audio CD Unabri); audio compact disk 79.97 (978-1-4418-5291-5(3), 9781441852915, BriAudCD Unabrid) Brilliance Audio.

Book Lady. unabr. ed. Malcolm Forsythe. Read by Michael Wade. 4 cass. (Running Time: 5 hrs. 15 mins.). (Storysound Ser.). (J). 2002. 44.95 (978-1-85903-521-4(3)) Pub: Mgna Lrg Print GBR. Dist(s): Ulverscroft US

Book Marketing for the Clueless(R) Created by Mike Rounds. Narrated by Mike Rounds. (ENG.). 2006. audio compact disk 24.95 (978-1-891440-49-6(7)) CPM Systems.

Book of a Thousand Days. unabr. ed. Shannon Hale. Read by Chelsea Mixon. (J). 2008. 39.99 (978-1-60514-680-5(3)) Find a World.

Book of Air & Shadows. unabr. ed. Michael Gruber. Read by Stephen Hoye. (YA). 2007. 74.99 (978-1-60252-878-9(0)) Find a World.

Book of Air & Shadows. unabr. ed. Michael Gruber. (Running Time: 18 hrs. 30 mins. 0 sec.). (ENG.). 2007. audio compact disk 34.99 (978-1-4001-5449-4(9)) Pub: Tantor Media. Dist(s): IngramPubServ

Book of Air & Shadows. unabr. ed. Michael Gruber. Read by Stephen Hoye. (Running Time: 18 hrs. 30 mins. 0 sec.). (ENG.). 2007. audio compact disk 49.99 (978-1-4001-0449-9(1)); audio compact disk 99.99 (978-1-4001-3449-6(8)) Pub: Tantor Media. Dist(s): IngramPubServ

***Book of American Heroes: Our Founders.** unabr. ed. Glenn Beck. (Running Time: 4 hrs. 0 mins. 0 sec.). (ENG.). (J). 2010. audio compact disk 24.99 (978-1-4423-4039-8(8)) Pub: S&S Audio. Dist(s): S and S Inc

Book of Ancestors see Poetry & Voice of Margaret Atwood

Book of Angels. Sylvia Browne. 2 cass. (ENG.). 2003. 18.95 (978-1-4019-0088-5(7), 0887); audio compact disk 18.95 (978-1-4019-0089-2(5), 0895) Hay House.

Book of Angels. Marigold Hunt. 4 cass. (J). 18.95 (515) Ignatius Pr.
Account of the presence & actions of angels in the Old & New Testaments by the well-known author of children's books.

Book of Colossians - Verse by Verse. Michael Pearl. 4 CDs. 2003. audio compact disk (978-1-892112-33-0(7)) No Greater Joy.

Book of Country Things. unabr. collector's ed. Walter Needham & Barrows Mussey. Read by Paul Shay. 4 cass. (Running Time: 4 hrs.). 1983. 24.00 (978-0-7366-0393-5(X), 1370) Books on Tape.
A book for people interested in crafts & in the current back-to-nature; also presents an accurate picture of life in New England.

Book of Daniel, Part 1, Part 2. Finis J. Dake, Sr. (J). (gr. k up). 5.95 (978-1-55829-033-4(8)) Dake Publishing.
Bible study.

Book of David: the Transition. Contrib. by Dave Hollister et al. 2006. audio compact disk 18.98 (978-5-558-18343-6(8)) GospoCen.

***Book of Days: A Novel.** unabr. ed. James L. Rubart. (Running Time: 10 hrs.). 2011. 14.99 (978-1-61106-435-3(X), 9781611064353, BAD); 39.97 (978-1-61106-436-0(8), 9781611064360, BADLE); audio compact disk 59.97 (978-1-61106-432-2(5), 9781611064322, BriAudCD Unabrid) Brilliance Audio.

***Book of Days: A Novel.** unabr. ed. James L. Rubart. Read by James L. Rubart. (Running Time: 10 hrs.). 2011. 14.99 (978-1-61106-433-9(3), 9781611064339, Brilliance MP3); 39.97 (978-1-61106-434-6(1), 9781611064346, Brlnc Audio MP3 Lib); audio compact disk 19.99 (978-1-61106-431-5(7), 9781611064315, Bril Audio CD Unabri) Brilliance Audio.

Book of Days: A Resource Book of Activities for Special Days in the Year. Adrian Wallwork. (Running Time: 1 hr. 54 mins.). (Cambridge Copy Collection). (ENG.). 1999. 43.00 (978-0-521-62611-8(0)) Cambridge U Pr.

***Book of Days Audio CDs (2) A Resource Book of Activities for Special Days in the Year.** Adrian Wallwork. (Running Time: 1 hr. 53 mins.). (Cambridge Copy Collection). (ENG.). 2010. audio compact disk 43.00 (978-0-521-18360-4(X)) Cambridge U Pr.

Book of Dead Days. unabr. ed. 4 cass. (Running Time: 5:48 hrs.). 2004. 32.00 (978-1-4000-9051-8(2), Listening Lib) Random Audio Pubg.

Book of Discipline & the Book of Resolutions 2005-2008. 2005. bk. 18.00 (978-0-687-06162-4(8)) Abingdon.

Book of Ephesians: In-Depth Commentary. Chuck Smith. (ENG.). 2003. 25.99 (978-1-932941-25-8(8)) Word For Today.

Book of Ephesians-Verse by Verse. Michael Pearl. 10 cass. 2000. (978-1-892112-36-1(1)) No Greater Joy.

Book of Evidence. unabr. ed. John Banville. Read by David Case. 6 cass. (Running Time: 1 hr. 30 min. per cass.). 1989. Rental 9.95 Set. (2854) Books on Tape.
Freddie Montgomery is a bad son, a worse husband, & a failed scientist. His expatriate life drags itself out in seedy resort bars. His one decisive act is to return home. But no sooner does he set foot on Irish soil than he steps in it. Trying robbery, he kills a servant. Freddie's lawyer proposes a plea: guilty to manslaughter, innocent to murder. That way, no trial. But Freddie wants drama. He seethes to tell his story.

Book of Evidence, unabr. collector's ed. John Banville. Read by David Case. 6 cass. (Running Time: 9 hrs.). 1991. 48.00 (978-0-7366-2040-6(0), 2854) Books on Tape.
Freddie Montgomery is a bad son, a worse husband & a failed scientist. His expatriate life drags itself out in seedy resort bars. His one decisive act is to return home. But no sooner does he set foot on Irish soil than he steps in it. Trying robbery, he kills a servant. Freddie's lawyer proposes a plea: guilty to manslaughter, innocent to murder. That way, no trial. But Freddie wants drama. He seethes to tell his story.

Book of Ezekial. Kelley Varner. 8 cass. 1992. 42.00 Set. (978-0-938612-77-3(8)) Destiny Image Pubs.

Book of Fate. abr. ed. Brad Meltzer. Read by Scott Brick. (Running Time: 7 hrs. 30 mins.). (ENG.). 2006. 14.98 (978-1-59483-542-1(X)) Pub: Hachet Audio. Dist(s): HachBkGrp

Book of Fate. abr. ed. Brad Meltzer. Read by Scott Brick. 6 CDs. (Running Time: 7 hrs. 30 mins.). (ENG.). 2008. audio compact disk 14.98 (978-1-60024-384-4(3)) Pub: Hachet Audio. Dist(s): HachBkGrp

Book of Fate. unabr. ed. Brad Meltzer. Read by Scott Brick. (YA). 2007. 69.99 (978-1-60252-670-9(2)) Find a World.

Book of Fate. unabr. ed. Brad Meltzer. Read by Scott Brick. (Running Time: 16 hrs.). (ENG.). 2006. 16.98 (978-1-59483-544-5(6)) Pub: Hachet Audio. Dist(s): HachBkGrp

Book of Fate. unabr. ed. Brad Meltzer. Read by Scott Brick. (Running Time: 16 hrs.). (ENG.). 2009. 74.98 (978-1-60788-142-1(X)) Pub: Hachet Audio. Dist(s): HachBkGrp

***Book of Five Rings.** unabr. ed. Miyamoto Musashi. Narrated by Scott Brick. (Running Time: 3 hrs. 0 mins. 0 sec.). (ENG.). 2010. 19.99 (978-1-4001-6852-1(X)); 11.99 (978-1-4001-8852-9(0)); audio compact disk 19.99 (978-1-4001-1852-6(2)); audio compact disk 47.99 (978-1-4001-4852-3(9)) Pub: Tantor Media. Dist(s): IngramPubServ

Book of Five Rings: Gorin No Sho the Accurate, Unabridged Translation the Greatest Samurai Musashi Speaks ! Musashi Miyamoto. Tr. by Urara Tsukamoto. Narrated by Ross M. Armetta. 2 CDs. (Running Time: 100 Mins. Aprox.). 2005. audio compact disk 16.99 (978-1-59733-205-7(4), Martial Strat) InfoFount.
The Book of 5 Rings Gorin No ShoThe accurate, unabridged translation ? Musashi speaks!Starting at 13 years old, Musashi fought over 60 life and death battles - never losing! Gorin No Sho - The Book of 5 Rings outlines the fundamentals of Kendo and marital training as proven successful in actual combat by Japan""""s Greatest Samurai - Musashi Miyamoto. You will readily understand how these strategies are useful for business, sports, and virtually any competitive situation. From black spots, to rhythms, to positioning, to psyching your opponent out and dozens more - you will learn practical strategies to win.This is a great audiobook for anybody interested in martial arts, competitive strategy, Samurai and their training and ethics, Japan, Japanese culture, Oriental culture and philosophy, and especially the Samurai and Bushido. This is especially helpful for martial artists in understanding the mental aspects of training and strategy in fighting. Once you read this book you will know where Bruce Lee developed most of his fighting philosophy and style from. Pay careful attention to the water and fire chapter and you will see it is similar to what Bruce Lee spoke of - except this was written in 1643 - 300 years before Bruce Lee was born.The strategies in The Book of 5 Rings can be applied to all challenges and conflicts of life.Based upon the to the death duels Musashi fought, knowledge gained from his samurai father warrior, and almost 20 years of study and reflection solely on martial strategy Musashi produced the most useful book ever made for one to one individual combat and a very useful book for group combat. This audiobook explains practical combat theories, training, and execution. It is an original translation and absolutely unique - IT IS ACCURATELY AND MINIMALLY INTERPRETED! We have looked at the other translations available and can say that most of them are abridged (even though they do not admit it) and are highly interpretive (read opinions of the translator / author added to the material - not from Musashi - how do you know what he actually wrote in these cases?)Martial Strategist?s translation is so accurate (we translated from a copy of the original 1645 manuscript that Musashi wrote) that we did very minimal correction/interpretation of the grammatical and verbal differences between these two very different languages, worlds, and ages in changing it to modern English. The result is an audiobook that is often grammatically incorrect in English, but much more vivid and accurate. Actually, the irony of this is that this translation is much less abstract than others. Because we did not worry about trying to rephrase things to make it pass the English teacher""""s inspection, we were able to maintain the direct, specific language and meaning that Musashi imparted.If you are a stickler for proper English, you may not enjoy this audiobook, however if you want to get the true text and meaning that Musashi wrote and are willing to listen to a few things a couple of times we are sure that you will be very pleased with this version.This is the only truly unabridged audiobook CD version available of this classic master work. It is complete, clear, and enjoyable. It is a quality production recorded in 2005 with music and sound effects. This audiobook has a real actor and is performed in a manner that is easy to understand and entertaining. It is a concise and accurate translation with the actor clearly and comprehensively articulating the text. It is not dry and boring as some other versions are. It has some levity in appropriate places. 2 Compact Disks: approx 1 hour 50 minutes running time. CONTENTS include The Ground Chapter, The Water Chapter, The Fire Chapter,The

Wind Chapter, The Ku / Sky Chapter. Gorin No Sho - The Book of 5 Rings you can understand and integrate the principles of winning into your life. This audiobook is energizing, informative, entertaining and very thought - Provoking.Martial Strategists are strategy specialists. They obtain, translate, and make the most useful military and strategy editions . They are unequaled for entertainment, practical application, and value.The Book of 5 Rings is also available discounted as part of the Samurai Pack or Martial Strategist?s Master Strategy Pack.More information available at www.InfoFount.comExcerpts from the Book of 5 Rings Translated by Urara TsukamotoThe Ground ChapterI name my martial strategy the way of NITOU-ICHIRYU (two swords one way). I write what I have been practicing many years in a book for the first time. It is in the beginning of October of Kanei 20 (1643) I climbed on the Iwatono Mountain in Higo in Kyushu, and I worship the sky and ka non [religious statue] and faced in front of the Buddha.I am a samurai named Shinmen Musashi No Kami, Fujiwara No Genshin. I was born in Harima. I am 60 years old now.I practiced the way of martial strategy since I was young. I fought for the first time at the age of 13. At tha

Book of Five Rings: The Classic Text of Principles, Craft, Skill & Samurai Strategy That Changed the American Way of Doing Business. abr. ed. Miyamoto Musashi. Read by Stanley Ralph Ross. Tr. by Victor Harris. 2 CDs. (Running Time: 1 hr. 30 mins. 0 sec.). (ENG.). 2005. audio compact disk 17.95 (978-1-59397-691-0(7)) Pub: Macmill Audio. Dist(s): Macmillan

Book of Galatians: In-Depth Commentary. Chuck Smith. (ENG.). 2003. 25.99 (978-1-932941-21-0(5)) Word For Today.

Book of Galatians - Verse by Verse. Michael Pearl. 6 CDs. 2003. audio compact disk (978-1-892112-35-4(3)) No Greater Joy.

Book of Genesis. Instructed by Gary Rendsburg. 12 cass. (Running Time: 12 hrs.). 2006. 129.95 (978-1-59803-188-1(0)) Teaching Co.

Book of God: The Bible as a Novel. unabr. ed. Walter Wangerin, Jr. (Running Time: 25 hrs. 23 mins. 0 sec.). (ENG.). 2003. 19.99 (978-0-310-26004-2(3)) Zondervan.

Book of Guys. unabr. abr. ed. Read by Garrison Keillor. 1 CD. (Running Time: 3 hrs.). (ENG.). 2003. audio compact disk 29.95 (978-1-56511-814-0(6), 1565118146) Pub: HighBridge. Dist(s): Workman Pub

Book of Hebrews. Scott Hahn. 8 cass. 1995. 39.95 Set. (5263-C) Ignatius Pr.
Scott tackles one of the most challenging & fascinating books of the New Testament. He describes what was at stake for the people of Israel, then facing a bloody confrontation with the world's most powerful empire. Scott shows you how it reveals God's plan of salvation in Christ.

***Book of Illusions.** unabr. ed. Paul Auster. Read by Paul Auster. (ENG.). 2004. (978-0-06-078436-2(9), Harper Audio) HarperCollins Pubs.

***Book of Illusions.** unabr. ed. Paul Auster. Read by Paul Auster. (ENG.). 2004. (978-0-06-081457-1(8), Harper Audio) HarperCollins Pubs.

***Book of Investing Wisdom: Classic Writings by Great Stock-Pickers & Legends of Wall Street.** unabr. ed. Peter Krass. Read by Stuart Langton. (Running Time: 14 hrs.). 2010. 29.95 (978-1-4417-1338-4(7)); audio compact disk 118.00 (978-1-4417-1335-3(2)) Blckstn Audio.

Book of Investing Wisdom: Classic Writings by Great Stock-Pickers & Legends of Wall Street. unabr. ed. Read by Jonathan Tindle. Ed. by Peter Krass. 10 cass. (Running Time: 14 hrs. 30 mins.). 2000. 69.95 (978-0-7861-1747-5(8), 2551) Blckstn Audio.
An anthology of 46 essays & speeches in which the legends of Wall Street share their best investment ideas & advice. You'll hear from Bernard Baruch on stock market slumps, Peter Bernstein on investing for the long term, Joseph E. Granville on market movements, to name just a few.

Book of Isaiah. Kelley Varner. 4 cass. 1992. 25.00 Set. (978-0-938612-79-7(4)) Destiny Image Pubs.

Book of Job. Read by The Full Cast Family & Cynthia Bishop. 2004. 20.00 (978-1-932076-64-6(6)) Full Cast Audio.

Book of Job. unabr. ed. Read by Peter Coyote. Tr. by Stephen Mitchell. 1 cass. (Running Time: 1 hr. 13 mins.). 1995. 10.95 (978-0-944993-08-8(7)) Audio Lit.
Penetrates deeply into the eternal question of why we are here & why we suffer.

Book of Job. unabr. ed. Perf. by Paul Scofield & Robert Harris. Adapted by Pamela Gravett. Composed by Terence Allbright. 1 cass. 12.95 (ECN 081) J Norton Pubs.
Gravett's selection & arrangement of this story has turned it into a powerful drama.

Book of Job. unabr. ed. Text From the King James Bible. Read by Full Cast Production Staff. (J). 2007. 34.99 (978-1-60252-550-4(1)) Find a World.

Book of John 1-8 - Verse by Verse. Michael Pearl. 24 cass. 2000. (978-1-892112-37-8(X)) No Greater Joy.

Book of Kings. unabr. ed. James Thackara. Read by Robert Whitfield. 3 CDs. (Running Time: 38 hrs.). 2002. audio compact disk 54.95 (978-0-7861-9119-2(8), 3023A, B) Blckstn Audio.

Book of Kings, Pt. 1. unabr. ed. James Thackara. Read by Robert Whitfield. 15 cass. (Running Time: 38 hrs.). 2002. 95.95 (978-0-7861-2364-3(8), 3023A, B) Blckstn Audio.
Set across the entire continent of Europe, as well as North and South America and North Africa, in the years shortly before and during World War II and leading up to the present day. While Europe drifts toward Nazism, four students share an apartment on the Rue de Fleurus. The stories of these four men whose lives mirror the large picture of events around the world are forged.

Book of Kings, Pt. 2 unabr. ed. James Thackara. Read by Robert Whitfield. 11 cass. (Running Time: 38 hrs.). 2002. 76.95 (978-0-7861-2338-4(9), 3023A, B) Blckstn Audio.

Book of Lies. abr. ed. Brad Meltzer. Read by Scott Brick. (Running Time: 7 hrs.). (ENG.). 2008. 14.98 (978-1-60024-379-0(7)) Pub: Hachet Audio. Dist(s): HachBkGrp

Book of Lies. abr. ed. Brad Meltzer. Read by Scott Brick. (Running Time: 7 hrs.). (ENG.). 2009. audio compact disk 14.98 (978-1-60024-663-0(X)) Pub: Hachet Audio. Dist(s): HachBkGrp

Book of Lies. unabr. ed. Brad Meltzer. Read by Scott Brick. (Running Time: 11 hrs. 30 mins.). (ENG.). 2008. 26.98 (978-1-60024-381-3(9)); audio compact disk 39.98 (978-1-60024-380-6(0)) Pub: Hachet Audio. Dist(s): HachBkGrp

Book of Lies. unabr. ed. Brad Meltzer. Read by Scott Brick. 10 CDs. 2008. audio compact disk 120.00 (978-1-4159-5991-6(9), BksonTape); 120.00 (978-1-4159-6040-0(2), BksonTape) Pub: Random Audio Pubg. Dist(s): Random
In chapter four of the Bible, Cain kills Abel. It is the world's most famous murder. But the Bible is silent about one key detail: the weapon Cain used to kill his brother. That weapon is still lost to history. In 1932, Mitchell Siegel was killed by two gunshots to the chest. While mourning, his son dreamed of a bulletproof man and created the world's greatest hero: Superman. And like Cain's murder weapon, the gun used in this unsolved murder has never been found. Today in Fort Lauderdale, Florida, Cal Harper comes face-to-face with his own family tragedy: His long-missing father has been shot with a gun that traces back to Mitchell Siegel's 1932 murder. But soon after their surprising reunion, Cal and his father are attacked by a ruthless killer tattooed with the ancient markings of Cain. So begins the chase for the world's first murder weapon. It is a race that will pull Cal back into his own past even as it propels him forward through the true story of Cain and Abel, an eighty-year-old unsolvable puzzle, and the deadly organization known for the past century as the Leadership.

book of Life: Transcribed by, the Archangel Michael. Michael Paige. (ENG., 2008. pap. bk. 30.00 (978-0-615-25723-5(2)) M Paige.

Book of Light. Light. Read by Sun. 1 cass. (Running Time: 40 min.). 1989. 7.00 (978-0-929274-17-1(2)) Gentle World.
Presents a spiritual collection of poetry, stories, sayings, haiku.

Book of Lost Things. unabr. ed. John Connolly. 10 CDs. (Running Time: 39600 sec.). 2006. audio compact disk 34.99 (978-1-4281-2040-2(8)) Recorded Bks.

Book of Mary. Henri Daniel-Rops. 8 cass. 32.95 (904) Ignatius Pr.
Deals with all the recorded facts about the Mother of Christ.

Book of Matthew. Michael Pearl. 3 CDs. (Running Time: 215 mins). 2004. audio compact disk (978-1-892112-65-1(5)) No Greater Joy.

Book of Miracles. unabr. ed. Gilbert Highet. Read by Gilbert Highet. 1 cass. (Running Time: 30 min.). 9.95 (23311-A) J Norton Pubs.

***Book of Miracles: 101 True Stories of Healing, Faith, Divine Intervention, & Answered Prayers.** unabr. ed. Jack L. Canfield et al. Read by Kathy Garver & Tom Parks. 1 Playaway. (Running Time: 9 hrs.). (Chicken Soup for the Soul (Audio Health Communications) Ser.). 2010. 39.99 (978-1-4418-8221-9(9)); audio compact disk 14.99 (978-1-4418-7781-9(9)) Brilliance Audio.

Book of Monsters. unabr. ed. Bruce Coville. 2 cass. (YA). 1999. 16.98 (FS9-31429) Highsmith.

Book of Mormon. 21 CDs. 2004. audio compact disk 49.95 (978-1-57734-694-4(7)) Covenant Comms.

Book of Mormon. Read by Rex Campbell. (Running Time: 25 hrs.). 2005. 25.95 (978-1-933092-97-3(1)) Iofy Corp.

Book of Mormon. Narrated by Lael J. Woodbury. 21 CDs. 2003. audio compact disk 29.95 (978-0-87579-054-1(2)) Deseret Bk.

Book of Mormon. unabr. ed. Read by Lael Woodbury. 16 cass. (Scriptures on Cassette Ser.). 1990. 25.95 Set. (978-1-887938-00-6(1)) Snd Concepts.
LDS scripture.

Book of Mormon, Set. Narrated by Rex Campbell. 17 cass. 2004. 24.95 (978-1-55503-206-7(0), 0500209) Covenant Comms.

Book of Mormon, Set. Narrated by Rex Campbell. 21 CDs. audio compact disk 49.95 (978-1-57734-058-4(2), 0200530) Covenant Comms.

Book of Mormon: A Marvelous Work or, I Wonder? Jack Marshall. 1 cass. 9.95 (978-1-57734-566-4(5), 06006124) Covenant Comms.
A witty look at the Book of Mormon.

Book of Mormon: Hallowed Journey, Set. 36 CDs. audio compact disk 99.95 (978-1-55503-946-2(4), 0200484) Covenant Comms.

Book of Mormon Set: Hallowed Journey. 30 cass. 69.95 (978-1-55503-947-9(2), 0500216) Covenant Comms.

Book of Mormon - CD Box Set. 21 CDs. 1984. audio compact disk 29.95 (978-1-887938-17-4(6)) Snd Concepts.

Book of Mormon & You. Jack R. Christianson. 1 cass. 7.98 (978-1-55503-359-0(8), 061979) Covenant Comms.
Powerful, convincing, motivating talk.

Book of Mormon, Doctrine & Covenants & Pearl of Great Price, Set. 33 CDs. audio compact disk 79.95 (978-1-57734-057-7(4), 0200522) Covenant Comms.

Book of Mormon Is the Word of God. collector's ed. Ezra Taft Benson. 1 cass. 4.98 (978-1-55503-081-0(5), 06003443) Covenant Comms.
Explains meaning & purpose.

Book of Mormon on CD-Box Set. Narrated by Rex Cambell. 21 CDs. 2004. bk. 29.95 (978-1-59156-346-4(1)) Covenant Comms.

Book of Mormon Songs. Lynn S. Lund. 1996. 9.95 (978-1-57008-274-0(X), Bkcraft Inc) Deseret Bk.

***Book of Murray: The Life, Teachings, & Kvetching of the Lost Prophet.** unabr. ed. David M. Bader. Read by Yash Kimmelfarb. (ENG.). 2010. audio compact disk 19.95 (978-1-61573-518-1(6), 1615735186) Pub: HighBridge. Dist(s): Workman Pub

Book of Names. abr. ed. Jill Gregory & Karen Tintori. Read by Christopher Graybill. (Running Time: 21600 sec.). 2007. audio compact disk 14.99 (978-1-4233-3085-1(4), 9781423330851, BCD Value Price) Brilliance Audio.

Book of Names. unabr. ed. Jill Gregory and Karen Tintori. Read by Christopher Graybill. (Running Time: 9 hrs.). 2007. 39.25 (978-1-4233-3083-7(8), 9781423330837, BADLE); 24.95 (978-1-4233-3082-0(X), 9781423330820, BAD) Brilliance Audio.

Book of Names. unabr. ed. Jill Gregory & Karen Tintori. Read by Christopher Graybill. (Running Time: 32400 sec.). 2007. 69.25 (978-1-4233-3077-6(3), 9781423330776, BrilAudUnabridg); audio compact disk 87.25 (978-1-4233-3079-0(X), 9781423330790, BriAudCD Unabrid); audio compact disk 39.25 (978-1-4233-3081-3(1), 9781423330813, Brinc Audio MP3 Lib); audio compact disk 34.95 (978-1-4233-3078-3(1), 9781423330783, Bril Audio CD Unabri); audio compact disk 24.95 (978-1-4233-3080-6(3), 9781423330806, Brilliance MP3) Brilliance Audio.

Book of Night Women. Marlon James. (Running Time: 16 hrs.). (ENG.). (gr. 12 up). 2009. audio compact disk 39.95 (978-0-14-314440-3(5), PengAudBks) Penguin Grp USA.

***Book of Night Women.** unabr. ed. Marlon James. Read by Robin Miles. 1 Playaway. (Running Time: 15 hrs. 45 mins.). 2009. 61.75 (978-1-4361-9845-5(3), Griot Aud) Recorded Bks.

***Book of Night Women.** unabr. ed. Marlon James & Marion James. Read by Robin Miles. 14 CDs. (Running Time: 15 hrs. 45 mins.). 2009. audio compact disk 123.75 (978-1-4361-9843-1(7)) Recorded Bks.

***Book of Night Women.** unabr. collector's ed. Marlon James. Read by Robin Miles. 14 CDs. (Running Time: 15 hrs. 45 mins.). 2009. audio compact disk 39.95 (978-1-4361-9844-8(5), Griot Aud) Recorded Bks.

Book of Nightmares: Under the Maud Moon see Poetry & Voice of Galway Kinnell

Book of Old Houses. unabr. ed. Sarah Graves. Narrated by Lindsay Ellison. 8 CDs. (Running Time: 10 hrs.). (Home Repair Is Homicide Mystery Ser.). 2008. audio compact disk 79.95 (978-0-7927-5242-4(2)) AudioGO.
When a mysterious book is unearthed from the foundation of Jake's 1823 fixer-upper, she immediately sends it off to local book historian Horace Robotham. After all, there must be a logical explanation for why the long-buried volume has her name in it - written in what looks suspiciously like blood. But all logic goes out the window when the book disappears, and Horace turns up dead. When two more victims turn up in a town better known for its scenic views and historic homes than its body count, Jake and her comrade-in-sleuthing, Ellie White, need to go on the prowl to find someone who may believe that the pages of an ancient book are the blueprint for a perfect murder.

Book of Old Houses. unabr. ed. Sarah Graves. Read by Lindsay Ellison. (YA). 2008. 64.99 (978-1-60514-939-4(X)) Find a World.

Book of Oneself. J. Krishnamurti. 1 cass. 8.50 (ABOO82) Krishnamurti.
In reading the book of oneself, which is the book of mankind, two questions arise: What is the nature of what is seen, & what is the instrument which sees? Krishnamurti discusses these questions with Pupul Jayakar & Achyut Patwardhan.

Book of Pirates. Howard Pyle. Read by Ralph Cosham. (Running Time: 8 hrs.). 2003. 24.95 (978-1-59912-045-4(3), Audiofy Corp) Iofy Corp.

Book of Pirates. Howard Pyle. Narrated by Ralph Cosham. (Running Time: 28800 sec.). (Unabridged Classics in MP3 Ser.). (ENG.). 2008. audio compact disk 14.95 (978-1-58472-584-8(2), In Aud); audio compact disk 24.00 (978-1-58472-585-5(0), In Aud) Sound Room.

Book of Pirates. unabr. ed. Howard Pyle. Read by Ralph Cosham. (J). 2007. 59.99 (978-1-59895-845-4(3)) Find a World.

Book of Psalms. Read by Marvin Miller. 6 cass. 35.70 (E-708) Audio Bk.
150 spiritual truths wrought from the emotions, experiences & hopes of the author of Biblical times.

Book of Psalms. unabr. ed. Read by Michael York. 4 cass. (Running Time: 6 hrs.). 2001. 25.00 (978-1-57453-460-3(2)) Audio Lit.
Inspiring, timeless in their wisdom and without compare in their soul-soothing beauty. Represents the diversity found in the 150 songs and poems collected throughout ancient Israel's history.

Book of Q. Jonathan Rabb. Read by Arthur Addison. 2001. 88.00 (978-0-7366-7048-7(3)); audio compact disk 104.00 (978-0-7366-8518-4(9)) Books on Tape.

Book of Revelation. 2002. audio compact disk (978-1-931713-24-5(3)) Word For Today.

Book of Revelation. Chuck Smith. (ENG.). 2001. 15.99 (978-1-932941-18-0(5)) Word For Today.

Book of Revelation. Gary V. Whetstone. Adapted by June Austin. (New Testament Ser.). 1996. 220.00 (978-1-928774-88-4(1), NT202) Gary Whet Pub.

Book of Revelation: Mystery Babylon, False Prophet, Sabbath Day. Finis J. Dake, Sr. (J). (gr. k up). 5.95 (978-1-55829-034-1(6)) Dake Publishing.
Bible study.

Book of Revelation: The Revelation of Jesus Christ. 505. audio compact disk 19.95 (978-0-9675577-7-9(1)) Puddleduck Pubg.

Book of Revelation: The Testifying of Christ. Richard D. Draper. 2004. 9.95 (978-1-57734-794-1(3)); audio compact disk 10.95 (978-1-57734-795-8(1)) Covenant Comms.

Book of Revelation Prophecy, Vol. 1. Speeches. Ronald G. Fanter. 16 cass. 2003. 80.00 (978-1-931215-39-8(1)) Cut Edge Min.
Tapes Included In This VolumeIntro. Book of RevelationThe TabernacleThe Existence of AngelsGoverning SpiritsGod's WitnessesThe Day of The LordThe MessiahFeast Days of IsraelSeven Historical ChurchesSmyrna And PergamosThyatira DispensationSardis and PhiladelphiaLaodicea DispensationLucifer's EarthPreAdamic CreationPreAdamic World.

Book of Revelation Tape Pack. 2002. (978-1-931713-14-6(6)) Word For Today.

Book of Romans. 12 cass. 49.98 Set, vinyl albums with display box. (1110-DB) Chrstn Dup Intl.

Book of Romans: In-Depth Commentary. Chuck Smith. (ENG.). 2003. 25.99 (978-1-932941-84-5(3)) Word For Today.

Book of Romans - Verse by Verse. Michael Pearl. 20 CDs. 2003. audio compact disk (978-1-892112-31-6(0)) No Greater Joy.

Book of Ruth. Jane Hamilton. 2004. 15.95 (978-0-7435-4213-5(4)) Pub: S&S Audio. Dist(s): S and S Inc

Book of Ruth. abr. ed. 2 cass. (Running Time: 3 hrs.). 2000. audio compact disk 15.99 (978-0-7435-0569-7(7), Audioworks) S&S Audio.

Book of Ruth. unabr. ed. Jane Hamilton. Narrated by Angela Jayne Rogers. 9 cass. (Running Time: 13 hrs. 15 mins.). 1997. 83.00 (978-0-7887-0912-8(7), 95052E7) Recorded Bks.
A bittersweet testament to the resilience of the human spirit, as it captures the enduring strength of a tortured, innocent soul.

Book of Salsa: A Chronicle of Urban Music from the Caribbean to New York City. César Miguel Rondón. Tr. by Frances R. Aparicio & Jackie White. (ENG.). 2008. 23.95 (978-0-8078-8642-7(4)); audio compact disk 23.95 (978-0-8078-8644-1(0)) U of NC Pr.

Book of Samson. unabr. ed. David Maine. Read by Simon Vance. (YA). 2007. 54.99 (978-1-60252-820-8(9)) Find a World.

Book of Samson. unabr. ed. David Maine. Narrated by Simon Vance. (Running Time: 7 hrs. 0 mins. 0 sec.). (ENG.). 2006. audio compact disk 19.99 (978-1-4001-5323-7(9)); audio compact disk 59.99 (978-1-4001-3323-9(8)) Pub: Tantor Media. Dist(s): IngramPubServ

Book of Samson. unabr. ed. David Maine. Read by Simon Vance. (Running Time: 7 hrs. 0 mins. 0 sec.). (ENG.). 2006. audio compact disk 29.99 (978-1-4001-0323-2(1)) Pub: Tantor Media. Dist(s): IngramPubServ

***Book of Scandal.** unabr. ed. Julia London. (Running Time: 11 hrs.). (Scandalous Ser.). 2011. 24.99 (978-1-4418-5115-4(1), 9781441851154, BAD); 39.97 (978-1-4418-5116-1(X), 9781441851161, BADLE) Brilliance Audio.

***Book of Scandal.** unabr. ed. Julia London. Read by Anne Flosnik. (Running Time: 11 hrs.). (Scandalous Ser.). 2011. 24.99 (978-1-4418-5113-0(5), 9781441851130, Brilliance MP3); 39.97 (978-1-4418-5114-7(3), 9781441851147, Brinc Audio MP3 Lib); audio compact disk 19.99 (978-1-4418-5111-6(9), 9781441851116, Bril Audio CD Unabri); audio compact disk 69.97 (978-1-4418-5112-3(7), 9781441851123, BriAudCD Unabrid) Brilliance Audio.

Book of Secrets. Perf. by Loreena McKennitt. 1 cass., 1 CD. 8.78 (WB 46719); audio compact disk 13.58 CD. (WB 46719) NewSound.

Book of Secrets: Unlocking the Hidden Dimensions of Your Life. abr. ed. Deepak Chopra. 3 cassettes. (Running Time: 2 hrs). 2004. 63.00 (978-1-4159-0442-8(1)) Books on Tape.

Book of Secrets: Unlocking the Hidden Dimensions of Your Life. abr. ed. Deepak Chopra. Read by Deepak Chopra. 3 CDs. (Running Time: 4 hrs.). (Deepak Chopra Ser.). (ENG.). 2004. audio compact disk 18.00 (978-0-7393-1397-8(5), RH-Aud Dim) Pub: Random Audio Pubg. Dist(s): Random

Book of Spies. unabr. ed. Gayle Lynds. (Running Time: 13 hrs. 30 mins.). 2010. 29.95 (978-1-4417-2692-6(6)); audio compact disk 39.95 (978-1-4417-2691-9(8)) Blckstn Audio.

***Book of Spies.** unabr. ed. Gayle Lynds. (Running Time: 13 hrs. 30 mins.). 2010. 79.95 (978-1-4417-2688-9(8)) Blckstn Audio.

***Book of Spies.** unabr. ed. Gayle Lynds. Read by Kate Reading. 12 CDs. (Running Time: 13 hrs. 30 mins.). 2010. audio compact disk 109.00 (978-1-4417-2689-6(6)) Blckstn Audio.

Book of Tea. 2001. audio compact disk 8.99 (978-0-923586-52-2(0)) Data Syst CA.

Book of the Dead. Patricia Cornwell. No. 15. (ENG.). (gr. 8). 2008. audio compact disk 14.95 (978-0-14-314381-9(6), PengAudBks) Penguin Grp USA.

Book of the Dead. abr. ed. Douglas Preston & Lincoln Child. Read by Rene Auberjonois. (Running Time: 6 hrs.). (Pendergast Ser.: No. 7). (ENG.). 2006. 14.98 (978-1-59483-521-6(7)) Pub: Hachet Audio. Dist(s): HachBkGrp

Book of the Dead. unabr. ed. Patricia Cornwell. 10 cass. (Running Time: 15 hrs.). (Kay Scarpetta Ser.: No. 15). 2007. 90.00 (978-1-4159-3127-1(5)); audio compact disk 96.00 (978-1-4159-3128-8(3)) Books on Tape.

Book of the Dead. unabr. ed. Patricia Cornwell. Read by Kate Reading. 11 CDs. (Running Time: 13 hrs.). No. 15. (ENG.). (gr. 8). 2007. audio compact disk 39.95 (978-0-14-305914-1(9), PengAudBks) Penguin Grp USA.

Book of the Dead. unabr. ed. Douglas Preston & Lincoln Child. Read by Scott Brick. (Pendergast Ser.: No. 7). (YA). 2006. 59.99 (978-1-59895-442-5(3)) Find a World.

Book of the Dead. unabr. ed. Douglas Preston & Lincoln Child. Read by Scott Brick. (Running Time: 13 hrs.). (Pendergast Ser.: No. 7). (ENG.). 2006. 16.98 (978-1-59483-522-3(5)) Pub: Hachet Audio. Dist(s): HachBkGrp

Book of the Dead. unabr. ed. Douglas Preston & Lincoln Child. Read by Scott Brick. (Running Time: 13 hrs.). (ENG.). 2009. 74.98 (978-1-60788-154-4(3)) Pub: Hachet Audio. Dist(s): HachBkGrp

***Book of the Dun Cow.** unabr. ed. Walter Wangerin Jr. Narrated by Paul Michael. (Yasmin Peace Ser.). (ENG.). 2007. 14.98 (978-1-59644-524-6(6), christaudio) christianaud.

Book of the Dun Cow. unabr. ed. Walter Wangerin, Jr.. Afterword by Walter Wangerin, Jr. Narrated by Paul Michael. (Running Time: 6 hrs. 0 mins. 0 sec.). (ENG.). 2007. audio compact disk 23.98 (978-1-59644-523-9(8), christaudio) christianaud.

Book of the Homeless. unabr. ed. Edith Wharton. 1995. 12.98 (978-1-57375-013-4(1)) Audioscope.

Book of the Law. unabr. ed. Aleister Crowley. Read by Steven Ashe & Carolyn Hucker. 1 cass. (Running Time: 40 min.). 1993. 9.95 (978-1-881532-00-2(3)) IllumiNet Pr.
British reading of Aleister Crowley's "Book of the Law." Accurately read from the original manuscript.

Book of the Lion. unabr. ed. Michael Cadnum. Narrated by Simon Prebble. 4 cass. (Running Time: 5 hrs. 45 min.). 2003. 37.00 (978-1-4025-5539-8(3)) Recorded Bks.
When 17-year-old Edmund is rescued from a harsh, violent punishment by a knight seeking a new squire, he suddenly finds himself making a dangerous journey toward the Holy Land to meet up with crusading King Richard. Michael Cadnum?s sweeping tale of medieval Crusaders unveils the harsh realities of an historical era that still echoes in the modern world.

Book of the Maidservant. unabr. ed. Rebecca Barnhouse. (J). (gr. 5). 2009. audio compact disk 34.00 (978-0-7393-8553-1(4), Listening Lib) Pub: Random Audio Pubg. Dist(s): Random

***Book of the Shepherd.** unabr. ed. Joann Davis. Read by Kirby Heyborne. (ENG.). 2009. (978-0-06-198160-9(5), Harper Audio); (978-0-06-198161-6(3), Harper Audio) HarperCollins Pubs.

Book of Thel. William Blake. Intro. by Hallam M. Tennyson. Narrated by Cecil Day Lewis. 1 cass. 10.95 (ECN 213) J Norton Pubs.
This poem was written in 1789. It was the first of Blake's which he took leave of the world of innocence for ever.

Book of Three. unabr. ed. Lloyd Alexander. Read by Chris King. 4 vols. (Running Time: 5 hrs. 25 mins.). (Chronicles of Prydain Ser.: Bk. 1). (J). (gr. 4-7). 1991. pap. bk. 38.00 (978-0-8072-7346-7(1), YA 834 SP, Listening Lib); 32.00 (978-0-8072-7347-0(3), YA 834 CX, Listening Lib) Random Audio Pubg.
Taran & a strange assortment of companions are on a dangerous mission to save their beloved land.

Book of Three. unabr. ed. Lloyd Alexander. Read by James Langton. (Running Time: 18240 sec.). (Chronicles of Prydain Ser.: Bk. 1). (ENG.). (J). (gr. 5-9). 2007. audio compact disk 28.00 (978-0-7393-5612-8(7), Listening Lib) Pub: Random Audio Pubg. Dist(s): Random

Book of Time. unabr. ed. Guillaume Prevost. Read by Holter Graham. (J). 2007. 54.99 (978-1-60252-821-5(7)) Find a World.

Book of Time. unabr. ed. Guillaume Prevost. Read by Holter Graham. 5 CDs. (Running Time: 6 hrs. 36 mins.). (ENG.). (J). (gr. 4-7). 2007. audio compact disk 54.95 (978-0-545-02492-1(7)) Scholastic Inc.

Book of Time. unabr. ed. Guillaume Prevost. Read by Holter Graham. 5 CDs. (Running Time: 23760 sec.). (ENG.). (J). (gr. 4-7). 2007. audio compact disk 29.95 (978-0-545-02467-9(6)) Scholastic Inc.

***Book of Tomorrow: A Novel.** unabr. ed. Cecelia Ahern. (ENG.). 2011. (978-0-06-202730-6(1), Harper Audio) HarperCollins Pubs.

Book of Unholy Mischief. abr. ed. Elle Newmark & Elle Newmark. Read by Raul Esparza. (Running Time: 6 hrs. 0 mins. 0 sec.). (ENG.). 2008. audio compact disk 29.99 (978-0-7435-7803-5(1)) Pub: S&S Audio. Dist(s): S and S Inc

Book of Unholy Mischief. unabr. ed. Elle Newmark. Read by Raul Esparza. 10 CDs. (Running Time: 11 hrs. 30 mins. 0 sec.). (ENG.). 2008. audio compact disk 39.99 (978-0-7435-7804-2(X)) Pub: S&S Audio. Dist(s): S and S Inc

Book of Virtues. William J. Bennett. Read by Barbara Bush et al. 8 cass. 49.95 Set incl. bklet. (12380PAM) Nightingale-Conant.
Here's a thought-provoking program everyone in your family will enjoy, for it will help children & adults alike develop the characters traits we will admire. William J. Bennett, former secretary of education, gathered dozens of stories about good character & positive values...then brought them together in a captivating collection that belongs in every home.

Book of Virtues, Vols. 1 & 2. unabr. ed. William J. Bennett. Read by William J. Bennett. 8 cass. (Running Time: 12 hrs.). 1997. audio compact disk 50.00 Set. (978-0-671-93447-7(3), Audioworks) S&S Audio.

Book of Virtues: A Treasury of Great Moral Stories, Vol. II. William J. Bennett. 2004. 10.95 (978-0-7435-4215-9(0)) Pub: S&S Audio. Dist(s): S and S Inc

Book of Virtues: An Audio Library of Great Moral Stories. William J. Bennett. 2004. 15.95 (978-0-7435-4214-2(2)) Pub: S&S Audio. Dist(s): S and S Inc

Book of Yahweh, the Holy Scriptures: Genesis. (Running Time: 4 hrs. 46 min.). 1999. 16.95 (978-1-890967-25-3(4)) Hse of Yahweh.
The first book in The Holy Scriptures tells the stories of Adam & Eve, Noah & the Flood, & the Coat of Many Colors. Told by the characters themselves.

Book on Bush: How George W. (Mis)Leads America. Eric Alterman & Mark J. Green. Read by Nick Sullivan. 13 vols. 2004. 99.95 (978-0-7927-3137-5(9), CSL 631, Chivers Sound Lib); audio compact disk 117.95 (978-0-7927-3138-2(7), SLD 631, Chivers Sound Lib); audio compact disk 49.95 (978-0-7927-3139-9(5), CMP 631, Chivers Sound Lib) AudioGO.

Book on Bush: How George W. (Mis)Leads America. unabr. ed. Eric Alterman & Mark Green. Read by Nick Sullivan. 16 CDs. (Running Time: 19 hrs. 30 mins.). 2004. audio compact disk 49.95 (978-1-57270-376-6(8)) Pub: Audio Partners. Dist(s): PerseuPGW

Book on Bush: How George W. (Mis)Leads America. unabr. ed. Eric Alterman & Mark Green. Read by Nick Sullivan. 13 cass. (Running Time: 19 hrs. 30 mins.). 2004. 44.95 (978-1-57270-375-9(X)) Pub: Audio Partners. Dist(s): PerseuPGW

Book on Tape. Barbara Rocha. Read by Barbara Rocha. 2 cass. (Running Time: 3 hrs.). 17.95 Set. Bouldin Hill.
Topics include: "How to manage your mind," How to manage your body," & How to prepare a well-organized presentation that excites your audience &, at the same time, reduces stress".

Book Promotion & Marketing: Success Strategies to Increase Your Sales. Marilyn Ross & Tom Ross. 6 cass. 1987. 69.95 Set. (978-0-918880-15-4(7)) Comm Creat.

Book Publishing in United Kingdom: A Strategic Reference 2006. Compiled by Icon Group International, Inc. Staff. 2007. ring bd. 195.00 (978-0-497-82451-8(5)) Icon Grp.

Book Store. Wiley US.

Book-Talk: Singable Songs for Lifelong Readers. Michelle O'Brien-Palmer. 1 cass. (J). 1994. 9.95 (978-1-879235-03-8(X)) MicNik Pubns.

Book That Cried, Vol. 1. Shirley A. Jackson Whitaker. (J). (gr. k-3). 1997. (978-0-9669017-2-6(X)) Whitaker Pr.

Book That Dripped Blood. Michael Dahl. Illus. by Bradford Kendall. (Library of Doom Ser.). (gr. 1-3). 2008. audio compact disk 14.60 (978-1-4342-0603-9(3)) CapstoneDig.

Book Thief. unabr. ed. Markus Zusak. Read by Allan Corduner. 11 CDs. (Running Time: 49800 sec.). (ENG.). (J). (gr. 7-12). 2006. audio compact disk 51.00 (978-0-7393-3727-1(0), Listening Lib) Pub: Random Audio Pubg. Dist(s): Random

Book Thief. unabr. ed. Markus Zusak. Read by Allan Corduner. 11 CDs. (Running Time: 13 hrs. 57 mins.). (YA). (gr. 9 up). 2006. audio compact disk 63.75 (978-0-7393-3800-1(5), Listening Lib) Pub: Random Audio Pubg. Dist(s): NetLibrary CO
It's just a small story really, about among other things: a girl, some words, an accordionist, some fanatical Germans, a Jewish fist-fighter, and quite a lot of thievery... Set during World War II in Germany, Markus Zusak's groundbreaking new novel is the story of Liesel Meminger, a foster girl living outside of Munich. Liesel scratches out a meager existence for herself by stealing when she encounters something she can't resist - books. With the help of her accordion-playing foster father, she learns to read and shares her stolen books with her neighbors during bombing raids as well as with the Jewish man hidden in her basement before he is marched to Dachau.

Book Without Words: A Fairy Tale of Medieval Magic. unabr. ed. Avi. Narrated by John Curliss. 4 CDs. (Running Time: 4 hrs. 30 mins.). 2005. audio compact disk 52.75 (978-1-4193-5557-8(0), C3403); 42.75 (978-1-4193-5055-9(2), 98112) Recorded Bks.
Hiding from a cadaverous stalker in 1046 England, Thorston races to unleash the magical charms from the diabolical Book Without Words. Suddenly - with success almost in his grasp - he slumps to the floor, muttering cryptic words. Newbery Award-winning author Avi adds this jewel to his many literary gems offered by Recorded Books.

Book Writing & Publishing. unabr. ed. Dan Poynter. Read by Dan Poynter. 1 cass. (Running Time: 1 hr. 16 min.). 1993. 9.95 (978-0-915516-75-9(6), P-101) Para Pub.
Dan Poynter on how to write & publish books. Reasons to write a book, what to write, how to write, publishing options, how to self-publish & the secrets of successful self-publishing. Includes resources.

Book You'll Actually Listen To (OT, NT, God, Church Leadership) unabr. ed. Mark Driscoll. Narrated by Johnny Heller. (Running Time: 7 hrs. 0 mins. 0 sec.). Orig. Title: Quitting the Mob. (ENG.). 2009. audio compact disk 24.98 (978-1-59644-739-4(7), christianSeed) christianaud.

Book Yourself Solid: The Fastest, Easiest, & Most Reliable System for Getting More Clients Than You Can Handle Even If You Hate Marketing & Selling. rev. unabr. ed. Michael Port. Read by Michael Port. (Running Time: 7 hrs. 30 mins.). (ENG.). 2008. audio compact disk 29.98 (978-1-59659-135-6(8), GildAudio) Pub: Gildan Media. Dist(s): HachBkGrp

Booked for Murder. Val McDermid. (Isis (CDs) Ser.). (J). 2005. audio compact disk 71.95 (978-0-7531-2396-6(7)) Pub: ISIS Lrg Prnt GBR. Dist(s): Ulverscroft US

Booked for Murder. unabr. ed. Val McDermid. Read by Vari Sylvester. 8 cass. (Running Time: 8 hrs. 40 min.). (Isis Cassettes Ser.). (J). 2005. 69.95 (978-0-7531-1163-5(2)) Pub: ISIS Lrg Prnt GBR. Dist(s): Ulverscroft US
Why would anyone want to kill Penny Varnavides, author of the teen dream Series?.

Booked to Die. unabr. ed. John Dunning. Narrated by George Guidall. 8 cass. (Running Time: 11 hrs.). (Cliff Janeway Novel Ser.). 1995. 70.00 (978-0-7887-0411-6(7), 94603E7) Recorded Bks.
The murder of a harmless book dealer draws Denver homicide detective, Cliff Janeway into an extraordinary quest.

Bookends. unabr. ed. Jane Green. Narrated by Jacqueline King. 9 cass. (Running Time: 13 hrs.). 2001. 82.00 (978-1-84197-194-0(4), H1177E7) Recorded Bks.
Cath may have a flash job with an advertising agency, but underneath she is still the scruffy student she was ten years ago. In many ways, she's yet to get her life together, but since she has such good friends to fill in the gaps, she's not too worried. Not until the beautiful, elusive Portia reappears, that is Portia, her best friend from college, faded out of Cath's life after a disastrous evening which no one could forget. Even ten years on, it seems Cath cannot keep up with her, &, as always, Portia's schedule is entirely her own.

Booker T. Washington. 10.00 Esstee Audios.
The famous leader of Tuskegee is explored.

Bookman's Wake. unabr. ed. John Dunning. Read by George Guidall. 8 Cass. (Running Time: 13 Hrs). (Cliff Janeway Novel Ser.). 34.95 (978-1-4025-6300-3(0)) Recorded Bks.

Bookman's Wake. unabr. ed. John Dunning. Narrated by George Guidall. 9 cass. (Running Time: 13 hrs.). (Cliff Janeway Novel Ser.). 2000. 78.00 (978-0-7887-0414-7(1), 94606E7) Recorded Bks.

Booknotes - Storytellers Vol. 1: Presidential Biographers. collector's ed. 6 cass. (Running Time: 6 hrs.). 1997. 36.00 (978-0-7366-3714-5(1), 4398) Books on Tape.
Includes complete booknotes interviews.

BookRoom. Compiled by Benchmark Education Staff. 2005. audio compact disk 10.00 (978-1-4108-5412-4(4)) Benchmark Educ.

Books see Children

Books. BMP Music.

Books: A Memoir. unabr. ed. Larry McMurtry. Narrated by William Dufris. 1 MP3-CD. (Running Time: 5 hrs. 30 mins. 0 sec.). (ENG.). 2008. audio compact disk 19.99 (978-1-4001-5805-8(2)); audio compact disk 49.99 (978-1-4001-3805-0(1)) Pub: Tantor Media. Dist(s): IngramPubServ

Books: A Memoir. unabr. ed. Larry McMurtry. Read by William Dufris. 5 CDs. (Running Time: 5 hrs. 30 mins. 0 sec.). (ENG.). 2008. audio compact disk 24.99 (978-1-4001-0805-3(5)) Pub: Tantor Media. Dist(s): IngramPubServ

Books Are Tremendous. Charlie Tremendous Jones. Read by Charlie Tremendous Jones. (Life-Changing Classics Ser.). (ENG.). 2007. audio compact disk 19.95 (978-1-933715-40-7(5)) Executive Bks.

Books in Argentina: A Strategic Reference 2007. Compiled by Icon Group International, Inc. Staff. 2007. ring bd. 195.00 (978-0-497-35796-2(8)) Icon Grp.

Books in Czech Republic: A Strategic Reference 2007. Compiled by Icon Group International, Inc. Staff. 2007. ring bd. 195.00 (978-0-497-35904-1(9)) Icon Grp.

Books in Greece: A Strategic Reference 2007. Compiled by Icon Group International, Inc. Staff. 2007. ring bd. 195.00 (978-0-497-35991-1(X)) Icon Grp.

Books of Wisdom. (23317-A) J Norton Pubs.

Books That Have Made History Vols. I-III: Books That Can Change Your Life. Instructed by J. Rufus Fears. 18 cass. (Running Time: 18 hrs.). 2005. bk. 79.95 (978-1-59803-022-8(1), 4600); bk. 99.95 (978-1-59803-024-2(8), 4600) Teaching Co.

Books 17 & 18 - Audio. Geronimo Stilton. (Geronimo Stilton Ser.). (ENG.). (J). (gr. 2-5). 2009. audio compact disk 29.95 (978-0-545-13881-9(7)) Scholastic Inc.

***Books #22 & #24: the Secret of Cacklefur Castle, & Field Trip to Niagra Falls - Audio.** Geronimo Stilton. (Geronimo Stilton Ser.). (ENG.). 2011. audio compact disk 19.99 (978-0-545-27375-6(7)) Scholastic Inc.

***Books #22 & #24: the Secret of Cacklefur Castle, & Field Trip to Niagra Falls - Audio Library Edition.** Geronimo Stilton. (Geronimo Stilton Ser.). (ENG.). 2011. audio compact disk 29.99 (978-0-545-27376-3(5)) Scholastic Inc.

Bookseller of Kabul. Asne Seierstad. Tr. by Ingrid Christophersen. Narrated by Joanna David. 2005. audio compact disk 22.99 (978-1-4193-3986-8(9)) Recorded Bks.

Booksigning at City Lights. Colin Wilson. 1 cass. 9.00 (A0267-87) Sound Photosyn.

Bookwoman's Last Fling. John Dunning. Narrated by George Guidall. (Running Time: 40500 sec.). (Cliff Janeway Novel Ser.). 2006. audio compact disk 34.99 (978-1-4193-8722-7(7)) Recorded Bks.

Bookwoman's Last Fling. unabr. ed. John Dunning. Read by George Guidall. 8 cass. (Running Time: 10 hrs. 45 mins.). (Cliff Janeway Novel Ser.). 2006. 79.75 (978-1-4193-8918-4(1)); audio compact disk 99.75 (978-1-4193-8920-7(3)) Recorded Bks.
Tempted out of his bookstore into the world of horseracing, Janeway accepts an invitation from wealthy horse trainer H.R. Geiger to travel to Idaho and look at some rare first-editions books. The books are stunning, flawless children's classics that render the usually eloquent Janeway speechless. It's a collection worth millions of dollars, a fact that Janeway would be happy to discuss with Mr. Geiger if the man wasn't dead. Janeway becomes convinced that someone has been cherry-picking the book collection for personal profit. Soon he's off on Geiger's cold trail, to the California Races at Golden Gates Fields and Santa Anita Park.

Boom. abr. ed. Bob Woodward. Read by James Naughton. 4 cass. (Running Time: 4 hrs. 30 mins.). 2000. 25.00; audio compact disk 30.00 S&S Audio.

Boom! unabr. ed. Mark Haddon. Read by Julian Rhind-Tutt. (ENG.). (J). 2010. audio compact disk 28.00 (978-0-7393-8137-3(7), Listening Lib) Pub: Random Audio Pubg. Dist(s): Random

Boom! Voices of the Sixties. unabr. ed. Tom Brokaw. Read by Robertson Dean. 12 CDs. (Running Time: 18 hrs.). 2007. audio compact disk 120.00 (978-1-4159-3264-3(6), BksonTape) Pub: Random Audio Pubg. Dist(s): Random
Now, in BOOM!, one of America's premier journalists gives us an epic portrait of another defining era in America as he brings to life the tumultuous Sixties, a fault line in American history. Brokaw takes us on a memorable journey through a remarkable time, exploring how individual lives and the national mindset were affected by a controversial era and showing how the aftershocks of the Sixties continue to resound in our lives today. BOOM! gives us what Brokaw sees as a virtual reunion of some members of "the class of '68." As they look back decades later, what do members of the Sixties generation think really mattered in that tumultuous time, and what will have meaning going forward? Race, war, politics, feminism, popular culture, and music are all explored here. Remarkable in its insights, this revealing portrait of a generation and of an era, and of the impact of the 1960s on our lives today, lets us be present at this reunion ourselves, and join in these frank conversations about America then, now, and tomorrow.

Boom! Voices of the Sixties Personal Reflections on the '60s & Tod. abr. ed. Tom Brokaw. Read by Tom Brokaw. 5 CDs. (Running Time: 6 hrs.). (ENG.). 2007. audio compact disk 29.95 (978-0-7393-4075-2(1), Random AudioBks) Pub: Random Audio Pubg. Dist(s): Random

Boom Dot Bust. Perf. by Firesign Theatre Firesign Theatre Staff. 1 CD. (Running Time: 46 mins.). 2001. audio compact disk 15.95 Lodestone Catalog.
This is pedal-to-the-metal Firesign...open-chest surgery on the heart basket America...a shoot out on the Yellow Brick Road. Welcome to Billville, the town that nature forgot to hate...where everybody's named Bill.

Boom Dot Bust. Perf. by Firesign Theatre Firesign Theatre Staff. 1 CD. (Running Time: 1 hr. 30 mins.). 2000. audio compact disk 16.98 (978-0-7379-0103-0(9), R2 75983) Rhino Enter.

Boom Town. unabr. ed. Sonia Levitin. Narrated by Kate Forbes. 1 cass. (Running Time: 30 mins.). (ps up). 2002. 10.00 (978-0-7887-9589-3(9)) Recorded Bks.
Mama, Baby Betsy, Billy, Joe, Ted, and Amanda are now reunited with Pa in California. But Pa spends so much time panning for gold, they see him only once a week. One day, Amanda is so bored that she decides to try baking a gooseberry pie in an iron skillet. After a few tries, the pie turns out perfect. When the pie becomes a favorite of the local miners, Amanda's pie-selling business takes off. Soon Cowboy Charlie, Miss Camilla, Mr. Hooper and Pa are returning to Boom Town to start businesses of their own.

Boom!: Voices of the Sixties: Personal Reflections on the '60s & Today. unabr. ed. Tom Brokaw. Read by Robertson Dean. (YA). 2007. 64.99 (978-0-7393-7121-3(5)) Find a World.

Boomerang: Bruce Carroll. Perf. by Bruce Carroll. 1 cass. 1997. 10.98 (978-0-7601-1572-5(9)); audio compact disk 16.98 Provident Mus Dist.

***Boomerang Bounty.** Peter Dawson. 2009. (978-1-60136-425-8(3)) Audio Holding.

Boomerang Bounty. Peter Dawson. (Running Time: 0 hr. 42 mins.). 2000. 10.95 (978-1-60083-533-9(3)) Iofy Corp.

Boomerang Joy: 60 Devotions to Brighten Your Day & Lighten Your Load. Barbara Johnson. 2 cass. 1998. 16.99 (978-0-310-22548-5(5)) Zondervan.

Boomers Bunk down for the 90's: Titus 2:4-5. Ed Young. 1991. 4.95 (978-0-7417-1859-4(6), 859) Win Walk.

BooMP Bop: Fun Songs that Inspire Movement. 1 CD. (Running Time: 1 hr. 30 min.). audio compact disk 15.95 (978-0-9720427-3-4(3)) OLLY Pubng Co.

Boomsday. abr. ed. Christopher Buckley. Read by Janeane Garofalo. (Running Time: 6 hrs.). (ENG.). 2007. 14.98 (978-1-59483-889-7(5), Twelve) Pub: GrandCentral. Dist(s): HachBkGrp

Boomsday. abr. ed. Christopher Buckley. Read by Janeane Garofalo. (Running Time: 6 hrs.). (ENG.). 2008. audio compact disk 14.98 (978-1-60024-215-1(4), Twelve) Pub: GrandCentral. Dist(s): HachBkGrp

Boomsday. unabr. ed. Christopher Buckley. Read by Janeane Garofalo. (Running Time: 10 hrs.). (ENG.). 2007. 16.98 (978-1-60024-003-4(8), Twelve) Pub: GrandCentral. Dist(s): HachBkGrp

Boomtown. unabr. ed. Larry D. Names. Read by Rusty Nelson. 6 cass. (Running Time: 6 hrs. 12 min.). 2001. 39.95 (978-1-58116-096-3(8)) Books in Motion.
A single newspaper article regarding a rich gold strike by a prospector creates a gold rush. Overnight the town blossoms into a boomtown, bringing with it saloons, women, gamblers and hustlers. The Cass brothers ride in with a single goal in mind, kill the men they are hired to kill, and win the mining claims for the man willing to pay their price.

Boone: A Biography. unabr. ed. Robert Morgan. Narrated by James Jenner. (Running Time: 20 hrs. 15 mins.). 2008. 61.75 (978-1-4407-0006-4(0)); 113.75 (978-1-4361-5579-3(7)); audio compact disk 123.75 (978-1-4361-5581-6(9)) Recorded Bks.

Boone Voice Program for Adults. Daniel R. Boone. 1 cass. 189.00 kit. (W496) PRO-ED.
Provides materials for diagnosis & remediation of adult voice disorders, based on the same philosophy & therapy as The Boone Voice Program for Children, but presented at an adult interest level.

Boone Voice Program for Children. Daniel R. Boone. 1 cass. 189.00 kit. (W360) PRO-ED.
Provides a cognitive approach to voice therapy & is designed to give useful step-by-step guidelines & materials for diagnosis & remediation of voice disorders in children.

Boone's Lick. unabr. ed. Larry McMurtry. Read by Will Patton. 6 vols. (Running Time: 9 hrs.). 2001. bk. 54.95 (978-0-7927-2463-6(1), CSL 352, Chivers Sound Lib) AudioGO.
A group of settlers, accompanied most of the way by a priest & Snake Indian. One of the settlers by the name of Mary Margaret wants to locate her husband & let him know that she is going to leave him.

Boone's Lick. unabr. ed. Larry McMurtry. Read by Will Patton. 2006. 18.95 (978-0-7435-6329-1(8), Audioworks) Pub: S&S Audio. Dist(s): S and S Inc

Boost Your Relationship IQ Set: Starting One, Building One - Or Give up on One. David Grudermeyer & Rebecca Grudermeyer. 2 cass. 18.95 Incl. handouts. (T-35) Willingness Wrks.

Boosting Your Energy. Speeches. Judit M. E. Rajhathy. Read by Judit M. E. Rajhathy. Ed. by Francis G. Mitchell & William Oulton. Des. by Francis G. Mitchell. Engineer William Oulton. Photos by Florian Kutchurean. 1 cassette. (Running Time: 1 hr.,15 min.). Dramatization. 1999. (978-1-895814-08-8(1), NWP114) NewWorld Pub CAN.

Boot. Lothar-Günther Buchheim. Read by Gordon Dulieu. 18 CDs. (Running Time: 20 hrs. 57 mins.). (Isis (CDs) Ser.). (ENG & LAV., (J). 2004. audio compact disk 116.95 (978-0-7531-1705-7(3)) Pub: ISIS Lrg Prnt GBR. Dist(s): Ulverscroft US

Boot. unabr. ed. Lothar-Günther Buchheim. Read by Gordon Dulieu. 16 cass. (Running Time: 21 hrs. 15 min.). (Isis Ser.). (GER., (J). 2003. 104.95 (978-0-7531-1455-1(0)) Pub: ISIS Lrg Prnt GBR. Dist(s): Ulverscroft US
Written by a survivor of the U-Boat fleet - of the 40,000 men who served on German submarines, 30,000 failed to return - Das Boot is a story of war told with a stunning force that grips from start to finish.

Boot Camp Success. Steven Gurgevich. (ENG.). 2002. audio compact disk 19.95 (978-1-932170-38-2(3), HWH) Tranceformation.

Boot Camp #3: Your Roll in the Church: Cor.12:13-14, Ephesians 2:11. Ed Young. 1980. 4.95 (978-0-7417-1138-0(9), A0138) Win Walk.

Boot Camp #4: The Wittness: John 1:1-3, Eph 4:13. Ed Young. 1980. 4.95 (978-0-7417-1140-3(0), A0140) Win Walk.

Bootleg. Alex Shearer. (Running Time: 3 hrs.). 2006. 25.95 (978-1-59912-954-9(X)) Iofy Corp.

Bootleg CD's: Another book of Poems. ed. 2005. audio compact disk (978-0-9747043-3-3(4)) K H Burton.

Bootlegger's Daughter. unabr. ed. Margaret Maron. Narrated by C. J. Critt. 7 cass. (Running Time: 9 hrs. 30 mins.). (Deborah Knott Mystery Ser.: No. 1). 1994. 60.00 (978-0-7887-0086-6(3), 94326E7) Recorded Bks.
Deborah Knott, small town lawyer curently seeking election to the judgeship, investigates a decades old murder.

Boots & Saddles. unabr. ed. Elizabeth Bacon Custer. Read by Flo Gibson. 6 cass. (Running Time: 9 hrs.). 1989. 24.95 (978-1-55685-145-2(6)) Audio Bk Con.
Custer's widow gives an account of life with the U. S. army in Sioux country in the Dakotas.

Boots & Saddles: Life in Dakota with General Custer. abr. ed. Elizabeth Bacon Custer. Read by Pat Gutensohn Ness. 2 cass. (Running Time: 3 hrs. 30 min.). 1993. 14.98 Set. (978-0-9650872-0-9(4), SC01074) Scoria.
Elizabeth (Libbie) Custer's experiences during her stay in the Dakotas with her husband, General George Armstrong Custer.

Boots, Buckles & Blades: Practical Self-Defense for the Urban Warrior. Sid Campbell. 2 cass. (Running Time: 1 hr. per cass.). cass. & video 169.95 incl. 2 1-hr. audio cass. & 1 1-hr. video cass. Gong Prods.

Boots on the Ground by Dusk: My Tribute to Pat Tillman. unabr. ed. Mary Tillman. Read by Mary Tillman. Told to Narda Zacchino. 1 MP3-CD. (Running Time: 12 hrs. 0 mins. 0 sec.). (ENG.). 2008. 24.99 (978-1-4001-5702-0(1)); audio compact disk 34.99 (978-1-4001-0702-5(4)) Pub: Tantor Media. Dist(s): IngramPubServ

Boots on the Ground by Dusk: My Tribute to Pat Tillman. unabr. ed. Mary Tillman & Narda Zacchino. Read by Mary Tillman & Narda Zacchino. (YA). 2008. 59.99 (978-1-60514-763-5(X)) Find a World.

Boots on the Ground by Dusk: My Tribute to Pat Tillman. unabr. ed. Mary Tillman & Narda Zacchino. 10 CDs. (Running Time: 12 hrs. 0 mins. 0 sec.). (ENG.). 2008. audio compact disk 69.99 (978-1-4001-3702-2(0)) Pub: Tantor Media. Dist(s): IngramPubServ

Boots Randolph: When the Spirit Moves You. Boots Randolph. 2005. pap. bk. 24.98 (978-1-59615-698-2(8), 586-029) Pub: Music Minus. Dist(s): H Leonard

***Bootstrap: Armed Forces Stress Management System.** Prod. by Yoga Pura Global Wellness. Created by Eric Walrabenstein. Eric Walrabenstein. (ENG.). 2010. spiral bd. 89.95 (978-0-615-37808-4(0)) Yoga Pura.

***Bootstrap to Big Time.** Susie Carder. 2010. audio compact disk 129.95 (978-1-4507-1030-5(1)) Indep Pub IL.

Booty Nomad. abr. ed. Scott Mebus. Read by Mark Feuerstein. 4 cass. (Running Time: 6 hrs.). 2004. 25.98 (978-1-4013-9810-1(3)) Pub: Hyperion. Dist(s): HarperCollins Pubs

Boppin' at the Blue Note. Perf. by Jon Hendricks. 1 cass., 1 CD. 7.98 (TA 33320); audio compact disk 12.78 CD Jewel box. (TA 83320) NewSound.

Border Art: Creative Neighboring. 1 cass. (Running Time: 30 min.). 9.95 (B0210B090, HarperThor) HarpC GBR.

Border Ballads: Sir Patrick Spense see Poetry of Robert Burns & Border Ballads

Border Crossing. Pat Barker. Narrated by Simon Prebble. 5 cass. (Running Time: 6 hrs. 30 mins.). 47.00 (978-1-4025-2487-5(0)); audio compact disk 62.00 (978-1-4025-3285-6(7)) Recorded Bks.

Border Crossing. Belen Garcia-Alvarado & Alan Venable. (Step into History Ser.). 2000. audio compact disk 18.95 (978-1-4105-0147-9(7)) D Johnston Inc.

Border Crossing. Alan Venable. Ed. by Belén Garcia-Alvarado. Illus. by Bob Stotts. Narrated by Jos Saro Sol s. (J). (gr. 5-6). 2000. audio compact disk 200.00 (978-1-58702-476-4(4)) D Johnston Inc.

Border Crossing. Alan Venable. Ed. by Belén Garcia-Alvarado et al. Illus. by Bob Stotts. Narrated by Jos Saro Sol s. Contrib. by Ted S. Hasselbring. (Start-to-Finish Books). (J). (gr. 2-3). 2000. 35.00 (978-1-58702-477-1(2)) D Johnston Inc.

Border Crossing. unabr. ed. Pat Barker. Read by James Wilby. 6 cass. (Running Time: 9 hrs.). 2002. 49.95 (978-0-7540-0762-3(6), CAB 2184) AudioGO.
Tom Seymour is a child psychologist who has worked in the north of England for many years. One day, while walking by a river near his home, he rescues a young man from drowning, and realizes that it's Danny Miller, a child murderer at whose trial he once gave evidence, evidence he has since come to regard as flawed. Danny has served his sentence and is out of prison. But now he is asking for Tom's help.

Border Crossing, Vol. 6. Alan Venable. Ed. by Belén Garcia-Alvarado et al. Illus. by Bob Stotts. Narrated by Jos Saro Sol s. Contrib. by Ted S. Hasselbring. (Start-to-Finish Books). (J). (gr. 2-3). 2002. 100.00 (978-1-58702-977-6(4)) D Johnston Inc.

Border Crossing, Vol. 6. unabr. ed. Alan Venable. Ed. by Belén Garcia-Alvarado et al. Illus. by Bob Stotts. Narrated by Jos Saro Sol s. Contrib. by Ted S. Hasselbring. 1 cass. (Running Time: 1 hr.). (Start-to-Finish Books). (J). (gr. 2-3). 2000. (978-1-893376-98-4(2), F20K2) D Johnston Inc.
This is the fictional but realistic story of a Mexican family that crosses the border illegally into Texas in the 1990s in search of a better economic life. Carlos Sanchez, the father, comes first after being laid off from a factory job in Mexico. Three years pass before he is able to bring his wife Linda, and their children Rico, Ana and Pedro.

Border Empire. abr. ed. Ralph Compton. Narrated by Jim Gough. 4 cass. (Running Time: 6 hrs.). (Gun Ser.). 2000. 24.95 (978-1-890990-55-8(8), 99055) Otis Audio.
Taking up the custom-made Colts of his late father, murdered in the streets of El Paso by Mexico's notorious Sandlin gang, Wes Stone trades his aspirations to be a lawman for his thirst for vengeance.

Border Legion. Zane Grey. Contrib. by John Bolen. (Playaway Adult Fiction Ser.). (ENG.). 2009. 64.99 (978-1-60775-771-9(0)) Find a World.

Border Legion. Zane Grey. Read by John Bolen. (Running Time: 10 hrs. 30 mins.). 2002. 29.95 (978-1-60083-624-4(0), Audiofy Corp) Iofy Corp.

Border Legion. Zane Grey. Read by John Bolen. (ENG.). 2005. audio compact disk 90.00 (978-1-4001-3055-9(7)) Pub: Tantor Media. Dist(s): IngramPubServ

Border Legion. unabr. ed. Zane Grey. Narrated by Zane Grey. (Running Time: 10 hrs. 27 mins.). (ENG.). 2002. audio compact disk 23.00 (978-1-4001-5055-7(8)) Pub: Tantor Media. Dist(s): IngramPubServ
Unabridged Audiobook. 1 MP3 CD - 10 hours, 27 minutes. Narrated by John Bolen.Jim Cleve has been deemed, ?a good guy? all of his life and it agitates him to no end. Even his girlfriend, Joan Randle has scorned him for this ?weakness? shouting, ?You haven't it in you even to be BAD!? Dejected and hurt, Jim abandons the life he has known for the gold mining camps along Alder Gulch in southern Montana. It is here, among the thieves and murderers, that he must make a new name for himself.Meanwhile, Joan realizes the danger that she has put Jim in and rushes off to save him. However, when she stumbles across the ruthless desperado gang leader, Jack Kells, it is soon Joan who is in need of rescue. When Kells tries to rape her, Joan grabs his gun and shoots him. But something keeps Joan from leaving him to die. In the face of Joan's loving spirit, Kells experiences his own change of heart. But it is too late, Kells outlaw gang arrives and keeps Joan hostage.So begins the border legion adventures of roving bandits, lust and greed. With Jim's search for a new identity, Jack's moral dilemma and the fight for Joan's freedom, this thrilling story portrays the epic theme of man's continual struggle between good and evil.This audiobook is on one CD, encoded in MP3 format and will only play on computers and CD players that have the ability to play this unique format.

Border Legion. unabr. ed. Zane Grey. Narrated by John Bolen. (Running Time: 10 hrs. 30 mins. 0 sec.). (Tantor Unabridged Classics Ser.). (ENG.). 2009. audio compact disk 32.99 (978-1-4001-0944-9(2)) Pub: Tantor Media. Dist(s): IngramPubServ

Border Legion. unabr. ed. Zane Grey. Read by John Bolen. (Running Time: 10 hrs. 30 mins. 0 sec.). (Tantor Unabridged Classics Ser.). (ENG.). 2009. 22.99 (978-1-4001-5944-4(X)); audio compact disk 65.99 (978-1-4001-3944-6(9)) Pub: Tantor Media. Dist(s): IngramPubServ

***Border Lords.** abr. ed. T. Jefferson Parker. (Running Time: 6 hrs.). (Charlie Hood Ser.). 2011. audio compact disk 24.99 (978-1-4418-2622-0(X), 9781441826220, BACD) Brilliance Audio.

***Border Lords.** unabr. ed. T. Jefferson Parker. Read by David Colacci. (Running Time: 11 hrs.). (Charlie Hood Ser.). 2011. 24.99 (978-1-4233-7923-2(3), 9781423379232, BAD); 39.97 (978-1-4233-7924-9(1), 9781423379249, BADLE); 24.99 (978-1-4233-7921-8(7), 9781423379218, Brilliance MP3); 39.97 (978-1-4233-7922-5(5), 9781423379225, Brinc Audio MP3 Lib); audio compact disk 34.99 (978-1-4233-7919-5(5), 9781423379195, Bril Audio CD Unabri); audio compact disk 92.97 (978-1-4233-7920-1(9), 9781423379201, BriAudCD Unabrid) Brilliance Audio.

***Border Lords: A Charlie Hood Novel.** abr. ed. T. Jefferson Parker. Read by David Colacci. (Running Time: 6 hrs.). (Charlie Hood Ser.). 2011. 9.99 (978-1-61106-111-6(3), 9781611061116, BAD) Brilliance Audio.

***Border Man.** Frank Bonham. 2009. (978-1-60136-390-9(7)) Audio Holding.

Border Man. Frank Bonham. (Running Time: 1 hr. 12 mins.). 1998. 10.95 (978-1-60083-477-6(9)) Iofy Corp.

Border Princes. unabr. ed. Dan Abnett. Narrated by Eve Myles. (Running Time: 4 hrs. 0 mins. 0 sec.). (ENG.). 2010. audio compact disk 29.95 (978-1-60283-828-4(3)) Pub: AudioGO. Dist(s): Perseus Dist

Border Showdown. Matthew S. Hart. Read by Charlton Griffin. 2 vols. No. 3. 2003. 18.00 (978-1-58807-245-0(2)); (978-1-58807-740-0(3)) Am Pubng Inc.

***Border Songs.** unabr. ed. Jim Lynch. Narrated by Richard Poe. 1 Playaway. (Running Time: 10 hrs. 15 mins.). 2009. 59.75 (978-1-4407-1332-3(4)); 72.75 (978-1-4407-1329-3(4)); audio compact disk 102.75 (978-1-4407-1330-9(8)); audio compact disk 51.95 (978-1-4407-1331-6(6)) Recorded Bks.

Border Trilogy: All the Pretty Horses; The Crossing; Cities of the Plain. Cormac McCarthy. Read by Brad Pitt. 6 cass. (Border Trilogy: Nos. 1-3). 1998. 33.70 Set. (978-0-00-105543-8(7)) Ulvrscrft Audio.

Borderland. Bud Shrake. Narrated by George Guidall. 14 cass. (Running Time: 18 hrs. 30 mins.). 104.00 (978-1-4025-0597-3(3)); audio compact disk 154.00 (978-1-4025-3488-1(4)) Recorded Bks.

Borderlands. Brian McGilloway & John Cormack. 2009. 54.95 (978-1-84652-391-5(5)); audio compact disk 71.95 (978-1-84652-392-2(3)) Pub: Magna Story GBR. Dist(s): Ulverscroft US

Borderlands: From Conjunto to Chicken Scratch: Music of the Rio Grande Valley of Texas & Southern Arizona. Contrib. by Cathy Ragland et al. 1 cass. or CD. 1993. (0-9307-404180-9307-40418-2-6); audio compact disk (0-9307-40418-2-6) Smithsonian Folkways.
Includes performances by Narisco Martinez, Lydia Mendoza, Ruben Vela, Beto Villa & others.

Borderlands of Science. unabr. ed. Michael Shermer. Read by Grover Gardner. 9 cass. (Running Time: 13 hrs. 30 mins.). 2001. 54.00 Books on Tape.
How to tell the difference between science, borderline science, and nonsense.

Borderlands of Science. unabr. ed. Michael Shermer. Read by Grover Gardner. 9 cass. (Running Time: 13 hrs. 30 mins.). 2001. 72.00 (978-0-7366-8090-5(X)) Books on Tape.

Borderline. Mark Schorr. Read by Michael Pritchard. (Running Time: 32400 sec.). 2007. 59.95 (978-1-4332-0131-8(3)); audio compact disk 63.00 (978-1-4332-0132-5(1)); audio compact disk 29.95 (978-1-4332-0133-2(X)) Blckstn Audio.

Borderline. abr. ed. Nevada Barr. Read by Joyce Bean. 1 MP3-CD. (Running Time: 6 hrs.). (Anna Pigeon Ser.). 2009. 24.99 (978-1-4233-2573-4(7), 9781423325734, Brilliance MP3); 39.97 (978-1-4233-2574-1(5), 9781423325741, Brinc Audio MP3 Lib); 39.97 (978-1-4233-2576-5(1), 9781423325765, BADLE); 24.99 (978-1-4233-2575-8(3), 9781423325758, BAD); audio compact disk 26.99 (978-1-4233-2570-3(2), 9781423325703); audio compact disk 74.97 (978-1-4233-2571-0(0), 9781423325710, BACDLib Ed) Brilliance Audio.

Borderline. abr. ed. Nevada Barr. Read by Joyce Bean. (Running Time: 6 hrs.). (Anna Pigeon Ser.). 2010. audio compact disk 14.99 (978-1-4233-2572-7(9), 9781423325727, BCD Value Price) Brilliance Audio.

Borderline. unabr. ed. Nevada Barr. Narrated by Barbara Rosenblat. 1 Playaway. (Running Time: 12 hrs.). 2009. 61.75 (978-1-4407-0361-4(2)); 92.75 (978-1-4407-0362-1(0)); audio compact disk 123.75 (978-1-4407-0359-1(0)) Recorded Bks.

Borderline. unabr. ed. Nevada Barr. Read by Barbara Rosenblat. 12 CDs. (Running Time: 10 hrs.). 2009. audio compact disk 39.99 (978-1-4407-1160-2(7)) Recorded Bks.

Borderline. unabr. ed. Janette Turner Hospital. Read by Stewart Morritt. 7 cass. (Running Time: 10 hrs. 30 mins.). 1998. (978-1-86340-725-0(1), 580641) Bolinda Pubng AUS.
Felicity had crossed more borders on more continents than anyone would want to keep a file on. In the ordinary course of events she would never have put herself on the wrong side of the law, nor been obliged to hide from knives & shadows. But at borders there is never an ordinary course of events.

Borderline Personality Disorder: Program from the Award Winning Public Radio Series. Interview. Hosted by Fred Goodwin. 1 CD. (Running Time: 1 Hour). 1999. audio compact disk 21.95 (978-1-932479-28-7(7), LCM 89) Lichtenstein Creat.
Statistics on Borderline Personality Disorder can be hard to come by. But reliable estimates indicate as many as one in fifty Americans may suffer from the disorder. It was first recognized in the 1930s, but therapists still argue over how to define and treat it. In fact, many object to the name itself, since personality disorders are often seen as less "serious" than the major mental illnesses like schizophrenia, depression, and bipolar disorder.This week on The Infinite Mind, we learn about the symptoms of BPD, why it is so frustrating for therapists to treat it, and a new form of therapy that has been effective.

Borderliners. Hoeg. 2004. 15.95 (978-0-7435-4052-0(2)) Pub: S&S Audio. Dist(s): S and S Inc

Borderliners, unabr. ed. Peter Hoeg. Narrated by George Guidall. 7 cass. (Running Time: 9 hrs. 15 mins.). 1995. 60.00 (978-0-7887-0263-1(7), 94472E7) Recorded Bks.
From the author of "Smilla's Sense of Snow," comes a stunning novel of psychological suspense. Peter, an orphan studying at a prestigious Danish boarding school, discovers that the headmaster is conducting a dangerous, government-approved experiment on controlling children.

Borderlines. rev. ed. Phil Carradice. 1994. 31.95 (978-1-873942-75-8(3)) Pub: P Chapman GBR. Dist(s): SAGE

Bordermen. unabr. ed. Lauran Paine. Read by John Keyworth. 3 cass. (Running Time: 4 hrs. 30 min.). 2001. 34.95 (61748) Pub: Soundings Ltd GBR. Dist(s): Ulverscroft US
The idea was to deliver a band of horses to their owner by taking them southward through hostile Indian country. For Mitchell & Alvarado, the challenge & the risk was worth the pay. They found out, however, that the Apaches would not be their only enemy. Mexico's Rurales, the deadliest killers of the border county, would also be out there.

Borders. (Timesaving Software Tools for Teachers Ser.). 2004. audio compact disk 19.99 (978-1-57690-695-8(7)) Tchr Create Ma.

***Borders of Infinity.** unabr. ed. Lois McMaster Bujold. Read by Grover Gardner. (Running Time: 11 hrs. 0 mins.). (Miles Vorkosigan Adventures Ser.). 2010. 29.95 (978-1-4332-3209-1(X)); 65.95 (978-1-4332-3205-3(7)); audio compact disk 100.00 (978-1-4332-3206-0(5)) Blckstn Audio.

Borders of Infinity. unabr. ed. Lois McMaster Bujold. 1 CD. (Running Time: 10 hrs.). (Vorkosigan Ser.). 1999. audio compact disk 19.95 (978-1-885585-09-7(8)) Readers Chair.

Borders of Infinity. unabr. ed. Lois McMaster Bujold. Perf. by Michael I. Ianson & Carol Cowan. 9 cass. (Running Time: 10 hrs. 15 min.). (Vorkosigan Ser.). 2000. 54.00 (978-1-885585-06-6(3), 90017) Readers Chair.
A trilogy of Miles Vorkosigan Adventures.

Bordersnakes. James Crumley. Read by Rob McQuay. 7 cass. (Running Time: 10 hrs. 30 min.). 1997. 56.00 (4489) Books on Tape.

Bordertown. Culture Clash. Contrib. by Culture Clash. (Running Time: 5040 sec.). 2001. audio compact disk 25.95 (978-1-58081-261-0(9), CDTPT166) Pub: L A Theatre. Dist(s): NetLibrary CO

Bordo Cassette 1. Spanish Course Team Staff. 2004. (978-0-415-20321-0(X)) Routledge.

Bordo Cassette 2. Spanish Course Team Staff. 2004. (978-0-415-20322-7(8)) Routledge.

Bordo Cassette 3. Spanish Course Team Staff. 2004. (978-0-415-20323-4(6)) Routledge.

Bordo Cassettes & Transcripts: Get Ready for Spanish. Open University Course Team & Spanish Course Team Staff. 8 cass. (Running Time: 12 hrs.). 1999. 53.95 (978-0-415-19900-1(X)) Pub: Routledge. Dist(s): Taylor and Fran

Focuses on both Spanish and Latin-American culture: Emphasis on communicating in everyday situations in Spanish: Extensive use of exercises for self-assessment, with key to exercises at the end of each unit, and more.

Boredom: Mal. 1:13. Ed Young. (J). 1981. 4.95 (978-0-7417-1180-9(X), A0180) Win Walk.

Borg: Experience the Collective. Hillary Bader. 2004. 7.95 (978-0-7435-4256-2(8)) Pub: S&S Audio. Dist(s): S and S Inc

Borges in 90 Minutes. unabr. ed. Paul Strathern. Read by Robert Whitfield. (Running Time: 2 hrs. NaN mins.). 2009. audio compact disk 22.95 (978-1-4332-1813-2(5)); audio compact disk 27.00 (978-1-4332-1814-9(3)) Blckstn Audio.

Borgias. unabr. ed. Marion Johnson. Narrated by Aviva Skell. 5 cass. (Running Time: 7 hrs. 15 mins.). 1986. 44.00 (978-1-55690-068-6(6), 86330E7) Recorded Bks.

The life & times of the infamous Borgia Family.

Boris Karloff. Read by Boris Karloff. (Running Time: 9 hrs.). 2003. 39.98 (978-1-57019-647-8(8)) Radio Spirits.

Boris Pasternak's In the Woods from "Imitations" see Twentieth-Century Poetry in English, No. 32-33, Recordings of Poets Reading Their Own Poetry

Bormann Brief, Set. unabr. ed. Clive Egleton. Read by Christopher Consani. 6 cass. (Running Time: 8 hrs.). 1986. 49.00 (978-1-55690-069-3(4), 86180) Recorded Bks.

A British force targets Martin Bormann for assassination.

Born a Davior Born a King. Stan Pethel. 1997. 11.98 (978-0-7673-3304-7(7)) LifeWay Christian.

Born a Savior Born a King. Stan Pethel. 1997. 8.00 (978-0-7673-3306-1(3)); 75.00 (978-0-7673-3303-0(9)); audio compact disk 85.00 (978-0-7673-3302-3(0)) LifeWay Christian.

Born Again. 1 cass. (Bullfrogs & Butterflies Ser.). (J). 9.95 (ABBA) Brdgstn Multimed Grp.

Floydd Frogg, that born again polywog, is back! This time, he imagines that he is a real boy with a desire to fill an empty place in his heart. This musical story of salvation will tug at your heart & get your toes tappin' too!.

Born Again: What Really Happened to the White House Hatchet Man. unabr. ed. Charles Colson. Narrated by Jon Gauger. (Running Time: 13 hrs. 27 mins. 21 sec.). (ENG.). 2008. 32.19 (978-1-60814-087-9(3)); audio compact disk 45.99 (978-1-59859-367-9(6)) Oasis Audio.

Born Confused. Tanuja Desai Hidier. Read by Marguerite Gavin. (Running Time: 54000 sec.). (YA). (gr. 7). 2006. 85.95 (978-0-7861-4561-4(7)) Blckstn Audio.

Born Confused. Tanuja Desai Hidier. Read by Marguerite Gavin. (Running Time: 54000 sec.). (YA). (gr. 8-12). 2006. audio compact disk 99.00 (978-0-7861-7080-7(8)) Blckstn Audio.

Born Confused. unabr. ed. Tanuja Desai Hidier. Read by Marguerite Gavin. (Running Time: 27000 sec.). (YA). (gr. 8-12). 2006. audio compact disk 29.95 (978-0-7861-7564-2(8)) Blckstn Audio.

Born Drunk: Fetal Alcohol Syndrome. Michael Dorris. Read by Michael Dorris. 1 cass. (Running Time: 45 min.). 9.95 (DO-030, HarperThor) HarpC GBR.

Born Free. (Running Time: 60 mins.). 2002. audio compact disk 15.99 (978-1-904972-56-3(X)) Global Jrny GBR GBR.

Born Free. Joy Adamson. Read by Veronika Hyks. 12 cass. (Running Time: 13 hrs. 10 min.). 2001. 45.95 (978-0-7540-0602-2(6)) AudioGO.

Includes the first book "Born Free" & the subsequent "Living Free" & "Forever Free." All three books had a tremendous impact on wildlife conservation & attitudes to the environment.

Born Guilty. unabr. ed. Reginald Hill. Read by Simon J. Williamson. 6 cass. (Running Time: 8 hrs.). (Joe Sixsmith Ser.). 1998. 69.95 Set. (978-1-85903-234-3(6)) Pub: Magna Story GBR. Dist(s): Ulverscroft US

Joe Sixsmith stumbles across a boy's corpse in a cardboard box & into more trouble than he's ever known. Joe threads his mild-mannered way through Luton's mean streets, fighting off angry cops, demented druggies, & the matchmaking machinations of his Aunt Mirabelle. But the truth he discovers does not set him free, for there's little joy in confirming that today's kids grow up so much faster than he did, & even the luckiest of them find out all too soon that they have been born guilty.

Born in Death. J. D. Robb, pseud. Read by Susan Ericksen. (In Death Ser.). 2009. 70.00 (978-1-60775-524-1(6)) Find a World.

Born in Death. abr. ed. J. D. Robb, pseud. Read by Susan Ericksen. (Running Time: 6 hrs.). (In Death Ser.). 2007. audio compact disk 14.99 (978-1-4233-0486-9(1), 9781423304869, BCD Value Price) Brilliance Audio.

Born in Death. unabr. ed. J. D. Robb, pseud. Read by Susan Ericksen. (Running Time: 11 hrs.). (In Death Ser.). 2006. 39.25 (978-1-4233-0482-1(9), 9781423304821, BADLE); 24.95 (978-1-4233-0481-4(0), 9781423304814, BAD); 82.25 (978-1-4233-0476-0(4), 9781423304760, BrilAudUnabridg); 32.95 (978-1-4233-0475-3(6), 9781423304753, BAU); audio compact disk 39.25 (978-1-4233-0480-7(2), 9781423304807, Brlnc Audio MP3 Lib); audio compact disk 97.25 (978-1-4233-0478-4(0), 9781423304784, BriAudCD Unabrid); audio compact disk 36.95 (978-1-4233-0477-7(2), 9781423304777, Bril Audio CD Unabri); audio compact disk 24.95 (978-1-4233-0479-1(9), 9781423304791, Brilliance MP3) Brilliance Audio.

Please enter a Synopsis.

Born in Fire. abr. ed. Nora Roberts. Read by Fiacre Douglas. (Running Time: 21600 sec.). (Concannon Sisters Trilogy: Vol. 1). 2007. audio compact disk 14.99 (978-1-4233-3187-2(7), 9781423331872, BCD Value Price) Brilliance Audio.

Born in Fire. unabr. ed. Nora Roberts. Read by Fiacre Douglas. (Running Time: 10 hrs.). (Concannon Sisters Trilogy: Vol. 1). 2007. 39.25 (978-1-4233-3191-9(5), 9781423331919, BADLE); 24.95 (978-1-4233-3190-2(7), 9781423331902, BAD); audio compact disk 29.95 (978-1-4233-3270-1(9), 9781423332701, Bril Audio CD Unabri); audio compact disk 24.95 (978-1-4233-3188-9(5), 9781423331889, Brilliance MP3); audio compact disk 92.25 (978-1-4233-3271-8(7), 9781423332718, BriAudCD Unabrid); audio compact disk 39.25 (978-1-4233-3189-6(3), 9781423331896, Brlnc Audio MP3 Lib) Brilliance Audio.

Born in Ice. abr. ed. Nora Roberts. Read by Fiacre Douglas. (Running Time: 6 hrs.). (Concannon Sisters Trilogy: Vol. 2). 2007. audio compact disk 14.99 (978-1-4233-3192-6(3), 9781423331926, BCD Value Price) Brilliance Audio.

Born in Ice. unabr. ed. Nora Roberts. Read by Fiacre Douglas. (Running Time: 12 hrs.). (Concannon Sisters Trilogy: Vol. 2). 2007. 39.25 (978-1-4233-3196-4(6), 9781423331964, BADLE); 24.95 (978-1-4233-3195-7(8), 9781423331957, BAD); audio compact disk 24.95 (978-1-4233-3193-3(1), 9781423331933, Brilliance MP3); audio compact disk 29.95 (978-1-4233-3272-5(5), 9781423332725, Bril Audio CD Unabri); audio compact disk 97.25 (978-1-4233-3273-2(3), 9781423332732, BriAudCD Unabrid); audio compact disk 39.25 (978-1-4233-3194-0(X), 9781423331940, Brlnc Audio MP3 Lib) Brilliance Audio.

Born in My Heart. 2000. 11.98 (978-0-633-02961-6(0)); audio compact disk 16.98 (978-0-633-02956-2(4)); audio compact disk 85.00 (978-0-633-00798-0(6)) LifeWay Christian.

Born in Shame. abr. ed. Nora Roberts. Read by Fiacre Douglas. (Running Time: 21600 sec.). (Concannon Sisters Trilogy: Vol. 3). 2007. audio compact disk 14.99 (978-1-4233-3197-1(4), 9781423331971, BCD Value Price) Brilliance Audio.

Born in Shame. unabr. ed. Nora Roberts. Read by Fiacre Douglas. (Running Time: 10 hrs.). (Concannon Sisters Trilogy: Vol. 3). 2007. 39.25 (978-1-4233-3201-5(6), 9781423332015, BADLE); 24.95 (978-1-4233-3200-8(8), 9781423332008, BAD); audio compact disk 29.95 (978-1-4233-3274-9(1), 9781423332749, Bril Audio CD Unabri); audio compact disk 24.95 (978-1-4233-3198-8(2), 9781423331988, Brilliance MP3); audio compact disk 39.25 (978-1-4233-3199-5(0), 9781423331995, Brlnc Audio MP3 Lib); audio compact disk 97.25 (978-1-4233-3275-6(X), 9781423332756, BriAudCD Unabrid) Brilliance Audio.

Born in the Tradition. Perf. by Obo Addy. 1 cass. (Running Time: 35 min.). 1990. 9.98 (978-1-877737-68-8(2), EB 2602) MFLP CA.

Traditional drum music of Ghana, West Africa by Ga master drummer.

Born Losers or Leaders? A Positive Spiritual Perspective on ADD. Jerry Seiden. 1. (Running Time: 7 hrs. 15 mins.). 2005. 9.95 (978-1-929753-19-2(5)) Spirit of Hope.

Born Naked: The Early Adventures of the Author of Never Cry Wolf. unabr. ed. Farley Mowat. Read by Alexander Adams. 7 cass. (Running Time: 7 hrs.). 1995. 42.00 (978-0-7366-2932-4(7), 3628) Books on Tape.

Farley Mowat, author of "Never Cry Wolf," chronicles his adventurous boyhood years. An unspoiled Canada calls to us over the decades.

Born of A Virgin: Matt. 1:18-25. Ed Young. 1990. 4.95 (978-0-7417-1835-8(9), 835) Win Walk.

Born of God. Derek Prince. 1 cass. 5.95 (120) Derek Prince.

How to receive the most profound, life-changing experience that can ever happen to any human being.

***Born of Ice.** unabr. ed. Sherrilyn Kenyon. 1 Playaway. (Running Time: 7 hrs. 30 mins.). 2010. 69.95 (978-0-7927-7209-5(1)) AudioGO.

***Born of Ice.** unabr. ed. Sherrilyn Kenyon. Narrated by Fred Berman. 6 CDs. (Running Time: 7 hrs. 30 mins.). 2010. audio compact disk 64.95 (978-0-7927-6658-2(X)) AudioGO.

Born of Love. Arleen Lorrance. 3 cass. (Running Time: 3 hrs. 30 min.). 1988. 14.95 (978-0-916192-58-7(X)) Teleos Inst.

A dramatic reading of the poetic tale of Arleen's rebirth.

***Born of Night.** unabr. ed. Sherrilyn Kenyon. Narrated by Kelly Fish. 12 CDs. (Running Time: 14 hrs. 45 mins.). 2009. audio compact disk 110.95 (978-0-7927-6654-4(7)) AudioGO.

***Born of Shadows.** Sherrilyn Kenyon. (Running Time: 10 hrs.). (ENG.). 2011. audio compact disk 54.99 (978-1-61113-824-5(8)) Pub: Hachet Audio. Dist(s): HachBkGrp

***Born of Shadows.** unabr. ed. Sherrilyn Kenyon. (Running Time: 11 hrs.). (ENG.). 2011. 24.98 (978-1-60788-584-9(0)); audio compact disk & audio compact disk 29.98 (978-1-60788-583-2(2)) Pub: Hachet Audio. Dist(s): HachBkGrp

Born on a Blue Day: Inside the Extraordinary Mind of an Autistic Savant. unabr. ed. Daniel Tammet. Narrated by Simon Vance. (Running Time: 6 hrs. 30 mins. 0 sec.). (ENG.). 2007. audio compact disk 29.99 (978-1-4001-0403-1(3)); audio compact disk 59.99 (978-1-4001-3403-8(X)) Pub: Tantor Media. Dist(s): IngramPubServ

Born on a Blue Day: Inside the Extraordinary Mind of an Autistic Savant. unabr. ed. Daniel Tammet. Read by Simon Vance. (Running Time: 6 hrs. 30 mins. 0 sec.). (ENG.). 2007. audio compact disk 19.99 (978-1-4001-5403-6(0)) Pub: Tantor Media. Dist(s): IngramPubServ

Born Round: The Secret History of a Full-Time Eater. unabr. ed. Frank Bruni. Read by Frank Bruni. 8 CDs. (Running Time: 10 hrs.). (ENG.). 2009. audio compact disk 39.95 (978-0-14-314524-0(X), PengAudBks) Penguin Grp USA.

Born Standing Up: A Comic's Life. unabr. ed. Steve Martin. Read by Steve Martin. 4 CDs. (Running Time: 4 hrs. 30 mins. 0 sec.). (ENG., 2007. audio compact disk 29.95 (978-0-7435-6972-9(5)) Pub: S&S Audio. Dist(s): S and S Inc

Born to Add. 1 cass. (J). 1995. 9.98 (Sony Wonder); audio compact disk 13.98 CD. Sony Music Ent.

Includes Bruce Stringbean & the S Street Band singing "Barn in the U.S.A." Mick Swagger & The Sesame Street Cobble Stones doing "(I Can't Get No) Co-Operation" & Chrissy & the Alphabeats performing "Count It Higher".

***Born to Be Business Savy.** James Timothy White. 2010. 24.95 (978-0-9825755-9-8(9)) Mot Prss.

Born to Be Wild. abr. ed. Catherine Coulter. Read by Susanna Burney. (Running Time: 21600 sec.). 2007. audio compact disk 14.99 (978-1-59600-889-2(X), 9781596008892, BCD Value Price) Brilliance Audio.

Please enter a Synopsis.

Born to Be Wild. unabr. ed. Catherine Coulter. Read by Susanna Burney. (Running Time: 11 hrs.). 2006. 39.25 (978-1-59710-853-9(7), 9781597108539, BADLE); 24.95 (978-1-59710-852-2(9), 9781597108522, BAD); 82.25 (978-1-59355-735-5(3), 9781593557355, BrilAudUnabridg); audio compact disk 36.95 (978-1-59355-737-9(X), 9781593557379, Bril Audio CD Unabri); audio compact disk 97.25 (978-1-59355-738-6(8), 9781593557386, BriAudCD Unabrid); audio compact disk 24.95 (978-1-59335-754-2(0), 9781593357542, Brilliance MP3); audio compact disk 39.25 (978-1-59335-888-4(1), 9781593358884, Brlnc Audio MP3 Lib) Brilliance Audio.

***Born to Bite: An Argeneau Novel.** unabr. ed. Lynsay Sands. Read by Kirby Heyborne. (ENG.). 2010. (978-0-06-204137-1(1), Harper Audio); (978-0-06-199890-4(7), Harper Audio) HarperCollins Pubs.

***Born to Kvetch.** unabr. ed. Michael Wex. Read by Michael Wex. (ENG.). 2006. (978-0-06-117324-0(X), Harper Audio); (978-0-06-117323-3(1), Harper Audio) HarperCollins Pubs.

Born to Kvetch: Yiddish Language & Culture in All of Its Moods. unabr. ed. Michael Wex. Read by Michael Wex. 8 CDs. (Running Time: 34200 sec.). 2006. audio compact disk 34.95 (978-0-06-113122-6(9)) HarperCollins Pubs.

Born to Rock. unabr. ed. Gordon Korman. Read by Billy Hammond. (Running Time: 5 hrs.). 2006. 39.25 (978-1-4233-1200-0(7), 9781423312000, BADLE); 24.95 (978-1-4233-1199-7(X), 9781423311997, BAD) Brilliance Audio.

Born to Rock. unabr. ed. Gordon Korman. Read by Billy Hammond. 4 cass. (Running Time: 18000 sec.). (YA). (gr. 8-12). 2006. 62.25 (978-1-4233-1194-2(9), 9781423311942, BriAudUnabridg); 24.95 (978-1-4233-1193-5(0), 9781423311935); audio compact disk 74.25 (978-1-4233-1196-6(5), 9781423311966, BriAudCD Unabrid); audio compact disk 39.25 (978-1-4233-1198-0(1), 9781423311980, Brlnc Audio MP3 Lib); audio compact disk 24.95 (978-1-4233-1197-3(3), 9781423311973, Brilliance MP3); audio compact disk 26.95 (978-1-4233-1195-9(7), 9781423311959) Brilliance Audio.

Leo Caraway - president of the Young Republicans Club, future Harvard student, holder of a 4.0 GPA - had his entire future perfectly planned out. That is, until the X factor - as in Marion X. McMurphy, aka King Maggot, the lead singer of Purge, the most popular, most destructive band punk rock has ever seen. As in Leo's biological father. At first, Leo is horrified to find out his real father is punk rock's most notorious bad boy. Not only is Leo not a punk rock fan, but he believes the X factor (the Maggot blood in his veins) is a dangerous time bomb just waiting to explode. And sure enough it does - when Leo stubbornly defends the unlikeliest of people, thereby getting himself falsely accused of cheating on a test. Because of the blemish on his record, the once-star pupil finds his scholarship to Harvard taken away. So he accepts a job as a roadie on Purge's summer revival tour, all the while secretly hoping to convince King Maggot to pay for his tuition. But life on the road is even crazier than Leo bargained for, and before the summer is out, he will finally discover the surprising truth about his dad, his friends, and most important, himself.

***Born to Run.** unabr. ed. James Grippando. Read by Jonathan Davis. (ENG.). 2008. (978-0-06-172955-3(8)); (978-0-06-172956-0(6)) HarperCollins Pubs.

Born to Run. unabr. ed. James Grippando. Read by Jonathan Davis. 2009. audio compact disk 19.99 (978-0-06-190627-5(1), Harper Audio) HarperCollins Pubs.

Born to Run: A Hidden Tribe, Superathletes, & the Greatest Race the World Has Never Seen. unabr. ed. Christopher McDougall. Read by Fred Sanders. 9 CDs. (Running Time: 11 hrs.). (ENG.). 2009. audio compact disk 39.95 (978-0-7393-8372-8(8), Random AudioBks) Pub: Random Audio Pubg. Dist(s): Random

***Born to Run: A Hidden Tribe, Superathletes, & the Greatest Race the World Has Never Seen.** unabr. ed. Christopher McDougall. Read by Fred Sanders. (ENG.). 2010. audio compact disk 19.99 (978-0-307-91455-2(0), Random AudioBks) Pub: Random Audio Pubg. Dist(s): Random

Born to Serve. unabr. ed. Josephine Cox. Read by Maggie Ollerenshaw. 10 cass. (Running Time: 10 hrs.). 1995. 84.95 Set. (978-0-7451-4387-3(3), CAB 1071) AudioGO.

When the love of her life is seduced by the mistress of the house, it's only the first trial that Jenny must bear from Claudia's vicious nature. Shamed, Frank leaves the household for a new life in Blackburn. And when Claudia gives birth to Frank's child, she cruelly disowns little Katie & relies on Jenny to take care of her. Now, ever protective of Katie, Jenny must fight for all she holds dear.

Born to Sing. Austin & Elizabeth Howard. 4 CDs. (Running Time: 3 hrs.). 1985. audio compact disk 49.95 (SCD124) J Norton Pubs.

Offers entire course in technique, another one in style, plus advanced exercises & sing aerobics (a 30 minute daily workout for all voice types). No prior music knowledge required. Produces immediate results in vocal control, power & range.

Born to Sing. unabr. ed. Howard Austin & Elisabeth Howard. 4 cass. (Running Time: 3 hrs.). 1985. pap. bk. 39.95 (978-0-934419-03-1(5), SO1985) J Norton Pubs.

Born to Sing. unabr. ed. Elizabeth Jane Howard & Howard Austin. 4 cass. 39.95 incl. bklt. (S01985) Vocal Power Inc.

Provides step-by-step instruction on all the basic & advance voice techniques as well as most vocal styles, including Broadway, classical, jazz, country, blues, rock & pop.

Born to Sing, 1 Bk. rev. ed. Elisabeth Howard & Howard Austin. Rev. by Elisabeth Howard. 4 CDs. (Running Time: 4 hrs). 2004. audio compact disk 49.95 (978-0-934419-14-7(0)) Vocal Power Inc.

4 CDs, with Born to Sing Revised book. (1) Singing Technique: power, range expansion, vibrato control, volume, dynamics, pitch. (2) Singing Styles: Pop, Rock, Country, Blues, R&B, Broadway, Phrasing, Improvisation, Personal Style. (3) Super Vocals: additional exercises, "Licks and Tricks," for every style. (4) Sing-Aerobics: 30 minute Daily Workout, Male and Female voice, warm-up at home or in your car.

Born to Sing: Complete Voice Training. Elisabeth Howard & Howard Austin. 4 cass. 1985. bk. 39.95 (VPC-3); 12.95 bk. (VP-BK) Vocal Power Inc.

Contains easy, step by step instructions, vocal demonstrations & accompaniments to sing with. Covers basic techniques; advanced techiques; styles; vocal excercises.

Born to Sing: Mother Goose Parodies. 1 cass. 1997. 5.98 (Warner Bro); 9.98 CD. (Warner Bro) Alfred Pub.

Twenty Mother Goose parodies are sung in the vocal style of the characters featured in the "Baby Looney Tunes" animated television program.

Born to Sing: Twenty Mother Goose Parodies. 1 cass. (J). 4.78 Blisterpack. (KID 72641); 4.78 Blisterpack. (KID 72641); audio compact disk 7.98 Longbox. (KID 72641); audio compact disk 7.98 Longbox. (KID 72641) NewSound.

Born to Sing: 20 Mother Goose Parodies. Rhino Records Staff. 1 cass. (Baby Looney Tunes Ser.). (J). (ps-3). 1998. 7.99 (978-1-56826-777-7(0)) Rhino Enter.

Born to Sing Foundation Set, Singing Lessons, Technique & Style. unabr. ed. Howard Austin & Elisabeth Howard. Perf. by Howard Austin. 2 CDs. (Running Time: 2 hrs.). 1999. audio compact disk 24.95 CD set incl. bklet. (978-0-934419-38-3(8), BTS-2-CD) Vocal Power Inc.

Technique & style exercises.

Born to Sing Foundation Set Technique & Style. unabr. ed. Howard Austin & Elisabeth Howard. Perf. by Howard Austin. 2 cass. (Running Time: 2 hrs.). 1999. 19.95 Set, incl. vinyl case. (978-0-934419-06-2(X), BTS-2) Vocal Power Inc.

Born to Sing Sing Aerobics/Workout CD. Scripts. Elisabeth Howard. Perf. by Elisabeth Howard. Perf. by Howard Austin. 1 CD. (Running Time: 1 hr). 1997. audio compact disk Rental 19.95 (978-0-934419-39-0(6)) Vocal Power Inc.

Singing Techniques examples and exercises to accompany Born to Sing book.

Born to Sing Singing Style. Scripts. Elisabeth Howard. Perf. by Elisabeth Howard. Perf. by Howard Austin. 1 CD. (Running Time: 1 hr.). 1997. audio compact disk 19.95 (978-0-934419-41-3(8)) Vocal Power Inc.

Examples and singing techniques applied to singing style, accompanies the Born to Sing book.

Born to Sing Singing Techniques. Scripts. Elisabeth Howard. Perf. by Elisabeth Howard. Perf. by Howard Austin. 1 CD. (Running Time: 1 hr.). 2004. audio compact disk 19.95 (978-0-934419-42-0(6)) Vocal Power Inc.
Born to Sing/Vocal Power Method examples and singing exercises, accompanies the Born to Sing book.

Born to Sing Super Vocals. Scripts. Elisabeth Howard. Perf. by Elisabeth Howard. Perf. by Howard Austin. 1 CD. (Running Time: 1 hr.). 1997. audio compact disk 19.95 (978-0-934419-40-6(X)) Vocal Power Inc.
Advanced singing techniques and exercises for the Vocal Power/Born to Sing method of singing.

Born to Sing Super Vocals & Sing Aerobics/Workout. Scripts. Elisabeth Howard. Perf. by Elisabeth Howard. Perf. by Howard Austin. 2 CDs. (Running Time: 2 hrs.). 2004. audio compact disk 34.95 (978-0-934419-43-7(4)) Vocal Power Inc.
Set of Born to Sing Super Vocals CD and Born to Sing Sing Aerobics/Workout CD.

Born to Sing Too: Twenty More Mother Goose Parodies. 1 cass. (Looney Tunes Ser.). (J). 4.78 Blisterpack. (KID 72931); audio compact disk 7.98 Longbox. (KID 72931) NewSound.
Includes: "If Your Happy," "My Bunny Lies Over the Ocean," "Paws & Feathers" & more.

Born to Steal: When the Mafia Hit Wall Street. abr. ed. Gary Weiss. Read by Frank Whaley. (ENG.). 2005. 14.98 (978-1-59483-346-5(X)) Pub: Hachet Audio. Dist(s): HachBkGrp

Born to Us. abr. ed. Lucien Deiss. 1 CD. 1999. audio compact disk 16.00 Remaster. (978-0-937690-65-9(1), 2584) Wrld Lib Pubns.
Christian religious music.

Born to Win. Muriel James & Dorothy Jongeward. 1988. SMI Intl.

Born to Worship. Contrib. by Sarah Kelly et al. Prod. by Mitch Dane. 2008. audio compact disk 13.99 (978-5-557-47119-0(7)) Gotee Records.

Borrowed Light. unabr. ed. Anna Fienberg. Read by Rebecca Macauley. 6 cass. (Running Time: 8 hrs. 15 mins.). 2000. 48.00 (978-1-74030-141-1(2), 500532) Pub: Bolinda Pubng AUS. Dist(s): Bolinda Pub Inc

***Borrowed Light.** unabr. ed. Anna Fienberg. Read by Rebecca Macauley. (Running Time: 8 hrs. 15 mins.). 2004. audio compact disk 56.00 (978-1-74093-513-5(6)) Pub: Bolinda Pubng AUS. Dist(s): Bolinda Pub Inc

Borrowed Time. unabr. ed. Robert Goddard. Read by Nicholas Farrell. 10 cass. (Running Time: 10 hrs.). 1996. 84.95 (978-0-7451-6589-9(3), CAB1205) AudioGO.

Borrowed Time. unabr. ed. Robert Goddard. Read by Nicholas Farrell. 10 cass. (Running Time: 15 hrs.). 2000. 69.95 (CAB 1205) Pub: Chivers Audio Bks GBR. Dist(s): AudioGO
On a summer evening in 1990, Robin Timariot is nearing the end of a six day hike when he encounters an elegant middle-aged woman, and they exchange a few enigmatic words. On returning, he learns that the woman, Louise Paxton, was raped and murdered nearby. Fascinated by the experience, he is drawn into the complex search for what really happened. But his search soon threatens many powerful people.

Borrowed Years 1938-1941 Pt. 1: America on the Way to War. collector's ed. Richard M. Ketchum. Read by Barrett Whitener. 15 cass. (Running Time: 22 hrs. 30 min.). 1999. 120.00 (978-0-7366-4719-9(8), 4976-A) Books on Tape.
In 1938, Americans saw sign of coming out of the Depression & come out they did, into war. The three years 1938-1941 were to be a time of profound permanent change. Ketchum tells of the high-water mark of isolation & of the woeful weakness of the U.S. military (our air corps had only nineteen late-model bombers) & meanwhile Americans watched the premier of "Gone with the Wind" & heard the devastating sound of Nazi rallies at Nuremberg. They saw miracles, too, like Dunkirk & the Battle of Britain. Brings to vibrant life that brief, borrowed time when America lost its innocence, that moment of history before we went to war to help save & later lead, the free world.

Borrowed Years 1938-1941 Pt. 2: America on the Way to War. unabr. collector's ed. Richard M. Ketchum. Read by Barrett Whitener. 13 cass. (Running Time: 19 hrs. 30 min.). 1999. 104.00 (978-0-7366-4569-0(1), 4976-B) Books on Tape.

Borrower of Salt see Twentieth-Century Poetry in English, No. 26, Recordings of Poets Reading Their Own Poetry

Borrower of the Night. unabr. ed. Elizabeth Peters, pseud. Read by Susan O'Malley. 5 cass. (Running Time: 7 hrs.). (Vicky Bliss Mystery Ser.). 2000. 39.95 (978-0-7861-1844-1(X), 2643) Blckstn Audio.
It begins as a game, a treasure hunt in an old German castle. For Vicky Bliss, tall, beautiful & brilliant, it is also a challenge, a chance to bring an arrogant young man down a notch or two. And all things considered, it will be no contest.

Borrower of the Night. unabr. ed. Elizabeth Peters, pseud. Read by Susan O'Malley. 5 cass. (Running Time: 7 hrs. 30 mins.). 2001. 27.95 (978-0-7861-1916-5(0)) Pub: Blckstn Audio. Dist(s): Penton Overseas
It begins as a game, a treasure hunt in an old German castle. For Vicky Bliss, tall, beautiful and brilliant, it is also a challenge, a chance to bring an arrogant young man down a notch or two. And all things considered, it will be no contest.

Borrower of the Night. unabr. ed. Elizabeth Peters, pseud. Read by Susan O'Malley. 6 CDs. (Running Time: 9 hrs.). (Vicky Bliss Mystery Ser.). 2001. audio compact disk 48.00 (z2643) Blckstn Audio.
It begins as a game, a treasure hunt in an old German castle. For Vicky Bliss, tall, beautiful & brilliant, it is also a challenge, a chance to bring an arrogant young man down a notch or two. And all things considered, it will be no contest.

Borrower of the Night. unabr. ed. Elizabeth Peters, pseud. Read by Susan O'Malley. 6 CDs. (Running Time: 7 hrs.). (Vicky Bliss Mystery Ser.). 2006. audio compact disk 48.00 (978-0-7861-9746-0(3), 2643) Blckstn Audio.

***Borrower of the Night.** unabr. ed. Elizabeth Peters, pseud. Read by Susan O'Malley. (Running Time: 7 hrs.). 2010. audio compact disk 19.95 (978-1-4417-3543-0(7)) Blckstn Audio.

***Borrower of the Night.** unabr. ed. Elizabeth Peters, pseud. Read by Susan O'Malley. (Running Time: 7 hrs.). 2010. 29.95 (978-1-4417-3544-7(5)) Blckstn Audio.

Borrower of the Night. unabr. ed. Elizabeth Peters, pseud. Narrated by Barbara Rosenblat. 5 cass. (Running Time: 7 hrs. 30 mins.). (Vicky Bliss Mystery Ser.). 1994. 44.00 (978-1-55690-986-3(1), 94125E7) Recorded Bks.
A Mysterious reference in an old & musty book sends art historian Vicky Bliss in pursuit of an ancient undiscovered relic buried deep in a spooky castle.

Borrowers. unabr. ed. Mary Norton. Read by Rowena Cooper. 4 CDs. (Running Time: 6 hrs.). (J). 2002. audio compact disk 34.95 (978-0-7540-6520-3(0), CHCD 020, Chivers Child Audio) AudioGO.

Borrowing Brilliance: The Six Steps to Business Innovation by Building on the Ideas of Others. David Kord Murray. Read by Patrick G. Lawlor. (Playaway Adult Nonfiction Ser.). (ENG.). 2009. 59.99 (978-1-4418-1015-1(3)) Find a World.

Borrowing Brilliance: The Six Steps to Business Innovation by Building on the Ideas of Others. unabr. ed. David Kord Murray. Read by Patrick G. Lawlor. (Running Time: 10 hrs.). 2009. 24.99 (978-1-4418-0142-5(1), 9781441801425, Brilliance MP3); 39.97 (978-1-4418-0143-2(X), 9781441801432, Brlnc Audio MP3 Lib); 24.99 (978-1-4418-0144-9(8), 9781441801449, BAD); 39.97 (978-1-4418-0145-6(6), 9781441801456, BADLE); audio compact disk 24.99 (978-1-4418-0140-1(5), 9781441801401, Bril Audio CD Unabri); audio compact disk 82.97 (978-1-4418-0141-8(3), 9781441801418, BriAudCD Unabrid) Brilliance Audio.

Borstal Boy. unabr. collector's ed. Brendan Behan. Read by Dan Lazar. 8 cass. (Running Time: 12 hrs.). 1978. 64.00 (978-0-7366-0132-0(5), 1138) Books on Tape.
This is an autobiographical record of Behan's experiences of his imprisonment, trial, remand to reform school, & final release. Schools for delinquents in England are called Borstal Institutions, & this is Behan's account of his years as a "Borstal Boy".

Bo's Cafe. unabr. ed. Bill Thrall et al. Narrated by Roger Mueller. (ENG.). 2009. 19.59 (978-1-60814-611-6(1)); audio compact disk 27.99 (978-1-59859-664-9(0)) Oasis Audio.

Bo's Lasting Lessons: The Legendary Coach Teaches the Timeless Fundamentals of Leadership. abr. ed. Bo Schembechler & John Bacon. Read by John H. Mayer. (Running Time: 3 hrs. 30 mins.). (ENG.). 2007. 19.98 (978-1-60024-022-5(4)) Pub: Hachet Audio. Dist(s): HachBkGrp

Bosco & the Rainbow Bridge. Perf. by Rita Ann Freeman. Based on a story by Rita Ann Freeman. 2002. audio compact disk 10.00 (978-0-9719944-1-6(2)) Celestial Consortium.
A delightful, theatrical presentation of the book, "Bosco and the Rainbow Bridge". A performance rich in characterizations, sound and music that delivers the lasting effect, for which the story was originally written. Therapeutic in value to all who have come to know the loss of a beloved pet. A heartwarming experience the whole family can share!.

Boscombe Valley Mystery see Adventures of Sherlock Holmes

Boscombe Valley Mystery. unabr. ed. Arthur Conan Doyle. Read by Walter Covell & Cindy Hardin. 1 cass. (Running Time: 52 min.). Dramatization. 1981. 7.95 (N-69) Jimcin Record.
Sherlock Holmes defends a man accused of killing his father.

Bosnia. 1 cass. (Leonard Peikoff Show Ser.). 1995. 12.95 (LPXXC2) Second Renaissance.

Bosnia: Echoes from an Endangered World, Music & Chant of the Bosnian Muslims. Anno. by Ted Levin & Ankica Petrovic. 1 cass. (Running Time: 49 min.). 1993. (0-9307-404070-9307-40407-2-0); audio compact disk (0-9307-40407-2-0) Smithsonian Folkways.
Beautiful examples of Muslim traditions document the rich confluence of Turkish & European music in the region. Compiled from commercial & field recordings.

Bosnian, Croatian, Serbian Audio Supplement: To Accompany Bosnian, Croatian, Serbian, a Textbook. Ronelle Alexander. Ed. by Ellen Elias-Bursac. 2006. audio compact disk 29.95 (978-0-299-22110-2(5)) Pub: U of Wis Pr. Dist(s): Chicago Distribution Ctr

Bosque de los Pigmeos see Forest of the Pygmies

bosque de Miel. (Saludos Ser.: Vol. 1). (SPA.). (gr. 2-3). 10.00 (978-0-7635-5883-3(4)) Rigby Educ.

Boss, Jaybird & Me. Jimmy Reed. 2006. audio compact disk 34.95 (978-0-9773774-1-1(5)) JR Bks LLC.

Boss of Lunch. unabr. ed. Barbara Park. Read by Lana Quintal. (Running Time: 48 mins.). (Junie B., First Grader Ser.: No. 2). (J). (gr. k-3). 2004. pap. bk. 17.00 (978-0-8072-1021-5(8), S FTR 259 SP, Listening Lib) Random Audio Pubg.

***Boss of the World.** Fran Manushkin. Illus. by Tammie Lyon. (Katie Woo Ser.). (ENG.). 2010. audio compact disk 8.95 (978-1-4048-6241-8(2)) CapstoneDig.

Bossa, Samba & Tango Duets for Flute & Guitar Plus Percussion. Katarzyna Bury. 2006. pap. bk. 29.98 (978-1-59615-723-1(2), 586-051) Pub: Music Minus. Dist(s): H Leonard

BOSSA, SAMBA & TANGO DUETS for GUITAR & FLUTE PLUS PERCUSSION. Christian Reichert. 2006. pap. bk. 34.98 (978-1-59615-731-6(3), 586-056) Pub: Music Minus. Dist(s): Bookworld

***Bossy Gallito.** Lucia Gonzalez. Read by Lucia Gonzalez. 1 CD. (Running Time: 39 mins.). (ENG & SPA., (J). (ps-2). 2009. pap. bk. & pap. bk. 15.95 (978-0-9842981-1-2(8)) Lorito Bks.

***Bossypants.** unabr. ed. Tina Fey. (Running Time: 8 hrs.). (ENG.). 2011. 26.99 (978-1-60941-971-4(5)); audio compact disk & audio compact disk 29.98 (978-1-60941-969-1(3)) Pub: Hachet Audio. Dist(s): HachBkGrp

Boston Audissey. Short Stories. (Running Time: 78 mins.). Dramatization. 2005. audio compact disk 19.95 (978-0-9771349-0-8(3)) Audissey Guides.

Boston Blackie, Set. Perf. by Dick Kilimar. 2 cass. (Running Time: 2 hrs.). vinyl bd. 10.95 (978-1-57816-045-7(6), BB2401) Audio File.
Includes: "Murder at the Movies" (1940's); "The Baseball Murder" (1940's); "Death Comes for the Harmonica Man" (1940's); "The Rockwell Diamond" (1940's).

Boston Blackie, Vol. 1. 1998th collector's ed. Perf. by Richard Kollmar. 6 cass. (Running Time: 9 hrs.). 1998. bk. 34.98 (978-1-57019-107-7(7), 4102) Radio Spirits.
Master thief turned detective, who is an "enemy to those who make him an enemy, friend to those who have no friend," in 18 episodes.

Boston Blackie, Vol. 2. collector's ed. Perf. by Richard Kollmar. 6 cass. (Running Time: 9 hrs.). 2000. bk. 34.98 (4397) Radio Spirits.
18 episodes of Boston Blackie, a former safecracker turned private eye. "An enemy to those who make him an enemy, friend to those who have no friends".

Boston Blackie, Vol. 3. collector's ed. Perf. by Richard Kollmer et al. 6 cass. (Running Time: 9 hrs.). 2001. bk. 34.98 (4428) Radio Spirits.
18 mystery adventures.

Boston Blackie: Austin Is Killed & Henry Dale Killed by Mary? unabr. ed. Perf. by Richard Kollmar. 1 cass. (Running Time: 1 hr.). 2001. 6.98 (1610) Radio Spirits.

Boston Blackie: Friend or Enemy. Perf. by Richard Kollmar & Maurice Tarplin. 2009. audio compact disk 31.95 (978-1-57019-879-3(9)) Radio Spirits.

Boston Blackie: Hypnotic Murder & Fred Arlen Murder. unabr. ed. Perf. by Richard Kollmar. 1 cass. (Running Time: 1 hr.). 2001. 6.98 (2511) Radio Spirits.

Boston Blackie: Jerry Williams Fixed Court Case & Jealous Partners & Arson. unabr. ed. Perf. by Richard Kollmar. 1 cass. (Running Time: 1 hr.). 2001. 6.98 (2252) Radio Spirits.

Boston Blackie: Mary's Stolen Car & Frances Feilding Murdered. unabr. ed. Perf. by Richard Kollmar. 1 cass. (Running Time: 1 hr.). 2001. 6.98 (2233) Radio Spirits.

Boston Blackie: Missing Millicent Bromley & Blackie Breaks into Prison. unabr. ed. Perf. by Richard Kollmar. 1 cass. (Running Time: 1 hr.). 2001. 6.98 (2571) Radio Spirits.

Boston Blackie: Mrs. Boston Blackie & Winthrope Diamond. unabr. ed. Perf. by Richard Kollmar. 1 cass. (Running Time: 1 hr.). 2001. 6.98 (1611) Radio Spirits.

Boston Blackie: Murder at the Rodeo & The Bill Thayer Mob. unabr. ed. Perf. by Richard Kollmar. 1 cass. (Running Time: 1 hr.). 2001. 6.98 (1972) Radio Spirits.

Boston Blackie: Nothing Up My Sleeve & Buy a Cat, Save a Life. unabr. ed. Perf. by Richard Kollmar. 1 cass. (Running Time: 1 hr.). 2001. 6.98 (2031) Radio Spirits.

Boston Blackie: On the Wrong Track & Carl Browning Murdered. unabr. ed. Perf. by Richard Kollmar. 1 cass. (Running Time: 1 hr.). 2001. 6.98 (1954) Radio Spirits.

Boston Blackie: Paul Blaine Murdered & Escaped Prisoner. unabr. ed. Perf. by Richard Kollmar. 1 cass. (Running Time: 1 hr.). 2001. 6.98 (2115) Radio Spirits.

Boston Blackie: Reynolds & the Stolen Goods & Kingston's Office Building. unabr. ed. Perf. by Richard Kollmar. 1 cass. (Running Time: 1 hr.). 2001. 6.98 (2175) Radio Spirits.

Boston Blackie: Stolen Rings at Christmas & Joe Barton Missing. unabr. ed. Perf. by Richard Kollmar. 1 cass. (Running Time: 1 hr.). 2001. 6.98 (2092) Radio Spirits.

Boston Blackie: Sunken Treasure & Barking up the Wrong Tree. unabr. ed. Perf. by Richard Kollmar. 1 cass. (Running Time: 1 hr.). 2001. 6.98 (2131) Radio Spirits.

Boston Blackie: The Case of the Unused Shoes. 1 cass. (Running Time: 60 min.). 7.95 (MM-2437) Natl Recrd Co.
In the story "The Case of the Unused Shoes" Blackie finds a dead man in the park & discovers the man is wearing a pair of shoes that has never been used, & Inspector Farraday accuses Blackie of the murder. "A Study In Horror" consists of six short horror stories.

Boston Blackie: The Deadly Grandfather Clock & Freighter Crew Plans Mutiny. unabr. ed. Perf. by Richard Kollmar. 1 cass. (Running Time: 1 hr.). 2001. 6.98 (1612) Radio Spirits.

Boston Blackie: The Fredricks Gang & The Crooked Carter Brother. unabr. ed. Perf. by Richard Kollmar. 1 cass. (Running Time: 1 hr.). 2001. 6.98 (2054) Radio Spirits.

Boston Blackie: The Ice Rink Murder & The Linda Crane Case. unabr. ed. Perf. by Richard Kollmar. 1 cass. (Running Time: 1 hr.). 2001. 6.98 (1540) Radio Spirits.

Boston Blackie: The Wentworth Diamonds & Mary at Sea. unabr. ed. Perf. by Richard Kollmar. 1 cass. (Running Time: 1 hr.). 2001. 6.98 (2472) Radio Spirits.

***Boston Blackie, Volume 1.** RadioArchives.com. (ENG.). 2003. audio compact disk 29.98 (978-1-61081-010-4(4)) Radio Arch.

***Boston Blackie, Volume 2.** RadioArchives.com. (Running Time: 600). (ENG.). 2009. audio compact disk 29.98 (978-1-61081-093-7(7)) Radio Arch.

***Boston Blackie, Volume 3.** RadioArchives.com. (Running Time: 600). (ENG.). 2009. audio compact disk 29.98 (978-1-61081-094-4(5)) Radio Arch.

***Boston Blackie, Volume 4.** RadioArchives.com. (Running Time: 600). (ENG.). 2009. audio compact disk 29.98 (978-1-61081-095-1(3)) Radio Arch.

Boston Fiddle. Frank Ferrel. 1999. pap. bk. 23.95 (978-0-7866-3850-5(8), 97231CDP) Mel Bay.

Boston Jane. unabr. ed. Jennifer L. Holm. Read by Jessalyn Gilsig. 4 vols. (Running Time: 6 hrs. 15 mins.). (Middle Grade Cassette Librariestm Ser.). (J). (gr. 5-9). 2004. pap. bk. 38.00 (978-0-8072-0787-1(X), S YA 307 SP, Listening Lib) Random Audio Pubg.

Boston Jane: A Young Lady's Journey. unabr. ed. Jennifer L. Holm. Read by Jessalyn Gilsig. 4 cass. (Running Time: 6 hrs. 15 mins.). (J). (gr. 5-9). 2004. 32.00 (978-0-8072-0510-5(9), Listening Lib) Random Audio Pubg.
Fresh from Miss Hepplewhite's Young Ladies' Academy, sixteen-year-old Jane Peck has come to the unknown wilds of the Northwest to be wedded to her true love, William Baldt, her idol from childhood. But her socially correct upbringing in straitlaced Philadelphia is hardly preparation for the colorful characters and crude life that await her in Shoal Water Bay in the Washington Territory.

Boston Jane: an Adventure. unabr. ed. Jennifer L. Holm. Read by Jessalyn Gilsig. (ENG.). (J). (gr. 5). 2010. 30.00 (978-0-307-70628-7(1), Listening Lib) Pub: Random Audio Pubg. Dist(s): Random

Boston Massacre. 1 cass. (Running Time: 46 min. per cass.). 1978. 10.00 (HV211) Esstee Audios.
Explanation of the events preceding the Boston Massacre, the massacre itself, & the ensuing trial of the British soldiers.

Boston Stranglers. unabr. ed. Susan Kelly. Read by Lorna Raver. (Running Time: 15 hrs. 50 mins.). (ENG.). 2009. 29.95 (978-1-4332-5682-0(7)); 85.95 (978-1-4332-5678-3(9)); audio compact disk 118.00 (978-1-4332-5679-0(7)) Blckstn Audio.

Boston Tea Party. Compiled by Benchmark Education Staff. 2005. audio compact disk 10.00 (978-1-4108-5503-9(1)) Benchmark Educ.

Bostonians. Henry James. Narrated by Flo Gibson. 2009. audio compact disk 42.95 (978-1-60646-077-1(3)) Audio Bk Con.

***Bostonians.** unabr. ed. Henry James. Narrated by Sands Xe. (Running Time: 18 hrs. 0 mins.). 2010. 29.99 (978-1-4526-5057-9(8)); 39.99 (978-1-4526-0057-4(0)); 95.99 (978-1-4526-3057-1(7)) Tantor Media.

***Bostonians.** unabr. ed. Henry James. Narrated by Xe Sands. (Running Time: 18 hrs. 0 mins.). 2010. 22.99 (978-1-4526-7057-7(9)) Tantor Media.

Bostonians, Set. unabr. ed. Henry James. Read by Flo Gibson. 11 cass. (Running Time: 16 hrs.). 1989. 34.95 (978-1-55685-150-6(2)) Audio Bk Con.
Triangle between a male chauvinist, an ardent feminist & the lovely, gifted Pawn, Verena Tarrant.

***Bostonians (Library Edition)** unabr. ed. Henry James. Narrated by Xe Sands. (Running Time: 18 hrs. 0 mins.). 2010. 39.99 (978-1-4526-2057-2(1)) Tantor Media.

Boswell in Search of a Wife. abr. ed. James Boswell. Perf. by Anthony Quayle. 1 cass. 12.95 (SWC 1475) HarperCollins Pubs.
This is a sequel to "London Journal." Boswell, now a man of the world, describes his love affairs & occasional visits to Dr. Johnson in London.

Boswell's Clap & Other Essays: Medical Analyses of Literary Men's Afflictions, unabr. ed. William B. Ober. Narrated by Ron Keith. 11 cass. (Running Time: 15 hrs. 45 mins.). 1994. 91.00 (978-0-7887-0045-3(6), 94244E7) Recorded Bks.
Dr. Ober delves into the public medical problems & private vices of some of literature's great writers. While some essays, including the first, are interesting only for the well-read physician, many of the later essays will provide the literary reader with an insightful look into how the private

demons of men like Cowper, Chekhov & Smart were put on highly public display in their writings.

Bosworth Field & the Wars of the Roses. unabr. ed. A. L. Rowse. Read by Bill Kelsey. 8 cass. (Running Time: 1 hr. 30 min. per cass.). 1988. 64.00 (978-0-7366-1302-6(1), 2209) Books on Tape.
Factual historical account of the struggle for power in late medieval England.

Botany of Desire: A Plant's-Eye View of the World. unabr. ed. Michael Pollan. Read by Scott Brick. (YA). 2008. 59.99 (978-1-60514-026-1(0)) Find a World.

Botany of Desire: A Plant's-Eye View of the World. unabr. rev. abr. ed. Michael Pollan. Read by Scott Brick. 8 CDs. (Running Time: 9 hrs.). (ENG.). 2007. audio compact disk 39.98 (978-1-59659-093-9(9), GildAudio) Pub: Gildan Media. Dist(s): HachBkGrp

Botany of Hallucinogens. Richard E. Schultes. 1 cass. 1999. 11.00 (13801) Big Sur Tapes.
1978 Esalen Institute.

Both Ends of the Night. unabr. ed. Marcia Muller. Read by Bernadette Dunne. 6 cass. (Running Time: 9 hrs.). (Sharon McCone Mystery Ser.: No. 17). 1997. 48.00 (978-0-7366-3802-9(4), 4473) Books on Tape.
P.I. Sharon McCone is back. A pilot for several years, McCone is due for a biannual flight review. Her former flight instructor, Matty Wildress, invites her to fly up to a small Sonoma County town for the evaluation. But McCone suspects Matty has more in mind than safe flying. Matty's live-in lover has been gone for a week, abandoning his mall son, Zach. In a desperate letter he entrusts the boy to Matty's care & urges them both to go into hiding. When Matty is killed in a suspicious flying accident, a missing person case becomes a personal vendetta. Sharon bypasses the authorities to hunt down the man responsible for her friend's death.

Both Ends of the Night. unabr. ed. Marcia Muller. Read by Jean Reed Bahle. (Running Time: 36000 sec.). (Sharon McCone Mystery Ser.: No. 17). 2008. 39.25 (978-1-4233-5328-7(5), 9781423353287, Brinc Audio MP3 Lib) Brilliance Audio.

Both Ends of the Night. unabr. ed. Marcia Muller. Read by Jean Reed-Bahle. (Running Time: 10 hrs.). (Sharon McCone Mystery Ser.: No. 17). 2008. 39.25 (978-1-4233-5330-0(7), 9781423353300, BADLE) Brilliance Audio.

Both Ends of the Night. unabr. ed. Marcia Muller. Read by Jean Reed Bahle. (Running Time: 36000 sec.). (Sharon McCone Mystery Ser.: No. 17). 2008. 24.95 (978-1-4233-5327-0(7), 9781423353270, Brilliance MP3) Brilliance Audio.

Both Ends of the Night. unabr. ed. Marcia Muller. Read by Jean Reed-Bahle. (Running Time: 10 hrs.). (Sharon McCone Mystery Ser.: No. 17). 2008. 24.95 (978-1-4233-5329-4(3), 9781423353294, BAD) Brilliance Audio.

Both Good & Evil in a Single Thought. Contrib. by Hua. (978-0-88139-605-8(2)) Buddhist Text.

Both Halves of the Brain. Eldon Taylor. 1 cass. (Running Time: 62 min.). (Inner Talk Ser.). 16.95 (978-1-55978-174-9(2), 53797N) Progress Aware Res.
Soundtrack - Contemporary Moments with underlying subliminal affirmations.

***Both Ways Is the Only Way I Want It.** unabr. ed. Maile Meloy. Read by Bronson, Kirsten; Pinchot Potter. (Running Time: 5 hrs.). 2010. 29.95 (978-1-4417-7004-2(6)); 54.95 (978-1-4417-7001-1(1)); audio compact disk 29.95 (978-1-4417-7003-5(8)); audio compact disk 76.00 (978-1-4417-7002-8(X)) Blckstn Audio.

Both Your Houses. unabr. ed. Sarah Harrison. Narrated by Judith Boyd. 10 cass. (Running Time: 13 hrs. 45 mins.). 2001. 92.00 (978-1-84197-187-2(1), H1171E7) Recorded Bks.
Despite their differences, the Blakes & the Armitages have been friends for more years than any of them care to remember. To begin with, the problems their children cause serve to provide a united, commiserating front. But when Giselle, the Blakes' most wayward child starts seeing one of the Armitages' sons, soon the parents discover that it is not just their offspring who end up taking sides.

Boticellian Trees see William Carlos Williams Reads His Poetry

Bottes de Sept Lieues, Set. Short Stories. Marcel Ayme. Read by Jose Artur. 2 cass. (FRE.). (J). (gr. 3 up). 1991. bk. 35.95 (1GA052) Olivia & Hill.
Ayme, who is a master at mixing fantasy & reality, tells three tales. The title story recounts the adventures of Antoine, his school friends & the seven league boots. In "A et B" we join the students of M. Jourdin in the lycee & in "Le Proverbe" we identify with Lucien as he struggles with his homework.

Bottle. unabr. ed. W. Bartow Wright. Read by Rusty Nelson. 6 cass. (Running Time: 6 hrs. 36 min.). 2001. 39.95 (978-1-58116-168-7(9)) Books in Motion.
Bucky is called upon to clear the name of retired Marine Sergeant Bron Skonie in a mysterious murder. The victim has fallen prey to a killer leaving behind a strange bottle of brandy.

Bottle Factory Outing. unabr. ed. Beryl Bainbridge. Read by Julia Franklin. 6 CDs. (Running Time: 6 hrs.). (Sound Ser.). (J). 2002. audio compact disk 64.95 (978-1-84283-231-8(X)) Pub: ISIS Lrg Prnt GBR. Dist(s): Ulverscroft US

Bottle Factory Outing. unabr. ed. Beryl Bainbridge. Read by Julian Franklyn. 5 cass. (Running Time: 6 hrs. 45 mins.). (Sound Ser.). 2000. 49.95 (978-1-86042-658-2(1), 26581) Pub: UlverLrgPrint GBR. Dist(s): Ulverscroft US
Freda & Brenda spend their days working in an Italian-run wine bottling factory & their nights in a dismal room. Little wonder, then, that the works outing offers such promise for Freda, determined to capture the heart of Vittorio, & such terror for Brenda, constantly escaping the clutches of Rossi. Passions run high on that chilly day of freedom, & life after the outing can - tragically - never return to normal.

Bottle Imp. Robert Louis Stevenson. Ed. by Raymond Harris. (Classics Ser.). (YA). (gr. 6-12). 1982. pap. bk. 13.00 (978-0-89061-261-3(7), 464) Jamestown.

Bottle Imp. unabr. ed. Robert Louis Stevenson. Read by Jim Killavey. 1 cass. (Running Time: 87 min). Dramatization. 1986. 7.95 (S-70) Jimcin Record.
Wishes galore - but with a catch.

Bottle Imp & Other Stories. unabr. ed. Robert Louis Stevenson. Read by Jim Killavey & John Chatty. 7 cass. (Running Time: 7 hrs.). 1989. 36.00 incl. album. (C-160) Jimcin Record.
Includes, "The Body Snatcher".

Bottle Imp & Other Stories. unabr. ed. Short Stories. Robert Louis Stevenson. Narrated by Alexander Spencer. 3 cass. (Running Time: 4 hrs. 30 mins.). (gr. 8 up). 1999. 26.00 (978-1-55690-070-9(8), 81281E7) Recorded Bks.
Short stories of the macabre & supernatural.

Bottle Imp & Other Stories. unabr. collector's ed. Robert Louis Stevenson. Read by Jim Killavey & John Chatty. 7 cass. (Running Time: 7 hrs.). Incl. Beach at Falesa. 1986. (9159); Body Snatcher. 1986. (9159); Lodging for the Night. 1986. (9159); Thrawn Janet. 1986. (9159); 1986. 42.00 (978-0-7366-3920-0(9), 9159) Books on Tape.
Includes: "The Body Snatcher," "The Beach at Falesa," "A Lodging for the Night," & "Thrawn Janet.".

Bottled Spider. John E. Gardner. Read by Patience Tomlinson. 12 cass. (Running Time: 57600 sec.). (Isis Cassettes Ser.). 2007. 94.95 (978-0-7531-3646-1(5)) Pub: ISIS Lrg Prnt GBR. Dist(s): Ulverscroft US

***Bottled Up.** Andrew Grey. (ENG.). 2010. 14.99 (978-1-61581-989-8(4)) Dreamspinner.

Bottom Dunker's Bible: How to Find & Fish for the Finest Finny Food. Roger Jarvis. 1 cass. 1998. 15.00 (978-1-888964-07-3(3)) Jones Riv Pr.

Bottom Line on Network Marketing. Patrick W. Higgins. 3 cass. (Running Time: 2 hrs. 45 min.). 1997. 29.95 Set. (978-0-9658978-2-2(6)) Unltd Horizons.
Network marketing training series.

Bottom Line, the Sharp End & Other Stories, Set. abr. ed. Short Stories. Fay Weldon. Read by Julie Christie. 2 cass. (Running Time: 3 hrs.). 1999. 12.00 (978-1-878427-30-4(X), 390436) Cimino Pub Grp.
This collection of seven short stories includes "Bottom Line," "The Sharp End," "Man with No Eyes," "Holy Stones," "School Run," "Whose Birthday," & "Mary, Don't You Cry.".

Bottom Liner Blues. unabr. ed. K. C. Constantine. Read by Lloyd James. 7 cass. (Running Time: 10 hrs. 30 min.). (Mario Balzic Ser.). 1997. 56.00 (978-0-7366-3691-9(9), 4370) Books on Tape.
The mines have shut down & the blue-collar dreams of Rocksburg's inhabitants are coming apart.

Bottom Live the Stage Show. R. Mayall & A. Edmonson. 2000. 17.99 (978-0-00-105700-5(6), HarpColl UK) Pub: HarpC GBR. Dist(s): Trafalgar

Bottom of the Boat. Bob Hartman & Mike McGuire. (What Was It Like Ser.). (J). 1994. 11.99 (3-0005) David C Cook.

Bottom of the Boat. Bob Hartman et al. 1 cass. (What Was It Like Ser.). (J). (ps-3). 1994. bk. 11.99 (978-1-56476-298-6(X), 6-3298) David C Cook.

Bottom of the Sky: A Novel. unabr. ed. William C. Pack. Read by Scott Brick. (Running Time: 22 hrs. 0 mins.). 2010. 44.95 (978-1-4417-2756-5(6)); 109.95 (978-1-4417-2752-7(3)); audio compact disk 123.00 (978-1-4417-2753-4(1)) Blckstn Audio.

Bottom-Up Marketing. Al Ries & Jack Trout. 1 cass. (Running Time: 88 min.). 1988. 9.95 (978-0-07-052734-8(2)) McGraw.
Provides step-by-step procedures for developing a marketing campaign; determining tactics, establishing strategy & launching campaigns.

Bottoms. unabr. ed. Joe R. Lansdale. Read by Don Jellerson. 10 vols. (Running Time: 15 hrs.). 2001. bk. 84.95 (978-0-7927-2459-9(3), CSL 348, Chivers Sound Lib) AudioGO.
Harry Crane discovers the black woman's body, mutilated & bound to a tree with barbed wire, he unleashes a storm of uncontrolled fear, thinly buried racial animosities & escalating violence. Harry's father & the town constable struggle to see that proper justice gets done.

Botulism. Stephen Ludwig. (Pediatric Emergencies: The National Conference for Practioners Ser.). 1986. 9.00 (978-0-932491-71-8(5)) Res Appl Inc.

Boucle D'or. (Plaisir de Lire Ser.). 5.95 (978-88-8148-701-1(2)) EMC-Paradigm.

Boucle d'Or et les Trois Ours. 1 cass. (Running Time: 1 hr., 30 mins.). (Musicontes Ser.).Tr. of Goldilocks. (FRE.). (J). 2000. bk. 24.95 (978-2-09-230441-9(0)) Pub: F Nathan FRA. Dist(s): Distribks Inc

Boucles d'Or et les Trois Ours. Tr. of Goldilocks & the Three Bears. (FRE.). pap. bk. 12.95 (978-2-89558-061-4(8)) Pub: Coffragants CAN. Dist(s): Penton Overseas

Boucles d'or et les trois ours (Goldilocks & the Three Bears) 1 cass. (Coffragants Ser.). (FRE.). (J). (ps-2). 1999. 9.95 Incl. bklet. & plastic case. Penton Overseas.

***Bought & Paid For: The Unholy Alliance Between Barack Obama & Wall Street.** unabr. ed. Charles Gasparino. (Running Time: 8 hrs. 0 mins. 0 sec.). (ENG.). 2010. 19.99 (978-1-4001-6901-6(1)); 15.99 (978-1-4001-8901-4(2)); audio compact disk 71.99 (978-1-4001-4901-8(0)); audio compact disk 29.99 (978-1-4001-1901-1(4)) Pub: Tantor Media. Dist(s): IngramPubServ

Bouillon de Poulet pour l'Ame. 1 CD. (Running Time: 1 hr.).Tr. of Chicken Soup for the Soul. 2001. bk. 18.95 (978-2-89558-023-2(5)) Pub: Coffragants CAN. Dist(s): Penton Overseas

Bouillon de Poulet pour l'Ame. Marie-Jose Beaudoin et al. 1 cass., bklet. (Running Time: 90 mins.).Tr. of Chicken Soup for the Soul. (FRE.). 2000. bk. 14.95 (978-2-89517-043-3(6)) Pub: Coffragants CAN. Dist(s): Penton Overseas
Recorded completely in international French language by well-known actors or speakers.

Bouillon de Poulet pour l'Ame de la Femme. Marie-Jose Beaudoin et al. 1 cass., bklet. (Running Time: 90 mins.). (Best-Sellers Ser.).Tr. of Chicken Soup for the Woman's Soul. (FRE.). 1999. bk. 14.95 (978-2-89517-038-9(X)) Pub: Coffragants CAN. Dist(s): Penton Overseas

Bouillon de Poulet pour l'Ame des Ados. Marie-Jose Beaudoin et al. Perf. by Michel Montignac. 1 cass., bklet. (Running Time: 90 mins.). (Best-Sellers Ser.).Tr. of Chicken Soup for the Teenage Soul. (FRE.). 1999. audio compact disk 14.95 (978-2-89517-039-6(8)) Pub: Coffragants CAN. Dist(s): Penton Overseas

Bouillon de Poulet pour l'Ame des Ados. Jack L. Canfield & Mark Victor Hansen. 1 CD. (Running Time: 1 hr.).Tr. of Chicken Soup for the Teenage Soul. (FRE., (J). 2002. pap. bk. 18.95 (978-2-89558-045-4(6)) Pub: Coffragants CAN. Dist(s): Penton Overseas

Bouillon de Poulet pour l'Ame d'Une Meres. Jack L. Canfield & Mark Victor Hansen. 1 CD. (Running Time: 1 hr.).Tr. of Chicken Soup for the Mother's Soul. (FRE.). 2002. pap. bk. 18.95 (978-2-89558-028-7(6)) Pub: Coffragants CAN. Dist(s): Penton Overseas

Bouken Desho Desho. Perf. by Aya Hirano. (YA). 2007. 9.98 (978-1-59409-840-6(9)) Bandai Ent.

Boulder, Colorado - A City That Plans & Controls Its Growth. Hosted by Nancy Pearlman. 1 cass. (Running Time: 28 min.). 10.00 (1417) Educ Comm CA.

Boule de Suif. Guy de Maupassant. 3 cass. (Running Time: 3 hrs.). (FRE.). 1996. pap. bk. 39.50 set. (978-1-58085-353-8(6)) Interlingua VA.
Includes dual French-English transcription. The combination of written text & clarity & pace of diction will open the door for intermediate & advanced students to genuine comprehension & the use of literary texts for advancement in rapid understanding of written & oral language materials. The audio text plus written text concept makes foreign languages accessible to a much wider range of students than books alone.

Boule de Suif, Set. Guy de Maupassant. Read by C. Jacquin. 2 cass. (FRE.). 1991. 26.95 (1078-OH) Olivia & Hill.
During the Franco-Prussian war, a prostitute nicknamed "Boule de Suif" escapes from Rouen with a small group of bourgeois. She shares her food with them & helps them when they are confronted by the enemy. Once their hunger is assuaged & the danger of the Prussians less imminent, their appreciation changes to disdain.

Boulevard. unabr. ed. Stephen Schwartz. Read by Ray Porter. (Running Time: 7 hrs. 30 mins.). (ENG.). 2009. 29.95 (978-1-4332-6273-9(8)) Blckstn Audio.

Boulevard. unabr. ed. Stephen Jay Schwartz. Read by Ray Porter. (Running Time: 7.5 hrs. 0 mins.). (ENG.). 2009. 54.95 (978-1-4332-6269-2(X)); audio compact disk 24.95 (978-1-4332-6272-2(X)); audio compact disk 69.00 (978-1-4332-6270-8(3)) Blckstn Audio.

Bouman - MacroEconomics Fall 07. rev. ed. John Bouman. (ENG.). 2010. 23.95 (978-1-60250-053-2(3)) Kendall-Hunt.

Bouman - MicroEconomics Fall 07. rev. ed. John Bouman. (ENG.). 2010. 23.95 (978-1-60250-052-5(5)) Kendall-Hunt.

***Bounce.** unabr. ed. Matthew Syed. Read by James Clamp. (ENG.). 2010. (978-0-06-201596-9(6), Harper Audio) HarperCollins Pubs.

***Bounce: Mozart, Federer, Picasso, Beckham, & the Science of Success.** unabr. ed. Matthew Syed. Read by James Clamp. (ENG.). 2010. (978-0-06-200901-2(X), Harper Audio) HarperCollins Pubs.

Bounce Back: Overcoming Setbacks to Succeed in Business & in Life. abr. ed. John Calipari. Read by John Calipari. (Running Time: 6 hrs. 0 mins. 0 sec.). (ENG.). 2009. audio compact disk 29.99 (978-0-7435-8235-3(7)) Pub: S&S Audio. Dist(s): S and S Inc

Bounce Back from Job Loss in Six Days - Guaranteed! Create the Career Comeback of Your Dreams with Mental Imagery Technology. Lynn Joseph. 1 CD. Orig. Title: After Job Loss - Moving On. 2002. pap. bk. 39.95 (978-0-9676615-1-3(X)) Discovery Dynamics.

Bouncy Mouse. Created by Kane Press. (Let's Read Together Ser.). 2005. audio compact disk 4.25 (978-1-57565-181-1(5)) Pub: Kane Pr. Dist(s): Lerner Pub

***Bound.** unabr. ed. Antonya Nelson. (Running Time: 7 hrs. 30 mins.). 2010. 29.99 (978-1-4001-9864-1(X)) Tantor Media.

***Bound.** unabr. ed. Antonya Nelson. Narrated by Cassandra Campbell. (Running Time: 9 hrs. 0 mins. 0 sec.). 2010. audio compact disk 71.99 (978-1-4001-4864-6(2)) Pub: Tantor Media. Dist(s): IngramPubServ

***Bound: A Novel.** unabr. ed. Antonya Nelson. (Running Time: 9 hrs. 0 mins. 0 sec.). 2010. 19.99 (978-1-4001-6864-4(3)); 14.99 (978-1-4001-8864-2(4)) Tantor Media.

***Bound: A Novel.** unabr. ed. Antonya Nelson. Narrated by Cassandra Campbell. (Running Time: 9 hrs. 0 mins. 0 sec.). 2010. audio compact disk 29.99 (978-1-4001-1864-9(6)) Pub: Tantor Media. Dist(s): IngramPubServ

Bound by Blood. unabr. ed. Cynthia Danielewski. Read by Gillian Styles. 8 cass. (Running Time: 9 hrs.). 2001. 49.95 (978-1-55686-933-4(9)) Books in Motion.
N.Y. Police Detective Brandon Cole is drawn into the grant crime family after he kills the younger Grant in the line of duty. While sister Lauren grant learns the truth, the mob wants Cole dead.

Bound by Honor. Bill Bonanno. 2004. 15.95 (978-0-7435-4216-6(9)) Pub: S&S Audio. Dist(s): S and S Inc

Bound by Honor. Virginia Weldon. 3 cass. 2004. 14.95 (978-1-59156-157-6(4)); audio compact disk 14.95 (978-1-59156-167-5(1)) Covenant Comms.

Bound Feet & Western Dress. abr. ed. Pang-Mei Natasha Chang. Read by Pang-Mei Natasha Chang. 2 cass. (Running Time: 3 hrs.). 1997. 17.95 (978-1-57453-093-3(3)) Audio Lit.
Unforgettable saga of a remarkable woman born in Shanghai at the turn of the century.

***Bound for Canaan.** abr. ed. Fergus Bordewich. Read by Fergus Bordewich. (ENG.). 2005. (978-0-06-089506-8(3), Harper Audio); (978-0-06-089507-5(1), Harper Audio) HarperCollins Pubs.

Bound for Canaan: The Underground Railroad & the War for the Soul of America. abr. ed. Fergus M. Bordewich. Read by Fergus M. Bordewich. 2005. audio compact disk 29.95 (978-0-06-076064-9(8)) HarperCollins Pubs.

Bound for Glory. Perf. by Bill Murk. 1 Tape. (Running Time: 40 mins). 1993. 9.99 (978-0-9725443-1-3(3)); audio compact disk 14.99 (978-0-9725443-0-6(5)) Pub: Myrrh Pub. Dist(s): STL Dist NA
A wonderful collection of music performed by Bill Murk.

Bound for Glory. abr. ed. Woody Guthrie. Read by Arlo Guthrie. 2 cass. (Running Time: 3 hrs.). 1995. 16.95 (978-0-944993-61-3(3)) Audio Lit.
A marvelous evocation of the American spirit in the post-depression years, the author's son, Arlo, who has carried on in his father's tradition as a singer & writer of "classic" folk music.

***Bound for Pleasure: Three Stories to Tease & Thrill: Includes: Looking Glass, the Music Lesson, & War Story from Pleasure Bound.** unabr. ed. Susan Swann. Read by Roseanna Green et al. (Running Time: 1 hr.). (ENG.). 2010. 4.98 (978-1-60788-513-9(1)) Pub: Hachet Audio. Dist(s): HachBkGrp

***Bound for Punishment: Three Stories of Strict Discipline: Includes: Domia, with Kid Gloves, & Therapy from Pleasure Bound.** unabr. ed. Susan Swann. Read by Roseanna Green et al. (Running Time: 1 hr.). (ENG.). 2010. 4.98 (978-1-60788-515-3(8)) Pub: Hachet Audio. Dist(s): HachBkGrp

***Bound for Sin: Three Stories of Wicked Temptation: Includes Succubus, Wet Nurse, & Charity Begins from Pleasure Bound.** unabr. ed. Susan Swann. Read by Priscilla Carson et al. (Running Time: 1 hr.). (ENG.). 2010. 4.98 (978-1-60788-514-6(X)) Pub: Hachet Audio. Dist(s): HachBkGrp

Bound for Vietnam. unabr. ed. Lydia Laube. Read by Deidre Rubenstein. 6 cass. (Running Time: 9 hrs.). 1999. (978-1-876584-29-0(7), 590789) Bolinda Pubng AUS.
A chance conversation on the Trans Siberian Express en route to Outer Mongolia causes Lydia Laube to veer off course & take a long way home. She heads south thousands of kilometers to the eerie mountains of South China, in search of a broachable pass into Vietnam. Lydia never takes no for an answer. Against all protests she finds ways to venture through rarely travelled parts of China, overcoming language barriers & standing her ground in crowded buses, boats & trains. She makes a meal of snake & submits to the ministrations of the Dental Department of your worst nightmare.

Bound Man: Why We Are Excited about Obama & Why He Can't Win. unabr. ed. Shelby Steele. Read by Richard Allen. 3 CDs. (Running Time: 3 hrs. 30 mins. 0 sec.). (ENG.). 2008. audio compact disk 19.99 (978-1-4001-0603-5(6)); audio compact disk 19.99 (978-1-4001-5603-0(3)); audio compact disk 39.99 (978-1-4001-3603-2(2)) Pub: Tantor Media. Dist(s): IngramPubServ

***Bound to Obey: Three Stories of Domination: Includes: Seven Year Itch, the Huntress, & Peep Show from Pleasure Bound.** unabr. ed. Susan Swann. Read by Priscilla Carson et al. (Running Time: 1 hr.). (ENG.). 2010. 4.98 (978-1-60788-516-0(6)) Pub: Hachet Audio. Dist(s): HachBkGrp

Boundaries. Pia Mellody. Read by Pia Mellody. 2 cass. 24.00 Set. (A6) Featuka Enter Inc.
Defines & discusses the nature of boundaries including their purpose, composition & how they function.

Boundaries: And Other Poems. Poems. Jeff Daniel Marion. Read by Jeff Daniel Marion. 1 cass. (Running Time: 48 mins.). 1996. 10.00 (978-0-916078-12-6(4), Iris) Iris Pub Group.
Appalachian poetry read by the poet.

Boundaries: When to Say Yes, How to Say No. abr. ed. Henry Cloud & John Townsend. (Running Time: 2 hrs. 0 mins. 0 sec.). (ENG.). 2003. 10.99 (978-0-310-26005-9(1)) Zondervan.

Boundaries: When to Say Yes, How to Say No. unabr. ed. Henry Cloud & John Townsend. (Running Time: 11 hrs. 40 mins. 0 sec.). (ENG.). 2001. audio compact disk 29.99 (978-0-310-24180-5(4)) Zondervan.

Boundaries: When to Say Yes, How to Say No. unabr. ed. Henry Cloud & John Townsend. (Running Time: 11 hrs. 40 mins. 0 sec.). (ENG.). 2003. 14.99 (978-0-310-26137-7(6)) Zondervan.

Boundaries: When to Say Yes When to Say No to Take Control of Your Life. unabr. ed. Henry Cloud & John Townsend. 1 cass. 1992. 17.99 (978-0-310-58598-5(8)) Zondervan.

***Boundaries at Work: When to Say Yes, How to Say No to Take Control of Your Work Life.** Henry Cloud. (ENG.). 2010. 16.99 (978-0-310-58694-4(1)) Zondervan.

***Boundaries in Dating: How Healthy Choices Grow Healthy Relationships.** unabr. ed. Henry Cloud & John Townsend. (Running Time: 8 hrs. 9 mins. 0 sec.). (ENG.). 2009. 14.99 (978-0-310-77132-6(3)) Zondervan.

Boundaries in Dating: Making Dating Work. abr. ed. Henry Cloud & John Townsend. (Running Time: 2 hrs. 0 mins. 0 sec.). (ENG.). 2003. 12.99 (978-0-310-26007-3(8)) Zondervan.

Boundaries in Dating: Making Dating Work. abr. ed. Henry Cloud et al. Read by Henry Cloud & John Townsend. (Running Time: 3 hrs. 0 mins. 0 sec.). (ENG.). 2006. audio compact disk 19.99 (978-0-310-27078-2(2)) Zondervan.

Boundaries in Marriage. Henry Cloud & John Townsend. 2006. audio compact disk 19.99 (978-0-310-27082-9(0)) Zondervan.

Boundaries in Marriage. Henry Cloud et al. Read by Dick Fredricks. (Running Time: 8 hrs. 0 mins. 0 sec.). (ENG.). (gr. 13). 2006. audio compact disk 24.99 (978-0-310-27083-6(9)) Zondervan.

Boundaries in Marriage. abr. ed. Henry Cloud & John Townsend. (Running Time: 3 hrs. 0 mins. 0 sec.). (ENG.). 2003. 10.99 (978-0-310-26008-0(6)) Zondervan.

Boundaries in Marriage. unabr. ed. Henry Cloud & John Townsend. (Running Time: 8 hrs. 0 mins. 0 sec.). (ENG.). 2003. 14.99 (978-0-310-26138-4(4)) Zondervan.

Boundaries with Kids: When to Say Yes, How to Say No. abr. ed. Henry Cloud & John Townsend. (Running Time: 3 hrs. 0 mins. 0 sec.). (ENG.). 2003. 12.99 (978-0-310-26009-7(4)) Zondervan.

Boundaries with Kids: When to Say Yes, When to Say No, to Help Your Children Gain Control of Their Lives. abr. ed. Henry Cloud et al. (Running Time: 3 hrs. 0 mins. 0 sec.). (ENG.). 2006. audio compact disk 19.99 (978-0-310-27079-9(0)) Zondervan.

Boundaries with Teens: When to Say Yes, How to Say No. unabr. ed. John Townsend. (Running Time: 8 hrs. 20 mins. 0 sec.). (ENG.). 2006. 14.99 (978-0-310-26907-6(5)) Zondervan.

Boundary Law in Pennsylvania. (Running Time: 4 hrs.). 1999. bk. 99.00 (ACS-2230) PA Bar Inst.
"Good fences make good neighbors," except when the fence is on the wrong side of the property line. Boundary disputes involving common walls, driveways, outbuildings, plantings, roads, & streams are all too common for the real estate & general practitioner. Despite the frequency of these emotionally charged cases, there are few good sources to which lawyers can turn for guidance.

Boundless Grace. unabr. ed. Mary Hoffman. Narrated by Andrea Johnson. 1 cass. (Running Time: 1 hr.). (J). 2001. pap. bk. & stu. ed. 32.99 Recorded Bks.
Grace lives with her mother & Nana. When her father sends her a ticket to visit him & his "perfect" new family in Africa, she is confused about her place in all this.

Boundless Grace. unabr. ed. Mary Hoffman. Narrated by Andrea Johnson. 1 cass. (Running Time: 15 mins.). (gr. 1 up). 2001. 10.00 (978-0-7887-4717-5(7), 96391E7) Recorded Bks.

Boundless Joy: OZO. Eldon Taylor. Read by Eldon Taylor. Ed. by Leslie Brice. 1 cass. (Running Time: 1 hr.). 1992. 19.95 (978-1-56705-011-0(5)) Gateways Inst.
Self improvement.

Boundless Love: Devotions to Celebrate God's Love for You. abr. ed. Thelma Wells et al. (Running Time: 2 hrs. 0 mins. 0 sec.). (ENG.). 2003. 12.99 (978-0-310-26011-0(6)) Zondervan.

Boundless Love: Devotions to Celebrate God's Love for You. unabr. ed. Patsy Clairmont et al. 2001. 17.99 (978-0-310-23572-9(3)) Zondervan.

Bountiful Earth. 1 CD. (Running Time: 28 min.). (J). 2005. audio compact disk 14.95 (978-0-9765887-7-1(3)) S Edu Res LLC.

Bounty Hunter. H. A. De Rosso. (Running Time: 1 hr. 54 mins.). 2000. 10.95 (978-1-60083-534-6(1)) Iofy Corp.

***Bounty Hunter.** H. A. DeRosso. 2009. (978-1-60136-405-0(9)) Audio Holding.

Bounty Hunter 2000. D'Andre Collins & Samuel M. A. Johnson. 2 cass. (Running Time: 60 min. per cass.). 1997. 89.95 (978-0-9636273-3-9(3)) ICR Pub.

***Bounty Hunters.** unabr. ed. Elmore Leonard. Read by Josh Clark. (ENG.). 2010. (978-0-06-199365-7(4), Harper Audio); (978-0-06-199747-1(1), Harper Audio) HarperCollins Pubs.

Bounty Man. abr. ed. Matthew S. Hart. Read by Charlton Griffin. Abr. by Edward McClure. 2 vols. No. 4. 2003. 18.00 (978-1-58807-246-7(0)); (978-1-58807-741-7(1)) Am Pubng Inc.

Bounty Mutiny: What Really Happened (audio CD) Ian Ball & Harry Shapiro. Interview with Heywood Hale Broun, Jr. (ENG.). 2007. audio compact disk 12.95 (978-1-57970-473-5(5), Audio-For) J Norton Pubs.

Bounty Trilogy Pt. 1: Mutiny on the Bounty. unabr. collector's ed. Charles Nordhoff & James Norman Hall. Read by Jonathan Reese. 8 cass. (Running Time: 12 hrs.). 1978. 64.00 (978-0-7366-0148-1(1), 1149-A) Books on Tape.
Retells the story of the mutiny aboard the English vessel Bounty on its return voyage from the South Seas in 1789.

Bounty Trilogy Pt. 2: Men Against the Sea & Pitcairn's Island. unabr. collector's ed. Charles Nordhoff & James Norman Hall. Read by Jonathan Reese. 11 cass. (Running Time: 16 hrs. 30 min.). 1978. 88.00 (978-0-7366-0149-8(X)) Books on Tape.
Parts two & three of the trilogy. Set adrift, Captain Bligh sailed 3600 miles. The mutineers remained aboard the "Bounty" & cast about for security. There was little respite for the crew.

Bouquet of Poison Ivy. (C23328) J Norton Pubs.

Bourgeois Gentilhomme. Molière. Contrib. by Arletty & Jacques Fabbri. 1 CD. (FRE.). 1991. audio compact disk 44.95 (1372-OH) Olivia & Hill.
Monsieur Joudain, a simple bourgeois, believes that one needs only to learn what gentlemen do (dancing, fencing, etc.) in order to become one.

Bourne Betrayal. abr. ed. Eric Lustbader. Read by Jeremy Davidson. (Running Time: 6 hrs.). (Bourne Ser.: Bk. 5). (ENG.). 2008. audio compact disk 14.98 (978-1-60024-280-9(4)) Pub: Hachet Audio. Dist(s): HachBkGrp

Bourne Betrayal. abr. ed. Eric Lustbader & Robert Ludlum. Read by Jeremy Davidson. (Running Time: 6 hrs.). (Bourne Ser.: Bk. 5). (ENG.). 2007. 14.98 (978-1-59483-917-7(4)) Pub: Hachet Audio. Dist(s): HachBkGrp

Bourne Betrayal. unabr. ed. Eric Lustbader & Robert Ludlum. Read by Jeremy Davidson. (Running Time: 18 hrs.). (Bourne Ser.: Bk. 5). (ENG.). 2007. 16.98 (978-1-59483-919-1(0)) Pub: Hachet Audio. Dist(s): HachBkGrp

Bourne Deception. abr. ed. Eric Lustbader & Robert Ludlum. Read by Jeremy H. Davidson. (Running Time: 6 hrs.). (Bourne Ser.: Bk. 7). (ENG.). 2009. 14.98 (978-1-60024-597-8(8)) Pub: Hachet Audio. Dist(s): HachBkGrp

Bourne Deception. abr. ed. Eric Lustbader & Robert Ludlum. Read by Jeremy Davidson. (Running Time: 6 hrs.). (Bourne Ser.: Bk. 7). 2010. audio compact disk 14.98 (978-1-60788-239-8(6)) Pub: Hachet Audio. Dist(s): HachBkGrp

Bourne Deception. unabr. ed. Eric Lustbader & Robert Ludlum. Narrated by Jeremy Davidson. 2 MP3-CDs. (Running Time: 14 hrs. 42 mins.). (Bourne Ser.: Bk. 7). 2009. 69.95 (978-0-7927-6488-5(9)); 112.95 (978-0-7927-6489-2(7)); audio compact disk 117.95 (978-0-7927-6367-3(X)) AudioGO.

Bourne Deception. unabr. ed. Eric Lustbader & Robert Ludlum. Read by Jeremy H. Davidson. (Running Time: 14 hrs. 45 mins.). (Bourne Ser.: Bk. 7). (ENG.). 2009. 32.98 (978-1-60024-600-5(1)); audio compact disk 49.98 (978-1-60024-599-2(4)) Pub: Hachet Audio. Dist(s): HachBkGrp

***Bourne Dominion.** abr. ed. Robert Ludlum & Eric Lustbader. (Running Time: 6 hrs.). 2011. 24.98 (978-1-60941-209-8(5)); audio compact disk & audio compact disk 29.98 (978-1-60941-208-1(7)) Pub: Hachet Audio. Dist(s): HachBkGrp

***Bourne Dominion.** unabr. ed. Robert Ludlum & Eric Lustbader. (Running Time: 14 hrs.). 2011. 29.98 (978-1-60941-215-9(X)); audio compact disk & audio compact disk 39.98 (978-1-60941-214-2(1)) Pub: Hachet Audio. Dist(s): HachBkGrp

Bourne Identity, Pts. 1 & 2. unabr. collector's ed. Robert Ludlum. Read by Michael Prichard. 13 cass. (Running Time: 19 hrs. 30 min.). Incl. Pt. I. Bourne Identity. 8 cass. (Running Time: 8 hrs.). Robert Ludlum. Read by Michael Prichard. (Bourne Ser.: Bk. 1). 1983. 64.00 (1760-A); Pt. II. Bourne Identity. 6 cass. (Running Time: 6 hrs.). Robert Ludlum. Read by Michael Prichard. (Bourne Ser.: Bk. 1). 1983. 48.00 (1760-B); (Bourne Ser.: Bk. 1). 1983. 104.00 (978-0-7366-0809-1(5), 1760) Books on Tape.
A man is shot, left for dead, but later rescued from the sea. Surviving, but with no memory, he is given a name: Jason Bourne. Physically & mentally agile, he retraces his past through a harrowing personal labyrinth. The discovery: he was a trained killer, & now in turn is being hunted by assassins.

Bourne Legacy. abr. ed. Eric Lustbader & Robert Ludlum. Read by Scott Brick. 5 CDs. (Running Time: 6 hrs. 0 mins. 0 sec.). Bk. 4. (ENG.). 2008. audio compact disk 14.95 (978-1-4272-0487-5(X)) Pub: Macmill Audio. Dist(s): Macmillan

Bourne Legacy. abr. rev. ed. Eric Lustbader & Robert Ludlum. Read by Scott Brick & Scott Sowers. 5 CDs. (Running Time: 6 hrs. 0 mins. 0 sec.). Bk. 4. (ENG.). 2004. audio compact disk 29.95 (978-1-59397-512-8(0)) Pub: Macmill Audio. Dist(s): Macmillan

Bourne Legacy. unabr. ed. Eric Lustbader & Robert Ludlum. Read by Scott Brick. 13 cass. (Running Time: 19 hr.s 30 mins.). (Bourne Ser.: Bk. 4). 2004. 90.00 (978-1-4159-0409-1(X)) Books on Tape.

Bourne Legacy. unabr. rev. ed. Eric Lustbader & Robert Ludlum. Read by Scott Brick & Scott Sowers. 14 CDs. (Running Time: 18 hrs. 0 mins. 0 sec.). Bk. 4. (ENG.). 2004. audio compact disk 49.95 (978-1-59397-514-2(7)) Pub: Macmill Audio. Dist(s): Macmillan

***Bourne Objective.** Eric Lustbader. Read by Scott Sowers. (Running Time: 6 hrs.). 2011. audio compact disk 14.98 (978-1-61113-816-0(7)) Pub: Hachet Audio. Dist(s): HachBkGrp

Bourne Objective. abr. ed. Eric Lustbader & Robert Ludlum. Read by Jeremy Davidson & Scott Sowers. (Running Time: 6 hrs.). (Bourne Ser.: Bk. 8). 2010. 19.98 (978-1-60788-225-1(6)); audio compact disk 29.98 (978-1-60788-224-4(8)) Pub: Hachet Audio. Dist(s): HachBkGrp

***Bourne Objective.** unabr. ed. Eric Lustbader. Narrated by Scott Sowers. 2 MP3-CDs. (Running Time: 14 hrs. 23 mins.). 2010. 79.99 (978-1-60788-537-5(9)) Pub: Hachet Audio. Dist(s): HachBkGrp

***Bourne Objective.** unabr. ed. Eric Lustbader & Robert Ludlum. Narrated by Scott Sowers. 12 CDs. (Running Time: 14 hrs. 23 mins.). 2010. audio compact disk 119.99 (978-1-60788-536-8(0)) Pub: Hachet Audio. Dist(s): HachBkGrp

Bourne Objective. unabr. ed. Eric Lustbader & Robert Ludlum. Read by Jeremy Davidson & Scott Sowers. (Running Time: 14 hrs. 30 mins.). (Bourne Ser.: Bk. 8). 2010. 32.98 (978-1-60788-227-5(2)); audio compact disk 49.98 (978-1-60788-226-8(4)) Pub: Hachet Audio. Dist(s): HachBkGrp

Bourne Sanction. abr. ed. Eric Lustbader & Robert Ludlum. Read by Jeremy Davidson. (Running Time: 6 hrs.). (Bourne Ser.: Bk. 6). (ENG.). 2009. audio compact disk 14.98 (978-1-60024-587-9(0)) Pub: Hachet Audio. Dist(s): HachBkGrp

Bourne Sanction. abr. ed. Eric Lustbader & Ludlum Robert. Read by Jeremy Davidson. (Running Time: 6 hrs.). (Bourne Ser.: Bk. 6). (ENG.). 2008. 14.98 (978-1-60024-295-3(2)) Pub: Hachet Audio. Dist(s): HachBkGrp

Bourne Sanction. unabr. ed. Eric Lustbader & Robert Ludlum. Read by Jeremy Davidson. 15 CDs. (Running Time: 18 hrs.). Bk. 6. (ENG.). 2008. audio compact disk 49.98 (978-1-60024-296-0(0)) Pub: Hachet Audio. Dist(s): HachBkGrp

Bourne Sanction. unabr. ed. Eric Lustbader & Ludlum Robert. Read by Jeremy Davidson. (Running Time: 18 hrs.). (Bourne Ser.: Bk. 6). (ENG.). 2008. 32.98 (978-1-60024-297-7(9)) Pub: Hachet Audio. Dist(s): HachBkGrp

Bourne Supremacy, Pt. 1. unabr. collector's ed. Robert Ludlum. Read by Michael Prichard. 9 cass. (Running Time: 13 hrs. 30 min.). (Bourne Ser.: Bk. 2). 1986. 72.00 (978-0-7366-0867-1(2), 1818-A) Books on Tape.
David Webb is an ordinary citizen living in a small university town... except he is under 24 hour personal surveillance. His memory is gone, but with his wife's care, his past is on the mend. Suddenly it returns, but not at his volition. From Hong Kong comes word that the assassin has struck again, that Bourne is back! But the U.S. government knows he never existed. Webb only posed as Bourne to unearth a notorious killer. Yet someone is killing again in Bourne's name... & he must be stopped or stability in the Far East will crumble. The decision is made-Jason Bourne must exist again & hunt his own imposter.

Bourne Supremacy, Pt. 2. unabr. collector's ed. Robert Ludlum. Read by Michael Prichard. 8 cass. (Running Time: 12 hrs.). (Bourne Ser.: Bk. 2). 1986. 64.00 (978-0-7366-0868-8(0), 1818-B) Books on Tape.

Bourne Ultimatum. abr. ed. Robert Ludlum. Read by Darren McGaven. (Playaway Adult Fiction Ser.). 2008. 54.99 (978-1-60640-573-4(X)) Find a World.

Bourne Ultimatum. abr. ed. Robert Ludlum. Read by Darren McGavin. 3 CDs. (Running Time: 12600 sec.). (Bourne Ser.: Bk. 3). (ENG.). 2007. audio compact disk 18.00 (978-0-7393-4299-2(1), Random AudioBks) Pub: Random Audio Pubg. Dist(s): Random

Bourne Ultimatum, Pt. 1. unabr. collector's ed. Robert Ludlum. Read by Michael Prichard. 8 cass. (Running Time: 12 hrs.). (Bourne Ser.: Bk. 3). 1990. 64.00 (978-0-7366-1702-4(7), 2547A) Books on Tape.
Summoned by telegrams signed Jason Bourne, two men who share the secret of Bourne's real identity witness a bizarre killing. They recognize the work of Carlos, known as the Jackal, the elusive terrorist. The murder is a signal from Carlos - he seeks a final confrontation with Bourne. David Webb must do what he hoped not to do again. He assumed the identity of Bourne, the deadly alter ego created in the jungles of Vietnam & the streets of Saigon years ago. He must confront the stalking Jackal, outsmart & destroy him. Bristling with high-voltage excitement on every page, The Bourne Ultimatum is Ludlum's greatest thriller so far, it engages the reader with mounting suspense as the deadly antagonists circle each other in a confrontation that must end in a fatal decision.

Bourne Ultimatum, Pt. 2. unabr. collector's ed. Robert Ludlum. Read by Michael Prichard. 8 cass. (Running Time: 12 hrs.). (Bourne Ser.: Bk. 3). 1990. 64.00 (978-0-7366-1703-1(5), 2547B) Books on Tape.

Bout My People. unabr. ed. Beverly A. Davis. 1 cass. (J). (gr. k-3). 1995. 8.00 B A Davis.
Poems & songs for children.

***Bow Down.** Created by Lillenas Publishing Company. (ENG.). 2008. audio compact disk 12.00 (978-5-557-38507-7(X)) Lillenas.

Bow Down. Perf. by True II Society. 1 cass. 1997. audio compact disk 15.99 CD. (D7521) Diamante Music Grp.
Their music portrays life from a Christian point of view & is geared toward teenagers who face problems with violence, gangs & drugs. The group is complete with singers, dancers, rappers & drama.

Bow Window Caper & Edith Hamilton. Perf. by Howard Duff. 1 cass. (Running Time: 60 min.). Dramatization. (Adventures of Sam Spade Ser.). 1949. 6.00 Once Upon Rad.
Radio broadcasts - mystery & suspense.

Bow Wow Baby. unabr. ed. Dennis Caraher. 1 cass. (Running Time: 40 min.). (J). (ps-4). 1991. 9.98 (978-0-9649933-2-7(5)) Mud Pie Prods.
Original songs for children ages 2-10.

Bowdrie Passes Through; Where Buzzards Fly; No Man's Man. unabr. ed. Louis L'Amour. Read by Dramatization Staff. (Running Time: 10800 sec.). (ENG.). 2008. audio compact disk 14.99 (978-0-7393-5885-6(5), Random AudioBks) Pub: Random Audio Pubg. Dist(s): Random

Bowie: The Unauthorised Biography of David Bowie. Ben Graham. (Maximum Ser.). (ENG.). 2001. audio compact disk 14.95 (978-1-84240-120-0(3)) Pub: Chrome Dreams GBR. Dist(s): IPG Chicago

Bowl of Cherries. unabr. ed. Millard Kaufman. (Running Time: 10 hrs. 0 mins.). 2008. 26.95 (978-1-4332-1526-1(8)); audio compact disk 26.95 (978-1-4332-1527-8(6)) Blckstn Audio.

Bowl of Cherries. unabr. ed. Millard Kaufman. Read by Bronson Pinchot. (Running Time: 11 hrs. 0 mins.). 2008. 29.95 (978-1-4332-1528-5(4)); 65.95 (978-1-4332-1524-7(1)); audio compact disk 90.00 (978-1-4332-1525-4(X)) Blckstn Audio.

Bowling. 1 cass. (Running Time: 60 min.). 10.95 (SP2) Psych Res Inst.
Mental sports conditioning.

Bowling. Eldon Taylor. 1 cass. (Running Time: 62 min.). (Inner Talk Ser.). 16.95 incl. script. (978-1-55978-190-9(4), 53803C) Progress Aware Res.
Soundtrack - Musical Themes with underlying subliminal affirmations.

Bowling: Babbling Brook. Eldon Taylor. 1 cass. 16.95 (978-1-55978-519-8(5), 53803F) Progress Aware Res.

Bowling: Rhythm. Eldon Taylor. Read by Eldon Taylor. Ed. by Leslie Brice. 1 cass. (Running Time: 1 hr.). 1992. 16.95 (978-1-56705-244-2(4)) Gateways Inst.
Self improvement.

Bowling: Stream. Eldon Taylor. Read by Eldon Taylor. Ed. by Leslie Brice. 1 cass. (Running Time: 1 hr.). 1992. 16.95 (978-1-56705-245-9(2)) Gateways Inst.

Bowling - Improve & Win. Norman J. Caldwell. Read by Norman J. Caldwell. Ed. by Achieve Now Institute Staff. 1 cass. (Running Time: 20 min.). (Sports Achievement Ser.). 1988. 9.97 (978-1-56273-085-7(1)) My Mothers Pub.
Your ball goes where you direct it from concentration.

Bowmaker Girls. unabr. ed. Margaret Yorke. Read by Elizabeth Proud. 12 cass. (Running Time: 18 hrs.). 2001. 94.95 (978-0-7531-1006-5(7), 001114) Pub: ISIS Audio GBR. Dist(s): Ulverscroft US
Lydia Cunningham, a respectable, solitary widow, knows she's in for trouble when her restless, twice married daughter, Thelma, returns home. Thelma has brought with her, a young man with an unsavory past, who quickly sets about ingratiating himself with Lydia. But it is Lydia's own past that finally overtakes her, sending her headlong to the very edge of sanity.

Bowmaker Girls. unabr. ed. Margaret Yorke. Read by Josephine Tewson. 9 CDs. (Running Time: 9 hrs. 18 mins.). (Isis Ser.). (J). 2002. audio compact disk 84.95 (978-0-7531-1203-8(5)) Pub: ISIS Lrg Prnt GBR. Dist(s): Ulverscroft US

Bowmar Orchestral Library. Ed. by Lucille Wood. (Bowmar Orchestral Library Ser.). (ENG.). 1994. audio compact disk 189.00 (978-0-89898-775-1(X), Warner Bro) Alfred Pub.

***Box: Tales from the Dark Room.** unabr. ed. Günter Grass. (Running Time: 7 hrs.). 2010. 29.95 (978-1-4417-6586-4(7)); 44.95 (978-1-4417-6583-3(2)); audio compact disk 69.00 (978-1-4417-6584-0(0)); audio compact disk 29.95 (978-1-4417-6585-7(9)) Blckstn Audio.

Box: You Are the Experiment. unabr. ed. Richard Matheson. Read by Grover Gardner. 4 CDs. (Running Time: 5 hrs. 0 mins. 0 sec.). (ENG.). 2009. audio compact disk 24.99 (978-1-4272-0561-2(2)) Pub: Macmill Audio. Dist(s): Macmillan

Box-Free Living. 2001. 8.95 (978-1-930514-16-4(6), BFL) Diana Waring.

***Box of Darkness: The Story of a Marriage.** unabr. ed. Sally Ryder Brady. (Running Time: 7 hrs. 0 mins.). 2011. 14.99 (978-1-4526-7056-0(0)); 19.99 (978-1-4526-5056-2(X)); audio compact disk 29.99 (978-1-4526-0056-7(2)) Pub: Tantor Media. Dist(s): IngramPubServ

***Box of Darkness (Library Edition) The Story of a Marriage.** unabr. ed. Sally Ryder Brady. (Running Time: 7 hrs. 0 mins.). 2011. 29.99 (978-1-4526-2056-5(3)); audio compact disk 71.99 (978-1-4526-3056-4(9)) Pub: Tantor Media. Dist(s): IngramPubServ

Box of Tricks. unabr. ed. Simon Brett. Narrated by Simon Brett. 4 cass. (Running Time: 5 hrs.). 2000. 40.00 (978-1-84197-156-8(1), H1150E7) Recorded Bks.
The collection runs the theme of murder in its many guises, With a cast of characters who plot sometimes for gain, sometimes for revenge.

Box Socials. unabr. ed. W. P. Kinsella. Read by Tom Parker. 4 cass. (Running Time: 5 hrs. 30 mins.). 1994. 32.95 (978-0-7861-0784-1(7), 1427) Blckstn Audio.
Here's the story of how "Truckbox" Al McClintock, a small-town greaser whose claim to fame was hitting a baseball clean across the Pembina River,

almost got a tryout with the genuine St. Louis Cardinals - but instead ended up batting against Bob Feller of Cleveland Indian fame in Renfrew Park, Edmonton, Alberta.

***Box Thirteen.** RadioArchives.com. (Running Time: 600). (ENG.). 2007. audio compact disk 29.98 (978-1-61081-060-9(0)) Radio Arch.

***Box Turtle at Silver Pond Lane.** Susan Korman. Illus. by Stephen Marchesi. (Smithsonian's Backyard Ser.). (ENG.). (J). 2009. bk. 24.95 (978-1-59249-825-3(6)) Soundprints.

Box Turtle at Silver Pond Lane. Susan Korman. Illus. by Stephan Marchesi. (Smithsonian's Backyard Ser.). (ENG.). (J). (ps-2). 2005. 8.95 (978-1-59249-065-3(4), SC5020) Soundprints.

Box 13, Vol. 1. collector's ed. Perf. by Alan Ladd. 6 cass. (Running Time: 9 hrs.). 1998. bk. 34.98 (4129) Radio Spirits.
1948-1949 detective adventure series in which mystery novel writer Dan Holiday seeks material for his books by running an ad that reads "Adventure wanted: will go anywhere, do anything - Box 13." 18 episodes.

Box 13, Vol. 2. collector's ed. Perf. by Alan Ladd. 6 cass. (Running Time: 9 hrs.). 2000. bk. 34.98 (4202) Radio Spirits.
Detective adventure series in which mystery novel writer, Dan Holiday seeks material for his books by running an ad that reads "Adventure wanted: will go anywhere, do anything - Box 13." 18 episodes.

Box 13: Death Is a Doll & Triple Cross. unabr. ed. Perf. by Alan Ladd. 1 cass. (Running Time: 1 hr.). 2001. 6.98 (1613) Radio Spirits.

Box 13: Delinquent's Dilemma & the Biter Bitten. unabr. ed. Perf. by Alan Ladd. 1 cass. (Running Time: 1 hr.). 2001. 6.98 (1923) Radio Spirits.

Box 13: One, One, Three, Point Five & Dan & the Wonderful Lamp. unabr. ed. Perf. by Alan Ladd. 1 cass. (Running Time: 1 hr.). 2001. 6.98 (1614) Radio Spirits.

Box 13: The Dead Man Walks & Killer at Large. unabr. ed. Perf. by Alan Ladd. 1 cass. (Running Time: 1 hr.). 2001. 6.98 (2005) Radio Spirits.

Box 13: The Perfect Crime & Archimedes & the Romans. unabr. ed. Perf. by Alan Ladd. 1 cass. (Running Time: 1 hr.). 2001. 6.98 (2454) Radio Spirits.

Boxcar Children. Gertrude Chandler Warner. Read by Phyllis Newman. 2 cass. (Running Time: 2 hrs.). (Boxcar Children Ser.: No. 1). (J). (gr. 2-5). 2000. 18.00 (978-0-7366-9109-3(X)) Books on Tape.

Boxcar Children. unabr. ed. Gertrude Chandler Warner. Read by Phyllis Newman. 2 cass. (Running Time: 2 hrs.). (Boxcar Children Ser.: No. 1). (J). (gr. 2-5). 1997. 23.00 (LL 0009, Chivers Child Audio) AudioGO.
Henry, Jessie, Violet & Benny, four orphaned brothers & sisters, suddenly appear in a small town. No one knows who these young wanderers are or where they have come from. Frightened to live with a grandfather they have never met, the children make a home for themselves in an abandoned red boxcar they discover in the woods. Henry, the oldest, goes to town to earn money & buy food & supplies.

Boxcar Children. unabr. ed. Gertrude Chandler Warner. Read by Phyllis Newman. 2 vols. (Running Time: 1 hr. 58 mins.). (Boxcar Children Ser.: No. 1). (J). (gr. 3-7). 1991. pap. bk. 29.00 (978-0-8072-7332-6(5), YA 830SP, Listening Lib); 23.00 (978-0-8072-7331-9(7), YA 830CX, Listening Lib) Random Audio Pubg.
Henry, Violet, Jessie & Benny Alden are orphans who face every challenge with perseverance & courage.

Boxcar Children. unabr. ed. Gertrude Chandler Warner. Read by Phyllis Newman. 2 CDs. (Running Time: 7080 sec.). (Boxcar Children Ser.: No. 1). (ENG.). (J). (gr. 1). 2006. audio compact disk 12.95 (978-0-307-28404-4(2), Listening Lib) Pub: Random Audio Pubg. Dist(s): Random

Boxcar Children, Vol. 3. unabr. ed. Gertrude Chandler Warner. Narrated by Aimee Lilly. (Running Time: 36000 sec.). (Boxcar Children Ser.). (ENG.). (J). 2007. audio compact disk 29.99 (978-1-59859-257-3(2)) Oasis Audio.

Boxcar Children: The Chocolate Sundae Mystery. unabr. ed. Gertrude Chandler Warner. Read by Aimee Lilly. (J). 2007. 34.99 (978-1-60252-671-6(0)) Find a World.

Boxcar Children: The Ghost Ship Mystery. unabr. ed. Gertrude Chandler Warner. Read by Aimee Lilly. (J). 2007. 34.99 (978-1-60252-672-3(9)) Find a World.

Boxcar Children: The Hockey Mystery. unabr. ed. Gertrude Chandler Warner. Read by Aimee Lilly. (J). 2007. 34.99 (978-1-60252-745-4(8)) Find a World.

Boxcar Children: The Mystery in the Fortune Cookie. unabr. ed. Gertrude Chandler Warner. Read by Aimee Lilly. (J). 2007. 34.99 (978-1-60252-879-6(9)) Find a World.

Boxcar Children: The Mystery of the Mummy's Curse. unabr. ed. Gertrude Chandler Warner. Read by Aimee Lilly. (J). 2007. 34.99 (978-1-60252-673-0(7)) Find a World.

Boxcar Children: The Mystery of the Star Ruby. unabr. ed. Gertrude Chandler Warner. Read by Aimee Lilly. (J). 2007. 34.99 (978-1-60252-823-9(3)) Find a World.

Boxcar Children: The Mystery on Blizzard Mountain. unabr. ed. Gertrude Chandler Warner. Read by Aimee Lilly. (J). 2007. 34.99 (978-1-60252-880-2(2)) Find a World.

Boxcar Children: The Pizza Mystery. unabr. ed. Gertrude Chandler Warner. Read by Aimee Lilly. (J). 2007. 34.99 (978-1-60252-881-9(0)) Find a World.

Boxcar Children: The Radio Mystery. unabr. ed. Gertrude Chandler Warner. Read by Aimee Lilly. (J). 2007. 34.99 (978-1-60252-882-6(9)) Find a World.

Boxcar Children: The Summer Camp Mystery. unabr. ed. Gertrude Chandler Warner. Read by Aimee Lilly. (J). 2007. 34.99 (978-1-60252-674-7(5)) Find a World.

Boxcar Children Collection, Vol. 2. unabr. ed. Gertrude Chandler Warner. Narrated by Aimee Lilly. (Running Time: 36000 sec.). (Boxcar Children Ser.). (ENG.). (J). 2007. audio compact disk 29.99 (978-1-59859-256-6(4)) Oasis Audio.

Boxcar Children Mysteries, Vol. 1. unabr. ed. Gertrude Chandler Warner. Read by Phyllis Newman. 7 cass. (Running Time: 7 hrs.). (Boxcar Children Ser.). (J). (gr. 2-5). 1996. 34.00 (978-0-7366-3508-0(4), 4147) Books on Tape.
In "Mystery Ranch" the Alden children visit their great aunt at her ranch out West to cheer her up. What they don't expect is that they're soon unraveling an intriguing mystery. In "Mike's Mystery" a friend the children make at their great aunt's ranch, stands accused of starting a fire in a nearby town. It's up to the children to find the real culprit. In "The Lighthouse Mystery" the children take notice when strange things happen at a lighthouse near Grandpa Alden's house. They'll encounter still more puzzles before they solve the mystery.

Boxcar Children Mysteries, Vol. 2. unabr. ed. Gertrude Chandler Warner. Read by Phyllis Newman. 6 cass. (Running Time: 6 hrs.). (Boxcar Children Ser.). (J). (gr. 2-5). 1996. 30.00 (978-0-7366-3509-7(2), 4148) Books on Tape.
The Alden children - Henry, Violet, Jessie & Bessie - find themselves orphaned & alone, so they make an abandoned boxcar their home. Here they learn to surmount every obstacle with perserverance & pluck.

Boxcar Childrens: The Mystery in the Computer Game. unabr. ed. Gertrude Chandler Warner. Read by Aimee Lilly. (J). 2007. 34.99 (978-1-60252-746-1(6)) Find a World.

***Boxer & the Spy.** unabr. ed. Robert B. Parker. Read by Scott Brick. 4 CDs. (Running Time: 4 hrs. 12 mins.). (YA). (gr. 9 up). 2009. audio compact disk 38.00 (978-0-7393-7304-0(8), Listening Lib) Pub: Random Audio Pubg. Dist(s): Random

Boxer & the Spy. unabr. ed. Robert B. Parker. Read by Scott Brick. (ENG.). (J). (gr. 6). 2009. audio compact disk 28.00 (978-0-7393-7302-6(1), Listening Lib) Pub: Random Audio Pubg. Dist(s): Random

Boxes & Bags see Carl Sandburg's Poems for Children

Boxful of Fun. abr. ed. Nina Mattikow. Perf. by Purple Balloon Players. 3 cass. (Running Time: 3 hrs.). (Triple Packs Ser.). (J). 11.95 Set. (978-1-55569-533-0(7), 23003) Great Am Audio.
Jokes & riddles, stories & sing-alongs guaranteed to keep children giggling, singing & listening during quiet or active playtime.

Boy. abr. ed. Roald Dahl. Read by Andrew Sachs. 3 CDs. (Running Time: 4 hrs. 30 mins.). 2003. audio compact disk 39.95 (978-0-7540-5556-3(6), CCD 247) AudioGO.

Boy. unabr. ed. Roald Dahl. Read by Andrew Sachs. 3 cass. (Running Time: 4 hrs. 30 mins.). 2000. 29.95 (978-0-7540-0550-6(X), CAB 1973) Pub: Chivers Audio Bks GBR. Dist(s): AudioGO
Into his description of an enchanted boyhood spent in Wales & Norway, counterpointed with his cruel, often barbaric experience at an English public school, he weaves a sparkling thread of reminiscence filled with wit, high spirits & more than a touch of the macabre.

***Boy.** unabr. ed. Roald Dahl. Read by Derek Jacobi. (ENG.). 2005. (978-0-06-088650-9(1)); (978-0-06-088649-3(8)) HarperCollins Pubs.

Boy, an Old Man & a Buck. abr. ed. Read by Richard Cassell. 1 cass. (Running Time: 1 hr.). (Outdoor Life; Classic Stories of the Great Outdoors Ser.: Vol. 3). 1998. 9.95 (978-1-886463-44-8(1)) Oasis Audio.
When an old-timer gives a young boy a chance to prove himself among a seasoned group of hunters, honors & respect span the generations.

***Boy & His Bot.** unabr. ed. Daniel H. Wilson. Read by David Ackroyd. (ENG.). (J). 2011. audio compact disk 28.00 (978-0-307-91523-8(9), Listening Lib) Pub: Random Audio Pubg. Dist(s): Random

Boy & the Samurai, unabr. ed. Erik Christian Haugaard. Narrated by George Guidall. 5 pieces. (Running Time: 7 hrs.). (gr. 7 up). 2001. 44.00 (978-1-55690-780-7(X), 93135E7) Recorded Bks.
This colorful, adventurous tale is a great way to introduce young listeners to the culture & history of Japan. A street urchin & a Samurai warrior take on a mighty warlord in this tale set in feudal Japan.

***Boy Audio-mp3 Book.** Sherry J. Campbell. 2010. 9.95 (978-1-4507-1285-9(1)) Indep Pub IL.

Boy Bands Have Won. Chumbawamba & Chumbawamba. (Running Time: 0 hr. 49 mins. 0 sec.). (PM Audio Ser.). (ENG.). 2008. audio compact disk 14.99 (978-1-60486-027-6(8)) Pub: Pm Pre. Dist(s): IPG Chicago

Boy Blue's Book of Beasts see Twentieth-Century Poetry in English, No. 31, Recordings of Poets Reading Their Own Poetry: William Jay Smith Reading His Poems for Children

Boy Clinton, unabr. ed. Emmett R. Tyrrell, Jr. Read by Jeff Riggenbach. 8 cass. (Running Time: 11 hrs. 30 mins.). 1998. audio compact disk 56.95 (978-0-7861-1086-5(4), 1857) Blckstn Audio.
Traces the informative influences on the young, fatherless Clinton. Shows how the influence-peddlers who dominated Arkansas politics served as Clinton's real political model. Reports dozens of fresh revelations about both Bill & Hillary Clinton & sheds important new light on their activities in Arkansas & Washington. This portrait of Clinton is far from flattering, but, sadly, it is true to life.

Boy Clinton: The Political Biography. unabr. ed. R. Emmett Tyrrell, Jr. Read by Jeff Riggenbach. (Running Time: 11 hrs. 50 mins.). (ENG.). 2009. 29.95 (978-1-4417-0298-2(9)); audio compact disk 100.00 (978-1-4417-0295-1(4)) Blckstn Audio.

Boy Detective Vol. 1: The Case of the Secret Pitch. unabr. ed. Donald J. Sobol. Read by Jason Harris. (Running Time: 2 hrs. 15 mins.). (Encyclopedia Brown Ser.: Nos. 1-2). (ENG.). (J). 2003. audio compact disk 19.99 (978-0-8072-1874-7(X), ImaginStudio) Pub: Random Audio Pubg. Dist(s): Random

Boy in Hob-Nailed Boots. unabr. ed. Edward Prynn & Steve Hodson. 3 cass. (Isis Ser.). (J). 2003. 34.95 (978-0-7531-1011-9(3)) Pub: ISIS Lrg Prnt GBR. Dist(s): Ulverscroft US

Boy in Me. Perf. by Glen Campbell. 1 cass. audio compact disk 15.99 CD. (D2025) Diamante Music Grp.
A message of encouragement to Christians in whatever circumstance they're facing, & the promise that "The Best is Yet to Come".

Boy in the Barn see Gathering of Great Poetry for Children

Boy in the Striped Pajamas. unabr. ed. John Boyne. Read by Michael Maloney. 4 CDs. (Running Time: 4 hrs. 58 mins.). (J). (gr. 4-7). 2006. audio compact disk 32.30 (978-0-7393-3774-5(2), Listening Lib) Pub: Random Audio Pubg. Dist(s): NetLibrary CO

Boy in the Striped Pajamas. unabr. ed. John Boyne. Read by Michael Maloney. 4 CDs. (Running Time: 17880 sec.). (ENG.). (J). (gr. 5-12). 2006. audio compact disk 24.95 (978-0-7393-3705-9(X), Listening Lib) Pub: Random Audio Pubg. Dist(s): Random

Boy in the Water. collector's ed. Stephen Dobyns. Read by Jonathan Marosz. 10 cass. (Running Time: 15 hrs.). 1999. 80.00 (978-0-7366-4665-9(5), 5047) Books on Tape.
The author probes the daily life of an ordinary community to reveal the depths of good & evil.

Boy Meets Boy. unabr. ed. David Levithan. Read by Full Cast Production Staff. (YA). 2007. 44.99 (978-1-60252-601-3(X)) Find a World.

Boy Next Door. Meg Cabot. Narrated by Barbara Rosenblat. 6 cass. (Running Time: 8 hrs. 15 mins.). (Boy Ser.). 55.00 (978-1-4025-3431-7(0)) Recorded Bks.

Boy No More. unabr. collector's ed. Paxton Davis. Read by Wolfram Kandinsky. 7 cass. (Running Time: 7 hrs.). 1993. 42.00 (978-0-7366-2419-0(8), 3186) Books on Tape.
Newspaperman describes the changed America he returned to at the end of WW II.

Boy of Good Breeding. abr. ed. Miriam Toews. 3 CDs. (Running Time: 14400 sec.). (ENG.). 2006. audio compact disk 24.95 (978-0-86492-464-3(X), Between Covers Coll) Pub: Goose Ln Eds CAN. Dist(s): U Toronto Pr

Boy Overboard. Morris Gleitzman. Read by Morris Gleitzman. (Running Time: 3 hrs. 20 mins.). (J). 2009. 54.99 (978-1-74214-381-1(4), 9781742143811) Pub: Bolinda Pubng AUS. Dist(s): Bolinda Pub Inc

Boy Overboard: The Play. unabr. ed. Morris Gleitzman. Read by Morris Gleitzman. 3 CDs. (Running Time: 3 hrs. 20 mins.). 2002. audio compact disk 54.95 (978-1-74030-814-4(X)) Pub: Bolinda Pubng AUS. Dist(s): Bolinda Pub Inc

Boy Overboard: The Play. unabr. ed. Narrated by Morris Gleitzman. 2 cass. (Running Time: 3 hrs. 20 mins.). 2002. 24.00 (978-1-74030-807-6(7)) Pub: Bolinda Pubng AUS. Dist(s): Bolinda Pub Inc
Jamal and Bibi have a dream. To lead Australia to soccer glory in the next World Cup. But first they must face landmines, pirates, storms and assassins. Can Jamal and his family survive their incredible journey and get to Australia? Sometimes, to save the people you love, you have to go overboard.

***Boy Scouts of America Wilderness First Aid Instructor's Toolkit CD-ROM.** 3rd rev. ed. American Academy of Orthopaedic Surgeons Staff & Wilderness Medical Society Staff. 2010. audio compact disk 55.75 (978-0-7637-9277-0(2)) Jones Bartlett.

Boy Still Missing. John Searles. Narrated by Scott Shina. 10 CDs. (Running Time: 12 hrs.). audio compact disk 97.00 (978-1-4025-2104-1(9)) Recorded Bks.

Boy Still Missing. John Searles. Narrated by Scott Shina. 9 cass. (Running Time: 12 hrs.). 2001. 81.00 (978-0-7887-8862-8(0), 96634) Recorded Bks.
While searching for his drunken father, 15-year-old Dominick Pindle meets Edie, his father's mistress. They begin a scandalous relationship that spirals out of control, leads to a shocking death and compels Dominick to place his own life on the line.

Boy vs. the Cynic. Contrib. by John Reuben. Prod. by John Reuben Zappin & C. R. pendleton. Contrib. by Toby McKeehan & Joey Elwood. 2005. audio compact disk 13.98 (978-5-558-97850-6(3)) Gotee Records.

Boy Who Burped Too Much. Scott Nickel. Illus. by Steve Harpster. (Graphic Sparks Ser.). (ENG.). (gr. 1-3). 2008. audio compact disk 14.60 (978-1-4342-0598-8(3)) CapstoneDig.

***Boy Who Came Back from Heaven.** unabr. ed. Kevin Malarkey & Alex Malarkey. 2010. audio compact disk 25.99 (978-1-4143-3609-1(8)) Tyndale Hse.

***Boy Who Climbed into the Moon.** unabr. ed. John Altman & David Almond. (Running Time: 2 hrs.). 2010. 39.97 (978-1-4418-9005-4(X), 9781441890054, Candlewick Bril); 14.99 (978-1-4418-9004-7(1), 9781441890047, Candlewick Bril) Brilliance Audio.

***Boy Who Climbed into the Moon.** unabr. ed. John Altman & David Almond. Read by Anne Flosnik. (Running Time: 2 hrs.). 2010. audio compact disk 14.99 (978-1-4418-9002-3(5), 9781441890023, Candlewick Bril); audio compact disk 19.99 (978-1-4418-9000-9(9), 9781441890009, Candlewick Bril); audio compact disk 39.97 (978-1-4418-9003-0(3), 9781441890030, Candlewick Bril); audio compact disk 39.97 (978-1-4418-9001-6(7), 9781441890016, Candlewick Bril) Brilliance Audio.

Boy Who Cried Wolf. 1 cass. (Bilingual Fables). 12.00 (978-0-8325-7297-5(7), Natl Textbk Co) M-H Contemporary.
Presents a story in Spanish & English.

Boy Who Cried Wolf. Arlene Capriola & Rigmor Swenson. Ed. by Cherisse Mastry. Illus. by Kathy Burns. (Once upon a Time Ser.). (J). (gr. k-2). 1998. 6.95 (978-1-57022-159-0(6), ECS1596) ECS Lrn Systs.

Boy Who Cried Wolf. Arlene Capriola & Rigmor Swenson. Ed. by Cherisse Mastry. Illus. by Kathy Burns. (Once upon a Time Ser.). (J). (gr. k-2). 1998. pap. bk. & wbk. ed. (978-1-57022-170-5(7)) ECS Lrn Systs.

Boy Who Cried Wolf. B. G. Hennessy. Illus. by Boris Kulikov. Narrated by Peter Scolari. 1 CD. (Running Time: 8 mins.). (J). (ps-2). 2008. bk. 29.95 (978-0-545-09452-8(6)) Weston Woods.

Boy Who Cried Wolf. B. G. Hennessy. Narrated by Peter Scolari. 1 CD. (Running Time: 8 mins.). (J). (ps-2). 2008. audio compact disk 12.95 (978-0-545-09442-9(9)) Weston Woods.

***Boy Who Cried Wolf.** Illus. by Jess Stockham. (Flip-up Fairy Tales Ser.). (ENG.). (J). 2011. audio compact disk 7.99 (978-1-84643-407-5(6)) Childs Play GBR.

Boy Who Cried Wolf/el Pastorcito Mentiroso: A Retelling of Aesop's Fable/Version de la Fabula de Esopo. Eric Blair. Illus. by Dianne Silverman. (Read-It! Readers: Folk Tales Yellow Level Ser.). (J). (gr. k-4). 2008. audio compact disk 9.27 (978-1-4048-4470-4(8)) CapstoneDig.

Boy Who Dared. unabr. ed. Susan Campbell Bartoletti. Read by David Ackroyd. (ENG.). (J). (gr. 5). 2009. audio compact disk 28.00 (978-0-7393-7405-4(2), Listening Lib) Pub: Random Audio Pubg. Dist(s): Random

Boy Who Drew Cats see Great American Short Stories, Vol. II, A Collection

***Boy Who Harnessed the Wind.** unabr. ed. William Kamkwamba & Bryan Mealer. Read by Chike Johnson. (ENG.). 2009. (978-0-06-199217-9(8), Harper Audio) HarperCollins Pubs.

***Boy Who Harnessed the Wind: Creating Currents of Electricity & Hope.** unabr. ed. William Kamkwamba & Bryan Mealer. Read by Chike Johnson. (ENG.). 2009. (978-0-06-199216-2(X), Harper Audio) HarperCollins Pubs.

Boy Who Laughed at Santa Claus see Christmas with Ogden Nash

Boy Who Liked Green. unabr. ed. Michele Sobel Spirn. 1 cass. (Running Time: 5 min.). (Read Along ... For Fun Ser.). (J). (ps-2). 1984. bk. 16.99 (978-0-934898-69-0(3)); pap. bk. 9.95 (978-0-934898-81-2(2)) Jan Prods.
One day Tom gets up & thinks about the color green. He likes green, it is a good color. It is the color of trees & grass. His father, mother, & sister also like the color green, so Tom paints this green: his hair, his sister's shoes, his mother's hat, & even his dog.

Boy Who Lived with the Bears & Other Iroquois Stories. abr. ed. Read by Joe Bruchac. 1 cass. (Running Time: 63 min.). (Storytime Ser.). (J). (ps-6). 1990. 9.95 (978-0-930407-19-3(9)) Parabola Bks.
This collection of six Native American tales is the first of a new series of traditional stories told by traditional storytellers. The myths, legends, & folktales passed on through storytelling hold valuable messages from our ancestors, messages that are easily lost in the babble of the modern world.

Boy Who Loved Frogs. Jay O'Callahan. 1 cass. (Running Time: 49 min.). (J). (ps up). 9.98 (311) MFLP CA.
Fascinating collection of five stories including a tale of a worm & a caterpillar whose living friendship gives each the strength to save a lonely orchard.

Boy Who Loved Frogs. unabr. ed. Jay O'Callahan. 1 cass. (Running Time: 49 min.). (Time for a Tale Storytelling Ser.). (J). (gr. k up). 1987. 9.98 (978-0-942303-02-5(4), HW 1204C) Pub: High Windy Audio. Dist(s): August Hse
Light-hearted, all original animal tales full of love, friendship, loyalty & self-acceptance. Parents' Choice winner.

Boy Who Loved Mammoths & Other Tales. 1 cass. (Running Time: 55 min.). (Storytelling Circle Ser.). (J). (gr. k-5). 1987. 8.95 (978-0-89719-973-5(1), 742C) Weston Woods.

Boy Who Made Dragonfly: A Zuni Myth. abr. ed. Tony Hillerman. Read by Debra Winger. 1 cass. (Running Time: 1 hr. 30 min.). 1995. bk. 10.95 (978-0-944993-44-6(3)) Audio Lit.
The hero of this enchanting Zuni Indian myth is a little boy who saves his people from an ecological disaster.

Boy Who Never Grew Up. unabr. ed. David Handler. Narrated by Tom Stechschulte. 10 cass. (Running Time: 13 hrs. 30 mins.). (Stewart Hoag

Mystery Ser.: Vol. 5). 1998. 85.00 (978-0-7887-2283-7(2), 95534E7) Recorded Bks.
When the cultured sleuth, Stewart Hoag & his sensitive Basset Hound Lulu take on Hollywood, no one is safe from lampoonery.

Boy Who Saved Baseball. unabr. ed. 5 cass. (Running Time: 6 hrs. 45 min.). (J). 2003. 45.00 (978-1-4025-6720-9(0)) Recorded Bks.

Boy Who Talked to Whales: A Musical. Michael Mish. 1 cass. (J). (gr. 2 up). 9.95 (978-0-9622465-8-6(1), MMM 2009) Mish Mash Music.
Young environmentalists will cheer at Michael Mish's musical whale tale.

Boy Who Taught the Beekeeper to Read. Susan Hill. Read by Anne Dover & Christopher Kay. 4 cass. (Running Time: 4 hrs.). (Soundings Ser.). (J). 2004. 44.95 (978-1-84283-710-8(9)) Pub: ISIS Lrg Prnt GBR. Dist(s): Ulverscroft US

Boy Who Taught the Beekeeper to Read. Susan Hill. 4 CDs. (Running Time: 4 hrs.). (Soundings (CDs) Ser.). (J). 2004. audio compact disk 51.95 (978-1-84283-968-3(3)) Pub: ISIS Lrg Prnt GBR. Dist(s): Ulverscroft US

Boy Who Was Raised by Librarians. Brad Sneed. Illus. by Brad Sneed. 1 cass. (Running Time: 12 mins.). (J). (gr. k-3). 2008. bk. 27.95 (978-0-8045-6965-1(7)); bk. 29.95 (978-0-8045-4188-6(4)) Spoken Arts.
Every day after school Melvin goes to the library where everything has its place. His favorite people - Marge, Betty and Leola - are always in their places, behind the reference desk. When something interests Melvin his librarian friends always help him find lots of books on the subject. When he collects creepy bugs in a jar they help him identify, classify and catalog the insects. As the years pass and Melvin begins college, he wonders will he ever return to his friends at his beloved library?.

Boy Who Would Be King, abr. ed. Earl Greenwood & Kathleen Tracy. Read by Earl Greenwood. 2 cass. (Running Time: 3 hrs.). 2000. 7.95 (978-1-57815-066-3(3), 1049, Media Bks Audio) Media Bks NJ.
A compellingly honest look at Presley family secrets.

Boy Who Would Be King, Set. abr. ed. Earl Greenwood & Kathleen Tracy. Read by Earl Greenwood. 2 cass. (Running Time: 3 hrs.). 1993. 16.95 (978-1-879371-50-7(2)) Pub Mills.
Earl Greenwood, Elvis' cousin recounts & examines Presley's family history based on the author's childhood memories of the late "King" & on his years spent as Presley's press agent & confidant.

boy who would live forever & Walter wants to be a Werewolf. unabr. ed. Richard Harland & Moya Simons. Read by Francis Greenslade. 2 cass. (Running Time: 2 hrs. 40 mins.). (Aussie Chomps: Ser.). (YA). 2003. audio compact disk 24.00 (978-1-74093-144-1(0)) Pub: Bolinda Pubng AUS. Dist(s): Bolinda Pub Inc

Boy Who Wouldn't Give Up. Janet Clark Shay. Illus. by Kevin Scott Collier. (Big Words for God's Little People Ser.). (ENG.). (J). 2009. audio compact disk 7.95 (978-0-9766823-4-9(6)) Pub: Sa Creek. Dist(s): STL Dist NA

Boy with the Cuckoo Clock Heart. unabr. ed. Mathias Malzieu. Read by Jim Dale. Tr. by Sarah Ardizzone. (Running Time: 6 hrs.). 2010. 29.95 (978-1-4417-2660-5(8)); audio compact disk 29.95 (978-1-4417-2659-9(4)) Blckstn Audio.

Boy with the Cuckoo-Clock Heart: A Novel. unabr. ed. Mathias Malzieu. Read by Jim Dale. Tr. by Sarah Ardizzone. (Running Time: 6 hrs.). 2010. 44.95 (978-1-4417-2656-8(X)); audio compact disk 55.00 (978-1-4417-2657-5(8)) Blckstn Audio.

Boy with the Magic Numbers. Sally Gardner. 2 CDs. 2005. audio compact disk 21.95 (978-0-7540-6704-7(1), Chivers Child Audio) AudioGO.

Boycott of Mitsubishi & Saving Ellsmere Canyon. Hosted by Nancy Pearlman. 1 cass. (Running Time: 28 min.). 10.00 (1116) Educ Comm CA.

Boyfriend List. unabr. ed. Prod. by Listening Library Staff. 4 cass. (Running Time: 5 hrs. 42 mins.). 2005. 35.00 (978-1-4000-9888-0(2), Listening Lib); audio compact disk 38.25 (978-0-307-20686-2(6), Listening Lib) Pub: Random Audio Pubg. Dist(s): NetLibrary CO

Boynton Canyon: Walkabout Audio Tours. Patrick T. Houlihan & Betsy Houlihan. 1 cass. (Running Time: 1 hr.). 2000. 9.00 (978-1-931544-05-4(0)); audio compact disk 16.00 (978-1-931544-04-7(2)) Walkabout Audio.
An historical description of cultural geological, archaeological floral & fauna facts of Boynton Canyon & Sedona area.

Boys Adrift: The Five Factors Driving the Growing Epidemic of Unmotivated Boys & Underachieving Young Men. unabr. ed. M.D, Ph. D., Leonard Sax. (Running Time: 9 hrs. NaN mins.). 2008. 59.95 (978-1-4332-4629-6(5)) Blckstn Audio.

Boys Adrift: The Five Factors Driving the Growing Epidemic of Unmotivated Boys & Underachieving Young Men. unabr. ed. Leonard Sax. (Running Time: 9 hrs. NaN mins.). 2008. 29.95 (978-1-4332-4632-6(5)); audio compact disk 80.00 (978-1-4332-4630-2(9)) Blckstn Audio.

Boys Adrift: The Five Factors Driving the Growing Epidemic of Unmotivated Boys & Underachieving Young Men. unabr. ed. Leonard Sax. (Running Time: 9 hrs. 0 mins.). 2008. audio compact disk & audio compact disk 29.95 (978-1-4332-4631-9(7)) Blckstn Audio.

***Boys & Girls Like You & Me.** unabr. ed. Aryn Kyle. (Running Time: 7 hrs. 0 mins.). 2010. 14.99 (978-1-4001-8677-8(3)) Tantor Media.

***Boys & Girls Like You & Me.** unabr. ed. Aryn Kyle. Narrated by Hillary Huber. (Running Time: 7 hrs. 0 mins. 0 sec.). (ENG.). 2010. 19.99 (978-1-4001-6677-0(2)); audio compact disk 29.99 (978-1-4001-1677-5(5)) Pub: Tantor Media. Dist(s): IngramPubServ

***Boys & Girls Like You & Me: Stories.** unabr. ed. Aryn Kyle. (Running Time: 7 hrs. 0 mins.). 2010. 29.99 (978-1-4001-9677-7(9)) Tantor Media.

***Boys & Girls Like You & Me: Stories.** unabr. ed. Aryn Kyle. Narrated by Hillary Huber. (Running Time: 7 hrs. 0 mins. 0 sec.). (ENG.). 2010. audio compact disk 59.99 (978-1-4001-4677-2(1)) Pub: Tantor Media. Dist(s): IngramPubServ

Boys Are Dogs. unabr. ed. Leslie Margolis. Read by Ellen Grafton. (Running Time: 5 hrs.). 2009. 39.97 (978-1-4233-7733-7(8), 9781423377337, BADLE); 39.97 (978-1-4233-7731-3(1), 9781423377313, Brlnc Audio MP3 Lib); 24.99 (978-1-4233-7732-0(X), 9781423377320, BAD); 24.99 (978-1-4233-7730-6(3), 9781423377306, Brilliance MP3); audio compact disk 48.97 (978-1-4233-7729-0(X), 9781423377290, BriAudCD Unabrid); audio compact disk 24.99 (978-1-4233-7728-3(1), 9781423377283) Brilliance Audio.

Boys at Work, unabr. ed. Gary Soto. Narrated by Robert Ramirez. 2 cass. (Running Time: 2 hrs. 30 mins.). (gr. 4 up). 1997. 19.00 (978-0-7887-0678-3(0), 94850E7) Recorded Bks.
A witty, action-packed story of ten-year-old Rudy Herrera & a broken Discman that causes more trouble than it's worth. Rudy works to replace the CD player & confronts the tattooed neighborhood bully.

***Boys, Bears, & a Serious Pair of Hiking Boots.** unabr. ed. Abby McDonald. (Running Time: 8 hrs.). 2010. 39.97 (978-1-4418-8981-2(7), 9781441889812, Candlewick Bril); 14.99 (978-1-4418-8980-5(9), 9781441889805, Candlewick Bril) Brilliance Audio.

***Boys, Bears, & a Serious Pair of Hiking Boots.** unabr. ed. Abby McDonald. Read by Stephanie Wolfe. (Running Time: 8 hrs.). 2010. audio compact disk 14.99 (978-1-4418-8978-2(7), 9781441889782, Candlewick Bril); audio compact disk 19.99 (978-1-4418-8976-8(0), 9781441889768, Candlewick Bril); audio compact disk 54.97 (978-1-4418-8977-5(9), 9781441889775, Candlewick Bril); audio compact disk 39.97 (978-1-4418-8979-9(5), 9781441889799, Candlewick Bril) Brilliance Audio.

Boys Beware. Jean Ure. Read by Clare Corbett. (Running Time: 12960 sec.). (J). (gr. 4-6). 2006. audio compact disk 29.95 (978-1-4056-5571-2(2)) AudioGo GBR.

Boys from Brazil. unabr. ed. Ira Levin. Read by Simon Vance. 6 cass. (Running Time: 8 hrs. 30 mins.). 1994. 44.95 (978-0-7861-0696-7(4), 1498) Blckstn Audio.
Harmless aging men have been marked for murder & there is a hidden link that binds them. The most famous Nazi still alive, the Angel of Death, has dispatched six former SS men from South America to hunt them down.

***Boys from Brazil.** unabr. ed. Ira Levin. Read by Simon Vance. (Running Time: 8 hrs. NaN mins.). (ENG.). 2010. 29.95 (978-1-4417-8297-7(4)); audio compact disk 76.00 (978-1-4417-8295-3(8)) Blckstn Audio.

Boys of Everest: Chris Bonington & the Tragedy of Climbing's Greatest Generation. unabr. ed. Clint Willis. (Running Time: 57600 sec.). 2007. audio compact disk 108.00 (978-1-4332-0746-4(X)); audio compact disk 29.95 (978-1-4332-0747-1(8)) Blckstn Audio.

Boys of Everest: Chris Bonington & the Tragedy of Climbing's Greatest Generation. unabr. ed. Clint Willis & James Adams. 2007. audio compact disk 89.95 (978-1-4332-0745-7(1)) Blckstn Audio.

***Boys of Pointe du Hoc.** abr. ed. Douglas Brinkley. Read by Douglas Brinkley. (ENG.). 2005. (978-0-06-085451-5(0), Harper Audio); (978-0-06-079682-2(0), Harper Audio) HarperCollins Pubs.

Boys of Pointe du Hoc: Ronald Reagan, D-Day, & the U. S. Army 2nd Ranger Battalion. unabr. ed. Douglas Brinkley. 5 CDs. (Running Time: 021600 sec.). 2005. audio compact disk 29.95 (978-0-06-075959-9(3)) HarperCollins Pubs.

Boys of St. Julien, Set. abr. ed. Lucian K. Truscott, IV. 2 cass. (Running Time: 3 hrs.). 2000. 17.95 (978-1-56740-846-1(X), Nova Audio Bks) Brilliance Audio.
During World War II, every man & boy in the tiny French village of St. Julien de Crempse was lined up at the edge of a ditch, while a young German captain personally delivered the coup de grace into each victim's temple. Only one young boy survived, Pierre Fargaudie, who witnessed the slaughter of his father & brother. Fifty years later a retired CIA agent Hank Mathias has bought a home in the village. One evening he invites the Fargaudies over for dinner. When he returns from a trip to the wine cellar, he finds Madame Fargaudie shot to death & Pierre, lying seconds away from death, whispers that the German captain who killed his family is back.

Boys of St. Julien, Set. unabr. ed. Lucian K. Truscott, IV. 8 cass. (Running Time: 12 hr.). Date not set. 73.25 (978-1-56740-661-0(0), Unabridge Lib Edns); 26.95 (978-1-56740-435-7(9), Bkcassette) Brilliance Audio.

Boys of Summer: The Classic Narrative of Growing up Within Shouting Distance of Ebbets Field, Covering the Jackie Robinson Dodgers, & What's Happened to Everybody Since. unabr. ed. Roger Kahn. Read by Michael Russotto. 12 cass. (Running Time: 18 hrs.). 1990. 96.00 (978-0-7366-1732-1(9), 2572) Books on Tape.
The Boys of Summer is the story of the Brooklyn Dodgers of the 1950s - one of the most exciting teams ever fielded, the team that broke the color barrier with Jackie Robinson & set many other records. It is also a book about the author's boyhood in the 30's & 40's, when he grew up within shouting distance of Ebbets Field. Imagine his feelings when, as a young reporter, he had the miraculous good fortune to cover the Dodgers during their legendary heyday. Finally, it is a book about what's happened since to Jackie Robinson, Carl Erskine, Preacher Roe, Pee Wee Reese, Roy Campanella, Carl Furillo & the others, no longer boys but men in their middle years when this book was written, now oldsters with their glory days long behind them.

Boys of Summer: The Classic Narrative of Growing up Within Shouting Distance of Ebbets Field, Covering the Jackie Robinson Dodgers, & What's Happened to Everybody Since. unabr. ed. Roger Kahn. Read by Phil Gigante. (Running Time: 15 hrs.). 2009. 39.97 (978-1-4233-7773-3(7), 9781423377733, BADLE); 39.97 (978-1-4233-7771-9(0), 9781423377719, Brlnc Audio MP3 Lib); 24.99 (978-1-4233-7772-6(9), 9781423377726, BAD); 24.99 (978-1-4233-7770-2(2), 9781423377702, Brilliance MP3); audio compact disk 99.97 (978-1-4233-7769-6(9), 9781423377696, BriAudCD Unabrid); audio compact disk 34.99 (978-1-4233-7768-9(0), 9781423377689, Bril Audio CD Unabri) Brilliance Audio.

Boy's Own Story, Nocturnes for the King of Naples, & the Beautiful Room Is Empty. Edmund White. Read by Edmund White. 1 cass. 1989. 13.95 (978-1-55644-340-4(4), 9071) Am Audio Prose.
The author reads excerpts from three of his works.

Boys R Us. unabr. ed. Lisi Harrison. (Running Time: 5 hrs.). (Clique Ser.: No. 11). (ENG.). 2009. 19.98 (978-1-60024-632-6(X)) Pub: Hachet Audio. Dist(s): HachBkGrp

Boys Should Be Boys: Seven Secrets to Raising Healthy Sons. unabr. ed. Meg Meeker. Read by Pam Ward. 7 CDs. (Running Time: 30600 sec.). (ENG.). 2008. audio compact disk 29.95 (978-1-4332-1398-4(2)) Blckstn Audio.

Boys Should Be Boys: Seven Secrets to Raising Healthy Sons. unabr. ed. Meg Meeker. Read by Pam Ward. (Running Time: 8.5 hrs. 0 mins.). (ENG.). 2008. 65.95 (978-1-4332-1395-3(8)) Blckstn Audio.

Boys Should Be Boys: 7 Secrets to Raising Healthy Sons. unabr. ed. Meg Meeker. 6 cass. (Running Time: 8 hrs.). (ENG.). 2008. 29.95 (978-1-4332-1397-7(4)) Blckstn Audio.

Boys Should Be Boys: 7 Secrets to Raising Healthy Sons. unabr. ed. Meg Meeker. Read by Pam Ward. 1 MP3-CD. (Running Time: 8.5 hrs. 0 mins.). 2008. 29.95 (978-1-4332-1399-1(0)); audio compact disk 70.00 (978-1-4332-1396-0(6)) Blckstn Audio.

Boy's Tale. Margaret Frazer. Read by Anne Cater. 6 cass. 2009. 54.95 (978-1-84559-567-8(X)) Pub: Soundings Ltd GBR. Dist(s): Ulverscroft US

Boys War. Jim Murphy. Read by Ed Sala. 2 cass. (Running Time: 2 hrs.). (YA). 1999. pap. bk. & stu. ed. 37.20 (978-0-7887-3791-6(0), 41035) Recorded Bks.
Thousands of Civil War soldiers ranged in age from 10 to 15. Their diaries & letters bring their story to life in a way that few historians could. Told in their own words, these everyday details of the war are an unforgettable history lesson.

Boy's War. unabr. collector's ed. Paxton Davis. Read by Wolfram Kandinsky. 6 cass. (Running Time: 9 hrs.). 1992. 48.00 (978-0-7366-2097-0(4), 2903) Books on Tape.
In his first book of memoirs, "Being a Boy," we met a young Paxton Davis growing up in North Carolina during the Depression. "A Boy's War" continues his story as he leaves for college & his "Rat Year" at the Virginia Military Institute. He was going not to prepare for war, simply to continue a family tradition.

Boys War, Class set. Jim Murphy. Read by Ed Sala. 2 cass. (Running Time: 2 hrs.). (YA). 1999. 121.30 (978-0-7887-3862-3(3), 47027) Recorded Bks.
Thousands of Civil War soldiers ranged in age from 10 to 15. Their diaries & letters bring their story to life in a way that few historians could. Told in their own words, these everyday details of the war are an unforgettable history lesson.

Boy's War: Confederate & Union Soldiers Talk about the Civil War. unabr. ed. Jim Murphy. Narrated by Ed Sala. 2 pieces. (Running Time: 2 hrs.). (gr. 9 up). 2000. 21.00 (978-0-7887-3834-0(8), 95924E7) Recorded Bks.

Boys' War Set: Confederate & Union Soldiers Talk about the Civil War. unabr. ed. Jim Murphy. Narrated by Ed Sala. 2 cass. (Running Time: 2 hrs.). (YA). 2000. pap. bk. 37.20 (41035X4) Recorded Bks.

Boys Will Be Boys: The Glory Days & Party Nights of the Dallas Cowboys Dynasty. unabr. ed. Jeff Pearlman. (Running Time: 14 hrs. 0 mins. 0 sec.). (ENG.). 2009. audio compact disk 37.99 (978-1-4001-1073-5(4)); audio compact disk 75.99 (978-1-4001-4073-2(0)); audio compact disk 24.99 (978-1-4001-6073-0(1)) Pub: Tantor Media. Dist(s): IngramPubServ

Boys Will Be Men: Masculinity in Troubled Times. unabr. collector's ed. Richard A. Hawley. Read by David Hilder. 5 cass. (Running Time: 5 hrs.). 1995. 30.00 (978-0-7366-2996-6(3), 3685) Books on Tape.
Boy's school headmaster counters politically correct version of sensitive, '90s man. Accept masculinity, don't fix it, he says.

Boys Will Put You on a Pedestal (So They Can Look up Your Skirt) A Dad's Advice for Daughters. unabr. ed. Philip Van Munching. Read by Philip Van Munching. 2005. 15.95 (978-0-7435-5240-0(7)) Pub: S&S Audio. Dist(s): S and S Inc

Bozo & Pals: Get Down with the Clown. 1 cass. (Running Time: 60 min.). (J). 2003. 10.95 (978-1-56628-370-0(1)) MFLP CA.

BPG Building Fabric Component Life Manual. Building Performance Group, Ltd. Staff. 2000. cd-rom 630.00 (978-0-419-25480-5(3), Spon) Pub: Routledge. Dist(s): Taylor and Fran

Brace of Bloodhounds. unabr. ed. Virginia Lanier. Read by Kate Forbes. 10 vols. (Running Time: 15 Hrs.). (Jo Beth Sidden Mystery Ser.). 2000. bk. 84.95 (978-0-7927-2405-6(4), CSL 294, Chivers Sound Lib) AudioGO.
When Gilly Ainsley shows up on Jo Beth Sidden's doorstep, she is stunned by the woman's bizarre tale of deception & manslaughter.

Braces. Donald Davis. (Running Time: 3420 sec.). 1999. audio compact disk 14.95 (978-0-87483-772-8(3)) Pub: August Hse. Dist(s): Natl Bk Netwk

Braces. unabr. ed. Donald Davis. Read by Donald Davis. 1 cass. (Running Time: 59 mins.). (American Storytelling Ser.). (gr. 3-7). 1999. 12.00 (978-0-87483-581-6(X)) Pub: August Hse. Dist(s): Natl Bk Netwk
A new coming-of-age story.

Brack, abr. ed. Johnny Quarles. Read by Dick Wilkinson. 4 cass. (Running Time: 6 hrs.). 1998. 24.95 (978-1-890990-13-8(2), 694792) Otis Audio.
Brack Haynes wants a homestead of his own a wife, family & peace from the memories of war & bounty hunting that haunted his soul. So he hires a half-breed rancher & leads his cattle to the edge of Indian territory, a hostile stretch of wilderness that no white man has ever dared to claim.

Brackenroyd Inheritance. unabr. ed. Aileen Armitage. Read by Patricia Jones. 8 cass. (Running Time: 12 hrs.). 2000. 69.95 (978-0-7531-0548-1(9), 000215) Pub: ISIS Audio GBR. Dist(s): Ulverscroft US
A young Victorian governess finds herself mistress of a brooding Yorkshire mansion on condition that she marry her extraordinary relative.

Brad Lansky & the Alien at Planet X. J. D. Venne. 1 CD. (Running Time: 56 min). Dramatization. (YA). 2005. audio compact disk 9.95 (978-0-9760459-0-8(7), protophonic) Integrated App.
Fully acted, with music and special effects.

Brad Lansky & the Alien Engineer. J. D. Venne. 1 CD. (Running Time: 58 mins). Dramatization. 2005. audio compact disk 9.90 (978-0-9760459-1-5(5), protophonic) Integrated App.
After their return from Planet X, Brad and Alex have a tough time trying to get their ship to pass its maintenance review. The alien?s viral onslaughts have left the Full Advantage riddled with software mutations and there are suspicions of even more invasive alterations. Dieter, whom they?d rescued from the moon-swamp at Planet X, is alive but struggling to shake off his infection. Even though their mission had been highly successful by many standards, no sentient press agents on Earth have shown the slightest interest at their return. Surely their findings were newsworthy?!Things take a turn for the worse when Dieter?s condition deteriorates. Just then one of the most powerful A.I.?s in the world requests their immediate presence and offers compelling arguments for a risky mission to an unchartered system twenty thousand light years away. Could this A.I.?s theory about the origin of the alien they found at Planet X be right? If so, can they trust a fragment of this A.I. aboard the Full Advantage to have their well-being at heart, and for that matter, can they still rely on their own ship to bring them back safely? And as if this mission didn?t have enough unknowns, Brad couldn?t deny the wishes of a dying man and has allowed Dieter to come along!.

Bradamant. Ron Miller. 11 cass. (Running Time: 16 hrs.). 2001. 34.95 (WOLF007); audio compact disk 39.95 (WOLF008) Lodestone Catalog.
Bradamant's further adventures: in the 7th century Europe of myths, gods & monsters, she vanquishes evil knights, rescues the unfortunate & fights black magic in her quest for her lost lover.

Bradbury Report. unabr. ed. Steven Polansky. (Running Time: 11 hrs. 0 mins.). 2010. 29.95 (978-1-4332-7273-8(3)); audio compact disk 32.95 (978-1-4332-7272-1(5)) Blckstn Audio.

***Bradbury Report.** unabr. ed. Steven Polansky. (Running Time: 11 hrs. 0 mins.). 2010. 65.95 (978-1-4332-7269-1(5)); audio compact disk 100.00 (978-1-4332-7270-7(9)) Blckstn Audio.

***Bradbury 13.** unabr. ed. Ray Bradbury. (Running Time: 6 hrs. 0 mins.). 2010. 29.95 (978-1-4417-1509-8(6)); 44.95 (978-1-4417-1505-0(3)); audio compact disk 24.95 (978-1-4417-1508-1(8)); audio compact disk 69.00 (978-1-4417-1506-7(1)) Blckstn Audio.

Bradford, You're Fired! William W. Woodbridge. Read by Charlie Tremendous Jones. (Life-Changing Classics Ser.). (ENG.). 2007. audio compact disk 19.95 (978-1-933715-33-9(2)) Executive Bks.

Bradley. unabr. ed. Alan Axelrod. Read by William Hughes. Frwd. by Wesley K. Clark. (Running Time: 25200 sec.). (Great Generals Ser.). 2008. 29.95 (978-1-4332-0538-5(6)); 54.95 (978-1-4332-0536-1(X)); audio compact disk 29.95 (978-1-4332-0539-2(4)); audio compact disk 29.95 (978-1-4332-0540-8(8)); audio compact disk & audio compact disk 55.00 (978-1-4332-0537-8(8)) Blckstn Audio.

Bradley & the Billboard. Mame Farrell. Read by L. J. Ganser. 4 cass. (Running Time: 5 hrs. 45 mins.). (YA). 1999. pap. bk. & stu. ed. 58.00 (978-0-7887-3060-3(6), 40894) Recorded Bks.
Bradley lives with a houseful of females. Still he manages to be average, except he is handsome. When he's offered a modeling job he decides it's time to take the role as man of the house.

Bradley & the Billboard, unabr. ed. Mame Farrell. Narrated by L. J. Ganser. 4 pieces. (Running Time: 5 hrs. 45 mins.). (gr. 5 up). 1999. 35.00 (978-0-7887-3059-7(2), 95669E7) Recorded Bks.
Illustrates what can happen when a young man lets his ego run away with him. Ever since his father died, Bradley has lived with a houseful of females. Still he manages to be the average, baseball-obsessed 6th grader - except he is incredibly handsome. When the local department store offers him big money for modeling, he decides it's time to step into his role as man of the family. That's when all the trouble begins.

Bradley & the Billboard, Class set. Mame Farrell. Read by L. J. Ganser. 4 cass. (Running Time: 5 hrs. 45 mins.). (YA). 1999. 203.30 (978-0-7887-3090-0(8), 46865) Recorded Bks.
Bradley lives with a houseful of females. Still he manages to be average, except he is handsome. When he's offered a modeling job he decides it's time to take the role as man of the house.

***Bradley Banana & the Jolly Good Pirate Audio CD.** Lila Devi. (ENG.). (J). 2010. audio compact disk 0.00 (978-1-4507-2518-7(X)) Indep Pub IL.

Bradshaw on Creating Love. unabr. ed. John Bradshaw. Read by John Bradshaw. Perf. by Richard Wagner. 10 cass. (Running Time: 10 hrs.). 1992. 60.00 Set. (978-1-57388-092-3(2)) J B Media.
Series of ten one-hour programs exploring the creation of healthy relationships in every aspect of life.

Bradshaw on: Creating Love: The Next Stage of Growth. John Bradshaw. (Running Time: 36000 sec.). 2008. audio compact disk 199.00 (978-1-57388-093-0(0)) J B Media.

Bradshaw on Eating Disorders. unabr. ed. John Bradshaw. 3 cass. (Running Time: 3 hrs.). 1994. 23.95 Set. (978-1-57388-009-1(4)) J B Media.
John explains why most diets don't work - examines 4 kinds of eating disorders & how they relate to family systems - he finally offers 10 components of non-addictive eating.

Bradshaw on Family Secrets. unabr. ed. John Bradshaw. 6 cass. (Running Time: 9 hrs.). 1998. 34.95 Set. (978-1-57388-055-8(8)) J B Media.
Takes listeners into the heart of the family's mysterious power to impact our lives. It explores how secrets are created, the influence they have on us, & the risks we take exploring them.

Bradshaw on: Family Secrets: What You Don't Know CAN Hurt You. John Bradshaw. (Running Time: 8400 sec.). 2008. audio compact disk 85.00 (978-1-57388-017-6(5)) J B Media.

Bradshaw on: Homecoming: Reclaiming & Championing Your Inner Child. John Bradshaw. (Running Time: 36000 sec.). 2008. audio compact disk 199.00 (978-1-57388-193-7(7)) J B Media.

Bradshaw on Homecoming: Reclaiming Your Inner Child. unabr. ed. John Bradshaw. Read by John Bradshaw. Perf. by Richard Wagner & Steven Halpern. 10 cass. (Running Time: 10 hrs.). 1990. 60.00 Set. (978-1-57388-061-9(2)) J B Media.
Ten one-hour programs designed to assist listeners in reclaiming the authentic self.

Bradshaw on the Family. unabr. ed. John Bradshaw. Interview with Terry Kellogg. 10 cass. (Running Time: 10 hrs.). 1986. 60.00 Set. (978-1-57388-058-9(2)) J B Media.
Ten one-hour programs focusing on family life & family systems as they relate to compulsive & addictive behavior.

Bradshaw on the Family: A New Way of Creating Solid Self-Esteem. John Bradshaw. Read by John Bradshaw. 1 cass. (Running Time: 60 min.). Dramatization. 1989. Rental 9.95 (978-1-55874-044-0(9)) Health Comm.
Based on the television series of the same name, John Bradshaw focuses on the dynamics of the family, how the attitudes learned while growing up become encoded within each family member. This positive life-affirming audio book teaches us that bad beginnings can be remedied.

Bradshaw on: the Family: A New Way of Creating Solid Self Esteem. John Bradshaw. (Running Time: 36000 sec.). 2008. audio compact disk 199.00 (978-1-57388-195-1(3)) J B Media.

Brady Bunch: Gen. 35:23-26. Ed Young. 1991. 4.95 (978-0-7417-1844-0(8), 844) Win Walk.

Brag! The Art of Tooting Your Own Horn Without Blowing It. abr. ed. Peggy Klaus. (ENG.). 2005. 14.98 (978-1-59483-282-6(X)) Pub: Hachet Audio. Dist(s): HachBkGrp

Brag! The Art of Tooting Your Own Horn without Blowing It. abr. ed. Peggy Klaus. (Running Time: 3 hrs.). (ENG.). 2009. 39.98 (978-1-60024-967-9(1)) Pub: Hachet Audio. Dist(s): HachBkGrp

Braggin' in Brass. Perf. by Empire Brass Quintet. 1 cass., 1 CD. 7.98 (TA 30249); audio compact disk 12.78 CD Jewel box. (TA 80249) NewSound.

Bragging Rights: 11 Cor. 10:7-18. Ed Young. 1990. 4.95 (978-0-7417-1796-2(4), 796) Win Walk.

Brahams: An Introduction to Piano Concerto No. 2. Jeremy Siepmann. 2 CDs. (Running Time: 3 hrs.). (Classics Explained Ser.). 2003. pap. bk. (978-1-84379-095-2(5)) NaxMulti GBR.

Brahma see Poetry of Ralph Waldo Emerson

Brahms: The Greatest Hits. 1 cass. 10.98 (978-1-57908-166-9(5), 3617) Platinm Enter.

Brahms / Schubert Companion CD. Compiled by Zeezok Publishing. (J). 2008. audio compact disk 7.95 (978-1-933573-17-5(1), 4834) Zeezok Pubng.

Brahms Concerto No. 1 in D Minor: Book/2-CD Pack. Composed by Johannes Brahms. 2006. pap. bk. 39.98 (978-1-59615-007-2(6), 1596150076) Pub: Music Minus. Dist(s): H Leonard

Braided Lives see Woman on the Edge of Time

Braille Rider-Waite Tarot. 2004. bk. 40.00 (978-1-57281-368-7(7), BRW78) US Games Syst.

Brain. unabr. ed. Robin Cook. Read by Donada Peters. 8 cass. (Running Time: 8 hrs.). 1993. 64.00 (978-0-7366-2461-9(9), 3225) Books on Tape.
Women patients suffer mental breakdowns & exhibit bizarre behavior in a medical world gone mad.

Brain. unabr. ed. Christopher Evans. 1 cass. 1990. 12.95 (TSE008) J Norton Pubs.

Brain: Repairs & Maintenance. Robert A. Monroe. Read by Robert A. Monroe. (Running Time: 30 min.). (Human Plus Ser.). 1989. 14.95 (978-1-56102-001-0(X)) Inter Indus.
Improve blood flow & electrical activity in the brain.

Brain & Colour Perception. unabr. ed. Semir Zeki. 1 cass. 1990. 12.95 (ECN212-B) J Norton Pubs.

Brain-Based Learning. Eric Jensen. 2 cass. bk. 36.95 Set. (B434-A); 26.95 bk. (B434) Learning Forum.
How emotions & stress impact the brain's chemistry; & how hormones, nutrition, sleep cycles, color & music affect learning.

Brain-Based Learning. David A. Sousa. 1999. 99.95 (978-0-7619-7522-9(5), 85416) Pub: Corwin Pr. Dist(s): SAGE

Brain Bloomers: Listening Adventures for Cognitive Development. Mark Cooper & Carl Johnson. Prod. by Imagination Development Group Staff. (J). 2000. audio compact disk 15.95 (978-1-931184-02-1(X)) Imagination Dev.

***Brain Center at Whipple's.** 2010. audio compact disk (978-1-59171-203-9(3)) Falcon Picture.

Brain Drug Mystery. unabr. ed. Peter Evans. 1 cass. 1990. 12.95 (ECN119-A) J Norton Pubs.
Endogenous opiates.

Brain Functioning & Human Behavior. Matthew Stubblefield. 1 cass. (Running Time: 1 hr. 24 min.). 1998. bk. 20.00 (978-1-58111-064-7(2)) Contemporary Medical.
Personal insights into ADHD, brain imaging, clinical & brain complexity of ADHD.

Brain Information Processing. E. J. Gold. 3 cass. (Running Time: 4 hrs.). 27.98 set. (TP177) Union Label.
Discussion on the inability of the brain to represent the universe in its field of interpretation. Life-form tracking through DNA & the ultimate weapon against death, examination of the sensory apparatus of the human biological machine.

Brain Injury Healing. Steven Gurgevich. (ENG.). 2005. audio compact disk 19.95 (978-1-932170-36-8(7), HWH) Tranceformation.

***Brain Lock.** abr. ed. Jeffrey M. Schwartz. Read by Jeffrey M. Schwartz. (ENG.). 2009. (978-0-06-196232-5(5), Harper Audio); (978-0-06-196231-8(7), Harper Audio) HarperCollins Pubs.

Brain Longevity. Dharma Singh Khalsa. 1999. (978-1-57042-705-3(4)) Hachet Audio.

Brain Longevity. Dharma Singh Khalsa & Cameron Stauth. 2001. (978-1-57042-890-6(5)) Hachet Audio.

Brain Longevity: The Breakthrough Medical Program that Improves Your Mind & Memory. unabr. ed. Dharma Singh Khalsa & Cameron Stauth. (Running Time: 4 hrs.). (ENG.). 2006. 14.98 (978-1-59483-667-1(1)) Pub: Hachet Audio. Dist(s): HachBkGrp

Brain Machine: How Does It Function? unabr. ed. John Maddox. 1 cass. 1990. 12.95 (ECN119-B) J Norton Pubs.

Brain Mania. E. Jensen. 2002. 64.95 (978-1-890460-20-4(6)) Pub: Corwin Pr. Dist(s): SAGE

Brain Massage: Revitalize Mind & Body. Kelly Howell. 1 CD. (Running Time: 60 mins.). (ENG.). 2004. audio compact disk 14.95 (978-1-881451-96-9(8)) Brain Sync.
Just slip on your headphones and listen to Brain Massage. Pure and precisely tuned sound waves gently massage brain activity into profound states and blissful reverie. Within minutes you'll tingle all over with a rush cleansing energy swirling through your mind and body. Soothing sound waves massage your brain and trigger your body's automatic relaxation response. Nagging aches and pains and pestering concerns wash away as a revitalizing flood of positive energy is released to help you overcome even the most stressful thoughts and feelings.

Brain Massage: Revitalize Mind & Body. unabr. ed. Kelly Howell. 1 cass. (Running Time: 1 hr.). 1991. 11.95 (978-1-881451-00-6(3)) Brain Sync.
You'll tingle all over with a rush of cleansing energy swirling through your mind & body. A combination of brain waves that feels like a holistic massage. A revitalizing flood of positive energy is released into your consciousness to help you overcome even the most stressful thoughts & feelings.

Brain-Mind & the Dimensions Beyond Space-Time. Jean Millay. 1 cass. 7.00 (A0089-85) Sound Photosyn.
ICS Shamanism '85.

Brain Power: Master your Mind. Kelly Howell. 1 cass. (Running Time: 60 min.). 1992. 11.95 (978-1-881451-13-6(5)) Brain Sync.
Effortlessly access up to 90% more of your untapped ability to learn, recall & create new ideas.

Brain Power: Master your Mind. unabr. ed. Kelly Howell. 1 CD. (Running Time: 60 min.). 1997. audio compact disk 14.95 (978-1-881451-91-4(7)) Brain Sync.

Brain Rot, Shopping at Costco & Other Joys of Middle Age. Doug Hurd. 2 cass. (Running Time: 1 hrs. 30 min.). 1996. 14.95 Set. QBS Publ.
Collection of Public Radio commentaries on relationships, marriage, parenting & living through middle age - very funny material.

Brain Rot, Shopping at Costco & Other Joys of Middle Age. abr. ed. Doug Hurd. Read by Doug Hurd. 1 cass. (Running Time: 1 hr. 30 min.). 1996. pap. bk. (978-0-9658630-0-1(X)); 16.50 (978-0-9658630-1-8(8)) QBS Publ.
Collection of humorous radio commentaries about relationships, marriage, parenting & living through middle age.

Brain Rules: 12 Principles for Surviving & Thriving at Work, Home, & School. John Medina. Read by John Medina. (Running Time: 25200 sec.). (ENG.). 2008. audio compact disk 34.95 (978-0-9797777-1-4(2)) Pub: Pear Pr. Dist(s): Perseus Dist

***Brain Rules for Baby: How to Raise a Smart & Happy Child from Zero to Five.** John Medina. Read by John Medina. 2010. 34.95 (978-0-9797777-9-0(8)) Pear Pr.

***Brain Rules for Baby: How to Raise a Smart & Happy Child from Zero to Five.** Read by John Medina. (Running Time: 7 hrs. 0 mins. 0 sec.). (ENG.). 2010. audio compact disk 34.95 (978-0-9797777-6-9(3)) Pub: Pear Pr. Dist(s): Perseus Dist

Brain Smart. 2001. audio compact disk 25.95 (978-1-889609-16-4(1)) Loving Guidnce.

Brain Smart, Set. unabr. ed. Becky Bailey & Sarah Sprinkel. 2 cass. (Running Time: 2 hrs.). 1998. 16.95 (978-1-889609-09-6(9), AT118) Loving Guidnce.
Learn how the self discipline system in the brain develops & three strategies needed to facilitate & boost brain power & how to "wire" your child's brain for success.

Brain Sprouts: Exercise Physiology for the Mind: Memory Training for the New Millennium. unabr. ed. Vicki Mizel. 6 cass. (Running Time: 3 hrs.). 2000. 50.00 (978-0-9654554-9-7(1)) Golden Treasures Int Inc.
Have you ever had trouble remembering a certain person's name? Or maybe it's the address where you're supposed to meet a friend? Worry no longer, there's hope for you yet. Mizel's new visual memory system may just be what the doctor ordered. By using visual images that each person creates for themselves, teaches the listener how to recall large amounts of information, memorize number quickly, increase vocabulary and remember names.

Brain Storm: A Novel. unabr. ed. Richard Dooling. Narrated by George Guidall. 12 cass. (Running Time: 18 hrs.). 1998. 97.00 (978-0-7887-1988-2(2), 95375E7) Recorded Bks.
In this fast-paced legal thriller, Dooling explores modern controversies, including the death penalty & scientific & moral questions about sex, crime & religion.

Brain Storm: A Novel, unabr. collector's ed. Richard Dooling. Read by John Edwardson. 13 cass. (Running Time: 19 hrs. 30 min.). 1998. 104.00 (978-0-7366-4335-1(4), 4816) Books on Tape.
Attorney Joe Watson does legal research for the lawyers in his firm. He's on track to become one of its youngest partners. Then he gets notice to defend James Whitlow, a small-time lowlife with a loser's rap sheet accused of a double hate crime killing his wife's deaf black lover. When Watson decides not to plead out his client, life takes a nasty turn: His boss fires him, his wife leaves him, the Whitlow case consumes him. Joe Watson finds himself fighting not only to save his marriage & his career but also to hold intact his conviction that a person is more than a series of chemical reactions.

Brain Systems. Frank Barr. 2 cass. 18.00 set. (A0007-85) Sound Photosyn.
Frank Barr is the foremost authority on melanin operation in brain/mind function.

Brain Teasers. (Timesaving Software Tools for Teachers Ser.). (J). 2004. audio compact disk 19.99 (978-1-57690-698-9(1)) Tchr Create Ma.

Brain That Changes Itself: Stories of Personal Triumph from the Frontiers of Brain Science. unabr. ed. Norman Doidge. Read by Jim Bond. (Running Time: 11 hrs.). 2008. 39.25 (978-1-4233-6804-5(5), 9781423368045, BADLE); 24.95 (978-1-4233-6803-8(7), 9781423368038, BAD) Brilliance Audio.

Brain That Changes Itself: Stories of Personal Triumph from the Frontiers of Brain Science. unabr. ed. Norman Doidge. Read by Jim Bond. Directed By Laurel Kelly Young. Contrib. by Cory Young. (Running Time: 39600 sec.). 2008. audio compact disk 39.25 (978-1-4233-6802-1(9), 9781423368021, Brlnc Audio MP3 Lib); audio compact disk 39.95 (978-1-4233-6799-4(5), 9781423367994); audio compact disk 24.95 (978-1-4233-6801-4(0), 9781423368014, Brilliance MP3) Brilliance Audio.

Brain That Changes Itself: Stories of Personal Triumph from the Frontiers of Brain Science. unabr. ed. Norman Doidge & Charles Doidge. Read by Jim Bond. Directed By Laurel Kelly Young. Contrib. by Cory Young. (Running Time: 11 hrs.). 2008. audio compact disk 112.25 (978-1-4233-6800-7(2), 9781423368007, BriAudCD Unabrid) Brilliance Audio.

Brain Vitality Meditation CD. Ilchi Lee. (ENG.). 2008. audio compact disk 16.98 (978-0-9799388-6-3(4)) Pub: BEST Life. Dist(s): SCB Distributors

Brain Warping. Ed. by Arthur Toga & Arthur W. Toga. (ENG., 1998. 316.00 (978-0-12-692535-7(6), Acad Press) Sci Tech Bks.

***Brain Wave.** unabr. ed. Poul Anderson. Read by To be Announced. (Running Time: 6 hrs. NaN mins.). (ENG.). 2011. 29.95 (978-1-4417-7808-6(X)); 44.95 (978-1-4417-7805-5(5)); audio compact disk 55.00 (978-1-4417-7806-2(3)) Blckstn Audio.

***Brain Wave Vibration Guided Training Audio Cd: Getting Back into the Rhythm of A Happy, Healthy Life.** Ilchi Lee. (Running Time: 1 hr. 1 min.). 2009. audio compact disk 17.95 (978-1-935127-31-4(4)) Pub: BEST Life. Dist(s): SCB Distributors

Brainstorm: Using Science to Spark Maximum Creativity. unabr. ed. Mariette Dichristina. Read by William Dufris & Helen Litchfield. 1 CD. (Running Time: 1 hr. 0 mins. 0 sec.). (ENG.). 2008. audio compact disk 14.95 (978-1-4272-0441-7(1)) Pub: Macmill Audio. Dist(s): Macmillan

Brainstorming. Howard S. Berg. 1 cass. 8.95 (607) Am Fed Astrologers.
An AFA Convention workshop tape.

Brainstorming - 1990. Howard S. Berg. 1 cass. 8.95 (751) Am Fed Astrologers.

BrainStyles: Be Who You Really Are. David Cherry & Marlane Miller. 1992. 18.95 (978-0-9634406-1-7(6)) BrainStyles.

Brainwash Projects. Perf. by Brainwash Projects Staff. 1 cass. 1997. audio compact disk 15.99 CD. (D8609) Diamante Music Grp.
This L. A. based outfit has been performing as a unit for over five years, creating a national buzz & fans across the country. Their unique jazz influenced Hip Hop sound has made them a truly respected group. Taking their name from those that would say that Christians are just brainwashed...they respond with "yes we are, but with the blood of Christ!".

Brainwave. 2004. audio compact disk (978-1-59250-370-4(5)) Gaiam Intl.

Brainwave - Alpha-theta. 2004. audio compact disk 9.98 (978-1-59250-367-4(5)) Gaiam Intl.

Brainwave III. 2004. audio compact disk 9.98 (978-1-59250-368-1(3)) Gaiam Intl.

Brainwave Journey. Jeffrey Thompson. 4 CDs. (Running Time: 4 hrs.). 1996. audio compact disk 29.95 (978-1-55961-393-4(9)) Relaxtn Co.

Brainwave Journey. unabr. ed. Jeffrey Thompson & Owen Morrison. 4 cass. (Running Time: 4 hrs.). 1996. 26.95 (978-1-55961-394-1(7)) Relaxtn Co.

Brainwave Meditation CD Set: Sound Waves that Move your Mind. unabr. ed. Kelly Howell. 2 CDs. (Running Time: 120 min.). (ENG.). 2005. audio compact disk 24.95 (978-1-881451-77-8(1)) Brain Sync.
Now you can quickly reach depths of meditation that would otherwise take years of practice to attain. Brain Sync?s precision-engineered frequencies massage your brain into blissful states of reverie. With this program 87% of research subjects who never meditated before were able to enter the theta state their very first session. Guided Meditation Kelly Howell guides you create your own inner healing sanctuary, a place where you can go to revitalize the very core of your being. You?ll learn how to generate states of being that nurture your sense of self, your creativity and the dynamic expression of your power in the world. Deep MeditationCompletely free of spoken words, this program delivers a unique combination of brainwave frequencies that produce an extraordinary ?mind-awake/body-asleep? state. Negative thoughts are dramatically swept away by brilliant flashes of insight and understanding as you experience untold depths of inner peace. Clinical studies show that theta meditation increases creativity, enhances cognition, deepens perception, aids in overcoming substance abuse and awakens intuition.In just 30 minutes you?ll reap the same powerful benefits meditation masters have documented for millennium. The results are profound. To experience the benefits of Brainwave Therapy headphones are required.

Brainwave Music. Jeffrey Thompson. 1 cass. (Running Time: 1 hr.). 29.95 (978-1-55961-609-6(1)) Relaxtn Co.

Brainwave Music. Prod. by Jeffrey Thompson. 3 CDs. (Running Time: 4 hrs. 30 mins.). 2000. audio compact disk 29.95 (978-1-55961-608-9(3)) Relaxtn Co.

Brainwave Music System. unabr. ed. Jeffrey Thompson. (Running Time: 6:00:00). 2009. audio compact disk 39.98 (978-1-60297-007-6(6)) Sounds True.

Brainwave Nature Suite: Soothing Natural Sounds Combined with Brainwave Pulses. unabr. abr. ed. Jeffrey Thompson. (Running Time: 1:00:00). 2007. audio compact disk 29.98 (978-1-55961-878-6(7)) Sounds True.

Brainwave Suite. Jeffrey Thompson. 4 cass. (Running Time: 6 hrs.). 1999. 24.95 Set. (45422); audio compact disk 29.95 CD. (45430) Courage-to-Change.
Combines natural brainwave frequencies with music to create a pattern to help you achieve a specific state of mind: Alpha (relaxation), Theta (insight), Delta (Stress release), or alpha-theta (Openess, communication).

Brainwave Suite. Jeffrey Thompson. 4 cass. (Running Time: 4 hrs.). 29.95 (978-1-55961-530-3(3)) Relaxtn Co.

Brainwave Suite. Jeffrey Thompson. 4 CDs. (Running Time: 4 hrs.). 1995. audio compact disk 29.95 (978-1-55961-309-5(2)) Relaxtn Co.

Brainwave Suite. unabr. ed. Jeffrey Thompson. (Running Time: 1:00:00). 2007. audio compact disk 29.98 (978-1-55961-723-9(3)) Sounds True.

Brainwave Symphony. Jeffrey Thompson. 4 CDs. (Running Time: 4 hrs.). 1999. audio compact disk 29.95 (978-1-55961-529-7(X)) Relaxtn Co.

Brainwave Symphony. abr. ed. Jeffrey Thompson. (Running Time: 1:00:00). 1999. audio compact disk 29.98 (978-1-55961-760-4(8)) Sounds True.
Combines carefully selected music from the baroque, classical, romantic, impressionistic, and twentieth-century eras with breakthrough audio technology to give you the best of classical wisdom and modern science.

Brainwaves, Relaxation & Music. Read by Steven Halpern. 1 cass. (Running Time: 60 min.). 1992. 9.98 (SRX 100) Inner Peace Mus.
Instructional & guided visualization for health & well-being.

Brakes, Steering, Front Suspension, Wheels & Tires. rev. ed. Bob Leigh et al. Ed. by Roger L. Fennema & Paul B. Shewan. Illus. by Ralph J. Butterworth. (Automobile Mechanics Refresher Course Ser.: Bk. 4). 1981. pap. bk. 13.90 (978-0-88098-071-5(0), H M Gousha) Prntice Hall Bks.

Bram Stoker Stories. unabr. ed. Bram Stoker. Read by Flo Gibson. 2 cass. (Running Time: 3 hrs. 6 min.). 1998. bk. 24.95 Set. (978-1-887645-01-0(2)) Audio Bk Con.
Includes: "The Secret of Growing Old," "Crooked Sands," "The Judge's House," & "Dracula's Guest".

Bram Stoker Stories, Set. Flo Gibson. 3 cass. (Running Time: 4 hrs.). 2000. 16.95 (978-1-55685-537-5(0)) Audio Bk Con.
"The Secret of Growing Gold", "Crooken Sands", "The Judge's House" & "Dracula's Guest" are bound to thrill & chill you.

Bran Hambric: The Farfield Curse. unabr. ed. Kaleb Nation. Read by Marc Thompson. (Running Time: 13 hrs.). 2009. 24.99 (978-1-4418-2633-6(5), 9781441826336, Brilliance MP3); 39.97 (978-1-4418-2634-3(3), 9781441826343, Brlnc Audio MP3 Lib); 39.97 (978-1-4418-2635-0(1), 9781441826350, BADLE) Brilliance Audio.

Bran Hambric: The Farfield Curse. unabr. ed. Kaleb Nation. Read by Marc Thompson. (Running Time: 13 hrs.). 2009. audio compact disk 29.99 (978-1-4418-2631-2(9), 9781441826312, Bril Audio CD Unabri); audio compact disk 79.97 (978-1-4418-2632-9(7), 9781441826329, BriAudCD Unabrid) Brilliance Audio.

***Bran Hambric: The Specter Key.** unabr. ed. Kaleb Nation. Read by Marc Thompson. (Running Time: 10 hrs.). 2010. 39.97 (978-1-4418-8258-5(8), 9781441882585, BADLE); audio compact disk 59.97 (978-1-4418-8255-4(3), 9781441882554, BriAudCD Unabrid) Brilliance Audio.

***Bran Hambric: The Specter Key.** unabr. ed. Kaleb Nation. Read by Marc Thompson. (Running Time: 9 hrs.). (YA). 2010. 24.99 (978-1-4418-8256-1(1), 9781441882561, Brilliance MP3); 39.97 (978-1-4418-8257-8(X), 9781441882578, Brlnc Audio MP3 Lib); audio compact disk 24.99 (978-1-4418-8254-7(5), 9781441882547, Bril Audio CD Unabri) Brilliance Audio.

***Bran Mak Morn: The Last King.** unabr. ed. Robert E. Howard. Narrated by Robertson Dean. (Running Time: 11 hrs. 30 mins.). 2010. 17.99 (978-1-4001-8226-8(3)) Tantor Media.

***Bran Mak Morn: The Last King.** unabr. ed. Robert E. Howard. Narrated by Robertson Dean. (Running Time: 12 hrs. 0 mins. 0 sec.). (ENG.). 2010. 24.99 (978-1-4001-6226-0(2)) Pub: Tantor Media. Dist(s): IngramPubServ

***Bran Mak Morn: The Last King.** unabr. ed. Robert E. Howard. Narrated by Robertson Dean & Dawkins Dean. (Running Time: 12 hrs. 0 mins. 0 sec.). (ENG.). 2010. audio compact disk 69.99 (978-1-4001-4226-2(1)); audio compact disk 34.99 (978-1-4001-1226-5(5)) Pub: Tantor Media. Dist(s): IngramPubServ

***Branch Rickey: A Life.** unabr. ed. Jimmy Breslin. (Running Time: 4 hrs. 0 mins.). 2011. 12.99 (978-1-4001-8959-5(4)); 19.99 (978-1-4001-6959-7(3)); audio compact disk 24.99 (978-1-4001-1959-2(6)) Pub: Tantor Media. Dist(s): IngramPubServ

***Branch Rickey (Library Edition) A Life.** unabr. ed. Jimmy Breslin. (Running Time: 4 hrs. 0 mins.). 2011. 24.99 (978-1-4001-9959-4(X)); audio compact disk 59.99 (978-1-4001-4959-9(2)) Pub: Tantor Media. Dist(s): IngramPubServ

Branche Entre Nous, Vol. 1. 1 cass., bklet. (FRE.). 1995. 19.95 (1498-AF) Olivia & Hill.
This intermediate-level program introduces students of French to colorful idioms & everyday expressions & emphasizes the informal tu used increasingly in France. The accompanying booklet provides transcripts of the lively branche dialogues & translations into both formal French & English. Review questions are recorded after four dialogues.

Branche Entre Nous, Vol. 2. 1 cass., bklet. (FRE.). 1995. 19.95 (1499-AF) Olivia & Hill.

Branché Entre Nous & Booklet Pt. 1. Colette Crosnier. 1 CD. (Running Time: 1 hr.). (FRE.). 2005. audio compact disk 21.95 (978-1-57970-184-0(1), FR0624D) J Norton Pubs.

Branche Entre Nous I. unabr. ed. Colette Crosnier. 1 cass. (Running Time: 60 min.). (FRE., (YA). (gr. 10 up). 1988. pap. bk. 21.95 (978-0-88432-256-6(4), FRO624) J Norton Pubs.
An intermediate level program for learning to listen & understand the new informal idioms of the French language. The booklet provides transcripts of the lively "branche" dialogs & translations into both academic French & English. The glossary is "branche" to academic French & English. After each group of four dialogs, a set of review questions is recorded to allow the learner to recall the "branche" expressions used.

Branche Entre Nous II. unabr. ed. Colette Crosnier. 1 cass. (Running Time: 1 hr.). (FRE., (YA). (gr. 10 up). 1992. pap. bk. 21.95 (978-0-88432-422-5(2), FR0625) J Norton Pubs.
Foreign Language Instruction. An additional intermediate-level program for learning contemporary French idioms through dialogs.

Branché Entre Nous II CD & Booklet. Colette Crosnier. 1 CD. (Running Time: 1 hr.). (FRE.). 2005. audio compact disk 21.95 (978-1-57970-120-8(5), FR0625D) J Norton Pubs.

Brand New Day. unabr. ed. Paul Vincent Nunes. Perf. by Paul Vincent Nunes. 1 cass. (Running Time: 39 min.). 1997. 9.98 (978-0-9634024-3-1(9), LR-3003-4); audio compact disk 15.98 CD. (978-0-9634024-4-8(7), LR-3003-2) Lighthse Recs.
Collection of twelve original songs including "Girls (Boys) Can Do Anything," "Martin (Luther King) Had a Dream," "Golden Rule Rap," "Stuck in the Middle Blues," "Amelia (Earhart)," "Special One," "Lighthouse (Shine On Me)" & Stephen Foster's "Oh! Susanna" with new lyrics & arrangement.

Brand New World: Ten Principles for Achieving Brand Leadership in the 21st-Century Marketplace. Scott Bedbury & Stephen Fenichell. Read by Scott Bedbury. 2 cass. (Running Time: 3 hrs.). 2000. 17.98 Hachet Audio.

Brand NFL: Making & Selling America's Favorite Sport. Michael Oriard. (ENG., 2007. 29.95 (978-0-8078-8585-7(1)); audio compact disk 34.95 (978-0-8078-8587-1(8)) U of NC Pr.

***Brand of Justice.** Luke Short. 2009. (978-1-60136-426-5(1)) Audio Holding.

Brand of Justice. Luke Short. (Running Time: 0 hr. 30 mins.). 1998. 10.95 (978-1-60083-451-6(5)) Iofy Corp.

Brand Warfare: 10 Rules for Building the Killer Brand. David F. D'Alessandro. 3 cass. (Running Time: 4 hrs. 30 min.). 2003. 24.00 (978-1-932378-04-7(9)); audio compact disk 28.00 (978-1-932378-05-4(7)) Pub: A Media Intl. Dist(s): Natl Bk Netwk

Branda's Great New Getup. Created by Gail Louise Anderson. (J). 2003. audio compact disk 7.99 (978-0-9740847-0-1(0)) GiGi Bks.
The clothes make the person - or do they? Find out in this story about a fashionable 8th grader who has it all, and her envious classmates that wish they did. But then again, maybe they don't.

Branded Clothing & Apparel in Hungary: A Strategic Reference 2007. Compiled by Icon Group International, Inc. Staff. 2007. ring bd. 195.00 (978-0-497-36005-4(5)) Icon Grp.

Branded in Blood. unabr. ed. Jon Black. Read by Michael Taylor & Marilyn Langbehn. 3 cass. (Running Time: 3 hrs. 24 min.). 1994. 21.95 (978-1-55686-526-8(0)) Books in Motion.
Contemporary ranchers in Eastern Oregon are mystified at the loss of cattle in their herds. Ross Singletary investigates his loss & suffers the bloody consequences.

Branded Man. unabr. ed. Catherine Cookson. Read by Gordon Griffin. 12 cass. (Running Time: 16 hrs.). 2001. 94.95 (978-1-86042-231-7(4), 22314) Pub: Soundings Ltd GBR. Dist(s): Ulverscroft US
Fourteen year old Marie Ann Lawson was running away from a sight she'd rather not have witnessed, she stumbled & fell to be discovered by a local man, who because of a disfigurement, was known as 'the branded man".

Branded Outlaw. unabr. ed. L. Ron Hubbard. Read by David O'Donnell. 2 CDs. (Running Time: 2 hrs.). (Stories from the Golden Age Ser.). 2008. audio compact disk 9.95 (978-1-59212-349-0(X)) Gala Pr LLC.

Branded World. Michael K. Levine. Read by Lloyd James. (Running Time: 11 hrs. 30 mins.). 2003. 30.95 (978-1-59912-371-4(1)) Iofy Corp.

Branded World. unabr. ed. Michael K. Levine. Read by Lloyd James. 8 cass. (Running Time: 11 hrs. 30 mins.). 2004. 56.95 (978-0-7861-2665-1(5), 3224); audio compact disk 72.00 (978-0-7861-8842-0(1), 3224) Blckstn Audio.

Brandeis. unabr. collector's ed. Lewis J. Paper. Read by Jonathan Marosz. 14 cass. (Running Time: 21 hrs.). 1994. 112.00 (978-0-7366-2716-0(2), 3446) Books on Tape.
Reflects the fulness of Supreme Court Justice Brandeis personal & professional life. Born in Kentucky before the Civil War, rose to fame as the first public interest lawyer & adviser to Woodrow Wilson.

Branden on Self-Esteem, Lectures 11-14. unabr. ed. Nathaniel Branden. 4 cass. (Running Time: 5 hrs. 21 min.). 1989. 39.00 (631-634) J Norton Pubs.
The processes in Biocentric Therapy through which personality change is achieved & self-esteem is enhanced - Self-awareness - Self-acceptance - Self-responsibility - Self-assertion.

Branden on Self-Esteem, Lectures 15-16. unabr. ed. Nathaniel Branden. 2 cass. (Running Time: 3 hrs.). 19.95 Set. (635-636) J Norton Pubs.
The Study of Psychology-Ethics-Morality-Anxiety-Depression.

Branden on Self-Esteem, Lectures 17-18. unabr. ed. Nathaniel Branden. 2 cass. (Running Time: 2 hrs. 32 min.). 19.95 Set. (637-638) J Norton Pubs.
Men-Women relationships - Psychological needs - Characteristics of a good relationship - The importance of a relationship enhancing one's own self-esteem - Self-esteem & the psychological meaning of productive work - Pride - The high potential - low performance syndrome.

Branden on Self-Esteem Lectures 1-2: The Goals of Psychology. unabr. ed. Nathaniel Branden. 2 cass. (Running Time: 3 hrs. 2 min.). 19.95 Set. (621-622) J Norton Pubs.
The role of a Psychotherapist - What psychotherapy means & what it entails - Biocentric Psychology - The concept of well-being & neurotic behavior - The foundation of the philosophical approach - The behind-the-scene substructure of the Biocentric approach.

Branden on Self-Esteem Lectures 3-6: The Importance of Understanding One's Needs & Motivations. unabr. ed. Nathaniel Branden. 4 cass. (Running Time: 3 hrs. 27 min.). 39.00 Set. (623-626) J Norton Pubs.
The exploration of some of the distinctive features of human consciousness which have relevance to growth, change, neurosis & psychotherapy - Reason & emotion in Biocentric therapy & psychology.

Branden on Self-Esteem Lectures 7-8: The Role of Self-Esteem in Human Life. unabr. ed. Nathaniel Branden. 2 cass. (Running Time: 2 hrs. 37 min.). 19.95 Set. (627-628) J Norton Pubs.
What self-esteem is - Why humans need it - How & why self-esteem - self-evaluation affects our thinking, emotions, desires, goals & values - The effects that inadequacies or deficiencies of self-esteem have on our thinking processes & lives - Defense Values - Myths.

Branden on Self-Esteem Lectures 9-10: Avoidance, Repression, Self-Deception & the Process of Self-Disowning-the Psychology of Autonomy. unabr. ed. Nathaniel Branden. 2 cass. (Running Time: 2 hrs. 33 min.). 19.95 Set. (629-630) J Norton Pubs.
What it means - What the absence of Autonomy or psychological dependency means, implies & entails.

Branden on Self-Esteem Lectures 19-20: Biocentric Therapy. unabr. ed. Nathaniel Branden. 2 cass. (Running Time: 2 hrs. 14 min.). 19.95 Set. (639-640) J Norton Pubs.
Its goals & techniques - Social implications - Concepts of Progress in Evolutionary terms, Industrial Scientific terms, Psychological terms & Political terms.

Brandenburg. unabr. ed. Glenn Meade. Read by David Case. 12 cass. (Running Time: 18 hrs.). 1999. 96.00 (978-0-7366-4490-7(3), 4921) Books on Tape.
Tipped off by a journalist to a possible drug smuggling scheme, Joseph Volkmann stumbles on a series of unsolved homicides throughout Germany & realizes that far more than narcotics are involved. Pressing on, he learns that the contraband he's been tracking is bomb-grade uranium that a band of neo-Nazis plan to use as part of a coup to take over reunified Germany. With time running out, a desperate Volkmann prepares to mount an assault on an abandoned monastery where the conspirators are preparing to launch a nuclear warhead aimed at the heart of Berlin.

Branding on the Net see 11 Immutable Laws of Internet Branding

***Brandon Bee: Surrendered.** 2009. audio compact disk 5.99 (978-0-9822699-2-3(7)) Rain On Me.

Brandon Bee: This Is the Revolution. Brandon Bee. (ENG.). 2009. audio compact disk 13.98 (978-0-9822699-0-9(0)) Rain On Me.

Brandons. unabr. ed. Angela Thirkell. Read by Nadia May. 9 CDs. (Running Time: 11 hrs. 30 mins.). 2002. audio compact disk 72.00 (978-0-7861-9479-7(0), 2959); 56.95 (978-0-7861-2235-6(8), 2959) Blckstn Audio.
Replete with youthful nonsense and middle-aged folly. People will fall in love with the wrong person, and all are determined to misunderstand each other. The Brandons and their friends and servants are irresistible.

Brandon's Posse. unabr. ed. Ray Hogan. Read by William Dufris. 4 cass. (Running Time: 6 hrs.). (Sagebrush Western Ser.). (J). 2005. 44.95 (978-1-57490-313-3(6)) Pub: ISIS Lrg Prnt GBR. Dist(s): Ulverscroft US

Brannocks. unabr. ed. Matt Braun. Narrated by George Guidall. 7 cass. (Running Time: 9 hrs. 15 mins.). 1996. 60.00 (978-0-7887-0498-7(2), 94691E7) Recorded Bks.
Three brothers seeking new lives in the untamed frontier. Each Brannock follows his own path to fame & romance, until a threat brings them together in a fight for the honor of their family.

Branson Bear & the Kite Contest. Ken Forsse & John Moore. Illus. by Jan Forsse. 1 cass. (J). 1997. bk. 12.95; 9.95 Color Portfolio. Xploractive.
Branson Bear teaches his forest friends how to build very unique kites. Feathers the owl flies & judges the kite contest in this charming story for children ages 3-4.

Bras & Broomsticks. unabr. ed. Sarah Mlynowski. Read by Ariadne Meyers. 7 CDs. (Running Time: 8 hrs.). (Magic in Manhattan Ser.: No. 1). (YA). 2005. audio compact disk 55.00 (978-0-307-20684-8(X), Listening Lib); 45.00 (978-1-4000-9879-8(3), Listening Lib) Random Audio Pubg.
Everyone needs a little magic. Especially 14-year-old Rachel. Not only did her younger sister inherit an ample bosom, she is also a witch.

Brass Bands & Snake Oil Stands: Colorful Glimpses of America's Early Entertainment. Dennis Goodwin. Read by Gwen Hughes. 3 cass. (Running Time: 4 hrs. 30 min.). 1995. 14.95 (978-0-936885-05-6(X)) Activity Factory.
Glimpses of medicine shows, Vaudeville, Wild West shows & more. A time when entertainment was served up in rough-edged slices of pure fun.

Brass Button see Black Museum

Brass Dolphin. unabr. ed. Joanna Trollope. Narrated by Virginia Leishman. 10 CDs. (Running Time: 11 hrs. 45 mins.). audio compact disk 97.00 (978-0-7887-4899-8(8), C1274E7) Recorded Bks.
Set on the exotic island of Malta during World War II, this passionate novel takes us through the many complexities of love, war & self-discovery. When Lila's artist father loses their house to the bank, kind benefactors offer them the use of a family villa on the ancient island of Malta. The twenty-year-old easily adapts to island life & even garners the affection of three intriguing young men. But a year later, German bombers begin daily raids on the island & fear & deprivation become a way of life. After the war, Lila has not only survived intact, but she has also learned some very insightful & unexpected lessons about life. Available to libraries only.

Brass Dolphin. unabr. ed. Joanna Trollope. Narrated by Virginia Leishman. 9 cass. (Running Time: 11 hrs. 45 mins.). 2000. 83.00 (978-0-7887-4310-8(4), 96224E7) Recorded Bks.
When Lila moves to Malta, she adapts to island life & wins the affection of three intriguing young men. But a year later, German bombers begin their daily raids & fear & deprivation become a way of life. Surviving intact, Lila learns some unexpected lessons.

Brass Eagle. unabr. ed. Margaret Duffy. 8 cass. 1998. 83.95 Set. (978-1-85903-017-2(3)) Pub: Magna Story GBR. Dist(s): Ulverscroft US

Brass Tacks: Integrated Skills in English. Lynne Gaetz. 2002. 21.85 (978-0-13-790205-7(0)) Longman.

Brass Verdict. abr. ed. Michael Connelly. Read by Peter Giles. (Running Time: 6 hrs.). (Mickey Haller Ser.). 2008. 19.98 (978-1-60024-398-1(3)) Pub: Hachet Audio. Dist(s): HachBkGrp

Brass Verdict. abr. ed. Michael Connelly. Read by Peter Giles. 5 CDs. (Running Time: 6 hrs.). (Mickey Haller Ser.). 2009. audio compact disk 14.98 (978-1-60024-821-4(7)) Pub: Hachet Audio. Dist(s): HachBkGrp

Brass Verdict. unabr. ed. Michael Connelly. Read by Peter Giles. (Running Time: 11 hrs.). (Mickey Haller Ser.). 2008. 26.98 (978-1-60024-400-1(9)); audio compact disk 39.98 (978-1-60024-401-8(7)) Pub: Hachet Audio. Dist(s): HachBkGrp

Brass Verdict. unabr. ed. Michael Connelly. Read by Peter Giles. 7 cass. (Mickey Haller Ser.). 2008. 110.00 (978-1-4159-6088-2(7), BksonTape); audio compact disk 110.00 (978-1-4159-6065-3(8), BksonTape) Pub: Random Audio Pubg. Dist(s): Random

Brassed Off. abr. ed. 2 cass. 1998. 15.00 Set. (978-1-86117-181-8(1)) Ulvrscrft Audio.
The miners of Grimley Colliery are facing uncertainty & the Crimley Colliery Band is on the verge of breaking up - that is until Gloria arrives.

Brat Farrar. unabr. ed. Josephine Tey. Read by Carole Boyd. 8 cass. (Running Time: 12 hrs.). 2000. 59.95 (978-0-7451-6320-8(3), CAB 499) Pub: Chivers Audio Bks GBR. Dist(s): AudioGO
Soon after the death of his parents, Patrick Ashby disappeared without a trace, leaving a suicide note on a lonely clifftop. It was a severe shock to the family, but the years passed and the memories gradually faded. Then, on the eve of Simon Ashby's coming of age, a young man turns up at Latchetts. He calls himself Brat Farrar, and his physical resemblance to Simon is so remarkable that even Ashby's solicitor is convinced of his right, as Patrick, to claim the family inheritance.

***Brava.** unabr. ed. Elmore Leonard. (ENG.). 2010. (978-0-06-206258-1(1), Harper Audio); (978-0-06-206272-7(7), Harper Audio) HarperCollins Pubs.

Brava, Valentine. unabr. ed. Adriana Trigiani. Read by Cassandra Campbell. 2010. audio compact disk 39.99 (978-0-06-179139-0(3), Harper Audio) HarperCollins Pubs.

***Brava, Valentine.** unabr. ed. Adriana Trigiani. Read by Cassandra Campbell. (ENG.). 2010. (978-0-06-196929-4(X), Harper Audio); (978-0-06-196928-7(1), Harper Audio) HarperCollins Pubs.

Brave. Contrib. by Nichole Nordeman. 2005. audio compact disk 16.98 (978-5-559-05796-5(7)) Pt of Grace Ent.

Brave. collector's ed. Gregory Mcdonald. Read by Alexander Adams. 3 cass. (Running Time: 4 hrs. 30 min.). 1999. 24.95 (978-0-7366-4661-1(2), 5043) Books on Tape.
Though he is not yet 21, Rafael is married, has three kids & lives next to the dump in a forgotten corner of America's Southwest. Alcoholic since boyhood, he is unemployed & hopeless. Then, a miracle: For $200 cash & a contract that promises $30,000 to his wife & children, he gets hired for a snuff film. It may be the end for him, but it will be the beginning for them. The $200 goes for a family feast in the trailer, then he's off to work. And did we mention that the contract is bogus.

***Brave: A Novel.** unabr. ed. Nicholas Evans. Read by Michael Emerson. (Running Time: 10 hrs.). (ENG.). 2010. 24.98 (978-1-60788-630-3(8)); audio compact disk 34.98 (978-1-60788-629-7(4)) Pub: Hachet Audio. Dist(s): HachBkGrp

Brave Cowboy: An Old Tale in a New Time. unabr. collector's ed. Edward Abbey. Read by Paul Shay. 7 cass. (Running Time: 10 hrs. 30 min.). 1988. 56.00 (978-0-7366-1255-5(6), 2169) Books on Tape.
Modern day Western, of a man who is jailed for refusing the draft. Became the movie "Lonely Are the Brave".

Brave Enemies. unabr. ed. Robert Morgan. 8 cass. (Running Time: 12 hrs.). 2003. 64.00 (978-0-7366-9641-8(5)) Books on Tape.

Brave Heart. Perf. by Kim Hill. 1 cass. 1991. audio compact disk Brentwood Music.
Taking home a Dove Award for music packaging, Kim's third release features the No. 1 song, Mysterious Ways.

Brave Hearts. 1 cass.; 9.98; audio compact disk 15.98 CD. Lifedance.
Celtic music infused with modern sensibilities, resulting in music that is rhythmic, exuberant, experimental, & just a whole lot of fun. Bagpipes, fiddles, vocals, percussion, & countless celtic instruments. Demo CD or cassette available. Demo CD or cassette available.

Brave Hearts: New Scots Music. 1 cass., 1 CD. 7.98 (NAR 45445); audio compact disk 12.78 CD. (NAR 45445) NewSound.

Brave Irene. 2004. pap. bk. 32.75 (978-1-55592-195-8(7)); 8.95 (978-0-7882-0053-3(4)); cass. & flmstrp 30.00 (978-0-89719-605-5(8)) Weston Woods.

Brave Irene. (J). 2004. bk. 24.95 (978-1-56008-006-0(X)) Weston Woods.

Brave Irene. William Steig. Narrated by Lindsay Crouse. 1 cass., 5 bks. (Running Time: 14 min.). (J). pap. bk. 32.75 Weston Woods.
Irene, the dressmaker's daughter, is the classic heroine who battles powerful wind & snow to deliver a ball gown promised to the Duchess.

Brave Irene. William Steig. Narrated by Lindsay Crouse. 1 cass. (Running Time: 14 min.). (J). (ps-4). bk. 24.95 Weston Woods.

Brave Irene. William Steig. Narrated by Lindsay Crouse. 1 cass. (Running Time: 14 min.). (J). (ps-4). 1989. pap. bk. 14.95 (978-1-56008-007-7(8), PRA331) Weston Woods.

Brave Irene. William Steig. Read by Lindsay Crouse. 1 cass. (Running Time: 14 min.). (J). (ps-4). 1989. 8.95 (978-0-89719-989-6(8), RAC331) Weston Woods.

Brave Lion, Scared Lion see Leon Valiente, Leon Miedoso

Brave Little Red & Other Tales: Folktales for the 21st Century. Perf. by LuAnn Adams. (Folktales For The 21st Century). 1998. 10.99 (978-0-9715341-0-0(1)) LuAnn Adams.

Brave Little Tailor see Goldilocks & the Three Bears & Other Stories

***Brave Little Tailor.** Anonymous. 2009. (978-1-60136-533-0(0)) Audio Holding.

Brave Mouse. Jill Eggleton. Illus. by Clive Taylor. (Sails Literacy Ser.). (gr. 1 up). 10.00 (978-0-7578-2657-3(1)) Rigby Educ.

Brave New World see Feliz Mundo Nuevo

Brave New World. Aldous Huxley. Read by Laura Garcia. (Running Time: 3 hrs.). 2005. 8.95 (978-1-60083-278-9(4), Audiofy Corp) Iofy Corp.

Brave New World. Aldous Huxley. Perf. by William Conrad. 1 cass. (Running Time: 60 min.). Dramatization. (CBS Radio Workshop Ser.). 1956. 6.00 Once Upon Rad.
Radio broadcasts - fantasy & science fiction.

Brave New World. Aldous Huxley. 1 cass. (Running Time: 1 hr.). (Radiobook Ser.). 1987. 4.98 (978-0-929541-03-7(0)) Radiola Co.

Brave New World. unabr. ed. Aldous Huxley. Read by Michael York. 6 cass. (Running Time: 8 hrs. 20 mins.). (gr. 9-12). 2004. 29.95 (978-1-57270-064-2(5), B61054u) Pub: Audio Partners. Dist(s): PerseusPGW
Cloning & feel-good drugs - has Huxley accurately predicted our future? Illustrates many controversies brought about science & technology.

Brave New World. unabr. ed. Aldous Huxley. Narrated by Michael York. 1 MP3-CD. (Running Time: 8 hrs 20 mins.). 2008. 44.95 (978-0-7927-5321-6(6)); audio compact disk 74.95 (978-0-7927-5225-7(2)) AudioGO.
On the 75th anniversary of its publication, this outstanding work of literature is more crucial and relevant today than ever before. Cloning, feel-good drugs, anti-aging programs, and total social control through politics, programming and media - has Aldous Huxley accurately predicted our future? With a storyteller's genius, he weaves these ethical controversies in a compelling narrative that dawns in the year 632 A. F. (After Ford, the deity). When Lenina and Bernard visit a savage reservation, we experience how Utopia can destroy humanity.

Brave New World. unabr. ed. Aldous Huxley. Read by Michael York. (YA). 2008. 64.99 (978-1-60514-874-8(1)) Find a World.

Brave New World. 75th unabr. ed. Aldous Huxley. Narrated by Michael York. (Running Time: 30000 sec.). (ENG.). 2007. audio compact disk 29.95 (978-1-60283-336-4(2)) Pub: AudioGO. Dist(s): Perseus Dist

Brave New World: Forecast of the Future. Aldous Huxley. Perf. by William Conrad. 1 cass. (Running Time: 60 min.). 1956. 7.95 (DD-7900) Natl Recrd Co.
The Director of Hatcheries & Conditioning is taking new students on a tour of the hatchery where human beings are bred & cultivated artificially. The tour continues to the bottling room, the pre-conditioning room & the nursery. The sound effects are outstanding.

Brave New World - after the Flood: A World of Devils, Demons, & Dinosaurs. 2005. 15.00 (978-1-933561-10-3(6)) BFM Books.

Braveheart. abr. ed. Randall Wallace. Read by Alan Shearman. 2 cass. (J). 1995. 16.95 (978-1-55935-166-9(7), 392934) Soundelux.
A story of passion & perseverance & the legendary life of William Wallace, the 13th century Scottish hero who struggled to restore the sovereignty of his Scottish homeland from British rule. The film version received several 1996 Academy Awards.

Bravest Kids in Town. (J). 2003. audio compact disk (978-1-930429-47-5(9)) Love Logic.

Bravest Man. William Tuohy. Read by E. H. Jones. 2002. 88.00 (978-0-7366-8918-2(4)) Books on Tape.

Braving the Brimstone. Maria K. Simms. 1 cass. 8.95 (183) Am Fed Astrologers.
Does the Bible really condemn astrology.

Bravo! Mormon Youth Chorus and Symphony. 1 cass. 2.97 (10001395); audio compact disk 12.95 (28001036) Covenant Comms.

Bravo. 4th ed. Muyskens. (C). 2001. bk., wbk. ed., lab manual ed. 29.50 (978-0-8384-1328-9(5)) Heinle.

Bravo. 4th ed. Judith Muyskens et al. 1 CD. (Running Time: 1 hr.). (ENG.). (C). 2001. 45.95 (978-0-8384-1347-0(1)) Pub: Heinle. Dist(s): CENGAGE Learn
One-volume intermediate French text that integrates communication, grammar, culture and literature.

Bravo: Testbank. Muyskens et al. 2001. audio compact disk 29.50 (978-0-8384-1357-9(9)) Heinle.
Intermediate French text that integrates communication, grammar, culture and literature. It was created to respond to the challenge of students entering intermediate classes with different levels of preparedness. Each chapter of BRAVO! opens with La grammaire à réviser (grammar to review) to provide students with the opportunity to review certain grammar points that they have already been exposed to in first-year courses.

Bravo! Beethoven. 1 cass. (Vox - Turnabout Classical Ser.). 3.98 (CTX 4803) VOX Music Grp.

Bravo Two Zero. unabr. ed. Andy McNab. Read by Christian Rodska. 10 cass. (Running Time: 15 hrs.). 2000. 69.95 (978-0-7451-6542-4(7), CAB 1158) Pub: Chivers Audio Bks GBR. Dist(s): AudioGO
The Gulf War. On a January night in 1991, eight men set off on a mission to sever links between Baghdad and north-west Iraq, and to destroy Scud missile launchers before Israel is provoked into the war. Within days, the patrol is stricken with hypothermia and other injuries. Four men were captured, three died, and only one escaped. But in their wake lay 250 Iraqi casualties. This is their commander's powerfully shocking story.

***Brazen Bride.** unabr. ed. Stephanie Laurens. Read by Simon Prebble. (Running Time: 13 hrs. 30 mins.). (Black Cobra Quartet, Book 3 Ser.). 2010. 29.95 (978-1-4417-4316-9(2)); 79.95 (978-1-4417-4312-1(X)); audio compact disk 109.00 (978-1-4417-4313-8(8)) Blckstn Audio.

***Brazen Bride.** unabr. ed. Stephanie Laurens. Read by Simon Prebble. (ENG.). 2010. (978-0-06-201597-6(4), Harper Audio); (978-0-06-199562-0(2), Harper Audio) HarperCollins Pubs.

Brazen Careerist. unabr. ed. Penelope Trunk. (Running Time: 4 hrs. 30 mins. 0 sec.). (ENG.). 2007. audio compact disk 19.99 (978-1-4001-5365-7(4)) Pub: Tantor Media. Dist(s): IngramPubServ

Brazen Careerist: The New Rules for Success. unabr. ed. Penelope Trunk. Read by Shelly Frasier. (Running Time: 4 hrs. 30 mins. 0 sec.). (ENG.). 2007. audio compact disk 24.99 (978-1-4001-0365-2(7)) Pub: Tantor Media. Dist(s): IngramPubServ

Brazen Careerist: The New Rules for Success. unabr. ed. Penelope Trunk. Read by Shelly Frasier. (Running Time: 4 hrs. 30 mins. 0 sec.). (ENG.). 2007. audio compact disk 49.99 (978-1-4001-3365-9(3)) Pub: Tantor Media. Dist(s): IngramPubServ

Brazen Laver & the Holiness of God. Rick Joyner. 1 cass. (Running Time: 90 mins.). (Foundation Ser.: Vol. 10). 2000. 5.00 (RJ05-010) Morning NC.
As an overview of God's plan for His church, this series contains essential truths for everyone who wants to see the church become all that she is called to be.

Brazil. Compiled by Benchmark Education Staff. 2006. audio compact disk 10.00 (978-1-4108-6649-3(1)) Benchmark Educ.

Brazil Story: An Experience with Ayahusca. W. Brugh Joy. 1 cass. 1999. 18.00 (35001) Big Sur Tapes.
1994 Arizona.

Brazilian Adventure. unabr. collector's ed. Peter Fleming. Read by Richard Green. 9 cass. (Running Time: 13 hrs. 30 mins.). 1987. 72.00 (978-0-7366-1116-9(9), 2039) Books on Tape.
In 1932, Peter Fleming joined a search for the celebrated English adventurer Colonel P.H. Fawcett, missing for 5 years in the jungles of central Brazil. With meager supplies, faulty maps, & rival newspapermen hot on their trail, Fleming & his companions marched through 3000 miles of savage country toward an uncertain rendezvous with the lost colonel!.

Brazilian Guitar Book. Nelson Faria. 1995. pap. bk. 26.00 (978-1-883217-02-0(4), 00242141) Pub: Sher Music. Dist(s): H Leonard

Brazilian Jazz Guitar. Mike Christiansen & John Zaradin. 1998. audio compact disk 19.95 (978-0-7866-7023-9(1), WMB010BCD) Mel Bay.

Brazilian Music for Acoustic Guitar. Carlos Barbosa-Lima. 1993. pap. bk. 18.95 (978-0-7866-1151-5(0), 94840P); pap. bk. 23.95 (978-0-7866-1150-8(2), 94840CDP); 10.98 (978-1-56222-794-4(7), 94840C); audio compact disk 15.98 (978-0-7866-0371-8(2), 95397CD) Mel Bay.

Brazilian Portuguese: Learn to Speak & Understand Brazilian Portuguese with Pimsleur Language Programs. 2nd abr. unabr. ed. Pimsleur Staff. 8 CDs. (Running Time: 80 hrs. 0 mins. 0 sec.). (Instant Conversation Ser.). (POR & ENG.). 2005. audio compact disk 49.95 (978-0-7435-5044-4(7), Audioworks) Pub: S&S Audio. Dist(s): S and S Inc

Brazilian Portuguese: Learn to Speak & Understand Brazilian Portuguese with Pimsleur Language Programs. 2nd unabr. ed. Pimsleur Staff. Created by Simon and Schuster Staff. 5 CDs. (Running Time: 50 hrs. 0 mins. 0 sec.). (Basic Ser.). (POR & ENG.). 2005. audio compact disk 24.95 (978-0-7435-5069-7(2), Pimsleur) Pub: S&S Audio. Dist(s): S and S Inc

Brazilian Portuguese Basic Course Vol. 2 (FSI) CDs & Text. 18 CDs. (Running Time: 16 hrs.). (Foreign Service Institute Basic Course Ser.). (POR.). 2005. audio compact disk 275.00 (978-1-57970-243-4(0), AFP180D) J Norton Pubs.

Brazilian Portuguese II: Learn to Speak & Understand Portuguese with Pimsleur Language Programs. Pimsleur Staff. (Running Time: 160 hrs. 0 mins. 0 sec.). (Comprehensive Ser.). (ENG.). 2001. audio compact disk 345.00 (978-0-671-77626-8(6), Pimsleur) Pub: S&S Audio. Dist(s): S and S Inc

Brazilian Rhythms for Drumset. Duduka Da Fonseca & Bob Weiner. Intro. by Emily Moorefield. Contrib. by John Riley & Edilberto Mendez. 1 cass. (Drummers Collective Ser.). pap. bk. 24.95 (BD080) DCI Music Video.
A guide to applying traditional Brazilian rhythms to drumset. Rhythms covered are samba, partido alto, bossa nova, baiao, caterete, maracatu, marcha & fredo.

Brazilian Rhythms for Solo Guitar. Flavio Henrique Medeiros & Carlos Almada. 1999. pap. bk. 17.95 (978-0-7866-4700-2(0), 98226BCD) Mel Bay.

Brazos. unabr. ed. Jory Sherman. Read by Michael Taylor. 6 cass. (Running Time: 7 hrs. 30 min.). 2001. 39.95 (978-1-58116-058-1(5)) Books in Motion.
Nancy Stafford left St. Louis with her husband and son, drawn by the promise of new life in Texas. But when her family is killed in a Comanche attack, Nancy finds herself alone in a desolate and unknown land, determined to build a home and a new life in honor of her family's memory.

Brazzaville Beach. unabr. ed. William Boyd. Read by Donada Peters. 8 cass. (Running Time: 12 hrs.). 1998. 64.00 (978-0-7366-4012-1(6), 4510) Books on Tape.
A primate researcher contemplates her recent past, chimps & the nature of good & evil. A witty, dark story by an acclaimed novelist.

***Breach.** unabr. ed. Patrick Lee. Read by Jeff Gurner. (ENG.). 2010. (978-0-06-200649-3(5), Harper Audio); (978-0-06-200998-2(2), Harper Audio) HarperCollins Pubs.

Breach of Duty. unabr. ed. J. A. Jance. Read by Gene Engene. 8 cass. (Running Time: 10 hrs. 12 min.). (J. P. Beaumont Mystery Ser.). 1999. 49.95 (978-1-55686-897-9(9)) Books in Motion.
A Seattle police detective investigates the death of an elderly woman burned in her bed & a series of incidents related to an apparent curse on the stolen bones of a Native American shaman.

Breach of Faith: Hurricane Katrina & the near Death of a Great American City. Jed Horne. 2008. audio compact disk 49.95 (978-0-9779883-6-5(8)) Legacy Audio Bks.

Breach of Faith: The Fall of Richard Nixon. unabr. collector's ed. Theodore H. White. Read by John MacDonald. 12 cass. (Running Time: 18 hrs.). 1987. 96.00 (978-0-7366-1215-9(7), 2134) Books on Tape.
Examination of the Watergate affair & the history of Nixon & his political advisors.

Breach of Promise. abr. ed. Perri O'Shaughnessy. Read by Laural Merlington. 3 CDs. (Running Time: 3 hrs.). (Nina Reilly Ser.). 2002. audio compact disk 62.25 (978-1-59086-466-1(2), 1590864662, CD Lib Edit) Brilliance Audio.
At glitzy Lake Tahoe, couples break up every day, but none quite so glamorous or successful as Lindy and Mike Markov. The scenario starts off in the standard way: Mike's met a younger woman and wants out. The problem? Mike and Lindy built a $200-million business together and Mike claims he doesn't owe Lindy a dime since they never married. Ready to fight, Lindy hires Nina Reilly to represent her in her palimony suit, and lacking the resources to handle a case with stakes so high, Nina turns to an expert litigator in palimony law who insists on hiring a jury consultant. The case is hardly open-and-shut, and complicating things further, a carefully chosen juror winds up dead. With a host of possible suspects and the biggest case of her career hanging in the balance, the pressure's on Nina to find the killer, win the case, and save the day.

***Breach of Promise.** abr. ed. Perri O'Shaughnessy. Read by Laural Merlington. (Running Time: 3 hrs.). 2010. audio compact disk 9.99 (978-1-4418-6270-9(6), 9781441862709, BCD Value Price) Brilliance Audio.

Breach of Promise. unabr. ed. Perri O'Shaughnessy. Read by Laural Merlington. 10 cass. (Running Time: 13 hrs.). 1998. 89.25 (978-1-56740-595-8(9), 1567405959, Unabridge Lib Edns) Brilliance Audio.

Breach of Promise. unabr. ed. Perri O'Shaughnessy. Read by Laural Merlington. (Running Time: 13 hrs.). 2007. 39.25 (978-1-4233-3064-6(1), 9781423330646, BADLE); 24.95 (978-1-4233-3063-9(3), 9781423330639, BAD) Brilliance Audio.

Breach of Promise. unabr. ed. Perri O'Shaughnessy. Read by Laural Merlington. (Running Time: 13 hrs.). 2007. 39.25 (978-1-4233-3062-2(5), 9781423330622, Brlnc Audio MP3 Lib); 24.95 (978-1-4233-3061-5(7), 9781423330615, Brilliance MP3) Brilliance Audio.

***Breach of Promise.** unabr. ed. Perri O'Shaughnessy. Read by Laural Merlington. (Running Time: 14 hrs.). 2010. audio compact disk 89.97 (978-1-4418-4028-8(1), 9781441840288, BriAudCD Unabrid) Brilliance Audio.

Breach of Promise. unabr. ed. Perri O'Shaughnessy. Read by Laural Merlington. 10 cass. 1999. 89.25 (FS9-43214) Highsmith.

***Breach of Promise.** unabr. ed. Perri O'Shaughnessy & Thriller-Legal Staff. Read by Laural Merlington. (Running Time: 14 hrs.). 2010. audio compact disk 29.99 (978-1-4418-4027-1(3), 9781441840271) Brilliance Audio.

Breach of Promise. unabr. ed. Anne Perry. Read by Terrence Hardiman. 10 vols. (Running Time: 15 hrs.). (William Monk Novel Ser.). 2000. bk. 84.95 (978-0-7927-2296-0(5), CSL 185, Chivers Sound Lib) AudioGO.
Killian Melville is a brilliant architect. Young and intelligent, he is liked by everyone. Despite his talent he maintains an honesty which endears him to Victorian Society. So when he visits Sir Oliver Rathbone, in need of the best lawyer there is to represent him over an alleged "breach of promise", Rathbone agrees despite his misgivings. However, Melville has nothing concrete in his defense.

Breach of Promise. unabr. ed. Anne Perry. Read by Terrence Hardiman. 14 CDs. (Running Time: 21 hrs.). (William Monk Novel Ser.). 2001. audio compact disk 115.95 (978-0-7927-9973-3(9), SLD 024, Chivers Sound Lib) AudioGO.
When Killian Melville seeks out Sir Oliver Rathbone's help in defending him over an alleged 'breach of promise', the case proves to be a very difficult one, especially when Melville has nothing concrete to offer in his defense.

Breach of Trust. unabr. ed. D. W. Buffa. Read by Buck Schirner. 8 cass. (Running Time: 14 hrs.). (Joseph Antonelli Ser.). 2004. 34.95 (978-1-59086-796-9(3), 1590867963, BAU); 97.25 (978-1-59086-797-6(1), 1590867971, BrilAudUnabridg) Brilliance Audio.
In Breach of Trust Antonelli is seduced into taking an old case that has dangerous implications for the upcoming United States presidential race, but also for a group of old friends who thought they had put the sudden death of a young woman years ago long behind them. When Antonelli attends a Harvard Law School reunion at Manhattan's Plaza Hotel, he doesn't suspect how disturbing his return will be - for it was at a party in this very hotel that a bright and lively young woman fell from a window to her death. The event was ruled an accident at the time, but the case is about to be reopened, and a potential witness is wary of its potential to ruin his political chances - a man with promise and ambition in equal measure - the vice president of the United States. When the trial begins, the nation's eyes turn to the accused, the downtrodden James Haviland, and to the unseen powers both within and without the White House who want to bury him. It's up to the shrewd and sharp Antonelli to uncover just where the secrets lie - and exactly who is playing whom.

Breach of Trust. unabr. ed. D. W. Buffa. Read by Buck Schirner. (Running Time: 14 hrs.). (Joseph Antonelli Ser.). 2004. 39.25 (978-1-59335-651-4(X), 159335651X, Brlnc Audio MP3 Lib); 24.95 (978-1-59335-288-2(3), 1593352883, Brilliance MP3) Brilliance Audio.

Breach of Trust. unabr. ed. D. W. Buffa. Read by Buck Schirner. (Running Time: 14 hrs.). (Joseph Antonelli Ser.). 2004. 39.25 (978-1-59710-109-7(5), 1597101095, BADLE); 24.95 (978-1-59710-108-0(7), 1597101087, BAD) Brilliance Audio.

Breach of Trust. unabr. ed. David Ellis. (Running Time: 15 hrs.). 2011. audio compact disk 32.99 (978-1-4233-7931-7(4), 9781423379317, Bril Audio CD Unabri) Brilliance Audio.

***Breach of Trust.** unabr. ed. David Ellis. Read by Luke Daniels. (Running Time: 15 hrs.). 2011. 39.97 (978-1-4233-7936-2(5), 9781423379362, BADLE); 24.99 (978-1-4233-7935-5(7), 9781423379355, BAD); 24.99 (978-1-4233-7933-1(0), 9781423379331, Brilliance MP3); 39.97 (978-1-4233-7934-8(9), 9781423379348, Brlnc Audio MP3 Lib); audio compact disk 84.97 (978-1-4233-7932-4(2), 9781423379324, BriAudCD Unabrid) Brilliance Audio.

Breach of Trust: How Washington Resists Reform & Makes Outsiders Insiders. unabr. ed. Tom A. Coburn & John Hart. Read by Richard Fredricks. 7 CDs. (Running Time: 8 hrs.). 2003. audio compact disk 29.95 (978-1-59355-281-7(5), 1593552815); 27.95 (978-1-59355-279-4(3), 1593552793) Brilliance Audio.
Tom A. Coburn, a congressional maverick who kept his promise to serve three terms and then leave Washington, offers a candid look at the inner workings of Congress - why the system changes politicians instead of vice versa. Breach of Trust shows listeners, through shocking behind-the-scenes stories, why Washington resists the reform our country desperately needs and how they can make wise, informed decisions about current and future political issues and candidates. This honest and critical look at "business as usual" in Congress reveals how and why elected representatives are quickly seduced into becoming career politicians who won't push for change. Along the way, Coburn offers listeners realistic ideas for how to make a difference.

Breach of Trust: How Washington Resists Reform & Makes Outsiders Insiders. unabr. ed. Tom A. Coburn & John Hart. Read by Tom A. Coburn & Richard Fredricks. 6 cass. (Running Time: 8 hrs.). 2003. 69.25 (978-1-59355-280-0(7), 1593552807); audio compact disk 87.25 (978-1-59355-282-4(3), 1593552823) Brilliance Audio.

Breach of Trust: How Washington Turns Outsiders into Insiders. unabr. ed. Tom A. Coburn & John Hart. Read by Richard Fredricks. (Running Time: 8 hrs.). 2004. 39.25 (978-1-59335-505-0(X), 159335505X, Brlnc Audio MP3 Lib) Brilliance Audio.

Breach of Trust: How Washington Turns Outsiders into Insiders. unabr. ed. Tom A. Coburn & John Hart. Read by Richard Fredricks. (Running Time: 14 hrs.). 2004. 39.25 (978-1-59710-106-6(0), 1597101060, BADLE); 24.95 (978-1-59710-107-3(9), 1597101079, BAD) Brilliance Audio.

Breach of Trust: How Washington Turns Outsiders into Insiders. unabr. ed. Tom A. Coburn & John Hart. Read by Richard Fredricks. (Running Time: 8 hrs.). 2004. 24.95 (978-1-59335-232-5(8), 1593352328) Soulmate Audio Bks.

Bread. unabr. ed. Ed McBain, pseud. Read by Michael Prichard. 7 cass. (Running Time: 7 hrs.). (87th Precinct Ser.: Bk. 29). 1987. 42.00 (978-0-7366-1198-5(3), 2116) Books on Tape.
An '87th Precinct' mystery-thriller: police, drugs, & murder.

Bread & Chocolate. unabr. ed. Philippa Gregory. Read by Jacqueline King & Richard Heffer. 6 CDs. (Running Time: 24300 sec.). (Isis Ser.). 2003. audio compact disk 64.95 (978-0-7531-2248-8(0)) Pub: ISIS Lrg Prnt GBR. Dist(s): Ulverscroft US
A delicious new collection of short stories.

Bread & Chocolate. unabr. ed. Philippa Gregory et al. 6 cass. (Isis Ser.). (J). 2003. 54.95 (978-0-7531-1009-6(1)) Pub: ISIS Lrg Prnt GBR. Dist(s): Ulverscroft US

Bread & Roses, Too. unabr. ed. Katherine Paterson. Read by Lorna Raver. 6 CDs. (Running Time: 6 hrs. 30 mins.). (J). (gr. 4-7). 2006. audio compact disk 42.50 (978-0-7393-3594-9(4), Listening Lib); 35.00 (978-0-7393-3593-2(6), Listening Lib) Pub: Random Audio Pubg. Dist(s): Random
Rosa's mother is singing again, for the first time since Papa died in an accident in the mills. But instead of filling their cramped tenement apartment with Italian lullabies, Mamma is out on the streets singing union songs. Rosa is terrified that her mother and older sister, Anna, are endangering their lives by marching against the corrupt mill owners. After all, didn't Miss Finch tell the class that the strikers are nothing but rabble-rousers - an uneducated, violent mob? Suppose Mamma and Anna are jailed or, worse, killed? What will happen to Rosa and little Ricci? When Rosa is sent to Vermont with other children to live with strangers until the strike is over, she fears she will never see her family again. Then, on the train, a boy begs her to pretend that he's her brother. Alone and far from home, she agrees to protect him... even though she suspects that he is hiding some terrible secret.

Bread & Roses, Too. unabr. ed. Katherine Paterson. Read by Lorna Raver. 6 CDs. (Running Time: 24600 sec.). (ENG.). (J). (gr. 5). 2006. audio compact disk 39.00 (978-0-7393-3107-1(8), Listening Lib) Pub: Random Audio Pubg. Dist(s): Random

Bread for Life Audio. Instructed by Beth Holland. (Running Time: 90 mins.). 1996. 5.00 (978-0-9753922-8-7(X)) Bread For Life.
90 minute audio excerpt from the 5 1/2 hour Bread For Life Video presentation covering the medically and scientifically documented links between the typical American diet and many of the diseases that are now common to us (heart attack, diabetes, cancer, constipation, appendicitis, diverticulitis, obesity, hiatal hernias, hemorrhoids, varicose veins, etc) and how tasty, simple, dietary changes to whole foods can prevent and many times reverse these deadly enemies of health.

Bread for the Journey. Contrib. by Shaina Noll & Russell Walden. (Running Time: 50 min.). 1995. audio compact disk 15.99 (978-5-559-68369-0(8)) Pub: Pt of Grace Ent. Dist(s): STL Dist NA

Bread from Heaven. Edward Hays. 2 cass. (Running Time: 60 min. per cass.). 14.95 set in vinyl album. (For Peace Pubng) Ave Maria Pr.
These four recorded "live" conferences reflect on the mystical words of Jesus, "I am the Bread from Heaven." Weaving together such images as Toasties, Graham crackers, Elijah's hearth cake & ancient manna. Father Hays both entertains & inner-attains. Expanding our horizons beyond the Holy Eucharist, these reflections call us to a broader view of Jesus as the New Manna, to how we are nourished by the life-giving word of the Gospels & by each other, since we together from the Living Bread of the Body of Christ. These conferences challenge us to not be half-baked, but fully fired in the hot oven of daily suffering & sacrifice.

Bread of Angels: A Journey to Love & Faith. unabr. ed. Stephanie Saldana. (Running Time: 10 hrs. 30 mins.). 2010. audio compact disk 100.00 (978-1-4417-2911-8(9)) Blckstn Audio.

Bread of Angels: A Journey to Love & Faith. unabr. ed. Stephanie Saldana. (Running Time: 10 hrs. 30 mins.). 2010. 29.95 (978-1-4417-2914-9(3)); 65.95 (978-1-4417-2910-1(0)); audio compact disk 32.95 (978-1-4417-2913-2(5)) Blckstn Audio.

bread of Life see Pan de Vida

Breadmaker's Carnival. unabr. ed. Andrew Lindsay. Read by Noel Hodda. 8 cass. (Running Time: 10 hrs.). 2004. 64.00 (978-1-74030-339-2(3)); audio compact disk 93.95 (978-1-74093-505-0(5)) Pub: Bolinda Pubng AUS. Dist(s): Bolinda Pub Inc

Breadwinner. Deborah Ellis. 2 cass. (Running Time: 3 hrs.). (J). (gr. 5-7). 2004. 23.00 (978-0-8072-0974-5(0), Listening Lib) Random Audio Pubg.
Parvana is forbidden by the Taliban government to earn money as a girl, so she must transform herself into a boy and become the breadwinner.

Breadwinner. unabr. ed. Deborah Ellis. Read by Rita Wolf. 2 vols. (Running Time: 3 hrs.). (J). (gr. 5-7). 2004. pap. bk. 29.00 (978-0-8072-0982-0(1), S YA 411 SP, Listening Lib) Random Audio Pubg.

Break & Enter. unabr. ed. Colin Harrison. Narrated by George Guidall. 10 cass. (Running Time: 13 hrs. 45 mins.). 1990. 85.00 (978-1-55690-071-6(6), 90092E7) Recorded Bks.
Philadelphia Assistant D. A., Peter Scattergood, lands the case of his career only to find that no one is left on his side - not even his wife.

Break Bad Habits & Addictions: Guided Meditation. Concept by Vicky Thurlow. Voice by Vicky Thurlow. (ENG.). 2008. audio compact disk 14.95 (978-0-9817055-5-2(3)) DVT Invest.

Break Dividing Walls. Keith Giles. 1 cass. 1996. 8.99 (978-0-7684-0042-7(2)); audio compact disk 12.99 CD. (978-0-7684-0043-4(0)) Destiny Image Pubs.

Break Free. Lynnita Mattock. 3 cass. (Running Time: 60 min.). bk. 24.95 Set. (BF-90) Psych Res Inst.
Designed to enable the listener through subliminal suggestion to end the destructiveness of substance abuse.

Break In. Dick Francis. Read by Simon Prebble. 8 CDs. (Running Time: 9.5 Hrs). (Kit Fielding Adventure Ser.: Bk. 1). audio compact disk 39.95 (978-1-4025-3708-0(5)) Recorded Bks.

Break In. unabr. ed. Dick Francis. Read by Tony Britton. 8 cass. (Running Time: 8 hrs.). (Kit Fielding Adventure Ser.: Bk. 1). 1994. 69.95 Set. (978-0-7451-4225-8(7), CAB 908) AudioGO.
Family ties mean trouble, & when steeplechase jockey Kit Fielding comes to aid his twin sister & her husband Bobby, even death threatens. A vicious newspaper campaign jeopardizes Bobby's career as a racehorse trainer. Kit tries to find out who is behind it all, but there are powerful people who think Kit should mind his own business.

Break In. unabr. ed. Dick Francis. Read by Tony Britton. 8 cass. (Running Time: 12 hrs.). (Kit Fielding Adventure Ser.: Bk. 1). 2000. 59.95 (CAB 908) Pub: Chivers Audio Bks GBR. Dist(s): AudioGO
Family ties mean trouble when steeplechase jockey Kit Fielding comes to aid his twin sister and her husband Bobby. When a vicious newspaper campaign jeopardizes Bobby's career, Kit tries to find out who is behind it all. But powerful people think Kit should mind his own business.

Break In. unabr. ed. Dick Francis. Read by Nigel Havers. 2 read-along cass. (Kit Fielding Adventure Ser.: Bk. 1). bk. 34.95 (S23913) J Norton Pubs.

Break In. unabr. ed. Dick Francis. Read by Simon Prebble. 6 Cass. (Running Time: 9.5 Hrs). (Kit Fielding Adventure Ser.: Bk. 1). 29.95 (978-1-4025-3707-3(7)) Recorded Bks.

Break In. unabr. ed. Dick Francis. Narrated by Simon Prebble. 8 CDs. (Running Time: 9 hrs. 30 mins.). (Kit Fielding Adventure Ser.: Bk. 1). 1999. audio compact disk 73.00 (978-0-7887-3717-6(1), C1074E7) Recorded Bks.
Jockey Kit Fielding's winning streak is interrupted when his twin sister calls him for help. Threatened with scandal, she & her husband may lose their training stables. Behind the threat, however, lurks danger that could permanently sever the bond between Kit & his sister.

Break In. unabr. ed. Dick Francis. Narrated by Simon Prebble. 7 cass. (Running Time: 9 hrs. 30 mins.). (Kit Fielding Adventure Ser.: Bk. 1). 1999. 60.00 (978-0-7887-2941-6(1), 95722E7) Recorded Bks.

Break in Your Cycle: The Medical & Emotional Causes & Effects of Amenorrhea. Theresa Francis-Cheung. 1998. pap. bk. 14.95 (978-1-56561-164-1(0)) Wiley US.

Break No Bones. abr. ed. Kathy Reichs. Read by Dorothee Berryman. (Temperance Brennan Ser.: No. 9). 2006. 17.95 (978-0-7435-6459-5(6), Audioworks); audio compact disk 29.95 (978-0-7435-5260-8(1), Audioworks) Pub: S&S Audio. Dist(s): S and S Inc

Break No Bones. unabr. ed. Kathy Reichs. (Temperance Brennan Ser.: No. 9). 2006. 23.95 (978-0-7435-6460-1(X), Audioworks) Pub: S&S Audio. Dist(s): S and S Inc

Break No Bones. unabr. ed. Kathy Reichs. Read by Dorothee Berryman. (Running Time: 12 hrs. 0 mins. 0 sec.). No. 9. (ENG.). 2006. audio compact disk 39.95 (978-0-7435-5262-2(8), Audioworks) Pub: S&S Audio. Dist(s): S and S Inc

Break Out & Become: A New Creature in Christ. Mary V. Parrish. 1978. bk. 9.95 (978-0-687-03973-9(8)) Abingdon.

Break the Smoking Habit with Hypnosis: A 3-Session Stop Smoking Program. Scripts. Michael Robinson. Voice by Michael Robinson. 3 CDs. (Running Time: 3 hrs.). 2005. audio compact disk 99.95 (978-0-9745230-4-0(6)) Loxias Audio Pub.
This stop smoking program is a 3-session approach to help you to develop newer, healthier associations to reprogram your mind. In just 3 days, you will learn a method that has helped many people break the addiction using the powers of their own mind. Each session is approximately an hour long and is designed to help you break the habit. Learn it. Use it. Stop smoking now!.

Break Their Bad Habits: (the Bugville Critters, Lass's Adventures Series #2) unabr. ed. Robert Stanek, pseud. Narrated by Ginny Westcott. (Running Time: 17 mins.). (ENG.). (J). 2008. 4.95 (978-1-57545-317-0(7), RP Audio Pubng) Pub: Reagent Press. Dist(s): OverDrive Inc

Break Through: From the Death of Environmentalism to the Politics of Possibilities. unabr. ed. Ted Nordhaus & Michael Shellenberger. Read by Jeff Cummings. (Running Time: 34200 sec.). 2007. 44.95 (978-1-4332-0424-1(X)); audio compact disk 45.00 (978-1-4332-0425-8(8)) Blckstn Audio.

Break Through: From the Death of Environmentalism to the Politics of Possibility. unabr. ed. Michael Shellenberger & Ted Nordhaus. Read by Jeff Cummings. (Running Time: 34200 sec.). 2007. 19.95 (978-1-4332-0426-5(6)); audio compact disk 19.95 (978-1-4332-0427-2(4)); audio compact disk 29.95 (978-1-4332-0428-9(2)) Blckstn Audio.

Break Through Difficult Emotions. Shinzen Young. 2 CDs. (Running Time: 2 Hrs 30 Mins). 2006. audio compact disk 19.95 (978-1-59179-487-5(0), AW00313D) Sounds True.
When mindfulness meditation was introduced as an aid for patients suffering from chronic pain, physicians were skeptical. Today, mindfulness meditation is used in hundreds of hospitals and clinics across the country. On Break through Difficult Emotions, meditation mentor Shinzen Young adapts the core principles of mindfulness training to the treatment of emotional suffering. You will learn powerful meditations for overcoming anger, grief, anxiety, shame, and the many other painful emotions we all experience. Four step-by-step exercises cover how to: deconstruct any emotion into its harmless components; identify the location, shape, and flow of your emotions; melt frozen emotions into their natural, fluid state; untangle emotional confusion by watching your thoughts; transform negative emotions into positive ones, and much more.

Break Through Pain: A Step-by-Step Mindfulness Meditation Program for Transforming Chronic & Acute Pain. Shinzen Young. (Running Time: 1 hr. 15 mins.). 2006. bk. 19.95 (978-1-59179-199-7(5), K849D) Sounds True.

Break-Ups of Professional Practices. 1997. bk. 99.00 (ACS-1276) PA Bar Inst.
The world of professional practice is no longer the stable place it once was. Individual professionals & groups leave firms to go out on their own, to join other groups or because they are forced to depart. Whether you are asked to advise clients or are personally experiencing the break-up of your practice, this book gives you a firm grasp of the unique & varied issues.

Breakaway. unabr. ed. B. J. Green. Read by Stephanie Brush. 8 cass. (Running Time: 10 hrs.). 2001. 49.95 (978-1-58116-008-6(9)) Books in Motion.
Appointed by her father as the Executive Assistant to the general Manager of the New Orleans Professional ice hockey team, Maggie Regan is distracted from her job, by both the teams' best player and the Russian Mafia's plans to force the big game's outcome.

***Breakdown Lane.** abr. ed. Jacquelyn Mitchard. Read by Jacquelyn Mitchard. (ENG.). 2005. (978-0-06-084288-8(1), Harper Audio); (978-0-06-084289-5(X), Harper Audio) HarperCollins Pubs.

Breakdown Lane. unabr. ed. Jacquelyn Mitchard. Read by Anna Fields. 8 cass. (Running Time: 45840 sec.). 2005. 74.95 (978-0-7927-3619-6(2), CSL 796); DVD, audio compact disk, audio compact disk 94.95 (978-0-7927-3621-9(4), SLD 796); audio compact disk 59.95 (978-0-7927-3622-6(2), CMP 796) AudioGO.

Breakdown Lane. unabr. ed. Jacquelyn Mitchard. Read by Anna Fields. 2005. audio compact disk 39.95 (978-0-06-075927-8(5)) HarperCollins Pubs.

***Breakdown Lane.** unabr. ed. Jacquelyn Mitchard. Read by Anna Fields. (ENG.). 2005. (978-0-06-084286-4(5), Harper Audio); (978-0-06-084287-1(3), Harper Audio) HarperCollins Pubs.

Breaker. Kit Denton. Read by Terence Donovan. 1 cass. 1998. Bolinda Pubng AUS.

Breaker. Kit Denton. Read by Terence Donovan. (Running Time: 11 hrs.). (Classic Ser.). 2009. 89.99 (978-1-74214-222-7(2), 9781742142227) Pub: Bolinda Pubng AUS. Dist(s): Bolinda Pub Inc

Breaker. Minette Walters. 2 cass. (Running Time: 3 hrs.). 1998. 15.00 (978-0-333-74614-1(7)) Pub: Macmillan UK GBR. Dist(s): Macmillan NJ
Twelve hours after a woman's broken body is washed up on a deserted shore, her traumatized three-year-old daughter is discovered twenty miles away.

Breaker. unabr. ed. Kit Denton. Read by Terence Donovan. 10 CDs. (Running Time: 11 hrs.). 2001. audio compact disk 80.00 (978-1-74030-380-4(6)) Pub: Bolinda Pubng AUS. Dist(s): Bolinda Pub Inc

Breaker. unabr. ed. Kit Denton. Read by Terence Donovan. 8 cass. (Running Time: 11 hrs.). 2004. 64.00 (978-1-86340-775-5(8), 571129) Bolinda Pubng AUS.
Breaker Morant was executed at Pietersburg on 27 February, 1902, for willful murder of civilians. Yet to this day his guilt remains in doubt. Does more than recount the facts & mystery surrounding Morant's death sentence. Set in three continents, it covers the entire range of Breaker's activities. See him as a champion horseman, a likeable larrikin, a popular balladist. See him in love & in war...then facing the firing squad that ends his life. Was he a cold-blooded killer or a scapegoat?.

Breaker. unabr. ed. Minette Walters. Read by Robert Powell. 10 CDs. (Running Time: 15 hrs.). 1999. audio compact disk 94.95 (978-0-7540-5315-6(6), CCD006, Chivers Sound Lib) AudioGO.
Twelve hours after a woman's broken body is washed up on a deserted shore on the south coast of England, her traumatized 3-year-old daughter is discovered twenty miles away walking the streets of Poole. But why was Kate killed & her daughter, a witness, allowed to live?.

Breaker. unabr. ed. Minette Walters. Read by Robert Powell. 10 cass. (Running Time: 15 hrs.). 1999. Rental 84.95 (978-0-7540-0373-1(6), Chivers Sound Lib) AudioGO.

Breaker. unabr. ed. Minette Walters. Narrated by Simon Prebble. 10 CDs. (Running Time: 11 hrs. 15 mins.). 2000. audio compact disk 90.00 (978-0-7887-4208-8(6), C1137E7) Recorded Bks.
Twelve hours after Kate Sumner's brutally murdered body washes up on the beach, her traumatized three year-old daughter is found wandering the streets alone. The prime suspect is a young actor, obsessed with pornography. But why does the child scream whenever her father tries to touch her?.

Breaker. unabr. ed. Minette Walters. Narrated by Simon Prebble. 8 cass. (Running Time: 11 hrs. 15 mins.). 1999. 67.00 (978-0-7887-3897-5(6), 96077E7) Recorded Bks.

breaker - Re-release. unabr. ed. Kit Denton. Read by Terence Donovan. (Running Time: 11 hrs.). (Classic Ser.). 2009. audio compact disk 98.95 (978-1-921415-82-1(7), 9781921415821) Pub: Bolinda Pubng AUS. Dist(s): Bolinda Pub Inc

***Breaker's Reef.** Terri Blackstock. (Running Time: 9 hrs. 59 mins. 0 sec.). (Cape Refuge Ser.). (ENG.). 2008. 14.99 (978-0-310-30428-9(8)) Zondervan.

Breakfast in Bed. (gr. k-3). 10.00 (978-0-7635-6367-7(6)) Rigby Educ.

Breakfast in Bed. unabr. ed. Sandra Brown. Narrated by Richard Poe. 4 cass. (Running Time: 5 hrs. 45 mins.). 1997. 35.00 (978-0-7887-0845-9(7), 94991E7) Recorded Bks.
When the charming, seductive Carter Madison arrives at Sloan Fairchild's bed & breakfast, he forces her into a dilemma. Will she choose to do the right thing or succumb to the temptation of forbidden love?.

Breakfast of Champions. unabr. ed. Kurt Vonnegut. Read by Stanley Tucci. 4 cass. (Running Time: 6 hrs.). 2004. 25.95 (978-0-06-056497-1(0)); audio compact disk 29.95 (978-0-06-058623-2(0)) HarperCollins Pubs.

***Breakfast of Champions.** unabr. ed. Kurt Vonnegut. Read by Stanley Tucci. (ENG.). 2004. (978-0-06-076423-4(6), Harper Audio); (978-0-06-081358-1(X), Harper Audio) HarperCollins Pubs.

Breakfast Session: Changes in Health Care Delivery Systems. Jan Ozga. 1 cass. 9.00 (TAPE 15) Recorded Res.

Breakheart Hill. unabr. ed. Thomas H. Cook. Narrated by George Guidall. 7 cass. (Running Time: 9 hrs. 45 mins.). 2000. 60.00 (978-0-7887-0424-6(9), 94616E7) Recorded Bks.

***Breaking Addiction.** unabr. ed. Lance M. Dodes. (ENG.). 2011. (978-0-06-206276-5(X)) HarperCollins Pubs.

***Breaking Addiction: A 7-Step Handbook for Ending Any Addiction.** unabr. ed. Lance M. Dodes. (ENG.). 2011. (978-0-06-206163-8(1)) HarperCollins Pubs.

Breaking & Entering. H. R. F. Keating. Read by H. R. F. Keating. 7 CDs. (Running Time: 7 hrs. 57 mins.). (Inspector Ghote Mystery Ser.: No. 24). (J). 2004. audio compact disk 71.95 (978-0-7531-2279-2(0)) Pub: ISIS Lrg Prnt GBR. Dist(s): Ulverscroft US

Breaking & Entering. unabr. ed. H. R. F. Keating. Read by H. R. F. Keating. 6 cass. (Running Time: 9 hrs.). (Inspector Ghote Mystery Ser.: No. 24). 2001. 54.95 (978-0-7531-0991-5(3), 010306) Pub: ISIS Audio GBR. Dist(s): ISIS Pub
All Bombay is buzzing with the murder of a millionaire found stabbed to death in his tightly secure mansion. Every inspector in the branch hopes to be the one to nail the killer, including Inspector Ganesh Ghote. Unfortunately he is the only officer not assigned to the case.

Breaking Back CD: My Most Difficult Yearâ€"and the Lessons That Helped Me Survive It. abr. ed. James Blake. 2007. audio compact disk 29.95 (978-0-06-136356-6(1), Harper Audio) HarperCollins Pubs.

Breaking Bad News: NACADA Webinar No. 31. Featuring José Rodriguez et al. (ENG.). 2010. audio compact disk 140.00 (978-1-935140-73-3(6)) Nat Acad Adv.

Breaking Belief Barriers. G. Michael Durst. Read by G. Michael Durst. 1 cass. 1987. 10.00 Train Sys.

Breaking Bread in the Gospel of Luke. Eugene LaVerdiere. 4 cass. (Running Time: 4 hrs.). 2001. vinyl bd. 32.95 (A6560) St Anthony Mess Pr.
Leads us through ten stories which celebrate the breaking of the bread in the Gospel of Luke.

Breaking Dawn. unabr. ed. Stephenie Meyer. Read by Ilyana Kadushin. 16 CDs. (Twilight Saga: No. 4). (YA). 2008. audio compact disk 90.00 (978-0-7393-6769-8(2), Listening Lib) Pub: Random Audio Pubg. Dist(s): Random

Breaking Dawn. unabr. ed. Stephenie Meyer. Read by Ilyana Kadushin & Matt Walters. 16 CDs. (Running Time: 20 hrs. 30 mins.). (Twilight Saga: No. 4). (ENG.). (J). (gr. 7). 2008. audio compact disk 60.00 (978-0-7393-6767-4(6), Listening Lib) Pub: Random Audio Pubg. Dist(s): Random

Breaking Eighty: A Journey Through the Nine Fairways of Hell, abr. ed. Lee Eisenberg. Read by Lee Eisenberg. 2 cass. (Running Time: 2 hrs.). 1997. 17.95 (978-1-57453-200-5(6)) Audio Lit.
Hilarious & memorable account of how to learn to play golf.

Breaking Faith: The Pope, the People & the Fate of Catholicism. unabr. ed. John Cornwell. Read by John Lee. 7 cass. (Running Time: 10 hrs. 30 mins.). 2001. 42.00 Books on Tape.
A former seminarian decries the conservative trend in the modern Catholic church, and offers suggestions for its liberalization.

Breaking Faith: The Pope, the People & the Fate of Catholicism. unabr. ed. John Cornwell. Read by John Lee. 7 cass. (Running Time: 10 hrs. 30 mins.). 2001. 56.00 (978-0-7366-8092-9(6)) Books on Tape.
Reflections on the state of the church in the final years of Pope John Paul II's reign. A liberal Catholic, Cornwell believes that the church has descended too far into conservatism. He claims that it has stigmatized millions of Catholics with its sexual teachings, has centralized authority ever more firmly in Rome, has squelched dissent among its members, and has ruled in a retrograde manner on a variety of other burning issues.

Breaking Free. 2004. (978-1-59024-149-3(5)); audio compact disk (978-1-59024-175-2(4)) B Hinn Min.

Breaking Free. unabr. ed. Susan Eisenhower. Read by Kate Reading. 9 cass. (Running Time: 13 hrs. 30 min.). 1996. 72.00 (978-0-7366-3249-2(2), 3907) Books on Tape.
With the political situation off-balance, wiretaps, hidden agendas & lurking suspicions threaten not only their romantic serenity, but Sagdeev's personal safety.

Breaking Free. unabr. ed. Lauraine Snelling. Read by Pam Ward. (Running Time: 34200 sec.). 2007. 19.95 (978-1-4332-0204-9(2)); audio compact disk 19.95 (978-1-4332-0205-6(0)) Blckstn Audio.

Breaking Free. unabr. ed. Lauraine Snelling. (Running Time: 34200 sec.). 2007. 59.95 (978-1-4332-0306-0(5)) Blckstn Audio.

Breaking Free. unabr. ed. Lauraine Snelling. Read by Pamela Ward. (Running Time: 34200 sec.). 2007. audio compact disk 29.95 (978-1-4332-0206-3(9)) Blckstn Audio.

Breaking Free. unabr. ed. Lauraine Snelling. Read by Pam Ward. (Running Time: 34200 sec.). 2007. audio compact disk 72.00 (978-1-4332-0307-7(3)) Blckstn Audio.

Breaking Free: My Life with Dissaociative Identity Disorder. unabr. ed. Herschel Walker. Narrated by Andre Teamer. (ENG.). 2008. 19.59 (978-1-60814-099-2(7), SpringWater) Oasis Audio.

Breaking Free: My Life with Dissociative Identity Disorder. Herschel Walker. Read by Andre Teamer. Told to Gary Brozek & Charlene Maxfield. Frwd. by Jerry Mungadze. (Playaway Adult Nonfiction Ser.). (ENG.). 2009. 60.00 (978-1-60775-594-4(7)) Find a World.

***Breaking Free: The Journey, the Stories.** Beth Moore. (ENG.). 2009. pap. bk. (978-1-4158-6920-8(0)) LifeWay Christian.

Breaking Free Day by Day. unabr. ed. Beth Moore. Narrated by Renee Ertl. (ENG.). 2007. 13.99 (978-1-60814-100-5(4)); audio compact disk 19.99 (978-1-59859-260-3(2)) Oasis Audio.

Breaking Free from the Power of Lust. 4 CDs. (Running Time: 5 hrs.). 2004. audio compact disk 23.95 (978-0-9758832-2-8(4)) Pure Life.

Breaking Free from the Victim Trap - the Audio Program. Diane Zimberoff. 2004. audio compact disk 15.00 (978-0-9622728-1-3(7)) Wellness Pr.

Breaking His Hold. Elbert Willis. 1 cass. (Understanding Satan's Strate Ser.). 4.00 Fill the Gap.

Breaking In, Breaking Out. unabr. collector's ed. Nicholas Monsarrat. Read by Chris Winfield. 12 cass. (Running Time: 18 hrs.). 1978. 96.00 (978-0-7366-0079-8(5), 1089) Books on Tape.
The autobiography of Monsarrat, in which we follow him to Cambridge, the Royal Navy, South Africa & Canada. We learn much about him, & much more about the world through which he traveled.

Breaking Intimidation CD Series. 2007. audio compact disk 24.99 (978-1-933185-16-3(3)) Messengr Intl.

***Breaking Intimidation Life Message Series.** John Bevere. 2010. audio compact disk 0.00 (978-1-933185-60-6(0)) Messengr Intl.

Breaking into the Travel Business. unabr. ed. Richard Berman. 1 cass. (Running Time: 48 min.). 12.95 (960) J Norton Pubs.
Where to get free advertising, assistance from airlines & foreign governments, sources of profits & commissions.

Breaking Negative Psychic Contracts: Releasing Limitation. Galexis. 2 cass. (Running Time: 3 hrs.). 1995. 17.95 Set. (978-1-56089-026-3(6)) Visionary FL.
Tap the powers & heal the issues left in other lifetimes, so that you can become whole. Includes meditation on Side 4.

Breaking News. abr. ed. Read by Stan Chambers. 4 cass. (Running Time: 6 hrs.). 2001. 24.95 (978-1-57511-097-4(0)) Pub Mills.
Stan Chambers began his television reporting career in 1947. His ability to capture a story, from the terror of the Sylmar earthquake to the solemnity of the first televised atomic bomb blast, quickly pushed him to the top of his field.

Breaking News: A Stunning & Memorable Account of Reporting from Some of the Most Dangerous Places in the World. unabr. ed. Martin Fletcher. Narrated by Stephen Hoye. 8 CDs. (Running Time: 9 hrs. 30 mins. 0 sec.). (ENG.). 2008. audio compact disk 34.99 (978-1-4001-0723-0(7)); audio compact disk 69.99 (978-1-4001-3723-7(3)); audio compact disk 24.99 (978-1-4001-5723-5(4)) Pub: Tantor Media. Dist(s): IngramPubServ

Breaking Out Breaking Through: Tales from Both Sides of the Glass Ceiling. Speeches. As told by Joan Koerber-Walker. 1 CD. (Running Time: 50 mins.). 2004. audio compact disk 19.95 (978-0-9747056-2-0(4), BOBT CD) CorePurpose.
Join CorePurpose founder, Joan Koerber-Walker, as she shares her personal experiences from both sides of the glass ceiling & shares three winning tactics YOU can use to break through.Recorded LIVE at Arizona State University in April of 2004, this one hour session illustrates that the Glass Ceiling is NOT just a women's issue but applies to all of us. The Glass Ceiling is whatever is between where you are and where you want to be."Joan shares her own experiences and journey over a 25 year career from student to employee - from team member to leaders and from corporate executive to entrepreneur with candor and humor.".

Breaking Out of the Prison of Guilt: Matthew 18:21-25. Ed Young. (J). 1980. 4.95 (978-0-7417-1114-4(1), A0114) Win Walk.

Breaking Point. Jennie L. Hansen. 3 cass. 2004. 14.95 (978-1-59156-214-6(7)) Covenant Comms.

Breaking Point. abr. ed. Suzanne Brockmann. Read by Melanie Ewbank & Patrick G. Lawlor. (Running Time: 21600 sec.). (Troubleshooter Ser.: No. 9). 2006. audio compact disk 16.99 (978-1-59737-350-0(8), 9781597373500, BCD Value Price) Brilliance Audio.
Please enter a Synopsis.

Breaking Point. unabr. ed. Suzanne Brockmann. Read by Patrick G. Lawlor & Melanie Ewbank. (Running Time: 13 hrs.). (Troubleshooter Ser.: No. 9). 2005. 39.25 (978-1-59710-833-1(2), 9781597108331, BADLE); 24.95 (978-1-59710-832-4(4), 9781597108324, BAD); 39.95 (978-1-59600-148-0(8), 9781596001480, BAU); 97.25 (978-1-59600-149-7(6), 9781596001497, BrilAudUnabridg); audio compact disk 39.95 (978-1-59600-150-3(X), 9781596001503, Bril Audio CD Unabri); audio compact disk 97.25 (978-1-59600-151-0(8), 9781596001510, BriAudCD Unabrid); audio compact disk 39.25 (978-1-59335-947-8(0), 9781593359478, Brinc Audio MP3 Lib); audio compact disk 24.95 (978-1-59335-946-1(2), 9781593359461, Brilliance MP3) Brilliance Audio.

Breaking Point. unabr. ed. Alex Flinn. 4 cass. (Running Time: 5 hrs. 30 mins.). (J). (gr. 7 up). 2004. 32.00 (978-0-8072-0812-0(4), LYA 373 CX, Listening Lib) Random Audio Pubg.
Paul is new to Gate, a school whose rich students make life miserable for anyone not like them. And Paul is definitely not like them. Then, one day something incredible happens. Charlie Good, a star student and athlete, invites Paul to join his elite inner circle. All Charlie wants are a few things in return, small things that paul does willingly. And then, one day, Charlie wants something big, really big. Now paul has to decide how far he'll go to be one of the gang.

Breaking Point: How Female Midlife Crisis Is Transforming Today's Women. unabr. ed. Sue Shellenbarger. Read by Beth Wernick. 6 CDs. (Running Time: 6 hrs. 30 mins.). 2005. audio compact disk 41.95 (978-1-59758-016-8(3)) Audis Libros Pub.
In the tradition of The Second Shifti, a groundbreaking work that identifies and explains the phenomenon poised to redefine our culture.b

When Sue Shellenbarger wrote about her midlife crisis in her award-winning Wall Street Journali "Work & Family" column, the volume and emotional intensity of the responses from her readers was stunning. As she heard story after story of middle-aged women radically changing course in search of greater fulfillment, a trend began to emerge: an entire generation of women was experiencing the tumultuous transition of midlife in ways not seen before.

To capture this paradigm shift, Shellenbarger combines original research data and interviews with more than fifty women who've navigated their own midlife crises. Long stereotyped as the province of men, today the midlife crisis is reported with greater frequency by women than men. Emboldened by the financial independence to act upon midlife desires, exhausted by decades of playing supermom and repressing the feminine sides of themselves to succeed at work, women are shedding the age roles of the past in favor of new pursuits in adventure, sports, sex, romance, education, and spirituality. And in the process they are rewriting all the rules.

Beyond defining a new phenomenon, The Breaking Pointi shows how various options women use to cope with the turmoil of midlife - from playing it safe to dynamiting their lives - have a profound impact on their families, careers, and our culture at large. Provocative, insightful, and resonant, The Breaking Pointi is sure to be one of the most controversial and talked-about publications of 2005.

Unabridged audiobook on 6 audio CDs, about 6.5 hours.b

.

***Breaking Point-ABR.** Suzanne Brockmann & #9 Troubleshooters Series. 2010. audio compact disk 9.99 (978-1-4418-5669-2(2)) Brilliance Audio.

Breaking Points. unabr. collector's ed. Jack Hinckley & Jo Ann Hinckley. Read by Dan Lazar. 8 cass. (Running Time: 12 hrs.). 1986. 64.00 (978-0-7366-0570-0(3), 1542) Books on Tape.
This is a step-by-step saga of the Hinckleys' son, John - who shot President Reagan & three other men in 1981 - his mental illness which is one of the most common & least understood of all diseases. The Hinckleys were scrutinized in one of the most public trials in history, a trial ending in the verdict "not guilty by reason of insanity".

Breaking Ranks: A Political Memoir. unabr. ed. Norman Podhoretz. Read by Phillip J. Sawtelle. 9 cass. (Running Time: 13 hrs.). 1989. 62.95 (978-0-7861-0047-7(8), 1045) Blckstn Audio.
This is the story of Norman Podhoretz' own intellectual & political odyssey which took him...from liberalism to radicalism & then to the neoconservative position... The intent of "Breaking Ranks" is to explain what has happened to America, how & why he believes it became a nation so deeply unhappy with itself that it seems almost to have lost its will to survive.

Breaking the Barriers to a Longer, Healthier Life. Roby Mitchell. 2 cass. 1997. 17.95 (978-1-56823-051-1(6)) Pub: Knowledge Prod. Dist(s): APG

Breaking the Bread. Eugene LaVerdiere. 4 cass. (Running Time: 4 hrs. 55 min.). 1995. 34.95 Set. (TAH354) Alba Hse Comns.
Fr. Eugene reveals some of the hidden meaning of the "multiplication" of the loaves, the blessing of the bread at meals, even the significance of the Barley loaves. Uplifting material for a quiet mini retreat. Excellent as a source of detailed study into this aspect of the gospels.

Breaking the Chain of Low Self-Esteem. abr. ed. Marilyn J. Sorensen. Read by Kitt Weagant. 2 cass. (Running Time: 3 hrs.). 1999. 17.95 (978-1-57453-300-3(7)) Audio Lit.
Dr. Sorensen illuminates the actual inner experience of the struggle with self-doubt and reveals her discoveries about how to improve our view of ourselves, a process that automatically begins to free us from harmful behaviors and reactions. Offers new understanding, hope and direction to anyone embarking on the journey of personal transformation.

Breaking the Chains: African American Slave Resistance. unabr. ed. William Loren Katz. Read by Peter Francis James. 4 pieces. (Running Time: 5 hrs. 45 mins.). (gr. 9 up). 1998. 35.00 (978-0-7887-2265-3(4), 95496E7) Recorded Bks.
Generations of American history students grew up believing that slave rebellion was relatively rare, that slaves accepted their lot & became attached to their masters & that they were ultimately liberated by little or no effort of their own. Liberally sprinkled with firsthand accounts from the Civil War era, this is an eye-opening look at a turbulent period of American History.

Breaking the Chains: African-American Slave Resistance, Class Set. unabr. ed. William Loren Katz. Read by Peter Francis James. 4 cass., 10 bks. (Running Time: 5 hrs. 45 min.). (YA). 1998. bk. 155.80 (978-0-7887-2556-2(4), 46726) Recorded Bks.
Liberally sprinkled with firsthand accounts from the Civil War era, this is an eye-opening look at a turbulent period of American history.

Breaking the Chains Homework Set: African-American Slave Resistance. unabr. ed. William Loren Katz. Read by Peter Francis James. 4 cass. (Running Time: 5 hrs. 45 min.). (YA). 1998. bk. 53.25 (978-0-7887-2252-3(2), 40736) Recorded Bks.

Breaking the Chains of Karma. Swami Amar Jyoti. 1 cass. 1991. 9.95 (F-18) Truth Consciousness.
Explanations & examples of the sometimes baffling workings of Karma. On Karma, reincarnation & Grace.

Breaking the Chains That Bind Us: Choice & Choicemaking. unabr. ed. Lee B. Rafe. 1 cass. (Running Time: 1 hr.). 1999. 12.95 (978-0-9675722-1-5(5)) Bravo Pubg Grp.
Learn to recognize & release patterns that keep you bound to bad relationships, stress, sadness, anger & fear.

Breaking the Da Vinci Code. unabr. ed. Darrell L. Bock. Read by Chris Fabry. 4 CDs. (Running Time: 5 hrs.). 2004. audio compact disk 25.99 (978-1-58926-687-2(0)) Oasis Audio.

Breaking the Da Vinci Code: Answers to the Questions Everyone's Asking. unabr. ed. Darrell L. Bock. Read by Chris Fabry. Prod. by Oasis Audio Staff. 3 cass. (Running Time: 4 hrs.). 2006. 23.95 (978-0-7861-2758-0(9), 3291); audio compact disk 32.00 (978-0-7861-8630-3(5), 3291) Blckstn Audio.

Breaking the Da Vinci Code: Answers to the Questions Everyone's Asking. unabr. ed. Darrell L. Bock. Read by Chris Fabry. 3 cass. (Running Time: 5 hrs.). 24.99 (978-1-58926-686-5(2)) Oasis Audio.

Breaking the Enigma: Triumph & Tragedy of the Polish-German Cipher War. Otmar Moritsch & Wolfgang Pensold. 2008. audio compact disk 24.95 (978-3-7065-4536-5(5)) Pub: StudienVerlag AUT. Dist(s): Transaction Pubs

Breaking the Food Seduction. Neal D. Barnard. (Running Time: 68 minutes). 2003. audio compact disk 10.00 (978-0-9664081-4-0(4)) Physcns Comm Resp Med.

Breaking the Ice: Your Introductory Guide to the Canadian Market. Ron Love. Read by Ron Love. 1 CD. (Running Time: 67min 3sec). 2004. pap. bk. 12.95 (978-1-932226-32-4(X)) Wizard Acdmy.

Breaking the Jewish Code. unabr. ed. Perry Stone. Narrated by Tim Lundeen. (Running Time: 8 hrs. 28 mins. 25 sec.). (ENG.). 2009. audio compact disk 29.99 (978-1-59859-546-8(6)) Oasis Audio.

Breaking the Jewish Code. unabr. ed. Perry Stone. Narrated by Tim Lundeen. (Running Time: 8 hrs. 28 mins. 25 sec.). (ENG.). 2009. 20.99 (978-1-60814-542-3(5)) Oasis Audio.

Breaking the Language Barrier with Spanish. Janice L. Logan. 1977. bk. 237.60 (978-0-89420-127-1(1), 176000) Natl Book.

Breaking the Laws of the Lord. Swami Amar Jyoti. 1 cass. 1982. 9.95 (B-12) Truth Consciousness.
Harmfulness of attachment & selfish isolation, seen in terms of God's working.

Breaking the Myths of Reality. unabr. ed. Cari Alter. Read by Cari Alter. 2 cass. (Running Time: 2 hrs.). 2000. 19.95 (978-0-9702445-0-5(9)) Soul Wks Pubng.
A near-death experience, coupled with other metaphysical experiences, push the author beyond the boundaries of ordinary reality. The author shares her new understanding of Reality as a result of these experiences, confirmed by research into Quantum Mechanics.

Breaking the Pattern. L. Jane Madey. 1 cass. 8.95 (876) Am Fed Astrologers.

Breaking the Ring. unabr. ed. John Barron. Read by Larry McKeever. 8 cass. (Running Time: 8 hrs.). 1990. 48.00 Set. (978-0-7366-1817-5(1), 2653) Books on Tape.
For nearly 20 years, John Anthony Walker sold the Soviets every secret that he, his brother Arthur, friend Jerry Whitworth & son Michael, could get their hands on. As Walker told interrogators, "If I had access to it, color it gone." What Walker had access to was almost every form of secret communications equipment the United States possessed. Loss of codes can mean life or death to a nation at war. As Vitaly Yurchenko, the Soviet KGB defector said, "It was the greatest case in KGB history. We deciphered millions of your messages. If there had been a war we would have won it." Breaking the Ring is different from any other book on the Walker case. It makes a sober assessment of the damage our national security suffered - damage that makes us vulnerable for years to come. It leaves us with the questions: How can our security services be so easily fooled? How many other moles are burrowing at this very moment?.

Breaking the Ring. unabr. ed. John Barron. Read by Multivoice Production Staff & J. Charles. (Running Time: 7 hrs.). 2009. 24.99 (978-1-4233-5929-6(1), 9781423359296, BAD); 24.99 (978-1-4233-5927-2(5), 9781423359272, Brilliance MP3); 39.97 (978-1-4233-5930-2(5), 9781423359302, BADLE); 39.97 (978-1-4233-5928-9(3), 9781423359289, Brinc Audio MP3 Lib) Brilliance Audio.

Breaking the Ring. unabr. ed. John Barron. Read by J. Charles. (Running Time: 8 hrs.). 2009. audio compact disk 29.99 (978-1-4418-0162-3(6), 9781441801623, Bril Audio CD Unabri); audio compact disk 87.97 (978-1-4418-0163-0(4), 9781441801630, BriAudCD Unabrid) Brilliance Audio.

Breaking the Rules. abr. ed. Barbara Taylor Bradford. Read by Katherine Kellgren. (Running Time: 6 hrs. 0 mins. 0 sec.). (ENG.). 2009. audio compact disk 29.99 (978-1-4272-0850-7(6)) Pub: Macmill Audio. Dist(s): Macmillan

Breaking the Rules. unabr. ed. Barbara Taylor Bradford. Read by Katherine Kellgren. (Running Time: 13 hrs. 0 mins. 0 sec.). (ENG.). 2009. audio compact disk 44.99 (978-1-4272-0848-4(4)) Pub: Macmill Audio. Dist(s): Macmillan

***Breaking the Rules.** unabr. ed. Suzanne Brockmann. (Running Time: 14 hrs.). (Troubleshooters Ser.). 2011. 24.99 (978-1-4418-5077-5(5), 9781441850775, BAD); 24.99 (978-1-4418-5075-1(9), 9781441850751, Brilliance MP3); 39.97 (978-1-4418-5076-8(7), 9781441850768, Brinc Audio MP3 Lib); 39.97 (978-1-4418-5078-2(3), 9781441850782, BADLE); audio compact disk 34.99 (978-1-4418-5073-7(2), 9781441850737, Bril Audio CD Unabri); audio compact disk 89.97 (978-1-4418-5074-4(0), 9781441850744, BriAudCD Unabrid) Brilliance Audio.

Breaking the Shackles: Bringing Joy Into Our Lives. Roy U. Schenk et al. Ed. by John Everingham. 1 CD. (Running Time: 1 hr. 30 mins.). Orig. Title: Men Healing Shame. 2002. audio compact disk 14.95 (978-0-9613177-7-5(9)) MPC Pr.
Examines how shame damages man's lives and how men are learning to move from shame to joy.

Breaking the Silence, Set. abr. ed. Mariette Hartley. Read by Mariette Hartley. 2 cass. (Running Time: 3 hrs.). 1990. 15.95 (978-0-9627187-3-1(4), 20030) Pub Mills.
Mariette Hartley's memoir of family secrets & personal courage. Stories about television, Hollywood & a life suffused with both tragedy & joy.

Breaking the Sound Barrier. Compiled by Benchmark Education Staff. 2006. audio compact disk 10.00 (978-1-4108-6679-0(3)) Benchmark Educ.

Breaking the Sound Barrier. Amy Goodman. (ENG.). 2009. audio compact disk 40.00 (978-1-931859-98-1(1)) Pub: Haymarket Bks. Dist(s): Consort Bk Sales

Breaking the Spanish Barrier, Level I (Beginner), Double Audio CD Set: The Language Series with All the Rules You Need to Know. John Conner. (SPA.). 2005. audio compact disk 15.00 (978-0-9758573-9-7(8)) Brkng the Barrier.

Breaking the Spanish Barrier, Level I (Beginner), Self Learner Special: The Language Series with All the Rules You Need to Know. John Conner. (SPA.). 2005. per. 50.00 (978-0-9758573-6-6(3)) Brkng the Barrier.

Breaking the Spanish Barrier, Level II (Intermediate), Double Audio CD Set. John Conner. 2 CDs. (Running Time: 2 hours). 2005. audio compact disk 15.00 (978-0-9758573-5-9(5)) Brkng the Barrier.

Breaking the Spanish Barrier, Level II (Intermediate), Self Learner Special: The Language Series with All the Rules You Need to Know. John Conner. (SPA.). 2005. per. 50.00 (978-0-9758573-7-3(1)) Brkng the Barrier.

Breaking the Spirit of Failure. T. D. Jakes. 2001. 6.00 (978-1-57855-250-4(8)) T D Jakes.

Breaking the Success Barrier. Paul J. Meyer. 1 cass. (Running Time: 56 min.). 1991. 11.00 (978-0-89811-273-3(7), SP100078) Meyer Res Grp.
How to choose to dream, believe in the reality of your dreams, believe in yourself, reject negative conditioning, & accept responsibility for your success.

Breaking the Success Barrier. Paul J. Meyer. 1 cass. 10.00 (SP100077) SMI Intl.
To reach your dreams - you must break your success barrier. In his live speech, Paul J. Meyer shares how he daily challenges his limits. This message will inspire you, no matter what your career.

Breaking Thought Barriers. unabr. ed. Robert A. Monroe. Read by Robert A. Monroe. (Running Time: 45 min.). (Explorer Ser.). 1983. 12.95 (978-1-56113-007-8(9), 8) Monroe Institute.
The importance of breaking thought barriers by putting knowledge into action.

Breaking Through. Francisco Jiménez & Robert Ramirez. (J). 2003. (978-1-4025-4677-8(7)) Recorded Bks.

Breaking Through Barriers to Quality. Innovation Groups Staff. Contrib. by Bruce Snell. 1 cass. (Transforming Local Government Ser.: Vol. 3). 1999. 10.00 (978-1-882403-59-2(2), IG9903) Alliance Innov.

Breaking Through Church Growth Barriers: From 75 to 375 & Beyond: Proceedings of the 45th Annual Convention National Association of Evangelicals Buffalo, New York. Read by James L. Nicodem. 1 cass. (Running Time: 60 min.). 1987. 4.00 (307) Nat Assn Evan.

Breaking Through the Access Barrier: How Academic Capital Formation Can Improve Policy in Higher Education. (Dovetales Ser.: Tape 3). pap. bk. 6.95 (978-0-944391-38-9(9)); 4.95 (978-0-944391-18-1(4)) DonWise Prodns.

Breaking Through the Roadblocks Between You & Your Goals. 2005. 17.00 (978-1-933475-01-1(3)) Great Mind.

Breaking Through Writer's Block: Every Letter & Template You'll Need for a Thriving Professional Services Practice. 12 CDs. 2003. audio compact disk 295.00 (978-1-928611-07-3(9), Las Bri) Summit Cons Grp.

Breaking Through Your Weight Loss Barriers. Shad Helmstetter. 1 cass. (Self-Talk Ser.). 10.95 (978-0-937065-46-4(3)) Grindle Pr.
Companion Self-Talk Cassettes as mentioned in the book, "What To Say When You Talk To Your Self".

Breaking Wave. unabr. ed. Nevil Shute. Narrated by Patrick Tull. 6 cass. (Running Time: 9 hrs.). 1988. 51.00 (978-1-55690-072-3(4), 88420E7) Recorded Bks.
Allan had been away from Coombaragana, flying in the Royal Air Force. Now he has returned, wounded & disillusioned, to his ancestral home. Days before, Jessie Proctor had taken her own life. Why? Allan looked at the young face in the photograph in Jessie's passport & froze. He knew who she really was.

Breaking Your Belief Barriers. G. Michael Durst. Read by G. Michael Durst. 1 cass. (Running Time: 40 min.). 12.00 Train Sys.

Breakneck. unabr. ed. Erica Spindler. Read by Lorelei King. 8 CDs. (Running Time: 9 hrs. 30 mins. 0 sec.). (ENG.). 2009. audio compact disk 39.95 (978-1-4272-0499-8(3)) Pub: Macmill Audio. Dist(s): Macmillan

Breakout. unabr. ed. 3 cass. (Running Time: 3 hrs. 30 min.). 2003. 29.00 (978-1-4025-6708-7(1)) Recorded Bks.

***Breakout Churches: Discover How to Make the Leap.** Thom S. Rainer. (Running Time: 5 hrs. 49 mins. 0 sec.). (ENG.). 2008. 22.99 (978-0-310-30425-8(3)) Zondervan.

Breakout Churches: Discover How to Make the Leap. abr. ed. Thom S. Rainer. 2005. audio compact disk 29.99 (978-0-310-25744-8(1)) Zondervan.

Breakout Principle: How to Activate the Natural Trigger That Maximizes Creativity, Athletic Performance, Productivity & Personal Well-Being. abr. ed. Herbert Benson & William Proctor. Read by Jeffrey DeMunn. 2004. 15.95 (978-0-7435-4884-7(1)) Pub: S&S Audio. Dist(s): S and S Inc

Breakout Session: Ambulatory Surgery: Legislative-Regulatory Update & Future Prospects. Gail D. Durant & Diane S. Millman. 1 cass. 9.00 (TAPE 9) Recorded Res.

Breakout Session: Effective Political Advocacy: Maximizing Your Influence in Washington, DC. Thomas Dawson et al. 1 cass. 9.00 (TAPE 8) Recorded Res.

Breakout Session: Graduate Medical Education: Legislative-Regulatory Update. Nancy Selene & Robert W. Heins. 1 cass. 9.00 (TAPE 10) Recorded Res.

Breakout Session: Laboratory Issues Update. Kenneth E. Ballinger, Jr. & Bernard Patashnik. 1 cass. 9.00 (TAPE 12) Recorded Res.

Breakout Session: Legislation-Regulations Affecting Prepaid Groups: HMO & Medicare Risk Update. Patricia H. Billings & Diane Maupai. 1 cass. 9.00 (TAPE 11) Recorded Res.

Breakout Session Part B: Medicare: Current Claims & Interpretaton Issues. Paulette Hodges & Timothy Keating. 1 cass. 9.00 (TAPE 6) Recorded Res.

Breakpoint. unabr. ed. Richard A. Clarke. 6 cass. (Running Time: 9 hrs.). 2007. 60.00 (978-1-4159-3460-9(6)); audio compact disk 80.00 (978-1-4159-3461-6(4)) Books on Tape.

Breaks. 1982. (2111) Am Audio Prose.

Breakthrough! Colin Wilson. 1 cass. 9.00 (A0626-90) Sound Photosyn.
Faustin chats with Colin in Cornwall, where he lives, houses his 30,000 volume library, & is writing his 86th book.

Breakthrough. unabr. ed. R. J. Pineiro. Read by Adams Morgan. 8 cass. (Running Time: 11 hrs. 30 mins.). 1999. 56.95 (978-0-7861-1283-8(2), 2178) Blckstn Audio.
Silicon Valley has become a battlefield. While giant computer companies compete on a dialy basis for technological superiority in the post-Cold War age, yet another enemy has entered the fray. As nuclear war is no longer a concern, it is the research produced by American computer companies that has caught the attention of the world's spies.

Breakthrough: Politics & Race in the Age of Obama. Gwen Ifill. Read by Gwen Ifill. (Playaway Adult Nonfiction Ser.). 2009. 49.99 (978-1-60812-508-1(4)) Find a World.

Breakthrough: Politics & Race in the Age of Obama. unabr. ed. Gwen Ifill. Read by Gwen Ifill. 7 CDs. (Running Time: 8 hrs. 45 mins.). (ENG.). 2009. audio compact disk 34.95 (978-1-59887-872-1(7), 1598878727) Pub: HighBridge. Dist(s): Workman Pub

Breakthrough: The Return of Hope to the Middle East. unabr. ed. Tom Doyle. Narrated by Tom Doyle. (Running Time: 5 hrs. 30 mins. 28 sec.). (ENG.). 2009. 16.09 (978-1-60814-497-6(6)); audio compact disk 22.99 (978-1-59859-504-8(0)) Oasis Audio.

Breakthrough Vol. 1: Training in the Zone. unabr. ed. Kelly Howell. 1 cass. (Running Time: 1 hr.). (Music & Frequencies for Training in the Zone Ser.). 1995. 11.95 (978-1-881451-41-9(0)) Brain Sync.
A fusion of jazz, rock & world beat music creates the soundscape for an extraordinary journey into the mysterious world of Zone 1.

Breakthrough Company: How Everyday Companies Become Extraordinary Performers. abr. unabr. ed. Keith McFarland. Read by Keith McFarland. (Running Time: 21600 sec.). (ENG.). 2008. audio compact disk 29.95 (978-0-7393-5853-5(7), Random AudioBks) Pub: Random Audio Pubg. Dist(s): Random

Breakthrough Dreaming. Gayle Delaney. 4 cass. (Running Time: 4 hrs.). 1995. 49.95 Set. (12360A) Nightingale-Conant.

Breakthrough Dreaming: How to Tap the Power of Your 24-Hour Mind. Gayle Delaney. 4 cass. 49.95 Set incl. 12p. wkbk. & bonus cass. (12360AM) Nightingale-Conant.
This fascinating program reveals step-by-step how to use your 24-hour mind to access your intuitive wisdom & tap a hidden reservoir of information. Harness the power of Breakthrough Dreaming & take yourself to a higher level of self-knowledge & understanding.

BREAKTHROUGH FACTOR: CREATING A LIFE of VALUE for SUCCESS& HAPPINESS CST: Creating a Life of Value for Success & Happiness. Henry Marsh. 2004. 7.95 (978-0-7435-4217-3(7)) Pub: S&S Audio. Dist(s): S and S Inc

Breakthrough French 2: The Successful Way to Speak, Read & Understand French. Stephanie Rybak. 1 cass. (Running Time: 90 mins.). (Breakthrough Ser.). (ENG & FRE.). 2000. pap. bk. 59.95 (978-0-658-00509-1(X), 00509X) M-H Contemporary.

Breakthrough Learning Skills. Scott J. Bornstien. 2 cass. (Running Time: 3 hrs.). 1996. 15.95 (978-1-55977-489-5(4)) CareerTrack Pubns.

Breakthrough Learning Skills: How to Make Quantum Leaps in Your Ability to Grasp & Remember Almost Anything. Created by Scott Bornstein. 6 cass. (Running Time: 6 hrs. 47 min.). 79.95 Set, incl. wkbk., 84p. (Q10191) CareerTrack Pubns.
Program highlights: Ways to learn hundreds of new words quickly; How to boost your reading-retention rate; 6 steps to remembering people's names; How to stay relaxed in situations demanding total concentration; Simple mental mechanisms that enable you to remember obscure facts, trivia & minutiae; A fast & efficient note-taking system that helps you capture key ideas in meetings, classrooms, training sessions & textbooks; An easy-to-use system for learning languages faster.

Breakthrough Navajo CDs & Text. Alan Wilson. 4 CDs. (Running Time: 3 hrs.). (NAV.). 2005. audio compact disk 49.00 (978-1-57970-197-0(3), AFNV10D) J Norton Pubs.

Breakthrough Prayer: The Secret of Receiving Everything You Need from God. unabr. ed. Jim Cymbala. 4 CDs. (Running Time: 5 hrs.). 2003. audio compact disk 29.99 (978-0-310-25440-9(X)) Zondervan.
A practical and visionary approach to the principles of prayer that will revolutionize our lives and enable us to receive all God has for us.

Breakthrough Prayer: The Secret of Receiving Everything You Need from God. unabr. ed. Zondervan Publishing Staff & Jim Cymbala. (Running Time: 7 hrs. 0 mins. 0 sec.). (ENG.). 2004. 13.99 (978-0-310-26139-1(2)) Zondervan.

Breakthrough Principles for Change. Taffi L. Dollar. 2008. audio compact disk 14.00 (978-1-59944-692-9(8)) Creflo Dollar.

Breakthrough Series Audios. Gwen Shamblin. 2009. audio compact disk (978-1-892729-06-4(7)) Weigh Down Work.

Breakthrough Strategies to Teach & Counsel Troubled Youth. Ruth Herman Wells. Read by Ruth Herman Wells. 2 cass., 1 video. 1999. 169.00 Set. (978-1-891881-20-6(5)) Youth Change.
200 powerful interventions to turnaround youth with problems.

Breakthrough Strategies to Teach & Counsel Troubled Youth Workshop. Ruth Herman Wells. Read by Ruth Herman Wells. 4 cass. (Running Time: 6 hrs.). 1990. 99.00 Set, incl. wkbks. & handouts.; Incl. wkbk. & handouts. (978-1-891881-15-2(9)); Incl. wkbk. & handouts. (978-1-891881-16-9(7)); Incl. wkbk. & handouts. (978-1-891881-17-6(5)); Incl. wkbk. & handouts. (978-1-891881-18-3(3)) Youth Change.
Learn dozens of the newest & best solutions to turn around troubled youths. Solve your worst "kid problems" including apathy, ADD, violence, delinquency & more.

Breakthrough Teamwork: Outstanding Results Using Structured Teamwork. Excerpts. Dennis A. Romig. Read by Dennis A. Romig. 1CD. 2006. audio compact disk 19.95 (978-0-9672350-1-1(4)) Perf Res Pr.

Breakthrough Thinking: Strategies for Winning Big in Business. Robert B. Tucker & Denis Waitley. Read by Robert B. Tucker & Denis Waitley. 6 cass. 59.95 Set. (714AD) Nightingale-Conant.
Skills for survival in a changing world.

Breakthrough to Purpose. Featuring John Eldredge et al. 2007. audio compact disk 20.00 (978-1-933207-27-8(2)) Ransomed Heart.

Breakthrough to the New Age. Swami Amar Jyoti. 1 dolby cass. 1984. 9.95 (M-47) Truth Consciousness.
The time of breakthrough is here; a sense of urgency is needed. Realistic dreaming of that golden shore.

Breakthrough Training in the Zone: Increase Energy & Motivation. Kelly Howell. 1 CD. (Running Time: 60 mins.). (ENG.). 2004. audio compact disk 14.95 (978-1-881451-98-3(4)) Brain Sync.
Just slip on your headphones, and start your workout. Within minutes you'll feel an exhilarating surge of power and energy as your mind transcends daily clutter. You'll soon enter timeless states of ecstasy as an intoxicating fusion of high-beta brain wave frequencies and primal rhythms stimulate your body to:-Boost beta-endorphin production-Blast through blocks-Burn more fat-Dramatically increase heart-health.

BreakTime. D. A. Tubesing. 1 cass. (Running Time: 52 min.). (Stressbreaks Ser.: No. 1). 11.95 (978-0-938586-84-5(X), BT) Whole Person.
Need a break from work or study? A creativity boost? A refocusing of attention? Try a short "energy break." These six revitalizing routines will help you return to work with renewed vigor. Eckels classical guitar accompaniment. Solar Power is the source of all energy - & the source of refueling in this personal visualization. Belly Breathing automatically soothes & relaxes. Mentally open a Fortune Cookie, & exercise creativity as you imagine the empowering message written inside. Wise, nurturing Mother Earth restores strength & vitality. The Big Yawn fills the lungs with oxygen & stretches the muscles. Use Affirmation to center yourself & renew your energy.

Breakup. collector's ed. Dana Stabenow. Read by Marguerite Gavin. 6 cass. (Running Time: 9 hrs.). (Kate Shugak Ser.). 2000. 48.00 (978-0-7366-5532-3(8)) Books on Tape.
April in Alaska is a period of spring thaw, what the locals call breakup. It is a time of rebirth, renewal - & the resurfacing of past debris. For Kate Shugak, this year's meltdown brings nothing but mayhem. She must deal not only with the April 15th deadline for taxes, but also with rampaging bears, family feuds & finally a jet engine that crashes into her backyard. Then the melting snow uncovers a dead body near Kate's home. And when a deadly bear attack raises suspicions, Kate in drawn further into the destruction of this year's breakup & into the path of a cunning murderer.

Breast. unabr. ed. Philip Roth. Read by David Colacci. (Running Time: 2 hrs.). 2010. 19.99 (978-1-4418-0553-9(2), 9781441805539, Brilliance MP3); 19.99 (978-1-4418-0555-3(9), 9781441805553, BAD); 39.97 (978-1-4418-0554-6(0), 9781441805546, Brlnc Audio MP3 Lib); 39.97 (978-1-4418-0556-0(7), 9781441805560, BADLE); audio compact disk 19.99 (978-1-4418-0551-5(6), 9781441805515, Bril Audio CD Unabri); audio compact disk 62.97 (978-1-4418-0552-2(4), 9781441805522, BriAudCD Unabrid) Brilliance Audio.

Breast Cancer - A Bibliography & Dictionary for Physicians, Patients, & Genome Researchers. Compiled by Icon Group International, Inc. Staff. 2007. ring bd. 28.95 (978-0-497-11341-4(4)) Icon Grp.

Breast Disease, 1986 - What the Obstetrician-Gynecologist & Patient Should Know: Interdisciplinary Panel Discussion. Moderated by Douglas J. Marchant. 2 cass. (Gynecology & Obstetrics Ser.: GO-2). 1986. 19.00 (8641) Am Coll Surgeons.

Breast Diseases. Contrib. by Douglas J. Marchant et al. 1 cass. (American College of Obstetrics & Gynecologists UPDATE: Vol. 24, No. 1). 1998. 20.00 Am Coll Obstetric.

Breast Health. 2003. audio compact disk 19.95 (978-0-9743448-9-8(3)) NMA Media Pr.

Breastfeeding - Current Thoughts. Contrib. by Lawrence M. Gartner et al. 1 cass. (American Academy of Pediatrics UPDATE: Vol. 16, No. 2). 1998. 20.00 Am Acad Pediat.

Breastfeeding Basics & Beyond Vol. 1: The Foundation of the Series. Scripts. Beverly Morgan. 2 CDs. (Running Time: 2 hrs.). (Breastfeeding Basics & Beyond Ser.). 2003. audio compact disk 29.95 (978-1-891768-12-5(3)) Pub: Milky Way Pr. Dist(s): Baker Taylor
The first CD covers the science of breastfeeding helping mothers learn how to monitor theirbaby's urine output and bowel movements, and how the feel of a mother?s breasts before and aftera nursing can show if their baby took their milk. Mothers will recognize the signs that nursing isgoing well and how to know breastfeeding may not be on track. This audiobook also providesanswers to some frequently asked questions: How about weight gain?, How often and longshould a baby nurse? And Should I wake him to nurse? (Narrated by Roberta Kennedy)The second CD takes breastfeeding mothers past the science into the relationship ofbreastfeeding. It can help a mother fall even more in love with her baby as she discovers she canread his subtle communication cues. Now breastfeeding mothers can benefit from BeverlyMorgan?s years of experience. Eminent lactation expert Jack Newman, IBCLC, MD, FRCP,Medical Director of the Breastfeeding Clinics in Toronto, Canada, commends the author on thiswork and praises her strong emphasis on the role that milk flow plays in breastfeeding. (Narrated by KathrynNymoen).

Breastfeeding Meditation. Scripts. Sheri Menelli. Voice by Sheri Menelli. 1. (Running Time: 51 minutes). 2004. audio compact disk 15.99 (978-0-9747853-0-1(X)) White Hrt Pub.
This guided meditation helps you to: improve your attitude toward breastfeeding* relax your mind and body completely* bring in breast milk through powerful visualizations* create a better bond with your baby.*

Breastfeeding's Number One Question: How Do I Know My Baby Is Getting Enough Milk?, unabr. ed. Beverly Morgan. Narrated by Roberta Kennedy. 1 cass. (Running Time: 50 min.). (Breastfeeding Basics & Beyond Ser.). 2000. 12.95 (978-1-891768-02-6(6)) Milky Way Pr.
Focuses on the first seven days, providing an easy-to-use format & clear guidelines to be sure breastfeeding is on track.

Breastplate: Ephesians 6:14, 643. Ed Young. 1987. 4.95 (978-0-7417-1643-9(7), 643) Win Walk.

Breastplate of Integrity: Protecting Yourself Against the Attacks of the Enemy. Mac Hammond. 1 cass. 1996. 12.00 (978-1-57399-021-9(3)) Mac Hammond.
Teaching on the importance of having the characteristic of integrity in your life.

***Breastplate of Integrity: Protecting Yourself Against the Attacks of the Enemy.** Mac Hammond. 2010. audio compact disk 12.00 (978-1-57399-459-0(6)) Mac Hammond.

Breath see Philip Levine

Breath. Tim Winton. Read by Dan Wyllie. (Running Time: 6 hrs. 20 mins.). 2009. 69.99 (978-1-74214-184-8(6), 9781742141848) Pub: Bolinda Pubng AUS. Dist(s): Bolinda Pub Inc

Breath. unabr. ed. Tim Winton. Read by Dan Wyllie. (Running Time: 6 hrs. 20 mins.). 2008. audio compact disk 57.95 (978-1-921415-61-6(4), 9781921415616) Pub: Bolinda Pubng AUS. Dist(s): Bolinda Pub Inc

Breath. unabr. ed. Tim Winton. Read by Dan Wyllie. (Running Time: 6 hrs. 20 mins.). 2008. 43.95 (978-1-921415-53-1(3), 9781921415531) Pub: Bolinda Pubng AUS. Dist(s): Bolinda Pub Inc

Breath Energy Ecstasy, CD 1 Beginners Course: Radiant Embodiment. Executive Producer Sabine Grandke-Taft. 1. (Running Time: 45 mins). 2005. audio compact disk 21.00 (978-1-59971-741-8(7)) AardGP.
This 40 minute Beginners CD will teach you how to gain energy and achieve ecstasy through breathing and gentle movement while having FUN.Radiant Embodiment, Breath Energy Ecstasy CD 1, Beginners Course. This 40 minute CD for women and men will give you energy to live ecstasy through gentle breath and movement. Rediscover and reconnect to your body's natural pleasure while having FUN.

Breath Energy Ecstasy, CD 2, Advanced Course: Radiant Embodiment. Executive Producer Sabine Grandke-Taft. 1. (Running Time: 50). 2005. audio compact disk 21.00 (978-1-59971-740-1(9)) AardGP.
This 42 minute Advanced CD for women and men will support you with fun to stretch your mind and to explore your body on deeper levels. By bringing awareness to every breath and sensation in your body, Life can be truly sacred.

Breath Meditations, Vol. 1 unabr. ed. Carla Woody. 1 cass. (Running Time: 60 min.). 1999. 12.00 (978-1-930192-01-0(0)) Kenosis.
These are meditations that use the breath as a conduit to still spaces against the backdrop of Tibetan bells. Side one "Chakra Breathing." Side two is "One.".

Breath of French Air. unabr. ed. H. E. Bates. Read by Bruce Montague. 4 cass. (Running Time: 6 hrs.). (Larkin Family Ser.: Bk. 2). 2001. 34.95

(978-0-7451-4002-5(5), CAB 699) Pub: Chivers Audio Bks GBR. Dist(s): AudioGO
They're here again, the indestructible Larkins! This time, they are headed to France!.

Breath of Fresh Air. unabr. ed. Erica James. 7 cass. (Isis Ser.). (J). 2002. 61.95 (978-0-7531-1365-3(1)) Pub: ISIS Lrg Prnt GBR. Dist(s): Ulverscroft US

Breath of God. Stephen Petruhak. 1 cass., 1 CD. 1998. 10.95 (CS-425); audio compact disk 15.95 (CD-425) GIA Pubns.

Breath of God. unabr. ed. Harry Turtledove. Narrated by William Dufris. (Running Time: 15 hrs. 0 mins. 0 sec.). (Opening of the World Ser.). (ENG.). 2009. audio compact disk 79.99 (978-1-4001-3784-8(5)) Pub: Tantor Media. Dist(s): IngramPubServ

Breath of God. unabr. ed. Harry Turtledove. Narrated by William Dufris. (Running Time: 15 hrs. 0 mins. 0 sec.). (Opening of the World Ser.). (ENG.). 2009. audio compact disk 39.99 (978-1-4001-0784-1(9)) Pub: Tantor Media. Dist(s): IngramPubServ

Breath of God: A Novel of the Opening of the World. unabr. ed. Harry Turtledove. Narrated by William Dufris. (Running Time: 15 hrs. 0 mins. 0 sec.). (Opening of the World Ser.). (ENG.). 2009. audio compact disk 29.99 (978-1-4001-5784-6(6)) Pub: Tantor Media. Dist(s): IngramPubServ

Breath of God: God's Promises, Vol. 1. 1 cass. (Breath of God Ser.). (C5302N) Brentwood Music.
The truth of the Father speaks boldly & tenderly through the powerful promises of this unique audio gift pack. You will be empowered by the Breath of God.

Breath of God: God's Promises, Vol. 1. gif. ed. 1 cass. (Breath of God Ser.). Date not set. (978-1-55897-879-9(8), CD-5302GP) Brentwood Music.

Breath of God: Loving Instructions from the Father, Vol. 2. gif. ed. audio compact disk (978-1-55897-881-2(X), CD-5460GP) Brentwood Music.

Breath of God Vol. 1: God's Promises, gif. ed. 1 cass. (Breath of God Ser.). Date not set. (978-1-55897-878-2(X), C-5302GP) Brentwood Music.

Breath of God Vol. 2: Loving Instructions from the Father. gif. ed. (978-1-55897-880-5(1), C-5302GP) Brentwood Music.

Breath of Heaven - ShowTrax. Perf. by Amy Grant. Arranged by Roger Emerson. 1 CD. (Running Time: 5 mins.). 2000. audio compact disk 19.95 (08595538) H Leonard.
The miracle of Christmas is expressively portrayed through the peaceful, reflective atmosphere of this lovely song.

Breath of Heaven (Mary's Song) Contrib. by Amy Grant. (Mastertrax Ser.). 2007. audio compact disk 9.98 (978-5-557-58528-6(1)) Pt of Grace Ent.

Breath of Life. David Binion. Read by David Binion. 1 cass. (Running Time: 90 mins.). 10.99 (978-0-7684-0188-2(7)); audio compact disk 15.99 (978-0-7684-0187-5(9)) Destiny Image Pubs.

Breath of Life: The Biblical Stress Management Series. Gail Bretan. Created by Gail Bretan. 1 CD. (Running Time: 15 min.). 2003. audio compact disk (978-0-9741064-1-0(0), Biblical Stress) G Bretan Assocs Inc.
One of the first things people do when they are stressed is hold their breath or breathe shallowly, creating a continuous negative cycle of lack of oxygen, inability to handle stress, and a sense of lifelessness. Learning and using proper breathing techniques is difficult for many people. However by listening to and practicing this relaxing and refreshing guided imagery of God breathing the ?Breath of Life? as experienced by Adam (the first human in the Bible), breathing can become an easy and spiritual way to transform stress and manifest peace. (Words and Piano).

Breath of Scandal. abr. ed. Sandra Brown. Read by Dick Hill. (Running Time: 21600 sec.). 2008. audio compact disk 14.99 (978-1-4233-2481-2(1), 9781423324812, BCD Value Price) Brilliance Audio.

Breath of Scandal. unabr. ed. Sandra Brown. Read by Dick Hill. (Running Time: 15 hrs.). 2007. 39.25 (978-1-4233-2477-5(3), 9781423324775, Brlnc Audio MP3 Lib); 24.95 (978-1-4233-2476-8(5), 9781423324768, Brilliance MP3); 39.25 (978-1-4233-2479-9(X), 9781423324799, BADLE); 24.95 (978-1-4233-2478-2(1), 9781423324782, BAD); 97.25 (978-1-4233-2473-7(0), 9781423324737, BrilAudUnabridg); audio compact disk 117.25 (978-1-4233-2475-1(7), 9781423324751, BriAudCD Unabrid); audio compact disk 38.95 (978-1-4233-2474-4(9), 9781423324744, Bril Audio CD Unabri) Brilliance Audio.

Breath of Snow & Ashes. Diana Gabaldon. Narrated by Davina Porter. (Running Time: 208800 sec.). (Outlander Ser.: Bk. 6). 2005. audio compact disk 79.99 (978-1-4193-6153-1(8)) Recorded Bks.

Breath of Snow & Ashes. abr. ed. Diana Gabaldon. Read by Geraldine James. (Running Time: 15 hrs.). (Outlander Ser.: Bk. 6). (ENG.). 2005. audio compact disk 39.95 (978-0-7393-2201-7(X), Random AudioBks) Pub: Random Audio Pubg. Dist(s): Random

Breath of Snow & Ashes. unabr. ed. Diana Gabaldon. Narrated by Davina Porter. 42 cass. (Running Time: 58 hrs.). (Outlander Ser.: Bk. 6). 2005. 109.75 (978-1-4193-4888-4(4), 98090) Recorded Bks.
Another spellbinding entry in the series, A Breath of Snow and Ashes continues the saga of 18th-century Scotsman Jamie Fraser and his 20th-century, time-traveling wife, Claire. The year is 1772, and the rift between Britain and its American colonies has put a frightening word into the minds of all concerned: revolution. In the backwoods of North Carolina, violence has already reared its ugly head, as cabins have been burned to the ground. To preserve the colony for King George III, the governor pleads with Jamie to bring the people together and restore peace. But Jamie has the privilege, although some might call it a burden, of knowing that war cannot be avoided. Claire has told him that the colonies will unite and rebel, and the result will be independence, with all British loyalists either dead or exiled. And there is an additional problem. Claire has discovered a newspaper clipping from 1776 that tells of Jamie's death. With its epic scope, historical details, and sweeping romance, A Breath of Snow and Ashes is everything Gabaldon's fans love and more.

Breath of Snow & Ashes. unabr. ed. Diana Gabaldon. Narrated by Davina Porter. 48 CDs. (Running Time: 58 hrs.). (Outlander Ser.: Bk. 6). 2005. audio compact disk 119.75 (978-1-4193-4890-7(6), C3364) Recorded Bks.

Breath of Suspicion. unabr. ed. Elizabeth Ferrars. Read by Nigel Graham. 6 cass. (Running Time: 6.5 hrs.). (Isis Ser.). (J). 2002. 54.95 (978-0-7531-0918-2(2)) Pub: ISIS Lrg Prnt GBR. Dist(s): Ulverscroft US

Breath of Suspicion. unabr. ed. Read by Nigel Graham. 6 CDs. (Running Time: 24000 sec.). (Isis Ser.). 2003. audio compact disk 64.95 (978-0-7531-1722-4(3)) Pub: ISIS Lrg Prnt GBR. Dist(s): Ulverscroft US

Breath of Tantric Love: Music for Ecstatic Practice. Perf. by Patrick J. Fitzgerald. Composed by Patrick J. Fitzgerald. Concept by Steve & Lokita Carter. 1 CD. (Running Time: 60 mins). 2005. audio compact disk 16.97 (978-0-9755511-3-4(2)) Institute for Ecstatic.

Breath of the Eternal: Awakening. Swami Chetanananda. 1 cass. (Running Time: 75 min.). (Breath of the Eternal Ser.). 1986. 8.95 (978-0-916356-69-9(8)) Vedanta Soc St Louis.
Selections from the Taittiriya Upanishad & the entire Isha Upanishad, chanted in Sanskrit with English translation.

Breath of the Eternal: Illumination. Swami Chetanananda. 1 cass. (Running Time: 70 min.). (Breath of the Eternal Ser.). 1986. 8.95 (978-0-916356-71-2(X)) Vedanta Soc St Louis.
Selections from the Bhagavad Gita chanted in Sanskrit with English translation.

Breath of the Eternal: Reflection. Swami Chetanananda. 1 cass. (Running Time: 62 min.). (Breath of the Eternal Ser.). 1986. 8.95 (978-0-916356-70-5(1)) Vedanta Soc St Louis.
Creation hymns from the Rig Veda & dialogue on the Self from the Brihadaranyaka Upanishad in Sanskrit with English translation.

Breath of the Eternal Series. unabr. ed. Music by Swami Chetanananda. 3 cass. (Running Time: 3 hrs. 27 min.). (SAN & ENG.). 1986. 22.00 Set. (978-0-916356-75-0(2)) Vedanta Soc St Louis.
Selections from the Upanishads, Vedas, & Bhagavad Gita were recorded in the domed shrine of the Ramakrishna Monastery at Trabuco Canyon, California; Sanskrit with English translation. Individual cassettes are also listed & available separately under the following subtitles: Awakening; Reflection; Illumination.

Breath of the Soul. Created by Adam Gainsburg. (ENG.). 2007. audio compact disk 14.95 (978-0-9788535-4-9(7)) Soulsign.

Breath of Your Life: Discovering Your Breath Prayer. Ron DelBene & Herb Montgomery. 1 cass. (Running Time: 60 min.). 1989. 9.95 HarperCollins Pubs.

Breath Sweeps Mind. Jakusho Kwong-Roshi. 2007. audio compact disk 79.95 (978-1-59179-045-7(X)) Sounds True.

Breath Sweeps Mind. Jakusho Kwong-Roshi. 2007. audio compact disk 69.95 (978-1-59179-594-0(X)) Sounds True.

Breathe. 2008. audio compact disk 19.99 (978-0-9818864-0-4(X)) Pub: Kairos Pubg. Dist(s): Destiny Image Pubs

***Breathe.** Penni Russon. Read by Melissa Eccleston. (Running Time: 7 hrs.). (YA). 2009. 49.99 (978-1-74214-353-8(9), 9781742143538) Pub: Bolinda Pubng AUS. Dist(s): Bolinda Pub Inc

Breathe. Perf. by Soulfood. 1 cass., 1 CD. 8.78 (RYKO 10394); audio compact disk 12.78 CD Jewel box. (RYKO 10394) NewSound.

Breathe. Perf. by Midge Ure. 1 cass., 1 CD. 8.78 (RCA 34629); 8.78 (RCA 34629); audio compact disk 12.78 CD Jewel box. (RCA 34629) NewSound.

Breathe: The Sequel to Undine. unabr. ed. Penni Russon. Read by Melissa Eccleston. 6 CDs. (Running Time: 7 hrs.). (YA). (gr. 9-12). 2007. audio compact disk 77.95 (978-1-921334-43-6(6), 9781921334436) Pub: Bolinda Pubng AUS. Dist(s): Bolinda Pub Inc

***Breathe & Meditate Collection.** Rodney Yee. Read by Rodney Yee. (Playaway Adult Nonfiction Ser.). (ENG.). 2009. 39.99 (978-1-61574-626-2(9)) Find a World.

Breathe & Unwind: With Alpha Brainwave Pulses. abr. ed. Jeffrey Thompson et al. (Running Time: 2:00:00). 2006. audio compact disk 19.98 (978-1-55961-798-7(5)) Sounds True.

Breathe... As If Your Life Depended on It. Kathleen Cairns. Read by Kathleen Cairns. 1 cass. (Running Time: 29 min.). 10.00 (978-1-891409-03-5(4)) Life Goes On.
Relaxation & self hypnois.

Breathe Better, Live in Wellness (audio Book) Winning Your Battle over Shortnes of Breath. Jane M. Martin. Narrated by Heidi Hayes. 5 CDs. (Running Time: 5 hrs., 40 mins., 52 secs.). 2006. audio compact disk 24.95 (978-1-60031-004-1(4)) Spoken Books.
his new book by respiratory therapist and teacher, Jane M. Martin, provides hope for those diagnosed with a chronic lung disease - Emphysema, COPD, Asthma, or other lung disorders. With stories by and about people who have been diagnosed, it offers education, support and encouragement. Hear stories about people like you or your loved one who are successfully using oxygen, stopping smoking, dealing with denial, participating in exercise, and acting as caregivers. There IS hope for people with lung disease. Whether you are a patient or a supporter, you will breathe better after listening to this highly inspirational book.

***Breathe Easy: Relieve Stress & Reclaim Balance.** unabr. ed. Made for Success. Read by Mache, M.D.; Ziglar, Zig, Brian; Siebel Tracy. (Running Time: 9 hrs.). (Made for Success Ser.). 2010. audio compact disk 32.95 (978-1-4417-6070-8(9)) Blckstn Audio.

***Breathe Easy (Library Edition) Relieve Stress & Reclaim Balance.** unabr. ed. Made for Success. Read by Mache Tracy. (Running Time: 9 hrs.). (Made for Success Ser.). 2010. audio compact disk 118.00 (978-1-4417-6068-5(7)) Blckstn Audio.

Breathe for Health. (Running Time: 45 min.). (Health Ser.). 9.98 (978-1-55909-139-8(8), 114) Randolph Tapes.
Lets you learn to make use of your breath for more energy, strength & total well-being.

Breathe for Life. 1 cass. (Health Ser.). 12.98 (114) Randolph Tapes.
This powerful tape lets you learn to make use of your breath for more energy, strength & total well-being.

Breathe to Beat the Blues: Manage Your Mood with Your Breath. Amy Weintraub. 1 CD. (Running Time: 58:57). 2003. audio compact disk 16.99 (978-0-9747380-0-0(X)) Amy Wein.
Author of YOGA FOR DEPRESSION, Amy Weintraub, leads ten Yogic Breathing exercises to help calm the mind and elevate the mood, followed by a guided relaxation. Music by Larry Redhouse with Cantrell Maryott and Phil Lipman.

Breathe with the Body: A Body Scan: Guided Imagery for Well-Being. Read by Catherine Sheen. 2006. audio compact disk 14.95 (978-0-9773381-0-8(X)) Reach In.

Breathing: Techniques to Reduce Tension & Benefit Health. Music by Hugh Fraser. 2000. audio compact disk (978-1-893238-10-7(5)) Doc Borrie.

Breathing: The Master Key to Self Healing. Andrew Weil. 2 CDs. (Running Time: 2 hrs.). (Self Healing Ser.). 1999. bk. & stu. ed. 24.95 (978-1-56455-726-1(X), W445) Sounds True.
Eight breathing exercises that Dr. Weil uses in his own life & has prescribed to hundreds of patients over the past two decades.

Breathing Box. Gay Hendricks. (Running Time: 2 hrs. 45 mins.). 2006. stu. ed. 26.95 (978-1-59179-234-5(7), W882D) Sounds True.

Breathing Colors. Read by Mary Richards. 1 cass. (Running Time: 45 min.). (Energy Break Ser.). 2007. audio compact disk 19.95 (978-1-56136-157-1(7)) Master Your Mind.

Breathing Easy: Meditation & Breathing Techniques to Relax, Refresh & Revitalize. unabr. ed. Michael F. Roizen & Mehmet C. Oz. Read by Michael F. Roizen et al. CDs 2. (Running Time: 2 hrs. 0 mins. 0 sec.). (ENG.). 2008. audio compact disk 19.95 (978-0-7435-7374-0(9)) Pub: S&S Audio. Dist(s): S and S Inc

Breathing for Life: The Principles & Practice of Ujjayi Pranayama. Miller Richard. (ENG.). 2010. 49.95 (978-1-893099-11-1(3)) Pub: Anahata Pr. Dist(s): Ctr of Timeless

Breathing Free. unabr. ed. Read by Gabrielle De Cuir. 6 cass. (Running Time: 9 hrs.). 2001. 32.00 (978-1-59040-147-7(6), Phoenix Audio) Pub: Amer Intl Pub. Dist(s): PerseuPGW

Breathing Grace: What You Need More Than Your Next Breath. Harry Kraus. Read by Wayne Shepherd. (Running Time: 3 hrs. 57 mins.). 2007. audio compact disk 26.99 (978-1-58134-914-6(9)) CrosswayIL.

Breathing Healthy, Breathing Free, Pt. 1. unabr. ed. Read by Peter Himmelman. Perf. by Peter Himmelman. 1 cass. (Running Time: 30 min.). Dramatization. (J). 1991. 8.95 (978-1-58452-008-5(6), 4380); 8.95 Spanish version. (978-1-58452-017-7(5), 5380) Spinoza Co.

Breathing Healthy, Breathing Free, Pt. 2. unabr. ed. Read by Peter Himmelman. Perf. by Peter Himmelman. 1 cass. (Running Time: 30 min.). Dramatization. (J). 1991. 8.95 (978-1-58452-009-2(4), 4385); 8.95 Spanish version. (978-1-58452-018-4(3), 5385) Spinoza Co.

Breathing into Oneness. Christopher Love. Read by Christopher Love. 1 cass. (Running Time: 30 min.). 1997. 10.95 (978-1-891820-12-0(5)) World Sangha Pubg.
Self-hypnosis meditation for healing, self-improvement & realizing our full & powerful potential as spiritual beings.

Breathing Lessons. Anne Tyler. Read by Alexandra O'Karma. 10 CDs. (Running Time: 12.25 Hrs). audio compact disk 39.95 (978-1-4025-2493-6(5)) Recorded Bks.

Breathing Lessons. unabr. ed. Anne Tyler. Read by Ruth Stokesberry. 8 cass. (Running Time: 12 hrs.). 1989. 64.00 (978-0-7366-1587-7(3), 2450) Books on Tape.
Maggie is scattered, impetuous, soft; Ira is competent, patient, infallible. They have been married for 28 years. A hot summer day finds them driving to Deer Lick, Pennsylvania, 90 miles from their home in Baltimore, to the funeral of Maggie's best friend's husband. But the journey is a metaphor for their own lives, with the tensions, disappointments & frustrations that a long marriage brings.

Breathing Lessons. unabr. ed. Anne Tyler. Read by Alexandra O'Karma. 7 Cass. (Running Time: 12.25 Hrs). 29.95 (978-1-4025-2369-4(6)) Recorded Bks.

Breathing Lessons. unabr. ed. Anne Tyler. Narrated by Alexandra O'Karma. 9 cass. (Running Time: 12 hrs. 15 mins.). 1994. 78.00 (978-1-55690-685-5(4), 92338E7) Recorded Bks.
A dissimilar & disenchanted middle-aged couple head out one morning for a friend's funeral & end up taking an hilarious collision course into the past.

Breathing Love. 1. 2003. audio compact disk (978-0-9748215-2-8(7)) Sensuous Myst.

Breathing Method. Stephen King. Read by Frank Muller. (Running Time: 3 hrs.). (ENG.). (gr. 12 up). 2009. audio compact disk 19.95 (978-0-14-314393-2(X), PengAudBks) Penguin Grp USA.

***Breathing Method.** unabr. ed. Stephen King. (Running Time: 3 hrs.). (ENG.). 2010. audio compact disk 14.95 (978-0-14-242805-4(1), PengAudBks) Penguin Grp USA.

Breathing Method, unabr. ed. Stephen King. Narrated by Frank Muller. 2 cass. (Running Time: 3 hrs.). (gr. 8 up). 1984. 18.00 (978-1-55690-073-0(2), 84066E7) Recorded Bks.
At an exclusive men's club in New York, an aging member tells a hypnotic story of survival.

Breathing Method, Set. unabr. ed. Stephen King. Read by Frank Muller. 2 cass. 1999. 17.95 (FS9-50944) Highsmith.

Breathing Rhythms. Glen Velez. 1 CD. (Running Time: 55 mins.). 2000. audio compact disk 16.98 (978-1-56455-821-3(5), MM00120D) Sounds True.
The author is a pioneer in the use of music to heal the body & calm the mind. With Breathing Rhythms, velez offers a multilayerer, interactive journey to attune you to the natural rhythms & energy flows of your own body.

***Breathing Room.** abr. ed. Susan Elizabeth Phillips. Read by Kate Forbes. (ENG.). 2005. (978-0-06-085311-2(5), Harper Audio); (978-0-06-085312-9(3), Harper Audio) HarperCollins Pubs.

Breathing Room. unabr. ed. Susan Elizabeth Phillips. Read by Kate Fleming. 1 CD. (Running Time: 10 hrs.). 2002. audio compact disk 29.95 (978-0-7927-2663-4(X), CMP 468, Chivers Sound Lib) AudioGO.
America's Diva of Self-Help, Dr. Isabel Favor, just lost her fiance to a disorganized earth mother, her accountant has absconded with her hard-earned money, and the empire she's built is in shambles. Seeking emotional shelter, she flees to Italy to find some peace. But for Isabel, the biggest disaster lies just ahead, in the gorgeous form of Lorenzo Gage, Hollywood's favorite villain. Before they know it, wine will flow, sparks will fly, and hearts will meld.

***Breathing Room.** unabr. ed. Susan Elizabeth Phillips. Read by Kate Forbes. (ENG.). 2007. (978-0-06-147265-7(4), Harper Audio); (978-0-06-147264-0(6), Harper Audio) HarperCollins Pubs.

Breathing Self Esteem. Michael G. White. Read by Michael G. White. 1 cass. (Running Time: 50 min.). Dramatization. (Somatic Education System Ser.). 1993. 12.00 (978-1-883417-22-2(8)) Balance Breath.
Guided breathing exercise accompanied by Tibetan singing bowls.

Breathing the Fire. Kimberly Dozier. Read by Kimberly Dozier. (Playaway Adult Nonfiction Ser.). 2008. 54.99 (978-1-60640-551-2(9)) Find a World.

Breathing the Fire: Fighting to Report - And Survive - The War in Iraq. unabr. ed. Kimberly Dozier. Read by Kimberly Dozier. 8 CDs. (Running Time: 10 hrs. 30 mins. 0 sec.). (ENG.). 2008. audio compact disk 34.99 (978-1-4001-0645-5(1)); audio compact disk 24.99 (978-1-4001-5645-0(9)) Pub: Tantor Media. Dist(s): IngramPubServ

Breathing the Fire: Fighting to Report - And Survive-The War in Iraq. unabr. ed. Kimberly Dozier. Read by Kimberly Dozier. 8 CDs. (Running Time: 10 hrs. 30 mins. 0 sec). (ENG.). 2008. audio compact disk 69.99 (978-1-4001-3645-2(8)) Pub: Tantor Media. Dist(s): IngramPubServ

Breathing Underwater. unabr. ed. Alex Flinn. 3 cass. (Running Time: 5 hrs. 8 mins.). (Young Adult Cassette Librariestm Ser.). (J). (gr. 7 up). 2004. 30.00 (978-0-8072-0686-7(5), S YA 346 CX, Listening Lib) Random Audio Pubg.

Breathing Underwater. unabr. ed. Alex Flinn. Read by Jon Cryer. 3 vols. (Running Time: 5 hrs. 8 mins.). (Young Adult Cassette Librariestm Ser.). (J). (gr. 7 up). 2004. pap. bk. 36.00 (978-0-8072-0992-9(9), S YA 346 SP, Listening Lib) Random Audio Pubg.

Breathing Underwater: Spirituality & the 12 Steps. Richard Rohr. 2 cass. (Running Time: 2 hrs.). 1989. vinyl bd. 17.95 (978-0-00-689611-1(1), A0150) St Anthony Mess Pr.
To survive in a world flooded with compulsive behavior and addictions Christians must learn to "breath under water" and discover God's love and compassion.

Breathless. 1 cass. (Running Time: 1 hr. 30 mins.). 2001. 11.95 (LTYH002) Lodestone Catalog.
Angelica wants revenge, but her target sways her.

***Breathless.** Dean Koontz. Contrib. by Jeff Cummings. (Playaway Adult Fiction Ser.). (ENG.). 2009. 69.99 (978-1-4418-2286-4(0)) Find a World.

Breathless. unabr. ed. Dean Koontz. (Running Time: 9 hrs.). 2009. 39.97 (978-1-4233-5708-7(6), 9781423357087, BADLE) Brilliance Audio.

Breathless. unabr. ed. Dean Koontz. Read by Jeff Cummings. (Running Time: 8 hrs.). 2009. 24.99 (978-1-4233-5707-0(8), 9781423357070, BAD); 24.99 (978-1-4233-5705-6(1), 9781423357056, Brilliance MP3); 39.97 (978-1-4233-5706-3(X), 9781423357063, Brinc Audio MP3 Lib); audio compact disk 39.99 (978-1-4233-5703-2(5), 9781423357032, Bril Audio CD Unabri); audio compact disk 99.97 (978-1-4233-5704-9(3), 9781423357049, BriAudCD Unabrid) Brilliance Audio.

Breathless. unabr. ed. J. P. Smith. Read by Michael Prichard. 8 cass. (Running Time: 12 hrs.). 1995. 64.00 (978-0-7366-3128-0(3), 3803); audio compact disk 12.95 Set. (3803) Books on Tape.
Jill Bowman, a history professor in Boston, leads a structured life full of obligations: to her academic research, to her autistic daughter, to her husband, Peter. Then her world gets scrambled when police find Peter dead - his throat cut - in a seedy motel. Oddly, helping solve the murder takes a back seat to Jill's personal mysteries which emerge as she struggles with the tragedy. The shadowy events in her past return to haunt her & an intimate view of this 42-year-old woman's life unfolds, painfully. A detective on the case may provide the only way for Jill to breathe again.

Breathless Summer. Mary Minton. 7 cass. (Running Time: 9 hrs. 15 mins.). (Story Sound Ser.). (J). 2004. 61.95 (978-1-85903-696-9(1)) Pub: Mgna Lrg Print GBR. Dist(s): Ulverscroft US

BreathSounds 4-16-8 Vol. 3: Measured Music for Breathing Practices in the Science of Pranayama. Sandra Kozak. (Running Time: 29.10). 2004. audio compact disk 12.95 (978-0-940985-65-0(9)) Lotus Pr.
BreathSounds makes pranayama easier and more effective. These CD's consist of 2 beautifully blended musical phrases for inhalation and exhalation and chime phrases for retentions. The pattern 4-16-8- denotes a 4-count inhalation, 16-count hold and an 8-count exhalation with no hold on the exhalation. This volume is ideal for those who wish to deepen their sitting meditation practice.

BreathSounds 6-3-12-3 Vol. 1: Measured Music for Breathing Practices in the Science of Pranayama. Sandra Kozak. (Running Time: 29.10). 2004. audio compact disk 12.95 (978-0-940985-66-7(7)) Lotus Pr.
BreathSounds makes pranayama easier and more effective. These CD's consist of 2 beautifully blended musical phrases for inhalation and exhalation and chime phrases for retentions. The pattern 6-3-12-3 denotes a 6-count inhalation, 3-count hold, a 12-count exhalation and a 3-count hold. This volume is ideal for starting pranayama practice and for those who can exhale for 7-10 seconds or less.

BreathSounds 8-4-16-4 Vol. II: Measured Music for Breathing Practices in the Science of Pranayama. Sandra Kozak. (Running Time: 29.10). 2004. audio compact disk 12.95 (978-0-940985-67-4(5)) Lotus Pr.
BreathSounds makes pranayama easier and more effective. These CD's consist of 2 beautifully blended musical phrases for inhalation and exhalation and chime phrases for retentions. The pattern 8-4-16-4 denotes an 8-count inhalation, 4-count hold, a 16-count exhalation and a 4-count hold. This volume is ideal for those who are intermediate in their practice and who can exhale for 12 or more seconds.

Breathtaker. unabr. ed. Alice Blanchard. Read by Peter Coyote. (ENG.). 2005. 14.98 (978-1-59483-312-0(5)) Pub: Hachet Audio. Dist(s): HachBkGrp

Breathwalks: Companion Tape Set for the Book "Breathwalk" Gurucharan Singh Khalsa & Yogi Bhajan. 1 cass. 2000. (978-0-9700967-0-8(4)) Khalsa Con.

Breezing Through the Storms of Life, Vol. 1. Mac Hammond. 7 cass. (Running Time: 7 hrs.). 1997. 42.00 Set. (978-1-57399-047-9(7)) Mac Hammond.
What to do when faced with life's adversities.

Breezing Through the Storms of Life, Vol. 1. Mac Hammond. (ENG.). 2007. audio compact disk 35.00 (978-1-57399-331-9(X)) Mac Hammond.

Breezing Through the Storms of Life, Vol. 2. Mac Hammond. 5 cass. (Running Time: 5 hrs.). 1997. 30.00 Set. (978-1-57399-048-6(5)) Mac Hammond.

Breezing Through the Storms of Life, Vol. 2. Mac Hammond. (ENG.). 2007. audio compact disk 25.00 (978-1-57399-332-6(8)) Mac Hammond.

Bremen Town Musicians see Favorite Children's Stories: A Collection

Bremen Town Musicians see Favorite Tales by the Brothers Grimm

Bremen Town Musicians. Ruth B. Gross. Illus. by Jack Kent. 1 cass. (Easy-to-Read Folktales Ser.). (J). (ps-2). 1985. Scholastic Inc.

Bremen Town Musicians. Ruth B. Gross & Jack Kent. Illus. by Jack Kent. 1 cass. (Easy-to-Read Folktales Ser.). (J). (ps-2). 1985. 5.95 (978-0-590-63065-8(2)) Scholastic Inc.

Bremen Town Musicians. Max Showalter. 1 cass. (Running Time: 35 min.). (J). (gr. k-6). 1990. 9.98 (978-1-879305-10-6(0), AM-C-109) Am Melody.
Traditional fairy tales with original songs & music, performed by famed character actor Max Showalter.

Brendan Behan. unabr. ed. Brendan Behan. 1 cass. (Author Speaks Ser.). 1991. 14.95 J Norton Pubs.
Archival recordings of 20th-century authors.

Brendan Behan Sings Irish Ballads. Perf. by Brendan Behan. 10.95 (978-0-8045-0760-8(0), SAC 760) Spoken Arts.

Brendan Buckley's Universe & Everything in It. unabr. ed. Sundee Tucker Frazier. Read by Mirron Willis. 5 CDs. (Running Time: 5 hrs. 15 mins.). (J). (gr. 4-7). 2008. audio compact disk 38.00 (978-0-7393-7912-7(7), Listening Lib) Pub: Random Audio Pubg. Dist(s): Random
Ten-year-old Tae Kwon Do blue belt and budding rock hound Brendan Buckley keeps a "Confidential" notebook for his top-secret scientific discoveries. And he's found something totally top secret. The grandpa he's never met, who his mom refuses to talk about or see, is an expert mineral collector and lives nearby! Secretly, Brendan visits Ed DeBose, whose skin is pink, not brown like Brendan's, his dad's, or that of Grampa Clem's, who recently died. Brendan sets out to find the reason behind Ed's absence, but what he discovers can't be explained by science, and now he wishes he'd never found him at all.

Brendan Buckley's Universe & Everything in It. unabr. ed. Sundee Tucker Frazier. Read by Mirron Willis. (ENG.). (J). (gr. 4). 2008. audio compact disk 35.00 (978-0-7393-7910-3(0), Listening Lib) Pub: Random Audio Pubg. Dist(s): Random

Brendan Gill. unabr. ed. Read by Brenda N. Gill. 1 cass. (Running Time: 29 min.). 1985. 10.00 New Letters.
Gill reads two stories from his book, "Ways of Loving".

Brentwood Jazz Revival. Perf. by Brentwood Jazz Quartet. 1 cass. 1999. 10.98 (978-0-7601-2685-1(2)) Provident Music.

Brer Deer n de Hot Peppas. Illus. by Jan Blackshire. (ENG.). (J). 2009. pap. bk. 25.00 (978-0-9842956-0-9(7)) MarshTales.

Brer Rabbit & Boss Lion. As told by Danny Glover. Music by Dr. John. Illus. by Bill Mayer. 1 cass. (Running Time: 1 hr.). 9.95 Weston Woods.
In this hilarious Southern folktale, Brer Rabbit outsmarts the mean old boss Lion, then saunters back to town as the local hero.

Brer Rabbit & Boss Lion. Joel Chandler Harris. Narrated by Danny Glover. Music by Dr. John. Illus. by Jeffrey J. Mayer. 1 cass. (J). (gr. k-3). 1996. 10.95 INCL. BK. (Little Simon) SandS Childrens.
The peaceful animals at Brer Village discover, their new neighbor, old Boss Lion, has a large appetite for fresh meat. When he starts feeding on the Brer folk, Brer rabbit steps in & teaches him a lesson he'll never forget.

Brer Rabbit & His Tricks. Ennis Rees. 1 cass. (Running Time: 43 min.). (J). 10.95 (978-0-8045-1070-7(9), SAC 1070) Spoken Arts.
A retelling of the Brer Rabbit stories, read by, Ennis Rees.

Brer Rabbit & the Wonderful Tar Baby. Joel Chandler Harris. Narrated by Danny Glover. Music by Taj Mahal. Illus. by Henrik Drescher. 1 cass. (J). (gr. k-3). 1992. bk. 10.95 (SSChildren); 10.95 INCL. BK. (SSChildren) SandS Childrens.
Brer Rabbit gets his comeuppance, thanks to Brer Fox and his kooky, gooey Tar Baby.

Bresilien sans Peine. 1 cass. (Running Time: 1 hr., 30 min.). (FRE & POR.). 2000. bk. 75.00 (978-2-7005-1318-9(5)) Pub: Assimil FRA. Dist(s): Distribks Inc

Brest Boys' & Young Men's Choir. Contrib. by Alla Igumnova. 2003. 10.00 (978-1-59033-670-0(4)) Nova Sci Pubs.

Bret Lott. unabr. ed. Ed. by Jim McKinley. Prod. by Rebekah Presson. 1 cass. (Running Time: 29 min.). (New Letters on the Air Ser.). 1994. 10.00 (120693) New Letters.
In his new novel, "Reed's Beach," Bret Lott tells a story of grief as a couple attempts to recover from the hit-&-run car death of their seven year-old son. The "Los Angeles Times" has called Lott "one of the most important & imaginative writers today" & the "New York Times" says "Mr. Lott knows how ordinary people work & love, or try to love, & knows how intractable, even perverse, human feelings can be".

Brethren. John Grisham. Read by Vincent Marzello. 10 cass. (Running Time: 11 hrs. 50 min.). 2001. 40.95 (978-0-7540-0594-0(1)) AudioGO.
Trumble is a minimum security federal prison, home to an assortment of criminals, including three former judges. One of their scams goes awry, it ensnares the wrong victim, an innocent on the outside, a man with dangerous friends.

Brethren. John Grisham. Read by Frank Muller. 2000. audio compact disk 80.00 (978-0-7366-8904-5(4)) Books on Tape.

Brethren. unabr. ed. John Grisham. Read by Frank Muller. 7 cass. (Running Time: 10 hrs. 30 mins.). 2000. 49.95 (H417) Blckstn Audio.
Trumble is a minimum security federal prison, a home to the usual assortment of relatively harmless criminals - drug dealers, bank robbers, swindlers, embezzlers, tax evaders, two Wall Street crooks, one doctor, at least five lawyers. And three former judges who call themselves The Brethren: one from Texas, one from California & one from Mississippi.

Brethren. unabr. ed. John Grisham. Read by Frank Muller. 7 cass. (Running Time: 10 hrs. 30 min.). 2000. 56.00 (978-0-7366-4907-0(7)) Books on Tape.
Three former judges accidentally snare an innocent man with dangerous friends when their jailhouse scheme goes awry.

Brethren. unabr. ed. Beverly Lewis. Read by Stina Nielsen. 8 cass. (Running Time: 9 hrs.). (Annie's People Ser.: No. 3). 2007. 61.75 (978-1-4281-3205-4(8)); audio compact disk 92.75 (978-1-4281-3207-8(4)) Recorded Bks.

Breton Sans Peine, Vol. 1. 1 cass. (Running Time: 1 hr., 30 min.). (BRE & FRE.). 2000. audio compact disk 75.00 (978-2-7005-1346-2(0)) Pub: Assimil FRA. Dist(s): Distribks Inc

Breton Sans Peine, Vol. 2. 1 cass. (Running Time: 1 hr., 30 min.). (BRE & FRE.). 2000. audio compact disk 75.00 (978-2-7005-1347-9(9)) Pub: Assimil FRA. Dist(s): Distribks Inc

Breuddwyd Madlen. Eleri Llewelyn Morris & Cwmni Iaith. 2005. 5.90 (978-0-00-067987-1(9)) Zondervan.

Brewing up a Storm. unabr. ed. Emma Lathen. Read by Garrick Hagon. 8 cass. (Running Time: 12 hrs.). (John Putnam Thatcher Mystery Ser.). 2000. 59.95 (978-0-7540-0030-3(3), CAB 1453) Pub: Chivers Audio Bks GBR. Dist(s): AudioGO
Quax, a non-alcoholic alternative to popular beers, becomes the center of a political feud when a 19-year-old dies in a drunken wreck. But NOBBY (No Beer-Buying Youngster) asserts that non-alcoholic beer primes youngsters for premature alcohol abuse and takes the Kichsel Brewery to court. Although he begins just as an observer, Wall Street Banker John Putnam Thatcher begins to uncover a brew of political intrigue and murder.

***Brewster's Millions.** unabr. ed. George Barr McCutcheon. Read by Bronson Pinchot. (Running Time: 5 hrs. 30 mins.). 2011. 29.95 (978-1-4417-6446-1(1)); 34.95 (978-1-4417-6443-0(7)); audio compact disk 24.95 (978-1-4417-6445-4(3)); audio compact disk 55.00 (978-1-4417-6444-7(5)) Blckstn Audio.

Brhaspati; The Importance of Earning. Ann Ree Colton & Jonathan Murro. 7.95 A R Colton Fnd.

Brian D. Mcclure Audio Book Collection, Vol. 1. Short Stories. Brian D. McClure. Read by Brian D. McClure. Des. by Aretta Swanson. Intro. by Aretta Swanson. Engineer Doug Durham. 1 CD. (Running Time: 30 minutes). (J). 2006. audio compact disk 8.95 (978-1-933426-02-0(0)) Universal Flag.
Volume I Stories Include:The RaindropThe Sun and the MoonWho Am I?The BubbleAll stories read by the authorUnabridged Audio CD.

Brian Friel: Philadelphia, Here I Come. unabr. ed. Read by Abbey Theatre Company Staff et al. 2 cass. (Running Time: 1 hr. 44 min.). (Abbey Theatre Reads Ser.). 1988. 21.95 Set. (978-0-88432-279-5(3), ABB 008) J Norton Pubs.
Abbey Theatre company perform a classic contemporary Irish drama first performed in 1964.

Brian Patten Reading His Poetry. unabr. ed. Brian Patten. Read by Brian Patten. 1 cass. Incl. Creature to Tell the Time by. (SWC 1300); January Gladsong. (SWC 1300); Little Johnny's Confession. (SWC 1300); Little Johnny's Final Letter. (SWC 1300); Making a Call. (SWC 1300); Maud. (SWC 1300); Now We Will Either Sleep, Lie Still or Dress Again. (SWC 1300); Projectionist's Nightmare. (SWC 1300); Prophet's Good Idea. (SWC 1300); Rauin into My Mirror Has Walked. (SWC 1300); Schoolboy. (SWC 1300); Small Dragon. (SWC 1300); Talk with a Wood. (SWC 1300); Telephonists. (SWC 1300); Theme for Various Murders. (SWC 1300); Travelling Between Places. (SWC 1300); Unisong. (SWC 1300); Winter Song. Jean-Claude Mourlevat. (SWC 1300); You Come to Me Quiet As Rain Not Yet Fallen. (SWC 1300); 1984. 12.95 (978-0-694-50204-2(9), SWC 1300) HarperCollins Pubs.

Brian Tracy's Action Strategies for Personal Achievement. Brian S. Tracy. 24 cass. 1993. 179.95 set. (10390A) Nightingale-Conant.

Brian Tracy's Advanced Selling Techniques & Advanced Selling in Action, Set. 6 cass. 1994. 69.95 (10660AX) Nightingale-Conant.
Customers, markets & the very act of selling itself are changing almost daily. In this program, you'll discover powerful new tactics & techniques employed by only the top 10 percent of the sales profession. Brian Tracy reveals the critical issues facing buyers today. He gives his unique perspective on concepts such as partnering, GAP analysis & risk management - concepts that are helping many Fortune 500 companies break sales records. And he teaches you how (& why) to become a problem-solving partner rather than just a "vendor" or "supplier." Includes workbook.

Brian Wildsmith's Birds. (J). 2004. pap. bk. 14.95 (978-1-56008-164-7(3)) Weston Woods.

Brian Wildsmith's Circus. (J). 2004. pap. bk. 14.95 (978-1-56008-165-4(1)) Weston Woods.

Brian Wildsmith's Circus; Brian Wildsmith's Fishes. 2004. 8.95 (978-1-56008-849-3(4)); cass. & flmstrp 30.00 (978-0-89719-659-8(7)) Weston Woods.

Brian Wildsmith's Circus; Brian Wildsmith's Fishes; Angus & the Cat; Changes, Changes; Funny Little Woman. 2004. (978-0-89719-833-2(6)); cass. & flmstrp (978-0-89719-741-0(0)) Weston Woods.

Brian Wildsmith's Fishes. (J). 2004. bk. 24.95 (978-1-56008-167-8(8)); pap. bk. 14.95 (978-1-56008-166-1(X)) Weston Woods.

Brian Wildsmith's Puzzles. 2004. 8.95 (978-1-56008-850-9(8)); cass. & flmstrp 30.00 (978-0-89719-660-4(0)) Weston Woods.

Brian Wildsmith's Wild Animals. (J). 2004. pap. bk. 14.95 (978-1-56008-168-5(6)) Weston Woods.

Brian Wizard's Nigerian 419 Scam "Game Over!" Brian Wizard. 2002. audio compact disk 32.00 (978-0-949702-99-9(4)) BrianWizards.

Brian's Hunt. Gary Paulsen. Read by Ron McLarty. 2 cass. (Running Time: 2 hrs. 23 mins.). (J). (gr. 5-9). 2004. 23.00 (978-0-8072-2339-0(5), Listening Lib); audio compact disk 24.00 (978-1-4000-8608-5(6), Listening Lib) Random Audio Pubg.
The fifth story about Brian, now 16, takes place two years after he had been stranded in the Canadian wilderness as the result of a plane crash. Brian is unable to adjust to living back in civilization and arranges to home school himself in the Canadian north woods. As he begins his new life, he encounters a wounded dog that appears to be domesticated. He starts to get a gut feeling that the dog may have come from a Cree camp in the north where friends of his live. After attending the dog's wounds, he decides to head toward the camp only to find that residents have experienced a savage bear attack.

Brian's Return. Gary Paulsen. Read by Peter Coyote. 2 cass. (Running Time: 3 hrs.). (J). 2000. 18.00 (978-0-7366-9054-6(9)) Books on Tape.
The gripping conclusion to the extraordinary story that began in "Hatchet" & continued in "The River" & "Brian's Winter." In this final tale, Brian Robeson returns to the woods & discovers his true path in life & where he really belongs.

Brian's Return. unabr. ed. Gary Paulsen. Read by Peter Coyote. 2 vols. (Running Time: 2 hrs. 26 mins.). (Middle Grade Cassette Librariestm Ser.). (J). (gr. 5-9). 2004. pap. bk. 29.00 (978-0-8072-0658-4(X), S YA 292 SP, Listening Lib); 23.00 (978-0-8072-0446-7(3), Listening Lib) Random Audio Pubg.
After surviving alone in the wilderness, Brian finds that he can no longer live in the city. High school leaves him feeling more isolated than he ever did in the wild. For Brian, returning to the woods, the place where he really belongs, is the answer.

Brian's Return. unabr. ed. Gary Paulsen. Read by Peter Coyote. (ENG.). (J). (gr. 4). 2009. audio compact disk 19.99 (978-0-307-58293-5(0), Listening Lib) Pub: Random Audio Pubg. Dist(s): Random

Brian's Winter. Gary Paulsen. Read by Richard Thomas. 2 cass. (Running Time: 3 hrs. 15 mins.). (J). 2000. 18.00 (978-0-7366-9053-9(0)) Books on Tape.
Begins where "Hatchet" might have ended. Brian is not rescued, but must rely on his survival skills to face his deadliest enemy, a northern winter.

Brian's Winter. unabr. ed. Gary Paulsen. 2 vols. (Running Time: 3 hrs. 14 mins.). (J). (gr. 5-9). 2004. pap. bk. 29.00 (978-0-8072-0464-1(1), Listening Lib) Random Audio Pubg.

Brian's Winter. unabr. ed. Gary Paulsen. Read by Richard Thomas. 2 cass. (Running Time: 3 hrs. 14 mins.). (J). (gr. 5-9). 2004. 23.00 (978-0-8072-0463-4(3), Listening Lib) Random Audio Pubg.
Brian Robeson, the sole survivor of a plane crash in the Canadian wilderness, has not been rescued. With only the survival pack from the plane & his hatchet, Brian must now face the most brutal winter he's ever known.

Brian's Winter. unabr. ed. Gary Paulsen. Read by Richard Thomas. (Running Time: 11460 sec.). (ENG.). (J). (gr. 5-6). 2008. audio compact disk 27.00 (978-0-7393-6275-4(5), Listening Lib) Pub: Random Audio Pubg. Dist(s): Random

Briar Rose, unabr. ed. Jane Yolen. Narrated by Linda Stephens. 5 pieces. (Running Time: 7 hrs.). (gr. 6 up). 44.00 (978-0-7887-0505-2(9), 94697E7) Recorded Bks.
The fairy tale of the Sleeping Beauty told anew, set this time against the terrifying backdrop of the Holocaust. Available to libraries only.

Briarpatch, unabr. ed. Ross Thomas. Narrated by Frank Muller. 6 cass. (Running Time: 8 hrs. 30 mins.). 1985. 51.00 (978-1-55690-074-7(0), 85110E7) Recorded Bks.
The red-headed homicide detective climbed into the two-door Honda at the corner, threw in the clutch & detonated a charge of C-4 plastic that obliterated car & detective. Harold Snow, the only witness, remarked: "Someone just blew away the landlady.".

Briar's Book. unabr. ed. Tamora Pierce. Read by Full Cast Production Staff. (Circle of Magic Ser.: No. 4). (YA). 2006. 39.99 (978-1-59895-506-4(3)) Find a World.

Bribery, Corruption Also. unabr. ed. H. R. F. Keating. Read by H. R. F. Keating. 8 cass. (Running Time: 10 hrs.). (Inspector Ghote Mystery Ser.: No. 23). 1999. 69.95 (978-0-7531-0580-1(2), 990509) Pub: ISIS Audio GBR. Dist(s): Ulverscroft US
Bombay detective Inspector Ghote is not a happy man as his wife is determined that they leave his beloved Bombay & live in luxurious retirement in a large house that she has just inherited in Calcutta. When the couple arrive they find it in disrepair & inhabited by squatters. Their lawyer advises them to sell it immediately but Ghote detects a whiff of corruption & is determined to get to the bottom of it. The Ghotes refuse to sell, however, the corruption extends to the top of the political ladder and soon they are putting themselves in very great danger.

Bribery, Corruption Also. unabr. ed. H. R. F. Keating. 8 CDs. (Running Time: 12 hrs.). (Inspector Ghote Mystery Ser.: No. 23). 2001. audio compact disk 79.95 (978-0-7531-1246-5(9), 1246-9) Pub: ISIS Audio GBR. Dist(s): ISIS Pub

Brice & Breezy: The Mall Adventure. unabr. ed. Marian L. Clish. 2 CDs. (Running Time: 4 hrs). (J). (gr. k-3). 2000. 14.95 (978-1-928632-49-8(1)) Writers Mrktpl.
Brice & Breezy get locked in the mall alone, or are they alone? They explore until they are discovered.

Brice & Breezy: The Mall Adventure. unabr. ed. Marian L. Clish. Read by Marian L. Clish. Illus. by Lori Clish Robinson. 1 cass. (Running Time: 4

mins.). (J). (gr. k-3). 2000. pap. bk. 10.95 (978-1-928632-47-4(5)) Writers Mrktpl.
Brice & Breezy get locked in the mall alone, or are they alone? They explore the mall until they are discovered.

Brice & Breezy: The Mall Adventure. unabr. ed. Marian L. Clish. Read by Marian L. Clish. Illus. by Lori Clish Robinson. 1 CD. (Running Time: 4 mins.). (J). (gr. k-3). 2000. pap. bk. 14.95 (978-1-928632-48-1(3)) Writers Mrktpl.
Brice & Breezy get locked in the mall alone, or are they alone? They explore until they are discovered.

Brick Lane: A Novel. Monica Ali. Read by Elizabeth Sastre. (Playaway Adult Fiction Ser.). (ENG.). 2009. 59.99 (978-1-60812-736-8(2)) Find a World.

Brick Lane: A Novel. unabr. abr. ed. Monica Ali. Read by Elizabeth Sastre. 10 CDs. (Running Time: 12 hrs.). (ENG.). 2003. audio compact disk 36.95 (978-1-56511-829-4(4), 1565118294) Pub: HighBridge. Dist(s): Workman Pub

Brick Mallery Episode II: The Bride of Mallery. 1 cass. (Running Time: 40 mins.). 2001. 12.95 (SPR0003) Lodestone Catalog.

Brick Mallery Episode III: The Case of the 'Down Alive' 1 cass. (Running Time: 45 mins.). 2001. 12.95 (SPR0005) Lodestone Catalog.

Brick Mallery Episode I: The Case of the Denim Cut Shiny Stainless Steel Mirrored Suit. 1 cass. (Running Time: 47 mins.). 2001. 12.95 (SPR0001) Lodestone Catalog.

Brick Mallery Private Investigator. 3 cass. (Running Time: 3 hrs). 2001. bk. 34.95 (SPR0126) Lodestone Catalog.

Brick Mallery Private Investigator. 3 cass. (Running Time: 2 hrs. 15 min.). 1999. bk. (978-1-894003-00-1(4)) Scenario Prods CAN.
Triple volume boxed set contains episode 1: "The Case of the Denim Cut Shiny Stainless Steel mirrored Suit," - episode 2: "The Case of the Bride of Mallery", & episode 3: "The Case of Down Alive" - winners of the Publishers Weekly "Listen Up" Award for Audio Mystery.

Brick Mallery Private Investigator Vols. 1-3: The Denim Cut Shiny Stainless Steel Mirrored Suit, the Bride of Mallery, Down Alive. abr. ed. Mark Bornstein. Photos by James Griffith. 3 pieces. (Running Time: 132 min.). 1999. reel tape 29.99 (978-1-894003-04-9(7)) Pub: Scenario Prods CAN. Dist(s): PerseuPGW

Brick Mallery Private Investigator - Episode 1: The Case of the Denim Cut Shiny Stainless Steel Mirrored Suit. 1 cass. (Running Time: 45 mins.). 1999. 11.99 (978-1-894003-02-5(0)) Pub: Scenario Prods CAN. Dist(s): PerseuPGW
Brick Mallery, private investigator, deals with the usual kidnappings, blackmail and stolen goods, but specializes in more bizarre evils involving clones, zombies, identical half-twins and, of course, cannibal vampire zombies.

Brick Mallery Private Investigator - Episode 2: The Case of the Bride of Mallery. 1 cass. (Running Time: 45 mins.). 1999. 11.99 (978-1-894003-01-8(2)) Pub: Scenario Prods CAN. Dist(s): PerseuPGW

Brick Mallery Private Investigator - Episode 3: The Case of Down Alive. 1 cass. (Running Time: 45 mins.). 1999. 11.99 (978-1-894003-03-2(9)) Pub: Scenario Prods CAN. Dist(s): PerseuPGW

***Bricklayer.** unabr. ed. Noah Boyd. Read by Michael Mcconnohie. (ENG.). 2010. (978-0-06-197749-7(7), Harper Audio) HarperCollins Pubs.

***Bricklayer: A Novel.** unabr. ed. Noah Boyd. Read by Michael Mcconnohie. 2010. (978-0-06-197434-2(X), Harper Audio) HarperCollins Pubs.

Brickmakers Journal: Surviving in the Flesh, Thriving in the Spirit. Lucy Y. Shaw. 1995. 19.95 (978-0-9647185-2-4(9)) Common Denom.

***Brida.** unabr. ed. Paulo Coelho. Read by Linda Emond. (ENG.). 2008. (978-0-06-170228-0(5)); (978-0-06-170229-7(3)) HarperCollins Pubs.

Brida. unabr. ed. Paulo Coelho. Read by Linda Emond. 5 CDs. (Running Time: 6 hrs.). 2008. audio compact disk 34.95 (978-0-06-167255-2(6), Harper Audio) HarperCollins Pubs.

Bridal Party see Babylon Revisited: And Other Stories

Bridal Party see Great Gatsby & Other Stories

Bridal Party see Fitzgerald Short Stories

Bridal Preparation. Larry Randolph. 1 cass,. (Running Time: 90 mins.). (Church in Transition Ser.: Vol. 4). 2000. 5.00 (LR01-004) Morning NC.
Larry prepares us for the needed changes we must accept in order to receive our bridegroom.

Bride. abr. ed. Julie Garwood. Read by Rosalyn Landor. (Running Time: 6 hrs.). 2009. audio compact disk 19.99 (978-1-4418-1211-7(3), 9781441812117, BACD) Brilliance Audio.

Bride. abr. ed. Julie Garwood. Read by Rosalyn Landor. (Running Time: 6 hrs.). 2010. audio compact disk 9.99 (978-1-4418-4800-0(2), 9781441848000, BCD Value Price) Brilliance Audio.

Bride. unabr. ed. Julie Garwood. Read by Rosalyn Landor. (Running Time: 12 hrs.). 2009. 24.99 (978-1-4418-1200-1(8), 9781441812001, Brilliance MP3); 24.99 (978-1-4418-1203-2(2), 9781441812032, BAD); 39.97 (978-1-4418-1202-5(4), 9781441812025, Brlnc Audio MP3 Lib); 39.97 (978-1-4418-1204-9(0), 9781441812049, BADLE); audio compact disk 29.99 (978-1-4418-1198-1(2), 9781441811981, Bril Audio CD Unabri); audio compact disk 87.97 (978-1-4418-1199-8(0), 9781441811998, BriAudCD Unabrid) Brilliance Audio.

Bride: Renewing Our Passion for the Church. Charles R. Swindoll. 2 cass. (Running Time: 60 min. per cass.). 1994. 18.99 Set. (978-0-310-42078-1(4)) Zondervan.
In ten stirring chapters, Chuck Swindoll calls for an alert, wide-awake church, ready to grasp the incredible opportunities at the close of the twentieth century.

Bride: Renewing Our Passion for the Church. abr. ed. Charles R. Swindoll. (Running Time: 3 hrs. 0 mins. 0 sec.). (ENG.). 2003. 9.99 (978-0-310-26012-7(4)) Zondervan.

Bride: Renewing Our Passion for the Church. unabr. ed. Charles R. Swindoll. 6 cass. (Running Time: 5 hrs. 15 mins.). 1998. 30.95 (978-1-57972-285-2(7)) Insight Living.

Bride & Groom see Poetry & Voice of Ted Hughes

Bride & the Beast. unabr. ed. Teresa Medeiros. Narrated by Virginia Leishman. 6 cass. (Running Time: 8 hrs. 30 mins.). 2001. 54.00 (978-0-7887-4880-6(7), L1008x7) Recorded Bks.
Deftly blending romance, suspense & comedy, a wonderfully imaginative retelling of Beauty & the Beast set in the Scottish Highlands of the 18th century. It is the story of a spirited maiden, Gwendolyn Wilder & the Dragon of Castle Wyercraig who captures her heart.

Bride Bed. collector's unabr. ed. Linda Needham. Narrated by Jenny Sterlin. 7 cass. (Running Time: 9 hrs. 45 min.). 2003. 37.95 (978-1-4025-4537-5(1)) Recorded Bks.

Bride Bed. unabr. ed. Linda Needham. Narrated by Jenny Sterlin. 2003. 61.00 (978-1-4025-4536-8(3)) Recorded Bks.
The fiery Lady Talia resides in a castle of great strategic importance. With his eye on the castle, King Stephen wants to see Lady Talia tamed. He assigns Lord Alex de Monteneau to protect the maiden and make certain she is properly married off, but Lord Alex quickly falls for his charge.

Bride Collector. unabr. ed. Ted Dekker. Read by John Glover. (Running Time: 14 hrs.). (ENG.). 2010. 24.98 (978-1-60788-188-9(8)); audio compact disk 34.98 (978-1-60788-187-2(X)) Pub: Hachet Audio. Dist(s): HachBkGrp

***Bride Collector.** unabr. ed. Ted Dekker. Read by John Glover. (Running Time: 14 hrs.). (ENG.). 2011. audio compact disk 19.98 (978-1-60788-699-0(5)) Pub: Hachet Audio. Dist(s): HachBkGrp

Bride Comes to Yellow Sky see Great American Short Stories, Vol. III, A Collection

Bride Comes to Yellow Sky see Red Badge of Courage & Other Stories

Bride Comes to Yellow Sky. unabr. ed. Stephen Crane. Read by Walter Zimmerman & Jim Killavey. 1 cass. (Running Time: 50 min.). Dramatization. 1983. 7.95 (S-47) Jimcin Record.
These two stories illustrate the contrasting sides of Crane's art - the humorous & the gruesome.

Bride Comes to Yellow Sky & A Mystery of Heroism. Stephen Crane. 1 cass. 1989. 7.95 (S-47) Jimcin Record.
Two contrasting sides of Crane's art.

Bride of Firesign. Firesign Theatre Firesign Theatre Staff. 2001. audio compact disk 17.98 Rhino Enter.

Bride of Lammermoor. Walter Scott, Sr. Read by Anais 9000. 2008. 27.95 (978-1-60112-160-8(1)) Babblebooks.

Bride of the Wilderness. unabr. ed. Charles McCarry. Read by Pam Ward. (Running Time: 72000 sec.). 2008. 79.95 (978-1-4332-1941-2(7)); audio compact disk 29.95 (978-1-4332-1945-0(X)); audio compact disk & audio compact disk 99.00 (978-1-4332-1942-9(5)) Blckstn Audio.

***Bride Who Pondered Too Much.** Anonymous. 2009. (978-1-60136-593-4(4)) Audio Holding.

Bridegroom Press Collection. Compiled by Steve Kellmeyer. 2005. audio compact disk 39.95 (978-0-9767368-2-0(9)) Bridegroom.

Bride's Farewell. Meg Rosoff. Contrib. by Susan Duerden. (Running Time: 6 hrs.). (ENG.). (gr. 12 up). 2009. audio compact disk 29.95 (978-0-14-314463-2(4), PengAudBks) Penguin Grp USA.

***Brides for Brothers.** unabr. ed. Debbie Macomber. Read by Dan John Miller. (Running Time: 5 hrs.). 2010. 14.99 (978-1-4418-5287-8(5), 9781441852878, BAD) Brilliance Audio.

***Brides for Brothers.** unabr. ed. Debbie Macomber. Read by Dan John Miller. (Running Time: 5 hrs.). (Midnight Sons Ser.: Bk. 1). 2010. 14.99 (978-1-4418-5285-4(9), 9781441852854, Brilliance MP3) Brilliance Audio.

***Brides for Brothers, Vol. 1.** unabr. ed. Debbie Macomber. Read by Dan John Miller. (Running Time: 5 hrs.). (Midnight Sons Ser.: Bk. 1). 2010. audio compact disk 14.99 (978-1-4418-5281-6(6), 9781441852816, Bril Audio CD Unabri) Brilliance Audio.

Brides for Brothers; The Marriage Risk. unabr. ed. Debbie Macomber. Read by Dan John Miller. (Running Time: 10 hrs.). (Midnight Sons Ser.: Bks. 1- 2). 2010. audio compact disk 29.99 (978-1-4418-1640-5(2), 9781441816405) Brilliance Audio.

Brides for Brothers; The Marriage Risk. unabr. ed. Debbie Macomber. Read by Dan John Miller. (Running Time: 10 hrs.). (Midnight Sons Ser.: Bks. 1- 2). 2010. 24.99 (978-1-4418-1644-3(5), 9781441816443, BAD) Brilliance Audio.

Brides for Brothers; The Marriage Risk. unabr. ed. Debbie Macomber. Read by Dan John Miller. (Running Time: 10 hrs.). (Midnight Sons Ser.: Bks. 1-2). 2010. 24.99 (978-1-4418-1642-9(9), 9781441816429, Brilliance MP3); 39.97 (978-1-4418-1643-6(7), 9781441816436, Brlnc Audio MP3 Lib); 39.97 (978-1-4418-1645-0(3), 9781441816450, BADLE) Brilliance Audio.

Brides for Brothers; The Marriage Risk, Vol. 1. unabr. ed. Debbie Macomber. Read by Dan John Miller. (Running Time: 10 hrs.). (Midnight Sons Ser.: Bks. 1 -2). 2010. audio compact disk 87.97 (978-1-4418-1641-2(0), 9781441816412, BriAudCD Unabrid) Brilliance Audio.

Brides of Dracula. unabr. ed. Bram Stoker. Adapted by Thomas E. Fuller. 1 cass. (Running Time: 60 min.). 2002. 12.95 Centauri Express Co.
In a moonlit garden, three women with disturbing smiles wait. Their eyes gleam like opals and the only color in the silver night is the red of their lips. They long for what they wait for. And what they wait for comes quickly.

Brideshead Revisited. unabr. ed. Evelyn Waugh. Narrated by Jeremy Irons. 10 CDs. (Running Time: 11 hrs. 30 mins.). 2008. audio compact disk 94.95 (978-0-7927-5794-8(7), Chivers Sound Lib) AudioGO.

***Brideshead Revisited.** unabr. ed. Evelyn Waugh. Narrated by Jeremy Irons. (Running Time: 11 hrs. 21 mins. 0 sec.). (ENG.). 2010. audio compact disk 39.95 (978-1-4084-0094-4(4)) Pub: AudioGO. Dist(s): Perseus Dist

Brideshead Revisited: The Sacred & Profane Memories of Captain Charles Ryder. abr. ed. Evelyn Waugh. (Running Time: 5 hrs. 0 mins. 0 sec.). (ENG.). 2008. audio compact disk 26.95 (978-1-934997-05-5(6)) Pub: CSAWord. Dist(s): PerseuPGW

Brideshead Revisited: The Sacred & Profane Memories of Captain Charles Ryder. movie tie-in ed. Evelyn Waugh. 2008. audio compact disk 33.59 (978-1-906147-26-6(4)) CSA Telltapes GBR.

Brideshead Revisited: The Sacred & Profane Memories of Captain Charles Ryder. unabr. ed. Evelyn Waugh. Read by Jeremy Irons. 10 cass. (Running Time: 11 hrs. 22 min.). 1989. 69.95 (978-0-7451-6346-8(7), CAB 350) Pub: Chivers Audio Bks GBR. Dist(s): AudioGO
Charles Ryder's friendship with the charming Sebastian Flyte and his family begins when they are both at Oxford in 1923. Carefree days of drinking champagne and driving in the country soon end, however, as Sebastian's health deteriorates. Questions about morality and religion are raised as the radiant tone gives way to a bleak atmosphere of shattered illusion.

Brideshead Revisited: The Sacred & Profane Memories of Captain Charles Ryder. unabr. ed. Evelyn Waugh. Read by Jeremy Irons. 10 CDs. 2000. audio compact disk 94.95 (978-0-7540-5370-5(9), CCD 061) Pub: Chivers Audio Bks GBR. Dist(s): AudioGO
Charles Ryder's friendship with Sebastian Flyte begins at Oxford in 1923. Carefree days of drinking champagne & driving in the country soon end, however, as Sebastian's health deteriorates. Questions about morality & religion are raised as the radiant tone gives way to a bleak atmosphere of shattered illusion.

Brideshead Revisited: The Sacred & Profane Memories of Captain Charles Ryder. unabr. ed. Evelyn Waugh. Read by Jeremy Irons. 8 cass. (Running Time: 11 hrs. 30 mins.). 2000. 39.95 (978-0-694-52378-8(X)) HarperCollins Pubs.

Brideshead Revisited: The Sacred & Profane Memories of Captain Charles Ryder. unabr. collector's ed. Evelyn Waugh. Read by David Case. 8 cass. (Running Time: 12 hrs.). 1990. 64.00 (978-0-7366-1850-2(3), 2683) Books on Tape.
This is the story of an aristocratic Marchmain family. Rich, beautiful & fatally charming, they struggle with inherited weariness, generational fatigue. Sebastian & Julia, of the youngest generation, are vivid & palpable. Their pain is ours, their dilemmas engage us & we share in their fate. The novel, a symbol of England & her decline, mirrors upper-class decadence at Oxford in the 1920s, the abdication of responsibility in the 1930s. It has become shorthand for a fantasy era of titled elegance, dead-end hedonism & fatuous wit.

Bridesmaid. unabr. ed. Ruth Rendell. Read by William Gaminara. 8 cass. (Running Time: 9 hrs. 30 min.). 1990. 69.95 set. (978-0-7451-6237-9(1), CAB 468) AudioGO.
Left to himself, Phillip would have taken no interest in the disappearance of Rebecca Neave. But his sister, Fee, knew her at school. Murder was suspected - but no body had been found. Then Fee got married & it was Phillip who gave her away, as their father was dead. At the wedding he met Senta Pelham, one of Fee's bridesmaids & soon found himself drawn into an erotic & disturbing relationship.

Bridesmaid. unabr. ed. Ruth Rendell. Read by Donada Peters. 7 cass. (Running Time: 10 hrs.). 2001. 29.95 (978-0-7366-6799-9(7)) Books on Tape.
A young man who fears violence falls in love with a woman who loves it. She asks him to prove his love... by killing.

Bridesmaid. unabr. ed. Ruth Rendell. Narrated by Barbara Rosenblat. 8 cass. (Running Time: 11 hrs.). 1991. 70.00 (978-1-55690-075-4(9), 91215K8) Recorded Bks.
Senta Pelham is a mirror image of Flora, the lovely marble bust Philip fantacized about for so long. But life, like art, is not always what its mere surface suggests. And Senta's strange world of make-believe, where truth & falsehood are eerily interchangeable, soon draws Philip into a shadowy cloister of vague & uncertain terror.

Bridesmaid. unabr. collector's ed. Ruth Rendell. Read by Donada Peters. 7 cass. (Running Time: 10 hrs. 30 min.). 1990. 56.00 (978-0-7366-1811-3(2), 2647) Books on Tape.
Philip Wardman, an ordinary young man, sports one eccentricity: a neurotic fear of violence & death. Like Ferdinand, he likes to smell the flowers, particularly those in his mother's garden, where stands a statue of the goddess Flora, who over time has come to represent to Philip all the female virtues. Imagine Philip's constemation when, at his sister's wedding, he encounters a living incarnation of the marble Flora: Senta Pelham, an actress happily contemptuous of conventional morality. She comes to him that night. But Senta has a dark side. Where death frightens Philip, it fascinates her. She proposes a wicked test: to prove his love he needs to kill.

Bridesmaids Revisited. unabr. ed. Dorothy Cannell. Narrated by Barbara Rosenblat. 7 CDs. (Running Time: 8 hrs. 15 mins.). (Ellie Haskell Mystery Ser.: No. 10). 2001. audio compact disk 78.00 (978-1-4025-0492-1(6)) Recorded Bks.
Ellie Haskell, heroine of The Trouble with Harriet, digs to the roots of her own family tree - where she uncovers a murderous tangle of secrets. While her husband and children are away, Ellie plans nothing more ambitious than some quiet home redecorating. But her instinct for mystery is aroused when she gets a letter from three old friends of her grandmother Sophie: friends Ellie remembers only as the bridesmaids. The three friends insist that Sophie wants to contact Ellie, even though Sophie has been dead for decades. With the help of her tart-tongued domestic, Mrs. Malloy, Ellie sets off to get to the bottom of things.

Bridesmaids Revisited. unabr. ed. Dorothy Cannell. Narrated by Barbara Rosenblat. 6 cass. (Running Time: 8 hrs. 15 mins.). (Ellie Haskell Mystery Ser.: No. 10). 2001. 54.00 (978-0-7887-5265-0(0), 96548x7) Recorded Bks.
Ellie Haskell's instinct for mystery is aroused when she gets a letter from three old friends of her grandmother Sophie: friends Ellie remembers only as "the bridesmaids." The three friends insist that Sophie wants to contact Ellie - even though Sophie has been dead for decades. With the help of her tart-tongued domestic, Mrs. Malloy, Ellie sets off to get to the bottom of things.

Bridge. Contrib. by Anthony Evans. Prod. by Nathan Nockels. 2008. audio compact disk 13.99 (978-5-557-42212-3(9)) Pt of Grace Ent.

Bridge. Myrrh. 2003. audio compact disk 14.99 (978-0-9729353-0-2(4)) Pub: Myrrh Pub. Dist(s): STL Dist NA

Bridge. Myrrh. (Running Time: 1 hr.). 2003. 9.99 (978-0-9729353-1-9(2)) Pub: Myrrh Pub. Dist(s): STL Dist NA

***Bridge: The Life & Rise of Barack Obama.** unabr. ed. David Remnick. Read by Mark Deakins. (ENG.). 2010. audio compact disk 50.00 (978-0-307-73432-7(3), Random AudioBks) Pub: Random Audio Pubg. Dist(s): Random

Bridge: To Brooklyn Bridge see Poetry of Hart Crane

Bridge at Andau. unabr. ed. James A. Michener. Read by Larry McKeever. 7 cass. (Running Time: 10 hrs. 30 min.). 1995. 56.00 (978-0-7366-3032-0(5), 3714) Books on Tape.
Obscure bridge becomes path to freedom for Hungarians fleeing the 1956 Russian assault on Budapest. High drama, rich in details.

Bridge Books: Series A. 2 CDs. (Language Development Ser.). 2002. pap. bk. 149.00 (978-0-9711372-3-3(4)); pap. bk. 149.00 (978-0-9711372-5-7(0)); pap. bk. 149.00 (978-0-9711372-7-1(7)) BridgeBooks.

Bridge Books: Series A Chinese. Created by Dee Gardner. 2 CDs. (Language Development Ser.). (ENG & CHI., (J). 2002. pap. bk. 149.00 (978-0-9711372-1-9(8)) BridgeBooks.

Bridge Books: Series A Spanish. Dee Gardner. 2 Cds. (Language Development Ser.). (SPA & ENG., (J). (gr. k-2). 2000. pap. bk. 118.00 (978-0-615-11585-6(3)) BridgeBooks.

Bridge Books: Series B. 2 CDs. (Language Development Ser.). (GER & ENG., 2002. pap. bk. 149.00 (978-0-9711372-6-4(9)); pap. bk. 149.00 (978-0-9711372-2-6(6)); pap. bk. 149.00 (978-0-9711372-4-0(2)); pap. bk. 149.00 (978-0-9711372-8-8(5)) BridgeBooks.

Bridge Books: Series B Spanish. Dee Gardner. 2 CDs. (Language Development Ser.). (SPA & ENG., (J). (gr. k up). 2001. pap. bk. 119.00 (978-0-9711372-0-2(X)) BridgeBooks.

Bridge Books Series B: Navajo/English. 2 CDs. (Language Development Ser.). (ENG & NAV., 2002. pap. bk. 149.00 (978-0-9711372-9-5(3)) BridgeBooks.

Bridge Builder's Story. unabr. collector's ed. Howard Fast. Read by Barrett Whitener. 6 cass. (Running Time: 6 hrs.). 1996. 36.00 (978-0-7366-3284-3(0), 3939) Books on Tape.
Scott & Martha Waring expect to live happily ever after, but they pick a bad spot to honeymoon. Vacationing in Germany, 1939, they watch a Nazi rally, to which Scott foolishly carries his grandfather's pistol. The Nazis accuse him of plotting to assassinate Hitler & threaten to kill Martha unless he confesses.

Bridge Building: Bridge Designs & How They Work. Diana Briscoe. (High Five Reading - Purple Ser.). (ENG.). (gr. 4-5). 2007. audio compact disk 5.95 (978-1-4296-1444-3(7)) CapstoneDig.

Bridge Building: Bridge Designs & How They Work. Diana C. Briscoe. (High Five Reading Ser.). (ENG.). (gr. 4 up). 2004. audio compact disk 5.95 (978-0-7368-3858-0(9)) CapstoneDig.

Bridge of Light, Vol. 1. 2nd ed. 1997. 49.95 (978-1-893027-02-2(3)) Path of Light.

Bridge of Light, Vol. 2. 2nd ed. 1996. 49.95 (978-1-893027-03-9(1)) Path of Light.

Bridge of San Luis Rey. unabr. ed. Thornton Wilder. Read by Sam Waterston. 3 cass. (Running Time: 4 hrs. 30 min.). 1997. 19.95 Pub: HighBridge. Dist(s): Workman Pub
Wilder's Pulitzer Prize-winning story of a humble Franciscan friar's attempt to uncover something about the lives of five individuals who fell to their deaths.

Bridge of San Luis Rey. unabr. ed. Thornton Wilder. Read by Sam Waterston. 4 CDs. (Running Time: 4 hrs.). (ENG.). 2004. audio compact disk 24.95 (978-1-56511-937-6(1), 1565119371) Pub: HighBridge. Dist(s): Workman Pub

Bridge of Sighs. unabr. ed. Richard Russo. Read by Arthur Morey. (YA). 2007. 74.99 (978-0-7393-7123-7(1)) Find a World.

Bridge of Sighs. unabr. ed. Richard Russo. Read by Arthur Morey. (Running Time: 97200 sec.). (ENG.). 2007. audio compact disk 44.95 (978-0-7393-1889-8(6)) Pub: Random Audio Pubg. Dist(s): Random

Bridge of Sighs: A Novel. unabr. ed. Olen Steinhauer. Read by Ned Schmidtke. 7 cass. (Running Time: 9 hrs. 30 mins.). 2003. 49.95 (978-0-7861-2378-0(8), 3055) Blckstn Audio.
In the volatile and shifting political atmosphere of Eastern Europe after World War II, an inexperienced homicide detective fresh out of the academy is assigned a homicide that no one wants to solve. Set in a bombed-out city in an unnamed country formerly occupied by the Germans and now by the Russians, the story follows Emil Brod as he unravels the threads of the cover-up of a brutal murder, while supporting his grandparents, his only family, in the equally brutal city.

Bridge of Sighs: A Novel. unabr. ed. Olen Steinhauer. Read by Ned Schmidtke. 8 CDs. (Running Time: 9 hrs. 30 mins.). 2003. audio compact disk 64.00 (978-0-7861-9327-1(1), 3055) Blckstn Audio.

Bridge of Sighs: A Novel. unabr. ed. Olen Steinhauer. 7 pieces. (Running Time: 10 hrs.). 2004. reel tape 35.95 (978-0-7861-2412-1(1)) Blckstn Audio.

Bridge of Sighs: A Novel. unabr. ed. Olen Steinhauer. Read by Ned Schmidtke. 8 CDs. 2004. audio compact disk 39.95 (978-0-7861-9329-5(8)) Blckstn Audio.

Bridge over the River Kwai. unabr. ed. Pierre Boulle. Read by John Mills. 4 cass. 23.80 (D-135) Audio Bk.
A story of a captured British officer & his men, who aid the Japanese in building a bridge during W.W.II.

Bridge over the River Kwai. unabr. ed. Pierre Boulle. Read by John Mills. 4 cass. (Running Time: 6 hrs.). 2000. 34.95 (978-0-7451-5797-9(1), CAB 021) Pub: Chivers Audio Bks GBR. Dist(s): AudioGO
In a prison camp deep in Siam, Colonel Nicholson and his men are ordered by the Japanese to build a bridge. The Colonel refuses, but after weeks of torture and solitary confinement, he agrees. Meanwhile, a group of the Allies have parachuted into Siam with orders to destroy the bridge.

Bridge to Communication. 34.95 (978-1-56014-433-5(5)) Santillana.

***Bridge to Cutter Gap.** unabr. ed. Catherine Marshall. Adapted by C. Archer. Narrated by Jaimee Draper. (Catherine Marshall's Christy Ser.). (ENG.). 2010. 7.00 (978-1-60814-700-7(2), SpringWater) Oasis Audio.

Bridge to Terabithia. Katherine Paterson. Narrated by Tom Stechschulte. 3 cass. (Running Time: 4 hrs.). (J). 1997. 90.50 Recorded Bks.
When the new student Leslie appears at school, her natural athletic ability keeps Jess from being the fastest student in the 5th grade. However, when she draws Jess into the imaginary world of Terabithia, they discover a rare friendship.

Bridge to Terabithia. Katherine Paterson. (J). 1986. 21.33 (978-0-394-76891-5(4)) SRA McGraw.

Bridge to Terabithia. unabr. ed. Katherine Paterson. Read by Robert Sean Leonard. (J). 2005. audio compact disk 25.95 (978-0-06-075833-2(3), HarperChildAud) HarperCollins Pubs.

***Bridge to Terabithia.** unabr. ed. Katherine Paterson. Read by Robert Sean Leonard. (ENG.). 2009. (978-0-06-112609-3(8)); (978-0-06-112608-6(X)) HarperCollins Pubs.

Bridge to Terabithia. unabr. ed. Katherine Paterson. Narrated by Tom Stechschulte. 3 pieces. (Running Time: 4 hrs.). (J). (gr. 5 up). 1997. 27.00 (978-0-7887-0693-6(4), 94867E7) Recorded Bks.
Paterson beautifully illustrates the joys & tragedies of growing up. When the new student Leslie appears at school, her natural athletic ability keeps Jess from being the fastest student in the fifth grade. However, when she draws Jess into the imaginary world of Terabithia, they discover a rare friendship.

Bridge to Terabithia. unabr. ed. Katherine Paterson. Narrated by Tom Stechschulte. 4 CDs. (Running Time: 4 hrs.). (J). (gr. 5). 2000. audio compact disk 36.00 (C1052E7) Recorded Bks.

Bridge to Terabithia. unabr. ed. Katherine Patterson. Read by Robert Sean Leonard. (J). 2007. 39.99 (978-1-59895-788-4(0)) Find a World.

Bridge to the Higher. Arthur Young. 1 cass. 9.00 (A0163-87) Sound Photosyn.

Bridge to the Stars. Henning Mankell. Read by Francis Greenslade. (Running Time: 5 hrs.). (Joel Gustafson Stories). (J). 2009. 59.99 (978-1-74214-411-5(X), 9781742144115) Pub: Bolinda Pubng AUS. Dist(s): Bolinda Pub Inc

Bridge to the Stars. unabr. ed. Henning Mankell. Read by Francis Greenslade. 4 CDs. (Running Time: 5 hrs.). (Joel Gustafson Stories). (YA). (gr. 6-9). 2008. audio compact disk 57.95 (978-1-921415-20-3(7), 9781921415203) Pub: Bolinda Pubng AUS. Dist(s): Bolinda Pub Inc

Bridge to Wiseman's Cove. unabr. ed. James Moloney. Read by Dino Marnika. 5 cass. (Running Time: 6 hrs. 10 mins.). 2002. (978-1-876584-62-7(9), 590701) Bolinda Pubng AUS.
Carl Matt, even his name mocks him. The people of Wattle Beach do their best to grind him under foot. Why are the Matts such pariahs? The answer lies in Wiseman's Cove, a short ride across the straight where Carl finds refuge in the most unlikely place. Wiseman's Cove has been waiting for Carl, waiting a long time.

Bridge to Wiseman's Cove. unabr. ed. James Moloney. Read by Dino Marnika. (Running Time: 22200 sec.). (J). 2006. audio compact disk 77.95 (978-1-74093-767-2(8)) Pub: Bolinda Pubng AUS. Dist(s): Bolinda Pub Inc

Bridge Too Far. unabr. collector's ed. Cornelius Ryan. Read by Bill Kelsey. 13 cass. (Running Time: 19 hrs. 30 min.). 1990. 104.00 (978-0-7366-1818-2(X), 2654) Books on Tape.
In A Bridge Too Far the subject is Arnhem, the greatest airborne operation of WW II, the masterstroke by which Field Marshal Bernard Montgomery proposed to end the war. His plan: drop the combined airborne forces of the American & British armies behind German lines, capture the crucial bridge across the Rhine at Arnhem & send an immense army on the run into German. But the brilliant plan went wrong & this daring operation ended in bitter defeat for the Allies - a defeat with twice the casualties of D-Day.

Bridges: Songs of Unity & Purpose. 1 cass., 1 CD. 1999. 10.98 (978-0-7601-2734-6(4)); audio compact disk 16.98 (978-0-7601-2735-3(2)) Provident Music.
The best of Contemporary Christian & Gospel in a collection of duets, plus a group song.

Bridges Across the World: A Multicultural Songfest. Sarah Barchas. Perf. by De Colores Chorus. Illus. by Elizabeth Gething. 1 CD. (Running Time: 1 hr. 14 mins.). (J). (gr. k-6). 1999. pap. bk. 16.98 (978-1-889686-14-1(X)) High Haven Mus.
Multicultural cassette for storytimes or classroom use. Barchas sings 30 songs with the help of the De Colores Chorus, a group of children vocalists.

Bridges Across the World: A Multicultural Songfest. Sarah Barchas. Perf. by De Colores Chorus. Illus. by Elizabeth Gething. 1 cass. (Running Time: 1 hr. 15 mins.). (J). (gr. k-6). 1999. pap. bk. 14.98 (978-1-889686-13-4(1)) High Haven Mus.

Bridges of Madison County. unabr. ed. Robert James Waller. Read by Mitch Greenburg. (Running Time: 3 hrs.). (ENG.). 2006. 14.98 (978-1-59483-649-7(3)) Pub: Hachet Audio. Dist(s): HachBkGrp

Bridges of Madison County. unabr. ed. Robert James Waller. Read by Mitch Greenburg. (Running Time: 3 hrs.). (ENG.). 2009. 19.98 (978-1-60788-153-7(5)) Pub: Hachet Audio. Dist(s): HachBkGrp

Bridges Out of Poverty: Strategies for Professionals & Communities. Phil Devol & Terie Druessi Smith. 2005. audio compact disk 35.00 (978-1-929229-42-0(9)) aha Process.

Bridges Out of Poverty: Strategies for Professionals & Communities. Ruby Payne et al. 1999. audio compact disk 40.00 (978-1-929229-29-1(1)) aha Process.

Bridges Out of Poverty Audio Workshop. Philip E. DeVol et al. 2008. audio compact disk 149.00 (978-1-934583-06-7(5)) aha Process.

Bridges to Asia. (Music Connection Ser.). (gr. k-4). 2000. tchr.'s training gde. ed. 62.55 (978-0-382-34091-8(4)) Silver.

Bridges to Asia. (Music Connection Ser.). (gr. 5-8). 2000. audio compact disk 62.55 (978-0-382-34092-5(2)) Silver.

Bridges to Literature, Level I. (gr. 6-12). 2002. lib. bdg. (978-0-618-14879-0(5), 2-80917); lib. bdg. (978-0-618-27467-3(7), 2-03973) Holt McDoug.

Bridges to Literature, Vol. 2. (gr. 6-12). 2002. lib. bdg. (978-0-618-16417-2(0), 2-03989); lib. bdg. (978-0-618-27471-0(5), 2-03976) Holt McDoug.

Bridges to Literature, Vol. 3. (gr. 6-12). 2002. lib. bdg. (978-0-618-16422-6(7), 2-03993); lib. bdg. (978-0-618-27477-2(4), 2-03979) Holt McDoug.

Bridget Jones: The Edge of Reason. Helen Fielding. 2 cass. (Running Time: 3 hrs.). 2001. (978-0-333-74611-0(2)) Macmillan UK GBR.

Bridget Jones: The Edge of Reason. unabr. ed. Helen Fielding. Narrated by Barbara Rosenblat. 8 cass. (Running Time: 10 hrs. 45 mins.). 1999. 76.00 (978-0-7887-4845-5(9), 96447E7) Recorded Bks.
Taking up where the Diary left off.The Edge of Reason follows the next year of Bridget's life. Over the months, she juggles her love for Mark Darcy, advice for her friends & rivalry with the willowy Rebecca, who is slyly pursuing Mark. Bridget's arsenal of self-help books reminds her to be an "assured, receptive responsive woman of substance" but chardonnay & chocolate are much more accessible.

Bridget Jones: The Edge of Reason. unabr. ed. Helen Fielding. Narrated by Barbara Rosenblat. 10 CDs. (Running Time: 10 hrs. 45 mins.). 2001. audio compact disk 97.00 (978-0-7887-6169-0(2), C1393) Recorded Bks.
Taking up where the Diary left off, The Edge of Reason follows the next year in Bridget's life. Over the months, she juggles her love for Mark Darcy, advice from her friends & rivalry with the willowy Rebecca, who is slyly pursuing Mark. Bridget's arsenal of self-help books reminds her to be an assured, receptive, responsive woman of substance. But Chardonnay & chocolate are much more accessible.

Bridget Jones's Diary. Helen Fielding. 2 cass. (Running Time: 3 hrs.). (ENG., 2001. (978-0-333-72217-6(5)) Macmillan UK GBR.

Bridget Jones's Diary. unabr. ed. Helen Fielding. Narrated by Barbara Rosenblat. 8 CDs. (Running Time: 8 hrs. 30 mins.). 2001. audio compact disk 78.00 (978-0-7887-6175-1(7), C1399) Recorded Bks.
Sunday 1 January: 129 lbs. (but post-Christmas), alcohol units 14 (but effectively covers 2 days as 4 hours of party was on New Year's Day), cigarettes 22, calories 5424. From its beginning as a weekly column in a British newspaper, Bridget Jones's Diary quickly became a best-seller in England. After gaining international popularity, it also shot to the top of the New York Times best-seller list. A 30-something single professional, Bridget Jones prefers a diary to a day planner for tracking her life.

Bridget Jones's Diary. unabr. ed. Helen Fielding. Narrated by Barbara Rosenblat. 6 cass. (Running Time: 8 hrs. 30 mins.). 1999. 56.00 (978-0-7887-2917-1(9), 95709E5) Recorded Bks.
A 30-something single professional, Bridget Jones tracks her life in her diary. Each entry is an honest & hilarious step in her endless quest for self-improvement. Originally a weekly column in a British newspaper.

Bridget Jones's Diary. 3rd abr. ed. Helen Fielding. Read by Tracie Bennett. 3 CDs. (Running Time: 3 hrs.). (ENG., 2001. audio compact disk (978-0-333-90353-7(6)) Macmillan UK GBR.

Bridging Science & Spirit: Common Elements in David Bohm's Physics, the Perennial Philosophy & Seth. Norman Friedman. 2 cass. 1994. 16.95 (978-1-889964-02-7(6)) Pub: Moment Pt Pr. Dist(s): Words Distrib

Bridging the Gap: Between the Christian & Metaphysical Worlds. Scott Christiansen. 3 CD. (Running Time: 3.5 hours). 2003. audio compact disk 19.95 (978-0-9761975-1-5(0)) Continued Search.

Bridie. unabr. ed. Christine Thomas. Read by Annie Aldington. 8 cass. (Running Time: 34200 sec.). (Sound Ser.). 2003. 69.95 (978-1-86042-724-4(3)) Pub: ISIS Lrg Prnt GBR. Dist(s): Ulverscroft US

Brief Chapter in My Impossible Life. unabr. ed. Dana Reinhardt. Read by Mandy Siegfried. 4 cass. (Running Time: 6 hrs.). (YA). (gr. 7 up). 2006. 35.00 (978-0-307-28565-2(0), Listening Lib); audio compact disk 38.25 (978-0-307-28566-9(9), Listening Lib) Pub: Random Audio Pubg. Dist(s): NetLibrary CO
Simone's starting her junior year in high school. Her mom's a lawyer for the ACLU, her dad's a political cartoonist, so she's grown up standing outside the organic food coop asking people to sign petitions for worthy causes. She's got a terrific younger brother and amazing friends. And she's got a secret crush on a really smart and funny guy - who spends all of his time with another girl. Then her birth mother contacts her. Simone's always known she was adopted, but she never wanted to know anything about it. She's happy with her family just as it is, thank you. She learns who her birth mother was - a 16-year-old girl named Rivka. Who is Rivka? Why has she contacted Simone? Why now? The answers lead Simone to deeper feelings of anguish and love than she has ever known, and to question everything she once took for granted about faith, life, the afterlife, and what it means to be a daughter.

Brief Debut of Tildy see Favorite Stories by O. Henry

***Brief Encounter: A Complete Adaptation.** abr. ed. Noel Coward. Read by Simon Jones. (ENG.). 2006. (978-0-06-125282-2(4), Harper Audio) HarperCollins Pubs.

***Brief History of Montmaray.** unabr. ed. Michelle Cooper. Narrated by Emma Bering. 7 CDs. (Running Time: 8 hrs. 39 mins.). (YA). (gr. 8-10). 2010. audio compact disk 55.00 (978-0-307-70780-2(6), Listening Lib) Pub: Random Audio Pubg. Dist(s): Random

Brief History of Montmaray. unabr. ed. Michelle Cooper. Read by Emma Bering. (Montmaray Journals). (ENG.). (J). (gr. 7). 2010. audio compact disk 37.00 (978-0-307-70778-9(4), Listening Lib) Pub: Random Audio Pubg. Dist(s): Random

Brief History of Roman State-Church Persecution. Richard Bennett. 1 cass. (Conference on Christianity & Roman Catholicism Ser.: No. 3). 5.00 Trinity Found.

Brief History of Slime. Susan P. Gates. Read by Nigel Lambert. 3 CDs. (J). 2004. audio compact disk 29.95 (978-0-7540-6618-7(5), Chivers Child Audio) AudioGO.

Brief History of the Dead. Kevin Brockmeier. Read by Richard Poe. (Running Time: 31500 sec.). 2006. audio compact disk 34.99 (978-1-4193-7169-1(X)) Recorded Bks.

Brief History of the World. Instructed by Peter N. Stearns. (ENG.). 2007. 199.95 (978-1-59803-324-3(7)); audio compact disk 99.95 (978-1-59803-325-0(5)) Teaching Co.

Brief History of Time: From the Big Bang to Black Holes. unabr. ed. Stephen W. Hawking. Read by Michael Jackson. 4 cass. (Running Time: 6 hrs.). 2001. 25.00 (978-1-57453-446-7(7)) Audio Lit.
This is the story of the ultimate quest for knowledge, the ongoing search for the secrets at the heart of time and space.

Brief History of Time: From the Big Bang to Black Holes. unabr. ed. Stephen W. Hawking. Read by Grover Gardner. 6 cass. (Running Time: 6 hrs.). 1989. 48.00 (978-0-7366-1480-1(X), 2356) Books on Tape.
Explores the outer limits of the knowledge of astrophysics & the nature of time & the universe.

Brief History of Time: From the Big Bang to Black Holes, unabr. ed. Stephen W. Hawking. Narrated by Nelson Runger. 5 cass. (Running Time: 7 hrs. 15 mins.). 1988. 44.00 (978-1-55690-076-1(7), 88980E7) Recorded Bks.
Stephen W. Hawking, widely regarded as the most brilliant physicist since Einstein, discusses in a friendly & self-deprecating manner age-old questions about the origin & fate of the universe. Difficult concepts are made simple by Hawking's familiar, accessible prose.

Brief Interviews with Hideous Men. abr. ed. David Foster Wallace. Read by Bobby Cannavale et al. (Running Time: 3 hrs.). (ENG.). 2006. 14.98 (978-1-59483-817-0(8)) Pub: Hachet Audio. Dist(s): HachBkGrp

Brief Interviews with Hideous Men. unabr. ed. David Foster Wallace. Read by John Krasinski et al. (Running Time: 4 hrs.). (ENG.). 2009. 16.98 (978-1-60024-738-5(5)) Pub: Hachet Audio. Dist(s): HachBkGrp

Brief Interviews with Hideous Men. unabr. ed. David Foster Wallace. Read by John Krasinski et al. (Running Time: 4 hrs.). (ENG.). 2009. 39.98 (978-1-60788-161-2(6)); audio compact disk 24.98 (978-1-60024-737-8(7)) Pub: Hachet Audio. Dist(s): HachBkGrp

Brief Lives see Cambridge Treasy Burton

Brief Lives. John Aubrey. Read by Brian Cox. (Running Time: 3 hrs. 30 mins.). 2001. 21.95 (978-1-60083-688-6(7)) Iofy Corp.

Brief Lives. abr. ed. John Aubrey. Read by Brian Cox. 2 cass. (Running Time: 2 hrs. 38 mins.). 1995. 13.98 (978-962-634-543-6(8), NA204314, Naxos AudioBooks) Naxos.
Probably English literature's greatest collector of gossip, anecdotes and personal trivia, Aubrey's compilation of the doings and sayings of the major and minor figures of the 16th and 17th centuries has survived in popular esteem.

Brief Lives. abr. ed. John Aubrey. 2 CDs. (Running Time: 9483 sec.). 2006. audio compact disk 17.98 (978-962-634-378-4(8), Naxos AudioBooks) Naxos.

Brief Shining. unabr. ed. Kathleen Rowntree. Read by Patricia Gallimore. 8 cass. (Running Time: 10 hrs. 12 mins.). (Isis Ser.). (J). 2002. 69.95 (978-0-7531-1151-2(9)) Pub: ISIS Lrg Prnt GBR. Dist(s): Ulverscroft US
As a young girl, Sally struggles through a minefield of pretension, sexual jealousy and conditional love. It opens in the years immediately after the war, at Willow Dassett Farm, a childhood dream of perfection. It closes in the present day, as Sally relives the intensity of her feelings for the plan, its 'brief shining', while viewing the farm in the light of a changed world.

Brief Strategic Intervention for School Behavior Problems. Ellen S. Amatea. (Social & Behavioral Science - Education Ser.). 1989. bk. 40.50 (978-1-55542-174-8(1), Jossey-Bass) Wiley US.

Brief Therapy in Action: A Clinical Demonstration. Simon H. Budman & Alan S. Gurman. 2 cass. (Running Time: 1 hr. 56 min.). (ENG.). 1989. 26.95 set. (978-0-89862-962-0(4)) Guilford Pubns.
With managed care dominating the treatment scene, this classic volume is as timely and important as ever. Noted experts analyze the major forms of brief therapy and offer explicit, data-based recommendations to help the clinician make sound decisions about patient care.

Brief Wondrous Life of Oscar Wao. unabr. ed. Junot Díaz. Read by Jonathan Davis. 13 CDs. (Running Time: 16 hrs.). (ENG.). (gr. 8). 2007. audio compact disk 39.95 (978-0-14-314280-5(1), PengAudBks) Penguin Grp USA.

Brief Wondrous Life of Oscar Wao. unabr. ed. Junot Díaz. Read by Jonathan Davis. 9 CDs. (Running Time: 11 hrs.). 2007. audio compact disk 100.00 (978-1-4159-4194-2(7)) Random.

Briefe Set: 1877-1904, Anton Cechov. (GER.). 1988. (978-3-257-06196-3(X)) Diogenes Verlag CHE.

Briefer & Better Ways of Helping Yourself Emotionally. Albert Ellis. 1 cass. (Running Time: 69 min.). 9.95 (C002) A Ellis Institute.
Dozens of popular techniques are critiqued in terms of helpfulness vs. palliativeness, followed by REBT techniques for producing long-lasting changes. Lively & humorous.

Briefer & Better Ways of Helping Yourself Emotionally. Albert Ellis. 1 cass. (Running Time: 69 min.). 9.95 (C002) Inst Rational-Emotive.

Briefer History of Time. Erik Davies. 2005. 34.99 (978-1-59895-012-0(6)) Find a World.

Briefer History of Time. Erik Davies. 2006. cd-rom 34.99 (978-1-59895-475-3(X)) Find a World.

Briefer History of Time. unabr. ed. Erik Davies. Read by Erik Davies. (YA). 2005. 44.99 (978-0-7393-7443-6(5)) Find a World.

Briefer History of Time. unabr. ed. Erik Davies & Leonard Mlodinow. 5 cass. (Running Time: 7 hrs.). 2005. 45.00 (978-1-4159-2443-3(0)); audio compact disk 38.25 (978-1-4159-2444-0(9)) Pub: Books on Tape. Dist(s): NetLibrary CO

Briefer History of Time. unabr. ed. Leonard Mlodinow & Stephen W. Hawking. Read by Erik Davies. (Running Time: 18000 sec.). (ENG.). 2005. audio compact disk 30.00 (978-0-7393-2187-4(0)) Pub: Random Audio Pubg. Dist(s): Random

Briefs Encountered: Searchable Database of Briefs & Phrases for Court Reporters. 1 CD. (Running Time: 1 HR.). 2001. audio compact disk 75.00 (978-1-888580-13-6(5)) Pub: White-Boucke. Dist(s): Baker Taylor

***Brigadier & the Golf Widow.** abr. ed. John Cheever. Read by Meryl Streep et al. (ENG.). 2009. (978-0-06-125283-9(2), Caedmon) HarperCollins Pubs.

***Brigadier & the Golf Widow.** unabr. ed. John Cheever. Read by Meryl Streep et al. (ENG.). 2009. (978-0-06-196856-3(0), Caedmon) HarperCollins Pubs.

Brigham Young: Dramatized Scenes from His Life & Ministry, Set. 2 CDs. audio compact disk 3.57 (978-1-57734-240-3(2), 2600544) Covenant Comms.
Discover Brigham Young.

Brigham Young Set: An Inspiring Personal Biography. Susan Evans McCloud. 2 cass. 11.95 (978-1-57734-242-7(9), 07001770) Covenant Comms.

Brigham Young Set: Dramatized Scenes from His Life & Ministry. 2 cass. 2.97 (978-1-57734-239-7(9), 07001762) Covenant Comms.

Brigham Young Vol. 1: Portrait of a Prophet, James Arrington. 2 cass. 9.98 Set. (978-1-55503-847-2(6), 07001150); 19.95 (978-1-57734-238-0(0), 0900141) Covenant Comms.
Brigham Young is brought to life in this delightful depiction.

Brigham Young Vol. 2: Portrait of a Prophet, James Arrington. 2 cass. 9.98 Set. (978-1-55503-848-9(4), 07001169) Covenant Comms.
Brigham's philosophy of life, Brigham's thoughts on Joseph Smith, Brigham explores pioneering.

Bright & the Dark Way. Swami Amar Jyoti. 1 cass. 1982. 9.95 (M-33) Truth Consciousness.
Our free will to choose the way. Reviving from the bottom line of darkness.

Bright Day Is Done. Judith Saxton. 6 cass. (Running Time: 7 hrs. 30 mins.). (Soundings Ser.). (J). 2004. 54.95 (978-1-84283-474-9(6)); audio compact disk 71.95 (978-1-84283-920-1(9)) Pub: ISIS Lrg Prnt GBR. Dist(s): Ulverscroft US

Bright Futures. unabr. ed. Stuart M. Kaminsky. Read by Michael McConnohie. (Running Time: 8 hrs.). 2009. 64.95 (978-0-7927-6174-7(X), Chivers Sound Lib); audio compact disk 74.95 (978-0-7927-5998-0(2), Chivers Sound Lib) AudioGO.

Bright Lights, Big Ass: A Self-Indulgent, Surly, Ex-Sorority Girl's Guide to Why It Often Sucks in the City, or Who Are All These Idiots & Why Do They All Live Next Door to Me? unabr. ed. Jen Lancaster. 2009. audio compact disk 39.95 (978-1-4406-4106-0(4), PengAudBks) Penguin Grp USA.

Bright Orange for the Shroud. unabr. collector's ed. John D. MacDonald. Read by Michael Prichard. 8 cass. (Running Time: 8 hrs.). (Travis McGee Ser.: Vol. 6). 1978. 48.00 (978-0-7366-0174-0(0), 1176) Books on Tape.
This is the story of an immensely clever confidence scheme run by a group of vicious doublecrossers. An old friend of McGee's is sucked into their trap & bled, financially & physically. Before the story ends McGee is forced to use dirtier tactics than ever before. He becomes more cunning & heartless than the men he is pursuing. Along the way he discovers an innocent-looking blonde whose treachery includes the blackest arts of love.

Bright Path of Knowing. Swami Amar Jyoti. 1 cass. 1983. 9.95 (R-48) Truth Consciousness.
Facing Truth on the Lord's bright, open way. Why we cling to illusory dreams. How to awaken.

"Bright" Revelation Series, Vol. 2. Adi Da Samraj. 2001. audio compact disk 24.95 (978-1-57097-122-8(6)) Dawn Horse Pr.

Bright Shadow, unabr. ed. Avi. Narrated by Virginia Leishman. 3 pieces. (Running Time: 3 hrs. 30 mins.). (gr. 3 up). 1998. 27.00 (978-0-7887-1686-7(7), 95286E7) Recorded Bks.
When Morwenna is given the gift of wizardry, she must guard the five wishes she has been granted & protect herself & the peasants from vengeful King Ruthvin.

Bright Shadow, Set unabr. ed. Avi. Read by Virginia Leishman. 3 cass. (Running Time: 3 hr. 30 min.). (J). 1998. 39.20 Homework. (978-0-7887-1959-2(9), 40660) Recorded Bks.
When Morwenna is given the gift of wizardry, she must guard the five wishes she has been granted.

Bright Shadow, Set unabr. ed. Avi. Read by Virginia Leishman. 3 cass. (Running Time: 3 hr. 30 min.). (J). (gr. 4). 1998. 87.30 Class set. (978-0-7887-3379-6(6), 46121) Recorded Bks.

Bright Shiny Morning. unabr. ed. James Frey. Read by Ben Foster. 1 MP3-CD. (Running Time: 16 hrs. 30 mins.). 2008. 29.95 (978-1-4332-4745-3(3)); audio compact disk & audio compact disk 110.00 (978-1-4332-4744-6(5)) Blckstn Audio.

***Bright Shiny Morning.** unabr. ed. James Frey. Read by Ben Foster. (ENG.). 2008. (978-0-06-168826-3(6)); (978-0-06-168828-7(2)) HarperCollins Pubs.

Bright Shiny Morning. unabr. ed. James Frey. Read by Ben Foster. 2009. audio compact disk 19.99 (978-0-06-178023-3(5), Harper Audio) HarperCollins Pubs.

Bright-Sided: How the Relentless Promotion of Positive Thinking Has Undermined America. unabr. ed. Barbara Ehrenreich. Read by Kate Reading. 6 CDs. (Running Time: 8 hrs. 0 mins. 0 sec.). (ENG.). 2009. audio compact disk 29.99 (978-1-4272-0836-1(0)) Pub: Macmill Audio. Dist(s): Macmillan

Bright Smiles & Blue Skies: "Sonrisas Radiantes y el Cielo Brillante" unabr. ed. Lisa M. Nelson. 1 cass. (Running Time: 40 min.). (Positive Music for Today's Kids Ser.: No. 2). (ENG & SPA.). (J). (gr. k-6). 1991. 9.95 (978-0-9627863-1-0(4)) Brght Ideas CA.
7 original songs, Spanish on one side, English on the other side - for children, designed to promote self-esteem.

Bright Star! Would I Were As Steadfast As Thou Art see Poetry of Keats

***Bright Young Things.** unabr. ed. Anna Godbersen. (ENG.). 2010. (978-0-06-199682-5(3)) HarperCollins Pubs.

Brighter Day. Rachel. (Running Time: 50 min.). 2004. audio compact disk 17.98 (978-5-559-77304-9(2)) Pub: Pt of Grace Ent. Dist(s): STL Dist NA

Brighter Garden. unabr. ed. Emily Dickinson. 1 cass. (Running Time: 15 min.). (J). (ps-8). 1992. pap. bk. 29.95 (978-0-8045-6587-5(2), 6587) Spoken Arts.
The poems and excerpts from poems are tantalizing bits and pieces from a prodigious life's work.

Brighter Than Fireflies. Amy Lowe. 1 CD. (Running Time: 38 mins.). (J). 2005. audio compact disk 14.98 (978-1-893967-27-4(1)) Emphasis Ent.
Amy Lowe is a multi award winning singer, songwriter, and storyteller. She has over 20 years experience as a performer in clubs, concert venues, theaters, festivals, coffeehouses, museums, historical societies, schools, libraries, galleries, pubs, and community centers throughout the world. She is a prolific songwriter with a recording career that dates back to 1980. Performances include: Second City, The Taste of Chicago and The Chicago Historical Society, The Winnipeg Folk Festival- Canada, Las Vegas Storytelling Festival and Winchester Children's Music Festival- Las Vegas-Nevada, Arizona Theater Works- Flagstaff , Maricopa County College tour-Arizona and a concert tour of Ecuador. Who's Next- Paris, France.

Brighter Than the Son: Acts 9:1-18. Ed Young. 1997. 4.95 (978-0-7417-2162-4(7), A1162) Win Walk.

Brightest Star in the Sky. Marian Keyes. Contrib. by Caitriona Keyes. (Running Time: 18 hrs.). (ENG.). (gr. 12 up). 2010. audio compact disk 39.95 (978-0-14-314553-0(3), PengAudBks) Penguin Grp USA.

Brighton Beach Memoirs. Neil Simon. Contrib. by Valerie Harper et al. 2 CDs. (Running Time: 7560 sec.). (L. A. Theatre Works Audio Theatre Collections). 2003. audio compact disk 25.95 (978-1-58081-273-3(2), CDTPT184) Pub: L A Theatre. Dist(s): NetLibrary CO

Brighton Beach Memoirs. unabr. ed. Neil Simon. Perf. by Max Casella et al. 2 cass. (Running Time: 1 hr. 46 mins.). 1993. 22.95 (978-1-58081-000-5(4), RDP17) L A Theatre.
Neil Simon's darkly funny memoir of his struggling family in 1930's Brooklyn is viewed through the eyes of fourteen year old Eugene Jerome, equally preoccupied by passion for the Yankees & lust for his beautiful cousin, Nora. Eugene's comic growing pains contrast with the darker issues troubling his family, including poverty, illness, sibling-held sibling resentment & the growing Nazi threat to relatives in Europe. With a deft & compassionate hand, Simon creates a Brooklyn universe full of memorable charters, humor & truth.

Brighton Rock, unabr. ed. Graham Greene. Read by Richard Brown. 7 cass. (Running Time: 10 hrs.). 1990. 49.95 (978-0-7861-0160-3(1), 1143) Blckstn Audio.
Set in Brighton among the criminal rabble, the book depicts the tragic career of a 17-year-old boy named Pinkie whose primary ambition is to lead a gang to rival that of the wealthy & established Colleoni. His calamitous childhood & repressed sexuality combine to create a force of evil which is both fascinating & repellent.

***Brighton Rock.** unabr. ed. Graham Greene. Read by Richard Brown. (Running Time: 10 hrs. NaN mins.). (ENG.). 2011. 29.95 (978-1-4417-0387-3(X)); audio compact disk 29.95 (978-1-4417-0386-6(1)); audio compact disk 90.00 (978-1-4417-0384-2(5)) Blckstn Audio.

Brighty: Of the Grand Canyon. Marguerite Henry. Read by John McDonough. 4 cass. (Running Time: 5 hrs. 30 mins.). (YA). 2000. stu. ed. 49.75 (978-0-7887-4157-9(8), 41115) Recorded Bks.
Brighty, a shaggy burro, lives wild & free in the Grand Canyon of Arizona. But one day he encounters a ruthless claim jumper. Will Brighty be able to bring the criminal to justice & make the wilderness safe again? Based on actual incidents in the life of a Grand Canyon burro.

Brighty: Of the Grand Canyon. unabr. ed. Marguerite Henry. Narrated by John McDonough. 4 pieces. (Running Time: 5 hrs. 30 mins.). (gr. 3 up). 2000. 37.00 (978-0-7887-4027-5(X), 96102E7) Recorded Bks.

Brighty: Of the Grand Canyon, Class set. Marguerite Henry. Read by John McDonough. 4 cass. (Running Time: 5 hrs. 30 mins.). (YA). 2000. 102.80 (978-0-7887-4158-6(6), 47108) Recorded Bks.

Brigid's Charge, Set. unabr. ed. Cynthia Lamb. Read by Cindy Hollenberg. 6 cass. (Running Time: 11 hrs. 20 min.). 2000. 32.95 (978-1-893530-09-6(4)) Arania Bks.

Brigitta. Adalbert Stifter. 3 cass. (Running Time: 3 hrs.). (GER.). 1996. pap. bk. 39.50 set. (978-1-58085-203-6(3)) Interlingua VA.
Includes German transcription. The combination of written text & clarity & pace of diction will open the door for intermediate & advanced students to genuine comprehension & the use of literary texts for advancement in rapid understanding of written & oral language materials. The audio text plus written text concept makes foreign languages accessible to a much wider range of students than books alone.

Brilliance. Rosalind Laker, pseud. 2008. 84.95 (978-1-4079-0075-9(7)); audio compact disk 89.95 (978-1-4079-0076-6(5)) Pub: Soundings Ltd GBR. Dist(s): Ulverscroft US

Brilliance of African Art. Rex A. Barnett. (Running Time: 22 min.). (J). 1990. 16.99 (978-0-924198-02-1(8)) Hist Video.
African artistry reviewed.

Brilliance of Jane Austen: A Light & Enlightening Lecture, Featuring Elliot Engel. 2000. bk. 15.00 (978-1-890123-21-5(8)) Media Cnslts.

Brilliance of the Moon. unabr. ed. Lian Hearn. Read by Aiko Nakasone & Kevin Grey. (Running Time: 12 hrs.). Bk. 3. (ENG.). 2004. audio compact disk 36.95 (978-1-56511-893-5(6), 1565118936) Pub: HighBridge. Dist(s): Workman Pub

Brilliant. unabr. ed. Marne Davis Kellogg. 6 cass. (Running Time: 9 hrs.). 2003. 64.00 (978-0-7366-9402-5(1)) Books on Tape.
At Ballantyne and Company, a genteel but failing auction house in the heart of London, Kick Keswick has been an expert on painting, furniture, and objets d'art for over thirty years. When Ballantyne falls victim to a corporate takeover by robber baron and womanizer Owen Brace, Kick is the next target for Brace's idea of romantic merger and acquisition.

Brilliant & Bizarre Brontes: A Light & Enlightening Lecture. Featuring Elliot Engel. 2000. bk. 15.00 (978-1-890123-19-2(6)) Media Cnslts.

Brilliant Beginnings Baby Brain Basics Parent Kit. Brilliant Beginnings, LLC Staff. 1 cass. (Running Time: 58 mins.). 1999. pap. bk. 39.95 (978-0-9665815-0-8(4)) Brlnt Begnngs.

Brilliant NLP [Neuro Linguistic Programming]: What the Most Successful People Know, Say & Do. David Molden & Pat Hutchinson. 2006. audio compact disk 39.50 (978-0-273-70993-0(3), FT Pren) Pearson EducLt GBR.

Brimstone. abr. ed. Douglas Preston & Lincoln Child. Read by Rene Auberjonois. (Pendergast Ser.: No. 5). (ENG.). 2005. 14.98 (978-1-59483-154-6(8)) Pub: Hachet Audio. Dist(s): HachBkGrp

Brimstone. abr. ed. Douglas Preston & Lincoln Child. Read by Rene Auberjonois. (Running Time: 6 hrs.). (ENG.). 2009. 49.98 (978-1-60024-624-1(9)) Pub: Hachet Audio. Dist(s): HachBkGrp

Brimstone. unabr. ed. Robert B. Parker. Read by Titus Welliver. (ENG.). 2009. audio compact disk 29.95 (978-0-7393-8295-0(0), Random AudioBks) Pub: Random Audio Pubg. Dist(s): Random

***Brimstone.** unabr. ed. Robert B. Parker. Read by Titus Welliver. 4 CDs. (Running Time: 5 hrs.). 2009. audio compact disk 40.00 (978-1-4159-6318-0(5), BksonTape) Pub: Random Audio Pubg. Dist(s): Random

Brimstone Journals. Al Petteway. 1995. bk. & pap. bk. (978-0-7866-1302-1(5), 95381CDP) Mel Bay.

Brimstone Wedding. unabr. ed. Barbara Vine, pseud. Read by Juliet Stevenson. 10 cass. (Running Time: 10 hrs.). 1996. 84.95 Set. (978-0-7451-6701-5(2), CAB1317) AudioGO.
Why has Stella kept possession of a house & the terrible secret that even her family doesn't know about? And will her friend, Jenny, be able to persuade her to reveal the shocking truth of her past?.

Bring Back the Glory. Jakes. 2004. audio compact disk 48.99 (978-1-57855-502-4(7)) T D Jakes.

Bring Back the Glory. T. D. Jakes. 2004. 29.99 (978-1-57855-501-7(9)) T D Jakes.

Bring 'Em Back: Dazzling Customer Service. Mark Mayfield. 1 cassette. (Running Time: 70 minutes). 2001. 15.00 (978-0-9700569-2-4(3)) Mayfield Present.
How to see customer service from a different perspective.....the customer's! Tips on how to create a dazzling customer experience and how to bring them back again and again.

Bring Forth Your Dead. J. M. Gregson. Read by Robbie MacNab. 6 cass. (Storysound Ser.). (J). 2003. 54.95 (978-1-85903-609-9(0)) Pub: Mgna Lrg Print GBR. Dist(s): Ulverscroft US

Bring Me the Head of Anne Boleyn: Historical Mysteries. unabr. ed. Read by Judy Geeson et al. 4 cass. (Running Time: 6 hrs.). 2001. 25.00 (978-1-59040-060-9(7), Phoenix Audio) Pub: Amer Intl Pub. Dist(s): PerseuPGW
Historical mysteries as you've never heard them before. Unforgettable mystery stories include: "The Blackmailer," "Busted Blossoms," "The Sun-Dog Trail," "The Dancing Bear," "The Hudson Chain," "No Room at the Inn," "Poison Peach," "A Black Death" and "Bring Me the Head of Anne Boleyn".

Bring Me the Ocean: The Natural World as Healer. abr. ed. Rebecca A. Reynolds. 1 cass. (Running Time: 125 min.). 1999. 18.95 (978-1-889242-01-9(2)) Pub: VanderWyk & Burnham. Dist(s): Natl Bk Netwk

Bring Me to Life. Contrib. by Bebo Norman. (Mastertrax Ser.). 2006. audio compact disk 9.98 (978-5-558-11352-5(9)) Pt of Grace Ent.

Bring on the Brass. Perf. by Hannaford Street Silver Band & Leo McKern. (J). (gr. k up). 9.98 (274); audio compact disk 14.98 (D274) MFLP CA.
Children love the rousing sounds of a big brass band! This exuberant production will have your entire family parading around the room to the varied moods of brass music.

***Bring the Classics to Life.** adpt. ed. EDCON Publishing Group Staff. (Bring the Classics to Life Ser.). (ENG.). 2008. audio compact disk 124.00 (978-1-55576-593-4(9)); audio compact disk 124.00 (978-1-55576-594-1(7)); audio compact disk 124.00 (978-1-55576-592-7(0)) EDCON Pubng.

Bring the Rain. Contrib. by MercyMe. (Christian World Soundtraks Ser.). 2007. audio compact disk 8.99 (978-5-557-60867-1(2)) Christian Wrld.

Bring the Rain. Contrib. by MercyMe. (Sound Performance Soundtracks Ser.). 2007. audio compact disk 5.98 (978-5-557-63289-8(1)) Pt of Grace Ent.

***Bring Us Back.** Contrib. by Mosie Lister. (ENG.). 2001. audio compact disk 12.99 (978-5-550-11702-6(9)) Lillenas.

Bring Your Dreams to Pass. Speeches. Joel Osteen. 1 Cass. (Running Time: 30 Mins.). 2000. 6.00 (978-1-59349-079-9(8), JA0079) J Osteen.

Bring Your New Product to Market: 10 Innovative & Practical Secrets to a More Successful New Product Introduction. Christina M. Brown. Intro. by Norma J. Rist. 2006. audio compact disk 39.99 (978-1-4276-0450-7(9)) AardGP.

Bringing a Course in Miracles into Application, Series II. Tara Singh. 3 cass. (Running Time: 3 hrs.). bk. 21.95 (978-1-55531-236-7(5), #A278) Life Action Pr.
Deals with Facts & man's inherent unwillingness to have "the ears to hear." A Course In Miracles is to be lived - APPLICATION is the next step.

Bringing Darkness to Light: The Vision of Forgiveness. Kenneth Wapnick. 1 CD. (Running Time: 3 hrs. 48 mins. 24 secs.). 2006. 18.00 (978-1-59142-285-3(X), 3m132); audio compact disk 23.00 (978-1-59142-284-6(1), CD132) Foun Miracles.

Bringing down the House: The Inside Story of Six M. I. T. Students Who Took Vegas for Millions. abr. ed. Ben Mezrich. (Running Time: 60 hrs. 0 mins. 0 sec.). (ENG.). 2005. audio compact disk 30.00 (978-0-7435-3061-3(6), Audioworks) Pub: S&S Audio. Dist(s): S and S Inc

Bringing down the House: The Inside Story of Six M. I. T. Students Who Took Vegas for Millions. unabr. ed. Ben Mezrich. 4 cass. (Running Time: 112 hrs. 50 mins. 0 sec.). (ENG.). 2004. 26.00 (978-0-7435-2654-8(6), Audioworks) Pub: S&S Audio. Dist(s): S and S Inc

Bringing Elizabeth Home: A Journey of Faith & Hope. unabr. ed. Ed and Lois Smart & Laura Morton. Read by Sandra Burr Mel Foster. (Running Time: 5 hrs.). 2005. 24.95 (978-1-59710-608-5(9), 9781597106085, BAD) Brilliance Audio.

Bringing Elizabeth Home: A Journey of Faith & Hope. unabr. ed. Ed Smart et al. Read by Sandra Burr Mel Foster. 4 cass. (Running Time: 5 hrs.). 2003. 62.25 (978-1-59355-575-7(X), 159355575X) Brilliance Audio.

Bringing Elizabeth Home: A Journey of Faith & Hope. unabr. ed. Ed Smart et al. Read by Mel Foster & Sandra Burr. 4 cass. (Running Time: 5 hrs.). 2003. 24.95 (978-1-59355-574-0(1), 1593555741); audio compact disk 26.95 (978-1-59355-576-4(8), 1593555768) Brilliance Audio.
At 3:58 in the morning of June 5, 2002, Ed and Lois Smart awoke to the sound of their nine-year-old daughter Mary Katherine's frightened voice. "She's gone. Elizabeth is gone." At first they thought she was having a bad dream about her older sister, but Mary Katherine's "bad dream" would quickly become their worst nightmare. Their daughter Elizabeth was gone. They were not sure why the media picked up on Elizabeth's story, but after their daughter was kidnapped she became the whole world's daughter. After nine months of a strange, hard, sometimes rewarding, but mostly painful journey, Elizabeth was miraculously returned to them. Just as millions throughout the world had grieved for her loss, now they celebrated her safe return. In Bringing Elizabeth Home, Ed and Lois share the pain of every parent's worst fear: "What would I do if my child was taken from me?" They also share a story of great hope, strong faith, and trust in God. The Smart family had always been devoted to their Mormon faith, but through their terribly painful experience they gained a tremendous inner strength, which became the key to their survival. They write, "Having our daughter back home, in our arms, is nothing short of a miracle. It is the ultimate proof that God answers prayers. Granted, sometimes the answer is not the one we pray for, but still it remains an answer. We feel truly blessed that He answered our prayers the way we had hoped for, although we realize, regretfully, that this is not always the outcome in kidnapping cases. We have met so many families with missing children and we've seen how deep their pain goes . . . But what we hope to convey through our journey of faith and hope is that with a strong belief in God, all things are possible. Miracles do happen." In the end, the Smarts' story brings one point poignantly home-nothing is more important in this world than family. Not money. Not work. Not a fancy new car or an expensive, big house. Family, the prayers of so many friends and strangers, and trust in God are what got them through this experience-and having survived, they have no doubt that they can persevere in any situation as long as those three things are in their lives. Though their story is filled with many incredible twists and turns, they never lost focus on what was important: bringing Elizabeth home.

Bringing Elizabeth Home: A Journey of Faith & Hope. unabr. ed. Ed Smart et al. Read by Sandra Burr Mel Foster. 5 CDs. (Running Time: 5 hrs.). 2003. audio compact disk 74.25 (978-1-59355-577-1(6), 1593555776) Brilliance Audio.

Bringing Elizabeth Home: A Journey of Faith & Hope. unabr. ed. Ed Smart et al. Read by Sandra Burr Mel Foster. (Running Time: 5 hrs.). 2004. 39.25 (978-1-59335-517-3(3), 1593355173, Brinc Audio MP3 Lib) Brilliance Audio.

Bringing Elizabeth Home: A Journey of Faith & Hope. unabr. ed. Ed Smart et al. Read by Sandra Burr Mel Foster. (Running Time: 5 hrs.). 2005. 39.25 (978-1-59710-776-1(X), 9781597107761, BADLE) Brilliance Audio.

Bringing Elizabeth Home: A Journey of Faith & Hope. unabr. ed. Ed Smart et al. Read by Sandra Burr & Mel Foster. (Running Time: 5 hrs.). 2004. 24.95 (978-1-59335-251-6(4), 1593352514) Soulmate Audio Bks.

Bringing Forth the Old & the New. Richard Rohr. 1 cass. (Running Time: 1 hr.). 2001. 8.95 St Anthony Mess Pr.
Two-thirds of Jesus' teaching is about letting go or forgiveness. We are living in the age of anxiety. Dealing with anxiety requires the act of letting go, of moving forward in faith - which is what all great spirituality is about.

Bringing Heaven into Hell. 4 cass. 11.95 Incl. album. (978-0-943026-18-3(0), A6) Carothers.

Bringing Heaven to Earth. unabr. ed. Andrew Cohen. 1 cass. (Running Time: 1 hr. 08 min.). 10.95 (978-1-883929-16-9(4)) Moksha Pr.
Shows that when we cease to be preoccupied with ourselves & make enormous room in our hearts & minds for others, then heaven will reveal itself as the experience of joy & well-being that is the natural & unfettered expression of life itself.

Bringing Home the Prodigals. unabr. ed. Rob Parsons. Narrated by Rob Parsons. (Running Time: 2 hrs. 21 mins. 48 sec.). (ENG.). 2008. 11.19 (978-1-60814-462-4(3)); audio compact disk 15.99 (978-1-59859-505-5(9)) Oasis Audio.

Bringing in Cosmic Force. Ormond McGill. 2000. (978-1-933332-18-5(2)) Hypnotherapy Train.

Bringing It To Print In The Digital Age: A Comprehensive Course On Buying Services Of The Graphic Arts. 2005. audio compact disk 579.00 (978-0-9670543-2-2(X)) Graphic Arts Ed.

Bringing Out the Best in Children. Michael N. Deranja. 1 cass. (Running Time: 80 min.). (Spiritual Child - Raising Ser.). 9.95 (AT-30) Crystal Clarity.
Topics include: How to make children more aware of their emotions & habits; what's wrong with public education; why teachers need to love their students.

Bringing Out the Best in People. Alan L. McGinnis. Read by Alan L. McGinnis. 6 cass. 1992. 59.95 set. (892A) Nightingale-Conant.
Dr. McGinnis has taught thousands of people & corporations to use the power of motivation, build group morale, build inner drive in others, to be the best that they can be.

Bringing Out the Best in People: How to Apply the Astonishing Power of Positive Reinforcement. Aubrey C. Daniels. 3 CDs. (Running Time: 4 hrs. 30 min.). 2003. audio compact disk 28.00 (978-1-932378-03-0(0)); 24.00 (978-0-9724889-9-0(5)) Pub: A Media Intl. Dist(s): Natl Bk Netwk
The classic bestseller on performance management, now updated with the latest and best motivational methods, perfected at such companies as Xerox, 3M, and Kodak.

Bringing Out the Best in Your Kids: Insights & Advice on Discipline. Warren Umansky et al. 1 cass. (Running Time: 45 min.). (Behavior Beasts Ser.: Vol. 1). 1998. Incl. game board, stickers, incentive charts, diplomas, coloring mats, award coupons for kids. (978-0-9664396-9-4(4)) PPP Enterp.
Advice & answers on cassette regarding behavior & discipline, packaged with "hands-on" tools for kids.

Bringing the Aloha Spirit into the Workplace. Linda A. Wheeler. Intro. by Jack Kellner. 1 cass. 1994. bk. 12.95 (978-0-9639713-0-2(1)) Human Connect.
Developing & nurturing the Aloha Spirit - that particular feeling which embraces & cultivates the uniqueness of every individual - through the understanding, accepting & appreciation of them.

Bringing up Baby, Vol. 1. Read by Joanie Bartels. 2 cass. (Running Time: 42 min.). (Magic Series Gift Collection). pap. bk. set. (978-1-881225-12-6(7)) Discov Music.
Full length audio cassette, full color lyric book with words to lullaby songs & Better Homes & Gardens: New Baby Book (parenting book).

Bringing up Baby, Vol. 2. Read by Joanie Bartels. 1 cass. (Running Time: 33 min.). (Magic Series Gift Collection). pap. bk. (978-1-881225-13-3(5)) Discov Music.
Full length audio cassette, full color lyric book with words to wake-up songs & Name Your Baby Book (parenting book).

Bringing up Baby, Vol. 3. Read by Joanie Bartels. 1 cass. (Running Time: 44 min.). (Magic Series Gift Collection). pap. bk. (978-1-881225-14-0(3)) Discov Music.
Full length audio cassette, full color lyric book with words to lullaby songs & The First Twelve Months of Life (parenting book).

Bringing up Baby, Vol. 4. Read by Joanie Bartels. 1 cass. (Running Time: 30 min.). (Magic Series Gift Collection). pap. bk. (978-1-881225-15-7(1)) Discov Music.
Full length audio cassette, full color lyric book with words to lullaby songs, & You & Your Baby's First Year (parenting book).

Bringing up Boys: Practical Advice & Encouragement for Those Shaping the Next Generation of Men. abr. ed. James C. Dobson. 6 CDs. (ENG.). 2001. audio compact disk 26.99 (978-0-8423-2297-3(3)) Tyndale Hse.

Bringing up Girls: Practical Advice & Encouragement for Those Shaping the Next Generation of Women. abr. ed. James C. Dobson. 6 CDs. (Running Time: 10 hrs.). (ENG.). 2010. audio compact disk 29.99 (978-1-4143-3650-3(0)) Tyndale Hse.

Bringing up Girls: Practical Advice & Encouragement for Those Shaping the Next Generation of Women. unabr. ed. James C. Dobson. 15 CDs. (Running Time: 18 hrs.). (ENG.). 2010. instr.'s gde. ed. 39.99 (978-1-4143-0128-0(6), Tyndale Audio) Tyndale Hse.

Bringing Water to People: Audiocassette. (Greetings Ser.: Vol. 3). (gr. 3-5). 10.00 (978-0-7635-1822-6(0)) Rigby Educ.

Brink of War. unabr. ed. Keith Douglass. Read by David Hilder. 6 cass. (Running Time: 6 hrs.). (Carrier Ser.: No. 13). 2001. 48.00 (978-0-7366-6834-7(9)) Books on Tape.
Admiral "Tombstone" Magruder and his men are sent to an airmanship competition against Russia.

Brisingr. unabr. ed. Christopher Paolini. Read by Gerard Doyle. (Inheritance Cycle Ser.: Bk. 3). (YA). 2009. 89.99 (978-1-60640-574-1(8)) Find a World.

Brisingr. unabr. ed. Christopher Paolini. Read by Gerard Doyle. 23 CDs. (Running Time: 29 hrs. 30 mins.). (Inheritance Cycle Ser.: Bk. 3). (ENG.). (J). (gr. 7). 2008. audio compact disk 60.00 (978-0-7393-6804-6(4), Listening Lib) Pub: Random Audio Pubg. Dist(s): Random

Brisingr. unabr. ed. Christopher Paolini. Read by Gerard Doyle. 23 CDs. (Running Time: 29 hrs. 35 mins.). (Inheritance Cycle Ser.: Bk. 3). (YA). (gr. 7 up). 2008. audio compact disk 90.00 (978-0-7393-6809-1(5), Listening Lib) Pub: Random Audio Pubg. Dist(s): Random

Britain 1500-1750 & Britain 1750-1900. 2006. audio compact disk 449.00 (978-0-340-91605-6(2), HodderMurray) Pub: Hodder Edu GBR. Dist(s): Trans-Atl Phila

Britannica Biographies: Great Minds. Compiled by Encyclopaedia Britannica, Inc. 2007. audio compact disk 14.95 (978-1-59339-539-1(6)) Ency Brit Inc.

Britannica Biographies: Heroes & Villians. Compiled by Encyclopaedia Britannica, Inc. 2007. audio compact disk 14.95 (978-1-59339-541-4(8)) Ency Brit Inc.

Britannica Biographies: World Leaders. Compiled by Encyclopaedia Britannica, Inc. 2007. audio compact disk 14.95 (978-1-59339-540-7(X)) Ency Brit Inc.

Britannica Brain Games. Compiled by Encyclopaedia Britannica, Inc. 2008. audio compact disk 39.95 (978-1-59339-434-9(9)) Ency Brit Inc.

Britannica Concise Edition. Compiled by Encyclopaedia Britannica, Inc. 2004. audio compact disk (978-1-59339-096-9(3)) Ency Brit Inc.

Britannica Premium Service. Compiled by Encyclopaedia Britannica, Inc. 2004. audio compact disk (978-1-59339-079-2(3)) Ency Brit Inc.

Britannica Quiz Show. Compiled by Encyclopaedia Britannica, Inc. 2008. audio compact disk 9.95 Ency Brit Inc.

Britannica Standard Edition. Compiled by Encyclopaedia Britannica, Inc. 2004. audio compact disk (978-1-59339-097-6(1)) Ency Brit Inc.

Britannica Sudoku Unlimited. Compiled by Encyclopaedia Britannica, Inc. 2008. audio compact disk 9.95 Ency Brit Inc.

Britannica Visual Dictionary. Compiled by Encyclopaedia Britannica, Inc. 2008. audio compact disk 29.95 Ency Brit Inc.

Britannica Word Search. Compiled by Encyclopaedia Britannica, Inc. 2008. audio compact disk 9.95 (978-1-59339-435-6(7)) Ency Brit Inc.

Britannica 2003 Deluxe. Compiled by Encyclopaedia Britannica, Inc. 2004. audio compact disk (978-1-59339-117-1(X)) Ency Brit Inc.

Britannica 2005 Children's. Compiled by Encyclopaedia Britannica, Inc. 2005. audio compact disk (978-1-59339-176-8(5)) Ency Brit Inc.

Britannica 2005 Deluxe. Compiled by Encyclopaedia Britannica, Inc. 2005. audio compact disk (978-1-59339-166-9(8)); audio compact disk (978-1-59339-167-6(6)); audio compact disk (978-1-59339-179-9(X)) Ency Brit Inc.

Britannica 2005 Standard. Compiled by Encyclopaedia Britannica, Inc. 2005. audio compact disk (978-1-59339-173-7(0)); audio compact disk (978-1-59339-178-2(1)); audio compact disk (978-1-59339-172-0(2)); audio compact disk (978-1-59339-164-5(1)) Ency Brit Inc.

Britannica 2005 Ultimate Reference Suite. Compiled by Encyclopaedia Britannica, Inc. 2005. audio compact disk 69.95 (978-1-59339-171-3(4)); audio compact disk 69.95 (978-1-59339-170-6(6)) Ency Brit Inc.

Britannica's Fairy Tales from Around the World. Compiled by Encyclopaedia Britannica, Inc. 2004. audio compact disk (978-1-59339-111-9(0)) Ency Brit Inc.

Britannicus, Set. Jean Racine. Perf. by Francoise Seigner. 2 cass. (FRE.). 1992. 26.95 (1602-RF) Olivia & Hill.
The scene is Rome at the time when Nero is rebelling against the authority of his mother Agrippina. Unable to win the love of Junia who is in love with his half-brother Britannicus, a marriage favored by his mother, he poisons him.

Brite Dreams. Janeen J. Brady & Diane Woolley. Illus. by Evan Twede. (J). (ps). 1988. pap. bk. 12.95 (978-0-944803-80-6(0)) Brite Music.

***British Bird Sounds.** Ron Kettle & Vrej Nersessian. (ENG.). 2010. instr.'s gde. ed. 25.00 (978-0-7123-0512-9(2)) Pub: Britis Library GBR. Dist(s): Chicago Distribution Ctr

British Columbia, Canada's Temperate Rainforests with a Look At: Clearcutting in "Legacy," Wilderness in "Raincoast North among the Fjords" & Demonstrations at Clayoquot Sound in the Music Video "Sulphur Passage" Hosted by Nancy Pearlman. 1 cass. (Running Time: 30 min.). 10.00 (1420) Educ Comm CA.

British Design & Art Direction. bk. 89.95 (978-0-06-018583-1(X)) HarperCollins Pubs.

British Literature. (gr. 12 up). 2001. (978-0-395-97166-6(7), 2-80702); audio compact disk (978-0-395-97144-4(6), 2-80690) Holt McDoug.

British Literature. (CRP.). (gr. 12 up). 2004. audio compact disk (978-0-618-28974-5(7), 2-04277); audio compact disk (978-0-618-28993-6(3), 2-04285) Holt McDoug.

***British Mammals: An Audio Introduction to the Mammals of Britain.** British Library Sound Archive Staff & Vrej Nersessian. 2010. audio compact disk 15.00 (978-0-7123-0589-1(0)) Pub: Britis Library GBR. Dist(s): Chicago Distribution Ctr

British Pharmacopoeia, Set. Department of Health Staff. 1999. bk. 1495.00 (978-0-11-322258-2(0), HM22580) Pub: Statnry Office GBR. Dist(s): Bernan Associates

***Brittle Clay in Tender Hands.** Featuring Ravi Zacharias. 1995. audio compact disk 9.00 (978-1-61256-051-9(2)) Ravi Zach.

Brittle Glass. unabr. ed. Norah Lofts. Read by Prue Clark & Stuart Fox. 5 cass. 1997. 49.95 Set. (978-1-86015-417-1(4)) T T Beeler.
A young woman inherits her estranged father's business & decides to manage it herself, much to the surprise & consternation of her friends.

Brittle Image. unabr. ed. Emma Stirling. Read by Elizabeth Henry. 3 cass. (Running Time: 4 hrs. 30 min.). 1996. 34.95 (978-1-86042-023-8(0), 20230) Pub: Soundings Ltd GBR. Dist(s): Ulverscroft US
Cailean takes a temporary position of nurse to Sonia, Alan Keen's sick wife, who hears the crying of a baby she lost. Why is Alan so unsympathetic, why won't he believe Cailean when she tries to tell him of the terrifying things that are happening.

Brittle Image, Set. Emma Stirling. Read by Elizabeth Henry. 3 cass. 1999. 34.95 (20230) Pub: Soundings Ltd GBR. Dist(s): ISIS Pub

Brixton Rock. unabr. ed. Alex Wheatle. Narrated by Joel Trill. 8 cass. (Running Time: 8 hrs. 15 mins.). 2003. 79.75 (978-1-84505-118-1(1), H1700MC, Clipper Audio) Recorded Bks.

Bro. Robert Newton Peck. Narrated by Scott Shina. 3 CDs. (Running Time: 3 hrs. 30 mins.). (J). 2004. audio compact disk 29.75 (978-1-4193-1777-4(6)) Recorded Bks.

Bro. unabr. ed. 3 cass. (Running Time: 3:30 hrs.). 2004. 28.75 (978-1-4025-9993-4(5)) Recorded Bks.

Bro Code. unabr. ed. Barney Stinson. Read by Neil Patrick Harris as Barney Stinson. (Running Time: 1 hr. 30 mins. 0 sec.). (ENG.). 2008. audio compact disk 19.99 (978-0-7435-8205-6(5)) Pub: S&S Audio. Dist(s): S and S Inc

***Bro Code.** unabr. ed. Barney Stinson. Read by Neil Patrick Harris as Barney Stinson. (Running Time: 1 hr. 30 mins. 0 sec.). (ENG.). 2010. audio compact disk 14.99 (978-1-4423-3958-3(6)) Pub: S&S Audio. Dist(s): S and S Inc

Bro. Pearry Green's Personal Testimony: 1933-1965. unabr. ed. Pearry Green. (ENG.). 2005. audio compact disk (978-1-60246-008-9(6)) Tucson Taber.

Broadband Equipment & Services in China: A Strategic Reference 2007. Compiled by Icon Group International, Inc. Staff. 2007. ring bd. 195.00 (978-0-497-35863-1(8)) Icon Grp.

Broadband Equipment & Services in Russia: A Strategic Reference 2007. Compiled by Icon Group International, Inc. Staff. 2007. ring bd. 195.00 (978-0-497-82399-3(3)) Icon Grp.

Broadcast Voice Handbook: How to Polish Your On-Air Delivery. 2nd ed. Ann S. Utterback. (J). (gr. 10-12). 1990. 19.95 (978-1-56625-039-9(0)) Bonus Books.

Broadcast Voice Handbook: How to Polish Your On-Air Delivery. 2nd ed. Ann S. Utterback. (J). (gr. 10-12). 1992. 19.95 (978-1-56625-038-2(2)) Bonus Books.

Broadcasting & Telecommunications Equipment & Services in Australia: A Strategic Reference 2007. Compiled by Icon Group International, Inc. Staff. 2007. ring bd. 195.00 (978-0-497-35807-5(7)) Icon Grp.

Broadcasting & Telecommunications Equipment & Services in China: A Strategic Reference 2007. Compiled by Icon Group International, Inc. Staff. 2007. ring bd. 195.00 (978-0-497-35864-8(6)) Icon Grp.

Broadcasting & Telecommunications Equipment & Services in Indonesia: A Strategic Reference 2007. Compiled by Icon Group International, Inc. Staff. 2007. ring bd. 195.00 (978-0-497-36026-9(8)) Icon Grp.

Broadcasting & Telecommunications Equipment & Services in Malaysia: A Strategic Reference 2007. Compiled by Icon Group International, Inc. Staff. 2007. ring bd. 195.00 (978-0-497-82342-9(X)) Icon Grp.

Broadcasting & Telecommunications Equipment & Services in New Zealand: A Strategic Reference 2007. Compiled by Icon Group International, Inc. Staff. 2007. ring bd. 195.00 (978-0-497-82368-9(3)) Icon Grp.

Broadcasting & Telecommunications Equipment & Services in Philippines: A Strategic Reference 2007. Compiled by Icon Group International, Inc. Staff. 2007. ring bd. 195.00 (978-0-497-82383-2(7)) Icon Grp.

Broadcasting & Telecommunications Equipment & Services in Singapore: A Strategic Reference 2007. Compiled by Icon Group International, Inc. Staff. 2007. ring bd. 195.00 (978-0-497-82410-5(8)) Icon Grp.

Broadcasting & Telecommunications Equipment & Services in Vietnam: A Strategic Reference 2007. Compiled by Icon Group International, Inc. Staff. 2007. ring bd. 195.00 (978-0-497-82471-6(X)) Icon Grp.

Broadcasting Equipment in Brazil: A Strategic Reference 2006. Compiled by Icon Group International, Inc. Staff. 2007. ring bd. 195.00 (978-0-497-35833-4(6)) Icon Grp.

Broadcasting in Singapore: A Strategic Reference 2006. Compiled by Icon Group International, Inc. Staff. 2007. ring bd. 195.00 (978-0-497-82411-2(6)) Icon Grp.

Broadside Tapes I: Broadside No. 14. Perf. by Phil Ochs & Eric Andersen. Anno. by Jane Friesen. 1 cass. 1989. (0-9307-400080-9307-40008-2-3); audio compact disk (0-9307-40008-2-3) Smithsonian Folkways.

Broadsides from the Other Orders: A Book of Bugs. unabr. ed. Sue Hubbell. Narrated by Barbara Caruso. 6 cass. (Running Time: 9 hrs.). 1994. 51.00 (978-1-55690-961-0(6), 94104E7) Recorded Bks.
Lifestyles of the six-legged; a mixture of facts about bugs & reflections on nature. Under the microscope of Sue Hubbell's keen eye emerges an exciting world we rarely take time to see.

Broadway. Friedman-Fairfax and Sony Music Staff. 1 CD. (Life, Times, & Music Ser.). 1995. pap. bk. 15.98 (978-1-56799-002-7(9), Friedman-Fairfax) M Friedman Pub Grp Inc.

Broadway Classics. David Glen Hatch & Diana Walker. 1 cass. 9.95 (10001158); audio compact disk 14.95 (2800799) Covenant Comms.
A variety of the most loved Broadway songs.

Broadway Classics for Solo Jazz Guitar. Created by Hal Leonard Corporation Staff. 2008. pap. bk. 19.99 (978-1-4234-3042-1(5), 1423430425) H Leonard.

Broadway for Solo Singers: Contemporary Arrangements of 10 Broadway Favorites. Composed by Sally K. Albrecht & Brian Fisher. (On Broadway Ser.). (ENG.). 2008. audio compact disk 15.95 (978-0-7390-4955-6(0)) Alfred Pub.

Broadway for Two: 10 Musical Theatre Duets. Composed by Sally K. Albrecht. Compiled by Brian Fisher & Andy Beck. (For Two Ser.). (ENG.). 2007. audio compact disk 9.95 (978-0-7390-4478-0(8)) Alfred Pub.

Broadway Is My Beat. Created by Radio Spirits. Contrib. by Larry Thor. (Running Time: 36000 sec.). 2004. 39.98 (978-1-57019-679-9(6)) Radio Spirits.

Broadway Is My Beat. collector's ed. Perf. by Larry Thor. 6 cass. (Running Time: 9 hrs.). 2000. bk. 34.98 (4178) Radio Spirits.
Detective Danny Clover in 18 crime drama stories "from Times Square to Columbus Circle - the gaudiest, the most violent, the lonesomest mile in the world".

Broadway Is My Beat: David Blaine & Howard Crawford. unabr. ed. Perf. by Larry Thor. 1 cass. (Running Time: 1 hr.). 2001. 6.98 (2234) Radio Spirits.

Broadway Is My Beat: Earl Lawson & Frank Dunn. unabr. ed. Perf. by Larry Thor. 1 cass. (Running Time: 1 hr.). 2001. 6.98 (2273) Radio Spirits.

Broadway Is My Beat: Ed Koster & Ricardo Miguel. unabr. ed. Perf. by Larry Thor. 1 cass. (Running Time: 1 hr.). 2001. 6.98 (2116) Radio Spirits.

Broadway Is My Beat: Harry Foster & Joe Gruber. unabr. ed. Perf. by Larry Thor. 1 cass. (Running Time: 1 hr.). 2001. 6.98 (2593) Radio Spirits.

Broadway Is My Beat: Johnny Hill & Joan Fuller. unabr. ed. Perf. by Larry Thor. 1 cass. (Running Time: 1 hr.). 2001. 6.98 (2075) Radio Spirits.

Broadway Is My Beat: Mary Demming & Ben Justin. unabr. ed. Perf. by Larry Thor. 1 cass. (Running Time: 1 hr.). 2001. 6.98 (2572) Radio Spirits.

Broadway Is My Beat: Paul Thomas & Dion Hartley. unabr. ed. Perf. by Larry Thor. 1 cass. (Running Time: 1 hr.). 2001. 6.98 (2093) Radio Spirits.

Broadway Is My Beat: Receipt for a Teapot & The Hudson Club Initiations. unabr. ed. Perf. by Larry Thor. 1 cass. (Running Time: 1 hr.). 2001. 6.98 (1616) Radio Spirits.

Broadway Is My Beat: Suicide of Jimmy Hunt & The Missing Julie Dixon. unabr. ed. Perf. by Larry Thor. 1 cass. (Running Time: 1 hr.). 2001. 6.98 (1943) Radio Spirits.

Broadway Is My Beat: The Mary Smith Case & The Lucille Baker Case. unabr. ed. Perf. by Larry Thor. 1 cass. (Running Time: 1 hr.). 2001. 6.98 (2192) Radio Spirits.

Broadway Is My Beat: The Thomas Hart Case & The Nick Norman Case. unabr. ed. Perf. by Larry Thor. 1 cass. (Running Time: 1 hr.). 2001. 6.98 (1615) Radio Spirits.

Broadway Is My Beat: Val Dane & Roberto Seguara. unabr. ed. Perf. by Larry Thor. 1 cass. (Running Time: 1 hr.). 2001. 6.98 (1955) Radio Spirits.

Broadway Jeeves? The Diary of a Theatrical Adventure. unabr. ed. Martin Jarvis. Read by Martin Jarvis. 7 cass. (Running Time: 10 hrs. 30 mins.). 2004. 32.95 (978-1-59007-567-8(6)); audio compact disk 55.00 (978-1-59007-568-5(4)) Pub: New Millenn Enter. Dist(s): PerseuPGW

Broadway Kids: Back on Broadway. 1 cass. (Running Time: 1 hr.). (J). 2002. 9.98 (978-1-56896-286-3(X), 54268-4); audio compact disk 15.98 (978-1-56896-285-6(1), 54268-2) Lightyear Entrtnmnt.
Introduce your children to the wonderful world of Broadway and more. Enjoy the youthful exuberance of actual Broadway performers, The Broadway Kids, as they perform your favorite songs from Broadway, movies and American traditional and popular songs. Featuring I Feel Pretty, Hair, Beauty and the Beast, You Gotta Have Heart.

Broadway Kids: The Best of Broadway. 1 cass. (Running Time: 1 hr.). (J). 2002. 11.98 (978-1-56896-600-7(8), 54467-4); audio compact disk 16.98 (978-1-56896-599-4(0), 54467-2) Lightyear Entrtnmnt.

Broadway Kids at the Movies. Perf. by Richard Jay-Alexander & Broadway Kids Staff. Prod. by Ned Ginsburg & Julius Shulman. 1 cass. 1997. 9.98 (978-1-56896-163-7(4), 54183-4); 9.98 Blister. (978-1-56896-165-1(0), 54184-4); audio compact disk 15.98 (978-1-56896-164-4(2), 54183-2); audio compact disk 15.98 CD Blister. (978-1-56896-166-8(9), 54184-2) Lightyear Entrtnmnt.
Follow-up release to "The Broadway Kids Sing Broadway".

Broadway Kids Sing America. 1 cass. (Running Time: 1 hr.). (J). 2002. 9.98 (978-1-56896-461-4(7), 54367-4); audio compact disk 15.98 (978-1-56896-432-4(3), 54367-2) Lightyear Entrtnmnt.
Introduce your children to the wonderful world of Broadway and more. Enjoy the youthful exuberance of actual Broadway performers, The Broadway Kids, as they perform your favorite songs from Broadway, movies and American traditional and popular songs. Featuring City of New Orleans, This Land is Your Land, America, Take Me Home, Country Road.

Broadway Kids Sing Broadway. Perf. by Broadway Kids Staff. Contrib. by Petula Clark. Prod. by Ned Ginsburg & Julius Shulman. 1 cass. 1996. 9.98 (978-1-56896-146-0(4), 54174-4); 8.98 Blister. (978-1-56896-148-4(0), 54175-4); audio compact disk 15.98 (978-1-56896-147-7(2), 54174-2); audio compact disk 15.98 CD Blister. (978-1-56896-149-1(9), 54175-2) Lightyear Entrtnmnt.
Features some of the most recognizable songs from classic shows originally sung by kids on broadway. The Broadway Kids are today's youngest performers, who have all appeared in featured roles in the hottest Broadway musicals.

Broadway Kids Sing Christmas. Perf. by Kathie Lee Gifford. 1 cass. 8.98 Norelco. (978-1-56896-219-1(3), 54226-4); 8.98 Blister. (978-1-56896-221-4(5), 54227-4); audio compact disk 15.98 CD. (978-1-56896-218-4(5), 54226-2); audio compact disk 15.98 CD blister. (978-1-56896-220-7(7), 54227-2) Lightyear Entrtnmnt.
Collection of holiday favorites sung by young performers with featured roles in Broadway musicals, TV shows & movies.

Broadway Legacy, Set. Michael Ballam. 8 cass. (Running Time: 12 hrs.). 49.95 (978-1-55503-877-9(8), 1100734) Covenant Comms.

Broadway Legacy, 1891-1928, No. 1. Michael Ballam. 2 cass. (Running Time: 3 hrs.). 2000. 14.98 (978-1-55503-878-6(6), 1100688) Covenant Comms.

Broadway Legacy, 1930-1947, No. 2. Michael Ballam. 2 cass. (Running Time: 3 hrs.). 2000. 14.98 (978-1-55503-879-3(4), 1100696) Covenant Comms.

Broadway Legacy, 1948-1961, No. 3. Michael Ballam. 2 cass. (Running Time: 3 hrs.). 14.98 (978-1-55503-880-9(8), 1100718) Covenant Comms.

Broadway Legacy, 1960-1995, No. 4. Michael Ballam. 2 cass. (Running Time: 3 hrs.). 14.98 (978-1-55503-881-6(6), 1100726) Covenant Comms.

Broadway Memory. unabr. ed. Kitty C. Hart. 1 cass. (Running Time: 1 hr.). 1997. 14.95 (978-1-885608-19-2(5)); audio compact disk 16.95 Airplay.
One-woman show gives first hand account of the artists & artistry that made Broadway Broadway, & recaptures the magic of the American Musical Theater.

Broadway Revisited. Christopher Leonard. 1 cass. 1992. 9.95 (978-1-887756-01-3(9)) Richmnd Hill.
Musical recording.

Broadway Rhythm Band: Sing & Play down the Great White Way! 10 Unison Showtunes with Optional Rhythm Band. Composed by Andy Beck & Tim Hayden. (ENG.). 2008. audio compact disk 34.95 (978-0-7390-5152-8(0)) Alfred Pub.

Broadway's My Beat. Perf. by Larry Thor & Charles Calvert. 2009. audio compact disk 31.95 (978-1-57019-904-2(3)) Radio Spirits.

***Broke, USA: From Pawnshops to Poverty, Inc. -How the Working Poor Became Big Business.** unabr. ed. Gary Rivlin. Read by Scott Sowers. 2010. (978-0-06-206210-9(7), Harper Audio); (978-0-06-204939-1(9), Harper Audio) HarperCollins Pubs.

Brokeback Mountain. unabr. ed. Annie Proulx. Read by Campbell Scott. 2005. 7.95 (978-0-7435-5411-4(6)) Pub: S&S Audio. Dist(s): S and S Inc

Broken. Daniel Clay. Read by Colin Moody. (Running Time: 9 hrs. 50 mins.). 2009. 79.99 (978-1-74214-171-8(4), 9781742141718) Pub: Bolinda Pubng AUS. Dist(s): Bolinda Pub Inc

***Broken.** Karin Slaughter. Read by Natalie Ross. 1 Playaway. (Running Time: 14 hrs.). 2010. 39.99 (978-1-4418-6891-6(7)) Brilliance Audio.

***Broken.** Karin Slaughter. 2011. audio compact disk 14.99 (978-1-4233-4246-5(1)) Brilliance Audio.

***Broken.** abr. ed. Karin Slaughter. Read by Natalie Ross. 5 CDs. (Running Time: 6 hrs.). (Grant County Ser.: Bk. 7). 2010. audio compact disk 26.99 (978-1-4233-4245-8(3), 9781423342458, BACD) Brilliance Audio.

Broken. unabr. ed. Kelley Armstrong. Read by Laural Merlington. Narrated by Laural Merlington. (Running Time: 12 hrs. 30 mins. 0 sec.). (Women of the Otherworld Ser.: Bk. 6). (ENG.). 2008. audio compact disk 24.99 (978-1-4001-5741-9(2)); audio compact disk 34.99 (978-1-4001-0741-4(5)); audio compact disk 69.99 (978-1-4001-3741-1(1)) Pub: Tantor Media. Dist(s): IngramPubServ

Broken. unabr. ed. Daniel Clay. Read by Colin Moody. (Running Time: 9 hrs. 50 mins.). 2008. audio compact disk 87.95 (978-1-921415-62-3(2), 9781921415623) Pub: Bolinda Pubng AUS. Dist(s): Bolinda Pub Inc

***Broken.** unabr. ed. Karin Slaughter. (Running Time: 14 hrs.). (Grant County Ser.: Bk. 7). 2010. 24.99 (978-1-4233-4243-4(7), 9781423342434, BAD); 39.97 (978-1-4233-4244-1(5), 9781423342441, BADLE) Brilliance Audio.

Broken. unabr. ed. Karin Slaughter. Read by Natalie Ross. 1 MP3-CD. (Running Time: 13 hrs.). (Grant County Ser.: Bk. 7). 2010. 24.99 (978-1-4233-4241-0(0), 9781423342410, Brilliance MP3); audio compact disk 99.97 (978-1-4233-4240-3(2), 9781423342403, BriAudCD Unabrid) Brilliance Audio.

***Broken.** unabr. ed. Karin Slaughter. Read by Natalie Ross. 1 MP3-CD. (Running Time: 13 hrs.). (Grant County Ser.: Bk. 7). 2010. 39.97 (978-1-4233-4242-7(9), 9781423342427, Brinc Audio MP3 Lib); audio compact disk 38.99 (978-1-4233-4239-7(9), 9781423342397, Bril Audio CD Unabri) Brilliance Audio.

Broken & Beautiful. Contrib. by Mark Schultz & Shaun Shankel. Prod. by Shaun Shankel et al. 2007. 17.99 (978-5-557-59878-1(2), Word Records) Word Enter.

Broken & Beautiful. Contrib. by Shaun Shankel & Mark Schultz. Prod. by Shaun Shankel. (Studio Ser.). 2006. audio compact disk 9.98 (978-5-558-14483-3(1), Word Music) Word Enter.

Broken & Blessed: A Retreat. Richard Rohr. Read by Richard Rohr. 10 cass. (Running Time: 11 hrs.). 59.95 incl. vinyl album. (AA1686) Credence Commun.
Illuminates ones own experience with the gospel message & calls you to a new growth.

Broken Angels. unabr. ed. Richard K. Morgan. Narrated by Todd McLaren. (Running Time: 16 hrs. 30 mins. 0 sec.). (Takeshi Kovacs Novels Ser.). (ENG.). 2005. audio compact disk 25.99 (978-1-4001-5138-7(4)); audio compact disk 42.99 (978-1-4001-0138-2(7)); audio compact disk 85.99 (978-1-4001-3138-9(3)) Pub: Tantor Media. Dist(s): IngramPubServ

Broken Appointment see Dylan Thomas Reading

Broken Arrow. abr. ed. 2 cass. (Running Time: 3 hrs.). 1995. 17.00 Set. (978-1-56876-048-3(5)) Soundlines Ent.

Broken Bike Boy & the Queen of 33rd Street. unabr. ed. Sharon G. Flake. Narrated by Bahni Turpin. 2 CDs. (Running Time: 2 hrs. 33 mins.). (J). (gr. 4-6). 2007. audio compact disk 24.00 (978-0-7393-4872-7(8), Listening Lib) Pub: Random Audio Pubg. Dist(s): Random

Broken Bodies. June Hampson. 2007. 84.95 (978-0-7531-3822-9(0)); audio compact disk 99.95 (978-0-7531-2804-6(7)) Pub: ISIS Audio GBR. Dist(s): Ulverscroft US

Broken Bones. Donald Davis. 2006. audio compact disk 14.95 (978-0-87483-822-0(3)) Pub: August Hse. Dist(s): Natl Bk Netwk

Broken Bones. unabr. ed. Donald Davis. Read by Donald Davis. (J). 2008. 34.99 (978-1-60252-954-0(X)) Find a World.

***Broken Bridge.** unabr. ed. Philip Pullman. (Running Time: 7 hrs.). (YA). 2011. 22.99 (978-1-4418-7571-6(9), 9781441875716, Brilliance MP3); 39.97 (978-1-4418-7572-3(7), 9781441875723, Brinc Audio MP3 Lib); 39.97 (978-1-4418-7574-7(3), 9781441875747, BADLE); audio compact disk 22.99 (978-1-4418-7569-3(7), 9781441875693, Bril Audio CD Unabri); audio compact disk 69.97 (978-1-4418-7570-9(0), 9781441875709, BriAudCD Unabrid) Brilliance Audio.

Broken but I'm Healed. Contrib. by Byron Cage. (Soundtraks Ser.). 2007. audio compact disk 8.99 (978-5-557-95427-3(9)) Christian Wrld.

Broken Chain see Whistler

Broken Doll A Christmas Story Narrative CD & Songs. Narrated by Diane Zuber. (J). 2006. audio compact disk 10.95 (978-0-9785551-2-2(0)) Zuber.

Broken Dreams see Poetry of William Butler Yeats

***Broken Eggs.** Eduardo Machado. Contrib. by Mehnlehseh Boayue et al. (Running Time: 4320 sec.). (L. A. Theatre Works Audio Theatre Collections). (ENG.). 2010. audio compact disk (978-1-58081-658-8(4)) L A Theatre.

Broken Feather: A Journey to Healing. Suzanne Stutman. 1 cass. 1997. 9.95 (978-0-9648261-2-0(7)) Man Hse PA.

Broken for You. Stephanie Kallos. Ed. by Anna Fields. 10 cass. (Running Time: 13 hrs.). 2004. 69.95 (978-0-7861-2869-3(0), 3359); audio compact disk 88.00 (978-0-7861-8343-2(8), 3359) Blckstn Audio.

Broken for You. Stephanie Kallos. Read by Anna Fields. (Running Time: 13 hrs.). 2004. 41.95 (978-1-59912-436-0(X)) Iofy Corp.

Broken for You. unabr. ed. Stephanie Kallos. Read by Anna Fields. 45 CDs. (Running Time: 13 hrs.). 2004. audio compact disk 24.95 (978-0-7861-8403-3(5), 3359); audio compact disk 34.95 (978-0-7861-8245-9(8), ZE3359) Blckstn Audio.

Broken for You. unabr. ed. Stephanie Kallos. Read by Anna Fields. 10 cass. (Running Time: 13 hrs. 30 mins.). 2005. reel tape 32.95 (978-0-7861-2905-8(0), E3359) Blckstn Audio.

Broken Gate, Set. unabr. ed. Eileen Ramsay. Read by Pamela Donald. 9 cass. (Running Time: 12 hrs.). 1999. 90.95 (978-1-85903-285-5(0)) Pub: Magna Story GBR. Dist(s): Ulverscroft US
Life for a miner's daughter in Scotland in 1910 was never easy, but young Kate Kennedy had it tougher than most. When tragedy snatched her mother from her, she put childhood joys aside & rolled up her sleeves. Kate became Charlie's wife & a mother, still looking after everyone except herself, but doing surprisingly well with her own bakery business. But what of the great plans she had for her family, her secret dreams? Sometimes it seemed as if it had all been in vain.

Broken Glass. Arthur Miller. Contrib. by JoBeth Williams et al. (Playaway Adult Fiction Ser.). (ENG.). 2009. 39.99 (978-1-60812-509-8(2)) Find a World.

Broken Glass. unabr. ed. Arthur Miller. Perf. by Jane Brucker et al. 2 CDs. (Running Time: 1 hr. 44 mins.). 1996. audio compact disk 25.95 (978-1-58081-001-2(2), CDTPT77) Pub: L A Theatre. Dist(s): NetLibrary CO
Set in Brooklyn, in 1938, this gripping psychological mystery begins when fourty-five year old Sylvia Gelburg suddenly loses her ability to walk. Phillip Gelburg is desperate to find out what is crippling his attractive, level-headed wife. The doctor can find nothing wrong. The prosperous Gelburgs have been contentedly married for decades. The only clue lies in Sylvia's growing obsession with news accounts from Germany. Even though she is safe in Brooklyn, Sylvia is terrified by Nazi violence - or is it something closer to home.

Broken Ground. unabr. ed. Kai Maristed. Read by Johanna Ward. 10 CDs. (Running Time: 13 hrs.). 2001. audio compact disk 80.00 (978-0-7861-8981-6(9), 3186) Blckstn Audio.

Broken Ground. unabr. ed. Kai Maristed. 9 cass. (Running Time: 13 hrs.). 2003. 62.95 (978-0-7861-2585-2(3), 3186) Blckstn Audio.
Kaethe Shalk has married into a family of disappearing German aristocracy. Having spent years in East Berlin, she faces a new life of boundless complexity when the Berlin Wall comes down and the ruin of the East stands in stark contrast to the exuberance of the West. Kaethe's journey from America to the broken ground of contemporary Germany becomes an act of recovery: of the lives intertwined by politics and passion, of memory and the invented self, and of Kaethe's search for a daughter lost to her, now grown and living in uncompromising isolation from her mother's past and present, somewhere in vast, resurgent Berlin.

***Broken Gun.** unabr. ed. Louis L'Amour. (Running Time: 5 hrs.). (ENG.). 2011. audio compact disk 20.00 (978-0-307-73762-5(4), Random AudioBks) Pub: Random Audio Pubg. Dist(s): Random

Broken Heart: Applying the Atonement to Life's Experiences. Bruce C. Hafen. 2005. audio compact disk 19.95 (978-1-59038-453-4(9)) Deseret Bk.

Broken Heartland. unabr. ed. Read by Lloyd James. (Running Time: 28800 sec.). (Mad Dog & Englishman Mysteries Ser.). 2007. 54.95 (978-1-4332-1129-4(7)); audio compact disk 29.95 (978-1-4332-1131-7(9)); audio compact disk 63.00 (978-1-4332-1130-0(0)) Blckstn Audio.

Broken Honor. Patricia Potter. Narrated by Alexandra O'Karma. 11 cass. (Running Time: 16 hrs.). 94.00 (978-1-4025-2150-8(2)) Recorded Bks.

Broken Journey. Janet Woods. 2008. 61.95 (978-1-84559-983-6(7)); audio compact disk 79.95 (978-1-84559-984-3(5)) Pub: Soundings Ltd GBR. Dist(s): Ulverscroft US

***Broken Kingdoms.** unabr. ed. N. K. Jemisin. Read by Casaundra Freeman. (Running Time: 11 hrs.). (Inheritance Trilogy). 2010. 24.99 (978-1-4418-8653-8(2), 9781441886538, Brilliance MP3); 24.99 (978-1-4418-8655-2(9), 9781441886552, BAD); 39.97 (978-1-4418-8654-5(0), 9781441886545, Brinc Audio MP3 Lib); 39.97 (978-1-4418-8656-9(7), 9781441886569, BADLE); audio compact disk 34.99 (978-1-4418-8651-4(6), 9781441886514, Bril Audio CD Unabri); audio compact disk 89.97 (978-1-4418-8652-1(4), 9781441886521, BriAudCD Unabrid) Brilliance Audio.

Broken on the Back Row: A Journey through Grace & Forgiveness. unabr. ed. Sandi Patty. 2005. 29.99 (978-1-58926-846-3(6), 6846) Pub: Oasis Audio. Dist(s): TNT Media Grp

Broken on the Back Row: A Journey through Grace & Forgiveness. unabr. ed. Sandi Patty. Narrated by Sandi Patty. (ENG.). 2005. 19.59 (978-1-60814-101-2(2)); audio compact disk 27.99 (978-1-58926-847-0(4), 6847) Oasis Audio.

Broken Places: A Rachel Goddard Mystery. unabr. ed. Sandra Parshall. (Running Time: 8 hrs. 30 mins.). 2010. 29.95 (978-1-4417-2566-0(0)); 54.95 (978-1-4417-2562-2(8)); audio compact disk 76.00 (978-1-4417-2563-9(6)) Blckstn Audio.

Broken Prey. abr. ed. John Sandford, pseud. Read by Eric Conger. (Running Time: 21600 sec.). (ENG.). (gr. 8). 2006. audio compact disk 14.95 (978-0-14-305885-4(1), PengAudBks) Penguin Grp USA.

Broken Prey. unabr. ed. John Sandford, pseud. Read by Richard Ferrone. 9 cass. (Running Time: 11 hrs.). (Prey Ser.). 2005. 79.75 (978-1-4193-4046-8(8), 98032) Recorded Bks.
Number one best-selling author John Sandford's Prey series consistently garners rave reviews for its breathtaking suspense. Lucas Davenport is on the trail of a gruesome killer. The main suspect, Charlie Pope, was recently released from a mental hospital, where he was locked up with a trio of sadistic murderers. But there are two problems: Charlie hardly seems intelligent enough to be a serial killer - and he has disappeared.

Broken Promise Land. unabr. ed. Marcia Muller. Read by Bernadette Dunne. 8 cass. (Running Time: 12 hrs.). (Sharon McCone Mystery Ser.: No. 16). 1996. 64.00 (978-0-7366-3383-3(9), 4033) Books on Tape.
The allure of the platinum disc & what a young woman won't do to win one. Just ask Trisha Terriss who tried sleeping her way to the top.

Broken Promise Land. unabr. ed. Marcia Muller. Read by Jean Reed-Bahle. (Running Time: 10 hrs.). (Sharon McCone Mystery Ser.: No. 16). 2008. 39.25 (978-1-4233-5278-5(5), 9781423352785, BADLE); 24.95 (978-1-4233-5277-8(7), 9781423352778, BAD); audio compact disk 39.25 (978-1-4233-5276-1(9), 9781423352761, Brinc Audio MP3 Lib); audio compact disk 24.95 (978-1-4233-5275-4(0), 9781423352754, Brilliance MP3) Brilliance Audio.

Broken Rainbows. Catrin Collier. Read by Helen Griffin. 12 cass. (Running Time: 18 hrs.). 2002. 96.95 (978-0-7540-0705-0(7), CAB 2127) AudioGO.

Broken Seal. unabr. collector's ed. Ladislas Farago. Read by Wolfram Kandinsky. 12 cass. (Running Time: 18 hrs.). 1984. 96.00 (978-0-7366-0747-6(1), 1702) Books on Tape.
The whole secret history of Japanese & American code-breaking operations between 1921 & 1941.

Broken Shore. unabr. ed. Peter Temple. Read by Peter Hosking. (Running Time: 36000 sec.). 2007. 29.95 (978-1-4332-0189-9(5)); audio compact disk 29.95 (978-1-4332-0190-5(9)) Blckstn Audio.

Broken Shore. unabr. ed. Peter Temple. (Running Time: 36000 sec.). 2007. 72.95 (978-1-4332-0296-4(4)); audio compact disk 90.00 (978-1-4332-0297-1(2)) Blckstn Audio.

Broken Shore. unabr. ed. Peter Temple. Read by Peter Hosking. (Running Time: 36000 sec.). 2007. audio compact disk 29.95 (978-1-4332-0191-2(7)) Blckstn Audio.

Broken Skin. Stuart Macbride. 2007. 84.95 (978-0-7531-3799-4(2)); audio compact disk 99.95 (978-0-7531-2780-3(6)) Pub: ISIS Audio GBR. Dist(s): Ulverscroft US

Broken Threads. Tessa Barclay. Read by Elizabeth Henry. 10 cass. (Running Time: 12 hrs.). (Sound Ser.). (J). 2001. 84.95 (978-1-84283-001-7(5)) Pub: ISIS Lrg Prnt GBR. Dist(s): Ulverscroft US

Broken Threads. Tessa Barclay. 10 CDs. (Running Time: 12 hrs. 30 mins.). (Soundings (CDs) Ser.). (J). 2005. audio compact disk 89.95 (978-1-84559-074-1(0)) Pub: ISIS Lrg Prnt GBR. Dist(s): Ulverscroft US

Broken Tower see Poetry of Hart Crane

Broken Toy. rev. ed. Thomas Brown et al. 1993. 46.95 (978-1-873942-23-9(0)) Pub: P Chapman GBR. Dist(s): SAGE

Broken Trust. Una mary Parker. Read by Juliet Prague. 12 CDs. (Running Time: 18 hrs.). 2001. audio compact disk 94.95 (108879) Pub: ISIS Audio GBR. Dist(s): Ulverscroft US

Broken Trust. unabr. ed. Una-Mary Parker. Read by Juliet Prague. 10 cass. (Running Time: 13 hrs. 30 mins.). 2000. 84.95 (978-0-7531-0659-4(0), 000303) Pub: ISIS Audio GBR. Dist(s): Ulverscroft US
Mark Driver wants his new wife & baby boy to have all that money can buy. But his four grown-up children from his first marriage have other ideas. When they discover that he has sold the family home & stolen money from their trust funds, tension mounts & it's only a matter of time before one of them does something they'll regret.

Broken Trust: Program from the award winning public radio Series. Interview. Hosted by Fred Goodwin. Comment by John Hockenberry. 1 CD. (Running Time: 1hr). (Infinite Mind Ser.). 2002. audio compact disk 21.95 (978-1-888064-78-0(1), LCM 220) Lichtenstein Creat.
Recent allegations against priests and educators are bringing new attention to the subject of child sexual abuse, but the majority of children who are victimized never tell an adult, much less report the abuse to police. Yet the opportunity to be heard, believed, and helped can be critical in decreasing a victim's risks for profound and lasting problems associated with this abuse. These risks include post traumatic stress disorder, suicidal depression, drug abuse, and the possibility that a victim will grow up to be a victimizer. In the first half of this program we hear from adult survivors of childhood sexual abuse and explore how therapy and art-making can help victims heal.Guests include psychologist Dr. Esther Deblinger, clinical director of the Center for Children's Support at The University of Medicine and Dentistry of New Jersey; filmmaker James Ronald Whitney, the director of the documentary Just, Melvin; and adult survivors of childhood sexual abuse.In the program's second half, we explore what we know about treatment for pedophilia with Nick, who has served time for molesting children and now works with an innovative educational organization called Stop It Now; Fran Henry, the president of Stop It Now; Dr. Carol Ball, a psychologist at New England Forensic Associates;and psychiatrist Dr. John Bradford, director of the forensic psychiatry program at Canada's Royal Ottawa Hospital. Commentary from John Hockenberry concludes the program.

Broken Window. abr. ed. Jeffery Deaver. Read by Dennis Boutsikaris. (Running Time: 6 hrs. 0 mins. 0 sec.). (Lincoln Rhyme Ser.: No. 8). 2010. audio compact disk 14.99 (978-1-4423-0469-7(3)) Pub: S&S Audio. Dist(s): S and S Inc

Broken Window. unabr. ed. Jeffery Deaver. Read by Dennis Boutsikaris. 12 CDs. (Running Time: 14 hrs. 0 mins. 0 sec.). (Lincoln Rhyme Ser.: No. 8). 2008. audio compact disk 49.95 (978-0-7435-7053-4(7)) Pub: S&S Audio. Dist(s): S and S Inc

*__Broken Wings.__ Terri Blackstock. (Running Time: 8 hrs. 29 mins. 0 sec.). (Second Chances Ser.). (ENG.). 2009. 14.99 (978-0-310-30512-5(8)) Zondervan.

Brokenness. 2002. (978-0-940110-34-2(2)); audio compact disk (978-0-940110-35-9(0)) Life Action Publishing.

Brokenness: The Heart God Revives, Vol. 1. Narrated by Nancy Leigh DeMoss. 1 cass. (Running Time: 1 hrs. 1 min.). 1995. 4.00 (978-1-57902-150-4(6), 2995-BRE) Integrtd Res.
Message to move the hearts of Christians.

Broker see Intermediario

Broker. John Grisham. Read by Michael Beck. 10 cds. 2005. audio compact disk 90.00 (978-1-4159-1646-9(2)) Books on Tape.

Broker. John Grisham & Michael Beck. 7 cass. 2005. 72.00 (978-1-4159-1559-2(8)) Books on Tape.

Broker. abr. ed. 2005. 34.99 (978-1-59895-041-0(X)) Find a World.

Broker. abr. ed. John Grisham. Read by Michael Beck. (YA). 2005. 44.99 (978-0-7393-7445-0(1)) Find a World.

Broker. abr. ed. John Grisham. Read by Dennis Boutsikaris. 5 CDs. (Running Time: 6 hrs.). (John Grisham Ser.). (ENG.). 2006. audio compact disk 14.99 (978-0-7393-3402-7(6), Random AudioBks) Pub: Random Audio Pubg. Dist(s): Random

Broker. unabr. ed. John Grisham. Read by Michael Beck. 10 CDs. (Running Time: 11 hrs. 30 mins.). (John Grisham Ser.). (ENG.). 2005. audio compact disk 59.95 (978-0-7393-1647-4(8), Random AudioBks) Pub: Random Audio Pubg. Dist(s): Random

Broker-Dealer Regulation. 9 cass. (Running Time: 12 hrs.). 1999. 345.00 Set; incl. study guide 253p. (MD44) Am Law Inst.
Advanced course offers views presented by leading practitioners, senior SEC staff members, & other officials of governmental & self-regulatory organizations.

Broker Exam Drill Series for the Customs Broker Exam. Excerpts. Created by Boskage Commerce Publications. 3 CDs. (Running Time: 3 hrs). 2003. audio compact disk (978-1-893495-31-9(0)) Boskage.
Three 60-minute drills with questions and answers to help build knowledge of U.S. Customs facts in preparation for the Customs Broker's Exam.

Bronchoplasty Techniques. 2 cass. (Thoracic Surgery Ser.: C85-TH2). 1985. 15.00 (8586) Am Coll Surgeons.

Bronco Buster. Susannah Brin. Narrated by Larry A. McKeever. (Thrillers Ser.). (J). 2001. audio compact disk 14.95 (978-1-58659-325-4(0)) Artesian.

Bronco Buster. unabr. ed. Susannah Brin. Narrated by Larry A. McKeever. 1 cass. (Running Time: 40 min.). (Thrillers Ser.). (J). 2001. 10.95 (978-1-58659-046-8(4), 54121) Artesian.

Bronk: A Selection. unabr. ed. William Bronk. Read by William Bronk. 1 cass. (Running Time: 1 hr.). (Watershed Tapes of Contemporary Poetry). 1979. 12.95 (23614) J Norton Pubs.

Bronte. abr. ed. Emily Brontë et al. Read by Hannah Gordon & Carole Boyd. 8 CDs. (Running Time: 10 hrs.). (ENG.). 2009. audio compact disk 35.95 (978-1-934997-41-3(2)) Pub: CSAWord. Dist(s): PerseuPGW

Bronte Collection: 4 Classic Stories. Charlotte Brontë et al. Read by Carole Boyd et al. (ENG.). 2009. audio compact disk 35.95 (978-1-906147-51-8(5), CSAW) Pub: CSA Telltapes GBR. Dist(s): PerseuPGW

Brontes. unabr. ed. Kathryn White. Read by Tracey Lloyd. 2 cass. (Running Time: 2 hrs. 20 min.). 1999. 24.95 (978-0-7531-0602-0(7), 990516) Pub: ISIS Audio GBR. Dist(s): Ulverscroft US
The Brontes are the world's most famous literary family & their novels are among the best-loved books in the English language. They have been translated into dozens of languages & dramatized on stage, screen & television many times.

Brontosaurus. Angela Shenan. (Angela Shenan Ser.). (J). (ps-6). 1988. bk. 25.95 (SAC 6513-A) Spoken Arts.

Brontosaurus Fun: Prehistoric Rock Sing-a-Longs, Stories, Games & Adventures. 1 cass. 1993. 14.95 (978-1-55569-636-8(8)) Great Am Audio.

Bronx Masquerade. unabr. ed. Nikki Grimes. 3 cass. (Running Time: 3 hrs. 15 mins.). (YA). (gr. 8 up). 2006. 29.75 (978-1-4193-9475-1(4), 98379) Recorded Bks.
Each of the 18 kids in Mr. Ward's inner city classroom has something important to say, but some don't even realize it. Then Mr. Ward begins to have "open mic" poetry slams once a month on Fridays. Young adult listeners will identify with the characters in Bronx Masquerade as they explore questions about life and self-expression.

Bronx Primitive: Portraits in a Childhood. unabr. ed. Kate Simon. Read by Barbara Rosenblat. 4 cass. (Running Time: 6 hrs.). 2001. 39.95 (978-1-893079-08-3(2), JCCAUDIOBOOKS) Jewish Contempry Classics.
A colorful & completely unsentimental revocation of the author's immigrant girlhood.

Bronze Axe. abr. ed. Jeffrey Lord. Read by Lloyd James. 2 vols. 2003. (978-1-58807-774-5(8)) Am Pubng Inc.

Bronze Axe. abr. ed. Jeffrey Lord. Read by Lloyd James. 2 vols. (Richard Blade Adventure Ser.: No. 1). 2003. 18.00 (978-1-58807-356-3(4)) Am Pubng Inc.

Bronze Axe. abr. ed. Jeffrey Lord. Read by Carol Eason. 3 CDs. (Running Time: 3 hrs.). (Richard Blade Adventure Ser.: No. 1). 2004. audio compact disk 25.00 (978-1-58807-492-8(7)) Am Pubng Inc.
British secret agent Richard Blade is propelled into an unknown parallel dimension where he finds himself helping a beautiful princess. While they run for their lives from a savage rival faction, Blade must endure unimaginable trials.

Bronze Bow. Elizabeth George Speare. Read by Mary Woods. (Playaway Children Ser.). (J). 2008. 49.99 (978-1-60640-756-1(2)) Find a World.

Bronze Bow. unabr. ed. Elizabeth George Spear. Read by Mary Woods. (Running Time: 25200 sec.). (J). (gr. 4-7). 2008. audio compact disk 19.95 (978-1-4332-1043-3(6)) Blckstn Audio.

Bronze Bow. unabr. ed. Elizabeth George Speare. Read by Mary Woods. 5 cass. (Running Time: 7 hrs.). 2001. 39.95 (978-0-7861-2081-9(9), 2842) Blckstn Audio.
After witnessing his father's crucifixion by Roman soldiers, Daniel bar Jamin is fired by a single passion: to avenge his father's death by driving the Roman legions from the land of Israel.

Bronze Bow. unabr. ed. Elizabeth George Speare. Read by Mary Woods. 5 cass. (Running Time: 7 hrs.). 2005. 24.95 (978-0-7861-3458-8(5), E2842) Blckstn Audio.

Bronze Bow. unabr. ed. Elizabeth George Speare. Read by Mary Woods. 13 vols. (Running Time: 25200 sec.). (J). (gr. 4-7). 2005. DVD & audio compact disk 29.95 (978-0-7861-8160-5(5), ZM2842); audio compact disk 29.95 (978-0-7861-8035-6(8), ZE2842) Blckstn Audio.

Bronze Bow. unabr. ed. Elizabeth George Speare. 6 CDs. (Running Time: 7 hrs.). 2005. audio compact disk 48.00 (978-0-7861-9714-9(5), 2842) Blckstn Audio.

Bronze Bow. unabr. ed. Elizabeth George Speare. Read by Pete Bradbury. 6 cass. (Running Time: 7 hrs. 45 min.). (YA). (gr. 9-12). 2001. 56.00 Recorded Bks.
Set at the time of Jesus, when the Jews were among many peoples dominated by Roman rule. Eighteen-year-old Daniel has lived for years with a band of Hebrew Zealots who plan small-scale insurgencies against Roman soldiers and foreign traders while awaiting the Messiah. When Daniel's grandmother dies, he returns to his former village to care for his younger sister.

Bronze Horseman. Mednyj Vsadnik. Poems. Alexander Pushkin. Read by Lora Paperno. 1 disc. (Running Time: 23 mins). (RUS.). 1999. audio compact disk 11.95 (978-1-58269-035-3(9)) Lxcon Brdge.
This audio recording has no background music or sound effects - just the pure sound of poetry, in a very personal delivery style.

Bronze Ring. unabr. ed. 1 cass. (Running Time: 20 min.). Dramatization. (Magic Looking Glass Ser.). (J). (gr. 2-6). 1989. 9.95 (978-0-7810-0034-5(3), NIM-CW-128-6-C) NIMCO.
A French folk tale.

Brood of Vipers: Being the Fourth Journal of Sir Roger Shallot Concerning Certain Wicked Conspiracies & Horrible Murders Perpetrated in the Reign of King Henry VIII. unabr. ed. Michael Clynes, pseud. 7 cass. 1998. 76.95 Set. (978-1-85903-164-3(1)) Pub: Magna Story GBR. Dist(s): Ulverscroft US

Brooke. unabr. ed. V. C. Andrews. Read by Laurel Lefkow. 3 cass. (Running Time: 4 hrs. 30 min.). (Orphans Ser.: No. 3). 2001. 34.95 (978-0-7531-0634-1(5), 990901) Pub: ISIS Audio GBR. Dist(s): ISIS Pub
Brooke never imagined a rich couple who looked like movie stars saying, "we'll take her," & whisking her away from the orphanage to be their daughter. The Thompsons seem thrilled to welcome her into their huge house & luxurious life-style. But soon every day is spent preparing her for beauty pageants, instead of playing on the school softball team where her real talents are appreciated. Only when playing can she escape the dreadful feeling that she must be obedient... or risk losing her golden chance for a name, a home & freedom from the terrible secrets of her past.

Brooke Sisters. Perf. by Radio Repertory Company Staff. 2 cass. (Running Time: 2 hrs.). 2001. 19.95 Lodestone Catalog.
Two delightful, slightly wacky little old ladies keep finding themselves bloomers-deep in mystery & murder. Also our heroines become inmates, contestants, linebackers & time-travellers.

Brooke Sisters. unabr. ed. Short Stories. Larry Weiner. Perf. by Radio Repertory Company Staff. 2 cass. (Running Time: 2 hrs.). Dramatization. (C). 1996. 17.95 (978-0-9660392-1-4(1), RRCA001) Pub: Radio Repertory. Dist(s): Penton Overseas
Two lovely, wacky seasoned citizens keep finding themselves bloomers-deep in murder & mystery in this series. Four great stories include: "The Night Club Murder," "The Superbowl Murder," "The Asylum Murders" & "The Beauty Pageant Murders." With sound effects & original orchestral score.

Brookings-Newport. Dan Heller. 1 cass. 1995. 9.95 (978-1-885433-03-9(4)) Takilma East.

Brookland. unabr. ed. Emily Barton. Read by Ruth Ann Phimister. 18 cass. (Running Time: 23 hrs. 15 mins.). 2006. 109.75 (978-1-4193-9646-5(3)); audio compact disk 119.75 (978-1-4193-9648-9(X)) Recorded Bks.
Brooklyn native Emily Barton has received many accolades for her fiction, including a grant from the NEA. Here she tells the story of Prudence Winship, a woman living in late 18th-century New York who has a vision of a great bridge spanning the East River. After inheriting a gin distillery from her father, Prue uses her resources to undertake one of America's greatest public works projects. But many hardships threaten to curtail her efforts, and realizing her dream will not be an easy task.

Brooklyn. unabr. ed. Colm Tóibín. (Running Time: 11 hrs. NaN mins.). 2009. audio compact disk 29.95 (978-1-4332-9190-6(8)) Blckstn Audio.

Brooklyn. unabr. ed. Colm Tóibín. Read by Kirsten Potter. (Running Time: 7.5 hrs. 0 mins.). 2009. 29.95 (978-1-4332-9191-3(6)); 65.95 (978-1-4332-9187-6(8)); audio compact disk 100.00 (978-1-4332-9188-3(6)) Blckstn Audio.

Brooklyn-Breukelen Poems. Leo Vroman. Ed. by Stanley H. Barkan. Tr. by Claire N. White. (Review Dutch Writers Chapbook Ser.). 1989. 10.00 (978-0-89304-179-3(3)) Cross-Cultrl NY.

Brooklyn Bridge. unabr. ed. Karen Hesse. Read by Fred Berman. Illus. by Chris Sheban. 4 CDs. (Running Time: 4 hrs. 30 mins.). (J). (gr. 5-9). 2008. audio compact disk 24.95 (978-1-4272-0546-9(9)) Pub: Macmill Audio. Dist(s): Macmillan

Brooklyn Bridge - Audio Guide: From City to Metropolis. Elizabeth Gaffney. Prod. by CityReads. 1 CD. (Running Time: Approx 45 Min). 2004. audio compact disk 14.95 (978-0-9768312-0-4(1), BB01C) CityReads.
An Entertaining and informative audio guide for New Yorkers and tourists alike. Walk across the Brooklyn Bridge with novelist Elizabeth Gaffney as she recounts the exciting story of the bridge. Opened in 1883, it was for a time the longest suspension bridge in the world. To build it required the invention of new technologies, the risk of injury and death, and most of all courage and drive. Learn about the ingenious wire-spinning machines that formed the cables; the dark underwater world of the caissons; the scandals, from industrial espionage to jumpers; the Roebling family, and discover how the bridge changed New York. An Audio Guide for the Cultured Traveler.

Brooklyn Doesn't Rhyme. unabr. ed. Joan W. Blos. Narrated by Barbara Rosenblat. 2 pieces. (Running Time: 2 hrs.). (gr. 5 up). 1994. 19.00 (978-0-7887-0079-8(0), 94312E7) Recorded Bks.
At the suggestion of her teacher, a young Jewish girl writes stories of her family life in Brooklyn in the early 20th century.

*__Brooklyn Follies.__ unabr. ed. Paul Auster. Read by Paul Auster. (ENG.). 2006. (978-0-06-087827-6(4), Harper Audio); (978-0-06-087828-3(2), Harper Audio) HarperCollins Pubs.

Brooklyn Follies. unabr. ed. Paul Auster. Read by Paul Auster. (Running Time: 28800 sec.). 2006. audio compact disk 39.95 (978-0-06-083878-2(7)) HarperCollins Pubs.

Brooklyn Rose. unabr. ed. Ann Rinaldi. Narrated by Kate Forbes. 3 CDs. (Running Time: 3 hrs. 50 mins.). (YA). 2005. audio compact disk 31.75 (978-1-4193-3852-6(8), C3278); 29.75 (978-1-4193-3579-2(0), 98015) Recorded Bks.
Historical fiction writer Ann Rinaldi has received the ALA Best Book for Young Adults. Brooklyn Rose is loosely based on the life of her own grandmother. Rose Frampton is content with life on her family¿s plantation in South Carolina, but the year 1900 brings many changes for the 15 year-old. She could never imagine that she would marry a Yankee and become the mistress of a New York City estate. Uprooted from the tranquil shores of Saint Helena's Island, she comes to know and love Rene, learns to make her own decisions, and finds an untapped inner strength.

Brooks Robinson: Infielding. Read by Brooks Robinson. 1 cass. (Running Time: 30 min.). 9.95 (978-0-89811-069-2(6), 7120) Lets Talk Assocs.
Brooks Robinson talks about the people & events which influenced his career, & his own approach to his speciality.

Broom of the System. unabr. ed. David Foster Wallace. Read by Robert Petkoff. (Running Time: 17 hrs.). (ENG.). 2010. 24.98 (978-1-60788-389-0(9)); audio compact disk 29.98 (978-1-60788-388-3(0)) Pub: Hachet Audio. Dist(s): HachBkGrp

Brother Anansi & the Cattle Ranch - El Hermano Anansi y el Rancho de Ganado. James De Sauza & Harriet Rohmer. Read by James De Sauza et al. Read by Anna Olivarez et al. Illus. by Stephen Von Mason. 1 cass. (Running Time: 30 min.). (Tales of the Americas Ser.). (SPA & ENG.). (J). (ps-3). 1997. 9.95 (978-0-89239-059-5(X)) Pub: Childrens Book Pr. Dist(s): PerseuPGW
Anansi the spider, traditional trickster of West African & Caribbean folklore, proves once again that cleverness can come in a very small package. When Tiger wins the lottery & buys a cattle ranch, Anansi outwits him & ends up with all the cattle.

Brother Anansi & the Cattle Ranch - El Hermano Anansi y el Rancho de Ganado: Read along Set. Harriet Roehmer. Read by Harriet Rohmer. Ed. by Anna Olivarez. Illus. by Stephen Von Mason. (ENG & SPA.). (YA). (ps-7). 1989. bk. 25.95 (978-0-89239-063-2(8)) Childrens Book Pr.

Brother & Sister. Joanna Trollope. Read by Lindsay Duncan. 8 cass. 69.95 (978-0-7927-3166-5(2), CAB 2654); audio compact disk 79.95 (978-0-7927-3167-2(0), CCD 405) AudioGO.

Brother Cadfael. Ellis Peters, pseud. Perf. by Derek Jacobi & Sean Pertwee. 4 cass. (Running Time: 5 hrs. 20 min.). Dramatization. 1999. 39.80 Enhanced audiotrack. (978-1-56938-264-6(6), AMP-2646) Acorn Inc.
Casting aside his serenity, the monk turns sleuth when trouble arises in 12th century England. With his partner Lord Beringar, he uses his medicinal skills & knowledge of botany to foil treachery & bring justice to Shrewsbury. Includes: "One Corpse Too Many," "Monk's Hood," "The Leper of St. Giles" & "The Sanctuary Sparrow.".

Brother Cadfael's Penance. unabr. ed. Ellis Peters, pseud. Read by Stephen Thorne. 6 cass. (Running Time: 8 hrs. 48 min.). (Chronicles of Brother Cadfael Ser.: Vol. 20). 2002. 29.95 (978-1-57270-282-0(6), Audio Editions) Pub: Audio Partners. Dist(s): PerseuPGW
In the autumn of 1145, Brother Cadfael finds himself in an awkward position. Receiving word that the son he had during the Crusades , before he was a monk is en peril, Cadfael decides to attend a peace conference that might result in the young man's freedom. But to get there, Cadfael must leave the monastery without his abbot's permission.

Brother Cadfael's Penance. unabr. ed. Ellis Peters, pseud. Read by Stephen Thorne. 8 cass. (Running Time: 12 hrs.). (Chronicles of Brother Cadfael Ser.: Bk. 20). 2000. 59.95 (978-0-7451-6652-0(0), CAB 1268) Pub: Chivers Audio Bks GBR. Dist(s): AudioGO
It is 1145, and a council is set up to settle the dispute between two cousins battling for the throne. Brother Cadfael attends, because it may involve a release of prisoners that could include Olivier de Bretagne, Cadfael's son. But the meeting erupts into violence, and a murder occurs. Will Cadfael find his son, and in the meantime solve a murder?.

Brother Cadfael's Penance. unabr. ed. Ellis Peters, pseud. Read by Stephen Thorne. 8 CDs. (Chronicles of Brother Cadfael Ser.: Vol. 20). 2000. audio compact disk 79.95 (978-0-7540-5364-4(4), CCD 055) Pub: Chivers Audio Bks GBR. Dist(s): AudioGO
It is 1145 & Brother Cadfael attends a council set up to settle the dispute between two cousins battling for the throne. But the meeting turns into a heated debate that spills over into violence & murder.

*__Brother Fish.__ Bryce Courtenay. Read by Humphrey Bower. (Running Time: 32 hrs.). 2009. 174.99 (978-1-74214-172-5(2), 9781742141725) Pub: Bolinda Pubng AUS. Dist(s): Bolinda Pub Inc

Brother Fish. unabr. ed. Bryce Courtenay. Read by Humphrey Bower. (Running Time: 115200 sec.). 2005. 168.00 (978-1-74093-641-5(8)); audio compact disk 54.95 (978-1-74093-642-2(6)) Pub: Bolinda Pubng AUS. Dist(s): Bolinda Pub Inc

Brother Fish. unabr. ed. Bryce Courtenay. Read by Humphrey Bower. (Running Time: 32 hrs.). 2008. audio compact disk 123.95 (978-1-74214-004-9(1), 9781742140049) Pub: Bolinda Pubng AUS. Dist(s): Bolinda Pub Inc

Brother for Sale. Perf. by Mary-Kate Olsen & Ashley Olsen. 1 cass., 1 CD. (J). 7.18 (LIGHT 54247); audio compact disk 12.98 CD Jewel box. (LIGHT 54247) NewSound.
Includes: "Peanut Butter," "Brother for Sale," "Gonna Stay in the Bathtub (Till the Soap Disappears)," "Cattle Drive" & more.

Brother for Sale 50 Cents. Perf. by Mary-Kate Olsen & Ashley Olsen. 1 cass. (Running Time: 1 hr.). (Mary-Kate & Ashley Series). (J). 2002. 8.98 (54247-4); audio compact disk 15.98 (978-1-56896-253-5(3), 54247-2) Lightyear Entrtnmnt.
America has watched the Olsen twins grow up from their TV series "Full House" to their current series "So Little Time". The whole family can enjoy this series of titles.

Brother, I'm Dying. unabr. ed. Edwidge Danticat. Read by Robin Miles. 7 cass. (Running Time: 8 hrs.). 2007. 61.75 (978-1-4281-6629-5(7)); audio compact disk 77.75 (978-1-4281-6631-8(9)) Recorded Bks.

Brother, I'm Dying. unabr. ed. Edwidge Danticat. 7 CDs. (Running Time: 28800 sec.). 2007. audio compact disk 34.99 (978-1-4281-6628-8(9)) Recorded Bks.

Brother John, Wake up! Audio CD. Adapted by Benchmark Education Company Staff. Based on a work by Brooke Harris. (Reader's Theater Nursery Rhymes & Songs Ser.). (J). (gr. k-1). 2008. audio compact disk 10.00 (978-1-60437-997-6(9)) Benchmark Educ.

Brother Mine Audio Book. Mike Odell. (ENG.). 2007. audio compact disk 24.95 (978-1-932278-31-6(1)) Pub: Mayhaven Pub. Dist(s): Baker Taylor

Brother, My Brother (from The Civil War) - ShowTrax. Contrib. by Frank Wildhorn. Arranged by Ed Lojeski. 1 CD. (Running Time: 90 mins.). 2000. audio compact disk 19.95 (08621164) H Leonard.
The haunting, timeless story of brother battling brother is the powerful message of this poignant song.

Brother Odd. unabr. ed. Dean Koontz. 8 cass. (Running Time: 12 hrs.). (Odd Thomas Ser.: No. 3). 2006. 72.00 (978-1-4159-3245-2(X)); audio compact disk 76.50 (978-1-4159-3246-9(8)) Pub: Books on Tape. Dist(s): NetLibrary CO

Brother Odd. unabr. ed. Dean Koontz. Read by David Aaron Baker. (Odd Thomas Ser.: No. 3). (YA). 2006. 59.99 (978-0-7393-7447-4(8)) Find a World.

Brother Odd. unabr. ed. Dean Koontz. Read by David Aaron Baker. (Running Time: 32400 sec.). (Odd Thomas Ser.: No. 3). (ENG.). 2008. audio compact disk 19.99 (978-0-7393-6942-5(3), Random AudioBks) Pub: Random Audio Pubg. Dist(s): Random

Brother Ray. Ray Charles & David Ritz. Read by Andrew Barnes. (Running Time: 13 hrs. 30 mins.). 2004. 41.95 (978-1-59912-437-7(8)) Iofy Corp.

Brother Ray: Ray Charles' Own Story. Ray Charles & David Ritz. Read by Andrew Barnes. 9 Tapes. (Running Time: 13 hrs. 30 mins.). 2005. 79.95 (978-0-7861-2948-5(4)); audio compact disk 99.00 (978-0-7861-8094-3(3)) Blckstn Audio.

Brother Ray: Ray Charles' Own Story. unabr. ed. Ray Charles & David Ritz. Read by Andrew L. Barnes. 9 cass. (Running Time: 13 hrs.). 2005. reel tape 29.95 (978-0-7861-2947-8(6)) Blckstn Audio.

Brother Ray: Ray Charles' Own Story. unabr. ed. Ray Charles & David Ritz. Read by Andrew Barnes. 11 CDs. (Running Time: 13 hrs.). 2005. audio compact disk 32.95 (978-0-7861-8095-0(1)) Blckstn Audio.

Brother Ray: Ray Charles' Own Story. unabr. ed. Ray Charles & David Ritz. Read by Andrew Barnes. 1 MP3. (Running Time: 13 hrs.). 2005. audio compact disk 29.95 (978-0-7861-8217-6(2)) Blckstn Audio.

Brother, Sister. Contrib. by Mewithoutyou. Prod. by Brad Wood. 2006. audio compact disk 16.99 (978-5-558-21029-3(X)) Tooth & Nail.

Brother to the Wind. 2004. cass. & flmstrp 30.00 (978-0-89719-572-0(8)) Weston Woods.

Brother to the Wind. (J). 2004. bk. 24.95 (978-1-56008-169-2(4)); 8.95 (978-0-7882-0075-5(5)) Weston Woods.

Brother to the Wind. Mildred Pitts Walter. Narrated by Terry Alexander. Prod. by Morton Schindel. 1 cass. (Running Time: 17 min.). (J). (gr. 4 up). 8.95 (978-0-89719-960-5(X), 313) Weston Woods.
African boy learns to fly with the help of the supernatural powers, Good Snake & the Wind.

Brother Wolf. unabr. ed. Jim Brandenburg. Read by John Maclean. 2 cass. (Running Time: 3 hrs.). Dramatization. 1993. 16.95 (978-0-939643-49-3(9), NrthWrd Bks) TandN Child.
Brandenburg, the pre-eminent wolf photographer, immerses himself deep in the woods of northern Minnesota to live close to wild packs of timber wolves.

Brother Zero: Life of St. John of God. Covelle Newcomb. 6 cass. 24.95 (736) Ignatius Pr.
A man whose vision carried him centuries beyond the time where he did his work.

***Brotherhood.** Jerry B. Jenkins. (ENG.). 2011. 14.98 (978-1-61045-073-7(6), christaudio); audio compact disk 26.98 (978-1-61045-072-0(8), christaudio) christianaud.

Brotherhood of Heroes: The Marines at Peleliu, 1944-the Bloodiest Battle of the Pacific War. unabr. ed. Bill Sloan. Read by Patrick G. Lawlor. 11 CDs. (Running Time: 12 hrs. 0 mins. 0 sec.). (ENG.). 2005. audio compact disk 37.99 (978-1-4001-0150-4(6)); audio compact disk 22.99 (978-1-4001-5150-9(3)); audio compact disk 75.99 (978-1-4001-3150-1(2)) Pub: Tantor Media. Dist(s): IngramPubServ

Brotherhood of the Rose. unabr. ed. David Morrell. (Running Time: 10 hrs.). 2005. 24.95 (978-1-59737-753-9(8), 9781597377539, BAD) Brilliance Audio.

Brotherhood of the Rose. unabr. ed. David Morrell. Read by Multivoice Production Staff. (Running Time: 10 hrs.). 2005. 39.25 (978-1-59737-754-6(6), 9781597377546, BADLE); audio compact disk 29.95 (978-1-59737-749-2(X), 9781597377492, Bril Audio CD Unabri); audio compact disk 24.95 (978-1-59737-751-5(1), 9781597377515, Brilliance MP3); audio compact disk 92.25 (978-1-59737-750-8(3), 9781597377508, BriAudCD Unabrid); audio compact disk 39.25 (978-1-59737-752-2(X), 9781597377522, Brinc Audio MP3 Lib) Brilliance Audio.
They were orphans, Chris and Saul - raised in a Philadelphia school for boys, bonded by friendship, and devoted to a mysterious man called Eliot. He visited them and brought them candy. He treated them like sons. He trained them to be assassins. Now he is trying desperately to have them killed. Spanning the globe, here is an astonishing novel of fierce loyalty and violent betrayal, of murders planned and coolly executed, of revenge bitterly, urgently desired.

Brotherhood of the Wolf: Runelords, Book Two. unabr. ed. David Farland. (Running Time: 23 hrs. 0 mins.). 2009. 44.95 (978-1-4332-2705-9(3)); audio compact disk 130.00 (978-1-4332-2702-8(9)) Blckstn Audio.

Brotherhood of the Wolf Bk. 2: Runelords. unabr. ed. David Farland. (Running Time: 12 hrs. 0 mins.). 2009. audio compact disk 109.95 (978-1-4332-2701-1(0)) Blckstn Audio.

Brotherhood of Valor: The Common Soldiers of the Stonewall Brigade, C. S. A. & the Iron Brigade, U. S. A. Jeffry D. Wert. Read by Dick Estell. 9 cass. (Running Time: 13 hrs. 30 min.). 1999. 72.00 (5078); 72.00 (978-0-7366-4740-3(6)) Books on Tape.

Brotherhood of Warriors. Aaron Cohen. Read by David Drummond. Told to Douglas Century. (Playaway Adult Nonfiction Ser.). 2008. 54.99 (978-1-60640-552-9(7)) Find a World.

Brotherhood of Warriors: Behind Enemy Lines with a Commando in One of the World's Most Elite Counterterrorism Units. unabr. ed. Aaron Cohen & Douglas Century. Narrated by David Drummond. (Running Time: 7 hrs. 0 mins. 0 sec.). (ENG.). 2008. audio compact disk 59.99 (978-1-4001-3701-5(2)) Pub: Tantor Media. Dist(s): IngramPubServ

Brotherhood of Warriors: Behind Enemy Lines with a Commando in One of the World's Most Elite Counterterrorism Units. unabr. ed. Aaron Cohen & Douglas Century. Read by David Drummond. (Running Time: 7 hrs. 0 mins. 0 sec.). (ENG.). 2008. audio compact disk 29.99 (978-1-4001-0701-8(6)) Pub: Tantor Media. Dist(s): IngramPubServ

Brotherhood of Warriors: Behind Enemy Lines with One of the World's Most Elite Counterterrorism Commandos. unabr. ed. Aaron Cohen & Douglas Century. Narrated by David Drummond. (Running Time: 7 hrs. 0 mins. 0 sec.). (ENG.). 2008. audio compact disk 19.99 (978-1-4001-5701-3(3)) Pub: Tantor Media. Dist(s): IngramPubServ

Brotherhoods: The True Story of Two Cops Who Murdered for the Mafia. unabr. ed. Guy Lawson & William Oldham. Read by Dick Hill. 20 CDs. (Running Time: 25 hrs. 30 mins. 0 sec.). (ENG.). 2006. audio compact disk 49.99 (978-1-4001-0352-2(5)); audio compact disk 99.99 (978-1-4001-3352-9(1)); audio compact disk 39.99 (978-1-4001-5352-7(2)) Pub: Tantor Media. Dist(s): IngramPubServ

***Brotherly Love.** abr. ed. Pete Dexter. Read by Chris Sarandon. (ENG.). 2007. (978-0-06-128733-6(4), Harper Audio); (978-0-06-128734-3(2), Harper Audio) HarperCollins Pubs.

***Brotherly Love.** unabr. ed. Catherine Marshall. Adapted by C. Archer. Narrated by Jaimee Draper. (Catherine Marshall's Christy Ser.). (ENG.). 2010. 7.00 (978-1-60814-711-3(8), SpringWater) Oasis Audio.

Brothers. unabr. ed. Da Chen. 12 CDs. (Running Time: 15 hrs.). 2006. audio compact disk 95.20 (978-1-4159-3389-3(8)) Pub: Books on Tape. Dist(s): NetLibrary CO
At the height of China's Cultural Revolution a powerful general fathered two sons. Tan was born to the general's wife and into a life of comfort and luxury. His half brother, Shento, was born to the general's mistress, who threw herself off a cliff in the mountains of Balan only moments after delivering her child. Growing up, each remained ignorant of the other's existence. In Beijing, Tan enjoyed the best schools, the finest clothes, and the prettiest girls. Shento was raised on the mountainside by an old healer and his wife until their deaths landed him in an orphanage, where he was always hungry, alone, and frightened. Though on divergent roads, each brother is driven by a passionate desire - one to glorify his father, the other to seek revenge against him.

Brothers & Keepers. 1985. (5081) Am Audio Prose.

Brothers & Sisters. Read by Christine Downing. 1 cass. (Running Time: 90 min.). 1982. 10.95 (978-0-7822-0058-4(3), 116) C G Jung IL.
A discussion of the varied representations of brotherly & sisterly relationships provided in Greek mythology.

Brothers & Sisters. unabr. ed. Bebe Moore Campbell. Read by Maxine Robinson. 14 cass. (Running Time: 21 hrs.). 1996. 112.00 (978-0-7366-3202-7(6), 3866) Books on Tape.
The L.A. riots made Esther Jackson, a bank executive & an African-American, think long & hard about race & fairness. But she has no complaints. She's done well & the bank just appointed a black man as senior vice president. It's heartening, until the new VP starts harassing a white employee, her good friend. Should she be loyal to friendship or race? Her choice gets muddier when internal looting creates suspicions along racial lines.

***Brothers Ashkenazi.** unabr. ed. I. J. Singer. (Running Time: 15 hrs. 30 mins.). 2010. 85.95 (978-1-4417-6390-7(2)); audio compact disk 118.00 (978-1-4417-6391-4(0)) Blckstn Audio.

***Brothers Ashkenazi: A Modern Classic.** unabr. ed. I. J. Singer. (Running Time: 15 hrs. 30 mins.). 2010. 29.95 (978-1-4417-6393-8(7)); audio compact disk 32.95 (978-1-4417-6392-1(9)) Blckstn Audio.

Brothers Bulger: How They Terrorized & Corrupted Boston for a Quarter Century. unabr. ed. Howie Carr. Narrated by Michael Prichard. 10 CDs. (Running Time: 12 hrs. 30 mins. 0 sec.). (ENG.). 2006. audio compact disk 34.99 (978-1-4001-0188-7(3)); audio compact disk 22.99 (978-1-4001-5188-2(0)); audio compact disk 69.99 (978-1-4001-3188-4(X)) Pub: Tantor Media. Dist(s): IngramPubServ

Brothers in Arms. unabr. ed. Lois McMaster Bujold. Read by Grover Gardner. (Running Time: 36000 sec.). (Vorkosigan Ser.). 2007. 59.95 (978-0-7861-4892-9(6)); audio compact disk 63.00 (978-0-7861-5988-8(X)); audio compact disk 29.95 (978-0-7861-7108-8(1)) Blckstn Audio.

Brothers in Arms. unabr. ed. Lois McMaster Bujold. Perf. by Michael Hanson & Carol Cowan. 1 CD (MP3). (Running Time: 10 hrs.). (Vorkosigan Ser.). 1999. audio compact disk 24.95 (978-1-885585-10-3(1)) Readers Chair.
The daring interspace rescue of an entire Cetagandan POW camp by the Dendarii mercenaries made for some deadly enemies. Having finally outrun the infuriated Cetagandans, Admiral Naismith (a.k.a. Lord Miles Vorkosigan) & the Dendarii arrive on Earth for battle shuttle repair & a well-deserved rest.

Brothers in Arms: The Kennedys, the Castros, & the Politics of Murder. unabr. ed. Gus Russo & Stephen Molton. Narrated by Paul Boehmer. 2 MP3-CDs. (Running Time: 24 hrs. 0 mins. 0 sec.). (ENG.). 2009. 39.99 (978-1-4001-5996-3(2)); audio compact disk 109.99 (978-1-4001-3996-5(1)); audio compact disk 54.99 (978-1-4001-0996-8(5)) Pub: Tantor Media. Dist(s): IngramPubServ

Brothers in Battle, Best of Friends: Two WWII Paratroopers from the Original Band of Brothers Tell Their Story. unabr. ed. William 'Wild Bill' Guarnere et al. Read by Dick Hill. (YA). 2008. 59.99 (978-1-60252-955-7(8)) Find a World.

Brothers in Battle, Best of Friends: Two WWII Paratroopers from the Original Band of Brothers Tell Their Story. unabr. ed. William Guarnere et al. Frwd. by Tom Hanks. Narrated by Dick Hill. 8 CDs. (Running Time: 10 hrs. 30 mins. 0 sec.). (ENG.). 2007. audio compact disk 69.99 (978-1-4001-3532-5(X)) Pub: Tantor Media. Dist(s): IngramPubServ

Brothers in Battle, Best of Friends: Two WWII Paratroopers from the Original Band of Brothers Tell Their Story. unabr. ed. William Guarnere et al. Narrated by Dick Hill. 8 CDs. (Running Time: 10 hrs. 30 mins. 0 sec.). (ENG.). 2007. audio compact disk 34.99 (978-1-4001-0532-8(3)) Pub: Tantor Media. Dist(s): IngramPubServ

Brothers in Battle, Best of Friends: Two WWII Paratroopers from the Original Band of Brothers Tell Their Story. unabr. ed. William Guarnere et al. Narrated by Dick Hill. Frwd. by Tom Hanks. 1 MP3-CD. (Running Time: 10 hrs. 30 mins. 0 sec.). (ENG.). 2007. audio compact disk 24.99 (978-1-4001-5532-3(0)) Pub: Tantor Media. Dist(s): IngramPubServ

Brothers in War. Michael Walsh. 2008. 94.95 (978-1-84559-629-3(3)); audio compact disk 104.95 (978-1-84559-851-8(2)) Pub: Soundings Ltd GBR. Dist(s): Ulverscroft US

Brother's Journey: Surviving a Childhood of Abuse. abr. ed. Richard B. Pelzer. Read by Joshua Gates. (ENG.). 2005. 14.98 (978-1-59483-133-1(5)) Pub: Hachet Audio. Dist(s): HachBkGrp

Brother's Journey: Surviving a Childhood of Abuse. abr. ed. Richard B. Pelzer. Read by Joshua Gates. Contrib. by Digby Diehl. (Running Time: 3 hrs. 30 mins.). (ENG.). 2009. 35.98 (978-1-60024-926-6(4)) Pub: Hachet Audio. Dist(s): HachBkGrp

Brothers K. unabr. ed. David James Duncan. Read by Robertson Dean. (Running Time: 100800 sec.). 2008. audio compact disk & audio compact disk 44.95 (978-1-4332-2601-4(4)); audio compact disk & audio compact disk 130.00 (978-1-4332-2598-7(0)) Blckstn Audio.

Brothers K, Pt. 1. unabr. ed. David James Duncan. Read by Robertson Dean. (Running Time: 55800 sec.). 2008. 109.95 (978-1-4332-2597-0(2)) Blckstn Audio.

Brothers Karamazov see Los Hermanos Karamazov

Brothers Karamazov. Fyodor Dostoyevsky. Read by Tim Pigott-Smith. (Running Time: 9 hrs. 30 mins.). 2004. 49.95 (978-1-60083-689-3(5)) Iofy Corp.

Brothers Karamazov. Fyodor Dostoyevsky. Read by Daniel Quintero. (Running Time: 3 hrs.). 2005. 16.95 (978-1-60083-279-6(2), Audiofy Corp) Iofy Corp.

Brothers Karamazov. Fyodor Dostoyevsky. Read by Walter Covell. 28 cass. (Running Time: 41 hrs.). 1989. 120.00 incl. album. (C-162) Jimcin Record.
Dostoevsky's masterpiece.

Brothers Karamazov. Fyodor Dostoyevsky. Read by Tim Pigott-Smith. 8 CDs. (Running Time: 9 hrs. 30 mins.). 2004. audio compact disk 54.98 (978-962-634-306-7(0)) Naxos.

Brothers Karamazov. Fyodor Dostoyevsky & Anthony Quayle. 2004. audio compact disk 11.99 (978-1-57050-034-3(7)) Multilingua.

Brothers Karamazov. abr. ed. Fyodor Dostoyevsky. Read by Anthony Quayle. 2 cass. (Running Time: 3 hrs.). 2000. 7.95 (978-1-57815-115-8(5), 1077, Media Bks Audio) Media Bks NJ.
Two brothers come under scrutiny for their heinous acts.

***Brothers Karamazov.** abr. ed. Fyodor Dostoyevsky. Narrated by Simon Vance. (ENG.). 2005. 19.98 (978-1-59644-077-7(5), Hovel Audio) christianaud.

Brothers Karamazov. abr. ed. Fyodor Dostoyevsky. Narrated by Simon Vance. 2 MP3CDs. (Running Time: 19 hrs. 15 mins. 0 sec.). (ENG.). 2005. lp 29.98 (978-1-59644-078-4(3), Hovel Audio) christianaud.
Dostoyevsky's crowning life work, The Brothers Karamazov, stands among the best novels in world literature. The book probes the possible roles of four brothers in the unresolved murder of their father, Fyodor Karamazov. At the same time, it carefully explores the personalities and inclinations of the brothers themselves. Their psyches together represent the full spectrum of human nature, the continuum of faith and doubt. Ultimately, this novel seeks to understand the real meaning of faith and existence and includes much beneficial philosophical and spiritual discussion that moves the reader towards faith. An incredibly enjoyable and edifying story!.

Brothers Karamazov. abr. ed. Fyodor Dostoyevsky. Abr. by Thomas Beyer. 16 CDs. (Running Time: 19 hrs. 15 mins. 0 sec.). (ENG.). 2005. audio compact disk 39.98 (978-1-59644-079-1(1), Hovel Audio) christianaud.

Brothers Karamazov. unabr. ed. Fyodor Dostoyevsky. Read by Frederick Davidson. 27 CDs. (Running Time: 126000 sec.). 2008. audio compact disk & audio compact disk 44.95 (978-1-4332-1384-7(2)) Blckstn Audio.

Brothers Karamazov. unabr. ed. Fyodor Dostoyevsky. Read by Frederick Davidson. (YA). 2008. 159.99 (978-1-60514-714-7(1)) Find a World.

Brothers Karamazov, Pt. 1. unabr. ed. Fyodor Dostoyevsky. Read by Frederick Davidson. 4 MP3-CDs. (Running Time: 36 hrs. 30 mins.). 2002. 54.95 (978-0-7861-9252-6(6), 2934A,B); 85.95 (978-0-7861-2183-0(1), 2934A,B) Blckstn Audio.
Tells the stirring tale of four brothers: the pleasure-seeking, impatient Dmitri; the brilliant and morose Ivan; the gentle, loving, and honest Alyosha; and the illegitimate Smerdyakov, shy, silent, and cruel. They are behind the murder of one of literature's most despicable characters: their father.

Brothers Karamazov, Pt. 1. unabr. ed. Fyodor Dostoyevsky. Read by Frederick Davidson. Tr. by Constance Garnett. 17 CDs. (Running Time: 79200 sec.). 2008. audio compact disk & audio compact disk 110.00 (978-1-4332-1383-0(4)) Blckstn Audio.

Brothers Karamazov, Pt. 2. unabr. ed. Fyodor Dostoyevsky. Read by Frederick Davidson. 12 cass. (Running Time: 36 hrs. 30 mins.). 2002. 83.95 (978-0-7861-2186-1(6), 2934A,B) Blckstn Audio.

Brothers Karamazov, Pt. 2. unabr. ed. Fyodor Dostoyevsky. Read by Frederick Davidson. Tr. by Constance Garnett. 17 CDs. (Running Time: 46800 sec.). 2008. audio compact disk & audio compact disk 110.00 (978-1-4332-0781-5(8)) Blckstn Audio.

Brothers Karamazov, Pt. C. unabr. collector's ed. Fyodor Dostoyevsky. Read by Walter Covell. 9 cass. (Running Time: 13 hrs. 30 min.). (Jimcin Recording Ser.). 1986. 72.00 (978-0-7366-3925-5(X), 9161C) Books on Tape.
A story of four brothers - Dmitri, pleasure-seeking, impatient, unruly; Ivan, brilliant & morose; Alyosha, gentle, loving, honest & the illegitimate Smerdyakov, sly, silent, cruel. These brothers play a part in their father's murder.

Brothers Karamazov, Pt. A. unabr. collector's ed. Fyodor Dostoyevsky. Read by Walter Covell. 10 cass. (Running Time: 15 hrs.). (Jimcin Recording Ser.). 1986. 80.00 (978-0-7366-3923-1(3), 9161A) Books on Tape.

Brothers Karamazov, Pt. B. unabr. collector's ed. Fyodor Dostoyevsky. Read by Walter Covell. 9 cass. (Running Time: 13 hrs. 30 min.). (Jimcin Recording Ser.). 1986. 72.00 (978-0-7366-3924-8(1), 9161B) Books on Tape.

Brothers Karamazov: The Idiot. unabr. ed. Fyodor Dostoyevsky. Perf. by Edward Asner et al. Contrib. by David Fishelson. 3 cass. (Running Time: 2 hrs. 20 mins.). 1994. 27.95 (978-1-58081-050-0(0), TPT46) L A Theatre.

Brothers Martin. Contrib. by Brothers Martin, The. 2007. audio compact disk 16.99 (978-5-558-00785-5(0)) Tooth & Nail.

***Brothers of Baker Street.** unabr. ed. Michael Robertson. Read by To be announced. (Running Time: 7 hrs. NaN mins.). (Baker Street Mysteries Ser.). (ENG.). 2011. 29.95 (978-1-4417-8165-9(X)) Blckstn Audio.

***Brothers of Baker Street.** unabr. ed. Michael Robertson. Read by To be Announced. (Running Time: 7 hrs. NaN mins.). (Baker Street Mysteries Ser.). (ENG.). 2011. 44.95 (978-1-4417-8162-8(5)) Blckstn Audio.

***Brothers of Baker Street.** unabr. ed. Michael Robertson. Read by To be announced. (Running Time: 7 hrs. NaN mins.). (Baker Street Mysteries Ser.). 2011. audio compact disk 24.95 (978-1-4417-8164-2(1)) Blckstn Audio.

***Brothers of Baker Street.** unabr. ed. Michael Robertson. Read by To be Announced. (Running Time: 7 hrs. NaN mins.). (Baker Street Mysteries Ser.). (ENG.). 2011. audio compact disk 69.00 (978-1-4417-8163-5(3)) Blckstn Audio.

Brothers of the Head. Poems. Ben Winch & Tim Sinclair. 1 CD. (Running Time: 40 mins). Dramatization. 2004. audio compact disk 19.95 (978-0-9752077-1-0(7)) Cottage AUS.

Brothers Schlemiel from Birth to Bar Mitzvah. Short Stories. Mark Binder. (Running Time: 60 mins). 2000. audio compact disk 14.95 (978-0-9702642-9-9(1), Chelm Tales) Light Pubns.

Brought in Dead. abr. ed. Jack Higgins. Perf. by Patrick Macnee. 4 cass. (Running Time: 6 hrs.). 2004. 25.00 (978-1-59007-070-3(4)) Pub: New Millenn Enter. Dist(s): PerseuPGW

***Brought in Dead.** unabr. ed. Jack Higgins. Read by Michael Page. (Running Time: 5 hrs.). (Nick Miller Ser.). 2010. 24.99 (978-1-4418-4453-8(8), 9781441844538, Brilliance MP3); 39.97 (978-1-4418-4454-5(6), 9781441844545, Brinc Audio MP3 Lib); 24.99 (978-1-4418-4455-2(4), 9781441844552, BAD); 39.97 (978-1-4418-4456-9(2), 9781441844569, BADLE); audio compact disk 29.99 (978-1-4418-4451-4(1), 9781441844514, Bril Audio CD Unabri); audio compact disk 87.97 (978-1-4418-4452-1(X), 9781441844521, BriAudCD Unabrid) Brilliance Audio.

Brought to Book. unabr. ed. Anthea Fraser. Read by Jacqueline Tong. 8 cass. (Running Time: 8.5 hrs.). 2004. 69.95 (978-0-7540-8449-5(3)) AudioGO.

Brow Beater. 1 CD. 1999. audio compact disk 16.98 (KMGD 9469) Provident Mus Dist.

Brow of the Gallowgate, Set. unabr. ed. Doris Davidson. Read by Pamela Donald. 11 cass. (Running Time: 14 hrs. 35 min.). 1999. 103.95 (978-1-85903-279-4(6)) Pub: Magna Story GBR. Dist(s): Ulverscroft US
Albert Ogilvie & his wife Bathie finally obtain the shop they have dreamed of for years, & as their babies are born, Albert employs three sisters, one after another, as nursemaids. Mary & Jeannie Wyness are more than satisfactory, but Bella, the youngest, is an impertinent, voluptuous girl who causes distress & is eventually dismissed. As the years go by, some of the family emigrate to New Zealand & it is there that Bella Wyness, her resentment of the family grown to black hatred, will wreak her terrible revenge.

Browbeats: Wither Wing. 1 CD. 1999. audio compact disk 16.98 (KMGD8644) Provident Mus Dist.

Brown & Beige. Ed. by Robert A. Monroe. 1 cass. (Running Time: 30 min.). (Meta Music Ser.). 1986. 12.95 (978-1-56102-203-8(9)) Inter Indus.
Words ordinarily used to describe shades of a color in a painting or cloth, reflective rather than radiant. Here, they are musical shades that attempt to develop radiant color in a mental mode behind closed eyes.

Brown Bear & Friends. unabr. ed. Bill Martin, Jr. & Eric Carle. Read by Gwyneth Paltrow. 1 CD. (Running Time: 1 hr. 0 mins. 0 sec.). (ENG.). (J). (ps-k). 2008. audio compact disk 14.95 (978-1-4272-0324-3(5)) Pub: Macmill Audio. Dist(s): Macmillan

Brown Cow Farm. 2004. 8.95 (978-1-56008-852-3(4)); cass. & flmstrp 30.00 (978-0-89719-662-8(7)) Weston Woods.

Brown Girl, Brownstones. Paule Marshall. Read by Paule Marshall. 1 cass. (Running Time: 55 min.). 13.95 (978-1-55644-115-8(0), 4131) Am Audio Prose.
Paule Marshall reads parts of her most recent novel & also from one of her earlier novels.

Brown Girl in the Ring. 1 CD. (Running Time: 40 min.). (J). (gr. k-6). 2001. audio compact disk 15.98 (978-1-56628-270-3(5)); 9.98 (978-1-56628-271-0(3), 74283) MFLP CA.
From the hills of Ireland to the island of Jamaica, from South Africa to Mexico and points beyond, here is a sampling of world music for the entire family. A blend of musical styles in 13 songs.

Brown Girl in the Ring. unabr. ed. Nalo Hopkinson. Narrated by Peter Jay Fernandez. 6 cass. (Running Time: 8 hrs.). 2001. 52.00 (978-0-7887-5228-5(6), F0027E7) Recorded Bks.
When the wealthy flee the city & leave it to crumble, those left behind turn to the old ways, including farming & barter.

Brown Hand see Tales of the Supernatural

Brown Honey in Broomwheat Tea. abr. ed. Joyce Carol Thomas. Narrated by Ruby Dee. 1 cass. (Running Time: 15 min.). 1997. pap. bk. 16.90 (978-0-8045-6839-5(1), 6839) Spoken Arts.
In this joyous and unusually moving collection of poems, African-American identity is explored through delicately interwoven images.

Brown-Nosing 101. 2006. audio compact disk (978-0-9758756-4-3(7)) Enlighten Internl.

Brown-Nosing 201. 2007. audio compact disk (978-0-9758756-9-8(8)) Enlighten Internl.

Brown of Calaveras see Luck of Roaring Camp & Other Stories

Brown Water, Black Berets. unabr. collector's ed. Thomas J. Cutler. Read by Wolfram Kandinsky. 10 cass. (Running Time: 15 hrs.). 1990. 80.00 (978-0-7366-1704-8(3), 2548) Books on Tape.
One significant aspect of America's involvement in Vietnam, the U. S. Navy's brown-water force, has received little attention. Often using converted pleasure boats & aging landing craft to partrol the narrow rivers & shallow coastal waters of South Vietnam, the men of this unorthodox navy played a vital role in the war effort. Thomas Cutler is both an historian teaching at the Naval Academy & a naval officer who served in Vietnam. He puts the reader in the midst of battle to convey the terror of nocturnal firefights. He goes into the camps to witness life in the tropics & the sudden perils of guerrilla warfare.

Brownie McGhee & Sonny Terry Sing. Perf. by Brownie McGhee & Sonny Terry. Anno. by Charles E. Smith. 1 cass. 1990. (0-9307-400110-9307-40011-2-7); audio compact disk (0-9307-40011-2-7) Smithsonian Folkways.
Tracks include "Dark Road," "John Henry," "Better Day" & "Can't Help Myself".

Brownies, Their Book, Set. Palmer Cox. Read by Flo Gibson. 2 cass. (Running Time: 2 hrs.). (J). 1995. 14.95 (978-1-55685-394-4(7)) Audio Bk Con.
The Brownies romp in rhyme in school, on bicycles, at lawn tennis, ballooning, canoeing, at baseball, in a circus, on the Fourth of July & have many other adventures.

Brownie's Vigil at Smith Mine. unab. ed. Wayne H. Freeman. Read by Jim Davis et al. 2 CDs. Dramatization. 1999. pap. bk. 19.95 set. (978-1-883466-00-8(8)) W Freeman & Assocs.
Audio Award Winner-1999 Fictionalized drama based upon a real event - the Smith Coal Mine Disaster of February 27, 1943.

Browning As a Painter. (23292-A) J Norton Pubs.

Brownings. 1 cass. 10.00 Esstee Audios.

Browning's Last Duchess. unabr. ed. Poems. Robert Browning. Perf. by James Mason. 1 cass. Incl. Childe Roland to the Dark Tower Came. (SWC 1201); Home-Thoughts from Abroad. (SWC 1201); How They Brought the Good News from Ghent to Aix. (SWC 1201); Lost Leader. (SWC 1201); Memorabilia. (SWC 1201); Pippa Passes. (SWC 1201); Prospice. (SWC 1201); Rabbi Ben Ezra. (SWC 1201); Soliloquy of the Spanish Cloister. (SWC 1201); 1970. 12.95 (978-0-694-50152-6(2), SWC 1201) HarperCollins Pubs.

Brownstone Theatre: Cyrano De Bergerac & The Prisoner of Zenda. unabr. ed. Perf. by Jackson Beck. 1 cass. (Running Time: 1 hr.). 2001. 6.98 (1617) Radio Spirits.

Brownsville Worship, Vol. 1. 1 cass. 1996. 10.99 (978-0-7684-0013-7(9)); audio compact disk 15.99 CD. (978-0-7684-0012-0(0)) Destiny Image Pubs.

Brownsville Worship, Vol. 2. 1 cass. 1996. 10.00 (978-0-7684-0015-1(5)); audio compact disk 15.99 CD. (978-0-7684-0014-4(7)) Destiny Image Pubs.

Bruach Blend. unabr. ed. Lillian Beckwith. Read by Hannah Gordon. 4 cass. (Running Time: 6 hrs.). 2000. 39.95 (978-0-7540-0460-8(0), CAB 1883) Pub: Chivers Audio Bks GBR. Dist(s): AudioGO
What can take the fire out of a fever & the ache out of loneliness? The answer according to Tealaich is whiskey! When he suggests to Lillian that the Islanders should have their own blend, Lillian can see his logic. Here is a pleasurable glimpse of the way the Islanders, with irreverent practicality, manage on the island of Bruach.

Bruach na Carraige Baine. Contrib. by Diarmuid O. Suilleabhain. (ENG.). 1995. 13.95 (978-0-8023-7115-7(9)); audio compact disk 20.95 (978-0-8023-8115-6(4)) Pub: Clo Iar-Chonnachta IRL. Dist(s): Dufour

Bruce. Narrated by Bobbie Frohman. Prod. by Alcazar AudioWorks. Engineer Scott Weiser. Music by David Thorn. Bedford. Albert Payson Terhune. (ENG.). (YA). 2009. audio compact disk 21.95 (978-0-9821853-7-7(5)) Alcazar AudioWorks.

Bruce: The Unauthorized Biography of Bruce Springsteen. Keith Rodway. (Maximum Ser.). (ENG., 2003. audio compact disk 14.95 (978-1-84240-199-6(8)) Pub: Chrome Dreams GBR. Dist(s): IPG Chicago

Bruce Coville's Book of Monsters: Tales to Give You the Creeps. unabr. ed. Bruce Coville. Read by Bruce Coville. 2 cass. (Running Time: 3 hrs. 24 mins.). Dramatization. (J). (gr. 3-6). 1996. pap. bk. 23.00 Incl. guide. (978-0-8072-7626-6(X), YA903SP, Listening Lib) Random Audio Pubg.
A monster-lover's dream anthology featuring 13 deliciously frightful tales by such popular children's authors as Bruce Coville, Jane Yolen, & Laura Simms.

Bruce Coville's Book of Monsters: Tales to Give You the Creeps. unabr. ed. Bruce Coville et al. Read by Bruce Coville. 2 cass. (Running Time: 2 hrs.). (J). 1997. 23.00 (LL 0083, Chivers Child Audio) AudioGO.

Bruce Cutler. unabr. ed. Bruce Cutler. Read by Bruce Cutler. 1 cass. (Running Time: 29 min.). 1986. 10.00 New Letters.
One of a weekly half-hour radio program with authors presenting their own works.

Bruce Di Marsico Presents the Option Method. Speeches. Created by Bruce M. Di Marsico. 1 cassette. (Running Time: 35 minutes). 2001. 10.00 (978-0-9704795-1-8(4)) White Raven.
Lecture by the author.

Bruce Goddard: Live & Kickin' Bruce Goddard. (ENG.). 2007. 13.00i (978-0-9785562-1-1(6)) Socio Pub.

Bruce Weigl. unabr. ed. Bruce Weigl. Read by Bruce Weigl. 1 cass. (Running Time: 29 min.). 1988. 10.00 New Letters.
Weigl reads Vietnam poems from Song of Napalm & is interviewed.

Bruce Williams: An Insider's Report: Choosing a College. Read by Bruce Williams. 1 cass. (Running Time: 60 min.). 1989. 7.95 Bonneville Media.

Bruce Williams: An Insider's Report: Landing a Job. Read by Bruce Williams. 1 cass. (Running Time: 60 min.). 1989. 7.95 Bonneville Media.

Bruce Williams One Hour Crash Course in Getting the Job. Bruce Williams & Dennis F. Regan. Read by Bruce Williams & Dennis F. Regan. 1 cass. (Running Time: 1 hr. 06 min.). (Audio Bks.). 1993. 12.95 (978-1-882991-02-0(8)) Mainst Pubs.
Practical advice on finding & getting the right job for you or changing careers. Narrated by Dennis Regan with practical advice from Bruce Williams - America's No. 1 Radio Talk Show Host - & job & career professionals.

Bruch - Violin Concerto No. 1 in G Minor, Op. 25. Composed by Max Bruch. 2006. pap. bk. 29.98 (978-1-59615-097-3(1), 1596150971) Pub: Music Minus. Dist(s): H Leonard

Brugada Syndrome - A Bibliography & Dictionary for Physicians, Patients, & Genome Researchers. Compiled by Icon Group International, Inc. Staff. 2007. ring bd. 28.95 (978-0-497-11342-1(2)) Icon Grp.

Bruges-la-Morte. unabr. ed. Georges Rodenbach. Read by Denis Wetterwald. (YA). 2007. 69.99 (978-2-35569-039-6(1)) Find a World.

Bruja de Portobello. Paulo Coelho. (SPA.). 2009. 59.99 (978-1-61545-565-2(5)) Find a World.

Bruja de Portobello. abr. ed. Paulo Coelho. 5 cds. (Running Time: 18000 sec.). (SPA.). 2007. audio compact disk 24.95 (978-1-933499-56-7(7)) Fonolibro Inc.

Brunelleschi's Dome. Ross King. Read by Richard Matthews. 2001. audio compact disk 40.00 (978-0-7366-8299-2(6)) Books on Tape.

Brunelleschi's Dome: How a Renaissance Genius Reinvented Architecture. Ross King. 2001. 32.00 (978-0-7366-7180-4(3)) Books on Tape.

Bruno Bettelheim: On Learning to Read. Interview with Bruno Bettelheim. 1 cass. (Running Time: 30 min.). 9.95 (D0300B090, HarperThor) HarpC GBR.

Bruno Munari's Abc. 2004. 8.95 (978-1-56008-853-0(2)); cass. & flmstrp 30.00 (978-0-89719-663-5(5)) Weston Woods.

Bruno Munari's Abc; See & Say; Picture Has a Special Look, A; Wind on a Flea. 2004. cass. & flmstrp (978-0-89719-727-4(5)) Weston Woods.

Bruno Munari's Abc; See & Say; Picture Has a Special Look, A; Wing on a Flea. 2004. (978-0-89719-819-6(0)) Weston Woods.

Bruno Munari's Zoo. 2004. cass. & flmstrp 30.00 (978-0-89719-664-2(3)) Weston Woods.

Bruno Munari's Zoo; It Looked Like Spilt Milk; Sleepy Book; Hole Is to Dig, A; Paint All Kinds of Pictures. 2004. (978-0-89719-822-6(0)); cass. & flmstrp (978-0-89719-730-4(5)) Weston Woods.

Bruno Walter & Hans Pfitzner: Sonatas for Violin & Piano. Bruno Walter et al. 1 cass., 1 CD. 1997. on CD. (VA1A 1155) VAI Audio.
World premiere recording of Bruno Walter's Sonata for Piano & Violin in A major (1910); also premiere compact disc release of Hans Pfitzner's Sonata for Violin & Piano in E minor (1918).

Brunswick Gardens. Anne Perry. Read by David McCallum. 2 cass. (Running Time: 180 min.). (Thomas Pitt Ser.). 2001. 9.99 (978-0-375-41673-6(0), Random AudioBks) Random Audio Pubg.

Brush up Your Shorthand. unabr. ed. Audio-Forum Staff et al. 2 cass. (Running Time: 90 min.). 1989. bk. 24.95 Set. (978-0-88432-263-4(7), S17070) J Norton Pubs.
Provides timed dictations for Gregg shorthand.

Brushback. unabr. collector's ed. K. C. Constantine. Read by Lloyd James. 8 cass. (Running Time: 12 hrs.). (Mario Balzic Ser.). 1998. 64.00 (978-0-7366-4216-3(1), 4714) Books on Tape.
In the rust-belt town of Rocksburg, Pennsylvania, Detective Sergeant Rugs Carlucci, the acting police chief, has a murder on his hands.

Brushfire. abr. ed. Louis Tridico. Abr. by Louis Tridico. Read by Carol Eason. 2 cass. (Running Time: 180 mins.). (Delta Code Ser.: No. 1). 2003. 18.00 (978-1-58807-369-3(6)) Am Pubng Inc.
Doug Malone is a former Special Forces officer with friends in strange places - from a former U.S. Senator to the owner of a tourist business in Mexico and a couple of aging DEA helicopter pilots in Peru. When South American narcoterrorists destroy a U.S. lab doing government biological research, one scientist survives by chance and flees with the last samples of the results of the research - bacteria that might just win a major battle in the war on illegal drugs. The corporation that owns the lab comes to Malone's industrial security company in Dallas, "High Ground" - specialists in hostage negotiations and recovery - to rescue the scientist and secure the bugs. But the scientist has other ideas, and Malone helps her take the war on drugs to the enemy's home turf in the face of the cartels' private armies - with a little help from his friends.

Brushfire. abr. ed. Louis Tridico. Abr. by Louis Tridico. Read by Carol Eason. 3 CDs. (Running Time: 3 hrs.). (Delta Code Ser.: No. 1). 2004. audio compact disk 25.00 (978-1-58807-320-4(3)) Am Pubng Inc.

Brushfire: Delta Code #1. Louis Tridico. Read by Charlie O'Dowd. 2 cass. (Running Time: 180 mins.). No. 1. 2003. (978-1-58807-637-3(7)) Am Pubng Inc.

***Brutal.** unabr. ed. Michael Harmon. Read by Kim Mai Guest. 5 CDs. (Running Time: 6 hrs.). (YA). (gr. 8 up). 2009. audio compact disk 45.00 (978-0-7393-7987-5(9), Listening Lib) Pub: Random Audio Pubg. Dist(s): Random

Brutal. unabr. ed. Michael Harmon. Read by Kim Mai Guest. (ENG.). (J). (gr. 9). 2009. audio compact disk 35.00 (978-0-7393-7985-1(2), Listening Lib) Pub: Random Audio Pubg. Dist(s): Random

Brutal Telling. unabr. ed. Louise Penny. Read by Ralph Cosham. (Running Time: 1 hr. 0 mins.). (Chief Inspector Armand Gamache Ser.: Bk. 5). 2009. 29.95 (978-1-4332-9712-0(4)); 72.95 (978-1-4332-9708-3(6)); audio compact disk 105.00 (978-1-4332-9709-0(4)); audio compact disk & audio compact disk 34.95 (978-1-4332-9711-3(6)) Blckstn Audio.

***Brute: The Life of Victor Krulak, U. S. Marine.** unabr. ed. Robert Coram. (Running Time: 12 hrs. 0 mins. 0 sec.). (ENG.). 2010. 24.99 (978-1-4001-6896-5(1)); 17.99 (978-1-4001-8896-3(2)); audio compact disk 34.99 (978-1-4001-1896-0(4)) Pub: Tantor Media. Dist(s): IngramPubServ

Brute & Suspense. unabr. collector's ed. Joseph Conrad. Read by Wolfram Kandinsky. 8 cass. (Running Time: 12 hrs.). 1993. 64.00 (978-0-7366-2511-1(9), 3267) Books on Tape.
Two stories - the first about a ship where someone dies on each voyage & the other Conrad's unfinished last work.

***Brute (Library Edition) The Life of Victor Krulak, U. S. Marine.** unabr. ed. Robert Coram. (Running Time: 12 hrs. 0 mins.). 2010. 34.99 (978-1-4001-9896-2(8)); audio compact disk 83.99 (978-1-4001-4896-7(0)) Pub: Tantor Media. Dist(s): IngramPubServ

Buachaill Dreoite. Contrib. by Joe Ryan. (ENG.). 1995. 13.95 (978-0-8023-7113-3(2)); audio compact disk 20.95 (978-0-8023-8113-2(8)) Pub: Clo Iar-Chonnachta IRL. Dist(s): Dufour

Bub: Or the Very Best Thing. Natalie Babbitt. (J). (ps-3). 2001. pap. bk. 15.95 (VX-465C) Kimbo Educ.
A young king & queen both want "the one & only best thing" for their son, but what would that be? Includes a read along book.

Bub: Or the Very Best Thing. Natalie Babbitt. Illus. by Natalie Babbitt. Read by Rita Gardner. 14 vols. (Running Time: 9 mins.). (J). (gr. k-3). 1998. pap. bk. & tchr. ed. 37.95 Reading Chest. (978-0-87499-467-4(5)) Live Oak Media.
A young king & gueen , both want 'the one & only very best thing' for their son, but what would that be?.

Bub: Or the Very Best Thing. unabr. ed. Natalie Babbitt. Illus. by Natalie Babbitt. Read by Rita Gardner. 1 cass. (Running Time: 9 mins.). (J). (gr. k-3). 1998. pap. bk. 15.95 (978-0-87499-465-0(9)) Live Oak Media.

Bubble of Light. Rudy Noel. 1988. CN Video Creations.
A guided imagery & relaxation audio tape.

Bubble of Light. unabr. ed. Rudy Noel. 1 cass. (Running Time: 1 hr.). (YA). 1989. 10.00 (978-0-925332-00-4(3)) CN Video Creations.

Bubble Trouble: Audiocassette. Jill Eggleton. Illus. by Philip Webb. (Sails Literacy Ser.). (gr. k up). 10.00 (978-0-7578-4045-6(0)) Rigby Educ.

Bubbles a Broad. unabr. ed. Sarah Strohmeyer. Narrated by Barbara McCulloh. 7 cass. (Running Time: 10 hrs. 15 mins.). 2004. 69.75 (978-1-4193-0768-3(1), 97872MC) Recorded Bks.

Bubbles Betrothed. unabr. ed. Sarah Strohmeyer. Narrated by Barbara McCulloh. 9 CDs. (Running Time: 10 hrs.). 2005. audio compact disk 99.75 (978-1-4193-4740-5(3), C3358) Recorded Bks.
Agatha Award-winning author Sarah Strohmeyer delights readers everywhere with this fifth installment in the popular Bubbles Yablonsky series. Armed with her trusty high heels and unflappable demeanor, Bubbles stumbles into trouble when she interviews Crazy Popeye, the chief suspect in a local murder. To her dismay, Popeye dies mid-interview, and everyone from a pesky police detective to a Polish mafioso wants to pick her brain. What's more, Bubbles' head is set spinning when long-time love interest Steve Stiletto asks her to pose as his fiance to avoid a job transfer.

Bubbles, Bubbles Everywhere. Sundance/Newbridge, LLC Staff. (Early Science Ser.). (gr. k-3). 2007. audio compact disk 12.00 (978-1-4007-6208-8(1)); audio compact disk 12.00 (978-1-4007-6210-1(3)); audio compact disk 12.00 (978-1-4007-6209-5(X)) Sund Newbrdge.

Bubbles in Trouble. Sarah Strohmeyer. Narrated by Barbara McCulloh. 8 cass. (Running Time: 10 hrs. 30 mins.). 2004. 79.75 (978-1-4025-3237-5(7)); audio compact disk 79.80 (978-1-4025-7186-2(0)) Recorded Bks.

Buccaneers. Iain Lawrence. Narrated by Ron Keith. 7 CDs. (Running Time: 7 hrs. 30 mins.). (gr. 5 up). audio compact disk 69.00 (978-1-4025-3307-5(1)) Recorded Bks.

Buccaneers. Edith Wharton. Narrated by Flo Gibson. (ENG.). 2008. audio compact disk 29.95 (978-1-55685-989-2(9)) Audio Bk Con.

Buccaneers. unabr. ed. Iain Lawrence. Narrated by Ron Keith. 6 pieces. (Running Time: 7 hrs. 30 mins.). (gr. 5 up). 2002. 55.00 (978-1-4025-2768-5(3)) Recorded Bks.
After 17 year old John Spencer sets out on his first voyage to foreign lands, he and his crew are wary when they come across a stranger named Horn rowing a lifeboat in the middle of nowhere. What is the man hiding?.

Buccaneers. unabr. ed. Edith Wharton. Read by Frances Cassidy. 9 cass. (Running Time: 13 hrs. 30 mins.). 1994. 72.00 (978-0-7366-2717-7(0), 3447) Books on Tape.
Set in the 1870s, about five young American women denied entry to New York society because their parents' money is too new. They sail for London, where they marry nobility who find their beauty charming & their wealth useful.

Buccaneers, Set. Edith Wharton. Read by Flo Gibson. 6 cass. (Running Time: 9 hrs.). 1996. 24.95 (978-1-55685-427-9(7)) Audio Bk Con.
Wealthy young American girls visit England & lay siege to the hearts of members of the nobility. This last, unfinished novel of Wharton's is witty, romantic & perceptive.

Buchwald Stops Here. unabr. ed. Art Buchwald. Read by Edmund Stoiber. 7 cass. 41.65 (B-117) Audio Bk.
An irreverant look at America by its best humorist-satirist.

Buck: Building up Christ's Kingdom. 1 cass., 1 CD. (J). 1999. 8.99; audio compact disk 13.99 CD. Brentwood Music.
Buck's mission is just that, to use the musical gifts God has blessed them with to break through Satan's ranks & spread the Good News of Jesus Christ to the unsaved youth of this world. This Detroit, MI based group of musicians ranges in age from 17 to 23. Blending traditional reggae with hard-hitting punk beats, a good dose of swing, a little rock & a pinch of jazz & rap, this ensemble is serving up a heaping bowl full of third-wave Ska. Songs include: "Fruit," "Understanding," "Lord I Lift," "My Alarm Goes Off," "70 X 7," "Superman Soup," "Follower" & many more.

***Buck Alice & the Actor-Robot.** unabr. ed. Walter Koenig. 1 MP3-CD. (Running Time: 7 hrs.). 2010. 39.97 (978-1-61106-468-1(6)); 14.99 (978-1-61106-467-4(8)); audio compact disk 9.99 (978-1-4418-9219-5(2)); audio compact disk 39.97 (978-1-61106-466-7(X)) Brilliance Audio.

Buck Fever. Ben Rehder. Narrated by Jonathan Davis. 6 cass. (Running Time: 7 hrs. 45 mins.). (Blanco County, Texas Ser.). 2002. 58.00 (978-1-4025-4499-6(5)) Recorded Bks.

Buck Meets the Monster Stick: Five Original Tall Tales. Bil Lepp. (Running Time: 51 mins.). 1999. audio compact disk 16.95 (978-0-87483-665-3(4)) Pub: August Hse. Dist(s): Natl Bk Netwk

Buck Meets the Monster Stick: Five Original Tall Tales. Bil Lepp. (Running Time: 51 mins.). (J). 2002. 12.00 (978-0-87483-664-6(6)) August Hse.

Bucking the Sarge. Christopher Paul Curtis. 4 cass. (J). 2004. 35.00 (978-1-4000-9036-5(9), Listening Lib); audio compact disk 45.00 (978-1-4000-9484-4(4), Listening Lib) Random Audio Pubg.

Bucking the Sarge. unabr. ed. Christopher Paul Curtis. Read by Michael Boatman. 5 CDs. (Running Time: 6 hrs. 10 mins.). (ENG.). (J). (gr. 5). 2004. audio compact disk 30.00 (978-1-4000-9097-6(0), Listening Lib) Pub: Random Audio Pubg. Dist(s): Random

Bucking the Sun. Ivan Doig. Read by Will Patton. 2004. 15.95 (978-0-7435-4053-7(0)) Pub: S&S Audio. Dist(s): S and S Inc

Buckingham Blowout. Axel Kilgore. Read by Carol Eason. 2 vols. No. 17. 2004. 18.00 (978-1-58807-173-6(1)); (978-1-58807-664-9(4)) Am Pubng Inc.

Buckingham Palace Gardens. abr. ed. Anne Perry. (Running Time: 6 hrs.). (Thomas Pitt Ser.). 2009. audio compact disk 14.99 (978-1-59737-678-5(7), 9781597376785, BCD Value Price) Brilliance Audio.

Buckingham Palace Gardens. unabr. ed. Anne Perry. Read by Michael Page. (Running Time: 13 hrs.). (Thomas Pitt Ser.). 2008. 39.25 (978-1-59710-920-8(7), 9781597109208, BADLE); 24.95 (978-1-59710-921-5(5), 9781597109215, BAD); 24.95 (978-1-59335-981-2(0), 9781593359812, Brilliance MP3); audio compact disk 107.25 (978-1-59600-277-7(8), 9781596002777, BriAudCD Unabrid); audio compact disk 40.95 (978-1-59600-276-0(X), 9781596002760, Bril Audio CD Unabri); audio compact disk 39.25 (978-1-59335-982-9(9), 9781593359829, Brlnc Audio MP3 Lib) Brilliance Audio.
Please enter a Synopsis.

Buckled Bag & Locked Doors. unabr. ed. Mary Roberts Rinehart. Read by Laurie Klein. 4 cass. (Running Time: 4 hrs. 18 min.). Dramatization. 1992. 26.95 (978-1-55686-436-0(1), 436) Books in Motion.
Beautiful, wealthy, & soon-to-be-married Clare March is missing, & Detective Patton is baffled. That is, until he teams up with Miss Adams, an independent & strong minded nurse called in to care for the girl's frantic parents.

Buckley's Firing Line. unabr. ed. William F. Buckley, Jr. 19 cass. (Running Time: 1 hr. per cass.). Incl. Albert Gore: Public vs. Private Power; Barry Goldwater: Conservatism; Clare Booth Luce: Future of G.O.P.; David Merrick: American Theatre; David Susskind: Media Blues; F. Clifton White: Presidential Politics; Harold Taylor: Academic Freedom; Harry Golden: States' Rights; James Pike: Prayer in Public Schools; Leo Cherne: McCarthyism; Mark Lane: Warren Commission Report; Murray Kempton: Bobby Kennedy; Norman Thomas: Vietnam; Paul Weis: Failure of Organized Religion; Pierre Salinger: President & the Press; Senator Thomas Dodd: Misconduct Charges; Seymour Melman: Disarmament; Victor Riesel: Organized Labor; William Sloan Coffin: Church Militant; 12.95 ea.; 12.95 ea. J Norton Pubs.
Recorded in 1966 & 1967, these are debates with some of the most provocative personalities of the times.

Buckminster Fuller: A Twentieth Century Renaissance. unabr. ed. Read by Heywood Hale Broun & R. Buckminster Fuller. 1 cass. (Heywood Hale Broun Ser.). 12.95 (40100) J Norton Pubs.
Fuller, in a down-to-earth conversation with Heywood Hale Broun describes some of his discoveries about the structure of what he calls Spaceship Earth.

Buckminster Fuller: An Audio Biography. Lloyd Steven Sieden. Based on a work by Lloyd Steven Sieden. Interview with Laura Lee. Hosted by Laura Lee. 3 cass. (Running Time: 3 hrs.). 2000. 24.95 (978-1-889071-14-5(5), 6235) Radio Bookstore.

Buckshot. Larry J. Martin. 1 cass. 1994. (978-1-885339-00-3(3)) Wolfpack Pub.
Western fiction.

Buckskin Brigades. abr. ed. L. Ron Hubbard. Read by Bruce Boxleitner. 2 cass. (Running Time: 3 hrs.). 1992. 15.95 (978-0-88404-709-4(1)) Bridge Pubns Inc.
The story centers on a brave Blackfoot warrior named Yellow Hair.

Buckskin Brigades. abr. ed. L. Ron Hubbard. Read by Bruce Boxleitner. 2 cass. (Running Time: 3 hrs.). 2002. 15.95 (978-1-59212-011-6(3)) Gala Pr LLC.

Buckskin Brigades. abr. ed. L. Ron Hubbard. Read by Bruce Boxleitner. 3 CDs. (Running Time: 10800 sec.). 2005. audio compact disk 19.95 (978-1-59212-221-9(3)) Gala Pr LLC.

Buckskin Line. abr. ed. Elmer Kelton. Read by Richard McGonagle. 4 cass. (Running Time: 6 hrs.). (Texas Rangers Ser.: No. 1). 2002. 25.00 (978-1-59040-244-3(8), Phoenix Audio) Pub: Amer Intl Pub. Dist(s): PerseuPGW
In 1861, Rusty Shannon rides out from the family homestead to join a company of the Texas volunteers dedicated to protecting settlers against Indian raids, but he carries a heavy burden. Yet, Rusty is determined to take up his adoptive father's work as a Texas Ranger even though his duties as a ranger conflict with his sense of justice.

Buckskin Mare. Poems. Baxter Black. 1 cass. 9.99 (978-0-939343-27-0(4)) Coyote Cowboy.
Baxter calls this poem "a cowboy's nightmare...Edgar Allen Poe in spurs." Also included is "Runnin' Wild Horses," "The Lost Dog," "Goodbye Old Man" & others.

Bucoliques, Set. Poems. Andre Marie Chenier. Read by G. Bejean et al. 2 cass. (FRE.). 1991. 26.95 (1409-VSL) Olivia & Hill.
The beautiful lyric poems of this 18th-century poet who was guillotined at the age of 32.

Bud: A New Home. W. Keith Courtney. Read by W. Keith Courtney. Ed. by Chris Acker & Jorge Acker. Illus. by Chip David. 1 cass. (Running Time: 11 min.). (Bud Bk.). (J). (ps-3). 1996. bk. 14.95 (978-1-888133-00-4(7)) Bud Pubs.
Includes background music & sound effects.

Bud, Not Buddy. Christopher Paul Curtis. 5 cass. (Running Time: 7 hrs.). (J). 2001. audio compact disk 36.00 (978-0-8072-0502-0(8), Listening Lib) Random Audio Pubg.

Bud, Not Buddy. collector's ed. Christopher Paul Curtis. Read by James Avery. 4 cass. (Running Time: 6 hrs.). (J). 2000. 24.00 (978-0-7366-9016-4(6)) Books on Tape.
Ten-year-old Bud may be a motherless boy on the run, but he's on a mission. His momma never told him who his father was, but she left a clue: posters of Herman E. Calloway & his famous band, the Dusky Devastators of the Depression! Bud's got an idea that those posters will lead him to his father. Once he decides to hit the road & find this mystery man, nothing can stop him.

Bud, Not Buddy. unabr. ed. Christopher Paul Curtis. 5 CDs. (Running Time: 5 hrs. 15 mins.). (Middle Grade Cassette Librariestm Ser.). (J). (gr. 4-7). 2004. audio compact disk 40.00 (978-0-8072-1045-1(5), S YA 140 CD, Listening Lib) Random Audio Pubg.

Bud, Not Buddy. unabr. ed. Christopher Paul Curtis. Read by James Avery. 3 cass. (Running Time: 5 hrs. 15 mins.). (J). (gr. 4-7). 2004. 30.00 (978-0-8072-8209-0(X), LL0165, Listening Lib); pap. bk. 36.00 (978-0-8072-8210-6(3), LYA 140 S{, Listening Lib) Random Audio Pubg.

Bud, Not Buddy. unabr. ed. Christopher Paul Curtis. Read by James Avery. (Running Time: 18900 sec.). (ENG.). (J). (gr. 3). 2006. audio compact disk 19.95 (978-0-7393-3179-8(5), Listening Lib) Pub: Random Audio Pubg. Dist(s): Random

Buddha. Karen Armstrong. Read by Kate Reading. 2001. audio compact disk 48.00 (978-0-7366-8060-8(8)); 40.00 (978-0-7366-6186-7(7)) Books on Tape.
This rich, timely & highly original portrait of the Buddha explores both the archetypal religious icon & Buddha the man. In lucid & compelling prose, Armstrong brings to life the Buddha's quest, from his renunciation of his privileged life to the discovery of a truth.

Buddha. unabr. ed. Karen Armstrong. Read by Kate Reading. 4 cass. (Running Time: 6 hrs.). 2001. 24.95 (978-0-7366-6814-9(4)) Books on Tape.
In compelling prose Armstrong brings to life the Buddha's quest: to discover a truth, that he believed would utterly transform human beings & enable them to live at peace in the midst of life's suffering.

Buddha: A Story of Enlightenment. Deepak Chopra. 2009. audio compact disk 9.99 (978-1-4418-2657-2(2)) Brilliance Audio.

Buddha: A Story of Enlightenment. unabr. ed. Deepak Chopra. Read by Deepak Chopra. (Running Time: 9 hrs.). 2007. 39.25 (978-1-4233-1231-4(7), 9781423312314, BADLE); 24.95 (978-1-4233-1230-7(9), 9781423312307, BAD); 74.25 (978-1-4233-1225-3(2), 9781423312253, BrilAudUnabridg); audio compact disk 39.25 (978-1-4233-1229-1(5), 9781423312291, Brlnc Audio MP3 Lib); audio compact disk 92.25 (978-1-4233-1227-7(9), 9781423312277, BriAudCD Unabrid); audio compact disk 24.95 (978-1-4233-1228-4(7), 9781423312284, Brilliance MP3); audio compact disk 34.95 (978-1-4233-1226-0(0), 9781423312260, Bril Audio CD Unabri) Brilliance Audio.
Please enter a Synopsis.

Buddha & Meditation. unabr. ed. 1 cass. (Running Time: 1 hr.). 1986. 7.95 (978-1-58638-508-8(9)) Nilgiri Pr.
Describes dhyana - meditation - for an end to suffering.

Buddha & the Bomb. Instructed by Manly P. Hall. 8.95 (978-0-89314-018-2(X), C820829) Philos Res.

Buddha Boy. unabr. ed. Kathe Koja. Read by Full Cast Production Staff. (J). 2007. 34.99 (978-1-60252-522-1(6)) Find a World.

Buddha Da. Anne Donovan. Read by Jonathan Hackett & Sally Armstrong. 8 CDs. (Running Time: 34200 sec.). (Isis (CDs) Ser.). 2005. audio compact disk 79.95 (978-0-7531-2429-1(7)) Pub: ISIS Lrg Prnt GBR. Dist(s): Ulverscroft US

Buddha Da. unabr. ed. Anne Donovan. Read by Sally Armstrong & Jonathan Hackett. 7 cass. (Running Time: 9 hrs. 27 mins.). (Isis Cassettes Ser.). (J). 2004. 61.95 (978-0-7531-1796-5(7)) Pub: ISIS Lrg Prnt GBR. Dist(s): Ulverscroft US

Buddha in the Palm of Your Hand. Osel Tendzin. Read by Osel Tendzin. 3 cass. 1983. 29.50 (A070) Vajradhatu.
Three talks. This seminar was given shortly after the publication of Osel Tendzin's first book, by the same title. It goes into depth about questions concerning basic meditation.

Buddha is As Buddha Does: The Ten Original Practices for Enlightened Living. Lama Surya Das. 4 CDs. (Running Time: 18000 sec.). 2007. audio compact disk 29.95 (978-1-59179-559-9(1), AW01122D) Sounds True.

Buddha-Nature: The Seed of Enlightenment. Read by Chogyam Trungpa. 3 cass. 1976. 29.50 (A013) Vajradhatu.
Four talks. Through meditation & renunciation of our personal reference point, the seed of buddha-nature can ripen into the heroism & vision of the Mahayana path.

Buddha of Brewer Street. unabr. ed. Michael Dobbs. Read by Michael Kitchen. 10 cass. (Running Time: 15 hrs.). 2000. 69.95 (978-0-7540-0194-2(6), CAB 1617) Pub: Chivers Audio Bks GBR. Dist(s): AudioGO
Tom Goodfellowe is the unlikeliest of political heroes. He's an MP with a descending career and a private life in chaos, and it's about to get worse. A new Dalai Lama is born in Tibet. This means nothing to Goodfellowe until a mysterious Tibetan monk walks into his chaotic life and draws him into a murderous race against time.

Buddha of Suburbia. Hanif Kureishi. Read by Christopher Simpson. 10 vols. (Running Time: 15 hrs.). 2003. 84.95 (978-0-7540-8382-5(9)) Pub: Chivers Audio Bks GBR. Dist(s): AudioGO

Buddha on the Cause & End of Suffering. Instructed by Manly P. Hall. 8.95 (978-0-89314-019-9(8), C820606) Philos Res.

Buddha Root Farm. Contrib. by Hua. (978-0-88139-660-7(5)) Buddhist Text.

Buddhadharma Without Credentials. Read by Chogyam Trungpa. 4 cass. 1973. 38.50 (A001) Vajradhatu.
Five talks: Spiritual materialism is the attempt to use spiritual practice as a credential for ego. Authentic practice demands more bravery & boredom.

Buddhadharma Without Credentials, NYC. Vajracarya. 4 cass. 1973. 38.50 Vajradhatu.
Five talks given in NYC: 1)Credentials As Spiritual Materialism. 2)The Dualistic Search for Credentials. 3)Boredom. 4)The Lion's Roar. 5)Charlatanism & Cynicism.

***Buddha's Brain: The Practical Neuroscience of Happiness, Love & Wisdom.** unabr. ed. Rick Hanson. (Running Time: 6 hrs.). 2010. 19.99 (978-1-4418-8755-9(5), 9781441887559, BAD); 39.97 (978-1-4418-8756-6(3), 9781441887566, BADLE) Brilliance Audio.

***Buddha's Brain: The Practical Neuroscience of Happiness, Love & Wisdom.** unabr. ed. Rick Hanson & Richard Mendius. Read by Alan B. Jones. (Running Time: 7 hrs.). 2010. 39.97 (978-1-4418-8754-2(7), 9781441887542, Brlnc Audio MP3 Lib) Brilliance Audio.

***Buddha's Brain: The Practical Neuroscience of Happiness, Love & Wisdom.** unabr. ed. Rick Hanson & Richard Mendius. Read by Alan Bomar Jones. (Running Time: 7 hrs.). 2010. 19.99 (978-1-4418-8753-5(9), 9781441887535, Brilliance MP3); audio compact disk 49.97 (978-1-4418-8752-8(0), 9781441887528, BriAudCD Unabrid) Brilliance Audio.

***Buddha's Brain: The Practical Neuroscience of Happiness, Love & Wisdom.** unabr. ed. Rick Hanson & Richard Mendius. Read by Alan Jones. (Running Time: 7 hrs.). 2010. audio compact disk 19.99 (978-1-4418-8751-1(2), 9781441887511, Bril Audio CD Unabri) Brilliance Audio.

Buddha's Child: My Fight to Save Vietnam. unabr. ed. Nguyen Cao Ky & Marvin J. Wolf. Read by Dick Hill. 8 cass. (Running Time: 12 hrs.). 2002. 32.95 (978-1-58788-798-7(3), 1587887983, BAU); 87.25 (978-1-58788-799-4(1), 1587887991, Unabridge Lib Edns) Brilliance Audio.
Even after 25 years in America, former South Vietnamese Prime Minister Nguyen Cao Ky is regarded as a national hero by three million fellow expatriots. He travels widely in the US and abroad, and is recognized and applauded by former US servicemen, to whom he remains a charismatic and admirable figure. Buddha's Child will flood the shadowy corners of South Vietnam's Byzantine political world with the bright light of truth. Ky will describe the Americans and their activities from the perspective of the Vietnamese patriot. Condemned by US Defense Secretary Robert McNamara as "the absolute bottom of the barrel," Ky was not expected to survive a week in the office into which he was thrust. Instead, he lasted three years, until he wrote himself out of office by penning the country's first constitution.

Buddha's Child: My Fight to Save Vietnam. unabr. ed. Nguyen Cao Ky & Marvin J. Wolf. Read by Dick Hill. (Running Time: 12 hrs.). 2004. 39.25 (978-1-59335-573-9(4), 1593355734, Brlnc Audio MP3 Lib) Brilliance Audio.

Buddha's Child: My Fight to Save Vietnam. unabr. ed. Nguyen Cao Ky & Marvin J. Wolf. Read by Dick Hill. (Running Time: 12 hrs.). 2004. 39.25 (978-1-59710-113-4(3), 1597101133, BADLE); 24.95 (978-1-59710-112-7(5), 1597101125, BAD) Brilliance Audio.

Buddha's Child: My Fight to Save Vietnam. unabr. ed. Nguyen Cao Ky & Marvin J. Wolf. Read by Dick Hill. (Running Time: 12 hrs.). 2004. 24.95 (978-1-59335-056-7(2), 1593350562) Soulmate Audio Bks.

Buddha's Noble Eightfold Path: An Introduction. Urgyen Sangharakshita. 2006. audio compact disk 34.98 (978-962-634-416-3(4), Naxos AudioBooks) Naxos.

Buddha's Teachings. unabr. ed. Bukkyo Dendo Kyokai. Narrated by Jonathan Reese. (Running Time: 3 hrs. 0 mins. 0 sec.). (ENG.). 2008. audio compact disk 17.99 (978-1-4001-0795-7(4)); audio compact disk 17.99 (978-1-4001-5795-2(1)); audio compact disk 35.99 (978-1-4001-3795-4(0)) Pub: Tantor Media. Dist(s): IngramPubServ

Buddha's Teachings. unabr. collector's ed. Buddha. Read by Jonathan Reese. 3 cass. (Running Time: 3 hrs.). 1995. 24.95 (978-0-7366-3046-7(5), 3728) Books on Tape.
Teachings of "The Enlightened One" carve the path to achieving peace, purity & virtue. Timeless principles for 450 million Buddhists.

Buddhism. unabr. ed. Winston King. Read by Ben Kingsley. Ed. by Walter Harrelson & Mike Hassell. 2 cass. (Running Time: 3 hrs.). Dramatization. (Religion, Scriptures & Spirituality Ser.). 1994. 17.95 (978-1-56823-013-9(3), 10456) Pub: Knowledge Prod. Dist(s): APG
Buddhism began with Gotama the Buddha in the 6th century B.C.E. & has developed two chief forms: Theravada (or Hinayana) is found especially in Sri Lanka, Burma, & Thailand; Mahayana is found in Japan, China, Korea, & Indochina. Zen, a more recent form of Buddhism, is found throughout the world. Some believe Buddhism is not properly understood as a religion, though this presentation describes its religious qualities; a belief in transcendent reality, sacred scriptures, monastic life, & views on a future life & the goal of human existence.

Buddhism, Pt. I-II. Instructed by Malcolm David Eckel. 12 cass. (Running Time: 12 hrs.). 54.95 (978-1-56585-190-0(0), 687) Teaching Co.

Buddhism, Pts. I-II. Instructed by Malcolm David Eckel. 12 CDs. (Running Time: 12 hrs.). 2001. bk. 69.95 (978-1-56585-369-0(5), 687) Teaching Co.

Buddhism, Vol. 2. Instructed by Malcolm David Eckel. 6 cass. (Running Time: 6 hrs.). 2001. 129.95 (978-1-56585-191-7(9)) Teaching Co.

Buddhism: A Personal Story. 70th ed. Jack Kornfield. 1 cass. (Running Time: 1 hr. 35 min.). 1983. 11.00 (03604) Big Sur Tapes.
Achaan Chah, one of Kornfield's teachers, spoke of two kinds of suffering: the kind that keeps going around & around, & the kind that leads to liberation, the end of suffering. "That's hopefully the kind that we practice here," says Kornfield in describing his formative experiences with Buddhist practice.

Buddhism: Knowledge Products Production. unabr. ed. Winston King. Read by Ben Kingsley. (Running Time: 4 mins.). (J). 2006. audio compact disk 25.95 (978-0-7861-6494-3(5)) Pub: Blckstn Audio. Dist(s): NetLibrary CO

Buddhism, Advaitism & the Way of Adidam. abr. ed. Ruchira Avatar Adi Da Samraj staff. 1 cass. (Dual Sensitivities Ser.). 1995. Dawn Horse Pr.

Buddhism for Beginners. Jack Kornfield. 8 CDs. (Running Time: 9 Hrs). 2005. audio compact disk 69.95 (978-1-59179-397-7(1), AF00988D) Sounds True.
Created specifically to address the questions and needs of first-time students, this full-length retreat on audio guides participants through Buddhism's cornerstone teachings, including the Four Noble Truths, the Eightfold Path to freedom, understanding karma, the Ten Perfections for opening the heart, the inner tools of samadhi and prajna (concentration and insight), and many other essential principles. Includes meditations, teaching parables, poetry, and inspiring true accounts gathered from Buddhism's 2,500-year-old legacy.

***Buddhism for Busy People.** David Michie. Read by Nicholas Bell. (Running Time: 6 hrs. 35 mins.). 2009. 49.99 (978-1-74214-180-0(3), 9781742141800) Pub: Bolinda Pubng AUS. Dist(s): Bolinda Pub Inc

Buddhism for Busy People. unabr. ed. David Michie. Read by Nicholas Bell. (Running Time: 6 hrs. 35 mins.). 2009. 43.95 (978-1-74214-508-2(6), 9781742145082) Pub: Bolinda Pubng AUS. Dist(s): Bolinda Pub Inc

Buddhism for Busy People: Finding Happiness in an Uncertain World. unabr. ed. David Michie. Read by Nicholas Bell. 7 CDS. (Running Time: 6 hrs. 35 mins.). 2008. audio compact disk 77.95 (978-1-74214-040-7(8), 9781742140407, Bolinda AudioAUS) Pub: Bolinda Pubng AUS. Dist(s): Bolinda Pub Inc

Buddhism for Mothers. unabr. ed. Sarah Napthali. Read by Rebecca Macauley. (Running Time: 7 hrs. 30 mins.). 2009. audio compact disk 77.95 (978-1-74214-070-4(X), 9781742140704) Pub: Bolinda Pubng AUS. Dist(s): Bolinda Pub Inc

***Buddhism for Mothers.** unabr. ed. Sarah Napthali. Read by Rebecca Macauley. (Running Time: 7 hrs. 30 mins.). 2010. 43.95 (978-1-74214-688-1(0), 9781742146881) Pub: Bolinda Pubng AUS. Dist(s): Bolinda Pub Inc

Buddhism in Eastern Europe. Ole Nydahl. 2 cass. 18.00 set. (A0623-90) Sound Photosyn.
Buddhist meditation master, international author & founder of more than 100 Tibetan Buddhist Meditation Centers around the world, Ole talks at Shared Visions, about his travels to countries that are just opening up to Buddhism, & what we can learn from them.

Buddhism in the Nineties: Active Compassion. Ole Nydahl. 2 cass. 18.00 set. (A0625-90) Sound Photosyn.
A Talking Thangkha, this video is an excellent exhortation to right living in the modern world & is lavishly illustrated with static & moving images.

Buddhist Drums, Bells & Chants. unabr. ed. 1 cass. 12.95 (7200) J Norton Pubs.

Buddhist Meditation for Beginners. Jack Kornfield. 6 CDs. (Running Time: 22500 sec.). 2006. audio compact disk 39.95 (978-1-59179-537-7(0), AW01093D) Sounds True.

Buddhist Path of Wisdom & Compassion. Read by T'ai Situ. 1 cass. 1982. 12.50 (A170) Vajradhatu.

Buddhist Practice in Everyday Life. Read by Osel Tendzin. 3 cass. 1977. 29.50 (A049) Vajradhatu.
Three talks: 1) The Wheel of Life; 2) This Precious Human Birth; 3) The Lonely Journey of Individual Salvation.

Buddhist Tantra. Vajracarya. Read by Chogyam Trungpa. 1 cass. 1975. 10.00 Vajradhatu.
A seminar by the scholar & meditation master trained in the philosophical & meditative traditions of buddhism in Tibet.

Buddhist Tantra: Teachings & Practices for Touching Enlightenment with the Body. Reginald A. Ray. 8 CDs. (Running Time: 9 hrs.). 2002. audio compact disk 89.95 (978-1-59179-017-4(4), AF00651D) Sounds True.
The popular or "exoteric" teachings of Tibetan Buddhism are known to millions, yet, the universe of its esoteric or "tantric" teachings remains hidden to all but a few. With this book, the author offers a landmark recording to address this need. in 12 sessions distilled from his years as a practitioner, meditation teacher, and scholar, he takes us into the secret heart of the Vajra World to explore: the tantric view of human nature and reality, detailed teachings on the major dimensions of Vajrayana practice, preparation for initiates, the role of the "tantric mentor," and much more.

Budding Prospects. T. C. Boyle. 1 cass. (Running Time: 30 min.). 8.95 (AMF-18) Am Audio Prose.
Reads from "Budding Prospects" & talks about marijuana growing in California & the comic narrative voice.

Budding Prospects. unabr. ed. T. C. Boyle. Read by Jonathan Reese. 10 cass. (Running Time: 15 hrs.). 1994. 80.00 (978-0-7366-2667-5(0), 3404) Books on Tape.
Million-dollar scheme to harvest marijuana in Northern California takes eccentric characters from one crisis to another.

Buddy & Buster. unabr. ed. Prod. by Joy Stories Staff. 1 CD. (Running Time: 20 min.). (J). 2004. audio compact disk 14.00 (978-0-9745977-1-3(6)) Joy Stories.
The story of Buddy, a golden retriever puppy, who is bullied by Buster, an aggressive Jack Russell terrier. Buddy's owner, a young boy named Dylan, experiences similar bullying at school. The subtle-as-a-brick message of the story is delivered by Dylan's mother, who tells Buddy "that deep within himself he would find the courage, his own inner strength, that would make him feel strong" and that "somehow, when he was able to feel his own strength, Buster would leave him alone." Of course, Buddy does find his strength, and provides a shining example for Dylan as well.

Buddy & Buster, Audio Story with Finger puppet of Golden Retriever. Short Stories. Joy Frost. 1 CD with Finger Pup. (Running Time: 20 Min.). (J). 2004. audio compact disk Rental 20.00 (978-0-9745977-0-6(8)) Joy Stories.
Exciting new audio stories by Joy B. Frost are original, metaphorical audio bedtime stories that are aimed at raising self-esteem. These stories are filled with positive messages with that are based on the principles of confidence building. These stories have won 7 awards in the past two years. "Buddy and Buster" is the story of an impressionable golden retriever puppy, Buddy, and an aggressive Jack Russell terrier, Buster. Buddy learns to develop values and, in doing so, becomes an example that makes a positive change in the lives of the dogs in his neighborhood, especially Buster. A child learns to use Buddy's example to deal with others who are more aggressive then himself/herself. Suggested age 4-9 years old.

Buddy Bond: Brothers & Sisters, Friends Forever. Troy Dunn. 1 cass. 2004. 9.95 (978-1-55503-856-4(5), 06005063); audio compact disk 10.95 (978-1-57734-454-4(5), 2500833) Covenant Comms.
Thoughts on being part of a family.

Buddy Butterfly - Butterfly's Life. Steck-Vaughn Staff. 1 cass. (Running Time: 90 mins.). (J). 1999. (978-0-7398-2437-5(6)) SteckVau.

Buddy Shell Pts. 1 - 2: Metaphysical Private Investigator, Prod. by Steve Carlson. 2 CDs. (Running Time: 2 hrs.). 1998. audio compact disk 24.95 (978-1-57677-106-8(7), FRIE001) Lodestone Catalog.

Budget Deficit: Two Creative Explanations. 1 cass. (Running Time: 23 min.). 9.95 (AT-82-02-05, HarperThor) HarpC GBR.

Budget Formulation, Justification, & Execution: Capitol Learning Audio Course: A How-to for Budget Analysts. James Capretta. Prod. by TheCapitol.Net. (ENG.). 2007. 47.00 (978-1-58733-060-5(1)) TheCapitol.

Budget Resolution in a Nutshell. Ray Meyers. Prod. by TheCapitol.Net. (ENG.). 2008. 47.00 (978-1-58733-085-8(7)) TheCapitol.

Budgie Book. Sarah Ferguson. Illus. by John Richardson. (J). bk. 20.00 (978-0-614-13218-2(5), 21-38036) EAA Aviation.

Budokon for Weightloss. 1. 2005. audio compact disk (978-1-59250-565-4(1)) Gaiam Intl.

Budokon for Weightloss Media Collection. 2005. DVD & audio compact disk (978-1-59250-566-1(X)) Gaiam Intl.

Buena Memoria. Betty L. Randolph. 1 cass. (Educational Ser.). (SPA.). 1989. bk. 9.98 (978-1-55909-183-1(5), 24E) Randolph Tapes.
Presents a program in Spanish. Features male-female voice tracks with the right-left brain.

***Buena Tierra.** abr. ed. Pearl S. Buck. Read by Laura Garcia. (SPA.). 2002. audio compact disk 17.00 (978-958-43-0187-1(X)) Pub: Yoyo Music COL. Dist(s): YoYoMusic

Buena Vista Social Club. Perf. by Ry Cooder et al. 1 cass., 1 CD. 8.78 (NONE 79478); audio compact disk 13.58 CD Jewel box. (NONE 79478) NewSound.
Includes an extraordinary variety of Cuban styles from the city sounds of Havana to the country style of Santiago & covers a range of the island's history.

Buenas Noches, Luna. abr. ed. Margaret Wise Brown. Illus. by Clement Hurd. 1 cass. (Running Time: 90 min.). (Tell Me a Story Bks.).Tr. of Goodnight Moon. (SPA.). (J). (ps-3). 1996. 10.95 (978-0-694-70021-9(5), HC2070, HarperTrophy) HarperCollins Pubs.

Bueno Es. unabr. ed. Torre Fuerte & Heriberto Hermosillo. (SPA.). 1999. 7.99 (978-0-8297-2526-1(1)) Pub: Vida Pubs. Dist(s): Zondervan

Bueno Es. unabr. ed. Heriberto Hermosillo. 1999. audio compact disk 11.99 (978-0-8297-2527-8(X)) Zondervan.

Buffalo Before Breakfast. Mary Pope Osborne. Read by Mary Pope Osborne. (Running Time: 38 mins.). (Magic Tree House Ser.: No. 18). (J). (gr. k-3). 2004. pap. bk. 17.00 (978-0-8072-0927-1(9), Listening Lib) Random Audio Pubg.

Buffalo Bill. unabr. ed. Ingri Parin D'Aulaire & Edgar Parin D'Aulaire. 1 cass. (Running Time: 6 min.). (J). (gr. 3-5). 1992. pap. bk. 15.00 (6512-B) Spoken Arts.

Buffalo Bird Woman: My Life on the Northern Plains 1840-1890. abr. ed. Waheenee. Read by Bonnie Good Bird Wells. 2 cass. (Running Time: 2 hrs. 30 min.). 1994. 14.98 Set. (978-0-9650872-1-6(2), SC01114) Scoria.
In a compelling narrative, Buffalo Bird Woman tells how the Hidatsa lived on the Missouri River in western North Dakota during the late 1800's.

Buffalo Dreaming: Ballads, Stories, & Music from the Dawn of Time. Created by Hawk Hurst. Featuring Sean Sweeney et al. 1 CD. (Running Time: 1 hr. 2 mins., 58 secs.). 2001. audio compact disk 15.00 (978-0-9710716-1-2(6)) Silv Watr Ret.
Traditional and original stories and folk songs, influenced by various indigenous tribes of North America, Africa, and Australia. Poetry, Stories, and Ballads accompanied by Native American flute, African percussion, guitar, and Australian didgeridoo.Lyrics included.

Buffalo Dusk see Carl Sandburg's Poems for Children

Buffalo Girls. Larry McMurtry. Read by Betty Buckley. 2004. 18.95 (978-0-7435-4218-0(5)) Pub: S&S Audio. Dist(s): S and S Inc

Buffalo Girls. unabr. collector's ed. Larry McMurtry. Read by Mary Peiffer. 7 cass. (Running Time: 10 hrs. 30 min.). 1990. 56.00 (978-0-7366-1851-9(1), 2684) Books on Tape.
Calamity Jane is the book's central figure, a reclusive legend content to remember the past & retell it in letters to her daughter. But Buffalo Bill Cody, an ageless promoter, wants her in his show & turns on the charm to get her there. The question is, does Jane want to relive the glory days?.

Buffalo Horns Adventure: With Buffalo Biff & Farley's Raiders. unabr. ed. Joe Loesch. Ed. by Cheryl J. Hutchinson. Illus. by Ott Denney. 1 CD. (Running Time: 43 min.). (Backyard Adventure Ser.: Vol. 1). (J). (gr. 1-5). 1995. pap. bk. 16.95 INCL. BK. (978-1-887729-01-7(1)) Toy Box Prods.
Pete & Ruby embark on an adventure to reunite Pete with his dog Farley. They encounter Little Big Dog, an Indian spirit, who teaches them about responsibility & taking care of one's pets.

Buffalo Horns Adventure: With Buffalo Biff & Farley's Raiders. unabr. ed. Joe Loesch. Ed. by Cheryl J. Hutchinson. Illus. by Ott Denney. 1 CD. (Running Time: 43 min.). (Backyard Adventure Ser.: Vol. 1). (J). (gr. 1-5). 1995. pap. bk. 14.95 (978-1-887729-00-0(3)) Toy Box Prods.

Buffalo Medicine. unabr. ed. Don Coldsmith. Read by Rusty Nelson. 6 cass. (Running Time: 6 hrs. 6 min.). 2001. 39.95; audio compact disk 39.00 (978-1-58116-169-4(7)) Books in Motion.
The coming of the Hair Faces and their "elk-dog" horses changed the ways of the People. Yet as the ways of the People change, they must also rediscover the ancient way of the great buffalo. Under the tutelage of an ancient medicine man, Owl embarks on his own vision quest through enemy territory where he faces capture and enslavement by the Hair Faces.

Buffalo Restoration on Indian Lands. Hosted by Nancy Pearlman. 1 cass. (Running Time: 28 min.). 10.00 (1109) Educ Comm CA.

Buffalo Skinners. Woody Guthrie et al. 1 CD. (Running Time: 74 min.). (Asch Recordings Ser.: Vol. 4). (YA). 1999. 14.00 Smithsonian Folkways.
Booklet contains historical & biographical information, song notes & artwork.

Buffalo Soldiers: A Novel. unabr. collector's ed. Tom Willard. Read by Dick Estell. 8 cass. (Running Time: 8 hrs.). (Black Sabre Chronicles). 1997. 48.00 (978-0-7366-3555-4(6), 4200) Books on Tape.
Depicts the distinguished military service of Augustus Sharps, one of the "Buffalo Soldiers" - African-American men who joined the U. S. Army after the Civil War. His excellence as a soldier & skill with a sabre ultimately elevate him to the rank of Sergeant Major in the 10th Cavalry. His adventures span the years from his duty with General Custer to the Charge up San Juan Hill with Teddy Roosevelt.

Buffalo Wagons. Elmer Kelton. Narrated by George Guidall. 5 cass. (Running Time: 6 hrs. 30 mins.). 48.00 (978-1-4025-2133-1(2)) Recorded Bks.

Buffalo Wagons. unabr. ed. Elmer Kelton. Narrated by George Guidall. 5 cass. (Running Time: 6 hrs. 30 mins.). 2002. 32.95 (978-0-7887-9481-0(7), RF346) Recorded Bks.

Buffettology Collection: Warren Buffett's Investing Techniques. abr. ed. Mary Buffett & David Clark. Read by Mary Buffett. (Running Time: 6 hrs. 0 mins. 0 sec.). (ENG.). 2008. audio compact disk 29.95 (978-0-7435-7609-3(8)) Pub: S&S Audio. Dist(s): S and S Inc

Buffettology: previously unexplained technique have made buffet famous Investr: The Previously Unexplained Techniques That Have Made Warren Buffett American's Most Famous Investor. Mary Buffett. Based on a work by David Clark. 2004. 10.95 (978-0-7435-4219-7(3)) Pub: S&S Audio. Dist(s): S and S Inc

Bug. unabr. ed. Richard Strand. 1999. 15.99 (978-1-889889-06-1(7)); audio compact disk 15.99 CD. (978-1-889889-07-8(5)) Plays On Tape.
A frustrated office worker is at his wit's end as he tries to determine his future at the company. In Kafkaesque manner, the author pokes fun at human's ungoing dependence on machinery & what happens when the tiniest of things go wrong. Part BRAZIL & part THE TRIAL. This story is not only entertaining but also quite thought provoking.

Bug Business. 2002. (978-0-7398-5158-6(6)) SteckVau.

Bug Business, Level 3. (J). 2002. audio compact disk (978-0-7398-5341-2(4)) SteckVau.

Bugalugs Bum Thief. unabr. ed. Tim Winton. Read by Stig Wemyss. (Running Time: 17 mins.). (J). 2004. audio compact disk 39.95 (978-1-74030-861-8(1)); 18.00 (978-1-876584-89-4(0), 590907) Bolinda Pubng AUS.
Skeeta Anderson wakes up one morning to find that part of him is gone, something he thought he'd never miss, his bum. He discovers that almost every single backside in the town of Bugalugs has been stolen & it's up to Skeeta to catch the thief.

Bugg Book Curriculum 1. Stephen Cosgrove. 2004. 75.00 (978-1-58804-369-6(X)) PCI Educ.

Bugged. Created by Saddleback Educational Publishing. 1 cass. (Running Time: 3823 sec.). (PageTurner Science Fiction Ser.). (J). 2002. audio compact disk 10.95 (978-1-56254-485-0(3), SP 4853) Saddleback Edu.
Word-for-word read-along of Bugged!.

Bugglar Brothers Cassette. Stephen Cosgrove. 2004. 5.00 (978-1-58804-395-5(9)) PCI Educ.

Bugles in the Afternoon. unabr. ed. Ernest Haycox. 8 cass. (Running Time: 12 hrs.). 2001. 64.00 (978-0-7366-6387-8(8)) Books on Tape.
General George Custer and his troublesome 7th Regiment take on the proud Sioux nation at Little Big Horn.

Bugs & Friends Sing Elvis. Rhino Records Staff. 1 cass. (J). (ps-3). 1998. 15.98 (978-1-56826-793-7(2)) Rhino Enter.

Bugs, Bugs, Bugs! Pam Schiller. (J). 2005. audio compact disk 14.95 (978-0-9765887-2-6(2)) S Edu Res LLC.

Bugs! Bugs! Bugs! unabr. ed. Bob Barner. 1 CD. (Running Time: 8 mins.). (J). (ps-2). 2008. bk. 29.95 (978-0-545-09453-5(4)); audio compact disk 12.95 (978-0-545-09445-0(3)) Weston Woods.
With whimsical verse and brightly colored collage images, everyone's favorite bugs come to life. Music and vocals by Crystal Taliefero. DVD includes an interactive "Bug-O-Meter" game, and DVD and audio CD both include bug facts in "Meet the Bugs," a segment created especially for this production by author/illustrator Bob Barner, plus a bonus interview with Barner.

Bugs Bunny Starring in Carrotblanca. Rhino Records Staff. 1 cass. (J). (ps-3). 1998. pap. bk. 7.99 (978-1-56826-820-0(3), KR8) Rhino Enter.

Bug's Life. Prod. by Walt Disney Records Staff. 1 CD. (J). 1998. audio compact disk 22.50 CD. (978-0-7634-0444-4(6)) W Disney Records.

Bug's Life Read Along. Prod. by Walt Disney Records Staff. 1 cass. (J). (ps-3). 1998. bk. 6.98 (978-0-7634-0441-3(1)) Walt Disney.

Bug's Life Sing Along. Prod. by Walt Disney Records Staff. 1 cass. (J). 1998. pap. bk. 12.98 (978-0-7634-0440-6(3)) Walt Disney.

Bugsters. Short Stories. Read by Tim Russ et al. Based on a story by Tim Russ & Jedda Roskilly. 1 CD. (Running Time: 20:88). Dramatization. (J). 2001. audio compact disk 11.78 (978-0-9660122-9-3(1)) Russ Invis.

Bugsters Tunes & Tales. Prod. by Russ Entertainment. (ENG.). (J). 2004. audio compact disk 14.99 (978-0-9747064-3-6(4), ABridge) Russ Invis.

Bugsy a death to Innocents. Based on a comic strip by warzone comics. Created by george lawson-easley & prince george. (ENG, APA, ARA, ARM & EGY.). (YA). 2010. DVD 10.95 (978-0-9785256-2-0(0), Trinity Vsn) Prince Zone Pub.

Bugsy Cartoons. Based on a comic strip by warzone comics. Prince George. Characters created by George Lawson-Easley. (ENG.). (YA). 2010. DVD 10.95 (978-0-9785256-5-1(5), Trinity Vsn) Prince Zone Pub.

Bugsy the Becoming. Based on a comic strip by warzone comics. (ENG, APA, ARA, ARM & EGY.). (YA). 2010. DVD 10.95 (978-0-9785256-8-2(X), Trinity Vsn) Prince Zone Pub.

Bugville Critters Audio Collection: Go on Vacation; Rush to the Hospital; Play Their First Big Game. unabr. ed. Robert Stanek, pseud. Read by Victoria Charters. (J). 2008. 34.99 (978-1-60514-561-7(0)) Find a World.

Bugville Critters Audio Collection: Visit Dad & Mom at Work; Go to School; Have a Sleepover; Visit Garden Box Farms. unabr. ed. Robert Stanek, pseud. Read by Victoria Charters. (J). 2008. 34.99 (978-1-60514-560-0(2)) Find a World.

Bugville Critters Audio Collection, Volume 3: Have Trouble at School; Break Their Bad Habits; Stay after School; Have a Bad Day. Robert Stanek, pseud. Narrated by Giny Westcott. (J). 2008. 34.99 (978-1-60514-629-4(3)) Find a World.

Bugville Critters Audio Collection, Volume 4: Visit City Hall; Have a Surprise Party; Have a Backyard Picnic; Compete in the Big Spelling Bee. Robert Stanek, pseud. Narrated by Giny Westcott. (J). 2008. 34.99 (978-1-60514-630-0(7)) Find a World.

Bugz: Level 3. 2002. (978-0-7398-5157-9(8)) SteckVau.

Bugz Level 3. (J). 2002. audio compact disk (978-0-7398-5340-5(6)) SteckVau.

Build-A-Word: Blends & Digraphs Set. Created by Steck Vaughan. (Build-A-Word Ser.). 2001. pap. bk. 139.35 (978-0-7398-4663-6(9)) SteckVau.

Build Financial Security. Judith L. Powell. Read by Judith L. Powell. 1 cass. (Running Time: 40 min.). (Balanced Living Ser.). 12.95 (978-0-914295-30-3(6)) Top Mtn Pub.
Break out of poverty thinking - claim what you desire now! Side A: Guided visualization; Side B: Subliminals in music.

Build Self-Confidence. 2 cass. (Running Time: 2 hrs.). (Self Hypnosis & Subliminal Reinforcement Ser.). 14.95 (978-1-55569-230-8(3), SUB-8006) Great Am Audio.
Presents tools for positive self-change.

Build Self-Confidence. Lee Pulos. Read by Lee Pulos. 1 cass. (Running Time: 60 min.). 9.95 (978-1-55569-430-2(6), 4016) Great Am Audio.
Subliminal self-help.

Build Self-Confidence: Subliminal. Lee Pulos. Read by Lee Pulos. 3 cass. (Running Time: 3 hrs.). 19.95 Set. (978-1-55569-403-6(9), 7159) Great Am Audio.
Contains: Build self-confidence, build self-esteem & be more positive.

Build Self-Confidence in Ten Days! Herbert Fensterheim. 1 cass. (Running Time: 60 min.). (Self-Improvement Through Self-Help Ser.). 9.95 (978-1-55569-197-4(8), SFH-6400) Great Am Audio.
Explains how in ten days one can learn how to feel self-assured & confident in all those situations that challenge self-esteem.

Build Self-Esteem. Lee Pulos. 2 cass. (Running Time: 60 min. per cass.). (Self Hypnosis & Subliminal Reinforcement Ser.). 14.95 (978-1-55569-229-2(X), SUB-8005) Great Am Audio.
Presents tools for positive self-change.

Build Self-Esteem. Lee Pulos. Read by Lee Pulos. 1 cass. (Running Time: 60 min.). 9.95 (978-1-55569-423-4(3), 4012) Great Am Audio.
Subliminal self-help.

Build Self-Esteem. Barry Tesar. 2 cass. 1998. 14.95 Set. (978-1-889800-15-8(5)) TNT Media Grp.

Build the Temple: 1T Samuel 7:3. Ed Young. 1983. 4.95 (978-0-7417-1299-8(7), 299) Win Walk.

Build up Poetry. ed. Compiled by Benchmark Education Staff. (Phonics Ser.). (J). 2004. audio compact disk 12.00 (978-1-4108-1502-6(1)) Benchmark Educ.

Build Your Baby's Brain - Through the Power of Music. Contrib. by Zell Miller. 1 cass. 1998. (SFK/SFT 60815) Sony Music Ent.
Contains 16 classical favorites, six by Mozart, an aria from "The Marriage of Figaro" & the duet from "Don Giovanni." Also included are works by Bach, Handel, Beethoven, Schubert, Vivaldi, & Pachelbel.

Build Your Brain Power. unabr. ed. Arthur Winter & Ruth Winter. Read by Nadia May. 4 cass. (Running Time: 5 hrs. 30 mins.). 1996. 32.95 (978-0-7861-0920-3(3), 1725) Blckstn Audio.
Until recently it was believed that as the years pass, our brains inevitably decline in function, but as Dr. Arthur Winter & Ruth Winter prove in this book, people who continue to actively use their brain power can actually improve their intelligence throughout their lives. Adapting techniques used in exercising damaged brains, the authors show us how to improve a variety of brain functions, from aiding memory & increasing the ability to learn, to protecting the brain from stress & attendant depression. This book gives you simple, interesting, & fun exercises that get your brain into tip-top shape.

Build Your Own Library & the Pleasures of Reading CD. Gilbert Highet. 1 CD. (Running Time: 26 mins.). (Gilbert Highet Ser.). 2006. audio compact disk 12.95 (978-1-57970-382-0(8), C23335D, Audio-For) J Norton Pubs.
2 lectures by the superb monologist Gilbert Highet. The first is about building your own library: encouragement and advice on building a personal library that reflects and develops your own taste. The second is on the pleasures of reading: the delights and rewards found only in reading.

Build Your Self Esteem. Glenn Harrold. 1 cass. (Running Time: 1 hr. 30 mins.). 2002. 11.95 (978-1-901923-06-3(1)) Pub: Divinit Pubing GBR. Dist(s): Bookworld

Build Your Self Esteem. Glenn Harrold. 2003. audio compact disk 17.95 (978-1-901923-26-1(6)) Pub: Divinit Pubing GBR. Dist(s): Bookworld

Builders & Heroes Vol. 3: 250th Chronicles Set, 1999. bk. 95.00 (978-1-929348-05-3(3)) York County Comm.

Building A Better Map Lecture Series #2: the Brief Future of Oil see Building A Better Map Lecture Series #2 the Brief Future of Oil, 2, The Brief Future of Oil

Building A Better Map Lecture Series #2 the Brief Future of Oil 2: The Brief Future of Oil. Speeches. 1 CD. (Running Time: 1 hr. 6 min.). Orig. Title: Building A Better Map Lecture Series #2: the Brief Future of Oil. 2004. audio compact disk 14.95 (978-0-9758698-0-2(9), 80-002) Fr The Wilderness.

Building a Better You - Starting Now. Dave Johnson. (Dave Johnson Educational Library). D Johnson.
Shows how to save time, money, & avoid mistakes & enjoy a great future.

Building a Bridge to the Other Side: The Secrets of Psychic & Mediumship Development. Lysa Moskowitz-Mateu. (ENG.). 2001. audio compact disk 15.95 (978-0-9707468-8-7(1)) Channeling Spirits.

Building a Contagious Church. unabr. ed. Mark Mittelberg & Bill Hybels. 2000. 17.99 (978-0-310-22972-8(3)) Zondervan.

Building a Contagious Church: Revolutionizing the Way We View & Do Evangelism. abr. ed. Mark Mittelberg & Bill Hybels. (Running Time: 2 hrs. 0 mins. 0 sec.). (ENG.). 2003. 10.99 (978-0-310-26014-1(0)) Zondervan.

Building a Customer-Driven Organization: The Manager's Role. Lisa Ford & Ron Meiss. 4 cass. (Running Time: 4 hrs. 8 min.). 59.95 Set incl. 24p. wkbk. (V10159) CareerTrack Pubns.
This is an advanced class in learning what your customers really want & how to deliver it...how to add those "extra touches"™ that set your customer service apart from your competitors'...how to improve your billing, delivery, inquiry response time, telephone communications, warranties & customer recovery...how to hire, train & keep service stars.

Building a Developmentally Appropriate Preschool Program, Set. Connie Hine. Read by Connie Hine. 6 cass. (Running Time: 4 hr. 15 min.). 1994. 75.00 (978-1-886397-01-9(5)) Bureau of Educ.
Live audio workshop including 6 cassettes & a comprehensive resource handbook.

Building a Family That Will Stand. Speeches. Featuring Douglas W. Phillips et al. 8 cass. 1999. 30.00 (978-0-9665233-9-3(3)) Vsn Forum.

Building a Family That Will Stand (CD) As told by Doug Phillips et al. 8 CDs. 2003. audio compact disk 35.00 (978-1-929241-81-1(X)) Vsn Forum.

***Building a Fortune in Business: Entrepreneurial Success by Trump University.** unabr. ed. Made for Success. Read by Donald J. Trump. (Running Time: 9 hrs.). (Made for Success Ser.). 2010. audio compact disk 59.95 (978-1-4417-6086-9(5)) Blckstn Audio.

***Building a Fortune in Business (Library Edition) Entrepreneurial Success by Trump University.** unabr. ed. Made for Success. Read by Donald J. Trump. (Running Time: 9 hrs.). (Made for Success Ser.). 2010. audio compact disk 123.00 (978-1-4417-6084-5(9)) Blckstn Audio.

Building a Free Society: Prospects & Possibilities. Read by George Smith et al. (Running Time: 120 min.). (FOF Con). 1985. 18.00 (F172A & B) Freeland Pr.
Included in this program is a recorded telephone message from Paul Jacob, a scheduled speaker, who was incarcerated in a federal prison & unable to attend the conference. Panel discussion.

Building a Functional Family: Gen. 32:28. Ed Young. 2000. 4.95 (978-0-7417-2263-8(1), 1263) Win Walk.

Building a Healthy Self-Concept. Frank Minirth & Paul Meier. Read by Frank Minirth & Paul Meier. 1 cass. (Running Time: 82 min.). (Minirth & Meier Home Counseling Audio Library). 1994. 9.95 (978-1-56707-035-4(3)) Dallas Christ Recs.
Factors for a healthy & balanced self-concept, from infancy through adulthood.

Building a Home with My Husband: A Journey Through the Renovation of Love. unabr. ed. Rachel Simon. Narrated by Laural Merlington. (Running Time: 9 hrs. 0 mins. 0 sec.). (ENG.). 2009. 24.99 (978-1-4001-6345-8(5)); audio compact disk 69.99 (978-1-4001-4345-0(4)); audio compact disk 34.99 (978-1-4001-1345-3(8)) Pub: Tantor Media. Dist(s): IngramPubServ

Building a Legendary Reputation. Andrew Wood. 1 cass. 2000. 69.95; audio compact disk 69.95 Personal Quest.
Contains the detailed step-by-step information necessary to succeed to get to the top of your profession in a matter of months.

Building a Management Philosophy. unabr. ed. Harold F. Puff. 1 cass. (Running Time: 29 min.). 12.95 (13040) J Norton Pubs.
Management, which is basically the accomplishment of an objective through others, requires professional leaders. This discusses the establishment of a managerial philosophy through your own ideas, beliefs & opinions.

Building a Musical First Aid Kit. Michael Ballam. 2 cass. 12.98 (119112) Covenant Comms.
Talk plus music about the healing power of music.

Building a Musical First Aid Kit, Set. Michael Ballam. 2 cass. 14.98 (978-1-55503-339-2(3), 119112) Covenant Comms.

Building a Professional Practice. Edward Kluska. 1 cass. 8.95 (197) Am Fed Astrologers.

Building a Quality Physical Education Program. Voice by Bonnie Mohnsen. 6 cass. (Running Time: 4 hrs. 2 mins.). (YA). (gr. 6-12). 2000. pap. bk. & wbk. ed. 85.00 (978-1-886397-34-7(1)) Bureau of Educ.
Live workshop.

Building a Second Career after Sixty. Instructed by Manly P. Hall. 8.95 (978-0-89314-020-5(1), C841028) Philos Res.

Building a Successful Business. Sue Apitz-Upwall. 1 cass. 1992. 8.95 (1004) Am Fed Astrologers.

Building a 21st Century Mind. unabr. ed. Jennifer James. Read by Jennifer James. 1 cass. (Running Time: 1 hr.). 9.95 Jennifer J.

Building Amazing Bass Technique. Chris Matheos. 2000. pap. bk. 5.95 (978-0-7866-4988-4(7), 98434BCD) Mel Bay.

Building an Enlightened Society. Vajracarya. Read by Chogyam Trungpa. 1982. 12.50 Vajradhatu.
A seminar by the scholar & mediatation master trained in the philosophical & meditative traditions of Buddhism in Tibet.

Building an Outstanding Second Grade Program, Set. Lisa Blau. Read by Lisa Blau. 6 cass. (Running Time: 3 hr. 47 min.). 1994. 75.00 (978-1-886397-02-6(3)) Bureau of Educ.
Live audio workshop including 6 cassettes & a comprehensive resource handbook.

Building & Maintaining High Energy. Vivan Quiring. 1995. 15.95 (978-1-55977-206-8(9)) CareerTrack Pubns.

Building & Managing a Profitable Practice. Allan S. Boress & Robert E. Miller, Jr. 12 cass. 1995. bk. 225.00 set. (CPE0055) Bisk Educ.
Monthly subscription that provides you with techniques & strategies which enable you to market more effectively, sell more business & increase client satisfaction.

Building & Nurturing Your Grassroots Campaign. Ed. by TheCapitol.Net. 2005. audio compact disk 107.00 (978-1-58733-019-3(9)) TheCapitol.

Building & Running a Tight Ship. unabr. ed. Dan Poynter. Read by Dan Poynter. 1 cass. (Running Time: 1 hr. 10 min.). 1993. 9.95 (978-0-915516-82-7(9), P-104) Para Pub.
Dan Poynter describes his eleven-point plan for successfully operating your publishing company. Learn the advantages to being a smaller publisher, why you must publish more than one book - in the same field, the importance of consistent packaging, should you pursue wholesale over retail sales, the secrets of low-cost book promotion & more. This tape is for both new & seasoned publishers. Includes resources.

Building Bass Lines. Chuck Archard. (ENG.). 1998. audio compact disk 10.00 (978-0-7390-2526-0(0)) Alfred Pub.

Building Better Boundaries. Martha B. Beveridge. 1 cass. (Running Time: 60 min.). 1989. 9.95 (978-1-889237-26-8(4)) Options Now.
Develop skills for setting personal limits & boundaries that are vital to healthy relationships & loving parenting.

Building Better Families: A Five-Step Plan. 1 CD. (Running Time: 1 hr.l). 2003. audio compact disk 6.95 (978-1-932631-73-9(9)) Ascensn Pr.

Building Better Families: A Practical Guide to Raising Amazing Children. abr. unabr. ed. Matthew Kelly. Read by Matthew Kelly. (Running Time: 18000 sec.). (ENG.). 2008. audio compact disk 29.95 (978-0-7393-4043-1(3), Random AudioBks) Pub: Random Audio Pubg. Dist(s): Random

Building Better Habits. Virgil B. Smith. Read by Virgil B. Smith. 1 cass. (Running Time: 15 min.). 1979. 5.95 (978-1-878507-07-5(9), 27C) Human Grwth Services.
Constructive self-talk on self confidence, accepting reality, ways of avoiding errors in following a program of habit-change training, positive attitude, reminders for building new lifestyle.

Building Better Relationships with People. unabr. ed. Charles Garrett. Read by Charles Garrett. 4 cass. 1996. 34.95 set. (978-1-57294-037-6(9), 11-0402) SkillPath Pubns.
Practical information on how to communicate clearly & assertively. Learn how to listen, give corrective feedback, use ice-breakers, & handle put-downs.

Building Blocks: Acts 1:6-14. Ed Young. 1997. 4.95 (978-0-7417-2147-1(3), 1147) Win Walk.

Building Blocks of Biblical Character, Charles R. Swindoll. 6 cass. (Running Time: 11 hrs.). 1994. 30.95 (978-1-57972-030-8(7)) Insight Living.
Bible study on building a life of character from God's eternal word.

Building Blocks of Self-Esteem. Michele Borba. 6 cass. (Running Time: 30 min. per cass.). 1994. bk. 89.95 incl. wkbk. (978-1-880396-22-3(X), JP9622-X) Jalmar Pr.

Building Bridges: Stephen King Live at the National Book Awards. unabr. ed. Stephen King. 2004. 7.95 (978-0-7435-4422-1(6)) Pub: S&S Audio. Dist(s): S and S Inc

Building Bridges: The Work of Common Ground. Richard Rohr. 6 cass. (Running Time: 6 hrs.). 2001. 49.95 (A7030) St Anthony Mess Pr.
How can we stand against evil and hatred in this world, against the destruction of life from womb to tomb, and not become attacking, righteous, hateful people ourselves? That is the heart of the Common Ground Project.

Building Bridges 2, Level 1. Anna Uhl Chamot et al. (YA). (gr. 8-12). 1991. 17.95 (978-0-8384-2230-4(6)) Heinle.

Building Bridges 2, Level 2. Anna Uhl Chamot et al. (J). 1991. 47.95 (978-0-8384-2231-1(4)) Pub: Heinle. Dist(s): CENGAGE Learn

Building Bridges 2, Level 3. Anna Uhl Chamot et al. (J). 1992. 17.95 (978-0-8384-2232-8(2)) Heinle.

Building Business Through In-Store Demonstrations. 1 cass. (America's Supermarket Showcase '96 Ser.). 1996. 11.00 (NGA96-005) Sound Images.

Building Champions: A Motivational Presentation (West Indies Cricket Edition) Emmanuel Guadeloupe & Augustine 'Gus' Logie. Narrated by Emmanuel Guadeloupe. 2 CDs. 2005. audio compact disk 19.95 (978-0-9761628-1-0(4)) Plain Vision.

Building Character. 1 cass. (Twin Sisters Ser.). (J). bk. 7.18 (TWIN 114); bk. 7.98 Blisterpack. (TWIN 414); Incl. 24 p. bk. set. (TWIN 414) NewSound.
Learn to make the right choices & teach life-long skills.

Building Character. (J). 1997. pap. bk. 13.99 (978-1-57583-328-6(X), Twin 414CD); 8.99 (978-1-57583-048-3(5), Twin 114); audio compact disk 12.99 (978-1-57583-306-4(9), Twin 114CD) Twin Sisters.

Building Character. Kim Mitzo Thompson & Karen Mitzo Hilderbrand. Illus. by Steve Rutter. 1 cass. (Running Time: 10 min.). (J). 1997. pap. bk. 9.98 (978-1-57583-049-0(3), TWIN 414) Twin Sisters.
Consists of a variety musical styles, catchy rhythm which are introduced to young children to help to develop solid, personal character.

Building Children's Self-Esteem. Ben Bissell. 1 cass. (Running Time: 43 min.). 15.00 C Bissell.
This brief but powerful presentation focuses on 10 special gifts to which every child is entitled in order to acquire self-esteem.

Building Children's Self-Esteem. Stephanie Marston. Read by Stephanie Marston. 1 cass. (Running Time: 45 min.). (Magic of Encouragement Audio Ser.). 1991. 10.95 (978-1-56170-014-1(2), 243) Hay House.
On this tape you will learn why self-esteem is so important for children, how it is formed, the negative effects of criticism & five tools for encouragement.

Building Cisco Scalable Networks. M. Thomas et al. (McGraw-Hill Technical Expert Ser.). 2000. bk. 60.00 (978-0-07-212477-4(6)) Pub: McGraw-Hill Osborne. Dist(s): McGraw

Building Communication Skills for Social Studies. Virginia Nelson. 1 cass. (Running Time: 1 hr.). 2000. 15.95 (P00086-1) M-H Contemporary.

***Building Confidence CD Set.** Jim Lohr. Narrated by Jim Lohr. (ENG.). 2010. audio compact disk 39.95 (978-0-9825720-0-9(X)) J Lohr Consult.

Building Confidence for Chairing Meetings! Scripts. Jim Lohr. 1. (Running Time: 55 min). 2005. audio compact disk 14.95 (978-0-9643142-4-5(X)) J Lohr Consult.
"Close your eyes and relax deeply following the author's voice on the cd and the slides on the PowerPoint. The PowerPoint contains the author's copyrighted "Ladder of Motions" for guiding the meeting. Relax and imagine yourself in 10 scenes from starting the meeting until adjourning it, understanding and practicing motions used in a fair and efficient meeting. If you repeat the relaxation and visualization cycle enough, you will overcome anxiety and chair meetings comfortably. Do not use while driving or operating machinery due to closed eyes and deep relaxation for your safety and the safety of others.

***Building Confidence for Instrumental Performance!** Jim Lohr. Narrated by Jim Lohr. (ENG.). 2010. audio compact disk 14.95 (978-0-9825720-2-3(6)) J Lohr Consult.

Building Confidence for Speeches & Talks! Scripts. Jim Lohr. 1. (Running Time: 55 min). 2005. audio compact disk 14.95 (978-0-9643142-3-8(1)) J Lohr Consult.
"Close your eyes and relax deeply following the author's voice on the cd and the slides on the PowerPoint. Then relax and imagine yourself in 10 scenes from being told/asked to give a speech to and through presenting the talk. If you repeat the relaxation and visualization cycles enough, you will no longer hear the anxious thoughts about giving your speech. Or you can consciously relax and refocus on sharing your expertise with your listeners. Do not use while driving or operating machinery because of the closed eyes and deep relaxation for your safety and the safety of others.

Building Confidence for Taking Tests! Scripts. Jim Lohr. 1. (Running Time: 55 min). 2005. audio compact disk 14.95 (978-0-9643142-2-1(3)) J Lohr Consult.
"Close your eyes and relax deeply following the author's voice on the cd and the slides on the PowerPoint. Then relax and imagine yourself in 10 scenes from the teacher going too fast in class through taking a test. If you repeat the relaxation and visualization cycles enough, you will no longer have the blocked mind while taking a test. Or you can consciously relax muscles and concentrate on the test. Not for use while driving or operating machinery because of closed eyes and deep relaxation for your own safety and the safety of others.

***Building Confidence for Vocal Performance!** Jim Lohr. Narrated by Jim Lohr. (ENG.). 2010. audio compact disk 14.95 (978-0-9825720-3-0(4)) J Lohr Consult.

Building Confidence with Horses. Julie Goodnight. 2004. 19.95 (978-0-9763619-0-9(6)) Goodnght Trning Stables.

***Building Courage to Have My Baby!** Jim Lohr. Narrated by Jim Lohr. (ENG.). 2010. audio compact disk 14.95 (978-0-9825720-4-7(2)) J Lohr Consult.

Building Customer Loyalty with Value Added & Specialty Departments. 1 cass. (America's Supermarket Showcase '96 Ser.). 1996. 11.00 (NGA96-036) Sound Images.

Building Customer Satisfaction. unabr. ed. Robert L. Desatnick. 8 cass. (Running Time: 30 min. per cass.). 1990. 69.95 Incl. action guide. (2001) Dartnell Corp.
Interviews with America's leading "Service Superstars", including top executives from Hewlett-Packard, Federal Express, Subaru, Prudential, AT&T & Dayton-Hudson.

Building Customer Satisfaction: A Blueprint for Your Business. unabr. ed. Robert L. Desatnick. 8 cass. (Running Time: 30 min. per cass.). 1990. pap. bk. 69.95 Dartnell Corp.

Building Customer Service in Health Organizations. Russell Giles. 3 cass. (Running Time: 2 hrs. 45 min.). 1997. bk. 65.00 (978-1-58111-021-0(9)) Contemporary Medical.
Fundamental definitions & concepts for customer service; specific examples, processes & procedures for health professionals, health care as a product & health care professionals as providers.

Building Design/Materials & Methods Mock Exam. Ed. by Architectural License Seminars Staff. 2004. audio compact disk 45.00 (978-0-7931-9395-0(8)) Kaplan Pubng.

Building Energy Exercises. Read by Mary Richards. (Short Strengthening Exercises Ser.). 6.00 (084) Master Your Mind.

Building Great Sentences: Exploring the Writer's Craft. Instructed by Brooks Landon. (ENG.). 2008. 129.95 (978-1-59803-446-2(4)); audio compact disk 69.95 (978-1-59803-447-9(2)) Teaching Co.

Building Happiness Series One. Virgil B. Smith. Read by Virgil B. Smith. 1 cass. (Running Time: 32 min.). 1990. 5.95 (978-1-878507-09-9(5), 21C1) Human Grwth Services.
Ten three-minute solutions for problems related to Confidence, Finding Lost Time, Depression, Smoking & Rights, Jumping to Conclusions, When to Change a Habit, Responsibility, Forgetting Problems, Organizing Multiple Goals, Affection & Drugs.

Building Happiness Series Three. Virgil B. Smith. Read by Virgil B. Smith. 1 cass. (Running Time: 30 min.). 1979. 5.95 (978-1-878507-11-2(7), 21C3) Human Grwth Services.
Ten three-minute solutions to problems related to Persuasion, Relaxation, Inflation, Behavior & Health, Overprotection, Dating, Nutrition & Behavior, Communicating, Efficiency, & Marriage.

Building Happiness Series Two. Virgil B. Smith. Read by Virgil B. Smith. 1 cass. (Running Time: 30 min.). 1990. 5.95 (978-1-878507-10-5(9), 21C2) Human Grwth Services.
Ten three-minute solutions to problems related to Social Barriers, Reality & Freedom, Goal Steps, Eating Behavior, Body Height, Fairness, Easier Learning, Exercise, Seeking Status, & Understanding "Normal.".

Building Healthy Adult Relationships. Earnie Larsen. 6 cass. (Running Time: 6 hrs.). 1988. 45.95 (978-1-56047-022-9(4), A603) E Larsen Enterprises.
Discusses what makes relationships work or fail; what skills are necessary; & how those skills are gained.

Building Healthy & Strong Self Esteem. Scott Sulak. 1998. 15.00 (978-1-932659-07-8(2)) Change For Gd.

Building Healthy Small Groups. Lance Witt & Steve Gladen. (ENG.). 2005. audio compact disk 20.00 (978-1-4228-0016-4(4)) Purpose Driven Pub.

Building Her House- Alternate Cover: Commonsensical Wisdom for Christian Women. Read by Nancy Wilson. 8 cass. 2006. 12.00 (978-1-59128-331-7(0)) Canon Pr ID.

Building Her House AudioBook: Commonsensical Wisdom for Christian Women. Nancy Wilson. Read by Karen Hieronymus. (ENG.). 2007. audio compact disk 20.00 (978-1-59128-275-4(6)) Canon Pr ID.

Building Houses of Glory Tape Set. As told by Frank Damazio. 4 Cass. 1998. 20.00 (978-1-886849-63-1(3)) CityChristian.

Building Life Skills: Powerpoint Presentations CD, Individual License. Louise A. Liddell & Yvonne S. Gentzler. (gr. 6-9). tchr. ed. 160.00 (978-1-59070-366-3(9)) Goodheart.

Building Life Skills: Teacher's Resource. Louise A. Liddell & Yvonne S. Gentzler. (gr. 6-9). 2003. tchr. ed. 200.00 (978-1-56637-890-1(7)) Goodheart.

Building Life Skills: Teaching Package Powerpoint Presentation, Site License. Louise A. Liddell & Yvonne S. Gentzler. (gr. 6-9). audio compact disk 480.00 (978-1-59070-367-0(7)) Goodheart.

Building Math Confidence! Scripts. Jim Lohr. 1. (Running Time: 55 min). 2005. audio compact disk 14.95 (978-0-9643142-1-4(5)) J Lohr Consult.
"Close your eyes and relax deeply following the author's voice on the cd and the slides on the PowerPoint. Then relax and imagine yourself in 10 scenes from signing up for a math class to taking a math exam. If you repeat the relaxation and visualization cycle enough, you will no longer hear the anxious thoughts about math. Or you can consciously reduce muscle tension and focus on doing the math. Do not play the cd while driving or operating machinery for your safety and the safety of others.".

Building of Character. (709) Yoga Res Foun.

Building of Character. Swami Jyotirmayananda. 1 cass. (Running Time: 1 hr.). 1990. 12.99 Yoga Res Foun.

Building of the Ship see Best Loved Poems of Longfellow

Building on Solid Ground: Authentic Values & How to Attain Them. Thomas Williams. Read by John Bartunek. 6 cassettes. (Running Time: 281 minutes). 1998. 29.00 (978-0-9651601-4-8(9)) Circle Pr CT.
The unabridged reading of Thomas Williams, LC's book "Building on Solid Ground". Williams examines how to apply authentic human and Christian values to the world around you and your family.

Building Our Own Conscience. unabr. ed. William O'Malley. 1 cass. (Running Time: 48 min.). 1999. 9.95 (TAH417) Alba Hse Comns.
For today's educator or for those who seek answers to the dilemmas that plague contemporary society.

Building Positive Self Esteem in Your Children. abr. ed. 1 cass. (Running Time: 60 min.). 1999. 10.00 (978-1-928652-02-1(6)) Motivational OH.

Building Praying, Looking: Jude 17-21. Ed Young. 1989. 4.95 (978-0-7417-1744-3(1), 744) Win Walk.

Building Produce Profits: What's in Your Future? 1 cass. (America's Supermarket Showcase '96 Ser.). 1996. 11.00 (NGA96-001) Sound Images.

Building Products in France: A Strategic Reference 2007. Compiled by Icon Group International, Inc. Staff. 2007. ring bd. 195.00 (978-0-497-35944-7(8)) Icon Grp.

Building Rapport: An Inspirational Overview of NLP. Paul M. Lisnek. Read by Paul M. Lisnek. 1 cass. (Running Time: 1 hr.). 1994. 17.95 (978-1-57654-200-2(9), CPA104) Creat Core.
An overview of the powerful communication patterns of NLP.

Building Regulations in Brief. 3rd rev. ed. Ray Tricker. 2005. 32.95 (978-0-7506-6703-6(6), Butter Sci Hein) Sci Tech Bks.

Building Relationships. G. Michael Durst. Read by G. Michael Durst. 3 cass. 45.00 Set, incl. wkbk. Train Sys.

Building Relationships. G. Michael Durst. Read by G. Michael Durst. 2 cass. 1987. 36.00 Train Sys.

Building Relationships. Duane H. Elmer & Muriel I. Elmer. 1 cass. 1984. 55.00 (978-0-942726-01-5(4)) Mission Trng.

Building Rich Relationships. unabr. ed. Eknath Easwaran. 1 cass. (Running Time: 60 min.). 1990. 7.95 (978-1-58638-509-5(7), BRR) Nilgiri Pr.
Here Easwaran reveals how we can create relationships that grow & endure. He discusses the importance of instilling high ideals in our children, & the value of overcoming differences to maintain loyalty in relationships.

Building Self-Esteem. Shad Helmstetter. 1 cass. (Self-Talk Cassettes Ser.). 10.95 (978-0-937065-29-7(3)) Grindle Pr.

Building Self-Esteem. Earnie Larsen. 6 cass. (Running Time: 6 hrs.). 1986. 53.95 (978-1-56047-020-5(8), A601) E Larsen Enterprises.
Discusses how shame affects one, how to change self-defeating behaviors, & how to build self-esteem. Includes workbook.

Building Self-Esteem. unabr. ed. Brad Caudle & Richard Caudle. Perf. by Brad Caudle et al. Illus. by Bart Harlan. 1 cass. (Running Time: 40 min.). (Rock 'N Learn Ser.). (J). (gr. 1 up). 1994. pap. bk. 9.95 (978-1-878489-43-2(7), RL943) Rock N Learn.
"Top 40" type songs with educational lyrics promote setting goals, making friends, maintaining a good attitude, & more. Includes reproducible book.

Building Self-Esteem in Your Child. Susan Baile. 4 cass. (Running Time: 6 hrs.). 1995. 19.95 (978-1-55977-161-0(5)) CareerTrack Pubns.

Building Self-Esteem in Your Child. Susan Baile. 2 cass. (Running Time: 102 min.). 1996. 15.95 (978-1-55977-493-2(2)) CareerTrack Pubns.

Building Self-Esteem in Your Child. PUEI. 1992. audio compact disk 89.95 (978-1-933328-37-9(1), CareerTrack) P Univ E Inc.

Building Self-Esteem in Your Child: How to Give Your Child a Healthy Foundation for Life. Susan Baile. 4 cass. (Running Time: 4 hrs. 5 min.). 39.95 Set incl. 32p. wkbk. (Q10131) CareerTrack Pubns.
In this program, Dr. Susan Baile teaches you to be more conscious of the ways you can unknowingly damage your child's self-esteem. Plus she gives you plenty of realistic techniques for giving your child control over his or her life.

Building Self-Esteem in Your Daughter. Julie White. 4 cass. (Running Time: 4 hrs. 23 min.). 39.95 Set. (Q10189) CareerTrack Pubns.
Respected child-development authority Julie White gives you the practical parenting skills & insights you'll need to help your daughter become a more independent, self-confident & self-assured young woman.

Building Self-Esteem Through Positive Discipline. Jane Nelsen. Ed. by Kenneth Ainge, Jr. (ENG.). 2006. audio compact disk 14.95 (978-0-9816250-0-3(2)) EmpoweringUT.

Building Self-Exteem: 1 Peter 3:8. Ed Young. 1991. Rental 4.95 (978-0-7417-1861-7(8), 861) Win Walk.

Building Self-Image. Earnie Larsen. 1 cass. (Running Time: 1 hr.). 1989. 10.95 (978-1-56047-006-9(2), A110) E Larsen Enterprises.
Explains how to be ones own best friend.

Building Skills for Understanding. Marc Helgesen et al. 2 cass. 34.95 Set. Midwest European Pubns.
Learn to listen through a careful balance of activities, including listening for gist, specific information, & making inferences.

***Building Social Business: The New Kind of Capitalism That Serves Humanity's Most Pressing Needs.** unabr. ed. Muhammad Yunus. (Running Time: 9 hrs. 0 mins.). 2010. 29.95 (978-1-4417-3533-1(X)); audio compact disk 29.95 (978-1-4417-3532-4(1)) Blckstn Audio.

***Building Social Business: The New Kind of Capitalism That Serves Humanity's Most Pressing Needs.** unabr. ed. Muhammad Yunus. (Running Time: 9 hrs. 0 mins.). 2010. 59.95 (978-1-4417-3529-4(1)); audio compact disk 90.00 (978-1-4417-3530-0(5)) Blckstn Audio.

Building the Image of Prosperity. Featuring Bill Winston. 8 cass. 2005. 20.00 (978-1-59544-159-1(X)); audio compact disk 40.00 (978-1-59544-160-7(3)) Pub: B Winston Min. Dist(s): Anchor Distributors

Building the Panama Canal. Kenneth Bruce. 1 cass. (Running Time: 1 hr.). Dramatization. (Excursions in History Ser.). 12.50 Alpha Tape.

Building the Right Stuff in Your Children: Deut. 6:6-7, 723. Ed Young. 1989. 4.95 (978-0-7417-1723-8(9), 723) Win Walk.

Building the Transcontinental Railroad, Pts. I & II. Kenneth Bruce. 2 cass. (Running Time: 2 hrs.). Dramatization. (Excursions in History Ser.). 12.50 Set. Alpha Tape.

Building Trust. unabr. ed. Eknath Easwaran. 1 cass. (Running Time: 60 min.). 1989. 7.95 (978-1-58638-510-1(0), BT) Nilgiri Pr.
When we lack trust, in ourselves & in others, personal relationships become difficult. The Buddha shows us that trust can be renewed.

Building Trust: Organized Labor's Role in the Change Process. Innovation Groups Staff. 1 cass. (Running Time: 2 hrs.). 1997. 21.50 (978-1-882403-40-0(1)) Alliance Innov.
Training information for those working in or with local government.

Building Trust for Community & Government. unabr. ed. Innovation Groups Staff. Contrib. by Peter Block & Joel Henning. 1 cass. (Running Time: 1 hr. 15 min.). (Transforming Local Government Ser.: Vol. 22). 1999. 10.00 (978-1-882403-78-3(9), IG9924) Alliance Innov.

Building Trust for Elected Officials & Managers. unabr. ed. Innovation Groups Staff. 1 cass. (Running Time: 1 hrs. 15 min.). (Transforming Local Government Ser.: Vol. 8). 1999. 10.00 (978-1-882403-64-6(9), IG9908) Alliance Innov.

Building Trust for Staff & Supervisors (Follow-Up to General Session) unabr. ed. Innovation Groups Staff. 1 cass. (Running Time: 1 hrs. 15 min.). (Transforming Local Government Ser.: Vol. 19). 1999. 10.00 (978-1-882403-75-2(4), IG9920) Alliance Innov.

Building Trust Within Schools. Interview. Susan Simon. 1. (Running Time: 60 mins). 2005. audio compact disk (978-0-9764153-3-6(X)) R James TV.
"Building Trust Within Schools" is an educational CD designed for teachers, administrators and parents. It provides discussion around the importance of creating trust in classrooms and schools. Strategies and action steps are provided to assist educators in implementing trust within school settings. The material presented on this CD is excerpted from a book entitled, Building A Schoolhouse...Laying The Foundation For Success.

Building up the Church. Rick Joyner. 1 cass. (Running Time: 90 mins.). (Vision Ser.: Vol. 2). 2000. 5.00 (RJ16-002) Morning NC.
This tape series will help to impart new vision or restore lost vision in the church.

Building Walking Bass Lines. Ed Friedland & Hal Leonard Corporation Staff. (Instrument Instruction). 1995. 19.99 (978-0-7935-4204-8(9), 0793542049) H Leonard.

Building Wealth One House at a Time. abr. ed. John W. Shaub. Read by William Dufris. (Running Time: 16200 sec.). 2006. audio compact disk 28.00 (978-1-932378-97-9(9)) Pub: A Media Intl. Dist(s): Natl Bk Netwk

Building Wealth Through Spirituality. (Running Time: 48 mins.). audio compact disk (978-1-59076-201-1(0)) DscvrHlpPubng.

Building Wings. Don Johnston & Jerry Stemach. 2006. audio compact disk 18.95 (978-1-4105-0783-9(1)) D Johnston Inc.

Building Winning Relationships. unabr. ed. Zig Ziglar. Narrated by Zig Ziglar. (Running Time: 7 hrs. 43 mins. 7 sec.). (Christian Motivation for Daily Living Ser.). (ENG.). 2009. 19.59 (978-1-60814-652-9(9)); audio compact disk 27.99 (978-1-59859-709-7(4)) Oasis Audio.

Building Witnesses Who Build the Church: Proceedings of the 45th Annual Convocational Association of Evagelicals Buffalo, New York. Read by Archie B. Parrish. 1 cass. (Running Time: 60 min.). 1987. 4.00 (324) Nat Assn Evan.

Building Your Energetic Currency: Learning How to Heal. Caroline Myss. (Building Your Energetic Currency). 1998. 55.00 (978-1-893869-60-8(1)) Celbrtng Life.

Building Your Family upon a Rock. Taffi L. Dollar. 2 cass. (Running Time: 3 hrs.). 2001. 10.00 (978-1-931172-18-9(8), TS 294, Kidz Faith) Pub: Creflo Dollar. Dist(s): STL Dist NA

Building Your Field of Dreams Step by Step. unabr. ed. Mary M. Morrissey. Read by Mary M. Morrissey. 10 cass. (Running Time: 10 hrs.). 1999. Set. (978-1-886491-22-9(4)) Tiger Mtn Pr.

Building Your Financial Future. unabr. ed. 6 cass. bk. 89.95 Set. (SO1910) J Norton Pubs.

Building Your Financial Future, Set. unabr. ed. 6 cass. (Running Time: 9 hrs.). 89.95 incl. text, 293p. (SO1910) J Norton Pubs.

Building Your Life Through Faith Confessions. Taffi L. Dollar. 20.00 (978-1-59089-003-5(5)) Pub: Creflo Dollar. Dist(s): STL Dist NA

Building Your Mate's Self-Esteem. abr. ed. Dennis Rainey & Barbara Rainey. Ed. by Keith Lynch. 8 cass. (Running Time: 8 hrs.). 1995. 39.95 Set. (978-1-57229-052-5(8)) FamilyLife.
Building up your mate's self-esteem & your marriage relationship.

Building Your Own Conscience. William O'Malley. 1 cass. (Running Time: 48 min.). 1999. 9.95 (TAH417) Alba Hse Comns.
Through his experiential knowledge as an educator, Fr. O'Malley investigates the immediate needs of modern society to understand morality as a system of objective truths directed to the creation of truly human lives.

Building Your Support Team. unabr. ed. Neal Pirolo. 2 cass. (Running Time: 2 hrs. 20 min.). 1992. 10.00 set. (978-1-880185-04-9(0)) Emmaus Rd Intl.
Teaches a missionary how to gather & train those who will care for him; correlates with the book, "Serving As Senders".

BuildUp Phonics Skill Bags. Compiled by Benchmark Education Staff. 2006. audio compact disk 10.00 (978-1-4108-6977-7(6)) Benchmark Educ.

***Built to Last.** abr. ed. Jim Collins. Read by Jim Collins. Read by Jerry I. Porras. (ENG.). 2008. (978-0-06-179125-3(3), Harper Audio) HarperCollins Pubs.

Built to Last: Successful Habits of Visionary Companies. Jim Collins & Jerry I. Porras. Narrated by Rick Rohan. 8 cass. (Running Time: 9 hrs. 15 mins.). 74.00 (978-0-7887-5289-6(8)); audio compact disk 78.00 (978-1-4025-1531-6(6)) Recorded Bks.

Built to Last: Successful Habits of Visionary Companies. abr. ed. Jim Collins. Read by Jim Collins. Read by Jerry I. Porras. 2004. audio compact disk 29.95 (978-0-06-058905-9(1)) HarperCollins Pubs.

Built to Last: Successful Habits of Visionary Companies. unabr. ed. James C. Collins & Jerry I. Porras. Read by Jonathan Reese. 8 cass. (Running Time: 12 hrs.). 1995. 64.00 (3790) Books on Tape.
What separates successful companies such as General Electric, 3M, & Wal-Mart from their rivals? Why do certain companies - the 3Ms, Motorolas, & Procter & Gambles of the world - seem to thrive year after year as management fads & fancies come & go? What makes a company the crown jewel of its industry?.

Built to Last: Successful Habits of Visionary Companies. unabr. ed. James C. Collins & Jerry I. Porras. 2001. (T1002L8) Recorded Bks.
What separates successful companies such as General Electric, 3M & Wal-Mart from their rivals? Why do certain companies - the 3Ms, Motorolas & Procter & Gambles of the world - seem to thrive year after year as management fads & fancies come & go? What makes a company the crown jewel of its industry?.

***Built to Win.** Ian Anderson. 2009. audio compact disk 49.95 (978-0-578-00717-5(7)) My Friend.

Buitres en la Playa, EDL Level 4. (SPA.). 2003. 11.50 (978-0-7652-1006-7(1)) Modern Curr.

Bukhara: Musical Crossroads of Asia. Otanazar Matyubov. Contrib. by Ted Levin. 1 cass. or CD. (Running Time: 58 min.). 1991. (0-9307-400500-9307-40050-2-6); audio compact disk (0-9307-40050-2-6) Smithsonian Folkways.

Bulfinch's Mythology: The Age of Fable. Thomas Bulfinch. Narrated by Flo Gibson. 2008. 29.95 (978-1-55685-982-3(1)); audio compact disk 39.95 (978-1-60646-039-9(0)) Audio Bk Con.

Bulgari Connection. Fay Weldon. Narrated by Patricia Gallimore. 6 CDs. (Running Time: 7 hrs.). audio compact disk 62.00 (978-1-4025-2919-1(8)) Recorded Bks.

Bulgari Connection. unabr. ed. Fay Weldon. Narrated by Patricia Gallimore. 5 cass. (Running Time: 7 hrs.). 2002. 47.00 (978-1-84197-262-6(2)) Recorded Bks.

Bulgari Connection. unabr. ed. Fay Weldon. Narrated by Patricia Gallimore. 5 cass. (Running Time: 7 hrs.). 2002. 32.95 (978-1-4025-2219-2(3), RG049) Recorded Bks.
Invites us into the world of a wealthy businessman, his passionate and successful wife, an artist, and two women wearing Bulgari necklaces. The resulting story is one of desire, envy, and a touch of the supernatural.

Bulgarian, Vol. 1. 15 CDs. (Running Time: 16 hrs.). (Foreign Service Institute Basic Course Ser.). (BUL.). 2005. audio compact disk 295.00 (978-1-57970-167-3(1), AFL450D) J Norton Pubs.

Bulgarian, Vol. 2 9 CDs. (Running Time: 5 hrs. 30 min.). (Foreign Service Institute Basic Course Ser.). (BUL.). 2005. audio compact disk 185.00 (978-1-57970-168-0(X), AFL500D) J Norton Pubs.

Bulgarian Basic Course, Vol. 1. unabr. ed. Foreign Service Institute Staff. 23 cass. (Running Time: 16 hrs.). (Foreign Service Institute Basic Course Ser.). (BUL.). 1970. pap. bk. 295.00 (978-0-88432-089-0(8), AFL450) J Norton Pubs.
Assumes no previous knowledge of Bulgarian or any other Slavic language. The Cyrillic alphabet is taught through side-by-side presentation of English translations & phonetics.

Bulgarian Basic Course, Vol. 2. Carleton T. Hodge. Prod. by Foreign Service Institute Staff. 11 cass. (Running Time: 5 hrs. 30 mins.). (Foreign Service Institute Basic Course Ser.). (BUL.). 2000. pap. bk. 185.00 (978-1-57970-080-5(2), AFL500) J Norton Pubs.
Presumes knowledge of Bulgarian from Basic Course Vol. 1 or equivalent.

Bulgarian Folk Music. unabr. ed. 1 cass. 1994. 12.95 (978-0-88432-353-2(6), C11148) J Norton Pubs.

***Bulgarian Poetess: A Selection from the John Updike Audio Collection.** unabr. ed. John Updike. Read by John Updike. (ENG.). 2009. (978-0-06-196234-9(1), Caedmon); (978-0-06-196233-2(3), Caedmon) HarperCollins Pubs.

Bulibasha: King of the Gypsies, abr. ed. Witi Ihimaera. Read by George Henare. 2 cass. (Running Time: 3 hrs.). 1997. 17.95 (978-1-57453-090-2(9)) Audio Lit.
On the East Coast of New Zealand, two patriarchs fight to win the title of Bulibasha & be proclaimed the King of the Gypsies. Takes the listener into the heart of contemporary Maori culture.

Bull from the Sea. unabr. ed. Mary Renault. Read by Peter McDonald. 7 cass. (Running Time: 10 hrs. 30 min.). 1985. 56.00 (978-0-7366-0869-5(9), 1819) Books on Tape.
Theseus, King of Athens, is torn between his genius for kingship & his craving for adventure. He joins the forays of the pirate prince, Pirithoos. While exploring Euxine, Theseus captures a warrior priestess, Hippolyta. She becomes the love of his life & the key to his fate. When Phaedra, his queen, meets Hippolyta, the Great Goddess whom Theseus had defied so often takes her full revenge.

Bull from the Sea. unabr. ed. Mary Renault. Narrated by Jamie Hanes. 6 cass. (Running Time: 8 hrs. 30 mins.). (gr. 10 up). 1988. 51.00 (978-1-55690-077-8(5), 88680E7) Recorded Bks.
Theseus becomes King of Athens & goes to war with the Amazons.

Bull Hunter. unabr. collector's ed. Max Brand. Read by Jonathan Marosz. 5 cass. (Running Time: 5 hrs.). 1994. 30.00 (978-0-7366-2806-8(1), 3520) Books on Tape.
The young Bull tracks down a famed gunfighter, discovers a dangerous trail leading to adventure & unexpected rewards.

Bull Hunter's Romance. unabr. collector's ed. Max Brand. Read by Jonathan Marosz. 6 cass. (Running Time: 6 hrs.). 1994. 36.00 (978-0-7366-2854-9(1), 3562) Books on Tape.
This sequel to Bull Hunter follows the y[illegible] giant, his horse & a dog on a series of gripping adventures in the Ol[illegible]

Bull in China: Investing Profitably in the [illegible]ld's Greatest Market. unabr. ed. Jim Rogers. Read by Johnny Heller. (YA). 2008. 54.99 (978-1-60514-875-5(X)) Find a World.

Bull in China: Investing Profitably in the World's Greatest Market. unabr. ed. Jim Rogers. 6 CDs. (Running Time: 7 hrs. 0 mins. 0 sec.). (ENG.). 2007. audio compact disk 29.99 (978-1-4001-0593-9(5)) Pub: Tantor Media. Dist(s): IngramPubServ

Bull in China: Investing Profitably in the World's Greatest Market. unabr. ed. Jim Rogers. Read by Johnny Heller. 1 MP3-CD. (Running Time: 7 hrs. 0 mins. 0 sec.). (ENG.). 2007. audio compact disk 19.99 (978-1-4001-5593-4(2)); audio compact disk 59.99 (978-1-4001-3593-6(1)) Pub: Tantor Media. Dist(s): IngramPubServ

Bull-Jean Stories (CD) Short Stories. Sharon Bridgforth. Read by Sharon Bridgforth. 1 CD. (Running Time: 60). Dramatization. 1999. audio compact disk 12.99 (978-0-9656659-2-6(5)) RedBone Pr.

Bull Moves in Bear Markets: How to Keep Your Portfolio up When the Market Is Down. unabr. ed. Peter D. Schiff. Read by Sean Pratt. (Running Time: 6 hrs. 30 mins.). (ENG.). 2008. 24.98 (978-1-59659-296-4(6), GildAudio) Pub: Gildan Media. Dist(s): HachBkGrp

Bull Moves in Bear Markets: How to Keep Your Portfolio up When the Market Is Down. unabr. ed. Peter D. Schiff. Read by Sean Pratt. (Running Time: 7 hrs.). (ENG.). 2009. audio compact disk 29.98 (978-1-59659-274-2(5)) Pub: Gildan Media. Dist(s): HachBkGrp

Bull Run. Paul Fleischman. Narrated by Paul Fleischman. 2 CDs. (Running Time: 2 hrs.). (gr. 4 up). audio compact disk 22.00 (978-1-4025-2293-2(2)) Recorded Bks.

Bull Run. unabr. ed. Paul Fleischman. Perf. by Paul Fleischman. 2 cass. (Running Time: 2 hrs.). (YA). 1999. 17.95 (978-1-883332-37-2(0)); audio compact disk 24.95 (978-1-883332-58-7(3)) Audio Bkshelf.
Sixteen voices woven together to produce a vivid portrayal of Bull Run, the first battle of the Civil War.

Bull Run, unabr. ed. Paul Fleischman. Narrated by Paul Fleischman. 2 pieces. (Running Time: 2 hrs.). (gr. 4 up). 1997. 19.00 (978-0-7887-0432-1(X), 94624E7) Recorded Bks.
Re-creates the Battle of Bull Run through the eyes of 16 participants - Yankee & Confederate, male & female, white & black.

Bulldog Drummond: Jockey Al Russo Case & The Oil Tanker Case. unabr. ed. Perf. by Ned Weaver. 1 cass. (Running Time: 1 hr.). 2001. 6.98 (1618) Radio Spirits.

Bullet. abr. ed. Charlaine Harris & Laurell K. Hamilton. (Running Time: 9 hrs.). (Anita Blake, Vampire Hunter Ser.: Bk. 19). (ENG.). 2010. audio compact disk 29.95 (978-0-14-314577-6(0), PengAudBks) Penguin Grp USA.

Bullet. unabr. ed. Laurell K. Hamilton. 11 CDs. (Running Time: 13 hrs.). (Anita Blake, Vampire Hunter Ser.: No. 19). (ENG.). 2010. audio compact disk 39.95 (978-0-14-314562-2(2), PengAudBks) Penguin Grp USA.

Bullet for a Star. Stuart M. Kaminsky. Read by Christopher Lane. (Running Time: 4 hrs.). (Toby Peters Mystery Ser.: No. 1). 2000. 22.95 (978-1-59912-438-4(6)) Iofy Corp.

Bullet for a Star. unabr. ed. Stuart M. Kaminsky. Read by Christopher Lane. 9 cass. (Running Time: 4 hrs.). (Toby Peters Mystery Ser.: No. 1). 1994. 23.95 (978-0-7861-0731-5(6), 1482) Blckstn Audio.
Toby Peters looked at the glossy photograph. Yes, that was Errol Flynn in the picture. Toby found the picture where he was supposed to find it. He wasn't planning to get hit on the head though, or to find a corpse when he awoke. The first of a series of corpses, scattered all over Hollywood. The trail Toby follows in order to clear Flynn & himself, takes him throughout the film colony & finally onto the set of "The Maltese Falcon," where Bogie, Lorre & Greenstreet find themselves playing roles that weren't rehearsed - but whose execution had to be picture perfect.

Bullet for a Star. unabr. ed. Stuart M. Kaminsky. Read by Christopher Lane. 4 CDs. (Running Time: 4 hrs.). (Toby Peters Mystery Ser.: No. 1). 2000. audio compact disk 32.00 (978-0-7861-9936-5(9), 1482) Blckstn Audio.
Toby Peters looked at the glossy photograph. Yes that was Errol Flynn in the picture. And, yes, there was a girl with him... a very young girl. They were both birthday naked, & seemed to be enjoying themselves. No wonder

Flynn & Warner Brothers were nervous, if the photograph wasn't a fake, the studio's investment in the star was in serious jeopardy.

Bullet for a Star. unabr. ed. Stuart M. Kaminsky. Read by Christopher Lane. 1 CD. (Running Time: 4 hrs.). (Toby Peters Mystery Ser.: No. 1). 2001. audio compact disk 19.95 (zm1482) Blckstn Audio.

Bullet in the Ballet. unabr. ed. Caryl Brahms & S. J. Simon. Read by Gretel Davis. 6 cass. (Running Time: 6 hrs. 35 min.). 2001. 54.95 (978-1-85089-838-2(3), 20791) Pub: ISIS Audio GBR. Dist(s): Ulverscroft US

Never has such an incompetent ballet company taken to the stage. Most unprofessional is Petroushka, who sees fit to drop dead in the middle of the performance. Inspector Adam Quill arrives to investigate.

Bullet Meant for Me. Jan Reid. Narrated by Ed Sala. 6 cass. (Running Time: 9 hrs.). 58.00 (978-1-4025-1352-7(6)) Recorded Bks.

Bullet Meant for Me: A Memoir. unabr. ed. Jan Reid. Narrated by Ed Sala. 6 cass. (Running Time: 9 hrs.). 2002. 34.95 (978-1-4025-1353-4(4), RF772) Recorded Bks.

One night in Mexico City, as he celebrates a friend's victory in the boxing ring, Reid is abducted by bandits. When he swings at his captor, he is shot and paralyzed. In this powerful memoir, Reid relates his account of the fight to regain his life.

Bullet Park. unabr. collector's ed. John Cheever. Read by Michael Prichard. 7 cass. (Running Time: 7 hrs.). 1986. 42.00 (978-0-7366-0831-2(1), 1781) Books on Tape.

Eliot Nailles & Paul Hammer meet, presumably by chance, on Sunday at church in Bullet Park. Nailles is open, a nice girl, no secrets. Hammer is, dangerously for her, not what he seems. The third character, Tony Nailles, is the one who holds the bag. How he got into it & how in the nick of time he appears to get out is the crux of this tale.

Bulletproof Love. Created by Sonny Black. (YA). 2009. audio compact disk 60.00 (978-0-9824920-0-0(6)) Black Dawn.

Bulletproof Love. unabr. ed. Sonny F. Black. Read by Angela Yee. (Running Time: 4 hrs. 30 mins.). 2009. 34.95 (978-1-4417-2077-1(4)); audio compact disk 49.00 (978-1-4417-2078-8(2)) Blckstn Audio.

Bulletproof Love: K'Wan Presents. unabr. ed. Sonny F. Black. Read by Angela Yee. (Running Time: 4 hrs. 30 mins.). 2009. 29.95 (978-1-4417-2081-8(2)); audio compact disk 29.95 (978-1-4417-2080-1(4)) Blckstn Audio.

Bulletproof Mascara: A Novel. unabr. ed. Bethany Maines. Read by Renée Raudman. (Running Time: 12 hrs.). 2010. 24.99 (978-1-4418-3704-2(3), 9781441837042, Brilliance MP3); 24.99 (978-1-4418-3706-6(X), 9781441837066, BAD); 39.97 (978-1-4418-3705-9(1), 9781441837059, Brlnc Audio MP3 Lib); 39.97 (978-1-4418-3707-3(8), 9781441837073, BADLE); audio compact disk 29.99 (978-1-4418-3702-8(7), 9781441837028, Bril Audio CD Unabri); audio compact disk 79.97 (978-1-4418-3703-5(5), 9781441837035, BriAudCD Unabrid) Brilliance Audio.

Bullets, Booze & Bandits: Chicago's Gangland Days. unabr. ed. Ron Jordan. Read by Ron Jordan. Ed. by James E. Gray. 1 cass. (Running Time: 60 min.). (Americana Ser.). 1995. 9.95 (978-1-887262-06-4(7)) Natl Tape & Disc.

The story of Chicago's gangland days in the twenties & thirties. John Dillinger, Al Capone, Baby Face Nelson...Elliot Ness & the G-Men.

Bullets, Booze & Bandits: Chicago's Gangland Days. unabr. ed. Ron Jordan. Prod. by Joe Loesch. 1 cass. (Running Time: 1 hr.). (Americana Ser.). 1999. lib. bdg. 12.95 (978-1-887729-62-8(3)) Toy Box Prods.

A fascinating look at the colorful history of Chicago during it's gangland days, with characters such as Al Capone, John Dillinger & Babyface Nelson.

***Bullets Off-Broadway: A Sam Jenkins Mystery.** Wayne Zurl. Read by David Colacci. (Running Time: 74). (ENG.). 2010. 2.99 (978-1-61114-021-7(8)); 2.99 (978-0-9827919-1-2(7)) Mind Wings Aud.

Bullfrog & Butterflies: God Loves Fun. 1 cass. (Running Time: 1 hr.). (J). 2000. 6.99 HARK Ent.

Will fill your home with fun-filled praise of the Lord. Provides wholesome messages that are sure to last a lifetime.

Bullfrog at Magnolia Circle. Deborah Dennard. Illus. by Kristin Kest. (Smithsonian's Backyard Ser.). (ENG.). (J). (ps-2). 2005. 8.95 (978-1-59249-073-8(5), SC5022) Soundprints.

Bullfrog Jumped: Children's Folksongs from the Byron Arnold Collection. Prod. by Joyce Cauthen. (J). 2006. bk. 17.00 (978-0-9672672-9-6(3)) AL Folk Assn.

Bullfrogs & Butterflies: God Is Great. 1 cass. (Running Time: 1 hr.). (J). 2000. 6.99 HARK Ent.

Bullfrogs & Butterflies Vol. 1: God Is My Friend. 1 cass. (Running Time: 1 hr.). (J). 2000. 6.99 HARK Ent.

Bullfrogs & Butterflies Vol. 4: I've Been Born Again. 1 cass. (Running Time: 1 hr.). (J). 2000. 6.99 HARK Ent.

Bullfrogs on Your Mind: Stories, Songs & Adventures from the Swamps to the Henhouse. unabr. ed. Doug Elliott. Perf. by Doug Elliott. 1 cass. 1997. audio compact disk 14.95 CD. Native Ground.

Bullfrogs on Your Mind: Stories, Songs & Adventures from the Swamps to the Henhouse. unabr. ed. Doug Elliott. Read by Doug Elliott. 1 cass. 1997. 9.95 (NG620) Native Ground.

Bullion. James Pattinson. 5 cass. (Running Time: 5 hrs. 30 mins.). (Soundings Ser.). (J). 2005. 49.95 (978-1-84283-985-0(3)); audio compact disk 59.95 (978-1-84559-005-5(8)) Pub: ISIS Lrg Prnt GBR. Dist(s): Ulverscroft US

***Bullpen Gospels: Major League Dreams of a Minor League Veteran.** unabr. ed. Dirk Hayhurst. (Running Time: 11 hrs. 15 mins.). 2010. audio compact disk 29.95 (978-1-4417-6308-2(2)) Blckstn Audio.

***Bullpen Gospels: Major League Dreams of a Minor League Veteran.** unabr. ed. Dirk Hayhurst. Read by Ray Porter. (Running Time: 11 hrs. 30 mins.). 2010. 29.95 (978-1-4417-6309-9(0)); 65.95 (978-1-4417-6306-8(6)); audio compact disk 100.00 (978-1-4417-6307-5(4)) Blckstn Audio.

***Bulls Island.** unabr. ed. Dorothea Benton Frank. Read by Julia Gibson & Joey Collins. (ENG.). 2008. (978-0-06-158287-5(5)); (978-0-06-163250-1(3)) HarperCollins Pubs.

Bulls Island. unabr. ed. Dorothea Benton Frank. Read by Julia Gibson & Joey Collins. 2009. audio compact disk 19.99 (978-0-06-172756-6(3), Harper Audio) HarperCollins Pubs.

Bulls Island. unabr. ed. Dorothea Benton Frank. Narrated by Julia Gibson & Joey Collins. (Running Time: 11 hrs. 30 mins.). 2008. 56.75 (978-1-4361-5784-1(6)); audio compact disk 123.75 (978-1-4361-0704-4(0)) Recorded Bks.

Dorothea Benton Frank is a New York Times best-selling author whose books are prized by fans who enjoy her heartfelt stories. In Bull's Island, she offers a fun and original twist on Shakespeare's classic, Romeo and Juliet. The blue-blooded Langley family and the new-money Barretts are at odds over the impending wedding of JD and Betts. And then a shocking event on the night of their engagement changes everything.

Bullseye. unabr. ed. Alf Harris. Read by Nancy Lee Painter. 6 cass. (Running Time: 6 hrs. 30 min.). 2001. 39.95 (978-1-55686-758-3(1)) Books in Motion.

Police Detective Sydney Kramer is convinced that suicide victim Tom Grant was actually murdered. But at the hands of Tom's own wife? Sydney seeks the evidence.

Bully Father: Theodore Roosevelt's Letters to His Children. unabr. ed. Theodore Roosevelt & Joan Paterson Kerr. Ed. by John P. Kerr. Narrated by John McDonough. 6 cass. (Running Time: 8 hrs.). 1996. 51.00 (978-0-7887-0652-3(7), 94829E7) Recorded Bks.

This collection of letters, written between 1898 & 1911, captures all the fascination & love Roosevelt felt for his four sons & two daughters.

Bully for Brontosaurus: Reflections in Natural History. unabr. collector's ed. Stephen Jay Gould. Read by Larry McKeever. 14 cass. (Running Time: 21 hrs.). 1991. 112.00 (978-0-7366-2002-4(8), 2819) Books on Tape.

A collection of 35 essays on language, the role of chance in history, the evolution of life & the family tree.

Bully Grows Up: Erik Meets the Wizard: Student Edition (Audio Book) Caryn Sabes Hacker. Narrated by Cooke Lainie. 1 CD. (Running Time: 70.14 mins.). Dramatization. (J). 2006. audio compact disk 12.95 (978-0-9791046-2-6(9)) Caryn Solutns.

Bully Grows Up: MP3 Download (Student Edition) Caryn Sabes Hacker. Narrated by Lainie Cooke. 20 MB. (Running Time: 70:14). Dramatization. (J). 2006. 9.95 (978-0-9791046-4-0(5)) Caryn Solutns.

Bully of Brocas Court see Tales of the Supernatural

Bullying: Program from the Award Winning Public Radio Series. Interview. Hosted by Fred Goodwin. 1 CD. (Running Time: 1 Hour). 2003. audio compact disk 21.95 (978-1-932479-29-4(5), LCM 273) Lichtenstein Creat.

In this hour, we explore Bullying. Beat up during recess? Teased on the school bus? New research shows bullying has serious consequences for children on both sides of the problem. Guests include Dr. Howard Spivak, the director of the Tufts University Center for Children and the chair of the American Academy of Pediatrics Task Force on Violence; Dr. Susan Limber, a developmental psychologist and a researcher at the Clemson University Institute on Family and Neighborhood Life in South Carolina; John Scagliotti, the award-winning director of Oliver Button is a Star - a new film that deals with building acceptance for kids who don't fit boy/girl stereotypes; and Dr. Gary Namie, a social psychologist who, with his wife Ruth Namie, co-founded The Workplace Bullying & Trauma Institute in Bellingham, WA and co-wrote The Bully at Work: What You Can Do to Stop the Hurt and Reclaim Your Dignity On the Job.

Bullying Prevention Handbook: A Guide for Principals, Teachers, & Counselors. 2nd ed. John H. Hoover & Ronald L. Oliver. 2008. pap. bk. 29.95 (978-1-934009-11-6(3)) Solution Tree.

Bulow Hammock: Mind of a Rain Forest. abr. ed. David R. Wallace. Read by Edward Markmann. 2 cass. (Running Time: 3 hrs.). 1995. 15.95 (978-0-944993-28-6(1)) Audio Lit.

Brilliant blend of ecological philosophy, history & personal reminiscence.

Bum Steer. unabr. ed. Nancy Pickard. Read by Nicola Sheara. 6 vols. (Running Time: 9 hrs.). (Jenny Cain Mystery Ser.). 2000. bk. 54.95 (978-0-7927-2238-0(8), CSL 127, Chivers Sound Lib) AudioGO.

Hours after the Port Frederick Civic Foundation got wind of a highly unusual bequest: a $4 million Kansas cattle ranch, director Jenny Cain hops a flight west. She arrives at the hospital room of the gravely ill benefactor, Charles W. "Cat" Benet, to find that he's already dead. Murdered. Could charming Quentin Harlan, the ranch hand, be Cat Benet's killer? Or did Cat's estranged daughters, unhappy ex-wives and their jealous second husbands have something to do with his death?.

Bumble Boogie & Other Wonderful Piano Pieces: Intermediate Piano Solos. Contrib. by Debra Wanless. (Debra Wanless Intermediate Piano Library). 2008. pap. bk. 14.95 (978-1-933657-58-5(8)) Pro Music In.

***Bumble Boogie & Other Wonderful Piano Pieces: The Debra Wanless Intermediate Piano Library.** Debra Wanless. (ENG.). 2010. pap. bk. 12.99 (978-1-4234-9750-9(3), 1423497503) H Leonard.

Bumblebee at Apple Tree Lane. Laura Gates Galvin. Illus. by Kristin Kest. 1 cass. (Running Time: 35 min.). (J). (gr. k-4). 2001. pap. bk. 19.95 (SP 5019C) Kimbo Educ.

Bumblebee emerges from her winter hibernation & begins searching for a nest site so she can lay her eggs. When her daughter's hatch, they keep the nest clean & care for the younger bees. Includes read along book.

Bumblebee at Apple Tree Lane. Laura Gates Galvin. Illus. by Kristin Kest. Narrated by Alexi Komistar. (J). 2000. bk. (978-1-56899-828-2(7)) Soundprints.

Bumblebee at Apple Tree Lane. Laura Gates Galvin. Illus. by Kristin Kest. (Smithsonian's Backyard Ser.). (ENG.). (J). (ps-2). 2005. 8.95 (978-1-59249-071-4(9), SC5019) Soundprints.

Bumface. unabr. ed. Morris Gleitzman. Read by Morris Gleitzman. (Running Time: 3 hrs. 25 mins.). (J). 2006. audio compact disk 57.95 (978-1-74093-802-0(X)) Pub: Bolinda Pubng AUS. Dist(s): Bolinda Pub Inc

Bumping & A-Jumping. 1 cass., 1 CD. (Bananas in Pajamas Ser.). (J). 7.98 (CAP 59109); audio compact disk 12.78 CD Jewel box. (CAP 59109) NewSound.

Bumping into Bankruptcy in a General Practice. Elizabeth Warren. 1 cass. 1990. 135.00 (3324) Natl Prac Inst.

Bums: An Oral History of the Brooklyn Dodgers. unabr. ed. Peter Golenbock. Read by Raymond Todd. 16 CDs. (Running Time: 20 hrs. 30 mins.). 2003. audio compact disk 128.00 (978-0-7861-9245-8(3), 3083); 89.95 (978-0-7861-2423-7(7), 3083) Blckstn Audio.

A fascinating oral history of the Ebbets Field heroes with recollections from former players, writers, front-office executives, and faithful fans. Dodgers' legends such as Pee Wee Reese, Leo Durocher, Duke Snider, Roy Campanella, Ralph Branca, and many others recall the ups and downs of that unforgettable ball club in their own words.

Bunbury: A Serious Play for Trivial People. unabr. ed. Tom Jacobson. Contrib. by Jean Gilpin et al. 2 CDs. (Running Time: 6600 sec.). 2007. audio compact disk 25.95 (978-1-58081-356-3(9)) Pub: L A Theatre. Dist(s): NetLibrary CO

Bundle from Britain. collector's ed. Alistair Horne. Read by Bill Kelsey. 10 cass. (Running Time: 15 hrs.). 2000. 80.00 (978-0-7366-5909-3(9)) Books on Tape.

Bundle from Britain. unabr. ed. Alistair Horne. Read by Bill Kelsey. 10 cass. (Running Time: 15 hrs.). 2000. 80.00 Books on Tape.

The story of a child evacuated to America from the war in Europe, told with wit & charm.

***Bundle up & Go.** Cunla. (ENG.). 1992. 11.95 (978-0-8023-7085-3(3)) Pub: Clo Iar-Chonnachta IRL. Dist(s): Dufour

Bungalow Mystery. unabr. ed. Carolyn Keene. Read by Laura Linney. (Running Time: 10620 sec.). (Nancy Drew Ser.). (ENG.). (J). (gr. 3-7). 2007. audio compact disk 14.95 (978-0-7393-5059-1(5), Listening Lib) Pub: Random Audio Pubg. Dist(s): Random

Bungalow Mystery Vol. 3. unabr. ed. Carolyn Keene. Read by Laura Linney. 2 cass. (Running Time: 2 hrs. 58 mins.). (Nancy Drew Mystery Stories). (J). (gr. 4-7). 2004. 23.00 (978-0-8072-0761-1(6), S YA 406 CX, Listening Lib) Random Audio Pubg.

"Nancy believes her friend's guardians are trying to steal her inheritance. As she investigates, she has a perilous experience near the deserted bungalow.".

Bungalow 2. abr. ed. Danielle Steel. Read by Michael Boatman. (Running Time: 21600 sec.). (Danielle Steel Ser.). (ENG.). 2008. audio compact disk 14.99 (978-0-7393-2872-9(7)) Pub: Random Audio Pubg. Dist(s): Random

Bungalow 2. unabr. ed. Danielle Steel. 8 cass. (Running Time: 12 hrs.). 2007. 90.00 (978-1-4159-3899-7(7)); audio compact disk 90.00 (978-1-4159-3900-0(4)) Books on Tape.

Bungalow 2. unabr. ed. Danielle Steel. Read by Michael Boatman. (YA). 2007. 59.99 (978-0-7393-7449-8(4)) Find a World.

Bungalow 2. unabr. ed. Danielle Steel. Read by Michael Boatman. (Running Time: 36000 sec.). (Danielle Steel Ser.). (ENG.). 2007. audio compact disk 44.95 (978-0-7393-1365-7(7)) Pub: Random Audio Pubg. Dist(s): Random

Bunker Hill. Perf. by Colonial Radio Theatre Staff. 1 cass. (Running Time: 1 hr.). Dramatization. 2001. 12.98 (978-1-929244-11-9(8)) Pub: Colonial Radio. Dist(s): Penton Overseas

The first set battle of the American Revolution pits veteran British troops against the untested Minutemen of New England. Your chest will fill with pride as the determined American army repels the finest fighting force in the world twice, before running out of ammunition & being overrun.

Bunnicula Collection, Bks. 1-3. unabr. ed. James Howe & Deborah Howe. Read by Victor Garber. 6 CDs. (Running Time: 6 hrs. 40 mins.). (ENG.). (J). (gr. 3). 2004. audio compact disk 19.99 (978-1-4000-9472-1(0), Listening Lib) Pub: Random Audio Pubg. Dist(s): Random

Bunnicula Meets Edgar Allan Crow. unabr. ed. James Howe. Read by Patrick Mulvihill. 3 CDs. (Running Time: 2 hrs. 51 mins.). (Bunnicula Ser.). (J). (gr. 4-7). 2007. audio compact disk 24.00 (978-0-7393-4847-5(7)) Books on Tape.

Bunnicula Meets Edgar Allan Crow. unabr. ed. James Howe. Read by Patrick Mulvihill. (Running Time: 10260 sec.). (Bunnicula Ser.). (ENG.). (J). (gr. 5-7). 2007. audio compact disk 27.00 (978-0-7393-3867-4(6), Listening Lib) Pub: Random Audio Pubg. Dist(s): Random

Bunnicula Strikes Again! James Howe. Read by Victor Garber. 2 cass. (Running Time: 2 hrs.). (Bunnicula Ser.). (J). (gr. 3-5). 2000. 18.00 (978-0-7366-9018-8(2)) Books on Tape.

It seems that Bunnicula, the vampire rabbit, is back to his old ways or so Chester thinks, having found pale vegetables drained of their juices & scattered about the Monroe family kitchen. This time Chester decides to take matters into his own hands (or rather paws).

Bunnicula Strikes Again! James Howe. Read by Victor Garber. 2 vols. (Running Time: 2 hrs. 4 mins.). (Bunnicula Ser.). (J). (gr. 3-7). 2004. pap. bk. 29.00 (978-0-8072-8213-7(8), Listening Lib) Random Audio Pubg.

Bunnicula Strikes Again! unabr. ed. James Howe. Read by Victor Garber. 2 cass. (Running Time: 2 hrs. 4 mins.). (Bunnicula Ser.). (J). (gr. 3-7). 2004. 23.00 (978-0-8072-8212-0(X), LL0167, Listening Lib) Random Audio Pubg.

It seems that Bunnicula, the vampire rabbit, is back to his old ways, or so Chester thinks, having found pale vegetables drained of their juices & scattered about the Monroe family kitchen. This time Chester decides to take matters into his own hands (or rather paws).

Bunny Rabbit & the Gardener. Louie Swift. Read by Barry McAlister. 1 cass. (Running Time: 30 min.). Dramatization. (Froggie's Tales: Vol. 4). (J). (ps-3). 2001. bk. 9.95 (978-0-9675577-6-2(3)) Puddleduck Pubg.

Six new original songs, stories & poems for children with character voices, music & sound effects.

Bunny Songs. Ed. by Publications International Staff. (J). 2007. audio compact disk 3.98 (978-1-4127-6195-6(6)) Pubns Intl Ltd.

Bunny Trouble. Hans Wilhelm. 1 read-along cass. (J). (ps-3). 1991. bk. 5.95 (978-0-590-63153-2(5)) Scholastic Inc.

Bunyan & Banjoes: Michigan Songs & Stories. Contrib. by Kitty Donohoe. (J). (ps-7). 1998. 9.00 (978-1-882376-62-9(5)) ThunderBay.

Bunyan & Banjoes: Michigan Songs & Stories. Kitty Donohoe & Pasqua Cekola Warstler. Perf. by Kitty Donohoe. Illus. by Pasqua Cekola Warstler. (J). 2004. pap. bk. 19.95 (978-1-882376-58-2(7)) ThunderBay.

Bunyip of Berkeley's Creek. 2004. pap. bk. 14.95 (978-1-56008-170-8(8)); 8.95 (978-1-56008-855-4(9)); cass. & flmstrp 30.00 (978-0-89719-665-9(1)) Weston Woods.

Buon Natale: Sing along & Learn Carols in Italian. (Teach Me Ser.). (ITA.). (J). (ps-13). 2007. audio compact disk 14.99 (978-1-59972-907-7(5), Tch Me) Teach Me.

Buongiorno Italia. audio compact disk 99.95 (978-0-8219-3638-2(7)) EMC-Paradigm.

Buongiorno Italia, Cassettes 1, 2 & 3. Joseph Cremona. (Running Time: 0 hr. 60 mins. 0 sec.). (ENG.). 2003. (978-0-563-36745-1(8)) BBC WrldWd GBR.

Burden of Bad Ideas. unabr. ed. Heather Mac Donald. 7 cass. (Running Time: 9 hrs.). 2001. 56.00 (978-0-7366-6365-6(7)) Books on Tape.

A collection of articles on urban problems and social policy from one of the nation's leading conservative intellectuals.

Burden of Bad Ideas: How Modern Intellectuals Misshape Our Society. Heather MacDonald. Read by Anna Fields. 2001. audio compact disk 64.00 (978-0-7366-8062-2(4)) Books on Tape.

Burden of Prometheus: Creativity & the "Suffering" Artist. Read by Keith Cunningham. 2 cass. (Running Time: 2 hrs. 30 min.). 1986. 18.95 Set. (978-0-7822-0049-2(4), 225) C G Jung IL.

Burden of Proof. Scott Turow. Read by Scott Turow. Prod. by Moveable Feast Staff. 1 cass. (Running Time: 30 min.). 1990. 8.95 (AMF-233) Am Audio Prose.

Scott Turow reads from "The Burden of Proof" & talks about Lawyers, legal reform, the language of the law & moral ambiguity.

Burden of Proof. Scott Turow. Read by Len Cariou. 2004. 10.95 (978-0-7435-4220-3(7)) Pub: S&S Audio. Dist(s): S and S Inc

Burden of Proof. unabr. ed. Scott Turow. Read by John Bedford Lloyd. (Running Time: 20 hrs.). (ENG.). 2010. 24.98 (978-1-60788-379-1(1)); audio compact disk 29.98 (978-1-60788-378-4(3)) Pub: Hachet Audio. Dist(s): HachBkGrp

Burden of Proof. unabr. collector's ed. Scott Turow. Read by Grover Gardner. 12 cass. (Running Time: 18 hrs.). 1990. 96.00 (978-0-7366-1786-4(8), 2623) Books on Tape.

Sandy Stern, defense lawyer, returns from a business trip to find that his wife Clara has committed suicide. But mourning must wait while Stern defends Dixon Hartnell, target of a federal grand jury investigation. As Stern ponders the mysteries of Clara's death & Dixon's tangled financial affairs, his whole world cracks in a kaleidoscope of change & uncertainty. In this vortex he must solve the greatest riddles of his personal & professional career.

Burden-Removing. Creflo A. Dollar. 15.00 (978-1-59089-093-6(0)) Pub: Creflo Dollar. Dist(s): STL Dist NA

Burdens Become Light. 1985. (0251) Evang Sisterhood Mary.

Bureau: The Secret History of the FBI. unabr. ed. Ronald Kessler. Read by Raymond Todd. 12 cass. (Running Time: 16 hrs.). 2002. 83.95 (978-0-7861-2232-5(3), 2956); audio compact disk 104.00 (978-0-7861-9529-9(0), 2956); audio compact disk 39.95 (978-0-7861-9211-3(9), 2956) Blckstn Audio.
Delves deep within the FBI, presenting the organization in its historical context and answering questions concerning its somewhat checkered past.

Bureau: The Secret History of the FBI. unabr. ed. Ronald Kessler. Read by Raymond Todd. 7 pieces. 2004. 44.95 (978-0-7861-2208-0(0)) Blckstn Audio.

Bureau of Professional & Occupational Affairs. 1 cass. (Running Time: 1 hr.). (Advocacy Before Administrative Agencies Ser.). 1986. 20.00 PA Bar Inst.

Bureaucracy. unabr. ed. Ludwig von Mises. Read by Robert Morris. 4 cass. (Running Time: 5 hrs. 30 mins.). 1989. 32.95 (978-0-7861-0080-4(X), 1074) Blckstn Audio.
In this classic work, he issues a timeless economic manifesto. In so doing he does not condemn bureaucracy as bad in & of itself. To the contrary, he sees bureaucracy as the appropriate technique for the conduct of select governmental agencies such as the courts of law, police departments & the IRS. However, when it comes to economic production & distribution, the bureaucratic method is an abomination spelling universal ruin & disaster.

Burger's Daughter. unabr. ed. Nadine Gordimer. Read by Nadia May. 9 cass. (Running Time: 13 hrs.). 1993. 62.95 Set. (978-0-7861-0417-8(1), 1369) Blckstn Audio.
It is hard to know whether "Burger's Daughter" will have greater impact as a depiction of South Africa today, more revealing than a thousand new dispatches, or as a universal celebration of the human spirit with the moving story of the unforgettable Ross Burger. She is a young woman cast in the mold of a revolutionary tradition, trying to uphold a heritage handed on by martyred parents & still carve out a sense of self.

Burglar in the Closet. unabr. ed. Lawrence Block. Read by Mike Jarmus. 6 vols. (Running Time: 9 hrs.). (Bernie Rhodenbarr Mystery Ser.: No. 2). 2000. bk. 54.95 (978-0-7927-2209-0(4), CSL 098, Chivers Sound Lib) AudioGO.
At a routine check-up, Bernie's dentist hires him to steal some valuable diamonds from his soon-to-be ex-wife. But after Bernie breaks into Crystal Sheldrake's apartment, someone comes home and Bernie slips into the closet. Time passes, and Bernie emerges, and there's lovely Crystal Sheldrake, only she's dead on the floor, a dental instrument to blame. To top it off, the diamonds are gone, and soon Bernie is too, chasing a killer's shadow and evading his nemesis, Detective Ray Kirschmann.

Burglar in the Closet. unabr. ed. Lawrence Block. Narrated by Richard Ferrone. 4 cass. (Running Time: 6 hrs.). (Bernie Rhodenbarr Mystery Ser.: No. 2). 1998. 35.00 (978-0-7887-0854-1(6), 95000E7) Recorded Bks.
Bernie Rhodenbarr does a favor for his dentist, only to discover mixing his personal & professional lives can be hazardous to his well-being.

Burglar in the Library. unabr. ed. Lawrence Block. Narrated by Richard Ferrone. 7 cass. (Running Time: 9 hrs. 45 mins.). (Bernie Rhodenbarr Mystery Ser.: No. 8). 1999. 65.00 (978-0-7887-4388-7(0), 96180E7) Recorded Bks.
Follows the adventures of the suave bookseller & crook, Bernie Rhodenbarr. Now, spending a snowy winter weekend at a country inn, Bernie is hoping to nab a rare, signed first edition of "The Big Sleep" from its library.

Burglar in the Rye. unabr. ed. Lawrence Block. Narrated by Richard Ferrone. 8 CDs. (Running Time: 9 hrs. 15 mins.). (Bernie Rhodenbarr Mystery Ser.: No. 9). 2001. audio compact disk 78.00 (978-0-7887-7165-1(5), C1418) Recorded Bks.
In this diverting caper, full-time bookstore owner & part-time burglar Bernie tries to do the right thing for a new friend, only to find himself accused of some terrible wrongs. All Bernie plans to do is steal some letters. A New York City literary agent is auctioning off her personal correspondence with enigmatic writer Gully Fairborn. Gully's attractive ex-girlfriend has asked Bernie to swipe the letters so she can return them to her old heartthrob. But when Bernie breaks in, the letters are missing & the literary agent is in bed with no hope of waking up. With the police watching him very closely, Bernie relies on jiggers of rye & Caroline, his lesbian best friend, to sharpen his deductive skills & find the killer.

Burglar in the Rye. unabr. ed. Lawrence Block. Narrated by Richard Ferrone. 7 cass. (Running Time: 9 hrs. 15 mins.). (Bernie Rhodenbarr Mystery Ser.: No. 9). 2000. 65.00 (978-0-7887-4928-5(5), 95856E7) Recorded Bks.
All Bernie does is offer to steal some letters as a favor but when he breaks into the apartment, the letters are missing & the owner is in bed with no hope of waking up. With police watching him very closely, Bernie relies on Jiggers of rye & Caroline, his lesbian best friend, to sharpen his deductive skills & find the killer.

Burglar in the Rye, Set. abr. ed. Lawrence Block. Read by Lawrence Block. 2 cass. (Bernie Rhodenbarr Mystery Ser.: No. 9). 1999. 18.95 (FS9-50947) Highsmith.

Burglar on the Prowl. Lawrence Block. Read by Nick Sullivan. 7 vols. (Bernie Rhodenbarr Mystery Ser.: No. 10). 2004. bk. 59.95 (978-0-7927-3200-6(6), CSL 649, Chivers Sound Lib); bk. 89.95 (978-0-7927-3201-3(4), SLD 649, Chivers Sound Lib); bk. 29.95 (978-0-7927-3202-0(2), CMP 649, Chivers Sound Lib) AudioGO.

***Burglar on the Prowl.** abr. ed. Lawrence Block. Read by Lawrence Block. (ENG.). 2004. (978-0-06-078317-4(6), Harper Audio) HarperCollins Pubs.

***Burglar on the Prowl.** abr. ed. Lawrence Block. Read by Lawrence Block. (ENG.). 2004. (978-0-06-081400-7(4), Harper Audio) HarperCollins Pubs.

Burglar Who Liked to Quote Kipling. Lawrence Block. Narrated by Richard Ferrone. 5 cass. (Running Time: 6 hrs. 15 mins.). (Bernie Rhodenbarr Mystery Ser.: No. 3). 1998. 44.00 (978-0-7887-0810-7(4), 94959E7) Recorded Bks.
Bernie takes over a secondhand bookstore in Greenwich Village. Hearing of a rare edition of Kipling's poetry, he can't resist practicing his criminal talents which land him in one dangerous scrape after another.

Burglar Who Painted Like Mondrian. unabr. ed. Lawrence Block. Narrated by Richard Ferrone. 5 cass. (Running Time: 7 hrs. 15 mins.). (Bernie Rhodenbarr Mystery Ser.: No. 5). 1993. 46.00 (978-0-7887-3214-0(5), 95846E7) Recorded Bks.
Bernie Rhodenbarr, the most likely suspect in an art burglary, murder & kidnap, finds himself up against an eccentric kidnapper with a taste for abstract Dutch art.

Burglar Who Studied Spinoza. abr. ed. Lawrence Block. Read by Lawrence Block. 2 cass. (Running Time: 3 hrs.). (Bernie Rhodenbarr Mystery Ser.: No. 4). 1997. 16.95 (PengAudBks) Penguin Grp USA.

Burglar Who Studied Spinoza. unabr. ed. Lawrence Block. Narrated by Richard Ferrone. 5 cass. (Running Time: 6 hrs. 45 mins.). (Bernie Rhodenbarr Mystery Ser.: No. 4). 1999. 46.00 (978-0-7887-1872-4(X), 95294E7) Recorded Bks.
When Bernie commits the "perfect" crime, he suddenly must match wits with a wily murderer & a host of housebreakers.

Burglar Who Thought He Was Bogart. unabr. ed. Lawrence Block. Narrated by Frank Muller. 6 cass. (Running Time: 7 hrs. 45 mins.). (Bernie Rhodenbarr Mystery Ser.: No. 7). 1997. 51.00 (978-0-7887-0476-5(1), 94669E7) Recorded Bks.
Bernie Rhodenbarr is a bookseller by day & a burglar by night. His passion for Humphrey Bogart movies lead him to a beautiful damsel in distress, a dangerous international conspiracy & more than a few incriminating bodies.

Burglar Who Traded Ted Williams. unabr. ed. Lawrence Block. Narrated by Richard Ferrone. 6 cass. (Running Time: 8 hrs. 15 mins.). (Bernie Rhodenbarr Mystery Ser.: No. 6). 1994. 51.00 (978-0-7887-1302-6(7), 95138E7) Recorded Bks.
Bernie is seriously considering retiring from his nocturnal activities, now that his Greenwich Village bookstore is finally turning a profit. But then his nasty landlord wants to raise the rent - by $10,000 a month - & Bernie is plunged into desperate times again. When the landlord's brother-in-law's million dollar baseball card collection is stolen, guess who is blamed for the job?.

Burglars Can't Be Choosers. unabr. ed. Lawrence Block. Read by Mike Jarmus. 6 vols. (Running Time: 9 hrs.). (Bernie Rhodenbarr Mystery Ser.: No. 1). 2000. bk. 54.95 (978-0-7927-2201-4(9), CSL 090, Chivers Sound Lib) AudioGO.
Bernie Rhodenbarr tends to work alone. He finds the risks lower and the company better. Some call him a sleuth, others call him a burglar. Who can resist being hired for a nice fee, all for a simple breakin? Not Bernie, but nothing's ever that simple. The item he's hired to take is missing, and a dead body is discovered! Accused of murder, Bernie hides out in a friend's apartment. Now Bernie must figure out what's going on, and just who set him up.

Burglars Can't Be Choosers. unabr. ed. Lawrence Block. Narrated by Richard Ferrone. 5 cass. (Running Time: 6 hrs. 45 mins.). (Bernie Rhodenbarr Mystery Ser.: No. 1). 1998. 44.00 (978-0-7887-1990-5(4), 95377E7) Recorded Bks.
An occasional, very discreet breaking & entering enables Bernie Rhodenbarr to maintain his comfortable New York City lifestyle. But when he discovers a corpse on a routine job, Bernie finds himself one of the NYPD's most wanted.

Burgmuller, op. 100. Valery Lloyd-Watts. Ed. by Willard A. Palmer. Composed by Johann Friedrich Burgmüller. 1 CD. (Running Time: 1 hr.). (Alfred Masterwork Edition Ser.). (ENG.). 1998. audio compact disk 10.95 (978-0-7390-1930-6(9), 16787) Alfred Pub.

Burials. Anne Schraff. Narrated by Larry A. McKeever. (Extreme Customs Ser.). (J). 2006. 10.95 (978-1-58659-128-1(2)); audio compact disk 14.95 (978-1-58659-362-9(5)) Artesian.

Buried Alive, Set. unabr. ed. Arnold Bennett. Read by Flo Gibson. 4 cass. (Running Time: 6 hrs.). 1997. 19.95 (978-1-55685-499-6(4), 499-4) Audio Bk Con.
In this funny tale, Henry Leek, valet to the reknowned painter Priam Farll, dies & they are mistakenly identified. The valet is buried with pomp & circumstance in Westminster Abbey while Priam poses as Leek. However, his talents will out.

Buried Book: The Loss & Rediscovery of the Great Epic of Gilgamesh. unabr. ed. David Damrosch. Read by William Hughes. (Running Time: 27000 sec.). 2007. 19.95 (978-1-4332-0685-6(4)); audio compact disk 19.95 (978-1-4332-0686-3(2)) Blckstn Audio.

Buried Book: The Loss & Rediscovery of the Great Epic of Gilgamesh. unabr. ed. David Damrosch. Read by William Hughes. (Running Time: 27000 sec.). 2008. 54.95 (978-1-4332-0683-2(8)); audio compact disk 29.95 (978-1-4332-0687-0(0)); audio compact disk & audio compact disk 55.00 (978-1-4332-0684-9(6)) Blckstn Audio.

Buried Caesars. unabr. ed. Stuart M. Kaminsky. Narrated by George Guidall. 5 cass. (Running Time: 6 hrs. 30 mins.). (Toby Peters Mystery Ser.: No. 14). 1997. 44.00 (978-0-7887-0401-7(X), 94593E7) Recorded Bks.
P.I. Toby Peters is reduced to taking orders from the U.S. Army during World War II. An aide has absconded with money & sensitive papers that could destroy General MacArthur's plans.

Buried Evidence. unabr. ed. Nancy Taylor Rosenberg. Read by Sandra Burr. 8 cass. (Running Time: 11 hrs.). 2000. 35.95 (978-1-56740-380-0(8), 1567403808, BAU) Brilliance Audio.
When the accuser becomes the accused . . . As a dedicated district attorney, Lily Forrester presents the perfect image of a defender of justice. Only she knows the dark secret of what happened six years ago, when a desperate crisis drove her to step outside the law and exact a horrifying personal vengeance. Now her ex-husband, faced with serious criminal charges, threatens to expose her unless she compromises her most cherished beliefs to help him. A violent rapist she put behind bars is back on the streets and looking for her. Her beloved daughter seems to be the target of a dangerous madman. And Lily must call on her deepest strength to face her accusers and ensure that the values she holds most dear will triumph. In this taut new thriller, Nancy Taylor Rosenberg displays the brilliant legal expertise and dramatic flair that have made her books classics of suspense.

Buried Evidence. unabr. ed. Nancy Taylor Rosenberg. Read by Sandra Burr. (Running Time: 11 hrs.). 2004. 39.25 (978-1-59600-458-0(4), 1596004584, BADLE); 24.95 (978-1-59600-457-3(6), 1596004576, BAD); 39.25 (978-1-59600-456-6(8), 1596004568, Brlnc Audio MP3 Lib); 24.95 (978-1-59600-455-9(X), 159600455X, Brilliance MP3) Brilliance Audio.

Buried Guilt Lives: Gen. 42:1-28. Ed Young. 1988. Rental 4.95 (978-0-7417-1683-5(6), 683) Win Walk.

***Buried in Clay.** Priscilla Masters. Ed. by Julia Franklin. 2010. audio compact disk 71.95 (978-1-84652-626-8(4)) Pub: Magna Story GBR. Dist(s): Ulverscroft US

***Buried in Clay.** Priscilla Masters. Read by Julia Franklin. 2010. 61.95 (978-1-84652-625-1(6)) Pub: Magna Story GBR. Dist(s): Ulverscroft US

Buried in the Bitter Waters: The Hidden History of Racial Cleansing in America. unabr. ed. Elliot Jaspin. Read by Elliot Jaspin. (YA). 2007. 49.99 (978-1-60252-824-6(1)) Find a World.

Buried in the Past. Elizabeth Lemarchand. Read by Gordon Griffin. 5 cass. (Running Time: 7 hrs. 30 mins.). 2001. 49.95 (67576) Pub: Soundings Ltd GBR. Dist(s): Ulverscroft US

Buried in the Past. unabr. ed. Elizabeth Lemarchand. Read by Gordon Griffin. 5 cass. (Sound Ser.). 2004. 49.95 (978-1-85496-757-2(6)) Pub: UlverLrgPrint GBR. Dist(s): Ulverscroft US

Buried Lies Companion Workbook. Marty Delmon. 2007. audio compact disk 24.99 (978-1-60247-725-4(6)) Tate Pubng.

Buried Onions. Gary Soto. Narrated by Robert Ramirez. 4 CDs. (Running Time: 4 hrs. 30 mins.). (gr. 7 up). audio compact disk 39.00 (978-1-4025-0473-0(X)) Recorded Bks.

Buried Onions. unabr. ed. Gary Soto. Narrated by Robert Ramirez. 3 pieces. (Running Time: 4 hrs. 30 mins.). (gr. 7 up). 2001. 28.00 (978-0-7887-5266-7(9), 96549E7) Recorded Bks.
"You can pray and sometimes God listens," says 19-year-old Eddie. 'Other times he's far away in India or Africa or maybe close to home in Fresno, his body sprawled on the floor, glass all around because of a drive-by".

***Buried Secrets.** unabr. ed. Joseph Finder. Read by Holter Graham. (Running Time: 11 hrs. 30 mins. 0 sec.). (ENG.). 2011. audio compact disk 39.99 (978-1-4272-0957-3(X)) Pub: Macmill Audio. Dist(s): Macmillan

Buried Too Deep: An Aurelia Marcella Mystery. unabr. ed. Jane Finnis. Read by Rebecca Rogers. (Running Time: 10 hrs. 0 mins.). 2008. 29.95 (978-1-4332-3529-0(3)); 59.95 (978-1-4332-3525-2(0)); audio compact disk 80.00 (978-1-4332-3526-9(9)) Blckstn Audio.

Buried Treasures of the Civil War. W. C. Jameson. 1 cass. (Running Time: 1 hr.). (Buried Treasures Ser.). (gr. 3-7). 1997. 12.00 (978-0-87483-492-5(9)) Pub: August Hse. Dist(s): Natl Bk Netwk

Burl Ives: A Twinkle in Your Eye. Perf. by Burl Ives. 1 cass. (Family Heritage Ser.). (J). 1997. 7.98 Incl. cass. blisterpack. (978-1-57330-826-7(9), Sony Wonder); audio compact disk 11.98 CD. (978-1-57330-827-4(7), Sony Wonder) Sony Music Ent.
Burl Ives was a leading folk & country singer, a Broadway & television star & an Academy Award winning actor in 1958, as well as a Grammy Award winner in 1962. Includes: The Lollipop Tree, Two Little Trains, Mr. Froggie Went A-Courtin' & Mother Goose Songs.

Burl Ives Children Album. Prod. by Walt Disney Records Staff. 1 cass. (J). (ps-3). 1998. 22.50 (978-0-7634-0401-7(2)) W Disney Records.

Burl Ives Sings Little White Duck. Perf. by Burl Ives. 1 cass. (J). (ps up). 7.98 (2288); audio compact disk 14.98 (D2288) MFLP CA.
Songs include: "Little White Duck," "The Little Engine That Could," "Mr. Froggie Went A-Courtin'," "The Tailor & the Mouse" & many more.

Burla de Don Pedro a Caballo see Poesia y Drama de Garcia Lorca

Burma Road. abr. ed. Donovan Webster. Read by Donovan Webster. 2003. audio compact disk 29.95 (978-0-06-057785-8(1)) HarperCollins Pubs.

Burmese. unabr. ed. 6 cass. (Running Time: 9 hrs.). pap. bk. 135.00 (AFBU10) J Norton Pubs.
The text uses Roman transcription & provides all the basic structures of the language & grammatical explanations. Native speakers have recorded the conversations, pronunciation exercises & response drills.

Burmese: A Course in Four Volumes. John Okell. 34 cass. (C). 1994. pap. bk. 179.95 (978-1-877979-49-1(X)) SE Asia.

Burmese: An Introduction to the Literary Style. John Okell. 1 cass. (Southeast Asian Language Text Ser.). (C). 1994. pap. bk. 23.00 (978-1-877979-44-6(9)) SE Asia.

Burmese: An Introduction to the Script. John Okell. 7 cass. (Southeast Asian Language Text Ser.). (C). 1994. pap. bk. 51.00 (978-1-877979-43-9(0)) SE Asia.

Burmese Bk. 1: An Introduction to the Spoken Language. John Okell. 12 cass. (Southeast Asian Language Text Ser.). (C). 1994. pap. bk. 56.00 (978-1-877979-41-5(4)) SE Asia.

Burmese Days. unabr. ed. George Orwell. Read by Frederick Davidson. 8 cass. (Running Time: 10 hrs.). 1992. 56.95 (978-0-7861-0295-2(0), 1259) Blckstn Audio.
Burmese Days presents a bitter & satirical picture of the white man's rule in Upper Burma. One thread of the story is a corrupt native politician's attempt to win membership in the white man's club, & the other is an Englishman's courtship of Elizabeth, a girl from home.

Burmese Days. unabr. ed. George Orwell. Narrated by Margaret Hilton. 8 cass. (Running Time: 11 hrs. 30 mins.). 1988. 70.00 (978-1-55690-078-5(3), 88440E7) Recorded Bks.
In a small settlement in upper Burma a group of English "colonials" strives to keep their club intact.

Burmese Days. unabr. collector's ed. George Orwell. Read by Stuart Langton. 7 cass. (Running Time: 10 hrs. 30 min.). 1996. 56.00 (978-0-7366-3441-0(X), 4085) Books on Tape.
Set in Burma in the 1920's, when British rule was still unchallenged, this novel is the story of Flory, a middle-aged Englishman who has led an "unexerted" life. Though he is not ready for love, it takes him by storm after he meets Elizabeth Lackerstein, a beautiful, recently orphaned English girl, & her need for a protector undoes him.

***Burn.** abr. ed. Nevada Barr. Read by Joyce Bean. 5 CDs. (Running Time: 6 hrs.). (Anna Pigeon Ser.). 2010. audio compact disk 24.99 (978-1-4418-1607-8(0), 9781441816078, BACD) Brilliance Audio.

***Burn.** abr. ed. Nevada Barr. (Running Time: 6 hrs.). (Anna Pigeon Ser.). 2011. audio compact disk 14.99 (978-1-4418-1608-5(9), 9781441816085, BCD Value Price) Brilliance Audio.

Burn. abr. ed. Linda Howard. Read by Joyce Bean & Laural Merlington. (Running Time: 6 hrs.). 2009. audio compact disk 26.99 (978-1-4233-1037-2(3), 9781423310372, BACD) Brilliance Audio.

Burn. abr. ed. Linda Howard. Read by Joyce Bean & Laural Merlington. (Running Time: 6 hrs.). 2010. audio compact disk 14.99 (978-1-4233-1038-9(1), 9781423310389, BCD Value Price) Brilliance Audio.

***Burn.** unabr. ed. Nevada Barr. Read by Joyce Bean. 1 MP3-CD. (Running Time: 12 hrs.). (Anna Pigeon Ser.). 2010. 24.99 (978-1-4418-1603-0(8), 9781441816030, Brilliance MP3); 39.97 (978-1-4418-1604-7(6), 9781441816047, Brlnc Audio MP3 Lib); 39.97 (978-1-4418-1606-1(2), 9781441816061, BADLE); 24.99 (978-1-4418-1605-4(4), 9781441816054, BAD); audio compact disk 36.99 (978-1-4418-1601-6(1), 9781441816016, Bril Audio CD Unabri); audio compact disk 89.97 (978-1-4418-1602-3(X), 9781441816023, BriAudCD Unabrid) Brilliance Audio.

Burn. unabr. ed. Ted Dekker. 2010. audio compact disk 29.99 (978-1-4003-1623-6(5)) Nelson.

Burn. unabr. ed. Linda Howard. Read by Joyce Bean. (Running Time: 13 hrs.). 2009. 24.99 (978-1-4233-1033-4(0), 9781423310334, Brilliance MP3); audio compact disk 36.99 (978-1-4233-1031-0(4), 9781423310310, Bril Audio CD Unabri); audio compact disk 97.97 (978-1-4233-1032-7(2), 9781423310327, BriAudCD Unabrid) Brilliance Audio.

***Burn.** unabr. ed. Linda Howard. Narrated by Joyce Bean. 1 Playaway. (Running Time: 12 hrs. 45 mins.). 2009. 69.99 (978-1-61545-522-5(1)) Find a World.

Burn, No. 4. unabr. ed. Linda Howard. Read by Joyce Bean. (Running Time: 13 hrs.). 2009. 24.99 (978-1-4233-1035-8(7), 9781423310358, BAD); 39.97 (978-1-4233-1034-1(9), 9781423310341, Brlnc Audio MP3 Lib); 39.97 (978-1-4233-1036-5(5), 9781423310365, BADLE) Brilliance Audio.

Burn Before Reading: Presidents, CIA Directors, & Secret Intelligence. Stansfield Turner. Read by Michael Prichard. (Playaway Adult Nonfiction Ser.). (ENG.). 2009. 65.00 (978-1-60775-653-8(6)) Find a World.

Burn Before Reading: Presidents, CIA Directors, & Secret Intelligence. unabr. ed. Stansfield Turner. Narrated by Michael Prichard. (Running Time: 10 hrs. 30 mins. 0 sec.). (ENG.). 2005. audio compact disk 34.99 (978-1-4001-0181-8(6)) Pub: Tantor Media. Dist(s): IngramPubServ

Burn Before Reading: Presidents, CIA Directors, & Secret Intelligence. unabr. ed. Stansfield Turner. Read by Michael Prichard. (Running Time: 10 hrs. 30 mins. 0 sec.). (ENG.). 2005. audio compact disk 22.99 (978-1-4001-5181-3(3)) Pub: Tantor Media. Dist(s): IngramPubServ

Burn Before Reading: Presidents, CIA Directors & Secret Intelligence. unabr. ed. Stansfield Turner. Narrated by Michael Prichard. (Running Time: 10 hrs. 30 mins. 0 sec.). (ENG.). 2005. audio compact disk 69.99 (978-1-4001-3181-5(2)) Pub: Tantor Media. Dist(s): IngramPubServ

Burn Care & Rehabilitation. Ronald M. Sato. 1 cass. (Running Time: 70 min.). 1997. bk. 22.00 (978-1-58111-004-3(9)) Contemporary Medical.
Description of types of burns & dressings utilized. Treatment for burns including whirlpool, range of motion, use of modalities, scar management, skin grafts.

Burn Factor. Kyle Mills. 8 cass. (Running Time: 12 hrs.). 2001. 64.00 (978-0-7366-6194-2(8)) Books on Tape.
Quinn Barry wants to be an FBI agent - someday. Right now she's a nobody, toiling in the basement of Quantico, revamping ancient computer programming against impossible deadlines. Until, one day, her creative computer savvy turns up a mysterious DNA link among five very high-profile & gruesome serial-killer cases.

Burn Factor. unabr. ed. Kyle Mills. Read by Michael Kramer. 8 cass. (Running Time: 8 hrs.). 2001. 64.00; audio compact disk 80.00 Books on Tape.
Bright, young & ambitious, Quinn Barry desperately wants to be an FBI agent. At the moment, however, she's just a low-level employee toiling in the basement at Quantico. But Quinn's career & her life are about to change wildly. Testing her new database program, Quinn's computer savvy turns up a mysterious DNA link among five gruesome murders...a link that the old FBI system had been carefully programmed to miss. The discovery lands her a demotion to the hinterlands, followed by a series of unfortunate "accidents" that nearly end her life.

Burn Factor. unabr. ed. Kyle Mills. Read by Michael Kramer. 8 cass. (Running Time: 12 hrs.). 2001. audio compact disk 80.00 (978-0-7366-6308-3(8)) Books on Tape.
Quinn Barry wants to be an FBI agent - someday. Right now she's a nobody, toiling in the basement of Quantico, revamping ancient computer programming against impossible deadlines. Until, one day, her creative computer savvy turns up a mysterious DNA link among five very high-profile & gruesome serial-killer cases.

Burn Journals. unabr. ed. Brent Runyon. Narrated by Christopher Evan Welch. 7 cass. (Running Time: 8 hrs.). (YA). (gr. 8 up). 2008. 56.75 (978-1-4361-3871-0(X)); audio compact disk 77.75 (978-1-4361-3876-5(0)) Recorded Bks.

Burn Marks. unabr. ed. Sara Paretsky. Read by Donada Peters. 8 cass. (Running Time: 12 hrs.). (V. I. Warshawski Novel Ser.). 1992. 64.00 (978-0-7366-2168-7(7), 2967) Books on Tape.
V. I. Warshawski investigates arson which soon involves her Aunt Elena & leads to death of Elena's best friend. What goes on?.

Burn Me Deadly: An Eddie Lacrosse Novel. unabr. ed. Alex Bledsoe. Read by Stefan Rudnicki. (Running Time: 10 hrs. 50 mins.). (ENG.). 2009. 29.95 (978-1-4332-7282-0(2)); 65.95 (978-1-4332-7278-3(4)); audio compact disk 100.00 (978-1-4332-7279-0(2)) Blckstn Audio.

Burned. abr. ed. Carol Higgins Clark. (Regan Reilly Mystery Ser.: No. 8). 2005. 15.95 (978-0-7435-5024-6(2)) Pub: S&S Audio. Dist(s): S and S Inc

***Burned.** unabr. ed. P. C. Cast & Kristin Cast. Narrated by Caitlin Davies. 9 CDs. (Running Time: 13 hrs.). 2010. audio compact disk 89.95 (978-0-7927-7245-3(8)) AudioGO.

Burned. unabr. ed. P. C. Cast & Kristin Cast. 10 CDs. (Running Time: 13 hrs. 0 mins. 0 sec.). (House of Night Ser.: Bk. 7). (ENG.). (YA). 2010. audio compact disk 17.99 (978-1-4272-0876-7(X)) Pub: Macmill Audio. Dist(s): Macmillan

Burned. unabr. ed. Ellen Hopkins. Read by Laura Flanagan. (ENG., 2009. audio compact disk 26.95 (978-1-59887-755-7(0), 1598877550) Pub: HighBridge. Dist(s): Workman Pub

Burning. unabr. ed. Kathryn Lasky. Read by Pamela Garelick. (Running Time: 5.5 hrs. NaN mins.). (Guardians of Ga'Hoole Ser.: Bk. 6). 2008. audio compact disk 50.00 (978-1-4332-2614-4(6)); audio compact disk 34.95 (978-1-4332-2613-7(8)) Blckstn Audio.

Burning. unabr. ed. Kathryn Lasky. Read by Pamela Garelick. (Running Time: 5 hrs. 30 mins.). (Guardians of Ga'Hoole Ser.: Bk. 6). 2010. 29.95 (978-1-4332-2617-5(0)) Blckstn Audio.

***Burning.** unabr. ed. Kathryn Lasky. Read by Pamela Garelick. (Running Time: 5 hrs. 30 mins.). (Guardians of Ga'Hoole Ser.: Bk. 6). 2010. audio compact disk 24.95 (978-1-4332-2616-8(2)) Blckstn Audio.

Burning Angel. James Lee Burke. 1 cass. (Dave Robicheaux Ser.). 1998. 9.98 (978-0-671-58254-8(2), Audioworks) S&S Audio.
Mystery & detective with police procedure.

Burning Angel. unabr. ed. James Lee Burke. Narrated by Mark Hammer. 10 cass. (Running Time: 14 hrs. 15 mins.). (Dave Robicheaux Ser.). 2000. 85.00 (978-0-7887-0345-4(5), 94537E7) Recorded Bks.

Burning Blue: A Sweeping Novel of Love, Loss & War. unabr. ed. James Holland. Narrated by Glen McCready. 12 cass. (Running Time: 17 hrs. 15 mins.). 2004. 99.75 (978-1-84505-208-9(0), H1754MC, Clipper Audio) Recorded Bks.

Burning Bridge. unabr. ed. John Flanagan. Read by John Keating. 7 CDs. (Running Time: 8 hrs. 30 mins.). (Ranger's Apprentice Ser.: Bk. 2). (J). (gr. 4-8). 2006. audio compact disk 77.75 (978-1-4281-1053-3(4)); 61.75 (978-1-4281-1048-9(8)) Recorded Bks.
Will, a promising Ranger apprentice, will need every ounce of his courage to thwart the evil lord Morgarath. With the help of his Battleschool friend Horace, he pursues a desperate plan to save the Kingdom of Araluen.

Burning Bush see Twentieth-Century Poetry in English, No. 28, Recordings of Poets Reading Their Own Poetry

Burning Daylight. unabr. ed. Jack London. Read by Tim Behrens. 12 cass. (Running Time: 13 hrs.). Dramatization. 1990. 64.95 (978-1-55686-357-8(8), 357) Books in Motion.
What at first seems a grandiose tale of man versus nature in the Yukon becomes slowly & delightfully London's finest love story.

Burning down My Masters' House: My Life at the New York Times. unabr. ed. Jayson Blair. Read by Jayson Blair. 9 CDs. (Running Time: 10 hrs. 30 mins.). 2004. audio compact disk 34.95 (978-1-59007-547-0(1)) Pub: New Millenn Enter. Dist(s): PerseuPGW

Burning down My Masters' House: My Life at the New York Times. unabr. ed. Jayson Blair Jayson. Read by Jayson Blair. 8 cass. 2004. 34.95 (978-1-59007-546-3(3)) Pub: New Millenn Enter. Dist(s): PerseuPGW

Burning Eddy. unabr. ed. Scot Gardner. Read by Stig Wemyss. 6 CDs. (Running Time: 20700 sec.). (YA). (gr. 7-13). 2005. audio compact disk 77.95 (978-1-74093-608-8(6)) Pub: Bolinda Pubng AUS. Dist(s): Bolinda Pub Inc

Burning for Revenge. John Marsden. Read by Suzi Dougherty. (Running Time: 7 hrs.). (Tomorrow Ser.). (YA). 2009. 69.99 (978-1-74214-333-0(4), 9781742143330) Pub: Bolinda Pubng AUS. Dist(s): Bolinda Pub Inc

Burning for Revenge. unabr. ed. John Marsden. 6 CDs. (Running Time: 7 hrs.). (Tomorow Ser.). (YA). 2001. audio compact disk 77.95 (978-1-74030-399-6(7)) Pub: Bolinda Pubng AUS. Dist(s): Bolinda Pub Inc

Burning for Revenge. unabr. ed. John Marsden. Read by Suzi Dougherty. 4 cass. (Running Time: 7 hrs.). (Tomorrow Ser.). (YA). 2004. 32.00 (978-1-876584-93-1(9), 591011) Bolinda Pubng AUS.
John Marsden has sold over two million books world-wide. John has won every major writing award in Australia for young people's fiction, as well as numerous awards both in the USA and Europe. John has three titles in the top ten list of all Australian books sold.

Burning for Revenge. unabr. ed. John Marsden. Read by Suzi Dougherty. (Running Time: 25200 sec.). (Tomorrow Ser.). 2008. audio compact disk 43.95 (978-1-921334-80-1(0), 9781921334801) Pub: Bolinda Pubng AUS. Dist(s): Bolinda Pub Inc

Burning Girl. unabr. ed. Mark Billingham. Read by Graeme Malcolm. 2005. 29.95 (978-0-7927-3715-5(6), CMP 829); 54.95 (978-0-7927-3713-1(X), CSL 829); audio compact disk 94.95 (978-0-7927-3714-8(8), SLD 829) AudioGO.

Burning Heart: Luke 24:32. Ed Young. (J). 1983. 4.95 (978-0-7417-1292-9(X), 292) Win Walk.

***Burning Lamp.** abr. ed. Amanda Quick, pseud. Read by Anne Flosnik. 4 CDs. (Running Time: 5 hrs.). (Arcane Society Ser.). 2010. audio compact disk 24.99 (978-1-4418-2556-8(8), 9781441825568, BACD) Brilliance Audio.

***Burning Lamp.** abr. ed. Amanda Quick, pseud. Read by Anne Flosnik. (Running Time: 5 hrs.). (Dreamlight Trilogy). 2010. 9.99 (978-1-4418-9354-3(7), 9781441893543, BAD) Brilliance Audio.

***Burning Lamp.** abr. ed. Amanda Quick, pseud. (Running Time: 5 hrs.). (Arcane Society Ser.). 2011. audio compact disk 14.99 (978-1-4418-2557-5(6), 9781441825575, BCD Value Price) Brilliance Audio.

Burning Lamp. unabr. ed. Amanda Quick, pseud. Read by Anne Flosnik. 1 MP3-CD. (Running Time: 9 hrs.). (Arcane Society Ser.). 2010. 24.99 (978-1-4233-8976-7(X), 9781423389767, Brilliance MP3); 24.99 (978-1-4233-8978-1(6), 9781423389781, BAD); 39.97 (978-1-4233-8977-4(8), 9781423389774, Brinc Audio MP3 Lib); 39.97 (978-1-4233-8979-8(4), 9781423389798, BADLE); audio compact disk 34.99 (978-1-4233-8974-3(3), 9781423389743, Bril Audio CD Unabri); audio compact disk 92.97 (978-1-4233-8975-0(1), 9781423389750, BriAudCD Unabrid) Brilliance Audio.

***Burning Land.** unabr. ed. Bernard Cornwell. Read by John Lee. (ENG.). 2010. (978-0-06-196747-4(5), Harper Audio); (978-0-06-195364-4(4), Harper Audio) HarperCollins Pubs.

Burning Man. unabr. ed. Phillip Margolin. Read by Michael Russotto. 9 cass. (Running Time: 13 hrs. 30 min.). 1996. 72.00 (978-0-913369-24-1(1), 4175) Books on Tape.
Peter Hale, a young lawyer trying to fill his father's shoes, makes an irrevocable decision: trying a million dollar case against his father's wishes. He loses the case, his job & the reputation of the firm. He moves to Oregon & takes a job as public defender, hoping to regain his father's respect.

Burning Moon. Richard Barre. Read by Patrick G. Lawlor. (Running Time: 10 hrs.). 2004. 30.95 (978-1-59912-439-1(4)) Iofy Corp.

Burning Moon. unabr. ed. Richard Barre. Read by Patrick G. Lawlor. 7 cass. (Running Time: 10 hrs.). 2004. 49.95 (978-0-7861-2798-6(8), 3325); audio compact disk 64.00 (978-0-7861-8496-5(5), 3325) Blckstn Audio.

Burning of the Peggy Stewart. Perf. by Lary Lewman & Doug Roberts. 1 cass. 1.00 (HS332) Esstee Audios.
Radio drama.

Burning Point. unabr. ed. Alan Axelrod. Narrated by Nelson Runger. 7 CDs. (Running Time: 8 hrs.). 2001. audio compact disk 69.00 (978-0-7887-7200-9(7)) Recorded Bks.
When Elizabeth ascended the throne in 1558, England was the laughing stock of Europe. Economic, political & religious calamities were numerous & Elizabeth endured constant criticism. But by the end of her 45-year reign, England was one of the world's mightiest nations. Axelrod uses the legendary Queen's life as a model for modern leadership & a powerful example of how one person can make an extraordinary difference. This is an indispensable guide for today's business managers & leaders. It is also inspiring for those taking their first steps up the corporate ladder, or those who simply love history.

Burning Point. unabr. ed. Mary Jo Putney. Narrated by Jack Garrett. 11 CDs. (Running Time: 12 hrs. 45 mins.). 2001. audio compact disk 111.00 (978-0-7887-6184-3(6), C1409) Recorded Bks.
A searing story of family, love & desire. Kate Corsi's lifelong dream has been to work for her family's world-famous explosive demolition business. Her stubborn father denied her this dream until he died. Now his will has promised Kate a fortune, but only if she can live for a year in the same house with her ex-husband, Donovan. As Kate & Donovan form an uneasy alliance to learn the truth about her father's mysterious death, they must confront the wrenching secrets of a past that nearly destroyed them. And they must face the perils of moving too close to the burning point, where their passion could once again catch fire.

Burning Point. unabr. ed. Mary Jo Putney. Narrated by Jack Garrett. 9 cass. (Running Time: 12 hrs. 45 mins.). 2000. 81.00 (978-0-7887-4871-4(8), 96286E7) Recorded Bks.
A burning story of family, love & desire. Kate Corsi's dream of working for her family's world-famous explosive demolition business is denied by her stubborn father until the day he dies. Now, his will promises Kate a fortune but only if she can live for a year in the same house with her ex-husband. Forming an uneasy alliance, the two must confront the wrenching secrets of their past & face the perils of moving too close to the point where their passion could once again catch fire.

Burning Prairie. unabr. ed. M. Lehman. Read by Gene Engene. 3 cass. (Running Time: 3 hrs. 15 min.). Dramatization. 1992. 21.95 set. (978-1-55686-419-3(1), 419) Books in Motion.
In the frontier days, 160 free acres drew many a hardy homesteader to the prairies of North Dakota. This is the story of one family that braved terrible ordeals to own a piece of land.

Burning Season: The Murder of Chico Mendes & the Fight for the Amazon Rain Forest. unabr. collector's ed. Andrew C. Revkin. Read by Grover Gardner. 8 cass. (Running Time: 12 hrs.). 1991. 64.00 (978-0-7366-1970-7(4), 2790) Books on Tape.
The title refers to the monstrous fires set each dry season in the Amazon rain forest by ranchers attempting to clear the land & to the Brazilian ecological labor activist who brought notice of their destruction to the world before his wasteful death in 1988.

Burning Shore. unabr. collector's ed. Elleston Trevor. Read by Michael Prichard. 5 cass. (Running Time: 7 hrs. 30 min.). 1984. 48.00 (978-0-7366-0733-9(1), 1690) Books on Tape.
Set in Malaya, where Hugh Copland is appointed manager of a jungle airstrip menaced by Communist guerillas. He soon becomes dangerously involved in a struggle for power between the Sultan of Tamarah & elusive enemies.

Burning Shore, Pt. 1. unabr. collector's ed. Wilbur Smith. Read by Richard Brown. 8 cass. (Running Time: 12 hrs.). (Courtney Novels). 1988. 64.00 (978-0-7366-1256-2(4), 2170-A) Books on Tape.
Romantic saga follows the love affair between a French country girl & a British World War I flying ace.

Burning Shore, Pt. 2. collector's ed. Wilbur Smith. Read by Richard Brown. 7 cass. (Running Time: 10 hrs. 30 min.). (Courtney Novels). 1988. 56.00 (978-0-7366-1257-9(2), 2170-B) Books on Tape.
How Russia looked in pre-Glasnost days. Written by New York Times Moscow Bureau Chief.

Burning the Dreams see Poetry & Voice of Muriel Rukeyser

Burning Time. abr. ed. Leslie Glass. Read by Jane E. Lawder. 4 vols. No. 1. 2003. (978-1-58807-756-1(X)) Am Pubng Inc.

Burning Time. abr. ed. Leslie Glass. Read by Jane E. Lawder. 4 vols. (Running Time: 6 hrs.). (April Woo Detective Ser.: No. 1). 2003. 25.00 (978-1-58807-060-9(3)) Am Pubng Inc.
A savage killer is on the loose in New York City. His calling card is a tattoo of flames; his trail of victims leads from the scorched sands of California to the blistering heart of Manhattan. Only Detective April Woo can block this vicious madmans next move. And with the help of psychiatrist Jason Frank, this NYPD policewoman will prove that the predator shes hunting is no ordinary killer but then, April Woo is no ordinary cop.

Burning Times. Perf. by Rumors of the Big Wave. 1 cass. (Running Time: 47 min.). 1992. 9.98 (978-1-56628-013-6(3), EB2398/WB42535-4) MFLP CA.
Fiercely poetic songwriting combined with electric cello & innovative keyboard. Adult alternative rock.

Burning Up. Caroline B. Cooney. Read by Christina Moore. 5 cass. (Running Time: 6 hrs.). (YA). 1999. pap. bk. & stu. ed. 68.99 (978-0-7887-3190-7(4), 40925) Recorded Bks.
When 15-year-old Macey Clare decides to research the history of a burned-out barn for a school project, no one wants to answer her questions. Her quest to learn the truth about the fire of 1959 reveals racist crimes of the past. Now Macey has to decide what she can do in the present.

Burning Up. unabr. ed. Caroline B. Cooney. Narrated by Christina Moore. 5 pieces. (Running Time: 6 hrs.). (gr. 7 up). 1999. 46.00 (978-0-7887-3167-9(X), 95840E7) Recorded Bks.

Burning Up, Class set. Caroline B. Cooney. Read by Christina Moore. 5 cass. (Running Time: 6 hrs.). (YA). 1999. 214.20 (978-0-7887-3236-2(6), 46892) Recorded Bks.

Burning Up, Set. unabr. ed. Caroline B. Cooney. Narrated by Christina Moore. 5 cass. (Running Time: 6 hrs.). (YA). 2000. 46.00 (95840X4) Recorded Bks.

Burning Wild. abr. ed. Christine Feehan. Read by Phil Gigante & Jeffrey Cummings. (Running Time: 4 hrs.). (Leopard Ser.). 2010. audio compact disk 14.99 (978-1-4418-1528-6(7), 9781441815286, BACD) Brilliance Audio.

Burning Wild. unabr. ed. Christine Feehan. Read by Phil Gigante & Jeffrey Cummings. (Running Time: 14 hrs.). (Leopard Ser.). 2010. 24.99 (978-1-4418-1524-8(4), 9781441815248, Brilliance MP3); 24.99 (978-1-4418-1526-2(0), 9781441815262, BAD); 39.97 (978-1-4418-1525-5(2), 9781441815255, Brinc Audio MP3 Lib); 39.97 (978-1-4418-1527-9(9), 9781441815279, BADLE); audio compact disk 29.99 (978-1-4418-1522-4(8), 9781441815224, Bril Audio CD Unabri); audio compact disk 97.97 (978-1-4418-1523-1(6), 9781441815231, BriAudCD Unabrid) Brilliance Audio.

Burning Wire. abr. ed. Jeffery Deaver. Read by Dennis Boutsikaris. (Running Time: 6 hrs. 0 mins. 0 sec.). (Lincoln Rhyme Ser.: No. 9). 2010. audio compact disk 29.99 (978-1-4423-0420-8(0)) Pub: S&S Audio. Dist(s): S and S Inc

Burning Wire. unabr. ed. Jeffery Deaver. Read by Dennis Boutsikaris. 12 CDs. (Running Time: 13 hrs. 30 mins. 0 sec.). No. 9. (ENG.). 2010. audio compact disk 39.99 (978-1-4423-0422-2(7)) Pub: S&S Audio. Dist(s): S and S Inc

Burning with Holy Spirit Fire. abr. ed. Reinhard Bonnke. (Running Time: Approx: 50 min.). (ENG.). 2001. audio compact disk 7.00 (978-0-9758789-8-9(0)) E-R-Productions.
Whether you are tackling family problems, business difficulties or matters of personal need, you are destined for victory in the sure knowledge that Satan has already been defeated by the power of Holy Spirit.

Burno Munari's Zoo. 2004. 8.95 (978-1-56008-854-7(0)) Weston Woods.

Burnout. Frank Minirth. Read by Frank Minirth. Read by Paul Meier. 1 cass. (Running Time: 86 min.). (Minirth & Meier Home Counseling Audio Library). 1994. 9.95 (978-1-56707-034-7(5)) Dallas Christ Recs.
The road to recovery & how to counter the stresses that can cause burnout in your life.

Burnout: Keeping the Fire. Ruth J. Luban. 2 cass. 1996. pap. bk. 19.95 Set, incl. 28p. guidebk. (978-1-55678-058-5(3), 3270, Lrn Inc) Oasis Audio.
An in-depth guide to job or career burnout. Covers how to recognize the symptoms, reduce your risk & reclaim your life. The author, a noted burnout therapist, offers compassionate guidance that comes out of her own struggle with burnout seven years ago.

Burnout: Prevention & Recovery Get Your Life Back on Track. Sally Fisher. 1 cass. 1996. 11.95 (978-1-881451-43-3(7)) Brain Sync.

Burnout & Inspiration in the Helping Vocations. unabr. ed. Paul Gorman. 2 cass. 18.00 (OC26L) Sound Horizons AV.

Burns & Allen. 2 CDs. (Running Time: 2 hrs.). 2004. audio compact disk 10.95 (978-1-57816-221-5(1)) Audio File.

Burns & Allen. Perf. by Jack Benny. 1 CD. (Running Time: 1 hr.). (Old-Time Radio Blockbusters Ser.). 2002. audio compact disk 4.98 (978-1-57019-390-3(8), OTR7701) Pub: Radio Spirits. Dist(s): AudioGO

Burns & Allen. Read by George Burns & Gracie Allen. 4 vols. (Running Time: 6 hrs.). (Smithsonian Legendary Performers Ser.). 2002. bk. 24.98 (978-1-57019-504-4(8), OTR40004) Pub: Radio Spirits. Dist(s): AudioGO

Burns & Allen, Set. unabr. ed. 2 cass. (Running Time: 2 hrs.). 10.95 (978-1-57816-042-6(1), BA2401) Audio File.
Four programs with outstanding guests & hilarious stories from the Burns & Allen radio show.

Burns & Allen, Vol. 1, set. Perf. by George Burns & Gracie Allen. 6 cass. (Running Time: 1 hr. 30 mins. per cass.). 34.98 (Q103) Blckstn Audio.
Burns & Allen Show ran on radio from 1933 until 1949. By 1942 they had their show firmly rooted in situation comedy.

Burns & Allen, Vol. 2, set. Perf. by George Burns & Gracie Allen. 6 cass. (Running Time: 1 hr. 30 mins. per cass.). 34.98 (Q110) Blckstn Audio.
Don't say "Goodnight Gracie" without listening to this great husband & wife team at the top of their form.

Burns & Allen: All Promises Are Ficticious & Biggest in the World. unabr. ed. Perf. by George Burns & Gracie Allen. 1 cass. (Running Time: 1 hr.). 2001. 6.98 (2297) Radio Spirits.

Burns & Allen: Aunt Clara Kangaroo & Rah! Rah! in Omaha! unabr. ed. Perf. by George Burns & Gracie Allen. 1 cass. (Running Time: 1 hr.). 2001. 6.98 (2298) Radio Spirits.

Burns & Allen: Burglar Reformation & George in Need of Recognition. unabr. ed. Perf. by George Burns et al. 1 cass. (Running Time: 1 hr.). 2001. 6.98 (1886) Radio Spirits.

Burns & Allen: Charles Laughton & Elsa Lanchester & John Garfield. unabr. ed. Perf. by George Burns et al. 1 cass. (Running Time: 1 hr.). 2001. 6.98 (2433) Radio Spirits.

Burns & Allen: Claudette Colbert & Jack Benny. Perf. by George Burns et al. 1 CD. (Running Time: 1 hr.). (Old-Time Radio Blockbusters Ser.). 2001. audio compact disk 4.98 (7701) Radio Spirits.

Burns & Allen: George Has Allergies & Tax Time. unabr. ed. Perf. by George Burns & Gracie Allen. 1 cass. (Running Time: 1 hr.). 2001. 6.98 (2611) Radio Spirits.

Burns & Allen: George Runs for Councilman & Gracie Feels Slighted. unabr. ed. Perf. by George Burns & Gracie Allen. 1 cass. (Running Time: 1 hr.). 2001. 6.98 (1837) Radio Spirits.

Burns & Allen: George's Malady & Sweeping into Office. unabr. ed. Perf. by George Burns & Gracie Allen. 1 cass. (Running Time: 1 hr.). 2001. 6.98 (2299) Radio Spirits.

Burns & Allen: Going on Quiz Shows to Win Appliances & Eddie Cantor Guest Stars. unabr. ed. Perf. by George Burns et al. 1 cass. (Running Time: 1 hr.). 2001. 6.98 (1621) Radio Spirits.

Burns & Allen: Government Jobs & Hats Off to Gracie. unabr. ed. Perf. by George Burns & Gracie Allen. 1 cass. (Running Time: 1 hr.). 2001. 6.98 (2294) Radio Spirits.

Burns & Allen: Gracie & Uplift Society Put on a Play & Harpo Marx Guest Stars. unabr. ed. Perf. by George Burns & Harpo Marx. 1 cass. (Running Time: 1 hr.). 2001. 6.98 (1620) Radio Spirits.

Burns & Allen: Gracie for President. Perf. by George Burns & Gracie Allen. (ENG.). 2008. audio compact disk 27.95 (978-1-57019-860-1(8)) Radio Spirits.

Burns & Allen: Gracie Has Romantic Notions & French Singer. unabr. ed. Perf. by George Burns & Gracie Allen. 1 cass. (Running Time: 1 hr.). 2001. 6.98 (1623) Radio Spirits.

Burns & Allen: Gracie Is Late for the Show & Gracie Signs a Singer to a Contract. unabr. ed. Perf. by George Burns & Gracie Allen. 1 cass. (Running Time: 1 hr.). 2001. 6.98 (2531) Radio Spirits.

Burns & Allen: Gracie Turns House into Office & Gracie Takes up Crime Solving. unabr. ed. Perf. by George Burns & Gracie Allen. 1 cass. (Running Time: 1 hr.). 2001. 6.98 (1622) Radio Spirits.

Burns & Allen: Gracie Writes Gossip Column & Christmas Gift Mix-Up. unabr. ed. Perf. by George Burns & Gracie Allen. 1 cass. (Running Time: 1 hr.). 2001. 6.98 (1838) Radio Spirits.

Burns & Allen: Gracie's Losing George & Brian Donlevy Guest Stars. unabr. ed. Perf. by George Burns et al. 1 cass. (Running Time: 1 hr.). 2001. 6.98 (2055) Radio Spirits.

Burns & Allen: Guessing Gracie's Gift & Open House. unabr. ed. Perf. by George Burns & Gracie Allen. 1 cass. (Running Time: 1 hr.). 2001. 6.98 (1944) Radio Spirits.

Burns & Allen: Hat Merchants' Prices & Gracie's Filing System. unabr. ed. Perf. by George Burns & Gracie Allen. 1 cass. (Running Time: 1 hr.). 2001. 6.98 (2006) Radio Spirits.

***Burns & Allen: Home Fires.** Perf. by George Burns & Grace Allen. 2010. audio compact disk 18.95 (978-1-57019-935-6(3)) Radio Spirits.

Burns & Allen: Hot Box Hostage & Victory Garden. unabr. ed. Perf. by George Burns & Gracie Allen. 1 cass. (Running Time: 1 hr.). 2001. 6.98 (2573) Radio Spirits.

Burns & Allen: Impressing Cubina Wright & George Goes to the Art Gallery. unabr. ed. Perf. by George Burns & Gracie Allen. 1 cass. (Running Time: 1 hr.). 2001. 6.98 (2512) Radio Spirits.

Burns & Allen: Kiddy Party & George Tries Out for a Movie. unabr. ed. Perf. by George Burns & Gracie Allen. 1 cass. (Running Time: 1 hr.). 2001. 6.98 (2493) Radio Spirits.

Burns & Allen: King George Becomes a Royal Pain & Good Help Is Hard to Find. unabr. ed. Perf. by George Burns & Gracie Allen. 1 cass. (Running Time: 1 hr.). 2001. 6.98 (2412) Radio Spirits.

Burns & Allen: Married but Single & Marriage Manual. unabr. ed. Perf. by George Burns & Gracie Allen. 1 cass. (Running Time: 1 hr.). 2001. 6.98 (2292) Radio Spirits.

Burns & Allen: Messy Mechanics & Being Neighborly. unabr. ed. Perf. by George Burns & Gracie Allen. 1 cass. (Running Time: 1 hr.). 2001. 6.98 (2253) Radio Spirits.

Burns & Allen: New Year's Resolution & The Uplifters Club. unabr. ed. Perf. by George Burns & Gracie Allen. 1 cass. (Running Time: 1 hr.). 2001. 6.98 (1568) Radio Spirits.

Burns & Allen: No to Salesmen & Spiritualism Swamp Real Estate. unabr. ed. Perf. by George Burns & Gracie Allen. 1 cass. (Running Time: 1 hr.). 2001. 6.98 (1839) Radio Spirits.

Burns & Allen: Painting Masterpieces & A Couple of Kleptomaniacs. unabr. ed. Perf. by George Burns & Gracie Allen. 1 cass. (Running Time: 1 hr.). 2001. 6.98 (2291) Radio Spirits.

Burns & Allen: Pooling Resources & 99 Year Lease. unabr. ed. Perf. by George Burns & Gracie Allen. 1 cass. (Running Time: 1 hr.). 2001. 6.98 (2154) Radio Spirits.

Burns & Allen: Society after George's Show & Can't Get Rid of Meredith. unabr. ed. Perf. by George Burns & Gracie Allen. 1 cass. (Running Time: 1 hr.). 2001. 6.98 (1619) Radio Spirits.

Burns & Allen: Swiss Family Robinson & Grandfather's Birthday. unabr. ed. Perf. by George Burns & Gracie Allen. 1 cass. (Running Time: 1 hr.). 2001. 6.98 (2473) Radio Spirits.

Burns & Allen: The Folly of Molly O'Malley & Charles Boyer Guest Stars. unabr. ed. Perf. by George Burns et al. 1 cass. (Running Time: 1 hr.). 2001. 6.98 (1846) Radio Spirits.

Burns & Allen: The Lady Killer & Caesar Romero as Guest Star. unabr. ed. Perf. by George Burns et al. 1 cass. (Running Time: 1 hr.). 2001. 6.98 (2594) Radio Spirits.

Burns & Allen: The Man from MGM & Expecting a Baby. unabr. ed. Perf. by George Burns & Gracie Allen. 1 cass. (Running Time: 1 hr.). 2001. 6.98 (2293) Radio Spirits.

Burns & Allen: Till the Cows Come Home & Gracie Wins Wisconsin. unabr. ed. Perf. by George Burns & Gracie Allen. 1 cass. (Running Time: 1 hr.). 2001. 6.98 (2296) Radio Spirits.

Burns & Allen: Triumphant Return & Surprise Party Platform. unabr. ed. Perf. by George Burns & Gracie Allen. 1 cass. (Running Time: 1 hr.). 2001. 6.98 (2295) Radio Spirits.

Burns & Allen: $5,000 Mink Coat & Walter Pidgeon Guest Stars. unabr. ed. Perf. by George Burns & Gracie Allen. 1 cass. (Running Time: 1 hr.). 2001. 6.98 (1836) Radio Spirits.

Burns & Allen Vol. 3: The Lost Shows of 1940. collector's ed. Perf. by George Burns & Gracie Allen. 6 cass. (Running Time: 9 hrs.). 2000. bk. 34.98 (4183) Radio Spirits.
18 "lost shows" from the 1940 season.

Burns & Allen Show. 1 cass. (Running Time: 60 min.). (Old Time Radio Classic Singles Ser.). 4.95 (978-1-57816-089-1(8), BA104) Audio File.
George & Gracie in two comedy broadcasts: 1) Guest Jack Benny enrolls with George at Beverly Hills Tech. 11/29/45. 2) Gracie wants guest Bing Crosby to retire so George can replace him. 1940s Maxwell House Coffee.

Burns & Allen Show. 1 cass. (Running Time: 1 hr.). 7.95 (CC4313) Natl Recrd Co.

Burns & Allen Show. Perf. by Jack Benny & Bing Crosby. 1 cass. (Running Time: 60 min.). 1945. 7.95 (CC-5900) Natl Recrd Co.
In the espisode with Jack Benny, George is left $5,000 by his late Uncle Marvin & Gracie insists George must attend college; Jack Benny & George enroll & both men become student contestants in the "most popular man" contest. In the episode with Bing Crosby, Gracie wants Bing to retire so George can take his place both as a singer & in the movies; she gets Bing to consider it until he hears George sing & "emote" a few lines. That does it!.

Burns & Allen Show, No. 2. unabr. ed. Perf. by Al Jolson & Mickey Rooney. 1 cass. (Running Time: 60 min.). Dramatization. 7.95 Norelco box. (9802) Natl Recrd Co.
Al Jolson: George & Gracie celebrate their 15th radio anniversary, & they recall how they got their start on the air. Guest Al Jolson, in a flashback, shows how he gave them their first job. With Mel Blanc & Bill Gordon. Maxwell House Coffee, 1947. Mickey Rooney: Gracie wants to adopt Mickey Rooney (she thinks he's a little boy) who agrees because he is hiding from his studio. Mickey's tired of playing little boy parts in pictures & wants to play tough guy roles. George is not happy - Gracie has slipped him a "mickey." Maxwell House Coffee, 1949.

Burns & Allen Show, Vol. 1. collector's ed. Perf. by George Burns et al. 6 cass. (Running Time: 9 hrs.). 2000. bk. 34.98 (978-1-57019-311-8(8), 4100) Radio Spirits.
Originally George delivered the funny lines, but it was Gracie who always got the laughs. So they switched parts and George became the world's foremost straight man with Gracies a s his "dizzy" wife. 18 episodes.

Burns & Allen Show, Vol. 2. collector's ed. Perf. by George Burns et al. 6 cass. (Running Time: 9 hrs.). 1998. bk. 34.98 (4137) Radio Spirits.

Burns & Allen Show: Christmas Show of 1940's. Perf. by Edna Mae Oliver & Paul Whiteman. (CC-9009) Natl Recrd Co.

Burns, Government by the People: Instructor's Resource CD. 20th ed. audio compact disk 18.97 (978-0-13-110185-2(4)) PH School.

***Burnt Creek.** Ernest Haycox. 2009. (978-1-60136-427-2(X)) Audio Holding.

Burnt Creek. Ernest Haycox. (Running Time: 0 hr. 36 mins.). 1999. 10.95 (978-1-60083-505-6(8)) Iofy Corp.

Burnt House. abr. ed. Faye Kellerman. Read by Mitchell Greenberg. (Running Time: 21600 sec.). (Peter Decker & Rina Lazarus Novel Ser.). 2007. audio compact disk 29.95 (978-0-06-125660-8(9), Harper Audio) HarperCollins Pubs.

***Burnt House.** abr. ed. Faye Kellerman. Read by Mitchell Greenberg. (ENG.). 2007. (978-0-06-154633-4(X)); (978-0-06-154634-1(8)) HarperCollins Pubs.

Burnt House. unabr. ed. Faye Kellerman. Read by George Guidall. 11 CDs. (Running Time: 46800 sec.). (Peter Decker & Rina Lazarus Novel Ser.). 2007. audio compact disk 39.95 (978-0-06-125659-2(5), Harper Audio) HarperCollins Pubs.

Burnt House. unabr. ed. Faye Kellerman. Read by George Guidall. 15 CDs. (Running Time: 18 hrs. 30 mins.). (Peter Decker & Rina Lazarus Novel Ser.). 2007. audio compact disk 123.75 (978-1-4281-5589-3(9)); 113.75 (978-1-4281-5587-9(2)) Recorded Bks.
When a mysterious plane crashes, it leaves the charred remains of four unidentified bodies. As LAPD Lieutenant Peter Decker and his wife Rina investigate, they soon must race to unravel crucial clues before something sinister happens to anyone else.

***Burnt House CD.** unabr. ed. Faye Kellerman. Read by George Guidall. (ENG.). 2007. (978-0-06-154631-0(3)); (978-0-06-154632-7(1)) HarperCollins Pubs.

Burnt Mountain. unabr. ed. Anne Rivers Siddons. (Running Time: 14 hrs.). (ENG.). 2011. 26.98 (978-1-60788-250-3(7)); audio compact disk 34.98 (978-1-60788-249-7(3)) Pub: Hachet Audio. Dist(s): HachBkGrp

Burnt Offerings. abr. ed. Laurell K. Hamilton. 5 CDs. (Running Time: 8 hrs.). (Anita Blake, Vampire Hunter Ser.: No. 7). (ENG.). 2010. audio compact disk 29.95 (978-0-14-314427-4(8), PenAudBks) Pub: Pnguin Bks Ltd GBR. Dist(s): Penguin Grp USA

Burnt Offerings. unabr. ed. Laurell K. Hamilton. Read by Kimberly Alexis. 11 CDs. (Running Time: 13 hrs.). (Anita Blake, Vampire Hunter Ser.: No. 7). (ENG.). 2010. audio compact disk 39.95 (978-0-14-314407-6(3), PenAudBks) Pub: Pnguin Bks Ltd GBR. Dist(s): Penguin Grp USA

Burnt Offerings. unabr. collector's ed. Robert Marasco. Read by Dan Lazar. 8 cass. (Running Time: 8 hrs.). 1978. 48.00 (978-0-7366-0119-1(8), 1126) Books on Tape.
The Rolfe family - Ben, Marian, their son, David & aunt, Elizabeth - are a pleasant family from New York seeking to escape the horrors of a summer in their Queens apartment. They find a beautiful old country mansion on Long Island. But their summer home is anything but calm & quiet. During that long summer the house becomes a mesmerizing nightmare from which there seems no escape.

Burnt Sienna. unabr. ed. David Morrell. Read by Gabrielle De Cuir. 6 cass. (Running Time: 9 hrs.). 2001. 32.00 (978-1-59040-180-4(8), Phoenix Audio) Pub: Amer Intl Pub. Dist(s): PerseuPGW
A tough ex-marine and world class painter who risks all for a beautiful woman is set in exotic locations in the Caribbean and on the French Riviera. The plot bristles with excitement and danger, as our hero fights the arch-villain Derek Bellasar.

Burnt Toast: And Other Philosophies of Life. abr. ed. Teri Hatcher. Read by Teri Hatcher. Read by Deanna Hurst. (Running Time: 10800 sec.). 2007. audio compact disk 14.98 (978-1-4013-8736-5(5)) Pub: Hyperion. Dist(s): HarperCollins Pubs

***BURNT TOAST [audio digital download].** Teri Hatcher. (ENG.). 2006. 14.99 (978-1-4013-8509-5(5)) Pub: Hyperion. Dist(s): HarperCollins Pubs

Burps, Sneezes, & Super Robots: The Boy Who Burped Too Much; the Super-Powered Sneeze; Robot Rampage. Scott Nickel. Read by Full Cast Production Staff. (Playaway Children Ser.). (J). 2008. 39.99 (978-1-60640-967-1(0)) Find a World.

Burr. unabr. ed. Gore Vidal. Read by Grover Gardner. 13 cass. (Running Time: 19 hrs. 30 min.). (American Chronicles Ser.). 1993. 104.00 (978-0-7366-2329-2(9), 3109) Books on Tape.
A fascinating fictional portrait of Aaron Burr, one of our most complex & contradictory historical figures.

Burst Forth in Song Sing-Along Tape. Christine Wyrtzen & Paula Bussard. Read by Christine Wyrtzen. 1 cass. (50-Day Spiritual Adventure Ser.). (J). (gr. k-2). 1995. 10.00 (978-1-879050-80-8(3)) Chapel of Air.

Burst, Poems Quickly. Richard Hague. (ENG.). 2005. 4.00 (978-1-933675-03-9(9)) Dos Madres Pr.

Burt Dow: Deep Water Man. 2004. audio compact disk 12.95 (978-1-55592-900-8(1)) Weston Woods.

Burt Dow: Deep Water Man. (J). 2004. bk. 24.95 (978-1-56008-021-3(3)); pap. bk. 18.95 (978-1-55592-374-7(7)); pap. bk. 38.75 (978-1-55592-376-1(3)); pap. bk. 32.75 (978-1-55592-197-2(3)) Weston Woods.

Burt Dow: Deep-Water Man. 2004. cass. & flmstrp 30.00 (978-0-89719-507-2(8)) Weston Woods.

Burt Dow: Deep-Water Man. Robert McCloskey. Narrated by Sherry Stringfield. Music by John Jennings. 1 cass., 5 bks. (Running Time: 17 min.). (J). pap. bk. 32.75 Weston Woods.
When Burt drops his baited hook over the side of his boat, the Tidely-Idley, he never dreams that on the other end there will be a whale.

Burt Dow: Deep-Water Man. Robert McCloskey. Narrated by Sherry Stringfield. Music by John Jennings. 1 cass. (Running Time: 17 min.). (J). (ps-4). bk. 24.95 Weston Woods.

Burt Dow: Deep-Water Man. Robert McCloskey. 1 cass. (Running Time: 15 min.). (J). (ps-4). 1990. pap. bk. 8.95 (978-1-56008-101-2(5), RAC262) Weston Woods.
Burt catches himself a lot more than a fish when he & his trusty boat, the Tidely-Idely, put out to sea. A whale of a tale!.

Burt Dow: Deep-Water Man. Robert McCloskey. Narrated by Sherry Stringfield. Music by John Jennings. 1 cass. (Running Time: 17 min.). (J). (ps-4). 1990. pap. bk. 14.95 (978-1-56008-022-0(1), PRA262) Weston Woods.
When Burt drops his baited hook over the side of his boat, the Tidely-Idley, he never dreams that on the other end there will be a whale.

Burt Dow; Deep Water Man. 2004. 8.95 (978-0-89719-907-0(3)) Weston Woods.

Burt Dow: Deep-Water Man: A Tale of the Sea in the Classic Tradition. Robert McCloskey. Narrated by John McDonough. (Running Time: 1 hr.). (ps up). 12.00 (978-0-7887-5361-9(4)) Recorded Bks.

Burt Dow: Deep Water Man; Each Peach Pear Plum; Shadow; Ernest & Celestine. 2004. (978-0-89719-853-0(0)) Weston Woods.

Burt Dow; Deep-Water Man; Each Peach Pear Plum; Shadwo; Ernest & Celestine. 2004. cass. & flmstrp (978-0-89719-753-3(4)) Weston Woods.

Burton. unabr. ed. Byron Farwell. Read by Simon Vance. 13 cass. (Running Time: 19 hrs.). 1996. 85.95 (978-0-7861-0922-7(X), 1703) Blckstn Audio.
Explorer & inventor, soldier & poet, archaeologist & diplomat, Richard Francis Burton (1821-1890) was the most versatile & remarkable man of his age. Byron Farwell brilliantly recreates the sheer excitement of Burton's achievements & astonishing range of interest. And yet, as the biography makes clear, Burton was primarily an adventurer. The pioneering traveler in Central Africa who discovered Lake Tanganyika was also the translator of "The African Nights," & the secret translator of Oriental sex manual like "The Perfumed Garden." The man who made a dangerous pilgrimage to Mecca in disguise also produced major writings on reptiles & religion, mining & mountain climbing, slavery & strange sexual practices.

Burton: A Biography of Sir Richard Frances Burton. unabr. ed. Byron Farwell. Read by Simon Vance. (Running Time: 19 hrs. 0 mins.). 2009. 44.95 (978-1-4332-6929-5(5)); audio compact disk 120.00 (978-1-4332-6926-4(0)) Blckstn Audio.

Burton: A Biography of Sir Richard Francis Burton. unabr. collector's ed. Byron Farwell. Read by David Case. 14 cass. (Running Time: 21 hrs.). 1992. 112.00 (978-0-7366-2098-7(2), 2904) Books on Tape.
No man can be all things at once, no matter how hard he tries, but no man ever tried harder than Richard Francis Burton. He made significant contributions in the fields of literature & geography & was also a poet, traveler, soldier, diplomat, inventor, explorer, archaeologist, student of religion & more. But above all, Burton was an adventurer in both the intellectual & spiritual worlds.

Bury Him among Kings. unabr. collector's ed. Elleston Trevor. Read by Victor Rumbellow. 10 cass. (Running Time: 15 hrs.). 1980. 80.00 (978-0-7366-0191-7(0), 1191) Books on Tape.
World War I & the lives of a variety of English soldiers are the setting & characters of this novel. The narrative centers around two brothers from the British aristocracy - Aubray & Victor Talbot. Through their experiences in the trenches of France, we enter the war & learn about its horrifying futility.

Bury in Haste. Jean Rowden. 2009. 69.95 (978-1-84652-367-0(2)) Pub: Magna Story GBR. Dist(s): Ulverscroft US

Bury in Haste. Jean Rowden & Geoff Annis. 2009. audio compact disk 79.95 (978-1-84652-368-7(0)) Pub: Magna Story GBR. Dist(s): Ulverscroft US

Bury It Deep, Set. unabr. ed. Sam Reaves. Read by Michael Hanson & Mary Dilts. 7 cass. (Running Time: 10 hrs. 8 mins.). (Cooper MacLeish Mystery Ser.: Vol. 3). 1993. 42.00 (978-0-9624010-5-3(6), 892558) Readers Chair.
While investigating a big scoop, Cooper & his reporter friend Moreland uncover behind-the-scenes political double-dealing & a mysterious tape that no one wants found.

***Bury My Heart at Conference Room B: What Truly Drives the World's Most Passionate Managers.** unabr. ed. Stan Slap. (Running Time: 8 hrs. 0 mins.). 2010. 15.99 (978-1-4001-8755-3(9)) Tantor Media.

***Bury My Heart at Conference Room B: What Truly Drives the World's Most Passionate Managers.** unabr. ed. Stan Slap. (Running Time: 7 hrs. 0 mins. 0 sec.). (ENG.). 2010. 19.99 (978-1-4001-6755-5(8)); audio compact disk 71.99 (978-1-4001-4755-7(7)); audio compact disk 29.99 (978-1-4001-1755-0(0)) Pub: Tantor Media. Dist(s): IngramPubServ

Bury My Heart at Wounded Knee. unabr. collector's ed. Dee Brown. Read by Dick Estell. 12 cass. (Running Time: 18 hrs.). 1992. 96.00 (978-0-7366-2242-4(X), 3032) Books on Tape.
Bury My Heart at Wounded Knee is an eloquent, fully documented account of the systematic destruction of American Indians during the second half of the 19th century. Using council records, autobiographies & other firsthand descriptions, Dee Brown allows the great chiefs & warriors of the Dakota, Ute, Sioux & Cheyenne to tell us about the battles, massacres & broken treaties that finally left them demoralized & defeated. Sadly, this is how the west was really won.

Bury My Heart at Wounded Knee: An Indian History of the American West. unabr. ed. Dee Brown. Read by Paul Michael Garcia & Grover Gardner. (Running Time: 23 hrs.). (ENG.). 2009. 44.95 (978-1-4332-9344-3(7)) Blckstn Audio.

Bury My Heart at Wounded Knee: An Indian History of the American West. unabr. ed. Dee Brown. Read by Grover Gardner. (Running Time: 23 hrs. 0 mins.). (ENG.). 2009. 109.95 (978-1-4332-9340-5(4)) Blckstn Audio.

Bury My Heart at Wounded Knee: An Indian History of the American West. unabr. ed. Dee Brown. Read by Paul Michael Garcia. (Running Time: 23 hrs.). (ENG.). 2009. audio compact disk 32.95 (978-1-4332-9343-6(9)) Blckstn Audio.

Bury My Heart at Wounded Knee: An Indian History of the American West. unabr. ed. Dee Brown. Read by Grover Gardner. (Running Time: 23 hrs. 0 mins.). (ENG.). 2009. audio compact disk 123.00 (978-1-4332-9341-2(2)) Blckstn Audio.

Bury the Lead. abr. ed. David Rosenfelt. 5 CDs. (Running Time: 6 hrs.). (What's New Ser.). 2004. audio compact disk 29.95 (978-1-59316-025-8(9)) Listen & Live.
Clever plot twists, deft legal maneuverings, and keen wit are hallmarks of Rosenfelt's third follow-up to his Edgar-nominated debut novel, featuring millionaire attorney, Andy Carpenter, who is irreverent, intelligent, sarcastic and dry.

Bury the Past; Be Ye Kind, One to Another; Does Prayer Work?; How Much Farther? John D. Jess. 1 cass. (Eternal Truths Ser.). 1993. 4.97 (978-1-55748-378-2(7)) Barbour Pub.

***Bury Your Dead.** unabr. ed. Louise Penny. Read by Paul Michael & Ralph Cosham. (Running Time: 12 hrs. 30 mins. 0 sec.). (Chief Inspector Gamache Novel Ser.: Bk. 6). 2010. audio compact disk 39.99 (978-1-4272-1071-5(3)) Pub: Macmill Audio. Dist(s): Macmillan

Burying Place. unabr. ed. Brian Freeman. Read by Joe Barrett. (Running Time: 12 hrs. 0 mins.). (Book 5 of the Lieutenant Jonathan Stride Ser.). 2010. 29.95 (978-1-4417-2684-1(5)); audio compact disk 34.95 (978-1-4417-2683-4(7)) Blckstn Audio.

***Burying Place.** unabr. ed. Brian Freeman. Read by Joe Barrett. (Running Time: 12 hrs. 0 mins.). (Book 5 of the Lieutenant Jonathan Stride Ser.). 2010. 72.95 (978-1-4417-2680-3(2)); audio compact disk 105.00 (978-1-4417-2681-0(0)) Blckstn Audio.

Bus Named Desire. Perf. by Ashley Cleveland. 1 cass. 1993. audio compact disk (978-7-01-008172-4(7)) Brentwood Music.
The former Atlantic recording artist's first Christian release showcases her powerful & dynamic vocals & songwriting prowess.

Buscadme y Vivireis. unabr. ed. Marcos Vidal. 1 CD. 1998. 14.99 (978-0-8297-2646-6(2)) Zondervan.

Bush: The Unauthorized Biography of Bush. Martin Harper. (Maximum Ser.). (ENG.). 2001. audio compact disk 14.95 (978-1-84240-046-3(0)) Pub: Chrome Dreams GBR. Dist(s): IPG Chicago

Bush at War: Inside the Bush White House. abr. ed. Bob Woodward. Read by James Naughton. 2006. 18.95 (978-0-7435-6142-6(2)) Pub: S&S Audio. Dist(s): S and S Inc

Bush Pilots: Legends of the Old & Bold. Bob Cary & Jack Hautala. 2003. per. 15.95 (978-1-59193-010-5(3)) Adventure Pubns.

Bush Tragedy. unabr. ed. Jacob Weisberg. Read by Robertson Dean. 5 cass. (Running Time: 34200 sec.). 2008. 24.95 (978-1-4332-0908-6(X)); 44.95 (978-1-4332-0906-2(3)); audio compact disk 24.95 (978-1-4332-0909-3(8)); audio compact disk 29.95 (978-1-4332-0910-9(1)); audio compact disk 45.00 (978-1-4332-0907-9(1)) Blckstn Audio.

Bush Warfare. Carol Eason. Read by Carol Eason. 3 CDs. (Running Time: 3 hrs.). (Mercenary Ser.: No. 10). 2005. audio compact disk (978-1-58807-900-8(7)); audio compact disk 25.00 (978-1-58807-334-1(3)) Am Pubng Inc.
Hank Frost, the fast-shooting, fast-talking mercenary, finds himself the target of a beautiful woman's revenge. Kidnapped, he awakens in a deep African jungle with a needle mark in his arm and a note that tells him he must fight his way through the jungle itself, its beasts, Communist terrorists, and his own poisoned body and penetrate his enemy's fortified home - because only she has the antidote. Unarmed, Frost makes tracks through the bush, with plans of giving his ruthless enemy a dose of her own medicine.

Bush Warfare. Axel Kilgore. Read by Carol Eason. Abr. by Odin Westgaard. 2 vols. No. 10. 2004. 18.00 (978-1-58807-166-8(9)); (978-1-58807-657-1(1)) Am Pubng Inc.

Bushes: Portrait of a Dynasty. unabr. ed. Peter Schweizer & Rochelle Schweizer. Read by Robertson Dean. 16 cass. (Running Time: 24 hrs.). 2004. 96.00 (978-0-7366-9728-6(4)) Books on Tape.
The Bushes presents an unprecedented look at America's most powerful-and private-political dynasty.

Bushido. 1 cass. (Running Time: 42 min.). 12.00 (L904) MEA A Watts Cass.

Bushido: The Way of the Warrior & the Soul of Japan: the Japanese Art of War. Inazo Nitobe. Narrated by Ross M. Armetta & Urara Tsukamoto. 3 CDs. (Running Time: 3 hours Approx.). 2005. audio compact disk 16.99 (978-1-59733-203-3(8), Martial Strat) InfoFount.
Become Wise, Win easily with grace, respectability, and style ! Bushido - The Japanese Art of War describes Oriental marital training, virtue, and philosophy. It?s useful for business, sports, and any competitive situation.For Centuries the code of Bushido has been the guiding force of strength and honor in Japan. With Bushido ? The Japanese Art of War you can understand and integrate the code of honor and success in competition into your own life. This audiobook is energizing, informative, and entertaining. Your edge to gaining respect and wisdom !Bushido is based upon the teachings of Confucius, Mencius, Shintoism and the practical needs of warriors. It encompasses the discipline, physical, and moral training of the Japanese warrior and its integration into Japanese culture. Use it to create successful, honorable, and respectable actions and campaigns.Bushido will increase your comprehension and help you acquire and develop the culture, ethics, and spirituality, of a professional warrior. The complimentary audiobook Gorin No Sho, The Book of 5 Rings (sold separately) is unequaled in learning about and dealing with the infinite details of competition especially in real combat (martial arts or war, individual or group). Contents include (partial list) Bushido as an Ethical System; Sources of Bushido; Rectitude or Justice; Courage, the Spirit of Daring and Bearing; Benevolence, the Feeling of Distress; Politeness; Veracity or Truthfulness; Honor; The Duty of Loyalty; Education and Training of a Samurai; Self-Control; The Institutions of Suicide and Redress; The Sword, the Soul of the Samurai; The Training and Position of Woman.This is a great audiobook for anybody interested in ethics / warrior""s ethics, Japan, Japanese culture, Oriental culture and philosophy, and particularly the Samurai and Bushido. This is especially helpful for martial artists in understanding the philosophy, training, and culture of their arts.Bushido is also available discounted as part of the Samurai Pack or Martial Strategist?s Master Strategy Pack.More information available at www.InfoFount.comAn excerpt from COURAGE, THE SPIRIT OF DARING AND BEARING. Courage was scarcely deemed worthy to be counted among virtues, unless: it was exercised in the cause of Righteousness. In his "Analects "Confucius defines Courage by explaining, as is often his wont what its negative is." Perceiving what is right," he says," and doing it not, argue lack of courage." Put this epigram into; positive statement, and it runs, "Courage is doing what is right."To run all kinds of hazards, to jeopardize one""""""""s self, to rush into the jaws of death-these are too often identified with Valor, and in the profession of arms such rashness of conduct-what Shakespeare calls, "valor misbegot" is unjustly applauded; but not so in the Precepts of Knighthood.Death for a cause unworthy of dying for, was called a "dog""""""""s death." " To rush into the thick of battle and to be slain in it," says a Prince of Mito, " is easy enough, and the merest churl is equal to the task; but," he continues, " it is true courage to live when it is right to live, and to die only when it is right to die," and yet the Prince had not even heard of the name of Plato, who defines courage as "the knowledge of things that a man should fear and that he should not fear." A distinction which is made in the West between moral and physical courage has long been recognized among us. What Samurai youth has not heard of "Great Valor" and the "Valor of a Villain?"Valor, Fortitude, Bravery, Fearlessness, Courage, being the qualities of soul which appeal most easily to juvenile minds, and which can be trained by exercise and example, were, so to speak, the most popular virtues, early emulated among the youth. Stories of military exploits were repeated almost before boys left their mother""""""""s breast. Does a little booby cry for any ache? The mother scolds him in this fashion: "What a coward to cry for a trifling pain! What will you do when your arm is cut off in battle? What when you are called upon to commit hara-kiri.".

Bushranger of the Skies. unabr. ed. Arthur W. Upfield. Read by Peter Hosking. 7 cass. (Running Time: 10 hrs. 30 mins.). (Inspector Napoleon Bonaparte Mysteries). 1999. (978-1-86442-387-7(0), 590378) Bolinda Pubng AUS.
An extraordinary case of Detective-Inspector Napoleon Bonaparte opens when a police car is bombed from the air on a lonely outback road by a mysterious pilot who plans to conquer a nation. The trail through the Land of Burning Water tests Bony's endurance to the limit & takes the detective as close to death as he has ever been.

Bushranger of the Skies. unabr. ed. Arthur W. Upfield. Read by Peter Hosking. (Running Time: 7 hrs. 45 mins.). (Inspector Napoleon Bonaparte Mysteries). 2009. audio compact disk 77.95 (978-1-74214-055-1(6), 9781742140551) Pub: Bolinda Pubng AUS. Dist(s): Bolinda Pub Inc

Bushwhacked: Life in George W. Bush's America. Molly Ivins & Lou DuBose. 9 CDs. 2004. audio compact disk 64.00 (978-0-7366-9520-6(6)) Books on Tape.

Bushwhacked: Life in George W. Bush's America. abr. ed. Lou DuBose & Molly Ivins. Read by Molly Ivins. 2 CDs. (Running Time: 6 hrs.). (ENG.). 2004. audio compact disk 14.99 (978-0-7393-1775-4(X), Random AudioBks) Pub: Random Audio Pubg. Dist(s): Random

Bushwhacked: Life in George W. Bush's America. unabr. ed. Molly Ivins & Lou DuBose. 8 cass. (Running Time: 12 hrs.). 2003. 56.00 (978-0-7366-9428-5(5)) Books on Tape.

Business. Iain Banks, pseud. Narrated by Barbara Rosenblat. 10 CDs. (Running Time: 12 hrs.). audio compact disk 97.00 (978-0-7887-9864-1(2)) Recorded Bks.

Business. Ed. by Oxford University Press Staff. 2009. audio compact disk 39.95 (978-0-19-457685-7(X)) OUP.

Business, Vol. 1. Harris Winitz. Illus. by Sydney M. Baker. (All about Language Ser.). 1986. 22.00 (978-0-939990-41-2(5)) Intl Linguistics.

Business - Auf Deutsch: Kopiervorlagen. Dietmar Roesler et al. (C). 1993. 42.25 (978-3-12-675222-0(5)) Pub: Klett Ernst Verlag DEU. Dist(s): Intl Bk Import

Business @ the Speed of Thought. 2000. (978-1-57042-896-8(4)) Hachet Audio.

Business @ the Speed of Thought. Bill Gates. Read by Jonathan Marosz. 1999. audio compact disk 96.00 (978-0-7366-5161-5(6)) Books on Tape.

Business @ the Speed of Thought. Bill Gates. 2000. (978-1-57042-897-5(2)); (978-1-57042-898-2(0)) Hachet Audio.

Business @ the Speed of Thought. unabr. ed. Bill Gates. Read by Jonathan Marosz. 12 CDs. (Running Time: 14 hrs.). 2001. audio compact disk 96.00 Books on Tape.
As the cofounder, chairman & chief executive officer of Microsoft, the world's leading provider of software for personal computers, the author played a prominent role in launching the Information Age. Now this modern visionary reveals how expanding technology is propelling the business world into an exciting new economic era .how every manager can & must stay ahead of the curve & how integrated information systems can help every organization achieve business.

Business @ the Speed of Thought: Using a Digital Nervous System. unabr. ed. Bill Gates. Read by Jonathan Marosz. 9 cass. (Running Time: 13 hrs. 30 min.). 1999. 72.00 (978-0-7366-4468-6(7), 4883) Books on Tape.
Microsoft chairman & CEO Bill Gates discusses how technology can help run business better today & how it will affect the future.

***Business & Career Toolkit.** unabr. ed. Various Authors. (Running Time: 1 hr. 30 mins.). (GetAbstract Ser.). 2009. 78.00 (978-1-4417-3362-7(0)); audio compact disk 80.00 (978-1-4417-3359-7(0)) Blckstn Audio.

Business & Estate Planning: Innovative Techniques for the Business Owners. Instructed by Terry Stanaland. 2 CDs. (Running Time: 120 mins.). 2004. audio compact disk 19.95 (978-1-59280-118-3(8)) Marketplace Bks.
Fair is not necessarily equal, and equal is not always fair,? notes estate planning pro Terry Stanaland, when it comes to designing an estate plans that address the needs of each client. Now, join Stanaland, as his entertaining new presentation walks you through the top estate-planning tools and demonstrates how to apply them in every scenario.Drawing on real-world cases studies, Stanaland explores in detail the wide variety of estate planning techniques available to achieve client goals - no matter what the particular circumstances. You'll be able to give your clients real value, time after time, as you discover:-The essentials elements of every estate plan-The significance of properly titling assets-The 3 strategic objectives of estate tax planning -7 estate reduction techniques -The importance of having the business appraised Plus, he covers: - New concepts and step-by-step methods for including a family business in an estate plan - And the all-important role of considering fairness and equality along with client goals, when formulating a plan.Stanaland's decades of hands-on experience and creative strategies provide financial professionals with a rich resource to tap into.

Business & Golf: The FREEDOM to Succeed. Suzanne Woo. 2008. cd-rom 15.00 (978-0-9702731-2-3(6)) SuccessWorks CA.

Business & Leadership Conference 1994, Vol. 1. Hosted by Bill Winston. 3 cass. 1994. 15.00 (978-1-931289-90-0(5)) B Winston Min.

Business & Leadership Conference 1995, Vol. 2. Hosted by Bill Winston. 2 cass. 1995. 10.00 (978-1-931289-91-7(3)) B Winston Min.

Business & Leadership Conference 1996, Vol. 3. Hosted by Bill Winston. 2 cass. 1996. 10.00 (978-1-931289-92-4(1)) B Winston Min.

Business & Leadership Conference 1997, Vol. 4. Hosted by Bill Winston. 3 cass. (Running Time: 2hr.36min.). 1997. 15.00 (978-1-931289-93-1(X)) B Winston Min.

Business & Leadership Conference 1998, Vol. 5. Hosted by Bill Winston. 4 cass. (Running Time: 4hr.12min.). 1998. 20.00 (978-1-931289-94-8(8)) B Winston Min.

Business & Leadership Conference 1999, Vol. 6. Hosted by Bill Winston. 3 cass. (Running Time: 3hr.40min.). 1999. 15.00 (978-1-931289-95-5(6)) B Winston Min.

Business & Leadership Conference 2000, Vol. 7. Hosted by Bill Winston. 4 cass. (Running Time: 4hr.16min.). 2000. 20.00 (978-1-931289-96-2(4)) B Winston Min.

Business & Leadership Conference 2001, Vol. 8. Hosted by Bill Winston. 3 cass. (Running Time: 3hr.12min.). 2001. 15.00 (978-1-931289-97-9(2)) B Winston Min.

Business & Leadership Conference 2002, Vol. 9. Hosted by Bill Winston. 5 cass. (Running Time: 5hr.13min.). 2002. 25.00 (978-1-931289-98-6(0)) B Winston Min.

Business As Unusual Audible. Price Pritchett & Ron Pound. Narrated by Eric Conger. (ENG.). 2007. 9.95 (978-0-944002-42-1(0)) Pritchett.

Business As Usual: Buck Enterprises. Buck Enterprises Staff. (Running Time: 47 min.). 2000. 10.98 (978-0-9700482-1-9(1)); audio compact disk 14.98 (978-0-9700482-0-2(3)) Sonlight Music.

Business Assignments. Ken Casler. 1989. 17.50 (978-0-19-451383-8(1)) OUP.

Business Astrology. Eugene Moore. 1 cass. 8.95 (240) Am Fed Astrologers.
When to buy, sell, introduce new product, invest, & more.

Business at the Speed of Thought: Succeeding in the Digital Economy. abr. ed. Bill Gates. (Running Time: 3 hrs. 30 mins.). (ENG.). 2006. 14.98 (978-1-59483-766-1(X)) Pub: Hachet Audio. Dist(s): HachBkGrp

Business Aviation Equipment & Services in Japan: A Strategic Reference 2006. Compiled by Icon Group International, Inc. Staff. 2007. ring bd. 195.00 (978-0-497-82322-1(5)) Icon Grp.

Business Basic Terms, Bk. 2. Harris Winitz. Illus. by Sydney M. Baker. (YA). (gr. 7 up). 1986. pap. bk. 22.00 (978-0-939990-46-7(6)) Intl Linguistics.

Business Basics. ed. David Grant & Robert McLarty. 2004. audio compact disk 35.95 (978-0-19-457362-7(1)) OUP.

Business Benchmark: BEC Higher Advanced. Guy Brook-Hart. (Running Time: 3 hrs. 15 mins.). (ENG., 2007. audio compact disk 43.05 (978-0-521-67299-3(6)) Cambridge U Pr.

Business Benchmark: BEC Vantage: Upper-Intermediate. Guy Brook-Hart. (Running Time: 2 hrs. 26 mins.). (ENG.). 2006. audio compact disk 41.00 (978-0-521-67293-1(7)) Cambridge U Pr.

Business Benchmark: BULATS Advanced. Guy Brook-Hart. (Running Time: 2 hrs. 49 mins.). (ENG.). 2007. audio compact disk 43.05 (978-0-521-67662-5(2)) Cambridge U Pr.

Business Benchmark Advanced. Guy Brook-Hart. (Running Time: 3 hrs.). (ENG.). 2007. 41.00 (978-0-521-67298-6(8)) Cambridge U Pr.

Business Benchmark Advanced Audio Cassette BULATS Edition. Guy Brook-Hart. (Running Time: 3 hrs.). (ENG.). 2007. 43.05 (978-0-521-67661-8(4)) Cambridge U Pr.

Business Benchmark Pre-Intermediate to Intermediate. Norman Whitby. (Running Time: 2 hrs. 15 mins.). (ENG.). 2006. 41.00 (978-0-521-67287-0(2)) Cambridge U Pr.

Business Benchmark Pre-Intermediate to Intermediate Audio Cassettes BULATS Edition. Norman Whitby. (Running Time: 1 hr. 46 mins.). (ENG.). 2006. 43.05 (978-0-521-67657-1(6)) Cambridge U Pr.

Business Benchmark Pre-Intermediate to Intermediate Audio CDs BULATS Edition. Norman Whitby. (Running Time: 1 hr. 46 mins.). (ENG.). 2006. audio compact disk 41.00 (978-0-521-67658-8(4)) Cambridge U Pr.

Business Benchmark Upper Intermediate Audio Cassette BEC & BULATS Edition. Guy Brook-Hart. (Running Time: 2 hrs. 26 mins.). (ENG.). 2006. 43.05 (978-0-521-67292-4(9)) Cambridge U Pr.

Business Benchmark Upper Intermediate Audio Cassette BULATS Edition. Guy Brook-Hart. (Running Time: 2 hrs. 6 mins.). (ENG.). 2006. 43.05 (978-0-521-67659-5(2)) Cambridge U Pr.

Business Benchmark Upper Intermediate Audio CD BULATS Edition. Guy Brook-Hart. (Running Time: 2 hrs. 6 mins.). (ENG.). 2006. audio compact disk 43.05 (978-0-521-67660-1(6)) Cambridge U Pr.

Business Bonding. Charles D. Brennan, Jr. 6 cass. (New Think Selling Ser.). 1999. 99.00 Set, incl. wkbk. (978-1-928821-03-8(0), 220) Brennan Sales Inst.
Techniques on how to: make Power Pin-Point Presentations, eliminate & handle customer objections & gain commitment on every meeting.

Business Cash Management - Maximizing Your Cash Flows. John S. Purtill, Jr. 1 cass. 129.00 incl. wkbk. & template. (751927KQ); 119.00 incl. 1 cass. & wkbk. (751931KQ) Am Inst CPA.
This course offers various methods for improving cash management. Discover ways to select & negotiate the best cash management structure for your clients, or your own firm. Find out how to best advise on planning cash flows & determining cash balances.

Business Chart. Bernice P. Grebner. 1 cass. 8.95 (767) Am Fed Astrologers.

Business Charts: Three Approaches. Weiss Kelly. 1 cass. 8.95 (192) Am Fed Astrologers.
Charts of three businesses and owners.

Business Chinese. rev. ed. Ed. by Huang Weizhi. (CHI & ENG.). 2004. reel tape 9.95 (978-7-88718-029-2(5), BUCHRT) China Bks.

Business Civilization in Decline. unabr. ed. Robert L. Heilbroner. 1 cass. (Running Time: 56 min.). 12.95 (40245) J Norton Pubs.
Author & economist, Heywood Lale Heilbroner, confirms that the success of capitalism has always depended on its growth; that with resources running out, we can expect more control of science & technology by the state; & will business civilization survive if there is an economic holocaust?.

Business Class: Etiquette Essentials for Success at Work. Interview. Jacqueline Whitmore. 9 CDs. 2006. audio compact disk (978-0-9789330-0-5(1)) Protocol Schl.

Business Co-op Panel. ACT Staff. 1 cass. 8.95 (475) Am Fed Astrologers.

Business Coach: A Parable of Small Business Breakthrough! abr. ed. Bradley J. Sugars. Read by Lloyd James. (Running Time: 14400 sec.). (Instant Success Ser.). 2008. audio compact disk 28.00 (978-1-933309-59-0(8)) Pub: A Media Intl. Dist(s): Natl Bk Netwk

Business Companion Series: Chinese. 1 CD. (Running Time: 1 hr.). (CHI.). 2001. pap. bk. 21.95 (LivingLang) Random Info Grp.

Business Companion Series: German. 1 CD. (Running Time: 1 hr.). (GER.). 2001. pap. bk. 21.95 (LivingLang) Random Info Grp.

Business Companion Series: Spanish. 1 CD. (Running Time: 1 hr.). (SPA.). 2001. pap. bk. 21.95 (LivingLang) Random Info Grp.

Business Corporation Law - Highlights, 1988. Read by Dean E. Sell. 1 cass. 1989. 20.00 (AL-67) PA Bar Inst.

Business Energy Professional Reference Library. Hordeski Michael F Staff. 2005. audio compact disk 424.95 (978-0-8493-9400-3(7)) Pub: Fairmont Pr. Dist(s): Taylor and Fran

Business Environment & Concepts, Set. 3rd ed. Anita L. Feller. (ENG.). 2008. audio compact disk 85.00 (978-0-470-32342-7(6), JWiley) Wiley US.

Business Ethics: Leadership by Example. unabr. ed. Ken Blanchard. Read by Ken Blanchard. 2 CDs. (Running Time: 3 hrs.). (Smart Audio Ser.). 2004. audio compact disk 19.99 (978-1-58926-338-3(3)); 19.99 (978-1-58926-337-6(5)) Oasis Audio.
Ken Bkanchard, New York Times best-selling author who penned The One Minute Manager, talkes with CEOs of leading companies about a subject he knows well: business ethics and leadership.

Business Ethics: Successful Business Practices. unabr. ed. Ken Blanchard. Read by Ken Blanchard. 2 cass. (Running Time: 3 hrs.). (Smart Audio Ser.). 2004. 19.99 (978-1-58926-630-8(7)); audio compact disk 19.99 (978-1-58926-631-5(5)) Oasis Audio.

Business Etiquette. Linda Hughes. 2 cass. (Running Time: 3 hrs.). 1995. 15.95 (978-1-55977-100-9(3)) CareerTrack Pubns.

Business Etiquette: Keys to Professional Success (CD) Featuring Jill Kamp Melton. Prod. by TheCapitol.Net. 2006. 107.00 (978-1-58733-038-4(5)) TheCapitol.

Business Explorer. Gareth Knight & Mark O'Neil. 3 cass. (Running Time: 1 hr. 2 mins.). (ENG.). 2004. 25.00 (978-0-521-75455-2(0)) Cambridge U Pr.

Business Explorer 1. Gareth Knight & Mark O'Neil. (Running Time: 52 mins.). (ENG.). 2001. 24.00 (978-0-521-77778-0(X)); audio compact disk 25.00 (978-0-521-77777-3(1)) Cambridge U Pr.

Business Explorer 2. Gareth Knight & Mark O'Neil. (Running Time: 44 mins.). (ENG., 2002. 24.00 (978-0-521-77774-2(7)); audio compact disk 25.00 (978-0-521-77773-5(9)) Cambridge U Pr.

Business Explorer 3. Gareth Knight & Mark O'Neil. 1 CD. (Running Time: 1 hr. 2 mins.). (ENG.). 2004. audio compact disk 24.00 (978-0-521-75456-9(9)) Cambridge U Pr.

Business Financing: 25 Keys to Raising Money. unabr. ed. Dileep Rao & Richard N. Cardozo. Read by Eric Conger. 2 cass. (Running Time: 2 hrs. 30 mins.). (New York Times Pocket MBA Ser.). 2001. 16.95 (978-1-885408-44-0(7), LL037) Listen & Live.
Learn the 25 keys to find & secure the funds to start a business & keep it going-including whether to go public & if so, when.

Business Forms. Ed. by Socrates Media Editors. 2005. audio compact disk 29.95 (978-1-59546-097-4(7)) Pub: Socrates Med LLC. Dist(s): Midpt Trade

Business French. Assimil Staff. 1 cass. (Running Time: 1 hr.). 1999. pap. bk. 59.95 (978-2-7005-1378-3(9)); pap. bk. 69.95 (978-2-7005-2014-9(9)) Pub: Assimil FRA. Dist(s): Distribks Inc

Business French. Brian Hill. 3 cass. (Running Time: 3 hrs. 30 min.). (Just Listen N' Learn Ser.). 1993. 29.95 set. (Passport Bks) McGraw-Hill Trade.

Business German. Dieter Wessels & Brian Hill. 3 cass. (Running Time: 3 hrs. 30 min.). 1993. 29.95 set. (Passport Bks) McGraw-Hill Trade.

Business Goals. Gareth Knight et al. 1 cass. (Running Time: 1 hr.). (ENG.). 2004. stu. ed. 19.95 (978-0-521-75539-9(5)) Cambridge U Pr.

Business Goals. 2nd ed. Gareth Knight et al. 2 cass. (Running Time: 1 hr.). (ENG.). 2004. stu. ed. 18.90 (978-0-521-75543-6(3)); stu. ed. 18.00 (978-0-521-75544-3(1)) Cambridge U Pr.

Business Goals 1: Professional English. Gareth Knight et al. 1 CD. (Running Time: 1 hr.). (ENG.). 2004. stu. ed. 18.90 (978-0-521-75540-5(9)) Cambridge U Pr.

Business Goals 3. Gareth Knight et al. (Running Time: 1 hr.). (ENG.). 2005. 19.00 (978-0-521-61318-7(3)) Cambridge U Pr.

Business Goals 3. Gareth Knight et al. (Running Time: 1 hr.). (ENG.). 2005. audio compact disk 19.00 (978-0-521-61319-4(1)) Cambridge U Pr.

Business Grammar & Usage for Professionals. Kathy Bote. 6 cass. wbk. ed. 69.95 Set, incl. 90p. wkbk. (129-C47) Natl Seminars.
Do you wish your spelling ability was on par with your selling ability? Do grammatical errors interfere with an otherwise solid presentation? No more faking it! This program is a must for anyone in a "people" position!.

Business Intelligence Software Leadership Seminar: The World's Top CEOs on Best Practices & Strategies for Client Success. Ed. by ReedLogic Staff. 2006. pap. bk. 499.95 (978-1-59701-083-2(9)) Aspatore Bks.

Business Is Combat: A Fighter Pilot's Guide to Winning in Modern Business Warfare. unabr. ed. James D. Murphy. Read by Patrick Cullen. 5 cass. (Running Time: 7 hrs.). 2001. 39.95 (978-0-7861-1985-1(3), 2755); audio compact disk 56.00 (978-0-7861-9739-2(0), 2755) Blckstn Audio.
Combines the cool calculation of a four-star general & the hot-blooded nerve of a combat pilot. Provides a blueprint for the kind of success every warrior seeks, absolute victory.

Business Law: Contracts. Instructed by Frank Cross. 4 cass. (Running Time: 6 hrs.). 1994. 39.95 (978-1-56585-154-2(4)) Teaching Co.

Business Law: Contracts. Instructed by Frank B. Cross. 8 CDs. (Running Time: 6 hrs.). 2006. 54.95 (978-1-59803-246-8(1)) Teaching Co.

Business Law: Negligence & Torts. Instructed by Frank Cross. 4 cass. (Running Time: 6 hrs.). 1994. 39.95 (978-1-56585-155-9(2)) Teaching Co.

Business Law: Negligence & Torts. Instructed by Frank B. Cross. 8 CDs. (Running Time: 6 hrs.). 2006. 54.95 (978-1-59803-247-5(X)) Teaching Co.

Business Law Pt. 2: Syllabus. Ronald W. Singleton et al. (J). 1973. bk. 471.20 (978-0-89420-128-8(X), 146700) Natl Book.

Business Law for Accountants. Richard M. Feldheim & Ivan Fox. 12 cass. (Running Time: 12 hrs.). 199.00 set, incl. textbk. & quizzer. (CPE1040) Bisk Educ.
Explains fundamental aspects of business law that pervade everyday business transactions.

Business Law Library. Ed. by Socrates Media Editors. 2005. audio compact disk 49.95 (978-1-59546-111-7(6)) Pub: Socrates Med LLC. Dist(s): Midpt Trade

Business Law Practice: Recent Developments (1992) Read by Robert Sullivan et al. (Running Time: 2 hrs. 45 min.). 1992. 89.00 Incl. 245p. tape materials. (BU-55247) Cont Ed Bar-CA.
Discusses & analyzes the most pressing issues facing business practice today, including bankruptcy; commercial law; competitive business practices; consumer protection; contracts; corporations; wrongful termination; sexual harassment; environmental law; franchises; partnerships; securities; taxation; & general business.

Business Lawyers under Fire: Liability & Ethical Risks Facing In-House & Outside Counsel. 3 cass. (Running Time: 3 hrs. 30 min.). 1996. 160.00 Set, incl. study materials. (D246) Am Law Inst.
This program emphasizes practical strategies & preventive measures for dealing with potential liability & ethical issues as either in-house or outside counsel to business entities. The discussions center on a series of real-life hypotheticals involving large & small businesses of all types.

Business Legal Forms & Agreements. Ed. by Socrates Media Editors. 2005. audio compact disk 29.95 (978-1-59546-094-3(2)) Pub: Socrates Med LLC. Dist(s): Midpt Trade

Business Map of Nigeria. Oxford University Press Staff & Graham and Trotman Conference Staff. 1980. 20.50 (978-0-86010-194-9(0)) Graham & Trotman GBR.

Business Map of the Arab World. Oxford University Press Staff. 1980. 20.50 (978-0-86010-211-3(4)) Graham & Trotman GBR.

Business Mystic: A Practical Guide to Being in Business & Having a Life. Lisa Gollan & Mardi Palmer. Prod. by Shaun O'Callaghan. (ENG.). 2009. 35.00 (978-0-9805983-1-5(1)) BusBal AUS.

Business Objectives. Ed. by Oxford Staff. (Business Objectives International Edition Ser.). 2006. audio compact disk 24.50 (978-0-19-457829-5(1)) OUP.

Business Objectives. ed. Vicki Hollett. 2004. audio compact disk 35.95 (978-0-19-451372-2(6)) OUP.

Business Objectives. 2nd rev. ed. Vicki Hollett. 1996. 17.95 (978-0-19-451394-4(7)) OUP.

Business of Forecasting. Lloyd Cope. 1 cass. (Running Time: 90 min.). 1990. 8.95 (815) Am Fed Astrologers.

Business of Practicing Law. Contrib. by Lawrence R. Bright et al. Moderated by Albert L. Cohn. (Running Time: 2 hrs. 30 min.). 1985. 30.00 incl. program handbook. NJ Inst CLE.
Focuses on how to start & build a practice, advertising, a solo practitioner's perspective, protecting fees, fee arbitration, judicial perspective, enforcement of liens, & when an attorney can withdraw from a case.

Business of Sewing, Vol. 1. Barbara Wright Sykes. 1 cass. (Running Time: 1 hr.). 16.95 Collins Pubns.

Business of Sewing Audio. Barbara Wright Sykes. 1 CD. 2004. audio compact disk 16.95 (978-0-9632857-0-6(X)) Pub: Collins Pubns. Dist(s): Baker Taylor

Business of Sewing Audio Album: How to Start, Maintain & Achieve Success, Barbara Wright Sykes. 3 CDs. (Running Time: 4 hrs.). 2004. audio compact disk 45.00 (978-0-9632857-1-3(8)) Pub: Collins Pubns. Dist(s): Baker Taylor
A complete step-by-step guide that will show you how to start, maintain & achieve success in your own sewing business.

Business One. Jane Hudson et al. 2009. audio compact disk 39.95 (978-0-19-457646-8(9)) OUP.

Business One: One Pre-Intermediate. Rachel Appleby et al. Ed. by Oxford Staff. 2009. audio compact disk 39.95 (978-0-19-457645-1(0)) OUP.

Business Opinions. unabr. ed. Contrib. by Donald W. Glazer & Arthur Norman Field. 4 cass. (Running Time: 5 hrs. 30 min.). 1989. pap. bk. 95.00 (T6-9105) PLI.

Business Opinions 1991: Recent Developments in Opinion Practice. 4 cass. (Running Time: 5 hrs. 30 min.). 1991. 125.00 Set. (T7-9326) PLI.

Business Opportunities. Vicki Hollett. 1995. 24.50 (978-0-19-452030-0(7)) OUP.

Business Options. Adrian Wallwork. 2007. audio compact disk 37.50 (978-0-19-457218-7(6)) OUP.

Business Partners in Russia. 6th rev. ed. BIA. (J). 2006. audio compact disk 289.00 (978-1-4187-5224-8(X)) Bus Info Agency.

Business Partners in Russia. 6th rev. ed. BIA. (J). 2006. audio compact disk 249.00 (978-1-4187-5223-1(1)) Bus Info Agency.

Business Planning. unabr. ed. Edward Williams. Narrated by Eric Conger. 2 CDs. (Running Time: 2 hrs. 30 mins.). (New York Times Pocket MBA Ser.). 2003. audio compact disk 19.95 (978-1-885408-98-3(6)) Listen & Live.

Business Planning: 25 Keys to a Sound Business Plan. unabr. ed. Edward Williams et al. Read by Eric Conger. 2 cass. (Running Time: 2 hrs. 30 mins.). (New York Times Pocket MBA Ser.). 2000. 16.95 (978-1-885408-39-6(0), LL032) Listen & Live.
Understanding the vital points that can make or break a great business plan, that will guide your business growth and attract necessary financing.

Business Plans. 2nd abr. ed. Paul Tiffany & Steven D. Peterson. Read by Brett Barry. (Running Time: 12600 sec.). 2007. audio compact disk 14.95 (978-0-06-137439-5(3), Harper Audio) HarperCollins Pubs.

***Business Plans for Dummies 2nd Ed.** 2nd abr. ed. Paul Tiffany & Steven Peterson. Read by Brett Barry. (ENG.). 2007. (978-0-06-155599-2(1)); (978-0-06-155600-5(9)) HarperCollins Pubs.

Business Principles: Syllabus. Ronald W. Singleton. (J). 1976. bk. 240.40 (978-0-89420-129-5(8), 102000) Natl Book.

Business Profile of Former Soviet Republics. 6th rev. ed. BIA. (J). 2006. audio compact disk 319.00 (978-1-4187-5398-6(X)) Bus Info Agency.

Business Profile of Russia. 6th rev. ed. BIA. (J). 2006. audio compact disk 319.00 (978-1-4187-5358-0(0)) Bus Info Agency.

Business Profile of the Bashkortostan Republic of Russia. 6th rev. ed. BIA. (J). 2006. audio compact disk 319.00 (978-1-4187-5391-7(2)) Bus Info Agency.

Business Profile of the Central Federal District of Russia. 6th rev. ed. BIA. (J). 2006. audio compact disk 319.00 (978-1-4187-5364-1(5)) Bus Info Agency.

Business Profile of the Chelyabinsk Region of Russia. 6th rev. ed. BIA. (J). 2006. audio compact disk 319.00 (978-1-4187-5383-2(1)) Bus Info Agency.

Business Profile of the Far Eastern Federal District of Russia. 6th rev. ed. BIA. (J). 2006. audio compact disk 319.00 (978-1-4187-5359-7(9)) Bus Info Agency.

Business Profile of the Irkutsk Region of Russia. 6th rev. ed. BIA. (J). 2006. audio compact disk 319.00 (978-1-4187-5395-5(5)) Bus Info Agency.

Business Profile of the Kemerovo Region of Russia. 6th rev. ed. BIA. (J). 2006. audio compact disk 319.00 (978-1-4187-5396-2(3)) Bus Info Agency.

Business Profile of the Krasnodar Region of Russia. 6th rev. ed. BIA. (J). 2006. audio compact disk 319.00 (978-1-4187-5385-6(8)) Bus Info Agency.

Business Profile of the Krasnoyarsk Region of Russia. 6th rev. ed. BIA. (J). 2006. audio compact disk 319.00 (978-1-4187-5384-9(X)) Bus Info Agency.

Business Profile of the Moscow Region of Russia. 6th rev. ed. BIA. (J). 2006. audio compact disk 319.00 (978-1-4187-5382-5(3)) Bus Info Agency.

Business Profile of the Nizhny Novgorod Region of Russia. 6th rev. ed. BIA. (J). 2006. audio compact disk 319.00 (978-1-4187-5393-1(9)) Bus Info Agency.

Business Profile of the Northwestern Federal District of Russia. 6th rev. ed. BIA. (J). 2006. audio compact disk 319.00 (978-1-4187-5365-8(3)) Bus Info Agency.

Business Profile of the Novosibirsk Region of Russia. 6th rev. ed. BIA. (J). 2006. audio compact disk 319.00 (978-1-4187-5386-3(6)) Bus Info Agency.

Business Profile of the Sakha (Yakut) Republic of Russia. 6th rev. ed. BIA. (J). 2006. audio compact disk 319.00 (978-1-4187-5392-4(0)) Bus Info Agency.

Business Profile of the Samara Region of Russia. 6th rev. ed. BIA. (J). 2006. audio compact disk 319.00 (978-1-4187-5394-8(7)) Bus Info Agency.

Business Profile of the Siberian Federal District of Russia. 6th rev. ed. BIA. (J). 2006. audio compact disk 319.00 (978-1-4187-5360-3(2)) Bus Info Agency.

Business Profile of the Southern Federal District of Russia. 6th rev. ed. BIA. (J). 2006. audio compact disk 319.00 (978-1-4187-5363-4(7)) Bus Info Agency.

Business Profile of the St. Petersburg Region of Russia. 6th rev. ed. BIA. (J). 2006. audio compact disk 319.00 (978-1-4187-5397-9(1)) Bus Info Agency.

Business Profile of the Sverdlovsk Region of Russia. 6th rev. ed. BIA. (J). 2006. audio compact disk 319.00 (978-1-4187-5387-0(4)) Bus Info Agency.

Business Profile of the Tatarstan Republic of Russia. 6th rev. ed. BIA. (J). 2006. audio compact disk 319.00 (978-1-4187-5388-7(2)) Bus Info Agency.

Business Profile of the Tyumen Region of Russia. 6th rev. ed. BIA. (J). 2006. audio compact disk 319.00 (978-1-4187-5389-4(0)) Bus Info Agency.

Business Profile of the Urals Federal District of Russia. 6th rev. ed. BIA. (J). 2006. audio compact disk 319.00 (978-1-4187-5361-0(0)) Bus Info Agency.

Business Profile of the Volga Federal District of Russia. 6th rev. ed. BIA. (J). 2006. audio compact disk 319.00 (978-1-4187-5362-7(9)) Bus Info Agency.

Business Profile of the Voronezh Region of Russia. 6th rev. ed. BIA. (J). 2006. audio compact disk 319.00 (978-1-4187-5390-0(4)) Bus Info Agency.

Business Sense. Jack Pachuta et al. 3 cass. (Running Time: 2 hrs. 15 min.). 1995. 29.95 set. (978-1-888475-04-3(8)) Mangmt Stratgies.
Topics include: Selling your ideas & yourself; Combating professional stupidity; Exploding the American workplace myth.

Business Spanish. 125.00 (1813, Lrn Inc) Oasis Audio.
Presents methods to learn a second language.

Business Spanish. Pili B. Matias & Brian Hill. 3 cass. (Running Time: 3 hrs. 30 min.). (Just Listen N' Learn Ser.). 1993. 29.95 set. (Passport Bks) McGraw-Hill Trade.

Business Spanish Speed. Mark Frobose. 3 cass. (Running Time: 3 hrs.). (SPA.). 2000. 19.99 (978-1-893564-79-4(7)) Macmill Audio.

Business Start-up. Mark Ibbotson & Bryan Stephens. 1 cass. (Running Time: 1 hr. 16 mins.). (ENG.). 2006. 45.15 (978-0-521-53467-3(4)) Cambridge U Pr.

Business Start-up. Mark Ibbotson & Bryan Stephens. 2 cass. (Running Time: 1 hr. 38 mins.). (ENG.). 2006. 45.15 (978-0-521-53471-0(2)) Cambridge U Pr.

Business Start-up 1: Student's Book. Mark Ibbotson & Bryan Stephens. (Running Time: 1 hr. 16 mins.). (ENG.). 2005. audio compact disk 45.15 (978-0-521-53468-0(2)) Cambridge U Pr.

Business Start-up 2: Student's Book. Mark Ibbotson & Bryan Stephens. (Running Time: 1 hr. 37 mins.). (ENG.). 2006. audio compact disk 45.15 (978-0-521-53472-7(0)) Cambridge U Pr.

Business Statistics in Practice. 4th ed. Bruce L. Bowerman & Richard T. O'Connell. Contrib. by J. B. Orris. (McGraw-Hill/Irwin Series in Operations & Decision Sciences). 2007. audio compact disk (978-0-07-319186-7(8)) McGraw.

***Business Stripped Bare.** Richard Branson. Read by Adrian Mulraney. (Running Time: 11 hrs. 45 mins.). 2010. 94.99 (978-1-74214-626-3(0), 9781742146263) Pub: Bolinda Pubng AUS. Dist(s): Bolinda Pub Inc

Business Stripped Bare: Adventures of a Global Entrepreneur. unabr. ed. Richard Branson. Read by Adrian Mulraney. 10 CDs. (Running Time: 11 hrs. 45 mins.). 2009. audio compact disk 98.95 (978-1-74214-463-4(2), 9781742144634) Pub: Bolinda Pubng AUS. Dist(s): Bolinda Pub Inc

***Business Stripped Bare: Adventures of a Global Entrepreneur.** unabr. ed. Richard Branson. Read by Adrian Mulraney. 1 MP3-CD. (Running Time: 11 hrs. 45 mins.). 2009. 43.95 (978-1-74214-489-4(6), 9781742144894) Pub: Bolinda Pubng AUS. Dist(s): Bolinda Pub Inc

Business Success. unabr. ed. Judith L. Powell. Read by Judith L. Powell. 1 cass. (Running Time: 40 min.). (Successfull Living Ser.). 1987. pap. bk. 12.95 (978-0-914295-32-7(2)) Top Mtn Pub.
Side A presents exercises designed to achieve business success by increasing efficiency, using intuition to solve problems & make decisions, creating ideas, communicating & enjoying work. Side B presents subliminal business suggestions hidden in New Thought Music.

Business Think. abr. ed. David Marcum. 2006. 15.95 (978-1-933976-12-9(8)) Pub: Franklin Covey. Dist(s): S and S Inc

Business Think: Rules for Getting It Right - Now & No Matter What! abr. unabr. ed. David Marcum & Mahan K. Khalsa. Read by David Marcum & Steve Smith. 4 CDs. (Running Time: 40 hrs. 0 mins. 0 sec.). (ENG.). 2002. audio compact disk 24.95 (978-1-929494-65-1(3)) Pub: Franklin Covey. Dist(s): S and S Inc

Business Trip to China 1: Conversation & Application. Zhang Wangxi & Sun Zude. (CHI & ENG.). 2005. bk. & wbk. ed. 25.95 (978-7-5619-1454-0(7), BUTRCH1) Pub: Beijing Lang CHN. Dist(s): China Bks

Business Trip to China 2: Conversation & Application. Zhang Wangxi & Sun Zude. (CHI & ENG.). 2005. bk. & wbk. ed. 25.95 (978-7-5619-1524-0(1), BUTRCH2) Pub: Beijing Lang CHN. Dist(s): China Bks

Business Use of Astrology. Weiss Kelly. Read by Weiss Kelly. 1 cass. (Running Time: 90 min.). 1994. 8.95 (1161) Am Fed Astrologers.

Business Valuation Discount Planning & Tax Dispute Techniques. 4 cass. (Running Time: 3 hrs. 47 min.). 225.00 Set, incl. study guides. (M240) Am Law Inst.
This three-program series is a fundamental resource for all lawyers & tax professionals interested in business valuation discount planning & tax dispute techniques. It provides clear explanations, useful tips, & cautionary notes on problem areas & eas & traps. The titles are: "Effective Transfer Tax Valuation Discount Planning," "How to Work with a Business Appraiser," & "Handling Business Valuations for Audits & Tax Disputes".

Business Valuation Methods. Alan Zipp. 1 cass. 155.00 incl. wkbk. (752344KQ) Am Inst CPA.
This thorough course presents the latest information on methods & techniques for performing competent, efficient appraisals. You will find out how to perform a business valuation, how to select from different methods & how to validate your results.

Business Venture. 2nd rev. ed. Roger Barnard & Jeff Cady. 2000. 39.95 (978-0-19-457246-0(3)); 24.50 (978-0-19-457328-3(1)) OUP.

Business Venture. 2nd rev. ed. Roger Barnard & Jeff Cady. 2004. audio compact disk 39.95 (978-0-19-457445-7(8)) OUP.

Business Venture, No. 2. 2nd rev. ed. Roger Barnard & Jeff Cady. 2004. audio compact disk 24.50 (978-0-19-457446-4(6)) OUP.

Business Vision. Adrian Wallwork. 2003. audio compact disk 35.95 (978-0-19-437984-7(1)) OUP.

Business Vision. Adrian Wallwork. 2003. 31.95 (978-0-19-437983-0(3)) OUP.

Business without Biceps: The Untold Truths of Women in Business & How to Make Them Work for You. Natalie Brecher. 1 CD. (Running Time: 75 minutes). 2004. audio compact disk 18.95 (978-0-9744990-1-7(3), CheetahExpress) Brecher Assocs.
An educational and humorous look at men and women in business, providing insight into gender work differences and specific techniques to improve professional success.

Business Writing. Fred Pryor. 6 cass. (Running Time: 6 hrs.). 1995. 59.95 Set. (12120A) Nightingale-Conant.

Business Writing: The Power Training Method. Margaret M. Bynum & Nate Rosenblatt. 4 cass. 74.95 Set incl. 108p. wkbk. & 37p. grammar guide. (780PAB) Nightingale-Conant.
Good business writing is a specific skill that is quite unlike any other form of communication. With this success-oriented, practical program, you can learn how to produce powerful, fluent business letters, reports & presentations that will benefit your organization as well as your own career.

***Business Writing & Editing for Professionals.** PUEI. 2009. audio compact disk 199.00 (978-1-935041-64-1(9), CareerTrack) P Univ E Inc.

Business Writing for Results. PUEI. 2006. audio compact disk 89.95 (978-1-933328-65-2(7), Fred Pryor) P Univ E Inc.

Business Writing for Results: Make Your Words Sizzle with Clarity & Impact! 6 cass. 59.95 Set incl. wkbk. (12121AS) Pryor Resources.
Acquire the basics of organizing your thoughts on paper, overcome writer's block. Choose words that elicit a positive response, establish credibility & trust with your reader. Cut unnecessary words, & write to appeal to the styles & preferences of varying personality types.

Business Writing Skills. Debra Smith. 4 cass. 64.95 set. (V10006) CareerTrack Pubns.
You'll learn such important & helpful skills as: tips for transforming long, laborious writing into short, simple sentences, how to choose the perfect word, how to write with your "natural voice".

***Busman's Honeymoon.** Dorothy L. Sayers. Narrated by Ian Carmichael & Full Cast Production Staff. (Running Time: 2 hrs. 25 mins. 0 sec.). (ENG.). 2010. audio compact disk 24.95 (978-0-563-52547-9(9)) Pub: AudioGO. Dist(s): Perseus Dist

Busman's Honeymoon. unabr. ed. Dorothy L. Sayers. Read by Ian Carmichael. 8 cass. (Running Time: 12 hrs. 44 mins.). (Lord Peter Wimsey Mystery Ser.). 2003. 34.95 (978-1-57270-317-9(2)) Pub: Audio Partners. Dist(s): PerseuPGW
Newlyweds Lord Peter Wimsey and harriet Vane are looking forward to a quiet, romantic honeymoon. Instead, after their first night in their new home, they discover its previous owner dead in the cellar, and with a pocketful of cash. Sayers's ingenious plotting and literate style make this mystery one of her best.

Busman's Honeymoon. unabr. ed. Dorothy L. Sayers. Read by Ian Carmichael. 10 cass. (Running Time: 15 hrs.). (Lord Peter Wimsey Mystery Ser.). 2000. 69.95 (978-0-7451-4313-2(X), CAB 996) Pub: Chivers Audio Bks GBR. Dist(s): AudioGO

Busted: Avoiding Scams & Fraud in Adoption. Hosted by Mardie Caldwell. (ENG.). 2008. audio compact disk 12.95 (978-1-935176-01-5(3)) Pub: Am Carrage Hse Pubng. Dist(s): STL Dist NA

Busted: Life Inside the Great Mortgage Meltdown. unabr. ed. Edmund L. Andrews. Narrated by Dick Hill. (Running Time: 8 hrs. 0 mins. 0 sec.). (ENG.). 2009. 19.99 (978-1-4001-6332-8(3)); audio compact disk 29.99 (978-1-4001-1332-3(6)); audio compact disk 59.99 (978-1-4001-4332-0(2)) Pub: Tantor Media. Dist(s): IngramPubServ

Buster. Denise Flemming. 1 CD. (Running Time: 10 mins.). (J). (gr. k-3). 2007. bk. 29.95 (978-0-8045-4182-4(5)); bk. 27.95 (978-0-8045-6959-0(2)) Spoken Arts.

Buster, Where Are You? Judith Lane. Read by Tom Chapin. Illus. by Nancy Lane. Narrated by Tom Chapin. 1 cass. (Running Time: 11 min.). (Humane Society of the United States Animal Tales Ser.). (J). (gr. 1-5). 1998. pap. bk. 9.95 (978-1-58021-023-2(6)); pap. bk. 19.95 (978-1-58021-021-8(X)) Benefactory.
Buster & his owner move in next door to Emma. Buster helps Emma overcome her fear of dogs & becomes a good friend. When he gets lost in the park, Emma is determined to find him.

Buster's Diaries. unabr. ed. Roy Hattersley. (ENG.). 2005. 14.98 (978-1-59483-453-0(9)) Pub: Hachet Audio. Dist(s): HachBkGrp

Buster's Dino Dilemma. unabr. ed. Marc Brown. Read by Mark Linn-Baker. Text by Stephen Krensky. 1 cass. (Running Time: 40 mins.). (Arthur Chapter Bks.: Bk. 7). (J). (gr. 2-4). 1999. pap. bk. 17.00 (978-0-8072-0397-2(1), EFTR198SP, Listening Lib) Random Audio Pubg.

***Busting Vegas: A True Story of Monumental Excess, Sex, Love, Violence, & Beating the Odds.** abr. ed. Ben Mezrich. Read by Ben Mezrich. (ENG.). 2005. (978-0-06-112109-8(6), Harper Audio); (978-0-06-112110-4(X), Harper Audio) HarperCollins Pubs.

Busting Vegas: The MIT Whiz Kid Who Brought the Casinos to Their Knees. Ben Mezrich. 2005. 34.99 (978-1-59895-011-3(8)) Find a World.

Busting Vegas: The MIT Whiz Kid Who Brought the Casinos to Their Knees. abr. ed. Ben Mezrich. Read by Ben Mezrich. (YA). 2005. 44.99 (978-1-59895-135-6(1)) Find a World.

Busting Vegas: The MIT Whiz Kid Who Brought the Casinos to Their Knees. abr. ed. Ben Mezrich. Read by Ben Mezrich. 2008. audio compact disk 14.95 (978-0-06-167352-8(8), Harper Audio) HarperCollins Pubs.

Busy As a Bee. Sundance/Newbridge, LLC Staff. (Early Science Ser.). (gr. k-3). 2007. audio compact disk 12.00 (978-1-4007-6596-6(X)); audio compact disk 12.00 (978-1-4007-6597-3(8)); audio compact disk 12.00 (978-1-4007-6598-0(6)) Sund Newbrdge.

Busy Bees: Cassette. (Song Box Ser.). (gr. 1-2). bk. 8.50 (978-0-7802-2269-4(5)) Wright Group.

Busy Bees: 1 Big Book, 6 Each of 1 Student Book, & 1 Cassette. (Song Box Ser.). (gr. 1-2). 68.95 (978-0-7802-3203-7(8)) Wright Group.

Busy Bodies. unabr. ed. Lee Burns. Read by Robert Morris. 10 cass. (Running Time: 14 hrs. 30 mins.). 1995. 69.95 (978-0-7861-0774-2(X), 1623) Blckstn Audio.
This book is a warning about the late twentieth-century American disease - the increasing time pressures that are eroding our quality of life. In our affluent society, technology was supposed to free us for greater leisure time & creativity. Instead, the demands of our increasingly complex lives have come up against the unyielding 24-hour day. As a result we have become "Busy Bodies", working frantically to maintain our standard of living, but not seeming to get much satisfaction. With humor & wit the author shows how this obsession with time has crept into every aspect of our lives, from our changing romantic & eating habits to the way we run our economy & politics.

***Busy Body.** M. C. Beaton, pseud. Narrated by Penelope Keith. (Running Time: 5 hrs. 30 mins. 0 sec.). (ENG.). 2010. audio compact disk 29.95 (978-1-60283-927-4(1)) Pub: AudioGO. Dist(s): Perseus Dist

Busy Executive Biblical Dad: Proverbs 4:3-4. Ed Young. 1987. 4.95 (978-0-7417-1611-8(9), 611) Win Walk.

Busy Toes, Audiocassette. C. W. Bowie. (Metro Reading Ser.). (J). (gr. k). 2000. 8.46 (978-1-58120-982-2(7)) Metro Teaching.

Busybodies & Overseers. Derek Prince. 1 cass. (Running Time: 60 min.). 5.95 (I-4030) Derek Prince.

Busybody Nora. unabr. ed. Johanna Hurwitz. Narrated by Barbara Caruso. 1 cass. (Running Time: 1 hr. 15 mins.). (gr. k up). 10.00 (978-0-7887-0330-0(7), 94522E7) Recorded Bks.
Introduces a spunky five-year-old who sets out to meet every person in her apartment building - all 200 of them! Available to libraries only.

Busyness Issues & Self-Esteem. Earnie Larsen. 1 cass. (Running Time: 1 hr.). 1993. 10.95 (978-1-56047-058-8(5), A124) E Larsen Enterprises.
How busyness issues affect self-esteem; what is at the core of busyness issues; your right to choose your identity; concrete steps for healing.

But, God... ! Kohake. (J). 2007. audio compact disk 14.99 (978-1-60247-207-5(6)) Tate Pubng.

But Have Not Love! Read by Basilea Schlink. 1 cass. (Running Time: 30 min.). 1985. (0204) Evang Sisterhood Mary.
Discusses the solution to a daily problem & sacrifice - a blessing?.

But not for Love. unabr. ed. Edwin Shrake. Narrated by George Guidall. 10 cass. (Running Time: 14 hrs. 15 mins.). (Tcu Press Texas Tradition Ser.). 2000. 89.75 (978-1-4193-1221-2(9), S1073MC); audio compact disk 109.75 (978-1-4193-1223-6(5), CS023MC) Recorded Bks.

But Not in Shame: The Six Months after Pearl Harbor. unabr. collector's ed. John Toland. Read by John MacDonald. 12 cass. (Running Time: 18 hrs.). 1988. 96.00 (978-0-7366-1435-1(4), 2319) Books on Tape.
Discusses events which determined the Pearl Harbor catastrophe; What were the last few days on Wake Island like; What really happened on the infamous Bataan Death March & why did it happen; How did MacArthur escape from Corregidor; And what the story is behind Wainwright's forced surrender of the Phillippines.

***But Now I See.** Kristen Belcher. 2010. audio compact disk 14.99 (978-1-60641-775-1(4)) Deseret Bk.

But Seriously... The American Comedy (1915-1994) 4 CDs. (Running Time: 6 hrs.). 2001. bk. 49.98 (R2 71617) Rhino Enter.

But Still Desire & Will... see Twentieth-Century Poetry in English, No. 26, Recordings of Poets Reading Their Own Poetry

But the Water Is Bad/NSM. George Bloomer. 2004. audio compact disk 14.99 (978-0-88368-448-1(9)) Whitaker Hse.

But Then, November. unabr. ed. Rand D. Johnson. Read by David Sharp. 2 cass. (Running Time: 2 hrs.). 1992. 16.95 (978-1-55686-558-9(9)) Books in Motion.
Hunting season opens & a confrontation between hunters & a landowner turn ugly when the hunters decide to get even in a steadily escalating case that results in death.

But Was It Murder?, Set,Level. 4. Jania Barrell. Contrib. by Philip Prowse. (Running Time: 2 hrs. 15 mins.). (Cambridge English Readers Ser.). (ENG.). 2000. 15.75 (978-0-521-78360-6(7)) Cambridge U Pr.

But We Love Each Other: Sex & the Single Life: 1 Cor 6:15-20. Ed Young. 1995. 4.95 (978-0-7417-2048-1(5), 1048) Win Walk.

Butch Baldassari's Appalachian Mandolin. Butch Baldassari & David Schnaufer. 2008. pap. bk. 19.95 (978-1-59773-255-0(9), 1597732559) Pub: Homespun Video. Dist(s): H Leonard

Butch Thompson. Read by Butch Thompson. 1 cass. (Running Time: 60 min.). (Marian McPartland's Piano Jazz Ser.). 13.95 (MM-87-02-26, HarperThor) HarpC GBR.

Butcher. Campbell Armstrong. Read by James Bryce. 10 cass. 2007. 84.95 (978-1-84559-407-7(X)) Pub: ISIS Audio GBR. Dist(s): Ulverscroft US

Butcher. Campbell Armstrong. 2007. audio compact disk 99.95 (978-1-84559-592-0(0)) Pub: Soundings Ltd GBR. Dist(s): Ulverscroft US

Butcher. unabr. ed. Alina Reyes. Read by Ruby Featherstone. 1 cass. (Running Time: 1 hr. 30 min.). 1995. 12.00 (978-1-886238-06-0(5)) Passion Press.

Butcher: Anatomy of a Mafia Psychopath. unabr. ed. Philip Carlo. Narrated by Dick Hill. (Running Time: 10 hrs. 30 mins. 0 sec.). (ENG.). 2009. 24.99 (978-1-4001-6313-7(7)); audio compact disk 34.99 (978-1-4001-1313-2(X)); audio compact disk 69.99 (978-1-4001-4313-9(6)) Pub: Tantor Media. Dist(s): IngramPubServ

***Butcher: Anatomy of a Mafia Psychopath.** unabr. ed. Philip Carlo. Narrated by Dick Hill. (Running Time: 10 hrs. 30 mins.). 2009. 16.99 (978-1-4001-8313-5(8)) Tantor Media.

Butcher Boy. Patrick McCabe. 2004. 10.95 (978-0-7435-4221-0(5)) Pub: S&S Audio. Dist(s): S and S Inc

Butcher's Boy. unabr. ed. Thomas Perry. Narrated by Michael Kramer. (Running Time: 10 hrs. 30 mins. 0 sec.). (ENG.). 2008. audio compact disk 34.99 (978-1-4001-1019-3(X)); audio compact disk 24.99 (978-1-4001-6019-8(7)); audio compact disk 69.99 (978-1-4001-4019-0(6)) Pub: Tantor Media. Dist(s): IngramPubServ

***Butcher's Crossing.** unabr. ed. John Williams. (Running Time: 9 hrs. 30 mins.). 2010. audio compact disk 29.95 (978-1-4417-5346-5(X)) Blckstn Audio.

***Butcher's Crossing.** unabr. ed. John Williams. Read by Anthony Heald. (Running Time: 9 hrs. 30 mins.). 2010. 29.95 (978-1-4417-5347-2(8)); 59.95 (978-1-4417-5343-4(5)); audio compact disk 90.00 (978-1-4417-5344-1(3)) Blckstn Audio.

***Butchers Hill: A Tess Monaghan Novel.** Laura Lippman. Narrated by Deborah Hazlett. (Running Time: 8 hrs. 47 mins. 0 sec.). (ENG.). 2010. audio compact disk 29.95 (978-1-60283-275-6(7)) Pub: AudioGO. Dist(s): Perseus Dist

Butcher's Moon. unabr. ed. Richard Stark, pseud. Read by Michael Kramer. 7 cass. (Running Time: 10 hrs.). 2001. 56.00 (978-0-7366-8386-9(0)) Books on Tape.
John Rossendale's home is the sea; in his 38-foot cutter, he is far away from his disagreeable family and his role as black sheep and heir to an earldom. Still, mystery and danger have a way of finding him even when he is far from any coast. He is obliged to return home to England on account of a mysterious painting which disappeared from the family's house years ago and which everyone suspects him of possessing. Blackmail and violence follow, and in the end Rossendale must contend with a deadly enemy at sea in the Channel Islands - an enemy he may not be able to survive.

Butler Shaffer: The Institutional Causes of Conflict. (Running Time: 60 min.). (Long Beach City College). 1983. 9.00 (F151) Freeland Pr.
The author refutes the idea of accepting institutional solutions to our problems today.

Butlerian Jihad. Brian Herbert & Kevin J. Anderson. Read by Scott Brick. 2002. 144.00 (978-0-7366-8770-6(X)) Books on Tape.

Butlerian Jihad. unabr. ed. Brian Herbert & Kevin J. Anderson. Read by Scott Brick. 2002. audio compact disk 160.00 (978-0-7366-8938-0(9)) Books on Tape.
Centuries-long confrontation between thinking machines and human beings. Xavier Harkonnen, the resolute and courageous leader of the planet Salusa Secundus, has managed to lead the humans to fight the forces of artificial intelligence to a standstill. Serena Butler, Xavier's fiancee, will, in her passion and grief, ignite the final stage of the war. Against the brute strength and faultless efficiency of their adversaries, the humans have only luck, ingenuity, and courage. It will have to be enough.

Butlerian Jihad. unabr. rev. ed. Brian Herbert & Kevin J. Anderson. Read by Scott Brick & Scott Sowers. 20 CDs. (Running Time: 22 hrs. 0 mins. 0 sec.). (Dune Ser.). (ENG., 2002. audio compact disk 60.00 (978-1-55927-755-6(6)) Pub: Macmill Audio. Dist(s): Macmillan

Butter-Ball & Other Stories see Bola de Sebo y Otras Narraciones

Butter-Ball & Other Stories. Guy de Maupassant. Read by Laura Garcia. (Running Time: 3 hrs.). 2002. 16.95 (978-1-60083-243-7(1), Audiofy Corp) Iofy Corp.

Butter Did It. unabr. ed. Phyllis C. Richman. Read by Susan O'Malley. 7 cass. (Running Time: 10 hrs.). (Chas Wheatley Mystery Ser.). 1998. 49.95 (978-0-7861-1293-7(X), 2197) Blckstn Audio.
In her eagerly awaited fiction debut, the "Washington Post's" best-loved, award-winning food writer has cooked up a tempting tale of mousse, mayhem, & murder.

Buttercup Has My Smile - Coping with Serious Illness. Lynne Massie. 1 cass. 12.50 (978-0-9669075-2-0(3)) Cymitar Inc.

Buttered Side Down: A Slice of Country Life. unabr. ed. Faith Addis. Narrated by Briony Sykes. 5 cass. (Running Time: 6 hrs. 15 mins.). 2000. 47.50 (978-1-84197-104-9(9), H1106E7) Recorded Bks.
It seems the Addises have not moved out of their lovely Devon farmhouse at the best of times. Indeed icicles on the inside of their windows & snow on their bed are two very convincing reasons to try some home improvements.

Buttered Side Down Set: Stories. Edna Ferber. Read by Flo Gibson. 3 cass. (Running Time: 1 hr. 30 min. per cass.). 1995. 16.95 (978-1-55685-381-4(5)) Audio Bk Con.
There is invariably something to laugh or cry about & a lot to think about in these short stories, which include: "The Frog & the Puddle," "The Man Who Came Back," "What She Wore," "A Bush League Hero," "The Kitchen side of the Door," "One of the Old Girls," "Maymeys from Cuba," "The Leading Lady," "That Home Town Feeling," "The Homely Heroine," "Sun Dried," & "Where the Car Turns at 18th".

Butterfield Overland Stage. Kenneth Bruce. (Running Time: 1 hr.). Dramatization. (Excursions in History Ser.). 12.50 Alpha Tape.

Butterflies. Noel Carroll. 1 MP3. (Running Time: 37 min.). 2003. audio compact disk; audio compact disk (978-0-9731596-8-4(5)) AudioRealms CN CAN.
On the way home form a routine shuttle mission, two astronauts are ordered to investigate an unidentified floating object. The husband and wife team of Noel Carroll spin a tale that leave you wondering just who or what is out there, and more precisely, who is watching who.

Butterflies Always Come Back. Emmett Smith. 1 cass. 5.98 (978-1-55503-291-3(5), 06003222); 3.95 (978-1-57734-399-8(9), 34441409) Covenant Comms.

Butterflies, Bullies & Bad, Bad Habits. Karen McCombie. 3 CDs. 2005. audio compact disk 29.95 (978-0-7540-6712-2(2), Chivers Child Audio) AudioGO.

Butterflies Die. unabr. ed. C. S. Fuqua. Read by Ron Varela. 8 cass. (Running Time: 8 hrs. 6 min.). (Deadlines Ser.: Bk. 4). 2001. 49.95 (978-1-58116-140-3(9)) Books in Motion.
Suspicions point to a neighborhood ex-con, when the daughter of a local author is found murdered. Reporter Dean Moore learns that the girl visited the con the day the child was killed.

Butterfly. unabr. ed. V. C. Andrews. Read by Laurel Lefkow. 3 cass. (Running Time: 4 hrs. 30 min.). (Orphan Ser.: Vol. 1). 2001. 34.95 (978-0-7531-0633-4(7), 990801) Pub: ISIS Audio GBR. Dist(s): ISIS Pub

Butterfly. unabr. ed. V. C. Andrews. Read by Laurel Lefkow. 4 CDs. (Running Time: 3 hrs. 55 min.). (Orphans Ser.: No. 1). (J). 2001. audio compact disk 51.95 (978-0-7531-1319-6(8)) Pub: ISIS Lrg Prnt GBR. Dist(s): Ulverscroft US
For as long as she can remember, Janet's world has been the orphanage. She can hardly believe it when handsome Sanford and elegant Celine Deloric choose her to be their daughter. Celine, confined to a wheelchair, is convinced Janet will one day dazzle audiences as a ballerina, just as she herself did before her accident. Eager to please, Janet tries with all her might, but she is dancing on a fragile web of happiness.

***Butterfly.** unabr. ed. Sonya Hartnett. Read by Rebecca Macauley. (Running Time: 6 hrs. 40 mins.). 2010. audio compact disk 77.95 (978-1-74214-154-1(4), 9781742141541) Pub: Bolinda Pubng AUS. Dist(s): Bolinda Pub Inc

Butterfly. unabr. ed. Patricia Polacco. Narrated by Patricia Polacco. 1 cass. (Running Time: 12 min.). (J). (gr. 1-6). 2001. bk. 27.95 (978-0-8045-6875-3(8), 6875) Spoken Arts.
Since the Nazis, with their tall boots, have marched into Monique's small French village, terrorizing it, nothing surprises her. It is war! Then, one night, Monique encounters "the little ghost" sitting at the end of her bed. When she turns out to be - not a ghost at all - but a young Jewish girl named Sevrine, who has been hiding from the Nazis in Monique's own basement, how could Monique not be surprised! Playing secretly after dark in Monique's room, the two become friends, until, in a terrifying moment, they are discovered, sending their families into a nighttime flight.

Butterfly Box. unabr. ed. Santa Montefiore. Narrated by Juanita McMahon. 15 cass. (Running Time: 21 hrs. 30 min.). 2003. 62.95 (978-1-4025-5913-6(5)) Recorded Bks.
In Chile, six-year-old Frederica eagerly awaits the return of her adventurous father Ramon, who is travelling abroad again. But Frederica's mother Helena has grown tired of Ramon's long absences and returns to Cornwall with the children. Frederica's only connection with her father is a crystalline butterfly in a box that he had given her as a gift.

Butterfly Effect see #1571;#1579;#1585; #1575;#1604;#1601;#1585;#1575;#1588;#1577;

***Butterfly in Flame: A Fred Taylor Art Mystery.** unabr. ed. Nicholas Kilmer. (Running Time: 8 hrs. 30 mins.). (Fred Taylor Art Mysteries Ser.). 2010. 29.95 (978-1-4417-6670-0(7)); 54.95 (978-1-4417-6667-0(7)); audio compact disk 76.00 (978-1-4417-6668-7(5)) Blckstn Audio.

Butterfly Is Born. Sundance/Newbridge, LLC Staff. (Early Science Ser.). (gr. k-3). 2007. audio compact disk 12.00 (978-1-4007-6227-9(8)); audio compact disk 12.00 (978-1-4007-6226-2(X)); audio compact disk 12.00 (978-1-4007-6228-6(6)) Sund Newbrdge.

Butterfly Kisses & Bedtime Prayers. 1 cass. 1999. 10.98 (978-0-7601-2090-3(0)); audio compact disk 16.98 (978-0-7601-2091-0(9)) Provident Music.

Butterfly Kisses & Bedtime Prayers, Vol. 2. Prod. by Bob Carlisle. 1 CD. (J). 1998. 10.98 Incl. calendar. (978-0-7601-2578-6(3), 84418-2383-484418-2383-2) Pub: Brentwood Music. Dist(s): Provident Mus Dist
Timeless lullabies, featuring a medley of "Father's Love-Butterfly Kisses," Vol. 2 again highlights beautiful original photographs of babies along with prayers designed to teach children how to pray.

Butterfly Kisses & Bedtime Prayers, Vol. 2. Prod. by Bob Carlisle. 1 CD. (J). 1998. audio compact disk 16.98 (978-0-7601-2579-3(1), 84418-2383-2) Provident Music.

Butterfly Kisses & Other Stories. Perf. by Bob Carlisle. 2002. audio compact disk 17.98 Provident Mus Dist.

butterfly Man. Heather Rose. Read by Humphrey Bower. (Running Time: 9 hrs. 25 mins.). 2009. 79.99 (978-1-74214-446-7(2), 9781742144467) Pub: Bolinda Pubng AUS. Dist(s): Bolinda Pub Inc

butterfly Man. unabr. ed. Heather Rose. Read by Humphrey Bower. (Running Time: 9 hrs. 25 mins.). 2006. audio compact disk 87.95 (978-1-74093-813-6(5)) Pub: Bolinda Pubng AUS. Dist(s): Bolinda Pub Inc

Butterfly Summers. Elizabeth Lord. 6 cass. (Running Time: 8 hrs.). (Story Sound Ser.). (J). 2005. 54.95 (978-1-85903-673-0(2)); audio compact disk 71.95 (978-1-85903-820-8(4)) Pub: Mgna Lrg Print GBR. Dist(s): Ulverscroft US

Buttermilk Hill. Ruth White. Narrated by Nancy Wu. 4 cass. (Running Time: 5 hrs. 15 mins.). (YA). 2004. 39.75 (978-1-4193-0833-8(5)) Recorded Bks.

Button Box: Stories about Mama. Barbara McBride-Smith. 1 CD. (Running Time: 48 mins.). 2005. audio compact disk 14.95 (978-0-87483-762-9(6)) Pub: August Hse. Dist(s): Natl Bk Netwk

Mama believed the woman who dies with the most fabric scraps wins. She saved scraps from odd sewing jobs for neighbors. She saved buttons from old winter coats and birthday dresses. Mama had a button from Daddy's first uniform and another from Grandma's cloth coat - and every button in the box came with a story. In her trademark Texas twang, award-winning storyteller Barbara McBride-Smith recounts stories from her family that speak to all of us.

Buttons. Brock Cole. Narrated by David Hyde Pierce. 1 cass. (Running Time: 14 min.). (J). (ps-3). 2001. bk. 26.90 (978-0-8045-6881-4(2), 6881) Spoken Arts.

Once there was an old man who ate so much his britches burst and his buttons popped one, two, three, into the fire. The man's three daughters are enlisted to try to replace his buttons. The eldest promises to find a rich man who will give her buttons in exchange for her hand in marriage. The second daughter decides to join the army for the buttons on the uniform. And the youngest will run through the meadows with her apron outstretched in hopes of catching any buttons that fall from the sky. It's the third who succeeds in getting them, of course, but all three daughters find themselves richer as a result of their adventures and the airy, comical watercolors bring all the characters vividly to life.

Buttons. Brock Cole. Read by David Hyde Pierce. 1 cass. (Running Time: 30 mins.). (J). (gr. k-4). 2001. bk. 26.90 (SAC6881) Spoken Word.

When Father busts the buttons from his pants, there is mayhem in the house. How will they ever solve this button problem? Each of his three daughters hatch a plan, but will any of these plans work?.

Buttons. unabr. ed. Brock Cole. Narrated by Jenny Sterlin. 1 cass. (Running Time: 20 mins.). (J). 2001. pap. bk. & stu. ed. 33.00 Recorded Bks.

One terrible day a man eats so much that his britches burst & the buttons pop off into the fire.

Buttons. unabr. ed. Brock Cole. Narrated by Jenny Sterlin. 1 cass. (Running Time: 15 mins.). (gr. k up). 2001. 10.00 (978-0-7887-4718-2(5), 96392E7) Recorded Bks.

Buttons for General Washington. Peter Roop & Connie Roop. Illus. by Peter E. Hanson. Narrated by Jason Harris. (J). (gr. k-3). 2007. 9.95 (978-1-59519-928-7(4)) Live Oak Media.

Buttons for General Washington. Peter Roop & Connie Roop. Read by Jason Harris. (J). (gr. k-3). 2007. audio compact disk 12.95 (978-1-59519-932-4(2)) Live Oak Media.

Buttons for General Washington. unabr. ed. Peter Roop & Connie Roop. Illus. by Peter E. Hanson. 1 cass. (Running Time: 15 mins.). (Readalongs for Beginning Readers Ser.). (J). (gr. 2-3). 2007. pap. bk. 16.95 (978-1-59519-929-4(2)) Live Oak Media.

Buttons for General Washington, Set. unabr. ed. Peter Roop & Connie Roop. Illus. by Peter E. Hanson. 1 CD. (Running Time: 15 mins.). (Readalongs for Beginning Readers Ser.). (J). (gr. 2-3). 2007. pap. bk. 39.95 (978-1-59519-935-5(7)) Live Oak Media.

Buttons for General Washington, Set. unabr. ed. Peter Roop & Connie Roop. Read by Peter E. Hanson. 1 cass. (Running Time: 15 mins.). (Readalongs for Beginning Readers Ser.). (J). (gr. 2-3). 2007. pap. bk. 37.95 (978-1-59519-931-7(4)) Live Oak Media.

Buy American Is Un-American. Harry Binswanger. 2 cass. (Running Time: 2 hrs. 30 min.). 1992. 24.95 Set. (978-1-56114-134-0(8), HB04D) Second Renaissance.

Buy & Hold 7 Steps to a Real Estate Fortune. abr. ed. Schumacher David. 2007. audio compact disk 0.00 (978-0-9701162-4-6(1)) Schumacher Enter.

***Buy-in: Saving Your Good Idea from Getting Shot Down.** unabr. ed. John P. Kotter. (Running Time: 4 hrs.). 2010. 39.97 (978-1-4418-7235-7(3), 9781441872357, BADLE); 24.99 (978-1-4418-7234-0(5), 9781441872340, BAD); 24.99 (978-1-4418-7232-6(9), 9781441872326, Brilliance MP3) Brilliance Audio.

***Buy-in: Saving Your Good Idea from Getting Shot Down.** unabr. ed. John P. Kotter. Read by Tim Wheeler. (Running Time: 4 hrs.). 2010. 39.97 (978-1-4418-7233-3(7), 9781441872333, Brinc Audio MP3 Lib); audio compact disk 69.97 (978-1-4418-7231-9(0), 9781441872319, BriAudCD Unabrid) Brilliance Audio.

***Buy-in: Saving Your Good Idea from Getting Shot Down.** unabr. ed. John P. Kotter & Lorne A. Whitehead. Read by Tim Wheeler. (Running Time: 4 hrs.). 2010. audio compact disk 24.99 (978-1-4418-7230-2(2), 9781441872302, Bril Audio CD Unabri) Brilliance Audio.

Buy the Numbers. abr. ed. Robert A. Monroe. Read by Robert A. Monroe. (Running Time: 30 min.). (Human Plus Ser.). 1989. 14.95 (978-1-56102-007-7(8)) Inter Indus.

Enhancer of Human Performance.

Buyers, Renters & Freeloaders: Turning Revolving-Door Romance into Lasting Love. Willard F. Harley, Jr.. Read by Willard F. Harley, Jr. 4 cass. (Running Time: 6 hrs.). 2002. 29.99 (978-0-8007-4427-4(6)) Revell.

Buying a Car for Dummies. abr. ed. Deanna Sclar. 1 cass. (Running Time: 90 mins.). (For Dummies Ser.). 1998. 12.00 (978-0-694-52062-6(4), CPN10164) HarperCollins Pubs.

Buying a Car For Dummies points out the rules you need to follow to successfully negotiate your next car purchase and warns you of circumstances that are either dangerous or could cost a fortune.

Buying a House: An Easy, Smart Guide to Buying a New Home. Chris Sandlund. (B & N Basics Ser.). 2003. audio compact disk 9.98 (978-0-7607-3770-5(3), Silver Lini) M Friedman Pub Grp Inc.

Buying a Piece of Paris: Finding a Key to the City of Love. unabr. ed. Ellie Nielsen. Read by Nicki Paull. 7 CDs. (Running Time: 8 hrs. 45 mins.). 2009. audio compact disk 83.95 (978-1-921415-16-6(9), 9781921415166) Pub: Bolinda Pubng AUS. Dist(s): Bolinda Pub Inc

Buying & Selling a Business. Ed. by Socrates Media Editors. 2005. audio compact disk 29.95 (978-1-59546-098-1(5)) Pub: Socrates Med LLC. Dist(s): Midpt Trade

Buying & Selling a Business. 2nd ed. 1990. 60.00 (AC-597) PA Bar Inst.

Buying & Selling a Business: Troubleshooting Taxable Acquisitions. Read by Christopher Cicconi. 1 cass. 1990. 20.00 (AL-92) PA Bar Inst.

Buying & Selling a Home. abr. ed. Shelley O'Hara. 2005. 25.99 (978-1-58926-820-3(2), 6820) Pub: Oasis Audio. Dist(s): TNT Media Grp

Buying & Selling a Home. abr. ed. Shelley O'Hara & Nancy D. Lewis. Narrated by Grover Gardner. (Running Time: 6 hrs. 0 mins. 0 sec.). (Complete Idiot's Guides). (ENG.). 2005. audio compact disk 27.99 (978-1-58926-821-0(0), 6821) Oasis Audio.

Buying & Starting a Small Business. Thomas R. Curran. 2 cass. 1996. 109.00 Set. (0930) Toolkit Media.

Focuses on the "start-up" phase of new business ventures & explores many of the issues every new business owner must face, including raising capital, federal income tax considerations, etc.

Buying Facilitation: The New Way to Sell that Influences & Expands Decisions. Sharon Drew Morgen. 2003. 25.00 (978-0-9643553-3-0(7)) Morgen Pubng.

Buying In: The Secret Dialogue Between What We Buy & Who We Are. Rob Walker. Narrated by Robert Fass. (Running Time: 33720 sec.). (ENG.). 2008. audio compact disk 29.95 (978-1-60283-430-9(X)) Pub: AudioGO. Dist(s): Perseus Dist

Buying Insurance. Ernest Yaniger. 1 cass. (Running Time: 32 min. per cass.). 1985. 10.00 (TC719) Esstee Audios.

Uses fundamental terms & definitions in its checklist of issues & caveats needed for assessing long-term economic needs & spreading their risks. Concentrates on auto, health, & life (term, whole life, & endowments) insurance.

Buying or Selling a Small Business. (Running Time: 6 hrs.). 1994. 92.00 Incl. 303p. coursebk. (20474) NYS Bar.

Highlights the most important tax & business considerations arising with the sale of a small business. The speakers consider the respective viewpoints of both seller & buyer in the course of an acquisition. The first few tapes review the common & recurring legal & practical situations present in most kinds of small business acquisitions. The later presentations concentrate on the techniques & practicalities of negotiating & drafting acquisition agreements, with a hypothetical negotiation session included to simulate the negotiating process involved in the sale & purchase of a small business.

Buying Secrets Retailers Don't Want You to Know. unabr. ed. Peter Wink. Read by Peter Wink. (Running Time: 11 hrs. 30 mins.). (ENG.). 2009. 29.98 (978-1-59659-399-2(7), GildAudio) Pub: Gildan Media. Dist(s): HachBkGrp

Buying Shelter. Ernest Yaniger. 1 cass. (Running Time: 30 min. per cass.). 1985. 10.00 (TC716) Esstee Audios.

Compares the pros & cons of purchasing as opposed to renting a home. Key topics are rental agreements, home location, & practical techniques for efficient evaluation of a prospective home.

Buying the Night Flight. unabr. ed. Georgie A. Geyer. Read by Mary Woods. 8 cass. (Running Time: 12 hrs.). 1986. 64.00 (978-0-7366-0895-4(8), 1839) Books on Tape.

In Geyer's autobiographical story she shares the experience of covering revolutions & reporting the hopes & tragedies they represent. She also reports another revolution, one that took place in her heart & soul - the "inner revolution of a whole watershed generation of women." She takes the reader behind the glamorous facade of foreign correspondent.

Buying Trances: A New Psychology of Sales & Marketing. unabr. rev. ed. Joe Vitale, Jr. (Running Time: 6 hrs.). (ENG.). 2007. audio compact disk 29.98 (978-1-59659-120-2(X), GildAudio) Pub: Gildan Media. Dist(s): HachBkGrp

Buyology: Truth & Lies about Why We Buy. unabr. ed. Martin Lindstrom. Read by Don Leslie. Frwd. by Paco Underhill. 6 CDs. (Running Time: 7 hrs. 30 mins.). 2008. audio compact disk 29.95 (978-0-7393-7601-0(2), Random AudioBks) Pub: Random Audio Pubg. Dist(s): Random

Buyology: Truth & Lies about Why We Buy & the New Science of Desire. unabr. ed. Martin Lindstrom. Read by Don Leslie. 2008. audio compact disk 90.00 (978-1-4159-5834-6(3), BksonTape) Pub: Random Audio Pubg. Dist(s): Random

Buzby. abr. ed. Julia Hoban. Illus. by John Himmelman. 1 cass. (Running Time: 10 min.). (I Can Read Bks.). (J). (gr. k-3). 1996. 8.99 (978-0-694-70044-8(4), HarperFestival) HarperCollins Pubs.

Buzon de Tiempo. Mario Benedetti. 3 cass. (Running Time: 4 hrs.). (SPA.). 29.75 (978-1-4025-6314-0(0)) Recorded Bks.

Buzz Cut. unabr. ed. James W. Hall. Narrated by Frank Muller. 12 CDs. (Running Time: 13 hrs. 30 mins.). (Thorn Ser.). 1999. audio compact disk 99.00 (978-0-7887-3413-7(X), C1019E7) Recorded Bks.

Off the coast of south Florida, a cruise ship becomes a prison for the rich & famous, all at the mercy of a madman's terrorism.

Buzz Cut. unabr. ed. James W. Hall. Narrated by Frank Muller. 10 cass. (Running Time: 13 hrs. 30 mins.). (Thorn Ser.). 1996. 85.00 (978-0-7887-0628-8(4), 94802E7) Recorded Bks.

Buzz One. unabr. ed. British Broadcasting Corporation Staff. 3 cass. 1994. 59.95 Set, ESL. (SEN405) J Norton Pubs.

Includes 96-page pupils book, 122-page teachers book, 55-page activity book.

Buzz Two. unabr. ed. British Broadcasting Corporation Staff. 3 cass. 1994. 59.95 Set, ESL. (SEN410) J Norton Pubs.

Buzzing Bugs. Tom Greve. (Rourke Discovery Library (CD-ROM) Ser.). (J). (gr. 4-7). 2008. audio compact disk 24.95 (978-1-60472-778-4(0)) Rourke FL.

Bwana. unabr. ed. Mike Resnick. Read by Pat Bottino. 2 cass. (Running Time: 2 hrs. 10 min.). (Tales of Kirinyaga Ser.: No. 3). 1998. 15.99 Set. (978-1-884612-29-9(6)) AudioText.

Due to an ecological imbalance on the planet Kirinyaga, the hyenas do not have enough to eat & are killing the children of this world of farmers. A hunter from Earth is brought in to save them from the hyenas but who will save them from the hunter.

BWH Talking Book: The Ballad of the White Horse. unabr. ed. Narrated by James M. Courtright. 2 cass. (Running Time: 2 hrs. 10 min.). 1996. 24.95 Set. Sstrs Srvnts.

This is a ballad of King Alfred's reign, & describes that monarch's noble exploits, his character, his struggle with the Danes, the story of the White Horse & the battle of Ethandune.

By a Promise Bound. unabr. ed. Barbara Francis. Read by Jean DeBarbieris. 12 cass. (Running Time: 13 hrs. 30 min.). Dramatization. 1991. 64.95 (978-1-55686-349-3(7), 349) Books in Motion.

The sweeping saga of the Carvel family of Rhode Island from the early 1900's to the 1920's.

By a Spider's Thread. abr. ed. Laura Lippman. Read by Linda Emond. (Tess Monaghan Ser.: No. 8). 2004. audio compact disk 29.95 (978-0-06-073861-7(8)) HarperCollins Pubs.

***By a Spider's Thread.** abr. ed. Laura Lippman. Read by Linda Emond. (ENG.). 2004. (978-0-06-081799-2(2), Harper Audio); (978-0-06-081800-5(X), Harper Audio) HarperCollins Pubs.

By a Spider's Thread. unabr. ed. Laura Lippman. Narrated by Barbara Rosenblat. 7 cass. (Running Time: 9 hrs. 45 mins.). (Tess Monaghan Ser.: No. 8). 2004. 69.75 (978-1-4193-0762-1(2), 97871MC) Recorded Bks.

By Any Means. abr. ed. Charley Boorman. Read by Rupert Degas. (Running Time: 2 hrs. 56 mins. 0 sec.). (ENG.). 2008. audio compact disk 19.95 (978-1-4055-0504-8(4)) Pub: Little BrownUK GBR. Dist(s): IPG Chicago

By Candlelight. Janelle Taylor. Narrated by Barbara McCulloh. 9 cass. (Running Time: 12 hrs. 30 mins.). 82.00 (978-1-4025-3664-9(X)) Recorded Bks.

By Canoe to Loon Lake. unabr. ed. 1 cass. (Solitudes Ser.). 9.95 (C11201) J Norton Pubs.

This tape tunes in the sounds & experiences of the natural environment.

By Courier see Favorite Stories by O. Henry

By Divine Design. Michael Pearl. 3 cass. 1999. (978-1-892112-14-9(0)) No Greater Joy.

By Fiat of Adoration see Twentieth-Century Poetry in English, No. 26, Recordings of Poets Reading Their Own Poetry

By Flowing Waters: Chant for the Liturgy. Paul F. Ford. 1 CD. (Running Time: 55 min.). 1999. audio compact disk 16.95 (978-0-8146-7949-4(8)) Liturgical Pr.

This recording of chant is an act of prayer and a perfect meditation tool and salve for the spirit.

***By Heresies Distressed.** unabr. ed. David Weber. Narrated by Jason Culp. 2 MP3-CDs. (Running Time: 25 hrs.). 2009. 84.95 (978-0-7927-6526-4(5)); audio compact disk 139.95 (978-0-7927-6381-9(5)) AudioGO.

By Heresies Distressed. unabr. ed. David Weber. Read by Oliver Wyman & Jason Culp. (Running Time: 25 hrs. 0 mins. 0 sec.). Bk. 3. (ENG.). 2009. audio compact disk 69.95 (978-1-4272-0679-4(1)) Pub: Macmill Audio. Dist(s): Macmillan

By His Wounds. Contrib. by Mac Powell et al. (Soundtraks Ser.). 2007. audio compact disk 8.99 (978-5-557-60869-5(9)) Christian Wrld.

By His Wounds. Contrib. by Mac Powell et al. (Praise Hymn Soundtracks Ser.). 2007. audio compact disk 8.98 (978-5-557-92880-9(4)); audio compact disk 9.98 (978-5-557-92871-7(5)) Pt of Grace Ent.

By Hook & by Crook. unabr. ed. Fred Archer. 5 cass. (Isis Cassettes Ser.). (J). 2005. 49.95 (978-0-7531-2040-8(2)) Pub: ISIS Lrg Prnt GBR. Dist(s): Ulverscroft US

***By King's Command.** Adapted by Siren Audio Studios. (ENG.). 2010. audio compact disk 32.99 (978-0-9844180-1-5(6)) Siiren Audio.

By-Line Pt. A: Ernest Hemingway. unabr. collector's ed. Ernest Hemingway. Read by Wolfram Kandinsky. 7 cass. (Running Time: 10 hrs. 30 min.). 1990. 56.00 (978-0-7366-1705-5(1), 2549A) Books on Tape.

Is a collection of Hemingway's articles & dispatches over a span of four decades. The first part consists of pieces written for the Toronto Star Weekly between 1920 & 1924; the second, of pieces from Esquire from 1933-1939. The third section deals mostly with the Spanish Civil War & the fourth covers the Chinese situation in June 1941 & WW II. The final part consists of pieces written after 1949.

By-Line Pt. B: Ernest Hemingway. unabr. collector's ed. Ernest Hemingway. Read by Wolfram Kandinsky. 6 cass. (Running Time: 9 hrs.). 1990. 48.00 (978-0-7366-1706-2(X), 2549-B) Books on Tape.

By-Line - Ernest Hemingway: Selected Articles & Dispatches of Four Decades. unabr. ed. Ernest Hemingway. Read by Alexander Adams. 13 cass. (Running Time: 18 hrs.). 2001. 34.95 (978-0-7366-5671-9(5)) Books on Tape.

These articles & dispatches written primarily during the author's early career show him to be a superb journalist.

By Love & Grace, Set. Anita Stansfield. 2 cass. 1996. 11.98 Set. (978-1-55503-991-2(X), 07001355) Covenant Comms.

A powerful novel of love, faith & redemption.

By Love Divided, Set. unabr. ed. Grace Goodwin. Read by Sarah Sherborne. 4 cass. (Running Time: 5 hrs. 15 min.). 1999. 57.95 (978-1-85903-298-5(2)) Pub: Magna Story GBR. Dist(s): Ulverscroft US

If her car hadn't been in for its MOT, then Jenny Weston would never have met Richard, a sophisticated, charismatic, whizz-kid. Handsome & worldly, nothing is the same for schoolteacher Jenny, even though her dearest friend, Roz, doesn't seem to like Richard at all! Eventually, Jenny flees to her Aunt Isobel's in Scotland, where a beautiful waterfall begins a different chapter in her life, a life changed by two chance meetings, teaching her that there are many different kinds of love.

By Love Unveiled. abr. ed. Deborah Martin, pseud. Read by Noel Taylor. 1 cass. (Running Time: 90 min.). 1995. 5.99 (978-1-57096-014-7(3), RAZ 915) Romance Alive Audio.

In the court of King Charles II, Marianne Winchilsea is fleeing for her life, accused of treason & disguised as a gypsy. She must enlist the help of her family's old enemy, Garrett Lyon, Earl of Falkham, to overcome treachery & discover love.

By My Spirit. Perf. by Lori Wilke. 1 cass. (Running Time: 8 min.). 1988. 9.98 Sound track. (978-1-891916-13-7(0)) Spirit To Spirit.

***By Myself & Then Some.** abr. ed. Lauren Bacall. Read by Lauren Bacall. (ENG.). 2005. (978-0-06-084046-4(3), Harper Audio); (978-0-06-084047-1(1), Harper Audio) HarperCollins Pubs.

***By Nightfall.** unabr. ed. Michael Cunningham. Read by Hugh Dancy. 7 CDs. (Running Time: 7 hrs. 45 mins. 0 sec.). 2010. audio compact disk 34.99 (978-1-4272-1057-9(8)) Pub: Macmill Audio. Dist(s): Macmillan

By Order of the President. abr. ed. W. E. B. Griffin. 5 CDs. (Running Time: 6 hrs.). No. 1. (ENG.). (gr. 8). 2004. audio compact disk 29.95 (978-0-14-280089-8(9), PengAudBks) Penguin Grp USA.

By Order of the President. unabr. ed. W. E. B. Griffin. Read by Dick Hill. (Running Time: 20 hrs.). (Presidential Agent Ser.: Bk. 1). 2004. 29.95 (978-1-59710-114-1(1), 1597101141, BAD) Brilliance Audio.

By Order of the President. unabr. ed. W. E. B. Griffin. Read by Dick Hill. (Running Time: 20 hrs.). (Presidential Agent Ser.: No. 1). 2004. 44.25 (978-1-59710-115-8(X), 159710115X, BADLE); audio compact disk 44.95 (978-1-59355-962-5(3), 1593559623); 44.25 (978-1-59335-910-2(1), 1593359101, BriAudCD Unabrid); 29.95 (978-1-59335-776-4(1), 1593357761, Brilliance MP3); 36.95 (978-1-59355-960-1(7), 1593559607); 107.25 (978-1-59355-961-8(5), 1593559615, BrilAudUnabridg); audio compact disk 127.25 (978-1-59355-963-2(1), 1593559631, BriAudCD Unabrid) Brilliance Audio.

Two armed men board a 727 all but forgotten at an airfield in Angola. Hijacking the jet, they then slit the throat of the lone crew and fly to parts unknown. The consternation is immediate, as the CIA, FBI, and other agencies race to find out what happened, in the process elbowing one another in the sides a little too vigorously. Fed up, the president of the United States turns to an outside investigator to determine the truth, an Army intelligence officer serving as special assistant to the secretary of homeland security. Delta Force major Carlos Guillermo Castillo, known as Charley, is the son of a German mother and a Tex-Mex father who was killed in the Vietnam War and awarded a Medal of Honor. A West Point graduate, a pilot, and a veteran of Desert Storm, Castillo has a sharp eye for the facts - and the reality behind them. Traveling undercover, he flies to Africa, and there, helped and hindered by unexpected allies and determined enemies, begins to untangle a story of frightening dimensions - a story that, unless he can do something about it, will end very, very badly indeed, not only for Castillo . . . but for all of America.

***By Royal Command.** unabr. ed. Charlie Higson. Read by Gerard Doyle. (Running Time: 10 hrs. 30 mins.). (Young Bond Ser.: Bk. 5). 2010. 29.95 (978-1-4417-3329-0(9)); 65.95 (978-1-4417-3325-2(6)); audio compact disk 100.00 (978-1-4417-3326-9(4)) Blckstn Audio.

By Schism Rent Asunder. unabr. ed. David Weber. Read by Oliver Wyman. 20 CDs. (Running Time: 25 hrs. 30 min. 0 sec.). Bk. 2. (ENG.). 2008. audio compact disk 69.95 (978-1-4272-0429-5(2)) Pub: Macmill Audio. Dist(s): Macmillan

By Small & Simple Things: Inspiring Stories of Christlike Service. Michele Romney Garvin. 1 cass. (Running Time: 1 hr. 30 min.). 1996. 7.98 Digital. (978-1-55503-909-7(X), 06005233) Covenant Comms.
Heart-touching accounts of love in action.

By Small Means. Emmett Smith. 1 cass. 3.95 (978-1-57734-400-1(6), 34441417) Covenant Comms.

By Small Means Are Great Things Brought to Pass. Emmett Smith. 1 cass. 7.98 (978-1-55503-415-3(2), 06004555) Covenant Comms.
Includes "Conversion!". Helps you see that we travel on the path to perfection one step at a time, not in leaps.

By Sorrow's River. unabr. ed. Larry McMurtry. Narrated by Henry Strozier. 11 CDs Lib. Ed. (Running Time: 12 hrs.). (Berrybender Narratives Ser.: Bk. 3). 2003. audio compact disk 109.75 (978-1-4025-7734-5(6)) Recorded Bks.

By Sorrow's River. unabr. ed. Larry McMurtry. Narrated by Henry Strozier. 9 cass. Lib. Ed. (Running Time: 12 hrs.). (Berrybender Narratives Ser.: Bk. 3). 2003. 79.75 (978-1-4025-7698-0(6)) Recorded Bks.

By Sorrow's River. unabr. collector's ed. Larry McMurtry. Narrated by Henry Strozier. 9 cass. (Running Time: 12 hrs.). (Berrybender Narratives Ser.: Bk. 3). 2003. 42.95 (978-1-4025-7699-7(4), RH069); audio compact disk 42.95 (978-1-4025-7736-9(2), CC032) Recorded Bks.
Traces the adventures of a wealthy but eccentric English family who hunt and travel across the Great Plains in the 1830s.

By Surprise. Perf. by Joy Williams. 2002. audio compact disk Reunion Recs.

By Ted Tred: Logos November 16, 1997. Ben Young. 1997. 4.95 (978-0-7417-6056-2(8), B0056) Win Walk.

By the Grand Canal. William Riviere. (Running Time: 27000 sec.). 2005. 44.95 (978-0-7861-3529-5(8)); audio compact disk 45.00 (978-0-7861-7798-1(5)); audio compact disk 29.95 (978-0-7861-8014-1(5)) Blckstn Audio.

By the Great Horn Spoon! unabr. ed. Sid Fleischman. Read by Full Cast Production Staff. (J). 2007. 39.99 (978-1-59895-789-1(9)) Find a World.

By the Green of the Spring, Pt. 1. unabr. collector's ed. John Masters. Read by Walter Zimmerman. 9 cass. (Running Time: 13 hrs. 30 min.). (Loss of Eden Ser.). 1986. 72.00 (978-0-7366-0787-2(0), 1740-A) Books on Tape.
This is the third & final volume in John Master's trilogy "Loss of Eden." It brings to its close & casts with survivors; half the war-time generations was killed on the barren shores of peace.

By the Green of the Spring, Pt. 2. collector's ed. John Masters. Read by Walter Zimmerman. 10 cass. (Running Time: 15 hrs.). 1986. 80.00 (978-0-7366-0788-9(9), 1740-B) Books on Tape.

By the Light of the Halloween Moon. 2004. pap. bk. 18.95 (978-1-55592-800-1(5)); audio compact disk 12.95 (978-1-55592-865-0(X)) Weston Woods.

By the Light of the Halloween Moon. (J). 2004. pap. bk. 38.75 (978-1-55592-817-9(X)); pap. bk. 32.75 (978-1-55592-198-9(1)) Weston Woods.

By the Light of the Halloween Moon. Narrated by Sherry Stringfield. Music by John Jennings. 1 readalong cass. (Running Time: 7 min.). (J). (ps-3). 2000. pap. bk. 12.95 Weston Woods.
Join the fun as a brave young girl, who would rather play a trick than be gobbled up as a treat, is the star of this spirited romp under an old wooden bridge by the light of the spooky Halloween moon.

By the Light of the Halloween Moon. Caroline Stutson. Illus. by Kevin Hawkes. 1 cass., 5 bks. (Running Time: 7 min.). (J). pap. bk. 32.75 Weston Woods.
A brave young girl, who would rather play a trick than be gobbled up as a treat, sits on an old bridge by the light of the Halloween moon.

By the Light of the Halloween Moon. unabr. ed. 1 cass. (Running Time: 7 min.). (J). (ps-3). 1998. 8.95 (978-1-56008-818-9(4), RAC370) Weston Woods.

By the Light of the Halloween Moon. unabr. ed. Caroline Stutson. Illus. by Kevin Hawkes. 1 cass. (Running Time: 7 min.). (J). (ps-3). 1998. bk. 24.95 (978-0-7882-0680-1(X), HRA370); pap. bk. 14.95 (978-0-7882-0667-2(2), PRA370) Weston Woods.

By the Light of the Moon. unabr. ed. Dean Koontz. Read by Stephen Lang. (Dean Koontz Ser.). (ENG.). 2007. audio compact disk 29.95 (978-0-7393-4139-1(1), Random AudioBks) Pub: Random Audio Pubg. Dist(s): Random

By the Light of the Moon. unabr. ed. Dean Koontz. Read by Stephen Lang. 8 cass. (Running Time: 12 hrs.). 2002. 88.00 (978-0-7366-8916-8(8)); audio compact disk 81.60 (978-0-7366-8920-5(6)) Pub: Books on Tape. Dist(s): NetLibrary CO
Two brothers & their traveling companion race to puzzle out a vicious violation committed against them, only steps ahead of deadly pursuers.

By the Light of the Moon: Campfire Songs & Cowboy Tunes. Perf. by Charlie Daniels. 1 cass. 1997. 9.98 (Sony Wonder); audio compact disk 13.98 CD. (Sony Wonder) Sony Music Ent.
Traditional tunes, reworked classics & several original songs about cowboys, miners & railroad people - hard working folks like Big John, John Henry & the people on the Chisolm Trail - working people who are heroes in Mr. Daniels' mind. Features: Cowboy Logic, Git Along, Little Dogies, Yippie Ki Yea & others.

By the Mast Divided. David Donachie. 2008. 94.95 (978-1-4079-0028-5(5)); audio compact disk 104.95 (978-1-4079-0029-2(3)) Pub: Soundings Ltd GBR. Dist(s): Ulverscroft US

By the North Gate. unabr. ed. Gwyn Griffin. Read by Wolfram Kandinsky. 6 cass. (Running Time: 9 hrs.). 1959. 48.00 Set. (978-0-7366-0617-2(3), 1579) Books on Tape.
The story of personal, political & amorous intrigue set in a British outpost in Northeast Africa after World War II. In an attempt to whip resentment into hysteria, a group of Rabid Nationalists seize on the bungled execution of a native terrorist as a means to thwart British occupation.

By the Pricking of My Thumbs. unabr. ed. Agatha Christie. Read by Alex Jennings. 5 cass. (Running Time: 7 hrs.). 2001. 27.95 (978-1-57270-233-2(8), N51233u) Pub: Audio Partners. Dist(s): PerseuPGW
Tommy & Tuppence Beresford have a modern marriage & a remarkable knack for solving crimes.

By the Pricking of My Thumbs. unabr. ed. Agatha Christie. Narrated by Alex Jennings. (Tommy & Tuppence Mystery Ser.). (ENG.). 2008. audio compact disk 29.95 (978-1-60283-338-8(9)) Pub: AudioGO. Dist(s): Perseus Dist

By the River. Rose Boucheron. 5 cass. (Running Time: 6 hrs. 35 mins.). (Story Sound Ser.). (J). 2004. 49.95 (978-1-85903-758-4(5)) Pub: Mgna Lrg Print GBR. Dist(s): Ulverscroft US

By the River Piedra I Sat down & Wept see A Orillas del Río Piedra Me Senté y Lloré

By the Rivers of Babylon. unabr. ed. Nelson DeMille. Read by Scott Brick. 14 CDs. (Running Time: 17 hrs. 30 mins.). 2006. audio compact disk 99.00 (978-1-4159-3185-1(2)) Books on Tape.

By the Rivers of Babylon Vol. II: American Psalmody. Gloriae Dei Cantores. 1 CD. 1999. audio compact disk 16.95 (978-1-55725-220-3(3), GDCD027) Paraclete MA.

By the Shores of Silver Lake. unabr. ed. Laura Ingalls Wilder. Read by Cherry Jones. 3 cass. (Running Time: 4 hrs. 30 min.). (J). 2004. 22.00 (978-0-06-056499-5(7), HarperChildAud) HarperCollins Pubs.

By the Shores of Silver Lake. unabr. ed. Laura Ingalls Wilder. Read by Cherry Jones. Ed. by Allessi. 4 CDs. (Running Time: 4 hrs.). (J). 2004. audio compact disk 25.95 (978-0-06-056501-5(2), HarperChildAud) HarperCollins Pubs.

By the Sword. unabr. ed. F. Paul Wilson. Read by Dick Hill. (Running Time: 12 hrs.). (Repairman Jack Ser.: Bk. 11). 2008. 39.25 (978-1-4233-7431-2(2), 9781423374312, BADLE); 39.25 (978-1-4233-7429-9(0), 9781423374299, Brlnc Audio MP3 Lib); 24.95 (978-1-4233-7430-5(4), 9781423374305, BAD); 24.95 (978-1-4233-7428-2(2), 9781423374282, Brilliance MP3); audio compact disk 97.25 (978-1-4233-7427-5(4), 9781423374275, BriAudCD Unabrid); audio compact disk 29.99 (978-1-4233-7426-8(6), 9781423374268, Bril Audio CD Unabri) Brilliance Audio.

By the Waters of Liverpool. unabr. ed. Helen Forrester. 6 cass. (Sound Ser.). 2004. 54.95 (978-1-85496-091-7(1)) Pub: UlverLrgPrint GBR. Dist(s): Ulverscroft US

By the Word of Their Testimony CD Pack. 2003. audio compact disk (978-1-931713-60-3(X)) Word For Today.

By the Word of Their Testimony MP3. 2003. audio compact disk (978-1-931713-67-2(7)) Word For Today.

By the Word of Their Testimony Tape Pack. 2003. (978-1-931713-59-7(6)) Word For Today.

By Then I Was Thirteen. unabr. ed. Derrick Rees. Read by Stanley McGeagh. 8 cass. (Running Time: 12 hrs.). 2004. 64.00 (978-1-74030-480-1(2)) Pub: Bolinda Pubng AUS. Dist(s): Lndmrk Audiobks

By Way of Deception: The Making of a Mossad Officer. 2nd ed. Victor Ostrovsky. 2 cass. (Running Time: 3 hrs.). 2002. pap. bk. 24.95 (978-0-9717595-0-3(2)) Wilshire Pr.

By Way of the World. Perf. by Spies. 1 cass., 1 CD. 7.98 (TA 33305); audio compact disk 12.78 CD Jewel box. (TA 83305) NewSound.

By What Authority Do We Minister? Myron Madden & Wilbur Schwartz. 1986. 10.80 (0210B) Assn Prof Chaplains.

Bye Bye Bad Moods: Introducing Thought Field Therapy, Set. David Grudermeyer & Rebecca Grudermeyer. 2 cass. 18.95 Incl. handouts. (T-55) Willingness Wrks.

Byeliye Nochi. Fyodor Dostoyevsky. Read by Angela Sarkissian. 4 cass. (Running Time: 4 hrs.). (RUS.). 1996. pap. bk. 49.50 set. (978-1-58085-551-8(2)) Interlingua VA.
Includes Russian text with notes. The combination of written text & clarity & pace of diction will open the door for intermediate & advanced students to genuine comprehension & the use of literary texts for advancement in rapid understanding of written & oral language materials. The audio text plus written text concept makes foreign languages accessible to a much wider range of students than books alone.

Byron: Letters. George Gordon Byron. 2001. 16.95 (978-1-85998-367-6(7), HoddrStoughton) Pub: Hodder General GBR. Dist(s): Trafalgar

Byron: Poets for Pleasure. George Gordon Byron. Narrated by John Hannah. 1999. 18.95 (978-1-85998-368-3(5), HoddrStoughton) Pub: Hodder General GBR. Dist(s): Trafalgar

Byron Berline - Jumpin the Strings. Byron Berline. Arranged by Skip Holmes. 1996. pap. bk. 24.95 (978-0-7866-1767-8(5)) Mel Bay.

Byron by Dancing Beetle. Perf. by Eugene Ely. 1 cass. (Running Time: 70 min.). (J). 1991. 10.00 Erthviibz.
Lord Byron, nature sounds & parody come together when Ms. Moon & the spunky musical humans read & sing with Dancing Beetle.

Byron Cage: Recorded Live at New Birth Cathedral, Atlanta, GA. Perf. by Byron Cage. 2003. audio compact disk GospoCen.

Byron's Rhetoric. unabr. ed. G. Wilson Knight. 1 cass. (Running Time: 24 min.). 1965. 12.95 (23068) J Norton Pubs.
Selected readings from Byron's poetry illustrate the range of Byron's poetic resources & the reliance upon the spoken voice for full understanding. Selections are linked by brief commentaries on the specific quality of the passages.

Byzantine Virgin. Poems. Read by David O. Offutt. (Running Time: 28 MINS.). Dramatization. 2003. audio compact disk (978-0-9663605-0-9(8)) Inflammable Pr.
Seventeen poems comprise this miniature drama, which tells of a young woman - pregnant, husbandless, spurned by her community - who believes "her lord, her lover is coming". An unobtrusive musical backdrop compliments the performance. Sound engineering by CD Marksman. "A wonderful affirmation," said one listener.

Byzantium see Poetry of William Butler Yeats

Byzantium Pt. 1. unabr. ed. Stephen R. Lawhead. Read by Stuart Langston. 12 cass. (Running Time: 26 hrs.). 2002. 83.95 (978-0-7861-2306-3(0), 2993A, B) Blckstn Audio.
Although born to rule, Aidan lives as a scribe in a remote Irish monastery on the far, wild edge of Christendom. Secure in work, contemplation, and dreams of the wider world, a miracle bursts into Aidan's quiet life. He is chosen to accompany a small band of monks on a quest to the farthest eastern reaches of the known world, to the fabled city of Byzantium, where they are to present a beautiful and costly hand-illuminated manuscript, the Book of Kells, to the Emperor of all Christendom.

Byzantium Pt. 2. unabr. ed. Stephen R. Lawhead. Read by Stuart Langston. 6 CDs. (Running Time: 26 hrs.). 2002. audio compact disk 44.95 (978-0-7861-2319-3(2), 2993A, B) Blckstn Audio.

Bzots - Powered Up! Music by Matt Meils. Prod. by Eat Your Lunch. Created by Dave Skwarczek. Executive Producer Dave Skwarczek. (J). 2004. audio compact disk 13.99 (978-0-9746085-4-9(8)) Eat Your Lu.
What happens when three assembly line robots decide they'd rather follow their dreams than follow their programming? They escape from the factory and start a band, of course! Bzots are a lovable trio of robots that have chosen to follow their dreams of becoming a band rather than follow their pre-programmed orders to build Globocrud's vast array of consumable consumer products. Bzots mix funk, rock, pop, dance, classical and electronica into the silly-dance inspiring sound of now and then some for kids and their cool parents alike. The Powered Up CD features all 13 funkelectrockalicious tunes from Bzots' smash full-length videos Escape A Go Go and A Gotta Get A Gig, PLUS a super sweet, never-before-released bonus track and a fold-out poster! Woohoo!.

C

***C.** unabr. ed. Tom McCarthy. (Running Time: 13 hrs. 30 mins.). 2010. 37.99 (978-1-4001-9812-2(7)); 18.99 (978-1-4001-8812-3(1)) Tantor Media.

***C.** unabr. ed. Tom McCarthy. Narrated by Stephen Hoye. (Running Time: 14 hrs. 0 mins. 0 sec.). 2010. 24.99 (978-1-4001-6812-5(0)); audio compact disk 90.99 (978-1-4001-4812-7(X)); audio compact disk 37.99 (978-1-4001-1812-0(3)) Pub: Tantor Media. Dist(s): IngramPubServ

C. A. S. A. (Court Appointed Special Advocate) A Basic Guide. Karen Jean Matsko Hood. 2006. 29.95 (978-1-59434-250-9(4)); audio compact disk 24.95 (978-1-59434-249-3(0)) Whsprng Pine.

C-Change Audio. 2006. audio compact disk 19.99 (978-0-9762151-8-9(7)) Lanphier Pr.

C-Chute see Best of Isaac Asimov

C Corporations. William J. Lindquist & William H. Olson. 8 cass. (Running Time: 12 hrs.). 1995. 139.00 set, incl. wkbk. (753482EZ) Am Inst CPA.
This course is a comprehensive study of the principles & concepts of C Corporation taxation. From start-up through liquidation, you get precise definitions, clearly explained procedures, & detailed insights on shareholder taxation, corporate tax planning & strategies, & dissolution.

C. Everett Koop: Educating America about AIDS. Narrated by C. Everett Koop. 1 cass. (Running Time: 60 min.). 10.95 (K0310B090, HarperThor) HarpC GBR.

C. G. Jung, Miss Frank Miller, & the Creative Imagination. Read by Sonu Shamdasani. 1 cass. (Running Time: 90 min.). 1990. 10.95 (978-0-7822-0252-6(7), 427) C G Jung IL.
The longest case study in Jung's published works, Frank Miller has curiously received little attention to date, despite the continued relevance to analytical psychology. This analysis of her life, career & creative work suggests ways in which this material may help us revision our understanding of Jung's work.

C. H. Spurgeon Autobiography Vol. 1: The Early Years 1834-1859. unabr. ed. Charles H. Spurgeon. Read by Robert Whitfield. 16 cass. (Running Time: 24 hrs.). 1999. 99.95 (978-0-7861-1523-5(8), 2373) Blckstn Audio.
At the age of seventeen, he became pastor of a handful of believers at Waterbeach, in Cambridgeshire, meeting in what had been a dovecote. Within five years he had become the best-known minister in the Metropolis, judged competent before another two years had passed to conduct a service of National Humiliation in the Crystal Palace, where almost 24,000 persons were assembled.

C. H. Spurgeon Autobiography Vol. 2: The Full Harvest. unabr. ed. Charles H. Spurgeon. Read by Robert Whitfield. 14 cass. (Running Time: 21 hrs.). 1999. 89.95 (978-0-7861-1559-4(9), 2389) Blckstn Audio.
His last thirty years, from the building of the Metropolitan Tabernacle to his death in 1892, saw no fulfillmen t of the newspaper prophecy of his early days. There is more than his as the preacher in this autobiography.

C. H. Spurgeon's Autobiography: Volume I: the Early Years. unabr. ed. C. H. Spurgeon. Read by Robert Whitfield. (Running Time: 20 hrs. 0 mins.). 2008. 44.95 (978-1-4332-5185-6(X)); audio compact disk 125.00 (978-1-4332-5184-9(1)) Blckstn Audio.

C. H. Spurgeon's Autobiography: Volume II: the Full Harvest. unabr. ed. C. H. Spurgeon. Read by Simon Vance. (Running Time: 19 hrs. 0 mins.). 2009. 44.95 (978-1-4332-6710-9(1)); audio compact disk 125.00 (978-1-4332-6707-9(1)) Blckstn Audio.

C Is for Cookie. 1 cass. (J). 1995. bk. 9.98 (Sony Wonder); audio compact disk 13.98 CD. Sony Music Ent.
Everyone's favorite blue monster sings some of the most loved songs. Your tummy will be rumbling after singing along with Cookie to "Good-bye Little Cookie" & "Gingerbread Man," two never-before-released songs, in addition to classics such as "C Is for Cookie," "If Moon Was Cookie" & "Me Gotta Be Blue".

C Is for Cookie: Cookie's Favorite Songs. 1 cass. (J). (ps-2). 1995. 9.98 (Sony Wonder); audio compact disk 13.98 CD. (Sony Wonder) Sony Music Ent.
The Big Blue star of the Sesame Street television show offers 14 songs that have been features on the program. The opening number, "C Is for Cookie," features abundant dialogue. "The Last Cookie Round-up" is a spoof of "On Top of Old Smoky." "C Is for Circle" pairs Cookie Monster with another of the Muppet characters. "If I Knew You Were Comin' I'd've Baked a Cake" is a duet with Cookie Monster & the Count, a fairly straightforward rendition of the 1950's hit by Georgia Gibbs. "Breakfast Time" is another duet, this time pairing Cookie with Kermit. "Healthy Food" is a rap that has an infectious beat, with Cookie Monster naming a variety of healthy foods backed up by a Supremes-like chorus. "Me Gotta Be Blue" is a blues anthem about Cookie's color, not his mood.

C Is for Corpse. abr. ed. Sue Grafton. Read by Judy Kaye. (Running Time: 10800 sec.). (Kinsey Millhone Mystery Ser.). (ENG.). 2007. audio compact disk 14.99 (978-0-7393-5791-0(3), Random AudioBks) Pub: Random Audio Pubg. Dist(s): Random

C Is for Corpse. unabr. collector's ed. Sue Grafton. Read by Mary Peiffer. 6 cass. (Running Time: 9 hrs.). (Kinsey Millhone Mystery Ser.). 1993. 48.00 (978-0-7366-2512-8(7), 3268) Books on Tape.
Bobby Callahan was struggling to get back to life after his Porsche was forced off the edge of a canyon. Desperate to find the stalker responsible, he hires Kinsey, but she is too late. Three days after she is hired, Bobby is found dead.

C. J. 's Fate. unabr. ed. Kay Hooper. (Running Time: 18000 sec.). 2007. 24.95 (978-1-4332-0748-8(6)); audio compact disk 36.00 (978-1-4332-0749-5(4)); audio compact disk 19.95 (978-1-4332-0750-1(8)) Blckstn Audio.

C-Level Secrets: Selling at the Highest Level. Created by Jeffrey Gitomer. 2007. DVD 199.00 (978-0-9719468-4-2(1)) Lito Pr.

C++ Plus Data Structures. 2nd ed. Nell B. Dale & David Teague. (C). 2001. audio compact disk 101.00 (978-0-7637-1543-4(3), 1543-3) Jones Bartlett.

C. S. A. Confederate States of America, Set. abr. ed. Howard Means. Read by Richard Gilliland. 4 cass. 1999. 25.00 (FS9-43320) Highsmith.

C. S. Lewis: Memories & Reflections. unabr. ed. John Lawlor. Read by Bernard Mayes. 4 cass. (Running Time: 5 hrs. 30 mins.). 2001. 32.95 (978-0-7861-1980-6(2), 2750) Blckstn Audio.
An unforgettable account of studying under Lewis & an enchanting depiction of undergraduate life at Oxford between the wars.

C. S. Lewis: Memories & Reflections. unabr. ed. John Lawlor & Bernard Mayes. (Running Time: 5 hrs. NaN mins.). 2008. 19.95

(978-1-4332-5400-0(X)); audio compact disk 40.00 (978-1-4332-5399-7(2)) Blckstn Audio.

C. S. Lewis: Mentor & Model. Robert F. Morneau. 5 cass. (Running Time: 6 hrs. 15 min.). 1992. 41.95 set. (TAH260) Alba Hse Comns.
In his learned & witty style, Bishop Morneau shows how the stories of C. S. Lewis can shape our emotions, guide & direct our energies & provide meaning of our journey through life.

C. S. Lewis Set: Screwtape Letters, Great Divorce, Problem of Pain, Mere Christianity. unabr. abr. ed. C. S. Lewis. 2005. audio compact disk 59.99 (978-0-06-082578-2(2)) HarperCollins Pubs.

C. S. Lewis & Narnia. abr. ed. Jon Kennedy. Narrated by Mark Warner. Frwd. by Lee Oser. (Running Time: 5 hrs. 0 mins. 0 sec.). (Everything (Oasis Audio) Ser.). (ENG.). 2008. audio compact disk 19.99 (978-1-59859-336-5(6)) Oasis Audio.

C-SPAN 1 Viewer's Guide: Making Sense of Watching the House of Representatives: Informed Citizen Series Audio Course. Elizabeth Rybicki. Prod. by TheCapitol.Net. (ENG.). 2008. 27.00 (978-1-58733-036-0(9)) TheCapitol.

C-SPAN 2 Viewer's Guide: Making Sense of Watching the Senate: Informed Citizen Series Audio Course: What's Behind the Classical Music. Elizabeth Rybicki. Prod. by TheCapitol.Net. (ENG.). 2008. 27.00 (978-1-58733-054-4(7)) TheCapitol.

***C Street: The Fundamentalist Threat to American Democracy.** unabr. ed. Jeff Sharlet. Read by Jeremy Guskin. (Running Time: 9 hrs.). (ENG.). 2010. 24.98 (978-1-60788-626-6(X)); audio compact disk 29.98 (978-1-60788-625-9(1)) Pub: Hachet Audio. Dist(s): HachBkGrp

C. U. P. Course, Set. Barrie Konicov. 12 cass. 199.98 Incl. study manual & storage binder. (CUP) Potentials.

C W - Lent & Easter. 1 CD. 1999. audio compact disk 12.99 (978-0-8100-0833-5(5)) Northwest Pub.

C-Word: August 15-16, 1998. Ben Young. 1998. 4.95 (978-0-7417-6094-4(0), B0094) Win Walk.

Cabal. unabr. ed. Michael Dibdin. Read by Michael Tudor Barnes. 7 cass. (Running Time: 9 hrs. 15 min.). (Aurelio Zen Mystery Ser.). (J). 1997. 61.95 (978-1-85695-890-5(6), 940809) Pub: ISIS Lrg Prnt GBR. Dist(s): Ulverscroft US

Cabal: And Other Stories. unabr. ed. Ellen Gilchrist. Read by Mary Peiffer. 6 cass. (Running Time: 9 hrs.). 2001. 29.95 (978-0-7366-5680-1(4)) Books on Tape.
Touching on all things Southern, this is a vivid collection of stories by one of the most delightful writers today.

Cabal & Other Stories. collector's unabr. ed. Ellen Gilchrist. Read by Mary Peiffer. 6 cass. (Running Time: 9 hrs.). 2000. 29.95 (978-0-7366-5523-1(9), 5363) Books on Tape.
The story of a group of prominent citizens of Jackson, Mississippi, whose psychiatrist suddenly goes mad, revealing their deepest secrets & embarrassing misdeeds to anyone who will listen. The whole town goes crazy trying to figure out what to do. The result is a bilingly ironic tale, revealing that our deepest secrets are invariably those best known by others.

Caballo de Troya: Jerusalen. Scripts. Based on a book by Juan Jose Benitez. Adapted by FonoLibro Inc. 9 CDs. (Running Time: 10 Hrs). Dramatization. (SPA.). 2004. audio compact disk 39.95 (978-0-9728598-2-0(9)) Fonolibro Inc.
Jerusalen. Caballo de Troya (Jerusalem. The Trojan Horse), audiobook dramatized in Spanish based on the International Bestseller from J.J. Benitez ?. In this extraordinary production, Benitez unveils the truth never told before about the figure and history of Jesus of Nazareth, and how super-potencies cover their military and space projects to the public; The Trojan Horse. In 1973, the US Air forces, after many years of preparation, executed one of their most secret projects, ?The Trojan Horse?s Operation.? A retired Air force Major in his last days gave to J.J. Benitez authentic documentation about this project, in which two pilots traveled in time to the year 30 of our time, and had direct contact with Jesus Christ and discovering how the sacred story really happened. Now, FonoLibro brings you a dramatized version in Spanish of the international bestseller in the audiobook format, with a full cast of more than 25 actors, original music, and sound effects that would make you feel as if you were present in the story.

Caballo de Troya 2. Masada. abr. ed. J. J. Benitez. 4 CDs. (Running Time: 18000 sec.). (Caballo de Troya (Fonolibro) Ser.). (SPA.). 2006. audio compact disk 24.95 (978-1-933499-25-3(7)) Fonolibro Inc.

Caballo de Troya 7. Nahum. 5 CDs. (Running Time: 21600 sec.). (Caballo de Troya (Fonolibro) Ser.). 2005. audio compact disk 29.95 (978-1-933499-04-8(4)) Fonolibro Inc.

Caballo de Troya 8. Jordan, Vol. 8. abr. ed. J. J. Benitez. Prod. by FonoLibro Inc. 3. (Running Time: 12600 sec.). (SPA.). 2007. audio compact disk 24.95 (978-1-933499-49-9(4)) Fonolibro Inc.

Cabana: Donde la Tragedia Se Encuentra Con la Eternidad. William Paul Young. Read by Frank Rodriguez. (Running Time: 10 hrs.). (SPA.). 2008. audio compact disk 24.98 (978-1-60024-686-9(9)) Pub: Hachet Audio. Dist(s): HachBkGrp

Cabaña: Donde la Tragedia Se Encuentra con la Eternidad. William Paul Young. Read by Frank M. Rodriguez. (Running Time: 10 hrs.). (SPA.). 2008. 16.98 (978-1-60024-687-6(7)) Pub: Hachet Audio. Dist(s): HachBkGrp

***Cabaña Del Tio Tom.** abr. ed. Harriet Beecher-Stowe. Read by Yadira Sanchez. (SPA.). 2008. audio compact disk 17.00 (978-958-8318-30-1(0)) Pub: Yoyo Music COL. Dist(s): YoYoMusic

Cabaret Berlin. Edel Staff. 2006. pap. bk. 59.95 (978-3-937406-16-9(6)) Pub: edel CLASS DEU. Dist(s): Natl Bk Netwk

Cabaret Violin Treasures - Solo Violin. Mary Ann Harbar. 1995. pap. bk. 24.95 (978-0-7866-0879-9(X), 95386CDP) Mel Bay.

Cabaret Violin Treasures/Solo Violin. Mary Ann Harbar. 1995. pap. bk. 18.95 (978-0-7866-0693-1(2), 95386P) Mel Bay.

Cabbage Patch Curse. unabr. ed. Paul Jennings & Paul Jennings. Read by Rebecca Macauley. (Running Time: 2100 sec.). (Cabbage Patch: Ser.). (J). (gr. 2-7). 2005. audio compact disk 39.95 (978-1-74093-583-8(7)) Pub: Bolinda Pubng AUS. Dist(s): Bolinda Pub Inc

Cabbage Patch Fib. unabr. ed. Paul Jennings. 2 cass. (Running Time: 24 mins.). (Cabbage Patch Ser.). (J). 2000. 18.00 (978-1-74030-264-7(8)) Pub: Bolinda Pubng AUS. Dist(s): Bolinda Pub Inc
Cabbage Patch Pong - The green baby is back, but this time with a great many companions, Chris and his sister are left with them in a forest when the babies mothers run away from a cow. Yes, it is a VERY odd situation! Fortunately the cow provides milk for the hungry babies, but food leads to some very nasty nappies. And how can Chris ensure the mothers find the babies?.

Cabbage Patch Fib. unabr. ed. Paul Jennings. (Running Time: 24 mins.). (Cabbage Patch: Ser.). (J). 2004. audio compact disk 39.95 (978-1-74093-329-2(X)) Pub: Bolinda Pubng AUS. Dist(s): Bolinda Pub Inc

Cabbage Patch Pong. unabr. ed. Paul Jennings. (Running Time: 35 mins.). (Cabbage Patch: Ser.). (J). 2004. audio compact disk 39.95 (978-1-74093-412-1(1)) Pub: Bolinda Pubng AUS. Dist(s): Bolinda Pub Inc

Cabbage Patch Pong. unabr. ed. Paul Jennings. 1 cass. (Running Time: 35 mins.). (Cabbage Patch Ser.). (J). 2004. 18.00 (978-1-74030-878-6(6)) Bolinda Pubng AUS.

Cabbage Patch War. unabr. ed. Paul Jennings. (Running Time: 40 mins.). (Cabbage Patch Ser.). (J). 2000. 18.00 (978-1-74030-265-4(6)) Pub: Bolinda Pubng AUS. Dist(s): Bolinda Pub Inc

Cabbage Patch War. unabr. ed. Paul Jennings. (Running Time: 40 mins.). (Cabbage Patch: Ser.). (J). 2004. audio compact disk 39.95 (978-1-74093-334-6(6)) Pub: Bolinda Pubng AUS. Dist(s): Bolinda Pub Inc

Cabbage Soup. Perf. by Children's Radio Theatre Staff. Text by Pat Harrison. Adapted by Sophy Burnham. (J). 1999. audio compact disk 14.95 (978-0-939065-94-3(0)) Gentle Wind.

Cabbage Soup: Children's Radio Theatre. 1 cass. (Running Time: 55 min.). (J). (gr. 2-7). 1986. 9.95 (978-0-939065-20-2(7), GW 1024) Gentle Wind.
Dramatizations include: the classic "Beauty & The Beast," & "Cabbage Soup," an updated musical play based on the Rapunzel story.

Cabbages & Kings. unabr. ed. O. Henry. Read by Lloyd James. 5 cass. (Running Time: 7 hrs.). 1997. 39.95 (978-0-7861-1173-2(9), 1961) Blckstn Audio.
Several stories, set in a fictional country called Coralio in Central America, a banana republic where larceny is rampant & revolution lurking. It is a cutting satire of contemporary politics & prejudices.

Cabbages & Kings. unabr. ed. O. Henry. Read by Sean Pratt. (Running Time: 25200 sec.). 2007. audio compact disk 29.95 (978-0-7861-6215-4(5)); audio compact disk & audio compact disk 55.00 (978-0-7861-6214-7(7)) Blckstn Audio.

Cabeza Y No Cola. Daniel Cipolla. 2004. audio compact disk 18.99 (978-0-88113-628-9(X)) Grupo Nelson.

Cabin B-13: Bill & Brenda Leslie & The Bride Vanishes. Perf. by Arnold Moss et al. 1 cass. (Running Time: 1 hr.). 2001. 6.98 (2193) Radio Spirits.

Cabin in the Clearing see Robert Frost in Recital

Cabinet of Curiosities. abr. ed. Douglas Preston & Lincoln Child. Read by Rene Auberjonois. (Pendergast Ser.: No. 3). (ENG.). 2005. 14.98 (978-1-59483-367-0(2)) Pub: Hachet Audio. Dist(s): HachBkGrp

Cabinet of Curiosities. abr. ed. Douglas Preston & Lincoln Child. Read by Rene Auberjonois. 5 CDs. (Running Time: 6 hrs.). No. 3. (ENG.). 2009. audio compact disk 19.98 (978-1-60024-213-7(8)) Pub: Hachet Audio. Dist(s): HachBkGrp

Cabinet of Curiosities. unabr. ed. Douglas Preston & Lincoln Child. 8 cass. (Running Time: 12 hrs.). (Pendergast Ser.: No. 3). 2002. 96.00 (978-0-7366-8643-3(6)); audio compact disk 120.00 (978-0-7366-8644-0(4)) Books on Tape.
A gruesome discovery has just been made - an underground charnel house containing the bones of dozens of murder victims. Research reveals that a serial killer was at work in New York's notorious Five Points neighborhood in the 1880s, bent on prolonging his lifespan by any means. When a newspaper story on the old murders appears to ignite a new series of horrifyingly similar killings, panic overtakes New York City. Now, FBI agent Pendergast, journalist Bill Smithback, and archaeologist Nora Kelly join forces to protect themselves from a vicious killer. . .before they become the next victims.

Cabinet of Doctor Caligari. unabr. ed. Read by John De Lancie. Ed. by Yuri Rasovsky. 2 cass. (Running Time: 1 hr.). 2004. 14.95 (978-0-7861-2801-3(1), 3328); audio compact disk 15.00 (978-0-7861-8492-7(2), 3328) Blckstn Audio.

Cabinet of Dr. Caligari. Prod. by Yuri Rasovsky. 1 cass. (Running Time: 70 mins.). 2001. 12.95 (HTOE003) Lodestone Catalog.

Cabinet of Dr. Caligari. Yuri Rasovsky. Narrated by John De Lancie and a full cast. (Running Time: 1 hr. 30 mins.). (C). 2004. 17.95 (978-1-59912-625-8(7)) Iofy Corp.

Cabinet of Wonders. unabr. ed. Marie Rutkoski. Read by Lorelei King. 6 CDs. (Running Time: 7 hrs. 0 mins. 0 sec.). (Kronos Chronicles: Bk. 1). (J). (gr. 5). 2008. audio compact disk 29.95 (978-1-4272-0548-3(5)) Pub: Macmill Audio. Dist(s): Macmillan

Cable Advertising: A Surprising & Exciting Alternative Medium. 1 cass. (America's Supermarket Showcase '96 Ser.). 1996. 11.00 (NGA96-048) Sound Images.

Cable Car Ride. abr. ed. Robert A. Monroe. Read by Robert A. Monroe. (Mind Food Ser.). 1984. 14.95 (978-1-56102-401-8(5)) Inter Indus.
Gently guides from sleep to wakefulness.

Caboose Who Got Loose. unabr. ed. Bill Peet. 1 cass. (Running Time: 15 min.). Dramatization. (Carry-Along Book & Cassette Favorites Ser.). (ENG., (J). (gr. k-3). 1993. pap. bk. 10.95 (978-0-395-66501-5(9), 493324) HM Harcourt.

Cabronas: De Tapete A Chica de Ensueno. abr. ed. Sherry Argov. Narrated by Anna Silvetti. 2007. audio compact disk 24.95 (978-1-933499-41-3(9)) Fonolibro Inc.

Cache of Jewels. unabr. ed. Ruth Heller. 1 cass. (Running Time: 10 min.). (J). (gr. k-5). 1989. bk. 17.95 (978-0-8045-6561-5(9), 6561) Spoken Arts.
A fine introduction to a specialized part of speech, the collective noun. Reading Rainbow Review Book. American Bookseller Pick of the Lists.

Cacophony: A Captain Sulu Adventure. J. J. Molloy. (Star Trek Ser.). 2004. 7.95 (978-0-7435-4253-1(3)) Pub: S&S Audio. Dist(s): S and S Inc

Cactus & Cowpies. Poems. Phil Kennington. Read by Phil Kennington. 1 cass. 1998. 8.00 (978-1-890672-12-6(2)) Phil Don.
Selected poems from "Trail Dust".

Cactus Cafe. 1 cass. (Running Time: 35 min.). (J). (gr. k-4). 2001. pap. bk. 19.95 (SP 7001C) Kimbo Educ.
As night falls, the desert comes alive. Meet kangaroo rats, kit foxes & long-nosed bats. Includes read along book.

Cactus Cafe: A Story of the Sonoran Desert. Kathleen Weidner Zoehfeld. Read by Randye Kaye. Illus. by Paul Mirocha. 1 cass. (Running Time: 12 min.). (Habitat Ser.). (J). (gr. 1-4). 1997. 5.00 (978-1-56899-431-4(1), C7001) Soundprints.
As the night falls, the Sonoran Desert comes alive around a giant saguaro cactus. Kangaroo rats hop across the sand in search of seeds; kit foxes slink through the sage brush; & long-nosed bats arrive from the hillside. This night is special as the giant saguaro is about to surprise them.

Cactus Cafe: A Story of the Sonoran Desert. Kathleen Weidner Zoehfeld. Illus. by Paul Mirocha. (Soundprints' Wild Habitats Ser.). (ENG.). (J). (gr. 1-4). 2005. 8.95 (978-1-59249-089-9(1), SC7001) Soundprints.

Cactus Island: A Stan Turner Mystery, bk. 7. William Manchee. Read by William Timnick. (ENG.). 2009. 12.00 (978-1-929976-59-1(3), TOP USA) Top Pubns.

Cada Nino (Every Child) Perf. by Tish Hinojosa. 1 cass. (Running Time: 41 mins.). (Family Ser.). (J). (ps-5). 1996. 9.98 (978-1-886767-11-9(4), 8032); audio compact disk 14.98 (978-1-886767-10-2(6), 8032) Rounder Records.
Acclaimed singer/songwriter Tish Hinojosa presents eleven bilingual songs for the younger generation. Some are playful, some tell stories & some are lullabies, but all of the songs will teach children & adults about Tex-Mex culture & traditions. Each song is sung in both Spanish & English & the printed lyrics in each language are also included.

CADASIL - A Bibliography & Dictionary for Physicians, Patients, & Genome Researchers. Compiled by Icon Group International, Inc. Staff. 2007. ring bd. 28.95 (978-0-497-11343-8(0)) Icon Grp.

Caddie Woodlawn. Carol Ryrie Brink. Narrated by Roslyn Alexander. 6 CDs. (Running Time: 6 hrs. 15 mins.). (gr. 5 up). audio compact disk 58.00 (978-1-4025-0470-9(5)) Recorded Bks.

Caddie Woodlawn, unabr. ed. Carol Ryrie Brink. Narrated by Roslyn Alexander. 5 pieces. (Running Time: 6 hrs. 15 mins.). (gr. 5 up). 1994. 44.00 (978-0-7887-0016-3(2), 94215E7) Recorded Bks.
In spite of her mother's best efforts, Caddie was as wild as the wind, playing freely & rambunctiously with her two brothers in the Wisconsin backwoods. But living on the edge of civilization has its risks, too. And when Indians threaten to attach the settlers, it is Caddie's resourcefulness & bravery that save the day.

Caddy for Life. abr. ed. John Feinstein. (ENG.). 2005. 14.98 (978-1-59483-231-4(5)) Pub: Hachet Audio. Dist(s): HachBkGrp

Caddy for Life: The Bruce Edwards Story. abr. ed. John Feinstein. (Running Time: 3 hrs.). (ENG.). 2009. 38.98 (978-1-60024-581-7(1)) Pub: Hachet Audio. Dist(s): HachBkGrp

Cadeau pour Toi. pap. bk. 16.95 (978-88-8148-815-5(9)) Pub: Europ Lang Inst ITA. Dist(s): Distribks Inc

Cadillac Desert Pt. 1: The American West & Its Disappearing Water. unabr. collector's ed. Marc P. Reisner. Read by Wolfram Kandinsky. 11 cass. (Running Time: 16 hrs. 30 min.). 1990. 88.00 (978-0-7366-1707-9(8), 2550-A) Books on Tape.
The story of the American West is one of the relentless quest to control & allocate nature's most common & the West's most precious, resource: water. The early settlers were lured by free land. But there was not enough water to sustain them & they drifted on.

Cadillac Desert Pt. 2: The American West & Its Disappearing Water. collector's ed. Marc P. Reisner. Read by Wolfram Kandinsky. 11 cass. (Running Time: 16 hrs 30 min.). 1990. 88.00 (978-0-7366-1708-6(6), 2550-B) Books on Tape.
The story of the American West is one of the relentless quest to control & allocate nature's most common, & the West's most precious, resource: water. Cadillac Desert recounts this dramatic saga. The early settlers were lured by free land. But there was not enough water to sustain them & they drifted on. Only the Mormons stayed, carefully tending a system of irrigation canals that tempered perpetual drought.

Cadillac Jack: A Novel. unabr. collector's ed. Larry McMurtry. Read by Wolfram Kandinsky. 10 cass. (Running Time: 15 hrs.). 1986. 80.00 (978-0-7366-0727-8(7), 1684) Books on Tape.
The hero of "Cadillac Jack" is a rodeo cowboy turned antique dealer whose gypsy life centers on his classic Cadillac. In it he wanders the Texas flatlands, roams back roads looking for flea markets, samples Washingtons's political high life. The cast of characters includes a beautiful social climber, a high-rolling Texan, D.C. politicians & the kind of attractive young women who seem to have their minds on something else when they're making love.

Cadillac Jukebox. abr. ed. James Lee Burke. Read by Will Patton. 2 cass. (Running Time: 3 hrs.). (Dave Robicheaux Ser.). 1998. 14.40 (978-0-671-57732-2(8), 908764, Audioworks) S&S Audio.

Cadillac Jukebox. unabr. ed. James Lee Burke. Narrated by Mark Hammer. 9 cass. (Running Time: 12 hrs. 30 mins.). (Dave Robicheaux Ser.). 1996. 83.00 (978-0-7887-0725-4(6), 94902E7) Recorded Bks.
Dave Robicheaux clashes with mob bosses, corrupt police chiefs & even dirtier politicians in this murder case nearly three decades old.

Cadillac Orpheus. unabr. ed. Solon Timothy Woodward. Read by Dion Graham. 7 CDs. (Running Time: 8 hrs. 45 mins.). (ENG., 2008. audio compact disk 32.95 (978-1-59887-584-3(1), 1598875841) Pub: HighBridge. Dist(s): Workman Pub

Caedmon Poetry Collection: A Century of Poets Reading Their Work. abr. ed. Poems. Compiled by Caedmon Players Staff. 3 CDs. (Running Time: 3 hrs. 30 mins.). 2000. audio compact disk 29.95 (978-0-694-52278-1(3)) HarperCollins Pubs.

Caedmon Treasury of Modern Poets Reading Their Own Poetry. unabr. ed. Poems. Contrib. by Joan Aiken et al. 2 cass. (Running Time: 1 hr. 35 mins.). Incl. After Apple-Picking. Robert Frost. Read by Robert Frost. (CDL5 2006); Birches. Robert Frost. Perf. by Robert Frost. (CDL5 2006); Coole & Ballylee. (CDL5 2006); Epistle to Be Left in the Earth. Archibald Macleish. Read by Archibald Macleish. (CDL5 2006); Fern Hill. Dylan Thomas. (CDL5 2006); Groundhog. Richard Eberhart. Read by Richard Eberhart. (CDL5 2006); I Think Continually of Those. Stephen Spender. Read by Stephen Spender. (CDL5 2006); Idea of Order at Key West. Wallace Stevens. Read by Wallace Stevens. (CDL5 2006); If I Told Him: A Completed Portrait of Picasso. Gertrude Stein. Read by Gertrude Stein. (CDL5 2006); In Memory of W. B. Yeats. W. H. Auden. Read by W. H. Auden. (CDL5 2006); Innisfree. (CDL5 2006); Love Calls Us to the Things of This World. Richard Wilbur. Perf. by Richard Wilbur. (CDL5 2006); Missing Dates. William Empson. Read by William Empson. (CDL5 2006); Moeurs Contemporaines. Ezra Pound. Read by Ezra Pound. (CDL5 2006); Poem to My Son: To Juan at the Winter Solstice. Robert Graves. Read by Robert Graves. (CDL5 2006); Refugees. (CDL5 2006); Refusal to Mourn the Death, by Fire, of a Child in London. Dylan Thomas. Read by Dylan Thomas. (CDL5 2006); Seafarer. William Carlos Williams. Read by William Carlos Williams. (CDL5 2006); Seascape. (CDL5 2006); Song of the Old Mother. W. B. Yeats. Read by W. B. Yeats. (CDL5 2006); Still Falls the Rain. Edith Sitwell. Read by Edith Sitwell. (CDL5 2006); Sweet Spring Is Your. e e cummings. Read by e e cummings. (CDL5 2006); Tetelestai. Conrad Aiken. Read by Conrad Aiken. (CDL5 2006); Turfstacks. Louis MacNeice. Perf. by Louis MacNeice. (CDL5 2006); Waste Land. T. S. Eliot. Read by T. S. Eliot. (CDL5 2006); What Are Years. Marianne Moore. Read by Marianne Moore. (CDL5 2006); What If a Much of a Which of a Wind. e e cummings. Read by e e cummings. (CDL5 2006); 1993. 18.00 (978-0-694-50370-4(3), CDL5 2006) HarperCollins Pubs.

Caedmon's Call: Forty Acres. Perf. by Caedmon's Call Staff. 1 cass. 1998. 10.98 (978-0-7601-2441-3(8)); audio compact disk 16.98 (978-0-7601-2442-0(6)) Provident Music.
The intense blend of acoustic folk, pop & alternative.

Caedmon's Hymn see Beowulf & Other Poetry

Caesar. Colleen McCullough. (Masters of Rome Ser.: No. 5). 2004. 15.95 (978-0-7435-4247-0(9)) Pub: S&S Audio. Dist(s): S and S Inc

Caesar, Pt. 1. unabr. ed. Colleen McCullough. Read by Donada Peters. 12 cass. (Running Time: 18 hrs.). (Masters of Rome Ser.: No. 5). 1998. 96.00 (978-0-7366-4086-2(X), 4595-A) Books on Tape.
Rome's greatest soldier prepares to crush the opposition.

Caesar, Pt. 2. unabr. ed. Colleen McCullough. Read by Donada Peters. 11 cass. (Running Time: 17 hrs. 30 min.). (Masters of Rome Ser.: No. 5). 1998. 88.00 (978-0-7366-4087-9(8), 4595-B) Books on Tape.

Caesar: On Deaf Ears. Loren Spiotta-DiMare. Read by Tom Chapin. (J). (gr. 1-4). 1997. bk. 34.95 (978-1-882728-89-3(0)) Benefactory.
An animal-shelter employee finds inventive ways to train a deaf dog.

Caesar: On Deaf Ears. Loren Spiotta-DiMare. Narrated by Tom Chapin. (Humane Society of the United States Animal Tales Ser.). (J). (gr. 1-4). 1997. pap. bk. 19.95 (978-1-882728-91-6(2)); pap. bk. 9.95 (978-1-882728-93-0(9)) Benefactory.

Caesar: The Life Story of a Panda-Leopard. unabr. ed. Patrick O'Brian. 2 cass. (Running Time: 3 hrs.). (J). 2001. 24.00 (978-0-7366-6367-0(3)) Books on Tape.

Caesar & Christ, Pt. B. unabr. collector's ed. Will Durant & Ariel Durant. Read by Alexander Adams. 11 cass. (Running Time: 16 hrs. 30 min.). (Story of Civilization Ser.: Vol. 3). 1994. 88.00 (978-0-7366-2856-3(8), 3563-B) Books on Tape.
The Roman age, from infancy to empire, with an account of the advent of Jesus of Nazareth.

Caesar & Cleopatra. George Bernard Shaw. Narrated by Kimberly Schraf. 3 cass. (Running Time: 4 hrs.). 2000. 16.95 (978-1-55685-651-8(2)) Audio Bk Con.
The Emperor of Rome & the Queen of the Nile as only Shaw could have imagined them! He is a self-questioning cynic in mid-life crisis; she is an imperious & impertinent child on the threshold of womanhood. Much mirth & scathing skewering ensue. The recording includes Shaw's brilliant prologues & post-text notes.

***Caesar & Me.** 2010. audio compact disk (978-1-59171-221-3(1)) Falcon Picture.

Caesaris Commentarii de Bello Gallico (From Books I (Partial) IV, & V) Hans Orberg. 2004. 8.95 (978-87-90696-06-1(9)) Pub: Domus Latina DNK. Dist(s): Focus Pub-R Pullins

Caesar's Legion -Lib. (Running Time: 11 hrs. 0 mins.). 2005. 65.95 (978-0-7861-3018-4(0)); audio compact disk 81.00 (978-0-7861-8085-1(4)) Blckstn Audio.

Caesar's Legion -Lib: Mp3. (Running Time: 11 hrs. 0 mins.). 2005. audio compact disk 29.95 (978-0-7861-8207-7(5)) Blckstn Audio.

Caesar's Women. Colleen McCullough. (Masters of Rome Ser.: No. 4). 2004. 15.95 (978-0-7435-4248-7(7)) Pub: S&S Audio. Dist(s): S and S Inc

Caesar's Women, Pt. 1. unabr. ed. Colleen McCullough. Read by Donada Peters. 11 cass. (Running Time: 16 hrs. 30 min.). (Masters of Rome Ser.: No. 4). 1996. 88.00 (978-0-7366-3311-6(1), 3964-A) Books on Tape.
Caesar was lover to Servilia, mother of young Brutus who did not escape the destructive influence of their affair. He was patriarch to his mother, his second wife, his daughter & Rome's revered Vestal Virgins - all of whom suffered the misfortune of loving a man who had no love to give them.

Caesar's Women, Pt. 2. unabr. ed. Colleen McCullough. Read by Donada Peters. 10 cass. (Running Time: 15 hrs.). (Masters of Rome Ser.: No. 4). 1996. 80.00 (3964-B) Books on Tape.

Cafe Nevo. collector's ed. Barbara Rogan. Read by Anna Fields. 7 cass. (Running Time: 10 hrs. 30 min.). 2000. 56.00 (978-0-7366-5514-9(X)) Books on Tape.
Cafe Nevo is a Tel Aviv gathering place for artists, politicians, lovers, Jews & Arabs, the old & the young, conservatives & radicals. It is presided over by Emmanuel Sternholz, the proprietor, waiter whose unblinking gaze takes in the tangled web of destinies & desires spun out around him. In this comic, tragic & compelling mosaic of intertwined lives, Barbara Rogan has created a dazzling work of fiction & a marvelously illuminating mirror of Israel today.

Cafe on the Nile. unabr. ed. Bartle Bull. Read by Fred Williams. (Running Time: 97200 sec.). (Anton Rider Trilogy). 2007. 124.95 (978-1-4332-0230-8(1)); audio compact disk 44.95 (978-1-4332-0232-2(8)); audio compact disk 140.00 (978-1-4332-0231-5(X)) Blckstn Audio.

Cafe Tempest: Adventures on a Small Greek Island. Barbara Bonfigli. 2010. audio compact disk 17.95 (978-0-9819835-0-9(2)) Tell Me Pr.

Cage of Delirium. F. Wesley Schneider. (Dungeon Crawl Classics Ser.). 2006. pap. bk. 24.99 (978-0-9779602-0-0(X)) Good Games.

Cage of Stars. abr. ed. Jacquelyn Mitchard. Read by Hope Davis. (Running Time: 6 hrs.). (ENG.). 2006. 14.98 (978-1-59483-513-1(6)) Pub: Hachet Audio. Dist(s): HachBkGrp

Cage of Stars. abr. ed. Jacquelyn Mitchard. Read by Hope Davis. (Running Time: 6 hrs.). (ENG.). 2009. 44.98 (978-1-60788-119-3(5)) Pub: Hachet Audio. Dist(s): HachBkGrp

Cagney: A Biography. unabr. collector's ed. John McCabe. Read by John Edwardson. 11 cass. (Running Time: 16 hrs. 30 mins.). 1999. 88.00 (978-0-7366-4442-6(3), 4887) Books on Tape.
Explosive on screen, biography reveals Cagney's other side; quiet & deeply private, a poet, painter & environmentalist.

CAI & BI: Effective, Efficient Instruction. 2 cass. (Running Time: 2 hrs.). 1990. 16.00 Recorded Res.

***Cailiffs of Baghdad, Georgia: A Novel.** unabr. ed. Mary Helen Stefaniak. (Running Time: 11 hrs. 5 mins.). (ENG.). 2010. 29.95 (978-1-4417-7221-3(9)); audio compact disk 32.95 (978-1-4417-7220-6(0)) Blckstn Audio.

***Cailiffs of Baghdad, Georgia: A Novel.** unabr. ed. Mary Helen Stefaniak. Read by To be Announced. (Running Time: 11 hrs. 5 mins.). (ENG.). 2010. 72.95 (978-1-4417-7218-3(9)); audio compact disk 105.00 (978-1-4417-7219-0(7)) Blckstn Audio.

Caillou's Favorite Songs. 1 cass. (Running Time: 34 min.). 2003. pap. bk. 9.98 (978-0-7379-0288-4(4)) Rhino Enter.

Caillou's Favorite Songs. 1 CD. (Running Time: 34 min.). (J). 2003. pap. bk. 13.98 (978-0-7379-0287-7(6)) Rhino Enter.

Cain. unabr. ed. James Byron Huggins. Read by Barrett Whitener. 12 cass. (Running Time: 18 hrs.). 1997. 96.00 (978-0-7366-3844-9(X), 4563) Books on Tape.
A recreation of the Frankenstein tale. Every general dreams of a soldier who can carry everything he needs, travel far & fast, kill multitudes, & survive to fight another day.

Cain & Abel, Vol. 2. Orlando Rodriguez. 1 cass. (Sabio Y Prudente Ser.). (SPA.). (J). 2002. 5.99 (978-0-8254-0988-2(8), Edit Portavoz) Kregel.

Cain Conversion. unabr. ed. Richard Aellen. Read by Bill Weideman. (Running Time: 13 hrs.). 2008. 39.25 (978-1-4233-7202-8(6), 9781423372028, BADLE); 24.95 (978-1-4233-7199-1(2), 9781423371991, Brilliance MP3); 39.25 (978-1-4233-7200-4(X), 9781423372004, Brinc Audio MP3 Lib); 24.95 (978-1-4233-7201-1(8), 9781423372011, BAD) Brilliance Audio.

Caine Mutiny Court-Martial. unabr. ed. Herman Wouk. Read by David Selby. (YA). 2008. 34.99 (978-1-60514-982-0(9)) Find a World.

Caine Mutiny Court-Martial. unabr. ed. Herman Wouk. Perf. by David Selby et al. 2 CDs. (Running Time: 2 hrs. 1 min.). Dramatization. 2001. audio compact disk 25.95 (978-1-58081-218-4(X), CDWTA12) Pub: L A Theatre. Dist(s): NetLibrary CO
Gives great insight of a sailor's life during the war. Read by full cast.

Caine Mutiny Court-Martial. unabr. ed. Herman Wouk. Perf. by David Selby et al. 2 cass. (Running Time: 2 hrs. 1 min.). Dramatization. 2001. 23.95 (978-1-58081-203-0(1), WTA12) L A Theatre.

Cairo Jim amidst the petticoats of Artemis. Geoffrey McSkimming. Read by Geoffrey McSkimming. (Running Time: 4 hrs. 55 mins.). (Cairo Jim Ser.). (J). 2009. 64.99 (978-1-74214-167-1(6), 9781742141671) Pub: Bolinda Pubng AUS. Dist(s): Bolinda Pub Inc

Cairo Jim amidst the petticoats of Artemis. unabr. ed. Geoffrey McSkimming. Read by Geoffrey McSkimming. (Running Time: 4 hrs. 55 mins.). (Cairo Jim Ser.). (J). 2008. audio compact disk 63.95 (978-1-74093-725-2(2)) Pub: Bolinda Pubng AUS. Dist(s): Bolinda Pub Inc

Cairo Jim & Doris in Search of Martenarter. unabr. ed. Geoffrey McSkimming. 4 CDs. (Running Time: 4 hrs. 8 mins.). (Cairo Jim Ser.). (YA). 2004. audio compact disk 57.95 (978-1-74093-117-5(3)) Pub: Bolinda Pubng AUS. Dist(s): Bolinda Pub Inc

Cairo Jim & the Alabastron of Forgotton Gods. unabr. ed. Geoffrey McSkimming. Read by Geoffrey McSkimming. 5 CDs. (Running Time: 5 hrs. 15 mins.). (Cairo Jim Ser.). (J). (gr. 3-5). 2008. audio compact disk 63.95 (978-1-74093-328-5(1)) Pub: Bolinda Pubng AUS. Dist(s): Bolinda Pub Inc

Cairo Jim & the Astragals of Angkor. unabr. ed. Geoffrey McSkimming. Read by Geoffrey McSkimming. (Running Time: 15600 sec.). (Cairo Jim Ser.). 2008. audio compact disk 57.95 (978-1-921334-58-0(4), 9781921334580) Pub: Bolinda Pubng AUS. Dist(s): Bolinda Pub Inc

Cairo Jim & the chaos from Crete. Geoffrey McSkimming. Read by Geoffrey McSkimming. (Running Time: 4 hrs. 30 mins.). (J). 2009. 59.99 (978-1-74214-415-3(2), 9781742144153) Pub: Bolinda Pubng AUS. Dist(s): Bolinda Pub Inc

Cairo Jim & the Chaos from Crete. unabr. ed. Geoffrey McSkimming. Read by Geoffrey McSkimming. 4 CDs. (Running Time: 4 hrs. 30 mins.). (Cairo Jim Ser.). (YA). 2003. audio compact disk 57.95 (978-1-74093-136-6(X)) Pub: Bolinda Pubng AUS. Dist(s): Bolinda Pub Inc

Cairo Jim & the quest for the Quetzal Queen - NYP on HOLD. unabr. ed. Geoffrey McSkimming. Read by Geoffrey McSkimming. (Running Time: 5 hrs.). (Cairo Jim Ser.). (J). 2009. audio compact disk 57.95 (978-1-74093-336-0(2)) Pub: Bolinda Pubng AUS. Dist(s): Bolinda Pub Inc

Cairo Jim & the rorting of Rameses' Regalia. unabr. ed. Geoffrey McSkimming. Read by Geoffrey McSkimming. (Running Time: 4 hrs. 30 mins.). (Cairo Jim Ser.). (YA). 2009. audio compact disk 57.95 (978-1-74093-706-1(6)) Pub: Bolinda Pubng AUS. Dist(s): Bolinda Pub Inc

***Cairo Jim & the secret sepulchre of the Sphinx.** Geoffrey McSkimming. Read by Geoffrey McSkimming. (Running Time: 5 hrs. 20 mins.). (Cairo Jim Ser.). (J). 2010. 64.99 (978-1-74214-637-9(6), 9781742146379) Pub: Bolinda Pubng AUS. Dist(s): Bolinda Pub Inc

Cairo Jim & the Secret Sepulchre of the Sphinx. unabr. ed. Geoffrey McSkimming. Read by Geoffrey McSkimming. (Running Time: 5 hrs. 20 mins.). (Cairo Jim Ser.). (YA). 2009. audio compact disk 63.95 (978-1-74093-566-1(7)) Pub: Bolinda Pubng AUS. Dist(s): Bolinda Pub Inc

Cairo Jim & the sumptuous stash of Silenus. Geoffrey McSkimming. Read by Geoffrey McSkimming. (Running Time: 4 hrs. 25 mins.). (Cairo Jim Ser.). (J). 2009. 59.99 (978-1-74214-416-0(0), 9781742144160) Pub: Bolinda Pubng AUS. Dist(s): Bolinda Pub Inc

Cairo Jim & the Sumptuous Stash of Silenus. unabr. ed. Geoffrey McSkimming. Read by Geoffrey McSkimming. 4 CDs. (Running Time: 4 hrs. 25 mins.). (Cairo Jim Ser.). (J). (gr. 3-8). 2008. audio compact disk 57.95 (978-1-74093-833-4(X)) Pub: Bolinda Pubng AUS. Dist(s): Bolinda Pub Inc

***Cairo Jim at the crossroads of Orpheus.** Geoffrey McSkimming. Read by Geoffrey McSkimming. (Running Time: 4 hrs. 5 mins.). (J). 2009. 39.99 (978-1-74214-417-7(9), 9781742144177) Pub: Bolinda Pubng AUS. Dist(s): Bolinda Pub Inc

Cairo Jim at the crossroads of Orpheus. unabr. ed. Geoffrey McSkimming. Read by Geoffrey McSkimming. (Running Time: 4 hrs. 5 mins.). (Cairo Jim Ser.). (J). 2008. audio compact disk 57.95 (978-1-74093-905-8(0)) Pub: Bolinda Pubng AUS. Dist(s): Bolinda Pub Inc

Cairo Jim on the Trail of Chacha Munchos. unabr. ed. Geoffrey McSkimming. Read by Geoffrey McSkimming. 4 CDs. (Running Time: 4 hrs. 50 mins.). (Cairo Jim Ser.). (YA). 2004. audio compact disk 57.95 (978-1-74093-121-2(1)) Pub: Bolinda Pubng AUS. Dist(s): Bolinda Pub Inc

Cairo Jim on the trail to Chacha Muchos. Geoffrey McSkimming. Read by Geoffrey McSkimming. (Running Time: 4 hrs. 50 mins.). (J). 2009. 59.99 (978-1-74214-414-6(4), 9781742144146) Pub: Bolinda Pubng AUS. Dist(s): Bolinda Pub Inc

Cairo Jim on the Trail to Chacha Munchos. unabr. ed. Geoffrey McSkimming. Read by Geoffrey McSkimming. 3 cass. (Running Time: 4 hrs. 50 mins.). (Cairo Jim Ser.). (YA). 2004. 28.00 (978-1-74030-874-8(3)) Pub: Bolinda Pubng AUS. Dist(s): Bolinda Pub Inc

Caise Ceoil: Classics from the CIC Traditional Irish Music Collection. (ENG.). 2001. audio compact disk 20.95 (978-0-8023-8146-0(4)) Pub: Clo Iar-Chonnachta IRL. Dist(s): Dufour

***Caislean Ui Neill.** Coilin Cliseam. (ENG.). 1989. 11.95 (978-0-8023-7018-1(7)) Pub: Clo Iar-Chonnachta IRL. Dist(s): Dufour

Caja de Herramientas. Robert E. Logan & Steve L. Ogne. (SPA.). ring bd. 61.45 (978-1-55883-110-0(X), 216785) Pub: CRC Wrld Lit. Dist(s): FaithAliveChr

Cajas de Carton see Circuit: Stories from the Life of a Migrant Child

Cajas de Carton. Francisco Jiménez. 4 cass. (Running Time: 3 hrs. 30 min.).Tr. of Circuit. (SPA.). (YA). (gr. 5 up). 2001. 24.95 (978-1-883332-45-7(1)) Audio Bkshelf.
Poignant stories about growing up in a migrant Mexican American family in California in the 1940's.

Cajas de Carton. unabr. ed. Francisco Jiménez. Read by Adrian Vargas. 4 cass. (Running Time: 3 hrs. 30 mins.).Tr. of Circuit. 2001. 24.95 Audio Bkshelf.

Cajas de Carton. unabr. ed. Francisco Jiménez. Read by Adrian Vargas. 3 CDs. (Running Time: 3 hrs.30 mins.).Tr. of Circuit. (SPA.). (YA). 2001. audio compact disk 29.95 (978-1-883332-72-3(9)) Audio Bkshelf.

Cajita De Hueso. Toledo. audio compact disk 12.95 (978-0-8219-3808-9(8)) EMC-Paradigm.

Cajun Country, U. S. A. 1 cass. (Running Time: 30 min.). (J). 1986. 9.95 BackPax Int.
The spirited Cajun lifestyle is captured in a visit to the bayous of Louisiana.

Cajun Country, U. S. A. Prod. by Janus Adams. 1 cass. (Running Time: 30 mins.). (J). 1986. 12.95 (978-0-930399-00-9(5)) BackPax Int.
The spirited Cajun lifestyle is captured in a visit to the bayous of Louisiana.

Cajun Dance Hall Special - Accordion Edition. Rounder Records Staff. 1995. pap. bk. 19.95 (978-0-7866-1148-5(0), 95313P); pap. bk. 24.95 (978-0-7866-1147-8(2), 95313CDP) Mel Bay.

Cajun Dance Hall Special - Fiddle Edition. Rounder Records Staff. 1995. pap. bk. 24.95 (978-0-7866-1286-4(X), 95364CDP); pap. bk. 19.95 (978-0-7866-1287-1(8), 95364P) Mel Bay.

Cajun Fairy Tales. J. J. Reneaux. 1 cass. (Running Time: 59 mins.). (J). 1996. 12.00 (978-0-87483-439-0(2)) Pub: August Hse. Dist(s): Natl Bk Netwk
Offers an insight into a colorful culture found entirely within our own borders. This distinctive people is a blend of French, Indian, Spanish, African & Irish cultures, creating a "gumbo of folklore unique in American culture".

Cajun Folktales. Perf. by J. J. Reneaux. 1 cass. (Running Time: 57 mins.). (American Storytelling Ser.). (gr. k-3). 1994. 12.00 (978-0-87483-383-6(3)) Pub: August Hse. Dist(s): Natl Bk Netwk
Eight spicy selections served up from the rich Louisiana "melting pot." Cajun stories incorporate characters & elements from French, Indian, Spanish, African & Irish culture, creating a "gumbo of folklore unique in American culture".

Cajun for Kids! Perf. by Papillion. 1 cass. (Running Time: 34 mins.). (J). (ps-5). 1998. 9.98 (978-1-56628-162-1(8)); audio compact disk 15.98 (978-1-56628-161-4(X)) MFLP CA.
Cajun musician "Papillion" sings 13 songs accompanied by several authentic Cajun instruments. On many songs, children also participate in the singing.

Cajun for Kids! Papillion. 1 cass., 1 CD. (J). 7.98 (MLP 75309); audio compact disk 11.98 (MLP 75309) NewSound.
Unique & unforgettable cultural celebration of life.

Cajun French Stories for Children: Clovis Crawfish & His Friends; Clovis Crawfish & Simeon Suce-Fleur. unabr. ed. Mary Alice Fontenot. 1 cass. (Running Time: 20 mins.). (J). 14.95 (CFR102) J Norton Pubs.
Introduces children to the natural world & the bayous. Simple French songs & French-Arcadian words of everyday Cajun life are interspersed throughout these stories read in English to the delight of adults & children alike.

Cajun French Stories for Children: Clovis Crawfish & Michelle Mantis; Clovis Crawfish & Etienne Escargot. unabr. ed. Mary Alice Fontenot. 1 cass. (Running Time: 20 mins.). (J). 14.95 (CFR103) J Norton Pubs.

Cajun Humor from the Heart. Narrated by Tommy J. Breaux. 2 cass. (Running Time: 115 mins.). (ENG.). 1997. 14.95 (978-1-56554-188-7(X)) Pelican.

Cajun Night Before Christmas: Gaston the Green-Nosed Alligator. David R. Davis. Illus. by James Rice. Narrated by Tommy Joe Breaux. 1 cass. (Running Time: 20 mins.). (Night Before Christm Ser.). (ENG.). (J). (gr. k-3). 1998. 9.95 (978-1-56554-189-4(8)) Pelican.

Cajun Night before Christmas: With Gaston the Green-Nosed Alligator. Narrated by Coleen Salley. (Night Before Christm Ser.). (J). 1996. 9.95 (978-1-56554-269-3(X)) Pelican.

Cajun Night before Christmas: With Gaston the Green-Nosed Alligator. Coleen Salley. 1 cass. (Night Before Christm Ser.). (J). 1998. 9.95 (978-1-56554-388-1(2)) Pelican.

Cajun Night before Christmas; Cajun Night after Christmas. Narrated by Coleen Salley. (Running Time: 20 mins.). (J). 2009. audio compact disk 15.95 (978-1-58980-722-8(7)) Pelican.

Cajun Night Before Christmas /Gaston the Green-Nosed Alligator CD. Narrated by Tommy Breaux. (Running Time: 25 mins.). (ENG.). (J). 2009. audio compact disk 15.95 (978-1-58980-706-8(5)) Pelican.

Cajun Self-Taught: Learning to Speak the Cajun Language. Excerpts. Jules O. Daigle. 4 cass. (Running Time: 3HRS.). 1992. 16.00 (978-0-9614245-5-8(9)) Swallow Pubns.

Cajun Self-Taught: Learning to Speak the Cajun Language. Excerpts. Jules O. Daigle. 3 CDs. (Running Time: 3HRS). 1996. audio compact disk 22.00 (978-0-9614245-6-5(7)) Swallow Pubns.
Provides listeners actual pronunciations of the words and phrases in the book.

Cajun Social Music. Gerard Dole. 1 cass. (Running Time: 35 mins.). 1990. (0-9307-400060-9307-40006-2-5); audio compact disk (0-9307-40006-2-5) Smithsonian Folkways.
Includes performances by Abshire, Duhon, Savoy, Courville & others.

Cajun Spice for Accordion. Rounder Records Staff. Arranged by Larry Hallar. 1 cass. 1996. pap. bk. 19.95 (978-0-7866-1690-9(3), 95711P); pap. bk. 24.95 (978-0-7866-1689-3(X), 95711CDP) Mel Bay.

Cajun Stories My Granpa Tole Me. Narrated by Tommy Breaux. 2 cass. (Running Time: 2 hrs.). (ENG.). 1999. 14.95 (978-1-56554-643-1(1)) Pelican.

Cakes & Ale. unabr. ed. W. Somerset Maugham. Read by James Saxon. 6 cass. (Running Time: 6 hrs.). 1993. bk. 54.95 (978-0-7451-6149-5(9)) AudioGO.

Cakes & Ale. unabr. collector's ed. W. Somerset Maugham. Read by Erik Bauersfeld. 7 cass. (Running Time: 10 hrs. 30 min.). 1980. 56.00 (978-0-7366-0217-4(8), 1215) Books on Tape.
"Cakes & Ale" is a short novel which dissects the English Literary world. "Up at the Villa" is the romantic tale of a beautiful young English widow who is living in a village outside Florence recovering after the death of her husband. This being Italy, the young & attractive widow receives proposals from two men in the same evening.

Cakes & Ale: The Skeleton in the Cupboard. unabr. ed. W. Somerset Maugham. Narrated by Neil Hunt. 5 cass. (Running Time: 6 hrs. 30 mins.). 1987. 44.00 (978-1-55690-079-2(1), 87190E7) Recorded Bks.
A writer finds life imitating art when researching a biography.

Cakewalk. unabr. ed. Peter Feibleman. Read by Elaine Stritch & Bruce Davidson. 1 cass. (Running Time: 1 hr. 25 mins.). 2001. 20.95 (978-1-58081-163-7(9), TPT140) L A Theatre.

Cakewalk. unabr. ed. Peter Feibleman. Read by Elaine Stritch & Bruce Davison. 2 CDs. (Running Time: 1 hr. 25 mins.). 2002. audio compact disk 25.95 (978-1-58081-232-0(5), CDTPT140) L A Theatre.
Chronicles the tumultuous love affair of playwright Lillian Hellman and Peter Feibleman, a novelist and playwright 25 years her junior. Spanning more than two decades, the relationship ricochets between tenderness and rage, humor and woe.

Cakewalk. unabr. ed. Short Stories. Lee Smith. Narrated by Linda Stephens & Tom Stechschulte. 7 cass. (Running Time: 10 hrs.). 2000. 60.00 (978-0-7887-4066-4(0), 96163E7) Recorded Bks.
A collection of nine stories of Southern women's lives.

Cakras. Read by Chogyam Trungpa. 1 cass. 1971. 12.50 (A077) Vajradhatu.

Cal. unabr. ed. Bernard MacLaverty. Read by David Threlfall. 4 cass. (Running Time: 4 hrs.). 1999. 39.95 (978-0-7540-0372-4(8), CAB 1795) AudioGO.
For Cal, some of the choices are devastatingly simple: he can work in the abattoir that nauseates him or join the dole queue; he can brood on his past or plan a future with Marcella. Set amid the fear & violence of Ulster, Cal is a haunting love story in a land where tenderness & innocence can only flicker briefly in the dark.

Cal & the Amazing Anti-Gravity Machine. unabr. ed. Richard Hamilton. Read by Russell Boulter. Illus. by Sam Hearn. 1 CD. (Running Time: 4620 sec.). (J). (gr. 3-5). 2007. audio compact disk 9.95 (978-1-4056-5583-5(6), Chivers Child Audio) AudioGO.

Cal Ripken, Jr. Play Ball! unabr. ed. Cal Ripken, Jr. & Mike Bryan. Narrated by Jeff Woodman. Adapted by Gail Herman. 1 cass. (Running Time: 30 mins.). (gr. 3 up). 2000. 10.00 (978-0-7887-4014-5(8), 96135M5) Recorded Bks.
Cal Ripken, Jr. is an extraordinary baseball player. In 1995, he broke the record for playing the most consecutive games. He has played in 16 All-Star games & has won many honors & awards. All young readers who love baseball will find inspiration in this account of his life & career.

Cal Ripkin, Jr. Class set: Play Ball! Cal Ripkin, Jr. & Mike Bryan. Read by Jeff Woodman. 1 cass. (Running Time: 30 mins.). (YA). 2000. pap. bk. & stu. ed. 22.24 (978-0-7887-4093-0(8), 41102); 70.70 (978-0-7887-4094-7(6), 47095) Recorded Bks.

Calamity Town, unabr. ed. Ellery Queen. Read by Scott Harrison. 7 cass. (Running Time: 10 hrs.). 1998. 49.95 (978-0-7861-1292-0(1), 2193) Blckstn Audio.
Ellery Queen likes sophistication, savoir faire, & all the swinging assets of Manhattan & its environs. So what in the world is he doing in this unearthly place? It is the job of the famous detective to find out which of the Wrights is the town's poisoner. He must match his wits with a diabolically cunning & ruthless killer, while defending himself against a charge of murder.

Calamus see Twentieth-Century Poetry in English, No. 17, Walt Whitman Speaks for Himself

Calcium Channel Blockers in Clinical Practice. Moderated by August M. Watanabe. Contrib. by Carl J. Pepine & Michael D. Winniford. 1 cass. (Running Time: 90 min.). 1986. 12.00 (A8606) Amer Coll Phys.
This topic is discussed by a moderator & experts who offer differing opinions.

Calculated Risk. unabr. ed. Collin Wilcox. Read by Larry McKeever. 6 cass. (Running Time: 9 hrs.). (Frank Hastings Ser.). 1996. 48.00 (978-0-7366-3203-4(4), 3867) Books on Tape.
Is any secret safe in politics today? Howard Best, a promising senatorial candidate, confronts this question in the latest of the popular Frank Hastings mystery series. Hastings maneuvers with skill & caution through the world of California power politics. He finds intense ambition, huge egos, blackmail & murder as he seeks to solve a case once suspected to be a random gay-bashing.

Calculer. unabr. ed. Robert A. Monroe. Read by Roland Simon. 1 cass. (Running Time: 30 mins.). (Human Plus Ser.). (FRE.). 1993. 14.95 (978-1-56102-060-7(5)) Inter Indus.
Learn to balance the budget more easily.

Calculus. 5th ed. (C). 2002. audio compact disk 28.95 (978-0-534-39347-2(0)) Pub: Brooks-Cole. Dist(s): CENGAGE Learn

Calculus for Chemists: Solving Chemistry Related Problems Mathematically. Instructed by Charles L. Perrin. 6 cass. (Running Time: 6 hrs.). 480.00 incl. 185pp. manual. (85) Am Chemical.
Presents examples & problems to illustrate how calculus is used to solve chemistry-related problems.

Calculus: Graphical Numerical, Algebraic: Teachers Resource CD. Martha I. Finney et al. audio compact disk 18.97 (978-0-13-067817-1(1)) PH School.

Calculus: Graphical Numerical, Algebraic: TestWorks CD. Martha I. Finney et al. audio compact disk 49.97 (978-0-13-067825-6(2)) PH School.

Calculus of Consent. James Buchanan & Gordon Tullock. 1 cass. (Running Time: 60 mins.). 1987. 9.95 (978-0-945999-12-6(7)) Independent Inst.
Government Political & Bureaucratic Processes Are Inherently Determined by the Self-Interest Motivations of the Individuals Involved, Which Lead to Reducing Government to a Massive Series of Special Interest Rivalries.

***Calcutta Chromosome: A Novel of Fevers, Delirium & Discovery.** unabr. ed. Amitav Ghosh. (Running Time: 7 hrs.). 2010. 24.99 (978-1-4418-3496-6(6), 9781441834966, Brilliance MP3) Brilliance Audio.

***Calcutta Chromosome: A Novel of Fevers, Delirium & Discovery.** unabr. ed. Amitav Ghosh. Read by Simon Vance. (Running Time: 9 hrs.). 2010. 24.99 (978-1-4418-3498-0(2), 9781441834980, BAD); 39.97 (978-1-4418-3497-3(4), 9781441834973, Brinc Audio MP3 Lib); 39.97 (978-1-4418-3499-7(0), 9781441834997, BADLE); audio compact disk 29.99 (978-1-4418-3494-2(X), 9781441834942, Bril Audio CD Unabri); audio compact disk 89.97 (978-1-4418-3495-9(8), 9781441834959, BriAudCD Unabrid) Brilliance Audio.

Calcutta One. unabr. ed. Julian C. Hollick. 1 cass. (Running Time: 60 mins.). 1990. 15.00 (978-1-56709-035-2(4), 1071) Indep Broadcast.
Why Calcutta Lives; The Sparrows of Tollygunge; Santalal: Portrait of a Rickshawwallah; Jack Preger: The Pavement Doctor.

Calcutta Two. unabr. ed. Julian C. Hollick. 1 cass. (Running Time: 60 mins.). 1992. 15.00 (978-1-56709-036-9(2), 1073) Indep Broadcast.
The Musicians of Ram Bhagan Slum; The Festival of Durga Puja.

Caldecott Award Collection. unabr. ed. Alice Provensen et al. 66 vols. (Running Time: 54 mins.). (J). 1999. pap. bk. 91.95 (978-0-87499-489-6(6)) Live Oak Media.
Includes: "The Glorious Flight." "Madeline's Rescue," "Make Way for Ducklings," "Ox-Cart Man" & "The Snowy Day.".

Caldecott Honor Collection. unabr. ed. Rachel Isadora et al. 1010 vols. (Running Time: 1 hr. 38 mins.). (J). 1999. pap. bk. 152.95 (978-0-87499-706-4(2)) Live Oak Media.
Includes: "Ben's Trumpet," "Blueberries for Sal," "Crow Boy," "Madeline," "Mr. Rabbit & the Lovely Present," "The Relatives Came," "Stone Soup" & "Umbrella.".

Calder Game. unabr. ed. Blue Balliett. Read by Deirdre Lovejoy. 5 CDs. (Running Time: 6 hrs. 17 mins.). (YA). (gr. 5-8). 2008. audio compact disk 45.00 (978-0-7393-6802-2(8), BksonTape) Pub: Random Audio Pubg. Dist(s): Random

Calder Pride, abr. ed. Janet Dailey. Read by Judith Ivey. 4 cass. (Running Time: 4 hrs.). 1999. 25.00 (FS9-50999) Highsmith.

Calder Pride. unabr. ed. Janet Dailey. Read by Kate Harper. 10 vols. (Running Time: 15 hrs.). (Calder Ser.). 2000. bk. 84.95 (978-0-7927-2355-4(4), CSL 244, Chivers Sound Lib) AudioGO.
Cat, a Calder through & through, has lost her fiance in an accident. She returns to the homestead to mourn, vowing never to give her heart to another. But a reckless night with a handsome grey-eyed stranger changes her life forever & gives her a son with striking grey eyes. Cat decides to raise the child on her own & live with her family on the Triple C Ranch. Then the new sheriff with striking grey eyes arrives in town, the man Cat thought she would never see again. Now he is part of her life, whether or not she wants him to be.

***Calder Pride Low Price.** abr. ed. Janet Dailey. Read by Judith Ivey. (ENG.). 2005. (978-0-06-089428-3(8), Harper Audio); (978-0-06-089429-0(6), Harper Audio) HarperCollins Pubs.

Calder Promise. unabr. ed. Janet Dailey. Read by Anna Fields. 8 CDs. (Running Time: 8 hrs.). 2004. audio compact disk 79.95 (978-0-7927-3283-9(9), SLD 679, Chivers Sound Lib); 54.95 (978-0-7927-3282-2(0), CSL 679, Chivers Sound Lib) AudioGO.
In this ninth episode in the series, a new generation of Calders is poised for romance, with Laura taking center stage. In Rome on a grand tour with her deceased father's first wife, Tara, she meets wealthy Texan Boone Rutledge. Later that day, she encounters Sebastian Dunshill, the Earl of Crawford, and falls hopelessly in lust. Following Sebastian to England, Laura learns that he is so impoverished that a rich wife is the only thing likely to save him. Hurt, she flees home to Montana where she falls prey to overbearing Boone. Accepting his offer of marriage on the rebound, she can't forget the handsome earl.

Calder Storm. unabr. ed. Janet Dailey. Read by Julie Briskman. (YA). 2008. 64.99 (978-1-60514-631-7(5)) Find a World.

Caleb: Lessons from a Dog's Life. Derek Prince. 1 cass. 5.95 (4393) Derek Prince.
Caleb (Hebrew "Dog"): after 40 years in the wilderness, as strong at 85 as at 40 - for peace or for war. What was his secret?.

Caleb's Story. unabr. ed. Patricia MacLachlan. Read by Glenn Close. (J). 2008. 34.99 (978-1-60514-562-4(9)) Find a World.

***Caleb's Story.** unabr. ed. Patricia Maclachlan. Read by Glenn Close. (ENG.). 2008. (978-0-06-179914-3(9), KTegenBooks); (978-0-06-179913-6(0), KTegenBooks) HarperCollins Pubs.

Calendar. Lubrecht & Cramer.

Calendar of State Papers, Colonial: North America & the West Indies 1574-1739. Ed. by Karen Ordahl Kupperman et al. 2000. cd-rom 4475.00 (978-0-415-21960-0(4)) Pub: Routledge. Dist(s): Taylor and Fran

Calendar Quest. Jennifer Johnson Garrity. Read by Lloyd James. (Running Time: 23400 sec.). (J). 2006. 44.95 (978-0-7861-4572-0(2)); audio compact disk 45.00 (978-0-7861-7042-5(5)) Blckstn Audio.

Calendar Quest. unabr. ed. Jennifer Johnson Garrity. Read by Lloyd James. (Running Time: 21600 sec.). (J). 2006. audio compact disk 29.95 (978-0-7861-7556-7(7)) Blckstn Audio.

***Calendars: Audio Book.** Annie Finch. 2010. audio compact disk 12.00 (978-1-932195-86-6(6)) Pub: Tupelo Pr Inc. Dist(s): SPD-Small Pr Dist

Calendula. 1 cass. (Running Time: 1 hr.). 9.95 (978-1-55961-437-5(4)) Relaxtn Co.

CalHouse - Leonis Manor. unabr. ed. Mark Paul Sebar. Voice by Mark Paul Sebar. Voice by Arlene Francis & Toni Attell. 2 CDs. (Running Time: 108 mins.). 2000. audio compact disk 12.99 (978-1-930246-02-7(1), CAIDOM) Sebar Pubng.
Horror science fiction set in the 23rd century. Cybers, jetcars, demons & an island they never return from.

CalHouse MP3. Mark Paul Sebar. 2001. 9.99 (978-1-930246-24-9(2), 1930246242) Sebar Pubng.

Calibre. unabr. ed. Ken Bruen. Narrated by Michael Deehy. 5 CDs. (Running Time: 13860 sec.). (Sound Library). 2006. audio compact disk 59.95 (978-0-7927-4073-5(4), SLD 980) AudioGO.

Calico Captive. Elizabeth George Speare. Narrated by Barbara Caruso. 5 pieces. (Running Time: 6 hrs. 30 mins.). (gr. 7 up). 45.00 (978-0-7887-9371-4(3)) Recorded Bks.

Calico Captive. unabr. ed. Elizabeth George Speare. Read by C. M. Herbert. 13 vols. (Running Time: 7 hrs.). 2005. audio compact disk 29.95 (978-0-7861-8162-9(1), ZM2868) Blckstn Audio.

Calidad Humana. Carlos Cuauhtemoc Sanchez. audio compact disk 15.95 (978-968-7277-55-4(6)) Pub: EdSelect MEX. Dist(s): Giron Bks

Califone Cassette Player. Created by Califone. 2005. 64.00 (978-1-59621-305-0(1)) Read Naturally.

Califone Cassette Player/Recorder. Created by Califone. 2005. 67.00 (978-1-59621-304-3(3)) Read Naturally.

Califone CD Player W/Headphones. Created by Califone. 2005. 55.00 (978-1-59621-307-4(8)) Read Naturally.

Califone Computer Headphones. Created by Califone. 2005. 20.00 (978-1-59621-325-8(6)) Read Naturally.

Califone Deluxe Headphones. Created by Califone. 2005. 16.00 (978-1-59621-306-7(X)) Read Naturally.

California. National Textbook Company Staff. 1 cass. (Discover America Ser.). 15.00 (978-0-8442-7493-5(3), Natl Textbk Co) M-H Contemporary.
Offers a fascinating introduction to key locations in the country. Especially designed for intermediate ESL students, combines language learning with American culture study.

California! Dana Fuller Ross, pseud. Read by Paul Ukena. 5 CDs. (Running Time: 6 hrs.). (Wagon West Ser.: No. 6). 2004. audio compact disk (978-1-58807-852-0(3)) Am Pubng Inc.
Violence is ignited by the glitter of gold, men are desperate to strike it rich, and families and farms are forsaken in a wild rush West to stake claims. Strong men and courageous women struggle across an untamed continent to gamble their few and precious dollars in overnight boom towns or die bushwacked by outlaws. Some become valiant fighters in places where six shooters keep the peace. No risk is too great, and no depravity is too low when men catch gold fever and dream of quick millions, strong whiskey and wanton women. CALIFORNIA! Men answer the siren song of gold while thier lonely wives fend off peril. Melissa, a red- haired Texas beauty, finds herself sold into shame by the man she loves. Former wagon master Whip Holt sets out to save her and joins Sheriff Rick Miller in a relentless search for two brutal murderers. Together they try to stem the tide of greed and violence, which theatens to destroy the new American territory.

California! abr. ed. Dana Fuller Ross, pseud. Read by Paul Ukena. 4 vols. (Wagons West Ser.: No. 6). 2003. (978-1-58807-520-8(6)); 25.00 (978-1-58807-011-1(5)) Am Pubng Inc.

California! abr. ed. Dana Fuller Ross, pseud. Read by Paul Ukena. 5 vols. (Wagons West Ser.: No. 6). 2004. audio compact disk 30.00 (978-1-58807-348-8(3)) Am Pubng Inc.

California! unabr. ed. Dana Fuller Ross, pseud. Read by Phil Gigante. (Running Time: 11 hrs.). (Wagons West Ser.: No. 6). 2010. audio compact disk 29.99 (978-1-4418-2460-8(X), 9781441824608, Bril Audio CD Unabri) Brilliance Audio.

California: Fresno to Monterey. 1 cass. (Running Time: 90 min.). 12.95 (CCI-5) Comp Comms Inc.
Visit the San Luis reservoir & power station. Travel the old stagecoach route to San Juan Bautista. Your guide explains how this town survived three periods in history.

California: Los Angeles & Area (overview) 1 cass. (Running Time: 60 mins.). 11.95 (CC201) Comp Comms Inc.
Intimate view of L.A. & all the surrounding areas. Tells you what to see... where to go... etc.

California: San Francisco to San Francisco. (Running Time: 90 mins.). 12.95 (CCI-9) Comp Comms Inc.
Your guide to take you on a one day circle tour. Yor visit Sausalto, the redwoods at Muir Woods & Somoma in the Valley of the Moon.

California Tape 1: San Francisco to Sacramento. 1 cass. (Running Time: 90 mins.). (Guided Auto Tape Tour). 12.95 (C1) Comp Comms Inc.

California Tape 2: Sacramento to South Lake Tahoe. 1 cass. (Running Time: 90 mins.). (Guided Auto Tape Tour). 12.95 (C2) Comp Comms Inc.

California Tape 3: South Lake Tahoe to Mariposa. 1 cass. (Running Time: 90 mins.). (Guided Auto Tape Tour). 12.95 (C3) Comp Comms Inc.

California Tape 4: Mariposa to Fresno (Yosemite National Park) 1 cass. (Running Time: 90 mins.). (Guided Auto Tape Tour). 12.95 (C4) Comp Comms Inc.

California Tape 5: Monterey to Fresno. 1 cass. (Running Time: 90 min.). (Guided Auto Tape Tour). 12.95 (C5) Comp Comms Inc.

California Tape 6: Monterey to San Luis Obispo. 1 cass. (Running Time: 90 min). (Guided Auto Tape Tour). 12.95 (C6) Comp Comms Inc.

California Tape 7: San Luis Obispo to Los Angeles. 1 cass. (Running Time: 90 mins.). (Guided Auto Tape Tour). 12.95 (C7) Comp Comms Inc.

California Tape 8: Fresno to Los Angeles. 1 cass. (Running Time: 90 mins.). (Guided Auto Tape Tour). 12.95 (C8) Comp Comms Inc.

California Tape 9: San Francisco-Wine Country Circle Tour. 1 cass. (Running Time: 90 mins.). (Guided Auto Tape Tour). 12.95 (C9) Comp Comms Inc.

California Tape 10: San Francisco to Monterey. 1 cass. (Running Time: 90 mins.). (Guided Auto Tape Tour). 12.95 (C10) Comp Comms Inc.

California Tape 11: Sacramento to Mariposa. 1 cass. (Running Time: 90 mins.). (Guided Auto Tape Tour). 12.95 (C11) Comp Comms Inc.

California Tape 12: Monterey to Mariposa. 1 cass. (Running Time: 90 min.). (Guided Auto Tape Tour). 12.95 (C12) Comp Comms Inc.

California Tape 13: Reno to South Lake Tahoe. 1 cass. (Running Time: 90 mins.). (Guided Auto Tape Tour). 12.95 (C13) Comp Comms Inc.

California Tape 14: Sacramento to Reno. 1 cass. (Running Time: 90 mins.). (Guided Auto Tape Tour). 12.95 (C14) Comp Comms Inc.

California Angel. unabr. ed. Nancy Taylor Rosenberg. Read by Frances Cassidy. 6 cass. (Running Time: 9 hrs.). 1996. 48.00 (978-0-7366-3510-3(6), 4149) Books on Tape.
Is Toy Johnson an angel of mercy & a gifted psychic? Or is she a kidnapper & a child killer? Even Toy, a teacher in Southern California, doesn't know the answer after a near-death experience leaves her bewildered.

California Association of Family Therapists (CAMFT) 8 cass. (AA & A Symposium Ser.). 80.00 set. (A0422-88) Sound Photosyn.
Including James Bugental, Aliyah Stein, Pat McCaffrey, Chrystal Engleman-Lampe, Linda Myers, Linda Lawless & others. Complete conference.

California Characters: An Array of Amazing People. unabr. ed. Charles Hillinger. Read by Dennis McKee. 8 cass. (Running Time: 11 hrs. 30 mins.). 2001. 56.95 (978-0-7861-2023-9(1), 2791) Blckstn Audio.
California Characters is a gathering of stories about a number of intriguing, eccentric, unusual, or simply amazing individuals profiled by Hillinger. Many of these people have strange occupations, or live solitary lives in remote locations, or collect, build, or design an assortment of odd things.

***California Characters: An Array of Amazing People.** unabr. ed. Charles Hillinger. Read by Dennis McKee. (Running Time: 11 hrs. 5 mins.). (ENG.). 2011. 29.95 (978-1-4417-8396-7(2)); audio compact disk 100.00 (978-1-4417-8394-3(6)) Blckstn Audio.

California Conservatorships & Guardianships. Read by Barbara Miller et al. (Running Time: 3 hrs.). 1992. 89.00 Incl. Ethics: 15 min., & 238p. tape materials. (ES-55249) Cont Ed Bar-CA.
Explains the roles of conservators & guardians, as well as suggesting substitutes. Covers pre-appointment counseling, pre-appointment disputes, the general plan, substituted judgment, temporary conservatorships & guardianships, court investigations & reports, termination of appointment, & attorney fees.

California Demon: The Secret Life of a Demon-Hunting Soccer Mom. Julie Kenner. Narrated by Laura Hicks. 9 CDs. (Running Time: 41100 sec.). (Sound Library). 2006. audio compact disk 89.95 (978-0-7927-3979-1(5), SLD 929) AudioGO.

California Desert. Hosted by Nancy Pearlman. 1 cass. (Running Time: 28 mins.). 10.00 (103) Educ Comm CA.

California Employer's Guide CD, Version 1.0: Version 1.0. Ed. by Aspen Publisher Staff. 2008. audio compact disk 177.50 (978-0-7355-7296-6(8)) WoltersKlu.

California Fever. unabr. ed. John Jacobson. Read by Grover Gardner. (Running Time: 18000 sec.). 2007. 24.95 (978-1-4332-1120-1(3)); audio compact disk 19.95 (978-1-4332-1122-5(X)); audio compact disk 36.00 (978-1-4332-1121-8(1)) Blckstn Audio.

California Fire & Life. Don Winslow. Narrated by Ron McLarty. 12 CDs. (Running Time: 12 hrs.). 2000. audio compact disk 116.00 (978-0-7887-4758-8(4), C1251E7) Recorded Bks.
Jack Wade is one of the best arson investigators in the insurance business. He's thorough & objective. But when he sees the charred body in the opulent oceanside mansion, he walks into a case that will get very personal & dangerous. Using his extensive experience as an arson investigator & P.I., Winslow has penned a suspenseful novel of murder & intrigue.

California Fire & Life, unabr. ed. Don Winslow. Narrated by Ron McLarty. 9 cass. (Running Time: 12 hrs.). 1999. 80.00 (978-0-7887-3770-1(8), 95987E7) Recorded Bks.

California Friends. unabr. ed. Gail Taylor. Read by Gail Taylor. Ed. by James B. Kirgan. 1 cass. (Running Time: 1 hr. 30 mins.). (Essence of Nature Ser.: Vol. 13). (J). 1989. 12.99 stereo. (978-1-878362-13-1(5)) Emerald Ent.
On this tape Thumper, the adventure dog, makes new friends at the San Diego Zoo in California. This tape includes actual recordings of the animals in the San Diego Zoo.

California Girl. abr. unabr. ed. Jefferson Parker. Read by Patrick G. Lawlor. 5 CDs. (Running Time: 11 hrs.). 2004. audio compact disk 102.25 (978-1-59086-974-1(5), 1590869745, BACDLib Ed) Brilliance Audio.
A different world then, a different world now...California in the 1960s, and the winds of change are raging. Orange groves uprooted for tract houses, people flooding into Orange County, and strange new ideas in the air about war, music, sex, and drugs, and new influences including Richard Nixon and Timothy Leary. But for the Becker brothers, the past is always present and it comes crashing back when the body of the lovely and mysterious Janelle Vonn is discovered in an abandoned orange packinghouse. The Beckers and Vonns have a history, beginning years ago in high school with a rumble between the brothers of each clan. But boys grow up. Now one Becker brother is a cop on his first homicide case. One's a minister yearning to perform just one miracle. One is a reporter drunk with ambition. And all three are about to collide with the changing world of 1968 as each brother, in his own special way, tries to find Janelle's killer. As the suspects multiply and

secrets are exposed, the Becker brothers are all drawn further into the case, deeper into the past, and closer to the danger.

California Girl. abr. unabr. ed. T. Jefferson Parker. Read by Patrick G. Lawlor. 9 CDs. (Running Time: 11 hrs.). 2004. audio compact disk 36.95 (978-1-59086-973-4(7), 1590869737, BACD) Brilliance Audio.
A different world then, a different world now...California in the 1960s, and the winds of change are raging. Orange groves uprooted for tract houses, people flooding into Orange County, and strange new ideas in the air about war, music, sex, and drugs, and new influences including Richard Nixon and Timothy Leary. But for the Becker brothers, the past is always present and it comes crashing back when the body of the lovely and mysterious Janelle Vonn is discovered in an abandoned orange packinghouse. The Beckers and Vonns have a history, beginning years ago in high school with a rumble between the brothers of each clan. But boys grow up. Now one Becker brother is a cop on his first homicide case. One's a minister yearning to perform just one miracle. One is a reporter drunk with ambition. And all three are about to collide with the changing world of 1968 as each brother, in his own special way, tries to find Janelle's killer. As the suspects multiply and secrets are exposed, the Becker brothers are all drawn further into the case, deeper into the past, and closer to the danger.

California Girl. unabr. ed. Jefferson Parker. Read by Patrick G. Lawlor. (Running Time: 11 hrs.). 2004. 24.95 (978-1-59335-694-1(3), 1593356943, Brilliance MP3); 39.25 (978-1-59710-116-5(8), 1597101168, BADLE); 24.95 (978-1-59710-117-2(6), 1597101176, BAD); 39.25 (978-1-59335-828-0(8), 1593358288, Brlnc Audio MP3 Lib); 32.95 (978-1-59086-970-3(2), 1590869702, BAU); 87.25 (978-1-59086-971-0(0), 1590869710, BrilAudUnabridg) Brilliance Audio.
A different world then, a different world now...California in the 1960s, and the winds of change are raging. Orange groves uprooted for tract houses, people flooding into Orange County, and strange new ideas in the air about war, music, sex, and drugs, and new influences including Richard Nixon and Timothy Leary. But for the Becker brothers, the past is always present and it comes crashing back when the body of the lovely and mysterious Janelle Vonn is discovered in an abandoned orange packinghouse. The Beckers and Vonns have a history, beginning years ago in high school with a rumble between the brothers of each clan. But boys grow up. Now one Becker brother is a cop on his first homicide case. One's a minister yearning to perform just one miracle. One is a reporter drunk with ambition. And all three are about to collide with the changing world of 1968 as each brother, in his own special way, tries to find Janelle's killer. As the suspects multiply and secrets are exposed, the Becker brothers are all drawn further into the case, deeper into the past, and closer to the danger.

California Gold, Pt. 1. unabr. ed. John Jakes. Narrated by George Guidall. 12 cass. (Running Time: 18 hrs.). 1990. 90.00 (978-1-55690-080-8(5), 90072E7) Recorded Bks.
An epic story of an orphan's fight to gain riches in turn-of-the century California. During his struggles he meets the greats of California history, which gives this not only a sense of historical accuracy that greatly adds to its fast moving plot, but also a you-are-there realism.

California Gold, Pt. 2. unabr. ed. John Jakes. Narrated by George Guidall. 9 cass. (Running Time: 12 hrs. 30 mins.). 75.00 (978-1-55690-081-5(3), 90078E7) Recorded Bks.
An epic story of an orphan's fight to gain riches in turn-of-the-century California. Available to libraries only.

California Gold Rush: And the Coming of the Civil War. Leonard L. Richards. Read by Jeff Riggenbach. (Running Time: 36000 sec.). 2007. 59.95 (978-0-7861-4822-6(5)); audio compact disk 72.00 (978-0-7861-6180-5(9)) Blckstn Audio.

California Gold Rush: And the Coming of the Civil War. unabr. ed. Leonard L. Richards. Read by Jeff Riggenbach. (Running Time: 36000 sec.). 2007. 29.95 (978-0-7861-4821-9(7)); audio compact disk 29.95 (978-0-7861-6179-9(5)); audio compact disk 29.95 (978-0-7861-7167-5(7)) Blckstn Audio.

California Golf. D. E. Traynor. 6 cass. (Running Time: 3 hrs.). 1986. 24.50 Alpha Tape.
Presents discussion on "How to Play Golf", golf courtesy, golf etiquette, putting chip & more.

California History Through Folksong Vols. 1 & 2: With Historical Narration. Keith McNeil & Rusty McNeil. Read by Keith McNeil & Rusty McNeil. (YA). (gr. 4 up). 1998. 37.45 (978-1-878360-19-9(1)); audio compact disk 42.95 (978-1-878360-23-6(X)) WEM Records.

California History Through Folksongs. Keith McNeil. Read by Rusty McNeil. 2 cass. (Running Time: 4 hrs.). 1998. 42.95 WEM Records.
This 80 song set explores the musical heritage of California. Project is divided into the following aspects of California history: Indian, Spanish & Mexican California; The Gold Rush; Railroaders; Farmers & Ranchers: Immigrants/Dust Bowl Refugees; & World War II; & a section on Temperance, Suffrage, Cars & The Movie Industry.

California Indians. unabr. ed. Peter M. Spizzirri. Read by Charles Fuller. Ed. by Linda Spizzirri. 1 cass. (Running Time: 15 mins.). Dramatization. (Educational Coloring Book & Cassette Ser.). (J). (gr. 1-8). pap. bk. 6.95 (978-0-86545-094-3(3)) Spizzirri.
Learn how the Yokutus, Chumash, Pomo Indians developed their cultures in this land of bountiful fish & game.

California Interview on the Believer's Security. Dan Corner. 2 cass. 6.00 Set. (CA) Evang Outreach.

California Latino - Chicano High School Dropout Prevention Project. 8 cass. (Running Time: 4 hrs.). (YA). (gr. 8-12). 1996. (978-1-889621-05-0(6)); (978-1-889621-04-3(8)) Hispnc Ed & Media.
The project consists of 3 components: a year long, 18 unit Language Arts & Social Science, culturally-based curriculum guide, (with historical musical cassettes, slides & historical documents); a resource directory that highlights exemplary drop out prevention programs in the state of California & a documentary film "Cada Cabeza Es Un Mundo-(Each Mind Is A World)," featuring original music by Carlos Santana & special narration by Edward James Olmos, Rita Moreno & Carlos Santana.

California Latino-Chicano High School Dropout Prevention Project. 8 cass. (Running Time: 4 hrs.). (YA). (gr. 8-12). 1996. (978-1-889621-01-2(3)); (978-1-889621-02-9(1)); (978-1-889621-03-6(X)) Hispnc Ed & Media.

California Latino-Chicano High School Dropout Prevention Project. Maria Natera et al. 8 cass. (Running Time: 4 hrs.). (YA). (gr. 9-12). 1996. ring bd. 79.99 (978-1-889621-00-5(5)) Hispnc Ed & Media.

California Nursing Practice Act with Regulations & Related Statutes. bk. 13.50 (978-0-8205-8707-3(9)) LEXIS Pub.

California Oaks see Twentieth-Century Poetry in English, No. 7, Recordings of Poets Reading Their Own Poetry

California Poems: Robinson Jeffers, Edwin Markham & Hildegarde Flanner. unabr. ed. Robinson Jeffers et al. Read by David Frost & Dorothy Jacobson. 1 cass. (Running Time: 60 mins.). (Poetic Heritage). 1981. 10.00 (105301) Summer Stream.

California Project. Perf. by Papa Doo Run Run. 1 cass. (Running Time: 1 hr.). 7.98 (TA 35501); audio compact disk 12.78 Jewel box. (TA 85501) NewSound.

California Real Estate Exam Review, Audio Course. 2005. audio compact disk (978-0-9743923-8-7(3), GCC Pubs) Lib Soldiers.

***California Roll.** unabr. ed. John Vorhaus. (Running Time: 9 hrs. 0 mins.). 2010. 15.99 (978-1-4001-8649-5(8)) Tantor Media.

***California Roll.** unabr. ed. John Vorhaus. Narrated by William Dufris. (Running Time: 8 hrs. 30 mins. 0 sec.). (ENG.). 2010. 24.99 (978-1-4001-6649-7(7)); audio compact disk 69.99 (978-1-4001-4649-9(6)); audio compact disk 34.99 (978-1-4001-1649-2(X)) Pub: Tantor Media. Dist(s): IngramPubServ

***California Roll: A Novel.** unabr. ed. John Vorhaus. (Running Time: 9 hrs. 0 mins.). 2010. 34.99 (978-1-4001-9649-4(3)) Tantor Media.

***California Saxon Matematicas, Intermedias 4.** Created by Saxon Publishers. (SPA.). 2007. audio compact disk 256.00 (978-1-60277-656-2(3)) Saxon Pubs.

***California Saxon Matematicas, Intermedias 5.** Created by Saxon Publishers. (SPA.). 2007. audio compact disk 256.00 (978-1-60277-655-5(5)) Saxon Pubs.

***California Saxon Matematicas, Intermedias 6.** Created by Saxon Publishers. (SPA.). 2007. audio compact disk 85.33 (978-1-60032-438-3(X)); audio compact disk 256.00 (978-1-60277-654-8(7)) Saxon Pubs.

***California Saxon Math, Intermediate 6.** Created by Saxon Publishers. (ENG.). 2007. audio compact disk 75.47 (978-1-60032-437-6(1)) Saxon Pubs.

***California Science: Grade 5.** Created by Harcourt School Publishers. (ENG.). 2006. audio compact disk 52.85 (978-0-15-355256-4(5)) Harcourt Schl Pubs.

California Songs Vol. 1: With Historical Narration. Keith McNeil & Rusty McNeil. Read by Keith McNeil & Rusty McNeil. 4 cass. (Running Time: 3 hrs. 75 mins.). (California History Through Folksong Ser.). (YA). (gr. 4-9). 1998. 19.95 (978-1-878360-18-2(3)); audio compact disk 22.95 (978-1-878360-21-2(3)) WEM Records.
This extensive collection of folksongs covers California history from earliest eras to modern times.

California Songs Vol. 2: With Historical Narration. Keith McNeil & Rusty McNeil. Read by Keith McNeil & Rusty McNeil. (California History Through Folksong Ser.). (YA). (gr. 4 up). 1998. 19.95 (978-1-878360-20-5(5)); audio compact disk 22.95 (978-1-878360-22-9(1)) WEM Records.

California Tales: From the Mountains to the Sea. Phila Rogers. Narrated by Laurel Lyle. 2 cass. (Running Time: 2 hrs. 16 mins.). 1999. bk. 36.95 (978-1-893366-00-8(6)); bk. 36.95 (978-1-893366-01-5(4)) Sola Pub.
"The Nature of California," a guide to state's regions & natural history & "Golden State Trivia" are included.

California Trail. abr. ed. Ralph Compton. Read by Jim Gough. 4 cass. (Running Time: 6 hrs.). (Trail Drive Ser.: Vol. 5). 1998. 24.95 (978-1-890990-04-6(3)) Otis Audio.
Gold fever hits California & suddenly the land is full of hungry pioneers. For Gil & Van Austin, two Texas brothers, it means the chance to sell well-grazed longhorns after years of hard ranching & a treacherous cattle drive through Mexico. The trouble is that California is on the other side of a searing desert, swollen rivers, a barrage of Indian attacks & a whole passel of outlaw trouble. While the Texans & their men are ready & willing to take it all on there's one thing they aren't prepared for - the ultimate act of treachery & deceit in a land of schemers, dreamers & gold.

Californians. unabr. ed. Gertrude Franklin Horn Atherton. Read by Flo Gibson. 6 cass. (Running Time: 9 hrs.). (Classic Books on Cassette). 1988. 24.95 (978-1-55685-106-3(5)) Audio Bk Con.
Life in California at the turn of the century as seen through the lives of the shy, plain daughter of a Spanish Grandee & the beautiful vivacious daughter of a San Francisco entrepreneur.

Californians for Population Stabilization (CAPS) Honors the Peoples Republic of China. Hosted by Nancy Pearlman. 1 cass. (Running Time: 30 mins.). 10.00 (416) Educ Comm CA.

Californian's Tale see Great American Short Stories, Vol. III, A Collection

***Californian's Tale.** Mark Twain. 2009. (978-1-60136-468-5(7)) Audio Holding.

Californian's Tale. Mark Twain. (Running Time: 0 hr. 30 mins.). 1998. 10.95 (978-1-60083-473-8(6)) Iofy Corp.

Californian's Tale. unabr. ed. Mark Twain. Perf. by Walter Zimmerman & Jim Killavey. 1 cass. (Running Time: 56 mins.). Dramatization. Incl. McWilliams & the Burglar Alarm. 1986. (S-74); Mrs. McWilliams & the Lightning. 1986. (S-74); 1986. 8.95 (S-74) Jimcin Record.

Californian's Tale, The McWilliams & the Burglar Alarm, & The McWilliams & the Lightning. Mark Twain. 1 cass. 1989. 7.95 (S-74) Jimcin Record.
Three of Twain's best.

Caliph, Cupid & the Clock see Favorite Stories by O. Henry

***Call.** unabr. ed. Michael Grant. Read by Ramon De Ocampo. (Magnificent 12 Ser.: Bk. 1). 2010. (978-0-06-206213-0(1), KTegenBooks); (978-0-06-199674-0(2), KTegenBooks) HarperCollins Pubs.

***Call.** unabr. ed. Oriah. Read by Oriah. (ENG.). 2004. (978-0-06-079995-3(1), Harper Audio); (978-0-06-074777-0(3), Harper Audio) HarperCollins Pubs.

Call Across the Valley of Not-Knowing see Poetry & Voice of Galway Kinnell

***Call after Midnight.** unabr. ed. Tess Gerritsen. Read by Angela Dawe. (Running Time: 8 hrs.). 2010. 19.99 (978-1-4418-7126-8(8), 9781441871268, Brilliance MP3); 39.97 (978-1-4418-7128-2(4), 9781441871282, BADLE); 39.97 (978-1-4418-7127-5(6), 9781441871275, Brlnc Audio MP3 Lib); audio compact disk 19.99 (978-1-4418-7124-4(1), 9781441871244, Bril Audio CD Unabri); audio compact disk 69.97 (978-1-4418-7125-1(X), 9781441871251, BriAudCD Unabrid) Brilliance Audio.

Call & Response. Ella Jenkins. 1 CD. (Running Time: 1 hr.). (J). 2001. audio compact disk 15.00 (FC 45030CD) Kimbo Educ.

Call & Response. T. R. Pearson. Read by T. R. Pearson. Prod. by Moveable Feast Staff. 1 cass. (Running Time: 30 min.). 8.95 (AMF-229) Am Audio Prose.
T. R. Pearson reads from his novel "Call & Response" & talks about comedy, love & passion among older people.

Call & Response: Rhythmic Group Singing. Perf. by Ella Jenkins. 1 cass. (J). (gr. k-4). 1990. (0-9307-45030-4-1) Smithsonian Folkways.
Explores rhythms of West African peoples on eight chants. Children accompany on conga drums, wood blocks & other simple instruments.

Call & Response: The Riverside Anthology of the African American Literary Tradition. Ed. by Patricia L. Hill. 1998. pap. bk. 50.00 (978-0-395-88404-1(7)) CENGAGE Learn.

Call CD: Discovering Why You Are Here. abr. unabr. ed. Oriah Mountain Dreamer Staff. Read by Oriah Mountain Dreamer Staff. 5 CDs. (Running Time: 6 hrs.). 2003. audio compact disk 29.95 (978-0-06-056766-8(X)) HarperCollins Pubs.

Call Center Management on Fast Forward: Succeeding in Today's Dynamic Inbound Environment. unabr. ed. Brad Cleveland & Julia Mayben. 6 cass. (Running Time: 6 hrs. 45 min.). 1998. bk. 49.95 Set. (978-0-9659093-1-0(X)) Call Cnter Pr.

Call Each River Jordan. unabr. ed. Owen Parry. Read by Paul Boehmer. 8 cass. (Running Time: 12 hrs.). 2001. 64.00 (978-0-7366-8311-1(9)) Books on Tape.
Investigating the murder of forty slaves, Abel Jones is drawn into the underworld of the Civil War's brutality.

Call for Character. Greg Zoschak. 2007. audio compact disk 37.99 (978-1-60247-614-1(4)) Tate Pubng.

Call for Convenient Christianity: Acts 24:1-27. Ed Young. 2000. 4.95 (978-0-7417-2251-5(8), 1251) Win Walk.

Call for the Dead. John le Carré. Narrated by Full Cast Production Staff. 2 CDs. (Running Time: 1 hr. 30 mins. 0 sec.). (ENG.). 2009. audio compact disk 19.95 (978-1-60283-637-2(X)) Pub: AudioGO. Dist(s): Perseus Dist

Call for the Dead. John le Carré. Read by John le Carré. 2 cass. (Running Time: 2 hrs. 14 mins.). 1999. (978-1-84032-113-5(X), HoddrStoughton) Hodder General GBR.
An anonymous letter had alleged that Foreign office man Samual Fenman had been a member of the Communist Party as a studen before the war. Next day he was dead with a note by his body.

Call for the Dead. John le Carré. Narrated by Frederick Davidson. (Running Time: 5 hrs. 30 mins.). 1991. 24.95 (978-1-59912-440-7(8)) Iofy Corp.

***Call for the Dead.** unabr. ed. John le Carré. (Running Time: 5 hrs. 30 mins.). 2010. audio compact disk 29.95 (978-1-4417-3561-4(5)) Blckstn Audio.

***Call for the Dead.** unabr. ed. John le Carré. Read by Ralph Cosham. (Running Time: 5 hrs. 30 mins.). 2010. 29.95 (978-1-4417-3562-1(3)); 34.95 (978-1-4417-4242-1(5)); audio compact disk 55.00 (978-1-4417-3559-1(3)) Blckstn Audio.

Call for the Dead. unabr. ed. John le Carré. Read by Rupert Keenlyside. 6 cass. (Running Time: 6 hrs.). (George Smiley Novels Ser.). 1982. 36.00 (978-0-7366-0560-1(6), 1532) Books on Tape.
The cast includes a brilliant, twisted former hero of the German underground, a once-beautiful woman with a terrifying secret, a suspect British civil servant, a high-ranking bureaucrat & an undercover operative named George Smiley. Smiley has seen & done more than he ever wanted to, but he can't refuse this one last call to duty.

Call for the Dead. unabr. ed. John le Carré. Read by Michael Jayston. 4 cass. (Running Time: 6 hrs.). (George Smiley Ser.: Bk. 1). 2000. 34.95 (978-0-7451-6851-7(5), CAB 668) Pub: Chivers Audio Bks GBR. Dist(s): AudioGO
George Smiley met with Samuel Fennan, a senior member of the Foreign Office, in order to clarify allegations made about him in an anonymous letter. Smiley reassured Fennan that the matter would not be pursued. So it came as a shock to Smiley upon learning that Fennan had committed suicide.

Call for the Dead. unabr. ed. John le Carré. Narrated by Frank Muller. 3 cass. (Running Time: 4 hrs. 30 mins.). (George Smiley Novels Ser.). 1987. 26.00 (978-1-55690-083-9(X), 87810E7) Recorded Bks.
Spy-master George Smiley's first case.

Call from Mount Sinai. 1985. Evang Sisterhood Mary.

Call from Tomorrow: A Message about Your Future from the God Whose Already Been There. Mac Hammond. 4 cass. 1998. 24.00 Set. (978-1-57399-074-5(4)) Mac Hammond.
God's plan for your tomorrows is in His Word.

Call It Courage. Armstrong Sperry. Read by Lou Diamond Phillips. 2 cass. (Running Time: 2 hrs. 30 mins.). (J). 2001. 18.00 Books on Tape.
Scorned by the other island children because he is afraid of the sea,12-year-old Mafatu, whose name means, stout heart secretly takes a canoe to prove to himself that he can conquer his terror of the water.

Call It Courage. collector's ed. Armstrong Sperry. Read by Dan Lazar. 7 cass. (Running Time: 10 hrs. 30 mins.). (J). 1987. 56.00 (978-0-7366-9063-8(8),) Books on Tape.

Call It Courage. unabr. ed. Armstrong Sperry. Read by Lou Diamond Phillips. 2 vols. (Running Time: 1 hr. 57 mins.). (J). (gr. 5-9). 2004. pap. bk. 29.00 (978-0-8072-8685-2(0), YA235SP, Listening Lib); 19.55 (978-0-8072-8684-5(2), YA235CX, Listening Lib) Pub: Random Audio Pubg. Dist(s): NetLibrary CO

Call It Courage, unabr. ed. Armstrong Sperry. Narrated by George Guidall. 2 pieces. (Running Time: 2 hrs. 15 mins.). (gr. 5 up). 1994. 19.00 (978-0-7887-0075-0(8), 94308E7) Recorded Bks.
Discover the culture & history of Polynesia with this classic tale of bravery & adventure in which a young boy struggles with his fear of the sea.

Call It Courage. unabr. ed. Armstrong Sperry. Narrated by George Guidall. 2 CDs. (Running Time: 2 hrs. 15 mins.). (gr. 5 up). 2000. audio compact disk 22.00 (978-0-7887-4648-2(0), C1199E7) Recorded Bks.

Call it Courage. unabr. ed. Armstrong Sperry. Read by Lou Diamond Phillips. (ENG.). (J). (gr. 4). 2009. audio compact disk 22.00 (978-0-7393-8232-5(2), Listening Lib) Pub: Random Audio Pubg. Dist(s): Random

Call It Courage. unabr. collector's ed. Short Stories. Armstrong Sperry. Read by Dan Lazar. 7 cass. (Running Time: 10 hrs. 30 mins.ss.). (J). 1987. 56.00 (978-0-7366-1199-2(1), 2117) Books on Tape.
Story for children & young people, tells how a polynesian boy finds courage & returns to his tribe.

Call It Sleep: A Novel. unabr. ed. Henry Roth. Narrated by George Guidall. 15 CDs. (Running Time: 17 hrs. 15 mins.). 1999. audio compact disk 133.00 (978-0-7887-3710-7(4), C1067E7) Recorded Bks.
Overly sensitive & fearful, hated by his father & doted on by his mother, Jewish immigrant David Schearl grows up in a New York ghetto in the years just prior to World War I.

Call It Sleep: A Novel. unabr. ed. Henry Roth. Narrated by George Guidall. 12 cass. (Running Time: 17 hrs. 15 mins.). 1994. 97.00 (978-0-7887-0091-0(X), 94332E7) Recorded Bks.

Call Me Burroughs. unabr. ed. William S. Burroughs. 1 CD. (Running Time: 1 hr. 30 mins.). 1996. audio compact disk 16.98 (R2 71848) Rhino Enter.

Call Me by My True Names. Thich Nhat Hanh. 2 cass. (Running Time: 180 min.). 2003. 18.95 (978-3-938093-11-5(0)) Parallax Pr.
Shares his life story, his poetry, and his vision for a more mindful, harmonious world community.

Call Me Francis Tucket, unabr. ed. Gary Paulsen. Narrated by John Randolph Jones. 2 pieces. (Running Time: 2 hrs.). (Tucket Adventures Ser.: Bk. 2). (gr. 5 up). 2001. 19.00 (978-0-7887-0385-0(4), 94576E7) Recorded Bks.
Continues the adventure that began in "Mr. Tucket." After spending a year in the mountain wilderness together, Mr. Grimes & Francis Tucket have parted ways & Francis is headed up the dangerous trail to Orgeon, where he hopes to find his family.

***Call Me Irresistible.** unabr. ed. Susan Elizabeth Phillips. (ENG.). 2011. (978-0-06-202723-8(9), Harper Audio) HarperCollins Pubs.

*Call Me Mrs. Miracle. unabr. ed. Debbie Macomber. Read by Jennifer Van Dyck. (Running Time: 5 hrs.). 2010. 24.99 (978-1-4418-0585-0(0), 9781441805850, BAD); 39.97 (978-1-4418-0584-3(2), 9781441805843, Brlnc Audio MP3 Lib); 39.97 (978-1-4418-0586-7(9), 9781441805867, BADLE); 24.99 (978-1-4418-0583-6(4), 9781441805836, Brilliance MP3); audio compact disk 74.97 (978-1-4418-0582-9(6), 9781441805829, BriAudCD Unabrid); audio compact disk 26.99 (978-1-4418-0581-2(8), 9781441805812, Bril Audio CD Unabri) Brilliance Audio.

Call Me Ted: The Autobiography of the Extraordinary Business Leader & Founder of CNN. abr. ed. Ted Turner & Bill Burke. Read by Ted Turner. (Running Time: 8 hrs.). (ENG.). 2008. 24.98 (978-1-60024-421-6(1)); audio compact disk 34.98 (978-1-60024-420-9(3)) Pub: Hachet Audio. Dist(s): HachBkGrp

Call Me Ted: The Autobiography of the Extraordinary Business Leader & Founder of CNN. unabr. ed. Ted Turner & Bill Burke. Read by Ted Turner. (Running Time: 15 hrs.). (ENG.). 2008. 19.98 (978-1-60024-423-0(8)) Pub: Hachet Audio. Dist(s): HachBkGrp

Call Me Ted: The Autobiography of the Extraordinary Business Leader & Founder of CNN. unabr. ed. Ted Turner & Bill Burke. Read by Ted Turner. (Running Time: 15 hrs.). (ENG.). 2009. audio compact disk 19.98 (978-1-60024-825-2(X)) Pub: Hachet Audio. Dist(s): HachBkGrp

Call No Man Father. collector's ed. William X. Kienzle. Read by Edward Holland. 7 cass. (Running Time: 10 hrs. 30 min.). (Father Koesler Mystery Ser.: No. 17). 2000. 56.00 (978-0-7366-5637-5(5)) Books on Tape.
An impending papal visit is wreaking havoc in Detroit. Rumors run rampant that the Pope comes bearing a pronouncement on birth control that will rock devout Catholics to the very foundations of their faith & Father Koesler can't help but get caught up on the religious controversy. But soon he'll be swept into the secular & dangerous business of protecting the pontiff's life. For among the throng of pilgrims lurks a host of predators, a devout man hopelessly twisted by grief, a washed up reporter desperate to make headlines & a faceless assassin within the Pope's inner circle, all hell bent on silencing His Holiness.

Call of Duty: My Life Before, During, & after the Band of Brothers. Lynn D. Compton. Read by Dick Hill. Told to Marcus Brotherton. Frwd. by John McCain. (Playaway Adult Nonfiction Ser.). 2008. 64.99 (978-1-60640-853-7(4)) Find a World.

Call of Duty: My Life Before, During, & after the Band of Brothers. unabr. ed. Lynn D. Compton & Marcus Brotherton. Narrated by Dick Hill. Frwd. by John McCain. (Running Time: 10 hrs. 0 mins. 0 sec.). (ENG.). 2008. audio compact disk 34.99 (978-1-4001-0734-6(2)) Pub: Tantor Media. Dist(s): IngramPubServ

Call of Duty: My Life Before, During, & after the Band of Brothers. unabr. ed. Lynn D. Compton & Marcus Brotherton. Read by Dick Hill. Narrated by Dick Hill. (Running Time: 10 hrs. 0 mins. 0 sec.). (ENG.). 2008. audio compact disk 24.99 (978-1-4001-5734-1(X)); audio compact disk 69.99 (978-1-4001-3734-3(9)) Pub: Tantor Media. Dist(s): IngramPubServ

Call of Earth Vol. 2: Homecoming. unabr. ed. Orson Scott Card & Stefan Rudnicki. (Running Time: 11 hrs. NaN mins.). 2008. 29.95 (978-1-4332-1881-1(X)); 65.95 (978-1-4332-1877-4(1)); audio compact disk 90.00 (978-1-4332-1878-1(X)) Blckstn Audio.

Call of Glengarron. Nancy Buckingham. 1992. pap. bk. 44.95 (978-1-85496-628-5(6)) Pub: UlverLrgPrint GBR. Dist(s): Ulverscroft US

Call of Glengarron. unabr. ed. Nancy Buckingham. Read by Judith Franklyn. 4 cass. (Running Time: 6 hrs.). 1999. 44.95 (66286) Pub: Soundings Ltd GBR. Dist(s): Ulverscroft US

Call of God. Derek Prince. 1 cass. (Running Time: 60 min.). 5.95 (I-4259) Derek Prince.

Call of God: A Call to All Believers. Gary V. Whetstone. 4 cass. (Running Time: 6 hrs.). (Empowerment Ser.). 1995. pap. bk. 35.00 (978-1-58866-178-4(4), VE002A) Gary Whet Pub.
Examines the Word of God in relationship to the call of God on your life & others. You will study & discover the believer's call, the specific call to service.

Call of My Blood Mysteries. Judith Barr. 1 cass. 1990. 12.32 (978-1-886264-01-4(5)) Mysteries of Life.
Women's spirituality - psychology.

Call of St. Clare. Henri Daniel-Rops. 4 cass. 18.95 (752) Ignatius Pr.
The first woman follower of St. Francis of Assisi.

Call of the Canyon. Zane Grey. Contrib. by John Bolen. (Unabridged Classics (Playaway) Ser.). (ENG.). 2009. 69.99 (978-1-60775-784-9(2)) Find a World.

Call of the Canyon. Zane Grey. Read by John Bolen. (Running Time: 7 hrs. 45 mins.). 2001. 27.95 (978-1-60083-579-7(1), Audiofy Corp) Iofy Corp.

Call of the Canyon. unabr. ed. Zane Grey. Read by Jim Gough. 5 cass. (Running Time: 7 hrs.). 2004. 44.95 (978-0-7861-2407-7(5), 3077); audio compact disk 45.00 (978-0-7861-8795-9(6), 3077) Blckstn Audio.

Call of the Canyon. unabr. ed. Zane Grey. Read by John Bolen. 1 CD. (Running Time: 8 hrs.). 2001. audio compact disk 25.00; audio compact disk 57.00 Books on Tape.
Carley Burch, a beautiful young woman must leave her high society life in New York City to follow her fiance to the rugged Wild West.

Call of the Canyon. unabr. ed. Zane Grey. Read by John Bolen. 7 CDs. (Running Time: 7 hrs. 45 mins.). (ENG.). 2001. audio compact disk 39.00 (978-1-4001-0006-4(2)); audio compact disk 20.00 (978-1-4001-5006-9(X)) Pub: Tantor Media. Dist(s): IngramPubServ
Carley Burch, a beautiful young woman must leave her glamorous high society life of New York to follow her fiance, Glenn Kilbourne, to the rugged Wild West. She braves fierce ruffians, brutal elements and lack of civilization in an attempt to reclaim him. Glenn, suffering from shell shock and the betrayal of his country following World War I, had moved west to recover.

Call of the Canyon. unabr. ed. Zane Grey. Narrated by John Bolen. (Running Time: 7 hrs. 30 mins. 0 sec.). (ENG.). 2009. lab manual ed. 55.99 (978-1-4001-3929-3(5)) Pub: Tantor Media. Dist(s): IngramPubServ

Call of the Canyon. unabr. ed. Zane Grey. Read by John Bolen. (Running Time: 7 hrs. 30 mins. 0 sec.). (Tantor Unabridged Classics Ser.). (ENG.). 2009. audio compact disk 27.99 (978-1-4001-0929-6(9)) Pub: Tantor Media. Dist(s): IngramPubServ

Call of the Canyon. unabr. ed. Zane Grey. Read by John Bolen. Narrated by John Bolen. (Running Time: 7 hrs. 30 mins. 0 sec.). (Tantor Unabridged Classics Ser.). (ENG.). 2009. audio compact disk 19.99 (978-1-4001-5929-1(6)) Pub: Tantor Media. Dist(s): IngramPubServ

***Call of the Heather.** Gwen Kirkwood. 2010. 61.95 (978-1-4079-0761-1(1)); audio compact disk 79.95 (978-1-4079-0762-8(X)) Pub: Soundings Ltd GBR. Dist(s): Ulverscroft US

***Call of the Horse.** 2010. audio compact disk (978-0-9760415-7-3(X)) Touched.

Call of the Wild see Appel de la Foret

Call of the Wild see Llamado de la Selva

Call of the Wild. Cynthia Heimel. 2000. 18.00 (978-0-671-58257-9(7), Audioworks) S&S Audio.
Sex tips.

Call of the Wild. Jack London. Narrated by Theodore Bikel. (Running Time: 2 hrs.). 2006. 14.95 (978-1-59912-973-0(6)) Iofy Corp.

Call of the Wild. Jack London. Retold by Gina D. B. Clemen. (Green Apple Step Two Ser.). (J). (gr. 4-7). 2005. pap. bk. 21.95 (978-88-7754-859-7(2)) Cideb ITA.

Call of the Wild. Jack London. Ed. by Jerry Stemach et al. Retold by Noe Venable. (Start-to-Finish Books). (J). (gr. 2-3). 2002. (978-1-58702-808-3(5)) D Johnston Inc.

Call of the Wild. Jack London. Retold by Noe Venable. (Classic Adventures Ser.). 2002. audio compact disk 18.95 (978-1-4105-0190-5(6)) D Johnston Inc.

Call of the Wild. Jack London. Read by Theodore Bikel. 2 cass. 19.95 set. (8109Q) Filmic Archives.
One of the most powerful dog stories ever told. It is the story of Buck, a dog born to luxury but stolen & sold as a sledge dog. Buck is a proud dog who escapes captivity & rises magnificently above all his enemies to become one of the most feared & admired dogs in the North.

Call of the Wild. Jack London. Read by Garrick Hagon. (Running Time: 2 hrs. 30 mins.). 1999. 20.95 (978-1-60083-690-9(9)) Iofy Corp.

Call of the Wild. Jack London. Read by Carlos J. Vega. (Running Time: 3 hrs.). 2002. 16.95 (978-1-60083-191-1(5), Audiofy Corp) Iofy Corp.

Call of the Wild. Jack London. Read by Michael Kramer. (Running Time: 3 hrs.). 2002. 19.95 (978-1-59912-046-1(1), Audiofy Corp) Iofy Corp.

Call of the Wild. Jack London. Read by Patrick G. Lawlor. (Running Time: 3 hrs. 24 mins.). 2003. 25.95 (978-1-60083-660-2(7), Audiofy Corp) Iofy Corp.

Call of the Wild. Jack London. Narrated by Michael Kramer. (Running Time: 10860 sec.). (Unabridged Classics in MP3 Ser.). (ENG.). (J). 2008. audio compact disk 24.00 (978-1-58472-634-0(2), In Aud) Sound Room.

Call of the Wild. Jack London. Narrated by Flo Gibson. (ENG.). 2008. audio compact disk 18.95 (978-1-60646-065-8(X)) Audio Bk Con.

Call of the Wild. abr. ed. Jack London. Narrated by Jeff Chandler. 2 cass. 12.95 (978-0-89926-123-2(X), 811) Audio Bk.

Call of the Wild. abr. ed. Jack London. Read by Ethan Hawke. (Running Time: 10800 sec.). 2008. audio compact disk 19.95 (978-1-4332-0958-1(6)); audio compact disk & audio compact disk 33.00 (978-1-4332-1357-1(5)) Blckstn Audio.

Call of the Wild. abr. ed. Jack London. Ed. by Jerry Stemach et al. Retold by Noe Venable. Contrib. by Ted S. Hasselbring. 1 cass. (Running Time: 1 hr.). (Start-to-Finish Books). (J). (gr. 2-3). 2002. (978-1-58702-793-2(3), H09) D Johnston Inc.
The tale is told through the eyes of a dog, Buck, who starts out his life as a domesticated animal, the loyal companion of a country gentleman. When gold is discovered in the Klondike, however, Buck is cruelly stolen form his comfortable life and sold into the harsh life of a sled dog in the frozen north. What follows is an incredible adventure. Faces with every imaginable trail. Buck comes into his own as a creature of savage instinct, great courage and fierce loyalty.

Call of the Wild. abr. ed. Jack London. Perf. by Ed Begley. 1 cass. 1984. 12.95 (978-0-89845-244-0(9), SWC 1219) HarperCollins Pubs.

Call of the Wild. abr. ed. Jack London. Read by Peter Marinker. Contrib. by Neville Teller. 2 cass. 15.95 (SCN 188) J Norton Pubs.
Relationship between Thorton & his dog Buck, stolen from his owners & transported to the Yukon during the gold-rush pf 1897.

Call of the Wild. abr. ed. Jack London. Read by Garrick Hagon. 2 CDs. (Running Time: 2 hrs. 30 mins.). (J). (gr. 6-12). 1995. audio compact disk 17.98 (978-962-634-064-6(9), NA206412) Naxos.

Call of the Wild. abr. ed. Jack London. Read by Garrick Hagon. 2 cass. (Running Time: 2 hrs. 30 mins.). (J). 1996. 13.98 (978-962-634-564-1(0), NA206414, Naxos AudioBooks) Naxos.

Call of the Wild. abr. ed. Jack London. Read by Larry McKeever. (Running Time: 90 mins.). (Saddleback Classics Ser.). (YA). 2001. pap. bk. 16.95 (978-1-56254-312-9(1), SP3121) Saddleback Edu.

Call of the Wild. adpt. ed. Jack London. (Bring the Classics to Life: Level 2 Ser.). (ENG.). 2008. audio compact disk 12.95 (978-1-55576-457-9(6)) EDCON Pubng.

Call of the Wild. unabr. ed. 4 cass. (Running Time: 4 hrs.). 1995. 89.95 (978-1-57574-001-0(X)) InteliQuest.
This collection includes Jack London's 1903 classic. It also includes a valuable replica of the original first edition of the book & a study guide.

Call of the Wild. unabr. ed. Jack London. Narrated by Patrick G. Lawlor. (Running Time: 3 hrs. 30 mins. 0 sec.). (Tantor Unabridged Classics Ser.). (ENG.). (J). (gr. 4-7). 2008. audio compact disk 17.99 (978-1-4001-0853-4(5)) Pub: Tantor Media. Dist(s): IngramPubServ

Call of the Wild. unabr. ed. Jack London. Read by Jeff Chandler. 4 cass. 23.80 (E-409) Audio Bk.
Tales of adventure on the Alaskan frontier during the Klondike Gold rush.

Call of the Wild, unabr. ed. Jack London. Read by Stuart Milligan. 2 cass. (Running Time: 2 hrs.). (J). (gr. 1-8). 1999. 18.95 (CTC 757, Chivers Child Audio) AudioGO.

Call of the Wild. unabr. ed. Jack London. Read by Gene Engene. 3 cass. (Running Time: 3 hrs. 45 mins.). 21.95 (978-1-55686-161-1(3), 161) Books in Motion.
A story that needs little introduction, this famous classic is exceptionally well read.

Call of the Wild. unabr. ed. Jack London. Read by Roger Dressler. 6 cass. (Running Time: 5 hrs.). (Bookcassette Classic Collection). 1992. 57.25 (978-1-56100-116-3(3), 1561001163, Unabridge Lib Edns) Brilliance Audio.

Call of the Wild. unabr. ed. Jack London. Read by Roger Dressler. 5 CDs. (Running Time: 5 hrs.). (Classic Collection). 2001. audio compact disk 29.95 (978-1-58788-604-1(9), 1587886049, CD Unabridged); audio compact disk 69.25 (978-1-58788-605-8(7), 1587886057, CD Unabrid Lib Ed) Brilliance Audio.

Call of the Wild. unabr. ed. Jack London. Read by Roger Dressler. 4 cass. (Running Time: 5 hrs.). 2001. 19.95 (978-1-58788-773-4(8), 1587887738, BAU) Brilliance Audio.

Call of the Wild. unabr. ed. Jack London. Read by Roger Dressler. (Running Time: 5 hrs.). 2004. 39.25 (978-1-59335-994-2(2), 1593359942, Brlnc Audio MP3 Lib); 24.95 (978-1-59335-993-5(4), 1593359934, Brilliance MP3) Brilliance Audio.

Call of the Wild. unabr. ed. Jack London. Read by Roger Dressler. (Running Time: 5 hrs.). 2004. 39.25 (978-1-59710-119-6(2), 1597101192, BADLE); 24.95 (978-1-59710-118-9(4), 1597101184, BAD) Brilliance Audio.

Call of the Wild. unabr. ed. Jack London. Read by Samuel W. Griffin. 2 pieces. (Running Time: 3 hrs.). lib. bdg. 26.95 (978-1-55656-099-6(0), DAB013) Pub: Dercum Audio. Dist(s): APG

Call of the Wild. unabr. ed. Jack London. 2 vols. (Running Time: 3 hrs.). (Classic Literature Ser.). (ps-7). 1997. bk. 16.95 (978-1-55656-198-6(9)) Pub: Dercum Audio. Dist(s): APG
The classic 1903 story of Buck, a courageous dog fighting for survival in the Alaskan wilderness. Vividly evokes the harsh & frozen Yukon during the Gold Rush. As Buck is ripped from his pampered surroundings & shipped to Alaska to be a sled dog, his primitive, wolflike nature begins to emerge.

Call of the Wild. unabr. ed. Jack London. Read by Frank Muller. 2006. 34.99 (978-1-59895-165-3(3)) Find a World.

Call of the Wild. unabr. ed. Jack London. Read by Stewart Granger. 2 cass. (Read-Along Ser.). (J). 34.95 Incl. read-along bk., learner's guide & exercises. (S23906) J Norton Pubs.

Call of the Wild. unabr. ed. Jack London. Read by William Roberts. 3 CDs. (Running Time: 4 hrs.). 2009. audio compact disk 22.98 (978-962-634-923-6(9), Naxos AudioBooks) Naxos.

Call of the Wild, unabr. ed. Jack London. Narrated by Frank Muller. 3 cass. (Running Time: 3 hrs. 45 mins.). (gr. 6). 1999. 26.00 (978-1-55690-082-2(1), 80110E7) Recorded Bks.
Story of Buck, the intrepid shepherd dog born & raised on a ranch in California & abducted & shipped off to work Alaskan gold fields.

Call of the Wild. unabr. ed. Jack London. Narrated by Frank Muller. 4 CDs. (Running Time: 3 hrs. 45 mins.). 2000. audio compact disk 36.00 (978-0-7887-3456-4(3), C1062E7) Recorded Bks.

Call of the Wild. unabr. ed. Jack London. Read by Michael Kramer. 3 cds. (Running Time: 3 hrs 1 min). (YA). 2002. pap. bk. (978-1-58472-221-2(5), In Aud) Sound Room.
The story of Buck, the mixed breed dog who is stolen from a good life and thrust into the savage Klondike, is a thrilling adventure of survival in the wild.

Call of the Wild. unabr. ed. Jack London. Read by Michael Kramer. 3 cds. (Running Time: 3 hrs 1 min). (YA). 2002. audio compact disk 22.95 (978-1-58472-219-9(3), 079, In Aud) Pub: Sound Room. Dist(s): Baker Taylor
The story of Buck, the mixed breed who is stolen from a good life and thrust into the savage Klondike, is a thrilling adventure of survival in the wild.

Call of the Wild. unabr. ed. Jack London. Narrated by Patrick G. Lawlor. (Running Time: 3 hrs. 30 mins. 0 sec.). (ENG.). (J). (gr. 4-7). 2008. 17.99 (978-1-4001-5853-9(2)); audio compact disk 35.99 (978-1-4001-3853-1(1)) Pub: Tantor Media. Dist(s): IngramPubServ

Call of the Wild. unabr. ed. Jack London. Read by Jeff Daniels. (ENG.). (J). (gr. 3). 2010. 25.00 (978-0-307-71026-0(2), Listening Lib) Pub: Random Audio Pubg. Dist(s): Random

Call of the Wild. unabr. ed. Running Press Staff. 4 CDs. (Running Time: 3 hrs.). (YA). (gr. 7 up). 2002. audio compact disk 43.00 (978-1-58472-162-8(6), Commuters Library) Sound Room.

Call of the Wild. unabr. abr. ed. Jack London. Read by Ethan Hawke. 2 cass. (Running Time: 3 hrs.). (Ultimate Classics Ser.). (gr. 6-12). 2004. 18.00 (978-1-931056-75-5(7), N Millennium Audio) New Millenn Enter.
Set in the frozen wastelands of the Yukon, this is the story of the magnificent dog Buck, who is a loyal pet until cruel man makes him a pawn of their feverish search for the gold of the klondike.

Call of the Wild. unabr. abr. ed. Jack London. Read by Brian Parry. 2 cass. (Running Time: 3 hrs.). 2001. pap. bk. 17.95 (978-1-882071-02-9(6), 003) B-B Audio.
Danger, Deceit, and Despair plague Lord and Lady Greystroke - alias Tarzan and his wife Jane - in the third Edgar Rice Burroughs thrilling adventure series. When arch villain Nikolas Rokoff escapes to wreak his twisted vengeance on the ape-man, he targets.

Call of the Wild. 2nd ed. Jack London. Contrib. by Jennifer Basset & Tricia Hedge. (Oxford Bookworms Ser.). 1998. 13.75 (978-0-19-422783-4(9)) OUP.

Call of the Wild: Abridged. (ENG.). 2007. (978-1-60339-039-2(1)); cd-rom & audio compact disk (978-1-60339-040-8(5)) Listenr Digest.

***Call of the Wild: Bring the Classics to Life.** adpt. ed. Jack London. (Bring the Classics to Life Ser.). 2008. pap. bk. 21.95 (978-1-55576-494-4(0)) EDCON Pubng.

Call of the Wild & Make Westing, unabr. ed. Jack London. Read by Flo Gibson. 3 cass. (Running Time: 4 hrs. 30 mins.). 1993. 16.95 (978-1-55685-304-3(1)) Audio Bk Con.
Buck, the dog hero, is sold into service in the Klondike. Abused by men & dogs, clubs & fangs, he becomes a ruthless fighter. He eventually meets a master he deeply loves & respects, whose murder causes Buck to answer the call of the wild where he becomes the leader of a pack of wolves. "Make Westing," a disturbing sea tale, is also included.

Call of the Wild & Other Stories, unabr. ed. Jack London. 6 cass. (Running Time: 6 hrs.). 1999. 44.98 (LL 0032) AudioGO.

Call of the Wild & Other Stories. unabr. ed. Jack London. Read by Jonathan Kent. 5 cass. (Running Time: 8 hrs.). 2001. 24.95 (978-0-7366-6777-7(6)) Books on Tape.
This is the story of a dog rediscovering his instincts in the Yukon. Other stories include "Moon-Face", "Brown Wolf", "That Spot" & "To Build a Fire".

Call of the Wild & Other Stories. unabr. ed. Jack London. Read by Jim Killavey & Walter Zimmerman. 5 cass. (Running Time: 6 hrs.). Incl. Man with the Gash. 1979. (C-6); To the Man on the Trail. 1979. (C-6); 1979. 35.00 (C-6) Jimcin Record.
Buck is a courageous & valiant dog, kidnapped from his comfortable home & forced to fight for survival in the frozen north country.

Call of the Wild & Other Stories. unabr. ed. Jack London. Read by Jack Dahlby & Arnold Moss. 6 cass. (Running Time: 5 hrs. 54 mins.). Incl. Piece of Steak. 1976. (CXL517CX); To Build a Fire. 1976. (CXL517CX); Told in the Drooling Ward. 1976. (CXL517CX); (Cassette Library). 1976. Set tchr.'s training gde. ed. 44.98 (978-0-8072-2984-2(9), CXL517CX, Listening Lib) Random Audio Pubg.
A collection of some of London's best-known novels, as well as five shorter pieces.

Call of the Wild & Other Stories. unabr. collector's ed. Jack London. Read by Jonathan Kent. 5 cass. (Running Time: 5 hrs.). (J). 1997. 40.00 (978-0-7366-3760-2(5), 4435) Books on Tape.
Buck is a courageous & valiant dog that is kidnapped from his comfortable life on a California estate & thrown into the wild north woods. Buck must fight for survival & turns almost wild. Yet, he receives unexpected kindness from a human & becomes devoted to his new master.

Call of the Wild Read Along. Jack London. (Saddleback's Illustrated Classics Ser.). (YA). 2005. audio compact disk (978-1-56254-889-6(1)) Saddleback Edu.

Call of the Wild, White Fang, & Other Stories. unabr. ed. Jack London. Read by John Lee. (Running Time: 41400 sec.). 2006. 72.95 (978-0-7861-4899-8(3)) Blckstn Audio.

Call of the Wild, White Fang & Other Stories. unabr. ed. Jack London. Read by John Lee. (Running Time: 12 hrs. 30 mins.). 2006. audio compact disk 90.00 (978-0-7861-5984-0(7)) Blckstn Audio.

Call of the Wolf. Ed. by Andrea Donner. Photos by Denver Bryan. 2008. bk. 19.95 (978-1-59543-815-7(7)) Willow Creek Pr.

Call of the Yukon see Poetry of Robert W. Service

Call on Jesus. Contrib. by Nicole C. Mullen. 2006. audio compact disk 8.98 (978-5-558-26958-1(8), Word Music) Word Enter.

Call the Dead Again: A Markby & Mitchell Mystery. unabr. ed. Ann Granger. Read by Bill Wallis. 8 cass. (Running Time: 8 hrs.). 1999. 69.95 (978-0-7540-0284-0(5), CAB 1707) AudioGO.

Call the Dead Again Set: A Markby & Mitchell Mystery. unabr. ed. Ann Granger. Read by Bill Wallis. 8 cass. (Superintendent Markby & Civil Servant Mitchell Mysteries Ser.). 1999. 69.95 (CAB 1707) AudioGO.

Call the Midwife: A True Story of the East End in the 1950s. unabr. ed. Jennifer Worth. Read by Annie Aldington. 10 cass. (Running Time: 46800 sec.). (Soundings Ser.). 2006. 84.95 (978-1-84559-426-8(6)) Pub: ISIS Lrg Prnt GBR. Dist(s): Ulverscroft US

Call the Next Witness. Neville Goddard. 1 cass. (Running Time: 62 mins.). 1964. 8.00 (73) J & L Pubns.
Neville taught Imagination Creates Reality. He was a powerfully influential teacher of God as Consciousness.

Call to Arms. Allan Mallinson. Narrated by Erick Graham. 9 cass. (Running Time: 12 hrs. 45 mins.). 82.00 (978-1-84197-379-1(3)) Recorded Bks.

Call to Arms. unabr. ed. Allan Mallinson. Narrated by Errick Graham. 9 cass. (Running Time: 12 hrs. 45 mins.). 2002. 42.95 (978-1-4025-3195-8(8), RG207) Recorded Bks.
It's 1819, and the last two years have been tough for Matthew Hervey-his beloved wife is dead and he has turned his back on the cavalry regiment. Hervey travels to Rome with his sister and meets one of England's most controversial figures who reminds him of why he joined the Light Dragoons. He rejoins, and is assigned a new troop and horses. They must travel to India and advance through the jungle-unaware that a large number of Burmese warboats are awaiting their arrival.

Call to Arms. unabr. collector's ed. W. E. B. Griffin. Read by Michael Russotto. 10 cass. (Running Time: 15 hrs.). (Corps Ser.: Bk. 2). 1992. 80.00 (978-0-7366-2206-6(3), 3001) Books on Tape.
The second book in The Corps series, deals realistically with the early days of the Raiders, specifically with their first tenuous combat operations.

Call to Awaken: A Multidimensional Story. 1 cass. (Running Time: 90 mins.). 1994. 12.95 (978-1-886594-01-2(5), Inner Harmon) Inner Harmonics.
A mutlidimensional story. With 54 original vibrational chants.

Call to Conscience: The Landmark Speeches of Dr. Martin Luther King, Jr. Ed. by Clayborne Carson & Kris Shepard. 2002. audio compact disk 42.98 (978-1-58621-130-1(7)) Hachet Audio.

Call to Conscience: The Landmark Speeches of Dr. Martin Luther King, Jr. abr. ed. Ed. by Clayborne Carson & Kris Shepard. 2002. 34.98 (978-1-58621-129-5(3)) Hachet Audio.

Call to Conscience: The Landmark Speeches of Dr. Martin Luther King, Jr. unabr. ed. Ed. by Clayborne Carson & Kris Shepard. 7 CDs. (Running Time: 8 hrs.). 2001. (978-1-58621-089-2(0)) Hachet Audio.
Expressing a deeply felt faith in democracy, the power of loving change, and a self-deprecating humor, is Dr. King speaking today. It is a unique, unforgettable record of the words that rallied millions, forever changed the face of America, and even today shape our deepest personal hopes and dreams for the future.

Call to Conscience: The Landmark Speeches of Dr. Martin Luther King, Jr. unabr. ed. Clayborne Carson & Kris Shepard. Contrib. by Andrew Young. (Running Time: 8 hrs.). (ENG.). 2009. 64.98 (978-1-60024-991-4(4)) Pub: Hachet Audio. Dist(s): HachBkGrp

Call to Conscience: The Landmark Speeches of Dr. Martin Luther King Jr. unabr. ed. Clayborne Carson & Kris Shepard. Contrib. by Andrew Young. (ENG.). 2005. 14.98 (978-1-59483-431-8(8)) Pub: Hachet Audio. Dist(s): HachBkGrp

Call to Conscience: The Landmark Speeches of Dr. Martin Luther King Jr. unabr. ed. Clayborne Carson et al. Read by Edward M. Kennedy. Contrib. by Andrew Young. 7 CDs. (Running Time: 8 hrs.). (ENG., 2001. audio compact disk 42.98 (978-1-58621-046-5(7)) Pub: Hachet Audio. Dist(s): HachBkGrp

Call to Corporate Fasting. Derek Prince. 1 cass. (I-4093) Derek Prince.

Call to Decision. 1 cass. (Running Time: 30 mins.). 1985. (0237) Evang Sisterhood Mary.
Topics are: Between Two Magnets; Saint Michael; When Jesus Returns.

Call to Faith: Isiah 6:9-13. Ed Young. (J). 1980. 4.95 (978-0-7417-1153-3(2), A0153) Win Walk.

Call to Faith Grades 7 And 8. Composed by David Haas & Marty Haugen. 2 CDs. (YA). 2006. audio compact disk 24.95 (978-1-57999-586-7(1), CD-689) GIA Pubns.

Call to Family Reformation. abr. ed. Dennis Rainey & Barbara Rainey. Ed. by Keith Lynch. 5 cass. (Running Time: 5 hrs.). 1996. 19.95 (978-1-57229-030-3(7)) FamilyLife.
Talks about what a family reformation is.

Call to Freedom. 3rd ed. Holt, Rinehart and Winston Staff. 2002. audio compact disk 208.73 (978-0-03-065364-3(9)); audio compact disk 208.73 (978-0-03-065366-7(5)) Holt McDoug.

Call to Freedom: Audio CD Summaries. 5th ed. Holt, Rinehart and Winston Staff. 2005. audio compact disk 212.93 (978-0-03-038304-5(8)); audio compact disk 212.93 (978-0-03-038306-9(4)) Holt McDoug.

Call to Freedom: Before 1877. Holt, Rinehart and Winston Staff. 2000. audio compact disk 208.73 (978-0-03-053522-2(0)); audio compact disk 208.73 (978-0-03-053523-9(9)) Holt McDoug.

Call to Freedom: Beginning 1877. 3rd ed. Holt, Rinehart and Winston Staff. 2002. audio compact disk 208.73 (978-0-03-065371-1(1)) Holt McDoug.

Call to Freedom: Beginning-1877. 3rd ed. Holt, Rinehart and Winston Staff. (SPA.). 2002. audio compact disk 208.73 (978-0-03-065369-8(X)) Holt McDoug.

Call to Freedom: Beginning-1914. Holt, Rinehart and Winston Staff. 1998. 45.60 (978-0-03-054506-1(4)); 45.60 (978-0-03-054507-8(2)) Holt McDoug.

Call to Freedom: Beginning 1914. 3rd ed. Holt, Rinehart and Winston Staff. 2002. audio compact disk 208.73 (978-0-03-065383-4(5)); audio compact disk 208.73 (978-0-03-065382-7(7)) Holt McDoug.
Will make history relevant with special features that help students discover how historical events influence the present, how common issues cross national boundaries, and how history is embedded in the arts, literature, and science.

Call to Freedom: 1865-Present. Holt, Rinehart and Winston Staff. 2000. audio compact disk 208.73 (978-0-03-053657-1(X)) Holt McDoug.

Call to Freedom: 1865-Present. Holt, Rinehart and Winston Staff. (SPA.). 2000. audio compact disk 208.73 (978-0-03-053658-8(8)) Holt McDoug.

Call to Freedom: 1865-Present. 3rd ed. Holt, Rinehart and Winston Staff. 2002. audio compact disk 208.73 (978-0-03-065376-6(2)); audio compact disk 208.73 (978-0-03-065377-3(0)) Holt McDoug.

Call to Heroism. Peter H. Gibbon. Read by Brian Emerson. (Running Time: 8 hrs. 30 mins.). 2004. 27.95 (978-1-59912-372-1(X)) Iofy Corp.

Call to Heroism: Renewing America's Vision of Greatness. unabr. ed. Peter H. Gibbon. Read by Brian Emerson. 6 cass. (Running Time: 8 hrs. 30 mins.). 2004. 44.95 (978-0-7861-2714-6(7), 3274); audio compact disk 56.00 (978-0-7861-8640-2(2), 3274) Blckstn Audio.

Call to Holiness, A Call to Action. Thomas J. Gumbleton. 1 cass. (Running Time: 1 hr.). 2001. 8.95 (A6901) St Anthony Mess Pr.
One can't have a call to holiness without a call to action for justice. Every disciple is called to both.

Call to Leadership Series. Rick Joyner. 3 cass. (Running Time: 4 hrs. 30 mins.). 2000. 15.00 (RJ01-000) Morning NC.
Incls: "A Coming Breed of Ministry," "Paying the Price" & "The Heavenly Perspective." Rick addresses the qualities required of spiritual leaders in these times.

Call to Live a Symbolic Life: Live Workshop. Caroline Myss. 4 CDs. 2004. audio compact disk 23.95 (978-1-4019-0206-3(5), 2065) Hay House.

Call to Motherhood. Elisabeth Elliot. Read by Elisabeth Elliot. 4 cass. (Running Time: 4 hrs.). 1989. 18.95 (978-0-8474-2008-7(6)) Back to Bible.
Features talks that will help one, as a mother, to understand the important role in the home. Includes advice on raising children.

Call to Radical Christianity. abr. ed. Paul Cain. 2004. 14.99 (978-0-7684-0214-8(X)) Destiny Image Pubs.

Call to Radical Christianity Series. Paul Cain. 2 cass. (Running Time: 3 hrs.). 2000. 10.00 (PC01-000) Morning NC.
"Radical Culture/Conservative Church" & "The Rest of God." This is a call for the church to become a revolutionary power on the earth once again.

Call to Shakabaz. Amy Wachpress. Narrated by Andrew L. Barnes. Music by Timothy Barnes. Illus. by JoAnn M. Mirlenbrink. (ENG.). (YA). 2008. audio compact disk 49.99 (978-0-9779883-9-6(2)) Pub: Legacy Audio Bks. Dist(s): Quality Bks IL

Call to Stewardship. Robert F. Morneau. 1 cass. (Running Time: 55 mins.). 1994. 7.95 (TAH299) Alba Hse Comns.
Good for clarifying basic doctrinal, pastoral, spiritual & social principles underlying the concept of stewardship. Indispensable for pastors, parish council members & stewardship committees. Excellent meditation material.

Call to Wholeness & Holiness. Chester P. Michael. 1985. 24.00 (978-0-940136-10-6(4)) Open Door Inc.

Call to Yahweh. 1 cass. (Running Time: 1 hr. 11 min.). 1990. 8.00 (978-1-890967-31-4(9)) Hse of Yahweh.
The songs of praise comfort us in knowing that those who sincerely call upon Yahweh's name in times of trouble will be saved.

Call upon Me. 1985. (0273) Evang Sisterhood Mary.

Call upon the Lord. Steve Amerson. 1991. 10.98 (978-0-00-153652-4(4)) Pub: Amerson Mus Min. Dist(s): STL Dist NA

Call upon the Lord. Steve Amerson. (ENG.). 2006. audio compact disk 15.98 (978-0-00-153633-3(8)) Pub: Amerson Mus Min. Dist(s): STL Dist NA

Callahan Chronicals. unabr. ed. Spider Robinson. Read by Barrett Whitener. 14 CDs. (Running Time: 17 hrs. 30 mins.). 2003. audio compact disk 112.00 (978-0-7861-9181-9(3), 3095); 83.95 (978-0-7861-2460-2(1), 3095) Blckstn Audio.
Contains the trio of books that introduced the world to Mike Callahan, Jake Stonebender, Doc Webster, Mickey Finn, Fast Eddie Costigan, Long-Drink McGonnigle, Ralph Von Wau Wau, and the rest of the regulars of Callahan's Place.

Callahan Cousins Bk. 1: Summer Begins. unabr. ed. Elizabeth Doyle Carey. Narrated by Stina Nielsen. 6 CDs. (Running Time: 6 hrs. 15 mins.). 2005. audio compact disk 58.75 (978-1-4193-5561-5(9), C3404); 32.95 (978-1-4193-5062-7(5), RH938) Recorded Bks.
Twelve-year-old cousins Phoebe, Hillary, Neeve, and Kate are spending the summer at their grandmother's beach house. They have heard stories about the Callahan-Bicket family rivalry. Now it's up to them to prove that the Callahans are the best family on the island! Fans of the American Girl books will love these spunky girls.

Callahan Cousins Bk. 2: Home Sweet Home. unabr. ed. Elizabeth Doyle Carey. Narrated by Stina Nielsen. 4 cass. (Running Time: 5 hrs. 15 mins.). 2005. 37.75 (978-1-4193-5238-6(5), 98127); audio compact disk 48.75 (978-1-4193-6773-1(0), C3506) Recorded Bks.
Elizabeth Doyle Carey pens an engaging story of the four Callahan cousins, Neeve, Hillary, Kate, and Phoebe, as they continue their summer vacation with their grandmother on beautiful Gull Island, Ireland. Grandmother Gee honors them with the privilege of taking over the Dorm, a stable that was converted into a guesthouse many years ago and needs redecorating. But before they move in, old family secrets need to be swept out of those closets.

Callahan's Con. Spider Robinson. Ed. by Barrett Whitener. 7 cass. (Running Time: 10 hrs.). 2004. 49.95 (978-0-7861-2813-6(5), 3338); audio compact disk 64.00 (978-0-7861-8347-0(0), 3338) Blckstn Audio.

Callahan's Con. Spider Robinson. Narrated by Barrett Whitener. (Running Time: 10 hrs.). 2005. 30.95 (978-1-59912-441-4(6)) Iofy Corp.

Callahan's Key. Spider Robinson. Narrated by Barrett Whitener. (Running Time: 12 hrs. 30 mins.). 2005. 34.95 (978-1-59912-442-1(4)) Iofy Corp.

Callahan's Key. unabr. ed. Spider Robinson. Read by Barrett Whitener. 10 CDs. (Running Time: 11 hrs. 30 mins.). 2003. audio compact disk 80.00 (978-0-7861-9128-4(7), 3158); 62.95 (978-0-7861-2551-7(9), 3158) Blckstn Audio.
The universe is in desperate peril. Due to a cluster of freakish phenomena, the United States' own defense system has become a doomsday machine, threatening the entire universe. And only one man can save everything-as-we-know-it from annihilation.

Callahan's Legacy. Spider Robinson. Read by Spider Robinson. (Running Time: 23400 sec.). 2006. 44.95 (978-0-7861-4522-5(6)); audio compact disk 55.00 (978-0-7861-7182-8(0)) Blckstn Audio.

Callahan's Legacy. unabr. ed. Spider Robinson. Read by Spider Robinson. (Running Time: 23400 sec.). 2006. audio compact disk 29.95 (978-0-7861-7616-8(4)) Blckstn Audio.

Callander Square. unabr. ed. Anne Perry. Narrated by Davina Porter. 7 cass. (Running Time: 10 hrs.). (Thomas Pitt Ser.). 2000. 63.00 (978-0-7887-4494-5(1), H1083E7) Recorded Bks.
The bodies of two newborn babies have been found in a park in the fashionable London neighborhood of Callander Square. While Inspector Thomas Pitt is fighting to get the squire's aristocratic residents to speak with him, his pretty, well-born wife Charlotte decides to do some detective work of her own. Soon she is unearthing secrets in every house on the square while Thomas tries to discover what would drive a person to murder.

Called Out of Darkness: A Spiritual Confession. unabr. ed. Anne Rice. Read by Anne Rice. 4 cass. 2008. 40.00 (978-1-4159-6089-5(5), BksonTape) Pub: Random Audio Pubg. Dist(s): Random

Called Out of Darkness: A Spiritual Confession. unabr. ed. Anne Rice. Read by Anne Rice. Narrated by Kirsten Potter. 6 CDs. (Running Time: 7 hrs.). 2008. audio compact disk 40.00 (978-1-4159-5671-7(5), BksonTape) Pub: Random Audio Pubg. Dist(s): Random

Called Out of Darkness: A Spiritual Confession. unabr. ed. Anne Rice. Read by Anne Rice. Read by Kirsten Potter. 6 CDs. (Running Time: 7 hrs.). (ENG.). 2008. audio compact disk 29.95 (978-0-7393-5896-2(0), Random AudioBks) Pub: Random Audio Pubg. Dist(s): Random

Called to a Cause. Steck-Vaughn Staff. 2003. (978-0-7398-8425-6(5)) SteckVau.

Called to Be a Christian Set: Grounding Spirituality in Sacrament, Community & Scripture. John Shea. 3 cass. (Running Time: 90 min. per cass.). 1998. 19.95 Vinyl binder. (978-0-87946-180-5(2), 334) ACTA Pubns.
Noted theologian & storyteller presents a foundation for contemporary spirituality that is practical, alive, rewarding & enriching. Considers the themes of initiation, forgiveness, commitment & Eucharist as well as service & ministry, prayer & fellowship. Each program divided into numerous segments by brief musical interludes to allow for reflection or discussion.

Called to Be a Parent: Genesis 1:27-28. Ed Young. (J). 1981. 4.95 (978-0-7417-1159-5(1), A0159) Win Walk.

Called to be Children. Tom Leonhardt. Read by Tom Leonhardt. Contrib. by Susan DeCrane. 5 cass. (Running Time: 4 hrs. 22 min.). 1986. 39.95 set; incl. shelf-case. (TAH160) Alba Hse Comns.
Detail the importance of resting in the arms of God (Abba & Ima) & allowing ourselves to be called "my child" by God.

Called to be Christians: Grounding Spirituality in Sacrament, Community & Scripture. John Shea. 1998. 19.95 ACTA Pubns.

Called to be God's Leader: Lessons from the Life of Joshua. abr. ed. Henry and Richard Blackaby. Read by J. Charles. (Running Time: 3 hrs.). 2006. 24.95 (978-1-4233-0307-7(5), 9781423303077, BAD) Brilliance Audio.

Called to be God's Leader: Lessons from the Life of Joshua. abr. ed. Henry Blackaby & Richard King. Read by J. Charles. (Running Time: 3 hrs.). 2006. 39.25 (978-1-4233-0308-4(3), 9781423303084, BADLE); 39.25 (978-1-4233-0306-0(7), 9781423303060, Brinc Audio MP3 Lib) Brilliance Audio.
What did God have in mind when He saw Joshua as a young slave in Egypt? How did He mold and shape Joshua to prepare him for service? Through Joshua and numerous examples from their own lives, the authors create a picture of God's ways, offering deep insight that listeners can apply to their own lives. Purpose, Obedience, Faith, Character, and Influence are among the themes that are included in the book; key truths are emphasized at the end of each chapter.

Called to Be God's Leader: Lessons from the Life of Joshua. abr. ed. Henry T. Blackaby & Richard King. 2 cass. (Running Time: 3 hrs.). 2004. 17.95 (978-1-59355-499-6(0), 1593554990) Brilliance Audio.

Called to Be God's Leader: Lessons from the Life of Joshua. abr. ed. Henry T. Blackaby & Richard King. Read by J. Charles. 2 cass. (Running Time: 3 hrs.). 2004. 44.25 (978-1-59355-500-9(8), 1593555008); audio compact disk 19.95 (978-1-59355-501-6(6), 1593555016); audio compact disk 62.25 (978-1-59355-502-3(4), 1593555024) Brilliance Audio.

Called to Be God's Leader: Lessons from the Life of Joshua. abr. ed. Richard King & Henry T. Blackaby. Read by J. Charles. (Running Time: 10800 sec.). (Biblical Legacy Ser.). 2006. audio compact disk 24.95 (978-1-4233-0305-3(9), 9781423303053, Brilliance MP3) Brilliance Audio.

Called to Be Mothers. unabr. ed. Elisabeth Elliot. Read by Elisabeth Elliot. 2 cass. (Running Time: 2 hrs.). 1990. 9.95 (978-0-8474-2017-9(5)) Back to Bible.
Practical insights on working mothers & what the Bible says about raising children today.

Called to Coaching? Discover if Coaching Is the Career for You. Created by Grace Durfee. 2 CDs. (Running Time: 2 hrs.). 2005. audio compact disk 29.00 (978-0-9766140-1-2(4)) Bal w Grace.
Called to Coaching? answers the many questions you might have about entering the ﬁeld of coaching. This two-houraudio program explores the beneﬁts and challenges ofbecoming a coach, pinpoints necessary developmentalsteps, and offers strategies for starting a coachingbusiness. You will learn about accredited training programs,certiﬁcation requirements, and how to select a mentorcoach. The accompanying e-book includes resources tofacilitate your research and a quiz to help you determine ifcoaching is right for you.

Called to Holiness. Mother Angelica & Father Michael. 1 cass. (Running Time: 60 min.). (Mother Angelica Live Ser.). 1989. 10.00 (978-1-55794-116-9(5), T67) Eternal Wrd TV.
Argues that people are all called to holiness & what that means - & personality changes that occur when they reach for holiness.

Called to Lead: CD Set. 2005. audio compact disk 325.00 (978-1-932927-53-5(0)) Ascensn Pr.

Called to Lead: CD Set. 2006. audio compact disk 250.00 (978-1-932927-90-0(5)) Ascensn Pr.

Called to Mutuality: Men & Women in Ministry. Evelyn Whitehead & James Whitehead. 2 cass. (Running Time: 2 hrs.). 2001. vinyl bd. 18.95 (A6420) St Anthony Mess Pr.
Men and women have left behind traditional ways of relating to each other and have entered a time of peril and possibility. Nowhere is the relationship of the two sexes more challenging than in the Church.

Called to Serve Him. Elaine Cannon & Ed J. Pinegar. 2 cass. 1993. 11.95 set. (978-1-57008-001-2(1), Bkcraft Inc) Deseret Bk.

Called to Spiritual Fatherhood. George Pearsons. (ENG.). 2008. audio compact disk 5.00 (978-1-57562-977-3(1)) K Copeland Pubns.

Called to Testify. Short Stories. Kenn J. Kremer. 2 CDs. 2003. audio compact disk 12.99 (978-0-8100-1561-6(7)) Northwest Pub.
audio of the book "Called to Testify".

Callender Papers, unabr. ed. Cynthia Voigt. Narrated by Barbara Caruso. 5 pieces. (Running Time: 6 hrs. 45 mins.). (gr. 8 up). 1992. 44.00 (978-1-55690-620-6(X), 92313E7) Recorded Bks.
Jean, a thirteen-year-old student at a 19th century Boston boarding school, spends a summer organizing a school trustee's personal files & stumbles across a terrifying mystery from the past.

Calligrapher's Daughter. unabr. ed. Eugenia Kim. Narrated by Lorna Raver. 2 MP3-CDs. (Running Time: 16 hrs. 30 mins. 0 sec.). (ENG.). 2009. audio compact disk 29.99 (978-1-4001-6354-0(4)); audio compact disk 39.99 (978-1-4001-1354-5(7)); audio compact disk 79.99 (978-1-4001-4354-2(3)) Pub: Tantor Media. Dist(s): IngramPubServ

Calling. 3 CDs. 2005. audio compact disk 21.00 (978-1-933207-05-6(1)) Ransomed Heart.

***Calling.** unabr. ed. David Gaider. Narrated by Stephen Hoye. (Running Time: 14 hrs. 30 mins.). (Dragon Age Ser.). 2010. 39.99 (978-1-4001-9620-3(5)); audio compact disk 79.99 (978-1-4001-4620-8(8)) Pub: Tantor Media. Dist(s): IngramPubServ

Calling. unabr. ed. Jane Goodall. Read by Nicki Paull. (Running Time: 42000 sec.). 2007. audio compact disk 98.95 (978-1-921334-40-5(1), 9781921334405) Pub: Bolinda Pubng AUS. Dist(s): Bolinda Pub Inc

Calling. unabr. ed. Inger Ash Wolfe. Narrated by Bernadette Dunne. 9 CDs. (Running Time: 11 hrs. 30 mins.). 2008. audio compact disk 89.95 (978-0-7927-5265-3(1)) AudioGO.

Calling: A Year in the Life of an Order of Nuns. abr. ed. Catherine Whitney. Read by Susie Breck. (Running Time: 6 hrs.). 2008. 39.25 (978-1-4233-5290-7(4), 9781423352907, BADLE); 24.95 (978-1-4233-5288-4(2), 9781423352884, BAD); audio compact disk 39.25

(978-1-4233-5289-1(0), 9781423352891, Brlnc Audio MP3 Lib) Brilliance Audio.

Calling: A Year in the Life of an Order of Nuns. abr. ed. Catherine Whitney. Read by Susie Breck. Directed By Laura Grafton. Contrib. by Jill Sovis. (Running Time: 6 hrs.). 2008. audio compact disk 24.95 (978-1-4233-5287-7(4), 9781423352877, Brilliance MP3) Brilliance Audio.

***Calling: Unabridged Value-Priced Edition.** Inger Ash Wolfe. Narrated by Bernadette Dunne. (Running Time: 11 hrs. 28 mins. 0 sec.). (ENG.). 2010. audio compact disk 14.95 (978-1-60283-997-7(2)) Pub: AudioGO. Dist(s): Perseus Dist

Calling Ahead of Time. Keith Winston. Read by Ralph Cosham. (Running Time: 1 hr.). 2003. 15.95 (978-1-59912-047-8(X), Audiofy Corp) Iofy Corp.

Calling All Cars: Flight to the Desert & Tobaccoville Road. 1 cass. (Running Time: 1 hr.). 2001. 6.98 (1865) Radio Spirits.

***Calling All Cars, Volume 1.** RadioArchives.com. (Running Time: 600). (ENG.). 2007. audio compact disk 29.98 (978-1-61081-058-6(9)) Radio Arch.

***Calling All Cars, Volume 2.** RadioArchives.com. (Running Time: 600). (ENG.). 2009. audio compact disk 29.98 (978-1-61081-096-8(1)) Radio Arch.

***Calling All Cars, Volume 4.** RadioArchives.com. (Running Time: 600). (ENG.). 2010. audio compact disk 29.98 (978-1-61081-168-2(2)) Radio Arch.

Calling All Disciples! Caryl Krueger. Read by Caryl Krueger. 1 cass. (Running Time: 1 hr. 30 min). 2001. pap. bk. 12.00 Belleridge.
Did you ever think of yourself as a disciple, one who shares the message of the Christ? Learn how the dedicated lives and memorable saying of Jesus' first followers are relevant to today's living. Hear their words and see their activities through the eyes of a young boy whose story is told in "The Legend of the Palm Leaf.".

Calling All Kids. Jim Kimball. (J). 1992. 9.98 (978-1-881214-00-7(1)) J Jangle Ent.

***Calling All the Nations Cd.** (ENG.). 2000. audio compact disk 13.98 (978-0-01-247046-6(5)) Pub: Cactus Game. Dist(s): STL Dist NA

Calling Americans to Islam: The Dawah Smart Pack. unabr. ed. Yahiya Emerick et al. Read by Yahiya Emerick. 6 cass. (Running Time: 5 hrs. 35 min.). (C). 1996. 18.95 Set. (978-1-889720-12-8(7), 311-103) Amirah Pubng.
An exposition on how to communicate Islam to non-Muslims. Interviews with converts & a detailed examination of Christianity are included.

Calling & Separation. David T. Demola. 1 cass. 4.00 (1-083) Faith Fellow Min.

Calling Catholics to Be "Bible Christians" Scott Hahn. 3 cass. 1995. 19.95 Set. (145-C) Ignatius Pr.
Titles include: "Discover Your Faith through Scripture:" Scott offers one of the most compelling presentations ever about why Catholics should learn about, love & study Sacred Scripture. "Deepen Your Faith with Scripture:" An in-depth study of the Bible should be the lifelong task of all Catholics. Scott presents key Scripture texts that clarify the issues at stake in Christian Faith. "Defend Your Faith from Scripture:" In this final tape, Scott explains that there is no inconsistency in being evangelical & Catholic. In fact, according to Scott, you can't be Catholic & not be evangelical.

Calling Kokopelli. Lance Auburn Everett. 3 CDs. (Running Time: 3 hrs.). (Michael Ser.). 2005. 25.00 (978-1-58943-062-4(X)) Am Pubng Inc.

Calling Mr. Callaghan. unabr. ed. Peter Cheyney. Read by Peter Wheeler. 3 cass. (Running Time: 4 hrs. 30 min.). (Sound Ser.). 2004. 34.95 (978-1-85496-042-9(3), 60423) Pub: UlverLrgPrint GBR. Dist(s): Ulverscroft US
A fast-moving story of detectives, gamesters, thieves & hard-living women. A glorious pattern of excitement & suspense, of crossing & double-crossing.

Calling Mr. Lonely Hearts. unabr. ed. Laura Benedict. Read by Emily Durante. (Running Time: 11 hrs.). 2008. 24.95 (978-1-4233-3442-2(6), 9781423334422, Brilliance MP3); 39.25 (978-1-4233-3443-9(4), 9781423334439, Brlnc Audio MP3 Lib); 39.25 (978-1-4233-3445-3(0), 9781423334453, BADLE); 24.95 (978-1-4233-3444-6(2), 9781423334446, BAD); audio compact disk 29.99 (978-1-4233-3440-8(X), 9781423334408, Bril Audio CD Unabri); audio compact disk 97.25 (978-1-4233-3441-5(8), 9781423334415, BriAudCD Unabrid) Brilliance Audio.

Calling of Apostles; The Holy War. Ann Ree Colton & Jonathan Murro. 1 cass. 7.95 A R Colton Fnd.

Calling of Dan Matthews. unabr. ed. Harold Bell Wright. Read by David Sharp. 6 cass. (Running Time: 8 hrs. 36 min.). 1994. 39.95 (978-1-55686-489-6(2)) Books in Motion.
Dan Matthews joins the ministry which he believes is his true calling. But deep seated feelings of discomfort reveal to Dan that there is a stronger calling than the ministry.

Calling on Dragons. unabr. ed. Patricia C. Wrede. 4 cass. (Running Time: 6 hrs. 4 mins.). (Enchanted Forest Chronicles: Bk. 3). (J). (gr. 6 up). 2004. 32.00 (978-0-8072-0636-2(9), Listening Lib); pap. bk. 38.00 (978-0-8072-0792-5(6), LYA 347 SP, Listening Lib) Random Audio Pubg.
This time the dastardly wizards have stolen King Mendanbar's magic sword, vital to the health of the forest, right out of the castle armory. Morwen joins Cimorene, Kazul, Telemain, several cats, and Killer on a quest to retrieve the sword. Meanwhile, the wizards are gathering their forces.

Calling the Roll: Romans 16:1-16. Ed Young. (J). 1984. 4.95 (978-0-7417-1406-0(X), 406) Win Walk.

Calling the Roll: Romans 16:17-20. Ed Young. 1997. 4.95 (978-0-7417-2143-3(0), 1143) Win Walk.

Calling upon Love. Eknath Easwaran. 1 cass. (Running Time: 56 min.). 1989. 7.95 (978-1-58638-511-8(9), CUL) Nilgiri Pr.
Describes the goal of meditation as union with the Lord of Love; upon discovering the Lord in our own consciousness, we simultaneously discover the divinity in everyone.

Callirobics. unabr. ed. Liora Laufer. Perf. by Liora Laufer. 1 cass. (Running Time: 56 min.). (J). (gr. 3-12). 1990. bk. 26.95 (978-0-9630478-0-9(9), CL500) Callirobics.
Handwriting exercises accompanied by music.

Callirobics: Advanced Handwriting Exercises with Music from Around the World. Perf. by Liora Laufer. 1 cass. (J). (gr. 2-9). pap. bk. 19.95 (978-0-9630478-3-0(3), CL550) Callirobics.
Continuation of "Handwriting Exercises to Music" features 10 exercises creating new abstract shapes with popular melodies from around the world. Improves eye-hand coordination, fine motor skills & handwriting.

Callirobics: Handwriting Exercises to Music. Contrib. by Liora Laufer. 1 cass. 16.95 Incl. wkbk. (LL112A) OptimaLearning.
Series of simple, enjoyable hand-writing exercises, set to music, which require only brief, self-guided daily sessions to improve handwriting skills. Designed for all people who wish to develop: better eye-hand coordination, fine-motor skills, self-esteem! Excellent for persons with stroke, head injury, Parkinsons, or developmental disability.

Callirobics: Handwriting Exercises to Music. Contrib. by Liora Laufer. 1 cass. (J). (gr. 2 up). 24.95 Incl. wkbk., guide. (LL112B) OptimaLearning.

Callirobics: Handwriting Exercises with Music. Liora Laufer. 1 cass. 29.95 Incl. wkbk., guide. (LL112C) OptimaLearning.

Callirobics-for-Adults: Handwriting Skills for Adults with Music in the Style of the Twenties, Thirties & Forties. 1 cass. (Running Time: 24 min.). 1995. 26.95 (978-0-9630478-2-3(5), CL600) Callirobics.
Designed to help adults regain the small-muscle coordination after temporary loss due to stroke, head injury, Parkinson's or Alzheimer's diseases.

Callirobics-for-Kids: Pre-Writing Skills with Music. abr. ed. Liora Laufer. Perf. by Liora Laufer. 1 cass. (Running Time: 46 min.). (J). (gr. k-2). 1993. 18.95 Incl. wkbk. (978-0-9630478-1-6(7), CL400) Callirobics.
Designed to introduce the basic elements of the writing movements in a "stress free" method.

***Callisto.** Torsten Krol. Read by Curt Skinner. (Running Time: 12 hrs. 15 mins.). 2010. 99.99 (978-1-74214-600-3(7), 9781742146003) Pub: Bolinda Pubng AUS. Dist(s): Bolinda Pub Inc

Callisto. unabr. ed. Torsten Krol. Read by Curt Skinner. (Running Time: 12 hrs. 15 mins.). 2009. audio compact disk 108.95 (978-1-921415-23-4(1), 9781921415234) Pub: Bolinda Pubng AUS. Dist(s): Bolinda Pub Inc

Calls of Frogs & Toads. Lang Elliott. 1 cass. (Running Time: 65 min.). 1994. audio compact disk 16.95 CD. (2657, Creativ Pub) Quayside.
A comprehensive audio guide to the breeding calls & other sounds made by 42 species of frogs & toads found east of the Great Plains. Includes 48-page booklet.

Calls of Frogs & Toads. Lang Elliott. 1 cass. (Running Time: 65 min.). 1994. 12.95 (2656, NrthWrd Bks) TandN Child.

Callusses of Poetry. Jack Collom & Ken Bernstein. 1996. audio compact disk 17.50 (978-0-9651878-0-0(2)) Pub: TreeHse Pr. Dist(s): SPD-Small Pr Dist

Cally's War. John Ringo & Julie Cochrane. Narrated by Christine Marshall & William Dufris. 1 CD. (Running Time: 13 Hrs. 15 Mins.). (Posleen War Ser.: No. 6). 2004. audio compact disk 28.50 (978-1-58439-003-9(4)) Pbk Dig Inc.
Look into the abyss - For as long as Cally O'Neal could remember, she had lived in danger. While her father was off fighting the invading Posleen, she had been raised by her grandfather, practically on the front lines of a war that had erased five billion humans from the face of the earth.The abyss looks back - In the final stages of the war, she had officially "died" and been recruited into the elite ranks of the Bane Sidhe, a group of underground warriors dedicated to breaking the stranglehold of the elf-like Darhel. A stranglehold the Darhel held on the Galactic Confederation before the war and now were extending to their human "allies."And you become the abyss - For forty years she has led a life of unremitting, unrecognized, unhallowed slaughter, wearing a constant stream of disguises, sending humans who support the Darhel off to meet their Maker, with her body, mind, and soul twisted and "improved" to serve the needs of her own "allies."Now, on the most important mission of her career, at odds with her superiors, hunting a mole that could destroy her at any moment, and inexorably falling in love with the enemy, for the first time in her life she has to wonder if it's worth it. If being a dragon is the best way to fight the dragon. And if there will be a morning after for the little girl who liked to play with guns and swim with the dolphins.Cally had been fighting for the future of the human race, but now she is in a war for survival: the survival of her soul. - - - - - - - - - - - - - This MP3-CD Audiobook can only be played on an MP3 compatible CD player or an MP3 device like an Apple iPod. Please make sure that your CD player is MP3 compatible before you purchase this audiobook.

Calm amid Chaos: Building a Practical Philosophy for a Challenging World. Barry Neil Kaufman. (ENG.). 2007. audio compact disk 29.50 (978-0-9798105-2-7(3)) Option Inst.

Calm & Loving It! Finding Peace of Mind in the Chaos. 2001. 19.95 (978-0-9671010-8-8(5)) Lifestrides Pubg.

Calm & Peaceful Mind. Dick Sutphen. 1 cass. (Running Time: 1 hr.). (RX17 Ser.). 1986. 14.98 (978-0-87554-294-2(8), RX103) Valley Sun.
You are at peace with yourself, the world & everyone in it; have a quietness of spirit in body & mind; accept the things you cannot change; allow negativity to flow through you without affecting you; rise above the need of approval or control & experience tranquility, peace, love, & joy.

Calm Answers for a Confused Church. unabr. ed. Charles R. Swindoll. 8 cass. (Running Time: 6 hrs. 15 mins.). 1998. 39.95 (978-1-57972-264-7(4)) Insight Living.

Calm at Sunset, Calm at Dawn: A Novel. unabr. ed. Paul Watkins. Narrated by Richard Poe. 7 cass. (Running Time: 9 hrs. 30 mins.). 1991. 60.00 (978-1-55690-084-6(8), 91107E7) Recorded Bks.
James Pfeiffer has a single desire - to own & operate his own boat.

Calm Beneath the Waves: A Program for Panic, Anxiety, Depression & Helplessness. 1 CD. (Running Time: 41 mins.). 2004. audio compact disk 15.00 (978-0-9764498-1-2(1)) O'H O'H Inc.

Calm Beneath the Waves: Help Relieve Panic, Anxiety & Desperation CD. Short Stories. Bill O'Hanlon. Narrated by Bill O'Hanlon. 1 CD. (Running Time: 45 mins.). 2009. audio compact disk 16.95 (978-0-9823573-2-3(X), 7323) Crown Hse GBR.

Calm Birth: Empowering Preparation for Childbirth. abr. ed. Robert Newman. Read by Dara Knerr. Contrib. by Michael Mish. (Running Time: 1 hr. 7 mins.). (ENG.). 2006. audio compact disk 19.95 (978-1-55643-588-1(6)) Pub: North Atlantic. Dist(s): Random

Calm Classroom. 2nd rev. ed. Created by Jai Luster & Joy8 Luster. (ENG., 2009. pap. bk. (978-0-9842423-0-6(9)) Still Moment.

Calm Commute: A: Calm Commute to Work B: Calm Commute Home. Cathrine D. Glashan. Read by Cathrine D. Glashan. Perf. by Tom Barabas & Dean Evenson. 1 cass. (Running Time: 42 mins.). (YA). (gr. 11 up). 1994. 12.98 (978-0-9642378-0-3(6), SRU274-813) Glashan & Assocs.
One hundred-seventy one affirmations soothingly spoken over peaceful music & ocean waves. Listening in the car while driving to & from work promotes a safe, calm, alert, confident commute. Carefully chosen words & rhythm balance the drivers mental, emotional, physical & spiritual well being.

Calm Down: Relaxation & Imagery Skills for Managing Stress, Anxiety & Panic. Read by Shirley Babior & Carol Goldman. 1 cass. (Running Time: 50 mins.). 1996. 11.95 (978-1-57025-106-1(1)) Whole Person.
Let go of anxiety - breathe away stress & experience total body relaxation. Techniques endorsed by leading clinical experts provide relief & help listeners manage anxiety before it gets out of control.

Calm My Anxious Heart: A Woman's Guide to Contentment. unabr. ed. Linda Dillow. Narrated by Christie O. King. (ENG.). 2007. 13.99 (978-1-60814-107-4(1)) Oasis Audio.

Calm My Anxious Heart: A Woman's Guide to Finding Contentment. unabr. ed. Linda Dillow. Read by Christy King. (Running Time: 21600 sec.). (ENG.). 2007. audio compact disk 19.99 (978-1-59859-282-5(3)) Oasis Audio.

Calm Parenting. unabr. ed. Ronald Soderquist & Lynn di Sarro. 2 CD. (Running Time: 1 hr. 30 min.). 2001. audio compact disk 49.77 (978-0-9712609-0-0(7)) Westlke Hyp.
Two great CDs in one package on teaching parenting skills.

Calming the Chaos. 3 CD Set. (Running Time: 210 mins). 2003. audio compact disk 21.95 (978-1-930429-32-1(0)) Pub: Love Logic. Dist(s): Penton Overseas

Calming the Chaos: Behavior Improvement Strategies for the Child with ADHD. unabr. ed. Jim Fay & Charles Fay. 2 cass. (Running Time: 3 hrs. 30 mins.). 1998. 18.95 (978-0-944634-95-0(8)) Pub: Love Logic. Dist(s): Penton Overseas
The Love & Logic approach hands adults simple & effective techniques which can be used to manage even the most chaotic & manipulative behaviors.

Calming the Storm: How to Distinguish & Deal with the Various Storms of Life. 3. (Running Time: 3 hrs.). 2002. 15.00 (978-1-57399-105-6(8)) Mac Hammond.
In this hope-inspiring series, Mac Hammond teaches the three ways storms can begin to brew in our lives and the way of excape for each one.

Calvario Triunfo. Terry Franklin & Barbi Franklin. (Running Time: 30 min.). (SPA.). 2002. 9.95 (978-7-901443-08-2(1)) Pub: Tylis Music. Dist(s): STL Dist NA

Calvario Triunfo. Terry Franklin & Barbi Franklin. (Running Time: 1 hr.). (SPA.). 2002. audio compact disk 14.95 (978-7-901443-15-0(4)) Pub: Tylis Pubng. Dist(s): STL Dist NA

Calvary Road Audio Book. Roy Hession. Read by Dave Birchall. (ENG.). 2008. audio compact disk 14.99 (978-0-87508-980-5(1)) CLC.

Calves see Poetry & Voice of Ted Hughes

Calvin: Selected Writings from the Institutes: of Prayer & the Christian Life: of Prayer & the Christian Life. unabr. ed. John Calvin. Tr. by Henry Beveridge. Narrated by James Adams. (Running Time: 4 hrs. 30 mins. 0 sec.). (ENG.). 2008. audio compact disk 18.98 (978-1-59644-608-3(0), Hovel Audio) christianaud.

***Calvin for Armchair Theologians.** unabr. ed. Christopher Elwood. Narrated by Simon Vance. (ENG.). 2005. 10.98 (978-1-59644-197-2(6), Hovel Audio) christianaud.

Calvin for Armchair Theologians. unabr. ed. Christopher Elwood. Narrated by Simon Vance. 3 CDs. (Running Time: 3 hrs. 48 mins. 0 sec.). (ENG.). 2005. audio compact disk 18.98 (978-1-59644-196-5(8), Hovel Audio) christianaud.

Calvin Murphy. 1 cass. (Running Time: 25 mins.). (Reading with Winners: Ser. 1). 1984. 32.95 (978-0-89811-122-4(6), 8803C) Lets Talk Assocs.
This is a "read-along" program with the athlete's own voice serving as the reader's tutor/guide.

Calvin Murphy. 1 cass. (Running Time: 25 min.). (Reading with Winners: Ser.1). 1984. Lets Talk Assocs.

Calvin Murphy: Basketball. Read by Calvin Murphy. 1 cass. (Running Time: 25 mins.). 9.95 (978-0-89811-085-2(8), 7136) Lets Talk Assocs.
He talks about the people & events which influenced his career & his own approach to his speciality.

***Calvin: of Prayer & the Christian Life: Selected Writings from the Institutes.** unabr. ed. John Calvin. Narrated by James Adams. (ENG.). 2008. 10.98 (978-1-59644-609-0(9), Hovel Audio) christianaud.

Calvin Trillin. Interview with Calvin Trillin. 1 cass. (Running Time: 35 mins.). 1982. 11.95 (L075) TFR.
The "New Yorker" writer talks about the values of downtown cooking, the tacky inelegant authentic stuff that people eat when they just want something good & don't care about putting on airs.

Calvin Trillin. unabr. ed. Ed. by Jim McKinley. Prod. by Rebekah Presson. 1 cass. (Running Time: 29 mins.). (New Letters on the Air Ser.). 1994. 10.00 (061193) New Letters.
A former staff writer for "The New Yorker, Trillin is also well-known for his comic, syndicated columns. In his latest book, "Remembering Denny," Trillin's voice is more somber as he recalls the life of a former classmate at Yale University, a golden boy whose life seemed perfect until he committed suicide.

Calvinist's Honest Doubts Resolved: By Reason & God's Amazing Grace. Hunt Dave. Read by Eric Martin. (Running Time: 6840 sec.). (ENG.). 2006. audio compact disk 7.99 (978-1-928660-54-5(1)) Pub: Berean Call. Dist(s): STL Dist NA

Calypso. unabr. ed. Ed McBain, pseud. Read by Jonathan Marosz. 7 cass. (Running Time: 7 hrs.). (87th Precinct Ser.: Bk. 33). 1998. 42.00 (978-0-7366-3775-6(3), 4448) Books on Tape.
To everyone at the 87th precinct, it looks like an ordinary-enough case. Investigate a couple of homicides & find out who stiffed C.J., the friendly hooker & George, the king of Calypso. Simple enough, right? Wrong. It is only a prelude to something much more complex, more sinister. For Detectives Carella & Meyer, it turns out to be a descent into hell, into a dark underworld of sex, sadism & death. And in the background, they can always hear it - the lilting strains of Calypso music. But it won't stop there. There's more to follow, & what comes next is going to totally blow their minds!.

Calypso Awakening: From the Emory Cook Collection. 1 CD. (Running Time: 67 mins.). 2000. audio compact disk 15.00 (40453) Smithsonian Folkways.

Calypso Chronicles (bind-up) Tyne O'Connell. Read by Tyne O'Connell. Read by Nicky Talacko. (Running Time: 27 hrs. 20 mins.). (Calypso Chronicles). (YA). 2009. 114.99 (978-1-74214-348-4(2), 9781742143484) Pub: Bolinda Pubng AUS. Dist(s): Bolinda Pub Inc

Calypso Chronicles (bind-up) unabr. ed. Tyne O'Connell. Read by Tyne O'Connell. Read by Nicky Talacko. (Running Time: 27 hrs. 20 mins.). (Calypso Chronicles). (YA). 2009. 54.95 (978-1-74214-076-6(9), 9781742140766) Pub: Bolinda Pubng AUS. Dist(s): Bolinda Pub Inc

CAM Design & Manufacturing Handbook. Created by Industrial Press Reference Library. 2005. audio compact disk 94.95 (978-0-8311-3219-4(1)) Indus Pr.

Cam Jansen & the Mystery of the Stolen Diamonds. David A. Adler. Narrated by Christina Moore. (Running Time: 45 mins.). (Cam Jansen Ser.: No. 1). 1997. 10.00 (978-1-4025-4213-8(5)) Recorded Bks.

Cambermere. unabr. ed. Aileen Armitage. Read by Josephine Tewson. 6 cass. (Running Time: 10 hrs.). 1999. 69.95 (978-0-7531-0550-4(0), 990614) Pub: ISIS Audio GBR. Dist(s): Ulverscroft US
Trying to escape an unhappy love affair, Pippa Korvak leaves paris & comes to Cambermere Hall, her fathers's country house. Cambermere does not prove to be the haven she had sought. Handsome journalist stephen Lorant seems determined to blacken the name of Pippa's father, Alexis Korvak & Pippa is equally determined to prove her fathers's innocence. When mysterious "accidents" begin to threaten Pippa's life, she becomes ever more anxious to uncover the shocking truth.

Cambodian Advanced Reader, Robert K. Headley, Jr. & Rath Chim. 3 cass. (Running Time: 4 hrs. 30 mins.). (CAM.). 1998. 24.00 (3173) Dunwoody Pr.
Twenty-five lessons, recorded by native speakers, are intended for anyone who has a good basic knowledge of Cambodian.

Cambodian Advanced Transcription Course, Robert K. Headley, Jr. & Rath Chim. 4 cass. (Running Time: 6 hrs.). (CAM.). 1999. 29.00 (3174) Dunwoody Pr.
Provides practice in aural comprehension & transcription of relatively difficult material. Candidates for this course should have completed a basic course, specifically the Dunwoody Press "Cambodian Intensive Basic Course" & have had some additional experience in listening to & using the spoken language. The material has been selected from Cambodian radio news broadcasts, interviews & commentaries as well as from studio recordings of conversations on a variety of topics. The style of language varies from carefully enunciated Standard Cambodian to the colloquial spoken language & includes royal & religious vocabulary.

Cambodian Complete Set. unabr. ed. University of Iowa, CEEDE Staff. 1 cass. (Running Time: 1 hr.). (People & Activities Around the World Ser.). (CAM.). 1989. tchr. ed. 70.00 (978-0-7836-0734-4(2), 8930) Triumph Learn.
A cultural awareness program told in Cambodian for intermediate LEP students, bilingual, ESL, sheltered English & social studies classes.

Cambodian for Beginners. abr. ed. Richard K. Gilbert. 2008. pap. bk. 15.00 (978-1-887521-83-3(6)) Paiboon Pubng.

Cambodian Intensive Basic Course. William Patterson et al. 16 cass. (Running Time: 1 hr. 30 mins. per cass.). (CAM.). 1998. 75.00 (3148) Dunwoody Pr.
Programmed to take a beginning student to Level 3 (minimum professional fluency) in about thirty weeks. The teaching methodology is based on the model used by the Defense Language Institute & the course is designed to be taught by a native speaker. Standard Cambodian throughout.

Cambodian (Khmer) unabr. ed. 19 cass. (CAM.). bk. 195.00 (KH01) J Norton Pubs.
Learn the same way that you learned English - by listening & repeating. Native speakers ensure that you hear the correct pronunciation, while the cassette player becomes your own private "tireless tutor," repeating the same phrase time after time until you have mastered it.

Cambodian (Khmer) Intensive Course. Richard Noss et al. (Intensive Cassette Ser.). 1998. spiral bd. 225.00 (978-1-58214-000-1(6)) Language Assocs.

Cambodian Set. unabr. ed. University of Iowa, CEEDE Staff. 1 cass. (Running Time: 1 hr.). (You & Others Ser.). (CAM.). 1989. tchr. ed. 17.00 (978-0-7836-0729-0(6), 8925) Triumph Learn.
Cambodian readings of fictional episodes which address common situations. An awareness program for interpersonal relationships & situations.

Cambodian Teaching Set. unabr. ed. University of Iowa, CEEDE Staff. 5 cass. (Running Time: 5 hrs.). (Tales of Marvel & Wonder Ser.). (CAM.). 1988. tchr. ed. 99.00 (978-0-7836-1090-0(4), 9990) Triumph Learn.
Twenty-three Indochinese fables.

Cambridge BEC Higher. Cambridge ESOL. 3 Cass. (BEC Practice Tests Ser.). (ENG.). 2006. 15.75 (978-0-521-67206-1(6)) Cambridge U Pr.

Cambridge Bec Higher 1: Practice Tests from University of Cambridge ESOL Examinations. Created by Cambridge University Press. (Running Time: 4058 sec.). (BEC Practice Tests Ser.). (ENG.). 2002. audio compact disk 15.75 (978-0-521-75291-6(4)) Cambridge U Pr.

Cambridge BEC Higher 2: Examination Papers from University of Cambridge ESOL Examinations. Cambridge ESOL Staff. (Running Time: 1 hr. 30 mins.). (BEC Practice Tests Ser.). (ENG.). 2004. 15.75 (978-0-521-54461-0(0)) Cambridge U Pr.

Cambridge BEC Higher 2: Examination Papers from University of Cambridge ESOL Examinations. Cambridge ESOL Staff. (Running Time: 1 hr. 17 mins.). (BEC Practice Tests Ser.). (ENG.). 2004. audio compact disk 15.75 (978-0-521-54460-3(2)) Cambridge U Pr.

Cambridge Bec Higher 3: Examination Papers Form University of Cambridge ESOL Examinations. Created by Cambridge University Press. (Running Time: 1 hr. 17 mins.). (BEC Practice Tests Ser.). (ENG., 2006. audio compact disk 15.75 (978-0-521-67205-4(8)) Cambridge U Pr.

Cambridge BEC Preliminary. Cambridge ESOL Staff. 3 Cass. (Running Time: 1 hr. 30 mins.). (BEC Practice Tests Ser.). (ENG.). 2006. 15.75 (978-0-521-67198-9(1)) Cambridge U Pr.

Cambridge Bec Preliminary: Practice Tests from the University of Cambridge Local Examinations Syndicate. Created by Cambridge University Press. (Running Time: 4314 sec.). (BEC Practice Tests Ser.). (ENG.). 2002. audio compact disk 15.75 (978-0-521-75303-6(1)) Cambridge U Pr.

Cambridge BEC Preliminary 2: Examination Papers from University of Cambridge ESOL Examinations. Cambridge ESOL Staff. (Running Time: 1 hr. 30 mins.). (BEC Practice Tests Ser.). (ENG.). 2004. 15.75 (978-0-521-54453-5(X)) Cambridge U Pr.

Cambridge Bec Preliminary 2: Examination Papers from University of Cambridge ESOL Examinations. 2nd ed. Created by Cambridge University Press. (Running Time: 1 hr. 17 mins.). (BEC Practice Tests Ser.). (ENG.). 2004. audio compact disk 15.00 (978-0-521-54452-8(1)) Cambridge U Pr.

Cambridge Bec Preliminary 3: Examination Papers from University of Cambridge ESOL Examinations. Created by Cambridge University Press. (Running Time: 4376 sec.). (BEC Practice Tests Ser.). (ENG., 2006. audio compact disk 15.00 (978-0-521-67197-2(3)) Cambridge U Pr.

Cambridge BEC Vantage: Examination papers from University of Cambridge ESOL Examinations. Cambridge ESOL Staff. 2 Cass. (Running Time: 1 hr. 30 mins.). (BEC Practice Tests Ser.). (ENG.). 2004. 15.75 (978-0-521-54457-3(2)) Cambridge U Pr.

Cambridge BEC Vantage: Examination papers from University of Cambridge ESOL Examinations. Cambridge ESOL Staff. Contrib. by Cambridge ESOL Staff. (Running Time: 2 hrs. 34 mins.). (BEC Practice Tests Ser.). (ENG.). 2004. audio compact disk 15.75 (978-0-521-54456-6(4)) Cambridge U Pr.

Cambridge Bec Vantage 1: Examination Papers from University of Cambridge ESOL Examinations. Created by Cambridge University Press. (Running Time: 4868 sec.). (BEC Practice Tests Ser.). (ENG.). 2002. audio compact disk 15.75 (978-0-521-75306-7(6)) Cambridge U Pr.

Cambridge BEC Vantage 3: Examination Papers from University of Cambridge ESOL Examinations, Set. Created by Cambridge ESOL Staff. (BEC Practice Tests Ser.). (ENG.). 2006. audio compact disk 15.75 (978-0-521-67201-6(5)) Cambridge U Pr.

***Cambridge BEC Vantage 3 Audio Cassette.** Cambridge ESOL. (BEC Practice Tests Ser.). (ENG.). 2006. 15.75 (978-0-521-67202-3(3)) Cambridge U Pr.

Cambridge BEC 4 Higher Audio CD: Examination Papers from University of Cambridge ESOL Examinations. Cambridge ESOL. (BEC Practice Tests Ser.). (ENG.). 2009. audio compact disk 15.75 (978-0-521-73921-4(7)) Cambridge U Pr.

Cambridge BEC 4 Preliminary Audio CD: Examination Papers from University of Cambridge ESOL Examinations. Cambridge ESOL. (Running Time: 1 hr. 15 mins.). (BEC Practice Tests Ser.). (ENG.). 2009. audio compact disk 15.75 (978-0-521-73924-5(1)) Cambridge U Pr.

Cambridge BEC 4 Vantage Audio CDs (2) Examination Papers from University of Cambridge ESOL Examinations. Cambridge ESOL. (BEC Practice Tests Ser.). (ENG.). 2009. audio compact disk 15.00 (978-0-521-73927-6(6)) Cambridge U Pr.

Cambridge Business Benchmark: Pre-Intermediate to Intermediate. Norman Whitby. (Running Time: 1 hr. 50 mins.). (ENG.). 2006. audio compact disk 43.05 (978-0-521-67288-7(0)) Cambridge U Pr.

***Cambridge Certificate in Advanced: Official Examination Papers from University of Cambridge Esol Examinations.** rev. ed. Cambridge ESOL Staff. (Running Time: 2 hrs. 34 mins.). (CAE Practice Tests Ser.). (ENG.). 2010. audio compact disk 40.00 (978-0-521-15691-2(2)) Cambridge U Pr.

Cambridge Certificate in Advanced English 1 for Updated Exam: Examination Papers from University of Cambridge Esol Examinations. Cambridge ESOL Staff. 2 CDs. (Running Time: 2 hrs. 24 mins.). (CAE Practice Tests Ser.). (ENG.). 2008. audio compact disk 41.00 (978-0-521-71445-7(1)) Cambridge U Pr.

Cambridge Certificate in Advanced English 2 for updated exam Audio CDs (2) Official Examination Papers from University of Cambridge ESOL Examinations. Cambridge ESOL Staff. (Running Time: 2 hrs. 32 mins.). (CAE Practice Tests Ser.). (ENG.). 2008. audio compact disk 43.05 (978-0-521-71449-5(4)) Cambridge U Pr.

Cambridge Certificate in Advanced English 3 for Updated Exam Audio CDs (2) Examination Papers from University of Cambridge ESOL Examinations. Cambridge ESOL. (CAE Practice Tests Ser.). (ENG.). 2009. audio compact disk 42.00 (978-0-521-73915-3(2)) Cambridge U Pr.

Cambridge Certificate of Proficiency in English: Examination Papers from the University of Cambridge Local Examinations Syndicate. 2nd ed. University of Cambridge, Local Examinations Syndicate Staff. (Running Time: 2 hrs. 50 mins.). (CPE Practice Tests Ser.). (ENG.). 2002. 42.00 (978-0-521-75106-3(3)) Cambridge U Pr.

Cambridge Certificate of Proficiency in English 1: Examination Papers from University of Cambridge ESOL Examinations, Set. Created by Cambridge University Press. (Running Time: 8760 sec.). (CPE Practice Tests Ser.). (ENG.). 2001. audio compact disk 40.00 (978-0-521-00991-1(X)) Cambridge U Pr.

Cambridge Certificate of Proficiency in English 1 Set: Examination Papers from the University of Cambridge Local Examinations Syndicate. University of Cambridge Local Examinations Syndicate Staff. (Running Time: 2 hrs. 46 mins.). (CPE Practice Tests Ser.). (ENG.). 2001. 42.00 (978-0-521-79996-6(1)) Cambridge U Pr.

Cambridge Certificate of Proficiency in English 2: Examination Papers from the University of Cambridge Local Examinations Syndicate. 2nd ed. Created by University of Cambridge Local Examinations Syndicate. 2 CDs. (Running Time: hrs. mins.). (CPE Practice Tests Ser.). (ENG., 2002. audio compact disk 42.00 (978-0-521-75105-6(5)) Cambridge U Pr.

Cambridge Certificate of Proficiency in English 3: Examination Papers from University of Cambridge ESOL Examinations. Created by Cambridge ESOL Staff. (Running Time: 2 hrs. 34 mins.). (CPE Practice Tests Ser.). (ENG., 2004. audio compact disk 42.00 (978-0-521-54389-7(4)) Cambridge U Pr.

Cambridge Certificate of Proficiency in English 3 Cassette Set: Examination Papers from University of Cambridge ESOL Examinations. Cambridge ESOL Staff. Contrib. by Cambridge ESOL Staff. (Running Time: 2 hrs. 34 mins.). (CPE Practice Tests Ser.). (ENG., 2004. 42.00 (978-0-521-54388-0(6)) Cambridge U Pr.

Cambridge Certificate of Proficiency in English 4: Examination Papers from University of Cambridge ESOL Examinations. Created by Cambridge ESOL Staff. (Running Time: 2 hrs. 34 mins.). (CPE Practice Tests Ser.). (ENG.). 2005. audio compact disk 42.00 (978-0-521-61156-5(3)) Cambridge U Pr.

Cambridge Certificate of Proficiency in English 4 Cassette Set. Cambridge ESOL Staff. (Running Time: 2 hrs. 34 mins.). (CPE Practice Tests Ser.). (ENG.). 2005. 42.00 (978-0-521-61155-8(5)) Cambridge U Pr.

Cambridge Certificate of Proficiency in English 5: Examination Papers from University of Cambridge ESOL Examinations. Created by Cambridge ESOL Staff. (Running Time: 2 hrs. 27 mins.). (CPE Practice Tests Ser.). (ENG.). 2006. audio compact disk 43.05 (978-0-521-67278-8(3)) Cambridge U Pr.

Cambridge Certificate of Proficiency in English 5 Cassette Set: Examination Papers from University of Cambridge ESOL Examinations. Cambridge ESOL Staff. (Running Time: 2 hrs. 27 mins.). (CPE Practice Tests Ser.). (ENG.). 2006. 45.15 (978-0-521-67277-1(5)) Cambridge U Pr.

Cambridge English for Schools. Andrew Littlejohn & Diana Hicks. 1 cass. (Running Time: hrs. mins.). (ENG.). 1998. wbk. ed. 12.60 (978-0-521-42133-1(0)); 40.00 (978-0-521-42129-4(2)) Cambridge U Pr.

Cambridge English for Schools, Set. Andrew Littlejohn & Diana Hicks. 3 cass. (ENG.). 1996. 42.00 (978-0-521-42181-2(0)) Cambridge U Pr.

Cambridge English for Schools, Set. 2nd ed. Andrew Littlejohn & Diana Hicks. 2 cass. (ENG.). 1996. 42.00 (978-0-521-42182-9(9)) Cambridge U Pr.

***Cambridge English for Schools Level 1 Class Audio CDs (2)** Andrew Littlejohn & Diana Hicks. (Running Time: 1 hr. 59 mins.). (ENG.). 2010. audio compact disk 40.00 (978-0-521-15711-7(0)) Cambridge U Pr.

***Cambridge English for Schools Level 2 Class Audio CDs (2)** Andrew Littlejohn & Diana Hicks. (Running Time: 2 hrs. 14 mins.). (ENG.). 2010. audio compact disk 44.00 (978-0-521-17812-9(6)) Cambridge U Pr.

***Cambridge English for Schools Level 3 Class Audio CDs (2)** Andrew Littlejohn & Diana Hicks. (Running Time: 2 hrs. 16 mins.). (ENG.). 2010. audio compact disk 43.00 (978-0-521-15410-9(3)) Cambridge U Pr.

***Cambridge English for Schools Level 4 Class Audio CDs (2)** Andrew Littlejohn & Diana Hicks. (Running Time: 1 hr. 46 mins.). (ENG.). 2010. audio compact disk 41.00 (978-0-521-18898-2(9)) Cambridge U Pr.

Cambridge English for Schools Starter. Andrew Littlejohn & Diana Hicks. (Running Time: hrs. mins.). (ENG.). 1997. wbk. ed. 12.60 (978-0-521-56791-6(2)); 24.15 (978-0-521-56792-3(0)) Cambridge U Pr.

***Cambridge English for Schools Starter Class Audio CDs (2)** Andrew Littlejohn & Diana Hicks. (Running Time: 1 hr. 58 mins.). (ENG.). 2010. audio compact disk 23.00 (978-0-521-18026-9(0)) Cambridge U Pr.

Cambridge English for Schools Starter Tests. Patricia Aspinall & George Bethell. (Running Time: 38 mins.). (ENG.). 2001. 23.00 (978-0-521-65649-8(4)) Cambridge U Pr.

Cambridge English for Schools Tests 1. Patricia Aspinall & George Bethell. (Running Time: 50 mins.). (ENG.). 2000. 23.00 (978-0-521-65647-4(8)) Cambridge U Pr.

Cambridge English for Schools Tests 2. Patricia Aspinall & George Bethell. (Running Time: 48 mins.). (ENG.). 2000. 23.00 (978-0-521-65645-0(1)) Cambridge U Pr.

Cambridge English for Schools Tests 3. Patricia Aspinall & George Bethell. (Running Time: 56 mins.). (ENG.). 2001. 23.00 (978-0-521-65643-6(5)) Cambridge U Pr.

Cambridge English for Schools Tests 4. Patricia Aspinall & George Bethell. (Running Time: 1 hr. 5 mins.). (ENG.). 2001. 24.15 (978-0-521-65641-2(9)) Cambridge U Pr.

Cambridge English for Schools 1. Andrew Littlejohn & Diana Hicks. 1 cass. (ENG.). 1996. wbk. ed. 12.00 (978-0-521-42130-0(6)) Cambridge U Pr.

Cambridge English for Schools 3. Andrew Littlejohn & Diana Hicks. 1 cass. (Running Time: hrs. mins.). (ENG.). 1997. wbk. ed. 12.60 (978-0-521-42132-4(2)) Cambridge U Pr.

Cambridge English for Schools 3, Set. Andrew Littlejohn & Diana Hicks. 2 cass. (Running Time: hrs. mins.). (ENG.). 1997. 40.00 (978-0-521-42128-7(4)) Cambridge U Pr.

Cambridge English for the Scuola Media Class, Set. Andrew Littlejohn & Diana Hicks. Adapted by Maristella Sena & Biagio Tedesco. 1997. pap. bk. 50.00 (978-0-521-58894-2(4)) Cambridge U Pr.
Starter unit; Theme A NEW FRIENDS; Units A1-A5; Theme B THE CIRCLE OF LIFE; Units B1-B5; Theme C; NORTH AND SOUTH; Units C1-C5; Theme D AROUND TOWN; Units D1-D5; Theme E THE NATURAL WORLD; Units E1-E5; Revision game; Theme F THE WAY WE LIVE; Units F1-F5; Special unit A Parcel of English; Theme G SCIENCE NOW; Units G1-G5; Theme H NATURAL FORCES; Units H1-H5; Theme I A GOOD LIFE; Units I1-I5; Theme J LIFE ON EARTH; Units J1-J5; Revision game; Theme K BACK IN TIME; Units K1-K5; Special unit A Parcel of English update; Theme L BELOW THE CLOUDS; Units L1-L5; Theme M ACROSS BORDERS; Units M1-M5; Theme N ENERGY IN OUR LIVES; Units N1-N5; Theme O THINK OF THE FUTURE; Units O1-O5; Songs; Tests.

Cambridge English for the Scuola Media 1. Andrew Littlejohn & Diana Hicks. Adapted by Maristella Sena & Biagio Tedesco. 1 cass. (Running Time: 1 hr. 29 mins. 48 sec.). 1997. wbk. ed. 6.00 (978-0-521-58893-5(6)) Cambridge U Pr.

Cambridge English for the Scuola Media 2. Andrew Littlejohn & Diana Hicks. Adapted by Maristella Sena & Biagio Tedesco. 1 cass. (Running Time: 1 hr. 3 mins.). 1997. wbk. ed. 6.00 (978-0-521-58892-8(8)) Cambridge U Pr.
Theme F THE WAY WE LIVE; Units F1-F5; Special unit A Parcel of English; Theme G SCIENCE NOW; Units G1-G5; Theme H NATURAL FORCES; Units H1-H5; Theme I A GOOD LIFE; Units I1-I5; Theme J LIFE ON EARTH; Units J1-J5; Songs.

Cambridge English for the Scuola Media 3, Set. Andrew Littlejohn & Diana Hicks. Adapted by Maristella Sena & Biagio Tedesco. 1 cass. (Running Time: 1 hr. 12 mins.). 1997. pap. bk. & wbk. ed. 6.00 (978-0-521-58891-1(X)) Cambridge U Pr.
Theme K BACK IN TIME; Units K1-K5; Special unit A Parcel of English update; Theme L BELOW THE CLOUDS; Units L1-L5; Theme M ACROSS BORDERS; Units M1-M5; Theme N ENERGY IN OUR LIVES; Units N1-N5; Theme O THINK OF THE FUTURE; Units O1-O5; Songs; exam practice.

Cambridge English for the World Starter with American Voices. Andrew Littlejohn & Diana Hicks. (Running Time: 1 hr. 27 mins.). 1999. wbk. ed. 12.60 (978-0-521-65639-9(7)) Cambridge U Pr.

Cambridge English for the World with American Voices. 4th ed. Andrew Littlejohn & Diana Hicks. (Running Time: hrs. mins.). 1999. wbk. ed. 12.60 (978-0-521-65631-3(1)) Cambridge U Pr.

Cambridge English for the World with American Voices, No. 2,Set. Andrew Littlejohn & Diana Hicks. (Running Time: hrs. mins.). 1999. 42.00 (978-0-521-65636-8(2)) Cambridge U Pr.

Cambridge English for the World with American Voices, No. 3. Andrew Littlejohn & Diana Hicks. (Running Time: 1 hr. 28 mins.). 1999. wbk. ed. 12.60 (978-0-521-65633-7(8)) Cambridge U Pr.

Cambridge English for the World 1 with American Voices. Andrew Littlejohn & Diana Hicks. (Running Time: 1 hr. 32 mins.). 1999. wbk. ed. 12.00 (978-0-521-65637-5(0)) Cambridge U Pr.

Cambridge English for the World 1 with American Voices, Set. Andrew Littlejohn & Diana Hicks. 1999. 40.00 (978-0-521-65638-2(9)) Cambridge U Pr.

Cambridge English for the World 2 with American Voices. Andrew Littlejohn & Diana Hicks. (Running Time: 1 hr. 26 mins.). 1999. wbk. ed. 12.00 (978-0-521-65635-1(4)) Cambridge U Pr.

Cambridge English for the World 3 with American Voices, Set. Andrew Littlejohn & Diana Hicks. (Running Time: hrs. mins.). 1999. 42.00 (978-0-521-65634-4(6)) Cambridge U Pr.

Cambridge English for the World 4 with American Voices, Set. Andrew Littlejohn & Diana Hicks. (Running Time: hrs. mins.). 1999. 42.00 (978-0-521-65632-0(X)) Cambridge U Pr.

Cambridge English Worldwide: American Voices. Andrew Littlejohn & Diana Hicks. 1. (Running Time: 1 hr. 23 mins.). (ENG.). 1999. 24.15 (978-0-521-64509-6(3)) Cambridge U Pr.

Cambridge English Worldwide: American Voices. Andrew Littlejohn & Diana Hicks. (Running Time: 1 hr. 19 mins.). (ENG.). 1999. 24.15 (978-0-521-64499-0(2)) Cambridge U Pr.

Cambridge English Worldwide: American Voices. 2nd ed. Andrew Littlejohn & Diana Hicks. 2. (Running Time: 1 hr. 28 mins.). (ENG.). 1999. 24.15 (978-0-521-64504-1(2)) Cambridge U Pr.

Cambridge English Worldwide: American Voices. 5th ed. Andrew Littlejohn & Diana Hicks. (Running Time: 55 mins.). (ENG.). 2000. 23.00 (978-0-521-78385-9(2)) Cambridge U Pr.

***Cambridge English Worldwide Level 1 Class Audio CDs (2) American Voices.** Andrew Littlejohn & Diana Hicks. (Running Time: 1 hr. 23 mins.). (ENG.). 2010. audio compact disk 43.00 (978-0-521-14475-9(2)) Cambridge U Pr.

***Cambridge English Worldwide Level 2 Class Audio CDs (2) American Voices.** Andrew Littlejohn & Diana Hicks. (Running Time: 1 hr. 29 mins.). (ENG.). 2010. audio compact disk 43.00 (978-0-521-16548-8(2)) Cambridge U Pr.

***Cambridge English Worldwide Level 3 Class Audio CDs (2) American Voices.** Andrew Littlejohn & Diana Hicks. (Running Time: 1 hr. 15 mins.). (ENG.). 2010. audio compact disk 41.00 (978-0-521-18710-7(9)) Cambridge U Pr.

***Cambridge English Worldwide Level 5 Class Audio CD American Voices.** Andrew Littlejohn & Diana Hicks. (Running Time: 53 mins.). (ENG.). 2010. audio compact disk 23.00 (978-0-521-17129-8(6)) Cambridge U Pr.

Cambridge English Worldwide Starter: American Voices. Andrew Littlejohn & Diana Hicks. (Running Time: 1 hr. 20 mins.). 1999. 24.15 (978-0-521-64514-0(X)) Cambridge U Pr.

Cambridge English Worldwide Starter Class (British Voices) Diana Hicks & Andrew Littlejohn. (Running Time: 1 hr. 22 mins.). (ENG.). 2001. 24.15 (978-0-521-00159-5(5)) Cambridge U Pr.

***Cambridge English Worldwide Starter Class CD American Voices.** Andrew Littlejohn & Diana Hicks. (Running Time: 1 hr. 20 mins.). (ENG.). 2010. audio compact disk 23.00 (978-0-521-14291-5(1)) Cambridge U Pr.

Cambridge English Worldwide 1 (British Voices) Andrew Littlejohn & Diana Hicks. (Running Time: 1 hr. 23 mins.). (ENG.). 2001. 24.15 (978-0-521-00162-5(5)) Cambridge U Pr.

Cambridge English Worldwide 2 (British Voices) Andrew Littlejohn & Diana Hicks. (Running Time: 1 hr. 21 mins.). (ENG.). 2001. 24.15 (978-0-521-00166-3(8)) Cambridge U Pr.

Cambridge English Worldwide 3 (British Voices) Andrew Littlejohn & Diana Hicks. (Running Time: 1 hr. 22 mins.). (ENG.). 2001. 24.15 (978-0-521-00171-7(4)) Cambridge U Pr.

Cambridge English Worldwide 4: American Voices. Andrew Littlejohn & Diana Hicks. 4 cass. (Running Time: 51 mins.). (ENG.). 2000. 23.00 (978-0-521-78380-4(1)) Cambridge U Pr.

Cambridge English Worldwide 4 (British Voices) Andrew Littlejohn & Diana Hicks. (Running Time: 51 mins.). (ENG.). 2001. 24.15 (978-0-521-00175-5(7)) Cambridge U Pr.

Cambridge Exams Extra PET, Set. Cambridge ESOL Staff. (Running Time: 2 hrs. 12 mins.). (PET Practice Tests Ser.). (ENG.). 2006. audio compact disk 42.00 (978-0-521-67669-4(X)) Cambridge U Pr.

***Cambridge First Certificate in English: Official Examination Papers from University of Cambridge ESOL Examinations.** Cambridge ESOL Staff. (Running Time: 2 hrs. 34 mins.). (FCE Practice Tests Ser.). (ENG.). 2010. audio compact disk 35.00 (978-0-521-15696-7(3)) Cambridge U Pr.

Cambridge First Certificate in English 1 for Updated Exam: Examination Papers from University of Cambridge Esol Examinations. Cambridge ESOL Staff. 2 CDs. (FCE Practice Tests Ser.). (ENG.). 2008. audio compact disk 43.05 (978-0-521-71452-5(4)) Cambridge U Pr.

Cambridge First Certificate in English 2 for updated exam Audio CDs (2) Official Examination papers from University of Cambridge ESOL Examinations. Cambridge ESOL Staff. (Running Time: 2 hrs. 34 mins.). (FCE Practice Tests Ser.). (ENG.). 2008. audio compact disk 43.05 (978-0-521-71456-3(7)) Cambridge U Pr.

Cambridge First Certificate in English 3 for Updated Exam Audio CDs (2) Examination Papers from University of Cambridge ESOL Examinations. Cambridge ESOL. (FCE Practice Tests Ser.). (ENG.). 2009. audio compact disk 42.00 (978-0-521-73931-3(4)) Cambridge U Pr.

Cambridge Flyers 2: Examination Papers from the University of Cambridge ESOL Examinations. 2nd ed. Created by Cambridge University Press. (Running Time: 1 hr. 7 mins.). (ENG.). 2007. 25.20 (978-0-521-69358-5(6)) Cambridge U Pr.

Cambridge Fun for Flyers. Anne Robinson. (Running Time: 1 hr. 27 mins.). (ENG.). (J). 2006. audio compact disk 23.00 (978-0-521-61369-9(8)) Cambridge U Pr.

Cambridge Fun for Movers. Anne Robinson. (Running Time: 1 hr. 19 mins.). (ENG.). 2006. audio compact disk 23.00 (978-0-521-61365-1(5)) Cambridge U Pr.

Cambridge Fun for Starters. Anne Robinson. (ENG.). 2006. 24.15 (978-0-521-61360-6(4)); audio compact disk 24.15 (978-0-521-61361-3(2)) Cambridge U Pr.

Cambridge IELTS. Cambridge ESOL. (Running Time: 2 hrs. 38 mins.). (IELTS Practice Tests Ser.). (ENG.). 2006. audio compact disk 44.00 (978-0-521-67704-2(1)) Cambridge U Pr.

Cambridge IELTS Audio CD Set 4: Examination Papers from University of Cambridge ESOL Examinations. abr. ed. Created by Cambridge University Press. 4 CDs. (Running Time: 2 hrs. 38 mins.). (IELTS Practice Tests Ser.). (ENG., 2005. audio compact disk 44.00 (978-0-521-54465-8(3)) Cambridge U Pr.

***Cambridge IELTS 1 Audio CDs (2)** Vanessa Jakeman & Clare McDowell. (Running Time: 1 hr. 48 mins.). (IELTS Practice Tests Ser.). (ENG.). 2010. audio compact disk 42.00 (978-0-521-14604-3(6)) Cambridge U Pr.

Cambridge IELTS 2 Set: Examination Papers from the University of Cambridge Local Examinations Syndicate, Set. University of Cambridge, Local Examinations Syndicate Staff. 2 cass. (Running Time: 1 hr. 49 mins.). (IELTS Practice Tests Ser.). (ENG., 2000. 44.00 (978-0-521-77530-4(2)) Cambridge U Pr.

***Cambridge IELTS 2 Audio CDs (2) Examination Papers from the University of Cambridge Local Examinations Syndicate.** Cambridge ESOL. (Running Time: 1 hr. 38 mins.). (IELTS Practice Tests Ser.). (ENG.). 2010. audio compact disk 42.00 (978-0-521-17674-3(3)) Cambridge U Pr.

Cambridge IELTS 2 Cassettes China Edition. UCLES. (IELTS Practice Tests Ser.). 2002. (978-7-88012-142-1(0)) Cambridge U Pr.

Cambridge Ielts 3: Examination Papers from University of Cambridge ESOL Examinations: with Answers, Set. Created by Cambridge University Press. 3 cass. (Running Time: 1 hr. 43 mins.). (IELTS Practice Tests Ser.). (ENG.). 2002. 44.00 (978-0-521-01335-2(6)) Cambridge U Pr.

Cambridge IELTS 3 Audio CD Set: Examination Papers from the University of Cambridge ESOL Examinations, Set. abr. ed. Created by Cambridge University Press. 3 CDs. (Running Time: 102 hrs. 3 mins.). (IELTS Practice Tests Ser.). (ENG., 2002. audio compact disk 42.00 (978-0-521-01336-9(4)) Cambridge U Pr.

Cambridge IELTS 4: Examination Papers from University of Cambridge ESOL Examinations. Created by Cambridge ESOL Staff. 4 cass. (Running Time: 2 hrs. 38 mins.). (IELTS Practice Tests Ser.). (ENG.). 2005. 44.00 (978-0-521-54464-1(5)) Cambridge U Pr.

Cambridge IELTS 6: Examination Papers from University of Cambridge ESOL Examinations. Created by Cambridge ESOL Staff. (Running Time: 2 hrs. 34 mins.). (IELTS Practice Tests Ser.). (ENG., 2007. 44.00 (978-0-521-69309-7(8)) Cambridge U Pr.

Cambridge IELTS 6 Audio CDs: Examination papers from University of Cambridge ESOL Examinations. Cambridge ESOL. (Running Time: 2 hrs. 34 mins.). (IELTS Practice Tests Ser.). (ENG., 2007. audio compact disk 44.00 (978-0-521-69310-3(1)) Cambridge U Pr.

Cambridge IELTS 7 Audio CDs (2) Examination Papers from University of Cambridge ESOL Examinations. Cambridge ESOL. (Running Time: 2 hrs. 38 mins.). (IELTS Practice Tests Ser.). (ENG., 2009. audio compact disk 44.00 (978-0-521-73918-4(7)) Cambridge U Pr.

Cambridge Insight into PET. Helen Naylor & Stuart Hagger. (Running Time: 2 hrs. 8 mins.). (ENG.). 2004. audio compact disk 44.10 (978-0-521-52757-6(0)) Cambridge U Pr.

***Cambridge KET for Schools 1 Audio CD: Official examination papers from University of Cambridge ESOL Examinations.** Cambridge ESOL Staff. (Running Time: 1 hr. 20 mins.). (KET Practice Tests Ser.). (ENG.). 2010. audio compact disk 25.00 (978-0-521-14569-5(4)) Cambridge U Pr.

Cambridge Key English Test. Cambridge ESOL Staff. 4 Cass. (Running Time: 1 hr. 17 mins.). (KET Practice Tests Ser.). (ENG., 2006. 24.15 (978-0-521-67085-2(3)) Cambridge U Pr.

Cambridge Key English Test: Examination Papers from the University of Cambridge ESOL Examinations. 2nd rev. ed. Cambridge ESOL Staff. (Running Time: hrs. mins.). (KET Practice Tests Ser.). (ENG.). 2003. audio compact disk 24.15 (978-0-521-52811-5(9)) Cambridge U Pr.

Cambridge Key English Test: Examination Papers from the University of Cambridge ESOL Examinations. 2nd rev. ed. Cambridge ESOL Staff. (Running Time: 1 hr. 25 mins.). (KET Practice Tests Ser.). (ENG.). 2003. 23.00 (978-0-521-52815-3(1)) Cambridge U Pr.

Cambridge Key English Test No. 1: Examination Papers from the University of Cambridge ESOL Examinations. 2nd rev. ed. Cambridge ESOL Staff. (Running Time: hrs. mins.). (KET Practice Tests Ser.). (ENG.). 2003. 24.15 (978-0-521-52810-8(0)) Cambridge U Pr.

Cambridge Key English Test Extra Audio CD. Cambridge ESOL Staff. (Running Time: 1 hr. 19 mins.). (KET Practice Tests Ser.). (ENG.). 2008. audio compact disk 19.95 (978-0-521-71436-5(2)) Cambridge U Pr.

Cambridge Key English Test 2: Examination Papers from the University of Cambridge ESOL Examinations, Set. 2nd rev. ed. Created by Cambridge ESOL Staff. (KET Practice Tests Ser.). (ENG., 2003. audio compact disk 23.00 (978-0-521-52816-0(X)) Cambridge U Pr.

Cambridge Key English Test 3: Examination Papers from the University of Cambridge ESOL Examinations. Contrib. by Cambridge ESOL Staff. (Running Time: 1 hr. 13 mins.). (KET Practice Tests Ser.). (ENG.). 2003. 24.15 (978-0-521-75481-1(X)) Cambridge U Pr.

Cambridge Key English Test 3: Examination Papers from University of Cambridge ESOL Examinations. 3rd ed. Created by Cambridge University Press. 1 CD. (Running Time: 4342 sec.). (KET Practice Tests Ser.). (ENG.). 2003. audio compact disk 23.00 (978-0-521-75482-8(8)) Cambridge U Pr.

Cambridge Key English Test 4: Examination Papers from University of Cambridge ESOL Examinations. Created by Cambridge University Press. (Running Time: 2 hrs. 34 mins.). (KET Practice Tests Ser.). (ENG., 2006. audio compact disk 23.00 (978-0-521-67084-5(5)) Cambridge U Pr.

Cambridge Key English Test 5 Audio CD: Official Examination Papers from University of Cambridge ESOL Examinations. Cambridge ESOL. (Running Time: 1 hr. 17 mins.). (KET Practice Tests Ser.). (ENG.). 2010. audio compact disk 19.00 (978-0-521-12310-5(0)) Cambridge U Pr.

Cambridge Latin Course, Units 1, 2A and 2B. Edward Phinney & Cambridge School Classics Project. 1 cass. (Cambridge Latin Course Ser.). (ENG.). 1986. 28.50 (978-0-521-24913-3(9)) Cambridge U Pr.

Cambridge Latin Course, Units 3A and 3B. Edward Phinney & Cambridge School Classics Project. 1 cass. (Running Time: 52 mins.). (Cambridge Latin Course Ser.). (ENG.). 1986. 28.50 (978-0-521-24914-0(7)) Cambridge U Pr.

Cambridge Latin Course Unit 4: Omnibus Workbook North American Edition. North American Cambridge Classics Project Staff. (North American Cambridge Latin Course Ser.). 1997. 35.00 (978-0-521-56778-7(5)) Cambridge U Pr.

Cambridge Making Progress to First Certificate: A Pre-First Certificate Course, Set. Leo Jones. (Running Time: 2 hrs. 40 mins.). (ENG., 2005. 42.00 (978-0-521-53707-0(X)) Cambridge U Pr.

Cambridge Nursery Rhymes. Singing Kettle Productions. Contrib. by Richard Brown et al. (Cambridge Reading Ser.). 1996. 20.50 (978-0-521-57451-8(X)) Cambridge U Pr.

Cambridge Objective CAE. 2nd rev. ed. Annie Broadhead & Felicity O'Dell. (Running Time: 2 hrs. 50 mins.). (Objective Ser.). (ENG.). 2008. audio compact disk 42.00 (978-0-521-70062-7(0)) Cambridge U Pr.

Cambridge Objective PET, Set. Louise Hashemi & Barbara Thomas. (Running Time: 11198 sec.). (Objective Ser.). 2006. audio compact disk 61.95 (978-0-521-67881-0(1)) Cambridge U Pr.

Cambridge Objective Proficiency, Set. Annette Capel & Wendy Sharp. 1 cass. (Running Time: 2 hrs. 50 mins.). (Cambridge Books for Cambridge Exams Ser.). (ENG.). 2002. 44.00 (978-0-521-00035-2(1)) Cambridge U Pr.

***Cambridge PET for Schools: Official Examination Papers from University of Cambridge ESOL Examinations.** Cambridge ESOL. (Running Time: 2 hrs. 34 mins.). (PET Practice Tests Ser.). (ENG.). 2010. audio compact disk 43.00 (978-0-521-16655-3(1)) Cambridge U Pr.

Cambridge Practice Tests for IELTS 1 Cassettes China Edition. Vanessa Jakeman & Clare McDowell. (Running Time: 1 hr. 30 mins.). (IELTS Practice Tests Ser.). 2002. (978-7-88012-141-4(2)) Cambridge U Pr.

Cambridge Practice Tests for IELTS 1 Self-Study Edition, Set. abr. ed. Vanessa Jakeman & Clare McDowell. (Running Time: hrs. mins.). (IELTS Practice Tests Ser.). (ENG.). 1996. 42.00 (978-0-521-49766-4(3)) Cambridge U Pr.

Cambridge Preliminary English Test: Examination Papers from the University of Cambridge ESOL Examinations. 2nd rev. ed. Cambridge ESOL Staff. (Running Time: 2 hrs. 34 mins.). (PET Practice Tests Ser.). (ENG.). 2003. audio compact disk 42.00 (978-0-521-75470-5(4)) Cambridge U Pr.

Cambridge Preliminary English Test: Examination Papers from the University of Cambridge ESOL Examinations, Set. 2nd rev. ed. Contrib. by Cambridge ESOL Staff. (Running Time: 2 hrs. 34 mins.). (PET Practice Tests Ser.). (ENG.). 2003. 42.00 (978-0-521-75469-9(0)) Cambridge U Pr.

Cambridge Preliminary English Test 3 Audio Cassette Set: Examination Papers from the University of Cambridge ESOL Examinations. 2nd rev. ed. Cambridge ESOL Staff. (PET Practice Tests Ser.). (ENG.). 2003. 42.00 (978-0-521-75475-0(5)) Cambridge U Pr.

Cambridge Preliminary English Test 3 Audio CD Set: Examination Papers from University of Cambridge ESOL Examinations. 2nd rev. ed. Created by Cambridge University Press. (Running Time: 6303 sec.). (PET Practice Tests Ser.). (ENG.). 2003. audio compact disk 42.00 (978-0-521-75476-7(3)) Cambridge U Pr.

Cambridge Preliminary English Test 4: Examination Papers from the University of Cambridge ESOL Examinations. Cambridge ESOL Staff. . (Running Time:). (PET Practice Tests Ser.). (ENG.). 2003. 42.00 (978-0-521-75530-6(1)) Cambridge U Pr.

Cambridge Preliminary English Test 4 Audio CD Set: Examination Papers from the University of Cambridge ESOL Examinations. Created by Cambridge University Press. (Running Time: 7200 sec.). (PET Practice Tests Ser.). (ENG.). 2003. audio compact disk 42.00 (978-0-521-75531-3(X)) Cambridge U Pr.

Cambridge Preliminary English Test 5 Audio CD Set. Cambridge ESOL Staff. (Running Time: 1 hr. 48 mins.). (PET Practice Tests Ser.). (ENG., 2008. audio compact disk 43.05 (978-0-521-71440-2(0)) Cambridge U Pr.

Cambridge Preliminary English Test 6 Audio CDs (2) Official Examination Papers from University of Cambridge ESOL Examinations. Cambridge ESOL. (Running Time: 2 hrs. 34 mins.). (ENG.). 2010. audio compact disk 50.00 (978-0-521-12321-1(6)) Cambridge U Pr.

Cambridge Preparation for the TOEFL Test. 3rd rev. ed. Jolene Gear & Robert Gear. 4 cass. (Cambridge Preparation for the TOEFL Test Ser.). (ENG., 2002. 53.00 (978-0-521-78400-9(X)); audio compact disk & audio compact disk 53.00 (978-0-521-78399-6(2)) Cambridge U Pr.

Cambridge Preparation for the TOEFL(r) Test. 4th rev. ed. Jolene Gear & Robert Gear. (Running Time: 9 hrs. 30 mins.). (ENG., 2006. audio compact disk 74.00 (978-0-521-75585-6(9)) Cambridge U Pr.

Cambridge Preparation for the TOEFL Test. 4th rev. abr. ed. Jolene Gear & Robert Gear. (Running Time: 9 hrs. 30 mins.). (ENG.). 2006. 74.00 (978-0-521-75586-3(7)) Cambridge U Pr.

Cambridge Secondary Course 1. Andrew Littlejohn & Diana Hicks. (SPA.). 1996. wbk. ed. 8.00 (978-0-521-55722-1(4)); wbk. ed. 8.00 (978-0-521-55723-8(2)) Cambridge U Pr.

Cambridge Starters 1. 2nd rev. abr. ed. Created by Cambridge University Press. (Running Time: 1 hr.). (ENG., (J). (gr. 2-7). 2007. 15.75 (978-0-521-69338-7(1)) Cambridge U Pr.

Cambridge Starters 3: Examination Papers from the University of Cambridge ESOL Examinations. 2nd rev. ed. Created by Cambridge University Press. (Running Time: 1 hr. 2 mins.). (ENG., (J). (gr. 2-7). 2007. 15.00 (978-0-521-69362-2(4)) Cambridge U Pr.

Cambridge Storybooks. Brenda Kent. Jean Glasberg. (Running Time: 1 hr. 15 mins.). (ENG.). 2004. 18.90 (978-0-521-54910-3(8)); 18.90 (978-0-521-54907-3(8)); 18.90 (978-0-521-54904-2(3)) Cambridge U Pr.

Cambridge Storybooks, Level 1. Brenda Kent. (Running Time: 1 hr. 15 mins.). (ENG., 2004. audio compact disk 18.90 (978-0-521-54905-9(1)) Cambridge U Pr.

Cambridge Storybooks, Level 2. Brenda Kent. 2 CDs. (Running Time: 1 hr. 15 mins.). (ENG., 2004. audio compact disk 18.90 (978-0-521-54908-0(6)) Cambridge U Pr.

Cambridge Storybooks: Level 3. Brenda Kent. (Running Time: 1 hr. 15 mins.). (ENG., 2004. audio compact disk 43.05 (978-0-521-54911-0(6)) Cambridge U Pr.

Cambridge Storybooks, Level 4. Brenda Kent. (ENG., 2005. audio compact disk 24.15 (978-0-521-67489-8(1)) Cambridge U Pr.

Cambridge Storybooks 4. (ENG.). 2005. 23.00 (978-0-521-67490-4(5)) Cambridge U Pr.

Cambridge Stratford Study Skills Course, 10 Hour Edition: A College Study Skills Manual - Ten Tips for Academic Success. June Crawford. Illus. by Mary Sullivan-Szarek. (Cambridge-Stratford Study Skills Course). (J). (gr. 11-12). 1988. pap. bk. 40.00 (978-0-935637-14-4(1)) Cambridge Strat.

Cambridge Stratford Study Skills Course, 20 Hour Edition. Mary E. Paterra. (J). (gr. 6-8). 1986. pap. bk. 40.00 (978-0-935637-01-4(X)) Cambridge Strat.

Cambridge Stratford Study Skills Course, 30 Hour Edition. Mary E. Paterra. (YA). (gr. 9-11). 1986. pap. bk. 40.00 (978-0-935637-05-2(2)) Cambridge Strat.

Cambridge Treasury of English Prose: Austen to Bronte. abr. ed. Perf. by Cambridge University Members. 1 cass. (Running Time: 1 hr.). Incl. Biographia Literaria: Biographical Sketches of My Literary Life & Opinions. Samuel Taylor Coleridge. (SWC 1057); Confessions of an English Opium-Eater. Thomas de Quincey. (SWC 1057); Critical & Historical Essays. Thomas Babington Macaulay. (SWC 1057); Emma. Jane Austen. (SWC 1057); French Revolution. Thomas Carlyle. (SWC 1057); Heart of Midlothian. Walter Scott, Sr. (SWC 1057); Imaginary Conversations. Walter Savage Landor. (SWC 1057); Last Essays of Elia. Charles Lamb. (SWC 1057); Letter to Richard Woodhouse. John Keats. (SWC 1057); Plain Speaker: Opinions on Books, Men, & Things. William Hazlitt. (SWC 1057); Villette. Charlotte Brontë. (SWC 1057); Wuthering Heights. Emily Brontë. (SWC 1057); 1985. 12.95 (978-0-694-50046-8(1), SWC 1057) HarperCollins Pubs.

Cambridge Treasury of English Prose: Dickens to Butler. unabr. ed. Perf. by Cambridge University Members. 1 cass. Incl. Apologia Pro Vita Sua & Six Sermons. John Henry Newman. (SWC 1058); Egoist: A Comedy in Narrative. George Meredith. (SWC 1058); Essays in Criticism. Matthew Arnold. (SWC 1058); Mill on the Floss. George Eliot. (SWC 1058); Modern Painters. John Ruskin. (SWC 1058); Pickwick Papers. Charles Dickens. (SWC 1058); Renaissance: Studies in Art & Poetry. Walter Pater. (SWC 1058); Tess of the D'Urbervilles. Thomas Hardy. (SWC 1058); Through the Looking-Glass. Lewis Carroll, pseud. (J). (SWC 1058); Treasure Island. Hamilton Tim. (SWC 1058); Vanity Fair. William Makepeace Thackeray. (SWC 1058); Way of All Flesh. Samuel Butler. (SWC 1058); 1985. 12.95 (978-0-694-50047-5(X), SWC 1058) HarperCollins Pubs.

Cambridge Treasy Burton. unabr. ed. Perf. by Cambridge University Members. 1 cass. Incl. Anatomy of Melancholy: Commentary from Part. 1, Sect. 2, Memb. 4, Subs. 1 to the End of the Second Partition. Robert Burton. (SWC 1055); Brief Lives. John Aubrey. (SWC 1055); Centuries of Meditations. Thomas Traherne. (SWC 1055); Compleat Angler. Izaak Walton. (SWC 1055); Diary. Samuel Pepys. (SWC 1055); Essay of Dramatic Poesy. John Dryden. (SWC 1055); History of the Rebellion & Civil Wars in England. Lord Clarendon. (SWC 1055); Lives of the Poets. Samuel Johnson. (SWC 1055); Rule & Exercises of Holy Dying. Jeremy Taylor. (SWC 1055); Urn Burial. Thomas Browne. (SWC 1055); 1977. 14.00 (978-0-694-50044-4(5), SWC 1055, Harper Audio) HarperCollins Pubs.

Cambridge Treasy Malory. unabr. ed. Perf. by Cambridge University Members. 1 cass. Incl. Apologie for Poetrie. Philip Sidney. (SWC 1054); Essays, of Counsel Civil & Moral. Francis Bacon. (SWC 1054); Euphues & His England. John Lyle. (SWC 1054); King James Version of the Bible: Ecclesiastes. (SWC 1054); LXXX Sermons. John Donne. (SWC 1054); Morte D'Arthur. Photos by Thomas Malory. (SWC 1054); Of the Chronicles of England. John Froissart & Lord Berners. (SWC 1054); Plutarch's Lives. Thomas North. (SWC 1054); Principal Navigations, Voyages & Discoveries of the English Nation. Richard Hakluyt. (SWC 1054); Unfortunate Traveller. Thomas Nashe. (SWC 1054); Utopia. Thomas More. (SWC 1054); Wonderful Year of 1603. Thomas Dekker. (SWC 1054); 1977. 14.00 (978-0-694-50043-7(7), SWC 1054) HarperCollins Pubs.

Cambridge Young Learners English Tests Flyers 2 Audio CD: Examination Papers from the University of Cambridge ESOL Examinations. 2nd rev. ed. Cambridge ESOL. (Running Time: 1 hr. 7 mins.). (ENG., 2007. audio compact disk 24.15 (978-0-521-69359-2(4)) Cambridge U Pr.

Cambridge Young Learners English Tests Flyers 3 Audio Cassette: Examination Papers from the University of Cambridge ESOL Examinations. 2nd ed. Cambridge ESOL Staff. (Running Time: 1 hr. 17 mins.). (ENG.). 2007. 15.75 (978-0-521-69371-4(3)) Cambridge U Pr.

Cambridge Young Learners English Tests Flyers 5 Audio CD: Examination Papers from the University of Cambridge ESOL Examinations. Cambridge ESOL. (Running Time: 1 hr. 17 mins.). (ENG.). 2007. audio compact disk 24.15 (978-0-521-69335-6(7)) Cambridge U Pr.

Cambridge Young Learners English Tests Movers 5 Audio Cassette: Examination Papers from the University of Cambridge ESOL Examinations. Cambridge ESOL. (Running Time: 1 hr. 17 mins.). (ENG.). 2007. 24.15 (978-0-521-69330-1(6)) Cambridge U Pr.

Cambridge Young Learners English Tests Movers 5 Audio CD: Examination Papers from the University of Cambridge ESOL Examinations. Cambridge ESOL. (Running Time: 1 hr. 17 mins.). (ENG., 2007. audio compact disk 24.15 (978-0-521-69331-8(4)) Cambridge U Pr.

Cambridge Young Learners English Tests Starters 1. 2nd rev. ed. Created by Cambridge University Press. (Running Time: 1 hr.). (ENG., (J). (gr. 2-7). 2007. audio compact disk 15.75 (978-0-521-69339-4(X)) Cambridge U Pr.

Cambridge Young Learners English Tests Starters 2: Examination Papers Cambridge ESOL. 2nd rev. ed. Created by Cambridge ESOL Staff. (Running Time: 56 mins.). (ENG., (J). (gr. 2-7). 2007. 15.75 (978-0-521-69350-9(0)); audio compact disk 15.75 (978-0-521-69351-6(9)) Cambridge U Pr.

Cambridge Young Learners English Tests Starters 3: Examination Papers Cambridge ESOL. 2nd rev. ed. Created by Cambridge ESOL Staff. (Running Time: 1 hr.). (ENG., (J). (gr. 2-7). 2007. audio compact disk 15.75 (978-0-521-69363-9(2)) Cambridge U Pr.

Cambridge Young Learners English Tests Starters 4: Examination Papers Cambridge ESOL. 2nd rev. ed. Created by Cambridge ESOL Staff. (Running Time: 1 hr. 4 mins.). (ENG., (J). (gr. 2-7). 2007. 15.75 (978-0-521-69399-8(3)); audio compact disk 15.75 (978-0-521-69400-1(0)) Cambridge U Pr.

Cambridge Young Learners English Tests Starters 5 Audio Cassette: Examination Papers from the University of Cambridge ESOL Examinations. Cambridge ESOL. (Running Time: 1 hr. 17 mins.). (ENG.). 2007. 24.15 (978-0-521-69326-4(8)) Cambridge U Pr.

Cambridge Young Learners English Tests Starters 5 Audio CD: Examination Papers from the University of Cambridge ESOL Examinations. Cambridge ESOL. (Running Time: 1 hr. 17 mins.). (ENG., 2007. audio compact disk 24.15 (978-0-521-69327-1(6)) Cambridge U Pr.

Cambridge Young Learners English Tests 6 Flyers Audio CD: Examination Papers from University of Cambridge ESOL Examinations. Cambridge ESOL. (Running Time: 1 hr. 18 mins.). (ENG.). 2009. audio compact disk 24.15 (978-0-521-73941-2(1)) Cambridge U Pr.

Cambridge Young Learners English Tests 6 Movers Audio CD: Examination Papers from University of Cambridge ESOL Examinations. Cambridge ESOL. (Running Time: 1 hr. 18 mins.). (ENG.). 2009. audio compact disk 23.00 (978-0-521-73938-2(1)) Cambridge U Pr.

Cambridge Young Learners English Tests 6 Starters Audio CD: Examination Papers from University of Cambridge ESOL Examinations. Cambridge ESOL. (Running Time: 1 hr.). (ENG.). 2009. audio compact disk 23.00 (978-0-521-73935-1(7)) Cambridge U Pr.

Camden Connection. unabr. ed. Laurena Gilbert. Read by Leitha Christie. 1 cass. (Running Time: 1 hr. 06 mins.). (YA). (gr. 7-12). 1995. 9.95 (978-1-889112-03-9(8)) Earbks.
A souvenir novella-mystery set in Maine.

Came back to show you I could Fly. Robin Klein. Read by Dino Marnika. (Running Time: 5 hrs.). (YA). 2009. 59.99 (978-1-74214-329-3(6), 9781742143293) Pub: Bolinda Pubng AUS. Dist(s): Bolinda Pub Inc

Came Back to Show You I Could Fly. unabr. ed. Robin Klein. 4 CDs. (Running Time: 5 hrs.). 2004. audio compact disk 57.95 (978-1-74030-606-5(6)) Pub: Bolinda Pubng AUS. Dist(s): Bolinda Pub Inc

Came Back to Show You I Could Fly. unabr. ed. Robin Klein. Read by Dino Marnika. 5 cass. (Running Time: 5 hrs.). 2004. 40.00 (978-1-74030-089-6(0), 500120) Pub: Bolinda Pubng AUS. Dist(s): Bolinda Pub Inc

Camel Club. David Baldacci. Read by Jonathan Davis. (Camel Club Ser.: No. 1). 2005. 90.00 (978-1-4159-2518-8(6)) Books on Tape.

Camel Club. abr. ed. David Baldacci. Read by James Naughton. (Camel Club Ser.: No. 1). (ENG.). 2005. 14.98 (978-1-59483-253-6(6)) Pub: Hachet Audio. Dist(s): HachBkGrp

Camel Club. abr. ed. David Baldacci. Read by James Naughton. (Running Time: 6 hrs.). No. 1. (ENG.). 2007. audio compact disk 14.98 (978-1-59483-951-1(4)) Pub: Hachet Audio. Dist(s): HachBkGrp

Camel Club. unabr. ed. David Baldacci. Read by Jonathan Davis. 10 cass. (Camel Club Ser.: No. 1). 2005. 72.00 (978-1-4159-2504-1(6)) Books on Tape.
David Baldacci takes listeners inside the nation's most elite power club and shows how far its members will go to protect their darkest secrets.

Camel Club. unabr. ed. David Baldacci. Read by Jonathan Davis. (Camel Club Ser.: No. 1). (ENG.). 2005. 16.98 (978-1-59483-254-3(4)) Pub: Hachet Audio. Dist(s): HachBkGrp

Camel Club. unabr. ed. David Baldacci. Read by Jonathan Davis. (Running Time: 16 hrs.). (ENG.). 2009. 74.98 (978-1-60788-066-0(0)) Pub: Hachet Audio. Dist(s): HachBkGrp

Camel Club. unabr. ed. David Baldacci. Read by Jonathan Davis. (YA). 2007. 69.99 (978-1-60252-603-7(6)) Find a World.

Camel Club, Set. abr. ed. David Baldacci. Read by James Naughton et al. (Running Time: 18 hrs.). (ENG.). 2008. 24.98 (978-1-60024-506-0(4)); audio compact disk 29.98 (978-1-60024-505-3(6)) Pub: Hachet Audio. Dist(s): HachBkGrp

Camel Who Took a Walk see Camello Que Se Fue de Paseo

Camel Who Took a Walk. 2004. 8.95 (978-1-56008-856-1(7)); cass. & flmstrp 30.00 (978-0-89719-666-6(X)) Weston Woods.

Camel Who Took a Walk, the; Circus Baby, the; Lentil; Little Red Lighthouse. 2004. (978-0-89719-802-8(6)); cass. & flmstrp (978-0-89719-711-3(9)) Weston Woods.

Camello Que Se Fue de Paseo. Tr. of Camel Who Took a Walk. (SPA.). 2004. 8.95 (978-0-7882-0259-9(6)) Weston Woods.

Camelot: Its Power to the Present Day. Instructed by Stuart Wilde. 2 cass. (Self-Help Tape Ser.). 21.95 (978-0-930603-16-8(8)) White Dove NM.
The legend of Camelot & the quest for the Holy Grail has fired the imagination of poets, artists & visionaries for generation upon generation & is still alive for us today. This legend shows us how to align ourselves with a power that is as old as time. Used properly, the power of quest brings our life & the light within us to their highest possible expansion.

Camelot Caper. Elizabeth Peters, pseud. Narrated by Grace Conlin. (Running Time: 7 hrs.). (C). 1995. 27.95 (978-1-59912-626-5(5)) Iofy Corp.

Camelot Caper, unabr. ed. Elizabeth Peters, pseud. Read by Grace Conlin. 5 cass. (Running Time: 7 hrs.). 1995. 39.95 (978-0-7861-0908-1(4), 1713) Blckstn Audio.
Jessica Tregarth went to England to visit her grandfather; an invitation which surprised and pleased her. The only link she had with her dead father's family was an antique ring he had brought with him to America. This would be a chance to learn more about who she is; it would be fun. She's barely off the boat before the chase begins and Jess finds herself playing a deadly game of cat and mouse through Cornwall, helped by David Randall, the ingenious author of a series of paperback gothic novels. But even Randall's cleverness may not be enough - the couple doesn't know what the pursuers want and it is not the obvious.

Camelot Caper. unabr. ed. Elizabeth Peters, pseud. Read by Grace Conlin. 6 CDs. (Running Time: 7 hrs.). 2005. audio compact disk 48.00 (978-0-7861-8944-1(4), 1713) Blckstn Audio.

Camels, Cats & Rainbows. Paul Strausman. (J). 1982. audio compact disk 14.95 (978-0-939065-81-3(9)) Gentle Wind.

Camels, Cats & Rainbows. Perf. by Paul Strausman. 1 cass. (Running Time: 30 mins.). (J). 1982. 9.95 (978-0-939065-09-7(6), GW1009) Gentle Wind.
Songs children can act out & dance to.

Camels Don't Fly. Dave Blevins. 1 cass. (Running Time: 1 hr.). (J). 2001. pap. bk. 8.99 David C Cook.
Honk is a camel who believes he can fly & tries ingenious ways to do so. Of course, camels are not supposed to be able to fly, so his friends in Noah's Park work together to help him learn to appreciate the gifts God gave him. Included: read-along book.

Camera My Mother Gave Me. unabr. ed. Susanna Kaysen. 4 CDs. (Running Time: 4 hrs.). 2004. audio compact disk 29.95 (978-1-59007-049-9(6)) Pub: New Millenn Enter. Dist(s): PerseuPGW

Camera My Mother Gave Me. unabr. ed. Susanna Kaysen. Perf. by Susanna Kaysen. 3 cass. (Running Time: 4 hrs.). 2004. 25.00 (978-1-59007-048-2(8)) Pub: New Millenn Enter. Dist(s): PerseuPGW
An astonishing, brave, darkly funny & revelatory odyssey across the terrains of sexual "normalcy" & "dysfunction".

Cameras on the Battlefield: Photos of War. Matt White. (High Five Reading Ser.). (ENG.). (gr. 4 up). 2001. audio compact disk 5.95 (978-0-7368-9509-5(4)) CapstoneDig.

Cameras on the Battlefield: Photos of War. Matt White. (High Five Reading - Purple Ser.). (ENG.). (gr. 4-5). 2007. audio compact disk 5.95 (978-1-4296-1424-5(2)) CapstoneDig.

Cameron, Clayton Brushworks. audio compact disk 24.95 (978-0-8258-4962-6(4)) Fischer Inc NY.

Cameron Comes Through. Philip McCutchan. Read by Geoffrey W. Oxley. 4 cass. (Running Time: 6 hrs.). 2001. 44.95 (67940) Pub: Soundings Ltd GBR. Dist(s): Ulverscroft US

Cameron Comes Through. unabr. ed. Philip McCutchan. Read by Peter Barker. 4 cass. (Sound Ser.). 2004. 44.95 (978-1-85496-794-7(0)) Pub: UlverLrgPrint GBR. Dist(s): Ulverscroft US

Cameron in Command. Philip McCutchan. Read by Christopher Scott. 5 cass. (Running Time: 7 hrs. 30 mins.). 2001. 49.95 (23507) Pub: Soundings Ltd GBR. Dist(s): Ulverscroft US

Cameron in the Gap, Philip McCutchan. Read by Christopher Scott. 4 cass. (Running Time: 4 hrs.). 1999. 44.95 (67584) Pub: Soundings Ltd GBR. Dist(s): Ulverscroft US

Cameron in the Gap. unabr. ed. Philip McCutchan. Read by Christopher Scott. 4 cass. (Sound Ser.). 2004. 44.95 (978-1-85496-758-9(4)) Pub: UlverLrgPrint GBR. Dist(s): Ulverscroft US

Cameron of the Castle Bay. unabr. ed. Philip McCutchan. Read by Christopher Scott. 4 cass. (Running Time: 6 hrs.). (Sound Ser.). 2004. 44.95 (978-1-85496-708-4(8), 67088) Pub: UlverLrgPrint GBR. Dist(s): Ulverscroft US
An old ocean boarding vessel, the Castle Bay, is to blow up a secret Nazi base in the Norwegian mountains. Their careful plan goes awry almost immediately though, despite Sub-lieutenant Donald Cameron's knowledge of the treacherous coastline. The flotilla of dinghies meet a minefield & are ambushed, & only a handful of soldiers remain to make the attack. In the meantime, can the captain of the Castle Bay stand by after the rendezvous time when he is certain that the Germans are aware of his ship.

Cameron's Chase. unabr. ed. Philip McCutchan. Read by Christopher Scott. 5 cass. (Running Time: 7 hrs. 30 mins.). 1994. 49.95 (978-1-85496-934-7(X), 6934X) Pub: Soundings Ltd GBR. Dist(s): Ulverscroft US
Cameron, commanding the destroyer Glenshiel, must outwit Hitler's most powerful battleship, the Atila. With the Atila moving in for the kill he must position himself between the battleship & its target, the Queen Mary.

Cameron's Convoy. unabr. ed. Philip McCutchan. Read by Christopher Kay. 4 cass. (Running Time: 6 hrs.). (Sound Ser.). 2004. 44.95 (978-1-85496-138-9(1), 61381) Pub: UlverLrgPrint GBR. Dist(s): Ulverscroft US

Cameron's Crossing. unabr. ed. Philip McCutchan. Read by Gordon Griffin. 6 cass. (Running Time: 9 hrs.). 2001. 54.95 (978-1-86042-434-2(1), 24341) Pub: Soundings Ltd GBR. Dist(s): Ulverscroft US

Cameron's Raid, unabr. ed. Philip McCutchan. Read by Christopher Scott. 6 cass. (Running Time: 8 hrs.). 1998. 54.95 (978-1-86042-388-8(4), 23884) Pub: Soundings Ltd GBR. Dist(s): Ulverscroft US
Right from the start the whole exercise seemed doomed. When he heard he was to take part in one of Churchill's most audacious, some would say foolhardy, operations, Lieutenant-Commander Donald Cameron reckoned expendability was in the air. With a reduced complement, minimal supplies & armament, Cameron is given the command of a shaky old P-class destroyer joining two others in a similar state for the short crossing to the French port of Brest. There they are to penetrate the port & land a detachment of commandos to blow up the huge German U-boat pens. When the Senior Officer's ship is blown up & the commandos fail to make the return rendezvous a the quayside, control of the operation falls to Cameron. Knowing that German warships are in the offing, he decides to creep inland, up the shallows of the Rade de Brest & make contact with the Resistance. It may seem hopeless but to attempt a dash to sea without support would be suicidal.

Cameroon. unabr. ed. Loreto Todd. 1 cass. (Running Time: 56 mins.). (Varieties of English Around the World Ser.). 1982. 51.00 J Benjamins Pubng Co.
Spoken examples of the book.

Camila & Clay-Old-Woman. (Greetings Ser.: Vol. 1). (gr. 3-5). 10.00 (978-0-7635-1746-5(1)) Rigby Educ.

Camila y la Anciana-del-Barro. (Saludos Ser.: Vol. 1). (SPA.). (gr. 3-5). 10.00 (978-0-7635-1753-3(4)) Rigby Educ.

Camilla. unabr. ed. Christopher Davis. Read by Olympia Dukakis. 4 cass. (Running Time: 5 hrs.). 1994. 22.95 (978-1-56876-033-9(7), Cinema Snds) Soundlines Ent.
Freda & Vince have taken a vacation on the Georgia coast to help rekindle their marriage, where they encounter an eccentric old woman, Camilla. When Freda & Camilla are left alone to their own devices, they decide to make a road trip to Toronto to see the Symphony. What entails is the development of one of the most endearing and enchanting relationships.

Camilla. unabr. ed. Madeleine L'Engle. 1 read-along cass. (Running Time: 1 hr. 13 mins.). (Young Adult Cliffhangers Ser.). (YA). (gr. 7 up). 1985. 15.98 incl. bk. & guide. (978-0-8072-1806-8(5), JRH 103 SP, Listening Lib) Random Audio Pubg.
A story about a young girl's first romance, her devastation over her parent's marital problems & the growth of her own sense of self.

***Camilla.** unabr. ed. Madeleine L'Engle. Narrated by Ann Marie Lee. 5 CDs. (Running Time: 7 hrs. 36 mins.). (YA). (gr. 7 up). 2009. audio compact disk 50.00 (978-0-7393-8093-2(1), Listening Lib) Pub: Random Audio Pubg. Dist(s): Random

Camilla. unabr. ed. Madeleine L'Engle. Read by Ann Marie Lee. (ENG.). (J). (gr. 7). 2009. audio compact disk 39.00 (978-0-7393-8091-8(5), Listening Lib) Pub: Random Audio Pubg. Dist(s): Random

Camilla's Roses. unabr. ed. Bernice L. McFadden. Narrated by Patricia R. Floyd. 5 cass. (Running Time: 6.25 hrs.). 2005. 49.75 (978-1-4025-9436-6(4)) Recorded Bks.

Camille. unabr. collector's ed. Alexandre Dumas. Read by David Case. 7 cass. (Running Time: 7 hrs.). 1995. 42.00 (978-0-7366-3116-7(X), 9506) Books on Tape.
Parental meddling destroys genuine love & leads to tragedy. Passionate & penetrating.

Camino: A Journey of the Spirit. Shirley MacLaine. Read by Shirley MacLaine. 2004. 15.95 (978-0-7435-1947-2(7)) Pub: S&S Audio. Dist(s): S and S Inc

Camino a la Felicidad: Una Guia Basada en el Sentido Comun para Vivir Mejor. L. Ron Hubbard. (Running Time: 1 hr. 31 mins. 0 sec.). (SPA.). 2007. audio compact disk 20.00 (978-1-4031-5134-6(2)) Bridge Pubns Inc.

***Camino al Autoconocimiento: Despierta Tu Poder Interior.** Anton Teruel. (SPA.). 2010. audio compact disk 15.99 (978-607-457-062-5(0)) Lectorum MEX.

Camino al Español: A Comprehensive Course in Spanish. Anthony Trippett et al. (SPA & ENG., 2004. 36.99 (978-0-521-53074-3(1)) Cambridge U Pr.

Camino al Español: A Comprehensive Course in Spanish, Set. Consuelo de Andrés Martinez et al. (ENG & SPA., 2004. audio compact disk 46.99 (978-0-521-54065-0(8)) Cambridge U Pr.

Camino del Éxito y Cómo Mejorar la Calidad de Vida. unabr. ed. Hugo Tapias. Read by Pedro Montoya. 3 CDs.Tr. of Road to Success & How to Improve the Quality of Life. (SPA.). 2001. audio compact disk 17.00 (978-958-9494-90-5(0)) YoYoMusic.

Camino Mas Facil: Conferencia en vivo con Dr. Ihaleakala y Mabel Katz. Mabel Katz. Hosted by Mabel Katz.Tr. of Live conference with Dr. Ihaleakala & Mabel Katz. (SPA.). 2008. audio compact disk 19.95 (978-0-9748820-3-1(8)) Your Business.

Camino Más Fácil: Conferencia en vivo con el Dr. Ihaleakala y Mabel Katz. Narrated by Mabel Katz & Ihaleakala. 2007. audio compact disk 39.95 (978-0-9748820-6-2(2)) Your Business.

***Camino Mas Facil - Edicion Especial.** Mabel Katz. (SPA.). 2010. pap. bk. 19.95 (978-0-9825910-5-5(5)) Your Business.

Camino Mas Facil a la Prosperidad. Hosted by Mabel Katz. (SPA.). 2009. audio compact disk 29.95 (978-0-9818210-0-9(6)) Your Business.

Camino Más Fácil para Entender Ho'oponopono: Las Respuestas Más Claras a Tus Preguntas Más Frecuentes-Volumen I, Vol. 1. Mabel Katz. (SPA.). 2009. 19.95 (978-0-9748820-8-6(9)) Your Business.

Camino Real Audio CD Road Trip: Albuquerque/Santa Fe Santa Fe/Albuquerque Deluxe 2 CD Pakage. Scripts. 2 CDs. (Running Time: 2 Hrs.). 2004. audio compact disk 19.50 (978-0-9759930-1-9(1)) Galloping Glries.
The Camino Real road trip brings to life the history and background of the pueblos along the way, geology of the Rio Grande valley, history & cultures of Albuquerque and Santa Fe as well as imparting myths and legends that add to the mystique of New Mexico's unique landscape.

Caminos Peligrosos. 7 cass. (Running Time: 10 hrs. 30 mins.). pap. bk. 89.95 (SSP260) J Norton Pubs.
Recorded by native professional actors, this short-episode thriller on the intermediate level, in a radio-play format, is especially created to develop your listening comprehension skills. Accompanying book provides a transcript of the recording, exercises & vocabulary.

Caminos Peligrosos. Emile de Harven. 89.95 (978-0-8219-3637-5(9)) EMC-Paradigm.

Caminos Student Audio CD. 2nd ed. Joy Renjilian-Burgy. (YA). 2001. cass. & cd-rom 15.96 (978-0-618-14396-2(3), 347521) CENGAGE Learn.

Caminos Three. Niobe O'Connor & Amanda Rainger. 7 cass. (ENG & SPA., 1998. cass. & audio compact disk 282.00 (978-0-7487-3891-5(6)) St Mut.

Caminos Two. Niobe O'Connor & Amanda Rainger. 5 cass. (J). 1998. cass. & audio compact disk 220.00 (978-0-7487-3150-3(4)) St Mut.

camisa de Guerrero. (Saludos Ser.: Vol. 2). (SPA.). (gr. 2-3). 10.00 (978-0-7635-5878-9(8)) Rigby Educ.

Camomile Lawn. unabr. ed. Mary Wesley. Read by Carole Boyd. 8 cass. (Running Time: 10 hrs.). (Audio Bks.). 1991. 69.95 (978-0-7451-6352-9(1)) AudioGO.
Behind the large house, the fragrant camomile lawn stretches down to the Cornish cliffs. Here, in the dizzying heat of August, 1939, five cousins have gathered for their annual ritual of a holiday. For most of them it is the last summer of their youth, with the heady exhilarations & freedoms of lost innocence, as well as the fears of the coming war.

***Camouflage: A Nameless Detective Novel.** Bill Pronzini. (Running Time: 6 hrs. 0 mins. 0 sec.). (ENG.). 2011. audio compact disk 29.95 (978-1-60998-176-1(6)) Pub: AudioGO. Dist(s): Perseus Dist

Camouflage & Lace: My Journey with A Windbender. Diane Ford Wood. 2 CDs. 2004. audio compact disk (978-1-886921-07-8(5)) Alaska Pr Prodns.

Camouflage & Lace: Script & Songbook. Diane Ford Wood. 2004. audio compact disk (978-1-886921-08-5(3)) Alaska Pr Prodns.

Camp. abr. ed. Michael D. Eisner. (ENG.). 2005. 14.98 (978-1-59483-168-3(8)) Pub: Hachet Audio. Dist(s): HachBkGrp

Camp. abr. ed. Michael D. Eisner. (Running Time: 3 hrs.). (ENG.). 2009. 39.98 (978-1-60788-045-5(8)) Pub: Hachet Audio. Dist(s): HachBkGrp

Camp Fear Ghouls. R. L. Stine. 1 cass. (Ghosts of Fear Street Ser.: No. 18). (J). (gr. 4-7). 1997. 95.67 (978-0-671-85756-1(8), AlaChild) SandS Childrens.
Horror & ghost stories.

Camp Ghost-Away. unabr. ed. Judy Delton. Narrated by Christina Moore. 1 cass. (Running Time: 45 mins.). (Pee Wee Scouts Ser.: No. 2). (gr. 2-5). 1997. 10.00 (978-0-7887-0751-3(5), 94928E7) Recorded Bks.
When six-year old Molly Duff & the other Pee Wee Scouts go to Camp Hide-Away, strange things happen. First, Molly hears spooky noises in the dark. Then she & the other Pee Wee Scouts see a ghost! Will Camp Hide-Away turn into Camp Ghost-Away?.

Camp Harmony & the Celebration House. Contrib. by Donut Man. (Donut Man Ser.). (J). (ps-3). 2004. 9.95 (978-5-559-50021-8(6)) Integrity Music.

Camp Meetin' Perf. by Gold City. 2002. audio compact disk Provident Mus Dist.

Camp Oven Cooking. Tommo. 2007. audio compact disk 19.99 (978-3-00-002098-8(5)) Pub: AFN AUS. Dist(s): Cardinal PubGr

Camp Sing-Along. 1 cass. (Running Time: 30 mins.). (J). 1998. bk. 9.95 (978-1-887120-02-9(5)) Prodn Assocs.
Collection of new & traditional sing-along & play-along camp songs for family & group fun.

Camp Wacki Kooki, Vol. 1. Lonny Kocina et al. 1 cass. (Running Time: 1 hr. 2 mins.). (J). (gr. k-6). 1996. 9.95 (978-0-9657166-0-4(0)) Mid-Amer Ent.
Seven stories about a fictional Camp Wacki Kooki narrated by Emmy-winner Brian Czock, known to children as Brian Z.

Camp Wacki Kooki II: Friendship. 2nd ed. Brian Czock et al. 1 cass. (Running Time: 55 mins.). (J). (gr. k-5). 1997. 9.95 (978-0-9657166-1-1(9)) Mid-Amer Ent.
Camp Wacki Kooki 2 stories are a delightful blend of kids'-style fun & value-based messages. These tapes are perfect for helping kids fall asleep at night & for keeping them quietly entertained in the car.

Camp Wacki Kooki III: Teamwork. Brian Czock et al. 1 cass. (Running Time: 55 mins.). (J). (gr. k-5). 1997. 9.95 (978-0-9657166-2-8(7)) Mid-Amer Ent.
A delightful blend of kids'-style fun & value-based messages. These are perfect for helping kids fall asleep at night & for keeping them quietly entertained in the car.

Campaign. Marilyn Tucker Quayle & Nancy T. Northcott. 2 cass. (Running Time: 3 hrs.). 1996. 14.99 (978-0-310-20999-7(4)) Zondervan.
Suspenseful thriller about a Christian politician.

Campaign. unabr. ed. Marilyn Tucker Quayle & Nancy T. Northcott. Read by Anna Fields. 13 cass. (Running Time: 19 hrs.). 1996. 85.95 (978-0-7861-0998-2(X), 1775) Blckstn Audio.
Campaign fever is in the air...& Robert Hawkins Grant is a shoe-in for reelection to the Senate. Grant, a conservative from Georgia, is a strong favorite in the next presidential race, on track to being the first black president of the United States. But nine days before the senatorial election, a reporter who had been publicly dogging him is murdered. Evidence points to Grant, & too many people are quick to believe the worst. Grant must clear his name, solve a murder, exonerate his son from trumped-up drug charges, & expose the White House corruption while maintaining his integrity & keeping himself in the race...& time is running out.

Campaign. unabr. ed. Marilyn Tucker Quayle & Nancy Tucker Northcott. (Running Time: 3 hrs. 10 mins. 0 sec.). (ENG.). 2005. 9.99 (978-0-310-26015-8(9)) Zondervan.

Campaign for A Better Life: 20 Tools to Enrich Your Life & Everyone Around You. Gary Bergenske. (Running Time: 60 mins). 2008. 11.99 (978-1-59755-169-4(4), Advant Self Help) Advant Bks FL.

Campaign Game. 1 cass. (Running Time: 30 mins.). 9.95 (PP-84-09-25, HarperThor) HarpC GBR.

Campaign Management. unabr. ed. F. Clifton White et al. 1 cass. (Running Time: 53 mins.). 12.95 (242) J Norton Pubs.

Campaign Mentality. Elbert Willis. 1 cass. (Moving Life's Mountains Ser.). 4.00 Fill the Gap.

Campaign of Chancellorsville. Theodore Ayrault Dodge. Read by Anais 9000. 2008. 27.95 (978-1-60112-190-5(3)) Babblebooks.

Campaigning, Innovative: Four Case Studies. unabr. ed. 4 cass. (Running Time: 4 hrs.). Incl. From Alienation to Cynicism: Effects of Watergate on the Voter. Peter Hart. (27029-27032); How to Get the Best Possible Media Exposure for a Candidate at No Cost. D. J. Leary. (27029-27032); Iowa Senate Race. Richard Clark. (27029-27032); John Lindsay-Nineteen Sixty-Nine & Nineteen Seventy-Three: Anatomy of a Replay. Tully Plesser. (27029-27032); 35.00 (27029-27032) J Norton Pubs.
The object of this conference was to show how imaginative planning can yield surprising electoral results.

Campaigning with Grant. unabr. ed. Horace Porter. Read by Noah Waterman. 9 cass. (Running Time: 13 hrs.). 1994. 62.95 (978-0-7861-0783-4(9), 1510) Blckstn Audio.
Horace Porter served as lieutenant colonel attached to Ulysses S. Grant's staff from April 1864 to the end of the Civil War. He accompanied Grant into battle in the Wilderness, Cold Harbor & Petersburg campaigns & was present at Lee's surrender at McLean's house. Throughout the war he kept extensive notes which capture Grant's conversations, as well as his own observations of military life.

Campbell's Kingdom, unabr. ed. Hammond Innes. Narrated by Ian Stuart. 6 cass. (Running Time: 9 hrs.). 1988. 51.00 (978-1-55690-085-3(6), 88993E7) Recorded Bks.
A man inherits a deed to oil drilling land in Canada from an ex-con & accompanied by a certified jinx.

Campbell's Kingdom. unabr. collector's ed. Hammond Innes. Read by Charles Garst. 7 cass. (Running Time: 10 hrs. 30 mins.). 1984. 56.00 (978-0-7366-0851-0(6), 1802) Books on Tape.
At the still vital age of 36, Bruce Wetheral, a London insurance clerk, finds he hasn't much time to live. Shocked & discomfitted, he resolutely determines that it's about time to put all the pieces of his scattered existence into perspective. However he also learns that he has become the sole heir to his grandfather's failing Canadian enterprise - Campbell's Rocky Mountain Oil Exploration Co.

Campfire Classics: Bb Instruments. James Curnow & Paul Curnow. 2005. pap. bk. 14.95 (978-90-431-2127-9(4), 9043121274) H Leonard.

Campfire Classics: BC Instruments. James Curnow & Paul Curnow. 2005. pap. bk. 14.95 (978-90-431-2124-8(X), 904312124X) H Leonard.

Campfire Classics: C Instruments. James Curnow & Paul Curnow. 2005. pap. bk. 14.95 (978-90-431-2128-6(2), 9043121282) H Leonard.

Campfire Classics: Eb Instruments. James Curnow & Paul Curnow. 2005. pap. bk. 14.95 (978-90-431-2126-2(6), 9043121266) H Leonard.

Campfire Classics: F/Eb Horn. James Curnow & Paul Curnow. 2005. pap. bk. 14.95 (978-90-431-2125-5(8), 9043121258) H Leonard.

Campfire Homecoming. Contrib. by Bill & Gloria Gaither and Their Homecoming Friends. (Gaither Gospel Ser.). 2008. 19.99 (978-5-557-50366-2(8)) Gaither Music Co.

Campfire Songs, Healthy Happy Songs, Mother Goose, Silly Songs. Ed. by Publications International Staff. (J). 2007. audio compact disk 9.98 (978-1-4127-8496-2(4)) Pubns Intl Ltd.

Camphor Laurel, unabr. ed. Sarah Walker. Read by Megan E. Rees. 2 cass. (Running Time: 3 hrs.). 2002. (978-1-876584-61-0(0), 950808) Bolinda Pubng AUS.
"Pretty please with sugar on top, come with me." Under the camphor laurel, bonds are made & broken even the special friendship between Melissa & Julietta can't escape the rusting winds of change. Anyone who has ever had a best friend will recognize the bittersweet moments of companionship captured with poignancy & affection in Camphor Laurel.

Camping Caper. Barbara Davoll & Dennis Hockerman. Illus. by Dennis Hockerman. 1 cass. (Christopher Churchmouse Ser.). (J). (ps-2). 1993. bk. 11.99 (978-1-56476-162-0(2), 6-3162) David C Cook.

Camping with Henry & Tom. unabr. ed. Mark St. Germain. Perf. by Alan Alda et al. 1 cass. (Running Time: 1 hr. 29 mins.). 2000. 19.95 (978-1-58081-002-9(0), TPT68) L A Theatre.
President Harding wants to be with his mistress. Industrialist Henry Ford wants to be President. And inventor Thomas Alva Edison wonders how the three of them ever got stuck in the woods together. Inspired by an actual camping trip taken by the three men in 1921, playwright Mark St. Germain creates a rollicking adventure filled with humor, insight & surprising relevance to the politics of our time.

Camping with Henry & Tom. unabr. ed. Mark St. Germain. Perf. by Alan Alda et al. 2 CDs. (Running Time: 1 hr. 29 mins.). 2000. audio compact disk 25.95 (978-1-58081-187-3(6), CDTPT68) Pub: L A Theatre. Dist(s): NetLibrary CO

Campmeetin' Live, Vol. 1. Perf. by Oak Ridge Boys, The et al. 1 cass. 1999. (978-0-7601-3129-9(5)); audio compact disk (978-0-7601-3128-2(7)) Brentwood Music.
Relive the sound & spirit of the old fashioned tent revival with classic live performances by the greatest groups of Southern Gospel Music.

Campmeetin' Live, Vol. 2. Perf. by Oak Ridge Boys, The et al. 1 cass. 1999. (978-0-7601-3131-2(7)); audio compact disk (978-0-7601-3130-5(9)) Brentwood Music.

Campmeetin' Live, Vol. 3. Perf. by Oak Ridge Boys, The et al. 1 cass. 1999. (978-0-7601-3133-6(3)); audio compact disk (978-0-7601-3132-9(5)) Brentwood Music.
Relive the sound & spirit of old fashioned tent revival with classic live performances by the greatest groups of Southern Gospel Music.

Campmeetin' Live, Vol. 4. Perf. by Oak Ridge Boys, The et al. 1 cass. 1999. (978-0-7601-3135-0(X)); audio compact disk (978-0-7601-3134-3(1)) Brentwood Music.
Relive the sound & spirit of the old fashioned tent revival with classic live performances by the greatest groups of Southern Gospel Music.

Campus Confidential. Robert A. Wilson. 2 cass. 18.00 (A0481-89) Sound Photosyn.
A hilarious rave that makes you want to take notes.

Campus Conservative Leadership Conference: Addresses. Read by Eric Brodin & Stephen M. Krason. 1 cass. Incl. Campus Conservative Leadership Conference: Conservatism & Student Activism. (126); Campus Conservative Leadership Conference: Presentations from Conservative Educational Groups. (126); 2.50 (126) ISI Books.

Campus Conservative Leadership Conference: Conservatism & Student Activism see Campus Conservative Leadership Conference: Addresses

Campus Conservative Leadership Conference: Presentations from Conservative Educational Groups see Campus Conservative Leadership Conference: Addresses

Camus Parle: L'Ecrivain. Excerpts. Albert Camus. Read by Albert Camus. 1 CD. (Running Time: 1 hr.). (FRE.). 1995. audio compact disk 29.95 (1322-AD) Olivia & Hill.
Camus's early career as an actor makes him well suited to read excerpts from L'Etranger. Recorded in April 1954.

Camus Parle: L'Ecrivain et le Theatre. Excerpts. Albert Camus. Read by Albert Camus. 1 CD. (Running Time: 1 hr.). (FRE.). 1995. audio compact disk 29.95 (1323-AD) Olivia & Hill.
Camus reads excerpts from Noces, La Peste, La Chute, also an interview he gave on the style & composition of La Peste.

Camus Parle: L'Homme. Albert Camus. Read by Albert Camus. 1 CD. (Running Time: 1 hr.). (FRE.). 1995. audio compact disk 29.95 (1321-AD) Olivia & Hill.
Camus reads from his archives, including the first editorial of Combat, a newspaper created in 1944. He also discusses the problems he encounters as a man & as a writer. An exceptional document.

Can a Cherry Pie Wave Goodbye? Perf. by Hap Palmer. 1 CD. (Running Time: 1 hr.). 2001. audio compact disk 14.95 (HP 103 CD) Hap-Pal Music.
Children learn best by doing & this upbeat music invites active involvement in mastering a wealth of vocabulary, including colors, numbers, letters, phonics, days of the week, animals, opposites, occupations, identifying body parts, actions & spatial elements. Lyrics & activities.

Can a Cherry Pie Wave Goodbye? Perf. by Hap Palmer. 1 cass. (Running Time: 1 hr.). (J). 2001. 9.95 (HP 103) Hap-Pal Music.

Can a Jumbo Jet Sing the Alphabet? 1 CD. (Running Time: 40 mins.). (J). (ps-2). 1999. audio compact disk 14.95 Rounder Kids Mus Dist.
Combines music, movement & other activities in the learning process. From the 16 short songs, children can learn numbers & phonics, identify tools & utensils & discern the difference between fantasy & reality, among other concepts.

Can a Jumbo Jet Sing the Alphabet? Hap Palmer. 1 cass. (Running Time: 1 hr.). (J). 1999. 11.95; audio compact disk 14.95 Ed Activities.
Sixteen original tunes that help children learn basic pre-reading & math concepts while having fun.

Can a Jumbo Jet Sing the Alphabet? Perf. by Hap Palmer. 1 cass. (Running Time: 1 hr.). (J). 2001. 9.95 (HP 110); audio compact disk 14.95 (HP 110 CD) Hap-Pal Music.
Using a variety of musical styles from around the world, these songs invite active involvement in mastering a wealth of vocabulary & concepts including, shapes & letters, numbers & counting, phonics, fractions, tools & utensils, cultural diversity & creative problem solving. The activities support the curriculum from pre-school through third grade. Up-beat musical arrangements also appeal to students in the intermediate grades, making the activities beneficial for review of basic concepts.

Can a Jumbo Jet Sing the Alphabet? Hap Palmer. 1 cass. (Running Time: 1 hr.). (J). 2001. pap. bk. 11.95 (EA 511C); pap. bk. 14.95 (EA 511CD) Kimbo Educ.
Instrumentals for rhythm instruments & movement activities. Taking a Walk, Sophisticated Popcorn, Rocking Robot, Funky Choo Choo & more. Includes guide.

Can a Jumbo Jet Sing the Alphabet? Hap Palmer. 1 cass. (Running Time: 40 mins.). (J). (ps-2). 1999. 10.95 Rounder Kids Mus Dist.
Combines music, movement & other activities in the learning process. From the 16 short songs, children can learn numbers & phonics, identify tools & utensils & discern the difference between fantasy & reality, among other concepts.

***Can America Survive? 10 Prophetic Signs That We Are the Terminal Generation.** unabr. ed. John Hagee. Read by John Hagee. (Running Time: 10 hrs. 0 mins. 0 sec.). 2010. audio compact disk 39.99 (978-1-4423-3403-8(7)) Pub: S&S Audio. Dist(s): S and S Inc

Can Another Dispel the Darkness in Oneself? J. Krishnamurti. 1 cass. (Krishnamurti & Swami Venkatesananda - 1969 Ser.: No. 1). 8.50 (ASV691) Krishnamurti.

Can Anyone Hide from Antichrist; The Day Heaven Is Evacuated. C. S. Lovett. 1 cass. 6.95 (7026) Prsnl Christianity.
Expands on truths of the book, "Latest Word on the Last Days".

Can Astrology Help Us to Understand Reincarnation & Karma? Instructed by Manly P. Hall. 8.95 (978-0-89314-022-9(8), C610813) Philos Res.

Can Capitalism Survive? Leonard Peikoff. Read by Leonard Peikoff. 1 cass. (Running Time: 60 mins.). 1986. 12.95 (978-1-56114-015-2(5), LP18C) Second Renaissance.
By means of an inventive analogy to two methods of financial forecasting, Dr. Peikoff tells a business audience why the outlook for capitalism appears "bearish." According to the method of "fundamental analysis," the political marketplace will not buy the stock of capitalism unless it first accepts reason, reality & the virtue of selfishness - & in today's world, Dr. Peikoff shows, both liberals & conservatives reject all three. According to the method of "technical analysis" - by which charted patterns of the past are extrapolated to predict future performance - a political graph would reveal that America's freedom peaked in 1776, remained constant until around 1860, then began moving in an ever-accelerating downward trend to its current dismal level. The evidence thus indicates, Dr. Peikoff concludes, that capitalism will "not" survive - unless the root cause of its decline, i.e., the entrenched influence of German philosophy in our colleges, is excised.

Can Catholics & Muslims Co-Exist? 1 cass. (Running Time: 1 hr.). 2003. 13.95 (978-1-932631-41-8(0)); audio compact disk 13.95 (978-1-932631-42-5(9)) Ascensn Pr.

Can Cockatoos Count by Twos? 1 cass. (Running Time: 1 hr.). (J). 2001. pap. bk. 11.95 (EA 525C) Kimbo Educ.
Rhyme Time Band, Jolly Clock, Colors in Motion, Seasons, Jumping to Add & Subtract & more. Includes guide.

Can Cockatoos Count by Twos? Perf. by Hap Palmer. 1 CD. (Running Time: 55 min.). (J). 2001. pap. bk. & tchr. ed. 14.95 (HP109E) Hap-Pal Music.
Combination of music and movement to facilitate comprehension by involving the whole child. Subjects include numbers, rhyming and phonics, colors, telling time, opposites and an appreciation of diversity. Includes five new original songs and expanded activity ideas in liner notes.

Can Cockatoos Count by Twos? Perf. by Hap Palmer. 1 cass. (Running Time: 55 min.). (J). (ps-3). 2001. pap. bk. & tchr. ed. 9.95 (HP109E) Hap-Pal Music.

Can Cockatoos Count by Twos? rev. ed. 1 CD. (Running Time: 1 hr.). (J). (ps-3). 2001. pap. bk. 14.95 (EA 525CD) Kimbo Educ.
Rhyme Time Band, Jolly Clock, Colors in Motion, Seasons, Jumping to Add & Subtract & more. Includes guide.

Can Evangelicals Learn from World Religions? Jesus, Revelation & Religious Traditions. unabr. ed. Gerald McDermott. 6 CDs. (Running Time: 6 hrs. 48 mins. 0 sec.). (ENG.). 2005. audio compact disk 24.98 (978-1-59644-094-4(5), Hovel Audio) christianaud.
What is the nature of revelation in other world religions? And what can evangelicals learn from it? In this provocative and thoughtful book Gerald McDermott explores the theological concept of revelation and how evangelicals have responded to world religions. He then makes a case for God's having revealed himself outside of Israel and the church. He also explores four case studies of how Buddhist, Daoist, Confucian and Islamic understandings have enriched his own concepts of scriptural concepts.

***Can Evangelicals Learn from World Religions? Jesus, Revelation & Religious Traditions.** unabr. ed. Gerald McDermott. Narrated by David Cochran Heath. (ENG.). 2005. 14.98 (978-1-59644-092-0(9), Hovel Audio) christianaud.

Can Evangelicals Learn from World Religions? Jesus, Revelations, & Religious Traditions. unabr. ed. Gerald McDermott. Narrated by David Cochran Heath. 1 MP3 CD. (Running Time: 6 hrs. 48 mins. 0 sec.). (ENG.). 2005. lp 19.98 (978-1-59644-093-7(7), Hovel Audio) christianaud.

Can God? God Can! Elbert Willis. 1 cass. (Spirit of a Finisher Ser.). 4.00 Fill the Gap.

Can I Be Good? unabr. ed. Livingston Taylor. Read by Livingston Taylor. 1 cass. (Running Time: 11 min.). (J). (gr. k-3). 1994. pap. bk. 16.95 (978-0-8045-6817-3(0), 6817) Spoken Arts.
Children will see themselves through the doleful brown eyes of a golden retriever puppy who tries to be good, but just can't help being what he is - a puppy.

Can I Find the Right One? Susan Aiu. 1 cass. 8.95 (487) Am Fed Astrologers.
Your most compatible partners - romantic or not.

Can I Really Believe? Elbert Willis. 1 cass. (Learning Divine Healing Ser.). 4.00 Fill the Gap.

Can I Rise above My Chart? Maxine Taylor. 1 cass. 8.95 (717) Am Fed Astrologers.
An AFA Convention workshop tape.

Can I Touch You: Love Poems & Affirmations. St James Synthia. 1997. 12.95 (978-1-890207-00-7(4)) Beckham Pubns.

Can I Use Frozen Bread Dough? William Wait. 1 cass. 7.98 (978-1-55503-733-8(X), 069404) Covenant Comms.
Dispelling latter-day myths.

Can Karma Be Changed? Kriyananda, pseud. 1 cass. 9.95 (ST-59) Crystal Clarity.
Karma & the Western mind; why we need to know the law of karma; typical American attitudes toward the law; specific ways to view karma & change its effect on you; the role of grace.

Can Land Use Preservation Coexist with Resource Development? Hosted by Nancy Pearlman. 1 cass. (Running Time: 29 min.). 10.00 (327) Educ Comm CA.

Can One Experience the Infinite? J. Krishnamurti. 1 cass. (Krishnamurti & Swami Venkatesananda - 1969 Ser.: No. 2). 8.50 (ASV692) Krishnamurti.

Can One Person Make a Difference? 2003. 25.95 (978-1-57972-508-2(2)) Insight Living.

Can One Person Make a Difference? 2003. audio compact disk 34.00 (978-1-57972-509-9(0)) Insight Living.

Can One Person Make a Difference? unabr. ed. Charles R. Swindoll. 5 cass. (Running Time: 4 hrs. 30 mins.). 1998. 25.95 (978-1-57972-275-3(X)) Insight Living.

Can This Be Love? Capel McCutcheon. 1 cass. 8.95 (562) Am Fed Astrologers.
Mars, Venus, Eros & Amor & romance.

Can This Relationship Be Saved? How to Make This Crucial Determination: How to Make This Crucial Determination. Michael Broder. 1 cass. 1996. 12.95 (C064) A Ellis Institute.
This unique interactive audio program helps you objectively evaluate your relationship by means of a 40-item self-assessment questionnaire. It then outlines specific options to experiment with in order to see if your relationship is salvageable; & finally provides helpful guidelines for deciding whether the positives outweigh the negatives in your relationship & whether to stay or leave.

Can Thought Give Human Being Security? J. Krishnamurti. 1 cass. (Running Time: 75 min.). (Madras, India Talks 1985 Ser.: No. 2). 1999. 8.50 (AMT852) Krishnamurti.
Krishnamurti addresses the timeless questions which mankind has always asked & he invites each one of us to suspend our beliefs & theories, to observe together, to walk together with the speakers as we inquire into the human condition.

Can Vedic Astrology Help Childless Couples? R. G. Krishnan. 1 cass. 8.95 (434) Am Fed Astrologers.

Can We Go Now? Victor Cockburn & Judith Steinbergh. Perf. by Troubadour Staff. 1 cass. (Running Time: 40 min.). (J). (gr. k-3). 1987. 9.95 (978-0-939065-37-0(1), GW1041) Gentle Wind.
Children's music about home, school & everyday life.

Can We Go Now. Victor Cockburn & Judith Steinbergh. Perf. by Troubadour Staff. (J). 1987. audio compact disk 14.95 (978-1-58467-003-2(7)) Gentle Wind.

Can We Have a Pet? Early Explorers Emergent Set A Audio CD. Benchmark Education Staff. (J). 2006. audio compact disk 10.00 (978-1-4108-7602-7(0)) Benchmark Educ.

Can We Really Do Anything about the Way We Are? Read by Mother Basilea Schlink. 1 cass. (Running Time: 30 min.). 1985. Evang Sisterhood Mary.
Includes: My Praying in Battle against My Sins; Is Annoyance a Sin? True Greatness; Behold the Lamb of God.

Can We Still Trust the Clergy? abr. ed. John Ortberg. Read by John Ortberg. 1 cass. (Running Time: 90 mins.). 2002. 8.99 (978-1-58926-046-7(5)) Oasis Audio.

Can We Talk to the Dead? Volume 5, Vol. 5. Speeches. Bhagat Singh Thind. (Running Time: 60 mins). (ENG.). 2003. audio compact disk 12.00 (978-1-932630-06-0(6)) Pub: Dr Bhagat Sin. Dist(s): Baker Taylor

Can We Talk to the Dead? Volume 5, Vol. 5. As told by Bhagat Singh Thind. (Running Time: 60). (ENG., 2003. 6.50 (978-1-932630-29-9(5)) Pub: Dr Bhagat Sin. Dist(s): Baker Taylor

Can We Uncondition Ourselves? J. Krishnamurti. 1 cass. (Running Time: 1 hr.). (Krishnamurti & Dr. Jonas Salk - 1982 Ser.). 1999. 8.50 (AJS83) Krishnamurti.

Can You Believe It? Bk. 3, Vol. 3: Stories & Idioms for Real Life. Jann Huizenga. 2000. 24.50 (978-0-19-437278-7(2)) OUP.

Can You Believe It? Vol. 2: Stories & Idioms from Real Life. Jann Huizenga. 2000. 24.50 (978-0-19-437280-0(4)) OUP.

Can You Believe It? Vol. 2: Stories & Idioms from Real Life. Jann Huizenga & Linda Huizenga. 2000. 24.50 (978-0-19-437277-0(4)) OUP.

Can You Command Love? Matthew 5:43-48. Ed Young. 1979. 4.95 (978-0-7417-1063-5(3)) Win Walk.

Can You Drink the Cup? Henri J. M. Nouwen. Read by Dan Anderson. 2 CDs. (Running Time: 7200 sec.). 2006. audio compact disk 19.95 (978-0-86716-824-2(2)) St Anthony Mess Pr.

Can You Feel the Love Tonight, Level 2. (Yamaha Clavinova Connection Ser.). 2004. disk 1.04 (978-0-634-09589-4(7)) H Leonard.

Can You Feel the Thunder? Lynn E. McElfresh. Read by Johnny Heller. 3 cass. (Running Time: 3 hrs. 30 mins.). (YA). 1999. pap. bk. & stu. ed. 52.00 (978-0-7887-3837-1(2), 41031) Recorded Bks.
Thirteen-year-old Mic Parsons is surrounded by weird people. His deaf & blind sister clunks noisily around the house & a truly strange boy has moved onto the street. Can either of them give Mic the help he needs to pass math?.

Can You Feel the Thunder?, unabr. ed. Lynn E. McElfresh. Narrated by Johnny Heller. 3 pieces. (Running Time: 3 hrs. 30 mins.). (gr. 5 up). 2000. 29.00 (978-0-7887-3825-8(9), 95877E7) Recorded Bks.

Can You Feel the Thunder?, Class Set. Lynn E. McElfresh. Read by Johnny Heller. 3 cass. (Running Time: 3 hrs. 30 mins.). (YA). 1999. 197.30 (978-0-7887-3836-4(4), 46998) Recorded Bks.

***Can You Forgive Her?** unabr. ed. Anthony Trollope. Read by Simon Vance. (Running Time: 14 hrs.). (Palliser Novels Ser.). 2010. 29.95 (978-1-4417-6820-9(3)); 79.95 (978-1-4417-6817-9(3)); audio compact disk 118.00 (978-1-4417-6818-6(1)) Blckstn Audio.

Can You Forgive Her?, Pt. 1. unabr. collector's ed. Anthony Trollope. Read by David Case. 11 cass. (Running Time: 16 hrs. 30 min.). 1993. 88.00 (978-0-7366-2560-9(7), 3312-A) Books on Tape.
Victorian society under the microscope in this first of the Palliser novels.

Can You Forgive Her?, Pt. 2. collector's ed. Anthony Trollope. Read by David Case. 11 cass. (Running Time: 16 hrs. 30 min.). 1993. 88.00 (978-0-7366-2561-6(5), 3312-B) Books on Tape.

Can You Forgive Her?, Pt. 2. unabr. ed. Anthony Trollope. Read by Flo Gibson. 11 cass. (Running Time: 15 hrs. 30 min.). 1993. 71.95 Set. Audio Bk Con.
In this, the first of the Palliser parliamentary novels, the plight of women in marriage, politics, & private life is seen through the eyes of Alice & Kate Vavasor, Lady Glencora, & the coquettish Mrs. Greenow.

Can You Forgive Her?, Pt. 2, set. unabr. ed. Anthony Trollope. 11 cass. (Running Time: 14 hrs.). 71.95 Audio Bk Con.
In this, the first of the Palliser parliamentary novels, the plight of women in marriage, politics & private life is seen through the eyes of Alice & Kate Vavasor, Lady Glencora & the coquettish Mrs. Greenow.

Can You Forgive Her? (Part 1), Vol. 11. unabr. ed. Anthony Trollope. Read by Flo Gibson. 10 cass. (Running Time: 15 hrs.). 1993. 29.95 (978-1-55685-311-1(4)) Audio Bk Con.
In this, the first of the Palliser parliamentary novels, the plight of women in marriage, politics, & private life is seen through the eyes of Alice & Kate Vavasor, Lady Glencora, & the coquettish Mrs. Greenow.

Can You Forgive Her? (Part 2), Vol. 2. unabr. ed. Anthony Trollope. Narrated by Flo Gibson. (Running Time: 14 hrs. 59 mins.). 1993. 34.95 (978-1-55685-798-0(5)) Audio Bk Con.

Can You Forgive Her? (Parts 1 And 2) unabr. ed. Anthony Trollope. Narrated by Flo Gibson. (Running Time: 29 hrs. 46 mins.). 1993. 59.95 (978-1-55685-799-7(3)) Audio Bk Con.

Can You Hear a Lullaby. Dee Carstensen & Julie Dansky. (Running Time: 40 mins.). 2001. audio compact disk (978-1-888795-27-1(1)) Sugar Beats.

Can You Hear Me Now? Raising the Bar in Family Communication. George Pearsons. (ENG.). 2006. audio compact disk 30.00 (978-1-57562-894-3(5)) K Copeland Pubns.

Can You Help Me Find My Smile? Short Stories. Carl Sommer. Narrated by Carl Sommer. 1 cass. Dramatization. (Another Sommer-Time Story Ser.). (J). (gr. 1-4). 2003. bk. 16.95 (978-1-57537-556-4(7)) Advance Pub.

Can You Help Me Find My Smile? Carl Sommer. Narrated by Carl Sommer. 1 cass. Dramatization. (Another Sommer-Time Story Ser.). (J). (gr. k-4). 2003. lib. bdg. 23.95 (978-1-57537-757-5(8)) Advance Pub.

***Can You Help Me Find My Smile? / Me puedes ayudar a encontrar mi Sonrisa?** ed. Carl Sommer. Illus. by Greg Budwine. (Another Sommer-Time Story Bilingual Ser.). (ENG & SPA.). (J). 2009. bk. 26.95 (978-1-57537-175-7(8)) Advance Pub.

Can You Imagine? 27 Scripture Songs for Young Voices. Arranged by Joseph Linn. 1 cass. (Running Time: 20 min.). (J). 1983. 12.99 (TA-9045C) Lillenas.
A collection of 27 rollicking, fun-filled Scriptures for children's choir in unison & optional 2-part arrangements. Each has a pointed message for singers & their audiences.

Can You Keep a Secret? abr. ed. Sophie Kinsella, pseud. Read by Emily Gray. 5 CDs. (Running Time: 6 hrs.). (ENG., 2005. audio compact disk 14.99 (978-0-7393-1810-2(1)) Pub: Random Audio Pubg. Dist(s): Random

Can You Keep a Secret: A Video Story Book. rev. ed. Simon Firth. 2002. 35.95 (978-1-873942-49-9(4)) Pub: P Chapman GBR. Dist(s): SAGE

Can You Make Your Home Ecological? Hosted by Nancy Pearlman. 1 cass. (Running Time: 29 min.). 10.00 (323) Educ Comm CA.

Can You Raise Your Child's IQ? James C. Dobson. 1 cass. (Life-Lifter Ser.). 1985. 10.99 Nelson.
Explores the basis of children's intelligence & the role of parents in its development.

Can You Sound Just Like Me? Red Grammer & Kathy Grammer. 1 CD. (J). audio compact disk 15.00 (978-1-886146-14-3(4)) Red Note Recs.

Can You Sound Just Like Me? Red Grammer & Kathy Grammer. 1 cass. (J). (ps-6). 10.00 (978-1-886146-01-3(2)) Red Note Recs.

Can You Sue Your Parents for Malpractice? Karen Cushman. Read by Karen Cushman. 2 cass. (Running Time: 3 hrs. 20 mins.). (J). 2000. 18.00 (978-0-7366-5113-4(6)) Books on Tape.
It is absolutely disgusting being fourteen. You've got no rights whatsoever. Your parents get to make all the decisions: Who gets the single bedroom. How much allowance is enough. What time you must come in. Who is a proper friend. What your report card is supposed to look like. And what your parents don't tell you to do, the school does. None of this seems fair to Lauren Allen, but then she finds a way to fight back. She can even sue her parents for malpractice, can't she?.

Can You Sue Your Parents for Malpractice? unabr. ed. Paula Danziger. Read by Paula Danziger. 2 cass. (J). (gr. 1-8). 1999. 23.00 (LL 0159, Chivers Child Audio) AudioGO.

Can You Sue Your Parents for Malpractice? unabr. ed. Paula Danziger. 1 read-along cass. (Running Time: 89 min.). (Young Adult Cliffhangers Ser.). (YA). (gr. 5 up). 1986. 15.98 incl. bk. & guide. (978-0-8072-1838-9(3), JRH121SP, Listening Lib) Random Audio Pubg.
When Lauren Allen takes a course in "Law for Children & Young People," she begins to see that all her problems can be resolved. But can she really sue her parents for malpractice?.

Can You Sue Your Parents for Malpractice? unabr. ed. Paula Danziger. Read by Paula Danziger. 2 cass. (Running Time: 3 hrs. 19 mins.). (J). (gr. 5-9). 2004. 23.00 (978-0-8072-7990-8(0), BWYA 960CX, Listening Lib); 29.00 (978-0-8072-7991-5(9), YA960SP, Listening Lib) Random Audio Pubg.
It's absolutely disgusting being fourteen. You've got no rights whatsoever. Your parents get to make all decisions. Who gets a single bedroom. How much allowance is enough. What time you must come in. Who is a proper friend. And what your parents don't tell you to do, the school does.

Can You Sue Your Parents for Malpractice?, Set. unabr. ed. Paula Danziger. Read by Paula Danziger. 2 cass. (YA). 1999. 16.98 (FS9-50959) Highsmith.

Can You Trust God's Word? Logos 09/27/98. 1998. 4.95 (978-0-7417-6100-2(9), B0100) Win Walk.

Can Your Relationship Be Saved? Michael Broder. 1 cass. 14.95 (C064) Inst Rational-Emotive.
Helps you objectively to evaluate your relationship by means of a 40-item self-assessment questionnaire; & provides helpful guidelines for deciding whether the positives outweigh the negatives in the relationship & whether to stay or leave.

Canaan Road. Jamica Flint. Read by Jamica Flint. 2009. audio compact disk 38.00 (978-0-9793960-0-7(X)) Malachi Hse.

Canada. Compiled by Benchmark Education Staff. 2006. audio compact disk 10.00 (978-1-4108-6650-9(5)) Benchmark Educ.

Canada: Kootenay Passages. (Running Time: 65 min.). 1990. 12.95 (CC253) Comp Comms Inc.
Leads you 100 km from Balfour to New Denver through many forgotten ghost towns. Discover the shipwreck of the mountain passages...the relics of old deserted mines which made millions.

Canada: Pioneers of Nelson. (Running Time: 60 min.). 1990. 12.95 (CC254) Comp Comms Inc.
The heritage of the "Queen City of the Kootenays" - Nelson - a beautiful, relaxing town which boasts 350 important historic buildings constructed before 1910.

Canada: The Sights & Sounds of Vancouver. 1 cass. (Running Time: 60 min.). 12.95 (CC252) Comp Comms Inc.
Narrates Vancouver's history with thoroughness. Tour begins with a drive through the semi-rain forest of Stanley Park & continues on to Vancouver's beaches.

Canada Geese Quilt. unabr. ed. Natalie Kinsey-Warnock. Narrated by Alyssa Bresnahan. 1 cass. (Running Time: 1 hr.). (gr. 3 up). 1998. 10.00 (978-0-7887-1906-6(8), 95327E7) Recorded Bks.
Ten-year-old Ariel & Grandma secretly plan a beautiful quilt for the new baby Mother will have, until Grandma gets sick.

Canada Geese Quilt. unabr. ed. Natalie Kinsey-Warnock. Read by Alyssa Bresnahan. 1 cass. (Running Time: 1 hr.). (J). (gr. 4). 1998. 21.75 Hmwk set. (978-0-7887-1934-9(3), 40641); 64.50 Class set. (978-0-7887-3291-1(9), 46131) Recorded Bks.
Ten-year-old Ariel & Grandma secretly plan a beautiful quilt for the new baby Mother will have until Grandma gets sick.

Canada Smarts by Dancing Beetle. Perf. by Eugene Ely. 1 cass. (Running Time: 87 mins.). (J). 1995. 10.00 Erthviibz.
Canadian science, myth, ecology & nature sounds come together when Ms. Porcupine & the spunky humans read & sing with Dancing Beetle.

Canada 2050. Compiled by Various. (ENG.). 2009. audio compact disk Rental 15.95 (978-0-660-19917-7(3), CBC Audio) Canadian Broadcasting CAN.

Canada's Green Plan; Noise Pollution in New York City; & Ecological Thinking & Consumerism. Hosted by Nancy Pearlman. 1 cass. (Running Time: 29 mins.). 10.00 (916) Educ Comm CA.

Canada's Gwitchin First Nation Opposes U. S. Arctic National Wildlife Refuge Oil Drilling Because of Negative Impacts on the Porcupine Caribou Herd. Hosted by Nancy Pearlman. 1 cass. (Running Time: 28 mins.). 10.00 (1504) Educ Comm CA.

Canada's Sustainable Design & Architecture. Hosted by Nancy Pearlman. 1 cass. (Running Time: 30 mins.). 10.00 (1120) Educ Comm CA.

Canadian Killing Ground. abr. ed. Axel Kilgore. Read by Charlton Griffin. 2 vols. No. 5. 2003. 18.00 (978-1-58807-161-3(8)); (978-1-58807-652-6(0)) Am Pubng Inc.

Canadian Killing Ground. abr. ed. Axel Kilgore. Read by Charlie Eason. Abr. by Odin Westgaard. 3 CDs. (Running Time: 3 hrs.). (Mercenary Ser.: No. 5). 2004. audio compact disk 25.00 (978-1-58807-329-7(7)) Am Pubng Inc.
Hank Frost, the wise-cracking, one-eyed mercenary captain, takes on an "easy" executive protection job. The assignment is to ride shotgun on a seven-year-old genius en route to rejoin his father, a U.S. military aircraft expert working on a top secret "mystery bomber" with the Canadian government. But the whiz-kid doesn't like Frost's eye patch jokes and the boy's father turns up missing, as does a mysterious plane. Add the PLO and some Baader-Meinhof gang alumns who have plans to introduce global terrorism to North America in a big, big way.

Canadian Who's Who 2002. 27th rev. ed. Ed. by Elizabeth Lumley. (gr. 13). 2002. disk 275.00 (978-0-8020-4971-1(0)) U Toronto Pr CAN.

Canal Builders: Making America's Empire at the Panama Canal. unabr. ed. Julie Greene. Narrated by Paul Boehmer. (Running Time: 17 hrs. 0 mins. 0 sec.). (ENG.). 2009. audio compact disk 39.99 (978-1-4001-1067-4(X)) Pub: Tantor Media. Dist(s): IngramPubServ

Canal Builders: Making America's Empire at the Panama Canal. unabr. ed. Julie Greene. Read by Karen White. Narrated by Paul Boehmer. (Running Time: 17 hrs. 0 mins. 0 sec.). (ENG.). 2009. lab manual ed. 79.99 (978-1-4001-4067-1(6)); audio compact disk 29.99 (978-1-4001-6067-9(7)) Pub: Tantor Media. Dist(s): IngramPubServ

Canapes for the Kitties. unabr. ed. Marian Babson. Read by Nadia May. 6 cass. (Running Time: 8 hrs. 30 mins.). 1999. 44.95 (978-0-7861-1565-5(3), 2396) Blckstn Audio.
The chaos that ensues when Lorinda Lucas tries to dispose of Miss Petunia & her siblings.

Canapes for the Kitties. unabr. ed. Marian Babson. Read by Nadia May. (Running Time: 28800 sec.). 2007. audio compact disk 63.00 (978-0-7861-6225-3(2)) Blckstn Audio.

Canape's for the Kitties. unabr. ed. Marian Babson. Read by Nadia May. (Running Time: 28800 sec.). 2007. audio compact disk 29.95 (978-0-7861-5911-6(1)) Blckstn Audio.

Canary Caper. unabr. ed. Ron Roy. Illus. by John Steven Gurney. (Running Time: 53 mins.). (A to Z Mysteries Ser.: No. 3). (J). (gr. k-3). 2004. pap. bk. 17.00 (978-0-8072-1705-4(0), S FTR 271 SP, Listening Lib) Random Audio Pubg.

Canary in the CoalMine: Blowing the Whistle in the Case of ¿American Taliban¿ John Walker Lindh. Jesselyn Radack. Executive Producer Susan Krueger. 2006. audio compact disk 16.95 (978-1-4276-0974-8(8)) AardGP.

Canary Trainer. unabr. collector's ed. Nicholas Meyer. Read by David Case. 7 cass. (Running Time: 7 hrs.). 1994. 42.00 (978-0-7366-2857-0(6), 3564) Books on Tape.
A missing manuscript by Dr. Watson in which Sherlock Holmes, employed as a violinist in the Paris Opera, meets the phantom of the same.

Canavan Disease - A Bibliography & Dictionary for Physicians, Patients, & Genome Researchers. Compiled by Icon Group International, Inc. Staff. 2007. ring bd. 28.95 (978-0-497-11344-5(9)) Icon Grp.

Cancel My Subscription: The Worst of N. P. R. unabr. ed. Moe Moskowitz. Read by Robert Kaplow et al. 1 CD. (Running Time: 1.5 hrs.). 2004. audio compact disk 15.00 (978-1-931056-28-1(5), N Millennium Audio) New Millenn Enter.
Assembled in mock-documentary format, traces the history of Moe & includes all his greatest hits.

Cancel My Subscription: The Worst of N. P. R. unabr. abr. ed. Moe Moskowitz. Read by Robert Kaplow et al. 1 cass. (Running Time: 1.5 hrs.). 2004. 15.00 (978-1-931056-27-4(7), N Millennium Audio) New Millenn Enter.

Canceled Czech. unabr. ed. Lawrence Block. Read by Nick Sullivan. 6 vols. (Running Time: 9 hrs.). (Evan Tanner Mysteries Ser.). 2000. bk. 54.95 (978-0-7927-2330-1(9), CSL 219, Chivers Sound Lib) AudioGO.
Janos Kotacek has been imprisoned by the Czech government & will no doubt be tried & hanged for his crimes, but to the secret intelligence agency that Tanner works for, Kotacek is worth more alive than dead. Tanner's orders are simple: go to Prague, storm a castle, free a criminal. That, of course, is the easy part. Keeping himself & his captive alive will take all of Tanner's waking hours.

Cancelling Sin's Control. Elbert Willis. 1 cass. (Outcome of Abiding in Jesus Ser.). 4.00 Fill the Gap.

Cancelling Your Order. Elbert Willis. 1 cass. (Growth Series). 4.00 Fill the Gap.

Cancer. Narrated by Patricia G. Finlayson. Music by Mike Cantwell. Contrib. by Marie De Seta & TMY Communications Staff. 1 cass. (Running Time: 30 mins.). (Astrologer's Guide to the Personality Ser.: Vol. 4). 1994. 7.99 (978-1-878535-15-3(3)) De Seta-Finlayson.
Astrological description of the sign of Cancer; individually customized, covering love, money, career, relationships & more.

Cancer. Francis Moore. 1 cass. (Running Time: 1 hr.). 2001. 9.95 (CA606) Pub: VisnQst Vid Aud. Dist(s): TMW Media

Cancer. Ingrid Naiman. 3 cass. (Running Time: 4 hrs. 30 mins.). 30.00 (978-1-882834-91-4(7)) Seventh Ray.
Penetrating view of the deeper causes of cancer & the issues faced by patients. Some therapeutic suggestions.

Cancer: A Positive Approach for Men. Matthew Manning. Read by Matthew Manning. Music by Enid. 1 cass. 11.95 (MM-105) White Dove NM.
An invaluable listening aid for those working on their own cancer or for those who want to give help & support in the best possible way. Side One identifies predisposing factors of the cancer personality. Side Two, a guided exercise with the inspirational music of the Enid, helps to symbolically overpower the cancer & fortify the system.

Cancer: A Positive Approach for Women. Matthew Manning. Read by Matthew Manning. Music by Enid. 1 cass. 11.95 (MM-104) White Dove NM.

Cancer: Ancient Truths, Natural Remedies & the Latest Findings for Your Health Today. unabr. ed. Don Colbert. 1 cass. (Running Time: 1 hr. 30 mins.). (Bible Cure Ser.). 2003. 7.99 (978-1-58926-192-1(5), S56L-0180) Oasis Audio.

Cancer: Discovering Your Healing Power. Louise L. Hay. Read by Louise L. Hay. 1 cass. (Running Time: 63 mins.). (ENG.). 1988. 10.95 (978-0-937611-06-7(9), 205) Hay House.
Designed for people with cancer who would like to take an active part in assisting their own healing.

Cancer: Discovering Your Healing Power. Louise L. Hay. 1 CD. 2004. audio compact disk 10.95 (978-1-4019-0409-8(2)) Hay House.

Cancer: June Twenty-First - July Twenty-Second. Barrie Konicov. 1 cass. 11.98 (978-0-87082-091-5(5), 017) Potentials.
The author explains how each sign of the Zodiac has its positive & negative aspects & that as individuals, in order to master our own destiny, we must enhance our positive traits.

Cancer: Touching Deep with Music. Howard Richman. 1 cass. (Running Time: 17 mins.). (Entrainment Music Ser.). 1988. 15.95 (978-0-929060-60-6(1)) Sound Feelings.
Transformational music to help release pain & anger.

Cancer: Unleash the Power of Your True Self. 1 cass. (Running Time: 1 hr.). 1999. 9.99 (978-1-928996-03-3(5)) MonAge.

Cancer: Your Relationship with the Energy of the Universe. Loy Young. 1993. 9.95 (978-1-882888-16-0(2)) Aquarius Hse.

Cancer - Embracing the Healing Journey: Relax into Healing Series (2 Spoken Audio CDs & Booklet) Nancy Hopps. (Relax Into Healing Ser.). 2007. pap. bk. 24.95 (978-0-9785985-0-1(4), Relas into Healing) Pub: Syner Systs. Dist(s): Baker Taylor

Cancer - Improving, Strengthening Immunity System. Norman J. Caldwell. Read by Norman J. Caldwell. Ed. by Achieve Now Institute Staff. 1 cass.

(Running Time: 20 mins.). (Health-Imaging Ser.). 1988. 9.97 (978-1-56273-070-3(3)) My Mothers Pub.
Rebuild & strengthen your own natural immune system.

Cancer & the American Diet. Read by Adelle Davis. 1 cass. (Running Time: 45 mins.). 10.00 (AC9) Am Media.
Discusses how certain vitamins & minerals are a bulwark against cancer; how the typical diet is deficient in these factors; how the addition of chemicals to foods is a cause of cancer; & how to overcome their effects.

Cancer & the Healing Power of Play: A Prescription for Living Joyously with Presence, Acceptance & Trust. Created by Izzy Gesell & Roz Trieber. (ENG., 2008. (978-0-9627329-3-5(1)) Trieber Assocs.

Cancer as a Turning Point. Sounds True Staff. 2007. audio compact disk 69.95 (978-1-59179-513-1(3)) Sounds True.

Cancer as a Turning Point, Vol. 2. Sounds True Staff. 2007. audio compact disk 69.95 (978-1-59179-598-8(2)) Sounds True.

Cancer as Initiation: Archetypal Aspects of Breast Cancer. Barbara Stone. 1 cass. (Running Time: 80 mins.). 1995. 10.95 (978-0-7822-0497-1(X), 573) C G Jung IL.
Examining the archetypal apsects of breast cancer sheds light on the current epidemic of this disease, which now claims the lives of 46,000 American women each year. Through her own personal experience with breast cancer, Dr. Barbara Stone found prominent themes of snakes, pregnancy & new birth woven into her dreams before diagnosis & throughout treatment & recovery.

Cancer as Initiation: Surviving the Fire. abr. ed. Barbara Stone. Read by Barbara Stone. 2 cass. (Running Time: 3 hrs.). 1994. bk. 17.95 (978-1-893129-00-9(4), 001) Stonepower.
Inspiring personal account of the author's journey through breast cancer diagnosed in 1991 at age 42.

Cancer Cells see Richard Eberhart Reading His Poetry

Cancer Control Conference. unabr. ed. 11 cass. (Running Time: 7 hrs.). 98.00 (931-942) J Norton Pubs.

Cancer-Free, Third Edition: Your Guide to Gentle, Non-toxic Healing. unabr. ed. Bill Henderson. (Running Time: 11 hrs. 0 mins.). (ENG.). 2009. 29.95 (978-1-4332-9534-8(2)); 65.95 (978-1-4332-9530-0(X)); audio compact disk 100.00 (978-1-4332-9531-7(8)) Blckstn Audio.

Cancer Involvement Program: An Integrative & Holistic Approach to Conventional Medical Treatment. unabr. ed. Sandy Jost. 9 cass. (Running Time: 3 hrs. 30 mins.). 2002. pap. bk. 139.95 (978-1-932153-21-7(7)); pap. bk. 169.95 (978-1-932153-22-4(5)) ONE Health Pubng.
This publication offers a complete program for integrating a holistic, mind/body approach with conventional medical treatments throughout the entire process of cancer prognosis.

Cancer Meditation. 1 cass. (Holistic Support Meditations Ser.). 14.98 (978-0-87554-580-6(7), MH103) Valley Sun.

Cancer Meets Inquiry: The Work with Byron Katie. 2005. audio compact disk 15.00 (978-1-890246-28-0(X)) B Katie Int Inc.

Cancer-Nutrition Link. unabr. ed. Paavo Airola. 1 cass. (Running Time: 43 mins.). 12.95 (937) J Norton Pubs.

Cancer of the Colon & the Rectum. Moderated by Alan D. Forward. 2 cass. (General Sessions Ser.: Spring 1986). 1986. 15.00 (8605) Am Coll Surgeons.
Addresses issues such as hepatic metasteses in colon cancer, colorectal cancer screening program & sphincter saving procedures in cancer of the rectum.

Cancer Research Update. Emylu Hughes & Robert Hughes. 1 cass. 8.95 (169); 8.95 (539) Am Fed Astrologers.
Evidence of natal links to specific types.

Cancer Residency for Clergy. Lowell Mays. 1986. 10.80 (0208B) Assn Prof Chaplains.

Cancer Salves: A Botanical Approach to Treatment. 1 cass. (Running Time: 90 mins.). 10.00 (978-1-882834-95-2(X)) Seventh Ray.
History & use of herbal salves to treat malignant tumors.

Cancer Schmancer. abr. ed. Fran Drescher. (ENG.). 2005. 14.98 (978-1-59483-373-1(7)) Pub: Hachet Audio. Dist(s): HachBkGrp

Cancer Support: Chemotherapy & Radiation. Steven Gurgevich. (ENG.). 2002. audio compact disk 19.95 (978-1-932170-12-2(X), HWH) Tranceformation.

Cancer Symposium: Melanoma: Patterns of Care & Perspectives for Management. 3 cass. (General Sessions Ser.: C84-SP8). 1984. 22.50 (8424) Am Coll Surgeons.

Cancer Symposium: The Surgeon's Role in the Management of Lymphoma. 3 cass. (General Sessions Ser.: C85-SP9). 22.50 (8552) Am Coll Surgeons.

Cancer, Your Diet & You. Michael Klaper. 1 cass. (Running Time: 30 mins.). (Help Yourself to Health Ser.). 7.00 (978-0-929274-06-5(7)) Gentle World.
One of a series of tapes discussing the relationship between a diet free of animal products & improving one's health or a particular disease.

Cancion de Jinete see Poesia y Drama de Garcia Lorca

***Cancion de Navidad.** Charles Dickens. (SPA.). 2010. audio compact disk (978-607-457-054-0(X)) Lectorum MEX.

Cancion de Navidad. abr. ed. Read by Thomas Chacon. Tr. by Jeff Longwell. Music by Billy Cowie. Illus. by Rhonda Steele. 2 cass. (Running Time: 1 hr. 50 mins.).Tr. of Christmas Carol. (SPA.). 1995. 12.00 (978-0-9649969-0-8(1)) Prducnes Ocotillo.
A reading in Spanish of Dickens' "A Christmas Carol".

Cancion de Navidad. abr. ed. Charles Dickens. Read by Laura García. 3 CDs.Tr. of Christmas Carol. (SPA.). 2002. audio compact disk 17.00 (978-958-8161-00-6(2)) YoYoMusic.

Cancion del Lagarto. 1 cass. (Running Time: 1 hr.).Tr. of Lizard's Song. (SPA.). (J). 2001. 15.95 (VXS-31C) Kimbo Educ.

Cancion del Lagarto. George Shannon. Illus. by Jose Aruego. 14 vols. (Running Time: 7 mins.).Tr. of Lizard's Song. 1995. pap. bk. 39.95 (978-1-59519-145-8(3)); 9.95 (978-1-59112-017-9(9)); audio compact disk 12.95 (978-1-59519-143-4(7)) Live Oak Media.

Cancion del Lagarto. George Shannon. Illus. by Jose Aruego. 11 vols. (Running Time: 7 mins.).Tr. of Lizard's Song. (SPA.). (J). 1995. pap. bk. 18.95 (978-1-59519-144-1(5)) Pub: Live Oak Media. Dist(s): AudioGO

Cancion del Lagarto. unabr. ed. George Shannon. Read by Willie Colon. Illus. by Jose Aruego & Ariane Dewey. 14 vols. (Running Time: 7 mins.).Tr. of Lizard's Song. (SPA.). (J). 1995. pap. bk. & tchr. ed. 37.95 Reading Chest. (978-0-87499-351-6(2)) Live Oak Media.
A forgetful & selfish bear, eager to learn the song a lizard neighbor constantly & happily sings, makes a pest of himself until the lizard tailors his song so that the bear can finally remember it.

Cancion del Lagarto. unabr. ed. George Shannon. Read by Willie Colon. Illus. by Jose Aruego & Ariane Dewey. 11 vols. (Running Time: 7 mins.).Tr. of Lizard's Song. (SPA.). (J). (gr. 2-4). 2005. pap. bk. 16.95 (978-0-87499-349-3(0), LK6492) Pub: Live Oak Media. Dist(s): AudioGO
A forgetful and selfish bear makes a pest of himself until the lizard tailors his song so that the bear can finally remember it.

Canciones, 1. 2 CDs. (SPA.). audio compact disk 64.95 (978-0-8219-2513-3(X)) EMC-Paradigm.

Canciones Vol. 2: Serie Heroes de la Fe. (SPA.). 2000. audio compact disk (978-1-57697-853-5(2)) Untd Bible Amrcas Svce.

Canciones Vol. 3: Serie Heroes de la Fe. 2000. (978-1-57697-950-1(4)) Untd Bible Amrcas Svce.

Canciones con Acción. Serie Vida para Niños. 1 CD. (Running Time: 30 min.). (Vida Para Ninos Ser.: Vol. 5). (SPA.). 2003. audio compact disk 4.99 (978-0-8297-3952-7(1)) Pub: Vida Pubs. Dist(s): Zondervan

Canciones con Acción. unabr. ed. (SPA.). 2003. 3.99 (978-0-8297-3954-1(8)) Zondervan.

Canciones de la Aurora. Perf. by Lucy Esquilín. Lyrics by Diego Duey. Music by Diego Duey. Arranged by Rafy Escudero & Mandy Visozo. Illus. by Mariana Diaz. (SPA.). (J). 2005. bk. 8.95 (978-0-8477-0394-4(0)) U of PR Pr.

Canciones de lo Alto. Perf. by Steve Green & Renee Garcia. 1 CD. (Running Time: 1 hr.). (SPA.). 1994. audio compact disk Brentwood Music.
A Spanish version of "Songs from the Loft".

Canciones de Patricia va a California, Casi se muere, el viaje de su vida y ¡Viva el Toro! (SPA.). (J). 2004. audio compact disk (978-0-929724-88-1(7)) Command Performance.

Canciones Dramatizadas. Pablo Ozaeta. 9.95 (Natl Textbk Co) M-H Contemporary.
Each Song deals with a specific letter-sound relationship.

Canciones Heroes de la Fe. (SPA.). 1999. audio compact disk (978-1-57697-778-1(1)) Untd Bible Amrcas Svce.

Canciones para Bebe. Tr. of Lullabies for Babies. (SPA.). 2001. (978-84-305-8590-8(7)) Lectorum Pubns.

Canciones para el Recreo: Children's Songs for the Playground. Perf. by Suni Paz. 1 cass. (Running Time: 26 mins.). (ENG & SPA.). (J). (ps-7). 1990. (0-9307-45013-4-4) Smithsonian Folkways.
Cross-cultural entertainment. Songs in Spanish & English with translations.

Canciones Tematicas para Aprender Idiomas. abr. ed. Agustina Tocalli-Beller. 1 CD. (Running Time: 30 min.). (Songs that Teach Spanish Ser.). (SPA.). (J). 2001. audio compact disk 13.95 (978-1-894262-44-6(1), JMP S20CD) Pub: S Jordan Publ. Dist(s): CrabtreePubCo

Canciones Temáticas para Aprender Idiomas: Apprende Cantando. Agustina Tocalli-Beller. Prod. by Sara Jordan. Composed by Sara Jordan. Engineer Mark Shannon. Illus. by Alex Filipov. 1 cass. (Running Time: 49 min. 4 secs.). (SPA.). (J). 2001. pap. bk. 14.95 (978-1-894262-46-0(8), JMP S20K) Jordan Music.

Canciones y Cuentos Infantiles. Penton Overseas, Inc. Staff. 1 CD. (Running Time: 1 hr.). (J). 2002. audio compact disk 4.99 (978-1-59125-155-2(9)) Penton Overseas.
Each contains a collection of 12 popular Spanish songs. Words and phrases are taught by using simple rhythms. A great way to learn Spanish.

Canciones y Rimas. Benchmark Education Staff. 2004. audio compact disk 10.00 (978-1-4108-3708-0(4)) Benchmark Educ.

Candida. 2 CDs. (Running Time: 5400 sec.). Dramatization. (Stratford Festival Ser.). 2006. audio compact disk 19.95 (978-0-660-19545-2(3), CBC Audio) Pub: Canadian Broadcasting CAN. Dist(s): Georgetown Term

Candida. George Bernard Shaw. Contrib. by JoBeth Williams et al. 2 CDs. (Running Time: 5100 sec.). 1993. audio compact disk 25.95 (978-1-58081-307-5(0), CTA18) Pub: L A Theatre. Dist(s): NetLibrary CO

Candida. unabr. ed. George Bernard Shaw. Read by Flo Gibson. 2 cass. (Running Time: 2 hrs. 24 mins.). 1992. 14.95 (978-1-55685-264-0(9)) Audio Bk Con.
In this poignant play Candida, the wife of the Rev. James Morell, is loved by the visionary & sensitive young poet, Eugene Marchbanks. The two men agree that Candida is to make her choice. She demands that they bid for her.

Candida. unabr. ed. George Bernard Shaw. Perf. by Tom Amandes et al. 1 cass. (Running Time: 1 hr. 25 mins.). 1993. 19.95 (978-1-58081-075-3(6), CTA18) L A Theatre.
Play that challenged conventional wisdom about male female relationships, concerns a beautiful wife's choice between the two men who love her.

Candidate Sourcing & Recruiting: How to Find Talent to Fill Your Jobs. Bill Radin. Voice by Bill Radin. (ENG.). 2008. audio compact disk 95.00 (978-1-929836-14-7(7)) Innovative Consulting.

Candidate's Wife. unabr. ed. Virginia Coffman. 5 cass. (Running Time: 5 hrs.). 1997. 47.95 (978-1-86015-411-9(5)) T T Beeler.
While attending a function in her capacity as, perhaps, the next Vice President's wife, Senator Jesica March overhears what sounds like plotting for an assassination. Although pursuit of the truth will bring more stress upon an already strained marriage & may even cost Jessica her life, she realizes that justice & integrity must prevail.

Candide see Treasury of French Prose

Candide. Voltaire. Narrated by Andrew Sachs. (CSA Word Classics (Playaway) Ser.). (ENG.). 2008. 59.99 (978-1-60640-927-5(1)) Find a World.

Candide. Francois Voltaire, pseud. Narrated by Flo Gibson. 2007. audio compact disk 19.95 (978-1-55685-980-9(5)) Audio Bk Con.

Candide. Francois Voltaire, pseud. pap. bk. 24.95 (978-88-7754-143-7(1)) Pub: Cideb ITA. Dist(s): Distribks Inc

Candide. Francois Voltaire, pseud. audio compact disk 12.95 (978-0-8219-3765-5(0)) EMC-Paradigm.

Candide. Francois Voltaire, pseud. Read by Monique Lebreton-Savigny. 4 cass. (Running Time: 4 hrs.). (FRE.). 1996. pap. bk. 59.50 (978-1-58085-350-7(1)) Interlingua VA.
Includes dual English-French transcription. The combination of written text & clarity & pace of diction will open the door for intermediate & advanced students to genuine comprehension & the use of literary texts for advancement in rapid understanding of written & oral language materials. The audio text plus written text concept makes foreign languages accessible to a much wider range of students than books alone.

Candide. Francois Voltaire, pseud. Read by Laura García. (Running Time: 3 hrs.). 2001. 16.95 (978-1-60083-169-0(9), Audiofy Corp) Iofy Corp.

Candide. Francois Voltaire, pseud. Read by Tom Whitworth. (Running Time: 4 hrs.). 2005. 25.95 (978-1-60083-615-2(1), Audiofy Corp) Iofy Corp.

Candide. Francois Voltaire, pseud. Read by Claude Beauclair. 3 cass. (Running Time: 3 hrs.). (FRE.). 1991. 29.95 (1302-OH) Olivia & Hill.
Candide is a gentle young man taught by the philosopher Pangloss that all is for the best in this, the best of all possible worlds. Separated from his love, Cunegonde, Candide undergoes every adventure from forced service in the Bulgarian army, to the Lisbon earthquake, followed by exile in South America.

Candide. abr. ed. Francois Voltaire, pseud. Read by Michael York. 2 cass. (Running Time: 3 hrs.). 2000. 7.95 (978-1-57815-119-6(8), 1081, Media Bks Audio) Media Bks NJ.
Candide encounters an array of humiliations & mishaps in his journey through 18th centruy Europe.

Candide. unabr. ed. Voltaire. Read by Tom Whitworth. (YA). 2008. 39.99 (978-1-60514-668-3(4)) Find a World.

***Candide.** unabr. ed. Voltaire. Read by Don Hagen. (Running Time: 3 hrs. 30 mins.). (ENG.). 2010. 4.98 (978-1-59659-671-9(6), GildAudio) Pub: Gildan Media. Dist(s): HachBkGrp

Candide. unabr. ed. Francois Voltaire, pseud. Narrated by Flo Gibson. 3 cass. (Running Time: 3 hrs. 22 mins.). 2001. 16.95 (978-1-55685-663-1(6)) Audio Bk Con.
The satirical, amusing and often violent misadventures of young Candide as he searches for love and the meaning of life. We meet the beautiful Cunegonde, the loyal Cacambo and philosophers Pangloss & Martin.

Candide. unabr. ed. Francois Voltaire, pseud. Narrated by Andrew Sachs. (Running Time: 3 hrs. 45 mins. 0 sec.). (ENG.). 2010. audio compact disk 26.95 (978-1-934997-52-9(8)) Pub: CSAWord. Dist(s): PerseuPGW

Candide, unabr. ed. Francois Voltaire, pseud. Narrated by Donal Donnelly. 3 cass. (Running Time: 4 hrs. 15 mins.). 1986. 26.00 (978-1-55690-086-0(4), 86540E7) Recorded Bks.
The guileless Candide & the good Dr. Pangloss suffer burning at the stake, the galleys & polite society itself in their comic search for first-hand answers to life's perennial mysteries.

Candide. unabr. ed. Francois Voltaire, pseud. Narrated by Tom Whitworth. (Running Time: 3 hrs. 30 mins. 0 sec.). (Tantor Unabridged Classics Ser.). (ENG.). 2009. audio compact disk 17.99 (978-1-4001-1108-4(0)) Pub: Tantor Media. Dist(s): IngramPubServ

Candide. unabr. ed. null Voltaire. Narrated by Tom Whitworth. (Running Time: 3 hrs. 30 mins. 0 sec.). (ENG.). 2009. audio compact disk 35.99 (978-1-4001-4108-1(7)) Pub: Tantor Media. Dist(s): IngramPubServ

Candide. unabr. ed. null Voltaire. Narrated by Tom Whitworth. (Running Time: 3 hrs. 30 mins. 0 sec.). (ENG., 2009. 17.99 (978-1-4001-6108-9(8)) Pub: Tantor Media. Dist(s): IngramPubServ

Candide. unabr. collector's ed. Francois Voltaire, pseud. Read by Thomas Whitworth. 4 cass. (Running Time: 4 hrs.). 1981. 24.00 (978-0-7366-2130-4(X), 2931) Books on Tape.
One of the world's best known satires, "Candide" refutes the optimistic but shallow "All's for the best in this best of all possible worlds," the philosophy of Candide's tutor, Dr. Pangloss. "Candide" is as funny & absurd today as when it was written more than 200 years ago.

Candide & Zadig. Francois Voltaire, pseud. Narrated by Jim Killavey. (Running Time: 6 hrs. 30 mins.). 1990. 22.95 (978-1-59912-804-7(7)) Iofy Corp.

Candide & Zadig, unabr. ed. Francois Voltaire, pseud. Read by Frederick Davidson. 5 cass. (Running Time: 7 hrs.). 2000. 39.95 (978-0-7861-1692-8(7), 2510) Blckstn Audio.
Candide is the story of a thoughtful man who, though pummeled by fate, holds to his belief that he lives "in the best of all possible worlds." On the surface, it appears to be a simple story, but all matter of wit, irony & influence lurk underneath. Zadig, a young man well endowed by nature & possessor of a fine education, is puzzled by the uncertainties of his destiny. He rises to the highest office but is unsuccessful in his ventures into love. He meets with a number of misfortunes & is actually enslaved in Egypt.

Candide & Zadig. unabr. ed. Francois Voltaire, pseud. Read by Frederick Davidson. (Running Time: 23400 sec.). 2008. audio compact disk 29.95 (978-1-4332-4574-9(4)); audio compact disk 60.00 (978-1-4332-4573-2(6)) Blckstn Audio.

Candide & Zadig, unabr. ed. Francois Voltaire, pseud. Read by Robert L. Halvorson. 4 cass. (Running Time: 6 hrs.). 28.95 (26) Halvorson Assocs.

Cándido. unabr. ed. Francois Voltaire, pseud. Read by Laura García. 3 CDs. (SPA.). 2001. audio compact disk 17.00 (978-958-9494-53-0(6)) YoYoMusic.

Candle in a Windless Place. Swami Amar Jyoti. 1 dolby cass. 1986. 9.95 (I-16) Truth Consciousness.
The joy of meditation, the heroic work of calmness. Doing nothing - being everything.

Candle in the Darkness. unabr. ed. Lynn Austin. 11 cass. (Running Time: 16 hrs.). (Refiner's Fire Ser.: No. 1). 2004. 99.75 (978-1-4025-7247-0(6)) Recorded Bks.

Candle in the Wind & the Book of Merlyn. unabr. ed. T. H. White. Read by Neville Jason. 9 CDs. (Running Time: 10 hrs.). 2008. audio compact disk 59.95 (978-962-634-880-2(1)) Naxos.

Candle Meditation - Crystal Cave, No. 2. Kathleen Milner. 1 cass. (Running Time: 40 mins.). 1994. 11.00 (978-1-886903-60-9(3)) K Milner.
Meditator guided into the "gap" between thought & breath through spiritual techniques taught in ancient mystery schools. Some meditators can hear & experience the qualities of Angeliclight. "Crystal Cave" is an inward journey to places of healing & self empowerment.

Candleford Green. unabr. ed. Flora Thompson. Read by Mollie Harris. 5 cass. (Running Time: 6 hrs. 30 mins.). (Isis Ser.). (J). 1994. 49.95 (978-1-85089-799-6(9), 941202) Pub: ISIS Lrg Prnt GBR. Dist(s): Ulverscroft US

Candleland. Martyn Waites. Read by Martyn Waites. 6 cass. (Running Time: 8 hrs.). (Story Sound Ser.). (J). 2004. 54.95 (978-1-85903-715-7(1)) Pub: Mgna Lrg Print GBR. Dist(s): Ulverscroft US

Candlelight Christmas. Michael Ballam. 1 cass. 9.95 (1100610); audio compact disk 14.95 (1100629) Covenant Comms.

Candlelight Christmas Garden: Accompaniment/Performance. Scott Schram. Composed by Ruth Elaine Schram. (ENG.). 2002. audio compact disk 49.95 (978-0-7390-2385-3(3)) Alfred Pub.

Candlelight Christmas Garden: Listening. Scott Schram. Composed by Ruth Elaine Schram. (ENG.). 2002. audio compact disk 14.95 (978-0-7390-2387-7(X)) Alfred Pub.

Candlelight in Quintero. David A. Petreman. (ENG.). 2007. 4.00 (978-1-933675-21-3(7)) Dos Madres Pr.

Candles at Dusk. unabr. ed. Celia Laurence. 6 cass. (Running Time: 6 hrs.). 1998. 69.95 (978-1-872672-05-2(1)) Pub: Magna Story GBR. Dist(s): Ulverscroft US

Candles Burning. unabr. ed. Tabitha King. Read by Carrington MacDuffie. (Running Time: 54000 sec.). 2006. 85.95 (978-0-7861-4737-3(7)) Blckstn Audio.

Candles Burning. unabr. ed. Tabitha King. Read by Carrington MacDuffie. (Running Time: 16 hrs. 55 mins.). (J). 2006. 29.95 (978-0-7861-4728-1(8)) Blckstn Audio.

Candles Burning. unabr. ed. Tabitha King & Michael McDowell. Read by Carrington MacDuffie. (Running Time: 57600 sec.). 2006. audio compact disk 44.95 (978-0-7861-7313-6(0)); audio compact disk 108.00 (978-0-7861-6428-8(X)) Blckstn Audio.

Candles Burning. unabr. ed. Tabitha King & Michael McDowell. Read by Carrington MacDuffie. (Running Time: 57600 sec.). 2006. audio compact disk 29.95 (978-0-7861-6543-8(X)) Blckstn Audio.

Candles for the Dead. unabr. ed. Frank Smith. Read by Michael Tudor Barnes. 8 cass. (Running Time: 12 hrs.). 2001. 69.95 (978-1-86042-723-7(5)) Pub: Soundings Ltd GBR. Dist(s): Ulverscroft US
When bank worker Beth Smallwood is found battered to death, Chief Neil Paget finds no shortages of suspects but little hard evidence.

Candles from the Dead. Frank Smith. Read by Michael Tudor Barnes. 8 cass. (Running Time: 12 hrs.). 2001. 69.95 (27235) Pub: Soundings Ltd GBR. Dist(s): Ulverscroft US

Candles on Bay Street, abr. ed. K. C. McKinnon, pseud. Read by Sam Freed. 2 cass. (Running Time: 2 hrs.). 1999. 18.00 (FS9-50886) Highsmith.

Candlestick Charting Basics. Instructed by Steve Nison. 2005. audio compact disk 19.95 (978-1-59280-229-6(X)) Marketplace Bks.

Candlestone. unabr. ed. Bryan Davis. (Dragons in Our Midst Ser.). (ENG.). (YA). 2007. 10.49 (978-1-60814-108-1(X)) Oasis Audio.

Candlestone. unabr. ed. Bryan Davis. Narrated by Peter Sandon. (Running Time: 10 hrs. 0 mins. 22 sec.). (Dragons in Our Midst Ser.). (ENG.). 2009. audio compact disk 39.99 (978-1-59859-492-8(3)) Oasis Audio.

Candy Classics. 1 cass. (Running Time: 90 mins.). (J). 2000. 7.98; audio compact disk 9.98 Peter Pan.
This sweet treat includes high energy hits like "Sugar, Sugar," "Chewy Chewy, Yummy Yummy," "Popcorn," "Do Wah Diddy Diddy" & other great bubblegum hits.

Candy Corn Contest. unabr. ed. Patricia Reilly Giff. 1 cass. (Running Time: 1 hr. 18 mins.). (Follow the Reader Ser.). (J). (gr. 1-2). 1984. pap. bk. 17.00 incls. guide. (978-0-8072-0094-0(8), FTR102SP, Listening Lib) Random Audio Pubg.
Follow the kids in Ms. Rooney's second grade class as they learn & grow through an entire school year filled with fun & surprises. Corresponding month: November.

Candy Shop War. Brandon Mull. 2008. audio compact disk 39.95 (978-1-59038-933-1(6), Shadow Mount) Deseret Bk.

Candyland: A Novel in Two Parts. abr. ed. Ed McBain, pseud & Evan Hunter. Read by Mark Blum & Linda Emond. 2006. 17.95 (978-0-7435-6372-7(7), Audioworks) Pub: S&S Audio. Dist(s): S and S Inc

Candyland: A Novel in Two Parts. unabr. ed. Ed McBain, pseud & Evan Hunter. Read by Alan Sklar. 6 vols. (Running Time: 9 hrs.). 2001. bk. 54.95 (978-0-7927-2470-4(4), CSL 359, Chivers Sound Lib); audio compact disk 79.95 (978-0-7927-9916-0(X), SLD 067, Chivers Sound Lib) AudioGO.
Benjamin Thorpe is married, a father, a successful New York architect & a man obsessed. Alone in New York City on business, he spends the empty hours of the night in a compulsive search for female companionship. His descent leads to an early morning confrontation in a midtown bordello & a searing self-revelation. Part II opens with three detectives discussing a homicide. The victim is a young prostitute who crossed Thorpe's path the night before. As the foggy events of the night before come into sharper focus, Thorpe becomes an ever more possible suspect.

Cane River. abr. ed. Lalita Tademy. Read by Shari Belafonte et al. (ENG.). 2005. 14.98 (978-1-59483-410-3(5)) Pub: Hachet Audio. Dist(s): HachBkGrp

Cane River: A Novel. unabr. ed. Lalita Tademy. Narrated by Robin Miles. 10 cass. (Running Time: 14 hrs. 30 mins.). 2002. 93.00 (978-0-7887-8849-9(3), 96742) Recorded Bks.
Cane River is an isolated community that lies on a small river in central Louisiana. There in the early 19th century, slaves, free people of color, and Creole French planters lived and worked, loved and bore children.

Cane River: A Novel. unabr. ed. Lalita Tademy. Narrated by Robin Miles. 10 cass. (Running Time: 14 hrs. 30 mins.). 2002. 44.95 (978-0-7887-8886-4(8), RF259) Recorded Bks.
Lalita Tademy was vice president of Sun Microsystems until she left corporate life to research the history of her family. The result of her two-year search is Cane River, a novel which quickly became both a New York Times best-seller and an Oprah's Book Club® selection. Cane River is an isolated community that lies on a small river in central Louisiana. There in the early 19th century, slaves, free people of color, and Creole French planters lived and worked, loved and bore children. And there, 165 years later, Tademy discovers her amazing heritage. Beginning with her great-great-great-great grandmother, a slave owned by a Creole family, Tademy chronicles four generations of strong, determined black women.

Caneuon Caffi Sali Mali 1. Caryl Parry Jones & Sain. 2005. 6.99 (978-0-00-077506-1(1)); audio compact disk 11.99 (978-0-00-077501-6(0)) Zondervan.

Caneuon i Blant 2. Fflach. 2005. audio compact disk 8.99 (978-88-88043-59-3(4)) Scuola Istruzione ITA.

Caneuon Tecwyn y Tractor. 2005. audio compact disk 8.99 (978-88-88043-79-1(9)) Scuola Istruzione ITA.

Cangrijito Ermitano see Cangrjito Ermitano

***Cangrijito Ermitano.** Emma Romeu. Orig. Title: El Cangrijito Ermitano. (SPA.). (J). 2009. 9.95 (978-1-61658-340-8(1)) Indep Pub IL.

Canguro en la Cocina!, EDL Level 10. (SPA.). 2003. 11.50 (978-0-7652-1022-7(3)) Modern Curr.

Canine Cineradiography: A Study of Bone & Joint Motion as Seen Through Moving X-Rays. Ed. by Rachel Page Elliott. (Running Time: 2700 sec.). 2005. DVD 34.95 (978-1-929242-26-9(3)) Dogwise Pubng.

Canine Radiographic Anatomy: An Interactive Instructional. Anton Hoffman et al. (ENG.). 2008. audio compact disk 25.00 (978-1-60344-106-3(9)) Tex AM Univ Pr.

Canned. unabr. ed. Katherine L. James. Read by Stephanie Brush. 4 cass. (Running Time: 5 hrs.). (Cait Dramis Mystery Ser.). 2001. 26.95 (978-1-55686-798-9(0)) Books in Motion.

Cannery Row, unabr. ed. John Steinbeck. Narrated by Jerry Farden. 4 cass. (Running Time: 6 hrs.). 1989. 35.00 (978-1-55690-087-7(2), 89390E7) Recorded Bks.
Life among the canneries in Monterey.

Cannibal Queen: A Flight into the Heart of America. unabr. ed. Stephen Coonts. Read by Michael Prichard. 9 cass. (Running Time: 13 hrs. 30 mins.). 1992. 72.00 (978-0-7366-2243-1(8), 3033) Books on Tape.
Exultant account of three months in the summer '91 spent exploring America from a vintage biplane with his 14-year-old son.

Cannibalism in the Cars see Man That Corrupted Hadleyburg & Other Stories

Cannibalism in the Cars see Favorite Stories by Mark Twain

Cannibals see Custom

Cannibals. unabr. ed. Iain Lawrence. Read by John Keating. 5 cass. (Running Time: 6 hrs. 45 mins.). (YA). (gr. 5-9). 2006. 49.75 (978-1-4193-7158-5(4)) Recorded Bks.
Tom Tin, an innocent convict, is aboard a ship bound for Australia where he will serve a lengthy sentence in prison. To avoid this horrible fate, Tom jumps ship to nearby islands, but finds that the refuge he hoped for may just be another struggle for his freedom, and his life. Acclaimed author Iain Lawrence delivers another exotic adventure tale for young readers.

Canning Season. unabr. ed. Polly Horvath. Read by Julie Dretzin. 4 cass.- Library Ed. (Running Time: 6 hrs.). 2003. 38.75 (978-1-4025-5894-8(5)) Recorded Bks.
While Ratchet Clark's life has never been precisely normal, her mother's decision to send her to visit two ancient great aunts in Maine for the summer is weird even by her family's standards. As the summer unfolds, her aunts fill Ratchet in on all the details of their memorable lives, including servants eaten by bears, a groom dumped at the altar, and their mother's gruesomely ingenious suicide.

Canning Season. unabr. rev. ed. Polly Horvath. Read by Julie Dretzin. 5 CDs. (Running Time: 7 hrs. 30 min.). 2003. audio compact disk 48.75 (978-1-4025-6606-6(9)) Recorded Bks.
While Ratchet Clark?s life has never been precisely normal, her mother?s decision to send her to visit two ancient great aunts in Maine for the summer is weird even by her family?s standards. As the summer unfolds, her aunts fill Ratchet in on all the details of their memorable lives, including servants eaten by bears, a groom dumped at the altar, and their mother?s gruesomely ingenious suicide.

Cannon Beach Poetry: A Collection of Poetry with Themes of Cannon Beach & the Oregon Coast. Karen Jean Matsko Hood. 2006. (978-1-59434-718-4(2)); audio compact disk 24.95 (978-1-59434-719-1(0)) Whsprng Pine.

Cannons. Contrib. by Phil Wickham. Prod. by Peter Kipley. 2007. audio compact disk 13.99 (978-5-557-60937-1(7)) INO Rec.

***Cannons at Dawn - Audio.** Kristiana Gregory. (Dear America Ser.). (ENG.). 2011. audio compact disk 19.99 (978-0-545-31526-5(3)) Scholastic Inc.

***Cannons at Dawn - Audio Library Edition.** Kristiana Gregory. (Dear America Ser.). (ENG.). 2011. audio compact disk 29.99 (978-0-545-31544-9(1)) Scholastic Inc.

Cannon's Call. unabr. ed. Adam Rutledge. Read by Charlie O'Dowd. 6 vols. No. 5. 2003. (978-1-58807-567-3(2)) Am Pubng Inc.

Cannon's Call. unabr. ed. Adam Rutledge. Read by Charlie O'Dowd. 6 cass. (Running Time: 6 hrs.). (Patriots Ser.: No. 5). 2003. 30.00 (978-1-58807-089-0(1)) Am Pubng Inc.
Determined to prove to his weary army of farmers and frontiersman that victory is possible, General Washington sets in motion his greatest plan - to transport Fort Ticonderoga's captured artillery across the Berkshires and into the field of battle.

Canon: A Whirligig Tour of the Beautiful Basics of Science. unabr. ed. Natalie Angier. Read by Nike Doukas. (YA). 2007. 54.99 (978-1-59895-977-2(8)) Find a World.

Canon Alberic's Scrapbook. unabr. ed. M. R. James. Read by Walter Covell. 1 cass. (Running Time: 58 min.). Dramatization. 1981. 7.95 (S-17) Jimcin Record.
Terror preserved from the ancient days in these spine-tingling horror stories.

Canon Alberic's Scrapbook & The Treasure of Abbot Thomas. M. R. James. 1 cass. 1989. 7.95 (S-17) Jimcin Record.
Terror preserved from ancient days.

Canon in D. 2004. disk 7.95 (978-0-634-08656-4(1)) H Leonard.

Canon Law One. Father Kricek. 14 cass. (Running Time: 14 hrs.). 56.00 (93C) IRL Chicago.

Canon Law Two. Father Kricek. 8 cass. (Running Time: 8 hrs.). 32.00 (93D) IRL Chicago.

Canon of Maverick Brands. Frank Bonham. (Running Time: 2 hrs. 24 mins.). 2000. 10.95 (978-1-60083-549-0(X)) Iofy Corp.

Canonization see Love Poems of John Donne

Canopy. abr. ed. Angela Hunt. Read by Bill Myers. 8 CDs. (Running Time: 10 hrs.). 2003. audio compact disk 34.99 (978-1-58926-235-5(2), W10M-010D); 29.99 (978-1-58926-234-8(4), W10M-0010) Oasis Audio.
Alexandra Pace and her team are searching the dangerous Peruvian rainforests for a cure for a deadly disease. A strain of the disease has already begun ravaging Alexandra's mind and body.

Canopy Crossing. 1 cass. (Running Time: 35 min.). (J). (gr. k-4). 2001. 19.95 (SP 7004C) Kimbo Educ.
An Atlantic rainforest! Pacas, agoutis, lizards, frogs, sloths, exotic birds. Includes read along book.

Canopy Crossing: A Story of an Atlantic Rainforest. Ann Whitehead Nagda. Read by Randye Kaye. Illus. by Thomas Buchs. 1 cass. (Running Time: 12 mins.). (Habitat Ser.). (J). (gr. 1-4). 1997. 5.00 (978-1-56899-455-0(9), C7004) Soundprints.
In the Atlantic rainforest, the lone, rare, black-faced lion tamarin leaps from vine to vine in search of a companion to accompany him on his hunt for food.

Can't Buy Me Love - ShowTrax. Arranged by Mac Huff. 1 CD. 2000. audio compact disk 19.95 (08551456) H Leonard.
The 1964 #1 hit by The Beatles in an accessible arrangement for young choirs that's fun to sing & sounds great.

Can't Help Falling in Love, Level 2. (Yamaha Clavinova Connection Ser.). 2004. disk 1.04 (978-0-634-09592-4(7)) H Leonard.

Can't Lose Sales Tips. unabr. abr. ed. Joe Girard. Read by Joe Girard. 1 CD. (Running Time: 1 hr. 30 mins.). 2002. audio compact disk 14.95 (978-0-06-008933-7(4)) HarperCollins Pubs.

Can't Remember What I Forgot: The Good News from the Front Lines of Memory Research. Sue Halpern. Read by Cassandra Campbell. (Playaway Adult Nonfiction Ser.). (ENG.). 2009. 64.99 (978-1-60812-798-6(2)) Find a World.

Can't Remember What I Forgot: The Good News from the Front Lines of Memory Research. unabr. ed. Sue Halpern. Narrated by Cassandra Campbell. (Running Time: 8 hrs. 30 mins. 0 sec.). (ENG.). 2008. audio compact disk 69.99 (978-1-4001-3754-1(3)) Pub: Tantor Media. Dist(s): IngramPubServ

Can't Remember What I Forgot: The Good News from the Frontlines of Memory Research. unabr. ed. Sue Halpern. Narrated by Cassandra Campbell. (Running Time: 8 hrs. 30 mins. 0 sec.). (ENG.). 2008. audio compact disk 34.99 (978-1-4001-0754-4(7)); audio compact disk 24.99 (978-1-4001-5754-9(4)) Pub: Tantor Media. Dist(s): IngramPubServ

Can't Stop Praising His Name. William G. Rowland. 2001. bk. 5.00 (978-0-687-33750-7(X)) Abingdon.

Can't Take My Eyes off of You. abr. ed. Judith McNaught. (ENG.). 2012. audio compact disk 30.00 (978-0-7393-1935-2(3)) Pub: Random Audio Pubg. Dist(s): Random

Can't Wait to Get to Heaven. abr. ed. Fannie Flagg. Read by Fannie Flagg. 5 cds. (Running Time: 6 hrs.). (ENG.). 2006. audio compact disk 29.95 (978-0-7393-0409-9(7)) Pub: Random Audio Pubg. Dist(s): Random

Can't Wait to Get to Heaven. unabr. ed. Fannie Flagg. Read by Cassandra Campbell. 8 CDs. (Running Time: 9 hrs.). 2006. audio compact disk 68.00 (978-1-4159-3068-7(6)); 72.00 (978-1-4159-3067-0(8)) Books on Tape.
Life is the strangest thing. One minute, Mrs. Elner Shimfissle is up in her tree, picking figs, and the next thing she knows, she is off on an adventure she never dreamed of, running into people she never in a million years expected to meet. Meanwhile, back home, Elner's nervous, high-strung niece Norma faints and winds up in bed with a cold rag on her head; Elner's neighbor Verbena rushes immediately to the Bible; her truck driver friend, Luther Griggs, runs his eighteen-wheeler into a ditch - and the entire town is thrown for a loop and left wondering, "What is life all about, anyway?" Except for Tot Whooten, who owns Tot's Tell It Like It Is Beauty Shop. Her main concern is that the end of the world might come before she can collect her social security.

Can't You Make Them Behave, King George? 2004. bk. 24.95 (978-1-56008-171-5(6)); 8.95 (978-1-56008-857-8(5)); audio compact disk 12.95 (978-1-55592-901-5(X)) Weston Woods.

Can't You Make Them Behave, King George? (J). 2004. pap. bk. 14.95 (978-1-56008-172-2(4)); pap. bk. 18.95 (978-1-55592-377-8(1)); pap. bk. 18.95 (978-1-55592-380-8(1)); pap. bk. 38.75 (978-1-55592-379-2(8)); pap. bk. 38.75 (978-1-55592-381-5(X)); pap. bk. 32.75 (978-1-55592-350-1(X)) Weston Woods.

Can't You Make Them Behave, King George? Jean Fritz. Illus. by Tomie dePaola. 1 cass., 5 bks. (Running Time: 1 hr.). pap. bk. 32.75 Weston Woods.
A charming, amiable biography of George III, which includes an approach to the American Revolution not usually found in children's books.

Can't You Make Them Behave, King George? Jean Fritz. Illus. by Tomie dePaola. 1 cass. (Running Time: 1 hr.). (J). bk. 24.95; pap. bk. 12.95 Weston Woods.

Can't You Sleep, Little Bear? CD. unabr. ed. Martin Waddell. Illus. by Barbara Firth. (Running Time: 51 mins.). (Little Bear Ser.). (ENG.). (J). (ps-2). 2004. audio compact disk 7.99 (978-0-7636-2424-8(1)) Pub: Candlewick Pr. Dist(s): Random

Canta con Justo: Products for all three levels: Intro, Book A, Book B. Schmitt et al. (SPA.). (J). (gr. 6-12). 2003. audio compact disk 27.32 (978-0-07-860654-0(3), 9780078606540) Pub: Glencoe. Dist(s): McGraw

Canta Conmigo: Panama to Peru, Plus Mexico, Too!, Vol. 2. Juanita Newland-Ulloa. 1 cass. (Running Time: 1 hr.). (J). 7.98 (SEND 102); audio compact disk 11.98 (SEND 102) NewSound.
Compositions are from Peru - in both "Vals" (a rhythmic waltz) style & "huayno" rhythms from the Andes covering themes of instruments, a fiesta, & an orphan llama.

Cantabile Woods. Music by Thomas A. Mitchell. (ENG.). 2008. audio compact disk 10.00 (978-0-9746003-5-2(0)) Byblos Pr.

Cantado y Jugando. Penton Overseas, Inc. Staff. 1 CD. (Running Time: 1 hr.). (J). 2002. audio compact disk 4.99 (978-1-59125-157-6(5)) Penton Overseas.
Each CD contains a collection of 12 popular Spanish songs. Words and phrases are taught by using simple rhythms. A great way to learn Spanish.

Cantando la Palabra. Prod. by Vino Nuevo. (SPA.). (J). 1999. 6.00 (978-1-885630-67-4(0)) Jayah Producc.

Cantando We Learn. Neraida Smith. 1 cass. (J). 9.95 (978-0-8442-7607-6(3), Natl Textbk Co) M-H Contemporary.
Collection of 20 different songs that are easy & fun to sing, making them an ideal way to introduce children to the words, accent & rhythms of the Spanish language.

Cantando y Aprendiendo con ANISA. ANISA, Inc. audio compact disk 14.95 (978-1-56835-076-9(7)) Prodns Anisa.

Cantar Quiero: Music of the California Missions. Prod. by John Flaherty & Keith Paulson-Thorp. (Running Time: 4140 sec.). 2006. audio compact disk 17.00 (978-1-58459-307-2(5)) Wrld Lib Pubns.

Cantaré Al Señor, Vol. III. unabr. ed. (SPA.). 1998. 5.99 (978-0-8297-2689-3(6)) Pub: Vida Pubs. Dist(s): Zondervan

Cantare de Tu Amor. Danilo Montero. 2003. audio compact disk 14.99 (978-0-8297-4322-7(7)) Zondervan.
In August 2000 we went to "The country of the rising Sun", Japan. A nation of the giant screen, multitudes in the streets, super fast trains, digital TV, perfect gardens and ancient palaces. Next to the accelerated modern lifestyle there is a society that is looking for spiritual relief...It was in the country of the rising sun were we recorded "I will Sing of your Love", a contemporary project of Praise and Worship under the direction of Danilo Montero and the production of Juan Salinas.

Cantare de Tu Amor. unabr. ed. Danilo Montero. 2003. 9.99 (978-0-8297-4324-1(3)) Pub: Vida Pubs. Dist(s): Zondervan

Cantare de Tu Amor por Siempre. unabr. ed. Ricardo Aquino. 1 CD. 2001. audio compact disk & audio compact disk 11.99 (978-0-8297-2568-1(7)) Zondervan.

Cantare de Tu Amor por Siempre. unabr. ed. Ricardo Aquino & Zondervan Publishing Staff. (SPA.). 2001. 7.99 (978-0-8297-2567-4(9)) Pub: Vida Pubs. Dist(s): Zondervan

***Cantare de tu Fama.** (SPA.). 2009. audio compact disk 14.99 (978-0-8297-6135-1(7)) Pub: CanZion. Dist(s): Zondervan

Cante Flamenco Paso A Paso I: Flamenco Singing Step by Step I, Por Merenguito. Contrib. by Antonio Izquierdo. (Running Time: 1 hr.). (SPA.). 2005. 39.95 (978-84-934452-0-1(7)) Mel Bay.

Cantemos Chiquitos, No. 2. Georgette Baker. (SPA., (J). (gr. k-12). pap. bk. 12.95 (978-0-9623930-2-0(9), TAL002) Pub: Cantemos-bilingual. Dist(s): Continental Bk

Cantemos Chiquitos: Songs & Fingerplays from Mexico & South America, No. 1. Georgette Baker. Illus. by Michael Mastorakis & James Mastorakis. (SPA & ENG.). (J). (gr. k-3). 1994. pap. bk. 8.95 (978-0-9623930-1-3(0), TAL001) Cantemos-bilingual.

Cantemos Como Profetas de Esperanza, abr. ed. Perf. by Carlos Castañeda et al. 1 cass. (Running Time: 57 mins.). (Prophets of Hope Ser.: Vol. 1). (SPA.). (J). 1999. 8.95 (978-0-88489-660-9(9)) St Marys.
Fifteen diverse songs that celebrate the commitment of Hispanic youth & young adults to the church & society. Delivers music that will move the body, stimulate the mind & nourish the soul. Beautiful harmonies, joyful rhythms & challenging messages.

Cantemos Como Profetas de Esperanza, Vol. 1. Perf. by Carlos Castañeda et al. 1 CD. (Running Time: 57 mins.). (J). 1999. audio compact disk 14.95 (978-0-88489-661-6(7)) St Marys.

Cantemos con Georgette Vol. 4: Songs & Fingerplays. 2nd ed. (Cantemos Ser.: Vol. 4). (J). 2000. audio compact disk 22.95 (978-0-9623930-6-8(1)) Cantemos-bilingual.

Cantemos en Español: Spanish Learning CD for Children. Susy Dorn. 1 CD. (SPA.). (J). 2004. audio compact disk 16.00 (978-0-9764010-1-8(0)) Susy Dorn Prodns.
¡Cantemos En Español! or "Let's Sing In Spanish", the music CD has twenty short easy to learn songs in Spanish composed by Susy Dorn....including

the basics...colors, shapes, vowels, alphabet, days of the week, months of the year, animals, instruments, and more fun songs! SONG TITLES AND DESCRIPTIONS: 1. Las Frutas (The Fruits) 2. Los Números (The Numbers) 3. Los Colores (The Colors) 4. Las Formas (The Shapes) 5. Los Dias de la Semana (The Days of the Week) 6. Las Vocales (The Vowels) 7. El Alfabeto (The Alphabet) 8. Las Partes del Cuerpo (The Parts of the Body) 9. Los Meses del Año (The Months of the Year) 10. Las Estaciones (The Seasons) 11. La Ropa (The Cloths) 12. Los Animales de la Granja (The Animals of the Farm) 13. Los Servidores de la Comunidad (The Servers of the Community) 14. El Oso (The Oso) 15. Los Animales Salvajes (The Animals of the Jungle) 16. Las Herramientas (The Tools) 17. ¿Dónde Viven? (Where Do They Live?) 18. ¡Vamos de Paseo! (Let's Go for a Ride) 19. Los Instrumentos (The Instruments) 20. Los Dinosaurios (The Dinosaurs) MORE ABOUT THE ARTIST: Besides a singer, author and song writer for children, Susy Dom is a Spanish Immersion teacher in the Bay Area, CA. With a bachelor's degree in early childhood development, Susy has managed to develop very original and amazing Spanish Immersion materials that are fun and effective such as books, music CDs, and DVDs for her students to supplement the learning of Spanish in her program.

Canterbury Tales. Geoffrey Chaucer. Narrated by Flo Gibson. (ENG.). 2007. audio compact disk 36.95 (978-1-55685-939-7(2)) Audio Bk Con.

Canterbury Tales. Geoffrey Chaucer. Read by Fred Williams. (Running Time: 19 hrs.). 2002. 50.95 (978-1-59912-627-2(3)) Iofy Corp.

Canterbury Tales. Geoffrey Chaucer. Read by David Cutler. (Running Time: 9 hrs. 30 mins.). 2003. 64.95 (978-1-59912-048-5(8), Audiofy Corp) Iofy Corp.

Canterbury Tales. Geoffrey Chaucer. Read by Philip Madoc et al. 3 cass. (Running Time: 3 hrs. 15 mins.). (Great Tales Ser.). (C). 1996. 17.98 (978-962-634-544-3(6), NA304414, Naxos AudioBooks) Naxos.

Canterbury Tales. Geoffrey Chaucer. 9 cass. (Running Time: 13 hrs.). 78.00 (978-0-7887-6090-7(4)) Recorded Bks.

Canterbury Tales. Geoffrey Chaucer. 2008. audio compact disk 29.95 (978-1-4332-4972-3(3)) Blckstn Audio.

Canterbury Tales. abr. ed. Geoffrey Chaucer. Narrated by Robert French. 2 cass. (Running Time: 2 hrs. 6 mins.). 12.95 (978-0-89926-171-3(X), 853) Audio Bk.
Seven tales by the Pilgrims on the way to Canterbury.

Canterbury Tales, unabr. ed. Geoffrey Chaucer. Read by Flo Gibson. Tr. by John Tatlock & Percy Mackaye. 8 cass. (Running Time: 12 hrs.). 1998. bk. 26.95 (978-1-55685-535-1(4)) Audio Bk Con.
Tales told by a Miller, Friar, Nun, Knight & many more are often bloody, bawdy & full of religious zeal.

Canterbury Tales. unabr. ed. Geoffrey Chaucer. Tr. by Burton Raffel. Intro. by John Miles Foley. Narrated by Ric Jerrom & Bill Wallis. 18 CDs. (Running Time: 22 hrs. 23 mins.). (ENG.). 2008. audio compact disk 39.95 (978-1-60283-485-9(7)) Pub: AudioGO. Dist(s): Perseus Dist

Canterbury Tales. unabr. ed. Geoffrey Chaucer. Read by Fred Williams, Jr. 2 CDs (MP3). (Running Time: 19 hrs.). 2002. audio compact disk 29.95 (978-0-7861-9208-3(9)); 85.95 (978-0-7861-2239-4(0)); audio compact disk 128.00 (978-0-7861-9497-1(9)) Blckstn Audio.
The poet tells of meeting at the Tabard Inn with thirty others to make the usual April pilgrimage to Becket's shrine at Canterbury. He describes his companions, who are of widely varying classes and occupations. It is agreed that each traveler will tell four tales during the course of the trip and the host of the inn will reward the best storyteller with a free supper upon their return.

Canterbury Tales. unabr. ed. Geoffrey Chaucer. Read by Philip Madoc et al. 3 CDs. (Running Time: 3 hrs. 15 mins.). (J). (gr. 9-12). 1995. audio compact disk 22.98 (978-962-634-044-8(4), NA304412) Naxos.
Chaucer's greatest work paints a brilliant picture of medieval life, society and values. Includes "The Prologue," "The Knight's Tale," "The Miller's Tale," "The Pardoner's Tale," "The Merchant's Tale" and "The Franklin's Tale".

Canterbury Tales, unabr. ed. Geoffrey Chaucer. Comment by Michael Murphy. 9 cass. (Running Time: 13 hrs.). (YA). 2001. 78.00 (978-1-55690-652-7(8), 92349E7) Recorded Bks.
The Prologue & the twelve major tales from Chaucer's original text, read by professional actors in modern pronunciation.

Canterbury Tales. unabr. ed. Short Stories. Geoffrey Chaucer. Read by David Butler. 5 cds. (Running Time: 9 hrs 8 mins). 2002. audio compact disk 29.95 (978-1-58472-355-4(6), 086, In Aud) Pub: Sound Room. Dist(s): Baker Taylor
Stories of common folk by the Father of English Poetry.

Canterbury Tales. unabr. ed. Geoffrey Chaucer. Read by David Butler. 1 cd. (Running Time: 9 hrs 8 min). 2002. audio compact disk 18.95 (978-1-58472-383-7(1), In Aud) Pub: Sound Room. Dist(s): Baker Taylor
MP3 format. Includes Prologue to the Canterbury Tales, The Miller's Prologue, the Miller's Tale, The Reeve's Prologue, The Reeve's Tale, the Franklin's Prologue, The Franklin's Tale, The Words of the Host, The Pardoner's Tale Prologue, The Pardoner's Tale, Words of the Host to the Prioress, the Prioress's Prologue, The Prioress's Tale, Prologue to the Nun's Priest's Tale, The Nun's Priest's Tale, Epilogue to the Nun's Priest's Tale, The Clerk's Prologue, the Clerk's Tale, the Knight's Tale, the Cook's Prologue, the Cook's Tale, The Wife of Bath's Prologue, The Friar's Prologue, The Friar's Tale, The Merchant's Prologue, The Merchants Tale, Chaucer's Farewell.

Canterbury Tales. unabr. ed. Geoffrey Chaucer. Read by David Cutler. (YA). 2006. 84.99 (978-1-59895-166-0(1)) Find a World.

Canterbury Tales, Vol. 3. unabr. ed. Geoffrey Chaucer. pap. bk. 22.98 (978-962-634-304-3(4)) Naxos.

Canterbury Tales: Classic Collection. unabr. ed. Geoffrey Chaucer. (Running Time: 21 hrs. 0 mins.). 2008. 29.95 (978-1-4332-4973-0(1)); audio compact disk 105.95 (978-1-4332-4970-9(7)); audio compact disk 125.00 (978-1-4332-4971-6(5)) Blckstn Audio.

Canterbury Tales II. Geoffrey Chaucer. Read by Frances Jeater et al. 3 cass. (Running Time: 3 hrs. 30 mins.). 2002. 17.98 (978-962-634-756-0(2), NA325614, Naxos AudioBooks) Naxos.
Though writing in the 13th century, the author's wit and observation comes down undiminished through the ages, especially in this accessible modern verse translation. These four delightful tales, from one of the most entertaining storytellers of all time, vary considerably, from the uproarious Wife of Bath's Tale, promoting the power of women, to the sober account of patient Griselda in The Clerk's Tale.

Canterbury Tales II. unabr. ed. Geoffrey Chaucer. Read by Frances Jeater et al. Tr. by Frank Ernest Hill. 3 CDs. (Running Time: 3 hrs. 30 mins.). 2002. audio compact disk 22.98 (978-962-634-256-5(0), NA325612, Naxos AudioBooks) Naxos.

Canterville Ghost see Classic Ghost Stories, Vol. 2, A Collection

Canterville Ghost see Great Ghost Stories, Volume II

Canterville Ghost. Oscar Wilde. (J). 1992. 7.95 Jimcin Record.

Canterville Ghost. Oscar Wilde. 2004. 12.95 (978-0-19-423298-2(0)) OUP.

Canterville Ghost. unabr. ed. Oscar Wilde. Read by Walter Covell. 1 cass. (Running Time: 78 mins.). Dramatization. (J). 1983. 7.95 (S-52) Jimcin Record.
Described by many critics as the best ghost story ever written. A rather inept ghost is helped to find peace by a little girl.

Canterville Ghost & Other Stories. Oscar Wilde. Read by Donada Peters. (Running Time: 16200 sec.). 2006. 34.95 (978-0-7861-4511-9(0)); audio compact disk 36.00 (978-0-7861-7193-4(6)) Blckstn Audio.

Canterville Ghost & Other Stories. unabr. ed. Oscar Wilde. Read by Donada Peters. (Running Time: 16200 sec.). 2006. audio compact disk 19.95 (978-0-7861-7652-6(0)) Blckstn Audio.

Canterville Ghost & Other Stories. unabr. collector's ed. Short Stories. Oscar Wilde. Read by Donada Peters. 5 cass. (Running Time: 5 hrs.). 1992. 30.00 (978-0-7366-2274-5(8), 3062) Books on Tape.
A collection of short stories, social comedies & fairy tales including the favorite "The Canterville Ghost".

Canterville Ghost: Volume 1 And 2. unabr. ed. Intro. by Douglas Fairbanks, Jr. & Douglas Fairbanks. 2 cass. (Running Time: 003373 sec.). (Family Classic Audio Bks.). 1998. 16.95 (978-1-892613-00-4(X), CG1998) NYS Theatre Inst.
Fully dramatized musical underscoring & song.

Canticle for Good Friday see Poetry of Geoffrey

Canticle for Leibowitz. unabr. collector's ed. Walter M. Miller, Jr. Read by Jonathan Marosz. 8 cass. (Running Time: 12 hrs.). 1998. 64.00 (978-0-7366-4267-5(6), 4766) Books on Tape.
Deep in the Utah desert, Brother Francis of the Albertian Order of Leibowitz has miraculously discovered the relics of the matyr Isaac Leibowitz.

Cánticos de Adoración. unabr. ed. (SPA.). 2000. 7.99 (978-0-8297-3335-8(3)) Pub: Vida Pubs. Dist(s): Zondervan

Canticos Inolvidables. Giovani Rios. 2003. 3.00 (978-0-8297-3795-0(2)); audio compact disk 4.00 (978-0-8297-3793-6(6)) Zondervan.

Cánticos Inolvidables. Giovani Rios. 1 CD. 2003. audio compact disk 9.99 (978-0-8297-3792-9(8)) Pub: Vida Pubs. Dist(s): Zondervan

Canto Amor see Twentieth-Century Poetry in English, No. 8, Recordings of Poets Reading Their Own Poetry

Canto (de Las Sombras) For clarinet & computer generated Tape. Composed by Robert Scott Thompson. 2006. audio compact disk 50.00 (978-1-934174-01-2(7)) Aucourant.

Canto del Agua. unabr. ed. Nelly Rosario. 6 cass. (Running Time: 480 mins.). (SPA.). 58.00 (978-1-4025-2465-3(X)) Recorded Bks.
Available to libraries only.

Canto del Mosquito. Alma Flor Ada. (Libros Para Contar Ser.). (SPA., (J). (gr. k-3). 4.95 (978-1-58105-256-5(1)) Santillana.

Canto for a Gypsy, unabr. ed. Martin Cruz Smith. Narrated by Walt MacPherson. 3 cass. (Running Time: 4 hrs. 30 mins.). (Roman Grey - Sergeant Isidore Mystery Ser.: Vol. 2). 1983. 26.00 (978-1-55690-088-4(0), 83056E7) Recorded Bks.
Gypsy antique dealer, Roman Grey, sets out to recover St. Stephen's crown, an ancient Hungarian treasure.

Canto Musica Ayahuasca en la Silva de Peru. Agustin Rivas. 1 cass. 9.00 (A0105-88) Sound Photosyn.
A shaman at work, singing & playing an instrument of his own invention.

Canto y Cuento. 1 CD. (Running Time: 1 hr. 30 mins.). bk. 16.00 (978-1-57417-037-5(6), AC7600) Arcoiris Recs.

Canto y Cuento. 1 cass. (Running Time: 1 hr. 30 mins.). (J). (ps-3). 12.00 (978-1-57417-038-2(4), AC6877) Arcoiris Recs.

Canton Spirituals Live in Washington. Perf. by Eddie Jackson et al. (J). 1997. 10.98; audio compact disk 15.98 Pub: Brentwood Music. Dist(s): Provident Mus Dist
Includes "Hallelujah Square," "Heaven's Looking," "Fly Away with Jesus," "I Know I've Been Changed," & more.

Cantonese. Berlitz Editors & Berlitz Publishing Staff. 2 CDs. (Running Time: 1 hr. 15 mins.). (CD Pack Ser.). (ENG & CHI., 2003. audio compact disk 21.95 (978-981-246-202-2(3), 462023) Pub: Berlitz Pubng. Dist(s): Langenscheidt

Cantonese: Short Course, Paul Pimsleur. 5 cass. (Running Time: 5 hrs.). (Pimsleur Language Learning Ser.). 1996. 149.95 (0671-57908-8) SyberVision.

Cantonese Basic Course FSI CDs & Text, Vol. 2. 15 CDs. (Running Time: 11 hrs.). (Foreign Service Institute Basic Course Ser.). (CHI.). 2005. audio compact disk 265.00 (978-1-57970-278-6(3), AFC140D, Audio-For) J Norton Pubs.

Cantonese Basic Course Vol. 1 FSI CDs & Text. 15 CDs. (Running Time: 11 hrs.). (CHI.). 2005. audio compact disk 225.00 (978-1-57970-108-6(6), AFC131D) J Norton Pubs.

Cantonese Chinese. Ed. by Berlitz Publishing. (PHRASE BOOK & CD Ser.). (CHI & ENG., 2008. 12.95 (978-981-268-478-3(6)) Pub: APA Pubns Serv SGP. Dist(s): IngramPubServ

Cantonese Chinese. unabr. ed. Created by Pimsleur Staff. 8 CDs. (Running Time: 80 hrs. 0 mins. 0 sec.). (Instant Conversation Ser.). (CHI & ENG.). 2006. audio compact disk 49.95 (978-0-7435-5116-8(8), Pimsleur) Pub: S&S Audio. Dist(s): S and S Inc

Cantonese Sounds & Tones. Po-Fei Huang. 3 cass. 1965. 8.95 ea. incl. suppl. materials. (978-0-88710-006-2(6)) Yale Far Eastern Pubns.

Cantor Meets Jolson. Perf. by Eddie Cantor & Al Jolson. 6 episodes on 3 cas. 19.98 Boxed set, Digitally Restored & Remastered. (4156); audio compact disk 24.98 CD Boxed set, Digitally Restored & Remastered. (4157) Radio Spirits.
Delight in all six appearances of Jolson on "The Eddie Cantor Radio Show".

Cantos al maiz: un poeta hopi habla del Maiz. (Saludos Ser.: Vol. 2). (SPA.). (gr. 3-5). 10.00 (978-0-7635-1814-1(X)) Rigby Educ.

Cantos Biblicos Gospel. (J). 2002. audio compact disk Provident Mus Dist.

Cantos Biblicos Gospel: 17 Cantos Biblicos Clasicos para Ninos. Directed By Sue M. Gay. Contrib. by Cedarmont Ninos. Prod. by Mike Gay. (Running Time: 33 mins.). (J). (ps-3). 2005. 9.99 (978-5-559-11257-2(7)) Pt of Grace Ent.

Cantos Calientes: Musically Accompanied Chants for the Spanish Student. Lonnie G. Daizovi. (SPA.). (YA). (gr. 7-12). 1998. pap. bk. 28.50 (978-0-935301-70-0(4)) Vibrante Pr.

Cantos de Gozo para Ninos. 2003. 1.30 (978-0-8297-3755-4(3)); audio compact disk 1.50 (978-0-8297-3753-0(7)) Zondervan.

Cantos de Gozo Para Ninos. Serie Vida para Niños. 1 CD. (Running Time: 30 min.). (SPA.). 2003. audio compact disk 4.99 (978-0-8297-3752-3(9)) Pub: Vida Pubs. Dist(s): Zondervan

Cantos de Gozo para Niños. unabr. ed. Zondervan Publishing Staff. (SPA.). 2003. 3.99 (978-0-8297-3754-7(5)) Pub: Vida Pubs. Dist(s): Zondervan

***Cantos para Nuestros Tiempos.** Charles R. Swindoll.Tr. of Songs for All Seasons. 2010. audio compact disk 18.00 (978-1-57972-873-1(1)) Insight Living.

Cantos, Rimos y Rimas. Lonnie Dai Zovi. (SPA.). (YA). (gr. 7 up). 1990. pap. bk. 28.50 (978-0-935301-73-1(9)) Vibrante Pr.

Cantos, Rimos y Rimas: Chants, Rhythms & Rhymes for the Spanish CLassroom. Lonnie Dai Zovi. (YA). (gr. 7 up). 1990. pap. bk. 30.50 (978-0-935301-79-3(8)) Vibrante Pr.

Cantus Christi Audio Guide. 4 CDs. (ENG.). 2004. audio compact disk 15.00 (978-1-59128-534-2(8)) Canon Pr ID.

Canvasser's Tale see $30,000 Bequest & Other Stories

Canyon & Old Ramon. unabr. collector's ed. Jack Schaefer. Read by Walter Zimmerman. 8 cass. (Running Time: 8 hrs.). 1989. 48.00 (978-0-7366-1568-6(7), 2435) Books on Tape.
The Canyon is the story of Little Bear, a Cheyenne. The canyon is his refuge from a world in which he wants no part. But Little Bear learns that canyon walls are not a barrier & that for better or worse, man must be with others of his own kind. Old Ramon is an old shepherd wise in the basics of human life. Ramon has been put in charge of his patron's small boy for a season with the sheep. As his father & grandfather before him, the boy watches & learns about fear, death & responsibility as well as sheep.

Canyon Dreams. Perf. by Tangerine Dream. 1 cass. 9.98 (MPC2801); audio compact disk 14.98 CD. Miramar Images.
The Grammy nominated musical accompaniment to the Platinum video Canyon Dreams. This magnificent & majestic soundtrack includes a previously unreleased bonus track.

Canyon Drums. Perf. by Peter Bender. 1 cass. (Running Time: 1 hr.). 7.98 (TT 135); audio compact disk 11.98 Jewel box. (TT 135) NewSound.

***Canyon of Maverick Brands.** Frank Bonham. 2009. (978-1-60136-406-7(7)) Audio Holding.

***Canyon Walls.** Zane Grey. 2009. (978-1-60136-391-6(5)) Audio Holding.

Canyons. Gary Paulsen. Read by Peter Coyote. 2 cass. (Running Time: 2 hrs. 50 mins.). (J). 2000. 18.00 (978-0-7366-9055-3(7)) Books on Tape.
Coyote Runs is a young Apache murdered by soldiers in the 1800s & a century later, fifteen-year-old Brennan finds the boy's skull while camping.

Canyons. Gary Paulsen. 2 cass. (Running Time: 3 hrs.). (J). (gr. 4-7). 2000. 16.99 (978-0-8072-8687-6(7), Listening Lib) Random Audio Pubg.

Canyons. unabr. ed. Gary Paulsen. Read by Peter Coyote. 2 cass. (J). 2000. pap. bk. 23.00 (978-0-8072-8688-3(5), YA236SP, Listening Lib); 18.00 (YA236CX, Listening Lib) Random Audio Pubg.

Canyons. unabr. abr. ed. Gary Paulsen. Read by Peter Coyote. (ENG.). (J). (gr. 4). 2009. audio compact disk 25.00 (978-0-307-58292-8(2), Listening Lib) Pub: Random Audio Pubg. Dist(s): Random

Canzoniere of Fransesco Petrarco: Multilingual Books Literature. Ed. by Maurizio Falyhera & Cristina Giocometti. 1 cass. (Running Time: 90). (Audio Anthology of Italian Literature Ser.: 2). (ITA.). 1999. spiral bd. 19.95 (978-1-58214-102-2(9)) Language Assocs.

Cap d'Antibes: Let You Not Say of Me When I Am Old see Poetry of Edna St. Vincent Millay

Cap d'Antibes: Moon, That Against the Lintel of the West see Poetry of Edna St. Vincent Millay

***Cape.** unabr. ed. Joe Hill. (ENG.). 2007. (978-0-06-155221-2(6)); (978-0-06-155222-9(4)) HarperCollins Pubs.

Cape Breton Road. D. R. MacDonald. Narrated by Paul Hecht. 9 CDs. (Running Time: 10 hrs.). audio compact disk 89.00 (978-1-4025-3500-0(7)) Recorded Bks.

Cape Breton Road. unabr. ed. D. R. MacDonald. Narrated by Paul Hecht. 7 cass. (Running Time: 10 hrs.). 2002. 66.00 (978-1-4025-0958-2(8), 96956) Recorded Bks.
This is the haunting story of Innis Corbett, a young man in trouble with the law, who is forced back to his birthplace on Cape Breton. Living with his uncle, he is pulled into a volatile and violent triangle when a bruised but beautiful woman comes to stay with them.

Cape Cod. Read by Casey Clark. Ed. by Adam Gamble. Frwd. by Adam Gamble. 2000. 19.95 (978-0-9653283-4-0(1)) On Cape Pub.

Cape Cod. Henry David Thoreau. Narrated by Jim Killavey. (Running Time: 8 hrs. 30 mins.). 1990. 32.95 (978-1-59912-854-2(3)) Iofy Corp.

Cape Cod. unabr. ed. Henry David Thoreau. (Running Time: 28800 sec.). 2007. audio compact disk 29.95 (978-0-7861-5869-0(7)) Blckstn Audio.

Cape Cod. unabr. ed. Henry David Thoreau. Read by Patrick Cullen. (Running Time: 28800 sec.). 2007. audio compact disk 63.00 (978-0-7861-5868-3(9)) Blckstn Audio.

Cape Cod: The Grand Tour. 1 cass. (Running Time: 1 hr.). 10.95 (G0090B090, HarperThor) HarpC GBR.

Cape Cod Fisherman. unabr. collector's ed. Phil Schwind. Read by Jonathan Reese. 8 cass. (Running Time: 8 hrs.). 1978. 48.00 (978-0-7366-0076-7(0), 1086) Books on Tape.
In 1934 Phil Schwind, a young man smarting from the sting of the Depression, took his family & left the city life. He turned, as have many in times of struggle, to the sea & settled at Cape Cod with the intention of making his livelihood by fishing. He was completely unskilled in his new trade, but he learned well & became in time a scalloper, clam digger, eeler, boatbuilder, fisherman, lobsterman & charterboat skipper - par excellence.

Cape Grimm. unabr. ed. Carmel Bird. Read by Humphrey Bower & Nicki Paull. 10 CDs. (Running Time: 10 hrs. 35 mins.). 2005. audio compact disk 98.95 (978-1-74093-545-6(4)) Pub: Bolinda Pubng AUS. Dist(s): Bolinda Pub Inc

***Cape May Court House.** abr. ed. Lawrence Schiller. Read by Sam Tsoutsouvas. (ENG.). 2006. (978-0-06-113535-4(6), Harper Audio); (978-0-06-113534-7(8), Harper Audio) HarperCollins Pubs.

Cape Perdido. unabr. ed. Marcia Muller. Read by Dick Hill & Joyce Bean. (Running Time: 7 hrs.). 2005. 39.25 (978-1-59737-088-2(6), 9781597370882, BADLE); 24.95 (978-1-59737-087-5(8), 9781597370875, BAD); 69.25 (978-1-59737-082-0(7), 9781597370820, BrilAudUnabridg); 27.95 (978-1-59737-081-3(9), 9781597370813, BAU); audio compact disk 39.25 (978-1-59737-086-8(X), 9781597370868, Brlnc Audio MP3 Lib); audio compact disk 24.95 (978-1-59737-085-1(1), 9781597370851, Brilliance MP3); audio compact disk 82.25 (978-1-59737-084-4(3), 9781597370844, BriAudCD Unabrid); audio compact disk 29.95 (978-1-59737-083-7(5), 9781597370837, Bril Audio CD Unabri) Brilliance Audio.
At the northernmost point of Soledad County lies Cape Perdido - once a lumber town, now a getaway for tourists and outdoor recreationists. But when the water harvesting plans of a North Carolina company threaten the residents' livelihoods, four people get caught up in the fight to save the town: Jessie Domingo, a community liaison specialist from New York City; Joseph Openshaw, an environmentalist forced to face ghosts of his past; Steph Pace, a restaurateur and former love of Openshaw's who must confront the same ghosts; and Timothy McNear, a former lumber mill owner who harbors secrets of his own. The arrival of the "waterbaggers" will drive otherwise peaceful people to desperate acts, and a dramatic series of events - including a sniper's bullet, a midnight inferno, and an abduction - will awaken the residents of Cape Perdido to unsavory truths about their town and each other.

Cape Refuge. Terri Blackstock. Narrated by Alan Nebelthau. 7 cass. (Running Time: 10 hrs 15 mins.). (Cape Refuge Ser.: Bk. 1). 62.00 (978-1-4025-3797-4(2)) Recorded Bks.

***Cape Refuge.** Terri Blackstock. (Running Time: 11 hrs. 6 mins. 0 sec.). (Cape Refuge Ser.). (ENG.). 2008. 14.99 (978-0-310-30429-6(6)) Zondervan.

Cape Town, South Africa. Compiled by Benchmark Education Staff. 2006. audio compact disk 10.00 (978-1-4108-6614-1(9)) Benchmark Educ.

Caperucita Roja. I.t. ed. Short Stories. Illus. by Graham Percy. 1 cass. (Running Time: 10 mins.). Dramatization.Tr. of Little Red Riding Hood. (SPA.). (J). (ps-3). 2001. bk. 8.99 (978-84-86154-06-6(5)) Pub: Peralt Mont ESP. Dist(s): imaJen

Caperucita Roja y Lobo/Los Lobos. Steck-Vaughn Staff. (SPA.). 1999. (978-0-7398-0752-1(8)) SteckVau.

Capital Collection, '85. 12 cass. (Running Time: 18 hrs.). 1985. vinyl bd. 120.00 Amer Coll Phys.
Includes Respiratory Failures & Sepsis; Chemotherapy of Viral Infections; Sexually Transmitted Disease: 1985; Treatment of Obesity; A "Sherlock Holmes" Approach to the Detection of Bleeding Disorders; The Clinical Spectrum of Vasculitis; Dietary Management of Early Renal Insufficiency; & more.

Capital Crimes. unabr. ed. Faye Kellerman & Jonathan Kellerman. 7 cass. (Running Time: 10 hrs.). 2006. 63.00 (978-1-4159-3432-6(0)); audio compact disk 68.85 (978-1-4159-3433-3(9)) Pub: Books on Tape. Dist(s): NetLibrary CO

Capital for Minority Business Owners Made Easy. Mervin L. Evans. 4 cass. (Running Time: 6 hr.). 2004. 49.99 (978-0-914391-51-7(8)) Comm People Pr.

Capital for Women & Minority Business Owners Made Easy Funding Workshop: Finding the Money! Mervin Evans. 4 CDs. (Running Time: 6 hrs.). 2004. 139.99 (978-0-914391-34-0(8)) Comm People Pr.
Step by Step Guide to locating investment capital for a Women & Minority Owned business.

Capital for Women & Minority Business Owners Made EZ: Finding the Money! Speeches. Mervin L. Evans. 1 60-Minute Audio CD. (Running Time: 60 M). 2003. 19.99 (978-0-914391-04-3(6)) Comm People Pr.

Capital Fund Raising: National Association of Evangelicals, 47th Annual Convention, Columbus, Ohio, March 7-9, 1989. Earl Murphy. 1 cass. (Workshops Ser.: No. 33-Thursda). 1989. 4.25 ea. 1-8 tapes.; 4.00 ea. 9 tapes or more. Nat Assn Evan.

Capital Ideas Evolving. unabr. ed. Peter L. Bernstein. Read by Sean Pratt. (Running Time: 10 hrs. 30 mins.). (ENG.). 2009. 29.98 (978-1-59659-336-7(9), GildAudio) Pub: Gildan Media. Dist(s): HachBkGrp

Capital, Interest & Profit. unabr. ed. Murray Newton Rothbard. 1 cass. (Running Time: 1 hr. 7 mins.). (Introduction to Free Market Economics Ser.). 12.95 (310) J Norton Pubs.
Covers long-run & short-run profit; the structure of production; & the economic function of interest.

Capital of the World see Stories of Ernest Hemingway

Capital Punishment. unabr. ed. R. J. Rushdoony. 1 cass. (Running Time: 1 hr.). 12.95 (717) J Norton Pubs.

Capitalism: The Unknown Ideal. Ayn Rand. Read by Anna Fields. 12 CDs. (Running Time: 14 hrs. 30 mins.). 2000. audio compact disk 96.00 (978-0-7861-9831-3(1), 2637) Blckstn Audio.
The foundations of capitalism are being battered by a flood of altruism, which is the cause of the modern world's collapse.This was the view of Ayn Rand, a view so radically opposed to prevailing attitudes that it constituted a major philosophic revolution.

Capitalism: The Unknown Ideal. unabr. ed. Ayn Rand. Read by Anna Fields. 10 cass. (Running Time: 14 hrs. 30 mins.). 2000. 69.95 (978-0-7861-1838-0(5), 2637) Blckstn Audio.

Capitalism: The Unknown Ideal. unabr. ed. Ayn Rand. Read by Anna Fields. (Running Time: 14 hrs. 30 mins.). 2003. 24.95 (978-0-7861-9454-4(5), 2637) Blckstn Audio.

***Capitalism: The Unknown Ideal.** unabr. ed. Ayn Rand. Read by Anna Fields. (Running Time: 14 hrs. 30 mins.). 2010. audio compact disk 29.95 (978-0-7861-9192-5(9)) Blckstn Audio.

***Capitalism & Freedom.** unabr. ed. Milton Friedman. Read by Michael Edwards. (Running Time: 7 hrs.). 2010. 29.95 (978-1-4417-4425-8(8)); audio compact disk 69.00 (978-1-4417-4422-7(3)) Blckstn Audio.

Capitalism & Freedom, unabr. ed. Milton Friedman. Read by Michael Edwards. 5 cass. (Running Time: 7 hrs.). 1989. 39.95 (978-0-7861-0049-1(4), 1047) Blckstn Audio.
Friedman argues that the appropriate role of competitive capitalism occurs when the majority of our economic activity flows through private enterprise within a free market environment.

Capitalism & Freedom. unabr. ed. Milton Friedman. Read by Francis Kelly. 6 cass. (Running Time: 1 hr. 30 mins. per cass.). 1989. 60.00 incl. outline. (978-0-942563-05-4(0)); Rental 15.00 incl. outline. (978-0-942563-10-8(7)) CareerTapes.
Friedman argues that capitalism, through its free competitive markets, is essential to the preservation of political freedom. This book is the intellectual foundation of the "Reagan Revolution" & is equally revelant to Perestroika & Glasnost.

Capitalism & Selfishness: Ayn Rand's Radical Code of Value. Peter Schwartz. 1 cass. (Running Time: 60 mins.). 1991. 9.95 (978-1-56114-141-8(0), HS09C) Second Renaissance.

Capitalism vs. Communism. Ayn Rand. 1 cass. (Running Time: 28 mins.). 1961. cass. & video 14.95 (978-1-56114-118-0(6), AR38C) Second Renaissance.

Capitalism vs. Socialism (Debate) Harry Binswanger et al. 2 cass. (Running Time: 2 hrs.). 1992. 19.95 (978-1-56114-133-3(X), HB03D) Second Renaissance.

***Capitalism 4. 0: The Birth of a New Economy in the Aftermath of Crisis.** unabr. ed. Anatole Kaletsky. Read by Scott Peterson. (Running Time: 13 hrs.). (ENG.). 2010. 49.98 (978-1-59659-652-8(X), GildAudio) Pub: Gildan Media. Dist(s): HachBkGrp

Capitalist Conspiracy: An Inside View of International Banking. G Edward Griffin. 1 cass. (Running Time: 60 mins.). 10.00 (AC2) Am Media.
The story of the richest people in the world who control the money systems of the non-Communist nations & who yield power, behind the scenes, over every aspect of our daily lives.

Capitalizing on the Nineteen Eighty-Six Tax Act. 45.00 Am Soc Chart.
Discusses deferred compensation plans, IRAs, Fringe Benefit Plans & Estate planning in 3 segments.

Capitalizing on Transits of Saturn & Pluto. Jan Spiller. 1 cass. (Running Time: 90 mins.). 1986. 8.95 (586) Am Fed Astrologers.

Capitán Blood. abr. ed. Rafael Sabatini. Read by Fabio Camero. 3 CDs.Tr. of Captain Blood. (SPA.). 2002. audio compact disk 17.00 (978-958-8161-07-5(X)) YoYoMusic.

Capitán Fracaso. abr. ed. Teofilo Gautier. Read by Santiago Munevar. 3 CDs. (SPA.). 2002. audio compact disk 17.00 (978-958-8161-04-4(5)) YoYoMusic.

Capitanskaya Dochka. Alexander Pushkin. 6 cass. (Running Time: 6 hrs.). (RUS.). 1996. pap. bk. 69.50 (978-1-58085-557-0(1)) Interlingua VA.
Includes Russian text, English vocabulary & notes. The combination of written text & clarity & pace of diction will open the door for intermediate & advanced students to genuine comprehension & the use of literary texts for advancement in rapid understanding of written & oral language materials. The audio text plus written text concept makes foreign languages accessible to a much wider range of students than books alone.

Capitol Punishment. Ryne Douglas Pearson. 2001. 18.00 (978-0-671-57037-8(4), Audioworks) S&S Audio.

CAPM Exam Success Series Terms & Definitions Audio CD. 2006. audio compact disk 24.99 (978-0-9787032-2-6(7)) Crosswind Proj Manag.

CAPM Exam Success Series Understanding the Processes Audio CD. 2006. audio compact disk 24.99 (978-0-9787032-3-3(5)) Crosswind Proj Manag.

Capoeira Angola from Salvador Brazil, Grupo de Capoeira Angola Pelourinho. Anno. by Mestre Morales & D. Daniel Dawsen. Contrib. by Metre C. Mansa et al. Anno. by GCAP Directive Council Staff. 1 cass. (Running Time: 1 hr.). 1996. (0-9307-404650-9307-40465-2-4); audio compact disk (0-9307-40465-2-4) Smithsonian Folkways.
Call-&-response singing accompanied by compelling rhythms played on berimbau & percussion instruments that express & control the performance of the Capoeira fight/dance.

Capone Pts. I & 2: The Man & the Era. unabr. ed. Laurence Bergreen. Read by Michael Kramer. 10 cass. (Running Time: 15 hrs.). 1995. 80.00 (3698-A); 88.00 (3698-B) Books on Tape.
Al Calpone Scarface was more than public enemy #1. He was also a generous, loving family man.

Capone Pts. I & 2: The Man & the Era, unabr. ed. Laurence Bergreen. Read by Michael Kramer. 21 cass. (Running Time: 31 hrs. 30 mins.). 1995. 168.00 (978-0-7366-3012-2(0), 3698A&B) Books on Tape.
Al Capone, "Scarface," was more than public enemy No. 1. He was also a generous, loving family man.

Capo's Mistress. abr. ed. Richard Harris. (Running Time: 21600 sec.). (ENG.). 2007. audio compact disk 24.95 (978-1-930754-97-3(3)) Pub: Durban Hse. Dist(s): Natl Bk Netwk

Cappella: Live Poetry. audio compact disk 29.95 (978-0-8023-9072-1(2)) Pub: Bloodaxe Bks GBR. Dist(s): Dufour

Cappella degli Scrovegni di Giotto see ARTineraries Tour Padova: Giotto¿s Scrovegni Family Chapel

Cappella Worship, Vol. 2. Perf. by Glad. 1 cass. 1999. 10.98 (978-0-7601-2896-1(0)); audio compact disk 16.98 (978-0-7601-2895-4(2)) Provident Music.

Caprice see Sir John Betjeman Reading His Poetry

Capricorn, Narrated by Patricia G. Finlayson. Music by Mike Cantwell. Contrib. by Marie De Seta & TMY Communications Staff. 1 cass. (Running Time: 30 mins.). (Astrologer's Guide to the Personality Ser.: Vol. 10). 1994. 7.99 (978-1-878535-21-4(8)) De Seta-Finlayson.
Astrological description of the sign of Capricorn; individually customized, covering love, money, career, relationships & more.

Capricorn: December Twenty-Two - January Nineteen. Barrie Konicov. 1 cass. 11.98 (978-0-87082-092-2(3), 018) Potentials.
The author, Barrie Konicov, explains how each sign of the Zodiac has its positive & negative aspects & that, as individuals, in order to master our own destiny we must enhance our positive traits.

Capricorn: Unleash the Power of Your True Self. 1 cass. (Running Time: 1 hr.). 1999. 9.99 (978-1-928996-09-5(4)) MonAge.

Capricorn: Your Relationship with the Energy of the Universe. Loy Young. 1993. 9.95 (978-1-882888-22-1(7)) Aquarius Hse.

Capricorn Transits. Carol Ruth. 1 cass. (Running Time: 90 mins.). 1988. 8.95 (710) Am Fed Astrologers.

Capricornia. unabr. ed. Xavier Herbert. Read by Humphrey Bower. (Running Time: 23 hrs. 40 mins.). 2009. audio compact disk 123.95 (978-1-74214-516-7(7), 9781742145167) Pub: Bolinda Pubng AUS. Dist(s): Bolinda Pub Inc

Caps for Sale. 2004. pap. bk. 18.95 (978-1-55592-768-4(8)); pap. bk. 38.75 (978-1-55592-783-7(1)); pap. bk. 32.75 (978-1-55592-179-8(5)); pap. bk. (978-1-55592-346-4(1)); pap. bk. 8.95 (978-1-55592-728-8(9)); 8.95 (978-1-56008-858-5(3)); cass. & flmstrp 30.00 (978-0-89719-542-3(6)); audio compact disk 12.95 (978-1-55592-866-7(8)) Weston Woods.

Caps for Sale. Esphyr Slobodkina. Read by Peter Fernandez. 1 cass. (Running Time: 30 mins.). (J). 2000. pap. bk. 19.97 (978-0-7366-9218-2(5)) Books on Tape.
An itinerant cap salesman awakens from a restful nap to find his wares confiscated by a band of feisty monkeys.

Caps for Sale. Esphyr Slobodkina. 1 cass. (Running Time: 35 min.). (J). (ps-4). 2001. bk. 15.95 (VX-77C) Kimbo Educ.
A cap salesman awakens from a restful nap to find his wares stolen by a group of feisty monkeys. See how he outwits the culprits. Includes book.

Caps for Sale. Esphyr Slobodkina. Illus. by Esphyr Slobodkina. 9.95 (978-1-59112-297-5(X)); 4.50 (978-1-59112-304-0(6)) Live Oak Media.

Caps for Sale. Esphyr Slobodkina. Illus. by Esphyr Slobodkina. (Running Time: 8 mins.). 2000. 9.95 (978-1-59112-018-6(7)); audio compact disk 12.95 (978-1-59112-696-6(7)) Live Oak Media.

Caps for Sale. Esphyr Slobodkina. Illus. by Esphyr Slobodkina. Read by Peter Fernandez. 11 vols. (Running Time: 8 mins.). (J). (gr. k-3). 2000. bk. 25.95 (978-0-87499-059-1(9)); pap. bk. & tchr. ed. 33.95 Reading Chest. (978-0-87499-060-7(2)) Live Oak Media.
An itinerant cap salesman awakens from a restful nap to find his wares confiscated by a band of feisty monkeys.

Caps for Sale. Esphyr Slobodkina. Read by Peter Fernandez. 11 vols. (Running Time: 8 mins.). (J). 2005. pap. bk. 18.95 (978-1-59112-697-3(5)) Pub: Live Oak Media. Dist(s): AudioGO

Caps for Sale. Esphyr Slobodkina. Illus. by Esphyr Slobodkina. Read by Peter Fernandez. 11 vols. (Running Time: 8 mins.). (J). (gr. k-3). 2005. pap. bk. 16.95 (978-0-87499-058-4(0)) Pub: Live Oak Media. Dist(s): AudioGO

Caps for Sale. Esphyr Slobodkina. 1 read-along cass. (Blue-Ribbon Listen-and-Read Ser.). (J). (ps-2). 1984. 4.95 (978-0-590-37664-8(0)); Scholastic Inc.

Caps for Sale. Esphyr Slobodkina. 1 read-along cass. (Running Time: 7 min.). (J). 8.95 (RAC012) Weston Woods.

Caps for Sale. Esphyr Slobodkina. (J). 2004. 8.95 (978-1-56008-124-1(4)); bk. 24.95 (978-0-89719-863-9(8), HRA012) Weston Woods.
A band of mischief-making monkeys steals a napping peddler's colorful caps & he must think of a way to get them back.

***Caps for Sale.** unabr. ed. Esphyr Slobodkina. (ENG.). 2007. (978-0-06-143481-5(7)) HarperCollins Pubs.

Caps for Sale. unabr. ed. Esphyr Slobodkina. Illus. by Esphyr Slobodkina. Tr. by Teresa Mlawer. 22 vols. (Running Time: 10 mins.). (ENG & SPA.). (J). (gr. k-3). 1999. pap. bk. 33.95 (978-0-87499-562-6(0)) Live Oak Media.

Caps for Sale: A Tale of a Peddler, Some Monkeys, & Their Monkey Business. abr. ed. Esphyr Slobodkina. Illus. by Esphyr Slobodkina. (Share a Story Ser.). (J). (ps-1). 2007. 9.99 (978-0-06-121512-4(0), HarperFestival) HarperCollins Pubs.

Caps for Sale: A Tale of a Peddler, Some Monkeys, & Their Monkey Business. unabr. abr. ed. Esphyr Slobodkina & Slobodkina. Read by Brian O'Sullivan. Perf. by Brian O'Sullivan. Illus. by Esphyr Slobodkina. 1 cass. (Running Time: 20 mins.). (J). (ps-2). 1995. 8.99 (978-0-694-70004-2(5)) HarperCollins Pubs.

Caps for Sale & other Storybook Classics: The Caps for Sale; Millions of Cats; Petunia; Leo the Late Bloomer; Little Red Hen. unabr. ed. Esphyr Slobodkina et al. Read by Owen Jordan et al. (J). 2008. 44.99 (978-1-60514-876-2(8)) Find a World.

Capstick: African Campfires. Narrated by Peter H. Capstick. (Running Time: 60 mins.). (African Hunting Ser.). 9.95 Sportsmen Film.
World famous hunting author answers Ken Wilson's questions about Africa & safaris around a campfire.

Capsule History of Music. Duane Shinn. 1 cass. 19.95 (MU-5) Duane Shinn.
Explains basic music periods: baroque, classical, romantic, nationalistic, expressionistic & contemporary then plays typical pieces from each period.

***Capt. Hook.** unabr. ed. J. V. Hart. Read by John Keating. (ENG.). 2005. (978-0-06-088308-9(1)); (978-0-06-088309-6(X)) HarperCollins Pubs.

Capt. Hook: The Adventures of a Notorious Youth. unabr. ed. J. V. Hart. Read by John Keating. 7 CDs. (Running Time: 8.5 Hrs). (J). 2005. audio compact disk 25.95 (978-0-06-082075-6(6), HarperChildAud) HarperCollins Pubs.

***Captain & Matey Set Sail.** unabr. ed. Daniel Laurence. (ENG.). 2008. (978-0-06-169394-6(4)); (978-0-06-171317-0(1)) HarperCollins Pubs.

Captain & the Enemy, unabr. ed. Graham Greene. Read by Kenneth Branagh. 4 cass. (Running Time: 4 hrs.). 2000. 39.95 (978-0-7451-6833-3(7), CAB 398) Pub: Chivers Audio Bks GBR. Dist(s): AudioGO
Victor Baxter is a loveless 12-year-old, won in a game of backgammon (or was it chess?) by the Captain. Victor, or Jim as he becomes known, is educated in the ways of the world by the Captain. The drama is seen through Jim's eyes but the central figure is the Captain, a devious criminal, whose beliefs contrast sharply with the barrenness of Jim's existence.

Captain at Arms. Philip McCutchan. 8 cass. (James Ogilvie Ser.). 2006. 69.95 (978-1-84283-758-0(3)) Pub: ISIS Lrg Prnt GBR. Dist(s): Ulverscroft US

***Captain at Arms.** Philip Mccutchan. 2010. audio compact disk 84.95 (978-1-4079-1885-3(0)) Pub: Soundings Ltd GBR. Dist(s): Ulverscroft US

Captain Bligh's Portable Nightmare: From the Bounty to Safety... 4,162 Miles Across the Pacific in a Rowing Boat. unabr. ed. John Toohey. Narrated by Erick Graham. 4 cass. (Running Time: 6 hrs.). 2000. 40.00 (978-1-84197-119-3(7), H1116E7) Recorded Bks.
Left in the middle of the Pacific Ocean, he & eighteen others were forced to sail an amazing 4,162 miles on a 23-foot boat. Illness, malnutrition, bad weather & attacks by hostile islanders are just some of the problems Bligh & his erst-while crew faced on their long, drawnout journey.

Captain Blood see Capitán Blood

Captain Blood. Perf. by Errol Flynn & Olivia De Havilland. Narrated by Herbert Marshall. 1 cass. (Running Time: 60 mins.). 1937. 7.95 (DD-5105) Natl Recrd Co.
A young physician named Peter Blood is sold as a slave in the West Indies. He is purchased by a beautiful young lady & a strange & changeable relationship takes place. Naturally romance enters the picture, but not until some exciting pirating by Captain Blood. Cast also includes Basil Rathbone & Donald Crisp.

Captain Blood. Rafael Sabatini. 1 CD. (Running Time: 11.6 hours). 2007. 16.95 (978-1-60112-009-0(5)) Babblebooks.

Captain Blood. Rafael Sabatini. Read by Fabio Camero. (Running Time: 3 hrs.). 2002. 16.95 (978-1-60083-229-1(6), Audiofy Corp) Iofy Corp.

Captain Blood. Rafael Sabatini. Read by Robert Whitfield. 8 cass. (Running Time: 11 hrs. 30 mins.). 2000. 56.95 (978-0-7861-1807-6(5), 2606) Blckstn Audio.
Dr. Peter Blood's quiet life is shattered when he is convicted of treason for helping a wounded nobleman in the 1685 rebellion against King James II. He's swept into a slave ship to Barbados but escapes from slavery & a brutal plantation owner during a Spanish Pirate attack. Peter becomes a pirate & before long becomes the greatest buccaneer of them all.

Captain Blood. unabr. ed. Rafael Sabatini. Read by Robert Whitfield. 10 CDs. (Running Time: 41400 sec.). 2000. audio compact disk 80.00 (978-0-7861-9862-7(1), 2606) Blckstn Audio.
Doctor Peter Blood's quiet life is shattered when he is convicted of treason for helping a wounded nobleman in the 1685 rebellion against King James II. He's swept into a slave ship to Barbados but escapes from slavery & a brutal plantation owner during a Spanish Pirate attack & becomes a pirate. Before long he is the greatest buccaneer of them all.

Captain Blood. unabr. collector's ed. Rafael Sabatini. Read by Dan Lazar. 8 cass. (Running Time: 12 hrs.). (J). 1981. 64.00 (978-0-7366-0580-9(0), 1550) Books on Tape.
Peter Blood is a gentlemanly freelancer who by a turn of fate becomes prisoner of the English, captive on an island stronghold. His escape & subsequent adventures have captivated generations of readers.

Captain Blood Complete Collection. Rafael Sabatini. (ENG.). 2008. audio compact disk 39.95 (978-1-60245-170-4(2)) GDL Multimedia.

Captain Blood Volume 1. Rafael Sabatini. (ENG.). 2008. audio compact disk 9.95 (978-1-60245-166-7(4)) GDL Multimedia.

Captain Blood Volume 2. Rafael Sabatini. (ENG.). 2008. audio compact disk 9.95 (978-1-60245-167-4(2)) GDL Multimedia.

Captain Blood Volume 3. Rafael Sabatini. (ENG.). 2008. audio compact disk 9.95 (978-1-60245-168-1(0)) GDL Multimedia.

Captain Blood Volume 4. Rafael Sabatini. (ENG.). 2008. audio compact disk Rental 9.95 (978-1-60245-169-8(9)) GDL Multimedia.

Captain Burle see Three by Zola

Captain Carpenter see Twentieth-Century Poetry in English, No. 5, Recordings of Poets Reading Their Own Poetry

Captain Clawbeak & the Red Herring. unabr. ed. Anne Morgan & Wayne Harris. Read by Stephen Phillips. (Running Time: 3600 sec.). 2008. audio compact disk 39.95 (978-1-74093-973-7(5), 9781740939737) Pub: Bolinda Pubng AUS. Dist(s): Bolinda Pub Inc

Captain Corelli's Mandolin. unabr. ed. Louis de Bernières. Read by Michael Maloney. 14 cass. (Running Time: 21 hrs.). 2001. 110.95 (978-0-7540-0403-5(1), CAB 1826, Chivers Sound Lib) AudioGO.

Captain Corelli's Mandolin. unabr. ed. Louis de Bernières. Read by Michael Maloney. 14 cass. (Running Time: 21 hrs.). 2000. 89.95 (978-0-7451-7382-5(9), SAB 149) Pub: Chivers Audio Bks GBR. Dist(s): AudioGO
It is 1941, and Captain Antonio Corelli, a young Italian officer, is posted to the Greek island of Cephallonia. At first he is ostracized by the locals, but as

a conscientious soldier, whose main aim is to be civilized, humorous and a consummate musician. But when the local doctor's daughter's letters to her fiance go unanswered, the working of a triangle is inevitable. Can this fragile love survive this savage war as the lines are drawn between invader and defender.

Captain Corelli's Mandolin. unabr. ed. Louis de Bernières. Read by Michael Maloney. 16 CDs. (Running Time: 24 hrs.). 2000. audio compact disk 119.95 (978-0-7540-5348-4(2), CCD 039) Pub: Chivers Audio Bks GBR. Dist(s): AudioGO

It is 1941 & Captain Antonio Corelli, a young Italian officer, is posted to the Greek Island of Cephallonia. At first he is ostracized by the locals, but as a conscientious soldier, whose main aim is to have a peaceful war, he proves to be civilized, humorous & a consummate musician.

Captain David Grief. unabr. ed. Jack London. Read by Brian Emerson. 4 cass. (Running Time: 6 hrs.). Orig. Title: Son of the Sun. 2001. 32.95 (978-0-7861-2025-3(8), P2793) Blckstn Audio.

This book includes eight long tales of danger and adventure, with titles like "The Proud Goat of Aloysius Pankburn," "The Feathers of the Sun" and "The Pearls of Parlay," told in Jack London's most graphic and colorful style.

Captain David Grief. unabr. ed. Jack London. (Running Time: 19800 sec.). Orig. Title: Son of the Sun. 2007. audio compact disk 45.00 (978-0-7861-6007-5(1)) Blckstn Audio.

Captain David Grief. unabr. ed. Jack London & Brian Emerson. Orig. Title: Son of the Sun. 2007. audio compact disk 29.95 (978-0-7861-6008-2(X)) Blckstn Audio.

Captain Fantastic: A Tribute to Elton John. 1 cass. (Running Time: 1 hr.). 7.98 (CMH 8027); audio compact disk 11.18 Jewel box. (CMH 8027) NewSound.

Captain Fiddle's Learning, Tape 1. Ryan J. Thomson. Music by Ryan J. Thomson. 1 cass. (Running Time: 1 hr.). 1985. 9.95 (978-0-931877-01-8(6)) Captain Fiddle Pubns.

Instructional tape in traditional folk fiddling for those with little or no experience with fiddle or violin playing.

Captain Fiddle's Learning, Tape 2. Ryan J. Thomson. Music by Ryan J. Thomson. 1 cass. (Running Time: 1 hr.). (YA). 1985. 9.95 (978-0-931877-02-5(4)) Captain Fiddle Pubns.

Instructional tape in traditional folk fiddling for those with experience in playing easy scales & simple melodies.

Captain Fiddle's Learning, Tape 3. Ryan J. Thomson. Music by Ryan J. Thomson. 1 cass. (Running Time: 1 hr.). 1985. 9.95 (978-0-931877-03-2(2)) Captain Fiddle Pubns.

Captain Fiddle's Learning, Tape 4. Ryan J. Thomson. Music by Ryan J. Thomson. 1 cass. (Running Time: 60 mins.). (YA). 1987. 9.95 (978-0-931877-04-9(0)) Captain Fiddle Pubns.

Captain Fiddle's Learning, Tape 5. Ryan J. Thomson. Music by Ryan J. Thomson. 1 cass. (Running Time: 1 hr.). (YA). 1995. 9.95 (978-0-931877-05-6(9)) Captain Fiddle Pubns.

Captain Fiddle's Tune, Vol. 1. Ryan J. Thomson. (C). 2001. audio compact disk 24.95 (978-0-931877-33-9(4)) Captain Fiddle Pubns.

Captain Fiddle's Tune, Vol. 2. Ryan J. Thomson. 2001. audio compact disk 24.95 (978-0-931877-34-6(2)) Captain Fiddle Pubns.

Captain Fiddle's Tunes & Variations, Bk. 1. Ryan J. Thomson. Perf. by Ryan J. Thomson. 2005. audio compact disk 24.95 (978-0-931877-13-1(X)) Captain Fiddle Pubns.

Captain Fracasse. Teofilo Gautier. Read by Santiago Munévar. (Running Time: 3 hrs.). 2002. 16.95 (978-1-60083-215-4(6), Audiofy Corp) Iofy Corp.

Captain from Connecticut. unabr. collector's ed. C. S. Forester. Read by Bill Whitaker. 7 cass. (Running Time: 10 hrs. 30 mins.). 1991. 56.00 (978-0-7366-1877-9(5), 2708) Books on Tape.

No one but a madman would put to sea in such conditions. A blizzard cut visibility to yards. Long Island Sound was galloping white caps. But in this second year of the War of 1812, conditions like these spelled opportunity to Captain Josiah Peabody, USN. His mission: break the British blockade. The only thing in his favor was surprise. Who would expect a Yankee frigate in Long Island Sound that night? Peabody is a fictional character & C. S. Forester's first American hero. Yet it was men like him who compensated for our tragic lack of warships & set the world sounding with the feats of our small navy.

Captain Grey, unabr. ed. Avi. Narrated by Ron Keith. 3 cass. (Running Time: 3 hrs. 45 mins.). (gr. 5 up). 2001. 27.00 (978-0-7887-0366-9(8), 94558E7) Recorded Bks.

In 1783, Kevin Cartwright is captured by colonial pirates. These lawless men of the sea have already killed Kevin's family. Will he be next?.

Captain Hook. unabr. ed. J. V. Hart. Read by John Keating. (J). 2008. 54.99 (978-1-60252-957-1(4)) Find a World.

Captain Horatio Hornblower. Gregory Peck. 1 cass. (Running Time: 60 mins.). 1999. 14.98 Radio Spirits.

Captain James Cook. unabr. collector's ed. Alan Villiers. Read by Richard Green. 8 cass. (Running Time: 12 hrs.). 1983. 64.00 (978-0-7366-0350-8(6), 1336) Books on Tape.

Alan Villers helps us come to grips with the scope of Cook's accomplishments.

Captain John & His New Mates. 2002. audio compact disk 7.99 (978-0-9726070-1-8(3)) James Ball.

Captain Murderer & the Devil's Bargain see Complete Ghost Stories

Captain Nemo, Set. abr. ed. Xavier Joseph Carbajal. Read by Joe H. Maylea. 3 cass. (Running Time: 5 hrs.). (Captain Nemo Legacy Ser.: Vol. 13). (YA). (gr. 6 up). 1999. pap. bk. 18.95 (978-0-9654507-7-5(5), 97-92534) New Future Pub.

Musical soundtrack & reading. In the sequel to "20,000 Leagues under the Sea" & "The Mysterious Island", Captain Nemo battles Uriah, an evil brother who wishes to capture Cuba, destroy coral that stops diseases & capture the Nautilus in 2012 AD.

***Captain Nobody.** unabr. ed. Dean Pitchford. Read by Dean Pitchford. 4 CDs. (Running Time: 4 hrs. 34 mins.). (J). (gr. 3-7). 2009. audio compact disk 30.00 (978-0-7393-8031-4(1), Listening Lib) Pub: Random Audio Pubg. Dist(s): Random

Captain Nobody. unabr. ed. Dean Pitchford. Read by Dean Pitchford. (ENG.). (J). (gr. 3). 2009. audio compact disk 28.00 (978-0-7393-8029-1(X), Listening Lib) Pub: Random Audio Pubg. Dist(s): Random

Captain of Her Heart. abr. ed. Anita Stansfield. 4 CDs. (Running Time: 5 hrs.). 2004. audio compact disk 15.95 (978-0-9746269-1-8(0)) Crosswlks Bks.

Captain of the Caryatid. unabr. ed. Richard Woodman. Read by Gordon Griffin. 5 cass. (Running Time: 7 hrs. 30 min.). 2001. 49.95 (978-1-86042-657-5(3), 26573) Pub: Soundings Ltd GBR. Dist(s): Ulverscroft US

A unique mixture of seamanship, rivalry & romance.

Captain of the Polestar see Tales of the Supernatural

Captain Pugwash. unabr. ed. John J. Ryan. Read by Peter Hawkins. 1 cass. (Running Time: 1 hr., 30 min.). (J). (gr. 1-8). 1999. 9.95 (CTC 068, Chivers Child Audio) AudioGO.

Captain Pugwash, Tom the cabin boy & the crew of the Black Pig cross wires & swords with Cut-throat Jake & his desperate band of bloodthirsty buccaneers in "The Fancy Dress Party," "The Mutiny," "The Wreckers" & "The Midnight Feast".

Captain Quake & Boss Bird. (Sails Literacy Ser.). (gr. 2 up). 10.00 (978-0-7578-6826-9(6)) Rigby Educ.

Captain Stormfield Goes to Heaven & the Diaries of Adam & Eve. Mark Twain. Narrated by Don Randall. (Running Time: 3 hrs. 21 mins.). 2006. audio compact disk 29.95 (978-0-9790364-7-7(X)) A Audiobooks.

Twain's favorite parlor tale, Captain Stormfield Goes to Heaven presents an entertaining version of the afterlife, full of the humor and irony we have come to expect from this master of American letters.The Diaries of Adam and Eve is Twain's humorous take on the myth of the Garden of Eden, as told by the participants. The joys and conflicts described will be familiar to all who labor with and love the opposite sex.

Captain Sulu Adventure Envoy. L. A. Graf. (Star Trek Ser.). 2004. 7.95 (978-0-7435-4255-5(X)) Pub: S&S Audio. Dist(s): S and S Inc

Captain Underhill Uncoils the Mystery: The Cobra in the Kindergarten & the Whirlpool. unabr. ed. Steven Thomas Oney. (Running Time: 1 hr. 45 mins.). (ENG.). 2005. audio compact disk 22.95 (978-1-56511-961-1(4), 1565119614) Pub: HighBridge. Dist(s): Workman Pub

Captain Underhill Uncovers the Truth: Behind Edgar Allan Crow & the Purloined, Purloined Letter. unabr. ed. Steven Thomas Oney. (Running Time: 1 hr. 20 mins.). (ENG.). 2005. audio compact disk 22.95 (978-1-56511-962-8(2), 1565119622) Pub: HighBridge. Dist(s): Workman Pub

Captain Underhill Unlocks the Enigma: The Queen Is in the Counting House & Don't Touch That Dial! unabr. ed. Steven Thomas Oney. (Running Time: 2 hrs.). (ENG.). 2005. audio compact disk 22.95 (978-1-56511-960-4(6), 1565119606) Pub: HighBridge. Dist(s): Workman Pub

Captain Underhill Unmasks the Murderer: The Legacy of Euriah Pillar & the Case of the Indian Flashlights. unabr. ed. Steven Thomas Oney. (Running Time: 2 hrs.). (ENG.). 2005. audio compact disk 22.95 (978-1-56511-959-8(2), 1565119592) Pub: HighBridge. Dist(s): Workman Pub

Captains. unabr. ed. W. E. B. Griffin. Read by Michael Russotto. 10 cass. (Running Time: 15 hrs.). (Brotherhood of War Ser.: No. 2). 1995. 80.00 (3629) Books on Tape.

A deadly assault across the 38th parallel is more than an incident; it sparks the Korean War. In a strong response, American calls legions of reserves. Many are veterans who once again man the trenches & sandbag bunkers. From Pusan to the Yalu, the troops drive forward in new combinations but with outdated tanks. Battle makes them the brothers they wouldn't be in peace.

Captains. unabr. collector's ed. W. E. B. Griffin. Read by Michael Russotto. 10 cass. (Running Time: 15 hrs.). (Brotherhood of War Ser.: No. 2). 1995. 80.00 (978-0-7366-2933-1(5), 3629) Books on Tape.

America recalls WWI veterans to man the trenches against invading North Koreans. Hard cheese for the reserves.

Captain's Blood. abr. ed. William Shatner. 2004. 12.95 (978-0-7435-4805-2(1)) Pub: S&S Audio. Dist(s): S and S Inc

Captains Courageous. Rudyard Kipling. Narrated by Flo Gibson. 2007. audio compact disk 24.95 (978-1-55685-909-0(0)) Audio Bk Con.

Captains Courageous. Rudyard Kipling. Retold by Alan Venable & Jerry Stemach. (Classic Adventures Ser.). 2005. pap. bk. 18.95 (978-1-4105-0260-5(0)) D Johnston Inc.

Captains Courageous. Rudyard Kipling. Read by David Stuart. (Playaway Adult Fiction Ser.). 2008. 54.99 (978-1-60640-894-0(1)) Find a World.

Captains Courageous. Rudyard Kipling. (Classics Ser.). (YA). 2006. audio compact disk (978-1-56254-870-4(0)) Saddleback Edu.

Captains Courageous, abr. ed. Rudyard Kipling. Perf. by St. Charles Players. 2 cass. (Running Time: 1 hr. 40 mins.). Dramatization. (Story Theatre for Young Readers Ser.). 1999. 16.95 (978-1-56994-502-5(0), 309224, Monterey SoundWorks) Monterey Media Inc.

A spoiled rich boy falls from an ocean liner & is rescued by fishermen. An exciting journey of discovery begins as he sails the open seas, learning about friendship & the rewards of hard work.

Captains Courageous. abr. ed. Rudyard Kipling. (Running Time: 1 hr.). Dramatization. (J). 10.95 (978-0-8045-1024-0(5), SAC 7018) Spoken Arts.

Captains Courageous. adpt. ed. Rudyard Kipling. (Bring the Classics to Life: Level 4 Ser.). 2008. audio compact disk 12.95 (978-1-55576-569-9(6)) EDCON Pubng.

Captains Courageous, unabr. ed. Rudyard Kipling. Read by Flo Gibson. 4 cass. (Running Time: 5 hrs. 30 mins.). (gr. 5-8). 1995. 19.95 (978-1-55685-598-6(2)) Audio Bk Con.

Poor little rich boy Harvey Cheyne falls overboard from a luxury liner & is rescued by a steamer from Gloucester. The perils of the sea & his adventures with the rugged crew teach him courage & loyalty.

Captains Courageous, unabr. ed. Rudyard Kipling. Read by Nadia May. 4 cass. (Running Time: 6 hrs.). 1988. 32.95 (978-0-7861-0018-7(4), 692165) Blckstn Audio.

This wonderful classic combines three unbeatable elements: a sea story, living characters & a protagonist who undergoes a character transformation.

Captains Courageous. unabr. ed. Rudyard Kipling. Read by Nadia May. (Running Time: 21600 sec.). 2007. audio compact disk 29.95 (978-0-7861-6115-7(9)); audio compact disk 45.00 (978-0-7861-6114-0(0)) Blckstn Audio.

Captains Courageous. unabr. ed. Rudyard Kipling. Read by Gene Engene. 4 cass. (Running Time: 5 hrs. 30 mins.). 26.95 (978-1-55686-179-6(6), 179) Books in Motion.

Young, spoiled Harvey Cheyne is rescued by the We're Here fishing schooner after falling from an ocean liner and is forced by the skipper to earn his way.

Captains Courageous. unabr. ed. Rudyard Kipling. Read by David Stuart. (Running Time: 5 hrs.). 2006. 39.25 (978-1-4233-1069-3(1), 9781423310693, BADLE); 24.95 (978-1-4233-1068-6(3), 9781423310686, BAD); audio compact disk 74.25 (978-1-4233-1065-5(9), 9781423310655, BriAudCD Unabrid); audio compact disk 39.25 (978-1-4233-1067-9(5), 9781423310679, Brinc Audio MP3 Lib); audio compact disk 24.95 (978-1-4233-1066-2(7), 9781423310662, Brilliance MP3); audio compact disk 26.95 (978-1-4233-1064-8(0), 9781423310648, Bril Audio CD Unabri) Brilliance Audio.

Young Harvey Cheyne is rich, spoiled, prejudiced, and totally lacking in the real experiences of life. When the fifteen-year-old is accidentally washed overboard a great ocean liner headed for Europe, he is picked up by a fisherman and brought aboard the fishing schooner "We're Here". Harvey's stories of privilege and wealth mean nothing aboard this hard-working vessel, and the boy receives many lessons in self-reliance, values, and hard-bitten reality - "things every man must know, blind, drunk, or asleep" - in the words of Long Jack. Harvey, Long Jack, Tom Platt, Manuel, and many more great characters come alive in this rich retelling of life aboard the "We're Home".

Captains Courageous, unabr. ed. Rudyard Kipling. Read by Cindy Hardin. 4 cass. (Running Time: 4 hrs.). (J). (gr. 5 up). 1994. vinyl bd. 24.00 (C-255) Jimcin Record.

Young, spoiled Harvey Cheyne falls overboard from his luxury liner & is picked up by a fishing boat bound for Georgia's Banks. His tantrums & demands of a swift return are ignored. Six months later when the boat returns he is a changed boy.

Captains Courageous, unabr. ed. Rudyard Kipling. Narrated by George Guidall. 4 cass. (Running Time: 6 hrs.). 1995. 35.00 (978-0-7887-0159-7(2), 94384E7) Recorded Bks.

The son of a millionaire, rescued from the sea by a fishing schooner, must work alongside the crew for his keep during the three month fishing season before returning to land.

Captains Courageous. unabr. ed. Rudyard Kipling. Read by John Chancer. 4 cass. (Running Time: 4 hrs.). 1994. 44.95 (978-1-86015-421-8(2)) Pub: UlverLrgPrint GBR. Dist(s): Ulverscroft US

The pampered son of a millionaire is swept overboard & learns about the harsh realities of life after being rescued by a group of New England fishermen.

Captains Courageous. unabr. collector's ed. Rudyard Kipling. Read by Cindy Hardin. 6 cass. (Running Time: 6 hrs.). (YA). (gr. 8 up). 1983. 36.00 (978-0-7366-3970-5(5), 9515) Books on Tape.

A rich, spoiled, 15-year-old American boy, Harvey Cheyne, is swept off an ocean liner bound for Europe. Rescued by a fishing crew, he must earn his way. Kipling's story calls up visions of the fishery industry at the turn of the century. The author peoples it with characters real enough to swagger out of the mists of time & step from the decks of wooden sailing ships, happily preserved for us in this great favorite.

Captains Courageous, Set. abr. ed. Rudyard Kipling. Perf. by St. Charles Players. 2 cass. Dramatization. 1999. 16.95 (FS9-50876) Highsmith.

***Captains Courageous: Bring the Classics to Life.** adpt. ed. Rudyard Kipling. (Bring the Classics to Life Ser.). 2008. pap. bk. 21.95 (978-1-55576-610-8(2)) EDCON Pubng.

Captains Courageous - A Story of the Grand Banks. Alan Venable. Rudyard Kipling. (Classic Adventures Ser.). 2005. pap. bk. 69.00 (978-1-4105-0262-9(7)) D Johnston Inc.

Captain's Doll, unabr. ed. D. H. Lawrence. Narrated by Davina Porter. 3 cass. (Running Time: 3 hrs. 30 mins.). 1988. 26.00 (978-1-55690-089-1(9), 88200E7) Recorded Bks.

Captain Hepburn had a wife he didn't love & a mistress who made hand-crafted dolls; in fact, she'd made one in the image of the captain, resplendent in his military uniform & now his wife wants to buy it. Love is a complicated battle & the soldier is outflanked.

***Captain's Duty: Somali Pirates, Navy Seals, & Dangerous Days at Sea.** unabr. ed. Richard Phillips & Stephan Talty. Narrated by George K. Wilson. (Running Time: 8 hrs. 30 mins.). 2010. 29.99 (978-1-4001-9686-9(8)); 15.99 (978-1-4001-8686-0(2)); 19.99 (978-1-4001-6686-2(1)); audio compact disk 59.99 (978-1-4001-4686-4(0)); audio compact disk 29.99 (978-1-4001-1686-7(4)) Pub: Tantor Media. Dist(s): IngramPubServ

Captain's Fury. unabr. ed. Jim Butcher. Read by Kate Reading. 16 CDs. (Running Time: 21 hrs.). Bk. 4. (ENG.). (gr. 8). 2008. audio compact disk 49.95 (978-0-14-314338-3(7), PengAudBks) Penguin Grp USA.

Captain's Glory. abr. ed. William Shatner et al. Read by William Shatner. 2006. 12.95 (978-0-7435-6230-0(5)) Pub: S&S Audio. Dist(s): S and S Inc

Captains Moon Updated 2008. (ENG., 2008. audio compact disk 12.95 (978-0-9776580-1-5(5)) Miller Astro.

Captains Outrageous. unabr. ed. Joe R. Lansdale. Read by Phil Gigante. (Running Time: 9 hrs.). (Hap & Leonard Ser.). 2009. 39.97 (978-1-4233-8453-3(9), 9781423384533, Brinc Audio MP3 Lib); 39.97 (978-1-4233-8455-7(5), 9781423384557, BADLE); 24.99 (978-1-4233-8452-6(0), 9781423384526, Brilliance MP3); 24.99 (978-1-4233-8454-0(7), 9781423384540, BAD); audio compact disk 87.97 (978-1-4233-8451-9(2), 9781423384519, BriAudCD Unabrid); audio compact disk 29.99 (978-1-4233-8450-2(4), 9781423384502, Bril Audio CD Unabri) Brilliance Audio.

Captiva. Contrib. by Falling Up. Prod. by Aaron Sprinkle. 2007. audio compact disk 13.99 (978-5-557-59285-7(7)) BEC Recordings.

***Captivate.** unabr. ed. Carrie Jones. Read by Julia Whelan. 1 MP3-CD. (Running Time: 8 hrs.). 2010. 39.97 (978-1-4418-5140-6(2), 9781441851406, Brinc Audio MP3 Lib); 24.99 (978-1-4418-5139-0(9), 9781441851390, Brilliance MP3); 24.99 (978-1-4418-5141-3(0), 9781441851413, BAD); 39.97 (978-1-4418-5142-0(9), 9781441851420, BADLE); audio compact disk 29.99 (978-1-4418-5137-6(2), 9781441851376, Bril Audio CD Unabri); audio compact disk 87.97 (978-1-4418-5138-3(0), 9781441851383, BriAudCD Unabrid) Brilliance Audio.

***Captivated.** unabr. ed. Nora Roberts. Read by Therese Plummer. (Running Time: 8 hrs.). (Donovan Legacy Ser.). 2010. 39.97 (978-1-4418-5711-8(7), 9781441857118, Brinc Audio MP3 Lib); 24.99 (978-1-4418-5710-1(9), 9781441857101, Brilliance MP3); 39.97 (978-1-4418-5712-5(5), 9781441857125, BADLE); audio compact disk 79.97 (978-1-4418-5709-5(5), 9781441857095, BriAudCD Unabrid); audio compact disk 24.99 (978-1-4418-5708-8(7), 9781441857088, Bril Audio CD Unabri) Brilliance Audio.

Captivating: Unveiling the Mystery of a Woman's Soul. abr. ed. John Eldredge & Stasi Eldredge. 5 CDs. (Running Time: 3 hrs. 30 mins.). 2005. audio compact disk 24.99 (978-0-7852-0909-6(3)) Nelson.

Captivating: Unveiling the Mystery of a Woman's Soul. unabr. ed. John Eldredge & Stasi Eldredge. Read by John Eldredge & Stasi Eldredge. (Running Time: 27000 sec.). 2006. audio compact disk 63.00 (978-0-7861-6733-3(5)) Blckstn Audio.

Captivating: Unveiling the Mystery of a Woman's Soul. unabr. ed. John Eldredge & Stasi Eldredge. 2005. 34.99 (978-1-58926-854-8(7), 6854) Pub: Oasis Audio. Dist(s): TNT Media Grp

Captivating: Unveiling the Mystery of a Woman's Soul. unabr. ed. John Eldredge & Stasi Eldredge. (Running Time: 8 hrs. 16 mins. 38 sec.). (ENG.). 2005. audio compact disk 27.99 (978-1-58926-855-5(5), 6855) Oasis Audio.

Captivating: Unveiling the Mystery of A Woman's Soul. unabr. ed. John Eldredge & Stasi Eldredge. (ENG.). 2005. 16.09 (978-1-60814-109-8(8)) Oasis Audio.

Captivating Live Conference Audio, Third Edition. 10 CDs. 2007. audio compact disk 49.00 (978-1-933207-19-3(1)) Ransomed Heart.

Captivating Live, Second Edition. 10 CDs. 2006. audio compact disk 69.00 (978-1-933207-10-0(8)) Ransomed Heart.

Captive. Marcel Proust. Read by Neville Jason. Tr. by C. K. Scott Moncrieff. Adapted by Neville Jason. 3 cass. (Running Time: 3 hrs. 45 mins.).

(Remembrance of Things Past Ser.: Vol. IX). 2000. 17.98 (978-962-634-690-7(6), NA319014, Naxos AudioBooks) Naxos.
Marcel's obsessive love for Albertine makes her virtually a captive in his Paris apartment.

Captive. abr. ed. Marcel Proust. Read by Neville Jason. Tr. by C. K. Scott Moncrieff. Adapted by Neville Jason. 3 CD. (Running Time: 3 hrs. 45 mins.). (Remembrance of Things Past Ser.: Vol. IX). 2000. audio compact disk 22.98 (978-962-634-190-2(4), NA319012) Naxos.

Captive. unabr. ed. Heather Graham. Narrated by George Guidall. 11 cass. (Running Time: 16 hrs.). 91.00 (978-0-7887-0714-8(0), 94890E7) Recorded Bks.
The lush Florida Territory is unlike any landscape Teela Warren has ever seen. Raised in the gentility of the South, she is overwhelmed by this wilderness. And when she sees halfbreed James McKenzie, her passions are aroused in ways that are as strange & wonderful as her new surroundings. But their love is perilous & the Indian Wars threaten to put them on opposite sides of the bloodshed. Available to libraries only.

Captive! unabr. ed. Gary Paulsen. Narrated by Jeff Woodman. 1 cass. (Running Time: 1 hr.). (Gary Paulsen's World of Adventure Ser.: Bk. 8). (gr. 4 up). 1997. 10.00 (978-0-7887-0881-7(3), 95019E7) Recorded Bks.
Roman Sanchez starts his boring school day with a test. But gunmen enter the classroom & he & three other boys become hostages in a dangerous scheme.

Captive. unabr. ed. B. Boyd Robinson. Read by Kevin Foley. 12 cass. (Running Time: 12 hrs. 30 mins.). 1997. 64.95 (978-1-55686-728-6(X)) Books in Motion.
Abused by her English aunt & uncle, orphan Martha Hazlett escapes to the American colonies, is auctioned as a colonial bride then struggles to survive when captured by Indians.

Captive. unabr. collector's ed. Heather Graham. Read by Mary Peiffer. 10 cass. (Running Time: 15 hrs.). 1997. 80.00 (978-0-7366-3596-7(3), 115110) Books on Tape.
In this romance set at the dawn of the nineteenth century, Teela Warren, a Southern beauty, falls in love with lush Florida territory - & with James McKenzie, half-Indian & the most attractive man she's ever met. but the Indian Wars intervene & their romance spells only danger.

Captive. unabr. collector's ed. Victoria Holt. Read by Donada Peters. 8 cass. (Running Time: 12 hrs.). 1991. 64.00 (978-0-7366-2041-3(9), 2855) Books on Tape.
It is midway through Queen Victoria's long reign. Proper children grow up sheltered & Rosetta Cranleigh, teenage rosebud, knows little of life beyond her London home. So when her parents book passage to Cape Town, Rosetta is ecstatic. Off Africa's west coast the ship turns turtle in a storm. Rosetta is rescued by a handsome deckhand, but the two are captured by pirates. Her they sell to a Turkish pasha. But harem life is not for Rosetta. She risks everything to escape...& to find the stranger who saved her.

Captive, Pt. 2. Marcel Proust. Read by Neville Jason. Tr. by C. K. Scott Moncrieff. Adapted by Neville Jason. Prod. by Nicolas Soames. 3 cass. (Running Time: 4 hrs.). (Remembrance of Things Past Ser.: Vol. X). 2000. 17.98 (978-962-634-703-4(1), NA320314, Naxos AudioBooks) Naxos.

Captive, Vol. 2. Marcel Proust. Read by Neville Jason. Tr. by C. K. Scott Moncrieff. Adapted by Neville Jason. Prod. by Nicolas Soames. 3 CDs. (Running Time: 4 hrs.). (Remembrance of Things Past Ser.: Vol. X). 2000. audio compact disk 22.98 (978-962-634-203-9(X), NA320312, Naxos AudioBooks) Naxos.

***Captive: My Time as a Prisoner of the Taliban.** unabr. ed. Jere Van Dyk. 8 CDs. (Running Time: 10 hrs.). (ENG.). 2010. audio compact disk 39.99 (978-1-4272-1043-2(8)) Pub: Macmill Audio. Dist(s): Macmillan

Captive - Two, Returning. unabr. ed. B. Boyd Robinson. Read by Kevin Foley. 12 cass. (Running Time: 12 hrs. 36 mins.). 1997. 64.95 (978-1-55686-738-5(7)) Books in Motion.
Though free of her Indian captors & expecting little acceptance of her half-breed children, Martha attempts to build her life outside the colonies but later returns to England.

Captive Audience. unabr. ed. Jessica Mann. Read by Paddy Glynn. 5 cass. (Running Time: 8 hrs.). 2000. 49.95 (978-0-7531-0555-9(1), 990508) Pub: ISIS Audio GBR. Dist(s): Ulverscroft US
Sylvester Crawford, the invalid husband of one of Buriton University's professors, watches as the ambitions, affairs & darkest secrets of the students & staff are revealed in the tense lead-up to a manslaughter trial.

Captive Bride. abr. ed. Johanna Lindsey. Read by Noel Taylor. 1 cass. (Running Time: 90 mins.). 1994. 5.99 (978-1-57096-008-6(9), RAZ 909) Romance Alive Audio.
Dreamspinner extraordinaire, bestselling author Lindsey writes this quintessential captive/captor romance created to stir the imagination & the heartstrings.

Captive Crown. unabr. ed. Nigel Tranter. Read by Joe Dunlop. 14 cass. (Running Time: 14 hrs.). (House of Stewart Trilogy: Bk. 3). (J). 1998. 99.95 (978-0-7531-0347-0(8), 980208) Pub: ISIS Lrg Prnt GBR. Dist(s): Ulverscroft US
With the heir to the throne murdered, King Robert the Third, a sick weakling, is left with his remaining son. Scotland & the Stewarts were in a bad way - three generations removed from the great Bruce. Nevertheless, two young men stood out: Alex Stewart & his cousin, Brave John of Coull. Their fortunes are all intertwined with those of Sir Jamie Douglas, the bastard son of the powerful Lord of Dalkeith. Jamie is still the landless outlaw that he had been made following his vow to avenge the suspicious death of his master. Unrelenting & with a conscience that could make life hard in such unscrupulous times, Jamie tells us the story of the Stewarts.

Captive of My Desires. abr. ed. Johanna Lindsey. Read by Laural Merlington. (Running Time: 6 hrs.). (Malory Ser.). 2007. audio compact disk 14.99 (978-1-59737-672-3(8), 9781597376723, BCD Value Price) Brilliance Audio.

Captive of My Desires. abr. ed. unabr. ed. Johanna Lindsey. Read by Laural Merlington. (Running Time: 36000 sec.). (Malory Ser.). 2006. audio compact disk 97.25 (978-1-59600-235-7(2), 9781596002357, BACDLib Ed) Brilliance Audio.
Please enter a Synopsis.

Captive of My Desires. unabr. ed. Johanna Lindsey. Read by Laural Merlington. (Running Time: 10 hrs.). (Malory Ser.). 2006. 39.25 (978-1-59710-909-3(6), 9781597109093, BADLE); 24.95 (978-1-59710-908-6(8), 9781597109086, BAD); 32.95 (978-1-59600-231-9(X), 9781596002319, BAU); 82.25 (978-1-59600-232-6(8), 9781596002326, BrilAudUnabridg); audio compact disk 39.25 (978-1-59335-965-2(9), 9781593359652, Brlnc Audio MP3 Lib); audio compact disk 24.95 (978-1-59335-964-5(0), 9781593359645, Brilliance MP3); audio compact disk 36.95 (978-1-4233-1234-5(1), 9781423312345, Bril Audio CD Unabri) Brilliance Audio.

***Captive Queen: A Novel of Eleanor of Aquitaine.** unabr. ed. Alison Weir. (Running Time: 15 hrs. 45 mins.). 2010. 29.95 (978-1-4417-5467-7(9)); audio compact disk 34.95 (978-1-4417-5466-0(0)) Blckstn Audio.

Captive Voice. unabr. ed. B. J. Hoff. Read by Jean DeBarbieris. 6 cass. (Running Time: 6 hrs.). (Daybreak Mystery Ser.: Bk. 2). 1998. 39.95 (978-1-55686-835-1(9)) Books in Motion.
Daniel & Jennifer hope to find peace on the shores of Lake Erie. Instead, they find Vali Tremayn, a famous singer hiding from a demented stalker, pulling them into a vortex of deception.

Captive's Trail. unabr. ed. Will C. Knott. Read by Maynard Villers. 4 cass. (Running Time: 4 hrs. 30 mins.). (Golden Hawk Ser.: Bk. 8). 1996. 26.95 (978-1-55686-703-3(4)) Books in Motion.
Hawk learns the whereabouts of his beautiful sister Annabelle, held captive since Bk. 1 & sold from hand to hand eluding his pursuit.

Captivity of the Oatman Girls. unabr. ed. Lorenzo D. Oatman & Olive A. Oatman. Read by Larry McKeever. 5 cass. (Running Time: 7 hrs.). 2000. 39.95 (978-0-7861-1694-2(3), 2516) Blckstn Audio.
The despairing life of the Oatman girls in captivity & their brothers five-year-long search for them is vividly described in this true-life story.

Captivity of the Oatman Girls. unabr. ed. Lorenzo D. Oatman & Olive A. Oatman. Read by Larry McKeever. 5 cass. (Running Time: 7 hrs. 30 min.). 2001. 27.95 (978-0-7861-1923-3(3)) Pub: Blckstn Audio. Dist(s): Penton Overseas
In 1851, nine members of the Oatman family, on their way to California, were savagely attacked by Apache Indians in Arizona. Two girls, Olive Ann, 14, and Mary Ann, 8, were taken captive by their attackers. An older brother, Lorenzo, 15, left for dead, made his way back to civilization. The rest of the family had been brutally massacred.

***Captivity of the Oatman Girls: Among the Apache & Mohave Indians.** unabr. ed. Lorenzo D. Oatman. Read by Larry McKeever. (Running Time: 7 hrs.). 2010. 29.95 (978-1-4417-4473-9(8)); audio compact disk 69.00 (978-1-4417-4470-8(3)) Blckstn Audio.

Capture. Kathryn Lasky. Read by Pamela Garelick. (Running Time: 360 hrs. NaN mins.). (Guardians of Ga'Hoole Ser.: Bk. 1). (J). (gr. 3-7). 2006. 34.95 (978-0-7861-4599-7(4)); audio compact disk 45.00 (978-0-7861-6989-4(3)) Blckstn Audio.

***Capture.** unabr. ed. Kathryn Lasky. Read by Pamela Garelick. (Running Time: 5 hrs. 30 mins.). (Guardians of Ga'Hoole Ser.: Bk. 1). 2010. audio compact disk 24.95 (978-1-4417-5553-7(5)) Blckstn Audio.

Capture. unabr. ed. Kathryn Lasky. Read by Pamela Garelick. (Running Time: 5 hrs. 30 mins.). (Guardians of Ga'Hoole Ser.: Bk. 1). (gr. 3-7). 2010. audio compact disk 29.95 (978-0-7861-7506-2(0)) Blckstn Audio.

Capture. unabr. ed. Kathryn Lasky. Read by Pamela Garelick. (Guardians of Ga'Hoole Ser.: Bk. 1). (J). 2007. 44.99 (978-1-60252-502-3(1)) Find a World.

***Capture.** unabr. ed. Robert K. Tanenbaum. Read by Charles Leggett. 13 CDs. (Running Time: 16 hrs. 30 mins.). 2009. audio compact disk 110.95 (978-0-7927-6493-9(5)) AudioGO.

***Capture Your Listeners' Minds: Your Presentation Persuasion Equation.** (ENG.). 2010. 14.95 (978-0-9701642-2-3(X)) Ah-Ha Bks.

Captured. Scott Zesch. Narrated by Grover Gardner. (Running Time: 10 hrs. 30 mins.). 2004. 30.95 (978-1-59912-628-9(1)) Iofy Corp.

Captured: A True Story of Abduction by Indians on the Texas Frontier. unabr. ed. Scott Zesch. 10 CDs. (Running Time: 12 hrs. 30 mins.). 2004. audio compact disk 80.00 (978-0-7861-8340-1(3), 3367); 62.95 (978-0-7861-2835-8(6), 3367) Blckstn Audio.
On New Year's Day in 1870, ten-year-old Adolph Korn was kidnapped by an Apache raiding party. Traded to Comanches, he thrived in the rough, nomadic existence, quickly becoming one of the tribe's fiercest warriors. Forcibly returned to his parents after three years, Korn never adjusted to life in white society. He spent his last years living in a cave, all but forgotten by his family.

***Captured by Grace: No One Is Beyond the Reach of a Loving God.** unabr. ed. David Jeremiah. (Running Time: 10 hrs. 0 mins. 0 sec.). (ENG.). 2011. audio compact disk 29.99 (978-1-59859-849-0(X)) Oasis Audio.

Captured by Indians. Mary Rowlandson. Narrated by Carrington MacDuffie. (Running Time: 6780 sec.). (Unabridged Classics in MP3 Ser.). (ENG.). (J). 2008. audio compact disk 24.00 (978-1-58472-628-9(8), In Aud) Sound Room.

Captured by Indians. unabr. ed. Mary Rowlands. Read by Carrington McDuffie. 2 cds. 2002. pap. bk. 37.00 (978-1-58472-224-3(X), In Aud) Pub: Sound Room. Dist(s): Baker Taylor
Mrs. Mary Rowlands was captured by Indians in 1676. This is a reading of her experiences.

Captured by Indians. unabr. ed. Mary Rowlands. Read by Carrington McDuffie. 2 cds. 2002. audio compact disk 18.95 (978-1-58472-222-9(3), In Aud) Pub: Sound Room. Dist(s): Baker Taylor

Captured by Indians: A True Account by Mary Rowlandson. unabr. ed. Mary Rowlandson. Read by Carrington McDuffie. (YA). 2007. 39.99 (978-1-59895-921-5(2)) Find a World.

Captured by Indians: A True Account by Mary Rowlandson: A True Account by Mary Rowlandson. Mary Rowlandson. Read by Carrington MacDuffie. (Running Time: 2 hrs. 18 mins.). 2003. 19.95 (978-1-59912-049-2(6), Audiofy Corp) Iofy Corp.

Captured Live & in the Act. Barry Louis Polisar. 1 cass. (Running Time: 90 min.). (J). 1978. pap. bk. 9.95 (978-0-9615696-9-3(7)) Pub: Rainbow Morn. Dist(s): IPG Chicago

Car Songs. Dennis Buck. 1 cass. (Running Time: 37 mins.). (J). (ps-5). 1990. bk. 10.95 (978-0-937124-42-0(7), KIM 9119C); pap. bk. 11.95 (KIM 9119) Kimbo Educ.
25 great songs ideal for parties, story hours, car rides & classroom fun. The Wheels on the Bus, Mr. Sun, This Old Man, Skinnamarink, Going to the Zoo, Bingo, Take Me Out to the Ball Game, Car Car Song & more. Includes lyric sheet.

Car Talk: The Hatchback of Notre Dame - More Car Talk Classics. unabr. ed. Ray Magliozzi et al. Executive Producer Doug Berman. 1 CD. (Running Time: 1 hr.). (ENG.). 2004. audio compact disk 13.95 (978-1-56511-880-5(4), 1565118804) Pub: HighBridge. Dist(s): Workman Pub

Car Talk: Why You Should Never Listen to Your Father When It Comes to Cars. unabr. ed. Tom Magliozzi & Ray Magliozzi. (Running Time: 1 hr.). (ENG.). 2001. audio compact disk 14.95 (978-1-56511-564-4(3), 1565115643) Pub: HighBridge. Dist(s): Workman Pub

Car Talk: Born Not to Run: More Disrespectful Car Songs. unabr. ed. Ray Magliozzi & Tom Magliozzi. (Running Time: 1 hr.). (ENG.). 2004. audio compact disk 16.95 (978-1-56511-881-2(2), 1565118812) Pub: HighBridge. Dist(s): Workman Pub

Car Talk Car Tunes Vol. 1: The Car Talk Compendium of Desrespectful Car Songs. Tom Magliozzi & Ray Magliozzi. 1 CD. (Running Time: 1 hr.). (ENG.). 2002. audio compact disk 16.95 (978-1-56511-661-0(5), 1565116615) Pub: HighBridge. Dist(s): Workman Pub

Car Talk Classics: Four Perfectly Good Hours. unabr. ed. Narrated by Tom Magliozzi & Ray Magliozzi. 4 CDs. (Running Time: 14400 sec.). (ENG.). 2007. audio compact disk 29.95 (978-1-59887-099-2(8), 1598870998) Pub: HighBridge. Dist(s): Workman Pub

Car Talk: Doesn't Anyone Screen These Calls? Calls about Animals & Cars. unabr. ed. Tom Magliozzi & Ray Magliozzi. (Running Time: 1 hr.). (ENG.). 2006. audio compact disk 14.95 (978-1-59887-019-0(X), 159887019X) Pub: Penguin-HghBrdg. Dist(s): Penguin Grp USA

Car Talk Fathers: Why You Should Never Listen to Your Father When It Comes to Cars. abr. ed. Tom Magliozzi & Ray Magliozzi. Read by Tom Magliozzi & Ray Magliozzi. 1 cass. (Running Time: 1 hr.). 1999. 11.95 (978-1-55935-320-5(1)); audio compact disk 14.95 (978-1-55935-321-2(X)) Soundelux.
The authors, better known as Click & Clock share their favorite calls over the years about auto repair & fatherly advice.

Car Talk Maternal Combustion: Calls about Moms & Cars. unabr. ed. Tom Magliozzi & Ray Magliozzi. (Running Time: 1 hr.). (ENG.). 2005. audio compact disk 13.95 (978-1-56511-980-2(0), 1565119800) Pub: HighBridge. Dist(s): Workman Pub

Car Talk: Tales of the Brothers Grime. unabr. ed. Contrib. by Ray Magliozzi & Tom Magliozzi. (ENG.). 2009. audio compact disk 16.95 (978-1-59887-895-0(6), 1598878956) Pub: HighBridge. Dist(s): Workman Pub

Car Talk: the Greatest Stories Ever Told: Once upon a Car Fire. unabr. ed. Ray Magliozzi & Tom Magliozzi. (Running Time: 3600 sec.). (ENG.). 2006. audio compact disk 14.95 (978-1-59887-057-2(2), 1598870572) Pub: HighBridge. Dist(s): Workman Pub

Car We Had to Push see World of James Thurber

Cara a Cara. unabr. ed. Marcos Vidal. 1 CD. 1998. 14.99 (978-0-8297-2642-8(X)) Zondervan.

Cara al Cielo. (Saludos Ser.: Vol. 3). (SPA.). (gr. 2-3). 10.00 (978-0-7635-5886-4(9)) Rigby Educ.

Caracteres see Treasury of French Prose

Caracteres, La Bruyere. Read by P. Lejour & C. Lecourt. 2 cass. (Running Time: 2 hrs.). (FRE.). 1991. 26.95 (1452-LV) Olivia & Hill.
Selections from the famous 17th-century author's witty & masterful collection of observations & portraits of human conduct.

Caracteres ou les Moeurs. La Bruyere. 2 cass. (Running Time: 2 hrs.). (FRE.). 1996. pap. bk. 29.50 (978-1-58085-361-3(7)) Interlingua VA.
Includes French transcription. The combination of written text & clarity & pace of diction will open the door for intermediate & advanced students to genuine comprehension & the use of literary texts for advancement in rapid understanding of written & oral language materials. The audio text plus written text concept makes foreign languages accessible to a much wider range of students than books alone.

Caramelo. unabr. ed. Sandra Cisneros. Read by Sandra Cisneros. 10 vols. (Running Time: 12 hrs.). 2002. bk. 84.95 (978-0-7927-2708-8(8), CSL 494, Chivers Sound Lib); audio compact disk 115.95 (978-0-7927-2735-4(5), SLD 494, Chivers Sound Lib) AudioGO.
As Lala Reyes and her family make the yearly journey from Chicago to her grandparents' house in Mexico City, she learns the story of her family. Caramelo portrays life inside and across borders - a story that combines history (including the "Paris of the New World" that was Mexico City, and Chicago at the dawn of the Roaring '20s) and family (a shameful secret in Lala's father's past will haunt her own future) to make a bridge among Mexican, American, and Mexican-American cultures.

***Caramelo.** unabr. ed. Sandra Cisneros. Read by Sandra Cisneros. (ENG.). 2006. (978-0-06-112743-4(4), Harper Audio) HarperCollins Pubs.

Caravan. unabr. ed. Dorothy Gilman. Narrated by Roslyn Alexander. 7 cass. (Running Time: 10 hrs.). 1992. 60.00 (978-1-55690-661-9(7), 92326E7) Recorded Bks.
Caressa & Jacob Bowman travel to pre-WWI Africa. When Jacob meets an untimely death Caressa is left in the midst of the desert where she struggles to survive.

Caravans. unabr. ed. James A. Michener. Read by Larry McKeever. 11 cass. (Running Time: 16 hrs. 30 mins.). 1994. 88.00 (978-0-7366-2668-2(9), 3405) Books on Tape.
Beautiful, bright & daring Ellen Jaspar leaves her privileged world of family for the remote territory of Afghanistan. After her impetuous marriage to a young Afghan, she disappears, sending her parents in search of her.

Caraveggio: Music of His Time. Hugh Griffith. 1 CD. (Running Time: 1 hr. 30 min.). (Art & Music Ser.). 2003. audio compact disk (Naxos AudioBooks) Naxos.

Carbamoyl Phosphate Synthetase I Deficiency - A Bibliography & Dictionary for Physicians, Patients, & Genome Researchers. Compiled by Icon Group International, Inc. Staff. 2007. ring bd. 28.95 (978-0-497-11345-2(7)) Icon Grp.

Carbo Recorded Books: Easy Primary. (J). (ps-2). 2003. pap. bk. 895.00 (978-1-883186-28-9(5), NAPS16) Natl Read Styles Inst.
Provides practice in vocabulary, fluency and comprehension.

Carbo Recorded Books: High Intermediate. (YA). (gr. 4-8). 2002. pap. bk. 1031.00 (978-1-883186-31-9(5), NHIS12) Natl Read Styles Inst.

Carbo Recorded Books: Primary. (J). (gr. 2-4). 2003. pap. bk. 1007.00 (978-1-883186-29-6(3), NAPS13) Natl Read Styles Inst.

Carbo Recorded Books: Primary/Intermediate. (J). (gr. 2-5). 2003. pap. bk. 729.00 (978-1-883186-30-2(7), NPIS9) Natl Read Styles Inst.

Carbon-Thirteen NMR Spectroscopy. Instructed by George C. Levy & Gordon L. Nelson. 6 cass. (Running Time: 6 hrs. 18 mins.). 175.00 Incl. manual. (31) Am Chemical.
Methods & characteristics are introduced.

Carcass Trade. unabr. ed. Noreen Ayres. Read by Mary Peiffer. 7 cass. (Running Time: 10 hrs. 30 mins.). 1995. 56.00 (978-0-7366-2934-8(3), 3630) Books on Tape.
Smokey Brandon goes undercover in a biker's bar to investigate her sister-in-law's gruesome death. It nearly does Smokey in!.

Carcinogens in Our Food. Tressa Drury. 2008. audio compact disk 12.95 (978-1-57970-530-5(8), Audio-For) J Norton Pubs.

Carcinogens in Our Food. unabr. ed. Tressa Drury. 1 cass. (Running Time: 27 mins.). 12.95 (931) J Norton Pubs.

Carcinoma of the Bladder - Invasive & Noninvasive. Moderated by Sam D. Graham, Jr. 2 cass. (Urologic Surgery Ser.: UR-1). 1986. 19.00 (8668) Am Coll Surgeons.

Carcinoma of the Breast. (Postgraduate Programs Ser.: C84-PG10). 1984. 85.00 (8490) Am Coll Surgeons.
Discusses concepts concerning the biology, diagnosis & treatment of carcinoma of the breast. 12 hours CME category 1 credit.

Carcinoma of the Mobile Tongue. 2 cass. (Otorhinolaryngology Ser.: C85-OT3). 1985. 15.00 (8575) Am Coll Surgeons.

Carciones. 2 CDs. (SPA.). audio compact disk 69.95 (978-0-8219-2621-5(7)) EMC-Paradigm.

Card. Arnold Bennett. Read by Peter Joyce. 6 cass. 1999. 54.95 (978-1-86015-461-4(1)) Ulverscroft US.

***Card: A Story of Adventure in the Five Towns.** Arnold Bennett. Read by Alfred von Lecteur. 2009. 27.95 (978-1-60112-961-1(0)) Babblebooks.

***Cardboard Gods: An All-American Tale Told through Baseball Cards.** unabr. ed. Josh Wilker. Read by Jim Meskimen. (Running Time: 7 hrs. 30 mins.). 2010. 29.95 (978-1-4417-6864-3(5)); 54.95 (978-1-4417-6861-2(0)); audio compact disk 24.95 (978-1-4417-6863-6(7)); audio compact disk 69.00 (978-1-4417-6862-9(9)) Blckstn Audio.

Cardcaptors: Songs from the Hit TV Series. Perf. by Froggy Mix. 1 CD. (Running Time: 1 hr.). (J). 2002. audio compact disk 13.98 (978-0-7379-0199-3(3), 74293) Rhino Enter.
It's the first album from the hit Kids WB series. John Sakura as she becomes the guardian of the cards in her fantastic musical journey to retrieve all the cards before they unleash their mischief. This upbeat pop collection features "No Nagging Anymore" Each CD also comes with a collectible trading game card.

Cardiac Interventions. Contrib. by Ziyad M. Hijazi et al. 1 cass. (American Academy of Pediatrics UPDATE: Vol. 18, No. 1). 1998. 20.00 Am Acad Pediat.

Cardiac Surgery. (Postgraduate Programs Ser.: C85-PG4). 85.00 (8514) Am Coll Surgeons.
Addresses problems encountered in the daily practice of the specialty. 12 hours CME category 1 credit.

Cardiac Surgery. (Postgraduate Programs Ser.: C84-PG4). 1984. 65.00 (8484) Am Coll Surgeons.
Covers the field of cardiac surgery with emphasis of results of accepted operative procedures & introduction of new therapeutic modalities. 9 hours CME category 1 credit.

Cardiac Surgery. Moderated by John L. Ochsner. (Postgraduate Courses Ser.: C86-PG4). 1986. 115.00 (8614) Am Coll Surgeons.
Covers the present state of the art of cardiac surgery. 12 hours CME Credit.

Cardinal, Fixed & Mutable Crosses. Mary Elness. 1 cass. (Running Time: 90 mins.). 1990. 8.95 (739) Am Fed Astrologers.

Cardinal Flower see Twentieth-Century Poetry in English, No. 25, Recordings of Poets Reading Their Own Poetry

Cardinal of the Kremlin. Tom Clancy. 1 cass. 1999. 18.00 (978-0-7435-0690-8(1), Audioworks) S&S Audio.

Cardinal of the Kremlin. unabr. ed. Tom Clancy. Read by Michael Prichard. 14 cass. (Running Time: 21 hrs.). 1988. 112.00 (978-0-7366-1408-5(7), 2297-A) Books on Tape.
In the rolling seas off the coast of South America, a target disappears in a puff of green light. In the Soviet hills of Dushanbe near the Afghanistan border, an otherwordly array of pillars & domes rises into the night.

Cardinal of the Kremlin. unabr. ed. Tom Clancy. 18 cass. (Running Time: 27 hrs.). 2002. 144.00 (978-0-7366-9112-3(X)) Books on Tape.

Cardinal Thomas Wolsey: His life & Death. George Cavendish. Read by David Thorn. Compiled by Roger Lockyer. Engineer Scott Weiser. Executive Producer Bobbie Frohman. (ENG.). 2009. audio compact disk 39.95i (978-0-9821853-4-6(0)) Alcazar AudioWorks.

Cardinal Trujillo on Humanae Vitae. 1 cass. (National Meeting of the Institute, 1993 Ser.). 4.00 (93N2) IRL Chicago.

Cardinal Virtues. 1 cass. (Running Time: 60 mins.). (Mother Angelica Live Ser.). 1986. 10.00 (978-1-55794-052-0(5), T3) Eternal Wrd TV.

Cardington Crescent. Anne Perry. Narrated by Davina Potter. 8 cass. (Running Time: 11 hrs. 25 mins.). (Thomas Pitt Ser.). 2004. 79.75 (978-1-4025-8760-3(0)); audio compact disk 109.75 (978-1-4025-8699-6(X)) Recorded Bks.

Cardington Crescent. unabr. ed. Anne Perry. Read by Kenneth Shanley. 8 cass. (Running Time: 10 hrs. 35 mins.). (Thomas Pitt Ser.). 1998. 83.95 (978-1-85903-217-6(6)) Pub: Magna Story GBR. Dist(s): Ulverscroft US
Lord Ashworth is found dead in his bed one morning in 1887 & suspicion falls on his young wife Emily. Fortunately for Emily, her spirited sister, Charlotte, is married to Inspector Thomas Pitt of Bow Street. With his knowledge of police procedure & Charlotte's understanding of Society & its intricacies, they make a formidable team. As fear & suspicion lay their chill hands on the household in Cardington Crescent, Charlotte & Pitt work furiously to discover the criminal before another tragedy darkens their lives.

Cardio in the Zone: Positive imaging & music for a focused & enjoyable Workout. Albina Tamalonis. Music by Thomas Tamalonis-Olofsson. (ENG.). 2007. audio compact disk 15.00 (978-0-9771008-4-2(7)) A M Tamalonis.

Cardiovascular Health in Women. Contrib. by Vivan M. Dickerson & Maida Taylor. 1 cass. (American College of Obstetrics & Gynecologists UPDATE: Vol. 24, No. 1). 1998. 20.00 Am Coll Obstetric.

Cardiovascular Infections. Contrib. by Stanford T. Schulman et al. 1 cass. (American Academy of Pediatrics UPDATE: Vol. 18, No. 2). 1998. 20.00 Am Acad Pediat.

Cardiovascular Principles & Instrumentation. Sidney K. Edelman. 1 cass. (C). 1992. 44.00 incl. quiz cards. (978-0-9626444-1-2(2)) ESP TX.

***Cards on the Table.** Agatha Christie. Narrated by John Moffatt. 2 CDs. (Running Time: 1 hr. 30 mins. 0 sec.). (ENG., 2010. audio compact disk 24.95 (978-0-563-53648-2(9)) Pub: AudioGO. Dist(s): Perseus Dist

Cards on the Table. unabr. ed. Agatha Christie. Read by Hugh Fraser. (Running Time: 21480 sec.). (Hercule Poirot Mystery Ser.). 2005. 27.95 (978-1-57270-491-6(8)) Pub: Audio Partners. Dist(s): PerseuPGW
Poirot is invited to a dinner party held by Mr. Shaitana, an eccentric man who informs him that four of his fellow guests are murderers who have pulled off their crimes without getting caught. After dinner the criminals assemble to play bridge in a separate room with their host, who is promptly killed. It's up to Poirot to ensure the murderer doesn't get off a second time.

Cards on the Table. unabr. ed. Agatha Christie. Narrated by Hugh Fraser. 5 CDs. (Running Time: 6 hrs.). 2008. audio compact disk 54.95 (978-0-7927-5291-2(0)) AudioGO.

Cards on the Table. unabr. ed. Agatha Christie. Read by Hugh Fraser. (Running Time: 21480 sec.). (Hercule Poirot Mystery Ser.). (ENG.). 2005. audio compact disk 27.95 (978-1-57270-492-3(6)) Pub: AudioGO. Dist(s): Perseus Dist

***Cardturner.** unabr. ed. Louis Sachar. Read by Louis Sachar. 6 CDs. 2010. audio compact disk 37.00 (978-0-307-71215-8(X), Listening Lib) Pub: Random Audio Pubg. Dist(s): Random

Cardturner: A Novel about Imperfect Partners & Infinite Possibilities. unabr. ed. Louis Sachar. Read by Louis Sachar. (ENG.). (J). 2010. audio compact disk 34.00 (978-0-307-71213-4(3), Listening Lib) Pub: Random Audio Pubg. Dist(s): Random

Care & Feeding of Expectancy: Stepping into God's Promises for Your Life. Mac Hammond. 2 CDs. (Running Time: 2 hours). 2005. audio compact disk 10.00 (978-1-57399-277-0(1)) Mac Hammond.
This two-message series will open your eyes to a key element that must work in conjunction with your faith in order for you to see the completed promises of God in your life.

Care & Feeding of Volunteers. Douglas W. Johnson. (Creative Leadership Ser.). 1978. bk. 45.00 (978-0-687-04669-0(6)) Abingdon.

Care for the Caregiver. Sue Vineyard. Read by Sue Vineyard. 1 cass. (Running Time: 45 mins.). 8.95 Heritage Arts.
She discusses symptoms of too little self-care, removing guilt about taking care of you, strategies for wellness, positive relationships, juggling multiple demands & refueling. A true survival guide from someone who's been there!.

Care of a Dying Person. (Caregiving to the Elderly Ser.). 1989. 9.95 (978-1-877843-11-2(3)) Elder Care Solutions.
The emotional crisis faced by the family. Working with a home nursing service or hospice organization. Making the final days the best they can be. Listening. Understanding dying person's mental status.

Care of Ischemic Foot Ulcerations: Interdisciplinary Panel Discussion. Moderated by F. William Wagner, Jr. 2 cass. (Orthopaedic Surgery Ser.: OR-1). 1986. 19.00 (8651) Am Coll Surgeons.

Care of Sick Children: A Basic Guide. Gerry Silk. 1 CD. (Ausmed Audiobooks Ser.). 2006. pap. bk. 29.95 (978-0-9752018-5-5(9)) Pub: Ausmed AUS. Dist(s): MPHC

Care of Specific Illnesses of the Older Person. 1989. 9.95 (978-1-877843-09-9(1)) Elder Care Solutions.
Illnesses common to the elderly. Emotional support. Food, exercise, massage & skin care.

Care of the Chronically Ill Older Person. 1989. 9.95 (978-1-877843-06-8(7)) Elder Care Solutions.
Dealing with physical disabilities & limitations. Chronic vs. acute illness. Denial, depression, etc.

Care of the Rape Victim. Rex Lewis. 1986. 10.80 (0103B) Assn Prof Chaplains.

***Care of the Soul.** abr. ed. Thomas Moore. Read by Peter Thomas. (ENG.). 2005. (978-0-06-089387-3(7), Harper Audio); (978-0-06-089388-0(5), Harper Audio) HarperCollins Pubs.

Care of the Soul: A Guide for Cultivating Depth & Sacredness in Everyday Life, unabr. ed. Thomas Moore. Narrated by Nelson Runger. 9 cass. (Running Time: 12 hrs. 15 mins.). 1995. 78.00 (978-0-7887-0151-1(7), 94373E7) Recorded Bks.
A leading lecturer & writer in North America & Europe in the areas of archetypal psychology, mythology & the imagination, explores ways of cultivating depth & sacredness in everyday life.

Care of the Soul: A Guide for Cultivating Depth & Sacredness in Everyday Life. unabr. ed. Thomas Moore. Narrated by Nelson Runger. 10 CDs. (Running Time: 12 hrs. 15 mins.). 2000. audio compact disk 90.00 (978-0-7887-3960-6(3), C1115E7) Recorded Bks.

Care of the Soul in Medicine: Healing Guidance for Patients & the People Who Care for Them. Thomas Moore. (ENG.). 2010. audio compact disk 23.95 (978-1-4019-2567-3(7)) Hay House.

Career Action Plan. Richard G. Hammes. Read by Richard G. Hammes. 1 cass. (Running Time: 60 mins.). 1992. 12.95 (978-1-882561-00-1(7)) Hammes & Assocs.
Provides framework for self-analysis of career interests, skills & abilities, work satisfiers & career plan.

Career Advantage, Ann Bass. 12 cass. (Running Time: 12 hrs.). 119.95 (652AX) Nightingale-Conant.
Do you have the job you really want? Or do you feel stuck in the right job, but not getting ahead as quickly as you'd like? Point your career toward success with this comprehensive program, packed with insights & ideas that will help you land the job you've always dreamed about. Includes workbook.

Career Advising in Action: NACADA Webinar Series 25. Featuring Joanne Damminger & Betsy McCalla-Wriggins. (ENG.). 2009. audio compact disk 140.00 (978-1-935140-67-2(1)) Nat Acad Adv.

Career & Vocational Techniques. Jeanne D. Lawlor. 1 cass. 1992. 8.95 (1059) Am Fed Astrologers.

Career Cure: How to Discover, Find or Create Your Perfect Job. Tom Welch. 1 cass. 1995. bk. 79.00 (978-1-884667-09-1(0)) Prime Concepts Grp.

Career Direct. Crown Financial Staff. 2004. cd-rom & audio compact disk 99.99 (978-1-56427-123-5(4)) Crown Fin Min Inc.

Career English Tourism: Managers, Etc. ELS, Inc. Staff. 1984. 15.00 (978-0-685-59487-2(4)) Heinle.

Career Guidance Through Astrology. Joanne Wickenburg. 1 cass. (Running Time: 90 mins.). 1984. 8.95 (362) Am Fed Astrologers.

Career of the Anti-Christ: Daniel 11:1-12:1. Ed Young. 1995. 4.95 (978-0-7417-2081-8(7), 1081) Win Walk.

Career Opportunities for the Liberal Arts Grad. unabr. ed. 3 cass. 29.95 (S15170) J Norton Pubs.
A step-by-step guide through the career search process. Teaches how to analyze your goals & values; discover your skills; identify your career options. The resume, the job hunt & the interview are also included.

Career Opportunities in Music. unabr. ed. Robert C. McSpadden. 1 cass. 12.95 (15032) J Norton Pubs.
Explores musical performances as a career & also related, non-performing areas of music.

Career Perspectives: Interviews with Blind & Visually Impaired Professionals. unabr. ed. Contrib. by Marie Attmore. 1 cass. (Running Time: 45 mins.). 19.95 (978-0-89128-171-9(1), 171-1) Am Foun Blind.

Career Planning. Rose Lineman. 1 cass. 8.95 (440) Am Fed Astrologers.
Choose rewarding career with chart factors.

Career Planning & Development. Jeanne D. Lawlor. 1 cass. 8.95 (628) Am Fed Astrologers.
An AFA Convention workshop tape.

Career Smarts: Career Portfolios with a Can Do Attitude. abr. ed. Interview. Anna Graf Williams & Karen J. Hall. Prod. by David E. Morrow. Directed By David E. Morrow. 1 cass. (Running Time: 45 mins.). 2002. 15.95 (978-0-9705790-2-7(0), 866-332-5905) Learnovation.
This audio tape features an interview with Anna Graf Williams, overviewing the contents of a Career Portfolio and the process of creating and assembling a portfolio. Anna focuses on how to select your best work samples, use your transferable skills to your advantage, and get that job, raise, or promotion you deserve.

***Career Success: Playing to Win the Donald Trump Way.** unabr. ed. Made For Success. (Running Time: 9 hrs.). (Made for Success Ser.). 2010. audio compact disk 39.95 (978-1-4417-5274-1(9)) Blckstn Audio.

***Career Success (Library Edition) Playing to Win the Donald Trump Way.** unabr. ed. Made for Success. (Running Time: 9 hrs. 0 mins.). (Made for Success Ser.). 2010. audio compact disk 123.00 (978-1-4417-5272-7(2)) Blckstn Audio.

Career Warfare: 10 Rules for Building a Successful Personal Brand on the Business Battlefield. David D'Alessando. 3 cass. 2004. 24.00 (978-1-932378-54-2(5)) Pub: A Media Intl. Dist(s): Natl Bk Netwk

Career Warfare: 10 Rules for Building a Successful Personal Brand on the Business Battlefield. David D'Alessando. 4 CDs. 2005. audio compact disk 28.00 (978-1-932378-55-9(3)) Pub: A Media Intl. Dist(s): Natl Bk Netwk

Careers for the English Major. unabr. ed. Daniel J. Steible. 1 cass. (Running Time: 22 mins.). 12.95 (15031) J Norton Pubs.
A discussion of the kinds of positions from teaching to government service, which offer opportunities to the English major.

Careers Without Reschooling: The Survival Guide to the Job Hunt for Liberal Arts Graduates. abr. ed. Interview with Dick Goldberg. 12 mono. cass. (Running Time: 12 hrs.). 1984. 95.00 ArGee Prods.
Interviews with career experts & professionals in 14 fields. Discusses concrete tools & practical information needed for job hunting for liberal arts grads, returning homemakers, career switchers, or recent college graduates.

Careertrack Collection. 6 cass. (Running Time: 6 hrs.). 79.95 (V10007) CareerTrack Pubns.
Features highlights from Careertrack's most popular audio seminars. They're ideal for previewing programs - or getting quick hits of motivation at department meetings.

Carefree Wedding: Postcards from Your Mind's Eye - Creative Stress Management. unabr. ed. Juliette Becker. 1 cass. (Running Time: 45 mins.). Dramatization. 1999. bk. 19.95 (978-1-928667-02-5(3)); bk. 19.95 (978-1-928667-00-1(7)) Postcards MindsEye.
An invitation to attend your own wedding feeling carefree, confident, radiant & relaxed. Dr. Becker tutors the listener through the process of guided imagery combined with relaxation techniques, teaching how to relax under the most overwhelming circumstances. Focuses on the bride.

Careful Use of Compliments. unabr. ed. Alexander McCall Smith. Read by Davina Porter. 7 cass. (Running Time: 8 hrs.). (Isabel Dalhousie Ser.: No. 4). 2007. 67.75 (978-1-4281-5528-2(7)); audio compact disk 77.75 (978-1-4281-5530-5(9)) Recorded Bks.

Careful Use of Compliments. unabr. ed. Alexander McCall Smith. 7 CDs. (Running Time: 28800 sec.). (Isabel Dalhousie Ser.: No. 4). 2007. audio compact disk 29.99 (978-1-4281-5527-5(9)) Recorded Bks.

***Caregiver: Families of Honor, Book One.** unabr. ed. Shelley Shepard Gray. (Running Time: 8.5 hrs. NaN mins.). (Families of Honor Ser.). (ENG.). 2011. 29.95 (978-1-4417-8005-8(X)); audio compact disk 29.95 (978-1-4417-8004-1(1)) Blckstn Audio.

***Caregiver: Families of Honor, Book One.** unabr. ed. Shelley Shepard Gray. Read by To be Announced. (Running Time: 8.5 hrs. NaN mins.). (Families of Honor Ser.). (ENG.). 2011. 54.95 (978-1-4417-8002-7(5)); audio compact disk 76.00 (978-1-4417-8003-4(3)) Blckstn Audio.

Careless Creek, unabr. abr. ed. Stan Lynde. Read by Stan Lynde. 4 pieces. (Running Time: 6 hrs.). 24.95 (978-1-886370-17-3(6), 1419) Cttnwd Pub.
In Careless Creek, the sequel to The Bodacious Kid, Merlin Fanshaw embarks on a quest for justice that takes him from the Yellowstone Territory to the goldfields of the Judith Range.

***Careless in Red.** abr. ed. Elizabeth George. Read by Charles Keating. (ENG.). 2008. (978-0-06-163063-7(2)); (978-0-06-163064-4(0)) HarperCollins Pubs.

Careless in Red. unabr. ed. Elizabeth George. Read by John Lee. 18 CDs. (Inspector Lynley Ser.). 2008. audio compact disk 129.00 (978-1-4159-5472-0(0), BksonTape) Pub: Random Audio Pubg. Dist(s): Random

Careless in Red. unabr. ed. Elizabeth George & Elizabeth George. Read by John Lee. 13 cass. (Inspector Lynley Ser.). 2008. 129.00 (978-1-4159-5501-7(8), BksonTape) Pub: Random Audio Pubg. Dist(s): Random
After the senseless murder of his wife, Detective Superintendent Thomas Lynley retreated to Cornwall, where he has spent six solitary weeks hiking the bleak and rugged coastline. But no matter how far he walks, no matter how exhausting his days, the painful memories of Helen's death do not diminish. On the forty-third day of his walk, at the base of a cliff, Lynley discovers the body of a young man who appears to have fallen to his death. The closest town, better known for its tourists and its surfing than its intrigue, seems an unlikely place for murder. However, it soon becomes apparent that a clever killer is indeed at work, and this time Lynley is not a detective but a witness and possibly a suspect. The head of the vastly understaffed local police department needs Lynley¿s help, though, especially when it comes to the mysterious, secretive woman whose cottage lies not far from where the body was discovered. But can Lynley let go of the past long enough to solve a most devious and carefully planned crime?.

Careless in Red. unabr. abr. ed. Elizabeth George & Elizabeth George. Read by Charles Keating. (Running Time: 41400 sec.). (Inspector Lynley Ser.). 2008. audio compact disk 39.95 (978-0-06-116120-9(9), Harper Audio) HarperCollins Pubs.

Careless Love: The Unmaking of Elvis Presley, abr. ed. Peter Guralnick. Read by J. Charles. 4 cass. (Running Time: 4 hrs.). 1999. 24.95 (FS9-43340) Highsmith.

Careless Love: The Unmaking of Elvis Presley. unabr. ed. Peter Guralnick. 2 cass. (Running Time: 2 hrs.). 1998. 36.95 (Bkcassette) Brilliance Audio.
The conclusion to the Elvis Presley biography.

Careless Widow & Other Stories. unabr. ed. V. S. Pritchett. Read by Robin Browne & Frances Jeater. 4 cass. (Running Time: 4 hrs. 40 mins.). (J). 1993. 44.95 (978-1-85089-583-1(X), 10492) Pub: ISIS Audio GBR. Dist(s): Ulverscroft US
Winner of the W. H. Smith Literary Award (1990), the stories in "A Careless Widow" are proof that V. S. Pritchett is still at the height of his powers. The stories are: "A Careless Widow," "Cocky Olly," "A Trip to the Seaside," "Things," "A Change of Policy," & "The Image Trade.".

Caress of Twilight. abr. ed. Laurell K. Hamilton. Read by Laural Merlington. (Running Time: 6 hrs.). (Meredith Gentry Ser.: No. 2). 2008. audio compact disk 14.99 (978-1-4233-6235-7(7), 9781423362357, BCD Value Price) Brilliance Audio.

Caress of Twilight. unabr. ed. Laurell K. Hamilton. Read by Laural Merlington. 8 cass. (Running Time: 11 hrs.). (Meredith Gentry Ser.: No. 2). 2002. 87.25 (978-1-59086-035-9(7), 1590860357, Unabridge Lib Edns); 32.95 (978-1-59086-034-2(9), 1590860349, BAU) Brilliance Audio.
I am Princess Meredith, heir to a throne - if I can stay alive long enough to claim it. My cousin, Prince Cel, is determined to see that I don't. As long as we both live, we are in a race for the crown: Whichever one of us reproduces first gets the throne. So now the men of my royal guard - frightening warriors skilled with blade, spell, and gun - have become my lovers, auditioning with pleasure for the role of future king and father of my child. And they must still protect me from assasination attempts - for unlike most fey, I am part human, and very mortal. All this royal backstabbing makes it difficult for me to pursue my living as a private investigator in Los Angeles, especially since the media made sure the whole world knows the Faerie princess is alive and well in sunny California. Now, in the City of Angels, people are dying in mysterious, frightening ways. What the human police don't realize is that the killer is hunting fey as well. Havoc lies on the horizon; the very existence of the place known as Faerie is at grave risk. So now, while I enjoy the greatest pleasures of my life with my guardians, I

must fend off an ancient evil that could destroy the very fabric of reality. And that's just my day job.

Caress of Twilight. unabr. ed. Laurell K. Hamilton. Read by Laural Merlington. (Running Time: 11 hrs.). (Meredith Gentry Ser.: No. 2). 2004. 39.25 (978-1-59335-568-5(8), 1593355688, Brlnc Audio MP3 Lib) Brilliance Audio.

Caress of Twilight. unabr. ed. Laurell K. Hamilton. Read by Laural Merlington. (Running Time: 11 hrs.). (Meredith Gentry Ser.: No. 2). 2004. 39.25 (978-1-59710-122-6(2), 1597101222, BADLE); 24.95 (978-1-59710-123-3(0), 1597101230, BAD) Brilliance Audio.

Caress of Twilight. unabr. ed. Laurell K. Hamilton. Read by Laural Merlington. (Running Time: 11 hrs.). (Meredith Gentry Ser.: No. 2). 2007. audio compact disk 102.25 (978-1-4233-3400-2(0), 9781423334002, BriAudCD Unabrid); audio compact disk 38.95 (978-1-4233-3399-9(3), 9781423333999, Bril Audio CD Unabri) Brilliance Audio.

Caress of Twilight. unabr. ed. Laurell K. Hamilton. Read by Laural Merlington. (Running Time: 11 hrs.). (Meredith Gentry Ser.: No. 2). 2004. 24.95 (978-1-59335-055-0(4), 1593350554) Soulmate Audio Bks.

Caressed. Perf. by Barry Weiss & Catherine Way. 1 cass. (Running Time: 50 mins.). 1998. (978-1-892450-28-9(3), 127) Promo Music.
Love songs on harp.

Caretaker. unabr. ed. Thomas W. Simpson. Read by Dale Hull. (Running Time: 15 hrs.). 2008. 39.25 (978-1-4233-7132-8(1), 9781423371328, Brlnc Audio MP3 Lib); 39.25 (978-1-4233-7134-2(8), 9781423371342, BADLE); 24.95 (978-1-4233-7131-1(3), 9781423371311, Brilliance MP3); 24.95 (978-1-4233-7133-5(X), 9781423371335, BAD) Brilliance Audio.

Cargo of Coffins. L. Ron Hubbard. Read by Tait Ruppert et al. Narrated by R. F. Daley. (Stories from the Golden Age Ser.). 2009. audio compact disk 9.95 (978-1-59212-170-0(5)) Gala Pr LLC.

Cargo of Eagles. unabr. ed. Margery Allingham. Read by Francis Matthews. 8 cass. (Running Time: 12 hrs.). (Albert Campion Ser.: Bk. 20). 2001. 59.95 (978-0-7451-4305-7(9), CAB 988) Pub: Chivers Audio Bks GBR. Dist(s): AudioGO
20 years ago, the village of Saltey was linked to a daring act of piracy. At the same time, the local undertaker was found dead in one of his coffins. Now, 20 years later, events are equally mysterious: a man killed by a silver bullet, an unexpected inheritance, and even a ghost or two. Campion enters the scene to uncover layers of deceit, malice and murder.

Caribbean. James A. Michener. Read by Alexander Adams. 1993. 96.00 (978-0-7366-2375-9(2)) Books on Tape.

Caribbean, Pt. 1. unabr. ed. James A. Michener. Read by Alexander Adams. 11 cass. (Running Time: 16 hrs. 30 mins.). 1993. 88.00 (978-0-7366-2374-2(4), 3147A) Books on Tape.
Seven hundred dramatic years in a tale teeming with revolution & romance, slavery & superstition.

Caribbean, Pt. 2. unabr. ed. James A. Michener. Read by Alexander Adams. 12 cass. (Running Time: 18 hrs.). 1993. 96.00 (3147B) Books on Tape.
Seven hundred dramatic years in a tale teeming with revolution & romance, slavery & superstition.

Caribbean Christmas. Contrib. by Don Boyer. Prod. by Chris McDonald. 2004. audio compact disk 11.99 (978-5-559-42446-0(3)) Sprg Hill Music Group.

Caribbean Coup. unabr. ed. Jonathan Lowe. Read by Rusty Nelson. 8 cass. (Running Time: 9 hrs. 36 min.). 2001. 49.95 (978-1-55686-926-6(6)) Books in Motion.
Travel writer Jack Stone's new assignment could be the biggest story of his career when he becomes involved in a coup attempt against the corrupt governor of Caribbean Palm Island.

Caribbean Fantasy for Acoustic Guitar. John Zaradin. 1 CD. (Running Time: 1 hr.). 1997. pap. bk. 19.95 (978-0-7866-3141-4(4), 96570BCD) Mel Bay.

Caribbean Mystery. Agatha Christie. Read by Rosalind Ayres. (Running Time: 21600 sec.). (Miss Marple Ser.: No. 12). 2006. 27.95 (978-1-57270-550-0(7)) Pub: Audio Partners. Dist(s): PerseuPGW

Caribbean Mystery. abr. ed. Agatha Christie. Narrated by Rosalind Ayres. (Running Time: 21600 sec.). (Miss Marple Ser.: No. 12). (ENG.). 2006. audio compact disk 27.95 (978-1-57270-549-4(3)) Pub: AudioGO. Dist(s): Perseus Dist

Caribbean Praise. Compiled by S. T. Kimbrough, Jr. 2008. audio compact disk 12.95 (978-1-933663-31-9(6), GBGMusik) Pub: Gnl Brd Glbl Minis. Dist(s): Cokesbury

Caribbean Revels: Haitian Rara & Dominican Gaga. Contrib. by Verna Gillis & Gage Averill. 1 cass. or CD. (Running Time: 74 mins.). 1991. (0-9307-404020-9307-40402-2-5); audio compact disk (0-9307-40402-2-5) Smithsonian Folkways.

Caribbean Steel Drums. (Running Time: 60 mins.). 2002. audio compact disk 15.99 (978-1-904972-26-6(8)) Global Jrny GBR GBR.

Caribbean Voyage: Brown Girl in the Ring. Perf. by Alan Lomax. 1 CD. (J). 1999. audio compact disk Rounder Records.
Collection of delightful & inventive game & pass play songs, sung by children & adults from Trinidad, Tobago, Dominica, St. Lucia, Anguilla, Nevis & Carriacou. Recorded by Alan Lomax in 1962 in the Lesser Antilles & Eastern Caribbean, this album is a joyful mix of African, British, French & Spanish rhythms & traditions - movement, song & preparation for life.

***Caribou Island: A Novel.** unabr. ed. David Vann. (Running Time: 11 hrs.). 2011. 29.95 (978-1-4417-7172-8(7)); 65.95 (978-1-4417-7169-8(7)); audio compact disk 32.95 (978-1-4417-7171-1(9)); audio compact disk 100.00 (978-1-4417-7170-4(0)) Blckstn Audio.

Caring. Tana Reiff. (That's Life Ser.: Bk. 6). 1994. 10.95 (978-0-7854-1100-0(3), 40716) Am Guidance.

Caring & Sharing. Blaine Yorgason. 1 cass. 5.98 (0600245) Covenant Comms.
Popular author & storyteller relates touching experiences.

Caring & Sharing. Brenton Yorgason. 1 cass. 2004. 3.95 (978-1-57734-411-7(1), 34441530) Covenant Comms.

Caring Customer Service. Emmet L. Robinson. Read by Emmet L. Robinson. 6 cass. (Running Time: 4 hrs.). 1991. 49.95 King Street.
How to prosper in business regardless of the economy.

Caring for an Endangered Planet. Comment by Helen Caldicott. (Running Time: 50 mins.). 1987. Original Face.
Outlines the global nature of our nuclear predicament & discusses dimensions of the work required to preserve & sustain a habitable planet.

Caring for Elderly Loved Ones, Vol. 1. Doug Manning. 1 cass. (Running Time: 20 mins.). 1995. 9.95 (978-1-892785-12-1(9)) In-Sight Bks Inc.
A live seminar dealing with the issues of caring for aging loved ones & the decisions that must be faced.

Caring for Missionaries. Contrib. by CCEF Faculty Staff. (ENG.). 2006. audio compact disk 40.00 (978-1-934885-57-4(6)) New Growth Pr.

Caring for Missionaries. Text by CCEF Faculty Staff. (ENG.). 2006. 40.00 (978-1-934885-58-1(4)) New Growth Pr.

Caring for Persons Who Are the Same... But Growing Older. Stephen Massie. 1986. 10.80 (0211) Assn Prof Chaplains.

Caring for the Caregiver, Vol. 1. Doug Manning. 1 cass. (Running Time: 20 mins.). 1991. 9.95 (978-1-892785-13-8(7)) In-Sight Bks Inc.
Focus on individuals or professionals who are involved in long-term care. It deals with caregiver burn-out & self-care.

Caring for the Confused or Memory Impaired Older Person, Pt. 1. 1989. 9.95 (978-1-877843-04-4(0)) Elder Care Solutions.
Dementia, memory loss & emotional upsets. Problems such as wandering, losing & hiding things. How gentleness & calmness help.

Caring for the Confused or Memory Impaired Older Person, Pt. 2. 1989. 9.95 (978-1-877843-05-1(9)) Elder Care Solutions.
A continuation of part one.

Caring for the Hemodialysis Patient. John Pumphrey & Cheryl Siegel. 1986. 10.80 (0301) Assn Prof Chaplains.

Caring for the Maternity Family. Pat Zimmel et al. 1986. 10.80 (0407) Assn Prof Chaplains.

Caring for Your Customers: A 3 Module Set of Materials for Home Study. rev. ed. James C. Campbell. (Skill Centered Leadership Ser.). 2001. pap. bk. & wbk. ed. 96.00 (978-1-891161-75-9(X)) ClamShell Pub.

Caring for Your Heart. abr. ed. Benjamin Lewis. 1 cass. (Running Time: 1 hr.). 1996. 10.95 (978-1-57453-024-7(0), 330092) Audio Lit.

Caring for Your Parents: The Complete AARP Guide. Hugh Delehanty. 2007. audio compact disk 22.95 (978-1-933310-18-3(9)) STI Certified.

Caring Parent, No. 1. 2 cass. 10.00 ea. (978-1-885357-80-9(X)) Rational Isl.
Shared experiences of parents about being parents & parenting & about parents using re-evaluation counseling.

Caring Parent, No. 2. 2 cass. 10.00 ea. . (978-1-885357-81-6(8)) Rational Isl.

Carioca Fletch. unabr. ed. Gregory Mcdonald. Read by Grover Gardner. 7 cass. (Running Time: 7 hrs.). (Fletch Ser.: No. 7). 1989. 42.00 (978-0-7366-1538-9(5), 2408) Books on Tape.
Fletch thinks he is one with the natives, but they think he is the reincarnation of a murdered Brazilian.

Carl Gustav Jung, Pt. 1. unabr. collector's ed. Frank McLynn. Read by Stuart Langton. 8 cass. (Running Time: 12 hrs.). 1997. 64.00 (978-0-7366-3761-9(3), 4436-A) Books on Tape.
A biography of an enduring icon, a one-time protege, of Freud who established his own following after a quarrel with his mentor.

Carl Gustav Jung, Pt. 2. unabr. collector's ed. Frank McLynn. Read by Stuart Langton. 8 cass. (Running Time: 12 hrs.). 1997. 64.00 (978-0-7366-3762-6(1), 4436-B) Books on Tape.
A biography of an enduring icon, a one-time protege of Freud, who established his own followers after a quarrel with his mentor.

Carl Hiaasen Collection: Sick Puppy; Lucky You. abr. ed. Carl Hiaasen. Read by Edward Asner. (Running Time: 30600 sec.). (ENG.). 2006. audio compact disk 29.95 (978-0-7393-4082-0(4), Random AudioBks) Pub: Random Audio Pubg. Dist(s): Random

Carl Jung: Analytical Psychology. Robert Stone. 1983. 10.00 (978-0-938137-05-4(0)) Listen & Learn.
Discusses the Psyche, Personal Unconscious, Collective Unconscious, Complexes, Archetypes, Anima, Animus, Persona, Shadow, Self, The Four Functions. Introversion, Extroversion, Personality Types, Dream Interpretation, Amplification of Symbols.

Carl Nicolai: How to Keep Privacy Private Through Cryptography. 1 cass. (Running Time: 60 mins.). (Cal State Univ., Long Beach). 1981. 9.00 (F123) Freeland Pr.

Carl Nicolai: The Future of Electronic Communication. 1 cass. (Running Time: 60 mins.). (Cypress College). 1980. 9.00 (F107) Freeland Pr.
Electronic devices are involved in changing our present reality, but the ramifications of the new communications, says the author, pose a threat to us just as the government does.

Carl Payne Tobey Revisited. Patricia Trubey. 1 cass. 8.95 (352) Am Fed Astrologers.
Basic teaching using equal houses.

Carl Rakosi. unabr. ed. Read by Carl Rakosi. 1 cass. (Running Time: 29 mins.). 1985. 10.00 New Letters.
Poet & psychotherapist Carl Rakosi was recorded in a public reading in San Francisco.

Carl Reiner see Movie Makers Speak: Directors

Carl Rogers: Client Centered Therapy. Robert Stone. 1 cass. (Running Time: 1 hr.). 1983. 10.00 (978-0-938137-04-7(2)) Listen & Learn.
View of Man, the Organism, Self & Phenomenal Field, the Need for Positive Regard, Congruence/Incongruence, Self-Actualization, the Six Necessary & Sufficient Therapeutic Conditions, Stages of Client Change, Group Therapy.

Carl Sandburg Reading Cool Tombs & Other Poems. unabr. ed. Carl Sandburg. Read by Carl Sandburg. 1 cass. Incl. Four Preludes on Playthings of the Wind. (SWC 1150); In Tall Grass. (SWC 1150); Night Stuff. (SWC 1150); Prairie Waters by Night. (SWC 1150); Prayers of Steel. (SWC 1150); Southern Pacific. (SWC 1150); White Ash. (SWC 1150); Windy City. (SWC 1150); 1984. 12.95 (978-0-694-50111-3(5), SWC 1150) HarperCollins Pubs.

Carl Sandburg Reading Fog & Other Poems. unabr. ed. Carl Sandburg. Read by Carl Sandburg. 1 cass. Incl. On a Flimmering Floom You Shall Ride. (SWC 1253); 1984. 12.95 (978-0-694-50180-9(8), SWC 1253) HarperCollins Pubs.

Carl Sandburg Reads, unabr. ed. Poems. Carl Sandburg. Read by Carl Sandburg. 2 cass. (Running Time: 1 hr. 34 mins.). 19.00 (H160) Blckstn Audio.
Includes "Fog," "Cool Tombs," "The Windy City," "The People," "Yes" & other of his poetry.

Carl Sandburg Reads. unabr. ed. Carl Sandburg. Read by Carl Sandburg. 2 cass. (Running Time: 1 hr. 34 mins.). 1992. 19.00 (978-1-55994-567-7(2), DCN 2288) HarperCollins Pubs.

Carl Sandburg's Poems for Children. unabr. ed. Carl Sandburg. Read by Carl Sandburg. 1 cass. (Running Time: 90 mins.). Incl. Anywhere & Everywhere People. (J). (CDL5 1124); Arithmetic. (J). (CDL5 1124); Changing Light Winds. (J). (CDL5 1124); Crossed Numbers. (J). (CDL5 1124); Foolish about Windows. (J). (CDL5 1124); Harmonica Humdrums. (J). (CDL5 1124); Little Candle. (J). (CDL5 1124); Love Letter to Hans Christian Andersen. (J). (CDL5 1124); Maybe. (J). (CDL5 1124); Meadow in Summer. (J). (CDL5 1124); Mysterious Biography. (J). (CDL5 1124); New Song for Indiana Ophelias. (J). (CDL5 1124); Night Bells. (J). (CDL5 1124); Number Man. (J). (CDL5 1124); Our Hills. (J). (CDL5 1124); Seventeen Months. (J). (CDL5 1124); Sleep Impression. (J). (CDL5 1124); Snatch of Sliphorn Jazz. (J). (CDL5 1124); This Street Never Sleeps. (J). (CDL5 1124); Wall Shadows. (J). (CDL5 1124); We Must Be Polite: Lessons for Children on How to Behave under Peculiar Circumstances. (J). (CDL5 1124); (J). 1985. 8.98 (CDL5 1124) HarperCollins Pubs.

Carl Sandburg's Poems for Children. unabr. ed. Carl Sandburg. Read by Carl Sandburg. 1 cass. Incl. Abracadabra Boys. (J). (CDL5 1124); Boxes & Bags. (J). (CDL5 1124); Buffalo Dusk. (J). (CDL5 1124); Chicago Poet. (J). (CDL5 1124); Doors. (J). (CDL5 1124); Early Moon. (J). (CDL5 1124); Evening Waterfall. (J). (CDL5 1124); Jazz Fantasia. (J). (CDL5 1124); Little Girl, Be Careful What You Say. (J). (CDL5 1124); Milk White Moon, Put the Cows to Sleep. (J). (CDL5 1124); Paper, I. (J). (CDL5 1124); Paper, II. (J). (CDL5 1124); Phizzog. (J). (CDL5 1124); Primer Lesson. (J). (CDL5 1124); Sky Talk. (J). (CDL5 1124); Small Homes. (J). (CDL5 1124); Small Talk. (J). (CDL5 1124); Sweeping Wendy: A Study in Fugue. (J). (CDL5 1124); Two Moon Fantasies. (J). (CDL5 1124); What Is Poetry? (J). (CDL5 1124); Wind on the Way. (J). (CDL5 1124); Worms & the Wind. (J). (CDL5 1124); Young Sea. (J). (CDL5 1124); (J). 1970. 9.95 (978-0-694-50661-3(3), CDL5 1124) HarperCollins Pubs.

Carl Watner & George Smith: Voluntaryist Workshop. (Running Time: 60 mins.). (Workshop Speeches). 1983. 9.00 (FW603) Freeland Pr.

***Carleton Hobbs Sherlock Holmes: Twelve Classic Full-Cast BBC Radio Dramas.** Narrated by Carleton Hobbs & Norman Shelley. (Running Time: 6 hrs. 0 mins. 0 sec.). (ENG.). 2010. audio compact disk 49.95 (978-1-4084-0064-7(2)) Pub: AudioGO. Dist(s): Perseus Dist

Carlino. unabr. collector's ed. Stuart Hood. Read by Ken Scott. 6 cass. (Running Time: 6 hrs.). 1989. 36.00 (978-0-7366-1520-4(2), 2391) Books on Tape.
This is a simple & gripping story of the eleven months of Stuart Hood flight, written from memory in a direct & evocative style.

Carlita Ropes the Twister/Storms! Steck-Vaughn Staff. 1997. (978-0-8172-7367-5(0)) SteckVau.

Carlito's Way - After Hours, abr. ed. Edwin Torres. Read by Edwin Torres. 4 cass. (Running Time: 6 hrs.). 1993. 24.95 (978-1-56876-017-9(5)) Soundlines Ent.
Two novels of the biographical journey of a Puerto Rican wiseguy who grew up on the streets of New York. He is a charming character who is a gangster who follows a strict code of ethics which land him it odds with a variety of hoods.

Carlos Castaneda's Tales of Fictive Power. Read by Daniel Noel. 1 cass. (Running Time: 90 mins.). 1977. 10.95 (978-0-7822-0221-2(7), 033) C G Jung IL.

Carlos Fuentes. unabr. ed. Ed. by Jim McKinley. Prod. by Rebekah Presson. 1 cass. (Running Time: 29 mins.). (New Letters on the Air Ser.). 1994. 10.00 (052394) New Letters.
Mexico's most celebrated novelist has a new book. "The Orange Tree" is composed of five novellas that combine history & imagination to tell such stories as that of Columbus' arrival in the Caribbean & the fate of Hernan Cortez's sons.

Carlos Maya's Paintings of the Amazon's Yanomamo Indians; Brazil's Golden Lion Tamarin Monkeys; Costa Rica's Rainforest; & The Judds Sing "Love Can Build a Bridge" Hosted by Nancy Pearlman. 1 cass. (Running Time: 29 mins.). 10.00 (1114) Educ Comm CA.

Carlsbad, CA: Strategic Planning. unabr. ed. Innovation Groups Staff. 1 cass. (Running Time: 1 hrs. 30 mins.). (Transforming Local Government Ser.: Vol. 17). 1999. 10.00 (978-1-882403-73-8(8), IG9918) Alliance Innov.

Carlton Fisk. 1 cass. (Reading With Winners: Ser. 2). 1984. 32.95 (978-0-89811-191-0(9), 9904D) Lets Talk Assocs.
This is a "read-along" story.

Carlton Fisk: Catching. Read by Carlton Fisk. 1 cass. (Running Time: 20 mins.). 9.95 (978-0-89811-071-5(8), 7122) Lets Talk Assocs.
He talks about the people & events that influenced his career & his own approach to his specialties.

Carly. unabr. ed. Lyn Cote. Read by Anna Fields. (Running Time: 27000 sec.). (Women of Ivy Manor Ser.). 2006. 54.95 (978-0-7861-4888-2(8)); audio compact disk 55.00 (978-0-7861-5992-5(8)); audio compact disk 29.95 (978-0-7861-7112-5(X)) Blckstn Audio.

Carmel: A Eucharistic Community. Keith J. Egan. 1 cass. (Running Time: 64 mins.). 8.95 I C S Pubns.
Eucharistic history lived & practiced for almost eight hundred years within the Carmelite Order.

Carmela the Italian Poodle: A Christmas Story by Pola Chapelle. Pola Chapelle. (Running Time: 16 mins). Dramatization. (J). 2005. audio compact disk 16.00 (978-0-9763967-5-8(0)) Hallelujah.

Carmel's Wellspring of Grace. Keith J. Egan. 1 cass. (Running Time: 1 hr.). 1992. 7.95 (TAH256) Alba Hse Comns.
Ideal for personal study, in the classroom & during retreat.

Carmen. Jouvet. audio compact disk 12.95 (978-0-8219-3773-0(1)) EMC-Paradigm.

Carmen. Merimee. audio compact disk 12.95 (978-0-8219-3818-8(5)) EMC-Paradigm.

Carmen. Prosper Merimee. Read by Monique Lebreton-Savigny. 2 cass. (Running Time: 2 hrs.). (FRE.). 1997. pap. bk. 29.50 (978-1-58085-351-4(X)) Interlingua VA.
Original short novel which inspired Bizet's opera, "Carmen".

Carmen. Próspero Merimée. Read by Guillermo Piedrahita. (Running Time: 3 hrs.). 2002. 16.95 (978-1-60083-185-0(0), Audiofy Corp) Iofy Corp.

Carmen. abr. ed. Próspero Merimée. Read by Guillermo Piedrahita. 3 CDs. (SPA.). 2002. audio compact disk 17.00 (978-958-9494-64-6(1)) YoYoMusic.

Carmen: An Introduction to Bizet's Opera. Thomson Smillie. Read by David Timson. 1 CD. (Running Time: 1 hr. 30 min.). (Opera Explained Ser.). 2003. audio compact disk 8.99 (978-1-84379-036-5(X)) NaxMulti GBR.

Carmen: Black Dog Opera Library. rev. ed. Composed by Bizet & Georges Bizet. 2 vols. (ENG., 2005. audio compact disk 19.95 (978-1-57912-508-0(5), 1579125085) Pub: Blck Dog & Leventhal. Dist(s): Workman Pub

Carmen & Other Stories. Prosper Mérimée. Read by Walter Covell. 3 cass. (Running Time: 4 hrs.). 1989. 18.00 incl. album. (C-90) Jimcin Record.
Classic stories of French Literature.

Carmen Tafolla. unabr. ed. Carmen Tafolla. Read by Carmen Tafolla. Prod. by Rebekah Presson. 1 cass. (Running Time: 29 mins.). 1991. 10.00 (041991) New Letters.
Tafolla is an educator & the author of three books of poems. A Mexican-American, she was raised in the barrios of San Antonio, Texas. Here she reads from her personal poems.

Carmen's Dance. Deininger & Jaugstetter. 2006. pap. bk. 49.95 (978-3-937406-03-9(4)) Pub: edel CLASS DEU. Dist(s): Natl Bk Netwk

Carmen's Men Stories. (Running Time: 51 mins.). 1989. 13.95 (G0710B090, HarperThor) HarpC GBR.

Carmilla. unabr. ed. J. Sheridan Le Fanu. Read by Walter Covell. 3 cass. (Running Time: 4 hrs.). 1980. 18.00 (C-30) Jimcin Record.
A female vampire & a horrifying spectre are the centers of these classic horror stories.

Carmilla: A Vampyre Tale. unabr. ed. J. Sheridan Le Fanu. Read by Megan Follows. 2 cass. (Running Time: 3 hrs.). 2000. 17.95 (978-1-57270-170-0(6), N21170u) Pub: Audio Partners. Dist(s): PerseuPGW
The innocent Laura has grown up in a solitary castle far from society & longs for a close friend. The arrival of a beautiful & mysterious stranger, Carmilla, delights Laura. However, as their friendship develops, frightening

events occur which mar Laura's happiness. The terrible secret of Carmilla's past unfolds as Laura sinks into a fatal illness.

Carmilla & Green Tea. J. Sheridan Le Fanu. Read by Walter Covell & Linda Vars. 3 cass. (Running Time: 4 hrs.). 1989. 18.00 incl. album. (C-30) Jimcin Record.
Female vampire & horrifying specter.

Carmine DeSapio: The Political Regular see Buckley's Firing Line

Carn, unabr. ed. Patrick McCabe. Narrated by Donal Donnelly. 6 cass. (Running Time: 7 hrs. 45 mins.). 1997. 51.00 (978-0-7887-1303-3(5), 95140E7) Recorded Bks.
Story of two women - one young & idealistic, the other world-weary - as they struggle in a town cursed with poverty & bloodshed.

Carnal Hours. abr. ed. Max Allan Collins. Read by Max Allan Collins. 2 cass. (Running Time: 3 hrs.). 1999. 16.95 Set. (978-1-882071-71-5(9)) B-B Audio.
The murder of multimillionaire Sir Harry Oaks in Nassau has remained one of the twentieth centurys most baffling and bizarre mysteries - -until now. Max Allan Collins and his fictional sleuth, Nathan Heller, have finally cracked the Oakes case in a gripp.

Carnal Innocence. Nora Roberts. Narrated by Tom Stechschulte. 16 CDs. (Running Time: 18 hrs. 15 mins.). audio compact disk 142.00 (978-0-7887-9882-5(0)) Recorded Bks.

Carnal Innocence. unabr. ed. Nora Roberts. Narrated by Tom Stechschulte. 14 cass. (Running Time: 18 hrs. 15 mins.). 1999. 109.00 (978-0-7887-3766-4(X), 95983E7) Recorded Bks.
Tale of murder & true love. After violinist Caroline Waverly breaks up with her conductor & lover, Luis, she escapes to her late grandmother's home in Innocence, Mississippi. Instead of solitude, however, she uncovers a murder victim & meets a dangerously handsome neighbor with a reputation for breaking hearts.

Carnal Prayer Mat, Set. 2 cass. (Running Time: 3 hrs.). 1995. 16.95 (978-1-886238-04-6(9)) Passion Press.
A classic Chinese fable that recounts the adventures of a brilliant young student, endowed with exceptional beauty & grace, who devotes himself to a life of pure eroticism. First published in 1634, this tale of one man & six women is designed to amuse & reform the listener, aptly demonstrating the time-honored words of Confucius, "Only one who has sinned can become a saint." Won a Best of 1995 Award from Publisher's Weekly.

Carnegie Learning(r) 2004 Module: Systems of Linear Equations & Inequalities. 2004. audio compact disk (978-1-932409-32-1(7)) Carnegie Learn.

Carnegie Maya: The Carnegie Institution of Washington Maya Research Program, 1913-1957. Ed. by John WEEKS. (ENG., 2006. audio compact disk 275.00 (978-0-87081-833-2(3)) Univ Pr Colo.

Carnets de Major Thompson. Pierre Daninos. Read by Pierre Daninos. 1 cass. (FRE.). 1991. 21.95 (1346-LQP) Olivia & Hill.
The notebooks of an Englishman who makes his home in Paris. Laugh with him as he pokes fun at all things French (and English!).

Carnitine-Acylcarnitine Translocase Deficiency - A Bibliography & Dictionary for Physicians, Patients, & Genome Researchers. Compiled by Icon Group International, Inc. Staff. 2007. ring bd. 28.95 (978-0-497-11348-3(1)) Icon Grp.

Carnitine Palmitoyltransferase I Deficiency - A Bibliography & Dictionary for Physicians, Patients, & Genome Researchers. Compiled by Icon Group International, Inc. Staff. 2007. ring bd. 28.95 (978-0-497-11346-9(5)) Icon Grp.

Carnitine Palmitoyltransferase II Deficiency - A Bibliography & Dictionary for Physicians, Patients, & Genome Researchers. Compiled by Icon Group International, Inc. Staff. 2007. ring bd. 28.95 (978-0-497-11347-6(3)) Icon Grp.

Carnival: Rainforest Foundation Concert (1997) 1 cass. (Running Time: 1 hr.). 8.78 (RCA 44769); audio compact disk 14.38 (RCA 44769) NewSound.
A collection of childhood songs selected & performed by top artists.

Carnival for the Gods, Ghost Dance: A Place of Voices & "The Rabbit in the Moon" Gladys Swan. Read by Gladys Swan. 1 cass. (Running Time: 88 mins.). 1993. 13.95 (978-1-55644-391-6(9), 13041) Am Audio Prose.
Excerpts from two novels & one complete short story.

Carnival in Motion. Perf. by William Janiak. 1 cass. (Running Time: 1 hr.). (J). 2001. pap. bk. 10.95 (KIM 0870C) Kimbo Educ.
Basic Body Movements involving head, hands, arms & legs. Includes Arms Up!, Point, Yes, Yes & more. Includes guide.

Carnival of Crime. unabr. ed. Mark Twain. Perf. by Larry Kenney. Contrib. by Laurie Altman. Intro. by Joyce Carol Oates & Peter Benchley. 1 cass. (Running Time: 1 hr.). 11.95 (978-1-56268-004-6(8)); audio compact disk 14.95 Spencer Library.
Mark Twain at his best - at his worst, as you will discover as you listen to a narration by a man who has grown comfortable with himself, his life & his values. Only one "thing" can call these things into question. As Twain confronts it, you will hope to never suffer the same encounter.

Carnival of Lost Souls. Concept by Joseph Vargo. Composed by Joseph Vargo. Composed by William Piotrowski. Nox Arcana. 1 disc. (Running Time: 63 mins). (ENG.). 2005. audio compact disk 13.99 (978-0-9675756-9-8(9)) Monolith.
"Carnival of Lost Souls" takes listeners inside an old-fashioned carnival that harbors sinister secrets and living nightmares. Musically, this album continues to deliver the dark symphonies, ghostly choirs and creepy narratives that define Nox Arcana's sound. Conceptually "Carnival of Lost Souls" offers a behind-the-scenes look into a traveling Vaudeville circus which exudes an eerie, unsettling atmosphere after darkness has descended on the grounds and the true faces of its diabolical denizens are revealed.

Carnival of the Animals. Jack Prelutsky. Illus. by Mary GrandPré. Created by Camille Saint-Saens. (Book & CD Ser.). (ENG.). (J). 2010. 19.99 (978-0-375-86458-2(X)); 22.99 (978-0-375-96458-9(4)) Pub: Knopf. Dist(s): Random

Carnival of the Animals. Camille Saint-Saens. 2008. pap. bk. 14.98 (978-962-634-900-7(X)) Naxos.

Carnival of the Animals & Children's Favourites. 1 cass. (Running Time: 65 mins.). (J). 7.98 (2197); audio compact disk 10.98 (D2197) MFLP CA.
A whole collection of classical music with animal themes! Perfect for inspiring your little dancer to be anything from a fly to an elephant.

Carnivocal: A Celebration of Sound Poetry. Ed. by Douglas Barbour & Stephen Scobie. (Running Time: 1 hr. 05 mins. 43 sec.). (Poetry Ser.). (ENG.). 2000. audio compact disk 12.95 (978-0-88995-210-2(8)) Pub: Red Deer CAN. Dist(s): IngramPubServ

Carnivorous Carnival. unabr. ed. Lemony Snicket, pseud. Narrated by Tim Curry. 5 CDs. (Running Time: 5 hrs.). (Series of Unfortunate Events Ser.: Bk. 9). (YA). (gr. 5 up). 2003. audio compact disk 45.00 (978-1-4025-3734-9(4)) Recorded Bks.

Carnivorous Carnival. unabr. ed. Lemony Snicket, pseud. Narrated by Tim Curry. 4 pieces. (Running Time: 5 hrs.). (Series of Unfortunate Events Ser.: Bk. 9). 2002. 35.00 (978-1-4025-3732-5(8)) Recorded Bks.
Even though this account of Violet, Klaus, and Sunny Baudelaire?s attempt to escape from Count Olaf by disguising themselves as circus freaks includes crowdpleasing features like violence and sloppy eating, I am sorry to report that it also contains hideous descriptions of many disagreeable things, including a pit of hungry lions, a contortionist, a man with pimples on his chin, and a job interview.

Carnivorous Carnival. unabr. abr. ed. Lemony Snicket, pseud. Read by Tim Curry. 3 cass. (Running Time: 4 hrs. 30 mins.). (Series of Unfortunate Events Ser.: Bk. 9). (J). (gr. 3-8). 2002. 20.00 (978-0-06-008781-4(1)) HarperCollins Pubs.

Carnivorous Carnival. unabr. ed. Lemony Snicket, pseud. Read by Tim Curry. 5 CDs. (Running Time: 3 hrs.). (Series of Unfortunate Events Ser.: Bk. 9). (J). (gr. 3-8). 2003. audio compact disk 25.95 (978-0-06-056626-5(4)) HarperCollins Pubs.

Carol Ann Duffy, 1985-1993: Selected Poems. unabr. ed. Carol Ann Duffy. Read by Carol Ann Duffy. (Running Time: 2 hrs. 0 mins. 0 sec.). (ENG.). 2006. audio compact disk 24.95 (978-1-4055-0220-7(7)) Pub: Little BrownUK GBR. Dist(s): IPG Chicago

Carol Britto. Read by Carol Britto. 1 cass. (Running Time: 60 min.). (Marian McPartland's Piano Jazz Ser.). 13.95 (MM-87-03-05, HarperThor) HarpC GBR.

Carol Channing the Year Without a Santa Claus. Phyllis McGinley & Clement C. Moore. (J). 1983. 8.98 (978-0-89845-199-3(X), HarperChildAud) HarperCollins Pubs.

Carol for Children see Christmas with Ogden Nash

***Carol for Christmas.** Robin Lee Hatcher. (Running Time: 2 hrs. 20 mins. 0 sec.). (ENG.). 2009. 14.99 (978-0-310-30434-0(2)) Zondervan.

Carol Hebald. unabr. ed. Read by Carol Hebald. 2 cass. (Running Time: 29 mins. per cass.). 1986. 10.00 ea. New Letters.
On the first program Carol reads from her novel, "Klara Kleinschmidt." On the second program she presents her poetry.

Carol Higgins Clark. Carol Higgins Clark. 1 cass. (Running Time: 1 hr.). 1998. 17.98 (978-1-57042-595-0(7)) Hachet Audio.

Carol Is Born. Terry. 2004. bk. 22.95 (978-1-57558-074-6(8)) Hearthstone OK.

***Carol of the Bagpipers: (Canzone D'l Zampognari)** Jill Gallina. (Running Time: 1 min.). (ENG.). 2010. audio compact disk 26.99 (978-1-4234-8587-2(4), 1423485874) Pub: Shawnee Pr. Dist(s): H Leonard

Carol of the Bells. 1 CD. (Running Time: 1 hr.). audio compact disk 10.98 (978-1-57908-395-3(1), 1668) Platinm Enter.

Carol Yacht's General Ledger & Peachtree Complete 2004: Fundamental Accounting Principles. 17th ed. Carol Yacht et al. 2004. audio compact disk 73.00 (978-0-07-287007-7(9)) McGraw.

***Carole King: Keyboard Play-along Volume 22.** Carole King. (ENG.). 2010. pap. bk. 14.99 (978-1-4234-9802-5(X), 142349802X) H Leonard.

Carole Oles. unabr. ed. Carol Oles. Read by Carol Oles. 1 cass. (Running Time: 29 mins.). 1986. 10.00 New Letters.
Carole Oles reads from "The Loneliness Factor" & "Night Watches: Inventions on the Life of Maria Mitchell".

Carolina Clawhammer: Lesson 1: The Piedmont & Western Mountains. Contrib. by Bob Carlin & Joe Thompson. (Running Time: 2 hrs. 20 mins.). 2006. 29.95 (978-5-558-11118-7(6)) Mel Bay.

Carolina Clawhammer: Lesson 2: Round Peak. Contrib. by Bob Carlin & Kirk Sutphin. (Running Time: 2 hrs. 20 mins.). 2006. 29.95 (978-5-558-11117-0(8)) Mel Bay.

Carolina Courage. abr. ed. Dana Fuller Ross, pseud. 4 cass. (Running Time: 6 hrs.). (Holts, an American Dynasty Ser.: Vol. 3). 2004. 25.00 (978-1-58807-452-2(8)) Am Pubng Inc.

Carolina Moon. abr. ed. Nora Roberts. Read by Dean Robertson. (Running Time: 21600 sec.). 2007. audio compact disk 14.99 (978-1-4233-2336-5(X), 9781423323365, BCD Value Price) Brilliance Audio.

Carolina Moon. unabr. ed. Nora Roberts. Read by Dean Robertson. (Running Time: 15 hrs.). 2004. 39.25 (978-1-59600-466-5(5), 1596004665, BADLE); 24.95 (978-1-59600-465-8(7), 1596004657, BAD); 39.25 (978-1-59600-464-1(9), 1596004649, Brinc Audio MP3 Lib); 24.95 (978-1-59600-463-4(0), 1596004630, Brilliance MP3) Brilliance Audio.
Tory Bodeen grew up in a small, rundown house where her father ruled with an iron fist and a leather belt - and where her dreams and talents had no room to flourish. But she had Hope - who lived in the big house, just a short skip away, and whose friendship allowed Tory to be something she wasn't allowed to be at home: a child. After young Hope's brutal murder, unsolved to this day, Tory's life began to fall apart. And now, as she returns to the tiny town of Progress, South Carolina, with plans to settle in and open a stylish home-design shop, she is determined to find a measure of peace and free herself from the haunting visions of that terrible night. As she forges a new bond with Cade Lavelle - Hope's older brother and the heir to the Lavelle fortune - she isn't sure whether the tragic loss they share will unite them or drive them apart. But she is willing to open her heart, just a little, and try. But living so close to unhappy memories will be more difficult and frightening than she ever expected. Because the killer of Hope is nearby as well.

Carolina Moon. unabr. ed. Nora Roberts. Read by Dean Robertson. (Running Time: 54000 sec.). 2006. audio compact disk 117.25 (978-1-4233-2334-1(3), 9781423323341, BriAudCD Unabrid); audio compact disk 38.95 (978-1-4233-2333-4(5), 9781423323334, Bril Audio CD Unabri) Brilliance Audio.

Carolina Moon. unabr. collector's ed. Jill McCorkle. Read by Kathleen O'Malley. 6 cass. (Running Time: 9 hrs.). 1997. 48.00 (978-0-7366-3723-7(0), 4404) Books on Tape.
Strange things are afoot in tiny Fulton, North Carolina. A woman entrusts her illicit love secrets to the dead letter file down at the post office. A philandering radio talk-show host turns up dead in a load of gardening topsoil.

Carolina Tarheels. 1 cass. 9.98 (C-24) Folk-Legacy.
A famous old-time strong band revisited, still making music.

Carolinda Clatter! unabr. ed. Mordicai Gerstein. Read by Mordicai Gerstein. 1 cass. (Running Time: 15 mins.). (J). (ps-2). 2006. bk. 25.95 (978-1-59519-954-6(3)) Live Oak Media.

Caroline Myss & Wayne Dyer Seminar. Caroline Myss & Wayne W. Dyer. 4 CDs. (Running Time: 6 hrs.). 2003. audio compact disk 23.95 (978-1-4019-0261-2(8), 2618) Hay House.

Caroline Myss Audio Collection: Spiritual Power, Spiritual Practice, Why People Don't Heal, Spiritual Madness. unabr. ed. Caroline Myss. 6 CDs. (Running Time: 7 hrs.). 2001. audio compact disk 49.95 (978-1-56455-948-7(3), AW00588D) Sounds True.
Explores the connections between mind, body & spirit by defining how stress & emotion contribute to disease. Suggests ways to harness our inherent spiritual powers & ultimately giving hope to patients whose illnesses have failed to respond to conventional treatment.

Caroline Myss' Chakra Meditation Music. abr. ed. Stevin McNamara. Music by Stevin McNamara. 1 CD. (Running Time: 1 hr. 13 mins.). 2001. audio compact disk 16.98 (978-1-56455-934-0(3), MM00125D) Sounds True.
Uses specific vibrational frequencies to influence the body's seven chakra centers. Listeners can use this exclusive music to complement morning and evening meditations, or simply listen to experience its beneficial effects. Composed and performed by acclaimed world music artist Stevin McNamara. With ethnic percussion instruments and drums, woodwinds, stringed instruments, voice, and bells.

Caroline Myss' Essential Guide for Healers. Caroline Myss. 4 CDs. (Running Time: 5 hrs.). 2006. audio compact disk 29.95 (978-1-59179-157-7(X), W792D) Sounds True.

Carols. 1 CD. (Running Time: 1 hr.). audio compact disk 10.98 (978-1-57908-387-8(0), 1551) Platinm Enter.

Carols & Candlelight. Mark Edwards. 2000. 11.98 (978-0-633-01208-3(4)); 40.00 (978-0-633-01207-6(6)) LifeWay Christian.

Carols of Christmas: A Windham Hill Classic Collection. 1 cass. 1999. (978-0-7601-3062-9(0)) Brentwood Music.
Instrumental light jazz & easy listening Christmas favorites include: "Oh, Come, All Ye Faithful" - W.G. Snuffy Walden; "Once in Royal David's City" - Liz Story; "Coventry Carol/What Child Is This" - Tuck Andress; "O Tannenbaum" - Steve Lukather; "It Came upon a Midnight Clear" - Steve Morse; "December Morning" - Jim Brickman; "Good King Wenceslas" - Robin Le Mesurier; "Accordion Bells" - Leo Kottke; "Angels from the Realms of Glory" - Joan Armatrading; "Carols of the Bells" - Steve Morse & Manuel Barruecco; "Simple Gifts" - Liz Story; "Hark the Herald Angels" - Nightnoise.

Carols of Christmas: A Windham Hill Classic Selection. 1 CD. (Running Time: 1 hr.). 1999. audio compact disk (978-0-7601-3061-2(2)) Brentwood Music.

Carolyn Arends: This Much I Understand. Perf. by Carolyn Arends. 1 cass. (Running Time: 1 hr.). 1999. 10.98 (978-0-7601-2469-7(8)); audio compact disk 16.98 (978-0-7601-2470-3(1)) Brentwood Music.
Songs that bring a fresh perspective to God's involvement in our everyday life experiences & offer encouragement for problems.

Carolyn Doty. unabr. ed. Carolyn Doty. 1 cass. (Running Time: 29 mins.). (New Letters on the Air Ser.). 1992. 10.00 (051592) New Letters.
She reads from "Whisper" & tells how she came to write the ghostly sleuth tale.

Carolyn Forche. unabr. ed. Carolyn Forche. Read by Carolyn Forche. 1 cass. (Running Time: 29 mins.). 1989. 10.00 New Letters.
She reads her poetry & is interviewed.

Carolyn Kizer. unabr. ed. Read by Carolyn Kizer. 1 cass. (Running Time: 29 mins.). Incl. Carolyn Kizer: Yin. 1987.; 1987. 10.00 New Letters.
Reads from her Pulitzer prize winning book & other works.

Carolyn Kizer: Yin see Carolyn Kizer

Carolyn Kizer II: Yin. unabr. ed. Carolyn Kizer. Read by Carolyn Kizer. 1 cass. (Running Time: 29 mins.). 1985. 10.00 (071285) New Letters.
Kizer won the 1984 Pulitzer Prize in poetry for "Yin". She reads poems from "Yin".

Carolyn 101: Business Lessons from the Apprentices Straight Shooter. abr. ed. Carolyn Kepcher. Told to Stephen Fenichell. 2004. 17.95 (978-0-7435-5114-4(1)) Pub: S&S Audio. Dist(s): S and S Inc

Carolyne Wright. unabr. ed. Read by Carolyne Wright. 1 cass. (Running Time: 29 mins.). 1985. 10.00 New Letters.
Wright includes poems from "Stealing The Children" & "Premonitions of An Uneasy Guest," as well as translations of a Mexican poet.

Carotid Case Studies Interactive CD. Featuring Cindy Owen. 2004. audio compact disk 150.00 (978-1-932680-25-6(X)) Gulfcoast Ultrasound.

Carousel. Richard Paul Evans. Read by Michael Gross. 2004. 10.95 (978-0-7435-1946-5(9)) Pub: S&S Audio. Dist(s): S and S Inc

Carousel. unabr. ed. Richard Paul Evans. Read by William Dufris. 6 vols. (Running Time: 9 hrs.). 2001. bk. 54.95 (978-0-7927-2453-7(4), CSL 342, Chivers Sound Lib); audio compact disk 79.95 (978-0-7927-9900-9(3), SLD 051, Chivers Sound Lib) AudioGO.
This is the love story of Michael Keddington & Faye Murrow, a story that takes place not in seclusion but in the real world, with the challenges that all lovers must face.

Carousel. unabr. ed. Rosamunde Pilcher. Read by Donada Peters. 5 cass. (Running Time: 5 hrs.). 1992. 40.00 (978-0-7366-2244-8(6), 3034) Books on Tape.
Young woman, restless in her safe world, journeys to Cornwall where her world turns upside down.

Carousel Keeps Turning. unabr. ed. Pamela Evans. Read by Heather Williams. 10 cass. (Running Time: 43620 sec.). (Detroit Ser.). 2004. 84.95 (978-0-7540-0394-6(9), CAB 1817) Pub: Chivers Audio Bks GBR. Dist(s): AudioGO
After escaping from a violent husband, Maddie Brown can only think about getting as far away from him as possible. Maddie wonders how she & her five-year-old daughter will survive. But on a hot day in 1960, Maddie follows the crowds to the river where a vibrant fairground is in full swing. An encounter there is about to change her life forever.

Carousel Painter. unabr. ed. Judith Miller. Narrated by Rebecca Gallagher. (Running Time: 7 hrs. 59 mins. 27 sec.). (ENG.). 2009. 19.59 (978-1-60814-572-0(7)); audio compact disk 27.99 (978-1-59859-619-9(5)) Oasis Audio.

Carp in the Bathtub. unabr. ed. Barbara Cohen. Read by Suzanne Toren. 1 cass. (Running Time: 24 mins.). (Follow the Reader Ser.). (J). (gr. 2-4). 1982. pap. bk. 17.00 Incls. guide. (978-0-8072-0022-3(0), FTR66 SP, Listening Lib) Random Audio Pubg.
With Passover only a week away, Leah & Harry are faced with a terrible dilemma. They've become good friends with Joe, the carp slated to become Mama's famous gefilte fish.

Carpal Tunnel Syndrome: The Invisible Threat. Kate Montgomery. 1 cass. (Running Time: 55 mins.). 19.95 (978-1-880688-03-8(4)) New Life Opt.

Carpe Corpus. unabr. ed. Rachel Caine. Narrated by Cynthia Holloway. (Running Time: 9 hrs. 0 mins. 0 sec.). (Morganville Vampires Ser.: Bk. 6). (ENG.). 2009. 19.99 (978-1-4001-6195-9(9)); audio compact disk 59.99 (978-1-4001-4195-1(8)) Pub: Tantor Media. Dist(s): IngramPubServ

Carpe Corpus. unabr. ed. Rachel Caine. Narrated by Cynthia Holloway. (Running Time: 9 hrs. 0 mins. 0 sec.). (Morganville Vampires Ser.: Bk. 6). (ENG.). (YA). (gr. 12-13). 2009. audio compact disk 29.99 (978-1-4001-1195-4(1)) Pub: Tantor Media. Dist(s): IngramPubServ

Carpe Demon. Julie Kenner. Read by Laura Hicks. 7 cass. 59.95 (978-0-7927-3804-6(7), CSL 868); audio compact disk 79.95 (978-0-7927-3805-3(5), SLD 868) AudioGO.

Carpe Diem. unabr. ed. Autumn Cornwell. Read by Lynde Houck. 7 CDs. (Running Time: 9 hrs. 5 mins.). (YA). (gr. 7 up). 2007. audio compact disk

50.00 (978-0-7393-6397-3(2), Listening Lib) Pub: Random Audio Pubg. Dist(s): Random
"I've got my entire life planned out for the next ten years - including my Ph.D. and Pulitzer Prize," claims sixteen-year-old overachiever Vassar Spore, the daughter of overachiever parents, who named her after an elite women's college. Vassar expects her sophomore summer to include both AP and AAP (Advanced Advanced Placement) classes. Surprise! Enter a world-traveling relative who sends her plans into a tailspin when she blackmails Vassar's parents into forcing their only child to backpack with her through Southeast Asia. On a journey from Malaysia to Cambodia to the remote jungles of Laos, Vassar is faced with things she isn't prepared for - adventure, danger, a Malaysian cowboy-slash-bodyguard her own age - and in learning to "live in the moment" uncovers a family secret that turns her world upside-down. Vassar Spore can plan on one thing: She'll never be the same again.

Carpe Diem: Put a Little Latin in Your Life. Harry Mount. Read by Stephen Hoye. (Playaway Adult Nonfiction Ser.). (ENG.). 2009. 50.00 (978-1-60775-620-0(X)) Find a World.

Carpe Diem: Put a Little Latin in Your Life. unabr. ed. Harry Mount. Read by Stephen Hoye. (Running Time: 5 hrs. 30 mins. 0 sec.). (ENG.). 2007. audio compact disk 24.99 (978-1-4001-0524-3(2)); audio compact disk 19.99 (978-1-4001-5524-8(X)); audio compact disk 49.99 (978-1-4001-3524-0(9)) Pub: Tantor Media. Dist(s): IngramPubServ

Carpe Diem: The Latest Frontiers of Personal Transformation. unabr. ed. Gary Arnold. 1 cass. (Running Time: 1 hr. 03 mins.). 1997. pap. bk. 12.95 (978-1-57867-275-2(9)) Windhorse Corp.
Learning to perceive your day as the creator of your experience. Explores the relationship between your beliefs & your daily reality.

Carpe Jugulum. Terry Pratchett. 2 cass. (Running Time: 3 hrs.). (Discworld Ser.). 1998. 16.99 (978-0-552-14653-1(6), Corgi RHG) Pub: Transworld GBR. Dist(s): Trafalgar

Carpe Jugulum. unabr. ed. Terry Pratchett. Read by Nigel Planer. 9 CDs. (Running Time: 10 hrs.). (Discworld Ser.). 2000. audio compact disk 84.95 (978-0-7531-0959-5(X)) Pub: ISIS Audio GBR. Dist(s): Ulverscroft US
Mightily Oats has not picked a good time to be a priest. He thought he'd come to the mountain kingdom of Lancre for a simple little religious ceremony. Now he's caught up in a war between vampires and witches, and he's not sure there is a right side. There are the witches - young Agnes, who is really in two minds about everything, Magrat, who is trying to combine witchcraft and nappies, Nanny Ogg, who is far too knowing . . . and Granny Weatherwax, who is big trouble.

Carpe Jugulum. unabr. ed. Terry Pratchett. Read by Nigel Planer. 8 cass. (Running Time: 10 hrs.). (Discworld Ser.). (J). 2001. 69.95 (978-0-7531-0838-3(0), 000603) Pub: ISIS Lrg Prnt GBR. Dist(s): Ulverscroft US

***Carpentaria.** Alexis Wright. Read by Isaac Drandich. (Running Time: 19 hrs. 15 mins.). 2009. 114.99 (978-1-74214-554-9(X), 9781742145549) Pub: Bolinda Pubng AUS. Dist(s): Bolinda Pub Inc

Carpentaria. unabr. ed. Alexis Wright. Read by Isaac Drandich. (Running Time: 19 hrs. 15 mins.). 2009. audio compact disk 123.95 (978-1-921415-43-2(6), 9781921415432) Pub: Bolinda Pubng AUS. Dist(s): Bolinda Pub Inc

Carpenter, Detective. unabr. ed. Hamilton T. Caine. Read by Daniel Chodos. 7 cass. 41.65 (B-134) Audio Bk.
With a gritty, slap-across-the-chops style, Caine kicks over that same slimy rock that Raymond Chandler & Ross MacDonald lift - the one covering the moist, rotting lifestyles of always-fascinating, always-threatening Southern California".

Carpenter's Apprentice. Matthew Price. 6 cass. 2004. (978-1-58807-300-6(9)) Am Pubng Inc.
In this most unusual coming-of-age story, the boy Jesus becomes a man amid the ordinary and extra-ordinary people of his youth. He is twelve years' old, learning the family trade, in the small Judean town of Nazareth. He is not an ordinary youngster, but he lives a normal life as the eldest child in a bustling family. But even in rural Judea, the times are becoming more unsettled. Roman invaders, highway robbers, extortionate tax collectors, rabble-rousing zealots, and a religion that seems to have lost touch with the people, all threaten his world. On his family's visit to Jerusalem for the Passover and his bar-Mitzvah, these forces change his life. He sees and is seen, hears and is heard, and an unremarkable carpenter's apprentice from nowhere changes the future. Matt Price has created a world of real people acting from all the normal human motives. Whatever your faith, you will find this story human and fascinating.

Carpenter's Apprentice: The Spiritual Biography of Jimmy Carter. Dan Ariail & Cheryl Heckler-Felz. 2 cass. (Running Time: 2 hrs.). 1996. 14.99 (978-0-310-20488-6(7)) Zondervan.
Explore the spiritual development of President Jimmy Carter.

***Carpenter's Children.** Maggie Bennett. Read by Anne Dover. 2010. 69.95 (978-1-84652-583-4(7)); audio compact disk 84.95 (978-1-84652-584-1(5)) Pub: Magna Story GBR. Dist(s): Ulverscroft US

Carpenter's Son. Brenton Yorgason. 2 cass. (Running Time: 2 hrs.). 11.98 (978-1-55503-766-6(6), 07001045) Covenant Comms.
Fictional portrayal of young Jesus.

Carpet People. Terry Pratchett. Read by Tony Robinson. 2 cass. (Running Time: 3 hrs.). (ENG.). (J). (gr. 4). 1997. 16.99 (978-0-552-54552-5(X), Corgi RHG) Pub: Transworld GBR. Dist(s): IPG Chicago

Carpool. unabr. ed. Mary Cahill. Narrated by Barbara Rosenblat & John Randolph Jones. 7 cass. (Running Time: 9 hrs. 15 mins.). 1992. 60.00 (978-1-55690-746-3(X), 92111E7) Recorded Bks.
Chauffeuring her three children to dozens of weekly appointments, Jenny Meade keeps her hand firmly on the wheel of her '79 Honda Accord. But her head is in the clouds, behind the controls of the Piper Cherokee she used to fly. Jenny's daily shuttle comes to a crashing halt when she stumbles into an unburied corpse.

Carrera Contra El Tiempo Y Como Ganarla. Camilo Cruz. 2003. (978-1-931059-48-0(9)) Taller del Exito.

Carriage for the Midwife. Maggie Bennett. (Story Sound Ser.). (J). 2005. 89.95 (978-1-85903-728-7(3)) Pub: Mgna Lrg Print GBR. Dist(s): Ulverscroft US

Carrie. unabr. ed. Stephen King. Read by Sissy Spacek. 6 CDs. (Running Time: 7 hrs. 15 mins.). 2005. audio compact disk 69.75 (978-1-4025-9383-3(X)); 59.75 (978-1-4025-9381-9(3)) Recorded Bks.
Carrie White is an awkward and unpopular high school teenager, bullied and beleaguered from all sides, who uses her burgeoning telekinetic powers to wreak vengeance on all who have teased or injured her. In her reading, Spacek reinhabits and reprises her film role as Carrie and impeccably voices all other characters as well.

Carrie. unabr. ed. Stephen King. Read by Sissy Spacek. 2005. 23.95 (978-0-7435-5023-9(4)) Pub: S&S Audio. Dist(s): S and S Inc

Carrie. unabr. ed. Stephen King. Read by Sissy Spacek. (Running Time: 73 hrs. 0 mins. 0 sec.). (ENG.). 2008. audio compact disk 19.99 (978-0-7435-8165-3(2)) Pub: S&S Audio. Dist(s): S and S Inc

Carrie Diaries. unabr. ed. Candace Bushnell. Read by Sarah Drew. (J). 2010. audio compact disk 29.99 (978-0-06-198394-8(2), HarperChildAud) HarperCollins Pubs.

***Carrie Diaries.** unabr. ed. Candace Bushnell. Read by Sarah Drew. (ENG.). 2010. (978-0-06-199164-6(3)); (978-0-06-199163-9(5)) HarperCollins Pubs.

Carried on the Wings of Angels. Victoria L. Hall. Narrated by Poppy Hill. Score by David Fabrizio. Directed By David Fabrizio. 2 CDs. (Running Time: 1 hr. 30 mins.). Dramatization. (ENG.). 2004. audio compact disk 16.95 (978-1-58124-763-3(X)) Pub: Fiction Works. Dist(s): Brodart

Carried on the Wings of Angels. abr. ed. Victoria L. Hall. Read by Poppy Hill. Contrib. by High Sierra Players Staff. 1 cass. (Running Time: 1 hrs. 30 min.). Dramatization. 1997. 12.95 Fiction Works.

Carrier see Twentieth-Century Poetry in English, No. 7, Recordings of Poets Reading Their Own Poetry

Carrier. unabr. ed. Holden Scott. Read by Dick Hill. 5 cass. (Running Time: 8 hrs.). 2000. 27.95 (978-1-56740-373-2(5), 1567403735, BAU) Brilliance Audio.
Jack Collier is a brilliant but troubled Ph.D. candidate at Harvard - the kid from the wrong side of the tracks. But he has an idea that will make medical history: train Strep A bacteria (also known as flesh eating bacteria) to attack tumors rather than healthy flesh. When his mentor, a renowned professor, steals Jack's idea and sets him up to get expelled from Harvard, Jack is devastated and nearly destroyed. But something has gone wrong with the cure and as Jack travels across the country, he unknowingly leaves a wake of deaths in his tracks. A sympathetic FBI agent wants to find Jack and stop him - before those that want to see his genius silenced find him first.

Carrier. unabr. ed. Holden Scott. Read by Dick Hill. (Running Time: 8 hrs.). 2004. 39.25 (978-1-59600-470-2(3), 1596004703, BADLE); 24.95 (978-1-59600-469-6(X), 159600469X, BAD); 39.25 (978-1-59600-468-9(1), 1596004681, Brlnc Audio MP3 Lib); 24.95 (978-1-59600-467-2(3), 1596004673, Brilliance MP3) Brilliance Audio.

Carrier. unabr. collector's ed. Keith Douglass. Read by David Hilder. 9 cass. (Running Time: 13 hrs. 30 mins.). 1995. 72.00 (978-0-7366-3052-8(X), 3734) Books on Tape.
The U.S. rushes its powerful carrier to slam the North Koreans for killing American intelligence agents. What if the Soviets meddle?.

Carrier 12. unabr. ed. Keith Douglass. 6 cass. (Running Time: 9 hrs.). 2001. 24.00 (978-0-7366-6193-5(X)) Books on Tape.
In North Vietnam, the Communist government is hiding something, & they're doing everything possible to protect it. But when the Communists launch a missile at an American plane, Admiral Wayne & the USS JEFFERSON plan a counterattack.

Carrier 16: Joint Operations. Keith Douglass. Read by David Hilder. 5 cass. (Running Time: 7 hrs. 30 mins.). 2001. 40.00 (978-0-7366-8072-1(1)) Books on Tape.
Tombstone Magruder leads his men, with the help of SEAL Team Seven, to repel a Chinese attack on Hawaii.

Carrier 2: Viper Strike. unabr. collector's ed. Keith Douglass. Read by David Hilder. 8 cass. (Running Time: 12 hrs.). 1995. 64.00 (978-0-7366-3093-1(7), 3769) Books on Tape.
Beijing called the operation Sheng-li, Mandarin for victory. The first objective: destabilize the Thai government through a covert airbase next door in Burma. General Hsiao's in charge, but he's working for himself now. Who cares about the honor of service to the People when he can have it all?.

Carrie's Comedy see Sampler of American Humor

Carrie's War. unabr. ed. Nina Bawden. Read by Zelah Clarke. 3 cass. (Running Time: 3 hrs.). (J). (gr. 1-8). 1995. 24.95 (978-1-85549-041-3(2), CTC 074, Chivers Child Audio) AudioGO.

Carrie's War. unabr. ed. Nina Bawden. Read by Zelah Clarke. 3 cass. (Running Time: 4 hrs. 20 mins.). 2002. (978-1-85549-302-5(0)) Cover To Cover GBR.
In her dreams Carrie is always running away from Druids Bottom, the house she visited as a war-time evacuee.

Carrion Death: Introducing Detective Kubu. Michael Stanley. Read by Simon Prebble. (Playaway Adult Fiction Ser.). 2008. 69.99 (978-1-60640-147-7(5)) Find a World.

Carrion Death: Introducing Detective Kubu. unabr. ed. Michael Stanley. Narrated by Simon Prebble. 2 MP3-CDs. (Running Time: 14 hrs. 30 mins. 0 sec.). (Detective Kubu Ser.). (ENG.). 2008. 29.99 (978-1-4001-5788-4(9)); audio compact disk 79.99 (978-1-4001-3788-6(8)) Pub: Tantor Media. Dist(s): IngramPubServ

Carrion Death: Introducing Detective Kubu. unabr. ed. Michael Stanley. Read by Simon Prebble. 12 CDs. (Running Time: 14 hrs. 30 mins. 0 sec.). (Detective Kubu Ser.). (ENG.). 2008. audio compact disk 39.99 (978-1-4001-0788-9(1)) Pub: Tantor Media. Dist(s): IngramPubServ

Carrot Cake Murder. unabr. ed. Joanne Fluke. Narrated by Suzanne Toren. 9 cass. (Running Time: 10 hrs. 15 mins.). (Hannah Swensen Mystery Ser.: No. 10). 2007. 46.95 (978-1-4281-7486-3(9)); 72.75 (978-1-4281-7485-6(0)); audio compact disk 102.75 (978-1-4281-7487-0(7)) Recorded Bks.

Carrot Principle: How the Best Managers Use Recognition to Engage Their Employees, Retain Talent, & Drive Performance. abr. unabr. ed. Adrian Gostick & Chester Elton. Read by Adrian Gostick & Chester Elton. 2007. 17.95 (978-0-7435-6362-8(X), Sound Ideas) Pub: S&S Audio. Dist(s): S and S Inc

Carrot Principle: How the Best Managers Use Recognition to Engage Their People, Retain Talent, & Accelerate Performance. abr. unabr. ed. Adrian Gostick & Chester Elton. Read by Adrian Gostick & Chester Elton. (Running Time: 5 hrs. 30 mins. 0 sec.). (ENG.). 2007. audio compact disk 29.95 (978-0-7435-6361-1(1), Sound Ideas) Pub: S&S Audio. Dist(s): S and S Inc

Carrot Seed. Ruth Krauss. Illus. by Crockett Johnson. 9.95 (978-1-59112-147-3(7)) Live Oak Media.

Carrot Seed. Ruth Krauss. Illus. by Crockett Johnson. 14 vols. (Running Time: 3 mins.). 1990. pap. bk. 35.95 (978-1-59112-707-9(6)); 9.95 (978-1-59112-019-3(5)); audio compact disk 12.95 (978-1-59112-704-8(1)) Live Oak Media.

Carrot Seed. Ruth Krauss. Read by Peter Fernandez. 11 vols. (Running Time: 3 mins.). (J). 2005. pap. bk. 18.95 (978-1-59112-705-5(X)) Pub: Live Oak Media. Dist(s): AudioGO

Carrot Seed. Ruth Krauss. Read by Peter Fernandez. Illus. by Crockett Johnson. Interview with Crockett Johnson. 11 vols. (Running Time: 3 mins.). (J). (gr. k-3). 1990. bk. 25.95 (978-0-87499-177-2(3)); pap. bk. 16.95 (978-0-87499-176-5(5)) Pub: Live Oak Media. Dist(s): AudioGO
After planting a carrot seed, a small boy ignores the nay-sayers in his family who say it won't come up & is handsomely rewarded for his labor & faith.

Carrot Seed. Ruth Krauss. Read by Peter Fernandez. Illus. by Crockett Johnson. Interview with Crockett Johnson. 14 vols. (Running Time: 3 mins.). (J). (ps-4). 1990. pap. bk. & tchr. ed. 33.95 Reading Chest. (978-0-87499-178-9(1)) Live Oak Media.

***Carrots & Sticks: Unlock the Power of Incentives to Get Things Done.** unabr. ed. Ian Ayres. Read by John H. Mayer. (ENG.). 2010. audio compact disk 35.00 (978-0-307-74895-9(2), Random AudioBks) Pub: Random Audio Pubg. Dist(s): Random

Carry Me Down. unabr. ed. Read by Gerard Doyle. (Running Time: 34200 sec.). 2006. 59.95 (978-0-7861-4654-3(0)); audio compact disk 72.00 (978-0-7861-6779-1(3)); audio compact disk 29.95 (978-0-7861-7412-6(9)) Blckstn Audio.

Carry Me Like Water: A Novel. abr. ed. Benjamin Alire Sáenz. Read by Edward James Olmos et al. 4 cass. (Running Time: 6 hrs.). 1995. 22.95 (978-1-56876-044-5(2), 694055) Soundlines Ent.
This illuminating novel bluntly confronts divisions of race, gender & class, fusing cultures & personal stories of people born in different Americas. Helen, who long ago abandoned her Chicano roots, lives an assimilated Yuppie life. Everything seems fine in their idyllic corner of the world until Lizzie, a dedicated AIDS nurse & Helen's best friend, meets a mysterious Chicano patient & discovers she has a remarkable gift. Lizzie's newfound power serves as a catalyst, bringing to light long-buried secrets causing the disparate worlds of privilege & pain to collide.

Carry on, Jeeves. P. G. Wodehouse. Read by Fredrick Davidson. 5 cass. (Running Time: 7 hrs.). (Jeeves & Wooster Ser.). 1999. 39.95 (978-0-7861-1614-0(5), 2442) Blckstn Audio.
Young Bertie Wooster needed help in life. His affairs were in a complete mess. When Jeeves, the incomparable manservant, offers his services as valet, Bertie takes him on. Soon Jeeves has everything running smoothly - even Bertie himself. At his best, Jeeves miraculously keeps Bertie & his helpless friends in the good graces of their rich uncles.

Carry on, Jeeves. P. G. Wodehouse. Read by Martin Jarvis. (CSA Word Classics (Playaway) Ser.). (ENG.). 2009. 60.00 (978-1-60775-553-1(X)) Find a World.

Carry on, Jeeves. P. G. Wodehouse. Narrated by Frederick Davidson. (Running Time: 5 hrs. 30 mins.). (Jeeves & Wooster Ser.). 2005. 26.95 (978-1-59912-443-8(2)) Iofy Corp.

Carry on, Jeeves. unabr. ed. Short Stories. P. G. Wodehouse. Read by Martin Jarvis. 4 cass. (Running Time: 6 hrs.). 1999. 22.95 (978-1-57270-109-0(9), C41109u) Pub: Audio Partners. Dist(s): PerseuPGW
In the first four stories, Jeeves is appointed as Bertie Wooster's valet & quickly sets about protecting his employer from numerous scrapes. The second four stories feature the befuddled Bertie exiled in 1920's New York. Jeeves is at hand, however, to extract his master from countless jams. In all, Bertie shows himself to be not much more than a helpless millionaire, but Jeeves rises to each challenge with astonishing ingenuity.

Carry on, Jeeves. unabr. ed. P. G. Wodehouse. Read by Martin Jarvis. (Jeeves & Wooster Ser.). 2006. audio compact disk 27.95 (978-1-57270-517-3(5)) Pub: Audio Partners. Dist(s): PerseuPGW
One of literature's most celebrated fictional duos, lovable fop Bertie Wooster and his clever valet Jeeves, take center stage in these hilarious tales. In the first four, Jeeves saves Bertie from some serious scrapes involving stolen manuscripts, unfortunate engagements, marital scandals, and jailbird friends. The other four find Bertie exiled to 1920s New York, where Jeeves rescues him from American aunts, visiting Brits, poetic chumps, and femme fatales. "Jeeves Takes Charge" is chronologically the first in the series, telling how the canny valet entered Wooster's life. "Jeeves and the Unbidden Guest" expands the canvas to include Bertie's young cousin who goes wild under his wing. "The Rummy Affair of Old Biffy," "Clustering Round Young Bingo," and "The Artistic Career of Corky" are variations on the Wodehousian theme of dastardly rascals who scheme to take advantage of Bertie's hopeless naivete. The author's witty wordplay, eccentric characters, and incisive comedics are well served by Martin Jarvis's pitch-perfect performance.

Carry on, Jeeves. unabr. ed. P. G. Wodehouse. Read by Frederick Davidson. 6 CDs. (Running Time: 7 hrs.). 2000. audio compact disk 48.00 (978-0-7861-9949-5(0), 2442) Blckstn Audio.
Jeeves miraculously keeps Bertie & his helpless friends in the good graces of their rich uncles. He deals knowingly with attractive, lovelorn young ladies - patching up their affairs of the heart just the way he thinks they should be mended.

Carry on, Jeeves. unabr. ed. P. G. Wodehouse. Read by Jonathan Cecil. 8 cass. (Running Time: 12 hrs.). (Jeeves & Wooster Ser.). 2000. 59.95 (978-0-7451-6366-6(1), CAB 570) Pub: Chivers Audio Bks GBR. Dist(s): AudioGO
From the moment that Jeeves walks through Bertie Wooster's door, Bertie gives up running his own affairs and lets Jeeves take charge. Whether it's the color of a tie, the style of a hat or a coat, Jeeves is always right. He is there to depend on in times of trouble, and such times are frequent in the lives of Bertie and his friends. Whether it's Corky's artistic career that needs boosting or Bingo Little's gloom that needs lifting, Jeeves can always be relied upon.

Carry on, Mr. Bowditch. unabr. ed. Jean Lee Latham. Read by Jim Weiss. 6 CDs. (Running Time: 6 hrs. 30 mins.). (J). (gr. 3-7). 2009. 32.95 (978-1-882513-62-8(2)) Pub: Greathall Prods. Dist(s): Allegro Dist

Carry the Light. Contrib. by Tom Fettke. (ENG.). 1990. 12.00 (978-0-00-503266-4(0)) Lillenas.

Carry the Light. Contrib. by Mark Harris. (Inoriginal Performance Trax Ser.). 2005. audio compact disk 9.98 (978-5-558-93085-6(3)) INO Rec.

Carry the Light: 27 Inspirational Classics. Contrib. by Tom Fettke. 1990. 19.99 (978-0-685-68234-0(X), TA-9126S) Lillenas.

Carry the Wind. abr. ed. Terry Johnston. (ENG.). 2006. 5.98 (978-1-59483-767-8(8)) Pub: Hachet Audio. Dist(s): HachBkGrp

Carry the Wind. abr. ed. Terry C. Johnston. Read by Ken Howard. 1 cass. (Running Time: 3 hrs.). (J). 1994. 9.98 (978-1-57042-075-7(0), 4-520750) Hachet Audio.
Slick with survival-and-gore heroics & thick with Northwest wilderness period detail, this gutsy adventure is a true "black powder" historical novel set in the Rocky Mountains, circa 1830.

Carry You. Contrib. by Amy Grant. Prod. by Brown Bannister & Vince Gill. (Studio Ser.). 2005. audio compact disk 9.98 (978-5-558-83774-2(8), Word Records) Word Enter.

Carryin' On. Read by Orville Hicks. 1 cass. (Running Time: 1 hr.). (YA). 8.00 (JA0062C) Appalshop.
Orville Hicks lives in Deep Gap, North Carolina & is in constant demand for storytelling events all over the Appalachian region. Orville is the second cousin of Ray Hicks.

Carrying Capacity - What Should It Be & How Do We Get It? Hosted by Nancy Pearlman. 1 cass. (Running Time: 29 mins.). 10.00 (503) Educ Comm CA.

Cars, Boats, Trains, Planes. 1 cass. (Running Time: 1 hr.). (Kidsongs Ser.). (J). 7.98 (SME 63459); audio compact disk 11.18 Jewel box. (SME 63459) NewSound.
Includes: "Riding in My Car," "I Got Wheels," "Oh Where Has My Little Dog Gone?" & more.

Cars, Trucks & Trains. 1 cass. (Running Time: 1 hr.). (J). 8.78 (KE 9140); audio compact disk 11.98 Jewel box. (KE 9140) NewSound.

Cars, Trucks & Trains. Perf. by Learning Station Staff. 1 CD. (Running Time: 1 hr.). (J). 2001. pap. bk. 14.95 (KIM 9140CD); cass. & lp 10.95 (KIM 9140C) Kimbo Educ.
Rattles, clickety clacks & whirring wheels make these songs about transportation vehicles a hit with children. Includes the fire engine, freight train, moving van, dump truck, ambulance, school bus & more & a song that teaches what makes the car go, from the engine to the crankshaft! This musical adventure stars The Learning Station! Freight Train, Whee, Whee, Whells, Blizzie the Snowplow, Cement Mixer & more. Includes song guide.

Carson City. Hank Mitchum. Read by Charlie O'Dowd. 4 vols. No. 13. 2004. 25.00 (978-1-58807-196-5(0)); (978-1-58807-597-0(4)) Am Pubng Inc.

Carta a Amy. Tr. of Letter to Amy. (SPA.). 2004. 8.95 (978-0-7882-0283-4(9)) Weston Woods.

Cartas a las Iglesias. Tr. of Letters to the Churches. 2007. audio compact disk 30.00 (978-1-57972-745-1(X)) Insight Living.

***Cartas A un Joven Poeta; Elegias Del Duino.** abr. ed. Rainer Maria Rilke. Read by Santiago Munevar. (SPA.). 2009. audio compact disk 17.00 (978-958-8313-98-6(8)) Pub: Yoyo Music COL. Dist(s): YoYoMusic

Carter Finally Gets It. unabr. ed. Brent Crawford. Read by Nick Podehl. (Running Time: 9 hrs.). 2009. 24.99 (978-1-4233-9182-1(9), 9781423391821, Brilliance MP3); 24.99 (978-1-4233-9184-5(5), 9781423391845, BAD); 39.97 (978-1-4233-9183-8(7), 9781423391838, Brlnc Audio MP3 Lib); 39.97 (978-1-4233-9185-2(3), 9781423391852, BADLE); audio compact disk 29.99 (978-1-4233-9180-7(2), 9781423391807); audio compact disk 87.97 (978-1-4233-9181-4(0), 9781423391814, BriAudCD Unabrid) Brilliance Audio.

Carter Years. (Presidency Ser.). 10.00 Esstee Audios.
About the man from Plains who came from nowhere to become President & how he operated the White House.

Cartoon Medley: A Hearty Serving of Cartoon Network's 38 Greatest Hits. 2002. 9.98 (978-0-7379-0040-8(7), R4 75692) Rhino Enter.
Thirty-eight delectable theme songs and musical snippets from recent Cartoon Network hit shows, including Dexter's Laboratory, Johnny Bravo, and classic favorites like The Flintstones and Underdog.

Cartoon Stickers. (Art Rom Create Your Own... Ser.). (J). 2004. pap. bk. 9.99 (978-1-84229-737-7(6)) Top That GBR.

Cartuja de Parma. abr. ed. Stendhal. Read by Pedro Montoya. 3 CDs.Tr. of Recluse of Parma. (SPA.). 2002. audio compact disk 17.00 (978-958-8161-03-7(7)) YoYoMusic.

***Carved in Sand.** unabr. ed. Cathryn Jakobson Ramin. Read by Cathryn Jakobson Ramin. (ENG.). 2007. (978-0-06-147585-6(8), Harper Audio) HarperCollins Pubs.

***Carved in Sand: When Attention Fails & Memory Fades in Midlife.** unabr. ed. Cathryn Jakobson Ramin. Read by Cathryn Jakobson Ramin. (ENG.). 2007. (978-0-06-146300-6(0), Harper Audio) HarperCollins Pubs.

Carver: A Great Soul. unabr. ed. Peter D. Burchard. Read by Peter D. Burchard. 2 cass. (Running Time: 1 hr. 41 mins.). 1998. 12.95 (978-0-9658023-1-4(0)) Serpent Wise.
George Washington Carver's character & vision.

Cary Grant, L. G. Godfrey. Read by Christopher Kay. 6 cass. (Running Time: 6 hrs.). 1999. 54.95 (61055) Pub: Soundings Ltd GBR. Dist(s): ISIS Pub

Cary Grant: A Class Apart. Graham McCann & Tom Parker. 6 cass. (Running Time: 8 hrs. 30 mins.). 2002. 44.95 (978-0-7861-1507-5(6), 2357) Blckstn Audio.

Cary Grant: A Class Apart, unabr. ed. Graham McCann. Read by Tom Parker. 6 cass. (Running Time: 9 hrs.). 1999. 44.95 (2357) Blckstn Audio.
A portrait of Cary Grant which tracks the transformation of a life & looks closely at the sources of Cary Grant's charms.

Cary Grant: The Light Touch. unabr. ed. L. G. Godfrey. Read by Christopher Kay. 6 cass. (Running Time: 9 hrs.). (Sound Ser.). 2004. 54.95 (978-1-85496-105-1(5), 61055) Pub: UlverLrgPrint GBR. Dist(s): Ulverscroft US

Cary Waterman. Read by Cary Waterman. 1 cass. (Running Time: 29 mins.). 1985. 10.00 New Letters.
This Minnesota poet reads from "The Salamander Migration" & other poems.

CAS Sum & Substance Audio on Constitutional Law. 6th rev. ed. Mary M. Cheh. 2005. 63.00 (978-0-314-16019-5(1), West Lglwrks) West.

CAS Sum & Substance Audio on Constitutional Law. 6th rev. ed. Mary M. Cheh. 2005. audio compact disk 74.00 (978-0-314-16018-8(3), West Lglwrks) West.

CAS Sum & Substance Audio on Sale & Lease of Goods. 2nd rev. ed. Douglas J. Whaley. 2005. 74.00 (978-0-314-15963-2(0), West Lglwrks) West.

CAS Tempest. William Shakespeare. Read by McKellen Ian. 2004. pap. bk. 13.98 (978-962-634-808-6(9), Naxos AudioBooks) Naxos.

Cas Treasure Seekers. E. Nesbit. Read by Teres Gallagher. 2 cass. (Running Time: 2 hrs. 30 min.). 2004. 13.98 (978-962-634-828-4(3), Naxos AudioBooks) Naxos.

Cas-Visions. unabr. ed. Donald R. Gallo. 6 cass. (YA). 1991. 44.98 (978-0-8072-3141-8(X), CXL544CX, Listening Lib) Random Audio Pubg.

Casa en Mango Street. unabr. ed. Sandra Cisneros. Read by Liliana Valenzuela. 2 CDs. (Running Time: 2 hrs. 18 mins.).Tr. of House on Mango Street. (SPA & ENG.). 2005. audio compact disk 14.99 (978-0-7393-2280-2(X), Random AudioBks) Pub: Random Audio Pubg. Dist(s): Random

Casa Grande. Hank Mitchum. Read by Charlie O'Dowd. 4 vols. No. 18. 2004. 25.00 (978-1-58807-201-6(0)); (978-1-58807-961-9(9)) Am Pubng Inc.

Casa Grande. Scripts. Hank Mitchum. 5 CDs. (Running Time: 6 hrs.). (Stagecoach Ser.: 18). 2005. 14.99 (978-1-58807-242-9(8)) Am Pubng Inc.
Someone framed Cooper Dundee. At stake were his life, his family, and the Dundee Transport Company he had sweated and struggled for years to operate. His wife next to him, Cooper heads into the final fight on the road to Casa Grande.

casa para Sergin. (Saludos Ser.: Vol. 2). (SPA.). (gr. 2-3). 10.00 (978-0-7635-5884-0(2)) Rigby Educ.

Casa sulla Scogliera. Cinza Medaglia. pap. bk. 19.95 (978-88-7754-918-1(1)) Pub: Cideb ITA. Dist(s): Distribks Inc

Casablanca. Perf. by Humphrey Bogart & Ingrid Bergman. 1943. 7.95 (DM-5110) Natl Recrd Co.

Casablanca: The Maltese Falcon. Perf. by Humphrey Bogart. 1999. pap. bk. 13.10 (978-1-900912-61-7(9)) Pub: Mr Punch Prodns GBR. Dist(s): Ulverscroft US
"Casablanca" tells the story of Rick Blaine & his former lover Ilse Lund. "The Maltese Falcon" is about a private detective Sam Spade who is entrusted with the safekeeping of the much-coveted black falcon statuette.

Casanegra: A Tennyson Hardwick Story. unabr. ed. Blair Underwood. Read by Richard Allen. Told to Tananarive Due & Steven Barnes. (Running Time: 14 hrs. 0 mins. 0 sec.). (Tennyson Hardwick Ser.). (ENG.). 2007. audio compact disk 75.99 (978-1-4001-3493-9(5)) Pub: Tantor Media. Dist(s): IngramPubServ

Casanegra: A Tennyson Hardwick Story. unabr. ed. Blair Underwood. Read by Richard Allen. Told to Steven Barnes & Tananarive Due. (Running Time: 14 hrs. 0 mins. 0 sec.). (Tennyson Hardwick Ser.). (ENG.). 2007. audio compact disk 24.99 (978-1-4001-5493-7(6)) Pub: Tantor Media. Dist(s): IngramPubServ

Casanegra: A Tennyson Hardwick Story. unabr. ed. Blair Underwood et al. Read by Richard Allen. 11 CDs. (Running Time: 14 hrs. 0 mins. 0 sec.). (Tennyson Hardwick Ser.). (ENG.). 2007. audio compact disk 37.99 (978-1-4001-0493-2(9)) Pub: Tantor Media. Dist(s): IngramPubServ

Casanova. unabr. ed. John Masters. Read by Robert Whitfield. 8 CDs. (Running Time: 7 hrs.). 2005. audio compact disk 72.00 (978-0-7861-7342-6(4)) Blckstn Audio.

Casanova, unabr. ed. John Masters. Read by Robert Whitfield. 7 cass. (Running Time: 10 hrs.). 1998. 49.95 (978-0-7861-1447-4(9), 2309) Blckstn Audio.
In chronicling the life of this bastard son of Venetian actors, Masters has drawn from Casanova's own highly expansive memoirs, unavailable until the 1960s. Many of the most racy & unlikely events have been corroborated by facts.

Casanova. unabr. ed. John Masters. Read by Robert Whitfield. 1 MP3. (Running Time: 10 hrs.). 2005. 19.95 (978-0-7861-7756-1(X)); audio compact disk 19.95 (978-0-7861-7387-7(4)); 19.95 (978-0-7861-4423-5(8)) Blckstn Audio.
Giacomo Casanova¿s reputation rests largely on his obsession with 'the mystery of exactly what was lurking between any particular woman¿s legs¿. But he was much more than the Great 18th century Lover: Lawyer, mathematician, poet, translator, librarian and fluent in several languages, he was described by one contemporary as 'the most civilized man in Europe¿.

Casanova: The Venetian Years. abr. ed. Giacomo Casanova. Narrated by Benedict Cumberbatch. (Running Time: 5 hrs. 0 mins. 0 sec.). (ENG.). 2010. audio compact disk 26.95 (978-1-934997-57-4(9)) Pub: CSAWord. Dist(s): PerseuPGW

Casanova: The Venetian Years. abr. ed. Giacomo Casanova. Read by Benedict Cumberbatch. (CSA Word Classics (Playaway) Ser.). (ENG.). 2009. 59.99 (978-1-60775-704-7(4)) Find a World.

Casanova in Bolzano. unabr. ed. Sándor Márai. Read by Richard Matthews. 6 cass. (Running Time: 9 hrs.). 2004. 72.00 (978-1-4159-0289-9(5)); audio compact disk 90.00 (978-1-4159-0785-6(4)) Books on Tape.
Sandor Marai, one of the leading Hungarian novelists, begins his story in 1756 when Giacomo Casanova, after having escaped from jail, stops at the Italian village of Bolzano, remembering a girl named Francesca, over whom he fought a duel with the duke of Parma & lost.

Casca: Casca: the eternal mercenary #25: halls of Montezuma. D. V Shattuck. 2006. audio compact disk 19.95 (978-1-4276-1209-0(9)) AardGP.

Casca Collector's Series. abr. ed. Barry Sadler. Read by Charlton Griffin. 6 vols. (Casca Ser.). 2003. (978-1-58807-919-0(8)) Am Pubng Inc.

Casca Collector's Series, Vol. 1. abr. ed. Barry Sadler. Read by Bruce Watson. 6 vols. (Casca Ser.). 2003. 35.00 (978-1-58807-466-9(8)) Am Pubng Inc.

Casca Collector's Series, Vol. 2. Barry Sadler. Read by Charlton Griffin. 6 vols. (Casca Ser.). 2004. (978-1-58807-920-6(1)) Am Pubng Inc.

Casca Collector's Series, Vol. 2. Barry Sadler. Read by Charlton Griffin. 6 vols. (Casca Ser.). 2004. 35.00 (978-1-58807-467-6(6)) Am Pubng Inc.

Casca Collector's Series, Vol. 3. Barry Sadler. Read by Charlton Griffin. 6 vols. (Casca Ser.). 2004. (978-1-58807-921-3(X)) Am Pubng Inc.

Casca Collector's Series, Vol. 3. Barry Sadler. Read by Charlton Griffin. 6 vols. (Casca Ser.). 2004. 35.00 (978-1-58807-468-3(4)) Am Pubng Inc.

Casca Collector's Series, Vol. 4. Barry Sadler. Read by Charlton Griffin. 6 vols. (Casca Ser.). 2004. (978-1-58807-922-0(8)) Am Pubng Inc.

Casca Collector's Series, Vol. 4. Barry Sadler. Read by Charlton Griffin. 6 vols. (Casca Ser.). 2004. 35.00 (978-1-58807-469-0(2)) Am Pubng Inc.

Casca Collector's Series, Vol. 5. abr. ed. Barry Sadler. Read by Bruce Watson. 6 cass. (Running Time: 9 hrs.). (Casca Ser.). 2004. 35.00 (978-1-58807-470-6(6)) Am Pubng Inc.
This special Collector's Edition includes the 13th, 14th, and 15th novels in Barry Sadler's Casca series. From the moment Roman soldier Casca Longinus ran his spear through the torso of the self-proclaimed 'Son of God,' he began an endless lifelong journey filled with war, death, love, and heartache. At every turn of his sword, at every miraculously healed wound on his body, at every escape from death, the words of Jesus echo madly through his mind, "Soldier, you are content with what you are. Then that you shall remain until we meet again." In The Assassin, Casca's latest captor, Hassan al Sabah, forces the soldier to murder in his name. Relentlessly facing death, but not his own, Casca has no real life. Unless he can fight his way out of the clutches of the maniac who holds him. Casca's only hope is to take on all the best of the madman and walk away with his own sanity intact. In The Phoenix, Viet Cong Commander Ho van Tuyen has a hit list and Casca is on it. Using his invincible Ke'satnhan assassins to spread death and terror among American ranks, Ho is certain he can take out any man any time. But Casca, alias Casey Romain, has powerful friends of his own, including a fierce tribe of Kamserai warriors and some unusual allies. In The Pirate, Casca find himself thrown out of a tropical paradise and into the service of Bluebeard, the infamous pirate. A beautiful woman is held captive by a vicious man. Casca's job is to rescue the woman and not be killed by the either her jailor or the cutthroats who accompany him. Whether he's trying to stay ahead of trouble, protect the women who enter his life, or just keep more blood from being shed, the eternal soldier never has rest from the violence that stalks the earth.

Casca Collector's Series, Vol. 6. abr. ed. Barry Sadler. 6 cass. (Running Time: 9 hrs.). (Casca Ser.). 2004. 35.00 (978-1-58807-471-3(4)) Am Pubng Inc.

Cascade. 1 cass. (Running Time: 1 hr.). 9.95 (978-1-55961-443-6(9)) Relaxtn Co.

Cascade. Laraaji. 1 CD. (Running Time: 1 hr.). (Healing Music Ser.). 1997. audio compact disk 14.95 (978-1-55961-441-2(2)) Relaxtn Co.

***Cascade Loop Heritage Tour - South: U. S. Route 2 - Everett/Mukilteo to Wenatchee/Entiat, Vol. 8.** Text by Jill Linzee. (Washington Heritage Tours Ser.: No. 8). (ENG., 2010. spiral bd. 17.95 (978-1-891466-08-3(9)) NW Heritage.

Cascanueces. l.t. ed. Short Stories. Illus. by Graham Percy. 1 cass. (Running Time: 10 mins.). Dramatization.Tr. of Nutcracker. (SPA.). (J). (ps-3). 2001. 9.95 (978-84-86154-51-6(0)) Peralt Mont ESP.

Cascanueces y la Suerte del Jugador. abr. ed. E. T. A. Hoffmann. Read by Laura García. 3 CDs.Tr. of Nutcracker - The Luck of the Gambler. (SPA.). 2002. audio compact disk 17.00 (978-958-8161-09-9(6)) YoYoMusic.

Case Acct Info Systms/Bus App. 2nd ed. (C). 2005. audio compact disk 34.95 (978-0-324-30164-9(2)) Pub: Course Tech. Dist(s): CENGAGE Learn

Case Against Environmentalism. Peter Schwartz. Read by Peter Schwartz. Read by Richard M. Salsman et al. 1 cass. (Running Time: 3 hrs.). 24.95 (978-1-56114-139-5(9), HS05D) Second Renaissance.
Moral, Economic & Scientific assault on environmentalism.

Case Against Hillary Clinton. Peggy Noonan. Read by Marguerite Gavin. 5 CDs. (Running Time: 5 hrs. 30 mins.). 2000. audio compact disk 40.00 (978-0-7861-9868-9(0), 2602) Blckstn Audio.
As the long, scandal-ridden trial of the Clinton years comes to an end & as the first lady mounts her own campaign for independent political office, it is time for a summation. What is the legacy of Clintonism? What is there in Hillary Clinton's background, talents, or record of achievement that qualifies her to represent New York in the U.S. Senate? What will happen if Hillary should win this fall? Where will her ambition lead her next?.

Case Against Hillary Clinton. unabr. ed. Peggy Noonan. Read by Marguerite Gavin. 4 cass. (Running Time: 5 hrs. 30 mins.). 2000. 32.95 (978-0-7861-1803-8(2), 2602) Blckstn Audio.

Case Against Hillary Clinton. unabr. ed. Peggy Noonan. Read by Marguerite Gavin. 1 CD. (Running Time: 9 hrs.). 2001. audio compact disk 19.95 (zm2602) Blckstn Audio.
The measure of the woman, the candidate, the striving politician - offers a convincing argument that her calculated bid for power will be the first truly important election of the new millennium.

Case Against Hillary Clinton. unabr. ed. Peggy Noonan. Read by Marguerite Gavin. 4 cass. (Running Time: 6 hrs.). 2001. (978-0-7861-1914-1(4)) Blckstn Audio.
Peggy Noonan, one of our most astute political observers and a speechwriter for the Reagan White House, argues in this passionate and compelling book that everyone in the United States must look closely at Hillary and the implications of her political aspirations.

Case Against Hillary Clinton. unabr. ed. Peggy Noonan. Read by Marguerite Gavin. 4 cass. (Running Time: 6 hrs.). 2001. 24.95 Penton Overseas.

Case against Hillary Clinton. unabr. ed. Peggy Noonan. Read by Marguerite Gavin. (Running Time: 5 hrs. 30 mins.). 2000. 24.95 (978-0-7861-9650-0(5), 2602) Blckstn Audio.

Case Against Hillary Clinton. unabr. collector's ed. Peggy Noonan. Read by Karesa McElheny. 4 cass. (Running Time: 6 hrs.). 2000. 32.00 (978-0-7366-5445-6(3)) Books on Tape.
As the long, scandal-ridden trial of the Clinton years comes to an end & as the first lady mounts her own campaign for independent political office, it is time for a summation. What is the legacy of Clintonism? What is there in Hillary Clinton's background, talents, or record of achievement that qualifies her to represent New York in the U.S. Senate? What will happen if Hillary should win this fall? Where will her ambition lead her next?.

Case Closed, abr. ed. Gerald L. Posner. Read by Gerald L. Posner. 2 cass. (Running Time: 3 hrs.). 1993. 16.95 (978-1-879371-62-0(6), 393028) Pub Mills.
After thirty years, "Case Closed" succeeds where hundreds of other books & investigations have failed: it resolves the greatest murder mystery of our time, the assassination of JFK. Nominated for a Pulitzer Price, "Case Closed" examines explosive never before documented interviews, secret files & the latest scientific & computer enhancement of evidence to put to rest the speculation that has surrounded this case for decades.

Case Closed. unabr. ed. Gerald Posner. Read by Alexander Adams. 13 cass. (Running Time: 19 hrs. 30 mins.). 1994. 104.00 (978-0-7366-2718-4(9), 3448) Books on Tape.
An antidote to conspiracy theorists. Concludes that Lee Harvey Oswald did it alone.

Case for a Creator: A Journalist Investigates Scientific Evidence That Points Toward God. unabr. ed. Lee Strobel. (Running Time: 11 hrs. 0 mins. 0 sec.). (ENG.). 2004. audio compact disk 29.99 (978-0-310-25439-3(6)) Zondervan.

Case for a Creator: A Journalist Investigates the New Scientific Evidence That Points Toward God. unabr. ed. Zondervan Publishing Staff & Lee Strobel. (Running Time: 10 hrs. 43 mins. 0 sec.). (ENG.). 2004. 14.99 (978-0-310-26142-1(2)) Zondervan.

Case for Black America: A Political Road Map. Speeches. Mervin Evans. 1 CD. (Running Time: 60 min.). (ENG.). 2010. audio compact disk (978-0-914391-58-6(5)) Comm People Pr.

Case for California: The Evans Agenda - the Roadmap to End Poverty in California. Mervin Evans. 1 Audio CD. (Running Time: 60). 2005. audio compact disk 29.99 (978-0-914391-38-8(0)) Comm People Pr.

Case for Celibacy: A Biblical Defense of Catholic Teaching. 1 cass. (Running Time: 1 hr.). 2003. 13.95 (978-1-932631-39-5(9)); audio compact disk 13.95 (978-1-932631-40-1(2)) Ascensn Pr.

Case for Christ. unabr. ed. Lee Strobel. 8 cass. (Running Time: 12 hrs.). 2002. 39.99 (978-0-310-24824-8(8)) Zondervan.
Uses the dramatic scenario of an investigative journalist pursuing his story and leads and his experience as a reporter for the Chicago Times to interview experts about the evidence for Christ from the fields of science, philosophy, and history.

Case for Christ: A Journalist's Personal Investigation of the Evidence for Jesus. abr. ed. Lee Strobel. (Running Time: 2 hrs. 0 mins. 0 sec.). (ENG.). 2003. 10.99 (978-0-310-26017-2(5)) Zondervan.

Case for Christ: A Journalist's Personal Investigation of the Evidence for Jesus. unabr. ed. Lee Strobel. (Running Time: 10 hrs. 5 mins. 0 sec.). (ENG.). 2002. audio compact disk 29.99 (978-0-310-24779-1(9)) Zondervan.

Case for Christ: A Journalist's Personal Investigation of the Evidence for Jesus. unabr. ed. Zondervan Publishing Staff & Lee Strobel. (Running Time: 10 hrs. 5 mins. 0 sec.). (ENG.). 2003. 14.99 (978-0-310-26143-8(0)) Zondervan.

Case for Christmas: A Journalist Investigates the Identity of the Child in the Manger. unabr. ed. Lee Strobel. (Running Time: 3 hrs. 35 mins. 0 sec.). (ENG.). 2005. 8.99 (978-0-310-26891-8(5)) Zondervan.

Case for Christ's Resurrection. David W. Balsiger & Michael Minor. (Faith Evidence Ser.). 2007. pap. bk. 19.99 (978-0-88270-431-9(1)) Bridge-Logos.

Case for Classical Christian Education AudioBook. Douglas Wilson. Read by Gentry Rench. (ENG.). 2008. audio compact disk 20.00 (978-1-59128-476-5(7)) Canon Pr ID.

Case for Democracy. Natan Sharansky with Ron Dermer. Narrated by Simon Vance. (Running Time: 8.5 hrs. NaN mins.). 2005. 37.95 (978-1-59912-629-6(X)) Iofy Corp.

Case for Democracy: The Power of Freedom to Overcome Tyranny & Terror. Natan Sharansky & Ron Dermer. 6 cass. (Running Time: 8 hrs. 30 mins.). 2005. 54.95 (978-0-7861-3475-5(5), 3458) Blckstn Audio.

Case for Democracy: The Power of Freedom to Overcome Tyranny & Terror. unabr. ed. Natan Sharansky. Read by Simon Vance. Told to Ron Dermer. 7 CDs. (Running Time: 30600 sec.). 2005. audio compact disk 29.95 (978-0-7861-7932-9(5), ZE3458) Blckstn Audio.

Case for Democracy: The Power of Freedom to Overcome Tyranny & Terror. unabr. ed. Natan Sharansky. 7 CDs. (Running Time: 8 hrs. 30 mins.). 2005. audio compact disk 63.00 (978-0-7861-7931-2(7), 3458) Blckstn Audio.

Case for Democracy: The Power of Freedom to Overcome Tyranny & Terror. unabr. ed. Natan Sharansky & Ron Dermer. Read by Simon Vance. 6 cass. (Running Time: 8 hrs. 30 mins.). 2005. 29.95 (978-0-7861-3449-6(6), E3458) Blckstn Audio.
In this brilliantly analytical yet personal book, non-democratic societies are put under a microscope to reveal the mechanics of tyranny that sustain them. In exposing the inner workings of a "fear society;" the authors explain why democracy is not beyond any nation's reach, why it is essential for our security and why there is much that can be done to promote it around the world.

Case for Democracy: The Power of Freedom to Overcome Tyranny & Terror. unabr. ed. Natan Sharansky & Ron Dermer. Read by Simon Vance. 1 MP3. (Running Time: 8 hrs. 30 mins.). 2005. audio compact disk 29.95 (978-0-7861-8108-7(7), 3458) Blckstn Audio.

Case for Faith. unabr. ed. Lee Strobel. 2002. 39.99 (978-0-310-24825-5(6)) Zondervan.

Case for Faith: A Journalist Investigates the Toughest Objections to Christianity. abr. ed. Lee Strobel. (Running Time: 2 hrs. 0 mins. 0 sec.). (ENG.). 2003. 12.99 (978-0-310-26022-6(1)) Zondervan.

Case for Faith: A Journalist Investigates the Toughest Objections to Christianity. unabr. ed. Lee Strobel. 2 cass. (Running Time: 2 hrs.). 2000. 17.99 (978-0-310-23475-3(1)) Zondervan.
Investigates the nettlesome issues and doubts of the heart that threaten anyone's faith, even if he or she believes the evidences of Strobel's first book, The Case for Christ.

Case for Faith: A Journalist Investigates the Toughest Objections to Christianity. unabr. ed. Lee Strobel. (Running Time: 11 hrs. 2 mins. 0 sec.). (ENG.). 2002. audio compact disk 29.99 (978-0-310-24787-6(X)) Zondervan.

Case for Faith: A Journalist Investigates the Toughest Objections to Christianity. unabr. ed. Lee Strobel. (Running Time: 11 hrs. 2 mins. 0 sec.). (ENG.). 2003. 26.99 (978-0-310-26144-5(9)) Zondervan.

Case for Free Trade & Elimination of Social Security. unabr. ed. W. M. Curtiss & Paul Poirot. 1 cass. (Running Time: 1 hr. 8 mins.). 12.95 (104) J Norton Pubs.

***Case for God: What Religion Really Means.** unabr. ed. Karen Armstrong. Read by Karen Armstrong. 14 CDs. (Running Time: 16 hrs. 45 mins.). 2009. audio compact disk 100.00 (978-0-307-70239-5(1), BksonTape) Pub: Random Audio Pubg. Dist(s): Random

Case for God: What Religion Really Means. unabr. ed. Karen Armstrong. Read by Karen Armstrong. (ENG.). 2009. audio compact disk 50.00 (978-0-307-70237-1(5), Random AudioBks) Pub: Random Audio Pubg. Dist(s): Random

Case for Gold. Ron Paul & Lewis Lehrman. 1 cass. (Running Time: 32 mins.). 1987. 9.95 (978-0-945999-16-4(X)) Independent Inst.
The History of Gold As Money & How Governments Have Created Social & Economic Havoc Through Central Banking & Regulation of Money & Banking.

***Case for Hillary Clinton.** abr. ed. Susan Estrich. Read by Susan Estrich. (ENG.). 2005. (978-0-06-089464-1(4), Harper Audio); (978-0-06-089465-8(2), Harper Audio) HarperCollins Pubs.

Case for Israel. unabr. ed. Alan Dershowitz. 6 cass. (Running Time: 9 hrs.). 2003. 48.00 (978-0-7366-9660-9(1)) Books on Tape.

Case for Jefferson see Robert Frost in Recital

***Case for Mecca.** Avi Lipkin. (ENG.). 2009. audio compact disk 19.95 (978-1-57821-454-9(8)) Koinonia Hse.

Case for Mix: A Case for Calling, a Case for Skill, a Case for Serving, & a Case for Character. Stephen Graves & Thomas Addington. 1997. 15.99 (978-0-8054-0187-5(3)) BH Pubng Grp.

Case for Parallels. Rita Francomano. 1 cass. 8.95 (117) Am Fed Astrologers.
Exploration of excess of parallels in natal chart.

Case for Peace: How the Arab-Israeli Conflict Can Be Resolved. Alan M. Dershowitz. Narrated by Alan M. Dershowitz. (Running Time: 23400 sec.). 2005. audio compact disk 29.99 (978-1-4193-5741-1(7)) Recorded Bks.

Case for Peace: How the Arab-Israeli Conflict Can Be Resolved. unabr. ed. Alan Dershowitz. Read by Alan Dershowitz. 6 CDs. (Running Time: 6.5 hrs.). 2005. audio compact disk 69.75 (978-1-4193-6334-4(4), C3460); 49.75 (978-1-4193-6332-0(8), 98217) Recorded Bks.
Alan Dershowitz presents a persuasive roadmap for achieving a lasting peace between Israel and Palestine. As he did in his widely acclaimed work The Case for Israel, the renowned defender of civil liberties offers compelling - and sometimes controversial - solutions for ending this bloody, divisive conflict. Dershowitz maintains that, following the death of Yassar Arafat and the democratic election of Mahmoud Abbas, the time is ripe to let go of old assumptions and embrace new solutions. The challenge, too, is not only to achieve peace, but to do it without further loss of life in the region. The answer, Dershowitz maintains, lies in a two-state solution, with Israel recognizing the rights of Palestinian refugees and Palestine making a concentrated effort to stamp out terrorism. Both sides must take bold steps toward peace - steps that ensure a continuing security in the region. With unflinching candor and rigorous logic, Dershowitz targets the opponents of Israel, including the United Nations, the media, and American academics who insist on a one-state solution. But he also attacks Israeli and Pelestinian extremists who oppose peace. By plotting out a realistic course of action, The Case for Peace demands the attention of anyone interested in the future of global politics.

Case for Right-to-Work. unabr. ed. Reed Larson. 1 cass. (Running Time: 43 mins.). 12.95 (143) J Norton Pubs.

Case for the Real Jesus. Lee Strobel. (Running Time: 10 hrs. 0 mins. 0 sec.). (ENG.). 2007. 12.99 (978-0-310-27541-1(5)) Zondervan.

Case for the Real Jesus: A Journalist Investigates Current Attacks on the Identity of Christ. unabr. ed. Lee Strobel. (Running Time: 10 hrs. 0 mins. 0 sec.). (ENG.). 2007. audio compact disk 24.99 (978-0-310-27539-8(3)) Zondervan.

Case Forhristurriculum. Lee Strobel. 2002. cass. & video 99.99 (978-0-310-24112-6(X)) Zondervan.

Case Has Altered. Martha Grimes. (Richard Jury Novel Ser.). 2000. 15.99 (978-0-7435-0577-2(8), Audioworks) S&S Audio.

Case Has Altered. unabr. ed. Martha Grimes. Read by Donada Peters. 9 cass. (Running Time: 13 hrs. 30 min.). (Richard Jury Novel Ser.). 1998. 72.00 (978-0-7366-4072-5(X), 4581) Books on Tape.
This Richard Jury case involves an antique dealer & the murder of two women in the Lincolnshire fens.

Case Histories. unabr. ed. Kate Atkinson. Read by Susan Jameson. 10 CDs. (Running Time: 11 hrs.). (ENG.). 2008. audio compact disk 24.98 (978-1-60024-500-8(5)) Pub: Hachet Audio. Dist(s): HachBkGrp

Case Histories. unabr. ed. Read by Susan Jameson. 7 cass. 59.95 (978-0-7927-3382-9(7)); audio compact disk 89.95 (978-0-7927-3383-6(5)) AudioGO.

Case Histories: A Novel. unabr. ed. Kate Atkinson. Read by Susan Jameson. (Running Time: 11 hrs.). (ENG.). 2008. 16.98 (978-1-60024-501-5(3)) Pub: Hachet Audio. Dist(s): HachBkGrp

Case of Abraham Lincoln. unabr. ed. Julie M. Fenster. 5 CDs. (Running Time: 6 hrs. 15 mins.). (J). 2007. audio compact disk 19.95 (978-1-4332-0444-9(4)) Blckstn Audio.

Case of Abraham Lincoln: A Story of Adultery, Murder & the Making of a Great President. unabr. ed. Julie M. Fenster. Read by Hilary Huber. Frwd. by Douglas Brinkley. (Running Time: 28800 sec.). 2007. 19.95 (978-1-4332-0443-2(6)) Blckstn Audio.

Case of Abraham Lincoln: A Story of Adultery, Murder & the Making of a Great President. unabr. ed. Julie M. Fenster. Read by Hillary Huber. Frwd. by Douglas Brinkley. (Running Time: 28800 sec.). 2007. 44.95 (978-1-4332-0441-8(X)); audio compact disk 29.95 (978-1-4332-0445-6(2)); audio compact disk 45.00 (978-1-4332-0442-5(8)) Blckstn Audio.

Case of Bugs Meaney. (J). 1982. 20.33 (978-0-394-63185-1(4)) SRA McGraw.

Case of Daniel Brown. Ernest Yaniger. 10.00 (LSS1119) Esstee Audios.

Case of ESP. unabr. ed. Lois Browning Bauer. Read by Stephanie Brush. 6 cass. (Running Time: 6 hrs.). 2001. 39.95 (978-1-58116-044-4(5)) Books in Motion.
Hillary is asked to investigate, when King's best friend loses her future son-in-law to murder. Hillary's talents for both investigation, and her unusual powers of ESP, help her dig deeper into the crime.

Case of Identity see Adventures of Sherlock Holmes

Case of Identity see Sherlock Holmes: Selected Stories

Case of Jennie Brice. Mary Roberts Rinehart. Narrated by Cindy Hardin Killavey. (Running Time: 3 hrs. 30 mins.). 1992. 21.95 (978-1-59912-866-5(7)) Iofy Corp.

Case of Jennie Brice, unabr. ed. Mary Roberts Rinehart. Read by Flo Gibson. 3 cass. (Running Time: 3 hrs. 30 mins.). 1997. 16.95 (978-1-55685-472-9(2), 472-2) Audio Bk Con.
Did Ladley murder his wife or was it all a hoax? A mind-boggling mystery.

Case of Jennie Brice, unabr. ed. Mary Roberts Rinehart. Read by C. M. Herbert. 3 cass. (Running Time: 4 hrs.). 1998. 23.95 (978-0-7861-1274-6(3), 2210) Blckstn Audio.
Mrs. Pittman ran a respectable establishment & she was not about to harbor a killer on the premises. If the police couldn't see what was in front of their noses, then she would just have to take matters into her own hands. As the landlady, after all, she had the perfect excuse to do a little snooping.

Case of Jennie Brice. unabr. ed. Mary Roberts Rinehart. Read by Laurie Klein. 3 cass. (Running Time: 4 hrs.). Dramatization. 1993. 21.95 (978-1-55686-463-6(9), 463) Books in Motion.
It is spring 1907 & early thaw has flooded the first floor of Bess Pittman's boarding house. That's when Bess discovers the stolen clock, the broken knife & the blood stained towel. But worst of all, Mr. Ladley's beautiful wife, Jennie Brice, is missing.

Case of Jennie Brice. unabr. ed. Mary Roberts Rinehart. Read by Cindy Hardin. 3 cass. (Running Time: 4 hrs. 30 mins.). (YA). (gr. 10-12). 1991. 21.00 (C-228) Jimcin Record.
A strange disappearance leads to mysterious goings-on in this fine example from the "Had-I-but-Known" school of mystery fiction.

***Case of Jennie Brice.** unabr. ed. Mary Roberts Rinehart. Read by C. M. Hebert. (Running Time: 3 hrs. 30 mins.). 2010. 19.95 (978-1-4417-2040-5(5)); audio compact disk 30.00 (978-1-4417-2037-5(5)) Blckstn Audio.

Case of Lies. abr. ed. Read by Laural Merlington. (Running Time: 21600 sec.). (Nina Reilly Ser.). 2006. audio compact disk 16.99 (978-1-59737-420-0(2), 9781597374200, BCD Value Price) Brilliance Audio.
For Nina Reilly, the mountain town of Lake Tahoe is home. It's where she forged a successful career as a tough, resourceful attorney - and raised her teenage son, Bob, alone. Back from a stint in Monterey, where her love life took a tumble, Nina has returned to her Tahoe law office with her old friends Sandy Whitefeather and Sandy's son, Wish. It isn't long before she has a new client whose wife was shot and killed during a casino-district robbery two years before. The police have no suspects, and the robbery victims, three students, lied about their identities and are hiding outside California and the reach of the court. Two of the witnesses have fled to a village not far from the home of Bob's father, Kurt Scott, in Germany. As Nina tries to unravel the mystery of one violent Tahoe night, a harrowing journey begins - one that takes her from the dark underworld of Tahoe's casinos to the halls of a prestigious East Coast university to Europe and an emotional reunion with Kurt. As old feelings are rekindled, Nina's case turns violent. Everyone has something to hide - the brilliant but unstable mathematics student who has made an astonishing discovery, the owner of a motel where the shooting took place, and the shooter, who has turned the whole case into a gigantic lie.

Case of Lies. unabr. ed. Read by Laural Merlington. (Running Time: 39600 sec.). (Nina Reilly Ser.). 2005. 87.25 (978-1-59737-416-3(4), 9781597374163, BrilAudUnabridg); 32.95 (978-1-59737-415-6(6), 9781597374156, BAU); DVD & audio compact disk 24.95 (978-1-59737-421-7(0), 9781597374217, Brilliance MP3); audio compact disk 39.25 (978-1-59737-422-4(9), 9781597374224, Brinc Audio MP3 Lib); audio compact disk 38.95 (978-1-59737-417-0(2), 9781597374170, Bril Audio CD Unabri) Brilliance Audio.

Case of Lies. unabr. ed. Perri O'Shaughnessy. Read by Laural Merlington. (Running Time: 11 hrs.). (Nina Reilly Ser.). 2005. 39.25 (978-1-59737-424-8(5), 9781597374248, BADLE); 24.95 (978-1-59737-423-1(7), 9781597374231, BAD) Brilliance Audio.

Case of Lies. unabr. ed. Perri O'Shaughnessy. Read by Laural Merlington. (Running Time: 11 hrs.). (Nina Reilly Ser.). 2005. audio compact disk 97.25 (978-1-59737-418-7(0), 9781597374187, BriAudCD Unabrid) Brilliance Audio.

Case of M. Valdemar see Edgar Allan Poe, Set, Short Stories and Poems

Case of Miss Elliott see Classic Detective Stories, Vol. III, A Collection

Case of Mr. Geldard's Elopement see Classic Detective Stories, Vol. III, A Collection

Case of Ockham's Razor: A Father Shrader Mystery. unabr. ed. Charles M. Kovich & Curtis L. Hancock. Read by Charles M. Kovich. 4 cass. (Running Time: 4 hrs. 34 mins.). (Father Shrader Mystery Ser.: Vol. 1). (YA). (gr. 7 up). 2000. 21.88 (978-0-9703877-0-7(9)) Liber Media & Pubng.

Case of R. S. Steamboat. (J). 1982. 17.33 (978-0-07-508740-3(5)) SRA McGraw.

Case of Sup Suc Hold. (J). 1982. 14.96 (978-0-394-07897-7(7)) SRA McGraw.

Case of the Bad Seed. Created by Saddleback Educational Publishing. 1 cass. (Running Time: 3965 sec.). (Saddleback Pageturners Detective Ser.). (J). 2002. audio compact disk 10.95 (978-1-56254-495-9(0), SP 4950) Saddleback Edu.
Word-for-word audio of The Case of the Bad Seed.

Case of the Baffled Bear. Cynthia Rylant. Read by William Dufris. 1 CD. (Running Time: 15 mins.). (High-Rise Private Eyes Ser.: Bk. 7). (J). (gr. k). 2007. pap. bk. 18.95 (978-1-4301-0060-7(5)) Live Oak Media.

Case of the Baffled Bear. Cynthia Rylant. Read by William Dufris. 1 cass. (Running Time: 15 mins.). (High-Rise Private Eyes Ser.: Bk. 7). (J). (gr. k-2). 2007. pap. bk. 16.95 (978-1-4301-0058-4(3)) Live Oak Media.

Case of the Baffled Bear, Set. Cynthia Rylant. Read by William Dufris. 1 CD. (Running Time: 15 mins.). (High-Rise Private Eyes Ser.: Bk. 7). (J). (gr. k-2). 2007. pap. bk. 31.95 (978-1-4301-0061-4(3)); pap. bk. 37.95 (978-1-4301-0059-1(1)) Live Oak Media.

Case of the Black-Hooded Hangmans. unabr. ed. John R. Erickson. 2 cass. (Running Time: 2 hrs.). (Hank the Cowdog Ser.: No. 24). 2001. 24.00 (978-0-7366-6157-7(3)) Books on Tape.
Hank, Drover and Little Alfred end up in the lair of the dreaded Black-Hooded Hangman when they go searching for Eddy the Raccoon.

Case of the Black-Hooded Hangmans. unabr. ed. John R. Erickson. Read by John R. Erickson. 2 cass. (Running Time: 3 hrs.). (Hank the Cowdog Ser.: No. 24). (J). (gr. 2-5). 2001. 16.95 (978-0-7366-6913-9(2)) Books on Tape.
Hank, Drover & Little Alfred end up in the lair of the dreaded Black Hooded Hangman when they go searching for Eddy the Raccoon.

Case of the Black-Hooded Hangmans. unabr. ed. John R. Erickson. 2 CDs. (Running Time: 2 hrs.). (Hank the Cowdog Ser.: No. 24). (J). 2001. audio compact disk 28.00 (978-0-7366-7546-8(9)) Books on Tape.
Hank, Drover and Little Alfred end up in the lair of the dreaded Black-Hooded Hangman when they go searching for Eddy the Raccoon.

Case of the Black-Hooded Hangmans. unabr. ed. John R. Erickson. Read by John R. Erickson. 2 cass. (Running Time: 3 hrs.). (Hank the Cowdog Ser.: No. 24). (J). 2002. 17.99 (978-1-59188-324-1(5)) Maverick Bks.
Hank assists Eddy the Rac in performing amazing feats of illusion. But the magic tricks backfire when Hank becomes a prime suspect in a felony and Eddy pulls a disappearing act.

Case of the Black-Hooded Hangmans. unabr. ed. John R. Erickson. Read by John R. Erickson. 3 CDs. (Running Time: Approx 3 hours). (Hank the Cowdog Ser.: No. 24). (J). 2002. audio compact disk 19.99 (978-1-59188-624-2(4)) Maverick Bks.
Tired of his reputation as a con artist, Eddy the Rac sets out to prove that he?s really a master magician. But the trick?s on Hank when Eddy pulls a disappearing act?and leaves the Head of Ranch Security perched in the henhouse with egg on his face.A search for the fugitive coon leads Hank, along with Drover and Little Alfred, to a spooky abandoned house where the dreaded Black-Hooded Hangmans lurk. Can Hank find a way to protect his comrades from these creepy creatures?and save his own tail in the process?Hear Hank sing ?What Good is a Flea or a Fly? and ?When She?s Angry.? Also hear Hank, Drover, Eddy, and Little Alfred render a rousing ?Famous Heroes? Battle Marching Song.?.

Case of the Black-Hooded Hangmans, unabr. ed. John R. Erickson. Read by John R. Erickson. 2 cass. (Running Time: 2 hrs.). (Hank the Cowdog Ser.: No. 24). (J). (gr. 2-5). 1998. 17.00 (21663) Recorded Bks.

Case of the Blazing Sky. John R. Erickson. Read by John R. Erickson. (Running Time: 10800 sec.). (Hank the Cowdog Ser.). (J). 2008. audio compact disk 19.99 (978-1-59188-651-8(1)) Maverick Bks.

Case of the Burrowing Robot. John R. Erickson. Read by John R. Erickson. 2 cassettes. (Running Time: Approx. 3 Hours). (Hank the Cowdog Ser.: No. 42). (J). 2003. 17.99 (978-1-59188-342-5(3)); audio compact disk 19.99 (978-1-59188-642-6(2)) Maverick Bks.

Case of the Candid Camera: The Consequences of Deception. 1 cass. (Running Time: 50 mins.). Dramatization. (Adventures in Odyssey Ser.). (J). (gr. 3-7). 5.99 (CC110) Focus Family.
Private Investigator Harlow Doyle gets pulled into a case involving a missing camera, a Bible contest & the always-suspect Rodney Rathbone.

Case of the Car-Barkaholic Dog. unabr. ed. John R. Erickson. Read by John R. Erickson. 2 cass. (Running Time: 3 hrs.). (Hank the Cowdog Ser.: No. 17). (J). (gr. 2-5). 2001. 16.95 (978-0-7366-6906-1(X)) Books on Tape.
Hank's sister & her children are the target of malicious threats from a Great Dane named Rambo.

Case of the Car-Barkaholic Dog. unabr. ed. John R. Erickson. 1 CD. (Running Time: 3 hr.). (Hank the Cowdog Ser.: No. 17). 2001. audio compact disk 19.99 Books on Tape.
Hank's sister and her children are the target of malicious threats from a Great Dane named Rambo.

Case of the Car-Barkaholic Dog. unabr. ed. John R. Erickson. Read by John R. Erickson. 2 cass. (Running Time: 3 hrs.). (Hank the Cowdog Ser.: No. 17). (J). 2002. 17.99 (978-1-59188-317-3(2)) Maverick Bks.
What happens when Hank the Cowdog finds himself stuck in town and facing the mean, monster Great Dane, "Rambo"? Rambo's only weakness is that he's a car-barkaholic. He just can't resist chasing and barking at passing cars.

Case of the Car-Barkaholic Dog. unabr. ed. John R. Erickson. Read by John R. Erickson. 3 CDs. (Running Time: Approx. 3 hours). (Hank the Cowdog Ser.: No. 17). (J). 2002. audio compact disk 19.99 (978-1-59188-617-4(1)) Maverick Bks.
After a brilliant use of the Syruptishus Laoderation maneuver, Hank the Cowdog wins himself a free ride into town. But when the ticket turns out to be one-way, the trouble begins for the Head of Ranch Security. It seems that Hank?s beloved sister and her children are the targets of malicious threats from the neighborhood bully, a Great Dane named Rambo. Honor-bound to defend his family, Hank devises an ingenious plan to ensnare the enemy. But will he sacrifice his own hide in the process?You?ll hear two original songs, ?The Chicken Bone Blues? and Hymn to the Home,? in this hilarious adventure for the whole family.

Case of the Car-Barkaholic Dog, unabr. ed. John R. Erickson. Read by John R. Erickson. 2 cass. (Hank the Cowdog Ser.: No. 17). (J). (gr. 2-5). 1998. 17.00 (21659) Recorded Bks.

Case of the Car-Barkaholic Dog. unabr. collector's ed. John R. Erickson. 2 cass. (Running Time: 3 hrs.). (Hank the Cowdog Ser.: No. 17). 2001. 24.00 (978-0-7366-6150-8(6)); audio compact disk 28.00 (978-0-7366-7539-0(6)) Books on Tape.
Hank's sister and her children are the target of malicious threats from a Great Dane named Rambo.

Case of the Car-Barkaholic Dog & the Case of the Hooking Bull. unabr. ed. John R. Erickson. Read by John R. Erickson. 4 cass. (Running Time: 6 hrs.). (Hank the Cowdog Ser.: Nos. 17-18). (J). 2002. 26.99

(978-0-916941-69-7(8)); audio compact disk 31.99 (978-0-916941-89-5(2)) Maverick Bks.
After a brilliant use of the Syruptishus Laoderation maneuver, Hank the Cowdog wins himself a free ride into town. But when the ticket turns out to be one-way, the trouble begins for the Head of Ranch Security. It seems that Hanks beloved sister and her children are the targets of malicious threats from the neighborhood bully, a Great Dane named Rambo.

Case of the Carnival Cash Level 1. 1 cass. (Running Time: 90 min.). (J). 2002. (978-0-7398-5091-6(1)); audio compact disk (978-0-7398-5328-3(7)) SteckVau.

***Case of the Case of Mistaken Identity.** unabr. ed. Mac Barnett. Narrated by Arte Johnson. 3 CDs. (Running Time: 2 hrs. 55 mins.). (Brixton Brothers Ser.: Bk. 1). (J). (gr. 3-5). 2010. audio compact disk 30.00 (978-0-307-71042-0(4), Listening Lib) Pub: Random Audio Pubg. Dist(s): Random

Case of the Case of Mistaken Identity. unabr. ed. Mac Barnett. Read by Arte Johnson. (Brixton Brothers Ser.: Bk. 1). (ENG.). (J). (gr. 3). 2010. audio compact disk 25.00 (978-0-307-71040-6(8), Listening Lib) Pub: Random Audio Pubg. Dist(s): Random

Case of the Chinese Boxes. unabr. ed. Marele Day. Read by Diana Greentree. 5 cass. (Running Time: 5 hrs.). 1998. (978-1-86340-792-2(8), 580132) Bolinda Pubng AUS.
The New Year starts with a bang in Sydney's Chinatown - the biggest bank job in Australia's history is taking place. In those missing safety deposit boxes is something much more valuable than money. A gold key with a dragon on it. Why does the Chen family want it back so badly?.

Case of the Climbing Cat. Cynthia Rylant. Illus. by G. Brian Karas. 11 vols. (Running Time: 17 mins.). (High-Rise Private Eyes Ser.: No. 2). (J). (gr. k-3). 2003. bk. 28.95 (978-1-59112-611-9(8)); pap. bk. 18.95 (978-1-59112-610-2(X)); 9.95 (978-1-59112-188-6(4)) Live Oak Media.

Case of the Climbing Cat. Cynthia Rylant. Illus. by G. Brian Karas. 11 vols. (Running Time: 17 mins.). (High-Rise Private Eyes Ser.: No. 2). (J). (ps-3). 2003. bk. 25.96 (978-1-59112-190-9(6)); pap. bk. 29.95 (978-1-59112-191-6(4)) Live Oak Media.

Case of the Climbing Cat. Cynthia Rylant. Read by William Dufris. Illus. by G. Brian Karas. 11 vols. (Running Time: 17 mins.). (High-Rise Private Eyes Ser.: No. 2). (J). (gr. k-3). 2003. pap. bk. 16.95 (978-1-59112-189-3(2)) Pub: Live Oak Media. Dist(s): AudioGO

Case of the Climbing Cat. Cynthia Rylant. Illus. by G. Brian Karas. (Running Time: 17 mins.). (High-Rise Private Eyes Ser.: No. 2). (J). (gr. k-3). 2003. 12.95 (978-1-59112-609-6(6)) Live Oak Media.

Case of the Cursed Chalet. Created by Saddleback Educational Publishing. 1 cass. (Running Time: 4057 sec.). (Saddleback Pageturners Detective Ser.). (J). 2002. audio compact disk 10.95 (978-1-56254-496-6(9), SP 4969) Saddleback Edu.
Word-for-word audio of The Case of the Cursed Chalet.

Case of the Dead Duck. Created by Saddleback Educational Publishing. 1 cass. (Running Time: 3999 sec.). (PageTurner Detective Ser.). (J). 2002. audio compact disk 10.95 (978-1-56254-497-3(7), SP 4977) Saddleback Edu.
Word-for-word read-along of The Case of the Dead Duck.

Case of the Deadly Ha-Ha Game. unabr. ed. John R. Erickson. 2 cass. (Running Time: 3 hrs.). (Hank the Cowdog Ser.: No. 37). (J). (gr. 2-5). 2001. 24.00 (978-0-7366-6252-9(9)) Books on Tape.
When Hank finds himself face-to-face with Rip and Snort, the ruthless coyote brothers, he devises a plan to outsmart them by unleashing his secret weapon - the deadly ha-ha game. Everything seems to be going according to plan until Hank and Drover find that even they can't resist the lure of this dangerous game. What happens next is no laughing matter!.

Case of the Deadly Ha-Ha Game. unabr. ed. John R. Erickson. Read by John R. Erickson. 2 cass. (Running Time: 3 hrs.). (Hank the Cowdog Ser.: No. 37). (J). (gr. 2-5). 2001. 16.95 (978-0-7366-6924-5(8)) Books on Tape.
Faced with the evil coyote brothers Rip & Snort, Hank decides to unleash the deadly Ha-Ha Game - but he & Drover find they cannot resist its deadly lure either.

Case of the Deadly Ha-Ha Game. unabr. ed. John R. Erickson. Read by John R. Erickson. 2 cass. (Running Time: 3 hrs.). (Hank the Cowdog Ser.: No. 37). (J). 2002. 17.99 (978-1-59188-337-1(7)) Maverick Bks.

Case of the Deadly Ha-Ha Game. unabr. ed. John R. Erickson. Read by John R. Erickson. 3 CDs. (Running Time: Approx. 3 hours). (Hank the Cowdog Ser.: No. 37). (J). 2002. audio compact disk 19.99 (978-1-59188-637-2(6)) Maverick Bks.
The bottom line was that I was in big trouble. The window slammed shut. The coyotes had gained a few steps on me and I was beginning to feel the strain and exhaustion of the chase. Didn?t coyotes get tired? Maybe not, but I was starting to wear down. Things were looking pretty grim, fellars. I was gasping for breath and I could hear the brothers behind me, laughing and chuckling and muttering threats about all the things they would do when they caught me. I had one last trick in my bag of tricks. Over my shoulder, I yelled, ?Hey Snort?HA!? Snort yelled back, ?Ha your own self! Rip and Snort not fall for dummy Ha-Ha Game one more time in a row, ho-ho!? Well, that did it. I was out of luck, out of time, and out of breath. My cook was goosed.

Case of the Deadly Ha-Ha Game. unabr. collector's ed. John R. Erickson. 3 CDs. (Running Time: 4 hrs. 30 mins.). (Hank the Cowdog Ser.: No. 37). (J). (gr. 2-5). 2001. audio compact disk 28.00 Books on Tape.
When Hank finds himself face-to-face with Rip and Snort, the ruthless coyote brothers, he devises a plan to outsmart them by unleashing his secret weapon - the deadly ha-ha game. Everything seems to be going according to plan until Hank and Drover find that even they can't resist the lure of this dangerous game. What happens next is no laughing matter!.

Case of the Desperate Duck. Cynthia Rylant. Narrated by William Dufris. 1 CD. (Running Time: 17 mins.). (High-Rise Private Eyes Ser.: Bk. 8). (J). (gr. k-2). 2007. pap. bk. 18.95 (978-1-4301-0066-9(4)); pap. bk. 16.95 (978-1-4301-0064-5(8)) Live Oak Media.
When it's time to serve high tea, missing sugar cubes create a disaster for the white duck with pink earrings who owns Mabel's Tea Room. Fortunately, Jack Jones and Bunny Brown appreciate sugar and are on the case immediately! Fast-paced and fun, this eighth mystery is sure to satisfy!.

Case of the Desperate Duck, Set. Cynthia Rylant. Narrated by William Dufris. 1 cass. (Running Time: 17 mins.). (High-Rise Private Eyes Ser.: Bk. 8). (J). (gr. k-2). 2007. pap. bk. 29.95 (978-1-4301-0065-2(6)); pap. bk. 31.95 (978-1-4301-0067-6(2)) Live Oak Media.

Case of the Dirty Bird; Dunc's Doll. unabr. ed. Gary Paulsen. Read by Bill Fantini. 2 cass. (Culpepper Adventures Ser.: Nos. 1-2). (gr. 3-5). lib. bdg. 16.95 set. (978-1-55656-183-2(0), DAB 075) Pub: Dercum Audio. Dist(s): APG

Case of the Dirty Bird; Dunc's Doll. unabr. ed. Gary Paulsen. Read by Bill Fantini. 2 cass. (Running Time: 3 hrs.). (Culpepper Adventures Ser.: Nos. 1-2). (gr. 3-5). 1993. pap. bk. 9.95 (978-1-55656-182-5(2)) Pub: Dercum Audio. Dist(s): APG
Includes The Case of the Dirty Bird & Dunc's Doll. Dunc Culpepper & his best friend Amos Binder look for buried treasure & track a stolen doll.

Case of the Dixon Torpedo see Martin Hewitt, Investigator

Case of the Dixon Torpedo. unabr. ed. Arthur Morrison. Read by Walter Covell. 1 cass. (Running Time: 52 mins.). Dramatization. 1981. 7.95 (N-78) Jimcin Record.
Martin Hewitt in a case of espionage.

Case of the Double Bumblebee Sting. unabr. ed. John R. Erickson. Read by John R. Erickson. 2 cass. (Running Time: 3 hrs.). (Hank the Cowdog Ser.: No. 22). (J). (gr. 2-5). 2001. 16.95 (978-0-7366-6911-5(6)) Books on Tape.
While Slim & Lopez are away from the ranch for three days, Hank suffers from - is it a double bumblebee sting, or much worse?.

Case of the Double Bumblebee Sting. unabr. ed. John R. Erickson. 3 CD. (Running Time: 3 hrs.). (Hank the Cowdog Ser.: No. 22). (J). 2001. audio compact disk 28.00 (978-0-7366-7544-4(2)) Books on Tape.
While Slim and Loper are away from the ranch, Hank suffers from - is it a double bumblebee sting, or much worse?.

Case of the Double Bumblebee Sting. unabr. ed. John R. Erickson. Read by John R. Erickson. 2 cass. (Running Time: 3 hrs.). (Hank the Cowdog Ser.: Vol. 22). (J). 2002. 17.99 (978-1-59188-322-7(9)) Maverick Bks.

Case of the Double Bumblebee Sting. unabr. ed. John R. Erickson. Read by John R. Erickson. 3 CDs. (Running Time: Approx. 3 hours). (Hank the Cowdog Ser.: Vol. 22). (J). 2002. audio compact disk 19.99 (978-1-59188-622-8(8)) Maverick Bks.
When Hank the Cowdog sticks his nose where it doesn?t belong?into an old pipe behind the machine shed?he gets more than he bargained for. Before he can say ?boy howdy,? Hank gets a nip that sets his eyes a-watering and his snout a-throbbing. Hank is sure that he?s the unlikely recipient of a dreaded double bumblebee sting. But when his snout swells up and he starts feeling woozy, it seems as though it might be something much worse. No matter what, Hank?s gonna need some help to survive?or his days as Head of Ranch Security will be over forever.New songs in the hilarious adventure for the whole family include ?I Was Bitten on the Nose by a Rattlesnake? and ?Eating Bugs is Lots of Fun.?.

Case of the Double Bumblebee Sting. unabr. ed. John R. Erickson. Read by John R. Erickson. 2 cass. (Running Time: 2 hrs.). (Hank the Cowdog Ser.: No. 22). (J). (gr. 2-5). 1998. 17.00 (21661) Recorded Bks.

Case of the Falling Sky. John R. Erickson. Read by John R. Erickson. 3 CDs. (Running Time: Approx 3 hours). (Hank the Cowdog Ser.: No. 45). (J). 2005. audio compact disk 19.99 (978-1-59188-645-7(7)) Maverick Bks.
When Hank hears a rumor that the sky is going to fall from the ranch's resident rooster, he is naturally a bit skeptical. But then a report from Pete the Barncat and a strange dream seem to support the theory, and Hank realizes that he'd better take the threat seriously. After all, as Head of Ranch Security, it's his job to protect the ranch from any and all potential danger. So Hank decides that he'll do whatever it takes to prevent the sky from falling on his beloved ranch. Even if it means getting into trouble with Sally May (again).

Case of the Falling Sky. John R. Erickson. Read by John R. Erickson. 2 cass. (Running Time: 3 hrs.). (Hank the Cowdog Ser.: No. 45). (J). 2005. 17.99 (978-1-59188-345-6(8)) Maverick Bks.

Case of the Fiddle-Playing Fox. John R. Erickson. 2 cass. (Running Time: 3 hrs.). (Hank the Cowdog Ser.: No. 12). (J). (gr. 2-5). 2001. (978-0-7366-6141-6(7)) Books on Tape.

Case of the Fiddle-Playing Fox. John R. Erickson. 2 cass. (Running Time: 2 hrs.). (Hank the Cowdog Ser.: No. 12). (J). (gr. 2-5). 1989. 16.95 (978-0-87719-171-1(9)) Lone Star Bks.

Case of the Fiddle-Playing Fox. unabr. ed. John R. Erickson. 2 cass. (Running Time: 3 hrs.). (Hank the Cowdog Ser.: No. 12). (J). (gr. 2-5). 2001. 24.00 (978-0-7366-6145-4(X)) Books on Tape.
Someone, or something, has been robbing eggs from the chicken house. Hank stakes it out and, to his surprise, sees a fiddle-playing fox hop in with the hens, play them some hot fiddle music and then accept several fresh eggs as his payment. Instead of arresting Frankie the Fox, Hank joins forces with him to try and win the heart of Beulah the Collie.

Case of the Fiddle-Playing Fox. unabr. ed. John R. Erickson. Read by John R. Erickson. 2 cass. (Running Time: 3 hrs.). (Hank the Cowdog Ser.: No. 12). (J). (gr. 2-5). 2001. 16.95 (978-0-7366-6901-6(9)) Books on Tape.
Noticing that Frankie the Fox's fiddle music charms the ladies, Hank asks Frankie to help him win the heart of Beulah the Collie.

Case of the Fiddle-Playing Fox. unabr. ed. John R. Erickson. Read by John R. Erickson. 2 cass. (Running Time: 3 hrs.). (Hank the Cowdog Ser.: No. 12). (J). 2002. 17.99 (978-1-59188-312-8(1)) Maverick Bks.

Case of the Fiddle-Playing Fox. unabr. ed. John R. Erickson. Read by John R. Erickson. 3 CDs. (Running Time: Approx. 3 hours). (Hank the Cowdog Ser.: No. 12). (J). 2002. audio compact disk 19.99 (978-1-59188-612-9(0)) Maverick Bks.
Who ever heard of a fiddle-playing fox? Not Hank the Cowdog, that?s for sure. But when several reports of unexplained fiddle music come in, Hank knows that it?s his job to check things out. And to his surprise, he finds that the ranch has indeed been invaded by a fox with a fiddle! Can Hank resist the lure of the music long enough to run that rascal off his territory? Or are his days as Head of Ranch Security numbered? Find out in this hilarious adventure!Included are two new songs and some great fiddle playing by Frankie McWhorter.

Case of the Fiddle-Playing Fox, unabr. ed. John R. Erickson. 2 cass. (Hank the Cowdog Ser.: No. 12). (J). (gr. 2-5). 1998. 17.00 (21654) Recorded Bks.

Case of the Fiddle-Playing Fox. unabr. collector's ed. John R. Erickson. 3 CDs. (Running Time: 4 hrs. 30 mins.). (Hank the Cowdog Ser.: No. 12). (J). (gr. 2-5). 2001. audio compact disk 28.00 Books on Tape.

Case of the Fidgety Fox. unabr. ed. Cynthia Rylant. Read by William Dufris. Illus. by G. Brian Karas. 1 cass. (Running Time: 21 mins.). (High-Rise Private Eyes Ser.: No. 6). (J). (gr. k-4). 2005. bk. 25.95 (978-1-59519-405-3(3)) Live Oak Media.
Melvin, the bus-driving skunk, refuses to drive the bus because his lucky fluffy dice were stolen the night before. Can Bunny Brown and Jack Jones help the frustrated passengers reach their destination by finding the culprit? With quick thinking and a little luck - and a lot of silliness, they can, to the glee of young listeners.

Case of the Fidgety Fox, Set. unabr. ed. Cynthia Rylant. Read by William Dufris. Illus. by G. Brian Karas. 1 cass. (Running Time: 21 mins.). (High-Rise Private Eyes Ser.: No. 6). (J). (gr. k-4). 2005. pap. bk. 29.95 (978-1-59519-406-0(1)); pap. bk. 31.95 (978-1-59519-410-7(X)) Live Oak Media.

Case of the Five Orange Pips see Adventures of Sherlock Holmes

Case of the Five Orange Pips see Famous Cases of Sherlock Holmes

Case of the Five Orange Pips see Selections from the Adventures of Sherlock Holmes

Case of the Five Orange Pips. unabr. ed. Arthur Conan Doyle. Read by Walter Covell. (Running Time: 82 min.). Dramatization. 1981. 7.95 (N-19) Jimcin Record.
Two classic Sherlock Holmes adventures. Holmes finds a missing lover & receives a deadly message. Components in package.

Case of the Golden Key. unabr. ed. Kenneth Thomas. Read by Renee Dennis & Mary More. 1 cass. (Running Time: 1 hr. 30 mins.). Dramatization. (Adventures of Minerva Holmes Ser.). 1993. 11.00 IDA Games.
Minerva Holmes, the half Indian, illegitimate daughter follows in her father, Sherlock Holmes' footsteps.

Case of the Halloween Ghost. John R. Erickson. Illus. by Gerald L. Holmes. 2 cass. (Running Time: 2 hrs.). (Hank the Cowdog Ser.: No. 9). (J). (gr. 2-5). 1990. 16.95 (978-0-87719-149-0(2)) Lone Star Bks.

Case of the Halloween Ghost. collector's unabr. ed. John R. Erickson. 3 CDs. (Running Time: 4 hrs. 30 mins.). (Hank the Cowdog Ser.: No. 9). (J). (gr. 2-5). 2001. audio compact disk 28.00 Books on Tape.
When darkness falls, Drover reports that he has seen a ghost, a pirate, and two skeletons on Slim's front porch. These terrifying creatures were saying something about "Tricker Trees." Hank goes to verify the report and the fun really starts.

Case of the Halloween Ghost. unabr. ed. John R. Erickson. Read by John R. Erickson. 2 cass. (Running Time: 3 hrs.). (Hank the Cowdog Ser.: No. 9). (J). (gr. 2-5). 2001. 16.95 (978-0-7366-6898-9(5)) Books on Tape.
On Halloween night, a car drove up to the house with some mighty suspicious looking passengers... & Drover saw the whole thing.

Case of the Halloween Ghost. unabr. ed. John R. Erickson. Read by John R. Erickson. Illus. by Gerald L. Holmes. 2 cass. (Running Time: 3 hrs.). (Hank the Cowdog Ser.: No. 9). (J). (gr. 2-5). 1987. 13.95 (978-0-916941-36-9(1)) Maverick Bks.
Hank & his cowardly companion, Drover, find themselves in a strange place on Halloween.

Case of the Halloween Ghost. unabr. ed. John R. Erickson. Read by John R. Erickson. 2 cass. (Running Time: 3 hrs.). (Hank the Cowdog Ser.: No. 9). (J). 2002. 17.99 (978-1-59188-309-8(1)) Maverick Bks.
When darkness falls, Drover reports that he has seen a witch, a ghost, a pirate, and two skeletons on Slim's front porch. These terrifying creatures were saying something about "Tricker Trees." Hank goes to verify the report and the fun really starts.

Case of the Halloween Ghost. unabr. ed. John R. Erickson. Read by John R. Erickson. 3 CDs. (Running Time: Approx. 3 hours). (Hank the Cowdog Ser.: No. 9). (J). 2002. audio compact disk 19.99 (978-1-59188-609-9(0)) Maverick Bks.
When Halloween arrives, Hank?the self-appointed Head of Ranch Security?has got his hands full of adventure. First there?s a problem with the Tricker Trees. Then the ranch is invaded by two skeletons, a witch, and a pirate. And when Hank goes to investigate a strange sound in the cake house, he?s sure it can only be one thing?a ghost. Can Hank rid the ranch of this unwanted visitor? Or is he destined to be spooked for good?Wallace the Buzzard makes his singing debut doing a number called ?Buzzard Love? and a chorus of ghosts sing an old Shaker hymn called ?Followers of the Lamb.?.

Case of the Halloween Ghost, unabr. ed. John R. Erickson. 2 cass. (Running Time: 2 hrs.). (Hank the Cowdog Ser.: No. 9). (J). (gr. 2-5). 1998. 17.00 (21651) Recorded Bks.

Case of the Halloween Ghost. unabr. collector's ed. John R. Erickson. 2 cass. (Running Time: 3 hrs.). (Hank the Cowdog Ser.: No. 9). (J). (gr. 2-5). 2001. 24.00 (978-0-7366-6144-7(1)) Books on Tape.
When darkness falls, Drover reports that he has seen a ghost, a pirate and two skeletons on Slim's front porch. These terrifying creatures were saying something about "Tricker Trees." Hank goes to verify the report and the fun really starts.

Case of the Halloween Ghost & Every Dog Has His Day. unabr. ed. John R. Erickson. Read by John R. Erickson. 4 cass. (Running Time: 6 hrs.). (Hank the Cowdog Ser.: Nos. 9-10). (J). 2002. 26.99 (978-0-916941-65-9(5)); audio compact disk 31.99 (978-0-916941-85-7(X)) Maverick Bks.
When Halloween arrives, Hank the self-appointed head of ranch security has got his hands full of adventure. First there's a problem with the Tricker Trees. Then the ranch is invaded by two skeletons, a witch, and a pirate. And when Hank goes to investigate a strange sound in the cake house, he's sure it can only be one thing, a ghost.

Case of the Haystack Kitties. John R. Erickson. Read by John R. Erickson. 3 CDs. (Running Time: 3 hrs. 36 mins.). (Hank the Cowdog Ser.: No. 30). (J). (gr. 4-7). 2001. audio compact disk 14.95 Books on Tape.
When a raging bull starts threatening a group of helpless kittens, Hank feels obligated to keep them safe, despite his hatred of cats.

Case of the Haystack Kitties. John R. Erickson. Read by John R. Erickson. 2 cass. (Running Time: 2 hrs.). (Hank the Cowdog Ser.: No. 30). (J). (gr. 4-7). 2001. 12.95 (978-0-7366-6919-1(1)) Books on Tape.

Case of the Haystack Kitties. John R. Erickson. Illus. by Gerald L. Holmes. 1 cass. 1998. bk. (978-0-87719-329-6(0)) Maverick Books.

Case of the Haystack Kitties. unabr. ed. John R. Erickson. Read by John R. Erickson. 2 cass. (Running Time: 1 hr.). (Hank the Cowdog Ser.: No. 30). (J). (gr. 4-7). 2001. 24.00 (978-0-7366-6163-8(8)) Books on Tape.
Hank has his paws full when he discovers a mother cat and six kittens trespassing in a haystack on his very own ranch. (Have we mentioned that cowdogs don't like cats?) Join Hank as he is trapped in a runaway pickup, surrounded by a herd of stray cats, and forced to battle a raging bull.

Case of the Haystack Kitties. unabr. ed. John R. Erickson. Read by John R. Erickson. 3 CDs. (Running Time: 1 hr. 12 mins.). (Hank the Cowdog Ser.: No. 30). (J). 2001. audio compact disk 28.00 (978-0-7366-7552-9(3)) Books on Tape.

Case of the Haystack Kitties. unabr. ed. John R. Erickson. Read by John R. Erickson. 2 cass. (Running Time: 3 hrs.). (Hank the Cowdog Ser.: No. 30). (J). 2002. 17.99 (978-1-59188-330-2(X)) Maverick Bks.

Case of the Haystack Kitties. unabr. ed. John R. Erickson. Read by John R. Erickson. 3 CDs. (Running Time: Approx. 3 hours). (Hank the Cowdog Ser.: No. 30). (J). 2002. audio compact disk 19.99 (978-1-59188-630-3(9)) Maverick Bks.
Hank the Cowdog doesn?t like cats. Not one bit. So when a mother cat and her kittens take up residence in the haystack, he does all he can get them to leave. But they?ve got nowhere to go. Unfortunately, neither does the gigantic bull who has knocked down the fence?and is headed right for the haystack! Hank knows that it?s up to him to run that bull off and keep the ranch safe for everyone?even if that includes a bunch of cats.Hear two new songs, ?Slim?s Boring Song? and ?Kitties Will Grow into Cats,? in this hilarious adventure for the whole family.

Case of the Hooking Bull. unabr. ed. John R. Erickson. Read by John R. Erickson. 2 cass. (Running Time: 3 hrs.). (Hank the Cowdog Ser.: No. 18). (J). (gr. 2-5). 2001. 16.95 (978-0-7366-6907-8(8)) Books on Tape.
Hank & Slim must stop a vicious bull from terrorizing the north pasture.

Case of the Hooking Bull. unabr. ed. John R. Erickson. Read by John R. Erickson. 2 cass. (Running Time: 3 hrs.). (Hank the Cowdog Ser.: No. 18). (J). 2002. 17.99 (978-1-59188-318-0(0)) Maverick Bks.

Case of the Hooking Bull. unabr. ed. John R. Erickson. Read by John R. Erickson. 2 CDs. (Running Time: Approx. 3 hours). (Hank the Cowdog Ser.: No. 18). (J). 2002. audio compact disk 19.99 (978-1-59188-618-1(X)) Maverick Bks.
When Sally May and Loper head out of town for a wedding, Hank the Cowdog, Head of Ranch Security, knows it?s up to him to keep things under control. After subjecting strawberry ice cream to rigorous product testing, test-driving a mysterious spaceship, and thwarting a sneak attack from a couch monster, Hank faces the fight of his life. A vicious hooking bull is terrorizing the north pasture, and he doesn?t take orders from cowboys or cowdogs. In fact, he delights in thrashing them. Can Hank and Slim prevail in the face of overwhelming odds?Hear two original songs, ?Just Another Cowboy Day? and ?Family Fugue,? in this hilarious adventure for the whole family.

Case of the Hooking Bull, unabr. ed. John R. Erickson. Read by John R. Erickson. 2 cass. (Running Time: 2 hrs.). (Hank the Cowdog Ser.: No. 18). (J). (gr. 2-5). 1998. 17.00 (21660) Recorded Bks.

Case of the Hooking Bull. unabr. collector's ed. John R. Erickson. 1 CD. (Running Time: 3 hrs.). (Hank the Cowdog Ser.: Bk. 18). (J). 2001. audio compact disk 19.99 Books on Tape.
Hank and Slim must stop a vicious bull from terrorizing the north pasture.

Case of the Hooking Bull. unabr. collector's ed. John R. Erickson. 2 cass. (Running Time: 3 hrs.). (Hank the Cowdog Ser.: No. 18). (J). 2001. 24.00 (978-0-7366-6151-5(4)); 24.00 (978-0-7366-7540-6(X)) Books on Tape.
Hank and Slim must stop a vicious bull from terrorizing the north pasture.

Case of the Hungry Stranger. Crosby N. Bonsall. 1 read-along cass. (Running Time: 15 mins.). (I Can Read Bks.). (J). (gr. 1-3). HarperCollins Pubs.
One side has a turn-the-page beep signal & the other side is uninterrupted narration for more experienced readers.

Case of the Hungry Stranger Book & Tape. abr. ed. Crosby N. Bonsall. Illus. by Crosby N. Bonsall. 1 cass. (I Can Read Bks.). (J). (gr. k-3). 1990. 8.99 (978-1-55994-223-2(1), TBC 2231) HarperCollins Pubs.

Case of the Indian Flashlights. unabr. ed. Steven Thomas Oney. Photos by David Ellsworth & Stephen Russell. 1 CD. (Running Time: 1 hr. 15 min.). (Cape Cod Mystery Radio Theater Ser.: 26). (YA). 2001. audio compact disk 12.50 (978-0-9745668-2-5(9)) Cape Cod Radio.
Captain Waverly Underhill and Doctor Scofield on the trail again, tracking down an eccentric millionaire's strong box.

Case of the Kidnapped Collie. John R. Erickson. 1 cass. (Running Time: 1 hr. 30 mins.). (Hank the Cowdog Ser.: No. 26). (J). 2001. 24.00 (978-0-7366-6159-1(X)) Books on Tape.
When Beulah, the Border Collie falls into the clutches of a ruthless cannibal, there's only one dog tough enough to save her - Hank.

Case of the Kidnapped Collie. John R. Erickson. 2 cass. (Running Time: 2 hrs.). (Hank the Cowdog Ser.: No. 26). (J). (gr. 2-5). 1995. 16.95 (978-0-87719-297-8(9), 9297) Lone Star Bks.

Case of the Kidnapped Collie. unabr. ed. John R. Erickson. 1 cass. (Running Time: 1 hr. 30 mins.). (Hank the Cowdog Ser.: No. 22). (J). 2001. 24.00 Books on Tape.

Case of the Kidnapped Collie. unabr. ed. John R. Erickson. Read by John R. Erickson. 2 cass. (Running Time: 3 hrs.). (Hank the Cowdog Ser.: No. 26). (J). (gr. 2-5). 2001. 16.95 (978-0-7366-6915-3(9)) Books on Tape.
When Beulah, the Border Collie, falls into the clutches of a ruthless cannibal, there's only one dog tough enough to save her - Hank.

Case of the Kidnapped Collie. unabr. ed. John R. Erickson. 2 CDs. (Running Time: 2 hrs.). (Hank the Cowdog Ser.: No. 26). (J). 2001. audio compact disk 28.00 (978-0-7366-7548-2(5)) Books on Tape.
When Beulah, the Border Collie falls into the clutches of a ruthless cannibal, there's only one dog tough enough to save her - Hank.

Case of the Kidnapped Collie. unabr. ed. John R. Erickson. Read by John R. Erickson. 2 cass. (Running Time: 3 hrs.). (Hank the Cowdog Ser.: No. 26). (J). 2002. 17.99 (978-1-59188-326-5(1)) Maverick Bks.

Case of the Kidnapped Collie. unabr. ed. John R. Erickson. Read by John R. Erickson. 3 CDs. (Running Time: Approx. 3 hours). (Hank the Cowdog Ser.: No. 26). (J). 2002. audio compact disk 19.99 (978-1-59188-626-6(0)) Maverick Bks.
It?s a dark day for Hank the Cowdog. First, Loper invites Hank?s archenemy Plato the Bird Dog over for some quail hunting on the ranch. Then Beulah, the collie of Hank?s dreams, snubs him in favor of watching Plato in action. But when Beulah finds herself caught in the clutches of a ruthless cannibal, Hank knows there?s only one dog tough enough to save her?and it isn?t a bird dog.Hank sings ?Punt of Love? and ?My Best for You? in this hilarious adventure for the whole family.

Case of the Kidnapped Collie, unabr. ed. John R. Erickson. Read by John R. Erickson. 2 cass. (Running Time: 2 hrs.). (Hank the Cowdog Ser.: No. 26). (J). (gr. 2-5). 1998. 17.00 (21665) Recorded Bks.

Case of the Late Pig. unabr. ed. Margery Allingham. Read by Francis Matthews. 4 cass. (Running Time: 4 hrs.). (Albert Campion Ser.). 2001. 24.95 (978-1-57270-157-1(9), N41157u, Audio Edits Mystry) Pub: Audio Partners. Dist(s): PerseuPGW
When Campion is summoned to attend a funeral for an old school bully, Roland "Pig" Peters, he attends the event with an extraordinary collection of other apparent mourners. Several months later an old friend asks him to investigate a murder committed at a local country club. The corpse turns out to be none other than Pig Peters, the now several months dead & buried Pig Peters... or so Campion had thought. The death toll grows, with Campion himself a target for termination as he works to sift truth from fiction.

Case of the Late Pig. unabr. ed. Margery Allingham. Read by Francis Matthews. 4 cass. (Running Time: 6 hrs.). (Albert Campion Ser.: Bk. 21). 2000. 34.95 (978-0-7540-0179-9(2), CAB 1602) Pub: Chivers Audio Bks GBR. Dist(s): AudioGO
Albert Campion recently attended the funeral of Pig Peters, whom he remembered only as a childhood bully. It was an unpleasant affair, with one or two dubious mourners. Campion had already forgotten it when he is called in to investigate a distasteful death. The body turns out to be that of Peters, freshly killed five months after his own funeral.

Case of the Left-Handed Lady. unabr. ed. Nancy Springer. Read by Katherine Kellgren. 5 cass. (Running Time: 5 hrs.). (Enola Holmes Mystery Ser.). (YA). (gr. 5-9). 2007. 41.75 (978-1-4281-4744-7(6)); audio compact disk 51.75 (978-1-4281-4749-2(7)) Recorded Bks.

Case of the Measled Cowboy. unabr. ed. John R. Erickson. Read by John R. Erickson. 2 cass. (Running Time: 1 hr.). (Hank the Cowdog Ser.: No. 33). (J). (gr. 4-7). 2001. 24.00 (978-0-7366-6248-2(0)) Books on Tape.
Sally May and Loper head off to visit relatives, leaving Slim in charge of Little Alfred. Hank knows that trouble is sure to come knocking; but not even Hank could have predicted what happens. First, Slim is struck down with the measles. Then a blizzard hits the ranch, trapping them in the house without heat or electricity. Somehow, Hank's got to find a way to get them out of this mess - before they're snowed in for good.

Case of the Measled Cowboy. unabr. ed. John R. Erickson. Read by John R. Erickson. 2 cass. (Running Time: 2 hrs.). (Hank the Cowdog Ser.: No. 33). (J). (gr. 4-7). 2001. 12.95 (978-0-7366-6922-1(1)) Books on Tape.
When Sally May and Loper head off to visit relatives - leaving Slim in charge of Little Alfred - Hank knows trouble is sure to come knocking.

Case of the Measled Cowboy. unabr. ed. John R. Erickson. Read by John R. Erickson. 3 CDs. (Running Time: 1 hr. 12 mins.). (Hank the Cowdog Ser.: No. 33). (J). (gr. 4-7). 2001. audio compact disk 28.00 (978-0-7366-7555-0(8)) Books on Tape.
Sally May and Loper head off to visit relatives, leaving Slim in charge of Little Alfred. Hank knows that trouble is sure to come knocking; but not even Hank could have predicted what happens. First, Slim is struck down with the measles. Then a blizzard hits the ranch, trapping them in the house without heat or electricity. Somehow, Hank's got to find a way to get them out of this mess - before they're snowed in for good.

Case of the Measled Cowboy. unabr. ed. John R. Erickson. Read by John R. Erickson. 2 cass. (Running Time: 3 hrs.). (Hank the Cowdog Ser.: No. 33). (J). 2002. 17.99 (978-1-59188-333-3(4)) Maverick Bks.
Hank knows that trouble is sure to come knocking. But not even the Head of Ranch Security could have predicted what would happen.First, Slim is struck down with the measles. Then a blizzard hits the ranch, trapping them in the house with no heat or electricity.

Case of the Measled Cowboy. unabr. ed. John R. Erickson. Read by John R. Erickson. 3 CDs. (Running Time: Approx. 3 hours). (Hank the Cowdog Ser.: No. 33). (J). 2002. audio compact disk 19.99 (978-1-59188-633-4(3)) Maverick Bks.
When Sally May and Loper head of to visit the relatives, leaving Slim in charge of Little Alfred, Hank knows that trouble is sure to come knocking. But not even the Head of Ranch Security could have predicted what would happen. First, Slim is stuck down with the measles. Then a blizzard hits the ranch, trapping them in the house with no heat or electricity. Somehow, Hank?s got to find a way to get them out of this mess?before they?re snowed in for good!Hank, Drover, and Alfred join to sing ?We?ll Never Pull This Stunt Again? in this hilarious adventure for the whole family.

Case of the Midnight Rustler. John R. Erickson. Illus. by Gerald L. Holmes. 2 cass. (Running Time: 2 hrs.). (Hank the Cowdog Ser.: No. 19). (J). (gr. 2-5). 1992. bk. 16.95 (978-0-87719-220-6(0), 9220) Lone Star Bks.

Case of the Midnight Rustler. unabr. ed. John R. Erickson. Read by John R. Erickson. 2 cass. (Running Time: 3 hrs.). (Hank the Cowdog Ser.: No. 19). (J). (gr. 2-5). 2001. 16.95 Books on Tape.
Hank & Slim get distracted while trying to nab a calf-snitching rustler.

Case of the Midnight Rustler. unabr. ed. John R. Erickson. 1 CD. (Running Time: 2 hr.). (Hank the Cowdog Ser.: Bk. 19). (J). 2001. audio compact disk 19.99 Books on Tape.
Hank and Slim get distracted while trying to nab a calf-snitching rustler.

Case of the Midnight Rustler. unabr. ed. John R. Erickson. Read by John R. Erickson. 2 cass. (Running Time: 3 hrs.). (Hank the Cowdog Ser.: No. 19). (J). 2002. 17.99 (978-1-59188-319-7(9)) Maverick Bks.

Case of the Midnight Rustler. unabr. ed. John R. Erickson. Read by John R. Erickson. 3 CDs. (Running Time: Approx. 3 hours). (Hank the Cowdog Ser.: No. 19). (J). 2002. audio compact disk 19.99 (978-1-59188-619-8(8)) Maverick Bks.
Someone has been stealing calves from Uncle Johnny?s pasture, and it?s up to Hank and Slim to put a stop to it. In the hopes of catching the ?criminals? in the act, they set up camp in the field just north of the canyon. But the stakeout isn?t all fun and games. Before the rustlers even make an appearance, Hank must overcome the poisoned weenies, weather a run-in with a larger-than-life guard dog, and survive a tussle with the dreaded coyote brothers. But despite all the distraction, when the time comes to nab the calf-snatchers, everyone?s favorite Head of Ranch Security is there to do the job.Hear two songs, ?See the Morning Sun Ascending? and ?Alas and Alack,? in this hilarious adventure for the whole family.

Case of the Midnight Rustler, unabr. ed. John R. Erickson. Read by John R. Erickson. 2 cass. (Running Time: 2 hrs.). (Hank the Cowdog Ser.: No. 19). (J). (gr. 2-5). 1998. 17.00 (21629) Recorded Bks.

Case of the Midnight Rustler. unabr. collector's ed. John R. Erickson. (Hank the Cowdog Ser.: No. 19). 2001. 24.00 (978-0-7366-6152-2(2)) Books on Tape.
Hank and Slim get distracted while trying to nab a calf-snitching rustler.

Case of the Midnight Rustler. unabr. collector's ed. John R. Erickson. 3 CDs. (Running Time: 3 hrs. 36 min.). (Hank the Cowdog Ser.: No. 19). (J). 2001. audio compact disk 28.00 (978-0-7366-7541-3(8)) Books on Tape.
Hank and Slim get distracted while trying to nab a calf-snitching rustler.

Case of the Midnight Rustler & the Phantom in the Mirror. unabr. ed. John R. Erickson. Read by John R. Erickson. 5 CDs. (Running Time: 6 hrs.). (Hank the Cowdog Ser.: Nos. 19-20). (J). 2002. audio compact disk 31.99 (978-0-916941-90-1(6)); 26.99 (978-0-916941-70-3(1)) Maverick Bks.
Someone has been stealing calves from Uncle Johnny's pasture, and it's up to Hank and Slim to put a stop to it. In the hopes of catching the criminals in the act, they set up camp in the field just north of the canyon. But the stakeout isn't all fun and games. Before the rustlers even make an appearance, Hank must overcome the poisoned weenies, weather a run-in with a larger-than-life guard dog, and survive a tussle with the dreaded coyote brothers.

Case of the Missing Bird Dog. unabr. ed. John R. Erickson. Read by John R. Erickson. 2 cass. (Running Time: 3 hrs.). (Hank the Cowdog Ser.: No. 40). (J). 2002. 17.99 (978-1-59188-340-1(7)); audio compact disk 19.99 (978-1-59188-640-2(6)) Maverick Bks.
In the first day of quail season Plato, the Bird Dog, is missing. At first, Hank is willing to let him stay lost. But when Beulah pleads for help, Hank caves in and takes off in search of Plato. Before he can catch a scent of a spotted bird dog, he finds himself face-to-face with an angry mother hog and her litter. Can Hank?s quick wits help him out of this fix? Our will he become hogmeat? Find out in this latest adventure starring everyone?s favorite Head of Ranch Security.Slim sings ?Hunting for Bird Dogs? and ?Jerky Symphony in Nothing Flat.?.

Case of the Missing Cat. John R. Erickson. 2 cass. (Running Time: 2 hrs.). (Hank the Cowdog Ser.: No. 15). (J). (gr. 2-5). 1991. 16.95 (978-0-87719-187-2(5)) Lone Star Bks.

Case of the Missing Cat. unabr. ed. John R. Erickson. Read by John R. Erickson. 2 cass. (Running Time: 3 hrs.). (Hank the Cowdog Ser.: No. 15). (J). (gr. 2-5). 2001. 16.95 (978-0-7366-6904-7(3)) Books on Tape.
Hank devises a plan to rid the ranch of Pete the Barncat but finds that sticking to it is more difficult than he imagined.

Case of the Missing Cat. unabr. ed. Read by John R. Erickson. Told to John R. Erickson. 2 cass. (Running Time: 3 hrs.). (Hank the Cowdog Ser.: No. 15). (J). 2002. 17.99 (978-1-59188-315-9(6)) Maverick Bks.
Hank makes a foolish bet with his arch-enemy, Pete the Barncat, that he can catch the Lumberpile Bunny. He loses the wager and with it go his job, his pride, and even his gunny sack bed under the gas tanks. Suffering a "nervous breakthrough," Hank begins plotting revenge. He must dispose of the cat.

Case of the Missing Cat. unabr. ed. John R. Erickson. Read by John R. Erickson. 2 CDs. (Running Time: Approx. 3 hours). (Hank the Cowdog Ser.: No. 15). (J). 2002. audio compact disk 19.99 (978-1-59188-615-0(5)) Maverick Bks.
Hank the Cowdog knows. After losing his post as Head of Ranch Security in a crooked bet with Pete the Barncat, Hank is finally pushed to the limit. Long having wanted to rid the ranch of Pete?s snide presence, Hank devises a plan to do just that. But sticking to his evil plot is more difficult than he imagined. Will good conscience prevail? Or will Little Alfred be fixing to find a new feline friend?Two new songs, ?I Must Dispose of the Cat? and ?Prairie Vespers,? are included in this hilarious adventure for the whole family.

Case of the Missing Cat, unabr. ed. John R. Erickson. Read by John R. Erickson. 2 cass. (Running Time: 2 hrs.). (Hank the Cowdog Ser.: No. 15). (J). (gr. 2-5). 1998. 17.00 (21657) Recorded Bks.

Case of the Missing Cat. unabr. collector's ed. John R. Erickson. 1 CD. (Running Time: 3 hrs.). (Hank the Cowdog Ser.: Bk. 15). (J). 2001. audio compact disk 19.99 Books on Tape.
Hank devises a plan to rid the ranch of Pete the Barncat but finds that sticking to it is more difficult than he imagined.

Case of the Missing Cat. unabr. collector's ed. John R. Erickson. 2 cass. (Running Time: 3 hrs.). (Hank the Cowdog Ser.: No. 15). 2001. 24.00 (978-0-7366-6148-5(4)) Books on Tape.

Case of the Missing Cat. unabr. collector's ed. John R. Erickson. 2 cass. (Running Time: 3 hrs.). (Hank the Cowdog Ser.: No. 15). (J). 2001. 24.00 (978-0-7366-7537-6(X)) Books on Tape.
Hank devises a plan to rid the ranch of Pete the Barncat but finds that stickng to it is more difficult than he imagined.

Case of the Missing Cat & Lost in the Blinded Blizzard. unabr. ed. John R. Erickson. Read by John R. Erickson. 4 cass. (Running Time: 6 hrs.). (Hank the Cowdog Ser.: Nos. 15-16). (J). 2002. 26.99 (978-0-916941-68-0(X)); audio compact disk 31.99 (978-0-916941-88-8(4)) Maverick Bks.
Hank the Cowdog knows. After losing his post as head of ranch security in a crooked bet with Pete the Barncat, Hank is finally pushed to the limit. Long having wanted to rid the ranch of Pete's snide presence, Hank devises a plan to do just that.

Case of the Missing Christmas. Lyrics by Nan Allen. Music by Dennis Allen. 1 cass. (Running Time: 1 hr.). (J). (gr. 3-6). 1988. 80.00 (MU-9095C) Lillenas.
When Baby Jesus turns up missing from the church's Nativity-scene, the kids turn detective to solve the mystery. Their investigation turns up the truth about Christmas. Lots of fun & meaning are packed into the musical for kids. Traditional carols & singable new songs are featured.accompaniment tapes are arranged in unison with optional 2-part. Designed for ages 8 to 11 but also suitable for older plus younger kids.

Case of the Missing Christmas. Nan Allen & Dennis Allen. 1 cass. (Running Time: 1 hr.). (J). (gr. 3-6). 1988. 12.99 (978-0-685-68522-8(5), TA-9095C) Lillenas.

Case of the Missing Hand see Martin Hewitt, Investigator

Case of the Missing Hand. unabr. ed. Arthur Morrison. Read by Walter Covell. 1 cass. (Running Time: 54 mins.). Dramatization. 7.95 (S-15) Jimcin Record.
Was it murder or suicide? Martin Hewitt takes this strange case to find out.

Case of the Missing Locket: Abbie Girl Spy Mystery. Darren J. Butler. Read by Olivia Klein. Ed. by Margaret Greer. Narrated by Dana McArthur. 2 cass. (Running Time: 2 hrs. 15 mins.). (Abbie, Girl Spy Ser.). (J). (gr. 3-9). 2000. audio compact disk 16.95 (978-0-9700752-2-2(7)) Onstage Pubng.

Case of the Missing Marquess. unabr. ed. Nancy Springer. Read by Katherine Kellgren. 5 CDs. (Running Time: 5 hrs.). (Enola Holmes Mystery Ser.). (J). (gr. 4-8). 2006. audio compact disk 49.75 (978-1-4193-8985-6(8), C3705); 39.75 (978-1-4193-8980-1(7)) Recorded Bks.
Two-time Edgar Award-winning author Nancy Springer introduces the sleuthing powers of Sherlock Holmes' sister in the captivating mystery Booklist and School Library Journal praise with starred reviews. Prompted by clues her missing mother cleverly left her, 14-year-old Enola races clutches of his captors. But how can Enola escape these slimy ruffians and find her mother?.

Case of the Missing Monkey. Cynthia Rylant. Illus. by G. Brian Karas. 11 vols. (Running Time: 14 mins.). (High-Rise Private Eyes Ser.: No. 1). 2003. bk. 28.95 (978-1-59112-615-7(0)) Live Oak Media.

Case of the Missing Monkey. Cynthia Rylant. Illus. by G. Brian Karas. 11 vols. (Running Time: 14 mins.). (High-Rise Private Eyes Ser.: No. 1). (J). 2003. bk. 25.95 (978-1-59112-194-7(9)); pap. bk. 29.95 (978-1-59112-195-4(7)); pap. bk. 18.95 (978-1-59112-614-0(2)); audio compact disk 12.95 (978-1-59112-613-3(4)) Live Oak Media.

Case of the Missing Monkey. Cynthia Rylant. Read by William Dufris. Illus. by G. Brian Karas. 14 vols. (Running Time: 14 mins.). (High-Rise Private Eyes Ser.: No. 1). (J). (gr. k-3). 2003. pap. bk. 16.95 (978-1-59112-193-0(0)) Pub: Live Oak Media. Dist(s): AudioGO

Case of the Missing Monkey. Cynthia Rylant. Illus. by G. Brian Karas. (Running Time: 14 mins.). (High-Rise Private Eyes Ser.: No. 1). (J). (gr. k-3). 2003. 9.95 (978-1-59112-192-3(2)) Live Oak Media.

Case of the Night-Stalking Bone Monster. John R. Erickson. Contrib. by Gerald L. Holmes. 2 cass. (Hank the Cowdog Ser.: No. 27). (J). (gr. 2-5). 1996. 16.95 (978-0-87719-305-0(3), 9305) Lone Star Bks.

Case of the Night-Stalking Bone Monster, unabr. ed. John R. Erickson. 2 cass. (Running Time: 2 hrs.). (Hank the Cowdog Ser.: No. 27). 2001. 24.00 (978-0-7366-6160-7(3)) Books on Tape.
Hank is the proud owner of three precious steak bones and protects his fortune by burying them in Sally May's garden. Shortly after meeting Dog Pound Ralph, Hank returns to the garden...The bones are gone! He finds an empty vienna sausage can in each hole. A night-stalking bone monster is loose on the ranch!.

Case of the Night-Stalking Bone Monster. unabr. ed. John R. Erickson. Read by John R. Erickson. 2 cass. (Running Time: 3 hrs.). (Hank the Cowdog Ser.: No. 27). (J). (gr. 2-5). 2001. 16.95 (978-0-7366-6916-0(7)) Books on Tape.
The dreaded Bone Monster must be loose on the ranch because Hank has lost three juicy T-bones.

Case of the Night-Stalking Bone Monster. unabr. ed. John R. Erickson. 3 CDs. (Running Time: 2 hrs.). (Hank the Cowdog Ser.: No. 27). (J). 2001. audio compact disk 28.00 (978-0-7366-7549-9(3)) Books on Tape.

Case of the Night-Stalking Bone Monster. unabr. ed. John R. Erickson. Read by John R. Erickson. 2 cass. (Running Time: 3 hrs.). (Hank the Cowdog Ser.: No. 27). (J). 2002. 17.99 (978-1-59188-327-2(X)) Maverick Bks.

Case of the Night-Stalking Bone Monster. unabr. ed. John R. Erickson. Read by John R. Erickson. 3 CDs. (Running Time: Approx. 3 hours). (Hank the

Cowdog Ser.: No. 27). (J). 2002. audio compact disk 19.99 (978-1-59188-627-3(9)) Maverick Bks.

Hank is the happiest cowdog in the universe when scraptime leaves him with not one but three juicy T-bones. But before Hank has a chance to enjoy his treasure, they disappear! It can only mean one thing?there?s a dreaded Bone Monster loose on the ranch. Can Hank put a stop to this devious creature?or will he lose his precious T-bones forever?Songs include ?Drover?s Wake-up Song,? and ?I?d Like To Be Your Pal,? which Hank sings to Miss Scamper.

Case of the Night-Stalking Bone Monster, unabr. ed. John R. Erickson. Read by John R. Erickson. 2 cass. (Running Time: 2 hrs.). (Hank the Cowdog Ser.: No. 27). (J). (gr. 2-5). 1998. 17.00 (21666) Recorded Bks.

Case of the One-Eyed Killer Stud Horse. John R. Erickson. 2 cass. (Running Time: 2 hrs.). (Hank the Cowdog Ser.: No. 8). (J). (gr. 2-5). 1989. 16.95 (978-0-87719-146-9(8)) Lone Star Bks.

Case of the One-Eyed Killer Stud Horse. unabr. ed. John R. Erickson. 2 cass. (Running Time: 3 hrs.). (Hank the Cowdog Ser.: No. 8). (J). (gr. 2-5). 2001. 24.00 (978-0-7366-6143-0(3)) Books on Tape.

It's Hank to the rescue when a one-eyed killer sets out to destroy the ranch.

Case of the One-Eyed Killer Stud Horse. unabr. ed. John R. Erickson. Read by John R. Erickson. 2 cass. (Running Time: 3 hrs.). (Hank the Cowdog Ser.: No. 8). (J). (gr. 2-5). 2001. 16.95 (978-0-7366-6897-2(7)) Books on Tape.

It's Hank to the rescue when a one eyed killer sets out to destroy the ranch.

Case of the One-Eyed Killer Stud Horse. unabr. ed. John R. Erickson. Read by John R. Erickson. Illus. by Gerald L. Holmes. (Hank the Cowdog Ser.: No. 8). (J). (gr. 2-5). 1987. 13.95 (978-0-916941-29-1(9)) Maverick Bks.

Case of the One-Eyed Killer Stud Horse. unabr. ed. John R. Erickson. Read by John R. Erickson. 2 cass. (Running Time: 3 hrs.). (Hank the Cowdog Ser.: No. 8). (J). 2002. 17.99 (978-1-59188-308-1(3)) Maverick Bks.

Case of the One-Eyed Killer Stud Horse. unabr. ed. John R. Erickson. Read by John R. Erickson. 3 CDs. (Running Time: Approx. 3 hours). (Hank the Cowdog Ser.: No. 8). (J). 2002. audio compact disk 19.99 (978-1-59188-608-2(2)) Maverick Bks.

Things are looking pretty bleak for Hank the Cowdog. First he gets sick on poisoned bacon grease. Then he accidentally trips Sally May?and she ends up with a broken ankle. And if that?s not bad enough, he gets stuck playing dress-up with Amy and Ashley, Little Alfred?s cousins. But when Tuerto the Killer Stud Horse breaks free and charges at the girls, Hank knows it?s up to him to protect them. He?ll show that one-eyed horse who?s boss?even if it means risking his own life!Hear two great new songs, ?A Fundamental Disagreement? and ?Thank You Lord For Making Gals,? in this hilarious adventure for the whole family.

Case of the One-Eyed Killer Stud Horse, unabr. ed. John R. Erickson. 2 cass. (Running Time: 2 hrs.). (Hank the Cowdog Ser.: No. 8). (J). (gr. 2-5). 1998. 17.00 (21650) Recorded Bks.

Case of the One-Eyed Killer Stud Horse. unabr. collector's ed. John R. Erickson. 3 CDs. (Running Time: 4 hrs. 30 mins.). (Hank the Cowdog Ser.: No. 8). (J). (gr. 2-5). 2001. audio compact disk 28.00 Books on Tape.

It's Hank to the rescue when a one-eyed killer sets out to destroy the ranch.

***Case of the Peculiar Pink Fan.** unabr. ed. Nancy Springer. Narrated by Katherine Kellgren. 4 cass. (Running Time: 4 hrs.). (YA). (gr. 5-8). 2009. 33.75 (978-1-4361-6157-2(6)); audio compact disk 46.75 (978-1-4361-6162-6(2)) Recorded Bks.

Case of the Puzzling Possum. Cynthia Rylant. Illus. by G. Brian Karas. 11 vols. (Running Time: 16 mins.). (High-Rise Private Eyes Ser.: No. 3). (J). (gr. k-3). 2003. bk. 28.95 (978-1-59112-619-5(3)); pap. bk. 29.95 (978-1-59112-199-2(X)); 9.95 (978-1-59112-196-1(5)) Live Oak Media.

Case of the Puzzling Possum. Cynthia Rylant. Illus. by G. Brian Karas. 11 vols. (Running Time: 16 mins.). (High-Rise Private Eyes Ser.: No. 3). (J). (ps-3). 2003. bk. 25.95 (978-1-59112-198-5(1)) Live Oak Media.

Case of the Puzzling Possum. Cynthia Rylant. Read by William Dufris. Illus. by G. Brian Karas. 11 vols. (Running Time: 16 mins.). (High-Rise Private Eyes Ser.: No. 3). (J). (gr. k-3). 2003. pap. bk. 16.95 (978-1-59112-197-8(3)) Pub: Live Oak Media. Dist(s): AudioGO

Case of the Puzzling Possum. Cynthia Rylant. Illus. by G. Brian Karas. (Running Time: 16 mins.). (High-Rise Private Eyes Ser.: No. 3). (J). (gr. k-3). 2003. 12.95 (978-1-59112-617-1(7)) Live Oak Media.

Case of the Raging Rottweiler. abr. ed. John R. Erickson. 2 cass. (Running Time: 3 hrs.). (Hank the Cowdog Ser.: No. 36). (J). (gr. 2-5). 2000. 18.00 (978-0-8072-6156-9(4), Listening Lib) Random Audio Pubg.

Case of the Raging Rottweiler. unabr. ed. John R. Erickson. 2 cass. (Running Time: 2 hrs.). (Hank the Cowdog Ser.: No. 36). (J). (gr. 2-5). 2001. 24.00 (978-0-7366-6251-2(0)); 28.00 (978-0-7366-6870-5(5)) Books on Tape.

A raging rottweiler is loose on the ranch and it's up to Hank to teach the visiting pooch some manners.

Case of the Raging Rottweiler. unabr. ed. John R. Erickson. Read by John R. Erickson. 2 cass. (Running Time: 3 hrs.). (Hank the Cowdog Ser.: No. 36). (J). (gr. 2-5). 2001. 16.95 (978-0-7366-6262-8(6)) Books on Tape.

A raging rottweiler is loose on the ranch & it's up to Hank to teach the visiting pooch some manners.

Case of the Raging Rottweiler. unabr. ed. John R. Erickson. Read by John R. Erickson. 2 cass. (Running Time: 3 hrs.). (Hank the Cowdog Ser.: No. 36). (J). 2002. 17.99 (978-1-59188-336-4(9)) Maverick Bks.

It's rumored that Bruiser is all talk and no action, but when Hanks gets a look at the rottweiler's sharp teeth and giant body, he's not sure what to think. Can Hank put this crazy canine in his place? Or are our hero's dog days numbered.

Case of the Raging Rottweiler. unabr. ed. John R. Erickson. Read by John R. Erickson. 3 CDs. (Running Time: Approx 3 hours). (Hank the Cowdog Ser.: No. 36). (J). 2002. audio compact disk 19.99 (978-1-59188-636-5(8)) Maverick Bks.

The ranch is in the grip of a sweltering summer heat wave, and to make matters worse, Bruiser the Rottweiler is on the loose. First Bruiser attacks a defenseless fawn, then he threatens to come after Hank the Cowdog, the Head of Ranch Security! It?s rumored that Bruiser is all talk and no action, but when Hank gets a look at the rottweiler?s sharp teeth and giant body, he?s not sure what to think. Can Hank put this crazy canine in his place? Or are our hero?s dog days numbered?Hank and Drover sing ?Let Us in the House Song.? Drover sings ?It?s Not Smart to Show Your Hiney to a Bear.?.

Case of the Raging Rottweiler. unabr. ed. John R. Erickson. Read by John R. Erickson. 2 cass. (Running Time: 2 hrs. 30 mins.). (Hank the Cowdog Ser.: No. 36). (J). (gr. 2-5). 2000. 18.00 (978-0-8072-8715-6(6), YA245CX, Listening Lib) Random Audio Pubg.

When a raging Rottweiler threatens the wildlife on the ranch, it's up to Hank the Cowdog, head of Ranch Security, to teach the visiting pooch some manners. It's rumored that Bruiser is all talk & no action, but Hank's not so sure. Has he got what it takes to take care of this crazy canine? Or are his dog days numbered?.

Case of the Raging Rottweiler. unabr. collector's ed. John R. Erickson. 3 CDs. (Running Time: 4 hrs. 30 mins.). (Hank the Cowdog Ser.: No. 36). (J). (gr. 2-5). 2001. audio compact disk 28.00 Books on Tape.

The ranch is in the grip of a sweltering summer heat wave and to make matters worse, Bruiser the Rottweiler is on the loose. First Bruiser attacks a defenseless fawn, then he threatens to come after Hank the Cowdog, the Head of Ranch Sercurity! It's rumored that Bruiser is all talk and no action, but when Hank gets a look at the Rottweiler's sharp teeth and giant body, he's not sure what to think. Can Hank put this crazy canine in his place? Or are our hero's dog days numbered?.

Case of the Saddle House Robbery. John R. Erickson. 2 cass. (Running Time: 1hr. 10 mins.). (Hank the Cowdog Ser.: No. 35). (J). (gr. 2-5). 2000. 18.00 (978-0-8072-8239-7(1), Listening Lib) Random Audio Pubg.

Case of the Saddle House Robbery. unabr. ed. John R. Erickson. 2 cass. (Running Time: 3 hrs.). (Hank the Cowdog Ser.: No. 35). (J). (gr. 2-5). 2001. 24.00 (978-0-7366-6250-5(2)) Books on Tape.

There's a new dog on the ranch & Hank the Cowdog is none too thrilled about it. He's supposed to keep an eye on Jake until his owner shows up, but Jake's got other plans. He has to get to Madagascar before someone makes off with his treasure!.

Case of the Saddle House Robbery. unabr. ed. John R. Erickson. Read by John R. Erickson. 2 cass. (Running Time: 3 hrs.). (Hank the Cowdog Ser.: No. 35). (J). (gr. 2-5). 2001. 16.95 (978-0-7366-6261-1(8)) Books on Tape.

A thief makes off with all of Loper's best saddles. Hank has to find the saddles - and protect his hide.

Case of the Saddle House Robbery. unabr. ed. John R. Erickson. Read by John R. Erickson. 2 cass. (Running Time: 3 hrs.). (Hank the Cowdog Ser.: No. 35). (J). 2002. 17.99 (978-1-59188-335-7(0)) Maverick Bks.

As Head of Ranch Security, Hank's supposed to keep an eye on Jake until his owner shows up. But Jake's got other plans - he's convinced he needs to get to Madagascar before some pirates make off with his treasure. As if that's not bad enough, while Hank's looking after Jake a thief makes off with all of Loper's best saddles.

Case of the Saddle House Robbery. unabr. ed. John R. Erickson. Read by John R. Erickson. 3 CDs. (Running Time: Approx. 3 hours). (Hank the Cowdog Ser.: No. 35). (J). 2002. audio compact disk 19.99 (978-1-59188-635-8(X)) Maverick Bks.

There?s a new dog on the ranch, and Hank the Cowdog is none too thrilled about it. He?s supposed to keep an eye on Jake until his owner shows up, but Jake?s got other plans. He has to get to Madagascar before someone makes off with his treasure! As if Hank doesn?t have enough to worry about, there?s a saddle thief on the loose. Is Jake in cahoots with the robber? Are there really monkeys under the toolshed?Rip and Snort sing ?The Coyote Howl-Up-The Sun Song? and Hank belts out ?I?m Trapped in Madagascar.?.

Case of the Saddle House Robbery. unabr. ed. John R. Erickson. Read by John R. Erickson. 2 cass. (Running Time: 2 hrs. 30 mins.). (Hank the Cowdog Ser.: No. 35). (J). (gr. 2-5). 2000. 18.00 (978-0-8072-8375-2(4), YA172CX, Listening Lib) Random Audio Pubg.

Case of the Saddle House Robbery. unabr. ed. John R. Erickson. Read by John R. Erickson. 2 cass. (Hank the Cowdog Ser.: No. 35). (J). (gr. 2-5). 2000. pap. bk. 23.00 (978-0-8072-8376-9(2), YA172SP, Listening Lib) Random Audio Pubg.

A stray dog has appeared on the ranch & he's missing more than a couple of his marbles. While crazy Jake has Hank running around to defend the ranch from marauding pirates from Madagascar, a thief makes off with all of Loper's best saddles! It's up to Hank to find the saddles & save his hide!.

Case of the Saddle House Robbery. unabr. collector's ed. John R. Erickson. 3 CDs. (Running Time: 4 hrs. 30 mins.). (Hank the Cowdog Ser.: No. 35). (J). (gr. 2-5). 2001. audio compact disk 28.00 (978-0-7366-6869-9(1)) Books on Tape.

A thief makes off with all of Loper's best saddles. Hank has to find the saddles - and protect his hide.

Case of the Scaredy Cats. abr. ed. Crosby N. Bonsall. Illus. by Crosby N. Bonsall. 1 cass. (I Can Read Bks.). (J). (gr. k-3). 1991. 8.99 (978-1-55994-434-2(X), TBC 434X) HarperCollins Pubs.

Case of the Shipwrecked Tree. John R. Erickson. Read by John R. Erickson. 2 cassettes. (Running Time: approx. 3 hours). (Hank the Cowdog Ser.: No. 41). (J). 2003. wbk. ed. 17.99 (978-1-59188-341-8(5)) Maverick Bks.

Hank the Cowdog and his trusty partner, Drover, are just beginning their latest investigation when a pirate suddenly appears on the front porch! Hank and Drover soon realize that the pirate is just Little Alfred in disguise. Who else would Little Alfred choose as his first mate but Hank? After Hank enthusiastically agrees to be hoisted up into the tree-house pirate ship, he suddenly remembers?dogs don?t belong in trees! Can Hank come up with a way to survive his adventure on the high seas and return to shore in one piece?Hear Hank sing ?The Turkey Song? and ?You Have to Grow Up, Boys.?.

Case of the Shipwrecked Tree. unabr. ed. John R. Erickson. Read by John R. Erickson. 3 CDs. (Running Time: 3 hrs.). (Hank the Cowdog Ser.: No. 41). (J). (gr. 4 up). 2003. audio compact disk 19.99 (978-1-59188-641-9(4)) Maverick Bks.

Case of the Sleepy Sloth. unabr. ed. Cynthia Rylant. Read by William Dufris. Illus. by G. Brian Karas. 1 cass. (Running Time: 20 mins.). (High-Rise Private Eyes Ser.: No. 5). (J). (gr. k-4). 2005. bk. 29.95 (978-1-59519-413-8(4)); bk. 28.95 (978-1-59519-417-6(7)); pap. bk. 18.95 (978-1-59519-416-9(9)); pap. bk. 16.95 (978-1-59519-412-1(6)) Live Oak Media.

Jack and Bunny are back in another exciting adventures as small crime fighters, this time trying to find a lawn chair that has mysteriously disappeared from the houseboat of a dog they meet down at the docks. Hijinks abound as usual in this witty mystery that will prompt some serious giggles!.

Case of the Sleepy Sloth, Set. unabr. ed. Cynthia Rylant. Read by William Dufris. Illus. by G. Brian Karas. 1 cass. (Running Time: 20 mins.). (High-Rise Private Eyes Ser.: No. 5). (J). (gr. k-4). 2005. pap. bk. 29.95 (978-1-59519-414-5(2)); pap. bk. 31.95 (978-1-59519-418-3(5)) Live Oak Media.

Case of the Swirling Killer Tornado. John R. Erickson. 2 cass. (Running Time: 2 hrs.). (Hank the Cowdog Ser.: No. 25). (J). (gr. 2-5). 1995. 16.95 (978-0-87719-280-0(4), 9280) Lone Star Bks.

Case of the Swirling Killer Tornado. unabr. ed. John R. Erickson. 2 cass. (Running Time: 2 hrs.). (Hank the Cowdog Ser.: No. 25). 2001. 24.00 (978-0-7366-6158-4(1)) Books on Tape.

A tornado is headed straight for the ranch and Hank and Drover are trapped in the house. Will they find a way out?.

Case of the Swirling Killer Tornado. unabr. ed. John R. Erickson. Read by John R. Erickson. 2 cass. (Running Time: 3 hrs.). (Hank the Cowdog Ser.: No. 25). (J). (gr. 2-5). 2001. 16.95 (978-0-7366-6914-6(0)) Books on Tape.

A tornado is headed straight for the ranch & Hank & Drover are trapped in the house. Will they find a way out?.

Case of the Swirling Killer Tornado. unabr. ed. John R. Erickson. 1 CD. (Running Time: 1 hr. 30 mins.). (Hank the Cowdog Ser.: No. 25). 2001. audio compact disk 28.00 (978-0-7366-7547-5(7)) Books on Tape.

Case of the Swirling Killer Tornado. unabr. ed. John R. Erickson. Read by John R. Erickson. 2 cass. (Running Time: 3 hrs.). (Hank the Cowdog Ser.: No. 25). (J). 2002. 17.99 (978-1-59188-325-8(3)) Maverick Bks.

Hank and Drover dodge the relentless attack of the terrible Charlie Monsters. Then, incredibly, they find themselves in the inner sanctum of Sally May's kitchen, with a polka-dot midget dangling raw bacon in front of their noses. As if that's not enough, they come face-to-face with the Swirling Killer Tornado, and must gather every ounce of courage they have to save the ranch from the tornado's course.

Case of the Swirling Killer Tornado. unabr. ed. John R. Erickson. Read by John R. Erickson. 3 CDs. (Running Time: Approx. 3 hours). (Hank the Cowdog Ser.: No. 25). (J). 2002. audio compact disk 19.99 (978-1-59188-625-9(2)) Maverick Bks.

Awakened by an attack from an invisible enemy, Hank the Cowdog knows that there?s only one thing for him to do?get inside the house and make sure that his family is safe. But when he arrives, Hank learns that the house is in the path of a swirling killer tornado! Even worse, the family has rushed into the storm cellar?leaving Hank and Drover, trapped inside the house. Will they be able to get out before it?s too late?Drover makes his singing debut with ?Never Ever Bark at a Funnel-Shaped Cloud? in this hilarious adventure for the whole family.

Case of the Swirling Killer Tornado, unabr. ed. John R. Erickson. Read by John R. Erickson. 2 cass. (Running Time: 2 hrs.). (Hank the Cowdog Ser.: No. 25). (J). (gr. 2-5). 1998. 17.00 (21664) Recorded Bks.

Case of the Tricky Trap. John R. Erickson. Read by John R. Erickson. 3 CDs. (Running Time: 10800 sec.). (Hank the Cowdog Ser.: No. 46). (J). (gr. 4-7). 2005. audio compact disk 19.99 (978-1-59188-646-4(5)); 17.99 (978-1-59188-346-3(6)) Maverick Bks.

Someone has been getting into the feed shed, and Slim puts out a trap. Hank, must check the trap and help Slim nab the culprit. Unfortunately, the trap is trickier than Hank thought, and he soon comes face to face with his old buddy, Eddy the Rac.

Case of the Troublesome Turtle. Cynthia Rylant. Illus. by G. Brian Karas. 11 vols. (Running Time: 18 mins.). (High-Rise Private Eyes Ser.: No. 4). (J). (gr. k-3). 2003. bk. 25.95 (978-1-59112-202-9(3)); bk. 28.95 (978-1-59112-623-2(1)); pap. bk. 29.95 (978-1-59112-203-6(1)); pap. bk. 31.95 (978-1-59112-624-9(X)) Live Oak Media.

Case of the Troublesome Turtle. Cynthia Rylant. Read by William Dufris. Illus. by G. Brian Karas. 11 vols. (Running Time: 18 mins.). (High-Rise Private Eyes Ser.: No. 4). (J). (gr. k-6). 2003. pap. bk. 16.95 (978-1-59112-201-2(5)) Pub: Live Oak Media. Dist(s): AudioGO

Case of the Troublesome Turtle. Cynthia Rylant. Illus. by G. Brian Karas. (Running Time: 18 mins.). (High-Rise Private Eyes Ser.: No. 4). (J). (gr. k-3). 2003. 12.95 (978-1-59112-200-5(7)); 12.95 (978-1-59112-621-8(5)) Live Oak Media.

Case of the Twisted Kitty. John R. Erickson. Read by John R. Erickson. 2 cassettes. (Running Time: Approx. 3 hours). (Hank the Cowdog Ser.: No. 43). (J). 2004. 17.99 (978-1-59188-343-2(1)) Maverick Bks.

Case of the Twisted Kitty, 43. John R. Erickson. Read by John R. Erickson. 3 CDs. (Running Time: Approx 3 hours). (Hank the Cowdog Ser.: No. 43). (J). 2004. audio compact disk 19.99 (978-1-59188-643-3(0)) Maverick Bks.

Case of the Vampire Cat. unabr. ed. John R. Erickson. Read by John R. Erickson. 2 cass. (Running Time: 3 hrs.). (Hank the Cowdog Ser.: No. 21). (J). (gr. 2-5). 2001. 16.95 (978-0-7366-6910-8(8)) Books on Tape.

When Hank is accidently abandoned at a neighbor's ranch, he finds himself with a very undesirable feline companion.

Case of the Vampire Cat. unabr. ed. John R. Erickson. Read by John R. Erickson. 2 cass. (Running Time: 3 hrs.). (Hank the Cowdog Ser.: No. 21). (J). 2002. 17.99 (978-1-59188-321-0(0)) Maverick Bks.

Case of the Vampire Cat. unabr. ed. John R. Erickson. Read by John R. Erickson. 3 CDs. (Running Time: Approx. 3 hours). (Hank the Cowdog Ser.: No. 21). (J). 2002. audio compact disk 19.99 (978-1-59188-621-1(X)) Maverick Bks.

When Slim accidentally abandons Hank at a neighbor?s ranch, the Head of Ranch Security finds himself with a very undesirable companion. This new sidekick?better known as Mary D Cat?is an overly affectionate cat with an affinity for cheese and a severe case of Skipsofrazzled Personality. What?s even worse, Hank is certain that Mary is a vampire. But when Hank and Mary find themselves face-to-face with two hungry coyotes, he realizes that a vampire cat might not be such a bad thing to have around after all.Songs in this hilarious adventure for the whole family include ?Ode to a Mother Skunk? and ?The Cannibal Way.?.

Case of the Vampire Cat, unabr. ed. John R. Erickson. Read by John R. Erickson. 2 cass. (Running Time: 2 hrs.). (Hank the Cowdog Ser.: No. 21). (J). (gr. 2-5). 1998. 17.00 (21627) Recorded Bks.

Case of the Vampire Cat. unabr. collector's ed. John R. Erickson. 1 CD. (Running Time: 2 hrs.). (Hank the Cowdog Ser.: Bk. 21). (J). 2001. audio compact disk 19.99 Books on Tape.

When Hank is accidentally abandoned at a neighbor's ranch, he finds himself with a very undesirable feline companion.

Case of the Vampire Cat. unabr. collector's ed. John R. Erickson. 2 cass. (Running Time: 2 hrs.). (Hank the Cowdog Ser.: No. 21). 2001. 24.00 (978-0-7366-6154-6(9)) Books on Tape.

Case of the Vampire Cat. unabr. collector's ed. John R. Erickson. 3 CDs. (Running Time: 3 hrs. 36 min.). (Hank the Cowdog Ser.: No. 21). (J). 2001. audio compact disk 28.00 (978-0-7366-7543-7(4)) Books on Tape.

Case of the Vampire Cat & the Case of the Double Bumblebee Sting. unabr. ed. John R. Erickson. Read by John R. Erickson. 4 cass. (Running Time: 6 hrs.). (Hank the Cowdog Ser.: No. 21-22). (J). 2002. 26.99 (978-0-916941-71-0(X)) Maverick Bks.

When Slim accidentally abandons Hank at a neighbor's ranch, the head of ranch security finds himself with a very undesirable companion. This new sidekick better known as Mary D Cat, is an overly affectionate cat with an affinity for cheese and a severe case of Skipsofrazzled Personality.

Case of the Vampire Cat & the Case of the Double Bumblebee Sting. unabr. ed. John R. Erickson. Read by John R. Erickson. 6 CDs. (Running Time: 6 hrs.). (Hank the Cowdog Ser.: Nos. 21-22). (J). 2002. audio compact disk 31.99 (978-0-916941-91-8(4)) Maverick Bks.

When Slim accidentally abandons Hank at a neighbor?s ranch, the Head of Ranch Security finds himself with a very undesirable companion. This new sidekick better known as Mary D Cat is an overly affectionate cat with an affinity for cheese and a severe case of Skipsofrazzled Personality.

Case of the Vampire Vacuum Sweeper. unabr. ed. John R. Erickson. Read by John R. Erickson. 2 cass. (Running Time: 1 hrs.). (Hank the Cowdog Ser.: No. 29). (J). (gr. 4-7). 2001. 24.00 (978-0-7366-6162-1(X)) Books on Tape.

Marauding trespassers are threatening to stampede the cattle. It's Hank the Cowdog, Head of Ranch Security, to the rescue as he: tracks down enemy

agent Mysterious Esther, escapes the relentless Vampire Vacuum Sweeper, and confronts Buster and his gang. Will Hank prevail and save the ranch.

Case of the Vampire Vacuum Sweeper. unabr. ed. John R. Erickson. Read by John R. Erickson. 2 cass. (Running Time: 2 hrs.). (Hank the Cowdog Ser.: No. 29). (J). (gr. 4-7). 2001. 12.95 (978-0-7366-6918-4(3)) Books on Tape.
Before Hank can run a pack of wild dogs off the ranch, he must deal with a vicious vacuum cleaner.

Case of the Vampire Vacuum Sweeper. unabr. ed. John R. Erickson. Read by John R. Erickson. 3 CDs. (Running Time: 1 hr. 12 mins.). (Hank the Cowdog Ser.: No. 29). (J). 2001. audio compact disk 28.00 (978-0-7366-7551-2(5)) Books on Tape.
Marauding trespassers are threatening to stampede the cattle. It's Hank the Cowdog, Head of Ranch Security, to the rescue as he: tracks down enemy agent Mysterious Esther, escapes the relentless Vampire Vacuum Sweeper, and confronts Buster and his gang. Will Hank prevail and save the ranch.

Case of the Vampire Vacuum Sweeper. unabr. ed. John R. Erickson. Read by John R. Erickson. 2 cass. (Running Time: 3 hrs.). (Hank the Cowdog Ser.: No. 29). (J). 2002. 17.99 (978-1-59188-329-6(6)) Maverick Bks.

Case of the Vampire Vacuum Sweeper. unabr. ed. John R. Erickson. Read by John R. Erickson. 3 CDs. (Running Time: Approx. 3 hours). (Hank the Cowdog Ser.: No. 29). (J). 2002. audio compact disk 19.99 (978-1-59188-629-7(5)) Maverick Bks.
A gang of marauding dogs is threatening the calf population on the ranch, and Hank knows that it?s up to the Head of Ranch Security to do something about it. But instead of being outside where he can fight off the fiends, Hank is trapped inside?at the mercy of Slim and his dreaded vampire sweeper! Will Hank be able to save the ranch?Hank and Drover sing ?Freezing on the Porch,? and Hank sings ?The Porcupine Blues? in this hilarious adventure for the whole family.

Case of the Vanishing Beauty. unabr. ed. Richard S. Prather. Read by Maynard Villers. 6 cass. (Running Time: 7 hrs.). (Shell Scott Ser.: Bk. 1). 2001. 39.95 (978-1-55686-890-0(1)) Books in Motion.
Scott searches for a missing woman, while another woman he's working with dies in a hail of bullets.

Case of the Vanishing Fishhook. John R. Erickson. Read by John R. Erickson. 1 MP3 CD. (Running Time: 3 hrs.). (Hank the Cowdog Ser.: No. 31). (J). (gr. 4-7). 2001. audio compact disk 19.99 Books on Tape.
While on a fishing trip, Hank swallows a fishhook. Is it curtains for everyone's favorite Cowdog?.

Case of the Vanishing Fishhook. John R. Erickson. Illus. by Gerald L. Holmes. 2 cass. 1998. bk. (978-0-87719-342-5(8)) Maverick Books.

Case of the Vanishing Fishhook. unabr. ed. John R. Erickson. Read by John R. Erickson. 2 cass. (Running Time: 1 hr.). (Hank the Cowdog Ser.: No. 31). (J). (gr. 4-7). 2001. 24.00 (978-0-7366-6164-5(6)) Books on Tape.
Hank's day begins defending the ranch against a vicious one-eyed robot. Even after that exhausting morning, Hank still has energy left to supervise Little Alfred's fishing trip. But what starts out as a routine expedition turns into a first-class crisis when Hank reels in more than he bargained for. A vanishing fishhook leads to bad news indeed. Is there hope for Hank or is it curtains for our hero.

Case of the Vanishing Fishhook. unabr. ed. John R. Erickson. Read by John R. Erickson. 2 cass. (Running Time: 2 hrs.). (Hank the Cowdog Ser.: No. 31). (J). (gr. 4-7). 2001. 12.95 (978-0-7366-6920-7(5)) Books on Tape.
While on a fishing trip, Hank swallows a fishhook. Is it curtains for everyone's favorite Cowdog?.

Case of the Vanishing Fishhook. unabr. ed. John R. Erickson. Read by John R. Erickson. 3 CDs. (Running Time: 1 hr. 12 mins.). (Hank the Cowdog Ser.: No. 31). (J). (gr. 4-7). 2001. audio compact disk 28.00 (978-0-7366-7553-6(1)) Books on Tape.
Hank's day begins defending the ranch against a vicious one-eyed robot. Even after that exhausting morning, Hank still has energy left to supervise Little Alfred's fishing trip. But what starts out as a routine expedition turns into a first-class crisis when Hank reels in more than he bargained for. A vanishing fishhook leads to bad news indeed. Is there hope for Hank or is it curtains for our hero.

Case of the Vanishing Fishhook. unabr. ed. John R. Erickson. Read by John R. Erickson. 2 cass. (Running Time: 3 hrs.). (Hank the Cowdog Ser.: No. 31). (J). 2002. 17.99 (978-1-59188-331-9(8)) Maverick Bks.

Case of the Vanishing Fishhook. unabr. ed. John R. Erickson. Read by John R. Erickson. 3 CDs. (Running Time: Approx. 3 hours). (Hank the Cowdog Ser.: No. 31). (J). 2002. audio compact disk 19.99 (978-1-59188-631-0(7)) Maverick Bks.
Even after an exhausting morning defending the ranch against a vicious one-eyed robot, Hank the Cowdog, Head of Ranch Security, still has energy left to supervise Little Alfred?s fishing trip. But what starts as a routine expedition turns into a first-class crisis when Hank reels in more than he bargained for. A fishhook finds its way into Hank?s stomach, which is bad news indeed. Is there hope for Hank, or is this curtains for our hero?Sally May sings ?Sally May?s Lament,? and Hank manages to croon ?I Will Never Eat Another Fishhook?' in this hilarious adventure for the whole family.

Case of the Wanted Man. Created by Saddleback Educational Publishing. 1 cass. (Running Time: 3893 sec.). (PageTurner Detective Ser.). (J). 2002. audio compact disk 10.95 (978-1-56254-498-0(5), SP 4985) Saddleback Edu.
Word-for-word read-along of The Case of the Wanted Man.

Case of the Watery Grave. Created by Saddleback Educational Publishing. 1 cass. (Running Time: 3930 sec.). (PageTurner Detective Ser.). (J). 2002. audio compact disk 10.95 (978-1-56254-499-7(3), SP 4993) Saddleback Edu.
Word-for-word read-along of The Case of the Watery Grave.

Case of Troublesome Turtle. Cynthia Rylant. Read by William Dufris. Illus. by G. Brian Karas. 11 vols. (Running Time: 18 mins.). (High-Rise Private Eyes Ser.: No. 4). (J). (ps-2). 2004. 18.95 (978-1-59112-622-5(3)) Pub: Live Oak Media. Dist(s): AudioGO

Case of William Smith. Patricia Wentworth. (Isis (CDs) Ser.). (J). 2006. audio compact disk 79.95 (978-0-7531-2572-4(2)) Pub: ISIS Lrg Prnt GBR. Dist(s): Ulverscroft US

Case of William Smith. unabr. ed. Patricia Wentworth. Read by Diana Bishop. 7 cass. (Running Time: 8 hrs. 20 mins.). (Isis Cassettes Ser.). (J). 2006. 61.95 (978-0-7531-3581-5(7)) Pub: ISIS Lrg Prnt GBR. Dist(s): Ulverscroft US

Case Samples in Chinese see Sixth Sense: RADIO DIVINITY

***Case Studies in Health Information Management.** Patricia Schnering. (ENG.). 2008. bk. 111.95 (978-1-4283-0345-4(6)) Delmar.

Case Studies in Hypocrisy: U. S. Human Rights Policy. Noam Chomsky. Read by Noam Chomsky. (ENG.). 2000. audio compact disk 20.00 (978-1-902593-27-2(8)) Pub: AK Pr GBR. Dist(s): Consort Bk Sales

Case Studies in Pediatric Emergency Medicine, Vol. 1. Ed. by Christopher King & Brent R. King. 4 cass. (Running Time: 6 hrs.). (Case Studies in Pediatric Emergency Medicine: 1). 2000. 125.00 (978-0-9720467-5-6(5)) TPEM.
Four 90-minute audiotapes, text summaries, and high resolution visual stimuli presented in a true oral boards format.

Case Studies in Pediatric Emergency Medicine, Vol. 2. Ed. by Christopher King & Brent R. King. 4 cass. (Running Time: 6 hrs.). (Case Studies in Pediatric Emergency Medicine: 2). 2000. 125.00 (978-0-9720467-6-3(3)) TPEM.
Four 90-minute audiotapes, text summaries, and high-resolution copies of visual stimuli presented in a true oral boards format.

Case Study, Nos. 1 & 2. Shivahi Bhattacharjee. 1 cass. 8.95 (383) Am Fed Astrologers.

Case to Answer. unabr. ed. Margaret Yorke. Read by Celia Montague. 8 cass. (Running Time: 12 hrs.). 2001. 69.95 (978-0-7540-0659-6(X), CAB 2081) Pub: Chivers Audio Bks GBR. Dist(s): AudioGO
The day Jerry Hunt met Charlotte Frost was the day he decided to go straight. Jerry had been running a successful scam with his friend, Pete, but something in Charlotte's smile made him take stock of his activities.

Casebook of Gregory Hood: Gregory Hood, Suspect & The Sad Clown. Perf. by Gale Gordon. 1 cass. (Running Time: 1 hr.). 2001. 6.98 (1924) Radio Spirits.

Casebook of Gregory Hood: The Forgetful Murderer & Double Diamond. Perf. by Gale Gordon. 1 cass. (Running Time: 1 hr.). 2001. 6.98 (1825) Radio Spirits.

Casebook of Gregory Hood: The Murder of Gregory Hood & Murder in Celluloid. Perf. by Gale Gordon. 1 cass. (Running Time: 1 hr.). 2001. 6.98 (1824) Radio Spirits.

Casebook of Gregory Hood: Three Silver Pesos & Black Museum. Perf. by Gale Gordon. 1 cass. (Running Time: 1 hr.). 2001. 6.98 (1887) Radio Spirits.

Casebook of Sherlock Holmes, Vol. 2. unabr. ed. Arthur Conan Doyle. Read by David Timson. 4 CDs. (Running Time: 5 hrs. 30 mins.). (Complete Classics Ser.). 2008. audio compact disk 28.98 (978-962-634-862-8(3), Naxos AudioBooks) Naxos.

Casebook of Sherlock Holmes 1, Vol. 1. unabr. ed. Arthur Conan Doyle. Read by David Timson. 4 CDs. (Running Time: 16892 sec.). (Complete Classics Ser.). 2007. audio compact disk 28.98 (978-962-634-465-1(2), Naxos AudioBooks) Naxos.

CaseKeeper. 2000. audio compact disk 1698.50 (978-0-85308-675-8(3)) Pub: Jordan Pubng GBR. Dist(s): Intl Spec Bk

Cases That Haunt Us: From Jack the Ripper to JonBenet Ramsey, the FBI's Legendary Mindhunter Sheds Light on the Mysteries That Won't Go Away. John E. Douglas & Mark Olshaker. 11 cass. (Running Time: 16 hrs. 30 mins.). 2001. 88.00 (978-0-7366-6213-0(8)) Books on Tape.
Of all the millions of horrendous crimes that have been committed over the years, certain cases seem to have lives of their own. Despite the passage of time, they continue their hold on our collective imagination, & our collective fears.

Casete la Biblia Canta. (SPA.). 2003. (978-1-931952-53-8(1)) Untd Bible Amrcas Svce.

Casey: Crime Photographer, collector's ed. Perf. by Staats Cotsworth. 6 cass. (Running Time: 9 hrs.). 1999. bk. 34.98 (4174) Radio Spirits.
Casey, ace cameraman for the "Morning Express" newspaper, along with his girlfriend Annie Williams, helps police solve baffling crime cases in 18 exciting mysteries.

Casey at the Bat see Fourteen American Masterpieces

Casey at the Bat. 2004. 8.95 (978-1-56008-860-8(5)); cass. & flmstrp 30.00 (978-0-89719-545-4(0)) Weston Woods.

Casey at the Bat: A Ballad of the Republic, Sung in the Year 1888 see Classic American Poetry

Casey at the Bat: A Ballad of the Republic, Sung in the Year 1888 see Favorite American Poems

Casey at the Bat: A Ballad of the Republic, Sung in the Year 1888. unabr. ed. Ernest Lawrence Thayer. Narrated by Richard Poe. 1 cass. (Running Time: 15 mins.). (gr. k up). 2001. 10.00 (978-0-7887-5359-6(2)) Recorded Bks.
With the Mudville baseball team behind by two runs in the ninth inning, things seem pretty grim. Then might Casey strolls to the plate.

Casey at the Bat: A Ballad of the Republic, Sung in the Year 1888. unabr. ed. Ernest Lawrence Thayer. Read by Curt Gowdy. 1 cass. (Running Time: 8 mins.). (J). (gr. k-4). 1994. pap. bk. 17.95 (978-0-8045-6822-7(7), 6822) Spoken Arts.
There will be plenty of joy in Mudville as popular sportscaster Curt Gowdy reads this contemporary update of the all-American classic baseball poem.

Casey, Crime Photographer. Created by Radio Spirits. (Running Time: 36000 sec.). (Legends of Radio Ser.). 2004. 39.98 (978-1-57019-691-1(5)) Radio Spirits.

Casey, Crime Photographer: King of the Apes & Box of Death. Perf. by Staats Cotsworth. 1 cass. (Running Time: 1 hr.). 2001. 6.98 (2056) Radio Spirits.

Casey Jones see Classic American Poetry

Casey Jones. 2004. 8.95 (978-1-56008-861-5(3)); cass. & flmstrp 30.00 (978-0-89719-667-3(8)) Weston Woods.

Casey's Code/All about Codes. Steck-Vaughn Staff. (J). 1999. (978-0-7398-0929-7(6)) SteckVau.

Cash & Business Management During Possible Double-Digit Inflation. unabr. ed. Richard Goff & C. Van Myers. 1 cass. (Running Time: 35 mins.). 12.95 (375) J Norton Pubs.

Cash Flow Planning. Featuring Dave Ramsey. 2002. audio compact disk (978-0-9720044-6-6(7)) Lampo Inc.

Cash Flow Statements: Preparation, Presentation & Use. Thomas Klammer & Professional Development Institute Staff. 3 cass. (Running Time: 3 hrs.). 1994. wbk. ed. 139.00 template. (751725VC); wbk. ed. 129.00 (751739VC) Am Inst CPA.
This course is specifically designed to illustrate & explain cash flow statement presentation problems. Numerous illustrations, examples & exercises help you develop a thorough understanding of the statement of cash flows & the technical problems of preparation & presentation. The helpful template, an optional feature, illustrates how a well-structured computer application can dramatically reduce the time necessary to prepare the statement of cash flows. Template is on a 5.25" disk, written in Lotus 1-2-3, & works on Lotus version 2.1 & higher.

Cash in a Flash: Fast Money in Slow Times. abr. ed. Robert G. Allen & Mark Victor Hansen. Read by Mark Victor Hansen & Daryl Allen. (ENG.). 2009. audio compact disk 24.00 (978-0-7393-8370-4(1), Random AudioBks) Pub: Random Audio Pubg. Dist(s): Random

Cash McCall. unabr. collector's ed. Cameron Hawley. Read by John MacDonald. 12 cass. (Running Time: 18 hrs.). 1984. 96.00 (978-0-7366-0573-1(8), 1545) Books on Tape.
Cash McCall is a vastly intriguing man, a 20th century adventurer who carries on his successful buying & selling of companies behind a suspiciously secret screen of anonymity. This is also an eloquent love story, a disceming journey into the hearts & minds of business wives.

Cash or Deferred 401(K) Plans. unabr. ed. Joel E. Horowitz. 7 cass. (Running Time: 10 hrs.). 1995. wbk. ed. 129.00 (749452EZ) Am Inst CPA.
If there was ever a time to sharpen your expertise in the area of 401(k) plans, it is now! With taxes taking a bigger bite out of higher incomes, tax-deferred retirement plans are more attractive than ever. You will discover how to tailor plans to meet an individual company's specific needs. You will also be alerted to pitfalls to beware of in plan operations, tax treatment, documentation & all the new & relevant tax rules.

Cash Quest - the Path Less Traveled: How to Beat Language Barriers & Improve Language Minority Customer Service to Make More Money. Speeches. Arron Grow. Voice by Arron Grow. 2. (Running Time: 90). 2000. per. 49.95 (978-0-9744737-0-3(7)) Grow Intl.
Two 45-min audio cassette tapes packaged with perfect bound paperback book in prepackaged, hard plastic case.

Cashing It In. abr. ed. Ethan Pope. Narrated by Ethan Pope. (ENG.). 2007. 9.09 (978-1-60814-110-4(1)); audio compact disk 12.99 (978-1-59859-229-0(7)) Oasis Audio.

Casino love & honor in las Vegas. Nicholas Pileggi. 2004. 10.95 (978-0-7435-4251-7(7)) Pub: S&S Audio. Dist(s): S and S Inc

Casino Moon. Peter Blauner. 2001. 18.00 (978-0-671-57042-2(0), Audioworks) S&S Audio.

Casino Royale. abr. ed. Ian Fleming. Read by Simon Vance. 4 cass. (Running Time: 16200 sec.). (James Bond 007 (Blackstone) Ser.). 2006. 17.95 (978-0-7861-4469-3(6)) Blckstn Audio.

Casino Royale. unabr. ed. Ian Fleming. Read by Robert Whitfield. 4 cass. (Running Time: 5 hrs. 30 mins.). 2000. 32.95 (978-0-7861-1817-5(2), 2616); audio compact disk 32.00 (978-0-7861-9854-2(0), 2616) Blckstn Audio.
At the Casino in Deauville, Bond's game is baccarat, for stakes that run into millions of francs. But away from the discreet salons, the caviar & champagne, it's 007 versus one of Russia's most powerful & ruthless agents & the prize is a bullet in the head from a S.M.E.R.S.H. assassin.

Casino Royale. unabr. ed. Ian Fleming. Read by Robert Whitfield. 4 cass. (Running Time: 6 hrs.). (James Bond Ser.). 2001. 24.95 (978-0-7861-1910-3(1)) Pub: Blckstn Audio. Dist(s): Penton Overseas
A friendly game of canasta turns out crooked & a golden girl ends up dead. Bond's first encounter with Auric Goldfinger, the world's cleverest, cruelest criminal, teaches him useful lessons. Soon the game will change & the stakes will rise to 15 billion dollars worth of U. S. gold bullion reserves. But 007 knows that Goldfinger's rules remain brutally simple.

Casino Royale. unabr. ed. Ian Fleming. Read by Robert Whitfield. 1 CD. (Running Time: 5 hrs.). 2001. audio compact disk 19.95 (zm2616) Blckstn Audio.
At the Casino in Deauville, Bond's game is baccarat, for stakes that run into millions of francs. But away from the discreet salons, the caviar & champagne, it's 007 versus one of Russia's most powerful & ruthless agents & the prize is a bullet in the head from a S.M.E.R.S.H. assassin.

Casino Royale. unabr. ed. Ian Fleming. Read by Robert Whitfield. (Running Time: 18000 sec.). (James Bond Ser.). 2006. audio compact disk 24.95 (978-0-7861-9667-8(X), 2616) Blckstn Audio.

Casino Royale. unabr. movie tie-in ed. Ian Fleming. Read by Simon Vance. 4 CDs. (Running Time: 16200 sec.). (James Bond 007 (Blackstone) Ser.). 2006. audio compact disk 17.95 (978-0-7861-7283-2(5)) Blckstn Audio.

Cask of Amontillado see Invisible Man & Selected Short Stories of Edgar Allan Poe

Cask of Amontillado see Tales of Terror

Cask of Amontillado see Pit & the Pendulum

Cask of Amontillado see Best of Edgar Allan Poe

Cask of Amontillado see Edgar Allan Poe, Set, Short Stories and Poems

Cask of Amontillado see Tales of Horror & Suspense

Cask of Amontillado see Interlopers

Cask of Amontillado see Mind of Poe

Cask of Amontillado. 1 cass. (Running Time: 1 hr. 30 mins.). (SmartReader Ser.). (J). 1999. pap. bk. & tchr. ed. 19.95 (978-0-7887-2852-5(0), 79669T3) Recorded Bks.
Join Montresor & his friend as they celebrate the carnival season long ago. While they search in the cellar for a cask of wine called Amontillado, the happy evening turns into a time of fear & danger.

Cask of Amontillado. Edgar Allan Poe. 10.00 (LSS1102) Esstee Audios.

Cask of Amontillado. rev. ed. Edgar Allan Poe. Ed. by Don Kisner. Adapted by Dottie Havlik. (YA). (gr. 7 up). 1998. ring bd. 38.00 (978-1-878298-15-7(1)) Balance Pub.

Cask of Amontillado. unabr. ed. Edgar Allan Poe. 1 cass. (Running Time: 52 mins.). Dramatization. Incl. Conversation of Eiros & Charmion. 1977. (D-4); Fall of the House of Usher. 1977. (D-4); 1977. 7.95 (D-4) Jimcin Record.
Three of Poe's most famous stories dramatized by a cast of characters. It's Poe at his terrifying best.

Cask of Amontillado. unabr. ed. Edgar Allan Poe. Read by Arthur L. Klein. (Running Time: 50 mins.). 10.95 (978-0-8045-0978-7(6)) Spoken Arts.

Casl Intro Mngd Care Ppt. Ed. by Kaplan Publishing Staff. 2005. cass. & audio compact disk (978-1-4195-1942-0(5)) Dearborn Financial.

Casl Undrst Oldr Clnt Ppt. Ed. by Kaplan Publishing Staff. 2005. cass. & audio compact disk (978-1-4195-1989-5(1)) Dearborn Financial.

Casl Undrst Oldr Clnt Terms. Ed. by Kaplan Publishing Staff. 2005. cass. & audio compact disk (978-1-4195-1988-8(3)) Dearborn Financial.

Caso de Cristo Audio Libro CD/Case for Christ Audio. unabr. ed. Strobel Lee. (SPA.). 2008. audio compact disk 14.99 (978-0-8297-5184-0(X)) Pub: Vida Pubs. Dist(s): Zondervan

Caso de la fe audio Labor. unabr. ed. Read by Lee Strobel. (SPA.). 2009. audio compact disk 14.99 (978-0-8297-5240-3(4)) Pub: Vida Pubs. Dist(s): Zondervan

Caspar Weinberger: America's Defense Philosophy & Strategy. Narrated by Caspar W. Weinberger. 1 cass. (Running Time: 1 hr.). 9.00 (K0250B090, HarperThor) HarpC GBR.

Casper - A Spirited Beginning: The Soundtrack. Prod. by EMI-Capitol Entertainment Properties Staff & Saban Entertainment Staff. 1 cass. (J). (gr. 1 up). 1997. 6.43 (978-0-9659725-1-2(8)); audio compact disk 10.30 CD. (978-0-9659725-0-5(X)) EMI-Capitol.
From the original direct-to-video movie.

Caspian Sea: A Quest for Environmental Security: Proceedings of the NATO Advanced Research Workshop, Venice, Italy, March 15-19, 199. Ed. by William Ascher & Natalia Mirovitskaya. (NATO Science Ser.). 2000. 209.00 (978-0-7923-6218-0(7)) Pub: Springer Lond GBR. Dist(s): Spri

CASS Salud Financiera Audio Series: Mi Sistema Financiero. Walter Dominguez. 2006. pap. bk. (978-1-883955-43-4(2)) Penmarin Bks.

Cassandra Compact. Robert Ludlum & Philip Shelby. 9 cass. (Running Time: 13.5 hrs.). (Covert-One Ser.). 2001. 72.00 (978-0-7366-6841-5(1)) Books on Tape.

Cassandra Compact. Robert Ludlum & Philip Shelby. Narrated by George Guidall. 9 CDs. (Running Time: 11 hrs.). (Covert-One Ser.). audio compact disk 91.00 (978-0-7887-9848-1(0)) Recorded Bks.

Cassandra Compact. abr. ed. Robert Ludlum & Philip Shelby. Read by Frank Muller. (Running Time: 7 hrs. 0 mins. 0 sec.). (Covert-One Ser.). (ENG.). 2007. audio compact disk 14.95 (978-1-4272-0130-0(7)) Pub: Macmill Audio. Dist(s): Macmillan

Cassandra Compact. unabr. ed. Robert Ludlum & Philip Shelby. Narrated by George Guidall. 8 cass. (Running Time: 11 hrs.). (Covert-One Ser.). 2001. 71.00 (978-0-7887-7151-4(5), 96712K8) Recorded Bks.
As American intelligence officer, Jonathan Smith, tries to discover why his Russian colleague was assassinated, he uncovers plans for biochemical warfare that could change the face of the globe.

Cassandra's Angel - the Musical. Prod. by Gina Otto. (J). 2002. audio compact disk 16.99 (978-0-9740454-2-9(X)) Ginas Ink.

Casse Noisette. Anne Dorval. 1 cass. (Running Time: 30 min.). (FRE.). (YA). 2001. bk. 9.95 (978-2-89517-063-1(0)) Pub: Coffragants CAN. Dist(s): Penton Overseas

Casse-Noisette. Lucie Papineau. Illus. by Stéphane Jorisch. 1 cass., bklet. (Running Time: 50 mins.). (Best-Sellers Ser.).Tr. of Nutcracker. (FRE.). (J). (ps-2). 2000. cass. & audio compact disk 9.95 (978-2-921997-40-9(1), PS8581 A6658) Pub: Coffragants CAN. Dist(s): Penton Overseas

Cassell Concise Dictionary. 2nd ed. Lesley Brown. 1998. reel tape (978-0-304-35012-4(5), Burns and O) Contnmlntl Grp GBR.

Cassette. 2nd rev. ed. K. Frazier et al. (Let's Go Second Edition Ser.). 2000. 22.75 (978-0-19-436448-5(8)) OUP.

Cassette Bible. Narrated by Samuel Montoya. 160 cass. (Running Time: 160 hrs.). (SPA.). 238.40 (1303S) Chrstn Dup Intl.

Cassette Collection, 6. Raintree Steck-Vaughn Staff. (Pair it Books Ser.). 2002. (978-0-7398-6226-1(X)) SteckVau.

Cassette for Piano for Pleasure. 3rd ed. (C). 1998. 21.95 (978-0-534-54103-3(8)) Pub: Wadsworth Pub. Dist(s): CENGAGE Learn

Cassia Nomame: The Natural Lipase Inhibitor for Losing Weight Safely & Effectively. Rita Elkins. (Woodland Health Ser.). 2000. 4.95 (978-1-58054-080-3(5)) Pub: Woodland UT. Dist(s): Midpt Trade

Cassian: Disposition for Prayer. Thomas Merton. 1 cass. (Running Time: 60 mins.). (Origins of Prayer Ser.). 8.95 (978-7-900780-07-2(6), AA2068) Credence Commun.
Merton at his richest, sharing the best of monastic contemplation.

Cassian: Trials & Belief. Thomas Merton. 1 cass. (Running Time: 60 min.). (Origins of Prayer Ser.). 8.95 (AA2067) Credence Commun.
Merton at his richest, sharing the best of monastic contemplation.

Cassidy. unabr. ed. Lori Wick. Narrated by Jill Shellabarger. (Running Time: 8 hrs. 15 mins. 42 sec.). (Big Sky Dreams Ser.). (ENG.). 2008. 19.59 (978-1-60814-111-1(X)); audio compact disk 27.99 (978-1-59859-429-4(X)) Oasis Audio.

Cast a Long Shadow. unabr. ed. Wayne D. Overholser. Read by William Dufris. 4 cass. (Running Time: 5 hrs.). (Sagebrush Western Ser.). (J). 1999. 49.95 (978-1-57490-223-5(7)) Pub: ISIS Lrg Prnt GBR. Dist(s): Ulverscroft US

Cast All Your Cares. Speeches. Joel Osteen. 1 Cass. (Running Time: 30 Mins.). (J). 2000. 6.00 (978-1-59349-059-1(3), JA0059) J Osteen.

Cast, in Order of Disappearance. unabr. ed. Simon Brett. Narrated by Simon Prebble. 4 cass. (Running Time: 5 hrs. 45 mins.). (Charles Paris Mystery Ser.: Vol. 1). 1997. 35.00 (978-0-7887-0858-9(9), 94984E7) Recorded Bks.
An aging but urbane actor Charlie Paris, still manages to turn on enough charm to attract minor film roles & aspiring actresses. But some naughty photos are about to land Charlie & his current girlfriend on the cutting room floor.

Cast Not Away Your Confidence. Speeches. Joel Osteen. 1 cass. (Running Time: 30 Mins). 2000. 6.00 (978-1-59349-082-9(8), JA0082) J Osteen.

Cast of Characters: Common People in the Hands of an Uncommon God. unabr. ed. Max Lucado. Narrated by Roger Mueller. (Running Time: 6 hrs. 0 mins. 0 sec.). (ENG.). 2009. audio compact disk 25.99 (978-1-59859-568-0(7)) Oasis Audio.

Cast of Characters: Common People in the Hands of an Uncommon God. unabr. ed. Max Lucado. Narrated by Roger Mueller. (Running Time: 6 hrs. 0 mins. 0 sec.). (ENG.). 2009. 18.19 (978-1-60814-493-8(3)) Oasis Audio.

Cast of Smiles. Amanda Brookfield. Narrated by Briony Sykes. 5 cass. (Running Time: 7 hrs. 15 mins.). 47.00 (978-1-84197-271-8(1)) Recorded Bks.

Castaneda. (978-1-57453-539-6(0)) Mar Co Prods.

Castaneda & the New Society. unabr. ed. Stephan Hoeller. 1 cass. (Running Time: 90 min.). 1980. 11.00 (40010) Big Sur Tapes.
Speaks of the differences between truth seekers concerned with abstract truths, & the magical, fluid, illusive, mercurial world of the shaman, who is a transformer.

Castaways see Twentieth-Century Poetry in English, No. 10, Recordings of Poets Reading Their Own Poetry

***Castaways.** Brian Keene. (Running Time: 8 mins.). 2009. 19.95 (978-1-897331-24-8(X), AudioRealms); audio compact disk 33.95 (978-1-897304-70-9(6), AudioRealms) Dorch Pub Co.

Castaways. unabr. ed. Elin Hilderbrand. Read by Katie Hale. (Running Time: 13 hrs.). 2009. 19.98 (978-1-60024-623-4(0)) Pub: Hachet Audio. Dist(s): HachBkGrp

Castaways. unabr. ed. Elin Hilderbrand. Read by Katie Hale. (Running Time: 13 hrs.). 2010. audio compact disk 19.98 (978-1-60788-238-1(8)) Pub: Hachet Audio. Dist(s): HachBkGrp

Castaways. unabr. ed. Iain Lawrence. Narrated by John Keating. 6 cass. (Running Time: 6 hrs. 45 mins.). (YA). (gr. 6-9). 2008. 61.75 (978-1-4193-8292-5(6)); audio compact disk 66.75 (978-1-4193-8294-9(2)) Recorded Bks.

Castaways of the Flying Dutchman. Brian Jacques. 6 cass. (Running Time: 8 hrs. 30 mins.). (Castaways of the Flying Dutchman Ser.: No. 1). 62.00 (978-1-4025-1589-7(8)) Recorded Bks.

Castaways of the Flying Dutchman. Brian Jacques & Brian Jacques. 5 cass. (Running Time: 8 hrs. 15 mins.). (Castaways of the Flying Dutchman Ser.: No. 1). 2004. 24.99 (978-1-4025-0521-8(3), 00854) Recorded Bks.

CAS/Temple of Shamanic Witchcr. Christo Penczak. (Penczak Temple Ser.). 2005. DVD & audio compact disk 26.95 (978-0-7387-0768-6(6)) Llewellyn Pubns.

Casting Crowns, Volume 1. Contrib. by Casting Crowns. (Mastertrax Premium Collection). 2007. audio compact disk 14.98 (978-5-557-60313-3(1)) Beach St.

Casting down Strongholds. Derek Prince. 1 cass. (Running Time: 1 hr.). 1991. 5.95 (I-4326) Derek Prince.
Why is there spiritual warfare? Who is fighting whom? Which side are we on? Learn how to arm yourself to gain victory over Satan's kingdom.

Casting Her Own Shadow: Eleanor Roosevelt & the Shaping of Postwar Liberalism. unabr. collector's ed. Allida M. Black. Read by Kimberly Schraf. 7 cass. (Running Time: 10 hrs. 30 mins.). 1996. 56.00 (978-0-7366-3384-0(7), 4034) Books on Tape.
During her years in the White House, Eleanor Roosevelt made great changes in the role of First Lady. But her life post-FDR made her earlier times look calm & contemplative by comparison.

Casting Lots. Perf. by Casting Lots. Prod. by Randy Ray. 1 CD. (Running Time: 1 hr.). 1997. audio compact disk 14.98 (978-1-57919-108-5(8)) Randolf Prod.

Casting Lots. Perf. by Casting Lots & Randy Ray. Prod. by Randy Ray. 1 cass. (Running Time: 1 hr.). 1997. 10.98 (978-1-57919-106-1(1)) Randolf Prod.

Casting Off. Elizabeth Jane Howard. 4 cass. (Running Time: 6 hrs.). (ENG., 2001. (978-0-333-67561-8(4)) Macmillan UK GBR.

Casting Off. unabr. ed. Nicole Dickson. Read by Emily Durante. (Running Time: 11 hrs.). 2009. 24.99 (978-1-4233-9764-9(9), 9781423397649, Brilliance MP3); 24.99 (978-1-4233-9766-3(5), 9781423397663, BAD); 39.97 (978-1-4233-9765-6(7), 9781423397656, Brlnc Audio MP3 Lib); 39.97 (978-1-4233-9767-0(3), 9781423397670, BADLE); audio compact disk 29.99 (978-1-4233-9762-5(2), 9781423397625, Bril Audio CD Unabri); audio compact disk 89.97 (978-1-4233-9763-2(0), 9781423397632, BriAudCD Unabrid) Brilliance Audio.

Casting Off. unabr. collector's ed. Elizabeth Jane Howard. Read by Donada Peters. 12 cass. (Running Time: 18 hrs.). (Cazalet Chronicles: Vol. 4). 1997. 96.00 (978-0-7366-4023-7(1), 4521) Books on Tape.
Fourth & final volume of the Cazalet Chronicle. It is July 1945, VE Day is behind, Japan has yet to surrender. Polly, Clary & Louise, girls on the brink of adolescence when the chronicle began in 1937, are now grown up. Painfully, they've discovered those things that adults never seemed to talk about, sexual passion, loneliness & loss. Rupert Cazalet, missing in France for several years, returns to find his wife, Zoe, curiously withdrawn. Still contriving to juggle a wife & a mistress, Edward will be forced to choose between them, while Hugh, estranged from Edward after discovering his duplicity, must finally come to terms with sybil's death & what of Archie Lestrange? Drawn to the center of the Cazalets' untidy circle, he decides escape may be the only means of survival.

Casting the First Stone. Kimberla Lawson Roby. Narrated by Caroline S. Clay. 8 cass. (Running Time: 11 hrs.). (Reverend Curtis Black Ser.: Bk. 1). 76.00 (978-0-7887-5311-4(8)) Recorded Bks.

Casting Your Cares upon the Lord. Kenneth E. Hagin. 3 cass. (Running Time: 3 hrs.). 1994. 12.00 (72H) Faith Lib Pubns.

Casting Your Cares upon the Lord. Lynne Hammond. 1 cass. (Running Time: 1 hr.). 2005. 5.00 (978-1-57399-213-8(5)); audio compact disk 5.00 (978-1-57399-273-2(9)) Mac Hammond.

Castings see Lola Haskins & Pattiann Rogers

Castle. unabr. ed. Franz Kafka. Read by Geoffrey Howard. Tr. by Mark Harman. 8 cass. (Running Time: 11 hrs. 30 mins.). 1998. 56.95 (978-0-7861-1424-5(X), 2300) Blckstn Audio.
The haunting tale of a man known only as K. & of his relentless, unavailing struggle with an inscrutable authority in order to gain entrance to the Castle. This new edition of the terrifying & comic masterpiece is the product of an international team of experts who returned to Kafka's original manuscript & notes to create a text that is as close as possible to the way the author left it.

Castle. unabr. ed. Franz Kafka. Read by Geoffrey Howard. Tr. by Mark Harman. 9 CDs. (Running Time: 12 hrs.). 2000. audio compact disk 72.00 (z2300) Blckstn Audio.

Castle. unabr. ed. Franz Kafka. Read by Geoffrey Howard. Tr. by Mark Harman. 9 CDs. (Running Time: 11 hrs. 30 mins.). 2002. audio compact disk 72.00 (978-0-7861-9878-8(8), 2300) Blckstn Audio.

Castle. unabr. ed. Franz Kafka. Read by Geoffrey Howard. (Running Time: 11 hrs. 0 mins.). 2008. audio compact disk & audio compact disk 19.95 (978-1-4332-4645-6(7)) Blckstn Audio.

Castle. unabr. ed. Franz Kafka. Tr. by Mark Harman. Narrated by George Guidall. 9 cass. (Running Time: 12 hrs.). 2000. 81.00 (978-0-7887-4929-2(3), 95762E7) Recorded Bks.
A man known only as K. faces increasingly frustrating setbacks while trying to meet face to face with an official from the Castle, but when K. arrives tin town to claim his position, he learns that owing to a clerical error his services aren't needed after all. Seeking an explanation, K. endures increasingly frustrating setbacks as he strives in vain to simply make contacts with someone - anyone - from the Castle.

Castle Corona. Sharon Creech. Read by Jennifer Wiltsie. 5 cass. (Running Time: 6 hrs.). (J). (gr. 3-6). 2007. 41.75 (978-1-4281-7166-4(5)) Recorded Bks.

***Castle Corona.** unabr. ed. Sharon Creech. Read by Jennifer Wiltsie. (ENG.). 2007. (978-0-06-155463-6(4)); (978-0-06-155464-3(2)) HarperCollins Pubs.

Castle Corona. unabr. ed. Sharon Creech. Read by Jennifer Wiltsie. 4 CDs. (Running Time: 5 hrs.). (J). (gr. 3-7). 2007. audio compact disk 22.95 (978-0-06-135533-2(X), HarperChildAud) HarperCollins Pubs.

Castle Corona. unabr. ed. Sharon Creech. Read by Jennifer Wiltsie. 5 CDs. (Running Time: 6 hrs.). (J). (gr. 3-6). 2007. audio compact disk 51.75 (978-1-4281-7171-8(1)) Recorded Bks.

Castle Craggs. unabr. ed. Virginia Maas. Read by Kelly Faulkner. 6 cass. (Running Time: 6 hrs.). 2001. 39.95 (978-1-55686-855-9(3)) Books in Motion.
At the turn of the century, young Irene Kendee finds that a stranger is passing herself off as the heiress to Irene's castle and business fortune. While fighting for her place, she falls in love.

***Castle in the Air.** unabr. ed. Diana Wynne Jones. Narrated by Jenny Sterlin. 1 Playaway. (Running Time: 8 hrs.). (YA). (gr. 6 up). 2009. 59.75 (978-1-4407-2773-3(2)); 56.75 (978-1-4361-6113-8(4)); audio compact disk 77.75 (978-1-4361-6118-3(5)) Recorded Bks.

Castle in the Attic. Elizabeth Winthrop. Read by Elizabeth Winthrop. 2 cass. (Running Time: 2 hrs. 20 mins.). (J). 2000. 18.00 (978-0-7366-9111-6(1)) Books on Tape.
Now that ten-year-old William's beloved nanny is returning to England, she entrusts him with a mysterious model castle. When the tiny silver knight magically springs to life, he takes William on a fantastical quest to another land & time.

Castle in the Attic. unabr. ed. Elizabeth Winthrop. 2 cass. (Running Time: 2 hrs.). (YA). 1999. 16.98 (FS9-31421) Highsmith.

Castle in the Attic. unabr. ed. Elizabeth Winthrop. Read by Elizabeth Winthrop. Read by Words Take Wing Repertory Company Staff. 2 vols. (Running Time: 3 hrs. 30 mins.). Dramatization. (J). (gr. 3-7). 1996. pap. bk. 29.00 (978-0-8072-7629-7(4), YA904SP, Listening Lib); 23.00 (978-0-8072-7628-0(6), YA904CX, Listening Lib) Random Audio Pubg.
The model castle William has been given is the most authentic he's ever seen - right down to the tiny knight who stands guard out front. When the nobleman magically springs to life he takes William on a mystical journey.

Castle in the Attic. unabr. ed. Elizabeth Winthrop. Read by Elizabeth Winthrop. Read by Full Cast Production Staff. 3 CDs. (Running Time: 3 hrs. 30 mins.). (ENG.). (J). (gr. 3). 2005. audio compact disk 14.99 (978-1-4000-9912-2(9), Listening Lib) Pub: Random Audio Pubg. Dist(s): Random

Castle in the Forest. unabr. ed. Norman Mailer. Read by Harris Yulin. (Running Time: 17 hrs. 30 mins. 0 sec.). (ENG.). 2008. audio compact disk 21.99 (978-0-7435-8167-7(9)) Pub: S&S Audio. Dist(s): S and S Inc

Castle in the Forest: A Novel. unabr. ed. Norman Mailer. Read by Harris Yulin. 15 cass. (Running Time: 16 hrs.). 2007. 113.75 (978-1-4281-4679-2(2)); audio compact disk 12.75 (978-1-4281-4681-5(4)) Recorded Bks.
A devil serving in Satan's bureaucracy - the very one assigned to nurture the young Hitler's perverse inclinations - sets out on a daring task: The rank-and-file devil will risk the Evil One's wrath by setting to paper an account of Hitler's birth and early childhood. Through the devil's eyes, Hitler as a boy displays impulses toward the murder campaign he will later orchestrate and proves a frightening, mind-boggling portrait of evil. Mailer's fictional treatment of an almost inconceivable passage in world history is as daring as it is provocative.

Castle of Inside Out. unabr. ed. David Henry Wilson. Read by Clive Mantle. 2 CDs. (Running Time: 9600 sec.). (J). (gr. 4-7). 2002. audio compact disk 21.95 (978-0-7540-6550-0(2), CHCD 050) AudioGO.

Castle of Llyr. Lloyd Alexander. Read by James Langdon. 3 vols. (Running Time: 5 hrs. 15 mins.). (Chronicles of Prydain Ser.: Bk. 3). (J). (gr. 4-7). 2004. pap. bk. 36.00 (978-1-4000-9019-8(9), Listening Lib); 29.75 (978-0-8072-2391-8(3), Listening Lib) Pub: Random Audio Pubg. Dist(s): NetLibrary CO

Castle of Otranto. Horace Walpole. Read by Anais 9000. 2008. 27.95 (978-1-60112-202-5(0)) Babblebooks.

Castle of Otranto: A Gothic Story. Horace Walpole. Read by Tony Jay. (Running Time: 14400 sec.). 2006. 24.95 (978-0-7861-4588-1(9)); audio compact disk 36.00 (978-0-7861-7025-8(5)) Blckstn Audio.

Castle of Otranto: A Gothic Story. Horace Walpole. Read by Neville Jason. (Running Time: 2 hrs. 30 mins.). 2001. 20.95 (978-1-60083-696-1(8)) Iofy Corp.

Castle of Otranto: A Gothic Story. abr. ed. Horace Walpole. Read by Neville Jason. 2 cass. (Running Time: 2 hrs. 30 mins.). 1995. 13.98 (978-962-634-534-4(9), NA203414, Naxos AudioBooks) Naxos.
Written in 1764, it's ghosts, skeletons, wild landscapes and supernatural horrors shocked the audience of the day and inspired all gothic literature which followed. Story of a buried secret and a dreadful revelation, in which a ghost seeks justice.

Castle of Otranto: A Gothic Story. abr. ed. Horace Walpole. Read by Neville Jason. 3 CDs. (Running Time: 9211 sec.). (Classic Literature with Classical Music Ser.). 2006. audio compact disk 17.98 (978-962-634-379-1(6), Naxos AudioBooks) Naxos.

Castle of Otranto: A Gothic Story. unabr. ed. Horace Walpole. Read by Tony Jay. (Running Time: 14400 sec.). 2006. audio compact disk 19.95 (978-0-7861-7515-4(X)) Blckstn Audio.

Castle of Otranto: A Gothic Story. unabr. ed. Horace Walpole. 3 cass. (Running Time: 3 hrs.). 1996. 34.95 (978-1-86015-433-1(6)) Pub: UlverLrgPrint GBR. Dist(s): Ulverscroft US
The action in the Castle of Otranto is set against the murky background of gothic battlements where enchanted helmets & swords fall as the villain rants & raves. The heroine escapes his clutches through a musty trapdoor into a chill underground cavern & is helped by a mysterious hero of strange origin & a friar who is not all he seems.

Castle of Personality. unabr. ed. Barbara D. DeVault. Read by Barbara D. DeVault. 1 cass. (Running Time: 1 hr.). (J). 1997. 9.95 (978-1-891536-06-9(0), P1705C) DeVault Ents.

Castle of Personality, Vol. P-1705. unabr. ed. Barbara D. DeVault. Read by Barbara D. DeVault. 1 cass. (Running Time: 1 hr.). (J). (gr. 1-6). 1997. pap. bk. 12.99 (978-1-891536-02-1(8), BD9197A) DeVault Ents.

Castle of the Carpathians. unabr. ed. Jules Verne. Read by Patrick Treadway. 4 cass. (Running Time: 5 hrs. 30 mins.). Dramatization. 1990. 26.95 (978-1-55686-352-3(7), 352) Books in Motion.
Mysterious entities take possession of a long-deserted castle creating fear among the residents of the adjacent village of Werst, in Transylvania.

Castle of the King see Classic Ghost Stories, Vol. 3, A Collection

Castle on the Hill. unabr. collector's ed. Elizabeth Goudge. Read by Wanda McCaddon. 15 cass. (Running Time: 15 hrs.). 1983. 90.00 (978-0-7366-0766-7(8), 1723) Books on Tape.
It is the summer of 1940 & England is fighting for her life. In a rural corner of England the war brings together a disparate group of people wrestling the enemy within fear, despair, cynicism & loss of faith.

Castle Rackrent. Maria Edgeworth. Read by Anais 9000. 2008. 27.95 (978-1-60112-164-6(4)) Babblebooks.

Castle Richmond. Anthony Trollope. Read by Anais 9000. 1 DVD. (Running Time: 19.4 hours). 2006. 19.95 (978-1-60112-001-4(X)) Babblebooks.

Castle Richmond, unabr. ed. Anthony Trollope. Read by Flo Gibson. 12 cass. (Running Time: 18 hrs.). 1997. 39.95 (978-1-55685-489-7(7), 489-7) Audio Bk Con.
The tragedy of the potato famine in Ireland, bigamy, changing fortunes & two cousins courting Lady Clara Desmond make this a fascinating multi-layered tale.

Castlemaine Murders. Kerry Greenwood. Read by Stephanie Daniel. (Running Time: 8 hrs. 15 mins.). (Phryne Fisher Mystery: Ser.). 2009. 74.99 (978-1-74214-233-3(8), 9781742142333) Pub: Bolinda Pubng AUS. Dist(s): Bolinda Pub Inc

Castlemaine Murders. unabr. ed. Kerry Greenwood. Read by Stephanie Daniel. (Running Time: 29700 sec.). (Phryne Fisher Ser.). 2006. audio compact disk 83.95 (978-1-74093-790-0(2)) Pub: Bolinda Pubng AUS. Dist(s): Bolinda Pub Inc

Castles: Towers, Dungeons, Moats, & More. Matt White. (High Five Reading Ser.). (ENG.). (gr. 4 up). 2002. audio compact disk 5.95 (978-0-7368-9560-6(4)) CapstoneDig.

Castles: Towers, Dungeons, Moats, & More. Matt White. (High Five Reading - Red Ser.). (ENG.). (gr. 2-3). 2007. audio compact disk 5.95 (978-1-4296-1414-6(5)) CapstoneDig.

Castles in the Sand. abr. ed. Janet Dailey. Read by Erin Leigh. 1 cass. (Running Time: 90 mins.). 1996. 6.99 (978-1-57096-043-7(7), RAZ 944) Romance Alive Audio.
Childhood sweethearts Bridget O'Dwyer & Reese Sullivan grew up together on the Sand Castle Pier, but tragedy & misunderstandings conspired to separate them. Years later, with the pier now in disrepair, they are brought together once more for a chance to mend the pier - & their broken hearts.

Castles, Knights & Unicorns: Action Songs for Fantasy & Fun. 1 cass. (Running Time: 40 min.). (J). (ps-2). 2001. pap. bk. & tchr. ed. 10.95 (KIM91620) Kimbo Educ.
Songs by Ronno about castles, princes, princesses, dragons and more.

Castles, Knights & Unicorns: Action Songs for Fantasy & Fun. Ronno. 1 CD. (Running Time: 40 min.). (J). (ps-2). 2001. pap. bk. & tchr. ed. 14.95 (KIM9162CD) Kimbo Educ.
Songs by Ronno about castles, princes, princesses, dragons and more.

Castles Made of Sand: The Jimi Hendrix Story. Geoffrey Giuliano. 2009. (978-1-60136-164-6(5)) Audio Holding.

Castles of Athlin & Dunbayne. Ann Radcliffe. Read by Anais 9000. 2009. 27.95 (978-1-60112-215-5(2)) Babblebooks.

Castration of Harry Bluethorn. Short Stories. R. V. Cassill. Read by R. V. Cassill. 1 cass. (Running Time: 36 mins.). 13.95 (978-1-55644-001-4(4), 1011) Am Audio Prose.

Castro & Cuba. 1 cass. (Running Time: 3 hrs.). 10.00 (HE818) Esstee Audios.
A visitor's view of what is going on in Fidel's island. Is the real revolution working?.

Castro's Curveball. Tim Wendel. Read by Tom Parker. 5 cass. (Running Time: 7 hrs. 30 mins.). 1999. 27.95 (978-0-7861-1700-0(1)) Pub: Blckstn Audio. Dist(s): Penton Overseas
Captures the passion of baseball & the vibrant flavor of Cuba.

Castro's Curveball, unabr. ed. Tim Wendel. Read by Tom Parker. 6 cass. (Running Time: 8 hrs. 30 mins.). 1999. 44.95 (978-0-7861-1553-2(X), 2383) Blckstn Audio.
The passion of baseball & the vibrant flavor of Cuba.

Castro's Curveball. unabr. ed. Tim Wendel. Read by Tom Parker. 7 CDs. (Running Time: 8 hrs. 30 mins.). 2000. audio compact disk 56.00 (978-0-7861-9938-9(5), 2383) Blckstn Audio.

***Castro's Curveball.** unabr. ed. Tim Wendel. Read by Tom Parker. (Running Time: 8 hrs. 0 mins.). 2010. 29.95 (978-1-4417-5561-2(6)) Blckstn Audio.

Castro's Curveball. unabr. ed. Tim Wendel. Narrated by L. J. Ganser. 6 cass. (Running Time: 8 hrs.). 2001. 57.00 (978-0-7887-4063-3(6), 96011x7) Recorded Bks.
In 1947, catcher Billy Bryan breaks up a political protest at his Cuban winter league game by asking a skinny student revolutionary named Fidel Castro to throw him a couple of pitches. To Billy's surprise, the kid has good stuff: a decent fastball & an unhittable curve. Soon, Billy is in the middle of a strange tangle of people, including revolutionaries, mobsters, major league scouts & a beguiling photographer, whose interests in the young Castro go far beyond his pitching abilities. The author skillfully mixes his pitches in a story that keeps listeners guessing until the final at-bat.

***Castrovalva.** unabr. novel ed. Christopher H. Bidmead. Narrated by Peter Davison. (Running Time: 4 hrs. 0 mins. 0 sec.). (Doctor Who Ser.). (ENG.). 2010. audio compact disk 34.95 (978-1-4084-2697-5(8)) Pub: AudioGO. Dist(s): Perseus Dist

Casual Rex: A Detective Story. abr. ed. Eric Garcia. 4 cass. (Running Time: 6 hrs.). 2001. 24.95 (978-1-57511-088-2(1)) Pub Mills.
Detective Vincent Rubio & his partner, Ernie, manage to maintain their anonymity thanks to special latex costumes that allow them to pass for humans. But many of their dinosaur brethren are tired of fitting in & have formed a back-to-basics cult - whose members are mysteriously dying.

Cat. Dorling Kindersley Publishing Staff. (Eyewitness Videos Ser.). (ENG.). (J). 2010. 12.99 (978-0-7566-6298-1(2)) DK Pub Inc.

Cat. unabr. ed. Freya North. Narrated by Phoebe James. 11 cass. (Running Time: 15 hrs. 30 mins.). 2000. 98.00 (978-1-84197-225-1(8), H1198L8) Recorded Bks.
Cat McCabe is a budding sports journalist who's been offered a chance of a lifetime - to cover the Tour de France for the Guardian. But, recently dumped by her boyfriend, she's feeling a little on the fragile side & lacking confidence. How will she survive the testosterone-fuelled cycling race?.

Cat. unabr. ed. Freya North. Narrated by Phoebe James. 13 CDs. (Running Time: 15 hrs. 30 mins.). 2001. audio compact disk 134.00 (978-1-4025-1017-5(9), C1595) Recorded Bks.
Cat McCabe is a budding sports journalist who's just been offered the chance of a lifetime, to cover the Tour de France for the Guardian. But, recently dumped by her boyfriend, she's feeling a little on the fragile side and lacking confidence. How will she survive the testosterone-fuelled cycling race? Will she succumb to the muscular thighs of the cyclists, and they to her English gorgeousness? Will her Ex show up? How will she survive as one of only a handful of women in the 1000 strong press corps? Set against the backdrop of the French countryside, with sex, drugs, lycra, large bulges and even larger egos, the Tour de France unfolds, with McCabe's life mirroring the peaks, perils and pace of the race.

Cat. unabr. collector's ed. Georges Simenon. Read by Michael Prichard. 5 cass. (Running Time: 5 hrs.). 1984. 30.00 (978-0-7366-0542-7(8), 1516) Books on Tape.
Why are Emile & Marguerite Bouin still married? They cannot stand each other which is evident when we meet them. Their only correspondence is an occasional invective jotted on a scrap of paper - this discreetly flicked across the room to the recipient's lap. Simenon makes hate almost as alluring as love.

Cat Abroad, unabr. ed. Peter Gethers. Narrated by David Laundra. 5 cass. (Running Time: 7 hrs. 30 mins.). 1994. 44.00 (978-1-55690-966-5(7), 94109E7) Recorded Bks.
From the author of "The Cat Who Went to Paris," comes another true-life adventure featuring the author & his Scottish Fold feline, Norton, seasoned world-traveler & renowned ice cream critic. Whether it is the trademark flattened ears of his breed or the personality quirks individual to Norton, this cat has an uncanny knack for attracting celebrity attention.

Cat among the Pigeons. unabr. ed. Agatha Christie. Narrated by Hugh Fraser. 6 CDs. (Running Time: 7 hrs.). (Hercule Poirot Mystery Ser.). (ENG.). 2008. audio compact disk 29.95 (978-1-60283-346-3(X)) Pub: AudioGO. Dist(s): Perseus Dist

Cat & Canary. 2004. cass. & flmstrp 30.00 (978-0-89719-570-6(1)); 8.95 (978-1-56008-391-7(3)) Weston Woods.
Cat's unlikely friend Canary shows him the greatest time when his master is away at work. You'll never look at your cat the same way again.

Cat & Mouse see Istwa Chat ak Sourit

Cat & Mouse. abr. ed. James Patterson. Read by Anthony Heald & Keith David. (Running Time: 6 hrs.). No. 4. (ENG.). 2007. audio compact disk 17.98 (978-1-60024-128-4(X)) Pub: GrandCentral. Dist(s): HachBkGrp

Cat & Mouse. abr. ed. James Patterson. (Alex Cross Ser.: No. 4). 1999. (978-1-57042-737-4(2)) Hachet Audio.
Two killers, one operating in America-one in Europe-believe Alex Cross is the only worthy opponent in the deadly game each has planned. Villian Gary Soneji is back. He vows his last act on earth will be taking the life of Alex Cross. But first he wants some fun, and Union Station, Washington, and Penn Station in New York are scenes of chaos as Soneji creates a train ride to hell.

Cat & Mouse. abr. ed. James Patterson. (Running Time: 4 hrs.). (Alex Cross Ser.: No. 4). (ENG.). 2006. 14.98 (978-1-59483-696-1(5)) Pub: Hachet Audio. Dist(s): HachBkGrp

Cat & Mouse. unabr. ed. James Patterson. Read by Michael Kramer. 7 cass. (Running Time: 10 hrs. 30 min.). (Alex Cross Ser.: No. 4). 1998. 56.00 (978-0-7366-4138-8(6), 4643) Books on Tape.
Alex Cross, psychologist, single father, homicide detective, returns to face two serial killers & his family is targeted for vengeance.

Cat & Mouse, unabr. ed. James Patterson. Narrated by Richard Ferrone & George Guidall. 8 cass. (Running Time: 10 hrs. 30 mins.). (Alex Cross Ser.: No. 4). 1998. 70.00 (978-0-7887-2022-2(8), 95395E7) Recorded Bks.
Two psychotic killers have chosen Detective Alex Cross as their worthy opponent in a deadly game of cat and mouse.

Cat & Mouse. unabr. ed. James Patterson. Narrated by Richard Ferrone & George Guidall. 9 CDs. (Running Time: 10 hrs. 30 mins.). (Alex Cross Ser.: No. 4). 1999. audio compact disk 69.00 (978-0-7887-3411-3(3), C1017E7) Recorded Bks.

Cat & Mouse: A Delicious Tale. Jiwon Oh. Narrated by Carine Montbertrand. (Running Time: 15 mins.). (J). 2003. audio compact disk 12.75 (978-1-4193-1757-6(1)) Recorded Bks.

Cat & the Collector. 2004. 8.95 (978-1-56008-862-2(1)); cass. & flmstrp 30.00 (978-0-89719-668-0(6)) Weston Woods.

Cat & the Curmudgeon: Polar Bear Strikes Back. abr. ed. Cleveland Amory. Read by Cleveland Amory. 1 cass. (Running Time: 60 min.). (J). (gr. 3 up). 1990. 17.95 Little.
Sequel to The Cat Who Came for Christmas.

Cat & the Moon see Poetry of William Butler Yeats

Cat & the Moon see Five One Act Plays

Cat Ate My Gymsuit. abr. ed. Paula Danziger. Read by Paula Danziger. 1 cass. (Running Time: 90 mins.). (J). 1984. 9.95 (978-1-55994-048-1(4), CP 1745) HarperCollins Pubs.
Marcy Lewis is bored by school & despairs of ever being thin. Her life changes after she meets her vital & very human teacher Ms. Finney.

Cat Ate My Gymsuit. unabr. ed. Paula Danziger. 1 read-along cass. (Running Time: 56 mins.). (Young Adult Cliffhangers Ser.). (J). (gr. 3-5). 1985. pap. bk. 15.98 guide. (978-0-8072-1826-6(X), JRH113SP, Listening Lib) Random Audio Pubg.
Life for Marcy Lewis begins to have a purpose when Ms. Finney, a remarkable English teacher, comes along. Suddenly her weight problem, her social life & her relationship with her parents seem more bearable.

Cat Ate My Gymsuit. unabr. ed. Paula Danziger. Read by Caitlin Brodnick. 2 cass. (Running Time: 2 hrs, 46 mins). (YA). (gr. 12 up). 2005. (978-1-932076-55-4(7)) Full Cast Audio.

Cat Ate My Gymsuit. unabr. ed. Paula Danziger. Read by Full Cast Production Staff. (J). 2006. 44.99 (978-1-59895-621-4(3)) Find a World.

Cat Breaking Free. Shirley Rousseau Murphy. Read by William Dufris. 7 cass. (Joe Grey Mystery Ser.). 59.95 (978-0-7927-3810-7(1), CSL 871) AudioGO.

Cat Breaking Free. unabr. ed. Shirley Rousseau Murphy. Read by William Dufris. 9 CDs. (Joe Grey Mystery Ser.). 2005. audio compact disk 89.95 (978-0-7927-3811-4(X), Chivers Sound Lib) AudioGO.
The feline P.I. in his audio debut and 11th caper by the Cat Writer's Association Award-winning Murphy.

Cat Burglar on the Prowl, unabr. ed. Peg Kehret. Narrated by Carine Montbertrand. 2 cass. (Running Time: 2 hrs. 30 mins.). (Frightmares Ser.: No. 1). (gr. 5 up). 1996. 19.00 (978-0-7887-0530-4(X), 94725E7) Recorded Bks.
The adventures of sixth-graders Kayo Benton & Rosie Saunders put them in spooky dilemmas, usually in the company of a furry pet or two.

Cat by Any Other Name. unabr. collector's ed. Lydia Adamson. Read by Anna Fields. 5 cass. (Running Time: 5 hrs.). (Alice Nestleton Ser.). 1997. 30.00 (978-0-7366-3597-4(1), 4248) Books on Tape.
Alice Nestleton attends a Manhattan garden party & a guest falls twenty-five floors to her death.

Cat Came Back. Perf. by Fred Penner. 1 cass. (J). (ps-5). 10.98 (978-0-945267-60-7(6), YM088-CN); audio compact disk 13.98 (978-0-945267-61-4(4), YM088-CD) Youngheart Mus.
Songs include: The Cat Came Back"; "I Had a Rooster"; "Sandwiches"; "Bob King"; "Winken, Blinken & Nod"; "John Russel Watkins"; "Teagan's Lullaby"; "Ghost Riders in the Sky"; "It Ain't Gonna Rain"; "Little White Duck"; & "The Story of Blunder.".

Cat Came Back: Mike Anderson "Live" unabr. ed. Perf. by Mike Anderson. 1 cass. (Running Time: 40 mins.). (J). (gr. k-6). 1984. 10.00 (978-1-929050-02-4(X)) MW Prods.
A collection of children's songs.

Cat Caterpillar & the Polliwog, the; Wilfred Gordon Gordon Mcdonald Partridge, Joey Runs Away. 2004. (978-1-56008-823-3(0)) Weston Woods.

Cat Caterpillar & the Polliwog, the; Wilfred Gordon Mcdonald Partridge; Joey Runs Away. 2004. cass. & flmstrp (978-0-89719-760-1(7)) Weston Woods.

***Cat Chaser.** unabr. ed. Elmore Leonard. Read by Frank Muller. (ENG.). 2010. (978-0-06-199375-6(1), Harper Audio); (978-0-06-206267-3(0), Harper Audio) HarperCollins Pubs.

Cat Chaser. unabr. ed. Elmore Leonard. Narrated by Frank Muller. 7 CDs. (Running Time: 7.75 hrs.). audio compact disk 34.95 (978-1-4025-3715-8(8)) Recorded Bks.

Cat Chaser. unabr. ed. Elmore Leonard. Read by Frank Muller. 5 Cass. (Running Time: 7.75 Hrs.). 24.95 (978-1-4025-3714-1(X)) Recorded Bks.

Cat Chaser. unabr. ed. Elmore Leonard. Narrated by Frank Muller. 6 cass. (Running Time: 7 hrs. 45 mins.). 1995. 51.00 (978-0-7887-0256-3(4), 94465E7) Recorded Bks.
When ex-leatherneck, George Moran falls in love with the wife of a Miami millionaire, he drops square in the middle of a dangerous con more deadly than sniper fire.

Cat Chaser. unabr. collector's ed. Elmore Leonard. Read by Alexander Adams. 8 cass. (Running Time: 8 hrs.). 1995. 48.00 (978-0-7366-3117-4(8), 3793) Books on Tape.
American wife of an exiled Dominican general. After visiting the Dominican Republic, he gets caught in a crossfire between con-men, private eyes & the General. Can he get out of this alive?.

Cat Chat Vol. 2: Jesus in My Heart. 2004. audio compact disk 13.95 (978-1-932631-96-8(8)) Ascensn Pr.

Cat Chat Vol. 3: Amazing Angels & Saints. 2004. 9.99 (978-1-932631-97-5(6)); audio compact disk 13.95 (978-1-932631-98-2(4)) Ascensn Pr.

Cat Chat - Christmas. Gerald MontPetit. 2005. audio compact disk 13.95 (978-1-932927-55-9(7)) Ascensn Pr.

Cat Chat - Volume #4: The Mass Comes Alive. Gerald MontPetit. 2005. 9.95 (978-1-932927-33-7(6)) Ascensn Pr.

Cat Chat - Volume #4: The Mass Comes Alive. Gerald Montpetit. 2005. audio compact disk 13.95 (978-1-932927-34-4(4)) Ascensn Pr.

Cat Chat (AC) Vol. 1: Mary Leads me Closer to Jesus. 2004. 9.95 (978-1-932631-93-7(3)) Ascensn Pr.

Cat Chat (CD) Vol. 1: Jesus in My Heart. 2004. 13.95 (978-1-932631-94-4(1)) Ascensn Pr.

Cat Chat 2 (AC) Jesus in My Heart. 2004. 9.99 (978-1-932631-95-1(X)) Ascensn Pr.

Cat Chat #6. 2006. audio compact disk 13.95 (978-1-932927-69-6(7)) Ascensn Pr.

Cat Dance. Harriet R. Ackert. 1 read along cass. (Running Time: 20 min.). 2000. pap. bk. 8.95 (978-1-58519-090-4(X)) BkOnDisc.

Cat Dancers. abr. ed. P. T. Deutermann. Read by Dick Hill. 5 CDs. (Running Time: 21600 sec.). 2006. audio compact disk 16.99 (978-1-59737-354-8(0), 9781597373548, BCD Value Price) Brilliance Audio.
Please enter a Synopsis.

Cat Dancers. abr. unabr. ed. P. T. Deutermann. Read by Dick Hill. (Running Time: 54000 sec.). 2005. audio compact disk 97.25 (978-1-59600-070-4(8), 9781596000704, BACDLib Ed) Brilliance Audio.

Cat Dancers. unabr. ed. P. T. Deutermann. Read by Dick Hill. (Running Time: 15 hrs.). 2005. 39.25 (978-1-59710-125-7(7), 9781597101257, BADLE); 24.95 (978-1-59710-124-0(9), 9781597101240, BAD); 97.25 (978-1-59600-067-4(8), 9781596000674, BrilAudUnabridg); audio compact disk 24.95 (978-1-59335-790-0(7), 9781593357900, Brilliance MP3); audio compact disk 39.25 (978-1-59335-924-9(1), 9781593359249, Brinc Audio MP3 Lib); audio compact disk 39.95 (978-1-4233-0616-0(3), 9781423306160, Bril Audio CD Unabri) Brilliance Audio.
When two lowlifes rob a gas station, murder the attendant, and then incinerate bystanders who are filling up their minivan, the Manceford County, North Carolina, police quickly arrest the killers at a nearby motel. But a stubborn judge throws out the case because the suspects were not read their rights, leaving Sheriff Bobby Lee Baggett and Lieutenant Cam Richter to face the anger of the victims' families. Soon thereafter, a mysterious e-mail arrives in the department: a link to a video of one of the murderers being executed in a homemade electric chair, ending with a voice announcing, "That's one." The shocking video spreads throughout the Internet, drawing the attention of local, state, and federal authorities and national media, and putting intense pressure on Bobby Lee and Cam to find the vigilante before he claims his second victim. Assigned to head the search, Cam finds himself resented by some of his fellow officers and subtly threatened by others. His job is further complicated by the fact that the offending judge is also his ex-wife and now - after years apart, and an uneasy reconciliation - his sometime lover. Cam's questions lead him to a remote mountain area in western North Carolina and a group of daredevils who call themselves "the cat dancers" - so named because they have tracked the last wild mountain lions in the region to their dens, where they have photographed the animals face-to-face, or died trying. Cam must hunt this group and the cats they seek, or become their next target.

***Cat Dancers: Spider Mountain.** abr. ed. P. T. Deutermann & 2-In-1 Cd Coll. Read by Dick Hill. (Running Time: 12 hrs.). 2010. audio compact disk 19.99 (978-1-4418-5042-3(2), 9781441850423) Brilliance Audio.

Cat-Goddesses see Robert Graves Reads from His Poetry & the White Goddess

Cat in a Chorus Line. unabr. ed. Lydia Adamson. Read by Anna Fields. 4 cass. (Running Time: 4 hrs.). (Alice Nestleton Ser.: Vol. 12). 1997. 24.00 (978-0-7366-4052-7(5), 4561) Books on Tape.
Murder strikes a musical theater troupe & the motive is a mystery.

Cat in a Glass House. unabr. ed. Lydia Adamson. Read by Anna Fields. 5 cass. (Running Time: 5 hrs.). (Alice Nestleton Ser.). 1997. 30.00 (978-0-7366-3675-9(7), 4354) Books on Tape.
Alice Nestleton's agent sent her to Tribeca to meet an almost-major film producer in a trendy Chinese eatery.

Cat in Fine Style. unabr. ed. Lydia Adamson. Read by Anna Fields. 5 cass. (Running Time: 5 hrs.). (Alice Nestleton Ser.: Vol. 10). 1997. 30.00 (978-0-7366-3831-9(8), 4551) Books on Tape.
Alice Nestleton is posing in elegant duds for a New York boutique's latest ad campaign & in the loft where they are shooting they find a corpse.

Cat in the Bag. unabr. ed. Susan Kempler. 1 cass. (Running Time: 7 mins.). (Read It Alone Ser.). (J). (ps-3). 1985. pap. bk. 16.99 (978-0-87386-007-9(1)) Jan Prods.
A Giant has captured Carlos the Cat. Barney the Bear, Leo the Lion & Tashi the Tiger set out to help.

Cat in the Hat & Other Dr. Seuss Favorites. unabr. ed. Dr. Seuss. (Running Time: 2 hrs. 15 mins.). (ENG.). (J). 2003. audio compact disk 19.99 (978-0-8072-1873-0(1), Listening Lib) Pub: Random Audio Pubg. Dist(s): Random

Cat in the Hat & Other Dr. Seuss Favorites. unabr. collector's ed. Prod. by Listening Library Staff. 2 CDs. (Running Time: 2 hrs.). (J). (ps-3). 2005. audio compact disk 20.40 (978-0-307-24670-7(1), BksonTape); 23.00 (978-0-307-24669-1(8), BksonTape) Random Audio Pubg.
9 complete stories at a great price! Featuring: The Cat in the Hat read by Kelsey Grammer; Horton Hears a Who read by Dustin Hoffman; How the Grinch Stole Christmas read by Walter Matthau; Did I Ever Tell You How Lucky You Are? read by John Cleese; The Lorax read by Ted Danson; Yertle the Turtle, Gertrude McFuzz, and The Big Brag read by John Lithgow; Thidwick, the Big-Hearted Moose read by Mercedes McCambridge; Horton Hatches the Egg read by Billy Crystal; The Cat in the Hat Comes Back read by Kelsey Grammer.

Cat in the Manger. unabr. collector's ed. Lydia Adamson. Read by Anna Fields. 5 cass. (Running Time: 5 hrs.). (Alice Nestleton Ser.: Vol. 1). 1997. 30.00 (978-0-7366-3556-1(4), 4201) Books on Tape.
When Alice Nestleton, actress & sleuth, goes to a friend's Long Island estate to cat-sit, she comes face-to-bloody face with a corpse.

Cat in the Wings. unabr. collector's ed. Lydia Adamson. Read by Anna Fields. 6 cass. (Running Time: 6 hrs.). (Alice Nestleton Ser.). 1997. 36.00 (978-0-7366-3598-1(X), 4249) Books on Tape.
Peter Dobrynin, former ballet great, has been shot dead backstage at the Lincoln Center. Alice Nestleton starts snooping for clues among New York's homeless.

Cat in Wolf's Clothing. unabr. collector's ed. Lydia Adamson. Read by Anna Fields. 5 cass. (Running Time: 5 hrs.). (Alice Nestleton Ser.: Vol. 3). 1997. 30.00 (978-0-7366-3558-5(0), 4203) Books on Tape.
New York City cops enlist Alice Nestleton to track down a serial killer who preys on cat owners, steals their pets & leaves a mouse toy at the scene.

Cat Lovers Only. Julian Padowicz. Read by Julian Padowicz. 2 cass. (Running Time: 1 hr. 50 mins.). 1994. 14.95 (978-1-881288-09-1(9), BFI AudioBooks) BusnFilm Intl.
A guide to a happy cat-human relationship, through understanding, respect & love. Also traces history of domestic cats. Explains nature & habits of cats.

Cat-Nappers. unabr. ed. P. G. Wodehouse. Read by Frederick Davidson. 3 cass. (Running Time: 4 hrs.). 1996. 23.95 (978-0-7861-1006-3(6), 1783) Blckstn Audio.
Bertie Wooster & his valet, Jeeves, join the racing set & are embroiled once again in a scheme of Bertie's redoubtable Aunt Dahlia. Two racehorses, Simla & Potato Chip, are favorites in the upcoming contest at

Birdmouth-on-Sea - & of course, Aunt Dahlia is betting. Now, it seems that Potato Chip has fallen in love with a cat that sleeps in his stall & becomes quite listless if the cat is missing. Naturally, to achieve a certain result, all one has to do is abduct the cat.

Cat-Nappers. unabr. ed. P. G. Wodehouse. Read by Frederick Davidson. 1 CD. (Running Time: 4 hrs. 30 mins.). 2001. audio compact disk 19.95 (zm1783) Blckstn Audio.

Cat-Nappers. unabr. ed. P. G. Wodehouse. Read by Frederick Davidson. 4 CDs. (Running Time: 4 hrs.). 2004. audio compact disk 32.00 (978-0-7861-9897-9(4), 1783) Blckstn Audio.

Cat of a Different Color. unabr. collector's ed. Lydia Adamson. Read by Anna Fields. 5 cass. (Running Time: 5 hrs.). (Alice Nestleton Ser.: Vol. 2). 1997. 30.00 (978-0-7366-3557-8(2), 4202) Books on Tape.
Alice Nestleton, starts snooping after someone kills a fellow student in her acting class & steals his gorgeous white kitty.

Cat of Bubastes. G. A. Henty. Read by John Bolen. (Running Time: 41640 sec.). (ENG.). (J). (gr. 4-7). 2005. audio compact disk 96.00 (978-1-4001-3058-0(1)) Pub: Tantor Media. Dist(s): IngramPubServ

Cat of Bubastes. Short Stories. Read by Jim Weiss. Prod. by Greathall Productions. 6 CDs. (Running Time: 6 hrs.). Dramatization. (YA). 2004. audio compact disk 32.95 (978-1-882513-94-9(0)) Greathall Prods.
Six hours of adventure in ancient Egypt wertten by GA Henty and read by Jim Weiss. Amid chariot battles and court intrigues, Nile crocodiles and desert bandits, a young man finds friendship, love, and his own destiny. Excellent historical fiction.

Cat of Bubastes. unabr. ed. G A Henty. Narrated by John Bolen. (Running Time: 11 hrs. 30 mins. 0 sec.). (ENG.). (J). (gr. 4-7). 2008. 22.99 (978-1-4001-5869-0(9)); audio compact disk 65.99 (978-1-4001-3869-2(8)) Pub: Tantor Media. Dist(s): IngramPubServ

Cat of Bubastes. unabr. ed. G A Henty. Narrated by John Bolen. (Running Time: 11 hrs. 30 mins. 0 sec.). (ENG.). (J). (gr. 4-7). 2008. audio compact disk 32.99 (978-1-4001-0869-5(1)) Pub: Tantor Media. Dist(s): IngramPubServ

Cat of Bubastes: A Tale of Ancient Egypt. G. A. Henty. Read by John Bolen. (Running Time: 11 hrs. 30 mins.). 2002. 29.95 (978-1-60083-627-5(5), Audiofy Corp) Iofy Corp.

Cat of Bubastes: A Tale of Ancient Egypt, abr. ed. G. A. Henty. Read by Jim Weiss. 6 cass., color bk. (Running Time: 8 hrs.). (YA). 2000. 28.99 (978-1-887159-58-6(4)) PrestonSpeed.
Amid chariot battles and court intrigues, Nile crocodiles and desert bandits, a young man finds friendship, love and his own destiny, in this adventure in ancient Egypt. Includes a coloring book.

Cat of Bubastes: A Tale of Ancient Egypt. abr. ed. G. A. Henty. 2000. audio compact disk 28.95 (978-1-887159-63-0(0)) PrestonSpeed.

Cat of Bubastes: A Tale of Ancient Egypt. abr. ed. G. A. Henty. Read by Jim Weiss. 5 CDs, color bk. (Running Time: 7 hrs. 30 mins.). (YA). 2000. 32.99 (978-1-887159-60-9(6)) PrestonSpeed.

Cat of Bubastes: A Tale of Ancient Egypt. unabr. ed. G. A. Henty. Narrated by G. A. Henty. (Running Time: 11 hrs. 34 mins.). (ENG.). 2002. audio compact disk 23.00 (978-1-4001-5058-8(2)) Pub: Tantor Media. Dist(s): IngramPubServ
Unabridged Audiobook. 1 MP3 CD - 11 hours, 34 minutes. Narrated by John Bolen.The sacred cat of Bubastes has accidentally been slain; now young Chebron must pay for the offense with his own life, as this is the law of the Pagans in Egypt, 1250 BC. Chebron, the son of a high Egyptian priest, flees for his life taking his sister Mysa, one of the household slaves Amuba and several companions with him. They escape through closely guarded Egyptian exits only to find themselves in unfamiliar and dangerous lands inhabited by a very different culture of people. Along the way, the roving band of refugees encounters and befriends a Hebrew girl, who exposes them to very strange ideas including the worship of ?one true God?.This arduous journey through time, customs and religion provides an adventurous and accurate insight into the ancient people of Egyptian history.This audiobook is on one CD, encoded in MP3 format and will only play on computers and CD players that have the ability to play this unique format.

Cat on a Beach Blanket. unabr. ed. Lydia Adamson. Read by Anna Fields. 5 cass. (Running Time: 5 hrs.). (Alice Nestleton Ser.). 1998. 30.00 (978-0-7366-4260-6(9), 4759) Books on Tape.
Alice Nestleton can't resist the offer to housesit off-season in an exclusive Long Island enclave.

Cat on a Winning Streak. unabr. ed. Lydia Adamson. Read by Anna Fields. 4 cass. (Running Time: 4 hrs.). (Alice Nestleton Ser.). 1997. 24.00 (978-0-7366-3746-6(X), 4421) Books on Tape.
Alice Nestleton is in Atlantic City for a gig & she finds a cat & takes it to her owner only to find her slashed to death.

Cat on Jingle Bell Rock. unabr. ed. Lydia Adamson. Read by Anna Fields. 3 cass. (Running Time: 4 hrs. 30 mins.). (Alice Nestleton Ser.). 1999. 24.95 (978-0-7366-4336-8(2), 4825) Books on Tape.
Once again everyone's favorite actress, catsitter & amateur sleuth, Alice Nestleton, finds herself in the middle of a not-so-merry mystery when she agrees to help an old friend track down his charity's anonymous benefactor. When the generous one is found dead, Alice soon becomes the target of a murderous scrooge determined to keep the "Bah! Humbug!" in Christmas & Alice away from the truth.

Cat on the Cutting Edge. unabr. ed. Lydia Adamson. Read by Anna Fields. 4 cass. (Running Time: 4 hrs.). (Alice Nestleton Ser.: Vol. 9). 1997. 24.00 (978-0-7366-3745-9(1), 4420) Books on Tape.
Alice Nestleton's cat is acting up & her representative from Village Cat People service is murdered at her front door.

Cat O'Nine Tales. unabr. ed. Jeffrey Archer. 1 MP3 CD. (Running Time: 6 hrs.). 2007. 39.95 (978-0-7927-4761-1(5)); 44.95 (978-0-7927-4784-0(4)); audio compact disk 59.95 (978-0-7927-4681-2(3)) AudioGO.

Cat O'Nine Tales. unabr. ed. Jeffrey Archer. Read by Anton Lesser. (Running Time: 7 hrs. 0 mins. 0 sec.). 2007. audio compact disk 29.95 (978-1-4272-0047-1(5)) Pub: Macmill Audio. Dist(s): Macmillan

Cat Paws: Collection for Moving & Playing. Lee Campbell-Towell & Judy Smith Murray. 1994. bk. 19.95 (978-0-7935-3607-8(3)) H Leonard.

Cat Running, unabr. ed. Zilpha Keatley Snyder. Narrated by Christina Moore. 4 cass. (Running Time: 5 hrs.). (J). (gr. 2). 1996. 34.00 (94556E7) Recorded Bks.

Cat Running. unabr. ed. Zilpha Keatley Snyder. Narrated by Christina Moore. 4 pieces. (Running Time: 5 hrs.). (gr. 2 up). 1997. 34.00 Set. (978-0-7887-0364-5(1), 94574) Recorded Bks.

Cat Sat on the Mat see Necklace of Raindrops & Other Stories

Cat That Ate the Candle. Contrib. by John Carty. (ENG.). 1994. 13.95 (978-0-8023-7099-0(3)) Pub: Clo Iar-Chonnachta IRL. Dist(s): Dufour

Cat That Ate the Candle. Contrib. by John Carty. (ENG.). 1994. audio compact disk 21.95 (978-0-8023-8099-9(9)) Pub: Clo Iar-Chonnachta IRL. Dist(s): Dufour

Cat That Saw Stars. unabr. ed. Lilian Jackson Braun. Narrated by George Guidall. 1 CD. (Running Time: 1 hr.). 1999. audio compact disk 38.00 (C1090) Recorded Bks.

Cat That Walked by Himself see Favorite Children's Stories: A Collection

Cat That Walked by Himself see Just So Stories, Set, For Little Children

Cat That Walked by Himself. abr. ed. Rudyard Kipling. 1 read-along cass. (Running Time: 22 mins.). (World of Just So Stories Ser.: No. 2). (J). bk. 15.00 (SAC 6504C) Spoken Arts.

Cat That Walked by Himself: And Other Stories see Complete Just So Stories

Cat under the Mistletoe. unabr. ed. Lydia Adamson. Read by Anna Fields. 5 cass. (Running Time: 5 hrs.). (Alice Nestleton Ser.). 1998. 30.00 (978-0-7366-4259-0(5), 4758) Books on Tape.
When Alice Nestleton takes Roberta, a cat, to her therapist, Dr. Wilma Tedescu, she finds her dead.

Cat Who Ate Danish Modern. Lilian Jackson Braun. Narrated by George Guidall. 5 CDs. (Running Time: 5 hrs.). (Cat Who... Ser.). 2001. audio compact disk 48.00 (978-0-7887-5180-6(8), C1342E7) Recorded Bks.
When the first issue of Gracious Abodes went to press without a hitch, it looked like a bad omen. So it really shouldn't have surprised anybody when the cover story became a statistic in crime.

Cat Who Ate Danish Modern. Lilian Jackson Braun. Read by George Guidall. 3 cass. (Running Time: 5 hrs.). (Cat Who... Ser.). 2004. 19.95 (978-0-7887-5428-9(9), 00124) Recorded Bks.

Cat Who Ate Danish Modern. unabr. ed. Lilian Jackson Braun. Narrated by George Guidall. 4 cass. (Running Time: 5 hrs.). (Cat Who... Ser.). 1990. 35.00 (978-1-55690-090-7(2), 90081E7) Recorded Bks.
Jim Qwilleran is aided by Koko the cat in solving a stylish murder.

Cat Who Blew the Whistle. Lilian Jackson Braun. Narrated by George Guidall. 5 cass. (Running Time: 6 hrs. 30 mins.). (Cat Who... Ser.). 52.00 (978-1-4025-1294-0(5)) Recorded Bks.

Cat Who Blew the Whistle. Lilian Jackson Braun. Contrib. by George Guidall. (Playaway Adult Fiction Ser.). 2008. 59.99 (978-1-60640-655-7(8)) Find a World.

Cat Who Blew the Whistle. abr. ed. Lilian Jackson Braun. Read by Mason Adams. 2 cass. (Running Time: 3 hrs.). (Cat Who... Ser.). 2004. 18.00 (978-1-59007-171-7(9)) Pub: New Millenn Enter. Dist(s): PerseuPGW
This is one of the beloved collection for lighthearted mystery lovers, particularly those who also happen to love cats! Newspaper columnist Jim Qwilleran and his crime-solving Siamese cats, Koko and Yum-Yum live in tiny Moose County and solve crimes together.

Cat Who Blew the Whistle. unabr. ed. Lilian Jackson Braun. Read by George Guidall. 5 cass. (Cat Who... Ser.). 2004. 27.95 (978-1-59007-482-4(3)); audio compact disk 39.95 (978-1-59007-483-1(1)) Pub: New Millenn Enter. Dist(s): PerseuPGW

Cat Who Brought down the House. unabr. ed. Lilian Jackson Braun. Narrated by George Guidall. 5 CDs Library Ed. (Running Time: 6 hrs.). (Cat Who... Ser.). 2003. audio compact disk 49.75 (978-1-4025-4224-4(0)); 29.95 (978-1-4025-3863-6(4), RG388) Recorded Bks.
Thelma Thackeray, an ancient movie star, has returned to her home in Moose County to have some fun before she dies. Her fame and fortune are put to good use as she renovates the old opera house and reopens it as a film club. But when the first performance turns deadly, Qwill and his feline snoops start to look behind the scenes for the culprit.

Cat Who Brought down the House. unabr. ed. Lilian Jackson Braun. Narrated by George Guidall. 4 cass. Library Ed. (Running Time: 5 hrs. 45 mins.). (Cat Who... Ser.). 2003. 43.00 (978-1-4025-3862-9(6)) Recorded Bks.

Cat Who Came for Christmas. unabr. ed. Cleveland Amory. Read by Alan Sklar. 6 CDs. (Running Time: 9 hrs.). 2002. audio compact disk 64.95 (978-0-7927-2739-2(8), SLD 499, Chivers Sound Lib); bk. 54.95 (978-0-7927-2713-2(4), CSL 499, Chivers Sound Lib) AudioGO.
'Tis the night before Christmas when a self-described curmudgeon rescues a bedraggled feline from a snowy New York City alley. . . Thus begins this touching, timeless, and inspiring tale of a man his cat - or, rather, of a cat and his man. It is a story that succeeds not only in illuminating the animal-human bond but in capturing the spirit of the holiday season.

Cat Who Came in from the Cold. Jeffrey Moussaieff Masson. Read by Erik Steele. 2 cass. 24.95 (978-0-7927-3370-6(3), CSL 714); audio compact disk 39.95 (978-0-7927-3371-3(1), SLD 714) AudioGO.

Cat Who Came Indoors: A Story from Nelson Mandela's Favorite African Folktales. Read by Helen Mirren. Compiled by Nelson Mandela. (Running Time: 3 mins.). (ENG.). 2009. 1.99 (978-1-60788-010-3(5)) Pub: Hachet Audio. Dist(s): HachBkGrp

Cat Who Came to Breakfast. Lilian Jackson Braun. Narrated by George Guidall. 5 cass. (Running Time: 7 hrs.). (Cat Who... Ser.). 52.00 (978-1-4025-1296-4(1)) Recorded Bks.

Cat Who Came to Breakfast. Lilian Jackson Braun. Contrib. by George Guidall. (Cat Who... Ser.). 2008. 59.99 (978-1-60640-656-4(6)) Find a World.

Cat Who Came to Breakfast. abr. unabr. ed. Lilian Jackson Braun. Perf. by Dick Van Patten. 6 CDs. (Running Time: 3 hrs.). (Cat Who... Ser.). 2004. 18.00 (978-1-59007-172-4(7)) Pub: New Millenn Enter. Dist(s): PerseuPGW
Trouble literally lands in Jim Qwilleran's own backyard when the local theatre's universally disliked director is found dead in Qwilleran's apple orchard. Qwilleran and his two feline detectives search for an actor who is playing the part of a killer. "Some of the most witty original fare in the genre." - New York Daily News.

Cat Who Came to Breakfast. unabr. ed. Lilian Jackson Braun. Read by George Guidall. 5 cass. (Cat Who... Ser.). 2004. 27.95 (978-1-59007-484-8(X)); audio compact disk 39.95 (978-1-59007-485-5(8)) Pub: New Millenn Enter. Dist(s): PerseuPGW

Cat Who Could Read Backwards. Lilian Jackson Braun. Narrated by George Guidall. 5 CDs. (Running Time: 5 hrs. 15 mins.). (Cat Who... Ser.). audio compact disk 49.75 (978-0-7887-4488-4(7)) Recorded Bks.

Cat Who Could Read Backwards. Lilian Jackson Braun. 3 cass. (Running Time: 5 hrs. 15 mins.). (Cat Who... Ser.). 2004. 19.95 (978-0-7887-5430-2(0), 00144) Recorded Bks.

Cat Who Could Read Backwards. unabr. ed. Lilian Jackson Braun. Narrated by George Guidall. 4 cass. (Running Time: 5 hrs. 15 mins.). (Cat Who... Ser.). 1990. 39.75 (978-1-55690-091-4(0), 90082) Recorded Bks.
Jim Qwilleran teams up with a Siamese cat to solve a mystery.

Cat Who Could Read Backwards. unabr. ed. Lilian Jackson Braun. Narrated by George Guidall. 1 CD. (Cat Who... Ser.). 2000. audio compact disk 48.00 (C1190W5) Recorded Bks.

Cat Who Couldn't Meow. unabr. ed. Doreen Rappaport & Michele Sobel Spirn. 1 cass. (Running Time: 5 mins.). (Happy Endings! Ser.). (J). (ps-1). 1988. pap. bk. 9.95 (978-0-87386-050-5(0)) Jan Prods.
Bruno, the King family's cat disappears during their family picnic. The search is made more difficult because Bruno is unable to Meow!!.

Cat Who Cried for Help. unabr. ed. Nicholas H. Dodman. Read by Michael Mitchell. 6 cass. (Running Time: 9 hrs.). 1997. 48.00 (978-0-7366-3793-0(1), 4467) Books on Tape.
A renowned animal psychologist explores the fascinating & often frustrating mind of one of our most popular animal companions.

Cat Who Had 14 Tales. unabr. ed. Lilian Jackson Braun. Narrated by George Guidall. 4 cass. (Running Time: 5 hrs.). (Cat Who... Ser.). 2000. 35.00 (978-0-7887-0312-6(9), 94504E7) Recorded Bks.

Cat Who Had 14 Tales. unabr. ed. Lilian Jackson Braun. Read by George Guidall. 4 cass. (Running Time: 5 hrs.45 min.). (Cat Who... Ser.). 2000. 49.00 (96504E7) Recorded Bks.
A courageous Siamese bags a cunning cat burglar. A country kitty proves a stumbling block in a violent murder. And an intuitive feline's premonition helps solve the case of the missing antique dealer. Here are 14 Braun "Cat" tales that are riveting & amusing whodunits.

Cat Who Had 60 Whiskers. unabr. ed. Lilian Jackson Braun & Lilian Jackson Braun. Read by George Guidall. 3 CDs. (Running Time: 4 hrs.). (ENG.). (gr. 8). 2007. audio compact disk 23.95 (978-0-14-305911-0(4), PengAudBks) Penguin Grp USA.

Cat Who Killed Lilian Jackson Braun: A Parody. unabr. ed. Scripts. Robert Kaplow. Read by Arte Johnson. 4 cass. (Running Time: 4 hrs. 30 mins.). 2004. 21.95 (978-1-59007-314-8(2)) Pub: New Millenn Enter. Dist(s): PerseuPGW

Cat Who Knew a Cardinal. Lilian Jackson Braun. Narrated by George Guidall. 6 CDs. (Running Time: 7 hrs.). (Cat Who... Ser.). audio compact disk 58.00 (978-1-4025-2913-9(9)) Recorded Bks.

Cat Who Knew a Cardinal. abr. ed. Lilian Jackson Braun. Read by Theodore Bikel. 2 cass. (Running Time: 3 hrs.). (Cat Who... Ser.). 2001. 18.00 (978-1-59040-135-4(2), Phoenix Audio) Pub: Amer Intl Pub. Dist(s): PerseuPGW

Cat Who Knew a Cardinal. abr. ed. Lilian Jackson Braun. Perf. by Theodore Bikel. 2 cass. (Running Time: 3 hrs.). (Cat Who... Ser.). 2004. 18.00 (978-1-59007-173-1(5)) Pub: New Millenn Enter. Dist(s): PerseuPGW

Cat Who Knew a Cardinal. unabr. ed. Lilian Jackson Braun. Read by George Guidall. 5 cass. (Running Time: 7 hrs. 30 min.). (Cat Who... Ser.). 2004. 27.95 (978-1-59007-486-2(6)); audio compact disk 39.95 (978-1-59007-487-9(4)) Pub: New Millenn Enter. Dist(s): PerseuPGW

Cat Who Knew a Cardinal. unabr. ed. Lilian Jackson Braun. Narrated by George Guidall. 5 cass. (Running Time: 6 hrs. 45 mins.). (Cat Who... Ser.). 2002. 49.00 (978-1-4025-1286-5(4), 96971) Recorded Bks.
When the director of Pickax Theatre Club's Shakespeare production is found dead in Qwilleran's apple orchard, so begins the mad search for clues to find out which player staged the murder. Qwilleran and his Siamese sleuths soon realize that they have entered the world of "All the world's a stage," when questioning the players proves to be most challenging.

Cat Who Knew Shakespeare. unabr. ed. Lilian Jackson Braun. Narrated by George Guidall. 4 cass. (Running Time: 6 hrs.). (Cat Who... Ser.). (gr. 10 up). 1991. 35.00 (978-1-55690-092-1(9), 91115E7) Recorded Bks.
Jim Qwilleran & his feline side-kick pry into some decidedly dirty doings in Moose County.

Cat Who Knew Shakespeare. unabr. ed. Lilian Jackson Braun. Read by George Guidall. 4 cass. (Running Time: 6 hrs.). (Cat Who... Ser.). 2004. 24.95 (978-0-7887-5431-9(9), 00154) Recorded Bks.

Cat Who Lived High. Lilian Jackson Braun. Read by George Guidall. 5 cass. (Running Time: 7 hrs. 30 mins.). (Cat Who... Ser.). 2004. 24.99 (978-0-7887-5492-0(0), 00284) Recorded Bks.

Cat Who Lived High. unabr. ed. Lilian Jackson Braun. Narrated by George Guidall. 5 cass. (Running Time: 7 hrs. 30 mins.). (Cat Who... Ser.). 1994. 44.00 (978-1-55690-992-4(6), 94131) Recorded Bks.
Reporter-turned millionaire, Jim Qwilleran, has the winter blues, so he decides to venture "Down Below" for a few months, moving into temporary quarters at the Casablanca, a colorful 1920s apartment building he hopes to save from the demolition crews. But things are off to dubious beginnings when Qwill gets trapped in the elevator shaft & is accosted by an irate matron wielding a lethal cane. Worse things are still to come when Qwill discovers that his penthouse is covered with wall-to-wall mushrooms.

Cat Who Moved a Mountain. Lilian Jackson Braun. Narrated by George Guidall. 5 cass. (Running Time: 7 hrs. 15 mins.). (Cat Who... Ser.). 48.00 (978-1-4025-1304-6(6)) Recorded Bks.

Cat Who Moved a Mountain. abr. ed. Lilian Jackson Braun. Perf. by Theodore Bikel. 2 cass. (Running Time: 3 hrs.). (Cat Who... Ser.). 2004. 18.00 (978-1-59007-174-8(3)) Pub: New Millenn Enter. Dist(s): PerseuPGW
After five years of legal formalities, Jim Qwilleran has officially inherited his freedom and a fortune, which leaves him with a serious dilemma. What should he do now? Seeking a place of peace and isolation to make up his mind, he heads to the Potato Mountains for the summer.

Cat Who Moved a Mountain. unabr. ed. Lilian Jackson Braun. Read by George Guidall. 5 cass. (Cat Who... Ser.). 2004. 27.95 (978-1-59007-488-6(2)); audio compact disk 45.00 (978-1-59007-489-3(0)) Pub: New Millenn Enter. Dist(s): PerseuPGW

Cat Who Played Brahms. unabr. ed. Lilian Jackson Braun. Narrated by George Guidall. 5 cass. (Running Time: 6 hrs. 30 mins.). (Cat Who... Ser.). 1992. 44.00 (978-1-55690-651-0(X), 92133) Recorded Bks.
Jim Qwilleran & his feline assistants solve a lakeside mystery.

Cat Who Played Brahms. unabr. ed. Lilian Jackson Braun. Read by George Guidall. 4 cass. (Running Time: 6 hrs. 30 mins.). (Cat Who... Ser.). 2004. 24.95 (978-0-7887-5489-0(0), 00254) Recorded Bks.

Cat Who Played Post Office. unabr. ed. Lilian Jackson Braun. Narrated by George Guidall. 5 cass. (Running Time: 6 hrs. 30 mins.). (Cat Who... Ser.). 2000. 44.00 (978-1-55690-689-3(7), 92343) Recorded Bks.
A bicycle accident presages a new mystery that puts Qwilleran & the two cats in danger.

Cat Who Played Post Office. unabr. ed. Lilian Jackson Braun. Read by George Guidall. 4 cass. (Running Time: 6 hrs. 30 mins.). (Cat Who... Ser.). 2004. 24.95 (978-0-7887-5432-6(7), 00164) Recorded Bks.

Cat Who Said Cheese. Lilian Jackson Braun. Narrated by George Guidall. 5 cass. (Running Time: 7 hrs.). (Cat Who... Ser.). 52.00 (978-1-4025-1292-6(9)) Recorded Bks.

Cat Who Said Cheese. abr. ed. Lilian Jackson Braun. Read by Mason Adams. 2 cass. (Running Time: 3 hrs.). (Cat Who... Ser.). 2001. 18.00 (978-1-59040-067-8(4), Phoenix Audio) Pub: Amer Intl Pub. Dist(s): PerseuPGW
Everything smells in Pickax when a killer invades the Great Food Expo. Luckily, Qwill is on the scene, his mustache twitching with suspicions, as he and the cats are on the trail that will demand all their feline intuition and mustachioed insight.

Cat Who Said Cheese. abr. ed. Lilian Jackson Braun. Read by Mason Adams. 2 cass. (Running Time: 3 hrs.). (Cat Who... Ser.). 2004. 18.00 (978-1-59007-175-5(1)) Pub: New Millenn Enter. Dist(s): PerseuPGW
Qwill agrees to join his beloved Polly on a group tour of Scotland to keep her safe from the Pickax Prowler. On their sixth day in Scotland, however,

the tour organizer - Polly's best friend Irma - dies of an apparent heart attack, and Qwill suspects foul play. Koko and Yum Yum may have been miles away from the scene of the crime, but they're just a whisker away from cracking the case. LG Alternate.

Cat Who Said Cheese. unabr. ed. Lilian Jackson Braun. Read by George Guidall. 5 cass. (Cat Who... Ser.). 2004. 27.95 (978-1-59007-490-9(4)); audio compact disk 39.95 (978-1-59007-491-6(2)) Pub: New Millenn Enter. Dist(s): PerseuPGW

Cat Who Said Cheese. unabr. ed. Lilian Jackson Braun. Narrated by George Guidall. 5 cass. (Running Time: 7 hrs. 15 mins.). (Cat Who... Ser.). 2002. 34.95 (978-1-4025-1293-3(7), RF754) Recorded Bks.
Moose County is bustling with activity as the hamlet prepares for the Great Food Explo. Restaurants are opening, recipes are being traded and all the townsfolk are squabbling over whose cooking is best. But the arrival of a mysterious woman sets more than tongues wagging when an explosion in her room rocks the New Pickax Hotel. It is readily apparent to Koko that there is more to this than meets the eye and soon he and Qwill find themselves hot on the trail of a murderer.

Cat Who Sang for the Birds. Lilian Jackson Braun. Read by George Guidall. 4 cass. (Running Time: 420 min.). (Cat Who... Ser.). 2001. 24.95 (978-0-7887-5493-7(9)) Recorded Bks.

Cat Who Sang for the Birds. unabr. ed. Lilian Jackson Braun. Narrated by George Guidall. 6 CDs. (Running Time: 7 hrs.). (Cat Who... Ser.). 1999. audio compact disk 54.00 (978-0-7887-3428-1(8), C1034E7) Recorded Bks.
Jim & his cats have some sleuthing to do when a newly opened art center is broken into & an elderly woman dies in a suspicious fire.

Cat Who Sang for the Birds. unabr. ed. Lilian Jackson Braun. Narrated by George Guidall. 5 cass. (Running Time: 7 hrs.). (Cat Who... Ser.). 1998. 49.00 (978-0-7887-1971-4(8), 95358) Recorded Bks.

Cat Who Saw Red. abr. ed. Lilian Jackson Braun. Read by George Guidall. 4 cass. (Running Time: 5 hrs. 45 mins.). (Cat Who... Ser.). 2004. 24.95 (978-0-7887-5488-3(2), 00244) Recorded Bks.
Jim Qwilleran & Koko are forced by Yun-yum to solve a "disk" of a mystery.

Cat Who Saw Red. unabr. ed. Lilian Jackson Braun. Narrated by George Guidall. 4 cass. (Running Time: 5 hrs. 45 mins.). (Cat Who... Ser.). (gr. 10 up). 1990. 35.00 (978-1-55690-093-8(7), 90083E7) Recorded Bks.
Jim Qwilleran & Koko are forced by Yum-yum to solve a "dish" of a mystery.

Cat Who Saw Stars, abr. ed. Lilian Jackson Braun. Read by George Guidall. 2 cass. (Running Time: 2 hrs.). (Cat Who... Ser.). 1999. 17.95 (FS9-43325) Highsmith.

Cat Who Saw Stars. unabr. ed. Lilian Jackson Braun. Narrated by George Guidall. 5 cass. (Running Time: 6 hrs. 15 mins.). (Cat Who... Ser.). 1999. 49.00 (978-0-7887-2913-3(6), 95706) Recorded Bks.
Qwill & his fabulous felines are on the trail of some very unusual "visitors." A back-packer has disappeared in Moose County & rumor has it extraterrestrials are responsible.

Cat Who Saw Stars. unabr. ed. Lilian Jackson Braun. Narrated by George Guidall. 6 CDs. (Running Time: 6 hrs. 15 mins.). (Cat Who... Ser.). 2001. audio compact disk 38.00 (978-0-7887-3971-2(9), C1090E7) Recorded Bks.
Finds Qwill & his fabulous felines on the trail of some very unusual visitors. A backpacker has disappeared in Moose County & rumor has it extraterrestrials are responsible.

Cat Who Smelled a Rat. unabr. ed. Lilian Jackson Braun. Narrated by George Guidall. 5 CDs. (Running Time: 5 hrs. 45 mins.). (Cat Who... Ser.). 2001. audio compact disk 48.00 Recorded Bks.
October finds Moose County, 400 miles north of everywhere, in the grips of a record-breaking drought. With the danger of a wildfire threatening the village of Pickax, the locals pray for the annual fall blizzard. But trouble comes unexpectedly with a case of arson and the shooting death of a volunteer fireman. When the crime wave continues, it takes reporter Jim Qwilleran and his clever felines, KoKo and Yum Yum, to sniff out the rat behind it all.

Cat Who Smelled a Rat. unabr. ed. Lilian Jackson Braun. Narrated by George Guidall. 4 cass. (Running Time: 5 hrs. 45 mins.). (Cat Who... Ser.). 2001. 48.00 (978-0-7887-4977-3(3), 964417) Recorded Bks.
Qwilleran & his whisker-twitching pets spring into action as trouble comes unexpectedly to Pickax with a case of arson & the shooting death of a volunteer fireman.

Cat Who Smelled a Rat. unabr. ed. Lilian Jackson Braun. Narrated by George Guidall. 5 CDs. (Running Time: 5 hrs. 45 mins.). (Cat Who... Ser.). 2001. audio compact disk 48.00 (978-1-4025-0490-7(X), C1546) Recorded Bks.
Trouble comes unexpectedly to Pickax with a case of arson and the shooting death of a volunteer fireman. It takes reporter Jim Qwilleran and his clever felines to sniff out the rat behind it all. The bemused Qwilleran and his whisker-twitching pets seem to spring from the pages to solve the case right in your very own living room.

Cat Who Smelled Smoke. Lilian Jackson Braun. (Cat Who... Ser.). (YA). (gr. 8). 2008. audio compact disk 25.95 (978-0-14-314286-7(0), PengAudBks) Penguin Grp USA.

Cat Who Sniffed Glue. unabr. ed. Lilian Jackson Braun. Narrated by George Guidall. 5 cass. (Running Time: 6 hrs. 45 mins.). (Cat Who... Ser.). 2000. 44.00 (978-1-55690-837-8(7), 93205E7) Recorded Bks.
A crime-solving Siamese cat's sudden predilection for licking stamps & sniffing glue lead to the apprehension of a killer.

Cat Who Sniffed Glue. unabr. ed. Lilian Jackson Braun. Read by George Guidall. 4 cass. (Running Time: 6 hrs. 45 mins.). (Cat Who... Ser.). 2004. 24.95 (978-0-7887-5490-6(4), 00264) Recorded Bks.

Cat Who Tailed a Thief. Lilian Jackson Braun. Narrated by George Guidall. 5 cass. (Running Time: 7 hrs.). (Cat Who... Ser.). 1997. 52.00 (978-1-4025-1302-2(X)) Recorded Bks.

Cat Who Tailed a Thief. abr. ed. Lilian Jackson Braun. Read by Mason Adams. 2 cass. (Running Time: 3 hrs.). (Cat Who... Ser.). 2004. 18.00 (978-1-59007-176-2(X)) Pub: New Millenn Enter. Dist(s): PerseuPGW
When small items disappear throughout the town, the residents are up in arms! Pickax has seldom fallen victim to "big city" crimes, particularly during the holiday season. But after the bridge club's money is stolen, the townspeople decide that there is more to this mystery. The rash of petty thievery started when banker Willard Carmichael and his much younger (and flashier) wife, Danielle, moved to Pickax from Down Below. Along with their big-city lifestyle, Willard brought plans to restore the Victorian houses on Gingerbread Alley (fondly known as Pleasant Street). Unfortunately, Willard is murdered in an apparent mugging Down Below. When a local man is accused of the thievery, newspaper columnist Jim Qwilleran has serious questions about the recent crimes plaguing Pickax.

Cat Who Tailed a Thief. unabr. ed. Lilian Jackson Braun. Read by George Guidall. 5 cass. (Cat Who... Ser.). 2004. 27.95 (978-1-59007-492-3(0)); audio compact disk 39.95 (978-1-59007-493-0(9)) Pub: New Millenn Enter. Dist(s): PerseuPGW

Cat Who Talked to Ghosts. abr. ed. Lilian Jackson Braun. Read by George Guidall. 5 cass. (Running Time: 7 hrs. 30 mins.). (Cat Who... Ser.). 2004. 24.99 (978-0-7887-5433-3(5), 00174) Recorded Bks.

Cat Who Talked to Ghosts. unabr. ed. Lilian Jackson Braun. Narrated by George Guidall. 5 cass. (Running Time: 7 hrs. 30 mins.). (Cat Who... Ser.). 1994. 44.00 (978-0-7887-0050-7(2), 94249E7) Recorded Bks.
Qwilleran's long-time housekeeper is murdered & Qwill & his Siamese cats are out to find the killer.

Cat Who Talked to Ghosts, unabr. ed. Lilian Jackson Braun. Read by George Guidall. 5 cass. (Running Time: 7 hrs. 30 mins.). (Cat Who... Ser.). 1994. 42.00 (94249E5) Recorded Bks.
Qwilleran's long-time housekeeper is murdered, & Qwill & his Siamese cats are out to find the killer.

Cat Who Talked Turkey. abr. ed. Lilian Jackson Braun. Narrated by George Guidall. 4 cass. Lib. Ed. (Running Time: 4 hrs. 15 min.). (Cat Who... Ser.). 2004. 39.75 (978-1-4025-7471-9(1), 97639) Recorded Bks.

Cat Who Talked Turkey. unabr. collector's ed. Lilian Jackson Braun. Narrated by George Guidall. 4 cass. (Running Time: 4 hrs. 15 min.). (Cat Who... Ser.). 2004. 24.95 (978-1-4025-7472-6(X), RH002); audio compact disk 29.95 (978-1-4025-7739-0(7), CC035) Recorded Bks.
What Pickax, the town 400 miles north of everywhere, needs is a new bookstore. Ever since the old one burned down, the townspeople have had to go elsewhere. As wealthy resident James Qwilleran says, A town without a bookstore is like a chicken with one leg. But just as Pickax prepares to celebrate the ground breaking for a new one, a body is discovered in a nearby wooded area. Turning their attention from books to clues, Qwill, Koko, and Yum Yum set off on a hunt that will entertain all Cat Who fans and newcomers alike.

Cat Who Turned on & Off. Lilian Jackson Braun. Narrated by George Guidall. 6 CDs. (Running Time: 6 hrs. 45 mins.). (Cat Who... Ser.). audio compact disk 59.00 (978-0-7887-9856-6(1)) Recorded Bks.

Cat Who Turned on & Off. unabr. ed. Lilian Jackson Braun. Narrated by George Guidall. 5 cass. (Running Time: 6 hrs. 45 mins.). (Cat Who... Ser.). 1991. 44.00 (978-1-55690-094-5(5), 91402E7) Recorded Bks.
Qwilleran & Koko go antiquing in search of a solution to their mystery.

Cat Who Turned on & Off. unabr. ed. Lilian Jackson Braun. Read by George Guidall. 4 cass. (Running Time: 6 hrs. 15 mins.). (Cat Who... Ser.). 2004. 24.95 (978-0-7887-5487-6(4), 00234) Recorded Bks.
Qwill moves his felines to "Junktown," a charming community of eccentric antique dealers. But before they?ve had a chance to settle in, Qwill finds himself embroiled in a mystery where a lot more than 19th century English bookcases are being shellacked.

Cat Who Walked by Himself see Favorite Just So Stories

Cat Who Walks Through Walls. unabr. ed. Robert A. Heinlein. Read by Tom Weiner. (Running Time: 48600 sec.). 2007. audio compact disk 29.95 (978-1-4332-1292-5(7)) Blckstn Audio.

Cat Who Walks Through Walls. unabr. ed. Robert A. Heinlein. Narrated by George Wilson. 11 cass. (Running Time: 16 hrs.). 1999. 91.00 (978-0-7887-2940-9(3), 95721E7) Recorded Bks.
This spicy, fast-paced sci-fi adventure delivers brave new worlds of humor & politics. In the novel's space-age future, it seems human foibles have multiplied as quickly as technological wonders.

Cat Who Walks Through Walls: A Comedy of Manners. unabr. ed. Robert A. Heinlein. Read by Tom Weiner. (Running Time: 48600 sec.). 2007. audio compact disk & audio compact disk 90.00 (978-1-4332-1291-8(9)) Blckstn Audio.

Cat Who Walks through Walls: A Comedy of Manners. unabr. ed. Robert A. Heinlein. Read by Tom Weiner. (Running Time: 12 hrs. NaN mins.). 2007. 72.95 (978-1-4332-1290-1(0)) Blckstn Audio.

Cat Who Wasn't There. Lilian Jackson Braun. Narrated by George Guidall. 5 cass. (Running Time: 7 hrs. 30 mins.). (Cat Who... Ser.). 48.00 (978-1-4025-1298-8(8)) Recorded Bks.

Cat Who Wasn't There. abr. ed. Lilian Jackson Braun. Perf. by Theodore Bikel. 2 cass. (Running Time: 3 hrs.). (Cat Who... Ser.). 2004. 18.00 (978-1-59007-177-9(8)) Pub: New Millenn Enter. Dist(s): PerseuPGW

Cat Who Wasn't There. unabr. ed. Lilian Jackson Braun. Read by George Guidall. 5 cass. (Cat Who... Ser.). 2004. 27.95 (978-1-59007-494-7(7)); audio compact disk 45.00 (978-1-59007-495-4(5)) Pub: New Millenn Enter. Dist(s): PerseuPGW

Cat Who Wasn't There. unabr. ed. Lilian Jackson Braun. Narrated by George Guidal. 5 cass. (Running Time: 7 hrs. 15 mins.). (Cat Who... Ser.). 2002. 29.95 (96979) Recorded Bks.
Jim Qwilleran, the perennially jobless, but always witty journalist, is completely at the mercy of his pair of blue-eyed Siamese cats, Koko and Yum Yum. While he pampers them with gourmet food, their whisker-twitching premonitions put Qwill on the track of some of the most intriguing and entertaining cases.

Cat Who Went Bananas. unabr. ed. Lilian Jackson Braun. Narrated by George Guidall. 4 CDs. (Running Time: 4 hrs. 45 mins.). (Cat Who... Ser.). 2005. audio compact disk 49.75 (978-1-4193-0531-3(X), C2842); 39.75 (978-1-4193-0529-0(8), 97849) Recorded Bks.
Lilian Jackson Braun has authored 27 best-selling Cat Who... novels, including The Cat Who Talked Turkey. Her amusing feline-sleuths, Koko and Yum Yum, make each installment to the series delightfully "purr-fect." The Cat Who Went Bananas continues in the tradition of the beloved series - finding Koko and Yum Yum paw-deep in a new mystery. The people of Pickax are in a state of eager anticipation. The Pirate's Chest, the long-awaited new bookstore, is finally set to open, and the Theatre Club is preparing to perform Oscar Wilde's The Importance of Being Earnest. However, the play is brought to an abrupt halt as a cast member is killed in a car accident. But was it really an accident? As suspicions rise, Qwill and his sleuthing Siamese cats have their work cut out for them.

Cat Who Went into the Closet. Lilian Jackson Braun. Narrated by George Guidall. 5 cass. (Running Time: 6 hrs. 45 mins.). (Cat Who... Ser.). 52.00 (978-1-4025-1300-8(3)) Recorded Bks.

Cat Who Went into the Closet. abr. ed. Lilian Jackson Braun. Perf. by Dick Van Patten. 2 cass. (Running Time: 3 hrs.). (Cat Who... Ser.). 2001. 18.00 (978-1-59040-134-7(4), Phoenix Audio) Pub: Amer Intl Pub. Dist(s): PerseuPGW

Cat Who Went into the Closet. abr. ed. Lilian Jackson Braun. Perf. by Dick Van Patten. 2 cass. (Running Time: 3 hrs.). (Cat Who... Ser.). 2004. 18.00 (978-1-59007-178-6(6)) Pub: New Millenn Enter. Dist(s): PerseuPGW

Cat Who Went into the Closet. unabr. ed. Lilian Jackson Braun. Read by George Guidall. 5 cass. (Cat Who... Ser.). 2004. 27.95 (978-1-59007-496-1(3)); audio compact disk 39.95 (978-1-59007-497-8(1)) Pub: New Millenn Enter. Dist(s): PerseuPGW

Cat Who Went Underground. abr. ed. Lilian Jackson Braun. Read by George Guidall. 4 cass. (Running Time: 7 hrs.). (Cat Who... Ser.). 2004. 19.99 (978-0-7887-5491-3(2), 00274) Recorded Bks.

Cat Who Went up the Creek. Lilian Jackson Braun. Narrated by George Guidall. 5 CDs. (Running Time: 5 hrs. 15 mins.). (Cat Who... Ser.). audio compact disk 52.00 (978-1-4025-1569-9(3)) Recorded Bks.

Cat Who Went up the Creek. Lilian Jackson Braun. 4 cass. (Running Time: 6 hrs.). (Cat Who... Ser.). 2002. 29.95 (96966) Recorded Bks.

Cat Who Went up the Creek. unabr. ed. Lilian Jackson Braun. Narrated by George Guidall. 4 cass. (Running Time: 5 hrs. 15 mins.). (Cat Who... Ser.). 2002. 46.00 (978-1-4025-1271-1(6), 96966) Recorded Bks.
The game is afoot at the Nutcracker Inn in the village of Black Creek, famous for it's black walnuts and for its squirrels, which keep Koko endlessly entertained as he fences with them.

Cat Who Wished to Be a Man. unabr. ed. Lloyd Alexander. Read by Words Take Wing Repertory Company Staff. 2 cass. (Running Time: 2 hrs. 25 mins.). (J). (gr. 3-5). 1997. pap. bk. 28.00 (978-0-8072-7847-5(5), YA933SP, Listening Lib); 23.00 (978-0-8072-7846-8(7), YA933CX, Listening Lib) Random Audio Pubg.
Magician Stephanus gave his cat the gift of voice; he now wants to be a human.

Cat with a Fiddle. unabr. collector's ed. Lydia Adamson. Read by Anna Fields. 6 cass. (Running Time: 6 hrs.). (Alice Nestleton Ser.: Vol. 6). 1997. 36.00 (978-0-7366-3676-6(5), 4355) Books on Tape.
Alice Nestleton's latest play has just bombed so she's turned to the kinder world of cat-sitting.

Cat with No Regrets. unabr. ed. Lydia Adamson. Read by Anna Fields. 5 cass. (Running Time: 5 hrs.). (Alice Nestleton Ser.). 1997. 30.00 (978-0-7366-3744-2(3), 4419) Books on Tape.
Alice Nestleton lands a part in a major motion picture, & to celebrate she takes off to Provence, France.

Cat with the Blues. unabr. ed. Lydia Adamson. Read by Anna Fields. 3 cass. (Running Time: 4 hrs. 30 mins.). (Alice Nestleton Ser.). 2001. 24.95 (978-0-7366-6207-9(3)) Books on Tape.
Alice Nestleton is cat-sitting a beautiful Russian Blue who also happens to be the center of a raging custody battle. Sidney & Beatrice Woburn are fighting over Frenchy & just about everything else, so Alice, at the request of the lawyers, is keeping the cat company in the couple's luxurious high-rise apartment.

***Catacombs: A Tale of the Barque Cats.** unabr. ed. Anne McCaffrey and Elizabeth Ann Scarborough. Read by Laural Merlington. (Running Time: 8 hrs.). (Barque Cats Ser.). 2010. audio compact disk 99.97 (978-1-4418-3834-6(1), 9781441838346, BriAudCD Unabrid) Brilliance Audio.

***Catacombs: A Tale of the Barque Cats.** unabr. ed. Anne McCaffrey & Elizabeth Ann Scarborough. Read by Laural Merlington. (Running Time: 8 hrs.). (Barque Cats Ser.). 2010. 39.97 (978-1-4418-3836-0(8), 9781441838360, Brinc Audio MP3 Lib) Brilliance Audio.

***Catacombs: A Tale of the Barque Cats.** unabr. ed. Anne McCaffrey & Elizabeth Ann Scarborough. Read by Laural Merlington. (Running Time: 8 hrs.). (Barque Cats Ser.). 2010. 24.99 (978-1-4418-3835-3(X), 9781441838353, Brilliance MP3) Brilliance Audio.

***Catacombs: A Tale of the Barque Cats.** unabr. ed. Read by Laural Merlington. (Running Time: 8 hrs.). (Barque Cats Ser.). 2010. 39.97 (978-1-4418-3838-4(4), 9781441838384, BADLE) Brilliance Audio.

***Catacombs: A Tale of the Barque Cats.** unabr. ed. Elizabeth Ann Scarborough & Anne McCaffrey. Read by Laural Merlington. (Running Time: 8 hrs.). (Barque Cats Ser.). 2010. 24.99 (978-1-4418-3837-7(6), 9781441838377, BAD) Brilliance Audio.

***Catacombs: A Tale of the Barque Cats.** unabr. ed. Elizabeth Ann Scarborough & Anne McCaffrey. Read by Laural Merlington. (Running Time: 8 hrs.). (Barque Cats Ser.). 2010. audio compact disk 29.99 (978-1-4418-3833-9(3), 9781441838339, Bril Audio CD Unabri) Brilliance Audio.

Catalan Sin Esfuerzo. 1 cass. (Running Time: 1 hr.). (CAT & SPA.). 2000. bk. 75.00 (978-2-7005-1303-5(7)) Pub: Assimil FRA. Dist(s): Distribks Inc

Catalans. unabr. ed. Patrick O'Brian. Read by Simon Vance. 6 CDs. (Running Time: 7 hrs.). 2007. audio compact disk 64.95 (978-0-7927-4738-3(0)) AudioGO.

Catalina, unabr. ed. W. Somerset Maugham. Narrated by Davina Porter. 6 cass. (Running Time: 8 hrs. 30 mins.). (gr. 10). 1987. 51.00 (978-1-55690-095-2(3), 87900E7) Recorded Bks.
A young girl, Catalina, dreams of becoming the greatest actress in Spain.

Catalogue of Stamping Patterns Embracing All of the Latest & Choicest Designs Used in Connection with the Ilustrated Catalogue Home Beautiful, A Treatise of Decorative Art Needlework & Embroidery Materials. T. G Farnham. Mary Worrall et al. (ENG., (YA). 2007. audio compact disk 21.00 (978-0-944311-23-3(7)) MSU Museum.

Catalyst. Laurie Halse Anderson. 4 cass. (Running Time: 6 hrs. 1 min.). (J). (gr. 7 up). 2004. 32.00 (978-0-8072-0940-0(6), Listening Lib) Random Audio Pubg.
Meet Kate Malone, excellent student, minster's daughter, ace long-distance runner, whose world spins out of control.

Catalyst: A Tale of the Barque Cats. unabr. ed. Anne McCaffrey & Elizabeth Ann Scarborough. Read by Laural Merlington. (Running Time: 9 hrs.). (Barque Cats Ser.). 2010. 39.97 (978-1-4418-3830-8(9), 9781441838308, Brinc Audio MP3 Lib); 24.99 (978-1-4418-3829-2(5), 9781441838292, Brilliance MP3); 39.97 (978-1-4418-3832-2(5), 9781441838322, BADLE) Brilliance Audio.

Catalyst: A Tale of the Barque Cats. unabr. ed. Elizabeth Ann Scarborough. Read by Laural Merlington. Told to Anne McCaffrey. (Running Time: 9 hrs.). (Barque Cats Ser.). 2010. 24.99 (978-1-4418-3831-5(7), 9781441838315, BAD); audio compact disk 29.99 (978-1-4418-3827-8(9), 9781441838278, Bril Audio CD Unabri) Brilliance Audio.

Catalyst: A Tale of the Barque Cats. unabr. ed. Elizabeth Ann Scarborough. Read by Laural Merlington. Anne McCaffrey. (Running Time: 9 hrs.). (Barque Cats Ser.). 2010. audio compact disk 99.97 (978-1-4418-3828-5(7), 9781441838285, BriAudCD Unabrid) Brilliance Audio.

Catamarans Cabanas. Rock Overstreet. 1 cass. (Running Time: 1 hr. 30 mins.). 1999. audio compact disk 9.80 (978-0-536-02690-3(4)) Pearson Custom.

Catapulting to the Best-Seller List: One Talk Show at a Time. Narrated by T. J. Walker. 2003. audio compact disk 39.00 (978-1-932642-17-9(X)) Media Training.

***Cataract Surgery Essentials: Trusted Cataract Surgeon Reveals What You Need to Know about Modern Eye Surgery & Your Ophthalmologist.** David Richardson. (ENG.). 2010. audio compact disk 17.97 (978-0-9844489-0-6(X)) St Lucy Press.

Catastrofe de la Punta del Diablo. Roman Calvo. (SPA.). 2001. 16.95 (CSP312) J Norton Pubs.
Roman Calvo is the Chilean Sherlock Holmes. The attention to detail & the method of unravelling clues are reminiscent of Arthur Conan Doyle.

Catastrophe. abr. ed. Dick Morris & Eileen McGann. Read by Peter Ganim. (Playaway Adult Nonfiction Ser.). (ENG.). 2009. 59.99 (978-1-61545-572-0(8)) Find a World.

***Catastrophe.** abr. ed. Dick Morris & Eileen Mcgann. Read by Peter Ganim. (ENG.). 2009. (978-0-06-190234-5(9), Harper Audio); (978-0-06-190235-2(7), Harper Audio) HarperCollins Pubs.

Catastrophe. abr. ed. Dick Morris & Eileen McGann. Read by Peter Ganim. 2009. audio compact disk 29.99 (978-0-06-177440-9(5), Harper Audio) HarperCollins Pubs.

Catch. Poems. Robert Francis. (J). (CDL5 1237) HarperCollins Pubs.

Catch. unabr. ed. Archer Mayor. Read by Christopher Graybill. 6 CDs. (Running Time: 7 hrs. 15 mins.). 2008. audio compact disk 64.95 (978-0-7927-5781-8(5)) AudioGO.

Catch a Falling Clown. Stuart M. Kaminsky. Narrated by Tom Parker. (Running Time: 7 hrs.). (Toby Peters Mystery Ser.: No. 7). 2000. 27.95 (978-1-59912-444-5(0)) Iofy Corp.

Catch a Falling Clown. unabr. ed. Stuart M. Kaminsky. Read by Tom Parker. 5 cass. (Running Time: 7 hrs.). (Toby Peters Mystery Ser.: No. 7). 2001. 39.95 (978-0-7861-2075-8(4), 2836); audio compact disk 48.00 (978-0-7861-9693-7(9), 2836) Blckstn Audio.
Toby Peters, the Hollywood private eye who has previously saved the likes of Judy Garland, Gary Cooper and the Marx Brothers, is back. This time there's trouble under the big top and his services are required by none other than Emmett Kelly. A circus elephant has been electrocuted and Kelly fears for his life. Toby goes undercover as a clown and becomes entangled with a cast of bizarre characters, including a 250 pound wrestler/poet, a beautiful snake charmer, an immaculately dressed Swiss midget and a baffling witness named Alfred Hitchcock. It's all in a day's work for Toby Peters and in another fast paced Forties era mad cap adventure for his fans.

Catch a Falling Star. Ken McCoy. Read by Ken McCoy. 8 cass. (Running Time: 10 hrs. 35 mins.). (Story Sound Ser.). (J). 2004. 69.95 (978-1-85903-676-1(7)) Pub: Mgna Lrg Print GBR. Dist(s): Ulverscroft US

Catch a Wave: Beach Songs for Kids. Lyrics by Beach Boys, The. 1 cass. (Running Time: 44 min.). (J). 2000. 9.98 (978-1-56628-238-3(1)) MFLP CA.
Collection of songs performed by a team of kid vocalists & accomplished musicians.

Catch a Wave: Beach Songs for Kids. Lyrics by Beach Boys, The. 1 CD. (Running Time: 44 min.). (J). (gr. k-1). 2000. audio compact disk 15.98 (978-1-56628-237-6(3)) MFLP CA.
Collection of songs performed by a team of kid vocalists & accomplished musicians.

Catch As Cat Can. Rita Mae Brown & Sneaky Pie Brown. Narrated by Kate Forbes. 7 cass. (Running Time: 9 hrs. 45 mins.). (Mrs. Murphy Mystery Ser.). 2002. 62.00 (978-0-7887-9612-8(7), 96822) Recorded Bks.
This time out, the agile-witted tiger puss Mrs. Murphy makes the round of parties where Virginia's Very Best People mingle with some of the worst. Together, she and her human must unravel a veritable cat's cradle of ambition, greed, and murder at the center of which waits a killer with the most tangled of motives.

Catch by the Hearth - ShowTrax. Music by Paula Foley Tillen. 1 CD. (Running Time: 5 mins.). 2000. audio compact disk 19.95 (08742342) H Leonard.
Set in an easy jazz-waltz feel, this holiday original, heard here in the SSA voicing, perfectly captures the magical atmosphere of a holiday romance.

Catch Me If You Can: The Amazing True Story of the Youngest & Most Daring Con Man in the History of Fun & Profit! unabr. ed. Frank W. Abagnale. Read by Barrett Whitener. 1 CD. (Running Time: 8 hrs. 30 mins.). 2002. audio compact disk 24.95 (978-0-7861-9469-8(3), 2738) Blckstn Audio.
Frank W. Abagnale, alias Frank Williams, Robert Conrad, Frank Adams & Robert Monjo, was one of the most daring con-men, forgers, imposters & escape artists in history. Now recognized as the nation's leading authority on financial foul play, Abagnale is a charming rogue whose hilarious, stranger-than-fiction international escapades & ingenious escapes make this an irresistible tale of deceit.

Catch Me If You Can: The Amazing True Story of the Youngest & Most Daring Con Man in the History of Fun & Profit! unabr. ed. Frank W. Abagnale. Read by Barrett Whitener. 6 cass. (Running Time: 8 hrs. 30 mins.). 2001. 44.95 (978-0-7861-1968-4(3), 2738); audio compact disk 64.00 (978-0-7861-9757-6(9), 2738) Blckstn Audio.

Catch Me If You Can: The Amazing True Story of the Youngest & Most Daring Con Man in the History of Fun & Profit! unabr. ed. Frank W. Abagnale. 8 CDs. 2004. audio compact disk 29.95 (978-0-7861-9482-7(0)) Blckstn Audio.

Catch Me If You Can: The Amazing True Story of the Youngest & Most Daring Con Man in the History of Fun & Profit! unabr. ed. Frank W. Abagnale. Read by Barrett Whitener. 6 pieces. 2004. reel tape 25.95 (978-0-7861-2217-2(X)) Blckstn Audio.

Catch Me When I Fall. abr. ed. Nicci French. Read by Anne Flosnik. (Running Time: 6 hrs.). 2006. audio compact disk 16.99 (978-1-59737-667-9(1), 9781597376679, BCD Value Price) Brilliance Audio.

Catch Me When I Fall. abr. unabr. ed. Nicci French. Read by Anne Flosnik. (Running Time: 9 hrs.). 2006. audio compact disk 92.25 (978-1-59600-053-7(8), 9781596000537, BACDLib Ed) Brilliance Audio.
Holly Krauss lives her life in the fast lane. A successful, happily married businesswoman, she is loved and admired by everyone she meets. But that's only one side of Holly. The other takes regular walks on the wild side and is making reckless mistakes. When the two sides of Holly's life collide, her world quickly spirals out of control. She thinks she's being stalked, that someone is trying to extort money from her, and that threats lurk around every corner. Soon the people closest to her are running out of patience... But are her fears due to paranoia and illness, or is the danger very, very real? And if Holly's judgment and mental health are not sound, who will catch her when she falls?.

Catch Me When I Fall. unabr. ed. Nicci French. Read by Anne Flosnik. (Running Time: 9 hrs.). 2006. 39.25 (978-1-59710-916-1(9), 9781597109161, BADLE); 24.95 (978-1-59710-917-8(7), 9781597109178, BAD); 39.25 (978-1-59335-811-2(3), 9781593358112, Brinc Audio MP3 Lib); 24.95 (978-1-59335-677-4(3), 9781593356774, Brilliance MP3); 82.25 (978-1-59086-193-6(0), 9781590861936, BrilAudUnabridg); audio compact disk 34.95 (978-1-4233-0090-8(4), 9781423300908, Bril Audio CD Unabri) Brilliance Audio.

Catch of the Day. Marcia Evanick. Narrated by Johanna Parker. 8 CDs. (Running Time: 9 hrs. 30 mins.). 2002. audio compact disk 78.00 (978-1-4025-3819-3(7)) Recorded Bks.

Catch of the Day. unabr. ed. Marcia Evanick. Narrated by Johanna Parker. 7 cass. (Running Time: 9 hrs. 30 mins.). 2002. 62.00 (978-1-4025-3245-0(8), RG225) Recorded Bks.
When Chef Gwen Fletcher moves to Misty Harbor, Maine to fulfill her dream of opening her own restaurant, she isn't prepared for the throng of suitors who want to pay homage to the town's only bachelorette. Much to the dismay of the town's gentlemen, Gwen has only two things on her mind-getting her restaurant open before the tourist season begins and seeing what carpenter Daniel Creighton is hiding in his blue jeans. But the uncooperative Creighton's odd behavior may preclude her from doing either of these.

Catch the Fallen Sparrow. Priscilla Masters. (Story Sound CD Ser.). (J). 2002. audio compact disk 64.95 (978-1-85903-568-9(X)) Pub: Mgna Lrg Print GBR. Dist(s): Ulverscroft US

Catch the Lightning. unabr. ed. Catherine Asaro. Read by Anna Fields. 9 CDs. (Running Time: 12 hrs.). 2002. audio compact disk 72.00 (978-0-7861-9445-2(6)); 56.95 (978-0-7861-2303-2(6)) Blckstn Audio.
A young girl from Earth falls in love with a handsome stranger - and becomes a pawn in an interstellar war. In the distant future, the Skolian Empire rules one third of the human galaxy, and is the most powerful of all. For the ruling family has the power of telepathy, and through it, the ability to communicate faster than light, across interstellar space. But their most determined enemy, the traders, who thrive on human pain, need to interbreed with a Skolian to gain their powers. And now they have her.

Catch the Mood. Neville Goddard. 1 cass. (Running Time: 62 mins.). 1970. 8.00 (86) J & L Pubns.
Neville taught Imagination Creates Reality. He was a powerfully influential teacher of God as Consciousness.

Catch the Spirit. Michael Ballam. 1 cass. 9.95 (978-1-57734-327-1(1), 1100815) Covenant Comms.

Catch the Spirit - ShowTrax. Cristi Cary Miller. 1 CD. (Running Time: 1 hr.). 2000. audio compact disk 19.95 H Leonard.
This upbeat original is a great showcase for two-part choirs with a positive message & easy-t-sing melody & harmony.

Catch the Vision. Perf. by Imani Project Staff. Prod. by Brian Cook & Eric Smith. 1 CD. (Running Time: 1 hr.). 1997. audio compact disk 15.98 (978-1-57908-172-0(X)) Platinm Enter.

Catch-Up Catechesis. Judith Dunlap. 1 cass. (Running Time: 1 hr.). 2001. 8.95 (A6991) St Anthony Mess Pr.
Walks catechist and parent through the "General Directory for Catechesis" and suggests different ways to evangelize in various situations.

Catch-22. Joseph Heller. Read by Jim Weiss. 2002. 104.00 (978-0-7366-8962-5(1)) Books on Tape.

Catch-22. abr. ed. Joseph Heller. 2 cass. (Running Time: 3 hrs.). 1995. 21.95 (8246Q) Filmic Archives.
"Catch 22" said that if Yossarian were crazy, he wouldn't have to fly any more dangerous combat missions, but since he was sane enough to know he'd be crazy to keep on flying, then he wasn't crazy & would have to continue. Joseph Heller's deeply serious, yet brilliantly funny story is one of the great novels of the century.

Catch-22. unabr. ed. Joseph Heller. Read by Wolfram Kandinsky. 12 cass. (Running Time: 18 hrs.). 1996. 96.00 (978-0-7366-0527-4(4), 1501) Books on Tape.
This black satire of the American air war in Italy is comedy all the way to its conclusion. The message is: life is good but frail, death is random & violent, wars are insane & a menace.

Catch-22. unabr. ed. Joseph Heller. Read by Peter Whitman. 14 cass. (Running Time: 21 hrs.). 2000. 89.95 (SAB 020) Pub: Chivers Audio Bks GBR. Dist(s): AudioGO
It was Catch-22 that kept the men of the 256th Squadron flying. The regulation was a paradox, but it made as much sense as anything else to the men. A hypochondriac doctor, a navigator who gets lost, and a chaplain with a faith crisis, are just some of the characters encountered in this brilliantly funny yet serious satire.

***Catch-22.** unabr. ed. Joseph Heller. Read by Jay O. Sanders. (ENG.). 2007. (978-0-06-126245-6(5), Harper Audio); (978-0-06-126246-3(3), Harper Audio) HarperCollins Pubs.

Catch-22. unabr. ed. Joseph Heller & Joseph Heller. Read by Jay O. Sanders. 16 CDs. (Running Time: 70200 sec.). 2007. audio compact disk 44.95 (978-0-06-089009-4(6)) HarperCollins Pubs.

Catching Fire. 1 cass. (Running Time: 60 min.). (Discovery Ser.). 10.00 (978-0-89486-664-7(8), 5618G) Hazelden.

Catching Fire. Suzanne Collins. Narrated by Carolyn McCormick. 9 CDs. (Running Time: 11 hrs. 0 mins. 0 sec.). (Hunger Games Ser.: No. 2). (J). (gr. 7). 2009. audio compact disk 39.95 (978-0-545-10141-7(7)) Scholastic Inc.

Catching Fire. unabr. ed. Suzanne Collins. 10 CDs. (Running Time: 11 hrs. 37 mins.). (Hunger Games Ser.: No. 2). (YA). (gr. 7 up). 2009. audio compact disk 84.95 (978-0-545-10143-1(3)) Scholastic Inc.

Catching on to American Idioms. 2nd ed. Esther Ellin-Elmakiss. (C). 1993. 15.00 (978-0-472-00237-5(6)) U of Mich Pr.

Catching the Big Fish: Meditation, Consciousness, & Creativity. unabr. ed. David Lynch. Read by David Lynch. 2 CDs. (Running Time: 2 hrs.). (ENG.). (gr. 8). 2006. audio compact disk 19.95 (978-0-14-314207-2(0), PengAudBks) Penguin Grp USA.

Catching the Visions of Eternity. Bernell Christensen. 1 cass. 2004. 7.98 (978-1-55503-698-0(8), 06004946) Covenant Comms.
Learning to live gospel principles.

Catching the Wolf of Wall Street: More Incredible True Stories of Fortunes, Schemes, Parties, & Prison. unabr. ed. Jordan Belfort. (Running Time: 14 hrs. 50 mins.). 2009. 29.95 (978-1-4332-8880-7(X)); 85.95 (978-1-4332-8876-0(1)); audio compact disk 118.00 (978-1-4332-8877-7(X)) Blckstn Audio.

Catchy Choruses for Children. 1999. audio compact disk 15.00 (978-1-58302-141-5(8)) One Way St.
A 20 sing-along collection of songs from across the country and around the world.

Cate Quiz Em. 1 CD. (YA). (gr. 7-8). 1998. audio compact disk 19.99 (978-0-8100-0683-6(9)) Northwest Pub.

Catechesis: The Mission - Mother of Sorrows. John A. Hardon. Read by John A. Hardon. 1 cass. (Running Time: 1 hr. 05 mins.). 2.50 (978-1-56036-021-6(6), 361578) AMI Pr.
Side 1 - An explanation of the catechetical mission of the World Apostolate of Fatima. Side 2 - Homily on the Mother of Sorrows.

Catechism & the Sacraments. David Liptak. 1 cass. (Inspiring Presentations from the National Rosary Congress Ser.). 2.50 (978-1-56036-090-2(9)) AMI Pr.

Catechumen Game. 2004. cd-rom & audio compact disk 19.99 (978-0-9700919-0-1(7)) N Lightning.

Category Management: Building the Retail Performance of the Confectionery Category. 1 cass. (America's Supermarket Showcase '96 Ser.). 1996. 11.00 (NGA96-027) Sound Images.

Category Management 101. 1 cass. (America's Supermarket Showcase '96 Ser.). 1996. 11.00 (NGA96-009) Sound Images.

Category Romance. Brenda Wilbee. 1 cass. (Running Time: 45 mins.). (How to Write Best-Selling Romance Ser.: Tape 2). 7.95 (978-0-943777-09-2(7)) byBrenda.
Explains how to write category romance novels.

Category 5 Storm: Acts 2:1-13. Ed Young. 1997. 4.95 (978-0-7417-2150-1(3), A1150) Win Walk.

Cater Street Hangman. unabr. ed. Anne Perry. Narrated by Davina Porter. 7 cass. (Running Time: 10 hrs. 15 mins.). (Thomas Pitt Ser.). 2000. 62.00 (978-0-7887-3997-2(2), H1078E7) Recorded Bks.
When a maid in the upper class Ellison household is strangled, Inspector Pitt is called in to investigate. He finds a world ruled by strict manners & social customs, where the inhabitants of the Ellison's neighborhood appear to be more outraged by the thought of scandal than they are by murder. Inspector Pitt finds a most unlikely ally in Charlotte, the Ellison's spirited daughter. But as the murders continue Charlotte & Pitt find themselves drawn together by more than the investigation.

Catering to Nobody. abr. ed. Diane Mott Davidson. Read by Mary Gross. 2 cass. (Goldy Schulz Culinary Mysteries Ser.: No. 1). 2001. 7.95 (978-1-57815-191-2(0), Media Bks Audio) Media Bks NJ.

Catering to Nobody. abr. ed. Diane Mott Davidson. Read by Mary Gross. 2 cass. (Running Time: 3 hrs.). (Goldy Schulz Culinary Mysteries Ser.: No. 1). 1996. 16.95 (978-1-57511-020-2(2)) Pub Mills.
Catering the wake of her son's favorite teacher is not Goldy's idea of fun. Particularly when her former father-in-law passes out, nearly felled from rat poison & Goldy's business is shut down. That's the last straw, so Goldy stops sauteing & starts sleuthing to save her business & perhaps even her life!.

Catering to Nobody. unabr. ed. Diane Mott Davidson. Read by Barbara Rosenblat. 6 cass. (Running Time: 9 hrs.). (Goldy Schulz Culinary Mysteries Ser.: No. 1). 2004. 29.95 (978-1-59007-350-6(9)); audio compact disk 49.95 (978-1-59007-436-7(X)) Pub: New Millenn Enter. Dist(s): PerseuPGW

Catering to Nobody. unabr. ed. Diane Mott Davidson. Narrated by Barbara Rosenblat. 8 CDs. (Running Time: 8 hrs. 45 mins.). (Goldy Schulz Culinary Mysteries Ser.: No. 1). 2001. audio compact disk 78.00 (978-0-7887-7163-7(9), C1416) Recorded Bks.
Get ready for a smorgasbord of delicious suspense prepared by Goldy Bear, an irrepressible mistress of menus & amateur sleuth. Goldy Bear, recently divorced, has made a home for herself & her young son in scenic Aspen Valley, Colorado. There, calls for Goldilock's Catering have been steady enough to pay the bills. But when a mourner is felled by rat poison during a funeral buffet Goldy is serving, the police quickly close her business. Now it's up to Goldy to find the rat who has tainted her food & her reputation. As the mystery unfolds, its tension is sweetened by delectable recipes, including Goldy's Dream Cake, Dungeon Bars & Honey Ginger Snaps.

Catering to Nobody. unabr. ed. Diane Mott Davidson. Narrated by Barbara Rosenblat. 6 cass. (Running Time: 8 hrs. 45 mins.). (Goldy Schulz Culinary Mysteries Ser.: No. 1). 1999. 51.00 (978-0-7887-0647-9(0), 94824E7) Recorded Bks.
Goldy bear makes a home for herself & her son in Colorado, where Goldilock's Catering has been a success. But when a guest dies at her buffet, she must find who tainted her food.

Caterpillar & the Polliwog. 2004. bk. 24.95 (978-0-89719-763-2(1)); 8.95 (978-0-7882-0074-8(7)); cass. & flmstrp 30.00 (978-0-89719-571-3(X)) Weston Woods.

Caterpillar & the Polliwog. Jack Kent. 1 cass. (J). (ps-3). 8.95 (978-0-89719-959-9(6), LTR312C) Weston Woods.
"When I grow up, I'm going to turn into something else," the caterpillar boasts to her friends. When polliwog discovers that he, too, will turn into something else, he tells caterpillar & off they go to change into butterflies. While the polliwog waits patiently for his friend to emerge from her cocoon, he doesn't notice that he is changing too - but not into a butterfly!.

Caterpillar & the Polliwog. Jack Kent. 1 readalong cass. (Running Time: 6 min.). (J). (ps-3). 2004. pap. bk. 14.95 (978-0-89719-762-5(3), PBC312) Weston Woods.

Caterpillar Can't Wait! Early Explorers Early Set A Audio CD. Benchmark Education Staff. (J). 2006. audio compact disk 10.00 (978-1-4108-7612-6(8)) Benchmark Educ.

Caterpillars see Tales of Terror

***Caterpillars: A Tale of Terror.** E. F. Benson. 2009. (978-1-60136-516-3(0)) Audio Holding.

Caterpillar's Wish. unabr. ed. Alexander R. Shepherd School Staff. 1 cass. (Running Time: 6 mins.). (J). (ps-3). 1993. pap. bk. 14.45 (978-0-8045-6754-1(9), 6754) Spoken Arts.

Catfish Cafe. unabr. ed. Earl Emerson. Narrated by Richard Poe. 6 cass. (Running Time: 9 hrs.). (Thomas Black Mystery Ser.: Vol. 10). 2000. 57.00 (978-0-7887-4875-2(0), 96029E7) Recorded Bks.
Banilda Little, daughter of Thomas' former police partner, vanishes & a bullet riddled school teacher is found in her car. Thomas' efforts to crack the case force him to sift through the extended Little family, leaving him with more questions than answers.

Catfish Row - Grand Canyon Suite. Perf. by George Gershwin et al. 1 cass. (Running Time: 1 hr.). 7.98 (TA 30086); audio compact disk 12.78 Jewel box. (TA 80086) NewSound.

Cathedral. unabr. ed. Nelson DeMille. Read by Scott Brick. (Running Time: 19 hrs.). (ENG.). 2009. 24.98 (978-1-60024-817-7(9)) Pub: Hachet Audio. Dist(s): HachBkGrp

Cathedral Classics. 2005. audio compact disk 16.98 (978-5-559-11275-6(5)) Pt of Grace Ent.

Cathedral of the Sea. Ildefonso Falcones. Read by Paul Michael. (Running Time: 82800 sec.). (ENG.). (gr. 8 up). 2008. audio compact disk 44.95 (978-0-14-314293-5(3), PengAudBks) Penguin Grp USA.

Cathedrals Precious Memories: A Cappella Favorites. Perf. by Cathedrals, The. 1 CD. (Running Time: 60 mins.). 2000. audio compact disk (978-0-7601-3617-1(3), SO42870) Brentwood Music.
Songs include: "Heavenly Parade," "Tell It to Jesus," "Abide with Me," "Dig a Little Deeper," "All Hail the Power" & more.

Cathedrals Precious Memories: Inspirational Hits. Perf. by Cathedrals, The. 1 CD. (Running Time: 60 mins.). 2000. audio compact disk (978-0-7601-3613-3(0), SO42870) Brentwood Music.
Songs include: "You Can Walk on Water," "Who Can Do Anything," "Bloodwashed Band," "Champion of Love," "This Ole House" & more.

Catherine, Called Birdy. Karen Cushman. Read by Kate Maberly. 2 cass. (Running Time: 3 hrs. 6 mins.). (J). 2000. 18.00 (978-0-7366-9031-7(X)) Books on Tape.
Catherine's mother wants her to become a lady; her father wants her to marry well; Catherine, called Birdy, has her own ideas & dreams only of painting & making songs.

Catherine, called Birdy. Karen Cushman. Narrated by Jenny Sterlin. 6 CDs. (Running Time: 6 hrs. 30 mins.). (gr. 6 up). audio compact disk 58.00 (978-0-7887-9520-6(1)) Recorded Bks.

Catherine, Called Birdy. unabr. ed. Karen Cushman. Narrated by Jenny Sterlin. 5 pieces. (Running Time: 6 hrs 30 mins.). (gr. 6 up). 1997. 44.00 (978-0-7887-0687-5(X), 94861E7) Recorded Bks.
In 1290, her fourteenth year, Catherine begins a diary that quickly fills with the irrespressible joys & frustrations of her days. Birdy's lively writing is sprinkled with the vivid details of life in medieval England.

Catherine Carmier, unabr. ed. Ernest J. Gaines. Read by S. Patricia Bailey. 4 cass. (Running Time: 6 hrs.). 1997. 32.95 (1892) Blckstn Audio.
A compelling love story set in a deceptively bucolic Louisiana countryside, where blacks, Cajuns & whites maintain an uneasy coexistence. After living in San Francisco for ten years, Jackson returns to his benefactor, Aunt Charlotte.

Catherine Carmier. unabr. ed. Ernest J. Gaines. Read by S. Patricia Bailey. 4 cass. (Running Time: 5 hrs. 30 mins.). 2001. 32.95 (978-0-7861-1127-5(5), 1892) Blckstn Audio.

Catherine Cookson. unabr. ed. Kathleen Jones. Read by Elizabeth Henry. 15 cass. (Running Time: 22 hrs. 30 min.). 2001. 104.95 (26794) Pub: Soundings Ltd GBR. Dist(s): Ulverscroft US

Catherine Cookson Set: The Biography. Kathleen Jones. Read by Elizabeth Henry. 15 CDs. (Sound Ser.). 2003. audio compact disk 104.95 (978-1-86042-926-2(2)) Pub: UlverLrgPrint GBR. Dist(s): Ulverscroft US

Catherine Cookson Set: The Biography. unabr. ed. Kathleen Jones. Read by Elizabeth Henry. 15 cass. (Running Time: 20 hrs.). 2000. 49.95 (978-1-86042-679-7(4), 26794) Pub: Soundings Ltd GBR. Dist(s): ISIS Pub

Catherine Coulter: Eleventh Hour, Blindside, & Blowout. abr. ed. Catherine Coulter. Read by Sandra Burr. (Running Time: 18 hrs.). 2006. audio compact disk 34.95 (978-1-4233-1676-3(2), 9781423316763, BACD) Brilliance Audio.
Eleventh Hour: When FBI agent Dane Carver's twin brother, Father Michael Joseph, is brutally murdered in his San Francisco church, husband-and-wife agents Lacey Sherlock and Dillon Savich take a personal interest in the investigation. Then Nicola "Nick" Jones, a homeless woman and the only witness to the shooting, is scared out of her mind because she is trying to hide from her own monsters - who are drawing closer and closer. Blindside: When six-year-old Sam Kettering is kidnapped and then manages to save himself, Savich and Sherlock join his father-former FBI agent Miles Kettering -to determine why Sam would be abducted and brought to eastern Tennessee. Though the local sheriff, Katie Benedict, catches up with Sam before the kidnappers do, the case isn't over -not by a long shot. Blowout: A long weekend in the Poconos is cut short when Sherlock and Savich are helicoptered back to Washington to lead the investigation into the brutal murder of a Supreme Court Justice. Savich allows Callie Markham, an investigative reporter for The Washington Post, to partner with local Metro Police liaison Ben Raven, since she's got the inside track - she's the stepdaughter of the murdered justice.

Catherine Coulter Bride: Mad Jack, the Courtship, the Scottish Bride. abr. ed. Catherine Coulter. Read by Anne Flosnik. (Running Time: 18 hrs.). (Bride Ser.). 2007. audio compact disk 34.95 (978-1-4233-3422-4(1), 9781423334224, BACD) Brilliance Audio.

Catherine Coulter Bride: The Sherbrooke Bride, the Hellion Bride, the Heiress Bride. abr. ed. Catherine Coulter. Read by Anne Flosnik. (Running Time: 18 hrs.). (Bride Ser.). 2007. audio compact disk 34.95 (978-1-4233-3364-7(0), 9781423333647, BACD) Brilliance Audio.

Catherine Coulter Bride CD Collection 3: Pendragon, the Sherbrooke Twins, Lyon's Gate. abr. ed. Catherine Coulter. Read by Anne Flosnik. (Running Time: 18 hrs.). (Bride Ser.). 2008. audio compact disk 34.95 (978-1-4233-5250-1(5), 9781423352501, BACD) Brilliance Audio.

Catherine Coulter FBI: Point Blank, Double Take, TailSpin. abr. collector's ed. Catherine Coulter. (Running Time: 18 hrs.). (FBI Thriller Ser.). 2009. audio compact disk 34.99 (978-1-4418-1196-7(6), 9781441811967) Brilliance Audio.

Catherine Doherty Talks to Families. Speeches. Perf. by Catherine Doherty. 1 cass. (Running Time: 75 mins.). 2001. 9.95 (978-0-921440-71-0(5)) Madonna Hse CAN.
For over five decades, Madonna House has been the host to a summer retreat vacation for families called "Cana Colony" on a lake in rural Ontario. For many years, a highlight of the week was the talk given by Catherine Doherty-this new cassette contains some inspiring and motivating selections, including: The holiness of family life, the family and the Eucharist, walking through trials in the light of the Gospel, Mary's fiat and the family.

Catherine Lim. unabr. ed. Catherine Lim. Read by Catherine Lim. Interview with Rebekah Presson. 1 cass. (Running Time: 29 mins.). 1990. 10.00 (113090) New Letters.
She is a best-selling author in her home of Singapore. In this interview Lim reads a short story about an old woman who is frightened that her children will not take care of her.

Catherine Mcevoy with Felix Dolan. Contrib. by Catherine McEvoy. (ENG.). 1996. 13.95 (978-0-8023-7117-1(5)); audio compact disk 20.95 (978-0-8023-8117-0(0)) Pub: Clo Iar-Chonnachta IRL. Dist(s): Dufour

***Catherine of Siena.** Sigrid Undset. 2010. audio compact disk 39.95 (978-1-58617-518-4(1)) Pub: Ignatius Pr. Dist(s): Midpt Trade

Catherine Tate Show. Catherine Tate. 2006. audio compact disk 12.99 (978-1-84607-095-2(3)) Pub: AudioGo GBR. Dist(s): AudioGO

Catherine the Great. unabr. ed. Henri Troyat. Read by Jill Masters. 15 cass. (Running Time: 22 hrs. 30 mins.). Incl. Pt. 1. Catherine the Great. 7 cass. (Running Time: 7 hrs.). Henri Troyat. Read by Jill Masters. 56.00 (1427-A); Pt. 2. Catherine the Great. 8 cass. (Running Time: 8 hrs.). Henri Troyat. Read by Jill Masters. 64.00 (1427-B); 1977. 120.00 (978-0-7366-0454-3(5), 1427A/B) Books on Tape.
This is the story of Russia's passionate empress & how she triumphed to become the most powerful woman in the world.

Catherine-Wheel. Patricia Wentworth. Read by Diana Bishop. (Running Time: 34800 sec.). 2007. 69.95 (978-0-7531-3725-3(9)) Pub: ISIS Audio GBR. Dist(s): Ulverscroft US

Catherine-Wheel. Patricia Wentworth. Read by Diana Bishop. (Running Time: 34800 sec.). 2007. audio compact disk 84.95 (978-0-7531-2692-9(3)) Pub: ISIS Audio GBR. Dist(s): Ulverscroft US

Catherine Wheels. abr. ed. Leif Peterson. (Running Time: 21600 sec.). 2005. audio compact disk 27.99 (978-1-59859-103-3(7)) Oasis Audio.

Catherine Wheels. abr. ed. Leif Peterson. Narrated by Scott Brick. (ENG.). 2006. 19.59 (978-1-60814-112-8(8)) Oasis Audio.

Catholic at Heart. 2004. 24.95 (978-1-888992-54-0(9)); audio compact disk 27.95 (978-1-888992-55-7(7)) Catholic Answers.

Catholic Bells see William Carlos Williams Reads His Poetry

Catholic Book of Prayers. 3 cass. 1997. 12.95 (978-0-89942-913-7(0), 913/00) Cathlic Bk Pub.

Catholic Catechism: Its Significance for Catholics, Non-Catholic Christians, for Non-Christians. Jose Sanchez. 1 cass. (National Meeting of the Institute, 1994 Ser.). 4.00 (94N1) IRL Chicago.

Catholic Catechism & the Sacraments. John A. Hardon. 10 cass. (Running Time: 90 min. per cass.). 40.00 Set. (95H) IRL Chicago.

Catholic Catechism Is for Everyone. Joseph Fessio. 1 cass. (National Meeting of the Institute, 1994 Ser.). 4.00 (94N7) IRL Chicago.

Catholic Church: A History. Instructed by William R. Cook. 2009. 199.95 (978-1-59803-595-7(9)); audio compact disk 269.95 (978-1-59803-596-4(7)) Teaching Co.

Catholic Classics, Vol. 1. Composed by Stuart Hine et al. 1 cass. (Running Time: 1 hr.). 1996. 10.95 (375); audio compact disk 15.95 (375) GIA Pubns.

Catholic Classics, Vol. 2. Composed by Bob Dufford et al. 1 cass. (Running Time: 1 hr.). 1996. 10.95 (376); audio compact disk 15.95 (376) GIA Pubns.

Catholic Classics: Simple Gift of Praise. Stephen Petrunak. Perf. by David Fischer. 2000. 10.95 (CS-488); audio compact disk 15.95 (CD-488) GIA Pubns.

Catholic Classics Vol. 3: Hymn Instrumental. Bobby Fisher. 1 cass. (Running Time: 1 hr.). 1998. 10.95 (CS-440) GIA Pubns.

Catholic Classics Vol. 3: Hymn Instrumental, Vol. 3. Bobby Fisher. 1 CD. (Running Time: 1 hr.). 1998. audio compact disk 15.95 (CD-440) GIA Pubns.

Catholic Digest, Words for Quiet Moments. unabr. ed. Read by Efrem Zimbalist. 1 cass. (Running Time: 1 hr. 30 min.). 2001. 13.00 (978-1-59040-155-2(7), Phoenix Audio) Pub: Amer Intl Pub. Dist(s): PerseuPGW

Catholic Edition New Testament of the New American Bible. 2006. audio compact disk 49.95 (978-0-89942-623-5(9)) Cathlic Bk Pub.

Catholic Eucharistic Ministry: Bridging Parish & Hospital. 1 cass. (Care Cassettes Ser.: Vol. 13, No. 2). 1986. 10.80 Assn Prof Chaplains.

Catholic Gospel. Scott Hahn. 8 cass. 39.95 (5273) Ignatius Pr.
One of the great ironies of the four-centuries old disagreement between Protestants & the Catholic Church is that both communities appeal, quite strongly, to the writings of St. Paul. Scott Hahn shows how profoundly Catholic are Paul's writings & how Protestant theologians, such as Martin Luther, often single out isolated themes in Paul's writings while ignoring other aspects of Paul's thought that balance out those themes. This is particularly true concerning the Redemption. Hahn shows how Christ's self-sacrifice on the Cross gives to human beings the grace - not merely a favor but a power - to share in the divine life of the Trinity.

Catholic Latin Classics. Cathedral Singers. 2000. 10.95 (CS-486); audio compact disk 15.95 (CD-486) GIA Pubns.

Catholic Morality & End-of-Life Issues: Euthanasia, Assisted Suicide & Life Support. Kenneth Overberg. 3 cass. (Running Time: 3 hrs.). 2001. 24.95 (A6690) St Anthony Mess Pr.
At a time when a growing numnber of states seek to legalize euthanasia and assisted suicide, Overberg defines the moral decision-making involved in these issues and explores the recent papal encyclical, "The Gospel of Life".

Catholic Prayer Companion: A Heartwarming Collection of 30 Best-Loved Catholic Prayers. Prod. by Sheldon Cohen. 1 CD. (Running Time: 50 mins.). 2004. audio compact disk 12.95 (978-0-87946-267-3(1), 409) ACTA Pubns.
The Catholic faith has a rich tradition of comforting and supportive prayers from which we can draw at will. This beautiful CD contains thirty of the best-known and most-loved devotions, intercessions and invocations, including prayers to God, Mary, the Saints, prayers from the Mass, and blessings for all sorts of occasions and locations. The reverent voices on this CD are accompanied by beautiful, original background music.

Catholic Response to Biblical Fundamentalism. Ronald Witherup. 1 cass. (Running Time: 1 hr. 21 mins.). 2001. 8.95 (A8051) St Anthony Mess Pr.
Reviews the unique Catholica approach to the Bible and contrasts the position of fundamentalist.

Catholic Sacramental Ministry to the Sick. Florence Smithe & James Moriarty. 1986. 10.80 (0311) Assn Prof Chaplains.

Catholic Teaching on the Coming of Antichrist. Perf. by John Vennari. 1 cass. (Running Time: 90 mins.). 7.00 (20205) Cath Treas.
In a period of reckless speculation on the "end times," gives solid Catholic principles based on Scripture, the Fathers & Church teaching. Helps to form sound judgements on this important topic. Learn what is certain, what is probable & what is indefinite regarding the man of sin.

Catholic to Charismatics: History of Worship: Logos July 4, 1999. Ben Young. 1999. 7.45 (978-0-7417-6140-8(8), B0140) Win Walk.

Catholic Traditions of Foundational Formative Spirituality. Adrian Van Kaam & Susan Muto. 8 cass. 1984. 61.95 incl. shelf-case. (TAH141) Alba Hse Comns.
Presents the basis for a new foundational human formation & spirituality.

Catholic Women's Response to Feminism. 1 cass. (Running Time: 1 hr.). 2003. 13.95 (978-1-932631-53-1(4)); audio compact disk 13.95 (978-1-932631-54-8(2)) Ascensn Pr.

Catholicism. 1 CD. (Running Time: 1 hr.). 2003. audio compact disk 6.95 (978-1-932631-77-7(1)) Ascensn Pr.

Catholicism: Eternity: Smoking or Non-Smoking. 1 cass. (Running Time: 1 hr.). 2003. 6.95 (978-1-932631-82-1(8)); audio compact disk 6.95 (978-1-932631-83-8(6)) Ascensn Pr.

Catholicism: More Than a Head Trip. Richard Rohr. 1 cass. (Running Time: 1 hr.). 2001. 8.95 (A8131) St Anthony Mess Pr.
How do we reclaim the richness of our tradition? Our Catholic incarnational tradition must reaffirm a worldview that all that is holy to counteract secular currents that often deny the inherent value of humanity and of the world.

Catholicism: Scripture & Tradition. 1 cass. (Running Time: 1 hr.). 2003. 6.95 (978-1-932631-80-7(1)); audio compact disk 6.95 (978-1-932631-81-4(X)) Ascensn Pr.

Catholicism: The Catholic Church. 1 cass. (Running Time: 1 hr.). 2003. 6.95 (978-1-932631-78-4(X)); audio compact disk 6.95 (978-1-932631-79-1(8)) Ascensn Pr.

Catholicism: The Divinity of Christ. 1 cass. (Running Time: 1 hr.). 2003. 6.95 (978-1-932631-76-0(3)) Ascensn Pr.

Catholicism No. 1: The Existence of God. 1 cass. (Running Time: 1 hr.). 2003. 6.95 (978-1-932631-74-6(7)); audio compact disk 6.95 (978-1-932631-75-3(5)) Ascensn Pr.

Catholicism & Fundamentalism. Karl Keating. Read by Al Covaia. 8 cass. (Running Time: 8 hrs.). 1988. pap. bk. 14.95 (978-0-89870-177-7(5), 107-C) Ignatius Pr.
A clear, detailed and charitable rebuttal to the Fundamentalist arguments against Catholicism.

Catholicism Dissolved: The New Evangelization. Perf. by John Vennari. 2 cass. (Running Time: 3 hrs.). 14.00 (20209) Cath Treas.
The "new Evangelization" is a further implementation of ecumenism, inculturation, pentecostalism & liberalism into the Church. Learn about its history, its principles & how to recognize its face. Be prepared for the next tidal wave of the Vatican II Revolution.

***Catholicism for Dummies.** abr. ed. John Trigilio. Read by Brett Barry. (ENG.). 2008. (978-0-06-176479-0(5), Harper Audio); (978-0-06-176478-3(7), Harper Audio) HarperCollins Pubs.

Catholicism 101: Essentials for the Journey. Jeff Cavins. (ENG.). 2007. audio compact disk 89.95 (978-1-934567-13-5(2)) Excorde Inc.

Catholicizing a Nation: The Six Points of Father Denis Fahey. Perf. by John Vennari. 1 cass. (Running Time: 45 mins.). 7.00 (20202) Cath Treas.
What constitutes a Catholic nation? The simple, profound Six Points outlines it for us. Gives a compressive Catholic world view solidly based on tradition Papal Teaching. This not only helps to understand the present crisis of Faith, but also offers a tried & true Catholic solution.

Cathy Alpert. Interview with Kay Bonetti. 1 cass. (Running Time: 1 hr.). (Author Interview Ser.). 13.95 (978-1-55644-409-8(5)); set. (978-1-55644-410-4(9), 15012) Am Audio Prose.
Lively & informative discussions of writer's life & work with Kay Bonetti.

Cathy & Marcy Collection for Kids. Perf. by Cathy Fink & Marcy Marxer. 1 cass. (Running Time: 44 mins.). (Family Ser.). (J). (ps-5). 1994. 9.98 (8029); audio compact disk 14.98 (8029) Rounder Records.
This collection will have you yodeling, laughing & dancing along with these two accomplished musicians. Beneath the fun, these songs teach self-respect & respect for others.

Cathy Barton & Dave Para: Ballad of the Boonslick. 1 cass. 9.98 (C-512) Folk-Legacy.
From the heart of the Central Missouri.

Cathy Barton & Dave Para: Movin' on down the River. 1 cass. 9.98 (C-511) Folk-Legacy.
Their first recording.

Cathy Barton & Dave Para: On a Day Like Today. 1 cass. 9.98 (C-107) Folk-Legacy.
A lovely program from the Heartland.

Cathy Freeman. unabr. ed. Adrian McGregor. 9 cass. (Running Time: 12 hrs. 40 mins.). 2004. 72.00 (978-1-74030-702-4(X)) Pub: Bolinda Pubng AUS. Dist(s): Lndmrk Audiobks

Catilina's Riddle, unabr. ed. Steven Saylor. Read by Scott Harrison. 13 cass. (Running Time: 19 hrs.). 1997. 85.95 (978-0-7861-1177-0(1), 1920) Blckstn Audio.
The year is 63 B.C. & Gordianus the Finder unexpectedly achieves the dream of every Roman-a farm in the Etruscan countryside. So he abandons the city.

Catnaper. abr. ed. Robert A. Monroe. Read by Robert A. Monroe. (Mind Food Ser.). 1988. 14.95 (978-1-56102-402-5(3)) Inter Indus.
Compresses 90 minute sleep cycle to 30.

Catnapped! abr. ed. Mildred Gordons. Read by Mary Dorr. 2 cass. (Running Time: 3 hrs.). 1995. 17.00 set. (978-0-9643324-2-3(6)) Dover Hill Pr.
The FBI has to solve the "kidnapping" of Darn Cat to save the lives of his "family." Sequel to Disney Film, "That Darn Cat".

Catnapper. unabr. ed. Robert A. Monroe. Read by Robert A. Monroe. 1 cass. (Running Time: 30 mins.). (TimeOut Ser.). 1991. 14.95 (978-1-56102-800-9(2)) Inter Indus.
Listen for 30 minutes & gain the refreshing benefits of a restful, 90 minute nap.

Catnapping Mystery. David A. Adler. Narrated by Christina Moore. 1 cass. (Running Time: 30 mins.). (Cam Jansen Ser.: No. 18). (gr. 2 up). 2001. 10.00 (978-0-7887-5018-2(6), 96196E7) Recorded Bks.
When Cam & her family go to the Royal Hotel, the last thing they have planned for the day is a mystery. But then they meet Mrs. Wright, a woman who gave her luggage & her cat to the bellhop while she checked in, but now can't find them. Can Cam's photographic memory help solve the mystery?.

Catriona. Robert Louis Stevenson. Read by David Case. (Running Time: 9 hrs. 30 mins.).Tr. of David Balfour. 2003. 27.95 (978-1-60083-664-0(X), Audiofy Corp) Iofy Corp.

Catriona. Robert Louis Stevenson. Read by David Case. (Running Time: 34440 sec.).Tr. of David Balfour. (ENG.). 2004. audio compact disk 34.99 (978-1-4001-0099-6(2)); audio compact disk 19.99 (978-1-4001-5099-1(X)) Pub: Tantor Media. Dist(s): IngramPubServ

Catriona. Robert Louis Stevenson. Read by David Case.Tr. of David Balfour. (ENG.). 2005. audio compact disk 69.99 (978-1-4001-3099-3(9)) Pub: Tantor Media. Dist(s): IngramPubServ

Catriona, unabr. ed. Robert Louis Stevenson. Read by Frederick Davidson. 7 cass. (Running Time: 10 hrs. 30 mins.).Tr. of David Balfour. 1999. 49.95 (2366) Blckstn Audio.
Continues the adventures of David Balfour & his friend Alan Breck. Balfour returns to the city in order to defend Breck against false charges in the Appin murder.

Catriona. unabr. ed. Robert Louis Stevenson. Read by Frederick Davidson. 7 cass. (Running Time: 10 hrs.).Tr. of David Balfour. 2001. 49.95 (978-0-7861-1516-7(5), 2366) Blckstn Audio.

Catriona. unabr. ed. Robert Louis Stevenson & Frederick Davidson. (Running Time: 9 hrs. NaN mins.).Tr. of David Balfour. 2008. 29.95 (978-0-7861-7224-5(X)); audio compact disk 70.00 (978-1-4332-5498-7(0)) Blckstn Audio.

Catriona. unabr. collector's ed. Robert Louis Stevenson. Read by David Case. 7 cass. (Running Time: 10 hrs. 30 mins.).Tr. of David Balfour. 1996. 56.00 (978-0-7366-3251-5(4), 3909) Books on Tape.
"Catriona" is the sequel to "Kidnapped" & one of Stevenson's own favorites. He considered it his "high water mark," saying he would "never do a better book".

Catriona, with EBook. unabr. ed. Robert Louis Stevenson. Narrated by David Case. (Running Time: 9 hrs. 30 mins. 0 sec.). (ENG.). 2009. 22.99 (978-1-4001-6122-5(3)); audio compact disk 32.99 (978-1-4001-1122-0(6)) Pub: Tantor Media. Dist(s): IngramPubServ

Catriona, with eBook. unabr. ed. Robert Louis Stevenson. Narrated by David Case. (Running Time: 9 hrs. 30 mins. 0 sec.). (ENG.). 2009. audio compact disk 65.99 (978-1-4001-4122-7(2)) Pub: Tantor Media. Dist(s): IngramPubServ

Cats. unabr. ed. Ed. by Linda Spizzirri. 1 cass. (Running Time: 15 mins.). Dramatization. (Educational Coloring Book & Cassette Package Ser.). (J). (gr. k-8). 1989. pap. bk. 6.95 (978-0-86545-160-5(5)) Spizzirri.
Includes famous breeds like the Siamese, Angora & more.

Cats: A Celebration of the Nation's Favourite Pet in Words. Read by Liza Goddard & Richard Griffiths. 2 cass. (Running Time: 2 hrs.). 1998. 16.85 (978-1-901768-25-1(2)) Pub: CSA Telltapes GBR. Dist(s): Ulverscroft US

Cats - Canines Can Communicate. unabr. ed. 2 cass. (Running Time: 3 hrs.). 10.95 (978-0-925589-03-3(9)) JPM Pubs.
Based on true stories & experiences of the author & others as they telepathically communicate with animals. Instructional guidelines are given on how to learn the technique used by the author.

Cats & More Cats. abr. ed. Jane Garmey. 2 cass. (Running Time: 2 hrs.). 1997. 16.95 HarperCollins Pubs.

Cats, Cats, & More Cats: An Audio Anthology - 20 Cat Tales from Great Writers. unabr. abr. ed. Catherine Aird & James Boswell. Read by Keith Baxter & Ensemble Cast Staff. Ed. by Jane Garmey. (Running Time: 9000 sec.). 2006. audio compact disk 19.95 (978-1-59887-045-9(9), 1598870459) Pub: HighBridge. Dist(s): Workman Pub

Cats, Cooks & Other Things. unabr. ed. Narrated by Gilbert Highet. 1 cass. 9.95 (C23338) J Norton Pubs.

Cat's Cradle. Chieko Okazaki. 2 cass. (Running Time: 2 hrs.). 1993. 11.95 (978-1-57008-082-1(8), Bkcraft Inc) Deseret Bk.

Cat's Cradle. unabr. ed. Kurt Vonnegut. Read by Tony Roberts. (Running Time: 25200 sec.). 2007. audio compact disk 29.95 (978-0-06-089873-1(9)) HarperCollins Pubs.

***Cat's Cradle.** unabr. ed. Kurt Vonnegut. Read by Tony Roberts. (ENG.). 2007. (978-0-06-113520-0(8), Harper Audio); (978-0-06-113521-7(6), Harper Audio) HarperCollins Pubs.

Cat's Cradle. unabr. collector's ed. Kurt Vonnegut. Read by Dan Lazar. 6 cass. (Running Time: 6 hrs.). 1978. 36.00 (978-0-7366-0105-4(8), 1113) Books on Tape.
Set on the Carribean island of San Lorenzo, Felix Hoenikker, a physicist & one of the fathers of the atomic bomb, discusses "Ice Nine," a substance that can turn all the liquid in the world into a solid block of ice.

Cat's Eye, unabr. ed. Margaret Atwood. Narrated by Barbara Caruso. 11 cass. (Running Time: 15 hrs. 15 mins.). 1995. 91.00 (978-0-7887-0171-9(1), 94396E7) Recorded Bks.
Returning to the city of her youth, a successful Canadian painter is engulfed by images of the past & the childhood friendships that haunt her still.

Cat's Eyewitness. Rita Mae Brown & Sneaky Pie Brown. (Mrs. Murphy Mystery Ser.). 2005. audio compact disk 29.99 (978-1-4193-1639-5(7)) Recorded Bks.

Cat's Eyewitness. unabr. ed. Rita Mae Brown & Sneaky Pie Brown. Narrated by Kate Forbes. 8 CDs. (Running Time: 9 hrs. 30 mins.). (Mrs. Murphy Mystery Ser.). 2005. audio compact disk 89.75 (978-1-4193-2060-6(2), C2927); 79.75 (978-1-4193-2058-3(0), 97941) Recorded Bks.
The New York Times best-selling Mrs. Murphy mysteries delight fans with an irresistible blend of suspense, engaging characters, and the entertaining high jinks of some quick-witted, four-legged friends. With more than two million copies in print, the series has made coauthors Rita Mae and Sneaky Pie Brown the most popular human/feline writing team in the world. The sleepy little town of Crozet, Virginia has seen its share of mischief and mayhem, but nothing like this. While visiting the Mt. Carmel monastery, Mary Minor "Harry" Haristeen witnesses a statue of the Virgin Mary cry tears of blood. Legend says this foretells crises, and soon a monk is found frozen to death near the statue. Before long the monk¿s body disappears, another Crozet citizen dies, and a shocking revelation to an ages-old mystery surfaces. Thankfully, Harry and her sleuthing animals are on the case - unofficially, of course.

Cat's Eyewitness. unabr. ed. Rita Mae Brown & Sneaky Pie Brown. (Mrs. Murphy Mystery Ser.). 2005. audio compact disk 34.99 (978-1-4193-2907-4(3)) Recorded Bks.

Cats in Concord. Doreen Tovey. Read by Diana Bishop. 4 cass. (Running Time: 4 hrs.). (Sound Ser.). 2001. 44.95 (978-1-84283-106-9(2)) Pub: UlverLrgPrint GBR. Dist(s): Ulverscroft US
After many years of keeping Siamese cats in a remote cottage in Somerset, Doreen Tovey has come to the conclusion that the breed grows more delinquent by the generation. Rama, a handsome young Seal Point who thinks, Tani, the Lilac Point matriarch who watches over him, and Tiah Tigerlily, the Tabby Point kitten who eventually arrives on the scene as his companion and hench-girl, are loveable characters in a hilarious account of country life.

Cats in the Belfry. unabr. ed. Doreen Tovey. Read by Diana Bishop. 4 cass. (Running Time: 6 hrs.). 1993. 39.95 (978-1-85496-845-6(9), 68459) Pub: Soundings Ltd GBR. Dist(s): Ulverscroft US
The author & her husband bought Sugieh, their first Siamese kitten, to deal with an invasion of mice. Sugieh brought bedlam to a quiet country home, & when she herself had kittens, life became more riotous than ever. After Sugieh's tragic death, her offspring Solomon & Sheba stayed on, doggedly determined to keep the Siamese flag flying.

Cats in the Coffee. unabr. ed. Joyce Fussey. Read by Anita Wright. 5 cass. (Running Time: 6 hrs.). 1999. 49.95 (978-0-7531-0622-8(1), 990915) Pub: ISIS Audio GBR. Dist(s): Ulverscroft US
Gallantly Joyce Fussey struggles for sanity among strong-willed cats, highly-strung cows, temperamental calves, recalcitrant hens, an aggressive drake & a host of animal personalities seeking attention. Even the muck-spreader has psychological problems, so what hope is there for "new-fangled" electricity.

***Cats in the Parsonage: Ask the Animals & They Will Teach You.** unabr. ed. Clair Shaffer. Narrated by Maurice England. (ENG.). 2010. 10.98 (978-1-59644-951-0(9)); audio compact disk 16.98 (978-1-59644-950-3(0)) christianaud.

Cats of the Wild. 1 cass. (J). pap. bk. 6.95 (978-0-86545-102-5(8)); Spizzirri.
The magnificent hunting cats are featured on this tape. The large Siberian tiger, the beautiful Pallas cat & the Cheetah included.

Cats of the Wild. Ed. by Linda Spizzirri. 1 cass. Dramatization. (J). (gr. 1-8). pap. bk. 4.98 (978-0-86545-045-5(5)) Spizzirri.

Cat's Paw. unabr. ed. L. L. Thrasher. Read by Ron Varela. 8 cass. (Running Time: 9 hrs. 54 min.). 2001. 49.95 (978-1-58116-061-1(5)) Books in Motion.
Arrow Investigation's Zach Smith is hired to find a missing teenager, only to become involved with a lovely young woman who just may be involved with murder, and the disappearance of the lost teen.

Cat's Purr. Ashley Bryan. 1 cass. (Running Time: 1 hr.). (J). 1987. 33.63 (978-0-676-31690-2(5)) SRA McGraw.

Catskill Eagle. unabr. collector's ed. Robert B. Parker. Read by Michael Prichard. 5 cass. (Running Time: 7 hrs. 30 min.). (Spenser Ser.). 1990. 40.00 (978-0-7366-1676-8(4), 2524) Books on Tape.
In the detective business, Spenser sometimes has to bend the law. Other times, to break it. But he lives by his own inviolate rules. And he loves just one woman - even though she is the one woman he's just lost. So when Susan's desperate letter arrives, Spenser doesn't think twice. His best friend, Hawk faces a life sentence. And Susan has gotten herself into even bigger trouble. Now Spenser has to free them both...even if it means breaking his own rules to do it.

Catskills on Broadway. unabr. abr. ed. 1 cass. (Running Time: 1 hr.). 2004. 15.00 (978-1-59007-223-3(5)) Pub: New Millenn Enter. Dist(s): PerseuPGW

Cattle Killing. unabr. ed. John Edgar Wideman. Read by Howard Weinberger. 5 cass. (Running Time: 7 hrs. 30 min.). 1998. 40.00 (978-0-7366-4074-9(6), 4583) Books on Tape.
In eighteenth century Philadelphia, a young black preacher searches for an African woman & encounters the horrors of a society splitting itself into white & black, white over black. The search for love & meaning spans two centuries & three continents.

***Cattle King for a Day.** unabr. ed. L. Ron Hubbard. Read by Corey Burton et al. Narrated by R. F. Daley. 2 CDs. (Running Time: 1 hr. 20 mins.). (YA). 2010. audio compact disk 9.95 (978-1-59212-365-0(1)) Gala Pr LLC.

Cattle Town: Forth Worth. Compiled by Benchmark Education Staff. 2006. audio compact disk 10.00 (978-1-4108-6619-6(X)) Benchmark Educ.

Catwalk: A Feline Odyssey. Kathie Freeman. Narrated by Kathie Freeman. 9 cassettes. (Running Time: 9 hrs.). (YA). 2006. 15.95 (978-0-9742062-4-0(5)) K McPugh.
"Catwalk" is the story of a young, comfort-loving tabby cat who, for reasons she cannot possibly understand, suddenly finds herself adrift in a big and sometimes dangerous world. Her odyssey ultimately takes her halfway across the continent, and brings her in contact with such diverse characters as a Cajun fisherman, a game warden and his wife, a trio of hoboes, and a Mexican-American family. She is befriended by many, abused by a few, but her indomitable spirit always carries her through. Her struggle for survival and her search for home and family is a story animal lovers of all ages will want to read and share.

Caught. abr. ed. Harlan Coben. Read by Carrington MacDuffie. (ENG.). 2010. audio compact disk 32.00 (978-0-7393-8520-3(8), Random AudioBks) Pub: Random Audio Pubg. Dist(s): Random

***Caught.** abr. ed. Harlan Coben. Read by Carrington MacDuffie. (ENG.). 2011. audio compact disk 14.99 (978-0-307-93312-6(1), Random AudioBks) Pub: Random Audio Pubg. Dist(s): Random

***Caught.** unabr. ed. Harlan Coben. Read by Carrington MacDuffie. 9 CDs. 2010. audio compact disk 100.00 (978-0-307-70483-2(1), BksonTape) Pub: Random Audio Pubg. Dist(s): Random

Caught. unabr. ed. Harlan Coben. Read by Carrington MacDuffie. 2010. audio compact disk 45.00 (978-0-7393-8522-7(4), Random AudioBks) Pub: Random Audio Pubg. Dist(s): Random

Caught Dead in Philadelphia. unabr. ed. Gillian Roberts. Narrated by Diane Warren. 5 cass. (Running Time: 7 hrs. 30 mins.). (Amanda Pepper Mystery Ser.). 1993. 44.00 (978-1-55690-900-9(4), 93342E7) Recorded Bks.
A Philadelphia schoolteacher finds herself drawn into the investigation of a co-worker's murder, & soon the murderer is coming after her.

Caught in a Casserole. Joni Hilton. 1 cass. 2004. 3.95 (978-1-57734-383-7(2), 34441220) Covenant Comms.

Caught in a Casserole; Replenishing the Inner Woman. Joni Hilton. 1 cass. 6.98 (978-1-55503-387-3(3), 06004466) Covenant Comms.
Fresh & fun ideas.

Caught in a Storm. Dan Corner. 1 cass. 3.00 (20) Evang Outreach.

Caught in the Crossfire. unabr. ed. Alan Gibbons. Read by Christopher J. Hoban. 7 CDs. (Running Time: 8 hrs.). 2006. audio compact disk 83.95 (978-1-74093-724-5(4)) Pub: Bolinda Pubng AUS. Dist(s): Bolinda Pub Inc

Caught in the Crossfire: Acts 9:23-31. Ed Young. 1997. 4.95 (978-0-7417-2163-1(5), A1163) Win Walk.

Caught in the Light. Robert Goddard. Read by Michael Kitchen. (Chivers Audio Bks.). 2003. audio compact disk 110.95 (978-0-7540-8782-3(4)) Pub: Chivers Audio Bks GBR. Dist(s): AudioGO

Caught in the Light. unabr. ed. Robert Goddard. Read by Michael Kitchen. 12 cass. (Running Time: 18 hrs.). 2000. 79.95 (CAB 1694) Pub: Chivers Audio Bks GBR. Dist(s): AudioGO
On assignment in Vienna, photographer Ian Jarrett falls desperately in love with a woman he meets by pure chance, Marian Esguard. Back in England, he separates from his wife and prepares to meet Marian. But she informs him that she will not be joining him. Then she vanishes from his life as mysteriously as she entered it. Who and where is the woman he met and fell in love with in Vienna?.

Caught in the Light. unabr. ed. Michael Kitchen. Read by Robert Goddard. 12 cass. (Running Time: 12 hrs.). 1999. 96.95 (978-0-7540-0271-0(3), CAB1694) AudioGO.
On assignment in Vienna, photographer Ian Jarrett falls desperately in love with Marian Esguard. Back in England, he separates from his wife & prepares to meet Marian. But she vanishes from his life mysteriously.

Caught me a big'un... & then i let him go! jimmy houston's bass fishing Tips 'n. Jimmy Houston. 2004. 7.95 (978-0-7435-4252-4(5)) Pub: S&S Audio. Dist(s): S and S Inc

Caught Out in Cornwall. unabr. ed. Janie Bolitho. Read by Patricia Gallimore. 6 CDs. (Running Time: 25200 sec.). (Soundings (CDs) Ser.). 2006. audio compact disk 64.95 (978-1-84559-307-0(3)) Pub: ISIS Lrg Prnt GBR. Dist(s): Ulverscroft US

Caught Out in Cornwall. unabr. ed. Janie Bolitho. Read by Patricia Gallimore. 6 cass. (Soundings Ser.). (J). 2006. 54.95 (978-1-84559-257-8(3)) Pub: ISIS Lrg Prnt GBR. Dist(s): Ulverscroft US

Caught Stealing. unabr. ed. Charlie Huston. Read by Christian Conn. 6 cass. 2005. 54.95 (978-0-7927-3666-0(4), CSL 813); audio compact disk 74.95 (978-0-7927-3667-7(2), SLD 813) AudioGO.

Caught up in the Rapture. unabr. ed. Sheneska Jackson. Narrated by Peter Francis James et al. 7 cass. (Running Time: 10 hrs. 30 mins.). 1996. 64.00 (978-0-7887-5478-4(5), F0042L8) Recorded Bks.
When fate brings college student Jazmine & gangsta rapper X-Man together, they have nothing in common but a dream to make it in the music business. Suddenly Black Tie Records discovers them both, & they discover each other. Can their passionate love survive a world scarred with street violence & cut-throat ambition?.

Cauldron. Colin Forbes. Read by William Franklyn. 2 cass. (Running Time: 3 hrs.). (ENG., 2001. 16.95 (978-0-333-69863-1(0)) Pub: Macmillan UK GBR. Dist(s): Trafalgar
With Germany and France locked in a deadly battle against the United States, massive dogfights occur in the skies, and the U.S. Navy struggles for survival in waters alive with U-boats.

Cauldron, Pt. 1. unabr. ed. Larry Bond. Read by Michael Prichard. 10 cass. (Running Time: 15 hrs.). 1993. 80.00 (978-0-7366-2513-5(5), 3269A) Books on Tape.
France, Germany & Russia line up against America, Britain & the new Eastern European democracies in global conflict.

Cauldron, Pt. 2. unabr. ed. Larry Bond. Read by Michael Prichard. 10 cass. (Running Time: 15 hrs.). 1993. 72.00 (3269-B) Books on Tape.

Cauldron Journey for Healing. unabr. ed. Nicki Scully. Perf. by Roland Barker & Jerry Garcia. 1 cass. 11.00 (978-0-9623365-2-2(1)) N Scully.
Journey takes you through the Cauldron alchemy to your Spirit Guide, & from there to the island of Kuan Yin to receive healing.

Cauldron Journey for Rebirth. unabr. ed. Nicki Scully. Perf. by Roland Barker & Jeff Mahoney. 1 cass. 11.00 (978-0-9623365-4-6(8)) N Scully.
Journey takes you through the Cauldron alchemy to Thoth, & from there to the river of life to re-experience birth with Tarat as your midwife.

Cauldron of Thoth: A Journey of Empowerment. Nicki Scully. 1 cass. 12.00 N Scully.
Designed to alter consciousness so that the listener can communicate in other realms. It is accompanied by a musical score created to enhance the journey. This work opens the way for communications with archetypes, deities & totems.

Cauldron of Thoth: A Journey of Empowerment. unabr. ed. Nicki Scully. Read by Nicki Scully. Perf. by John Sergeant. 1 cass. 11.00 (978-0-9623365-0-8(5)) N Scully.
Journey teaches the alchemy that allows you to travel out of the body safely. You will be introduced to Thoth, Mut & the Crone.

Cauldron Teachings: Eagle & Elephant. Nicki Scully. 1 cass. 10.98 N Scully.
Designed to alter consciousness so that the listener can communicate in other realms. It is accompanied by a musical score created to enhance the journey. This work opens the way for communications with archetypes, deities & totems.

Cauldron Teachings: Eagle & Elephant. unabr. ed. Nicki Scully. Perf. by Roland Barker. 1 cass. 11.00 (978-0-9623365-1-5(3)) N Scully.
Gives the Cauldron initiation into communication with the spirit realms. Visit Eagle to make choices & Elephant to clear obstacles & solve problems.

Caulk Boots & Marlin Spikes, Set. unabr. ed. 2 cass. (Running Time: 2 hrs. 30 mins.). (ENG.). 24.95 (978-1-55017-138-9(0)) Harbour Pub Co CAN.

Cause & Cure of Fear. Swami Amar Jyoti. 1 cass. 1980. 9.95 (K-32) Truth Consciousness.
A common sense look at what fear reallly is. Facing our mind. Truthfulness & boldness, faith & love.

Cause & Effect see May Swenson

***Cause & Effect.** AIO Team. (Running Time: 5 hrs.). (Adventures in Odyssey Ser.). (ENG.). (J). 2010. audio compact disk 24.99 (978-1-58997-638-2(X)) Tyndale Hse.

Cause & Effect. Kenneth Wapnick. 8 CDs. 2006. audio compact disk 51.00 (978-1-59142-237-2(X), CD123) Foun Miracles.

Cause & Effect. Kenneth Wapnick. 1 CD. (Running Time: 8 hrs. 27 mins. 22 secs.). 2006. 41.00 (978-1-59142-243-3(4), 3m123) Foun Miracles.

Cause & Remedy for Losing Heart. Dan Corner. 1 cass. 3.00 (100) Evang Outreach.

Cause Celeb. abr. ed. Helen Fielding. Read by Bernadette Quigley. 5 cass. (Running Time: 6 hrs.). 2001. audio compact disk 69.25 (978-1-58788-187-9(X), 158788187X) Brilliance Audio.
Cause Celeb - the critically acclaimed debut novel from a writer with a boundless grasp of the existential and the uproarious - has just landed in America. Deftly skewering the world of celebrity fundraising, Fielding has created an alternately comic and moving satire that straddles the glitter of media London and the horrors of an African refugee crisis. Rosie Richardson, a twenty-something literary puffette, is in a totally non-functional relationship with an unevolved but irresistible adult male - a hotshot TV presenter who plunges her into the glitzy, bitchy, inane lifestyle of London's It people. Disillusioned with the celebrity world, Rosie escapes to run a refugee camp in the African jungle. When famine strikes and a massive refugee influx heads for the camp, governments and agencies drag their heels. Bringing her former media savvy to the fore, realizing the only way to get food out fast is to bring celebrities first, Rosie turns to the life and man she fled to organize a star-studded emergency appeal from famine-racked Africa. Seamlessly bridging cataclysm and farce through the insights of a modern-day everywoman, Cause Celeb crackles with insight into fame, passion, and altruism in our time.

Cause Celeb. unabr. ed. Helen Fielding. Read by Bernadette Quigley. 7 cass. (Running Time: 10 hrs.). 2001. 78.25 (978-1-58788-134-3(9), 1587881349) Brilliance Audio.
Disillusioned by her glitzy life in London, Rosie Richardson chucks it all and ends up running a refuge camp in Africa. When famine strikes a nearby province and an influx of refugees threatens to overwhelm the camp, Rosie - frustrated by the cautious response of aid agencies - decides on a drastic short-term solution. She returns to London, breaks back into the celebrity circuit, and brings the celebs out to Africa for a star-studded TV emergency appeal. Hilarious and humane, Cause Celeb is a literary satire - full of insights into fame, passion, and altruism in our times.

Cause Celeb. unabr. ed. Helen Fielding. Read by Bernadette Quigley. (Running Time: 10 hrs.). 2005. 39.25 (978-1-59600-691-1(9), 9781596006911, BADLE); audio compact disk 39.25 (978-1-59600-689-8(7), 9781596006898, Brlnc Audio MP3 Lib); audio compact disk 24.95 (978-1-59600-688-1(9), 9781596006881, Brilliance MP3) Brilliance Audio.

Cause Celeb. unabr. ed. Helen Fielding. Read by Bernadette Quigley. (Running Time: 10 hrs.). 2005. 24.95 (978-1-59600-690-4(0), 9781596006904, BAD) Brilliance Audio.

Cause Celeb. unabr. ed. Helen Fielding & Helen Fielding. Read by Bernadette Quigley. 7 cass. (Running Time: 10 hrs.). 2001. 32.95 (978-1-58788-133-6(0), 1587881330, BAU) Brilliance Audio.

Cause for Alarm. unabr. collector's ed. Eric Ambler. Read by Richard Brown. 6 cass. (Running Time: 9 hrs.). 1987. 48.00 (978-0-7366-1182-4(7), 2102) Books on Tape.
He was desperate. Otherwise Marlow never would have ended up running for his life.

Cause for Concern. unabr. ed. Margaret Yorke. Read by Sheila Mitchell. 4 cass. (Running Time: 6 hrs.). 2002. 54.95 (978-0-7540-0834-7(7), CAB 2256) Pub: Chivers Pr GBR. Dist(s): AudioGO

***Cause Inside of You: Finding the One Great Thing You Were Created to Do in This World.** Matthew Barnett. Told to George Barna. (ENG.). 2011. audio compact disk 25.99 (978-1-4143-4851-3(7)) Tyndale Hse.

Cause of Conflict in Relatiohship. J. Krishnamurti. 1 cass. (Running Time: 75 min.). (Brockwood Talks - 1984 Ser.: No. 1). 1999. 8.50 (ABT841) Krishnamurti.
Krishnamurti addresses the timeless questions which mankind has always asked & he invites each one of us to suspend our beliefs & theories, to observe together, to walk together with the speakers as we inquire into the human condition.

Cause of Death. Patricia Cornwell. Narrated by C. J. Critt. 8 cass. (Running Time: 11 hrs. 30 mins.). (Kay Scarpetta Ser.: No. 7). 78.00 (978-1-4025-3401-0(9)) Recorded Bks.

Cause of Death. abr. unabr. ed. Patricia Cornwell. Read by Kate Reading. 6 cass. (Running Time: 9 hrs.). (Kay Scarpetta Ser.: No. 7). 2004. 29.95 (978-1-59007-300-1(2)) Pub: New Millenn Enter. Dist(s): PerseuPGW

Cause of Death. unabr. ed. Patricia Cornwell. Read by Kate Reading. 7 cass. (Running Time: 10 hrs. 30 min.). (Kay Scarpetta Ser.: No. 7). 1996. 56.00 (978-0-7366-3372-7(3), 4022) Books on Tape.
Celebration usually marks New Year's Eve, but on this night Kay Scarpetta, medical examiner, gets some unhappy news: Ted Eddings, a reporter & a friend, has died scuba diving in the Elizabeth River in December? What was he on to? Scarpetta questions the verdict of accidental death & nearly gets shot for her pains. That sets off an investigation that's even more dangerous & sucks her into a trap that's nearly fatal.

Cause of Death, unabr. ed. Patricia Cornwell. Read by Kate Reading. 12 cass. (Running Time: 12 hrs.). (Kay Scarpetta Ser.: No. 7). 1999. 39.95 (FS9-34621) Highsmith.

Cause of Death. unabr. ed. Patricia Cornwell. Read by C. J. Critt. 7 cass. (Running Time: 11 hrs. 45 mins.). (Kay Scarpetta Ser.: No. 7). 2004. 24.99 (978-1-4025-2893-4(0), 02294); audio compact disk 34.99 (978-1-4025-2894-1(9), 00562) Recorded Bks.
Award-winning, #1 New York Times best-selling author Patricia Cornwell plumbs the icy depths of the Inactive Naval Ship Yard in the thrilling Cause of Death. On New Year's Eve, Dr. Kay Scarpetta receives a disturbing phone call. Thirty feet deep in the murky waters of Virginia's Elizabeth River, scuba diver and investigative reporter Ted Eddings lies dead. Was he searching for Civil War relics, or probing the restricted area for a bigger

story? Scarpetta has another question. Why did she learn of this death before the police were informed? When a second murder hits closer to home, Scarpetta is hot on the trail of a conspiracy.

Cause of Death. unabr. abr. ed. Patricia Cornwell. Read by C. J. Critt. 8 CDs. (Running Time: 4 hrs.). (Kay Scarpetta Ser.: No. 7). 2004. audio compact disk 49.95 (978-1-59007-467-1(X)) Pub: New Millenn Enter. Dist(s): PerseuPGW

Cause Stone Said So! abr. ed. Stone Cold Steve Austin, pseud. Read by Stone Cold Steve Austin, pseud. 1 cass. (Running Time: 1 hr. 30 mins.). 2000. 12.00 (978-0-694-52293-4(7)) HarperCollins Pubs.

"Cause Stone Cold Said So!" tells Steve Austin's story in all its bone-crushing glory. From his humble beginnings on a loading dock to his rise to become one of the World Wrestling Federation's hottest superstars, here are all the gritty details in between, including his firing from the WCW & his tumultuous relationship with Federation owner Vince McMahon. "Cause Stone Cold Said So!" will introduce wrestling fans to the man behind the legend.

Cause Us to Glorify Jesus. Elbert Willis. 1 cass. (Purpose of the Holy Spirit Ser.). 4.00 Fill the Gap.

Cause Worth Living For. unabr. ed. Myrtle Smyth. 1 cass. (Running Time: 1 hrs. 5 mins.). (Myrtle Smyth Audiotapes Ser.: Vol. 26). 1999. 8.95 (978-1-893107-28-1(0), M26) Healing Unltd.

Lecture on the cause of Christian Science & includes experiences with ministering to IRA terrorists in Irish prisons.

Causeries sur la Poesie et les Elements, Gaston Bachelard. 2 CDs. (Running Time: 2 hrs.). (FRE.). 1995. audio compact disk 44.95 (1781-RF) Olivia & Hill.

A leading French philosopher, literary critic of this century discusses his theories.

Causes of Prejudice CD. Interview. Martin Luther King, Jr. Interview with Lee R. Steiner. 1 CD. (Running Time: 25 mins.). (Sound Seminars Ser.). 2006. audio compact disk 12.95 (978-1-57970-408-7(5), C29381D, Audio-For) J Norton Pubs.

Causes of War - United Nations, 1984. J. Krishnamurti. Read by J. Krishnamurti. 1 cass. (Running Time: 90 mins.). 8.50 (AUN84) Krishnamurti.

Causes Won, Lost, & Forgotten: How Hollywood & Popular Art Shape What We Know about the Civil War. Gary W. Gallagher. (ENG., 2008. 30.00 (978-0-8078-8628-1(9)); audio compact disk 30.00 (978-0-8078-8630-4(0)) U of NC Pr.

Cautionary Verses. Hilaire Belloc. Read by Rosalind Ayres & Martin Jarvis. (Running Time: 1 hr. 20 mins. 0 sec.). (ENG.). (gr. k). 2009. audio compact disk 15.00 (978-1-934997-43-7(9)) Pub: CSAWord. Dist(s): PerseuPGW

Cautionary Verses. Hilaire Belloc. Contrib. by Rosalind Ayres & Martin Jarvis. (CSA Word Classics (Playaway) Ser.). (ENG.). (J). (gr. k). 2009. 39.99 (978-1-60775-703-0(6)) Find a World.

Cavalcade of America: America for Christmas & The Day They Gave Babies Away. 1 cass. (Running Time: 1 hr.). 2001. 6.98 (2212) Radio Spirits.

Cavalcade of America: Going Up & The Melody Man. Perf. by Robert Cummings. 1 cass. (Running Time: 1 hr.). 2001. 6.98 (2595) Radio Spirits.

Cavalcade of America: Grandpa & the Statue & Wire to the West. 1 cass. (Running Time: 1 hr.). Dramatization. 2001. 6.98 (1866) Radio Spirits.

Cavalcade of America: The Grand Design & Ulysses in Love. 1 cass. (Running Time: 1 hr.). 2001. 6.98 (2434) Radio Spirits.

Cavalcade of America: The Philippines Never Surrendered & Petticoat Jury. 1 cass. (Running Time: 1 hr.). 2001. 6.98 (2413) Radio Spirits.

Cavaliers & Roundheads: The English Civil War, 1642-1649. Christopher Hibbert. 9 cass. (Running Time: 13.5 hrs.). 2001. 72.00 (978-0-7366-6356-4(8)) Books on Tape.

Cavaliers & Roundheads: The English Civil War, 1642-1649. unabr. ed. Christopher Hibbert. Narrated by Steven Crossley. 10 cass. (Running Time: 13 hrs. 45 mins.). 1996. 85.00 (978-0-7887-0405-5(2), 94597E7) Recorded Bks.

The vivid social & military history of this bloody struggle between Crown & Parliament are brought to life by Hibbert in this account of civil war.

Cavalryman of the Lost Cause: A Biography of J. E. B. Stuart. unabr. ed. Jeffry D. Wert. Read by Michael Prichard. Narrated by Michael Prichard. (Running Time: 17 hrs. 30 mins. 0 sec.). (ENG.). 2008. audio compact disk 39.99 (978-1-4001-0725-4(3)); audio compact disk 29.99 (978-1-4001-5725-9(0)); audio compact disk 79.99 (978-1-4001-3725-1(X)) Pub: Tantor Media. Dist(s): IngramPubServ

Cavanaugh's Luck. unabr. ed. Orville D. Johnson. Read by Gene Engene. 6 cass. (Running Time: 6 hrs. 30 mins.). 1995. 39.95 (978-1-55686-629-6(1)) Books in Motion.

This is the prequel to "Dead Man's Mine". In a 1920's poker game, Matt Cavanaugh wins a paying gold mine from Woody Doolin who vows revenge. The mine contains more than gold.

Cave Boy of the Age of Stone. unabr. ed. Margaret A. McIntyre. Read by Nancy Lee. (J). 2007. 34.99 (978-1-60252-883-3(7)) Find a World.

Cave Girl. Edgar Rice Burroughs. Read by Patrick G. Lawlor. (Running Time: 7 hrs.). 2004. 27.95 (978-1-59912-630-2(3)) Iofy Corp.

Cave Girl. unabr. ed. Edgar Rice Burroughs. Read by Patrick G. Lawlor. (Running Time: 8 hrs. 30 mins.). 2004. audio compact disk 24.95 (978-0-7861-8466-8(3)); audio compact disk 56.00 (978-0-7861-8483-5(3)); 44.95 (978-0-7861-2793-1(7)) Blckstn Audio.

Back in Boston, Massachusetts, U.S.A., he was a blueblood named Waldo Smith-Jones. But when he found himself in a desperate effort to survive on a lost island of primitive men and beasts, he won not only a new name but also the hand of the cave princess, Nadara.

Cave Man. unabr. ed. Ed. by Linda Spizzirri. 48 cass. (Running Time: 15 mins.). Dramatization. (Educational Coloring Book & Cassette Package Ser.). (J). (gr. k-8). 1989. pap. bk. 6.95 (978-0-86545-085-1(4)) Spizzirri.

Discusses man at the end of the ice age including his weapons, tools & clothing.

Cave of the Dark Wind. unabr. ed. Dave Barry & Ridley Pearson. (Running Time: 7200 sec.). (Never Land Ser.). (J). (gr. 3-7). 2007. audio compact disk 39.25 (978-1-4233-0961-1(8), 9781423309611, Brinc Audio MP3 Lib); audio compact disk 62.25 (978-1-4233-0959-8(6), 9781423309598, BriAudCD Unabrid) Brilliance Audio.

Cave of the Dark Wind. unabr. ed. Dave Barry & Ridley Pearson. (Running Time: 7200 sec.). (Never Land Ser.). (J). (gr. 3-7). 2007. 44.25 (978-1-4233-0957-4(X), 9781423309574, BrilAudUnabridg) Brilliance Audio.

Cave of the Dark Wind. unabr. ed. Dave Barry & Ridley Pearson. Read by Jim Dale. (Running Time: 2 hrs.). (Never Land Ser.). 2007. 14.95 (978-1-4233-0960-4(X), 9781423309604, Brilliance MP3); 39.25 (978-1-4233-0963-5(4), 9781423309635, BADLE); 14.95 (978-1-4233-0962-8(6), 9781423309628, BAD) Brilliance Audio.

***Cave of the Dark Wind: A Never Land Book.** unabr. ed. Dave Barry and Ridley Pearson. Read by Jim Dale. (Running Time: 2 hrs.). (Never Land Adventure Ser.). 2010. audio compact disk 9.99 (978-1-4418-7122-0(5), 9781441871220, Bril Audio CD Unabri) Brilliance Audio.

Cave of the Heart. Sister Ishpriya. 6 cass. (Running Time: 5 hrs.). 39.95 (AA2314) Credence Commun.

Techniques of relaxation & meditation using Yoga & Christianity.

***Cavender Is Coming.** 2010. audio compact disk (978-1-59171-188-9(6)) Falcon Picture.

Caves of Steel. unabr. ed. Isaac Asimov. Read by William Dufris. 6 CDs. (Running Time: 7 hrs. 30 mins. 0 sec.). (Robot Ser.). (ENG.). 2007. audio compact disk 29.99 (978-1-4001-0421-5(1)); audio compact disk 59.99 (978-1-4001-3421-2(8)); audio compact disk 19.99 (978-1-4001-5421-0(9)) Pub: Tantor Media. Dist(s): IngramPubServ

Cay. Theodore Taylor. Read by LeVar Burton. 2 cass. (Running Time: 3 hrs.). (J). 2000. 18.00 (978-0-7366-9065-2(4)) Books on Tape.

A German torpedo leaves young Phillip blind & stranded on an island with Timothy, an old West Indian man whom he initially distrusts.

Cay. unabr. ed. Theodore Taylor. Read by Michael Boatman. 3 CDs. (Running Time: 3 hrs.). (J). 2005. audio compact disk 25.50 (978-1-4000-9908-5(0)) Pub: Books on Tape. Dist(s): NetLibrary CO

Cay. unabr. ed. Theodore Taylor. Read by Michael Boatman. 2 cass. (Running Time: 3 hrs.). (J). 2005. 23.00 (978-1-4000-9907-8(2), Listening Lib) Random Audio Pubg.

A German torpedo leaves young Phillip blind and stranded on an island with Timothy, an old West Indian man whom he initially distrusts.

Cay. unabr. ed. Theodore Taylor. Read by Michael Boatman. 3 CDs. (Running Time: 3 hrs.). (ENG.). (J). (gr. 3). 2005. audio compact disk 25.00 (978-1-4000-9906-1(4), Listening Lib) Pub: Random Audio Pubg. Dist(s): Random

Cay. unabr. ed. Theodore Taylor. Narrated by LeVar Burton. 2 cass. (Running Time: 2 hr. 45 mins.). (J). (gr. 2). 1998. 21.00 (21626) Recorded Bks.

Uplifting tale of survival & friendship during World War II.

CB Libronix Compubiblia Profesional L. (SPA.). 2003. audio compact disk (978-1-931952-81-1(7)) Untd Bible Amrcas Svce.

CBC Radio's Award Winning Documentaries. (Running Time: 1 hr.). 2005. audio compact disk 15.95 (978-0-660-19383-0(3)) Canadian Broadcasting CAN.

CBC Radio's Award Winning Documentaries, 3. Compiled by Neil Sandell. 1 CD. (Running Time: 1 Hour). 2007. audio compact disk 15.95 (978-0-660-19674-9(3), CBC Audio) Canadian Broadcasting CAN.

1. The Cause of ThunderA glimpse into the remarkable world of Eliot Grant...a five year old with Asperger's Syndrome, a form of autism. Winner: Grand Award & Gold Medal, New York Festivals. Producers: Stewart Young & Neil Sandell2. Who is Vern Nash?Thelon Oeming befriends a neighbour - musically gifted, but tormented by demons. Thelon decides to help him. But how? Winner: Special Mention, Prix Italia, 2006; Finalist, New York Festivals 2006. Producer: Steve Wadhams.3. A Red Rocket to the Old World As Damiano Pietropaolo rides a streetcar through the Toronto neighbourhood of his childhood, his mind drifts to a time and place, and characters that exist only in memory. Winner: Jury?s Special Mention, Prix Italia, 2006; Finalist, New York Festivals 2006. Producer: Damiano Pietropaolo.4. Flanking on the Far DayAfter Kelly McCarthy's Dad had a heart attack his recovery focused on just one thing: getting back on his Harley. This time Kelly comes along for the ride. Winner: Bronze Medal, New York Festivals, 2006. Producer: Kent Hoffman.5. Between FriendsA secret that begins as a whisper at a pajama party winds up as testimony in a sexual assault trial. Jody Porter comes to understand the burden telling the secret placed on her life-long friend. Winner: Gabriel Award, 2006; Third Coast International Audio Festival Award, 2006. Producer: Neil Sandell & Jody Porter.6. He Just Can?t Help It15-year-old Marybeth Whalen offers a painfully honest view of life at home with a younger brother who has attention deficit hyperactivity disorder. In the end, her inquiry helps her make sense of the situation. Winner: Radio Television News Directors Association Award (RTNDA), 2006. Producer: Marie Wadden & Neil Sandell.

CBC Radio's Most Requested Documentaries. Interview. Created by Canadian Broadcasting Corporation. 1 CD. (Running Time: 3600 sec.). 2006. audio compact disk 15.95 (978-0-660-19547-6(X), CBC Audio) Canadian Broadcasting CAN.

CBS Radio Workshop: Brave New World. Narrated by Aldous Huxley. 1 cass. (Running Time: 60 mins.). (Old Time Radio Classic Singles Ser.). 4.95 (978-1-57816-088-4(X), BW105) Audio File.

Premiere broadcast of the series.

CBS Radio Workshop: Cops & Robbers & The Legend of Jimmy Blue Eyes. 1 cass. (Running Time: 1 hr.). 2001. 6.98 (2393) Radio Spirits.

CBS Radio Workshop: Storm & Season of Disbelief. 1 cass. (Running Time: 1 hr.). 2001. 6.98 (2032) Radio Spirits.

CBS Radio Workshop Pts. 1 & 2: The Space Merchants. 1 cass. (Running Time: 1 hr.). 2001. 6.98 (1624) Radio Spirits.

CBT Volume, Set. Deborah Phillips. 2002. 45.50 (978-0-201-38520-5(1)) Longman.

***CCBA Exam Prep.** Crosswind Project Management Inc. & Tony Johnson. Created by Crosswind Project Management Inc. (ENG.). 2010. audio compact disk 24.95 (978-1-936483-00-6(9)) Crosswind PM.

CCI - April 2008. RSMeans. 2008. audio compact disk 81.25 (978-0-87629-062-0(4)) R S Means.

CCI - January 2008. RSMeans. 2008. audio compact disk 81.25 (978-0-87629-061-3(6)) R S Means.

CCI - July 2008. RSMeans. 2008. audio compact disk 81.25 (978-0-87629-070-5(5)) R S Means.

CCI - October 2008. RSMeans. 2008. audio compact disk 81.25 (978-0-87629-071-2(3)) R S Means.

CCNA Erouter Learning Networks. Data Train. 2002. stu. ed. 70.95 (978-0-619-13058-9(X)) Course Tech.

CCNA Virtual Lab, Professional Edition. Todd Lammle & William Tedder. 2003. bk. 199.99 (978-0-7821-3036-2(4), SybWiley) Wiley US.

CCRN Prep. Instructed by Jill S. Flateland & JoAnn C. Tess-Pibum. 21 cass. (Running Time: 38 hrs.). 1992. bk. 229.00 (HT74) Ctr Hlth Educ.

Retaking the CCRN exam to recertify? Or maybe this is your first time taking the exam. With 60% passing ratio, studying the core curriculum is not enough. CCRN Prep provides all the tools needed to pass. All the research has been done for you, in this well designed study guide written & produced by CCRN exam "survivors.".

CCRN Prep: The Pulmonary System. unabr. ed. Instructed by Jill S. Flateland. 4 cass. (Running Time: 10 hrs.). 1990. bk. 79.00 (HT71) Ctr Hlth Educ.

The Pulmonary Section of the CCRN Prep has been updated & enhanced from the original course. It is 18% of the CCRN exam. The course thoroughly covers: detailed ABG interpretation; airway management; normal & abnormal breath sounds & much more.

***Cd.** Michael Taylor. 2009. audio compact disk 9.99 (978-0-578-04713-3(6)) EndtimeHrst TX.

CD: A Gatear. Matilde Cintron. 2006. audio compact disk (978-1-59608-268-7(2)) Ediciones Situm.

CD: Compilacion edad Temprana. Compiled by Matilde Cintron. 2006. audio compact disk (978-1-59608-265-6(8)) Ediciones Situm.

CD: La gallinita que Procastino. Lucas Rios-Cintron. 2006. audio compact disk (978-1-59608-266-3(6)) Ediciones Situm.

CD: Palabras en Saltitos. Matilde Cintron. 2006. audio compact disk (978-1-59608-267-0(4)) Ediciones Situm.

CD: Palabritas Danzarinas, Vol. 1. Matilde Cintron. 2006. audio compact disk (978-1-59608-269-4(0)) Ediciones Situm.

Cd-App Math F/Mlss 3e. 3rd ed. (C). 2005. audio compact disk 16.95 (978-0-495-01536-9(9)) Pub: Brooks-Cole. Dist(s): CENGAGE Learn

***CD Book - Needs Title.** Eli B. Toresen. (J). 2011. audio compact disk 11.95 (978-1-934983-92-8(6), Pny) Staben Inc.

***Cd Crisp Custom Course 1.0.** Crisp Learning Staff. audio compact disk (978-0-619-26075-0(0)) Course Tech.

Cd-Engage W/Hard-to-Reach 5e. 5th ed. (C). 2005. audio compact disk 34.95 (978-0-495-03093-5(7)) Pub: Wadsworth Pub. Dist(s): CENGAGE Learn

CD for Art Deco Patterns & Designs. unabr. ed. Phoebe Ann Erb. Illus. by Phoebe Ann Erb. 2005. audio compact disk 12.95 (978-0-88045-158-1(0)) Stemmer Hse.

CD for Arts & Crafts Patterns & Designs. unabr. ed. Phoebe Ann Erb. Illus. by Phoebe Ann Erb. 2005. audio compact disk 12.95 (978-0-88045-157-4(2)) Stemmer Hse.

CD for Swinger of Birches. Read by Clifton Fadinan. Tr. by Clifton Fadinan. 2006. audio compact disk 9.95 (978-0-88045-162-8(9)) Stemmer Hse.

CD for under the Greenwood Tree. Read by Claire Bloom & Derek Jacob. Tr. by Claire Bloom & Derek Jacob. Tr. by Folger Consort. Music by Folger Consort. (YA). 2006. audio compact disk 9.95 (978-0-88045-161-1(0)) Stemmer Hse.

Cd-from Black & White to Living in Color. Donald Davis. 2008. audio compact disk 16.95 (978-0-87483-824-4(X)) Pub: August Hse. Dist(s): Natl Bk Netwk

CD Great Poets Robert Service. Robert Service & Urgelt. 2007. bk. 14.98 (978-962-634-491-0(1), Naxos AudioBooks) Naxos.

CD Hazme un Instrumento. (SPA.). (J). 2003. audio compact disk (978-1-931952-70-5(1)) Untd Bible Amrcas Svce.

CD Historia de David y Jeremías. (SPA.). (J). 2004. audio compact disk (978-1-932507-97-3(3)) Untd Bible Amrcas Svce.

CD Historia de Jesús, un rey ha nacido y Jesús, el mejor Amigo. (SPA.). (J). 2004. audio compact disk (978-1-932507-99-7(X)) Untd Bible Amrcas Svce.

CD Historia de Pablo y José. (SPA.). (J). 2004. audio compact disk (978-1-932507-77-5(9)) Untd Bible Amrcas Svce.

CD Historia de Pedro I y Pedro II. (SPA.). (J). 2004. audio compact disk (978-1-932507-98-0(1)) Untd Bible Amrcas Svce.

CD Intentional Interview 5e. 5th ed. Allen Ivey. (C). 2003. audio compact disk 40.95 (978-0-534-52046-5(4)) Pub: Wadsworth Pub. Dist(s): CENGAGE Learn

CD Inter Conc Env Sci 2.0. 14th ed. G. Tyler Miller, Jr. 2005. audio compact disk (978-0-534-99732-8(5)) Brooks-Cole.

CD la Biblia Canta. (SPA.). 2003. audio compact disk (978-1-931952-50-7(7)) Untd Bible Amrcas Svce.

Cd-Live from Fearrington Village. Donald Davis. 2008. audio compact disk 16.95 (978-0-87483-885-5(1)) Pub: August Hse. Dist(s): Natl Bk Netwk

CD Managrl Acct Info for Dec. 5th ed. (C). 2005. audio compact disk 27.95 (978-0-324-22244-9(0)) Pub: South-West. Dist(s): CENGAGE Learn

CD Maria Jones y la Biblia. (SPA.). (J). 2003. audio compact disk (978-1-932507-14-0(0)) Untd Bible Amrcas Svce.

***Cd Mis Companion.** (C). 2004. audio compact disk 26.95 (978-0-619-21606-1(9)) Pub: Course Tech. Dist(s): CENGAGE Learn

CD Nutrition Explorer CD 10e. 10th ed. (C). 2004. audio compact disk 25.95 (978-0-534-62227-5(5)) Pub: Brooks-Cole. Dist(s): CENGAGE Learn

Cd-Nutritional Sciences: An Integrated Approach. (C). 2006. audio compact disk 26.95 (978-0-495-12663-8(2)) Pub: Brooks-Cole. Dist(s): CENGAGE Learn

CD Release Party Strategies: Insider Secrets for Independent Bands, Musicians, & Songwriters - How to Have a Major Label Event on a Shoestring Budget. David Hooper. Read by David Hooper. 2004. audio compact disk 22.95 (978-0-9754361-0-3(4)) K Ray Enterprses.

***CD-ROM.** Lu Lanlan. (CHI.). 2005. audio compact disk 6.95 (978-7-88703-180-8(X)) Pub: Beijing Lang CHN. Dist(s): China Bks

CD-ROM, an Interactive Study Guide for Soccio's Archetypes of Wisdom. 3rd ed. Douglas J. Soccio. (C). 1998. audio compact disk 12.95 (978-0-534-52445-6(1)) Pub: Wadsworth Pub. Dist(s): CENGAGE Learn

CD-ROM: Confronting Today's Issues, Pt. II: Products. 2 cass. (Running Time: 2 hrs.). 1990. 16.00 Recorded Res.

CD-ROM Networks in Libraries. 2 cass. (Running Time: 2 hrs.). 1990. 16.00 Recorded Res.

***CD Rope & a Prayer, A (Unabr CD)** David Rohde & Kristen Mulvihill. 2010. 29.95 (978-0-14-242843-6(4)) Pub: Pnguin Bks Ltd GBR. Dist(s): Penguin Grp USA

Cd T/A Intro to Statistics. Gargano & Paul L. DeVito. (C). 2007. 26.95 (978-0-15-500895-3(1)) Pub: Wadsworth Pub. Dist(s): CENGAGE Learn

***Cd Using Adobe In-Design Cs.** (C). 2004. audio compact disk 6.95 (978-0-619-26783-4(6)) Pub: Course Tech. Dist(s): CENGAGE Learn

CD Wayne & Shuster Radio Years, Vol. 2. Johnny Wayne. 2 CDs. (Running Time: 2 hrs. 30 mins.). 2004. audio compact disk 24.99 (978-1-894003-38-4(1)) Pub: Scenario Prods CAN. Dist(s): PerseuPGW

CDL Combination Vehicles Test. unabr. ed. Robert M. Calvin. Read by Jericho Productions, Inc. Staff. Ed. by Marilyn Martin. 6 cass. (Running Time: 28 mins.). (Truck Driver's CDL Audio Tape Ser.). (SPA.). 1991. pap. bk. 15.99 Spanish Version. (978-0-89262-290-0(3), 8) Career Pub.

All questions & answers to the CDL Combination Vehicles Test that all drivers of combination vehicles must take. Easy-to-understand explanations for the answers included. Test Study Book supports & enhances the tape.

CDL Combination Vehicles Test: Audiotape. unabr. ed. Robert M. Calvin. Read by Jericho Productions, Inc. Staff. Ed. by Marilyn Martin. 6 cass. (Running Time: 1 hr. 38 mins.). (Truck Driver's CDL Audio Tape Ser.). 1991. pap. bk. 15.99 (978-0-89262-267-2(9), CDLTCVTAT-738) Career Pub.

CDL Doubles - Triples Test. unabr. ed. Robert M. Calvin. Read by Jericho Productions, Inc. Staff. Ed. by Marilyn Martin. 6 cass. (Running Time: 22 mins.). (Truck Driver's CDL Audio Tape Ser.). (SPA.). 1991. pap. bk. 15.99 Spanish Version. (978-0-89262-294-8(6), 1) Career Pub.

All questions & answers to the CDL Doubles-Triples Test that all drivers of combination vehicles with double or triple trailers must take. Easy-to-understand explanations of the answers included. Test Study Book supports & enhances the tape.

CDL Doubles - Triples Test: Audiotape. unabr. ed. Robert M. Calvin. Read by Jericho Productions, Inc. Staff. Ed. by Marilyn Martin. 6 cass. (Running Time: 1 hr. 05 mins.). (Truck Driver's CDL Audio Tape Ser.). 1991. 15.99 (978-0-89262-271-9(7), CDLTDTTAT-741) Career Pub.

CDL General Knowledge Test. unabr. ed. Robert M. Calvin. Read by Jericho Productions, Inc. Staff. Ed. by Marilyn Martin. 3 cass. (Running Time: 3 hrs.). (Truck & Bus Driver's CDL Audio Tape Ser.). (SPA.). 1991. 16.99 Spanish Version. (978-0-89262-288-7(1)) Career Pub.
Questions & answers to the CDL General Knowledge Test all truck & bus drivers must take. Easy-to-understand explanations of the answers included. Test Study Book supports & enhances the tape.

CDL General Knowledge Test: Audiotape. unabr. ed. Robert M. Calvin. Read by Jericho Productions, Inc. Staff. Ed. by Marilyn Martin. 3 cass. (Running Time: 3 hrs.). (Truck & Bus Driver's CDL Audio Tape Ser.). 1991. pap. bk. 17.99 (978-0-89262-265-8(2), CDLBGKTAT-730) Career Pub.

CDL Hazardous Materials Test. unabr. ed. Robert M. Calvin. Read by Jericho Productions, Inc. Staff. Ed. by Marilyn Martin. 6 cass. (Running Time: 2 hrs. 58 mins.). (Truck Driver's CDL Audio Tape Ser.). 1991. 17.99 (978-0-89262-269-6(5), CDLTHMTAT-740) Career Pub.
All questions & answers to the CDL Hazardous Materials Test that all drivers who transport hazardous materials must take. Easy-to-understand explanations of the answers included. Test Study Book supports & enhances the tape.

CDL Passenger Transport Test. unabr. ed. Robert M. Calvin. Read by Jericho Productions, Inc. Staff. Ed. by Marilyn Martin. 6 cass. (Running Time: 20 min.). (Bus Driver's CDL Audio Tape Ser.). (SPA.). 1991. pap. bk. 15.99 Spanish Version. (978-0-89262-293-1(8)) Career Pub.
All questions & answers to the CDL Passenger Transport Test that all drivers of commercial vehicles that carry 15 or more passengers must take. Easy-to-understand explanations for the answers included. Test Study Book supports & enhances the tape.

CDL Passenger Transport Test: Audiotape. unabr. ed. Robert M. Calvin. Read by Jericho Productions, Inc. Staff. Ed. by Marilyn Martin. 6 cass. (Running Time: 1 hr. 20 mins.). (Bus Driver's CDL Audio Tape Ser.). 1991. pap. bk. 15.99 (978-0-89262-361-7(6), CDLBPTAT-732) Career Pub.

CDL Study Program. David Kushner. 1 cass. 1991. 10.95 (978-0-8273-4782-3(0)) Delmar.

CDL Tank Vehicles Test. unabr. ed. Robert M. Calvin. Read by Jericho Productions, Inc. Staff. Ed. by Marilyn Martin. 6 cass. (Running Time: 21 mins.). (Truck Driver's CDL Audio Tape Ser.). 1991. 15.99 (978-0-89262-268-9(7), CDLTTVT-739) Career Pub.
All questions & answers to the CDL Tank Vehicles Test that all drivers of tank vehicles must take. Easy-to-understand explanations for the answers included. Test Study Book supports & enhances the tape.

***CDQU-6-CTP Ultra PASS CD Exam Review: Adult Echocardiography.** Instructed by Christie Jordan. 2012. audio compact disk 74.95 (978-1-934864-22-7(6)) Gulfcoast Ultrasound.

C.E. Visminas Clip Art CD. C. E. Visminas. 2001. audio compact disk 29.95 (978-0-8192-2143-8(0), MoreHse Pubng) Church Pub Inc.

***Ceann Golaim.** Sonai Choilm Learai. (ENG.). 11.95 (978-0-8023-7041-9(1)) Pub: Clo Iar-Chonnachta IRL. Dist(s): Dufour

Ceann Golaim. Contrib. by Sonai Choilm Learai. (ENG.). 1997. audio compact disk 21.95 (978-0-8023-8041-8(7)) Pub: Clo Iar-Chonnachta IRL. Dist(s): Dufour

Cebuano Newspaper Reader. 1987. 13.00 (978-0-931745-42-3(X)) Dunwoody Pr.

Cebuano Newspaper Reader, R. David Zorc. 2 cass. (Running Time: 2 hrs.). (MIS.). 1987. 13.00 (3069) Dunwoody Pr.
Twenty-five selections provide the student with a broad range of articles together with necessary lexical & grammatical information. Every effort has been made to offer the widest range of genres encountered in Cebuano literature.

Cecil Dawkins. Interview. Interview with Cecil Dawkins & Kay Bonetti. 1 cass. (Running Time: 55 mins.). 13.95 (978-1-55644-172-1(X), 3062) Am Audio Prose.
The author of "The Live Goat" discusses her Southern roots & their relation to her craft & vision.

Cecil Rhodes & the Shard see $30,000 Bequest & Other Stories

Cecil Taylor. Read by Cecil Taylor. 1 cass. (Running Time: 60 mins.). (Marian McPartland's Piano Jazz Ser.). 13.95 (MM-87-02-05, HarperThor) HarpC GBR.

Cecily Parsley's Nursery Rhymes. (Running Time: 15 mins.). (Beatrix Potter's Tales Ser.). (ps up). 10.00 (978-1-4025-1687-0(8)) Recorded Bks.

Cedar Cove: 16 Lighthouse Road; 204 Rosewood Lane; 311 Pelican Court. abr. ed. Debbie Macomber. Read by Sandra Burr. (Running Time: 18 hrs.). (Cedar Cove Ser.: Bks. 1-3). 2009. audio compact disk 34.99 (978-1-4233-9735-9(5), 9781423397359, BACD) Brilliance Audio.

Cedar Cove Christmas. unabr. ed. Debbie Macomber. (Running Time: 5 hrs.). (Cedar Cove Ser.). 2008. 39.25 (978-1-4233-4807-8(9), 9781423348078, Brinc Audio MP3 Lib); audio compact disk 74.25 (978-1-4233-4805-4(2), 9781423348054, BriAudCD Unabrid) Brilliance Audio.

Cedar Cove Christmas. unabr. ed. Debbie Macomber. Read by Sandra Burr. (Running Time: 5 hrs.). (Cedar Cove Ser.). 2008. 39.25 (978-1-4233-4809-2(5), 9781423348092, BADLE); 24.95 (978-1-4233-4808-5(7), 9781423348085, BAD); 24.95 (978-1-4233-4806-1(0), 9781423348061, Brilliance MP3); audio compact disk 26.99 (978-1-4233-4804-7(4), 9781423348047, Bril Audio CD Unabri) Brilliance Audio.

***Cedar Green.** Rose Boucheron. 2010. cass. & cass. 49.95 (978-1-84652-851-4(8)); audio compact disk & audio compact disk 64.95 (978-1-84652-852-1(6)) Pub: Magna Story GBR. Dist(s): Ulverscroft US

Ceiliuradh / Celebration. (ENG.). 1995. 13.95 (978-0-8023-7112-6(4)); audio compact disk 21.95 (978-0-8023-8112-5(X)) Pub: Clo Iar-Chonnachta IRL. Dist(s): Dufour

Cel Hymnal Windows Softwr - Hy. 2004. 29.95 (978-3-01-034573-6(9)) Osterr AUT.

Celebrate. Mitch Cedar. 2008. audio compact disk 15.00 (978-1-4276-2946-3(3)) AardGP.

Celebrate! Jack Grunsky Live. Perf. by Jack Grunsky. 1 cass. (J). (gr. 4 up). 1993. 10.98 (978-0-945267-19-5(3), YM034-CN); audio compact disk 13.98 (978-0-945267-20-1(7), YM034-CD) Youngheart Mus.
Songs include: "Carnival Parade"; "The More We Get Together"; "Siyanibingelela"; "Moose & Caribou"; "Chili Chili, Hot Hot Hot"; "My Window"; "Let's Play"; "One Special Favourite Toy"; "Street Beat"; "Children of the Morning" & more.

Celebrate: Jesus down to Earth. unabr. ed. (Running Time: 1 hr. 5 mins. 0 sec.). (Kidz Rock Ser.). (ENG.). (J). 2008. 6.29 (978-1-60814-005-3(9)) Oasis Audio.

Celebrate: Jesus down to Earth. unabr. ed. HCSB. (Running Time: 1 hr. 5 mins. 0 sec.). (Kidz Rock Ser.). (ENG.). (J). 2008. audio compact disk 8.99 (978-1-59859-436-2(2)) Oasis Audio.

Celebrate! Songs of Worship. 2007. audio compact disk 11.99 (978-5-557-63791-6(5)) Columba GBR GBR.

Celebrate America. (J). 2002. audio compact disk 12.99 (978-1-57583-587-7(8)) Twin Sisters.

Celebrate America - ShowTrax. Arranged by Kirby Shaw. 1 CD. (Running Time: 5 mins.). 2000. audio compact disk 19.95 (08711259) H Leonard.
"What better place is there to be..." This Latin-flavored original celebrates what makes America great: hard work, tolerance, shared goals & loving hearts. Exciting from beginning to end!.

Celebrate His Grace, 1998. W. Ian Thomas. 1 cass. (Running Time: 1 hr. 40 mins.). 1998. 6.00 (978-1-57838-122-7(3)) CrossLife Express.
Christian living.

Celebrate Holidays. Sara Jordan. 1 CD. (Running Time: 1 hr.). (J). 2001. pap. bk. 16.95 (KIM 119CD) Kimbo Educ.
Sing & learn about the history of many of our holidays including Halloween, Easter, Thanksgiving, Chanukah, Christmas, New Years, Our Country's Birthday, Valentine's Day & more. Includes reproducible worksheets in lyric book & music only performance tracks.

Celebrate Holidays. Sarah Jordan. 1 cass. (Running Time: 1 hr.). (J). 2001. pap. bk. 14.94 (KIM 119C) Kimbo Educ.

Celebrate Holidays. Susan Pratt et al. Ed. by Joan Howard. Lyrics by Susan Pratt & Kim Smith. Composed by Sara Jordan. Contrib. by Darko Todic. Voice by Jennifer Moore & Peter DeBuis. 1 cass. (Running Time: 52 mins. 46 secs.). (J). (gr. k-3). 1999. pap. bk. 14.95 (978-1-894262-23-1(9), JMP119K) Jordan Music.
Sing and learn about the history of many of our holidays including Halloween, Thanksgiving, Chanukah, Christmas, New Year's Celebrations, Valentine's Day, St. Patrick's Day, Easter, and a patriotic song for our country's birthday. The lyrics book includes activities which teachers are free to reproduce for classroom use. Side B of the tape includes a complement of "music-only" tracks, allowing students to become performers, boosting literacy skills and making performances a breeze!.

Celebrate Holidays. abr. ed. Susan Pratt. Prod. by Sara Jordan. Composed by Sara Jordan. 1 CD. (Running Time: 30 min.). (Songs of Celebration Ser.). (ENG.). (J). (gr. 4-7). 1999. audio compact disk 13.95 (978-1-894262-22-4(0), JMP 119CD) Pub: S Jordan Publ. Dist(s): CrabtreePubCo

Celebrate! Jack Grunsky Live. (Running Time: 45 mins.). 1997. 10.98; audio compact disk 13.98 CD. Creat Teach Pr.
In this family concert Jack Grunsky celebrates animals, food, language, toys & everything that makes life fun for kids.

Celebrate Jesus. Marty Hamby. 1999. 75.00 (978-0-7673-9890-9(4)); 8.00 (978-0-7673-9885-5(8)); 11.98 (978-0-7673-9883-1(1)); audio compact disk 85.00 (978-0-7673-9889-3(0)); audio compact disk 12.00 (978-0-7673-9887-9(4)); audio compact disk 16.98 (978-0-7673-9882-4(3)) LifeWay Christian.

Celebrate Jesus. Contrib. by Elmo Mercer. 1997. 11.98 (978-0-00-514066-6(8), 75608776); 90.00 (978-0-00-514067-3(6), 75608777) Pub: Brentwood Music. Dist(s): H Leonard

Celebrate Jesus! Adventure Worship Music. unabr. ed. 1 cass. (Running Time: 60 mins.). (J). 1999. 11.00 (978-1-57849-178-0(9)) Mainstay Church.

Celebrate Jesus! Sing-Along Songs for Children's Worship. 1 cass. (Running Time: 60 mins.). (J). 1999. 8.00 (978-1-57849-187-2(8)) Mainstay Church.

Celebrate Jesus Christ: A Package of Praise for Easter Sunday: Satb. Tom Fettke. 2002. audio compact disk 10.00 (978-5-557-69298-4(3)) Allegis.

Celebrate Life. Ragan Courtney. 1990. audio compact disk 85.00 (978-0-7673-1288-2(0)) LifeWay Christian.

Celebrate Life! Ragan Courtney. 1990. audio compact disk 16.98 (978-0-7673-1281-3(3)) LifeWay Christian.

Celebrate Life. Ragan Courtney & Buryl Red. 1989. 11.98 (978-0-7673-1326-1(7)) LifeWay Christian.

Celebrate Life! Ragan Courtney & Buryl Red. 1989. 75.00 (978-0-7673-1348-3(8)) LifeWay Christian.

Celebrate New Life. Penton. 1 CD. (Running Time: 90 mins.). (Best of Contemporary Christian Ser.). 1999. audio compact disk 16.95 (978-1-56015-725-0(9)) Penton Overseas.
Contemporary Christian music including "For the Sake of the Call," "Go There with You," "Lay It Down" & "Oh How the Years Go By.".

***Celebrate Recovery: A Recovery Program based on Eight Principles from the Beatitudes.** ed. Zondervan. (Running Time: 5 hrs. 45 mins. 0 sec.). (Celebrate Recovery Ser.). (ENG.). 2009. 24.99 (978-0-310-39618-5(2)) Zondervan.

Celebrate Seasons. Sara Jordan. Lyrics by Sara Jordan. Ed. by Joan Howard. Arranged by Mark Shannon. Engineer Mark Shannon. Illus. by Alex Filipov. Contrib. by Hector Obando. 1 cass. (Running Time: 1 hr. 6 min.). (J). (gr. k-4). 1999. pap. bk. 14.95 (978-1-894262-02-6(6), JMP118K) Jordan Music.
A delightful collection of ten songs and activities to celebrate and learn about the seasons including fall and deciduous trees, migration and hibernation, how animals prepare for winter, spring and maple syrup, flowers and pollination, solstices and equinoxes and how seasons differ in different parts of the world. A bonus complement of ten "instrumental" tracks can be used to boost literacy (by having kids perform karaoke style) or for class performances.

Celebrate Seasons. Sara Jordan. 1 cass. (Running Time: 1 hr.). (J). (ps-3). 2001. 14.95 (KIM 118C); audio compact disk 16.95 (RT 118CD) Kimbo Educ.
Ten songs with activities teach about fall & deciduous trees, migration & hibernation, spring & maple syrup, flowers & polination, solstices/equinoxes & how the seasons differ around the world. Instrumental tracks included with song activity book.

Celebrate Seasons. abr. ed. Sara Jordan. Lyrics by Sara Jordan. 1 CD. (Running Time: 30 min.). (Songs of Celebration Ser.). (ENG.). (J). (gr. k up). 1999. audio compact disk 13.95 (978-1-894262-01-9(8), JMP 118CD) Pub: S Jordan Publ. Dist(s): CrabtreePubCo

Celebrate! Songs of Praise. Prod. by Joseph Burney. 2007. audio compact disk 11.99 (978-5-557-72182-0(7)) Legacy Publng.

Celebrate the Future Hand in Hand - ShowTrax. Arranged by Roger Emerson. 1 CD. (Running Time: 5 mins.). 2000. audio compact disk 19.95 (08742388) H Leonard.
From the Disney World Millennium Celebrations & featured at Super Bowl 2000, this powerful song just builds & builds into an uplifting gospel-style chorus. Fantastic for all kinds of festival performances.

Celebrate the Human Race: Multicultural Songs & Activities for Children. Sara Jordan. Prod. by Sara Jordan. Illus. by Hector Obando. Engineer Mark Shannon. Contrib. by Ishrat Rahim & James LaTrobe. 1 cass. (Running Time: 45 min. 8 secs.). (J). (gr. k-3). 1993. pap. bk. 14.95 (978-1-895523-32-4(X), JMP106K) Jordan Music.
Multicultural Songs and Activities! Award winning songs based on the lives and cultures of children whose homelands boast the Seven Natural Wonders of the World. This is an incredible cassette kit. Each song is musically representative of the culture. Paper dolls and costumes are included in the lyrics book. Ages: SK - Grade 3.

Celebrate the Human Race: Multicultural Songs for Children. Sara L. Jordan & Sara Jordan. (Running Time: 44 minutes). (Songs of Celebration Ser.). (ENG.). (J). 1993. audio compact disk 13.95 (978-1-894262-53-8(0), JMP106CD) Pub: S Jordan Publ. Dist(s): CrabtreePubCo

Celebrate with Us: Shabbat Chanukah & Passover. Prod. by Jewish Family Productions. 2 CDs. (Running Time: 3 hrs.). (ENG & HEB.). (J). 2003. audio compact disk 19.95 (978-1-890161-50-7(0)) Sounds Write.

Celebrated Cases of Judge Dee: An Authentic Eighteenth-Century Chinese Detective Novel. unabr. ed. Gulik and Yuri Rasovsky. Read by Mark Bramhall. (Running Time: 8 hrs. 0 mins.). (ENG.). 2009. 29.95 (978-1-4332-8871-5(0)); 54.95 (978-1-4332-8867-8(2)); audio compact disk 76.00 (978-1-4332-8868-5(0)) Blckstn Audio.

Celebrated Cases of Judge Dee: An Authentic Eighteenth Century Chinese Detective Novel. unabr. ed. Short Stories. Robert H. Van Gulik. Narrated by Frank Muller & Norman Dietz. 6 cass. (Running Time: 8 hrs. 30 mins.). (Judge Dee Mysteries Ser.). 1989. 51.00 (978-1-55690-096-9(1), 89560E7) Recorded Bks.
Based upon actual criminal investigations, each of these three stories deals with a different level of Chinese culture & society.

***Celebrated Jumping Frog & Other Sketches.** unabr. ed. Mark Twain. Narrated by Robin Field. (ENG.). 2010. 12.98 (978-1-59644-740-0(0), MissionAud); audio compact disk 21.98 (978-1-59644-911-4(X), MissionAud) christianaud.

Celebrated Jumping Frog of Calavares County see Favorite Stories by Mark Twain

Celebrated Jumping Frog of Calaveras County see Best of Mark Twain

Celebrated Jumping Frog of Calaveras County. Mark Twain. 10.00 (LSS1121) Esstee Audios.

Celebrated Jumping Frog of Calaveras County. rev. ed. Mark Twain. Ed. by Don Kisner. Adapted by Kathleen Chamberlain. (Read-Along Radio Dramas Ser.). (YA). (gr. 7 up). 1999. ring bd. 38.00 (978-1-878298-18-8(6)) Balance Pub.

Celebrated Jumping Frog of Calaveras County. unabr. ed. Mark Twain. 1 cass. (Running Time: 26 mins.). (Creative Short Story Audio Library Ser.). (YA). (gr. 7-12). 1995. 11.00 (978-0-8072-6103-3(3), CS901CX, Listening Lib) Random Audio Pubg.
When a stranger tells Jim Smiley that his frog Dan'l Webster isn't anything special, Jim offers to catch another frog & show off what Dan'l can do - for a small wager.

Celebrated Museums of Florence. Scripts. Created by WhiteHot Productions. 2 CDs. (Running Time: 33780 sec.). (Great Discoveries Personal Audio Guides: Florence Ser.). 2006. audio compact disk 21.95 (978-1-59971-117-1(6)) AardGP.
One hour and nineteen minutes of playtime provide today's independent traveler with an unparalleled audio tour of the Piazza della Signoria, the centuries old heart of Florentine political life. Professional narrators delight, inform and amuse the listener as they explain the piazza's great history and discuss the wonderful works of art contained in this one-of-a-kind outdoor museum. This 14 track audio tour is in standard CD format, on 2 CD's, ready for play on any CD player. Not for use on MP3 players.

Celebrating American Heroes: Plays for Students of English. Text by Anne Siebert. 1 cass. (gr. 4-12). 2001. 20.00 (978-0-86647-141-1(3)) Pro Lingua.

Celebrating American Heroes: Plays for Students of English. Anne Siebert. Illus. by Marilynne K. Roach. 1 cassette. (gr. 4-12). 2002. pap. bk. & tchr. ed. 35.00 (978-0-86647-212-8(6)) Pro Lingua.

Celebrating American Heroes: Plays for Students of English. Anne Siebert. Illus. by Marilynne Roach. 1 CD. (gr. 4-12). 2005. pap. bk. & tchr ed. 39.00 (978-0-86647-213-5(4)) Pro Lingua.

Celebrating American Heroes: Plays for Students of English. Anne Siebert. Illus. by Marilynne Roach. 1 CD. (gr. 4-12). 2005. audio compact disk 18.00 (978-0-86647-204-3(5)) Pro Lingua.

Celebrating Christian Initiation: Liturgical, Catechetical & Musical Dimensions. David Haas & Thomas H. Morris. 4 cass. (Running Time: 4 hrs.). 2001. 39.95 (A6000) St Anthony Mess Pr.
Helps RCIA teams understand and implement the rites.

Celebrating Christmas. 3 CDs. 2004. audio compact disk 24.95 (978-1-57734-891-7(5)) Covenant Comms.

Celebrating Christmas. Friedman-Fairfax and Sony Music Staff. 1 CD. (Life, Times, & Music Ser.). 1995. pap. bk. 15.98 (978-1-56799-004-1(5), Friedman-Fairfax) M Friedman Pub Grp Inc.

Celebrating Christmas. Contrib. by Hillsong. 2006. audio compact disk 19.98 (978-5-558-20057-7(X)) Hillsong Pubng AUS.

Celebrating in Tough Times: Romans 5:3-11. Ed Young. 1996. 4.95 (978-0-7417-2113-6(9), 1113) Win Walk.

Celebrating Life: Conversations about Choices That Heal. Ron Roth & Paul J. Funfsinn. 6 cass. (Running Time: 4 hrs. 30 mins.). 1994. 49.95 (978-1-893869-04-2(0)) Celbrtng Life.
How to deal with "Dark Night" experiences.

Celebrating Life: Songs of Joy & Jubilation to Open the Heart & Rekindle the Spirit. 1 cass. 1998. 7.98 (978-1-56826-947-4(1)); audio compact disk 11.98 (978-1-56826-948-1(X)) Rhino Enter.

Celebrating Life in Liturgy. Andre Papineau. 2 cass. (Running Time: 2 hrs.). 2001. 17.95 (A6840) St Anthony Mess Pr.
Focuses on the interaction between liturgy and life and challenges ministers to serve with gratitude, humility and faith.

Celebrating Our Faith: Music for Sacraments of Eucharist, Reconcilitation & Confirmation. Compiled by Robert W. Piercy. 1 cass. 1999. 19.95 (CS-451); audio compact disk 24.95 (CD-451) GIA Pubns.

Celebrating Our Seasons & Saints. 1 cass. 1994. 11.40 GRS 1&2. (978-0-8215-1531-0(4)); 11.40 GRS 3&4. (978-0-8215-1532-7(2)) W H Sadlier.

Celebrating Our Spiritual Heritage: Traditional Folk Melodies. Contrib. by Collecting Consort. 1 cass. (Running Time: 60 mins.). 2003. 9.95 (978-0-87793-885-9(7), A885COSH) Ave Maria Pr.

Celebrating Ten Years. Jerry Barnes. audio compact disk 15.95 (978-0-8198-1554-5(3), 332-041) Pauline Bks.

Celebrating the Earth. Hosted by Nancy Pearlman. 1 cass. (Running Time: 29 mins.). 10.00 (303) Educ Comm CA.

Celebrating the Mother Goddess Durga. unabr. ed. Julian C. Hollick & Marilyn Turkovich. 1 cass. (Running Time: 60 mins.). 1985. pap. bk. 30.00 (978-1-56709-050-5(8), 1030) Indep Broadcast.
Many in the West may be familiar with Kali, the Goddess of Destruction, from movies such as "Gunga Din" or "Indiana Jones & the Temple of Doom." But in India, Kali is better known as Durga, the Goddess of Creation & Renewal. This program is a radio portrait of the four-day festival of Durga Puja recorded on location in Calcutta. The accompanying booklet examines the importance of ritual & festivals in Indian culture, contains text about the mythology of the Mother Goddess & serves as a basic introduction to Hinduism & the basic duality of the Divine within Hindu thought.

Celebrating the Music of Janice Kapp Perry. Robert C. Bowden. 1 cass. (Running Time: 1 hr.). 9.95 (10001255); audio compact disk 14.95 (2800918) Covenant Comms.

Celebrating Thomas McGrath. Read by Thomas McGrath et al. 1 cass. (Running Time: 29 mins.). 1987. 10.00 New Letters.
Readings at the 1986 AWP meeting in honor of McGrath.

Celebration see James Dickey Reads His Poetry & Prose

Celebration. (K. I. D. S. Church Ser.: Vol. 1). (J). (gr. 1-6). 1998. ring bd. 119.99 (978-1-57405-035-6(4)) CharismaLife Pub.

Celebration. Jonathan Murro. 1 cass. 1990. 7.95 A R Colton Fnd.

Celebration! Dana Fuller Ross, pseud. Read by Lloyd James. 4 vols. (Wagons West Ser.: No. 24). 2004. 25.00 (978-1-58807-156-9(1)); (978-1-58807-625-0(3)) Am Pubng Inc.

***Celebration.** abr. ed. Fern Michaels. Read by Laural Merlington. (Running Time: 3 hrs.). 2010. audio compact disk 9.99 (978-1-4418-6694-3(9), 9781441866943, BCD Value Price) Brilliance Audio.

Celebration. unabr. ed. Fern Michaels. Read by Laural Merlington. (Running Time: 14 hrs.). 2008. 39.25 (978-1-4233-5414-7(1), 9781423354147, BADLE); 39.25 (978-1-4233-5412-3(5), 9781423354123, Brinc Audio MP3 Lib); 24.95 (978-1-4233-5411-6(7), 9781423354116, Brilliance MP3); 24.95 (978-1-4233-5413-0(3), 9781423354130, BAD) Brilliance Audio.

***Celebration.** unabr. ed. Fern Michaels. Read by Laural Merlington. (Running Time: 13 hrs.). 2010. audio compact disk 29.99 (978-1-4418-4049-3(4), 9781441840493, Bril Audio CD Unabri); audio compact disk 89.97 (978-1-4418-4050-9(8), 9781441840509, BriAudCD Unabrid) Brilliance Audio.

Celebration: Exodus 20:8-11. Ed Young. 1985. 4.95 (978-0-7417-1431-2(0), 431) Win Walk.

Celebration: The Life of Father Ramdon Estivill, a Renaissance Man of God. abr. ed. Mary R. Padilla & Nelson L. Haggerson, Jr. Read by Nelson L. Haggerson, Jr. 1 cass. (Running Time: 2 hrs.). 1999. 19.95 (978-0-9637606-3-0(7)) Nornel Assocs.

Celebration: With 32 Antique Postcards You Can Use: the Christmas Angel Book. Deidre J. Fogg. (FAN., 2005. 9.95 (978-0-9714372-9-6(7)) Pub: Red Rock. Dist(s): Natl Bk Netwk

Celebration in Song - A Children's Choir Christmas Around the World: SoundTrax. Ed. by Sally K. Albrecht. (ENG.). 2002. audio compact disk 34.95 (978-0-7390-2716-5(6)) Alfred Pub.

Celebration of Country. 1 CD. (Running Time: 37 min.). (J). 2001. 15.98 MFLP CA.

Celebration of Country. 1 cass. (Running Time: 37 min.). (J). (ps-6). 2001. 9.98 (978-1-56628-276-5(4)) MFLP CA.

***Celebration of Discipline.** abr. ed. Richard J. Foster. Read by Richard J. Foster. (ENG.). 2004. (978-0-06-078454-6(7), Harper Audio) HarperCollins Pubs.

***Celebration of Discipline.** abr. ed. Richard J. Foster. Read by Richard J. Foster. (ENG.). 2004. (978-0-06-081479-3(9), Harper Audio) HarperCollins Pubs.

***Celebration of Discipline: The Path to Spiritual Growth.** unabr. ed. Richard Foster. Narrated by Richard Rohan. (ENG.). 2007. 16.98 (978-1-59644-455-3(X), Hovel Audio) christianaud.

Celebration of Discipline: The Path to Spiritual Growth, unabr. ed. Richard J. Foster. Read by Tom Parker. 6 cass. (Running Time: 9 hrs.). 2000. 44.95 (2431) Blckstn Audio.
Expands on the inward Disciplines of meditation & prayer, the outward Discipline of simplicity & the corporate Discipline of celebration. He provides a wealth of examples, demonstrating how these Disciplines can become part of our daily activities.

Celebration of Discipline: The Path to Spiritual Growth. unabr. ed. Richard J. Foster. Read by Tom Parker. 6 cass. (Running Time: 8 hrs. 30 mins.). 2003. 44.95 (978-0-7861-1603-4(X), 2431) Blckstn Audio.

Celebration of Discipline: The Path to Spiritual Growth. unabr. ed. Richard J. Foster. Read by Tom Parker. (Running Time: 7.5 hrs. 0 mins.). 2008. 29.95 (978-1-4332-5034-7(9)); audio compact disk 60.00 (978-1-4332-5033-0(0)) Blckstn Audio.

Celebration of Discipline: The Path to Spiritual Growth. unabr. ed. Richard J. Foster. Read by Richard Rohan. (Running Time: 25200 sec.). 2007. audio compact disk 29.95 (978-0-06-133695-9(5), Harper Audio) HarperCollins Pubs.

***Celebration of Discipline: The Path to Spiritual Growth.** unabr. ed. Richard J. Foster. Read by Richard Rohan. (ENG.). 2007. (978-0-06-199989-5(X), Harper Audio); (978-0-06-133700-0(5), Harper Audio) HarperCollins Pubs.

Celebration of Discipline: The Path to Spiritual Growth. unabr. ed. Richard J. Foster. Narrated by Richard Rohan. (Running Time: 7 hrs. 0 mins. 0 sec.). (ENG.). 2007. lp 19.98 (978-1-59644-454-6(1)) christianaud.

Celebration of Discipline: The Path to Spiritual Growth. unabr. ed. Richard J. Foster. Read by Richard Rohan. (Running Time: 7 hrs. 0 mins. 0 sec.). (ENG.). 2007. audio compact disk 29.98 (978-1-59644-453-9(3)) christianaud.

Celebration of Fairy Tales, a Gathering of Archetypes, a Telling of Images. Leland Roloff. Read by Leland Roloff. 10 cass. (Running Time: 14 hrs. 30 mins.). 1993. 66.95 (978-0-7822-0416-2(3), 502) C G Jung IL.
Jungian analyst Lee Roloff presents an intensive & entertaining exploration into fairy tales - those stories of archetypal resonance which have become commonplace short-hand images for the complexities of psychological life.

Celebration of Love. Perf. by Mari Devon & Roger Rees. 1 cass. (Running Time: 40 mins.). (J). (gr. 3 up). 1994. 14.95 (978-1-883446-02-4(3)) Poet Tree CA.
A collection of 32 love-themed poems performed by Tony Award winner Roger Rees & Actress Mari Devon & accompanied by music. William Shakespeare, Ella Wheeler Wilcox & James Whitcomb Riley are among the poets who awaken feelings & emotions of anyone who has been - or hopes to be - in love.

Celebration of Peter Gzowski. Peter Gzowski. 2 CDs. (Running Time: 3 hrs). 2005. audio compact disk 19.95 (978-0-660-18780-8(9)) Pub: Canadian Broadcasting CAN. Dist(s): Georgetown Term

Celebration of Womanhood. Annie Chapman. 1 cass. 1990. 5.98 (978-7-901440-21-0(X)) S&A Family.
Spirituality.

Celebration Song. Contrib. by Geron Davis & Michael Burt. 1997. 24.95 (978-0-7601-2076-7(5), 75700195) Pub: Brentwood Music. Dist(s): H Leonard

Celebration with Maya Angelou, Guy Johnson, Janice Mirikitani: A Spoken Word Event on the Occasion of Guy Johnson's 50th Birthday. unabr. ed. Poems. Perf. by Maya Angelou et al. (Running Time: 1 hr. 28 mins.). Dramatization. 1995. 7.99 (978-1-893803-03-9(1), DQYD5-0005) Dont Quit.
Reading poetry in front of a live audience.

Celebrations: Rituals of Peace & Prayer. unabr. ed. Maya Angelou. Read by Maya Angelou. 1 CD. (Running Time: 43 mins.). 2006. audio compact disk 13.01 (978-1-4159-3256-8(5)) Pub: Books on Tape. Dist(s): NetLibrary CO

Celebrations Around the World: Soundtrax. Marti Lunn Lantz et al. (ENG.). 2001. audio compact disk 34.95 (978-0-7390-1715-9(2), 20150) Alfred Pub.

Celebrations Around the World - Again! SoundTrax. Sally K. Albrecht & Lois Brownsey. (ENG.). 2002. audio compact disk 34.95 (978-0-7390-2275-7(X)) Alfred Pub.

Celebrations at Thrush Green. unabr. ed. Miss Read. Read by Gwen Watford. 4 cass. (Running Time: 4 hrs. 4 min.). 2001. 24.95 (978-1-57270-185-4(4), M41185u, Audio Editions) Pub: Audio Partners. Dist(s): PerseuPGW
The townfolk combine the centennial anniversary of the village school with several other reasons for rejoicing.

Celebremos Unidos: Proceedings of the 45th Annual Convention of the National Association of Evangelicals Buffalo, New York. Read by John Gimenez. 1 cass. (Running Time: 60 mins.). (SPA.). 1987. 4.00 (319) Nat Assn Evan.

Celebrities That Helped Shape History: Voices & Sounds from Some of the Most Well Knows Celebrities in Modern History. Created by Soundworks. (Running Time: 3600 sec.). 2006. audio compact disk 15.95 (978-1-885959-84-3(2)) Soundworks Intl.

***Celebrity Chekhov.** unabr. ed. Ben Greenman. Read by Kathleen Mcinerney & Jeff Woodman. (ENG.). 2010. (978-0-06-206241-3(7), Harper Audio); (978-0-06-200701-8(7), Harper Audio) HarperCollins Pubs.

Celebutantes. unabr. ed. Amanda Goldberg & Ruthanna Khalighi Hopper. Read by Gigi Bermingham. (YA). 2008. 54.99 (978-1-60514-688-1(9)) Find a World.

Celebutantes. unabr. ed. Amanda Goldberg et al. Read by Gigi Bermingham. 8 CDs. (Running Time: 9 hrs. 30 mins.). (ENG., 2008. audio compact disk 34.95 (978-1-59887-583-6(3), 1598875833) Pub: HighBridge. Dist(s): Workman Pub

Celery Stalks at Midnight. James Howe. Perf. by Al Simmons. 1 cass. (Bunnicula Ser.). (J). (gr. 3-5). 1995. 10.98 (978-0-945267-39-3(8), YM048-CN); audio compact disk 13.98 (978-0-945267-40-9(1), YM048-CD) Youngheart Mus.
Songs include: "Discover Me"; "Vegetation Migration"; "Celery Stalks at Midnight"; "I.M.4.U"; "La Vie en Rose"; "My Hat's on the Side of My Head"; "Where Did You Get That Hat?"; "Sam's Men's Wear/Sam, You Made the Pants Too Long"; "Open the Door, Richard" & more.

Celery Stalks at Midnight. abr. ed. James Howe. Perf. by George S. Irving. 1 cass. (Running Time: 1 hr. 03 mins.). (Bunnicula Ser.). (J). (gr. 3-5). 1987. 11.95 (978-0-89845-745-2(9), CPN 1814) HarperCollins Pubs.
"Where is Bunnicula?" Thats What Chester the cat, Harold the dog & Howie the dachshund puppy would like to know.

Celery Stalks at Midnight. unabr. ed. James Howe. Read by Victor Garber. 2 vols. (Running Time: 1 hr. 40 mins.). (Bunnicula Ser.). (J). (gr. 3-7). 2004. pap. bk. 29.00 (978-0-8072-8357-8(6), YA173SP, Listening Lib); 23.00 (978-0-8072-8356-1(8), LL 0192, Listening Lib) Random Audio Pubg.
When Chester discovers Bunnicula has vanished from his cage, he fears the ultimate horror, but can he save Bunnicula's victims, or will they become vampires themselves?.

***Celestial Buffet.** Susan Dunlap. 2009. (978-1-60136-545-3(4)) Audio Holding.

Celestial Dating in a Telestial World. Scott Simmons. 1 cass. 1996. 9.95 (978-1-57008-228-3(6), Bkcraft Inc) Deseret Bk.

Celestial Toymaker. Doctor Who. 2 CDs. (Running Time: 1 hr. 40 mins.). 2001. audio compact disk 13.99 (978-0-563-47855-3(1)) London Brdge.

Celestial Voyagers. Contrib. by Rhino Records Staff. 1 cass. (New Visions Ser.). 1998. 16.98 (978-1-56826-934-4(X)) Rhino Enter.

Celestial Whispers. 1 cass. (Running Time: 60 mins.). (Interludes Music Ser.). 1989. 8.95 (978-1-55569-295-7(8), MOD-3908) Great Am Audio.

Celestina. Miguel de Cervantes Saavedra. (SPA.). pap. bk. 20.95 (978-88-7754-810-8(X)) Pub: Cideb ITA. Dist(s): Distribks Inc

Celestina. Rojas. audio compact disk 12.95 (978-0-8219-3745-7(6)) EMC-Paradigm.

Celestine see Twentieth-Century Poetry in English, No. 10, Recordings of Poets Reading Their Own Poetry

Celestine Meditations: A Guide to Meditation Based on "The Celestine Prophecy" Salle Merrill Redfield. 1999. (978-1-57042-758-9(5)) Hachet Audio.

Celestine Meditations: A Guide to Meditation Based on the Celestine Prophecy. unabr. ed. Salle Merrill Redfield. (Running Time: 1 hr.). (ENG.). 2009. 24.98 (978-1-60788-095-0(4)) Pub: Hachet Audio. Dist(s): HachBkGrp

Celestine Meditations: A Guide to Meditation Based on the Celestine Prophecy. unabr. ed. Salle Merrill Redfield. (ENG.). 2005. 5.98 (978-1-59483-353-3(2)) Pub: Hachet Audio. Dist(s): HachBkGrp

Celestine Prophecy see Prophetie des Andes

Celestine Prophecy. Salle Merrill Redfield. 2001. (978-1-57042-755-8(0)) Hachet Audio.

Celestine Prophecy. abr. ed. James Redfield. Read by Jesse Corti. (ENG.). 2005. 14.98 (978-1-59483-189-8(0)) Pub: Hachet Audio. Dist(s): HachBkGrp

Celestine Prophecy. unabr. ed. James Redfield. Read by Michael Kramer. 8 cass. (Running Time: 8 hrs.). 1996. 64.00 (978-0-7366-3205-8(0), 3869) Books on Tape.
A modern parable that begins with the disappearance of an ancient Peruvian manuscript that contains an important secret. The secret is a list of nine insights that, if understood, provide a positive vision of how we can save this planet & its creatures & preserve its beauty.

Celestine Prophecy. unabr. ed. James Redfield. Read by Lou Diamond Phillips. (Running Time: 7 hrs.). (ENG.). 2006. 16.98 (978-1-59483-499-8(7)); audio compact disk 29.98 (978-1-59483-195-9(5)) Pub: Hachet Audio. Dist(s): HachBkGrp

Celestine Prophecy, unabr. ed. James Redfield. Narrated by Tom Stechschulte. 7 cass. (Running Time: 9 hrs. 15 mins.). 1999. 60.00 (978-0-7887-0440-6(0), 94632E7) Recorded Bks.
Experience the best-seller that became a spiritual guidebook for the new millennium. It will give you chills & hope, as you perceive its predictions unfolding around you.

Celestine Prophecy. unabr. ed. James Redfield. Read by Lou Diamond Phillips. (Running Time: 8 hrs.). (ENG.). 2009. 44.98 (978-1-60788-085-1(7)) Pub: Hachet Audio. Dist(s): HachBkGrp

Celestine Prophecy: A Concise Guide to the Nine Insights Featuring Original Essays & Lectures by the Author. unabr. ed. James Redfield. (Running Time: 30 mins.). (ENG.). 2006. 9.99 (978-1-59483-697-8(3)) Pub: Hachet Audio. Dist(s): HachBkGrp

Celestine Vision: Living the New Spiritual Awareness. unabr. ed. James Redfield. Read by LeVar Burton. 4 cass. (Running Time: 6 hrs.). 1998. 32.00 (978-0-7366-4068-8(1), 4579) Books on Tape.
The historical & scientific background of a modern day renaissance. It's a rebirth of spirit that will shape us & our world in the new millennium.

Celia: My Life. Ana Christina Reymundo. 4 cass. (Running Time: 6 hrs.). 2004. 25.95 (978-0-06-073023-9(4)); audio compact disk 29.95 (978-0-06-073027-7(7)) HarperCollins Pubs.

Celia Cruz, Queen of Salsa. Veronica Chambers. Read by Michelle Manzo. Illus. by Julie Maren. 1 CD. (Running Time: 46 mins.). (J). (ps-3). 2008. bk. 28.95 (978-1-4301-0284-7(5)); bk. 25.95 (978-1-4301-0281-6(0)); pap. bk. 18.95 (978-1-4301-0283-0(7)); pap. bk. 16.95 (978-1-4301-0280-9(2)) Live Oak Media.

Celia, My Life see Celia SPA: Mi Vida

Celia SPA: Mi Vida. abr. ed. Ana Cristina Reymundo & Celia Cruz. Read by Cristina Saralegui.Tr. of Celia, My Life. (SPA.). 2004. audio compact disk 22.00 (978-0-06-073388-9(8)) HarperCollins Pubs.

Celibacy Is for the Birds, Or Is It? Cor. 6:12-20. Ed Young. 1993. 4.95 (978-0-7417-1960-7(6), 960) Win Walk.

***Celibato Audio Libro.** Daniel Garza. 2009. (978-1-61623-335-8(4)) Indep Pub IL.

Celine, unabr. ed. Brock Cole. Narrated by C. J. Critt. 5 pieces. (Running Time: 6 hrs. 15 mins.). (gr. 11 up). 1998. 44.00 (978-0-7887-2133-5(X), 95442 E7) Recorded Bks.
An unconventional high school girl is creative & bright, but flunking English. To pass, she has to avoid distraction & the lonely little boy in the apartment across the hall, long enough to rewrite a sloppy essay.

Cell. Stephen King. 2006. cd-rom 39.99 (978-1-59895-484-5(9)) Find a World.

Cell. unabr. ed. Stephen King. Read by Campbell Scott. 11 CDs. (Running Time: 12 hrs.). 2006. audio compact disk 119.75 (978-1-4193-8537-7(2), C3665); 79.75 (978-1-4193-8535-3(6), 98328) Recorded Bks.
Stephen King was born to write horror. His monumental catalog of novels has already assured his place in history as one of the most popular authors of all time. With the goresplattered literary bludgeon that is Cell, King conjures a startling horror tale of popular technology and the supernatural. On October 1, a single pulse is simultaneously transmitted through every active cell phone on the planet, causing people to transform into mindless killing machines.

Cell. unabr. ed. Stephen King. Read by Campbell Scott. 2006. 29.95 (978-0-7435-5570-8(8)); audio compact disk 49.95 (978-0-7435-5433-6(7), Audioworks) Pub: S&S Audio. Dist(s): S and S Inc

Cell: Inside the 9/11 Plot, & why the FBI & CIA Failed to Stop It. abr. ed. John Miller & Michael Stone. Told to Chris Mitchell. 2004. 15.95 (978-0-7435-4254-8(1)) Pub: S&S Audio. Dist(s): S and S Inc

Cell Perfection. Rick Brown. Read by Rick Brown. Ed. by John Quatro. 1 cass. (Running Time: 30 mins.). (Subliminal - New Age Ser.). 1993. 10.95 (978-1-57100-066-8(6), N145); 10.95 (978-1-57100-090-3(9), S145); 10.95 (978-1-57100-114-6(X), W145); 10.95 (978-1-57100-138-2(7), H145) Sublime Sftware.
Emphasizes the perfection at conception.

Cell Perfection, No. E145. Rick Brown. Read by Rick Brown. Ed. by John Quatro. 1 cass. (Running Time: 30 mins.). (Subliminal - Easy Listening Ser.). 1993. 10.95 (978-1-57100-018-7(6)) Sublime Sftware.
"Cell Perfection" emphasizes the perfection at conception.

Cell Perfection, No. J145. Rick Brown. Read by Rick Brown. Ed. by John Quatro. 1 cass. (Running Time: 30 mins.). (Subliminal - Jazz Ser.). 1993. 10.95 (978-1-57100-042-2(9)) Sublime Sftware.

Cell Phones: Program from the Award Winning Public Radio Series. Interview. Hosted by Fred Goodwim. 1 CD. (Running Time: 1 Hour). 2000. audio compact disk 21.95 (978-1-932479-30-0(9), LCM 134) Lichtenstein Creat.
One hundred million Americans are using them. Are they safe for you and your children? We'll hear the latest science and the politics behind the science.There is a lot of indications in the published scientific literature, that we may have a problem on our hands. We'll hear from the federal regulator in charge of cell phones. He says don't look to the federal government for guarantees of absolute safety.

***Cellist of Sarajevo.** unabr. ed. Steven Galloway. Read by Gareth Armstrong. 6 CDs. (Running Time: 5 hrs. 28 mins.). 2010. audio compact disk 34.98 (978-962-634-333-3(8)) Naxos.

Cello Method. 1999. audio compact disk 15.98 (978-0-7866-2922-0(3)) Mel Bay.

Cello Method: Beginning Level. Christine Watts. 1999. pap. bk. 24.95 (978-0-7866-2923-7(1), 96459CDP) Mel Bay.

Cello School Vol. 3 & 4: Leonard. Shinichi Suzuki. (Suzuki Method Core Materials Ser.). (ENG.). 1994. audio compact disk 15.95 (978-0-87487-941-4(8), Warner Bro) Alfred Pub.

Cello School Vols. 1 & 2: Tsutsumi. Shinichi Suzuki. (Suzuki Method Core Materials Ser.). (ENG.). 1994. audio compact disk 15.95 (978-0-87487-940-7(X), Warner Bro) Alfred Pub.

Cello School Cd V-5 Tsutsumi. Shinichi Suzuki. (Suzuki Method Core Materials Ser.). (ENG.). 1994. audio compact disk 15.95 (978-0-87487-942-1(6), Warner Bro) Alfred Pub.

Cello School Cd V-6 Tsutsumi. Shinichi Suzuki. (Suzuki Method Core Materials Ser.). (ENG.). 1994. audio compact disk 15.95 (978-0-87487-943-8(4), Warner Bro) Alfred Pub.

Cello School CD V-7 Tsutsumi. rev. ed. Shinichi Suzuki. (Suzuki Method Core Materials Ser.). (ENG.). 1994. audio compact disk 15.95 (978-0-87487-944-5(2), Warner Bro) Alfred Pub.

Cello School Cd V-8 Tsutsumi. Shinichi Suzuki. (Suzuki Method Core Materials Ser.). (ENG.). 1994. audio compact disk 15.95 (978-0-87487-945-2(0), Warner Bro) Alfred Pub.

***Cells: CD add-on Set.** Perf. by Millmark Education Staff. (ConceptLinks Ser.). 2009. audio compact disk 50.00 (978-1-61618-343-1(8)) Millmark Educ.

Cells, Anatomy & Physiology. Milady Publishing Company Staff. 1 cass. (Standard Ser.: Chapter 23). 1995. 15.95 (978-1-56253-295-6(2), Milady) Delmar.

***Cells Audio CD.** Perf. by Millmark Education Staff. (ConceptLinks Ser.). 2007. audio compact disk 28.00 (978-1-4334-0019-3(7)) Millmark Educ.

***Cells SB1 Audio CD the Smallest Unit of Life.** Perf. by Millmark Education Staff. (Content Literacy Libraries Ser.). 2008. audio compact disk (978-1-4334-0392-7(7)) Millmark Educ.

***Cells SB2 Audio CD Animal Cells & Plant Cells.** Perf. by Millmark Education Staff. (Content Literacy Libraries Ser.). 2008. audio compact disk (978-1-4334-0393-4(5)) Millmark Educ.

***Cells SB3 Audio CD Organization & Function.** Perf. by Millmark Education Staff. (Content Literacy Libraries Ser.). 2008. audio compact disk (978-1-4334-0394-1(3)) Millmark Educ.

***Cells SB4 Audio CD Growing & Dividing.** Perf. by Millmark Education Staff. (Content Literacy Libraries Ser.). 2008. audio compact disk (978-1-4334-0395-8(1)) Millmark Educ.

Cellular Telecommunications Equipment in Uruguay: A Strategic Reference 2006. Compiled by Icon Group International, Inc. Staff. 2007. ring bd. 195.00 (978-0-497-82461-7(2)) Icon Grp.

Cellular Telecommunications in Indonesia: A Strategic Reference 2007. Compiled by Icon Group International, Inc. Staff. 2007. ring bd. 195.00 (978-0-497-36027-6(6)) Icon Grp.

Celtic Airs, Jigs, Hornpipes, & Reels. Compiled by Stefan Grossman. (Guitar Workshop Ser.). 1997. bk. 17.95 (978-0-7866-2876-6(6), 94504BCD) Mel Bay.

Celtic Album. Perf. by Keith Lockhart & Boston Pops Orchestra. 1 cass. (Running Time: 1 hr.). 8.78 (RCA 68901); audio compact disk 13.58 Jewel box. (RCA 68901) NewSound.

Celtic Awakenings. Perf. by Solitudes. 1 cass. (Running Time: 1 hr.). 7.98 (DG 140); audio compact disk 12.78 Jewel box. (DG 140) NewSound.

Celtic Book of Days. Perf. by David Arkenstone. 1 cass. (Running Time: 1 hr.). 1998. 9.98; audio compact disk 16.98 Lifedance.
Electronic instruments, winds, fiddles, some vocals, & percussion. This contemporary take on ancient music behaves like a soundtrack, if you will, rather than focusing on individual songs. Sometimes the music is haunting & gentle, other times it is robust & upbeat.

Celtic Book of Days. Perf. by David Arkenstone. 1 cass. (Running Time: 1 hr.). 8.78 (WH 11246); audio compact disk 13.58 Jewel box. (WH 11246) NewSound.

Celtic Christmas. Jordan Peters. (Running Time: 1 hr.). 2002. audio compact disk 15.99 (978-1-904972-36-5(5)) Global Jrny GBR GBR.

Celtic Christmas. Windham Hill Staff. 1 cass. 1998. 15.00 (978-1-56170-559-7(4)) Hay House.

Celtic Christmas, Vol. 1. Perf. by Kim Robertson. 1 cass. (Running Time: 1 hr.). 9.98 (405); audio compact disk 17.98 (D405) MFLP CA.
A virtuoso on the Celtic harp, Kim weaves magic into Old World Christmas songs with her warm, inventive & nimble style.

Celtic Christmas, Vol. 2. Perf. by Kim Robertson & Virginia Kron. 1 cass. (Running Time: 1 hr.). 9.98 (406); audio compact disk 17.98 (D406) MFLP CA.
Kim is joined by renowned cellist Virginia Kron in this collection of International Christmas music. Features songs from France, Spain, Italy & Czechoslovakia, the Huron Indian & medieval music as well.

***Celtic Christmas: Beloved Christmas Songs - Celtic Celebrations in Vocal & Instrumental Styles.** Compiled by Barbour Publishing, Inc. (ENG.). 2010. audio compact disk 9.99 (978-1-61626-061-3(0), Barbour Bks) Barbour Pub.

Celtic Christmas II. 1 cass. (Running Time: 1 hr.). 1996. 10.98; audio compact disk 15.98 BMG Distribution.

Celtic Circles. Bonnie Rideout. 1996. pap. bk. 17.95 (978-0-7866-0668-9(1), 95572P); pap. bk. 22.95 (978-0-7866-0670-2(3), 95572CDP) Mel Bay.

Celtic Crossing-Guitar. William Coulter. 1998. pap. bk. 24.95 (978-0-7866-2763-9(8), 96316P) Mel Bay.

Celtic Crystal. Perf. by Dean Shostak. 1 cass. (Running Time: 1 hr.). 8.78 (DSM 121); audio compact disk 13.58 Jewel box. (DSM 121) NewSound.

Celtic Dance. 1 CD. (Running Time: 1 hr.). audio compact disk 19.98 Jewel box, double. (REL 28775) NewSound.

Celtic Dreams: With Booklet. Prod. by Ellipsis Arts Staff. 1 CD. (Running Time: 1 hr.). (J). 2003. audio compact disk 15.98 (978-1-55961-721-5(7), Ellipsis Arts) Relaxtn Co.

Celtic Echoes. Jordan Peters. (Running Time: 1 hr.). 2002. audio compact disk 15.99 (978-1-904972-15-0(2)) Global Jrny GBR GBR.

***Celtic Expressions: Hymns & Worship Vol 3 And 4.** (ENG.). 2006. audio compact disk 17.99 (978-92-822-2542-4(9)) Pub: Kingsway Pubns GBR. Dist(s): STL Dist NA

***Celtic Expressions (Box Set Vol. 1-2)** (ENG.). 2006. audio compact disk 17.99 (978-0-01-236839-8(3)) Pub: Kingsway Pubns GBR. Dist(s): STL Dist NA

***Celtic Expressions (vol 5 And 6)** (ENG.). 2007. audio compact disk 19.99 (978-5-557-90598-5(7)) Pub: Kingsway Pubns GBR. Dist(s): STL Dist NA

Celtic Fair. Maggie Sansone. (ENG.). 2009. pap. bk. 19.99 (978-0-7866-4994-5(1)) Mel Bay.

Celtic Fiddle Festival Encore. Perf. by Kevin Burke et al. 1 cass. (Running Time: 1 hr.). 8.78 (SIF 1189); audio compact disk 12.78 Jewel box. (SIF 1189) NewSound.

Celtic Folksongs for All Ages: Bb Instruments. James Curnow & Timothy Campbell. 2006. pap. bk. 14.95 (978-90-431-2293-1(9), 9043122939) H Leonard.

Celtic Folksongs for All Ages: BC Instruments. James Curnow & Timothy Campbell. 2006. pap. bk. 14.95 (978-90-431-2295-5(5), 9043122955) H Leonard.

Celtic Folksongs for All Ages: C Instruments. James Curnow & Timothy Campbell. 2006. pap. bk. 14.95 (978-90-431-2290-0(4), 9043122904) H Leonard.

Celtic Folksongs for All Ages: Eb Instruments. James Curnow & Timothy Campbell. 2006. pap. bk. 14.95 (978-1-4234-1663-0(5), 1423416635) H Leonard.

Celtic Folksongs for All Ages: F/Eb Horn. James Curnow & Timothy Campbell. 2006. pap. bk. 14.95 (978-90-431-2294-8(7), 9043122947) H Leonard.

Celtic Folksongs for All Ages: Violin (First Position) with Piano Accompaniment. James Curnow & Timothy Campbell. 2006. pap. bk. 14.95 (978-90-431-2328-0(5), 9043123285) H Leonard.

Celtic Hymns. 1 cass. (Running Time: 1 hr.). 1997. 9.98; audio compact disk 14.98 Brentwood Music.
Celtic songs are usually circular, or written is such a way that they can be repeated indefinitely or played back to back with several other tunes. Fiddle, flute, tin whistle, & pipes were favorite solo instruments & later joined together to form the unmistakable sounds of Irish bands.

Celtic Hymns. Created by Visions of Worship. 2007. audio compact disk 19.99 (978-5-557-53278-5(1)) Vision Vid PA.

Celtic Journey. Jordan Peters. (Running Time: 1 hr.). 2002. audio compact disk 15.99 (978-1-904972-16-7(0)) Global Jrny GBR GBR.

Celtic Lamentations. Aine Minogue. 1 CD. (Running Time: 3480 sec.). 2005. audio compact disk 16.98 (978-1-59179-351-9(3), M952D) Sounds True.

Celtic Legacy. 1 cass. (Running Time: 1 hr.). 9.98; audio compact disk 15.98 Lifedance.
Instrumental & vocal anthology that leans toward the quiet & gentle side of contemporary Celtic with a few peppier pieces included to liven things up. Demo CD or Cassette available. Demo CD or cassette available.

Celtic Love Songs. 1 cass., 1 CD. 7.98 (SH 78016); audio compact disk 12.78 CD Jewel box. (SH 78016) NewSound.

Celtic Lullaby. bk. 9.95 (978-1-55961-496-2(X)) Relaxtn Co.

Celtic Lullaby. 1 CD. (Running Time: 1 hr.). (J). 2001. audio compact disk 16.00 (93-0212) Relaxtn Co.
Cradlesongs from Ireland, Scotland and Wales coax children to sleep. Lovely multi-part harmonies, a cappella solos and instrumentals on harps and flutes provide a treasury of poetic celtic sound.

Celtic Meditation Music. Aine Minogue. 1 CD. (Running Time: 1 hr. 1 min.). 2006. audio compact disk 16.98 (978-1-59179-152-2(9), M787D) Sounds True.

Celtic Moods. 1 cass. (Running Time: 1 hr.). (Moods Ser.). 8.78 (VIR 44951); audio compact disk 12.78 Jewel box. (VIR 44951) NewSound.

Celtic Music Collection: Ballards. Traditional. (Running Time: 1 hr.). 2002. audio compact disk 15.99 (978-1-904972-08-2(X)) Global Jrny GBR GBR.

Celtic Music Collection: Jigs & Reels. Keith Halligan. (Running Time: 1 hr.). 2002. audio compact disk 15.99 (978-1-904972-10-5(1)) Global Jrny GBR GBR.

Celtic Music Collection: Rhythms. Jordan Peters. (Running Time: 1 hr.). 2002. audio compact disk 15.99 (978-1-904972-09-9(8)) Global Jrny GBR GBR.

Celtic Music Collection: Serenity. Keith Halligan. (Running Time: 1 hr.). 2002. audio compact disk 15.99 (978-1-904972-11-2(X)) Global Jrny GBR GBR.

Celtic Passage: A Musical Journey to the Depths of the Celtic Spirit. Deirdre Ni Chinneide. (Running Time: 53 mins.). 2007. audio compact disk 17.98 (978-1-59179-547-6(8), M1102D) Sounds True.

Celtic Poets. Read by Ralph Cosham. (Running Time: 2 hrs.). (C). 2003. 16.95 (978-1-59912-050-8(X), Audiofy Corp) Iofy Corp.

Celtic Poets. Narrated by Ralph Cosham. Selected by Keith Winston. (Running Time: 7200 sec.). (Unabridged Classics in MP3 Ser.). (ENG.). 2008. audio compact disk 24.00 (978-1-58472-647-0(4), In Aud) Sound Room.

Celtic Poets. unabr. ed. Poems. Read by Ralph Cosham. 2 cds. (Running Time: 2 hrs). 2002. audio compact disk 18.95 (978-1-58472-225-0(8), 061, In Aud) Pub: Sound Room. Dist(s): Baker Taylor
This is a collection of poems, old and modern, by Yeats, Swift, Burns and others.

Celtic Psalms: Music to Soothe the Soul. 1 cass. (Running Time: 1 hr.). 10.98 (978-0-7601-2582-3(1)) Brentwood Music.

Celtic Psalms: Music to Soothe the Soul. Contrib. by Brentwood / Provident Staff. 1 CD. (Running Time: 1 hr.). audio compact disk (978-0-7601-2583-0(X)) Brentwood Music.

Celtic Queen: An Epic Poem. Cynthia M. Bateman. (Running Time: 5400 sec.). 2007. audio compact disk 17.99 (978-1-60462-135-8(4)) Tate Pubng.

Celtic Requiem. Perf. by William Coulter & Mary McLaughlin. 1 cass. (Running Time: 1 hr.). 8.78 (WH 11314); audio compact disk 13.58 Jewel box. (WH 11314) NewSound.

Celtic Roads. 1 CD. (Running Time: 1 hr.). (J). 1999. audio compact disk 14.95 Revels Recs.
Celtic music from Ireland, Scotland & Britany. Twenty-six selections featuring Breton Bombards, evocation street cries & children's songs.

Celtic Romance. Perf. by Mychael Danna & Jeff Danna. 1 cass. (Running Time: 1 hr.). 1998. 9.98; audio compact disk 17.98 Lifedance.
Guitar, winds, mandolin, pipes, harp, vocals, et al. Traditional Celtic instruments intertwined with Gregorian chants & ethereal, vocal solos evoke the mythical feel of that time long ago.

Celtic Romance. Perf. by Mychael Danna & Jeff Danna. 1 cass. (Running Time: 1 hr.). 7.98 (HOS 11084); audio compact disk 12.78 Jewel box. (HOS 11084) NewSound.

Celtic Sanctuary. Jordan Peters. (Running Time: 1 hr.). 2002. audio compact disk 15.99 (978-1-904972-14-3(4)) Global Jrny GBR GBR.

Celtic Spirit. 1 cass. . 9.98; audio compact disk 15.98 CD. Lifedance.
Compilation of quiet Celtic spiritual music, from ancient Gregorian chants to contemporary Celtic hymns. Some songs are in Latin & some in Gaelic. Demo CD or cassette available.

Celtic Spirit. Jordan Peters. (Running Time: 1 hr.). 2002. audio compact disk 15.99 (978-1-904972-12-9(8)) Global Jrny GBR GBR.

Celtic Spirit Meditations. Mara Freeman. 2001. audio compact disk 16.00 (978-1-890851-05-7(1)) Chalice Prods.

Celtic Sunday: A Collection of Traditional Irish Hymns. Created by Spring Hill Music. Prod. by Craig Duncan. Contrib. by Greg Howard. 2005. audio compact disk 11.98 (978-5-558-94702-1(0)) Sprg Hill Music Group.

Celtic Sunrise: Stories & Music. Retold by Claudine Gandolfi. Illus. by Jo Gershman. (BookNotes Ser.). 1999. bk. 13.95 (978-0-88088-410-5(X)) Peter Pauper.

Celtic Sunset. Jordan Peters. (Running Time: 1 hr.). 2002. audio compact disk 15.99 (978-1-904972-13-6(6)) Global Jrny GBR GBR.

Celtic Tales of Birds & Beasts. Mara Freeman. Read by Mara Freeman. 1 CD. (Running Time: 1 hr.). (Stories from the Otherworld Ser.). (J). (gr. k-10). 2001. audio compact disk 16.00 (978-1-890851-04-0(3)) Chalice Prods.
"The Selkie," "The Legend of the Oldest Animals," "The Black Wolf," "The Prince, the Fox and the Sword of Light".

Celtic Tales of Birds & Beasts. Mara Freeman. Read by Mara Freeman. Music by Gerry Smida. 1 cass. (Running Time: 1 hr.). (Stories from the Otherworld Ser.). (J). (gr. k-10). 1997. 10.00 (978-1-890851-01-9(9)) Chalice Prods.
Celtic storytelling tape: myths & legends told by British storyteller set to the music of harp, whistle & pipes.

Celtic Tales of Birds & Beasts: Stories from the Otherworld. As told by Mara Freeman. Music by Gerry Smida. 1 cass. (Running Time: 57 min.). (J). 2001. 9.95; audio compact disk 16.95 Parabola Bks.
Tales from the British Isles, including the mysterious tale of "The Selkie," "The Legend of the Black Wolf" and the magical story of "The Children of Lir," featuring that most otherworldy of birds, the swan.

Celtic Treasures. Short Stories. As told by Jim Weiss. Music by Paul Machlis. 1 CD. (Running Time: 1 hr.). Dramatization. (Storyteller's Version Ser.). (J). (gr. 2 up). 2000. audio compact disk 14.95 (978-1-882513-48-2(7), 1124-023) Greathall Prods.
Ancient stories of bards and warriors told with passion and sensitivity, enhanced with music. Includes; "The Bard," "Dectera and Fifty Maidens," "Cuchulain's Name," "The Wooing of Emer," "Angus's Dream," "Oisin's Journey" and "Finn MacCoul & the Battle for Tara".

Celtic Treasures. unabr. ed. Read by Jim Weiss. (J). 2001. 9.86; audio compact disk 13.46 Books on Tape.
Ancient tales of bards and warriors, star-crossed lovers and daring feats of arms, all told with passion and sensitivity, and interspersed with traditional Irish music from Paul Machlis, Master Pianist of that genre. Jim Weiss has picked up the bard's mantle and made these tales his own.

Celtic Treasures. unabr. ed. Short Stories. As told by Jim Weiss. Music by Paul Machlis. 1 cass. (Running Time: 1 hr.). Dramatization. (Storyteller's Version Ser.). (J). (gr. 2 up). 2000. 10.95 (978-1-882513-23-9(1), 1124-23) Greathall Prods.
Ancient stories of bards and warriors told with passion and sensitivity, enhanced with music. Includes; "The Bard," "Dectera and Fifty Maidens," "Cuchulain's Name," "The Wooing of Emer," "Angus's Dream," "Oisin's Journey" and "Finn MacCoul & the Battle for Tara".

Celtic Twilight. Perf. by Loreena McKennitt. 1 cass. 9.98; audio compact disk 17.98 Lifedance.
Summons forth a powerful mystic sense of the ancient land & culture of the Celts. Demo CD or cassette available.

Celtic Twilight: Ireland & Its Mysteries. Robert A. Wilson. 2 cass. (Running Time: 2 hrs.). 18.00 (A0146-88) Sound Photosyn.

Celtic Twilight Four: Celtic Planet. 1 CD. (Running Time: 1 hr.). audio compact disk 17.98; 9.98 Lifedance.
Demo CD or cassette available.

Celtic Twilight Four: Celtic Planet. 1 cass. (Running Time: 1 hr.). 7.98 (HOS 11108); audio compact disk 12.78 (HOS 11108) NewSound.

Celtic Twilight II. Perf. by Loreena McKennitt. 1 cass. 9.98; audio compact disk 17.98 CD. Lifedance.
Demo CD or cassette available.

Celtic Twilight Three: Lullabies. 1 cass. (Running Time: 1 hr.). (J). 9.98; audio compact disk 17.98 Lifedance.
Soft-hearted lullabies from the British Isles. Demo CD or cassette available.

Celtic Twilight Three: Lullabies. 1 cass. (Running Time: 1 hr.). (J). 7.98 (HOS11107); audio compact disk 12.78 (HOS11107) NewSound.
A collection of vocal & instrumental lullabies. Featured artists include Arcady (with Frances Black) Talitha MacKenzie, Maireid Sullivan, Noirin Ni Riain, Kate Power, Julie Last, Linda Arnold, Anuna, Bill Douglas & the Ars Nova Singers, Alasdair Fraser, Jeff Johnson & Brian Dunning, Barbara Higbie & William Coulter.

Celtic Voices. 1 cass. 9.98; audio compact disk 15.98 Lifedance.
Guitar, uillean pipes, harp & recorder. The haunting, mystical voices of four women bring qualities both raw & ethereal to songs of love, separation, parting & peace. Demo CD or cassette available.

Celtic Wave. 1 cass. (Running Time: 1 hr.). 7.18 (RCA 68985); audio compact disk 12.78 Jewel box. (RCA 68985) NewSound.

Celtic Wedding: Music of Brittany. Perf. by Chieftains, The. 1 cass. (Running Time: 1 hr.). 7.98 (RCA 63120); audio compact disk 12.78 Jewel box. (RCA 63120) NewSound.

Cemetery Dance. abr. ed. Douglas Preston & Lincoln Child. Read by Rene Auberjonois. (Running Time: 6 hrs.). (Pendergast Ser.: No. 9). 2009. 14.98 (978-1-60024-264-9(2)) Pub: Hachet Audio. Dist(s): HachBkGrp

Cemetery Dance. abr. ed. Douglas Preston & Lincoln Child. Read by Rene Auberjonois. (Running Time: 7 hrs.). (Pendergast Ser.). 2010. audio compact disk 14.98 (978-1-60788-190-2(X)) Pub: Hachet Audio. Dist(s): HachBkGrp

Cemetery Dance. unabr. ed. Douglas Preston & Lincoln Child. Read by Rene Auberjonois. (Running Time: 13 hrs.). (Pendergast Ser.: No. 9). 2009. 29.98 (978-1-60024-266-3(9)); audio compact disk 44.98 (978-1-60024-265-6(0)) Pub: Hachet Audio. Dist(s): HachBkGrp

Cemetery Yew. unabr. ed. Cynthia Riggs. Read by Davina Porter. (Running Time: 10 mins.). (Martha's Vineyard Mystery Ser.). (J). 2006. 29.95 (978-0-7861-7267-2(3)) Blckstn Audio.

Cemetery Yew. unabr. ed. Cynthia Riggs. Read by Davina Porter. (Running Time: 27000 sec.). (Martha's Vineyard Mystery Ser.). 2006. 59.95 (978-0-7861-4764-9(4)); audio compact disk 72.00 (978-0-7861-6348-9(8)) Blckstn Audio.

Cemetry Nights see Stephen Dobyns

CEN Prep. unabr. ed. Instructed by Scott Bourn. 16 cass. (Running Time: 20 hrs.). 1992. 199.00 Set incl. cass. & soft-bound bks. (HT84) Ctr Hlth Educ.
The demand for well-trained Certified Emergency Nurses is growing each day. Being a qualified CEN is more than just knowing the material well enough to pass a written exam. With our Stat audio course, CEN Prep, listening to actual case histories will transform theory into vivid reality.

Cendrillon. Tr. of Cinderella. (FRE.). pap. bk. 12.95 (978-2-89558-065-2(0)) Pub: Coffragants CAN. Dist(s): Penton Overseas

Cendrillon (Cinderella) see Contes de Perrault

Cendrillon/Petite Rouge CD. Sheila Hébert-Collins. (Running Time: 24 hrs. NaN mins.). (ENG.). (J). 2008. audio compact disk 15.95 (978-1-58980-448-7(1)) Pelican.

Cenicienta. Charles Perrault. 1 cass. (Running Time: 1 hr. 30 min.).Tr. of Cinderella. (SPA., (J). 2000. 12.95 (978-84-207-6727-7(1)) Pub: Grupo Anaya ESP. Dist(s): Distribks Inc

Cenicienta. l.t. ed. Short Stories. Illus. by Graham Percy. 1 cass. (Running Time: 10 mins.). Dramatization.Tr. of Cinderella. (SPA.). (J). (ps-3). 2001. 8.99 (978-84-87650-13-0(9)) Pub: Peralt Mont ESP. Dist(s): imaJen

Cenicienta y Muchos Cuentos Mas, Vol. 2. abr. ed.Tr. of Cinderella, the Cat with Boots, the Sleeping Beauty & Many More Tales. (SPA.). 2001. audio compact disk 13.00 (978-958-9494-29-5(3)) YoYoMusic.

Cenni Sull'arte Italian Dall'XI al XV Secolo. 1 cass. (Running Time: 30 mins.). (ITA.). pap. bk. 16.95 (SIT210) J Norton Pubs.
Intermediate-level readings with accompanying cassettes can improve both reading & listening comprehension. Texts include exercises & answer key.

Censored Viets: Stories You Couldn't Read in the Paper. unabr. ed. Elaine Viets. Read by Elaine Viets. 2 cass. (Running Time: 80 mins.). 9.95 (978-1-882467-00-6(0)) Wildstone Media.
Elaine Viets is a syndicated columnist whose work goes to over 300 papers on the United Features Syndicate. On "Censored Viets" you will hear the columns that "were too racy...too tasteless...too wild for a dignified paper".

Censoring an Iranian Love Story: A Novel of Love's Triumph over Tyranny. unabr. ed. Shahriar Mandanipour. Read by Naila Azad & Sunil Malhotra. 2009. audio compact disk 39.95 (978-0-7393-8427-5(9)) Pub: Random Audio Pubg. Dist(s): Random

Censorship. Otto Preminger. Interview with William F. Buckley, Jr. 2007. audio compact disk 12.95 (978-1-57970-480-3(8), Audio-For) J Norton Pubs.

Censorship. unabr. ed. Otto Preminger. 1 cass. (Running Time: 1 hr.). 1967. 12.95 (23054) J Norton Pubs.
From William Buckley's "Firing Line" program, this is a conversation with Otto Preminger on censorship in the movies.

Censorship: Local & Express. Ayn Rand. Read by Ayn Rand. 1 cass. (Running Time: 90 mins.). 12.95 (978-1-56114-075-6(9), AR15C) Second Renaissance.
A penetrating analysis of the Supreme Court's decision to uphold anti-pornography laws. Examines the connection between the "marketplace of goods" & the "marketplace of ideas." Incisively explains why conservatives support government control over the intellectual realm, while liberals want to control the material realm.

An Asterisk (*) at the beginning of an entry indicates that the title is appearing for the first time.

Censorship: Local & Express. Comment by Ayn Rand. 1 cass. (Running Time: 90 mins.). (Ford Hall Forum Ser.). 1973. 12.95 (AR15C) Second Renaissance.
Analysis of the Supreme Court's upholding of anti-pornography laws. The "marketplace of goods" & the "marketplace of ideas". Why conservatives want to control the intellectual realm & liberals the material realm. Includes Q&A.

Censorship: The Threat to Silence Talk Radio. unabr. ed. Brian Jennings. Brian Jennings. Read by Jesse Boggs. (Running Time: 8 hrs. 0 mins. 0 sec.). (ENG.). 2009. audio compact disk 29.99 (978-0-7435-9907-8(1)) Pub: S&S Audio. Dist(s): S and S Inc

Censorship from Within. SERCON Panel. 1 cass. 9.00 (A0117-87) Sound Photosyn.
At the Science Fiction writers convention with Mona Clee, Brown, Meacham & Rose Kaufman.

Censorship from Without. SERCON Panel. 1 cass. 9.00 (A0126-87) Sound Photosyn.
A discussion at the SF writers convention with John Kessel, McKenna, Pohl, Schnatmeier, Douglas & Spinrad.

Centaur. unabr. collector's ed. John Updike. Read by John MacDonald. 9 cass. (Running Time: 9 hrs.). 1984. 72.00 (978-0-7366-0692-9(0), 1655) Books on Tape.
According the Greek mythology, a centaur is one of the race of monsters having the head, arms & trunk of a man & the body & legs of a horse. This story retells the myth of Chiron.

Centaurs see Gathering of Great Poetry for Children

Centenary Ode see Poetry & Voice of James Wright

Centennial. James A. Michener. Read by Larry McKeever.Tr. of Centennial. 1995. 96.00 (978-0-7366-2905-8(X)); 88.00 (978-0-7366-2906-5(8)) Books on Tape.

Centennial. abr. ed. James A. Michener. Read by David Dukes. 4 cass. (Running Time: 6 hrs.).Tr. of Centennial. 1993. 24.95 (978-1-879371-46-0(4), 692167) Pub Mills.
The epic drama of the winning of the West, told as only Michener can tell it. The story of the land & the Indians who inhabited it & of the people of many nations who came to drive them out.

Centennial, Pt. 1. unabr. ed. James A. Michener. Read by Larry McKeever. 12 cass. (Running Time: 18 hrs.).Tr. of Centennial. 1995. 96.00 (978-0-7366-2904-1(1), 3603A) Books on Tape.
Story of trappers, traders, homesteaders & gold seekers all caught up in the drama of the legendary American West.

Centennial, Pt. 2. James A. Michener. Read by Larry McKeever. 12 cass. (Running Time: 18 hrs.).Tr. of Centennial. 1995. 96.00 (3603-B) Books on Tape.

Centennial, Pt. 3. James A. Michener. Read by Larry McKeever. 11 cass. (Running Time: 16 hrs. 30 min.).Tr. of Centennial. 1995. 88.00 (3603-C) Books on Tape.

Centennial Commissions. UW Sch of Music. 2003. audio compact disk 25.00 (978-1-931569-02-6(9)) Pub: U of Wis Pr. Dist(s): Chicago Distribution Ctr

Centennial History of the Civil War Pt. 1: The Coming Fury. unabr. ed. Bruce Catton. Read by Michael Prichard. 14 cass. (Running Time: 21 hrs.). 1980. 112.00 (1202-A) Books on Tape.
Draws heavily on battlefield correspondence & published recollections of survivors. The book opens with the Democratic convention of 1860 & ends with the Battle of Bull Run in July, 1861, the first major encounter of the Civil War.

Centennial History of the Civil War Pt. II: Terrible Swift Sword. unabr. ed. Bruce Catton. Read by Michael Prichard. 13 cass. (Running Time: 20 hrs. 30 min.). 1963. 104.00 (1202-B) Books on Tape.
Examines two turning points which changed the scope & meaning of the war. First, Catton describes how events seemed to take charge, & then how the sweeping force of all-out conflict changed the war's purpose, making it into a war for human freedom.

Centennial History of the Civil War Pt. III: Never Call Retreat. unabr. ed. Bruce Catton. Read by Michael Prichard. 13 cass. (Running Time: 20 hrs. 30 min.). 1965. 104.00 (978-0-7366-0202-0(X), 1202-C) Books on Tape.
Fort Sumter & the war begins.

Center Cannot Hold. unabr. ed. Elyn R. Saks. 2007. audio compact disk 34.99 (978-1-4281-7004-9(9)) Recorded Bks.

Center Cannot Hold: My Journey Through Madness. unabr. ed. Elyn R. Saks. Read by Alma Cuervo. 10 cass. (Running Time: 12 hrs. 50 mins.). 2007. 82.75 (978-1-4281-7005-6(7)); audio compact disk 123.75 (978-1-4281-7007-0(3)) Recorded Bks.

Center of Everything: A Novel. unabr. ed. Laura Moriarty. Narrated by Julie Dretzin. 9 cass. Library ed. (Running Time: 13 hrs. 15 min.). 2003. 85.00 (978-1-4025-4816-1(8)); audio compact disk 116.00 (978-1-4025-5744-6(2), C2282) Recorded Bks.

Center of Everything: A Novel. unabr. ed. Laura Moriarty. Narrated by Julie Dretzin. 8 cass. (Running Time: 13 hrs. 15 mins.). 2004. 34.99 (978-1-4025-4514-6(2), 03024) Recorded Bks.
Story of 10-year-old math prodigy Evelyn Bucknow. Living in Kansas with her single mother and deeply religious grandmother, Evelyn believes she is destined to marry Travis, the boy next door. But as she grows up, she experiences the heartbreak of a love not meant to be.

Center Stage. Irene Frankel et al. 2006. (978-0-13-187495-4(0)); (978-0-13-194783-2(4)); audio compact disk (978-0-13-187489-3(6)); audio compact disk (978-0-13-194798-6(2)) Pearson Educ.

Center Within. Gyomay M. Kubose. Read by Gene Honda. 2 cass. (Running Time: 3 hrs.). 1987. 14.95 (978-0-944663-00-4(1)) Bullington Laird.
Classical Buddhist teachings on ego, ambition, behavior & personal responsibility.

Centerburg Tales: More Adventures of Homer Price. Robert McCloskey. Narrated by John McDonough. 4 CDs. (Running Time: 4 hrs. 15 mins.). (gr. 3 up). audio compact disk 39.00 (978-1-4025-1958-1(3)) Recorded Bks.

Centerburg Tales: More Adventures of Homer Price. Robert McCloskey. Narrated by John McDonough. 3 pieces. (Running Time: 4 hrs. 15 mins.). (gr. 3 up). 2001. 28.00 (978-0-7887-5364-0(9)) Recorded Bks.
Takes an affectionate look at small-town America. Something unusual is always going on in Centerburg. But Homer Price is in the middle of things, putting them right with his own brand of common sense.

Centered Life: A Practical Course on Centering Prayer. M. Basil Pennington. Read by M. Basil Pennington. 8 cass. (Running Time: 5 hrs. 30 mins.). 49.95 incl. study guide & vinyl album. (AA1040) Credence Commun.
Traces the rich history of contemplative prayer, explains how it has come to be called centering prayer & provides a step-by-step instruction on how to pray it.

Centering. Eldon Taylor. Read by Eldon Taylor. Ed. by Leslie Brice. 1 cass. (Running Time: 1 hr.). 1992. 16.95 (978-1-56705-294-7(0)) Gateways Inst.
Self improvement.

Centering. Eldon Taylor. Read by Eldon Taylor. 1 cass. (Running Time: 62 mins.). (Inner Talk Ser.). 16.95 incl. script. (978-1-55978-004-9(5), 5404C) Progress Aware Res.
Soundtrack with underlying subliminal affirmations.

Centering: Babbling Brook. Eldon Taylor. 1 cass. 16.95 (978-1-55978-768-0(6), 5404F) Progress Aware Res.

Centering: Lessons from Mescalero Apaches. Read by Claire Farrer. 1 cass. (Running Time: 2 hrs.). 1987. 12.95 (978-0-7822-0064-5(8), 299) C G Jung IL.

Centering Set: A Guide to Inner Growth. Sanders G. Laurie & Melvin J. Tucker. Read by Sanders G. Laurie. 1 cass. (Running Time: 1 hr.). 1995. pap. bk. 9.95 (978-0-89281-521-0(3), Heal Arts VT) Inner Tradit.

Centering Meditation. 1. (Running Time: 33 minutes). 2004. 14.95 (978-0-9779472-3-2(8)) Health Wealth Inc.
alm the mind and still the thoughts. This recording will gently guide you into your center, the very core of your being. Experience what it's like to be free from the babble of the thought stream so you may become centered and focused on your Higher Self. Then you will understand the meaning of the words "Peace, be still, I am in quiet meditation." This is a great recording to help you unwind from a hectic day. Find a comfortable place, turn off the phone - and let go!.

Centering Prayer: A Training Course for Opening to the Presence of God. unabr. ed. Thomas Keating. 2 CDs. (Running Time: 104:48). 2009. pap. bk. 149.95 (978-1-59179-736-4(5)) Sounds True.

Centering Prayer: Renewing an Ancient Christian Prayer Form. M. Basil Pennington. Read by David L. Abbott. 6 cass. (Running Time: 9 hrs.). 2004. 49.95 (978-0-86716-654-5(1)) St Anthony Mess Pr.

CENTERLESS CORPORATION: Transforming Your Organization for Growth & Prosperity. Bruce A. Pasternack. 2004. 10.95 (978-0-7435-4257-9(6)) Pub: S&S Audio. Dist(s): S and S Inc

***Centimetro y metro Audio CD.** April Barth. Adapted by Benchmark Education Co., LLC. (Content Connections Ser.). (SPA.). (J). 2010. audio compact disk 10.00 (978-1-61672-209-8(6)) Benchmark Educ.

Central America: A 25-Year Retrospective on U. S. Policy. (Running Time: 1 hr.). 11.95 (H0280B090, HarperThor) HarpC GBR.

Central America: Knowledge Products. unabr. ed. Stromberg Joseph. Read by Reasoner Harry. 2006. audio compact disk 25.95 (978-0-7861-6697-8(5)) Pub: Blckstn Audio. Dist(s): NetLibrary CO

Central American English. unabr. ed. John Holm. 1 cass. (Running Time: 90 mins.). (Varieties of English Around the World Ser.). 1982. 59.00 J Benjamins Pubng Co.
Spoken examples of the book "Central American English".

Central Europe. unabr. ed. Ralph Raico. Read by Richard C. Hottelet. (Running Time: 10800 sec.). (World's Political Hot Spots Ser.). 2006. audio compact disk 25.95 (978-0-7861-6440-0(9)) Pub: Blckstn Audio. Dist(s): NetLibrary CO

Central Texas. Doc Ball et al. Read by Kimberly Schraf. 2 cass. (Running Time: 2 hrs. 37 mins.). (Ride with Me Ser.). 1997. 17.95 (978-0-942649-30-7(3)) RWM Assocs.
Stories of Central Texas along Interstate-35 between Dallas & Laredo.

Central Washington Heritage Corridor: Leavenworth to Maryhill. Text by Jens Lund. (ENG., 1997. spiral bd. 12.00 (978-1-891466-00-7(3)) NW Heritage.

Centrality of Christ in the Life of the Believer. Ian Thomas. (Running Time: 59 mins.). (ICEL Three Ser.). 1996. 6.00 (978-1-57838-053-4(7)) CrossLife Express.
Christian living.

Centre of Magic. unabr. ed. Pamela Freeman. Read by Stanley McGeagh. 4 cass. (Running Time: 4 hrs. 10 mins.). (gr. 4-8). 2002. (978-1-74030-144-2(7), 500637) Bolinda Pubng AUS.

Centrifuge Games. (J). (gr. 7-12). 2002. audio compact disk 16.95 (978-0-633-01176-5(2)) LifeWay Christian.

Centro de la Esfera. Carlos Gonzalez. 1 CD. (Running Time: 42 mins.).Tr. of Sphere Center. (SPA.). 2003. audio compact disk 15.00 (978-1-56491-101-8(2)) Imagine Pubs.

Cents & Sensibility. unabr. ed. Maggie Alderson. Read by Nicky Talacko. (Running Time: 13 hrs. 10 mins.). 2007. audio compact disk 108.95 (978-1-74093-927-0(1), 9781740939270) Pub: Bolinda Pubng AUS. Dist(s): Bolinda Pub Inc

Centuries. unabr. ed. Thomas Traherne. Read by John Westbrook. 8 cass. (Running Time: 10 hrs. 30 mins.). (Isis Ser.). (J). 1990. 69.95 (978-1-85089-761-3(1), 90013) Pub: ISIS Lrg Prnt GBR. Dist(s): Ulverscroft US

Centuries of Meditations see Cambridge Treasy Burton

Centurion. Simon Scarrow. Read by Steven Pacey. (Running Time: 6 hrs. 8 mins. 0 sec.). (ENG.). 2008. audio compact disk 22.95 (978-1-4055-0554-3(0)) Pub: Little BrownUK GBR. Dist(s): IPG Chicago

Centurion's Wife. abr. ed. Davis Bunn & Janette Oke. Narrated by Aimee Lilly. (Running Time: 7 hrs. 34 mins. 5 sec.). (Acts of Faith Ser.). (ENG.). 2008. audio compact disk 27.99 (978-1-59859-471-3(0)) Oasis Audio.

Centurion's Wife. unabr. ed. Janette Oke & Davis Bunn. Narrated by Aimee Lilly. (Running Time: 7 hrs. 34 mins. 5 sec.). (Acts of Faith Ser.). (ENG.). 2008. 19.59 (978-1-60814-459-4(3)) Oasis Audio.

Century. unabr. ed. Peter Jennings & Todd Brewster. Read by Peter Jennings. 15 cass. (Running Time: 15 hrs.). (J). (gr. 7 up). 2004. 90.00 (978-0-8072-8337-0(1), LL0189, Listening Lib) Random Audio Pubg.
Sweeping retrospective of the events & people that have shaped this century. Featuring extensive audio footage. Brings the events of the past hundred years into contemporary focus.

Century Dictionary. Ed. by Tom Johnson. 2003. audio compact disk 49.99 (978-0-9721709-1-8(X)) Royal Fireworks.

Century of Dreiser. unabr. ed. Ellen Moers. 1 cass. (Running Time: 18 mins.). 1969. 12.95 (23051) J Norton Pubs.
A thorough & comprehensive discussion of Theodore Dreiser as spokesman for & shaper of the new America: middling in region; speech & social position; immigrants in origin; urban in feeling & fate.

Century of Great Suspense Stories. unabr. ed. Jeffery Deaver. 9 cass. (Running Time: 13 hrs. 30 mins.). 2002. 72.00 (978-0-7366-8575-7(8)) Books on Tape.
A great collection of the best suspense stories from the past century.

Century of Lionel Trains 1900-2000. Tm Books & Video Inc. 2002. audio compact disk 24.95 (978-0-937522-96-7(1)) Pub: TM Bks Video. Dist(s): MBI Dist Svcs

***Century Rain.** unabr. ed. Alastair Reynolds. Narrated by John Lee. (Running Time: 26 hrs. 30 mins.). 2010. 59.99 (978-1-4001-2959-1(1)); 39.99 (978-1-4001-5959-8(8)); 28.99 (978-1-4001-7959-6(9)); audio compact disk 119.99 (978-1-4001-3959-0(7)); audio compact disk 59.99 (978-1-4001-0959-3(0)) Pub: Tantor Media. Dist(s): IngramPubServ

Century Turns: New Fears, New Hopes - America 1988 to 2008. unabr. ed. William J. Bennett. Narrated by Jon Gauger. (Running Time: 10 hrs. 57 mins. 31 sec.). (America: the Last Best Hope Ser.). (ENG.). 2010. 24.49 (978-1-60814-639-0(1)); audio compact disk 34.99 (978-1-59859-696-0(9)) Oasis Audio.

***Century #2: Star of Stone.** unabr. ed. Pierdomenico Baccalario. Read by Carrington MacDuffie. (ENG.). (J). 2010. audio compact disk 37.00 (978-0-307-74576-7(7), Listening Lib) Pub: Random Audio Pubg. Dist(s): Random

CEO Boot Kamp: The Audio Review. unabr. ed. Perf. by Planned Marketing Staff. 12 cass. (Running Time: 12 hrs.). 1995. 195.00 (978-1-882306-07-7(4)) Planned Mktg.
A complete system with a balanced approach to increasing your productivity, increasing your effectiveness & living a balanced life.

***CEO Communication Skills: Verbal Skills to Inspire Passion.** unabr. ed. Made for Success. Read by Various Readers. (Running Time: 7 hrs. NaN mins.). (Made for Success Ser.). 2011. audio compact disk 32.95 (978-1-4417-7608-2(7)); audio compact disk 118.00 (978-1-4417-7607-5(9)) Blckstn Audio.

CEO of the Sofa. abr. ed. P. J. O'Rourke. Read by Dick Hill. 4 CDs. (Running Time: 4 hrs.). 2001. audio compact disk 61.25 (978-1-58788-934-9(X), 158788934X, CD Lib Edit) Brilliance Audio.

CEO of the Sofa. unabr. ed. P. J. O'Rourke. Read by Dick Hill. 6 cass. (Running Time: 9 hrs.). 2001. 29.95 (978-1-58788-930-1(7), 1587889307, BAU); 69.25 (978-1-58788-931-8(5), 1587889315, CD Unabrid Lib Ed) Brilliance Audio.
New York Times bestselling author P.J. O'Rourke has toured the fighting in Bosnia, visited the West Bank disguised as P.J. of Arabia, lobbed one-liners on the battlefields of the Gulf War, and traded quips with Communist rebels in the jungles of the Philippines. Now in The CEO of the Sofa, he embarks on a mission to the most frightening place of all - his own home. Ensconced on the domestic boardroom's throne (although not supposed to put his feet on the cushions), he faces a three-year-old who wants a cell phone, a freelance career devoted to writing articles like "Chewing-Mouth Dogs Bring Hope to People with Eating Disorders," and neighbors who smell like Democrats ("That is, using smell as a transitive verb. When I light a cigar they wave their hands in front of their faces and pretend to cough."). Undaunted - with the help of martinis - by middle age, P.J. holds forth on everything from getting toddlers to sleep ("Advice to parents whose kids love the story of the dinosaurs: Don't give away the surprise ending") to why Hillary Clinton's election victory was a good thing ("We Republicans were almost out of people to hate in the Senate. Teddy Kennedy is just too old and fat to pick on"). And P.J. leaps (well, groans and pushes himself up) from the couch to pursue assignments such as a high-speed drive across the ugliest part of India at the hottest time of the year, a blind (drunk) wine tasting with Christopher Buckley, and a sojourn at the U.N. Millennial Summit, where he runs the risk of perishing from boredom and puts readers in peril of laughing themselves to death.

CEO of the Sofa. unabr. ed. P. J. O'Rourke. Read by Dick Hill. (Running Time: 9 hrs.). 2004. 39.25 (978-1-59335-567-8(X), 159335567X, Brlnc Audio MP3 Lib) Brilliance Audio.

CEO of the Sofa. unabr. ed. P. J. O'Rourke. Read by Dick Hill. (Running Time: 9 hrs.). 2004. 39.25 (978-1-59710-126-4(5), 1597101265, BADLE); 24.95 (978-1-59710-127-1(3), 1597101273, BAD) Brilliance Audio.

***CEO of the Sofa.** unabr. ed. P. J. O'Rourke. Read by Dick Hill. (Running Time: 10 hrs.). 2010. audio compact disk 89.97 (978-1-4418-4013-4(3), 9781441840134, BriAudCD Unabrid) Brilliance Audio.

CEO of the Sofa. unabr. ed. P. J. O'Rourke. Read by Dick Hill. (Running Time: 9 hrs.). 2004. 24.95 (978-1-59335-054-3(6), 1593350546) Soulmate Audio Bks.

***CEO of the Sofa.** unabr. ed. P. J. O'Rourke. Read by Dick Hill. (Running Time: 10 hrs.). 2010. audio compact disk 29.99 (978-1-4418-4012-7(5), 9781441840127) Brilliance Audio.

***CEO Secrets to Team Building: Leading Loyal Teams to Achieve Amazing Results.** Made for Success. Read by John Maxwell et al. (Running Time: 8.5 hrs. NaN mins.). (Made for Success Ser.). (ENG.). 2011. audio compact disk 39.95 (978-1-4417-8076-8(9)); audio compact disk 123.00 (978-1-4417-8075-1(0)) Blckstn Audio.

***Ceol Na Dtead.** Mickey Byrne. Francie Byrne. (ENG.). 1992. 11.95 (978-0-8023-7078-5(0)) Pub: Clo Iar-Chonnachta IRL. Dist(s): Dufour

Ceramic Architecture for Low-Cost Housing. Hosted by Nancy Pearlman. 1 cass. (Running Time: 27 mins.). 10.00 (723) Educ Comm CA.

Ceramist Beatrice Wood see I'm Too Busy to Talk Now

***Cerca de Mi.** Contrib. by Yamil Ledesma. (SPA.). 2009. audio compact disk 14.99 (978-0-8297-6121-4(7)) Pub: CanZion. Dist(s): Zondervan

Cerddoriaeth Cymru / the Music of Wales. Sioned Webb Curiad. 2005. audio compact disk 19.99 (978-1-897664-90-2(7)) Cyhoeddiadau GBR.

Cereal Murders. abr. ed. Diane Mott Davidson. Read by Barbara Rosenblat. 2 cass. (Goldy Schulz Culinary Mysteries Ser.: No. 3). 2001. 7.95 (978-1-57815-192-9(9), Media Bks Audio) Media Bks NJ.

Cereal Murders. abr. ed. Diane Mott Davidson. Read by Barbara Rosenblat. 2 cass. (Running Time: 3 hrs.). (Goldy Schulz Culinary Mysteries Ser.: No. 3). 1994. 16.95 Pub Mills.
Goldy Bear, caterer extradordinaire is drawn into a web of intrigue & murder within the Ivy covered walls of Elk Park Prep School, one of Denver's most prestigious schools. College boards & high school graduation can be murder. As her catering business is starting to take off, a murder sends her life into yet another tailspin.

Cereal Murders. unabr. ed. Diane Mott Davidson. Read by Barbara Rosenblat. 7 cass. (Running Time: 9 hrs. 30 mins.). (Goldy Schulz Culinary Mysteries Ser.: No. 3). 2004. 32.95 (978-1-59007-346-9(0)); audio compact disk 49.95 (978-1-59007-437-4(8)) Pub: New Millenn Enter. Dist(s): PerseuPGW

Cereal Murders. unabr. ed. Diane Mott Davidson. Narrated by Barbara Rosenblat. 7 cass. (Running Time: 9 hrs. 15 mins.). (Goldy Schulz Culinary Mysteries Ser.: No. 3). 1997. 60.00 (978-0-7887-0721-6(3), 94898E7) Recorded Bks.
Goldy Bear stumbles upon a murdered student while catering an affair at her son's school.

Cerebral Cavernous Malformation - A Bibliography & Dictionary for Physicians, Patients, & Genome Researchers. Compiled by Icon Group International, Inc. Staff. 2007. ring bd. 28.95 (978-0-497-11349-0(X)) Icon Grp.

Cerebro, el Gran Arquitecto. Ramtha. (SPA.). 2003. audio compact disk 25.00 (978-0-9740337-1-6(5)) Voxrames.

Cerebrospinal Fluid Otorrhea & Rhinorrhea. 2 cass. (Neurological Surgery Ser.: C85-NS2). 1985. 15.00 (8567) Am Coll Surgeons.

Ceremonial Shamanism & the Mental Health Professional. Royal E. Allsup. 1 cass. 9.00 (A0388-88) Sound Photosyn.
Royal poignantly presents the problems of the Native American from a professional care givers perspective. ICSS '88 with Carroll, Norton, & Lyon on tape.

Ceremony. unabr. ed. Leslie Marmon Silko. Read by Adam Henderson. 8 vols. (Running Time: 12 hrs.). 2000. bk. 69.95 (978-0-7927-2380-6(5), CSL 269, Chivers Sound Lib) AudioGO.
Tayo, a young Native American, has been a prisoner of the Japanese during World War II & the horrors of captivity have almost eroded his will to survive. His return to the Laguna Pueblo reservation only increases his feeling of estrangement & alienation. While other returning soldiers find easy refuge in alcohol & senseless violence, Tayo searches for another kind of comfort & resolution. His quest leads him back to his Indian past & its traditions, to beliefs about witchcraft & evil & to the ancient stories of his people.

Ceremony. unabr. collector's ed. Robert B. Parker. Read by Michael Prichard. 5 cass. (Running Time: 5 hrs.). (Spenser Ser.). 1989. 40.00 (978-0-7366-1628-7(4), 2486) Books on Tape.
Pretty teenager April Kyle is in grown-up trouble, involved with people who'd beat her up for a dollar & kill her for five. Now she's disappeared, last seen in the Combat Zone, that side of Boston where nothing's proper, especially the sex for sale. With Hawk, his sidekick, Spenser takes on the whole X-rated industry. From a specialty whorehouse in Providence to stylish Back Bay bordellos, he pits muscle & wit against bullets & brawn until he finds what he's looking for: April Kyle, little girl lost.

Ceremony after a Fire Raid see Child's Christmas in Wales

Ceremony after a Fire Raid see Dylan Thomas Reading His Poetry

Ceremony in Death. abr. ed. J. D. Robb, pseud. Read by Susan Ericksen. (Running Time: 6 hrs.). (In Death Ser.). 2007. audio compact disk 14.99 (978-1-4233-1400-4(X), 9781423314004, BCD Value Price) Brilliance Audio.

Ceremony in Death. unabr. ed. J. D. Robb, pseud. Read by Susan Ericksen. (Running Time: 10 hrs.). (In Death Ser.). 2006. 39.25 (978-1-4233-0032-8(7), 9781423300328, BADLE); 24.95 (978-1-4233-0031-1(9), 9781423300311, BAD); audio compact disk 24.95 (978-1-4233-0029-8(7), 9781423300298, Brilliance MP3); audio compact disk 36.95 (978-1-4233-1371-7(2), 9781423313717, Bril Audio CD Unabri); audio compact disk 39.25 (978-1-4233-0030-4(0), 9781423300304, Brinc Audio MP3 Lib); audio compact disk 97.25 (978-1-4233-1372-4(0), 9781423313724, BriAudCD Unabrid) Brilliance Audio.
Conducting a top secret investigation into the death of a fellow police officer has Lieutenant Eve Dallas treading on dangerous ground. She must put professional ethics before personal loyalties. But when a dead body is placed outside her home, Eve takes the warning personally. With her husband, Roarke, watching her every move, Eve is drawn into the most dangerous case of her career. Every step she takes makes her question her own sense of right and wrong - and brings her closer to a confrontation with humanity's most seductive form of evil.

Ceremony of Innocence. Nick Bantock. 1 cass. 1998. 59.99 (978-0-9520864-7-5(6)) Penton Overseas.

Cereus Blooms at Night. unabr. ed. Shani Mootoo. Narrated by Peter Jay Fernandez. 7 cass. (Running Time: 9 hrs. 30 mins.). 2000. 63.00 (978-1-84197-102-5(2), H1091E7) Recorded Bks.
Tells of a demented old woman's past, as discovered by her male nurse. Set on a tiny Caribbean island, where the scent of flowers & the buzz of insects thicken the air.

***Cero Limites.** Joe Vitale. 2010. audio compact disk 24.95 (978-1-933499-96-3(6)) Fonolibro Inc.

Certain Girls. abr. ed. Jennifer Weiner. Read by Michele Pawk & Zoe Kazan. (Running Time: 6 hrs. 0 mins. 0 sec.). (Cannie Shapiro Ser.: Bk. 2). 2009. audio compact disk 14.99 (978-0-7435-8300-8(0)) Pub: S&S Audio. Dist(s): S and S Inc

Certain Girls. unabr. ed. Jennifer Weiner. Narrated by Rachel Botchan & Julie Dretzin. (Running Time: 14 hrs. 45 mins.). (Cannie Shapiro Ser.: Bk. 2). 2008. 61.75 (978-1-4361-3269-5(X)) Recorded Bks.

Certain Girls. unabr. ed. Jennifer Weiner. Narrated by Rachel Botchan & Julie Dretzin. 12 cass. (Running Time: 14 hrs. 45 mins.). (Cannie Shapiro Ser.: Bk. 2). 2008. 92.75 (978-1-4281-6916-6(4)) Recorded Bks.

Certain Girls. unabr. ed. Jennifer Weiner. Narrated by Rachel Botchan & Julie Dretzin. 12 cass. (Running Time: 14 hrs. 45 mins.). (Cannie Shapiro Ser.: Bk. 2). 2008. 51.95 (978-1-4281-6917-3(2)); audio compact disk 56.95 (978-1-4281-6919-7(9)); audio compact disk 123.75 (978-1-4281-6918-0(0)) Recorded Bks.

Certain Justice. abr. ed. John Lescroart. Read by David Colacci. (Running Time: 7 hrs.). 2009. audio compact disk 14.99 (978-1-4233-5726-1(4), 9781423357261, BCD Value Price) Brilliance Audio.

Certain Justice. unabr. ed. P. D. James. Read by Michael Jayston. 12 CDs. (Running Time: 18 hrs.). (Adam Dalgliesh Mystery Ser.). 2002. audio compact disk 110.95 (978-0-7540-5459-7(4), CCD 150) AudioGO.
For her last case, Venetia Aldridge defends Gary Ashe, accused of the brutal murder of his aunt, for one more chance to triumph in a distinguished career as a criminal lawyer. But the case sets in motion a chain of events as terrifying as they are unpredictable. And when, four weeks later, Miss Aldridge is found dead at her desk in her Middle Temple chambers, Dalgliesh and his team are called in to a case that promises to as sensitive as intriguing.

Certain Justice. unabr. ed. P. D. James. Read by Penelope Dellaporta. 13 cass. (Running Time: 19 hrs. 30 min.). (Adam Dalgliesh Mystery Ser.). 1998. 104.00 (978-0-7366-4067-1(3), 4578) Books on Tape.
Venetia Aldridge, a distinguished criminal lawyer, defends young Gary Ashe for the brutal murder of his aunt. Within weeks Aldridge is found dead at her desk. As Dalgliesh & his team attempt to make sense of events, the murders continue.

Certain Justice. unabr. ed. P. D. James. Read by Michael Jayston. 12 cass. (Running Time: 18 hrs.). (Adam Dalgliesh Mystery Ser.). 2000. 79.95 (978-0-7540-0079-2(6), CAB 1502) Pub: Chivers Audio Bks GBR. Dist(s): AudioGO
For the last case of her career, Venetia Aldridge defends Gary Ashe, accused of the brutal murder of his aunt. But the case sets in motion a chain of events as terrifying as they are unpredictable. And when Miss Aldridge is found dead, Dalgliesh and his team are called in to a case that promises to be as sensitive as intriguing.

Certain Justice. unabr. ed. P. D. James. Read by Michael Jayston. (Running Time: 54000 sec.). (Adam Dalgliesh Mystery Ser.). (ENG.). 2007. audio compact disk 34.95 (978-0-7393-4380-7(7), Random AudioBks) Pub: Random Audio Pubg. Dist(s): Random

Certain Justice. unabr. ed. P. D. James. Narrated by Michael Jayston & Simon Prebble. 12 cass. (Running Time: 16 hrs. 30 mins.). (Adam Dalgliesh Mystery Ser.). 1998. 97.00 (978-0-7887-1966-0(1), 95354E7) Recorded Bks.
Adam Dalgliesh is called in to solve the mysterious murder of a distinguished trial lawyer.

Certain Justice. unabr. ed. John Lescroart. Read by David Colacci. (Running Time: 16 hrs.). 2008. 39.25 (978-1-4233-5720-9(5), 9781423357209, Brinc Audio MP3 Lib); 39.25 (978-1-4233-5722-3(1), 9781423357223, BADLE); 24.95 (978-1-4233-5719-3(1), 9781423357193, Brilliance MP3); 24.95 (978-1-4233-5721-6(3), 9781423357216, BAD); audio compact disk 122.25 (978-1-4233-5718-6(3), 9781423357186, BriAudCD Unabrid); audio compact disk 38.99 (978-1-4233-5717-9(5), 9781423357179, Bril Audio CD Unabri) Brilliance Audio.

Certain Man see Bodies in Motion

Certain Prey. abr. ed. John Sandford, pseud. Read by Eric Conger. 4 cass. (Prey Ser.). 1999. 24.95 (FS9-50890) Highsmith.

Certain Prey. unabr. ed. John Sandford, pseud. Narrated by Richard Ferrone. 8 cass. (Running Time: 10 hrs. 45 mins.). (Prey Ser.). 1999. 75.00 (978-0-7887-3096-2(7), 95807E7) Recorded Bks.
Clara Rinker, the best hitwoman in the business, has been hired by a prominent defense attorney for a hit on Lucas' turf. She's prepared to eliminate anyone who get's in her way, including Lucas.

Certain Prey. unabr. ed. John Sandford, pseud. Narrated by Richard Ferrone. 9 CDs. (Running Time: 10 hrs. 45 mins.). (Prey Ser.). 1999. audio compact disk 83.00 (978-0-7887-3974-3(3), C1093E7) Recorded Bks.

***Certain Risk: Living Your Faith at the Edge.** unabr. ed. Paul Andrew Richardson. (Running Time: 6 hrs. 10 mins. 58 sec.). (ENG.). 2010. 13.99 (978-0-310-39561-4(5)) Zondervan.

Certain Slant of Light. unabr. ed. Laura Whitcomb. Read by Lauren Molina. 5 cass. (Running Time: 8 hrs. 32 mins.). (YA). 2006. 40.00 (978-0-7393-3574-1(X), Listening Lib); audio compact disk 55.00 (978-0-7393-3575-8(8), Listening Lib) Pub: Random Audio Pubg. Dist(s): Random

Certain Smile. abr. ed. Judith Michael. Read by Mary Beth Quillin-Gregor. 2 cass. (Running Time: 2 hrs.). 1999. 17.95 (FS9-43417) Highsmith.

Certain Smile. unabr. ed. Judith Michael. Read by Mary Beth Quillin-Gregor. (Running Time: 11 hrs.). 2008. 39.25 (978-1-4233-5774-2(4), 9781423357742, BADLE); 39.25 (978-1-4233-5772-8(8), 9781423357728, Brinc Audio MP3 Lib); 24.95 (978-1-4233-5771-1(X), 9781423357711, Brilliance MP3) Brilliance Audio.

Certain Smile. unabr. ed. Judith Michael. Read by Mary Beth Quillin Gregor. (Running Time: 11 hrs.). 2008. 24.95 (978-1-4233-5773-5(6), 9781423357735, BAD) Brilliance Audio.

Certainty & Happiness: Achieving Success in Thought & in Action. Leonard Peikoff. Read by Leonard Peikoff. 2 cass. 1988. 24.95 (978-1-56114-038-1(4), LP02D) Second Renaissance.
An analysis of the fundamental contrast between Objectivism's "philosophy of success" & the culturally dominant "philosophy of failure." Dr. Peikoff examines the link between epistemological success - i.e., certainty - & ethical success - i.e., happiness. The question period include an impassioned analysis of why Khomeini's death threats against the author Salmon Rushdie represent the most insidious danger to individual rights in America since the New Deal; a description of the five philosophic points that, at a minimum, the movie version of Atlas Shrugged would have to touch on.

Certainty of Judgment Day. Dan Corner. 1 cass. 3.00 (21) Evang Outreach.

Certifiable Salesperson: The Ultimate Guide to Help Any Salesperson Go Crazy with Unprecedented Sales! Tom Hopkins & Laura Laaman. Narrated by L. J. Ganser. 3 CDs. 2003. audio compact disk 29.00 (978-1-4025-4265-7(8)) Recorded Bks.

Certificates & Awards. (Timesaving Software Tools for Teachers Ser.). 2004. audio compact disk 19.99 (978-1-57690-697-2(3)) Tchr Create Ma.

Certificates On. Morehouse Publishing Staff. 2006. audio compact disk 49.95 (978-0-8192-2217-6(8), MoreHse Pubng) Church Pub Inc.

Cerulean Sins. abr. ed. Laurell K. Hamilton. Read by Cynthia Holloway. (Running Time: 6 hrs.). (Anita Blake, Vampire Hunter Ser.: No. 11). 2008. audio compact disk 14.99 (978-1-4233-6227-2(6), 9781423362272, BCD Value Price) Brilliance Audio.

Cerulean Sins. unabr. ed. Laurell K. Hamilton. Read by Cynthia Holloway. 7 cass. (Running Time: 16 hrs.). (Anita Blake, Vampire Hunter Ser.: No. 11). 2003. 36.95 (978-1-59086-200-1(7), 1590862007, BAU); 102.25 (978-1-59086-201-8(5), 1590862015, CD Unabrid Lib Ed); audio compact disk 46.95 (978-1-59086-271-1(6), 1590862716); audio compact disk 122.25 (978-1-59086-272-8(4), 1590862724) Brilliance Audio.
With her New York Times bestselling Anita Blake, Vampire Hunter novels, Laurell K. Hamilton wraps readers up in stories of suspense and sensuality. Cerulean Sins is no exception. Now, Anita learns what it's like to be at the new end of a centuries-old bloodline - and just how far she'll let herself get pushed around... How the mighty have fallen! Once a sworn enemy of all vampires, Anita is now the human consort of both Jean-Claude, the Master Vampire, and Micah, the leopard shapeshifter. But her love life doesn't stop there. It can't. For Anita - not quite as human as she once was - is consumed by both the lusts of the vampire and the primal hungers of the wereleopards. Desires that must be sated - time and time again... But it is Jean-Claude who needs her now. His oldest ancestor has sent one of her vicious and powerful underlings to St. Louis, putting Jean-Claude and his clan on the defensive. Unsure of where she stands with the interloper, Anita finds herself tested as never before - needing all the dark forces her passion can muster to save the ones she loves the most.

Cerulean Sins. unabr. ed. Laurell K. Hamilton. Read by Cynthia Holloway. (Running Time: 57600 sec.). (Anita Blake, Vampire Hunter Ser.: No. 11). 2004. audio compact disk 39.25 (978-1-59335-576-0(9), 1593355769, Brinc Audio MP3 Lib) Brilliance Audio.

Cerulean Sins. unabr. ed. Laurell K. Hamilton. Read by Cynthia Holloway. (Running Time: 16 hrs.). (Anita Blake, Vampire Hunter Ser.: No. 11). 2004. 39.25 (978-1-59710-129-5(X), 159710129X, BADLE); 24.95 (978-1-59710-128-8(1), 1597101281, BAD) Brilliance Audio.

Cerulean Sins. unabr. ed. Laurell K. Hamilton. Read by Cynthia Holloway. (Running Time: 16 hrs.). (Anita Blake, Vampire Hunter Ser.: No. 11). 2004. 24.95 (978-1-59335-069-7(4), 1593350694) Soulmate Audio Bks.

Cervantes y Su Obra. Slabon Software, Ltd. Staff. (SPA., 2000. audio compact disk (978-1-56409-041-6(8)) EBP Latin Am.

Cerveau: Reparation et Entretien. unabr. ed. Robert A. Monroe. Read by Roland Simon. 1 cass. (Running Time: 30 mins.). (Human Plus Ser.). (FRE.). 1993. 14.95 (978-1-56102-059-1(1)) Inter Indus.
Improve blood flow & electrical activity in the brain.

Cesar Chavez: Fighter in the Fields. J. L. Matthews. (High Five Reading - Red Ser.). (ENG.). (gr. 2-3). 2007. audio compact disk 5.95 (978-1-4296-1415-3(3)) CapstoneDig.

Cesar Chavez: Fighting for Farmworkers. Eric Braun. Illus. by Harry Roland et al. (Graphic Biographies Ser.). (ENG.). (gr. 3-4). 2007. audio compact disk 6.95 (978-1-4296-1466-5(8)) CapstoneDig.

Cesar Chavez (INK Audiocassette) Fighting for Farmworkers. (Graphic Library Biographies I Ser.). (ENG.). 2006. audio compact disk 5.95 (978-0-7368-7449-6(6)) CapstoneDig.

***Cesar Franck - Sonata for Violin & Piano in A Major: For Violin.** Composed by Cesar Franck. Mario Hossen. 2009. pap. bk. 29.98 (978-1-59615-757-6(7), 1596157577) Pub: Music Minus. Dist(s): H Leonard

Cesarean Section: Will it Reach 100 Percent. 2 cass. (Gynecology & Obstetrics Ser.: C85-GO6). 15.00 (8564) Am Coll Surgeons.

Cesar's Way: The Natural, Everyday Guide to Understanding & Correcting Common Dog Problems. abr. ed. Cesar Millan & Melissa Jo Peltier. Read by Cesar Millan. 4 CDs. (Running Time: 18000 sec.). (ENG.). 2006. audio compact disk 27.95 (978-0-7393-2499-8(3), Random AudioBks) Pub: Random Audio Pubg. Dist(s): Random

Cesnola Collection: Terracottas. Vassos Karageorghis et al. (Metropolitan Museum of Art Ser.). (ENG., 2004. audio compact disk 45.00 (978-0-300-10284-0(4)) Yale U Pr.

Cessation of Pain. Swami Amar Jyoti. 1 cass. 1988. 9.95 (R-91) Truth Consciousness.
Application of the Highest Wisdom to the solution of our pain & misery. What is the essential difference between all the pairs of opposites? Solving the illusion of isolation.

C'est a Toi! Level One: Assessment Program. 2nd ed. Karla Winther Fawbush et al. (FRE.). 2006. audio compact disk 158.00 (978-0-8219-3271-1(3)) EMC-Paradigm.

C'est a Toi! Level One: Audio CD Program. 2nd ed. Karla Winther Fawbush et al. (FRE.). audio compact disk 329.95 (978-0-8219-3278-0(0)) EMC-Paradigm.

C'est a Toi! Level One: Audio CD Program Manual. 2nd ed. Karla Winther Fawbush et al. (FRE.). audio compact disk (978-0-8219-3279-7(9)) EMC-Paradigm.

C'est a Toi! Level One: Exam View Testing/Assessment Program. audio compact disk 150.95 (978-0-8219-4036-5(8)) EMC-Paradigm.

C'est a Toi! Level One: Lesson Planner. audio compact disk 129.95 (978-0-8219-4031-0(7)) EMC-Paradigm.

C'est a Toi! Level One: Listening Activities. 2nd ed. Karla Winther Fawbush et al. (FRE.). audio compact disk 129.95 (978-0-8219-3269-8(1)) EMC-Paradigm.

C'est a Toi! Level One: Test Generator CD, IBM/Mac. 2nd ed. Karla Winther Fawbush et al. (FRE.). 2006. audio compact disk 92.00 (978-0-8219-3276-6(4)) EMC-Paradigm.

C'est a Toi! Level One: Tests. 2nd ed. Karla Winther Fawbush et al. (FRE.). 2006. audio compact disk (978-0-8219-3332-9(9)) EMC-Paradigm.

C'est a Toi! Level Three: Assessment Program. 2nd ed. Karla Winther Fawbush et al. (FRE.). 2006. audio compact disk 169.00 (978-0-8219-3320-6(5)) EMC-Paradigm.

C'est a Toi! Level Three: Audio CD Program. 2nd ed. Karla Winther Fawbush et al. (FRE.). audio compact disk 339.95 (978-0-8219-3327-5(2)) EMC-Paradigm.

C'est a Toi! Level Three: Audio CD Program Manual. 2nd ed. Karla Winther Fawbush et al. (FRE.). audio compact disk 315.00 (978-0-8219-3328-2(0)) EMC-Paradigm.

C'est a Toi! Level Three: Listening Activities. 2nd ed. Karla Winther Fawbush et al. (FRE.). audio compact disk 139.95 (978-0-8219-3318-3(3)) EMC-Paradigm.

C'est a Toi! Level Three: Test Generator CD, IBM/Mac. 2nd ed. Karla Winther Fawbush et al. (FRE.). 2006. audio compact disk 98.00 (978-0-8219-3325-1(6)) EMC-Paradigm.

C'est a Toi! Level Three: Tests. 2nd ed. Karla Winther Fawbush et al. (FRE.). 2006. audio compact disk (978-0-8219-3335-0(3)) EMC-Paradigm.

C'est a Toi! Level Two: Assessment Program. 2nd ed. Karla Winther Fawbush et al. (FRE.). 2006. audio compact disk 159.00 (978-0-8219-3296-4(9)) EMC-Paradigm.

C'est a Toi! Level Two: Audio CD Program. 2nd ed. Karla Winther Fawbush et al. (FRE.). audio compact disk 339.95 (978-0-8219-3303-9(5)) EMC-Paradigm.

C'est a Toi! Level Two: Exam View Testing/Assessment Program. 2nd ed. audio compact disk 150.95 (978-0-8219-4037-2(6)) EMC-Paradigm.

C'est a Toi! Level Two: Lesson Planner. 2nd ed. audio compact disk 129.95 (978-0-8219-4032-7(5)) EMC-Paradigm.

C'est a Toi! Level Two: Listening Activities. 2nd ed. Karla Winther Fawbush et al. (FRE.). audio compact disk 139.95 (978-0-8219-3294-0(2)) EMC-Paradigm.

C'est a Toi! Level Two: Multimedia Technology Audio CD Program Manual. 2nd ed. Karla Winther Fawbush et al. (FRE.). audio compact disk (978-0-8219-3304-6(3)) EMC-Paradigm.

C'est a Toi! Level Two: Test Generator CD, IBM/Mac. 2nd ed. Karla Winther Fawbush et al. (FRE.). 2006. audio compact disk 95.00 (978-0-8219-3301-5(9)) EMC-Paradigm.

C'est a Toi! Level Two: Tests. 2nd ed. Karla Winther Fawbush et al. (FRE.). 2006. audio compact disk (978-0-8219-3334-3(5)) EMC-Paradigm.

C'est a Vous. Boston. 1988. pap. bk. 23.00 (978-0-582-35570-5(2), 78046) Longman.

C'est Ca! Essentials of French. unabr. ed. Phyllis Golding. 6 cass. (Running Time: 9 hrs.). (FRE.). 1995. 34.80 (978-0-07-912192-9(6), Mc-H Human Soc) McGrw-H Hghr Educ.

***C'est chouette la Vie!** abr. ed. Giovanni Tempesta. (Collection Decouverte). (FRE.). 2007. audio compact disk (978-2-09-032695-6(6)) Cle Intl FRA.

C'est Français. Kathy Williams. 2004. pap. bk. 70.00 (978-1-903853-02-3(8)) Brilliant Pubns GBR.

C'Est la Folie. Michael Wright. 2008. 84.95 (978-0-7531-2988-3(4)); audio compact disk 99.95 (978-0-7531-2989-0(2)) Pub: ISIS Audio GBR. Dist(s): Ulverscroft US

C'est si Bon: Easy-to-Learn French Songs for Children. Lyrics by Alain Le Lait. Music by Alain Le Lait. Des. by Christy Pitts. 1CD & 1 bk. (Running Time: 30 minutes). (FRE & ENG., (J). (ps-7). 2002. audio compact disk 15.95 (978-0-9747122-3-9(X), FRCD200) Yadeeda.
Original songs in French by Alain Le Lait.

C'esta a Toi! Level Three: Exam View Testing/Assessment Program. audio compact disk 150.95 (978-0-8219-4038-9(4)) EMC-Paradigm.

C'esta a Toi! Level Three: Lesson Planner. audio compact disk 129.95 (978-0-8219-4033-4(3)) EMC-Paradigm.

Cetaganda. Read by Grover Gardner. (Running Time: 34200 sec.). (Vorkosigan Ser.). 2006. 65.95 (978-0-7861-4593-5(5)); audio compact disk 81.00 (978-0-7861-6995-5(8)) Blckstn Audio.

Cetaganda. unabr. ed. Lois McMaster Bujold. 1 CD (MP3). (Running Time: 10 hrs.). (Vorkosigan Ser.). 1999. audio compact disk 24.95 (978-1-885585-12-7(8)) Readers Chair.
Miles Vorkosigan exposes a scheme to control the Cetagandan Empire & clears Barrayar as the conspirator.

Cetaganda. unabr. ed. Lois McMaster Bujold. Perf. by Michael Hanson & Carol Cowan. 8 cass. (Running Time: 9 hrs. 54 mins.). (Vorkosigan Ser.). 1999. 48.00 (978-1-885585-04-2(7)) Readers Chair.
When the Cetagandan Empress dies, Barrayar dispatches Miles Vorkosigan & his cousin Ivan to the funeral ceremonies on Eta Ceta as official representatives. Upon their arrival, a stranger attacks, leaving behind a rod-shaped electronic device, which puts Miles & Barrayar in danger.

Cetaganda. unabr. ed. Read by Grover Gardner. (Running Time: 34200 sec.). (Vorkosigan Ser.). 2006. audio compact disk 29.95 (978-0-7861-7511-6(7)) Blckstn Audio.

CEV Bible. 2004. cd-rom & audio compact disk 12.99 (978-1-58516-005-1(9)) Am Bible.

CEV Kid's Dramatized New Testament with Padded Zipper Case. 15 CDs. Dramatization. (J). 2004. audio compact disk 24.99 (978-0-88368-824-3(7)) Pub: Whitaker Hse. Dist(s): Anchor Distributors

CEV Kids New Testament Discus. (J). 2004. audio compact disk 39.99 (978-1-930034-25-9(3)) Casscomm.

CEV New Testament. Narrated by Stephen Johnston. 13. (Running Time: 1014). 2005. audio compact disk 19.97 (978-0-89957-959-7(0)) AMG Pubs.

Cev'armiut Qanemciit Qulirait-llu: Eskimo Narratives & Tales from Chevak, Alaska. As told by Tom Imgalrea et al. Compiled by Anthony C. Woodbury. (C). 1984. 4.00 (978-0-933769-10-6(5)) Alaska Native.

CFA Institute Webcast Resource Pack - September 2007. Ed. by CFA Institute. 2008. audio compact disk (978-1-932495-72-0(X)) CFA Institute.

CFA Institute Webcast Resource Pack March 2008. Compiled by CFA Institute. 2008. audio compact disk (978-1-932495-76-8(2)) CFA Institute.

CFC Living by Faith, Vol. 6. Featuring Bill Winston. 6. 2003. 30.00 (978-1-59544-060-0(7)) Pub: B Winston Min. Dist(s): Anchor Distributors
Pastor Bill Winston, Founder of Bill Winston Ministries, host the annual Chicago Faith Conference which brings people fromall walks of life together in one place to hear anointed teachers share the life-changing message of faith from the Word of God. Listen to lessons on faith, love, financial increase, restoration and deliverance like your've never heard before!.

CFC Update - The Future Is Here! 1 cass. (America's Supermarket Showcase '96 Ser.). 1996. 11.00 (NGA96-020) Sound Images.

CFM Review Pt. 2: Corporate Financial Management. 10th ed. Irvin N. Gleim & Dale L. Flesher. 2001. 64.95 (978-1-58194-163-0(3)) Gleim Pubns.

***CG Jung & the Future.** Ira Progoff. 2010. audio compact disk 15.00 (978-1-935859-12-3(9)) Dialogue Assoc.

Chad's Triumph: The Story of the Life of Chad Green. Diana J. Meyer. 2007. audio compact disk 37.99 (978-1-60247-392-8(7)) Tate Pubng.

Chain Gang: One Newspaper vs. the Gannett Empire, unabr. ed. Richard McCord. Read by Richard McCord. 8 cass. (Running Time: 11 hrs. 30 mins.). 1999. 56.95 (978-0-7861-1650-8(1), 2478) Blckstn Audio.
In this sequel to "The Painted Word," that caused such a furor in the art world five years before, Wolfe once again shows how social & intellectual fashions have determined aesthetic form in our time & how willingly the creators have abandoned personal vision & originality in order to work a la mode.

Chain of Blame: How Wall Street Caused the Mortgage & Credit Crisis. unabr. ed. Mathew Paul & Padilla Muolo. Read by Walter Dixon. (Running Time: 11 hrs. 40 mins.). (ENG.). 2009. 29.98 (978-1-59659-335-0(0), GildAudio) Pub: Gildan Media. Dist(s): HachBkGrp

Chain of Command. Contrib. by Walter Goff. 1 cass. 1998. 16.99 (978-0-8499-6298-1(6)) Nelson.

***Chain of Command: The Road from 9/11 to Abu Ghraib.** abr. ed. Seymour M. Hersh. Read by Peter Friedman. (ENG.). 2004. (978-0-06-079534-4(4), Harper Audio); (978-0-06-081430-4(6), Harper Audio) HarperCollins Pubs.

Chain of Command: The Road from 9/11 to Abu Ghraib. unabr. abr. ed. Seymour M. Hersh. Read by Peter Friedman. 7 CDs. (Running Time: 10 hrs.). 2004. audio compact disk 29.95 (978-0-06-078056-2(8)) HarperCollins Pubs.

Chain of Evidence. unabr. ed. Ridley Pearson. Read by Michael Russotto. 9 cass. (Running Time: 13 hrs. 30 min.). 1996. 72.00 (978-0-7366-3377-2(4), 4027) Books on Tape.
Three years back, Lt. Joe Dartelli looked the other way when a rapist/killer died in police custody, supposedly a suicide. But Dartelli learned later that a rare hormonal imbalance turned up in the man's blood. Now comes a carbon copy. A wife beater dies, similarly ruled a suicide. The problem is, these two violent men share the same blood chemistry. Can Dartelli let this one go, too.

Chain of Fools. unabr. ed. Steven Womack. Read by Ron Varela. 8 cass. (Running Time: 8 hrs. 42 min.). (Harry Denton Ser.). 2001. 49.95 (978-1-58116-034-5(8)) Books in Motion.
Devastating family secrets are laid bare when Harry signs on to find missing person Stacey Jameson. Denton's search centers on the hypnotic underworld of the sex industry, where Stacy's estranged boyfriend "Red Dog" still works at a strip club.

Chain of Hearts. unabr. ed. Maureen McCarthy. Read by Lucy Taylor. 6 cass. (Running Time: 10 hrs.). 2002. (978-1-74030-215-9(X), 500958) Bolinda Pubng AUS.

Chain of Hearts. unabr. ed. Maureen McCarthy. Read by Lucy Taylor. (Running Time: 10 hrs. 15 mins.). (YA). 2007. audio compact disk 93.95 (978-1-74093-939-3(5), 9781740939393) Pub: Bolinda Pubng AUS. Dist(s): Bolinda Pub Inc

Chainfire. unabr. ed. Terry Goodkind. Read by Jim Bond. (Running Time: 26 hrs.). (Sword of Truth Ser.). 2005. 29.95 (978-1-59710-130-1(3), 9781597101301, BAD) Brilliance Audio.

Chainfire. unabr. ed. Terry Goodkind. Read by Jim Bond. (Running Time: 26 hrs.). (Sword of Truth: Bk. 1). 2005. 44.25 (978-1-59710-131-8(1), 9781597101318, BADLE); 29.95 (978-1-59335-686-2(2), 9781593356866, Brilliance MP3); 44.25 (978-1-59335-820-4(2), 9781593358204, Brlnc Audio MP3 Lib); 39.95 (978-1-59086-307-7(0), 9781590863077, BAU); 117.25 (978-1-59086-308-4(9), 9781590863084, BAudLibEd); audio compact disk 142.25 (978-1-59086-310-7(0), 9781590863107, CD Unabrid Lib Ed); audio compact disk 49.95 (978-1-59086-309-1(7), 9781590863091, Bril Audio CD Unabri) Brilliance Audio.
Please enter a Synopsis.

Chains. Laurie Halse Anderson. Read by Madison Leigh. (Playaway Children Ser.). (J). 2008. 54.99 (978-1-60640-588-8(8)) Find a World.

Chains. unabr. ed. Laurie Halse Anderson. Read by Madison Leigh. (Running Time: 8 hrs.). 2008. 39.25 (978-1-4233-6735-2(9), 9781423367352, BADLE); 39.25 (978-1-4233-6733-8(2), 9781423367338, Brlnc Audio MP3 Lib) Brilliance Audio.

Chains. unabr. ed. Laurie Halse Anderson. Read by Madisun Leigh & David Joe Wirth. (Running Time: 8 hrs.). 2008. 24.95 (978-1-4233-6734-5(0), 9781423367345, BAD) Brilliance Audio.

Chains. unabr. ed. Laurie Halse Anderson. Read by Madison Leigh. 1 MP3-CD. (Running Time: 8 hrs.). 2008. 24.95 (978-1-4233-6732-1(4), 9781423367321, Brilliance MP3); audio compact disk 74.25 (978-1-4233-6731-4(6), 9781423367314, BriAudCD Unabrid); audio compact disk 29.99 (978-1-4233-6730-7(8), 9781423367307, Bril Audio CD Unabri) Brilliance Audio.

Chains of Command. William J. Caunitz. Narrated by Frank Muller. 11 CDs. (Running Time: 12 hrs. 15 mins.). 2000. audio compact disk 111.00 (978-0-7887-4744-1(4), C1230E7) Recorded Bks.
When detective Matt Stuart goes underground to weed out some bent cops, a trail of blood & money leads him back through his won chain of command.

Chains of Command. abr. ed. Dale Brown. Perf. by Robert Culp. 4 cass. (Running Time: 6 hrs.). 2004. 25.00 (978-1-59007-168-7(9)) Pub: New Millenn Enter. Dist(s): PerseuPGW
When a volatile Russian leader tries to reclaim the former Soviet republics, Lt. Col. Daren Mace finds himself back in the cockpit of the sleek RF-111G "Vampire" bomber with Rebecca Furness, the military's first woman combat flier. Now Mace and Rebecca are in danger of being pulled into a war beyond borders.

Chains of Command, unabr. ed. William J. Caunitz. Narrated by Frank Muller. 9 cass. (Running Time: 12 hrs. 15 mins.). 1999. 80.00 (978-0-7887-4036-7(9), 96000E7) Recorded Bks.
When detective Matt Stuart goes underground to weed out some bent cops, a trail of blood & money leads him back through his won chain of command.

Chains of Sarai Stone. abr. ed. Cynthia Haseloff. Read by Laural Merlington. (Running Time: 3 hrs.). (Five Star Westerns Ser.). 2007. 39.25 (978-1-4233-3550-4(3), 9781423335504, BADLE); 24.95 (978-1-4233-3549-8(X), 9781423335498, BAD) Brilliance Audio.

Chains of Sarai Stone. abr. ed. Cynthia Haseloff. Read by Laural Merlington. (Running Time: 10800 sec.). (Five Star Westerns Ser.). 2007. audio compact disk 24.95 (978-1-4233-3547-4(3), 9781423335474, Brilliance MP3); audio compact disk 39.25 (978-1-4233-3548-1(1), 9781423335481, Brlnc Audio MP3 Lib) Brilliance Audio.

Chains of Sarai Stone. unabr. ed. Cynthia Haseloff. Read by Bernadette Dunne. 7 cass. (Running Time: 7 hrs.). 1996. 42.00 (978-0-7366-3344-4(8), 3994) Books on Tape.
It's 1836 & Indian raiders destroy Silas Stone's family, taking his grandchildren. One of them is Sarai, age 10, whom a Comanche family adopts. She grows up, marries a Comanche man & has three children. Her youngest, Summer, goes with her to a trading post, where a Texas Ranger insists on returning her to her white family. But Sarai's torn. She knows she can fit into her old world, just as she did with the Comanches. But how can she move on without her husband & two sons? These are the powerful chains that bind her.

Chair Dancing Through the Decades: Moves & Music for the Best of Times. Perf. by Jodi Stolove. Prod. by Jodi Stolove. Composed by Michael Silversher. 1 cass. (Running Time: 45 min.). 2002. 9.95 (978-0-9630939-5-0(9)) Chair Dancing.

***Chair for Always.** unabr. ed. Vera B. Williams. Read by Martha Plimpton. (ENG.). 2009. (978-0-06-180589-9(0), GreenwillowBks); (978-0-06-176244-4(X), GreenwillowBks) HarperCollins Pubs.

Chair for My Mother **see Sillon para Mi Mama, Grades 1-6**

Chair for My Mother. Vera B. Williams. (Running Time: 10 mins.). (J). (ps-6). 1988. pap. bk. 9.95 (978-0-688-08400-4(1)) HarperCollins Pubs.

Chair for My Mother. Vera B. Williams. (J). 1940. 14.00 (978-0-676-30686-6(1)) SRA McGraw.

***Chair for My Mother.** unabr. ed. Vera B. Williams. Read by Martha Plimpton. (ENG.). 2009. (978-0-06-180588-2(2), GreenwillowBks); (978-0-06-176241-3(5), GreenwillowBks) HarperCollins Pubs.

Chair for My Mother. unabr. ed. Vera B. Williams. Illus. by Vera B. Williams. 1 cass. (Running Time: 10 mins.). (Picture Book Read-Along Ser.). (J). (gr. k-3). 1991. pap. bk. 17.00 (978-0-8072-6031-9(2), MR 24SP, Listening Lib) Random Audio Pubg.
Daughter, mother & grandmother all share the dream of buying a wonderful, soft armchair to replace the one that burned up in a terrible fire.

Chair for My Mother & Other Stories. unabr. ed. Vera B. Williams. Read by Martha Plimpton. 1 CD. (Running Time: 1 hr.). (J). 2009. 13.99 (978-0-06-176121-8(4), HarperChildAud) HarperCollins Pubs.

***Chair for My Mother & Other Stories.** unabr. ed. Vera B. Williams. Read by Martha Plimpton. (ENG.). 2009. (978-0-06-180586-8(6), GreenwillowBks); (978-0-06-180587-5(4), GreenwillowBks) HarperCollins Pubs.

Chair Yoga: Stretching & Relaxation from the Comfort of Your Chair. Perf. by Jodi Stolove. Prod. by Jodi Stolove. Composed by Michael Silversher. 1 cass. (Running Time: 40 min.). 2002. 9.95 (978-0-9630939-9-8(1)) Chair Dancing.

Chairman of the Bored: Ecc. 4:4-8. Ed Young. 1993. 4.95 (978-0-7417-1983-6(5), 983) Win Walk.

Chairs. abr. ed. Eugène Ionesco. Perf. by Eugène Ionesco. Perf. by Siobhan McKenna et al. Tr. by Donald Watson. 2 cass. (Running Time: 4 hrs.). Dramatization. 1984. 17.96 (CDL5 323) HarperCollins Pubs.

Chakra Animal Meditation. Dmitriy Gushchin. 1 CD. (Running Time: 62 mins). 2003. audio compact disk 19.95 (978-0-9713650-5-6(9)) Inst of Russian Healing.
The meditation technique presented on this CD is based on ancient psycho-energetic techniques of India and Tibet. This meditation will help balance your psycho-emotional sphere, reduce stress level and recuperate your bio-energetic system. You can use this unique practice as an excellent tool for your spiritual development or simply for achieving a good health.

Chakra Balance. 1 CD. (Running Time: 55 mins.). 2005. audio compact disk 17.95 (978-0-9701207-6-2(1)) Age of Aware.
Chakra Balance includes 2 powerful meditations to balance your energy fields and clear your body and mind. Both meditations will improve your daily energy and create a stronger balance in your life.

Chakra Balance. unabr. ed. Kim Falcone & Steven Falcone. Read by Kim Falcone. 1 cass. (Running Time: 64 mins.). 1994. 10.95 (978-1-887799-01-0(X), 1-843-276) Creat Aware.
This program is a guided journey into the energy centers of the body, where balancing & activation of this energy can occur.

Chakra Balancing. Judith Anodea. 2 CDs. (Running Time: 2 hrs. 30 mins.). 2006. audio compact disk 29.95 (978-1-59179-088-4(3), W721D) Sounds True.

Chakra Balancing. Dick Sutphen. 1 cass. (Running Time: 1 hr.). 14.98 (978-0-87554-356-7(1), RX203) Valley Sun.

Chakra Balancing: Chakra Measurement, Chakra Healing, Healing with Crystals. 4th ed. Wendy Lambert. 1 cass. (Running Time: 30 min.). 1997. pap. bk. (978-0-9681249-0-1(9)) Erthtopia CAN.

Chakra Balancing Song of the Soul: To Develop Psychic Ability & Higher Consciousness. Stacy Dean. Interview with Stacy Dean. 1 cass. (Running Time: 60 mins.). (C). 1988. 9.99 (978-1-877760-01-3(3)) MY Las Vegas.
Side A: Features a guided meditation of the ancient method of balancing and cleansing the seven major chakra centers. Side B: Performs original compositions demostrating the concept of transposing the movement of planets at one's. Earth into music.

Chakra Breathing: A Guide to Energy, Harmony & Self-Healing. Helmut G. Sieczka. 1993. 12.95 (978-0-940795-15-0(9)) LifeRhythm.

Chakra Breathing Meditations. Layne Redmond. (Running Time: 1 hr. 15 mins.). 2006. bk. 16.98 (978-1-59179-094-5(8), W727D) Sounds True.

Chakra Clearing: A Morning & Evening Meditation to Awaken Your Spiritual Power. Doreen Virtue. 1 cass. (Running Time: 45 mins.). 1997. 10.95 (978-1-56170-394-4(X), 348) Hay House.
Experiential guide to activating your natural spiritual powers of psychic & spiritual healing through the opening, cleansing & balancing of the body's energy centers.

Chakra Clearing: A Morning & Evening Meditation to Awaken Your Spiritual Power. abr. ed. Doreen Virtue. 1 CD. 2003. audio compact disk 10.95 (978-1-4019-0138-7(7), 1387) Hay House.

Chakra Delight: Singing Bowls for Balancing the Energy Centers. Dick de Ruiter & Rainer Tillmann. (Running Time: 1 hr. 13 mins.). 2005. bk. 19.95 (978-90-74597-49-4(1)) Pub: Binkey Kok NLD. Dist(s): Red Wheel Weiser

Chakra Exercises. Read by Jack Schwarz. 1 cass. 15.00 (#102) Aletheia Psycho.
As given in his classes & book, "Voluntary Controls".

Chakra Healing. Bruce Goldberg. (ENG.). 2005. audio compact disk 17.00 (978-1-57968-075-6(5)) Pub: B Goldberg. Dist(s): Baker Taylor

Chakra Healing. Bruce Goldberg. Read by Bruce Goldberg. 1 cass. (Running Time: 25 mins.). (ENG.). 2007. 13.00 (978-1-885577-42-9(7)) B Goldberg.
Balance the energy centers in the body and return to optimum health and well-being through self-hypnosis.

Chakra Healing. Patricia O'Malley. Perf. by Barry Weiss. 1 cass. (Running Time: 50 mins.). 1998. 11.95 (978-1-892450-15-9(1), 132) Pub: Promo Music. Dist(s): Penton Overseas
Focus is on putting back in balance each of the Chakras & beginning the process of healing.

Chakra Healing. Sarah Shapiro. 1997. 12.00 (978-0-9703366-0-6(8)) Chakra Healing.

Chakra Healing. rev. unabr. ed. Rosalyn L. Bruyere et al. Read by Rosalyn L. Bruyere. (Running Time: 1 hr. 0 mins. 0 sec.). (ENG.). 2004. audio compact disk 14.99 (978-1-55927-996-3(6)) Pub: Macmill Audio. Dist(s): Macmillan

Chakra Healing I. Jonathan Parker. Read by Jonathan Parker. 2 CDs . (Running Time: 2 hrs.). (Guided Meditation Ser.). 1999. audio compact disk (978-1-58400-056-3(2)) QuantumQuests Intl.

Chakra Healing II. Jonathan Parker. Read by Jonathan Parker. 2 CDs. (Running Time: 2 hrs.). (Guided Meditation Ser.). 1999. audio compact disk (978-1-58400-057-0(0)) QuantumQuests Intl.

Chakra Journey CD. Music by ThunderBeat ThunderVision Record. 2007. (978-0-9814651-1-1(0)) ThunderVision.

Chakra Meditation. Glenn Harrold. 2007. audio compact disk 17.95 (978-1-901923-69-8(X)) Pub: Divinit Pubing GBR. Dist(s): Bookworld

Chakra Meditation. Barrie Konicov. 1 cass. 11.98 (978-0-87082-398-5(1), 019) Potentials.
Explains how balancing & harmonizing the energies of your chakras, you unleash incredible cosmic & psychic powers that benefit all mankind.

Chakra Meditation. Barrie Konicov. 2 CDs. 1980. audio compact disk 27.98 (978-1-56001-970-1(0)) Potentials.
By balancing and harmonizing the energies of your chakras, you unleash incredible cosmic and psychic powers that benefit all humankind.This 2-CD program from our Super Consciousness series is our newest, most powerful format. On the self-hypnosis CD, SC programs have the Subliminal Persuasion soundtrack added under Barrie?s voice. And the 17th Century Baroque music on the Subliminal CD has the same beat as your body's natural rhythm, thereby allowing the suggestions to enter deeply and effortlessly.

Chakra Meditation. Barrie Konicov. 1 CD. 2003. audio compact disk 16.98 (978-0-87082-965-9(3)) Potentials.
By balancing and harmonizing the energies of your chakras, unleash incredible cosmic and psychic powers that benefit all humankind.You will find the self-hypnosis on track 1 and the subliminal on track 2. The easy-listening music of the subliminal, together with the self-hypnosis, is the original format which most people love and with which they are most familiar.

Chakra Meditation. Layne Redmond. (Running Time: 1 hr. 15 mins.). 2006. bk. 19.95 (978-1-59179-178-2(2), K813D) Sounds True.

Chakra Meditation: Morning & Evening Meditations to Open & Balance Your Chakras. rev. ed. Aretta Swanson. 1 cass., bklet. (Running Time: 20 mins.). 1999. 12.00 (978-1-930380-02-8(X)) Performance IL.

Chakra Meditation: Morning & Evening Meditations to Open & Balance Your Chakras. unabr. ed. Aretta Swanson. 1 cass. (Running Time: 20 mins.). 2000. 12.00 (978-1-930380-05-9(4)) Performance IL.

Chakra Opening (Hypnosis), Vol. 21. Jayne Helle. 1 cass. (Running Time: 28 mins.). 1997. 15.00 (978-1-891826-20-7(4)) Introspect.
Open up energy centers & discover how wonderful it feels to have healing energy flowing with a divine purpose.

Chakra Soul. Created by Karen Jolly. Narrated by Karen Jolly. 1 CD. (Running Time: 55 mins.). 2005. audio compact disk 17.95 (978-0-9701207-9-3(6)) Age of Aware.
Includes 2 powerful meditations to open the sixth Chakra, the eye of the soul, allowing you to clear your attachments to the past and create your life moment by moment.

Chakra Sounds. unabr. ed. 1 cass. (Running Time: 1 hr. 30 mins.). (Meditations from Osho Ser.). 1992. 10.95 (TRR-0008) Oshos.
A meditation uses vocal sounds made by the meditator along with music to open & harmonize the chakras while bringing awareness to them.

Chakra System. Judith Anodea. 2003. audio compact disk 69.95 (978-1-59179-125-6(1)) Sounds True.

Chakras. Vajracarya. 1 cass. 1971. 12.50 Vajradhatu.
A seminar by the scholar & meditation master trained in the philosophical & meditative traditions of Buddhism in Tibet.

Chakras: Key to Spiritual Opening. rev. ed. Mary Ellen Flora. 1 cass. (Running Time: 1 hr. 12 mins.). (Key Ser.). 1999. reel tape 10.00 (978-1-886983-05-2(4)) CDM Pubns.
Shows how you can use your chakras to unlock your spiritual potential. Clearly presents information & instruction in terms that are easy to understand & fun to practice.

Chakras: Purify, Strengthen, Awaken. Swami Shankardev Saraswati & Jayne Stevenson. (ENG.). 2005. audio compact disk 22.00 (978-0-9803496-2-7(1)) Big Shakti AUS.

Chakras: Purifying the Subtle Body. unabr. ed. Swami Rama. Read by Pandit R. Tigunait. 1 cass. (Running Time: 30 mins.). 1995. 12.00 (978-0-89389-144-2(4), Yoga Joyful) Himalayan Inst.
This is an interactive yoga practice. The set comes with a poster, a cassette & a booklet.

Chakras for Beginners Audiobook: A Guide to Balancing Your Chakra Energies. David Pond. (ENG.). 2010. audio compact disk 26.95 (978-0-7387-1917-7(X)) Llewellyn Pubns.

Chakras for Starters. Savitri Simpson. 2004. audio compact disk 10.95 Crystal Clarity.

Chakras for Starters: Unlock the Hidden Doors to Peace & Well-Being. Savriti Simpson. 1 CD. (Running Time: 1 hr.). 2004. audio compact disk 10.95 (978-1-56589-200-2(3)) Pub: Crystal Clarity. Dist(s): Natl Bk Netwk

Chakras Series. 5 cass. 44.95 incl. vinyl storage album. (LS-8) Crystal Clarity.
Discusses: First Chakra - key to loyalty, discipline & focus; Second Chakra - key to flexibility, contentment & getting into the flow; Third Chakra - key to fiery self-control & overcoming obstacles; Fourth Chakra - key to love & expansiveness; Fifth Chakra - key to calmness & keeness of understanding.

Chalice Praise. audio compact disk 15.00 (978-0-8272-8042-7(4)) Chalice Pr.

Chalk Box Kid. Clyde Robert Bulla. Narrated by Johnny Heller. 1 cass. (Running Time: 30 mins.). (gr. 2 up). 2001. 10.00 (978-0-7887-5497-5(1)) Recorded Bks.
Tale of a boy finding a way to cope with his new surroundings.

Chalk Whispers. unabr. ed. Paul Bishop. Read by Stephanie Brush. 12 cass. (Running Time: 12 hrs. 6 min.). (Fey Croaker Mystery Ser.: Bk. 4). 2001. 64.95 (978-1-55686-951-8(7)) Books in Motion.
Detective Fey Croaker has been promoted to her first case at L.A. Robbery-Homicide, where the victim is identified as the sister of an outspoken police commissioner. The investigation leads to a daunting array of high-profile suspects, and an unsolved, 30-year-old murder.

Chalktown. abr. ed. Melinda Haynes. 2004. 26.00 (978-0-7435-4258-6(4)) Pub: S&S Audio. Dist(s): S and S Inc

Chalktown: A Novel. Melinda Rucker Haynes. Read by Barrett Whitener. 8 vols. (Running Time: 12 hrs.). 2001. bk. 69.95 (978-0-7927-2476-6(3), CSL 365, Chivers Sound Lib) AudioGO.
The story about Chalktown, a small village of folks who communicate mostly through the chalkboards set up in the front yard of their houses. Down the road lives the Sheehand family: sixteen-year-old Hezekiah, his older sister, Arena, his mentally disabled younger brother, Yellababy & their disaffected & often cruel mother & Susan Blair, whose husband has abandoned both the house & the family. It is the story of a mysterious town & its inhabitants, each with their own afflictions & joys, each with their own secrets.

Chalktown: A Novel. unabr. ed. Melinda Rucker Haynes. Read by Barrett Whitener. 12 CDs. (Running Time: 18 hrs.). 2001. audio compact disk 110.95 (978-0-7927-9918-4(6), SLD 069, Chivers Sound Lib) AudioGO.

Challenge. abr. ed. Jerry Ahern. Read by Alan Zimmerman. 3 vols. (Running Time: 4 hrs. 30 mins.). (Defender Ser.: No. 11). 2003. 22.00 (978-1-58807-031-9(X)) Am Pubng Inc.
The usurper government of the United States has been established. At its helm, a President who was never elected and who murdered legitimate heads of state, initiates his government's ultimate plan to throttle freedom. Once again, the liberty of America rests in the capable hands of David Holden and Rosie Shepherd. But this time, will they be able to thwart the devastating plans of the FLNA?.

Challenge. unabr. ed. Jerry Ahern. Read by Alan Zimmerman. 2 vols. No. 11. 2003. (978-1-58807-540-6(0)) Am Pubng Inc.

Challenge. unabr. ed. Jerry Ahern. Read by Alan Zimmerman. 4 vols. No. 11. 2004. audio compact disk 28.00 (978-1-58807-273-3(8)); audio compact disk (978-1-58807-704-2(7)) Am Pubng Inc.

Challenge. unabr. ed. Ridley Pearson. Read by William Dufris. 5 CDs. (Running Time: 6 hrs.). (J). 2008. audio compact disk 26.95 (978-1-4233-3857-4(X), 9781423338574, Bril Audio CD Unabri); audio compact disk 39.25 (978-1-4233-3860-4(X), 9781423338604, Brlnc Audio MP3 Lib) Brilliance Audio.

Challenge. unabr. ed. Ridley Pearson. Read by William Dufris. 1 MP3-CD. (Running Time: 6 hrs.). 2008. 24.95 (978-1-4233-3859-8(6), 9781423338598, Brilliance MP3); 24.95 (978-1-4233-3861-1(8), 9781423338611, BAD); 39.25 (978-1-4233-3862-8(6), 9781423338628, BADLE) Brilliance Audio.

Challenge. unabr. ed. Ridley Pearson. Read by William Dufris. 5 CDs. (Running Time: 6 hrs.). (J). (gr. 5). 2008. audio compact disk 74.25 (978-1-4233-3858-1(8), 9781423338581, BriAudCD Unabrid) Brilliance Audio.

Challenge: Hamdan V. Rumsfeld & the Fight over Presidential Power. unabr. ed. Jonathan Mahler. (Running Time: 10 hrs. NaN mins.). (ENG.). 2008. 29.95 (978-1-4332-4403-2(9)); 29.95 (978-1-4332-4401-8(2)); 65.95 (978-1-4332-4399-8(7)); audio compact disk 29.95 (978-1-4332-4402-5(0)); audio compact disk 80.00 (978-1-4332-4400-1(4)) Blckstn Audio.

Challenge: Theology of Christian Marriage: a Three-Part Workshop with Dr. Thomas Martin. Redemptorist Pastoral Communications Staff. Read by Thomas Martin. 3 cass. (Running Time: 60 mins. per cass.). 1992. 22.95 (978-0-89243-458-9(9)) Liguori Pubns.
He examines the causes & results of modern marriage trends by putting them into historical perspective. He focuses on what difference faith makes to a marriage of the past. These tapes show what today's actual marriage patterns are & what they mean from a Christian perspective.

Challenge & Consolidation of Christianity. unabr. ed. Samuel Sandmel. 1 cass. (Running Time: 30 mins.). 12.95 (31007) J Norton Pubs.
Describes the role of early Christian writings in the unity of the church.

Challenge at Second Base. unabr. ed. Matt Christopher. Narrated by Norman Dietz. 2 pieces. (Running Time: 2 hrs.). (gr. 2 up). 19.00 (978-0-7887-0409-3(5), 94601E7) Recorded Bks.
As young Stan Norman tries to move into the second base position on his team, he finds he must also search for the true meaning of sportsmanship. Available to libraries only.

***Challenge for Africa.** unabr. ed. Wangari Maathai. Narrated by Chinasa Ogbuagu. 1 Playaway. (Running Time: 11 hrs.). 2009. 64.75 (978-1-4407-0816-9(9)); 92.75 (978-1-4407-0813-8(4)); audio compact disk 123.75 (978-1-4407-0814-5(2)) Recorded Bks.

***Challenge for Africa.** unabr. collector's ed. Wangari Maathai. Read by Chinasa Ogbuagu. 9 CDs. (Running Time: 11 hrs.). 2009. audio compact disk 56.95 (978-1-4407-0815-2(0)) Recorded Bks.

Challenge of AIDS. Elisabeth Kubler-Ross. (AIDS: The National Conference for Practitioners). 1986. 9.00 (978-0-932491-47-3(2)) Res Appl Inc.

Challenge of Jesus: Rediscovering Who Jesus Was & Is. unabr. ed. Read by Simon Vance. 6 CDs. (Running Time: 6 hrs. 30 mins. 0 sec.). (ENG.). 2006. audio compact disk 24.98 (978-1-59644-411-9(8)) christianaud.
Today a renewed and vigorous scholarly quest for the historical Jesus is underway. In the midst of well publicized and controversial books on Jesus, N. T. Wright's lectures and writings have been widely recognized for providing a fresh, provocative and historically credible portrait.The Challenge of Jesus poses a double-edged challenge: to grow in our understanding of the historical Jesus within the Palestinian world of the first century, and to follow Jesus more faithfully into the postmodern world of the twenty-first century.

***Challenge of Jesus: Rediscovering Who Jesus Was & Is.** unabr. ed. N. T. Wright. Narrated by Simon Vance. (ENG.). 2006. 14.98 (978-1-59644-412-6(6), Hovel Audio) christianaud.

Challenge of Masculinity & Femininity. unabr. ed. Nathaniel Branden. 1 cass. (Running Time: 1 hr. 3 mins.). 12.95 (607) J Norton Pubs.
Discusses the biological basis of male & female sex roles, aggressiveness & passivity in man & woman.

Challenge of Personal Change. Tom Rusk. Read by Tom Rusk. 1 cass. (Running Time: 48 mins.). 1991. 10.95 (978-1-56170-026-4(6), 253N) Hay House.
Discusses the inner & outer process you face when you decide to change.

Challenge of Spiritual Marriage. Interview. Kriyananda, pseud. 1 cass. (Running Time: 80 mins.). (Relationship Ser.). 9.95 (QA-3) Crystal Clarity.
Discusses: Why it takes a successful human being to make a successful marriage partner; the impermanence of romance; why a truly good marriage is a spiritual marriage; the importance of moderation & balance in married life; the inner side of sexuality.

Challenge of Synthesis: Techniques & Strategies. unabr. ed. Read by Barry M. Trost & Edwin Vedejs. 6 cass. (Running Time: 7 hrs.). 535.00 manual. (99) Am Chemical.

Challenge to Women. Ruth Prince. 1 cass. (Running Time: 60 mins.). 5.95 (I-8003) Derek Prince.

Challenged see Bible in Living Sound: Life and Times of the Old Testament; Life and Times of Jesus; Life and Times of Paul

Challenger. Sandra D. Bricker. Narrated by Larry A. McKeever. (Disaster Ser.). (J). 2003. audio compact disk 14.95 (978-1-58659-285-1(8)) Artesian.

Challenger. unabr. ed. Sandra D. Bricker. Narrated by Larry A. McKeever. 1 cass. (Running Time: 40 mins.). (Take Ten Ser.). (J). (gr. 3-12). 2003. 10.95 (978-1-58659-026-0(X), 54111) Artesian.

Challenger: Power of the Enneagram Individual Type Audio Recording. Scripts. Based on a work by Enneagram Institute Staff. 1 CD. (Running Time: 60 mins.). 2004. audio compact disk 10.00 (978-0-9755222-7-1(2)) Enneagr.
Type Seven Individual Type Audio Recording (ITAR) in CD format from the audio tapeset The Power of the Enneagram. Includes a 25 minute introduction to the system as a whole, as well as a 35 minute exposition on Type Seven. An excellent way for therapists or business consultants to introduce the Enneagram to clients, or to work with the Enneagram in ongoing situations.

Challenger Park. unabr. ed. Stephen Harrigan. Read by Robertson Dean. 11 cass. (Running Time: 16 hrs.). 2006. 99.00 (978-1-4159-2727-4(8)); audio compact disk 104.00 (978-1-4159-2728-1(6)) Books on Tape.

Challenger Phonics Fun Vol. 1: Letters & Sounds. unabr. ed. Contrib. by Barbara B. Baker. 1 cass. (J). (ps). 1990. 7.95 (978-1-57812-004-8(7)) Learng Crew.
Songs that teach children to read.

Challenger Phonics Fun Vol. 2: Vowels & Reading. unabr. ed. Contrib. by Barbara B. Baker. 1 cass. (J). (gr. k-1). 1991. 7.95 (978-1-57812-005-5(5)) Learng Crew.

Challenger Phonics Fun Vol. 3: Irregular Vowel Families. Contrib. by Barbara B. Baker. 1 cass. (J). (gr. k-2). 1993. 7.95 (978-1-57812-006-2(3)) Learng Crew.

Challenges & Crosses. Benjamin T. Layton. Ed. by Interspace Books Staff. (978-0-930061-18-0(7)) Interspace Bks.
Dramatic reading from author's autobiography. He is an accomplished orator & toastmaster & his autobiography will be of inspiration & interest to minorities.

Challenges for the Sunday School in the '90s: National Association of Evangelicals, 47th Annual Convention, Columbus, Ohio, March 7-9, 1989. Phil Riley. 1 cass. (Workshops Ser.: No. 12-Wednesd). 1989. 4.25 ea. 1-8 tapes.; 4.00 ea. 9 tapes or more. Nat Assn Evan.

Challenges in Health Care Management: Strategic Perspectives for Managing Key Stakeholders. John D. Blair & Myron D. Fottler. (Health Management Ser.). 1990. bk. 50.00 (978-1-55542-288-2(8), Jossey-Bass) Wiley US.

Challenges in Production of Document Databases: Approaches to Document Image Database Retrieval. 1 cass. 1990. 8.50 Recorded Res.

Challenges of Contemporary Priesthood. Stephen J. Rossetti. 3 cass. (Running Time: 4 hrs. 5 min.). 1997. 28.95 Set. (TAH379) St Pauls Alba.
Directed to today's priest & addresses the issues that face the contemporary priesthood.

Challenging Parties, Changing Parliaments: Women & Elected Office in Contemporary Western Europe. Miki Caul Kittilson. (Parliaments & Legislatures Ser.). 2006. audio compact disk 9.95 (978-0-8142-9091-0(4)) Pub: Ohio St U Pr. Dist(s): Chicago Distribution Ctr

Challenging the Unmotivated Bachur in the Yeshiva Setting. Yechiel Cohen. 1 cass. (Running Time: 90 mins.). 1999. 6.00 (W60FQ) Torah Umesorah.

Chamber. John Grisham. Read by Alexander Adams. 1994. audio compact disk 112.00 (978-0-7366-8909-0(5)) Books on Tape.

Chamber. unabr. ed. John Grisham. Read by Alexander Adams. 12 cass. (Running Time: 18 hrs.). 1994. 96.00 (978-0-7366-2767-2(7), 3488) Books on Tape.
In 1967, Mississippi Klan member Sam Cayhill's trial for bombing the law offices of Jewish civil rights Activist Marvin Kramer & killing Kramer's two sons that ends in an all-white hung jury is held. In 1979, an ambitious DA reopens the case.

Chamber. unabr. ed. John Grisham. Narrated by George Guidall. 15 cass. (Running Time: 21 hrs. 30 mins.). 1994. 120.00 (978-0-7887-0061-3(8), 94317E7) Recorded Bks.
A young lawyer tries desperately to defend his grandfather, an inmate on Louisiana's death row.

Chamber, Set. unabr. ed. John Grisham. Read by Michael Beck. 12 cass. 1999. 49.95 (FS9-43345) Highsmith.

Chamber Music see James Joyce Reads James Joyce

Chamber Music. Doris Grumbach. Read by Doris Grumbach. 1 cass. (Running Time: 1 hr. 15 min.). Incl. Ladies. (4071); Missing Person. (4071); 13.95 (978-1-55644-103-5(7), 4071) Am Audio Prose.
Grumbach reading excerpts from all three of her recent novels.

Chamber Music of Mozart, Vol. I-II. Instructed by Robert Greenberg. 8 cass. (Running Time: 12 hrs.). bk. 54.95 (978-1-56585-932-6(4), 7237) Teaching Co.

Chamber Music of Mozart, Vol. I-II. Instructed by Robert Greenberg. 16 CDs. (Running Time: 12 hrs.). 2004. audio compact disk 69.95 (978-1-56585-934-0(0), 7237) Teaching Co.

Chambers of Death: A Medieval Mystery. unabr. ed. Priscilla Royal. (Running Time: 8.5 hrs. 0 mins.). (ENG.). 2009. 29.95 (978-1-4332-8836-4(2)); 54.95 (978-1-4332-8832-6(X)); audio compact disk 76.00 (978-1-4332-8833-3(8)) Blckstn Audio.

Chameleon. collector's ed. William X. Kienzle. Read by Edward Holland. 7 cass. (Running Time: 10 hrs. 30 min.). (Father Koesler Mystery Ser.: No. 13). 2000. 56.00 (978-0-7366-5585-9(9), 5399) Books on Tape.
A hooker dressed in a nun's habit is shot dead at the shrine of her sister's convent. No clues, no motive & scant leads present the police with a parish puzzler. Father Robert Koesler attends the woman's wake & soon finds himself swept into a bizarre & chilling case of multiple murders that begins with a nun under the gun & ends with Koesler under a cardinal's cassock.

Chameleon Wore Chantreuse; The Mystery of Mr. Nice. unabr. ed. Bruce Hale. Read by Jon Cryer. 2 cass. (Running Time: 2 hrs. 34 mins.). (Chet Gecko Mystery Ser.: Vol. 1). (J). (gr. 3-6). 2004. 23.00 (978-0-8072-8860-3(8), Listening Lib) Random Audio Pubg.
"The Chameleon Wore Chartreuse." Shirley Chameleon's friend Billy has disappeared & it's up to Chet, super sleuth, to find him. "The Mystery of Mister Nice." What has happened to Principal Zero? All of a sudden he's nice. One thing is certain: Principal Zero is not a nice guy. It's up to Chet to prove he's an imposter.

Chameleon Wore Chartreuse. unabr. ed. Bruce Hale. 1 cass. (Running Time: 1 hr. 19 mins.). (Chet Gecko Mystery Ser.: No. 1). (J). (gr. 3-6). 2004. pap. bk. 17.00 (978-0-8072-0342-2(4), Listening Lib) Random Audio Pubg.

Chameleon's Shadow. unabr. ed. Minette Walters. Narrated by Simon Vance. 9 CDs. (Running Time: 11 hrs. 0 mins. 0 sec.). (ENG.). 2008. audio compact disk 34.99 (978-1-4001-0598-4(6)); audio compact disk 24.99 (978-1-4001-5598-9(3)); audio compact disk 69.99 (978-1-4001-3598-1(2)) Pub: Tantor Media. Dist(s): IngramPubServ

Chamorro - English Min-Book Set with Audio. Claudia Schwalm. 2000. pap. bk. 21.95 (978-1-57371-035-0(0)) Cultural Cnnect.

Champagne for One. unabr. ed. Rex Stout. Read by Michael Prichard. 4 cass. (Running Time: 6 hrs.). (Nero Wolfe Ser.). 2001. 24.95 (978-1-57270-207-3(9), N41207u) Pub: Audio Partners. Dist(s): PerseuPGW
Faith Usher tells anyone willing to listen that she wants to kill herself. So when she dies after drinking champagne at the annual gala for unwed mothers, everyone insists that it was suicide. Everyone except Archie Goodwin, the perennial wise guy, who was watching her drink.

Champagne for One. unabr. ed. Rex Stout. Narrated by Michael Prichard. (Running Time: 21600 sec.). (Nero Wolfe Ser.). (ENG.). 2006. audio compact disk 27.95 (978-1-57270-520-3(5)) Pub: AudioGO. Dist(s): Perseus Dist

Champagne for One. unabr. collector's ed. Rex Stout. Read by Michael Prichard. 6 cass. (Running Time: 6 hrs.). (Nero Wolfe Ser.). 1996. 48.00 (978-0-7366-3345-1(6), 3995) Books on Tape.
There's nothing like murder to spoil a good meal. That's what Archie Goodwin, the able assistant to Nero Wolfe, discovers at a lavish dinner party hosted by a billionaire. It was a casual evening among gorgeous society girls...until champagne became a murder weapon. Luckily for Archie, his boss knows champagne - & other gourmet fare. He also happens to be a genius at deduction. That combination could mean the last call for a killer who spiked the bubbly with cyanide.

Champion. Max Brand. (Running Time: 0 hr. 42 mins.). 1998. 10.95 (978-1-60083-478-3(7)) Iofy Corp.

***Champion.** Max Brand. 2009. (978-1-60136-469-2(5)) Audio Holding.

Champion. unabr. ed. Elizabeth Chadwick. Narrated by Gerri Halligan. 14 cass. (Running Time: 19 hrs. 15 mins.). 1999. 116.00 (978-1-84197-003-5(4), H1003E7) Recorded Bks.
Beginning in the spring of 1193, this is the story of Monday de Cerizay & her involvement with two powerful men. One, the young Alexander de Montroi is a jousting champion amongst the knights of Normandy who promises excitement & passion, but delivers only betrayal. The Count of Mortain is heir to Coeur de Lion's empire & can deliver Monday from her life of squalor but there is a price to pay. From the mud-soaked fields of France to the refined environs of the royal court, from moments of breathtaking passion to the cold-hearted machination of medieval politics, this is an epic & unforgettable tale of love, injustice & revenge.

***Champion of IDEAS Yellow Level: Reader Audio CD.** Perf. by Ballard & Tighe Publishers Staff. 2010. cd-rom 25.00 (978-1-59989-307-5(X)) BallardTighe.

Champion of Love. Perf. by Gold City et al. 2002. audio compact disk Provident Mus Dist.

Champion of the Weather see O. Henry Favorites

Champion of the Weather see O. Henry Library

Champion, Success is Within Your Reach. Gary V. Whetstone. 4 cass. (Running Time: 6 hrs.). (Finance Ser.). 1993. pap. bk. 35.00 (978-1-58866-233-0(0), VIOO1A) Gary Whet Pub.
Jesus victory is ours! This series deals with how to reach the unseen resources of heaven & work with God's ability to reach His goals. You will never see defeat.

Champions Body for Life. abr. ed. Art Carey et al. Read by Michelle Lee. (Running Time: 16200 sec.). 2008. audio compact disk 22.95 (978-0-06-156201-3(7), Harper Audio) HarperCollins Pubs.

***Champions Body-for-LIFE.** unabr. ed. Art Carey. Read by Michelle Lee. (ENG.). 2008. (978-0-06-163248-8(1)); (978-0-06-163249-5(X)) HarperCollins Pubs.

Champions for Life. 1 cass. (Running Time: 1 hr. 30 mins.). 2001. 15.00 (978-0-9666412-3-3(X)) Bill Glass Minist.

Champion's Mind: Lessons from a Life in Tennis. abr. ed. Pete Sampras & Peter Bodo. Read by Mark Deakins. (Running Time: 19800 sec.). (ENG.). 2008. audio compact disk 29.95 (978-0-7393-2875-0(1), Random AudioBks) Pub: Random Audio Pubg. Dist(s): Random

***Championship Contest Fiddling Book/CD Set: 44 Transcriptions from 15 Championship Rounds.** Nate Olson. 2010. spiral bd. 24.99 (978-0-7866-7785-6(6)) Mel Bay.

Championship Flatpicking Guitar. Steve Kaufman. 1996. bk. 19.95 (978-0-7866-2644-1(5), 94533BCD) Mel Bay.

Championship Skeet Shooting. 2 cass. (Running Time: 2 hrs.). 1998. 29.95 Set, shrink wrap. (978-1-893417-06-9(9), SKT-01) Vector Studios.
Tape 1: instructions on the secrets of skeet shooting. Tape 2: relaxation/hypnosis program on mental reprogramming.

Champs d'Honneur, Set. Jean Rouaud. Read by Jean Rouaud. 3 cass. (FRE.). 1996. 34.95 (1801-LV) Olivia & Hill.
Prix Goncourt 1990. The history of 20th century France through the lives of a French family in Vendee: the traumas of war & times of joy & sadness.

Chance & Chaos: A Selection from Princeton University Press. David Ruelle. 2 cass. (Running Time: 2 hrs. 30 min.). 1996. 17.95 (978-1-879557-39-0(8)) Audio Scholar.
Listen to one of the founders of Chaos Theory, David Reulle. His more technical works on Chaos Theory have become classics in the field.

Chance or the Dance. unabr. ed. Thomas Howard. Read by Maureen O'Leary. 4 cass. 18.95 set. (125) Ignatius Pr.
A spirited contrast of the Christian & secular world-views, this inspiring work reveals how all activities of daily life - great & small - have meaning only if illuminated by the light of the "old" Christian perspective.

Chance to Die. unabr. ed. Elisabeth Elliot. Read by Elisabeth Elliot. 6 cass. (Running Time: 4 hrs. 45 min.). 1990. 25.95 (978-0-8474-2020-9(5)) Back to Bible.
The story of missionary Amy Carmichael, with a close look at what discipleship is all about.

Chance to See Egypt. unabr. ed. Sandra Scofield. Read by Mary Helen Fisher. 6 vols. (Running Time: 9 hrs.). 2000. bk. 54.95 (978-0-7927-2244-1(2), CSL 133, Chivers Sound Lib) AudioGO.
The death of Tom Riley's wife prompts him to travel to Mexico, where they honeymooned, as a pilgrimage to love's memory. An American writer also escaping from a painful past, befriends him, sensing he has a story to tell. "Change the plot," she advises. "Introduce new characters." Enter Consolata Aripse, a Mexican woman, and her daughter Divina. Their mystery and beauty draw Riley into their lives as fates converge.

Chancellor Manuscript. unabr. collector's ed. Robert Ludlum. Read by Michael Prichard. 11 cass. (Running Time: 16 hrs. 30 min.). 1984. 88.00 (978-0-7366-0807-7(9), 1757) Books on Tape.
Peter Chancellor, a novelist known for his deadly accurate & dangerously controversial political "fictions" makes a dangerous discovery in the course of his research: J. Edgar Hoover did not die a natural death. He was assasinated.

Chancellorsville. James Reasoner. Read by Lloyd James. (Running Time: 11 hrs. 30 mins.). (Civil War Battle Ser.: Bk. 4). 2003. 34.95 (978-1-59912-445-2(9)) Iofy Corp.

Chancellorsville. unabr. ed. James Reasoner. Read by Lloyd James. 8 cass. (Running Time: 11 hrs. 30 mins.). (Civil War Battle Ser.: Bk. 4). 2003. 56.95 (978-0-7861-2549-4(7), 3181); audio compact disk 80.00 (978-0-7861-8997-7(5), 3181) Blckstn Audio.

Chancellorsville. unabr. ed. Stephen W. Sears. Narrated by Richard M. Davidson. 17 cass. (Running Time: 23 hrs. 30 mins.). 1997. 136.00 (978-0-7887-0662-2(4), 94839E7) Recorded Bks.
Chancellorsville has been touted as Robert E. Lee's greatest victory. Sears examines the personal & military cost of this historic clash of armies.

Chances: Part 1, Gino's Story. Jackie Collins. (Lucky Santangelo Ser.: Bk. 1). 2004. 10.95 (978-0-7435-4259-3(2)) Pub: S&S Audio. Dist(s): S and S Inc

Chances: Part 2, Lucky's Story. Jackie Collins. (Lucky Santangelo Ser.: Bk. 1). 2004. 10.95 (978-0-7435-4260-9(6)) Pub: S&S Audio. Dist(s): S and S Inc

Chances of a Lifetime. Warren Christopher. Narrated by Warren Christopher. 8 cass. (Running Time: 11 hrs.). 2001. 71.00 (978-1-4025-0694-9(5), 96926) Recorded Bks.
Tells the story of how a quiet boy from a small prairie town in North Dakota rose to become one of the most powerful men in Washington, D.C. Christopher reached his pinnacle as U.S. Secretary of State in the Clinton administration.

Chances of a Lifetime. Warren Christopher. 7 cass. (Running Time: 9 hrs.). 2004. 29.99 (978-1-4025-0406-8(3), 00834) Recorded Bks.

Chandail de Hockey see Hockey Sweater & Other Stories

***Chanda's Secrets.** unabr. ed. Allan Stratton. (Running Time: 7 hrs.). 2011. 39.97 (978-1-4558-0393-4(6), 9781455803934, BADLE); 19.99 (978-1-4558-0391-0(X), 9781455803910, Brilliance MP3); 39.97 (978-1-4558-0392-7(8), 9781455803927, Brinc Audio MP3 Lib); audio compact disk 59.97 (978-1-4558-0390-3(1), 9781455803903, BriAudCD Unabrid); audio compact disk 19.99 (978-1-4558-0389-7(8), 9781455803897, Bril Audio CD Unabri) Brilliance Audio.

Chaneysville Incident see David Bradley

Chaneysville Incident. David Bradley. Read by David Bradley. 2 cass. (Running Time: 1 hr. 44 min.). 1992. 13.95 set. (978-1-55644-372-5(2), 12011) Am Audio Prose.
Bradley spent ten years researching & writing this highly complex historical mystery novel, winner of the 1982 PEN/Faulkner award. Here he reads one of Old Jack's stories & the story of Old Jack's funeral.

Chaneysville Incident. David Bradley. Read by David Bradley. 1 cass. (Running Time: 29 min.). 1984. 10.00 New Letters.
This award winning novel concerns a Black historian's search for truth among slave legends.

Change. Brothers in Unity. (Running Time: 45 min.). 2004. audio compact disk 17.98 (978-5-559-67763-7(9)) Pub: Pt of Grace Ent. Dist(s): STL Dist NA

Change. Earnie Larsen. 1 cass. (Running Time: 1 hr.). 1989. 10.95 (978-1-56047-009-0(7), A113) E Larsen Enterprises.
Discusses the secret of personal growth & self management.

Change: Companion music to the EXODUS Out of Egypt Seminar. Michael Shamblin. (ENG.). 2006. audio compact disk (978-1-892729-03-3(2)) Weigh Down Work.

Change: Women, Aging & the Menopause. unabr. ed. Germaine Greer. Read by Donada Peters. 11 cass. (Running Time: 16 hrs. 30 min.). 1993. 88.00 (978-0-7366-2462-6(7), 3226) Books on Tape.
Germaine Greer challenges all our accepted notions about the effects of menopause & aging.

Change & Acceptance. Edd Anthony. Read by Edd Anthony. 2007. audio compact disk 16.95 (978-1-881586-17-3(0)) Canticle Cass.

Change & Transition: Moving from a State of Fear into a State of Love. Louise L. Hay. Read by Louise L. Hay. 1 cass. (Running Time: 1 hr.). (Conversations on Living Lecture Ser.). 1992. reel tape 10.00 (978-1-56170-024-0(X), 251) Hay House.
Louise explains to us the difficulties we may encounter when we are going through our period of "change & transition". She assures us that sometimes we fall into old patterns whenever we are learning anything new.

Change & Transition: Moving from a State of Fear into a State of Love. Louise L. Hay. 1 CD. (Running Time: 90 min.). 2005. audio compact disk 10.95 (978-1-4019-0427-2(0)) Hay House.

***Change Anything: The New Science of Personal Success.** unabr. ed. Kerry Patterson et al. (Running Time: 9 hrs.). (ENG.). 2011. 26.98 (978-1-60941-988-2(X)); audio compact disk & audio compact disk 29.98 (978-1-60941-987-5(1)) Pub: Hachet Audio. Dist(s): HachBkGrp

Change at the Speed of Thought! Louise LeBrun & Roger Ellerton. 2000. ring bd. 209.00 (978-0-9685566-9-6(8)) Par3tners Renewal CAN.

Change Eating Habits. Read by Mary Richards. 12.95 (201) Master Your Mind.
Presents a willingness to create new healthy behavior that supports a slender, physically fit body.

Change for a Farthing. unabr. ed. Ken McCoy. Contrib. by Ken McCoy. 8 cass. (Story Sound Ser.). (J). 2006. 69.95 (978-1-85903-866-6(2)); audio compact disk 84.95 (978-1-85903-989-2(8)) Pub: Mgna Lrg Print GBR. Dist(s): Ulverscroft US

Change for the Better: Poetry & the Reimagination of Midlife - a Talk by David Whyte. Speeches. Featuring David Whyte. one. 2002. audio compact disk 15.00 (978-1-932887-01-3(6)) Many Rivers Pr.
On "A Change for the Better: Poetry and the Reimagination of Midlife", David speaks to an increasing sense of vulnerability as a key experience of midlife - a vulnerability not to be truned from, but inhabited almost as a new faculty of perception - a doorway to the next stage of life and a sixth sense that can put us into a new converation with the world.

Change in Altitude. unabr. ed. Anita Shreve. Read by Anita Shreve. Read by Emma Walton Hamilton et al. (Running Time: 9 hrs.). (ENG.). 2009. 19.98 (978-1-60024-765-1(2)) Pub: Hachet Audio. Dist(s): HachBkGrp

Change in Altitude. unabr. ed. Anita Shreve. Read by Anna Stone. (Running Time: 9 hrs.). (ENG.). 2010. audio compact disk 19.98 (978-1-60788-213-8(2)) Pub: Hachet Audio. Dist(s): HachBkGrp

***Change in Altitude.** unabr. ed. Anita Shreve. Read by Anna Stone. 8 CDs. (Running Time: 9 hrs.). 2009. audio compact disk 80.00 (978-1-4159-6417-0(3), BksonTape) Pub: Random Audio Pubg. Dist(s): Random

Change in the Weather: Life after Stroke. unabr. ed. Mark McEwen. Told to Daniel Paisner. Narrated by Richard Allen. 1 MP3-CD. (Running Time: 7 hrs. 0 mins. 0 sec.). (ENG.). 2008. 19.99 (978-1-4001-5716-7(1)) Pub: Tantor Media. Dist(s): IngramPubServ

Change in the Weather: Life after Stroke. unabr. ed. Mark McEwen & Daniel Paisner. Narrated by Richard Allen. Frwd. by Bill Cosby. 6 CDs. (Running Time: 7 hrs. 0 mins. 0 sec.). (ENG.). 2008. audio compact disk 29.99 (978-1-4001-0716-2(4)); audio compact disk 59.99 (978-1-4001-3716-9(0)) Pub: Tantor Media. Dist(s): IngramPubServ

Change Management in Action: The InfoManage Interviews, December, 1993-November, 1998: Industry Leaders Describe How They Manage Change in Information Services. Guy St. Clair. 1 cass. 1999. pap. bk. 59.00 (978-0-87111-500-3(X)) SLA.

Change Masters. Rosabeth Moss Kanter. Intro. by A. E. Whyte. 1 cass. (Running Time: 42 min.). (Listen & Learn USA! Ser.). 8.95 (978-0-88684-017-4(1)) Listen USA.
Explains how to make innovation work to effectively influence workers & the corporate workplace.

Change Me Now. Contrib. by Babbie Mason. (Spring Hill Studio Tracks Plus Ser.). 2006. audio compact disk 9.98 (978-5-558-14308-9(8)) Sprg Hill Music Group.

Change of Command Part 1. Elizabeth Moon. 2009. audio compact disk 19.99 (978-1-59950-571-8(1)) GraphicAudio.

Change of Command Part 2. Elizabeth Moon. (Serrano Legacy Ser.: Bk. 6). 2009. audio compact disk 19.99 (978-1-59950-580-0(0)) GraphicAudio.

Change of Gravity. unabr. ed. George V. Higgins. Read by Adams Morgan. 13 cass. (Running Time: 19 hrs.). 1998. 85.95 (978-0-7861-1300-2(6), 2212) Blckstn Audio.
For Ambrose Merrion, life was a matter of people taking care of one another, with society picking up the slack when family & friends weren't enough. For Danny Hilliard, politics was a matter of gaining & using power to make sure that society did just that. But then something went wrong. The law of political gravity had changed, & what was good clean wickedness in 1960 had become a felony in 1996.

Change of Gravity. unabr. ed. George V. Higgins. Read by Michael Kramer. 14 cass. (Running Time: 21 hrs.). 1998. 112.00 (978-0-7366-4050-3(9), 4549) Books on Tape.
A political candidate's past connections are examined in a larceny investigation. A lively & ironic look at local politics.

Change of Heart. Lucile Johnson. 1 cass. 9.95 (978-1-57734-317-2(4), 06005853) Covenant Comms.
Reliance on the Lord is the key to true growth & change.

Change of Heart. unabr. ed. Jodi Picoult. 12 cass. (Running Time: 15 hrs. 15 mins.). 2008. 113.75 (978-1-4281-8056-7(7)); audio compact disk 123.75 (978-1-4281-8058-1(3)); 61.95 (978-1-4281-8057-4(5)) Recorded Bks.
Change of Heart explores capital punishment and organized religion through the tale of death row inmate Shay Bourne. Bourne's last request is to donate his heart to his victim's ailing sister. The situation gets more complicated when Bourne begins performing miracles in full view of witnesses - including his Catholic spiritual advisor.

Change of Heart. unabr. ed. Jodi Picoult. Narrated by Nicole Poole et al. 12 CDs. (Running Time: 15 hrs. 15 mins.). 2008. audio compact disk 39.99 (978-1-4281-9817-3(2)) Recorded Bks.

Change of Mind: How to Change Your Life by Changing Your Thoughts. Mac Hammond. 6 cds. (Running Time: 6 hours). 2005. audio compact disk 30.00 (978-1-57399-196-4(1)) Mac Hammond.
Discover how a distored perception can lock you into bad situations, the three levels of mental activity and how to put them to work, keys to pulling down mental strongholds, how to "plug-in" to God's power source for change, and much more.

Change of Mind: How to Change Your Life by Changing Your Thoughts. Mac Hammond. 6 cass. 1996. 36.00 Set. (978-1-57399-052-3(3)) Mac Hammond.
How to change your behavior by changing your thoughts.

***Change or Die.** unabr. ed. Alan Deutschman. Read by Brian Keeler. (ENG.). 2006. (978-0-06-128723-7(7), Harper Audio); (978-0-06-128724-4(5), Harper Audio) HarperCollins Pubs.

Change or Die: The Three Keys to Change at Work & in Life. unabr. ed. Alan Deutschman. Read by Brian Keeler. 2007. audio compact disk 29.95 (978-0-06-123086-8(3)) HarperCollins Pubs.

Change Rearrange. Read by Janet Kuypers. 2002. audio compact disk 6.22 (978-1-891470-50-9(7)) Scars Pubns.
This CD is of original poetry by Janet Kuypers, read with music sampled in the background.

Change the Atmosphere with Encouraging Words. Compiled by Tonya Whiteside. (ENG.). 2008. audio compact disk 12.95 (978-0-9797393-1-6(4)) Whiteside CA.

Change the Channel on Pain. 1 cassette. 1983. 12.95 (978-1-55841-046-6(5)) Emmett E Miller.
Two thoroughly relaxing and soothing experiences teach you to use techniques to tune out pain and tune in relief. For chronic or acute pain - "Change the Channel".

Change the Channel on Pain. 1 CD. 1983. audio compact disk 16.95 (978-1-55841-123-4(2)) Emmett E Miller.
Two thoroughly relaxing and soothing guided meditations teach you to use techniques to tune out pain and tune in relief. For chronic or acute pain - "Change the channel.".

Change the World or Change Yourself Series. 3 cass. 23.00 Crystal Clarity.
Discusses: Is the World Getting Better?; Karma: What it is & How to change It; Tapping Your Inner Power.

Change Through Success & Anger Management Workshop. James W. Parrott, Jr. 2004. audio compact disk 12.00 (978-0-9742312-5-9(8)) Treasure The Monemt.

Change-Up. unabr. ed. John Feinstein. Read by John Feinstein. (ENG.). (J). (gr. 5). 2009. audio compact disk 34.00 (978-0-7393-8099-4(0), Listening Lib) Pub: Random Audio Pubg. Dist(s): Random

***Change-Up: Mystery at the World Series.** unabr. ed. John Feinstein. Read by John Feinstein. 6 CDs. (Running Time: 6 hrs. 33 mins.). (J). (gr. 5-7). 2009. audio compact disk 55.00 (978-0-7393-8101-4(6), Listening Lib) Pub: Random Audio Pubg. Dist(s): Random

Change We Can Believe In: Barack Obama's Plan to Renew America's Promise. unabr. ed. Read by Andre Blake. Frwd. by Barack Obama. 6 CDs. (Running Time: 6 hrs.). (ENG.). 2008. audio compact disk 19.95 (978-0-7393-8322-3(1), Random AudioBks) Pub: Random Audio Pubg. Dist(s): Random

Change We Can Believe In: Barack Obama's Plan to Renew America's Promise. unabr. ed. Barack Obama. Read by Andre Blake. 6 CDs. 2008. audio compact disk 70.00 (978-1-4159-6268-8(5), BksonTape) Pub: Random Audio Pubg. Dist(s): Random
At this defining moment in our history, Americans are hungry for change. After years of failed policies and failed politics from Washington, this is our chance to reclaim the American dream. Barack Obama has proven to be a new kind of leader - one who can bring people together, be honest about the challenges we face, and move this nation forward. Change We Can Believe In outlines his vision for America. In these pages you will find bold and specific ideas about how to fix our ailing economy and strengthen the middle class, make health care affordable for all, achieve energy independence, and keep America safe in a dangerous world. Change We Can Believe In asks you not just to believe in Barack Obama's ability to bring change to Washington, it asks you to believe in yours.

***Change Your Age: Audio CD Series, vol. 1.** Frank Wildman. Prod. by Change Your Age. (Running Time: 3 hrs). 2010. audio compact disk 49.95 (978-1-889618-05-0(5), The Intell Body Pr) Feldenkrais Move.

Change Your Aura, Change Your Life. Barbara Martin & Dimitr Moraitis. 2004. wbk. ed. 22.95 (978-0-9702118-2-8(1)) Pub: Spiritual Arts. Dist(s): AtlasBooks

Change Your Body, Change Your Life! The Diet Boot Camp Program. Jonny Bowden. 2006. audio compact disk 64.95 (978-0-9787416-0-0(9)) Jonny Bowden.

Change Your Brain, Change Your Body: Use Your Brain to Get & Keep the Body You Have Always Wanted. unabr. ed. Daniel G. Amen. Read by Marc Cashman. 2010. audio compact disk 40.00 (978-0-7393-8491-6(0), Random AudioBks) Pub: Random Audio Pubg. Dist(s): Random

***Change Your Brain, Change Your Body Cookbook: Cook Right to Live Longer, Look Younger, Be Thinner & Decrease Your Risk of Obesity, Depression, Alzheimer?s Disease, Heart Disease, Cancer & Diabetes.** Daniel G. Amen. 2010. audio compact disk 50.00 (978-1-886554-25-2(0)) MindWrks.

Change Your Brain, Change Your Life: The Breakthrough Program for Conquering Anxiety, Depression, Obsessiveness, Anger, & Impulsiveness. unabr. ed. Daniel G. Amen. Read by Daniel G. Amen. (Running Time: 46800 sec.). (ENG.). 2008. audio compact disk 29.95 (978-0-7393-7693-5(4), Random AudioBks) Pub: Random Audio Pubg. Dist(s): Random

Change Your Destiny. Richard A. Zarro & Mary Orser. Illus. by Robin Sherrer. 12 cass. (Running Time: 40 min. per cass.). Dramatization. 1988. 120.00 Set. (978-0-944812-20-4(1)) Trans Tech NY.
Features astrological advice.

Change Your Destiny: Aquarius. Richard A. Zarro & Mary Orser. Illus. by Robin Sherrer. (Running Time: 40 min.). Dramatization. 1988. 10.95 (978-0-944812-18-1(X)) Trans Tech NY.
Astrological advice for those born under the zodiac sign of Aquarius.

Change Your Destiny: Aries. Richard A. Zarro & Mary Orser. Illus. by Robin Sherrer. 1 cass. (Running Time: 40 min.). Dramatization. 1988. 10.95 (978-0-944812-08-2(2)) Trans Tech NY.
Astrological advice for those under the zodiac sign of Aries.

Change Your Destiny: Cancer. Richard A. Zarro & Mary Orser. Illus. by Robin Sherrer. 1 cass. (Running Time: 40 min.). Dramatization. 1988. 10.95 (978-0-944812-11-2(2)) Trans Tech NY.
Astrological advice for those under the zodiac sign of Cancer.

Change Your Destiny: Capricorn. Richard A. Zarro & Mary Orser. Illus. by Robin Sherrer. 1 cass. (Running Time: 40 min.). Dramatization. 1988. 10.95 (978-0-944812-17-4(1)) Trans Tech NY.
Astrological advice for those born under the zodiac sign of Capricorn.

Change Your Destiny: Gemini. Richard A. Zarro & Mary Orser. Illus. by Robin Sherrer. 1 cass. (Running Time: 40 min.). Dramatization. 1988. 10.95 (978-0-944812-10-5(4)) Trans Tech NY.
Astrological advice fro those born under the zodiac sign of Gemini.

Change Your Destiny: Leo. Richard A. Zarro & Mary Orser. Illus. by Robin Sherrer. 1 cass. (Running Time: 40 min.). Dramatization. 1988. 10.95 (978-0-944812-12-9(0)) Trans Tech NY.
Astrological advice for those born under the zodiac sign of Leo.

Change Your Destiny: Libra. Richard A. Zarro & Mary Orser. Illus. by Robin Sherrer. 1 cass. (Running Time: 40 min.). Dramatization. 1988. 10.95 (978-0-944812-14-3(7)) Trans Tech NY.
Astrological advice for those born under the zodiac sign Libra.

Change Your Destiny: Pisces. Richard A. Zarro & Mary Orser. Illus. by Robin Sherrer. 1 cass. (Running Time: 40 min.). Dramatization. 1988. 10.95 (978-0-944812-19-8(8)) Trans Tech NY.
Astrological advice for those born under the zodiac sign of Pisces.

Change Your Destiny: Sagittarius. Richard A. Zarro & Mary Orser. Illus. by Robin Sherrer. (Running Time: 40 min.). Dramatization. 1988. 10.95 (978-0-944812-16-7(3)) Trans Tech NY.
Astrological advice for those born under the zodiac sign of Sagittarius.

Change Your Destiny: Scorpio. Richard A. Zarro & Mary Orser. Illus. by Robin Sherrer. (Running Time: 40 min.). Dramatization. 1988. 10.95 (978-0-944812-15-0(5)) Trans Tech NY.
Astrological advice for those born under the zodiac sign of Scorpio.

Change Your Destiny: Taurus. Richard A. Zarro & Mary Orser. Illus. by Robin Sherrer. 1 cass. (Running Time: 40 min.). Dramatization. 1988. 10.95 (978-0-944812-09-9(0)) Trans Tech NY.
Astrological advice for those born under the sign of Taurus.

Change Your Destiny: Virgo. Richard A. Zarro & Mary Orser. Illus. by Robin Sherrer. 1 cass. (Running Time: 40 min.). Dramatization. 1988. 10.95 (978-0-944812-13-6(9)) Trans Tech NY.
Astrological Advice for those born under the zodiac sign of Virgo.

Change Your Life... And Do It Now! Seven Secret Strategies to Help You Design & Live! The Life of Your Dreams. unabr. ed. Tom K. Puderbaugh. Read by Tom K. Puderbaugh. 1 cass. (Running Time: 1 hr.). 1996. 14.95 (978-1-889132-02-0(0)) Dev Dynamics.
Lif change & goal setting strategies made easy through a customized "change plan" made especially for you.

Change Your Life in 30 Days. unabr. ed. Rhonda Britten. Read by Rhonda Britten. (Running Time: 8 hrs.). (ENG.). 2004. audio compact disk 29.95 (978-1-56511-884-3(7), 1565118847) Pub: HighBridge. Dist(s): Workman Pub

Change Your Life in 30 Days: A Journey to Finding Your True Self. Rhonda Britten. Read by Rhonda Britten. (Playaway Adult Nonfiction Ser.). (ENG.). 2008. 44.99 (978-1-60640-932-9(8)) Find a World.

Change Your Metabolism: Hypnotic & Subliminal Learning. David Illig. 1985. 14.99i (978-0-86580-002-1(2)) Success World.

Change Your Mind & Life, Set. unabr. ed. Scripts. Teri D. Mahaney. Read by Teri D. Mahaney. 11 cass. (Running Time: 18 hrs.). (Self Empowerment Ser.). 1992. 100.00 (978-0-9624140-9-1(3), 7000) Supertraining Pr.
Introduction, Your First Step, Releasing Your Past, Healing Your Childhood, Claiming Your Personal Power, Speaking Up For Yourself, Making Decisions & Taking Action, Accepting Changes & Facing Your Future, Achieving Success 1, Achieving Success - Women, Achieving Success - Men.

Change Your Mind & Life: Attaining Inner Peace. rev. ed. Scripts. Teri D. Mahaney. Read by Teri D. Mahaney. 1 cass. (Running Time: 1 hr. 35 min.). (Spirituality Ser.: 6). 2002. 20.00 (978-1-893158-22-1(5), SP 6) Supertraining Pr.
Life Changing on Statements on Attaining Inner Peace, Simplicity/Living in the Present, Spiritual Practices/Meditation, Congruence/Coherence, Surrender.

Change Your Mind & Life: Living Your Spiritual Purpose. rev. ed. Scripts. Teri D. Mahaney. Read by Teri D. Mahaney. 1 cass. (Running Time: 1 hr. 35 min.). (Spirituality Ser.: 4). 2001. 20.00 (978-1-893158-17-7(9), SP 4) Supertraining Pr.
Life Changing Statements on Opening to Life/Awakening, Being Whole, Spiritual Courage, Spiritual Purpose/Purification, Special Gifts & Talents, Personal Path, Mastery/Spiritual Fellowship, Serving, Being, Served.

Change Your Mind/Life: Accepting Changes & Facing Your Future. rev. ed. Scripts. Teri D. Mahaney. Read by Teri D. Mahaney. 1 cass. (Running Time: 1 hr. 35 min.). (Self Empowerment Ser.: 6). 2001. 20.00 (978-1-893158-05-4(5), EM 6) Supertraining Pr.
Life Changing Statements on Change, Having Expectations, Being Certain & Secure, Establishing Order/Flowing with Chaos, Having Faith & Trust, Facing the Future.

Change Your Mind/Life: Achieving Right Livelihood. (Money Ser.: 3). 2001. 20.00 (978-1-893158-45-0(4), MO 3) Supertraining Pr.

Change Your Mind/Life: Achieving Success. (Success Ser.: 6). 2002. 20.00 (978-1-893158-54-2(3), SU 6) Supertraining Pr.

Change Your Mind/Life: Balancing Your Energy Centers. rev. ed. Scripts. Teri D. Mahaney. Read by Teri D. Mahaney. 1 cass. (Running Time: 1 hr. 35 min.). (Spirituality Ser.: 2). 2001. 20.00 (978-1-893158-14-6(4), HE 2) Supertraining Pr.
Life Changing Statements on Root Center Sexual Center, Power Center, Heart Center, Throat Center, Third Eye Center, Crown Center.

Change Your Mind/Life: Being Organized. (Success Ser.: 2). 2002. 20.00 (978-1-893158-50-4(0), SU 2) Supertraining Pr.

Change Your Mind/Life: Being Proactive. (Success Ser.: 1). 2002. 20.00 (978-1-893158-49-8(7), SU 1) Supertraining Pr.

Change Your Mind/Life: Claiming Your Personal Power, rev. ed. Scripts. Teri D. Mahaney. Read by Teri D. Mahaney. 1 cass. (Running Time: 1 hr. 35 min.). (Self Empowerment Ser.: 4). 2001. 20.00 (978-1-893158-04-7(7), EM 4) Supertraining Pr.
Life Changing Statements on Empowerment, Being Taken Seriously, Setting Limits/Boundaries, Serving Others/Being Needed, Being a Martyr.

Change Your Mind/Life: Communicating Effectively. (Success Ser.: 4). 2002. 20.00 (978-1-893158-52-8(7), SU 4) Supertraining Pr.

Change Your Mind/Life: Empowerment SuperSleep Series. (Empowerment Ser.). 2001. 100.00 (978-0-9624140-4-6(2), EMS) Supertraining Pr.

Change Your Mind/Life: Giving Purposefully. (Money Ser.: 6). 2001. 20.00 (978-1-893158-48-1(9), MO 6) Supertraining Pr.

Change Your Mind/Life: Grounding Your Spirituality. rev. ed. Teri D. Mahaney. Read by Teri D. Mahaney. 1 cass. (Running Time: 1 hr. 35 min.). (Spirituality Ser.: 1). 1995. 20.00 incl. script . (978-1-893158-13-9(6), SP 1) Supertraining Pr.
Life Changing Statements on Grounding, Spirituality & Divinity, Soul, Personality, Guidance & Gurus, Dark Mind, Light Mind.

Change Your Mind/Life: Healing Money Wounds. (Money Ser.: 2). 2001. 20.00 (978-1-893158-44-3(6), MO 2) Supertraining Pr.

Change Your Mind/Life: Healing Your Childhood. rev. ed. Scripts. Teri D. Mahaney. Read by Teri D. Mahaney. 1 cass. (Running Time: 1 hr. 35 min.). (Empowerment Ser.: 2). 2001. 20.00 (978-1-893158-03-0(9), EM 2) Supertraining Pr.
Life Changing Statements on Childhood, Having a Troubled Family, Bonding/Being Intimate, Being Visible, Being Abused/Abandoned, Expressing Feelings, Shame.

Change Your Mind/Life: Introduction to the SuperSleep Program. Scripts. Teri D. Mahaney. Read by Teri D. Mahaney. 1 cass. (Running Time: 1 hr. 35 min.). (Self Empowerment Ser.). (J). 1992. 3.00 (978-1-893158-00-9(4), IN 1) Supertraining Pr.
Lecture on how the program began & developed, summary of subliminal research, case studies, & most commonly asked questions.

Change Your Mind/Life: Investing Profitably. (Money Ser.: 5). 2001. 5.00 (978-1-893158-47-4(0), MO 5) Supertraining Pr.

Change Your Mind/Life: Loving Commitment. Scripts. Teri D. Mahaney. Read by Teri D. Mahaney. 1 cass. (Running Time: 1 hr. 35 min.). (Loving Relationship Ser.: 3). 1999. 20.00 (978-1-893158-30-6(6), LO 3) Supertraining Pr.
Affirmations for self improvement.

Change Your Mind/Life: Loving Communication. Scripts. Teri D. Mahaney. Read by Teri D. Mahaney. 1 cass. (Running Time: 1 hr. 35 min.). (Loving Relationship Ser.: 5). 1998. 20.00 (978-1-893158-31-3(4), LR 5) Supertraining Pr.

Change Your Mind/Life: Loving Conflict. Scripts. Teri D. Mahaney. Read by Teri D. Mahaney. 1 cass. (Running Time: 1 hr. 35 min.). (Loving Relationship Ser.: 6). 1998. 20.00 (978-1-893158-32-0(2), LR 6) Supertraining Pr.

Change Your Mind/Life: Loving Courtship. Scripts. Teri D. Mahaney. Read by Teri D. Mahaney. 1 cass. (Running Time: 1 hr. 35 min.). (Loving Relationship Ser.: 2). 1999. 20.00 (978-1-893158-29-0(2), LO 2) Supertraining Pr.

Change Your Mind/Life: Loving Family. Scripts. Teri D. Mahaney. Read by Teri D. Mahaney. 1 cass. (Running Time: 1 hr. 30 min.). (Loving Relationship Ser.: 3). 1998. 20.00 (978-1-893158-28-3(4), LR 3) Supertraining Pr.

Change Your Mind/Life: Loving Friendships. Teri D. Mahaney. Read by Teri D. Mahaney. (Running Time: 1 hr. 35 min.). (Loving Relationship Ser.: 4). 1998. 20.00 incl. script 1 cass. (978-1-893158-26-9(8), LR 4) Supertraining Pr.

Change Your Mind/Life: Loving Intimacy. Scripts. Teri D. Mahaney. Read by Teri D. Mahaney. 1 cass. (Running Time: 1 hr. 35 min.). (Loving Relationship Ser.: 4). 1999. 20.00 (978-1-893158-33-7(0), LO 4) Supertraining Pr.

Change Your Mind/Life: Loving Partnership I. Scripts. Teri D. Mahaney. Read by Teri D. Mahaney. 1 cass. (Running Time: 1 hr. 35 min.). (Loving Relationship Ser.: 5). 1999. 20.00 (978-1-893158-34-4(9), LO 5) Supertraining Pr.

Change Your Mind/Life: Loving Partnership SuperSLeep Series. (Loving Partnership Ser.). 2002. 100.00 (978-0-9624140-6-0(9)) Supertraining Pr.

Change Your Mind/Life: Loving Partnership 2. Scripts. Teri D. Mahaney. Read by Teri D. Mahaney. 1 cass. (Running Time: 1 hr. 35 min.). (Loving Relationship Ser.: 6). 1999. 20.00 (978-1-893158-35-1(7), LO 6) Supertraining Pr.

Change Your Mind/Life: Loving Relationships SuperSleep Series. rev. ed. (Loving Relationship Ser.). 2002. 100.00 (978-0-9624140-5-3(0), LRS) Supertraining Pr.

Change Your Mind/Life: Managing Information & Technology. (Success Ser.: 5). 2002. 20.00 (978-1-893158-53-5(5), SU 5) Supertraining Pr.

Change Your Mind/Life: Managing Money Flow. (Money Ser.: 4). 2001. 20.00 (978-1-893158-46-7(2), MO 4) Supertraining Pr.

Change Your Mind/Life: Manifesting with Ease. (Spirituality Ser.: 5). 2002. 20.00 (978-1-893158-58-0(6), SP 5) Supertraining Pr.

Change Your Mind/Life: Money SuperSleep Series. (Money Ser.). 2001. 100.00 (978-0-9624140-3-9(4), MOS) Supertraining Pr.

Change Your Mind/Life: Opening to Healing. Scripts. Teri D. Mahaney. Read by Teri D. Mahaney. 1cass. (Running Time: 1 hr. 35 min.). (Spirituality Ser.: 1). 1998. 20.00 (978-1-893158-20-7(9), HE 1) Supertraining Pr.
Life Changing Statements on Healing, Taking Responsibility, Faith & Prayer, Spiritual Healing, Mental Healing, Emotional Healing, Physical Healing.

Change Your Mind/Life: Opening to Love. Scripts. Teri D. Mahaney. Read by Teri D. Mahaney. 1 cass. (Running Time: 1 hr. 35 min.). (Loving Relationship Ser.: 1). 1998. 20.00 (978-1-893158-24-5(1), LR 1) Supertraining Pr.
Affirmations for self improvement.

Change Your Mind/Life: Opening to Wealth. (Money Ser.: 1). 2001. 20.00 (978-1-893158-43-6(8), MO 1) Supertraining Pr.

Change Your Mind/Life: Opening Your Heart. Scripts. Teri D. Mahaney. Read by Teri D. Mahaney. 1 cass. (Running Time: 1 hr. 35 min.). (Spirituality Ser.: 3). 1995. 20.00 (978-1-893158-15-3(2), HE 3) Supertraining Pr.
Life Changing Statements on Opening Your Heart, Loving & Being Loved, Being Nourished, Unconditional Love, Compassion, Death Urge & Life Force, Radiance.

Change Your Mind/Life: Releasing Past Relationships. Teri D. Mahaney. Read by Teri D. Mahaney. 1 cass. (Running Time: 1 hr. 35 min.). (Loving Relationship Ser.: 1). 1999. 20.00 incl. script. (978-1-893158-27-6(6), LO 1) Supertraining Pr.

Change Your Mind/Life: Releasing Your Past, rev. ed. Scripts. Teri D. Mahaney. Read by Teri D. Mahaney. 1 cass. (Running Time: 1 hr. 35 min.). (Self Empowerment Ser.: 3). 2002. 20.00 (978-1-893158-02-3(0), EM 3) Supertraining Pr.
Life Changing Statements on Releasing & Forgiving Self & Others, Releasing Guilt, Grieving/The Grieving Process.

Change Your Mind/Life: Solving Problems Wisely. (Success Ser.: 3). 2002. 20.00 (978-1-893158-51-1(9), SU 3) Supertraining Pr.

Change Your Mind/Life: Speaking up for Yourself. rev. ed. Scripts. Teri D. Mahaney. Read by Teri D. Mahaney. 1 cass. (Running Time: 1 hr. 35 min.). (Self Empowerment Ser.: 5). 2001. 20.00 (978-1-893158-07-8(1), EM 5) Supertraining Pr.
Life Changing Statements on Speaking Up, Being Assertive, Asking for What you Want & Need, Saying No, Being Passive - Aggressive.

Change Your Mind/Life: Spirituality SuperSleep Series. (Spirituality Ser.). 2002. 100.00 (978-1-893158-55-9(1), SPS) Supertraining Pr.

Change Your Mind/Life: Success SuperSleep Series. (Success Ser.). 2002. 100.00 (978-0-9624140-2-2(6), SUS) Supertraining Pr.

Change Your Mind/Life: Transcending Cause & Effect. (Spirituality Ser.: 2). 2002. 20.00 (978-1-893158-56-6(X), SP 2) Supertraining Pr.

Change Your Mind/Life: Trusting Your Guidance. (Spirituality Ser.: 3). 2002. 20.00 (978-1-893158-57-3(8), SP 3) Supertraining Pr.

Change Your Mind/Life: Your First Step. rev. ed. Scripts. Teri D. Mahaney. Read by Teri D. Mahaney. 1 cass. (Running Time: 1 hr. 35 min.). (Empowerment Ser.: 1). 2001. 20.00 (978-1-893158-01-6(2), EM 1) Supertraining Pr.
Life Changing Statements on Change, Self Esteem, Receiving/Being Supported, Control & Authority, Using Change Your Mind.

Change Your Mind/Life Set: Loving Yourself. Scripts. Teri D. Mahaney. Read by Teri D. Mahaney. 2 cass. (Running Time: 1 hr. 35 min.). (Loving Relationship Ser.: 2). 1998. 20.00 (978-1-893158-25-2(X), LR 2) Supertraining Pr.
Life Changing Statements on Self Hatred, Punishment, Vectimgation, Being Dishonored, Perfectionism, Unrealistic Expectations, Losing yourself.

Change Your Thoughts - Change Your Life: Living the Wisdom of the Tao. unabr. ed. Wayne W. Dyer. Read by Wayne W. Dyer. 8 CDs. (Running Time: 8 hrs.). (ENG., 2007. audio compact disk 39.95 (978-1-4019-1185-0(4)) Hay House.

Change Your Thoughts - Change Your Life, Live Seminar! Living the Wisdom of the Tao. Wayne W. Dyer. (ENG.). 2009. audio compact disk 45.00 (978-1-4019-1973-3(1)) Hay House.

Change Your Thoughts, Change Your Life: Living the Wisdom of the Tao. unabr. ed. Wayne W. Dyer. Read by Wayne W. Dyer. (YA). 2008. 59.99 (978-1-60514-877-9(6)) Find a World.

Change Your Thoughts Meditation: Do the Tao Now! unabr. abr. ed. Wayne W. Dyer. 1 CD. (Running Time: 1 hr.). 2007. audio compact disk 15.00 (978-1-4019-1910-8(3)) Hay House.

Change Your World. Prod. by Michael W. Smith. 1 CD. 1992. audio compact disk Brentwood Music.
Michael's best-selling release to date, nearing platinum, features the No. 1 mainstream radio hit, I Will Be Here for You & the anthem, Give it Away.

Change Your World. Contrib. by Darlene Zschech. Prod. by David Holmes & Andy Sorenson. 2005. audio compact disk 13.97 (978-5-558-73806-3(5)) INO Rec.

Changed Life & Dealing with Doubt. unabr. ed. Henry Drummond. 1 CD. (Running Time: 1 hr. 15 mins. 0 sec.). (ENG.). 2004. audio compact disk 12.98 (978-1-59644-031-9(7), Hovel Audio) christianaud.
Professor of the natural sciences, world lecturer, and missionary, Henry Drummond was a man of multiple talents and interests. His penetrating scientific mind enabled him to tackle topics such as the way to become like Christ (The Changed Life) and objections to faith (Dealing with Doubt) with clarity and accuracy.

***Changed Life & Dealing with Doubt.** unabr. ed. Henry Drummond. Narrated by Paul Eggington. (Running Time: 1 hr. 15 mins. 0 sec.). (ENG.). 2004. 8.98 (978-1-59644-029-6(5), Hovel Audio) christianaud.

Changed Life & The Greatest Thing in the World. Henry Drummond. Narrated by Pamela Garelick. 2 CDs. (Running Time: 2 hrs. 30 mins.). 2001. audio compact disk 16.00 (978-0-7861-9627-2(0), 2909) Blckstn Audio.
The Writings of nineteenth-century Scottish Evangelist Henry Drummond can be enjoyed as originally planned, as sermons designed to inspire positive change within the listener.

Changed Life & the Greatest Thing in the World. Henry Drummond. Narrated by Pamela Garelick. (Running Time: 3 hrs.). 2001. 20.95 (978-1-59912-631-9(1)) Iofy Corp.

Changed Life & The Greatest Thing in the World. unabr. ed. Henry Drummond. Narrated by Pamela Garelick. 2 cass. (Running Time: 2 hrs. 30 mins.). 2001. 17.95 (978-0-7861-2136-6(X), 2909) Blckstn Audio.

Changed Man. unabr. ed. Francine Prose. Read by Eric Conger. 2005. audio compact disk 39.95 (978-0-06-077651-0(X)) HarperCollins Pubs.

***Changed Man.** unabr. ed. Francine Prose. Read by Eric Conger. (ENG.). 2005. (978-0-06-083938-3(4), Harper Audio); (978-0-06-083937-6(6), Harper Audio) HarperCollins Pubs.

Changeless Dwelling Place. Kenneth Wapnick. 4 CDs. 2005. audio compact disk 25.00 (978-1-59142-218-1(3), CD76) Foun Miracles.

Changeling see Evil, Exploration Of

Changeling. unabr. ed. Yasmine Galenorn. Narrated by Cassandra Campbell. (Running Time: 11 hrs. 0 mins. 0 sec.). (Sisters of the Moon Ser.). (ENG.). 2009. audio compact disk 34.99 (978-1-4001-1002-5(5)); audio compact disk 69.99 (978-1-4001-4002-2(1)); audio compact disk 24.99 (978-1-4001-6002-0(2)) Pub: Tantor Media. Dist(s): IngramPubServ

Changes. unabr. ed. Jim Butcher. Read by James Marsters. 13 CDs. (Running Time: 16 hrs.). Bk. 12. (ENG.). (gr. 12 up). 2010. audio compact disk 49.95 (978-0-14-314534-9(7), PengAudBks) Penguin Grp USA.

***Changes.** unabr. ed. Jim Butcher. Narrated by James Marsters. 13 cass. (Running Time: 15 hrs. 45 mins.). (Dresden Files Ser.: Bk. 12). 2010. 113.75 (978-1-4498-1661-2(4)); audio compact disk 123.75 (978-1-4498-1662-9(2)) Recorded Bks.

***Changes.** unabr. ed. Jim Butcher. Narrated by James Marsters. 1 Playaway. (Running Time: 15 hrs. 45 mins.). (Dresden Files Ser.: Bk. 12). 2010. 64.75 (978-1-4498-1664-3(9)) Recorded Bks.

***Changes.** unabr. collector's ed. Jim Butcher. Narrated by James Marsters. 13 CDs. (Running Time: 15 hrs. 45 mins.). (Dresden Files Ser.: Bk. 12). 2010. audio compact disk 61.95 (978-1-4498-1663-6(0)) Recorded Bks.

Changes at Fairacre. Miss Read Staff. Read by June Barrie. 6 CDs. (Running Time: 26040 sec.). 2005. audio compact disk 64.95 (978-0-7927-3801-5(2), SLD 866) AudioGO.

Changes at Fairacre. Miss Read. Read by June Barrie. 5 cass. 49.95 (978-0-7927-3800-8(4), CSL 866) AudioGO.

Changes, Changes. 2004. 8.95 (978-1-56008-863-9(X)); cass. & flmstrp 30.00 (978-0-89719-549-2(3)) Weston Woods.

Changes, Changes. (J). 2004. bk. 24.95 (978-1-56008-176-0(7)); pap. bk. 14.95 (978-1-56008-177-7(5)) Weston Woods.

Changes, Changes. Pat Hutchins. 1 cass. (Running Time: 6 min.). (J). (ps-3). 2000. pap. bk. 12.95 Weston Woods.
Two enterprising wooden dolls solve a series of problems by arranging & rearranging a set of wooden blocks to music performed solely on wooden instruments. A nonverbal classic.

Changes in Latitudes, unabr. ed. William Hobbs. Narrated by Johnny Heller. 3 pieces. (Running Time: 4 hrs. 15 mins.). (gr. 7 up). 1997. 27.00 (978-0-7887-0890-9(2), 95028E7) Recorded Bks.
Travis is looking for a good time. But his vacation to Mexico becomes a rite of passage as he finds himself dealing with his parents' impending divorce & his little brother's worrisome obsession with saving the endangered sea turtles.

Changes Intro: English for International Communication. Jack C. Richards. (Running Time: hrs. mins.). (Changes Ser.). 1998. stu. ed. 42.00 (978-0-521-62641-5(2)) Cambridge U Pr.

***Changes That Heal: How to Understand the Past to Ensure a Healthier Future.** abr. ed. Henry Cloud. (Running Time: 2 hrs. 0 mins. 0 sec.). (ENG.). 2003. 10.99 (978-0-310-26234-3(8)) Zondervan.

Changes That Heal: How to Understand the Past to Ensure a Healthier Future. unabr. ed. Henry Cloud. (Running Time: 11 hrs. 2 mins. 0 sec.). (ENG.). 2003. 23.99 (978-0-310-26145-2(7)) Zondervan.

Changes That Heal: How to Understand Your Past to Ensure a Healthier Future. Henry Cloud. 2 cass. (Running Time: 60 min.). 1996. 16.99 (978-0-310-20567-8(0)) Zondervan.

Changes Within You. abr. ed. Lee Carroll. Read by Lee Carroll. 1 cass. (Running Time: 1 hr.). (Kryon Tapes Ser.). 1995. 10.00 (978-0-9636304-9-0(0)) Kryon Writings.
Live recording of channelled event.

Changes 1: English for International Communication. Jack C. Richards et al. 1 cass. (Running Time: hrs. mins.). (Changes Ser.). 1994. stu. ed. 24.15 (978-0-521-44938-0(3)) Cambridge U Pr.

Changing Channels: Songs for TV & Media Smart Kids, Creative Conflict Resolution & More. Cathy Fink & Marcy Marxer. (J). 1998. 9.98 (978-1-57940-021-7(3)); audio compact disk 14.98 (978-1-57940-020-0(5)) Rounder Records.
Series of thematic recordings designed to help nurture & educate children with social awareness. These songs have an almost music-class sound to them, which makes them easy for parents & teachers to incorporate into children's everyday lives.

Changing Concepts in Cancer Surgery. (Postgraduate Programs Ser.: C85-PG10). 85.00 (8520) Am Coll Surgeons.
Reviews new diagnostic & treatment methods for cancer patients. 12 hours CME category 1 credit.

Changing Directions Without Losing Your Way: Manging the Six Stages of Change at Work & in Life. Paul Edwards & Sarah Edwards. 2004. 10.95 (978-0-7435-4261-6(4)) Pub: S&S Audio. Dist(s): S and S Inc

Changing Directions 1. Perf. by Gemini. 1 cass. (Running Time: 90 mins.). 10.95 (978-0-931114-73-1(X), M2101-C) High-Scope.
International folk music to accompany the dances described in Phyllis Weikart's "Teaching Movement & Dance: Intermediate Folk Dance." Melodies include: Bat Arad, Hora Nirkoda, Sapari, Eretz Zavat, Shiru Hashir, Debka Chag, Hora Chadera, Erev Ba, plus more!.

Changing Directions 1. Perf. by Gemini. Directed By Phyllis S. Weikart. 1 CD. (Running Time: 90 mins.). 1986. audio compact disk 15.95 (978-0-929816-48-7(X), M2301) High-Scope.

Changing Directions 2. Perf. by Gemini. 1 cass. (Running Time: 90 mins.). 10.95 (978-0-931114-74-8(8), M2102-C) High-Scope.
International folk music to accompany the dances described in Phyllis Weikart's "Teaching Movement & Dance: Intermediate Folk Dance." Melodies include: La Bastringue, Trata, Soultana, Tsamiko, Debka Druz, Sulam Ya'Akov, Ki Hivshiloo, Ahavat Hadasseh, plus more!.

Changing Directions 2. Perf. by Gemini. Directed By Phyllis S. Weikart. 1 CD. (Running Time: 90 mins.). 1987. audio compact disk 15.95 CD. (978-0-929816-49-4(8), M2302) High-Scope.

Changing Directions 3. Perf. by Gemini. Directed By Phyllis S. Weikart. 1 CD. (Running Time: 90 mins.). 1988. audio compact disk 15.95 CD. (978-0-929816-50-0(1), M2303) High-Scope.
International folk music to accompany the dances described in Phyllis Weikart's "Teaching Movement & Dance: Intermediate Folk Dance." Melodies include: Milanovo Kolo, Lemonaki, Dragaicuta, Sauerlaender Quadrille No. 5, Karagouna, Ivanica, Harmonica, Sharm A'Sheikh, & more!.

Changing Directions 4. Perf. by Gemini. 1 cass. (Running Time: 90 mins.). 10.95 (978-0-929816-10-4(2), M2104-C); 10.95 record. (978-0-929816-09-8(9), M2104) High-Scope.
International folk music to accompany the dances described in Phyllis Weikart's "Teaching Movement & Dance: Intermediate Folk Dance." Melodies include: Danis Masquerade, Pentozalis, Sheikani, Kalamatianos, Rav B'rachot, Hadarim, Bat Tsurim, Al Gemali, & more!.

Changing Directions 4. Perf. by Gemini. Directed By Phyllis S. Weikart. 1 CD. (Running Time: 90 mins.). 1989. audio compact disk 15.95 (978-0-929816-51-7(X), M2304) High-Scope.

Changing Directions 5. Perf. by Gemini. 1 cass. (Running Time: 90 mins.). 10.95 (978-0-929816-20-3(X), M2105-C); 10.95 record. (978-0-929816-19-7(6), M2105) High-Scope.
International folk music to accompany the dances described in Phyllis Weikart's "Teaching Movement & Dance: Intermediate Folk Dance." Melodies include: Santa Rita, Azul Cielo, Kulsko Horo, Pasarelska, Kritikos, Syrtaki No. 7, Silivriano, Argo Hasapikos, & more!.

Changing Directions 5. Perf. by Gemini. Directed By Phyllis S. Weikart. 1 CD. (Running Time: 90 mins.). 1990. audio compact disk 15.95 (978-0-929816-52-4(8), M2305) High-Scope.

Changing Directions 6. Phyllis S. Weikart. 1 cass. or 1 CD. 10.95 (978-1-57379-051-2(6), M2106-C); audio compact disk 15.95 (978-1-57379-050-5(8), M2306) High-Scope.

Changing Emotions: A Stress-Management Program. Lloyd Glauberman. 2 cass. (Hypno-Peripheral Processing Tapes Ser.). 34.95 Set. (851PA-3M) Nightingale-Conant.
This breakthrough psychotechnology program combines the methods of hypnotherapy with the latest teachings of Neuro-Linguistic Programming. Each high-impact tape gently overloads your conscious mind with messages on two channels at once, creating a synergistic whole that unleashes both hemispheres of your brain.

Changing English. unabr. ed. 1 cass. 12.95 (ECN134) J Norton Pubs.
Looks at the developments that have taken place in the English language over the centuries & in modern times.

Changing Face of the Meat Department. 1 cass. (America's Supermarket Showcase '96 Ser.). 1996. 11.00 (NGA96-002) Sound Images.

Changing Faces. Kimberla Lawson Roby. Read by Tracey Leigh. 2006. audio compact disk 29.95 (978-0-7927-3963-0(9), CMP 899) AudioGO.

Changing Faces. Kimberla Lawson Roby. Read by Tracey Leigh. 6 cass. (Running Time: 31020 sec.). 2006. 54.95 (978-0-7927-3894-7(2), CSL 899); audio compact disk 74.95 (978-0-7927-3895-4(0), SLD 899) AudioGO.

***Changing Faces.** abr. ed. Kimberla Lawson Roby. Read by Lynn Chavis et al. (ENG.). 2006. (978-0-06-113455-5(4), Harper Audio); (978-0-06-113456-2(2), Harper Audio) HarperCollins Pubs.

Changing Faces. abr. ed. Kimberla Lawson Roby. Read by Lynn Chavis et al. 5 CDs. (Running Time: 21600 sec.). 2006. audio compact disk 29.95 (978-0-06-087637-1(9)) HarperCollins Pubs.

Changing First Amendment. unabr. ed. David Barton. Read by David Barton. 1 cass. (Running Time: 1 hrs.). 1996. bk. (978-0-925279-52-1(8)) Wallbuilders.
The current interpretation of the First Amendment as the "separation of church & state" is a modern phenomenon. Learn what our Founders originally intended for this Amendment & how its meaning has dramatically changed in the last half-century.

Changing for Good. J. Prochaska. Read by David Brand. 2004. 10.95 (978-0-7435-4262-3(2)) Pub: S&S Audio. Dist(s): S and S Inc

Changing Habit Patterns: A Meditation on Weight-Loss - A Typical Day As the New You. Diana Keck. Read by Diana Keck. 1 cass. 1985. 9.95 (978-0-929653-09-9(2), TAPE 402) Mntn Spirit Tapes.

Changing Habit Patterns: Healing the Emotions - Transforming Mental Habits. Diana Keck. Read by Diana Keck. 1 cass. 1985. 9.95 (978-0-929653-08-2(4), TAPE 401) Mntn Spirit Tapes.

Changing Habit Patterns: On Becoming a Non-Smoker - Imaging a New You. Diana Keck. Read by Diana Keck. 1 cass. 1985. 9.95 (978-0-929653-07-5(6), TAPE 400) Mntn Spirit Tapes.

***Changing Habits.** abr. ed. Debbie Macomber. Read by Trini Alvarado. (ENG.). 2004. (978-0-06-081819-7(0), Harper Audio); (978-0-06-081820-3(4), Harper Audio) HarperCollins Pubs.

Changing Habits. abr. ed. Debbie Macomber. Read by Trini Alvarado. 2005. audio compact disk 14.95 (978-0-06-082097-8(7)) HarperCollins Pubs.

Changing Hearts Changing Lives. Paul David Tripp & David Powlison. (ENG.). 2006. audio compact disk 87.95 (978-1-934885-60-4(6)) New Growth Pr.

Changing Light Winds see Carl Sandburg's Poems for Children

Changing My Mind. unabr. ed. Zadie Smith. Contrib. by Barbara Rosenblat. (Running Time: 13 hrs.). (ENG.). (gr. 12 up). 2009. audio compact disk 39.95 (978-0-14-314521-9(5)) Penguin Grp USA.

***Changing My Mind.** unabr. ed. Zadie Smith. Narrated by Barbara Rosenblat. 1 Playaway. (Running Time: 12 hrs. 30 mins.). 2009. 59.75 (978-1-4407-5403-6(9)); 82.75 (978-1-4407-5400-5(4)); audio compact disk 123.75 (978-1-4407-5401-2(2)) Recorded Bks.

***Changing My Mind.** unabr. collector's ed. Zadie Smith. Narrated by Barbara Rosenblat. 10 CDs. (Running Time: 12 hrs. 30 mins.). 2009. audio compact disk 51.95 (978-1-4407-5402-9(0)) Recorded Bks.

***Changing of the Guard.** 2010. audio compact disk (978-1-59171-209-1(2)) Falcon Picture.

Changing of the Guard. unabr. abr. ed. Steve Pieczenik et al. Read by Sam Tsoutsouvas. Created by Tom Clancy. 5 CDs. (Running Time: 6 hrs.). (Tom Clancy's Net Force Ser.: No. 8). 2004. audio compact disk 29.95 (978-0-06-050829-6(9)) HarperCollins Pubs.

Changing Our Mind Patterns. Swami Amar Jyoti. 1 cass. 1980. 9.95 (J-35) Truth Consciousness.
Not conditions but our mental patterns determine our mind's state. Higher values give higher energy. Intensity & longing for the Goal.

Changing Ourselves & the World. Swami Amar Jyoti. 1 cass. 1987. 9.95 (A-50) Truth Consciousness.
How can mankind change? The easiest course for change. Why we cannot truly help anyone unless we know ourselves first. The Divine as a way of living.

Changing Paradigms. unabr. ed. Fritjof Capra. 4 cass. 36.00 (OC88) Sound Horizons AV.

Changing Places: Cassette. Alan Hines. (Dominoes Ser.). 2004. 14.25 (978-0-19-424413-8(X)) OUP.

Changing Planes: Stories. unabr. ed. Ursula K. Le Guin. 5 cass. (Running Time: 7 hrs. 30 mins.). 2004. 27.95 (978-1-59007-519-7(6)) Pub: New Millenn Enter. Dist(s): PerseuPGW

Changing Planes: Stories. unabr. ed. Ursula K. Le Guin. Read by Gabrielle de Cuir. 7 CDs. (Running Time: 7 hrs. 30 mins.). 2004. audio compact disk 45.00 (978-1-59007-520-3(X)) Pub: New Millenn Enter. Dist(s): PerseuPGW

Changing Seasons/Insects Change. Steck-Vaughn Staff. 2002. (978-0-7398-5987-2(0)) SteckVau.

Changing Sky. unabr. collector's ed. Norman Lewis. Read by Richard Brown. 6 cass. (Running Time: 9 hrs.). 1990. 48.00 (978-0-7366-1852-6(X), 2685) Books on Tape.
"Travel came before writing. There was a time when I felt that all I wanted from life was to be allowed to remain a perpetual spectator of changing scenes. I managed my meager supply of money as to be able to surrender myself as much as possible to this addiction, & charged with a wonderful ignorance I went abroad by third class train, country bus, on foot, by canoe, by tramp steamer & by Arab dhow." With this credo, Norman Lewis took off for places far removed from our world. He sojourned in Belize, a surviving Caribbean colony of the last century; Guatemala, the last home of the unmodernized native - the Mayan Indian; & Ibiza, where men who wear shorts are arrested. His adventures are of the highest order.

Changing the Channel: 12 Easy Ways to Make Millions for Your Business. unabr. ed. MaryEllen Michael & Tribby Masterson. Read by Walter Dixon. (Running Time: 7 hrs. 30 mins.). (ENG.). 2008. 24.98 (978-1-59659-306-0(7), GildAudio) Pub: Gildan Media. Dist(s): HachBkGrp

Changing the Game: The New Way to Sell. Larry Wilson. Read by Larry Wilson. 6 cass. 59.95 Set. (466AD) Nightingale-Conant.
Start earning a six-figure income.

Changing the Picture, Set. unabr. ed. Zig Ziglar. Read by Zig Ziglar. Ed. by Bert Newman. 6 cass. (Running Time: 6 hrs.). (How to Stay Motivated Ser.: Vol. II). 1993. 69.95 (978-1-56207-233-9(1)) Zig Ziglar Corp.
Differentiate between being a Responder & a Reactor. This program gives you the eight steps to building a good self-image. Build a better, more productive, satisfying life for yourself & your family.

Changing the Rules of Our Lives: From High School to Midlife & Beyond. Layne A. Longfellow. Read by Layne A. Longfellow. 4 cass. 1986. 47.00 incl. article, graphs, bibliography Set. Lect Theatre.
Lecture on communication principles, "elevator etiquette" & psychological contracts; plus the complete Life Transitions seminar.

Changing the Workplace. Contrib. by Genevieve A. Chornenki. 1 CD. (Running Time: 1 hr.). 2005. audio compact disk 15.95 (978-0-660-19043-3(5)) Pub: Canadian Broadcasting CAN. Dist(s): Georgetown Term

Changing Times. AIO Team Staff. Prod. by Focus on the Family Staff. 4 CDs. (Running Time: 6 hrs.). (Adventures in Odyssey Ser.: Vol. 22). (ENG.). (J). (gr. 3-7). 1995. audio compact disk 24.99 (978-1-56179-380-8(9)) Pub: Focus Family. Dist(s): Tyndale Hse

Changing Times & the Arts. unabr. ed. Fannie Hurst. 1 cass. (Running Time: 15 min.). 1967. 12.95 (11001) J Norton Pubs.
A discussion of the changing times in the arts from Miss Hurst's special vantage point.

Changing Values: A Look at the Future. unabr. ed. Jennifer James. Read by Jennifer James. 1 cass. (Running Time: 1 hr.). 9.95 (978-0-915423-52-1(9)) Jennifer J.

Changing View of ADHD: Rules for Speech-Language Pathologists in Evaluation & Treatment in Students. Carol E. Westby. 1 cass. (Running Time: 1 hr.). 2000. pap. bk. 79.00 (978-1-58041-053-3(7), 0112250) Am Speech Lang Hearing.
Examine ADHD & explore implications for assessing & treating students with this disorder.

Changing Wanderers into Worshipers. 2002. 39.95 (978-1-57972-379-8(9)) Insight Living.

Changing Wanderers into Worshipers. 2002. audio compact disk 49.00 (978-1-57972-439-9(6)) Insight Living.

Changing Words. (23324) J Norton Pubs.

Changing World. 10.00 (HD418) Esstee Audios.

Chang's Paper Pony. Eleanor Coerr. Read by Jeff Woodman. 1 cass. (Running Time: 15 mins.). (YA). 2000. pap. bk. & stu. ed. 22.20 (978-0-7887-4099-2(7), 41104) Recorded Bks.
Every day Chang helps his Grandfather Li in the kitchen of the Gold Ditch Hotel. He feels lonely, until Big Pete, the tallest, strongest man Chang has ever seen, comes to town.

Chang's Paper Pony, Class set. Eleanor Coerr. Read by Jeff Woodman. 1 cass. (Running Time: 15 mins.). (YA). 2000. 70.30 (978-0-7887-4150-0(0), 47097) Recorded Bks.

Chang's Paper Pony: An I Can Read Book. unabr. ed. Eleanor Coerr. Narrated by Jeff Woodman. 1 cass. (Running Time: 15 mins.). (gr. 2 up). 2000. 10.00 (978-0-7887-4016-9(4), 96137E7) Recorded Bks.

Channel Capacity: Absolute Judgment. unabr. ed. Harold D. Fishbein. 1 cass. (Running Time: 21 min.). 1968. 12.95 (29050) J Norton Pubs.
A demonstration experiment dealing with the determination of our channel capacity for tones which vary along one & two dimensions (pitch & loudness). Included are introductory material, experimental instructions, & 7 subexperiments, employing the method of absolute judgment.

Channel Firing see Poetry of Thomas Hardy

Channeled Messages of Simon Peter. Kevin R. Emery & Thomas A. Hensel. 6 cass. 1996. 54.95 (978-1-890405-08-3(6)) LightLines.
Channeled teaching from Simon Peter as channeled through Rev. Kevin Ross Emery.

Channeling & the Nature of the Self. Jon Klimo. 2 cass. 18.00 set. (A0287-88) Sound Photosyn.
He writes the book each time anew.

Channeling Grace: Invoking the Power of the Divine. unabr. abr. ed. Caroline Myss. (Running Time: 9000 sec.). 2008. audio compact disk 19.95 (978-1-59179-953-5(8)) Sounds True.

Channeling Your Higher Self. Barrie Konicov. 4 cass. 11.98 (978-1-56001-528-4(4), 161) Potentials.
Guides step-by-step to consciously make contact with your higher self.

Channeling Your Higher Self. Barrie Konicov. 1 CD. 2003. audio compact disk 16.98 (978-0-87082-981-9(5)) Potentials.
On this program Barrie guides you step-by-step to consciously make contact with your higher self.You will find the self-hypnosis on track 1 and the subliminal on track 2. The easy-listening music of the subliminal, together with the self-hypnosis, is the original format which most people love and with which they are most familiar.

Channeling Your Higher Self: A Practical Method to Tap into Higher Wisdom & Creativity. unabr. rev. ed. Edgar Cayce. 1 CD. (Running Time: 1 hr. 0 mins. 0 sec.). (ENG.). 2004. audio compact disk 11.95 (978-1-55927-997-0(4)) Pub: Macmill Audio. Dist(s): Macmillan

Channeling Your Highter Self. Barrie Konicov. 2 CDs. 2003. audio compact disk 27.98 (978-1-56001-971-8(9)) Potentials.
On this program Barrie guides you step-by-step to consciously make contact with your higher self.This 2-CD program from our Super Consciousness series is our newest, most powerful format. On the self-hypnosis CD, SC programs have the Subliminal Persuasion soundtrack added under Barrie?s voice. And the 17th Century Baroque music on the Subliminal CD has the same beat as your body's natural rhythm, thereby allowing the suggestions to enter deeply and effortlessly.

Chansons. 2 CDs. (FRE.). audio compact disk 69.95 (978-0-8219-2619-2(5)) EMC-Paradigm.

Chansons, 1. 2 CDs. (FRE.). audio compact disk 64.95 (978-0-8219-2511-9(3)) EMC-Paradigm.

Chansons Autour du Monde pour les Grandes. 1 CD. (Running Time: 1 hr. 30 mins.). (Prelude Ser.).Tr. of Songs from Around the World. (FRE., (J). 2000. pap. bk. 19.95 (978-2-7005-0218-3(3)) Pub: Assimil FRA. Dist(s): Distribks Inc

Chansons de la Vieille France. Perf. by Ensemble Vocal Contrepoint of Paris. 1 cass. (Running Time: 1 hr.). (FRE.). pap. bk. 14.95 (SFR450) J Norton Pubs.
A collection of songs popular during the 12th to 15th centuries. Includes notes & lyrics.

Chansons de Tous le Jours pour les Petits. 1 CD. (Running Time: 1 hr. 30 mins.). (Prelude Ser.).Tr. of Nursery Songs for Little Ones. (FRE.). (J). (ps-1). 2000. pap. bk. 19.95 (978-2-7005-0216-9(7)) Pub: Assimil FRA. Dist(s): Distribks Inc

Chansons Dorees, Vol. 1. 1 cass. (FRE.). (J). 1995. bk. 14.95 (1AD081) Olivia & Hill.
Maman, les p'tits bateaux, Il court le furet, La tour, prends garde, Mon beau sapin, Frere Jacques, A la volette, Polichinelle, Mon pere m'a donne un etang.

Chansons Dorees, Vol. 2. 1 cass. (FRE.). (J). 1995. bk. 14.95 (1AD082) Olivia & Hill.
Il etait une bergere, Le Roi Dagobert, Joli tambour, La Boulangere a des ecus, Le bon fromage au lait, Cadet Rousselle, L'apprenti pastoureau, Nuit Etoilee.

Chansons Dorees, Vol. 3. 1 cass. (FRE.). (J). 1995. bk. 14.95 (1AD083) Olivia & Hill.
Au clair de la lune, Plantons la vigne, Il etait un petit navire, Le vieux chalet, Meunier tu dors, Sur let pont d'Avignon, J'ai perdu le do de ma clarinette, Mon pere a 600 moutons.

Chansons Enfantines et Comptines. 1 cass. (Running Time: 30 min.). (J). (ps-1). 2000. 7.99 (978-1-894677-08-0(0)); audio compact disk 9.99 (978-1-894677-07-3(2)) Kidzup Prodns.
A collection of favorite French toddler songs. They include "Three Blind Mice," "Old MacDonald," "Mary Had a Little Lamb" and more.

Chansons Thématiques pour Apprendre la Langue. Tracy Irwin. Prod. by Sara Jordan. Composed by Sara Jordan. Engineer Mark Shannon. Rev. by Marjelaine Caya. Illus. by Alex Filipov. 1 cass. (Running Time: 48 min. 28 secs.). (FRE.). (J). 2000. pap. bk. 14.95 (978-1-894262-38-5(7), JMP F20K) Jordan Music.

Chansons Thematiques pour Apprendre la Langue. abr. ed. Tracy Ayotte-Irwin. 1 CD. (Running Time: 30 min.). (Songs That Teach French Ser.). (FRE.). (J). 2000. audio compact disk 13.95 (978-1-894262-36-1(0), JMP F20CD) Pub: S Jordan Publ. Dist(s): CrabtreePubCo

Chant. 1 cass. (Running Time: 1 hr.). 11.95 (C0570B090, HarperThor) HarpC GBR.

Chant. Ed. by Choirs of St Vladimir's Seminary. 1909. audio compact disk 18.00 (978-0-88141-332-8(1)) St Vladimirs.

Chant & Forgiveness: A Huna Odyssey. unabr. ed. Belinda Farrell. 1 cass. (Running Time: 42 min.). 1997. 15.95 (978-0-9671893-0-7(6)) Perf Enhance CA.
Ancient Hawaiian chants & drumming as a forgiveness process - closed eye guided meditation for cutting negative cords from past.

Chant & Spirituality. The Schola Cantorum of St. Peter the Apostle. Directed By J. Michael Thompson. 1 CD. (Running Time: 53 mins.). 2005. audio compact disk 16.95 (978-0-8146-7914-2(5)) Liturgical Pr.

Chant & Spirituality of Christmas. Perf. by Schola Cantorum of St. Peter the Apostle Staff. Directed By J. Michael Thompson. 2005. audio compact disk 16.95 (978-0-8146-7946-3(3)) Liturgical Pr.

Chant from the Hermitage. Perf. by John Michael Talbot. 1 cass. (Running Time: 52 mins.). 1999. 10.95 (T8262); audio compact disk 15.95 (K1120) Liguori Pubns.
Sung in both English & Latin, contains 12 Psalms, six canticles & six Latin Chants including: "Kyrie (de Angelis)," "Psalm II," "Psalm 15," "Psalm 15" & more.

Chant Mosaic. Alison Luedecke. 1 cass. 16.00 (978-1-58459-018-7(1)) Wrld Lib Pubns.
Liturgical Chants for Organ.

Chant of Jimmie Blacksmith. unabr. ed. Thomas Keneally. Read by Bruce Kerr. 5 cass. (Running Time: 7 hrs.). 1998. (978-1-86340-648-2(4), 561218) Bolinda Pubng AUS.
Jimmie is the son of an Aboriginal mother & a white father. A missionary shows him what it means to be white - already he is only too aware of what it means to be black. Exploited by his white employers & betrayed by his white wife, Jimmie cannot take any more. He must find a way to express his rage.

***chant of Jimmie Blacksmith - Re-release.** unabr. ed. Thomas Keneally. Read by Bruce Kerr. (Running Time: 7 hrs.). 2008. audio compact disk 48.00 (978-1-921415-84-5(3), 9781921415845) Pub: Bolinda Pubng AUS. Dist(s): Bolinda Pub Inc

Chant Spirit in Sound: The Best of World Chant. Perf. by Robert Gass. 1 CD. (Running Time: 1 hr. 35 min.). 1999. audio compact disk (978-1-891319-18-1(3)) Spring Hill CO.

Chantey Irish. unabr. ed. Christopher L. Woods. Read by Mark Luce & Rick Moock. Ed. by Julie Elaine Fleming. 2 cass. (Running Time: 2 hrs.).

Dramatization. (Civil War Era Songs Ser.: Vol. 3). 1994. 19.95 set. (978-1-884649-01-1(7)) Nouveau Glass.
Cassette (A) has 21 popular sea & immigrant songs of the Civil War Era sung by the 97th Regimental String Band without interruption. Cassette (B) has the history of each of the songs popular in both the North & South with anecdotes, parodies & sidelights on their creation, plus an overview of Civil War Era music.

Chanticleer & the Fox. 2004. 8.95 (978-1-56008-864-6(8)); cass. & flmstrp 30.00 (978-0-89719-669-7(4)) Weston Woods.

Chanticleer & the Fox. (J). 2004. bk. 24.95 (978-1-56008-178-4(3)); pap. bk. 14.95 (978-1-56008-179-1(1)) Weston Woods.

Chanticleer & the Fox; Finders Keepers; Time of Wonder; Tree Is Nice. (J). 2004. (978-0-89719-806-6(9)); cass. & flmstrp (978-0-89719-715-1(1)) Weston Woods.

Chanting Breath by Breath: With the Monks & Nuns of Plum Village. Thich Nhat Hanh & Parallax Press Staff. Told to Monks and Nuns of Plum Village Staff. 1 CD. (Running Time: 30 mins.). (ENG.). 2002. audio compact disk 15.00 (978-1-888375-29-9(9), 75299) Pub: Parallax Pr. Dist(s): PerseuPGW

***Chanting for Peace: Praying with the Earth.** John Philip Newell. Read by John Philip Newell. Perf. by Suzanne Butler. Composed by Linda Larkin. (Running Time: 60 minutes approximately). (ENG.). 2010. audio compact disk 23.00 (978-0-9819800-5-8(8), NewBeg) Mat Media.

Chanting from Plum Village. Chan Khong & Thich Nhat Hanh. 1 cass. (Running Time: 76 min.). 2003. 11.00 (99026) Parallax Pr.

Chanting the Chakras. Layne Redmond. 1 CD. (Running Time: 46 mins.). 2002. pap. bk. & stu. ed. 16.98 (978-1-56455-927-2(0), M124D) Sounds True.
In India's nada yoga (sound yoga) tradition, sacred music is revered for its power to attune and balance our physical, mental and spiritual energies. Combines trance drumming with authentic yogic chant to retune the body's seven vital energy centers and encourage inner awareness. Chant along, or simply listen, whenever you need to rejuvenate and center yourself.

Chanting the Hebrew Bible. Excerpts. Joshua R. Jacobson. 1CD. (ENG & HEB., 2005. pap. bk. & stu. ed. 25.00 (978-0-8276-0816-0(0)) JPS Phila.
Joshua Jacobson's masterpiece-the comprehensive 1000-page guide to cantillation-is now available in this condensed, 300-page, user-friendly paperback edition. It is an ideal instructional guide for adult and young-adult students of Torah, for b'nai mitzvah students; and for cantors, rabbis, and Jewish educators of all denominations. Like the original edition, it includes an explanation of the tradition and a description of the practice of chanting, with all its regional variations and grammatical rules. There is detailed instruction, with musical notation, on chanting of Torah, and shorter instructions for chanting the haftarah, the megillot, and readings for the High Holy Days. Over 85 links to the audio CD throughout make it easy for readers to follow examples in sound as well as in print and is invaluable for those who cannot read music. Charts, helpful hints, pronunciation guide, glossary, and indexes to the book and the CD complete the book.

Chanting the Holy Name. Swami Amar Jyoti. 1 cass. 1989. 9.95 (H-8) Truth Consciousness.
Chanting or repeating the Holy Name as a way of life. Behind everything we seek joy, our inherent nature.

Chanting with Tamboura & Dulcimer. unabr. ed. Ram Dass & Tenney Kimmel. 1 cass. (Running Time: 90 min.). 1970. 11.00 Big Sur Tapes.

Chants. Jake Berry. Read by Jake Berry. 1 cass. (Running Time: 1 hr.). Dramatization. 1990. 6.00 (978-0-944215-09-8(2), EAD 009) Ninth St Lab.
Dramatic readings & performances of pieces from the longpoem Brambu Drezi.

Chants & Prayers. Paramhansa Yogananda. 1984. 7.00 (2002) Self Realization.
Recording of Paramahansa Yogananda chanting & praying. Selections include: "Prayer at Dawn"; "What Lightning Flash"; "In the Temple of Silence"; "Song of India" (instrumental); "Prayer at Eventide"; "O God Beautiful"; "He Hari Sundara" (Hindi); "God, Christ, Gurus"; "Shanti Mundiray" (Bengali).

Chants Corpus Christi. Schola Cantorum. 1 cass. 1999. 11.00 (978-0-937690-89-5(9), 2400); audio compact disk 16.00 CD. (978-0-937690-88-8(0), 2402) Wrld Lib Pubns.
Latin chant.

Chants de Noel. 1 cass. (Running Time: 1 hr., 30 mins.). (Musicontes Ser.).Tr. of Christmas Songs. (FRE.). (J). 2000. bk. 24.95 (978-2-09-230369-6(4)) Pub: F Nathan FRA. Dist(s): Distribks Inc

Chants from the Christmas Season. Misericord. Read by Misericord. Perf. by Paul Turner. 2 cass. (Running Time: 1 hr. 51 min.). 1992. 17.95 Set. (978-7-900782-19-9(2), AA2554) Credence Commun.
Gregorian chants for the Christmas season accompanied by Paul Turner on the organ.

Chants from Valaam. Perf. by Brotherhood of Valaam Monastery Choir Staff. 1 cass., 1 CD. 11.95 Church Slavonic. (000067); audio compact disk 16.95 CD. (000068) Conciliar Pr.
Selected hymns from the services & Trodia & hymns of the all-night vigil.

Chants of a Ghost: Hidden Drives Impovisational Jazz & Poetry Ensemble. P. R-Smith. 1 cass. 1999. 12.95 (978-1-930149-02-1(6), Writ Pub Coop) Beech River.
Improvisational Jazz Poetry, recorded live in studios & performance, including a piece from New York's Knitting Factory.

Chants of Christmas. Gloriae Dei Cantores. 1 CD. 1992. audio compact disk 16.95 (978-1-55725-075-9(8), 930-092) Paraclete MA.

Chants of Christmas. Perf. by Gloriae Dei Cantores Schola. 1 CD. 2005. audio compact disk 16.95 (978-1-55725-470-2(2), GDCD112) Paraclete MA.

Chants of Easter. Gloriae Dei Cantores. 1 CD. 1994. audio compact disk 16.95 (978-1-55725-095-7(2), GDCD015) Paraclete MA.

***Chants of Easter.** Gloriae Dei Cantores Schola. (ENG.). 2006. audio compact disk 16.95 (978-1-55725-499-3(0)) Paraclete MA.

Chants of Illumination: Ten Sanskrit Mantras. Imre Vallyon. (ENG.). 2006. 11.95 (978-0-909038-73-1(2)) Sounding Light NZL.

Chants of the Church. Perf. by Benedictine Sisters of Mount Saint Scholastical Staff. 1 cass. (Running Time: 45 min.). 10.95 (AA2252) Credence Commun.
For those who really know & love chant. Directed by Sister Joachim Holthaus. Salve Sancte Parens, Ave Maria, Tu es Petrus, Veni Sancte Spiritus, Omnes Gentes & 10 other chant favorites, along with two sacred choral works, Jesu Dulcis Memoria & Hodie Christus.

Chants to the Divine Mother. I. G. Vallyon. (ENG.). 2007. 11.95 (978-0-909038-74-8(0)) Sounding Light NZL.

Chants to the Sun & Moon: Japa for Energizing the Planets Within. Harish Johari. 1 cass. (Running Time: 1 hr.). 1996. 9.95 (978-0-89281-563-0(9), Heal Arts VT) Inner Tradit.

Chanukah: A Joyous Celebration. Daniel S. Wolk. Illus. by Jo Gershman. 1 CD. (Running Time: 1 hr.). (BookNotes Ser.). 1998. bk. 14.99 (978-0-88088-402-0(9)) Peter Pauper.

Chanukah at Grover's Corner. Read by David Grover. 1 cass. (J). 1993. 6.98 (978-1-56628-028-0(1), MLP4139) MFLP CA.
Chanukah for Children. Companion video.

Chanukah at Home. Perf. by Dan Crow et al. 1 cass. (Running Time: 34 min.). (Family Ser.). (J). (ps-7). 1988. 9.98 (8017); audio compact disk 14.98 (8017) Rounder Records.
This joyful celebration in song features some of the West Coast's top children's performers. Combination of traditional Jewish & Yiddish material.

Chanukah at Home: Holiday Songs for Children. Perf. by Marcia Berman et al. 1 cass. (J). 9.98 (444); audio compact disk 17.98 (D444) MFLP CA.
Traditional & original Chanukah songs in a joyful folk style.

Chaos. abr. ed. James Gleick. Read by Michael Jackson. 2 cass. (Running Time: 3 hrs.). 2004. 18.00 (978-1-59007-112-0(3)) Pub: New Millenn Enter. Dist(s): PerseuPGW

Chaos. unabr. ed. Ted Dekker. Narrated by Adam Verner. (Books of History Chronicles: Bk. 4). (ENG.). (YA). 2008. 13.99 (978-1-60814-113-5(6)); audio compact disk 19.99 (978-1-59859-347-1(1)) Oasis Audio.

Chaos & Change: Using the Unconscious in the Workplace. Read by James Hall. 1 cass. (Running Time: 90 min.). 1989. 10.95 (978-0-7822-0087-4(7), 394) C G Jung IL.
Part of the "chaos & change" conference.

Chaos & Change in Organizational Life Conference. 5 cass. (Running Time: 7 hrs. 30 min.). 1989. 44.95 Set. (978-0-7822-0004-1(4), CCOL) C G Jung IL.

Chaos Code. unabr. ed. Justin Richards. Read by John Lee. 8 CDs. (Running Time: 9 hrs. 27 mins.). (YA). (gr. 7 up). 2007. audio compact disk 50.00 (978-0-7393-6171-9(6)) Pub: Random Audio Pubg. Dist(s): Random

chaos Connection. A. J. Butcher. Read by Richard Aspel. (Running Time: 7 hrs. 50 mins.). (Spy High Ser.). (YA). 2009. 74.99 (978-1-74214-302-6(4), 9781742143026) Pub: Bolinda Pubng AUS. Dist(s): Bolinda Pub Inc

Chaos Connection. unabr. ed. Aj Butcher. Read by Richard Aspel. (Running Time: 28200 sec.). (Spy High Ser.). (J). 2007. audio compact disk 83.95 (978-1-74093-738-2(4)) Pub: Bolinda Pubng AUS. Dist(s): Bolinda Pub Inc

Chaos, Gaia & Eros Awakened. Ralph H. Abraham. 1 cass. 9.00 (A0559-90) Sound Photosyn.
We've waited a long time for this - good pattern recognition. A mathematician/philosopher/historian in storyteller's clothing.

Chaos, Gaia, Eros: A Chaos Pioneer Uncovers the Three Great Streams of History. unabr. ed. Ralph H. Abraham & Elizabeth Gips. 1 cass. (Running Time: 90 min.). 1998. 11.00 (32003) Big Sur Tapes.

Chaos King. unabr. ed. Laura Ruby. Read by Renée Raudman. (Running Time: 7 hrs.). 2007. 24.95 (978-1-4233-0553-8(1), 9781423305538, Brilliance MP3); 39.25 (978-1-4233-0556-9(6), 9781423305569, BADLE); 24.95 (978-1-4233-0555-2(8), 9781423305552, BAD); 74.25 (978-1-4233-0550-7(7), 9781423305507, BrilAudUnabridg) Brilliance Audio.

Chaos King. unabr. ed. Laura Ruby & Renée Raudman. (Running Time: 7 hrs.). 2007. 39.25 (978-1-4233-0554-5(X), 9781423305545, Brlnc Audio MP3 Lib); audio compact disk 29.95 (978-1-4233-0551-4(5), 9781423305514, Bril Audio CD Unabri) Brilliance Audio.

Chaos King. unabr. ed. Laura Ruby & Renée Raudman. 7 CDs. (Running Time: 7 hrs.). (J). (gr. 5-7). 2007. audio compact disk 87.25 (978-1-4233-0552-1(3), 9781423305521, BriAudCD Unabrid) Brilliance Audio.

Chaos Mode. abr. ed. Piers Anthony. Read by Mark Winston. 2 cass. (Running Time: 3 hrs.). (Mode Ser.). 2000. 7.95 (978-1-57815-005-2(1), 1011, Media Bks Audio) Media Bks NJ.
A dangerous but thrilling intergalactic adventure from one universe to the next.

Chaos Mode. unabr. ed. Piers Anthony. Read by Mark Winston. (Running Time: 12 hrs.). (Mode Ser.). 2008. 24.95 (978-1-4233-5395-9(1), 9781423353959, Brilliance MP3); 24.95 (978-1-4233-5397-3(8), 9781423353973, BAD); 39.25 (978-1-4233-5396-6(X), 9781423353966, Brlnc Audio MP3 Lib); 39.25 (978-1-4233-5398-0(6), 9781423353980, BADLE) Brilliance Audio.

Chaos or Creativity? Marion Woodman. Read by Marion Woodman. 1 cass. (Running Time: 90 min.). 1991. 10.95 (978-1-880155-04-2(4), OTA201) Oral Trad Arch.
Is there a connection between chaos & creativity? Using dream-images as her roadmap, this passionate author, lecturer & Jungian analyst addresses the problems of living in a world full of chaos & confusion. She shows how the energy of chaos may be transformed into a creative, fulfilling life.

Chapel of the Ravens, Bk. 3. unabr. ed. Paul Bishop. Read by Gene Engene. 12 cass. (Running Time: 12 hrs. 30 min.). 1998. 64.95 (978-1-55686-781-1(6)) Books in Motion.
Ian is at the peak of his soccer career when an injury sidelines him. Taking a position coaching, he gets more than he bargained for when he learns his predecessor was murdered.

Chaplain-Physician Relationship. 1 cass. (Care Cassettes Ser.: Vol. 14, No. 3). 1987. 10.80 Assn Prof Chaplains.

Chaplain, Who Needs Him? Ray Carey. 1986. 10.80 (0104B) Assn Prof Chaplains.

Chaplain's Role in Organ Donation & Procurement. 1 cass. (Care Cassettes Ser.: Vol. 15, No. 1). 1988. 10.80 Assn Prof Chaplains.

Chaplet of Divine Mercy. Perf. by Still Waters and Friends. 1 cass. (Running Time: 40 min.). 1993. 10.00 (978-1-884479-00-7(6)) Spirit Song.
Christian religious music.

Chaplet of Divine Mercy. Perf. by Still Waters and Friends. 1 CD. (Running Time: 40 min.). 1995. audio compact disk 14.00 (978-1-884479-02-1(2)) Spirit Song.

Chaplet of Divine Mercy: Featuring I Am a Voice Crying for Mercy. Marian Helpers. (ENG.). 2005. audio compact disk 15.99 (978-0-944203-67-5(1)) Pub: Marian Pr. Dist(s): STL Dist NA

Chaplet of Divine Mercy in Song. 1997. 14.95 (978-0-944203-74-3(4)) Marian Pr.

***Chaplet of Saint Michael the Archangel.** Narrated by Shauna Nouhra. Prod. by Jonathan Halls. Susie Francis-Jimenez. (Running Time: 16:52). (ENG.). 2009. audio compact disk 11.95 (978-0-615-37202-0(3)) Panis Angelicus.

Chapter Eleven Business Reorganizations: Advanced ALI-ABA Course of Study, May 8-10, 1997. 11 cass. (Running Time: 15 hrs. 50 min.). 1997. 315.00 Incl. course materials. (MB37) Am Law Inst.
Explores new ground to acquaint registrants with cutting edge developments & emerging issues in chapter 11 law.

Chapter Seven Bankruptcy Case. 1 cass. bk. 55.00 (AC-635) PA Bar Inst.

Chapter Thirteen Plan. 1 cass. bk. 55.00 (AC-636) PA Bar Inst.

Chapter Two. Neil Simon. Read by David Dukes & Sharon Gless. (Playaway Adult Fiction Ser.). (ENG.). 2009. 39.99 (978-1-60775-737-5(0)) Find a World.

Chapter Two. unabr. ed. Neil Simon. Perf. by David Dukes et al. 2 cass. (Running Time: 2 hrs. 8 mins.). 1999. 23.95 (978-1-58081-144-6(2), RDP24) L A Theatre.
Comedy & pathos mingle in this portrait of a widowed New York novelist who fears he'll never love again.

Chapter Two. unabr. ed. Neil Simon. Perf. by David Dukes et al. 2 CDs. (Running Time: 2 hrs. 8 mins.). (L. A. Theatre Works). 2001. audio compact disk 25.95 (978-1-58081-200-9(7), CDRDP24) Pub: L A Theatre. Dist(s): NetLibrary CO
Based on the author's second marriage, which began in the wake of his first wife's death from cancer. Comedy & pathos intermingle in this incisive portrait of a widowed New York novelist who fears he will never love again until a grudging five-minute meeting with a recent divorcee blooms into a passionate romance.

Chapterhouse: Dune. collector's ed. Frank Herbert. Read by John Edwardson. 13 cass. (Running Time: 19 hrs. 30 min.). (Dune Chronicles: Bk. 6). 1998. 104.00 (978-0-7366-4344-3(3), 4834) Books on Tape.
The desert planet Arrakis, called Dune, has been destroyed. Now the Bene Gesserit, heirs to Dune's powers, have colonized a green world & are turning it into a desert, mile by scorched mile. In this, the final book in the Dune Chronicles, Herbert again creates a world of breathtakingly evolved characters & the contexts in which to appreciate them. The richness riveting from end to end, the legend lives on in the greatest science fiction epic of all time.

Chapterhouse Dune. unabr. ed. Frank Herbert. Read by Simon Vance et al. 2 MP3-CDs. (Running Time: 17 hrs.). 2008. 69.95 (978-0-7927-6181-5(2), Chivers Sound Lib); audio compact disk 115.95 (978-0-7927-6006-1(9), Chivers Sound Lib) AudioGO.

Chapterhouse Dune. unabr. ed. Frank Herbert. Read by Simon Vance et al. 13 CDs. (Running Time: 16 hrs. 30 mins. 0 sec.). (ENG.). 2009. audio compact disk 49.95 (978-1-4272-0317-5(2)) Pub: Macmill Audio. Dist(s): Macmillan

***Chapters from My Autobiography.** Mark Twain. (Running Time: 12 hrs. 0 mins. 0 sec.). (ENG.). 2010. audio compact disk 29.95 (978-1-60998-061-0(1)) Pub: AudioGO. Dist(s): Perseus Dist

Character, Vol. 2. Richard Gorham & Orison Swett Marden. Narrated by Richard Gorham. (ENG.). 2006. audio compact disk 14.95 (978-0-9791934-1-5(9)) LshipTools.

Character: Program from the Award Winning Public Radio Series. Hosted by Fred Goodwin. Comment by John Hockenberry. Contrib. by Marline Martin et al. 1 cass. (Running Time: 1 hr.). (Infinite Mind Ser.). 1999. audio compact disk 21.95 (978-1-888064-20-9(X), LCM 51) Lichtenstein Creat.
Character is a word we hear often from our political and religious leaders. But what does it really mean? And what can we do to make sure young people develop it? Join Dr. Goodwin as he speaks with an elementary school principal, an expert in adolescent psychology, and an evolutionary biologist who studies the science behind unselfish behavior. Hear an Afro-Caribbean folktale that teaches character. Also commentary on character by John Hockenberry. And on another topic, we hear about a disturbing report on psychiatric patients dying while in restraints.

Character & Confidence, Set. unabr. ed. Trenna Daniells. 2 cass. (Running Time: 80 min.). Dramatization. (One to Grow On! Ser.). (J). (gr. k-8). 1999. 19.95 (978-0-918519-21-4(7)) Trenna Prods.
Four stories that promote character, confidence, high self-esteem & self-responsibility. Action packed, non-violent audio tapes promoting morals & values.

Character & Destiny: Authentic Threads in Life. James Hillman & Michael Meade. Read by James Hillman & Michael Meade. Prod. by Richard Chelew. 2 cass. (Running Time: 3 hrs.). 1997. 18.95 Bookpack set. (978-1-880155-16-5(8)) Oral Trad Arch.
What if we could learn to view our "dysfunctions" in a new way? As messages from our soul - calling us to a more authentic life? Join psychologist James Hillman & mythologist Michael Meade in a live session of their "temporary learning community" where myth connects to psyche in a lively, passionate & slyly humorous exploration of the mysteries encoded in the soul. Here poems, stories & philosophies from many cultures, continents & centuries come alive.

Character Building. Booker T. Washington. Read by Charlie Tremendous Jones. (Laws of Leadership Ser.). (ENG.). 2007. audio compact disk 19.95 (978-1-933715-41-4(3)) Executive Bks.

Character Building Through Power. unabr. ed. Ralph Waldo Trine. (ENG.). 2005. 2.98 (978-1-59659-057-1(2), GildAudio) Pub: Gildan Media. Dist(s): HachBkGrp

Character Counts: Build a Life That Pleases God. 2000. 30.95 (978-1-57972-362-0(4)) Insight Living.

Character Counts: Build a Life That Pleases God. Charles R. Swindoll. 2007. audio compact disk 42.00 (978-1-57972-747-5(6)) Insight Living.

Character Counts: Building a Life that Pleases God. Charles R. Swindoll. 2008. audio compact disk 42.00 (978-1-57972-818-2(9)) Insight Living.

Character Defects. 1 cass. (Around the Tables Ser.). 1986. 6.50 (978-0-933685-09-3(2), TP-31) A A Grapevine.
Includes articles from AA Grapevine magazine on coping with anger, fear, resentment, & other problems in sobriety.

Character Education. Steck-Vaughn Staff. 1 cass. (Running Time: 1 hr. 30 min.). 2002. 9.00 (978-0-7398-6209-4(X)) SteckVau.

***Character Makeover: 40 Days with a Life Coach to Create the Best You.** unabr. ed. Katie Brazelton & Shelley Leith. (Running Time: 11 hrs. 4 mins. 0 sec.). (ENG.). 2009. 14.99 (978-0-310-77146-3(3)) Zondervan.

Character of God. Gary V. Whetstone. Adapted by June Austin. (Theology Ser.). 1996. 140.00 (978-1-58866-119-7(9)) Gary Whet Pub.

Character of God. Gary V. Whetstone. Instructed by June Austin. (Theology Ser.: Vol. TH 203). (C). 1996. 280.00 (978-1-58866-118-0(0)) Gary Whet Pub.

Characteristics of a Religious Spirit. Jack Deere. 1 cass. (Running Time: 90 mins.). (Exposing the Religious Spirit Ser.: Vol. 1). 2000. 5.00 (JD11-001) Morning NC.
This series exposes one of the greatest enemies of every move of God.

Characteristics of Animals. Compiled by Benchmark Education Staff. 2006. audio compact disk 10.00 (978-1-4108-6673-8(4)) Benchmark Educ.

Characteristics of Love, Pt. 1. Elbert Willis. 1 cass. (Oasis of Love Guidelines Ser.). 4.00 Fill the Gap.

Characteristics of Love, Pt. 2. Elbert Willis. 1 cass. (Oasis of Love Guidelines Ser.). 4.00 Fill the Gap.

Characteristics of People. Compiled by Benchmark Education Staff. 2006. audio compact disk 10.00 (978-1-4108-6674-5(2)) Benchmark Educ.

Characteristics of Plants. Compiled by Benchmark Education Staff. 2006. audio compact disk 10.00 (978-1-4108-6672-1(6)) Benchmark Educ.

Characteristics of Spiritual Progress. 1 cass. (Running Time: 1 hr.). 12.99 (203) Yoga Res Foun.

***Charade.** Gilbert Morris. (Running Time: 8 hrs. 23 mins. 0 sec.). (ENG.). 2009. 14.99 (978-0-310-30435-7(0)) Zondervan.

***Charade.** abr. ed. Sandra Brown. Read by Natalie Ross. (Running Time: 6 hrs.). 2010. 14.99 (978-1-4418-8084-0(4), 9781441880840, BAD); audio compact disk 14.99 (978-1-4418-1397-8(7), 9781441813978, BACD) Brilliance Audio.

***Charade.** unabr. ed. Sandra Brown. Read by Natalie Ross. (Running Time: 13 hrs.). 2010. 24.99 (978-1-4418-1395-4(0), 9781441813954, BAD); 39.97 (978-1-4418-1394-7(2), 9781441813947, Brlnc Audio MP3 Lib); 39.97 (978-1-4418-1396-1(9), 9781441813961, BADLE); 24.99 (978-1-4418-1393-0(4), 9781441813930, Brilliance MP3); audio compact disk 97.97 (978-1-4418-1392-3(6), 9781441813923, BriAudCD Unabrid); audio compact disk 34.99 (978-1-4418-1391-6(8), 9781441813916, Bril Audio CD Unabri) Brilliance Audio.

Charades. unabr. ed. Janette Turner Hospital. Read by Kate Hosking. 8 cass. (Running Time: 12 hrs.). 1998. 64.00 (978-1-86442-323-5(4), 581260) Pub: Bolinda Pubng AUS. Dist(s): Lndmrk Audiobks
Speaks of passion & obsession, ranging in setting from an Australian rainforest to Boston & Toronto. A mysterious & elusive love affair haunts the lives of three women in Australia. Twenty years later, on the other side of the world, Charade Ryan sorts through story & counter-story for her father, the legendary Nicholas, & the truth about her origins.

***Charango Method Book/CD Set: Metodo de Charango.** Italo Pedrotti & Horacio Duran. (ENG & SPA.). 2010. lib. bdg. 22.99 (978-0-7866-8172-3(1)) Mel Bay.

Charcot-Marie-Tooth Disease - A Bibliography & Dictionary for Physicians, Patients, & Genome Researchers. Compiled by Icon Group International, Inc. Staff. 2007. ring bd. 28.95 (978-0-497-11350-6(3)) Icon Grp.

Chard Witlow: Mr. T. S. Elliot's Sunday Evening Broadcast Postscript see Dylan Thomas Reading

Charena: Spider Woman. 2nd ed. Short Stories. G. Saul Snatsky. 1. (Running Time: 24 mins.). Dramatization. (ENG.). 2005. audio compact disk (978-0-9761674-2-6(5)) Sauls Audio.
In a biotech, cybernetic age, Charena, woman turned spider, adds new meaning to "Getting Close and Personal with the Enemy.".

Charge of the Light Brigade see Treasury of Alfred Lord Tennyson

Charge of the Light Brigade see Classics of English Poetry for the Elementary Curriculum

Charging the Body Electric Music. Tag Powell & Peter Abood. 1 cass. 1988. 12.95 (978-0-914295-73-0(X)) Top Mtn Pub.
Relaxing music designed to build pride & restore self-confidence. Sublitone music.

Charioteer. unabr. ed. Mary Renault. Narrated by Davina Porter. 10 cass. (Running Time: 14 hrs. 30 mins.). 1988. 85.00 (978-1-55690-097-6(X), 88760E7) Recorded Bks.
Revelations rarely come to those who are content with their lives. For Laurie, a survivor of Dunkirk, it took months of pain, loss & uncertainty to arrive at a truth which had been there all along.

Chariots Can't Swim: Exodus 14. Ed Young. 1984. 4.95 (978-0-7417-1423-7(X), 423) Win Walk.

Chariots in the Smoke. unabr. ed. Gilbert Morris. Read by Maynard Villers. 8 cass. (Running Time: 10 hrs. 12 min.). (Appomattox Ser.: Bk. 9). 2001. 49.95 (978-1-55686-852-8(9)) Books in Motion.
Wealthy Richmond planter David Rocklin is finally touched by the Civil War: fight for the South and defend the slavery he abhors, or lose the woman he loves.

Chariots of Fire. Mark Chironna. 1 cass. 1992. 7.00 (978-1-56043-928-8(9)) Destiny Image Pubs.

Charisma: Drawing People to You. Dick Sutphen. 1 cass. (Running Time: 1 hr.). (RX17 Ser.). 1986. 14.98 (978-0-87554-325-3(1), RX134) Valley Sun.
You project an inner warmth & friendliness; are self-assured & independent; project self-confidence to everyone you meet; are open, approachable, sensitive & allow others to know it; are confident enough to let your vulnerability show; project charisma & draw people to you. Every day, you become more charismatic.

Charismatic Chaos. John MacArthur, Jr. & John F. MacArthur. 2 cass. (Running Time: 2 hrs.). 1992. 14.99 (978-0-310-57578-8(8)) Zondervan.
Recognizing the importance of the charismatic movement & the need for a biblical evaluation of it, MacArthur analyzes the doctrinal differences between charismatics & non-charismatics in the light of Scripture.

Charismatic Gifts. Vincent M. Walsh. 1 cass. 1986. 4.00 Key of David.
Personal stories & examples told to promote a full understanding of the basic powers of the Renewal.

Charismatic Movement: Something More or Something Less. 12 cass. 35.95 (2053, HarperThor) HarpC GBR.

Charismatic Renewal & Priesthood. Vincent M. Walsh. 1 cass. 1986. 4.00 Key of David.

Charitable End. unabr. ed. Jessica Mann. Read by Wanda McCaddon. 6 cass. (Running Time: 9 hrs.). (Isis Ser.). (J). 1999. 54.95 (978-0-7531-0556-6(X), 990311) Pub: ISIS Lrg Prnt GBR. Dist(s): Ulverscroft US
Someone was sending the comfortable citizens of Edinburgh poison-pen letters, but the recipients thought it politic to say nothing about them. Dilly Gosset, the French-born wife of a judge, had received one of the letters & blurted out the details of her husband's not so blameless life to anyone who would listen. Spurred on by the appparently accidental, death of Lady Gosset, Diana Drummond began to investigate. Her discoveries led her to wonder if Lady Gosset's death had indeed been an accident.

Charitable Giving Techniques. 8 cass. (Running Time: 12 hrs.). 1999. 295.00 Set; incl. study guide 402p. (AD69) Am Law Inst.

Charitable Trusts. George B. Jewell. 2005. bk. 189.00 (978-0-8080-8928-5(5)) Toolkit Media.

Charity. (208); (710) Yoga Res Foun.

Charity. Swami Jyotirmayananda. 1 cass. (Running Time: 1 hr.). 1990. 12.99 Yoga Res Foun.

Charity: The Pure Love of Christ. Bernell Christensen. 1 cass. 5.98 (978-1-55503-098-8(X), 06002854) Covenant Comms.
A moving, motivating presentation.

***Charity in Truth.** Benedict XVI, pseud. 2008. audio compact disk 19.95 (978-1-58617-425-5(8)) Pub: Ignatius Pr. Dist(s): Midpt Trade

Charity of Perfection. Swami Amar Jyoti. 1 cass. 1983. 9.95 (E-26) Truth Consciousness.
Value of rituals & ceremonies comes only from following the Principle. Perfect Ones work in perfect Charity, Compassion & Oneness - never "duty bound".

Charlatan: America's Most Dangerous Huckster, the Man Who Pursued Him, & the Age of Flimflam. unabr. ed. Pope Brock. Read by Johnny Heller. (YA). 2008. 59.99 (978-1-60514-860-1(1)) Find a World.

Charlatan: America's Most Dangerous Huckster, the Man Who Pursued Him, & the Age of Flimflam. unabr. ed. Pope Brock. Read by Johnny Heller. (Running Time: 9 hrs. 0 mins. 0 sec.). (ENG.). 2008. audio compact disk 34.99 (978-1-4001-0607-3(9)); audio compact disk 24.99 (978-1-4001-5607-8(6)); audio compact disk 69.99 (978-1-4001-3607-0(5)) Pub: Tantor Media. Dist(s): IngramPubServ

***Charlemagne Pursuit.** abr. ed. Steve Berry. Read by Scott Brick. (ENG.). 2010. audio compact disk 14.99 (978-0-307-75084-6(1), Random AudioBks) Pub: Random Audio Pubg. Dist(s): Random

Charlemagne Pursuit. unabr. ed. Steve Berry. Read by Scott Brick. 13 CDs. 2008. audio compact disk 129.00 (978-1-4159-5679-3(0), BksonTape) Pub: Random Audio Pubg. Dist(s): Random
As a child, former Justice Department agent Cotton Malone was told his father died in a submarine disaster in the North Atlantic, but now he wants the full story and asks his ex-boss, Stephanie Nelle, to secure the military files. What he learns stuns him: His father's sub was a secret nuclear vessel lost on a highly classified mission beneath the ice shelves of Antarctica. But Malone isn't the only one after the truth. Twin sisters Dorothea Lindauer and Christl Falk are fighting for the fortune their mother has promised to whichever of them discovers what really became of their father - who died on the same submarine that Malone's father captained. The sisters know something Malone doesn't: Inspired by strange clues discovered in Charlemagne's tomb, the Nazis explored Antarctica before the Americans, as long ago as 1938. Now Malone discovers that cryptic journals penned in "the language of heaven," inscrutable conundrums posed by an ancient historian, and the ill-fated voyage of his father are all tied to a revelation of immense consequence for humankind. In an effort to ensure that this explosive information never rises to the surface, Langford Ramsey, an ambitious navy admiral, has begun a brutal game of treachery, blackmail, and assassination. As Malone embarks on a dangerous quest with the sisters - one that leads them from an ancient German cathedral to a snowy French citadel to the unforgiving ice of Antarctica - he will finally confront the shocking truth of his father's death and the distinct possibility of his own.

Charlemagne Pursuit. unabr. ed. Steve Berry. Read by Scott Brick. 13 CDs. (Running Time: 16 hrs. 30 mins.). (Cotton Malone Ser.: Bk. 4). (ENG.). 2008. audio compact disk 49.95 (978-0-7393-6943-2(1), Random AudioBks) Pub: Random Audio Pubg. Dist(s): Random

Charles Albert Tindley CD. Compiled by GBGMusik. (ENG.). 2006. audio compact disk Rental 12.95 (978-1-933663-04-3(9), GBGMusik) Gnl Brd Glbl Minis.

Charles & Emma: The Darwins' Leap of Faith. unabr. ed. Deborah Heiligman. Narrated by Rosalyn Landor. 6 CDs. (Running Time: 7 hrs. 38 mins.). (YA). (gr. 8 up). 2009. audio compact disk 50.00 (978-0-7393-8049-9(4), Listening Lib) Pub: Random Audio Pubg. Dist(s): Random

***Charles & Emma: the Darwins' Leap of Faith.** unabr. ed. Deborah Heiligman. Read by Rosalyn Landor. (ENG.). (J). 2010. audio compact disk 34.00 (978-0-307-74603-0(8), Listening Lib) Pub: Random Audio Pubg. Dist(s): Random

Charles & Taylor. Contrib. by Charles & Taylor. Prod. by Travon Potts. Contrib. by Chris Thomason & Jackie Patillo. 2005. audio compact disk 13.99 (978-5-558-97543-7(1)) Integrity G.

Charles Baxter. Charles Baxter. Read by Charles Baxter. 1 cass. (Running Time: 29 min.). 1989. 10.00 New Letters.
Baxter reads poetry & fiction & is interviewed.

Charles Bell: Delta Return. Charles Bell. Read by Charles Bell. 1 cass. (Running Time: 29 min.). 1991. 10.00 (040480) New Letters.

Charles Bell: Love. Charles Bell. Read by Charles Bell. 1 cass. (Running Time: 29 min.). 1991. 10.00 (051280) New Letters.

Charles Bell 1 & 2. Read by Charles Bell. 2 cass. (Running Time: 29 min. per cass.). Incl. Delta Return; Love. Running Press Staff.; 1985. 10.00 ea. One-sided cass.; 18.00 ea. Two-sided cass. New Letters.
Charles Bell of New Mexico reads about childhood memories in the American South & about love.

Charles Chaplin: My Autobiography. unabr. collector's ed. Charles Chaplin. Read by Grover Gardner. 12 cass. (Running Time: 18 hrs.). 1986. 96.00 (978-0-7366-1056-8(1), 1983) Books on Tape.
Charles Chaplin's career in films started in 1914 with a string of single-reelers for Keystone Comedy Film Company. Success was immediate, but his life was full of controversy, from his memorable arguments with the government about taxes to his marriage late in life to Oona O'Neill, daughter of playwright Eugene & two generations his junior.

Charles Curley: Hanging Ten on the Forthe Wave. (Running Time: 60 min.). (Freeland III Ser.). 1985. 9.00 (FL15) Freeland Pr.
Technology is presented with humour & intellect by the author.

Charles Curley Interviews of Hardmoney Experts. unabr. ed. 6 cass. (Running Time: 7 hrs.). 56.00 (411-416) J Norton Pubs.

Charles Darwin. unabr. ed. 1 cass. (Running Time: 1 hr. 17 min.). (History Maker Ser.). 12.95 (41004) J Norton Pubs.
The author of "The Origin of the Species" is depicted as a quiet, patient & gentle man who suffered chronic ill-health most of his life. His trials & tribulation as well as his accomplishments are discussed.

Charles Darwin: The Man Who Looked at Life. Alan Venable. (World Around Us Ser.). 2003. pap. bk. 69.00 (978-1-4105-0016-8(0)); audio compact disk 18.95 (978-1-4105-0198-1(1)) D Johnston Inc.

Charles de Gaulle. Henri Guillemin. 1 cass. (FRE.). 1991. 22.95 (1202-VSL) Olivia & Hill.

Charles de Gaulle: A Biography. unabr. ed. Don Cook. Read by Frederick Davidson. 16 cass. (Running Time: 23 hrs. 30 mins.). 1997. 99.95 (978-0-7861-1245-6(X), 2152) Blckstn Audio.
Biography of de Gaulle. Sheds new light on Europe's most controversial & enigmatic general, politician, & statesman.

Charles de Gaulle: A Biography. unabr. ed. Don Cook. Read by Frederick Davidson. (Running Time: 82800 sec.). 2008. audio compact disk & audio compact disk 44.95 (978-1-4332-3419-4(X)); audio compact disk & audio compact disk 130.00 (978-1-4332-3418-7(1)) Blckstn Audio.

Charles DeGaulle: 24 Juillet 1967 - at Montreal. unabr. ed. 1 cass. (Running Time: 1 hr). (FRE.). 1995. 16.95 (1738-RF) Olivia & Hill.
Vive le Quebec libre. With this statement DeGaulle made one of the most surprising & controversial statements of the Fifth Republic. Recordings of the time.

Charles Dickens. Catherine Peters. Read by Richard Derrington. 2 cass. (Running Time: 3 hrs.). 2001. 24.95 (981117) Pub: ISIS Audio GBR. Dist(s): Ulverscroft US

Charles Dickens. unabr. ed. Charles Dickens. 4 cass. Dramatization. (Classic Author Ser.). (J). 1995. 16.95 (978-1-55935-169-0(1)) Soundelux.
Includes "A Christmas Carol" & "Great Expectations".

Charles Dickens. unabr. ed. Jane Smiley. 5 cass. (Running Time: 7 hrs. 30 mins.). 2002. 40.00 (978-0-7366-8621-1(5)) Books on Tape.
Jane Smiley details the uncommon life, works and mind of Charles Dickens.

Charles Dickens. unabr. ed. Angus Wilson. 1 cass. (Running Time: 1 hr. 21 min.). 1967. 12.95 (23075) J Norton Pubs.
Discussion on English contributions to the growth of the novel.

Charles Dickens: Three Short Stories. unabr. collector's ed. Charles Dickens. Read by Donada Peters. 7 cass. (Running Time: 10 hrs. 30 min.). 1991. 56.00 (978-0-7366-1943-1(7), 2764) Books on Tape.
Charles Dickens is known not only for his novels, but also for his short stories, particularly "A Christmas Carol." In the latter genre, interestingly, these stories had a powerful commercial impulse, for they were serialized in magazines at the Christmas season. "The Cricket on the Hearth," "The Battle of Life" & "The Haunted Man" were written for the Christmas market, & all lay emphasis on family love & the delights of home. But there is more to these stories than surface sentimentality: their eager anticipation by a whole nation tells us much about the age Dickens lived in. And these stories never would have survived without roots & power.

Charles Dickens Set: A Concise Biography. unabr. ed. Catherine Peters. Read by Catherine Peters. 2 cass. 1999. 24.95 (978-0-7531-0499-6(7), 981117) Pub: ISIS Audio GBR. Dist(s): ISIS Pub
This short biography provides an excellent introduction to Dickens, from his disturbed childhood with a traumatic period working in a blacking factory, his instant success as a young writer & his tumultuous acclaim in both England & american, the major novels of the 1850's & 60's.

Charles Dickens & Other Essays. unabr. ed. George Orwell. Narrated by Patrick Tull. 3 cass. (Running Time: 3 hrs. 30 mins.). 1989. 26.00 (978-1-55690-098-3(8), 89170E7) Recorded Bks.
Essays: "Charles Dickens, Why I Write: in Defense of the Novel" & "New Words".

Charles Dickens Classics Volume 1. Charles Dickens. (ENG.). 2008. audio compact disk Rental 9.95 (978-1-60245-174-2(5)) GDL Multimedia.

Charles Dickens Classics Volume 2. Charles Dickens. (ENG.). 2008. audio compact disk 9.95 (978-1-60245-175-9(3)) GDL Multimedia.

Charles Dickens Quartet: Great Expectations , Oliver Twist , A Christmas Carol & the Cricket on the Hearth / the Signal Man. Charles Dickens. Narrated by Flo Gibson. (ENG.). 2008. 68.95 (978-1-60646-044-3(7)) Audio Bk Con.

Charles Dickens Three Short Stories. Charles Dickens. Read by Donada Peters. (Running Time: 34200 sec.). (ENG.). 2005. audio compact disk 19.99 (978-1-4001-5127-1(9)) Pub: Tantor Media. Dist(s): IngramPubServ

Charles Dickens' Three Short Stories. Charles Dickens. Narrated by Donada Peters. 2005. audio compact disk 34.99 (978-1-4001-0127-6(1)); audio compact disk 69.99 (978-1-4001-3127-3(8)) Pub: Tantor Media. Dist(s): IngramPubServ

Charles Dickens (1812-1870) unabr. ed. 1 cass. (Running Time: 1 hr.). (History Maker Ser.). 1977. 12.95 (41014) J Norton Pubs.
This audio biography, with music & dramatization, highlights the times in which Dickens lived & illustrates how some of his most famous characters are derived from his own family & contemporaries.

Charles d'Orleans, Ronsard, Apollinaire. Poems. Read by Jean Vilar. 1 cass. (Golden Treasury of Poetry & Prose Ser.). 1991. bk. 16.95 (1054-SA) Olivia & Hill.

Charles Finney. Barbour. 1998. 4.97 (978-1-57748-360-1(X)) Barbour Pub.

Charles Gordone. unabr. ed. Charles Gordone. Read by Charles Gordone. 1 cass. (Running Time: 29 min.). 1991. 10.00 (123078) New Letters.
Pulitzer prize winning author reads poems about the experience of being black in America.

Charles Gusewelle. Interview. Interview with Charles Gusewelle & Kay Bonetti. 1 cass. (Running Time: 58 min.). 13.95 (978-1-55644-073-1(1), 3072) Am Audio Prose.
Distinguished journalist & award-winning short story writer discusses art of prose from unique perspective, including cross influences of two differing genres.

Charles Hanzlicek. unabr. ed. Read by Charles Hanzlicek. 1 cass. (Running Time: 29 min.). 1985. 10.00 New Letters.
Charles Hanzlicek reads from "Stars" & newer poems.

Charles Hillinger's America. unabr. ed. Charles Hillinger. Read by Dennis McKee. 8 cass. (Running Time: 11 hrs. 30 mins.). 2003. 56.95 (978-0-7861-1590-7(4), 2419) Blckstn Audio.

Charles Hillinger's America: People & Places in All Fifty States. unabr. ed. Charles Hillinger. Read by Dennis McKee. Frwd. by Charles Kuralt. 8 cass. (Running Time: 12 hrs.). 1999. 56.95 (2419) Blckstn Audio.
This is the fruit of Hillinger's nearly 46 years of a dream job - traveling anywhere he wanted in the U.S. as a feature writer & columnist for the "Los Angeles Times." The result: 6,000 human & general interest stories that were syndicated to 600 newspapers.

Charles II, the Merry Monarch see Diary of Samuel Pepys

Charles Kuralt's Christmas. abr. ed. Charles Kuralt. 2004. 7.95 (978-0-7435-4266-1(5)) Pub: S&S Audio. Dist(s): S and S Inc

Charles Kingsford Smith. unabr. ed. Peter FitzSimons. Read by Richard Aspel. (Running Time: 26 hrs. 45 mins.). 2009. audio compact disk 123.95 (978-1-74214-465-8(9), 9781742144658) Pub: Bolinda Pubng AUS. Dist(s): Bolinda Pub Inc

***Charles Kingsford Smith.** unabr. ed. Peter FitzSimons. Read by Richard Aspel. (Running Time: 26 hrs. 45 mins.). 2010. 54.95 (978-1-74214-507-5(8), 9781742145075) Pub: Bolinda Pubng AUS. Dist(s): Bolinda Pub Inc

Charles Kuralt Collection. unabr. ed. Charles Kuralt. Read by Charles Kuralt. 6 cass. (Running Time: 7 hrs.). 1998. 42.00 Gift Set. (978-0-671-97019-2(4), Audioworks) S&S Audio.

Charles Kuralt's America. abr. ed. Charles Kuralt. 2 cass. 21.95 Set. (79745) Books on Tape.
Latest journey took him to delightful, way-out places at perfect times - from Montana's plains in the fall to North Carolina's mountains in the spring.

Charles Kuralt's America. abr. ed. Charles Kuralt. 2004. 15.95 (978-0-7435-4263-0(0)) Pub: S&S Audio. Dist(s): S and S Inc

Charles kuralt's american Moments. abr. ed. Charles Kuralt. 2004. 7.95 (978-0-7435-4264-7(9)) Pub: S&S Audio. Dist(s): S and S Inc

Charles kuralt's Autumn. Charles Kuralt. 2004. 7.95 (978-0-7435-4265-4(7)) Pub: S&S Audio. Dist(s): S and S Inc

Charles kuralt's Spring. Charles Kuralt. 2004. 7.95 (978-0-7435-4267-8(3)) Pub: S&S Audio. Dist(s): S and S Inc

Charles Kuralt's Spring & Summer, Set. abr. ed. Charles Kuralt. Read by Charles Kuralt. 2 cass. (Running Time: 2 hrs.). 1999. (395079) S&S Audio.
Drawing on pieces from his years at CBS News as well as new never-before-recorded material, Kurait takes us on an unforgettable journey through the beauty of spring & his favorite summertime adventures.

Charles kuralt's Summer. Charles Kuralt. 2004. 7.95 (978-0-7435-4268-5(1)) Pub: S&S Audio. Dist(s): S and S Inc

Charles Langton & Paul Engle. unabr. ed. Read by Charles Langton & Paul Engle. 1 cass. (Running Time: 29 min.). 1986. 10.00 New Letters.
A reading by two Iowa poets.

Charles Osgood: More of See You on the Radio. abr. ed. Charles Osgood. Read by Charles Osgood. 1 cass. (Running Time: 1 hr. 30 mins.). 2000. 17.95 (978-1-55935-334-2(1)) Soundelux.
Shares his essays over the last eight years at CBS Radio. Witty & often poetic.

Charles Ryder's School Days & Other Stories. unabr. ed. Evelyn Waugh. Read by Octavius Black. 6 cass. (Running Time: 6 hrs.). 1987. 36.00 (978-0-7366-1149-7(5), 2073) Books on Tape.
Likely intended as the first chapter of a novel tracing the Brideshead Revisited narrator's emotional roots, the story sheds new light on the elusive figure of Charles Ryder.

Charles Simic, No. 1. Read by Charles Simic. 1 cass. (Running Time: 29 min.). 1983. 10.00 New Letters.
Simic's reading includes poems from the award winning book "Classic Ballroom Dances".

Charles Simic II. unabr. ed. Charles Simic. Prod. by Rebekah Presson. 1 cass. (Running Time: 29 min.). 1990. 10.00 (112390) New Letters.
The winner of the 1990 Pulitzer Prize in poetry reads from both his winning book, "The World Doesn't End" & from a more recent work, "The Book of Gods & Devils".

Charles Simic Two. unabr. ed. Charles Simic. 1 cass. (Running Time: 29 min.). 1991. 10.00 (112390) New Letters.
The World Doesn't End; The Book of Gods & Devils.

Charles Spurgeon. Barbour Books Staff. 1998. 4.97 (978-1-57748-398-4(7)) Barbour Pub.

Charles Spurgeon: Boy Preacher to Christian Theologian. unabr. ed. Kathy Triggs. Read by Lloyd James. (Running Time: 9000 sec.). (Men of Faith Ser.). 2007. 23.95 (978-0-7861-2429-9(6)); audio compact disk 32.00 (978-0-7861-8828-4(6)) Blckstn Audio.

Charles Wesley at 300 CD. Compiled by GBGMusk. 2007. audio compact disk (978-1-933663-11-1(1), GBGMusik) Gnl Brd Glbl Minis.

Charles Wick: The Power of Freed Information. 1 cass. (Running Time: 1 hr.). 10.95 (NP-88-10-12, HarperThor) HarpC GBR.

Charleston. John Jakes. Narrated by George Guidall. 13 cass. (Running Time: 18 hrs. 30 mins.). 112.00 (978-1-4025-3331-0(4)) Recorded Bks.

Charleston. abr. ed. John Jakes. John Jakes. Read by Dylan Baker. 2006. 17.95 (978-0-7435-6166-2(X)) Pub: S&S Audio. Dist(s): S and S Inc

Charleston. unabr. ed. John Jakes. Narrated by George Guidall. 14 cass. (Running Time: 18 hrs. 15 mins.). 2002. 59.95 (978-1-4025-3332-7(2), RG239) Recorded Bks.
Charleston is the epic saga of an aristocratic South Carolina family's century-long role in American history. From the American Revolution to the Civil War, the Bell family survives, enduring shifting fortunes, dark secrets, and tragedies of the heart.

Charley, Charlotte & the Golden Canary. 2004. 8.95 (978-1-56008-865-3(6)); cass. & flmstrp 30.00 (978-0-89719-670-3(8)) Weston Woods.

Charley Skedaddle. Patricia Beatty. Read by Jeff Woodman. 4 cass. (Running Time: 5 hrs. 30 mins.). (J). 1999. pap. bk. & stu. ed. 51.20 (978-0-7887-3792-3(9), 41036) Recorded Bks.
Charlie Quinn, a 12-year-old street tough Bowery Boy from New York City, during the Civil War, runs away from home & enlists as a drummer boy with the Union Army. Seeking to avenge his older brother's death at Gettysburg, he is proud to be a soldier until he gets his first taste of battle. Then, terrified he skedaddles" into the Blue Ridge Mountains where he is befriended by an old cantakerous, abolitionist mountain woman. Characters, dialogue & descriptive settings are based on actual Civil War records & memoirs.

Charley Skedaddle. unabr. ed. Patricia Beatty. Narrated by Jeff Woodman. 4 cass. (Running Time: 5 hrs. 30 mins.). (gr. 5 up). 1999. 38.00 (978-0-7887-3823-4(2), 96051E7) Recorded Bks.

Charley Skedaddle, Class Set. Patricia Beatty. Read by Jeff Woodman. 4 cass. (Running Time: 5 hrs. 30 mins.). (J). (gr. 5 up). 1999. 108.30 (978-0-7887-3863-0(1), 47028) Recorded Bks.

Charley's Web. abr. ed. Joy Fielding. Read by Susan Ericksen. (Running Time: 6 hrs.). 2009. audio compact disk 14.99 (978-1-4233-2559-8(1), 9781423325598, BCD Value Price) Brilliance Audio.

Charley's Web. unabr. ed. Joy Fielding. Read by Susan Ericksen. 1 MP3-CD. (Running Time: 13 hrs.). 2008. 39.25 (978-1-4233-2555-0(9), 9781423325550, Brlnc Audio MP3 Lib); 39.25 (978-1-4233-2557-4(5), 9781423325574, BADLE); 24.95 (978-1-4233-2556-7(7), 9781423325567, BAD); 102.25 (978-1-4233-2551-2(6), 9781423325512, BrilAudUnabridg); audio compact disk 24.95 (978-1-4233-2554-3(0), 9781423325543, Brilliance MP3); audio compact disk 36.95 (978-1-4233-2552-9(4), 9781423325529, Bril Audio CD Unabri); audio compact disk 107.25 (978-1-4233-2553-6(2), 9781423325536, BriAudCD Unabrid) Brilliance Audio.

Charlie. unabr. ed. Kate Chopin. Read by Jacqueline Kinlow. 2 cass. (Running Time: 2 hrs. 34 min.). 1994. lib. bdg. 18.95 set incl. vinyl case with notes, author's picture & biography. (978-1-883049-34-8(2)) Sound Room.
A collection of heart-warming Louisiana stories: "Charlie", "Tante Cat'rinette", "A Matter of Prejudice", "Beyond the Bayou", "A Pair of Silk Stockings" & "Regret".

Charlie, Set. unabr. ed. Short Stories. Kate Chopin. Read by Jacqueline Kinlow. 2 cass. (Running Time: 2 hrs. 30 mins.). (Kate Chopin Ser.). 1994. bk. 16.95 Set, trade ed. (978-1-883049-14-0(8)) Sound Room.
Wonderful stories of early Louisiana. "Charlie," a heart warming story of a tomboy's transformation; "Beyond the Bayou," an old Creole woman must cross the bayou.

***Charlie All Night.** unabr. ed. Jennifer Crusie, pseud. Read by Aimee Jolson. (Running Time: 7 hrs.). 2011. 39.97 (978-1-4418-8313-1(4), 9781441883131, BADLE); 19.99 (978-1-4418-8315-5(0), 9781441883155, Brilliance MP3); 39.97 (978-1-4418-8312-4(6), 9781441883124, Brlnc Audio MP3 Lib); audio compact disk 19.99 (978-1-4418-8310-0(X), 9781441883100, Bril Audio CD Unabri); audio compact disk 69.97 (978-1-4418-8311-7(8), 9781441883117, BriAudCD Unabrid) Brilliance Audio.

Charlie & the Chocolate Factory. Roald Dahl. 2005. 39.99 (978-1-59895-007-6(X)) Find a World.

Charlie & the Chocolate Factory see Roald Dahl

Charlie & the Chocolate Factory. movie tie-in unabr. ed. Roald Dahl. Read by Eric Idle. 3 CDs. (Running Time: 3.5 Hrs). 2005. audio compact disk 25.95 (978-0-06-085280-1(1)) HarperCollins Pubs.

***Charlie & the Chocolate Factory.** unabr. ed. Roald Dahl. (ENG.). 2004. (978-0-06-079975-5(7)) HarperCollins Pubs.

***Charlie & the Chocolate Factory.** unabr. ed. Roald Dahl. Read by Eric Idle. (ENG.). 2004. (978-0-06-074605-6(X)) HarperCollins Pubs.

Charlie & the Chocolate Factory. unabr. abr. ed. Roald Dahl. Read by Eric Idle. 3 cass. (Running Time: 1 hr. 07 min.). (J). (gr. 3-5). 2002. audio compact disk 25.95 (978-0-06-051065-7(X)) HarperCollins Pubs.

Charlie & the Chocolate Factory & Charlie & the Glass Elevator. unabr. ed. Roald Dahl. Read by Eric Idle. (J). 2005. 44.99 (978-1-59895-131-8(9)) Find a World.

Charlie & the Chocolate Factory & Charlie & the Great Glass Elevator. Roald Dahl. Perf. by Eric Idle. 2006. 39.99 (978-1-59895-471-5(7)) Find a World.

Charlie & the Great Glass Elevator see Charlie et le Grand Ascenseur de Verre

Charlie & the Great Glass Elevator. abr. ed. Roald Dahl. Read by Eric Idle. (J). 2004. audio compact disk 25.95 (978-0-06-059784-9(4)) HarperCollins Pubs.

Charlie & the Great Glass Elevator. unabr. ed. Roald Dahl. Read by Eric Idle. (J). 2004. 24.00 (978-0-06-053629-9(2)) HarperCollins Pubs.

***Charlie & the Great Glass Elevator.** unabr. ed. Roald Dahl. Read by Eric Idle. (ENG.). 2004. (978-0-06-078261-0(7)); (978-0-06-081386-4(5)) HarperCollins Pubs.

Charlie & the Sir. unabr. ed. Frank Roderus. Read by Cameron Beierle. 4 cass. (Running Time: 5 hrs. 18 min.). 2001. 26.95 (978-1-58116-086-4(0)) Books in Motion.
Charlie Roy and skinny Sir Arthur, an English gentleman, arrive at the Crown B Ranch to help Charlie's sister resume control of the spread, after her husband's death. But forces are forming to take Elizabeth's ranch, with the threat of a range war in the balance.

Charlie Bone & the Beast. Jenny Nimmo. Narrated by Simon Jones. (ENG.). (J). (gr. 4-7). 2008. audio compact disk 24.95 (978-0-545-07220-5(4)) Scholastic Inc.

Charlie Bone & the Beast. unabr. ed. Jenny Nimmo & Jenny Nimmo. Narrated by Simon Jones. (ENG.). (J). (gr. 4-7). 2008. audio compact disk 64.95 (978-0-545-07240-3(9)) Scholastic Inc.

Charlie Bone & the Beast: Children of the Red King, Book 6. unabr. ed. Jenny Nimmo. Read by Simon Jones. (J). 2008. 54.99 (978-1-60514-879-3(2)) Find a World.

Charlie Bone & the Castle of Mirrors. unabr. ed. Jenny Nimmo. Read by Simon Russell Beale. 5 cass. (Running Time: 7 hrs. 11 mins.). (Children of the Red King Ser.: Bk. 4). (J). (gr. 4-7). 2006. 40.00 (978-0-307-28459-4(X), Listening Lib); audio compact disk 50.00 (978-0-307-28460-0(3), Listening Lib) Pub: Random Audio Pubg. Dist(s): Random

Charlie Bone & the Castle of Mirrors. unabr. ed. Jenny Nimmo. Read by Simon Russell Beale. 6 CDs. (Running Time: 25860 sec.). (Children of the Red King Ser.: Bk. 4). (ENG.). (J). (gr. 3-7). 2006. audio compact disk 34.00 (978-0-307-28427-3(1), Listening Lib) Pub: Random Audio Pubg. Dist(s): Random

Charlie Bone & the Hidden King. unabr. ed. Jenny Nimmo. Read by Simon Russell Beale. 7 CDs. (Running Time: 7 hrs. 58 mins.). (Children of the Red King Ser.: Bk. 5). (YA). (gr. 5-8). 2006. audio compact disk 55.00 (978-0-7393-3606-9(1), Listening Lib); 40.00 (978-0-7393-3605-2(3), Listening Lib) Pub: Random Audio Pubg. Dist(s): Random
In Charlie's most perilous adventure yet, the shadow from the Red King's portrait has escaped. Strange things start to happen at Bloor's Academy. But, with the help of a mysterious force, Charlie and his friends are closer to discovering the truth about Charlie Bone's father.

Charlie Bone & the Hidden King. unabr. ed. Jenny Nimmo. Read by Simon Russell Beale. (Running Time: 28680 sec.). (Children of the Red King Ser.: Bk. 5). (ENG.). (J). (gr. 5). 2006. audio compact disk 45.00 (978-0-307-28606-2(1), Listening Lib) Pub: Random Audio Pubg. Dist(s): Random

Charlie Bone & the Invisible Boy. unabr. ed. Jenny Nimmo. Read by Simon Russell Beale. 5 cass. (Running Time: 7 hrs. 17 mins.). (Children of the Red King Ser.: Bk. 3). (J). (gr. 4-7). 2005. 40.00 (978-0-8072-2364-2(6), Listening Lib); audio compact disk 45.00 (978-0-307-24567-0(5), Listening Lib) Random Audio Pubg.
In this third installment in the series, another semester at Bloor Academy is about to begin, and, as usual, chaos ensues. At home, Charlie's Uncle Paton disappears, then returns ill and powerless. Charlie's friend Benjamin heads off to Hong Kong, and his grandmother Maisie leaves to take care of her sick sister. At the same time, a new and sinister student named Belle arrives and quickly establishes herself as a force to be reckoned with. A new art teacher has joined the staff to find his younger brother, Ollie Sparks, turned invisible by a blue boa (snake, though there are feathers involved) controlled by the evil Ezekiel Bloor. Charlie and his friends try to come up with ways to help Ollie and Billy Raven, the poor orphan being manipulated and tormented by the Bloor clan. One of the strengths of this story (and the whole series) is the way both regular people and those who are magically endowed work toward common goals. A weakness is the lack of progress toward identifying and rescuing Charlie's father, who is barely mentioned in this outing.

Charlie Bone & the Red Knight. Jenny Nimmo. (Children of the Red King Ser.). (ENG.). (J). 2010. audio compact disk 64.99 (978-0-545-07880-1(6)) Scholastic Inc.

Charlie Bone & the Red Knight. Jenny Nimmo. Narrated by Simon Jones. (Running Time: 7 hrs.). (Children of the Red King Ser.). (ENG.). (J). 2010. audio compact disk 34.99 (978-0-545-07856-6(3)) Scholastic Inc.

Charlie Bone & the Shadow. Jenny Nimmo. Read by Simon Jones. (Playaway Children Ser.). (J). 2008. 59.99 (978-1-60640-547-5(0)) Find a World.

Charlie Bone & the Shadow. Jenny Nimmo. (Children of the Red King Ser.: Bk. 7). (ENG.). (J). (gr. 4-7). 2008. audio compact disk 64.95 (978-0-545-07879-5(2)) Scholastic Inc.

Charlie Bone & the Shadow. Jenny Nimmo. Narrated by Simon Jones. (Children of the Red King Ser.: Bk. 7). (ENG.). (J). (gr. 4-7). 2008. audio compact disk 24.95 (978-0-545-07855-9(5)) Scholastic Inc.

Charlie Bone & the Shadow. unabr. ed. Jenny Nimmo. 6 CDs. (Running Time: 7 hrs. 16 mins.). (Children of the Red King Ser.: Bk. 7). (YA). (gr. 5-8). 2008. audio compact disk 64.95 (978-0-545-14282-3(2)) Scholastic Inc.

Charlie Bone & the Time Twister. Prod. by Listening Library Staff. 4 cass. (Running Time: 6 hrs. 42 mins.). (J). (gr. 3 up). 2004. 32.00 (978-0-8072-1899-0(5), Listening Lib) Random Audio Pubg.

Charlie Byrd Guitar Stylings. Charlie Byrd & John Griggs. 1998. pap. bk. 17.95 (978-0-7866-3848-2(6), 97337BCD) Mel Bay.

Charlie Byrds Sugarloaf Suite. Charlie Byrd. Ed. by John Griggs. 2001. bk. 14.95 (978-0-7866-4667-8(5)) Mel Bay.

Charlie Chaplin & His Times. unabr. ed. Kenneth S. Lynn. Read by Adams Morgan. 15 cass. (Running Time: 22 hrs.). 1998. 95.95 (978-0-7861-1340-8(5), 2237) Blckstn Audio.
Probes beneath the mystique of the "Little Tramp," the first true world celebrity, whose unmatched comic genius masked a complex, sometimes tragic life.

***Charlie Chaplin & His Times.** unabr. ed. Kenneth S. Lynn. Read by Adams Morgan. (Running Time: 21 hrs. 30 mins.). 2010. 44.95 (978-1-4417-5946-7(8)); audio compact disk 123.00 (978-1-4417-5944-3(1)) Blckstn Audio.

Charlie Company. unabr. collector's ed. Peter Cochrane. Read by Rupert Keenlyside. 7 cass. (Running Time: 7 hrs.). 1985. 42.00 (978-0-7366-0834-3(6), 1785) Books on Tape.
This is the story of the Cameron Highlanders whose record of service fully deserves this tribute to their courage & endurance. Peter Cochrane joined the company as a young platoon commander in 1940. After winning the DS0, he rejoins the Highlanders as company commander at Monte Cassino. This is his story.

Charlie Company: What Vietnam Did to Us. unabr. collector's ed. Peter Goldman & Tony Fuller. Read by John MacDonald. 8 cass. (Running Time: 12 hrs.). 1987. 64.00 (978-0-7366-1200-5(9), 2118) Books on Tape.
A chronicle of a front-line infantry unit in Vietnam, giving personal accounts of war & its aftermath.

Charlie Daniels: the Ultimate Collection. Contrib. by Charlie Daniels & Steve Blair. 2007. audio compact disk 21.99 (978-5-558-00804-3(0)) Pt of Grace Ent.

Charlie et le Grand Ascenseur de Verre, Set. abr. ed. Roald Dahl. Read by Luc Alexander et al. 2 cass.Tr. of Charlie & the Great Glass Elevator. (FRE.). (J). 1995. bk. 35.95 (1GA075) Olivia & Hill.
Charlie Bucket, now the owner of Willy Wonka's chocolate factory, flies above the factory in a glass elevator. As Charlie & his family climb to outer space they discover a world of fantastic beings.

Charlie McCarthy. Perf. by Richard Widmark. 1945. (CC8400) Natl Recrd Co.

Charlie McCarthy: Last Program for Chase & Sanborn. Perf. by Edgar Bergen. 1952. (CC-2779) Natl Recrd Co.

Charlie McCarthy Show. 1 cass. (Running Time: 60 min.). (Old Time Radio Classic Singles Ser.). 4.95 (978-1-57816-091-4(X), CM106) Audio File.
Includes: 1) Guests Abbott & Costello & Edward Everett Horton from 5/3/42. 2) Guests Walt Disney & Donald Duck from 9/21/47.

Charlie McCarthy Show. Perf. by Edgar Bergen et al. 1 cass. (Running Time: 60 min.). 7.95 (CC-5121) Natl Recrd Co.
Nelson Eddy sings the "new song," The Happy Wanderer, & Mortimer Snerd & Jimmy Stewart appear in a sketch. Other guests includes Don Ameche, John Barrymore, Arthur Godfrey, Marilyn Monroe, & Rudy Vallee. In Fibber McGee & Molly, McGee becomes "Mysterious McGee, the Mental Marvel." With guests Arthur B. Brian, Jess Kirkpatrick & Bill Mill's Orchestra.

Charlie McCarthy Show. Perf. by Edgar Bergen & Abbott and Costello. 1 cass. (Running Time: 60 min.). 1942. 7.95 (CC-7020) Natl Recrd Co.
The first show features Abbott & Costello in a very funny skit about Uncle Guessit; & guest Edward Everett Horton in a skit about a kangaroo loose in a garden. In the second show, guest Walt Disney gets into a discussion with Charlie about his new movie "Fun & Fancy Free" & Donald Duck has a few remarks to add.

Charlie McCarthy Show, Vol. 1. collector's ed. Perf. by Edgar Bergen et al. 6 cass. (Running Time: 9 hrs.). 1998. bk. 34.98 (4098) Radio Spirits.
You'll love the well-crafted comedy dialogue from this superb team of ventriloquist Edgar Bergen and his dummy, Charlie McCarthy as well as Bergen's other dummy, the dimwitted Mortimer Snerd. 18 episodes.

Charlie McCarthy Show, Vol. 2. collector's ed. Perf. by Edgar Bergen et al. 6 cass. (Running Time: 9 hrs..). 1998. bk. 34.98 (4115) Radio Spirits.

Charlie McCarthy Show, Vol. 3. Perf. by Charlie McCarthy & Edgar Bergen. 6 cass. (Running Time: 9 hrs.). 2002. 34.98 (4688) Radio Spirits.

Charlie McCarthy Show: An Hour of Fun With Edgar Bergen, Mortimer Snerd & All the Gang. Perf. by Mortimer Snerd. Hosted by Edgar Bergen. 1 cass. (Running Time: 1 hr.). 2001. 6.98 (1956) Radio Spirits.

Charlie McCarthy Show: Answer to Personal Ad & Planetarium Trip. Hosted by Edgar Bergen. 1 cass. (Running Time: 1 hr.). 2001. 6.98 (1736) Radio Spirits.

Charlie McCarthy Show: Barbara Stanwyck & Irene Dunn. Perf. by Barbara Stanwyck et al. Hosted by Edgar Bergen. 1 cass. (Running Time: 1 hr.). 2001. 6.95 (1734) Radio Spirits.

Charlie McCarthy Show: Ben Him. Hosted by Edgar Bergen. 1 cass. (Running Time: 1 hr.). 2001. 6.98 (2315) Radio Spirits.

Charlie McCarthy Show: Cavalcade of Flops. Hosted by Edgar Bergen. 1 cass. (Running Time: 1 hr.). 2001. 6.98 (2312) Radio Spirits.

Charlie McCarthy Show: Charlie Marries Marilyn Monroe & Charlie Needs Tooth Pulled. Hosted by Edgar Bergen. 1 cass. (Running Time: 1 hr.). 2001. 6.98 (2010) Radio Spirits.

Charlie McCarthy Show: Devilish Dreams. Hosted by Edgar Bergen. 1 cass. (Running Time: 1 hr.). 2001. 6.98 (2301) Radio Spirits.

Charlie McCarthy Show: Dick Powell & Alec Templeton. Perf. by Dick Powell & Alec Templeton. Hosted by Edgar Bergen. 1 cass. (Running Time: 1 hr.). 2001. 6.98 (2156) Radio Spirits.

Charlie McCarthy Show: Don Ameche, W. C. Fields, Nelson Eddy & Ida Lupino. Perf. by Don Ameche et al. Hosted by Edgar Bergen. 1 cass,. (Running Time: 1 hr.). 2001. 6.98 (2134) Radio Spirits.

Charlie McCarthy Show: Egg Cup Awards. Hosted by Edgar Bergen. 1 cass. (Running Time: 1 hr.). 2001. 6.98 (2308) Radio Spirits.

Charlie McCarthy Show: Fearless McCarthy, City Editor. Hosted by Edgar Bergen. 1 cass. (Running Time: 1 hr.). 2001. 6.98 (2310) Radio Spirits.

Charlie McCarthy Show: Fugitives from the F. B. I. Hosted by Edgar Bergen. 1 cass. (Running Time: 1 hr.). 2001. 6.98 (2311) Radio Spirits.

Charlie McCarthy Show: Gertrude Neisen & Billie Burke. Perf. by Gertrude Neison & Billie Burke. Hosted by Edgar Bergen. 1 cass. (Running Time: 1 hr.). 2001. 6.95 (1735) Radio Spirits.

Charlie McCarthy Show: Interplanetary Western. Hosted by Edgar Bergen. 1 cass. (Running Time: 1 hr.). 2001. 6.98 (2314) Radio Spirits.

Charlie McCarthy Show: Juicy Gossip. Hosted by Edgar Bergen. 1 cass. (Running Time: 1 hr.). 2001. 6.98 (2302) Radio Spirits.

Charlie McCarthy Show: Klondike Charlie. Hosted by Edgar Bergen. 1 cass. (Running Time: 1 hr.). 2001. 6.98 (2306) Radio Spirits.

Charlie McCarthy Show: Lost in the Woods. Hosted by Edgar Bergen. 1 cass. (Running Time: 1 hr.). 2001. 6.98 (2316) Radio Spirits.

Charlie McCarthy Show: Maureen O'Sullivan. Perf. by Maureen O'Sullivan. Hosted by Edgar Bergen. 1 cass. (Running Time: 1 hr.). 2001. 6.98 (2612) Radio Spirits.

Charlie McCarthy Show: Mortimer's Fuzzy Friend. Hosted by Edgar Bergen. 1 cass. (Running Time: 1 hr.). 2001. 6.98 (2305) Radio Spirits.

Charlie McCarthy Show: Mortimer's New Year's Eve. Hosted by Edgar Bergen. 1 cass. (Running Time: 1 hr.). 2001. 6.98 (2307) Radio Spirits.

Charlie McCarthy Show: Mortimer's Ups & Downs. Hosted by Edgar Bergen. 1 cass. (Running Time: 1 hr.). 2001. 6.98 (2313) Radio Spirits.

Charlie McCarthy Show: New Year's Party Play & How Do You Feel. Hosted by Edgar Bergen. 1 cass. (Running Time: 1 hr.). 2001. 6.98 (1925) Radio Spirits.

Charlie McCarthy Show: Oliver "Charlie" Twist. Hosted by Edgar Bergen. 1 cass. (Running Time: 1 hr.). 2001. 6.98 (2304) Radio Spirits.

Charlie McCarthy Show: Rainbow Sweater. Hosted by Edgar Bergen. 1 cass. (Running Time: 1 hr.). 2001. 6.98 (2309) Radio Spirits.

Charlie McCarthy Show: Spencer Tracy. Perf. by Spencer Tracy. Hosted by Edgar Bergen. 1 cass. (Running Time: 1 hr.). 2001. 6.98 (2553) Radio Spirits.

Charlie McCarthy Show: Vacation with Jack Benny. Perf. by Jack Benny. Hosted by Edgar Bergen. 1 cass. (Running Time: 1 hr.). 2001. 6.98 (2303) Radio Spirits.

Charlie McCarthy Show: 100th Anniversary Chase & Sanborn Show. Hosted by Edgar Bergen. 1 cass. (Running Time: 1 hr.). 2001. 6.98 (1737) Radio Spirits.

Charlie McCarthy Show: 1955 Christmas Show with Candice Bergen. Perf. by Candice Bergen. Hosted by Edgar Bergen. 1 cass. (Running Time: 1 hr.). 2001. 6.98 (2213) Radio Spirits.

Charlie McCarthy Show & James Cagney & Olivia de Haviland. unabr. ed. 1 cass. Dramatization. 7.95 Norelco box. (CC 1644) Natl Recrd Co.
Charlie McCarthy Show: with Edgar Bergen, Judy Garland & Abbott & Costello. Why does a moth eat a hole in the rug? To see the floor show! That starts the show rolling. It continues with a hilarious comedy routine by Abbott & Costello & with Judy Garland doing a comedy skit with Charlie. Mortimer Snerd also has a funny skit. A Chase & Sanborn Show...Father's Day 1942. The Strawberry Blonde: A delightful turn-of-the-century comedy romance based on the 1941 movie of the same name. The stars re-create their screen roles with James Cagney as Biff, Olivia De Havilland as Amy & Jack Carson as Hugo. Presented by Gulf Oil.

Charlie McCarthy vs. Fred Allen. 1 cass. (Running Time: 60 min.). (Old Time Radio Classic Singles Ser.). 4.95 (978-1-57816-092-1(8), CF119) Audio File.
Clips from Charlie & Fred's month long feud from the 1945 season. Added attraction "Jack & the Beanstalk" presented by Charlie, Bergen & Donald Duck (9/21/47).

Charlie McCarthy vs. Fred Allen. Perf. by Edgar Bergen & Ray Nobel. 1 cass. (Running Time: 60 min.). 7.95 (CC-5035) Natl Recrd Co.
Charlie & Fred engage in a month-long feud, with help from Mortimer Snerd, on both of their shows in the fall of 1945. These shows have been put together as one hour of feuding fun. Also a special 1947 radio show where Edgar Bergen & Charlie McCarthy tell their version of Jack & the Beanstalk; with Donald Duck.

Charlie Muffin. Brian Freemantle. Read by Hayward Morse. 5 cass. (Running Time: 5 hrs 30 min.). (Sound Ser.). 2001. 49.95 (978-1-84283-021-5(X)) Pub: UlverLrgPrint GBR. Dist(s): Ulverscroft US
Charlie Muffin is an oddity - an over-tired, over-drawn, over-hung, middle-aged anachronism. To the army colonel, Charlie is the final inherited embarrassment from a disgraced Department he is committed to revitalize. Who better than to sacrifice in the capture of a KGB general? All Charlie hopes to do is survive.

Charlie Muffin. unabr. ed. Brian Freemantle. Read by Hayward Morse. 5 CDs. (Running Time: 5 hrs. 34 mins.). (Sound Ser.). (J). 2002. audio compact disk 59.95 (978-1-84283-230-1(1)) Pub: ISIS Lrg Prnt GBR. Dist(s): Ulverscroft US

Charlie Muffin & Russian Rose. unabr. ed. Brian Freemantle. Read by Hayward Morse. 8 cass. (Running Time: 9 hrs. 33 min.). (Sound Ser.). (J). 2003. 69.95 (978-1-84283-425-1(8)); audio compact disk 79.95 (978-1-84283-691-0(9)) Pub: ISIS Lrg Prnt GBR. Dist(s): Ulverscroft US

Charlie Muffin's Uncle Sam. unabr. ed. Brian Freemantle. Read by Peter Wickham. 7 cass. (Running Time: 7.5 hrs.). (Sound Ser.). (J). 2002. 61.95 (978-1-84283-189-2(5)) Pub: ISIS Lrg Prnt GBR. Dist(s): Ulverscroft US

Charlie Necesita Una Capa. Tr. of Charlie Needs a Cloak. (SPA.). 2004. 8.95 (978-0-7882-0292-6(8)) Weston Woods.

Charlie Needs a Cloak see Charlie Necesita Una Capa

Charlie Needs a Cloak. 2004. bk. 24.95 (978-1-56008-023-7(X)); pap. bk. 18.95 (978-1-55592-382-2(8)); pap. bk. 18.95 (978-1-55592-384-6(4)); pap. bk. 38.75 (978-1-55592-383-9(6)); pap. bk. 38.75 (978-1-55592-385-3(2)); pap. bk. 32.75 (978-1-55592-200-9(7)); pap. bk. 32.75 (978-1-55592-201-6(5)); pap. bk. 14.95 (978-1-55592-719-6(X)); 8.95 (978-1-56008-866-0(4)); audio compact disk 12.95 (978-1-55592-902-2(8)) Weston Woods.

Charlie Needs a Cloak. Tomie dePaola. 1 cass., 5 bks. (Running Time: 6 min.). (J). pap. bk. 32.75 Weston Woods.
A shepherd with a worn-out cloak shears his sheep, cards, spins wool, weaves, dyes the cloth & sews a beautiful new red cloak.

Charlie Needs a Cloak. Tomie dePaola. 1 cass. (Running Time: 6 min.). (J). (ps-4). 1990. pap. bk. 14.95 (978-1-56008-024-4(8)); 8.95 (978-1-56008-102-9(3), PRA167) Weston Woods.

Charlie Needs a Cloak; Apt 3; Ten What?; Henry the Explorer. 2004. (978-0-89719-842-4(5)) Weston Woods.

Charlie Parker Played Be Bop. Chris Raschka. Read by Charles Turner. 11 vols. (Running Time: 7 mins.). (Music Makers Ser.). (J). (gr. 1-6). 2000. pap. bk. 16.95 (978-0-87499-669-2(4)); pap. bk. & tchr. ed. 33.95 Reading Chest. (978-0-87499-671-5(6)) Live Oak Media.
Raschka has created a memorable tribute to jazz great Charlie Parker in this rhymic, syncopated, compelling, funny celebration of a man & a musical form. The brief text sings & swings & skips along, practically of its own volition, while the pictures add humor & just the right amount of jazziness to the mix. One of the most innovative picture books of recent times.

Charlie Parker Played Be Bop. Chris Raschka. Read by Charles Turner. 11 vols. (Running Time: 7 mins.). (Music Makers Ser.). (J). (gr. 2-6). 2000. bk. 25.95 (978-0-87499-670-8(8)) Live Oak Media.
Raschka has created a memorable tribute to jazz great Charlie Parker in this rhymic, syncopated, compelling, funny celebration of a man & a musical form. The brief text sings & swings & skips along, practically of its own volition, while the pictures add humor & just the right amount of jazziness to the mix. One of the most innovative picture books of recent times.

Charlie Parker Played Be Bop. Chris Raschka. Illus. by Chris Raschka. (Running Time: 7 mins.). 2000. 9.95 (978-0-87499-668-5(6)); audio compact disk 12.95 (978-1-59112-418-4(2)) Live Oak Media.

Charlie Parker Plays Be-Bop. Perf. by Charlie Parker. 1 cass. (Running Time: 35 min.). (J). (ps-3). 2001. pap. bk. 15.95 (VX-669C) Kimbo Educ.
Memorable tribute to jazz great Charlie Parker in this rhythmic, syncopated, compelling, funny celebration. Includes book.

Charlie Wilson's War. George Crile. Narrated by Christopher Lane. (Running Time: 20 hrs. 30 mins.). 2003. 50.95 (978-1-59912-446-9(7)) Iofy Corp.

Charlie Wilson's War: The Extraordinary Story of the Largest Covert Operation in History. abr. ed. George Crile. Read by Christopher Lane. 6 cass. (Running Time: 45000 sec.). 2005. 29.95 (978-0-7861-3445-8(3)); audio compact disk 29.95 (978-0-7861-7995-4(3)); audio compact disk 29.95 (978-0-7861-8112-4(5)) Blckstn Audio.

Charlie Wilson's War: The Extraordinary Story of the Largest Covert Operation in History. unabr. ed. George Crile. Read by Christopher Lane. 17 CDs. (Running Time: 20 hrs. 30 mins.). 2001. audio compact disk 136.00 (978-0-7861-9027-0(2), 3178) Blckstn Audio.

Charlie Wilson's War: The Extraordinary Story of the Largest Covert Operation in History. unabr. ed. George Crile. Read by Christopher Lane. 14 cass. (Running Time: 20 hrs. 30 mins.). 2002. 89.95 (978-0-7861-2546-3(2), 3178) Blckstn Audio.

Charlie Wilson's War: The Extraordinary Story of the Largest Covert Operation in History. unabr. ed. George Crile. Read by Christopher Lane. 2 MP3-CDs. (Running Time: 20 hrs. 30 mins.). 2003. 39.95 (978-0-7861-8852-9(9), 3178) Blckstn Audio.

Charlie Wilson's War: The Extraordinary Story of the Largest Covert Operation in History. unabr. ed. George Crile. Read by Christopher Lane. 14 cass. (Running Time: 20 hrs. 30 mins.). 2007. 44.95 (978-1-4332-0412-8(6)); audio compact disk 44.95 (978-1-4332-0413-5(4)) Blckstn Audio.

Charlie York: Maine Coast Fisherman. unabr. collector's ed. Harold B. Clifford. Read by Harold B. Clifford. 6 cass. (Running Time: 6 hrs.). 1976. 36.00 (978-0-7366-0020-0(5), 1031) Books on Tape.
Here, in his own words, are fifty years in the life of a Maine coast sailor & fisherman.

Charlie's Apprentice. unabr. ed. Brian Freemantle. Read by Hayward Morse. 12 cass. 2007. 94.95 (978-1-84559-347-6(2)) Pub: ISIS Audio GBR. Dist(s): Ulverscroft US

Charlie's Bones. unabr. ed. L. L. Thrasher. Read by Stephanie Brush. 6 cass. (Running Time: 7 hrs. 12 min.). 2001. 39.95 (978-1-58116-009-3(7)) Books in Motion.
While digging a hole for the new swimming pool for heiress Lizbeth Lange, workmen discover a human skeleton. And if that isn't enough, a mystical figure appears asking for Lizbeth's help in solving a 30-year-old crime.

Charlie's Chance. unabr. ed. Brian Freemantle. Read by Hayward Morse. 14 cass. 2007. 99.95 (978-1-84559-348-3(0)) Pub: Soundings Ltd GBR. Dist(s): Ulverscroft US

Charlies Needs a Cloak. 2004. cass. & flmstrp 30.00 (978-0-89719-671-0(6)) Weston Woods.

Charlies Needs a Cloak; Apt 3; Then What?; Henry the Explorer. 2004. cass. & flmstrp (978-0-89719-750-2(X)) Weston Woods.

Charlie's Raven. Jean Craighead George. Narrated by Ramon de Ocampo. 4 cass. (Running Time: 5 hrs.). (J). 2004. 39.75 (978-1-4193-0571-9(9)) Recorded Bks.

Charlie's Web. unabr. ed. L. L. Thrasher. Read by Stephanie Brush. 6 cass. (Running Time: 6 hrs. 42 min.). 2001. 39.95 (978-1-58116-099-4(2)); audio compact disk 39.00 (978-1-58116-119-9(0)) Books in Motion.
Charlie's back! The mystical figure again visits Lizbeth Lange with a summons to help expose ten-year-old Rachel Wright's killer on Halloween night 27 years ago. Charlie believes that another child might be murdered if the killer is not found.

Charlotte. Norah Lofts. 2009. 76.95 (978-1-4079-0048-3(X)); audio compact disk 89.95 (978-1-4079-0049-0(8)) Pub: Soundings Ltd GBR. Dist(s): Ulverscroft US

Charlotte & the White Horse. 2004. 8.95 (978-0-7882-0277-3(4)) Weston Woods.

Charlotte & the White Horse. (J). 2004. bk. 24.95 (978-1-56008-180-7(5)) Weston Woods.

Charlotte Bronte's Villette. Charlotte Brontë. 2 cass. (Running Time: 3 hrs.). 1998. 16.85 Set. (978-0-563-55713-5(3)) BBC WrldWd GBR.
Villette was the author's last novel & is often regarded as her most emotionally & aesthetically satisfying work. As in Jane Ayre, the theme is one of passionate personal integrity, the individual to preserve an independent spirit in the face of adverse circumstances.

Charlotte Church: Voice of an Angel. Perf. by Charlotte Church. 1 cass. (Running Time: 60 mins. per cass.). 1999. audio compact disk 16.98 (E6432) Video Collection.
In her first-ever solo concert, the Welsh schoolgirl with the incredible voice performs the songs that have thrilled the world.

***Charlotte Fairlie.** D. E. Stevenson. 2010. 69.95 (978-1-4079-0410-8(8)); audio compact disk 84.95 (978-1-4079-0411-5(6)) Pub: Soundings Ltd GBR. Dist(s): Ulverscroft US

Charlotte Gray. Sebastian Faulks. Read by Jamie Glover. 14 CDs. (Running Time: 60120 sec.). 2001. audio compact disk 115.95 (978-0-7540-5438-2(1), CCD 129) Pub: Chivers Audio Bks GBR. Dist(s): AudioGO
In 1942 with London blacked out and France under Nazi pressure, Charlotte Gray travels south where she falls for an English airman. When she goes to France on an errand for a British organization, she is unaware that she is being manipulated.

Charlotte Greenwood Show: Barton Estate & Thanksgiving Show. Perf. by Edward Arnold. 1 cass. (Running Time: 1 hr.). 2001. 6.98 (1738) Radio Spirits.

Charlotte Porte Bonheur. Macha Grenon. 1 CD. (Running Time: 60 min.). Dramatization. (FRE.). (J). (ps up). 2001. audio compact disk 12.95 (978-2-89558-002-7(2)) Pub: Coffragants CAN. Dist(s): Penton Overseas
Told entirely in French with a full cast production.

Charlotte Temple. Susanna Rowson. Read by Anais 9000. 2009. 27.95 (978-1-60112-148-6(2)) Babblebooks.

Charlotte Temple Set. unabr. ed. Susanna Haswell Rowson. Read by Flo Gibson. 3 cass. (Running Time: 4 hrs. 30 min.). 1993. 16.95 (978-1-55685-260-2(6)) Audio Bk Con.
This satirical novella, published in more than 200 editions, was the biggest seller in the United States prior to Uncle Tom's Cabin. A young English girl is lured to america by a dashing lieutenant who cruelly abandons her.

Charlotte the Lucky Charm. Macha Grenon. Illus. by Genevieve Despres. 1 cass. (Running Time: 1 hr.). (J). 2000. audio compact disk 12.95 (978-2-89517-022-8(3)) Pub: Coffragants CAN. Dist(s): Penton Overseas
Follows Charlotte, a ladybug on her journey of discovery.

Charlotte's Friends. Sarah Kennedy. 2 cass. (Running Time: 3 hrs.). (ENG., 1997. 18.00 (978-1-85998-631-8(5), HoddrStoughton) Pub: Hodder General GBR. Dist(s): IPG Chicago
Compelling psychological chiller examines the devasting effects of a damaged childhood.

Charlotte's Friends. unabr. ed. Sarah Kennedy. Read by Norma West. 6 cass. (Running Time: 8 hr. 30 min.). (Isis Ser.). (J). 1998. 54.95 (978-0-7531-0336-4(2), 980511) Pub: ISIS Lrg Prnt GBR. Dist(s): Ulverscroft US
Charlotte Pierce has had a solitary childhood, eked out in large houses with empty people doing empty things; the only person who ever remembered her birthday was Cook. Charlotte has two close friends from her schooldays: Bary, an acclaimed photographer & Therese, who now runs an animal sanctuary. Blissfully ignorant, the two girls don't know it, but Barty & Therese are the most important people in Charlie's life. Sarah Kennedy's first novel is a compelling psychological chiller that examines the devastating effects of a damaged childhood. A mixture of Highsmith & Rendall, a new style in suspense.

Charlotte's Web. unabr. ed. E. B. White. Read by E. B. White. 3 cass. (Running Time: 3 hrs.). (J). 2001. 30.00 (LL0172, Chivers Child Audio) AudioGO.
An affectionate, sometimes bashful pig named Wilbur befriends a spider named Charlotte, who lives in the rafters above his pen. A prancing, playful bloke, Wilbur is devastated when he learns of the destiny that befalls all those of porcine persuasion. Determined to save her friend, Charlotte spins a web that reads "Some Pig," convincing the farmer & surrounding community that Wilbur is no ordinary animal & should be saved.

Charlotte's Web. unabr. ed. E. B. White. 3 CDs. (Running Time: 4 hrs. 30 min.). (J). 2000. audio compact disk 25.00 (978-0-7366-9069-0(7)) Books on Tape.

Charlotte's Web. unabr. ed. E. B. White. Read by E. B. White. (J). 2006. 39.99 (978-0-7393-7451-1(6)) Find a World.

Charlotte's Web. unabr. ed. E. B. White. Read by E. B. White. 3 CDs. (Running Time: 3 hrs. 16 mins.). (J). (gr. 3-7). 2004. audio compact disk 25.50 (978-0-8072-8605-0(2), Listening Lib); pap. bk. 36.00 (978-0-8072-8304-2(5), YYA156SP, Listening Lib); 30.00 (978-0-8072-8303-5(7), LL0172, Listening Lib) Random Audio Pubg.
Charming, bittersweet tales of friendship & adventure have enchanted audiences young & old alike.

Charlotte's Web. unabr. ed. E. B. White. Narrated by Julie Harris. 3 cass. (Running Time: 3 hrs. 15 min.). (J). (gr. 2). 1998. 24.00 (21611) Recorded Bks.
Classic tale of the unusual relationship between a spider & a pig.

Charlotte's Web. unabr. ed. E. B. White. 3 cass. (Running Time: 3 hrs.). (J). pap. bk. 29.00 (LL1029AC) Weston Woods.
Wilbur the pig is destined for the annual fall slaughtering, but his resourceful friend, a spider named Charlotte, tries to save him.

Charlotte's Web. 50th unabr. anniv. ed. E. B. White. Read by E. B. White. 3 CDs. (Running Time: 3 hrs. 38 mins.). (ENG.). (J). (gr. 4-7). 2002. audio compact disk 27.00 (978-0-8072-0852-6(3), Listening Lib) Pub: Random Audio Pubg. Dist(s): Random

Charm City. Laura Lippman. Read by Deborah Hazlett. 1. (Running Time: 9 hrs. 50 mins.). (Tess Monaghan Ser.: No. 2). 2007. 49.95 (978-0-7927-4766-6(6)); 64.95 (978-0-7927-4787-1(9)) AudioGO.

Charm City. unabr. ed. Laura Lippman. Read by Deborah Hazlett. 8 CDs. (Running Time: 9 hrs. 50 mins.). (Tess Monaghan Ser.: No. 2). 2007. audio compact disk 79.95 (978-0-7927-4489-4(6)) Pub: AudioGO. Dist(s): AudioGo

***Charm City: A Tess Monaghan Novel.** Laura Lippman. Narrated by Deborah Hazlett. (Running Time: 9 hrs. 35 mins. 0 sec.). (ENG.). 2010. audio compact disk 29.95 (978-1-60998-133-4(2)) Pub: AudioGO. Dist(s): Perseus Dist

Charm of Maya. Swami Amar Jyoti. 1 cass. 1983. 9.95 (M-37) Truth Consciousness.
We are all intoxicated by Maya's hypnotic charm. The ways to go beyond it.

Charm School. Anne Fine. Read by Prunella Scales. 3 CDs. (Running Time: 4 hrs. 30 mins.). (J). 2003. audio compact disk 29.95 (978-0-7540-6588-3(X), CHCD 088) AudioGO.

Charm School. unabr. ed. Nelson DeMille. Read by Scott Brick. (Running Time: 21 hrs.). (ENG.). 2009. 24.98 (978-1-60024-816-0(0)) Pub: Hachet Audio. Dist(s): HachBkGrp

***Charmed & Dangerous: The Clique Prequel.** Lisi Harrison. Read by Cassandra Morris. (Clique Prequel (Playaway) Ser.). (ENG.). (J). 2009. 49.99 (978-1-60788-415-6(1)) Find a World.

Charmed & Dangerous: The Clique Prequel. unabr. ed. Lisi Harrison. Read by Cassandra Morris. (Running Time: 4 hrs.). (ENG.). 2009. 19.98 (978-1-60024-844-3(6)) Pub: Hachet Audio. Dist(s): HachBkGrp

Charmed Circle Pt. 1: Gertrude Stein & Company. unabr. ed. James R. Mellow. Read by C. M. Herbert. 9 cass. (Running Time: 26 hrs.). 1995. 62.95 (978-0-7861-0904-3(1), 1716A,B) Blckstn Audio.
Through the Paris salon of Gertrude Stein passed the luminous talents of an era: Picasso, Hemingway, Matisse, Cocteau, Fitzgerald, Apollinaire. With her devoted friend, Alice B. Toklas, Gertrude Stein presided over a table heavy with good food & alive with sparkling conversation. In "Charmed Circle," James R. Mellow has re-created this glorious world & the fascinating woman who dominated it. His compelling narrative is rich with insight into both Stein's celebrated career as a writer & her enduring relationship with Toklas. Spanning the years from 1903, when she first went to Paris, to her last days at the close of World War II, "Charmed Circle" is a penetrating & lively picture of this literary giant & her exciting times.

Charmed Circle Pt. 2: Gertrude Stein & Company. unabr. ed. James R. Mellow. Read by C. M. Herbert. 9 cass. (Running Time: 26 hrs.). 1995. 62.95 (978-0-7861-0905-0(X), 1716A,B) Blckstn Audio.

Charmed Life. unabr. rev. ed. Diana Wynne Jones. Read by Gerard Doyle. 6 cass. (Running Time: 9 hrs.). (Chrestomanci Ser.). 2004. 54.75 (978-1-4025-7622-5(6)) Recorded Bks.
At first, orphan Cat Chant isn¿t jealous of his magically gifted sister Gwendolen. After all, she is the only family he has left. But, then the mysterious sorcerer Chrestomanci adopts them and changes their lives forever. In this book, which won the Guardian Award for Children¿s books, author Diana Wynne Jones¿ characters come fully alive as narrator Gerard Doyle takes listeners into a wondrous world.

Charming Billy. unabr. ed. Alice McDermott. Read by Roses Prichard. 6 cass. (Running Time: 9 hrs.). 1999. 29.95 (978-0-7366-4425-9(3)) Books on Tape.
The late Billy Lynch's family & friends have gathered at a small bar. They have come to comfort his widow & to eulogize one of the last great romantics, trading tales of his famous humor, immense charm, & unfathomable sorrow.

Charming Billy. unabr. collector's ed. Alice McDermott. Read by Roses Prichard. 6 cass. (Running Time: 9 hrs.). 1998. 48.00 (978-0-7366-4357-3(5)) Books on Tape.

Charming Grace. Deborah Smith. Read by William Dufris. 7 vols. 2004. 59.95 (978-0-7927-3135-1(2), CSL 630, Chivers Sound Lib) AudioGO.

Charming Grace. unabr. ed. Deborah Smith. Read by William Dufris & Moira Driscoll. 6 cass. (Running Time: 9 hrs. 48 mins.). 2004. 34.95 (978-1-57270-379-7(2)) Pub: Audio Partners. Dist(s): PerseuPGW

Charming Grace. unabr. ed. Deborah Smith. Narrated by William Dufris & Moira Driscoll. 8 CDs. (Running Time: 48 mins.). (Audio Editions Ser.). (ENG.). 2004. audio compact disk 39.95 (978-1-57270-380-3(6)) Pub: AudioGO. Dist(s): Perseus Dist

Charming Grace. unabr. ed. Deborah Smith. Read by William Dufris & Moira Driscoll. 8 CDs. 2004. audio compact disk 99.95 (978-0-7927-3136-8(0), SLD 630, Chivers Sound Lib) AudioGO.

Charming Lily. unabr. ed. Fern Michaels. Read by Melissa Hughes. 6 vols. (Running Time: 9 hrs.). 2001. bk. 54.95 (978-0-7927-2465-0(8), CSL 354, Chivers Sound Lib) AudioGO.
Professional mountaineer Maggie Harper is building a new life for herself in ways she never would have expected. She's traded the wilderness of Wyoming for the lush river country of the deep South, where she is busy

restoring a fine old Natchez, Mississippi house. And she's rediscovered happiness with Matt Starr, the man she has always loved. But Maggie's dreams for the future are suddenly threatened when Matt disappears without a trace.

Charming Lily. unabr. ed. Fern Michaels. Read by Melissa Hughes. 10 CDs. (Running Time: 15 hrs.). 2002. audio compact disk 94.95 (978-0-7927-9851-4(1), SLD 102, Chivers Sound Lib) AudioGO.
Professional mountaineer Maggie Harper is building a new life for herself. She's traded the wilderness of Wyoming for the lush river country of the deep South. And she's rediscovered happiness with Matt Starr, the man she has always loved. But her dreams for the future are suddenly threatened when Matt disappears without a trace.

*__Charming Quirks of Others.__ Alexander McCall Smith. (Isabel Dalhousie Ser.: No. 7). 2010. audio compact disk 29.99 (978-1-4498-4276-5(3)) Recorded Bks.

Charming Your Way to the Top. Michael K. Levine. Read by Lloyd James. (Running Time: 6 mins. 30 sec.). 2005. 44.95 (978-0-7861-3687-2(1)); audio compact disk 55.00 (978-0-7861-7648-9(2)) Blckstn Audio.

Charming Your Way to the Top. unabr. ed. Michael K. Levine. Read by Lloyd James. (Running Time: 6 mins. 30 sec.). 2005. 29.95 (978-0-7861-7912-1(0)) Blckstn Audio.

Charms for the easy Life. Kaye Gibbons. 2004. 10.95 (978-0-7435-4273-9(8)) Pub: S&S Audio. Dist(s): S and S Inc

Charms for the Easy Life. unabr. ed. Kaye Gibbons. Read by Kate Fleming. 6 vols. (Running Time: 9 hrs.). 2000. bk. 54.95 (978-0-7927-2352-3(X), CSL 241, Chivers Sound Lib) AudioGO.
A family without men, the Birches live glorious offbeat lives in the lush backwoods of North Carolina. In a sad & singular era, they are unique among women of their time. For radiant, headstrong Sophia & her shy & brilliant daughter Margaret possess powerful charms to ward off loneliness & despair. They are protected by the wisdom & love of the most stalwart Birch of all: a solid, uncompromising self-taught healer, a remarkable matriarch who calls herself Charlie Kate.

Charms for the Easy Life. unabr. ed. Kaye Gibbons. Read by Kate Fleming. 6 CDs. (Running Time: 9 hrs.). 2001. audio compact disk 64.95 (978-0-7927-9991-7(7), SLD 042, Chivers Sound Lib) AudioGO.

Charon's Landing. unabr. ed. Jack Du Brul. Read by J. Charles. (Running Time: 17 hrs.). 2008. 44.25 (978-1-4233-5874-9(0), 9781423358749, BADLE); 44.25 (978-1-4233-5872-5(4), 9781423358725, Brlnc Audio MP3 Lib); 29.95 (978-1-4233-5871-8(6), 9781423358718, Brilliance MP3); 29.95 (978-1-4233-5873-2(2), 9781423358732, BAD) Brilliance Audio.

Charon's Landing. unabr. ed. Jack Du Brul. Read by J. Charles. 2 cass. 1999. 17.95 (FS9-50889) Highsmith.

Chart as a Counseling Tool. Ruth Eichler. 1 cass. 8.95 (106) Am Fed Astrologers.
Alternatives and ways out of dilemmas through awareness.

Chart Auditing Package. Medical Management Institute Staff. 1 CD. (Running Time: 1 hr.). audio compact disk 305.00 (978-1-58383-099-4(5)) Med Mgmt.
This module covers all areas & techniques required to successfully & accurately audit your practice's records. Each component of an evaluation & management visit is explained in detail & tools are provided to assist the student as well. The course manual include coding exercises while the audios concentrate on performing your audit.

Chart Comparisons - Relationships. Julie O'Toole. 1 cass. 8.95 (265) Am Fed Astrologers.
What to look for in relationships, business, marriage, etc.

Chart Reading. Bonnie Armstrong. 1 cass. 8.95 (022) Am Fed Astrologers.
Catherine Grant's method made simple for beginners.

Chart Reading. Mae R. Wilson-Ludlam. 1 cass. 8.95 (368) Am Fed Astrologers.
Individual charts done on blackboard.

Chart Throb. Ben Elton. 2007. 94.95 (978-0-7531-3727-7(5)); audio compact disk 99.95 (978-0-7531-2693-6(1)) Pub: ISIS Audio GBR. Dist(s): Ulverscroft US

Chart Throb. Ben Elton. Read by Adam Godley. (Running Time: 3 hrs. 28 mins.). (ENG., 2006. audio compact disk 26.95 (978-1-84657-073-5(5)) Pub: Transworld GBR. Dist(s): IPG Chicago

Charterhouse of Parma. Stendhal. Read by Pedro Montoya. (Running Time: 3 hrs.). 2002. 16.95 (978-1-60083-204-8(0), Audiofy Corp) Iofy Corp.

Charting Parallels of Declination. Bonnie Armstrong. 1 cass. 8.95 (023) Am Fed Astrologers.
Missing methods: Charting parallels and points of loneliness.

Charting the End Times: A Visual Guide to Understanding Bible Prophecy. Tim LaHaye & Thomas Ice. (Tim LaHaye Prophecy Library). 2006. audio compact disk 19.99 (978-0-7369-1762-9(4)) Harvest Hse.

Chase. unabr. ed. Clive Cussler. Read by Scott Brick. 10 CDs. (Running Time: 13 hrs.). No. 1. (ENG.). 2007. audio compact disk 39.95 (978-0-14-314243-0(7), PengAudBks) Penguin Grp USA.

Chase. unabr. ed. Clive Cussler. Read by Scott Brick. 10 CDs. (Isaac Bell Ser.: No. 1). 2007. audio compact disk 100.00 (978-1-4159-4186-7(6), BksonTape) Pub: Random Audio Pubg. Dist(s): Random
April 1950: The rusting hulk of a steam locomotive rises from the deep waters of a Montana lake. Inside is all that remains of three people who died forty-four years before. But it is neither the engine nor its grisly contents that interest the people watching nearby. It is what is about to come next... 1906: For two years, the western states of America have been suffering an extraordinary crime spree: a string of bank robberies by a single man who then cold-bloodedly murders any and all witnesses and vanishes without a trace. Fed up by the depredations of "The Butcher Bandit," the U.S. government brings in the best man it can find - a tall, lean, no-nonsense detective named Isaac Bell, who has caught thieves and killers from coast to coast. But he has never had a challenge like this one. From Arizona to Colorado to the streets of San Francisco during its calamitous earthquake and fire, he pursues the best criminal mind he has ever encountered, and the woman who seems to hold the key to the man's identity. He repeatedly draws near, only to grasp at empty air, but at least he knows his pursuit is having an effect. Because his quarry is getting angry now, and has turned the chase back on him. And soon, it will take all of Bell's skills not merely to prevail... but to survive.

*__Chase.__ unabr. ed. L. J. Smith. Read by Khristine Hvam. (Running Time: 6 hrs.). (Forbidden Game Ser.: Bk. 2). 2010. audio compact disk 19.99 (978-1-4418-7541-9(7), 9781441875419, Bril Audio CD Unabri) Brilliance Audio.

Chase & Sanborn Hour. Perf. by Mae West et al. 1 cass. (Running Time: 60 min.). (Old Time Radio Classic Singles Ser.). 4.95 (978-1-57816-093-8(6), CS132) Audio File.
Skits (12/12/37).

Chase & Sanborn Hour. unabr. ed. Perf. by Mae West et al. 1 cass. (Running Time: 60 min.). Dramatization. 1937. 7.95 Norelco box. (CC-8780) Natl Recrd Co.
This show features the infamous "Adam & Eve" skit, written by Arch Oboler. The skit had the approval of the NBC censor, but the way Mae West read her part, with such a strong sexual tone, it caused a storm of protest. Hundreds of protests came in, & even the Federal Communications Commission got into the act. Mae West was banned from the air for 15 years. On NBC it was forbidden to even mention her name! Charlie explains to Bergen about a chemistry set he bought for his friend, Skinny Dugan. Charlie & Mae West also have a skit. Nelson Eddy & Dorothy Lamour sing a few songs. Sponsor is Chase & Sanborn Coffee.

Chase Happy Family (Special Broadcast Edition) Contrib. by Slina Lam. Directed By Adam Shiu. Prod. by Nichol Liao. Hosted by Clare Mou. 6 discs. (CHI.). 2004. audio compact disk (978-1-59694-026-0(3)) EDI Media.

*__Chaser.__ (ENG.). 2010. audio compact disk (978-1-59171-266-4(1)) Falcon Picture.

Chaser. Contrib. by Dave Stryker. 2006. audio compact disk 14.98 (978-5-558-28753-0(5)) Mel Bay.

Chaser. unabr. ed. Jon Guenther. Read by Gene Engene. 6 cass. (Running Time: 7 hrs. 6 min.). 2001. 39.95 (978-1-55686-870-2(7)) Books in Motion.
Bail Enforcement Agent Chad Remington is asked to assist in the search for a dangerous and sadistic terrorist who has robbed an armored car of two million dollars in counterfeit currency.

*__Chaser: A Novel.__ unabr. ed. Miasha. (Running Time: 5 hrs.). 2010. audio compact disk 19.95 (978-1-4417-3962-9(9)) Blckstn Audio.

*__Chaser: A Novel.__ unabr. ed. Miasha. Read by Erica Peeples. (Running Time: 5 hrs. 0 mins.). 2010. 29.95 (978-1-4417-3963-6(7)); 44.95 (978-1-4417-3959-9(9)); audio compact disk 55.00 (978-1-4417-3960-5(2)) Blckstn Audio.

*__Chasers: Unabridged Value-Priced Edition.__ Lorenzo Carcaterra. Narrated by L. J. Ganser. (Running Time: 11 hrs. 47 mins. 0 sec.). (ENG.). 2010. audio compact disk 14.95 (978-1-60283-998-4(0)) Pub: AudioGO. Dist(s): Perseus Dist

Chaser's Return. unabr. ed. Jon Guenther. Read by Rusty Nelson. 6 cass. (Running Time: 7 hrs.). 2001. 39.95 (978-1-55686-896-2(0)) Books in Motion.
The world of Bail Enforcement Agent Chad Remington has turned upside down. First Heather's uncle has disappeared, followed by two other people, including Heather. Now Remington must crack the 'veneer' of a doctor's deadly deception.

Chasing Butterflies & Finding Rainbows. Leta N. Childers. Read by Leta N. Childers. 1 cass. (Running Time: 20 min.). (J). (gr. k-3). 1999. bk. 6.50 (978-1-58495-023-3(4)) DiskUs Publishing.

Chasing Cezanne. unabr. ed. Peter Mayle. Read by David Case. 6 cass. (Running Time: 9 hrs.). 1998. 48.00 (978-0-7366-4113-5(0), 4618) Books on Tape.
Photographer Andre Kelly, assigned to take glossies of the treasures of the rich & famous, happens to have his camera ready when he spots a Cezanne being loaded into a plumber's truck near the home of an absent collector. In no time he's on the trail of a state-of-the-art scam.

Chasing Cool: Standing Out in Today's Cluttered Marketplace. unabr. ed. Noah Kerner & Gene Pressman. Read by Johnny Heller. (Running Time: 5 hrs. 0 mins. 0 sec.). (ENG.). 2007. audio compact disk 24.99 (978-1-4001-0424-6(6)); audio compact disk 49.99 (978-1-4001-3424-3(2)) Pub: Tantor Media. Dist(s): IngramPubServ

Chasing Cool: Standing Out in Today's Cluttered Marketplace. unabr. ed. Noah Kerner & Gene Pressman. Read by Jonathan Heller. (Running Time: 5 hrs. 0 mins. 0 sec.). (ENG.). 2007. audio compact disk 19.99 (978-1-4001-5424-1(3)) Pub: Tantor Media. Dist(s): IngramPubServ

*__Chasing Darkness.__ Robert Crais. Read by James Daniels. (Elvis Cole Ser.). 2009. 64.99 (978-1-4418-2388-5(3)) Find a World.

Chasing Darkness. abr. ed. Robert Crais. Read by James Daniels. (Running Time: 5 hrs.). (Elvis Cole Ser.). 2009. audio compact disk 14.99 (978-1-4233-4444-5(8), 9781423344445, BCD Value Price) Brilliance Audio.

Chasing Darkness. unabr. ed. Robert Crais. Read by James Daniels. 1 MP3-CD. (Running Time: 7 hrs.). (Elvis Cole Ser.). 2008. 39.25 (978-1-4233-4440-7(5), 9781423344407, Brlnc Audio MP3 Lib); 24.95 (978-1-4233-4439-1(1), 9781423344391, Brilliance MP3); 49.97 (978-1-4233-4442-1(1), 9781423344421, BADLE); 24.95 (978-1-4233-4441-4(3), 9781423344414, BAD); audio compact disk 92.25 (978-1-4233-4438-4(3), 9781423344384, BriAudCD Unabrid); audio compact disk 34.95 (978-1-4233-4437-7(5), 9781423344377, Bril Audio CD Unabri) Brilliance Audio.

Chasing Daylight: How My Forthcoming Death Transformed My Life. 2008. audio compact disk 28.00 (978-1-933309-37-8(7)) Pub: A Media Intl. Dist(s): Natl Bk Netwk

Chasing Destiny. abr. ed. Eric Jerome Dickey. Read by Kimberly JaJuan. (Running Time: 6 hrs.). 2007. audio compact disk 14.99 (978-1-4233-0641-2(4), 9781423306412, BCD Value Price) Brilliance Audio.

Chasing Destiny. unabr. ed. Eric Jerome Dickey. Read by Kimberly JaJuan. (Running Time: 14 hrs.). 2006. 39.25 (978-1-59710-869-0(3), 9781597108690, BADLE); 24.95 (978-1-59710-868-3(5), 9781597108683, BAD) Brilliance Audio.

Chasing Destiny. unabr. ed. Eric Jerome Dickey. Read by Edye Evans Hyde & Kimberly JaJuan. 1 Disc. (Running Time: 14 hrs.). 2006. 39.25 (978-1-59335-913-3(6), 9781593359133, Brlnc Audio MP3 Lib) Brilliance Audio.
Please enter a Synopsis.

Chasing Destiny. unabr. ed. Eric Jerome Dickey. Read by Kimberly Jajuan. 9 cass. (Running Time: 50400 sec.). 2006. 97.25 (978-1-59600-005-6(8), 9781596000056, BrilAudUnabridg); audio compact disk 38.95 (978-1-59600-007-0(4), 9781596000070); audio compact disk 112.25 (978-1-59600-008-7(2), 9781596000087, BriAudCD Unabrid) Brilliance Audio.

Chasing Destiny. unabr. ed. Eric Jerome Dickey. Read by Edye Evans Hyde et al. 1 MP3 CD. (Running Time: 14 hrs.). 2006. 24.95 (978-1-59335-779-5(6), 9781593357795, Brilliance MP3) Brilliance Audio.

Chasing Destiny. unabr. ed. Stephen Overholser. Read by Paul Michael Garcia. (Running Time: 23400 sec.). 2006. audio compact disk 72.00 (978-0-7861-6344-1(5)); audio compact disk 29.95 (978-0-7861-7263-4(0)) Blckstn Audio.

Chasing Destiny: A Western Story. unabr. ed. Stephen Overholser. Read by Paul Michael Garcia. (Running Time: 23400 sec.). 2006. 59.95 (978-0-7861-4760-1(1)) Blckstn Audio.

*__Chasing down the Dawn.__ abr. ed. Jewel. Read by Jewel. (ENG.). 2006. (978-0-06-114197-3(6), Harper Audio); (978-0-06-114196-6(8), Harper Audio) HarperCollins Pubs.

Chasing Fireflies. unabr. ed. Charles Martin. Narrated by Andrew Peterson. (ENG.). 2007. 17.49 (978-1-60814-114-2(4)); audio compact disk 24.99 (978-1-59859-222-1(X)) Oasis Audio.

*__Chasing Francis: A Pilgrim's Tale.__ unabr. ed. Ian Morgan Cron. (Running Time: 8 hrs. 0 mins. 0 sec.). (ENG.). 2011. audio compact disk 27.99 (978-1-59859-885-8(6)) Oasis Audio.

*__Chasing Goldman Sachs: How the Masters of the Universe Melted Wall Street Down . . . And Why They'll Take Us to the Brink Again.__ unabr. ed. Suzanne McGee. (Running Time: 12 hrs. 0 mins.). 2010. 17.99 (978-1-4001-8751-5(6)) Tantor Media.

*__Chasing Goldman Sachs: How the Masters of the Universe Melted Wall Street Down . . . And Why They'll Take Us to the Brink Again.__ unabr. ed. Suzanne McGee. Narrated by Hillary Huber. (Running Time: 14 hrs. 0 mins. 0 sec.). 2010. 24.99 (978-1-4001-6751-7(5)); audio compact disk 34.99 (978-1-4001-1751-2(8)); audio compact disk 83.99 (978-1-4001-4751-9(4)) Pub: Tantor Media. Dist(s): IngramPubServ

Chasing Harry Winston. abr. ed. Lauren Weisberger. Read by Lily Rabe. (Running Time: 6 hrs. 0 mins. 0 sec.). 2010. audio compact disk 14.99 (978-1-4423-0013-2(2)) Pub: S&S Audio. Dist(s): S and S Inc

Chasing Life: New Discoveries in the Search for Immortality to Help You Age Less Today. abr. ed. Sanjay Gupta. (Running Time: 3 hrs.). (ENG.). 2007. 14.98 (978-1-59483-881-1(X)) Pub: Hachet Audio. Dist(s): HachBkGrp

Chasing Lincoln's Killer: The Search for John Wikes Booth. James L. Swanson. Narrated by Will Patton. 4 CDs. (Running Time: 4 hrs.). (J). (ps-3). 2009. 44.99 (978-1-60775-491-6(6)) Find a World.

Chasing Lincoln's Killer: The Search for John Wikes Booth. James L. Swanson. Read by Will Patton. (Playaway Young Adult Ser.). (ENG.). (YA). (gr. 7). 2009. 49.99 (978-1-60775-987-4(X)) Find a World.

Chasing Lincoln's Killer: The Search for John Wikes Booth. James L. Swanson. (J). 2009. audio compact disk 29.95 (978-0-545-11813-2(1)) Scholastic Inc.

Chasing Lincoln's Killer: The Search for John Wikes Booth. unabr. ed. James L. Swanson. Narrated by Will Patton. 4 CDs. (Running Time: 4 hrs.). (YA). (gr. 7 up). 2009. audio compact disk 49.95 (978-0-545-11943-6(X)) Scholastic Inc.

*__Chasing Perfect.__ unabr. ed. Susan Mallery. Read by Tanya Eby. (Running Time: 9 hrs.). (Fool's Gold Ser.). 2010. 19.99 (978-1-4418-3979-4(8), 9781441839794, BAD); 39.97 (978-1-4418-3978-7(X), 9781441839787, Brlnc Audio MP3 Lib); 39.97 (978-1-4418-3980-0(1), 9781441839800, BADLE); 19.99 (978-1-4418-3977-0(1), 9781441839770, Brilliance MP3); audio compact disk 79.97 (978-1-4418-3976-3(3), 9781441839763, BriAudCD Unabrid); audio compact disk 19.99 (978-1-4418-3975-6(5), 9781441839756, Bril Audio CD Unabri) Brilliance Audio.

*__Chasing Rainbows.__ Rowena Summers. 2010. cass. & cass. 54.95 (978-1-84652-833-0(X)); audio compact disk & audio compact disk 71.95 (978-1-84652-834-7(8)) Pub: Magna Story GBR. Dist(s): Ulverscroft US

Chasing Redbird. Sharon Creech. Read by Kate Harper. 4 cass. (Running Time: 5 hrs. 42 mins.). (J). 2000. 30.00 (978-0-7366-9139-0(1)) Books on Tape.
A young girl discovers that life is a mysterious journey & is "intriguing, delightful & touching.".

Chasing Redbird. unabr. ed. Sharon Creech. Read by Kate Harper. 4 cass. (Running Time: 6 hrs.). (J). (gr. 1-8). 1999. 32.00 (LL 0141, Chivers Child Audio) AudioGO.

Chasing Redbird. unabr. ed. Sharon Creech. Read by Kate Harper. 4 cass. (YA). 1999. 29.98 (FS9-43385) Highsmith.

Chasing Redbird. unabr. ed. Sharon Creech. Read by Kate Harper. 4 vols. (Running Time: 5 hrs. 18 mins.). (J). (gr. 4-7). 1999. pap. bk. 38.00 (978-0-8072-8057-7(7), YA989SP, Listening Lib); 32.00 (978-0-8072-8056-0(9), YA989CX, Listening Lib) Random Audio Pubg.
A young girl discovers that life is a tangle of mysteries, surprises & everyday occurrences - a journey that oftens needs unraveling & sometimes must be traveled alone.

*__Chasing Redbird.__ unabr. ed. Sharon Creech. Read by Jenna Lamia. (ENG.). 2009. (978-0-06-176867-5(7)); (978-0-06-176233-8(4)) HarperCollins Pubs.

Chasing Rubi: The Truth about Porfirio Rubirosa, the Last Playboy. unabr. ed. Marty Wall & Isabella Wall. Read by Tom Weiner. (Running Time: 21600 sec.). 2007. audio compact disk 55.00 (978-0-7861-6739-5(4)) Blckstn Audio.

Chasing Rubi: The Truth about Porfirio Rubirosa the Last Playboy. unabr. ed. Marty Wall & Isabella Wall. Read by Tom Weiner. (Running Time: 21600 sec.). 2007. 54.95 (978-0-7861-4668-0(0)) Blckstn Audio.

Chasing Rubi: The Truth about Porfirio Rubirosa, the Last Playboy. unabr. ed. Marty Wall & Robert Bruce Woodcox. (Running Time: 7 mins. 30 sec.). 2007. audio compact disk 29.95 (978-0-7861-7403-4(X)) Blckstn Audio.

Chasing Shadows: Two Novellas from Transgressions. Joyce Carol Oates & Walter Mosley. Read by Michael Boatman & Anne Twomey. Ed. by Ed McBain. 2005. 20.95 (978-1-59397-702-3(6)) Pub: Macmill Audio. Dist(s): Macmillan

*__Chasing Stars: The Myth of Talent & the Portability of Performance.__ unabr. ed. Boris Groysberg. Read by Don Hagen. (Running Time: 13 hrs. 20 mins.). (ENG.). 2010. 39.98 (978-1-59659-595-8(7), GildAudio) Pub: Gildan Media. Dist(s): HachBkGrp

*__Chasing the Bear.__ unabr. ed. Robert B. Parker. Narrated by Daniel Parker. 2 CDs. (Running Time: 2 hrs. 37 mins.). (YA). (gr. 7 up). 2009. audio compact disk 38.00 (978-0-307-58249-2(3), Listening Lib) Pub: Random Audio Pubg. Dist(s): Random

Chasing the Dead. unabr. ed. Joe Schreiber. Read by Renée Raudman. 5 CDs. (Running Time: 6 hrs. 30 mins. 0 sec.). (ENG.). 2006. audio compact disk 29.99 (978-1-4001-0296-9(0)); audio compact disk 59.99 (978-1-4001-3296-6(7)); audio compact disk 19.99 (978-1-4001-5296-4(8)) Pub: Tantor Media. Dist(s): IngramPubServ

Chasing the Devil: My Twenty-Year Quest to Capture the Green River Killer. abr. ed. Sheriff David Reichert. Read by Dennis Boutsikaris. (ENG.). 2005. 14.98 (978-1-59483-153-9(X)) Pub: Hachet Audio. Dist(s): HachBkGrp

Chasing the Devil: My Twenty-Year Quest to Capture the Green River Killer. abr. ed. Sheriff David Reichert. Read by Dennis Boutsikaris. (Running Time: 6 hrs.). (ENG.). 2009. [illegible] (978-1-60024-628-9(1)) Pub: Hachet Audio. Dist(s): HachBkGrp

Chasing the Devil's Tail: A Mystery of St[illegible]ille, New Orleans. unabr. ed. David Fulmer. Read by Dion Graham. (Running Time: 30600 sec.). 2007. 72.95 (978-1-4332-0248-3(4)); audio compact disk 90.00 (978-1-4332-0249-0(2)); audio compact disk 29.95 (978-1-4332-0250-6(6)) Blckstn Audio.

Chasing the Dime. abr. ed. Michael Connelly. Read by Alfred Molina. (ENG.). 2005. 14.98 (978-1-59483-359-5(1)) Pub: Hachet Audio. Dist(s): HachBkGrp

Chasing the Dime. abr. ed. Michael Connelly. Read by Alfred Molina. 5 CDs. (Running Time: 6 hrs.). (ENG.). 2006. audio compact disk 14.98 (978-1-59483-330-4(3)) Pub: Hachet Audio. Dist(s): HachBkGrp

Chasing the Dime. unabr. ed. Michael Connelly. Read by Jonathan Davis. (ENG.). 2005. 16.98 (978-1-59483-360-1(5)) Pub: Hachet Audio. Dist(s): HachBkGrp

Chasing the Dime. unabr. ed. Michael Connelly. Read by Jonathan Davis. (Running Time: 12 hrs.). (ENG.). 2009. 59.98 (978-1-60788-077-6(6)) Pub: Hachet Audio. Dist(s): HachBkGrp

Chasing the Monsoon: A Modern Pilgrimage Through India. unabr. ed. Alexander Frater. Read by Bernard Mayes. 9 cass. (Running Time: 13 hrs.). 1999. 62.95 (978-0-7861-1616-4(1), 2444) Blckstn Audio.
Frater was able to realize his dream of witnessing firsthand the most dramatic of meteorological events - the Indian monsoon - in 1987. He followed it from its "burst" on the beaches of Trivandrum, through Delhi & Calcutta, across Bangladesh, to its finale in the town of Cherrapunji, dubbed by the Guinness Book of World Records as "The Wettest Place on Earth." Illustrates the towering influence of nature over the lives & culture of India & her people.

***Chasing the Night.** abr. ed. Iris Johansen. Read by Jennifer Van Dyck. (Running Time: 6 hrs.). (Eve Duncan Ser.). 2010. 14.99 (978-1-4418-8546-3(3), 9781441885463, BAD) Brilliance Audio.

***Chasing the Night.** abr. ed. Iris Johansen. Read by Jennifer Van Dyck. 5 CDs. (Running Time: 5 hrs.). (Eve Duncan Ser.). 2010. audio compact disk 24.99 (978-1-4418-8545-6(5), 9781441885456, BACD) Brilliance Audio.

***Chasing the Night.** unabr. ed. Iris Johansen. Read by Jennifer Van Dyck. 1 MP3-CD. (Running Time: 10 hrs.). (Eve Duncan Ser.). 2010. 24.99 (978-1-4418-8540-1(4), 9781441885401, Brilliance MP3); 24.99 (978-1-4418-8542-5(0), 9781441885425, BAD); 39.97 (978-1-4418-8541-8(2), 9781441885418, Brinc Audio MP3 Lib); 39.97 (978-1-4418-8543-2(9), 9781441885432, BADLE) Brilliance Audio.

***Chasing the Night.** unabr. ed. Iris Johansen. Read by Jennifer Van Dyck. 9 CDs. (Running Time: 10 hrs.). (Eve Duncan Ser.). 2010. audio compact disk 36.99 (978-1-4418-8360-5(6), 9781441883605, Bril Audio CD Unabri) Brilliance Audio.

***Chasing the Night.** unabr. ed. Iris Johansen. Read by Jennifer Van Dyck. 9 CDs. (Running Time: 10 hrs.). (Eve Duncan Ser.). 2010. audio compact disk 97.97 (978-1-4418-8539-5(0), 9781441885395, BriAudCD Unabrid) Brilliance Audio.

Chasing Vermeer. unabr. ed. Blue Balliett. Read by Ellen Reilly. (J). 2006. 59.99 (978-0-7393-7457-3(5)) Find a World.

Chasing Vermeer. unabr. ed. Blue Balliett. Read by Ellen Reilly. 4 CDs. (Running Time: 4 hrs. 47 mins.). (ENG.). (J). (gr. 5). 2004. audio compact disk 28.00 (978-0-307-20673-2(4), Listening Lib) Pub: Random Audio Pubg. Dist(s): Random

Chasm City. unabr. ed. Alastair Reynolds. Narrated by John Lee. (Running Time: 23 hrs. 0 mins. 0 sec.). (ENG.). 2009. 39.99 (978-1-4001-5956-7(3)); audio compact disk 119.99 (978-1-4001-3956-9(2)); audio compact disk 59.99 (978-1-4001-0956-2(6)) Pub: Tantor Media. Dist(s): IngramPubServ

***Chasm City.** unabr. ed. Alastair Reynolds. Narrated by John Lee. (Running Time: 23 hrs. 0 mins.). 2009. 59.99 (978-1-4001-2956-0(7)); 25.99 (978-1-4001-7956-5(4)) Tantor Media.

***Chaste Clarissa.** abr. ed. John Cheever. Read by Meryl Streep et al. (ENG.). 2009. (978-0-06-125284-6(0), Caedmon) HarperCollins Pubs.

***Chaste Clarissa.** unabr. ed. John Cheever. Read by Meryl Streep et al. (ENG.). 2009. (978-0-06-196858-7(7), Caedmon) HarperCollins Pubs.

Chaste White & Blush Red. David Novak. (C). 2002. audio compact disk 15.00 (978-0-9714059-0-5(5)) A Telling Exp Inc.

***Chastened: The Unexpected Story of My Year Without Sex.** unabr. ed. Hephzibah Anderson. Narrated by Justine Eyre. (Running Time: 9 hrs. 0 mins.). 2010. 15.99 (978-1-4001-8782-9(6)); 24.99 (978-1-4001-6782-1(5)); audio compact disk 83.99 (978-1-4001-4782-3(4)); audio compact disk 34.99 (978-1-4001-1782-6(8)) Pub: Tantor Media. Dist(s): IngramPubServ

Chastity Challenge. Mother Angelica & Father Michael. 1 cass. (Running Time: 60 min.). (Mother Angelica Live Ser.). 1989. 10.00 (978-1-55794-120-6(3), T71) Eternal Wrd TV.
Offers a 5 step plan for parents to help with their teens, shares personal experiences, & discuss available books & videotapes to help.

Chat Botte. Tr. of Puss in Boots. (FRE.). pap. bk. 12.95 (978-2-89558-062-1(6)) Pub: Coffragants CAN. Dist(s): Penton Overseas

Chat Botte. 1 cass.Tr. of Puss in Boots. (FRE.). (J). (gr. 3 up). 1991. bk. 14.95 (1AD021) Olivia & Hill.

Chat Derriere la Vitre. l.t. ed. Gilbert Bordes. (French Ser.). 1995. bk. 30.99 (978-2-84011-101-6(2)) Pub: UlverLrgPrint GBR. Dist(s): Ulverscroft US

Chat with Challa. 2005. audio compact disk (978-0-9743883-8-0(6)) KS Med Pub.

Chataqua County, NY - Performance Measures in Action. unabr. ed. Innovation Groups Staff. 1 cass. (Running Time: 1 hrs. 15 min.). (Transforming Local Government Ser.: Vol. 11). 1999. 10.00 (978-1-882403-67-7(3), IG9911) Alliance Innov.

Chateau de Babar. Laurent de Brunhoff. 1 cass. (Babar Ser.).Tr. of Babar's House. (FRE.). (J). (ps-3). 1991. bk. 14.95 (1AD075) Olivia & Hill.
Babar & his family move to Goodtrunk Castle.

Chateau de Ma Mere. l.t. ed. Marcel Pagnol. (French Ser.).Tr. of My Mother's House. 2001. bk. 30.99 (978-2-84011-394-2(5)) Pub: UlverLrgPrint GBR. Dist(s): Ulverscroft US

Chateaubriand & Rousseau. Marc Fumaroli. 1 cass. (Running Time: 60 mins.). (College de France Lectures). (FRE.). 1996. 21.95 (1857-LQP) Olivia & Hill.

Chateaux of the Loire Valley: A Narrated Auto Tour of the Loire Valley. Brian N. Morton. 1 cass. (Running Time: 90 min.). (Touring France with Brian Morton Ser.). 1993. 12.95 (978-0-934034-24-1(9)) Olivia & Hill.
Autoroute from Paris to Chartres & on to the valley of the Loire. Along the way, the historic tapestry of the region is revealed. Combines history, local legends & anecdotes to enrich your tour. You'll discover how the Renaissance was introduced to the Loire Valley & how the Huguenots were banished. Visit Blois & learn about the assassination of the Duc de Guise. Enjoy Chenonceaux where women ruled. Hear the hunting horns at Chambord. Admire Cheverny where the Mona Lisa was hidden during WWII. See the castle at Chinon where the Knight Templars were imprisoned, the Jews were burned, & Joan of Arc arrived disguised as a man.

Chatham School Affair. unabr. ed. Thomas H. Cook. Narrated by George Guidall. 7 cass. (Running Time: 10 hrs.). 2000. 60.00 (978-0-7887-0622-6(5), 94796E7) Recorded Bks.

Chato & the Party Animals. 2004. bk. 29.95 (978-1-55592-703-5(3)); bk. 24.95 (978-1-55592-693-9(2)); pap. bk. 14.95 (978-1-55592-687-8(8)); 8.95 (978-1-55592-545-1(6)); audio compact disk 12.95 (978-1-55592-552-9(9)) Weston Woods.

Chato & the Party Animals. Gary Soto. Illus. by Susan Guevara. 11 vols. bk. 25.95 (978-1-59112-460-3(3)); bk. 28.95 (978-1-59112-920-2(6)); pap. bk. 37.95 (978-1-59112-461-0(1)); pap. bk. 39.95 (978-1-59112-921-9(4)); 9.95 (978-1-59112-458-0(1)); audio compact disk 12.95 (978-1-59112-918-9(4)) Live Oak Media.

Chato & the Party Animals. Gary Soto. Read by Willie Colon. (J). 2005. pap. bk. 18.95 (978-1-59112-919-6(2)) Pub: Live Oak Media. Dist(s): AudioGO

Chato & the Party Animals. Gary Soto. Read by Willie Colon. 11 vols. (J). 2005. pap. bk. 16.95 (978-1-59112-459-7(X)) Pub: Live Oak Media. Dist(s): AudioGO

Chato Goes Cruisin' Gary Soto. Read by Willie Colon. Illus. by Susan Guevara. (J). 2008. bk. 25.95 (978-1-59519-906-5(3)); pap. bk. 18.95 (978-1-59519-909-6(8)) Live Oak Media.

Chato y los Amigos Pachangueros. Gary Soto. Read by Willie Colon. Illus. by Susan Guevara. (J). (ps-3). 2006. pap. bk. 43.95 (978-1-59519-669-9(2)); pap. bk. 41.95 (978-1-59519-668-2(4)); pap. bk. 18.95 (978-1-59519-667-5(6)); pap. bk. 16.95 (978-1-59519-666-8(8)) Live Oak Media.

Chato Y Su Cena. (J). 2004. pap. bk. 32.75 (978-1-55592-342-6(9)) Weston Woods.

Chato y Su Cena. Gary Soto. Illus. by Susan Guevara. 14 vols. (Running Time: 12 mins.). 1998. pap. bk. 43.95 (978-1-59519-148-9(8)); audio compact disk 12.95 (978-1-59519-146-5(1)) Live Oak Media.

Chato y Su Cena. Gary Soto. Illus. by Susan Guevara. 11 vols. (Running Time: 12 mins.). (SPA.). (J). 1998. pap. bk. 18.95 (978-1-59519-264-6(6)) Pub: Live Oak Media. Dist(s): AudioGO

Chato y Su Cena. Gary Soto. Read by Willie Colon. Tr. by Alma Flor Ada. Illus. by Susan Guevara. 14 vols. (Running Time: 12 mins.). (SPA.). (gr. k-3). 1998. pap. bk. & tchr. ed. 41.95 Reading Chest. (978-0-87499-439-1(X)) Live Oak Media.
Chato, the coolest cat in East L.A. is thrilled when a family of plump mice move into the barrio. He & his pal Novio Boy invite the new neighbors for a feast, but their plan to turn their guest into the main course goes awry when the mice bring along a surprise friend.

Chato y Su Cena. Gary Soto. Illus. by Susan Guevara. 1 cass., 5 bks. (Running Time: 10 min.). (SPA.). (J). pap. bk. 32.75 Weston Woods.
Feeling hungry & somewhat sneaky, Chato invites a family of mice to his house to share a tasty meal of salsa & enchiladas. Wisely, the mice bring along a canine friend who ensures that Chato eats tortillas & not them for dinner.

Chato y Su Cena. Gary Soto. Illus. by Susan Guevara. 1 cass. (Running Time: 15 min.). (SPA.). (J). pap. bk. 12.95 Weston Woods.

Chato y Su Cena. Gary Soto. (SPA.). (J). (gr. 2-3). 2004. 8.95 (978-0-7882-0133-2(6)) Weston Woods.

Chato y Su Cena. unabr. ed. Gary Soto. Perf. by Willie Colon. 1 cass. (Running Time: 12 mins.). (J). 1998. 9.95 (978-0-87499-440-7(3)) Live Oak Media.
Chato, the coolest cat in East L.A. is thrilled when a family of plump mice move into the barrio. He & his pal Novio Boy invite the new neighbors for a feast, but their plan to turn their guest into the main course goes awry when the mice bring along a surprise friend.

Chato y Su Cena. unabr. ed. Gary Soto. Read by Willie Colon. Tr. by Alma Flor Ada. Illus. by Susan Guevara. 11 vols. (Running Time: 12 mins.). (SPA.). (J). (gr. k-3). 1998. pap. bk. 16.95 (978-0-87499-437-7(3)) Pub: Live Oak Media. Dist(s): AudioGO

Chato's Kitchen. 2004. audio compact disk 12.95 (978-1-55592-903-9(6)) Weston Woods.

Chato's Kitchen. (J). 2004. bk. 24.95 (978-0-7882-0696-2(6)); pap. bk. 18.95 (978-1-55592-386-0(0)); pap. bk. 18.95 (978-1-55592-389-1(5)); pap. bk. 38.75 (978-1-55592-388-4(7)); pap. bk. 38.75 (978-1-55592-390-7(9)); pap. bk. 32.75 (978-1-55592-202-3(3)); pap. bk. 32.75 (978-1-55592-203-0(1)); pap. bk. 14.95 (978-0-7882-0134-9(4)); pap. bk. 14.95 (978-0-7882-0697-9(4)) Weston Woods.

Chato's Kitchen. Gary Soto. Illus. by Susan Guevara. 11 vols. (Running Time: 11 mins.). 2002. bk. 25.95 (978-1-59112-206-7(6)); bk. 28.95 (978-1-59112-528-0(6)); pap. bk. 37.95 (978-1-59112-207-4(4)); audio compact disk 12.95 (978-1-59112-335-4(6)) Live Oak Media.

Chato's Kitchen. Gary Soto. Read by Willie Colon. 11 vols. (Running Time: 11 mins.). (Live Oak Readalong Ser.). (J). 2002. pap. bk. 16.95 (978-1-59112-205-0(8)); pap. bk. 18.95 (978-1-59112-336-1(4)) Pub: Live Oak Media. Dist(s): AudioGO

Chato's Kitchen. Gary Soto. Illus. by Susan Guevara. Narrated by Cheech Marin. 1 cass., 5 bks. (Running Time: 30 min.). (J). pap. bk. 32.75 Weston Woods.

Chato's Kitchen. Gary Soto. Illus. by Susan Guevara. Narrated by Cheech Marin. 1 cass. (Running Time: 30 min.). (J). (gr. k-4). bk. 24.95 Weston Woods.

Chato's Kitchen. Gary Soto. Illus. by Susan Guevara. Narrated by Cheech Marin. Music by Jerry Dale McFadden. 1cass. (Running Time: 11 min.). (J). (gr. k-4). pap. bk. 12.95 Weston Woods.
Feeling hungry & somewhat sneaky, Chato invites a family of mice to his house to share a tasty meal of salsa & enchiladas. Wisely, the mice bring along a canine friend who ensures that Chato eats tortillas & not them for dinner.

Chato's Kitchen. Gary Soto. (J). 2004. 8.95 (978-0-7882-0092-2(5)) Weston Woods.

Chato's Kitchen. Gary Soto. Illus. by Susan Guevara. (Running Time: 11 mins.). (J). (gr. k-3). 2003. 9.95 (978-1-59112-204-3(X)) Live Oak Media.

Chato's Kitchen; Chato y Su Cena. Gary Soto. Illus. by Susan Guevara. 22 vols. (Running Time: 23 mins.). 2002. pap. bk. 33.95 (978-1-59112-208-1(2)) Live Oak Media.

Chatte. Colette. audio compact disk 12.95 (978-0-8219-3755-6(3)) EMC-Paradigm.

Chatte. Sidonie-Gabrielle Colette. pap. bk. 24.95 (978-88-7754-163-5(6)) Pub: Cideb ITA. Dist(s): Distribks Inc

Chatterton. Peter Ackroyd. Read by James Wilby. 6 cass. 54.95 (978-0-7927-3318-8(5), CSL 693); audio compact disk 79.95 (978-0-7927-3319-5(3), SLD 693) AudioGO.

Chatterton. unabr. collector's ed. Peter Ackroyd. Read by David Case. 8 cass. (Running Time: 12 hrs.). 1998. 64.00 (978-0-7366-4013-8(4), 4511) Books on Tape.
A mystery novel on the "suicide" of English literature's most famous prodigy.

Chattery Teeth: And Other Stories. unabr. ed. Stephen King. Read by Kathy Bates et al. (Running Time: 4 hrs. 30 mins. 0 sec.). (ENG.). 2009. audio compact disk 14.99 (978-0-7435-9822-4(9)) Pub: S&S Audio. Dist(s): S and S Inc

Chaucer. unabr. ed. Peter Ackroyd. Narrated by Simon Vance. (Running Time: 5 hrs. 30 mins. 0 sec.). (Ackroyd's Brief Lives Ser.). (ENG.). 2005. audio compact disk 19.99 (978-1-4001-5160-8(0)); audio compact disk 49.99 (978-1-4001-3160-0(X)) Pub: Tantor Media. Dist(s): IngramPubServ

Chaucer: Ackroyd's Brief Lives. unabr. ed. Peter Ackroyd. Narrated by Simon Vance. (Running Time: 5 hrs. 30 mins. 0 sec.). (Ackroyd's Brief Lives Ser.). (ENG.). 2005. audio compact disk 24.99 (978-1-4001-0160-3(3)) Pub: Tantor Media. Dist(s): IngramPubServ

Chaucer & Religion. unabr. ed. Edward Wagenknecht. 1 cass. (Running Time: 44 min.). 12.95 (23080) J Norton Pubs.
A reading from Professor Wagenknecht's book, "The Personality of Chaucer".

Chaucer by Dancing Beetle. Perf. by Eugene Ely. 1 cass. (Running Time: 70 min.). (J). 1993. 10.00 Erthviibz.
Geoffrey Chaucer, nature sounds & parody come together when Ms. Alligator & the spunky humans read & sing with Dancing Beetle.

Chaucer on Love & Virtue. unabr. ed. Edward Wagenknecht. 1 cass. (Running Time: 44 min.). 1968. 12.95 (23081) J Norton Pubs.
A reading from Professor Wagenknecht's book, "The Personality of Chaucer".

Chavez Ravine. Culture Clash. Contrib. by Richard Montoya et al. (Running Time: 4560 sec.). 2004. audio compact disk 25.95 (978-1-58081-295-5(3)) Pub: L A Theatre. Dist(s): NetLibrary CO

Che Guevara: A Concise Biography. unabr. ed. Andrew Sinclair. Read by Peter Wickham. 2 cass. (Running Time: 2 hrs. 20 mins.). 2000. 24.95 (978-0-7531-0641-9(8), 990815) Ulverscroft US.
"I was born in Argentina, I fought in Cuba & I began to be a revolutionary in Guatemala." Che Guevara was the most admired & beloved revolutionary of his time, the first man since Simon Bolivar seriously to plan to unite the countries of Latin America. This concise biography unravels Che's life, from his birth in 1928, the child of free-thinking radical Argentinian aristocrats, his youthful membership of Accion Argentina & his training as a doctor in Buenos Aires, through witnessing of the fall of the new revolutionary government in Guatemala alongside its leader, Arbenz, his action as a commander in the guerrilla war in Cuba with Fidel Castro & his part in the reforming Marxist Cuban government, to his fight for liberation of the Congo &, finally, of Bolivia, where he was executed.

Che Guevara: A Revolutionary Life. unabr. ed. John Lee Anderson. (Running Time: 32 hrs. 0 mins.). (ENG.). 2008. audio compact disk 59.95 (978-1-4332-7068-0(4)) Blckstn Audio.

Che Guevara: A Revolutionary Life. unabr. ed. John Lee Anderson. (Running Time: 35 hrs. 0 mins.). (ENG.). 2009. 44.95 (978-1-4332-7069-7(2)) Blckstn Audio.

Che Guevara: A Revolutionary Life. unabr. ed. Jon Lee Anderson. Read by Armando Durán. (Running Time: 16 hrs. 50 mins.). (ENG.). 2009. 105.95 (978-1-4332-7806-8(5)); 109.95 (978-1-4332-7065-9(X)); audio compact disk 159.00 (978-1-4332-7066-6(8)) Blckstn Audio.

Che Guevara: A Revolutionary Life. unabr. ed. Jon Lee Anderson. Read by Edward Lewis. 23 cass. (Running Time: 34 hrs. 30 mins.). 1997. 184.00 (978-0-7366-3707-7(9), 4392-A&B) Books on Tape.
Guevara was an idealist who turned his back on middle-class comfort to fight for the interests of the poor & oppressed in Cuba, Bolivia, & the Congo.

Che Guevara Pt. 1: A Revolutionary Life. unabr. ed. Jon Lee Anderson. Read by Edward Lewis. 14 cass. (Running Time: 21 hrs.). 1997. 112.00 (4392-B) Books on Tape.

Che Guevara Pt. 2: A Revolutionary Life. unabr. ed. Jon Lee Anderson. Read by Edward Lewis. 9 cass. (Running Time: 13 hrs. 30 mins.). 1997. 72.00 (4392-B) Books on Tape.

Cheap: The High Cost of Discount Culture. unabr. ed. Ellen Ruppel Shell. (Running Time: 11 hrs. 30 mins. 0 sec.). (ENG.). 2009. audio compact disk 69.99 (978-1-4001-4279-8(2)) Pub: Tantor Media. Dist(s): IngramPubServ

Cheap: The High Cost of Discount Culture. unabr. ed. Ellen Ruppel Shell. Narrated by Lorna Raver. (Running Time: 11 hrs. 30 mins. 0 sec.). (ENG.). 2009. audio compact disk 24.99 (978-1-4001-6279-6(3)); audio compact disk 34.99 (978-1-4001-1279-1(6)) Pub: Tantor Media. Dist(s): IngramPubServ

***Cheap Excursion.** abr. ed. Noel Coward. Read by Simon Jones. (ENG.). 2006. (978-0-06-125285-3(9), Harper Audio) HarperCollins Pubs.

Cheaper by the Dozen. Frank B. Gilbreth, Jr. & Ernestine Gilbreth Carey. Read by Dana Ivey. 4 cass. (Running Time: 6 hrs. 12 mins.). (YA). (gr. 7 up). 2000. 30.00 (978-0-7366-9036-2(0)) Books on Tape.
With the twelve Gilbreth kids, Dad has plenty of chances to use his efficiency expertise. Mom's work as a psychologist comes in handy, too. Stories of dating, household emergencies, tonsillectomies & excursions to the movies by the dozen make for lively entertainment.

Cheaper by the Dozen. unabr. ed. Frank B. Gilbreth, Jr. & Ernestine Gilbreth Carey. Read by Dana Ivey. 4 vols. (Running Time: 6 hrs. 4 mins.). (J). (gr. 4-7). 2004. pap. bk. 38.00 (978-0-8072-8307-3(X), YA157SP, Listening Lib); 32.00 (978-0-8072-8306-6(1), LL0179, Listening Lib) Random Audio Pubg.

Cheaper by the Dozen. unabr. ed. Frank B. Gilbreth, Jr. & Ernestine Gilbreth Carey. Contrib. by Dana Ivey. 5 CDs. (Running Time: 6 hrs. 5 mins.). (ENG.). (J). (gr. 3-7). 2005. audio compact disk 24.95 (978-0-307-24324-9(9), Listening Lib) Pub: Random Audio Pubg. Dist(s): Random

Cheaper by the Dozen, unabr. ed. Frank B. Gilbreth, Jr. & Ernestine Gilbreth Carey. Narrated by George Guidall. 5 pieces. (Running Time: 6 hrs. 15 mins.). (gr. 8 up). 1994. 44.00 (978-0-7887-0007-1(3), 94206E7) Recorded Bks.
When Mr. Gilbreth, a rather large, often loud business efficiency expert tries to apply business techniques to his own family, hilarity ensues. This charming memoir of a large & loving family, written by two of the twelve Gilbreths, is a priceless piece of early 20th century-Americana.

Cheater. unabr. ed. Nancy Taylor Rosenberg. (Running Time: 10 hrs. 50 mins.). 2009. 29.95 (978-1-4332-7782-5(4)); 65.95 (978-1-4332-7778-8(6)); audio compact disk 29.95 (978-1-4332-7781-8(6)); audio compact disk 100.00 (978-1-4332-7779-5(4)) Blckstn Audio.

Cheaters. Eric Jerome Dickey. 15 CDs. (Running Time: 16 hrs. 15 mins.). audio compact disk 142.00 (978-0-7887-9872-6(3)) Recorded Bks.

Cheaters. unabr. ed. Eric Jerome Dickey. 12 cass. (Running Time: 16 hrs. 15 mins.). 2001. 95.00 (978-0-7887-4041-1(5), F0019E7) Recorded Bks.
When Stephan & Chante meet, their initial attraction is unsettling. Can they learn to trust each other despite their well meaning friends?.

Cheatin' & Hurtin' with the Plasmates from Altair IV. Jim Brown. Read by Steve Scherf. 2 cass. 1998. 17.99 Set. (890065) Penton Overseas.
The aliens have finally landed - due to their love of country music! Discovering he is hightly allergic to the country music loving Altarians, music critic John Jamieson has fled the big city to his home-town where he continues to write reviews on the net. But when a former girlfriend joins him, soon followed by her shapeshifting Altarian lover, Undular, they become the center of a galactic conflict. Before he & Tasha can settle down to a life of domestic bliss, John & his new Altarian pals must discover - & defeat - a nest of unfriendly people-eating aliens in his backyard.

Cheatin' & Hurtin' with the Plasmates from Altair IV, Set. abr. ed. Jim Brown. 2 cass. (Running Time: 180 min.). 1998. 17.95 (978-1-894144-02-5(3)) Penton Overseas.

Cheating: Program from the Award Winning Public Radio Series. Interview. Hosted by Fred Goodwin. Comment by John Hockenberry. 1 CD. (Running Time: 1 Hour). 2003. audio compact disk (978-1-932479-31-7(7), LCM 294) Lichtenstein Creat.
Four out of five high school students say they've cheated. More than half of medical school students say the same thing. Even The New York Times has cribbed from somebody else's paper. Is everybody doing it? Guests include Dr. Howard Gardner, professor in Cognition and Education at the Harvard Graduate School of Education and co-director of a large-scale research study called the GoodWork Project; renowned primate researcher Dr. Frans de Waal, professor of psychology at Emory University; Dr. Helen Fisher, research professor in the department of anthropology at Rutgers University and author of Anatomy of Love: A Natural History of Mating, Marriage, and Why We Stray; and country music group BR5-49, who perform the Hank Williams classic, "Your Cheatin' Heart."Plus, commentator John Hockenberry wonders, just what defines cheating these days?.

Cheating Culture: Why More Americans Are Doing Wrong to Get Ahead. David Callahan. Narrated by Richard M. Davidson. 10 CDs. (Running Time: 12 hrs.). 2004. audio compact disk 29.99 (978-1-4025-7926-4(8), 01552) Recorded Bks.

Cheating Death. unabr. ed. Marvin Cetron & Owen Davies. Read by C. M. Herbert. 6 cass. (Running Time: 8 hrs. 30 mins.). 1998. 44.95 (978-0-7861-1311-8(1), 2235) Blckstn Audio.
Examines every side of the dilemma - from the promises of science to the consequences of living an extended lifespan beyond any previous experience.

Cheating Death. unabr. ed. H. R. F. Keating. Read by Garard Green. 5 cass. (Running Time: 7 hrs. 15 min.). (Inspector Ghote Mystery Ser.: No. 20). 2001. 49.95 (978-1-85695-835-6(3), 940810) Pub: ISIS Audio GBR. Dist(s): Ulverscroft US
Under orders from New Delhi, Inspector Ghote is sent to look into the theft & sale of examination papers from one of the most deplorable outlying colleges of Bombay University. At first glance, all seems straightforward - the chief suspect has attempted suicide & the Principal has admitted leaving his office safe unlocked. However, life is never easy for Ghote & he soon finds himself head-over-heels in the often farcical world of Indian college life.

Cheating Death: The Doctors & Medical Miracles That Are Saving Lives Against All Odds. unabr. ed. Sanjay Gupta. Read by Sanjay Gupta. (Running Time: 7 hrs. 30 mins.). (ENG.). 2009. 24.98 (978-1-60024-797-2(0)); audio compact disk 34.98 (978-1-60024-795-8(4)) Pub: Hachet Audio. Dist(s): HachBkGrp

Cheating Death: The Promise & the Future Impact of Trying to Live Forever. unabr. ed. Marvin Cetron & Owen Davies. Read by C. M. Herbert. 6 cass. (Running Time: 9 hrs.). 1999. 29.95 (978-0-7861-1544-0(0)) Blckstn Audio.
Examines every side of the dilemma of aging - from the promises of science to the consequences of living an extended lifespan beyond any previous experience. Topics include the science of aging & how melatonin is guiding the drive to extend life, new gene research, environmental concerns, gaps between poor/wealthy nations, religious concerns.

Chechen Jihad: Al Qaeda's Training Ground & the Next Wave of Terror. unabr. ed. Yossef Bodansky. Read by James Adams. (Running Time: 64800 sec.). 2007. 24.95 (978-1-4332-0649-8(8)); 65.95 (978-1-4332-0647-4(1)); audio compact disk 24.95 (978-1-4332-0650-4(1)); audio compact disk 29.95 (978-1-4332-0651-1(X)); audio compact disk & audio compact disk 81.00 (978-1-4332-0648-1(X)) Blckstn Audio.

Check All Excess Baggage. Precious Jamail. Read by Precious Jamail. 1 cass. 1996. 14.00 (978-0-9649681-0-3(X), 634226) Precious Prodns.

Checker & the Derailleurs. unabr. ed. Lionel Shriver. Read by MacLeod Andrews. (Running Time: 11 hrs.). 2009. 39.97 (978-1-4233-9716-8(9), 9781423397168, Brlnc Audio MP3 Lib); 39.97 (978-1-4233-9718-2(5), 9781423397182, BADLE); 24.99 (978-1-4233-9717-5(7), 9781423397175, BAD); 24.99 (978-1-4233-9715-1(0), 9781423397151, Brilliance MP3); audio compact disk 97.97 (978-1-4233-9714-4(2), 9781423397144, BriAudCD Unabrid); audio compact disk 36.99 (978-1-4233-9713-7(4), 9781423397137, Bril Audio CD Unabri) Brilliance Audio.

Checker Playing Hound Dog. abr. ed. Joe Hayes. Read by Joe Hayes. 1 cass. (J). (gr. 4-8). 1986. 10.95 (978-0-939729-13-5(X), CPP913X) Pub: Trails West Pub. Dist(s): Continental Bk
Features ten Southwestern tall tales.

***Checkerboard of Nights: An Audio Book, Vol. 1.** Created by Pinnacle Courseware. (YA). 2010. audio compact disk 24.99 (978-0-9826205-0-2(0)) Judmar.

Checklist for Designating a Minor's Guardian. 1 cass. (Running Time: 1 hr. 30 min.). 1994. 17.40 (M163) Am Law Inst.
This tape teaches lawyers how to counsel clients who must select a guardian for the minor children, & how to adequately document testamentary & lifetime designations.

Checklist Manifesto: How to Get Things Right. unabr. ed. Atul Gawande. Read by John Bedford Lloyd. 5 CDs. (Running Time: 6 hrs. 30 mins. 0 sec.). 2010. audio compact disk 29.99 (978-1-4272-0898-9(0)) Pub: Macmill Audio. Dist(s): Macmillan

Checklist of CITES Species 2008: A Reference to the Appendices to the Convention on International Trade in Endangered Species of Wild Fauna & Flora. United Nations Environment Programme, World Conservation Monitoring Centre Staff. (ENG, FRE & SPA.). 2009. audio compact disk 17.00 (978-2-88323-029-3(3)) Untd Nat Pubns.

Checkmate. unabr. ed. Dorothy Dunnett. Narrated by Andrew Napier. 22 cass. (Running Time: 30 hrs. 45 mins.). (Lymond Chronicles: Bk. 6). 1997. 99.75 (978-1-84197-692-1(X), H1438MC, Clipper Audio) Recorded Bks.

Checkmates. Ron Milner. 2 cass. (Running Time: 2 hrs.). 1999. 16.99 (978-0-9673967-0-5(0)) Right Prodns.
Focuses on two couples: retirees Mattie & Frank Cooper & Laura & Sylvester Williams, the young marrieds who rent the Coopers second-floor apartment. At first glance Mattie & Frank have an idyllic relationship, a sharp contrast to Laura & Sylvester's competitiveness, fighting & infidelity. Through a mix of flashbacks & current scenes, the audience comes to learn that these four people aren't so unalike in their troubles.

***CheckPro 2003: Windows Site License for VanHuss/Forde/Woo/Hefferin's Keyboarding & Word Processing.** 16th ed. Connie Forde et al. (ENG.). (C). 2005. 481.95 (978-0-538-72913-0(9)) Pub: South-West. Dist(s): CENGAGE Learn

Checkride Tips: From Flying's Eye of the Examiner. Howard J. Fried. Read by Howard J. Fried. 6 cass. 1997. bk. 39.95 Set. (978-0-9653640-7-2(0)) Odyssey Aviation.
Tips on taking FAA Checkrides for new license or upgrade.

Chee-Chalker. unabr. ed. L. Ron Hubbard. Read by Tamara Meskimen & Tait Ruppert. 2 CDs. (Running Time: 2 hrs.). (Stories from the Golden Age Ser.). (ENG.). (gr. 6). 2009. audio compact disk 9.95 (978-1-59212-174-8(8)) Gala Pr LLC.

***Cheer along with Dr. Jean Ebook: 63 Cheers & Attention Grabbers to Motivate & Engage Children.** Jean Feldman. (J). 2009. 14.99 (978-1-60689-945-8(7)) Creat Teach Pr.

Cheer Leader. unabr. collector's ed. Jill McCorkle. Read by Leanor Reizen. 8 cass. (Running Time: 8 hrs.). 1988. 48.00 (978-0-7366-1258-6(0), 2171) Books on Tape.
Late 1960's coming-of-age novel concerning an all-American girl who falls for an older man.

Cheerful by Request, Set. Edna Ferber. Read by Flo Gibson. 6 cass. (Running Time: 8 hrs. 30 min.). 1995. 24.95 (978-1-55685-368-5(8)) Audio Bk Con.
Many of these moving stories are set against the backdrop of World War II. The title story is accompanied by "The Gay Old Dog," "The Tough Guy," "The Eldest," "That's Marriage," "The Woman Who Tried to Be Good," "The Girl Who Went Right," "The Hooker-up-the-Back," "The Guiding Miss Gowd," "Sophy As She Might Have Been," "The Three of Them," & "Shore Leave".

Cheerful Giving: 11 Cor. 9:1-15. Ed Young. 1997. 4.95 (978-0-7417-2130-3(9), 1130) Win Walk.

***Cheerful Money: Me, My Family, & the Last Days of Wasp Splendor.** unabr. ed. Tad Friend. Read by William Dufris. (Running Time: 12 hrs. 0 mins.). 2010. 29.95 (978-1-4417-3193-7(8)); 72.95 (978-1-4417-3189-0(X)); audio compact disk 105.00 (978-1-4417-3190-6(3)) Blckstn Audio.

Cheerfulness Breaks In. unabr. ed. Angela Thirkell. Read by Nadia May. 7 cass. (Running Time: 10 hrs.). 2002. 49.95 (978-0-7861-2327-8(3), 3035); audio compact disk 64.00 (978-0-7861-9377-6(8), 3035) Blckstn Audio.

Cheering CD. (CHI.). 1999. audio compact disk 15.00 (978-0-9721862-5-4(5)) Lamb Music & Min.

Cheerleading Series. (ENG.). 2008. 137.47 (978-0-9792996-6-7(7)) Summit Dynamics.

Cheers for Ears. unabr. ed. Terence Tobin. 3 cass. 29.95 (978-0-88432-496-6(6), S05002) J Norton Pubs.
This program by psychologist Terence Tobin has been created to develop basic listening skills in children, ages 6-8. The cassettes provide a variety of sounds: animals in the zoo, work on the farm, transportation, etc.

Cheers for Ears CDs & Booklet. Terence Tobin. 3 CDs. (Running Time: 2 hrs. 30 mins.). (J). 2005. audio compact disk 39.95 (978-1-57970-169-7(8), S05002D) J Norton Pubs.

Cheese Monkeys: A Novel in Two Semesters. unabr. ed. Chip Kidd. Read by Bronson Pinchot. (Running Time: 6 hrs. NaN mins.). 2009. 29.95 (978-1-4332-5151-1(5)); audio compact disk 50.00 (978-1-4332-5149-8(3)); audio compact disk 44.95 (978-1-4332-5148-1(5)) Blckstn Audio.

Cheese Runners. Chris A. Jackson. 2005. audio compact disk 15.00 (978-1-59975-126-9(7)) Indep Pub IL.

Cheever: A Life. unabr. ed. Blake Bailey. (Running Time: 25 hrs. 0 mins.). 2009. audio compact disk 140.00 (978-1-4332-6397-2(1)) Blckstn Audio.

Cheever: A Life. unabr. ed. Blake Bailey. Read by Grover Gardner. (Running Time: 25 hrs. 0 mins.). 2009. 44.95 (978-1-4332-6400-9(5)); audio compact disk 49.95 (978-1-4332-6399-6(8)) Blckstn Audio.

Cheever: A Life, Part A. unabr. ed. Blake Bailey. (Running Time: 12 hrs. 5 mins.). 2009. audio compact disk 72.95 (978-1-4332-6396-5(3)) Blckstn Audio.

Cheever: A Life, Part B. unabr. ed. Blake Bailey. (Running Time: 12 hrs. 5 mins.). 2009. audio compact disk 72.95 (978-1-4332-6977-6(5)) Blckstn Audio.

Cheever: The Enormous Radio & the Swimmer. unabr. ed. John Cheever. Read by John Cheever. Read by Meryl Streep & Ben Cheever. (Running Time: 3600 sec.). (Caedmon Essentials Ser.). 2006. audio compact disk 12.95 (978-0-06-112646-8(2)) HarperCollins Pubs.

Chekhov. unabr. ed. Henri Troyat. Read by Wolfram Kandinsky. 12 cass. (Running Time: 1 hr. 30 mins. per cass.). 1986. 96.00 (978-0-7366-1629-4(2), 2487) Books on Tape.
After a nightmarish childhood ruled by a tyrannical father, Anton Chekhov, one of the four greatest Russian novelists, forged for himself a stoical code of self-mastery. He placed medicine & literature as the twin pillars of his life, a life haunted by the tuberculosis that would finally kill him. Balancing between commitment (to family & medicine) & freedom (from politics & religion), Chekhov seemed cautious & wary. He was skeptical of his own success. He feared women & fended them off until the end of his life. Then, truly in love, he married a young actress. But even this did not bring him happiness.

Chekhov: Humanity's Advocate. unabr. ed. Ernest J. Simmons. 1 cass. (Running Time: 46 min.). (Classics of Russian Literature Ser.). 1968. 12.95 (23137) J Norton Pubs.
Explores various facets of Chekhov's works - the originality of his works as he moved from a depiction of life as it is to life as it should be; his artistic position of detached objectivity to final acceptance of the need for a moral purpose.

Chekhov Stories, Set. unabr. ed. Anton Chekhov. Read by Grover Gardner et al. 2 cass. (Running Time: 2 hrs.). 1993. 14.95 (978-1-55685-271-8(1)) Audio Bk Con.
Selections from Stories of Russian Life including: "Childer," "At Home," "The Troublesome Guest," "Lean & Fat," "Hush," "The Trousseau," "Agatha," "Not Wanted," & "Little Jack".

Chekhov Stories - Selections from Stories of Russian Life. Anton Chekhov. Narrated by Flo Gibson et al. (ENG.). 2009. audio compact disk 16.95 (978-1-60646-131-0(1)) Audio Bk Con.

Chekhov: 11 Stories. Anton Chekhov. Narrated by Ralph Cosham. (Running Time: 17040 sec.). (Unabridged Classics in MP3 Ser.). (ENG.). 2008. audio compact disk 24.00 (978-1-58472-609-8(1), In Aud); audio compact disk 14.95 (978-1-58472-610-4(5), In Aud) Sound Room.

Chelovek v Futlyare. Anton Chekhov. 1 cass. (Running Time: 1 hrs.). Orig. Title: A Man in a Case. (RUS.). 1996. pap. bk. 19.50 (978-1-58085-569-3(5)) Interlingua VA.

Chelsea Dreaming: A Play about Dylan Thomas. D. J. Britton. (Running Time: 1 hr. 30 mins. 0 sec.). (ENG.). 2009. audio compact disk 24.95 (978-1-60283-740-9(6)) Pub: AudioGO. Dist(s): Perseus Dist

Chelsea Murders. unabr. collector's ed. Lionel Davidson. Read by Richard Green. 6 cass. (Running Time: 9 hrs.). 1987. 48.00 (978-0-7366-1104-6(5), 2030) Books on Tape.
Horrendous murders by a killer who played games with the police, always mailing them cryptic bits of poetry-baffling clues to the identity of his next victim.

Chem Office 3.1. Cambridge Soft Corporation Staff. (C). 1997. audio compact disk 74.95 (978-0-7637-0611-1(6), 0611-6) Jones Bartlett.

Chem Tv: Organic Chemistry CD-ROM 3. 0. B. A. Luceigh. (C). 2004. audio compact disk 70.95 (978-0-7637-4703-9(3), 0763747033) Jones Bartlett.

Chem TV: Student Mac II 2.0. B. A. Luceigh. (C). 1996. audio compact disk 29.95 (978-0-7637-0034-8(7), 0034-7) Jones Bartlett.

***Chemical Changes: CD add-on Set.** Perf. by Millmark Education Staff. (ConceptLinks Ser.). 2009. audio compact disk 50.00 (978-1-61618-355-4(1)) Millmark Educ.

***Chemical Changes Audio CD.** Perf. by Millmark Education Staff. (ConceptLinks Ser.). 2008. audio compact disk 28.00 (978-1-4334-0220-3(3)) Millmark Educ.

***Chemical Changes SB1 Audio CD Forming New Substances.** Perf. by Millmark Education Staff. (Content Literacy Libraries Ser.). 2008. audio compact disk (978-1-4334-0440-5(0)) Millmark Educ.

***Chemical Changes SB2 Audio CD Transfer of Energy.** Perf. by Millmark Education Staff. (Content Literacy Libraries Ser.). 2008. audio compact disk (978-1-4334-0441-2(9)) Millmark Educ.

***Chemical Changes SB3 Audio CD Breaking Bonds.** Perf. by Millmark Education Staff. (Content Literacy Libraries Ser.). 2008. audio compact disk (978-1-4334-0442-9(7)) Millmark Educ.

***Chemical Changes SB4 Audio CD Acids & Bases.** Perf. by Millmark Education Staff. (Content Literacy Libraries Ser.). 2008. audio compact disk (978-1-4334-0443-6(5)) Millmark Educ.

Chemical Ecstasy. Walter B. Clark. 1 cass. 9.00 (A0021-83) Sound Photosyn.
Psychedelics Conference '83.

Chemical Engineering for Chemists: A Practical Problem-Solving Course with an Industry-Oriented Approach. Instructed by Richard G. Griskey. 7 cass. (Running Time: 7 hrs. 6 min.). 255.00 incl. 170pp. manual. (69) Am Chemical.
Focuses on each of the three major areas of chemical engineering - fluid flow, heat transfer, & mass transfer.

Chemical Hair Relaxing & Soft Curl Permanent. Milady Publishing Company Staff. 1 cass. (Standard Ser.: Chapter 13). 1995. 11.95 (978-1-56253-285-7(5), Milady) Pub: Delmar. Dist(s): CENGAGE Learn

Chemical Marketing Management. Instructed by Carl R. Pacifico & Robert J. Polacek. 10 cass. (Running Time: 11 hrs. 30 min.). 340.00 incl. 280pp. manual. (72) Am Chemical.
Discusses the selection & implementation of methods to attain specific marketing goals.

Chemical Production Machinery in Germany: A Strategic Reference 2007. Compiled by Icon Group International, Inc. Staff. 2007. ring bd. 195.00 (978-0-497-35967-6(7)) Icon Grp.

Chemical Revolution in Medicine. unabr. ed. Alexander Mennie. 1 cass. 1990. 12.95 (TSE012) J Norton Pubs.

Chemical Thermodynamics: A Practical View of Thermodynamics Applications. Instructed by Henry A. Bent. 8 cass. (Running Time: 10 hrs.). 280.00 incl. 416pp. manual. (60) Am Chemical.
Examines the physical meanings & practical applications of thermodynamics.

Chemical Thermodynamics of Selenium. Ed. by Jane Perrone. Contrib. by Organisation for Economic Co-operation and Development Staff. (Chemical Thermodynamics Ser.). (ENG., 2005. 353.00 (978-0-444-51403-5(1), ElseSci) Sci Tech Bks.

Chemicals in China: A Strategic Reference 2006. Compiled by Icon Group International, Inc. Staff. 2007. ring bd. 195.00 (978-0-497-35865-5(4)) Icon Grp.

Chemicals in India: A Strategic Reference 2007. Compiled by Icon Group International, Inc. Staff. 2007. ring bd. 195.00 (978-0-497-36007-8(1)) Icon Grp.

Chemicals in the Workplace. 1 cass. (Running Time: 23 min.). 9.95 (I0530B090, HarperThor) HarpC GBR.

Chemin du Retour. H. Jay Siskin et al. (C). 2001. tchr. ed. 107.81 (978-0-07-253245-6(9), Mc-H Human Soc) Pub: McGrw-H Hghr Educ. Dist(s): McGraw

Chemins Dangereux. 7 cass. (Running Time: 7 hrs.). (Mystery Thrillers in French Ser.). (FRE.). pap. bk. 89.95 (SFR270) J Norton Pubs.
Short-episode thriller, intermediate level, in a radio-play format, especially created to develop listening comprehension skills. Accompanying book provides a transcript of the recording, exercises & French vocabulary.

Chemins Dangereux. Emile De Harven. 95.95 (978-0-8219-3625-2(5)) EMC-Paradigm.

Chemist. 1 cass. (Science Ser.). (J). bk. Incl. 24p. bk. (TWIN 424) NewSound.

Chemistry. Prod. by Kevin Cadogan. 2005. audio compact disk 13.99 (978-5-559-01487-6(7)) Pt of Grace Ent.

Chemistry. Milady Publishing Company Staff. 1 cass. (Standard Ser.: Chapter 25). 1995. 15.95 (978-1-56253-297-0(9), Milady) Delmar.

Chemistry. Kim Mitzo Thompson & Karen Mitzo Hilderbrand. Illus. by Mark Paskiet. 1 cass. (Running Time: 30 min.). (I'd Like to Be a Ser.). (J). (ps-4). 1996. bk. & stu. ed. 9.98 (978-1-57583-019-3(1), TWIN 424) Twin Sisters.
Through twelve entertaining & educational songs, children learn the many jobs of being a chemist. Children discover that whether researching new medicines or developing fuels for space travel, the work of a chemist is always challenging.

Chemistry, Set. Myers. 2004. audio compact disk 598.33 (978-0-03-038092-1(8)) Holt McDoug.

Chemistry Vol. 124: Get Kids Excited about Chemistry! unabr. ed. Kim Mitzo Thompson & Karen Mitzo Hilderbrand. 1 CD. (Running Time: 32 min.). (Get Kids Excited about Ser.). (J). (ps-4). 1999. audio compact disk 12.99 (978-1-57583-204-3(6)) Twin Sisters.
Through 12 easy-to-understand songs, kids take an adventure to learn the basics of chemistry.

Chemistry & the Enlightenment. unabr. ed. Ian Jackson. Read by Edwin Newman. (Running Time: 9000 sec.). (Audio Classics: Science & Discovery Ser.). 2006. audio compact disk 25.95 (978-0-7861-6433-2(6)) Pub: Blckstn Audio. Dist(s): NetLibrary CO

Chemistry & the Enlightenment. unabr. ed. Ian Jackson. Read by Edwin Newman. Ed. by Jack Sommer & Mike Hassell. 2 cass. (Running Time: 2 hrs. 45 min.). Dramatization. (Science & Discovery Ser.). (YA). (gr. 11 up). 1993. 17.95 set. (978-0-938935-72-8(0), 10407) Knowledge Prod.
In the 17th & 18th centuries, scientists went beyond Aristotle's four elements (Earth, Wind, Fire, & Water) to catalogue nature's many basic elements. New materials & potions stimulated visions of wealth & healing; soon, new theories of atomic structure & combustion laid the foundation for practical applications that blossomed into the Industrial Revolution.

Chemistry Audio CD Theme Set: Set of 6 Set B. Adapted by Benchmark Education Staff. (English Explorers Ser.). (J). (gr. 3-6). 2007. audio compact disk 60.00 (978-1-4108-9825-8(3)) Benchmark Educ.

Chemistry Experiements on File. Diagram Group. (gr. 6-12). 2002. audio compact disk 149.95 (978-0-8160-4447-4(3)) Facts On File.

Chemistry for Beginners: A Novel. unabr. ed. Anthony Strong. (Running Time: 9.5 hrs. 0 mins.). (ENG.). 2009. 29.95 (978-1-4332-9526-3(1)); 59.95 (978-1-4332-9522-5(9)); audio compact disk 90.00 (978-1-4332-9523-2(7)) Blckstn Audio.

Chemistry for the Non-Chemist. Instructed by W. F. Oettle. 8 cass. (Running Time: 8 hrs.). 235.00 incl. 170pp. manual. (67) Am Chemical.
Chemical principles & applications for non-chemist professionals & support staff.

Chemistry I. Worldwise Education Staff. 1 cass. (Running Time: 1 hr. 10 min.). (Rap Notes Ser.). (YA). (gr. 9-12). 1993. 9.98 (978-0-9643439-1-7(6)) Wrld Wise Educ.
Chemistry curriculum set to rap music.

Chemistry: Matter & Its Changes: Instructor's Resource CD. 4th ed. James Brady & Frederick Senese. (YA). 2004. tchr. ed. (978-0-471-64901-4(5)) Wiley US.

Chemistry of Mescaline. Alexander Shulgin. 1 cass. (Running Time: 50 Min.). 1999. 11.00 (13704) Big Sur Tapes.
1978 San Francisco.

Chemistry of the Blood: God's Precious Provision for Power. Mac Hammond. 3 cass. (Running Time: 3 hrs). 2005. 15.00 (978-1-57399-237-4(2)) Mac Hammond.
Few believers truly understand the power available to them through the blood of Jesus. This series will open your eyes to a whole new source of strength for change, protection, healing and provision.

Chemistry of the Blood: God¿s Precious Provision for Power. Mac Hammond. 2008. audio compact disk 18.00 (978-1-57399-341-8(7)) Mac Hammond.

Chemistry Problem Solving. James W. Wheeler. (J). 1979. bk. & stu. ed. 342.20 (978-0-89420-133-2(6), 237000) Natl Book.

Chemistry Reprints. Ed. by Marco A. V. Bitetto. 1 cass. 2000. (978-1-58578-032-7(4)) Inst of Cybernetics.

Chemistry Songs. Leo Wood. 2 cass. 10.00 Incl. bklet. (LW111A); 10.00 Incl. bklet. (LW111B) OptimaLearning.
Singing enhances long-term memory with information being invested with the greatest of ease, grace, & joy. Contains short & easy songs, with simple melodies designed for the "non-singer." Students say they sing the songs mentally during a quiz & the information of the song is quickly recalled with minimum effort.

Chemistry: the Central Science: Instructor's Resource CD W/TestGen. 10th rev. ed. Kate Brown et al. audio compact disk 18.97 (978-0-13-146487-2(6)) PH School.

Chemistry: the Central Science: Replacement CD. 9th ed. Kate Brown. audio compact disk 14.97 (978-0-13-123935-7(X)) PH School.

Chemistry: the Central Science: Replacement CD. 10th ed. Kate Brown et al. audio compact disk 14.97 (978-0-13-194644-6(7)) PH School.

Chemotherapy. 1 cass. (Running Time: 1 hr.). 2001. 9.95 (CA607) Pub: VisnQst Vid Aud. Dist(s): TMW Media

Chemotherapy - A Healing Solution: Relax into Healing Series (Spoken Audio CD & Booklet) Nancy Hopps. (Relax Into Healing Ser.). 2007. pap. bk. 19.95 (978-0-9785985-1-8(2), Relas into Healing) Pub: Syner Systs. Dist(s): Baker Taylor

Chemotherapy Companion. unabr. ed. 1 cass. (Running Time: 1 hr.). (Mind Food Ser.). 2001. 14.95 (978-1-56102-431-5(7)) Inter Indus.
Supports a positive outcome for chemotherapy.

Chemotherapy of Viral Infections. Moderated by R. Gordon Douglas, Jr. Contrib. by Arnold S. Monto et al. 1 cass. (Running Time: 9 min.). 1985. 12.00 (A8503) Amer Coll Phys.
This topic is discussed by a moderator & experts who offer differing opinions.

ChemReact10: Info Chem Chemical Reaction Search System. Ed. by InfoChem GmbH Staff. 1994. bk. & tchr. ed. 2250.00 (978-0-387-14180-0(4)) Spri.

Chen mo de gao yang see Silence of the Lambs

Cheney. unabr. ed. Stephen F. Hayes. Read by Alan Sklar. (YA). 2007. 74.99 (978-1-60252-825-3(X)) Find a World.

Cheney. unabr. ed. Stephen F. Hayes. Read by Alan Sklar. 17 CDs. (Running Time: 22 hrs. 0 mins. 0 sec.). (ENG.). 2007. audio compact disk 49.99 (978-1-4001-0525-0(0)) Pub: Tantor Media. Dist(s): IngramPubServ

Cheney: The Untold Story of America's Most Powerful & Controversial Vice President. unabr. ed. Stephen F. Hayes. Narrated by Alan Sklar. (Running Time: 22 hrs. 0 mins. 0 sec.). (ENG.). 2007. audio compact disk 99.99 (978-1-4001-3525-7(7)); audio compact disk 34.99 (978-1-4001-5525-5(8)) Pub: Tantor Media. Dist(s): IngramPubServ

Chequered Life: Tales of a New England Upbringing. Merton L. Griswold. 1 cass. (Running Time: 45 min.). 1994. 9.95 (978-0-9630498-0-3(1)) Westminster CO.
Stories of New England life near the beginning of this century - includes stories about trains, cows, farm life, country doctor, tales from Amherst College & more.

Chere Francoise: Revision de la Grammaire Francaise. 2nd ed. Jeannette D. Bragger & Robert Ariew. (FRE.). (C). 1984. pap. bk. 17.50 (978-0-685-08250-8(4)) HM.

Cherish. Catherine Anderson. Narrated by Ruth Ann Phimister. 12 cass. (Running Time: 16 hrs. 15 mins.). 104.00 (978-0-7887-5981-9(7)) Recorded Bks.

Cherish. unabr. ed. Catherine Anderson. Narrated by Ruth Ann Phimister. 14 CDs. (Running Time: 16 hrs. 15 mins.). 2002. audio compact disk 134.00 (978-1-4025-1535-4(9)) Recorded Bks.
Race Spencer leads a lonely life out west until he stumbles upon Rebecca Morgan, the only survivor of a terrifying robbery. Sweeping the helpless beauty into his powerful arms, Race carries her away to safety. Rebecca's life is no longer in danger, but her virtue is decidedly threatened. Race arouses feelings in her she never knew she could experience - especially toward such a hardened man.

Cherished Freedom. Joyce Stranger. 7 cass. (Running Time: 9 hrs. 15 mins.). (Story Sound Ser.). (J). 2005. 61.95 (978-1-85903-788-1(7)) Pub: Mgna Lrg Print GBR. Dist(s): Ulverscroft US

Cherishing Our Soul... Enhancing Our Society. Robert F. Morneau. 2 cass. (Running Time: 2 hrs. 14 min.). 1996. 17.95 Set. (TAH366) Alba Hse Comns.
These two lectures deal with the need for balance within our lives, a contemplative stance in a fragmented world. He deals with some of the crises we face in our time & some possible solutions. This is contemplative, yet thought-provoking material in the inimitable Morneau style.

Cherokee. Donald Clayton Porter. Read by Lloyd James. Abr. by Odin Westgaard. 5 vols. No. 10. 2004. audio compact disk 30.00 (978-1-58807-410-2(2)) Am Pubng Inc.

Cherokee. abr. ed. Donald Clayton Porter. Read by Lloyd James. Abr. by Odin Westgaard. 4 vols. No. 10. 2004. (978-1-58807-757-8(8)); audio compact disk (978-1-58807-849-0(3)) Am Pubng Inc.

Cherokee. abr. ed. Donald Clayton Porter. Read by Lloyd James. Abr. by Odin Westgaard. 4 vols. No. 10. 2004. 25.00 (978-1-58807-226-9(6)) Am Pubng Inc.

Cherokee & Seneca, Songs & Dances. unabr. ed. 1 cass. (Running Time: 60 mins.). 12.95 (C11155) J Norton Pubs.

Cherokee Ceremonial Songs & Dances. 1 cass. (Running Time: 60 mins.). 12.95 (C11152) J Norton Pubs.

Cherokee Hymns, History & Hmm! Willena H. Robinson. Des. by Willena H. Robinson. Tr. by Prentice Robinson. (CHR.). 2005. audio compact disk 30.00 (978-1-882182-22-0(7)) Cherokee Lang & Cult.

Cherokee Hymns, History & Hmm. Willena H. Robinson. Des. by Willena H. Robinson. Tr. by Prentice Robinson. (CHR.). 2005. 30.00 (978-1-882182-21-3(9)) Cherokee Lang & Cult.

Cherokee Lighthorse. unabr. ed. Gary McCarthy. Read by Maynard Villers. 4 cass. (Running Time: 5 hrs. 18 min.). (Horsemen Ser.: Bk. 2). 1994. 26.95 (978-1-55686-528-2(7)) Books in Motion.
The Ballou family is forced to gather their horses & flee west as the Civil War bears down on their plantation.

Cherokee Messenger. Read by George Casey. Ed. by Willena Robinson. Contrib. by Willena Robinson. 2005. 30.00 (978-1-882182-16-9(2)) Cherokee Lang & Cult.

Cherokee Study Course: Cherokee Study I. Prentice Robinson. Des. by Willena Robinson. (CHR.). 2005. spiral bd. 29.95 (978-1-882182-03-9(0)) Cherokee Lang & Cult.

***Cherries & Cherry Pits.** unabr. ed. Vera B. Williams. Read by Martha Plimpton. (ENG.). 2009. (978-0-06-176238-3(5), GreenwillowBks); (978-0-06-180592-9(0), GreenwillowBks) HarperCollins Pubs.

Cherries & Cherry Pits. unabr. ed. Vera B. Williams. 1 cass. (Running Time: 15 min.). (J). (gr. k-4). 1993. pap. bk. 16.90 (978-0-8045-6673-5(9), 6673) Spoken Arts.
Ala Notable Book. New York Times Best Illustrated Book. Boston Globe/Hom Book Honor Book for Illustrations.

Cherries in Winter: My Family's Recipe for Hope in Hard Times. unabr. ed. Suzan Colon. Read by Suzan Colon. (ENG.). 2009. audio compact disk 25.00 (978-0-307-70287-6(1), Random AudioBks) Pub: Random Audio Pubg. Dist(s): Random

Cherry: A Memoir. Mary Karr. Read by Mary Karr. 4 cass. (Running Time: 6 hrs.). 2000. 25.95 (Random AudioBks) Random Audio Pubg.
Mary Karr told the prize-winning tale of her hardscrabble Texas childhood with enough literary verve to spark a renaissance in memoir. She is ultimately trying to run from the thrills & terrors of her sexual awakening by butting against authority in all its forms. she lands all too often in the principal's office & in one instance, a jail cell. Looking for a lover or heart's companion who'll make her feel whole, she hooks up with an outrageous band of surfers & heads, wannabe yois & bona fide geniuses.

Cherry: A Memoir. unabr. collector's ed. Mary Karr. Read by Karen White. 7 cass. (Running Time: 10 hrs. 30 min.). 2000. 56.00 (978-0-7366-5919-2(6)) Books on Tape.
The author of The Liars' Club explores a girl's stormy, ardent adolescence with humor & courage.

Cherry Bomb. unabr. ed. J. A. Konrath. Read by Dick Hill & Susie Breck. (Running Time: 9 hrs.). (Jacqueline "Jack" Daniels Mystery Ser.). 2009. 24.99 (978-1-4233-1264-2(3), 9781423312642, Brilliance MP3) Brilliance Audio.

Cherry Bomb. unabr. ed. J. A. Konrath. Read by Susie Breck & Dick Hill. (Running Time: 9 hrs.). (Jacqueline "Jack" Daniels Mystery Ser.). 2009. 24.99 (978-1-4233-1266-6(X), 9781423312666, BAD); 39.97 (978-1-4233-1265-9(1), 9781423312659, Brinc Audio MP3 Lib); 39.97 (978-1-4233-1267-3(8), 9781423312673, BADLE); audio compact disk 82.97 (978-1-4233-1263-5(5), 9781423312635, BriAudCD Unabrid) Brilliance Audio.

***Cherry Bomb.** unabr. ed. J A Konrath & Jacqueline Jack Daniels. (Running Time: 9 hrs.). (Jacqueline Jack Daniels Ser.). 2010. audio compact disk 14.99 (978-1-4418-8750-4(4), 9781441887504) Brilliance Audio.

Cherry Orchard: A Comedy in Four Acts. Anton Chekhov. Narrated by Flo Gibson. (ENG.). 2007. audio compact disk 16.95 (978-1-55685-955-7(4)) Audio Bk Con.

Cherry Orchard: A Comedy in Four Acts. Anton Chekhov. 2 CDs. (Running Time: 2 hrs.). 2005. audio compact disk 19.95 (978-0-660-19388-5(4)) Canadian Broadcasting CAN.

Cherry Orchard: A Comedy in Four Acts. Anton Chekhov. Read by Full Cast Production Staff. Tr. by Frank Dwyer & Nicholas Sanders from RUS. Contrib. by Jordan Baker & John Chardiet. (Playaway Adult Fiction Ser.). (ENG.). 2008. 39.99 (978-1-60640-943-5(3)) Find a World.

Cherry Orchard: A Comedy in Four Acts. Anton Chekhov. Perf. by Michael Cristofer et al. Tr. by Nicholas Saunders et al. 2 cass. (Running Time: 1 hr. 45 mins.). 2002. 22.95 (978-1-58081-227-6(9), TPT158); audio compact disk 25.95 (978-1-58081-235-1(X), CDTPT158) Pub: L A Theatre. Dist(s): NetLibrary CO
A work of timeless, bittersweet beauty about the fading fortunes of an aristocratic Russian family and their struggle to maintain their status in a changing world.

Cherry Orchard: A Comedy in Four Acts. unabr. ed. Anton Chekhov. Narrated by Flo Gibson. 2 cass. (Running Time: 2 hrs. 12 min.). (gr. 9 up). 2002. 14.95 (978-1-55685-682-2(2),) Audio Bk Con.
Madame Lyubov Ranevsky has to sell the dear old family estate for debts to a merchant who plans to cut down the orchard to turn it into suburban lots.

Cherry Orchard: A Comedy in Four Acts. unabr. ed. Anton Chekhov & Tyrone Guthrie. Perf. by Jessica Tandy & Hume Cronyn. Tr. by Leonid Kipnis. 3 cass. (Running Time: 5 hrs.). Dramatization. 1965. 26.94 (CDL5 314) HarperCollins Pubs.
Cast includes: Robert Pastene, Lee Richardson, Paul Ballantyne, Ed Flanders, Sandy McCallum, Nancy Wickwire, Kristina Callahan, Ken Ruta, Ruth Nelson, & Ellen Geer.

Chesapeake. James A. Michener. Read by Larry McKeever. 1993. 96.00 (978-0-7366-2421-3(X)); 96.00 (978-0-7366-2422-0(8)) Books on Tape.

Chesapeake, Pt. 1. unabr. ed. James A. Michener. Read by Larry McKeever. 12 cass. (Running Time: 18 hrs.). 1993. 96.00 (978-0-7366-2420-6(1), 3187A) Books on Tape.
Saga, spanning four centuries, of seven families living on Maryland's Chesapeake Bay.

Chesapeake, Pt. 2. unabr. ed. James A. Michener. Read by Larry McKeever. 12 cass. (Running Time: 18 hrs.). 1993. 96.00 (3187B) Books on Tape.

Chesapeake, Pt. 3. unabr. ed. James A. Michener. Read by Larry McKeever. 12 cass. (Running Time: 18 hrs.). 1993. 96.00 (3187-C) Books on Tape.

Chesapeake Affair. Kenneth Bruce. 1 cass. (Running Time: 1 hr.). Dramatization. (Excursions in History Ser.). 12.50 Alpha Tape.

Chesapeake Bay CD Collection: Sea Swept; Rising Tides; Inner Harbor; Chesapeake Blue. abr. ed. Nora Roberts. Read by David Stuart et al. (Running Time: 15 hrs.). (Chesapeake Bay Ser.: Bks. 1-4). 2006. audio compact disk 34.95 (978-1-59737-721-8(X), 9781597377218, BACD) Brilliance Audio.
SEA SWEPT A champion boat racer, Cameron Quinn traveled the world. But when his dying father calls him home to care for Seth, a troubled young boy not unlike Cameron once was, his life changes overnight. . . In the end, a social worker, as tough as she is beautiful, will decide Seth's fate. RISING TIDES Ethan Quinn is determined to make the family boatbuilding business a success. But amidst his achievements lie the most important challenges of his life. There is young Seth, who needs him more than ever. And a woman he has always loved but never believed he could have. INNER HARBOR Phillip Quinn has the scars from his own rough and tumble childhood on the streets of Boston. Now a high-powered advertising executive, he figures he's found his perfect match in educated, cultured Sybill. And when he discovers she has a family connection to young Seth, they join forces to secure the boy's future. CHESAPEAKE BLUE Now a grown man returning from Europe as a successful painter, Seth Quinn is settling down on Maryland's Eastern Shore. Still, a lot has changed in St. Christopher - and the most intriguing change of all is the presence of Dru Whitcomb Banks. But a secret Seth's kept hidden for years threatens to explode, destroying his new life and his new love.

Chesapeake Blue. Nora Roberts. Read by James Daniels. (Chesapeake Bay Ser.: Bk. 4). 2008. 64.99 (978-1-60640-800-1(3)) Find a World.

Chesapeake Blue. abr. ed. Nora Roberts. Read by James Daniels. (Running Time: 21600 sec.). (Chesapeake Bay Ser.: Bk. 4). 2006. audio compact disk 16.99 (978-1-4233-2765-3(9), 9781423327653, BCD Value Price) Brilliance Audio.

Chesapeake Blue. unabr. ed. Nora Roberts. Read by James Daniels. 7 cass., Library ed. (Running Time: 9 hrs.). (Chesapeake Bay Ser.: Bk. 4). 2002. 82.25 (978-1-59086-332-9(1), 1590863321, Unabridge Lib Edns); audio compact disk 36.95 (978-1-59086-333-6(X), 159086333X, CD Unabridged); audio compact disk 92.25 (978-1-59086-334-3(8), 1590863348, CD Unabrid Lib Ed) Brilliance Audio.
Seth Quinn is finally home. It's been a long journey. After a harrowing boyhood with his drug-addicted mother, he'd been taken in by the Quinn family, growing up with three older brothers who'd watched over him with love. Now a grown man returning from Europe as a successful painter, Seth is settling down on Maryland's Eastern Shore, surrounded once again by Cam, Ethan, and Phillip, their wives and children, all the blessed chaos of the extended Quinn clan. Finally, he's back in the little blue-and-white house where there's always a boat at the dock, a rocker on the porch, and a dog in the yard. Still, a lot has changed in St. Christopher since he's been gone - and the most intriguing change of all is the presence of Dru Whitcomb Banks. A city girl who has opened a florist shop in this seaside town, she craves independence and the challenge of establishing herself without the influence of her wealthy connections. In Seth, she sees another kind of challenge - a challenge she can't resist. But storms are brewing that are about to put their relationship to the test. Dru's past has made her sensitive to deception - and slow to trust. And Seth's past has made him a target of blackmail - as a secret he's kept hidden for years threatens to explode, destroying his new life and his new love.

Chesapeake Blue. unabr. ed. Nora Roberts. Read by James Daniels. (Running Time: 9 hrs.). (Chesapeake Bay Ser.: Bk. 4). 2004. 39.25 (978-1-59335-569-2(6), 1593355696, Brinc Audio MP3 Lib) Brilliance Audio.

Chesapeake Blue. unabr. ed. Nora Roberts. Read by James Daniels. (Running Time: 9 hrs.). (Chesapeake Bay Ser.: Bk. 4). 2004. 39.25 (978-1-59710-132-5(X), 159710132X, BADLE); 24.95 (978-1-59710-133-2(8), 1597101338, BAD) Brilliance Audio.

Chesapeake Blue. unabr. ed. Nora Roberts. Read by James Daniels. (Running Time: 9 hrs.). (Chesapeake Bay Ser.: Bk. 4). 2004. 24.95 (978-1-59335-053-6(8), 1593350538) Soulmate Audio Bks.

***Chesapeake Shores Christmas.** unabr. ed. Sherryl Woods. Read by Christina Traister. (Running Time: 6 hrs.). (Chesapeake Shores Ser.). 2010. 19.99 (978-1-4418-7675-1(8), 9781441876751, Brilliance MP3); 19.99 (978-1-4418-7677-5(4), 9781441876775, BAD); 39.97 (978-1-4418-7678-2(2), 9781441876782, BADLE); 39.97 (978-1-4418-7676-8(6), 9781441876768, Brinc Audio MP3 Lib); audio compact disk 19.99 (978-1-4418-7673-7(1), 9781441876737, Bril Audio CD Unabri); audio compact disk 79.97 (978-1-4418-7674-4(X), 9781441876744, BriAudCD Unabrid) Brilliance Audio.

Cheshire Cat's Eye. unabr. ed. Marcia Muller. Read by Bernadette Dunne. 6 cass. (Running Time: 6 hrs.). (Sharon McCone Mystery Ser.: No. 3). 1996. 48.00 (978-0-7366-3490-8(8), 4130) Books on Tape.
Intuitive San Francisco P.I., hurries to an old friend's house in the "Painted Ladies" district after she receives his urgent call. But she's too late. Her friend lies dead in a pool of red paint.

Chess Hotel. Contrib. by Elms. Prod. by David Bianco. Contrib. by Van Fletcher. 2006. audio compact disk 10.99 (978-5-558-45875-6(5)) Sigma F RUS.

Chess Machine. unabr. ed. Robert Lohr. Read by Stephen Hoye. Tr. by Anthea Bell. (Running Time: 13 hrs. 30 mins. 0 sec.). (ENG.). 2007. audio compact disk 37.99 (978-1-4001-0513-7(7)); audio compact disk 24.99 (978-1-4001-5513-2(4)); audio compact disk 75.99 (978-1-4001-3513-4(3)) Pub: Tantor Media. Dist(s): IngramPubServ

Chessie, the Travelin' Man. Randy Houk. Read by Tom Chapin. Illus. by Paula Bartlett. Narrated by Tom Chapin. 1 cass. (Running Time: 11 min.). (Humane Society of the United States Animal Tales Ser.). (J). (gr. 1-5). 1997. pap. bk. 9.95 (978-1-882728-60-2(2)) Benefactory.
Does an endangered manatee who swims all the way up the eastern seaboard to Rhode Island need to be rescued, or will he return to Florida waters on his own? Find out about Chessie, who was named for his trip to the Chesapeake Bay in 1994.

Chessie, the Travelin' Man, Incl. plush animal. Randy Houk. Read by Tom Chapin. Illus. by Paula Bartlett. Narrated by Tom Chapin. 1 cass. (Running Time: 11 min.). (Humane Society of the United States Animal Tales Ser.). (J). (gr. 1-5). 1997. bk. 34.95 (978-1-882728-57-2(2)); pap. bk. 19.95 (978-1-882728-62-6(9)) Benefactory.

Chessmen of Mars. Edgar Rice Burroughs. Read by John Bolen. (Running Time: 8 hrs. 30 mins.). 2001. 27.95 (978-1-60083-593-3(7), Audiofy Corp) Iofy Corp.

Chessmen of Mars. Edgar Rice Burroughs. Read by John Bolen. (Martian Tales of Edgar Rice Burroughs Ser.). (ENG.). 2005. audio compact disk 84.00 (978-1-4001-3021-4(2)) Pub: Tantor Media. Dist(s): IngramPubServ

Chessmen of Mars. unabr. ed. Edgar Rice Burroughs. Narrated by John Bolen. 1 CD (MP3). (Running Time: 8 hrs. 40 mins.). (Mars Ser.: Vol. 5). (ENG.). 2001. audio compact disk 20.00 (978-1-4001-5021-2(3)) Pub: Tantor Media. Dist(s): IngramPubServ

Chessmen of Mars. unabr. ed. Edgar Rice Burroughs. Narrated by John Bolen. 8 CDs. (Running Time: 8 hrs. 40 mins.). (Mars Ser.: Vol. 5). (ENG.). 2001. audio compact disk 42.00 (978-1-4001-0021-7(6)) Pub: Tantor Media. Dist(s): IngramPubServ

Chessmen of Mars. unabr. ed. Edgar Rice Burroughs. Narrated by John Bolen. (Running Time: 8 hrs. 30 mins. 0 sec.). (Barsoom Ser.). (ENG.).

2009. lab manual ed. 65.99 (978-1-4001-3925-5(2)); audio compact disk 22.99 (978-1-4001-5925-3(3)) Pub: Tantor Media. Dist(s): IngramPubServ

Chessmen of Mars. unabr. ed. Edgar Rice Burroughs. Read by John Bolen. (Running Time: 8 hrs. 30 mins. 0 sec.). (Barsoom Ser.). (ENG.). 2009. audio compact disk 32.99 (978-1-4001-0925-8(6)) Pub: Tantor Media. Dist(s): IngramPubServ

Chest: Its Signs & Sounds. unabr. ed. George Druger. 12 cass. (Running Time: 20 hrs.). 1973. bk. 275.00 Humetrics Corp.

Chest of Joash: 11 Kings 12:1-19. Ed Young. 1988. 4.95 (978-0-7417-1652-1(6), 652) Win Walk.

Chest Trauma Emergencies. unabr. ed. Instructed by Kristan Stewart. 4 cass. (Running Time: 8 hrs.). 1990. 79.00 cass. & soft-bound bk. (HT46) Ctr Hlth Educ.

Here at last-just what you asked for! An up-to-date, complete guide to assessment & treatment of chest trauma. This course is based on the latest ATLS guidelines. And the content is rated as excellent by over 90% of your peers who have taken this seminar.

Chester Is the Ant. Alan Seeley. Ed. by Andrea Ross. (J). (gr. k-4). 2001. 8.95 (978-1-887683-46-3(1)) Strybook Pr.

Chester's Way. Kevin Henkes. 11 vols. bk. 25.95 (978-1-59112-968-4(0)); bk. 28.95 (978-1-59112-972-1(9)); pap. bk. 33.95 (978-1-59112-969-1(9)); pap. bk. 35.95 (978-1-59112-973-8(7)) Live Oak Media.

Chester's Way. Kevin Henkes. (J). (gr. k-3). 2004. audio compact disk 9.95 (978-1-59112-966-0(4)); audio compact disk 12.95 (978-1-59112-970-7(2)) Live Oak Media.

Chester's Way. Kevin Henkes. Read by Laura Hamilton. 11 vols. (J). 2005. pap. bk. 16.95 (978-1-59112-967-7(2)); pap. bk. 18.95 (978-1-59112-971-4(0)) Pub: Live Oak Media. Dist(s): AudioGO

Chestnut King. unabr. ed. N. D. Wilson. Read by Russell Horton. (100 Cupboards Ser.). (ENG.). (J). (gr. 4). 2010. audio compact disk 54.00 (978-0-307-70590-7(0), Listening Lib) Pub: Random Audio Pubg. Dist(s): Random

Chestnut Lane. Anna Jacobs. 2009. 69.95 (978-1-4079-0609-6(7)); audio compact disk 79.95 (978-1-4079-0610-2(0)) Pub: Soundings Ltd GBR. Dist(s): Ulverscroft US

Chestnut Mare, Beware. unabr. collector's ed. Jody Jaffe. Read by Frances Cassidy. 8 cass. (Running Time: 12 hrs.). 1997. 64.00 (978-0-7366-3599-8(8), 4250) Books on Tape.

Josane Ashmore is trampled to death by her prize mare. The police think it's an accident. But Nattie Gold knows there's more to the story. It's true: Josane had a coke habit & chose to ride a crazy horse. But what about her abusive boyfriend? Why was someone so quick to dispose of her personal belongings? And most important, who keep trying to kill Nattie.

Chestnut Pan: A Christmas Story. Don Horton. 1 cass. 12.95 (978-0-9663750-1-5(7), Pumpkin Bread) Heartland MN.

Chestnut Soldier. unabr. ed. Jenny Nimmo. Read by John Keating. 5 CDs. (Running Time: 22080 sec.). (Snow Spider Trilogy: Bk. 3). (ENG.). (J). (gr. 5-8). 2007. audio compact disk 54.95 (978-0-439-02339-9(4)) Scholastic Inc.

Chestnut Soldier. unabr. ed. Jenny Nimmo. Read by John Keating. (J). 2007. 44.99 (978-1-60252-675-4(3)) Find a World.

Chesty: The Story of Lieutenant General Lewis B. Puller. Jon T. Hoffman. Read by Michael Prichard. 2002. 126.00 (978-0-7366-8917-5(6)) Books on Tape.

Chet Gecko - Private Eye Vol. 2: The Big Nap & Farewell, My Lunchbag. Prod. by Listening Library Staff. 3 CDs. (Running Time: 3 hrs. 8 mins.). (Chet Gecko Mystery Ser.). (J). (gr. 3-6). 2004. audio compact disk 30.00 (978-0-8072-1782-5(4), Listening Lib) Pub: Random Audio Pubg. Dist(s): Random

***cheval pour la Vie.** abr. ed. Dominique Renaud. (Collection Decouverte). (FRE.). 2007. audio compact disk (978-2-09-032669-7(7)) Cle Intl FRA.

Chevre de Monsieur Seguin. 1 cass. (Running Time: 1 hr., 30 mins.). (Musicontes Ser.). (FRE.). (J). 2000. bk. 24.95 (978-2-09-230431-0(3)) Pub: F Nathan FRA. Dist(s): Distribks Inc

Chevre de Monsieur Seguin. Perf. by Alphonse Daudet. 1 CD. (Running Time: 50 mins.). 2003. audio compact disk 14.95 (978-2-89558-074-4(X)) Pub: Coffragants CAN. Dist(s): Penton Overseas

Chevron Conservation Award Honorees, 1992. Hosted by Nancy Pearlman. 1 cass. (Running Time: 30 min.). 10.00 (1111) Educ Comm CA.

Chevron Conservation Award Honorees, 1993. Hosted by Nancy Pearlman. 1 cass. (Running Time: 30 min.). 10.00 (1119) Educ Comm CA.

Chevron Conservation Awards, 1987. Hosted by Nancy Pearlman. 1 cass. (Running Time: 29 min.). 10.00 (707) Educ Comm CA.

Chevron Conservation Awards, 1989. Hosted by Nancy Pearlman. 1 cass. (Running Time: 30 min.). 10.00 (706) Educ Comm CA.

Chevron Conservation Awards, 1990. Hosted by Nancy Pearlman. 1 cass. (Running Time: 28 min.). 10.00 (804) Educ Comm CA.

Chevron Conservation Awards, 1991. Hosted by Nancy Pearlman. 1 cass. (Running Time: 30 min.). 10.00 (904) Educ Comm CA.

Chewing Tabacco (Freedom From) Eldon Taylor. 1 cass. (Running Time: 62 min.). (Inner Talk Ser.). 16.95 (978-1-55978-072-8(X), 5335C) Progress Aware Res.

Soundtrack - Musical Themes with underlying subliminal affirmations.

Chewing the Cud: An Unexpected Life from Farmyard to Hollywood. unabr. ed. Dick King-Smith. Narrated by Dick King-Smith. 4 cass. (Running Time: 5 hrs. 30 mins.). 2004. 39.75 (978-1-84197-486-6(2), H1414MC, Clipper Audio) Recorded Bks.

Chewing the Objectivist Virtues. Gary Hull. 6 cass. (Running Time: 7 hrs.). 1994. 59.95 Set. (978-1-56114-355-9(3), CH05D) Second Renaissance.

The application of the virtues of integrity, productivity, justice & pride.

Cheyenne. unabr. ed. Hank Mitchum. Read by Charlie O'Dowd. 4 vols. No. 3. 2003. (978-1-58807-587-1(7)) Am Pubng Inc.

Cheyenne. unabr. ed. Hank Mitchum. Read by Charlie O'Dowd. 4 cass. (Running Time: 6 hrs.). (Stagecoach Ser.: No. 3). 2003. 25.00 (978-1-58807-186-6(3)) Am Pubng Inc.

The magnificent Wells Fargo stage speeds along the perilous trail from Billings, Montana to Cheyenne, Wyoming carrying a secret cargo of gold. Riding on board is the beautiful, strong-willed Caroline Wells, a young woman who will risk the dangers of marauding Indians, the treacherous frontier, and the darkest corners of Cheyenne to bring her runaway brother back home. She finds help in the proud, rugged rancher Kyle Warner, who has a debt to pay to the man who once saved his life and a score to settle with a band of bloodthirsty, revenge-seeking highwaymen who are planning a vicious showdown on the backstreets of Cheyenne.

Cheyenne Dawn. abr. ed. Will Brennan. Read by John Keyworth. 3 cass. (Running Time: 4 hrs. 30 mins.). (Sound Ser.). 2004. 34.95 (978-1-85496-028-3(8), 60288) Pub: UlverLrgPrint GBR. Dist(s): Ulverscroft US

Cheyenne Justice. unabr. ed. Larry D. Names. Read by Maynard Villers. 6 cass. (Running Time: 7 hrs. 30 min.). (Creed Ser.: Bk. 9). 2001. 39.95 (978-1-55686-823-8(5)) Books in Motion.

Creed has signed the confession that finally clears his name. But the trail to Texas is filled with danger. It won't do Creed much good to regain his reputation, if he loses his life.

Cheyenne Raiders. unabr. ed. Jackson O'Reilly, pseud. 6 cass. (Running Time: 9 hrs.). 2001. 48.00 (978-0-7366-7046-3(7)) Books on Tape.

Cheyenne Raiders. unabr. ed. Jackson O'Reilly, pseud. 8 cass. (Running Time: 11 hrs.). 2001. 29.95 (978-0-7366-6743-2(1)) Books on Tape.

Thomas McCabe is a Yale graduate on his way to a brilliant career as a lawyer when, in 1837, he gives up everything to take a job with the Bureau of Indian Affairs. Sent to live with a little-known tribe in the wilds of Missouri, McCabe soon finds that nothing could have prepared him for the rigors of the untamed West.

Chez Toots. Perf. by Toots Thielemans. 1 cass., 1 CD. audio compact disk 13.58 CD. (PM 82160) NewSound.

Chez Toots. Perf. by Toots Thielemans et al. 1 cass., 1 CD. 8.78 (PM 82160) NewSound.

Chi Gong One Finger Ch'an Melody. Perf. by Shanghai Chinese Traditional Orchestra. Composed by Chen Dawei. Conducted by Song Kwang-Hai. 1 CD. (Running Time: 50 min.). audio compact disk (978-1-57606-113-8(2)) Wind Recs.

This musical composition was composed in Mainland China expressly to stimulate & enhance the free flow of Chi during meditative practice.

Chi Gung for the Sexes: Balancing Yin & Yang Relationships. Bruce Frantzis. Narrated by Bruce Frantzis. (ENG.). 2008. audio compact disk 25.00 (978-1-55643-825-7(7)) Pub: North Atlantic. Dist(s): Random

Chi Kung: Health & Martial Arts. Jwing-Ming Yang. Read by Guy Peartree. 2 cass. (Running Time: 1 hr. 37 min.). 1997. bk. 15.95 (978-1-886969-39-1(6), A002) Pub: YMAA Pubn. Dist(s): Natl Bk Netwk

A general description of Chinese Qigong theory & how it applies to traditional Chinese medicine & martial arts.

Ch'i Pai-shih. Charles Chu. 2 cass. 1967. 8.95 ea. incl. suppl. materials. (978-0-88710-011-6(2)) Yale Far Eastern Pubns.

Chi Running: A Training Program for Effortless, Injury-Free Running. Danny Dreyer. 3 CDs. (Running Time: 3 hrs. 45 mins.). 2008. audio compact disk 24.95 (978-1-59179-653-4(9)) Sounds True.

Chicago. National Textbook Company Staff. 1 cass. (Discover America Ser.). 15.00 (978-0-8442-7491-1(7), Natl Textbk Co) M-H Contemporary.

Offers a fascinating introduction to key locations in the country. Especially designed for intermediate ESL students, combines language learning with American culture study.

Chicago Brass & Mormon Symphony. 1 cass. 9.95 (100977) Covenant Comms.

Chicago Conspiracy Trial. abr. ed. Peter Goodchild. 2 CDs. (Running Time: 7560 sec.). (L. A. Theatre Works Audio Theatre Collections). 1993. audio compact disk 25.95 (978-1-58081-325-9(9)) Pub: L A Theatre. Dist(s): NetLibrary CO

Chicago Conspiracy Trial. unabr. ed. Peter Goodchild. Perf. by Tom Amandes et al. 1 cass. (Running Time: 2 hrs. 7 mins.). 1993. 22.95 (978-1-58081-056-2(X), RDP16) L A Theatre.

Reality is stranger than fiction when seven '60's radicals refuse to behave in Judge Julius Hoffman's courtroom. Starring a cast of top Chicago actors & reminiscences from people involved in the actual events of 1968-1969.

Chicago Economics vs. Austrian Economics. unabr. ed. Murray Newton Rothbard. 1 cass. (Running Time: 59 min.). 12.95 (158) J Norton Pubs.

Rothbard compares the 2 schools of the free market economics & shows how the Chicago school, both historically & at present, has failed to adopt a consistent view. Rothbard characterizes them as "technical advisers to the State" & illustrates their basic disregard of genuine property rights.

Chicago Faith Conference 1998, Vol. 1. Hosted by Bill Winston. 3 cass. (Running Time: 2hr.55min.). (C). 1998. 15.00 (978-1-931289-46-7(8)) Pub: B Winston Min. Dist(s): Anchor Distributors

Chicago Faith Conference 1999, Vol. 2. Hosted by Bill Winston. 6 cass. (Running Time: 6hr.15min.). 1999. 25.00 (978-1-931289-86-3(7)) B Winston Min.

Chicago Faith Conference 2000, Vol. 3. Hosted by Bill Winston. 6 cass. (Running Time: 9hr.19min.). 2000. 30.00 (978-1-931289-87-0(5)) B Winston Min.

Chicago Faith Conference 2001, Vol. 4. Hosted by Bill Winston. 6 cass. (Running Time: 7hr.50min.). 2001. 30.00 (978-1-931289-88-7(3)) B Winston Min.

Chicago Faith Conference 2002, Vol. 5. Hosted by Bill Winston. 6 cass. (Running Time: 8hr.29min.). 2002. 30.00 (978-1-931289-89-4(1)) B Winston Min.

Chicago Faith Conference 2003. Hosted by Bill Winston. 7 CDs. (C). 2003. audio compact disk 40.00 (978-1-931289-85-6(9)) Pub: B Winston Min. Dist(s): Anchor Distributors

Chicago Faith Conference 2003, Vol. 6. Hosted by Bill Winston. 7 cass. (Running Time: 10hr.08min.). (C). 2003. 30.00 (978-1-931289-84-9(0)) Pub: B Winston Min. Dist(s): Anchor Distributors

Chicago Poet see Carl Sandburg's Poems for Children

Chicago Sings Gospel's Greatest Hits. 1 cass. 10.98 (978-1-57908-295-6(5), 1379); audio compact disk 15.98 CD. (978-1-57908-294-9(7), 1379) Platinm Enter.

Chicago Way. abr. ed. Michael T. Harvey. Read by Stephen Hoye. 5 CDs. (Running Time: 23400 sec.). (ENG.). 2007. audio compact disk 29.95 (978-0-7393-5466-7(3), Random AudioBks) Pub: Random Audio Pubg. Dist(s): Random

Chicano Culture in Los Angeles. (Running Time: 30 min.). 10.95 (F0610B090, HarperThor) HarpC GBR.

Chick: His Unpublished Memoirs & the Memories of Those Who Loved Him. Steve Springer & Chick Hearn. Frwd. by Jerry West. Afterword by Bill Walton. 2004. bk. 27.95 (978-1-57243-618-3(2)) Triumph Bks.

Chick Corea. Read by Chick Corea. 1 cass. (Running Time: 60 min.). (Marian McPartland's Piano Jazz Ser.). 13.95 (MM-87-05-07, HarperThor) HarpC GBR.

Chicka Chicka Boom Boom & Other Coconutty Songs. 1998. 14.99 (978-1-60689-176-6(6)) Pub: Youngheart Mus. Dist(s): Creat Teach Pr

Chicka Chicka 1, 2, 3. Bill Martin, Jr. & Michael Sampson. Illus. by Lois Ehlert. 1 cass. (Running Time: 12 mins.). (J). (ps-3). 2005. bk. 24.95 (978-0-439-76675-3(3), WHRA669); bk. 29.95 (978-0-439-76677-7(X), WHCD669) Weston Woods.

One hundred and one numbers race each other up the apple tree. As the numerals pile up, suddenly bad bumblebees come buzzing. Which number will save the day? Fun-filled music and vocals by Crystal Taliefero will have children singing about numbers long after the bumblebees have gone.

Chickamauga see Great American Short Stories, Vol. II, A Collection

Chickamauga see Selected American Short Stories

Chickamauga. James Reasoner. Contrib. by Lloyd James. (Running Time: 039600 sec.). (Civil War Battle Ser.: Bk. 7). 2005. DVD & audio compact disk 81.00 (978-0-7861-8088-2(9)) Blckstn Audio.

Chickamauga. James Reasoner. Narrated by Lloyd James. (Running Time: 11 hrs.). (Civil War Battle Ser.: Bk. 7). 2005. 34.95 (978-1-59912-447-6(5)) Iofy Corp.

Chickamauga. unabr. ed. Short Stories. Ambrose Bierce. 1 cass. (Running Time: 70 min.). Dramatization. 1981. 7.95 (S-58) Jimcin Record.

There is horror of mind & body in these famous short stories.

Chickamauga -Lib. (Running Time: 12 hrs. 0 mins.). 2005. 65.95 (978-0-7861-3021-4(0)) Blckstn Audio.

Chickamauga -Lib: Mp3. (Running Time: 12 hrs. 0 mins.). 2005. audio compact disk 29.95 (978-0-7861-8210-7(5)) Blckstn Audio.

Chickamauga, The Damned Thing, The Coup de Grace. Ambrose Bierce. 1 cass. 1989. 7.95 (S-58) Jimcin Record.

Horror of the mind & body.

Chickasaw. unabr. ed. Gregg Howard. 2 cass. (Running Time: 2 hrs.). pap. bk. 49.95 (AFCH20) J Norton Pubs.

Chicken Boy. unabr. ed. Frances O'Roark Dowell. Read by Stephen Hoye. 3 cass. (Running Time: 3 hrs. 51 mins.). (YA). 2005. 30.00 (978-0-307-24619-6(1), BksonTape); audio compact disk 38.00 (978-0-307-24620-2(5), BksonTape) Random Audio Pubg.

***Chicken-Chasing Queen of Lamar County.** unabr. ed. Janice N. Harrington. Narrated by Sisi Aisha Johnson. 1 cass. (Running Time: 15 mins.). (J). 2009. 15.75 (978-1-4361-8971-2(3)); audio compact disk 15.75 (978-1-4361-8975-0(6)) Recorded Bks.

Chicken Dance. unabr. ed. Jacques Couvillon. Narrated by Steven Boyer. 8 CDs. (Running Time: 8 hrs. 30 mins.). (YA). (gr. 6-9). 2008. audio compact disk 87.75 (978-1-4281-6707-0(2)); 56.75 (978-1-4281-6702-5(1)) Recorded Bks.

Acclaimed children's author Jacques Couvillon grew up on a Louisiana chicken farm just like the young protagonist in The Chicken Dance. Don Schmidt's birthday is coming fast! He can't wait to find out what kind of surprises his mom and dad are sure to have in store for him. But when Don's special day finally arrives, he is saddened when his weird parents get into another argument. What can Don do to make his mom see that he is a good son?.

Chicken Doesn't Skate. Gordon Korman. 4 cass. (Running Time: 4 hrs. 30 mins.). (J). (gr. 5). 1999. pap. bk. & stu. ed. 47.75 (978-0-7887-3637-7(X), 41002) Recorded Bks.

Sixth-grader Milo Neal plans to do a science project on "The Complete Life Cycle of a Link in the Food Chain." But when he brings his specimen - a baby chick - to class, everyone falls in love with the cute ball of fluff. How can Milo finish his project, which calls for cooking his specimen for the judges of the science fair?.

Chicken Doesn't Skate, unabr. ed. Gordon Korman. 4 pieces. (Running Time: 4 hrs. 30 mins.). (gr. 5 up). 2000. 35.00 (978-0-7887-3519-6(5), 95855E7) Recorded Bks.

Chicken Doesn't Skate, Class set. Gordon Korman. 4 cass. (Running Time: 4 hrs. 30 mins.). (J). (gr. 5). 1999. 100.80 (978-0-7887-3666-7(3), 46969) Recorded Bks.

Chicken Fat: Go, You Chicken Fat, Go. Meridith Wilson. Perf. by Bernie Vinee. 1 cass . (Running Time: 1 hr.). (J). 2001. pap. bk. 5.95 (KIM209C); pap. bk. 7.95 (KIM 209CD) Kimbo Educ.

Number 1 on the nation's physical fitness "Hit Parade." Stimulating commands allow individuals, at any age level, to be motivated to exercise. Includes guide.

Chicken Food. (Sails Literacy Ser.). (gr. 2 up). 10.00 (978-0-7578-2667-2(9)) Rigby Educ.

***Chicken Fun.** Created by Mary Jo Huff. (ENG.). (YA). 2008. audio compact disk 15.00 (978-0-9722213-7-5(9)) Storytellin Time.

Chicken Licken. Arlene Capriola & Rigmor Swenson. Ed. by Cherisse Mastry. Illus. by Kathy Burns. 1 cass. (Once upon a Time Ser.). (J). (gr. k-2). 1998. 6.95 (978-1-57022-160-6(X)) ECS Lrn Systs.

Chicken Licken. Arlene Capriola & Rigmor Swenson. Ed. by Cherisse Mastry. Illus. by Kathy Burns. 1 cass. (Once upon a Time Ser.). (J). (gr. k-2). 1998. pap. bk. & wbk. ed. (978-1-57022-171-2(5)) ECS Lrn Systs.

Chicken Little. 2004. audio compact disk 12.95 (978-1-55592-904-6(4)) Weston Woods.

Chicken Little. (J). 2004. pap. bk. 18.95 (978-1-55592-391-4(7)); pap. bk. 18.95 (978-1-55592-393-8(3)); pap. bk. 38.75 (978-1-55592-392-1(5)); pap. bk. 38.75 (978-1-55592-394-5(1)); pap. bk. 32.75 (978-1-55592-204-7(X)); pap. bk. 32.75 (978-1-55592-205-4(8)) Weston Woods.

Chicken Little. Retold by Steven Kellogg. Narrated by Helen Hunt & Hank Azaria. 1 cass., 5 bks. (Running Time: 11 min.). (J). pap. bk. 32.75 Weston Woods.

When an acorn falls on her head, Chicken Little convinces herself & friends the sky is falling.

Chicken Little. unabr. ed. Narrated by Helen Hunt. 1 cass. (Running Time: 11 min.). (J). (ps-4). 1998. bk. 24.95 (978-0-7882-0673-3(7), HRA372) Weston Woods.

Chicken Little. unabr. ed. Narrated by Helen Hunt. Illus. by Steven Kellogg. Narrated by Steven Kellogg. 1 cass. (Running Time: 11 min.). (J). (ps-4). 1998. pap. bk. 14.95 (978-0-7882-0678-8(8), PRA372) Weston Woods.

Chicken Little. unabr. ed. Steven Kellogg. Narrated by Helen Hunt & Hank Azaria. 1 cass. (Running Time: 6 min.). (J). (ps-4). 1998. pap. bk. 8.95 (978-0-7882-0084-7(4), RAC372) Weston Woods.

Chicken Little. unabr. ed. Read by Lionel Wilson. Retold by Steven Kellogg. 1 cass. (Running Time: 10 mins.). (Picture Book Read-Along Ser.). (J). (gr. k-3). 1991. pap. bk. 17.00 (978-0-8072-6033-3(9), MR 25SP, Listening Lib) Random Audio Pubg.

"The sky is falling!" cried Chicken Little as she got a mysterious bump on the head. A timeless, classic tale of chain-reaction panic.

Chicken Little/Pollita Pequenita. Christianne C. Jones. (Running Time: 387 sec.). (Read-It! Readers: Folklore Audio Ser.). (J). (gr. k-4). 2008. audio compact disk 9.27 (978-1-4048-4466-7(X)) CapstoneDig.

Chicken School. Jeremy Strong. 2 CDs. 2006. audio compact disk 21.95 (978-0-7540-6735-1(1), Chivers Child Audio) AudioGO.

Chicken Sisters. Laura Joffe Numeroff. Illus. by Sharleen Collicott. Narrated by Barbara Rosenblat. (Running Time: 10 mins.). (J). (ps-2). 2002. audio compact disk 12.95 (978-1-59112-309-5(7)) Live Oak Media.

Chicken Sisters. Laura Joffe Numeroff. Illus. by Sharleen Collicott. 14 vols. (Running Time: 10 mins.). 2002. pap. bk. 39.95 (978-1-59112-532-7(4)) Live Oak Media.

Chicken Sisters. Laura Joffe Numeroff. Illus. by Sharleen Collicott. 11 vols. (Running Time: 10 mins.). (J). 2002. pap. bk. 18.95 (978-1-59112-310-1(0)) Pub: Live Oak Media. Dist(s): AudioGO

Chicken Sisters. Laura Joffe Numeroff. Illus. by Sharleen Collicott. (Running Time: 10 mins.). 2002. 9.95 (978-0-87499-889-4(1)); 9.95 (978-1-59112-300-2(3)) Live Oak Media.

Chicken Sisters. abr. ed. Laura Joffe Numeroff. Illus. by Sharleen Collicott. 14 vols. (Running Time: 10 mins.). (J). 2002. pap. bk. & tchr.'s planning gde. ed. 37.95 (978-0-87499-892-4(1)) Live Oak Media.
Three chicken sisters unwittingly outsmart a wolf in this twist on the big bad wolf tale with 4 soft covered books.

Chicken Sisters. abr. ed. Laura Joffe Numeroff. Illus. by Sharleen Collicott. 11 vols. (Running Time: 10 mins.). (J). (ps-3). 2002. bk. 25.95 (978-0-87499-891-7(3)) Pub: Live Oak Media. Dist(s): AudioGO
Three chicken sisters unwittingly outsmart a wolf in this twist on the big bad wolf tale.

Chicken Sisters. abr. ed. Laura Joffe Numeroff. Read by Barbara Rosenblat. 11 vols. (Running Time: 10 mins.). (Live Oak Readalong Ser.). (J). 2002. pap. bk. 16.95 (978-0-87499-890-0(5)) Pub: Live Oak Media. Dist(s): AudioGO

Chicken Socks. unabr. ed. Poems. Brod Bagert. Read by Brod Bagert. 1 cass. (Running Time: 38 min.). (ENG.). (J). (gr. 1-5). 1995. reel tape Rental 9.00 (978-0-9614228-9-9(0)) Juliahouse Pubs.
Book of performance poetry for children.

Chicken Soup for Little Christian Souls: Songs to Build Your Christian Faith. 1 cass. (Running Time: 1 hr. 30 mins.). (J). 2002. 7.98 (R4 75531) Rhino Enter.
Performances by today's top children's artists as well as timeless recordings, including Raffi, Bobby McFerrin and Louis Armstrong.

Chicken Soup for Little Christian Souls: Songs to Build Your Christian Faith. Perf. by Jodi Benson et al. (J). 2002. 7.98 (978-0-7379-0109-2(8), 79760) Rhino Enter.

Chicken Soup For Little Souls: Mother's Love - Songs To Celebrate the Love & Wisdom of Mothers. Perf. by Doris Day et al. (J). 2002. 7.98 (978-0-7379-0112-2(8), 79762) Rhino Enter.

Chicken Soup for Little Souls: What a Wonderful World - Songs to Celebrate the Magic of Life. Jack L. Canfield & Mark Hanson. 1 CD. (Running Time: 1 hr. 30 mins.). (J). 2002. audio compact disk 11.98 (R2 75532) Rhino Enter.

Chicken Soup for Little Souls: What a Wonderful World - Songs to Celebrate the Magic of Life. Perf. by Raffi et al. (J). 2002. 7.98 (978-1-56826-960-3(9), 75531) Rhino Enter.

Chicken Soup for the Mother's Soul see Bouillon de Poulet pour l'Ame d'Une Meres

Chicken Soup for the Baseball Fan's Soul: Inspirational Stories of Baseball, Big-League Dreams & the Game of Life. Jack L. Canfield et al. Read by Jack L. Canfield et al. 1 cass. (Running Time: 1 hr. 30 min.). 2001. 9.95; audio compact disk 11.95 Health Comm.

Chicken Soup for the Baseball Fan's Soul: 101 Stories of Insights, Inspiration & Laughter from the World of Baseball. Jack L. Canfield. 2001. 9.95 (978-1-55874-968-9(3)) Health Comm.

Chicken Soup for the Baseball Fan's Soul: 101 Stories of Insights, Inspiration & Laughter from the World of Baseball. abr. ed. Jack L. Canfield et al. 2001. audio compact disk 11.95 (978-1-55874-967-2(5)) Health Comm.

Chicken Soup for the Cat & Dog Lover's Soul: Celebrating Pets as Family with Stories about Cats, Dogs & Other Critters. abr. ed. Jack L. Canfield et al. Read by Jack L. Canfield & Mark Victor Hansen. 1 cass. (Running Time: 90 mins.). (Chicken Soup for the Soul Ser.). 1999. 9.95 (978-1-55874-713-5(3)); audio compact disk 11.95 (978-1-55874-712-8(5)) Health Comm.
This collection is sure to capture the hearts of all cat & dog lovers.

Chicken Soup for the Christian Family Soul: Stories to Open the Heart & Rekindle the Spirit. abr. ed. Jack L. Canfield et al. 1 cass. (Running Time: 70 min.). (Chicken Soup for the Soul Ser.). 2000. audio compact disk 11.95 (978-1-55874-716-6(8)); 9.95 (978-1-55874-717-3(6)) Health Comm.
In a touching story of faith, an old tablecloth, remarkable timing & the resulting reunion of a husband & wife separated by many years & a cruel war, leaves little doubt that all factors were not just "coincidence." The gift of love is depicted in a Christmas story. Here a sad, lonely widower of only weeks was given the gift of happy memories & the joy of children by kind, concerned & caring neighbors. Family love is told in a story about the love a father shows for his children. Plus more stories for family enjoyment.

Chicken Soup for the College Soul: Inspiring & Humorous Stories about College. Jack L. Canfield et al. (Running Time: 90 mins.). (Chicken Soup for the Soul Ser.). 1999. 9.95 (978-1-55874-705-0(2)) Health Comm.

Chicken Soup for the College Soul: Inspiring & Humorous Stories about College. abr. ed. Jack L. Canfield et al. Read by Jack L. Canfield & Mark Victor Hansen. 1 CD. (Running Time: 90 min.). (Chicken Soup for the Soul Ser.). (C). 1999. bk. 11.95 (978-1-55874-704-3(4)) Health Comm.
Collection to guide, inspire, support & encourage students through their college experience.

Chicken Soup for the Country Soul: Stories Served up Country-Style & Straight from the Heart. abr. ed. Jack L. Canfield et al. 1 cass. (Running Time: 90 min.). (Chicken Soup for the Soul Ser.). 1998. 9.95 (978-1-55874-564-3(5)); audio compact disk 11.95 CD. (978-1-55874-565-0(3)) Health Comm.
Selections of the best from the bestseller.

Chicken Soup for the Couple's Soul: Inspirational Stories about Love & Relationships. Jack L. Canfield et al. Read by Jack L. Canfield & Mark Victor Hansen. 1 cass. (Running Time: 90 min.). (Chicken Soup for the Soul Ser.). 1999. 9.95 (978-1-55874-647-3(1)) Health Comm.
True stories about love, commitment, intimacy, family, overcoming obstacles & keeping a relationship alive year after year.

Chicken Soup for the Couple's Soul: Inspirational Stories about Love & Relationships. abr. ed. Short Stories. Jack L. Canfield et al. Read by Jack L. Canfield & Mark Victor Hansen. 1 CD. (Running Time: 90 min.). (Chicken Soup for the Soul Ser.). 1999. audio compact disk 11.95 (978-1-55874-648-0(X)) Health Comm.

Chicken Soup for the Expectant Mother's Soul: 101 Stories to Inspire & Warm the Hearts of Soon-to-Be-Mothers. abr. ed. Jack L. Canfield et al. Read by Jack L. Canfield et al. 1 cass. (Running Time: 90 mins.). (Chicken Soup for the Soul Ser.). 2000. 9.95 (978-1-55874-799-9(0)) Health Comm.
Every year, millions of women wait with anticipation as they watch their test strip change from white to pink, thus beginning the awesome adventure of becoming a mother. Some stories offer hope when the pregnancy isn't medically perfect; others offer light-hearted humor to cope with weight gain, morning sickness & other pregnancy woes & still others offer words of wisdom for the seemingly daunting responsibilities of choosing a name, going through labor & bringing a new life into the world.

Chicken Soup for the Expectant Mother's Soul: 101 Stories to Inspire & Warm the Hearts of Soon-to-Be-Mothers. abr. ed. Jack L. Canfield et al. Read by Jack L. Canfield et al. 1 CD. (Running Time: 70 mins.). (Chicken Soup for the Soul Ser.). 2000. audio compact disk 11.95 (978-1-55874-798-2(2)) Health Comm.
Every year, millions of women wait with anticipation as they watch their test strip change form white to pink, thus beginning the awesome adventure of becoming a mother. Some stories offer hope when the pregnancy isn't medically perfect; others offer light-hearted humor to cope with weight gain, morning sickness & other pregnancy woes & still others offer words of wisdom for the seemingly daunting responsibilities of choosing name, going through labor & bringing a new life into the world.

Chicken Soup for the Father's Soul: 101 Stories to Open the Hearts & Rekindle the Spirit of Fathers. abr. ed. Short Stories. Jack L. Canfield & Mark Victor Hansen. 1 CD. (Running Time: 90 min.). (Chicken Soup for the Soul Ser.). 2001. audio compact disk 11.95 (978-1-55874-896-5(2)) Health Comm.
For new dads, granddads, single dads & dads-to-be. Offers an inspiring collection of stories on the triumphs & trials of the amazing journey called fatherhood. Chapters include: Special Moments, Overcoming Obstacles, Insights & Lessons, The Joys of Fatherhood, Across the Generations & Achieving Dreams. By sharing true experiences & insights, this provides reassurance to fathers & a reminder to cherish the special moments in life.

Chicken Soup for the Father's Soul: 101 Stories to Open the Hearts & Rekindle the Spirits of Fathers. abr. ed. Short Stories. Jack L. Canfield et al. 1 cass. (Running Time: 90 mins.). (Chicken Soup for the Soul Ser.). 2001. 9.95 (978-1-55874-897-2(0)) Health Comm.

Chicken Soup for the Gardener's Soul: 101 Stories to Nurture the Spirits of Gardeners. abr. ed. Short Stories. Jack L. Canfield et al. 1 cass. (Running Time: 90 mins.). (Chicken Soup for the Soul Ser.). 2001. 9.95 (978-1-55874-889-7(X)); audio compact disk 11.95 (978-1-55874-888-0(1)) Health Comm.
Celebrates all the magic of gardening, the feeling of satisfaction that comes from creating something from nothing, the physical & spiritual renewal the earth provides & the special moments shared with friends & family only nature can bestow.

Chicken Soup for the Golden Soul: Heartwarming Stories for People 60 & Over. abr. ed. Jack L. Canfield et al. 1 cass. (Running Time: 90 min.). (Chicken Soup for the Soul Ser.). 2000. audio compact disk 9.95 (978-1-55874-728-9(1)); audio compact disk 11.95 (978-1-55874-727-2(3)) Health Comm.

Chicken Soup for the Golfer's Soul: 101 Stories of Insight, Inspiration & Laughter on the Links. Compiled by Jack L. Canfield et al. (Chicken Soup for the Soul Ser.). 2002. audio compact disk 11.95 (978-1-55874-984-9(5)) Health Comm.

Chicken Soup for the Golfer's Soul: 101 Stories of Insight, Inspiration & Laughter on the Links. abr. ed. Short Stories. Jack L. Canfield et al. Read by Jack L. Canfield & Mark Victor Hansen. 1 CD. (Running Time: 90 min.). (Chicken Soup for the Soul Ser.). 1999. audio compact disk 9.95 (978-1-55874-660-2(9)) Health Comm.
Especially for & about the millions of avid & novice readers.

Chicken Soup for the Golfer's Soul: 101 Stories of Insight, Inspiration & Laughter on the Links. abr. ed. Short Stories. Jack L. Canfield et al. Read by Jack L. Canfield & Mark Victor Hansen. 1 cass. (Running Time: 90 min.). (Chicken Soup for the Soul Ser.). 1999. 11.95 (978-1-55874-661-9(7)) Health Comm.

Chicken Soup for the Golfer's Soul, the 2nd Round: 101 More Stories of Insight, Inspiration & Laughter on the Links. Compiled by Jack L. Canfield et al. (Chicken Soup for the Soul Ser.). 2002. 9.95 (978-1-55874-985-6(3)) Health Comm.

Chicken Soup for the Grieving Soul: Stories about Life, Death & Overcoming the Loss of a Loved One. Jack L. Canfield & Mark Victor Hansen. (Chicken Soup for the Soul Ser.). 2001. 9.95 (978-1-55874-905-4(5)); audio compact disk 11.95 (978-1-55874-904-7(7)) Health Comm.

Chicken Soup for the Jewish Soul: 101 Stories to Open the Heart & Rekindle the Spirit. Jack L. Canfield. 1 CD. (Running Time: 1 hr. 10 mins.). 2001. audio compact disk 11.95 (978-1-55874-900-9(4)) Health Comm.

Chicken Soup for the Jewish Soul: 101 Stories to Open the Heart & Rekindle the Spirit. unabr. ed. Jack L. Canfield et al. Read by Jack L. Canfield et al. 1 cass. (Running Time: 1 hrs. 30 mins.). 2001. 9.95 (978-1-55874-901-6(2)) Health Comm.

Chicken Soup for the Kid's Soul: 101 Stories of Courage, Hope & Laughter. abr. ed. Jack L. Canfield et al. 1 cass. (Running Time: 90 min.). (Chicken Soup for the Soul Ser.). (J). (gr. 4-7). 1998. audio compact disk 11.95 (978-1-55874-611-4(0), CD) Health Comm.
Selections of the best from the bestseller.

Chicken Soup for the Kid's Soul: 101 Stories of Courage, Hope & Laughter. abr. ed. Jack L. Canfield et al. 1 cass. (Running Time: 90 min.). (Chicken Soup for the Soul Ser.). (J). (gr. 4-7). 1998. 9.95 (978-1-55874-610-7(2)) Health Comm.

Chicken Soup for the Mother's Soul: 101 Stories to Open the Heart & Rekindle the Spirit. abr. ed. Jack L. Canfield et al. Contrib. by Barbara Bush et al. 1 cass. (Running Time: 90 min.). (Chicken Soup for the Soul Ser.). 1997. 9.95 (978-1-55874-528-5(9)); audio compact disk 11.95 CD. (978-1-55874-529-2(7)) Health Comm.
Stories to open the hearts & rekindle the spirits of mothers.

Chicken Soup for the Mother's Soul: 101 Stories to Open the Heart & Rekindle the Spirits of Mothers. Jack L. Canfield & Mark Victor Hansen. 8 cass. 49.95 Set. (11060-C47) Natl Seminars.
This captivating collection brings together the carefully selected short stories of America's most inspirational writers & speakers - including Les Brown, Art Buchwald, Robert Fulghum, Dan Millman, Anthony Robbins & Gloria Steinem.

Chicken Soup for the Mother's Soul: 101 Stories to Open the Heart & Rekindle the Spirits of Mothers. Short Stories. Jack L. Canfield & Mark Victor Hansen. 8 cass. 1994. 49.95 (11060PAX) Nightingale-Conant.
A captivating, heartfelt collection of short stories bringing together the carefully selected works of America's most inspirational writers & speakers - including Les Brown, Art Buchwald, Roy Campanella, Pablo Casals, Robert Fulghum, Abraham Lincoln, Dan Millman, Anthony Robbins, Theodore Roosevelt & Gloria Steinem. This program provides powerful ideas & insights you can use to improve every aspect of your life.

Chicken Soup for the Mother's Soul: 101 Stories to Open the Heart & Rekindle the Spirits of Mothers. abr. ed. Jack L. Canfield et al. Contrib. by Corrie ten Boom et al. 1 CD. (Running Time: 90 min.). (Chicken Soup for the Soul Ser.). 1997. audio compact disk 11.95 (978-1-55874-531-5(9)) Health Comm.
Will show readers how to forgive others & themselves, encourage readers to stand up for what they believe in & be a reminder that no one is ever alone or without hope no matter how painful & challenging the situation.

Chicken Soup for the Mother's Soul: 101 Stories to Open the Heart & Rekindle the Spirits of Mothers. abr. ed. Jack L. Canfield et al. Contrib. by Corrie ten Boom et al. 1 cass. (Running Time: 90 min.). (Chicken Soup for the Soul Ser.). 1997. 9.95 (978-1-55874-530-8(0)) Health Comm.

Chicken Soup for the Mother's Soul: 101 Stories to Open the Heart & Rekindle the Spirits of Mothers. unabr. ed. Ed. by Jack L. Canfield & Mark Victor Hansen. 8 cass. 43.95 Set. (99421) Books on Tape.
Two of America's best-known inspirational speakers present stories to open the heart & rekindle the spirit. One will find permission to be human & see the path one should walk more clearly.

Chicken Soup for the Mother's Soul: 101 Stories to Open the Heart & Rekindle the Spirits of Mothers. unabr. ed. Jack L. Canfield & Mark Victor Hansen. Read by Jack L. Canfield et al. 8 cass. (Running Time: 11 hrs.). (Chicken Soup for the Soul Ser.). 1994. 29.95 (978-1-55874-310-6(3), 102579) Health Comm.
Based on the bestselling book, Chicken Soup for the Soul, in a gift set package containing three individual volumes of the audio series.

Chicken Soup for the Mother's Soul II: 101 More Stories to Open the Heart & Rekindle the Spirit. abr. ed. Jack L. Canfield et al. 1 cass. (Running Time: 90 mins.). (Chicken Soup for the Soul Ser.). 2001. 9.95 (978-1-55874-893-4(8)); audio compact disk 11.95 (978-1-55874-892-7(X)) Health Comm.
Collection of stories for & about the most important person in your life. Features chapters on Love, Becoming a Mother, Mothers & daughters, Miracles, Special Moments, Letting Go & more.

Chicken Soup for the Nurse's Soul: 101 Stories to Celebrate, Honor & Inspire the Nursing Profession. Jack L. Canfield et al. Read by Jack L. Canfield et al. 1 cass. (Running Time: 1 hr. 30 min.). 2001. 9.95 (978-1-55874-936-8(5)); audio compact disk 11.95 (978-1-55874-935-1(7)) Health Comm.
This collection of true stories champions the daily contributions, commitments and sacrifices of nurses and portrays the compassion, intellect and wit necessary to meet the challenging demands of the profession.

Chicken Soup for the Parent's Soul: 101 Stories of Loving, Learning & Parenting. Jack L. Canfield et al. Read by Jack L. Canfield et al. 1 cass. (Running Time: 90 mins.). (Chicken Soup for the Soul Ser.). 2000. 9.95 (978-1-55874-749-4(4)); audio compact disk 11.95 (978-1-55874-750-0(8)) Health Comm.
Offers a collections of inspiring & entertaining stories that relate of the triumphs, tribulations, challenges & joys of raising a family. Chapters include: The Joys of Parenting; A Mother's Love; A Father's Love; Special Connections; Special Moments; Insights & Lessons; Overcoming Obstacles; Surviving Loss; Across the Generations & Letting Go.

Chicken Soup for the Pet Lover's Soul: Stories about Pets as Teachers, Healers, Heroes & Friends. abr. ed. Jack L. Canfield et al. 1 cass. (Running Time: 90 min.). (Chicken Soup for the Soul Ser.). 1998. 9.95 (978-1-55874-573-5(4)); audio compact disk 11.95 CD. (978-1-55874-574-2(2)) Health Comm.
Selections of the best from the NY Times Bestseller, "Chicken Soup for the Pet Lover's Soul".

Chicken Soup for the Preteen Soul: 101 Stories of Changes, Choices & Growing Up. Jack L. Canfield et al. Read by Jack L. Canfield et al. 1 CD. (Running Time: 1 hr. 10 min.). (Chicken Soup for the Soul Ser.). (J). (gr. 5-7). 2000. audio compact disk 11.95 (978-1-55874-802-6(4)) Health Comm.

Chicken Soup for the Preteen Soul: 101 Stories of Changes, Choices & Growing Up. abr. ed. Jack L. Canfield et al. Read by Jack L. Canfield et al. 1 cass. (Running Time: 1 hr. 30 min.). (Chicken Soup for the Soul Ser.). (J). (gr. 5-7). 2000. 9.95 (978-1-55874-803-3(2)) Health Comm.

Chicken Soup for the Single's Soul: Stories of Love & Inspiration for the Single, Divorced & Widowed. abr. ed. Jack L. Canfield et al. Read by Jack L. Canfield & Mark Victor Hansen. 1 cass. (Running Time: 90 min.). (Chicken Soup for the Soul Ser.). 1999. 9.95 (978-1-55874-709-8(5)); audio compact disk 11.95 (978-1-55874-708-1(7)) Health Comm.
Stories of love & inspiration for all singles whether widowed, divorced, single & satisfied or still searching for the perfect mate.

Chicken Soup for the Soul see Bouillon de Poulet pour l'Ame

***Chicken Soup for the Soul: Happily Ever after - 30 Stories about Making it Work & Not Giving Up.** Jack Canfield & Mark Victor Hansen. 2011. audio compact disk 9.99 (978-1-61106-009-6(5)) Brilliance Audio.

***Chicken Soup for the Soul: Happily Ever after - 37 Stories about the Power of Love, Patience, Laughter & It Was Meant to Be.** Jack Canfield & Mark Victor Hansen. 2011. audio compact disk 9.99 (978-1-61106-049-2(4)) Brilliance Audio.

***Chicken Soup for the Soul: My Resolution - 31 Stories of Support, Making Your Dream a Reality & Liking It.** unabr. ed. Jack Canfield & Mark Victor Hansen. 2010. audio compact disk 9.99 (978-1-61106-035-5(4)) Brilliance Audio.

***Chicken Soup for the Soul: My Resolution - 33 Stories about First Steps, Possibilities & New Beginnings.** Jack Canfield & Mark Victor Hansen. 2010. audio compact disk 9.99 (978-1-61106-031-7(1)) Brilliance Audio.

***Chicken Soup for the Soul: My Resolution - 37 Stories of Discovering Your Worth & Just Doing It.** unabr. ed. Jack Canfield & Mark Victor Hansen. 2010. audio compact disk 9.99 (978-1-61106-033-1(8)) Brilliance Audio.

***Chicken Soup for the Soul: Shaping the New You, Vol. 1.** Jack Canfield & Mark Victor Hansen. 2011. audio compact disk 9.99 (978-1-61106-054-6(0)) Brilliance Audio.

***Chicken Soup for the Soul: Shaping the New You, Vol. 2.** Jack Canfield & Mark Victor Hansen. 2011. audio compact disk 9.99 (978-1-61106-056-0(7)) Brilliance Audio.

***Chicken Soup for the Soul: Shaping the New You, Vol. 3.** Jack Canfield & Mark Victor Hansen. 2011. audio compact disk 9.99 (978-1-61106-058-4(3)) Brilliance Audio.

***Chicken Soup for the Soul: Think Positive - 21 Inspirational Stories about Overcoming Adversity & Attitude Adjustments.** Jack Canfield & Mark Victor Hansen. 2010. audio compact disk 9.99 (978-1-4418-9414-4(4)) Brilliance Audio.

***Chicken Soup for the Soul: Think Positive - 21 Inspirational Stories about Role Models & Counting Your Blessings.** Jack Canfield & Mark Victor Hansen. 2010. audio compact disk 9.99 (978-1-4418-9412-0(8)) Brilliance Audio.

***Chicken Soup for the Soul: Think Positive - 29 Inspirational Stories about Silver Linings, Gratitude & Moving Forward.** unabr. ed. Jack Canfield & Mark Victor Hansen. 2010. audio compact disk 9.99 (978-1-4418-9416-8(0)) Brilliance Audio.

***Chicken Soup for the Soul: Think Positive - 30 Inspirational Stories about Words That Changed Lives, Health Challenges & Making Every Day Special.** Jack Canfield & Mark Victor Hansen. 2010. audio compact disk 9.99 (978-1-4418-9676-6(7)) Brilliance Audio.

***Chicken Soup for the Soul: True Love - 30 Stories about Proposals, Weddings & Keeping Love Alive.** Jack Canfield & Mark Victor Hansen. 2011. audio compact disk 9.99 (978-1-61106-042-3(7)) Brilliance Audio.

***Chicken Soup for the Soul: True Love - 31 Stories about First Meetings, Adventures in Dating & It Was Meant to Be.** Jack Canfield & Mark Victor Hansen. 2011. audio compact disk 9.99 (978-1-61106-040-9(0)) Brilliance Audio.

***Chicken Soup for the Soul: True Love - 40 Stories about Gifts from the Heart, Laughter & Love Everlasting.** Jack Canfield & Mark Victor Hansen. 2011. audio compact disk 9.99 (978-1-61106-044-7(3)) Brilliance Audio.

***Chicken Soup for the Soul: What I Learned from the Cat - 20 Stories About Laughter & Accepting Help-UAB.** Jack Canfield. 2010. audio compact disk 9.99 (978-1-61106-022-5(2)) Brilliance Audio.

***Chicken Soup for the Soul: What I Learned from the Cat - 20 Stories About Love & Letting Go-UAB.** Jack Canfield. 2010. audio compact disk 9.99 (978-1-61106-026-3(5)) Brilliance Audio.

***Chicken Soup for the Soul: What I Learned from the Cat - 30 Stories About Play, What's Important, & Belief-UAB.** Jack Canfield. 2010. audio compact disk 9.99 (978-1-61106-024-9(9)) Brilliance Audio.

***Chicken Soup for the Soul: What I Learned from the Cat - 31 Stories About Who's in Charge, How to Love a Cat & Be Your Best-UAB.** Jack Canfield. 2010. audio compact disk 9.99 (978-1-61106-020-1(6)) Brilliance Audio.

***Chicken Soup for the Soul: What I Learned from the Dog - 31 Stories About Family, Courage & How to Listen-UAB.** Jack Canfield. 2010. audio compact disk 9.99 (978-1-4418-9670-4(8)) Brilliance Audio.

***Chicken Soup for the Soul: What I Learned from the Dog - 34 Stories About Overcoming Adversity, Healing & How to Say Goodbye-UAB.** Jack Canfield. 2010. audio compact disk 9.99 (978-1-4418-9672-8(4)) Brilliance Audio.

***Chicken Soup for the Soul: What I Learned from the Dog - 36 Stories About Putting Things in Perspective, Kindness & Unconditional Love-UAB.** Jack Canfield. 2010. audio compact disk 9.99 (978-1-4418-9674-2(0)) Brilliance Audio.

Chicken Soup for the Soul - Live! Jack L. Canfield & Mark Victor Hansen. 6 cass. (Running Time: 6 hrs.). 59.95 Set. (Q10190) CareerTrack Pubns.
The stories you'll hear are filled with powerful, life-affirming messages on topics like these: Love; Learning to love yourself; Parenting; Learning & teaching; Living your dreams; Overcoming obstacles; Death & dying.

***Chicken Soup for the Soul: A Book of Miracles: 101 True Stories of Healing, Faith, Divine Intervention, & Answered Prayers.** Jack Canfield et al. Contrib. by Kathy Garver & Tom Parks. (Running Time: 34200 sec.). (Chicken Soup for the Soul (Audio Health Communications) Ser.). (ENG.). 2010. audio compact disk 39.97 (978-1-4418-8219-6(7)) Brilliance Audio.

Chicken Soup for the Soul at Work: 101 Stories of Courage, Compassion & Creativity in the Workplace. abr. ed. Jack L. Canfield et al. 1 cass. (Running Time: 90 min.). (Chicken Soup for the Soul Ser.). 1996. 9.95 (978-1-55874-442-4(8)); audio compact disk 11.95 CD. (978-1-55874-443-1(6)) Health Comm.
Selections of the best from the NY Times Bestseller, "Chicken Soup for the Soul at Work".

Chicken Soup for the Soul on Love & Learning. unabr. ed. Jack L. Canfield & Mark Victor Hansen. Read by Jack L. Canfield & Mark Victor Hansen. 2 cass. (Running Time: 3 hrs.). (Chicken Soup for the Soul Ser.). 1999. 12.95 (978-1-55874-307-6(3)) Health Comm.
Will open the heart & rekindle the spirit.

Chicken Soup for the Sports Fan's Soul: Stories of Insight, Inspiration & Laughter in the World of Sports. abr. ed. Jack L. Canfield et al. Read by Jack L. Canfield et al. 1 cass. (Running Time: 90 mins.). (Chicken Soup for the Soul Ser.). 2000. 9.95 (978-1-55874-878-1(4)); audio compact disk 11.95 (978-1-55874-877-4(6)) Health Comm.

Chicken Soup for the Surviving Soul: 101 Stories of Courage & Inspiration from Those Who Have Survived Cancer. abr. ed. Jack L. Canfield & Mark Victor Hansen. Read by Jack L. Canfield & Mark Victor Hansen. 1 cass. (Running Time: 90 min. per cass.). (Chicken Soup for the Soul Ser.). 1998. pap. bk. 9.95 (978-1-55874-532-2(7)) Health Comm.
Heartwarming accounts of courageous people who have found power to battle cancer in their endless hope, unwaivering faith & steadfast determination. #Includes bibliographical references and indexes.

Chicken Soup for the Surviving Soul: 101 Stories of Courage & Inspiration from Those Who Have Survived Cancer. abr. ed. Jack L. Canfield & Mark Victor Hansen. Read by Jack L. Canfield & Mark Victor Hansen. 1 CD. (Running Time: 90 min.). (Chicken Soup for the Soul Ser.). 2002. audio compact disk 11.95 (978-1-55874-527-8(0)) Health Comm.
Heartwarming accounts of courageous people who found power to battle cancer in their endless hope, unwavering faith & steadfast determination.

Chicken Soup for the Teenage Soul see Bouillon de Poulet pour l'Ame des Ados

Chicken Soup for the Teenage Soul: 101 Stories of Life, Love & Learning. abr. ed. Jack L. Canfield et al. 1 cass. (Running Time: 90 min.). (Chicken Soup for the Soul Ser.). (YA). (gr. 7-12). 1997. audio compact disk 11.95 CD. (978-1-55874-474-5(6)) Health Comm.
Selections of the best from the NY Times Bestseller, "Chicken Soup for the Teenage Soul".

Chicken Soup for the Teenage Soul: 101 Stories of Life, Love & Learning, Set. abr. ed. Jack L. Canfield et al. 1 cass. (Running Time: 90 min.). (Chicken Soup for the Soul Ser.). (YA). (gr. 7-12). 1997. 9.95 (978-1-55874-473-8(8), AF17R) Health Comm.
A teen guide for surviving & succeeding during the teen & pre-teen years with both sanity & sense of humor intact.

Chicken Soup for the Teenage Soul II: 101 More Stories of Life, Love & Learning. abr. ed. Jack L. Canfield et al. 1 cass. (Running Time: 90 min.). (Chicken Soup for the Soul Ser.). (YA). (gr. 7-12). 1998. audio compact disk 11.95 (978-1-55874-618-3(8), CD) Health Comm.
Selections of the best from the latest in the series.

Chicken Soup for the Teenage Soul II: 101 More Stories of Life, Love & Learning. abr. ed. Jack L. Canfield et al. 1 cass. (Running Time: 90 min.). (Chicken Soup for the Soul Ser.). (YA). (gr. 7-12). 1998. 9.95 (978-1-55874-617-6(X)) Health Comm.

Chicken Soup for the Teenage Soul III: More Stories of Life, Love & Learning. abr. ed. Jack L. Canfield et al. 1 cass. (Running Time: 70 mins.). (Chicken Soup for the Soul Ser.). (YA). (gr. 7-12). 2000. 9.95 (978-1-55874-763-0(X)); audio compact disk 11.95 (978-1-55874-764-7(8)) Health Comm.
More & more, life is a strugge for teens. Not just dealing with the tragedies that seem to plague them so often, but also handling the daily pressures that prevade their lives. This series will help them & will serve as their guide & constant companion.

Chicken Soup for the Teenage Soul on Tough Stuff: Stories of Tough Times & Lessons Learned. unabr. ed. Jack L. Canfield et al. Read by Jack L. Canfield et al. 1 cass. (Running Time: 1 hrs. 30 min.). (Chicken Soup for the Soul Ser.). (YA). 2001. 9.95 (978-1-55874-945-0(4)); audio compact disk 11.95 (978-1-55874-944-3(6)) Health Comm.
This latest offering in the bestselling Teenage Soul series explores a host of challenges faced by today's teens. Teens rank stress as one of their top concerns. The pressure can feel overwhelming, whether it involves worring about an upcoming test, competitive sports, family responsibilities, dating or more extreme issues such as depression, suicide or school violence.

Chicken Soup for the Unsinkable Soul: Stories of Triumph & Overcoming Life's Obstacles. abr. ed. Jack L. Canfield et al. Read by Jack L. Canfield & Mark Victor Hansen. 1 cass. (Running Time: 90 min.). (Chicken Soup for the Soul Ser.). 1999. 9.95 (978-1-55874-701-2(X)); audio compact disk 11.95 (978-1-55874-700-5(1)) Health Comm.
Will guide listeners through hardships in their lives & help them realize their dreams.

Chicken Soup for the Veteran's Soul: Stories to Stir the Pride & Honor the Courage of Our Veterans. unabr. ed. Jack L. Canfield et al. Read by Jack L. Canfield et al. 1 cass. (Running Time: 1 hr. 30 mins.). 2001. 9.95 (978-1-55874-940-5(3)) Health Comm.

Chicken Soup for the Veteran's Soul: Stories to Stir the Pride & Honor the Courage of Our Veterans. unabr. ed. Jack L. Canfield et al. Read by Jack L. Canfield et al. 1 CD. (Running Time: 1 hr. 30 mins.). 2001. audio compact disk 11.95 (978-1-55874-939-9(X)) Health Comm.

Chicken Soup for the Woman's Soul see Bouillon de Poulet pour l'Ame de la Femme

Chicken Soup for the Woman's Soul: 101 Stories to Open the Hearts & Rekindle the Spirits of Women. Contrib. by Rhino Records Staff. 1999. audio compact disk 11.98 (978-0-7379-0051-4(2)) Rhino Enter.

Chicken Soup for the Woman's Soul: 101 Stories to Open the Hearts & Rekindle the Spirits of Women. abr. ed. Jack L. Canfield et al. 1 cass. (Running Time: 90 min.). (Chicken Soup for the Soul Ser.). 1996. 9.95 (978-1-55874-440-0(1)); audio compact disk 11.95 CD. (978-1-55874-441-7(X)) Health Comm.
Selections of the best from the NY Times Bestseller, "Chicken Soup for the Woman's Soul".

Chicken Soup for the Writer's Soul: Stories to Open the Heart & Rekindle the Spirit of Writers. Jack L. Canfield et al. 1 CD. (Running Time: 70 min.). (Chicken Soup for the Soul Ser.). 2000. audio compact disk 11.95 (978-1-55874-772-2(9), Simcha Press) Health Comm.

Chicken Soup for the Writer's Soul: Stories to Open the Heart & Rekindle the Spirit of Writers. abr. ed. Jack L. Canfield et al. 1 cass. (Running Time: 90 min.). (Chicken Soup for the Soul Ser.). 2000. 9.95 (978-1-55874-771-5(0), Simcha Press) Health Comm.

Chicken Soup Teenage Triology: Stories of Life, Love & Learning. Jack L. Canfield et al. 3 cass. (Running Time: 270 min.). (Chicken Soup for the Soul Ser.). (J). 2000. 24.95 (978-1-55874-874-3(1)) Health Comm.

Chicken Soup with Rice. 2004. 8.95 (978-1-56008-868-4(0)); 8.95 (978-1-56008-125-8(2)); cass. & flmstrp 30.00 (978-0-89719-672-7(4)); audio compact disk 12.95 (978-1-55592-867-4(6)) Weston Woods.

Chicken Soup with Rice. (J). 2004. bk. 24.95 (978-0-89719-865-3(4)); pap. bk. 18.95 (978-1-55592-801-8(3)); pap. bk. 18.95 (978-1-55592-769-1(6)); pap. bk. 38.75 (978-1-55592-818-6(8)); pap. bk. 38.75 (978-1-55592-784-4(X)); pap. bk. 32.75 (978-1-55592-206-1(6)); pap. bk. 32.75 (978-1-55592-207-8(4)); pap. bk. 14.95 (978-1-56008-049-7(3)); pap. bk. 14.95 (978-1-55592-720-2(3)) Weston Woods.

Chicken Soup with Rice: A Book of Months. Maurice Sendak. 1 cass., 5 bks. (Running Time: 5 min.). (J). pap. bk. 32.75 Weston Woods.
Rhyme & repetition in this guided tour through the months of the year help give the young viewer help in learning the names of the months.

Chicken Soup with Rice: A Book of Months. Maurice Sendak. 1 cass. (Running Time: 5 min.). (J). (ps-3). 8.95 (RAC223) Weston Woods.

Chicken Soup with Rice: A Book of Months. Maurice Sendak. Illus. by Maurice Sendak. 1 cass. (Running Time: 5 min.). (J). (ps-3). bk. 24.95; pap. bk. 12.95 (PRA223) Weston Woods.

Chicken Sunday. unabr. ed. Patricia Polacco. Narrated by Patricia Polacco. 1 cass. (Running Time: 14 min.). (J). (gr. k-3). 1993. pap. bk. 17.95 (978-0-8045-6699-5(2), 6699) Spoken Arts.
A beautiful Easter bonnet for a special friend is at the root of this story about three children mistakenly accused of throwing eggs at a shop window.

Chickenhawk. Robert Mason. Narrated by L. J. Ganser. 13 CDs. (Running Time: 14 hrs. 30 mins.). audio compact disk 124.00 (978-0-7887-9891-7(X)) Recorded Bks.

Chickenhawk. unabr. ed. Robert Mason. Read by Walter Zimmerman. 12 cass. (Running Time: 18 hrs.). 1990. 96.00 (978-0-7366-1709-3(4), 2551) Books on Tape.
All Robert Mason knew when he entered the U. S. Army was that he wanted to fly helicopters. And as one of the first wave of assault helicopter pilots to ship out to South Vietnam in 1965, he did just that, flying more than 1000 combat missions in the space of a year's tour of duty. In this affecting, detailed memoir, he gives us that war in all its banality, terror & transcendent stupidity, from a perspective unique to the literature of the Vietnam War - the air.

Chickenhawk. unabr. ed. Robert Mason. Narrated by L. J. Ganser. 10 cass. (Running Time: 14 hrs. 30 mins.). 2001. 92.00 (978-0-7887-4380-1(5), 96319E7) Recorded Bks.
The Vietnam War, as told from a helicopter pilot & the traumatic experience that he lived.

Chickens Aren't the Only Ones. unabr. ed. Ruth Heller. 1 cass. (Running Time: 7 min.). (J). (gr. 1-4). 1989. pap. bk. 17.95 (978-0-8045-6551-6(1), 6551-A) Spoken Arts.
Reading Rainbow Feature Book. Childrens Science Book Award Honor Book.

Chicken's Guide to Talking Turkey with Your Kids about Sex. abr. ed. Kevin Leman & Kathy Flores Bell. 1 cass. (Running Time: 3 hrs. 0 mins. 0 sec.). (ENG.). 2003. 11.99 (978-0-310-26023-3(X)) Zondervan.

Chickens in the Garden. Perf. by Phil Rosenthal. 1 cass. (Running Time: 35 min.). (J). (gr. k-6). 1990. 9.98 (978-1-879305-08-3(9), AM-C-107) Am Melody.
Traditional & original folk & bluegrass songs. Song lyrics included. 1991 ALA Notable Children's Recording.

Chickens on Vacation. Rick Charette. Read by Rick Charette. 1 cass. (Running Time: 45 min.). (J). (gr. k-5). 1990. 9.98 (978-1-884210-05-1(8), PPC-005) Pine Pt Record.
A collection of original songs for children including the title song about some crazy chickens who needed a vacation. Includes: "Lemonade", "I Spilled My Juice", & many more. Lyrics & activities included.

Chickens, Oranges, & Other Funny Stuff. 1 cass. (Running Time: 32 min.). (J). (gr. k-5). 1997. 7.98 (UPC 7-9382-70607-4) Melonball Music.
A collection of jokes, riddles, & anecdotes presented by children. Adults Mel & Melony interject brief songs, sound effects & short musical interludes.

Chickie. Jay O'Callahan. Perf. by Jay O'Callahan. 1 CD. (Running Time: 37:15). (YA). 2004. audio compact disk 15.00 (978-1-877954-46-7(2)) Pub: Artana Prodns. Dist(s): Yellow Moon
Some friendships are made only at certain places and at certain times. This is a story of a friendship of two boys who come from different worlds and meet at the parochial school, St. Mary's. In that school, a relevo game becomes as epic as the Trojan War. The older boys, Flood and MacIntyre, are as large as Ajax and Hector. An old school janitor is like a wise Zeus. The friendship of the boys is sealed forever in the great relevo game.

Chicks with Sticks: Knit Two Together. Elizabeth Lenhard. Read by Liz Morton. 7. (Running Time: 8 hrs. 50 mins.). (Chicks with Sticks Ser.: Bk. 2). 2007. 61.75 (978-1-4281-3697-7(5)); audio compact disk 77.75 (978-1-4281-3702-8(5)) Recorded Bks.

Chideachd Mo Ghaoil: Dain Spioradail Air an Seinn le Cairistiona Sheadha. Ed. by Acair Ltd. Staff. 1986. (978-0-7855-2558-5(0)) Acair Ltd GBR.

Chief Designer. Andy Duncan. Narrated by Jared Doreck. (Great Science Fiction Stories Ser.). 2007. audio compact disk 17.99 (978-1-884612-54-1(7)) AudioText.

Chief Joseph. Grant Staff. (J). 1974. 8.95 (Creative Eds) Creative Co.

Chief Justice. A. J. Franze. Narrated by Ron Knowles. (Running Time: 9 hrs. 30 mins.). 2009. audio compact disk 59.95 (978-1-57545-394-1(0), RP Audio Pubng) Reagent Press.

Chiefs. Stuart Woods. Narrated by Mark Hammer. 15 CDs. (Running Time: 17 hrs. 30 mins.). (Will Lee Ser.: No. 1). audio compact disk 142.00 (978-0-7887-4759-5(2)) Recorded Bks.

Chiefs. Stuart Woods. Narrated by Mark Hammer. 15 CDs. (Running Time: 17 hrs. 30 min.). (Will Lee Ser.: No. 1). 2000. audio compact disk 142.00 (C1252E7) Recorded Bks.
Inspired by his grandfather's life, Stuart Woods creates a riveting tale that spans three generations of Georgia lawmen. Probing deep into life in a small southern town, it traces the path of a wily serial murderer.

Chiefs. unabr. ed. Stuart Woods. Narrated by Mark Hammer. 12 cass. (Running Time: 17 hrs. 30 mins.). (Will Lee Ser.: No. 1). 1981. 97.00 (978-0-7887-4055-8(5), 96105E7) Recorded Bks.

Chiefs. 3rd abr. ed. Stuart Woods. Read by Arte Johnson. 4 cass. (Running Time: 6 hrs.). (Will Lee Ser.: No. 1). 2001. 25.00 (978-1-59040-080-7(1), Phoenix Audio) Pub: Amer Intl Pub. Dist(s): PerseuPGW
During the bitter winter of 1920, the naked body of an unidentified teenaged boy is discovered in a wooded area of a small Georgia town. There is no direct evidence of murder, but the body bears marks of what seems to be a ritual beating. The investigation falls into the inexperienced hands of the newly appointed chief of police. His intelligent, obsessive hunt for the boy's tormentor begins a story that ultimately weaves through decades of deceit, hatred, perversion and political drama that inexorably envelops the lives of two other chiefs - one himself a murderer, the other hiding a secret that, if revealed, might destroy not only himself but also the promising career of a rising political figure.

Chieftains: An Authorized Biography. unabr. ed. John Glatt. Read by Nanci Griffith. 4 CDs. (Running Time: 6 hrs.). 1999. audio compact disk 35.00 (978-1-57511-043-1(1)) Pub Mills.
Interviews with the traditional music ensemble's founding members.

Chieftains - The Authorized Biography, Set. abr. ed. Read by Nanci Griffith. Ed. by John Glatt. 3 cass., 3 CD's. (Running Time: 4 hrs. 30 min.). 1999. 24.95 (978-1-57511-033-2(4)) Pub Mills.
The biography of the legendary best selling Celtic band told from the perspective of each member & the amazing roster of superstar musicians who they have worked & collaborated with over their 35 year history in the music business.

Chien des Baskerville, Set. Arthur Conan Doyle. 4 cass.Tr. of Hound of the Baskervilles. 1992. 36.95 (1561-LV) Olivia & Hill.
Sherlock Holmes & his faithful Watson solve the mystery of the dog who haunts the moors & kills all the members of the Baskerville family.

Chihuly Installations Postcard Book: This Accompanies the Hardcover Book, Chihuly Projects, ISBN# 0-8109-6708-1. 1999. cass. & audio compact disk 12.00 (978-1-57684-083-2(2)) Portland Pr.

Child Abuse. Thomas Eisentrout. 1986. 10.80 (0602B) Assn Prof Chaplains.

Child Abuse. Eliana Gil. Read by Eliana Gil. 5 cass. (Running Time: 5 hrs.). 1991. 45.00 Set. (978-1-877872-04-4(0), 0017) Launch Pr.
(1) Impact of abuse on children (2) Therapeutic evaluations of allegations of child abuse (3) Adults abused as children (4) Assessment & treatment (5) Family dynamics in child abuse.

Child Abuse: Policies, Procedures, Pastoral Care. 1 cass. (Care Cassettes Ser.: Vol. 11, No. 7). 1984. 10.80 Assn Prof Chaplains.

Child Abuse; Lessons in Detection. Shirley Lebovics. 1 cass. (Running Time: 90 mins.). 1999. 6.00 (S60SI) Torah Umesorah.

Child & Adolescent Development. 2nd ed. Kelvin Seifert & Robert J. Hoffnung. (C). 1987. bk. 125.96 (978-0-395-44467-2(5)) CENGAGE Learn.

Child & Adolescent Psychiatry for the Specialty Board Review. 2nd rev. ed. Robert L. Hendren & Robert Wood. (Continuing Education in Psychiatry & Psychology Ser.: Vol. 6). 1997. audio compact disk 105.00 (978-0-87630-849-3(3)) Pub: Brunner-Routledge. Dist(s): Taylor and Fran

Child & Adolescent Psychology. Hendren. 1997. audio compact disk 125.00 (978-0-87630-971-1(6)) Taylor and Fran.

Child & Adolescent Psychopharmacology. Contrib. by Lawrence F. Nazarian et al. 1 cass. (American Academy of Pediatrics UPDATE: Vol. 17, No. 2). 1998. 20.00 Am Acad Pediat.

Child & the Law. 1985. bk. 35.00; 30.00 PA Bar Inst.

Child Archetype & Violence: Genesis & Healing. Read by John Giannini. 1 cass. (Running Time: 90 min.). 1984. 10.95 (978-0-7822-0068-3(0), 156) C G Jung IL.

Child Buyer. unabr. collector's ed. John Hersey. Read by Dan Lazar. 8 cass. (Running Time: 8 hrs.). 1981. 48.00 (978-0-7366-0317-1(4), 1305) Books on Tape.
This is the story of an imaginary investigation into activities of Mr. Wissey Jones, who has come to the town of Pequot on urgent defense business. His business is to buy for his corporation children of a certain sort, in this case a ten-year-old named Barry Rudd, who has the precocity of a potential genius.

Child Called Freedom. unabr. ed. Maureen Peters. Read by Marie McCarthy. 4 cass. (Running Time: 6 hrs.). 2000. 44.95 (978-0-7531-0532-0(2), 991108) Pub: ISIS Audio GBR. Dist(s): ISIS Pub
When Tansy Malone first looks into the eyes of Tom Wolf, she falls in love. But Wolf is a half-breed Native American returning to his father's tribe & Tansy has an elderly husband & a delicate sister, with whom she is setting out for the New World.

Child Called "It" One Child's Courage to Survive. Dave Pelzer. Narrated by Brian Keeler. 2 cass. (Running Time: 3 hrs. 45 mins.). 2004. 12.99 (978-1-4025-0527-0(2), 00914) Recorded Bks.
This is the astonishing, disturbing story of Dave Pelzer's early years, one of the most severe child abuse cases in California history. Dave was in first grade when his unstable alcoholic mother began attacking him. Until he was in fifth grade, she starved, beat and psychologically ravaged her son. Eventually denying even his identity, Dave's mother called him an "it" instead of using his name. Relentlessly, she drove him to the brink of death before authorities finally stepped in. With faith and hope, Dave grew determined to survive.

Child Called "It" One Child's Courage to Survive. unabr. ed. Dave Pelzer. Narrated by Brian Keeler. 3 cass. Library ed. (Running Time: 4 hrs.). 1995. 34.00 (978-1-4025-0675-8(9), 96919) Recorded Bks.

Child Called "It" One Child's Courage to Survive. unabr. ed. Dave Pelzer. Narrated by Brian Keeler. 3 CDs. (Running Time: 4 hrs.). 2001. audio compact disk 39.00 (978-1-4025-1005-2(5), C1584) Recorded Bks.
This is the astonishing, disturbing story of Dave Pelzer's early years - one of the most severe child abuse cases in California history. A Child Called "It" was nominated for the Pulitzer Prize, and Dave Pelzer is now recognized as one of the nation's most effective and respected speakers about child abuse.

Child Care: Opportunities for the Pediatrician to Make a Difference. Contrib. by Susan S. Aronson et al. 1 cass. (American Academy of Pediatrics UPDATE: Vol. 19, No. 2). 1998. 20.00 Am Acad Pediat.

Child Care Discipline: Choosing Your Battles. Daniel Armstrong. 1 cass. (Running Time: 1 hr. 30 min.). 15.00 (5019) Natl Inst Child Mgmt.
The four styles of discipline predominant among care givers are analyzed for effectiveness & resulting characteristics of the children raised under them. Examines the decision-making process most child care givers go through to properly respond to a child involved in misbehavior. The developmentally appropriate approach to discipline is presented in regard to handling specific problems, such as biting in toddler classrooms, & temper tantrums. Also addressed are ways of communicating discipline problems & outcomes to parents.

Child Custody Litigation. 1984. bk. 55.00 incl. book.; 30.00 cass. only.; 25.00 book only. PA Bar Inst.

Child Development. Robert Stone. 1 cass. 1986. 10.00 (978-0-938137-14-6(X)) Listen & Learn.
Physical development, cognitive & language development, emotional & social development, role of play, personality & moral development.

Child Development: The Essentials. Dora C. Fowler. 1 cass. (Running Time: 60 min.). 1990. 9.95 (978-1-57323-024-7(3)) Natl Inst Child Mgmt.
Staff training materials for child care.

Child Discipline Process: Essentials for love-based, successful guidance of child Behavior. Bob Lancer. (Running Time: 60 mins.). (ENG.). 1997. audio compact disk 9.95 (978-0-9628666-7-8(9)) Parent Sol.

Child from the Sea, Pt. 1. unabr. collector's ed. Elizabeth Goudge. Read by Penelope Dellaporta. 10 cass. (Running Time: 15 hrs.). 1979. 80.00 (978-0-7366-0141-2(4), 1144A) Books on Tape.
The story of Lucy Walter, a child of transcendent beauty & spirituality, who grows up to become the secret wife of Charles II.

Child from the Sea, Pt. 2. collector's ed. Elizabeth Goudge. Read by Penelope Dellaporta. 9 cass. (Running Time: 13 hrs. 30 min.). 1979. 72.00 (978-0-7366-0142-9(2), 1144-B) Books on Tape.

Child Guidance Through Astrology. Gloria Star. 1 cass. 8.95 (330) Am Fed Astrologers.
Keys to talents & motivations of child.

Child in the Forest. unabr. ed. Winifred Foley. Read by Sarah Sherborne. 6 cass. (Running Time: 7 hr. 30 min.). 1998. 34.95 (978-0-7531-0090-5(8), 961214) Pub: ISIS Audio GBR. Dist(s): Ulverscroft US
Account of a childhood in the Forest of Dean in the first half of this century. Describes how life in a small mining community was one of economic hardship, faced with humor & overcome with fortitude.

Child Lovers see Dylan Thomas Reading

Child Next Door see Robert Penn Warren Reads Selected Poems

Child of Dandelions. unabr. ed. Shenaaz Nanji. Read by Vaishali Sharma. (Running Time: 6 hrs.). 2008. 39.25 (978-1-4233-7069-7(4), 9781423370697, BADLE); 39.25 (978-1-4233-7067-3(8), 9781423370673, Brlnc Audio MP3 Lib); 24.95 (978-1-4233-7066-6(X), 9781423370666, Brilliance MP3); 24.95 (978-1-4233-7068-0(6), 9781423370680, BAD); audio compact disk 69.25 (978-1-4233-7065-9(1), 9781423370659, BriAudCD Unabrid); audio compact disk 24.99 (978-1-4233-7058-1(9), 9781423370581, Bril Audio CD Unabri) Brilliance Audio.

Child of Fortune. unabr. ed. Jeffrey St. John. Read by Jeff Riggenbach. 8 cass. (Running Time: 11 hrs. 30 mins.). 1999. 56.95 (978-0-7861-1635-5(8), 2463) Blckstn Audio.
With his simulated day-by-day reportage, prize-winning journalist-historian St. John makes you an eyewitness to the 1787-1788 political battle to ratify the U.S. Constitution. Discover how the Federalists sought to stampede the states into early ratification with violence & rigged elections; how close some Anti-Federalists came to opposing the new Constitution with armed force.

Child of God. Dameans, The. Perf. by Gary Ault et al. 1995. 10.95 (347); audio compact disk 15.95 (347) GIA Pubns.

Child of God for Happy Dreams. unabr. ed. Mary Richards. Read by Mary Richards. 1 cass. (Running Time: 45 min.). (Children's I Am Ser.). (J). 2007. audio compact disk 19.95 (978-1-56136-205-9(0)) Master Your Mind.
An exciting ride into space where child senses the wonder of the Universe. "I am thankful for all the good in my life." Both sides fanciful journey.

Child of Happy Valley: A Memoir. unabr. ed. Juanita Carberry & Nicola Tyrer. Narrated by Briony Sykes. 5 cass. (Running Time: 8 hrs. 30 mins.). 1999. 44.00 (978-0-7887-3950-7(6), 96080E7) Recorded Bks.
Natives called the part of 1930's colonial Kenya where the British live "happy valley" & the river that flows through it "booze." It is into this decadent society that Juanita Carberry is born. Her memoir reflects both her undying love of the untamed land & the grim consequences of unbridled excess. As a young woman, Carberry becomes intimately involved with the infamous Lord Errol murder case. This betrays the ugly realities that lay beneath the glitzy veneer.

Child of My Heart. unabr. ed. Alice McDermott. 6 cass. (Running Time: 9 hrs.). 2002. 40.00 (978-0-7366-8923-6(0)) Books on Tape.

Child of Promise. 6 cass. (Running Time: 9 hrs.). 1997. 30.00 (978-0-00-525747-0(6)) Standard Pub.

Child of Storm. H. Rider Haggard. Read by Shelly Frasier. (Running Time: 9 hrs. 45 mins.). 2002. 27.95 (978-1-60083-601-5(1), Audiofy Corp) Iofy Corp.

Child of Storm. H. Rider Haggard. Read by Shelly Frasier. (Zulu (Tantor) Ser.). (ENG.). 2005. audio compact disk 84.00 (978-1-4001-3029-0(8)) Pub: Tantor Media. Dist(s): IngramPubServ

Child of Storm. unabr. ed. H. Rider Haggard. Narrated by Shelly Frasier. 8 CDs. (Running Time: 9 hrs. 49 mins.). (Zulu (Tantor) Ser.). (ENG.). 2002. audio compact disk 42.00 (978-1-4001-0029-3(1)); audio compact disk 20.00 (978-1-4001-5029-8(9)) Pub: Tantor Media. Dist(s): IngramPubServ

Child of Storm. unabr. ed. H. Rider Haggard. Narrated by Shelly Frasier. (Running Time: 10 hrs. 0 mins. 0 sec.). (Zulu Ser.). (ENG.). 2009. audio compact disk 32.99 (978-1-4001-1103-9(X)); audio compact disk 65.99 (978-1-4001-4103-6(6)); audio compact disk 22.99 (978-1-4001-6103-4(7)) Pub: Tantor Media. Dist(s): IngramPubServ

Child of the Century see Crimson Ramblers of the World, Farewell

Child of the Jago. unabr. ed. Arthur Morrison. Read by Peter Joyce. 4 cass. 1996. 44.95 (978-1-86015-441-6(7)) Pub: UlverLrgPrint GBR. Dist(s): Ulverscroft US
Young Dicky Perrott has a heart of gold, but growing up in the East End slums of London ensures his downfall.

Child of the Morning, Pt. 1. unabr. collector's ed. Pauline Gedge. Read by Donada Peters. 8 cass. (Running Time: 12 hrs.). 1985. 64.00 (978-0-7366-0874-9(5), 1824A) Books on Tape.
Thirty-five hundred years ago a woman sat on the throne of the Pharoahs of Egypt. She was Hatshepsut. She wore the kilts of a man & the regalia of a king. She received the schooling & military training of a boy, led her war chariot & her troops into battle. Her 22-year reign was one of superb administration, exploration, peace & the beautification of her empire. Yet dark forces were at work to destroy her & erase her name from history.

Child of the Morning, Pt. 2. collector's ed. Pauline Gedge. Read by Donada Peters. 7 cass. (Running Time: 10 hrs. 30 min.). 1985. 56.00 (978-0-7366-0875-6(3), 1824-B) Books on Tape.

Child on the Cliffs see Dylan Thomas Reading

Child Safety Book on Tape. Andrea Gravatt. 1 cass. (Running Time: 15 min.). (J). 2000. 4.99 (978-1-56664-098-5(9)) WorldComm.
Comprehensive child safety lesson that is specifically designed for preschool & primary school children.

Child Saint Dhruva (A); The Child Saint Prahlada (B) 1 cass. (Spiritual Stories Ser.). 5.00 Bhaktivedanta.

***Child Scientology.** L. Ron Hubbard. (ENG.). 2002. audio compact disk 15.00 (978-1-4031-1120-3(0)) Bridge Pubns Inc.

***Child, the State & the Victorian Novel.** Laura C. Berry. (Victorian Literature & Culture Ser.). (ENG.). 27.50 (978-0-8139-2929-3(6)) U Pr of Va.

***Child Thief.** unabr. ed. Brom. (ENG.). 2010. (978-0-06-206165-2(8), Harper Audio); (978-0-06-206278-9(6), Harper Audio) HarperCollins Pubs.

Child with NLD: Dealing with Secondary Emotional Outcomes. Kathryn Stewart. 1 cass. (Running Time: 1 hr. 25 min.). 1998. bk. 20.00 (978-1-58111-060-9(X)) Contemporary Medical.
Problems for NLD children & teens, distinctions between Bipolar, OLD & ADHD. Anxiety, cognitive behavioral interventions.

Child Within. 1 cass. (Running Time: 1 hr. 30 mins.). (Mendocino Ser.). 1990. 10.95 (978-1-56557-001-6(4), T04) Delos Inc.
Within each of us lives an Inner child who carries our essential being & who embodies our sensitivity to the world around us. It is this self which our other selves develop to protect. In this tape, you will be introduced to this child. You will hear it speak & will learn how to listen for the almost inaudible voice of your own Inner Child.

Child Within. Laurel Elizabeth Keyes. Voice by Laurel Elizabeth Keyes. 1 cass. (Running Time: 90 mins.). 1983. 10.00 (978-0-9791360-9-2(1)) Gentle Living.
Laurel Keyes leading a visual imagery for inner healing. Our childhood traumas cannot be healed by "talk therapy" and it is important to go into the unconscious emotional nature and heal the hurts and traumas that are blocking our relationships and spiritual growth.

Child Within: 1 Cor. 13:10-11. Ed Young. (J). 1980. 4.95 (978-0-7417-1118-2(4), A0118) Win Walk.

Child Within; Two Anathemas That Changed the World. Jonathan Murro & Ann Ree Colton. 1 cass. 7.95 A R Colton Fnd.

Child X. Lee Weatherly. Read by Claire Corbett. 5 CDs. (J). 2004. audio compact disk 49.95 (978-0-7540-6662-0(2), Chivers Child Audio) AudioGO.

Child 44. unabr. ed. Tom Rob Smith. Read by Dennis Boutsikaris. (Running Time: 12 hrs. 30 mins.). (ENG.). 2008. 14.98 (978-1-60024-160-4(3)) Pub: Hachet Audio. Dist(s): HachBkGrp

Child 44. unabr. ed. Tom Rob Smith. Read by Dennis Boutsikaris. (Running Time: 12 hrs. 30 mins.). (ENG.). 2009. audio compact disk 19.98 (978-1-60024-561-9(7)) Pub: Hachet Audio. Dist(s): HachBkGrp

Childbearing: A Period of Emotional Stress. Ann Seagrave & Faison Covington. Read by Ann Seagrave & Faison Covington. (Anxiety Treatment Ser.). 15.50 CHAANGE.
Discusses emotional & physical features of child-bearing & contains a dialogue between Dr. Selby & a new mother who has, herself, dealt with these changes.

Childbirth Preparation One Vol. I: Physical, Emotional, Mental Preparation for Childbirth. Mark Bancroft. Read by Mark Bancroft. 1 cass., bklet. (Running Time: 60 min.). (Pregnancy & Childbirth Ser.). 1998. 12.95 (978-0-9665539-4-9(2), 501, EnSpire Aud) EnSpire Pr.
Two complete sessions plus printed instructionmanual/guidebook. With healing music soundtrack.

Childbirth Preparation One Vol. I: Physical, Emotional, Mental Preparation for Childbirth. Mark Bancroft. Read by Mark Bancroft. 1 CD, bklet. (Running Time: 60 min.). (Pregnancy & Childbirth Ser.). 2006. audio compact disk 20.00 CD & bklet. (978-0-9665539-5-6(0)) EnSpire Pr.

Childbirth Preparation Two: Prepare for the Stages of Childbirth Labor & Delivery. Mark Bancroft. Read by Mark Bancroft. 1 CD, 1 bklet. (Running Time: 1 hr.). (Pregnancy & Childbirth Ser.). 2006. audio compact disk 20.00 (978-1-58522-062-5(0)) EnSpire Pr.

Childbirth Preparation Two Vol. II: Prepare for the Stages of Childbirth Labor & Delivery. Mark Bancroft. Read by Mark Bancroft. 1 cass., bklet. (Running Time: 1 hr.). (Pregnancy & Childbirth Ser.). 1999. 12.95 (978-1-58522-022-9(1), 502) EnSpire Pr.

Childcare: Space & Costs. (Running Time: 30 min.). 10.95 (D0170B090, HarperThor) HarpC GBR.

Childe Harold (selections) see Treasury of George Gordon, Lord Byron

Childe Harold's Pilgrimage: Cantos III & IV see Poetry of Byron

Childe Roland see Favorite Children's Stories: A Collection

Childe Roland to the Dark Tower Came see Browning's Last Duchess

Childe Rowland & Other British Fairy Tales. unabr. ed. Perf. by Claire Bloom. Ed. by Amabel Williams-Ellis. 1 cass. (Running Time: 90 min.). Incl. Black Bull of Norroway. (J). (CDL5 1278); Lake Lady. (J). (CDL5 1278); Midnight Hunt. (J). (CDL5 1278); (J). 1972. 9.95 (978-0-694-50683-5(4), CDL5 1278) HarperCollins Pubs.

Childes Project. 2000. audio compact disk 39.95 (978-0-8058-3637-0(3)) Pub: L Erlbaum Assocs. Dist(s): Taylor and Fran

Childhood: The Biography of a Place. Read by Harry Crews. 1 cass. (Running Time: 40 min.). 13.95 (978-1-55644-042-7(1), 2051) Am Audio Prose.
Reading of a hog-butchering episode & related tragic childhood accidents.

Childhood as a Stage on the Spiritual Path. Michael N. Deranja. 1 cass. (Running Time: 70 min.). (Spiritual Child-Raising Ser.). 9.95 (ND-2) Crystal Clarity.
Explains: How to help children meet the challenge of worldy influences, special problems posed by teenagers, basic principles of spiritual child-raising.

Childhood in Scotland. unabr. ed. Christian Miller. 4 cass. (Running Time: 4 hrs. 25 min.). (Isis Ser.). (J). 2003. 44.95 (978-0-7531-1184-0(5)) Pub: ISIS Lrg Prnt GBR. Dist(s): Ulverscroft US

Childhood Legends. unabr. ed. Read by Elinor G. Hoffman & Michael Eye. 5 cass. Incl. Great Stone Face. Nathaniel Hawthorne. (J). (D-306); King of the Golden River. Jane Ruskin. (J). (D-306); Legend of Sleepy Hollow. Ed. by Tod Smith. (J). (D-306); Merry Adventures of Robin Hood. Howard Pyle. (J). (D-306); Rip Van Winkle. Washington Irving. (J). (D-306); (J). 29.75 (D-306) Audio Bk.

Childhood Lying, Stealing & Cheating. 2004. audio compact disk 13.95 (978-1-930429-67-3(3)) Love Logic.

Childhood Lying, Stealing & Cheating: Guiding Children Towards Honesty & Integrity. unabr. ed. Foster W. Cline. 1 CD. (Running Time: 1 hr. 30 min.). 1999. audio compact disk 12.95 (978-0-944634-58-5(3), 0194401) Pub: Love Logic. Dist(s): Penton Overseas
Techniques which improve communication, avoid confrontations and guide children toward trust and honesty.

Childhood Remembered: A Musical Tribute to the Wonder of Childhood. Claude Clement et al. 1991. audio compact disk 16.97 (978-0-934245-14-2(2)) Narada Prodns.

Childhood Remembered: A Musical Tribute to the Wonder of Childhood. Claude Clement et al. 1991. 9.98 (978-0-934245-15-9(0)) Narada Prodns.

Childhood Soft Tissue Sarcoma. 2 cass. (Pediatric Surgery Ser.: C85-PE1). 1985. 15.00 (8579) Am Coll Surgeons.

Childhood Songs. Perf. by Jean Ritchie. 1 cass. (J). 1999. Rounder Records.
Some of the songs are from Jean's childhood; others from the young years of her own children, Peter & Jon. These songs, although personal to this family, are universal in appeal, some already widely used in music textbooks ("Shady Grove" & "Skin & Bones"). Greatly enjoyed by children of all ages, this album will be especially enjoyed by children aged three to 10.

Childhood's End see Arthur C. Clarke

Childhood's End. unabr. ed. Arthur C. Clarke. Read by Robert J. Sawyer & Summerer Eric Michael. (Running Time: 8 hrs.). 2009. 24.99 (978-1-4233-9505-8(0), 9781423395058, Brilliance MP3) Brilliance Audio.

Childhood's End. unabr. ed. Arthur C. Clarke. Read by Eric Michael Summerer & Robert J. Sawyer. (Running Time: 8 hrs.). 2009. 39.97 (978-1-4233-9506-5(9), 9781423395065, Brlnc Audio MP3 Lib) Brilliance Audio.

Childhood's End. unabr. ed. Arthur C. Clarke. Read by Eric Michael Summerer. (Running Time: 8 hrs.). 2009. 39.97 (978-1-4233-9507-2(7), 9781423395072, BADLE); audio compact disk 29.99 (978-1-4233-9503-4(4), 9781423395034, Bril Audio CD Unabri) Brilliance Audio.

Childhood's End. unabr. ed. Arthur C. Clarke. Read by Eric Michael Summerer & Robert J. Sawyer. (Running Time: 8 hrs.). 2009. audio compact disk 87.97 (978-1-4233-9504-1(2), 9781423395041, BriAudCD Unabrid) Brilliance Audio.

Childhood's End. unabr. collector's ed. Arthur C. Clarke. Read by Dan Lazar. 8 cass. (Running Time: 8 hrs.). 1979. 48.00 (978-0-7366-0167-2(8), 1169) Books on Tape.
This novel tells the tale of the last generation of mankind on earth. All of man's developments in space & travel are stopped by the alien "Overlords" who take over earth, establishing a benevolent dictatorship which eliminates poverty, ignorance & disease.

Childhood's End: Program from the Award Winning Public Radio Series. Hosted by Fred Goodwin. 1 CD. (Running Time: 1 hr). (Infinite Mind Ser.). 2003. audio compact disk 21.95 (978-1-932479-07-2(4), LCM 255) Lichtenstein Creat.
When our grandparents were young, adolescence was thought of as a short passage between childhood and adulthood. Now it starts early.... and does it ever end? Today's program, Childhood's End, explores the sometimes blurry lines between child and adult. Dr. Goodwin's guests include Ms. Kay Hymowitz, a fellow at the Manhattan Institute and contributing editor of "City Journal"; Dr. Reed Larson, professor of Human Development and Family Studies at the University of Illinois at Urbana-Champaign; Dr. Jeffrey Arnett, a researcher in developmental psychology at the University of Maryland; Dr. Laurence Steinberg, Professor of Psychology at Temple University; and Dr. Ronald Dahl, professor of psychiatry and pediatrics at the University of Pittsburgh School of Medicine. Eighteen-year-old reporters Jessica Margolis-Pineo and Valerie Randall of the Blunt/Youth Radio Project in Portland, Maine, contribute a report on what they think it might mean to be an adult today. We also hear from a 13-year-old boy, Zachary Charles, as he prepares for and later recalls his bar mitzvah.

Childlike Simplicity. Swami Amar Jyoti. 1 cass. Orig. Title: Guru's Story. 1976. 9.95 (K-69) Truth Consciousness.
Outer clouds reflect our mental weather. When we become a child before Mother Nature, She reveals Her true meaning. On mind, disease & reincarnation.

Childlikeness of the Believer. 2 cass. 7.95 (22-9, HarperThor) HarpC GBR.

Children, Set. unabr. ed. Michel de Montaigne. Read by Robert L. Halvorson. 2 cass. (Running Time: 180 min.). Incl. Books. (21); Solitude. (21); 14.95 (21) Halvorson Assocs.

Children, Set. unabr. ed. Edith Wharton. Read by Flo Gibson. 6 cass. (Running Time: 9 hrs.). (J). 1998. bk. 24.95 (978-1-55685-512-2(5)) Audio Bk Con.
The Wheater children & step-children, victims of many divorces live in various deluxe hotels, cling together under the guardianship of a caring bachelor.

Children & Marriage. Hal Stone & Sidra Stone. 1 cass. (Running Time: 1 hr.). (Mendocino Ser.). 1993. 10.95 (978-1-56557-016-0(2), T10) Delos Inc.
Children bring great gifts & at the same time, can introduce severe stress into the marriage relationship. In this tape, Hal & Sidra Stone give a down to earth explanation of some of the difficulties parents encounter & have practical suggestions as to how to maintain a healthy & romantic marriage.

Children & the Vegan Diet. Michael Klaper. Read by Michael Klaper. Ed. by Cynthia Klaper. 1 cass. (Running Time: 30 min.). 1987. 7.00 (978-0-929274-09-6(1)); 3.15 rental. Gentle World.
An overview of nutrition for children & how pure vegetarian (vegan) foods can produce optimal health.

***Children are from Heaven.** abr. ed. John Gray. Read by John Gray. (ENG.). 2005. (978-0-06-085642-7(4), Harper Audio); (978-0-06-085643-4(2), Harper Audio) HarperCollins Pubs.

***Children are from Heaven.** unabr. ed. John Gray. Read by John (reader) Gray. (ENG.). 2005. (978-0-06-085640-3(8), Harper Audio); (978-0-06-085641-0(6), Harper Audio) HarperCollins Pubs.

Children as Children? What Are the Needs Of. unabr. ed. Robert H. Steinkellner. 1 cass. (Running Time: 34 min.). 12.95 (29151) J Norton Pubs.
This probes into childhood & children as the pawns, & promises of human & humane society.

Children at Risk Part 1: Through the Eyes of the Child. 1 cass. (Running Time: 30 min.). 9.95 (D001AB090, HarperThor) HarpC GBR.

Children at Risk Part 2: Parenting - The World's Toughest Job. 1 cass. (Running Time: 30 min.). 9.95 (HO-84-06-06, HarperThor) HarpC GBR.

Children at Risk Part 3: Hush Little Baby. 1 cass. (Running Time: 30 min.). 9.95 (D001CB090, HarperThor) HarpC GBR.

Children at Risk Part 4: The Adolescent Self. 1 cass. (Running Time: 30 min.). 9.95 (D001DB090, HarperThor) HarpC GBR.

Children at Risk Part 5: Stolen Childhood. 1 cass. (Running Time: 30 min.). 9.95 (D001EB090, HarperThor) HarpC GBR.

Children at Risk Part 6: Out of Harm's Way. 1 cass. (Running Time: 30 min.). 9.95 (HD-85-01-02, HarperThor) HarpC GBR.

Children at Risk Part 7: For the Love of Children. 1 cass. (Running Time: 30 min.). 9.95 (D001GB090, HarperThor) HarpC GBR.

Children... Be Your Best. Created by Ellen Chernoff Simon. 1 CD. (Running Time: 15 min.). 2004. audio compact disk 18.00 (978-0-9765587-6-7(9)) Imadulation.
This introduction to guided imagery for children of primary shcool age is a 15 minute program desigend to enhance learning and academic performance. It teaches the method of guided imagery, the steps to building inner strength and self control in a step by step method for gaining competency and building skills through experiential learning. Help your child discover their many talents and abilities through the power of their creative imagination. When they master their own inner power they will naturally do their best.

Children Can Learn with Their Shoes Off! Supporting Young People with Asperger's Syndrome in Mainstream Schools & Colleges. rev. ed. Barbara Maines & George Robinson. 2002. 74.95 (978-1-873942-89-5(3)) Pub: P Chapman GBR. Dist(s): SAGE

Children, Five to Eleven: Instruction on Deliverance for Children & Their Parents. Derek Prince. 1 cass. (B-6008) Derek Prince.

Children from Dysfunctional Families (Hypnosis), Vol. 20. Jayne Helle. 1 cass. (Running Time: 29 min.). 1997. 15.00 (978-1-891826-19-1(0)) Introspect.
Stop finding the future in the past, forgive & move on to the wonderful healthy life you deserve.

Children in the Hands of a Mighty Mom. Susie Stone. 2008. audio compact disk 19.99 (978-1-60247-721-6(3)) Tate Pubng.

Children in the One-Parent Home. unabr. ed. Howard B. Lyman. 1 cass. (Running Time: 21 min.). (Single Again Ser.). 12.95 (35026) J Norton Pubs.

Children learn German - Songs from the Collection CD see Kinder lernen Deutsch Lieder aus der Loseblattsammlung CD

Children Learn Instant Spanish, Set. AMR Staff. 2 cass. (AMR Language Ser.). (SPA.). (J). 1999. 13.95 (978-1-886463-74-5(3)) Oasis Audio.

Children Love to Sing & Dance. 1 cass. (Running Time: 1 hr.). (J). 2001. 10.95 (KUB 5000C) Kimbo Educ.
Children sing, dance & more while learning valuable concepts. Counting Together, The Nutrition Song, Occupations, Move With Me, The Science Song & more.

Children Must Be Liberated. abr. ed. Adi Da Love-Ananda Samiraj. 1 cass. 1978. 11.95 (AT-CL) Dawn Horse Pr.
Adi Da considers basic principles of how to serve children's spiritual practice as they grow through the stages of life, & answers to questions from children.

Children Need Books. 1 cass. (Running Time: 8 min.). 1989. Cleary Connection.

Children of Christmas & Every Living Thing. Cynthia Rylant. Read by Sally Darling et al. 13 cass. (J). 2000. 64.00 (978-0-7366-9148-2(0)) Books on Tape.
Two collections of short stories. "Every Living Thing" features 12 stories about special relationships between people & animals. "Children of Christmas" presents six tales of Christmas that capture the heart of this season.

Children of Christmas & Every Living Thing. unabr. ed. Cynthia Rylant. 2 cass. (Running Time: 2 hrs. 36 min.). (Young Adult Cassette Library). (J). (gr. 4-7). 1989. 16.98 (978-0-8072-7268-8(X), YA 818 CX, Listening Lib) Random Audio Pubg.

Children of Christmas & Every Living Thing, Set. unabr. ed. Ed. by Cynthia Rylant. 2 cass. (Running Time: 2 hrs. 36 min.). (Young Adult Cassette Library). (J). (gr. 4-6). 2000. bk. 27.98 (978-0-8072-7325-8(2), YA8185SP, Listening Lib) Random Audio Pubg.

Children of Divorce. Carole Riley. 3 cass. (Running Time: 2 hrs. 33 min.). 1996. 27.95 Set. (TAH365) Alba Hse Comns.
Sr. Carole deals with all the important issues of separation & divorce, & how they impact upon the lives of the most vulnerable facets of the marital union. Understanding the sense of loss & dealing with the life-long issues that remain after divorce allow spiritual growth & healing to replace the pain of separation & loss.

Children of Divorce. unabr. ed. Ruth Frank. 1 Cass. (Running Time: 50 min.). 1983. 9.95 Newtown Psychological Ctr.
A lecture dealing with a variety of problems that children & parents face following a divorce.

Children of Divorce: A Guide for Parents. unabr. ed. Larry Losoncy. 10.95 (AF1901) J Norton Pubs.
Itemizes common mistakes many parents make in dealing with their children during divorce. Includes practical & sound advice in the form of ten commandments for divorcing parents.

Children of Dune. unabr. ed. Frank Herbert. Narrated by Simon Vance & Scott Brick. 2 MP3-CDs. (Running Time: 14 hrs.). 2008. 69.95 (978-0-7927-5304-9(6)); audio compact disk 115.95 (978-0-7927-5232-5(5)) AudioGO.
The bestselling science fiction series of all time continues! In this third installment, the sand-blasted world of Arrakis has become green, watered and fertile. Old Paul Atreides, who led the desert Fremen to political and religious domination of the galaxy, is gone. But for the children of Dune, the very blossoming of their land contains the seeds of its own destruction. The altered climate is destroying the giant sandworms, and this in turn is disastrous for the planet's economy. Leto and Ghanima, Paul Atreides's twin children and his heirs, can see possible solutions - but fanatics begin to challenge the rule of the all-powerful Atreides empire, and more than economic disaster threatens.

Children of Dune. unabr. ed. Frank Herbert & Frank Herbert. Read by Simon Vance & Scott Brick. 14 CDs. (Running Time: 17 hrs. 0 mins. 0 sec.). (ENG.). 2008. audio compact disk 49.95 (978-1-4272-0291-8(5)) Pub: Macmill Audio. Dist(s): Macmillan

Children of Dune. unabr. collector's ed. Frank Herbert. Read by Connor O'Brien. 10 cass. (Running Time: 15 hrs.). (Dune Chronicles: Bk. 3). 1998. 80.00 (978-0-7366-4019-0(3), 4517) Books on Tape.
This third installment finds the desert planet Arrakis in a state of unprecedented stability & prosperity. With the Herculean efforts of the Imperium, it has begun to grow green & lush. The life-giving spice is abundant& the nine year old royal twins are coming into their own. Possessed of their father's supernormal powers, they are being groomed as Messiahs but there are those who think the Imperium does not need omnipotent rulers & they'll stop at nothing to make their point.

Children of Dunseverick. unabr. ed. Vivienne Draper. Read by Paddy Glynn. 3 cass. (Running Time: 4 hrs.). (Isis Ser.). (J). 1999. 34.95 (978-0-7531-0678-5(7), 991216) Pub: ISIS Lrg Prnt GBR. Dist(s): Ulverscroft US
This enchanting & evocative book paints a vivid portrait of a happy childhood in the 1920s.

Children of Fatima. Mary F. Windeatt. 5 cass. (J). 22.95 (511) Ignatius Pr.
Mary's appearances at Fatima, based on historical records.

Children of God. unabr. collector's ed. Mary Doria Russell. Read by Anna Fields. 13 cass. (Running Time: 19 hrs. 30 min.). 1999. 104.00 (978-0-7366-4393-1(1), 4855) Books on Tape.
This continues the story of Father Emilio Sandoz, the Jesuit priest whose faith was severely tested when he was maimed & raped, & witnessed the death of his friends on the planet Rakhat. Sandoz has begun the long, slow work of healing both body & soul. Renouncing the priesthood, he has married & has found a measure of happiness. Now, however, the Jesuits want to go back to Rakhat, a planet on the verge of genocidal destruction, & they want Sandoz aboard the new mission.

***Children of God Storybook Bible.** Desmond Tutu. (Running Time: 1 hr. 50 mins. 24 sec.). (ENG.). (J). 2010. 15.99 (978-0-310-57834-5(5)) Pub: Zondkidz. Dist(s): Zondervan

Children of Green Knowe. L. M. Boston. Read by Simon Vance. 4 CDs. (Running Time: 14400 sec.). (Green Knowe Chronicles). (J). (ps-7). 2005. audio compact disk 27.95 (978-1-59316-060-9(7), LL152) Listen & Live.
L. M. Boston's thrilling and chilling tales of Green Knowe, a haunted manor deep in an overgrown garden in the English countryside, have been entertaining readers for half a century. There are three children: Toby, who rides the majestic horse Feste; his mischievous little sister, Linnet; and their brother, Alexander, who plays the flute. The children warmly welcome Tolly to Green Knowe... even though they've been dead for centuries. But that's how everything is at Green Knowe. The ancient manor hides as many stories as it does dusty old rooms. And the master of the house is great-grandmother Oldknow, whose storytelling mizes present and past with the oldest magic in the world.

Children of Green Knowe. unabr. ed. L. M. Boston. Read by Simon Vance. (J). 2007. 39.99 (978-1-60252-884-0(5)) Find a World.

Children of Húrin. unabr. ed. J. R. R. Tolkien. Read by Christopher Lee. Ed. by Christopher Tolkien. 8 CDs. (Running Time: 9 hrs. 30 mins. 0 sec.). (ENG.). 2007. audio compact disk 49.95 (978-0-00-726345-5(7)) Pub: HarpC GBR. Dist(s): IPG Chicago

Children of Jihad: A Young American's Travel's Among the Youth of the Middle East. unabr. ed. Jared Cohen. Read by Jason Collins. (Running Time: 34200 sec.). 2007. 29.95 (978-1-4332-0377-0(4)); audio compact disk 29.95 (978-1-4332-0378-7(2)) Blckstn Audio.

Children of Jihad: A Young American's Travel's Among the Youth of the Middle East. unabr. ed. Jared Cohen. Read by Jason Collins. (Running Time: 34200 sec.). 2007. 65.95 (978-1-4332-0375-6(8)); audio compact disk 29.95 (978-1-4332-0379-4(0)) Blckstn Audio.

Children of Jihad: A Young American's Travel's Among the Youth of the Middle East. unabr. ed. Jared Cohen & Jason Collins. (Running Time: 34200 sec.). 2007. audio compact disk 72.00 (978-1-4332-0376-3(6)) Blckstn Audio.

Children of Light. 2004. 10.99 (978-7-5124-0024-5(1)); 15.99 (978-7-5124-0031-3(4)) Mrning Str.

Children of Light. Heather Macauley. 5 cass. (Running Time: 4 hrs. 30 min.). 1996. 25.00 Set. (978-0-9648093-1-4(1)) HOME Pubng.

Children of Light. unabr. ed. Swami Amar Jyoti. 1 cass. (Satsangs of Swami Amar Jyoti Ser.). 1995. 9.95 (K-153) Truth Consciousness.
Remembering who we are & the purpose of our life on earth. Serving the cause of Light. Dealing with the dark forces.

Children of Light: Affirmations. Heather Macauley. Perf. by William Schimmel. . (Running Time:). 1996. cass. & video 9.99 (978-0-9648093-6-9(2)) Traci Rae Pubns.

Children of Men. unabr. ed. P. D. James. Read by David Case. 7 cass. (Running Time: 10 hrs. 30 min.). 1993. 56.00 (978-0-7366-2463-3(5), 3227) Books on Tape.
The human race is coming to an end in 2021 England in this departure from P. D. James's usual crime novel.

Children of Men. unabr. ed. P. D. James. Read by Julian Glover. 8 cass. (Running Time: 12 hrs.). 2000. 59.95 (978-0-7451-4275-3(3), CAB 958) Pub: Chivers Audio Bks GBR. Dist(s): AudioGO
The year is 2021, and no babies have been born for 25 years. The elderly succumb to despair and suicide, while the young are violent and cruel. The middle-aged try to sustain normality under the absolute rule of Xan Lyppiatt, Warden of England. His cousin, Theo, lives a solitary life under Lyppiatt's reign. By chance, Theo meets a woman in a small group seeking to challenge the Warden's regime, and the route to unimaginable disaster begins!.

Children of Men, unabr. ed. P. D. James. Narrated by John Franklyn-Robbins. 7 cass. (Running Time: 10 hrs. 30 mins.). 60.00 (978-1-55690-861-3(X), 93303E7) Recorded Bks.
It is 2025 & the human race faces imminent extinction. When mankind suddenly & universally finds it is unable to have children, the world turns into a bizarre & dangerous place. Available to libraries only.

Children of Nazis. 1 cass. (Running Time: 23 min.). 9.95 (AT-87-08-19, HarperThor) HarpC GBR.

Children of Prometheus: The Accelerating Pace of Human Evolution, unabr. ed. Christopher Wills. Narrated by Richard M. Davidson. 8 cass. (Running Time: 12 hrs.). 1999. 70.00 (978-0-7887-3595-0(0), 95659E7) Recorded Bks.
Professor Wills addresses three basic but intriguing questions: Are we still evolving? If so, how? What are we evolving into? Filled with fascinating examples for anyone curious about the future of our species.

Children of Pure Consciousness. Swami Amar Jyoti. 1 cass. 1990. 9.95 (R-101) Truth Consciousness.
Creation is infinite, yet all of Reality is in every particle. "You are That & That is within you.".

Children of the Candlelight. Scripts. Harry Stephens. Perf. by High Sierra Players Staff. Narrated by Poppy Hill. Score by David Fabrizio. Directed By David Fabrizio. Illus. by Michael Cox. 2 CDs. (Running Time: 1 hr. 30 mins.). Dramatization. (ENG.). 2004. audio compact disk 16.95 (978-1-58124-767-1(2)) Pub: Fiction Works. Dist(s): Brodart

Children of the Dust. unabr. ed. Clancy Carlile. Read by Christopher Lane. 13 cass. (Running Time: 1 hr. 30 mins. per cass.). 1995. 104.00 (978-0-7366-3168-6(2), 3838) Books on Tape.
Two inter-connected stories of doomed romance & ugly prejudice. They concern Gypsy Smith, a black-Cherokee mix & leader of a "colored" wagon train & John Maxwell, a white teacher on a reservation whose true beliefs emerge when his daughter falls for a Cheyenne boy.

Children of the Dust, Set. abr. ed. Clancy Carlile. Read by Courtney B. Vance. 2 cass. (Running Time: 3 hrs.). 1999. 16.95 (978-1-879371-91-0(X), 392832) Pub Mills.
In this sweeping & historically accurate account of the Oklahoma land rush of the 1880s, Gypsy Smith, mixed-blood black-Cherokee, a gunfighter & lawman, agrees to lead a caravan of black settlers into untamed Oklahoma territory. When he is attacked by the KKK, Gypsy vows revenge & sets out on a killing spree.

Children of the Father. 1 cass. (Running Time: 30 min.). 1985. (0284) Evang Sisterhood Mary.
The way to a true father-child relationship with god. Also talks on the riches of poverty.

Children of the Frost. unabr. ed. Jack London. Read by Walter Zimmerman. 5 cass. (Running Time: 7 hrs. 30 min.). 1995. 39.95 (978-0-7861-0629-5(8), 2119) Blckstn Audio.
A collection of stories dealing with Indian themes - the Indians of the frozen Northland that London was familiar with from his travels to that region during the gold rush. The book drew immediate praise. Its immense popularity was not expected because London described Indians as noble people - not savages - a treatment which was unorthodox for the period. As with his other books, these stories are sometimes brutal, & always exciting & evocative.

Children of the Frost. unabr. ed. Jack London. Read by Walter Zimmerman. 5 cass. (Running Time: 7 hrs. 30 min.). 1985. 28.00 (C-130) Jimcin Record.
Short stories dealing with Indian themes, the Yukon.

Children of the Frost. unabr. collector's ed. Jack London. Read by Walter Zimmerman. 7 cass. (Running Time: 7 hrs.). (J). 1984. 42.00 (978-0-7366-3898-2(9), 9130) Books on Tape.
A collection of ten stories based entirely upon Indian themes.

Children of the King: Read-Along Sing-Along. Max Lucado. 1 cass. (J). 1995. 9.99 (978-0-89107-895-1(9), Crossway Audio) CrosswayIL.
5 sing-along songs based on the story "The Children of the King." Story is also read. About 5 orphans who find out that the king who is to adopt them wants them to spend time with him, not try to impress him.

Children of the Lamp, No. 5. P. B. Kerr. (Children of the Lamp Ser.). (J). (gr. 4-7). 2010. audio compact disk 84.95 (978-0-545-16087-2(1)) Scholastic Inc.

Children of the Mind. Orson Scott Card. Narrated by John Rubinstein & Gabrielle De Cuir. 11 CDs. (Running Time: 48600 sec.). (Ender Ser.: Bk. 4). 2006. audio compact disk 99.95 (978-0-7927-4023-0(8), SLD 940) AudioGO.

Children of the Mind. Orson Scott Card. Narrated by Gabrielle DeCuir et al. 2 CDs. (Ender Ser.: Bk. 4). 2006. audio compact disk 49.95 (978-0-7927-4260-9(5), CMP 940) AudioGO.

Children of the Mind. Orson Scott Card. Read by Gabrielle De Cuir & John Rubinstein. (Ender Ser.: Bk. 4). 2004. 29.95 (978-1-59397-485-5(X)) Pub: Macmill Audio. Dist(s): Macmillan

Children of the Mind. unabr. ed. Orson Scott Card. Read by Gabrielle De Cuir et al. 11 CDs. (Running Time: 13 hrs. 30 mins. 0 sec.). (Ender Ser.: Bk. 4). (ENG.). 2006. audio compact disk 44.95 (978-1-59397-484-8(1), Rena Bks) Pub: St Martin. Dist(s): Macmillan

Children of the Morning. Perf. by Jack Grunsky. 1 cass. (J). (gr. 4 up). 10.98 (YM030-CN); lp 12.98 (YM030-R); audio compact disk 13.98 (YM030-CD) Youngheart Mus.
Songs include: "Day-O"; "Children of the Morning"; "Let's Paint a Picture"; "When the Rain Comes down"; "Michael Row the Boat Ashore"; "Cello"; "My Name is Jack"; "Playground"; "At the Hop"; "Little Samba Girl" & more.

Children of the New Forest, unabr. ed. Frederick Marryat. Read by Flo Gibson. 7 cass. (Running Time: 10 hrs.). (J). 1998. 25.95 (978-1-55685-530-6(3)) Audio Bk Con.
After their father died fighting for the Royalists in the British Civil War, four orphaned children hide in a cottage disguised as a forester's grandchildren, where they learn to support & fend for themselves.

Children of the Night. unabr. ed. Dan Simmons. Read by George Ralph. (Running Time: 15 hrs.). 2008. 39.25 (978-1-4233-5318-8(8), 9781423353188, BADLE); 24.95 (978-1-4233-5317-1(X), 9781423353171, BAD); audio compact disk 39.25 (978-1-4233-5316-4(1), 9781423353164, Brlnc Audio MP3 Lib); audio compact disk 14.99 (978-1-4233-5315-7(3), 9781423353157, Brilliance MP3) Brilliance Audio.

***Children of the Night.** unabr. ed. Dan Simmons. Read by George Ralph. (Running Time: 15 hrs.). 2010. audio compact disk 19.99 (978-1-4418-4105-6(9), 9781441841056, Bril Audio CD Unabri); audio compact disk 79.97 (978-1-4418-4106-3(7), 9781441841063, BriAudCD Unabrid) Brilliance Audio.

Children of the River. Linda Crew. Read by Christina Moore. 5 cass. (Running Time: 6 hrs. 15 mins.). (YA). 1999. pap. bk. & stu. ed. 59.24 (978-0-7887-3193-8(9), 40928) Recorded Bks.
To escape the Khmer Rouge army, Sundara fled Cambodia with her aunt, leaving her parents behind. Now she is a high school student in Oregon. As Sundara moves towards adulthood, reconciling American values with Cambodian traditions is not going to be easy.

Children of the River, unabr. ed. Linda Crew. Narrated by Christina Moore. 5 pieces. (Running Time: 6 hrs. 15 mins.). (gr. 10 up). 1999. 46.00 (978-0-7887-3210-2(2), 95793E7) Recorded Bks.

Children of the River, Class set. Linda Crew. Read by Christina Moore. 5 cass. (Running Time: 6 hrs. 15 mins.). (YA). 1999. 116.70 (978-0-7887-3239-3(0), 46895) Recorded Bks.

Children of the Storm. Elizabeth Peters, pseud. 11 cass. (Running Time: 15 hrs.). (Amelia Peabody Ser.: No. 15). 96.00 (978-1-4025-4243-5(7)) Recorded Bks.

***Children of the Storm.** abr. ed. Elizabeth Peters. Read by Barbara Rosenblat. (ENG.). 2004. (978-0-06-081382-6(2), Harper Audio); (978-0-06-077908-5(X), Harper Audio) HarperCollins Pubs.

Children of the Tracks: And Other San Antonio Ghost Stories. Tim Tingle. 1 cass. (Running Time: 48 min.). 1994. 12.00 (978-1-886334-00-7(5)) Storytribe.
Include urban folklore & well-documented "hauntings".

Children of the World: Folk Songs & Fun Facts from Many Lands, Arranged for Beginning 2-Part Voices. Ed. by Andy Beck & Brian Fisher. Composed by Tim Hayden. (ENG.). 2009. audio compact disk 39.95 (978-0-7390-5837-4(1)) Alfred Pub.

Children of the World: Multi-Cultural Rhythmic Activities for Preschool. Georgiana Stewart. 1 CD. (Running Time: 1 hr.). (J). (ps). pap. bk. 14.95 CD. (KIM9123CD) Kimbo Educ.
A unique combination of authentic activities from around the world. Cultures represented include, Mexican, Russian, African, Japanese, Puerto Rican, Greek, Chinese, Haitian, Brazilian, Indian, Israeli, French, German & more!.

Children of the World: Multi-Cultural Rhythmic Activities for Preschool. Georgiana Stewart. 1 cass. (Running Time: 1 hr.). (J). (ps). 2001. pap. bk. 10.95 (KIM 9123) Kimbo Educ.

Children of War: The Second World War Through the Eyes of a Generation. Susan Goodman. 2008. audio compact disk 99.95 (978-1-84559-594-4(7)) Pub: Soundings Ltd GBR. Dist(s): Ulverscroft US

Children of War: The Second World War Through the Eyes of a Generation. Susan Goodman. Read by Anne Dover. 12 cass. 2008. 94.95 (978-1-84559-566-1(1)) Pub: Soundings Ltd GBR. Dist(s): Ulverscroft US

Children on the Witness Stand. 1 cass. (Running Time: 30 min.). 9.95 (D0260B090, HarperThor) HarpC GBR.

Children, Parents, Lollipops. unabr. ed. Vladimir A. Tsesis M D. Read by Pat Bottino. (Running Time: 41400 sec.). 2007. audio compact disk 29.95 (978-0-7861-5901-7(4)) Blckstn Audio.

Children, Parents, Lollipops: Tales of Pediatrics. unabr. ed. Vladimir A. Tsesis. Read by Pat Bottino. 8 cass. (Running Time: 11 hrs. 30 mins.). 1998. 56.95 (978-0-7861-1321-7(9), 2246) Blckstn Audio.
Children universally take it for granted that their parents love them & will never abandon them. Not by bread alone, children need not only food, water & shelter but also a loving family to provide these things to them. Dealing with a child not only as a patient but also as a person helps a pediatrician become a part of the flowing river of life with its constant stories, the content & complexity of which are many times more fantastic & thrilling than the most sophisticated science-fiction novel.

Children, Parents, Lollipops: Tales of Pediatrics. unabr. ed. Vladimir A. Tsesis. Read by Pat Bottino. (Running Time: 41400 sec.). 2007. audio compact disk 90.00 (978-0-7861-5900-0(6)) Blckstn Audio.

Children Past & Present Audio CD. Adapted by Benchmark Education Company Staff. Based on a work by Margaret McNamara. (Content Connections Ser.). (J). (gr. k-2). 2008. audio compact disk 10.00 (978-1-60634-907-6(4)) Benchmark Educ.

Children Playing Before a Statue of Hercules: An Anthology of Outstanding Short Stories. unabr. ed. Read by Cherry Jones et al. Ed. by David Sedaris. 2005. 11.95 (978-0-7435-5166-3(4)) Pub: S&S Audio. Dist(s): S and S Inc

Children Songs in French & Creole (CD) Educa Vision Inc. (FRE & CRP.). (J). 2006. audio compact disk 12.00 (978-1-58432-311-2(6)) Educa Vision.

Children the Early Years: Teaching Package. Celia Anita Decker. (gr. 9-12). tchr. ed. 200.00 (978-1-56637-950-2(4)) Goodheart.

Children Who Excel. Read by Pinchas Zukerman et al. 1 cass. (Running Time: 1 hr.). 10.95 (D0250B090, HarperThor) HarpC GBR.

Children 18:3. Contrib. by Children 18 3. 2008. audio compact disk 13.99 (978-5-557-48887-7(1)) Tooth & Nail.

Children's All Star Rhythm Hits. Jank Capon & Rosemary Hallum. (J). 1989. 11.95 Ed Activities.

Children's All Time Mother Goose Favorites. Rosemary Hallum & Henry Buzz Glass. (J). 1990. bk. 11.95 Ed Activities.

Children's Anger: Triggers & Solutions for Coping. abr. ed. Toni Schutta. (Running Time: 4200 sec.). 2006. audio compact disk (978-0-9785426-4-1(9)) Ultimate Wealth.

Children's Book. unabr. ed. A. S. Byatt. Read by Rosalyn Landor. (ENG.). 2009. audio compact disk 50.00 (978-0-307-57752-8(X), Random AudioBks) Pub: Random Audio Pubg. Dist(s): Random

Children's Book of America. William J. Bennett. 2004. 7.95 (978-0-7435-4275-3(4)) Pub: S&S Audio. Dist(s): S and S Inc

Children's Book of Faith. unabr. ed. William J. Bennett. 2 cass. Library ed. (Running Time: 2 hrs.). (J). (gr. 3-5). 2001. 23.00 (978-0-8072-0569-3(9), Listening Lib) Random Audio Pubg.
A wonderful, inspirational treasury of beloved prayers, stories, hymns, Bible passages, and more. A must have for every family.

Children's Book of Heroes. William J. Bennett. 2004. 7.95 (978-0-7435-4277-7(0)) Pub: S&S Audio. Dist(s): S and S Inc

Children's Book of Virtues Audio Treasury. William J. Bennett. 2004. 7.95 (978-0-7435-4276-4(9)) Pub: S&S Audio. Dist(s): S and S Inc

Children's Brain Surgery: A Miracle of Medicine & Faith. 1 cass. (Running Time: 30 min.). 9.95 (D0120B090, HarperThor) HarpC GBR.

Children's Catechesis: Alternative Models for Faith Formation. Judith Dunlap. 1 cass. (Running Time: 1 hr.). 2001. 8.95 (A6641) St Anthony Mess Pr.

Children's Chanukah. 1 cass. (Running Time: 31 min.). (J). 1992. 9.98 (978-1-880528-92-1(4), 4-45027) Warner Bros.

Childrens Choir. 1999. audio compact disk 7.98 (978-0-633-04554-8(3)) LifeWay Christian.

Children's Christmas. 1 cass. (Running Time: 1 hr.). (J). 2001. 10.95 (KUB 2000C) Kimbo Educ.
Travel to many lands, celebrate other customs, visit Santa's Workshop & dance to a jolly holiday beat. Frosty the Snowman, Jingle Bells, Dancing Around the Christmas Tree, Me & Santa's Elves & more.

Children's Christmas Classics: The Millennia Collection. Ronald M. Clancy. 1 CD. (Running Time: 1 hr., 13 mins.). 2002. bk. 39.95 (978-0-615-12098-0(9)) Christ Class.
Enjoy 26 tracks of classic recordings from the world of carols, opera, and ballet, such as excerpts from The Nutcracker (Philadelphia Orchestra), Hansel and Gretel (Mormon Tabernacle Choir), and A Ceremony of Carols (Westminster Abbey Choir), and more.

Children's Christmas Sampler. unabr. ed. Louisa May Alcott et al. 1 cass. (Running Time: 60 min.). (Classic Literature Ser.). (J). 1997. pap. bk. 10.95 (978-1-55656-204-4(7)) Dercum Audio.
Includes "The Fir Tree," "Becky's Christmas Dream" & "T'was the Night Before Christmas".

Children's Christmas Sampler. unabr. ed. Read by Carolyn Noone. 1 cass. (J). 24.95 (978-1-55656-171-9(7), DAB 005) Pub: Dercum Audio. Dist(s): APG

Children's Church Leader's Guide: Facing the Fearigators with Critter County Friends. Judy Gillispie et al. Illus. by Larry Nolte. (50-Day Spiritual Adventure Ser.). (J). (gr. k-2). 1994. cass. & cd-rom 19.99 (978-1-879050-52-5(8)) Chapel of Air.

Children's Classic Audio Book. Prod. by PC Treasures Staff. (J). 2007. (978-1-60072-050-5(1)) PC Treasures.

Children's Classics. unabr. ed. 4 cass. (Running Time: 4 hr.). (Crated Gift Cassette Ser.). (J). 1985. 16.95 (978-1-55569-080-9(7), 5750-02) Great Am Audio.
Dramatized productions of "Wizard of Oz," "Pinnochio," "Jack & the Beanstalk," "Rumplestilskin," "Puss n' Boots" & "Hansel & Gretel".

Children's Classics I. unabr. ed. Marjorie Flack et al. 55 vols. (Running Time: 30 mins.). (J). 1999. pap. bk. 76.95 (978-0-87499-494-0(2)) Live Oak Media.
Includes: "Ask Mr. Bear," "The Carrot Seed," "Good Night Moon," "A Hole is to Dig" & "Runaway Bunny.".

Children's Classics II. unabr. ed. Marcia Brown et al. 55 vols. (Running Time: 56 mins.). (J). (ps-3). 1999. pap. bk. 76.95 (978-0-87499-495-7(0)) Live Oak Media.
Includes: "Caps for Sale," "Cloudy with a Chance of Meatballs," "Stone Soup," "The Story about Ping" & "The Story of Ferdinand.".

Children's Confidence. Glenn Harrold. 1 cass. (Running Time: 1 hr. 30 mins.). 2002. 11.95 (978-1-901923-15-5(0)) Pub: Divinit Pubing GBR. Dist(s): Bookworld

Children's Confidence. Glenn Harrold. 2002. audio compact disk 17.95 (978-1-901923-35-3(5)) Pub: Divinit Pubing GBR. Dist(s): Bookworld

Children's Coping - Information for Self Care Series: Asa Goes to School. Gail C. Feldman. 1 cass. (Running Time: 30 min.). (J). (gr. k-8). 1990. 9.95 (978-0-945054-14-6(9)) Speaking Health.

Children's Coping - Information for Self Care Series: Asa's Potty Learning. 1 cass. (Running Time: 20 min.). 1987. 9.95 (978-0-945054-11-5(4)) Speaking Health.

Children's Coping - Information for Self Care Series: Asa's Sick Day. 1 cass. (Running Time: 35 min.). (J). (gr. 3 up). 1987. 9.95 (978-0-945054-12-2(2)) Speaking Health.

Children's Coping - Information for Self Care Series: Asa's Sweet Dreams. 1 cass. (Running Time: 35 min.). 1987. 9.95 (978-0-945054-10-8(6)) Speaking Health.

Children's Course - School Version (10-Lesson Edition) Books 1-4 CD: English Language Teaching. 2005. audio compact disk (978-0-7428-1526-1(9)) CCLS Pubg Hse.

Children's Course - School Version (10-Lesson Edition) Introductory Book CD: English Language Teaching. 2005. audio compact disk (978-0-7428-1050-1(X)) CCLS Pubg Hse.

Children's Course - School Version (8-Lesson Edition) Books 1-4 CD: English Language Teaching. 2005. audio compact disk (978-0-7428-1514-8(5)) CCLS Pubg Hse.

Children's Easter. (J). 1994. cass. & video 9.98 (978-89-02-03001-1(6)) Chrstn Dup Intl.

Children's Fairy Tales World-Wide by Dancing Beetle. Perf. by Eugene Ely. 1 cass. (Running Time: 72 min.). (J). 1992. 10.00 Erthviibz.
Fairy tales, nature sounds & ecology come together when Ms. Doodle Bug & the spunky musical humans read & sing with Dancing Beetle.

Children's Favorites. (J). 1997. 6.98 CD. MFLP CA.

Children's Favorites, Vol. 1. 1 cass. (J). 7.99 (978-1-55723-026-3(9)); 7.99 Norelco. (978-1-55723-232-8(6)); audio compact disk 13.99 CD. (978-1-55723-040-9(4)); audio compact disk 13.99 (978-1-55723-503-9(1)) W Disney Records.

Children's Favorites, Vol. 2. unabr. ed. 1 cass. (J). 7.99 (978-1-55723-027-0(7)); 7.99 Norelco. (978-1-55723-233-5(4)); audio compact disk 13.99 CD. (978-1-55723-041-6(2)); audio compact disk 13.99 (978-1-55723-504-6(X)) W Disney Records.

Children's Favorites, Vol. 3. unabr. ed. 1 cass. (J). 7.99 (978-1-55723-028-7(5)); 7.99 Norelco. (978-1-55723-234-2(2)); audio compact disk 13.99 CD. (978-1-55723-042-3(0)); audio compact disk 13.99 (978-1-55723-576-3(7)) W Disney Records.

Children's Favorites, Vol. 4. unabr. ed. 1 cass. (J). 7.99 (978-1-55723-029-4(3)); 7.99 Norelco. (978-1-55723-235-9(0)); audio compact disk 13.99 CD. (978-1-55723-043-0(9)); audio compact disk 13.99 (978-1-55723-505-3(8)) W Disney Records.

Children's Fiddling Method. Carol Ann Wheeler. 1992. 9.98 (978-1-56222-453-0(0), 94817C) Mel Bay.

Children's Fiddling Method, Vol. 1. Carol Ann Wheeler. 1992. bk. 17.95 (978-0-7866-1120-1(0), 94817P) Mel Bay.

Children's Fiddling Method, Vol. 2. Carol Ann Wheeler & Roy Bredy. 1996. spiral bd. 19.95 (978-0-7866-1252-9(5), 95279P) Mel Bay.

Children's Fiddling Method, Volume 1. Carol Ann Wheeler. 2002. audio compact disk 19.95 (978-0-7866-6195-4(X)) Mel Bay.

Children's Finances. Larry Burkett. 1986. 5.00 (978-1-56427-090-0(4)) Crown Fin Min Inc.

Children's Folk Dances. Perf. by Georgiana Stewart. 1 cass. (Running Time: 1 hr.). (J). (ps-3). 2001. pap. bk. 10.95 (KIM 9149C); pap. bk. 14.95 (KIM 9149CD) Kimbo Educ.
Collection of creative folk dances that offer opportunities for movement, increasing coordination & rhythm, developing social skills & introducing the cultures of many countries. Includes guide.

Children's French. unabr. ed. Conversa-Phone Institute Staff. 2 cass. (Running Time: 1 hr. 17 min.). (Children's Language Programs Ser.). (J). (gr. 4-8). 1991. 15.95 Set, incl. illus. manual. (978-1-56752-005-7(7)) Conversa-phone.
Conversational lessons teaching basic French sentences, words & phrases through the day in the life of two fun loving children, Peter & Alice. The cassette also contains several popular French children's songs.

Children's German. unabr. ed. Conversa-Phone Institute Staff. 2 cass. (Running Time: 1 hr. 17 min.). (Children's Language Programs Ser.). (J). (gr. 4-8). 1991. 15.95 Set, incl. illus. manual. (978-1-56752-006-4(5)) Conversa-phone.
Conversational lessons teaching basic German sentences, words & phrases through the day in the life of two fun loving children, Peter & Alice. The cassette also contains several popular German children's songs.

Children's Ghost Stories World-Wide by Dancing Beetle. Perf. by Eugene Ely. 1 cass. (Running Time: 70 min.). (J). 1990. 10.00 Erthviibz.
Ghost stories, nature sounds & ecology come together when Ms. Squid & the spunky musical humans read & sing with Dancing Beetle.

Children's Guitar Method, Vol. 1. William Bay. (J). 1993. bk. 14.95 (978-0-87166-388-7(0), 93833P) Mel Bay.

Children's Guitar Method, Vol. 1. William Bay. 1982. pap. bk. 21.95 (978-0-7866-0810-2(2), 93833CDP) Mel Bay.

Children's Guitar Method, Vol. 1. William Bay. 1986. audio compact disk 15.98 (978-0-7866-0809-6(9), 93833CD) Mel Bay.

Children's Guitar Method, Vol. 1. William Bay. (J). 1986. 9.98 (978-0-87166-387-0(2), 93833C) Mel Bay.

Children's Homer. Padraic Colum. Narrated by Robert Whitfield. (Running Time: 5 hrs. 30 mins.). (J). 1999. 24.95 (978-1-59912-632-6(X)) Iofy Corp.

Children's Homer. unabr. ed. Padraic Colum. Read by Robert Whitfield. 4 CDs. (Running Time: 16200 sec.). (J). (gr. 4-7). 2006. audio compact disk 36.00 (978-0-7861-8131-5(1), 2515); audio compact disk 19.95 (978-0-7861-9560-2(6), 2515) Blckstn Audio.

Children's Homer: The Adventures of Odysseus & the Tale of Troy. unabr. ed. Padraic Colum. Read by Robert Whitfield. 4 cass. (Running Time: 5 hrs. 30 mins.). (gr. 4-7). 2000. 32.95 (978-0-7861-1693-5(5), 2515) Blckstn Audio.
Reissue of the 1919 classic combines the immortal stories from Homer's Ilaid & Odyssey into one glorious saga of heroism & magical adventure.

Children's Homer: The Adventures of Odysseus & the Tale of Troy, Set. unabr. ed. Padraic Colum. Read by Flo Gibson. 4 cass. (Running Time: 5 hrs.). (J). (gr. 4 up). 1994. 19.95 (978-1-55685-338-8(6)) Audio Bk Con.
Odysseus went with King Agamemnon to the wars of Troy; planned the Wooden Horse by which Priam's city was taken; sailed to the land of the Lotus-eaters & the dread Cyclopes, as well as Circe the Enchantress; heard the song of the Sirens; came to the Rocks Wandering & to the Terrible Charybdis & Scylla; & stayed at the home of the nymph Calypso who would have made him immortal if he had not yearned to return to this family & home.

Children's Hour see Best Loved Poems of Longfellow

Children's Hour see Classic American Poetry

Children's Hour, Set. Read by Flo Gibson. 2 cass. (Running Time: 3 hrs.). (J). 1996. 14.95 (978-1-55685-406-4(4)) Audio Bk Con.
A varied collection including: "The Curly Fish," "Bun, the Squirrel," "The Bird & the Field Mouse," "The Wolf That Wanted a Doctor," "Little Bobby Redbreast," "Tomorrow Will be Christmas," "Old Wine in a New Bottle," "Naughty Harry," "Harry's Birthday," "Real Magic," "Careless Sophia," "Tommy's Rivals," "Little Mabel," & "The Tale of the Great Giant, Smokey Bear".

Children's Hour (A Poem from the Poets' Corner) The One-and-Only Poetry Book for the Whole Family. unabr. ed. Henry Wadsworth Longfellow & John Lithgow. Read by John Lithgow. (Running Time: 10 mins.). (ENG.). 2008. 0.99 (978-1-60024-324-0(X)) Pub: Hachet Audio. Dist(s): HachBkGrp

Children's Italian. unabr. ed. Conversa-Phone Institute Staff. 2 cass. (Running Time: 1 hr. 17 min.). (Children's Language Programs Ser.). (J). (gr. 4-8). 1991. 15.95 Set, incl. illus. manual. (978-1-56752-007-1(3)) Conversa-phone.
Conversational lessons teaching basic Italian sentences, words & phrases through the day in the life of two fun loving children, Peter & Alice. The cassette also contains several popular Italian children's songs.

Children's Jazz Chants Old & New. Carolyn Graham. (Jazz Chants Ser.). 2002. 24.50 (978-0-19-433723-6(5)) OUP.

Children's Jazz Chants Old & New. Carolyn Graham. (Jazz Chants Ser.). 2003. audio compact disk & audio compact disk 24.50 (978-0-19-433724-3(3)) OUP.

Children's Krsna Book. 8 cass. 32.00 Set, incl. 1 vinyl album. Bhaktivedanta.
Based on Parvati Devi Dasi's wonderful adaptation of Krsna, the supreme personality of godhead. This will help your child develop spiritual values.

Children's Library see Biblioteca de los Ninos

Children's Living Bible Story Book. Joanne. Read by Joanne. 1 cass. (Running Time: 1 hr. 10 min.). (J). 1998. pap. bk. 19.95 (978-0-9663621-8-3(7)); incl. script. (978-0-9663621-9-0(5)) Sweetnote Rec.
Fifteen stories accompanied by an original music score. Sixty-four page paperback has seventeen full color original watercolor illustrations.

Children's Luau Event, Vol. II, Bk. 31. Vicki Corona. (Celebrate the Cultures Ser.). 1989. pap. bk. 16.95 (978-1-58513-021-4(4)) Dance Fantasy.

Children's Meditation Tape. Janalea Hoffman. 1 cass. (Running Time: 30 min.). 1985. 9.95 (978-1-886051-03-4(8)) Rhythmic Med.
A Tape specifically for children to learn about relaxation using music.

Children's Meditations with Music. unabr. ed. Dawn Buckholz. 1 cass. (Running Time: 1 hr.). (J). (ps-3). 1996. 9.95 (978-1-885608-07-9(1)) Airplay.
Getting energized is the theme for this highly original children's tape. Words & music to inspire the elementary school set.

Children's Ministry. Herb Owen. 3 cass. bk. 99.95 Set, incl. planning & teaching helps, reproducible promotional materials & textbk. (422) Chrch Grwth VA.
A plan of action for starting or refurbishing a children's ministry.

Children's Music Collection. Perf. by Langston Hughes et al. 1 cass., 1 CD. (J). 8.78 Incl. 28p. bklet. (FW 45043); audio compact disk 10.38 CD Jewel box, incl. 28p. bklet. (FW 45043) NewSound.

Children's Original Hanukkah Music & Coloring Book. Dora B. Krakower. Illus. by G. Steiner. (J). 1987. spiral bd. 10.95 (978-0-9643273-3-7(3)) AZURE CA.

Children's Physics by Dancing Beetle. Perf. by Eugene Ely. 1 cass. (Running Time: 71 min.). (J). 1995. 10.00 Erthviibz.
Children's physics, nature sounds & ecology come together when Ms. Gnu & the spunky musical humans read & sing with Dancing Beetle.

Children's Poems & Stories. unabr. ed. Read by Gene Lockhart et al. 5 cass. Incl. Child's Garden of Verses. Robert Louis Stevenson. Ed. by Robert Louis Stevenson. (J). (D-304); Just So Stories Set: For Little Children. Rudyard Kipling. (J). (D-304); (J). 29.75 (D-304); 6.95 rental. Audio Bk.
Includes 90 well-known children's stories.

Children's Poetry by Dancing Beetle. Perf. by Eugene Ely. 1 cass. (Running Time: 70 min.). (J). 1993. 10.00 Erthviibz.
Children's poetry & nature sounds come together when Ms. Ocelot & the spunky musical humans read & sing with Dancing Beetle.

Children's Rights. Perf. by John Vennari. 1 cass. 7.00 (20199); 7.00 (20199) Cath Treas.
The Children's Rights Movement & the "U.N. Convention on the Rights of the Child" is working to drive a wedge between parent & child, so that parents will lose practically all parental rights over the children.

Children's Science by Dancing Beetle. Perf. by Eugene Ely. 1 cass. (Running Time: 70 min.). (J). 1994. 10.00 Erthviibz.
Children's science & nature sounds come together when Ms. Fire Toad & the spunky musical humans read & sing with Dancing Beetle.

Children's Shakespeare. abr. ed. E. Nesbit. Narrated by Flo Gibson. (J). 2001. 14.95 (978-1-55685-753-9(5)) Audio Bk Con.
Presenting eleven stories to children.

Children's Shakespeare. unabr. ed. William Shakespeare & E. Nesbit. Read by John Belushi et al. 1 cass. (Running Time: 1 hr. 30 mins.). 2002. 9.95 (978-1-57453-508-2(0)) Audio Lit.
Seven of the most celebrated plays have been specifically adapted to introduce young listeners (and reintroduces adults) to his works. Based on the homespun storytelling of a literary turn-of-the-century mom, these classic retellings capture the drama and flavor of each original play, while simplifying plot and detail. Included are King Lear, As You Like It, A Midsummer Night's Dream, Pericles, Hamlet, Romeo and Juliet, and The Winters's Tale.

Children's Songs for Banjo Made Easy. Ross Nickerson. 2009. pap. bk. 14.99 (978-0-7866-4400-1(1)) Mel Bay.

***Children's Songs for Guitar Strummers: 38 Fun Songs for Singing, Playing & Listening.** Created by Hal Leonard Corp. (ENG.). 2010. pap. bk. 14.99 (978-1-4234-9153-8(X), 142349153X) H Leonard.

Children's Songs of Inspiration. 1 cass. (Running Time: 90 mins.). (J). 2000. 7.98; audio compact disk 9.98 Peter Pan.
For those quiet times, the positive & loving messages on this recording will make kids smile. Some of Broadway's brightest young stars sing tunes like "The Wind Beneath My Wings," "Somewhere Out There," "Lean on Me" & "Over the Rainbow".

Children's Spanish. unabr. ed. Conversa-Phone Institute Staff. 2 cass. (Running Time: 1 hr. 17 min.). (Children's Language Programs Ser.). (J). (gr. 4-8). 1991. 15.95 Set, incl. illus. manual. (978-1-56752-004-0(9)) Conversa-phone.
Conversational lessons teaching basic Spanish sentences, words & phrases through the day in the life of two fun loving children, Peter & Alice. The cassette also contains several popular Spanish children's songs.

Children's Stories. Rick Steber. Illus. by Don Gray. 1 cass. (Tales of the Wild West Ser.: Vol. 6). (J). 1989. pap. bk. 9.95 (978-0-945134-56-5(8)) Bonanza Pub.

Children's Stories from Africa, Vol. 3. Perf. by Nandi Nyembo & Mahlatsi Pre-School Dancers Staff. Directed By Linda Korsten. Composed by John Rothman. 1 cass. (Running Time: 26 min.). (AFR.). (J). (ps-3). 1997. 12.95 (978-1-56994-278-9(1), 30833, Monterey SoundWorks) Monterey Media Inc.
Charming original songs & delightful African fables entertain as well as teach youngsters with help from the likes of Warthog & Bushpig, Kafumbi & the Crocodile & many others. Enchantingly told by Nandi Nyembe with dancers from the Mahlatsi Pre-School in their colorful African garb.

Children's Story Hour: Famous Favorites for Bedtime Anytime. unabr. ed. Read by A. J. Redelsperger. Ed. by Marilyn Kay. 1 cass. (Running Time: 40 min.). (J). (gr. 3). 1995. 7.95 (978-1-882071-14-2(X), 016) B-B Audio.
Famous favorites for bedtime, anytime. Discreet editing conveys the authors intent in less frightening language. Includes: Snow White, Goldilocks and the Three Bears, The Three Little Pigs, The Tortoise and the Hare, The Ugly Duckling and the Little Po.

***Children's Ukulele Method Book/CD Set.** Lee (Drew) Andrews. (ENG.). 2010. pap. bk. 14.99 (978-0-7866-8208-9(6)) Mel Bay.

Children's Vision of the Future: 2007/2008 Crayola Juried Art Exhibition. Ed. by Susan L. Williams. 2008. per. 24.99 (978-0-86696-330-5(8)) Binney & Smith.

Children's Wear in Germany: A Strategic Reference 2006. Compiled by Icon Group International, Inc. Staff. 2007. ring bd. 195.00 (978-0-497-35968-3(5)) Icon Grp.

Children's Wear in Japan: A Strategic Reference 2006. Compiled by Icon Group International, Inc. Staff. 2007. ring bd. 195.00 (978-0-497-82323-8(3)) Icon Grp.

Children's Writer at Work: Jane Yolen. unabr. ed. Billie Judy & Jonathan T. Stratman. Read by Jane Yolen. Featuring Jane Yolen. 1 cass. (Running Time: 57 min.). (Writer at Work Ser.). cass. & video 19.95 Incl. public performance rights. (978-1-884016-05-9(7), 151) Reel Life Prods.
In her Hatfield, MA home & studio, this prolific childrens' writer talks about her work.

Child's Book of Faeries. Narrated by Tanya Robyn Batt. (Running Time: 50 mins. 47 sec.). (J). 2003. bk. 15.99 (978-1-84148-781-6(3)) BarefootBksMA.

Child's Book of True Crime: A Novel. unabr. ed. Chloe Hooper. Read by Kate Hosking. 4 cass. (Running Time: 6 hrs. 48 mins.). 2004. 32.00 (978-1-74030-863-2(8)); audio compact disk 77.95 (978-1-74030-954-7(5)) Pub: Bolinda Pubng AUS. Dist(s): Bolinda Pub Inc

Child's Calendar. John Updike. 11 vols. (Running Time: 13 mins.). (Live Oak Readalong Ser.). (J). 2004. pap. bk. 16.95 (978-1-59112-471-9(9)) Pub: Live Oak Media. Dist(s): AudioGO

Child's Calendar. John Updike. Illus. by John Updike. Illus. by Trina Schart Hyman. 1 CD. (Running Time: 13 mins.). (J). (gr. k-4). 2004. bk. 28.95 (978-1-59112-932-5(X)) Live Oak Media.

Child's Calendar. John Updike. Read by John Updike. Illus. by Trina Schart Hyman. 1 cass. (Running Time: 13 mins.). (J). (gr. k-4). 2004. pap. bk. 37.95 (978-1-59112-473-3(5)) Live Oak Media.

Child's Calendar. Read by John Updike. Compiled by John Updike. Illus. by Trina Schart Hayman. (Running Time: 13 mins.). (J). 2004. 9.95 (978-1-59112-470-2(0)); audio compact disk 12.95 (978-1-59112-930-1(3)) Live Oak Media.

Child's Calendar. unabr. ed. John Updike. Read by John Updike. Illus. by Trina Schart Hyman. 1 cass. (Running Time: 13 mins.). (J). (gr. k-4). 2004. bk. 25.95 (978-1-59112-472-6(7)); pap. bk. 18.95 (978-1-59112-931-8(1)); pap. bk. 39.95 (978-1-59112-933-2(8)) Live Oak Media.

Child's Celebration of Broadway. 1 cass. (Running Time: 40 min.). (J). 1995. 9.98 (978-1-56628-057-0(5), MLP 2531B/WBMLP 2531/WB MLP D25331/WB 42567-2); 9.98 Norelco. (978-1-56628-055-6(9), MLP 2531/WB MLP D25331/WB 42567-2); audio compact disk 15.98 CD. (978-1-56628-056-3(7), MLP D25331/WB 42567-2) MFLP CA.
A compilation of broadway showtunes for children.

Child's Celebration of Broadway. 1 cass.; 1 CD. 1998. 9.98 (978-1-56628-110-2(5), 42567); audio compact disk 15.98 CD. (978-1-56628-109-6(1), 42567D) MFLP CA.

Child's Celebration of Christmas. 1 cass.; 1 CD. 1998. 9.98 (978-1-56628-134-8(2), 72878); audio compact disk 15.98 CD. (978-1-56628-133-1(4), 72878D) MFLP CA.

Child's Celebration of Classical Music. 1 cass. (Running Time: 54 mins.). (J). (ps-4). 1999. 9.98 (978-1-56628-204-8(7)) MFLP CA.
Classical music recordings.

Child's Celebration of Classical Music. Music for Little People Band. 1999. (978-1-56628-205-5(5)) MFLP CA.

Child's Celebration of Dance. 1 cass.; 1 CD. (J). (gr. 8 up). 1998. 9.98 (978-1-56628-179-9(2), 75542); audio compact disk 15.98 CD. (978-1-56628-180-5(6), 75542D) MFLP CA.
A mixture of popular tunes from the 1950s to the 1990s.

Child's Celebration of Folk Music. Perf. by Pete Seeger & Woody Guthrie. (Running Time: 45 min.). (J). 9.98; audio compact disk 15.98 CD. MFLP CA.
Fine compilation of folk music for children.

Child's Celebration of Lullaby. (J). 1998. 15.98 CD. MFLP CA.
Top-notch performers from a variety of musical genres contribute soothing, quiet-time songs with appeal for the whole family.

Child's Celebration of Lullaby. Perf. by Jerry Garcia et al. 1 cass. (Running Time: 1 hr.). (J). 1998. 9.98 MFLP CA.

Child's Celebration of Showtunes. 1 cass. (Running Time: 38 min.). (J). 1992. bk. 10.98 (978-1-56628-000-6(1), MLP6318/WB42530-4); 9.98 (978-1-877737-99-2(2), MLP2390/WB42MLP6318/WB42530-4) MFLP CA.
Favorite songs from Broadway Musicals by original artists.

Child's Celebration of Song, Vol. 2. 1 cass.; 1 CD. 1998. 9.98 (978-1-56628-113-3(X), 72574); audio compact disk 15.98 CD. (978-1-56628-112-6(1), 72574D) MFLP CA.

Child's Celebration of Songs. 1 cass. (Running Time: 45 min.). (J). 1992. bk. 10.98 (978-1-56628-026-6(5), MLP6169/WB42529-4); 9.98 (978-1-877737-43-5(7), MLP2546/WB42MLP6169/WB42529-4) MFLP CA.
Popular favorites by original artists: Peter, Paul & Mary, Burl Ives, James Taylor, Sweet Honey in the Rock, Loggins & Messina, The Doobie Bros., Raffi, Taj Mahal, Maria Muldaur.

Child's Celebration of Soul. Perf. by Otis Redding et al. 1 cass. (Running Time: 45 min.). (J). 2000. 9.98 (978-1-56628-249-9(7)); audio compact disk 15.98 (978-1-56628-248-2(9)) MFLP CA.
Classics selected from Motown's extensive catalogue of songs & artists.

Child's Celebration of the World. 1 cass.; 1 CD. 1998. 9.98 (978-1-56628-166-9(0), 75341) MFLP CA.

Child's Celebration of the World. 1 cass., 1 CD. (J). 7.98 (MLP 75341); audio compact disk 11.98 CD. (MLP 75341) NewSound.
Various artists: Raffi; Joan Baez; Miriam Makeba; The Irish Rovers; The Chenille Sisters; Maria Muldaur; Jim Springer; Sweet Honey in the Rock; Ladysmith Black Mambazo; Bill Miller; Freyda Epstein; & Papillion.

Child's Celebration of the World. Rhino Records Staff. 1 cass.; 1 CD. 1998. audio compact disk 15.98 CD. (978-1-56628-165-2(2), 75341D) MFLP CA.

Child's Christmas: Festive Stories for Children of All Ages. unabr. ed. Read by Julie Alexander. Ed. by Marilyn Kay. 1 cass. (Running Time: 45 min.). (J). (gr. 3-6). 1994. 7.95 (978-1-882071-19-7(0), 021) B-B Audio.
Delightful, festive stories for children of all ages. These five classics will keep kids starry-eyed with wonder and enchantment during the holiday season and throughout the year. Includes: The Night Before Christmas, Santa Claus Sleepy Story, Christm.

Child's Christmas in Brooklyn. unabr. ed. Frank Crocitto. 1 cass. (Running Time: 1 hr. 30 mins.). 2001. 15.95 (978-0-9677558-4-7(0)); audio compact disk 15.95 (978-0-9677558-5-4(9)) Candlepower.

Child's Christmas in Wales see Dylan Thomas

***Child's Christmas in Wales.** abr. ed. Dylan Thomas. Read by Dylan Thomas. (ENG.). 2003. (978-0-06-074303-1(4), Harper Audio); (978-0-06-079962-5(5), Harper Audio) HarperCollins Pubs.

Child's Christmas in Wales. unabr. ed. Dylan Thomas. Read by Dylan Thomas. 1 cass. (Running Time: 46 mins.). (J). 12.00 (H162) Blckstn Audio.
The nostalgic recollection of Dylan Thomas's childhood that has become a classic among Christmas tales.

Child's Christmas in Wales. unabr. ed. Dylan Thomas. Read by Dylan Thomas. 1 cass. (Running Time: 46 min.). Incl. Ballad of the Long-Legged Bait. (J). 1987. (CPN 1002); Ceremony after a Fire Raid. (J). 1987. (CPN 1002); Do Not Go Gentle into That Good Night. (J). 1987. (CPN 1002); Fern Hill. Dylan Thomas. (J). 1987. (CPN 1002); In the White Giant's Thigh. (J). 1987. (CPN 1002); Child's Christmas in Wales. Dylan Thomas. (J). 1987. (CPN 1002); (J). 1987. 9.95 (978-0-89845-100-9(0), CPN 1002) HarperCollins Pubs.

Child's Christmas in Wales. unabr. ed. Poems. Dylan Thomas. Read by Dylan Thomas. 1 CD. (Running Time: 47 mins.). 1994. audio compact disk 14.95 (978-0-89845-648-6(7), CD 1002) HarperCollins Pubs.
The nostalgic recollection of Dylan Thomas' childhood that has become a classic among Christmas tales. With powerful grace, Thomas performs this renowned work along with five of his most well known poems.

Child's Christmas in Wales. 50th unabr. anniv. abr. ed. Dylan Thomas. Read by Dylan Thomas. 1 CD. (Running Time: 1 hr.). (gr. 6-12). 2002. audio compact disk 14.95 (978-0-06-051467-9(1)) HarperCollins Pubs.

***Child's Day Out.** unabr. ed. Mary Sheldon. Read by Betty White. (Running Time: 5 hrs. 30 mins.). (Classics Read by Celebrities Ser.). 2010. 29.95 (978-1-4417-6572-7(7)); 34.95 (978-1-4417-6569-7(7)); audio compact disk 55.00 (978-1-4417-6570-3(0)); audio compact disk 24.95 (978-1-4417-6571-0(9)) Blckstn Audio.

Child's Garden of Songs: The Poetry of Robert Louis Stevenson in Song. Perf. by Ted Jacobs. 1998. 9.98 (978-1-56628-189-8(X)); audio compact disk 15.98 MFLP CA.
Catchy rhymes recommended for listeners who are familiar with Robert Stevenson's classic collection.

Child's Garden of Verses see Children's Poems & Stories

Child's Garden of Verses. Robert Louis Stevenson. Read by Grandma Barbara Blewster. (J). 2006. audio compact disk 9.95 (978-0-9815788-0-4(2)) Amer Two.

Child's Garden of Verses. abr. ed. Robert Louis Stevenson. Ed. by Robert Louis Stevenson. Narrated by Elinor G. Hoffman. 2 cass. (Running Time: 1 hr. 4 min.). (J). 1999. 12.95 (978-0-89926-132-4(9), 820) Audio Bk.
52 autobiographical poems create a wonderful world of make believe.

Child's Garden of Verses. unabr. ed. Robert Louis Stevenson. Ed. by Robert Louis Stevenson. Perf. by Basil Langton & Nancy Wickwire. 1 cass. (Running Time: 45 min.). (J). 10.95 (978-0-8045-0905-3(0), SAC 905) Spoken Arts.
"The Unseen Playmate," My Ship & I," "My Kingdom," "The Land of Story Books," 17 others.

Child's Garden of Verses. unabr. ed. Robert Louis Stevenson. Ed. by Robert Louis Stevenson. Read by Nancy Wickwire & Basil Langton. 1 cass. (Running Time: 45 min.). Incl. Bed in Summer. (J). (SAC 904); Land of Counterpane. (J). (SAC 904); Land of Nod. (J). (SAC 904); Rain. (J). (SAC 904); Where Goes the Boats? (J). (SAC 904). (J). 10.95 (978-0-8045-0904-6(2), SAC 904) Spoken Arts.
Includes verses listed & others.

Child's Garden of Verses, Set. Robert Louis Stevenson. Ed. by Robert Louis Stevenson. 1 cass. (J). 1996. bk. & pap. bk. 5.95 (29305-X) Dover.

Child's Garden of Verses & Potpourri of Poetry, Set. unabr. ed. Robert Louis Stevenson. Read by Flo Gibson. 2 cass. (Running Time: 2 hrs.). (J). 1984. 14.95 (978-1-55685-047-9(6)) Audio Bk Con.
Stevenson catches the spirit of childhood experiences in such charming poems as "At The Seaside," "Foreign Land," "Bed in Summer," "The Land of Counterpane," "The Lamplighter," "My Ship & I" & many more.

Child's Gift of Lullabies. David R. Lehman. Perf. by Tanya Goodman. Created by J. Aaron Brown. Illus. by Jim Vienneau. 1 cass. (Running Time: 60 min.). (J). (ps). 1987. bk. 12.95 (978-0-927945-01-1(0)) Someday Baby.
A collection of nine original lullabies with positive, loving messages. This Grammy Award Finalist includes a full color lyric book. Fully orchestrated, Side One has a vocalist, Side Two is instrumental only. Also awarded American Library Assoc.'s Notable Children's Recording.

Child's Gift of Lullabies. David R. Lehman. Perf. by Tanya Goodman. Created by J. Aaron Brown. Illus. by Jim Vienneau. 1 cass. (Running Time: 60 min.). (J). (ps). 1991. bk. 15.95 CD. (978-0-927945-05-9(3)) Someday Baby.

Child's Gift of Lullabyes. 1 cass. 10.98; audio compact disk 4.25 demo CD. Lifedance.
Stories & songs are both fun & gentle, with the comforting sounds of nature sprinkled throughout. Demo CD or cassette available.

Child's Gift of Lullabyes. J. Aaron Brown. (Running Time: 1 hr.). (J). (ps-6). 1988. 12.95 JTG Nashville.

Child's Gift of Lullabyes. Created by J. Aaron Brown. 2003. audio compact disk 10.99 (978-5-553-49235-9(1)) Pt of Grace Ent.

Child's Gift of Lullabyes. Created by J. Aaron Brown. 1 cass. (Running Time: 1 hr.). (J). 2002. 9.98; audio compact disk 13.98 Rhino Enter.
This Grammy nominated collection of precious melodies and lyrics set the standard for lullaby albums in the baby gift market.

Child's Hanukkah. Perf. by Jewish Wedding Band. 1 cass.; 1 CD. 1998. 9.98 (978-1-56628-172-0(5), 75537); audio compact disk 15.98 CD. (978-1-56628-171-3(7), 75537D) MFLP CA.
Dance and sing traditional Hanukkah favorites and joyous new songs performed in English with Hebrew, Yiddish and Ladino. Old favorites include; I Have a Little Dreidel, Hanukkah, Oh, Hanukkah, Hey, It's Hanukkah and Hanukkah Waltz.

Child's History of England. Speeches. As told by Renee R. Ellison. 12 CD's. (Running Time: 13+ hours). Dramatization. (YA). 2004. audio compact disk 45.00 (978-0-9749455-7-6(9), 82) Cross Over.
Imagine teaching (or learning) all of British history (it goes on and on, you know) without ever having to crack a book! You and the kids can just listen to it, while you wash dishes or run errands... 10 minutes at a time. No one could ever write it quite like Dickens. Fascinating. At last, England's parade of kings easy enough to understand. Dickens (the master storyteller) at his finest. More than 13 hours, on 12 CD's.

Child's Introduction to American Folk Songs. Perf. by Ed McCurdy. 1 cass. (Music Ser.). (J). 1987. 10.95 (978-0-8045-0223-8(4), SAC 223) Spoken Arts.

Child's Play. unabr. ed. Reginald Hill. Read by Colin Buchanan. 8 CDs. (Running Time: 8 hrs.). (Dalziel & Pascoe Ser.). 2000. audio compact disk 84.95 (978-0-7540-5372-9(5), CCD063) AudioGO.
Andy Dalziel was preoccupied with the illegal book being run on who was to be appointed as the new Chief Constable. But when a Ford Escort containing one very dead Italian turned up in the police car park, Pascoe & his bloated superior were plunged into an investigation that made internal police politics look like child's play.

Child's Play. unabr. ed. Reginald Hill. Read by Colin Buchanan. 8 cass. (Running Time: 12 hr.s). (Dalziel & Pascoe Ser.). 2000. 69.95 (978-0-7540-0465-3(1), CAB 1888) Pub: Chivers Audio Bks GBR. Dist(s): AudioGO
Gwendoline Lomas's son had gone missing in Italy during World War II. Now she is dead & her funeral is interrupted by a man crying 'Mama!' When a battered car containing one very dead Italian turns up in the police car park, Peter Pascoe & Andy Dalziel are plunged into an overwhelming investigation.

Child's Spirit. Bunny Hull. Illus. by Synthia Saint-James. 1 CD. (Running Time: 35 mins.). (J). 2003. pap. bk. 15.95 (978-0-9673762-5-7(4), BH101CD, Kids Creative Classics) BrassHeart.

Child's Spirit. Bunny Hull. Illus. by Synthia Saint-James. 1 cass. (Running Time: 35 mins.). (J). (gr. k-4). 2003. pap. bk. 10.95 (978-0-9673762-4-0(6), BH101CA, Kids Creative Classics) BrassHeart.
Spiritual development through music. A collection of original songs for children of all ages, which goes beyond religion, race & color.

Child's View of Reality. unabr. ed. Hosted by David Elkind. 1 cass. (Famous Authorities Talk about Children Ser.). 12.95 (C29472) J Norton Pubs.

Child's World of Lullabies. Perf. by Hap Palmer. 1 cass. (Running Time: 1 hr.). (J). 2001. 9.95 (HP105); audio compact disk 14.95 Hap-Pal Music.
Gentle songs weave a theme of appreciation & respect for the diversity of life. Original songs are combined with lullabies from many lands. Soothing voices accompanied by acoustic guitar, piano, string quartet, woodwind ensemble & instruments from around the world.

Chile: Promise of Freedom. Speeches. Ed. by Freedom Archives Staff. 1 CD. (Running Time: 60 mins.). (AK Press Audio Ser.). 2003. audio compact disk 14.98 (978-0-9727422-3-8(9)) Pub: AK Pr GBR. Dist(s): Consort Bk Sales

Chile & Argentina. unabr. ed. Mark Szuchman. Read by Richard C. Hottelet. (Running Time: 10800 sec.). (World's Political Hot Spots Ser.). 2006. audio compact disk 25.95 (978-0-7861-6444-8(1)) Pub: Blckstn Audio. Dist(s): NetLibrary CO

Chili Peppers: The Unauthorized Biography of the Red Hot Chili Peppers. Harry Drysdale-Wood. (Maximum Ser.). (ENG.). 2001. audio compact disk 14.95 (978-1-84240-044-9(4)) Pub: Chrome Dreams GBR. Dist(s): IPG Chicago

Chill. unabr. ed. Ross MacDonald. Read by Tom Parker. (Running Time: 8 hrs. 30 mins.). 2000. 24.95 (978-0-7861-9408-7(1), 1837) Blckstn Audio.

Chill, unabr. ed. Ross MacDonald, pseud. Read by Tom Parker. 6 cass. (Running Time: 8 hrs. 30 mins.). (Lew Archer Mystery Ser.). 1996. 44.95 (978-0-7861-1066-7(X), 1837) Blckstn Audio.
Lew Archer knew he shouldn't have taken the case but Alex Kincaid seemed so desperate. Kincaid's loving new bride Dolly had just inexplicably walked out on him, leaving Kincaid more than a little fearful for his sanity & her safety. So, Archer reluctantly agreed to help Kincaid find his wife. But what he found instead was enough to send a chill down anyone's spine - a new fresh corpse & evidence linking Dolly not only to this murder, but to a series of others dating back to before she was even born.

Chill. unabr. ed. Ross MacDonald, pseud. Read by Tom Parker. 8 CDs. (Running Time: 8 hrs. 30 mins.). (Lew Archer Mystery Ser.). 2000. audio compact disk 64.00 (978-0-7861-9802-3(8), 1837) Blckstn Audio.
Lew Archer knew he shouldn't have taken the case, but Alex Kincaid seemed so desperate. Kincaid's loving new bride dolly had just inexplicably walked out on him, leaving Kincaid more than a little fearful for her sanity & her safety. So Archer reluctantly agreed to help Kincaid find his wife but what he found instead was enough to send a chill down anyone's spine, a new fresh corpse & evidence linking Dolly not only to this murder, but to a series of others dating back to before she was even born.

Chill, Bk. 1. unabr. ed. Jory Sherman. Read by Kevin Foley. 6 cass. (Running Time: 6 hrs. 36 min.). 2001. 39.95 (978-1-55686-935-8(5)) Books in Motion.
Dr. "Chill" Chillders and Psychic Laura Littlefawn accept investigation into the ritualistic death of a rancher's son. Chillders and Laura question if the perpetrators could be linked to Satan.

***Chill: A Lew Archer Novel.** unabr. ed. Ross Macdonald. Read by Tom Parker. (Running Time: 8 hrs. 30 mins.). 2010. audio compact disk 19.95 (978-1-4417-4001-4(5)) Blckstn Audio.

Chill Factor. Stuart Pawson. 9 cass. (Running Time: 12 hrs.). (Story Sound Ser.). (J). 2004. 76.95 (978-1-85903-735-5(6)) Pub: Mgna Lrg Print GBR. Dist(s): Ulverscroft US

Chill Factor. abr. ed. Sandra Brown. Read by Stephen Lang. 2005. 15.95 (978-0-7435-5444-2(2)) Pub: S&S Audio. Dist(s): S and S Inc

Chill Factor. abr. ed. Sandra Brown. Read by Stephen Lang. 2005. 9.95 (978-0-7435-5490-9(6)) Pub: S&S Audio. Dist(s): S and S Inc

Chill Factor. abr. ed. Sandra Brown. Read by Stephen Lang. (Running Time: 6 hrs. 0 mins. 0 sec.). (ENG.). 2008. audio compact disk 14.99 (978-0-7435-7207-1(6)) Pub: S&S Audio. Dist(s): S and S Inc

Chill Factor. unabr. ed. Sandra Brown. Read by Stephen Lang. 11 CDs. (Running Time: 13 hrs.). 2005. audio compact disk 119.75 (978-1-4193-7548-4(2), C3616) Recorded Bks.

Chill Factor. unabr. ed. Sandra Brown. Read by Stephen Lang. 2005. 23.95 (978-0-7435-5446-6(9)); audio compact disk 39.95 (978-0-7435-4439-9(0), Audioworks) Pub: S&S Audio. Dist(s): S and S Inc

Chill Factor. unabr. ed. Read by Stephen Lang. Ed. by Sandra Brown. 10 cass. (Running Time: 13 hrs.). 2005. 79.75 (978-1-4193-7546-0(6), 98280) Recorded Bks.
Set against a backdrop of snowy, North Carolina mountains, Chill Factor melts through the ice with generous doses of scorching romance and searing suspense. During a bad snowstorm, Lilly Martin skids off the road into the handsome but mysterious Ben Tierney, chief suspect in a string of recent disappearances. With nowhere else to go, the two are forced to take shelter in an isolated cabin and wait for the blizzard to weaken.

Chill of Fear. abr. ed. Kay Hooper. Read by Dick Hill. (Running Time: 21600 sec.). (Fear Trilogy: Bk. 2). 2006. audio compact disk 16.99 (978-1-59737-345-6(1), 9781597373456, BCD Value Price) Brilliance Audio.
FBI Agent Noah Bishop and his extrasensory Special Crimes Unit are at the deadly axis of imagination and chilling, unknown evil. Twenty-five years ago, at a secluded Victorian resort known as The Lodge, Quentin Hayes stumbled upon the body of a young girl - a tragedy no one should ever experience, let alone a 12-year-old boy. Now, on the eve of another disappearance, Quentin teams up with FBI Agent Bishop and artist Diana Brisco, whose "seeing" gifts have been misdiagnosed as mental illness. When it's discovered that many have fallen victim to an evil force that seems to possess the resort, Noah counts on Quentin and Diana to overcome their past trauma to bring a terrifying killer to justice.

Chill of Fear. unabr. ed. Kay Hooper. Read by Dick Hill. 8 CDs. (Running Time: 9 hrs.). (Fear Trilogy). 2005. audio compact disk 31.95 (978-1-59600-336-1(7), 9781596003361, Bril Audio CD Unabri) Brilliance Audio.
For twenty years, FBI agent Quentin Hayes has been haunted by an unsolved murder that took place at the Lodge. Now he's returned to the secluded resort one final time to put the mystery at rest. Diana Brisco has come there hoping to unlock the secrets in her troubled past. Instead she is assailed by nightmares and the vision of a child who vanished years ago. And an FBI agent is trying to convince her that she isn't crazy, but that she has a rare gift, a gift that could help him catch a killer. With an ever-growing readership and over five million copies of her thrillers in print, Kay Hooper has proven the power of her bestselling prowess time and again. Following the sensational hardcover releases of Sense of Evil and Hunting Fear, Hooper puts her readers back in the very capable hands of FBI agent Noah Bishop and his extrasensory Special Crimes Unit for another edge-of-your-seat adventure through the crossroads of criminal forensics and the chilling realm of what lies beyond the imagination.

Chill of Fear. unabr. ed. Kay Hooper. Read by Dick Hill. (Running Time: 9 hrs.). (Fear Trilogy: Bk. 2). 2005. 39.25 (978-1-59710-134-9(6), 9781597101349, BADLE); 24.95 (978-1-59710-135-6(4), 9781597101356, BAD); 74.25 (978-1-59600-334-7(0), 9781596003347, BrilAudUnabridg); 29.95 (978-1-59600-333-0(2), 9781596003330, BAU); audio compact disk 92.25 (978-1-59600-337-8(5), 9781596003378, BriAudCD Unabrid); audio compact disk 24.95 (978-1-59600-338-5(3), 9781596003385, Brilliance MP3); audio compact disk 39.25 (978-1-59600-339-2(1), 9781596003392, Brlnc Audio MP3 Lib) Brilliance Audio.

Chill of Summer Blue: A Collection of Poetry. Karen Jean Matsko Hood. 2006. 29.95 (978-1-59210-528-1(9)); audio compact disk 24.95 (978-1-59210-529-8(7)) Whsprng Pine.

Chill of Summer Blue Catholic Edition. Karen Jean Matsko Hood. 2010. audio compact disk 24.95 (978-1-59210-937-1(3)) Whsprng Pine.

Chill of Summer Blue Christian Edition. Karen Jean Matsko Hood. 2010. audio compact disk 24.95 (978-1-59210-931-9(4)) Whsprng Pine.

Chill Out-Stress Kit: Trainer Workshop Guide. 1 CD. (Running Time: 1 hr.). wbk. ed. 49.00 Prof Pride.
This fun workbook & informative CD follow a unique stress management workshop that is a favorite.

Chill Out-Stress Kit: Trainer Workshop Guide. 1 cass. (Running Time: 1 hr.). 2000. wbk. ed. 24.95 Prof Pride.
Follows a unique stress management workshop that is a favorite.

Chilling Tales of Bygone Days, Set. Read by Flo Gibson. 3 cass. (Running Time: 1 hr. 30 min. per cass.). 1996. 16.95 (978-1-55685-446-0(3)) Audio Bk Con.
Such outstanding authors as Charlotte Bronte, Mary Braddon, Mrs. Henry Wood, Gertrude Atherton, Mary Wilkins Freeman, Willa Cather, & Edith Nesbit, among others, have given these fourteen stories a memorable haunting quality.

Chilly Scenes of Winter. unabr. collector's ed. Ann Beattie. Read by Michael Prichard. 8 cass. (Running Time: 8 hrs.). 1979. 48.00 (978-0-7366-0162-7(7), 1164) Books on Tape.
Charles is 27 years old & working at a boring job he can't afford to leave. He endures a crazy mother & an idiot stepfather. Charles lives in a dream world, fantasizing his reunion with Laura, the woman he loves & had an affair with 10 years before.

Chimaera. abr. ed. Nathaniel Hawthorne. Read by Julie Harris. (Running Time: 49 min.). 10.95 (SAC 1105) Spoken Arts.
The story of Bellerophon & the magic horse Pegasus & how they defeat the three-headed monster.

***Chime.** unabr. ed. Franny Billingsley. (ENG.). (J). 2011. audio compact disk 40.00 (978-0-307-91519-1(0), Listening Lib) Pub: Random Audio Pubg. Dist(s): Random

Chimes. Charles Dickens. Read by Anais 9000. 2008. 27.95 (978-1-60112-200-1(4)) Babblebooks.

Chimes. unabr. collector's ed. Charles Dickens. Read by Cindy Hardin & Walter Covell. 5 cass. (Running Time: 5 hrs.). (J). 1982. 30.00 (978-0-7366-3963-7(2), 9501) Books on Tape.
"The Chimes" & "The Holly Tree" along with "A Christmas Carol," form a trilogy. In "The Holly Tree," the narrator is an old man who relates his Christmas story, which is that he came close to forsaking his bride; "The Chimes" celebrates New Year's Eve rather than Christmas. It tells us that whatever our state, there is always reason to be grateful.

Chimney Pond Tales: Yarns Told by Leroy Dudley. Ed. by Clayton Hall et al. Narrated by John McDonald. 2 cass. (Running Time: 3 hrs.). 1995. 19.95 Set. (978-0-9631718-1-8(X)) Pamola Pr.
A collection of tales told during the first half of this century by the legendary guide & storyteller from Maine's Mount Katahdin. Appropriate for all ages.

Chimney Sweeper's Boy. unabr. ed. Barbara Vine, pseud. Narrated by Jenny Sterlin. 11 cass. (Running Time: 16 hrs.). 1998. 91.00 (978-0-7887-2171-7(2), 95467E7) Recorded Bks.
When literary celebrity Gerald Candless suddenly dies, the beautiful facade he has carefully created begins to crumble & a mesmerizing story unfolds.

Chimney Sweeper's Boy. unabr. collector's ed. Barbara Vine, pseud. Read by Bernadette Dunne. 9 cass. (Running Time: 13 hrs. 30 min.). 1998. 72.00 (978-0-7366-4533-1(0), 4719) Books on Tape.
Bestselling novelist Gerald Candless dies suddenly of a heart attack, leaving behind a wife & two adoring daughters.

China. unabr. ed. Murray Sayle. Read by Richard C. Hottelet. (Running Time: 10800 sec.). (World's Political Hot Spots Ser.). 2006. audio compact disk 25.95 (978-0-7861-6441-7(7)) Pub: Blckstn Audio. Dist(s): NetLibrary CO

China: Understanding Its Past (teacher's manual & CD) Eileen H. Tamura et al. 1997. bk. & tchr. ed. 46.00 (978-0-8248-1996-5(9)) UH Pr.

China & Japan, Venerated Patterns Of. unabr. ed. 1 cass. 12.95 (7395) J Norton Pubs.

China Bloodhunt. Axel Kilgore. Read by Carol Eason. 2 vols. No. 16. 2004. 18.00 (978-1-58807-172-9(3)); (978-1-58807-663-2(6)) Am Pubng Inc.

China Bride. Mary Jo Putney. Narrated by Davina Porter. 9 cass. (Running Time: 12 hrs.). 81.00 (978-1-4025-0911-7(1)); audio compact disk 111.00 (978-1-4025-3077-7(3)) Recorded Bks.

China Calls: Paving the Way for Nixon's Historic Journey to China, abr. ed. Anne Collins Walker. Read by Joseph Campanella et al. 2 cass. (Running Time: 3 hrs.). 2000. 7.95 (978-1-57815-141-7(4), 1100, Media Bks Audio) Media Bks NJ.
This is the story of Walker & his team. Based on the actual transcripts of telephone calls between the advance team in Peking & the White House in Washington.

China Fantasy: How Our Leaders Explain Away Chinese Repression. Jim Mann. Read by Jeff Riggenbach. (Running Time: 16200 sec.). 2007. 24.95 (978-0-7861-6911-5(7)); audio compact disk 36.00 (978-0-7861-6910-8(9)) Blckstn Audio.

China Fantasy: How Our Leaders Explain Away Chinese Repression. unabr. ed. Jim Mann. Read by Jeff Riggenbach. (Running Time: 16200 sec.). 2007. audio compact disk 19.95 (978-0-7861-7003-6(4)) Blckstn Audio.

China Fantasy: How Our Leaders Explain Away Chinese Repression. unabr. ed. Jim Mann. Read by Jeff Riggenbach. (Running Time: 16200 sec.). 2007. 19.95 (978-0-7861-4952-0(3)); audio compact disk 19.95 (978-0-7861-5841-6(7)) Blckstn Audio.

China Folk Dance Booklet w/Music CD & Dance DVD. Vicki Corona. Composed by Vicki Corona. Merelika Shamash. (Celebrate the Cultures Ser.: 6-11C). 1989. pap. bk. 32.95 (978-1-58513-142-6(3)) Dance Fantasy.

China Garden. unabr. ed. Liz Berry. Narrated by Virginia Leishman. 7 cass. (Running Time: 10 hrs.). (gr. 9 up). 2001. 60.00 (978-0-7887-1801-4(0), 95273E7) Recorded Bks.
Ancient English custom & legend magically blend with contemporary life when 17-year-old Clare moves to historic Ravensmere estate only to find herself stalked by a leather clad motorcyclist.

China Garden. unabr. ed. Liz Berry. Read by Virginia Leishman. 7 cass. (Running Time: 10 hrs.). (J). (gr. 6). 1997. bk. 85.00 (978-0-7887-1843-4(6), 40623) Recorded Bks.

China Inc: How the Rise of the Next Superpower Challenges America & the World. unabr. ed. Ted C. Fishman. Narrated by Alan Sklar. (Running Time: 13 hrs. 30 mins. 0 sec.). (ENG.). 2005. audio compact disk 22.99 (978-1-4001-5159-2(7)); audio compact disk 79.99 (978-1-4001-3159-4(6)) Pub: Tantor Media. Dist(s): IngramPubServ

China Inc: How the Rise of the Next Superpower Challenges America & the World. unabr. ed. Ted C. Fishman. Read by Alan Sklar. (Running Time: 13 hrs. 30 mins. 0 sec.). (ENG.). 2005. audio compact disk 39.99 (978-1-4001-0159-7(X)) Pub: Tantor Media. Dist(s): IngramPubServ

China Lake. Meg Gardiner. Read by Tanya Eby Sirois. (Playaway Adult Fiction Ser.). 2008. 94.99 (978-1-60640-910-7(7)) Find a World.

China Lake. unabr. ed. Meg Gardiner. Read by Tanya Eby. (Running Time: 12 hrs.). (Evan Delaney Ser.). 2008. 24.95 (978-1-4233-6119-0(9), 9781423361190, Brilliance MP3) Brilliance Audio.

China Lake. unabr. ed. Meg Gardiner. Read by Tanya Eby Sirois. (Running Time: 12 hrs.). (Evan Delaney Ser.). 2008. 39.25 (978-1-4233-6122-0(9), 9781423361220, BADLE) Brilliance Audio.

China Lake. unabr. ed. Meg Gardiner. Read by Tanya Eby. (Running Time: 12 hrs.). (Evan Delaney Ser.). 2008. 24.95 (978-1-4233-6121-3(0), 9781423361213, BAD); audio compact disk 36.95 (978-1-4233-6117-6(2), 9781423361176, Bril Audio CD Unabri); audio compact disk 102.25 (978-1-4233-6118-3(0), 9781423361183, BriAudCD Unabrid) Brilliance Audio.

China Lake. unabr. ed. Meg Gardiner. Read by Tanya Eby. Directed By Sandra Burr. Contrib. by Troy Harrison. (Running Time: 12 hrs.). (Evan Delaney Ser.). 2008. 39.25 (978-1-4233-6120-6(2), 9781423361206, Brlnc Audio MP3 Lib) Brilliance Audio.

China Long Ago. Compiled by Benchmark Education Staff. 2005. audio compact disk 10.00 (978-1-4108-5497-1(3)) Benchmark Educ.

China Men. unabr. collector's ed. Maxine Hong Kingston. Read by Kate Reading. 9 cass. (Running Time: 13 hrs. 30 min.). 1995. 72.00 (978-0-7366-2975-1(0), 3666) Books on Tape.
Three generations of Chinese men embrace the harsh realities & joys of a new culture. Magical & mythical.

China Now: Doing Business in the World's Most Dynamic Market. abr. ed. N. Mark Lam & John L. Graham. (Running Time: 16200 sec.). 2008. audio compact disk 28.00 (978-1-933309-38-5(5)) Pub: A Media Intl. Dist(s): Natl Bk Netwk

China Price. unabr. ed. Alexand Harney. (Running Time: 11 hrs. 0 mins. 0 sec.). (ENG.). 2008. audio compact disk 34.99 (978-1-4001-0609-7(5)) Pub: Tantor Media. Dist(s): IngramPubServ

China Price: The True Cost of Chinese Competitive Advantage. abr. unabr. ed. Alexandra Harney. Read by Josephine Bailey. (Running Time: 11 hrs. 0 mins. 0 sec.). (ENG.). 2008. audio compact disk 24.99 (978-1-4001-5609-2(2)) Pub: Tantor Media. Dist(s): IngramPubServ

China Price: The True Cost of Chinese Competitive Advantage. unabr. ed. Alexandra Harney. Read by Josephine Bailey. (Running Time: 11 hrs. 0 mins. 0 sec.). (ENG.). 2008. audio compact disk 69.99 (978-1-4001-3609-4(1)) Pub: Tantor Media. Dist(s): IngramPubServ

China Road: A Journey into the Future of a Rising Power. unabr. ed. Rob Gifford. Read by Simon Vance. 10 CDs. (Running Time: 37800 sec.). 2007. audio compact disk 32.95 (978-0-7861-5790-7(9)); 32.95 (978-0-7861-4975-9(2)) Blckstn Audio.
National Public Radio's Beijing correspondent Rob Gifford recounts his travels along Route 312, the Chinese Mother Road, the longest route in the world's most populous nation. Based on his successful NPR radio series, China Road draws on Gifford's twenty years of observing first-hand this rapidly transforming country, as he travels east to west, from Shanghai to China's border with Kazakhstan. As he takes the reader on this journey, he will also take us through China's past and present while he tries to make sense of this complex nation's potential future.

China Road: A Journey into the Future of Rising Power. unabr. ed. Rob Gifford. 1 MP3-CD. (Running Time: 37800 sec.). 2007. audio compact disk 29.95 (978-0-7861-6962-7(1)) Blckstn Audio.

China Road: A Journey into the Future of Rising Power. unabr. ed. Rob Gifford. Read by Simon Vance. (Running Time: 37800 sec.). 2007. 72.95 (978-0-7861-6818-7(8)); audio compact disk 90.00 (978-0-7861-6817-0(X)) Blckstn Audio.

China Run. unabr. ed. David Ball. Narrated by George Guidall. 11 cass. (Running Time: 15 hrs. 45 mins.). 2002. 99.00 (978-1-4025-2569-8(9), RG241) Recorded Bks.
A compelling story of six American families and their desperate attempt to keep their newly adopted Chinese children. Before leaving China, authorities demand the infants be returned without offering the slightest explanation. What if three of the families refuse? What if they risk everything and attempt a renegade run through China with the babies.

China Scene. Hong Gang Jin et al. 2007. 31.95 (978-0-88727-603-3(2)) Cheng Tsui.

China Scene: An Advanced Chinese Multimedia Course. Hong Gang Jin et al. 2 cass. (CHI & ENG.). (gr. k up). 2002. 39.95 (978-0-88727-332-2(7)) Cheng Tsui.

China Seas. Perf. by Clark Gable et al. 1944. (DD-5090) Natl Recrd Co.

China Smarts by Dancing Beetle. Perf. by Eugene Ely. 1 cass. (Running Time: 86 min.). (J). 1994. 10.00 Erthviibz.
Chinese science, myth, ecology & nature sounds come together when Ms. Pheasant & the spunky musical humans read & sing with Dancing Beetle.

China Talks. unabr. ed. John K. Fairbank. 6 cass. (Running Time: 6 hrs.). pap. bk. 69.95 (S19033) J Norton Pubs.
This classic historical chronicle of China (in English) is an introduction to the traditional Chinese state & society as shaped by Confucian ideology. Discusses the impact of Western trade, technology & thought on China; the remolding of traditional patterns by the forces of the revolution; the interplay of tradition & modernization in contemporary China. Cassettes & pamphlet in album.

China, the History & the Mystery. Cerebellum Academic Team Staff. Executive Producer Ronald M. Miller. (Running Time: 2 hrs.). (Just the Facts Ser.). 2010. 39.95 (978-1-59163-604-5(3)) Cerebellum.

China White, unabr. ed. Peter Maas. Narrated by George Guidall. 8 cass. (Running Time: 10 hrs. 45 mins.). 1994. 70.00 (978-0-7887-0156-6(8), 94378E7) Recorded Bks.
Y.K. Deng, the ruthless mastermind of an international heroin ring, is poised to shatter the Mafia with a daring maneuver: transfer all of the assets of his crime syndicate's to the United States in one shipment of pure heroin.

***Chinaberry Sidewalks.** unabr. ed. Rodney Crowell. Read by Rodney Crowell. (ENG.). 2011. audio compact disk 35.00 (978-0-307-91204-6(3), Random AudioBks) Pub: Random Audio Pubg. Dist(s): Random

Chinaman. Stephen Leather. 2007. 84.95 (978-0-7531-3815-1(8)); audio compact disk 99.95 (978-0-7531-2796-4(2)) Pub: ISIS Audio GBR. Dist(s): Ulverscroft US

Chinaman's Chance. unabr. ed. Ross Thomas. Narrated by Frank Muller. 7 cass. (Running Time: 10 hrs. 30 mins.). (Durant & Wu Ser.). 1985. 60.00 (978-1-55690-100-3(3), 85450E7) Recorded Bks.
Artie Wu & Quincy Durant skillfully uncover the connection between a congressman's death & a plot to take over the seedy town of Pelican Bay.

Chinamen see Woman Warrior: Memoirs of a Girlhood among Ghosts

China's Megatrends: The 8 Pillars of a New Society. unabr. ed. John Naisbitt & Doris Naisbitt. Narrated by Lloyd James. (Running Time: 9 hrs. 30 mins. 0 sec.). (ENG.). 2010. 24.99 (978-1-4001-6444-8(3)); audio compact disk 69.99 (978-1-4001-4444-0(2)); audio compact disk 34.99 (978-1-4001-1444-3(6)) Pub: Tantor Media. Dist(s): IngramPubServ

***China's Megatrends: The 8 Pillars of a New Society.** unabr. ed. John Naisbitt & Doris Naisbitt. Narrated by Lloyd James. (Running Time: 9 hrs. 30 mins.). 2010. 16.99 (978-1-4001-8444-6(4)) Tantor Media.

China's Pandas & Driftnets Killing Marine Life. Hosted by Nancy Pearlman. 1 cass. (Running Time: 28 min.). 10.00 (614) Educ Comm CA.

Chinese. Elizabeth Scurfield. 1 cass. (Running Time: 60 min.). (Language Complete Course Packs Ser.). 1993. 19.95 (Passport Bks) McGraw-Hill Trade.

Chinese. Peter Terrell. 2 cass. (Running Time: 80 min.). (Language - Thirty Library). bk. 16.95 set in vinyl album. Moonbeam Pubns.
Using the proven method based on the famous U.S. Military accelerated language learning program, Language/30 courses stress conversationally useful words & phrases.

Chinese. unabr. ed. Behind the Wheel. (Running Time: 8 hrs. 0 mins. 0 sec.). (ENG.). 2009. audio compact disk 49.95 (978-1-4272-0629-9(5)) Pub: Macmill Audio. Dist(s): Macmillan

Chinese. unabr. ed. Linguistics Staff. Narrated by Linguistics Staff. Ed. by Oasis Audio Staff. 2 cass. (Running Time: 3 hrs.). (Complete Idiot's Guide to Languages Ser.). (ENG & CHI.). 2005. audio compact disk 9.99 (978-1-59859-121-7(5)) Oasis Audio.

Chinese. unabr. ed. Oasis Audio Staff & Linguistics Staff. Narrated by Linguistics Staff. (Complete Idiot's Guides). (ENG.). 2005. audio compact disk 39.99 (978-1-59859-065-4(0)) Oasis Audio.

Chinese. unabr. ed. Harold Stearns. 4 cass. (Running Time: 6 hrs.). (Accent English Ser.). (CHI & ENG.). 1991. bk. 89.50 set, incl. visual aids cards. J Norton Pubs.
English as a second language instructional program.

Chinese, Set. abr. ed. Mike Packevicz & Mengjun Liu. (For Dummies Ser.). (CHI & ENG.). 2007. audio compact disk 19.99 (978-0-470-12766-7(X), For Dummies) Wiley US.

Chinese: All the Chinese You Need to Get Started in a Simple Audio-Only Program. unabr. l.t. ed. Living Language Staff. (Starting Out In Ser.). (ENG.). 2008. audio compact disk 15.95 (978-1-4000-2466-7(8)) Pub: Random Info Grp. Dist(s): Random

***Chinese Acrobats DVD.** audio compact disk 44.95 (978-7-88518-086-7(7)) China Bks.

Chinese-American - Jewish-American. Joe Giordano. Narrated by George Guidall. Contrib. by Evelyn Lee & Elliot Rosen. 6 cass. (Running Time: 30 min.). (Growing Up in America Ser.: Vol. 3). 1997. 12.00 Set. Ethnic Prods.

Chinese & Japanese. Contrib. by Berlitz Publishing Staff. (NOVA PREMIER Ser.). (ENG.). 2008. audio compact disk 49.95 (978-0-8416-0039-3(2)) Pub: APA Pubns Serv SGP. Dist(s): IngramPubServ

Chinese & Oriental Herbs, Vol. 3. Jonathan Parker. 2 cass. (Running Time: 2 hrs.). 1998. 17.00 (978-1-58400-001-3(5)) QuantumQuests Intl.

Chinese Art of Paper-Cutting. Zhang Fengqin. (CHI & ENG.). 2004. 14.95 (978-7-88718-095-7(3), CHARPA) China Bks.

Chinese Audio Vocabulary Builder. unabr. ed. 1 cass. 12.95 (SCH010) J Norton Pubs.
Dictionary of 101 essential words & phrases for the traveler.

Chinese Breakthrough: Learning Chinese Through TV & Newspapers. Hong Gang Jin & De Bao Xu. 4 cass. (CHI & ENG.). (gr. k up). 1995. 56.95 (978-0-88727-211-0(8)) Cheng Tsui.

Chinese Cantonese. 2nd ed. Pimsleur Staff. 4 CDs. (Running Time: 400 hrs. 0 mins. NaN sec.). (Quick & Simple Ser.). (ENG.). 2001. audio compact disk 19.95 (978-0-7435-0016-6(4), Pimsleur) Pub: S&S Audio. Dist(s): S and S Inc

Chinese Cantonese: Learn to Speak & Understand Cantonese Chinese. Pimsleur Staff & Pimsleur. (Running Time: 160 hrs. 0 mins. 0 sec.). (Comprehensive Ser.). (ENG.). 2001. audio compact disk 345.00 (978-0-7435-0017-3(2), Pimsleur) Pub: S&S Audio. Dist(s): S and S Inc

Chinese Checkers. unabr. ed. Carol Doumani. Read by Frances Cassidy. 7 cass. (Running Time: 10 hrs. 30 min.). 2001. 29.95 (978-0-7366-4477-8(6)) Books on Tape.
Karen Armstrong's husband cheats on her, gets accused of murder, leaves the country & claims to work for the CIA.

Chinese Checkers. unabr. collector's ed. Carol Doumani. Read by Frances Cassidy. 7 cass. (Running Time: 10 hrs. 30 min.). 1996. 56.00 (978-0-7366-3378-9(2), 4028) Books on Tape.
On her first wedding anniversary, Karen Matthews, a young, unassuming dental student, overhears a passionate exchange between her husband Peter & his former girlfriend. Before she can confront Peter, he vanishes. That's hard enough to swallow, but it gets worse. The old girlfriend's fiance turns up dead & police want Peter for questioning.

Chinese Cinderella: The True Story of an Unwanted Daughter. unabr. ed. 5 cassettes. (Running Time: 7 hrs). (J). 2004. 45.75 (978-1-4025-9006-1(7)) Recorded Bks.

Chinese Classic Stories. Lu Hsun. Read by Martin Jarvis. 2 cass. (Running Time: 3 hrs.). 1999. 16.95 (978-0-9532509-0-5(3)) Penton Overseas.
Regarded as the founder of contemporary Chinese literature, Lu Xun used the pen as a weapon to wage an heroic struggle against imperialism, feudalism & bureaucratic capitalism. The rich heritage he has left behind is a treasure in the literature of the Chinese people.

Chinese Culture Capsules. unabr. ed. 1 cass. (Running Time: 1 hr.). 14.95 (978-0-88432-503-1(2), CCCH01) J Norton Pubs.
The brief culture capsules recorded in English at the end of each lesson unit of the introductory courses are available separately. They cover the traditions, holidays & customs such as the Chinese "siesta" in contemporary Chinese society.

Chinese Dance see Christmas with Ogden Nash

Chinese Dialogs. Fred Fang-Yu Wang. 5 cass. (Running Time: 5 hrs.). 1981. pap. bk. 95.00 (978-0-88432-981-7(X), CHOF03) J Norton Pubs.
Records the experiences of an American visiting Shanghai. Starting with arrival, the lessons take you through the daily activities of the visitor, renting a house, hiring a cook, making a phone call. Each lesson includes key vocabulary, sentence patterns & pronunciation guide. The Yale transcription system is used throughout the text.

Chinese Dialogues. Fred Fang-Yu Wang. 5 cass. 1953. 8.95 ea. incl. suppl. materials. (978-0-88710-015-4(5)) Yale Far Eastern Pubns.

Chinese Dumplings. Xiang Jun. (CHI & ENG.). 2003. 17.95 (978-7-88718-046-9(5), CHDU) China Bks.

Chinese Fairy Tales. unabr. ed. Read by Siobhan McKenna. 1 cass. (Running Time: 90 mins.). Incl. Chinese Red Riding Hood. (J). (CDL5 1328); Discontented Mason. (J). (CDL5 1328); Faithful One. (J). (CDL5 1328); How Some Animals Became As They Are. (J). (CDL5 1328); Sparrow & the Phoenix. (J). (CDL5 1328); Teardrop Dragon. (J). (CDL5 1328); Tiger's Teacher. (J). (CDL5 1328); (J). 1984. 9.95 (978-0-694-50687-3(7), CDL5 1328) HarperCollins Pubs.

Chinese Festivals. Beijing Percussion Group. 1995. cass. & cd-rom 16.95 (978-1-57606-061-2(6)) Wind Recs.

Chinese Folk & Art Songs. unabr. ed. Perf. by Wonona W. Chang & Anna Mi Lee. 1 cass. (Running Time: 90 mins.). 14.95 (CCH100) J Norton Pubs.
The distinguished Chinese soprano has recorded this unique anthology of 22 songs that represent many periods & regions in China & in some instances, date back thousands of years.

Chinese for Children. Sinolingua Press Staff. 3 cass. (Running Time: 4 hrs. 30 mins.). (CHI & ENG., (J). 1987. bk. 49.95 (978-7-80052-188-1(5)) Pub: New World Pr CHN. Dist(s): Cheng Tsui

Chinese for Dummies. unabr. ed. Mengjun LIU. Read by Becky Wilmes & Tao Zhang. (YA). 2008. 34.99 (978-1-60514-563-1(7)) Find a World.

Chinese for Everyone, Bk.1. Su David Liqun et al. 2 vols. (CHI & ENG., 2004. bk. 39.95 (978-1-84570-000-3(7), CHEV) Pub: China Lang Univ CHN. Dist(s): China Bks

Chinese for Martial Arts with Cassette. Carol M. Derrickson. 1 cass. (Running Time: 90 min.). (CHI & ENG., 1996. 16.95 (978-0-8048-2044-8(9)) Tuttle Pubng.

Chinese for Tourism. Wang Hailong. (Series of Practical Chinese Ser.). (CHI & ENG.). 2003. audio compact disk 6.95 (978-7-88703-181-5(8), CHTOCD) Pub: China Lang Univ CHN. Dist(s): China Bks

Chinese Gifts see Twentieth-Century Poetry in English, No. 24, Recordings of Poets Reading Their Own Poetry

Chinese Home Cooking. Chef Zhang Bo. (CHI & ENG.). 2004. audio compact disk 10.95 (978-7-88718-079-7(1), CHHCOV) China Bks.

Chinese in a Minute. 1 cass. (Language in a Minute Cassette Ser.). 5.95 (978-1-878427-02-1(4), XC1025) Cimino Pub Grp.
Feel at home in any foreign country with these 101 esssential words & phrases. Hear each word introduced in English, hear them pronounced by a Voice of America instructor. Practice at your own pace, you can check yourself with the wallet sized dictionary included.

Chinese in Action (DVD) Jennifer Li-Chia Liu & Indiana University Instructional Staff. (Chinese in Context Language Learning Ser.). (ENG.). 2003. 42.95 (978-0-253-34331-4(3)) Ind U Pr.

Chinese in Action 2 (DVD) "Instructional Support Services Media Production, Indiana University Staff" & Jennifer Li-Chia Liu. 2 DVDs. (Chinese in Context Language Learning Ser.). (ENG.). 2005. 27.95 (978-0-253-34584-4(7)) Ind U Pr.

Chinese in America: A Narrative History. unabr. ed. Iris Chang. Narrated by Jade Wu. 12 cass. (Running Time: 17 hrs.). 2005. 109.75 (978-1-4025-7165-7(8), 97616) Recorded Bks.
The suicide of acclaimed author Iris Chang, who has received numerous accolades for her work, has brought considerable attention to this encompassing creation. She employed meticulous research in this epic of Chinese- American history. The Chinese made outstanding achievements in politics, economics, and science. Despite 150 years of repression, their emotionally charged stories reveal their determination to avert racism and exclusionary laws. Their dreams, struggles and triumphs exemplify the spirit of America.

Chinese Knot Craft. Cao Haimei. (CHI & ENG.). 2003. audio compact disk 17.95 (978-7-88718-035-3(X), CHKNCR) China Bks.

Chinese Lullabies. 1 cass. (Running Time: 48 mins). (J). audio compact disk 16.95 (978-1-57606-064-3(0)) Pub: Wind Recs. Dist(s): Shens Bks

Chinese Made Easy. Yamin Ma & Li Xinying. (CHI & ENG.). 2004. pap. bk. & tchr. ed. 12.95 (978-962-04-2364-2(X), CMEI1) Pub: Joint Pub HKG. Dist(s): China Bks

Chinese Made Easy, Vol. 2. Yamin Ma & Li Xinying. (CHI & ENG.). 2004. pap. bk. & tchr. ed. 12.95 (978-962-04-2382-6(8), CMEI2) Pub: Joint Pub HKG. Dist(s): China Bks

Chinese Made Easy, Vol. 3. Yamin Ma & Li Xinying. (CHI & ENG.). 2004. pap. bk. & tchr. ed. 12.95 (978-962-04-2369-7(0), CMEI3) Pub: Joint Pub HKG. Dist(s): China Bks

Chinese Made Easy, Vol. 4. Yamin Ma & Li Xinying. (CHI & ENG.). 2004. pap. bk. & tchr. ed. 12.95 (978-962-04-2298-0(8), CMEI4) Pub: Joint Pub HKG. Dist(s): China Bks

Chinese Made Easy, Vol. 5. Yamin Ma & Li Xinying. (CHI & ENG.). 2004. pap. bk. & tchr. ed. 12.95 (978-962-04-2335-2(6), CMEI5) Pub: Joint Pub HKG. Dist(s): China Bks

Chinese Mandarin: Language 30. Educational Services Corporation Staff. 2004. audio compact disk 21.95 (978-1-931850-01-8(1)) Educ Svcs DC.

Chinese Mandarin: Language 30. rev. ed. Educational Services Corporation Staff. Intro. by Charles Berlitz. 2 cass. (CHI.). 1993. pap. bk. 21.95 (978-0-910542-65-4(1)) Educ Svcs DC.
Chinese (Mandarin) self-teaching language course.

Chinese (Mandarin) Learn to Speak & Understand Mandarin with Pimsleur Language Programs. 2nd ed. Pimsleur Staff & Pimsleur. 4 CDs. (Running Time: 400 hrs. 0 mins. NaN sec.). (Pimsleur Language Program Ser.). (ITA & ENG.). 2001. audio compact disk 19.95 (978-0-671-79033-2(1), Pimsleur) Pub: S&S Audio. Dist(s): S and S Inc

Chinese (Mandarin) - English: Level III. SER VOCABULEARN. 2 cass. (Running Time: 3 hrs.). (VocabuLearn Ser.). 1993. bk. 15.95 (978-0-939001-12-5(8)) Penton Overseas.

Chinese (Mandarin) for Speakers of English, One. unabr. ed. 16 cass. (Running Time: 15 hrs.). (Pimsleur Tapes Ser.). (CHI.). 345.00 set. (18100, Pimsleur) S&S Audio.
Spoken foreign-language proficiency training. Thirty, half-hour, intensive, spoken-language lesson units to be completed at the rate of one lesson per day for 30 days. By achieving eighty-percent correct answers to the questions in each unit, the Pimsleur Spoken Language Programmed Instructional Method will enable the learner to achieve the ACTFL Intermediate-Low Spoken Proficiency Level.

Chinese (Mandarin) I: Learn to Speak & Understand Mandarin with Pimsleur Language Programs. 2nd ed. Martin Hardingham & Pimsleur Staff. (Running Time: 400 hrs. 0 mins. NaN sec.). (Pimsleur Language Program Ser.). (ENG.). 2000. audio compact disk 345.00 (978-0-671-79061-5(7), Pimsleur) Pub: S&S Audio. Dist(s): S and S Inc
With Pimsleur Language Programs you don't just study a language, you learn it - the same way you mastered English! And because the technique relies on interactive spoken language training, the Pimsleur Language Programs are totally audio - no book is needed! The Pimsleur programs provide a method of self-practice with an expert teacher and native speakers in lessons specially designed to work with the way the mind naturally acquires language information. The various components of language - vocabulary, pronunciation and grammar - are all learned together without rote memorization and drills. Using a unique method of memory recall developed by renowned linguist, Dr. Paul Pimsleur, the programs teach listeners to combine words and phrases to express themselves the way native speakers do. By listening and responding to thirty minute recorded lessons, students easily and effectively achieve spoken proficiency. No other language program or school is as quick, convenient, and effective as the Pimsleur Language Programs. The Comprehensive Program is the ultimate in spoken language learning. For those who want to become proficient in the language of their choice, the Comprehensive programs go beyond the Basic Programs to offer spoken-language fluency. Using the same simple method of interactive self-practice with native speakers, these comprehensive programs provide a complete language learning course. The Comprehensive Program is available in a wide variety of languages and runs through three levels (thirty lessons each) in French, German, Italian, Japanese, Russian and Spanish. At the end of a full Comprehensive Program listeners will be conducting complete conversations and be well on their way to mastering the language. The Comprehensive Programs are all available on cassettes and are also on CD in the six languages in which we offer the Basic Program on CD.

Chinese (Mandarin) II: Learn to Speak & Understand Mandarin with Pimsleur Language Programs. unabr. ed. Pimsleur Staff & Pimsleur. 16 CDs. (Running Time: 400 hrs. 0 mins. NaN sec.). (Comprehensive Ser.). (ENG.). 2002. audio compact disk 345.00 (978-0-7435-0661-8(8), Pimsleur) Pub: S&S Audio. Dist(s): S and S Inc

Chinese (Mandarin) III: Learn to Speak & Understand Mandarin with Pimsleur Language Programs. Pimsleur Staff. (Running Time: 160 hrs. 0 mins. 0 sec.). (Comprehensive Ser.). (ENG.). 2003. audio compact disk 345.00 (978-0-7435-2546-6(9), Pimsleur) Pub: S&S Audio. Dist(s): S and S Inc

Chinese (Mandarin) Language Study Level 2. George Holod. Voice by Shu-Yun Shih. 1 CD. (Running Time: 60 mins). 2003. audio compact disk 16.00 (978-0-923586-55-3(5)) Data Syst CA.
Sentence structure and pronunciation practice.

Chinese New Testament. T. W. Kuo. 16 cass. (Running Time: 24 hrs.). (CHI.). 1994. 39.98 (978-7-902030-08-3(2)) Chrstn Dup Intl.

Chinese New Testament. Narrated by Tang D. Kuo. 16 cass. 39.98 (9001A) Chrstn Dup Intl.

Chinese New Testament: Union Version. 2002. 25.95 (978-1-57449-132-6(6), 107706) Pub: Hosanna NM. Dist(s): Am Bible

Chinese New Testament Bible on Cassette (Spoken Word) Mandarin-Union Version. Read by Tang Ding Kuo. 1 cass. 1997. 39.97 (978-1-58968-072-2(3)) Chrstn Dup Intl.

Chinese Odyssey. 2006. audio compact disk 295.00 (978-0-88727-553-1(2)); audio compact disk 295.00 (978-0-88727-518-0(4)) Cheng Tsui.

Chinese Odyssey. Xueying Wang. (C). 2008. stu. ed. 43.95 (978-0-88727-517-3(6)) Cheng Tsui.

Chinese Odyssey. Xueying Wang et al. 2005. audio compact disk 150.00 (978-0-88727-504-3(4)) Cheng Tsui.

Chinese Odyssey, Vol. 1. Xueying Wang et al. 2005. audio compact disk 150.00 (978-0-88727-464-0(1)) Cheng Tsui.

Chinese Odyssey, Vol. 2. Xueying Wang et al. 2005. cd-rom 150.00 (978-0-88727-489-3(7)) Cheng Tsui.

Chinese Odyssey, Vol. 2. Xueying Wang et al. (C). 2006. stu. ed. 48.95 (978-0-88727-488-6(9)) Cheng Tsui.

Chinese Odyssey, Vol. 3. Xueying Wang et al. (C). 2006. stu. ed. 54.95 (978-0-88727-503-6(6)) Cheng Tsui.

Chinese Odyssey: Ideal for: Beginning. 5 CDs. audio compact disk 150.00 (978-0-88727-562-3(1)) Cheng Tsui.

Chinese Odyssey: Ideal for: Intermediate. audio compact disk (978-0-88727-551-7(6)) Cheng Tsui.

Chinese Odyssey: Ideal for: Low Intermediate, Vol. 2. 5 CDs. audio compact disk 150.00 (978-0-88727-550-0(8)) Cheng Tsui.

Chinese Orange Mystery. unabr. collector's ed. Ellery Queen. Read by Michael Prichard. 8 cass. (Running Time: 8 hrs.). 1977. 48.00 (978-0-7366-0096-5(5), 1104) Books on Tape.
An unknown dead man is found in the office of a prosperous publisher. His clothes are on backward, & all of the furniture in the room has been reversed. Ellery Queen continues to uncover "backward" clues - leading him to the identity of this puzzling victim.

Chinese Paradise. Liu Fuhua et al. (CHI & ENG.). (J). (gr. 4-6). 2005. bk. & tchr. ed. 17.95 (978-7-5619-1441-0(5), CHPAI1) Pub: Beijing Lang CHN. Dist(s): China Bks

Chinese Paradise, Vol. 1. Liu Fuhua et al. (CHI & ENG.). (J). (gr. 4-6). 2005. bk. & stu. ed. 10.95 (978-7-5619-1439-7(3), CHPA1A); bk. & stu. ed. 9.95 (978-7-5619-1467-0(9), CHPA1B); bk. & wbk. ed. 8.95 (978-7-5619-1440-3(7), CHPAW1A); bk. & wbk. ed. 7.95 (978-7-5619-1468-7(7), CHPAW1B) Pub: Beijing Lang CHN. Dist(s): China Bks

Chinese Paradise, Vol. 2. Liu Fuhua et al. (CHI & ENG.). (J). (gr. 4-6). 2005. bk. & tchr. ed. 19.95 (978-7-5619-1445-8(8), CHPAI2); bk. & stu. ed. 10.95 (978-7-5619-1443-4(1), CHPA2A); bk. & stu. ed. 9.95 (978-7-5619-1469-4(5), CHPA2B); bk. & wbk. ed. 9.95 (978-7-5619-1444-1(X), CHPAW2A); bk. & wbk. ed. 8.95 (978-7-5619-1470-0(9), CHPAW2B) Pub: Beijing Lang CHN. Dist(s): China Bks

Chinese Paradise, Vol. 3. Liu Fuhua et al. (CHI & ENG.). (J). (gr. 4-6). 2005. bk. & stu. ed. 10.95 (978-7-5619-1465-6(2), CHPA3B); bk. & wbk. ed. 11.95 (978-7-5619-1437-3(7), CHPAW3A); bk. & wbk. ed. 10.95 (978-7-5619-1466-3(0), CHPAW3B) Pub: Beijing Lang CHN. Dist(s): China Bks

Chinese Paradise: Cards for Words & Expression. Liu Fuhua et al. (CHI & ENG.). (J). (gr. 4-6). 2005. bk. 22.95 (978-7-5619-1520-2(9), CHPAC3) Pub: Beijing Lang CHN. Dist(s): China Bks

Chinese Paradise 1: Cards of Words & Expression. Liu Fuhua et al. (CHI & ENG.). (J). (gr. 4-6). 2005. bk. 22.95 (978-7-5619-1495-3(4), CHPAC1) Pub: Beijing Lang CHN. Dist(s): China Bks

Chinese Paradise 2: Cards for Words & Expression. Liu Fuhua et al. (CHI & ENG.). (J). (gr. 4-6). 2005. bk. 22.95 (978-7-5619-1496-0(2), CHPAC2) Pub: Beijing Lang CHN. Dist(s): China Bks

Chinese Paradise 3, Vol. 3. Liu Fuhua et al. (CHI & ENG.). (J). (gr. 4-6). 2005. bk. & stu. ed. 11.95 (978-7-5619-1436-6(9), CHPA3A) Pub: Beijing Lang CHN. Dist(s): China Bks

Chinese Red Riding Hood see Chinese Fairy Tales

Chinese Revolution. unabr. ed. 1 cass. 12.95 (C19704) J Norton Pubs.

Chinese Secrets of Health & Longevity. 6 cass. (Running Time: 9 hrs.). 1999. 59.95 Set. (83-0065) Explorations.
Teaches strategies to increase energy & lifespan. Topics include diet for maximum vitality & immunity, regulating daily life to prevent illness, stress reduction & exercises.

Chinese Siamese Cat. unabr. ed. Amy Tan. Read by Amy Tan. 1 CD. (Running Time: 1.5 hrs.). 2004. audio compact disk 15.00 (978-1-931056-93-9(5), N Millennium Audio) New Millenn Enter.
The author's airy voice includes the listener as if sharing a bedtime story. The naughty white kitten, Sagwa, comes from a long line of royal Chinese cats. Her mischief changes the spirit of the cruel magistrate and future for her ancestors. A beautifully written story about why siamese cats are really Chinese cats and why their faces, ears, paws and tails turn darker as they grow up.

Chinese Siamese Cat. unabr. abr. ed. Amy Tan. Read by Amy Tan. 1 cass. (Running Time: 1.5 hrs.). 2004. 15.00 (978-1-931056-38-0(2), N Millennium Audio) New Millenn Enter.

Chinese Speakers: Learning the Sounds of American English. unabr. ed. 4 cass. (Accent English Ser.). bk. 89.50 incl. 144-pg bk, 42 visual aid cards, mirror. (SEN150) J Norton Pubs.

Chinese Takeout. Judith Cutler. (Isis (CDs) Ser.). 2007. audio compact disk 89.95 (978-0-7531-2627-1(3)) Pub: ISIS Lrg Prnt GBR. Dist(s): Ulverscroft US

Chinese Takeout. Judith Cutler. Read by Diana Bishop. 9 cass. (Running Time: 10 hrs. 45 mins.). (Isis Cassettes Ser.). 2007. 76.95 (978-0-7531-3610-2(4)) Pub: ISIS Lrg Prnt GBR. Dist(s): Ulverscroft US

Chinese Text for a Changing China. Irene Liu & Li Xiaoqi. 8 cass. (Running Time: 8 hrs.). (C & T Asian Language Ser.). (CHI.). 1992. bk. 99.95 set. (978-0-88727-186-1(3)) Cheng Tsui.
Audio recording of companion Chinese language text book.

Chinese Text for a Changing China. rev. ed. Irene Liu & Li Xiaoqi. 7 cass. (Running Time: 60 min. per cass.). 1995. 99.95 Set. (978-0-88727-207-3(X)) Cheng Tsui.

Chinese Top 100. 2 CDs. (Running Time: 2 hrs.). 2001. bk. 59.95 (SCH305) J Norton Pubs.
Each of the ten unique units teaches how to write & say 10 Chinese characters which have been identified to be the most frequently used words in daily life. Each character is accompanied by five sentences using the character in common daily conversation. After learning only 10 characters, the learner will be able to speak 50 sentences. Includes calligraphy brush.

Chinese Traditional Medicine. (Running Time: 30 min.). 10.95 (HO 880131, HarperThor) HarpC GBR.

Chinese Vocabulary, Set. 4 cass. (Running Time: 0 hr. 60 min.). (Foreign Language Vocabulary Builder Ser.). 43.95 VINYL ALBUM. (978-1-55536-148-8(X)) Oasis Audio.
Vocabulary words provided by categories of travel, health, money, music & science not covered in basic program. Boost your language vocabulary by 2000 words.

Chinese Vol 2 Earworms. (EARWORMS Ser.). 2009. audio compact disk 24.95 (978-0-8416-1068-2(1)) Pub: Berlitz Pubng. Dist(s): Langenscheidt

Chinese with Ease see Chinessisch Ohne Muhe

Chinese Women's Stories. abr. ed. Read by Miriam Margolyes. Interview with Zhang Xin Xin & Sang Ye. 2 cass. (Running Time: 2 hrs. 30 min.). 1999. 16.95 (978-0-9532509-1-2(1)) Penton Overseas.
Three short profiles based on individual interviews of three Chinese women; also a fictional novella, "The Story of Qiuju," which depicts one woman's painstaking search for justice.

Chinese Word Book. 1 cass. (Running Time: 30 mins.). (YA). (gr. 10-12). 1990. pap. bk. & wbk. ed. 24.95 (978-0-614-01441-9(7), SCH205) J Norton Pubs.
Illustrates 200 words from categories including the human body, food, clothing, numbers, nature, school, home & Chinese life & customs. Each illustrated word is captioned with Mand Chinese written characters, pinyin translation & English.

Chinese Word Book. Read by Fu Sita. 1 cass. (Rainbow International Word Book Ser.). 1990. 19.95 Bess Pr.
A native speaker pronounces each word in the accompanying book twice.

Chinessisch Ohne Muhe, Vol. 1. 1 cass. (Running Time: 1 hr. 30 min.).Tr. of Chinese with Ease. (CHI & GER.). 2000. bk. 75.00 (978-2-7005-1350-9(9)) Pub: Assimil FRA. Dist(s): Distribks Inc

Chinessisch Ohne Muhe, Vol. 2. 1 cass. (Running Time: 1 hr. 30 min.).Tr. of Chinese with Ease. (CHI & GER.). 2000. bk. 75.00 (978-2-7005-1351-6(7)) Pub: Assimil FRA. Dist(s): Distribks Inc

Chingis Khan. unabr. ed. Demi. 1 cass. (Running Time: 16 min.). (J). (gr. 3-5). 1993. bk. 30.90 (978-0-8045-6681-0(X), 6681) Spoken Arts.

Chinois sans Peine, Vol. 1. 1 cass. (Running Time: 1 hr., 30 min.). (CHI & FRE.). 2000. bk. 75.00 (978-2-7005-1319-6(3)); bk. 95.00 (978-2-7005-1091-1(7)) Pub: Assimil FRA. Dist(s): Distribks Inc

Chinois sans Peine, Vol. 2. 1 cass. (Running Time: 1 hr., 30 min.). (CHI & FRE.). 2000. bk. 75.00 (978-2-7005-1320-2(7)); bk. 95.00 (978-2-7005-1092-8(5)) Pub: Assimil FRA. Dist(s): Distribks Inc

Chinook. John D. Heisner. Read by Maynard Villers. 4 cass. (Running Time: 5 hrs. 5 min.). (Chinook Ser.: Bk. 2). 1995. 26.95 (978-1-55686-592-3(9)) Books in Motion.
After learning the identity of two men who raped & killed his wife, Jackson Kane, better known as "Chinook", takes to the vengeance trail. He's a man with a gun & knows how to use it.

Chinuch Habanos. Mattisyahu Salomon. 1 cass. (Running Time: 90 mins.). 1999. 6.00 (T60MA) Torah Umesorah.
Sh'ailos U'Teshuvos (Motzei Shabbos).

Chinuch Habonim. Reuven Feinstein. 1 cass. (Running Time: 90 mins.). 1999. 6.00 (T60MC) Torah Umesorah.

Chinyanja. unabr. ed. Foreign Service Institute Staff. 12 cass. (Running Time: 11 hrs. 30 mins.). (Language Science Monographs: Vol. 5). (YA). (gr. 10-12). 1992. pap. bk. 275.00 (978-0-88432-374-7(9), AFCY10) J Norton Pubs.
Also known as Nyanja, is the principal language of Malawi & is also spoken by large numbers of Malawians in neighboring countries. Compiled & published with the assistance of the Peace Corps.

Chinyanja Basic Course FSI CDs & Text. 12 CDs. (Running Time: 11 hrs. 30 mins.). (Foreign Service Institute Basic Course Ser.). (NYA.). 2005. audio compact disk 275.00 (978-1-57970-280-9(5), AFCY10D, Audio-For) J Norton Pubs.
Compiled and published with the assistance of the Peace Corps.

Chip Champions a Lady & Carcajou's Trial. abr. ed. Max Brand. Read by Barry Corbin. 2 cass. (Running Time: 3 hrs.). 2000. 7.95 (978-1-57815-091-5(4), 1059, Media Bks Audio) Media Bks NJ.
Captures the old West.

Chip Harrison Scores Again. unabr. ed. Lawrence Block. Read by Gregory Gorton. 6 vols. (Running Time: 9 hrs.). (Chip Harrison Mystery Ser.). 2000. bk. 54.95 (978-0-7927-2279-3(5), CSL 168, Chivers Sound Lib) AudioGO.
When young, broke, and single Chip Harrison finds a bus ticket to Bordentown, South Carolina, he knows it was sent by the hand of fate. It's his way out of wintry New York City, and a way into the warm welcome of the Bordentown sheriff! But before long, Chip charms his way into the sheriff's good graces and into the arms of Lucille, the preacher's daughter. Even Chip should see he is heading for trouble with a capital T!.

Chip 'n' Dale Rangers: Rootin' Tootin' Rangers. 1 cass. (Running Time: 15 min.). (Disney Afternoon Read-Along Ser.). (J). bk. 5.98 Disney Prod.

Chip off the New Block. Perf. by Tom Smith. (J). (ps-6). 1986. 9.95 (978-0-939065-05-9(3), GW 1005) Gentle Wind.
Stories & songs! for children including, "Here's to Cheshire," "John Jacob Jingleheimer Schmidt," "A Kangaroo Sat on an Oak," "It's Only an Old Beer Bottle," "Can You Dig That Crazy Jibberish," "Barney Mcabe," "Christmas Cake".

Chip, the Little Computer. unabr. ed. Valerie M. Hope. Read by Russ T. Nailz. Illus. by Dan Hamilton. 1 cass. (Running Time: 28 mins.). (Life Lessons Ser.). (SPA & ENG.). (J). (gr. k-4). 1999. 9.99 (978-1-885624-58-1(1)) Alpine Pubng.
The bi-lingual story of Chip is accompanied by 5 original children's songs.

Chipko Movement; The Green Revolution; Bamburi; The Money Launderer. unabr. ed. Julian C. Hollick. 1 cass. (Running Time: 60 min.). 1989. 15.00 (978-1-56709-030-7(3), 1061) Indep Broadcast.
"The Chipko Movement." This program takes a look at this grassroots organization in the Himalayas which teaches villagers to protect the forests. "The Green Revolution." This program examines the Green Revolution, which has been hailed as a miracle cure for Third World hunger. "Bamburi." A look at how the Wasteland is being made to bloom in Kenya. "The Money Launderer." Takes a humorous look at the informal sector of Indian banking.

Chipmunk Adventure (OST) 1 cass., 1 CD. (J). 7.18 (HIPO 40088); audio compact disk 11.18 CD Jewel box. (HIPO 40088) NewSound.

Chipmunk at Hollow Tree Lane. Victoria Sherrow. 1 cass. (Running Time: 35 min.). (J). (gr. k-4). 2001. 19.95 (SP 5001C) Kimbo Educ.
Chipmunk hurries to find food to store in her underground burrow.

Chipmunk at Hollow Tree Lane. Victoria Sherrow. Illus. by Allen Davis. 1 cass. (Smithsonian's Backyard Ser.). (J). (ps-2). 1994. bk. 32.95 TOY. (978-1-56899-042-2(1)) Soundprints.

Chipmunk at Hollow Tree Lane. unabr. ed. Victoria Sherrow. Read by Alexi Komisar. Illus. by Allen Davis. Narrated by Alexi Komisar. 1 cass. (Running Time: 7 min.). Dramatization. (Smithsonian's Backyard Ser.). (J). (ps-2). 1994. 5.00 (978-1-56899-041-5(3)) Soundprints.
Cassette is a read-a-long storybook, with authentic sound effects added. It consists of two sides - one with & one without page turning signals.

Chippendale Factor. John Malcolm. 2009. 61.95 (978-1-4079-0657-7(7)); audio compact disk 79.95 (978-1-4079-0658-4(5)) Pub: Soundings Ltd GBR. Dist(s): Ulverscroft US

Chiron, Halley's Comet & the Goddess Mysteries. Robert Thibodeau. 1 cass. 8.95 (343) Am Fed Astrologers.
An AFA Convention workshop tape.

Chiropractic-Healthcare for Life: Theory of Chiropractic for the Lay Person. 1 cass. (Running Time: 15 min.). 1999. 7.95 (978-1-881288-22-0(6), BFI AudioBooks) BusnFilm Intl.
An explanation of chiropractic for the lay person.

Chisellers. Brendan O'Carroll. Read by Donada Peters. 5 CDs. (Running Time: 6 hrs.). 2001. audio compact disk 40.00 Books on Tape.
The family is about to be forced out of their tenement home in the name of urban renewal. Pierre, Agnes' persistent suitor, is thankfully on hand to console her. Like all good Irish stories, includes a wedding & a funeral, much laughter & some tears & iy is sure to please all who enjoy a good tale.

Chisellers. collector's unabr. ed. Brendan O'Carroll. Read by Donada Peters. 4 cass. (Running Time: 6 hrs.). 2000. 32.00 (978-0-7366-5004-5(0)) Books on Tape.
The story of a brother & sister living alone together on their family farm & of the newcomer who threatens their land & more.

Chisellers. collector's ed. Brendan O'Carroll. Read by Donada Peters. 5 cass. (Running Time: 5 hrs.). 2000. 40.00 (978-0-7366-5229-2(9)) Books on Tape.

Chisellers. collector's unabr. ed. Brendan O'Carroll. Read by Donada Peters. 4 cass. (Running Time: 6 hrs.). 2000. 24.95 (978-0-7366-4948-3(4)) Books on Tape.

Chisholm Trail. abr. ed. Ralph Compton. Read by Jim Gough. 4 cass. (Running Time: 6 hrs.). Dramatization. (Trail Drive Ser.: Vol. 3). 1998. 24.95 (978-1-890990-02-2(7)) Otis Audio.
Young Tenatse Chisholm, half-breed son of Indian scout Jesse Chisholm, is a top-notch warrior with a Colt, a Henry rifle, a Bowie knife & his fists. In New Orleans, Ten falls hopelessly in love with beautiful Priscilla LeBeau. Her father hates him & manages to drive him from New Orleans with a price on his head. But Ten Chisholm vows to clear his name & win Priscilla from a father who has promised her in payment of his gambling debt.

Chitty Chitty Bang Bang. 40th anniv. ed. Ian Fleming. Read by Andrew Sachs. 2 cass. (Running Time: 2 hrs. 15 mins.). (J). (gr. 3-7). 2004. 19.55 (978-0-8072-1687-3(9), Listening Lib) Pub: Random Audio Pubg. Dist(s): NetLibrary CO

Chloe. Lyn Cote. (Running Time: 30600 sec.). (Women of Ivy Manor Ser.). 2005. 54.95 (978-0-7861-3772-5(X)); audio compact disk 63.00 (978-0-7861-7595-6(8)) Blckstn Audio.

Chloe, Vol. 1. unabr. ed. Lyn Cote. 8 cass. (Running Time: 30600 sec.). (Women of Ivy Manor Ser.). 2005. 29.95 (978-0-7861-3652-0(9), E3521); audio compact disk 29.95 (978-0-7861-7741-7(1), E3521); audio compact disk 29.95 (978-0-7861-7967-1(8), E3521) Blckstn Audio.

Chlordane. Daniel Zwerdling. 1 cass. (Running Time: 50 min.). 11.95 (I0550B090, HarperThor) HarpC GBR.

Chlorination: A Link Between Heart Disease & Cancer. 1 cass. (Running Time: 10 min.). 1986. 5.00 (978-0-9617432-1-5(2)) Health Water Res.
Chlorination & drinking water.

Chocky. unabr. ed. John Wyndham. Narrated by Full Cast. (Running Time: 1 hr. 30 mins. 0 sec.). (ENG.). 2010. audio compact disk 24.95 (978-1-60283-814-7(3)) Pub: AudioGO. Dist(s): Perseus Dist

Chocolate. 1 cass. (Running Time: 30 min.). 8.00 (NJ-82-11-02, HarperThor) HarpC GBR.

Chocolate: And Other Multicultural Stories. (J). 1998. 9.95 (978-0-9623930-8-2(8)) Cantemos-bilingual.

Chocolate: Songs for Children. Meghan Collins. Perf. by Linda Schrade et al. 1 cass. (Running Time: 31 min.). (J). (gr. k-4). 1997. 9.95 (978-0-9647805-0-7(X), Gentle Wnd) Nova Prodns.
Melodies are simple. Performances vary in quality.

Chocolate, a Glacier Grizzly. Peggy Christian. Read by Tom Chapin. Illus. by Carol Cottone-Kolthoff. Narrated by Tom Chapin. 1 cass. (Running Time: 13 min.). (Humane Society of the United States Animal Tales Ser.). (J). (gr. 1-5). bk. 34.95 Incl. plush animal. (978-1-882728-64-0(5)); pap. bk. 9.95 (978-1-882728-67-1(X)); pap. bk. 19.95 (978-1-882728-69-5(6)) Benefactory.
Why would a young grizzly go for a helicopter ride? Find out in this tale of a grizzly growing up in Glacier National Park.

CHOCOLATE & other Multicultural Stories see Multi-ethnic Stories

Chocolate Fever. Robert Kimmel Smith. Read by Lionel Wilson. 2 cass. (Running Time: 1 hr.). (J). 2000. 18.00 (978-0-7366-9106-2(5)) Books on Tape.
Henry's a chocolate maven, first class. He can't get enough, until aaarrfh! Brown spots, brown bumps all over Henry.

Chocolate Fever. unabr. ed. Robert Kimmel Smith. 1 read-along cass. (Running Time: 53 min.). (Children's Cliffhangers Ser.). (J). (gr. 2-5). 1984. 15.98 incl. bk. & guide. (978-0-8072-1104-5(4), SWR 33 SP, Listening Lib) Random Audio Pubg.
Henry is the ultimate chocoholic. He even turns into a walking candy bar, a medical case-history. It takes a nutty hijacking to teach Henry a hard lesson about life & chocolate.

Chocolate Fever. unabr. ed. Robert Kimmel Smith. Read by Lionel Wilson. 2 cass. (Running Time: 1 hr. 15 mins.). (J). (gr. 2-4). 1996. 23.00 (978-0-8072-7784-3(3), YA917CX, Listening Lib) Random Audio Pubg.
Henry loved chocolate probably more than anybody in the world. So much so, that he made medical history when he contacted chocolate fever.

Chocolate Fever. unabr. ed. Robert Kimmel Smith. Read by Lionel Wilson. (Running Time: 4500 sec.). (ENG.). (YA). (ps). 2007. audio compact disk 12.99 (978-0-7393-4889-5(2), Listening Lib) Pub: Random Audio Pubg. Dist(s): Random

Chocolate Fever. unabr. ed. Read by Lionel Wilson. Ed. by Robert Kimmel Smith. 2 vols. (Running Time: 1 hr. 15 mins.). (Middle Grade Cassette Librariestm Ser.). (J). (gr. 2-4). 2004. pap. bk. 29.00 (978-0-8072-7785-0(1), S YA 917 SP, Listening Lib) Random Audio Pubg.
"Henry Green was a boy who loved chocolate. He liked it bitter, sweet, dark, light. and daily; for breakfast, lunch, dinner, and snacks; in cakes, candy bars, milk, and every other form you could possibly imagine. One day Henry found that strange things were happening to him...".

Chocolate files (mr Pin 2) The Chocolate Files. unabr. ed. Mary Elise Monsell. Narrated by John McDonough. 1 cass. (Running Time: 1 hr.). (gr. 3 up). 1997. 10.00 (978-0-7887-1117-6(2), 95111E7) Recorded Bks.
Lovable Mr. Pin waddles across Chicago as he follows the chocolate trails in two puzzling mysteries. In the first case, someone is trying to kidnap Chicago's famous opera conductor. Mr. Pin rushes to the theater, but as he gathers clues, fog suddenly swirls over the stage. When the air clears, the conductor is gone! Will Mr. Pin be able to find him?.

Chocolate for a Womans Heart: Stories of Love, Kindness & Compassion to Nourish Your Soul & Sweeten Your Dreams. Kay Allenbaugh. 2004. 10.95 (978-0-7435-4279-1(7)) Pub: S&S Audio. Dist(s): S and S Inc

Chocolate for a Womans soul stories feed your Sp: Stories to Feed Your Spirit & Warm Your Heart. Kay Allenbaugh. 2004. 10.95 (978-0-7435-4280-7(0)) Pub: S&S Audio. Dist(s): S and S Inc

Chocolate Fudge Mystery. David A. Adler. Read by Christina Moore. 1 cass. (Running Time: 30 mins.). (YA). 2000. pap. bk. & stu. ed. 23.24 (978-0-7887-4326-9(0), 41121) Recorded Bks.
Cam & her friend Eric are selling chocolate fudge & rice cakes door-to-door for charity. When Cam sees a woman coming from a deserted yellow house, she knows something is wrong. Will Cam be able to solve the mystery with her amazing photographic memory?.

Chocolate Fudge Mystery. unabr. ed. David A. Adler. Narrated by Christina Moore. 1 cass. (Running Time: 30 mins.). (Cam Jansen Ser.: No. 14). (gr. 2 up). 2000. 11.00 (978-0-7887-4228-6(0), 96197E7) Recorded Bks.

Chocolate Fudge Mystery, Class set. David A. Adler. Read by Christina Moore. 1 cass. (Running Time: 30 mins.). (Cam Jansen Ser.: No. 14). (YA). 2000. 71.70 (978-0-7887-4427-3(5), 47118) Recorded Bks.

Chocolate Man: A Children's Horror Tale/ CD Story. Waide Riddle. Based on a book by Riddle. Narrated by Ron Geren. (Running Time: 38:05). 2003. cd-rom & audio compact disk 15.00 (978-0-615-24430-3(0)) Green Ghost.

Chocolate, Please: My Adventures in Food, Fat, & Freaks. unabr. ed. Lisa Lampanelli. Read by Lisa Lampanelli. 7 CDs. (Running Time: 8 hrs. 0 mins. 0 sec.). (ENG.). 2009. audio compact disk 29.99 (978-0-7435-9785-2(0)) Pub: S&S Audio. Dist(s): S and S Inc

Chocolate Sundae Mystery. Gertrude Chandler Warner. (Running Time: 5400 sec.). (Boxcar Children Ser.: No. 46). (J). 2005. audio compact disk 14.95 (978-0-7861-7486-7(2)) Blckstn Audio.

Chocolate Sundae Mystery. unabr. ed. Gertrude Chandler Warner. Read by Aimee Lilly. 2 cass. (Running Time: 3 hrs.). (Boxcar Children Ser.: No. 46). (J). 12.99 (978-1-58926-296-6(4)) Oasis Audio.

Chocolate Sundae Mystery. unabr. ed. Gertrude Chandler Warner. Narrated by Aimee Lilly. (Boxcar Children Ser.). (ENG.). (J). 2004. 10.49 (978-1-60814-092-3(X)) Oasis Audio.

Chocolate Sunday Mystery. unabr. ed. Gertrude Chandler Warner. Narrated by Aimee Lilly. (Running Time: 27000 sec.). (Boxcar Children Ser.). (ENG.). (J). (gr. 4-7). 2005. audio compact disk 29.99 (978-1-59859-052-4(9)) Oasis Audio.

Chocolate Touch. unabr. ed. Patrick Skene Catling. Read by Francis O'Leary. 2 vols. (Running Time: 1 hr. 18 mins.). Dramatization. (J). (gr. 3-7). 1992. pap. bk. 29.00 (978-0-8072-7362-3(7), YA 837 SP, Listening Lib); 23.00 (978-0-8072-7361-6(9), YA 837 CX, Listening Lib) Random Audio Pubg.
After an encounter with a mystical candyman, everything John puts to his lips turns to chocolate. Through this experience, he leams important lessons about greed & compassion.

Chocolate Touch, Set. unabr. ed. Patrick Skene Catling. Read by G. Francis O'Leary. 2 cass. (YA). 1999. 16.98 (FS9-34159) Highsmith.

Chocolate War. Robert Cormier. Read by Frank Muller. 5 CDs. (Running Time: 5 hrs. 38 mins.). (J). (gr. 7 up). 2004. audio compact disk 38.25 (978-1-4000-8996-3(4), Listening Lib) Pub: Random Audio Pubg. Dist(s): NetLibrary CO

Chocolate War. Robert Cormier. Narrated by George Guidall. 6 CDs. (Running Time: 6 hrs. 30 mins.). (gr. 8 up). audio compact disk 58.00 (978-1-4025-2294-9(0)) Recorded Bks.

Chocolate War. unabr. ed. Robert Cormier. Read by Frank Muller. 4 cass. (Running Time: 4 hrs.). (J). 1997. 29.98 (LL 3127, Chivers Child Audio) AudioGO.

Chocolate War. unabr. ed. Robert Cormier. Read by Frank Muller. 4 cass. (Running Time: 6 hrs.). (J). (gr. 1-8). 1999. 32.00 (LL 3127, Chivers Child Audio) AudioGO.

Chocolate War. unabr. ed. Robert Cormier. Read by Frank Muller. 4 vols. (Running Time: 5 hrs. 38 mins.). (J). (gr. 7 up). 1988. pap. bk. 38.00 (978-0-8072-7305-0(8), YA 801 SP, Listening Lib); 32.00 (978-0-8072-7221-3(3), YA801CX, Listening Lib) Random Audio Pubg.
In a tale of intimidation at a boy's prep school, Trinity is having a chocolate sale. The Vigils, the secret society of students that run Trinity, have banded with the power-hungry Brother Leon to make it a record-breaking sale. For Jerry Renaul, resisting the Vigils could cost him his life.

Chocolate War. unabr. ed. Robert Cormier. Read by Frank Muller. (Running Time: 20280 sec.). (ENG.). (J). (gr. 7-12). 2007. audio compact disk 26.00 (978-0-7393-5015-7(3), Listening Lib) Pub: Random Audio Pubg. Dist(s): Random

Chocolate War, unabr. ed. Robert Cormier. Narrated by George Guidall. 5 pieces. (Running Time: 6 hrs. 30 mins.). (gr. 8 up). 44.00 (978-1-55690-774-6(5), 93139E7) Recorded Bks.
Jerry Renault, a new student at the preppie Trinity School, must cope with a sadistic teacher & all-too-real threats of a student secret society. An unflinching portrait of cruelty & conformity in an exclusive prep school. Available to libraries only.

Chocolate War, Set. unabr. ed. Robert Cormier. Read by Frank Muller. 4 cass. (YA). 1999. 29.98 (FS9-25217) Highsmith.

Choctaw. 2 cass. (Running Time: 2 hrs. 20 mins.). (CHO.). 1991. ring bd. 49.95 (978-0-88465-502-2(4), SCT100) J Norton Pubs.

Choctaw. Donald Clayton Porter. Read by Lloyd James. 4 vols. No. 11. 2004. 25.00 (978-1-58807-227-6(4)); (978-1-58807-758-5(6)); audio compact disk 30.00 (978-1-58807-411-9(0)); audio compact disk (978-1-58807-875-9(2)) Am Pubng Inc.

Choctaw Way. Tim Tingle. 1 cass. (Running Time: 58 min.). 1997. 12.00 (978-1-886334-02-1(1)) Storytribe.
These tales recount the exodus of the Choctan people through the eyes of a single family - from tribal beginnings in Mississippi to urbanization in metropolitan Houston, Texas.

Chod. Perf. by Lama Wangdu Rinpoche. 1 CD. (Running Time: 44 mins.). (TIB.). 2001. audio compact disk 15.00 (978-0-915801-94-7(9)) Rudra Pr.

Choice. 2003. 6.00 (978-1-58602-171-9(0)); audio compact disk 10.00 (978-1-58602-172-6(9)) E L Long.

Choice. abr. ed. Nicholas Sparks. Read by Holter Graham. (Running Time: 5 hrs.). (ENG.). 2007. 14.98 (978-1-60024-082-9(8)) Pub: Hachet Audio. Dist(s): HachBkGrp

Choice. abr. ed. Nicholas Sparks. Read by Holter Graham. (Running Time: 5 hrs.). (ENG.). 2009. audio compact disk 14.98 (978-1-60024-669-2(9)) Pub: Hachet Audio. Dist(s): HachBkGrp

Choice. unabr. ed. Nicholas Sparks. Read by Holter Graham. (Running Time: 9 hrs.). (ENG.). 2007. 19.98 (978-1-60024-016-4(X)); audio compact disk 39.98 (978-1-60024-017-1(8)) Pub: Hachet Audio. Dist(s): HachBkGrp

Choice. unabr. ed. Nicholas Sparks. Read by Holter Graham. 8 CDs. 2007. audio compact disk 80.00 (978-1-4159-4494-3(6), BksonTape) Pub: Random Audio Pubg. Dist(s): Random
Travis Parker has everything a man could want: a good job, loyal friends, even a waterfront home in small-town North Carolina. In full pursuit of the good life - boating, swimming, and regular barbecues with his close buddies - he holds the vague conviction that a serious relationship with a woman would only cramp his style. That is until Gabby Holland moves in next door. Despite his attempts to be neighborly, the attractive redhead seems to have a grudge against him . . . and the presence of her longtime boyfriend doesn't help. Still, Travis can't stop trying to ingratiate himself with his new neighbor, and his persistent efforts lead them both to the doorstep of a journey that neither could have foreseen. Spanning the eventful years of young love, marriage, and family, THE CHOICE ultimately confronts us with the most heart-wrenching question of all: How far should you go to keep the hope of love alive?.

***Choice: A Novel.** unabr. ed. Suzanne Woods Fisher. Narrated by Jill Shellabarger & Cassandra Campbell. (Running Time: 10 hrs. 2 mins. 19 sec.). (Lancaster County Secrets Ser.). (ENG.). 2010. 20.99 (978-1-60814-766-3(5)); audio compact disk 29.99 (978-1-59859-784-4(1)) Oasis Audio.

Choice - The Truth about Cause & Effect. unabr. ed. Carol Howe. 3 cass. (Running Time: 4 hrs.). 1996. 24.95 Set. (978-1-889642-07-9(X)) C Howe.
Once & for all, see how today's choices for happiness are not limited or controlled by the events in one's personal history. As the true relationship between cause & effect, past & present is revealed, one finds that: (1) Cause & effect is a package deal. Today's experience is born from today's purpose & focus, rather than from past events long since gone. (2) One must choose, over & over again, the new purpose of letting go of memories

of past injury, inviting an entirely new pattern of happy experience to emerge.

***Choice Audio CD.** Susan Diane Matz. Read by Susan Diane Matz. (ENG.). 2010. 15.95 (978-0-9841054-7-2(6)) Abriev Ent.

Choice Cuts: A Savory Selection of Food Writing from Around the World & Throughout History. unabr. ed. Mark Kurlansky. 11 cass. (Running Time: 6 hrs.). 2004. 42.95 (978-1-59007-283-7(9)); audio compact disk 69.95 (978-1-59007-284-4(7)) New Millenn Enter.
This work was at least 3,000 years in the making as essays about food make your mouth water, your appetite build, and your appreciation for the art and history of cuisine grow by leaps and bounds. Mark Kurlansky, food historian and writer for Food and Wine magazine, comments about and introduces historical thoughts on everything from scrambled eggs to roast ribs of beef, souffles, and every category of food you can imagine. Some of the contributors include: Aristotle, Julia Child, James Beard, Gertrude Stein, and other famous authors, and historians. This enticing look at food is entertaining, amusing and fun.

Choice Cuts: A Savory Selection of Food Writing from Around the World & Throughout History. unabr. ed. Ed. by Mark Kurlansky. 11 cass. (Running Time: 15 hrs. 30 mins.). 2002. 99.75 (978-1-4025-6251-8(9), 97537MC, Griot Aud) Recorded Bks.

Choice in Packaging - Paper Versus Plastic. Hosted by Nancy Pearlman. 1 cass. (Running Time: 29 min.). 10.00 (524) Educ Comm CA.

Choice of Business Entity: More Options for New & Operating Businesses. 3 cass. (Running Time: 3 hrs. 30 min.). 1995. 155.00 Set; incl. study guide. (D235) Am Law Inst.
Reviews the factors to consider for both new & existing businesses, then applies those factors to 20 hypothetical fact situations for various types of business ventures.

Choice of Business Entity under the New Pennsylvania Business Code: Effects of Recent Legislation. Read by Robert H. Zimmerman & Sol B. Genauer. 1 cass. 1990. 20.00 (AL-83) PA Bar Inst.

Choice of Evil. unabr. ed. Andrew Vachss. Read by Phil Gigante. (Running Time: 11 hrs.). (Burke Ser.). 2010. audio compact disk 29.99 (978-1-4418-2151-5(1), 9781441821515, Bril Audio CD Unabri) Brilliance Audio.

***Choice of Evil.** unabr. ed. Andrew Vachss. Read by Phil Gigante. (Running Time: 11 hrs.). (Burke Ser.). 2010. 24.99 (978-1-4418-2155-3(4), 9781441821553, BAD); 39.97 (978-1-4418-2156-0(2), 9781441821560, BADLE); 24.99 (978-1-4418-2153-9(8), 9781441821539, Brilliance MP3); 39.97 (978-1-4418-2154-6(6), 9781441821546, Brinc Audio MP3 Lib); audio compact disk 79.97 (978-1-4418-2152-2(X), 9781441821522, BriAudCD Unabrid) Brilliance Audio.

Choice of Evils. unabr. ed. Elizabeth Ferrars. Read by Garard Green. 5 cass. (Running Time: 7 hrs.). (Isis Ser.). (J). 1995. 49.95 (978-1-85695-223-1(1), 951209) Pub: ISIS Lrg Prnt GBR. Dist(s): Ulverscroft US

Choice of the Cat. unabr. ed. E. E. Knight. Read by Christian Rummel. (Running Time: 12 hrs.). (Vampire Earth Ser.). 2010. audio compact disk 29.99 (978-1-4418-1561-3(9), 9781441815613) Brilliance Audio.

***Choice of the Cat.** unabr. ed. E. E. Knight. Read by Christian Rummel. (Running Time: 12 hrs.). (Vampire Earth Ser.). 2010. 39.97 (978-1-4418-1564-4(3), 9781441815644, Brinc Audio MP3 Lib); 39.97 (978-1-4418-1565-1(1), 9781441815651, BADLE) Brilliance Audio.

***Choice of the Cat.** unabr. ed. E. e. Knight. Read by Christian Rummel. (Running Time: 12 hrs.). (Vampire Earth Ser.). 2010. 24.99 (978-1-4418-1563-7(5), 9781441815637, Brilliance MP3) Brilliance Audio.

***Choice of the Cat.** unabr. ed. E. E. Knight. Read by Christian Rummel. (Running Time: 12 hrs.). (Vampire Earth Ser.). 2010. audio compact disk 92.97 (978-1-4418-1562-0(7), 9781441815620, BriAudCD Unabrid) Brilliance Audio.

Choice of Victims. J. F. Straker. Read by Diana Bishop. 5 cass. (Running Time: 6 hrs.). (Soundings Ser.). (J). 2004. 49.95 (978-1-84283-557-9(2)) Pub: ISIS Lrg Prnt GBR. Dist(s): Ulverscroft US

Choice Readings Bk. 1: International Edition. Mark A. Clarke et al. (C). 1999. 15.00 (978-0-472-00289-4(9)) U of Mich Pr.

Choice Readings Bk. 2: International Edition. Mark A. Clarke et al. (C). 1999. 15.00 (978-0-472-00290-0(2)) U of Mich Pr.

Choice: The New Age Movement: John 10:1-10. Ed Young. 1998. 4.95 (978-0-7417-2190-7(2), A1190) Win Walk.

Choice, Utility & Demand. unabr. ed. Murray Newton Rothbard. 1 cass. (Running Time: 1 hr. 9 min.). (Introduction to Free Market Economics Ser.). 11.95 (301) J Norton Pubs.
Resources, scarcity; technology & production; consumer & capital goods; time preference; specialization & the division of labor.

Choice: World Religions: Titus 3:3-7. Ed Young. 1998. 4.95 (978-0-7417-2189-1(9), A1189) Win Walk.

Choiceless Awareness. unabr. ed. Jiddu Krishnamurti & Eugene Schallert. Read by Eugene Schallert. Ed. by Krishnamurti Foundation of America Staff. 1 cass. (Running Time: 60 min.). 1992. 8.50 (ARES722) Krishnamurti.
J. Krishnamurti & Rev. Eugene Schallert discuss choiceless awareness. This dialogue was recorded February 17, 1972 at KPBS-TV in San Diego. This is the 2nd of a two part dialogue.

Choices. Susan Sallis. Read by Karen Cass. 10 cass. (Running Time: 15 hrs.). 2001. 84.95 (23272) Pub: Soundings Ltd GBR. Dist(s): Ulverscroft US

Choices. unabr. ed. Susan Sallis. Read by Karen Cass. 10 cass. (Running Time: 15 hrs.). 2000. 84.95 (978-1-86042-327-7(2), 23272) Pub: Soundings Ltd GBR. Dist(s): ISIS Pub
On a happy expedition to choose her wedding dress, accompanied by her fiancee Miles & her parents, Helen Wilson's life changed. A devastating car crash left Helen with only memories to console her. Yet as she came to terms with her loss, she discovered that Miles had kept something from her which made her see him in a very different light.

Choices: And Other Poems Read by the Poet. Poems. Dana Wildsmith. 1 cass. (Running Time: 48 min.). 1997. 10.00 (978-0-916078-13-3(2), Iris) Iris Pub Group.

Choices: Making Right Decisions in a Complex World. abr. ed. Lewis B. Smedes. Read by Lewis B. Smedes. 1 cass. (Running Time: 60 min.). 1986. 8.95 (978-0-06-067417-5(2)) HarperCollins Pubs.
Clear & sensible guidelines from bestselling author Lewis B. Smedes on how to make the most of life's many choices.

Choices: The Irreversible Moment: A Workbook & Diary for Those Who Are Depressed or Despondent. Gerald R. Griffin. 2000. pap. bk. 24.95 (978-0-939303-12-0(4)) Educ Lrn Syst.

Choices & Changes Using Gestalt. unabr. ed. Anne N. Simkin. 1 cass. (Running Time: 90 min.). 1989. 11.00 (10501) Big Sur Tapes.
In work with members of the Findhorn community, Simkin demonstrates her particularly loving & delightful practice of the process of Gestalt Therapy.

Choir, unabr. ed. Joanna Trollope. Read by Nadia May. 7 cass. (Running Time: 10 hrs.). 2000. 49.95 (978-0-7861-1030-8(9), 1805) Blckstn Audio.
Focuses on a crisis in one of England's beautiful old Cathedral Towns. The cathedral is in need of major repair & the community is divided on whether or not to disband the boys' choir in order to finance the work & Trollope's wonderfully drawn characters are all dragged into the battle.

Choir & Praise Team: Sing of His Love. Contrib. by Camp Kirkland. (ENG.). 2001. audio compact disk 12.99 (978-5-550-11709-5(6)) Allegis.

Choir Collection Vol. 1: Split Track. Terry Franklin & Barbi Franklin. 2002. 24.95 (978-7-901443-01-3(4)); audio compact disk 29.95 (978-7-901442-94-8(8)) Pub: Tylis Music. Dist(s): STL Dist NA

***Choir Collection Vol. 1: Splittrack of the Songs of Terry & Barbi Franklin for Solos & Duets.** Composed by Terry Franklin & Barbi Franklin. (ENG.). 2006. audio compact disk 29.95 (978-0-01-237069-8(X)) Pub: Tylis Pubng. Dist(s): STL Dist NA

Choir "Let it Fly" 1997. 8.99; audio compact disk 12.99 Pub: Brentwood Music. Dist(s): Provident Mus Dist
Recorded live during the "Free Flying Soul" tour in the spring of '96. Includes "Sad Face," "Sled Dog," "About Love," "To Cover You," & many more.

Choirboys. unabr. ed. Joseph Wambaugh. Read by Daniel Grace. 8 cass. (Running Time: 12 hrs.). 1976. 64.00 (978-0-7366-0014-9(0), 1024) Books on Tape.
Introduces the five teams of policemen who form the nightwatch patrol. In pre-dawn hours, these men gather for liquor & sex, sessions they emphatically call "choir practice".

***Choirboys.** unabr. ed. Joseph Wambaugh. Read by Oliver Wyman. (Running Time: 14 hrs.). 2010. 39.97 (978-1-4418-7485-6(2), 9781441874856, BADLE); 24.99 (978-1-4418-7483-2(6), 9781441874832, Brilliance MP3); 39.97 (978-1-4418-7484-9(4), 9781441874849, Brinc Audio MP3 Lib); audio compact disk 29.99 (978-1-4418-7481-8(X), 9781441874818, Bril Audio CD Unabri); audio compact disk 79.97 (978-1-4418-7482-5(8), 9781441874825, BriAudCD Unabrid) Brilliance Audio.

***Choke.** abr. ed. Stuart Woods. Read by Jay O. Sanders. (ENG.). 2005. (978-0-06-084190-4(7), Harper Audio); (978-0-06-084191-1(5), Harper Audio) HarperCollins Pubs.

Choke. unabr. ed. Stuart Woods. Read by Barrett Whitener. 7 cass. (Running Time: 10 hrs. 30 min.). 1995. 56.00 (978-0-7366-3192-1(5), 3858) Books on Tape.
Chuck Chandler, a former top tour tennis professional, moves to Key West & meets Claire Carras who is married to an enigmatic older man. Suddenly Chuck is suspected of murder & is on the verge of losing not only his modest career, but his freedom as well.

Choke, unabr. ed. Stuart Woods. Narrated by Richard Ferrone. 7 cass. (Running Time: 9 hrs. 45 mins.). 60.00 (978-0-7887-0446-8(X), 94642E7) Recorded Bks.
Chuck Chandler, one-time international tennis star, is a racquet club instructor when he meets Clare Carras, the stunning young wife of a mysterious millionaire. When Clare's husband disappears in a suspicious diving accident, Chuck becomes the prime suspect in a murderous plot that stretches from California's seedy mob headquarters to Florida's luxurious manors. Available to libraries only.

Choke. unabr. movie tie-in ed. Chuck Palahniuk. Read by Chuck Palahniuk. (ENG.). 2008. audio compact disk 19.99 (978-0-7393-6672-1(6), Random AudioBks) Pub: Random Audio Pubg. Dist(s): Random

Choker. unabr. ed. Frederick Ramsay. (Running Time: 7.5 hrs. 0 mins.). (ENG.). 2009. 29.95 (978-1-4332-9004-6(9)); 54.95 (978-1-4332-9000-8(6)); audio compact disk 69.00 (978-1-4332-9001-5(4)) Blckstn Audio.

Chonda Pierce on Her Soapbox. abr. ed. Chonda Pierce. (Running Time: 3 hrs. 0 mins. 0 sec.). (ENG.). 2003. 10.99 (978-0-310-26024-0(8)) Zondervan.

Chonda Pierce on Her Soapbox. unabr. ed. Chonda Pierce. 1999. 17.99 (978-0-310-22978-0(2)) Zondervan.

Choo Choo at the Zoo. (J). (ps-1). 2002. 10.95 (978-0-8126-0175-6(0)) Pub: Cricket Bks. Dist(s): PerseuPGW

Choo Choo Boogaloo. Perf. by Buckwheat Zydeco. 1 cass. (Running Time: 53 min.). (J). 1994. 9.98 (978-1-56628-042-6(7), MLP 2069/WB MLP 2069/WB MLP D2069/WB 42556-2); 9.98 Norelco. (978-1-56628-040-2(0), MLP 2069/WB MLP D2069/WB 42556-2); audio compact disk 13.98 CD. (978-1-56628-041-9(9), MLP D2069/WB 42556-2) MFLP CA.
Upbeat, musical tour of the Bayou country, music & narration.

Choose Life. Gloria Copeland. 2 cass. 1985. 10.00 Set. (978-0-88114-774-2(5)) K Copeland Pubns.
Biblical teaching on victorious living.

Choose Life. Kenneth Copeland. 1 cass. 1985. 5.00 (978-0-88114-924-1(1)) K Copeland Pubns.
Biblical teaching on powerful living.

Choose Once Again: Selections from a Course in Miracles. unabr. ed. Read by Charles Tart. 2 cass. (Running Time: 2 hrs.). 1993. 15.95 (978-0-944993-41-5(9)) Audio Lit.

Choose Something Like a Star see Robert Frost Reads

Choose Something Like a Star see Twentieth-Century Poetry in English, No. 6, Recordings of Poets Reading Their Own Poetry

Choose Them Wisely: Thoughts Become Things! unabr. ed. Mike Dooley. Read by Mike Dooley. (Running Time: 3 hrs. 30 mins. 0 sec.). (ENG.). 2009. audio compact disk 19.99 (978-0-7435-8000-7(1)) Pub: S&S Audio. Dist(s): S and S Inc

Choose to Live a Balanced Life. S. Jones. reel tape 20.00 (978-0-87516-729-9(2)) DeVorss.

Choose to Live & Love. Wayne W. Dyer. 1 cass. (Running Time: 60 min.). 1986. 8.95 (978-0-88684-095-2(3)) Listen USA.
Explores & discusses how to make those necessary choices to live & love the life you truly want.

Choose to Live Peacefully. abr. ed. Susan Smith Jones. 3 cass. (Running Time: 4 hrs. 30 mins.). 1999. 22.95 (978-0-87159-843-1(4)) Unity Schl Christ.

Choose to Love Yourself. Joan Fericy. 1 cass. (Running Time: 60 min.). 1988. 8.95 (978-0-9622371-3-3(2)) J Fericy.
Self-help.

Choose to Love Yourself Workshop. Joan Fericy. 1 cass. (Running Time: 60 min.). 1990. 8.00 (978-0-9622371-4-0(0)) J Fericy.
Self-help, motivational.

Choose You This Day. Ed Young. (J). 1979. 4.95 (978-0-7417-1045-1(5), A0046) Win Walk.

Choose Your Pardner. Scripts. Liz VonSeggen. 2. (J). 2001. spiral bd. 50.00 (978-1-58302-198-9(1)) One Way St.

Choose Your Partners! Contra Dance & Square Dance Music of New Hampshire. Perf. by Lamprey River Band Staff. 1 CD. (Running Time: 67 min.). 1999. 14.00 Smithsonian Folkways.
Notes discuss history of New England, social dance & line calls.

Choosing. unabr. ed. Diana Farr. Read by Norma West. 7 cass. (Running Time: 8 hrs. 34 min.). (Isis Ser.). (J). 1990. 61.95 (978-1-85089-702-6(6), 90026) Pub: ISIS Lrg Prnt GBR. Dist(s): Ulverscroft US

Choosing A Church. Mac Hammond. 1 cass. (Running Time: 1 hour). 2005. 5.00 (978-1-57399-201-5(1)) Mac Hammond.

Choosing a College. unabr. ed. Thomas Sowell. Read by Robert Morris. 5 cass. (Running Time: 7 hrs.). 1989. 39.95 (978-0-7861-0091-0(5), 1084) Blckstn Audio.
Starts at "square one" before you know what questions to ask, what colleges to read about, or what statistics to look up. Sowell candidly describes the inner & outer workings of scores of American colleges & universities, big & small. He gives special attention to special programs, financial aid & the academic environment.

Choosing a Mate: Alone & Lonely: Matt.19:10-12. Ed Young. 1991. 4.95 (978-0-7417-1882-2(0), 882) Win Walk.

Choosing a Mate: Necessary Basics: 11 Cor. 6:14. Ed Young. 1991. 4.95 (978-0-7417-1880-8(4), 880) Win Walk.

Choosing a Partner: 11 Cor. 6:11;7:1. Ed Young. 1990. 4.95 (978-0-7417-1789-4(1), 789) Win Walk.

Choosing Forgiveness: Your Journey to Freedom. unabr. ed. Nacy Leigh DeMoss. Frwd. by David Jeremiah. Narrated by Christine Dente. (Running Time: 18000 sec.). (ENG.). 2006. audio compact disk 21.99 (978-1-59859-168-2(1)) Oasis Audio.

Choosing Forgiveness: Your Journey to Freedom. unabr. ed. Nancy Leigh DeMoss. Narrated by Christine Dente. (ENG.). 2006. 15.39 (978-1-60814-115-9(2)) Oasis Audio.

Choosing Gratitude: Your Journey to Joy. unabr. ed. Nancy Leigh DeMoss. Narrated by Christian Taylor. (Running Time: 5 hrs. 37 mins. 55 sec.). (ENG.). 2009. 16.09 (978-1-60814-589-8(1)); audio compact disk 22.99 (978-1-59859-637-3(3)) Oasis Audio.

Choosing Happiness: The Art of Living Unconditionally. Veronica Ray. 1 cass. (Running Time: 60 min.). 10.00 (978-0-89486-726-2(1), 5635) Hazelden.
Listen to ideas from the popular book that reinforce your ability to stay in touch with your spirituality, see people & events in new ways, & choose happiness.

Choosing Kindness. unabr. ed. Perf. by Eknath Easwaran. 1 cass. (Running Time: 1 hr.). 1981. 7.95 (978-1-58638-512-5(7)) Nilgiri Pr.

Choosing Life: One Day at a Time. abr. ed. Dodie Osteen. Read by Dodie Osteen. (Running Time: 2 hrs. 0 mins. 0 sec.). (ENG.). 2006. audio compact disk 19.95 (978-0-7435-6739-8(0)) Pub: S&S Audio. Dist(s): S and S Inc

Choosing to Awaken & Moving History Forward. Marianne Williamson. Read by Marianne Williamson. 1 cass. (Running Time: 90 mins.). (Lectures on a Course in Miracles). 1999. 10.00 (978-1-56170-178-0(5), M706) Hay House.

Choosing to Be Single: 1 Cor. 7:28. Ed Young. 1991. 4.95 (978-0-7417-1878-5(2), 878) Win Walk.

***Choosing to SEE: A Journey of Struggle & Hope.** Mary Beth Chapman & Ellen Vaughn. Frwd. by Steven Curtis Chapman. (Running Time: 5 hrs. 57 mins.). 2010. audio compact disk 24.99 (978-0-8007-2006-3(7)) Pub: Revell. Dist(s): Baker Pub Grp

Choosing up Sides, unabr. ed. John Ritter. Narrated by Johnny Heller. 3 pieces. (Running Time: 4 hrs. 30 mins.). (gr. 7 up). 28.00 (978-0-7887-2630-9(7), 95634E7) Recorded Bks.
Luke Bledsoe has a wicked fastball, but he shouldn't be pitching left-handed. That's the side of the devil, his preacher father says. All his life this young teen has been trying to please his pa. Now, in sorting out what he wants for himself, Luke will need the same steely determination he calls upon when running for home plate. Available to libraries only.

Choosing Your Client's State of Incorporation. 1989. 55.00 (AC-524) PA Bar Inst.

Choosing Your English for Arabic Speakers. unabr. ed. 2 cass. 1994. bk. 44.50 (978-0-88432-671-7(3), S32591) J Norton Pubs.
Bilingual.

Choosing Your English for French Speakers. unabr. ed. British Broadcasting Corporation Staff. 2 cass. 1994. bk. 44.50 (978-0-88432-672-4(1), S32592) J Norton Pubs.

Choosing Your Own Greatness: Your Life, Your Choice. Wayne W. Dyer. Read by Wayne W. Dyer. (Running Time: 6 hrs.). 2005. 36.95 (978-1-59912-156-7(5)) Iofy Corp.

Choosing Your Own Greatness: Your Life, Your Choice. unabr. ed. Wayne W. Dyer. Read by Wayne W. Dyer. 6 CDs. (Running Time: 6 hrs.). (ENG.). 2005. audio compact disk 19.98 (978-1-59659-009-0(2), GildAudio) Pub: Gildan Media. Dist(s): HachBkGrp

Chop-Monster. Shelly Berg. (ENG.). 2002. audio compact disk 120.00 (978-0-7390-2924-4(X)); audio compact disk 7.00 (978-0-7390-2918-3(5)); audio compact disk 70.00 (978-0-7390-2922-0(3)) Alfred Pub.

Chop-Monster. Shelly Berg. (ENG.). 2002. audio compact disk 12.00 (978-0-7390-2923-7(1)) Alfred Pub.

Chop-Monster: Teacher's Score. Shelly Berg. (ENG.). 2002. audio compact disk 39.95 (978-0-7390-2969-5(X)) Alfred Pub.

Chop-Monster, Bk 1: Teacher's Score, Score & CD. Shelly Berg. (ENG.). 2002. audio compact disk 29.95 (978-0-7390-2970-1(3)) Alfred Pub.

Chopin: Frederic the Great. (Vox - Turnabout Classical Ser.). 3.98 (CTX 4817); audio compact disk (ACD 8743) VOX Music Grp.

Chopin: The Greatest Hits. 1 cass. 10.98 (978-1-57908-163-8(0), 3609) Platinm Enter.

Chopin - Dvorak. Gordon Jeffries. 1 cass. (Running Time: 52 min.). 9.95 (978-1-55961-130-5(8)) Relaxtn Co.

Chopin in Paris. unabr. collector's ed. Tad Szulc. Read by Alexander Adams. 12 cass. (Running Time: 18 hrs.). 1998. 96.00 (978-0-7366-4332-0(X), 4803) Books on Tape.
During Chopin's eighteen years in Paris, he shone at the center of the talented artists who were defining their time-Hugo, Balzac, Stendhal, Delacroix, Liszt, Berlioz & of course, George Sand, a rebel feminist writer who became Chopin's lover & protector. When Chopin left his homeland ten years later, he moved first to Vienna, then to Paris, where he quickly gained fame & circle of powerful friends & acquaintances. Chopin made his mark as a musical genius.

Chopin Manuscript. Jeffery Deaver. Narrated by Alfred Molina. (Playaway Adult Fiction Ser.). 2009. 84.99 (978-1-60812-654-5(4)) Find a World.

Chopin Manuscript. Jeffery Deaver et al. Ed. by Jim Fusilli. Narrated by Alfred Molina. 2007. 19.95 (978-1-60393-064-2(7)) Audible.

Chopin Manuscript. unabr. ed. Jeffery Deaver et al. Read by Alfred Molina. (Running Time: 6 hrs.). 2008. 39.97 (978-1-4233-7908-9(X), 9781423379089, Brinc Audio MP3 Lib); 24.99 (978-1-4233-7907-2(1), 9781423379072, Brilliance MP3); 49.97 (978-1-4233-7989-8(6), 9781423379898, BADLE); audio compact disk 82.25 (978-1-4233-7703-0(6), 9781423377030, BriAudCD Unabrid); audio compact disk 29.95 (978-1-4233-7702-3(8), 9781423377023, Bril Audio CD Unabri) Brilliance Audio.

Chopper Ops. abr. ed. Mack Maloney. Read by Charlie O'Dowd. 2 vols. No. 1. 2003. (978-1-58807-570-3(2)) Am Pubng Inc.

Chopper Ops. abr. ed. Mack Maloney. Read by Charlie O'Dowd. 4 cass. (Running Time: 6 hrs.). (Chopper Ops Ser.: No. 1). 2003. 25.00 (978-1-58807-095-1(6)) Am Pubng Inc.
At 0230 hours, ArcLight 4, the most technically advanced armed cargo plane ever created, embarks on a midnight Scud hunt from an isolated American base in the Saudi desert. Then the ArcLight 4 vanishes off the face of the earth. For nine years, the fate of the Allied craft - its elite crew of U.S. Army Green Berets, Air Force top brass, and Defense Intelligence Agents - has remained a mystery. Until now. Fifty miles northeast of Baghdad, hidden behind the impenetrable walls of a guarded fortress is the key to one man's plan for world domination: the AC-130 ArcLight gunship. There's only one team in the world fearless enough to retrieve it - a special-forces squadron of America's bravest: trained, armed, and equipped for dead-on attack and assault. Their first chance at the ArcLight is their only chance, and the countdown to take-over has begun. Delivering high-pitch military action and hard-hitting techno suspense, CHOPPER OPS is the thrilling new series of the world's superpowers at war.

Choppers. David Armentrout & Patricia Armentrout. (Motorcycle Mania (CD-ROM) Ser.). (J). 2008. audio compact disk 24.95 (978-1-60472-768-5(3)) Rourke FL.

Chopping Spree. unabr. ed. Diane Mott Davidson. Read by Joyce Bean. 7 cass. (Running Time: 10 hrs.). (Goldy Schulz Culinary Mysteries Ser.: No. 11). 2002. 32.95 (978-1-59086-141-7(8), 1590861418, BAU); 82.25 (978-1-59086-142-4(6), 1590861426, Unabridge Lib Edns) Brilliance Audio.
For Colorado caterer Goldy Schulz, business isn't just booming - it's skyrocketing. But as her friend Marla is constantly warning her, "success can kill you." Goldy knows she needs to slow down before she breaks down, and she vows she'll do it - right after her next booking: a cocktail party for the Westside Mall's Elite Shoppers Club. It's the event of the shopping season: the Princess Without a Pricetag party for the wealthy shopaholics who drop at least a thousand dollars a week at the mall. Goldy has been hired by charming mall manager Barry Dean to cater the jewel-encrusted affair. But she has hardly begun setting up when she finds herself in the path of a truck that has no intention of stopping until both she and Barry are crushed beneath it. Muddied, bruised, embarrassed, but determined to do her job, Goldy manages to get the party started on time with the help of her trusted assistants Julian Teller and Liz Fury. But with the outbreak of an ugly spat among the guests, the behavior of Barry's flighty young girlfriend, and Barry's own strange actions after the truck incident, the event is - by Goldy's standards - a catastrophe. And it's about to get worse. When she goes to pick up the check, she finds an old friend lying dead in a pile of sale shoes - stabbed with one of Goldy's new knives. Hours later, Julian is the prime suspect in the murder. To prove Julian's innocence, Goldy must catch the real killer. But to do that, she will have to figure out why the victim was carrying a powerful narcotic. And why was a private investigator called in shortly before the murder? Was the killer connected to a mall renovation project - or the eviction of a disgruntled tenant? Or was the villian the odd lover out in a violent love triangle? Between whipping up Sweethearts' Swedish Meatballs, Quiche Me Quick, and Diamond Lovers' Hot Crab Dip, and digging up clues, Goldy knows this is going to be one tough case to crack. And her gourmet sleuth's instinct tells her the final course will be a real killer.

Chopping Spree. unabr. ed. Diane Mott Davidson. Read by Joyce Bean. (Running Time: 36000 sec.). (Goldy Schulz Culinary Mysteries Ser.: No. 11). 2004. audio compact disk 39.25 (978-1-59335-342-1(1), 1593353421, Brinc Audio MP3 Lib) Brilliance Audio.

Chopping Spree. unabr. ed. Diane Mott Davidson. Read by Joyce Bean. (Running Time: 10 hrs.). (Goldy Schulz Culinary Mysteries Ser.: No. 11). 2004. 39.25 (978-1-59710-137-0(0), 1597101370, BADLE); 24.95 (978-1-59710-136-3(2), 1597101362, BAD) Brilliance Audio.

Chopping Spree. unabr. ed. Diane Mott Davidson. Read by Joyce Bean. (Running Time: 10 hrs.). (Goldy Schulz Culinary Mysteries Ser.: No. 11). 2004. 24.95 (978-1-59335-012-3(0), 1593350120) Soulmate Audio Bks.

Choral Club. bk. (978-0-687-08552-1(7)); bk. (978-0-687-08612-2(4)); bk. (978-0-687-08641-2(8)); bk. 12.00 (978-0-687-08828-7(3)); bk. 12.00 (978-0-687-08934-5(4)); bk. 12.00 (978-0-687-08947-5(6)); bk. 12.00 (978-0-687-09124-9(1)); bk. 12.00 (978-0-687-09128-7(4)); bk. 12.00 (978-0-687-09129-4(2)); bk. (978-0-687-09873-6(4)); bk. (978-0-687-09903-0(X)); bk. (978-0-687-09943-6(9)) Abingdon.

Choral Club. 2004. bk. 2.00 (978-0-687-32619-8(2)) Abingdon.

Choral Club CD Set. 2005. bk. 10.00 (978-0-687-32639-6(7)) Abingdon.

Choral Club CD 143. Composed by Cathy Bryant. 2004. bk. (978-0-687-07467-9(3)) Abingdon.

Choral Club 141 Rehearsal/Accompaniment. Ken Harold Dosso. 2004. bk. 10.00 (978-0-687-06241-6(1)) Abingdon.

Choraltrax CD 3. Created by Allegis Publications. 1995. audio compact disk 24.99 (978-5-557-68453-8(0)) Allegis.

Chord Melody Solos. 2 CDs. (Jazz Guitar Standards Ser.). 2004. audio compact disk 24.95 (978-0-7866-7024-6(X), WMB011BCD) Mel Bay.

Chord Progression & the Runs & Riffs That Flow Out of Them. Duane Shinn. Read by Duane Shinn. 6 cass. (Running Time: 6 hrs.). bk. 199.00 set. (CPRR-1) Duane Shinn.

Chord Substitutions. Duane Shinn. 1 cass. 19.95 (CP-12) Duane Shinn.
Presents 3 basic principles that will keep one busy substituting chords.

Chords & Thyme. Edward Flower. 1999. pap. bk. 32.95 (978-0-7866-4470-4(2), 97054CDP) Mel Bay.

Chords Complete! Bert Konowitz. 1 CD. (ENG.). 1999. audio compact disk 10.00 (978-0-7390-0276-6(7), 18482) Alfred Pub.

***Chords of Grace.** Fletcher Nick. (ENG.). 2007. audio compact disk 17.99 (978-92-822-6892-6(6)) Pub: Kingsway Pubns GBR. Dist(s): STL Dist NA

Chords, Progressions, Substitutions & Pieces. John Griggs. 2001. per. 22.95 (978-0-7866-3838-3(9)) Mel Bay.

Chorus for Survival: Poem Fourteen see Twentieth-Century Poetry in English, No. 8, Recordings of Poets Reading Their Own Poetry

Chorus of Cultures Music Tapes: Developing Literacy Through Multicultural Poetry. Poems. 4 cass. (Chorus of Cultures Ser.). (J). (gr. 1-6). 1993. 45.00 set. (978-1-56334-328-5(2)) Hampton-Brown.
Fresh musical arrangements of 28 songs & poems from the Poetry Anthology.

Chorus of Stones: The Private Life of War. Susan Griffin. Read by Susan Griffin. 1 cass. (Running Time: 95 min.). 1993. 10.95 (978-0-7822-0452-0(X), 530) C G Jung IL.
Drawing from her award-winning book A Chorus of Stones, Ms. Griffin challenges the apparent duality between private & public realms & restores a larger dimension of meaning to private life while revealing the secret significance of public events. In fusing the two realms she creates a radical new vision of both war & gender. Part of the conference set Who Do We Think We Are?: The Mystery & Muddle of Gender.

Chorus of Stones: The Private Life of War. unabr. ed. Susan Griffin. 2 cass. 1992. 18.00 set. (OC307-67) Sound Horizons AV.

Choruses: The Greatest Hits. 1 cass. 1997. 10.98 (978-1-57908-165-2(7), 3614) Platinm Enter.

***Chosen.** P. C. Cast. Read by Edwina Wren. (Running Time: 8 hrs. 20 mins.). (house of Night: Ser.). (YA). 2009. 64.99 (978-1-74214-188-6(9), 9781742141886) Pub: Bolinda Pubng AUS. Dist(s): Bolinda Pub Inc

Chosen. Chaim Potok. Read by Jim Weiss. 2002. 64.00 (978-0-7366-8814-7(5)) Books on Tape.

Chosen. Chaim Potok. 2005. audio compact disk 29.99 (978-1-4193-5017-7(X)) Recorded Bks.

Chosen. unabr. ed. P. C. Cast & Kristin Cast. Read by Edwina Wren. 7 CDs. (Running Time: 8 hrs. 20 mins.). (House of Night Ser.: No. 3). (YA). 2008. audio compact disk 83.95 (978-1-74214-087-2(4), 9781742140872) Pub: Bolinda Pubng AUS. Dist(s): Bolinda Pub Inc

***Chosen.** unabr. ed. P. C. Cast & Kristin Cast. Read by Edwina Wren. (Running Time: 8 hrs. 20 mins.). (House of Night Ser.). (YA). 2010. 43.95 (978-1-74214-676-8(7), 9781742146768) Pub: Bolinda Pubng AUS. Dist(s): Bolinda Pub Inc

Chosen. unabr. ed. Ted Dekker. Narrated by Adam Verner. (Books of History Chronicles: Bk. 1). (ENG.). (YA). 2008. 16.09 (978-1-60814-456-3(9)) Oasis Audio.

Chosen. unabr. ed. Ted Dekker. Narrated by Adam Verner. (Running Time: 5 hrs. 28 mins. 18 sec.). (Books of History Chronicles: Bk. 1). (ENG.). (YA). (gr. 8-13). 2008. audio compact disk 22.99 (978-1-59859-270-2(X)) Oasis Audio.

Chosen. unabr. ed. Chaim Potok. Narrated by Jonathan Davis. 8 pieces. (Running Time: 10 hrs. 45 mins.). (YA). 2003. 71.00 (978-1-4025-2199-7(5)) Recorded Bks.

Chosen. unabr. ed. L. J. Smith. (Running Time: 6 hrs.). (Night World Ser.: Vol. 5). 2010. 39.97 (978-1-4418-2054-9(X), 9781441820549, BADLE); 19.99 (978-1-4418-2053-2(1), 9781441820532, BAD) Brilliance Audio.

Chosen. unabr. ed. L. J. Smith. Read by Julia Whelan. (Running Time: 5 hrs.). (Night World Ser.: Vol. 5). 2010. 39.97 (978-1-4418-2052-5(3), 9781441820525, Brinc Audio MP3 Lib); 19.99 (978-1-4418-2051-8(5), 9781441820518, Brilliance MP3); audio compact disk 19.99 (978-1-4418-2049-5(3), 9781441820495, Bril Audio CD Unabri); audio compact disk 59.97 (978-1-4418-2050-1(7), 9781441820501, BriAudCD Unabrid) Brilliance Audio.

Chosen. unabr. collector's ed. Chaim Potok. Read by Dan Lazar. 6 cass. (Running Time: 9 hrs.). 1986. 48.00 (978-0-7366-1069-8(3), 1996) Books on Tape.
Set in New York toward the end of WW II, this is the story of two teenage Jewish boys, one the son of a Zionist, the other of a Russian Hassidic. They turn to each other in a fine show of male bonding.

Chosen by a Horse: How a Broken Horse Fixed a Broken Heart. unabr. ed. Susan Richards. Read by Lorna Raver. (Running Time: 23400 sec.). 2007. 54.95 (978-1-4332-1282-6(X)); audio compact disk 29.95 (978-1-4332-1284-0(6)); audio compact disk & audio compact disk 63.00 (978-1-4332-1283-3(8)) Blckstn Audio.

Chosen by a Horse: How a Broken Horse Fixed a Broken Heart. unabr. ed. Susan Richards. Read by Lorna Raver. (Running Time: 23400 sec.). 2008. 19.95 (978-1-4332-1405-9(9)); audio compact disk 19.95 (978-1-4332-1406-6(7)) Blckstn Audio.

Chosen Forever: A Memoir. unabr. ed. Susan Richards. Read by Lorna Raver. (Running Time: 7 hrs. 0 mins.). 2008. 29.95 (978-1-4332-4376-9(8)); 44.95 (978-1-4332-4372-1(5)); audio compact disk 60.00 (978-1-4332-4373-8(3)) Blckstn Audio.

Chosen Forever: A Memoir. unabr. ed. Susan Richards. (Running Time: 7 hrs. 0 mins.). 2008. cass. & cass. 29.95 (978-1-4332-4374-5(1)) Blckstn Audio.

Chosen Forever: A Memoir. unabr. ed. Susan Richards. Read by Lorna Raver. 6 CDs. (Running Time: 7 hrs.). 2008. audio compact disk 26.95 (978-1-4332-4375-2(X)) Blckstn Audio.

Chosen One. unabr. ed. Carol Lynch Williams. Read by Jenna Lamia. 5 CDs. (Running Time: 5 hrs. 30 mins. 0 sec.). (ENG.). (YA). (gr. 7). 2009. audio compact disk 24.99 (978-1-4272-0706-7(2)) Pub: Macmill Audio. Dist(s): Macmillan

***Chosen One.** unabr. ed. Carol Lynch Williams. Read by Jenna Lamia. 2009. 12.99 (978-1-4272-0707-4(0)) Pub: Macmill Audio. Dist(s): Macmillan

Chosen Prey. John Sandford, pseud. Narrated by Richard Ferrone. 11 CDs. (Running Time: 11 hrs. 45 mins.). (Prey Ser.). audio compact disk 97.00 (978-1-4025-0483-9(7)) Recorded Bks.

Chosen Prey. unabr. ed. John Sandford, pseud. Narrated by Richard Ferrone. 9 cass. (Running Time: 11 hrs. 45 mins.). (Prey Ser.). 2001. 81.00 (978-0-7887-5984-0(1), 96260K8) Recorded Bks.
James Qatar fancies himself an artist, though his most compelling work comes from using his computer to combine photos of unsuspecting women with pornographic images from the Internet. But when one of his "models" discovers his secret, Qatar develops a more stimulating artistic talent: murder. Only Lucas Davenport has the skill to track down Qatar before he creates another masterpiece.

Chosen to Be God's Prophet: Lessons from the Life of Samuel. unabr. ed. Henry T. Blackaby. 4 cass. (Running Time: 7 hrs.). 2003. 24.99 (978-1-58926-256-0(5), T10M-0150) Oasis Audio.
Shows from the Scriptures how God worked through the life of Samuel, taking him from a young lad asleep in the tabernacle and shaping him into becoming God's powerful voice for his age.

Chosen to Be God's Prophet: Lessons from the Life of Samuel. unabr. ed. Henry T. Blackaby. Narrated by Wayne Shepherd. (Biblical Legacy Ser.). (ENG.). 2004. 18.89 (978-1-60814-116-6(0)) Oasis Audio.

Chosen to Be God's Prophet: Lessons from the Life of Samuel. unabr. abr. ed. Henry T. Blackaby. Narrated by Wayne Shepherd. 6 CDs. (Running Time: 7 hrs.). (Biblical Legacy Ser.). (ENG.). 2004. audio compact disk 26.99 (978-1-58926-257-7(3), T10M-015D) Oasis Audio.

Chosen Vessel. Chuck Smith. 6 cass. (Running Time: 6 hrs. 15 mins.). (Leadership Ser.). 2001. 13.99 (978-0-936728-95-7(7)) Word For Today.
Messages directed for those who are interested in leadership.

Chosen Vessel Vol. 2: Leadership Series. 2003. audio compact disk (978-1-931713-89-4(8)) Word For Today.

Chosen Voices: The Story of the American Cantorate. Mark Slobin. (Music in American Life Ser.). 1990. 11.00 (978-0-252-01566-3(5)) Pub: U of Ill Pr. Dist(s): Chicago Distribution Ctr

Chris Hanburger. 1 cass. (Reading With Winners Ser.). 1984. 32.95 (978-0-89811-124-8(2), 8805C); Lets Talk Assocs.

Chris Hanburger: Linebacker. Read by Chris Hanburger. 1 cass. 9.95 (978-0-89811-099-9(8), 7150) Lets Talk Assocs.
Chris Hanburger talks about the people & events which influenced his career, & his own approach to his speciality, discussion format.

Chris Heimerdinger's Adventures with the Book of Mormon. Chris Heimerdinger. 1 cass. 7.98 (978-1-55503-424-5(1), 06004539) Covenant Comms.
Fireside talk about the research that gave substance to his novels.

Chris Mazza. unabr. ed. Read by Chris Mazza & Rebekah Presson. Ed. by James McKinley. 1 cass. (Running Time: 29 min.). (New Letters on the Air Ser.). 1992. 10.00 (112092); 18.00 2-sided cass. New Letters.
Mazza is interviewed by Rebekah Presson & reads from her book, How to Leave a Country.

Chris Mouse & the Christmas House Audio Story Book. Deanna Luke. Read by Eric Martin. Adapted by Oakridge Recording Staff. (J). 2001. 5.95 (978-1-928777-34-2(1), BOW Bks) Blessing Our Wrld.

Chris Offut. unabr. ed. Ed. by Jim McKinley. Prod. by Rebekah Presson. 1 cass. (Running Time: 29 min.). (New Letters on the Air Ser.). 1994. 10.00 (091093) New Letters.
At age 34, Offut's memoir "The Same River Twice" has been called by one critic "road autobiography at its Kerouackian best." Offut reads from his book & reflects on his Appalachian upbringing & work as a dishwasher & traveling carnival employee.

Chris Proctor/Only Now. Chris Proctor. 1999. pap. bk. 19.95 (978-0-7866-3841-3(9), 96903BCD) Mel Bay.

Chris Tomlin: Live from Austin Music Hall. Contrib. by Chris Tomlin et al. Prod. by Ed Cash. 2005. audio compact disk 9.99 (978-5-558-68480-3(1)) Pt of Grace Ent.

Christ: A Crisis in the Life of God. unabr. ed. Jack Miles. 9 CDs. (Running Time: 11 hrs. 20 mins.). 2001. audio compact disk 72.00 (978-0-7366-8462-0(X)) Books on Tape.
Jack Miles takes a provocative and revisionary look at the life of Christ.

Christ: A Crisis in the Life of God. unabr. ed. Jack Miles. Read by Grover Gardner. 8 cass. (Running Time: 12 hrs.). 2001. 64.00 (978-0-7366-8328-9(3)) Books on Tape.
A provocative and revisionary look at the life of Jesus, in which many of the most well-worn truths about Christ are recontextualized and revisited. It does not look for the historical Jesus, but takes the Gospels as the sole source about his life. The "crisis" to which the title refers is the continued subjugation of the Jews after five hundred years. God has not come to save them in a conventional way, but instead causes his son to appear as a Jew, inflicting upon himself in advance the fate that was destined for the Jews. By rising from the dead, he sidesteps this fate, and offers the promise of cosmic victory. This complex book will cause you to see Christ's life and passion anew.

Christ: Lessons from His Life. Don J. Black. 1 cass. 7.98 (978-1-55503-032-2(7), 060011) Covenant Comms.
Stories from the scriptures.

Christ: Meditation Scriptures on Who Christ Is & What He Did for You. Excerpts. Compiled by Steven B. Stevens. Voice by Steven B. Stevens. Engineer Thomas A. Webb. Executive Producer Thomas A. Webb. 1 CD. (Running Time: 38 mins.). (Promises for Life Ser.). 2005. audio compact disk 14.95 (978-0-9726363-4-6(X), CD-109, Promises for Life) Brite Bks.
Selected meditation scriptures focused on who Christ is and what he did for you. Un-unabridged, non-commentary, non-denominational audio reading of like topic bible promises from multiple translations all on the subject of the Christ.

***Christ above All.** Gordon Ferguson. (ENG.). 2009. 12.00 (978-0-9842006-2-7(2)) Illumination MA.

Christ & Antichrist: Understanding the Awesome Power of the Anointing & Its Enemies in Your Life. Mac Hammond. 6 cass. (Running Time: 60 min.). (Annointing Ser.: Vol. 1). 1998. 36.00 Set. (978-1-57399-064-6(7)) Mac Hammond.

Christ & the Eucharist. James S. Sullivan. 1 cass. (Inspiring Presentations from the National Rosary Congress Ser.). 2.50 (978-1-56036-097-1(6)) AMI Pr.

Christ Arose. Contrib. by Lari Goss. 1996. 24.95 (978-0-00-513570-9(2), 75608641) Pub: Brentwood Music. Dist(s): H Leonard

Christ Arose with He's Alive. Contrib. by Mike Speck & Cliff Duren. 2007. audio compact disk 24.99 (978-5-557-54325-5(2)) Lillenas.

Christ As a Revolutionary Figure. unabr. ed. James Pike. 1 cass. (Running Time: 1 hr. 27 min.). 1969. 11.00 (04501) Big Sur Tapes.
A look at Palestine before & after Christ & the considerable evidence for the thesis that Christ was a leader of revolution in a time in history with remarkable similarities to the present.

Christ As Master. Elbert Willis. 1 cass. (Learning Lordship Ser.). 4.00 Fill the Gap.

Christ at the Crossroads, Set. Charles R. Swindoll. 9 cass. 1998. 44.95 (978-1-57972-115-2(X)) Insight Living.

Christ-Centered Living. Robert L. Millet. 2 cass. 1994. 11.95 Set. (978-1-57008-087-6(9), Bkcraft Inc) Deseret Bk.

Christ Displays His Glory. John MacArthur, Jr. 4 cass. 15.95 (20150, HarperThor); 3.50 study guide. (405150, HarperThor) HarpC GBR.

Christ Has Conquered All. Contrib. by Michael Lawrence & Gary Rhodes. Created by Kristie Braselton. 2007. audio compact disk 24.98 (978-5-557-53097-2(5), Word Music) Word Enter.

Christ Has Risen, Alleluia. Contrib. by Joe E. Parks. 1992. 7.98 (978-0-00-543873-2(X), 75607908) Pub: Brentwood Music. Dist(s): H Leonard

***Christ, His Church & the Apostles.** Benedict XVI, pseud. Read by Deacon Toby Gaines. (ENG.). 2010. audio compact disk 18.95 (978-1-936231-20-1(4)) Cath Audio.

Christ in All the Scriptures. 2005. 15.00 (978-1-933561-06-6(8)) BFM Books.

Christ in Flanders see Great French & Russian Stories, Vol. 1, A Collection

Christ in Flanders. 1979. (N-29) Jimcin Record.

Christ in Gethsemane. Monks of Solesmes Staff. 1 CD. 1989. audio compact disk 16.95 (978-1-55725-124-4(X)) Paraclete MA.

Christ in the Life of the Soul: 12 Tape Audio Retreat. Perf. by John Vennari. 12 cass. (Running Time: 12 hrs.). 2000. 49.95 (20224) Cath Treas.
These outstanding conferences are based upon the classic spiritual teachings of Don Marmion (1858-1923), one of the greatest masters of the spiritual life in the 20th century. His writings have been a source of education & inspiration for thousands of priests, religious & laymen for decades. Abbot Marmion's cause for canonization has been introduced in Rome. Now that the famous book, "Christ in the Life of the Soul" is out of print, Mr. Vennari does a great service for Catholics by using it as the basis for 12 talks on Christ & his plan for the Divine Supernatural Adoption of souls, Christ as Cause of All Grace, as Mystical Body, author of our redemption & the Holy Spirit, the Spirit of Jesus.

Christ in the Realms of the Dead. Instructed by Manly P. Hall. 8.95 (978-0-89314-024-3(4), C860330) Philos Res.

Christ in You: The Anointed One & His Anointing, 2. Bill Winston. 3 cass. (Running Time: 2hr.27min.). (C). 2003. 15.00 (978-1-931289-37-5(9)) Pub: B Winston Min. Dist(s): Anchor Distributors

Christ in You: The Hope of Glory. Gloria Copeland. 4 cass. 1990. 20.00 Set incl. study guide. (978-0-88114-831-2(8)) K Copeland Pubns.
Biblical teaching on Christ's glory.

Christ in You: The Power of Holiness. Bill Winston. 2 cass. (Running Time: 1hr.45min.). (C). 2002. 10.00 (978-1-931289-36-8(0)) Pub: B Winston Min. Dist(s): Anchor Distributors

Christ in You: The Spirit of Counsel. Bill Winston. 4 cass. (Running Time: 3hr.01min.). (C). 2003. 20.00 (978-1-931289-58-0(1)) Pub: B Winston Min. Dist(s): Anchor Distributors

Christ in You: The Spirit of Knowledge. Bill Winston. 3 cass. (Running Time: 3hr.01min.). (C). 2003. 15.00 (978-1-931289-35-1(2)) Pub: B Winston Min. Dist(s): Anchor Distributors

Christ in You: The Spirit of the Lord. Bill Winston. 3 cass. (Running Time: 2hr.09min.). (C). 2003. 15.00 (978-1-931289-81-8(6)) Pub: B Winston Min. Dist(s): Anchor Distributors

Christ in You: The Spirit of Understanding. Bill Winston. 2 cass. (Running Time: 1hr.54min.). (C). 2003. 10.00 (978-1-931289-34-4(4)) Pub: B Winston Min. Dist(s): Anchor Distributors

Christ in You: The Spirit of Wisdom. Bill Winston. 3 cass. (Running Time: 1hr.53min.). (C). 2003. 15.00 (978-1-931289-33-7(6)) Pub: B Winston Min. Dist(s): Anchor Distributors

Christ in You Vol. 2,Pt. 2I: The Spirit of Knowledge-Power of Revelation. Bill Winston. 4 cass. (Running Time: 3hr.30min.). (C). 2003. 20.00 (978-1-931289-39-9(5)) Pub: B Winston Min. Dist(s): Anchor Distributors

Christ in You the Anointed One. Featuring Bill Winston. 3. 2003. audio compact disk 24.00 (978-1-59544-061-7(5)) Pub: B Winston Min. Dist(s): Anchor Distributors
Is there a noticeable difference in your lifestyle as a Believer versus when you were unsaved? If the answer is yes that's good news. If the answer is no, then there is cause for concern.

Christ Is Risen, Truly Risen: Easter Chants & Anthems. Directed By Paul French. Contrib. by William Ferris Chorale. 2007. audio compact disk 17.00 (978-1-58459-358-4(X)) Wrld Lib Pubns.

Christ Like Living Series, Set. Elbert Willis. 4 cass. 13.00 Fill the Gap.

Christ Lives: Chanted by Kriyananda. J. Donald Walters. 2000. audio compact disk 15.95 (978-1-56589-776-2(5)) Pub: Crystal Clarity. Dist(s): Natl Bk Netwk

Christ Mastery Teachings: 'Christ Reveals the True Essence of His Teachings' Speeches. Lea Chapin. 6 cass. (Running Time: 6 hrs). 2003. 70.00 (978-0-9762974-1-3(8)) Health Altern.
In the fall of 2003, Christ channeled His inspirational teachings through medium and intuitive counselor Lea Chapin. The Twelve Mastery Teachings are the truth principles Christ taught during His ministry on earth over two thousand years ago. With God's Grace, Christ's desire is for humanity to reawaken to their own divinity and to embrace and embody His teachings in the fullest essence. Each Mastery Lesson holds and carries the vibrational essence of Christ's Healing Power of Love.Christ Mastery TeachingsI. LoveII. PowerIII. TruthIV. OnenessV. EnlightenmentVI. ForgivenessVII. HopeVIII. FaithIX. RejuvenationX. RemembranceXI. PeaceXII. Joy.

Christ, My Life: Philippians. Robert A. Cook. 4 cass. (Running Time: 6 hrs.). 2000. 9.99 (978-7-902031-55-4(0)) Chrstn Dup Intl.

Christ, My Life - Philippians. Narrated by Robert A. Cook. 4 cass. (Dr. Robert A. Cook's Teaching Ser.). 9.98 ea. (RC21) Chrstn Dup Intl.

Christ of the Celts: The Healing of Creation. J. Philip Newell. Read by J. Philip Newell. Music by Kirkwall City Pipe Band. (ENG.). 2008. (978-0-9798958-7-6(1), NewBeg) Mat Media.

Christ of the Celts (Unabridged Audio) Healing of Creation. J. Philip Newell. Read by J. Philip Newell. (ENG.). 2008. audio compact disk 36.95 (978-0-9798958-6-9(3), NewBeg) Mat Media.

Christ Our Refuge: The Safest Spot in the Universe. 2005. 15.00 (978-1-933561-00-4(9)) BFM Books.

***Christ Plays in Ten Thousand Places: A Conversation in Spiritual Theology.** unabr. ed. Eugene H. Peterson. Narrated by Grover Gardner. (ENG.). 2005. 19.98 (978-1-59644-305-1(7), Hovel Audio) christianaud.

Christ Plays in Ten Thousand Places: A Conversation in Spiritual Theology. unabr. ed. Eugene H. Peterson. Narrated by Grover Gardner. 2 MP3 CDs. (Running Time: 15 hrs. 0 mins. 0 sec.). (ENG.). 2005. lp 24.98 (978-1-59644-303-7(0), Hovel Audio); audio compact disk 32.98 (978-1-59644-304-4(9), Hovel Audio) christianaud.
In this first book in a five-volume series on spiritual theology, Eugene Peterson firmly grounds spirituality once more in Trinitarian theology and offers a clear, practical statement of what it means to actually live out the Christian life.

Christ Revealed. 2003. 6.00 (978-1-58602-167-2(2)); audio compact disk 10.00 (978-1-58602-168-9(0)) E L Long.

Christ Rules in the Midst of His Enemies. Derek Prince. 1 cass. (B-7005) Derek Prince.

Christ saves, heals & frees the Family see Cristo salva, sana y libera a la Familia

Christ the Deliverer. Kenneth E. Hagin. 1 cass. 4.95 (SH29) Faith Lib Pubns.

Christ the Icon. Created by World Library Publications. 2005. audio compact disk 17.00 (978-1-58459-240-2(0)) Wrld Lib Pubns.

Christ the Lord: Out of Egypt. unabr. ed. Anne Rice. 8 cass. (Running Time: 12 hrs.). 2005. 72.00 (978-1-4159-2505-8(4)); audio compact disk 84.15 (978-1-4159-2506-5(2)) Pub: Books on Tape. Dist(s): NetLibrary CO

Christ the Lord: Out of Egypt. unabr. ed. Anne Rice. Read by Josh Heine. (Running Time: 9 hrs. 30 mins.). (Anne Rice Ser.). (ENG.). 2006. audio compact disk 19.99 (978-0-7393-4092-9(1), Random AudioBks) Pub: Random Audio Pubg. Dist(s): Random

Christ the Lord: The Road to Cana. unabr. ed. Anne Rice. Narrated by James Naughton. 6 CDs. (Running Time: 6 hrs. 45 mins.). 2008. audio compact disk 70.00 (978-1-4159-4627-5(2), BksonTape) Pub: Random Audio Pubg. Dist(s): Random

Christ the Lord: The Road to Cana. unabr. ed. Anne Rice. Read by James Naughton. (Running Time: 7 hrs.). (Anne Rice Ser.). (ENG.). 2008. 17.50 (978-0-7393-1604-7(4), Random AudioBks); audio compact disk 34.95 (978-0-7393-1603-0(6), Random AudioBks) Pub: Random Audio Pubg. Dist(s): Random

Christ the Messenger. unabr. ed. Vivekananda. Read by John Abbot. 1 cass. (Running Time: 37 min.). 1988. 7.95 (978-1-882915-07-1(0)) Vedanta Ctr Atlanta.
Universal aspects of Christ & His message.

Christ, the Saviour, Is Born! Read by Mother Basilea Schlink. 1 cass. (Running Time: 30 min.). 1985. (0215) Evang Sisterhood Mary.
A Christmas message for those who are seeking the Saviour; The Name of Jesus; a refuge in distress & trouble.

Christ the Tiger. unabr. ed. Thomas Howard. Read by Mark Taheny. 3 cass. 14.95 set. (337) Ignatius Pr.
In this semi-autobiography, Thomas Howard is able to bring out the true vitality of what the Christian faith is & should be, a redemptive faith that changes us.

Christ X-rays His Church. unabr. ed. Warren W. Wiersbe. Read by Warren W. Wiersbe. 4 cass. (Running Time: 4 hrs. 45 min.). 1989. 18.95 (978-0-8474-2356-9(5)) Back to Bible.
A study from the letters to the churches in Revelation, to challenge & encourage believers.

Christantemo. 2004. pap. bk. 32.75 (978-1-55592-343-3(7)) Weston Woods.

Christian Acts of Kindness, unabr. ed. Random Acts of Kindness Foundation Staff. Read by Edward Asner & Meredith MacRae. 2 cass. (Running Time: 3 hrs.). 1999. 17.95 (978-1-57453-338-5(X)) Audio Lit.
At the heart of Christianity is a very simple message of love & kindness, the most powerful tools people have to affect their lives & the lives of those around them. These inspiring stores present shining examples of everyday Samaritans around the world living the Christian credo to "love thy neighbor as thyself".

Christian & Catholic: The Catholic Identity. Eugene LaVerdiere. 1 cass. (Running Time: 55 min.). 1995. 8.95 (TAH345) Alba Hse Comns.
In this refreshing & informative audio cassette discussion, Fr. Laverdiere relates with sincerity to the three aspects of our faith that make the Catholic unique - the universal nature of our church, the depth of tradition, & the sacramental aspect.

Christian & Catholic Family Enjoying the New Millennium. Andrew Cusack. 1 cass. (Running Time: 42 min.). 1999. 9.95 (TAH414) Alba Hse Comns.
Presents moving insights in an experiential way that may provide the catalyst for reforming ourselves in preparation for the next chapter in our salvation history.

Christian & Government. 6 cass. 19.95 (20127, HarperThor) HarpC GBR.

Christian & His Money. Derek Prince. 1 cass. 1989. 5.95 (I-4266) Derek Prince.
Right handling of our money determines our relationship with God & is a key to spiritual progress.

Christian & Wealth. unabr. ed. Warren W. Wiersbe. Read by Warren W. Wiersbe. 2 cass. (Running Time: 2 hrs. 30 min.). 1989. 9.95 (978-0-8474-2344-6(1)) Back to Bible.
An examination of different aspects of wealth, exhorting biblical stewardship.

Christian Approach to Business Economics. unabr. ed. Charles Wolff. 1 cass. (Running Time: 1 hr. 29 min.). 12.95 (724) J Norton Pubs.
An explanation of profit, property rights, production, & other fundamentals of the free market. The relationship between business & society & the fallacies of socialism receive emphasis.

Christian Approach to Business Management. unabr. ed. Art Meier. 1 cass. (Running Time: 59 min.). 12.95 (725) J Norton Pubs.
Offers practical advice on how to make decisions in a wide range of areas, including negotiation, delegation of authority, hiring & firing, payments, customer servicing, & obtaining repeating business.

Christian Approach to Family Financial Problems. unabr. ed. Scott Cummings. 1 cass. (Running Time: 1 hr. 11 min.). 12.95 (722) J Norton Pubs.

Christian Approach to Family Problems. unabr. ed. Millard Sall. 1 cass. (Running Time: 1 hr. 9 min.). 12.95 (718) J Norton Pubs.

Christian Approach to Parent-Teen Relations. unabr. ed. Rex Rook. 1 cass. (Running Time: 1 hr. 11 min.). 12.95 (721) J Norton Pubs.

Christian Approach to Raising Children. unabr. ed. Hosted by Millard Sall. 1 cass. (Famous Authorities Talk about Children Ser.). 12.95 (AF0720) J Norton Pubs.

***Christian Atheist: When You Believe in God but Live As If He Doesn't Exist.** Craig Groeschel. (Running Time: 5 hrs. 52 mins. 11 sec.). (ENG.). 2010. 19.99 (978-0-310-59742-1(0)) Zondervan.

***Christian Atheist: When You Believe in God but Live As If He Doesn't Exist.** unabr. ed. Craig Groeschel. (Running Time: 5 hrs. 52 mins. 11 sec.). (ENG.). 2010. audio compact disk 24.99 (978-0-310-32792-9(X)) Zondervan.

Christian Basis of Motivation & Success in Business. unabr. ed. Bill Butler. 1 cass. (Running Time: 52 min.). 12.95 (726) J Norton Pubs.
Keys to success for the Christian businessman, Bill Butler illustrates his points with a wealth of interesting & entertaining personal anecdotes.

Christian Commitment: The Responsibility to the Cross. Jawanza Kunjufu. 1 cass. (Running Time: 60 mins.). 1999. 5.95 (AT5) African Am Imag.

Christian Communal Life. Olga Wittekind. 3 cass. (Running Time: 3 hrs. 30 min.). (Common Territory, Different Maps: the Archetypal Underpinnings of Religious Practice Ser.). 1994. 22.95 set. (978-0-7822-0479-7(1), 555) C G Jung IL.

Christian Construction, Pt. 1. Gordon Clark. 1 cass. (Lectures on Apologetics: No. 15). 5.00 Trinity Found.

Christian Construction, Pt. 2. Gordon Clark. 1 cass. (Lectures on Apologetics: No. 16). 5.00 Trinity Found.

Christian Counseling for Pastors & Laymen. Frank Minirth & Paul Meier. Read by Frank Minirth & Paul Meier. 2 cass. (Running Time: 2 hrs.). (Minirth & Meier Home Counseling Audio Library). 1994. 14.95 set. (978-1-56707-041-5(8)) Dallas Christ Recs.
Counseling & leadership skills for all areas of ministry.

Christian Dilemma: The Sin Within. John MacArthur, Jr. 2 cass. pap. bk. 8.25 (HarperThor) HarpC GBR.

Christian Dior: The Man Who Made the World Look New. unabr. ed. Marie-France Pochna. Read by Nadia May. 9 cass. (Running Time: 13 hrs.). 1997. 62.95 (978-0-7861-1423-8(1), 2299) Blckstn Audio.
The legendary French fashion designer caused a worldwide sensation in 1947, in a Paris still groping to recover from the devastations of wartime occupation. Reintroducing the flowing, ankle-length skirt, gave women back their long-lost sense of freedom, femininity, & joie de vivre. The collection, with its pinched waist & generous folds of fabric, also reestablished Paris as the center of world fashion.

Christian Dior: The Man Who Made the World Look New. unabr. ed. Marie-France Pochna. Read by Nadia May. Tr. by Joanna Savill. (Running Time: 45000 sec.). 2007. audio compact disk 29.95 (978-0-7861-0371-3(X)) Blckstn Audio.

Christian Dior: The Man Who Made the World Look New. unabr. ed. Marie-Franch Poshna. Tr. by Joanna Savill. (Running Time: 45000 sec.). 2007. audio compact disk 90.00 (978-0-7861-0370-6(1)) Blckstn Audio.

Christian Discernment. unabr. ed. H. Edward Rowe. 1 cass. (Running Time: 40 min.). 12.95 (715) J Norton Pubs.

Christian Doctrine of New Creation. Bede Griffiths. 1 cass. (Running Time: 1 hr. 22 min.). 1982. 11.00 (03302) Big Sur Tapes.
Coming from his ashram in India, Father Bede Griffiths addresses the 7th International Transpersonal Association meetings in Bombay regarding Christian doctrine & modern science & mysticism.

Christian Duplications International. 12 cass. 1994. 29.98 Set. Chrstn Dup Intl.
Bibles.

Christian Education - A Family Approach: National Association of Evangelicals, 47th Annual Convention, Columbus, Ohio, March 7-9, 1989. Donald M. Joy. 1 cass. (Workshops Ser.: No. 21-Wednesd). 1989. 4.25 ea. 1-8 tapes.; 4.00 ea. 9 or more tapes. Nat Assn Evan.

Christian Factor in Anti-Semitism. Derek Prince. 1 cass. 5.95 (4391) Derek Prince.
By 400 A.D. the Church had propagated three false interpretations of Scripture which incited 16 centuries of vicious anti-Semitism. One outcome was the holocaust, but the end is not yet.

Christian Family. unabr. ed. Deborah L. Butler. 1 cass. (Running Time: 1 hr. 30 mins.). 2001. 5.00 (A123) Word Faith Pubng.

Christian Fatherhood: The Eight Comitments of St. Joseph's Covenant Keepers. Stephen Wood. Read by Stephen Wood. Contrib. by James Burnham. 2 cass. (Running Time: 4 hrs. 30 min.). 1997. 19.95 (978-0-9658582-2-9(7)) Family Life Ctr.

Christian for All Christians: Essays in Honor of C. S. Lewis. unabr. ed. Andrew Walker. Ed. by Robin Lawson & James Patrick. 7 cass. (Running Time: 10 hrs. 30 min.). 1994. 49.95 (978-0-7861-0681-3(6), 1467) Blckstn Audio.
Looks at the influence & friendships that helped shape the real Clive Staples Lewis - Christian apologist, moral philosopher, literary critic, poet & fantasy writer. Examines the reasons for his enduring popularity with virtually all types of Christians by analyzing the true meaning of his teaching & faith.

Christian Formation for the Single Life. Susan Muto. 3 cass. (Running Time: 3 hrs.). 1983. 24.95 incl. shelf case. (TAH138) Alba Hse Comns.
Speaks of the invitation & the challenge to live alone with God while being fully immersed in building up his kingdom here on earth.

Christian Foundations. Lester Sumrall. 12 cass. (Running Time: 18 hrs.). 1999. 48.00 (978-1-58568-014-6(1)) Sumrall Pubng.

Christian Fundamentals: The Building Blocks of our Faith. 2006. audio compact disk 25.00 (978-1-59933-003-7(2)) Morning NC.

Christian Gospels That Were Never in the Bible. Instructed by Manly P. Hall. 8.95 (978-0-89314-025-0(2), C821219) Philos Res.

Christian Higher Education: A Critique: National Association of Evangelicals, 47th Annual Convention, Columbus, Ohio, March 7-9, 1989. David L. McKenna. 1 cass. (Luncheons Ser.: No. 112-Thursd). 1989. 4.25 ea. 1-8 tapes.; 4.00 ea. 9 tapes or more. Nat Assn Evan.

Christian Hit Music. Contrib. by VeggieTales. (VeggieTales (EMI-CMG Audio) Ser.). (J). (ps-3). 2007. audio compact disk 13.99 (978-5-557-59275-8(X)) Big Idea.

Christian Home. 1978. 4.95 (978-0-7417-1006-2(4)) Win Walk.

Christian in Business. unabr. ed. Jake Tollefse. 1 cass. (Running Time: 49 min.). 12.95 (723) J Norton Pubs.

Christian Initiation: Baptism, Confirmation & Eucharist. Kenan Osborne. 1 cass. (Running Time: 1 hr.). 2001. 8.95 (A6981) St Anthony Mess Pr.
Presents a historical view of Baptism, Confirmation and Eucharist and how our understanding and celebration of the Sacraments of Initiation have changed in the last two centuries.

Christian Life Patterns. Evelyn Whitehead & James Whitehead. 6 cass. 1988. 46.95 (TAH198) Alba Hse Comns.
The traditional expectation seems to have been that adulthood is a relatively stable state achieved once & for all after the unstelled time of childhood & adolescence. This program explores the stages of adult development; young adulthood & the search for identity & intimacy: the midlife "crisis" with its opportunities for a whole new stage of human development.

***Christian Manifesto.** unabr. ed. Francis A. Schaeffer. Narrated by David Cochran Heath. (ENG.). 2007. 10.98 (978-1-59644-428-7(2), Hovel Audio) christianaud.

Christian Manifesto. unabr. ed. Francis A. Schaeffer. Read by David C. Heath. (Running Time: 3 hrs. 0 mins. 0 sec.). (ENG.). 2007. audio compact disk 18.98 (978-1-59644-427-0(4)) christianaud.

Christian Marriage. unabr. ed. Millard Sall. 1 cass. (Running Time: 1 hr. 30 min.). 12.95 (719) J Norton Pubs.

Christian Marriage: Partnership & Journey. Evelyn Whitehead & James Whitehead. 2 cass. 1988. 16.95 (TAH197) Alba Hse Comns.
What is the deepest, the best wisdom of Christianity about marriage, love, sex, fruitfulness - about men & women? This husband & wife team show what the Christian vision of marriage means personally & sacramentally.

Christian Meaning of Human Sexuality. Paul M. Quay. Read by Mark Taheny. 3 cass. 1988. pap. bk. 11.95 (978-0-89870-212-5(7), 123) Ignatius Pr.
A work for Christian adults that offers true and approachable insights into why there is right and wrong sexual behavior.

Christian Meditation. unabr. ed. Hans Urs Von Balthasar. Read by Mark Taheny. 2 cass. 9.95 set. (950) Ignatius Pr.
A short, approachable & practical guide to that form of prayer which God's revelation in Jesus Christ has made indispensable: meditation on the word of God. Provides a guide for making the meditation & points the way to the union that prayer achieves.

Christian Meditation: Practice & Teachings for Entering the Mind of Christ. abr. ed. Jim Finley. 6 cass. (Running Time: 7.5 Hours). 2003. audio compact disk 69.95 (978-1-59179-047-1(6)) Sounds True.

Christian Meditation & Personal Growth. Joseph A. Grassi. 8 cass. 1982. 57.95 incl. shelf-case. (TAH086) Alba Hse Comns.
Combines how-to, biblical validation & developed exercises to enable one to acquire techniques of meditation.

Christian Meditation & Relaxation- Vol. 1: Taking Control of your Thought Life, One. Scripts. Jones Jones. 1. (Running Time: 75 minutes). 2006. audio compact disk 14.95 (978-0-9641008-4-8(3)) Serenity Ent.
Christian Meditation and Relaxation Audio Cds helps listeners overcome negative thoughts, deepen relationship with God and restore their peace of mind. Volume One contains the two biblically-based guided meditations "Taking Control of Your Thought Life" and "Morning Devotion," an invitation to salvation, and meditative music for prayer. There are a total of 4 volumes available.

Christian Meditation & Relaxation -Vol. 2: Overcoming Restlessness. Scripts. Rhonda Jones. 1. (Running Time: 75 minutes). 2006. audio compact disk 14.95 (978-0-9641008-5-5(1)) Serenity Ent.
Christian Meditation and Relaxation Audio Cds helps listeners overcome negative thoughts, deepen relationship with God and restore their peace of mind. Volume Two contains the two meditations "Overcoming Restlessness"

An Asterisk (*) at the beginning of an entry indicates that the title is appearing for the first time.

and "Interceding for Loved Ones," an invitation to salvation, and meditative music for prayer. There are a total of 4 volumes available.

Christian Meditation & Relaxation- Vol. 3: Eliminating Stress & Toxic Emotions, Three. Scripts. Rhonda Jones. 4. (Running Time: 75 minutes). 2006. audio compact disk 14.95 (978-0-9641008-2-4(7)) Serenity Ent.
Christian Meditation and Relaxation Audio Cds helps listeners overcome negative thoughts, deepen relationship with God and restore their peace of mind. Volume Three contains the two biblically-based guided meditations "Eliminating Stress and Toxic Emotions" and "Timeout- Let God Fight Your Battles," an invitation to salvation, and meditative music for prayer. There are a total of 4 volumes available.

Christian Meditation & Relaxation- Vol. 4: Divine Delay, Four. Scripts. Rhonda Jones. 1. (Running Time: 75 minutes). 2006. audio compact disk 14.95 (978-0-9641008-7-9(8)) Serenity Ent.
Christian Meditation and Relaxation Audio Cds helps listeners overcome negative thoughts, deepen relationship with God and restore their peace of mind. Volume Four contains the two biblically-based guided meditations "Devine Delay" and "Faith in God for Success and Prosperity," an invitation to salvation, and meditative music for prayer. There are a total of 4 volumes available.

Christian Mind. unabr. ed. Harry Blamires. Read by Nadia May. 5 cass. (Running Time: 7 hrs.). 1996. 39.95 (978-0-7861-0918-0(1), 1719) Blckstn Audio.
Blamires, a noted British Christian thinker who started writing through the encouragement of C. S. Lewis, his tutor at Oxford, makes a perceptive diagnosis of some of the weaknesses besetting the church today. He argues that the distinctively Christian intellect is being swept away by secular modes of thought & secular assumptions about reality.

Christian Mind. unabr. ed. Warren W. Wiersbe. Read by Warren W. Wiersbe. 3 cass. (Running Time: 4 hrs. 30 min.). 1989. 14.95 (978-0-8474-2341-5(7)) Back to Bible.
The key to a balanced Christian life - a submissive, renewed, loving & disciplined mind.

Christian Mission in the Modern World. unabr. ed. John Stott. 4 CDs. (Running Time: 5 hrs. 30 mins. 0 sec.). (ENG.). 2005. audio compact disk 21.98 (978-1-59644-115-6(1), Hovel Audio) christianaud.
In this classic book, John Stott shows that a Christian mission must encompass both evangelism and social action. He begins with careful definitions of five key terms-mission, evangelism, dialogue, salvation and conversion. Then, through a thorough biblical exploration of these concepts, Stott provides a model for ministry to peoplea??s spiritual and physical needs alike.

***Christian Mission in the Modern World.** unabr. ed. John Stott. Narrated by Simon Vance. (ENG.). 2005. 12.98 (978-1-59644-113-2(5), Hovel Audio) christianaud.

Christian Mission in the Modern World. unabr. ed. John Stott. Narrated by Simon Vance. 1 MP3CD. (Running Time: 5 hrs. 30 mins. 0 sec.). (ENG.). 2005. lp 19.98 (978-1-59644-114-9(3), Hovel Audio) christianaud.

***Christian Motivation for Daily Living: The Complete Series.** unabr. ed. Zig Ziglar. Narrated by Zig Ziglar. (Running Time: 23 hrs. 21 mins. 29 sec.). (Christian Motivation for Daily Living Ser.). (ENG.). 2010. audio compact disk 59.99 (978-1-59859-767-7(1)) Oasis Audio.

Christian Perspectives on Capital Punishment: Proceedings of the 45th Annual Conventional Association of Evangelicals Buffalo, New York. Read by Myron Augsburger et al. 1 cass. (Running Time: 60 min.). 1987. 4.00 (347) Nat Assn Evan.

Christian Philosophy: New Updated Audio Cass. 3. 2005. Rental 15.00 (978-1-59548-009-5(9)) A Wommack.

Christian Philosophy II: Cd Album. Created by Awmi. (ENG.). 2009. audio compact disk 30.00 (978-1-59548-138-2(9)) A Wommack.

Christian Philosophy Volume I. Created by Awmi. (ENG.). 2009. audio compact disk 35.00 (978-1-59548-137-5(0)) A Wommack.

Christian Philosophy 2: New Updated Compact Disk. 3. 2005. audio compact disk 21.00 (978-1-59548-008-8(0)) A Wommack.

Christian Principles of Finance. Derek Prince. 1 cass. (B-4013) Derek Prince.

***Christian Privilege.** Featuring Ravi Zacharias. 2006. audio compact disk 9.00 (978-1-61256-066-3(0)) Ravi Zach.

Christian Response to Terrorism & Evil. 6. (Running Time: 6 hrs.). 2001. 20.00 (978-1-57399-118-6(X)) Mac Hammond.
On Tuesday, September 11, 2001, America was touched by evil. Those who have a personal relationship with God know He was not responsible for this terrorist attack against America. But many still struggle with how a Christian should view and respond to terrorism , evil, government, and using military might to kill. As you listen to Mac Hammond's patrotic series, you'll be delighted to learn how "you" can be a part in establishing and supporing God's will during these tumultuous times.

Christian Rock: Guitar Play-along Volume 71. Created by Hal Leonard Corporation Staff. 2007. pap. bk. 14.95 (978-1-4234-1434-6(9), 1423414349) H Leonard.

Christian Rock Hits! The Videos 2005. 2005. 10.98 (978-5-559-05590-9(5)) BEC Recordings.

Christian Scriptures & the Battles over Authentication, Pts. I-II. Instructed by Bart D. Ehrman. 12 cass. (Running Time: 12 hrs.). 2002. bk. 54.95 (978-1-56585-555-7(8), 6593); bk. 69.95 (978-1-56585-557-1(4), 6593) Teaching Co.

Christian Shamanism: Visions of Nikolas of Flue. Thomas P. Lavin. 5 cass. (Running Time: 6 hrs. 30 min.). 1995. 39.95 set. (978-0-7822-0484-1(8), 560) C G Jung IL.
A shaman is a person who has been forced by fate to take an inner, awe-filled journey which ultimately gives a new form to the person & to the culture. This journey demands sacrifice, isolation from the collective's expectations, & a particular form of courage which is able to accept new forms of awareness & new forms of the divine.

Christian Sing-Along Vol. 1: Tape One. Armand Aronson. Read by Armand Aronson. 1 cass. (Running Time: 50 min.). 1997. 9.95 (978-1-889844-02-2(0)) Christian Sing-Along.
Demonstration of all songs including tuning notes.

Christian Sing-Along Guitar & Tape One, Vol. 1. Armand Aronson. Read by Armand Aronson. 1 cass. (Running Time: 50 min.). 1997. bk. 16.95 (978-1-889844-03-9(9)) Christian Sing-Along.

Christian Single: Colossians 3:2. Ed Young. (J). 1981. 4.95 (978-0-7417-1202-8(4), A0202) Win Walk.

Christian Singleness. Dan Corner. 1 cass. 3.00 (23) Evang Outreach.

Christian Spirituality & the Old Testament. Lawrence Boadt. 1 cass. (Running Time: 48 min.). 1999. 9.95 (TAH415) Alba Hse Comns.
Assists in a better appreciation of the power & presence of God in salvation history, revealed through scripture & made present in the person of Christ.

Christian Stress Management for Health & Healing. Darrell Franken. 6 cass. 1985. 49.95 (978-0-934957-09-0(6)) Wellness Pubns.
These cassettes use Jacobson Relaxation exercises, Autogenic Training exercises, hymns, meditations, walking & repetition of Biblical material to transcend illness & promote health.

Christian Survival Kit. Created by Awmi. (ENG.). 2007. 75.00 (978-1-59548-116-0(8)); audio compact disk 75.00 (978-1-59548-114-6(1)) A Wommack.

Christian Theology; Private Property. John Robbins. 1 cass. (Introduction to Economics Ser.: No. 11). 5.00 Trinity Found.

Christian University. John Robbins. 1 cass. (Christianity & Education Ser.: No. 2). 5.00 Trinity Found.

Christian Woman in the Modern World. Alice Von Hildebrand. Read by Alice Von Hildebrand. 5 cass. (Running Time: 5 hrs.). 17.00 (978-1-56036-009-4(7), 361576) AMI Pr.
Five-Cassette album recorded at Fatima, Portugal. 1. The Life of Edith Stein. 2. The Role of Women in the Church. (Part I) 3. The Role of Women in the Church (Part II). 4. The Role of Women in the Church (Part III). 5. The Virtue of Purity.

Christian Woman's Home Management Seminar. Bonnie Ferris. Read by Bonnie Ferris. 2 cass. (Running Time: 1 hr. 30 min.). 1992. 24.95 set. (978-1-881404-40-8(4)) Brightwtr Bks.
Home management seminar, packaged in 3-ring binder containing loose-leaf workbook & planning sheets.

***Christianity: The First Three Thousand Years.** unabr. ed. Diamaid MacCulloch. Read by Walter Dixon. (Running Time: 46 hrs. 30 mins.). (ENG.). 2010. 49.98 (978-1-59659-554-5(X), GildAudio) Pub: Gildan Media. Dist(s): HachBkGrp

Christianity Set: Fact or Fantasy? Gregory Koukl. 3 cass. 1999. 16.95 (978-0-9673584-5-1(0)) Stand to Reason.
Any old God won't do, you bet your life: A simple case against atheism & hell, yes! The terrifying truth.

Christianity: A Definition: 1 John 1:1-4. Ed Young. 1984. 4.95 (978-0-7417-1360-5(8), 360) Win Walk.

Christianity & Economics Series. John Robbins. 2 cass. 10.00 Set. Trinity Found.

Christianity & Education Series. John Robbins. 2 cass. 10.00 Set. Trinity Found.

Christianity & Full Humanity. unabr. ed. David Steindl-Rast. 4 cass. 36.00 (OC46) Sound Horizons AV.

Christianity & Islam: A Second Battle of Tours. Douglas Wilson. (ENG.). 2007. audio compact disk 22.00 (978-1-59128-234-1(9)) Canon Pr ID.

Christianity & Science Series. John Robbins. 3 cass. 15.00 Set. Trinity Found.

Christianity As Viewed by an Outsider. unabr. ed. Samuel Sandmel. 3 cass. (Running Time: 2 hrs. 47 min.). 49.50 Set. (978-0-88432-497-3(4), S31024) J Norton Pubs.

Christianity Beyond Belief. unabr. ed. Todd Hunter. Narrated by Todd Hunter. (Running Time: 5 hrs. 14 mins. 25 sec.). (ENG.). 2009. 16.09 (978-1-60814-495-2(X)) Oasis Audio.

Christianity Beyond Belief. unabr. ed. Todd Hunter. Narrated by Todd Hunter. (Running Time: 5 hrs. 14 mins. 25 sec.). (ENG.). 2009. audio compact disk 22.99 (978-1-59859-499-7(0)) Oasis Audio.

Christianity Explored. Rico Tice. 8 cass. 2002. 3.99 (978-1-85078-382-4(9)) Pub: AuthenticMedia. Dist(s): Gabriel Res

***Christianity in Action: The International History of the Salvation Army.** unabr. ed. Henry Gariepy. Narrated by Raymond Todd. (ENG.). 2009. 12.98 (978-1-59644-756-1(7), Hovel Audio) christianaud.

Christianity in Action: The Story & Saga of the International Salvation Army. unabr. ed. Henry Gariepy. (Running Time: 9 hrs. 0 mins. 0 sec.). (ENG.). 2009. audio compact disk 21.98 (978-1-59644-755-4(9), Hovel Audio) christianaud.

Christianity, Science & Mysticism. Bede Griffiths. 1 cass. (Running Time: 39 min.). 1983. 11.00 (03301) Big Sur Tapes.
A Catholic monk-priest from India speaks on the convergence of the new world view of physics with the ancient mystical traditions of the East & Christianity.

Christianity's Greatest Scandal. Ben Young. (Faith Worth Dying for Ser.). (YA). 2000. 4.95 (978-0-7417-6227-6(7), B0227) Win Walk.

Christian's Accomplishment: Phillipians 4:8-23. Ed Young. (J). 1980. 4.95 (978-0-7417-1102-1(8), A0102) Win Walk.

Christian's Adornment: Philippians 4:1-7. Ed Young. (J). 1980. 4.95 (978-0-7417-1100-7(1), A0100) Win Walk.

Christians Advancement: Philippians. Ed Young. 1 cass. (Running Time: 90 mins.). (J). 1979. 4.95 (978-0-7417-1076-5(5), A0076) Win Walk.

Christians Ambition: Philippians 2:19-30. Ed Young. (J). 1979. 4.95 (978-0-7417-1084-0(6), A0084) Win Walk.

Christians & the Lions. (23312-A) J Norton Pubs.

Christian's Anticipation: Philippians 3:17-21. Ed Young. (J). 1979. 4.95 (978-0-7417-1097-0(8), A0097) Win Walk.

Christians Application: Philippians 2:12-18. Ed Young. (J). 1979. 4.95 (978-0-7417-1082-6(X), A0082) Win Walk.

Christians Approximation: Philippians 3:1-9. Ed Young. (J). 1979. 4.95 (978-0-7417-1089-5(7), A0089) Win Walk.

***Christians Are Hate-Filled Hypocrites... & Other Lies You've Been Told: A Sociologist Shatters Myths from the Secular & Christian Media.** unabr. ed. Bradley R. E. Wright. Narrated by Bradley R. E. Wright. (Running Time: 4 hrs. 39 mins. 44 sec.). (ENG.). 2010. 16.09 (978-1-60814-714-4(2)); audio compact disk 22.99 (978-1-59859-759-2(0)) Oasis Audio.

Christians Aspiration: Philippians 2:1-11. Ed Young. (J). 1979. 4.95 (978-0-7417-1080-2(3), A0080) Win Walk.

Christians Assignment: Philippians 1:19-30. Ed Young. (J). 1979. 4.95 (978-0-7417-1078-9(1), A0078) Win Walk.

Christian's Assurance: Philippians 1:1-8. Ed Young. 1 cass. (Running Time: 90 mins.). (J). 1979. 4.95 (978-0-7417-1074-1(9), A0074) Win Walk.

Christian's Attainment: Philippians 3:10-16. Ed Young. (J). 1979. 4.95 (978-0-7417-1094-9(3), A0094) Win Walk.

Christians Cooperating with the Public Schools: Proceedings of the 45th Annual Conventional Association of Evangelicals, Buffalo, New York. Read by Walter C. Hobbs. 1 cass. (Running Time: 60 min.). 1987. 4.00 (337) Nat Assn Evan.

Christian's Debts. Perf. by Johann Lai. 1 cass. (Running Time: 90 mins.). (CHI.). (C). 2000. 5.00 (978-1-930490-13-0(5), 10B-206) CCM Pubs.
Everyone has a different aesthetic standard. However, it is truly a beautiful thing when Jesus recognized Mary's act of anointing Him with an expensive perfume as an act of selfless & Christ-centered love. This beautiful act is characterized by doing her best, seeing the unseen & asking for nothing in return.

Christians Growth Through Understanding & Caring. H. Dale Wright. 1986. 10.80 (0307) Assn Prof Chaplains.

Christian's Response to a Broken World: National Association of Evangelicals, 47th Annual Convention, Columbus, Ohio, March 7-9, 1989. Richard F. Schubert. 1 cass. (Luncheons Ser.: No. 3). 1989. 4.25 ea. 1-8 tapes.; 4.00 ea. 9 tapes or more. Nat Assn Evan.

Christian's Responsibility to Walk in Love. Creflo A. Dollar. 4 cass. (Running Time: 6 hrs.). 1999. 20.00 (978-1-931172-46-2(3), TS229, Kidz Faith) Pub: Creflo Dollar. Dist(s): STL Dist NA

Christian's Secret of a Happy Life. Hannah Whitall Smith. 1 cass. (Running Time: 96 min.). (Christian Audio Classics Ser.). 1996. 4.97 (978-1-55748-714-8(6)) Barbour Pub.

Christian's Secret of a Happy Life. Hannah Whitall Smith. Read by Marguerite Gavin. 6 CDs. (Running Time: 7 hrs.). 2000. audio compact disk 48.00 (978-0-7861-9835-1(4), 2640) Blckstn Audio.
I believe, the fundamental truths of life & experience, the truths that underlie all theologies & that are in fact their real & vital meaning. They will fit in with every creed, simply making it possible for those who hold the creed to live up to their own beliefs & to find in them the experimental realities of a present Savior & a present salvation.

Christian's Secret of a Happy Life. Hannah Whitall Smith. Read by Marguerite Gavin. 5 cass. (Running Time: 7 hrs.). 2000. 39.95 (978-0-7861-1841-0(5), 2640) Blckstn Audio.
The fundamental truths of life & experience, the truths that underlie all theologies & that are in fact their real & vital meaning.

Christian's Secret of a Happy Life. Hannah Whitall Smith. Read by Marguerite Gavin. (Running Time: 7 hrs.). 2000. 27.95 (978-1-59912-633-3(8)) Iofy Corp.

Christian's Secret of a Happy Life. unabr. ed. Hannah Whitall Smith. Read by Marguerite Gavin. (Running Time: 7 hrs. 0 mins. 0 sec.). (ENG.). 2007. audio compact disk 24.98 (978-1-59644-387-7(1)) christianaud.

***Christian's Secret of a Happy Life.** unabr. ed. Hannah Whitall Smith. Narrated by Marguerite Gavin. (ENG.). 2007. 14.98 (978-1-59644-388-4(X), Hovel Audio) christianaud.

Christians vs. Deists. Joe Morecraft. 1 CD. (Running Time: 1 hr. 2 mins.). 2001. audio compact disk 10.00 (978-1-929241-67-5(4)) Pub: Vsn Forum. Dist(s): STL Dist NA
These days, it is not surprising to hear leading Christian thinkers refer to our Founding Fathers as Deists. In so doing, they mimic the gobbledeegook being spouted by the architects of historical confusion which dominate modern academia. The time has come to set the record straight, and no one is better suited to handle the jobe than historian and theologian Joe Morecraft. Morecraft presents the founders as real men, but men who operated in a distinctively Christian and Calvinistic cultural consensus.

Christians vs. Deists. Joe Morecraft. 1 cass. (Running Time: 1 hr. 2 mins.). 2001. 7.00 (978-1-929241-28-6(3)) Pub: Vsn Forum. Dist(s): STL Dist NA

Christie Caper. unabr. ed. Carolyn G. Hart. Read by Kate Reading. 8 cass. (Running Time: 12 hrs.). (Death on Demand Mystery Ser.: No. 7). 1996. 64.00 (978-0-7366-3457-1(6), 4101) Books on Tape.
Annie Laurence organizes a rousing 100th birthday to commemorate her idol, Agatha Christie. It's smashing - until an uninvited guest, Neil Bledsoe, intrudes. Bledsoe, a writer of down & dirty true-life crime stories, carries with him a manuscript for a cruel & scurrilous biography of the venerated Dame Agatha.

Christie Pak: A Mysterious Affair at Styles & Two Christie Shorts. abr. ed. Agatha Christie. Read by Stan Winiarski. 2 cass. (Running Time: 3 hrs.). 2001. 34.95 (978-0-929071-27-5(1)) B-B Audio.
POL.

Christina Aguilera: The Unauthorized Audio Biography. unabr. ed. Interview. Chris Herring. Read by Chris Herring. Read by Susan Van Dusen. 1 CD. (Running Time: 1 hr.). (J). (gr. 2-9). 2000. audio compact disk 14.99 (978-0-9660180-9-7(5)) Scholarly Audio.
This biography uses Christina Aguilera's own words & music to tell her story, to address rumors & to reveal secrets & little known facts.

Christina's Ghost. Betty Ren Wright. Read by Carol Jordan Stewart. (Playaway Children Ser.). (J). 2008. 34.99 (978-1-60640-636-6(1)) Find a World.

Christina's Ghost. Betty Ren Wright. Illus. by Betty Ren Wright. 2002. 9.95 (978-0-87499-933-4(2)); 9.95 (978-0-87499-934-1(0)) Live Oak Media.

Christina's Ghost. Betty Ren Wright. Read by Carol Jordan Stewart. (Running Time: 7320 sec.). (Live Oak Mysteries Ser.). (J). 2006. audio compact disk 22.95 (978-1-59519-838-9(5)) Live Oak Media.

Christina's Ghost. unabr. ed. Betty Ren Wright. 2 vols. (Running Time: 2 hrs.). (J). (ps-3). 2002. bk. 39.95 (978-0-87499-937-2(5)) Live Oak Media.

Christina's Ghost. unabr. ed. Betty Ren Wright. Read by Carol Jordan Stewart. 2 cass. (Running Time: 2 hrs. 2 mins.). (J). (gr. 4-7). 2002. 18.95 (978-0-87499-947-1(2)) Pub: Live Oak Media. Dist(s): AudioGO
Christina and her Uncle forge a reluctant but touching relationship when the young girl spends the summer in his isolated mansion and get caught up on a ghost hunt that may be linked to murders that took place in the house 30 years later.

***Christine.** unabr. ed. Stephen King. (Running Time: 19 hrs. 0 mins.). 2010. 44.95 (978-1-4417-3897-4(5)); 99.95 (978-1-4417-3893-6(2)); audio compact disk 90.00 (978-1-4417-3894-3(0)) Blckstn Audio.

Christine. unabr. ed. Stephen King. (Running Time: 20 hrs.). (ENG.). 2010. audio compact disk 49.95 (978-0-14-242822-1(1), PengAudBks) Penguin Grp USA.

Christine Falls. unabr. ed. Benjamin Black. 1 MP3-CD. 2007. 54.95 (978-0-7927-4759-8(3), Chivers Sound Lib) AudioGO.

Christine Falls. unabr. ed. Benjamin Black. Read by Timothy Dalton. 8 CDs. (Running Time: 9 hrs. 30 mins.). 2007. audio compact disk 89.95 (978-0-7927-4682-9(1), Chivers Sound Lib) AudioGO.

Christine Falls. unabr. ed. Benjamin Black. Read by Timothy Dalton. 8 CDs. (Running Time: 9 hrs. 30 mins. 0 sec.). (ENG.). 2007. audio compact disk 39.95 (978-1-4272-0072-3(6)) Pub: Macmill Audio. Dist(s): Macmillan

***Christine Feehan: Dark Possession, Dark Curse.** abr. ed. Christine Feehan. Read by Jane C. Brown & Phil Gigante. (Running Time: 12 hrs.). 2010. audio compact disk 19.99 (978-1-4418-5048-5(1), 9781441850485) Brilliance Audio.

Christl & Robb: The Barley Grain for Me. 1 cass., 1 CD. 9.98 (C-62); audio compact disk 14.98 CD. (CD-62) Folk-Legacy.
Well chosen Canadian songs, powerfully sung.

Christman in Egypt. Kathie Hill. 1995. audio compact disk 85.00 (978-0-7673-0811-3(5)) LifeWay Christian.

Christmas. 1 cass. 9.95 (119117) Covenant Comms.
Favorite Christmas songs.

Christmas. Michael Ballam. 1 CD. audio compact disk 14.95 (978-1-55503-341-5(5), 119123) Covenant Comms.

Christmas. John Chisum. 2001. 75.00 (978-0-633-01688-3(8)); 11.98 (978-0-633-01686-9(1)); audio compact disk 85.00 (978-0-633-01689-0(6)); audio compact disk 16.98 (978-0-633-01687-6(X)) LifeWay Christian.

Christmas. Contrib. by Amy Grant. (Mastertrax Ser.). 2007. audio compact disk 14.98 (978-5-557-58517-0(6)) Pt of Grace Ent.

Christmas. Prod. by Danny McGuffey & Todd Burkhalter. Contrib. by Don Moen et al. (Reader's Digest Faith Ser.). 2005. audio compact disk 12.99 (978-5-558-78713-9(9)) RD Assn.

Christmas. Monks of Solesmes Staff. 1 CD. 1985. audio compact disk 16.95 (978-1-55725-100-8(2), 930-093) Paraclete MA.

Christmas. Ed. by Publications International Staff. (J). 2007. audio compact disk 22.98 (978-1-4127-8476-4(X)) Pubns Intl Ltd.

Christmas. Ed. by Publications International Staff. (J). 2007. audio compact disk 15.98 (978-1-4127-8480-1(8)) Pubns Intl Ltd.

Christmas. Perf. by Michael W. Smith. 1 cass. 1989. audio compact disk Brentwood Music.
The critically acclaimed & best selling Christmas collection features self-penned originals & timeless classic Christmas songs.

Christmas, No. 1. 1 cass. (Running Time: 29 min.). 1991. 10.00 (122479) New Letters.

Christmas, No. 2. Poems. 1 cass. (Running Time: 29 min.). 1991. 10.00 (121986) New Letters.
A celebration of Christmas through poetry.

Christmas, Vol. 1. (Running Time: 6 hrs.). 2004. audio compact disk 29.95 (978-1-57816-189-8(4)) Audio File.

Christmas, Vol. 2. (Running Time: 6 hrs.). 2004. audio compact disk 29.95 (978-1-57816-190-4(8)) Audio File.

Christmas: A Time for Family. Compiled by Lois L. Kaufman. Illus. by Barbara Chiantia. 1 CD. (Running Time: 1 hr.). (BookNotes Ser.). 1998. bk. 14.99 (978-0-88088-403-7(7)) Peter Pauper.

Christmas: A Time for Friends. Compiled by Lois L. Kaufman. Illus. by Wendy Wegner. (BookNotes Ser.). 1998. bk. 14.99 (978-0-88088-404-4(5)) Peter Pauper.

***Christmas: Easy Pieces for Acoustic Guitar.** Created by Hal Leonard Corp. (ENG.). 2010. pap. bk. 12.99 (978-1-84938-327-1(8), 1849383278) Pub: Music Sales. Dist(s): H Leonard

Christmas: The Message. abr. ed. Eugene H. Peterson. Narrated by Mark Lowry. (Running Time: 3600 sec.). (ENG.). 2006. audio compact disk 12.99 (978-1-59859-155-2(X)) Oasis Audio.

Christmas: The Night Office. Monks of Solesmes Staff. 1 CD. 1990. audio compact disk 16.95 (978-1-55725-122-0(3), 930-090) Paraclete MA.

Christmas Album. Narrated by Flo Gibson. (ENG.). 2007. audio compact disk 16.95 (978-1-55685-922-9(8)) Audio Bk Con.

Christmas Album. Contrib. by Amy Grant. Prod. by Brown Bannister. 2007. audio compact disk 9.99 (978-5-557-59289-5(X)) Pt of Grace Ent.

Christmas Album. unabr. ed. Clement C. Moore et al. Read by Flo Gibson. 2 cass. (Running Time: 3 hrs.). (J). (gr. 2-8). 1987. 14.95 (978-1-55685-088-2(3)) Audio Bk Con.
Stories for the twelve days of Christmas including: "The Nativity, a Visit from Saint Nicholas," "The Gift of the Magi," "Christmas Everywhere," & excerpts from "A Christmas Carol," "Pickwick Papers," "The Mill on the Floss" & others.

Christmas Album: Yuletide Favorites. Perf. by Janice Buckner. 1 CD. (Running Time: 1 hr.). (Learn along Song Ser.). (J). 2001. audio compact disk 15.00 Moonlight Rose.
Includes full song lyrics and features a karaoke-style Sing-It-Yourself instrumental version of each tune. The feature is designed for classrooms, children's choirs and budding performers.

Christmas Album: Yuletide Favorites. Perf. by Janice Buckner. 1 cass. (Running Time: 1 hr.). (Learn along Song Ser.: Vol. 5). (J). 1992. 9.98 (978-1-56479-111-5(4), MR111-4) Moonlight Rose.
Excellent for sing alongs, carolling, choral use & background holiday music. Includes a sing-it-yourself side.

Christmas & New Year Messages see Mensajes de Navidad y Año Nuevo

Christmas Angel. Kaye Jacobs Volk. 1 cass. 1.77 (978-1-55503-634-8(1), 06004830); 3.98 (06004830) Covenant Comms.
A warm Christmas story.

Christmas Angels: 20 Treasured Songs of the Season. Created by Barbour Publishing. 2006. audio compact disk 4.97 (978-1-59789-425-8(7), Barbour Bks) Barbour Pub.

Christmas Around the World. Arranged by Joe E. Parks. 1 cass. (Running Time: 20 min.). (J). 1982. 80.00 (MU-9034C) Lillenas.
Sing along cassette.

Christmas Around the World: A Cantata for Children's Voices. Joe E. Parks. 1 cass. (Running Time: 20 min.). (J). 1981. 12.99 (TA-9034C) Lillenas.
Cantata for children's choir. May also be used as a collection of individual songs. Unison, with optional 2-part voicing & keyboard. Consists of traditional carols of seven foreign countries, along with a brief narration summarizing the unique Christmas customs of that country. This has the makings of a tradition with color & tasteful orchestrations.

Christmas Around the World: 20 Treasured Songs of the Season. Created by Barbour Publishing. 2006. audio compact disk 4.97 (978-1-59789-427-2(3), Barbour Bks) Barbour Pub.

Christmas at Bethlehem Gulch. Contrib. by John DeVries. Created by Pam Andrews. 2007. audio compact disk 90.00 (978-5-557-69932-7(5)) Lillenas.

Christmas at Bethlehem Gulch: An 'Old West' Children's Musical about the Coming of the Savior. Pam Andrews. 2007. audio compact disk 12.00 (978-5-557-69930-3(9)) Lillenas.

Christmas at Grandma's. Donald Davis. (Running Time: 2700 sec.). (J). (gr. 5-9). 1994. audio compact disk 14.95 (978-0-87483-751-3(0)) Pub: August Hse. Dist(s): Natl Bk Netwk

Christmas at Grandma's. unabr. ed. Donald Davis. Read by Donald Davis. 1 cass. (Running Time: 45 mins.). (J). (gr. 2 up). 1994. 12.00 (978-0-87483-391-1(4)) August Hse.

Christmas at Hope Central: A Musical for Kids. Barny C. Robertson & Carter Robertson. 1 cass. (Running Time: 55 min.). (YA). 2001. 12.99 (TA-9256C) Lillenas.
Older elementary & middle school choirs will find a relevant message of hope, as timely today as ever. A humorous experience of a young discipleship group as they struggle with political correctness, an upcoming church musical that is a disaster in the making & their genuine concern over the salvation of a gifted classmate. Interesting characters, loads of humor, innovative songs in a variety of contemporary styles & a strong, message-centered theme.

Christmas at Hope Central: A Musical for Kids. Carter Robertson & Barny C. Robertson. 10 cass. (Running Time: 3 hrs. 30 min.). (J). 2001. bk. 54.99 (TA-9256PK) Lillenas.

Christmas at St. Francis. Barbara O'Donnell. 2000. audio compact disk 15.00 (978-0-89914-501-3(9)) Third Party Pub.

Christmas at the Homeplace: Stories & Songs. Connie Regan-Blake & Barbara Freeman. 1 cass. (Running Time: 36 min.). 1992. 10.99 (978-1-929415-02-1(8)) StoryWindow Prodns.
Sweet old timey memories.

Christmas Beginning. unabr. ed. Anne Perry. Narrated by Terrence Hardiman. 4 CDs. (Running Time: 4 hrs. 7 mins.). 2007. audio compact disk 49.95 (978-0-7927-5040-6(3)) AudioGO.
Superintendent Runcorn - who Anne Perry fans will remember as William Monk's ex-boss - is feeling rather lonely during his holiday on the remote, snowy island of Anglesey, off the north coast of Wales. However, he is suddenly called into action when the sister of the local vicar is discovered murdered and draped over a gravestone in her brother's churchyard. Investigating this tragic crime with the assistance of the beautiful Melisande gives him just the opportunity he needs to spend time with an upper class woman who normally wouldn't give him the time of day. Interweaving the original Christmas story with her own holiday tale, Perry also explores the meaning of Joseph's secondary role compared to that of Mary and Jesus. The novel ultimately shows that the seemingly less important people in our lives are sometimes more crucial than we realize.

Christmas Beginning. unabr. ed. Anne Perry. Narrated by Terrence Hardiman. (Running Time: 14820 sec.). (Christmas Stories Ser.). (ENG.). 2007. audio compact disk 19.95 (978-1-60283-301-2(X)) Pub: AudioGO. Dist(s): Perseus Dist

Christmas Beginning. unabr. ed. Anne Perry. Read by Terrence Hardiman. (YA). 2008. 39.99 (978-1-60514-564-8(5)) Find a World.

Christmas Blizzard. unabr. ed. Garrison Keillor. Read by Garrison Keillor. 5 CDs. (Running Time: 5 hrs.). 2009. audio compact disk 26.95 (978-1-59887-927-8(8), 1598879278) Pub: HighBridge. Dist(s): Workman Pub

Christmas Book. unabr. collector's ed. Elizabeth Goudge. Read by Wanda McCaddon. 6 cass. (Running Time: 9 hrs.). (J). 1983. 48.00 (978-0-7366-0904-3(0), 1847) Books on Tape.
Children & animals are central in this story, with Miss Goudge's usual warm blend of humor, love and joy & that special magic each new christmas brings.

***Christmas Book: Memories of Family, Friends, & Faith.** unabr. ed. Joel Osteen. Read by Joel Osteen. 2 CDs. (Running Time: 3 hrs. 0 mins. 0 sec.). (ENG.). 2010. audio compact disk 14.99 (978-1-4423-3636-0(6)) Pub: S&S Audio. Dist(s): S and S Inc

Christmas Box see Regalo de Navidad

Christmas Box. abr. unabr. ed. Richard Paul Evans. Read by Richard Thomas. (Running Time: 13 hrs. 0 mins. 0 sec.). Bk. 1. (ENG.). 2006. audio compact disk 9.95 (978-0-7435-6504-2(5)) Pub: S&S Audio. Dist(s): S and S Inc

Christmas Box. unabr. ed. Richard Paul Evans. Read by Richard Thomas. (Christmas Box Ser.: Bk. 1). 2004. 7.95 (978-0-7435-4281-4(9)) Pub: S&S Audio. Dist(s): S and S Inc

Christmas Box. unabr. ed. Alison Uttley. 1 cass. (Running Time: 6 min.). (J). (gr. 2-5). 1987. bk. 16.95 (978-0-8045-6580-6(5), 6580) Spoken Arts.

Christmas Box Collection: The Christmas Box; Timepiece; The Letter. abr. ed. Richard Paul Evans. Read by Richard Thomas. 4 cass. (Running Time: 6 hrs.). (Christmas Box Ser.: Bks. 1, 2, & 3). 1998. 30.00 (978-0-671-93446-0(5), 595612, Audioworks) S&S Audio.
The three novels that make up the Parkin family saga are included here. They are "Christmas Box," "Timepiece," & "The Letter".

Christmas Brass. 1 cass., 1 CD. audio compact disk 10.98 CD. (978-1-57908-384-7(6), 1548) Platinm Enter.

Christmas by the Book. Beverly King. 2 cass. 9.98 Set. (978-1-55503-846-5(8), 07001207) Covenant Comms.
A daring Christmas charade leads to love.

Christmas Candle. unabr. ed. Max Lucado. Read by Greg Whalen. (Running Time: 5400 sec.). 2006. audio compact disk 24.00 (978-0-7861-6034-1(9)) Blckstn Audio.

Christmas Candle. unabr. ed. Max Lucado. Narrated by Greg Whalen. (ENG.). 2006. 11.89 (978-1-60814-117-3(9)); audio compact disk 16.99 (978-1-59859-164-4(9)) Oasis Audio.

Christmas Carol see Cancion de Navidad

Christmas Carol see Cancion de Navidad

Christmas Carol. Short Stories. 2 CDs. (Running Time: 1hr. 37mins.). Dramatization. (J). 2005. 15.00 (978-0-9773525-1-7(X)) Hollywood Cliche.
On a cold, blustery Christmas Eve, Ebenezer Scrooge toils into the night, greedily counting his money, unable to give a kind word to a single soul. He cares nothing for the spirit of giving, shouting "Bah!" and "Humbug!" at the very mention of the holiday. But four ghostly visitors come to show him a different way, opening Scrooge's heart to kindness and charity, fraternity and goodwill - a lesson he takes to Christmas and beyond. Michael McFall, narrator of this unforgettable tale, creates an amazing journey for audiences of all ages. He is a natural story teller with a rich narrative voice. His recordings are sound and music enhanced, keeping his listeners mesmerized and free to engage the imagination in wondrous ways. McFall was classically trained at the prestigious American Conservatory Theatre and has worked consistently in television, film and regional theater. Running Time: 1 hour 37 minutes.

Christmas Carol. 1 cass. (Running Time: 1 hr.). (Christmas at Radio Spirits Ser.). 4.98 (978-1-57019-379-8(7), OTR7006) Pub: Radio Spirits. Dist(s): AudioGO

Christmas Carol. Perf. by Lionel Barrymore. 1 cass. (J). 3.98 Clamshell. (978-1-55886-144-2(0), BB/PT 451) Smarty Pants.

Christmas Carol. Perf. by Steve de C. Cook. (YA). 2008. audio compact disk 29.95 (978-0-9821616-0-9(3)) Five Talents.

Christmas Carol. Charles Dickens. Narrated by Paul Albertson. (ENG.). 2008. 12.95 (978-0-9801087-7-4(2)) Alpha DVD.

Christmas Carol. Charles Dickens. 1 cass. (Running Time: 50 mins.). 1999. Art of Hearing.

***Christmas Carol.** Charles Dickens. 2009. (978-1-60136-573-6(X)) Audio Holding.

Christmas Carol. Charles Dickens. Read by John Lee. 3 cass. (Running Time: 4 hrs. 30 mins.). (J). 2001. 28.00 (978-0-7366-8071-4(3)) Books on Tape.
We can all remember the miserly Scrooge, the humble Cratchett, the piteous Tiny Tim, and the mysterious and foreboding visitation of the three spirits. Nonetheless, it is only in listening to the work on tape, in a live reading such as Dickens himself used to do, that we can appreciate the fine details. The cold and fog of London at Christmastime, the grimacing knocker on Scrooge's house, and the pealing joy of a town transformed in the eyes of a repentant Scrooge - all these fine-grained visions bring back the merriness of our own Christmases.

Christmas Carol. Charles Dickens. Perf. by Michael Enright et al. Prod. by Judy Madden. Music by Toronto Mendelssohn Youth Choir. 2 CDs. (Running Time: 2 hrs.). 2005. audio compact disk 15.95 (978-0-660-17878-3(8)) Pub: Canadian Broadcasting CAN. Dist(s): Georgetown Term

Christmas Carol. Charles Dickens. 2 cass. (J). (gr. 3). 2006. 11.98 (978-0-660-17877-6(X)) Pub: Canadian Broadcasting CAN. Dist(s): Georgetown Term

Christmas Carol. Charles Dickens. Read by Alan Maitland. (ENG.). 2009. audio compact disk 24.95 (978-0-660-19920-7(3)) Canadian Broadcasting CAN.

Christmas Carol. Charles Dickens. Perf. by Michael Bennett. 1 cass. Dramatization. 4.98 (0400408) Covenant Comms.

Christmas Carol. Charles Dickens. Ed. by Jerry Stemach. Retold by Alan Venable. Narrated by Nick Sandys. 2000. audio compact disk 200.00 (978-1-58702-509-9(4)) D Johnston Inc.

Christmas Carol. Charles Dickens. 1 cass. 1996. pap. bk. 5.95 Boxed set. (29103-0) Dover.

Christmas Carol. Charles Dickens. Read by Ralph Cosham. (Playaway Young Adult Ser.). 2008. 44.99 (978-1-60640-834-6(8)) Find a World.

Christmas Carol. Charles Dickens. Read by Robert L. Halvorson. 2 cass. 14.95 (52) Halvorson Assocs.

***Christmas Carol.** Charles Dickens. 2005. 14.95 (978-1-61658-174-9(3)) Indep Pub IL.

Christmas Carol. Charles Dickens. Read by Laura García. (Running Time: 3 hrs.). 2002. 16.95 (978-1-60083-197-3(4), Audiofy Corp) Iofy Corp.

Christmas Carol. Charles Dickens. Read by Ralph Cosham. (Running Time: 2 hrs. 45 mins.). 2003. 17.95 (978-1-59912-052-2(6), Audiofy Corp) Iofy Corp.

Christmas Carol. Charles Dickens. Narrated by Peter Bartlett. (Running Time: 1 hr. 30 mins.). 2006. 14.95 (978-1-60083-002-0(1)) Iofy Corp.

Christmas Carol. Charles Dickens. 1 cass. (Running Time: 1 hr.). Dramatization. 2001. 12.95 (SNDX001) Lodestone Catalog.
Ebenezer Scrooge learns the real meaning of Christmas as the spirits move him.

Christmas Carol. Charles Dickens. (J). 1985. 4.95 (978-0-913675-40-3(7)) McGraw.

Christmas Carol. Charles Dickens. Perf. by Orson Welles. Narrated by Lionel Barrymore. 1 cass. (Running Time: 60 min.). 7.95 (DD-9493) Natl Recrd Co.

Christmas Carol. Charles Dickens. Read by Anton Lesser. 2 cass. (Running Time: 2 hrs. 30 mins.). (Works of Charles Dickens). 1999. 13.98 (978-962-634-682-2(5), NA218214, Naxos AudioBooks) Naxos.
This has become the most famous Christmas story of all, with the miserly figure of Scrooge, the epitome of the callous employer, sadly crippled Tiny Tim and the three specters - the ghost of Christmas Past, Christmas Present and Christmas Future.

Christmas Carol. Charles Dickens. Read by Anton Lesser. 2005. audio compact disk 22.98 (978-962-634-329-6(X)) Naxos UK GBR.

Christmas Carol. Charles Dickens. Perf. by Orson Welles & Arthur Anderson. 1 cass. (Running Time: 1 hr.). (Adventures in Old-Time Radio Ser.). 2001. 4.98 (7006); audio compact disk 4.98 (7007) Radio Spirits.
Presentation of Dickens' legendary tale of the ghosts of Christmas past, present and future visit the miserly Ebenezer Scrooge and help him discover the true spirit of the Christmas season.

Christmas Carol. Charles Dickens. 1 cass. (Running Time: 1 hr.). (Radiobook Ser.). 1987. 4.98 (978-0-929541-21-1(9)) Radiola Co.

Christmas Carol. Charles Dickens. 2 vols. (Running Time: 2 hrs. 59 mins.). (YA). 2004. pap. bk. 29.00 (978-1-4000-9005-1(9), Listening Lib) Random Audio Pubg.

Christmas Carol. Charles Dickens. Read by Jim Dale. 2 cass. (Running Time: 2 hrs. 59 mins.). (YA). 2004. 23.00 (978-1-4000-8605-4(1), Listening Lib); audio compact disk 30.00 (978-1-4000-8606-1(X), Listening Lib) Random Audio Pubg.

Christmas Carol. Charles Dickens. Read by R. J. Lupo. Arranged by SSI Records Staff. 2 CDs. (Running Time: 2 hrs. 20 mins.). 2001. audio compact disk (978-0-9725163-1-0(X)) SSI Pubng.
The original Charles Dickens story adapted to an audio CD read by Mr. R. J. Lupo, a well-known broadcast announcer. This 2 hour and 20 minute CD story is intertwined with Christmas songs including the words to be enjoyed with family and friends.

Christmas Carol. Charles Dickens. Narrated by Ralph Cosham. (Running Time: 10200 sec.). (Unabridged Classics in MP3 Ser.). (ENG.). 2008. audio compact disk 14.95 (978-1-58472-680-7(6), In Aud); audio compact disk 24.00 (978-1-58472-635-7(0), In Aud) Sound Room.

Christmas Carol. Charles Dickens. Read by Dan Toohey. Des. by John Burr. 2 CDs. (Running Time: 1 hr. 34 mins.). 2001. audio compact disk 19.95 (978-0-9728060-0-8(8)) John Burr.
This Charles Dickens classic is told in a radio-drama approach to truly bring life to one of the most heart warming stories of the last two centuries.

Christmas Carol. Perf. by MacDuff Entertainment. 2 CDs. (Running Time: 2 hrs. 20 mins.). 2001. audio compact disk 24.95 (MACD002) Lodestone Catalog.
A skillful blend of acting & narration to tell Scrooge's tale with much of the original language intact.

Christmas Carol. Retold by Alan Venable. Charles Dicken. (Classic Literature Ser.). 2000. audio compact disk 18.95 (978-1-4105-0158-5(2)) D Johnston Inc.

Christmas Carol. Read by Jim Weiss. 1 cass., 1 CD. (Running Time: 1 hr.). (J). NewSound.

Christmas Carol. abr. ed. Charles Dickens. Narrated by Dan O'Herlihy. 2 cass. (Running Time: 3 hrs. 4 min.). 12.95 (978-0-89926-140-9(X), 828) Audio Bk.

Christmas Carol. abr. ed. Charles Dickens. Read by Ralph Richardson. (Running Time: 3600 sec.). (Caedmon Essentials Ser.). 2007. audio compact disk 12.95 (978-0-06-137650-4(7), Caedmon) HarperCollins Pubs.

Christmas Carol. abr. ed. Charles Dickens. Read by Paul Scofield. 3 CDs. (Running Time: 3 hrs.). 2004. audio compact disk 24.95 (978-1-59007-570-8(6)); 18.00 (978-1-931056-54-0(4), N Millennium Audio) New Millenn Enter.
Ever since it's first publication in 1843, the tale of stingy Ebenezer Scrooge, humble Bob Crachit and beloved Tiny Tim has taken a special place in the heart of Christmas tradition. The most famous celebration of Christmas, and family love, in the English language shows us the nature of true charity, the power of tenderness and the wisdom of innocence in a coldhearted world. The story of Scrooge's transformation is a fable of hope and the true meaning of sharing that will be enjoyed over and over again. A timeless delight for young and old alike, this recording will become a cherished family tradition.

Christmas Carol. abr. ed. Charles Dickens. Read by Frederick Sinden. 3 cass. (Running Time: 4 hrs. 30 min.). 2001. 34.95 (60776) Pub: Soundings Ltd GBR. Dist(s): Ulverscroft US

Christmas Carol. abr. ed. Charles Dickens. Read by Frank Pettingell. (Running Time: 47 min.). 10.95 (978-0-8045-0728-8(7), SAC 728) Spoken Arts.

Christmas Carol, abr. ed. Charles Dickens. Perf. by St. Charles Players. 2 cass. (Running Time: 110 min.). (Story Theatre for Young Readers Ser.). (gr.

5-9). 2000. 16.95 (978-1-56994-523-0(3), 309584, Monterey SoundWorks) Monterey Media Inc.
T'was the night before Christmas, Ebenezer Scrooge was alone, when suddenly he heard a ghostly moan. A ghost took him back to the past, then to present & future days in hope that Scrooge would mend his ways.

***Christmas Carol.** abr. ed. Charles Dickens. Read by Sir Ralph Richardson. (ENG.). 2003. (978-0-06-079951-9(X), Harper Audio); (978-0-06-074304-8(2), Harper Audio) HarperCollins Pubs.

Christmas Carol. abr. ed. Charles Dickens. Read by Patrick Stewart. 2 CDs. (Running Time: 2 hrs. 0 mins. 0 sec.). (ENG.). 2006. audio compact disk 14.95 (978-0-7435-6379-6(4)) Pub: S&S Audio. Dist(s): S and S Inc

Christmas Carol. abr. adpt. ed. Charles Dickens. (Bring the Classics to Life: Level 1 Ser.). 2008. audio compact disk 12.95 (978-1-55576-425-8(8)) EDCON Pubng.

Christmas Carol. adpt. ed. Adapted by Paul McCusker & Dave Arnold. Created by Focus on the Family Staff. Charles Dickens. (Running Time: 1 hr. 30 mins. 0 sec.). (Radio Theatre Ser.). (ENG.). 2008. audio compact disk 14.97 (978-1-58997-544-6(8), Tyndale Ent) Tyndale Hse.

Christmas Carol see Complete Ghost Stories

Christmas Carol. unabr. ed. 3 CDs. (Running Time: 3 hrs.). 2002. audio compact disk 34.00 (978-1-58472-102-4(2), Commuters Library) Sound Room.

Christmas Carol. unabr. ed. Charles Dickens. Read by Miriam Margolyes. 2 cass. (Running Time: 3 hrs.). (gr. 6-8). 1999. 17.95 (978-1-57270-115-1(3), F21115u) Pub: Audio Partners. Dist(s): PerseuPGW
A beloved holiday classic. Margolyes brings this memorable cast to life: Tiny Tim, Bob Cratchit & Ebenezer Scrooge teach the true meaning of Christmas.

Christmas Carol. unabr. ed. Charles Dickens. Read by Simon Prebble. (Running Time: 10800 sec.). 2007. audio compact disk 19.95 (978-1-4332-1422-6(9)); audio compact disk & audio compact disk 27.00 (978-1-4332-1421-9(0)) Blckstn Audio.

Christmas Carol. unabr. ed. Charles Dickens. Read by Simon Prebble. (Running Time: 10800 sec.). (J). (gr. 3). 2007. 24.95 (978-1-4332-1420-2(2)) Blckstn Audio.

Christmas Carol. unabr. ed. Charles Dickens. Read by Simon Prebble. (Running Time: 3 hrs.). 2009. audio compact disk 14.95 (978-1-4417-1116-8(3)) Blckstn Audio.

Christmas Carol. unabr. ed. Charles Dickens. Read by Gene Engene. 2 cass. (Running Time: 3 hrs.). (J). 16.95 (978-1-55686-138-3(9), 138) Books in Motion.
Dicken's classic Christmas tale about Ebenezer Scrooge who learns the true spirit of Christmas by confronting the Ghosts of Christmas Past, Present and Future.

Christmas Carol. unabr. ed. Charles Dickens. Read by John Lee. 3 cass. (Running Time: 4 hrs. 30 mins.). 2001. 14.95 Books on Tape.
An inveterate miser is driven to repentance on Christmas Eve by the visit of three spirits.

Christmas Carol. unabr. ed. Charles Dickens. Read by Richard Green. 3 cass. (Running Time: 4 hrs.). 2001. 17.95 (978-0-7366-6763-0(6)) Books on Tape.
The much repeated but always touching story of the Cratchit family & Ebenezer Scrooge, the miser who confronts the ghosts of Christmas.

Christmas Carol. unabr. ed. Charles Dickens. Read by John Lee. 3 CDs. (Running Time: 4 hrs.). (J). 2001. audio compact disk 28.00 (978-0-7366-8273-2(2)) Books on Tape.
An inveterate miser is driven to repentance on Christmas Eve by the visit of three spirits.

Christmas Carol. unabr. ed. Charles Dickens. Read by Anton Lesser. (J). 2006. 34.99 (978-1-59895-628-3(0)) Find a World.

Christmas Carol. unabr. ed. Charles Dickens. Read by Gary N. Johnson. Ed. by Martin English & Bill Warren. 1 cass. 1997. 12.00 (978-0-9662157-0-0(2)) Grey Matter CO.

Christmas Carol. unabr. ed. Charles Dickens. Read by Robert L. Halvorson. 2 cass. (Running Time: 180 min.). 14.95 (52) Halvorson Assocs.

Christmas Carol. unabr. ed. Charles Dickens. Told to Susan Stamberg. Contrib. by Jonathan Winters & Mimi Kennedy. 1 CD. (Running Time: 3600 sec.). (ENG.). 2007. audio compact disk 14.95 (978-1-59887-532-4(9), 1598875329) Pub: HighBridge. Dist(s): Workman Pub

Christmas Carol. unabr. ed. Charles Dickens. 1 cass. (Running Time: 56 min.). Dramatization. 1978. 7.95 (D-9) Jimcin Record.
The most famous Christmas story of all is dramatized by a cast of characters.

Christmas Carol, unabr. ed. Charles Dickens. Narrated by Frank Muller. 2 cass. (Running Time: 3 hrs.). (gr. 6 up). 1981. 18.00 (978-1-55690-101-0(1), 80200E7) Recorded Bks.
The spirit of Christmas cannot touch the ice around old Scrooge's heart until four ghostly spirits change his mind just in time.

Christmas Carol. unabr. ed. Charles Dickens. Narrated by Frank Muller. 3 CDs. (Running Time: 3 hrs.). 2000. audio compact disk 29.00 (978-0-7887-4480-8(1), C1182E7) Recorded Bks.

Christmas Carol. unabr. ed. Charles Dickens. Read by Ralph Cosham. 3 cds. (Running Time: 2 hrs 50 mins). (YA). 2002. pap. bk. 45.00 (978-1-58472-229-8(0), In Aud) Pub: Sound Room. Dist(s): Baker Taylor

Christmas Carol. unabr. ed. Charles Dickens. Read by Ralph Cosham. 3 cds. (Running Time: 2 hrs 50 mins). (YA). 2002. audio compact disk 22.95 (978-1-58472-227-4(4), 015, In Aud) Pub: Sound Room. Dist(s): Baker Taylor

Christmas Carol. unabr. ed. Charles Dickens. Read by Jim Dale. 3 cass. (Running Time: 3 hrs.). (ENG.). (J). (gr. 3-3). 2003. audio compact disk 19.00 (978-1-4000-8603-0(5), Listening Lib) Pub: Random Audio Pubg. Dist(s): Random

Christmas Carol. unabr. ed. Charles Dickens. Narrated by Flo Gibson. (Running Time: 2 hrs. 56 mins.). (gr. 2-10). 2004. audio compact disk 16.95 (978-1-55685-777-5(2)) Audio Bk Con.

Christmas Carol. unabr. ed. Naomi Fox. Narrated by Robert Guillaume. Music by Michael Carpenter. 1 cass. (Running Time: 15 min.). Dramatization. (J). 1993. pap. bk. 9.95 (978-1-882179-17-6(X)) Confetti Ent.
The Confetti Company, a cast of multi-ethnic children, reenact the classic fairytale told in a modern, upbeat tempo.

Christmas Carol. unabr. abr. ed. Charles Dickens. Read by Paul Scofield. (Running Time: 9000 sec.). 2007. audio compact disk 27.00 (978-1-4332-0543-9(2)) Blckstn Audio.

Christmas Carol. unabr. abr. ed. Charles Dickens. Read by Paul Scofield. (Running Time: 9000 sec.). 2007. audio compact disk 19.95 (978-1-4332-0544-6(0)) Blckstn Audio.

Christmas Carol. unabr. collector's ed. Charles Dickens. Read by Richard Green. 3 cass. (Running Time: 3 hrs.). (J). 1979. 18.00 (978-0-7366-0953-1(9), 1897) Books on Tape.
Who can forget Tiny Tim & "God Bless Us Everyone!".

Christmas Carol, Set. Charles Dickens. Read by Frederick Sinden. 3 cass. 1999. 34.95 (60776) Pub: Soundings Ltd GBR. Dist(s): ISIS Pub

Christmas Carol, Set. unabr. ed. Charles Dickens. Read by Flo Gibson. 2 cass. (Running Time: 3 hrs.). (J). 1984. 14.95 (978-1-55685-048-6(4)) Audio Bk Con.
Miserly Scrooge is taken on journeys by the Ghosts of Christmas Past, Present & Future into the lives of such unforgettable characters as Tiny Tim, Bob Cratchit & the Fezziwigs. Their spirits gradually transform Scrooge's selfish heart.

Christmas Carol, Set. unabr. ed. Charles Dickens. Read by Michael Low. 3 cass. 1999. 23.95 (FS9-34214) Highsmith.

Christmas Carol, Vol. 6. Charles Dickens. Ed. by Jerry Stemach et al. Retold by Alan Venable. Illus. by Jeff Ham. Narrated by Nick Sandys. Contrib. by Ted S. Hasselbring. (Start-to-Finish Books). (J). (gr. 2-3). 2000. 35.00 (978-1-58702-510-5(8)) D Johnston Inc.

Christmas Carol, Vol. 6. Charles Dickens. Ed. by Jerry Stemach et al. Retold by Alan Venable. Illus. by Jeff Ham. Narrated by Nick Sandys. Contrib. by Ted S. Hasselbring. (Start-to-Finish Books). (J). (gr. 2-3). 2002. 100.00 (978-1-58702-949-3(9)) D Johnston Inc.

Christmas Carol, Vol. 6. abr. ed. Charles Dickens. Ed. by Jerry Stemach et al. Retold by Alan Venable. Illus. by Jeff Ham. Narrated by Nick Sandys. Contrib. by Ted S. Hasselbring. 1 cass. (Running Time: 1 hr.). (Start-to-Finish Books). (J). (gr. 2-3). 2000. (978-1-58702-371-2(7), F31K2) D Johnston Inc.
The story takes place at Christmastiime in 19th century London, where the lower class suffers at the hands of a brutal winter. Miserly Ebenezer Scrooge couldn't care less about the poor however, and he hates Christmas. Then, one Christmas eve, four ghostly visitors take Scrooge on a guided tour of his past, present,a and future. Scrooge is forced to face himself, and by the time the last ghost leaves, he's begging for the chance to change is life.

***Christmas Carol: A Performance Reading by Roy Lantz.** Narrated by Roy Lantz. (Running Time: 65). (ENG.). 2009. audio compact disk 14.95 (978-0-615-34464-5(X)) Magnolia Pines.

Christmas Carol: Accompaniment/Performance. Anna Laura Page & Jean Anne Shafferman. (ENG.). 2004. audio compact disk 45.00 (978-0-7390-3514-6(2)) Alfred Pub.

Christmas Carol: Preview Pack. Anna Laura Page & Jean Anne Shafferman. (ENG.). 2004. audio compact disk 12.95 (978-0-7390-3513-9(4)) Alfred Pub.

Christmas Carol: Radio Days Starring George Tirebiter. David Ossman. Read by David Ossman. 1 CD. audio compact disk 15.95 (978-1-57677-110-5(5), SPME002) Lodestone Catalog.

Christmas Carol: The Radio Play. abr. ed. Charles Dickens. Read by Lynn Segall et al. Ed. by John Williams. 2 cass. (Running Time: 1 hr. 33 min.). Dramatization. 1992. 14.95 set in vinyl case. (978-0-9634652-1-4(X)) Radio Theatre.
Fully underscored radio drama with multiple character voices, sound effects & richly orchestrated music.

Christmas Carol - Scrooge in Bethlehem (A Musical for Children Based upon a Story by Charles Dickens) Accompaniment/Performance. Composed by Anna Laura Page et al. (ENG.). 2008. audio compact disk 59.95 (978-0-7390-5063-7(X)) Alfred Pub.

Christmas Carol - Scrooge in Bethlehem (A Musical for Children Based upon a Story by Charles Dickens) Listening. Composed by Anna Laura Page et al. (ENG.). 2008. audio compact disk 14.95 (978-0-7390-5062-0(1)) Alfred Pub.

Christmas Carol & Other Favorites. Short Stories. Read by Jim Weiss. 1 CD. (Running Time: 1 hr.). Dramatization. (Storyteller's Version Ser.). (J). (gr. k up). 1996. audio compact disk 14.95 (978-1-882513-41-3(X), 1124-016) Greathall Prods.
The human spirit is wonderfully depicted through Ebenezer Scrooge's glorious transformation from miser to humanitarian, a young couple's poignant lesson in giving and receiving and with uproarious humor of Christmas in the Old West.

Christmas Carol & Other Favorites. Short Stories. Read by Jim Weiss. 1 cass. (Running Time: 1 hr.). (Storyteller's Version Ser.). (J). (gr. k up). 1996. 10.95 (978-1-882513-16-1(9), 1124-16) Greathall Prods.

Christmas Carol & Other Stories by Charles Dickens. Charles Dickens. Narrated by Jim Killavey. (Running Time: 3 hrs.). 1978. 18.95 (978-1-59912-776-7(8)) Iofy Corp.

Christmas Carol in Bethlehem: Listening. Alfred Publishing Staff. (ENG.). 2008. audio compact disk 16.95 (978-0-7390-5692-9(1)) Alfred Pub.

Christmas Carol (Reissue) abr. ed. Charles Dickens. Read by Patrick Stewart. 2006. 9.95 (978-0-7435-6380-2(8)) Pub: S&S Audio. Dist(s): S and S Inc

***Christmas Carol-UAB.** Charles Dickens. 2010. audio compact disk 9.99 (978-1-4418-9216-4(8)) Brilliance Audio.

Christmas Carol (Unabridged) Charles Dickens. Read by Anton Anton. (Running Time: 4 hrs.). 2005. 24.95 (978-1-60083-698-5(4)) Iofy Corp.

Christmas Carole. 1 CD. (Running Time: 1 hr.). (Christmas at Radio Spirits Ser.). audio compact disk 4.98 (978-1-57019-380-4(0), OTR7007) Pub: Radio Spirits. Dist(s): AudioGO

***Christmas Caroline.** abr. ed. Kyle Smith. Read by Nanette Savard. (ENG.). 2006. (978-0-06-123057-8(X), Harper Audio); (978-0-06-123058-5(8), Harper Audio) HarperCollins Pubs.

Christmas Carol/Radio Daze. David Ossman. Perf. by George Leroy Tirebiter. 1 CD. (Running Time: 1 hr.). 2001. audio compact disk 15.95 (SPME002) Lodestone Catalog.

Christmas Carols. (E-Z Play Today Ser.: Vol. 6). 2003. pap. bk. 14.95 (978-0-634-06653-5(6)) H Leonard.

Christmas Carols Around the World. Mormon Tabernacle Choir. 1 cass. 2.37 (3111393); audio compact disk 4.17 (3333108) Covenant Comms.

Christmas Carols for the Native American Flute. Dick Claassen. 2007. audio compact disk 22.95 (978-1-58749-643-1(7)) Awe-Struck.

Christmas Carols in Latin. (LAT.). 2003. audio compact disk (978-0-86516-551-9(3)) Bolchazy-Carducci.

Christmas Celebration: A Christmas Carol & the Christmas Collection. unabr. abr. ed. 2005. audio compact disk & audio compact disk 34.98 (978-962-634-330-2(3)) Naxos UK GBR.

Christmas Celebrations: A Windham Hill Selection. 1 cass. 1999. (978-0-7601-3068-1(X)); audio compact disk (978-0-7601-3067-4(1)) Brentwood Music.
Instrumental light jazz & easy listening Christmas favorites include: "The Christmas Song" - Braxton Brothers; "O Christmas Tree" - Snuffy Walden; "Felix Navidad" - Spyro Gyra; "I'll Be Home for Christmas" - Tom Grant; "Magic" - Chieli Minucci; "We Three Kings" - Earl Klugh; "In the City" - Ricky Peterson; "Island Christmas" - Michael Franks; "Joyous" - Special Effx; "Deck the Halls" - Larry Coryell; "Please Come Home for Christmas" - Etta James; "Seasons Greetings" - Tim Weisberg.

Christmas Chair. Short Stories. Read by Seth Williamson. 1. (Running Time: 54). (J). 2005. audio compact disk 14.95 (978-0-9763633-2-3(1)) Thomas W.

Christmas Chants - Santo Domin - K. 1 cass. 1996. 7.69 BMG Distribution.

Christmas Chants - Santo Domingo. 1 cass. 1996. 11.89 BMG Distribution.

***Christmas Cheer: 101 Stories about the Love, Inspiration, & Joy of Christmas.** unabr. ed. Jack L. Canfield et al. Read by Sandra Burr & Dan John Miller. 1 MP3-CD. (Running Time: 10 hrs.). (Chicken Soup for the Soul (Audio Health Communications) Ser.). 2010. 14.99 (978-1-4418-7780-2(0)); 39.97 (978-1-4418-8210-3(3)); 39.99 (978-1-4418-8212-7(X)) Brilliance Audio.

Christmas Child: A Story of Coming Home. abr. ed. Max Lucado. (Running Time: 1 hr.). 2004. 9.99 (978-1-58926-343-7(X), Oasis Kids) Oasis Audio.

Christmas Child: A Story of Coming Home. abr. unabr. ed. Max Lucado. Narrated by Reg Grant. 1 CDs. (Running Time: 1 hr. 30 min.). (ENG.). 2003. audio compact disk 9.99 (978-1-58926-344-4(8)) Oasis Audio.
A Chicago journalist finds himself in a small Texas town on Christmas Eve. Lonely, he encounters old faces and new facts...a hand carved manger, a father's guilt, a young girl's faith. The trip into the past holds his key to the future, and a scarlet cross shows him the way home.

Christmas Child: A Story of Coming Home. unabr. ed. Max Lucado. Narrated by Reg Grant. (ENG.). 2003. 6.99 (978-1-60814-118-0(7)) Oasis Audio.

Christmas Child: A Story of Coming Home. unabr. ed. Max Lucado. Read by Reg Grant. Prod. by Oasis Audio Staff. (Running Time: 1 hr.). 2000. audio compact disk 15.00 (978-0-7861-8839-0(1), 3225) Blckstn Audio.

Christmas Child: A Story of Coming Home. unabr. ed. Max Lucado. Read by Reg Grant. Prod. by Oasis Audio Staff. (Running Time: 1 hr.). 2006. 14.95 (978-0-7861-2666-8(3), 3225) Blckstn Audio.

Christmas Chorus. 1 cass., 1 CD. audio compact disk 10.98 CD. (978-1-57908-380-9(3), 1544) Platinm Enter.

***Christmas Chronicles: The Legend of Santa Claus.** unabr. ed. Tim Slover. (Running Time: 3 hrs. 30 mins.). 2010. 19.99 (978-1-4001-9865-8(8)); 19.99 (978-1-4001-6865-1(1)); 11.99 (978-1-4001-8865-9(2)); audio compact disk 19.99 (978-1-4001-1865-6(4)); audio compact disk 47.99 (978-1-4001-4865-3(0)) Pub: Tantor Media. Dist(s): IngramPubServ

Christmas Classics. 1 CD. audio compact disk 10.98 (978-1-57908-389-2(7), 1662) Platinm Enter.

Christmas Classics. AIO Team Staff. Created by Focus on the Family Staff. 4 cass. (Adventures in Odyssey Ser.). (ENG.). (J). (gr. 3-7). 2005. audio compact disk 24.99 (978-1-58997-351-0(8)) Pub: Focus Family. Dist(s): Tyndale Hse

Christmas Classics, Set. unabr. ed. 2 cass. (Running Time: 2 hrs.). 10.95 (978-1-57816-011-2(1), CC2401) Audio File.
Four heartwarming classics from radio's warmest season.

Christmas Classics: F Horn or Eb Horn. Created by Hal Leonard Corporation Staff. 2005. pap. bk. 14.95 (978-90-431-2143-9(6), 9043121436) H Leonard.

Christmas Classics: Stories for the Whole Family. unabr. ed. (Running Time: 7 hrs.). 2006. 24.95 (978-1-4233-1387-8(9), 9781423313878, BAD) Brilliance Audio.

Christmas Classics: Stories for the Whole Family. unabr. ed. Read by Multivoice Production Staff. (Running Time: 7 hrs.). 2006. 39.25 (978-1-4233-1388-5(7), 9781423313885, BADLE); 39.25 (978-1-4233-1386-1(0), 9781423313861, Brinc Audio MP3 Lib); 24.95 (978-1-4233-1385-4(2), 9781423313854, Brilliance MP3); audio compact disk 29.95 (978-1-4233-1383-0(6), 9781423313830, Bril Audio CD Unabri) Brilliance Audio.
Listen to a collection of classic short stories by the world's most beloved writers. Here are the complete stories, unabridged, for you and your family to enjoy together this Christmas and for many Christmases to come. Family favorites and remembered treasures are in this collection, as well as a few light-hearted surprises.

Christmas Classics: Stories for the Whole Family. unabr. ed. Read by Multivoice Production Staff. 6 CDs. (Running Time: 7 hrs.). (YA). (gr. k up). 2006. audio compact disk 82.25 (978-1-4233-1384-7(4), 9781423313847, BriAudCD Unabrid) Brilliance Audio.

Christmas Classics - Easy: Piano Accompaniment. Created by Hal Leonard Corporation Staff. 2005. pap. bk. 12.95 (978-90-431-2145-3(2), 9043121452) H Leonard.

Christmas Classics - Easy Instrumental Solos or Duets for Any Combination of Instruments: Bass Cleff Instruments (Bassoon, Trombone, Euphonium, & Others) Ed. by James Curnow. Created by Hal Leonard Corporation Staff. 2005. pap. bk. 14.95 (978-90-431-2144-6(4), 9043121444) H Leonard.

Christmas Classics - Easy Instrumental Solos or Duets for Any Combination of Instruments: Bb Instruments (Bb Clarinet, Bb Tenor Saxophone, Bb Trumpet, & Others) Ed. by James Curnow. Created by Hal Leonard Corporation Staff. 2005. pap. bk. 14.95 (978-90-431-2141-5(X), 904312141X) H Leonard.

Christmas Classics - Easy Instrumental Solos or Duets for Any Combination of Instruments: Eb Instruments (Eb Alto Sax, Eb Baritone Sax & Others) Ed. by James Curnow. Created by Hal Leonard Corporation Staff. 2005. pap. bk. 14.95 (978-90-431-2142-2(8), 9043121428) H Leonard.

Christmas Collection. C. Hardyment. (Running Time: 2 hrs. 30 mins.). 2001. 20.95 (978-1-60083-700-5(X)) Iofy Corp.

Christmas Collection. abr. ed. Stuart McLean. 2 CDs. (Vinyl Cafe Ser.). 2006. audio compact disk 24.99 (978-0-9738965-0-3(7), CBC Audio) Canadian Broadcasting CAN.

Christmas Collection: Poetry, Prose, Tales & Song in Celebration of the Holiday Season. Read by Peter Jeffrey et al. Selected by Christina Hardyment. 2 cass. (Running Time: 2 hrs. 30 mins.). 1998. 13.98 (978-962-634-649-5(3), NA214914, Naxos AudioBooks) Naxos.
Compilation of traditional holiday favorites, poems and music.

Christmas Collection: Poetry, Prose, Tales & Song in Celebration of the Holiday Season. unabr. ed. Read by Peter Jeffrey et al. Selected by Christina Hardyment. 2 CDs. (Running Time: 2 hrs 34 mins.). 1997. audio compact disk 17.98 (978-962-634-149-0(1), NA214912, Naxos AudioBooks) Naxos.

Christmas Collection: Shepherds Abiding, the Mitford Snowmen & Esther's Gift. unabr. ed. Jan Karon. Read by John McDonough. 4 cass. (Running Time: 5 hrs.). 2003.; audio compact disk (PenginMM) Penguin Grp USA.

Christmas Comes to Lone Star Gulch. Contrib. by Paul Miller. Arranged by Joseph Linn. 1 cass. (Running Time: 35 min.). (J). (gr. 3-6). 1989. 80.00 (MU-9106C) Lillenas.
Kids will love pretending to be adults in this colorful story set in a small western town, Lone Star Gulch. When the town grump adopts a baby abandoned on his doorstep, eh is transformed & the whole town sees

Christmas in a new light. The songs are fun to sing, varied in style & easily learned, for unison or 2-part choir.

Christmas Community Worship Service: Logos Dec. 20,1998. Ben Young. 1998. 4.95 (978-0-7417-6112-5(2), B0112) Win Walk.

***Christmas Companion: Stories, Songs, & Sketches.** unabr. ed. Garrison Keillor. Contrib. by Garrison Keillor. (ENG.). 2010. audio compact disk 14.99 (978-1-61573-511-2(9), 1615735119) Pub: HighBridge. Dist(s): Workman Pub

Christmas Cookie Club. unabr. ed. Ann Pearlman. Read by Gabra Zackman. 7 CDs. (Running Time: 8 hrs. 0 mins. 0 sec.). (ENG.). 2009. audio compact disk 29.99 (978-0-7435-9828-6(8)) Pub: S&S Audio. Dist(s): S and S Inc

Christmas Country. 1 cass., 1 CD. audio compact disk 10.98 CD. (978-1-57908-383-0(8), 1547) Platinm Enter.

Christmas Cradle. Kaye Jacobs Volk. 1 cass. 1.77 (978-1-57734-030-0(2), 06005403) Covenant Comms.

Christmas Crossroads. Contrib. by Dennis Allen. 1995. 90.00 (978-0-00-508773-2(2), 75608257) Pub: Brentwood Music. Dist(s): H Leonard

Christmas Crossroads. Contrib. by Dennis Allen. 1995. 11.98 (978-0-00-508772-5(4), 75608256) Pub: Brentwood Music. Dist(s): H Leonard

Christmas Day in the Morning. Pearl S. Buck. 1 cass. (Running Time: 52 min.). (J). 7.95 (CA 1087); audio compact disk 14.95 (CD 1087) Revels Recs.
Medieval instruments & synthesizer tie the old to the new in this joyous pageant of songs & dance. A Jubilant & robust celebration on the winter solstice.

Christmas Doll. Elvira Woodruff. Narrated by Bernadette Dunne. (Running Time: 3 hrs.). 2004. 20.95 (978-1-59912-634-0(6)) Iofy Corp.

Christmas Doll. Elvira Woodruff. Read by Bernadette Dunne. 5 cass. (Running Time: 6 hrs.). 2004. 44.95 (978-0-7861-2924-9(7), 3402); audio compact disk 55.00 (978-0-7861-8192-6(3), 3402) Blckstn Audio.

Christmas Dozen: Christmas Stories to Warm the Heart. Short Stories. Steven E. Burt. Read by Steven E. Burt. 2 CDs. (Running Time: 1 hr. 20 mins.). 2001. audio compact disk 16.95 (978-0-9649283-3-6(7)) Pub: Burt Creations. Dist(s): AtlasBooks
Twelve read-aloud stories that have long been part of the author's traveling program for church gatherings, senior centers, nursing homes, schools & libraries during the holidays.

Christmas Dream. Patti Teel. Perf. by Patti Teel. (J). 2002. 9.95 (978-0-9724962-3-0(8)); audio compact disk 12.95 (978-0-9724962-0-9(3)) Pub: Dream Flight Prods. Dist(s): Follett Med Dist
This recording helps kids rest during the hectic holiday season and plants the seeds of world peace. This CD contains two routines for quiet time or bedtime. The first routine teaches children to relax as they take part in Reindeer Flight Training. On the second routine, young listeners help Santa deliver presents. On the global journey children visit the moon, fly over mountains & oceans, hear prayers from children around the world, visit Bethlehem, and learn to care for all people.

Christmas Dream. unabr. ed. Louisa May Alcott. Read by Lauren Ambrose. (Running Time: 3600 sec.). (J). 2007. audio compact disk 14.95 (978-0-06-137350-3(8), HarperChildAud) HarperCollins Pubs.

***Christmas Dream.** unabr. ed. Louisa May Alcott. Read by Lauren Ambrose. (ENG.). 2007. (978-0-06-155461-2(8)); (978-0-06-155462-9(6)) HarperCollins Pubs.

Christmas Dreams. Sonya Nori. 2004. audio compact disk 11.99 (978-0-7684-0208-7(5)) Destiny Image Pubs.

Christmas Eve. Sunita Staneslow. 1997. pap. bk. 24.95 (978-0-7866-3184-1(8), 96481CDP) Mel Bay.

Christmas Eve. Sunita Staneslow. 2002. bk. 24.95 (978-0-7866-6847-2(4), 96481BCD) Mel Bay.

***Christmas Eve at Friday Harbor.** unabr. ed. Lisa Kleypas. Read by Tanya Eby. (Running Time: 4 hrs.). (Friday Harbor Ser.). 2010. 24.99 (978-1-4418-4763-8(4), 9781441847638, BAD); 39.97 (978-1-4418-4764-5(2), 9781441847645, BADLE); 24.99 (978-1-4418-4761-4(8), 9781441847614, Brilliance MP3); 39.97 (978-1-4418-4762-1(6), 9781441847621, Brlnc Audio MP3 Lib); audio compact disk 24.99 (978-1-4418-4759-1(6), 9781441847591, Bril Audio CD Unabri); audio compact disk 74.97 (978-1-4418-4760-7(X), 9781441847607, BriAudCD Unabrid) Brilliance Audio.

Christmas Eve Caper. 2 cass. (Running Time: 3 hrs.). (SmartReader Ser.). (J). 1999. pap. bk. & tchr. ed. 19.95 (978-0-7887-0118-4(5), 79306T3) Recorded Bks.
The Christmas show money has been stolen from the Rialto theater's safe. Join Officer Baker as he takes notes & pieces the evidence together. Can you identify the burglar before he does?.

Christmas Eve under Hooker's Statue see Twentieth-Century Poetry in English: Recordings of Poets Reading Their Own Poetry

Christmas Fairy. deluxe unabr. ed. Mary N. Wheeler. 1 cass. (Running Time: 1 hr.). (J). 2000. lib. bdg. 12.00 (978-0-932079-01-5(6), 79016) TimeFare AudioBks.

Christmas Family Tragedy: Original Motion Picture Soundtrack. Prod. by Break of Dawn Productions. Featuring Katherine Whalen. (ENG.). 2007. audio compact disk 15.00 (978-0-9791690-2-1(X)) Break of Dawn.

Christmas Family Tree. Kathie Hill. 1997. 75.00 (978-0-7673-3280-4(6)); audio compact disk 85.00 (978-0-7673-3279-8(2)) LifeWay Christian.

Christmas Fantasias. Michael Cox. 1998. 11.98 (978-0-7673-9191-7(8)); audio compact disk 16.98 (978-0-7673-9208-2(6)) LifeWay Christian.

Christmas Favorites. 1 cass.; 1 CD. 1998. 7.98 (978-1-56628-175-1(X), 75539); audio compact disk 11.98 CD. (978-1-56628-199-7(7), 75539D) MFLP CA.

Christmas Favorites. Jerry Barnes. 1960. audio compact disk 16.95 (978-0-8198-1558-3(6), 332-042) Pauline Bks.

Christmas Favorites: Essential Elements for Strings. 1997. audio compact disk 12.95 (978-0-634-05335-1(3)) H Leonard.

Christmas Favorites for Solo Guitar: Best-Loved Traditional Songs for Bluegrass Guitar. Dix Bruce. (ENG.). 2009. pap. bk. 17.99 (978-0-7866-8176-1(4)) Mel Bay.

Christmas Festival. Mormon Youth Symphony. 1 cass. 2.37 (1000608) Covenant Comms.
Twelve classical Christmas songs.

Christmas for Kids. Friedman-Fairfax and Sony Music Staff et al. 1 cass. (CD Ser.). (gr. 4-7). 1993. pap. bk. 15.98 (978-1-56799-038-6(X), Friedman-Fairfax) M Friedman Pub Grp Inc.

Christmas for Two: 8 Duets on Traditional Carols & Folk Songs. Ed. by Jean Anne Shafferman. (ENG.). 2003. audio compact disk 11.95 (978-0-7390-3025-7(6)) Alfred Pub.

Christmas from Radio's Golden Age, Vol. 1. collector's ed. Perf. by Lionel Barrymore et al. 6 cass. (Running Time: 9 hrs.). 1998. bk. 34.98 (4028) Radio Spirits.
Traditional stories of Christmas. "A Christmas Carol," "Amos 'n' Andy," "Burns and Allen," "The Cavalcade of America," "The Charlie McCarthy Show," "Duffy's Tavern," "Family Theater," "Escape", "Family Theater," "Fibber McGee & Molly," "First Nighter Program," "The Great Gildersleeve," "Gunsmoke," "The Jack Benny Program," "the Jimmy Durante Show," "Let's Pretend," "The Life of Riley," "The Lone Ranger." 18 episodes.

Christmas from Radio's Golden Age, Vol. 2. collector's ed. Perf. by Bud Abbott et al. 6 cass. (Running Time: 9 hrs.). 2000. bk. 34.98 (4184) Radio Spirits.
18 old-time radio Christmas stories. "The Abbott and Costello Show," "The Aldrich Family," "Archie Andrews," "Dragnet," "The Falcon," "Fibber McGee & Molly," "Grand Central Station," "The Great Gildersleeve," "The Greatest Story Ever Told," "The Jack Benny Program," "The Lone Ranger," "Mr. President," "Our Miss Brooks," "Philco Radio Time," "The Six Shooter," "Stars over Hollywood," "Suspense" and "Tales of the Texas Rangers".

Christmas from the Cozy Cottage. Read by Clair LeBear. Perf. by Clair LeBear. 1 CD. (Running Time: 1 hr.). (Clair's Cozy Cottage Music Ser.). 2000. audio compact disk 14.95 (978-0-9706321-6-6(9), CC004) Cozy Cottage.
Traditional Christmas hymns & songs.

Christmas... from the Realms of Glory. Contrib. by Bebo Norman. Prod. by Jason Ingram & Rusty Varenkamp. 2007. audio compact disk 13.99 (978-5-557-59287-1(3)) BEC Recordings.

Christmas Garland (Medley) - ShowTrax. Arranged by John Leavitt. 1 CD. (Running Time: 4 mins.). 2000. audio compact disk 25.00 (08742264) H Leonard.
A sparkling medley of German carols for choir & optional orchestra. Includes: "Kling, Glockchen"; "Oh How Joyfully"; "Still, Still, Still." German & English lyrics.

Christmas Gift. Perf. by Charlotte Diamond. 1 cass., 1 CD. (J). NewSound.

Christmas Greetings. Mormon Tabernacle Choir. 1 cass. 2.37 (3111385); audio compact disk 8.98 (333395) Covenant Comms.

Christmas Guest see Women in Literature, the Short Story: A Collection

Christmas Guest. 1980. (N-49) Jimcin Record.

Christmas Guest. unabr. ed. Anne Perry. 3 CDs. 2005. audio compact disk 39.95 (978-0-7927-3785-8(7), SLD 858) AudioGO.

Christmas Guest. unabr. ed. Anne Perry. Read by Terrence Hardiman. 3 cass. (Running Time: 13980 sec.). 2005. 34.95 (978-0-7927-3784-1(9), CSL 858) AudioGO.
This is a new Christmas novella from international bestselling author Anne Perry.

Christmas Guitar. Perf. by John Fahey. 2002. audio compact disk Rounder Records.

Christmas Hawaiian-Style: 3 New Christmas Songs CD. Prod. by Robert Westerman. Composed by Robert Westerman. Pru Westerman. Eleykaa Tahleh. (ENG., (J). 2008. audio compact disk 5.95 (978-0-9761992-3-6(8)) Gold Boy Mus.

Christmas Heart. Kaye Jacobs Volk. 1 cass. 2004. 2.95 (978-1-55503-890-8(5), 06005160) Covenant Comms.
A tender story of love & spiritual renewal.

Christmas Hope. abr. ed. Donna VanLiere. Read by Oliver Wyman. 2005. 11.95 (978-1-59397-803-7(0)) Pub: Macmill Audio. Dist(s): Macmillan

Christmas Hope. abr. ed. Told to Oliver Wyman. (Running Time: 10800 sec.). 2005. audio compact disk 19.99 (978-1-59859-094-4(4)) Oasis Audio.

Christmas I Love to Tell the Story. Contrib. by Russell Mauldin. 1994. 11.98 (978-1-55897-039-7(8), 75602211) Pub: Brentwood Music. Dist(s): H Leonard

Christmas in Camelot. unabr. ed. Mary Pope Osborne. Read by Mary Pope Osborne. Read by Will E. Osborn. 2 cass. (Running Time: 1 hr. 57 mins.). (Magic Tree House Ser.: No. 29). (J). (gr. k-3). 2004. 23.00 (978-0-8072-0587-7(7), Listening Lib) Random Audio Pubg.
The intrepid Jack and Annie are invited to come to Camelot for Christmas Eve. Without a research book for the first time ever, the two kids set off in the Magic Tree House. No sooner do they arrive at the castle, when a dark knight appears and freezes King Arthur and all his court - including Jack and Annie's friend Morgan le Fay. Jack and Annie set off to the Otherworld to find the Caldron of Poetry and Imagination, which is the only thing that can save Camelot.

Christmas in Camelot. unabr. ed. Mary Pope Osborne. Read by Mary Pope Osborne. (Running Time: 4620 sec.). (Magic Tree House Ser.: No. 29). (ENG.). (J). (gr. 1-3). 2006. audio compact disk 14.95 (978-0-7393-3688-5(6), ImaginStudio) Pub: Random Audio Pubg. Dist(s): Random

***Christmas in Cedar Cove.** unabr. ed. Debbie Macomber. Read by Sandra Burr. (Running Time: 8 hrs.). 2010. audio compact disk 92.97 (978-1-4418-1957-4(6), 9781441819574, BriAudCD Unabrid) Brilliance Audio.

Christmas in Cedar Cove: A Cedar Cove Christmas. unabr. ed. Debbie Macomber. Read by Sandra Burr. (Running Time: 8 hrs.). (Cedar Cove Ser.). 2010. audio compact disk 26.99 (978-1-4418-1949-9(5), 9781441819499, Bril Audio CD Unabri) Brilliance Audio.

***Christmas in Cedar Cove: A Cedar Cove Christmas.** unabr. ed. Debbie Macomber. Read by Sandra Burr. (Running Time: 12 hrs.). 2010. 39.97 (978-1-4418-1959-8(2), 9781441819598, Brlnc Audio MP3 Lib); 24.99 (978-1-4418-1958-1(4), 9781441819581, Brilliance MP3); 24.99 (978-1-4418-1960-4(6), 9781441819604, BAD); 39.97 (978-1-4418-1961-1(4), 9781441819611, BADLE) Brilliance Audio.

Christmas in Egypt. Kathie Hill. 1995. 75.00 (978-0-7673-0810-6(7)) LifeWay Christian.

Christmas in Egypt: Matthew 2:13-15. Ed Young. 1988. 4.95 (978-0-7417-1698-9(4), 698) Win Walk.

Christmas in My Heart, Bk. 2. Short Stories. Joe L. Wheeler. Read by Joe L. Wheeler. 2 cass. (Running Time: 3 hrs.). (Christmas in My Heart Ser.: audio bk 2). 1993. 12.99 (978-0-8280-0840-2(X), 33-696) Review & Herald.

Christmas in My Heart, Bk. 3. Short Stories. Joe L. Wheeler. Read by Joe L. Wheeler. 2 cass. (Running Time: 3 hrs.). (Christmas in My Heart Ser.: audio bk 3). 1994. 12.99 (978-0-8280-0937-9(6), 33-697) Review & Herald.

Christmas in My Heart, Bk. 4. Short Stories. Joe L. Wheeler. Read by Joe L. Wheeler. 2 cass. (Running Time: 3 hrs.). (Christmas in My Heart Ser.: audio bk 4). 1995. 12.99 (978-0-8280-0994-2(5)) Review & Herald.

Christmas in My Heart, Bk. 5. abr. ed. Short Stories. Read by Joe L. Wheeler. Compiled by Joe L. Wheeler. 2 cass. (Running Time: 3 hrs). (Christmas in My Heart Ser.: audio bk 5). 1996. 12.99 (978-0-8280-1261-4(X)) Review & Herald.

Christmas in Norway: A Timeless Tradition. Narrated by Astrid K. Scott & Brent Marshall. 1 cass. (Running Time: 57 min.). 1997. (978-1-891096-01-3(X)) Nordic Advent.
Christmas traditions of Norway with people participating, music, etc. English narrations; soundtrack from video, "Christmas in Norway".

Christmas in Plains: Memories. Contrib. by Jimmy Carter. 3 CDs. (Running Time: 2 hrs. 30 mins.). audio compact disk 29.00 (978-1-4025-1367-1(4)) Recorded Bks.

Christmas in Plains: Memories. Jimmy Carter. Narrated by Jimmy Carter. 2 cass. (Running Time: 2 hrs. 30 mins.). 2001. 19.00 (978-1-4025-1288-9(0), 96972) Recorded Bks.
Jimmy Carter, the 39th president of the United States, captivated readers with his childhood memoir. He returns to his birthplace of Plains, Georgia for a stirring collection of yuletide remembrances.

Christmas in Plains: Memories. unabr. ed. Jimmy Carter. 2006. 13.95 (978-0-7435-6371-0(9), Audioworks) Pub: S&S Audio. Dist(s): S and S Inc

Christmas in South Africa. Contrib. by Bill & Gloria Gaither and Their Homecoming Friends et al. Prod. by Bill Gaither. (Running Time: 1 hr. 35 mins.). 2006. 19.99 (978-5-558-21053-8(2)) Gaither Music Co.

Christmas in South Africa. Directed By Ben Speer. Contrib. by Bill & Gloria Gaither and Their Homecoming Friends & Bill Gaither. 2006. audio compact disk 17.99 (978-5-558-21039-2(7)) Gaither Music Co.

Christmas in the Adirondacks. unabr. ed. Short Stories. William H. H. Murray. Narrated by John McDonough. 3 cass. (Running Time: 3 hrs. 45 mins.). 1997. 26.00 (978-0-7887-1745-1(6), 95223E7) Recorded Bks.
Two stories by an American naturalist writer who popularized outdoor activities like hiking & camping for the first time.

Christmas in the City. Arrow Records. 2008. audio compact disk 9.99 (978-1-59944-733-9(9)) Creflo Dollar.

Christmas in the Stable. 2004. pap. bk. 14.95 (978-1-56008-083-1(3)); 8.95 (978-1-56008-439-6(1)) Weston Woods.

Christmas in Two Acts: Two Stories by O. Henry, Including the Gift of the Magi. adpt. ed. O. Henry. Contrib. by Full Cast Production Staff. Adapted by Dave Arnold & Paul McCusker. (Running Time: 43 mins.). (Radio Theatre Ser.). (ENG.). (J). (gr. 1-7). 2007. audio compact disk 4.97 (978-1-58997-519-4(7), Tyndale Ent) Tyndale Hse.

Christmas in Wildwood. 2004. 13.00 (978-1-57972-602-7(X)) Insight Living.

Christmas Is. 10.98 (978-1-57908-240-6(8), 1297); audio compact disk 15.98 CD. (978-1-57908-239-0(4)) Platinm Enter.

***Christmas Is.** Composed by Jay Rouse. (Running Time: 4 mins.). (ENG.). 2010. audio compact disk 26.99 (978-1-4234-8700-5(1), 1423487001) Pub: Shawnee Pr. Dist(s): H Leonard

Christmas Is a Birthday: A Musical for Senior Adult Choir. Contrib. by Paul Ferrin. 2008. audio compact disk 90.00 (978-5-557-42032-7(0)); audio compact disk 12.00 (978-5-557-42031-0(2)) Lillenas.

***Christmas Is a Birthday: A Musical for Senior Adult Choir.** Contrib. by Paul Ferrin. (Running Time: 2100 sec.). (ENG.). 2008. audio compact disk 90.00 (978-5-557-42033-4(9)); audio compact disk 16.99 (978-5-557-42029-7(0)) Lillenas.

Christmas Is a Feeling. Mormon Youth Chorus and Symphony. 1 cass. 9.95 (10001107); audio compact disk 14.95 (2800756) Covenant Comms.
A combination of traditional & spiritual songs.

***Christmas Is a Sad Season for the Poor.** abr. ed. John Cheever. Read by Meryl Streep et al. (ENG.). 2009. (978-0-06-125286-0(7), Caedmon) HarperCollins Pubs.

***Christmas Is a Sad Season for the Poor.** unabr. ed. John Cheever. Read by Meryl Streep et al. (ENG.). 2009. (978-0-06-196859-4(5), Caedmon) HarperCollins Pubs.

Christmas Is All in the Heart. Perf. by Steven Curtis Chapman. 1 cass. 1999. Provident Music.

***Christmas Is Here.** Composed by Janet Gardner. (ENG.). 2010. audio compact disk 26.99 (978-1-4234-8774-6(5), 1423487745) Pub: Shawnee Pr. Dist(s): H Leonard

Christmas Is Love. Patti Teel. 2002. audio compact disk 12.95 (978-0-9656156-5-5(0)) Dream Flight Prods.

Christmas Is Love. Perf. by Patti Teel. 2002. 12.95 (978-0-9656156-4-8(2)) Dream Flight Prods.

Christmas Jars. Jason F. Wright. Read by Jason F. Wright. (Running Time: 14400 sec.). 2006. audio compact disk 17.95 (978-1-59038-677-4(9), Shadow Mount) Deseret Bk.

Christmas Jars Reunion. Wrightjason F. 2009. audio compact disk 29.95 (978-1-60641-170-4(5), Shadow Mount) Deseret Bk.

***Christmas Journey.** unabr. ed. Donna VanLiere. (Running Time: 1 hr. 0 mins. 0 sec.). (ENG.). 2010. audio compact disk 9.99 (978-1-4272-1030-2(6)) Pub: Macmill Audio. Dist(s): Macmillan

Christmas Joy. David Glen Hatch. 1 cass. 6.98 (1000349) Covenant Comms.
Fourteen favorite Christmas carols on piano.

Christmas Joy: Eb Alto Saxophone - Grade 3 - Book/CD Pack. Stephen Bulla. 2000. pap. bk. 12.95 (978-90-431-0924-6(X), 904310924X) H Leonard.

Christmas Joy: The Greatest Christmas Worship Songs of All Time. Contrib. by Don Moen. (Songs 4 Worship Ser.). 2007. audio compact disk 16.98 (978-5-557-58776-1(4)) Integrity Music.

Christmas Joy - Instrumental Solos for the Holiday Season: Bb Clarinet - Grade 3 - Book/CD Pack. Stephen Bulla. 2000. pap. bk. 12.95 (978-90-431-0923-9(1), 9043109231) H Leonard.

Christmas Joy - Instrumental Solos for the Holiday Season: Bb Trumpet - Grade 3 - Book/CD Pack. Stephen Bulla. 2000. pap. bk. 12.95 (978-90-431-0925-3(8), 9043109258) H Leonard.

Christmas Joy - Instrumental Solos for the Holiday Season: Flute - Grade 3 - Book/CD Pack. Stephen Bulla. 2000. pap. bk. 12.95 (978-90-431-0922-2(3), 9043109223) H Leonard.

Christmas Joy Let Heaven & Nature Sing. George H. Back. 2007. audio compact disk 14.95 (978-0-9800520-1-5(7)) Spirit &Intel.

***Christmas Lamp: A Novella.** Lori Copeland. (Running Time: 2 hrs. 48 mins. 0 sec.). (ENG.). 2009. 14.99 (978-0-310-77286-6(9)) Zondervan.

Christmas Legacy. Bill Wolaver. 1993. audio compact disk 85.00 (978-0-7673-1291-2(0)) LifeWay Christian.

Christmas Legacy. Bill Wolaver. 1993. 75.00 (978-0-7673-1251-6(1)) LifeWay Christian.

Christmas Legacy Choir Cassette. Bill Wolaver. 1993. 11.98 (978-0-7673-1310-0(0)) LifeWay Christian.

Christmas Letter. Contrib. by Johnathan Crumpton & Camp Kirkland. Prod. by Ed Kee. (ENG.). 2008. audio compact disk 24.99 (978-5-557-38258-8(5), Brentwood-Benson Music) Brentwood Music.

Christmas Letters. unabr. ed. Debbie Macomber. Read by Renée Raudman. (Running Time: 5 hrs. 0 mins. 0 sec.). (ENG.). 2006. audio compact disk 24.99 (978-1-4001-0320-1(7)); audio compact disk 19.99 (978-1-4001-5320-6(4)); audio compact disk 49.99 (978-1-4001-3320-8(3)) Pub: Tantor Media. Dist(s): IngramPubServ

Christmas Letters: A Timeless Story for Every Generation. Read by Bret Nicholaus. Based on a book by Bret Nicholaus. Intro. by Greg Wheatley. Prod. by Jay Paylaitner. 1 CD. (Running Time: 23 mins, 33 secs). Dramatization. 2003. audio compact disk 9.95 (978-0-9634251-8-8(8), CLA) Questmarc Pub.
Unabridged audio version of the book read by the author with background music and sound effects.

Christmas Lights. unabr. ed. Christine Pisera Naman. Read by Pam Ward. (Running Time: 12600 sec.). 2007. 14.95 (978-1-4332-0453-1(3)); audio compact disk 14.95 (978-1-4332-0454-8(1)); audio compact disk 19.95 (978-1-4332-0455-5(X)) Blckstn Audio.

Christmas Lights. unabr. ed. Christine Pisera Naman. Read by Pamela Ward. (Running Time: 12600 sec.). 2007. audio compact disk 24.00 (978-1-4332-0452-4(5)) Blckstn Audio.

Christmas Lights. unabr. ed. Christine Pisera Naman & Pam Ward. (Running Time: 12600 sec.). 2007. 22.95 (978-1-4332-0451-7(7)) Blckstn Audio.

Christmas Lights: A Concordia Celebration of Christmas. 2006. audio compact disk 14.00 (978-0-9786707-4-0(4)) Concord I Minis.

Christmas List: A Novel. unabr. ed. Richard Paul Evans. Read by John Dossett. 5 CDs. (Running Time: 5 hrs. 0 mins. 0 sec.). (ENG.). 2009. audio compact disk 29.99 (978-0-7435-9728-9(1)) Pub: S&S Audio. Dist(s): S and S Inc

Christmas Lullaby (I Will Lead You Home) - ShowTrax. Arranged by Mac Huff. Contrib. by Amy Grant. 1 CD. (Running Time: 5 mins.). 2000. audio compact disk 19.95 (08595542) H Leonard.
This Amy Grant original is exquisite! With simple yet elegant harmonies & a wonderful expressive text, you will create an unforgettable concert effect.

Christmas Magic. Read by Joanie Bartels. Prod. by David Wohlstadter & Ellen Wohlstadter. 1 cass. (Running Time: 30 min.). (Magic Ser.). (J). (gr. k-4). 1990. 9.95 Discov Music.
Celebrate the magic, fun, & spirit of the holiday season with this unique selection of playful holiday songs. Joanie Bartels will get everyone rockin' & rollin' with songs such as "Little Saint Nick," "Rockin' Around the Christmas Tree," & "Jingle Bells.".

Christmas Magic. Read by Joanie Bartels. 1 cass. (Running Time: 32 min.). (Magic Ser.). (J). 1990. 8.95 incl. lyric bk. (978-1-881225-07-2(0)) Discov Music.
New packaging includes full length audio cassette & complete full color lyric book with words to holiday hits & photos of Joanie & kids.

Christmas Magic. Read by Joanie Bartels. 1 cass. (J). (ps-5). 9.98 (422) MFLP CA.
Discovery Music presents this fun & playful collection of holiday songs for kids, including "Little Saint Nick," "Rockin' Around the Christmas Tree," "Frosty the Snowman," "Jingle Bell Rock," "Rudolph the Red-Nosed Reindeer," & more.

Christmas Melody, Set. Anita Stansfield. 2 cass. 9.95 (978-1-57734-336-3(0), 07001959) Covenant Comms.

Christmas Memories: Selected Sketches. unabr. ed. 1 cass. (Running Time: 60 min.). Dramatization. 7.95 Norelco box. (DD 7912) Natl Recrd Co.
Spencer Tracy: Tracy tells the classic story of a small 14 year old donkey that is to be sold to a tanner...until the miracle of Christmas happens. With Lee J. Cobb & Howard Duff. 1994. Lum & Abner: Their traditional Christmas show, first told in 1933. A Nativity story as seen in a real life incident in Pine Ridge, Arkansas. A warm Christmas story, 1940's. Orson Welles & Bing Crosby: The beloved Oscar Wilde Christmas Story, The Happy Prince, about a statue & a little swallow that made his home in the statue. 1944. Bing Crosby, Dixie Lee & Family: Bing's first family...Gary, Dennis, Phillip & Lindsey. Bing insists on being Santa, but of course no one is fooled. Lot of wise cracks, & the singing of another generation. 1950.

Christmas Message from Myrtle Smyth. unabr. ed. Myrtle Smyth. 1 cass. (Running Time: 1 hrs.). (Myrtle Smyth Audiotapes Ser.: Vol. 24). 1999. 8.95 (978-1-893107-26-7(4), M24) Healing Unltd.
Lecture on peace.

Christmas Message 2006. 2006. audio compact disk 9.99 (978-1-57972-698-0(4)) Insight Living.

***Christmas Miracle.** Norma Garza. 2007. audio compact disk 19.99 (978-1-59886-958-3(2)) Tate Pubng.

Christmas Miracle of Jonathan Toomey. James Earl Jones. (J). 2000. bk. 24.99 (978-0-8499-7682-7(0)) Nelson.

Christmas Mood: Instrumental Contemporary Christian Classics. Perf. by Dan Cutrona. 2004. pap. bk. 11.99 (978-0-7684-0209-4(3)) Destiny Image Pubs.

Christmas Mouse & No Holly for Miss Quinn. unabr. ed. Miss Read. Read by Gwen Watford. 6 cass. (Running Time: 9 hrs.). 2000. 49.95 (978-0-7451-6221-8(5), CAB 639) Pub: Chivers Audio Bks GBR. Dist(s): AudioGO
In No Holly for Miss Quinn, the three young children of Miss Quinn's brother are staying with her while their mother is in the hospital. In The Christmas Mouse, a mouse's appearance on Christmas Eve in an old widow's bedroom leads to a chance encounter with a small boy; a meeting that would be remembered by both of them for a long time.

Christmas Music. Contrib. by Tom Fettke. (ENG.). 1997. audio compact disk 12.00 (978-0-00-523194-4(9)) Lillenas.

Christmas Music for Banjo Made Easy. Contrib. by Ross Nickerson. 2007. pap. bk. 14.95 (978-0-7866-7702-3(3)) Mel Bay.

Christmas Music for Electric Guitar: This Collection Includes Music Arranged for One, Two, or Three Guitars. John Kiefer. (ENG.). 2001. audio compact disk 14.95 (978-0-7866-0096-0(9), 98673BCD) Mel Bay.

Christmas Music for Guitar from the Sixteenth & Seventeenth Centuries: Intermediate Level. E. James Kalal. 1987. audio compact disk 15.98 (978-0-7866-0132-5(9), 94181CD) Mel Bay.

Christmas Mystery. unabr. ed. Jostein Gaarder. Narrated by John McDonough. 5 cass. (Running Time: 6 hrs. 15 mins.). 1997. 44.00 (978-0-7887-1312-5(4), 95044E7) Recorded Bks.
A unique Advent calendar becomes the catalyst for a mystifying backward journey through space & time at angelic speed.

Christmas Night. Karyn Henley. Perf. by Karyn Henley. (ENG.). (J). 2006. audio compact disk 8.99 (978-1-933803-17-3(7)) Child Sens Comm.

Christmas Night Murder. unabr. ed. Lee Harris. Read by Susan O'Malley. 5 cass. (Running Time: 7 hrs.). (Christine Bennett Mystery Ser.). 1999. 39.95 (978-0-7861-1672-0(2), 2500) Blckstn Audio.
Christine Bennett, a former St. Stephen's nun, arrives to investigate the disappearance. But the nuns are mum until an old scandal involving the priest & a St. Stephen's novice rears its ugly head. Has Father McCormick, unable to face the scene of his sins, gone underground? Or has someone taken belated revenge ensuring that the truth will never be known?.

***Christmas Night Murder: A Christine Bennett Mystery.** unabr. ed. Lee Harris. Read by Susan O'Malley. (Running Time: 7 hrs.). 2010. 29.95 (978-1-4417-1358-2(1)); audio compact disk 69.00 (978-1-4417-1355-1(7)) Blckstn Audio.

***Christmas Odyssey: A Novel.** Anne Perry. Narrated by Terrence Hardiman. (Running Time: 5 hrs. 0 mins. 0 sec.). (ENG.). 2010. audio compact disk 19.95 (978-1-60998-103-7(0)) Pub: AudioGO. Dist(s): Perseus Dist

Christmas Odyssey: 12 Stories Celebrating the True Meaning of Christmas. AIO Team Staff. Created by Tyndale House Publishers Staff. (Running Time: 4 hrs. 30 mins.). (Adventures in Odyssey Ser.). (ENG.). (J). (gr. 1-7). 2007. audio compact disk 24.99 (978-1-58997-472-2(7), Tyndale Ent) Tyndale Hse.

Christmas of the Angels. unabr. ed. Dora Van Gelder. 2 cass. (Running Time: 1 hr.). 1989. pap. bk. 5.95 (978-0-8356-2095-6(6), Quest) Pub: Theos Pub Hse. Dist(s): Natl Bk Netwk
The heightened role that angels play during the Christmas season. Includes the popular booklet of the same title.

Christmas Offering: A Praise & Worship Celebration for Any Choir. Contrib. by Marty Parks. 2008. audio compact disk 90.00 (978-5-557-42027-3(4)); audio compact disk 16.99 (978-5-557-42021-1(5)) Lillenas.

***Christmas Offering: A Praise & Worship Celebration for Any Choir.** Contrib. by Marty Parks. (ENG.). 2008. audio compact disk 90.00 (978-5-557-42026-6(6)) Lillenas.

***Christmas Offering: A Praise & Worship Celebration for Any Choir: SATB.** Contrib. by Marty Parks. (ENG.). 2008. audio compact disk 60.00 (978-5-557-42025-9(8)) Lillenas.

Christmas on Miracle Lane. Kaye Jacobs Volk. 1 cass. 1.77 (978-1-55503-763-5(1), 06004970); 3.98 (06004970) Covenant Comms.
An inspiring Christmas story.

Christmas on the Back Porch: 20 Treasured Songs of the Season. Created by Barbour Publishing. 2006. audio compact disk 4.97 (978-1-59789-426-5(5), Barbour Bks) Barbour Pub.

Christmas Oranges. Linda Bethers. (J). 2004. audio compact disk 9.95 (978-1-57734-756-9(0)) Covenant Comms.

Christmas Oranges. Linda Bethers. 2004. 7.95 (978-1-57734-755-2(2)) Covenant Comms.

Christmas Oratorio - Johann Se. Edel Staff. 2006. pap. bk. 49.95 (978-3-937406-02-2(6)) Pub: edel CLASS DEU. Dist(s): Natl Bk Netwk

***Christmas Pearl.** unabr. ed. Dorothea Benton Frank. Read by Celia Weston. (ENG.). 2007. (978-0-06-155530-5(4)); (978-0-06-155531-2(2)) HarperCollins Pubs.

Christmas Pearl. unabr. ed. Dorothea Benton Frank. Read by Celia Weston. 2007. audio compact disk 14.95 (978-0-06-145791-3(4), Harper Audio) HarperCollins Pubs.

Christmas Piano Ensembles: Level 1. Phillip Keveren. 2003. audio compact disk 10.95 (978-0-634-06776-1(1), 0634067761) H Leonard.

Christmas Piano Ensembles: Level 2. Phillip Keveren. 2003. audio compact disk 10.95 (978-0-634-06774-7(5), 0634067745) H Leonard.

Christmas Piano Ensembles: Level 4. Phillip Keveren. 2004. audio compact disk 10.95 (978-0-634-08993-0(5), 0634089935) H Leonard.

Christmas Piano Ensembles: Level 5. Phillip Keveren. 2004. audio compact disk 10.95 (978-0-634-08996-1(X), 063408996X) H Leonard.

Christmas Piano Ensembles - Level 3. Phillip Keveren. 2004. audio compact disk 10.95 (978-0-634-06772-3(9), 0634067729) H Leonard.

Christmas Piano Solos. Phillip Keveren. (ENG.). 1998. audio compact disk 10.95 (978-0-7935-9674-4(2), 0793596742) H Leonard.

Christmas Piano Solos, Level 3. Phillip Keveren. 1998. pap. bk. 10.95 (978-0-7935-9676-8(9), 0793596769) H Leonard.

Christmas Piano Solos, Level 5. Phillip Keveren. (Hal Leonard Student Piano Library). 2000. audio compact disk 10.95 (978-0-634-02535-8(X), 063402535X) H Leonard.

Christmas Piano Solos: Level 2. Phillip Keveren. 1998. pap. bk. 10.95 (978-0-7935-9675-1(0), 0793596750) H Leonard.

Christmas Piano Solos: Level 4. Phillip Keveren. 1998. pap. bk. 10.95 (978-0-7935-9677-5(7), 0793596777) H Leonard.

Christmas Poems. Mary M. Slappey. Read by Mary M. Slappey. (Running Time: 30 min). 1986. 10.00 Interspace Bks.

Christmas Pops. 1 cass., 1 CD. audio compact disk 10.98 CD. (978-1-57908-378-6(1), 1542) Platinm Enter.

Christmas Praise. Perf. by Gospel Kids Present. 1 cass., 1 CD. 10.98 (978-1-57908-333-5(1), 1409); audio compact disk 15.98 CD. (978-1-57908-332-8(3), 1409) Platinm Enter.

Christmas Praise. Perf. by Leonard Scott. 1 cass., 1 CD. 10.98 (978-1-57908-402-8(8), 1411); audio compact disk 15.98 CD. (978-1-57908-401-1(X), 1411) Platinm Enter.

Christmas Prayer. Contrib. by Aaron Neville. Prod. by Milton Davis. 2005. audio compact disk 17.98 (978-5-559-48635-2(3)) Pt of Grace Ent.

Christmas Presence. 1 CD. audio compact disk 16.98 (978-1-57908-490-5(7), 5349) Platinm Enter.

Christmas Presence. Short Stories. Contrib. by Tom McGrath et al. 1 CD. (Running Time: 68 min.). 2003. audio compact disk 12.95 (978-0-87946-251-2(5), 414) ACTA Pubns.
Now enjoy some of the beautiful stories from the bestselling book CHRISTMAS PRESENCE as an audiobook!.

Christmas Presence, Set. unabr. ed. 1 cass., 1 CD. 10.98 (978-1-57908-491-2(5), 5349) Platinm Enter.

Christmas Present. Contrib. by John DeVries. Created by Pam Andrews. 2007. audio compact disk 12.00 (978-5-557-69924-2(4)) Lillenas.

***Christmas, Present.** unabr. ed. Jacquelyn Mitchard. Read by Jacquelyn Mitchard. (ENG.). 2003. (978-0-06-073608-8(9), Harper Audio); (978-0-06-079945-8(5), Harper Audio) HarperCollins Pubs.

Christmas Present: An Easy-to-Sing, Easy-to-Stage Christmas Musical for Children. Contrib. by John DeVries. Created by Pam Andrews. 2007. audio compact disk 49.99 (978-5-557-69925-9(2)) Lillenas.

Christmas Prime Mover Cd Listening Cd. Dennis Allen & Nan Allen. 2000. audio compact disk 3.00 (978-0-633-01556-5(3)) LifeWay Christian.

***Christmas Promise.** unabr. ed. Anne Perry. Read by Terrence Hardiman. 1 Playaway. (Running Time: 3 hrs. 30 mins.). 2009. 64.95 (978-0-7927-6821-0(3)); audio compact disk 59.95 (978-0-7927-6709-1(8)) AudioGO.

Christmas Promise. unabr. ed. Donna VanLiere. Read by Donna VanLiere. (Running Time: 14400 sec.). (ENG.). 2007. audio compact disk 19.95 (978-1-4272-0189-8(7)) Pub: Macmill Audio. Dist(s): Macmillan

Christmas Promise. unabr. ed. Donna VanLiere. Narrated by Donna VanLiere. (Running Time: 6 hrs. 0 mins. 0 sec.). (ENG.). 2007. audio compact disk 19.99 (978-1-59859-304-4(8)) Oasis Audio.

Christmas Promise: Accompaniment/Performance. Composed by Lloyd Larson. 1 CD. (Running Time: 1 hr. 30 mins.). (ENG.). 2000. audio compact disk 45.00 (978-0-7390-0535-4(9), 19078) Alfred Pub.

Christmas Promise: Preview Pack. Composed by Lloyd Larson. (ENG.). 2000. audio compact disk 12.95 (978-0-7390-0534-7(0)) Alfred Pub.

Christmas Quilt. Jennifer Chiaverini. Narrated by Christina Moore. (Running Time: 23400 sec.). (Elm Creek Quilts Ser.: No. 8). 2007. audio compact disk 29.99 (978-1-4281-7003-2(0)) Recorded Bks.

Christmas Radio Classics. (Running Time: 2 hrs.). 2004. audio compact disk 12.95 (978-1-57816-195-9(9)) Audio File.

Christmas Rat. Avi. Narrated by Jeff Woodman. 3 CDs. (Running Time: 2 hrs. 45 mins.). (gr. 7 up). audio compact disk 29.00 (978-0-7887-6166-9(8)) Recorded Bks.

Christmas Rat. unabr. ed. Avi. Narrated by Jeff Woodman. 2 cass. (Running Time: 2 hrs. 45 mins.). (YA). 2001. pap. bk. & stu. ed. 46.00 Recorded Bks.
With his parents having to work & his friends out of town & also the town is snowed in, Eric is finding his vacation boring until he meets Anje Babrail, who takes him on an adventure of his life.

Christmas Rat. unabr. ed. Avi. Narrated by Jeff Woodman. 2 pieces. (Running Time: 2 hrs. 45 mins.). (gr. 7 up). 2001. 23.00 (978-0-7887-4724-3(X), 96398E7) Recorded Bks.

Christmas Rat. unabr. ed. Avi. Narrated by Jeff Woodman. 2 CDs. (Running Time: 2 hrs. 45 min.). (YA). (gr. 5-8). 2001. audio compact disk 29.00 (C1390) Recorded Bks.
It's the week before Christmas & Eric is already bored with his vacation. His parents have to work, his friends are out of town & the city is snowed under. Then he opens his apartment door for an exterminator & is dragged into the adventure of his life. Anje Gabrail carries a crossbow & lives for his work. When he discovers a rat in the basement of Eric's apartment building, he asks the boy to help him kill it. At first Eric agrees, after all, he doesn't have anything better to do. But as the week progresses, Eric finds himself in a fight to save not only the rat but himself as well.

Christmas Revels. 1 cass. (Running Time: 41 min.). 1978. 7.95 (CA 1078); audio compact disk 14.95 (CD 1078) Revels Recs.
Presents Medieval/Renaissance celebration of the winter solstice in song, carols, processionals, drama, dance, poetry and folk ritual by a Revels chorus of children and adults.

Christmas Rose. abr. ed. Arthur Silber, Jr.. Read by Arthur Silber, Jr. Contrib. by Klaus Ernst & Selma Lagerlöf. 1 cass. (Running Time: 25 min.). (YA). (gr. 3 up). 1996. 3.00 (978-0-9655675-0-3(8)) Samart.
Christmas stories from around the world for all ages.

Christmas Sampler #2 Cass. 2004. 99.00 (978-1-58997-039-7(X)) Nelson.

Christmas Secret. unabr. ed. Anne Perry. Narrated by Terrence Hardiman. 3 CDs. (Running Time: 14400 sec.). (J). (gr. 3-7). 2006. audio compact disk 39.95 (978-0-7927-4477-1(2), SLD 1007) AudioGO.

Christmas Secret. unabr. ed. Anne Perry. Read by Terrence Hardiman. 3 cass. (Running Time: 14400 sec.). 2006. 34.95 (978-0-7927-4541-9(8), CSL 1007) AudioGO.

Christmas Secret. unabr. ed. Donna VanLiere. (Running Time: 6 hrs. 0 mins. 0 sec.). (ENG.). 2009. audio compact disk 29.99 (978-1-4272-0765-4(8)) Pub: Macmill Audio. Dist(s): Macmillan

Christmas Shoes. Contrib. by Newsong. 2001. audio compact disk 9.98 (978-5-550-10628-0(0)) Pt of Grace Ent.

Christmas Shoes. unabr. rev. ed. Donna VanLiere. Read by Paul Michael. 3 CDs. (Running Time: 3 hrs. 0 mins. 0 sec.). (FRE & ENG., 2002. audio compact disk 19.95 (978-1-55927-775-4(0)) Pub: Macmill Audio. Dist(s): Macmillan

Christmas Shows, Vol. 1, Set. 6 cass. (Running Time: 6 hrs.). (Best of Old Time Radio Ser.). 24.95 in bookshelf album. (978-1-57816-030-3(8), CS1013) Audio File.
Includes: "Cavalcade of America" (12-25-44); "Challenge of the Yukon" (12-22-48); "Charlie McCarthy Show" (12-19-48); "Dragnet" (12-22-53); "Great Gildersleeve" (12-22-48); "Gunsmoke" (12-20-52); "Jack Benny Program" (12-19-48); "Life of Riley" (12-24-44); "Our Miss Brooks" (12-24-50); "Phil Harris - Alice Faye Show" (12-26-48); "Six Shooter" (12-20-50); "Truth or Consequences" (12-20-47).

Christmas Shows, Vol. 2, Set. 6 cass. (Running Time: 6 hrs.). 24.95 in bookshelf album. (978-1-57816-031-0(6), CS2023) Audio File.
Includes: "Amos 'n' Andy" (12-24-50); "Bing Crosby" (12-25-46); "Burns & Allen" (12-18-44); "Fibber McGee & Molly" (12-22-42); "Jack Benny" (12-26-43); "Life with Luigi" (12-20-48); "Adventures of Nero Wolfe" (12-22-50); "Red Skelton" (12-24-46); "Richard Diamond, Private Detective" (12-19-51); "The Whistler" (12-24-50); "A Christmas Carol" (12-24-39).

Christmas Sing-Along Songbook. 1 cass. or CD. (Running Time: 49 min.). (J). 2001. pap. bk. 12.99 (978-1-894281-80-5(2)) Kidzup Prodns.
The Inspirational Kids sing some of their favorite Christmas songs. Includes: "Twelve Days of Christmas", "Jingle Bells", "Deck the Halls" & more.

Christmas! Sing of the Wonder. Contrib. by Ted Wilson. 1994. 11.98 (978-1-55897-534-7(9), 75602279) Pub: Brentwood Music. Dist(s): H Leonard

Christmas Sleigh Ride. Perf. by White Brothers. 1 cass. (Running Time: 60 min.). 1994. audio compact disk 15.95 CD. (2645, Creativ Pub) Quayside.
Winter sounds highlight music performed by The White Brothers.

Christmas Sleigh Ride. Perf. by White Brothers. 1 cass. (Running Time: 60 min.). 1994. 9.95 (2644, NrthWrd Bks) TandN Child.

***Christmas Snow.** Jim Stovall. (ENG.). 2010. audio compact disk 24.99 (978-0-7684-0258-2(1)) Destiny Image Pubs.

***Christmas Snow.** Jim Stovall. Narrated by Vickie Daniels. (ENG.). 2010. audio compact disk 19.99 (978-1-936081-27-1(X)) Casscomm.

Christmas Solos for Beginning Pan Flute: Beginning-Intermediate Level. Costel Puscoiu. 1997. pap. bk. 14.95 (978-0-7866-2076-0(5), 95972BCD) Mel Bay.

Christmas Sonata. unabr. ed. Gary Paulsen. Narrated by Johnny Heller. 1 cass. (Running Time: 1 hr.). Rental 6.50 (94628) Recorded Bks.

Christmas Sonata. unabr. ed. Gary Paulsen. Narrated by Johnny Heller. 1 cass. (Running Time: 1 hr.). (gr. 3 up). 2001. 10.00 (978-0-7887-0436-9(2), 94628E7) Recorded Bks.

Christmas Songbook. 1 cd. audio compact disk 10.98 (978-1-57908-392-2(7), 1665) Platinm Enter.

Christmas Songs see Chants de Noel

***Christmas Songs.** Ed. by Anna Joyce. (Take the Lead Ser.). 2009. pap. bk. 14.99 (978-1-84328-830-5(3)) IMP GBR.

Christmas Songs. Bil Keane. 1 cass. (Running Time: 30 min.). (Family Circus Sings! Ser.). (J). 1994. pap. bk. 5.95 ea. Penton Overseas.
Here's a series that brings the whole family together to sing along & enjoy catchy, good-time tunes. Sure to capture the heart & imagination of any child.

***Christmas Songs: Ukulele Play-along Series Volume 5.** Created by Hal Leonard Corp. (ENG.). 2010. pap. bk. 12.99 (978-1-4234-9474-4(1), 1423494741) H Leonard.

Christmas Songs for Beginning Guitar: Learn to Play 15 Complete Holiday Classics. Composed by Peter Penhallow. (ENG.). 2001. pap. bk. 9.99 (978-1-4234-8475-2(4), 1423484754) Pub: String Letter. Dist(s): H Leonard

Christmas Songs for Folk Harp. Chuck Bird & Susan Peters. 1994. spiral bd. 21.95 (978-0-7866-1140-9(5), 95307P) Mel Bay.

Christmas Songs for 5-String Banjo. Janet Davis. 1995. pap. bk. 24.95 (978-0-7866-0690-0(8), 95444CDP) Mel Bay.

Christmas Star. 1 cass. (Running Time: 27 min.). 14.95 (23573) MMI Corp.
Astronomers speculate about the star the shepherds saw. Venus, comets, other possibilities are explored.

Christmas Star. Mary Thienes-Schunemann. Illus. by Lura Schwarz Smith. Intro. by René Querido. (J). 2001. bk. 21.95 (978-0-9708397-2-5(3)) Pub: Naturally You. Dist(s): SteinerBooks Inc

Christmas Star. Perf. by CeCe Winans. 1 cass. 1999. Provident Music.

Christmas Store. unabr. ed. Short Stories. Ray Sipherd. Read by Christopher Lane. 7 cass. (Running Time: 7 hrs.). 1994. 42.00 (978-0-7366-2858-7(4), 3565) Books on Tape.
In 12 interwoven short stories, a retired department store employee tells what goes on during the Christmas holidays.

Christmas Stories. Charles Dickens. Narrated by Robert Whitfield. (Running Time: 4 hrs.). (J). 2000. 22.95 (978-1-59912-635-7(4)) Iofy Corp.

Christmas Stories. Vincent Douglas. 1 cass. (Running Time: 60 min.). Incl. Desert Shall Rejoice. Read by John Hodiak. (DD-7911); Silent Night. James Hilton. (DD-7911); 7.95 (DD-7911) Natl Recrd Co.
Silent Night is the radio version of how the song, "Silent Night" came to be written in the year 1818. It was composed by a father & a schoolteacher & sung for the first time on Christmas Eve. "The Desert Shall Rejoice" is the story of Nick, the tough guy, "with a big heart." He hates Christmas. He puts 700 light bulbs in a sign only to discover that is doesn't work, has several other things upset him, but at the end his faith in Christmas is restored.

Christmas Stories. Vincent Douglas. 1 cass. (Running Time: 39 min.). (Picture Book Parade Ser.). (J). (ps-4). 1981. 8.95 (978-0-89719-947-6(2), WW715C) Weston Woods.
This anthology includes "The Little Drummer Boy," "The Holy Night," "The Twelve Days of Christmas," "Christmas in the Stable," "The Clown of God" & "M orris's Disappearing Bag".

Christmas Stories. unabr. ed. Charles Dickens. Narrated by Robert Whitfield. 4 CDs. (Running Time: 4 hrs.). 2001. audio compact disk 32.00 (978-0-7861-9631-9(9), 2885) Blckstn Audio.
These stories are recollections of childhood, reflections on past holidays and old friends, as well as tales of misunderstandings and lost opportunities. They offer a master storyteller's vision of the real meaning of Christmas.

Christmas Stories. unabr. ed. Charles Dickens. Narrated by Robert Whitfield. 3 cass. (Running Time: 4 hrs.). 2001. 23.95 (978-0-7861-2125-0(4), 2885) Blckstn Audio.

Christmas Stories: Two Stories about Christmas: The First Christmas & The Glittering Cathedral. Gordon Sullivan. Perf. by Rick Olmos et al. Comment by Pat Bottino. 1 cass. (Running Time: 65 mins.). Dramatization. (J). 1997. 9.95 (978-0-9655275-1-4(4)) Vis Aud Pub Inc.
Includes: "The First Christmas," a dramatization from a modern version of the King James Bible, with Traditional Christmas music underscoring story highlights. Also: "The Glittering Cathedral," a modern tale of the power of the Christmas spirit. An annual pilgrimage to the temple of the "great green god of materialism," where they discover a remote corner of the temple they had not explored before. What they found there takes them by surprise & has a profound effect upon them.

Christmas Stories to Warm the Heart. Jan Carlberg & Margaret Jensen. Read by Jan Carlberg & Margaret Jensen. 1 CD. (Running Time: 60 min.). 2001. audio compact disk 10.00 (978-0-9707487-3-7(6)) Gor Coll.
An original colleciton of inspirational Christmas storiesO.

Christmas Story. Contrib. by Mike Gay & Sue Gay. 1995. 90.00 (978-0-00-508779-4(1), 75608250) Pub: Brentwood Music. Dist(s): H Leonard

Christmas Story. Contrib. by Mike Gay & Sue Gay. 1996. audio compact disk 90.00 (978-0-00-513493-1(5), 75608248) Pub: Brentwood Music. Dist(s): H Leonard

Christmas Story. Neville Goddard. 1 cass. (Running Time: 62 min.). 1964. 8.00 (59) J & L Pubns.
Neville taught Imagination Creates Reality. He was a powerfully influential teacher of God as Consciousness.

Christmas Story. Narrated by Max E. McLean. 1 CD. (Running Time: 25 mins.). 2002. audio compact disk 9.95 (978-1-931047-31-9(6)) Pub: Fellow Perform Arts. Dist(s): Spring Arbor Dist

Christmas Story. unabr. ed. Read by Nerys Hughes & Stephen Thorne. 1 cass. (Running Time: 1 hr., 30 min.). (J). (gr. 1-8). 1999. 9.95 (CTC 779, Chivers Child Audio) AudioGO.

Christmas Story: Cedarmont Kids. 1 cass., 1 CD. (J). 1998. 5.99 Provident Mus Dist.
The story of Christ's birth in story and in song.

Christmas Story: What Really Happened? Chuck Missler. 2 cass. (Running Time: 2.5 hours plus). (Briefing Packages by Chuck Missler). 1994. vinyl bd. 14.95 Incls. notes. (978-1-880532-62-1(X)) Koinonia Hse.
** What really happened in Bethlehem two thousand years ago? * Who were the "Magi?" * Why a virgin birth?* What does a Christmas Tree have to do with it?Each year at Christmas we celebrate the birth of Jesus Christ.After the New Year, we struggle to remember to add a year as we date our checks, which should remind us that the entire Western World reckons its calendar from the birth of the One who changed the world more than any other before or since.It is disturbing to discover that much of what we have been taught about the Christmas season seems to be more tradition than truth. Santa Claus isn't the only myth or legend that has arisen out of this season.On what "loophole" does the Messianic hope rest? Who were the Maji? And why a "virgin birth?" Find out what really happened in Bethlehem two thousand years ago.*

Christmas Story: What Really Happened in Bethlehem Two Thousand Years Ago? Chuck Missler. 2 CD's. (Running Time: 2 hrs.). (Briefing Packages by Chuck Missler). 1994. audio compact disk 19.95 (978-1-57821-318-4(5)) Koinonia Hse.
What really happened in Bethlehem two thousand years ago? Who were the "Magi?" Why a virgin birth? What does a Christmas Tree have to do with it? Each year at Christmas we celebrate the birth of Jesus Christ.After the New Year, we struggle to remember to add a year as we date our checks, which should remind us that the entire Western World reckons its calendar from the birth of the One who changed the world more than any other before or since. It is disturbing to discover that much of what we have been taught about the Christmas season seems to be more tradition than truth. Santa Claus isn't the only myth or legend that has arisen out of this season.On what "loophole" does the Messianic hope rest? Who were the Maji? And why a "virgin birth?" Find out what really happened in Bethlehem two thousand years ago.

Christmas Story & The Three Wisemen. abr. ed. Laura Williams. 1 cass. (Running Time: 1 hr.). Dramatization. (Best Loved Bible Stories Ser.). (J). (ps-3). 1995. 9.99 (978-0-8423-6077-7(8)) Tyndale Hse.
Fully dramatized Bible stories for kids with original music & songs. Two stories & a 48-page activity booklet.

Christmas Story from the NIV & KJV Audio Bibles. unabr. ed. 2002. 71.64 (978-0-310-95686-0(2)) Zondervan.

Christmas Story Rhymes. unabr. ed. Alfreda C. Doyle. Read by Alfreda C. Doyle. 1 cass. (Running Time: 35 min.). (Alfreda's Radio Ser.: Vol. 6). (J). (gr. 5-9). 1998. 15.95 (978-1-56820-310-2(1)) Story Time.
Stories that educate, entertain, inform & rhyme.

Christmas Suite. Mark Brymer. 2003. pap. bk. 69.95 (978-0-634-05699-4(9)); audio compact disk 59.95 (978-0-634-05696-3(4)); audio compact disk 14.95 (978-0-634-05700-7(6)) H Leonard.

***Christmas Sweater.** unabr. ed. Glenn Beck. Read by Glenn Beck. (Running Time: 5 hrs. 0 mins. 0 sec.). (ENG.). 2010. audio compact disk 14.99 (978-1-4423-3617-9(X)) Pub: S&S Audio. Dist(s): S and S Inc

Christmas Sweater. unabr. ed. Glenn Beck et al. Read by Glenn Beck. 4 CDs. (Running Time: 5 hrs. 0 mins. 0 sec.). (ENG.). 2008. audio compact disk 29.99 (978-0-7435-7815-8(5)) Pub: S&S Audio. Dist(s): S and S Inc

Christmas Tales: From the Hearth of Catherine Doherty. Short Stories. Catherine Doherty. Featuring Catherine Doherty. Read by Madonna House Apostolate Staff. 1 cass. (Running Time: 1 hr.). 2001. 9.95 (978-0-921440-73-4(1)) Madonna Hse CAN.
Catherine tells the story of "The Donkey" and the old custom of wearing donkey bells during Advent. Adults and children alike will be inspired by her reminder that the first church bells were really the bells the humble donkey wore as he carried Mary to Bethlehem. Also includes readings of holiday stories, including "Christmas in Harlem," "A Woman, A Child, and Christmas," "How Pride Became Humble," and Eddie Doherty's story, "The Christmas Angel O'Ryan.".

Christmas Talk Story. Honolulu Theatre for Youth Staff. (J). 2003. bk. 14.95 (978-1-57306-172-8(7)) Bess Pr.

Christmas Tapestry. Contrib. by Bruce Greer. 1996. audio compact disk 15.98 (978-0-00-513532-7(X), 75608429) Pub: Brentwood Music. Dist(s): H Leonard

Christmas Tells the Truth: John 1:14; Luke 2:1-14. Ed Young. (J). 1980. 4.95 (978-0-7417-1152-6(4), A0152) Win Walk.

Christmas That Almost Wasn't see Christmas with Ogden Nash

Christmas, the Day When Divine Love was Made Flesh. Instructed by Manly P. Hall. 8.95 (978-0-89314-026-7(0), C8412230) Philos Res.

***Christmas: the Message.** abr. ed. Eugene H. Petersen. Narrated by Mark Lowry. (ENG.). 2006. 9.09 (978-1-60814-740-3(1)) Oasis Audio.

Christmas Thief. unabr. ed. Mary Higgins Clark & Carol Higgins Clark. (Regan Reilly Mystery Ser.). 2004. 15.95 (978-0-7435-4498-6(6)) Pub: S&S Audio. Dist(s): S and S Inc

Christmas Through Candlemas Vol. 2: Music for Feasts of Light. Michael Thompson. 2005. audio compact disk 16.95 (978-0-8146-7929-6(3)) Liturgical Pr.

Christmas Tides. Perf. by Don McCune. 1 cass, 1 CD. 1992. 7.95 Digitally Recorded. (A102); audio compact disk 12.95 CD. (C102) Don McCune Library.
Includes McCune's own Puget Sound Christmas ballad, "Christmas Tides," plus "Silver Bells," "Frosty the Snowman," "What Child is This?" "We Three Kings," "Do You Hear What I Hear?" & "It's Beginning to Look a Lot Like Christmas".

Christmas Time. Gail Gibbons. Illus. by Gail Gibbons. (J). (gr. k-3). 1985. bk. 22.95 (978-0-941078-84-9(1)) Live Oak Media.

(Christmas Time Is) No Time to Diet. Contrib. by Johnathan Crumpton & David Huntsinger. (ENG.). 2004. audio compact disk 24.99 (978-5-559-66418-7(9), Brentwood-Benson Music) Brentwood Music.

Christmas Time of Year: Sing, Color'n Say. Lenore Paxton & Phillip Siadi. Read by Lenore Paxton & Phillip Siadi. 1 cass. (Running Time: 46 min.). (World of Language Ser.). (J). (ps-4). 1995. 5.95 (978-1-880449-30-1(7)) Wrldkids Pr.
Sing-along song, musical effects, teach "Merry Christmas" in 10 languages along with entertaining narrative presenting Christmas customs, folklore, celebrations in many countries around the world. Companion coloring book included.

Christmas Time of Year: Sing, Color'n Say. 2nd ed. Lenore Paxton & Phillip Siadi. Read by Lenore Paxton & Phillip Siadi. 1 cass. (Running Time: 46 min.). (World of Language Ser.). (J). (ps up). 1994. pap. bk. 7.95 (978-1-880449-10-3(2)) Wrldkids Pr.

Christmas to Remember. Robert C. Bowden. 1 cass. 8.95 (10001470); audio compact disk 12.95 (28001120) Covenant Comms.
Beautiful Christmas carols.

Christmas to Remember. Contrib. by Brandon Egerton. Prod. by Myron Butler et al. 2006. audio compact disk 17.99 (978-5-558-21031-6(1)) Pt of Grace Ent.

Christmas Traditions: 20 Treasured Songs of the Season. Created by Barbour Publishing. 2006. audio compact disk 4.97 (978-1-59789-424-1(9), Barbour Bks) Barbour Pub.

Christmas Train. David Baldacci. 2002. audio compact disk 48.00 (978-0-7366-8882-6(X)) Books on Tape.

Christmas Train. unabr. ed. David Baldacci. Read by Tim Matheson. (ENG.). 2005. 14.98 (978-1-59483-317-5(6)) Pub: Hachet Audio. Dist(s): HachBkGrp

Christmas Train. unabr. ed. David Baldacci. Read by Tim Matheson. (Running Time: 7 hrs.). (ENG.). 2009. 54.98 (978-1-60024-909-9(4)) Pub: Hachet Audio. Dist(s): HachBkGrp

Christmas Train. unabr. ed. David Baldacci. Read by Tim Matheson. 6 CDs. (Running Time: 7 hrs.). (ENG.). 2004. audio compact disk 14.98 (978-1-59483-050-1(9)) Pub: Hachet Audio. Dist(s): HachBkGrp

Christmas Treasures. David Glen Hatch. 1 cass. 9.95 (3111288); audio compact disk 14.95 (333328) Covenant Comms.
Twelve favorite songs & medleys with Marden Pond conducting a full orchestra.

Christmas Tree. Rick Charette. Read by Rick Charette. 1 cass. (Running Time: 44 min.). (J). (gr. k-5). 1988. 9.98 (978-1-884210-03-7(1), PPC-003); 9.98 (978-1-884210-04-4(X)) Pine Pt Record.
A wonderful holiday recording for children, the album features seven original Christmas songs as well as some traditional favorites by singer/songwriter Rick Charette.

Christmas Troll. 2005. audio compact disk 24.00 (978-0-7861-7386-0(6)) Blckstn Audio.

Christmas Troll. Eugene H. Peterson. Read by Eugene H. Peterson. (Running Time: 3600 sec.). (J). (ps-3). 2005. audio compact disk 9.99 (978-1-59859-051-7(0)) Oasis Audio.

Christmas Visitor. Anne Perry. Read by Terrence Hardiman. 3 cass. 29.95 (978-0-7927-3361-4(4), CSL 710); audio compact disk 49.95 (978-0-7927-3362-1(2), SLD 710) AudioGO.

Christmas Wedding. collector's ed. Andrew M. Greeley. Read by Jonathan Marosz. 9 cass. (Running Time: 13 hrs. 30 min.). (O'Malley Family Saga). 2000. 72.00 (978-0-7366-5922-2(6)) Books on Tape.
Chuckie O'Malley & his foster sister, Rosemarie, come of age in post-World War II Chicago.

Christmas Wedding. unabr. ed. Andrew M. Greeley. Read by Jonathan Marosz. 10 CDs. (Running Time: 15 hrs.). (O'Malley Family Saga). 2001. audio compact disk 80.00 Books on Tape.
Chuckie O'Malley and his foster sister, Rosemarie, come of age in post-World War II Chicago.

Christmas with Annie May: Christmas Poems & a Christmas Carol. Anne Costello. Read by Anne Costello. 1 cass. (Running Time: 52 min.). (Annie May & Friends Ser.). (J). (gr. 2-6). 1997. 10.99 (978-1-890719-02-9(1), 71902) Jo-An Pictures.
Side 1: Annie May says Christmas poems to friends Dorothy & Jimmy. Everyone learns the names of Santa's reindeer together & then do stretch exercises. Side 2: Annie May tells about Charles Dickens' boyhood & then proceeds to tell his story, "A Christmas Carol".

Christmas with Johnny Cash. Contrib. by Johnny Cash. Prod. by Al Quaglieri & Bob Irwin. 2007. audio compact disk 9.99 (978-5-557-58784-6(5)) Legacy Publng.

Christmas with Jose-Luis Orozco see Pancho Claus con Jose-Luis Orozco

Christmas with Joseph & Emma. Michael Ballam. 1 cass. 2004. 9.95 (978-1-57734-329-5(8), 1100866) Covenant Comms.

Christmas with Ogden Nash. abr. ed. Ogden Nash. Perf. by Ogden Nash. 1 cass. (Running Time: 90 min.). Incl. Arabian Dance. (CPN 1323); Boy Who Laughed at Santa Claus. (CPN 1323); Carol for Children. (CPN 1323); Chinese Dance. (CPN 1323); Christmas That Almost Wasn't. (CPN 1323); Flutes. (CPN 1323); I Remember Yule. (CPN 1323); I'm a Pleasure to Shop For. (CPN 1323); Miraculous Count-Down. (CPN 1323); Nutcracker Suite. 1 cass. (Running Time: 1 hr.). (CPN 1323); Russian Dance. (CPN 1323); Sugarplum Dance. (CPN 1323); Untold Adventure of Santa Claus. (CPN 1323); Waltz of the Flowers. (CPN 1323); (J). 1989. 9.95 (978-1-55994-007-8(7), CPN 1323) HarperCollins Pubs.

Christmas with the Mormon Tabernacle Organ & Chimes. Mormon Tabernacle Choir. 1 cass. 4.98 (3111407); audio compact disk 8.98 (3333116) Covenant Comms.

Christmas with the Mormon Youth Chorus & Symphony. 1 cass. 6.98 (100314) Covenant Comms.
Thirteen best-loved Christmas carols.

***Christmas with Tucker.** unabr. ed. Greg Kincaid. (Running Time: 5 hrs. 30 mins.). 2010. 29.95 (978-1-4417-6565-9(4)); 34.95 (978-1-4417-6562-8(X)); audio compact disk 55.00 (978-1-4417-6563-5(8)); audio compact disk 24.95 (978-1-4417-6564-2(6)) Blckstn Audio.

Christmas with You. Contrib. by Anthony Burger & Luann Burger. (Gaither Gospel Ser.). 2007. audio compact disk 13.99 (978-5-557-57014-5(4)) Sprg Hill Music Group.

Christmastime for Kids. 1 cass. (J). (C25048N) Brentwood Music.
30 kids Christmas favorites sung by kids. Includes: Joy to the World, Hark! The Herald Angels Sing, Rudolph the Red Nosed Reindeer, Deck the Halls & many more.

Christopher & His Kind. unabr. ed. Christopher Isherwood. Read by James Clamp. (ENG.). 2010. audio compact disk 34.95 (978-1-61573-072-8(9), 1615730729) Pub: HighBridge. Dist(s): Workman Pub

Christopher Carolan: The Spiral Calendar, Redefining the Dimension of Time. Read by Christopher Carolan. 1 cass. 30.00 Dow Jones Telerate.
In his workshop, Christopher will define the Spiral Calendar & demonstrate how he has used it to construct forecasts. He will draw examples from prior successful forecasts as well as from future time periods that he expects to produce major market turns. Christopher will stress the Spiral Calendar's unique practical ability to increase a trader's reward/risk ratio & likewise, their bottom line.

Christopher Churchmouse. unabr. ed. Barbara Davoll. Read by Susan Butcher. (J). 2007. 39.99 (978-1-60252-886-4(1)) Find a World.

Christopher Churchmouse. unabr. ed. Barbara Davoll. Narrated by Susan Butcher. (ENG.). (J). 2003. 9.09 (978-1-60814-119-7(5)) Oasis Audio.

Christopher Churchmouse. unabr. ed. Barbara Davoll. Narrated by Susan Butcher. (ENG.). (J). 2003. audio compact disk 12.99 (978-1-58926-303-1(0)) Oasis Audio.

Christopher Churchmouse Treasure Chest of Tapes. Barbara Davoll & Dennis Hockerman. 3 cass. (J). (ps-2). 1992. 11.99 Set. (3-12) David C Cook.

Christopher Columbus. Peter Riviere. Read by Martyn Read. 2 cass. (Running Time: 4 hrs.). 2001. 24.95 (990816) Pub: ISIS Audio GBR. Dist(s): Ulverscroft US

Christopher Columbus. unabr. ed. Ingri Parin D'Aulaire & Edgar Parin D'Aulaire. 1 cass. (Running Time: 6 min.). (J). (gr. 3-5). 1989. pap. bk. 10.00 (6512-D) Spoken Arts.
Trace young Columbus' life from birth, including his many trips to the "New World".

Christopher Columbus. unabr. ed. Ingri Parin D'Aulaire & Edgar Parin D'Aulaire. 1 cass. (Running Time: 15 min.). (J). (gr. 3-5). 2001. pap. bk. 20.00 (978-0-8045-6716-9(6)) Spoken Arts.
Trace young Columbus' life from birth, including his many trips to the "New World." Includes 6 books.

Christopher Columbus. unabr. ed. Justin Winsor. Read by Nadia May. 12 cass. (Running Time: 17 hrs. 30 mins.). 1992. 83.95 (978-0-7861-0328-7(0), 1288) Blckstn Audio.
Justin Winsor, an historian, poet, literary critic & fiction writer, retraces every important aspect of Columbus's fascinating life, from his family origins to his beliefs & convictions. He provides us with a myriad of facts, as well as intriguing suppositions & deductions which provide important insights into the life of this great mariner. Columbus emerges as a living, breathing human being with passions & ideas - a man possessing intellect & imagination - able to believe that the earth was round, not flat.

Christopher Columbus. unabr. collector's ed. Ernle Bradford. Read by Walter Zimmerman. 7 cass. (Running Time: 10 hr. 30 mins. per cass.). 1988. 56.00 (978-0-7366-1436-8(2), 2320) Books on Tape.
In Columbus' day no one believed the earth was flat. To the end of his days Columbus insisted that he was in the Indies, even when it became clear to his contemporaries that they were in fact in an area of world unknown to Europeans. All that aside, & granted the irony, Columbus was nevertheless the foremost sailor & pilot the world has ever known.

Christopher Columbus, Set. unabr. ed. Peter Riviere. Read by Martyn Read. 2 cass. (Running Time: 2 hrs. 20 mins.). 2000. 24.95 (978-0-7531-0642-6(6), 990816) Ulverscroft US.

Christopher Columbus: And How He Received & Imparted the Spirit of Discovery. unabr. ed. Justin Winsor. (Running Time: 59400 sec.). 2007. audio compact disk 44.95 (978-0-7861-6101-0(9)) Blckstn Audio.

Christopher Columbus: And How He Received & Imparted the Spirit of Discovery. unabr. ed. Justin Winsor. Read by Nadia May. (Running Time: 59400 sec.). 2007. audio compact disk & audio compact disk 108.00 (978-0-7861-6100-3(0)) Blckstn Audio.

Christopher Columbus, Mariner. unabr. ed. Samuel Eliot Morison. Read by Frederick Davidson. 5 cass. (Running Time: 7 hrs.). 1997. 39.95 (978-0-7861-1223-4(9), 2159) Blckstn Audio.
Story of Columbus the seaman. Navigator followed Columbus's courses under sail.

Christopher Columbus, Mariner. unabr. ed. Samuel Eliot Morison. Read by John MacDonald. 7 cass. (Running Time: 7 hrs.). 1986. 42.00 (978-0-7366-0829-9(X), 1779) Books on Tape.
This is the story of Columbus the seaman, told by Admiral Morison who actually followed Columbus's original courses under sail. Morison rewrites the entire story of the discoverer's life & voyages, giving his own conclusions to the numerous controversial points in Columbus's career.

Christopher Howell. unabr. ed. Read by Christopher Howell. 1 cass. (Running Time: 29 min.). 1985. 10.00 New Letters.
Howell, author of "Why Shouldn't I" & "The Crime of Luck," includes poems about his Vietnam War experience.

Christopher Isherwood. unabr. ed. Read by Heywood Hale Broun & Christopher Isherwood. 1 cass. (Running Time: 56 mim.). (Broun Radio Ser.). 12.95 (40263) J Norton Pubs.
The author speaks about his life & his book "Christopher & His Kind".

Christopher Isherwood Reads Two Lectures on the Bhagavad Gita CD. Swami Vivekananda. Read by Christopher Isherwood. (ENG.). 2007. audio compact disk 11.95 (978-0-87481-959-5(8)) Vedanta Pr.

Christopher Marlowe: His Life & Times. unabr. ed. A. L. Rowse. Read by Bill Kelsey. 7 cass. (Running Time: 7 hrs.). 1988. 42.00 (978-0-7366-1259-3(9), 2172) Books on Tape.
Marlowe, a towering figure in the Elizabethan theatre & after Shakespeare, the most highly regarded playwright in the English language.

Christopher Merrill. unabr. ed. Read by Christopher Merrill & Rebekah Presson. Ed. by James McKinley. 1 cass. (Running Time: 29 min.). (New Letters on the Air Ser.). 1994. 10.00 (060694); 18.00 2-sided cass. New Letters.
Merrill is interviewed by Rebekah Presson & reads from the third part of his poetic trilogy.

Christopher Norton - Microswing: 20 New Pieces Based on Swing Rhythms for the Beginner Pianist. Composed by Christopher Norton. 2009. pap. bk. 19.95 (978-0-85162-584-3(3), 0851625843) H Leonard.

Christopher Norton Concert Collection for Cello: With a CD of performances & backing Tracks. Composed by Christopher Norton. 2009. pap. bk. 24.99 (978-0-85162-585-0(1), 0851625851) H Leonard.

Christopher's Ghosts. unabr. ed. Charles McCarry. Read by Stefan Rudnicki. (Running Time: 41400 sec.). 2007. 29.95 (978-0-7861-4976-6(0)); 59.95 (978-0-7861-6816-3(1)); audio compact disk 29.95 (978-0-7861-5789-1(5)); audio compact disk 29.95 (978-0-7861-6961-0(3)); audio compact disk 72.00 (978-0-7861-6815-6(3)) Blckstn Audio.

Christ's Ambassadors in the World. Dan Corner. 1 cass. 3.00 (22) Evang Outreach.

Christ's Call: "Follow My Footsteps" K. P. Yohannan. 1 cass. (Running Time: 41 mins.). 1999. 19.95 (978-1-56599-995-4(9)) ACW Pr.

Christ's Last Days. Asha Praver. 1 cass. (Second Coming of Christ Ser.). 9.95 (AT-57) Crystal Clarity.
Discusses: Why Jesus wept at Gethsemane; the teaching of the Last Supper; what Christ meant by "I am the way"; Christ on the cross; the meaning of the resurrection.

Christ's Last Order. Derek Prince. 1 cass. (B-4108) Derek Prince.

Christ's Mission. 1 cass. (Second Coming of Christ Ser.). 9.95 (AT-55) Crystal Clarity.
Includes: John the Baptist as Christ's guru; why Christ fasted; the lesson of his temptation in the wilderness; the purpose of miracles; how Christ healed the sick; Christ's need to talk in parable.

Christ's Object Lessons on MP3 CD. Ellen G. White. Narrated by Tony James Harriman. (ENG.). 2008. (978-0-9767533-3-9(2)) T Harriman.

Christ's Object Lessons on 10 Audio CDs. Ellen G. White. Narrated by Tony J. Harriman. (ENG.). 2008. audio compact disk 39.95 (978-0-9767533-6-0(7)) T Harriman.

Christ's Victory in Our Lives. 1985. (0259) Evang Sisterhood Mary.

Christs with Amnesia. Raymond Karczewski. 3 cass. (Running Time: 90 min. per cass.). 1996. 30.00 Set, bookpack container. (978-0-9638391-6-9(0)); 30.00 Set, individually pkgd. in dustcovers. (978-0-9638391-7-6(9)) Ark Enter.
A comprehensive examination of the conditioning of the human mind through psychological pressure. The subjects addressed under the sections Authority & Power, Freedom or Enslavement, Government & Religion, & The Spiritual Way, touch upon all aspects of societal conditioning from the political & religious to the spiritual & metaphysical.

Christy. unabr. ed. Catherine Marshall. Read by Frances Cassidy. 14 cass. (Running Time: 21 hrs.). 1996. 112.00 (978-0-7366-3206-5(9), 3870) Books on Tape.
One woman's story continues to inspire millions. At 19, Christy Huddleston left the security of home to teach school in the Smokies. For strength & inspiration, she drew on her deep faith - not only to see her through but to make a difference. What she doesn't need, but gets, is a heart that's torn between two men.

***Christy.** unabr. ed. Catherine Marshall. Narrated by Kellie Martin. (Running Time: 19 hrs. 2 mins. 10 sec.). (ENG.). 2010. 34.99 (978-1-60814-693-2(6), SpringWater); audio compact disk 49.99 (978-1-59859-745-5(0), SpringWater) Oasis Audio.

***Christy Collection Books 1-3: The Bridge to Cutter Gap, Silent Superstitions, the Angry Intruder.** unabr. ed. Catherine Marshall. Adapted by C. Archer. Narrated by Jaimee Draper. (Running Time: 8 hrs. 0 mins. 0 sec.). (Catherine Marshall's Christy Ser.). (ENG.). 2010. audio compact disk 29.99 (978-1-59859-753-0(1), SpringWater) Oasis Audio.

***Christy Collection Books 10-12: Stage Fright, Goodbye Sweet Prince, Brotherly Love.** unabr. ed. Catherine Marshall. Adapted by C. Archer. Narrated by Jaimee Draper. (Running Time: 6 hrs. 21 mins. 16 sec.). (Catherine Marshall's Christy Ser.). (ENG.). 2010. audio compact disk 29.99 (978-1-59859-756-1(6), SpringWater) Oasis Audio.

***Christy Collection Books 4-6: Midnight Rescue, the Proposal, Christy's Choice.** unabr. ed. Catherine Marshall. Adapted by C. Archer. Narrated by Jaimee Draper. (Running Time: 7 hrs. 10 mins. 19 sec.). (Catherine Marshall's Christy Ser.). (ENG.). 2010. audio compact disk 29.99 (978-1-59859-754-7(X), SpringWater) Oasis Audio.

***Christy Collection Books 7-9: The Princess Club, Family Secrets, Mountain Madness.** unabr. ed. Catherine Marshall. Adapted by C. Archer. Narrated by Jaimee Draper. (Running Time: 6 hrs. 38 mins. 35 sec.). (Catherine Marshall's Christy Ser.). (ENG.). 2010. audio compact disk 29.99 (978-1-59859-755-4(8), SpringWater) Oasis Audio.

Christy Lane's Authentic African & Caribbean Rhythms. 2000. audio compact disk 19.95 (978-1-889127-42-2(6)) C Lane Ent.

Christy Lane's Celebrate America Cd-rom: Patriotic Music for Singing, Dancing & Celebrating Our American Pride. 2001. audio compact disk 19.95 (978-1-889127-57-6(4)) C Lane Ent.

Christy Lane's Complete Guide to Latin Dancing Music. 2001. audio compact disk 19.95 (978-1-889127-47-7(7)) C Lane Ent.

Christy Lane's Dare to Dance Music, Vol. 1. Perf. by Christy Lane. Composed by Michael Capitanelli. 1 CD. (Running Time: 40 min.). 1999. audio compact disk 19.95 (978-1-889127-39-2(6)) C Lane Ent.
Music CD consisting of ten dance songs.

Christy Lane's Sports & Novelty Themes. Perf. by Christy Lane. (Running Time: 1 hr. 4 mi). 2001. audio compact disk 19.95 (978-1-889127-50-7(7)) C Lane Ent.

Christy Lane's Square Dancing Today Music. 2000. audio compact disk 19.95 (978-1-889127-44-6(2)) C Lane Ent.

***Christy's Choice.** unabr. ed. Catherine Marshall. Adapted by C. Archer. Narrated by Jaimee Draper. (Catherine Marshall's Christy Ser.). (ENG.). 2010. 7.00 (978-1-60814-706-9(1), SpringWater) Oasis Audio.

Chromosome 6. unabr. ed. Robin Cook. Read by Arthur Addison. 10 cass. (Running Time: 15 hrs.). (Jack Stapleton Ser.: No. 3). 1997. 80.00 (978-0-913369-74-6(8), 4328) Books on Tape.
Pathologist Jack Stapleton is troubled when an unidentifiable corpse arrives at the morgue missing its head, hands & liver. His search for the truth leads him to Africa, where a sinister group is practicing surgical techniques a step beyond accepted medical ethids.

Chronic & the Waking State. E. J. Gold. 2 cass. (Running Time: 3 hrs.). 18.98 set. (TP120) Union Label.
Qualities of the waking & sleeping states, & moving between. Ritual, theatre, hypnotism, the bardos, psychosomatic diseases. The work & the function of the Chronic in preventing the waking state.

Chronic Fatigue. Deepak Chopra. 4 cass. 49.95 Set incl. wkbk. (11380PAB) Nightingale-Conant.
Unlock Dr. Deepak Chopra's secrets to conquering one of America's most misunderstood medical syndromes. With Dr. Chopra's expertise, you'll tap into reservoirs of energy & dynamism hidden deep within you. Learn to eat energizing foods, counteract stress, identify your mind/body patterns, use the circadian rhythm for maximum energy & balance the five senses as a major source of vital energy.

Chronic Fatigue & Fibromyalgia: Ancient Truths, Natural Remedies & the Latest Findings for Your Health Today. unabr. ed. Don Colbert. Narrated by Steve Hiller. (Bible Cure Ser.). (ENG.). 2003. 6.99 (978-1-60814-051-0(2)) Oasis Audio.

Chronic Fatigue-EBV. 1 cass. (Running Time: 1 hr.). 2001. 9.95 (CA608) Pub: VisnQst Vid Aud. Dist(s): TMW Media

Chronic Fatigue Syndrome: Possible Causes, Testing & Therapies. unabr. ed. Gary S. Ross. Interview with Kathleen S. Ross. 1 cass. (Running Time: 77 min.). (Natural Treatment Ser.). 1994. 15.00 (978-1-891875-03-8(5)) Creat Hlth Wrks.
Explains chronic fatigue syndrome, possible root causes, testing, & effective natural treatments.

Chronic Fatigue Syndrome: Program from the Award Winning Public Radio Series. Featuring Gudrun Lange. (Infinite Mind Ser.). 2002. audio compact disk 21.95 (978-1-888064-59-9(5), LCM 239) Lichtenstein Creat.
Imagine coming down with a bad case of the flu - the kind where your whole body aches and it's hard to think straight - and that the flu NEVER GOES AWAY. That's how many people describe what it feels like to live with Chronic Fatigue Syndrome. Guests include author Laura Hillenbrand, explaining why she had to write part of her bestseller, Seabiscuit, with her eyes closed; Dr. Nancy Klimas, professor of medicine and director of the Chronic Fatigue Syndrome research center at the University of Miami School of Medicine; Dr. Gudrun Lange, a neuropsychologist at the University of Medicine and Dentistry of New Jersey; Kim Kenney, president of the Chronic Fatigue and Immune Dysfunction Syndrome Association of America; and singer-songwriter Janis Ian, performing a song that she wrote months after her diagnosis with chronic fatigue syndrome. Plus, Marlene Sanders reports on why some patients and advocates think the name of this illness should be changed. Her report includes interviews with filmmaker Kim Snyder, psychologist Dr. Leonard Jason, and Dr. Anthony Komaroff. And commentary by John Hockenberry.

Chronic Hepatitis: B & non-A, non-B. Read by Harold J. Fallon. 1 cass. (Running Time: 90 min.). 1985. 12.00 (C8555) Amer Coll Phys.

Chronic Pain. Read by Robert S. Friedman & Kelly Howell. 1 cass. (Running Time: 60 min.). (Sound Techniques for Healing Ser.). 1993. 11.95 (978-1-881451-22-8(4)) Brain Sync.
A release of "endorphins," the body's natural painkiller, is stimulated to ease discomfort & dissolve negative pressure buildup that causes chronic pain.

Chronic Pelvic Pain. Contrib. by John F. Steege et al. 1 cass. (American College of Obstetrics & Gynecologists UPDATE: Vol. 24, No. 4). 1998. 20.00 Am Coll Obstetric.

Chronicles, Set. Read by Joss Ackland. 4 cass. 1999. 56.00 (978-1-900912-12-9(0)) Ulvrscrft Audio.
An epic anthology of the most interesting & revealing diaries & journals written during the last 500 years, providing a fascinating & intriguing record of life as witnessed by some of history's most colourful characters. Arranged as a calendar, we are taken on a daily journey from January 1st to December 31st.

Chronicles, Vol. 1. abr. ed. Bob Dylan. Read by Sean Penn. 5 cass. (Running Time: 60 hrs. 0 mins. 0 sec.). 2004. audio compact disk 29.95 (978-0-7435-4309-5(2)) Pub: S&S Audio. Dist(s): S and S Inc

Chronicles I. Read by Joss Ackland. 1999. pap. bk. 16.85 (978-1-900912-91-4(0)) Ulvrscrft Audio.

Chronicles I & II Commentary. Chuck Missler. 1 CD Rom. (Running Time: 16 hours). (Chuck Missler Commentaries). 2006. cd-rom 29.95 (978-1-57821-364-1(9)); audio compact disk 69.95 (978-1-57821-362-7(2)) Koinonia Hse.

Chronicles II. abr. ed. Read by Joss Ackland. 1 cass. 1999. 16.85 (978-1-900912-96-9(1)) Ulvrscrft Audio.

Chronicles III. abr. ed. Read by Joss Ackland. 1 cass. 1999. 16.85 (978-1-900912-02-0(3)) Ulvrscrft Audio.

Chronicles IV. abr. ed. Read by Joss Ackland. 1 cass. 1999. 16.85 (978-1-900912-07-5(4)) Ulvrscrft Audio.

***Chronicles of Ancient Darkness #1: Wolf Brother.** unabr. ed. Michelle Paver. Read by Ian Mckellan. (ENG.). 2005. (978-0-06-083894-2(9), KTegenBooks); (978-0-06-083895-9(7), KTegenBooks) HarperCollins Pubs.

***Chronicles of Ancient Darkness #4: Outcast.** unabr. ed. Michelle Paver. Read by Ian Mckellen. (ENG.). 2008. (978-0-06-157549-5(6)); (978-0-06-163055-2(1)) HarperCollins Pubs.

***Chronicles of Ancient Darkness #5: Oath Breaker.** unabr. ed. Michelle Paver. Read by Ian Mckellen. (ENG.). 2009. (978-0-06-176518-6(X), KTegenBooks); (978-0-06-190191-1(1), KTegenBooks) HarperCollins Pubs.

***Chronicles of Ancient Darkness #6: Ghost Hunter.** unabr. ed. Michelle Paver. Read by Ian Mckellan. (ENG.). 2010. (978-0-06-199748-8(X), KTegenBooks); (978-0-06-198401-3(9), KTegenBooks) HarperCollins Pubs.

Chronicles of Avonlea. L. M. Montgomery. Narrated by Grace Conlin. (Running Time: 7 hrs.). (J). 1995. 27.95 (978-1-59912-448-3(3)) Iofy Corp.

Chronicles of Avonlea. unabr. ed. L. M. Montgomery. Read by Grace Conlin. 5 cass. (Running Time: 7 hrs.). (Avonlea Ser.: No. 3). (gr. 5-8). 1997. 39.95 (978-0-7861-1078-0(3), 1848) Blckstn Audio.
Old friend Anne Shirley is present in this gently sentimental & enjoyably humorous book. But readers are also introduced to Ludovic & Theodora, "Old Lady Lloyd" & Sylvia Gray, Felix Moore & his grandfather, Little Jocelyn & Aunty Nan, Lucinda Penhallow, Old Man Shaw's Blossom, Olivia Sterling & many, many others.

Chronicles of Avonlea. unabr. ed. L. M. Montgomery. Read by Grace Conlin. (Running Time: 7 hrs.). (J). 1998. 24.95 (978-0-7861-8709-6(3)) Blckstn Audio.

Chronicles of Avonlea. unabr. ed. L. M. Montgomery. Read by Grace Conlin. (J). 2008. 49.99 (978-1-60514-715-4(X)) Find a World.

Chronicles of Avonlea, Set. unabr. ed. L. M. Montgomery. Read by Grace Conlin. 5 cass. (Avonlea Ser.: No. 3). (YA). (gr. 5-8). 1999. 44.95 (FS9-29824) Highsmith.

Chronicles of Carlingford, Set. unabr. ed. Margaret Oliphant. Read by Flo Gibson. 5 cass. (Running Time: 6 hr. 30 min.). (gr. 8 up). 1989. 20.95 (978-1-55685-130-8(8)) Audio Bk Con.
Two novellas, "The Rector" & "The Doctor's Family," peopled with Clergy, tradesmen & the aristocracy in a small town near London in the mid-1800's.

Chronicles of Clovis, Set. unabr. ed. Saki. Read by Richard Brown. 4 cass. (Running Time: 5 hrs. 30 min.). (Classic Books on Cassette). 1988. 19.95 (978-1-55685-109-4(X)) Audio Bk Con.
The blend of stories, featuring the witty & sometimes machiavellian clovis, range from the supernatural & sinister to hilarious comedy.

Chronicles of Narnia see Complete Chronicles of Narnia

Chronicles of Narnia. C. S. Lewis. 2005. 34.99 (978-1-59895-006-9(1)) Find a World.

Chronicles of Narnia. C. S. Lewis. Prod. by Focus on the Family Staff. 19 CDs. (Running Time: 22 hrs.). (Radio Theatre Ser.). (ENG.). (J). (gr. 4-7). 2005. audio compact disk 29.97 (978-1-58997-299-5(6)) Pub: Focus Family. Dist(s): Tyndale Hse

Chronicles of Narnia. C. S. Lewis. 2 cass. (Running Time: 2 hrs.). (Chronicles of Narnia Ser.: Vol. 2). (J). 2001. 16.99 (BMDD016) Lodestone Catalog.

Chronicles of Narnia. C. S. Lewis. 2 cass. (Chronicles of Narnia Ser.: Bk.2). (J). (gr. 4-8). 1999. 16.99 (BMDD016, Random AudioBks) Random Audio Pubg.

Chronicles of Narnia. unabr. ed. C. S. Lewis. 2 cass. (Running Time: 3 hrs.). (Chronicles of Narnia Ser.: Bk.2). (J). (gr. 4-8). 16.99 (D101) Blckstn Audio.
Wicked King Miraz's regime is evil. His nephew and heir, Prince Caspion, vows to revive Narnia's glorious past.

Chronicles of Narnia. unabr. ed. C. S. Lewis. Read by Patrick Stewart et al. 33 cds. (Running Time: 31 hours). (Chronicles of Narnia Ser.). (J). 2004. bk. 75.00 (978-0-694-52475-4(1), HarperChildAud) HarperCollins Pubs.

***Chronicles of Narnia.** unabr. ed. C. S. Lewis. 2005. (978-0-06-113981-9(5)) HarperCollins Pubs.

Chronicles of Narnia. unabr. ed. Sbc123 Cae. 4 cass. (Running Time: 6 hrs.). Incl. Lion, the Witch & the Wardrobe. C. S. Lewis. (Chronicles of Narnia Ser.: Bk.1). (J). (gr. 4-8). (SBC 123); Silver Chair. C. S. Lewis. (Chronicles of Narnia Ser.). (J). (gr. 4-8). (SBC 123); Voyage of the Dawn Treader. C. S. Lewis. (Chronicles of Narnia Ser.). (J). (gr. 4-8). (SBC 123); Chronicles of Narnia. C. S. Lewis. (Chronicles of Narnia Ser.: Bk.2). (J). (gr. 4-8). (SBC 123); (J). 1985. 29.95 (978-0-89845-027-9(6), SBC 123) HarperCollins Pubs.

Chronicles of Narnia. unabr. movie tie-in ed. C. S. Lewis. Read by Lynn Redgrave. (Chronicles of Narnia Ser.). (J). 2008. audio compact disk 27.50 (978-0-06-143527-0(9), HarperChildAud) HarperCollins Pubs.

Chronicles of Narnia, Set. 14 cass. (J). 99.95 (BMDD020, Random AudioBks) Random Audio Pubg.

Chronicles of Narnia, Set. Prod. by Focus on the Family Staff. 19 CDs. (Running Time: 23 hrs.). (Radio Theatre Ser.). 2003. audio compact disk 99.99 (978-1-58997-149-3(3)) Pub: Focus Family. Dist(s): Tyndale Hse

Chronicles of Narnia: The Complete Collection. C. S. Lewis. 14 cass. (Running Time: 16 hrs.). 2001. 99.95 (BMDD020) Lodestone Catalog.

Chronicles of Narnia: The Complete Collection. C. S. Lewis. Read by Claire Bloom et al. 7 cass. (J). (gr. k up). 50.00 (330) MFLP CA.
A literary classic, includes: The Lion, The Witch & The Wardrobe, Prince Caspian - Voyage of the Dawn Treader, & The Silver Chair.

***Chronicles of Narnia Adult Box Set.** unabr. ed. C. S. Lewis. Read by Kenneth Branagh. (ENG.). 2005. (978-0-06-199988-8(1), Harper Audio) HarperCollins Pubs.

Chronicles of Narnia Audio Collection. abr. ed. C. S. Lewis. Read by Ian Richardson. 7 cass. (Running Time: 7 hrs.). (J). 2000. 50.00 HarperCollins Pubs.
The mystical land of Narnia is a glorious place where good & evil battle, beasts & creatures talk & magic reigns & it is entered through the wardrobe in the professor's home. Peter, Susan, Edmund & Lucy visit Narnia & meet Aslan, the Great Lion.

Chronicles of Narnia Audio Collection. unabr. abr. ed. C. S. Lewis. Read by Ian Richardson et al. 7 cass. (Running Time: 1 hr.). (Chronicles of Narnia Ser.). (J). (gr. 6-8). 2000. 50.00 (978-0-694-52466-2(2)) HarperCollins Pubs.

Chronicles of Narnia Super-Soundbook. unabr. ed. 7 cass. (Running Time: 10 hrs. 30 min.). Incl. Horse & His Boy. Prod. by Paul Scofield. (Chronicles of Narnia Ser.: Bk.5). (J). (gr. 4-8).; Last Battle. C. S. Lewis. (Chronicles of Narnia Ser.). (J). (gr. 4-8).; Lion, the Witch & the Wardrobe. 3 cass. (Running Time: 4 hrs. 30 mins.). C. S. Lewis. Read by Michael York. (Chronicles of Narnia Ser.: Bk.1). (J). (gr. 4-8). 2000. 50.00; Magician's Nephew. C. S. Lewis. (Chronicles of Narnia Ser.). (J). (gr. 4-8).; Silver Chair. C. S. Lewis. (Chronicles of Narnia Ser.). (J). (gr. 4-8).; Voyage of the Dawn Treader. C. S. Lewis. (Chronicles of Narnia Ser.: Bk.3). (J). (gr. 4-8).; (J). 1985. 49.95 (978-0-89845-049-1(7), SSBC 701) HarperCollins Pubs.

Chronicles of Narnia Travel Visor Pack. Created by Focus. 2008. bk. 49.97 (978-1-58997-426-5(3), Tyndale Ent) Tyndale Hse.

Chronicles of Pleasant Grove (as read by the Author) Short Stories. A. M. Johnston-Brown. 2 CDs. (Running Time: 140 min.). (J). 2006. audio compact disk 12.95 (978-0-9760718-7-7(8)) Retriever Pr.

Chronicles of the Frigate Macedonian, 1809-1922. unabr. ed. James T. de Kay. Read by Jonathan Reese. 7 cass. (Running Time: 10 hrs. 30 min.). 1996. 56.00 (978-0-7366-3315-4(4), 3967) Books on Tape.
During the War of 1812 many early land battles ended terribly for the United States. Our soldiers were volunteers who lacked the training to sustain the

fierce attacks of the seasoned British troops who had just defeated Napoleon. America needed a boost of confidence to thwart those in the land who would capitulate to the British rather than fight what they saw as a loosing battle.

Chronicles of the Frigate Macedonian, 1809-1922. unabr. ed. James T. de Kay. Read by Jonathan Reese. 7 cass. (Running Time: 10 hrs. 30 min.). 1996. 56.00 Set. (3967); Rental 9.95 Set. (3967) Books on Tape.
She was the most important prize ever taken by the American navy. Her capture from the British in the War of 1812 was proof of American daring & skill. She was His Majesty's frigate Macedonian, a tough, 1,300-ton gun platform.

Chronicles Through Malachi & Job Bible. Ty Fischer & Emily Fischer. Perf. by Steve Scheffler. 1998. 6.95 (978-1-930710-87-0(9)) Veritas Pr PA.

Chronique du Temps du Charles IX see Treasury of French Prose

Chronological Prophecies. Michael Pearl. 1 CD. 2005. audio compact disk (978-1-892112-72-9(8)) No Greater Joy.

Chronology: Volume 1: 1996-2000. Contrib. by Third Day. 2007. audio compact disk 18.98 (978-5-557-88215-6(4)) Essential Recs.

Chronology: Volume Two: 2001-2006. Contrib. by Third Day. 2007. audio compact disk 18.98 (978-5-557-63545-5(9)) Essential Recs.

Chrysalis. Prod. by Ray Gross. Engineer Ray Gross. (Running Time: 2 hrs. 6 minutes). Dramatization. 2006. 6.95 (978-0-9788044-0-4(6)) Audiocine.
Struggling genius Graham Godfrey, together with his select team of young discoverers, is led from Georgetown University to the mysterious Bainbridge Institute by his ambitious uncle in a quest to harness a new quantum energy source. But the project takes an unexpected turn and unfolding events thrust Graham into his haunted past where a dark secret shrouds an unspoken family tragedy.This full cast audio feature, including UK star Samantha Jane Robson as the provocative and calculating Dr. Delilah Mercer, forges a mystical journey where principles of science and faith converge to embody an ultimate truth.

Chrysalis: The Psychology of Transformation. Read by Marion Woodman. 1 cass. (Running Time: 90 min.). 1984. 10.95 (978-0-7822-0331-8(0), 155) C G Jung IL.

Chrysanthemum see Crisantemo

Chrysanthemum. 2004. audio compact disk 12.95 (978-1-55592-905-3(2)) Weston Woods.

Chrysanthemum. (SPA.). (J). 2004. bk. 24.95 (978-1-55592-162-0(0)); pap. bk. 18.95 (978-1-55592-395-2(X)); pap. bk. 18.95 (978-1-55592-398-3(4)); pap. bk. 38.75 (978-1-55592-397-6(6)); pap. bk. 38.75 (978-1-55592-399-0(2)); pap. bk. 32.75 (978-1-55592-208-5(2)); pap. bk. 32.75 (978-1-55592-209-2(0)); pap. bk. 32.75 (978-0-7882-0248-3(0)); pap. bk. 14.95 (978-1-55592-654-0(1)) Weston Woods.

Chrysanthemum. Kevin Henkes. Narrated by Meryl Streep. 1 cass., 5 bks. (Running Time: 30 min.). (J). pap. bk. 32.75 Weston Woods.
A little mouse thinks her name is perfect until kids make fun - except for Mrs. Twinkle, music teacher, who thinks Chrysanthemum's name is perfect too.

Chrysanthemum. unabr. ed. Kevin Henkes. Narrated by Meryl Streep. 1 cass. (J). (ps-2). 1998. bk. 24.95 (978-0-7882-0672-6(9), HRA369); pap. bk. 14.95 (978-0-7882-0675-7(3), PRA369) Weston Woods.

Chrysanthemum. unabr. ed. Narrated by Meryl Streep. 1 cass. (SPA.). (J). (ps-2). 1998. pap. bk. 14.95 Spanish. (978-0-7882-0126-4(3), PRA369SP) Weston Woods.

Chrysanthemum. unabr. ed. Narrated by Meryl Streep. Music by Ernest V. Troost. 1 cass. (Running Time: 15 min.). (J). (ps-2). 1998. pap. bk. 8.95 (978-1-56008-817-2(6), RAC369) Weston Woods.

Chrystallia & the Source of Light. Paul M. Glaser. Narrated by Paul M. Glaser. Ed. by Pamela M. Meserve. Pamela M. Meserve. (ENG., (J). 2010. audio compact disk 35.00 (978-0-9823604-3-9(6)) SITMOIA Prod.

Chuang Tsu - Inner Chapters: A Companion Volume to Tao Te Ching. abr. ed. Read by Chungliang Al Huang. Tr. by Gia-Fu Feng & Jane English. 2 cass. (Running Time: 3 hrs.). 1998. 17.95 (978-1-57453-271-5(5)) Audio Lit.
Addresses every man & woman seeking enlightenment in the midst of all the problems of life.

Chuchoteur. Brian Lumley. Read by Daniel Ceccaldi. 1 cass. (FRE.). 1991. 21.95 (1250-VSL) Olivia & Hill.
This tale is a mixture of the fantastic & the banal. An evil little hunchback insinuates himself, as might a ghost, into the uneventful life of an ordinary man.

Chuck & Danielle. Peter Dickinson. Read by Andrew Sachs. 2 cass. (Running Time: 2 hrs.). (J). 2000. 18.00 (978-0-7366-4969-8(7)) Books on Tape.
Set in England introduces Danielle & her dog, Chuck. A wellbred, high-strung whippet, Chuck is terrified of everything. Each chapter involves Danielle & chuck in a different set of circumstances (foiling a purse snatcher, setting loose a herd of cows, befriending an unpromising new neighbor.

Chuck & Danielle. unabr. ed. Peter Dickinson. Read by Andrew Sachs. 2 cass. (Running Time: 3 hrs.). (J). (gr. 1-8). 1999. 23.00 (LL 0101, Chivers Child Audio) AudioGO.

Chuck & Danielle. unabr. ed. Peter Dickinson. Read by Andrew Sachs. 2 cass. (Running Time: 2 hrs.). (YA). (gr. 8 up). 1997. 16.98 (978-0-8072-7834-5(3), 396015, Listening Lib) Random Audio Pubg.
Chuck is Danielle's dog, & Danielle understands her whippit well. She just wishes her mother could see the good in Chuck & would stop talking about giving Chuck away. To keep him, Danielle must prove that one day Chuck will save the universe.

Chuck & Danielle, Set. unabr. ed. Read by Andrew Sachs. Ed. by Peter Dickinson. 2 cass. (Running Time: 2 hrs.). (J). (gr. 8 up). 1997. bk. 21.98 (978-0-8072-7835-2(1), YA929SP, Listening Lib) Random Audio Pubg.
In a set of vignettes, Danielle & her pet whippet share some charming, often hilarious adventures.

Chuck Foreman: Running Back. Read by Chuck Foreman. 1 cass. (Running Time: 30 min.). 9.95 (7134) Lets Talk Assocs.
Chuck Foreman talks about the people & events which influenced his career, & his own approach to his speciality.

Chuck Klosterman Vol. 4: A Decade of Curious People & Dangerous Ideas. abr. ed. Chuck Klosterman. Read by Chuck Klosterman. 2006. 17.95 (978-0-7435-6382-6(4), Audioworks) Pub: S&S Audio. Dist(s): S and S Inc

***Chuck Norris Fact Book: 101 of Chuck's Favorite Facts & Stories.** unabr. ed. Chuck Norris & Todd duBord. Narrated by Johnny Heller. (ENG.). 2009. 10.98 (978-1-59644-822-3(9)) christianaud.

***Chuck-Wagon Jamboree, Volume 1.** RadioArchives.com. (Running Time: 600). (ENG.). 2007. audio compact disk 29.98 (978-1-61081-057-9(0)) Radio Arch.

***Chuck Wagon Jamboree, Volume 2.** RadioArchives.com. (Running Time: 600). (ENG.). 2007. audio compact disk 29.98 (978-1-61081-062-3(7)) Radio Arch.

Church. Standard Publishing Staff. 2006. cd-rom 24.99 (978-0-7847-1883-4(0)) Standard Pub.

Church. abr. ed. Carol Crook. 1 cass. (Running Time: 1 hr.). (YA). (gr. 10 up). 1998. pap. bk. 5.00 (978-0-939399-24-6(5)) Bks of Truth.
Instruction of what God intended it to be & how it grows. Gives scriptural teaching on where it meets, its structure, authority of leadership.

Church & Its Ministries, Album 1: The Church: Universal & Local. Derek Prince. 6 cass. 29.95 (I-TC1) Derek Prince.

Church & Its Ministries, Album 2: The Church: True & False. Derek Prince. 6 cass. 29.95 (I-TC2) Derek Prince.

Church & Pop Culture (2006) 10. 2006. 28.00 (978-1-59128-581-6(X)); 35.00 (978-1-59128-583-0(6)) Canon Pr ID.

Church & the Millenium. George Rutler. 1 cass. (National Meeting of the Institute, 1990 Ser.). 4.00 (90N5) IRL Chicago.

Church & Youth in the Eighties: Proceedings of the 45th Annual Convention National Association of Evangelicals Buffalo, New York. Read by Jay Kesler. 1 cass. (Running Time: 60 min.). 1987. 4.00 (320) Nat Assn Evan.

Church As a Psychological Crucible. Read by William Dols. 1 cass. (Running Time: 90 min.). 1985. 10.95 (978-0-7822-0055-3(9), 171) C G Jung IL.
Part of the conference set "Jung's Challenge to Contemporary Religion.".

Church as It Should Be: The Book of Acts. abr. ed. Doug Fields. (Sermon-Ser.). 2006. audio compact disk 42.00 (978-5-558-25703-8(2)) Group Pub.

***Church Awakening: An Urgent Call for Renewal.** Charles R. Swindoll. 2010. audio compact disk 38.00 (978-1-57972-902-8(9)) Insight Living.

***Church Awakening: An Urgent Call for Renewal.** unabr. ed. Charles R. Swindoll. (Running Time: 8 hrs. 30 mins.). (ENG.). 2010. 22.98 (978-1-60788-714-0(2)) Pub: Hachet Audio. Dist(s): HachBkGrp

Church Breaks Bread. Gary Daigle & Marty Haugen. 1 cass., 1 CD. 1998. 10.95 (CS-410); audio compact disk 15.95 (CD-410) GIA Pubns.

Church Child Care: The Problems & Solutions in Ministry. Daniel Armstrong. 2 cass. (Running Time: 2 hrs. 30 min.). 25.00 Set. (5020) Natl Inst Child Mgmt.
This seminar looks at: "The winning combination of ministry & business in balance," "Creating cooperation with the Sunday morning church program," "The Church board: friend or foe?" Also explored are the potential solutions to the unique problems encountered in a church-based child care program such as wages for staff members, expenses to the church, sharing the space, & effective evangelism.

Church Family Values. (RAJ.). 2004. 14.00 (978-1-57972-670-6(4)); audio compact disk 14.00 (978-1-57972-669-0(0)) Insight Living.

***Church Fathers.** Benedict XVI, pseud. Read by Jeff Blackwell. (ENG.). 2010. audio compact disk 20.95 (978-1-936231-19-5(0)) Cath Audio.

Church Finances: National Association of Evangelicals, 47th Annual Convention, Columbus, Ohio, March 7-9, 1989. Earl Murphy. 1 cass. (Workshops Ser.: No. 15-Wednesd). 1989. 4.25 ea. 1-8 tapes.; 4.00 ea. 9 tapes or more. Nat Assn Evan.

Church Folk. Michele Andrea Bowen. Narrated by Denise Burse. 8 cass. (Running Time: 11 hrs.). 74.00 (978-1-4025-1606-1(1)) Recorded Bks.

Church God Blesses. unabr. ed. Jim Cymbala. 2002. audio compact disk 34.99 (978-0-310-24800-2(0)) Zondervan.

Church God Blesses. unabr. ed. Jim Cymbala & Sorenson. 2002. 17.99 (978-0-310-24801-9(9)) Zondervan.

Church Growth: How to Increase the Influence of Your Ministry. Mac Hammond. 2008. audio compact disk 24.00 (978-1-57399-386-9(7)) Mac Hammond.

Church Growth Evangelism: Proceedings of the 45th Annual Conventional Association of Evangelicals Buffalo, New York. Read by Roland E. Griswold. 1 cass. (Running Time: 60 min.). 1987. 4.00 (335) Nat Assn Evan.

Church History: Fifteen Hundred Seventeen to the Present. Fr. Hardon. 9 cass. (Running Time: 90 min. per cass.). 36.00 Set. (94G) IRL Chicago.

Church History: Logos March 1, 1998. Ben Young. 1998. Rental 4.95 (978-0-7417-6075-3(4), B0075) Win Walk.

***Church History: Understanding its Influence & Impact on Us.** John M. Oakes. (ENG.). 2010. 10.00 (978-0-9844974-4-7(7)) Illumination MA.

Church History & the Coming Move of God Series. Rick Joyner. 6 cass. (Running Time: 9 hrs.). 2000. 30.00 (RJ11-000) Morning NC.
Church history is brought to life with practical applications & insights into how the enemy uses the same strategy against every new move of God.

Church-House: Romans 16: 3-5. Ed Young. (J). 1979. 4.95 (978-0-7417-1042-0(0)) Win Walk.

Church Hymnal 2. Greater Vision Staff. 2004. audio compact disk 15.98 (978-7-83491-263-1(1)) Great Vision.

Church in the New Millennium. Rosemary Luling Haughton. 1 cass. (Running Time: 1 hrs. 33 min.). 1999. 9.95 (TAH413) Alba Hse Comns.
As Haughton states, no one can really speak of the church in the next millennium. By relying on wisdom we will be able to read the signs of the times, to recognize both the gifts & needs of the church.

Church in the 21st Century: Finding Hope for Its Future in the Wisdom of Its Past. Speeches. 4. (Running Time: 90 mins). 2003. 29.95 (978-0-7648-1145-6(2)) Liguori Pubns.

Church in the 21st Century: Hebrews 11:23-29. Ed Young. 1992. 4.95 (978-0-7417-1922-5(3), 922) Win Walk.

Church in Transition Series. unabr. ed. Larry Randolph. 4 cass. (Running Time: 6 hrs.). 2000. 20.00 (LR01-000) Morning NC.
"New Wineskin," "Spirit-Led Ministry," Elisha: "Giver of Life" & "Bridal Preparation." Larry prepares us for the needed changes we must accept in order to receive our bridegroom.

Church of Dead Girls. unabr. collector's ed. Stephen Dobyns. Read by Jonathan Marosz. 9 cass. (Running Time: 13 hrs. 30 min.). 1998. 72.00 (978-0-7366-4116-6(5), 4620) Books on Tape.
One by one, three girls vanish from a small town in upstate New York. With the third disappearance, panic among the townsfolk mounts & the citizens take the law into their own hands. Old rumors & old angers surface, revealing the shadowy history of a seemingly genteel town.

Church of Doom. Alva Busch. 2 cass. (Running Time: 90 min.). (Inspector Files Ser.: Vol. 3). 1996. Set. Mystic Fire.

***Church of Facebook: How the wireless generation Is redefining Community.** unabr. ed. Jesse Rice. Narrated by Adam Verner. (ENG.). 2009. 12.98 (978-1-59644-762-2(1)) christianaud.

Church of Facebook: What Digging around the Social Networking Site Reveals about the Human Heart. unabr. ed. Jesse Rice. Narrated by Adam Verner. (Running Time: 5 hrs. 0 mins. 0 sec.). (ENG.). 2009. audio compact disk 21.98 (978-1-59644-761-5(3)) christianaud.

Church of Love. Contrib. by Lari Goss. 1996. 11.98 (978-0-00-512907-4(9), 75608495) Pub: Brentwood Music. Dist(s): H Leonard

Church of Rhythm. Perf. by Church of Rhythm. 1 cass. 1995. audio compact disk Brentwood Music.
This stunning debut is a diverse musical collection of vibrant soulful harmonies mixed with the best of pop, r&b & a little bit of hip hop. Features: Take Back, The Beat, Free & I Still Believe.

Church of the Dog. unabr. ed. Kaya McLaren. Read by Israel R. Potter. Contrib. by Arthur Morey et al. 6 CDs. (Running Time: 6 hrs.). (ENG.). (gr. 12 up). 2009. audio compact disk 29.95 (978-0-14-314470-0(7), PengAudBks) Penguin Grp USA.

Church on Fire: Igniting Leadership for the 21st Century. Perf. by T. D. Jakes. 5 cass. (Running Time: 7 hrs. 30 mins.). 1999. 25.00 (978-1-57855-463-8(2)) T D Jakes.

***Church on the Couch: Does the Church Need Therapy?** Zondervan. (Running Time: 5 hrs. 24 mins. 41 sec.). (ENG.). 2010. 9.99 (978-0-310-86942-9(0)) Zondervan.

Church Operations Manual. Stan Toler. 3 cass. pap. bk. 76.95 Set, incl. forms & appendixes. (435) Chrch Grwth VA.
Empower your laity to help carry out the day-to-day operations of your ministry.

Church Organization: At Open Gate. unabr. ed. Myrtle Smith. Prod. by David Keyston. 1 cass. (Running Time: 1 hrs. 5 min.). (Myrtle Smyth Audiotapes Ser.). 1998. , CD. (978-1-893107-08-3(6), M8, Cross & Crown) Healing Unltd.

Church People: The Lutherans of Lake Wobegon. unabr. ed. Garrison Keillor. Contrib. by Garrison Keillor. Read by Ensemble Cast Staff. 2009. audio compact disk 24.95 (978-1-59887-929-2(4), 1598879294) Pub: HighBridge. Dist(s): Workman Pub

Church Sings Her Saints I: Apostle, Martyrs & Virgins. Monks of Solesmes Staff. 1 CD. 1991. audio compact disk 16.95 (978-1-55725-112-1(6), 930-067) Paraclete MA.

Church Sings Her Saints II: Bishops, Doctors of the Church. Monks of Solesmes Staff. 1 CD. 1991. audio compact disk 16.95 (978-1-55725-114-5(2), 930-068) Paraclete MA.

Church Year & the Art of Clemens Schmidt. Ed. by Placid Stuckenschneider. Des. by Clemens Schmidt. (Virgil Michel Ser.). 2005. pap. bk. 24.95 (978-0-8146-2905-5(9)) Liturgical Pr.

Churches of Israel. 10.00 (RME101) Esstee Audios.

Churches Paul Left Behind. Raymond E. Brown. 2004. 26.50 (978-1-904756-07-1(7)) STL Dist NA.

Churchill. Instructed by J. Rufus Fears. 6 CDs. (Running Time: 6 hrs.). bk. 39.95 (978-1-56585-386-7(5), 807); 29.95 (978-1-56585-230-3(3), 807) Teaching Co.

Churchill. unabr. ed. Roy Jenkins & Roy Jenkins. Read by Robert Whitfield. 3 pieces. (Running Time: 142200 sec.). 2002. audio compact disk 54.95 (978-0-7861-9207-6(0), 2703A,B) Blckstn Audio.
A narrative account of Churchill's astounding career.

Churchill. unabr. ed. Paul Johnson. Narrated by Simon Prebble. 4 CDs. (Running Time: 4 hrs. 45 mins.). 2009. audio compact disk 29.99 (978-1-4407-6285-7(6)) Recorded Bks.

***Churchill.** unabr. ed. Paul Johnson. Narrated by Simon Prebble. 4 cass. (Running Time: 4 hrs. 45 mins.). 2009. 33.75 (978-1-4407-5416-6(0)); audio compact disk 51.75 (978-1-4407-5417-3(9)) Recorded Bks.

***Churchill.** unabr. ed. Paul Johnson. Narrated by Simon Prebble. 1 Playaway. (Running Time: 4 hrs. 45 mins.). 2010. 54.75 (978-1-4407-5419-7(5)) Recorded Bks.

Churchill: A Biography: Part 1. unabr. ed. Roy Jenkins & Robert Whitfield. (Running Time: 73800 sec.). 2007. audio compact disk 120.00 (978-0-7861-6054-9(3)) Blckstn Audio.

Churchill Pt. 1: A Biography. unabr. ed. Roy Jenkins. Read by Robert Whitfield. 16 cass. (Running Time: 39 hrs. 30 mins.). 2002. 99.95 (978-0-7861-2243-1(9), 2703A,B) Blckstn Audio.
A narrative account of Churchill's astounding career that is unmatched in its shrewd insights, its unforgettable anecdotes, the clarity of its overarching themes, and the author's nuanced appreciation of his extraordinary subject.

Churchill Pt. 2: A Biography. unabr. ed. Roy Jenkins. Read by Robert Whitfield. 11 cass. (Running Time: 39 hrs. 30 mins.). 2002. 76.95 (978-0-7861-2284-4(6), 2703A,B) Blckstn Audio.
A narrative account of Churchill's astounding career that is unmatched in its shrewd insights, its unforgettable anecdotes, the clarity of its overarching themes, and the author's nuanced appreciation of his extraordinary subject.

Churchill Pt. C: A Life. unabr. collector's ed. Martin Gilbert. Read by David Case. 12 cass. (Running Time: 18 hrs.). 1992. 96.00 (978-0-7366-2209-7(8), 3002C) Books on Tape.
The best one-volume life of Churchill to be found. Sweeps the reader up in great deeds & dark moments of one of history's most tumultuous eras.

Churchill Pt. A: A Life. unabr. collector's ed. Martin Gilbert. Read by David Case. 12 cass. (Running Time: 18 hrs.). 1992. 96.00 (978-0-7366-2207-3(1), 3002A) Books on Tape.
From his childhood, Churchill enjoyed uncommon vitality. Sometimes it even got in his way. But as he matured, he harnessed it to his service. Combined with a profound understanding of men, political acumen both realistic & visionary & interests that were far-ranging & multi-faceted, it made him the most important man of his time, probably of this century.

Churchill Pt. B: A Life. unabr. collector's ed. Martin Gilbert. Read by David Case. 11 cass. (Running Time: 16 hrs. 30 min.). 1992. 88.00 (978-0-7366-2208-0(X), 3002B) Books on Tape.
The best one-volume life of Churchill to be found. Sweeps the reader up in great deeds & dark moments of one of history's most tumultuous eras.

Churchill & America. unabr. ed. Martin Gilbert. Narrated by Simon Vance. (Running Time: 16 hrs. 0 mins. 0 sec.). (ENG.). 2005. audio compact disk 39.99 (978-1-4001-0193-1(X)); audio compact disk 79.99 (978-1-4001-3193-8(6)); audio compact disk 29.99 (978-1-4001-5193-6(7)) Pub: Tantor Media. Dist(s): IngramPubServ

Churchill & Secret Service. unabr. ed. David Stafford. Read by Frederick Davidson. 12 cass. (Running Time: 17 hrs. 30 mins.). 1998. 83.95 (978-0-7861-1410-8(X), 2281) Blckstn Audio.
Exploring for the first time Churchill's career in light of his passion for secret intelligence, makes the compelling case that one cannot understand Churchill's success as a modern day statesman without reference to his deep involvement in the world of espionage.

Churchill & Secret Service. unabr. ed. Davis Stafford. Read by Frederick Davidson. (Running Time: 16 hrs. 0 mins.). 2010. 29.95 (978-1-4417-1751-1(X)); audio compact disk 118.00 (978-1-4417-1748-1(X)) Blckstn Audio.

***Churchill Defiant: Fighting On: 1945-1955.** unabr. ed. Barbara Leaming. (ENG.). 2010. (978-0-06-204712-0(4), Harper Audio); (978-0-06-206244-4(1), Harper Audio) HarperCollins Pubs.

Churchill in His Own Voice. abr. ed. Winston Churchill. Read by Winston Churchill. 2 cass. (Running Time: 2 hrs.). 1994. 18.00 (978-1-55994-999-6(6), CPN 2018) HarperCollins Pubs.

Churchill in His Own Voice: And the Voices of His Contemporaries. abr. ed. Read by Winston L. S. Churchill et al. 2 cass. (Running Time: 4 hrs.). 1977. 19.95 (978-0-694-50379-7(7), SWC 2018) HarperCollins Pubs.
Cemented by narration from Churchill's memoirs, the story of the great prime minister & his era is retold through quotations selected from speeches delivered in his own voice, & from comments in the voices of his contemporaries, including Roosevelt, Eisenhower, Truman, Chamberlain, George VI & others.

Churchill in His Own Voice: And the Voices of His Contemporaries, unabr. ed. Read by Winston L. S. Churchill. 2 cass. (Running Time: 3 hrs.). 1999. 17.95 (H135) Blckstn Audio.
The story of the great prime minister & his era is retold through selections from his major speeches & those of his contemporaries, with selections from his memoirs read by Laurence Olivier & Sir John Gielgud.

Churchill on Leadership. unabr. collector's ed. Steven F. Hayward. Read by Stuart Langton. 4 cass. (Running Time: 6 hrs.). 1999. 32.00 (978-0-7366-4305-4(2), 4796) Books on Tape.
This examines Churchill's executive side. Here he's portrayed not as a mythic historical figure but rather as a role model for today's executives & managers. With wit & insight, the author, a historian reveals Churchill's secrets for business success.

Churchill Part 2: A Biography. unabr. ed. Roy Jenkins. Read by Robert Whitfield. (Running Time: 64800 sec.). 2007. audio compact disk 120.00 (978-0-7861-6055-6(1)) Blckstn Audio.

Churchills. unabr. ed. A. L. Rowse. Read by Richard Green. 15 cass. (Running Time: 22 hrs. 30 mins.). Incl. Pt. I. Churchills. 8 cass. (Running Time: 8 hrs.). A. L. Rowse. Read by Richard Green. 64.00 (1080-A); Pt. II. Churchills. 7 cass. (Running Time: 7 hrs.). A. L. Rowse. Read by Richard Green. 1978. 56.00 (1080-B); 1978. 120.00 (978-0-7366-0069-9(8), 1080A/B) Books on Tape.
Relates the history of one of England's First Families. Part I deals with the origins of the Churchill Family. Part II highlights the family's most distinguished member, Sir Winston.

***Churchill's Empire: The World That Made Him & the World He Made.** unabr. ed. Richard Toye. (Running Time: 13 hrs. 30 mins. 0 sec.). 2010. 24.99 (978-1-4001-6871-2(6)); 37.99 (978-1-4001-9871-9(2)); 18.99 (978-1-4001-8871-0(7)); audio compact disk 37.99 (978-1-4001-1871-7(9)); audio compact disk 90.99 (978-1-4001-4871-4(5)) Pub: Tantor Media. Dist(s): IngramPubServ

Churchill's Generals. unabr. collector's ed. Read by David Case. Ed. by John Keegan. 11 cass. (Running Time: 16 hrs. 30 min.). 1993. 88.00 (978-0-7366-2562-3(3), 3313) Books on Tape.
Churchill's generals hold the key to victory in WW II...& to the elusive character of their chief.

Churchmouse Birthday. Barbara Davoll. Illus. by Dennis Hockerman. (Christopher Churchmouse Classics Ser.). (J). 1994. 11.99 (3-1218) David C Cook.

Churchmouse Christmas. Barbara Davoll. Illus. by Dennis Hockerman. 1 cass. (Christopher Churchmouse Classics Ser.). (J). 1994. 11.99 David C Cook.

Churchmouse Christmas. Music by Barbara Davoll. 1 CD. (Running Time: 1 hr.). (J). (gr. k-6). 2001. audio compact disk 80.00 (MU-9173T) Lillenas.
Based on the series Christopher Churchmouse Classics, this story-within-a-story describes the Christmas adventures of Christopher Churchmouse & his very special gift for the church. Throughout the musical, Amy & her grandmother discuss the true meaning of Christmas & present the plan of salvation. Accompaniment cassette, Side A, stereo trax, Side B, split-channel.

Churchmouse Christmas. Music by Barbara Davoll. Arranged by Don Wyrtzen. 1 cass. (Running Time: 1 hr.). (J). (gr. k-6). 2001. 80.00 (MU-9173C) Lillenas.

Churchmouse Christmas. Barbara Davoll & Dennis Hockerman. 1 cass. (Christopher Churchmouse Ser.). (J). (ps-2). 1994. 11.99 (3-1217) David C Cook.

Churchmouse Christmas. Music by Don Wyrtzen. Lyrics by Barbara Davoll. 1 cass. (Running Time: 1 hr.). (J). 2001. 12.99 (TA-9173C) Lillenas.

ChurchpreneurTV. com present Allowyn Price Live: Promotional Edition. Prod. by Allowyn Price. 2008. audio compact disk (978-1-4276-3417-7(3)) AardGP.

Chute see Albert Camus: Reading from His Novel and Essays

Chute the Works. 2 cass. (Running Time: 2 hrs.). (J). (ps-5). 2001. pap. bk. 18.95 (KEA 9095C); pap. bk. & stu. ed. 20.95 (KEA 9095) Kimbo Educ.
Designed for students with previous parachute experience, these exercises progress from easy to more challenging. Do the twist, the bump, the grapevine, & play call ball, chute soccer, chute ball & more. Includes instructional manual.

CIA - FBI Threat to Privacy. unabr. ed. Morton Halperin. 1 cass. (Running Time: 53 min.). 12.95 (736) J Norton Pubs.

CIA Files: Defector Reveals Russia's Secret War Plans. 2001. 19.95 (978-0-9704029-6-7(1)) NewsMax Media.

Ciao. 4th ed. Federici. (C). bk. 171.95 (978-0-8384-8117-2(5)); bk. 114.95 (978-0-8384-8132-5(9)); bk. & stu. ed. 174.95 (978-0-8384-8069-4(1)) Heinle.

Ciao! 4th ed. Carla Federici. (C). bk. 128.95 (978-0-8384-7164-7(1)); bk. 146.95 (978-0-8384-7044-2(0)) Heinle.

Ciao! 4th ed. Carla Federici & Carla Riga. (ITA.). 1999. lab manual ed. (978-0-03-020698-6(7)); lab manual ed. (978-0-03-022272-6(9)) Harcourt Coll Pubs.

Ciao! 5th ed. Carla Federici & Riga. (C). bk. 140.95 (978-0-8384-7073-2(4)) Heinle.

***Ciao, I Am Poetino Audio CD.** Giusti-Gambini Publishing. (ENG.). 2010. audio compact disk 10.95 (978-0-9829496-0-3(X)) J M Gambini.

Ciao! Italian Dance w/Music CD. Vicki Corona. (Celebrate the Cultures Ser.: 8-11A). 2004. pap. bk. 24.95 (978-1-58513-118-1(0)) Dance Fantasy.

Ciao 5e-Multimedia Cd-Rom. 5th ed. Federici. (C). 2003. audio compact disk 13.95 (978-0-8384-0530-7(4)) Pub: Heinle. Dist(s): CENGAGE Learn

Ciardi, John. unabr. ed. John Ciardi. 1 cass. (Author Speaks Ser.). 1991. 14.95 J Norton Pubs.
Archival recordings of 20th-century authors.

Cibola. unabr. ed. Connie Willis. Read by Amy Bruce. Ed. by Allan Kaster. 1 cass. (Running Time: 50 min.). (Great Science Fiction Stories Ser.). 1996. 10.99 (978-1-884612-15-2(6)) AudioText.
A reporter for the "Denver Record" is assigned to cover the supposed great-granddaughter of Coronado & her claim to know where the Seven Cities of Gold are. The skeptical reporter soon gets caught up in the search.

***Cicada Summer.** unabr. ed. Andrea Beaty. Narrated by Maria Cabezas. 1 Playaway. (Running Time: 2 hrs. 45 mins.). (J). (gr. 4-6). 2009. 54.75 (978-1-4407-6189-8(2)); 33.75 (978-1-4407-6180-5(9)); audio compact disk 30.75 (978-1-4407-6184-3(1)) Recorded Bks.

***Cicada Summer.** unabr. collector's ed. Andrea Beaty. Narrated by Maria Cabezas. 3 CDs. (Running Time: 2 hrs. 45 mins.). (J). (gr. 4-6). 2009. audio compact disk 26.95 (978-1-4407-6188-1(4)) Recorded Bks.

Cicadas: Audio Book. Shawn Penning. Read by Shawn Penning. Music by Kevin McLeod. Bonnie Comella. (ENG.). 2009. audio compact disk 29.97 (978-0-9841063-0-1(8)) Pennimation Pub.

Cicero's de Amicitia AP Selections: A Digital Tutor. Anthony Hollingsworth. (Digital Scholia Ser.). bk. (978-0-86516-647-9(1)) Bolchazy-Carducci.

Cicero's Pro Archia: A Digital Tutor. Anthony Hollingsworth. (Digital Scholia Ser.). bk. (978-0-86516-646-2(3)) Bolchazy-Carducci.

***Ciclo de Vida de la Mariposa Audio Cd.** Margaret Mcnamara. Adapted by Benchmark Education Company, LLC. (Content Connections Ser.). (SPA.). (J). 2009. audio compact disk 10.00 (978-1-935472-58-2(5)) Benchmark Educ.

***Ciclo de Vida de la Rana Audio Cd.** Margaret Mcnamara. Adapted by Benchmark Education Company, LLC. (Content Connections Ser.). (SPA.). (J). 2009. audio compact disk 10.00 (978-1-935472-59-9(3)) Benchmark Educ.

***Ciclo de Vida Del Roble Audio Cd.** Debra Castor. Adapted by Benchmark Education Company, LLC. (Content Connections Ser.). (SPA.). (J). 2009. audio compact disk 10.00 (978-1-935472-54-4(2)) Benchmark Educ.

Cid, Set. Corneille. Perf. by Michel Etcheverry & Claude Winter. 2 cass. (FRE.). 1991. 26.95 (1037-RF) Olivia & Hill.
Don Rodrigue is called upon to avenge his father who has been slapped by the father of Chimene, the woman he loves. Both are torn between honor & love.

***Cider House Rules.** abr. ed. John Irving. Read by Grover Gardner. (ENG.). 2005. (978-0-06-079003-5(2), Harper Audio); (978-0-06-082451-8(4), Harper Audio) HarperCollins Pubs.

Cider House Rules, Pt. 1. unabr. collector's ed. John Irving. Read by Grover Gardner. 8 cass. (Running Time: 12 hrs.). 1985. 64.00 (978-0-7366-0988-3(1), 1927-A) Books on Tape.
St. Cloud is a train station, an orphanage & an abandoned lumber camp, but the place is busy with a steady stream of pregnant women arriving at the station & walking up the long hill to Dr. Wilbur Larch's office at the orphanage. Dr. Larch delivers unwanted babies & finds homes for them, he also performs abortions. This novel deals with the fragility of rules & rituals of everyday life.

Cider House Rules, Pt. 2. collector's ed. John Irving. Read by Grover Gardner. 9 cass. (Running Time: 13 hrs. 30 min.). 1985. 72.00 (978-0-7366-0989-0(X), 1927-B) Books on Tape.

Cider with Rosie. unabr. ed. Laurie Lee. Read by Laurie Lee. 7 CDs. (Running Time: 7 hrs. 50 min.). (Isis Ser.). (J). 2001. audio compact disk 71.95 (978-0-7531-0729-4(5)) Pub: ISIS Lrg Prnt GBR. Dist(s): Ulverscroft US
This loving and intimate record of childhood and growing up in a remote Cotswold village is a testament to a vanished world. Life was hard, but with all that can happen to a family of 3 sisters and 4 brothers, not to mention the other people of the village, it was also interesting and very funny.

Cider with Rosie. unabr. ed. Laurie Lee. 8 cass. (Isis Cassettes Ser.). (J). 2004. 69.95 (978-1-85089-688-3(7)) Pub: ISIS Lrg Prnt GBR. Dist(s): Ulverscroft US

Cider with Rosie: A Boyhood in the West of England, Set. unabr. ed. Laurie Lee. Read by Laurie Lee. 6 cass. (Running Time: 8 hrs.). 1989. 49.00 (978-1-55690-103-4(8), 89580) Recorded Bks.
Boyhood in the west of England just after WW I.

Cielito Lindo. David Martin del Campo. Narrated by Francisco Rivela. 5 cass. (Running Time: 6 hrs. 45 mins.). 47.00 (978-1-4025-1669-6(X)) Recorded Bks.

***Cielo: The Enchanted Mountain.** Composed by John Hunter. (C). 1995. 9.95 (978-1-61584-508-8(9)) Indep Pub IL.

Cielos de la Tierra. Carmen Boullosa. 8 cass. (Running Time: 11 hrs. 45 mins.). 72.00 (978-1-4025-1599-6(5)) Recorded Bks.

Cien Anos de Soledad see One Hundred Years of Solitude

Cien Rancheras. Cuco Sanchez. (SPA.). 2001. bk. 9.89 (978-970-651-523-0(2), 1150) Edit Oceano De Mex MEX.

***Ciencia Asombrosa.** (Ciencia Asombrosa Ser.). (SPA.). 2008. audio compact disk 116.80 (978-1-4048-4532-9(1)) CapstoneDig.

Cigale et la Fourmi see Fables de La Fontaine

Cigar Roller. Pablo Medina. Read by Stefan Rudnicki. (Running Time: 19800 sec.). 2005. audio compact disk 29.95 (978-0-7861-8059-2(5)) Blckstn Audio.

Cigar Roller: A Novel. Pablo Medina. Read by Stefan Rudnicki. (Running Time: 5 hrs.). 2005. reel tape 34.95 (978-0-7861-3507-3(7)); audio compact disk 45.00 (978-0-7861-7844-5(2)) Blckstn Audio.

Cigar Roller: A Novel. Pablo Medina. Narrated by Stefan Rudnicki. (Running Time: 5 hrs. 30 mins.). 2005. 24.95 (978-1-59912-636-4(2)) Iofy Corp.

Cigarette Case see Widdershins: The First Book of Ghost Stories

CigarQuest Vol. 1: Conversations in Smoke. abr. ed. Richard Carleton Hacker. 2 cass. (Running Time: 3 hrs.). 1997. 19.95 (978-0-931253-07-2(1)) Autumngold Pub.
Includes in-depth discussions with some of the world's top cigar makers, answers to the most frequently asked questions, & cigar smoking trivia.

Cigogne et le Renard. (Plaisir de Lire Ser.). 5.95 (978-88-8148-706-6(3)) EMC-Paradigm.

CIIS Commencement '89. Ram Dass. 2 cass. (AA & A Symposium Ser.). 18.00 set. (A0445-89) Sound Photosyn.
Ram Dass, introduced by Ralph Metzner, offers a warm address within this entire commencement proceedings.

Cilia-of-Gold. Short Stories. 1 CD. (Running Time: 70 mins.). (Great Science Fiction Stories Ser.). 2004. audio compact disk 10.99 (978-1-884612-32-9(6)) AudioText.

Cilia-of-Gold. unabr. ed. Stephen Baxter. Read by Amy Bruce. Ed. by Allan Kaster. 1 cass. (Running Time: 1 hr. 11 min.). (Great Science Fiction Stories Ser.). 1996. 10.99 (978-1-884612-12-1(1)) AudioText.
Larionova had had no intention of visiting Mercury. The planet was a piece of junk. But within days of landing exploratory teams on the planet, anomalies had been reported. A "Xeelee" story.

Cilla Fisher & Artie Trezise: For Foul Day & Fair. 1 cass. 9.98 (C-69) Folk-Legacy.
Dynamic duo doing great Scots songs.

Cimarron. Hank Mitchum. Read by Charlie O'Dowd. 4 vols. No. 14. 2004. 25.00 (978-1-58807-197-2(9)); (978-1-58807-957-2(0)) Am Pubng Inc.

Cimarron. unabr. collector's ed. Edna Ferber. Read by Flo Gibson. 8 cass. (Running Time: 12 hrs.). 1983. 64.00 (978-0-7366-0665-3(3), 1627) Books on Tape.
Restless Yancey Cravat, a pioneer newspaper editor & lawyer, settles in Osage, a muddy town thrown together overnight when Oklahoma territory opens in 1889. To this place he brings his wife Sabra, a woman both conventional & well-bred.

Cimarron, Set. unabr. ed. Edna Ferber. Read by Flo Gibson. 8 cass. (Running Time: 12 hrs.). (Classic Books on Cassettes Coll.). 1998. 64.00 Audio Bk Con.
A novel of ambition, western frontier adventures, newspaper business & politics.

Cimarron Rose. unabr. ed. James Lee Burke. Narrated by Tom Stechschulte. 8 cass. (Running Time: 11 hrs.). (Billy Bob Holland Ser.). 1998. 75.00 (978-0-7887-1746-8(4), 95224E7) Recorded Bks.
Billy Bob Holland, a lawyer in the small town of Deaf Smith, Texas, is gathering evidence to defend a local musician charged with murder.

Cincinnati Red Stalkings, unabr. ed. Troy Soos. Narrated by Johnny Heller. 6 cass. (Running Time: 8 hrs.). (Mickey Rawlings Baseball Ser.: Vol. 5). 1998. 52.00 (978-0-7887-2478-7(9), 95553E7) Recorded Bks.
It's 1921 & utility infielder Mickey Rawlings is thrilled to be playing for the Cincinnati Reds. But when he helps set up an exhibit honoring the team, he uncovers explosive clues to a 50-year-old mystery.

Cinco Crayones: Ingles. Created by Berlitz Publishing. 1. (Running Time: 1 hr.). (Berlitz Adventures with Nicholas Ser.). (ENG & SPA., (ps-3). 2006. audio compact disk 9.95 (978-981-246-829-1(3)) Pub: Berlitz Pubng. Dist(s): Langenscheidt

Cinco Hermanos Chicos. Tr. of Five Chinese Brothers. (SPA.). 2004. 8.95 (978-0-7882-0264-3(2)) Weston Woods.

Cinco Idiomas del Amor: Como Expresar un Verdadero Compromiso a Tu Pareja. abr. ed. Gary Chapman. Read by Cindy Rojas. Narrated by David Rojas. (Running Time: 18000 sec.). (SPA.). 2007. audio compact disk 17.99 (978-1-59859-288-7(2)) Oasis Audio.

Cinco Idiomas del Amor: Como Expresar un Verdadero Compromiso a Tu Pareja. unabr. ed. Gary Chapman. Read by David Rojas & Cindy Rojas. (Running Time: 16200 sec.). 2007. audio compact disk 36.00 (978-1-4332-1101-0(7)) Blckstn Audio.

Cinco Lenguajes de la Disculpa. abr. ed. Gary Chapman & Jennifer Thomas. Narrated by David Garcia & Cindy Rojas. (SPA.). 2006. audio compact disk 14.99 (978-1-59859-150-7(9)) Oasis Audio.

Cinco Lenguajes de la Disculpa. unabr. ed. Gary Chapman & Jennifer Thomas. (Running Time: 3 mins.). 2007. audio compact disk 27.00 (978-1-4332-1140-9(8)) Blckstn Audio.

Cinco Personas Que Encontraras en el Cielo. unabr. ed. Mitch Albom. Read by Francisco Rivela.Tr. of Five People You Meet in Heaven. 2006. 24.98 (978-1-4013-8742-6(X)) Pub: Hyperion. Dist(s): HarperCollins Pubs

Cincos Lenguajes de la Disculpa. abr. ed. Gary Chapman & Jennifer Thomas. Narrated by Cindy Rojas et al. (SPA.). 2006. 10.49 (978-1-60814-295-8(7)) Oasis Audio.

Cinder-Elly. unabr. ed. Frances Minters. 1 cass. (Running Time: 8 min.). (J). (gr. k-3). 1994. pap. bk. 16.95 (978-0-8045-6826-5(X), 6826) Spoken Arts.
When a modern day Cinderella attempts to win Prince Charming, a local basketball player, she gets help from a shopping-cart Fairy Godmother.

Cinder Path. unabr. ed. Catherine Cookson. Read by Susan Jameson. 2000. 49.95 (978-0-7451-5857-0(9)) Pub: Chivers Audio Bks GBR. Dist(s): AudioGO
Brilliantly portrays the life of Charlie MacFell, a man in search of himself; from rural Northumberland to the atrocities of World War I. At the root of MacFell's life is the cinder path of his childhood home, a place of harsh associations that will come to symbolize struggle with destiny itself.

Cinderella see Cenicienta

Cinderella see Cendrillon

Cinderella. Read by Charles Biddle, Jr. Illus. by Annabel Malak. 1 cass. (Running Time: 15 mins.). (Classic Stories Ser.). (J). (ps-2). bk. 9.95 (978-2-921997-75-1(4)) Coffragants CAN.
Kids know that fairies do not really exist, but the story of Cinderella reminds them that some adults can be as nice as the fairy godmother.

Cinderella. Read by Marjorie Westbury. 1 cass. (J). (ps-2). 3.98 incl. poster. (978-1-55886-020-9(7)) Smarty Pants.
A children's fairy tale of a girl, her stepmother & stepsisters & a fairy godmother.

***Cinderella.** Weston Woods Staff. (J). audio compact disk 12.95 (978-0-439-84878-7(4)) Weston Woods.

Cinderella, abr. ed. Perf. by St. Charles Players. 2 cass. (Running Time: 98 min.). (Story Theatre for Young Readers Ser.). 2000. 16.95 (978-1-56994-521-6(7), 309634, Monterey SoundWorks) Monterey Media Inc.
Once upon a time...there was a wicked stepmother with two wicked stepsisters, a glorious castle with a king & queen, a handsome prince, his horse named Steed, a grand ball, a fairy godmother, mice who could talk, &...a dream. Once upon a time...there was Cinderella.

Cinderella. I.t. ed. Short Stories. Illus. by Graham Percy. 1 cass. (Running Time: 10 mins.). Dramatization. (J). (ps-2). 2001. bk. 8.99 (978-84-87650-25-3(2)) Pub: Peralt Mont ESP. Dist(s): imaJen

Cinderella. unabr. ed. 1 cass. (Read-Along Ser.). (J). bk. 7.99 (978-1-55723-007-2(2)) W Disney Records.

Cinderella. unabr. ed. Barbara Karlin. Narrated by Stephanie J. Block. Illus. by James Marshall. 1 cass. (Running Time: 12 mins.). (J). (ps-4). 2006. pap. bk. 14.95 (978-0-439-84889-3(X), WPRA671) Weston Woods.

Cinderella. unabr. ed. Barbara Karlin. Narrated by Stephanie J. Block. Illus. by James Marshall. 1 CD. (Running Time: 12 mins.). (J). (ps-4). 2006. bk. 29.95 (978-0-439-84888-6(1), WHCD671); pap. bk. 18.95 (978-0-439-84890-9(3), WPCD671); bk. 24.95 (978-0-439-84887-9(3), WHRA671) Weston Woods.
The classic children¿s story of triumph over adversity is entertainingly re-told by Barbara Karlin and brought to life with James Marshall¿s signature illustrations. Sparkling narration provided by Stephanie J. Block, with music by Ernest V. Troost and animation by Virginia Wilkos.

Cinderella. unabr. ed. Ed McBain, pseud. Read by Paul Shay. 6 cass. (Running Time: 9 hrs.). (Matthew Hope Mystery Ser.: No. 6). 1992. 48.00 (978-0-7366-2245-5(4), 3035) Books on Tape.
Middle-aged barfly & P. I. turns up dead spoiling a great evening for Matthew Hope.

Cinderella - That Awful Cinderella. Alvin Granowsky. 1 cass. (Point of View Stories Ser.). (J). (gr. 4-6). 1993. 8.49 (978-0-8114-2212-3(7)) SteckVau.
Two versions of the traditional story & a retelling from the viewpoint of a story character motivate students to read & analyze literature through critical thinking. Flip-book presentation emphasizes the difference in the two story versions & encourages students to complete both & compare.

Cinderella Affidavit, unabr. ed. Michael Fredrickson. Narrated by Ron McLarty. 11 cass. (Running Time: 15 hrs. 30 mins.). 1999. 96.00 (978-0-7887-3764-0(3), 95981E7) Recorded Bks.
After a Chinatown drug raid goes bad, a judge suspects it was based on a phony informant. But attorney Michael Boer believes his client, a small-time hustler, is the real snitch. As Michael struggles to protect the terrified client, he faces off with mobsters, crooked politicians & enemies within his own firm. Includes an exclusive interview with the author.

Cinderella Affidavit. unabr. ed. Michael Fredrickson. Narrated by Ron McLarty. 13 CDs. (Running Time: 15 hrs. 30 mins.). 2000. audio compact disk 119.00 (978-0-7887-4210-1(8), C1139E7) Recorded Bks.

Cinderella & Other Children's Favorites. (J). 2005. audio compact disk (978-1-933796-31-4(6)) PC Treasures.

Cinderella & Other Fairy Tales. unabr. ed. Perf. by Claire Bloom. Ed. by Walter de la Mare. 1 cass. (Running Time: 90 mins.). Incl. Bluebeard. (J). (CDL5 1330); Cinderella & the Glass Slipper. (J). (CDL5 1330); Musicians of Bremen. (J). (CDL5 1330); (J). 1972. 9.95 (978-0-694-50689-7(3), CDL5 1330) HarperCollins Pubs.

Cinderella & the Glass Slipper see Cinderella & Other Fairy Tales

Cinderella Classic Read along Audio Book. Prod. by PC Treasures Staff. (J). 2007. (978-1-60072-060-4(9)) PC Treasures.

***Cinderella Deal.** Jennifer Crusie, pseud. Narrated by Susan Boyce. (Running Time: 5 hrs. 58 mins. 0 sec.). (ENG.). 2010. audio compact disk 19.95 (978-1-60283-908-3(5)) Pub: AudioGO. Dist(s): Perseus Dist

***Cinderella Deal.** unabr. ed. Jennifer Crusie, pseud. Narrated by Susan Boyce. 1 Playaway. (Running Time: 5 hrs. 58 mins.). 2010. 64.95 (978-0-7927-6883-8(3), Chivers Sound Lib); 39.95 (978-0-7927-6882-1(5), Chivers Sound Lib); audio compact disk 64.95 (978-0-7927-6881-4(7), Chivers Sound Lib) AudioGO.

CINDERELLA (Japanese to English - Level 1) Learn ENGLISH Through Fairy Tales. David Burke. (JPN & ENG.). (J). 2007. per. 14.95 (978-1-891888-03-8(X)) Slangman Pubng.

CINDERELLA (Korean to English - Level 1) Learn ENGLISH Through Fairy Tales. David Burke. (KOR & ENG.). (J). 2007. per. 14.95 (978-1-891888-07-6(2)) Slangman Pubng.

Cinderella Man: James J. Braddock, Max Baer, & the Greatest Upset in Boxing History. unabr. ed. Jeremy Schaap. Read by Grover Gardner. 9 CDs. (Running Time: 9 hrs.). 2005. audio compact disk 81.00 (978-1-4159-2179-1(2)); 63.00 (978-1-4159-2173-9(3)) Books on Tape.
This book is as much about Baer, the funloving playboy who won a championship, as it is about Braddock, the Irish American fighter who came off the relief rolls during the Depression to take the crown. Cinderella Man places this title match in the context not only of boxing but also of American sports, sports writing, and the larger framework of life during the Depression. Having beaten the overconfident Baer, Braddock promptly lost the title to Joe Louis, but for a short while he was a symbol of hope - a people;'s champion - for millions of struggling Americans.

Cinderella, Rumpelstiltskin. Charles Perrault. Read by Rebecca C. Burns. (Running Time: 5 hrs.). 2005. 25.95 (978-1-60083-618-3(6), Audiofy Corp) Iofy Corp.

Cinderella, Rumpelstiltskin: And Other Stories. Charles Perrault et al. (Running Time: 18000 sec.). (ENG.). (J). (ps-3). 2005. audio compact disk 19.99 (978-1-4001-5048-9(5)); audio compact disk 49.99 (978-1-4001-3048-1(4)); audio compact disk 24.99 (978-1-4001-0048-4(8)) Pub: Tantor Media. Dist(s): IngramPubServ

Cinderella, Rumpelstiltskin & Other Stories. unabr. ed. Charles Perrault et al. Read by Rebecca Burns. (J). 2007. 39.99 (978-1-59895-790-7(2)) Find a World.

Cinderella, Rumpelstiltskin, & Other Stories. unabr. ed. Charles Perrault et al. Narrated by Rebecca C. Burns. (Running Time: 4 hrs. 30 mins. 0 sec.). (ENG.). (J). (ps-3). 2008. 19.99 (978-1-4001-5913-0(X)); audio compact disk 39.99 (978-1-4001-3913-2(9)) Pub: Tantor Media. Dist(s): IngramPubServ

Cinderella Rumpelstiltskin & Other Stories. unabr. ed. Charles Perrault et al. Narrated by Rebecca C. Burns. (Running Time: 4 hrs. 30 mins. 0 sec.). (ENG.). (J). (ps-3). 2008. audio compact disk 19.99 (978-1-4001-0913-5(2)) Pub: Tantor Media. Dist(s): IngramPubServ

Cinderella, Rumpelstiltskin & Other Stories. unabr. collector's ed. Wilhelm K. Grimm & Jacob W. Grimm. Read by Rebecca C. Burns. 5 cass. (Running Time: 5 hrs.). (J). (ps-3). 1997. 30.00 (978-0-7366-3559-2(9), 4204) Books on Tape.
This cornucopia of traditional stories of magic & lore overflow with fantasy, sorrow, gaiety, courage, wit, wisdom, poetry & common sense.

Cinderella Soundtrack. 1 cass. (Classics Ser.). (J). 1997. 21.98 (978-1-55723-801-6(4)) W Disney Records.

Cinderella Soundtrack. Prod. by Walt Disney Productions Staff. 1 cass. (J). 1997. 12.98 (978-0-7634-0221-1(4)) W Disney Records.
Classics.

Cinderella Story in Psychological Folklore. Instructed by Manly P. Hall. 8.95 (978-0-89314-027-4(9), C571027) Philos Res.

Cinderella, the Cat with Boots, the Sleeping Beauty & Many More Tales see Cenicienta y Muchos Cuentos Mas

Cinderella, the Cat with Boots, the Sleeping Beauty & Many More Tales. (Running Time: 1 hr.). 2001. 14.95 (978-1-60083-131-7(1), Audiofy Corp) Iofy Corp.

***Cindy & the Prince.** unabr. ed. Debbie Macomber. Read by Teri Clark Linden. (Running Time: 5 hrs.). (Legendary Lovers Ser.: Bk. 1). 2010. 14.99 (978-1-4418-5350-9(2), 9781441853509, Brilliance MP3); 14.99 (978-1-4418-5351-6(0), 9781441853516, BAD); audio compact disk 14.99 (978-1-4418-5349-3(9), 9781441853493, Bril Audio CD Unabri) Brilliance Audio.

***Cindy Colley - Home & Hearth.** Arranged by Polishing the Pulpit. 2010. audio compact disk 25.00 (978-1-60644-107-7(8)) Heart Heart.

***Cindy Colley - Living Water for Thirsty Souls.** Arranged by Polishing the Pulpit. 2010. 25.00 (978-1-60644-109-1(4)) Heart Heart.

***Cindy Colley - Women in the Church.** Arranged by Polishing the Pulpit. 2010. 25.00 (978-1-60644-108-4(6)) Heart Heart.

Cindy Kallet: Cindy Two. 1 cass. 9.98 (C-98) Folk-Legacy.
The second recording of a lovely singer & songmaker & great guitarist.

Cindy Kallet: Dreaming down a Quiet Line. 1 cass., 1 CD. 9.98 (C-505); audio compact disk 14.98 CD. (CD-505) Folk-Legacy.
Very lovely self-produced recording.

Cindy Kallet: Working on Wings to Fly. 1 cass., 1 CD. 9.98 (C-83); audio compact disk 14.98 CD. (CD-83) Folk-Legacy.
Cindy's debut recording & it's wonderful.

Cindy Morgan: the Definitive Collection. Contrib. by Cindy Morgan. 2007. audio compact disk 7.97 (978-5-558-14539-7(0), Word Records) Word Enter.

Cinematique: Erotic Audio Screenplays. Sydney Irons. 1 cass. (Running Time: 1 hr.). 1999. 11.95 (978-1-886238-31-2(6)); audio compact disk 16.95 (978-1-886238-30-5(8)) Passion Press.

Cinna, Set. Corneille. Contrib. by Christine Fersen & Lucienne LeMarchand. 2 CDs. (FRE.). 1991. audio compact disk 26.95 (1685-H) Olivia & Hill.
Cinna, the leader of a conspiracy to assassinate the emperor Augustus, is in love with Aemilie. Maxime, a fellow conspirator, chooses to reveal the plot to Augustus in hopes of winning Aemilie's love upon Cinna's imprisonment.

***Cinnamon.** abr. ed. Neil Gaiman. Read by Neil Gaiman. (ENG.). 2006. (978-0-06-123236-7(X)) HarperCollins Pubs.

Cinnamon. unabr. ed. V. C. Andrews. Read by Laurel Lefkow. 4 cass. (Running Time: 5 hrs.). (Shooting Star Ser.). (J). 2002. 44.95 (978-0-7531-1508-4(5)); audio compact disk 59.95 (978-0-7531-1585-5(9)) Pub: ISIS Lrg Prnt GBR. Dist(s): Ulverscroft US
Cinnamon loves the shadows because that's where no one can find her... Dreaming of imaginary worlds and characters is Cinnamon's only escape from her mother's breakdowns, her grandmother's overbearing control, her family's turmoil. But she is discovering something special about herself, a gift from deep within that sets her apart: a talent for the theatre that would finally give her a chance to truly escape.

***Cinnamon.** unabr. ed. Neil Gaiman. Read by Neil Gaiman. (ENG.). 2009. (978-0-06-198734-2(4)) HarperCollins Pubs.

Cinnamon Bear. 6 cass. (Running Time: 15 min. ea. chapter (26 chapters)). (J). 41.70 (CB8939) Natl Recrd Co.
The adventures of Judy & Jimmy Barton, who can't find the Silver Star for the top of their Christmas tree. While searching they meet Paddy O'Cinnamon, the Cinnamon Bear who offers to help & shows Judy & Jimmy how to "de-grow" so he can take them with him on one adventure after another seeking the Silver Star. They meet many people along the way like Willy the Stork, the Roly Poly Policeman, the Singing Tree in the Golden Grove, Fee Foo the friendly giant, Jack Frost, & finally, Santa Claus himself!.

Cinnamon Bear. (Running Time: 6 hrs.). 2004. audio compact disk 29.95 (978-1-57816-182-9(7)) Audio File.

Cinnamon Bear. collector's ed. 5 CDs. (Running Time: 6 hrs.). Dramatization. (Smithsonian Historical Performances Ser.). (J). 1998. bk. 34.98 (978-1-57019-068-1(2), 4037) Radio Spirits.
Adventure story of Judy and Jimmy Barton and their search for the Silver Star that goes on top of their Christmas tree, led by Paddy O'Cinnamon, a stuffed bear come to life. In 26 episodes they meet such characters as Fraidy Cat, Fee-Fo the Giant, the Muddlers and Queen Melissa. First heard on radio in 1937. Includes cast list. Digitally restored and remastered.

Cinnamon Bear. collector's ed. 5 cass. (Running Time: 6 hrs.). Dramatization. (Smithsonian Historical Performances Ser.). (J). (ps-3). 1998. bk. 24.98 (978-1-57019-067-4(4), 4036) Radio Spirits.

Cinnamon Bear, Set. 6 cass. (J). vinyl bd. 24.95 (978-1-57816-038-9(3), CB1003) Audio File.
The exciting adventures of Judy & Jimmy Barton as they search for the silver star for the top of their Christmas tree. They meet Paddy O'Cinnamon, the Cinnamon Bear & travel to Maybe Land for adventure after cliff-hanging adventure with the Crazy Quilt Dragon, The Wintergreen Witch, Snapper Snick the Crocodile, Captain Tin Top, Fe Fo the Giant, Queen Melissa, Jack Frost & even Santa Claus!.

Cinnamon Bear MP3. ed. Short Stories. 1 CD. (Running Time: 6 hrs). (ENG.). (J). 2006. 13.95 (978-1-893437-08-1(6)) Amazing Grace Pubg.

Cinnamon Kiss. unabr. ed. Walter Mosley. Read by Michael Boatman. 5 cass. (Running Time: 7 hrs.). (Easy Rawlins Mystery Ser.). 2005. 45.00 (978-1-4159-0820-4(6)) Books on Tape.

Cinnamon Kiss. unabr. ed. Walter Mosley. Read by Michael Boatman. 6 CDs. (Running Time: 7.5 hrs.). (Easy Rawlins Mystery Ser.). 2005. audio compact disk 54.00 (978-1-4159-0821-1(4)) Books on Tape.

Cinnamon Kiss. unabr. ed. Walter Mosley. (Easy Rawlins Mystery Ser.). (ENG.). 2005. 14.98 (978-1-59483-252-9(8)) Pub: Hachet Audio. Dist(s): HachBkGrp

Cinnamon Kiss. unabr. ed. Walter Mosley. Read by Michael Boatman. (Running Time: 7 hrs.). (ENG.). 2009. 49.98 (978-1-60788-061-5(X)) Pub: Hachet Audio. Dist(s): HachBkGrp

Cinnamon Skin. unabr. collector's ed. John D. MacDonald. Read by Michael Prichard. 8 cass. (Running Time: 8 hrs.). (Travis McGee Ser.: Vol. 20). 1982. 48.00 (978-0-7366-0689-9(0), 1649) Books on Tape.
In this episode of Travis McGee, our perpetual hero undertakes to avenge his friend Meyer's personal tragedy. While Mayer is on a lecture tour, he lends his boat to his newly married niece. But the boat explodes & a Chilean terrorist group claims responsibility. Following a trail that leads from Florida to Mexico, Meyer & McGee uncover evidence of a drug connection as a possible reason for the fatal explosion.

Cinnamon Sky. Janet Woods. 2007. 61.95 (978-1-84559-833-4(4)); audio compact disk 79.95 (978-1-84559-834-1(2)) Pub: Soundings Ltd GBR. Dist(s): Ulverscroft US

Cinq Semaines en Ballon. Jules Verne. (FRE.). bk. 14.95 (978-2-09-032977-3(7), CL9777E) Pub: Cle Intl FRA. Dist(s): Continental Bk

***Cinq Semaines en Ballon.** Jules Verne. Tr. by Elyette Roussel. (Lectures Cle en Francais Facile: Niveau 1 Ser.). (FRE., 2007. pap. bk. 21.95 (978-2-09-031844-9(9)) Cle Intl FRA.

Circe's Palace see Tanglewood Tales

Circe's Palace. unabr. ed. Nathaniel Hawthorne. 1 cass. (Running Time: 68 min.). Dramatization. 1981. 7.95 (N-68) Jimcin Record.
Ulysses encounters a powerful sorceress in one of Hawthorne's adaptations of a classic myth.

Circe's Wand: Enigmas of Ancient Pharmacology. Alison Kennedy. 2 cass. 18.00 set. (A0427-89) Sound Photosyn.
This one is breathlessly amusing & idiosyncratically weird...but good.

Circle. Peter Lovesey. Narrated by Simon Prebble. 10 CDs. (Running Time: 37440 sec.). (Sound Library). 2006. audio compact disk 94.95 (978-0-7927-4056-8(4), SLD 963) AudioGO.

Circle, Set. unabr. ed. W. Somerset Maugham. Read by Flo Gibson. 2 cass. (Running Time: 2 hrs. 30 mins). 1998. bk. 14.95 (978-1-55685-543-6(5)) Audio Bk Con.
A tragi-comedy as history repeats itself in marital breakups.

Circle Around. Perf. by Tickle Tune Typhoon Staff. 1 cass. (J). 8.98 (214) MFLP CA.
Songs include: "Tree Dancing," "Muscle Music," "Vega Boogie," "Hug Bug," "Monster Song" & many more.

Circle Around. Tickle Tune Typhoon Staff. 1 cass. (Running Time: 37 min.). (J). 1984. 9.98 (978-0-945337-01-0(9), SRU 55-922) Tickle Tune Typhoon.
Features a collection of mostly original songs.

Circle Dances for Today. Instructed by Rudy Franklin. 1 cass. (Running Time: 1 hr.). (J). (gr. 5 up). 2001. pap. bk. 10.95 (KEA 1146C) Kimbo Educ.
These fun-to-do dances are ideal for co-ed settings. Fun for grades 5 & up. Seven Jumps, Five Foot Two, Jiffy Mixer & more. Includes instructional guide.

Circle Game: Folk Music for Kids. (J). 9.98 (978-1-56628-280-2(2)) MFLP CA.

Circle Game: Folk Music for Kids. 1 CD or 1 cass. (Running Time: 30 min.). (J). 2001. audio compact disk 15.98 (978-1-56628-279-6(9), 74339) MFLP CA.
Introduction to folk music. These 13 interactive, lyrically-driven songs were chosen especially for families. Child singers put a whole new spin on these timeless favorites.

Circle Games, Level 2. Frank Brennan. Contrib. by Philip Prowse. (Running Time: 1 hr. 30 mins.). (Cambridge English Readers Ser.). (ENG.). 2005. 9.45 (978-0-521-63071-9(1)) Cambridge U Pr.

Circle of Care: A Systems Approach to Spirituality. 1 cass. (Care Cassettes Ser.: Vol. 20, No. 2). 1993. 10.80 Assn Prof Chaplains.

***Circle of Flight.** John Marsden. Read by Mikaela Martin. (Running Time: 9 hrs. 15 mins.). (Ellie Chronicles). (YA). 2009. 64.99 (978-1-74214-334-7(2), 9781742143347) Pub: Bolinda Pubng AUS. Dist(s): Bolinda Pub Inc

Circle of Flight. unabr. ed. John Marsden. Read by Mikaela Martin. (Running Time: 9 hrs. 15 mins.). (Ellie Chronicles: Bk. 3). (YA). 2007. audio compact disk 87.95 (978-1-74093-864-8(X)) Pub: Bolinda Pubng AUS. Dist(s): Bolinda Pub Inc

Circle of Flight. unabr. ed. John Marsden. Read by Mikaela Martin. (Running Time: 9 hrs. 15 mins.). (Ellie Chronicles). (YA). 2009. 43.95 (978-1-74214-131-2(5), 9781742141312) Pub: Bolinda Pubng AUS. Dist(s): Bolinda Pub Inc

Circle of Friends. Perf. by Parachute Express Staff. 1 cass., 1 CD. (J). 7.98 (TLR 1005); audio compact disk 11.18 CD Jewel box. (TLR 1005) NewSound.

Circle of Grace: A Novel. unabr. ed. Penelope J. Stokes. 9 cass. (Running Time: 13 hrs. 30 min.). 2004. 81.00 (978-1-4159-0115-1(5)); 63.00 (978-1-4159-0083-3(3)) Books on Tape.
According to the "circle journal" they've used to keep in touch, they seem to have the lives they dreamed of. Liz, the hippie activist, fights for justice in Washington, D.C. Tess who always wanted to be a writer teaches literature in the Midwest and is married to another professor. Amanda, considered the prettiest by the group, enjoys a perfect marriage to her college boyfriend. And then there is Grace. As the moral compass of the group, she never planned on deceiving anyone; but afraid of telling the truth, she presented a life that was anything but hers. Now, she is fighting for her life, and when her friends gather around her to lend their support, she is not the only one who is forced to disclose - and face - the truth.

Circle of Healing. Paul Ferrini. Read by Paul Ferrini. Perf. by Michael Gray. 1 cass. (Running Time: 1 hr.). 1991. 10.00 (978-1-879159-08-2(2)) Heartways Pr.
This gentle meditation opens the heart to love's presence & extends that love to all the beings in your experience.

Circle of Healing: Suicide Prevention for Young Native Americans. 1 cass. (Running Time: 30 min.). 10.95 (I0380B090, HarperThor) HarpC GBR.

Circle of Innovation: You Can't Shrink Your Way to Greatness. abr. ed. Tom Peters. Read by Tom Peters. 2 cass. (Running Time: 3 hrs.). 1999. 16.85 Set. (978-1-85998-992-0(6)) Ulvrscrft Audio.
The world's most respected business thinker is a practical guide for the evolving organisation.

Circle of Love. Patricia O'Malley. Perf. by Barry Weiss. 1 cass. (Running Time: 50 min.). 1998. (978-1-892450-18-0(6), 113) Promo Music.
Guided imagery.

Circle of Nations: Voices & Visions of American Indians. abr. ed. Read by Joy Harjo & Simon Ortiz. Ed. by John Gattuso. 2 cass. (Running Time: 3 hrs.). 1995. 16.95 (978-0-944993-79-8(6)) Audio Lit.
Native Americans speak their dreams, hopes, visions & realities & show us how they see themselves.

Circle of Quilters. Jennifer Chiaverini. Read by Christina Moore. (Running Time: 36900 sec.). (Elm Creek Quilts Ser.: No. 9). 2006. audio compact disk 34.99 (978-1-4193-5778-7(6)) Recorded Bks.

***Circle of Reason.** unabr. ed. Amitav Ghosh. Read by Simon Vance. (Running Time: 17 hrs.). 2011. 24.99 (978-1-4418-3514-7(8), 9781441835147, Brilliance MP3); 39.97 (978-1-4418-3515-4(6), 9781441835154, Brlnc Audio MP3 Lib); audio compact disk 29.99 (978-1-4418-3512-3(1), 9781441835123, Bril Audio CD Unabri); audio compact disk 89.97 (978-1-4418-3513-0(X), 9781441835130, BriAudCD Unabrid) Brilliance Audio.

Circle of Song: Chants & Songs for Ritual & Celebration. unabr. ed. Kate Marks. Perf. by Douglas Hewitt. 1 cass., 1 CD. (Running Time: 1 hr.). (YA). 2000. 10.95 (978-0-9637489-4-2(7)) Pub: Full Circle MA. Dist(s): ACCESS Pubs Network
A companion to the songbook of the same name. It includes 16 songs, chants & sounds from many spiritual traditions as well as contemporary earth-based ritual/circle songs.

Circle of Song: Songs, Chants & Dances for Ritual & Celebration. unabr. ed. Perf. by Kate Marks & Douglas Hewitt. 1 CD. (Running Time: 1 hr.). 1999. audio compact disk 15.95 (978-0-9637489-3-5(9)) Full Circle MA.

Circle of Song - ShowTrax. Emily Crocker. 1 CD. 2000. audio compact disk 19.95 H Leonard.
Easy echo harmonies & a positive message make this upbeat song a perfect choice for any concert.

Circle of Stars. Anna Lee Waldo. Read by Kate Reading. (Druid Circle Ser.: Vol. 2). 2001. 64.00 (978-0-7366-7629-8(5)); 64.00 (978-0-7366-8028-8(4)) Books on Tape.

Circle of Stones. collector's ed. Anna Lee Waldo. Read by Kate Reading. 13 cass. (Running Time: 19 hrs. 30 min.). (Druid Circle Ser.: Vol. 1). 1999. 104.00 (978-0-7366-4562-1(4), 4969) Books on Tape.
As the favorite mistress of Prince Owain in twelfth-century Wales, Brenda finds herself at the center of an ever-changing world. In a Wales torn between the old ways of the druids & the new teachings of Christianity, Brenda gives birth because of a superstitious prophecy. Madoc is raised in safety, but Brenda is caught & brought back to Gwynedd castle where she rises to become a chief adviser & confidante to the most powerful prince in Wales. Her courage & indomitable spirit transform the course of history, while her child grows to be the savior of his people, leading the druids out of Wales & into the New World.

Circle of Three. unabr. ed. Patricia Gaffney. Read by Dean Robertson & Laural Merlington. 9 cass. (Running Time: 13 hrs.). 2000. 37.95 (978-1-56740-388-6(3), 1567403883, BAU) Brilliance Audio.
Patricia Gaffney's sensational national bestseller, The Saving Graces, won the hearts of readers everywhere and propelled her into the first ranks of contemporary women writers. Now this gifted author illuminates the silken bonds of family through the interconnected lives of three generations of women in a small town in rural Virginia. "Can grief last for a person's whole life?" That is the question Carrie struggles to answer after the sudden death of her husband. She also mourns the death of their love - an emotional erosion that began long before her husband's heart gave out. Complicating matters is Carrie's mother, Dana, a snobbish yet sympathetic woman who tries to do what she thinks best. Dana, too, mourns a painful loss - the disintegration of her relationship with Carrie. "I'd give anything for the closeness we used to have, but she won't let me in." At the end point of these two generations is Carrie's daughter Ruth, who silently copes with a double tragedy of her own, the loss of her father and the emotional abandonment of her mother. "She's still got me, but she's about half the mother I used to have." Through their stories, Patricia Gaffney explores all women's relationships - the things that sometimes divide them, but

ultimately bind them together. Wise, moving, and heartbreakingly real, Circle of Three creates the perplexing and invigorating magic that is life itself.

Circle of Three. unabr. ed. Patricia Gaffney. Read by Laural Merlington. (Running Time: 13 hrs.). 2005. 39.25 (978-1-59600-783-3(4), 9781596007833, BADLE); 24.95 (978-1-59600-782-6(6), 9781596007826, BAD); audio compact disk 24.95 (978-1-59600-780-2(X), 9781596007802, Brilliance MP3); audio compact disk 39.25 (978-1-59600-781-9(8), 9781596007819, Brlnc Audio MP3 Lib) Brilliance Audio.

Circle of Wisdom: Songs of Hildegard Von Bingen. Perf. by Hildegard Von Bingen & Anima Misa. 1 cass., 1 CD. audio compact disk 11.98 CD Jewel box. (SAP 2) NewSound.
This medieval nun, abbess & mystic is joined by instrumentalists Robert Mealy & Na'ama Lion.

Circle of Women. Perf. by Circle of Women. 1 cass.; 1 CD. 1998. 10.98 (978-1-56628-137-9(7), 72879); audio compact disk 15.98 CD. (978-1-56628-136-2(9), 72879D) MFLP CA.

Circle of Wonder: A Native American Christmas Story. Read by N. Scott Momaday. 2001. reel tape 5.95 (978-0-8263-2797-0(4)) U of NM Pr.

Circle the World. Dana Blanck & Bill Peterson. 1 cass., 1 CD. 1998. 10.95 (CS-441); audio compact disk 15.95 (CD-441) GIA Pubns.

Circle Time: Songs & Rhymes for the Very Young. Lisa Monet. 1 CD. (Running Time: 1 hr.). (J). 2002. audio compact disk 15.98 (R2 75594) MFLP CA.
Every preschooler looks forward to "circle time" more than any other time of day. The author's sunny soprano voice and brightly strummed guitar combine with an incredible 30 songs including If You're Happy and You Know It, Little Red Caboose, Where is Thumbkin?, Itsy Bitsy Spider, The Little Teapot, and The Muffin Man.

Circle Time: Songs & Rhymes for the Very Young. Lisa Monet. 1 cass. (J). (ps). 1989. 6.98 Norelco. (978-1-877737-05-3(4), MFLP #215) MFLP CA.
Lullabies for children.

Circle Time: Songs & Rhymes for the Very Young. Read by Lisa Monet. 1 cass. (Running Time: 35 min.). (J). (gr. 1). 1994. 9.98 (978-1-56628-043-3(5), MLP 215B/WB 42560-4) MFLP CA.
Fun & play songs for toddlers.

Circle Trilogy. unabr. ed. Ted Dekker. Narrated by Rob Lamont & Tim Gregory. (Running Time: 52 hrs. 26 mins. 0 sec.). (Books of History Chronicles: Bks. 1, 2, & 3). 2009. audio compact disk 89.99 (978-1-59859-106-4(1)) Oasis Audio.

Circle Trilogy: Morrigan's Cross; Dance of the Gods; Valley of Silence. abr. ed. Nora Roberts. Read by Dick Hill. (Running Time: 18 hrs.). (Circle Trilogy: Bks. 1-3). 2008. audio compact disk 34.95 (978-1-4233-3202-2(4), 9781423332022, BACD) Brilliance Audio.

Circles. unabr. ed. Doris Mortman. Read by Frances Cassidy. 10 cass. (Running Time: 15 hrs.). 1996. 80.00 (978-0-7366-3338-3(3), 3988) Books on Tape.
Jennifer Crenshaw, beautiful & brilliant, has it all - a handsome husband, a successful career. She had dreamed of this life when she traded a comforting circle of family & friends for ambition. But Jennifer will soon discover that ambition is a tightrope walk she'll have to take solo. A lost love will return to torment her - & the woman with everything must account for the price she paid to get to the top. She'll get a second chance. Will she seize it?.

Circles & Squares. John Malcolm. 2007. 54.95 (978-1-84559-795-5(8)); audio compact disk 71.95 (978-1-84559-796-2(6)) Pub: Soundings Ltd GBR. Dist(s): Ulverscroft US

Circles in the Stream. unabr. ed. Rachel Roberts. Read by Mandy Moore. 4 cass. (Running Time: 3 hrs. 47 mins.). (Avalon Ser.: Bk. 1). (J). (gr. 4-7). 2004. 35.00 (978-0-8072-0905-9(8), S YA 392 CD, Listening Lib) Random Audio Pubg.

Circles of Deceit. unabr. ed. Nina Bawden. Read by Richard Owens. 6 cass. (Running Time: 9 hrs.). 2001. 54.95 (90083) Pub: ISIS Audio GBR. Dist(s): Ulverscroft US

Circles of Seven. Bryan Davis. Read by Peter Sandon. (Dragons in Our Midst Ser.). (ENG.). (YA). (gr. 7). 2009. 64.99 (978-1-60812-767-2(2)) Find a World.

Circles of Seven. unabr. ed. Bryan Davis. Narrated by Peter Sandon. (Dragons in Our Midst Ser.). (ENG.). (YA). 2007. 10.49 (978-1-60814-120-3(9)) Oasis Audio.

Circles of Seven. unabr. ed. Bryan Davis. Narrated by Peter Sandon. (Running Time: 10 hrs. 58 mins. 5 sec.). (Dragons in Our Midst Ser.). (ENG.). 2009. audio compact disk 39.99 (978-1-59859-489-8(3)) Oasis Audio.

Circuit see Cajas de Carton

Circuit: Stories from the Life of a Migrant Child. unabr. ed. Francisco Jiménez. Read by Adrian Vargas. 3 CDs. (Running Time: 3 hrs.).Tr. of Cajas de Carton. 2001. audio compact disk 29.95 (978-1-883332-71-6(0)) Audio Bkshelf.
Poignant stories about growing up in a migrant Mexican American family in California in the 1940's.

Circuit: Stories from the Life of a Migrant Child. unabr. ed. Francisco Jiménez. Read by Adrian Vargas. 2 cass. (Running Time: 3 hrs.).Tr. of Cajas de Carton. (YA). (gr. 6 up). 2001. 21.95 (978-1-883332-44-0(3)) Audio Bkshelf.

Circular Staircase. Mary Roberts Rinehart. Read by Anais 9000. 2008. 27.95 (978-1-60112-204-9(7)) Babblebooks.

Circular Staircase. Mary Roberts Rinehart. Narrated by Cindy Hardin Killavey. (Running Time: 7 hrs.). 1986. 26.95 (978-1-59912-867-2(5)) Iofy Corp.

Circular Staircase. Mary Roberts Rinehart. Read by Cindy Hardin. 6 cass. (Running Time: 8 hrs. 30 min.). 1989. 32.00 incl. album. (C-135) Jimcin Record.
Her first novel.

Circular Staircase. Mary Roberts Rinehart. Read by Rebecca C. Burns. (ENG.). 2006. audio compact disk 59.99 (978-1-4001-3204-1(5)); audio compact disk 29.99 (978-1-4001-0204-4(9)); audio compact disk 19.99 (978-1-4001-5204-9(6)) Pub: Tantor Media. Dist(s): IngramPubServ

Circular Staircase. unabr. ed. Mary Roberts Rinehart. Read by Cindy Hardin. 6 cass. (Running Time: 8 hrs. 30 mins.). 1992. 44.95 (978-0-7861-0619-6(0), 2109) Blckstn Audio.
This is the story of how a middle-aged spinster lost her mind, deserted her domestic gods in the city, took a furnished house for the summer out of town, & found herself involved in one of these mysterious crimes that keep our newspapers & detective agencies happy & prosperous.

Circular Staircase. unabr. ed. Mary Roberts Rinehart. Read by Laurie Klein. 6 cass. (Running Time: 7 hrs. 50 min.). Dramatization. 1993. 39.95 (978-1-55686-469-8(8), 469) Books in Motion.
Miss Rachel Innes, a spry & opinionated spinster rents the Sunnyside mansion for the summer holidays to relax with her niece & nephew. Unfortunately, they are subjected to a string of break-ins, murders, & a kidnapping.

Circular Staircase. unabr. ed. Mary Roberts Rinehart. Narrated by Rebecca C. Burns. (Running Time: 6 hrs. 30 mins. 0 sec.). (ENG.). 2009. 19.99 (978-1-4001-6082-2(0)); audio compact disk 27.99 (978-1-4001-1082-7(3)) Pub: Tantor Media. Dist(s): IngramPubServ

Circular Staircase. unabr. ed. Mary Roberts Rinehart. Narrated by Rebecca C. Burns. (Running Time: 6 hrs. 30 mins. 0 sec.). (Tantor Unabridged Classics Ser.). (ENG., 2009. audio compact disk 55.99 (978-1-4001-4082-4(X)) Pub: Tantor Media. Dist(s): IngramPubServ

Circular Staircase. unabr. collector's ed. Mary Roberts Rinehart. Read by Rebecca C. Burns. 5 cass. (Running Time: 7 hrs. 30 min.). 1997. 40.00 (978-0-7366-3647-6(1), 4312) Books on Tape.
Miss Cornelia Van Gorder takes a summer house with her niece & nephew. A series of eerie events follow as a criminal tries to retrieve stolen securities hidden in the house & the aunt attempts to solve the mystery.

Circular Staircase, Set. unabr. ed. Mary Roberts Rinehart. Read by Flo Gibson. 5 cass. (Running Time: 7 hrs. 30 min.). 1989. 20.95 (978-1-55685-151-3(0)) Audio Bk Con.
Rachel Innes rents a summer house in the country full of hidden rooms & sinister happenings. Chilling romance & rollicking humor permeate this suspenseful mystery novel.

Circulation. abr. ed. Robert A. Monroe. Read by Robert A. Monroe. (Running Time: 30 min.). (Human Plus Ser.). 1989. 14.95 (978-1-56102-003-4(6)) Inter Indus.
Develop smooth & optimum blood flow throughout the body.

Circulation of Thought-1949 Cassettes. Eugen Rosenstock-Huessy. 6 cass. (Running Time: 1 hr. 30 min.). (Eugen Rosenstock-Huessy Lectures: 1). 1997. 21.00 (978-0-912148-59-5(4)) Argo Bks.
"Circulation of Thought" is a description of the way thought moves over time. Another word Rosenstock-Huessy uses for the process of thought and inspiration moving between generations is ?spirit.? Speech among men is a form in which this appears.Rosenstock-Huessy accepts the division of reality into logos (the word of God), physis (nature), and ethos (relationships among people). According to the Scholastics, the three areas differ in the position of their subject matter with respect to truth: Does the truth precede the subject matter, does truth follow the subject matter, or is truth within the subject matter? The three areas of reality are researched by three types of disciplines. Logos is the subject of theology, physis that of natural science, and ethos that of ethics or social sciences. The method used to study each discipline is a result of its relationship to truth. Established and successful methods exist for theology and the natural sciences. The social sciences, however, although occupying their own relationship to truth, to date have only mimicked the research methodology of the natural sciences. They need their own method, one that reflects that their truth shifts as a result of what people in the societies are doing."Circulation of Thought" outlines some of the foundations on which Rosenstock-Huessy bases his suggested method for the study of the third area of reality, the social sciences.

Circulatory System. Compiled by Benchmark Education Staff. 2006. audio compact disk 10.00 (978-1-4108-6702-5(1)) Benchmark Educ.

Circum-Gulf of Mexico & the Caribbean: Hydrocarbon Habitats, Basin Formation & Plate Tectonics. Ed. by Claudio Bartolini et al. (Memoir Ser.: Vol. 79). 2003. bk. 69.00 (978-0-89181-360-6(8)) AAPG.

Circumstances. Peter Jeppson. 1 cass. 5.98 (978-1-55503-290-6(7), 06003214) Covenant Comms.
Stories of others faced with tragedy, & how they triumphed.

Circumstances. Peter Jeppson. 1 cass. 2004. 3.95 (978-1-57734-384-4(0), 34441239) Covenant Comms.

Circus. unabr. ed. Alistair MacLean. Read by Simon Ward. 6 cass. (Running Time: 9 hrs.). 2000. 49.95 (978-0-7451-6126-6(X), CAB 047) Pub: Chivers Audio Bks GBR. Dist(s): AudioGO
Bruno Wildermann is the world's greatest trapeze artist, but also an enemy of the communist regime that arrested his family and murdered his wife. The CIA needs Bruno for an impossible raid: the Lubyan fortress where his family is being held. Under the cover of a circus tour, Bruno begins his mission, but within the circus is a Communist agent with orders to stop Bruno at any cost.

Circus. unabr. collector's ed. Nigel West. Read by Richard Brown. 6 cass. (Running Time: 9 hrs.). 1988. 48.00 (978-0-7366-1395-8(1), 2284) Books on Tape.
Details the failures of British Intelligence to detect Soviet spies in its own ranks, a failure the author argues continues to this day.

Circus Animals see Dylan Thomas Reads the Poetry of W. B. Yeats & Others

Circus Baby. 2004. bk. 24.95 (978-1-56008-181-4(3)); 8.95 (978-1-56008-870-7(2)); cass. & flmstrp 30.00 (978-0-89719-674-1(0)) Weston Woods.

Circus Baby, the see Elefantito Del Circo

Circus Fire: A True Story. unabr. ed. Stewart O'Nan. Read by Dick Hill. 7 cass. (Running Time: 11 hrs.). 2000. 32.95 (978-1-56740-392-3(1), 1567403921, BAU) Brilliance Audio.
One of America's most acclaimed novelists turns to nonfiction in this powerful re-creation of the great Hartford circus fire, which took the lives of 167 people and forever changed the city and its people. On July 6, 1944, in Hartford, Connecticut, the big top of Ringling Bros. Barnum & Bailey Circus caught fire during the middle of the afternoon performance. Nine thousand people were inside. The canvas of the big tent had been waterproofed with a mixture of paraffin and gasoline. In seconds, the big top was burning out of control. Bleacher seats were fronted by steel railings with narrow openings; the main exits were blocked by caged chutes in which leopards and lions, having just performed, raged, maddened by the fire. In re-creating the horrific events of one of America's most cataclysmic civic tragedies, Stewart O'Nan has fashioned both an incomparably gripping narrative and a profound, measured glimpse into the extremes of human behavior under duress. In the madness of the inferno, some like animal trainer May Kovar and the tragic Bill Curlee (who tossed dozens of children to safety over the lion's chute), would act with superhuman bravery. Others, like the sailor who broke a woman's jaw to get past her, would become beasts. The toll of the fire, and its circumstances, haunt Hartford to the present day - the identity of one young victim, known only as Little Miss 1565, remains an enduring mystery and a source of conflict in the city. But it is the intense, detailed narrative - before, after, and especially during the panic under the burning tent - that will remain with readers long after they finish this exceptional book.

Circus Fire: A True Story. unabr. ed. Stewart O'Nan. Read by Dick Hill. (Running Time: 11 hrs.). 2004. 39.25 (978-1-59600-486-3(X), 159600486X, BADLE); 24.95 (978-1-59600-485-6(1), 1596004851, BAD); 39.25 (978-1-59600-484-9(3), 1596004843, Brlnc Audio MP3 Lib); 24.95 (978-1-59600-483-2(5), 1596004835, Brilliance MP3) Brilliance Audio.

Circus Magic - Under the Big Top. Perf. by Linda Arnold. 1 cass. (J). 1999. 10.98 (978-1-57471-437-1(6), YM128-CN); audio compact disk 13.98 (978-1-57471-440-1(6), YM128-CD) Youngheart Mus.
Songs include: "Midway"; "Circus Train"; "Singing Ringmaster"; "Circus Poodles"; "Teddy Bears' Picnic"; "Ponies"; "Being for the Benefit of Mr. Kite"; "Clover the Clown"; "Peter's Trampoline Act"; "Try, Try Again"; "Circus of the World" & more.

Circus of the Damned. abr. ed. Laurell K. Hamilton. Read by Kimberly Alexis. (Running Time: 7 hrs.). (Anita Blake, Vampire Hunter Ser.: No. 3). (ENG.). (gr. 12 up). 2009. audio compact disk 29.95 (978-0-14-314514-1(2), PengAudBks) Penguin Grp USA.

Circus of the Damned. unabr. ed. Laurell K. Hamilton. Read by Kimberly Alexis. (Running Time: 10 hrs.). (Anita Blake, Vampire Hunter Ser.: No. 3). (ENG.). (gr. 12 up). 2009. audio compact disk 39.95 (978-0-14-314403-8(0), PengAudBks) Penguin Grp USA.

Circus Surprise. unabr. ed. 1 cass. (Running Time: 90 min.). (Romper Room Sing & Read-Alongs Ser.). (J). 1986. 5.95 incl. bk. & sheet music. (978-0-89845-313-3(5), RRC 3135) HarperCollins Pubs.

CIS Citizenship Interview. audio compact disk (978-0-9741737-6-4(2)) Citizenship Res.

CIS Citizenship Interview. 1 CD. (Running Time: 1 hr.). 2003. (978-0-9741737-5-7(4)) Citizenship Res.
Designed by experienced professionals to help in the classroom and to help the individual applicant prepare for the INS interview.

CIS Citizenship Interview. Created by Delta Systems. 2003. audio compact disk 12.95 (978-1-932748-63-5(6), DeltPubng) Delta Systems.

Cisco Kid: Poncho Escapes 1955 & The Duel. 1 cass. (Running Time: 1 hr.). 2001. 6.98 (1541) Radio Spirits.

Cisco Kid: Secret Mission & Fire in the Night. 1 cass. (Running Time: 1 hr.). 2001. 6.98 (2596) Radio Spirits.

Cisco Kid: The Cattlemen's War & Contraband. 1 cass. (Running Time: 1 hr.). 2001. 6.98 (2554) Radio Spirits.

***Cisco Kid, Volume 1.** RadioArchives.com. (ENG.). 2004. audio compact disk 29.98 (978-1-61081-026-5(0)) Radio Arch.

***Cisco Kid, Volume 2.** RadioArchives.com. (ENG.). 2005. audio compact disk 29.98 (978-1-61081-040-1(6)) Radio Arch.

***Cisco Kid, Volume 3.** RadioArchives.com. (Running Time: 600). (ENG.). 2009. audio compact disk 29.98 (978-1-61081-099-9(6)) Radio Arch.

***Cisco Kid, Volume 4.** RadioArchives.com. (Running Time: 600). (ENG.). 2010. audio compact disk 29.98 (978-1-61081-167-5(4)) Radio Arch.

Cisco Three. Clenny Terrell. 2008. audio compact disk 29.99 (978-1-60462-403-8(5)) Tate Pubng.

Cistercian Chants for the Feast of the Visitation. Comment by D. Martin Jenni. (Running Time: 3600 sec.). (Hors de Ser.). 2006. audio compact disk 16.95 (978-0-87907-980-2(0), CV012) Pub: Cistercian Pubns. Dist(s): Liturgical Pr

Citadel Run, Bk. 1. unabr. ed. Paul Bishop. Read by Maynard Villers. 6 cass. (Running Time: 8 hrs. 30 min.). 1996. 39.95 (978-1-55686-693-7(3)) Books in Motion.
Introducing "Calico" Jack Walker, thirty year veteran of the L.A.P.D., & his female partner of Japanese descent, a rookie.

CITE Collection. 2004. audio compact disk (978-1-55883-555-9(5)) CRC Wrld Lit.

Cite de Verre, Set. Paul Auster. Read by Claude Lesko. 4 cass.Tr. of City of Glass. (FRE.). 1995. 39.95 (1774-TH) Olivia & Hill.
A telephone call in the middle of the night throws Quinn, a mystery story writer, into an incredible adventure. The humor of Kafka & the suspense of Hitchcock, with the city of New York as the backdrop. A thriller by an American writer who has taken France by storm.

Cities see Poetry & Voice of Marilyn Hacker

Cities. Contrib. by Anberlin. Prod. by Aaron Sprinkle. 2007. 19.99 (978-5-557-94932-3(1)); audio compact disk 16.99 (978-5-557-94933-0(X)) Tooth & Nail.

Cities - States Horoscopes. Carolyn Dodson. 1 cass. 8.95 (874) Am Fed Astrologers.

Cities in the Wilderness: A New Vision of Land Use in America. Bruce E. Babbitt. (ENG.). 2007. audio compact disk 17.95 (978-1-59726-160-9(2)) Pub: Island Pr. Dist(s): Chicago Distribution Ctr

Cities of the Plain. abr. ed. Cormac McCarthy. Read by Brad Pitt. 2 cass. (Running Time: 3 hrs.). (Border Trilogy: No. 3). 1998. 16.85 Set. (978-0-00-105537-7(2)) Ulvrscrft Audio.
Friendship & passion with most of all the women they love and moum, men & their persistence, memories & dreams.

Cities of the Plain. unabr. ed. Cormac McCarthy. Narrated by Frank Muller. 7 cass. (Running Time: 9 hrs. 15 mins.). (Border Trilogy: No. 3). 1998. 60.00 (978-0-7887-2365-0(0), 95544E7) Recorded Bks.
Conclusion of the trilogy brings together two lifelong friends - John Grady Cole & Billy Parham. As they work a remote New Mexico range, Grady embarks on a quest that will demand ultimate sacrifices for both young men.

Cities of the Plain. unabr. collector's ed. Cormac McCarthy. Read by Alexander Adams. 6 cass. (Running Time: 9 hrs.). (Border Trilogy: No. 3). 1998. 48.00 (978-0-7366-4244-6(7), 4743) Books on Tape.
In the fall of 1952, John Grady Cole & Billy Parham, nine years apart, but bound by a powerful boyhood kinship, are on a New Mexico ranch just north of El Paso. To the north, the military is already encroaching upon the ranch. To the south, always on the horizon are the mountains of Mexico, looming over El paso, Cuidad Jaurez & all the cities of the plain. Indeed, Mexico is the beckoning far country, boasting many of the qualities that the American West has lost. And what draws one of them across the border again & again is his love for a young Mexican girl, in fact a teenage prostitute, whom he vows to rescue at any cost.

Cities of the Red Night. William S. Burroughs. Read by William S. Burroughs. 1 cass. (Running Time: 30 min.). 8.95 (AMF-4) Am Audio Prose.
Burroughs reads from "Cities of the Red Night" & talks about plagues, nuclear holocaust & writing.

Citizen Cyd: A Programme of Work to Develop Citizenship & Emotional Literacy for 5 to 7 Year Olds. Eve Wilson. 2003. 65.95 (978-1-904315-11-7(9)) Pub: P Chapman GBR. Dist(s): SAGE

Citizen Girl. abr. ed. Emma McLaughlin & Nicola Kraus. 2004. 15.95 (978-0-7435-4903-5(1)) Pub: S&S Audio. Dist(s): S and S Inc

Citizen Hearst, Pt. 1. unabr. collector's ed. W. A. Swanberg. Read by Wolfram Kandinsky. 11 cass. (Running Time: 16 hrs. 30 mins.). 1992. 88.00 (978-0-7366-2246-2(2), 3036-A) Books on Tape.
William Randolph Hearst: just a name today, but once the mightiest force in American journalism. His income was 15 million dollars a year (when it meant something) - yet he teetered constantly on the brink of financial disaster. He was a paradox: conservative on some issues, a radical reformer on others (he advocated eight-hour workdays & women's rights).

Citizen Hearst, Pt. 2. unabr. collector's ed. W. A. Swanberg. Read by Wolfram Kandinsky. 11 cass. (Running Time: 16 hrs. 30 min.). 1992. 88.00 (978-0-7366-2247-9(0), 3036-B) Books on Tape.

Citizen of the Galaxy. unabr. ed. Robert A. Heinlein. 8 CDs. (Running Time: 9 hrs.). 2004. audio compact disk 72.00 (978-0-7861-8381-4(0)) Blckstn Audio.

Citizen of the Galaxy. unabr. ed. Robert A. Heinlein. Read by Lloyd James. 6 cass. (Running Time: 9 hrs.). 2004. 54.95 (978-0-7861-2832-7(1)) Blckstn Audio.

Citizen of the Galaxy. unabr. ed. Robert A. Heinlein. 7 cass. (Running Time: 9 hrs. 30 mins.). 2005. reel tape 29.95 (978-0-7861-2744-3(9), E3324); audio compact disk 34.95 (978-0-7861-8479-8(5)); audio compact disk 24.95 (978-0-7861-8463-7(9), ZM3324) Blckstn Audio.
Citizen of the Galaxy takes place far in the future, when the human race has spread out to colonize other planets. In a slave market in the capital of Jubbul and of the Nine Worlds, an auctioneer announces, "Lot ninety-seven. A boy." Slavery is commonplace in Jubbul, and the sight of the ragged, starving boy, Thorby, on the auction block is not unusual. What does puzzle bystanders and Thorby himself is his purchase by crippled Baslim, the beggar who sits every day in a corner of the marketplace. Thorby soon discovers that Baslim is no ordinary beggar. Master of languages and superb teacher, Baslim leads a mysterious undercover life that brings Thorby eventually to his own adventure on the Free Trading starship Sisu and finally to the truth about Baslim's identity and his own.

Citizen Perot. unabr. ed. Gerald Posner. Read by Christopher Lane. 11 cass. (Running Time: 16 hrs.). 1997. 76.95 (978-0-7861-1109-1(7), 1883) Blckstn Audio.
The result of meticulous research & based on hundreds of news interviews & documents, Citizen Perot strips away the mythology & unmasks the real Ross Perot for the first time. Discloses the inside story of how Perot made his fortune; uncovers the tremendous influence he wielded with different presidents; presents the complete saga of his rescue mission to Iran; exposes the private wars he waged against government officials & more.

Citizen Soldiers: The U. S. Army from the Normandy Beaches to the Bulge to the Surrender of Germany - June 7, 1944-May 7, 1945. abr. ed. Stephen E. Ambrose. Read by Cotter Smith. 2004. 15.95 (978-0-7435-4282-1(7)) Pub: S&S Audio. Dist(s): S and S Inc

Citizen Soldiers: The U. S. Army from the Normandy Beaches to the Bulge to the Surrender of Germany - June 7, 1944-May 7, 1945. unabr. ed. Stephen E. Ambrose. Read by Barrett Whitener. 14 cass. (Running Time: 21 hrs.). 1998. 112.00 (978-0-7366-4088-6(6), 4596) Books on Tape.
Drawing on hundreds of interviews & oral histories from men & women who fought the battles, on both sides of the conflict, the author captures the tales of medics, nurses & doctors; of sad sacks, cowards & criminals; of men who struggled night after terrifying night on the front lines. Even when writing about Ike, Monty, Patton & Bradley, the author never strays from the perspective of the men who did the dirty work, focusing on how the decisions of the brass affected the rank & file.*

Citizen Soldiers: The U. S. Army from the Normandy Beaches to the Bulge to the Surrender of Germany - June 7, 1944-May 7, 1945. unabr. ed. Stephen E. Ambrose. Narrated by George Wilson. 15 cass. (Running Time: 21 hrs. 30 mins.). 2004. 109.75 (978-1-4025-3515-4(5)) Recorded Bks.
A breathtaking account of what faced the U.S. Army after the Normandy invasion of World War II. Told largely through personal accounts, Citizen Soldiers captures the stunning reality of the citizens who summoned the courage to become soldiers and save the world.

Citizen Soldiers: The U. S. Army from the Normandy Beaches to the Bulge to the Surrender of Germany - June 7, 1944-May 7, 1945. unabr. ed. Stephen E. Ambrose. Narrated by Cotter Smith. 5 CDs. (Running Time: 5 hrs.). 2002. audio compact disk 32.00 (D1021) Recorded Bks.
Traces the events of the Second World War from June 7, 1941 to May 7, 1945. Drawing on hundreds of interviews and oral histories from commanders and enlisted men, he creates a stunning account of how these citizens became soldiers in the best army in the world.

Citizens. Simon Shama. Read by Allison Green. 23 cass. (Running Time: 35 hrs.). 1993. 137.20 Set. (978-1-56544-011-1(0), 150002); Rental 24.50 30 day rental Set. (150002) Literate Ear.
Presents a startling new view of Louis XVI's France & her glorious & terrifying French Revolution.

Citizens Pt. I: A Chronicle of the French Revolution. unabr. ed. Simon Schama. Read by Frederick Davidson. 13 cass. (Running Time: 39 hrs. 30 mins.). 1990. 85.95 (978-0-7861-0155-9(5), 1140A,B) Blckstn Audio.
Schama deftly refutes the contemporary notion that the French Revolution represented a courageous & noble uprising of the poor & oppressed against a decadent aristocracy & the corrupt court of Louis XVI. He argues instead that the revolution was born of the aristocracy's, & the court's, "infatuation with modernity," scientific research, & social & economic change.

Citizens Pt. II: A Chronicle of the French Revolution. unabr. ed. Simon Schama. Read by Frederick Davidson. 14 cass. (Running Time: 39 hrs. 30 mins.). 1990. 89.95 (978-0-7861-0156-6(3), 1140A,B) Blckstn Audio.

***Citizens of London: The Americans Who Stood with Britain in Its Darkest, Finest Hour.** unabr. ed. Lynne Olson. (Running Time: 12 hrs. 0 mins.). 2010. 17.99 (978-1-4001-8595-5(5)) Tantor Media.

***Citizens of London: The Americans Who Stood with Britain in Its Darkest, Finest Hour.** unabr. ed. Lynne Olson. Narrated by Arthur Morey. (Running Time: 12 hrs. 0 mins.). 2010. 34.99 (978-1-4001-9595-4(0)) Tantor Media.

***Citizens of London: The Americans Who Stood with Britain in Its Darkest, Finest Hour.** unabr. ed. Lynne Olson. Narrated by Arthur Morey. 2 MP3-CDs. (Running Time: 18 hrs. 0 mins. 0 sec.). 2010. 24.99 (978-1-4001-6595-7(4)); audio compact disk 34.99 (978-1-4001-1595-2(7)); audio compact disk 69.99 (978-1-4001-4595-9(3)) Pub: Tantor Media. Dist(s): IngramPubServ

Citizenship. AIO Team Staff. Created by Focus on the Family Staff. (Running Time: 1 hr. 10 mins. 0 sec.). (Adventures in Odyssey Life Lessons Ser.). (ENG.). (J). 2006. audio compact disk 5.99 (978-1-58997-373-2(9)) Pub: Focus Family. Dist(s): Tyndale Hse

Citizenship: Passing the Test - Literacy - Low Beginning. 2001. 17.00 (978-1-56420-283-3(6)) New Readers.

Citizenship: Passing the Test - Literacy - Low Beginning. Lynne Weintraub. 2 CDs. (Running Time: 3 hrs.). 2001. audio compact disk 17.00 (978-1-56420-297-0(6)) New Readers.

Citizenship: Ready for the Interview - High Beginning - Intermediate. 2001. 17.00 (978-1-56420-228-4(3)) New Readers.

Citizenship Audio CD: Ready for the Interview. Lynne Weintraub. 2001. audio compact disk 18.00 (978-1-56420-299-4(2)) New Readers.

Citizenship Now. 2nd rev. ed. Aliza Becker. (C). 2003. 23.13 (978-0-07-282608-1(8), 9780072826081, ESL/ELT) Pub: McGrw-H Hghr Educ. Dist(s): McGraw

Citizenship Now: A Guide for Naturalization. Aliza Becker & Laurie Edwards. 1 cass. (Running Time: 1 hr.). 1999. 22.50 (P3271-5) M-H Contemporary.
Students have the opportunity for audio INS practice, sample dictations & other oral exercises for citizenship test.

Citizenship Q & A: Practice Questions & Answers on U. S. History & Government - Multilevel. 2001. audio compact disk 18.00 (978-1-56420-298-7(4)) New Readers.

Citraketu's Son Resurrected (A); Lord Siva Delivered (B) 1 cass. (Spiritual Stories Ser.). 5.00 Bhaktivedanta.

Citrullinemia - A Bibliography & Dictionary for Physicians, Patients, & Genome Researchers. Compiled by Icon Group International, Inc. Staff. 2007. ring bd. 28.95 (978-0-497-11351-3(1)) Icon Grp.

City & the Stars. Perf. by Dennis F. Regan & Michelle Regan-Dumelle. Executive Producer Geoffrey Williams. Composed by Stephen J. O'Connor. (ENG.). 2008. (978-0-9801671-1-5(6)) Geoffrey Williams.

City Divided. Steck-Vaughn Staff. 2003. (978-0-7398-8435-5(2)) SteckVau.

City Dog & Country Dog. unabr. ed. Susan Stevens Crummel & Dorothy Donohue. Illus. by Dorothy Donohue. 1 CD. (Running Time: 8 mins.). (J). (gr. k-3). 2006. bk. 29.95 (978-0-8045-4156-5(6)); bk. 27.95 (978-0-8045-6942-2(8), SAC6942) Spoken Arts.
Henry T. LaPooch is from the city. Vincent van Dog is from the country. And while at art school, they become very good friends. Good friends can be very different - especially if one likes living in the country and the other, the city. A new and original twist on a popular Aesop's fable.

City Foursquare: Rev. 21:1-22:7. Ed Young. 1987. 4.95 (978-0-7417-1586-9(4), 586) Win Walk.

City Girl. Lori Wick. Narrated by Ed Sala. 6 cass. (Running Time: 8 hrs. 30 mins.). (Yellow Rose Trilogy: No. 3). 54.00 (978-0-7887-5309-1(6)); audio compact disk 78.00 (978-1-4025-3082-1(X)) Recorded Bks.

City Girl. unabr. ed. Patricia Scanlan. Read by Brett O'Brien. 10 cass. (Running Time: 13 hrs.). (Isis Ser.). (J). 2000. 84.95 (978-0-7531-0661-7(2), 990912) Pub: ISIS Lrg Prnt GBR. Dist(s): Ulverscroft US
The story of three young women whose enduring friendship sustains them through thick & thin. Beautiful Devlin, rich & spoiled & content, until she meets the seductive, but married, Colin Cantrell-King. Her life is turned upside-down by this lying rat & then the unthinkable happens. Fat, frumpy Caroline is terrified at being left on the shelf until she meets Richard, who has a secret to hide. She makes a decision that has disastrous consequences for both of them. Maggie, flame-haired & fun-loving, lives life to the fullest & then she marries. Has she made the biggest mistake of her life?.

City Grows. (Metro Reading Ser.). (J). (gr. 12). 1999. 1.12 (978-1-58120-425-4(6)) Metro Teaching.

City in the Sea see Raven & Other Works

City in the Sky, Set. unabr. ed. Max Brand. Read by William Dufris. 6 cass. (Running Time: 6 hrs.). (Sagebrush Western Ser.). (J). 1999. 54.95 (978-1-57490-229-7(6)) Pub: ISIS Lrg Prnt GBR. Dist(s): Ulverscroft US

City in Winter. unabr. ed. Mark Helprin. Narrated by Alyssa Bresnahan. 3 cass. (Running Time: 3 hrs. 15 mins.). (gr. 3 up). 1998. 29.00 (978-0-7887-2218-9(2), 95517E7) Recorded Bks.
A young heroine's quest to avenge the murder of her royal parents.

City in Winter, Class Set. unabr. ed. Mark Helprin. Read by Alyssa Bresnahan. 3 cass., 10 bks. (Running Time: 3 hrs. 15 min.). (J). 1998. bk. 262.30 (978-0-7887-2540-1(8), 46710) Recorded Bks.
A young heroine's quest to avenge the murder of her royal parents.

City in Winter, Homework Set. unabr. ed. Mark Helprin. Read by Alyssa Bresnahan. 3 cass. (Running Time: 3 hrs. 15 min.). (J). (gr. 6). 1998. bk. 58.50 (978-0-7887-2235-6(2), 40719) Recorded Bks.

City Lives. Patricia Scanlan. (Isis (CDs) Ser.). (J). 2006. audio compact disk 99.95 (978-0-7531-2565-6(X)) Pub: ISIS Lrg Prnt GBR. Dist(s): Ulverscroft US

City Lives. unabr. ed. Patricia Scanlan & Brett O'Brien. 10 cass. (Running Time: 12 hrs. 5 mins.). (Isis Cassettes Ser.). (J). 2005. 84.95 (978-0-7531-1089-8(X)) Pub: ISIS Lrg Prnt GBR. Dist(s): Ulverscroft US

City Living. (Laubach Way to Reading Ser.). 1993. 12.00 (978-0-88336-938-8(9)) New Readers.

City Mouse & Country Mouse & Seventeen More Aesop's Fables. 1 cass. (J). 3.98 Clamshell. (BB/PT449) Smarty Pants.

City Mouse & the Country Mouse. l.t. ed. Short Stories. Illus. by Graham Percy. 1 cass. (Running Time: 10 mins.). Dramatization. (J). (ps-3). 2001. bk. 8.99 (978-84-86154-62-2(6)) Pub: Peralt Mont ESP. Dist(s): imaJen

City Mouse Country Mouse. Ed. by Dorothy S. Bishop. 1 cass. (Bilingual Fables). (J). 12.00 (Natl Textbk Co) M-H Contemporary.
Features stories in English & French.

City Noises/Working. Created by Steck-Vaughn Staff. (Running Time: 357 sec.). (Primary Take-Me-Home Books Level K Ser.). 1998. 9.80 (978-0-8172-8652-1(7)) SteckVau.

City Not Forsaken: Cheney Duvall. Lynn Morris & Gilbert Morris. Narrated by Kate Forbes. 8 cass. (Running Time: 11 hrs.). (Cheney Duvall, M. D. Ser.: No. 3). 2000. 73.00 (978-0-7887-4953-7(6), K0008E7) Recorded Bks.
The father/daughter writing team returns to the compelling characters & intriguing situations of their earlier best sellers for this thrilling adventure into the most compelling frontier, the human heart. Dr. Cheney Duvall has had her fill of places where people distrust her skills simply because she is a woman, so she has returned to New York for a more civilized practice but an outbreak of cholera causes Cheney to look to God to discover how she can best use her talents.

City, Not Long After -Lib. (Running Time: 8.3 hrs. 0 mins.). 2005. 54.95 (978-0-7861-3019-1(9)); audio compact disk 63.00 (978-0-7861-8086-8(2)); audio compact disk 29.95 (978-0-7861-8208-4(3)) Blckstn Audio.

City of Ashes. unabr. ed. Cassandra Clare. Read by Natalie Moore. (Running Time: 13 hrs. 0 mins. 0 sec.). (Mortal Instruments Ser.: Bk. 2). (ENG.). (YA). (gr. 9). 2008. audio compact disk 39.95 (978-0-7435-7275-0(0)) Pub: S&S Audio. Dist(s): S and S Inc

City of Bells. unabr. collector's ed. Elizabeth Goudge. Read by Donada Peters. 8 cass. (Running Time: 12 hrs.). 1988. 64.00 (978-0-7366-1281-4(5), 2190) Books on Tape.
An introduction of the Fordyce family, an odd collection of characters. There is Grandfather, small & twinkly, slightly uneasy being Canon of the Cathedral after a lifetime of slum ministry; Grandmother, a stickler for the proprities; Hugh Anthony, an orphaned grandson & a curious incorrigible at eight; Henrietta, ten, an orphan with a loving nature; & Jocelyn, a grown grandson, newly home from the Boer War.

City of Bones. Cassandra Clare. Read by Ari Graynor. 12 CDs. (Running Time: 14 hrs.). (Mortal Instruments Ser.: Bk. 1). (YA). (gr. 8 up). 2007. audio compact disk 108.75 (978-1-4281-5451-3(5)) Recorded Bks.

City of Bones. abr. ed. Michael Connelly. Read by Len Cariou. 5 CDs. (Running Time: 6 hrs.). (Harry Bosch Ser.: No. 8). (ENG.). 2002. audio compact disk 31.98 (978-1-58621-202-5(8)) Pub: Hachet Audio. Dist(s): HachBkGrp

City of Bones. abr. ed. Michael Connelly. Read by Len Cariou. (Harry Bosch Ser.: No. 8). (ENG.). 2005. 14.98 (978-1-59483-386-1(9)) Pub: Hachet Audio. Dist(s): HachBkGrp

City of Bones. unabr. ed. Cassandra Clare. Read by Ari Graynor. 12 cass. (Running Time: 14 hrs.). (Mortal Instruments Ser.: Bk. 1). (YA). (gr. 8 up). 2007. 97.75 (978-1-4281-5446-9(9)) Recorded Bks.

City of Bones. unabr. ed. Cassandra Clare. Read by Ari Graynor. 12 CDs. (Running Time: 14 hrs. 0 mins. 0 sec.). Bk. 1. (YA). (gr. 9 up). 2007. audio compact disk 39.95 (978-0-7435-6657-5(2)) Pub: S&S Audio. Dist(s): S and S Inc

City of Bones. unabr. ed. Cassandra Clare. (Mortal Instruments Ser.: Bk. 1). (J). 2007. 23.95 (978-0-7435-6658-2(0)) Pub: S&S Audio. Dist(s): S and S Inc

City of Bones. unabr. ed. Michael Connelly. Read by Peter Jay Fernandez. (Harry Bosch Ser.: No. 8). (ENG.). 2005. 16.98 (978-1-59483-387-8(7)) Pub: Hachet Audio. Dist(s): HachBkGrp

City of Bones. unabr. ed. Michael Connelly. Read by Peter Jay Fernandez. (Running Time: 12 hrs.). (Harry Bosch Ser.: No. 8). (ENG.). 2009. 59.98 (978-1-60788-078-3(4)) Pub: Hachet Audio. Dist(s): HachBkGrp

City of Desolation. unabr. ed. John Ward. Read by Colin Moody. 7 CDs. (Running Time: 27900 sec.). (Fate of the Stone Ser.). (YA). (gr. 8-12). 2006. audio compact disk 83.95 (978-1-74093-785-6(6)) Pub: Bolinda Pubng AUS. Dist(s): Bolinda Pub Inc

***City of Dragons.** unabr. ed. Kelli Stanley. (Running Time: 14 hrs. 0 mins.). 2010. 39.99 (978-1-4001-9664-7(7)); 19.99 (978-1-4001-8664-8(1)) Tantor Media.

***City of Dragons.** unabr. ed. Kelli Stanley. Narrated by Cynthia Holloway. (Running Time: 13 hrs. 0 mins. 0 sec.). 2010. 29.99 (978-1-4001-6664-0(0)); audio compact disk 39.99 (978-1-4001-1664-5(3)); audio compact disk 79.99 (978-1-4001-4664-2(X)) Pub: Tantor Media. Dist(s): IngramPubServ

***City of Dreaming Books.** unabr. ed. Walter Moers. Read by Paul Michael Garcia. (Running Time: 16 hrs.). 2011. 29.95 (978-1-4417-5793-7(7)); 85.95 (978-1-4417-5789-0(9)); audio compact disk 118.00 (978-1-4417-5790-6(2)) Blckstn Audio.

City of Dreams. unabr. ed. Read by Brad Lavelle. 8 CDs. 2004. audio compact disk 29.99 (978-1-57683-520-3(0)) NavPress.

City of Dreams. unabr. ed. William Martin. Read by Phil Gigante. (Running Time: 18 hrs.). (Peter Fallon Adventure Ser.). 2010. 29.99 (978-1-4233-8504-2(7), 9781423385042, BAD); 44.97 (978-1-4233-8505-9(5), 9781423385059, BADLE); 29.99 (978-1-4233-8502-8(0), 9781423385028, Brilliance MP3); 44.97 (978-1-4233-8503-5(9), 9781423385035, Brlnc Audio MP3 Lib); audio compact disk 97.97 (978-1-4233-8501-1(2), 9781423385011, BriAudCD Unabrid); audio compact disk 38.99 (978-1-4233-8500-4(4), 9781423385004, Bril Audio CD Unabri) Brilliance Audio.

City of Ember. Jeanne DuPrau. 4 cass. (Running Time: 6 hrs. 30 mins.). (Books of Ember Ser.: Bk. 1). (J). (gr. 5 up). 2004. 32.00 (978-0-8072-2076-4(0), Listening Lib); audio compact disk 45.00 (978-1-4000-8983-3(2), Listening Lib) Random Audio Pubg.

City of Ember. unabr. ed. Jeanne DuPrau. Read by Wendy Dillon. 6 CDs. (Running Time: 24660 sec.). (Books of Ember Ser.: Bk. 1). (ENG.). (J). (gr. 5-8). 2006. audio compact disk 30.00 (978-0-7393-3167-5(1), Listening Lib) Pub: Random Audio Pubg. Dist(s): Random

City of Evenings see Poetry & Voice of James Wright

City of Fading Light. unabr. ed. Jon Cleary. Read by Nigel Graham. 10 cass. (Running Time: 15 hrs.). 2001. 84.95 (22918) Pub: Soundings Ltd GBR. Dist(s): Ulverscroft US

***City of Fallen Angels.** unabr. ed. Cassandra Clare. (Running Time: 15 hrs. 0 mins. 0 sec.). (Mortal Instruments Ser.). (ENG.). (YA). 2011. audio compact disk 39.99 (978-1-4423-3466-3(5)) Pub: S&S Audio. Dist(s): S and S Inc

City of Falling Angels. unabr. ed. John Berendt. Read by Holter Graham. 12 CDs. (Running Time: 13 hrs.). 2005. audio compact disk 81.60 (978-1-4159-2476-1(7)); 72.00 (978-1-4159-2475-4(9)) Books on Tape.
THE CITY OF FALLING ANGELS opens on the evening of January 29, 1996, when a dramatic fire destroys the historic Fenice opera house. The loss of the Fenice, where five of Verdi's operas premiered, is a catastrophe for Venetians. Arriving in Venice three days after the fire, Berendt becomes a kind of detective - inquiring into the nature of life in this remarkable museum-city - while gradually revealing the truth about the fire. In the course of his investigations, Berendt introduces us to a rich cast of characters: a prominent Venetian poet whose shocking 'suicide' prompts his skeptical friends to pursue a murder suspect on their own; the First Family of American expatriates who lose possession of the family palace after four generations of ownership; an organization of high-society, party-going Americans who raise money to preserve the art and architecture of Venice, while quarreling in public among themselves, questioning each other's motives and drawing startled Venetians into the fray; a contemporary Venetian surrealist painter and outrageous provocateur; the master glassblower of Venice; and numerous others - stool-pigeons, scapegoats, hustlers, sleepwalkers, believers in Martians, the Plant Man, the Rat Man, and Henry James.

City of Falling Angels. unabr. ed. John Berendt. Read by Holter Graham. 12 CDs. (Running Time: 46800 sec.). (ENG.). 2005. audio compact disk 44.95 (978-0-7393-0878-3(5)) Pub: Random Audio Pubg. Dist(s): Random
It was seven years ago that Midnight in the Garden of Good and Evil achieved a record-breaking four-year run on the New York Times bestseller list. John Berendt's inimitable brand of nonfiction brought the dark mystique of Savannah so startlingly to life for millions of people that tourism to Savannah increased by 46%. It is Berendt and only Berendt who can capture Venice - a city of masks, a city of riddles, where the narrow, meandering passageways form a giant maze, confounding all who have not grown up wandering into its depths. Venice, a city steeped in a thousand years of history, art and architecture, teeters in precarious balance between endurance and decay. Its architectural treasures crumble - foundations shift, marble ornaments fall - even as efforts to preserve them are underway. THE CITY OF FALLING ANGELS opens on the evening of January 29, 1996, when a dramatic fire destroys the historic Fenice opera house. The loss of the Fenice, where five of Verdi's operas premiered, is a catastrophe for Venetians. Arriving in Venice three days after the fire, Berendt becomes a kind of detective - inquiring into the nature of life in this remarkable museum-city - while gradually revealing the truth about the fire. In the course of his investigations, Berendt introduces us to a rich cast of characters: a prominent Venetian poet whose shocking 'suicide' prompts his skeptical friends to pursue a murder suspect on their own; the First Family of American expatriates who lose possession of the family palace after four generations of ownership; an organization of high-society, party-going Americans who raise money to preserve the art and architecture of Venice, while quarreling in public among themselves, questioning each other's motives and drawing startled Venetians into the fray; a contemporary Venetian surrealist painter and outrageous provocateur; the master glassblower of Venice; and numerous others - stool-pigeons, scapegoats, hustlers, sleepwalkers, believers in Martians, the Plant Man, the Rat Man,

and Henry James. Berendt tells a tale full of atmosphere and surprise as the stories build, one after the other, ultimately coming together to reveal a world as finely drawn as a still-life painting. The fire and its aftermath serve as a leitmotif that runs throughout, adding to the elements of chaos, corruption and crime, and contributing to the ever-mounting suspense of this brilliant audiobook. Bonus feature includes an exclusive interview with the author!.

City of Fire. abr. ed. Robert Ellis. Read by Renée Raudman. (Running Time: 6 hrs.). (Lena Gamble Ser.). 2008. audio compact disk 14.99 (978-1-4233-3694-5(1), 9781423336945, BCD Value Price) Brilliance Audio.

City of Fire. unabr. ed. Robert Ellis. Read by Renée Raudman. (Running Time: 12 hrs.). (Lena Gamble Ser.). 2007. 39.25 (978-1-4233-3692-1(5), 9781423336921, BADLE); 24.95 (978-1-4233-3691-4(7), 9781423336914, BAD); 87.25 (978-1-4233-3686-0(0), 9781423336860, BrilAudUnabridg); audio compact disk 107.25 (978-1-4233-3688-4(7), 9781423336884, BriAudCD Unabrid); audio compact disk 39.25 (978-1-4233-3690-7(9), 9781423336907, Brinc Audio MP3 Lib); audio compact disk 24.95 (978-1-4233-3689-1(5), 9781423336891, Brilliance MP3); audio compact disk 38.95 (978-1-4233-3687-7(9), 9781423336877, Bril Audio CD Unabri) Brilliance Audio.

***City of Ghosts.** unabr. ed. Stacia Kane. (Running Time: 12 hrs.). 2010. audio compact disk 29.95 (978-1-4417-3673-4(5)) Blckstn Audio.

***City of Ghosts.** unabr. ed. Stacia Kane. Read by Bahni Turpin. (Running Time: 12 hrs. 30 mins.). 2010. 29.95 (978-1-4417-3674-1(3)); 72.95 (978-1-4417-3670-3(0)); audio compact disk 105.00 (978-1-4417-3671-0(9)) Blckstn Audio.

City of Glass see Cite de Verre

City of Glass. unabr. ed. Cassandra Clare. Read by Natalie Moore. (Running Time: 15 hrs. 0 mins. 0 sec.). (Mortal Instruments Ser.: No. 3). (ENG.). (YA). 2009. audio compact disk 39.99 (978-0-7435-7963-6(1)) Pub: S&S Audio. Dist(s): S and S Inc

City of God. unabr. ed. Saint Augustine & Bernard Mayes. Tr. by Marcus Dods. (Running Time: 48 hrs. NaN mins.). 2008. 69.95 (978-1-4332-5426-0(3)); audio compact disk 130.00 (978-1-4332-5425-3(5)); audio compact disk 130.00 (978-1-4332-5424-6(7)) Blckstn Audio.

City of God. unabr. ed. E. L. Doctorow. Read by Nick Sullivan. 10 vols. (Running Time: 15 Hrs.). 2000. bk. 84.95 (978-0-7927-2403-2(8), CSL 292, Chivers Sound Lib) AudioGO.
The large brass cross that hung behind the altar of St. Timothy's, a rundown Episcopal church in lower Manhattan, has disappeared & even more mysteriously reappeared on the roof of the Synagogue for Evolutionary Judaism, on the Upper West Side.

City of God. unabr. ed. Perf. by Eknath Easwaran. 1 cass. (Running Time: 1 hr.). 1992. 7.95 (978-1-58638-513-2(5)) Nilgiri Pr.

City of God, Pt. 1. unabr. ed. Saint Augustine. Read by Bernard Mayes. 16 cass. (Running Time: 47 hrs.). 1995. 99.95 (978-0-7861-0817-6(7), 1640-A,B) Blckstn Audio.
Written between 413 & 426 A. D., this book is one of the great cornerstones in the history of Christian thought & vital to the understanding of modern Western society. Originally intended to be an apology for Christianity against the accusation that the Church was responsible for the decline of the Roman Empire, it became an interpretation of history in terms of the conflict between good & evil.

City of God, Pt. 2. unabr. ed. Saint Augustine. Read by Bernard Mayes. 16 cass. (Running Time: 47 hrs.). 1995. 99.95 (978-0-7861-0818-3(5), 1640-A,B) Blckstn Audio.

City of God Beckons. 1 cass. (Running Time: 30 min.). 1985. (0251) Evang Sisterhood Mary.
Discusses a foretaste of heavenly joy & suffering need no longer depress us.

City of Gold & Shadows. unabr. ed. Ellis Peters, pseud. Narrated by Simon Prebble. 6 cass. (Running Time: 8 hrs. 15 mins.). (Inspector George Felse Mystery Ser.: Vol. 12). 1991. 51.00 (978-1-55690-104-1(6), 91207E7) Recorded Bks.
In search of a missing uncle, Charlotte Rossignol travels to the ancient Roman site of Aurae Phiala on the Welsh border, where she is assisted in her search & the solution to a murder by Inspector Felse.

City of Kings see Ciudad Real

City of Light. Tom Fettke. 1993. audio compact disk 85.00 (978-0-7673-1290-5(2)) LifeWay Christian.

City of Light. Tom Fettke. 1995. 75.00 (978-0-7673-0698-0(8)) LifeWay Christian.

City of Light. Tom Fettke. 1993. 11.98 (978-0-7673-1308-7(9)); 75.00 (978-0-7673-1247-9(3)); audio compact disk 16.98 (978-0-7673-1283-7(X)) LifeWay Christian.

City of Light - Easy Voicing. Tom Fettke. 1995. audio compact disk 85.00 (978-0-7673-0717-8(8)) LifeWay Christian.

City of Light - Easy Voicing. Tom Fettke. 1995. 11.98 (978-0-7673-0662-1(7)) LifeWay Christian.

City of Masks. Daniel Hecht. Narrated by Anna Fields. (Running Time: 16 hrs.). (Cree Black Thriller Ser.: No. 1). 2003. 44.95 (978-1-59912-449-0(1)) Iofy Corp.

City of Masks. unabr. ed. Daniel Hecht. 11 cass. (Running Time: 16 hrs.). (Cree Black Thriller Ser.: No. 1). 2003. 76.95 (978-0-7861-2541-8(1), 3169) Blckstn Audio.
Introducing Cree Black, a parapsychologist with a haunted past. When Lila Beauforte takes up residence in her ancestral home, the 150-year-old Beauforte House in the Garden District of New Orleans, she is terrified by ghostly apparitions. The family reluctantly calls Cree Black for help. Based out of Seattle, Cree, a parapsychologist with a degree from Harvard, is a "ghost buster." But as Cree gets closer to the truth, the proverbial skeletons in the closet of the prestigious Beauforte family come crashing down on her, and she must struggle to keep her own ghosts at bay.

City of Masks. unabr. ed. Daniel Hecht. Read by Anna Fields. 11 cass. 2000. 39.95 (978-0-7861-4405-1(X)) Blckstn Audio.

City of Masks. unabr. ed. Daniel Hecht. Read by Anna Fields. 13 CDs. (Running Time: 16 hrs.). (Cree Black Thriller Ser.: No. 1). 2001. audio compact disk 104.00 (978-0-7861-9036-2(1), 3169) Blckstn Audio.

City of Masks. unabr. ed. Daniel Hecht. Read by Anna Fields. (Running Time: 16 hrs.). (Cree Black Thriller Ser.: No. 1). 2001. audio compact disk 24.95 (978-0-7861-8860-4(X), 3169) Blckstn Audio.

City of Masks. unabr. ed. Daniel Hecht. Narrated by Anna Fields. 13 CDs. (Running Time: 16 hrs.). (Cree Black Thriller Ser.: No. 1). 2004. audio compact disk 49.95 (978-0-7861-9081-2(7), 130273) Blckstn Audio.

City of Masks. unabr. ed. Daniel Hecht. Read by Anna Fields. 11 pieces. (Running Time: 16 hrs.). (Cree Black Thriller Ser.: No. 1). 2004. reel tape 40.00 (978-0-7861-2572-2(1), 130337) Pub: Blckstn Audio. Dist(s): Lndmrk Audiobks
Detective First Grade Brian McKenna and his partner Cisco Sanchez are chasing a killer that all of New York City is rooting for, a vigilante of supreme technical skill, physical power, and intelligence who signs himself "Justice." Justice is executing drug dealers, helping the police close unsolved cases, and providing those in need with stolen drug money-creating a nightmare for the police commissioner, the mayor, and the two detectives. McKenna and Sanchez must work to outsmart the killer, discover his next victim, and find out who is helping Justice in his quest for revenge.

City of Masks. unabr. ed. Daniel Hecht. Read by Anna Fields. 13 CDs. (Running Time: 57600 sec.). (Cree Black Thriller Ser.). 2007. audio compact disk 49.95 (978-0-7861-7431-7(5)) Blckstn Audio.

City of Masks. unabr. ed. Mary Hoffman. 6 cass. (Running Time: 9 hrs. 40 mins.). (J). (gr. 5 up). 2004. 36.00 (978-0-8072-1702-3(6), S YA 1021 CX, Listening Lib) Pub: Random Audio Pubg. Dist(s): Random

City of Night. Dean Koontz & Kevin J. Anderson. 5 cass. (Running Time: 7 hrs.). (Dean Koontz's Frankenstein Ser.: Bk. 2). 2005. 45.00 (978-1-4159-2022-0(2)); audio compact disk 53.55 (978-1-4159-2139-5(3)) Pub: Books on Tape. Dist(s): NetLibrary CO

City of Stars. 1 cass. (Running Time: 23 min.). 14.95 (8369) MMI Corp.
Discusses solar system, galaxy, radio astronomy, Milky Way, binary stars, show astronomers work.

City of Stars. unabr. ed. Mary Hoffman. Read by Kathe Mazur. 8 cass. (Running Time: 12 hrs.). (YA). (gr. 9-12). 2004. 50.00 (978-1-4000-9479-0(8), Listening Lib) Pub: Random Audio Pubg. Dist(s): Random
Georgia, an ordinary girl living in London, steps into the world of the Stravagante and travels to Remora, the Talian parallel to Siena.

City of the Dead. 4 cass. (Running Time: 5 hrs.). (Tales of Mystery & Suspense Ser.: No. 3). 1991. 14.95 Set. Greatapes.

City of the Dead. 6 episodes on 3 cas. (Running Time: 60 min. per cass.). (Adventures by Morse Collection). 1998. 19.98 Boxed set. (4303) Radio Spirits.
The city of the dead is a cemetery & its caretaker is the mayor. When a young couple is stranded there, fear is not the only thing that clutches at their throats!.

City of the Dead. Brian Keene. Read by Peter Delloro. 8 CDs. (Running Time: 8 mins.). 2009. audio compact disk 34.95 (978-1-897304-67-9(6)) Dorch Pub Co.

***City of the Dead.** Brian Keene. Read by Peter Delloro. 1 MP3-CD. (Running Time: 8 mins.). 2009. 19.95 (978-1-897331-01-9(0), AudioRealms) Dorch Pub Co.

City of the Dead. Ian Morson. 2009. 54.95 (978-1-4079-0538-9(4)); audio compact disk 71.95 (978-1-4079-0539-6(2)) Pub: Soundings Ltd GBR. Dist(s): Ulverscroft US

City of the Dead. unabr. ed. Tony Abbott. Read by Nick Podehl. 1 MP3-CD. (Running Time: 3 hrs.). (Haunting of Derek Stone Ser.). 2009. 39.97 (978-1-4233-9478-5(X), 9781423394785, Brinc Audio MP3 Lib); 14.99 (978-1-4233-9477-8(1), 9781423394778, Brilliance MP3); 14.99 (978-1-4233-9479-2(8), 9781423394792, BAD); 39.97 (978-1-4233-9480-8(1), 9781423394808, BADLE); audio compact disk 14.99 (978-1-4233-9475-4(5), 9781423394754, Bril Audio CD Unabri) Brilliance Audio.

City of the Dead. unabr. ed. Tony Abbott. Read by Nick Podehl. 2 CDs. (Running Time: 3 hrs.). (Haunting of Derek Stone Ser.: Bk. 1). (YA). (gr. 5-8). 2009. audio compact disk 39.97 (978-1-4233-9476-1(3), 9781423394761, BriAudCD Unabrid) Brilliance Audio.

City of the Dead & A City of the Living. unabr. ed. Nadine Gordimer. Read by Nadine Gordimer. Ed. by Christopher King. Contrib. by Arthur L. Klein. 1 cass. (Running Time: 58 min.). 10.95 (978-0-8045-1168-1(3), SAC 1168) Spoken Arts.
Gordimer, reads a "City of the Dead", "A City of the Living" & "The Termitary" poignant stories which reveals the complexity of life in modern Africa.

City of the Mind. unabr. ed. Penelope Lively. Read by Nadia May. 5 cass. (Running Time: 7 hrs.). 1992. 39.95 Set. (978-0-7861-0347-8(7), 1304) Blckstn Audio.
Poignant love story & a meditation on the city of London, which has seen destruction, loss & quest over several centuries. The protagonist is an architect, intimately involved with the new face of the city while haunted by earlier times in its history.

City of the Soul: A Walk in Rome. unabr. ed. William Murray. 2 cass. (Running Time: 3 hrs.). 2004. 28.00 (978-0-7366-9773-6(X)) Books on Tape.

City of Thieves. unabr. ed. David Benioff. Read by Ron Perlman. 1 MP3-CD. 2008. 29.95 (978-1-4332-4750-7(X)); 54.95 (978-1-4332-4748-4(8)); audio compact disk & audio compact disk 70.00 (978-1-4332-4749-1(6)) Blckstn Audio.

City of Thieves. unabr. ed. David Benioff. Read by Ron Perlman. (Running Time: 9 hrs.). (ENG.). (gr. 12 up). 2008. audio compact disk 34.95 (978-0-14-314347-5(6), PengAudBks) Penguin Grp USA.

City of Time. unabr. ed. Eoin McNamee. Read by Kirby Heyborne. 7 CDs. (Running Time: 8 hrs. 10 mins.). (Navigator Trilogy: Bk. 2). (YA). (gr. 5-9). 2008. audio compact disk 55.00 (978-0-7393-6480-2(4), Listening Lib) Pub: Random Audio Pubg. Dist(s): Random
CATI, THE BOLD Watcher readers met in The Navigator, returns from the shadows of time to summon Owen and Dr. Diamond, for time is literally running out. The moon is coming closer to the earth, causing havoc with weather, tides, and other natural cycles; people fear the world will end. To discover what's gone wrong, Cati, Owen, and the Doctor must take an astonishing journey to the City of Time, where time is bought and sold. There, Owen begins to understand his great responsibility and power as the Navigator.

City of Time. unabr. ed. Eoin McNamee. Read by Kirby Heyborne. (Navigator Trilogy: No. 2). (ENG.). (J). (gr. 4-7). 2008. audio compact disk 45.00 (978-0-7393-6478-9(2), Listening Lib) Pub: Random Audio Pubg. Dist(s): Random

***City of Tranquil Light: A Novel.** unabr. ed. Bo Caldwell. (Running Time: 10 hrs.). 2010. 29.95 (978-1-4417-6885-8(8)); 65.95 (978-1-4417-6882-7(3)); audio compact disk 29.95 (978-1-4417-6884-1(X)); audio compact disk 90.00 (978-1-4417-6883-4(1)) Blckstn Audio.

***City of Veils.** unabr. ed. Zoe Ferraris. (Running Time: 15 hrs. 0 mins.). 2010. 39.99 (978-1-4001-9837-5(2)) Tantor Media.

***City of Veils.** unabr. ed. Zoe Ferraris. Narrated by Kate Reading. (Running Time: 15 hrs. 0 mins. 0 sec.). 2010. audio compact disk 95.99 (978-1-4001-4837-0(5)) Pub: Tantor Media. Dist(s): IngramPubServ

***City of Veils: A Novel.** unabr. ed. Zoe Ferraris. (Running Time: 15 hrs. 0 mins.). 2010. 20.99 (978-1-4001-8837-6(7)) Tantor Media.

***City of Veils: A Novel.** unabr. ed. Zoe Ferraris. Narrated by Kate Reading. (Running Time: 15 hrs. 0 mins. 0 sec.). 2010. 29.99 (978-1-4001-6837-8(6)); audio compact disk 39.99 (978-1-4001-1837-3(9)) Pub: Tantor Media. Dist(s): IngramPubServ

City of Vultures. unabr. ed. Ron Ellis. Read by Graham Padden. 7 cass. (Running Time: 9 hrs. 15 mins.). (Story Sound Ser.). (J). 2005. 61.95 (978-1-85903-858-1(1)) Pub: Mgna Lrg Prnt GBR. Dist(s): Ulverscroft US

City of Words. Alberto Manguel. (Running Time: 18000 sec.). (Massey Lectures). (ENG.). 2007. audio compact disk 39.95 (978-0-660-19729-6(4)) Canadian Broadcasting CAN.

***City on Our Knees: If You Gotta Start Somewhere, Why Not Here.** unabr. ed. Toby Mac. Narrated by Lloyd James. (ENG.). 2010. 12.98 (978-1-59644-935-0(7)); audio compact disk 21.98 (978-1-59644-934-3(9)) christianaud.

***City Primeval: High Noon in Detroit.** unabr. ed. Elmore Leonard. Read by Frank Muller. 2010. (978-0-06-206203-1(4), Harper Audio); (978-0-06-199372-5(7), Harper Audio) HarperCollins Pubs.

City Primeval: High Noon in Detroit. unabr. ed. Elmore Leonard. Narrated by Frank Muller. 5 cass. (Running Time: 6 hrs. 45 mins.). 1993. 44.00 (978-1-55690-919-1(5), 93415E7) Recorded Bks.
Clement Mansell didn't count on a cop like Raymond Cruz taking the case when he murdered Judge Guy. Cruz has some pretty conventional notions about justice & isn't going to see Clement walk again. The stage is set & the battle is on in an old-fashioned gunfight of stamina & wits.

City Primeval: High Noon in Detroit. unabr. collector's ed. Elmore Leonard. Read by Alexander Adams. 7 cass. (Running Time: 7 hrs.). 1996. 42.00 (978-0-7366-3285-0(9), 3940) Books on Tape.
Some killers are more daring because they know cops have to feed the D.A. air-tight cases. That's why Clement Mansell figures he's home-free after his latest murder-spree: all he leaves behind are the bodies of a judge & a girl.

City Reach Strategy. 2 cass. 1998. 10.00 (978-1-886849-62-4(5)) CityChristian.

City to City: Seattle reads New York. Poems. Contrib. by W. H. Auden. 1 CD. (Running Time: 1 hr. 20 mins.). 2006. audio compact disk 13.95 (978-0-9720205-2-7(7)) Pub: Whit Pr. Dist(s): SPD-Small Pr Dist

City Transformed. Innovation Groups Staff. Contrib. by Chuck Schwabe. Alliance Innov.

City Trees see Poetry of Edna St. Vincent Millay

City Woman. unabr. ed. Patricia Scanlan. Read by Brett O'Brien. 14 cass. (Running Time: 18 hrs.). (Isis Ser.). (J). 2000. 99.95 (978-0-7531-0722-5(8), 991213) Pub: ISIS Lrg Prnt GBR. Dist(s): Ulverscroft US
Entrepreneur Devlin is expanding her health & leisure complex & finding love along the way. Caroline is still coming to terms with her husband's revelations & is trying to be independent. But will she resort to the crutches of drugs & drink that have always carried her through? Maggie is torn between motherhood & her career & now finds her marriage under threat. After years of putting other people's needs before her own, Maggie has to decide if it's time to put herself first. Sequel to "City Girl.".

City's Concerns about Wildlife, Waste & Overpopulation. Hosted by Nancy Pearlman. 1 cass. (Running Time: 29 min.). 10.00 (414) Educ Comm CA.

Cityside. unabr. ed. William Heffernan. Narrated by L. J. Ganser. 8 cass. (Running Time: 10 hrs. 30 mins.). 2001. 78.00 (978-0-7887-5002-1(X), 96379E7) Recorded Bks.
A stirring tale of dangerous hospital policies & when a reporter covers a story of a hospital that refuses a dying boy life-saving care.

Ciudad de los Dioses. Luis Maria Carrero. (Coleccion Leer en Espanol: Nivel 2 Ser.). 2008. pap. bk. 13.99 (978-84-9713-060-8(X)) Santillana.

Ciudad Real. Rosario Castellanos. Narrated by Francisco Rivela. 4 cass. (Running Time: 5 hrs.).Tr. of City of Kings. 38.00 (978-1-4025-1628-3(2)) Recorded Bks.

Ciudad sin Sueno see Poesia y Drama de Garcia Lorca

***Ciudadaía Americana Inglés en Español Nuevo Examen,cds y Dvds.** 2010. pap. bk. 69.95 (978-0-9826663-4-0(9)) Audio Vis Lang.

Ciudadania: Exito en Su Entrevista con el C. I. S. Created by Delta Systems. 2006. audio compact disk 12.95 (978-1-932748-67-3(9), DeltPubng) Delta Systems.

***Ciudadanía Americana Inglés en Español Nuevo Examen y Cds.** (ENG & SPA.). 2009. pap. bk. 39.95 (978-0-9647863-5-6(4)) Audio Vis Lang.

Civic Journalism. unabr. ed. Innovation Groups Staff. 1 cass. (Running Time: 2 hrs.). (Transforming Local Government Ser.: No. 5). 1997. 21.50 (978-1-882403-41-7(X)) Alliance Innov.
Training information for those working in or with local government.

Civics: Student Edition on Audio CD. James E. Davis et al. cass. & audio compact disk 207.97 (978-0-13-181825-5(2)) PH School.

Civics & Economics: Interactive Textbook CD + 6 Year Online Access. audio compact disk 10.00 (978-0-13-116103-0(2)) PH School.

Civil Action. abr. ed. Jonathan Harr. Read by John Shea. 4 cass. (Running Time: 6 hrs.). 1998. 24.00 Set. (978-0-375-40525-9(9), Random AudioBks) Random Audio Pubg.

Civil Action. abr. ed. Jonathan Harr. Read by John Shea. 4 CDs. (Running Time: 12600 sec.). (ENG.). 2005. audio compact disk 14.99 (978-0-7393-2149-2(8), RH Aud Price) Pub: Random Audio Pubg. Dist(s): Random

Civil Action. unabr. ed. Jonathan Harr. Read by Alan Sklar. 14 vols. (Running Time: 21 hrs.). (American Collection). 2000. bk. 110.95 (978-0-7927-2271-7(X), CSL 160, Chivers Sound Lib) AudioGO.
This is the true story of an epic courtroom showdown. Two of the nation's largest corporations stand accused of causing the deaths of children. Representing the bereaved parents, the unlikeliest of heroes emerges: a young, flamboyant Porsche-driving lawyer who hopes to win millions. But he ends up losing nearly everything, including his sanity.

Civil Aviation Equipment & Services in France: A Strategic Reference 2006. Compiled by Icon Group International, Inc. Staff. 2007. ring bd. 195.00 (978-0-497-35945-4(6)) Icon Grp.

Civil Blood. Ann McMillan. 2001. 56.00 (978-0-7366-7054-8(8)) Books on Tape.

Civil Blood. unabr. ed. Ann McMillan. Read by Kimberly Schraf. 7 cass. (Running Time: 10 hrs.). 2001. 29.95 (978-0-7366-5712-9(6)) Books on Tape.
A white nurse, Narcissa Powers, and Judah Daniels, a freed slave, battle smallpox in war-torn Richmond, Virginia.

Civil Campaign. unabr. ed. Lois McMaster Bujold. (Running Time: 68400 sec.). (Vorkosigan Ser.). 2007. 99.95 (978-1-4332-0708-2(7)); audio compact disk 44.95 (978-1-4332-0710-5(9)); audio compact disk 120.00 (978-1-4332-0709-9(5)) Blckstn Audio.

Civil Conflict. Marina Oliver. Read by Kathryn M. Hunt. 4 cass. (Running Time: 6 hrs.). 1999. 44.95 (66650) Pub: Soundings Ltd GBR. Dist(s): Ulverscroft US

Civil Disobedience see Great American Essays: A Collection

Civil Disobedience. Henry David Thoreau. 1980. (N-48) Jimcin Record.

Civil Disobedience & The Liberator: Henry David Thoreau, William Lloyd Garrison, Set. unabr. ed. Wendy McElroy. Perf. by Bill Middleton. Narrated by Craig Deitschman. 2 cass. (Running Time: 2 hr. 50 mins.). Dramatization. (Giants of Political Thought Ser.: Vol. 2). 1985. 17.95 (978-0-938935-02-5(X), 390267) Knowledge Prod.
The practice of slavery spawned one of America's first protest movements. Thoreau & Garrison in reaction developed the techniques of civil disobedience & moral persuasion. This presentation includes the essential ideas of these classic works, with a narrative explanation of the author's

character, his times, the controversies he faced & the opinions of critics & supporters.

Civil Disobedience/the Liberator. Henry David Thoreau & William Lloyd Garrison. Read by Craig Deitschman. (Running Time: 7200 sec.). (Giants of Political Thought Ser.). 2006. audio compact disk 25.95 (978-0-7861-6987-0(7)) Pub: Blckstn Audio. Dist(s): NetLibrary CO

Civil Liberties & the Bill of Rights. Instructed by John E. Finn. 18 cass. (Running Time: 18 hrs.). 149.95 (978-1-59803-194-2(5)) Teaching Co.

Civil Liberties & the Bill of Rights. Instructed by John E. Finn. 18 CDs. (Running Time: 18 hrs.). 2006. audio compact disk 99.95 (978-1-59803-196-6(1)) Teaching Co.

Civil Litigation Practice: Recent Developments (1992) Read by Julia Molander et al. (Running Time: 2 hrs. 45 min.). 1992. 89.00 Incl. 162p. tape materials. (CP-55233) Cont Ed Bar-CA.
Experts identify & review the important state & federal decisions & legislation of the past year, & analyze their impact on your practice. They cover procedural hurdles & bars to maintaining causes of action; jurisdiction; pleadings; discovery; privileges; pretrial motion practice; arbitration; settlement; trial; judgments; & appeals & writs.

Civil Litigation Update. 1987. bk. 100.00 incl. book.; 50.00 cass. only.; 50.00 book only. PA Bar Inst.

Civil Litigation Update. 1991. 45.00 (AC-605) PA Bar Inst.

Civil Orders: What Can You Appeal? 1 cass. 1987. 65.00 PA Bar Inst.

Civil Practice & Litigation Techniques in the Federal Courts. 14 cass. (Running Time: 21 hrs. 50 min.). 1998. 315.00 Set incl. course materials. (MD15) Am Law Inst.
Designed to deal with the most important & controversial areas of civil practice, procedure, & litigation techniques in federal & state courts. Affords both experienced & newly admitted counsel the opportunity to keep abreast of the latest trends.

Civil Practice Before District Justices. 1997. bk. 99.00 (ACS-1351) PA Bar Inst.
Designed to serve experienced practitioners who may be unfamiliar with the usefulness of the Pennsylvania "small claims" process, as well as movice attorneys who are just beginning a collection practice, or who have landlords as clients.

Civil Procedure. Lisa A. Kloppenberg. 4 cass. (Blond's Audio Lectures). 1994. 49.99 (978-0-945819-72-1(2)) Sulzburger & Graham Pub.
Audio lectures summarizing the laws of civil procedure for law students.

Civil Procedure. unabr. ed. Doug Blaze. 5 cass. (Running Time: 6 hrs.). (Outstanding Professor Audio Tape Ser.). 1994. 49.95 (978-0-314-24186-3(8)) Sum & Substance.
Lecture by a prominent American law school professor on the subjects of Civil Procedure, Contracts, Criminal, Real Property, Torts, Exam Skills: Essay Writing.

Civil Procedure. 2nd rev. ed. Doug Blaze. 1 cass. (Running Time: 90 mins.). (Audio Tape Ser.). 1999. 63.00 (978-0-314-24339-3(9), 28479) Pub: West Pub. Dist(s): West

Civil Procedure, 5th ed. Arthur Raphael Miller. 7 cass. (Running Time: 10 hrs., 20 mins.). (Audio Tape Ser.). 1997. 59.95 (978-1-57793-047-1(9), 28393) Pub: Sum & Substance. Dist(s): West Pub

Civil Procedure: Sum & Substance. 6th rev. ed. Arthur Raphael Miller. (Running Time: 630 min.). 2002. 74.00 (978-0-314-24275-4(9), West Lglwrks) West.

Civil Procedure (Law School Legends Audio Series) 3rd rev. ed. Richard D. Freer. (Law School Legends Audio Ser.). 2009. 62.00 (978-0-314-19978-2(0)) West.

Civil Procedure, 2005 ed. (Law School Legends Audio Series) 2005th rev. ed. Richard D. Freer. 2005. 61.95 (978-0-314-16075-1(2), gilbert) West.

Civil Procedure, 2005 ed. (Law School Legends Audio Series) 2005th rev. ed. Richard D. Freer. 2006. audio compact disk 61.95 (978-0-314-16076-8(0), gilbert) West.

Civil Rico. 1990. 60.00 (AC-558) PA Bar Inst.

Civil Rico: Current Issues. 1 cass. (Running Time: 1 hr.). 1987. bk. 100.00 incl. book.; 55.00 cass. only.; 45.00 book only. PA Bar Inst.

Civil Rico: What General Practitioners Should Know. Read by Stephen D. Brown. 1 cass. 1989. 20.00 (AL-69) PA Bar Inst.

Civil Rico 1990. 5 cass. (Running Time: 6 hrs. 30 min.). 175.00 (T7-9311) PLI.
In this recording of the November 1990 program, a panel of experienced practitioners who have worked with the RICO statute in both the criminal & civil arenas discuss all of the relevant elements of a Civil RICO action.

Civil Rights: Rhetoric or Reality. unabr. ed. Thomas Sowell. Read by James Bundy. 3 cass. (Running Time: 4 hrs.). 1988. 23.95 (978-0-7861-0001-9(X), 1002) Blckstn Audio.
The economist's immense statistical research deftly refutes the key assumptions on which the Civil Rights movement was erected. He surgically probes the fundamental racial issues, e.g. affirmative action & busing, as well as women's issues, including the Equal Rights Amendment.

Civil to Strangers: And Other Writings. unabr. ed. Barbara Pym & Gretel Davis. 10 cass. (Running Time: 14 hrs. 45 min.). (Isis Ser.). (J). 1998. 84.95 (978-0-7531-0188-9(2), 970412) Pub: ISIS Lrg Prnt GBR. Dist(s): Ulverscroft US
Brings together one complete novel, & sections of three others which have been edited to form self-standing novellas. The title novel is a story of Cassandra & her self-absorbed writer husband Adam, a young couple from a small British village. Cassandra panders to her husband's whims, wondering if this is the right thing to do. Viewed locally as some sort of genius, Adam is not, in fact, particularly talented. However, both the village & Cassandra's marriage are thrown into upheaval when a mysterious Hungarian moves into town.

Civil War see Twentieth-Century Poetry in English, No. 1, Recordings of Poets Reading Their Own Poetry

Civil War. Kenneth Bruce. 2 cass. (Running Time: 2 hrs.). Dramatization. (Excursions in History Ser.). 12.50 Set. Alpha Tape.
Description of Civil War battles.

Civil War. Bruce Catton. (Running Time: 28800 sec.). 2005. audio compact disk 29.95 (978-0-7861-7973-2(2)) Blckstn Audio.

Civil War. abr. ed. Ken Burns & Geoffrey C. Ward. Read by Ken Burns. (Running Time: 10800 sec.). (ENG.). 2007. audio compact disk 19.99 (978-0-7393-5733-0(6), Random AudioBks) Pub: Random Audio Pubg. Dist(s): Random

Civil War. unabr. ed. Bruce Catton. Read by Barret Whitener. 6 pieces. (Running Time: 8 hrs. 30 mins.). 2004. reel tape 29.95 (978-0-7861-2682-8(5)); audio compact disk 32.95 (978-0-7861-8693-8(3)) Blckstn Audio.

Civil War. unabr. ed. Bruce Catton. Read by Barrett Whitener. (Running Time: 8 hrs.). 2005. 44.95 (978-0-7861-2773-3(2)) Blckstn Audio.

Civil War. unabr. ed. Jeffery Rogers Hummel. Read by George C. Scott. 5 CDs. (Running Time: 19800 sec.). (United States at War Ser.). 2000. audio compact disk 19.95 (978-0-7861-6897-2(8), z1783) Blckstn Audio.
Bertie Wooster & his valet, Jeeves, join the racing set & are embroiled once again in a scheme of Bertie's redoubtable Aunt Dahlia. Two racehorses, Simla & Potato Chip, are favorites in the upcoming contest at Birdmouth-on-Sea - & of course, Aunt Dahlia is betting. Now, it seems that Potato Chip has fallen in love with a cat that sleeps in his stall & becomes quite listless if the cat is missing. Naturally, to achieve a certain result, all one has to do is abduct the cat.

Civil War, Pt. 1, Set. unabr. ed. Jeffrey R. Hummel. Ed. by Wendy McElroy. Narrated by George C. Scott. 2 cass. (Running Time: 2 hrs. 30 mins.). Dramatization. (United States at War Ser.). (gr. 9 up). 1989. 17.95 (978-0-938935-55-1(0), 692170) Pub: Knowledge Prod. Dist(s): APG
No historical event, short of the American Revolution itself, has affected the United States as deeply as the Civil War. But much more than slavery was at stake. Was the United States one nation, indivisible under God? Or, were the United States a group of sovereign states who could choose to disassociate?.

Civil War, Vol. 1,Pt. 1. Shelby Foote. Narrated by Grover Gardner. (Running Time: 19 hrs.). 2004. 85.95 (978-1-59912-637-1(0)) Iofy Corp.

Civil War, Vol. 1,Pt. 2. Shelby Foote. Narrated by Grover Gardner. (Running Time: 20 hrs. 5 mins.). 2004. 80.95 (978-1-59912-638-8(9)) Iofy Corp.

Civil War, Vol. 2. unabr. ed. Jeffrey R. Hummel. Ed. by Wendy McElroy. Narrated by George C. Scott. 2 cass. (Running Time: 2 hrs. 30 mins.). Dramatization. (United States at War Ser.). (gr. 9 up). 1989. 17.95 (978-0-938935-56-8(9), 692170) Pub: Knowledge Prod. Dist(s): APG
With the surrender of General Lee in 1865, American government was severely altered: America was not one nation under God. A strong federal structure steered the nation & imposed its will on the conquered South. Colonial America had fought against taxes, tariffs & non-representative government; postwar America now seemed to embrace them. This is the story of the results - & the cost - of America's Civil War.

Civil War, Vol. 2,Pt. 1 Shelby Foote. Narrated by Grover Gardner. (Running Time: 23 hrs. 30 mins.). 2005. 98.95 (978-1-59912-639-5(7)) Iofy Corp.

Civil War, Vol. 2,Pt. 2. Shelby Foote. Narrated by Grover Gardner. (Running Time: 23 hrs. 5 mins.). 2005. 88.95 (978-1-59912-640-1(0)) Iofy Corp.

Civil War, Vol. 3,Pt. 1. Shelby Foote. Narrated by Grover Gardner. (Running Time: 20 hrs. 30 mins.). 2005. 104.95 (978-1-59912-641-8(9)) Iofy Corp.

Civil War, Vol. 3,Pt. 2. Shelby Foote. Narrated by Grover Gardner. (Running Time: 14 hrs. 5 mins.). 2005. 60.95 (978-1-59912-642-5(7)) Iofy Corp.

Civil War, Vol. 3,Pt. 3. Shelby Foote. Narrated by Grover Gardner. (Running Time: 16 hrs. NaN mins.). 2005. 63.95 (978-1-59912-643-2(5)) Iofy Corp.

Civil War: A Firsthand Look. unabr. ed. Nelson A. Miles. Read by Ernie Winstanley. 1 cass. (Running Time: 1 hr.). 1994. 7.95 (978-1-882071-15-9(8), 017) B-B Audio.
In a truly remarkable personal diary, this singular Union General details his commission, the formation of the army he commanded, and the battles he fought. So compellingly vivid, youll almost smell the pungent aroma of black powder drifting over the ba.

Civil War: A Short History. unabr. ed. Bruce Catton. Read by Norman Dietz. 6 cass. (Running Time: 8 hrs.). 1990. 44.95 (978-0-7861-0251-8(9), 3261) Blckstn Audio.
For a person seeking a single volume to serve as a captivating introduction & a dependable guide through the maze of battles & issues of the Civil War, this is a book without parallel. Bruce Catton understood the Civil War - its participants & battles - & he unfolds it with skill & simplicity.

***Civil War: Fort Sumter to Perryville.** unabr. ed. Shelby Foote. Read by Grover Gardner. (Running Time: 37 hrs. 30 mins.). 2010. audio compact disk 140.00 (978-1-4417-3742-7(1)) Blckstn Audio.

***Civil War: Fredericksburg to Meridian.** unabr. ed. Shelby Foote. Read by Grover Gardner. (Running Time: 45 hrs. 30 mins.). 2010. audio compact disk 150.00 (978-1-4417-3743-4(X)) Blckstn Audio.

***Civil War: Red River to Appomattox.** unabr. ed. Shelby Foote. Read by Grover Gardner. (Running Time: 48 hrs. 0 mins.). 2010. audio compact disk 160.00 (978-1-4417-3744-1(8)) Blckstn Audio.

Civil War: 50-48 BC. unabr. ed. Julius Caesar. Narrated by Larry McKeever. 3 cass. (Running Time: 4 hrs. 30 mins.). 1989. 26.00 (978-1-55690-106-5(2), 89860E7) Recorded Bks.
The Roman Emperor's account of his triumph over Pompey to capture control of the Empire.

Civil War Vol. 1: A Narrative:Fort Sumter to Perryville. unabr. ed. Shelby Foote. Read by Grover Gardner. (Running Time: 39 hrs. 0 mins.). 2009. audio compact disk 49.95 (978-1-4332-5759-9(9)) Blckstn Audio.

Civil War Vol. 1: The Battle of Bull Run & Blockade-Runners, unabr. ed. Julie Fenster. 2 cass. (Running Time: 3 hrs.). (American Heritage Voices from the Front Ser.). 1998. 16.95 (978-1-882071-72-2(7), 393915) B-B Audio.
Voices From The Front, delivers the past as if it were as urgent as todays mail: listeners will experience the major events of The Civil War, and World War I, through the simplicity and honesty, the clarity and color, of letters written from this country.

Civil War Vol. 2: The Fall of New Orleans & the Battle of Shiloh, unabr. ed. Henry N. Raymond. 2 cass. (Running Time: 3 hrs.). (American Heritage Voices from the Front Ser.). 1998. 17.95 (978-1-882071-78-4(6), 394312) B-B Audio.

Civil War: A Narrative: Vol. II: Fredericksburg to Meridian. unabr. ed. Shelby Foote. Read by Grover Gardner. (Running Time: 45 hrs. 5 mins.). (ENG.). 2009. audio compact disk 54.95 (978-1-4332-9136-4(3)) Blckstn Audio.

Civil War: A Narrative: Vol. III: Red River to Appomattox. unabr. ed. Shelby Foote. Read by Grover Gardner. (Running Time: 48 hrs. NaN mins.). (ENG.). 2009. audio compact disk & audio compact disk 54.95 (978-1-4417-0559-4(7)) Blckstn Audio.

Civil War: A Narrative Vol. 1: Fort Sumter to Perryville. unabr. ed. Shelby Foote. Read by Grover Gardner. 13 cass. (Running Time: 47 hrs.). 2003. 85.95 (978-0-7861-0112-2(1), 1102A,B) Blckstn Audio.
Here begins one of the most remarkable works of history ever fashioned. All the great battles are here, of course, from Bull Run through Shiloh, the Seven Days, Second Manassas to Antietam & Perryville in the fall of 1862, but so are the smaller & often equally important engagements on both land & sea: Ball's Bluff, Fort Donelson, Pea Ridge, Island Ten, New Orleans, "Monitor" versus "Merimac," & Stonewall Jackson's Valley Campaign - to mention only a few.

Civil War: A Narrative Vol. 1, Pt. 1: Fort Sumter to Perryville. unabr. collector's ed. Shelby Foote. Read by Dick Estell. 12 cass. (Running Time: 18 hrs.). 1991. 96.00 (978-0-7366-1878-6(3), 2709-A) Books on Tape.
Jefferson Davis resigns from the Senate, Lincoln leaves Springfield for Washington. Foote puts scores of leading personalities in a collage that becomes a multiple biography.

Civil War: A Narrative Vol. 1, Pt. 2: Fort Sumter to Perryville. collector's ed. Shelby Foote. Read by Dick Estell. 10 cass. (Running Time: 15 hrs.). 1991. 80.00 (978-0-7366-1879-3(1), 2709-B) Books on Tape.
Yaffa Eliach, the author of this book, was born in a small Jewish market town in Lithuania. In september 1941, the Germans killed almost 3,500 Jews there. The experience provided Ms. Eliach with her life work: bearing witness to the destruction of her birthplace & the near eradication of European Jewry.

Civil War: A Narrative Vol. 1, Pt. 3: Fort Sumter to Perryville. collector's ed. Shelby Foote. Read by Dick Estell. 9 cass. (Running Time: 13 hrs. 30 min.). 1991. 96.00 (978-0-7366-1880-9(5), 2709-C) Books on Tape.

Civil War: A Narrative Vol. 1,Pt. 2: Fort Sumter to Perryville. unabr. ed. Shelby Foote. Read by Grover Gardner. 14 cass. (Running Time: 47 hrs.). 2003. 89.95 (978-0-7861-0113-9(X), 1102A,B) Blckstn Audio.
Here begins one of the most remarkable works of history ever fashioned. All the great battles are here, of course, but so are the smaller ones: Ball's Bluff, Fort Donelson, Pea Ridge, Island Ten, New Orleans & Monitor versus Merrimac.

Civil War: A Narrative Vol. 2, Pt. 1: Fredericksburg to Meridian. unabr. ed. Shelby Foote. Read by Grover Gardner. 16 cass. (Running Time: 47 hrs.). 1997. 99.95 (978-0-7861-0114-6(8), 1103A,B) Blckstn Audio.
This volume is dominated by the almost continual confrontation of great armies. For the fourth time, the Army of the Potomac (now under the control of Burnside) attempts to take Richmond, resulting in the blood-bath at Fredericksburg. Then Joe Hooker tries again, only to be repulsed at Chancellorsville as Stonewall Jackson turns his flank - a bitter victory for the South, paid for by the death of Lee's foremost lieutenant.

Civil War: A Narrative Vol. 2, Pt. 1: Fredericksburg to Meridian. unabr. collector's ed. Shelby Foote. Read by Dick Estell. 12 cass. (Running Time: 18 hrs.). 1991. 96.00 (978-0-7366-1913-4(5), 2739-A) Books on Tape.
Though the events of the Civil War's midpassage have been recounted many times, they have rarely been told with the vigor & detail Shelby Foote brings to his authoritative trilogy, The Civil War. Volume II begins two years after the first guns were fired on Ft. Sumter. Federals & Confederates are both weary, but the fight rages on, increasingly focused on control of the Mississippi River, one of other strategic necessities of the war. All the battles of the middle years are here, told by those who fought them. Their vivid memories recall Vicksburg, Chancellorsville, the fall of Charleston & the bloodiest battle of all, in a small Pennsylvania town - Gettsburg.

Civil War: A Narrative Vol. 2, Pt. 2: Fredericksburg to Meridian. collector's ed. Shelby Foote. Read by Dick Estell. 12 cass. (Running Time: 18 hrs.). 1991. 96.00 (978-0-7366-1914-1(3), 2739-B) Books on Tape.

Civil War: A Narrative Vol. 2, Pt. 2: Fredericksburg to Meridian. unabr. ed. Shelby Foote. Read by Grover Gardner. 16 cass. (Running Time: 47 hrs.). 1997. 99.95 (978-0-7861-0115-3(6), 1103A,B) Blckstn Audio.
This volume is dominated by the almost continual confrontation of great armies. For the fourth time, the Army of the Potomac (now under the control of Burnside) attempts to take Richmond, resulting in the blood-bath at Fredericksburg. Then Joe Hooker tries again, only to be repulsed at Chancellorsville as Stonewall Jackson turns his flank - a bitter victory for the South, paid for by the death of Lee's foremost lieutenant.

Civil War: A Narrative Vol. 2, Pt. 3: Fredericksburg to Meridian. collector's ed. Shelby Foote. Read by Dick Estell. 13 cass. (Running Time: 19 hrs. 30 min.). 1991. 104.00 (978-0-7366-1915-8(1), 2739-C) Books on Tape.
Though the events of the Civil War's midpassage have been recounted many times, they have rarely been told with the vigor & detail Shelby Foote brings to his authoritative trilogy, The Civil War. Volume II begins two years after the first guns were fired on Ft. Sumter. Federals & Confederates are both weary, but the fight rages on, increasingly focused on control of the Mississippi River, one of other strategic necessities of the war. All the battles of the middle years are here, told by those who fought them. Their vivid memories recall Vicksburg, Chancellorsville, the fall of Charleston & the bloodiest battle of all, in a small Pennsylvania town - Gettsburg.

Civil War: A Narrative Vol. 3, Pt. 1: Red River to Appomattox. unabr. collector's ed. Shelby Foote. Read by Dick Estell. 14 cass. (Running Time: 21 hrs.). 1991. 112.00 (978-0-7366-1971-4(2), 2791-A) Books on Tape.
Foote's crowning achievement is his trilogy The Civil War: A Narrative, the most acclaimed work of our time about the war between the states. Vol. 3 begins two years after the first guns were fired on Ft. Sumter. It ends with Lee's surrender & the final extirpation of Southern hope.

Civil War: A Narrative Vol. 3, Pt. 2: Red River to Appomattox. collector's ed. Shelby Foote. Read by Dick Estell. 13 cass. (Running Time: 19 hrs. 30 min.). 1991. 104.00 (978-0-7366-1972-1(0), 2791-B) Books on Tape.

Civil War: A Narrative Vol. 3, Pt. 2: Red River to Appomattox. unabr. ed. Shelby Foote. Read by Grover Gardner. 10 cass. (Running Time: 41 hrs.). 1997. 69.95 (978-0-7861-0117-7(2), 1104A,B) Blckstn Audio.
The story of turmoil & strife which altered American life forever. A vivid narrative captures both sides climatic struggles, great & small, on & off the battlefield.

Civil War: A Narrative Vol. 3, Pt. 3: Red River to Appomattox. collector's ed. Shelby Foote. Read by Dick Estell. 14 cass. (Running Time: 21 hrs.). 1991. 112.00 (978-0-7366-1973-8(9), 2791-C) Books on Tape.
Foote's crowning achievement is his trilogy The Civil War: A Narrative, the most acclaimed work of our time about the war between the states. Vol. 3 begins two years after the first guns were fired on Ft. Sumter. It ends with Lee's surrender & the final extirpation of Southern hope.

Civil War: A Narrative Vol. 3, Pt. 3: Red River to Appomattox. unabr. ed. Shelby Foote. Read by Grover Gardner. 11 cass. (Running Time: 16 hrs. 30 mins.). 1997. 76.95 (978-0-7861-0118-4(0), 1104-C) Blckstn Audio.
The story of turmoil & strife which altered American life forever. The vivid narrative captures both sides, climactic struggle, great & small, on & off the battlefield.

Civil War Collection. unabr. ed. Jimmy Gray. Read by Dennis Stone. (YA). 2007. 34.99 (978-1-60252-887-1(X)) Find a World.

Civil War Collection Set. Stephen Crane et al. (ENG.). 2008. audio compact disk 44.95 (978-1-60245-181-0(8)) GDL Multimedia.

Civil War Draft Riots. Ernest Yaniger. 1 cass. (Running Time: 26 min. per cass.). 10.00 (AV1117) Esstee Audios.
Presents a look at the riots that shook New York City in July 1863 & recounts the events leading to the draft, provides a chronological narration of the riots themselves, & argues that the riots were not antidraft so much as they were reactions against blacks & the wealthy.

***Civil War Fantastic.** Ed. by Martin Greenberg. 2009. (978-1-60136-499-9(7)) Audio Holding.

Civil War in the American West. unabr. collector's ed. Alvin M. Josephy, Jr. Read by Dick Estell. 12 cass. (Running Time: 18 hrs.). 1993. 96.00 (978-0-7366-2515-9(1), 3270) Books on Tape.
History of the Civil War as it was fought from the western fringe of the Mississippi Valley to the Pacific Ocean.

Civil War on Sunday. unabr. ed. Mary Pope Osborne. Read by Mary Pope Osborne. (Running Time: 41 mins.). (Magic Tree House Ser.: No. 21). (J).

(gr. k-3). 2004. pap. bk. 17.00 (978-0-8072-0930-1(9), S FTR 253 SP, Listening Lib) Random Audio Pubg.

Civil War, Part 1: Knowledge Products. unabr. ed. Jeffrey Rogers Hummel. Read by George C. Scott. 2006. audio compact disk 25.95 (978-0-7861-6926-9(5)) Pub: Blckstn Audio. Dist(s): NetLibrary CO

Civil War, Part 2. unabr. ed. Jeffrey Rogers Hummel. Read by George C. Scott. (Running Time: 9000 sec.). (United States at War Ser.). 2006. audio compact disk 25.95 (978-0-7861-7126-2(X)) Pub: Blckstn Audio. Dist(s): NetLibrary CO

Civil War Songs: Songs of the Union Army. 1 cass. (Running Time: 1 hr.). 11.95 (CCWS313) Comp Comms Inc.
Features Battle Cry of Freedom, The Army of the Free, New York Volunteer, May God Save the Union, We'll Fight for Uncle Abe & Others.

Civil War Songs: With Historical Narration. Keith McNeil & Rusty McNeil. Read by Keith McNeil & Rusty McNeil. 2 cass. (Running Time: 3 hrs.). (American History Through Folksong Ser.). (YA). (gr. 4 up). 1989. pap. bk. 19.95 (978-1-878360-03-8(5), 507C) WEM Records.
The sixty songs & the dialogue on these two tapes reflect the pathos, tragedy, irony, humor, pride, hope & frustration which accompanied the War between the States.

Civil War Songs: With Historical Narration. Keith McNeil & Rusty McNeil. Read by Keith McNeil & Rusty McNeil. (American History Through Folksong Ser.). (YA). (gr. 4 up). 1996. audio compact disk 26.95 (978-1-878360-11-3(6)) WEM Records.

Civil War Stories. Colonial Radio Theatre Staff. 10 cass. (Running Time: 12 hrs.). (Battles, Ships & Glory Ser.). (YA). 2001. 39.95 (978-1-56015-923-0(5)) Penton Overseas.
Chronicles the heroic events in the history of our great nation. Includes "Gettysburg," "The Red Badge of Courage," "The Blockade Runners," "Shiloh," "Alabama" and "Advance and Retreat".

Civil War Tales of Ambrose Bierce. Adapted by Timothy P. Miller. 2 cass. (Running Time: 3 hrs.). 22.50 (978-0-9649040-0-2(4)) Am Listeners.
From Antietam to Shiloh, from Bloody Chickamauga & Kennesaw Moutain to the Rage at Gettysburg & on to the stillness at Appomattox, the great 19th century journalist Ambrose Bierce knew the Civil War like no other writer of his generation. He was there. He saw it all as a warrior on the blood-soaked battle fields where modern America was born.

Civil War, the Audio CD Theme Set: Set of 6 Set B. Adapted by Benchmark Education Staff. (English Explorers Ser.). (J). (gr. 3-6). 2007. audio compact disk 60.00 (978-1-4108-9820-3(2)) Benchmark Educ.

Civility & Community. unabr. ed. Brian Schrag. Read by Robert Guillaume. Ed. by John Lachs & Mike Hassell. 2 cass. (Running Time: 3 hrs.). Dramatization. (Morality in Our Age Ser.). 1995. 17.95 Set. (978-1-56823-031-3(1), 10510) Knowledge Prod.
Concern for others is the basis of human decency; without it, our communities are increasingly degraded by selfishness & corruption. Some think that crime & racial conflict naturally follow the breakdown of shared community values. In a world of violence & deviancy, how can we build a caring community? Have courtesy & civility disappeared - & if so, how can we regain them? Does a diverse population share enough concerns & values to sustain a tolerant yet unified society?.

Civility & Community. unabr. abr. ed. Read by Robert Guillaume. (Running Time: 10800 sec.). (Morality in Our Age Ser.). 2006. audio compact disk 25.95 (978-0-7861-6629-9(0)) Pub: Blckstn Audio. Dist(s): NetLibrary CO

Civilization & Addiction. unabr. ed. Gregory Bateson. 2 cass. (Running Time: 2 hrs. 42 min.). (Informal Esalen Lectures). 1979. 18.00 Set. (02808) Big Sur Tapes.

Civilization & Decay, Set. unabr. ed. Henry Adams. Read by Robert L. Halvorson. 8 cass. (Running Time: 720 min.). 56.95 (66) Halvorson Assocs.

Civilization & Its Discontents. unabr. collector's ed. Sigmund Freud. Read by Michael Prichard. 4 cass. (Running Time: 4 hrs.). 1987. 24.00 (978-0-7366-1201-2(7), 2119) Books on Tape.
A late work from the founding father of psychology, centering on the struggle between instinctive human drives & the constraints of modern society.

Civilization & Its Enemies: The Next Stage of History. Lee Harris. Read by Barrett Whitener. 7 cass. (Running Time: 9 hrs. 30 mins.). 2005. 59.95 (978-0-7861-3013-9(X), 3422); audio compact disk 72.00 (978-0-7861-8080-6(3), 3422) Blckstn Audio.

Civilization & Its Enemies: The Next Stage of History. Lee Harris. Narrated by Barrett Whitener. (Running Time: 9 hrs. 30 mins.). 2005. 30.95 (978-1-59912-450-6(5)) Iofy Corp.

Civilization Begins with Us. Instructed by Manly P. Hall. 8.95 (978-0-89314-028-1(7), C8611090) Philos Res.

Civilization in Europe, Set. abr. ed. Francois Guizot. Read by Robert L. Halvorson. 8 cass. (Running Time: 720 min.). 56.95 (43) Halvorson Assocs.

Civilization in Transition Conference. 7 cass. (Running Time: 10 hrs.). 1987. 64.95 Set. (978-0-7822-0003-4(6), CIT) C G Jung IL.

Civilization of Innocence. Swami Amar Jyoti. 1 dolby cass. 1984. 9.95 (K-65) Truth Consciousness.
A concious link with the Divine Mother. An understanding of the golden wealth of innocence. Achievements do not speak of Being. Changing our crude, primitive nature to something higher.

Civilization of the Middle Ages, Pt. I. unabr. ed. Norman F. Cantor. Read by Frederick Davidson. 11 cass. (Running Time: 30 hrs. 30 mins.). 1994. 76.95 (978-0-7861-0782-7(0), 1516A,B) Blckstn Audio.
This book incorporates current research, recent trends an interpretation, & novel perspectives, especially on the foundations of the Middle Ages to A. D. 450 & the Later Middle Ages of the fourteenth & fifteenth centuries, as well as a sharper focus on social history, Jewish history, women's roles in society, & popular religion & heresy.

Civilization of the Middle Ages, Pt. II. unabr. ed. Norman F. Cantor. Read by Frederick Davidson. 10 cass. (Running Time: 30 hrs. 30 mins.). 1994. 69.95 (978-0-7861-0841-1(X), 1516A,B) Blckstn Audio.

Civilization of the Renaissance in Italy. unabr. ed. Jacob Burckhardt. Read by Geoffrey Howard. 10 cass. (Running Time: 54000 sec.). 2006. 69.95 (978-0-7861-2022-2(3), 2790) Blckstn Audio.
Jacob Burckhardt chronicles the rise of Florence and Venice as powerful city-states, and the breakup of the medieval worldview that came with the rediscoveries of Greek and Roman culture and the new emphasis on the role of the individual.

***Civilization of the Renaissance in Italy.** unabr. ed. Jacob Burckhardt. Read by Geoffrey Howard. (Running Time: 14 hrs. 5 mins.). (ENG.). 2011. 29.95 (978-1-4417-8401-8(2)); audio compact disk 118.00 (978-1-4417-8399-8(7)) Blckstn Audio.

Civilizations of the Americas Audio CD Theme Set: Set of 6 Set A. Adapted by Benchmark Education Staff. (English Explorers Ser.). (J). (gr. 3-6). 2007. audio compact disk 60.00 (978-1-4108-9841-8(5)) Benchmark Educ.

CJ & Ahab. (Paws & Tales Ser.: No. 38). 2002. 3.99 (978-1-57972-494-8(9)); audio compact disk 5.99 (978-1-57972-495-5(7)) Insight Living.

Cjs Closet. 2004. cd-rom & audio compact disk 24.95 (978-0-9707201-0-8(6)) Kay Product.

Claim. Rob Robles. 2 cass. 9.98 Set. (978-1-55503-744-4(5), 079402) Covenant Comms.
A gripping tale of greed & deception in the old West.

Claim the Name Multimedia Teaching Tools. 2005. audio compact disk 30.00 (978-0-687-33124-6(2)) Abingdon.

Claim Your Victory Today: 10 Steps That Will Revolutionize Your Life. abr. unabr. ed. Creflo A. Dollar. Read by Karen Chilton & Roscoe Orman. (Running Time: 3 hrs.). (ENG.). 2007. audio compact disk 19.98 (978-1-59483-597-1(7)) Pub: FaithWords. Dist(s): HachBkGrp

Claim Your Victory Today: 10 Steps That Will Revolutionize Your Life. abr. unabr. ed. Creflo A. Dollar. Read by Karen Chilton & Roscoe Orman. (Running Time: 3 hrs.). (ENG.). 2007. 14.98 (978-1-59483-598-8(5)) Pub: Hachet Audio. Dist(s): HachBkGrp

Claimed by Shadow. unabr. ed. Karen Chance. Narrated by Cynthia Holloway. (Running Time: 13 hrs. 30 mins. 0 sec.). (Cassandra Palmer Ser.). (ENG.). 2008. audio compact disk 34.99 (978-1-4001-0818-3(7)); audio compact disk 69.99 (978-1-4001-3818-0(3)) Pub: Tantor Media. Dist(s): IngramPubServ

Claimed by Shadow. unabr. ed. Karen Chance. Read by Cynthia Holloway. (Running Time: 13 hrs. 30 mins. 0 sec.). (Cassandra Palmer Ser.). (ENG.). 2008. audio compact disk 24.99 (978-1-4001-5818-8(4)) Pub: Tantor Media. Dist(s): IngramPubServ

***Claiming of Sleeping Beauty.** abr. ed. Anne Rice. Read by Genvieve Bevier. (ENG.). 2004. (978-0-06-078290-0(0), Harper Audio) HarperCollins Pubs.

***Claiming of Sleeping Beauty.** abr. ed. Anne Rice. Read by Genvieve Bevier. (ENG.). 2004. (978-0-06-081489-2(6), Harper Audio) HarperCollins Pubs.

Claiming Our Inheritance. Derek Prince. 2 cass. 11.90 Set. (022-023) Derek Prince.
Jesus redeemed us from Satan's slave market, setting us free to discover & claim our full inheritance as Christians.

Claire. unabr. ed. Read by Cassandra Morris. Created by Lisi Harrison. (Running Time: 3 hrs. 30 mins.). (Clique Summer Collection: No. 5). (ENG.). 2009. 9.98 (978-1-60024-700-2(8)) Pub: Hachet Audio. Dist(s): HachBkGrp

Clairvoyance. rev. ed. Mary Ellen Flora. 2001. reel tape 10.00 (978-1-886983-14-4(3)) CDM Pubns.

Clairvoyance: Key to Spiritual Perspective. Mary Ellen Flora. 1 cass. (Running Time: 60 min.). (Key Ser.). 1994. 10.00 (978-0-9631993-9-3(0)) CDM Pubns.
Side one teaches spiritual techniques to stay in tune with your body & the planet. Side two applies those techniques to opening your clairvoyance to see yourself & your creations clearly.

Clairvoyant Countess. unabr. ed. Dorothy Gilman. Narrated by Ruth Ann Phimister. 5 cass. (Running Time: 6 hrs. 45 mins.). 2000. 44.00 (978-0-7887-2927-0(6), 95597E7) Recorded Bks.
Exotic Madame Karitska is a genuine countess, but is foremost a psychic. When one of her client turns up dead, Madame Karitska makes the acquaintance of Detective Lieutenant Pruden & an uncanny partnership is born.

Clamemos a Jesus. (SPA.). (J). 2003. audio compact disk 12.00 (978-1-885630-66-7(2)) Jayah Producc.

***Clamo a Ti in Times of Trouble.** Contrib. by Donna Pena. (Running Time: 3208 sec.). (SPA.). 2010. audio compact disk 17.00 (978-1-58459-487-1(X)) Wrld Lib Pubns.

Clan of the Cave Bear see Jean Auel

Clan of the Cave Bear. unabr. ed. Jean M. Auel. Read by Sandra Burr. 14 cass. (Running Time: 20 hrs.). (Earth's Children Ser.: Vol. 1). 1999. 44.95 (978-1-56740-471-5(5), 1567404715, BAU) Brilliance Audio.
A remarkable epic of one woman's odyssey - filled with mystery and magic. Here is the saga of a people who call themselves the Clan of the Cave Bear; how they lived; the animals they hunted; the great totems they revered. But mostly it is the story of Ayla, the girl they found and raised, who was not like them. To the Clan, her fair looks make her different - ugly. And she has odd ways: she laughs, she cries, she has the ability to speak. But even more, she struggles to be true to herself and, with her advanced intelligence, is curious about the world around her. Although Ayla is clearly a member of the Others, she is nurtured by her adoptive parents, befriended by members of the Clan, and gradually accepted into the family circle. But there are those who would cast her out for her strange, threatening ways. So the conflict between the ancient Clan, bound by heredity to its traditions, and the girl in its midst, of a newer breed destined to alter the face of earth, could never be resolved. And it is this same struggle that leads Ayla to venture where no Clan woman has ever dared. Driven by destiny and a will to survive, Ayla breaks the forbidden taboo.

Clan of the Cave Bear. unabr. ed. Jean M. Auel. Read by Sandra Burr. 17 CDs Library ed. (Running Time: 20 hrs.). (Earth's Children Ser.: Vol. 1). 2002. audio compact disk 155.25 (978-1-59086-087-8(X), 159086087X, CD Unabrid Lib Ed); audio compact disk 49.95 (978-1-59086-086-1(1), 1590860861, CD Unabridged) Brilliance Audio.

Clan of the Cave Bear. unabr. ed. Jean M. Auel. Read by Sandra Burr. (Running Time: 72000 sec.). (Earth's Children Ser.: Vol. 1). 2004. audio compact disk 44.25 (978-1-59335-385-8(5), 1593353855, Brinc Audio MP3 Lib) Brilliance Audio.

Clan of the Cave Bear. unabr. ed. Jean M. Auel. Read by Sandra Burr. (Running Time: 20 hrs.). (Earth's Children Ser.). 2004. 44.25 (978-1-59710-138-7(9), 1597101389, BADLE); 24.99 (978-1-59710-139-4(7), 1597101397, BAD) Brilliance Audio.

***Clan of the Cave Bear.** unabr. ed. Jean M. Auel. Read by Sandra Burr. (Running Time: 20 hrs.). (Earth's Children Ser.). 2011. 19.99 (978-1-61106-452-0(X), 9781611064520, Brilliance MP3); audio compact disk 29.99 (978-1-61106-447-6(3), 9781611064476, Bril Audio CD Unabri); audio compact disk 99.97 (978-1-61106-451-3(1), 9781611064513, BriAudCD Unabrid) Brilliance Audio.

Clan of the Cave Bear. unabr. ed. Jean M. Auel. Read by Rowena Cooper. 16 cass. (Running Time: 24 hrs.). (Earth's Children Ser.: Vol. 1). 2001. 99.95 (978-0-7451-4001-8(7), CAB 698) Pub: Chivers Audio Bks GBR. Dist(s): AudioGO
Five-year-old Ayla is adopted by a clan of Neanderthals. More advanced than they are, her differences and quick mind create a mixture of fear, suspicion and admiration. But Ayla is a survivor intent on overcoming the threat to her life and clan traditions.

Clan of the Cave Bear. unabr. ed. Jean M. Auel. Read by Sandra Burr. (YA). 2008. 139.99 (978-1-60514-812-0(1)) Find a World.

Clan of the Cave Bear. unabr. ed. Jean M. Auel. Read by Sandra Burr. (Running Time: 20 hrs.). (Earth's Children Ser.: Vol. 1). 2004. 29.95 (978-1-59335-105-2(4), 1593351054) Soulmate Audio Bks.
A remarkable epic of one woman's odyssey - filled with mystery and magic. Here is the saga of a people who call themselves the Clan of the Cave Bear; how they lived; the animals they hunted; the great totems they revered. But mostly it is the story of Ayla, the girl they found and raised, who was not like them. To the Clan, her fair looks make her different - ugly. And she has odd ways: she laughs, she cries, she has the ability to speak. But even more, she struggles to be true to herself and, with her advanced intelligence, is curious about the world around her. Although Ayla is clearly a member of the Others, she is nurtured by her adoptive parents, befriended by members of the Clan, and gradually accepted into the family circle. But there are those who would cast her out for her strange, threatening ways. So the conflict between the ancient Clan, bound by heredity to its traditions, and the girl in its midst, of a newer breed destined to alter the face of earth, could never be resolved. And it is this same struggle that leads Ayla to venture where no Clan woman has ever dared. Driven by destiny and a will to survive, Ayla breaks the forbidden taboo.

Clan of the Cave Bear, Pt. 2. collector's unabr. ed. Jean M. Auel. Read by Donada Peters. 8 cass. (Running Time: 12 hrs.). (Earth's Children Ser.: Vol. 1). 1986. 64.00 (978-0-7366-0638-7(6), 1597-B) Books on Tape.
When an earthquake destroys an Ice Age Cro-Magnon dwelling, the only one to escape is a 5-year-old girl, Ayla. Her survival & adoption by a band of cave-dwelling Neanderthal hunter-gatherers launches this fascinating tale of Pleistocene Epoch people 30,000 years ago.

Clan of the Cave Bear, Set. unabr. ed. Jean M. Auel. Read by Sandra Burr. 12 cass. (Earth's Children Ser.: Vol. 1). 1999. 105.25 (FS9-51038) Highsmith.

Clancy of the Mounted Police see Poetry of Robert W. Service

Clancy's Crossing. unabr. ed. Evan Green. Read by Richard Aspel. 14 cass. (Running Time: 21 hrs.). 1998. (978-1-86442-287-0(4), 580744) Bolinda Pubng AUS.
Quick-witted Clancy Fitzgerald, escaped the convict settlement of Sydney Town & crossed the steep ranges of the Blue Mountains, dragging with him the proud, but reluctant, Eliza Philips. Faced with constant danger & wrenching isolation, they find themselves pale-skinned strangers in a land of ancient traditions & spiritual beliefs. But their destiny is altered when Clancy discovers a golden road to fortune & makes a triumphant return.

Clandestine. unabr. ed. James Ellroy. Read by Jeremy Gage. 8 vols. (Running Time: 12 hrs.). 2000. bk. 69.95 (978-0-7927-2336-3(8), CSL 225, Chivers Sound Lib) AudioGO.
Fred Underhill is a young cop on the rise in Los Angeles in the early 1950's, a town blinded by Hollywood glitter. a chance lead on a possible serial killing is all it takes to fuel his reckless ambition & it propels him into a dangerous alliance with unstable elements in the law enforcement hierarchy. When the case implodes, it is Fred who takes the fall. But even without the authority of a badge, Fred Underhill knows that his only hope for redemption lies in following the investigation to its grim conclusion.

Clandestine. unabr. ed. James Ellroy. Read by Jeremy Gage. 12 CDs. (Running Time: 18 hrs.). 2002. audio compact disk 110.95 (978-0-7927-9864-4(3), SLD 115, Chivers Sound Lib) AudioGO.
Fred Underhill is a young cop in Los Angeles in the early 1950s. A Chance lead on a possible serial killing is all it takes to fuel Underhill's reckless ambition. When the case implodes, it is Fred who ultimately takes the fall. But Fred Underhill knows that his only hope for redemption lies in following the investigation to its grim conclusion.

Clap Hands, Here Comes Charlie. unabr. ed. Brian Freemantle. Read by Hayward Morse. 6 cass. (Running Time: 6 hrs. 30 min.). (Sound Ser.). 2002. 54.95 (978-1-84283-127-4(5)) Pub: UlverLrgPrint GBR. Dist(s): Ulverscroft US
Scruffy and down-at-heel, Charlie is a far cry from popular idea of an esponiage agent. Two years ago, Charlie was "set up", but managed both the American and the British agents sent to destroy him. Since then he has been holed up in Switzerland dreaming of retirement.

Clap, Snap & Tap. 1 LP. (J). stu. ed. 11.95 (EA 48); 11.95 incl. manual. (EA 48C) Kimbo Educ.
Finger snapping, rhythmic hand & arm movements, finger exercises & more. Hand Jive, Marching Fingers & others.

Clapton: The Autobiography. abr. ed. Eric Clapton. Read by Bill Nighy. 5 CDs. (Running Time: 21600 sec.). (ENG.). 2007. audio compact disk 29.95 (978-0-7393-3433-1(6), Random AudioBks) Pub: Random Audio Pubg. Dist(s): Random

***Clara & Mr. Tiffany: A Novel.** unabr. ed. Susan Vreeland. (ENG.). 2011. audio compact disk 40.00 (978-0-307-87670-6(5), Random AudioBks) Pub: Random Audio Pubg. Dist(s): Random

Clara Barton. unabr. ed. Stevenson Augusta. Read by Gavin Marguerite. 2006. audio compact disk 24.00 (978-0-7861-6642-8(8)); audio compact disk 19.95 (978-0-7861-7359-4(9)) Blckstn Audio.

Clara Barton, Set I. unabr. ed. Robert Hogrogian. 1 cass. (Running Time: 15 min.). (People to Remember). (J). (gr. 4-7). 1979. bk. 16.99 (978-0-934898-33-1(2)); pap. bk. 9.95 (978-0-934898-07-2(3)) Jan Prods.
The heartwarming story of a woman who devoted her life to helping others.

Clara Barton: Founder of the American Red Cross. unabr. ed. Augusta Stevenson. Read by Marguerite Gavin. 2 cass. (Running Time: 4 hrs.). 2001. 17.95 (978-0-7861-2128-1(9), 2820) Blckstn Audio.
Children will enjoy listening to early evidence of young Clara Barton's calling as when Patch, her beloved dog, is run over by a wagon and Clara nurses him back to health. They will sympathize with her early days in boarding school where she is snubbed because she is too shy to talk to the other girls. But her shyness disappears when she has the opportunity to assist the local doctor.

Clara Barton: Founder of the American Red Cross. unabr. ed. Augusta Stevenson. Read by Marguerite Gavin. 3 cass. (Running Time: 16200 sec.). (J). (gr. 4-7). 2002. 35.95 (978-0-7861-2059-8(2), K2820) Blckstn Audio.

Clare Booth Luce: Future of G.O.P. see Buckley's Firing Line

Clare's War. unabr. ed. Anita Burgh. Read by Jilly Bond. 12 cass. (Running Time: 18 hrs.). 2001. 94.95 (978-0-7531-1096-6(2), 010409) Pub: ISIS Audio GBR. Dist(s): Ulverscroft US
Set in 1938, seventeen-year-old Clare Springer is sent to Paris to complete her education. Relishing freedom, she's too busy to notice the onset of war. France is invaded & Clare is trapped, though happy to be so, when her French lover Fabien is reported missing. She is determined to find him. Yet despite her wish not to become involved, Clare is sucked into the chaos & suffering around her, for how can she not help this country & people she has come to love & in the process she pays a terrible price.

Clare's War. unabr. ed. Anita Burgh. Read by Jilly Bond. 13 CDs. (Running Time: 19 hrs. 30 min.). (Isis Ser.). (J). 2001. audio compact disk 99.95 (978-0-7531-1282-3(5), 1282-5) Pub: ISIS Lrg Prnt GBR. Dist(s): Ulverscroft US

Claribel Alegria. unabr. ed. Claribel Alegria. Read by Claribel Alegria. Interview with Tim Richards. Prod. by Rebekah Presson. 1 cass. (Running Time: 29 min.). 1991. 10.00 (040591) New Letters.
Nicaraguan poet & writer, Claribel Alegria, talks about her autobiographical novel, "Luisa in Reality Land".

Clarinet. Peter Gelling. (Progressive Ser.). 2004. pap. bk. 19.95 (978-1-86469-224-2(3), 256-050) Kolala Music SGP.

Clarinet Collection: 15 Pieces by 14 Composers: Easy to Intermediate Level. Created by G Schirmer Inc. (G. Schirmer Instrumental Library). 2007. pap. bk. 19.95 (978-1-4234-0649-5(4), G Schirmer) H Leonard.

Clarinet Method. Andrew Scott. (Progressive Ser.). 1997. pap. bk. (978-0-947183-07-3(8)) Kolala Music SGP.

Clarinet with Piano Accompaniment: An Exciting Collection of Ten Swing Tunes Expertly Arranged for the Beginning Soloist with Piano Accompaniment. Perf. by David Pearl. Arranged by David Pearl. 1 cass. (Running Time: 32 min.). (Solo Plus Ser.). 1999. pap. bk. 12.95 (978-0-8256-1676-1(X), AM947397, Amsco Music) Music Sales.

clarinetist (2 CD Set) Anton Hollich. 2 vols. 2006. pap. bk. 29.98 (978-1-59615-740-8(2), 1596157402) Pub: Music Minus. Dist(s): H Leonard

Clarion's Cell. abr. ed. Robert Vaughn. Read by Jim Gough. 4 cass. (Running Time: 6 hrs.). (Sundown Riders Ser.). 2002. 24.95 (978-1-890990-94-7(9), 99094) Otis Audio.
Western with sound effects.

Clarissa Oakes see Truelove

Clarity, Set. John Ramsey. Illus. by L. M. Kinnee et al. 1985. 22.00 (978-0-317-14112-2(0)) Brainchild Bks.

Clarity of Intention: The Foundation of Enlightenment. Andrew Cohen. 2 cass. (Running Time: 2 hrs. 50 min.). (Bodhgaya Ser.: Vol. 1). 1996. 16.00 Set. (978-1-883929-09-1(1)) Moksha Pr.
Lays the foundation for the pursuit & attainment of a profound & lasting spiritual transformation. In order to suceed, the serious seeker of liberation must deeply inquire into the question, "Do I want to be free here & now".

Clark Clifford Remembers: Why Truman Dropped the Bomb. Narrated by Clark Clifford. 1 cass. (Running Time: 1 hr.). 10.95 (K0230B090, HarperThor) HarpC GBR.

Clark Gable: Portrait of a Misfit. unabr. ed. Jane Ellen Wayne. Read by S. Patricia Bailey. 7 cass. (Running Time: 10 hrs.). 1997. 49.95 (978-0-7861-1101-5(1), 1865) Blckstn Audio.
"He was an alcoholic, an egotist & an opportunist who used the casting couch for sexual encounters to get into films. He married women to further his career. But he was the most enduring actor in the history of motion pictures." So begins this incisive & revealing portrait of one of Hollywood's greatest luminaries.

Clark-Hoover Debate. Gordon H. Clark & David Hoover. 2 cass. 10.00 Set. Trinity Found.
Debate on philosophy.

Clark-Hoover Debate, Set. Perf. by Gordon H. Clark & David Hoover. 2 cass. 10.00 Trinity Found.
Philosophy debate.

Clark Sisters: The Definitive Gospel Collection. Contrib. by Clark Sisters. (Definitive Gospel Collection). 2008. audio compact disk 7.99 (978-5-557-49741-1(2), Word Records) Word Enter.

Clarke Tin Whistle. Bill Ochs. 2000. pap. bk. 12.95 (978-0-9623456-3-0(6)) Pub: Pnnywhstlrs Pr. Dist(s): Bk Clearing Hse

Clarke Tin Whistle: Includes Clarke Original C Tin Whistle. Bill Ochs. 1 CD. (Running Time: 74 mins.). (gr. 3 up). 1988. pap. bk. 24.95 (978-0-9623456-2-3(8)) Pub: Pnnywhstlrs Pr. Dist(s): Bk Clearing Hse

Clarke Tin Whistle: Includes Clarke Original D Tin Whistle. Bill Ochs. 1 CD. (Running Time: 74 mins.). 1991. pap. bk. 24.95 (978-0-9623456-1-6(X)) Pub: Pnnywhstlrs Pr. Dist(s): Bk Clearing Hse

Clarke Tin Whistle: Includes Clarke Original D Whistle, deluxe ed. Bill Ochs. 1 CD. (Running Time: 74 mins.). 2000. pap. bk. 26.95 (978-0-9623456-9-2(5)) Pub: Pnnywhstlrs Pr. Dist(s): Bk Clearing Hse

Clarke Tin Whistle: Includes Clarke Sweetone D. Whistle. deluxe ed. Bill Ochs. 1 CD. (Running Time: 74 mins.). 2000. pap. bk. 24.95 (978-0-9623456-8-5(7)) Pub: Pnnywhstlrs Pr. Dist(s): Bk Clearing Hse

Clash of Civilizations & the Remaking of World Order. unabr. ed. Samuel P. Huntington. 11 cass. (Running Time: 16 hrs. 30 mins.). 2002. 88.00 (978-0-7366-8657-0(6)) Books on Tape.
For anyone interested in foreign affairs, this book will catalyze debate, and not only for Mr. Huntington's concluding scenario for World War III. He sees how this could happen if the U.S. mishandles an increasingly xenophobic and truculent China. Chinese assertiveness, Huntington argues, rises out of its felt grievances against a relatively weakening West. After China, the gravest challenge to the West is resurgent Islamic identity. So what to do? The West should ensure the survival of its values within a stronger European-North American alliance that can offset the emerging Sino-Islamic grouping.

Clash of the Titans: How the Unbridled Ambition of Ted Turner & Rupert Murdoch Has Created Global Empires That Control What We Read & Watch. unabr. ed. Richard Hack. Read by Scott Brick. 10 cass. (Running Time: 15 hrs.). 2004. 39.95 (978-1-59007-240-0(5)); audio compact disk 69.95 (978-1-59007-241-7(3)) Pub: New Millenn Enter. Dist(s): PerseuPGW
When Robert Edward (Ted) Turner III started out in business, he owned a small billboard company in rural Georgia. What he has ended up with is the vice-chairmanship of AOL Time Warnter through the sale of his $3 billion empire. Risk-taking, careful planning and steely determination are the hallmarks of this brash, out-spoken and wildly successful media mogul. On the other side of the world his counterpart Keith Rupert Murdoch began with one small Australian newspaper and parlayed it into 125 newspapers and magazines around the globe, the Fox, Inc. motion picture and television conglomerate, and news satellites on four continents.

Clash of Titans: WWII at Sea, unabr. ed. Walter J. Boyne. Read by Barrett Whitener. 11 cass. (Running Time: 16 hrs. 30 min.). 1998. 88.00 (978-0-7366-4014-5(2), 4512) Books on Tape.
From the sneak attack on Pearl Harbor to the bloody conflicts in the North Atlantic, Boyne brings us a comprehensive & marvelously narrated history of the naval battles of WW II. While all the major encounters at sea are here, Clash of Titans does more than tally wins & losses. It focuses on the qualities that made each navy important in its own right: the stalwart courage of the German U-Boat crews, the brilliant commanders of the Japanese navy, our own navy's Yankee tenacity as it recovered from a routing at pearl Harbor. This is military history written with panache, an exhilarating account of war as seen from the deck of a battleship.

Clash of Wings: Air Power in World War II. unabr. ed. Walter J. Boyne. Read by Barrett Whitener. 11 cass. (Running Time: 16 hrs. 30 min.). 1998. 88.00 (978-0-7366-4033-6(9), 4532) Books on Tape.
Retired Air Force Colonel Walter J. Boyne tells the story of air combat in WW II. He brings us a readable, authoritative history of the air war waged in the skies over land & sea. Colonel Boyne masterfully recounts the decisive battles & elucidates the strategies of each commander. He also gives critical evaluations of the machines themselves & the technological advances that made air power such a key element in the war.

Clashing Mountains: Heb. 12:18-29. Ed Young. 1992. 4.95 (978-0-7417-1940-9(1), 940) Win Walk.

clásicos de Benny Hinn: Colección #2. unabr. ed. Benny Hinn. (Running Time: 4 hrs. 40 mins.). (SPA.). 2006. audio compact disk 19.99 (978-0-88113-098-0(2)) Pub: Grupo Nelson. Dist(s): Nelson

Clasificar en el centro botánico Audio CD: Emergent Set A. Benchmark Education Staff. Ed. by Cynthia Swain. (Early Explorers Ser.). (J). 2008. audio compact disk 10.00 (978-1-60437-253-3(2)) Benchmark Educ.

Clasificar en el parque Audio CD: Emergent Set A. Benchmark Education Staff. Ed. by Cynthia Swain. (Early Explorers Ser.). (J). 2008. audio compact disk 10.00 (978-1-60437-250-2(8)) Benchmark Educ.

Class. unabr. ed. Paul Fussell. Read by Nick Bernard. 5 cass. (Running Time: 7 hrs. 30 min.). 1993. 39.95 (1388) Blckstn Audio.
The anxiety created by a lack of a convenient system of inherited titles, ranks & honors has led to a plethora of national idiocies: British street names in Houston, an alligator on every sock.

Class. unabr. ed. Paul Fussell. Read by Nick Bernard. 5 cass. (Running Time: 7 hrs.). 2000. 39.95 (978-0-7861-0436-9(8), 1388) Blckstn Audio.

Class Action: The Landmark Case That Changed Sexual Harassment. 2005. 85.95 (978-0-7861-4427-3(0)) Blckstn Audio.

Class Action: The Landmark Case That Changed Sexual Harassment. unabr. ed. Clara Bingham & Laura Leedy Gansler. Read by Gabrielle De Cuir. 1 MP3. (Running Time: 55800 sec.). 2005. audio compact disk 29.95 (978-0-7861-7757-8(8), ZM3632) Blckstn Audio.

Class Action: The Landmark Case That Changed Sexual Harassment Law. Clara Bingham & Laura Leedy-Gansler. Read by Gabrielle De Cuir. (Running Time: 55800 sec.). 2005. audio compact disk 99.00 (978-0-7861-7383-9(1)) Blckstn Audio.

Class Action: The Landmark Case That Changed Sexual Harassment Law. unabr. ed. Clara Bingham & Laura Leedy Gansler. Read by Gabrielle De Cuir. 24 CDs. (Running Time: 55800 sec.). 2002. audio compact disk 29.95 (978-0-7861-7388-4(2), ZE3632); 29.95 (978-0-7861-4422-8(X), E3632) Blckstn Audio.
In the coldest reaches of northern Minnesota, a group of women endured a shocking degree of sexual harrassment-until one of them stepped forward and sued the company that had turned a blind eye to their pleas for help. Jenson vs. Eveleth Mines, the first sexual harrassment class action in America, permanently changed the legal landscape as well as the lives of the women who fought the battle. In 1975, Lois Jenson, a single mother on welfare, heard that the local iron mine was now hiring women. From her first day on the job, through three intensely humiliating trials, to the emotional day of the settlement, it would take Jenson twenty-five years and most of her physical and mental health to fight the battle with the mining company. But with the support of other women miners and her luck at finding perhaps the finest legal team for class action law, Jenson would eventually prevail. The roller-coaster ride that became Jenson vs. Eveleth shows us that Class Action is not just one woman's story, it's every woman's legacy.

Class Brass: On the Edge. Perf. by Empire Brass Quintet. 1 cass., 1 CD. 7.98 (TA 30305); audio compact disk 12.78 CD Jewel box. (TA 80305) NewSound.

Class Clown, unabr. ed. Johanna Hurwitz. Narrated by Barbara Caruso. 2 pieces. (Running Time: 2 hrs.). (gr. 1 up). 19.00 (978-0-7887-0381-2(1), 94572E7) Recorded Bks.
When Lucas Cott, the clown of Mrs. Hockaday's third grade class, decides to get serious about school, the funniest things begin to happen. Available to libraries only.

Class Issues. SERCON Panel. 1 cass. 9.00 (A0125-87) Sound Photosyn.
At the SF writers convention with Samuel R. Delany, Edison, Charnas, Russo, & Paleo.

Class Legal Manual & Tape. 1 cass. (Running Time: 1 hr.). 2002. 5.00 (CLP89515) Christian Liberty.
Legal concerns are often on the minds of parents who make the commitment to home school. This will help to provide practical guidance to parents who truly desire to know how to protect and advance their parental rights.

Class of 1846, From West Point to Appomattox: Stonewall Jackson, George McClellan & Their Brothers. unabr. ed. John C. Waugh. Narrated by Paul Hecht. 2003. 62.95 (978-1-4025-2207-9(X)) Recorded Bks.
True story of the legendary West Point class of 1846. With members like Stonewall Jackson, A.P. Hill, George ickett, and George B. McClellan, this class left an indelible mark on history. Through letters, diaries and personal accounts, their extraordinary stories come to life.

Class of 1846, from West Point to Appomattox: Stonewall Jackson, George MCIellan & Their Brothers. unabr. ed. John C. Waugh. Narrated by Paul Hecht. 15 cass. Library ed. (Running Time: 21 hrs.). 2003. 62.95 (978-1-4025-2200-0(2)) Recorded Bks.

Class Reunion. unabr. ed. Nicola Thorne. Read by Joanna David. 6 cass. (Running Time: 9 hrs.). 2001. 54.95 (978-0-7540-0571-1(2), CAB1987) Pub: Chivers Audio Bks GBR. Dist(s): AudioGO
A story of three very different girls. Clare is pretty, clever & a conformist. Pippa is artistic & a dreamer & Eleanor, the skeptic.

Class Trip. unabr. ed. Emanuel Carrere. Narrated by Simon Prebble. 3 cass. (Running Time: 3 hrs. 45 mins.). 1997. 26.00 (978-0-7887-0910-4(0), 95049E7) Recorded Bks.
What should be a carefree two-week school trip to a ski resort, instead becomes a journey fraught with anxiety & displacement for little Nicholas.

Class with Drucker: The Lost Lessons of the World's Greatest Management Teacher. unabr. ed. William A. Cohen. Read by William A. Cohen. (Running Time: 9 hrs. 30 mins.). (ENG.). 2008. 24.98 (978-1-59659-251-3(6), GildAudio) Pub: Gildan Media. Dist(s): HachBkGrp

Class 11: Inside the CIA's First Post-9/11 Spy Class. unabr. ed. Patrick G. Lawlor. Read by Patrick G. Lawlor. (Running Time: 11 hrs. 0 mins. 0 sec.). (ENG.). 2006. audio compact disk 69.99 (978-1-4001-3226-3(6)); audio compact disk 24.99 (978-1-4001-5226-1(7)) Pub: Tantor Media. Dist(s): IngramPubServ

Class 11: Inside the CIA's First Post-9/11 Spy Class. unabr. ed. Read by Patrick G. Lawlor. (Running Time: 11 hrs. 0 mins. 0 sec.). (ENG.). 2006. audio compact disk 34.99 (978-1-4001-0226-6(X)) Pub: Tantor Media. Dist(s): IngramPubServ

Classes on the Manual for Teachers of a Course in Miracles, Vol. I. Kenneth Wapnick. 10 CDs. 2003. audio compact disk 58.00 (978-1-59142-107-8(1), CD83-1) Foun Miracles.
Reflecting the structure of symphonic compositions, these classes are organized around the two major themes in the manual for teachers, along with their variations and subsidiary themes. The line-by-line commentary presented in each class shows the masterful way in which Jesus weaves together his basic message, in this form of themes and variations.The first major theme is that of separate verrsus shared interests, which evolves from the larger theme permeating the entire Course of the oneness of God's Son and His perfect unity with His Creator and Source. This first theme unifies all of the seemingly disparate questions that comprise the manual for teachers, and is the basis of the Course's unique definition of a teacher of God. One important variation is the relationship between mind and body.The second and equally important theme is that of asking the Holy Spirit for help, which is central to the process of understanding and integrating the principles of A Course in Miracles into one's daily life, and without which one cannot transcend the self-centered perception of separate interests, nor truly become a teacher of God.

Classes on the Manual for Teachers of a Course in Miracles, Vol. II. Kenneth Wapnick. 10 CDs. 2003. audio compact disk 58.00 (978-1-59142-108-5(X), CD83-2) Foun Miracles.

Classes on the Text of a Course in Miracles, Vol. I. Kenneth Wapnick. 8 CDs. (Running Time: 6 hrs. 32 mins.). 2003. audio compact disk 45.00 (978-1-59142-059-0(8), CD61-1) Foun Miracles.

Classes on the Text of a Course in Miracles, Vol. II. Kenneth Wapnick. 8 CDs. 2003. audio compact disk 39.00 (978-1-59142-060-6(1), CD61-2) Foun Miracles.

Classes on the Text of a Course in Miracles, vol. III. Kenneth Wapnick. 8 CDs. 2003. audio compact disk 36.00 (978-1-59142-061-3(X), CD61-3) Foun Miracles.

Classes on the Text of a Course in Miracles, Vol. IV. Kenneth Wapnick. 8 CDs. 2003. audio compact disk 44.00 (978-1-59142-062-0(8), CD61-4) Foun Miracles.

Classes on the Text of a Course in Miracles, Vol. V Kenneth Wapnick. 8 CDs. 2003. audio compact disk 44.00 (978-1-59142-063-7(6), CD61-5) Foun Miracles.

Classes on the Text of a Course in Miracles, Vol. VI. Kenneth Wapnick. 8 CDs. 2003. audio compact disk 45.00 (978-1-59142-064-4(4), CD61-6) Foun Miracles.

Classes on the Text of a Course in Miracles, Vol. VII. Kenneth Wapnick. 8 CDs. 2003. audio compact disk 46.00 (978-1-59142-065-1(2), CD61-7) Foun Miracles.

Classes on the Text of a Course in Miracles, Vol. VIII. Kenneth Wapnick. 8 CDs. 2003. audio compact disk 47.00 (978-1-59142-066-8(0), CD61-8) Foun Miracles.

Classic Adventures of Sherlock Holmes, Vol. 1. Arthur Conan Doyle. 2008. audio compact disk 9.95 (978-1-60245-099-8(4)) GDL Multimedia.

Classic Adventures of Sherlock Holmes, Vol. 2. Arthur Conan Doyle. 2008. audio compact disk 9.95 (978-1-60245-160-5(5)) GDL Multimedia.

Classic American Folk Blues Themes. Duck Baker. 1995. pap. bk. 24.95 (978-0-7866-1192-8(8), 95068CDP) Mel Bay.

Classic American Nursery Rhymes: American Nursery Rhymes English & Spanish. ed. Cindy Parker Martinez. 1 CD. (Running Time: 45 mins.). (ENG & SPA., (ps-2). 2009. audio compact disk 9.99 (978-0-615-30593-6(8)) CANR.

Classic American Poetry. (Running Time: 2 hrs. 30 mins.). (C). 2004. 20.95 (978-1-60083-701-2(8)) Iofy Corp.

Classic American Poetry. Poems. Emily Dickinson et al. Read by Garrick Hagon et al. 2 CDs. (Running Time: 2 hrs. 30 mins.). 2000. audio compact disk 17.98 (978-962-634-198-8(X), NA219812, Naxos AudioBooks) Naxos.
Poetry, by definition, achieves its effects by rhythm, sound pattern and imagery. One of the most popular areas of audiobooks, spoken poetic form, evokes emotions.

Classic American Poetry. Poems. Emily Dickinson et al. Read by Garrick Hagon et al. 2 cass. (Running Time: 2 hrs. 30 mins.). 2000. 13.98 (978-962-634-698-3(1), NA219814, Naxos AudioBooks) Naxos.

Classic American Poetry. unabr. ed. Poems. Perf. by Eddie Albert & Hal Holbrook. 2 cass. (Running Time: 4 hrs.). Incl. Annabel Lee. Edgar Allan Poe. (J). (SWC 2041); Anonymous: John Henry. Ralph Waldo Emerson. (J). (SWC 2041); Barbara Frietchie. John Greenleaf Whittier. (J). (SWC 2041); Barefoot Boy. John Greenleaf Whittier. (J). (SWC 2041); Birches. Robert Frost. Perf. by Robert Frost. (J). (SWC 2041); Casey at the Bat: A Ballad of the Republic, Sung in the Year 1888. Ernest Lawrence Thayer. (J). (SWC 2041); Casey Jones. Ralph Waldo Emerson. (J). (SWC 2041); Children's Hour. Henry Wadsworth Longfellow. (J). (SWC 2041); Concord Hymn & Other Poems. Ralph Waldo Emerson. (J). (SWC 2041); Deacon's Masterpiece, or The Wonderful "One-Hoss Shay" Oliver Wendell Holmes. (J). (SWC 2041); Dorado. Edgar Allan Poe. (J). (SWC 2041); Fog. Carl Sandburg. Perf. by Carl Sandburg. (J). (SWC 2041); House by the Side of the Road. Sam Walter Foss. (J). (SWC 2041); I Hear America Singing. Walt Whitman. (J). (SWC 2041); In Flanders Fields. John McCrae. (J). (SWC 2041); Let My People Go. James Weldon Johnson. (J). (SWC 2041); Man with the Hoe. Edwin Charles Markham. (J). (SWC 2041); Narrow Fellow in the Grass. Emily Dickinson. (J). (SWC 2041); Negro Speaks of Rivers. Langston Hughes. (J). (SWC 2041); New Colossus. Emma Lazarus. (J). (SWC 2041); O Captain! My Captain! Walt Whitman. (J). (SWC 2041); Old Ironsides. Oliver Wendell Holmes. (J). (SWC 2041); Snow-Bound. John Greenleaf Whittier. (J). (SWC 2041); Tales of a Wayside Inn: Paul Revere's Ride. Henry Wadsworth Longfellow. (J). (SWC 2041); Village Blacksmith. Henry Wadsworth Longfellow. (J). (SWC 2041); Wreck of the Hesperus. Henry Wadsworth Longfellow. (J). (SWC 2041); (J). 1988. 22.00 (978-0-694-50766-5(0), SWC 2041) HarperCollins Pubs.
Other performers include: Basil Rathbone, Brock Peters, Ed Begley, Frederick O'Neal, Vincent Price, Julie Harris, Helen Gahagan Douglas & Eartha Kitt.

Classic American Poetry. unabr. ed. Emily Dickinson et al. Read by Garrick Hagon & Liza Ross. (YA). 2007. 34.99 (978-1-60252-496-5(3)) Find a World.

Classic American Short Stories. Read by William Roberts. (Running Time: 2 hrs. 30 mins.). (C). 2005. 20.95 (978-1-60083-702-9(6)) Iofy Corp.

Classic American Short Stories. Short Stories. Mark Twain et al. Read by William Roberts. 2 cass. (Running Time: 2 hrs. 30 mins.). (YA). (gr. 8 up). 2001. 13.98 (978-962-634-712-6(0), NA221214, Naxos AudioBooks); audio compact disk 17.98 (978-962-634-212-1(9), NA221212, Naxos AudioBooks) Naxos.
Nine classic stories by five late 19th and early 20th century American writers. With the exception of Mark Twain's "The Notorious jumping Frog of Calavaras County," the unifying theme among the selection is one of suspense. "An Occurrence at Owl Creek Bridge" recounts the hanging of a Confederate sympathizer during the American Civil War. "The Veteran" takes place a few years later and features a man who survived that war, in spite of his fearfulness, and now demonstrates his real bravery on a firey night when horses must be rescued from a burning barn.

Classic American Short Stories. unabr. ed. O. Henry et al. Read by William Roberts. (YA). 2007. 39.99 (978-1-60252-551-1(X)) Find a World.

Classic American Short Stories, Vol. 1. unabr. ed. Edith Wharton et al. 3 cass. (Running Time: 4 hrs. 30 mins.). 2002. 24.00 (978-1-929718-09-2(8), 1701-4) Audio Conn.
Selections include: A Journey, Impulse, Barn Burning, Paul's Case, A Christian Education, The Devil and Daniel Webster, Only the Dead Know Brooklyn.

Classic Bible Stories: Moses in Egypt, Moses the Lawgiver. unabr. abr. ed. Listening Library Staff & Rabbit Ears Books Staff. Read by Ben Kingsley & Danny Glover. (Running Time: 3600 sec.). (Rabbit Ears Ser.). (ENG.). (J). (gr. 1). 2006. audio compact disk 11.95 (978-0-7393-3707-3(6), Listening Lib) Pub: Random Audio Pubg. Dist(s): Random

Classic Big Game Encounters. Read by Dinsdale Landen. 2 cass. (Running Time: 2 hrs. 30 min.). 12.00 Set. (978-1-878427-44-1(X), XC435) Cimino Pub Grp.
Classic old-fashioned adventure stories told in a classic old-fashioned style suitable for any age who enjoys the excitement & thrill of the chase. With the exception of Kipling's "Tiger! Tiger!" & "The White Wolf" by Guy de Maupassant, these are largely Indian hunting stories from the time of the British Raj written by those who actually took part. Contains: "A Close Shot with a Charge of Sixpence," "The Tiger That Climbed a Tree," "At Close Quarters with a Tiger," "A Good Bag Before Breakfast," "Peer Bux," "The Terror of Hunsur".

Classic Blues Guitar Licks. Rikky Rooksby. 1 CD. (Running Time: 1 hr.). (Fast Forward Ser.). 1997. bk. 15.95 (978-0-7119-4527-2(6)) Pub: Music Sales. Dist(s): H Leonard

Classic Bob & Ray, Vol. 1. 4 cass. (Running Time: 60 min. per cass.). 1998. 29.98 Boxed set. (4325) Radio Spirits.
Tasty tidbits of wry humor gathered from 1946 through 1976.

Classic Bob & Ray, Vol. 2. 4 cass. (Running Time: 60 min. per cass.). 1998. 29.98 Boxed set. (4326) Radio Spirits.

Classic Bob & Ray, Vol. 3. 4 cass. (Running Time: 60 min. per cass.). 1998. 29.98 Boxed set. (4327) Radio Spirits.

Classic Bob & Ray, Vol. 4. 4 cass. (Running Time: 60 min. per cass.). 1998. 29.98 Boxed set. (4328) Radio Spirits.

Classic Bob & Ray: Selections from a Career, 1946-1976. 4 cass. (Running Time: 4 hrs.). 2000. 29.95 (978-1-892091-63-5(1), RadioArt) Radio Found.

Classic Bob & Ray Vol. 1: Selections from a Career: 1946-1976. Featuring Ray Goulding & Bob Elliot. 1982. audio compact disk (978-1-892091-29-1(1)) Radio Found.

Classic Bob & Ray Vol. 1: Selections from a Career, 1946-1976. Featuring Mary McGoon et al. 4 cass. (Running Time: 4 hrs.). 1999. 29.95 (978-1-892091-10-9(0), RadioArt) Radio Found.
Recipe for Frozen Ginger Ale Salad, Grub, The Story of Food & many zany routines from Bob & Ray.

Classic Bob & Ray Vol. 2: Selections from a Career, 1946-1976. 4 cass. (Running Time: 4 hrs.). 2000. 29.95 (978-1-892091-64-2(X), RadioArt) Radio Found.

Classic Bob & Ray Vol. 2: Selections from a Career: 1946-1976. Featuring Ray Goulding & Bob Elliot. 1991. audio compact disk (978-1-892091-30-7(5)) Radio Found.

Classic Bob & Ray Vol. 3: Selections from a Career, 1946-1976. 4 cass. (Running Time: 4 hrs.). 2000. 29.95 (978-1-892091-65-9(8), RadioArt) Radio Found.

Classic Bob & Ray Vol. 3: Selections from a Career: 1946-1976. Featuring Ray Goulding & Bob Elliot. 1993. audio compact disk (978-1-892091-31-4(3)) Radio Found.

Classic Bob & Ray Vol. 4: Selections from a Career, 1946-1976. 4 cass. (Running Time: 4 hrs.). 2000. 29.95 (978-1-892091-66-6(6), RadioArt) Radio Found.

Classic Bob & Ray Vol. 4: Selections from a Career: 1946-1976. Ray Goulding & Bob Elliot. 1993. audio compact disk 36.95 (978-1-892091-32-1(1)) Radio Found.

Classic Bob & Ray Vol. 4: Selections from a Career, 1946-1976. Featuring Mary McGoon et al. 4 cass. (Running Time: 4 hrs.). 1999. (978-1-892091-13-0(5)) Radio Found.
68 zany Bob & Ray routines collected from their 40-year career.

Classic Bush Yarns. Warren Fahey. (Running Time: 3 hrs.). 2001. cass. & cass. (978-0-7322-7454-2(0)) HarperAUS AUS.

Classic Car. abr. ed. Nina Mattikow. 4 cass. (Running Time: 4 hrs.). (Wood Classic Car Ser.). 1992. 34.95 Set. (978-1-55569-576-7(0), 44201) Great Am Audio.
Our beautifully made classic car contains a celebration of swing, 40 superstars of the Big Band Era.

Classic Cartoon Christmas. 1 cass. (Running Time: 1 hr.). 2000. 7.98 (Sony Wonder) Sony Music Ent.

Classic Cartoon Christmas. 1 CD. (Running Time: 1 hr.). (J). 2000. audio compact disk 11.98 (Sony Wonder) Sony Music Ent.

Classic Cartoon Christmas, Too. 1 cass. (Running Time: 1 hr.). 2000. 7.98 (Sony Wonder) Sony Music Ent.

Classic Cartoon Christmas, Too. 1 CD. (Running Time: 1 hr.). (J). 2000. audio compact disk 11.98 (Sony Wonder) Sony Music Ent.

Classic Case of Moral Decline: Genesis 19:1-14. Ed Young. 1994. 4.95 (978-0-7417-2033-7(7), 1033) Win Walk.

Classic Children's Tales. Read by Jackie Torrence. 1 cass. (Running Time: 44 min.). (Family Ser.). (J). (gr. k-7). 1989. 9.98 (8015); audio compact disk 14.98 (8015) Rounder Records.
This recording offers definitive interpretations of classic children's stories, from "Goldilocks & the Three Bears" to "The Gingerbread Man".

Classic Children's Tales, Vol. 10. EDCON Publishing Group Staff. (ENG.). 2008. audio compact disk 12.95 (978-0-8481-0421-4(8)) EDCON Pubng.

Classic Children's Tales: Rip Van Winkle, Gulliver's Travels, Hans Brinker & the Silver Skates. unabr. ed. LL Audio Staff. 2 cass. (Running Time: 3 hrs.). (Full - Cast Productions Ser.). (J). 2002. 19.95 (978-1-931953-14-6(7), AA106) Listen & Live.
They're stories that we've heard for generations, the kind of tales that children will remember for the rest of their lives. Listen as this full-cast production brings to life the characters of three of the most popular fables of our time: Rip Van Winkle, Jonathan Swift's Gulliver's Travels, Hans Brinker and the Silver Skates. Timeless and entertaining, these classic tales never grow old!.

***Classic Children's Tales Collection.** EDCON Publishing Group Staff. 2008. pap. bk. 199.00 (978-1-55576-659-7(5)); audio compact disk 123.00 (978-0-8481-0439-9(0)) EDCON Pubng.

***Classic Children's Tales Volume 1.** EDCON Publishing Group Staff. 2008. pap. bk. 21.00 (978-1-55576-428-9(2)) EDCON Pubng.

***Classic Children's Tales Volume 10.** EDCON Publishing Group Staff. 2008. pap. bk. 21.00 (978-1-55576-437-1(1)) EDCON Pubng.

***Classic Children's Tales Volume 2.** EDCON Publishing Group Staff. 2008. pap. bk. 21.00 (978-1-55576-429-6(0)); audio compact disk 12.95 (978-0-8481-0422-1(6)) EDCON Pubng.

***Classic Children's Tales Volume 3.** EDCON Publishing Group Staff. 2008. pap. bk. 21.00 (978-1-55576-430-2(4)) EDCON Pubng.

***Classic Children's Tales Volume 4.** EDCON Publishing Group Staff. 2008. pap. bk. 21.00 (978-1-55576-431-9(2)) EDCON Pubng.

***Classic Children's Tales Volume 5.** EDCON Publishing Group Staff. 2008. pap. bk. 21.00 (978-1-55576-432-6(0)) EDCON Pubng.

***Classic Children's Tales Volume 6.** EDCON Publishing Group Staff. 2008. pap. bk. 21.00 (978-1-55576-433-3(9)) EDCON Pubng.

***Classic Children's Tales Volume 7.** EDCON Publishing Group Staff. 2008. pap. bk. 21.00 (978-1-55576-434-0(7)) EDCON Pubng.

***Classic Children's Tales Volume 8.** EDCON Publishing Group Staff. 2008. pap. bk. 21.00 (978-1-55576-435-7(5)) EDCON Pubng.

Classic Children's Tales, Volume 9. Created by Edcon Publishing. (Classic Children's Tales Ser.). (ENG.). (J). 2009. audio compact disk 12.95 (978-1-55576-654-4(X)) EDCON Pubng.

***Classic Children's Tales Volume 9.** EDCON Publishing Group Staff. 2008. pap. bk. 21.00 (978-1-55576-436-4(3)); audio compact disk 12.95 (978-0-8481-0425-2(0)) EDCON Pubng.

Classic Chilling Tales Vol. 1: The Tell-Tale Heart; The Mark of the Beast; Lost Hearts; The Horla; The Furnished Room; Sredni Vashtar. Edgar Allan Poe et al. Read by Dermot Kerrigan. 2 cass. (Running Time: 2 hrs. 30 mins.). 1996. 13.98 (978-962-634-523-8(3), NA202314, Naxos AudioBooks) Naxos.

Classic Chilling Tales Vol. 2: The Raven; Rats; A Tough Tussle; The Birthday of the Infanta; No. 1 Branch Line; The Signalman; Berenice, 2. abr. ed. Edgar Allan Poe et al. Read by Anthony Donovan. 2 cass. (Running Time: 2 hrs. 30 mins.). 1996. 13.98 (978-962-634-549-8(7), NA204914, Naxos AudioBooks) Naxos.
The vengeful dead, premonition, ghosts, pacts with the devil & a strange madness - these are the themes of this collection. Includes: "Rats," "The Raven," "The Birthday of the Infanta," "A Tough Tussle," " Berenice".

Classic Chilling Tales Vol. 2: The Raven; Rats; A Tough Tussle; The Birthday of the Infanta; No. 1 Branch Line; The Signalman; Berenice, Vol. 2. abr. ed. Edgar Allan Poe et al. Read by Anthony Donovan. 2 CDs. (Running Time: 2 hrs. 30 mins.). 1995. audio compact disk 15.98 (978-962-634-049-3(5), NA204912, Naxos AudioBooks) Naxos.

Classic Chilling Tales Vol. 3: An Account of Some Strange Disturbances in Aungier Street, That Damned Thing, The Moonlit Road, The Upper Berth, To Let, Vol. 3. Ambrose Bierce et al. Read by Jonathan Keeble et al. 2 cass. (Running Time: 2 hrs. 30 mins.). 1999. 13.98 (978-962-634-664-8(7), NA216414, Naxos AudioBooks) Naxos.
Five fine ghost stories in the classic 19th century tradition. An Account of Some Strange Disturbances in Aungier Street; That Damned Thing; The Moonlit Road; The Upper Berth; To Let.

Classic Chilling Tales Vol. 3: An Account of Some Strange Disturbances in Aungier Street, That Damned Thing, The Moonlit Road, The Upper Berth, To Let, Vol. 3. abr. ed. Ambrose Bierce et al. Read by Jonathan Keeble et al. 2 CDs. (Running Time: 2 hrs. 30 min.). 1998. audio compact disk 15.98 (978-962-634-164-3(5), NA216412, Naxos AudioBooks) Naxos.
These stories date from the mid to late nineteenth century. Includes: "An Account of Some Strange Disturbances in Aungier Street," "That Damned Thing," "The Moonlit Road," "The Upper Berth," " To Let".

Classic Chilling Tales, Vol. 1. Read by Dermot Kerrigan. (Running Time: 2 hrs. 30 mins.). 1998. 20.95 (978-1-60083-703-6(4)) Iofy Corp.

Classic Chilling Tales, Vol. 2. Read by Anthony Donovan. (Running Time: 2 hrs. 30 mins.). 1999. 20.95 (978-1-60083-704-3(2)) Iofy Corp.

Classic Chilling Tales, Vol. 3. (Running Time: 2 hrs. 30 mins.). 2002. 20.95 (978-1-60083-705-0(0)) Iofy Corp.

***Classic Christianity: Life's Too Short to Miss the Real Thing.** abr. ed. Bob George. Narrated by Bob George. (Running Time: 2 hrs. 56 mins. 37 sec.). (ENG.). 2010. 11.89 (978-1-60814-671-0(5)); audio compact disk 16.99 (978-1-59859-720-2(5)) Oasis Audio.

Classic Christmas Carols: 30 Sing-along Favorites. Contrib. by Eric Wyse. Prod. by Eric Wyse & Brenda Boswell. 2005. audio compact disk 9.97 (978-5-558-92596-8(5)) Hendrickson MA.

Classic Christmas Carols: 30 Sing-Slong Favorites. Contrib. by Eric Wyse. Prod. by Eric Wyse & Brenda Boswell. 2005. audio compact disk 14.95 (978-5-558-85961-4(X)) Hendrickson MA.

Classic Clark Collection. abr. ed. Mary Higgins Clark. Read by Kate Burton et al. (Running Time: 120 hrs. 0 mins. 0 sec.). (ENG.). 2008. audio compact disk 21.99 (978-0-7435-8157-8(1)) Pub: S&S Audio. Dist(s): S and S Inc

Classic Comic Verse. (Running Time: 2 hrs. 15 mins.). 2003. 22.95 (978-1-60083-706-7(9)) Iofy Corp.

Classic Comic Verse. unabr. ed. Read by David Timson et al. Ed. by Anthony Anderson. 2 CDs. (Running Time: 2 hrs. 30 mins.). 1999. audio compact disk 15.98 (978-962-634-180-3(7), NA218012, Naxos AudioBooks) Naxos.
Straddling several centuries and including poetry by figures such as Shakespeare, Rochester, Donne, Gay, Byron, Keats and many more, these collections cover the pantheon of humorous verse - includes 150 poems in all.

Classic Comic Verse. unabr. ed. Read by David Timson et al. Ed. by Anthony Anderson. 2 cass. (Running Time: 2 hrs. 30 mins.). 1999. 13.98 (978-962-634-680-8(9), NA218014, Naxos AudioBooks) Naxos.

Classic Composers: Beethoven. 2002. audio compact disk (978-1-932013-08-5(3)) Intl Masters Pub.

Classic Composers: Mozart. 2002. audio compact disk (978-1-932013-07-8(5)) Intl Masters Pub.

Classic Composers: Tchaikovsky. 2002. audio compact disk (978-1-932013-05-4(9)) Intl Masters Pub.

Classic Country Set: 1960-1964. 2 CDs. audio compact disk 16.99 (YIA067) Time-Life.

Classic Country Hymns. 1 CD. audio compact disk 9.98 (978-1-57908-496-7(6), 5359) Platinm Enter.

Classic Country Hymns. unabr. ed. 1 cass. 7.98 (978-1-57908-497-4(4), 5359) Platinm Enter.

Classic Country 1960-1964, Set. 14.99 (YZA069) Time-Life.

Classic Crime Short Stories. Ruth Rendell et al. Read by Jack Shepherd & Patrick Malahide. (Playaway Adult Fiction Ser.). (ENG.). 2009. 59.99 (978-1-60775-705-4(2)) Find a World.

Classic Crime Short Stories. unabr. ed. Patrick Malahide. Read by Jack Shepherd. (Running Time: 5 hrs. 0 mins. 0 sec.). (ENG.). 2009. audio compact disk 26.95 (978-1-934997-17-8(X)) Pub: CSAWord. Dist(s): PerseuPGW

Classic Crime Short Stories. unabr. ed. Read by Patrick Malahide & Jack Shepherd. 4 cass. (Running Time: 6 hrs.). 2002. (978-1-901768-64-0(3)) CSA Telltapes GBR.

Classic Crime Stories. Read by Jack Shepherd. 2 cass. (Running Time: 3 hrs.). 12.00 Set. (978-1-878427-46-5(6), XC443) Cimino Pub Grp.
This selection of crime stories all feature a major criminal from the world of classic fiction. We have an elusive master of disguise, the 6' 4" Frenchman, Flambeau, who comes to England after escaping the clutches of the police in the Netherlands & France in "The Blue Cross," a classic Father Brown story. There is another Frenchman, Arsene Lupin, who masterminds the most audacious of crimes from his prison cell. Also includes: "The Missing Romney" by Edgar Wallace, "The Complete Criminal" by Edgar Wallace & "Markheim" by Robert Louis Stevenson.

Classic Crime Stories. Read by Jack Shepherd. 2 cass. (Running Time: 3 hrs.). 2002. 7.95 (978-1-57815-279-7(8), Media Bks Audio) Media Bks NJ.
Features major criminals from the world of classic fiction.

Classic Crimes of Passion. Read by Derek Jacobi. 2 cass. 1998. 16.85 Set. (978-1-901768-26-8(0)) Ulvrscrft Audio.

Classic Crimes of Passion, Set. Wilkie Collins. 2 cass. 1998. bk. 16.95 (978-1-896552-25-5(0)) Tangled Web CAN.

Classic Detective Stories. Read by Edward Hardwicke. 1 cass. 12.00 (978-1-878427-19-9(9), XC412) Cimino Pub Grp.

Classic Detective Stories. Read by Edward Hardwicke. (Playaway Adult Fiction Ser.). (ENG.). 2009. 59.99 (978-1-60775-706-1(0)) Find a World.

Classic Detective Stories. abr. ed. G. K. Chesterton. 2001. 7.95 (978-1-57815-257-5(7), 1111) Media Bks NJ.

Classic Detective Stories. unabr. ed. G. K. Chesterton et al. Read by Edward Hardwicke. 4 CDs. (Running Time: 4 hrs. 23 mins. 54 sec.). (ENG.). 2009. audio compact disk 26.95 (978-1-934997-16-1(1)) Pub: CSAWord. Dist(s): PerseuPGW

Classic Detective Stories, Vol. 1. Read by Multi Voice. (Running Time: 10 hrs.). 1988. 43.95 (978-1-59912-855-9(1)) Iofy Corp.

Classic Detective Stories, Vol. 1. unabr. ed. Read by Clifford Ashdown et al. 9 cass. (Running Time: 13 hrs.). 1994. 62.95 (978-0-7861-0622-6(0), 2112) Blckstn Audio.
Some of the treasures included in this collection are: "The Assyrian Rejuvenator," "The Ripening Rubies," "The Murder at Troyte's Hill," "The Absent-Minded Coterie," "The Problem of Cell 13," "The Case of the Dixon Torpedo," "The Glasgow Mystery.".

Classic Detective Stories, Vol. 1. unabr. collector's ed. 9 cass. (Running Time: 13 hrs. 30 min.). 1982. 72.00 (978-0-7366-3872-2(5), 9082) Books on Tape.
Contains: "The Problem of Cell 13" by Jacques Futrelle, "The Lenton Croft Robberies" by Arthur Morison, "The Adventure of the Six Napoleons" & "The Adventure of the Empty House" by Sir Arthur Conan Doyle, "The Absent Minded Coterie" by Robert Barr, "Madame Sara" by L.T. Meade, "How He Cut His Stick" by M. Bodkin, "The Glasgow Mystery" & "The Dublin Mystery" by Baroness Orczy.

Classic Detective Stories, Vol. 2. Read by Multi Voice. (Running Time: 11 hrs.). 1985. 43.95 (978-1-59912-856-6(X)) Iofy Corp.

Classic Detective Stories, Vol. 2. unabr. ed. Read by Bret Harte et al. 9 cass. (Running Time: 13 hrs.). 1994. 62.95 (978-0-7861-0739-1(1), 2125) Blckstn Audio.
Among the gems in this classic collection are: "The Stolen Cigar Case," "The Nicobar Bullion Case" & "The Affair of the Tortoise," "The Blood-Red Cross," "The Fatal Cipher" "The Duchess of Wilshire's Diamonds," "The Mystery of Mrs. Dickinson," "The Stolen White Elephant" & "A Double-Barreled Detective Story," "The Red-Headed League" & "The Adventure of the Noble Bachelo,r" "The Purloined Letter" & "The Murders in the Rue Morgue" & "Mrs. Policeman & the Cook.".

Classic Detective Stories, Vol. 2. unabr. collector's ed. 9 cass. (Running Time: 13 hr. 30 mins.). 1998. 72.00 (978-0-7366-3887-6(3), 9115) Books on Tape.
Includes: "The Stolen Cigar Case" by Bret Harte, "The Nicobar Bullion Case" & "The Blood Red Cross" by L.T. Meade & Robert Eustace, "The Fatal Cipher" by Jacques Futrelle, "The Duchess of Wilshire's Diamonds" by Guy Boothby, "The Mystery of Mrs. Dickenson" by Nicholas Carter, "The Stolen White Elephant" & "A Doubled-Barrelled Detective Story" by Mark Twain, "The Red-Headed League" & "The Adventure of the Noble Bachelor" by Sir Arthur Conan Doyle, "The Purloined Letter" & "The Murders in the Rue Morgue" by Edgar Allen Poe & "Mr. Policeman & the Cook" by Wilkie Collins.

Classic Detective Stories, Vol. 3. unabr. ed. Read by R. Austin Freeman et al. 7 cass. (Running Time: 10 hrs.). 1994. 49.95 (978-0-7861-0786-5(3), 2130) Blckstn Audio.
Selections included in this volume are: "The Mandarin's Pearl" & "The Blue Sequin," "The Chicago Heiress," "The Case of Mr. Geldard's Elopement" & "The Case of the Ward Lane Tabernacle," "The Liverpool Mystery" & "The Case of Miss Elioit," "The Little Old Man of Batignolle," "The Secret of the Fox Delight" & "The Adventure of the Naval Treaty.".

Classic Detective Stories Vol. I: A Collection. unabr. ed. 9 cass. (Running Time: 1 hr. 30 min. per cass.). Dramatization. Incl. Absent-Minded Coterie. Robert Barr. 1981. (C-82); Adventure of the Empty House. Arthur Conan Doyle. 1981. (C-82); Adventure of the Six Napoleons. Arthur Conan Doyle. 1981. (C-82); Dublin Mystery. Emmuska Orczy. 1981. (C-82); Glasgow Mystery. Emmuska Orczy. 1981. (C-82); How He Cut His Stick. M. Bodkin. 1981. (C-82); Lenton Croft Robberies. Arthur Morrison. 1981. (C-82); Problem of Cell 13. Jacques Futrelle. 1981. (C-82); 1981. 63.00 (C-82) Jimcin Record.
Stories from the vintage era of mystery writings.

Classic Detective Stories Vol. II: A Collection. unabr. ed. 9 cass. (Running Time: 13 hrs. 28 min.). Incl. Adventure of the Noble Bachelor. Arthur Conan Doyle. 1984. (C-115); Affair of the Tortoise. Arthur Morrison. 1984. (C-115); Blood Red Cross. Arthur Meade & Robert Eustace. 1984. (C-115); Double-Barreled Detective Story. Mark Twain. 1984. (C-115); Duchess of Wilshire's Diamonds. Guy Boothbay. 1984. (C-115); Fatal Cipher. Jacques Futrelle. 1984. (C-115); Mr. Policeman & the Cook. Wilkie Collins. 1984. (C-115); Murders in the Rue Morgue. Edgar Allan Poe. 1984. (C-115); Mystery of Mrs. Dickenson. Nicholas Carter. 1984. (C-115); Nicobar Bullion Case. Arthur Morrison. 1984. (C-115); Purloined Letter. Edgar Allan Poe. 1984. (C-115); Red-Headed League. Arthur Conan Doyle. 1984. (C-115); Stolen Cigar Case. Bret Harte. 1984. (C-115); Stolen White Elephant. Mark Twain. 1984. (C-115); 1984. 63.00 (C-115) Jimcin Record.
More great mystery stories from the vintage age of mystery writing.

Classic Detective Stories Vol. III: A Collection. Read by Walter Zimmerman & Walter Covell. 7 cass. (Running Time: 10 hrs. 16 min.). Dramatization. Incl. Adventure of the Naval Treaty. Arthur Conan Doyle. 1986. (C-146); Blue Sequin. R. Austin Freeman. 1986. (C-146); Case of Miss Elliott. Emmuska Orczy. 1986. (C-146); Case of Mr. Geldard's Elopement. Arthur Morrison. 1986. (C-146); Little Old Man of Batignolles. Ed. by Emile Gaboriau. 1986. (C-146); Liverpool Mystery. Emmuska Orczy. 1986. (C-146); Mandarin's Pearl. R. Austin Freeman. 1986. (C-146); Secret of the Foxhunter. William Le Queux. 1986. (C-146); Staircase at the Hearts Delight. Anna Katharine Green. 1986. (C-146); Ward Land Tabernacle. Arthur Morrison. 1986. (C-146); 1986. 42.00 (C-146) Jimcin Record.
More short stories from the vintage age of mystery writing.

Classic Disney. unabr. ed. 1 cass. (Classic Collections: Vol. 1). (J). 11.99 (978-1-55723-642-5(9)); 11.99 Norelco. (978-1-55723-643-2(7)); audio compact disk 19.99 CD. (978-1-55723-644-9(5)); audio compact disk 19.99 (978-1-55723-645-6(3)) W Disney Records.

Classic Disney. unabr. ed. 1 cass. (Classic Collections: Vol. 2). (J). 11.99 (978-1-55723-646-3(1)); 11.99 Norelco. (978-1-55723-647-0(X)); audio compact disk 19.99 CD. (978-1-55723-648-7(8)); audio compact disk 19.99 (978-1-55723-649-4(6)) W Disney Records.

Classic Disney. unabr. ed. 1 cass. (Classic Collections: Vol. 3). (J). 11.99 (978-0-7634-0076-7(9)); 11.99 Norelco. (978-0-7634-0075-0(0)); audio compact disk 19.99 CD. (978-0-7634-0077-4(7)); audio compact disk 19.99 (978-0-7634-0078-1(5)) W Disney Records.

Classic Disney, Vol. 1-4, set. Prod. by Walt Disney Productions Staff. 4 cass. (J). 1997. 69.95 Set. W Disney Records.

Classic Disney, Vol. 4. (J). 1997. 11.99 (978-0-7634-0269-3(9)); 11.99 Norelco. (978-0-7634-0268-6(0)); audio compact disk 19.99 W Disney Records.
This compilation include songs from Pinocchio & Bedknobs & Broomsticks.

Classic Disney, Vol. 4. (J). (ps-3). 1997. audio compact disk 19.99 CD. (978-0-7634-0270-9(2)) W Disney Records.

Classic Disney Five. Prod. by Walt Disney Records Staff. 1 CD. (Classic Collections). (J). 1998. audio compact disk 22.50 (978-0-7634-0543-4(4)) W Disney Records.

Classic Disney Five. Prod. by Walt Disney Records Staff. 1 cass . (Classic Collections). (J). (ps-3). 1998. 12.98 (978-0-7634-0542-7(6)) W Disney Records.

Classic Double Feature. Incl. Classic Double Feature: The Count of Monte Cristo. (879); Classic Double Feature: The Three Musketeers. (879); 10.95 (978-0-89926-219-2(8), 879) Audio Bk.
Two classic tales of adventure are dramatically retold with full musical accompaniment.

Classic Double Feature: The Count of Monte Cristo see Classic Double Feature

Classic Double Feature: The Three Musketeers see Classic Double Feature

Classic Erotic Verse, Set. abr. ed. Anthony Anderson. 2 cass. (Running Time: 2 hrs.). 1999. 16.85 Ulvrscrft Audio.
Collection of erotic verse. This anthology is merely a selection of such verse by writers such as Herrick, Marlowe, Jonson, Byron, Verlaine, Whitman & John Betjemen.

Classic Fairy Stories. Traditional Tales. Read by Bernard Cribbins. (Running Time: 2 hrs. 30 mins.). 2005. 20.95 (978-1-60083-707-4(7)) Iofy Corp.

Classic Fairy Stories: Traditional Tales. Read by Bernard Cribbins. Adapted by Nicholas Soames. 2 cass. (Running Time: 2 hrs. 30 min.). (J). 2001. 13.98 (978-962-634-722-5(8), NA222214, Naxos AudioBooks) Naxos.
From the brave little tailor who ends up a king, to Goldilocks and the three little pigs, and the English story of Dick Whittington.

Classic Fairy Stories: Traditional Tales. Read by Bernard Cribbins. 2 CDs. (Running Time: 2 hrs. 30 min.). (J). 2001. audio compact disk 17.98 (978-962-634-222-0(6), NA222212, Naxos AudioBooks) Naxos.

Classic Fairy Tales. unabr. ed. Peter Combe. Read by Peter Combe. 1 cass. (Running Time: 1 hr.). (J). 2004. 18.00 (978-1-74093-036-9(3)); audio compact disk 39.95 (978-1-74093-037-6(1)) Pub: Bolinda Pubng AUS. Dist(s): Bolinda Pub Inc

Classic Fairy Tales. unabr. ed. Jacob W. Grimm. 2 cass. (Running Time: 3 hrs.). (Full - Cast Productions Ser.). (J). 2002. 19.95 (978-1-931953-13-9(9)) Listen & Live.
Relive the most beloved stories of our time as you huff and puff with the Big Bad Wolf, escape the clutches of giants, follow breadcrumb trails through the forest, and much more! Listen as a full-cast of actors perform The Three Little Pigs, Tom Thumb, The Emperor's New Clothes, Hansel and Gretel, Little Red Riding Hood, Jack and the Beanstalk, and Rumpelstiltskin. Timeless and entertaining, these classic tales never grow old!.

Classic Fairy Tales, Vol. 1. Jacob W. Grimm et al. Narrated by Michael Stevens et al. Prod. by Ralph LaBarge. (J). 2006. 12.95 (978-0-9798626-5-6(5)) Alpha DVD.

Classic Fairy Tales, Vol. 2. Jacob W. Grimm et al. Narrated by Michael Stevens et al. Prod. by Ralph LaBarge. (J). 2006. 12.95 (978-0-9798626-6-3(3)) Alpha DVD.

Classic Fairy Tales, Vol. 2. unabr. ed. Peter Combe. Read by Peter Combe. 1 CD. (Running Time: 50 mins.). (J). (ps-3). 2005. audio compact disk 39.95 (978-1-74093-569-2(1)) Pub: Bolinda Pubng AUS. Dist(s): Bolinda Pub Inc

Classic Fairy Tales, Vol. 3. Jacob W. Grimm et al. Narrated by Michael Stevens et al. Prod. by Ralph LaBarge. (J). 2006. 12.95 (978-0-9798626-7-0(1)) Alpha DVD.

Classic Fairy Tales, Vol. 3. unabr. ed. Peter Combe. Read by Peter Combe. 1 CD. (Running Time: 50 mins.). (J). (ps-3). 2007. audio compact disk 39.95 (978-1-74093-899-0(2)) Pub: Bolinda Pubng AUS. Dist(s): Bolinda Pub Inc

Classic Fairy Tales Vol. 1: An Enchanting Collection of Magical Adventures. R. H. Bauman. 4 cass. (Running Time: 3 hrs.). (J). (ps-3). 2001. 9.95 (978-1-56015-692-5(9), Penton Kids) Penton Overseas.
Volume One includes: "Jack & the Beanstalk," "The Tortoise & the Hare," "Little Red Riding Hood," Pinocchio," "The Three Little Pigs" & more.

Classic Fairy Tales Vol. 2: An Enchanting Collection of Magical Adventures. R. H. Bauman. 4 cass. (Running Time: 3 hrs.). (J). (ps-3). 2001. 9.95 (978-1-56015-693-2(7), Penton Kids) Penton Overseas.
Volume Two includes: "Alice in Wonderland," "Ali Baba & the Forty Thieves," "Aladdin & His Magic Lamp," "Cinderella," "Sleeping Beauty" & more.

Classic Fairy Tales Collection. Peter Combe. Read by Peter Combe. (Running Time: 2 hrs. 30 mins.). (J). 2009. 39.99 (978-1-74214-370-5(9), 9781742143705) Pub: Bolinda Pubng AUS. Dist(s): Bolinda Pub Inc

Classic Favorites. Kenneth E. Hagin. 6 cass. 24.00 (17H) Faith Lib Pubns.

***Classic Fiction en Espanol 1 (Playaway)** (Playaway Ser.). (SPA.). audio compact disk 29.20 (978-1-4342-3002-7(3)) CapstoneDig.

***Classic Fiction en Espanol 2 (Playaway)** (Playaway Ser.). (SPA.). audio compact disk 29.20 (978-1-4342-3003-4(1)) CapstoneDig.

Classic Fm Shakespeare. William Shakespeare & J. Brunning. (Running Time: 2 hrs.). (ENG.). audio compact disk 27.50 (978-1-84032-186-9(5), HoddrStoughton) Pub: Hodder General GBR. Dist(s): Trafalgar

Classic German Short Stories, Vol. 1. unabr. ed. Johann Wolfgang von Goethe et al. 3 cass. (Running Time: 4 hrs. 30 mins.). 2002. 24.00 (978-1-929718-12-2(8), 2101-4) Audio Conn.
Selections include: The Attorney, The Sport of Destiny, Bassompierre, Little Herr Friedemann, Unexpected Reunion, Kannitverstan, The Hussar, The Enchanted Cabinet and The Bachelor.

Classic Ghost & Horror Stories: An Anthology. unabr. ed. 4 cass. (Running Time: 3 hrs.). 2004. 25.00 (978-1-59007-113-7(1)) Pub: New Millenn Enter. Dist(s): PerseuPGW
Close the windows, lock the doors, turn on the lights, and please do not listen to this chilling collection alone! Masters of supernatural fiction take perverse pleasure in evoking hair-raising horrors that feature ghostly characters, forbidding landscapes, occult phenomena, and gloomy manors.

Classic Ghost Stories. Read by Richard Pasco. 4 cass. (Running Time: 6 hrs.). 19.95 Boxed set. (978-1-878427-39-7(3), XC602) Cimino Pub Grp.
Contains fourteen of the best ghost stories in the world. "The Judge's House" - Bram Stoker, "The Upper Berth" - F. Marion Crawford, "Narrative of the Ghost of a Hand" - J. Sheridan Le Fanu, "To Be Taken with a Grain of Salt" - Charles Dickens, "The Tell-Tale Heart" - Edgar Allan Poe, "Gabriel - Ernest" - Saki, "The Furnished Room" - O. Henry, "My Own True Ghost" - Rudyard Kipling, "Lost Hearts" - M. R. James, "Called" - P. C. Wren, "Who Knows?" - Guy De Maupassant, "When I Was Dead" - Vincent O'Sullivan, "The Face" - E. F. Benson, "The Open Window" - Saki.

Classic Ghost Stories. Read by Richard Pasco. (Playaway Adult Fiction Ser.). (ENG.). 2009. 59.99 (978-1-60812-701-6(X)) Find a World.

Classic Ghost Stories. Read by Richard Pasco. 2 cass. (Running Time: 3 hrs.). 7.95 (978-1-57815-280-3(1), 1168, Media Bks Audio) Media Bks NJ.

Classic Ghost Stories. unabr. ed. Bram Stoker et al. Read by Richard Pasco. (Running Time: 4 hrs. 46 mins. 15 sec.). (ENG.). 2009. audio compact disk 26.95 (978-1-934997-18-5(8)) Pub: CSAWord. Dist(s): PerseuPGW

Classic Ghost Stories. unabr. ed. Bram Stoker et al. Read by Richard Pasco. 2001. 12.99 (978-1-57815-246-9(1), Media Bks Audio) Media Bks NJ.

Classic Ghost Stories, Vol. 1. Read by Richard Pasco. 1 cass. 1993. 12.00 (978-1-878427-32-8(6), XC403) Cimino Pub Grp.

Classic Ghost Stories, Vol. 2. Read by Richard Pasco. 1 cass. 12.00 (978-1-878427-33-5(4), XC417) Cimino Pub Grp.

Classic Ghost Stories: The Signal-Man, the Mezzotint & Others. Charles Dickens & M. R. James. 2. (Running Time: 9051 sec.). 2007. audio compact disk 17.98 (978-962-634-459-0(8), Naxos AudioBooks) Naxos.

Classic Ghost Stories: The Signalman & the Mezzotint & Others. unabr. ed. Charles Dickens & M. R. James. Read by Stephen Critchlow. (YA). 2007. 34.99 (978-1-60252-808-6(X)) Find a World.

Classic Ghost Stories Vol. 1: A Collection. unabr. ed. Read by Cindy Hardin. Ed. by Walter Zimmerman. 8 cass. (Running Time: 11 hrs. 30 min.). Dramatization. Incl. Apparition of Mrs. Veal. Daniel Defoe. 1982. (C-63); Furnished Room. O. Henry. 1982. (C-63); Green Tea. Amelia B. Edwards. 1982. (C-63); Middle Toe of the Right Foot. Ambrose Bierce. 1982. (C-63); Moonlit Road. Ambrose Bierce. 1982. (C-63); Mrs. Zant & the Ghost. Wilkie Collins. 1982. (C-63); Old Mrs. Jones. Clara Riddell. 1982. (C-63); Red Room & Other Stories. H. G. Wells. 1982. (C-63); Signalman. Charles Dickens. 1982. (C-63); Stranger. Ambrose Bierce. 1982. (C-63); Trial for Murder. Charles Dickens. 1982. (C-63); 1982. 54.00 (C-63) Jimcin Record.
A potpourri of ghost stories of different lands & languages.

Classic Ghost Stories Vol. 1: A Collection. unabr. collector's ed. Read by Walter Zimmerman & Cindy Hardin. 8 cass. (Running Time: 12 hrs.). 1982. 64.00 (978-0-7366-3860-9(1), 9063) Books on Tape.
Includes: "Mrs. Zant & the Ghost" by Wilkie Collins; "The Red Room" by H. G. Wells; "Old Mrs. Jones" by Clara Riddell; "The Moonlit Road," "The Middle Toe of the Right Foot" & "The Stranger" by Ambrose Bierce; "Green Tea" by Amelia Edwards; "The Signalman" & "The Trial for Murder" by Charles Dickens; "The Apparition of Mrs. Veal" by Daniel Defoe & "The Furnished Room" by O. Henry.

Classic Ghost Stories Vol. 2: A Collection. unabr. ed. 7 cass. (Running Time: 10 hrs. 30 min.). Incl. Canterville Ghost. Oscar Wilde. (J). 1984. (C-113); Doll's Ghost. F. Marion Crawford. 1984. (C-113); Familiar. J. Sheridan Le Fanu. 1984. (C-113); Ghost Story. E. T. A. Hoffmann. 1984. (C-113); Ghost Story. Mark Twain. 1984. (C-113); Hall Bedroom. Mary E. Wilkins Freeman. 1984. (C-113); Haunted House. Charles Dickens. 1984. (C-113); Hertford O'Donnell's Warning. Charlotte Riddell. 1984. (C-113); Inhabitant of Carcosa. Ambrose Bierce. 1984. (C-113); Old Mansion. 1984. (C-113); Old Nurse's Story. Elizabeth Gaskell. 1984. (C-113); Phantom Hag. Guy de Maupassant. 1984. (C-113); Phantom Woman. 1984. (C-113); Philosophy of Relative Existences. Frank Richard Stockton. 1984. (C-113); Spectre Bride. 1984. (C-113); Staley Fleming's Hallucination. Ambrose Bierce. 1984. (C-113); Story of the Bagman's Uncle. Charles Dickens. 1984. (C-113); 1984. 49.00 (C-113) Jimcin Record.
A collection of classic ghost stories.

Classic Ghost Stories Vol. 2: A Collection. unabr. collector's ed. 7 cass. (Running Time: 10 hrs. 30 min.). 1984. 56.00 (978-0-7366-3885-2(7), 9113) Books on Tape.
This second volume offers more of the world's best mysteries & ghost stories. Titles include: "The Hall Bedroom" by Mary E. Wilkins Freeman; "The Story of the Bagman's Uncle" & "The Haunted House" by Charles Dickens; "The Familiar" by Joseph Sheridan LeFanu; "Staley Fleming's Hallucination" & "An Inhabitant of Carcosa" by Ambrose Bierce; "The Old Nurse's Story" by Elizabeth Guskell; "The Philosophy of Relative Existences" by Frank Stockton; "The Phantom Hag" by Guy de Maupassant; "The Doll's Ghost" by F. Marion Crawford; "Hertford O'Donnell's Warning" by Charlotte Riddell; "Ghost Story" by E. T. Hoffman; "A Ghost Story" by Mark Twain; "The Canterville Ghost" by Oscar Wilde; "The Phantom Woman," "The Spectre Bride" & "The Old Mansion" - all three anonymous.

Classic Ghost Stories Vol. 3: A Collection. unabr. ed. 7 cass. (Running Time: 10 hrs. 32 min.). Incl. Castle of the King. Bram Stoker. 1984. (C-122); Conn Kilrea. J. H. Riddell. 1984. (C-122); Dead Woman's Photograph. 1984. (C-122); Eveline's Visit. Elizabeth Braddon. 1984. (C-122); Ghost, the Gallant, the Gael, & the Goblin. William S. Gilbert. 1984. (C-122); Ghostly Rental. Henry James. 1984. (C-122); Miss Dulane & My Lord. Wilkie Collins. 1984. (C-122); Mr. Justice Harbottle. J. Sheridan Le Fanu. 1984. (C-122); My Tapestried Chamber. Walter Scott, Sr. 1984. (C-122); Open Door. Margaret Oliphant. 1984. (C-122); Seventh Man. Joseph Quiller-Couch. 1984. (C-122); Some Haunted Houses. Ambrose Bierce. 1984. (C-122); 1984. 49.00 (C-122) Jimcin Record.

Classic Ghost Stories Vol. 3: A Collection. unabr. collector's ed. 8 cass. (Running Time: 12 hrs.). 1983. 64.00 (978-0-7366-3893-7(8), 9122) Books on Tape.
Thirteen of the world's best mystery & ghost stories. Includes: "Mr. Justice Harbottle" by J. S. LeFanu; "The Seventh Man" by Arthur Quiller-Couch; "Some Haunted Houses" by Ambrose Bierce; "Miss Dulane & My Lord" by Wilkie Collins; "The Tapestried Chamber" by Sir Walter Scott; "The Open Door" by Margaret Oliphant; "The Ghostly Rental" & "Sir Edmond Orme" by Henry James; "Eveline's Visitant" by Elizabeth Braddon; "The Dead Woman's Photograph," anonymous; "Conn Kilrea" by Mrs. J. H. Riddell; "The Castle of the King" by Bram Stoker; & "The Ghost, the Gallant, the Gael & the Goblin" by W. S. Gilbert.

Classic Grapevine, Vol. 1. 1 CD. (Running Time: 1 hr. 30 mins.). 2002. audio compact disk 10.00 (978-0-933685-34-5(3)) A A Grapevine.
Articles originated and read from our magazine.

Classic Grapevine, Vol. 2. 1 CD. (Running Time: 1 hr. 30 mins.). 2002. audio compact disk 10.00 (978-0-933685-35-2(1)) A A Grapevine.
The articles are read from our magazine.

Classic Grapevine, Vol. 3. 1 CD. (Running Time: 1 hr. 30 mins.). 2002. audio compact disk 10.00 (978-0-933685-36-9(X)) A A Grapevine.
Articles originally from our magazine read by different people.

Classic Guitar Method. Mel Bay Staff. 1996. audio compact disk 15.98 (978-0-7866-1699-2(7), 93207CD) Mel Bay.

Classic Guitar Method, Vol. 1. Mel Bay Staff. 1960. pap. bk. 14.95 (978-0-87166-334-4(1), 93207P); 9.98 (978-0-87166-333-7(3), 93207C) Mel Bay.

Classic Hits. Contrib. by Imperials. (Gospel Legacy Ser.). 2006. audio compact disk 13.99 (978-5-558-16552-4(9)) Pt of Grace Ent.

Classic Hoagy Carmichael. John E. Hasse. 1990. pap. bk. 42.00 (978-0-87195-051-2(0)) Ind Hist Soc.

Classic Horse & Pony Stories. Diana Pullein-Thompson & Neal Puddephatt. (Read & Listen Ser.). (J). 2000. pap. bk. (978-0-7894-6362-3(8)) DK Pub Inc.

Classic Hundred. unabr. ed. William Harmon. 5 CDs. (Running Time: 6 hrs.). 2001. audio compact disk 39.95 Books on Tape.
The "top 100" poems of all time in their order of popularity. The novelty of this collection lies in its completely original format, resulting in a compact anthology which ranges from Shakespeare to Frost, from love & death to crime & punishment.

Classic Hundred Poems: All Time Favorites. unabr. abr. ed. Ed. by William Harmon. Contrib. by Alice Quinn. Created by Workman Publishing Company, Inc. Staff. (Running Time: 21600 sec.). (ENG., 2007. audio compact disk 29.95 (978-1-59887-578-2(7), 1598875787) Pub: HighBridge. Dist(s): Workman Pub

Classic Irish Short Stories. Read by T. P. McKenna. 4 cass. 2002. (978-1-901768-71-8(6)) CSA Telltapes GBR.

Classic Irish Short Stories. Read by T. P. McKenna. 2 cass. (Running Time: 3 hrs.). 1996. 12.00 Set. (978-1-878427-51-9(2), XC457) Cimino Pub Grp.
Stories range from Gerald Griffin's chilling tale, "The Brown Man," to the delicate & closely observed Araby, taken from James Joyce's "Dubliners," about adolescent sexual awakening. Oscar Wilde's stylish & witty story, "The Model Millionaire" about a young man on whom good fortune smiles, Oliver Goldsmith's "Adventures of a Strolling Player" a compressed narrative of a peripatetic existence; Sheridan Le Fanu's "Faustian" Sir Dominick Sarsfield; William Carleton's willy distiller, Bob Pentland & his outwitting of the excise man & Agnes Castle's romantic Rosanna.

Classic Irish Short Stories, Vol. 1. unabr. ed. George Moore et al. Read by Charlton Griffin. 3 cass. (Running Time: 5 hrs.). 2002. 24.00 (978-1-929718-14-6(4)) Audio Conn.
Ten works by nine authors make up this enjoyable collection. The highlight is the short novel, "the Weaver's Grave." A solo violin adds weight and poignancy to the setting for the comic clash between the two old men in the O'Kelly selection.

Classic John Buchan Stories. John Buchan. Read by Iain Cuthbertson. 2 cass. 1998. 16.85 Set. (978-1-901768-18-3(X)) Pub: CSA Telltapes GBR. Dist(s): Ulverscroft US

Classic Kids Classroom Collection. Susan Hammond. (J). 1995. 159.98 Consort Bk Sales.

Classic Love Stories. abr. ed. Read by Rosalind Ayres & Martin Jarvis. 2 cass. (Running Time: 3 hrs.). 2002. 7.95 (978-1-57815-283-4(6), 1175, Media Bks Audio) Media Bks NJ.
This is a great collection of short stories based on the theme of love. They are not the typical stories steeped in sentimentality but the clever, poignant, humorous and even romantic stories set during an age when chivalry and honour abound.

Classic Love Stories. abr. ed. Read by Martin Jarvis & Rosalind Ayres. 1 cass. 1994. 12.00 (978-1-878427-37-3(7), XC402) Cimino Pub Grp.
Contains: "Mr. & Mrs. Dave" - Katherine Mansfield, "Genefer," - Sabine Baring-Gould, "The Sphinx Without a Secret" - Oscar Wilde, "The Bagman's Story" - from Pickwick Papers by Charles Dickens, "Angela" - W. S. Gilbert, "The Melancholy Hussar of the German Legion" - Thomas Hardy, "The Stinging Lesson" - Katherine Mansfield, "Perilous Play" - Louisa May Alcott.

Classic Love Stories. unabr. ed. Charles Dickens et al. 2001. 12.99 (978-1-57815-249-0(6), Media Bks Audio) Media Bks NJ.

Classic Love Stories, No. 1. Read by Rosalind Ayre & Martin Jarvis. 2 cass. (Running Time: 3 hrs.). 1999. 16.85 Set. (978-1-901768-29-9(5)) Pub: CSA Telltapes GBR. Dist(s): Ulverscroft US

Classic Love Stories, No. 2. Read by Joanna David & Edward Fox. 2 cass. (Running Time: 3 hrs.). 2002. (978-1-901768-55-8(4)) CSA Telltapes GBR.

Classic Mark Twain. unabr. ed. Mark Twain. 2 cass. (Running Time: 3 hrs.). (Full - Cast Productions Ser.). (J). 2002. 19.95 (978-1-931953-11-5(2)) Listen & Live.
Raft along the river with Tom and Huck on their boyhood escapades and misadventures in this full-cast classic production.

Classic Metal Bass. Phil Mulford. 1 CD. (Running Time: 1 hr.). 1997. audio compact disk 15.95 (978-0-7119-4505-0(5)) Music Sales.

Classic Moments: The Bill Gaither Trio - For Kids. Perf. by Bill Gaither. 1 cass. 1999. (978-0-7601-3162-6(7)) Brentwood Music.
Original performances includes: "I Am a Promise," "Jesus Loves Me," & "This Little Light of Mine.".

Classic Moments: The Bill Gaither Trio - Live. Perf. by Bill Gaither. 1 cass. 1999. (978-0-7601-3177-0(5)); audio compact disk (978-0-7601-3178-7(3)) Brentwood Music.
Original performances includes: "He Touched Me," "Get All Excited," & "Joy In the Camp.".

Classic Moments Vol. 1: The Gaither Vocal Band. 1 cass. (Running Time: 40 mins.). 1999. (978-0-7601-3158-9(9)) Brentwood Music.
Original performance includes: "Lamb of God," "No Other Name But Jesus," & "Your First Day In Heaven.".

Classic Moments Vol. 2: The Bill Gaither Trio. Perf. by Bill Gaither. 1 cass. 1999. (978-0-7601-3175-6(9)); (978-0-7601-3164-0(3)) Brentwood Music.
Relive the power & promise of 12 classic songs from these original performances.

Classic Moments Vol. 2: The Gaither Vocal Band. 1 cass. (Running Time: 45 mins.). 1999. (978-0-7601-3160-2(0)) Brentwood Music.
Original performances include: "Living Sacrifice," "Passin' the Faith Along," & "New Point of View.".

Classic Moments from the Bill Gaither Trio, Vol. 1. Perf. by Bill Gaither. 1 CD. 1999. audio compact disk (978-0-7601-3176-3(7)) Brentwood Music.
Relive the power & promise of 12 classics songs from these original performances. Includes: "Because He Lives," "Get All Excited," "Sweet, Sweet Spirit," "The Longer I Serve Him" & many more.

Classic Moments from the Bill Gaither Trio, Vol. 2. Perf. by Bill Gaither Trio, The. 1 CD. (Running Time: 43 mins.). 1999. audio compact disk (978-0-7601-3165-7(1)) Brentwood Music.
Includes "The King Is Coming," "The Family of God," "Something Beautiful" & more.

Classic Moments from the Gaither Vocal Band, Vol. 1. 1 CD. 1999. audio compact disk (978-0-7601-3174-9(0)) Brentwood Music.
Original performance includes: "Lamb of God," "No Other Name but Jesus" & "Your First Day In Heaven.".

Classic Moments from the Gaither Vocal Band, Vol. 2. 1 CD. (Running Time: 45 mins.). 1999. audio compact disk (978-0-7601-3161-9(9)) Brentwood Music.
Original performances includes: "Living Sacrifice," "Passin' the Faith Along" & "New Point of View.".

Classic Novels: Meeting the Challenge of Great Literature. Instructed by Arnold Weinstein. 2008. 199.95 (978-1-59803-386-1(7)); audio compact disk 99.95 (978-1-59803-387-8(5)) Teaching Co.

Classic Nursery Rhymes. unabr. ed. Read by Vanessa Maroney. (J). 2006. 39.99 (978-1-59895-171-4(8)) Find a World.

Classic Poe. Edgar Allan Poe. Narrated by Ralph Cosham. (Running Time: 9000 sec.). (Unabridged Classics in MP3 Ser.). (ENG.). 2008. audio compact disk 24.00 (978-1-58472-640-1(7), In Aud) Sound Room.

Classic Poe. unabr. ed. Edgar Allan Poe. Read by Ralph Cosham. 2 cass. (Running Time: 3 hrs. 10 min.). 1994. lib. bdg. 18.95 Set. (978-1-883049-45-4(8)) Sound Room.
Seven of Poe's masterworks of horror & suspense, including his immortal poem, "The Raven," the gruesome mystery, "The Murders in the Rue Morgue," & one of the most brilliantly crafted short stories ever written, "The Fall of the House of Usher.".

Classic Poe. unabr. ed. Short Stories. Edgar Allan Poe. Read by Ralph Cosham. 2 cds. (YA). 2002. audio compact disk 18.95 (978-1-58472-230-4(4), 007, In Aud) Pub: Sound Room. Dist(s): Baker Taylor
The Raven, The Bells, Annabel Lee, Tell-Tale Heart, The Black Cat, The Cask of Ammontillado, MS. Found in A Bottle, The Pit and the Pendulum.

Classic Poe. unabr. ed. Edgar Allan Poe. 2 CDs. (Running Time: 2 hrs. 30 mins.). (YA). (gr. 5-12). 2002. pap. bk. 37.00 (978-1-58472-232-8(0), In Aud) Sound Room.
Includes The Raven, The Bells, Annabel Lee, Tell-Tale Heart, The Black Cat, The Cask of Ammontillado, MS. Found in a Bottle, The Pit and the Pendulum. Includes book.

Classic Poe, Set. unabr. ed. Edgar Allan Poe. Read by Ralph Cosham. 2 cass. (Running Time: 3 hrs. 15 mins.). (Poe Ser.). 1994. bk. 16.95 (978-1-883049-39-3(3), 390525, Commuters Library) Sound Room.
Poe's masterworks of horror & suspense, including his immortal poem, "The Raven," the gruesome mystery, "The Murders in the Rue Morgue," & one of the most brilliantly crafted short stories ever written, "The Fall of the House of Usher." Also "The Tell-Tale Heart," "The Cask of Amontillado" "The Black Cat" & "The Black Cat.".

Classic Pooh Treasury Vol. 3: The House At Pooh Corner, Set. Short Stories. A. A. Milne. Prod. by Peter Dennis. Illus. by Ernest H. Shepard. 3 cass. (J). 1997. bk. (978-1-57375-465-1(X)) Audioscope.
Ten stories, including: "In Which a House Is Built At Pooh Corner for Eeyore," "In Which It Is Shown that Tiggers Don't Climb Trees," & "In Which Tigger Is Unbounced.".

Classic Praise: B Flat Clarinet. James Curnow & Timothy Johnson. 2009. pap. bk. 12.99 (978-1-4234-6857-8(0), 1423468570) H Leonard.

Classic Praise: B Flat Tenor Saxophone. James Curnow & Timothy Johnson. 2009. pap. bk. 12.99 (978-1-4234-6859-2(7), 1423468597) H Leonard.

Classic Praise: B Flat Trumpet. James Curnow & Timothy Johnson. 2009. pap. bk. 12.99 (978-1-4234-6861-5(9), 1423468619) H Leonard.

Classic Praise: E Flat Alto Saxophone. James Curnow & Timothy Johnson. 2009. pap. bk. 12.99 (978-1-4234-6858-5(9), 1423468589) H Leonard.

Classic Praise: E Flat Horn. James Curnow & Timothy Johnson. 2009. pap. bk. 12.99 (978-1-4234-6863-9(5), 1423468635) H Leonard.

Classic Praise: F Horn. James Curnow & Timothy Johnson. 2009. pap. bk. 12.99 (978-1-4234-6862-2(7), 1423468627) H Leonard.

Classic Praise: Flute. James Curnow & Timothy Johnson. 2009. pap. bk. 12.99 (978-1-4234-6855-4(4), 1423468554) H Leonard.

Classic Praise: Trombone/Euphonium/Bassoon. James Curnow & Timothy Johnson. 2009. pap. bk. 12.99 (978-1-4234-6865-3(1), 1423468651) H Leonard.

***Classic Punk: Guitar Play-along Volume 102.** Created by Hal Leonard Corp. 2010. pap. bk. 14.99 (978-1-4234-4325-4(X), 142344325X) H Leonard.

Classic Rags of Scott Joplin. Mel Bay Staff. 1996. spiral bd. 22.95 (978-0-7866-2563-5(5)) Mel Bay.

Classic Ragtime Guitar Solos. Compiled by Stefan Grossman. (Guitar Workshop Ser.). 1995. bk. 19.95 (978-1-56222-067-9(5), 94505BCD) Mel Bay.

Classic Railway Murders: Four Mysteries. Read by Patrick Malahide. 2002. pap. bk. (978-1-873859-71-1(6)) CSA Telltapes GBR.

Classic Railway Murders: Four Mysteries. 4th unabr. ed. Emmuska Orczy et al. Read by Patrick Malahide. 2 cass. (Running Time: 3 hrs.). 2001. 17.95 (978-1-57270-196-0(X), N21196u) Pub: Audio Partners. Dist(s): PerseuPGW
A murder committed in full view of the passengers, yet no one can identify the killer. A notorious villain dupes the police & escapes with ingenuity & audacity. A murderer who escapes from a moving train while his victims & an innocent bystander are locked in their compartment. A man's body found on the tracks could not have been thrown out of the train as supposed by the police. How did it get there?.

Classic Redemption. Kenneth Copeland. 4 cass. 1983. 20.00 Set incl. study guide. (978-0-938458-58-6(2)) K Copeland Pubns.
Biblical redemption.

Classic Religion & Myths of the Mediterrean. unabr. ed. Jon David Solomon. Read by Ben Kingsley. Ed. by Walter Harrelson & Mike Hassell. Prod. by Pat Childs. (Running Time: 10800 sec.). (Religion, Scriptures, & Spirituality Ser.). 2006. audio compact disk 25.95 (978-0-7861-6479-0(4)) Pub: Blckstn Audio. Dist(s): NetLibrary CO

Classic Rock: 1968. 1999. 9.99 (M7GN21); audio compact disk 9.99 (M8G371) Time-Life.

Classic Romance. abr. ed. Jane Eyre & Anna Karenina. Intro. by Alex Jennings. (Running Time: 17377 sec.). (Classic Fiction Collections). 2006. audio compact disk 28.98 (978-962-634-430-9(X), Naxos AudioBooks) Naxos.

Classic Russian Short Stories, Vol. 1. unabr. ed. Alexander Pushkin et al. 3 cass. (Running Time: 4 hrs. 30 mins.). 2002. 24.00 (978-1-929718-10-8(1), 2201-4) Audio Conn.
Selections include: The Shot, The Overcoat, The Tryst, The Wedding, A Prisoner in the Caucasus and An Upheaval.

Classic Science Fiction Stories. Read by Nicky Henson. 2 cass. 1998. 16.85 Set. (978-1-901768-16-9(3)) Pub: CSA Telltapes GBR. Dist(s): Ulverscroft US

Classic Science Fiction Stories. abr. ed. Read by Nicky Henson. 1 cass. 1993. 12.00 (978-1-878427-18-2(0), XC406) Cimino Pub Grp.

***Classic Series.** Kenneth Copeland & Gloria Copeland. (ENG.). 2010. 30.00 (978-1-60463-082-4(5)) K Copeland Pubns.

Classic Sermons. Ian R. K. Paisley. 4 CDs. (Running Time: 6 hrs.). 1999. audio compact disk 24.99 (978-1-889893-34-1(X)) Emerald House Group Inc.

Classic Short Stories. unabr. ed. Read by George Guidall & Frank Muller. 3 cass. (Running Time: 2 hrs.). 1998. 26.00 Set. (95219) Recorded Bks.
Includes: "The Gift of the Magi" "The Last Leaf" "The Bride Comes to Yellow Sky" & "The Lady with the Toy Dog".

Classic Short Stories, unabr. ed. Short Stories. O. Henry et al. Narrated by George Guidall & Frank Muller. 3 cass. (Running Time: 2 hrs.). 1998. 26.00 (978-0-7887-0995-1(X), 95219E7) Recorded Bks.
Includes:"The Gift of the Magi", "The Last Leaf", "The Bride Comes to Yellow Sky" & "The Lady with a Toy Dog.".

Classic Short Stories for Women. abr. ed. Read by Harriet Walter. 2 cass. (Running Time: 3 hrs.). 1996. 12.00 Set. (978-1-878427-52-6(0), XC451) Cimino Pub Grp.
Six classic stories - six marital relationships! Isobel in Katherine Mansfield's "Marriage a la Mode" embraces fashionable "Bloomsbury" values & sacrifices the most important thing of all...the Thorburns who only survive in their fantasy world of "rabbits" in Lappin & Lapinova by Virginia Woolf...Edith Wharton shows a deft comic touch in the heart-warming story of the lethbury's problems in marrying off their daughter in "The Mission of Jane"...passion, betrayal & murder in "The Red Room" by L. M. Montgomery...a poor country girl marries into a tilted & wealthy family with unfortunate results in Mary Shelley's "The Parvenue...& a woman's terrifying descent into madness in Charlotte Perkins Gilman's famous story, "The Yellow Wallpaper".

Classic Short Stories for Women, Set. Short Stories. Contrib. by Cimino Staff. 4 cass. 1997. 19.95 (978-1-878427-55-7(5)) Cimino Pub Grp.

Classic Short Story Collection. Read by Emma Hignett. (Running Time: 1 hr.). 2005. 16.95 (978-1-59912-921-1(3)) Iofy Corp.

Classic Sing Along, Vol. 1. unabr. ed. 1 cass. (Sing-Along Ser.). (J). bk. 11.99 (978-0-7634-0019-4(X)) W Disney Records.

Classic Sing Along, Vol. 2. unabr. ed. 1 cass. (Sing-Along Ser.). (J). bk. 11.99 (978-0-7634-0020-0(3)) W Disney Records.

***Classic Songs: Accordion Play-along Volume 3.** Created by Hal Leonard Corp. (ENG.). 2010. pap. bk. 14.99 (978-1-4234-9559-8(4), 1423495594) H Leonard.

Classic Speeches. Irving Younger. 7 cass. 90.00 Set. PEG MN.

Classic Stories for Boys & Girls. Short Stories. Mark Binder. As told by Mark Binder. 1 CD. (Running Time: 60 mins.). (J). 2004. audio compact disk 14.95 (978-0-9702642-1-3(6)) Light Pubns.
Winner of the Children's Music Web Award and the iParenting Media Award, "Classic Stories for Boys and Girls" contains 10 original and traditional stories that children and parents will listen to again and again. Includes: Jack and the Beanstalk, Golidlocks and the Three Bears, The Three Little Pigs, George Washington and the Cherry Tree, Paul Bunyan and more.

Classic Stories of Crime & Murder. Read by Jack Shepherd & Brian Cox. 4 cass. (Running Time: 6 hrs.). 2002. 12.99 (978-1-57815-247-6(X), 4426, Media Bks Audio) Media Bks NJ.

Classic Tales: Goldilocks & the Three Bears - Little Red Riding Hood Cassette. Sue Arengo. (Classic Tales Ser.). 1999. 14.75 (978-0-19-422033-0(8)) OUP.

***Classic Tales: Thumbelina & Jack & the Beanstalk Cassette (American English)** Sue Arengo. 2005. 13.25 (978-0-19-422540-3(2)) Pub: OUP-GBR GBR. Dist(s): OUP

Classic Tales of Horror. Read by Patrick Malahide. 2 cass. (Running Time: 3 hrs.). 12.00 Set. (978-1-878427-45-8(8), XC445) Cimino Pub Grp.
This collection includes the first ever recorded version of one of the most famous horror stories of all time, "The Monkey's Paw" by W. W. Jacobs. What collection would not be complete without a Poe, the macabre happenings at a party involving a man in "The Masque of the Red Death," a rare M. R. James which features the trial of Martin by the hanging judge & Bram Stoker's tale of the black cat gaining his revenge-not for the squemish. Also includes: "Timber" by John Galsworthy, "Caterpillars" by E. F. Benson, "A Tale of Terror" by Thomas Hood, & "The Man in the Bell" by W. E. Aytoun.

Classic Tales of Horror & Vampires. abr. ed. Robert Louis Stevenson & Arthur Conan Doyle. 1 cass. (Running Time: 1 hr. 30 mins.). 2001. 12.99 (978-1-57815-248-3(8), Media Bks Audio) Media Bks NJ.

Classic Tales of Humour. Read by Nigel Hawthorne. 2 cass. (Running Time: 3 hrs.). 1998. 16.85 Set. (978-1-901768-21-3(X)) Pub: CSA Telltapes GBR. Dist(s): Ulverscroft US

Classic Tales of Humour. Read by Nigel Hawthorne. 2 cass. (Running Time: 3 hrs.). 12.00 Set. (978-1-878427-49-6(0), XC432) Cimino Pub Grp.
British humour at its best. These stories have been chosen based on literary merit, their capacity to sound even funnier when read aloud & above all because there is much to laugh about. So from Kipling's inebriated characters journeying from the London dock to Hammersmith in a wheel barrow to the classic village cricket match from England their England. From Saki's sardonic view of upper-middle class house parties to Dickens' classic case of mistaken identity. Contains: "Brugglesmith," "The Cricket Match from England Their England," "Macdonell, Reginald on House Parties," "The Great Winglebury Duel," "The Celebrated Jumping Frog of Calaveras County," "A Photographer's Day Out" & "Jeff Veters is a Personal Magnet".

Classic Tales of Murder. Read by Brian Cox. 1 cass. 12.00 (978-1-878427-31-1(8), XC413) Cimino Pub Grp.

Classic Tales of Mystery & the Supernatural. abr. ed. Read by Robin Bailey. 1 cass. 1993. 12.00 (978-1-878427-17-5(2), XC404) Cimino Pub Grp.

Classic Tales of the Paranormal. Read by Robin Bailey. 2 cass. 1998. 16.85 Set. (978-1-901768-17-6(1)) Pub: CSA Telltapes GBR. Dist(s): Ulverscroft US

Classic Tales of the Paranormal. unabr. ed. Edgar Wallace. 2001. 7.95 (978-1-57815-256-8(9)) Media Bks NJ.

Classic Tape, No. 1. 1 cass. (Classic Tapes Ser.). 1983. 6.50 (978-0-933685-04-8(1), TP-01) A A Grapevine.
Features readings of articles from the AA Grapevine magaxine.

Classic Tape, No. 2. 1 cass. (Classic Tapes Ser.). 1984. 6.50 (978-0-933685-05-5(X), TP-02) A A Grapevine.
Includes readings of articles from the AA Grapevine magazine.

Classic Tape, No. 3. 1 cass. (Classic Tapes Ser.). 1985. 6.50 (978-0-933685-03-1(3), TP-03) A A Grapevine.
Features readings of articles from the AA Grapevine magazine.

Classic Thrillers: Dracula - Frankenstein. Bram Stoker & Mary Wollstonecraft Shelley. Read by Daniel Philpott et al. Perf. by Brian Cox et al. 5 cass. (Running Time: 6 hrs. 30 min.). 2001. 27.98 (978-962-634-741-6(4), NA524114, Naxos AudioBooks); audio compact disk 34.98 (978-962-634-241-1(2), NA524112, Naxos AudioBooks) Naxos.
Dracula - This classic horror story expressing the most persistent nightmare of the human condition, is brought to life by a skilled and imaginative cast, coupled with authentic 'monster music'. Frankenstein - Gothic tale of a human being, which runs amok, one of the most vivid horror stories.

Classic Thrillers: Dracula - Frankenstein. abr. ed. Bram Stoker & Mary Wollstonecraft Shelley. Read by Brian Cox et al. 5 cass. (Running Time: 6 hrs. 30 min.). 2001. 27.98 (Naxos AudioBooks) Naxos.

Classic Thrillers (Dracula/Frankenstein) Bram Stoker et al. (Running Time: 6 hrs. 30 mins.). 2005. 36.95 (978-1-60083-708-1(5)) Iofy Corp.

Classic Tracks. Perf. by Ladysmith Black Mambazo. 1 cass. (J). 9.98 (2511); audio compact disk 15.98 (D2511) MFLP CA.
Highly talented a capella singers presenting their majestic Zulu harmonies.

Classic Treasury of Nursery Songs & Rhymes. Tracey Moroney. 1 CD. (J). 2005. audio compact disk (978-1-86503-696-0(X)) Five MileAUS AUS.

Classic Twain: 10 Stories. Mark Twain. Narrated by Thomas Becker. (Running Time: 19800 sec.). (Unabridged Classics in MP3 Ser.). (ENG.). 2008. audio compact disk 24.00 (978-1-58472-636-4(9), In Aud) Sound Room.

Classic Vampire Short Stories. Read by Richard Pasco. 2 cass. (Running Time: 3 hrs.). 1996. 12.00 Set. (978-1-878427-50-2(4), XC454) Cimino Pub Grp.
This chilling selection of vampire stories makes no apology for its broad interpretation of the genre. The stories range from traditional bloodsuckers - the "undead" who sustain a deadly existence by preying on the life-blood of the living - like Bram Stoker's seminal Dracula's Guest & E. F. Benson's Mrs. Amworth - to others rich in vampire imagery, as in Poe's Gothic tale, Ligeia, in which a dead woman takes possession of a living soul, the story of the dreadful appetites of Hoffman's "Aurelia" & Rudyard Kipling's "The Mark of the Beast" in which a deadly bite revenges a desecrated Indian God with fearful consequences. Richard Pasco's deep & resonant tones will be sure to send chills down your spine with this ghoulish potpourri of vampirism.

Classic Weight Release. Created by Victoria Wizell. Voice by Victoria Wizell. 2 CDs. 2004. audio compact disk 39.00 (978-0-9679176-1-0(1)) Hyptalk.
Hypnosis for weight management is proven effective and supportive to your general health and well-being. Successful weight reduction can be accomplished once you put the power of your mind to work in managing your body.

Classic Wizard of Oz. 1 cass. (Running Time: 1 hr.). 2002. 19.95 Listen & Live.

Classic Wizard of Oz: The Wizard of Oz, the Land of Oz. unabr. ed. Original Script. 2 cass. (Running Time: 3 hrs.). (Full - Cast Productions Ser.). (J). 2002. 19.95 (978-1-931953-12-2(0), AA103) Listen & Live.
Join Dorothy, Toto, Scarecrow, Tin Man and the Cowardly Lion as they journey down the yellow brick road in search of the great and powerful Wizard of Oz. Marvel at the magical ruby slippers, shudder at the evil Wicked Witch of the West, and giggle along with the munchkins. This full-cast production brings new life to one of the best-known stories of our time.

Classic Women's Short Stories. Read by Harriet Walter. 2 cass. 1999. 16.85 Set. (978-1-901768-30-5(9)) Pub: CSA Telltapes GBR. Dist(s): Ulverscroft US
Includes "The Legacy," "Virginia Woolf," "The Violet Car," "E.E. Nesbitt," & many more.

Classic Women's Short Stories. Read by Harriet Walter. 1 cass. 12.00 (978-1-878427-36-6(9), XC429) Cimino Pub Grp.
Contains: "The Wronged Woman" - Winifred Holtby, "The Violet Car" - E. E. Nesbitt, "The Legacy" - Virginia Woolf, "The Bliss" - Katherine Mansfield, "Atrophy" - Edith Wharton, "The Half Brothers" - Elizabeth Gaskell.

Classic Women's Short Stories. Read by Harriet Walter. 2 cass. (Running Time: 3 hrs.). 7.95 (978-1-57815-284-1(4), 1177, Media Bks Audio) Media Bks NJ.

Classic Women's Short Stories. unabr. ed. Mary Wollstonecraft Shelley et al. 2001. 12.99 (978-1-57815-250-6(X), Media Bks Audio) Media Bks NJ.

Classic Women's Short Stories, No. 1-2. Read by Harriet Walter. 2002. pap. bk. (978-1-873859-91-9(0)) CSA Telltapes GBR.

Classic Women's Short Stories, No. 2. Read by Harriet Walter. 2 cass. 1999. 16.85 Set. (978-1-901768-31-2(7)) Pub: CSA Telltapes GBR. Dist(s): Ulverscroft US
Includes "Marriage a la Mode," "Katherine Mansfield," "Lapin & Lappinove" & many more.

Classic Women's Short Stories, No. 3. Read by Harriet Walter. 2 cass. (Running Time: 3 hrs.). 2002. (978-1-901768-35-0(X)) CSA Telltapes GBR.

Classic Women's Short Stories: The Garden Party - Daughters of the Late Colonel - Lilacs - Ma'ame Pelagie - A Mark on the Wall. Katherine Mansfield et al. Read by Carole Boyd et al. (Running Time: 2 hrs. 30 mins.). 2005. 20.95 (978-1-60083-709-8(3)) Iofy Corp.

Classic Women's Short Stories: The Garden Party - Daughters of the Late Colonel - Lilacs - Ma'ame Pelagie - A Mark on the Wall. Short Stories. Katherine Mansfield et al. Read by Liza Ross & Teresa Gallagher. 2 cass. (Running Time: 3 hrs.). 2001. 13.98 (978-962-634-738-6(4), NA223814, Naxos AudioBooks); audio compact disk 17.98 (978-962-634-238-1(2), NA223812, Naxos AudioBooks) Naxos.
Collection by influential women writers from the close of the 19th century and the first decades of the 20th century.

Classic Women's Short Stories: The Garden Party - Daughters of the Late Colonel - Lilacs - Ma'ame Pelagie - A Mark on the Wall. unabr. ed. Katherine Mansfield et al. Read by Liza Ross & Teresa Gallagher. 2 cass. (Running Time: 3 hrs.). 2001. 13.98 (Naxos AudioBooks); audio compact disk 15.98 (Naxos AudioBooks) Naxos.

Classic 100 Poems. unabr. ed. Read by Ensemble of Contemporary Poets. (YA). 2006. 44.99 (978-1-59895-211-7(0)) Find a World.

Classical Animals. 1 CD. (Running Time: 30 min.). (J). 2001. audio compact disk 12.98 (978-1-892309-86-0(6)) Pub: Baby Einstn. Dist(s): Penton Overseas

Classical Archaeology of Ancient Greece & Rome. Instructed by John R. Hale. 18 cass. (Running Time: 18 hrs.). 149.95 (978-1-59803-211-6(9)) Teaching Co.

Classical Archaeology of Ancient Greece & Rome. Instructed by John R. Hale. 18 CDs. (Running Time: 18 hrs.). 2006. audio compact disk 99.95 (978-1-59803-212-3(7)) Teaching Co.

Classical Baby Vol. 1: Awake Time. Arranged by James Incorvaia. 1 cass., 1 CD. (Baby Tunes Ser.). (J). 4.78 (KID 72948); audio compact disk 7.98 CD Jewel box. (KID 72948) NewSound.
Addresses researchers' recent findings that early exposure to classical music increases children's mathematics & logic skills.

Classical Baby Vol. 2: Sleepy Time. 1 cass., 1 CD. (Baby Tunes Ser.). (J). 4.78 (KID 72950); audio compact disk 7.98 CD Jewel box. (KID 72950) NewSound.

Classical Baby Mozart: Sleepy Time Mozart for Babies. (Baby Tunes Ser.). (J). (ps). 1998. audio compact disk 10.98 (978-1-56826-883-5(1)) Masquerade.

Classical Baby Mozart: Sleepy Time Mozart for Babies. unabr. ed. 1 cass. (Running Time: 35 min.). 1999. 5.98 (978-1-56826-882-8(3), 72949) Rhino Enter.
Develop your infant's mind as they drift off to sleep with the soothing side of Mozart's music.

Classical Baby: Mozartz: Awake Time. unabr. ed. 1 CD. (Running Time: 35 min.). 1999. audio compact disk 10.98 (978-1-56826-880-4(7)) Rhino Enter.

Classical Cats: A Children's Introduction to the Orchestra with Book. David Chesky. 1 cass. (Running Time: 58 min.). (J). (ps-3). 1997. 11.95 CD. (978-0-9658787-0-8(8)); 9.95 (978-0-9658787-1-5(6)) Chesky Recs.
Felines Maestro Leopold, Fidelo, Christina, and Furbert talk about the instruments that make up the orchestra. Brief demonstrations are given of 23 instruments.

Classical Civilisation for OCR AS Oxbox CD-ROM. Julian Morgan. (YA). 2010. audio compact disk 300.00 (978-0-19-912660-6(7)) OUP.

Classical Civilisation for OCR A2 Oxbox CD-ROM. Julian Morgan. (ENG.). (YA). 2010. audio compact disk 300.00 (978-0-19-912661-3(5)) OUP.

Classical Dolphin. Perf. by Gary Clausing. Ed. by Randy E. Beres & Charles W. Beres. 1 cass. (Running Time: 45 min.). 1993. 9.95 (978-1-883152-02-4(X)); 15.95 compact disc. (978-1-883152-03-1(8)) Amirra Pr.
A hypnotic blending of harmony & nature combines the soothing sounds of light classical & original music with the sounds of wild dolphins at rest & play.

Classical Economists. Read by Louis Rukeyser. (Running Time: 10800 sec.). (Great Economic Thinkers Ser.). 2006. audio compact disk 25.95 (978-0-7861-6975-7(3)) Pub: Blckstn Audio. Dist(s): NetLibrary CO

Classical Economists. unabr. ed. E. G. West. Ed. by Israel M. Kirzner & Mike Hassell. Narrated by Louis Rukeyser. 2 cass. (Running Time: 80 min. per cass.). Dramatization. (Great Economic Thinkers Ser.). (YA). (gr. 10 up). 1988. 17.95 (978-0-938935-31-5(3), 10201) Knowledge Prod.
In the 18th century, some viewed economics as a branch of moral philosophy, while others called it "political arithmetic." These cassettes examine the breakthrough of the classical school, which included Adam Smith, David Ricardo, Thomas Malthus & John Stuart Mill.

Classical Economists: Beginning a New World of Economic Insight. unabr. ed. Read by Louis Rukeyser. 3 CDs. (Running Time: 10800 sec.). (Great Economic Thinkers Ser.). 2006. audio compact disk 17.95 (978-0-7861-6893-4(5)) Blckstn Audio.

Classical Education & the Homeschool AudioBook. Wesley Callihan et al. Read by Aaron Wells. (ENG.). 2007. audio compact disk 10.00 (978-1-59128-200-6(4)) Canon Pr ID.

Classical Favorites on Piano. David Glen Hatch. 1 cass. 9.95 (109401); audio compact disk 14.95 (289401) Covenant Comms.

Classical FUN Sing-A-Longs. Lyrics by Robert N. Franki. Prod. by Classical Fun Music Inc. Lyrics by Claire Li Franki. 1. (Running Time: 55). (J). 2004. audio compact disk 14.95 (978-0-9759927-2-2(4)) Classical Fun.

Classical Gas. Ed. by Aaron Stang. Arranged by Bill Purse. (Warner Bros. Publications 21st Century Guitar Ensemble Ser.). (ENG.). 2002. audio compact disk 19.95 (978-0-7579-9726-6(0), Warner Bro) Alfred Pub.

Classical Greats: Easy Playalong for Recorder. Daniel Scott. 2004. bk. 14.95 (978-0-7119-9144-6(8)) Pub: Music Sales. Dist(s): H Leonard

Classical Greats: Easy Playalong for Clarinet. Arranged by Daniel Scott. 2004. audio compact disk 12.95 (978-0-7119-9142-2(1)) Pub: Music Sales. Dist(s): H Leonard

Classical Greats: Easy Playalong for Flute. Arranged by Daniel Scott. 2004. bk. 14.95 (978-0-7119-9143-9(X)) Pub: Music Sales. Dist(s): H Leonard

Classical Greeks. unabr. ed. Michael Grant. Read by Nadia May. 8 cass. (Running Time: 11 hrs. 30 mins.). 1991. 56.95 set. (978-0-7861-0242-6(X), 1212) Blckstn Audio.
The "Golden Age" of Greek civilization, the period from the first wars against Persia & Carthage in the early fifth century B. C. to Alexander the Great's accession in 336 B. C. Never have so many varied talents & so much genius flourished within so short a period. This was the time of Sophocles, Aristophanes, Herodotus, Aristotle, Socrates & Plato. This is an ideal historical introduction to very early Greece.

Classical Guitar. 2004. bk. 12.95 (978-0-7119-9180-4(4)) Music Sales.

Classical Guitar for Beginners. Nathaniel Gunod. (ENG.). 1996. audio compact disk 9.95 (978-0-7390-1789-0(6)) Alfred Pub.

Classical Guitar Method for Young Beginners Book 2. Connie Bull. (J). 2008. pap. bk. 14.95 (978-1-86469-200-6(6)) Kolala Music SGP.

Classical Guitar Method I. 1 CD. (Running Time: 1 hr.). audio compact disk (978-0-7390-1984-9(8), 19488) Alfred Pub.

Classical Guitar Method 2. 1 CD. (Running Time: 1 hr.). audio compact disk (978-0-7390-1987-0(2), 19491) Alfred Pub.

Classical Guitar Method 3. 1 CD. (Running Time: 1 hr.). audio compact disk (978-0-7390-1990-0(2), 19494) Alfred Pub.

Classical Guitar Method 4. 1 CD. (Running Time: 1 hr.). audio compact disk (978-0-7390-1993-1(7), 19497) Alfred Pub.

Classical Guitar Standards. (iSong Ser.). 1999. audio compact disk 24.95 (978-0-634-01110-8(3), 00451026) Pub: iSong. Dist(s): H Leonard

Classical Guitar Standards, Vol. 2. 1999. audio compact disk 24.95 (978-0-634-01150-4(2)) Pub: iSong. Dist(s): H Leonard

Classical Kids. Susan Hammond. 4 cass. (Running Time: 6 hrs.). (J). 1991. 31.94 (978-1-895404-49-4(5)) Pub: Child Group CAN. Dist(s): Consort Bk Sales

Classical Kids Music Box, Vol. 1. Susan Hammond. Perf. by Classical Kids. 3 cass., 1 CD. (J). 22.38 Set. (CG 84274); audio compact disk 38.38 CD Set, Jewel box. (CG 84274) NewSound.
A little bit of history & the world's best loved classical music set the scene for musical adventures. Includes "Beethoven Lives Upstairs," "Vivaldi's Ring of Mystery," & "Hallelujah Handel".

Classical Kids Music Box, Vol. 2. Susan Hammond. Perf. by Classical Kids. 3 cass., 3 CDs. (J). 22.38 Set. (CG 84275); audio compact disk 38.38 CD Set, Jewel box. (CG 84275) NewSound.
Includes "Mozart's Magic Fantasy," a young girl finds herself in the world of Mozart's "Magic Flute." "Tchaikovsky Discovers America," Tchaikovsky arrives in New York in 1891 for the grand opening of Carnegie Hall & takes a surprise adventure by train to Niagara Falls. "Mr. Bach Comes to Call," Bach visits a little girl at the piano & brings along his magical orchestra & choir featuring (among others) pieces Bach wrote specifically for children.

Classical Loon. 1 cass. (Running Time: 60 min.). 1994. audio compact disk 15.95 CD. (0289, Creativ Pub) Quayside.
Unique & memorable sounds of the loon drift through a series of richly orchestrated classical themes.

Classical Loon. 1 cass. (Running Time: 60 min.). 1994. 9.95 (0288, NrthWrd Bks) TandN Child.

Classical Loon Two. 1 cass. (Running Time: 60 min.). 1994. audio compact disk 15.95 CD. (2014, Creativ Pub) Quayside.
Classical works of the Masters meet the calls of the loons.

Classical Loon Two. 1 cass. (Running Time: 60 min.). 1994. 9.95 (2012, NrthWrd Bks) TandN Child.

Classical Love Poetry. (Running Time: 2 hrs. 15 mins.). 2002. 22.95 (978-1-60083-710-4(7)) Iofy Corp.

Classical Lullabies. Kidzup Productions Staff. 1 cass. (Running Time: 30 min.). (Lullabies Ser.). (J). 2000. 7.99 (978-1-894281-03-4(9)); audio compact disk 9.99 (978-1-894281-04-1(7)) Pub: Kidzup Prodns. Dist(s): Penton Overseas
Mind soothing collection of the world's best loved classic pieces. Includes musical masterpieces by Mozart, Bach, Beethoven, Brahms and more.

Classical Masterpieces for Bass. Josquin DesPeres. 1997. pap. bk. 19.95 (978-0-7866-2890-2(1), 96307BCD) Mel Bay.

Classical Masters, Vol. 1. Penton. 1 CD. (Running Time: 1 hr. 30 mins.). (Baby's First Ser.). (ENG.). (J). 2003. audio compact disk 7.95 (978-1-59125-329-7(2)) Penton Overseas.

Classical Masters, Vol. 2. Penton. 1 cass. (Running Time: 1 hr. 30 mins.). (Baby's First Ser.). (ENG.). (J). 2003. audio compact disk 7.95 (978-1-59125-330-3(6)) Penton Overseas.

Classical Music. 1 cass., 1 CD. (Running Time: 1 hr.). (Lullaby Ser.). (J). (TWIN 163); audio compact disk (TWIN 163) NewSound.

Classical Music. Compact Disc Staff. 1 cass.; 1 CD. (Running Time: 60 min.). (Growing Minds with Music Ser.). (J). 1998. audio compact disk 12.99 CD. (978-1-57583-071-1(X)) Twin Sisters.
Featuring fourteen original arrangements of the renowned music of Bach, Mozart, Pachelbel, Beethoven, Strauss, Haydn, Brahms, & other famous composers.

Classical Music. Twin Sisters Productions Staff. 1 cass.; 1 CD. (Running Time: 60 min.). (Growing Minds with Music Ser.). (J). 1998. 8.99 (978-1-57583-072-8(8)) Twin Sisters.

Classical Music. unabr. ed. Twin Sisters Productions. Read by Twin Sisters. (YA). 2008. 59.99 (978-1-60514-880-9(6)) Find a World.

Classical Music for Clarinet & Piano. Perf. by Vladislav Celik. 1 cass. (Running Time: 30 min.). 6.95 (978-1-883993-03-0(2)) Music Inst CA.

Classical Music for Clarinet & Piano. Vladislav Celik. 1 cass. (Running Time: 30 min.). 1991. 9.95 Music Inst CA.
Side A: G. Bonnard: Rondo; Z. Vauda: Sonata Brevis. Side B: H. Gagnebin: Andante Et Allegro; A. Messager: Solo De Concours.

Classical Music for Sleep. Jeffrey Thompson. (Running Time: 1:09:00). 2003. audio compact disk 11.95 (978-1-55961-669-0(5)) Sounds True.

Classical Music of Iran: Dastgah Systems. Contrib. by Ella Zonis & Ruhollah Khaleqi. 1 cass. or CD. (Running Time: 71 min.). 1991. (0-9307-400390-9307-40039-2-3); audio compact disk (0-9307-40039-2-3) Smithsonian Folkways.

Classical Music 101. Fred Plotkin. Read by Fred Plotkin. 14 cass. (Running Time: 19 hrs. 30 mins.). 2004. 89.95 (978-0-7861-2636-1(1), 3242) Blckstn Audio.

Classical Music 101. Fred Plotkin. Read by Fred Plotkin. (Running Time: 19 hrs. 30 mins.). 2004. 50.95 (978-1-59912-451-3(3)) Iofy Corp.

Classical Music 101. unabr. ed. Fred Plotkin. Read by Fred Plotkin. 16 CDs. (Running Time: 19 hrs. 30 mins.). 2004. audio compact disk 128.00 (978-0-7861-8733-1(6), 3242) Blckstn Audio.

Classical Mythology, Pts. I-II. Instructed by Elizabeth Vandiver. 12 CDs. (Running Time: 12 hrs.). 2000. bk. 69.95 (978-1-56585-292-1(3), 243); 89.95 (978-1-56585-413-0(6), 243) Teaching Co.

Classical Mythology, Pts. I-II, Vol. 1. Instructed by Elizabeth Vandiver. 12 cass. (Running Time: 12 hrs.). 2000. 54.95 (978-1-56585-037-8(8), 243) Teaching Co.

Classical Mythology, Vol. 2. Instructed by Elizabeth Vandiver. 6 cass. (Running Time: 6 hrs.). 2000. 129.95 (978-1-56585-038-5(6)); audio compact disk 179.95 (978-1-56585-293-8(1)) Teaching Co.

Classical Nature. 1 cass. (Running Time: 60 min.). 1994. 15.95 (2204, Creativ Pub) Quayside.
Classical pieces, masterfully melded with the tone & tenor of nature's most glorious wildlife sounds.

Classical Nature. 1 cass. (Running Time: 60 min.). 1994. 9.95 (2202, NrthWrd Bks) TandN Child.

Classical Nature Two. 1 cass. (Running Time: 60 min.). 1994. audio compact disk 15.95 CD. (2208, Creativ Pub) Quayside.
Music of the great composers in favorite outdoor setting.

Classical Nature Two. 1 cass. (Running Time: 60 min.). 1994. 9.95 (2206, NrthWrd Bks) TandN Child.

Classical Piano Solos for Worship Settings. Compiled by Gail Smith. 1992. bk. 17.95 (978-0-7866-1084-6(0), 94672P) Mel Bay.

Classical Praise from the Heart. Compiled by Denise Renner. 1993. audio compact disk 14.95 (978-0-9621436-8-7(5)) Teach All Nat.

Classical Religions & Myths of the Mediterranean Basin, Set. unabr. ed. Jon D. Solomon. Read by Ben Kingsley. Ed. by Walter Harrelson & Mike Hassell. 2 cass. (Running Time: 3 hrs.). Dramatization. (Religion, Scriptures & Spirituality Ser.). 1994. 17.95 (978-1-56823-017-7(6), 10460) Knowledge Prod.
Mesopotamia, Egypt, Asia Minor, Canaan, Greece, & Rome have greatly & continuously influenced all of Western culture & civilization. Today, theological interest is resurging in goddess worship, in mythologies & technical sciences from Egypt & Mesopotamia. This presentation also discusses how the literature & culture of these religions have influenced Hebrew & Christian scriptures.

Classical Russian Poetry. abr. ed. Perf. by Yevgeny Yevtushenko & Morris Carnovsky. 2 cass. (Running Time: 4 hrs.). Incl. Aleksandr Pushkin. Anna Andreevena Akhmatova. (SWC 2036); All That Lives, from the Earliest Hour. Sergey Yessenin. (SWC 2036); Cloud in Trousers. Vladimir Mayakovsky. (SWC 2036); Farewell, My Friend, Adieu. Sergey Yessenin. (SWC 2036); Gratitude. Mikhail Lermontov. (SWC 2036); I Loved You Once. Alexander Pushkin. (SWC 2036); Last Cataclysm. Fyodor Tyutchev. (SWC 2036); Longing for Motherland-a Fraud. Marina Tzvetaeva. (SWC 2036); Mid Letters Heaped upon the Floor. Fyodor Tyutchev. (SWC 2036); Music Resounds. Anna Andreevena Akhmatova. (SWC 2036); Rebirth. Alexander Pushkin. (SWC 2036); Russia. Fyodor Tyutchev. (SWC 2036); Soldier's Testament. Mikhail Lermontov. (SWC 2036); Thought. Mikhail Lermontov. (SWC 2036); To Chaadayev. Alexander Pushkin. (SWC 2036); Twelve. Alexander Blok. (SWC 2036); Unknown Woman. Alexander Blok. (SWC 2036); Years of My Youth & Glory, Now Quite Askew. Sergey Yessenin. (SWC 2036); (RUS & ENG.). 1977. 19.95 (978-0-694-50393-3(2), SWC 2036) HarperCollins Pubs.

Classical Studies for Clarinet. Himie Voxman. (ENG.). 2005. pap. bk. 19.95 (978-0-634-08681-6(2), 0634086812) H Leonard.

Classical Themes: Level 1. Phillip Keveren. 2003. audio compact disk 10.95 (978-0-634-05108-1(3), 0634051083) H Leonard.

Classical Themes: Level 3. Phillip Keveren. 2003. audio compact disk 10.95 (978-0-634-05110-4(5), 0634051105) H Leonard.

Classical Themes Vol. 2: Level 2. Phillip Keveren. 2003. audio compact disk 10.95 (978-0-634-05109-8(1), 0634051091) H Leonard.

Classical Themes - Level 4: Instrumental Accompaniments. Phillip Keveren. 2003. audio compact disk 10.95 (978-0-634-05111-1(3), 0634051113) H Leonard.

Classical Themes - Level 5. Phillip Keveren. 2003. audio compact disk 10.95 (978-0-634-05112-8(1), 0634051121) H Leonard.

Classical Voice: More Performance Pieces for Male Singers. Created by Chester Music. 2009. pap. bk. 22.95 (978-1-84609-700-3(2)) Chester Music GBR.

Classical Wolf. 1 cass. (Running Time: 60 min.). 1994. audio compact disk 15.95 CD. (2304, Creativ Pub) Quayside.
Songs of wolves in tune with the music of the Masters.

Classical Wolf. 1 cass. (Running Time: 60 min.). 1994. 9.95 (2302, NrthWrd Bks) TandN Child.

Classics: A Very Short Introduction. abr. ed. Mary Beard & John Henderson. 3 CDs. 2005. audio compact disk 22.98 (978-962-634-345-6(1)) Naxos UK GBR.

Classics: A Very Short Introduction: A Very Short Introduction. Mary Beard & John Henderson. Read by Tim Bentinck. (Running Time: 4 hrs.). 2005. 24.95 (978-1-60083-711-1(5)) Iofy Corp.

Classics Anthology Collection: Disc One. Compiled by Red Planet Audiobooks. (ENG.). (J). 2007. audio compact disk 12.99 (978-1-934814-01-7(6)) Red Planet Au.

Classics Anthology Collection: Disc Two. Compiled by Red Planet Audiobooks. (ENG.). (YA). 2007. audio compact disk 12.99 (978-1-934814-02-4(4)) Red Planet Au.

Classics Collection: Gingerbread Man, the; Little Red Hen; & the Velveteen Rabbit. unabr. ed. Karen Schmidt & Margery Williams. Read by Bruce Bailey Johnson & Kathleen McInerney. (J). 2007. 34.99 (978-1-60252-826-0(8)) Find a World.

Classics for Relaxation. (Running Time: 60 mins.). 2002. audio compact disk 15.99 (978-1-904972-49-5(7)) Global Jrny GBR GBR.

Classics for the Young Player: Clarinet - Grade 1. 5. James Curnow. 2003. pap. bk. 12.95 (978-90-431-1407-3(3), 9043114073) H Leonard.

Classics for the Young Player: Flute - Grade 1. 5. James Curnow. 2003. pap. bk. 12.95 (978-90-431-1406-6(5), 9043114065) H Leonard.

Classics for the Young Player: Saxophone - Grade 1. 5. James Curnow. 2003. pap. bk. 12.95 (978-90-431-1408-0(1), 9043114081) H Leonard.

Classics for the Young Player: Trumpet - Grade 1. 5. James Curnow. 2003. pap. bk. 12.95 (978-90-431-1410-3(3), 9043114103) H Leonard.

Classics for Two. Ed. by Patrick Liebergen. Compiled by Patrick Liebergen. (For Two Ser.). (ENG.). 2007. audio compact disk 12.95 (978-0-7390-4389-9(7)) Alfred Pub.

Classics of American Literature. Instructed by Arnold Weinstein. 7 cass. (Running Time: 42 hrs.). 2000. 399.95 Teaching Co.
Course 250, 7 parts, 84 lectures.

Classics of American Literature, Pts. I-VII. Instructed by Arnold Weinstein. 42 CDs. (Running Time: 42 hrs.). 1998. bk. 199.95 (978-1-56585-298-3(2), 250); 149.95 (978-1-56585-044-6(0), 250) Teaching Co.

Classics of American Literature, Vol. 2. Instructed by Arnold Weinstein. 6 cass. (Running Time: 6 hrs.). 1998. 399.95 (978-1-56585-045-3(9)); audio compact disk 549.95 (978-1-56585-299-0(0)) Teaching Co.

Classics of American Literature, Vol. 3. Instructed by Arnold Weinstein. 6 cass. (Running Time: 6 hrs.). 1998. 399.95 (978-1-56585-046-0(7)); audio compact disk 549.95 (978-1-56585-300-3(8)) Teaching Co.

Classics of American Literature, Vol. 4. Instructed by Arnold Weinstein. 6 cass. (Running Time: 6 hrs.). 1998. 399.95 (978-1-56585-047-7(5)); audio compact disk 549.95 (978-1-56585-301-0(6)) Teaching Co.

Classics of American Literature, Vol. 5. Instructed by Arnold Weinstein. 6 cass. (Running Time: 6 hrs.). 1998. 399.95 (978-1-56585-048-4(3)); audio compact disk 549.95 (978-1-56585-302-7(4)) Teaching Co.

Classics of American Literature, Vol. 6. Instructed by Arnold Weinstein. 6 cass. (Running Time: 6 hrs.). 1998. 399.95 (978-1-56585-049-1(1)); audio compact disk 549.95 (978-1-56585-303-4(2)) Teaching Co.

Classics of American Literature, Vol. 7. Instructed by Arnold Weinstein. 6 cass. (Running Time: 6 hrs.). 1998. 399.95 (978-1-56585-050-7(5)); audio compact disk 549.95 (978-1-56585-304-1(0)) Teaching Co.

Classics of British Literature. Instructed by John Sutherland. 2008. 249.95 (978-1-59803-412-7(X)); audio compact disk 129.95 (978-1-59803-413-4(8)) Teaching Co.

Classics of Childhood, Vol. 1: Classic Stories & Tales Read by Celebrities. unabr. ed. (Running Time: 4.5 hrs. NaN mins.). 2008. 19.95 (978-1-4332-6163-3(4)); audio compact disk 40.00 (978-1-4332-6160-2(X)); audio compact disk 34.95 (978-1-4332-6159-6(6)) Blckstn Audio.

Classics of Childhood, Vol. 2: Classic Stories & Tales Read by Celebrities. unabr. ed. Read by celebrity narrators. (Running Time: 4 hrs. 0 mins.). 2009. 19.95 (978-1-4417-1600-2(9)); 24.95 (978-1-4417-1596-8(7)); audio compact disk 49.00 (978-1-4417-1597-5(5)) Blckstn Audio.

***Classics of Childhood, Vol. 3: A Christmas Collection.** (Running Time: 3 hrs. 30 mins.). (Classics Read by Celebrities Ser.). 2010. 19.95 (978-1-4417-6330-3(9)); 24.95 (978-1-4417-6327-3(9)); audio compact disk 30.00 (978-1-4417-6328-0(7)) Blckstn Audio.

Classics of English Poetry for the Elementary Curriculum. unabr. ed. Perf. by Jeremy Brett & Katherine Cornell. 1 cass. (Running Time: 90 min.). Incl. Charge of the Light Brigade. Alfred Lord Tennyson. (J). (CDL5 1301); Gunga Din. Rudyard Kipling. (J). (CDL5 1301); Highwayman. Alfred Noyes. (J). (CDL5 1301); How Do I Love Thee? Elizabeth Barrett Browning. (J). (CDL5 1301); How They Brought the Good News from Ghent to Aix. Robert Browning. (J). (CDL5 1301); Incident of the French Camp. Robert Browning. (J). (CDL5 1301); Law of the Jungle. Rudyard Kipling. (J). (CDL5 1301); Lay of the Last Minstrel - Breathes There a Man. Walter Scott, Sr. (J). (CDL5 1301); Lochinvar. Walter Scott, Sr. (J). (CDL5 1301); My Last Duchess. Robert Browning. (J). (CDL5 1301); Owl & the Pussycat. Edward Lear. (J). (CDL5 1301); Rime of the Ancient Mariner. Samuel Taylor Coleridge. (J). (CDL5 1301); (J). 1984. 8.98 (CDL5 1301) HarperCollins Pubs.
Other performers include: Ronald Fraser, George Grizzard, Boris Karloff, James Mason, Frederick O'Neal, Sir Ralph Richardson, & Cyril Ritchard.

Classics of Russian Literature. Instructed by Irwin Weil. 18 cass. (Running Time: 18 hrs.). 79.95 (978-1-59803-183-6(X)) Teaching Co.

Classics of Russian Literature. Instructed by Irwin Weil. 18 CDs. (Running Time: 18 hrs.). 2006. audio compact disk 99.95 (978-1-59803-185-0(6)) Teaching Co.

Classics of the Christian Faith. Narrated by Max McLean. 2007. audio compact disk 59.95 (978-1-931047-59-3(6)) Fellow Perform Arts.

Classroom, No. 5. 3 cass. 10.00 ea. (978-1-885357-82-3(6)) Rational Isl.
About learning & educational change & the shared experiences of educators using re-evaluation counseling.

Classroom, No. 6. 8 cass. 10.00 ea. (978-1-885357-83-0(4)) Rational Isl.
About learning & educational change, & the shared experiences of educators using re-evaluation counseling.

Classroom, No. 7. 3 cass. 10.00 ea. (978-1-885357-85-4(0)) Rational Isl.
About learning & educational change, & about educators using re-evaluation counseling.

Classroom, No. 8. 4 cass. 10.00 ea. (978-1-885357-86-1(9)) Rational Isl.

Classroom Connections Teacher Guides. Benchmark Education Staff. 2005. audio compact disk 10.00 (978-1-4108-5062-1(5)); audio compact disk 10.00 (978-1-4108-5063-8(3)) Benchmark Educ.

*Classroom Music for Little Mozarts: Student CD, Bk 3: 22 Songs to Bring out the Music in Every Young Child. Alfred Publishing Staff. (Music for Little Mozarts Ser.). (ENG.). (J). 2010. audio compact disk 9.95 (978-0-7390-6524-2(6)) Alfred Pub.

*Classroom Music for Little Mozarts 1: Student CD. Contrib. by Donna Brink Fox et al. (Music for Little Mozarts Ser.). (ENG.). (J). 2009. audio compact disk 9.95 (978-0-7390-6505-1(X)) Alfred Pub.

*Classroom Music for Little Mozarts 2: Student CD. Contrib. by Donna Brink Fox et al. (Music for Little Mozarts Ser.). (ENG.). (J). 2009. audio compact disk 9.95 (978-0-7390-6506-8(8)) Alfred Pub.

Classroom TOEFL Teacher's Kit. Lloyd Precious et al. 4 cass. (Running Time: 6 hrs.). 1993. bk. & tchr. ed. 79.95 set. (978-0-8120-8027-8(0)) Barron.
Program designed specifically for classroom use will meet expanding demands by teachers of English as a foreign language.

Classroom TOEFL Test, Set. Lloyd Precious et al. 4 cass. 1993. 40.00 (978-0-8120-1516-4(9)) Barron.

Claude Bolling. Read by Claude Bolling. 1 cass. (Running Time: 1 hr.). (Marian McPartland's Piano Jazz Ser.). 13.95 (MM-88-04-09, HarperThor) HarpC GBR.

Claude Bolling - Suite for Flute & Jazz Piano Trio. Claude Bolling & Jean-Pierre Rampal. 2008. audio compact disk 16.95 (978-1-4234-3653-9(9), 1423436539) H Leonard.

Claude Chabrol, Autoportrait, Set. Featuring Claude Chabrol. 2 cass. (FRE.). 1996. 26.95 (1807-RF) Olivia & Hill.
Chabrol, one of France's leading movie directors, tells the story of his youth & adolescence in Paris & the provinces. Followed by his reading of seven short mystery stories.

Claude Money. (Language of Mathematics Ser.). 1989. 7.92 (978-0-8123-6428-6(7)) Holt McDoug.

Claude Pepper: The Elderly, Health Care, & the Election. Claude Pepper. Read by Claude Pepper. 1 cass. (Running Time: 1 hr.). 10.95 (K0400B090, HarperThor) HarpC GBR.

Claudel, Valery, Mauriac, Saint-John Perse. Poems. 1 cass. (Golden Treasury of Poetry & Prose Ser.). 1991. 16.95 (1057-SA) Olivia & Hill.

Claudel, Valery, Mauriac, Saint-John Perse. unabr. ed. 1 cass. (FRE.). 15.95 (CFR420) J Norton Pubs.

Claudette Colvin: Twice Toward Justice. unabr. ed. Phillip Hoose. Read by Channie Waites. (Running Time: 4 hrs.). 2009. 19.99 (978-1-4418-0238-5(X), 9781441802385, Brilliance MP3); 39.97 (978-1-4418-0239-2(8), 9781441802392, Brlnc Audio MP3 Lib); 39.97 (978-1-4418-0241-5(X), 9781441802415, BADLE); 19.99 (978-1-4418-0240-8(1), 9781441802408, BAD); audio compact disk 59.97 (978-1-4418-0237-8(1), 9781441802378, BriAudCD Unabrid); audio compact disk 19.99 (978-1-4418-0236-1(3), 9781441802361, Bril Audio CD Unabri) Brilliance Audio.

Claudia Black: Don't Talk, Don't Trust, Don't Feel. 4 cass. (Family & Friends Discussion Tape Ser.). 1988. 32.95 (5779G) Hazelden.

*Claudia, Volume 1. RadioArchives.com. (Running Time: 600). (ENG.). 2007. audio compact disk 29.98 (978-1-61081-059-3(7)) Radio Arch.

*Claudia, Volume 2. RadioArchives.com. (Running Time: 600). (ENG.). 2007. audio compact disk 29.98 (978-1-61081-065-4(1)) Radio Arch.

*Claudia, Volume 3. RadioArchives.com. (Running Time: 600). (ENG.). 2009. audio compact disk 29.98 (978-1-61081-098-2(8)) Radio Arch.

Claudine at School. unabr. ed. Sidonie-Gabrielle Colette. Narrated by Barbara McCulloh. 6 cass. (Running Time: 8 hrs.). 1989. 51.00 (978-1-55690-107-2(0), 89590E7) Recorded Bks.
Claudine is a mischievous 15-year-old, full of her sex & rampaging through the dusty corridors of a parochial school in provincial France.

Claudine's Daughter. unabr. ed. Rosalind Laker, pseud. Read by Anne Dover. 12 cass. (Running Time: 14 hrs.). (Sound Ser.). (J). 2003. 94.95 (978-1-84283-426-8(6)); audio compact disk 99.95 (978-1-84283-452-7(5)) Pub: ISIS Lrg Prnt GBR. Dist(s): Ulverscroft US

Claudius the God. Robert Graves. (ENG.). 2009. audio compact disk 33.07 (978-1-906147-38-9(8), CSAW) CSA Telltapes GBR.

Claudius the God. abr. ed. Robert Graves. Narrated by Derek J. Jacobi. (Running Time: 5 hrs. 0 mins. 0 sec.). (I, Claudius Ser.). (ENG.). 2009. audio compact disk 26.95 (978-1-934997-29-1(3)) Pub: CSAWord. Dist(s): PerseuPGW

Claudius the God. unabr. ed. Robert Graves. Read by Frederick Davidson. 12 cass. (Running Time: 20 hrs. 30 mins.). 1995. 89.95 (978-0-7861-0884-8(3), 1523) Blckstn Audio.
Shows us the splendor, vitality & decadence of the Roman Empire through the eyes of the bemused & wry Claudius, who describes himself as a cripple, a stammerer, the fool of the royal family, whom none of his ambitious & blood-thirsty relatives considered worth the trouble of killing. Although this is a continuation of the fictional autobiography begun in "I Claudius", it is a complete & compelling novel in itself - a book that can be enjoyed even by those unfamiliar with its companion volume.

Claudius the God. unabr. ed. Robert Graves. Read by Nelson Runger. 44.95 (978-1-4025-5594-7(6)) Recorded Bks.

Claudius the God. unabr. ed. Robert Graves. Narrated by Nelson Runger. 15 cass. (Running Time: 19 hrs.). 1987. 120.00 (978-1-55690-108-9(9), 87490E7) Recorded Bks.
Sequel to Graves' fictional recreation of the life of the Roman Emperor Claudius, I, Claudius. Tells of the epic adulteries of Messalina, King Herod Agrippa's betrayal of his old friend & the final arrival of that bloodthirsty teenager, Nero.

Claudius the God. unabr. collector's ed. Robert Graves. Read by David Case. 14 cass. (Running Time: 21 hrs.). 1993. 112.00 (978-0-7366-2516-6(X), 3271) Books on Tape.
Captures the vitality, splendor & decadence of Rome just entering its decline. It is a superb re-creation of a colorful moment in history & through the eyes of the bemused & wry Claudius, a compelling & ironic account of human nature.

Claudius the God: And His Wife, Messalina. unabr. ed. Robert Graves. Read by Frederick Davidson. (Running Time: 19 hrs. 50 mins.). 2008. 44.95 (978-1-4332-5004-0(7)); audio compact disk 120.00 (978-1-4332-5003-3(9)) Blckstn Audio.

Claudius the God: And His Wife, Messalina. unabr. ed. Robert Graves. Read by Frederick Davidson. (Running Time: 19 hrs. 30 mins.). 2010. audio compact disk 39.95 (978-1-4417-1513-5(4)) Blckstn Audio.

Clause Contracts for Gold & Its Future. unabr. ed. Nicholas L. Deak & Henry M. Holzer. 1 cass. (Running Time: 51 min.). 12.95 (374) J Norton Pubs.

Clausewitz's on War: A Biography. unabr. ed. Hew Strachan. Narrated by Simon Vance. (Running Time: 5 hrs. 30 mins. 0 sec.). (Books That Changed the World Ser.). (ENG.). 2007. audio compact disk 24.99 (978-1-4001-0389-8(4)); audio compact disk 19.99 (978-1-4001-5389-3(1)); audio compact disk 49.99 (978-1-4001-3389-5(0)) Pub: Tantor Media. Dist(s): IngramPubServ

Claverings, Set. Anthony Trollope. Read by Flo Gibson. 14 cass. (Running Time: 19 hrs.). 1995. 42.95 (978-1-55685-366-1(1)) Audio Bk Con.
Harry Clavering struggles with his conscience over his love for & commitments to two women. In this turbulent, often rollicking romance, Trollope is at his funniest.

Claves del Triunfo y el Exito - Las Siete Actitudes para el Triunfo y las 20 Claves para el Exito. unabr. ed. Mario Elnerz. Read by Daniel Quintero. 3 CDs.Tr. of Clues for Achievement & Success. (SPA.). 2003. audio compact disk 13.00 (978-958-8218-29-8(2)) YoYoMusic.

Clawhammer Banjo from Scratch A Guide for the Claw-less! Dan Levenson. (ENG.). 2003. spiral bd. 26.95 (978-0-7866-7133-5(5)) Mel Bay.

Claws & Effect. Rita Mae Brown & Sneaky Pie Brown. Narrated by Kate Forbes. 8 CDs. (Running Time: 9 hrs.). (Mrs. Murphy Mystery Ser.). audio compact disk 78.00 (978-1-4025-3476-8(0)) Recorded Bks.

Claws & Effect. unabr. ed. Rita Mae Brown & Sneaky Pie Brown. Narrated by Kate Forbes. 6 cass. (Running Time: 9 hrs.). (Mrs. Murphy Mystery Ser.). 2001. 58.00 (978-0-7887-5462-3(9)) Recorded Bks.
In this clever tale, nobody pays much mind to rumors of bad blood among the staff of Crozet Hospital. That is, until one of the staff turns up dead.

Clay & Water. Perf. by Margaret Becker. 1 cass. 1998. 7.98 HiLo Plus. (978-0-7601-2575-5(9)) Brentwood Music.

Clay Crosse: Stained Glass. Contrib. by Mark Heimermann. 1997. 10.98 (978-0-7601-1431-5(5), C10005); audio compact disk 16.98 CD. (978-0-7601-1432-2(3), CD10005) Brentwood Music.
Contemporary pop. Progressive sound coupled with bold lyrics.

Clay Marble. unabr. ed. Minfong Ho. Narrated by Christina Moore. 4 pieces. (Running Time: 4 hrs. 45 mins.). (gr. 6 up). 1998. 37.00 (978-0-7887-2263-9(8), 95453E7) Recorded Bks.
Early in 1980, 12-year-old Dara & her family flee their war-torn Cambodian village for safety in a refugee camp on the Thai border. But fighting continues even there. When shelling suddenly separates Dara from her family, she fears she will never find them again.

Clay Marble. unabr. ed. Minfong Ho. Read by Christina Moore. 4 cass., 10 bks. (Running Time: 4 hrs. 45 min.). (J). 1998. bk. 107.30 (978-0-7887-2554-8(8), 46724) Recorded Bks.

Clay Marble. unabr. ed. Minfong Ho. Read by Christina Moore. 4 cass. (Running Time: 4 hrs. 45 min.). (J). (gr. 6). 1998. bk. 50.20 (978-0-7887-2250-9(6), 40734) Recorded Bks.

Clayton Eshleman. unabr. ed. Read by Clayton Eshleman. 1 cass. (Running Time: 29 min.). 1985. 10.00 New Letters.
National Book Award winner Eshleman reads poems from "Hades in Manganese".

Clea. abr. ed. Lawrence Durrell. Read by Nigel Anthony. 3 CDs. (Running Time: 4 hrs.). (Alexandria Quartet Ser.: Vol. IV). 1995. audio compact disk 22.98 (978-962-634-066-0(5), NA306612, Naxos AudioBooks) Naxos.
The fourth and final volume of The Alexandria Quartet. Clea and Darley's love for her provides the dominant theme of this volume, which begins to draw the threads together.

Clea. abr. ed. Lawrence Durrell. Read by Nigel Anthony. 3 cass. (Running Time: 4 hrs.). (Alexandria Quartet Ser.: Vol. IV). 1996. 17.98 (978-962-634-566-5(7), NA306614, Naxos AudioBooks) Naxos.
Clea, and Darley's love for her, provides the dominant theme of this volume, which begins to draw the threads together.

Clea. unabr. ed. Lawrence Durrell. Read by Richard Brown. 8 cass. (Running Time: 12 hrs.). (Alexandria Quartet Ser.: Vol. IV). 1994. 64.00 (978-0-7366-2808-2(8), 3522) Books on Tape.
Decades later, an Irish emigre meets Clea who gives him perspective on forgotten liaisons in wartime Alexandria.

Clean Air Act - New Amendments, 1990. 1991. 85.00 (AC-623) PA Bar Inst.

Clean, Straight & Sober Raising Drug-Free Kids in a Drug-Filled World. Zig Ziglar. Read by Zig Ziglar. 2 cass. (Zig Ziglar Presents Ser.). 1990. 19.95 (978-1-56207-200-1(5)) Zig Ziglar Corp.
Parents are facing one of their toughest challenges in trying to keep their kids off drugs. Zig shares his ideas, formulas & specific steps that parents can take to help their children get and - or stay drug-free.

Clean Sweep. abr. unabr. ed. Alf Silver. 3 cass. (Running Time: 3 hrs.). (Full Cast Mysteries Ser.). (ENG.). 1999. 24.95 (978-1-55017-217-1(4)) Harbour Pub Co CAN.

*Clean up Power Up. Katie Souza. (ENG.). 2011. audio compact disk 10.00 (978-0-7684-0265-0(4)) Pub: Expected End. Dist(s): Destiny Image Pubs

Clean Water, Red Wine, Broken Bread AudioBook. Douglas Wilson. Read by Aaron Wells. (ENG.). 2007. audio compact disk 10.00 (978-1-59128-206-8(3)) Canon Pr ID.

Clean, Well-Lighted Place see Stories of Ernest Hemingway

Clean Your Room, Harvey Moon! unabr. ed. Pat Cummings. 1 cass. (Running Time: 5 min.). (J). (gr. k-3). 1993. pap. bk. 16.95 (978-0-8045-6667-4(4), 6667) Spoken Arts.
Harvey Moon's room is a MESS! His mother won't let him watch cartoons until he finishes his Saturday morning cleaning.

*Cleanse: A Meditation CD. (ENG.). 2005. 15.00 (978-0-9753910-3-7(8)) Hawk Pr CA.

Cleanse 2004: Taking Medication/HIV Positive & God's Guidance & Mother's Approval. 2005. audio compact disk 24.00 (978-1-890246-33-4(6)) B Katie Int Inc.

Cleansing Our Hearts. Francis Frangipane. 1 cass. (Running Time: 90 mins.). (Basics of Spiritual Warfare Ser.: Vol. 7). 2000. 5.00 (FF02-007) Morning NC.
Francis combines years of practical experience with a soundbiblical perspective in this popular & important series.

Cleansing the House. Francis Frangipane. 1 cass. (Running Time: 90 mins.). (Strategies for our Cities Ser.: Vol. 8). 2000. 5.00 (FF06-008) Morning NC.
This series provides practical, biblical solutions that have been tested & have born fruit for those with a vision for their cities.

Cleansing the Lens. Richard Rohr. 1 cass. (Running Time: 46 min.). 8.95 (AA2850) Credence Commun.
Contemplation begins with discipline, but we go beyond discipline to a point where effort & techniques of prayer fall away & we see the world in God clearly. Then we can see & love fully. Rohr leads you a few steps & encourages you to trust yourself to take the next ones.

Clear & Convincing Proof. Kate Wilhelm & Anna Fields. 6 cass. (Running Time: 8 hrs. 30 mins.). 2002. 44.95 (978-0-7861-2588-3(8), 3189) Blckstn Audio.

Clear & Convincing Proof. unabr. ed. Kate Wilhelm. Read by Anna Fields. 2004. audio compact disk 35.95 (978-0-7861-8943-4(6)) Blckstn Audio.
The Kelso-McIvey rehabilitation center is a place of hope and healing for both its patients and dedicated staff. And for its directors, it¿s a lifelong dream that¿s about to be destroyed, if David McIvey has his way. A brilliant surgeon but a man whose ego rivals his skill with a scalpel, David McIvey now plans to close the clinic and replace it with a massive new surgery center, with himself at the helm.

Clear & Convincing Proof. unabr. ed. Kate Wilhelm. Read by Anna Fields. 7 CDs. (Running Time: 8 hrs. 30 mins.). 2004. audio compact disk 56.00 (978-0-7861-8978-6(9), 3189) Blckstn Audio.

Clear & Convincing Proof. unabr. ed. Kate Wilhelm. Read by Anna Fields. 6 pieces. (Running Time: 9 hrs.). 2004. reel tape 29.95 (978-0-7861-2597-5(7)) Blckstn Audio.

Clear & Present Danger. Tom Clancy. Read by Michael Prichard. 2002. 152.00 (978-0-7366-9113-0(8)) Books on Tape.

Clear & Present Danger. abr. ed. Tom Clancy. 2 cass. (Running Time: 3 hrs.). 2000. 18.00 (978-0-7435-0692-2(8), Audioworks) S&S Audio.
The U.S. ambassador to Columbia has been murdered by drug lords. Enemy covert agents filter into the jungles of South America, & Central America is ready to explode.

Clear & Present Danger. unabr. ed. Tom Clancy. Read by J. C. Howe & J. Charles. 16 cass. (Running Time: 24 hrs.). 1990. 162.55 (978-1-56100-055-5(8), 1561000558, Unabridge Lib Edns) Brilliance Audio.
The sudden and surprising assassination of three American officials in Colombia. Many people in many places, moving off on missions they all mistakenly thought they understood. The future was too fearful for contemplation, and beyond the expected finish lines were things that, once decided, were better left unseen. Tom Clancy's thriller is based on America's war on drugs . . . and the covert - and shocking - U. S. response. "The issues raised are real ones, and a jump ahead of the headlines." The New York Times "Rousing adventure...A crackling good yarn." The Washington Post.

Clear & Present Danger. unabr. ed. Tom Clancy. Read by J. Charles. 2 CDs. (Running Time: 24 hrs.). 2004. 29.95 (978-1-59335-798-6(2), 1593357982, Brilliance MP3) Brilliance Audio.

Clear & Present Danger. unabr. ed. Tom Clancy. Read by J. Charles. (Running Time: 24 hrs.). 2004. 44.25 (978-1-59710-141-7(9), 1597101419, BADLE); 29.95 (978-1-59710-140-0(0), 1597101400, BAD) Brilliance Audio.

*Clear & Present Danger. unabr. ed. Tom Clancy. Read by J. Charles. (Running Time: 26 hrs.). 2010. 19.99 (978-1-4418-5059-1(7), 9781441850591, Brilliance MP3); 39.97 (978-1-4418-5060-7(0), 9781441850607, Brlnc Audio MP3 Lib); audio compact disk 29.99 (978-1-4418-5057-7(0), 9781441850577); audio compact disk 99.97 (978-1-4418-5058-4(9), 9781441850584, BriAudCD Unabrid) Brilliance Audio.

Clear & Present Danger, Pt. 1. unabr. ed. Tom Clancy. Read by Michael Prichard. 10 cass. (Running Time: 15 hrs.). 1989. 80.00 (978-0-7366-1630-0(6), 2488-A) Books on Tape.
Leaping out of today's headlines, Clear & Present Danger focuses on coke & crack. Columbian drug lords, bored with Uncle Sam's hectoring, assassinate the head of the FBI. The message is clear: bug off. At what point do these druggies threaten national security? When can a nation act against its enemies? These are questions Jack Ryan must answer because someone has quietly stepped over the line, deploying covert-action teams in Columbia. Does anyone know who the real enemy is? How much action is too much? Which lines have been crossed? Ryan & his "dark side," a shadowy field officer known only as Mr. Clark, are charged with finding out. They expect danger from without...but the danger from within may be the greatest of all.

Clear & Present Danger, Pt. 2. unabr. ed. Tom Clancy. Read by Michael Prichard. 9 cass. (Running Time: 13 hrs. 30 mins.). 1989. 72.00 (978-0-7366-1631-7(4), 2488-B) Books on Tape.
A Columbian drug lord kills the FBI chief. Jack Ryan looks for the culprits in South America, but are the real enemies at home? Ryan and his "dark side," a shadowy field officer known only as Mr. Clark, are charged with finding out. They expect danger from without, but the danger from within may be the greatest of all.

*Clear & Shining Instant of Time. Kenneth Wapnick. 2010. 41.00 (978-1-59142-485-7(2)); audio compact disk 51.00 (978-1-59142-484-0(4)) Foun Miracles.

Clear As the Moon. Chris Stewart. (Great & Terrible Ser.: Vol. 6). 2008. audio compact disk 39.95 (978-1-59038-995-9(6)) Deseret Bk.

Clear Case of Suicide. Michael Underwood. Read by Christopher Kay. 5 cass. (Running Time: 7 hrs. 30 min.). 1999. 49.95 (65085) Pub: Soundings Ltd GBR. Dist(s): Ulverscroft US

Clear Conscience. unabr. ed. Frances Fyfield. Read by Rula Lenska. 8 cass. (Running Time: 8 hrs.). 1995. 69.95 Set. (978-0-7451-6547-9(8), CAB 1163) AudioGO.
Prosecutor Helen West, her apartment & her relationship with Geoffrey Bailey are all in need of a little attention. Just up the road lives Cath, the treasure, who begins cleaning for Helen. But Cath's life has been struck with tragedy, with the death of her brother. Something about it makes Geoffrey very uneasy. Then Helen becomes a witness to the destructive forces of love & guilt & finds herself applying her own version of justice.

Clear Conscience. unabr. ed. Frances Fyfield. Read by Rula Lenska. 8 cass. (Running Time: 12 hrs.). (West & Bailey Mystery Ser.). 2000. 59.95 (CAB 1163) Pub: Chivers Audio Bks GBR. Dist(s): AudioGO
Prosecutor Helen West, her apartment and her relationship with Geoffrey Bailey are all in need of a little attention. Just up the road lives Cath, the treasure who begins cleaning for Helen. But Cath's life has been struck with tragedy, with the death of her brother. Something about it makes Geoffrey very uneasy. Then Helen becomes a witness to the destructive forces of love and guilt and finds herself applying her own version of justice.

Clear Implants & Spiritual Limitation Devices. August Stahr. Read by August Stahr. 1 cass. (Running Time: 1 hr. 30 min.). (Planetary Issues Ser.). 1993. 33.00 (978-1-884686-02-3(8)) Celestl Guardn.
Guided meditation.

Clear Mind, Open Heart Meditation. Brian Sheen. 2004. audio compact disk 108.00 (978-1-928787-09-9(6)) Quan Pubg.

Clear Mind, Wild Heart. unabr. ed. David Whyte. 6 CDs. (Running Time: 6 hrs.). 2002. audio compact disk 69.95 (978-1-56455-995-1(5)) Sounds True.
Discover how to "apprentice yourself to beauty" and find a place of belonging where you can hold loss and grief, the challenges of change, and the wonder of new discovery and adventure.

Clear Minded Children's Program: A Healthy Non-Medication Choice to Heal ADD, ADHD & Dpression. Brian Sheen. 2006. audio compact disk 249.00 (978-1-928787-10-5(X)) Quan Pubg.

Clear Set One. (Running Time:). (J). (gr. k-3). 1989. cass. & flmstrp 185.00 (CP-5001) Crystal.

Clear Skin. Eldon Taylor. 1 cass. (Running Time: 62 min.). (Inner Talk Ser.). 16.95 incl. script. (978-1-55978-185-5(8), 5362A) Progress Aware Res.
Soundtrack - Tropical Lagoon with underlying subliminal affirmations.

Clear Skin: Harmonies. Eldon Taylor. Read by Eldon Taylor. Ed. by Leslie Brice. 1 cass. (Running Time: 1 hr.). 1992. 16.95 (978-1-56705-232-9(0)) Gateways Inst.
Self improvement.

Clear Skin: Music Theme. Eldon Taylor. 1 cass. 16.95 (978-1-55978-127-5(0), 5362C) Progress Aware Res.

Clear Skin: Ocean. Eldon Taylor. Read by Eldon Taylor. Ed. by Leslie Brice. 1 cass. (Running Time: 1 hr.). 1992. 16.95 (978-1-56705-233-6(9)) Gateways Inst.

Clear Speech. unabr. ed. 2 cass. bk. 39.50 Set, with tchr's. resource bk. (SEN155); bk. 39.50 Set, with student bk. (SEN156); 11.95 student bk. (BEN154); bk. 34.50 (SEN155) J Norton Pubs.
Provides intermediate & advanced students practice in pronunciation & listening comprehension.

Clear Speech: Pronunciation & Listening Comprehension in North American English. 2nd ed. Judy B. Gilbert. 2 cass. 34.95 Set. Midwest European Pubns.
Revised & expanded edition with an emphasis on the "Musical Aspects" of English: rhythm, stress, & intonation.

Clear Speech: Pronunciation & Listening Comprehension in North American English. 3rd rev. ed. Judy B. Gilbert. (ENG.). 2004. audio compact disk 61.00 (978-0-521-54357-6(6)) Cambridge U Pr.

Clear Speech Cassettes: Pronunciation & Listening Comprehension in American English. 3rd rev. ed. Judy B. Gilbert. (Running Time: 2 hrs. 44 mins.). (ENG.). 2005. 61.00 (978-0-521-54356-9(8)) Cambridge U Pr.

Clear Speech from the Start: Basic Pronunciation & Listening Comprehension in North American English. Judy B. Gilbert. 2 cass. (Running Time: 3 hrs. 34 mins.). (ENG., 2001. stu. ed. 61.00 (978-0-521-63736-7(8)) Cambridge U Pr.

Clear Speech from the Start: Basic Pronunciation & Listening Comprehension in North American English. Judy B. Gilbert. (Running Time: 7980 sec.). (ENG., 2001. stu. ed. 61.00 (978-0-521-79966-9(X)) Cambridge U Pr.

Clear Speech Student's Book: Pronunciation & Listening Comprehension in American English. 2nd ed. Judy B. Gilbert. 2 cass. 1993. bk. & tchr. ed. 10.95 Cambridge U Pr.

***Clear Wave Creativity.** Kelly Howell. (ENG.). 2010. audio compact disk Rental 14.95 (978-1-60568-063-7(X)) Brain Sync.

Clear Word about Judgement: Romans 3:1-16. Ed Young. 1983. 4.95 (978-0-7417-1351-3(9), 351) Win Walk.

Clear Your Clutter with Feng Shui, Set. abr. ed. Karen Kingston. Read by Karen Kingston. 2 cass. (Running Time: 3 hrs.). 2000. 18.95 (978-1-56170-761-4(9), 4057) Hay House.

Cleared for Take-Off. unabr. ed. Dirk Bogarde. Read by Dirk Bogarde. 8 cass. (Running Time: 8 hrs.). 1996. 69.95 Set. (978-0-7451-6650-6(4), CAB 1266) AudioGO.
On his many reconnaissance missions in Europe, young Dirk Bogarde experienced the terror of enemy attack along with the intense camaraderie of the battlefield. And at the war's end, he & many other soldiers were dispersed to find a traumatized world.

Cleared for Takeoff: English for Pilots, Bk. 1. Liz Mariner. 2007. per. & wbk. ed. 48.95 (978-0-9795068-0-2(8)) A E Link.

Cleared for Takeoff: English for Pilots, Bk. 1 and 2. Liz Mariner. (ENG., 2007. per. 74.95 (978-0-9795068-2-6(4)) A E Link.

Cleared for Takeoff: English for Pilots, Bk. 2. Liz Mariner. (ENG., 2007. per. 48.95 (978-0-9795068-1-9(6)) A E Link.

Clearer View: What We Know Now That We Didn't Know Thirty Years Ago: the Thirtieth Anniversary Lectures, Set. unabr. ed. Daniel Greenberg. 6 cass. (Running Time: 6 hr.). 1998. 25.00 (978-1-888947-59-5(4)) Sudbury Valley.
Series of six talks: The Meaning of Play; Conversation - the Staple Ingredient; What Is the Role of Parents?; The Significance of the Democratic Model; Developing Each Child's Unique Destiny; Why the School Doesn't Work for Everyone.".

Clearing for the Millenium. abr. ed. Albert Clayton Gaulden. (ENG.). 2006. 9.99 (978-1-59483-831-6(3)) Pub: Hachet Audio. Dist(s): HachBkGrp

Clearing in the Wild. unabr. ed. Jane Kirkpatrick. (Running Time: 11 hrs. 0 mins. 0 sec.). (ENG.). 2007. audio compact disk 28.98 (978-1-59644-505-5(X), christaudio) christianaud.

***Clearing in the Wild.** unabr. ed. Jane Kirkpatrick. Narrated by Kirsten Potter. (Yasmin Peace Ser.). (ENG.). 2007. 16.98 (978-1-59644-506-2(8), christaudio) christianaud.

Clearing Karma, Set. Jonathan Parker. Read by Jonathan Parker. 2 CDs. (Running Time: 2 hrs.). (Guided Meditation Ser.: Vol. 6). 1999. audio compact disk (978-1-58400-063-1(5)) QuantumQuests Intl.

Clearwater, FL: One City, One Future. unabr. ed. Innovation Groups Staff. 1 cass. (Running Time: 1 hrs. 15 min.). (Transforming Local Government Ser.: Vol. 24). 1999. 10.00 (978-1-882403-80-6(0), IG9926) Alliance Innov.

Cleave. unabr. ed. Nikki Gemmel. 5 cass. (Running Time: 7 hrs.). 2004. 40.00 (978-1-74030-538-9(8)) Pub: Bolinda Pubng AUS. Dist(s): Lndmrk Audiobks

Cleaving: A Story of Marriage, Meat, & Obsession. abr. unabr. ed. Julie Powell. Read by Julie Powell. (Running Time: 10 hrs. 30 mins.). (ENG.). 2009. 24.98 (978-1-60024-570-1(6)) Pub: Hachet Audio. Dist(s): HachBkGrp

Cleaving: A Story of Marriage, Meat, & Obsession. unabr. ed. Julie Powell. Read by Julie Powell. 9 CDs. (Running Time: 10 hrs. 30 mins.). (ENG.). 2009. audio compact disk 29.98 (978-1-60024-569-5(2)) Pub: Hachet Audio. Dist(s): HachBkGrp

Clem the Detective Dog: Join Clem, the Crooked Tailed Detective Dog, as He Tracks down the Bad Guys. unabr. ed. 1 CD. (Running Time: 3000 sec.). (J). (gr. k-6). 2006. audio compact disk 12.95 (978-1-933781-02-0(5)) TallTales Aud.

Clematis Tree. unabr. ed. Ann Widdecombe. Read by Carole Boyd. 8 CDs. (Running Time: 36420 sec.). 2001. 79.95 (978-0-7540-5418-4(7), CCD 109) Pub: Chivers Audio Bks GBR. Dist(s): AudioGO
It started on a happy day with friends celebrating the christening of Mark & Claire's new daughter, Pippa. When tragedy strikes as their son Jeremy spots a pet rabbit racing across the garden & gives chase, Jeremy forgets & rushes through the gate & out into the lane. A speeding sports car knocks him down & although he survives, he has brain damage.

Clemency Pogue: Fairy Killer. unabr. ed. J. T. Petty. Narrated by L. J. Ganser. 2 CDs. (Running Time: 2 hrs. 15 mins.). 2005. audio compact disk 12.75 (978-1-4193-5573-8(2), C3407); 19.75 (978-1-4193-4354-4(8), 98052) Recorded Bks.
When she is attacked by a nasty fairy, Clemency Pogue remembers a lesson from Peter Pan. "I don't believe in fairies!" she shouts - seven times before the creature finally drops dead. But then a hobgoblin appears and gives Clemency the bad news. Seven fairies have died, and most of them were good. Now it's up to Clemency to travel the world and make things right.

Clement of Alexandria - Origen. Thomas Merton. 1 cass. (Running Time: 60 min.). (Early Christian Spirituality Ser.). 8.95 (AA2082) Credence Commun.
Commentary on early Christianity, specifically the early church fathers.

Clemente: The Passion & Grace of Baseball's Last Hero. abr. ed. David Maraniss. Read by David Maraniss. 2006. 17.95 (978-0-7435-5414-5(0), Audioworks) Pub: S&S Audio. Dist(s): S and S Inc

Clemente: The Passion & Grace of Baseball's Last Hero. unabr. ed. David Maraniss. Read by Jonathan Davis. 13 CDs. (Running Time: 15 hrs. 50 mins.). 2006. audio compact disk 123.75 (978-1-4193-7759-4(0)) Recorded Bks.

Clementine. 1 cass. (FRE.). 1998. 12.95 Plastic case, incl. text bklet. Pub: Coffragants CAN. Dist(s): Penton Overseas

Clementine. 2004. 8.95 (978-1-56008-871-4(0)); cass. & flmstrp 30.00 (978-1-56008-650-5(5)) Weston Woods.

Clementine. rev. unabr. ed. Sara Pennypacker. Read by Jessica Almasy. 2 CDs. (Running Time: 1 hr. 50 mins.). (Clementine Ser.: No. 1). (J). (gr. 2-4). 2007. audio compact disk 30.75 (978-1-4281-4589-4(3)) Recorded Bks.

Clementine. unabr. ed. Institut Fran Cais de Recherche Pour Lexploitation de La Mer. Read by Mikaela Martin. 5 CDs. (Running Time: 18900 sec.). (YA). (gr. 7-16). 2006. audio compact disk 63.95 (978-1-74093-560-9(8)) Pub: Bolinda Pubng AUS. Dist(s): Bolinda Pub Inc

Clementine. unabr. ed. Sara Pennypacker. Read by Jessica Almasy. 2 cass. (Running Time: 1 hr. 50 mins.). (Clementine Ser.: No. 1). (J). (gr. 2-4). 2007. 25.75 (978-1-4281-4584-9(2)) Recorded Bks.

Clementine's Letter. unabr. ed. Sara Pennypacker. Narrated by Jessica Almasy. 2 cass. (Running Time: 2 hrs. 30 mins.). (Clementine Ser.: No. 3). (J). (gr. 2-4). 2008. 25.75 (978-1-4281-8232-5(2)); audio compact disk 25.75 (978-1-4281-8237-0(3)) Recorded Bks.

Cleopatra. E. E. Rice. Read by Anita Wright. 2 CDs. (Running Time: 2 hrs. 31 mins.). (Isis (CDs) Ser.). (J). 2004. audio compact disk 34.95 (978-0-7531-2278-5(2)) Pub: ISIS Lrg Prnt GBR. Dist(s): Ulverscroft US

Cleopatra. unabr. ed. George B. Harrison. 1 cass. (Running Time: 43 min.). (Shakespeare's Critics Speak Ser.). 1965. 12.95 (23103) J Norton Pubs.
A discussion, with extended readings from the play, on how Shakespeare created one of his most fascinating & complex characters.

Cleopatra: A Concise Biography. unabr. ed. E. E. Rice. Read by Anita Wright. 2 cass. (Running Time: 2 hrs. 31 mins.). (Isis Ser.). (J). 2002. 24.95 (978-0-7531-0724-9(4)) Pub: ISIS Lrg Prnt GBR. Dist(s): Ulverscroft US
Taking as its subject the most famous queen in history, this biography reveals the troubled times, political upheaval and the charismatic personality of the ruler of Ancient Egypt. Famously romantically involved with two Roman leaders, Julius Caesar and Mark Antony, her story has long passed into legend. Her personal life led to war between two great countries, and finally to her own death. Fleeing Egypt in 31BC, pursued by Romans, Antony and Cleopatra both committed suicide, and together became one of the world's most enduring love stories. The life and times of this remarkable and powerful woman make a fascinating tale.

***Cleopatra: A Life.** unabr. ed. Stacy Schiff. Read by Robin Miles. (Running Time: 14 hrs. 30 mins.). 2010. 24.98 (978-1-60788-702-7(9)) Pub: Hachet Audio. Dist(s): HachBkGrp

***Cleopatra: A Life.** unabr. ed. Stacy Schiff. Read by Robin Miles. (Running Time: 14 hrs. 30 mins.). (ENG., 2010. audio compact disk 34.98 (978-1-60788-701-0(0)) Pub: Hachet Audio. Dist(s): HachBkGrp

Cleopatra: Being an Account of the Fall & Vengeance of Harmachis, the Royal Egyptian, as Set Forth by His Own Hand. unabr. ed. H. Rider Haggard. Read by William Sutherland. 8 cass. (Running Time: 11 hrs. 30 mins.). 1999. 56.95 (978-0-7861-1624-9(2), 2452) Blckstn Audio.
Cleopatra lies asleep: Harmachis looks down at the most gorgeous woman he had ever seen. The sight of Cleopatra's beauty strikes the young Egyptian with all the power of a mortal blow. And for a moment he aches with grief because he has to kill a thing that is so lovely.

Cleopatra: Queen of the Nile. Alan Venable. (Ancient History Ser.). 2002. audio compact disk 18.95 (978-1-4105-0176-9(0)) D Johnston Inc.

Cleopatra Gold. unabr. ed. William J. Caunitz. Read by John Michalski. 8 vols. (Running Time: 12 hrs.). 2000. bk. 69.95 (978-0-7927-2228-1(0), CSL 117, Chivers Sound Lib) AudioGO.
An undercover New York cop is trying to put an end to the newest and deadliest drug: Cleopatra Gold. To the party goers of the late-night club scene, Alejandro Monahan is just a singer, but to others he's a good cop. He knows that Cleopatra is also the code name for the head of the Latin drug-ring: a ruthless female assassin who years earlier killed his father. Aware that a single mistake could kill him, Monahan makes a perilous journey to the heart of the Cleopatra syndicate.

Cleopatra, Queen of the Nile. Ed. by Jerry Stemach et al. Contrib. by Ted S. Hasselbring. (Start-to-Finish Books). (J). (gr. 2-3). 2002. (978-1-58702-831-1(X)) D Johnston Inc.

Cleopatra, Queen of the Nile. unabr. ed. Ed. by Jerry Stemach et al. Contrib. by Ted S. Hasselbring. 1 cass. (Running Time: 1 hr.). (Start-to-Finish Books). 2002. (978-1-58702-816-8(6), F49) D Johnston Inc.
Cleopatra VII (circa 70 B.C to 30 B.C) ruled Egypt from the Greco-Egyptian city of Alexandria for 20 years, just before Egypt was swallowed by the Roman Empire. Through personal and political alliances, first with Julius Caesar and then with Mark Antony, she maintained the independent power of Egypt as long as she was able to do so. But her luck ran out when Julius Caesar's nephew Octavian (later known as the emperor Caesar Augustus) forced Mark Antony into civil war after Julius Caesar's assassination.

Cleopatra VII: Daughter of the Nile. unabr. ed. Kristiana Gregory. Read by Josephine Bailey. (J). 2007. 39.99 (978-1-60252-552-8(8)) Find a World.

Cleopatra's Daughter. unabr. ed. Michelle Moran. Narrated by Wanda McCaddon. 1 MP3-CD. (Running Time: 12 hrs. 30 mins. 0 sec.). (ENG.). 2009. 29.99 (978-1-4001-6429-5(X)); audio compact disk 79.99 (978-1-4001-4429-7(9)); audio compact disk 39.99 (978-1-4001-1429-0(2)) Pub: Tantor Media. Dist(s): IngramPubServ

***Cleopatra's Daughter.** unabr. ed. Michelle Moran. Narrated by Wanda McCaddon. (Running Time: 12 hrs. 30 mins.). 2009. 18.99 (978-1-4001-8429-3(0)) Tantor Media.

Cleopatra's Nose: Essays on the Unexpected. unabr. ed. Daniel J. Boorstin. Read by Noah Waterman. 5 cass. (Running Time: 7 hrs.). 1995. 39.95 (978-0-7861-0671-4(9), 1573) Blckstn Audio.
A compilation of essays illustrating specific subjects that have preoccupied Daniel Boorstin for several decades. Provocative themes all: How sometimes discovery only increases our ignorance. What were the specific historical opportunities in the New World? How has the fourth kingdom - the kingdom of machines - contradicted Darwinian expectations, contributed to a confusion of statistics, seated a need for the unnecessary, & highlighted the paradoxes of science & the politics of common sense?.

Cleopatra's Nose: Essays on the Unexpected. unabr. ed. Daniel J. Boorstin. Read by Michael Prichard. 6 cass. (Running Time: 9 hrs.). 1995. 48.00 (978-0-7366-3047-4(3), 3729) Books on Tape.
Daniel Boorstin, Pulitzer Prize author, shows how the accidental & unexpected stimulate civilization. Intellectually powerful.

Cleopatra's Sister. unabr. ed. Penelope L[illegible]. Read by Nadia May. 6 cass. (Running Time: 9 cass.). 44.95 Set. (1[illegible] [illegible]lckstn Audio.
Howard Beamish, paleontologist, is fly[illegible] Nairobi on a professional mission when his plane is forced to land [illegible] Callimbia. On assignment to write a travel piece for a Sunday magazine, journalist Lucy Faulkner has embarked on the same flight. What happens to them in Callimbia is one of those accidents that determine fate, that bring love & can take away joy, that reveal to us the precariousness of our existence & the trajectory of our lives.

Cleopatra's Sister. unabr. ed. Penelope Lively. Read by Nadia May. 6 cass. (Running Time: 8 hrs. 30 mins.). 2000. 44.95 (978-0-7861-0448-2(1), 1400) Blckstn Audio.

Cleopatra's Sister. unabr. ed. Penelope Lively. Narrated by Davina Porter. 7 cass. (Running Time: 9 hrs. 15 mins.). 1994. 60.00 (978-1-55690-996-2(9), 94135E7) Recorded Bks.
Howard Beamish, a somewhat short-sighted paleontologist & Lucy Faulkner, a driven, rather arch journalist, make separate plans for a trip to Nairobi. En route, their plane runs into engine trouble, forcing them to land in Callimbia, a country in the throes of revolution & in the clutches of a megalomaniacal despot with a passion for board games, as well as games of state. What happens next is rendered with suspense & intelligence.

CLEP College Algebra. Comex Systems Staff. 1991. audio compact disk 750.00 (978-1-56030-219-3(4)) Comex Systs.

CLEP General CD-ROM Set. Comex Systems Staff. 2000. audio compact disk 3750.00 (978-1-56030-194-3(5)) Comex Systs.

CLEP History I. Comex Systems Staff. 1998. audio compact disk 750.00 (978-1-56030-216-2(X)) Comex Systs.

CLEP History II. Comex Systems Staff. 1998. audio compact disk 750.00 (978-1-56030-217-9(8)) Comex Systs.

CLEP Principles of Management. Comex Systems Staff. 1990. audio compact disk 750.00 (978-1-56030-218-6(6)) Comex Systs.

CLEP Psychology. Comex Systems Staff. 2001. audio compact disk 750.00 (978-1-56030-215-5(1)) Comex Systs.

Clergy - Physician Relationships. Harold Nelson. 1986. 10.80 (0108B) Assn Prof Chaplains.

Clergy & Laity in Ministry Together. 1 cass. (Care Cassettes Ser.: Vol. 15, No. 9). 1988. 10.80 Assn Prof Chaplains.

Clergy & the Medical Record. Lowell Mays. 1986. 10.80 (0208A) Assn Prof Chaplains.

Clergyman's Daughter. unabr. ed. George Orwell. Read by Richard Brown. 8 cass. (Running Time: 11 hrs. 30 mins.). 1991. 56.95 (978-0-7861-0271-6(3), 1237) Blckstn Audio.
Dorothy Hare, the dutiful daughter of a rector in Suffolk, spends her days performing good works, cultivates good thoughts, & pricks her arm with a pin when a bad thought arises. And she does her best to reconcile her father's fanciful view of his position in the world with such realities as the butcher's bill. But even Dorothy's strength has its limits, & one night as she works feverishly on costumes for the church-school play, she blacks out. When she comes to, she finds herself on a London street, clad in a sleazy dress & unaware of her identity.

Clergyman's Daughter. unabr. collector's ed. George Orwell. Read by Richard Green. 7 cass. (Running Time: 10 hrs. 30 min.). 1983. 56.00 (978-0-7366-0564-9(9), 1536) Books on Tape.
Dorothy Hare, the clergyman's daughter of the title, grew up super-subservient to her tyrannical father. But submission has its limits & Dorothy rebels, or at least her psyche does. She blacks out & reappears as an amnesiac whose adventures show us life as it is, from the underside.

Clerk Saunders see Poetry of Robert Burns & Border Ballads

Cleveland Local. abr. ed. Les Roberts. 4 cass. (Running Time: 360 min.). (Milan Jacovich Mystery Ser.). 2000. 25.00 (978-1-58807-034-0(4)) Am Pubng Inc.
When hot shot Cleveland real estate attorney Joel Kerner Jr. is killed on a Caribbean holiday, only his angry sister Patrice thinks It's more than a botched robbery. The corrupt island police have nothing, and the Cleveland cops don't have the jurisdiction. So It's up to private eye Milan Jacovich to swim through the mire on his own.

Cleveland Years. (Presidency Ser.). 10.00 Esstee Audios.
A dramatization of Cleveland in action as well as an illustration of a man with integrity.

Clever Bill. 2004. 8.95 (978-1-56008-872-1(9)); cass. & flmstrp 30.00 (978-1-56008-651-2(3)) Weston Woods.

Clever Bill; Musicians of Bremen, the; David & Dog; Fool of the World & the Flying Ship. 2004. (978-0-89719-845-5(X)) Weston Woods.

Clever Bill; Musicians of Bremen, the; David & the Dog; Fool of the World & the Flying Ship. 2004. cass. & flmstrp (978-0-89719-701-4(1)) Weston Woods.

Clever Boy & the Dangerous Animal/el Muchachito Listo y el Terrible y Peligroso Animal. Idries Shah. Tr. by Rita Wirkala. Illus. by Rose Mary Santiago. (J). (ps-3). 2006. pap. bk. 18.95 (978-1-883536-66-4(9), Hoopoe Books) ISHK.

Clever Duck & The Swoose. unabr. ed. Dick King-Smith. Narrated by June Whitfield. 2 cass. (Running Time: 2 hrs.). (J). 1998. 18.95 (CCA3480, Chivers Child Audio) AudioGO.

Clever Polly & the Stupid Wolf. Catherine Storr. Read by Derek Griffiths. 1 cass. (Running Time: 1 hr. 30 min.). (J). (gr. 1-3). 6.95 (CC/024) C to C Cassettes.
When a wolf rings on the doorbell & tells Polly that he has come to eat her up she is not dismayed but gives him slices of delicious pie instead.

Clever Polly & the Stupid Wolf. unabr. ed. Catherine Storr. Read by Derek Griffiths. 1 cass. (Running Time: 1 hrs.). (J). 1995. 9.95 (978-1-85549-284-4(9), CTC 110) AudioGO.
One day the front door bell rings & Polly opens it. And there before her eyes, is a great black wolf who says he has come to eat her! But Clever Polly isn't frightened, & has plans to foil the wolf.

Clever Polly & the Stupid Wolf. unabr. ed. Catherine Storr. Read by Derek Griffiths. 1 cass. (Running Time: 1 hr. 35 mins.). 2002. (978-1-85549-352-0(7)) Cover To Cover GBR.

Clever Snake Charmer: A Story from Nelson Mandela's Favorite African Folktales. Read by Samuel L. Jackson. Compiled by Nelson Mandela. (Running Time: 5 mins.). (ENG.). 2009. 1.99 (978-1-60024-852-8(7)) Pub: Hachet Audio. Dist(s): HachBkGrp

Clic, Clac, Muu: Vacas Escritoras. Doreen Cronin.Tr. of Click, Clack, Moo: Cows That Type. (SPA.). (J). (ps-4). 2004. bk. 24.95 (978-1-55592-155-2(8)) Weston Woods.

Click: The Magic of Instant Connections. unabr. ed. Ori Brafman & Rom Brafman. Read by Rob Shapiro. (ENG.). 2010. 35.00 (978-0-307-73509-6(5), Random AudioBks) Pub: Random Audio Pubg. Dist(s): Random

***CLICK: What Millions of People Are Doing Online & Why it Matters.** Bill Tancer. (ENG.). 2008. 18.99 (978-1-4013-9031-0(5)); 18.99 (978-1-4013-9032-7(3)) Pub: Hyperion. Dist(s): HarperCollins Pubs

Click: What Millions of People Are Doing Online & Why It Matters. unabr. ed. Bill Tancer. Read by Bill Tancer. 5 CDs. (Running Time: 5 hrs.). 2008. audio compact disk 29.95 (978-1-4013-9030-3(7)) Pub: Hyperion. Dist(s): HarperCollins Pubs

Click, Clack, Moo: Cows That Type. (SPA.). (J). 2004. pap. bk. 14.95 (978-1-55592-653-3(3)) Weston Woods.

Click, Clack, Moo: Cows That Type. Doreen Cronin. (SPA.). 2004. 8.95 (978-1-55592-825-4(0)) Weston Woods.

Click, Clack, Moo: Cows That Type. Doreen Cronin. (J). 2004. pap. bk. 18.95 (978-1-55592-139-2(6)); pap. bk. 38.75 (978-1-55592-630-4(4)); pap. bk. 32.75 (978-1-55592-183-5(3)); pap. bk. 32.75 (978-1-55592-347-1(X)); pap. bk. 14.95 (978-1-55592-171-2(X)); audio compact disk 12.95 (978-1-55592-954-1(0)) Weston Woods.

Click, Clack, Moo: Cows That Type. Doreen Cronin. 1 cass. (Running Time: 6 min.). (J). (gr. k-3). 2004. 8.95 (978-1-55592-973-2(7)) Weston Woods.
A bunch of literate cows go on strike after Farmer Brown refuses to give in to their demands for electric blankets when the barn gets too cold.

Click, Clack, Moo: Cows That Type. Doreen Cronin. Illus. by Betsy Lewin. (J). 2004. bk. 24.95 (978-1-55592-077-7(2)) Weston Woods.

Click Clack Moo: Cows That Type. Doreen Cronin. (SPA.). (J). 2004. pap. bk. 32.75 (978-1-55592-652-6(5)) Weston Woods.

Click, Clack, Moo: Cows That Type see Clic, Clac, Muu: Vacas Escritoras

Click, Clack Moo: Cows That Type & other Barnyard Stories: Click, Clack, Moo Cows That Type, Giggle, Giggle, Quack, Duck for President. unabr. ed. Doreen Cronin. Read by Randy Travis. (J). 2007. 44.99 (978-1-60252-641-9(9)) Find a World.

Click Song. John A. Williams. Read by John A. Williams. 1 cass. 1989. 13.95 (978-1-55644-343-5(9), 9081) Am Audio Prose.
The author reads excerpts.

Click 4 Psych. 8th ed. Spencer A. Rathus. (C). 2001. audio compact disk 32.95 (978-0-15-506141-5(0)) Pub: Wadsworth Pub. Dist(s): CENGAGE Learn

Clicking of Cuthbert. unabr. ed. P. G. Wodehouse. Read by Frederick Davidson. 5 cass. (Running Time: 7 hrs. 30 min.). 1999. 39.95 (2365) Blckstn Audio.
Cuthbert Banks is young, handsome, & plus four on the Wood Hills links, but he can make no impression on the soulful girl of his heart. When the eminent Russian novelist kisses him on both cheeks, however, Adeline's attitude changes from scorn to adoration.

Clicking of Cuthbert. unabr. ed. P. G. Wodehouse. Read by Frederick Davidson. 5 cass. (Running Time: 7 hrs.). 2001. 39.95 (978-0-7861-1515-0(7), 2365) Blckstn Audio.

***Clicking of Cuthbert.** unabr. ed. P. g. Wodehouse. Read by Frederick Davidson. (Running Time: 7 hrs.). 2010. 29.95 (978-1-4417-4480-7(0)); audio compact disk 69.00 (978-1-4417-4477-7(0)) Blckstn Audio.

Clicking of Cuthbert, Set. unabr. ed. P. G. Wodehouse. Read by Frederick Davidson. 5 cass. 1999. 39.95 (FS9-50913) Highsmith.

Client. John Grisham. Read by John MacDonald. 1993. audio compact disk 96.00 (978-0-7366-8910-6(9)) Books on Tape.

Client. unabr. ed. John Grisham. Read by John MacDonald. 10 cass. (Running Time: 15 hrs.). 1993. 80.00 (978-0-7366-2464-0(3), 3228) Books on Tape.
In New Orleans an attorney, depressed & suicidal, does himself in. But it is witnessed by Mark Sway, a bright 11-year-old, who hears from the dying man a deadly secret about a Louisiana senator's murder. The accused killer, Mafia thug Barry Muldanno, is about to go on trial. Everyone wants to know the attorney's last words. But Mark dissembles. He knows that he knows to much, maybe too much to live. Streetsmart & wise beyond his years, he hires a lawyer: Reggie Love, a feisty 52-year-old divorcee who realizes she's in over her head. Then Mark comes up with a plan, a crazy plan in Reggie's opinion, but it's their only hope. And it just might work.

Client-Astrologer Relationship. Theresa Gurlacz. 1 cass. 8.95 (411) Am Fed Astrologers.
Establish rapport & handle difficult situations.

***Client Care Techniques.** Linda Maytum-Wilson. 1995. 65.80 (978-1-85811-110-0(2)) Pub: EMIS GBR. Dist(s): Intl Spec Bk

Client Satisfaction & Your Firm's Bottom Line. 1992. bk. 99.00 (AL-123) PA Bar Inst.
Learn how to identify client needs & meet them, even beyond the client's expectations. Learn how to tap all your firm's resources to systematically build an atmosphere that promotes client satisfaction. Discover how good planning, tied to effective communications with your staff & colleagues, can lead to more satisfied customers & a more satisfying bottom line.

Client-Server Computing. unabr. ed. Dawna T. Dewire. Read by Tom Scott. 9 cass. (Running Time: 9 hrs. 8 min.). (James Martin Productivity Ser.). 1993. 72.00 set. (978-1-884387-01-2(2)) Tech Bks-On-Tape.
This important new audio book provides information managers with a working overview of one of the most important trends in enterprise client/server computing. As part of the popular James Martin/McGraw Hill Productivity series, the book explains not only the basics of networking between mainframes & desktop computers, but also gives extensive & detailed description of how these systems can work in various network environments.

Clients du Bon Chien Jaune, Set. Pierre Mac Orland. Read by Arnaud Bedouet. 2 cass. (FRE.). 1991. bk. 35.95 (1GA057) Olivia & Hill.
The seaport of Brest in the 18th century, an inn of ill repute, a ship bearing a black flag, a curious young Breton - exciting adventures of the Flying Dutchman.

Cliff Drysdale: Tennis Tips. Read by Cliff Drysdale. 1 cass. 9.95 (978-0-89811-114-9(5), 7165) Lets Talk Assocs.
Cliff Drysdale talks about the people & events which influenced his career, & his own approach to his speciality.

Cliff Haslam: The Clockwinder. 1 cass. 9.98 (C-93) Folk-Legacy.
English singer with a smashing voice & a roguish air.

Cliff House Strangler. unabr. ed. Shirley Tallman. Read by Carrington MacDuffie. (Running Time: 39600 sec.). (Sarah Woolson Mystery Ser.: Bk. 3). 2007. 59.95 (978-1-4332-1302-1(8)); audio compact disk 29.95 (978-1-4332-1304-5(4)); audio compact disk & audio compact disk 72.00 (978-1-4332-1303-8(6)) Blckstn Audio.

Cliff Walk: A Memoir of a Job Lost & a Life Found. unabr. ed. Don J. Snyder. Read by Alan Sklar. 6 vols. (Running Time: 9 hr.). 1999. bk. 54.95 (978-0-7927-2327-1(9), CSL 216, Chivers Sound Lib) AudioGO.
Don Snyder was a professor of English, married with three children, when he got his pink slip. After years of fruitless searching for a comparable job, Snyder hit bottom; desperate, nearly broke, his sense of self dismantled. But when he landed a job as an unskilled construction worker, Snyder discovered the grace & dignity in the kind of work that he had run from all his life.

Cliffhanger. Skip Press & Skip Press Staff. Narrated by Larry A. McKeever. (Adventure Ser.). (J). 2000. audio compact disk 14.95 (978-1-58659-280-6(7)) Artesian.

Cliffhanger. abr. ed. Skip Press Staff. Narrated by Larry A. McKeever. 1 cass. (Running Time: 40 min.). (Take Ten Ser.). (J). (gr. 3-12). 2000. 10.95 (978-1-58659-016-1(2), 54106) Artesian.

Cliffhanger, Set. abr. ed. Jeff Rovin. Read by Ralph Waite. 2 cass. (Running Time: 3 hrs.). 1993. 16.95 (978-1-56876-003-2(5)) Soundlines Ent.
Gabe Walker, an expert Mountain Rescue Ranger, must do everything possible to rescue his former partner from the hands of an evil group who hijack a Treasury Jet containing $100 million & crash into the Rocky Mountains.

Clifford & the Grouchy Neighbors. Norman Bridwell. (Clifford, the Big Red Dog Ser.). (J). (gr. k-2). 1988. 6.95 (978-0-589-63437-7(2)) Scholastic Inc.

Clifford at the Circus. Norman Bridwell. (ENG.). (J). (ps-3). 2008. audio compact disk 18.95 (978-0-545-07325-7(1)); audio compact disk 9.95 (978-0-545-07324-0(3)) Scholastic Inc.

Clifford D. Simak & Felix Pollak. Read by Felix Pollak. Interview with Clifford Simak. 1 cass. (Running Time: 29 min.). 1986. 10.00 New Letters.
Science Fiction writer Clifford Simak is interviewed & his story, "Ghost of a Model T," is dramatized. Also Viennese born writer Felix Pollak reads his poetry.

Clifford the Big Red Dog: A Really Big Musical Tribute. 1 CD. (Running Time: 37 mins). (J). (ps). 2005. audio compact disk 9.98 (978-1-56628-408-0(2)) MFLP CA.

Clifford the Big Red Dog: A Really Big Musical Tribute. 1 cass. (Running Time: 37 mins). (J). (ps-k). 2005. 5.98 (978-1-56628-409-7(0)) MFLP CA.

Clifford the Big Red Dog & Other Clifford Stories: Clifford the Big Red Dog, Clifford the Small Red Puppy, Clifford Takes A Trip, Clifford's Good Deeds. unabr. ed. Norman Bridwell. Read by Stephanie D'Abruzzo & Kirsten Krohn. (J). 2007. 39.99 (978-1-60252-676-1(1)) Find a World.

Clifford's Birthday Party. Norman Bridwell. Narrated by Stephanie D'Abruzzo. (Clifford Ser.). (ENG.). (J). (ps-3). 2009. audio compact disk 9.95 (978-0-545-11756-2(9)); audio compact disk 18.95 (978-0-545-11945-0(6)) Scholastic Inc.

Clifford's Christmas. Norman Bridwell. Read by Judie Bazinger. 1 cass. (Running Time: 16 min.). (Clifford, the Big Red Dog Ser.). (J). (gr. k-2). 1987. pap. bk. 5.95 Scholastic Inc.

Clifford's Christmas. Norman Bridwell. (ENG.). (J). (ps-3). 2008. audio compact disk 18.95 (978-0-545-09137-4(3)) Scholastic Inc.

Clifford's Christmas. Norman Bridwell. Illus. by Norman Bridwell. Narrated by Stephanie D'Abruzzo. (ENG.). (J). (ps-3). 2008. audio compact disk 9.95 (978-0-545-09099-5(7)) Scholastic Inc.

Clifford's Christmas & Other Holiday Stories. Norman Bridwell. Narrated by Stephanie D'Abruzzo. (Playaway Children Ser.). (J). 2008. 34.99 (978-1-60640-548-2(9)) Find a World.

Clifford's Pals. unabr. ed. Norman Bridwell. (Clifford, the Big Red Dog Ser.). (J). (ps-3). 2008. pap. bk. 18.95 (978-0-545-05249-8(1)) Scholastic Inc.
Clifford and his pals just can't stay out of trouble! After a full day of mischief, they decide that next time they'll play somewhere safe - and a lot more fun.

CliffsNotes - Hamlet. unabr. ed. CliffsNotes. Read by Mark Jennings. (YA). 2007. 34.99 (978-1-60252-888-8(8)) Find a World.

CliffsNotes - Huckleberry Finn. unabr. ed. CliffsNotes. Read by John Tye. (YA). 2007. 34.99 (978-1-60252-889-5(6)) Find a World.

CliffsNotes - the Scarlet Letter. unabr. ed. CliffsNotes. Read by Shelly Frasier. (YA). 2007. 34.99 (978-1-60252-892-5(6)) Find a World.

Clifton Chenier - King of Zydeco. Clifton Chenier. Tr. by Gary Dahl. 1997. bk. 9.95 (978-0-7866-1780-7(2)) Mel Bay.

Climate Studies Reprints. Ed. by Marco A. V. Bitetto. 1 cass. 2000. (978-1-58578-035-8(9)) Inst of Cybernetics.

Climb. Susannah Brin. Narrated by Larry A. McKeever. (Thrillers Ser.). (J). 2004. audio compact disk 14.95 (978-1-58659-326-1(9)) Artesian.

Climb, unabr. ed. Anatoli Boukreev & G. Weston De Walt. Narrated by Richard M. Davidson & Nelson Runger. 7 cass. (Running Time: 10 hrs.). 1998. 62.00 (978-0-7887-1985-1(8), 95372E7) Recorded Bks.
As two commercial expeditions climbed Mt. Everest in May, 1996, poor planning, miscommunication & an unpredictable blizzard conspired to defeat them. Thirty-three people went up, but only 28 returned. Written by the hero of this desperate situation, Boukreev's first-hand account will hold listeners spellbound.

Climb. unabr. ed. Anatoli Boukreev & G. Weston DeWalt. Read by Lloyd James. 7 cass. (Running Time: 10 hrs.). 1998. 49.95 (978-0-7861-1272-2(7), 2207) Blckstn Audio.
On May 10, 1996, two commercial expeditions headed by experienced leaders attempted to climb Mt. Everest. Crowed conditions on the mountain, miscommunications, unexplainable delays, poor leadership, bad decisions & a blinding storm conspired to kill. Twenty-three men & women, disoriented & out of oxygen, struggled to find their way down the southern side of the mountain. Some of the climbers became hopelessly lost & resigned themselves to death. The head climbing guide for the West Seattle-based Mountain Madness expedition, refused to give up hope & brought climbers back from the edge of certain death.

Climb. unabr. ed. Susannah Brin. Narrated by Larry A. McKeever. 1 cass. (Running Time: 40 min.). (Thrillers Ser.). (J). 2004. 10.95 (978-1-58659-047-5(2), 54122) Artesian.

Climb: Stories of Survival from Rock, Snow & Ice. unabr. ed. Read by Terence Aselford et al. Ed. by Clint Willis. 4 cass. (Running Time: 6 hrs.). (Adrenaline Ser.). 2001. 24.95 (978-1-885408-61-7(7), LL053) Listen & Live.
Offers harrowing accounts of extreme mountaineering & its sometimes fatal consequences.

Climb: Tragic Ambitions on Everest. unabr. ed. Anatoli Boukreev & G. Weston Dewalt. Read by Lloyd James. (Running Time: 34200 sec.). 2008. audio compact disk & audio compact disk 29.95 (978-1-4332-3421-7(1)); audio compact disk & audio compact disk 80.00 (978-1-4332-3420-0(3)) Blckstn Audio.

Climb of Your Life: Reaching the Peak of Your Potential. Read by Robert Christopher Stephens. 2008. audio compact disk 15.00 (978-0-9817812-1-1(7)) Chris Stephens.

Climb to the Top: Client Development for Lawyers. Hildebrandt-Coulter Legal Products Staff. 1 cass. 1994. 195.00 (5000) Natl Prac Inst.

Climbing Mount Kasikasima in Surname's Amazon Rainforest; Roger Fielding of Amtour Vacations Promotes Ecotourism; La Salle's La Belle Archaeological Site. Hosted by Nancy Pearlman. 1 cass. (Running Time: 29 min.). 10.00 (1501) Educ Comm CA.

Climbing Mt. Rainier: The Inner Struggle. Read by Douglas A. Wakefield. 1 cass. (Running Time: 30 min.). 9.95 (G0190B090, HarperThor) HarpC GBR.

Climbing Olympus. unabr. ed. Kevin J. Anderson. Read by Larry McKeever. 8 cass. (Running Time: 12 hrs.). 1995. 64.00 (978-0-7366-3094-8(5), 3770) Books on Tape.
Raychel Dycek, M.D., was just following orders. Using convicts as fodder, she surgically transforms them for the Mars environment. The government needs the overhauled beings called "adin" to build the red planet for human colonists.

Climbing the Himalayas. unabr. ed. Perf. by Eknath Easwaran. 1 cass. (Running Time: 1 hr.). 1990. 7.95 (978-1-58638-514-9(3)) Nilgiri Pr.

Climbing the Ladder Home. Kenneth Wapnick. 7 CDs. 2007. audio compact disk 43.00 (978-1-59142-321-8(X), CD49) Foun Miracles.

Climbing the Ladder Home. Kenneth Wapnick. 1 CD. (Running Time: 7 hrs. 11 mins. 15 secs.). 2007. 34.00 (978-1-59142-322-5(8), 3m49) Foun Miracles.

Climbing the Mountain: My Search for Meaning. unabr. collector's ed. Kirk Douglas. Read by Michael Mitchell. 6 cass. (Running Time: 9 hrs.). 1997. 48.00 (978-0-7366-3829-6(6), 4522) Books on Tape.
The author discusses his devastating stroke & crippling injuries from a helicopter crash.

Climbing up on the Rough Side. abr. ed. Composed by Hopeful Gospel Quartet Staff. Told to Garrison Keillor et al. 1 CD. (Running Time: 41 mins.). (ENG.). 1997. audio compact disk 16.95 (978-1-56511-255-1(5), 1565112555) Pub: HighBridge. Dist(s): Workman Pub

Clinging to the Wreckage: A Part of Life, unabr. ed. John Mortimer. Narrated by Patrick Tull. 6 cass. (Running Time: 8 hrs. 45 mins.). 1997. 51.00 (978-0-7887-1333-0(7), 95179E7) Recorded Bks.
Author draws a quirky portrait of his own colorful life. With wit & style, he takes readers from his austere childhood in 1930s British boarding school through his successful middle-aged years with careers in law & writing.

Clinic. Jonathan Kellerman. Read by Alexander Adams. (Alex Delaware Ser.: No. 11). 1997. audio compact disk 72.00 (978-0-7366-8534-4(0)) Books on Tape.

Clinic. unabr. ed. Jonathan Kellerman. Read by Alexander Adams. 8 cass. (Running Time: 12 hrs.). (Alex Delaware Ser.: No. 11). 1997. 64.00 (978-0-913369-47-0(0), 4251) Books on Tape.
For three months, the police find no clues in the stabbing death of Hope Devane, the author of a pop-psychology bestseller. So they turn to Dr. Alex Delaware to study the case for insights that might point to a killer.

Clinical Advances in Gastroenterology. 6 cass. (Gastroenterology Ser.). 145.00 set, 6 cass. per year (every other month). (1046-7165) Ed Reviews.
Updates by experts on key issues, trends & clinical advances in gastroenterology.

Clinical & Immunologic Effects of Allergy Immunotherapy. Read by Ross E. Rocklin. 1 cass. (Running Time: 90 min.). 1986. 12.00 (C8632) Amer Coll Phys.

Clinical Application of Active Imagination Techniques. Read by Lois Khan. 2 cass. (Running Time: 3 hrs.). 1987. 18.95 Set. (978-0-7822-0115-4(6), 269) C G Jung IL.

Clinical Aspects of Memory. Speeches. Narrated by Paul Nussbaum. 3 CDs. (Running Time: 3 hrs. 49 mins). 2003. audio compact disk 59.00 (978-1-932609-03-5(2)) Cortext.
Learn how the brain processes and retrieves images in this dynamic new course. Brain pathology, amnesias, dementias and techniques to facilitate learning are explored with renowned neuropsychologist and author Paul Nussbaum.

Clinical Aspects of Perinatal Asphyxia. Contrib. by William J. Keenan et al. 1 cass. (American Academy of Pediatrics UPDATE: Vol. 17, No. 1). 1998. 20.00 Am Acad Pediat.

Clinical Basic Science Problems in Surgery: Endocrine Surgery. (Postgraduate Programs Ser.: C85-PG16). 45.00 (8526) Am Coll Surgeons.
Provides an overview of recent advances in basic science endocrinology as applied to clinical surgery. 6 hours CME category 1 credit.

Clinical Basic Science Problems in Surgery; Gastrointestinal Endoscopy for the Surgeon. Moderated by C. Thomas Bombeck, III. (Postgraduate Programs Ser.: C86-PG16). 1986. 57.00 (8626) Am Coll Surgeons.
Provides an outline of advances of upper & lower gastrointestinal endoscopy. 6 hours CME credit.

Clinical Chemistry. unabr. ed. Read by Richard F. Dods. 8 cass. (Running Time: 8 hrs.). 625.00 Set, incl. 420p. manual. (A9) Am Chemical.

Clinical Chemistry in France: A Strategic Reference 2006. Compiled by Icon Group International, Inc. Staff. 2007. ring bd. 195.00 (978-0-497-35946-1(4)) Icon Grp.

Clinical Diagnostic Equipment in Mexico: A Strategic Reference 2007. Compiled by Icon Group International, Inc. Staff. 2007. ring bd. 195.00 (978-0-497-82349-8(7)) Icon Grp.

Clinical Hypnosis: Brief Treatment with Restructuring & Self-Management. Herbert Spiegel & David Speigel. 6 cass. (Running Time: 5 hr. 37 min.). Incl. Clinical Hypnosis: Clinical Demonstrations: Alleviating Insomnia, Smoking Cessation, Weight Control, Pain Control, Controlling Conversion Reactions. 1989.; Clinical Hypnosis: Hypnosis: Myths & Facts about Clinical Applications. 1989.; Clinical Hypnosis: Restructuring Procedures: Guide to Clinical Applications. 1989.; Clinical Hypnosis: The Hypnotic Induction Profile: Assessing Trance Capacity. 1989.; (ENG.). 1989. 75.00 set. (978-0-89862-804-3(0)) Guilford Pubns.
One of the most scholarly & comprehensive courses available in clinical hypnosis. Distinguished by its innovative use of trance as a diagnostic tool, setting the stage for effective, short term treatment. Encourages self-instructions for patients.

Clinical Hypnosis: Clinical Demonstrations: Alleviating Insomnia, Smoking Cessation, Weight Control, Pain Control, Controlling Conversion Reactions see Clinical Hypnosis: Brief Treatment with Restructuring and Self-Management

Clinical Hypnosis: Hypnosis: Myths & Facts about Clinical Applications see Clinical Hypnosis: Brief Treatment with Restructuring and Self-Management

Clinical Hypnosis: Restructuring Procedures: Guide to Clinical Applications see Clinical Hypnosis: Brief Treatment with Restructuring and Self-Management

Clinical Hypnosis: The Hypnotic Induction Profile: Assessing Trance Capacity see Clinical Hypnosis: Brief Treatment with Restructuring and Self-Management

Clinical Laboratories in China: A Strategic Reference 2006. Compiled by Icon Group International, Inc. Staff. 2007. ring bd. 195.00 (978-0-497-35866-2(2)) Icon Grp.

Clinical Laboratory Equipment in Philippines: A Strategic Reference 2007. Compiled by Icon Group International, Inc. Staff. 2007. ring bd. 195.00 (978-0-497-82384-9(5)) Icon Grp.

Clinical Laboratory Testing Devices & Equipment in Thailand: A Strategic Reference 2007. Compiled by Icon Group International, Inc. Staff. 2007. ring bd. 195.00 (978-0-497-82438-9(8)) Icon Grp.

Clinical Management of Swallowing Disorders. Thomas Murry. (C). 2009. audio compact disk 29.95 (978-1-59756-380-2(3)) Plural Pub Inc.

Clinical Phonetics. 3rd abr. ed. Lawrence D. Shriberg & Raymond D. Kent. 2002. 49.20 (978-0-205-37778-7(5)) Allyn.

Clinical Sciences Pack B see 6 Clinical Sciences Lectures Absolutely Simple & Easy: Pack B Usmle, Step II, III, Spex, Complex Canadian Qualifaine

Clinical Spectrum of Vasculitis. Read by Anthony S. Fauci. 1 cass. (Running Time: 90 min.). 1985. 12.00 (C8559) Amer Coll Phys.

Clinical Strategies in Bronchospasm. Read by Thomas L. Petty. 1 cass. (Running Time: 90 min.). 1985. 12.00 (C8557) Amer Coll Phys.

Clinical Use of Oxaliplatin: Case Studies & Roundtable Discussion. Ed. by John L. Marshall. 2004. pap. bk. 19.95 (978-1-891483-28-8(5)) PRR.

Clinical Workshop, Package F 9000 Q/A: Usmle Step 2; Usmle Step 3, Spex, Comlex. Ljubo Skrbic. (Running Time: 20 hrs.). (C). 2003. bk. 250.00 (978-1-932622-06-5(3)) Postgraduate Med Rev Ed.

Clinton Chart. Nancy Rampendahl. Read by Nancy Rampendahl. 1 cass. (Running Time: 90 min.). 1994. 8.95 (1155) Am Fed Astrologers.
Horoscope of Bill Clinton.

***Clinton Tapes.** unabr. ed. Taylor Branch. Narrated by Boyd Gaines. 1 Playaway. (Running Time: 28 hrs. 45 mins.). 2009. 64.75 (978-1-4407-2755-9(4)); audio compact disk 123.75 (978-1-4407-6251-2(1)) Recorded Bks.

***Clinton Tapes.** unabr. collector's ed. Taylor Branch. Narrated by Boyd Gaines. 24 CDs. (Running Time: 28 hrs. 45 mins.). 2009. audio compact disk 61.95 (978-1-4407-2754-2(6)) Recorded Bks.

Clinton Tapes: Wrestling History with the President. abr. ed. Taylor Branch. Read by Taylor Branch. 8 CDs. (Running Time: 11 hrs. 0 mins. 0 sec.). (ENG.). 2009. audio compact disk 39.99 (978-0-7435-7674-1(8)) Pub: S&S Audio. Dist(s): S and S Inc

Clintonomics & the Lessons of the 1980s. unabr. ed. Robert L. Bartley. Read by Robert L. Bartley. 1 cass. (Running Time: 1 hr.). (Policy Forum Ser.). 1993. bk. 14.95; 9.95 (978-0-945999-32-4(1)) Independent Inst.
Based upon his book, "The Seven Fat Years: And How to Do It Again," in this speech Mr. Bartley discusses how the economy grew by one-third in the 1980s. He also discusses how the current political & economic myopia threaten to push the U.S. into a collective crisis of confidence of its own making, & that the current recession has resulted from an abandonment of the earlier "new classical economic" policies.

Clintonomics, the Information Revolution & the New Global Market Economy. unabr. ed. Walter B. Wriston. Read by Walter B. Wriston. 1 cass. (Running Time: 1 hr.). (Policy Forum Ser.). 1993. bk. 14.95 (978-0-945999-31-7(3)); 9.95 (978-0-945999-30-0(5)) Independent Inst.
Based upon his book, "The Twilight of Sovereignty", in this speech Mr. Wriston focuses on how the information revolution has eroded the control of government leaders & how the structure of the business firm is changing as well.

Clinton's Trip to China. Leonard Peikoff. 1 cass. (Philosophy: Who Needs It? Ser.). 1998. 12.95 (LPXXC63) Second Renaissance.

Clinton's Trip to China II. Leonard Peikoff. 1 cass. (Philosophy: Who Needs It? Ser.). 1998. 12.95 (LPXXC64) Second Renaissance.

Clip Art, Decorating & Publicity. Created by Group Publishing. (Power Lab Ser.). 2008. audio compact disk 19.99 (978-5-557-52144-4(5)) Group Pub.

Clipper Ships see Twentieth-Century Poetry in English, No. 4, Recordings of Poets Reading Their Own Poetry

Clippity-Clop - Clippity-Clop. Silvia Silk. 1982. (978-0-938861-10-2(7)) Jasmine Texts.

Clique Instinct: A Prescient Conscience. Ann Ree Colton & Jonathan Murro. 1 cass. 7.95 (978-0-917189-12-8(4)) A R Colton Fnd.

Clique Summer Collection Box Set. unabr. ed. Read by Cassandra Morris. Created by Lisi Harrison. (Running Time: 17 hrs. 30 mins.). (Clique Summer Collection: Nos. 1-5). (ENG.). 2009. 29.98 (978-1-60024-701-9(6)) Pub: Hachet Audio. Dist(s): HachBkGrp

***Cliques?** Cerebellum Academic Team. (Running Time: 18 mins.). (Lesson Booster Ser.). 2010. cd-rom 79.95 (978-1-59443-697-0(5)) Cerebellum.

Clive Barker's the History of the Devil, Set. Perf. by Dylan Baker et al. 2 cass. (Running Time: 3 hrs.). 1999. 17.98 (4421) Radio Spirits.

Clive Jenkins: Role of the Unions see Buckley's Firing Line

CLO Feeder Watshers Gd to Backyard. Thayer Birding Staff. 2003. audio compact disk 19.95 (978-1-887148-17-7(5)) Thayer Birding.

Cloak & Dagger: Swastika on the Windmill & Recommendation from Rommell. 1 cass. (Running Time: 1 hr.). 2001. 6.98 (1625) Radio Spirits.

***Clochar Ban.** Treasa Ni Mhiollain. (ENG.). 1989. 11.95 (978-0-8023-7022-8(5)) Pub: Clo Iar-Chonnachta IRL. Dist(s): Dufour

Clock, unabr. ed. James Lincoln Collier. Narrated by Alexandra O'Karma. 3 pieces. (Running Time: 4 hrs. 15 mins.). (gr. 6 up). 1994. 27.00 (978-1-55690-600-8(5), 92205E7) Recorded Bks.
Fifteen-year-old Annie Steele longs to become a teacher, but her spendthrift father throws the family into debt when he buys the workings of a clock. Now Annie must find work at the local mill to support her family. She soon finds that the bullying overseer, Mr. Hoggart, is stealing bags of wool. Can Annie convince the mill's owner of her discovery?.

***Clock: Bad Dreams.** Perf. by Alice Frost et al. 2010. audio compact disk 18.95 (978-1-57019-938-7(8)) Radio Spirits.

Clock: The Bank Vault & Hollywood Heartache. 1 cass. (Running Time: 1 hr.). 2001. 6.98 (1561) Radio Spirits.

Clock: The Hunter & the Hunted & A Helping Hand. Perf. by Charles Tingle. 1 cass. (Running Time: 1 hr.). 2001. 6.98 (2555) Radio Spirits.

Clock: The Manicurist & The Ride to Tijuana. 1 cass. (Running Time: 1 hr.). 2001. 6.98 (2132) Radio Spirits.

***Clock Strikes Twelve.** Patricia Wentworth. 2010. 54.95 (978-0-7531-4219-6(8)); audio compact disk 71.95 (978-0-7531-4220-2(1)) Pub: Isis Pubng Ltd GBR. Dist(s): Ulverscroft US

Clock This: My Life as an Inventor. unabr. ed. Trevor Baylis. Narrated by Gordon Griffin. 7 cass. (Running Time: 9 hrs. 45 mins.). 2000. 64.00 (978-1-84197-233-6(9), H1189L8) Recorded Bks.
Trevor Baylis has been inventing things nearly all of his life, his ambition always to solve problems & help others. Trevor takes us through his life, from memories of his jobs as swimming pool salesman, Berlin circus escape artist, & full-time stuntman, to his award-winning inventions that have given him celebrity status. His personal goal is to inspire & inform future inventors. His success has won him an OBE, the Presidential Gold & Silver medals from the Institution of Mechanical Engineers.

Clock Winder. unabr. ed. Anne Tyler. Read by Mary Peiffer. 7 cass. (Running Time: 10 hrs. 30 min.). 1994. 56.00 (978-0-7366-2719-1(7), 3449) Books on Tape.
The Emersons are a fragmented Baltimore family on the verge of destruction. The free-spirited Elizabeth drifts into their lives & Mrs. Emerson & the two sons become dependent on her. Elizabeth makes a tragic error in mistaking dependence for love & shatters their universe.

Clocks. unabr. ed. Agatha Christie. Read by Robin Bailey. 5 cass. (Running Time: 7 hrs. 41 mins.). 2004. 27.95 (978-1-57270-393-3(8)) Pub: Audio Partners. Dist(s): PerseuPGW

Clocks. unabr. ed. Agatha Christie. Read by Robin Bailey. 7 CDs. (Running Time: 9 hrs.). (Mystery Masters Ser.). (ENG.). 2004. audio compact disk 29.95 (978-1-57270-394-0(6)) Pub: AudioGO. Dist(s): Perseus Dist

Clocks & More Clocks. 2004. 8.95 (978-1-56008-873-8(7)); cass. & flmstrp 30.00 (978-1-56008-652-9(1)) Weston Woods.

Clocks Symphony. unabr. ed. Narrated by Janet E. Osen. Composed by Janet E. Osen. 1 CD. (Running Time: 40 mins.). (Clock Ser.). (J). (ps-k). 2000. bk. 9.95 (978-0-9700489-2-9(0)) Little Fiddle.
Features the Mini Maestro Theme Song with narration of The Tic-Toc Clocks. Classical music selections from Haydn's "The Clock" & "The Surprise Symphony".

***Clockwork Angel.** unabr. ed. Cassandra Clare. Read by Jennifer Ehle. (Running Time: 15 hrs. 30 mins. 0 sec.). (Infernal Devices Ser.). (ENG.). (YA). 2010. audio compact disk 39.99 (978-1-4423-3460-1(6)) Pub: S&S Audio. Dist(s): S and S Inc

***Clockwork Heart.** unabr. ed. Druann Pagliassotti. (Running Time: 13 hrs.). (Clockwork Heart Ser.). 2011. audio compact disk 29.99 (978-1-4418-6367-6(2), 9781441863676, Bril Audio CD Unabri) Brilliance Audio.

Clockwork or All Wound Up. unabr. ed. Philip Pullman. Read by Anton Lesser. 1 cass. (Running Time: 1 hr., 30 min.). (J). (gr. 1-8). 1999. 9.95 (CTC 793, Chivers Child Audio) AudioGO.

Clockwork Orange. unabr. ed. Anthony Burgess. Read by Tom Hollander. 7 CDs. (Running Time: 8 hrs.). 2007. audio compact disk 34.95 (978-0-06-117062-1(3), Caedmon) HarperCollins Pubs.

Clockwork Orange: Play with Music. abr. ed. Anthony Burgess. Read by Anthony Burgess. 1 cass. (Running Time: 51 min.). 10.95 (978-0-8045-1120-9(9), SAC 1120) Spoken Arts.
Tour de force of images, music, words & feelings, includes chapters from "A Clockwork Orange" & "Enderby".

***Clockwork Orange CD.** unabr. ed. Anthony Burgess. Read by Tom Hollander. (ENG.). 2007. (978-0-06-145089-1(8), Harper Audio); (978-0-06-145087-7(1), Harper Audio) HarperCollins Pubs.

***Clockwork Three.** Matthew Kirby. (ENG.). 2010. audio compact disk 79.99 (978-0-545-24958-4(9)); audio compact disk 39.99 (978-0-545-24955-3(4)) Scholastic Inc.

Cloister Walk, abr. ed. Kathleen Norris. Read by Debra Winger. 2 cass. (Running Time: 3 hrs.). 1996. 17.95 (978-1-57453-033-9(X), 330102) Audio Lit.

Cloister Walk. unabr. collector's ed. Kathleen Norris. Read by Kimberly Schraf. 8 cass. (Running Time: 12 hrs.). 1996. 64.00 (978-0-7366-3511-0(4), 4150) Books on Tape.
What could a married woman learn from a Benedictine monastery? This is what Kathleen Norris asks herself as she begins an extended stay at one in Minnesota. Yet upon leaving the monastery, the daily events in her secular life take on new meaning.

Cloning Christ. Peter Senese. 5 CDs. (Running Time: 7 hrs.). 2004. audio compact disk 34.99 (978-1-58926-137-2(2)) Oasis Audio.
Cloning Christ spins a tangled web of deceit, blackmail, violence, loss, faith, forgiveness, truth and acceptance. It is a story that questions the right to clone, killing one man to save another, while responding to the needs and harsh realities of life as we know it.

Cloning Christ. abr. ed. Peter Senese & Robert Geis. Read by Eric Synnestvedt. 2004. 29.99 (978-1-58926-136-5(4)) Oasis Audio.

Cloning of Joanna May. unabr. ed. Fay Weldon. Read by Norma West. 8 cass. (Running Time: 9 hrs. 30 min.). 2001. 69.95 (978-1-85695-487-7(0), 92091) Pub: ISIS Audio GBR. Dist(s): Ulverscroft US

Cloquet - Changes in Time. Timothy J. Krohn. 2004. audio compact disk 14.95 (978-0-9618959-9-0(3)) Carlton County Historical Society.

Close. abr. ed. Martina Cole. Read by Nicola Duffett. (Running Time: 6 hrs.). (ENG.). 2008. 24.98 (978-1-60024-269-4(3)) Pub: Hachet Audio. Dist(s): HachBkGrp

Close. abr. ed. Martina Cole. Read by Nicola Duffett. (Running Time: 5 hrs. 52 mins.). 2009. audio compact disk (978-1-4055-0614-4(8)) Little BrownUK GBR.

Close Call. J. M. Gregson. 2008. 61.95 (978-1-84559-863-1(6)); audio compact disk 71.95 (978-1-84559-864-8(4)) Pub: Soundings Ltd GBR. Dist(s): Ulverscroft US

Close Call. unabr. ed. John McEvoy. Read by Tom Weiner. (Running Time: 30600 sec.). 2008. 54.95 (978-1-4332-1157-7(2)); audio compact disk & audio compact disk 29.95 (978-1-4332-1159-1(9)); audio compact disk & audio compact disk 70.00 (978-1-4332-1158-4(0)) Blckstn Audio.

Close Case. Alafair Burke. Read by Betty Bobbitt. (Running Time: 10 hrs. 30 mins.). 2009. 84.99 (978-1-74214-194-7(3), 9781742141947) Pub: Bolinda Pubng AUS. Dist(s): Bolinda Pub Inc

Close Case: A Samantha Kincaid Mystery. unabr. ed. Alafair Burke. Read by Betty Bobbitt. (Running Time: 37800 sec.). 2006. audio compact disk 72.00 (978-1-74093-799-3(6)) Pub: Bolinda Pubng AUS. Dist(s): Bolinda Pub Inc

Close Combat. unabr. ed. W. E. B. Griffin. Read by Michael Russotto. 10 cass. (Running Time: 15 hrs.). (Corps Ser.: Bk. 6). 1993. 80.00 (978-0-7366-2423-7(6), 112719) Books on Tape.
The Marine Corps prepares for the defense of Guadalcanal against the Japanese.

Close Encounters. Sandra Kitt. Narrated by J. D. Jackson. 7 cass. (Running Time: 9 hrs. 45 mins.). 64.00 (978-0-7887-5122-6(0)) Recorded Bks.

Close Encounters of the Fourth Kind: Alien Abduction, UFOs & the Conference at M. I. T. abr. ed. C. D. Bryan & C. D. B. Bryan. Read by C. D. B. Bryan. 2 cass. (Running Time: 3 hrs.). 1996. 17.95 (978-1-57453-035-3(6), 330104) Audio Lit.
Is anybody out there & what do they want with us? Veteran reporter & author of "Friendly Fire," Bryan examines the enduring mysteries of alien abductions & UFOs & comes to some startling conclusions.

Close Encounters of the Holy Kind: Logos Sept. 21, 1997. Ben Young. 1997. 4.95 (978-0-7417-6048-7(7), B0048) Win Walk.

Close Encounters with the Hubble. unabr. ed. Elaine Scott. Narrated by Nelson Runger. 1 cass. (Running Time: 1 hr. 30 mins.). (gr. 2 up). 1998. 10.00 (978-0-7887-0901-2(1), 95039E7) Recorded Bks.
Guided tour of the incredible cosmos, from our own solar system neighborhood to the outer reaches of the universe.

Close Her Eyes. unabr. ed. Dorothy Simpson. Read by Terrence Hardiman. 6 cass. (Running Time: 9 hrs.). (Inspector Thanet Mystery Ser.). 2000. 49.95 (978-0-7451-6711-4(X), CAB 1327) Pub: Chivers Audio Bks GBR. Dist(s): AudioGO
Inspector Thanet is on the case of Charity Pritchard, a young girl who has been missing for some time now. But his concern deepens when her family, religious fundamentalists, leaves the matter in God's hands. Thanet doesn't pay much heed to first impressions, but it will be a good while after he finds Charity's poor broken body before he realizes just how wrong his preconceptions can be.

Close Kin. Clare B. Dunkle. Narrated by Jenny Sterlin. 6 cass. (Running Time: 7 hrs. 15 mins.). (Hollow Kingdom Trilogy: Vol. 2). (YA). 2004. 54.75 (978-1-4025-8503-6(9)) Recorded Bks.

Close Like a Pro: Selling Strategies for Success. unabr. rev. ed. Nido R. Qubein. Read by Nido R. Qubein. (Running Time: 4 hrs.). (ENG.). 2006. audio compact disk 19.98 (978-1-59659-075-5(0), GildAudio) Pub: Gildan Media. Dist(s): HachBkGrp

Close More Sales. Lee Boyan. Read by Lee Boyan. 6 cass. (Running Time: 6 hrs.). 1987. 65.00 Set. (978-1-881302-25-4(3), 050) L Boyan Assocs.
An audio program that combines all the most successful, tried & true principles & techniques of selling into one quick, clear, concise sales-producing program, conducted by sales trainer, Lee Boyan.

Close Quarters. Larry Heinemann. Read by Richard Ferrone. (Running Time: 39600 sec.). 2006. 65.95 (978-0-7861-4585-0(4)); audio compact disk 81.00 (978-0-7861-7030-2(1)) Blckstn Audio.

Close Quarters. abr. unabr. ed. Larry Heinemann. Read by Richard Ferrone. (Running Time: 39600 sec.). 2006. audio compact disk 29.95 (978-0-7861-7704-2(7)) Blckstn Audio.

Close Quarters. abr. ed. Larry Heinemann. Read by Richard Ferrone. 9 cass. (Running Time: 39600 sec.). 2006. 26.95 (978-0-7861-4477-8(7)); audio compact disk 26.95 (978-0-7861-7277-1(0)) Blckstn Audio.

Close Quarters. unabr. collector's ed. Larry Heinemann. Read by Walter Zimmerman. 10 cass. (Running Time: 15 hrs.). 1988. 80.00 (978-0-7366-1409-2(5), 2298) Books on Tape.
Like many other high school graduates in the 1960s Philip Dosier found that if he didn't have plans for himself, his country certainly did. Shipped off to fight in a war he knew nothing about, he found himself in a world of violence, fear, heat, & squalor unlike anything he ever dreamed could exist.

Close Quarters, Bk. 2. unabr. ed. William Golding. Read by William Golding. 8 cass. (Running Time: 9 hrs.). (Isis Ser.). (J). 2004. 69.95 (978-1-85089-790-3(5), 90061) Pub: ISIS Lrg Prnt GBR. Dist(s): Ulverscroft US

Close Range: Wyoming Stories. unabr. ed. Annie Proulx. Read by William Dufris. 6 vols. (Running Time: 9 hrs.). 2001. bk. 54.95 (978-0-7927-2479-7(8), CSL 368, Chivers Sound Lib) AudioGO.
Masterful language & fierce love of Wyoming shape these breathtaking tales of loneliness, quick violence & the wrong kinds of love. Set in a landscape both stark & magnificent, these are stories of brutal & unforgettable beauty.

Close Range: Wyoming Stories. unabr. ed. Annie Proulx. 2004. 15.95 (978-0-7435-4283-8(5)) Pub: S&S Audio. Dist(s): S and S Inc

Close Run Thing. Allan Mallinson. Narrated by Erick Graham. 12 CDs. (Running Time: 14 hrs. 45 mins.). 2001. audio compact disk 120.00 (978-1-84197-198-8(7), C1350E7) Recorded Bks.
It's 1814 & Napoleon is hard-pressed to defend France from a combination of Russia, Prussia, Austria & Britain. Nor is he the only one in a quandary. Matthew Hervey, a young British comet, is in a rather unusual situation. As far as he knows, it's highly irregular to be arrested on a battlefield after a successful action. Still, it's hardly the first time politics has interrupted war, & as Hervey's career progresses, he increasingly balances both, sometimes more successfully than others!.

Close Run Thing. unabr. ed. Allan Mallinson. Narrated by Erick Graham. 11 cass. (Running Time: 14 hrs. 45 mins.). 2000. 98.00 (978-1-84197-108-7(1), H1104E7) Recorded Bks.

Close That Sale! Virden J. Thornton. (Self-Directed Learning Program Ser.). 2000. pap. bk. 249.00 (978-1-56052-407-6(3)) Crisp Pubns.

Close to Death. 2 cass. (Running Time: 3 hrs.). (SmartReader Ser.). (J). 1999. pap. bk. & tchr. ed. 19.95 (978-0-7887-0557-1(1), 79337T3) Recorded Bks.
What happens during a near-death experience? How does it affect a person's life? Now you can find out.

Close to Home. Peter Robinson. Narrated by Ron Keith. 12 cass. (Running Time: 16 hrs.). (Inspector Banks Mystery Ser.). 2003. 108.00 (978-1-4025-3860-5(X)) Recorded Bks.

Close to Home. Poems. Featuring David Whyte. Music by Eastwest. one. 1992. audio compact disk 17.00 (978-1-932887-02-0(4)) Many Rivers Pr.
A selection of 12 poems written and recited by David Whyte, with a musical background. The poems are taken from the books titled "Where Many Rivers Meet", and "Fire in the Earth", both by David Whyte.

Close to Home. unabr. ed. Deborah Moggach. Read by Garard Green. 7 cass. (Running Time: 8 hrs. 15 min.). 2001. 61.95 (978-1-85695-423-5(4), 92114) Pub: ISIS Audio GBR. Dist(s): Ulverscroft US
Kate Cooper is almost content. Her husband James is handsome & successful, but imprisoned in his own reserve. Their neighbors, the Greens, are far too preoccupied with their respective careers to pay any attention to their family. During one summer, their lives converge in unexpected ways, & the results threaten their tranquil, everyday lives.

Close to Shore: The Terrifying Shark Attacks of 1916. unabr. ed. Michael Capuzzo. Read by Taylor Mali. 3 CDs. (Running Time: 14400 sec.). (YA). (gr. 7 up). 2007. audio compact disk 39.95 (978-0-9761932-6-5(4)) Audio Bkshelf.

Close to the Bone. unabr. ed. William G. Tapply. Read by David Brand. 6 vols. (Running Time: 9 hrs.). (Brady Coyne Ser.). 2000. bk. 54.95 (978-0-7927-2212-0(4), CSL 101, Chivers Sound Lib) AudioGO.
Brady Coyne has a thriving law practice. When an old client needs a defense lawyer for his son, Brady enlists his fishing buddy, Paul Cizek. Cizek is called in to defend Glen Falconer, who killed a woman while driving drunk. The case looks open and shut against Glen, but Cizek works miracles and gets him off. Not long after his victory, Cizek disappears when the Coast Guard finds his empty boat drifting at sea. Brady decides to take a closer look. Was it an accident, suicide or even murder?.

Close to the Bone: Life-Threatening Illness & the Search for Meaning. abr. ed. Jean Shinoda Bolen. Read by Jean Shinoda Bolen. 2 cass. (Running Time: 3 hrs.). 1996. 17.95 (978-1-57453-125-1(5)) Audio Lit.
Weaves myth, experience & story to show that facing one's mortality can be a life-transforming & even a life-saving, process.

Close to the Wind. Warren Salinger. 1 cass. 1999. 14.00 Incl. 213 p. (978-0-9660325-2-9(7), 99-70892) Trillium Bks.

Close to You. unabr. ed. Mary Jane Clark. Read by Carrington MacDuffie. 6 vols. (Running Time: 9 hrs.). (KEY News Ser.: Bk. 4). 2002. bk. 54.95 (978-0-7927-2528-2(X), CSL 417, Chivers Sound Lib); audio compact disk 79.95 (978-0-7927-9857-6(0), SLD 108, Chivers Sound Lib) AudioGO.
It begins innocently enough: A fan letter. A request for an autograph. Someone wants to get close to news anchor Eliza Blake. Someone who will kill to get what they want. In order to stay one step ahead of a psychopath, she has to answer five questions. Who is no longer content with just seeing her on TV? What can she do to protect herself? Where is the stalker hiding? When should she take matters into her own hands? Why have so many people become obsessed with getting close to her? it could be anyone with a television set.

Close to You. unabr. ed. Christina Dodd. Read by Natalie Ross. (Running Time: 11 hrs.). (Lost Texas Hearts Ser.: No. 3). 2010. 39.97 (978-1-4418-2509-4(6), 9781441825094, Brinc Audio MP3 Lib); 24.99 (978-1-4418-2508-7(8), 9781441825087, Brilliance MP3); 39.97 (978-1-4418-2511-7(8), 9781441825117, BADLE); 24.99 (978-1-4418-2510-0(X), 9781441825100, BAD); audio compact disk 89.97

(978-1-4418-2507-0(X), 9781441825070, BriAudCD Unabrid); audio compact disk 29.99 (978-1-4418-2506-3(1), 9781441825063, Bril Audio CD Unabri) Brilliance Audio.

***Close Your Eyes: A Novel.** unabr. ed. Amanda Eyre Ward. (ENG.). 2011. audio compact disk 30.00 (978-0-307-91296-1(5), Random AudioBks) Pub: Random Audio Pubg. Dist(s): Random

Close Your Eyes & Time to Rise. Read by Joanie Bartels. 2 cass. (Running Time: 75 min.). (Magic Series Gift Collection). (J). pap. bk. set incl. 2 lyric bks. (978-1-881225-10-2(0)) Discov Music.
Two full length audio cassettes, plus two full color lyric books with words to lullaby & wake-up songs.

Closed Circle. Jonathan Coe. Read by Colin Buchanan. 9 cass. 79.95 (978-0-7927-3780-3(6), CSL 856); audio compact disk 99.95 (978-0-7927-3781-0(4), SLD 856) AudioGO.

Closed Circle, Set. unabr. ed. Robert Goddard. 10 CDs. (Running Time: 45240 sec.). (Sound Library). 2000. 99.95 (978-0-7540-5323-1(7), CCD 014) Pub: Chivers Audio Bks GBR. Dist(s): AudioGO
It is 1931 & the luxurious liner Empress of Britain is on her transatlantic passage, bearing among its passengers two English confidence trixters. A chance meeting on deck brings a tempting new target in the shape of Diana Charnwood, only daughter of wealthy Fabian Charnwood. The plot is to charm the daughter into an engagement, then get the father to buy her way out of it.

Closed Circle, Set. unabr. ed. Robert Goddard. Read by Bill Wallis. 10 cass. (Running Time: 45240 sec.). (1930's Ser.). 2004. 84.95 (978-0-7540-0410-3(4), CAB 1833) Pub: Chivers Audio Bks GBR. Dist(s): AudioGO

Closed for Good see Robert Frost in Recital

***Closed for the Season.** unabr. ed. Mary Downing Hahn. (Running Time: 5 hrs.). 2011. 39.97 (978-1-61106-145-1(8), 9781611061451, BADLE); 24.99 (978-1-61106-144-4(X), 9781611061444, BAD); 24.99 (978-1-61106-142-0(3), 9781611061420, Brilliance MP3); 39.97 (978-1-61106-143-7(1), 9781611061437, Brinc Audio MP3 Lib); audio compact disk 24.99 (978-1-61106-140-6(7), 9781611061406, Bril Audio CD Unabri); audio compact disk 54.97 (978-1-61106-141-3(5), 9781611061413, BriAudCD Unabrid) Brilliance Audio.

Closed on Account of Rabies: Poems & Tales of Edgar Allan Poe, Set. unabr. ed. Poems. Read by Christopher Walken et al. 2 cass. (Running Time: 6 hr.). 1997. 20.00 (978-0-9662042-0-9(4)) Mouth Almighty.
Readings of poems & tales with musical accompaniment.

Closely Held Business: Estate Freezes & Other Planning Considerations. 4 cass. (Running Time: 5 hrs. 30 min.). 1991. 125.00 (T7-9341) PLI.

Closer. Perf. by Myrrh. 1 Tape. (Running Time: 58 mins.). 2002. 9.99 (978-0-9725443-9-9(9)) Pub: Myrrh Pub. Dist(s): STL Dist NA
Bill Murk and daughter Heather, of the music group Myrrh, join together to create a soothing blend of praise and worship. Between Bill?s sensitive touch on the violin, and Heather?s amazing vocal flexibility and contemporary style, this album is one to be enjoyed by all. Closer is being released to commemorate the three-year anniversary of their nearly fatal head-on collision.

Closer. Perf. by Myrrh. 1 CD. (Running Time: 58 mins.). 2003. audio compact disk 14.99 (978-0-9725443-8-2(0)) Pub: Myrrh Pub. Dist(s): STL Dist NA
"Bill Murk and daughter Heather, of the music group Myrrh, join together to create a soothing blend of praise and worship. Between Bill's sensitive touch on the violin, and Heather's amazing vocal flexibility and contemporary style, this album is one to be enjoyed by all.".

Closer Look. (Paws & Tales Ser.: Vol. 8). (J). 2001. 3.99 (978-1-57972-400-9(0)); audio compact disk 5.99 (978-1-57972-401-6(9)) Insight Living.

Closer Look at Golden Parachutes, 1989. unabr. ed. Ed. by James P. Klein. 1 cass. (Running Time: 25 min.). (Quarterly Employee Benefits Audio Reports). 1989. 55.00 series of 4. (T7-9240) PLI.
The Employee Benefits Reports, a quarterly series of audiocassettes, is designed to keep practitioners & their clients informed of key litigation, legislation & regulatory actions. This audio series annually provides twenty to thirty minute reports, by experts on the most recent developmnebts affecting employee benefitsecting employee benefits.

Closer Look at Peter Rabbit. (J). 2004. 8.95 (978-1-56008-874-5(5)); cass. & flmstrp 30.00 (978-0-89719-588-1(4)) Weston Woods.

Closer Look at Peter Rabbit, A; Tale of Peter Rabbit. 2004. cass. & flmstrp 30.00 (978-1-56008-805-9(2)) Weston Woods.

Closer to the Start. Created by Fellowship Church. (ENG.). 2008. 15.00 (978-1-934146-86-6(2)) Creality Pub.

Closer Walk with God. Jim Rosemergy. 2 cass. (Running Time: 3 hrs.). 1999. 13.95 (978-0-87159-804-2(3)) Unity Schl Christ.

Closer Walk with Jesus. 1 cass. (Running Time: 30 min.). 1985. (0224) Evang Sisterhood Mary.
Topics are: Treasure in Nazareth; Bearing a Crown of Thorns; Cross-bearer for the World; Encounter with the Risen Lord.

Closer Walk with Thee. Martin Simpson. 1994. pap. bk. 19.95 (978-0-7866-1256-7(8), 95285P); pap. bk. 24.95 (978-0-7866-1255-0(X), 95285CDP) Mel Bay.

Closers. unabr. ed. Michael Connelly. 7 cassettes. (Running Time: 12 hrs.). (Harry Bosch Ser.: No. 11). 2005. 63.00 (978-1-4159-0818-1(4)); audio compact disk 81.00 (978-1-4159-0819-8(2)) Books on Tape.

Closers. unabr. ed. Michael Connelly. Read by Len Cariou. (Harry Bosch Ser.: No. 11). (YA). 2007. 69.99 (978-1-60252-604-4(4)) Find a World.

Closers. unabr. ed. Michael Connelly. Read by Len Cariou. (Harry Bosch Ser.: No. 11). (ENG.). 2005. 14.98 (978-1-59483-165-2(3)) Pub: Hachet Audio. Dist(s): HachBkGrp

Closers. unabr. ed. Michael Connelly. Read by Len Cariou. (Running Time: 12 hrs.). (Harry Bosch Ser.: No. 11). (ENG.). 2009. 70.98 (978-1-60788-044-8(X)) Pub: Hachet Audio. Dist(s): HachBkGrp

Closers Pt. 2, Set: Sales Closers Bible. Ben Gay, III. 11 cass. 1996. 99.95 (978-0-942645-09-5(X)) LJR Group.

Closers Set: Sales Closer's Bible. 2nd ed. Jim Pickens. Ed. by Ben Gay, III. 1988. 99.95 (978-0-942645-01-9(4)) LJR Group.

***Closing Announcements: Selection from Things I've Learned from Women Who've Dumped Me.** abr. ed. Ben Karlin. (Running Time: 3 mins.). (ENG.). 2010. 1.98 (978-1-60788-801-7(7)) Pub: Hachet Audio. Dist(s): HachBkGrp

Closing Exits - Opening Hearts Set: A Guide to Enhancing Relationships. Bill Kerley. 2 cass. 2000. 14.95 (978-1-886298-03-3(3)) Bayou Pubng.
This program is based on the belief that our intimate relationships are in our lives to teach us how to love - not how to be loved. Only as we place ourselves firmly in our relationships - close the exits - can we see how to use the relationship for our emotional & spiritual growth - open our hearts.

Closing In. Kerry Blair. 3 cass. 2004. 14.95 (978-1-59156-024-1(1)) Covenant Comms.

Closing of Haverford State: Program from the Award Winning Public Radio Series. Hosted by Fred Goodwin. Comment by John Hockenberry. Contrib. by Joanne Silberner et al. 1 cass. (Running Time: 1 hr.). (Infinite Mind Ser.). 1999. audio compact disk 21.95 (978-1-888064-17-9(X), LCM 54) Lichtenstein Creat.
What happens when a psychiatric hospital closes down? Veteran radio correspondent Joanne Silberner took a year off from National Public Radio news to investigate the closing of one such hospital near Philadelphia. In this one-hour documentary, exclusive to The Infinite Mind, she follows the stories of patients and staff as they start their new lives. This special report has won three major journalism awards since it was first broadcast in 1999, including a Clarion Award from the Association of Women in Communication, an EDI Award from National Easter Seals and a Deadline Award from Sigma Delta Chi, the Society of Professional Journalists.

Closing of the American Border: Terrorism, Immigration & Security Since 9/11. unabr. ed. Edward Alden. (Running Time: 11 hrs. NaN mins.). 2008. 65.95 (978-1-4332-4705-7(4)); audio compact disk 90.00 (978-1-4332-4706-4(2)) Blckstn Audio.

Closing of the American Border: Terrorism, Immigration, & Security since 9/11. unabr. ed. Edward Alden. (Running Time: 11 hrs. NaN mins.). 2008. 29.95 (978-1-4332-4708-8(9)); audio compact disk 32.95 (978-1-4332-4707-1(0)) Blckstn Audio.

Closing of the American Mind. unabr. ed. Allan Bloom. Read by Christopher Hurt. 11 cass. (Running Time: 16 hrs.). 1993. 76.95 (978-0-7861-0386-7(8), 1338) Blckstn Audio.
One of the great & vitally important books of our time. Allan Bloom, a professor of social thought at the University of Chicago & a noted translator of Plato & Rousseau, argues that the social & political crisis of twentieth century America is really an intellectual crisis. From the universities' lack of purpose to their students' lack of learning, from the jargon of liberation to the supplanting of reason by "creativity," Bloom shows how American democracy has unwittingly played host to vulgarized Continental ideas of nihilism & despair, of relativism disguised as tolerance. He demonstrates that the collective mind of the American university is closed to the principles of the Western tradition & that it is especially closed to the spiritual heritage of the West, which gave rise to the university in the first place.

***Closing of the American Mind.** unabr. ed. Allan Bloom. Read by Christopher Hurt. (Running Time: 16 hrs.). 2010. 29.95 (978-1-4417-4614-6(5)); audio compact disk 118.00 (978-1-4417-4611-5(0)) Blckstn Audio.

Closing Open Doors. Francis Frangipane. 1 cass. (Running Time: 90 mins.). (Basics of Spiritual Warfare Ser.: Vol. 8). 2000. 5.00 (FF02-008) Morning NC.
Francis combines years of practical experience with a soundbiblical perspective in this popular & important series.

Closing Session. Innovation Groups Staff. Contrib. by Peter Block. 1 cass. (Transforming Local Government Ser.: Vol. 7). 1999. 10.00 (978-1-882403-63-9(0), IG9907) Alliance Innov.

Closing the Achievement Gap, Vol. 1201. Glenn Singleton. 3 cass. (Running Time: 2 hrs. 11 mins.). (Leaving No Child Behind Ser.: Vol. 1200). 2005. 445.00 (978-1-58740-122-0(3)) Pub: Corwin Pr. Dist(s): SAGE

Closing the Sale. (Running Time: 41 min.). 12.95 (203) Salenger.
Provides advice on determining when to close a sale.

Closing Time: A Memoir. unabr. ed. Joe Queenan. Narrated by Johnny Heller. (Running Time: 12 hrs. 30 mins. 0 sec.). (ENG.). 2009. audio compact disk 75.99 (978-1-4001-4216-3(4)); audio compact disk 37.99 (978-1-4001-1216-6(8)); audio compact disk 24.99 (978-1-4001-6216-1(5)) Pub: Tantor Media. Dist(s): IngramPubServ

Closing Time: The Sequel to Catch-22. Joseph Heller. 2004. 15.95 (978-0-7435-4284-5(3)) Pub: S&S Audio. Dist(s): S and S Inc

Closing Time: The Sequel to Catch-22. unabr. ed. Joseph Heller. Read by Michael Kramer. 12 cass. (Running Time: 12 hrs.). 1995. 96.00 (978-0-7366-2974-4(2), 3665) Books on Tape.
Sequel to Catch 22. Yossarian & friends, now 70, face a dwindling future. Funny & provocative.

***Closing with the Enemy: How GIs Fought the War in Europe, 1944-1945.** unabr. ed. Michael D. Doubler. Narrated by Mel Foster. (Running Time: 15 hrs. 0 mins.). 2010. 20.99 (978-1-4001-8949-6(7)); 29.99 (978-1-4001-6949-8(6)); audio compact disk 39.99 (978-1-4001-1949-3(9)) Pub: Tantor Media. Dist(s): IngramPubServ

***Closing with the Enemy (Library Edition) How GIs Fought the War in Europe, 1944-1945.** unabr. ed. Michael D. Doubler. Narrated by Mel Foster. (Running Time: 15 hrs. 0 mins.). 2010. 39.99 (978-1-4001-9949-5(2)); audio compact disk 95.99 (978-1-4001-4949-0(5)) Pub: Tantor Media. Dist(s): IngramPubServ

Clothes & Your Appearance. Louise A. Liddell & Carolee S. Samuels. (gr. 7-12). tchr. ed. 200.00 (978-1-59070-139-3(9)) Goodheart.

Clothes Audio CD. Adapted by Benchmark Education Company Staff. Based on a work by Cynthia Swain. (Early Explorers Set C Ser.). (J). (gr. k). 2008. audio compact disk 10.00 (978-1-60437-513-8(2)) Benchmark Educ.

Clothes Long Ago Audio CD. Adapted by Benchmark Education Company Staff. Based on a work by Katherine Scraper. (Early Explorers Set C Ser.). (J). (gr. 1). 2008. audio compact disk 10.00 (978-1-60437-539-8(6)) Benchmark Educ.

Clothes of Sand. Stuart Manning. 2009. audio compact disk 15.95 (978-1-84435-371-2(0)) Pub: Big Finish GBR. Dist(s): Natl Bk Netwk

Clothes Then & Now Audio CD. Adapted by Benchmark Education Company Staff. Based on a work by Vickey Herold. (Early Explorers Set C Ser.). (J). (gr. 2). 2008. audio compact disk 10.00 (978-1-60437-546-6(9)) Benchmark Educ.

Clothing & Apparel in Belgium: A Strategic Reference 2006. Compiled by Icon Group International, Inc. Staff. 2007. ring bd. 195.00 (978-0-497-35824-2(7)) Icon Grp.

Cloud see Treasury of Percy Bysshe Shelley

Cloud Chamber. collector's unabr. ed. Joyce Maynard. Read by Joel Johnstone. 5 CDs. (Running Time: 5 hrs. 39 mins.). (YA). 2005. audio compact disk 45.00 (978-0-307-24618-9(3), BksonTape); 35.00 (978-0-307-24617-2(5), BksonTape) Random Audio Pubg.
The minute the school bus carrying Nate Chance and his little sister, Junie, pulls up in front of his family's farmhouse, Nate can tell something's terribly wrong: Somehow his father has been wounded by a gunshot. Nate sees him stagger across the yard, then watches as the police take him away. Then, nothing. Nobody in the family will say what happened, or where Nate's dad has gone. At school, his best friend, Larry, won't talk to him, and kids whisper that his dad's a "psycho." Back home, police keep showing up with questions for his mom; and then there's Junie, worried that Mom will sell her beloved pony and counting on her big brother to figure out a way to reach their dad. But the science fair is coming up, and Nate has a plan. If he can just win first prize with his amazing cloud chamber project, he'll get to go to the state finals, near the hospital where his dad's been locked away. And since it was his dad who taught him to love science - and the stars - it seems like maybe the magic of the cloud chamber can bring the family together again, too. Too bad he has to work on it with the weirdest, most unpopular girl in school, Naomi, with her goofy hair and nutty idea that the two of them should be best friends. The craziest part is, she just might be right.

Cloud Forest: A Chronicle of the South American Wilderness. unabr. ed. Peter Matthiessen. Read by Stefan Rudnicki. (Running Time: 10 hrs. 0 mins.). 2009. 29.95 (978-1-4417-1063-5(9)); 59.95 (978-1-4417-1059-8(0)); audio compact disk 90.00 (978-1-4417-1060-4(4)) Blckstn Audio.

Cloud Forest: A Chronicle of the South American Wilderness. unabr. ed. Peter Matthiessen. Read by Stefan Rudnicki. (Running Time: 10 hrs.). 2010. audio compact disk 34.95 (978-1-4417-1062-8(0)) Blckstn Audio.

Cloud in Trousers see Classical Russian Poetry

Cloud Mountain. abr. ed. Aimee Liu. Read by B. D. Wong. (ENG.). 2006. 14.98 (978-1-59483-833-0(X)) Pub: Hachet Audio. Dist(s): HachBkGrp

Cloud Mountain. abr. ed. Aimee E. Liu. Read by B. D. Wong. (YA). 2001. 7.95 (978-1-57815-215-5(1), Media Bks Audio) Media Bks NJ.

***Cloud Nine.** abr. ed. Luanne Rice. Read by Sandra Burr. (Running Time: 3 hrs.). 2010. audio compact disk 9.99 (978-1-4418-6695-0(7), 9781441866950, BCD Value Price) Brilliance Audio.

Cloud Nine. unabr. ed. Luanne Rice. Read by Sandra Burr. (Running Time: 10 hrs.). 2008. 24.95 (978-1-4233-7197-7(6), 9781423371977, BAD); 24.95 (978-1-4233-7195-3(X), 9781423371953, Brilliance MP3); 39.25 (978-1-4233-7198-4(4), 9781423371984, BADLE); 39.25 (978-1-4233-7196-0(8), 9781423371960, Brinc Audio MP3 Lib) Brilliance Audio.

***Cloud Nine.** unabr. ed. Luanne Rice. Read by Sandra Burr. (Running Time: 10 hrs.). 2010. audio compact disk 29.99 (978-1-4418-4047-9(8), 9781441840479, Bril Audio CD Unabri); audio compact disk 89.97 (978-1-4418-4048-6(6), 9781441840486, BriAudCD Unabrid) Brilliance Audio.

Cloud of Sparrows. unabr. ed. Takashi Matsuoka. 5 cass. (Running Time: 7 hrs. 30 mins.). 2002. 40.00 (978-0-7366-8858-1(7)) Books on Tape.
A penurious journalist takes a Christmastime cross-country train trip.

Cloud of Sparrows. unabr. ed. Takashi Matsuoka. Read by Ron Rifkin. 11 cass. (Running Time: 16 hrs. 30 mins.). 2002. 88.00 (978-0-7366-8819-2(6)) Books on Tape.
A Japanese lord with the gift of prophecy must prepare with his friends for a final battle.

Cloud of Unknowing. Thomas H. Cook. Read by Stephen Hoye. (Playaway Adult Fiction Ser.). 2008. 59.99 (978-1-60640-975-6(1)) Find a World.

Cloud of Unknowing. Ed. by William Johnson. 8 cass. 32.95 (923) Ignatius Pr.
An anonymous work of the 14th Century by an English mystic.

Cloud of Unknowing. Arthur Young. 1 cass. 9.00 (A0382-88) Sound Photosyn.

Cloud of Unknowing. abr. ed. Read by Alan Jones. Tr. by James Walsh. 2 cass. (Running Time: 3 hrs.). 1995. 16.95 (978-0-944993-05-7(2)) Audio Lit.
Written in the 14th century as a guide to contemplative Christianity, reveals the universality at the heart of Christianity.

***Cloud of Unknowing.** unabr. ed. Anonymous. Narrated by Susan Denaker. (ENG.). 2007. 14.98 (978-1-59644-530-7(0), Hovel Audio) christianaud.

Cloud of Unknowing. unabr. ed. Anonymous. Narrated by Susan Denaker. (Running Time: 4 hrs. 30 mins. 0 sec.). (ENG.). 2007. audio compact disk 23.98 (978-1-59644-529-1(7), Hovel Audio) christianaud.

Cloud of Unknowing. unabr. ed. Thomas H. Cook. Read by Stephen Hoye. (Running Time: 8 hrs. 30 mins. 0 sec.). (ENG.). 2007. audio compact disk 29.99 (978-1-4001-0409-3(2)); audio compact disk 19.99 (978-1-4001-5409-8(X)); audio compact disk 59.99 (978-1-4001-3409-0(9)) Pub: Tantor Media. Dist(s): IngramPubServ

Cloud on Sand. unabr. ed. Gabriella DeFarrai. Read by Susan O'Malley. 9 cass. (Running Time: 13 hrs.). 2000. 62.95 (978-0-7861-1765-9(6), 2568) Blckstn Audio.
It is 1920. On the Italian Riviera, lives Dora, the only woman who has married her way out of poverty & into luxury. She is ignorant, imperious, volcanic, & frightening. Swooping off to Paris or Monte Carolo on mysterious assignations, only to return to sit in her vacant rooms by candlelight, she rules in lonely, widowed splendor over her fading kingdom.

Cloud over Malverton. unabr. ed. Nancy Buckingham. Read by Margaret Holt. 5 cass. (Running Time: 7 hrs. 30 mins.). (Sound Ser.). 2004. 49.95 (978-1-85496-469-4(0), 64690) Pub: UlverLrgPrint GBR. Dist(s): Ulverscroft US

Cloud Princess: A Story from Nelson Mandela's Favorite African Folktales. Read by Matt Damon. Compiled by Nelson Mandela. (Running Time: 14 mins.). (ENG.). 2009. 1.99 (978-1-60788-009-7(1)) Pub: Hachet Audio. Dist(s): HachBkGrp

Cloudburst, unabr. ed. Ryne Douglas Pearson. Narrated by Frank Muller. 10 cass. (Running Time: 14 hrs. 30 mins.). 1993. 85.00 (978-1-55690-901-6(2), 93343E7) Recorded Bks.
The President of the United States & his chief of staff are killed in a rain of gunfire & explosions. Immediately, a worldwide CIA/FBI investigation is launched. Is it a random terrorist incident, or the beginning of a complex plot to topple the government?.

Cloudcastle. abr. ed. Nan Ryan. Read by Jane Allen. 1 cass. (Running Time: 90 min.). 1994. 5.99 (978-1-57096-009-3(7), RAZ 910) Romance Alive Audio.
Exquisite Natalie Vallance has been rescued by the Indians & made mistress of a ranch high in the majestic Colorado Rockies. Kane Covington - was he outlaw, swindler, or charming rogue? Could she ever forget the blazing passion they had shared?.

Clouds see Philip Levine

Clouds & Nine Other Stories. unabr. ed. Story Time Staff. Read by Alfreda C. Doyle. 2 cass. (Running Time: 1 hr. 30 min.). (J). (gr. 4-8). 1992. 15.95 set. (SRC 0017PLUS9) Sell Out Recordings.
An introduction followed by a story about a group of clouds. The listener is introduced to clouds & their homeland. Other educational, entertaining, informative & inspirational stories are also found on this tape.

Clouds of Glory. Dan Hess. 1 cass. 1996. 9.95 (978-1-57008-242-9(1), Bkcraft Inc) Deseret Bk.

***Clouds of Witness.** Dorothy L. Sayers. Narrated by Full Cast Production Staff. (Running Time: 3 hrs. 5 mins. 0 sec.). (ENG., 2010. audio compact disk 29.95 (978-1-84607-149-2(6)) Pub: AudioGO. Dist(s): Perseus Dist

Clouds of Witness. unabr. ed. Dorothy L. Sayers. Read by Ian Carmichael. 6 cass. (Running Time: 8 hrs. 5 mins.). (Lord Peter Wimsey Mystery Ser.). 2002. 29.95 (978-1-57270-265-3(6)) Pub: Audio Partners. Dist(s): PerseuPGW

Clouds of Witness. unabr. ed. Dorothy L. Sayers. Narrated by Ian Carmichael. (Lord Peter Wimsey Mystery Ser.). (ENG.). 2008. audio compact disk 29.95 (978-1-60283-347-0(8)) Pub: AudioGO. Dist(s): Perseus Dist

Clouds of Witness. unabr. ed. Dorothy L. Sayers. Read by Ian Carmichael. 8 cass. (Running Time: 12 hrs.). (Lord Peter Wimsey Mystery Ser.). 2000.

59.95 (978-0-7451-4008-7(4), CAB 705) Pub: Chivers Audio Bks GBR. Dist(s): AudioGO
Lord Peter Wimsey, noted scholar and detective calls upon all his skills when murder strikes close to home. The victim: His sister's fiance. The accused: The Duke of Denver, Lord Peter's brother. As the Duke goes on trial for his life, Lord Peter, must come up with the real culprit.

Clouds of Witness. unabr. ed. Dorothy L. Sayers. Read by Ian Carmichael. (Lord Peter Wimsey Mystery Ser.). (YA). 2008. 64.99 (978-1-60514-955-4(1)) Find a World.

Clouds Roll Away: A Raleigh Harmon Novel. unabr. ed. Sibella Giorello. Narrated by Cassandra Campbell. (Running Time: 10 hrs. 14 mins. 17 sec.). (ENG.). 2010. 20.99 (978-1-60814-646-8(4)); audio compact disk 29.99 (978-1-59859-703-5(5)) Oasis Audio.

Cloud's Veil: The Song of the Celtic Soul. Liam Lawton. 1997. 10.95 (415); audio compact disk 15.95 (415) GIA Pubns.

Clouds Without Water: Jude 8-13. Ed Young. 1989. 4.95 (978-0-7417-1742-9(5), 742) Win Walk.

Cloudscapes. Ed. by Robert A. Monroe. 1 cass. (Running Time: 30 min.). (Meta Music Artist Ser.). 1989. 14.95 (978-1-56102-204-5(7)) Inter Indus.
Let go & flow with a musical spiral up, into, & among the cloud towers while you feel them pass in stately grace. An ideal composition for inspiring contemplative state or abstract meditation.

Cloudsplitter. Russell Banks. 2004. audio compact disk 14.95 (978-0-8258-5348-7(6)) Fischer Inc NY.

Cloudsplitter. abr. ed. Russell Banks. Read by George DelHoyo. 4 cass. (Running Time: 6 hrs.). 1998. 25.95 (978-1-57453-270-8(7)) Audio Lit.
A story of generational struggle as well as racial & cultural division, rich in incident & historic detail.

Cloudsplitter. unabr. collector's ed. Russell Banks. Read by John Edwardson. 9 cass. (Running Time: 13 hrs. 30 mins.). 1998. 72.00 (978-0-7366-4252-1(8), 4751-A) Books on Tape.
Takes a real person, Owen Brown, the last surviving son of John Brown & through Owen's experience lets us imagine the life he lived, the father he had, the country as it was in those years that led up to the Civil War.

Cloudsplitter, Pt. 2. collector's ed. Russell Banks. Read by John Edwardson. 10 cass. (Running Time: 15 hrs.). 1998. 80.00 (978-0-7366-4253-8(6), 4751-B) Books on Tape.

Cloudstreet. Tim Winton. Read by Peter Hosking. (Running Time: 13 hrs.). 2009. 94.99 (978-1-74214-292-0(3), 9781742142920) Pub: Bolinda Pubng AUS. Dist(s): Bolinda Pub Inc

Cloudstreet. unabr. ed. Tim Winton. 11 CDs. (Running Time: 13 hrs.). 2001. audio compact disk 103.95 (978-1-74030-389-7(X)) Pub: Bolinda Pubng AUS. Dist(s): Bolinda Pub Inc

Cloudy. 9.95 (978-1-59112-148-0(5)) Live Oak Media.

Cloudy Chinaberry. 9.95 (978-1-59112-020-9(9)) Live Oak Media.

Cloudy in the West. abr. ed. Elmer Kelton. Read by Elmer Kelton. 2 cass. (Running Time: 2 hrs. 50 mins.). 1997. 16.95 (978-1-55935-244-4(2), 395291) Soundelux.
When his Pa dies under mysterious circumstances, Joey is forced to live with his stepmother, Dulcie, & a slick-talking 'cousin'. When his best friend is found dead & Joey is nearly killed, he runs away, believing Dulcie is trying to get rid of him in order to inherit the farm.

Cloudy with a Chance of Meatballs. Judi Barrett. Read by Linda Terheyden & Jerry Terheyden. Illus. by Ron Barrett. 1 cass. (Running Time: 30 mins.). (J). 2000. pap. bk. 19.97 (978-0-7366-9210-6(X)) Books on Tape.
The tiny town of Chewandswallow enjoys being served breakfast, lunch & dinner from its benevolent skies, until the weather suddenly changes.

Cloudy with a Chance of Meatballs. Judi Barrett. Illus. by Ron Barrett. (Running Time: 13 mins.). (J). (gr. k-3). 1985. 9.95 (978-1-59112-143-5(4)) Live Oak Media.

Cloudy with a Chance of Meatballs. Judi Barrett. Illus. by Ron Barrett. 14 vols. (Running Time: 13 mins.). 1985. pap. bk. 39.95 (978-1-59112-703-1(3)); audio compact disk 12.95 (978-1-59112-700-0(9)) Live Oak Media.

Cloudy with a Chance of Meatballs. unabr. ed. Judi Barrett. Read by Jerry Terheyden & Linda Terheyden. Illus. by Ron Barrett. 11 vols. (Running Time: 13 mins.). (J). (gr. 1-6). 1985. bk. 25.95 (978-0-941078-93-1(0)); pap. bk. 16.95 (978-0-941078-91-7(4)); pap. bk. 37.95 Reading Chest. (978-0-941078-92-4(2)) Live Oak Media.
The tiny town of Chewandswallow enjoys getting breakfast, lunch & dinner from its benevolent skies - until the weather suddenly changes.

Cloudy/Pickles. 4.75 (978-0-87499-888-7(3)) Live Oak Media.

Cloven. unabr. ed. Sally Spedding. Read by Margaret Sircom. 11 cass. (Running Time: 14 hrs. 35 min.). (Storysound Ser.). (J). 2003. 89.95 (978-1-85903-633-4(3)) Pub: Mgna Lrg Print GBR. Dist(s): Ulverscroft US

Clover. unabr. ed. Dori Sanders. Narrated by Michele-Denise Woods. 4 cass. (Running Time: 5 hrs. 15 mins.). 1994. 35.00 (978-0-7887-0105-4(3), 94346E7) Recorded Bks.
A warm friendship kindles & grows between a 10 year old black girl & the white stepmother she hardly knows after the death of her father.

Clovis Crawfish & Batiste Bete Puante with Clovis Crawfish & Bertile's Bon Voyage. Narrated by Mary Alice Fontenot. 6 cass. (Running Time: 30 min. per cass.). (Clovis Crawfish Ser.). (J). 9.95 (978-0-88289-981-7(3)) Pelican.

Clovis Crawfish & Batiste Bete Puante/Clovis Crawfish & Bertile's Bon Voyage CD. Mary Alice Fontenot. Narrated by Mary Alice Fontenot. (Running Time: 46 mins.). (Clovis Crawfish Ser.). (ENG & FRE.). (J). 2009. audio compact disk 19.95 (978-1-58980-736-5(7)) Pelican.

Clovis Crawfish & Bidon Box Turtle: Clovis Crawfish & Paillasse Poule d'Eau. Narrated by Julie F. Landry & Mary Alice Fontenot. 1 cass. (Running Time: 30 min.). (Clovis Crawfish Ser.). (ENG.). (J). (ps-3). 1997. 9.95 (978-1-56554-287-7(8)) Pelican.

Clovis Crawfish & Bidon Box Turtle/Clovis Crawfish & Paillasse Poule d'Eau CD. Narrated by Mary Alice Fontenot. (Running Time: 41 mins.). (Clovis Crawfish Ser.). (ENG & FRE.). (J). 2009. audio compact disk 19.95 (978-1-58980-735-8(9)) Pelican.

Clovis Crawfish & His Friends With Clovis Crawfish & Simeon Suce-Fleur. Narrated by Mary Alice Fontenot. 6 cass. (Running Time: 30 min. per cass.). (Clovis Crawfish Ser.). (J). 9.95 (978-0-88289-976-3(7)) Pelican.

Clovis Crawfish & His Friends/Clovis Crawfish & Simeon Suce-Fleur CD. Mary Alice Fontenot. Narrated by Mary Alice Fontenot. (Running Time: 46 mins.). (Clovis Crawfish Ser.). (ENG & FRE.). (J). 2009. audio compact disk 19.95 (978-1-58980-718-1(9)) Pelican.

Clovis Crawfish & Michelle Mantis with Clovis Crawfish & Etienne Escargot. Narrated by Mary Alice Fontenot. 6 cass. (Running Time: 30 min. per cass.). (Clovis Crawfish Ser.). (J). 9.95 (978-0-88289-979-4(1)) Pelican.

Clovis Crawfish & Michelle Mantis/Clovis Crawfish & Etienne Escargot. Narrated by Mary Alice Fontenot. (Running Time: 1500 sec.). (Clovis Crawfish Ser.). (ENG.). (J). 1990. 9.95 (978-1-56554-381-2(5)) Pelican.

Clovis Crawfish & Michelle Mantis/Clovis Crawfish & Etienne Escargot CD. Mary Alice Fontenot. Narrated by Mary Alice Fontenot. (Running Time: 47 mins.). (Clovis Crawfish Ser.). (ENG & FRE.). (J). 2009. audio compact disk 19.95 (978-1-58980-734-1(0)) Pelican.

Clovis Crawfish & the Big Betail with Clovis Crawfish & the Orphan Zo-Zo. Narrated by Mary Alice Fontenot. 6 cass. (Running Time: 30 min. per cass.). (Clovis Crawfish Ser.). (J). 9.95 (978-0-88289-980-0(5)) Pelican.

Clovis Crawfish & the Singing Cigales with Clovis Crawfish & Petit Papillon. Narrated by Mary Alice Fontenot. 6 cass. (Running Time: 30 min. per cass.). (Clovis Crawfish Ser.). (J). 9.95 (978-0-88289-977-0(5)) Pelican.

Clovis Crawfish & the Singing Cigales/Clovis Crawfish & Petit Papillon. Narrated by Mary Alice Fontenot. (Clovis Crawfish Ser.). (ENG.). (J). 1998. 9.95 (978-1-56554-379-9(3)) Pelican.

Clovis Crawfish & the Singing Cigales/Clovis Crawfish & Petit Papillon CD. Narrated by Mary Alice Fontenot. (Running Time: 51 mins.). (Clovis Crawfish Ser.). (ENG & FRE.). (J). 2009. audio compact disk 19.95 (978-1-58980-733-4(2)) Pelican.

Clovis Crawfish & the Spinning Spider with Clovis Crawfish & the Curious Crapaud. Narrated by Mary Alice Fontenot. 6 cass. (Running Time: 30 min. per cass.). (Clovis Crawfish Ser.). (J). 9.95 (978-0-88289-978-7(3)) Pelican.

Clovis Crawfish & the Spinning Spider/Clovis Crawfish & the Curious Crapaud. Narrated by Mary Alice Fontenot. (Clovis Crawfish Ser.). (ENG.). (J). 1998. 9.95 (978-1-56554-380-5(7)) Pelican.

Clovis Crawfish & the Spinning Spider/Clovis Crawfish & the Curious Crapaud CD. Mary Alice Fontenot. Narrated by Mary Alice Fontenot. (Running Time: 44 mins.). (Clovis Crawfish Ser.). (ENG & FRE.). (J). 2009. audio compact disk 19.95 (978-1-58980-717-4(0)) Pelican.

Clovis Crawiish & His Friends/Clovis Crawfish & Simeon Suce-fleur. Narrated by Mary Alice Fontenot. (Clovis Crawfish Ser.). (ENG.). (J). 1998. 9.95 (978-1-56554-363-8(7)) Pelican.

Clovis Ecrevisse et Batiste Bete Puante - Clovis Ecrevisse et le Bon Voyage a Pauline. Mary Alice Fontenot. Narrated by Julie F. Landry. 1 cass. (Running Time: 30 min.). (Clovis Ecrivesse AudioCassette Ser.). (FRE.). (J). (gr. 4-7). 1997. 9.95 (978-1-56554-108-5(1)) Pelican.

Clovis Ecrevisse et Bidon Tortue Terrestre - Clovis Ecrevisse et Paillasse Poule d'Eau. Mary Alice Fontenot. Narrated by Julie F. Landry. 1 cass. (Running Time: 30 min.). (Clovis Ecrivesse AudioCassette Ser.). (FRE.). (J). (gr. 4-7). 1997. 9.95 (978-1-56554-284-6(3)) Pelican.

Clovis Ecrevisse et Charlotte Cheval de Diable: Clovis Ecrevisse et Etienne Escargot. Narrated by Julie F. Landry & Mary Alice Fontenot. 1 cass. (Running Time: 30 min.). (Clovis Ecrivesse AudioCassette Ser.). (FRE.). (J). (gr. 4-7). 1997. 9.95 (978-1-56554-106-1(5)) Pelican.

Clovis Ecrevisse et la Grosse Betail - Clovis Ecrevisse et l'Oiseau Orphelin. Mary Alice Fontenot. Narrated by Julie F. Landry. 1 cass. (Running Time: 30 min.). (Clovis Ecrivesse AudioCassette Ser.). (FRE.). (J). (gr. 4-7). 1997. 9.95 (978-1-56554-107-8(3)) Pelican.

Clovis Ecrevisse et l'Araignee Qui File - Clovis Ecrevisse et le Crapaud Curieux. Mary Alice Fontenot. Narrated by Julie F. Landry. 1 cass. (Running Time: 30 min.). (Clovis Ecrivesse AudioCassette Ser.). (FRE.). (J). (gr. 4-7). 1997. 9.95 (978-1-56554-105-4(7)) Pelican.

Clovis Maksoud: Rights & Myths of the Palestinians. 1 cass. (Running Time: 1 hr.). 10.95 (NP-88-03-17, HarperThor) HarpC GBR.

***Clown.** Verne Athanas. 2009. (978-1-60136-470-8(9)) Audio Holding.

Clown. Verne Athanas. (Running Time: 0 hr. 30 mins.). 1998. 10.95 (978-1-60083-476-9(0)) Iofy Corp.

Clown Is Right Vol. I: Fulton J. Sheen. unabr. ed. Fulton J. Sheen. 7 cass. (Running Time: 30 min.). (Life Is Worth Living Ser.: 0004). 1985. 29.95 F Sheen Comm.
The late Bishop Sheen explains the duality of our nature, our inner senses of tragedy & comedy, which are really work & play.

Clown of God. 2004. bk. 24.95 (978-0-89719-766-3(6)); pap. bk. 32.75 (978-1-55592-181-1(7)); 8.95 (978-1-56008-381-8(6)); cass. & flmstrp 30.00 (978-0-89719-530-0(2)) Weston Woods.

Clown of God. Tomie dePaola. 1 cass. (Running Time: 30 min.). (J). bk. 24.95; pap. bk. 32.75 Weston Woods.

Clown of God. Tomie dePaola. 1 cass. (J). (gr. k-5). 2004. pap. bk. 14.95 (978-0-89719-767-0(4), PRA260); 8.95 (978-0-89719-975-9(8), RAC260) Weston Woods.
He details the legend about the poor & homeless little juggler who returns in his old age to the city of his birth & takes refuge in the church on Christmas Eve.

Clowns & Zoos & Hippos Too. Lyrics by Janet Smith Post. Moderated by Janet Smith Post. (J). 2002. audio compact disk 20.00 (978-0-9702826-8-2(0)) BTSBRBE.

Clowns of God. unabr. ed. Morris West. 9 cass. (Running Time: 17 hrs.). (Vatican Trilogy). 2004. 72.00 (978-1-74030-583-9(3)) Pub: Bolinda Pubng AUS. Dist(s): Lndmrk Audiobks

Clssrm Interactivity-Earth Sys. (C). 2005. audio compact disk 69.95 (978-1-4018-9893-9(9)) Pub: Delmar. Dist(s): CENGAGE Learn

Clu Est Plnng Applic Terms Cd. Ed. by Kaplan Publishing Staff. 2005. (978-1-4195-1851-5(8)) Dearborn Financial.

Clu Fin Dcsn Mkng Ppt Cd. Ed. by Kaplan Publishing Staff. 2005. (978-1-4195-1948-2(4)) Dearborn Financial.

Clu Fin Dcsn Mkng Terms Cd. Ed. by Kaplan Publishing Staff. 2005. (978-1-4195-1929-1(8)) Dearborn Financial.

Clu Fin Plnng Applic Ppt Cd. Ed. by Kaplan Publishing Staff. 2005. (978-1-4195-1854-6(2)) Dearborn Financial.

Clu Fin Plnng Applic Terms Cd. Ed. by Kaplan Publishing Staff. 2005. (978-1-4195-1855-3(0)) Dearborn Financial.

Clu Fin Sys in Econ Ppt Cd. Ed. by Kaplan Publishing Staff. 2005. (978-1-4195-1893-5(3)) Dearborn Financial.

Clu Fin Sys in Econ Terms Cd. Ed. by Kaplan Publishing Staff. 2005. (978-1-4195-1892-8(5)) Dearborn Financial.

Clu Fund Estate Pln Ppt Cd. Ed. by Kaplan Publishing Staff. 2005. (978-1-4195-1846-1(1)) Dearborn Financial.

Clu Fund Estate Pln Terms Cd. Ed. by Kaplan Publishing Staff. 2005. (978-1-4195-1844-7(5)) Dearborn Financial.

Clu Group Benefits Ppt Cd. Ed. by Kaplan Publishing Staff. 2005. (978-1-4195-1934-5(4)) Dearborn Financial.

Clu Group Benefits Terms Cd. Ed. by Kaplan Publishing Staff. 2005. (978-1-4195-1926-0(3)) Dearborn Financial.

Clu Income Taxation Ppt Cd. Ed. by Kaplan Publishing Staff. 2005. (978-1-4195-1872-0(0)) Dearborn Financial.

Clu Income Taxation Terms Cd. Ed. by Kaplan Publishing Staff. 2005. (978-1-4195-1873-7(9)) Dearborn Financial.

Clu Indiv Lf Ins Ppt Cd. Ed. by Kaplan Publishing Staff. 2005. (978-1-4195-1903-1(4)) Dearborn Financial.

Clu Indiv Lf Ins Ppt Cd 2. Ed. by Kaplan Publishing Staff. 2005. (978-1-4195-1922-2(0)) Dearborn Financial.

Clu Indiv Lf Ins Terms Cd. Ed. by Kaplan Publishing Staff. 2005. (978-1-4195-1905-5(0)) Dearborn Financial.

Clu Ins & Fin Plnng Ppt Cd. Ed. by Kaplan Publishing Staff. 2005. (978-1-4195-1875-1(5)) Dearborn Financial.

Clu Ins & Fin Plnng Terms Cd. Ed. by Kaplan Publishing Staff. 2005. (978-1-4195-1876-8(3)) Dearborn Financial.

Clu Investments Ppt Cd. Ed. by Kaplan Publishing Staff. 2005. (978-1-4195-1928-4(X)) Dearborn Financial.

Clu Investments Terms Cd. Ed. by Kaplan Publishing Staff. 2005. (978-1-4195-1921-5(2)) Dearborn Financial.

Clu Life Ins Law Ppt Cd. Ed. by Kaplan Publishing Staff. 2005. (978-1-4195-1879-9(8)) Dearborn Financial.

Clu Life Ins Law Terms Cd. Ed. by Kaplan Publishing Staff. 2005. (978-1-4195-1923-9(9)) Dearborn Financial.

Clu Plnng Bus Owners Ppt Cd. Ed. by Kaplan Publishing Staff. 2005. (978-1-4195-1840-9(2)) Dearborn Financial.

Clu Plnng Bus Owners Terms Cd. Ed. by Kaplan Publishing Staff. 2005. (978-1-4195-1841-6(0)) Dearborn Financial.

Clu Plnng Rtrmnt Ppt Cd. Ed. by Kaplan Publishing Staff. 2005. (978-1-4195-1931-4(X)) Dearborn Financial.

Clu Plnng Rtrmnt Terms Cd. Ed. by Kaplan Publishing Staff. 2005. (978-1-4195-1932-1(8)) Dearborn Financial.

Clu the Sign of the Beaver. Elizabeth George Speare. (J). 1988. 21.33 (978-0-676-31090-0(7)) SRA McGraw.

Club Chipmunk: The Dance Mixes. (Running Time: 40 min.). (J). (ps-4). 1996. 9.98; audio compact disk 13.98 CD. Sony Music Ent.
Alvin & the boys sing "Macarena" (in English & again in Spanish), Madonna's "Vogue," "Stayin' Alive," "Play that Funky Music,"Turn the Beat Around," "love Shack," "Witch Doctor," & "Shout.".

Club de Amiguitos, Vol. 3. 1 CD. (Sabio & Prudente Ser.). (SPA.). 1998. audio compact disk 12.99 (978-0-8254-0953-0(5), Edit Portavoz) Kregel.

Club de amiguitos de sabio y prudente, Canciones, Vol. 3. (Sabio Y Prudente Ser.).Tr. of Friends of Sabio & Prudente, Songs. (SPA.). 2004. 7.99 (978-0-8254-0952-3(7), Edit Portavoz) Kregel.

Club de Aventura 2. Dan Aanderud. (SPA.). 2009. audio compact disk 8.99 (978-0-8297-5478-0(4)) Pub: Vida Pubs. Dist(s): Zondervan

Club de la Aventura. unabr. ed. Nathan Aanderud. 1 cass. (Running Time: 30 min.). (SPA.). 2000. 7.99 (978-0-8297-3274-0(8)) Pub: Vida Pubs. Dist(s): Zondervan

Club de la Aventura. unabr. ed. Nathan Aanderud. (SPA.). 2002. 7.99 (978-0-8297-3534-5(8)) Pub: Vida Pubs. Dist(s): Zondervan

Club de la Aventura 1. Created by Vida Publishers. (SPA.). (gr. 13). 2008. audio compact disk 8.99 (978-0-8297-5477-3(6)) Pub: Vida Pubs. Dist(s): Zondervan

Club J Spin. Contrib. by Club J. Prod. by Kurt Goebel et Al. Contrib. by Don Moen. (J). (gr. 2-7). 2005. audio compact disk 12.99 (978-5-558-80676-2(1)) Integrity Music.

Club of Queer Trades. G. K. Chesterton. Read by Alfred von Lecteur. 2009. 27.95 (978-1-60112-988-8(2)) Babblebooks.

Club of Queer Trades. unabr. collector's ed. G. K. Chesterton. Read by Stuart Courtney. 6 cass. (Running Time: 6 hrs.). 1985. 36.00 (978-0-7366-0468-0(5), 1443) Books on Tape.
Chesterton's first attempt at mystery fiction. It is the story of an English club with one typically eccentric membership requirement; no one can join unless he has created a brand new profession.

Club Sandwich - Goes Great with Chicken Soup; Best-Loved Stories from Jess Moody. Jess Moody. 1999. 15.99 (978-0-8054-2064-7(9)) BH Pubng Grp.

Club Social de las Chicas Temerarias. unabr. ed. Alisa Valdes-Rodriguez. Narrated by Adriana Sananes. 9 cass. (Running Time: 13 hrs.).Tr. of Dirty Girls Social Club. (ENG & SPA.). 2003. 79.75 (978-1-4193-2848-0(4), E1095MC) Recorded Bks.

Clubbable Woman. unabr. ed. Reginald Hill. Read by Brian Glover. 8 cass. (Running Time: 12 hrs.). (Dalziel & Pascoe Ser.). 2000. 59.95 (978-0-7451-6613-1(X), CAB 1230) Pub: Chivers Audio Bks GBR. Dist(s): AudioGO
When Connon returned from his match at the Rugby Club, his wife was more uncommunicative than usual. So he went upstairs to bed as she watched TV. Five hours later, the TV was still on, but his wife had been bludgeoned to death! Superintendent Dalziel knew exactly what happened, but Sergeant Pascoe had a few ideas of his own.

Clubbed to Death. unabr. ed. Ruth Dudley Edwards. Read by Bill Wallis. 6 cass. (Running Time: 9 hrs.). 2002. 49.95 (978-0-7540-0768-5(5), CAB 2190, Chivers Sound Lib) AudioGO.
Robert Amiss is working under cover as a waiter for a gentleman's club at the request of his friend, DS Pooley. The club secretary has allegedly jumped to his death from the club's gallery, but Pooley believe he was murdered. Amiss finds himself in a bizarre caricature of a club run by, and for, debauched geriatrics, with skeletons in every closet. Why are there so few members? And did they murder the reforming secretary.

Clubbed to Death. unabr. ed. Ruth Dudley Edwards. Read by Bill Wallis. 6 cass. (Running Time: 9 hrs.). 2002. audio compact disk 64.95 (978-0-7540-5482-5(9), CCD 173) AudioGO.

Clue at the Bottom of the Lake. unabr. ed. Kristiana Gregory. (Running Time: 1 hr. 45 mins. 0 sec.). (Cabin Creek Mysteries Ser.). (ENG.). (J). 2008. 10.49 (978-1-60814-104-3(7), SpringWater) Oasis Audio.

Clue at the Bottom of the Lake. unabr. ed. Kristiana Gregory. Read by Various Artists. (Running Time: 1 hr. 40 mins. 44 sec.). (Cabin Creek Mysteries Ser.). (ENG.). (J). 2008. audio compact disk 14.99 (978-1-59859-345-7(5)) Oasis Audio.

Clue in the Diary. Carolyn Keene. (Nancy Drew Mystery Stories: No. 7). (J). 2003. 23.00 (978-0-8072-1677-4(1), Listening Lib) Pub: Random Audio Pubg. Dist(s): Random

Clue in the Zoo. unabr. ed. Roni S. Denholtz. 1 cass. (Running Time: 20 min.). (Fun to Read Ser.). (J). (gr. 3-6). 1983. bk. 16.99 (978-0-934898-38-6(3)); pap. bk. 9.95 (978-0-934898-26-3(X)) Jan Prods.
When Patti Johnson began her visit to the Houston Zoo, she had no idea she would play a key role in the arrest of a kidnapper.

Clue of the Linoleum Lederhosen. unabr. ed. M. T. Anderson. Read by Marc Cashman. 4 CDs. (Running Time: 13920 sec.). (M. T. Anderson's Thrilling Tales Ser.). (ENG.). (J). (gr. 3). 2006. audio compact disk 30.00 (978-0-307-28431-0(X), Listening Lib) Pub: Random Audio Pubg. Dist(s): Random

Clue of the New Shoe. unabr. ed. Arthur W. Upfield. Read by Peter Hosking. 6 CDs. (Running Time: 24300 sec.). (Inspector Napoleon Bonaparte Mysteries). 2005. audio compact disk 77.95 (978-1-74030-860-1(3)) Pub: Bolinda Pubng AUS. Dist(s): Bolinda Pub Inc

Clues for Achievement & Success see Claves del Triunfo y el Exito - Las Siete Actitudes para el Triunfo y las 20 Claves para el Exito

Clues to the Nature of Jesus. unabr. ed. Read by Gayle D. Erwin. 1 cass. (Running Time: 1 hr.). 1992. 4.95 (978-1-56599-517-8(1), C-17) Yahshua Pub.

Clumsy Crocodile. Felicity Everett & Rebecca Treays. Read by Melinda Walker. (Young Reading CD Packs Ser.). (J). (gr. k-3). 2006. pap. bk. 9.99 (978-0-7945-1208-8(9), UsborneU) EDC Pubng.

Clung. unabr. collector's ed. Max Brand. Read by Jonathan Marosz. 7 cass. (Running Time: 7 hrs.). 1994. 42.00 (978-0-7366-2720-7(0), 3450) Books on Tape.
Solo gunfighter flees his small Arizona town with a posse in hot pursuit.

***Clutch: Why Some People Excel under Pressure & Others Don't.** unabr. ed. Paul J. Sullivan. Read by Don Hagen. (Running Time: 9 hrs.). (ENG.). 2010. 29.98 (978-1-59659-629-0(5), GildAudio) Pub: Gildan Media. Dist(s): HachBkGrp

Clutter-Free Christianity: What God Really Desires for You. Robert Jeffress. (ENG.). 2009. audio compact disk 26.99 (978-1-934384-32-9(1)) Pub: Treasure Pub. Dist(s): STL Dist NA

CMA Review Pt. 2CMA: Financial Accounting & Reporting. 10th ed. Irvin N. Gleim & Dale L. Flesher. 2001. 64.95 (978-1-58194-162-3(5)) Gleim Pubns.

CME,Intro Ocean Sciences. 3rd ed. Alan S. Tussy & R. David Gustafson. (C). 2005. audio compact disk 16.95 (978-0-534-40283-9(6)) Pub: Brooks-Cole. Dist(s): CENGAGE Learn

CME,Unders nor/Clin Nut Inftr. 10th ed. Sizer & Whitney. (C). 2005. audio compact disk 13.95 (978-0-534-39498-1(1)) Pub: Brooks-Cole. Dist(s): CENGAGE Learn

C'mon an' Swing in My Tree! Perf. by The Sunflowers. Illus. by Giselle Potter. Lyrics by Michael Taylor Fontaine. Music by Michael Taylor Fontaine. 1 CD. (Running Time: 30 mins.). (J). 2005. bds. 16.95 (978-0-9763012-0-2(2)) Cow Heard.
C'mon an' Swing in My Tree! is a twelve song children's music CD by The Sunflowers, packaged in a delightful board book featuring eight illustrations by Giselle Potter. This is a fun and sophisticated recording that parents will enjoy just as much as their children. The song lyrics talk about personal values, optimisim and friendship.

Cmplt Java Trng&Jbldr&CD. 5th ed. 2003. audio compact disk 116.50 (978-0-13-127104-3(0)) Pub: P-H. Dist(s): Pearson Educ

Cnn Cd-Everyday Chemistry. 3rd ed. (C). 2003. audio compact disk 41.95 (978-0-534-42219-6(5)) Pub: Brooks-Cole. Dist(s): CENGAGE Learn

***CNUDCI Annuaire: Volume XXXV: 2004.** United Nations Staff. (FRE.). 2009. audio compact disk 75.00 (978-92-1-233450-9(4)) Untd Nat Pubns.

Co-Addicted Relationships. Pia Mellody. Read by Pia Mellody. 4 cass. 35.00 Set. (A2) Featuka Enter Inc.
The journey from addiction to recovery in relationships.

Co. Aytch. unabr. ed. Sam R. Watkins. Read by Pat Bottino. 7 cass. (Running Time: 10 hrs. 30 min.). 1997. 49.95 (1895); audio compact disk 11.95 Blckstn Audio.
Balances the horror of war with irrepressible humor. Among Civil War memoirs, it stands as a living testament to one man's enduring humanity, courage & wisdom in the midst of death & destruction.

Co Aytch. unabr. ed. Sam R. Watkins. Read by Pat Bottino. 7 cass. (Running Time: 10 hrs.). 2001. 49.95 (978-0-7861-1130-5(5), 1895) Blckstn Audio.

Co. Aytch: A Side Show of the Big Show. abr. ed. Sam R. Watkins. Read by Gregory Daimwood. Prod. by William B. Styple. 4 cass. (Running Time: 5 hrs. 50 min.). (Classic Civil War Audio Bks.: Vol. I). 1996. 27.95 Set. (978-1-883926-08-3(4)) Belle Grv Pub.
The classic Civil War Confederate memoir of Sam Watkins, 1st Tennessee Infantry.

Co. Aytch: The Classic Memoir of the Civil War by a Confederate Soldier. unabr. ed. Sam R. Watkins. Read by Pat Bottino. (Running Time: 9 hrs. NaN mins.). 2009. 29.95 (978-1-4332-6694-2(6)); audio compact disk 80.00 (978-1-4332-6691-1(1)) Blckstn Audio.

Co-Creation in the New Age. Kryon. Read by Lee Carroll. 1 cass. (Running Time: 1 hr. 05 min.). 1996. 10.00 (978-1-888053-04-3(6)) Kryon Writings.
Recording of live event. Channeling of spiritual information.

Co-Dependency. Sue Apitz-Upwall. Read by Sue Apitz-Upwall. 1 cass. (Running Time: 90 min.). 1994. 8.95 (1116) Am Fed Astrologers.
Co-dependency as indicated in the horoscope.

Co-Dependency. John E. Bradshaw. (Running Time: 18000 sec.). 2008. audio compact disk 120.00 (978-1-57388-112-8(0)) J B Media.

Co-Dependency & Astrology. Sue Apitz-Upwall. 1 cass. 8.95 (760) Am Fed Astrologers.

Co-Dependency in Relationships. Sue Apitz-Upwall. 1 cass. 1992. 8.95 (1005) Am Fed Astrologers.

Co-Dependency Issues in Ministry. 1 cass. (Care Cassettes Ser.: Vol. 20, No. 6). 1993. 10.80 Assn Prof Chaplains.

Co-dependency to Self-Discovery. 2 CDs. 1982. audio compact disk 27.98 (978-1-56001-955-8(7)) Potentials.
By Melody Beattie's definition, a co-dependent person is one who has let another person's behavior affect him or her, and who is obsessed with controlling that person's behavior. If you find yourself in this situation and are ready to take a journey to self-discovery, this is the program for you.This 2-CD program from our Super Consciousness series is our newest, most powerful format. On the self-hypnosis CD, SC programs have the Subliminal Persuasion soundtrack added under Barrie?s voice. And the 17th Century Baroque music on the Subliminal CD has the same beat as your body's natural rhythm, thereby allowing the suggestions to enter deeply and effortlessly.

Co-Leaders: The Power of Great Partnerships. unabr. ed. David A. Heenan & Warren Bennis. Read by Jeff Riggenbach. 8 cass. (Running Time: 11 hrs. 30 mins.). 2000. 56.95 (978-0-7861-1847-2(4), 2646); audio compact disk 80.00 (978-0-7861-9823-8(0), 2646) Blckstn Audio.
The heart & soul of every organization are those leaders below the CEO. Today's celebrity CEO has become either a figurehead or an egomaniac & often too public a personality to get the real work done. The authors believe we must look beyond the Bill Gateses of the world to understand what makes an organization excel.

Co-Operation & Conflict, 1919-1945. Ben Walsh. 3 pieces. (YA). 2005. cd-rom 575.00 (978-0-7195-7972-1(4), HodderMurray) Pub: Hodder Edu GBR. Dist(s): Trans-Atl Phila

Co-Teaching That Works: Effective Strategies for Working Together in Today's Inclusive Classrooms. Anne M. Beninghof. 6 cass. (Running Time: 3 hrs. 56 min.). 2003. 89.00 (978-1-886397-52-1(X)) Bureau of Educ.

Co-Workers with God. 1 cass. (Running Time: 30 min.). 1985. (0222) Evang Sisterhood Mary.
Their blessings & responsibilities; the compass for my life.

Coach. unabr. ed. Stephen E. Heiman. Interview with Diane Sanchez. 2 cass. (Running Time: 1 hr. 29 min.). (Strategic Selling Advanced Ser.: Vol. 2). 1995. Set. (978-0-9619073-5-8(5)); audio compact disk (978-1-889888-01-9(X)) Miller Heiman.
Over the years many of our clients have told us that trying to identify & develop a strong coach is one of the most difficult concepts they've learned in strategic selling. Diane & Steve discuss the Coach in great detail.

Coach: Lessons on the Game of Life. unabr. ed. Michael Lewis. Read by Michael Lewis. 1 cass. (Running Time: 1 hr.). 2005. 18.00 (978-1-4159-2116-6(4)); audio compact disk 20.40 (978-1-4159-2131-9(8)) Pub: Books on Tape. Dist(s): NetLibrary CO

Coach Popp Fly Cassette. Stephen Cosgrove. 2004. 5.00 (978-1-58804-428-0(9)) PCI Educ.

Coach Training Package: How to Create Breakthrough Results with Your Clients So Your Practice Overflows. David Wood. 2007. audio compact disk 497.00 (978-0-9817647-4-0(6)) SolBox.

Coach Vince Lombardi's Power to Motivate with Jerry Kramer & Dick Schaap. 1 cass. (Running Time: 47 min.). 8.95 Listen USA.

***Coach Wooden's Pyramid of Success: Building Blocks for a Better Life.** unabr. ed. John Wooden & Jay Carty. Narrated by Sean Runnette. (ENG.). 2010. 12.98 (978-1-59644-998-5(5)); audio compact disk 18.98 (978-1-59644-997-8(7)) christianaud.

Coaching: The Best Kept Secret. unabr. ed. Debra Whiddon. Read by Debra Whiddon. Read by Doug Bailey et al. Ed. by David Osbourn & Zimmersmith Studios Staff. 1 cass. (Running Time: 1 hr. 30 min.). 1995. 8.95 (978-1-886112-05-6(3)) Global Dharma Ctr.

Coaching & Teambuilding Skills for Managers & Supervisors, Set. abr. ed. Jeffrey L. Magee. Read by Jeffrey L. Magee. 2 cass. (Running Time: 3 hrs.). 1996. bk. 21.95 (978-1-878542-71-7(0),) SkillPath Pubns.
Apply the nine indicators of successful teams.

Coaching from the Heart. unabr. ed. Ken Blanchard & Don Shula. Ed. by Dave Kuenstle. 5 cass. (Running Time: 5 hrs.). 1995. 39.95 Set, incl. pamphlet. Nightingale-Conant.
The winningest coach in the NFL & the One Minute manager team up to give the secrets of how to inspire anyone to be a winner.

Coaching Skills for Managers & Supervisors. Fred Pryor. 6 cass. (Running Time: 6 hrs.). 1993. 59.95 set. (10440A) Nightingale-Conant.

Coaching Skills for Managers & Supervisors. PUEI. 1993. audio compact disk 89.95 (978-1-933328-67-6(3), Fred Pryor) P Univ E Inc.

Coaching Skills for Managers & Supervisors: Turn Your Work Group into a Super-Productive, Successful, High-Morale Team. 6 cass. 59.95 Set incl. wkbk. (10441AS) Pryor Resources.
Now you can use the same proven management techniques perfected by the most successful men & women in coaching to inspire, motivate, counsel, lead, & create winners. Witness an exciting synergy among your employees, mutual support within your group, a sense of interdependence & exchange, as well as incredible productivity. Know what lineup is best for whatever situation you face, & devise a winning game plan for unstoppable success.

Coaching to Deep Level Change: Secrets to Permanently Changing Behavior. Speeches. Ben Saltzman & Donna Fowler. 3 CDs. 2002. 29.95 (978-0-9671010-1-9(8)) Lifestrides Pubg.
Two dynamic coaches teach methods to change behavior. Join Donna and Ben and learn to recognize legitimate coaching openings, connect authentically with your clients, and shift the manner in which they pay attention to the world.

Coach's Son. Jeffrey Hickey. 2007. 24.95 (978-1-933918-25-9(X)); 24.95 (978-1-933918-26-6(8)); audio compact disk 44.95 (978-1-933918-24-2(1)) Bloomimg Twig Bks.

Coal. Barbara Freese. Read by Shelly Frasier. (Running Time: 7 hrs. 36 mins.). 2003. 27.95 (978-1-60083-653-4(4), Audiofy Corp) Iofy Corp.

Coal: A Human History. unabr. ed. Barbara Freese. Narrated by Shelly Frasier. 7 CDs. (Running Time: 7 hrs. 37 mins. 12 sec.). (ENG.). 2003. audio compact disk 39.00 (978-1-4001-0087-3(9)); audio compact disk 19.99 (978-1-4001-5087-8(6)) Pub: Tantor Media. Dist(s): IngramPubServ

Coal: A Human History. unabr. ed. Barbara Freese. Read by Shelly Frasier. (Running Time: 7 hrs. 37 mins. 12 sec.). (ENG.). 2003. audio compact disk 78.00 (978-1-4001-3087-0(5)) Pub: Tantor Media. Dist(s): IngramPubServ

Coal Digging Blues: Songs of West Virginia Miners. Created by West Virginia University. 1. (West virginia sound Archives Ser.). 2006. audio compact disk 15.95 (978-1-933202-11-2(4)) Pub: West Va U Pr. Dist(s): Chicago Distribution Ctr
EightH addition to the West Virginia University Press Sound Archive. Nineteen field recordings made in the 1940s by folklorist George Korson represent a range of blues, country, and black gospel-quartet musical styles. Digitally remastered. Compiled and produced by Mark Allen Jackson."Coal Digging Blues makes a powerful statement about the importance of the union in the working lives of these singers, at a time when the 8-hr. day and basic safety issues were still a matter of heated debate." - John Lilly, GOLDENSEAL.

Coal Gatherer. Janet Woods. 2008. 61.95 (978-1-4079-0254-8(7)); audio compact disk 71.95 (978-1-4079-0255-5(5)) Pub: Soundings Ltd GBR. Dist(s): Ulverscroft US

Coal Strike of 1902. Kenneth Bruce. 1 cass. (Running Time: 1 hr.). Dramatization. (Excursions in History Ser.). 12.50 Alpha Tape.

Coalwood Way: A Memoir. unabr. ed. Homer H. Hickam, Jr. Narrated by Frank Muller. 8 cass. (Running Time: 11 hrs.). 2000. 76.00 (978-0-7887-5320-6(7), 96567K8) Recorded Bks.
In this memoir, as Homer & his high school buddies build & launch ingeniously designed rockets, their West Virginia hometown is slowly fading away. No matter how brilliant their rocketry experiments are, they can do little to help preserve Coalwood's way of life.

Coalwood Way: A Memoir. unabr. ed. Homer H. Hickam, Jr. Narrated by Frank Muller. 10 CDs. (Running Time: 11 hrs.). 2001. audio compact disk 97.00 (978-1-4025-0488-4(8), C1544) Recorded Bks.
Homer and his close buddies, who call themselves the Rocket Boys, are high school seniors in 1959. Their rocket building experiments amaze the locals, thanks to top-quality moonshine for fuel, liberated materials, and Homer's self-taught understanding of higher math. But no matter how brilliant their experiments are, they can do little to help preserve Coalwood's way of life. With the coal mine on its last legs, prospects for the town are unpredictable at best. For anyone who's ever dreamed of greatness or wondered what an uncertain future might bring, this book will seem warmly familiar.

Coast of Incense. unabr. collector's ed. Freya Stark. Read by Donada Peters. 8 cass. (Running Time: 12 hrs.). 1990. 64.00 (978-0-7366-1677-5(2), 2525) Books on Tape.
The Coast of Incense is the third book in Freya Stark's autobiography. It covers the middle years (1933-1939). The author emerges as an intelligent & gifted woman, a sensitive observer & a courageous traveler. Her vivid, intimate descriptions of Egypt, the Persian Gulf, Greece, Italy & the Middle East allow us to travel vicariously with every turn of the page. A sunset in Aden, the treasures of Tutankhamen, dinner with the Sheikh of Kuwait, a visit to the Queen of Iraq, a journey on the Orient Express - all are brought to life. The real focus of this book, however, is the author's introduction to South Arabia, "whose distant, severe & unimaginable beauty lives in my heart".

Coast Road. unabr. ed. Barbara Delinsky. Read by Laura Hicks. 8 vols. (Running Time: 35040 sec.). (Sound Library). 2000. 69.95 (978-0-7927-2362-2(7), CSL 251, Chivers Sound Lib) AudioGO.
Because Jack McGill chose his career as an architect over his family, his wife Rachel had left him. But now, six years later, a car accident has left Rachel clinging to life & she & their two daughters need him. Putting his work on hold for the first time in his life, he sits by his ex-wife's bedside. There he learns about a woman he never really knew & the secret that made her leave.

Coast Road. unabr. ed. Barbara Delinsky. Read by Laura Hicks. 12 CDs. (Running Time: 18 hrs.). 2001. audio compact disk 110.95 (978-0-7927-9908-5(9), SLD 059, Chivers Sound Lib) AudioGO.

Coast to Coast Story Service. 2005. audio compact disk (978-0-660-19484-4(8)) Canadian Broadcasting CAN.

***Coastal Birds: Bird Sounds of the British Coastline.** British Library Staff & Vrej Nersessian. (ENG.). 2010. audio compact disk 15.00 (978-0-7123-0588-4(2)) Pub: Britis Library GBR. Dist(s): Chicago Distribution Ctr

Coastal Marine Life. Hosted by Nancy Pearlman. 1 cass. (Running Time: 29 min.). 10.00 (110) Educ Comm CA.

Coastal Sediments 2003. Ed. by Richard A. Davis & Asbury Sallenger. 2003. cd-rom & audio compact disk 45.00 (978-981-238-422-5(7)) World Scientific Pub.

Coasting. unabr. collector's ed. Jonathan Raban. Read by David Case. 8 cass. (Running Time: 12 hrs.). 1989. 64.00 (978-0-7366-1632-4(2), 2489) Books on Tape.
In 1982, Jonathan Raban set sail on a voyage around his native land. He furnished a small boat with books & pictures & took to the sea, making a looping journey around the British Isles - a journey he describes as "a test, a reckoning, a voyage of territorial conquest, a homecoming." The voyage took him deep into history, his own & his country's, & put him in touch with unfashionable figures out of the past...Hillaire Belloc, for example, who wrote The Cruise of the Nona in 1925 about his own adventures at sea. Raban is at his best in these encounters, & they cut across all classes...poets, priests, bums, politicians, tourists. He even met Paul Theroux, but the two of them were wary, mining as it were the same material.

Coastliners. Joanne Harris. Read by Julia Franklin. 11 cass. (Sound Ser.). (J). 2003. 89.95 (978-1-84283-249-3(2)) Pub: ISIS Lrg Prnt GBR. Dist(s): Ulverscroft US

Coastliners. unabr. ed. Joanne Harris. Read by Vivien Benesch. 9 vols. (Running Time: 12 hrs.). 2002. bk. 79.95 (978-0-7927-2700-2(2), CSL 486, Chivers Sound Lib); audio compact disk 110.95 (978-0-7927-2725-5(8), SLD 486, Chivers Sound Lib) AudioGO.
The tiny island of Le Devin is a place where the salt of the sea is always on one's lips, the breeze never stops blowing, and nothing has changed for a hundred years. It is to this world that Madeleine returns after spending a decade in Paris. She has been haunted by this place - this island lost in time - but now she finds many things have changed. Madeleine's quiet father, a former boat builder, has almost completely withdrawn into an interior world.

***Coastliners.** unabr. ed. Joanne Harris. Read by Vivien Benesch. (ENG.). 2005. (978-0-06-085989-3(X), Harper Audio); (978-0-06-085990-9(3), Harper Audio) HarperCollins Pubs.

Coat, a Pharaoh, & a Family Reunion. (J). (ps-3). 2000. 7.98 (978-1-887729-28-4(3)) Toy Box Prods.

Coat, a Pharaoh & a Family Reunion: "The Story of Joseph" unabr. ed. Joe Loesch. Ed. by Cheryl J. Hutchinson. Illus. by Ott Denney. 1 cass. (Bible Stories for Kids Ser.). (J). (gr. 1-13). 1997. pap. bk. 14.95 (978-1-887729-19-2(4)) Toy Box Prods.
God's animals tell the story about the evil of jealousy & the joy of forgiving, as they travel from Canaan to Egypt in this amazing story of Joseph.

Coat, a Pharaoh & a Family Reunion: "The Story of Joseph" unabr. ed. Joe Loesch. Ed. by Cheryl J. Hutchinson. Illus. by Ott Denney. 1 CD. (Bible Stories for Kids Ser.). (J). (ps-3). 1997. pap. bk. 16.95 (978-1-887729-20-8(8)) Toy Box Prods.

Coat, a Pharoah & a Family Reunion. unabr. ed. Joe Loesch. Ed. by Cheryl J. Hutchinson. Illus. by Ott Denney. 1 cass. (Bible Stories for Kids Ser.). (J). (gr. k-6). 1997. 6.98 Toy Box Prods.

Coat of Many Colors. Kenneth G. Mills. Perf. by Earth-Stage Actors Staff. Composed by Michael Small. 1 cass., 1 CD. (Running Time: 1 hrs. 8 min.). Dramatization. 1996. 8.98 (978-0-919842-19-9(4), KGOC34); audio compact disk 14.98 CD. (978-0-919842-20-5(8), KGOD34) Ken Mills Found.
Dramatization of a lecture given by Kenneth G. Mills, as well as 7 poems; accompanied by music originally composed & performed by Kenneth Mills.

Coat of Varnish. unabr. ed. C. P. Snow. Read by Peter MacDonald. 8 cass. (Running Time: 12 hrs.). 1981. 64.00 (978-0-7366-0519-9(3), 1493) Books on Tape.
Aylestone Square is virtually the last bastion of upper-class gentleness & decorum. When a shockingly gruesome murder occurs there it takes everyone by surprise.

Cobain: The Secret Museum. unabr. ed. Charles Cross. (Running Time: 6 hrs. 30 mins.). 2010. audio compact disk 29.98 (978-1-60024-458-2(0)) Pub: Hachet Audio. Dist(s): HachBkGrp

Cobain Unseen. unabr. ed. Charles R. Cross. (Running Time: 6 hrs. 30 mins.). 2008. 24.98 (978-1-60024-459-9(9)) Pub: Hachet Audio. Dist(s): HachBkGrp

Cobb. unabr. ed. Al Stump. Read by Ian Esmo. 14 cass. (Running Time: 21 hrs.). 1996. 89.95 (1915) Blckstn Audio.
Stump tells how he was given a fascinating window into the Georgia Peach's life & times when the dying Cobb hired him in 1960 to ghostwrite his autobiography.

Cobb. unabr. ed. Al Stump. Read by Ian Esmo. 14 cass. (Running Time: 20 hrs. 30 mins.). 2006. 89.95 (978-0-7861-1147-3(X), 1915) Blckstn Audio.

Cobblestone Heroes. Ken McCoy. Read by Mary Gardner. 9 cass. (Storysound Ser.). (J). 2001. 76.95 (978-1-85903-415-6(2)) Pub: Mgna Lrg Print GBR. Dist(s): Ulverscroft US

***Cobra.** unabr. ed. Frederick Forsyth. Contrib. by Jonathan Davis. (Running Time: 13 hrs.). (ENG.). 2010. audio compact disk 39.95 (978-0-14-242846-7(9), PengAudBks) Penguin Grp USA.

***COBRA Compliance Update.** Created by Park University Enterprises. 2010. audio compact disk 199.95 (978-1-60959-009-3(0)) P Univ E Inc.

Cobra King of Kathmandu. Philip Kerr & P. B. Kerr. Narrated by Ron Keith. 9 CDs. (Running Time: 11 hrs.). (Children of the Lamp Ser.: Vol. 3). (ENG.). (J). (gr. 4-7). 2008. audio compact disk 39.95 (978-0-545-05245-0(9)) Scholastic Inc.

Cobra King of Kathmandu. unabr. ed. P. B. Kerr. Read by Ron Keith. (Children of the Lamp Ser.). (J). 2008. 59.99 (978-1-60252-958-8(2)) Find a World.

Cobra King Strikes Back. 6 episodes on 3 cas. (Running Time: 60 min. per cass.). (Adventures by Morse Collection). 1998. 19.98 Boxed set. (4306) Radio Spirits.
In the dense jungles of Cambodia, a long dormant culture of snake worshippers plots a return to greatness.

Cobra King Strikes Back. Carlton E. Morse. 5 cass. (Running Time: 60 min. per cass.). Dramatization. (Adventures by Morse Ser.). 6.00 ea. Once Upon Rad.
A complete story in 10 chapters - radio broadcasts - mystery & suspense.

Cobweb. Margaret Duffy. 2008. 69.95 (978-1-4079-0081-0(1)); audio compact disk 79.95 (978-1-4079-0082-7(X)) Pub: Soundings Ltd GBR. Dist(s): Ulverscroft US

Cocaine. David L. Ohlms. Read by David L. Ohlms. Ed. by JoAnn Moore. 1 cass. (Running Time: 1 hr.). 1994. 10.95 (978-1-56168-001-6(X), A9402) GWC Inc.
Dr. Ohlms explains the physical, mental, emotional, social & legal reasons why being a cocaine addict or user in the 1990s is becoming an increasingly miserable & life-threatening existence.

Cocaine: The Audio-Subliminal Guide to Self Help Treatment. unabr. ed. Alan Meyers. Read by Alan Meyers. 3 cass. (Running Time: 45 min.). 1991. 60.00 Set. Meyers Pub.
Cocaine: The Treatment System audio-subliminal set of 3 medically approved tapes for use with cocaine & crack patients. Complete scripts accompany tape set.

Cocaine: The Colombian Connection. 1 cass. (Running Time: 40 min.). 10.95 (ME-87-03-05, HarperThor) HarpC GBR.

Cocaine & Karma. Instructed by Manly P. Hall. 8.95 (978-0-89314-029-8(5), C8504210) Philos Res.

Cocaine Blues. Kerry Greenwood. Read by Stephanie Daniel. (Running Time: 5 hrs. 50 mins.). (Phryne Fisher Ser.). 2009. 64.99 (978-1-74214-231-9(1), 9781742142319) Pub: Bolinda Pubng AUS. Dist(s): Bolinda Pub Inc

Cocaine Blues. unabr. ed. Kerry Greenwood. Read by Stephanie Daniel. 4 cass. (Running Time: 6 hrs.). (Phryne Fisher Ser.). 2000. (978-1-74030-092-6(0), 500116) Bolinda Pubng AUS.
It's the end of the roaring twenties & the exuberant & Honorable Phyrne Fisher is dancing & gaming with gay abandon. But she becomes bored with London & the endless round of parties. In search of excitement, she sets her sights on a spot of detective work in Melbourne.

Cocaine Blues. unabr. ed. Kerry Greenwood. Read by Stephanie Daniel. (Running Time: 21000 sec.). (Phryne Fisher Ser.). 2006. audio compact disk 63.95 (978-1-74093-840-2(2)) Pub: Bolinda Pubng AUS. Dist(s): Bolinda Pub Inc

Cocaine Epidemic. Mark S. Gold. 1 cass. 1986. 7.95 (1697) Hazelden.
The founder of the National Cocaine Helpline & author of "800-Cocaine" discusses cocaine use & abuse in America.

Cocaine Nights. J. G. Ballard. Narrated by Gordon Griffin. 8 cass. (Running Time: 11 hrs. 30 mins.). 72.00 (978-1-84197-388-3(2)) Recorded Bks.

Cochlear Implant - Update. 2 cass. (Otorhinolaryngology Ser.: C85-OT5). 1985. 15.00 (8577) Am Coll Surgeons.

Cochrane: The Life & Exploits of a Fighting Captain. Robert Harvey. Read by Richard Matthews. 2001. 56.00 (978-0-7366-6046-4(1)); audio compact disk 72.00 (978-0-7366-7078-4(5)) Books on Tape.

Cochrane: The Real Master & Commander. unabr. ed. David Cordingly. Read by John Lee. (YA). 2008. 59.99 (978-1-60514-565-5(3)) Find a World.

Cochrane: The Real Master & Commander. unabr. ed. David Cordingly. Read by John Lee. (Running Time: 13 hrs. 30 mins. 0 sec.). (ENG.). 2007. audio compact disk 37.99 (978-1-4001-0542-7(0)); audio compact disk 24.99 (978-1-4001-5542-2(8)); audio compact disk 75.99 (978-1-4001-3542-4(7)) Pub: Tantor Media. Dist(s): IngramPubServ

***Cock & the Hen.** Anonymous. 2009. (978-1-60136-596-5(9)) Audio Holding.

Cockapoo: A Basic Guide to this Canine Hybrid. Karen Jean Matsko Hood. 2006. 29.95 (978-1-59434-825-9(1)); audio compact disk 24.95 (978-1-59434-822-8(7)) Whsprng Pine.

Cockatoo. (Choices & Decisions Ser.). 1990. 7.92 (978-0-8123-6436-1(8)) Holt McDoug.

Cockatoo Christmas. 1. (Running Time: 12 mins). 2002. audio compact disk 7.95 (978-0-9716093-4-1(9)) World Ctr for Exotic Birds.

Cockayne Syndrome - A Bibliography & Dictionary for Physicians, Patients, & Genome Researchers. Compiled by Icon Group International, Inc. Staff. 2007. ring bd. 28.95 (978-0-497-11352-0(X)) Icon Grp.

Cockie Lockie, Henny Penny & Mr. Korbes the Fox see Puss in Boots & Other Fairy Tales from Around the World

Cockleshell Girl. unabr. ed. Emma Stirling. 11 cass. 1994. 89.95 (978-1-85496-898-2(X), 5787X) Pub: Soundings Ltd GBR. Dist(s): Ulverscroft US
Orphan Alys Hughes gathered cockles from the beaches & sold them to add to the paltry wages her step-father earned & spent in the pub. Then Alys met Evan Jenkins, the son of a wealthy pit-owner. They fell deeply in love, meeting in secret. However, Evan's father, Thomas Jenkins, was determined to remove his son from the clutches of this cockleshell girl.

Cockney see Acting with an Accent

Cockney Family. unabr. ed. Elizabeth Waite. Read by Diana Bishop. 12 cass. (Running Time: 18 hrs.). 2001. 94.95 (978-1-86042-466-3(X), 2466X) Pub: Soundings Ltd GBR. Dist(s): Ulverscroft US
Patsy Kent thought she would never belong to a real family, after her mother died & she was nearly sent to the orphanage. But the market trader of Strathmore Street stood by her & Ollie, Florrie & the others became the best relatives anyone could wish for.

Cockney Waif. unabr. ed. Elizabeth Waite. Read by Annie Aldington. 11 cass. (Running Time: 16 hrs.). 2000. 89.95 (978-1-86042-438-0(4), 24384) Pub: Soundings Ltd GBR. Dist(s): Ulverscroft US
Patsy Kent is only thirteen years old when her dear mother dies & leaves her an orphan. As she becomes a young woman & starts work in the local market like her mother before her, Patsy discovers all too soon the pain of first love.

Cockroach Party. abr. ed. Margaret Read MacDonald. (Running Time: 3540 sec.). (J). (ps). 2005. audio compact disk 14.95 (978-0-87483-769-8(3)) Pub: August Hse. Dist(s): Natl Bk Netwk

Cocktail Time. unabr. ed. P. G. Wodehouse. Read by Frederick Davidson. 5 cass. (Running Time: 7 hrs.). 2003. 39.95 (978-0-7861-1071-1(6), 1841) Blckstn Audio.
If Lord Ickenham had not succumbed to the temptation to dislodge the hat of Beefy Bastable, the irascible Q'C, with a well-aimed Brazil nut, the latter's famous legal mind might never have been stimulated to literature. But the incident provoked Beefy to write his expose of the younger generation, a novel so shocking that it caused endless repercussions for its hapless author & sparked off a whole series of outrageous misunderstandings that it would take the inventive talents of Lord Ickenham himself to resolve.

Cocktail Time. unabr. ed. P. G. Wodehouse. Read by Jonathan Cecil. 6 cass. (Running Time: 9 hrs.). 2000. 54.95 (978-0-7540-0531-5(3)) Pub: Chivers Audio Bks GBR. Dist(s): AudioGO

Cocktail Time. unabr. ed. P. G. Wodehouse. Read by Jonathan Cecil. 6 CDs. (Running Time: 9 hrs.). 2002. audio compact disk 64.95 (978-0-7540-5549-5(3), CCD 240) Pub: Chivers Audio Bks GBR. Dist(s): AudioGO

Cocktails for Three. abr. ed. Madeleine Wickham. Read by Katherine Kellgren. 4 CDs. (Running Time: 5 hrs. 0 mins. 0 sec.). (ENG.). 2008. audio compact disk 14.95 (978-1-4272-0474-5(8)) Pub: Macmill Audio. Dist(s): Macmillan

Coco Loco y Amigos en el Suroeste see Humpty Dumpty & Friends in the Southwest

***Cocoanut Grove Ambassadors, Volume 1.** RadioArchives.com. (Running Time: 600). (ENG.). 2007. audio compact disk 29.98 (978-1-61081-070-8(8)) Radio Arch.

***Cocoanut Grove Ambassadors, Volume 2.** RadioArchives.com. (Running Time: 600). (ENG.). 2008. audio compact disk 29.98 (978-1-61081-075-3(9)) Radio Arch.

***Coconut.** Na Shandies. (ENG.). 1989. 11.95 (978-0-8023-7014-3(4)) Pub: Clo Iar-Chonnachta IRL. Dist(s): Dufour

Coconut Moon. Green Chili Jam Band. Read by Green Chili Jam Band. 1 cass. (Running Time: 45 min.). (J). 1997. 9.98 (978-0-9656393-0-9(4), GC030); audio compact disk 14.98 CD. (978-0-9656393-1-6(2), GC031) Squeaky Wheel.
Music & story based on imagination.

Coconut Oil: The New Health Food of the 21st Century. Speeches. Bruce Fife. 1 cass. (Running Time: 50 mins.). 2004. 5.95 (978-0-941599-54-2(X)); audio compact disk 6.95 (978-0-941599-61-0(2)) Piccadilly Bks.
Describes many of the health benefits of coconut oil.

Cocorico. unabr. ed. 1 cass. (Running Time: 1 hr.). (FRE & ENG.). 1992. pap. bk. 16.95 (978-0-88432-464-5(8), SFR135) J Norton Pubs.
Fifteen delightful stories featuring simple vocabulary in the present tense for beginning students.

Cocorico CD & Booklet. 1 CD. (Running Time: 56 mins.). (FRE.). 2006. audio compact disk 16.95 (978-1-57970-415-5(8), SFR135D, Audio-For) J Norton Pubs.
15 delightful stories featuring simple vocabulary in the present tense for beginning French students. 1 CD with booklet.

Cocteau Rodeo & the Myth of Absolute Time. 1 CD. (Running Time: 1 hr.). 2001. audio compact disk 15.95 (HEAD001) Lodestone Catalog.
After marring Eurydice in Las Vegas, Prometheus, the bodacious guitarist, goes to hell & back for his woman & loses her anyway.

Cod: A Biography of the Fish That Changed the World. Mark Kurlansky. Narrated by Richard M. Davidson. 7 CDs. (Running Time: 7 hrs. 45 mins.). audio compact disk 69.00 (978-1-4025-1566-8(9)) Recorded Bks.

Cod: A Biography of the Fish That Changed the World. unabr. ed. Mark Kurlansky. Narrated by Richard M. Davidson. 6 cass. (Running Time: 7 hrs. 45 mins.). 2001. 58.00 (978-0-7887-8866-6(3)) Recorded Bks.
This is the story of the codfish - object of wars, inspiration for revolutions, basis of economies, and the reason Europeans set sail across the Atlantic. Also a story of tragic environmental disregard.

Cod: A Biography of the Fish that Changed the World. unabr. ed. Mark Kurlansky. Read by Richard M. Davidson. 6 cass. (Running Time: 8 hrs.). 2004. 34.95 (978-1-59007-245-5(6)) Pub: New Millenn Enter. Dist(s): PerseuPGW
This is about a fish that altered diets, brought about the development of the new world, and provoked fishing rules internationally. This intriguing insight is well-researched and interestingly written with references back as far in history as the seafarers of the Mediterranean.

Code. Ernest Haycox. (Running Time: 0 hr. 30 mins.). 1998. 10.95 (978-1-60083-448-6(5)) Iofy Corp.

Code Name: Death. abr. ed. William W. Johnstone. 2 cass. (Running Time: 3 hrs.). (Code Name Ser.: No. 3). 2004. 18.00 (978-1-58807-430-0(7)) Am Pubng Inc.
Today, when bomb-throwing madmen rule nations and crime cartels strangle the globe, justice demands extreme measures. For twenty years, ex-CIA operations officer John Barrone fought his country's dirty back-alley wars. Now, he leads a secret strike force of former law enforcement, intelligence, and special operations professionals against America's enemies.Code Name: Death. In Los Angeles, a teenage prostitute disappears. Months later, her billionaire industrialist grandfather watches as she stars in a porn flick that ends with her brutal murder. Now, Marist J. Quinncannon has hired Barrone to penetrate a viper's nest of sex for sale and murder for kicks. What Barrone and his team find is a snuff film kingpin with a 20-year grudge against Quinncannon - a depraved killer to powerful he can only be taken down with maximum force.

Code Name God. Mani Bhaumik. Read by Stefan Rudnicki. (Running Time: 23400 sec.). 2006. 44.95 (978-0-7861-4583-6(8)) Blckstn Audio.

Code Name God. unabr. ed. Mani Bhaumik. Read by Stefan Rudnicki. (Running Time: 23400 sec.). 2006. audio compact disk 29.95 (978-0-7861-7521-5(4)) Blckstn Audio.

Code Name God: The Spiritual Odyssey of a Man of Science. Mani Bhaumik. Read by Stefan Rudnicki. (Running Time: 23400 sec.). 2006. audio compact disk 45.00 (978-0-7861-7031-9(X)) Blckstn Audio.

Code of Honor see Codigo de Honor

Code of Honor. unabr. ed. Harold Coyle. Read by Christopher Lane. 12 cass. (Running Time: 17 hrs. 30 mins.). 1994. 83.95 Set. (978-0-7861-0827-5(4), 1521) Blckstn Audio.
Captain Nancy Kazak's story is set against the decision to send U.S. troops to Columbia as a "peacekeeping" force to prevent anarchy, a decision that leads to a vicious full-scale war in which the American forces, at first out-fought, battle desperately for survival - a scenario with disturbing echoes of the current controversies about putting U.S. forces into foreign countries.

Code of Motherhood. Elbert Willis. 1 cass. (Tribute to Mothers Ser.). 4.00 Fill the Gap.

Code of Silence: Piercing the Veil. Ricardo A. Scott. 1 cass. (Running Time: 90 min.). (Silent No More Ser.). (J). 1999. pap. bk. (978-1-58470-055-5(6), GRTS 7391) Crnerstone GA.
Shows how the trail of blood money can lead to the real killers of our reggae prophets & our people.

Code of Silence: Piercing the Veil, GRTS 7391. Ricardo A. Scott. 1 cass. (Running Time: 90 min.). (Silent No More Ser.). (YA). 1999. cass. & video (978-1-58470-056-2(4)) Crnerstone GA.

***Code of the Woosters.** P. G. Wodehouse. Narrated by Richard Briers & Michael Hordern. (Running Time: 3 hrs. 0 mins. 0 sec.). (ENG., 2010. audio compact disk 29.95 (978-1-84607-136-2(4)) Pub: AudioGO. Dist(s): Perseus Dist

Code of the Woosters. unabr. ed. P. G. Wodehouse. Read by Simon Prebble. (Running Time: 27000 sec.). (Jeeves & Wooster Ser.). 2006. 54.95 (978-0-7861-4661-1(3)); audio compact disk 55.00 (978-0-7861-6747-0(5)); audio compact disk 29.95 (978-0-7861-7407-2(2)) Blckstn Audio.

Code of the Woosters. unabr. ed. P. G. Wodehouse. Read by Jonathan Cecil. 6 cass. (Running Time: 9 hrs.). (Jeeves & Wooster Ser.). 2000. 49.95 (978-0-7451-6372-7(6), CAB 497) Pub: Chivers Audio Bks GBR. Dist(s): AudioGO
Take Gussie Fink-Nottle, the soupy Madeline Bassett, old Pop Bassett, the unscrupulous Stuffy Byng, the Rev. H.P. 'Stinker' Pinker, an 18th century cowcreamer, a small brown notebook and mix well with a liberal dose of the aged relative Aunt Dahlia, and there you have it: a dangerous brew that spells toil and trouble for Bertie Wooster and some serious thinking for Jeeves!.

Code of the Woosters. unabr. ed. P. G. Wodehouse. Perf. by Rosalind Ayres et al. 2 cass. (Running Time: 2 hrs.). (Jeeves & Wooster Ser.). 1997. 22.95 (978-1-58081-060-9(8), CTA60) L A Theatre.
Bertie's beloved Aunt Dahlia pressures him into stealing a cow-shaped silver creamer. At the same time, Bertie attempts to patch up the shaky romance between Gussie Fink-Nottle, the newt expert, & Madeline Bassett, a four-star drip. The results of Bertie's efforts are, as always, a financial disaster. He nearly gets lynched, arrested & engaged by mistake. And as always, Jeeves is on hand with a last minute brainstorm to set everything straight.

Code of the Woosters, unabr. ed. P. G. Wodehouse. Narrated by Alexander Spencer. 6 cass. (Running Time: 8 hrs.). (Jeeves & Wooster Ser.). 1989. 51.00 (978-1-55690-109-6(7), 89600E7) Recorded Bks.
Upper class Englishman & his manservant in light-hearted adventure.

Code of the Woosters: Jeeves to the Rescue. unabr. ed. P. G. Wodehouse. Read by Jonathan Cecil. 6 cass. (Running Time: 7 hrs.). (Jeeves & Wooster Ser.). 2001. 29.95 (978-1-57270-182-3(X), C61182u) Pub: Audio Partners. Dist(s): PerseuPGW

Code of the Woosters: Jeeves to the Rescue. unabr. ed. P. G. Wodehouse. Read by Jonathan Cecil. (Running Time: 25680 sec.). (Jeeves & Wooster Ser.). (ENG.). 2006. audio compact disk 29.95 (978-1-57270-548-7(5)) Pub: AudioGO. Dist(s): Perseus Dist

Code of Woosters. unabr. ed. P. G. Wodehouse. Narrated by Richard Briers & Michael Hordern. 3 CDs. (Running Time: 3 hrs.). 2008. audio compact disk 39.95 (978-0-7927-5414-5(X)) AudioGO.
Who would think that an eighteenth-century silver cow-creamer could cause so much trouble? Uncle Tom wants it, Sir Watkyn Bassett has it, and Aunt Dahlia is blackmailing Bertie to steal it. With relations between Bertie and Sir Watkyn being far from cordial (ever since the Boat Race night when Sir Watkyn fined the young Wooster five pounds for pinching a policeman's helmet), the situation looks tricky. Arriving at Totleigh Towers, Sir Watkyn's country seat, matters get progressively worse. The nightmare crew includes not only that fierce old magistrate but his right-hand man, the frightful Roderick Spode. Add to that Madeline Bassett, Gussie Fink-Nottle, Stiffy Byng and Harold "Stinker" Pinker and there's only one thing to say, "What Ho, Jeeves!".

Code Talker. unabr. ed. Joseph Bruchac. Read by Derrick Henry. 5 cass. (Running Time: 6 hrs.). (YA). (gr. 5 up). 2006. 39.75 (978-1-4193-5121-1(4)) Recorded Bks.
Although the mission school bans all that is Navajo, Ned secretly clings to his native language and culture. Proudly joining the U.S. Marines in 1943, he becomes a top-secret Navajo Code Talker. During bloody battles for Japanese islands, Ned and his brave band of code-talking brothers save thousands of lives using Navajo encryption the enemy never cracks.

Code to Zero. Ken Follett. Read by George Guidall. 8 cass. (Running Time: 12 hrs.). 1999. 35.96 Blckstn Audio.
Bound together by the past, separated by the war & caught up in the mighty struggle between the superpowers, four old friends from Harvard sit at the very center in this dangerous heart of the Cold War & as Luke Lucas releams the story of his life, he uncovers long kept secrets about his wife, his best friend, the woman he once loved more than life itself & realized that his fate is tied to the rocket that stands ready on launch pad 26B at the Cape. Luke knew something that someone was desperate for him to forget & unless he is able to discover that terrible deadly secret, Luke may be left powerless to save the launch of Explorer & with it, America's future.

Code to Zero. unabr. ed. Ken Follett. 8 cass. (Running Time: 12 hrs.). 2000. 39.99 (766, PengAudBks) Penguin Grp USA.
On launch pad 26B sits Explorer I, America's best hope to match the Soviet Sputnik and regain the lead in the race for the skies. Bound together by the past, separated by the war, and caught up in the mighty struggle between the superpowers, four old friends from Harvard sit at the very center in this dangerous heart of the Cold War.

Code to Zero. unabr. ed. Ken Follett. Narrated by George Guidall. 7 cass. (Running Time: 9 hrs. 45 mins.). 2000. 61.00 (978-0-7887-4944-5(7), 96462E7) Recorded Bks.
America in 1958, riddled with suspicion & tension, as scientists struggle desperately to overtake Russia in a race to control outer space.

Code to Zero. unabr. ed. Ken Follett. Narrated by George Guidall. 9 CDs. (Running Time: 9 hrs. 45 mins.). 2001. audio compact disk 89.00 (978-0-7887-6168-3(4)) Recorded Bks.
Transports you to America of 1958, riddled with suspicion & tension, as scientists struggle desperately to overtake Russia in the race to control outer space. A man wakes up shaking with fear on the cold rest room floor in Union Station, Washington, D. C. He doesn't know how he got there, or even his own name. His ragged, dirty clothes imply that he's a bum, probably getting over a bender. But something seems terribly wrong & shadowy figures follow his every move. Searching for answers, the man uncovers a shocking truth that threatens to derail America's space program, even while Cape Canaveral counts down to liftoff.

Codependence: An Audio Spiritual Experience. Robert Burney. Read by Robert Burney. 2 cass. (Running Time: 4 hrs.). 1996. 19.95 (978-0-9648383-0-7(3)) Joy To You.
This is a slightly abridged version of the book Codepenence: The Dance of Wounded Souls written and spoken by Robert Burney. Subtitle: An Audio Spiritual Experience.

Codependence Recovery, Spirituality & Self Care. Pia Mellody. Read by Pia Mellody. 4 cass. 35.00 Set. (A3) Featuka Enter Inc.
Discusses child abuse & its relationship to spiritual growth & development.

Codependency. 1 cass. (Running Time: 60 min.). 10.95 (057) Psych Res Inst.
Designed to enable to become free from destructive relationships & approach life with happiness & confidence by letting go of compulsive behaviors.

Codependency Seminar. Earnie Larsen. 6 cass. 1986. 45.00 Set. (4035) Hazelden.
Popular speaker Earnie Larsen gives tips on codependency & explains what it is, where it comes from, how it affects one & what to do about it.

Codependency to Self-Discovery. Barrie Konicov. 1 cass. 11.98 (978-1-56001-526-0(8), 162) Potentials.
By definition, a codependent person is one who has let another person's behavior effect him or her, & who is obsessed with controlling that person's behavior. If this is the situation & a journey to self-discovery is needed, here it is.

Codependent No More: How to Stop Controlling Others & Start Caring for Yourself. Melody Beattie. 1 cass. (Running Time: 60 min.). (Discovery Ser.). 1987. 10.00 (978-0-89486-470-4(X), 5610G) Hazelden.

Codependent No More: How to Stop Controlling Others & Start Caring for Yourself. Melody Beattie. 1 cass. (Running Time: 60 min.). 1994. 10.00 (978-0-89486-633-3(8)) Hazelden.

Codependent No More: How to Stop Controlling Others & Start Caring for Yourself. abr. ed. Melody Beattie. Read by Melody Beattie. 1 cass. (Running Time: 1 hr.). 1998. 11.95 (978-1-57453-266-1(9)) Audio Lit.
Will help you take care of yourself.

Codependent No More: How to Stop Controlling Others & Start Caring for Yourself. abr. ed. Melody Beattie. 1 cass. (Running Time: 70 min.). 1999. 12.00 (35206) Courage-to-Change.
Describes codependency, its origins, & effects on ourselves & others, & discusses ways to change.

Codependent No More: How to Stop Controlling Others & Start Caring for Yourself. unabr. ed. Melody Beattie. 6 cass. (Running Time: 9 hrs.). 1999. 34.95 (978-1-57453-305-7(3)) Audio Lit.
For anyone struggling with a relationship involving alcoholism or other compulsive behaviors, this program points the way to healing & the renewal of hope.

Codependents' Guide to the Twelve Steps. Melody Beattie. Read by Melody Beattie. 1 cass. (Running Time: 60 min.). 1990. 11.00 (978-0-671-72606-5(4), Sound Ideas) S&S Audio.

Codes of Love: Rethink Your Family, Remake Your Life. Mark Bryan. 2004. 10.95 (978-0-7435-4285-2(1)) Pub: S&S Audio. Dist(s): S and S Inc

***Codes of Power Meditation.** Diana Cooper. Andrew Brel. (Running Time: 1 hr. 18 mins. 0 sec.). (ENG.). 2010. audio compact disk 14.95 (978-1-84409-524-7(X)) Pub: Findhorn Pr GBR. Dist(s): IPG Chicago

Codex. abr. rev. ed. Douglas Preston. Read by Scott Sowers. 5 CDs. (Running Time: 6 hrs. 0 mins. 0 sec.). (ENG.). 2004. audio compact disk 29.95 (978-1-59397-362-9(4)) Pub: Macmill Audio. Dist(s): Macmillan

Codex. unabr. ed. Douglas Preston. Read by Scott Brick. 8 cass. (Running Time: 12 hrs.). 2004. 72.00 (978-0-7366-9873-3(6)) Books on Tape.
The race is on for a notorious tomb raider's priceless collection of treasures-including an invaluable Mayan codex.

Codex 632: A Novel about the Secret Identity of Christopher Columbus. unabr. ed. Jose Rodrigues Dos Santos. Read by George Guidall. 10 cass. (Running Time: 11 hrs. 30 mins.). 2007. 46.95 (978-1-4281-6513-7(4)); 82.75 (978-1-4281-6512-0(6)); audio compact disk 123.75 (978-1-4281-6514-4(2)) Recorded Bks.

Codex 632: A Novel about the Secret Identity of Christopher Columbus. unabr. ed. Jose Rodrigues Dos Santos. Narrated by George Guidall. 10 CDs. (Running Time: 11 hrs. 30 mins.). 2008. audio compact disk 34.99 (978-1-4281-6511-3(8)) Recorded Bks.

Codicil. unabr. ed. Tom Topor. Read by Dale Hull. (Running Time: 14 hrs.). 2008. 39.25 (978-1-4233-5826-8(0), 9781423358268, BADLE); 39.25 (978-1-4233-5824-4(4), 9781423358244, Brlnc Audio MP3 Lib); 24.95 (978-1-4233-5823-7(6), 9781423358237, Brilliance MP3); 24.95 (978-1-4233-5825-1(2), 9781423358251, BAD) Brilliance Audio.

Codigo Da Vinci. Dan Brown. Read by Raul Amundaray.Tr. of Da Vinci Code. (SPA.). 2009. 64.99 (978-1-60775-716-0(8)) Find a World.

Codigo Da Vinci. Dan Brown. Narrated by Raul Amundaray. 19 CDs. (Running Time: 86400 sec.).Tr. of Da Vinci Code. (SPA.). 2005. audio compact disk 39.95 (978-0-9728598-8-2(8)) Fonolibro Inc.
Qué misterio se oculta tras la sonrisa de la celebre Mona Lisa?. Durante siglos, la Iglesia ha conseguido mantener oculta la verdad¿ hasta ahora. Uno de los libros con mas tiempo en el tope de la lista de los Best Sellers del New York Times!.... El Código Da Vinci, ahora en un audiolibro narrado en español del bestseller internacional de Dan Brown, producido exclusivamente por FONOLIBRO, el cual no podrá dejar de escuchar hasta que llegue al inesperado final. Mientras se encontraba en un viaje de negocios en Paris, Robert Langdon, experto en simbologia de la universidad de Harvard, recibe una llamada urgente a media noche. Jacques Saunière, el último Gran Maestre de una sociedad secreta que se remonta a la fundación de los Templarios, ha sido asesinado en el museo del Louvre. Saunière antes de morir transmite a su nieta Sofia una misteriosa clave. Saunière y sus predecesores, entre los que se encontraban hombres como Isaac Newton o Leonardo Da Vinci, han conservado durante siglos un conocimiento que puede cambiar completamente la historia de la humanidad. Ahora Sofía, con la ayuda Robert Langdon, comienza la búsqueda de ese secreto, en una trepidante carrera que les lleva de una clave a otra, descifrando mensajes ocultos en los más famosos cuadros del genial pintor y en las paredes de antiguas catedrales. Un rompecabezas que deberán resolver pronto, ya que no están solos en el juego: una poderosa e influyente organización católica está dispuesta a emplear todos los medios para evitar que el secreto salga a la luz. FonoLibro, lider en audiolibros en espanol, les trae una afamada historia sobre un apasionante juego de claves escondidas, sorprendentes revelaciones, acertijos ingeniosos, verdades, mentiras, realidades históricas, mitos, símbolos, ritos, misterios y suposiciones en una trama llena de giros inesperados narrada con un ritmo imparable que conduce al oyente hasta el secreto más celosamente guardado del inicio de nuestra era.

Codigo Da Vinci. abr. ed. Scripts. Dan Brown. Read by Raul Amundaray. 6 CDs. (Running Time: 28800 sec.).Tr. of Da Vinci Code. (SPA.). 2006. audio compact disk 24.95 (978-1-933499-05-5(2)) Fonolibro Inc.
?Que misterio se oculta tras la sonrisa de la celebre Mona Lisa? . Durante siglos, la Iglesia ha conseguido mantener oculta la verdad? hasta ahora. Uno de los libros con mas tiempo en el tope de la lista de los Best Sellers del New York Times!.... El Codigo Da Vinci, ahora en un audiolibro narrado en espa?ol del bestseller internacional de Dan Brown, producido exclusivamente por FONOLIBRO, en una version resumida la cual no podra dejar de escuchar hasta que llegue al inesperado final. Mientras se encontraba en un viaje de negocios en Paris, Robert Langdon, experto en simbologia de la universidad de Harvard, recibe una llamada urgente a media noche. Jacques Sauniere, el ultimo Gran Maestre de una sociedad secreta que se remonta a la fundacion de los Templarios, ha sido asesinado en el museo del Louvre. Sauniere antes de morir transmite a su nieta Sofia una misteriosa clave. Sauniere y sus predecesores, entre los que se encontraban hombres como Isaac Newton o Leonardo Da Vinci, han conservado durante siglos un conocimiento que puede cambiar completamente la historia de la humanidad. Ahora Sofia, con la ayuda Robert Langdon, comienza la busqueda de ese secreto, en una trepidante carrera que les lleva de una clave a otra, descifrando mensajes ocultos en los mas famosos cuadros del genial pintor y en las paredes de antiguas catedrales. Un rompecabezas que deberan resolver pronto, ya que no estan solos en el juego: una poderosa e influyente organizacion catolica esta dispuesta a emplear todos los medios para evitar que el secreto salga a la luz. FonoLibro, lider en audiolibros en espanol, les trae una afamada historia sobre un apasionante juego de claves escondidas, sorprendentes revelaciones, acertijos ingeniosos, verdades, mentiras, realidades historicas, mitos, simbolos, ritos, misterios y suposiciones en una trama llena de giros inesperados narrada con un ritmo imparable que conduce al oyente hasta el secreto mas celosamente guardado del inicio de nuestra era. Tambien disponible en una version completa de FonoLibro.

Codigo de Honor. Carlos Cuauhtemoc Sanchez.Tr. of Code of Honor. audio compact disk 15.95 (978-968-7277-57-8(2)) Pub: EdSelect MEX. Dist(s): Giron Bks

Codigo de Honor. Carlos Cuauhtemoc Sanchez. 1 cass. (Running Time: 40 mins.).Tr. of Code of Honor. (SPA.). 2002. 14.98 (978-968-7277-32-5(7)) Taller del Exito.
Ethics are concerned with what encourages a man on the inside...it isn't anything other than the Code of Honor that guides our destiny; a code to know that each one of the performances in our lives must have a clear line of conduct, a guide to live by, without cheating ourselves or others.

código del campeón audio libro CD. unabr. ed. Dante Gebel. (SPA & ENG.). 2009. audio compact disk 14.99 (978-0-8297-5732-3(5)) Pub: Vida Pubs. Dist(s): Zondervan

Coding for Optimal Reimbursement. Medical Management Institute Staff. 6 cass. (Running Time: 9 hrs.). 305.00 (978-1-58383-101-4(0)) Med Mgmt.
The course focuses on CPT & ICD coding for reimbursement for physician services. Everything from procedural coding to evaluation & management documentation guidelines. A strong emphasis is also placed on the proper use of modifiers & their effect on reimbursement.

Coding, Reporting & Documentation Guidance for Home Health Services, Nursing Facilities & Hospices. Ingenix. 2008. audio compact disk 119.95 (978-1-60151-134-8(5)) Ingenix Inc.

Cod's Tale. Mark Kurlansky. Narrated by John McDonough. (Running Time: 1 hr.). (gr. 3 up). 10.00 (978-1-4025-2885-9(X)) Recorded Bks.

Cody's Law Collector's Series. Matthew S. Hart. Read by Charlton Griffin. 6 vols. No. 2. 2004. (978-1-58807-916-9(3)) Am Pubng Inc.

Cody's Law Collector's Series. Matthew S. Hart. Read by Charlton Griffin. 4 vols. No. 3. 2004. (978-1-58807-917-6(1)) Am Pubng Inc.

Cody's Law Collector's Series. Matthew S. Hart. Read by Charlton Griffin. 4 vols. No. 4. 2004. (978-1-58807-918-3(X)) Am Pubng Inc.

Cody's Law Collector's Series. abr. ed. Matthew S. Hart. Read by Charlton Griffin. 6 vols. 2003. (978-1-58807-915-2(5)) Am Pubng Inc.

Cody's Law Collector's Series: I. abr. ed. Matthew S. Hart. Read by Charlton Griffin. 6 vols. (Cody's Law Collector's Ser.: No. 1). 2003. 35.00 (978-1-58807-462-1(5)) Am Pubng Inc.

Cody's Law Collector's Series: II. Matthew S. Hart. Read by Charlton Griffin. 6 vols. (Cody's Law Collector's Ser.: No. 2). 2004. 35.00 (978-1-58807-463-8(3)) Am Pubng Inc.

Cody's Law Collector's Series: III. Matthew S. Hart. Read by Charlton Griffin. 4 vols. (Cody's Law Collector's Ser.: No. 3). 2004. 35.00 (978-1-58807-464-5(1)) Am Pubng Inc.

Cody's Law Collector's Series: IV. Matthew S. Hart. Read by Charlton Griffin. 4 vols. (Cody's Law Collector's Ser.: No. 4). 2004. 35.00 (978-1-58807-465-2(X)) Am Pubng Inc.

Coeur: Reparation et Entretien. unabr. ed. Robert A. Monroe. Read by Roland Simon. 1 cass. (Running Time: 30 min.). (Human Plus Ser.). (FRE.). 1993. 14.95 (978-1-56102-067-6(2)) Inter Indus.
Establish improvement in heart function.

Coeur Simple. Gustave Flaubert. Read by E. Lecucq. 1 cass. (FRE.). 1991. 13.95 (1051-OH) Olivia & Hill.
The exquisitely simple story of Felicite, who at age 16 becomes a servant in the village of Pont-L'Eveque in Normandy. Her daily life centers upon her widowed mistress, the widow's children, her own sailor nephew & finally a parrot.

Coffee Break - A Time to Retreat. 1 cass. (Coffee Break Ser.). 10.98 (C70006); audio compact disk 15.98 (CD 70006) Pub: Brentwood Music. Dist(s): Provident Mus Dist
This series provides the perfect backdrop for a few moments of peace in the midst of life's chaos. Listeners are led in a guided devotion time incorporating soothing instrumental music & scripture-based meditations for personal moments of quiet reflection.

Coffee Break - Rediscover the Wonders of Your Creator. 1 cass. (Coffee Break Ser.). 10.98 (ERCS5665); audio compact disk 15.98 (ERCD5665) Pub: Brentwood Music. Dist(s): Provident Mus Dist

***Coffee Shop Conversations: Making the Most of Spiritual Small Talk.** unabr. ed. Dale Fincher and Jonalyn Fincher. (Running Time: 7 hrs. 1 mins. 54 sec.). (ENG.). 2010. 15.99 (978-0-310-39564-5(X)) Zondervan.

Coffeehouse Classics. abr. ed. 1 cass. 24.98 (978-1-57908-206-2(8), 1221) Platinm Enter.

Coffin Dancer. Jeffery Deaver. (Lincoln Rhyme Ser.: No. 2). 2000. audio compact disk 15.99 (978-0-7435-0548-2(4), Audioworks) S&S Audio.

Coffin Dancer. abr. ed. Jeffery Deaver. (Lincoln Rhyme Ser.: No. 2). 2004. 15.95 (978-0-7435-4286-9(X)) Pub: S&S Audio. Dist(s): S and S Inc

Coffin Dancer. abr. ed. Jeffery Deaver. Read by Joe Mantegna. (Running Time: 5 hrs. 0 mins. 0 sec.). (Lincoln Rhyme Ser.: No. 2). 2006. audio compact disk 14.95 (978-0-7435-6540-0(1)) Pub: S&S Audio. Dist(s): S and S Inc

Coffin Dancer. unabr. ed. Jeffery Deaver. Read by Alexander Adams. 9 cass. (Running Time: 13 hrs. 30 min.). (Lincoln Rhyme Ser.: No. 2). 1999. 72.00 (978-0-7366-4603-1(5), 4990); audio compact disk 88.00 Books on Tape.
Quadriplegic detective Lincoln Rhyme & protoge Amelia Sachs are on the trail of a chameleon-like assassin loose on the streets of NYC.

Coffin for Baby. unabr. ed. Gwendoline Butler. Read by Nigel Graham. 4 cass. (Running Time: 4 hrs.). 2000. 39.95 (978-0-7540-0477-6(5), CAB1899) AudioGO.
Mary Ellen worked in a baby clinic in south-east London where her days were busy & her cases were small. Until the Bishop baby was kidnapped, before Mrs. Cox was murdered & before the gruesome discovery of a mummified child in a suitcase. It would take all of Inspector Coffin's skill to discover the identity of the kidnapper murderer.

Coffin for Dimitrios. unabr. ed. Eric Ambler. Narrated by Alexander Spencer. 6 cass. (Running Time: 7 hrs. 30 mins.). 1981. 51.00 (978-1-55690-110-2(0), RD684) Recorded Bks.
Through the cafes, trains & nighttime cities of Europe, Charles Latimer follows a twisting trail of drug-smugglers, thieves & assassins that will lead him to Dimitrios.

Coffin for Dimitrios. unabr. collector's ed. Eric Ambler. Read by Richard Brown. 8 cass. (Running Time: 8 hrs.). 1987. 48.00 (978-0-7366-1186-2(X), 2106) Books on Tape.
Mystery about a mystery writer in search of a story.

Coffin for Two. Quintin Jardine. Read by Joe Dunlop. 9 cass. (Running Time: 10 hrs. 30 mins.). (Soundings Ser.). (J). 2004. 76.95 (978-1-84283-485-5(1)); audio compact disk 84.95 (978-1-84283-783-2(4)) Pub: ISIS Lrg Prnt GBR. Dist(s): Ulverscroft US

Coffin in Fashion. unabr. ed. Gwendoline Butler. Read by Phil Garner. 6 cass. (Running Time: 6 hrs. 37 min.). (Isis Ser.). (J). 2003. 54.95 (978-1-85695-428-0(5)) Pub: ISIS Lrg Prnt GBR. Dist(s): Ulverscroft US

Coffin-Lowry Syndrome - A Bibliography & Dictionary for Physicians, Patients, & Genome Researchers. Compiled by Icon Group International, Inc. Staff. 2007. ring bd. 28.95 (978-0-497-11353-7(8)) Icon Grp.

Coffin on Murder Street. Gwendoline Butler. (Soundings (CDs) Ser.). 2006. audio compact disk 79.95 (978-1-84559-437-4(1)) Pub: ISIS Lrg Prnt GBR. Dist(s): Ulverscroft US

Coffin on Murder Street. unabr. ed. Gwendoline Butler. Read by Michael Tudor Barnes. 7 cass. (Soundings Ser.). 2006. 61.95 (978-1-84559-420-6(7)) Pub: ISIS Lrg Prnt GBR. Dist(s): Ulverscroft US

Coffin Tree. unabr. ed. Gwendoline Butler. Read by Phil Garner. 6 cass. (Running Time: 6 hrs. 45 min.). (Isis Ser.). (J). 2004. 54.95 (978-1-85695-844-8(2), 941205) Pub: ISIS Lrg Prnt GBR. Dist(s): Ulverscroft US

Cogitape. John Lilly. 1 cass. 10.00 (A0450-89) Sound Photosyn.
An audio hallucination experiment in word repetition.

Cogitate Tape. John C. Lilly. 1 cass. (Running Time: 1 hr.). 1988. 15.00 (MT026) Union Label.
Authorized sound trade recording used for experiments at Esalen Institute in '70s, as described in "Center of the Cyclone." Second side is Gold's music with repeating word trade used as percussion.

Cogito Pt. 2: The Dream. Liliana Franco. Narrated by Lou Savage. 2008. (978-0-9794618-7-3(1)) AJL Pub.

Cognitive Core of Character. Claudio Naranjo. 1 cass. 9.00 (A0337-89) Sound Photosyn.
The introductory lecture.

Cognitive Exercises for the Renewed Mind: The Audio Book. unabr. ed. Olivia M. McDonald. Olivia M. McDonald. 2006. 19.95 (978-0-9778294-7-7(2), CADIPS) Grace Hse USA.

***Cognitive Surplus: Creativity & Generosity in a Connected Age.** unabr. ed. Clay Shirky. (Running Time: 8 hrs. 30 mins.). 2010. 29.99 (978-1-4001-9681-4(7)); 15.99 (978-1-4001-8681-5(1)) Tantor Media.

***Cognitive Surplus: Creativity & Generosity in a Connected Age.** unabr. ed. Clay Shirky. Narrated by Kevin Foley. (Running Time: 7 hrs. 0 mins. 0 sec.). 2010. 19.99 (978-1-4001-6681-7(0)); audio compact disk 29.99 (978-1-4001-1681-2(3)); audio compact disk 59.99 (978-1-4001-4681-9(X)) Pub: Tantor Media. Dist(s): IngramPubServ

Cognitive Therapy of an Avoidant Personality. unabr. ed. Aaron T. Beck. 2 cass. (Running Time: 1 hr. 39 min.). (ENG.). 1990. 29.00 (978-0-89862-966-8(7)) Guilford Pubns.

Cognitive Therapy of Anxiety & Panic Disorders: First Interview. unabr. ed. Aaron T. Beck. 1 cass. (Running Time: 44 min.). (ENG.). 1989. 15.00 (978-0-89862-874-6(1), 2874) Guilford Pubns.

Cognitive Therapy of Depression: Demonstration of an Initial Interview. Aaron T. Beck. Comment by Jeffrey T. Young. 1 cass. (Running Time: 56 mins.). 1990. 13.95 (2837) Guilford Pubns.

Cognitive Therapy of Depression: Demonstration of an Initial Interview. Aaron T. Beck et al. 1 cass. (Guilford Clinical Psychology & Psychopathology Ser.). (ENG.). 1980. 15.00 (978-0-89862-837-1(7), 8370) Guilford Pubns.

Coherent Emotion CBrain (Heart Synchronization) Eldon Taylor. 1 CD. (Running Time: 52 min.). (Whole Brain Innertalk Ser.). 1998. audio compact disk (978-1-55978-874-8(7)) Progress Aware Res.

Coherent Life. Thomas Merton. 1 cass. 1995. 8.95 (AA2802) Credence Commun.
Merton uses Rilke's elegies to explore the question of meaning. Rilke says we learn through suffering, but Merton adds that we find meaning only in giving ourselves to love.

Coin of Carthage. unabr. ed. Winifred Bryher. Read by Nadia May. 5 cass. (Running Time: 1 hr. 30 min. per cass.). 1997. audio compact disk 39.95 (1844) Blckstn Audio.
Brilliantly evoking the world of the Roman Republic during the Second Punic War through her description of the lives of two Greek traders, Bryher creates a common man's view of the greatest struggle in which ancient Rome engaged. Born Winifred Ellerman in England in 1894, Bryher became part of the literary circle associated with Sylvia Beach's Paris bookstore, Shakespeare & Company.

Coin of Carthage. unabr. ed. Winifred Bryher. Read by Nadia May. 5 cass. (Running Time: 5 hrs. 30 mins.). 1997. 39.95 (978-0-7861-1074-2(0), 1844) Blckstn Audio.

Coincidence: Program from the Award Winning Public Radio Series. Interview. Hosted by Fred Goodwin. 1 CD. (Running Time: 1 Hour). 2003. audio compact disk 21.99 (978-1-932479-32-4(5), LCM 301) Lichtenstein Creat.
We've all experienced it - a friend calls just as we are thinking of him, or a romantic partner has the same birthday we do. Some coincidences are small, and seemingly inconsequential, but others have the potential to change lives. What causes a coincidence to happen, and what does it mean? Is every coincidence meaningful? And what are the odds of a particular coincidence happening? This week we explore the nature of coincidence with scientists, psychotherapists, mathematicians, and people like you. Guests include: Jungian analyst and psychotherapist Robert Hopcke, who has authored books on coincidence and the related theory of synchronicity ("Coincidences are meaningful for what they tell us about ourselves"); cognitive scientist Josh Tenenbaum at the Massachusetts Institute of Technology, who studies how coincidences work in the brain ("They seem to be the source of some of our greatest irrationalities"); and statistician Karl Sigman at Columbia University, who computes the odds that coincidences will happen. The program also includes quirky first-person accounts of coincidence from writers, filmmakers, identical twins, and others, and from the producer of this show, who experienced an unusual coincidence while working on it.

Cois Abhann na Sead. Contrib. by Eilis Ni Shuilleabhain. (ENG.). 1997. 13.95 (978-0-8023-7132-4(9)); audio compact disk 20.95 (978-0-8023-8132-3(4)) Pub: Clo Iar-Chonnachta IRL. Dist(s): Dufour

***Coke Machine: The Dirty Truth Behind the World's Favorite Soft Drink.** unabr. ed. Michael Blanding. (Running Time: 11 hrs. 0 mins.). 2010. 17.99 (978-1-4001-8894-9(6)); audio compact disk 34.99 (978-1-4001-1894-6(8)) Pub: Tantor Media. Dist(s): IngramPubServ

*****Coke Machine: The Dirty Truth Behind the World's Favorite Soft Drink.** unabr. ed. Michael Blanding. Narrated by George K. Wilson. (Running Time: 13 hrs. 30 mins. 0 sec.). 2010. 24.99 (978-1-4001-6894-1(5)) Pub: Tantor Media. Dist(s): IngramPubServ

*****Coke Machine The Dirty Truth Behind the World's Favorite Soft Drink.** unabr. ed. Michael Blanding. Narrated by George K. Wilson. (Running Time: 13 hrs. 30 mins. 0 sec.). (ENG.). 2010. audio compact disk 83.99 (978-1-4001-4894-3(4)) Pub: Tantor Media. Dist(s): IngramPubServ

Colby's Missing Memory. Created by Maranatha! Music. (J). (gr. 4-7). 2008. audio compact disk 3.99 (978-5-557-41364-0(2)) Maranatha Music.

Cold & Golden Death. unabr. ed. Michael K. Jamison. Read by Jerry Sciarrio. 6 cass. (Running Time: 6 hrs. 36 min.). 2001. 39.95 (978-1-58116-022-2(4)) Books in Motion.

Chad Macklin answers a summons from a well-known political lobbyist, whose husband has disappeared with most of her jewelry and savings. The three-week old trail leads from Florida to Juneau, Alaska, where Chad faces peril of the deep.

Cold, Bleak Hill. abr. ed. Ron Carter. (Prelude to Glory Ser.: Vol. 5). 2002. 19.95 (978-1-57345-967-9(4)) Deseret Bk.

Cold Blood. unabr. ed. Lynda La Plante. Read by Lorelei King. 14 cass. (Running Time: 21 hrs.). (Lorraine Page Mystery Ser.). 2000. 89.95 (978-0-7451-8782-2(X), CAB 1417) Pub: Chivers Audio Bks GBR. Dist(s): AudioGO

Ex-Lieutenant Lorraine Page buried her past to start the Page Investigation Agency in Los Angeles. The Caley's are determined to find their daughter, dead or alive. The search for a missing girl becomes a deadly murder hunt, and in her desperation to succeed, Lorraine is caught in a web of deceit and violence that threatens to drag her back into the murky world she fought so hard to escape.

Cold Blooded. Lisa Jackson. Narrated by Alyssa Bresnahan. 12 cass. (Running Time: 17 hrs.). (New Orleans Ser.: Bk. 2). 94.00 (978-1-4025-1684-9(3)) Recorded Bks.

Cold-Blooded Business. collector's ed. Dana Stabenow. Read by Marguerite Gavin. 5 cass. (Running Time: 7 hrs. 30 min.). (Kate Shugak Ser.). 1999. 40.00 (978-0-7366-4861-5(5)) Books on Tape.

Aleut private eye Kate Shugak travels north of the Arctic Circle to investigate a rise in cocaine use among Alaskan oil field workers.

Cold Blue Sky. unabr. ed. Jack Novey. Perf. by Gary Arnold. Ed. by Yvette McCann. 2 cass. (Running Time: 2 hrs.). 1997. pap. bk. 16.95 Set. (978-1-57867-311-7(9)) Windhorse Corp.

Account of Jack Novey & his experiences during World War II as a bomber.

*****Cold Calling.** Will Kingdom. 2010. 94.95 (978-0-7531-4671-2(1)); audio compact disk 104.95 (978-0-7531-4672-9(X)) Pub: Isis Pubng Ltd GBR. Dist(s): Ulverscroft US

Cold Case. Stephen White. Read by Scott Brick. (Dr. Alan Gregory Ser.). 2000. audio compact disk 88.00 (978-0-7366-5218-6(3)) Books on Tape.

Cold Case. Stephen White. Read by Scott Brick. 11 CDs. (Running Time: 12 hrs.). (Dr. Alan Gregory Ser.). 2001. audio compact disk 39.95 Books on Tape.

A decade after the grisly murder of two teenage girls, an organization, Locard - an elite group of prosecutors, federal agents, forensic specialists & others - is reopening the case. Alan Gregory, clinical psychologist, joins them. Reconstructing the girls' lives, Alan finds they had been shadowed by secrets. An exercise in psychological detection evolves into a dangerous game of cat & mouse between Gregory & Dr. Raymond Welle, a therapist turned U.S. Congressman, with a connection to one of the victims. Someone investigating Welles' campaign contributions is killed & Alan steps up his own search for answers.

Cold Case. collector's ed. Stephen White. Read by Scott Brick. 9 cass. (Running Time: 13 hrs. 30 min.). (Dr. Alan Gregory Ser.). 2000. 72.00 (978-0-7366-4905-6(0), 5211) Books on Tape.

Alan Gregory's investigation of a ten-year-old case leads to a U.S. Congressman with a secret Gregory may not survive discovering.

Cold Case. unabr. ed. Linda Barnes. Narrated by C. J. Critt. 10 cass. (Running Time: 13 hrs. 45 mins.). (Carlotta Carlyle Mystery Ser.). 1997. 90.00 (978-0-7887-1316-3(7), 95174E7) Recorded Bks.

A mysterious client confronts Carlotta with a new novel by a literary sensation - the only trouble is the author disappeared 14 years ago. As Carlotta searches for the writer, she unearths a web of lies & scandal that rocks the foundations of Boston's high society.

Cold Case. unabr. ed. Philip Gourevitch. 4 cass. (Running Time: 6 hrs.). 2002. 24.95 (978-1-57511-110-0(1)) Pub Mills.

In this true story, the author follows Andy Rosenzweig, a Manhattan investigator, as he tracks down the killer of his childhood friend. Like Capote and Mailer, Gourevitch transforms a criminal investigation into a literary reckoning with the urges that drive one man to murder and another to pursue the murderer.

Cold Case. unabr. ed. Stephen White. Read by Scott Brick. 11 CDs. (Running Time: 12 hrs.). (Dr. Alan Gregory Ser.). 2001. audio compact disk 39.95 (978-0-7366-5705-1(3)) Books on Tape.

Alan Gregory's investigation of a ten-year-old case leads to a U.S. Congressman with a secret Gregory may not survive discovering.

Cold Case. unabr. ed. Stephen White. Read by Scott Brick. 9 cass.. (Running Time: 13 hrs. 30 min.). (Dr. Alan Gregory Ser.). 2000. 72.00 (978-0-7366-4937-7(9)) Books on Tape.

Alan Gregory's investigation of a ten-year-old case leads to a U. S. Congressman with a secret, Gregory may not survive discovering.

Cold Case. unabr. ed. Kate Wilhelm. Read by Carrington MacDuffie. 11 CDs. (Running Time: 14 hrs.). 2008. audio compact disk 99.00 (978-1-4332-5363-8(1)) Blckstn Audio.

Cold Case. unabr. ed. Kate Wilhelm & Carrington MacDuffie. (Running Time: 14 hrs. NaN mins.). 2008. 29.95 (978-1-4332-5364-5(X)); 79.95 (978-1-4332-5362-1(3)) Blckstn Audio.

Cold Choices. unabr. ed. Larry Bond. Read by Dick Hill. (Running Time: 20 hrs.). 2009. 44.97 (978-1-4233-4661-6(0), 9781423346616, BADLE); 44.97 (978-1-4233-4659-3(9), 9781423346593, Brlnc Audio MP3 Lib); 29.99 (978-1-4233-4660-9(2), 9781423346609, BAD); 29.99 (978-1-4233-4658-6(0), 9781423346586, Brilliance MP3); audio compact disk 97.97 (978-1-4233-4657-9(2), 9781423346579, BriAudCD Unabrid); audio compact disk 32.99 (978-1-4233-4656-2(4), 9781423346562, Bril Audio CD Unabri) Brilliance Audio.

Cold Coffin. unabr. ed. Gwendoline Butler. Read by Michael Tudor-Barnes. 7 CDs. (Running Time: 7 hs. 30 mins.). (Sound Ser.). (J). 2002. audio compact disk 71.95 (978-1-84283-304-9(9)) Pub: ISIS Lrg Prnt GBR. Dist(s): Ulverscroft US

Cold Coffin. unabr. ed. Gwendoline Butler. Read by Michael Tudor Barnes. 6 cass. (Running Time: 9 hrs.). (Sound Ser.). 2001. 54.95 (978-1-86042-985-9(8), 2-985-8) Pub: UlverLrgPrint GBR. Dist(s): Ulverscroft US

London has been the scene of many a terrifying crime, but the discovery of a pile of infant skulls unearthed near police headquarters is particularly horrifying. Another major worry for John Coffin, Chief Commander, is a triple murder, that of a midwife & her two daughters.

Cold, Cold Shoulder. Anne Schraff. (Running Time: 3970 sec.). (Pageturners Ser.). (J). 2004. 10.95 (978-1-56254-710-3(0), SP7100) Saddleback Edu.

Cold Comfort Farm. unabr. ed. Stella Gibbons. Read by Anna Massey. 8 cass. (Running Time: 12 hrs.). 2000. 59.95 (SAB 039) Pub: Chivers Audio Bks GBR. Dist(s): AudioGO

When the orphaned Flora Poste descends on her relatives at Cold Comfort Farm, she finds nothing but chaos. Judith is in grief, Amos has been called by God, Seth is smoldering with sensuality & of course, the Great Aunt Ada Doom, who witnesses something nasty in the woodshed. Naturally, Flora sees it her duty to restore order.

Cold Company. Sue Henry. 7 CDs. (Running Time: 9 hrs.). (Jessie Arnold Mystery Ser.). 2002. audio compact disk 56.00 (978-0-7366-8724-9(6)) Books on Tape.

Cold Company. unabr. ed. Sue Henry. 6 cass. (Running Time: 9 hrs.). (Jessie Arnold Mystery Ser.). 2002. 48.00 (978-0-7366-8723-2(8)) Books on Tape.

A murderer comes dangerously close to musher Jessie Arnold. When a body is discovered during the renovation of her home, Jessie learns it may be a victim of Alaska's most notorious serial killer. Soon after, another woman disappears in the same vicinity; Jessie suspects the killer is back at work...and that she may be the next victim.

Cold Day for Murder. collector's ed. Dana Stabenow. Read by Marguerite Gavin. 4 cass. (Running Time: 6 hrs.). (Kate Shugak Ser.). 1999. 32.00 (978-0-7366-4358-0(3), 4830) Books on Tape.

When a young national park ranger disappears during the long Alaskan winter, everyone assumes the cold got him. But when the investigator sent to find him disappears as well, it appears the weather may not be all that's killing.

Cold Day for Murder. unabr. ed. Dana Stabenow. Read by Marguerite Gavin. 4 cass. (Running Time: 6 hrs.). (Kate Shugak Ser.). 1999. 24.95 (978-0-7366-4423-5(7), 4830) Books on Tape.

Cold Day in Paradise. unabr. ed. Steve Hamilton. Read by Nick Sullivan. 8 CDs. (Running Time: 12 hrs.). (Alex McKnight Mystery Ser.). 2001. audio compact disk 79.95 (978-0-7927-9968-9(2), SLD 019, Chivers Sound Lib) AudioGO.

The pycho responsible for the bullet lodged in McKnight's heart has been in prison now for almost thirteen years. But then he finds a rose in the snow at the entrance to his cabin, he knows it's the killer's calling card.

Cold Day in Paradise. unabr. ed. Steve Hamilton. Read by Dan John Miller. (Running Time: 8 hrs.). (Alex Mcknight Ser.). 2010. 39.97 (978-1-4418-1743-3(3), 9781441817433, Brlnc Audio MP3 Lib); 24.99 (978-1-4418-1742-6(5), 9781441817426, Brilliance MP3); 24.99 (978-1-4418-1744-0(1), 9781441817440, BAD) Brilliance Audio.

Cold Day in Paradise. unabr. ed. Steve Hamilton. Read by Jim Bond & Dan John Miller. (Running Time: 8 hrs.). (Alex Mcknight Ser.). 2010. audio compact disk 29.99 (978-1-4418-1740-2(9), 9781441817402, Bril Audio CD Unabri) Brilliance Audio.

Cold Day in Paradise. unabr. ed. Steve Hamilton. Read by Dan John Miller. (Running Time: 8 hrs.). (Alex Mcknight Ser.). 2010. audio compact disk 87.97 (978-1-4418-1741-9(7), 9781441817419, BriAudCD Unabrid) Brilliance Audio.

*****Cold Day in Paradise.** unabr. ed. Steve Hamilton. Read by Dan John Miller. (Running Time: 9 hrs.). (Alex Mcknight Ser.). 2010. 39.97 (978-1-4418-1745-7(X), 9781441817457, BADLE) Brilliance Audio.

Cold Day in Paradise, Set. unabr. ed. Steve Hamilton. Read by Nick Sullivan. 6 vols. (Running Time: 9 hrs.). (Chivers Sound Library American Collections). 1999. bk. 54.95 (978-0-7927-2326-4(0), CSL 215, Chivers Sound Lib) AudioGO.

The bullet has been lodged next to Alex McKnight's heart for fourteen years now, his partner is fourteen years dead & the psycho named Rose, who shot them both, has been in prison for nearly thirteen years, but when McKnight finds a rose in the snow at the entrance to his cabin, he knows it's the killer's calling card. In the meantime, he is hired to protect Edwin Fulton, a compulsive gambler, whose bookie has been murdered. As both mysteries evolve, McKnight begins to think there is a connection between the bookie's murder & the return of Rose.

Cold Dog Soup. unabr. collector's ed. Stephen Dobyns. Read by Jonathan Marosz. 5 cass. (Running Time: 7 hrs. 30 min.). 1999. 40.00 (978-0-7366-4783-0(X)) Books on Tape.

Latchmer & a philosophically reckless Haitian cab driver have to get rid of a dead dog.

Cold Facts. unabr. ed. Janet Boling. Read by Stephanie Brush. 6 cass. (Running Time: 7 hrs. 24 min.). 2001. 39.95 (978-1-55686-800-9(6)) Books in Motion.

When a resort town newspaper editor and the handsome new Under Sheriff investigate the same suspicious lake death, mutual attraction occurs just as the case heats up.

Cold Fire. unabr. ed. Dean Koontz. Read by Carol Cowan & Michael Hanson. (Running Time: 16 hrs.). 2004. 39.25 (978-1-59335-847-1(4), 1593358474, Brlnc Audio MP3 Lib); 39.25 (978-1-59710-143-1(5), 1597101435, BADLE) Brilliance Audio.

Cold Fire. unabr. ed. Dean Koontz. Read by Carol Cowan and Michael Hanson. (Running Time: 16 hrs.). 2004. 24.95 (978-1-59710-142-4(7), 1597101427, BAD) Brilliance Audio.

Cold Fire. unabr. ed. Dean Koontz. Read by Carol Cowan & Michael Hanson. (Running Time: 16 hrs.). 2004. 24.95 (978-1-59335-713-9(3), 1593357133, Brilliance MP3); 29.95 (978-1-59355-336-4(6), 1593553366, BAU) Brilliance Audio.

Reporter Holly Thorne is intrigued by Jim Ironheart, who has saved 12 lives in the past three months. Holly wants to know what kind of power drives him, why terrifying visions of a churning windmill haunt his dreams, and just what he means when he whispers in his sleep that an enemy who will kill everyone is coming. "A master storyteller, sometimes humorous, sometimes shocking, but always riveting. His characters sparkle with life. And his fast-paced plots are wonderfully fiendish, taking unexpected twists and turns." - The San Diego Union-Tribune.

Cold Fire. unabr. ed. Dean Koontz. Read by Michael Hanson & Carol Cowan. 9 cass. (Running Time: 16 hrs.). 2004. 92.25 (978-1-59355-337-1(4), 1593553374, BrilAudUnabridg) Brilliance Audio.

Cold Fire. unabr. ed. Dean Koontz. Read by Carol Cowan & Michael Hanson. 11 cds. (Running Time: 16 hrs.). 2004. audio compact disk 40.95 (978-1-59355-338-8(2), 1593553382, Bril Audio CD Unabri) Brilliance Audio.

Cold Fire. unabr. ed. Dean Koontz. Read by Michael Hanson & Carol Cowan. 11 cds. (Running Time: 16 hrs.). 2004. audio compact disk 112.25 (978-1-59355-339-5(0), 1593553390, CD Unabrid Lib Ed) Brilliance Audio.

Cold Fission. unabr. ed. W. Bartow Wright. Read by Rusty Nelson. 6 cass. (Running Time: 6 hrs. 48 min.). 2001. 39.95 (978-1-55686-974-7(6)) Books in Motion.

Bucky Dolan lands in the middle of a terrorist problem. Some bad guys see a way to use a new nuclear concept to build tiny nuclear weapons with intentions to sell them to terrorists in the Middle East. Bucky is assigned to the team to stop them.

Cold Flat Junction. Martha Grimes. 10 cass. (Running Time: 15 hrs.). (Emma Graham Mysteries Ser.). 2001. 80.00 (978-0-7366-6361-8(4)) Books on Tape.

Emma Graham, the heroine of Hotel Paradise, continues her compelling inquiry into the suspicious drowning forty years ago of another twelve-year-old in Spirit Lake, near the Hotel Paradise. She is determined to find answers to the questions that surround not only the "accidental" drowning, but also to two unsolved murders that wind back to it.

Cold Flat Junction. unabr. ed. Martha Grimes. Read by Bernadette Dunne. 10 cass. (Running Time: 13 hrs.). (Emma Graham Mysteries Ser.). 2001. 29.95 (978-0-7366-5832-4(7)) Books on Tape.

Twelve-year-old Emma continues her inquiry into the suspicious drowning forty years ago near the Hotel Paradise.

Cold Frosty Morning: A Celebration of Christmas on Hammered & Mountain Dulcimer. Perf. by Katie La Raye Waldren. 1 cass. (Running Time: 42 min.). 9.95 (978-1-883206-01-7(4), NG021); audio compact disk 14.95 CD. (978-1-883206-02-4(2), NG-CD-200) Native Ground.

This instrumental rendition of Christmas & winter favorites is enough to warm anyone's heart.

Cold Genius of Robert Frost: A Light & Enlightening Lecture. Featuring Elliot Engel. 2000. bk. 15.00 (978-1-890123-29-1(3)) Media Cnslts.

Cold Granite. Stuart Macbride. (Isis (CDs) Ser.). (J). 2006. audio compact disk 99.95 (978-0-7531-2562-5(5)) Pub: ISIS Lrg Prnt GBR. Dist(s): Ulverscroft US

Cold Granite. unabr. ed. Stuart MacBride & Stuart Macbride. Read by Kenny Blyth. 10 cass. (Running Time: 13 hrs. 25 mins.). (Isis Cassettes Ser.). (J). 2006. 84.95 (978-0-7531-3493-1(4)) Pub: ISIS Lrg Prnt GBR. Dist(s): Ulverscroft US

Cold Harbour. Jack Higgins. Read by David McCallum. 2004. 10.95 (978-0-7435-4287-6(8)) Pub: S&S Audio. Dist(s): S and S Inc

*****Cold Harbour.** unabr. ed. Jack Higgins. Read by Michael Page. (Running Time: 8 hrs.). (Dougal Munro/Jack Carter Ser.). 2010. 24.99 (978-1-4418-4394-4(9), 9781441843944, BAD); 24.99 (978-1-4418-4392-0(2), 9781441843920, Brilliance MP3); 39.97 (978-1-4418-4397-5(3), 9781441843975, BADLE); 39.97 (978-1-4418-4393-7(0), 9781441843937, Brlnc Audio MP3 Lib); audio compact disk 29.99 (978-1-4418-4390-6(6), 9781441843906, Bril Audio CD Unabri); audio compact disk 87.97 (978-1-4418-4391-3(4), 9781441843913, BriAudCD Unabrid) Brilliance Audio.

Cold Heart. unabr. ed. Lynda La Plante. Read by Lorelei King. 10 cass. (Running Time: 10 hrs.). 1998. 84.95 (978-0-7540-0213-0(6), CAB 1636) AudioGO.

Harry Nathan's widow is charged with the murder of his death. She strongly believes that conspiracy is linked to his death, & by believing her story, private investigator Lorraine Paige runs into conflict with her ex-colleagues.

Cold Hit. Stephen J. Cannell. Read by Scott Brick. 8 CDs. (Shane Scully Ser.: No. 5). 2005. audio compact disk 44.95 (978-0-7927-3741-4(5), SLD 836); audio compact disk 29.95 (978-0-7927-3831-2(4), CMP 836, Chivers Sound Lib) AudioGO.

Cold Hit. Stephen J. Cannell. Read by Scott Sowers. (Shane Scully Ser.: No. 5). 2005. 23.95 (978-1-59397-798-6(0)) Pub: Macmill Audio. Dist(s): Macmillan

Cold Hit. Linda Fairstein. Read by Allison Janney. (Alexandra Cooper Mysteries Ser.). 2004. 15.95 (978-0-7435-4288-3(6)) Pub: S&S Audio. Dist(s): S and S Inc

Cold Hit. abr. ed. Stephen J. Cannell. Read by Scott Sowers. (Shane Scully Ser.: No. 5). 2005. 14.95 (978-1-59397-797-9(2)) Pub: Macmill Audio. Dist(s): Macmillan

Cold in the Earth: A Mitchell & Markby Mystery. unabr. ed. Ann Granger. Narrated by Judith Boyd. 8 cass. (Running Time: 10 hrs. 15 mins.). (Mitchell & Markby Mystery Ser.). 2000. 72.00 (978-1-84197-130-8(8), H1128E7) Recorded Bks.

It doesn't take Meredith Mitchell long to regret giving up her lovely Cotswold cottage in favour of living in London. Her job gives a whole new meaning to the word tedious does little to improve her mood. She needed a holiday. So, when Alan Markby's sister wants a housesitter, she jumps at the chance.

Cold in the Earth: A Mitchell & Markby Mystery. unabr. ed. Ann Granger. Narrated by Judith Boyd. 9 CDs. (Running Time: 10 hrs. 15 mins.). 2001. audio compact disk 89.00 (978-1-84197-249-7(5), C1413) Recorded Bks.

Cold Iron (Malkin) unabr. ed. Sophie Masson. Read by Esther Van Doornum. 5 CDs. (Running Time: 5 hrs. 50 mins.). (YA). 2005. audio compact disk 63.95 (978-1-74093-559-3(4)) Pub: Bolinda Pubng AUS. Dist(s): Bolinda Pub Inc

Cold Is the Grave. Peter Robinson. 3 cass. (Running Time: 4 hrs. 30 mins.). (Inspector Banks Mystery Ser.). 2001. (978-0-333-90378-0(1)) Macmillan UK GBR.

Cold Is the Grave. Peter Robinson. Narrated by Ron Keith. 12 cass. (Running Time: 16 hrs. 30 mins.). (Inspector Banks Mystery Ser.). 104.00 (978-0-7887-9498-8(1)) Recorded Bks.

Cold Is the Grave. unabr. ed. Peter Robinson. Narrated by Ron Keith. 12 cass. (Running Time: 16 hrs. 30 mins.). (Inspector Banks Mystery Ser.). 2002. 53.95 (978-0-7887-9511-4(2), RF377) Recorded Bks.

Cold Is the Grave takes the inspector from his cozy Yorkshire cottage into the dark underworld of London. The assignment is a favor, asked of him by his greatest enemy-his boss, the Chief Constable.

Cold Is the Sea. unabr. ed. Edward L. Beach, Jr. & Wolfram Kandinsky. 11 cass. (Running Time: 16 hrs. 30 mins.). 1989. 88.00 (978-0-7366-1566-2(0), 2432) Books on Tape.

The most advanced nuclear submarine in history, the Cushing carries more explosive power than all the munitions used in the two World Wars. She is secretly probing the Arctic waters north of the USSR when a collision sends her reeling. Skipper & crew desperately prepare to fend off a fatal attack, one that threatens not only the sub & the lives of the men on board, but the fate of an entire nation.

Cold Kill. Stephen Leather. (Isis (CDs) Ser.). 2006. audio compact disk 99.95 (978-0-7531-2558-8(7)) Pub: ISIS Lrg Prnt GBR. Dist(s): Ulverscroft US

Cold Kill. unabr. ed. Stephen Leather. Read by Martyn Read. 11 cass. (Running Time: 14 hrs. 50 mins.). (Isis Cassettes Ser.). 2006. 89.95 (978-0-7531-3589-1(2)) Pub: ISIS Lrg Prnt GBR. Dist(s): Ulverscroft US

*****Cold Kiss.** unabr. ed. John Rector. (Running Time: 10 hrs. 30 mins.). 2010. 29.95 (978-1-4417-4839-3(3)); 65.95 (978-1-4417-4835-5(0)); audio compact disk 29.95 (978-1-4417-4838-6(5)); audio compact disk 90.00 (978-1-4417-4836-2(9)) Blckstn Audio.

Cold Light. unabr. ed. John Harvey. Read by Jonathon Oliver. 8 cass. (Running Time: 11 hrs. 15 min.). 1997. 69.95 (978-1-85695-970-4(8), 950507) Pub: ISIS Audio GBR. Dist(s): Ulverscroft US

Suspenseful story in clipped, faintly sardonic style.

Cold Light. unabr. ed. John Harvey. Read by Jonathan Oliver. 10 CDs. (Running Time: 11 hrs. 22 mins.). (Isis Ser.). 2002. audio compact disk 89.95 (978-0-7531-1482-7(8)) Pub: ISIS Audio GBR. Dist(s): Ulverscroft US

Cold Light. unabr. ed. John Harvey. Narrated by Ron Keith. 8 cass. (Running Time: 11 hrs. 30 mins.). (Charlie Resnick Mystery Ser.: Vol. 6). 2000. 70.00 (978-0-7887-0483-3(4), 94676E7) Recorded Bks.

Cold Moon. abr. ed. Jeffery Deaver. Read by Joe Mantegna. (Lincoln Rhyme Ser.: No. 7). 2006. 17.95 (978-0-7435-6457-1(X), Audioworks) Pub: S&S Audio. Dist(s): S and S Inc

Cold Moon. abr. ed. Jeffery Deaver. Read by Joe Mantegna. (Running Time: 6 hrs. 0 mins. 0 sec.). No. 7. (ENG.). 2008. audio compact disk 14.99 (978-0-7435-7618-5(7)) Pub: S&S Audio. Dist(s): S and S Inc

Cold Moon. unabr. ed. Jeffery Deaver. Read by Joe Mantegna. (Lincoln Rhyme Ser.: No. 7). 2006. 29.95 (978-0-7435-6458-8(8), Audioworks); audio compact disk 49.95 (978-0-7435-5268-4(7), Audioworks) Pub: S&S Audio. Dist(s): S and S Inc

Cold Mountain. Charles Frazier. Read by Charles Frazier. 12 cass. (Running Time: 14 hrs. 30 mins.). 1998. (978-1-84032-176-0(8), HoddrStoughton) Hodder General GBR.
One man's epic voyage is woven together with an incredible love story.

Cold Mountain. unabr. ed. Charles Frazier. Read by Charles Frazier. 10 cass. (Running Time: 15 hrs.). 1998. 80.00 (978-0-7366-4137-1(8), 4642) Books on Tape.
A confederate soldier makes a harrowing journey home to his sweetheart's side.

Cold Paradise. unabr. ed. Stuart Woods. Read by Dick Hill. 6 cass. (Running Time: 8 hrs.). (Stone Barrington Ser.: No. 7). 2001. 29.95 (978-1-58788-577-8(8), 1587885778, BAU); 69.25 (978-1-58788-578-5(6), 1587885786, Unabridge Lib Edns); audio compact disk 35.95 (978-1-58788-579-2(4), 1587885794, CD Unabridged); audio compact disk 87.25 (978-1-58788-580-8(8), 1587885808, Unabridge Lib Edns) Brilliance Audio.
Stone Barrington hunts his most clever nemesis yet - a master of disguise and deceit. Cop-turned-lawyer Stone Barrington, he of street smarts, dry wit, and debonair charm, becomes reacquainted with a case he thought was buried years ago, and must settle romantic entanglements that haunt him still. Allison Manning, the beautiful and enigmatic woman Stone defended against a murder charge in Dead in the Water, mysteriously reappears to request his help with a set of problems she has never resolved, which involve millions of dollars. She fears, too, that somebody might be stalking her, but she's not sure who - or why. She knows of no one better than Stone, who has both the legal experience and the investigative instincts to guarantee her safety. Stone is happy to enjoy a few days in Palm Beach - and to have left frigid New York and the tempestuous Dolce Bianchi behind - but before he can dig into this latest case, he comes face to face again with Arrington Calder, the one woman who still holds a key to his affections. Stone and his partner, Dino, comb the glittering streets of Palm Beach and begin to suspect that more than one person might be after Allison: one so clever he manages never to show his face, but even more frightening, another man everybody has long forgotten. In a search that ranges from the boardrooms of Manhattan to the sumptuous villas that line the Gold Coast, Stone uncovers the sly and greedy plan to steal millions of dollars - and reveals the crafty killer behind it - in this electrifying thriller.

Cold Paradise. unabr. ed. Stuart Woods. Read by Dick Hill. (Running Time: 8 hrs.). (Stone Barrington Ser.: No. 7). 2004. 39.25 (978-1-59335-408-4(8), 1593354088, Brlnc Audio MP3 Lib) Brilliance Audio.

Cold Paradise. unabr. ed. Stuart Woods. Read by Dick Hill. (Running Time: 8 hrs.). (Stone Barrington Ser.: No. 7). 2004. 39.25 (978-1-59710-145-5(1), 1597101451, BADLE); 24.95 (978-1-59710-144-8(3), 1597101443, BAD) Brilliance Audio.

Cold Paradise. unabr. ed. Stuart Woods. Read by Dick Hill. (Running Time: 8 hrs.). (Stone Barrington Ser.: No. 7). 2004. 24.95 (978-1-59335-070-3(8), 1593350708) Soulmate Audio Bks.

***Cold Pizza for Breakfast: A Mem-wha??** Christine Lavin. Read by Christine Lavin. Frwd. by Jeff Daniels. 2010. audio compact disk 59.95 (978-0-9819835-2-3(9)) Tell Me Pr.

Cold Pursuit. Judith Cutler. 2007. 61.95 (978-0-7531-3736-9(4)); audio compact disk 79.95 (978-0-7531-2702-5(4)) Pub: ISIS Audio GBR. Dist(s): Ulverscroft US

Cold Pursuit. abr. ed. T. Jefferson Parker. Read by Patrick G. Lawlor. 5 CDs, Library ed. (Running Time: 6 hrs.). 2003. audio compact disk 74.25 (978-1-59086-852-2(8), 1590868528, BACDLib Ed) Brilliance Audio.
Homicide cop Tom McMichael is on the rotation when an 84-year-old city patriarch named Pete Braga is found bludgeoned to death. Not good news, especially since the Irish McMichaels and Portuguese Bragas share a violent family history dating back three generations. Years ago Braga shot McMichael's grandfather in a dispute over a paycheck; soon thereafter Braga's son was severely beaten behind a waterfront bar - legend has it that it was an act of revenge by McMichael's father. McMichael must put aside the old family blood feud, and find the truth about Pete Braga's death. Braga's beautiful nurse is a suspect - she says she stepped out for some firewood, but key evidence suggests otherwise. The investigation soon expands to include Braga's business, his family, the Catholic diocese, a multimillion dollar Indian casino, a prostitute, a cop, and, of course, the McMichael family.

Cold Pursuit. abr. ed. T. Jefferson Parker. Read by Patrick G. Lawlor. (Running Time: 21600 sec.). 2005. audio compact disk 16.99 (978-1-59600-437-5(1), 9781596004375, BCD Value Price) Brilliance Audio.

Cold Pursuit. unabr. ed. T. Jefferson Parker. Read by Patrick G. Lawlor. 7 cass. (Running Time: 10 hrs.). 2003. 32.95 (978-1-59086-137-0(X), 159086137X, BAU); 82.25 (978-1-59086-138-7(8), 1590861388, BrilAudUnabridg) Brilliance Audio.

Cold Pursuit. unabr. ed. T. Jefferson Parker. Read by Patrick G. Lawlor. (Running Time: 10 hrs.). 2004. 39.25 (978-1-59335-409-1(6), 1593354096, Brlnc Audio MP3 Lib) Brilliance Audio.

Cold Pursuit. unabr. ed. T. Jefferson Parker. Read by Patrick G. Lawlor. (Running Time: 10 hrs.). 2004. 39.25 (978-1-59710-147-9(8), 1597101478, BADLE); 24.95 (978-1-59710-146-2(X), 159710146X, BAD) Brilliance Audio.

Cold Pursuit. unabr. ed. T. Jefferson Parker. Read by Patrick G. Lawlor. (Running Time: 10 hrs.). 2004. 24.95 (978-1-59335-071-0(6), 1593350716) Soulmate Audio Bks.

Cold Quarry. Andy Straka. Read by Charlton Griffin. 4 vols. No. 3. 2003. (978-1-58807-612-0(1)) Am Pubng Inc.

Cold Quarry. unabr. ed. Andy Straka. Read by Charlton Griffin. 4 vols. (Running Time: 6 hrs.). (Frank Pavicek Mystery Ser.: No. 3). 2003. 25.00 (978-1-58807-141-5(3)) Am Pubng Inc.
When master falconer Chester Carew is found dead in the woods, private investigator Frank Pavlicek doesn't buy the official report of an accidental shooting. Hunting for clues, Frank stumbles across evidence of a toxic agent contaminating the area something the authorities refuse to discuss.The trail leads to a shadowy group of domestic terrorists and to Frank's former NYPD partner, Jake Toronto, who is accused of being involved with their plot. To prove Jake's innocence, Frank will have to trap the real killers before they can carry out their terrifying agenda.

Cold Rain in Berlin. Julian Jay Savarin. Read by Terry Wale. 6 cass. (Running Time: 8 hrs.). (Soundings Ser.). (J). 2004. 54.95 (978-1-84283-561-6(0)) Pub: ISIS Lrg Prnt GBR. Dist(s): Ulverscroft US

Cold Red Sunrise. unabr. ed. Stuart M. Kaminsky. Narrated by Mark Hammer. 6 cass. (Running Time: 7 hrs. 45 mins.). (Inspector Porfiry Rostnikov Mystery Ser.: No. 4). 1992. 51.00 (978-1-55690-677-0(3), 92330) Recorded Bks.
Inspector Porfiry Rostinikov is dispatched to Siberia to investigate the murder of a high-ranking commissar.

Cold Relations. Gerald Hammond & Cathleen McCarron. (Story Sound Ser.). 2007. 49.95 (978-1-84652-020-4(7)); audio compact disk 59.95 (978-1-84652-021-1(5)) Pub: Mgna Lrg Print GBR. Dist(s): Ulverscroft US

Cold Room. unabr. ed. J. T. Ellison. Read by Joyce Bean. 10 CDs. (Running Time: 11 hrs.). (Taylor Jackson Ser.). 2010. audio compact disk 29.99 (978-1-4418-3845-2(7), 9781441838452, Bril Audio CD Unabri) Brilliance Audio.

***Cold Room.** unabr. ed. J. T. Ellison. Read by Joyce Bean. (Running Time: 11 hrs.). (Taylor Jackson Ser.). 2010. 39.97 (978-1-4418-3848-3(1), 9781441838483, Brlnc Audio MP3 Lib); 24.99 (978-1-4418-3847-6(3), 9781441838476, Brilliance MP3); 39.97 (978-1-4418-3850-6(3), 9781441838506, BADLE); 24.99 (978-1-4418-3849-0(X), 9781441838490, BAD); audio compact disk 79.97 (978-1-4418-3846-9(5), 9781441838469, BriAudCD Unabrid) Brilliance Audio.

Cold Sassy Tree. Olive Ann Burns. Read by Tom Parker. (Running Time: 13 hrs.). 1993. 41.95 (978-1-59912-452-0(1)) Iofy Corp.

Cold Sassy Tree. unabr. ed. Olive Ann Burns. Read by Tom Parker. 9 cass. (Running Time: 13 hrs.). 2003. 62.95 (978-0-7861-0402-4(3), 1354) Blckstn Audio.
The one thing you can depend on in Cold Sassy, Georgia, is that word gets around - fast. On July 5, 1906, things took a scandalous turn. E. Rucker Blakeslee, proprietor of the general store & barely three weeks a widower, eloped with Miss Love Simpson - a woman half his age & worse yet, a Yankee! On that day, fourteen year old Will Tweedy's adventures began & an unimpeachably pious, deliciously irreverent town came to life.

Cold Sassy Tree. unabr. ed. Olive Ann Burns. Read by Tom Parker. 11 CDs. (Running Time: 13 hrs.). 2000. audio compact disk 88.00 (978-0-7861-9924-2(5), 1354) Blckstn Audio.

Cold Sassy Tree. unabr. ed. Olive Ann Burns. Read by Tom Parker. 9 cass. (Running Time: 13 hrs.). 2005. 32.95 (978-0-7861-3471-7(2), E1354); audio compact disk 24.95 (978-0-7861-9519-0(3), 1354) Blckstn Audio.

Cold Sassy Tree. unabr. ed. Olive Ann Burns. Read by Tom Parker. 11 CDs. (Running Time: 46800 sec.). 2005. audio compact disk 34.95 (978-0-7861-8048-6(X), ZE1354) Blckstn Audio.

Cold Sassy Tree. unabr. ed. Olive Ann Burns. Read by Tom Parker. (Running Time: 45000 sec.). 2008. audio compact disk 19.95 (978-1-4332-1040-2(1)) Blckstn Audio.

Cold Sassy Tree. unabr. collector's ed. Olive Ann Burns. Read by Dick Estell. 11 cass. (Running Time: 16 hrs. 30 mins.). 1987. 88.00 (978-0-7366-1207-4(6), 2125) Books on Tape.
Cold Sassy, Georgia, had never been a whirlpool of excitement. But on July 5, 1906, things took a scandalous turn. That was the day E. Rucker Blakeslee, proprietor of the general store & barely three weeks a widower, eloped with Miss Love Simpson - a woman half his age & a Yankee!.

Cold Sassy Tree, Set. unabr. ed. Olive Ann Burns. Read by Tom Parker. 9 cass. 1999. 62.95 (FS9-23900) Highsmith.

Cold Service. unabr. ed. Robert B. Parker. Read by Joe Mantegna. 5 CDs. (Running Time: 6 hrs.). (Spenser Ser.). 2005. audio compact disk 38.25 (978-1-4159-1665-0(9)); 36.00 (978-1-4159-1579-0(2)) Books on Tape.
Boston P.I. Spenser and his redoubtable sidekick, Hawk, seek revenge on a cold-blooded killer.

Cold Shoulder. unabr. ed. Lynda La Plante. Read by Lorelei King. 12 cass. (Running Time: 18 hrs.). (Lorraine Page Mystery Ser.). 2000. 79.95 (978-0-7451-6511-0(7), CAB 1127) Pub: Chivers Audio Bks GBR. Dist(s): AudioGO
It was a shock to learn that a cop like Lubrinski could die, and that his partner in the Pasadena Homicide Squad, Lt. Lorraine Page, could be thrown off the force. The hunt for a vicious serial killer spirals into an all-out search for a missing witness; a victim who escaped and is on the run from her life. Lorraine Page is that witness, and against her will she is drawn into the investigation and forced to face her tainted past.

***Cold Spot.** unabr. ed. Tom Piccirilli. (Running Time: 10 hrs.). 2011. 29.95 (978-1-4417-7018-9(6)); 59.95 (978-1-4417-7015-8(1)); audio compact disk 90.00 (978-1-4417-7016-5(X)) Blckstn Audio.

Cold Tangerines: Celebrating the Extraordinary Nature of Everyday Life. unabr. ed. Shauna Niequist. (Running Time: 4 hrs. 30 mins. 0 sec.). (ENG.). 2007. 16.99 (978-0-310-28397-3(3)) Zondervan.

Cold Truth. Mariah Stewart. Read by Anna Fields. (Running Time: 32400 sec.). 2006. 54.95 (978-0-7861-4597-3(8)); audio compact disk 63.00 (978-0-7861-6991-7(5)) Blckstn Audio.

Cold Truth. abr. unabr. ed. Mariah Stewart. Read by Anna Fields. 6 pieces. (Running Time: 32400 sec.). 2006. 29.95 (978-0-7861-4481-5(5)); audio compact disk 29.95 (978-0-7861-7248-1(7)); audio compact disk 29.95 (978-0-7861-7700-4(4)) Blckstn Audio.

***Cold Vengeance.** unabr. ed. Douglas Preston & Lincoln Child. (Running Time: 13 hrs.). (ENG.). 2011. 26.98 (978-1-60941-391-0(1)); audio compact disk & audio compact disk 39.98 (978-1-60941-386-6(5)) Pub: Hachet Audio. Dist(s): HachBkGrp

Cold War: A New History. unabr. ed. John Lewis Gaddis & John Lewis Gladdis. Read by Jay Gregory & Alan Sklar. 8 CDs. (Running Time: 9 hrs. 45 mins.). (ENG.). 2006. audio compact disk 39.95 (978-1-56511-995-6(9), 1565119959) Pub: Penguin-HghBrdg. Dist(s): Penguin Grp USA

Cold Zero. abr. ed. Christopher Whitcomb. (ENG.). 2005. 14.98 (978-1-59483-406-6(7)) Pub: Hachet Audio. Dist(s): HachBkGrp

Cold Zero: Inside the FBI Hostage Rescue Team. unabr. ed. Christopher Whitcomb. 10 cass. (Running Time: 15 hrs.). 2001. 80.00 (978-0-7366-8326-5(7)) Books on Tape.
The story of a career FBI agent's move up to the elite Hostage Rescue Team, and his view of FBI operations.

Colder War. Short Stories. Charles Stross. Read by Pat Bottino. 1 CD. (Running Time: 80 mins.). (Great Science Fiction Stories Ser.). 2005. audio compact disk 10.99 (978-1-884612-48-0(2)) AudioText.

Coldest Day in the Zoo & the Wildest Day at the Zoo. unabr. ed. Alan Rusbridger. Read by Brian Bowles. 2 CDs. (Running Time: 1 hr. 4 mins.). (J). (gr. 2-4). 2006. audio compact disk 21.95 (978-1-4056-5533-0(X), Chivers Sound Lib) AudioGO.

Coldest Winter: America & the Korean War. unabr. ed. David Halberstam. Read by Scott Brick. 21 CDs. 2007. audio compact disk 129.00 (978-1-4159-4414-1(8), BksonTape) Pub: Random Audio Pubg. Dist(s): Random
Up until now, the Korean War has been the black hole of modern American history. THE COLDEST WINTER changes that. David Halberstam gives us a masterful narrative of the political decisions and miscalculations on both sides. He charts the disastrous path that led to the massive entry of Chinese forces near the Yalu River, and that caught Douglas MacArthur and his soldiers by surprise. He provides astonishingly vivid and nuanced portraits of all the major figures, including Truman and Eisenhower, Kim Il Sung and Mao Zedong; and General MacArthur. At the same time, Halberstam provides us with his trademark highly evocative narrative journalism, chronicling the crucial battles with reportage of the highest order.

Coldest Winter: America & the Korean War. unabr. abr. ed. David Halberstam. Read by Edward Herrmann. (Running Time: 50400 sec.). 2007. 44.95 (978-1-4013-8485-2(4), Hyperion Audio) Pub: Hyperion. Dist(s): HarperCollins Pubs

Coldfire. abr. ed. William W. Johnstone. 2 cass. (Running Time: 3 hrs.). (Code Name Ser.: No. 4). 2004. 18.00 (978-1-58807-431-7(5)) Am Pubng Inc.
Today, when bomb-throwing madmen rule nations and crime cartels strangle the globe, justice demands extreme measures. For twenty years, ex-CIA operations officer John Barrone fought his country's dirty back-alley wars. Now, he leads a secret strike force of former law enforcement, intelligence, and special operations professionals against America's enemies.Code Name: Coldfire. Someone has shipped a tactical nuclear device to the U.S.A. For John Barrone, the way to knock out the nuke is to go undercover into two deadly terrorist organizations. But when Barrone's best operators penetrate one force on the Far Right and another on the Radical Left, the true terror is revealed. Now, a warhead hidden somewhere in the heartland of America is set to go off, and one strike force is all that stands in the way.

Coldheart Canyon: A Hollywood Ghost Story. unabr. ed. Clive Barker. Read by Frank Muller. 20 cass. (Running Time: 30 hrs.). 2001. 49.95 (978-0-694-52401-3(8)) HarperCollins Pubs.

Colditz Story. unabr. ed. P. R. Reid. Read by Tim Woodward. 6 cass. (Running Time: 9 hrs.). 2000. 49.95 (978-0-7451-6229-4(0), CAB 577) Pub: Chivers Audio Bks GBR. Dist(s): AudioGO
Colditz was the dreaded German P.O.W. camp from which there was no escape. It was escape-proof during World War I, and was to be again in World War II, according to the Germans. This is the true story that passed into legend: the story of the incredible courage and ingenuity of those who refused to admit defeat, the story of the finest escape attempt of World War II.

Colds & Flu, & Sinus Infections: Ancient Truths, Natural Remedies & the Latest Findings for Your Health Today. unabr. ed. Don Colbert. (Bible Cure Ser.). 2004. 7.99 (978-1-58926-705-3(2)) Oasis Audio.

Colds & Flu, & Sinus Infections: Ancient Truths, Natural Remedies & the Latest Findings for Your Health Today. unabr. ed. Don Colbert. Narrated by Tim Lundeen. 1 CD. (Running Time: 1 hr). (Bible Cure Ser.). 2004. audio compact disk 9.99 (978-1-58926-706-0(0)) Oasis Audio.

Cole... I Love You to the Moon & Back: A Family's Journey with Childhood Cancer. unabr. ed. Aaron Dean Ruotsala. Narrated by Aaron Dean Ruotsala. (Running Time: 5 hrs. 37 mins. 51 sec.). (ENG.). 2009. 18.19 (978-1-60814-610-9(3)); audio compact disk 25.99 (978-1-59859-663-2(2)) Oasis Audio.

Cole Porter. unabr. ed. William McBrien. Read by John Edwardson. 12 cass. (Running Time: 18 hrs.). 1999. 96.00 (4991) Books on Tape.
A beguiling composer & lyricists of the century.

Cole Protocol. unabr. ed. Tobias S. Buckell. Read by Jonathan Davis. (Running Time: 10 hrs. 30 mins. 0 sec.). (Halo Ser.: No. 6). (ENG.). 2008. audio compact disk 39.95 (978-1-4272-0528-5(0)) Pub: Macmill Audio. Dist(s): Macmillan

Colección de Adoración. unabr. ed. Haul Box. (SPA.). 2003. 9.99 (978-0-8297-3664-9(6)) Pub: Vida Pubs. Dist(s): Zondervan

Colección de Adoración. unabr. ed. Zondervan Publishing Staff. (SPA.). 2004. audio compact disk 14.99 (978-0-8297-4622-8(6)) Zondervan.

Coleccion de Alabanza y Adoracion. unabr. ed. (SPA.). 2001. 9.99 (978-0-8297-3404-1(X)) Pub: Vida Pubs. Dist(s): Zondervan

***Colección de Álbumes Infantiles.** (SPA.). (J). 2009. audio compact disk 15.99 (978-0-8297-6154-2(3)) Pub: CanZion. Dist(s): Zondervan

Coleccion de Fabulas y Cuentos: Oscar Wilde, Esopo, Tomas de Iriarte. Oscar Wilde. (Playaway Young Adult Ser.). (SPA.). 2009. 60.00 (978-1-60775-578-4(5)) Find a World.

***Colección en Vivo.** (SPA.). 2009. audio compact disk 15.99 (978-0-8297-6157-3(8)) Pub: CanZion. Dist(s): Zondervan

Coleman Balls. abr. ed. David Coleman. 1 cass. (Running Time: 1 hr.). 1998. 11.25 (978-0-563-55737-1(0)) BBC WrldWd GBR.
Memorable commentating blunders.

Colette Collection, Set. Read by Flo Gibson. 2 cass. (Running Time: 1 hr. 30 min. per cass.). 1995. 14.95 (978-1-55685-382-1(3)) Audio Bk Con.
Glimpses "On Tour" of behind the curtains lives of performers & stage hands & other tales told with a deft pen, such as: "Clever Dogs," "The Master," "Nostalgia" & "La Fenice".

Colette Inez. Read by Colette Inez. 1 cass. (Running Time: 29 min.). 1987. 10.00 New Letters.
The author reads poems about the world of orphans.

Colette, par elle-meme, Set. Sidonie-Gabrielle Colette. 4 cass. (FRE.). 1991. 39.95 (1438-RF) Olivia & Hill.
Colette was at the height of her success when, in 1949, she accepted to do a series of interviews on Radio France. She recounts her childhood, her discovery of Paris, the writings of the Claudine series which her writer husband, "Monsieur Willy," had published under his own name...she also reveals her tastes, her mood swings & her humor.

Colfax. abr. ed. Robert J. Conley. 4 cass. (Running Time: 6 hrs.). 1997. 25.00 (978-1-883268-26-8(5), 694300) Spellbinders.
Hired gun Oliver Colfax searches for the would-be killers of the only man he'd ever wanted to call a friend, Sergeant Bluff Luton.

Colibri. Ann Cameron. 3 cass. (Running Time: 5 hrs.). (J). (gr. 5 up). 2004. 30.00 (978-1-4000-8536-1(5), Listening Lib); audio compact disk 45.00 (978-1-4000-8993-2(X), Listening Lib) Random Audio Pubg.

Colic Stop. Created by Wendy Leigh. 1 cass. (Running Time: 60 min.). (Smart Baby Ser.). 1997. 9.99 (978-1-890680-03-9(6)) Smart Baby.
Quality recordings of white noise to calm babies, featuring lawn mower & vacuum cleaner sounds.

Colin Powell. Read by Sonny Buxton. 2 cass. (Running Time: 2 hrs. 20 min.). (Black Americans of Achievement Ser.). (YA). (gr. 9 up). 1995. 15.95 set. (978-1-879557-23-9(1)) Audio Scholar.
This set presents the life & career of the popular former National Security Advisor & Chairman of the Joint Chiefs of Staff. The personal information is limited to the facts such as can be found in reference sources, but recollections & quoted conversations make it more interesting.

Colin Powell. unabr. ed. 2 cass. (Running Time: 2 hrs. 30 min.). (Black Americans of Achievement Audiobook Collection). (J). 15.95 Set. (978-1-879557-09-3(6)) Audio Scholar.

Colin Powell: It Can Be Done! Mike Strong. (High Five Reading - Green Ser.). (ENG.). (gr. 4 up). 2002. audio compact disk 5.95 (978-0-7368-9562-0(0)) CapstoneDig.

Colin Powell: It Can Be Done! Mike Strong. (High Five Reading - Green Ser.). (ENG.). (gr. 3-4). 2007. audio compact disk 5.95 (978-1-4296-1419-1(6)) CapstoneDig.

Colin Powell: Soldier-Statesman - Statesman-Soldier. unabr. collector's ed. Howard Means. Read by Michael Kramer. 9 cass. (Running Time: 13 hrs. 30 mins.). 1994. 72.00 (978-0-7366-2859-4(2), 113264) Books on Tape.
Colin Powell is a man of grit, drive, determination & talent. His biography recounts the rise of a man the author says is the first African-American in a position of major national prominence whom the general public seems ready to judge on merit alone.

Collaboration. Arleen LaBella & Dolores Leach. 1986. 9.75 (978-0-932491-34-3(0)) Res Appl Inc.
Learn how to develop working relationships & capitalize on your strengths. Explore the benefits on your shared problem-solving, decision-making, risk & workload.

Collaborations, 3. Jann Huizenga. (Adult ESL Ser.). 1997. pap. bk., tchr. ed., suppl. ed. 17.75 (978-0-8384-6424-3(6)) Heinle.

Collaborations: Beginners 1. Jann Huizenga. (Adult ESL Ser.). (J). 1995. stu. ed. & suppl. ed. 23.95 (978-0-8384-4112-1(2)) Heinle.

Collaborations: Beginners 2. Jann Huizenga. (Adult ESL Ser.). (J). 1995. stu. ed. & suppl. ed. 23.95 (978-0-8384-4113-8(0)) Heinle.

Collaborations: Intermediate 1. Huizenga. (Adult ESL Ser.). 1996. stu. ed. & suppl. ed. 23.95 (978-0-8384-4114-5(9)) Heinle.

Collaborations: Intermediate 2. Lynda Terrill et al. 1 cass. (Running Time: 1 hr.). pap. bk. 30.95 (978-0-8384-5706-1(1)) Heinle.

Collaborations Beginners 2. Jann Huizenga. 1 cass. (Running Time: 1 hr.). 2000. pap. bk. 28.95 (978-0-8384-6422-9(X)) Heinle.
Organized around six relevant contexts: self, school, family, work, local community, and global community. The stories serve as springboards for lively activities which develop linguistic skills, vocabulary, and lifeskills competencies.

Collaborations Literacy. Cathy Shank. pap. bk. 53.95 (978-0-8384-8964-2(8)) Heinle.

Collaborations Literacy. Cathy C. Shank et al. (Global ESL/ELT Ser.). (J). 1997. stu. ed. & suppl. ed. 23.95 (978-0-8384-6626-1(5)) Heinle.

Collaborative Classroom Management. Contrib. by Robert Sylwester. 2001. 99.95 (978-0-7619-7766-7(X), 87464) Pub: Corwin Pr. Dist(s): SAGE

Collaborators. Reginald Hill. Read by Michael Tudor Barnes. (Running Time: 51000 sec.). (Isis (CDs) Ser.). 2006. audio compact disk 99.95 (978-0-7531-2619-6(2)) Pub: ISIS Lrg Prnt GBR. Dist(s): Ulverscroft US

Collaborators. Reginald Hill. Read by Michael Tudor Barnes. 11 cass. (Running Time: 14 hrs. 10 mins.). (Isis Cassettes Ser.). 2006. 89.95 (978-0-7531-3647-8(3)) Pub: ISIS Lrg Prnt GBR. Dist(s): Ulverscroft US

Collage: Performances by Students of the University of Wisconsin-Madison School of Music. UW Sch of Music. 2001. audio compact disk 25.00 (978-1-931569-00-2(2)) Pub: U of Wis Pr. Dist(s): Chicago Distribution Ctr

Collage: Student Set. unabr. ed. Baker. 4 cass. (Running Time: 6 hrs.). 1996. 31.95 (978-0-07-911762-5(7), Mc-H Human Soc) McGrw-H Hghr Educ.

Collage - A Portrait. Perf. by Sixpence None the Richer. 1 cd. audio compact disk 15.98 (978-1-57908-398-4(6), 1439) Platinm Enter.

***Collage Cat.** Anonymous. 2009. (978-1-60136-586-6(1)) Audio Holding.

Collage from the Life & Art of Romare Bearden. 1 cass. (Running Time: 30 min.). 10.95 (F0540B090, HarperThor) HarpC GBR.

Collana Longobarda. Mar Bernardo. pap. bk. 19.95 (978-88-7754-940-2(8)) Pub: Cideb ITA. Dist(s): Distribks Inc

Collapse: How Societies Choose to Fail or Succeed. abr. ed. Jared M. Diamond. Read by Christopher Murney. 8 CDs. (Running Time: 9 hrs.). (ENG.). (gr. 12 up). 2004. audio compact disk 34.95 (978-0-14-305718-5(9), PengAudBks) Penguin Grp USA.

Collapse: How Societies Choose to Fail or Succeed. unabr. ed. Jared M. Diamond. Read by Michael Prichard. 19 cass. (Running Time: 27 hrs.). 2005. 120.00 (978-1-4159-1726-8(4)); audio compact disk 144.00 (978-1-4159-1727-5(2)) Books on Tape.
From a Pulitzer Prize-winning author comes an examination of what caused the downfall of some of the greatest civilizations in history.

Collapse of the Third Republic, Pt. 1. unabr. collector's ed. William L. Shirer. Read by Larry McKeever. 12 cass. (Running Time: 18 hrs.). 1988. 96.00 (978-0-7366-1410-8(9), 2299-A) Books on Tape.
Discusses the collapse of the French Third Republic in 1940. In a span of six weeks this parliamentary democracy, the world's second largest empire, one of Europe's principal powers, went down to catastrophic military defeat. Its citizens, heirs to a long & glorious history, were left dazed & completely demoralized.

Collapse of the Third Republic, Pt. 2. collector's ed. William L. Shirer. Read by Larry McKeever. 12 cass. (Running Time: 18 hrs.). 1988. 96.00 (978-0-7366-1411-5(7), 2299-B) Books on Tape.

Collapse of the Third Republic, Pt. 3. collector's ed. William L. Shirer. Read by Larry McKeever. 12 cass. (Running Time: 18 hrs.). 1988. 96.00 (978-0-7366-1412-2(5), 2299-C) Books on Tape.

Collar see Hearing Great Poetry: From Chaucer to Milton

Collar de la Familia Albar. (SPA.). 6.95 (978-88-8148-603-8(2)) EMC-Paradigm.

Collateral Actions in Family Law: Tax Fraud, Criminal Actions & Bankruptcy. 1997. bk. 99.00 (ACS-1275) PA Bar Inst.
What do you, as a family lawyer, need to know about criminal law, tax fraud & bankruptcy? Top-notch family lawyers with a criminal lawyer, a bankruptcy judge or lawyer & a tax lawyer join together so you get answers to the nagging questions which plague you about these collateral issues. The focus is on giving you practical, workable techniques for handling these increasingly more common client issues.

Collateral Damage. abr. ed. Fern Michaels. Read by Laural Merlington. (Running Time: 3 hrs.). (Sisterhood Ser.: No. 11). 2010. audio compact disk 9.99 (978-1-4233-4511-4(8), 9781423345114) Brilliance Audio.

Collateral Damage. unabr. ed. Fern Michaels. Read by Laural Merlington. 1 MP3-CD. (Running Time: 7 hrs.). (Sisterhood Ser.: No. 11). 2008. 39.25 (978-1-4233-4507-7(X), 9781423345077, Brlnc Audio MP3 Lib); 39.25 (978-1-4233-4509-1(6), 9781423345091, BADLE); 24.95 (978-1-4233-4506-0(1), 9781423345060, Brilliance MP3); 24.95 (978-1-4233-4508-4(8), 9781423345084, BAD); audio compact disk 87.25 (978-1-4233-4505-3(3), 9781423345053, BriAudCD Unabrid); audio compact disk 29.99 (978-1-4233-4504-6(5), 9781423345046, Bril Audio CD Unabri) Brilliance Audio.

Collateral Damage: America's War Against Iraqi Civilians. unabr. ed. Chris Hedges & Laila Al-Arian. Read by Chris Hedges. Narrated by Lloyd James. (Running Time: 3 hrs. 30 mins. 0 sec.). (ENG.). 2008. audio compact disk 19.99 (978-1-4001-5666-5(1)); audio compact disk 39.99 (978-1-4001-3666-7(0)) Pub: Tantor Media. Dist(s): IngramPubServ

Collateral Damage: America's War Against Iraqi Civilians. unabr. ed. Chris Hedges & Laila Al-Arian. Read by Lloyd James. 3 CDs. (Running Time: 3 hrs. 30 mins. 0 sec.). (ENG.). 2008. audio compact disk 19.99 (978-1-4001-0666-0(4)) Pub: Tantor Media. Dist(s): IngramPubServ

Colleague, No. 3. 4 cass. 10.00 ea. (978-1-885357-87-8(7)) Rational Isl.
Shared experiences of college universtiy faculty & other interested people using re-evaluation counseling.

Collected Bowdrie Dramatizations. unabr. ed. Louis L'Amour. Read by Louis L'Amour. (YA). 2007. 49.99 (978-0-7393-7459-7(1)); 49.99 (978-0-7393-7461-0(3)) Find a World.

Collected Bowdrie Dramatizations, Vol. 1. unabr. ed. Louis L'Amour. 6 CDs. (Running Time: 21600 sec.). (ENG.). 2005. audio compact disk 29.95 (978-0-7393-2360-1(1), Random AudioBks) Pub: Random Audio Pubg. Dist(s): Random

Collected Bowdrie Dramatizations, Vol. 3. unabr. ed. Louis L'Amour. Read by Dramatization Staff. (Running Time: 25200 sec.). (ENG.). 2007. audio compact disk 30.00 (978-0-7393-2374-8(1), Random AudioBks) Pub: Random Audio Pubg. Dist(s): Random

Collected Bowdrie Dramatizations Vol. 2: More Brains Than Bullets; The Road to Casa Piedras; Bowdrie Passes Through; Where Buzzards Fly; South of Deadwood; Too Tough to Brand. unabr. ed. Louis L'Amour. (Running Time: 21600 sec.). (ENG.). 2006. audio compact disk 29.95 (978-0-7393-2372-4(5), Random AudioBks) Pub: Random Audio Pubg. Dist(s): Random

***Collected Chekhov: Five Tales of Childhood.** Anton Chekhov. Narrated by William Coon. (Running Time: 55). (ENG.). 2009. 4.95 (978-0-9844138-1-2(2)) Pub: Eloq Voice. Dist(s): OverDrive Inc

***Collected Chekhov: Five Tales of Men & Women.** Anton Chekhov. Narrated by William Coon. (Running Time: 52). (ENG.). 2009. 4.95 (978-0-9844138-2-9(0)) Pub: Eloq Voice. Dist(s): OverDrive Inc

***Collected Chekhov: Twelve Tales from Life's Passing Parade.** Anton Chekhov. Narrated by William Coon. (Running Time: 131). (ENG.). 2009. 8.95 (978-0-9844138-6-7(3)) Pub: Eloq Voice. Dist(s): OverDrive Inc

***Collected Fiction.** unabr. ed. Jorge Luis Borges. Read by George Guidall. Tr. by Andrew Hurley. 5 CDs. (Running Time: 5 hrs.). (ENG.). 2010. audio compact disk 29.95 (978-0-14-242808-5(6), PengAudBks) Penguin Grp USA.

***Collected George Smiley Radio Dramas: Eight BBC Full-Cast Productions Starring Simon Russell Beale.** John le Carré. Narrated by Full Cast & Simon Russell Beale. (Running Time: 23 hrs. 0 mins. 0 sec.). (ENG.). 2011. audio compact disk 139.95 (978-1-4084-2774-3(5)) Pub: AudioGO. Dist(s): Perseus Dist

Collected Short Stories of Edith Wharton. unabr. ed. Edith Wharton. Ed. by R. W. B. Lewis. 55 cass. (Running Time: 82 hrs. 30 mins.). Incl. Pt. 1. Collected Short Stories of Edith Wharton. 12 cass. (Running Time: 18 hrs.). Edith Wharton. Ed. by R. W. B. Lewis. 1984. 96.00 (978-0-7366-0409-3(X), 1385-A); Pt. 2. Collected Short Stories of Edith Wharton. 12 cass. (Running Time: 18 hrs.). Edith Wharton. Ed. by R. W. B. Lewis. 1984. 96.00 (978-0-7366-0410-9(3), 1385-B); Pt. 3. Collected Short Stories of Edith Wharton. 12 cass. (Running Time: 18 hrs.). Edith Wharton. Ed. by R. W. B. Lewis. 1984. 96.00 (978-0-7366-0411-6(1), 1385-C); Pt. 4. Collected Short Stories of Edith Wharton. 9 cass. (Running Time: 13 hrs. 30 mins.). Edith Wharton. Ed. by R. W. B. Lewis. 1984. 72.00 (978-0-7366-0412-3(X), 1385-D); Pt. 5. Collected Short Stories of Edith Wharton. 10 cass. Edith Wharton. Ed. by R. W. B. Lewis. 1984. 80.00 (978-0-7366-0413-0(8), 1385-E); 440.00 Books on Tape.
The author's characters accurately reflect the attitudes of her era, but their hurts are as real as our own. Nor did she skirt the grim issues of her day.

Collected Short Stories of Jack Schaefer, Pt. 1. unabr. collector's ed. Jack Schaefer. Read by Walter Zimmerman. 9 cass. (Running Time: 13 hrs. 30 min.). 1988. 72.00 (978-0-7366-1371-2(4), 2267-A) Books on Tape.
Thirty-two stories by the author of Shane.

Collected Short Stories of Jack Schaefer, Pt. 2. collector's ed. Jack Schaefer. Read by Walter Zimmerman. 9 cass. (Running Time: 13 hrs. 30 min.). 1988. 72.00 (978-0-7366-1372-9(2), 2267-B) Books on Tape.

Collected Short Stories of Louis L'Amour, Vol. 1. abr. ed. Louis L'Amour. Read by John Bedford Lloyd. 2 CDs. (Running Time: 3 hrs. 30 mins.). (Louis L'Amour Ser.). (ENG.). 2003. audio compact disk 21.95 (978-0-7393-0781-6(9)) Pub: Random Audio Pubg. Dist(s): Random

Collected Short Stories of Louis L'Amour, Vol. 5. unabr. abr. ed. Louis L'Amour. Read by Jason Culp. (ENG.). 2007. audio compact disk 21.95 (978-0-7393-4433-0(1), Random AudioBks) Pub: Random Audio Pubg. Dist(s): Random

Collected Short Stories of Louis L'Amour Vol. 2: What Gold Does to a Man; The Ghosts of Buckskin Run; The Drift; No Man's Man. unabr. abr. ed. Louis L'Amour. Read by Jason Culp. 3 CDs. (Running Time: 3 hrs.). 2004. audio compact disk 21.95 (978-0-7393-1368-8(1), Random AudioBks) Pub: Random Audio Pubg. Dist(s): Random

Collected Short Stories of Louis L'Amour Vol. 4: Unabridged Selections from the Adventure Stories. abr. ed. Louis L'Amour. Read by Jason Culp. (Running Time: 10800 sec.). (Louis L'Amour Ser.). (ENG.). 2006. audio compact disk 21.95 (978-0-7393-4011-0(5), Random AudioBks) Pub: Random Audio Pubg. Dist(s): Random

Collected Short Stories of Louis L'Amour Vol. 7: The Frontier Stories. abr. ed. Louis L'Amour. Read by Jason Culp. (ENG.). 2009. audio compact disk 22.00 (978-0-307-57707-8(4), Random AudioBks) Pub: Random Audio Pubg. Dist(s): Random

Collected Short Stories of Robert Graves. unabr. collector's ed. Short Stories. Robert Graves. Read by David Case. 8 cass. (Running Time: 12 hrs.). 1993. 64.00 (978-0-7366-2376-6(0), 3148) Books on Tape.
Beautifully varied & widely eclectic selections, all written between 1924 & 1962.

Collected Stories. unabr. ed. Short Stories. Richard Kennedy. Read by Christopher King. 2 cass. (Running Time: 3 hrs.). (J). (gr. 1-8). 1999. 23.00 (LL 0050, Chivers Child Audio) AudioGO.

Collected Stories. unabr. ed. Paul Theroux. Read by David Birney. 4 cass. (Running Time: 6 hrs.). 2001. 25.00 (978-1-59040-070-8(4), Phoenix Audio) Pub: Amer Intl Pub. Dist(s): PerseuPGW

Collected Stories of Edith Wharton, Pt. 1. Edith Wharton. 12 cass. (Running Time: 18 hrs.). 96.00 (1385-A) Audio Bk Con.
A remarkable collection of 86 stories to make you laugh, cry, bask in the warm glow of romance or shiver over ghosts.

Collected Stories of Edith Wharton, Pt. 2. Edith Wharton. 12 cass. (Running Time: 18 hrs.). 96.00 (1385-B) Audio Bk Con.

Collected Stories of Edith Wharton, Pt. 3. Edith Wharton. 12 cass. (Running Time: 18 hrs.). 96.00 (1385-C) Audio Bk Con.

Collected Stories of Edith Wharton, Pt. 4. Edith Wharton. 9 cass. (Running Time: 13 hrs. 30 mins.). 72.00 (1385-D) Audio Bk Con.

Collected Stories of Edith Wharton, Pt. 5. Edith Wharton. 10 cass. (Running Time: 15 hrs.). 80.00 (1935-E) Audio Bk Con.

Collected Stories of William Faulkner, Pt. 1. unabr. ed. William Faulkner. Read by Wolfram Kandinsky. 11 cass. (Running Time: 16 hrs. 30 mins.). 1996. 88.00 (978-0-7366-3207-2(7), 3871-A) Books on Tape.
Love & compassion, honor & sacrifice, pity & pride... Faulkner brings these universal qualities to life in this collection of stories, from the macabre in "A Rose for Emily" to the relationships between the races in "Dry September" & "A Justice" Faulkner deals with the "problems of the human heart in conflict with itself." Faulkner used short stories to develop characters that later appeared in his novels.

Collected Stories of William Faulkner, Pt. 2. unabr. ed. William Faulkner. Read by Michael Kramer. 11 cass. (Running Time: 1 hr. 30 min. per cass.). 1996. 88.00 (3871-B) Books on Tape.

***Collected Stories of Winnie-the-Pooh.** unabr. ed. A. A. Milne. Read by Stephen Fry et al. 4 CDs. (Running Time: 4 hrs. 28 mins.). (J). (ps-3). 2009. audio compact disk 38.00 (978-0-307-70610-2(9), BksonTape) Pub: Random Audio Pubg. Dist(s): Random

Collected Thoughts of Thomas Berry. Thomas Berry. Interview with Brian Swimme. 4 cass. (Running Time: 6 hrs.). 1998. 45.00 Set. (978-0-9650365-1-1(0)) Ctr Story Unvrse.
Thoughts & ideas of 20th century historian Thomas Berry on cosmology, religion, science, psychology.

Collected Voices of New Felons: No. 8 in the River Road Poetry Series. Ed. by Carol Jenkins. Executive Producer Carol Jenkins. (ENG.). 2008. audio compact disk 18.00 (978-0-9804148-7-5(3)) RivRoad AUS.

Collected Works of Billy the Kid. unabr. ed. Michael Ondaatje. (Running Time: 3.5 hrs. 0 mins.). (ENG.). 2009. 19.95 (978-1-4332-8950-7(4)); 24.95 (978-1-4332-8946-0(6)); audio compact disk 30.00 (978-1-4332-8947-7(4)) Blckstn Audio.

Collecting & Enforcing Judgments. 1998. bk. 99.00 (ACS-2190) PA Bar Inst.
Designed for every practitioner who represents clients with debts to collect. Not only an introduction to the basic structure of execution practice in Pennsylvania, but a wealth of tips & forms, & how-to-do-it interactions for enforcing judgments against real estate & personal property.

Collecting & Enforcing Judgments. 1991. 45.00 (AC-617) PA Bar Inst.

Collecting Child Support & Alimony. Robert S. Sigman. Read by Robert S. Sigman. 1 cass. (Running Time: 60 min.). (Law for the Layman Ser.). 1990. 16.95 (978-1-878135-03-2(1)) Legovac.
What you need to know before you see a lawyer!.

Collection. Contrib. by Steve Amerson. (ENG.). 2001. audio compact disk 15.98 (978-5-550-11441-4(0)) Pub: Amerson Mus Min. Dist(s): STL Dist NA

Collection. Contrib. by Katinas et al. 2006. audio compact disk 9.99 (978-5-558-15498-6(5)) Gotee Records.

Collection. Contrib. by Jennifer Knapp et al. 2005. audio compact disk 9.98 (978-5-559-72466-9(1)) Gotee Records.

Collection, Vol. 1. Perf. by Ken Rarick et al. 1 cass. (Running Time: 45 min.). (New Covenant Ser.). 1989. 5.98 (978-0-570-09657-3(X), 79-7907) Family Films.
A collection of favorite selections from each of the other seven New Covenant titles. Each selection features one of the following instrumental sounds - woodwinds, piano, guitar, electronic keyboards, or strings.

Collection Development & Technical Services Sections - Management of Internet Resources. 1 cass. (Medical Library Association 1998 Annual Meeting & Exhibit Ser.). 1998. 12.00 (22) Med Lib Assn.

Collection Development Section - Alphabet Soup or All Your Ducks in a Row: Selection Models for Purchase vs. Access in Collection Development. 1 cass. (Medical Library Association 1998 Annual Meeting & Exhibit Ser.). 1998. 12.00 (01) Med Lib Assn.

Collection Development Section - Peer Review in the Electronic Age. 1 cass. (Medical Library Association 1998 Annual Meeting & Exhibit Ser.). 1998. 12.00 (13) Med Lib Assn.

Collection of Haunting Tales, Set. unabr. ed. Mary Roberts Rinehart et al. Read by Flo Gibson. 3 cass. (Running Time: 4 hrs.). (YA). (gr. 8 up). 1991. 16.95 (978-1-55685-209-1(6)) Audio Bk Con.
"The Buckled Bag," "The Tapestried Room," "The Lady in the Sacque," "The New Catacomb," & "The Lost Ghost" are guaranteed to haunt you.

Collection of Just So Stories. Read by Jim Weiss. (ENG.). (J). 2008. audio compact disk 14.95 (978-1-882513-59-8(2)) Pub: Greathall Prods. Dist(s): Allegro Dist

Collection of My Poetry. Poems. Composed by Paul Sybert. Voice by Paul Sybert. 1 CD. (Running Time: 50 minutes). 2005. audio compact disk 15.00 (978-0-9767842-3-4(8)) Paul Syb.
Poetry written and spoken by Paul Sybert on CD: peoms about love, lyrics, cards, friends, pets, family and work.

Collection of Personal Test Pilot Stories. Marco A. V. Bitetto. Read by Marco A. V. Bitetto. 1 cass. 2000. (978-1-58578-286-4(6)) Inst of Cybernetics.

Collection of Sermons. Batsell Barrett Baxter. Read by Batsell Barrett Baxter. 24.99 (978-0-89098-117-7(5)) Twent Cent Christ.
Twelve sermons by one of the most beloved preachers of the Gospel of this century. Asleep in Jesus - yet he speaks!.

Collection of Speeches & Sermons. Jim Bill McInteer. Read by Jim Bill McInteer. 24.99 (978-0-89098-112-2(4)) Twent Cent Christ.
Contains the lessons of a gifted & beloved preacher of more than 50 years. His love for God's truth & loving spirit are reflected as he preaches God's Word.

Collection of the World's Shortest Stories. unabr. ed. (YA). 2006. 44.99 (978-1-59895-196-7(3)) Find a World.

Collection of Traditional Christmas Carols. 1 cass. 1995. 9.95 Liguori Pubns.
This classic collection of favorite Christmas carols includes: "Away in a Manger," "Joy to the World," "The First Noel," & 9 others.

Collection of Traditional Marian & Eucharistic Hymns. 1 cass. 1995. 9.95 Liguori Pubns.
This devotional collection of Marian & Eucharistic hymns includes: "Ave Maria," "Mother Dearest, Mother Fairest," "Panis Angelicus," & 15 more.

***Collection of Wednesdays: Creating a Whole from the Parts.** Zondervan. (ENG.). 2011. 17.99 (978-0-310-41194-9(7)) Zondervan.

Collection 2: Rapture in Death; Ceremony in Death; Vengeance in Death. abr. ed. J. D. Robb, pseud. Read by Susan Ericksen. (Running Time: 18 hrs.). (In Death Ser.). 2008. audio compact disk 34.95 (978-1-4233-4648-7(3), 9781423346487, BACD) Brilliance Audio.

Collection 991: Music & Art. Perf. by Paul Speer. 1 cass. 1992. 9.98 (MPC3002); audio compact disk 14.98 CD. Miramar Images.
Miramars award winning producer (Natural States, Desert Vision) steps out in his debut solo album which demonstrates his virtuosity. Several surprise guest musicians bless this compelling & melodic recording.

Collections. IBD Ltd.

Collections. Perf. by Fred Penner. 1 cass. (J). (ps-5). 1989. 10.98 (978-0-945267-46-1(0), YM081-CN); audio compact disk 13.98 (978-0-945267-47-8(9), YM081-CD) Youngheart Mus.
Songs include: "If I Knew You Were Comin'"; "Car Car"; "Rollerskating"; "Sandwiches"; "The Bump"; "The Cat Came Back"; "A House Is a House for Me"; "Collections"; "Ghost Riders in the Sky"; "Marvelous Toy"; "Poco"; "Teagan's Lullaby"; "Otto the Hippo" & "Holiday.".

Collections & the Enforcement of Money Judgments. (Running Time: 5 hrs. 30 min.). 1995. 92.00 Incl. 474p. coursebk. (20645) NYS Bar.
Basic-to-intermediate-level presentation addresses the practical needs, as well as the legal rights, of both judgment debtors & judgment creditors. The materials & speakers review the legal, statutory & regulatory framework for collections work & what the lawyer should know about the practical, nuts-&-bolts operation of this area of law.

Collective Consciousness: The Unity of the Universe. unabr. ed. Robert A. Monroe. Read by Robert A. Monroe. (Running Time: 45 min.). (Explorer Ser.). 1985. 12.95 (978-1-56113-027-6(3), 28) Monroe Institute.
A discussion encompassing the "Big Bang" theory.

Collective Unconscious & Astrology. unabr. ed. Alice Howell. 2 cass. 18.00 (OC96) Sound Horizons AV.

Collective Unconscious & the Shape of Psychopathology: A Perspective from Jungian Structural Analysis. Robert Moore. Read by Robert Moore. 5 cass. (Running Time: 7 hrs.). 1997. 39.95 Set. (978-0-7822-0531-2(3), 597) C G Jung IL.
Theodore Millon's understanding of the shape of psychopathology is interpreted & evaluated from the perspective of Moore's approach to a Jungian structural psychoanalysis & integrative psychotherapy.

Collectors. David Baldacci. 2006. 39.99 (978-1-59895-383-1(4)) Find a World.

Collectors. abr. ed. David Baldacci. Read by Maggi-Meg Reed & Tom Wopat. (Running Time: 6 hrs.). No. 2. (ENG.). 2006. audio compact disk 29.98 (978-1-59483-580-3(2)) Pub: GrandCentral. Dist(s): HachBkGrp

Collectors. abr. ed. David Baldacci. Read by Tom Wopat & Daphne Maxwell Reed. (Running Time: 6 hrs.). (ENG.). 2006. 14.98 (978-1-59483-581-0(0)) Pub: Hachet Audio. Dist(s): HachBkGrp

Collectors. unabr. ed. David Baldacci. Read by L. J. Ganser et al. (YA). 2006. 54.99 (978-1-59895-441-8(5)) Find a World.

Collectors. unabr. ed. David Baldacci. Read by L. J. Ganser et al. (Running Time: 13 hrs.). (ENG.). 2006. 14.98 (978-1-59483-583-4(7)) Pub: Hachet Audio. Dist(s): HachBkGrp

Collectors. unabr. ed. David Baldacci. Read by L. J. Ganser et al. (Running Time: 13 hrs.). (ENG.). 2009. 59.98 (978-1-60788-278-7(7)) Pub: Hachet Audio. Dist(s): HachBkGrp

Collector's Classics. 2 cass. 9.98 (978-1-55503-200-5(1), 0700118) Covenant Comms.

Collector's Trilogy. unabr. ed. William C. Dietz. 6 CDs. (Running Time: 6 hrs.). Dramatization. Bks. 1-3. (ENG.). (gr. 5 up). 1998. audio compact disk 49.95 (978-1-56511-278-0(4), 1565112784) Pub: HighBridge. Dist(s): Workman Pub

Colleen McCullough. Interview with Colleen McCullough. 1 cass. (Running Time: 25 min.). 1978. 12.95 (L047) TFR.
McCullough talks about her bestseller, The Thorn Birds, describes her early life in Australia, discusses her weight & family problems & tells how she turned out 20,000 words a day.

Colleen's Doll House. Short Stories. Lee Ann Butler-Owens. Music by Lee Ann Butler-Owens. 1 CD. (Running Time: 10 Mins.). (J). 2003. audio compact disk (978-0-9758529-0-3(6)) Lullalee Pubns.
"Colleen's Dollhouse" is a refreshing approach to teach children the importance of education, basic humanitarian value, emphasizing their specific contribution and awareness to their surroundings.

College Admissions Mystique. abr. ed. Bill Mayher. 2 CDs. (Running Time: 3 hrs.). 2000. audio compact disk 15.00 (978-1-885608-48-2(9)) Airplay.
An admissions pro demystifies the difficult process of applying for college. With humor & an insider's knowledge, he untangles the web of emotions & misinformation that makes the process so hazardous.

College Algebra: Enhanced with Graphing Utilities. 4th ed. Created by Pearson/Prentice Hall. (Math XL Ser.). 2005. audio compact disk 26.67 (978-0-13-154339-3(3)) Pearson Educ CAN CAN.

College Chinese: A First-Year. rev. ed. Shou-ying Lin. 10 cass. (CHI & ENG.). (C). (gr. 13 up). 1993. 141.95 (978-0-88727-189-2(8)) Cheng Tsui.

College Confidence with ADD ¿ the Unabridged Audiobook: The Ultimate Success Manual for ADD Students, from Applying to Academics, Preparation to Social Success & Everything Else You Need to Know. Michael Sandler. 2008. audio compact disk 29.95 (978-0-615-21187-9(9)) Create CO.

College English & Communication. 8th ed. Sue C. Camp & Marilyn L. Satterwhite. 2002. stu. ed. 31.33 (978-0-07-828273-7(X), 9780078282737, Irwn McGrw-H) Pub: McGrw-H Hghr Educ. Dist(s): McGraw

College Glee Club Songs. unabr. ed. 1 cass. 12.95 (978-0-88432-289-4(0), C11054) J Norton Pubs.
New England college songs from 1928-1962.

College Student Mental Health: NACADA Webinar Series 08. Featuring Dan Wilcox et al. (ENG.). 2007. audio compact disk 140.00 (978-1-935140-50-4(7)) Nat Acad Adv.

College Writing. 1 cass. (Running Time: 1 hr). 9.00 (G0400B090, HarperThor) HarpC GBR.

Colleges & Universities, Pt. 2. Read by J. Donald Monan et al. 1 cass. 3.00 (146) ISI Books.

Collegiate Business Series: Syllabus. Richard R. Gallagher. (J). 1977. bk. 120.25 (978-0-89420-135-6(2), 104000) Natl Book.

Collier see Dylan Thomas Reading

Collier De Famille. audio compact disk 6.95 (978-88-8148-584-0(2)) EMC-Paradigm.

Collier's Encyclopedia 1997, Set. Collier Staff. 1997. bk. 499.00 (978-0-02-864874-3(9), Macmillan Ref) Gale.

Collin Raye: The Gift Christmas. Perf. by Collin Raye. Contrib. by Ronn Huff. 1 cass. 1998. 9.99 (978-0-7601-2679-0(8)); audio compact disk 13.99 CD. (978-0-7601-2680-6(1)) Brentwood Music.
This masterpiece collection of songs whispers, celebrates & thunders the message of our Savior's birth. Includes: "The Christmas Song," "I'll Be Home for Christmas," "It Could Happen Again," "The First Noel," "Away in a Manger," "White Christmas," "Winter Wonderland," "Angels We Have Heard on High," "Little Drummer Boy," "Silent Night," The First Noel" (instrumental reprise) & "Holy Night.".

Colline, Set. Jean Giono. Read by Jacques Bonnaffe. 2 cass. (FRE.). 1991. 28.95 (1452-H) Olivia & Hill.
All set in the lower mountain-slopes of Provence, Giono depicts a pastoral life that is simple, beautiful & poetic.

Collins English Dictionary. 3rd ed. Collins Publishers Staff. 2003. audio compact disk (978-0-00-714235-4(8)) Zondervan.

Collins German Language Pack. HarperCollins UK Staff. (ENG & GER., 2005. audio compact disk 19.99 (978-0-00-769938-4(7)) Pub: HarpC GBR. Dist(s): Trafalgar

Collins Greek Phrase Book & Dictionary. HarperCollins UK Staff. (ENG & GRE., 2005. bk. 19.99 (978-0-00-769935-3(2)) Pub: HarpC GBR. Dist(s): Trafalgar

Collins Portuguese Phrase Book. 2nd ed. HarperCollins UK Staff. (POR & ENG., 2005. pap. bk. 19.99 (978-0-00-769936-0(0)) Pub: HarpC GBR. Dist(s): Trafalgar

Collins Robert French Dictionary. 2nd ed. Collins Publishers Staff. 2003. audio compact disk (978-0-00-714234-7(X)) Zondervan.

Collision. Contrib. by David Crowder Band. Prod. by Tedd T. Contrib. by Louie Giglio & Brad O'Donnell. 2005. audio compact disk 16.98 (978-5-558-86743-5(4)) Pt of Grace Ent.

Collision. unabr. ed. Jeff Abbott. Read by Phil Gigante. (Running Time: 12 hrs.). 2008. 39.25 (978-1-4233-6221-0(7), 9781423362210, BADLE); 24.95 (978-1-4233-6220-3(9), 9781423362203, BAD); audio compact disk 102.25 (978-1-4233-6217-3(9), 9781423362173, BriAudCD Unabrid); audio compact disk 38.95 (978-1-4233-6216-6(0), 9781423362166, Bril Audio CD Unabri) Brilliance Audio.

Collision. unabr. ed. Jeff Abbott. Read by Phil Gigante. Directed By Matthew Christilaw. (Running Time: 12 hrs.). 2008. audio compact disk 39.25 (978-1-4233-6219-7(5), 9781423362197, Brinc Audio MP3 Lib); audio compact disk 24.95 (978-1-4233-6218-0(7), 9781423362180, Brilliance MP3) Brilliance Audio.

Collision with the Earth see Poetry & Voice of Ted Hughes

Colloquial Afrikaans Pack: The Complete Course for Beginners. Bruce C. Donaldson. (Colloquial Ser.). 2002. audio compact disk 34.95 (978-0-415-30072-8(X)) Pub: Routledge. Dist(s): Taylor and Fran

Colloquial Albanian: The Complete Course for Beginners. 2nd ed. Isa Zymberi. (Colloquial Ser.). 2004. audio compact disk 44.95 (978-0-415-30133-6(5)) Pub: Routledge. Dist(s): Taylor and Fran

Colloquial Amharic: A Complete Language Course. David L. Appleyard. (Colloquial Ser.). 2003. audio compact disk 54.95 (978-0-415-30134-3(3)) Pub: Routledge. Dist(s): Taylor and Fran

Colloquial Arabic (Levantine) Leslie McLoughlin. 2007. audio compact disk (978-0-415-45044-7(6), Rout) Tay Francis Ltd GBR.

Colloquial Arabic of Egypt. Russell McGuirk. 1 cass. (Running Time: 60 min.). 1988. bk. 14.95 (978-0-7102-0581-0(3), 05813) Routledge.

Colloquial Arabic of Egypt: The Complete Course for Beginners. 2nd rev. ed. Jane Wightwick. Frwd. by Mahmoud Gaafar. (Colloquial Ser.). 2003. audio compact disk 44.95 (978-0-415-28694-7(8)) Pub: Routledge. Dist(s): Taylor and Fran

Colloquial Arabic of the Gulf & Saudi Arabia. Clive Holes. 1 cass. (Running Time: 60 min.). 1988. bk. 15.00 (978-0-7100-9769-4(7), 97697) Routledge.

Colloquial Azerbaijani: CDs, text & reference Cards. Kurtulus Öztopçu. Voice by Farida Zamanzade. 3 CD. (Running Time: 3 hrs. 30 min.). (AZE.). 2005. audio compact disk 75.00 (978-1-57970-165-9(5), AFAZ10D) J Norton Pubs.

Colloquial Bengali. 2nd rev. ed. Mithun Nasrin & Wim Van der Wurff. (Colloquial Ser.). (BEN & ENG., 2006. ring bd. 34.95 (978-0-415-30254-8(4)) Pub: Routledge. Dist(s): Taylor and Fran

Colloquial Breton. Ian Press & Herve Ar Bihan. Frwd. by Ian Press & Herve Ar Bihan. (Colloquial Ser.). (BRE & ENG., 2003. audio compact disk 54.95 (978-0-415-30255-5(2)) Pub: Routledge. Dist(s): Taylor and Fran

Colloquial Bulgarian. George D. Papantchev. (Colloquial Ser.). (ENG & BUL., (YA). (gr. 13). 1994. 29.95 (978-0-415-07964-8(0)) Pub: Routledge. Dist(s): Taylor and Fran

Colloquial Cambodian: Complete Language Course. David Smyth. (Colloquials Ser.). 1997. bk. 44.95 (978-0-415-15538-0(X)) Pub: Routledge. Dist(s): Taylor and Fran

Colloquial Cantonese. 2nd rev. ed. Dana Scott Bourgerie. (CHI & ENG.). 2010. audio compact disk 34.95 (978-0-415-47888-5(X), Rout) Pub: Tay Francis Ltd GBR. Dist(s): Taylor and Fran

Colloquial Catalan: The Complete Course for Beginners. Alexander Ibarz. (Colloquial Ser.). (CAT., 2005. audio compact disk 34.95 (978-0-415-30256-2(0)) Pub: Routledge. Dist(s): Taylor and Fran

Colloquial Chinese. (Colloquial Ser.). (J). 1982. 29.95 (978-0-415-01855-5(2)) Pub: Routledge. Dist(s): Taylor and Fran

Colloquial Chinese. P. C. T'ung & D. E. Pollard. 1 cass. (Running Time: 60 min.). (Colloquials Ser.). (ENG & CHI.). 1988. bk. 14.95 (978-0-7100-9428-5(0), 94280, Routledge Thoemms) Routledge.

Colloquial Chinese: A Multimedia Language Course. Kan Qian. (Colloquial Ser.). 1998. cd-rom 100.00 (978-0-415-14291-5(1)) Pub: Routledge. Dist(s): Taylor and Fran

Colloquial Chinese 2 CD. Qian Kan. 2006. audio compact disk 31.95 (978-0-415-32817-3(9)) Pub: Routledge. Dist(s): Taylor and Fran

Colloquial Croatian: The Complete Course for Beginners. abr. ed. Celia Hawkesworth. Contrib. by Dragan Milovic & Ivana Jovic. (Running Time: 120 sec.). (Colloquial Ser.). (ENG, CRO & SER., 2005. audio compact disk 34.95 (978-0-415-34895-9(1), RU42433) Pub: Routledge. Dist(s): Taylor and Fran

Colloquial Danish. 2nd rev. ed. Gly W. Jones & Kirsten Gade. 3 cass. (Running Time: 5 hrs.). (Colloquial Ser.). 2003. audio compact disk 34.95 (978-0-415-30180-0(7)) Pub: Routledge. Dist(s): Taylor and Fran

Colloquial Dutch: A Complete Language Course. 2nd rev. ed. Bruce Donaldson. (DUT & ENG., 2008. audio compact disk 34.95 (978-0-415-43575-8(7)) Pub: Routledge. Dist(s): Taylor and Fran

Colloquial Dutch 2: The Next Step in Language Learning. 2nd ed. Bruce Donaldson & Gerda Bodegom. Contrib. by Sicco E. Heyligers et al. (Colloquial 2 Ser.). (ENG & DUT., 2005. audio compact disk 27.95 (978-0-415-31075-8(X)) Pub: Routledge. Dist(s): Taylor and Fran

Colloquial English: The Complete Course for Beginners. Gary King & Gareth King. (Colloquial Ser.). 2005. bk. 34.95 (978-0-415-29952-7(7)) Pub: Routledge. Dist(s): Taylor and Fran

Colloquial Estonian. 2nd rev. ed. Christo Moseley. (EST & ENG., 2008. audio compact disk 34.95 (978-0-415-45289-2(9)) Pub: Routledge. Dist(s): Taylor and Fran

Colloquial Filipino CDs. Teresita V. Ramos & Ruth Mabanglo. (Colloquial Ser.). 2006. audio compact disk 28.95 (978-0-415-30613-3(2)) Pub: Routledge. Dist(s): Taylor and Fran

***Colloquial Finnish.** 2nd ed. Daniel Abondolo. (ENG.). 2010. audio compact disk 34.95 (978-0-415-48627-9(0)) Pub: Routledge. Dist(s): Taylor and Fran

Colloquial Finnish: The Complete Course for Beginners. Daniel M. Abondolo. (Colloquial Ser.). 2003. bk. 34.95 (978-0-415-28689-3(1)) Pub: Routledge. Dist(s): Taylor and Fran

Colloquial French. 3rd rev. ed. Valérie Demouy & Alan Moys. (Colloquial Ser.). (ENG & FRE., 2006. 21.95 (978-0-415-34015-1(2), RU0152X) Pub: Routledge. Dist(s): Taylor and Fran

Colloquial French: A Multimedia Language Course. Alan Moys. (Colloquial Ser.). 1998. cd-rom 95.00 (978-0-415-14290-8(3)) Pub: Routledge. Dist(s): Taylor and Fran

Colloquial French: The Complete Course for Beginners. 2nd rev. ed. Alan Moys & Valerie Demouy. Contrib. by Yves Aubert. (Colloquial Ser.). (ENG & FRE., 2006. 21.95 (978-0-415-34014-4(4), RU0144X) Pub: Routledge. Dist(s): Taylor and Fran

Colloquial French 2. Elspeth Broady. (Colloquial Ser.). (ENG & FRE., 2003. audio compact disk 23.95 (978-0-415-30257-9(9)) Pub: Routledge. Dist(s): Taylor and Fran

Colloquial German 2 CD. 2nd ed. HOFFGEN. 2010. cd-rom 32.95 (978-0-415-30258-6(7)) Pub: Routledge. Dist(s): Taylor and Fran

Colloquial Greek: The Complete Course for Beginners. 2nd rev. ed. Niki Watts. (Colloquial Ser.). (ENG & GRE., 2004. audio compact disk 34.95 (978-0-415-32512-7(9)) Pub: Routledge. Dist(s): Taylor and Fran

Colloquial Gujarati. Jagdish Dave. 2007. audio compact disk 44.95 (978-0-415-44944-1(8)) Pub: Routledge. Dist(s): Taylor and Fran

Colloquial Hausa. Malami Buba. (ENG.). 2009. audio compact disk 44.95 (978-0-415-45882-5(X)) Pub: Routledge. Dist(s): Taylor and Fran

Colloquial Hebrew. Tamar Wang. Frwd. by Zippi Lyttleton. (Colloquial Ser.). (ENG & HEB., 2003. audio compact disk 34.95 (978-0-415-30260-9(9)) Pub: Routledge. Dist(s): Taylor and Fran

***Colloquial Hebrew.** 2nd rev. ed. Zippi Lyttleton. (ENG.). 2010. audio compact disk 34.95 (978-0-415-61798-7(7)) Pub: Routledge. Dist(s): Taylor and Fran

Colloquial Hindi: The Complete Course for Beginners. 2nd rev. ed. Tej K. Bhatia. Contrib. by Anjali Ahuja et al. (Colloquial Ser.). (HIN & ENG., 2008. audio compact disk 34.95 (978-0-415-39528-1(3)) Pub: Routledge. Dist(s): Taylor and Fran

Colloquial Hindi, 2e. Bhatia. 2006. (978-0-415-39529-8(1), Rout) Tay Francis Ltd GBR.

Colloquial Hungarian. Jerry Payne. (Colloquials Ser.). (ENG & HUN., 1987. 15.95 (978-0-7102-0984-9(3), 09843, Routledge Thoemms) Routledge.

Colloquial Hungarian. 2nd rev. ed. Erika Solyom & Carol Rounds. (Colloquial Ser.). (ENG & HUN., (YA). (gr. 13). 2002. audio compact disk 34.95 (978-0-415-28829-3(0)) Pub: Routledge. Dist(s): Taylor and Fran

***Colloquial Hungarian: The Complete Course for Beginners.** 3rd rev. ed. Carol Rounds & Erika SÃ³lyom. 2011. audio compact disk 44.95 (978-0-415-56742-8(4)) Pub: Routledge. Dist(s): Taylor and Fran

Colloquial Icelandic: The Complete Course for Beginners. Daisy Neijmann. (Colloquial Ser.). (ICE & ENG., 2001. bk. 25.95 (978-0-415-20707-2(X)) Pub: Routledge. Dist(s): Taylor and Fran

Colloquial Icelandic: The Complete Course for Beginners. Daisy Neijmann. (Colloquial Ser.). (ICE & ENG., 2002. audio compact disk 34.95 (978-0-415-28690-9(5)) Pub: Routledge. Dist(s): Taylor and Fran

Colloquial Indonesian. Sutanto Atmosumarto. (Colloquial Ser.). 2003. audio compact disk 44.95 (978-0-415-30161-9(0)) Pub: Routledge. Dist(s): Taylor and Fran

Colloquial Indonesian CDs, text & reference Cards. Tony Lapsley. 3 CDs. (Running Time: 2 hrs. 30 mins.). Orig. Title: Survival Indonesian. (IND.). 2005. audio compact disk 75.00 (978-1-57970-259-5(7), AFIN10D, Audio-For) J Norton Pubs.
This mini-course in colloquial Indonesian features basic vocabulary on a variety of practical topics, such as introductions, food and drink, accommodations, money, communications, transportation, key words, and questions. The reference cards help reinforce newly acquired vocabulary.

Colloquial Irish: The Complete Course for Beginners. Thomas Ihde et al. (ENG., 2008. audio compact disk 34.95 (978-0-415-38131-4(2)) Pub: Routledge. Dist(s): Taylor and Fran

Colloquial Italian. 2nd rev. ed. Sylvia Lymbery. (Colloquial Ser.). (ENG & ITA., 2005. audio compact disk 20.95 (978-0-415-36270-2(9)) Pub: Routledge. Dist(s): Taylor and Fran

Colloquial Italian 2. Sylvia Lymbery & Sandra Silipo. (Colloquial Ser.). (ENG & ITA., 2003. audio compact disk 23.95 (978-0-415-28157-7(1)) Pub: Routledge. Dist(s): Taylor and Fran

Colloquial Japanese: The Complete Course for Beginners. 2nd rev. ed. H. D. B. Clarke & Motoko Hamamura. (Colloquial Ser.). (YA). (gr. 13). 2003. 22.95 (978-0-415-19479-2(2)) Pub: Routledge. Dist(s): Taylor and Fran

Colloquial Japanese: The Complete Course for Beginners. 2nd rev. ed. Motoko Hamamura. Ed. by H. D. B. Clarke. (Colloquial Ser.). (YA). (gr. 13). 2003. audio compact disk 34.95 (978-0-415-27911-6(9)) Pub: Routledge. Dist(s): Taylor and Fran

Colloquial Kazakh CDs, text & reference Cards. Kurtulus Öztopçu. Voice by Zhoumagaly Abuov & Sawliye Tajibayeva. 3 CDs. (Running Time: 3 hrs. 25 mins.). (KAZ.). 2005. audio compact disk 75.00 (978-1-57970-134-5(5), AFKA10D) J Norton Pubs.

Colloquial Korean. Andrew Inseok-Kim. (Colloquial Ser.). (VIE., 2003. audio compact disk 34.95 (978-0-415-28691-6(3)) Pub: Routledge. Dist(s): Taylor and Fran

Colloquial Korean. 2nd rev. ed. Kim In-Seok & Danielle Ooyoung Pyun. (ENG & KOR., 2009. audio compact disk 34.95 (978-0-415-44479-8(9)) Pub: Routledge. Dist(s): Taylor and Fran

Colloquial Latvian: A Complete Language Course. Christopher Moseley. (Colloquial Ser.). 2002. audio compact disk 44.95 (978-0-415-28687-9(5)) Pub: Routledge. Dist(s): Taylor and Fran

Colloquial Latvian: The Complete Course for Beginners. 2nd rev. ed. Ed. by Christopher Moseley. 2009. 44.95 (978-0-415-45807-8(2)) Pub: Routledge. Dist(s): Taylor and Fran

Colloquial Lithuanian: A Complete Language Course. Ian Press & Meilute Ramoniene. (Colloquial Ser.). 1996. audio compact disk 44.95 (978-0-415-28684-8(0)) Pub: Routledge. Dist(s): Taylor and Fran

Colloquial Malay: Book & Reference Cards. Tony Lapsley. 3 CDs. (Running Time: 2 hrs. 30 min.). (MAY.). 2005. audio compact disk 75.00 (978-1-57970-135-2(3), AFMA20D) J Norton Pubs.

Colloquial Malay CD. Zaharah Othman & Sutanto Atmosumarto. (Colloquial Ser.). 2005. audio compact disk 44.95 (978-0-415-30163-3(7)) Pub: Routledge. Dist(s): Taylor and Fran

Colloquial Mongolian: The Complete Course for Beginners. Alan J. K. Sanders & Jantsangiyn Bat-Ireedui. (Colloquial Ser.). 2002. audio compact disk 54.95 (978-0-415-28949-8(1)) Pub: Routledge. Dist(s): Taylor and Fran

***Colloquial Norwegian.** 2nd rev. ed. Torunn Strand Andresen et al. (ENG.). 2013. audio compact disk 26.95 (978-0-415-48626-2(2), Rout) Pub: Tay Francis Ltd GBR. Dist(s): Taylor and Fran

Colloquial Norwegian: A Complete Language Course. Kari Bratveit et al. (Colloquial Ser.). 2002. audio compact disk 34.95 (978-0-415-28685-5(9)) Pub: Routledge. Dist(s): Taylor and Fran

Colloquial Panjabi. Bhardwaj. 2007. audio compact disk 44.95 (978-0-415-43945-9(0)) Pub: Routledge. Dist(s): Taylor and Fran

***Colloquial Persian.** 2nd ed. Abdi Rafiee. (PER & ENG.). 2010. audio compact disk 44.95 (978-0-415-56046-7(2)) Pub: Routledge. Dist(s): Taylor and Fran

Colloquial Persian: The Complete Course for Beginners. 2nd rev. ed. Abdi Rafiee. (Colloquial Ser.). 2002. audio compact disk 44.95 (978-0-415-28907-8(6)) Pub: Routledge. Dist(s): Taylor and Fran

Colloquial Portuguese: A Complete Language Course. 2nd rev. ed. João Sampaio & Barbara McIntyre. (Colloquial Ser.). 2002. audio compact disk 34.95 (978-0-415-27776-1(0)) Pub: Routledge. Dist(s): Taylor and Fran

Colloquial Portuguese: A Multimedia Language Course. Barbara McIntyre & Joao Sampaio. (Colloquial Ser.). 1998. cd-rom 95.00 (978-0-415-14289-2(X)) Pub: Routledge. Dist(s): Taylor and Fran

Colloquial Portuguese of Brazil: The Complete Course for Beginners. 2nd rev. ed. Esmenia Simões Osborne et al. (Colloquial Ser.). (POR & ENG., 2002. audio compact disk 34.95 (978-0-415-28090-7(7)) Pub: Routledge. Dist(s): Taylor and Fran

Colloquial Portuguese of Brazil 2. Esmenia S. Osborne. Ed. by Barbara McIntyre. (Colloquial Ser.). (POR & ENG., 2008. audio compact disk 26.95 (978-0-415-43099-9(2)) Pub: Routledge. Dist(s): Taylor and Fran

Colloquial Romanian. 3rd rev. ed. Dennis Deletant & Ramona Gönczöl-Davies. (Colloquial Ser.). (ENG & RUM., (YA). (gr. 13). 2002. audio compact disk 34.95 (978-0-415-28803-3(7)) Pub: Routledge. Dist(s): Taylor and Fran

***Colloquial Romanian: A Complete Language Course.** 4th rev. ed. Ramona Gonczol & Dennis Deletant. (Colloquial Ser.). (ENG.). 2010. audio compact disk 34.95 (978-0-415-54953-0(1)) Pub: Routledge. Dist(s): Taylor and Fran

Colloquial Russian. Svetlana Le Fleming & Susan E. Kay. (Colloquial Ser.). 1995. audio compact disk 26.95 (978-0-415-12683-0(5)) Pub: Routledge. Dist(s): Taylor and Fran

Colloquial Russian: The Complete Course for Beginners. 3rd ed. Svetlana Le Fleming & Susan E. Kay. (Colloquial Ser.). (RUS & ENG., 2009. 34.95 (978-0-415-48629-3(7)) Pub: Routledge. Dist(s): Taylor and Fran

Colloquial Russian 2: The Next Step in Language Learning. Svetlana Le Fleming & Susan E. Kay. (Colloquial Ser.). 2003. bk. 25.95 (978-0-415-30250-0(1)) Pub: Routledge. Dist(s): Taylor and Fran

Colloquial Scottish Gaelic: The Complete Course for Beginners. Katherine M. Spadaro & Katie Graham. (Colloquial Ser.). 2002. audio compact disk 34.95 (978-0-415-28692-3(1)) Pub: Routledge. Dist(s): Taylor and Fran

Colloquial Serbian: The Complete Course for Beginners. Celia Hawkesworth & Jelena Calic. (Colloquial Ser.). 2006. audio compact disk 34.95 (978-0-415-34891-1(9), RU42429) Pub: Routledge. Dist(s): Taylor and Fran

Colloquial Slovak. James Naughton. (Colloquial Ser.). 1997. 29.95 (978-0-415-11541-4(8)) Pub: Routledge. Dist(s): Taylor and Fran

Colloquial Slovak. James Naughton. (Colloquial Ser.). (SLO.). 2003. audio compact disk 44.95 (978-0-415-30490-0(3)) Pub: Routledge. Dist(s): Taylor and Fran

Colloquial Slovene. Andrea Albretti. (Colloquial Ser.). 2003. audio compact disk 34.95 (978-0-415-30491-7(1)) Pub: Routledge. Dist(s): Taylor and Fran

Colloquial Somali. Orwin. 2007. audio compact disk 54.95 (978-0-415-45270-0(8)) Pub: Routledge. Dist(s): Taylor and Fran

Colloquial Spanish: A Multimedia Language Course. Untza Oatala Alday. (Colloquial Ser.). 1998. cd-rom 95.00 (978-0-415-14195-6(8)) Pub: Routledge. Dist(s): Taylor and Fran

Colloquial Spanish of Latin America. 2nd ed. Roberto Rodriquez-Saona. (Colloquial Ser.). (ENG & SPA., 2003. audio compact disk 34.95 (978-0-415-30049-0(5)) Pub: Routledge. Dist(s): Taylor and Fran

Colloquial Spanish of Latin America: The Complete Course for Beginners. 2nd rev. ed. Roberto Rodriquez-Saona. (Colloquial Ser.). (ENG & SPA., 2001. 25.95 (978-0-415-23787-1(4)) Pub: Routledge. Dist(s): Taylor and Fran

Colloquial Spanish of Latin America: The Next Step in Language Learning, Vol. 2. Roberto Rodriquez-Saona. (Colloquial 2 Ser.). (ENG & SPA., 2005. audio compact disk 30.95 (978-0-415-28198-0(9)) Pub: Routledge. Dist(s): Taylor and Fran

Colloquial Spanish 2: The Next Step in Language Learning. 2nd ed. Untza Otaola Alday. (Colloquial 2 Ser.). (ENG & SPA., 2003. audio compact disk 23.95 (978-0-415-30262-3(5)) Pub: Routledge. Dist(s): Taylor and Fran

Colloquial Swahili: The Complete Course for Beginners. Lutz Marten & Donovan McGrath. Contrib. by Gareth King et al. (Running Time: 20160 sec.). (Colloquial Ser.). (SWA.). 2003. audio compact disk 44.95 (978-0-415-28947-4(5)) Pub: Routledge. Dist(s): Taylor and Fran

Colloquial Swedish. 3rd rev. ed. Gunilla Serin et al. (Colloquial Ser.). (SWE & ENG., 2006. audio compact disk 34.95 (978-0-415-36273-3(3)) Pub: Routledge. Dist(s): Taylor and Fran

Colloquial Swedish: The Complete Course for Beginners. 2nd ed. Philip Holmes & Gunilla Serin. (Colloquial Ser.). (C). 2003. audio compact disk 26.95 (978-0-415-30493-1(8)) Pub: Routledge. Dist(s): Tay Francis Ltd

Colloquial Tamil: The Complete Course for Beginners. R. E. Asher & E. Annamalai. (Colloquial Ser.). (TAM & ENG., 2002. bk. 44.95 (978-0-415-27677-1(2)) Pub: Routledge. Dist(s): Taylor and Fran

***Colloquial Tamil: The Complete Course for Beginners.** 2nd rev. ed. E. Annamalai & R. E. Asher. (ENG.). 2012. audio compact disk 44.95 (978-0-415-61952-3(1)) Pub: Routledge. Dist(s): Taylor and Fran

Colloquial Thai: The Complete Course for Beginners. 2nd rev. abr. ed. John Moore & Saowalak Rodchue. Contrib. by Anukul Kosanantachai et al. (Colloquial Ser.). 2005. audio compact disk 34.95 (978-0-415-32979-8(5)) Pub: Routledge. Dist(s): Taylor and Fran

Colloquial Turkish: The Complete Course for Beginners. 2nd rev. ed. Ad Backus & Jeroen Aarssen. (Colloquial Ser.). (TUR., 2003. audio compact disk 34.95 (978-0-415-30494-8(6)) Pub: Routledge. Dist(s): Taylor and Fran

Colloquial Ukrainian. Ian Press. Ed. by Stefan Pugh. (Colloquial Ser.). 2003. bk. 44.95 (978-0-415-30495-5(4)) Pub: Routledge. Dist(s): Taylor and Fran

Colloquial Ukrainian. Ian Press. Ed. by Stefan Pugh. (Colloquial Ser.). 1994. 31.95 (978-0-415-09203-6(5)) Pub: Routledge. Dist(s): Taylor and Fran

Colloquial Urdu: The Complete Course for Beginners. Tej K. Bhatia & Ashok Koul. 2006. audio compact disk 34.95 (978-0-415-28950-4(5)) Pub: Routledge. Dist(s): Taylor and Fran

Colloquial Uzbek: CDs, text & reference Cards. Kurtulus Öztopçu. Voice by Komron Khakimov. 4 CDs. (Running Time: 4 hrs.). (UZB.). 2005. audio compact disk 75.00 (978-1-57970-217-5(1), AFUZ10D) J Norton Pubs.

Colloquial Vietnamese: Complete Language Course. John Moore & Tuan D. Vuong. (Colloquials Ser.). 1997. bk. 44.95 (978-0-415-15536-6(3)) Pub: Routledge. Dist(s): Taylor and Fran

Colloquial Yoruba CD. SCHLEICHER. (Colloquial Ser.). (YOR & ENG.). 2007. audio compact disk 44.95 (978-0-415-70059-7(0)) Taylor and Fran.

***Colloquial Zulu.** Audrey Mbeje. 2010. audio compact disk 24.95 (978-0-415-49748-0(5)) Pub: Routledge. Dist(s): Taylor and Fran

Colloquial Bulgarian: The Complete Course for Beginners. 2nd rev. ed. Yovka Tisheva & Kjetil Ra Hauge. Contrib. by Valentin Borissov. (Colloquial Ser.). (BUL & ENG., 2006. audio compact disk 34.95 (978-0-415-31623-1(5), RU6235X) Pub: Routledge. Dist(s): Taylor and Fran

Colomba, Set. Prosper Merimee. Read by C. Truche. 2 cass. (FRE.). 1991. 26.95 (1086-VSL) Olivia & Hill.

The story of a vendetta & of an inner conflict. Merimee's passionate character Orsa Antonia della Rebbia is torn between his "continental" education & his Corsican instinct. He is forced to choose between the woman he loves & a sister eager for vengeance.

Colombia & Its Satellite Countries. unabr. ed. Joseph Stromberg. Read by Richard C. Hottlet. Ed. by Wendy McElroy. 2 cass. (Running Time: 3 hrs.). Dramatization. (World's Political Hot Spots Ser.). (YA). (gr. 11 up). 1992. 17.95 (978-0-938935-49-0(6), 10367) Knowledge Prod.

Colombia in the 1980s became known for its role in the illegal drug trade, & for political instability & violence caused by this problem. But much of this is a recent development in Colombia's history that began in the 1530s, when Spain conquered local Indian kingdoms.

Colombia & Panama. unabr. ed. Joseph Stromberg. Read by Richard C. Hottelet. (Running Time: 10800 sec.). (World's Political Hot Spots Ser.). 2006. audio compact disk 25.95 (978-0-7861-6443-1(3)) Pub: Blckstn Audio. Dist(s): NetLibrary CO

Colombian Mule. unabr. ed. Massimo Carlotto. 4 cass. (Running Time: 5 hrs. 33 mins.). (Isis Cassettes Ser.). (J). 2005. 44.95 (978-0-7531-2146-7(8)) Pub: ISIS Lrg Prnt GBR. Dist(s): Ulverscroft US

Colon & Rectal Surgery. (Postgraduate Programs Ser.: C85-PG12). 45.00 (8522) Am Coll Surgeons.

Covers concepts in the management of an array of clinical problems encountered by surgeons dealing with the colon, rectum & perineum. 6 hours CME category 1 credit.

Colon & Rectal Surgery. (Postgraduate Programs Ser.: C84-PG12). 1984. 45.00 (8492) Am Coll Surgeons.

Describes current methods of evaluation & treatment of certain disease process affecting the colon & rectum. 6 hours CME category 1 credit.

Colon & Rectal Surgery. Moderated by Lee E. Smith. (Postgraduate Courses Ser.: C86-PG12). 1986. 57.00 (8622) Am Coll Surgeons.

Examines methods for the newly demanded ambulatory surgery for anorectal disease, reviews specific pathologic entities, presents operative emergencies of colon & rectal surgery, & reviews the status of ileoanal pouch pull. 6 hours CME credit.

Colon Cancer Survivors' Guide: Living Stronger, Longer. Curtis Pesmen. 2006. audio compact disk 17.95 (978-0-9661847-9-2(3)) Pub: Tatra Pr. Dist(s): Natl Bk Netwk

Colonel. unabr. ed. Patrick A. Davis. Read by Robert Lawrence. 6 cass. (Running Time: 9 hrs.). 2001. 29.95 (978-1-58788-414-6(3), 1587884143, BAU) Brilliance Audio.

A former Air Force investigator comes out of retirement to find a killer, only to discover a massive government cover-up. Retired Air Force investigator Martin Collins lives a quiet life in rural Virginia, working as a local chief of police and consulting on military homicides. When he's called in to assist on a grisly triple murder, nothing can prepare him for the crime scene: Colonel Margaret Wildman and her two young children, their throats slashed, left to die in pools of their own blood. At first, there seems to be no motive for the murders. But as Collins digs through an increasingly puzzling maze of clues, he reveals a secret that leads to the highest levels of the government - and the military. Buried files reveal a link between Colonel Wildman and series of fatal airline crashes; political pressure to keep a secret grows, as does the body count. Collins finds his own life jeopardized as he closes in on the truth, culminating in a shocking confrontation on the floors of Congress.

Colonel. unabr. ed. Patrick A. Davis. Read by Robert Lawrence. (Running Time: 9 hrs.). 2004. 39.25 (978-1-59335-566-1(1), 1593355661, Brlnc Audio MP3 Lib) Brilliance Audio.

Colonel. unabr. ed. Patrick A. Davis. Read by Robert Lawrence. (Running Time: 9 hrs.). 2004. 39.25 (978-1-59710-149-3(4), 1597101494, BADLE); 24.95 (978-1-59710-148-6(6), 1597101486, BAD) Brilliance Audio.

Colonel. unabr. ed. Patrick A. Davis. Read by Robert Lawrence. (Running Time: 9 hrs.). 2004. 24.95 (978-1-59335-052-9(X), 159335052X) Soulmate Audio Bks.

Colonel & Little Missie: Buffalo Bill, Annie Oakley, & the Beginnings of Superstardom in America. unabr. ed. Larry McMurtry. Narrated by Michael Prichard. (Running Time: 7 hrs. 30 mins. 0 sec.). (ENG.). 2005. audio compact disk 19.99 (978-1-4001-5163-9(5)) Pub: Tantor Media. Dist(s): IngramPubServ

Colonel & Little Missie: Buffalo Bill, Annie Oakley, & the Beginnings of Superstardom in America. unabr. ed. Larry McMurtry. Read by Michael Prichard. 6 cds. (Running Time: 7 hrs. 30 mins. 0 sec.). (ENG.). 2005. audio compact disk 59.99 (978-1-4001-3163-1(4)); audio compact disk 29.99 (978-1-4001-0163-4(8)) Pub: Tantor Media. Dist(s): IngramPubServ

Colonel Chabert, Set. Honoré de Balzac. 2 cass. (FRE.). 1995. 26.95 (1765-VSL) Olivia & Hill.

One day, a Paris lawyer is visited by a poor old man who claims to be Colonel Chabert, a man assumed to have been killed ten years earlier at the battle of Eylau. Read by a cast of actors.

***Colonel Roosevelt.** unabr. ed. Edmund Morris. Read by Mark Deakins. (Running Time: 24 hrs. 30 mins.). (ENG.). 2010. audio compact disk 50.00 (978-0-307-75040-2(X), Random AudioBks) Pub: Random Audio Pubg. Dist(s): Random

Colonel Starbottle's Client. Bret Harte. Read by John Bolen. (Running Time: 5 hrs. 36 mins.). 2001. 25.95 (978-1-60083-604-6(6), Audiofy Corp) Iofy Corp.

Colonel Starbottle's Client. unabr. ed. Bret Harte. Narrated by John Bolen. 5 CDs. (Running Time: 5 hrs. 40 mins.). (ENG.). 2001. audio compact disk 33.00 (978-1-4001-0032-3(1)); audio compact disk 20.00 (978-1-4001-5032-8(9)) Pub: Tantor Media. Dist(s): IngramPubServ

Colonel Starbottle's Client. unabr. ed. Bret Harte. Narrated by John Bolen. (Running Time: 5 hrs. 30 mins. 0 sec.). (ENG.). 2008. 19.99 (978-1-4001-5856-0(7)); audio compact disk 22.99 (978-1-4001-0856-5(X)); audio compact disk 45.99 (978-1-4001-3856-2(6)) Pub: Tantor Media. Dist(s): IngramPubServ

Colonel Sun. unabr. ed. Robert Markham. Read by Robert Whitfield. Contrib. by Kingsley Amis. 6 CDs. (Running Time: 7 hrs.). 2001. audio compact disk 48.00 (978-0-7861-9692-0(0), 2837) Blckstn Audio.

James Bond is enjoying a convivial round of golf at Sunningdale when the news comes in: M has been kidnapped. The violence has been extreme. M's servants are dead, coldly shot down without mercy. And on a deceptively calm Greek island, a most ungenial colonel Sun is waiting to welcome Bond to a new game. To be played without rules. To be played to the death.

Colonel Sun. unabr. ed. Robert Markham. Read by Robert Whitfield. Created by Kingsley Amis. 5 cass. (Running Time: 7 hrs.). 2001. 39.95 (978-0-7861-2076-5(2), 2837) Blckstn Audio.

Colonels. W. E. B. Griffin. Read by Michael Russotto. 13 cass. (Running Time: 19 hrs. 30 min.). (Brotherhood of War Ser.: No. 4). 1995. 104.00 (3673) Books on Tape.

In Indochina, in Greece, in Korea & in the mine covered European terrain, they were the men who were chiseled into fighting professionals. Now, as a decade flickers to an end, they must return to the States to sculpt a new kind of soldier, one that's rigorously tested in a new, simmering war.

Colonels. unabr. collector's ed. W. E. B. Griffin. Read by Michael Russotto. 13 cass. (Running Time: 19 hrs. 30 mins.). (Brotherhood of War Ser.: No. 4). 1995. 104.00 (978-0-7366-2982-9(3), 3673) Books on Tape.

Hardened soldiers return to the U.S. to command soldiers in a new kind of war. Authentic & vivid war life.

Colonel's Lady & No Man's Gun: Unabr[illegible] Stories from the Tonto Woman & Other Western Stories. ab[illegible] Elmore Leonard. 2004. 5.95 (978-0-7435-4671-3(7)) Pub: S&S Audio. Dist(s): S and S Inc

Colonial & Revolution Songbook: With Historical Commentary. Keith McNeil & Rusty McNeil. Read by Keith McNeil & Rusty McNeil. (YA). (gr. 4 up). 1996. bk. 32.95 (978-1-878360-16-8(7)); pap. bk. 29.95 (978-1-878360-17-5(5)) WEM Records.

Forty songs which accompanied the shaping of the country as it evolved from thirteen struggling colonies to prosperity & rebellion, & finally, to nationhood.

Colonial & Revolution Songs: With Historical Narration. Keith McNeil & Rusty McNeil. Read by Keith McNeil & Rusty McNeil. (American History Through Folksong Ser.). (YA). (gr. 4 up). 1996. audio compact disk 22.95 (978-1-878360-09-0(4)) WEM Records.

Colonial & Revolution Songs: With Historical Narration, Set. Keith McNeil & Rusty McNeil. Read by Keith McNeil & Rusty McNeil. 2 cass. (Running Time: 2 hrs.). (American History Through Folksong Ser.). (J). (gr. 4 up). 1989. 19.95 (978-1-878360-01-4(9), 503C) WEM Records.

Colonial Experience 1607-1774. unabr. ed. Clarence B. Carson. (Running Time: 28800 sec.). (Basic History of the United States Ser.). 2007. audio compact disk 29.95 (978-0-7861-6013-6(6)); audio compact disk 63.00 (978-0-7861-6012-9(8)) Blckstn Audio.

Colonial Fair. 1 cass. (Running Time: 56 mins.). (J). (gr. 3-7). 1999. 10.00 (978-0-9672927-1-7(9)); audio compact disk 15.00 (978-0-9672927-0-0(0)) Coastline Music.

A brief introduction tells a story about three people who meet musicians, dancers, fortune-tellers & others while traveling to an eighteenth-century country fair. 23 songs, stories & riddles are boisterously presented by male & female singers with musical accompaniment by historic instruments, including the unusual glass armonica. Includes such familiar nursery rhymes as "Old King Cole," "Three Blind Mice" & "Simple Simon," as well as folk songs "Michael Finnigin" & "Lavender's Blue.".

Colonies. unabr. ed. Ed. by Linda Spizzirri. 48 cass. (Running Time: 15 min.). Dramatization. (Educational Coloring Book & Cassette Package Ser.). (J). (gr. k-8). 1989. pap. bk. 6.95 (978-0-86545-150-6(8)) Spizzirri.

Explores the beginnings of America.

***Colonization: Down to Earth.** unabr. ed. Harry Turtledove. Narrated by Patrick G. Lawlor. (Running Time: 28 hrs. 30 mins. 0 sec.). (Colonization Ser.). (ENG.). 2010. audio compact disk 119.99 (978-1-4001-4399-3(3)) Pub: Tantor Media. Dist(s): IngramPubServ

***Colonization: Aftershocks.** unabr. ed. Harry Turtledove. Narrated by Patrick Lawlor. (Running Time: 28 hrs. 30 mins. 0 sec.). (Colonization Ser.). (ENG.). 2010. 39.99 (978-1-4001-6400-4(1)); 28.99 (978-1-4001-8400-2(2)); audio compact disk 59.99 (978-1-4001-1400-9(4)) Pub: Tantor Media. Dist(s): IngramPubServ

***Colonization: down to Earth.** unabr. ed. Harry Turtledove. Narrated by Patrick G. Lawlor. (Running Time: 26 hrs. 30 mins.). (Colonization Ser.). 2010. 28.99 (978-1-4001-8399-9(5)) Tantor Media.

***Colonization: down to Earth.** unabr. ed. Harry Turtledove. Narrated by Patrick G. Lawlor. (Running Time: 28 hrs. 30 mins. 0 sec.). (Colonization Ser.). (ENG.). 2010. 39.99 (978-1-4001-6399-1(4)); audio compact disk 59.99 (978-1-4001-1399-6(7)) Pub: Tantor Media. Dist(s): IngramPubServ

***Colonization: Second Contact.** unabr. ed. Harry Turtledove. Narrated by Patrick G. Lawlor. (Running Time: 25 hrs. 0 mins.). (Colonization Ser.). 2010. 27.99 (978-1-4001-8398-2(7)) Tantor Media.

***Colonization: Second Contact.** unabr. ed. Harry Turtledove. Narrated by Patrick G. Lawlor. (Running Time: 28 hrs. 0 mins. 0 sec.). (Colonization Ser.). (ENG.). 2010. 39.99 (978-1-4001-6398-4(6)); audio compact disk 54.99 (978-1-4001-1398-9(9)) Pub: Tantor Media. Dist(s): IngramPubServ

Colonoscopy for Surgeons. Moderated by Gerald Marks. 2 cass. (Colon & Rectal Surgery Ser.: CR-1). 1986. 19.00 (8636) Am Coll Surgeons.

Colony. unabr. ed. Anne Rivers Siddons. Narrated by Sally Darling & Alyssa Bresnahan. 16 cass. (Running Time: 23 hrs. 30 mins.). 1999. 128.00 (978-1-55690-867-5(9), 93309E7) Recorded Bks.

A summer colony in Maine, where for generations the same wealthy families have come to spend the season, is the setting for a woman's story of love, tragedy & rebirth.

Colony: The Harrowing True Story of the Exiles of Molokai. unabr. ed. John Tayman. Read by Simon Vance. 13 CDs. (Running Time: 15 hrs. 30 mins. 0 sec.). (ENG.). 2006. audio compact disk 79.99 (978-1-4001-3227-0(4)) Pub: Tantor Media. Dist(s): IngramPubServ

In 1866, twelve men and women and one small child were forced aboard a leaky schooner and cast away to a natural prison on the Hawaiian island of Molokai. Two weeks later, a dozen others were exiled, and then forty more, and then a hundred more. Tracked by bounty hunters and torn screaming from their families, the luckless were loaded into shipboard cattle stalls and abandoned in a lawless place where brutality held sway. Many did not have leprosy, and most of those who did were not contagious, yet all were caught in a shared nightmare. The colony had little food, little medicine, and very little hope. Exile continued for more than a century, the longest and deadliest instance of medical segregation in American history. Nearly nine thousand people were banished to the colony, trapped by pounding surf and armed guards and the highest sea cliffs in the world. Twenty-eight live there still. John Tayman tells the fantastic saga of this horrible and hopeful place - at one time the most famous community in the world - and of the individuals involved. The narrative is peopled by presidents and kings, cruel lawmen and pioneering doctors, and brave souls who literally gave their lives to help. A stunning cast includes the martyred Father Damien, Robert Louis Stevenson, Jack London, Mark Twain, Teddy Roosevelt, John Wayne, and more. The result is a searing tale of survival and bravery, and a testament to the power of faith, compassion, and heroism.

Colony: The Harrowing True Story of the Exiles of Molokai. unabr. ed. John Tayman. Read by Simon Vance. (Running Time: 15 hrs. 30 mins. 0 sec.). (ENG.). 2006. audio compact disk 39.99 (978-1-4001-0227-3(8)) Pub: Tantor Media. Dist(s): IngramPubServ

Colony: The Harrowing True Story of the Exiles of Molokai. unabr. ed. John Tayman. Read by Simon Vance & Patrick G. Lawlor. (Running Time: 15 hrs. 30 mins. 0 sec.). (ENG.). 2006. audio compact disk 29.99 (978-1-4001-5227-8(5)) Pub: Tantor Media. Dist(s): IngramPubServ

***Colony Adventures: Exploring the Park, no. 1.** David M. Smuin. Perf. by David M. Smuin. Perf. by Angela M. Smuin. Contrib. by Angela M. Smuin. 1. (ENG.). 2010. audio compact disk 11.95 (978-0-9830983-0-0(1)) Faith Counsel.

***Colony Low Price.** abr. ed. Anne Rivers Siddons. Read by Judith Ivey. (ENG.). 2006. (978-0-06-087928-0(9), Harper Audio); (978-0-06-087929-7(7), Harper Audio) HarperCollins Pubs.

Colony of Cats see Pied Piper

Color & Shading in the Rorschach Test. unabr. ed. Samuel J. Beck. 1 cass. (Running Time: 25 min.). 1967. 12.95 (29238) J Norton Pubs.
An interpretation of color & shading response in the Rorschach phenomenon.

***Color at Forty-Mile.** Tim Champlin. 2009. (978-1-60136-428-9(8)) Audio Holding.

Color Atlas & Synopsis of Clinical Dermatology. 3rd ed. Thomas B. Fitzpatrick. 1997. 89.00 (978-0-07-852969-6(7), M-H Apple & Lange) McGraw-Hill Prof.

Color Atlas of the Autopsy. Wagner Scott A. 2004. audio compact disk 259.95 (978-0-8493-3059-9(9), 3059) Taylor and Fran.

Color Breathing. unabr. ed. Robert A. Monroe. Read by Robert A. Monroe. (Running Time: 45 min.). (Gateway Experience - Threshold Ser.). 1983. 14.95 (978-1-56113-259-1(4)) Monroe Institute.
Link mind & body to recharge, heal & balance.

Color Breathing & Affirmations. Joyce Morris. Music by Will Morris. 1 cass. (Running Time: 45 min.). (978-1-888196-02-3(5)) Ctr Bkstore.
Accompanied by soothing music by Will Morris, Reiki Master Teacher Joyce Morris helps you to get "in the pink" with her guided visualization & affirmations. They are skillfully & lovingly designed to help you get rid of disease & replace it with perfect health in your body as well as in your relationships with others & your outlook on life. Side two contains a subliminal version of side one, with music to soothe you.

Color Healing. unabr. ed. Judith L. Powell. 1 cass. (Running Time: 40 min.). (Powell Life Improvement Programs Ser.). 1987. pap. bk. 12.95 (978-0-914295-36-5(5)) Top Mtn Pub.
Side A presents a Mental Training Exercise designed to mentally support & strengthen the body's immune mechanism, revitalize & rejuvenate the body & to alter & improve one's health. Side B presents subliminal rapid healing suggestions hidden in an ocean-type sound.

Color Healing Guided Meditations, Vol. 5. Jonathan Parker. 2 cass. (Running Time: 2 hrs.). 1998. 17.00 Set. (978-1-58400-003-7(1)) QuantumQuests Intl.

Color Healing Meditations, Vol. 12, Set. Jonathan Parker. Read by Jonathan Parker. 2 CDs. (Running Time: 2 hrs.). (Guided Meditation Ser.: Vol. 6). 1999. audio compact disk (978-1-58400-070-9(8)) QuantumQuests Intl.

Color Image Process: Optical Storage & the Macintosh, Ins & Out of Color Scanning. 1 cass. 1990. 8.50 Recorded Res.

Color in a Grey World see When the Sky Is Red

Color It Christmas. Greg Skipper. 1998. 40.00 (978-0-7673-9249-5(3)); 11.98 (978-0-7673-9246-4(9)) LifeWay Christian.

Color It Christmas Cassette Kit. Greg Skipper. 1998. 54.95 (978-0-7673-9048-4(2)) LifeWay Christian.

Color It Christmas Cassette Promo Pack. Greg Skipper. 1998. 8.00 (978-0-7673-9054-5(7)) LifeWay Christian.

Color, Light & Sound. Read by Jack Schwarz. 3 cass. 35.00 (#401) Aletheia Psycho.

Color Me Poetry: Sound Track to a Dream. Poems. Daniel R. Queen. 1 CD. (Running Time: 90 mins.). 2000. audio compact disk 15.00 (978-1-881328-03-2(1), DQ1227) Queens Palace.
Danny Queen's poetry soars with personal power & conviction. He believes that language can change us, or that's what we believe when we read his work. His act of magic takes what we read in the newspapers & makes us able to bear a world which is sometimes hard to love. Through his own alchemy, thought & intentions, he makes us understand how we treat each other & what we need to save ourselves.

Color Meditations. unabr. ed. Louise Taylor. Read by Louise Taylor. Prod. by Lisa M. Nelson. 1 cass. (Running Time: 45 min.). 1991. 9.95 (978-0-9627863-4-1(9), BIP201) Brght Ideas CA.
Side one for adults - for relaxation, health, & peace of mind. Side two for children - for positive thoughts & self-esteem.

Color My Chess World. I.t. ed. Stephen A. Schneider. Lyrics by Pat Schneider. Music by Eric Litwin. 1. (Running Time: 18 mins). (J). 2004. act. bk. ed. 19.50 (978-0-9729456-9-1(5)) Championship.

Color of Culture. Mona L. Jones. Read by Mona Lake Jones. 1 cass. (Running Time: 60 min.). 1993. pap. bk. 12.00 (978-0-9635605-7-5(3)) IMPACT Comm.
Read with musical instrumentation.

Color of Death. Elizabeth Lowell. Narrated by Carrington MacDuffie. 8 vols. 2004. bk. 69.95 (978-0-7927-3255-6(3), CSL 669, Chivers Sound Lib) AudioGO.

Color of Death. Elizabeth Lowell. Read by Carrington MacDuffie. 1 MP3 CD. (Running Time: 11 hrs.). 2004. 29.95 (978-0-7927-3257-0(X), CMP 669, Chivers Sound Lib) AudioGO.

***Color of Death.** abr. ed. Elizabeth Lowell. (ENG.). 2004. (978-0-06-081370-3(9), Harper Audio) HarperCollins Pubs.

Color of Death. abr. ed. Elizabeth Lowell. Read by Maria Tucci. 2004. audio compact disk 29.95 (978-0-06-075760-1(4)) HarperCollins Pubs.

***Color of Death.** abr. ed. Elizabeth Lowell. Read by Maria Tucci. (ENG.). 2004. (978-0-06-077906-1(3), Harper Audio) HarperCollins Pubs.

Color of Death. unabr. ed. Bruce Alexander. 8 cass. (Running Time: 12 hrs.). 2001. 64.00 (978-0-7366-6360-1(6)) Books on Tape.
Suspicion & fear are running high in London as a ruthless gang of black criminals terrorizes the town in a spree of robbery and murder. When Sir John & Jeremy set out to find out who is behind the menace, they discover that the difference between black & white is not as simple as it seems.

Color of Death. unabr. ed. Elizabeth Lowell. Narrated by Carrington MacDuffie. 10 vols. 2004. bk. 94.95 (978-0-7927-3256-3(1), SLD 669, Chivers Sound Lib) AudioGO.

***Color of Lightning.** unabr. ed. Paulette Jiles. Read by Jack Garrett. (ENG.). 2009. (978-0-06-180549-3(1), Harper Audio); (978-0-06-180547-9(5), Harper Audio) HarperCollins Pubs.

***Color of Love.** 2010. cd-rom 13.99 (978-0-9793927-4-0(8), RR&R) Posit Prints.

Color of Love. unabr. ed. Gene Cheek. (ENG.). 2006. 14.98 (978-1-59659-111-0(0), GildAudio) Pub: Gildan Media. Dist(s): HachBkGrp

Color of My Words. unabr. ed. Lynn Joseph. Read by Lisa Vidal. 2 vols. (Running Time: 2 hrs. 6 mins.). (J). (gr. 3-7). 2004. pap. bk. 29.00 (978-0-8072-0659-1(8), Listening Lib); 23.00 (978-0-8072-0511-2(7), Listening Lib) Random Audio Pubg.
Ana-Rosa is a blossoming young writer growing up in a poor seaside village in the Dominican Republic. At the young age of 12, she finds herself faced with turning points that will make up who she is. But in a country where words are feared, Ana-Rosa must struggle to find her own voice & the means for it to be heard.

Color of Night. abr. ed. David Lindsey. Read by Stanley Tucci. (ENG.). 2006. 14.98 (978-1-59483-851-4(8)) Pub: Hachet Audio. Dist(s): HachBkGrp

Color of Night. unabr. ed. David Lindsey. Narrated by Paul Hecht. 9 cass. (Running Time: 12 hrs. 45 mins.). 1999. 80.00 (978-0-7887-3535-6(7), 95866E7) Recorded Bks.
Before he retired, Harry Strand was an intelligence agent, and Schrade was his nemesis. A ruthless international criminal, Schrade arranged the "accident" that killed Harry's wife. Now Harry has met a beautiful, mysterious woman who may have information about Schrade, and he begins to see a way to stop this enemy.

Color of Night, Set. abr. ed. David Lindsey. Read by Stanley Tucci. 4 cass. 1999. 24.98 (FS9-43426) Highsmith.

Color of Night, Set. unabr. ed. Harriet Greenberg. Read by Brad Dourif. 2 cass. (Running Time: 3 hrs.). 1994. 16.95 (978-1-56876-030-8(2), 390542) Soundlines Ent.
An erotic-thriller about a psychologist who must find out who is murdering his Monday therapy group before he himself becomes a victim. What he finds sexual obsession & deceit.

Color of Night, Set. unabr. ed. David Lindsey. Narrated by Paul Hecht. 9 cass. (Running Time: 12.75 Hrs.). 1999. 80.00 (95866H4) Recorded Bks.
Before he retired, Harry Strand was an intelligence agent, and Schrade was his nemesis. A ruthless international criminal, Schrade arranged the "accident" that killed Harry's wife. Now Harry has met a beautiful, mysterious woman who may have information about Schrade, and he begins to see a way to stop this enemy.

Color of Water: A Black Man's Tribute to His White Mother. James McBride. Contrib. by Andre Braugher & Lainie Kazan. 2008. 59.99 (978-1-60640-657-1(4)) Find a World.

Color of Water: A Black Man's Tribute to His White Mother. unabr. ed. James McBride. Perf. by Andre Braugher & Lanie Kazan. 4 cass. (Running Time: 6 hrs.). 2001. 25.00 (978-1-59040-015-9(1), Phoenix Audio) Pub: Amer Intl Pub. Dist(s): PerseuPGW
A powerful portrait of growing up, a meditation on race and identity and a poignant, beautifully crafted hymn from a son to his mother.

Color Printing. Bob Nadler. Interview with Bob Nadler. Interview with David Vestal. 1 cass. (Running Time: 60 min.). 10.95 (978-0-933596-38-2(3)) F-Twenty-Two.
Explains how to make color prints in the photographic darkroom.

***Color Purple.** Alice Walker. 2010. audio compact disk 29.99 (978-1-4407-9249-6(6)) Recorded Bks.

***Color Purple.** Alice Walker. 2010. audio compact disk 29.99 (978-1-4407-9230-4(5)) Recorded Bks.

Color Really Doesn't Matter. Carol Wood. Illus. by Joe Glisson. (J). 2001. pap. bk. 9.95 (978-0-9662378-6-3(2)); bds. 14.95 (978-0-9662378-1-8(1)) Astoria Prodns.

Color Scheme. unabr. ed. Ngaio Marsh. Narrated by Nadia May. 3 CDs. (Running Time: 3 hrs.). 2001. audio compact disk 72.00 (zp2654); audio compact disk 19.95 (zm2654) Blckstn Audio.
Maurice Questing was lured into a pool of boiling mud and left there to die. Chief Inspector Roderick Alleyn, far from home on a wartime quest for German agents, knew that any number of people could have killed him.

Color Stones & Healing. Eileen Nauman. 1 cass. 8.95 (703) Am Fed Astrologers.
An AFA Convention workshop tape.

Color Therapy & Healing, Vol. 4. Jonathan Parker. 2 cass. (Running Time: 2 hrs). 1998. 17.00 Set. (978-1-58400-002-0(3)) QuantumQuests Intl.

Color Therapy & Healing Vol. 4, Set: Mini Course. Jonathan Parker. Read by Jonathan Parker. 2 CDs. (Running Time: 2 hrs.). (Natural Health Ser.: Vol. 5). 1999. audio compact disk (978-1-58400-055-6(4)) QuantumQuests Intl.

Color Tones. Duane Shinn. 1 cass. 19.95 (CP-14) Duane Shinn.
Explains what color tones are & how to use them.

Color Vision Deficiency - A Bibliography & Dictionary for Physicians, Patients, & Genome Researchers. Compiled by Icon Group International, Inc. Staff. 2007. ring bd. 28.95 (978-0-497-11354-4(6)) Icon Grp.

Color Your Listings SOLD. 2 CD's. 2003. audio compact disk (978-1-932616-10-1(1)) Feng Shui Para.
Feng Shui Your Home with the Hottest Feng Shui Program in the Industry!!Designed for Realtors? to help homeowners sell their properties in record time, COLOR YOUR LISTINGS SOLD is also a useful tool for homeowners who are not interested in selling their home but would like to enhance its beauty and energy.In this empowerment program you will learn how to use Feng Shui to attract positive energy and MAXIMIZE the physical, emotional and visual appeal of your property. Suzee will teach you, step-by-step, how to evaluate and Feng Shui your home. Discover fun and inexpensive remedies and enhancements that will amaze and thrill you and those who visit your home. This audio program will show you how to utililize the art of Feng Shui to save decorating dollars...while creating a healthy living environment for life!.

Color Your Property SOLD. 1 CD. 2003. audio compact disk (978-1-932616-11-8(X)) Feng Shui Para.
Transform Your Home into a Positive, Life-Affirming Place!!This audio CD is designed to educate you on the basic principles of Feng Shui and how they can assist you in enhancing the appeal of your property. Whether you're in the market for a home, selling your home, or simply looking for ways to beautify and energize your current home, Feng Shui Master Suzee Miller will guide you step-by-step along the way to creating a happier and healthier home!.

Colorado! abr. ed. Dana Fuller Ross, pseud. Read by Paul Ukena. 4 vols. (Wagons West Ser.: No. 7). 2003. (978-1-58807-524-6(9)) Am Pubng Inc.

Colorado! abr. ed. Dana Fuller Ross, pseud. Read by Paul Ukena. 4 vols. (Running Time: 6 hrs.). (Wagon West Ser.: No. 7). 2003. 25.00 (978-1-58807-012-8(3)) Am Pubng Inc.
As the guns of the Civil War rumble, Gen. Lee Blake stakes his life on the biggest challenge of his career - to keep Colorado as part of the Union. And Cathy Blake, who is threatened by a voluptuous rival for her husband's heart, is forced to summon all the fire in her blood to fight for her man. The 7th book in the Wagons West series.

Colorado! abr. ed. Dana Fuller Ross, pseud. Read by Paul Ukena. 5 vols. (Wagons West Ser.: No. 7). 2004. audio compact disk 30.00 (978-1-58807-349-5(1)); audio compact disk (978-1-58807-853-7(1)) Am Pubng Inc.

Colorado. unabr. ed. Gary McCarthy. Read by Maynard Villers. 12 cass. (Running Time: 12 hrs. 6 min.). (Rivers West Ser.: Bk. 3). 1996. 64.95 (978-1-55686-658-6(5)) Books in Motion.
Burly, Issac Beard lived by a private code of honor & swift justice. He forged a place of safety in the Colorado upcountry for generations of Beards.

Colorado! unabr. ed. Dana Fuller Ross, pseud. Read by Phil Gigante. (Running Time: 12 hrs.). (Wagons West Ser.: No. 7). 2011. 24.99 (978-1-4418-2469-1(3), 9781441824691, Brilliance MP3) Brilliance Audio.

Colorado Gold. unabr. ed. Douglas Hirt. Read by Rusty Nelson. 6 cass. (Running Time: 7 hrs.). 2001. 39.95 (978-1-58116-053-6(4)) Books in Motion.
Harrison Mandall comes to an Arizona outpost on the mighty Colorado River to find out who was stealing money from an upriver mining company. His trek to the mine requires a dangerous boat ride, accompanied by misfits and pretenders, who could quickly cause this boat ride to become a place of death.

Colorado Gold Dust Set: Short Stories & Profiles. Dave Southworth. Read by Dave Southworth. 4 cass. (Running Time: 5 hrs.). 1998. 24.95 (978-1-890778-04-0(4)) Wld Horse Pub.

Colorado Kid. unabr. ed. Stephen King. Read by Jeffrey DeMunn. 2005. 15.95 (978-0-7435-5243-1(1)) Pub: S&S Audio. Dist(s): S and S Inc

Colorado Kid. unabr. ed. Stephen King. Read by Jeffrey Demunn. (Running Time: 40 hrs. 0 mins. 0 sec.). (ENG.). 2008. audio compact disk 14.99 (978-0-7435-7091-6(X)) Pub: S&S Audio. Dist(s): S and S Inc

Colorado Prey. unabr. ed. Larry D. Names. Read by Maynard Villers. 6 cass. (Running Time: 6 hrs. 6 min.). (Creed Ser.: Bk. 8). 2001. 39.95 (978-1-55686-821-4(9)) Books in Motion.
The trail for the men who framed Creed leads to Colorado, where Slate finds Quade, one of those responsible. But can Creed avoid a lynching and get Quade back to Texas?.

Colorado Radio Interview on the Believer's Security. Dan Corner. 1 cass. 4.00 (CO) Evang Outreach.

Colorado's Gunnison River & Columbia's City Growth. Hosted by Nancy Pearlman. 1 cass. (Running Time: 28 min.). 10.00 (519) Educ Comm CA.

Colorblind: John P. Kee. Perf. by John P. Kee. 1 cass., 1 CD. Provident Mus Dist.

Colored People: A Memoir. unabr. collector's ed. Henry Louis Gates, Jr. Read by Dick Estell. 7 cass. (Running Time: 7 hrs.). 1996. 42.00 (978-0-7366-3385-7(5), 4035) Books on Tape.
Henry Louis Gates ushers us into a now-vanished "colored" world of hellfire religion, gossip & segregation. Splendid memoirs.

Colored Woman in a White World see Black Pioneers in American History, Vol. 2, 19th - 20th Centuries

Colorful Borders. (Timesaving Software Tools for Teachers Ser.). 2004. audio compact disk 21.99 (978-0-7439-3450-3(4)) Tchr Create Ma.

Colorful Comedies. (ENG.). 2007. 15.00 (978-0-9785562-2-8(4)) Socio Pub.

Colorful Coral Reefs Audio CD. Adapted by Benchmark Education Company Staff. Based on a work by Katherine Scraper. (Early Explorers Set C Ser.). (J). (gr. 1). 2008. audio compact disk 10.00 (978-1-60437-527-5(2)) Benchmark Educ.

Colorful Present with Book. (Pooh Learning Ser.). (J). (ps-3). 2000. pap. bk. 6.98 (978-0-7634-0474-1(8)) W Disney Records.

Colorful Sleepy Sheep. Rory Zuckerman. Illus. by Maryn Roos. 1 CD. (Running Time: 18 mins.). (Sleepy Sheep Ser.). (J). (ps). 2007. bds. 7.95 (978-0-9796393-2-6(8)) Little Lion Pr.

Colors & Shapes. Vincent Douglas. (J). 1994. audio compact disk 12.99 (978-1-57583-301-9(8), Twin108CD) Twin Sisters.

Colors & Shapes. Kim Mitzo Thompson & Karen Mitzo Hilderbrand. Arranged by Hal Wright. (J). 1994. pap. bk. 13.99 (978-1-57583-298-2(4), Twin 408) Twin Sisters.

Colors & Shapes: Early Learning Series. 1 cass. (Early Learning Ser.). (J). bk. (TWIN 408) NewSound.

Colors Black-Audio Book. (Colors Ser.). (ENG.). 2009. audio compact disk 5.95 (978-1-4329-3226-8(2), AcornHR) Heinemann Rai.

Colors-Blue-Audio Book. (Colors Ser.). (ENG.). 2009. audio compact disk 5.95 (978-1-4329-3227-5(6), AcornHR) Heinemann Rai.

Colors-Brown-Audio Book. (Colors Ser.). (ENG.). 2009. audio compact disk 5.95 (978-1-4329-3228-2(4), AcornHR) Heinemann Rai.

Colors-Green-Audio Book. (Colors Ser.). (ENG.). 2009. audio compact disk 5.95 (978-1-4329-3229-9(2), AcornHR) Heinemann Rai.

Colors of Spirit. Rick Nichols. Read by Rick Nichols. 1 cass. (Running Time: 1 hr.). 1999. 11.95 (978-1-893705-07-4(2)) Hlth Horiz.
Chakra balancing visualization with soothing background music.

Colors of the Mountain. abr. ed. Da Chen. Read by Daxing Zhang. 4 cass. (Running Time: 6 hrs.). 2002. 25.00 (978-1-57453-463-4(7)) Audio Lit.
In 1962, as millions of Chinese citizens were gripped by Mao Zedong's Cultural Revolution and the Red Guards enforced a brutal regime of communism, a boy was born to a poor family in southern China. Da Chen seemed destined for a life of poverty, shame, and hunger." "But winning humor and an indomitable spirit can be found in the most unexpected places. Colors of the Mountain is a story of triumph, a memoir of a boyhood full of spunk, mischief, and love. The young Da Chen is part Horatio Alger, part Holden Caulfield; he befriends a gang of young hoodlums as well as the elegant, elderly Chinese Baptist woman who teaches him English and opens the door to a new life.

Colors-Orange-Audio Book. (Colors Ser.). (ENG.). 2009. audio compact disk 5.95 (978-1-4329-3230-5(6), AcornHR) Heinemann Rai.

Colors Read-Aloud Audio Book. 2009. audio compact disk 5.95 (978-1-4329-3269-5(1), Acorn Read) Heinemann Rai.

Colors-Red-Audio Book. (Colors Ser.). (ENG.). 2009. audio compact disk 5.95 (978-1-4329-3231-2(4), AcornHR) Heinemann Rai.

Colors, Shapes & Counting. unabr. ed. Rock 'N Learn, Inc. Staff et al. Perf. by Brad Caudle et al. Illus. by Bart Harlan. 1 cass. (Running Time: 50 min.). (Rock n' Learn Ser.). (J). (ps-k). 1994. pap. bk. 12.99 (978-1-878489-32-6(1), RL932) Rock N Learn.
Catchy songs, lively sound effects, & fun dialogue teach basic & advanced colors, shapes, & counting (up to 20). A full-color "follow-along" book of pictures allows playful interaction with characters on tape.

Colors, Shapes & Sizes. abr. ed. Penton Overseas, Inc. Staff. 1 cass. (Running Time: 58 mins.). (J). (ps-3). 2003. bk. 12.99 (978-1-894677-24-0(2)) Pub: Kidzup Prodns. Dist(s): Penton Overseas

Colors-Violet-Audio Book. (Colors Ser.). (ENG.). 2009. audio compact disk 5.95 (978-1-4329-3232-9(2), AcornHR) Heinemann Rai.

Colors-White-Audio Book. (Colors Ser.). (ENG.). 2009. audio compact disk 5.95 (978-1-4329-3233-6(0), AcornHR) Heinemann Rai.

Colors-Yellow-Audio Book. (Colors Ser.). (ENG.). 2009. audio compact disk 5.95 (978-1-4329-3234-3(9), AcornHR) Heinemann Rai.

***Colossians Commentary.** Chuck Missler. (ENG.). 2009. Rental 29.95 (978-1-57821-468-6(8)) Koinonia Hse.

Colossians #1: Col.1:1-7. Ed Young. 1982. 4.95 (978-0-7417-1247-9(4), 247) Win Walk.

***Colossus: Hoover Dam & the Making of the American Century.** unabr. ed. Michael A. Hiltzik. (Running Time: 18 hrs. 0 mins.). 2010. 49.99 (978-1-4001-9678-4(7)); 22.99 (978-1-4001-8678-5(1)) Tantor Media.

***Colossus: Hoover Dam & the Making of the American Century.** unabr. ed. Michael A. Hiltzik. Narrated by Norman Dietz. 2 MP3-CDs. (Running Time: 18 hrs. 30 mins. 0 sec.). 2010. 34.99 (978-1-4001-6678-7(0)); audio compact disk 99.99 (978-1-4001-4678-9(X)); audio compact disk 49.99 (978-1-4001-1678-2(3)) Pub: Tantor Media. Dist(s): IngramPubServ

Colossus of New York: A City in Thirteen Parts. Colson Whitehead. Narrated by Colson Whitehead. 3 CDs. (Running Time: 3 hrs. 15 mins.). 2004. audio compact disk 19.99 (978-1-4025-6343-0(4), 01272) Recorded Bks.

Colossus of Rhodes. Caroline Lawrence. As told by Michael Praed. 3 CDs. (Running Time: 3 hrs. 0 mins. 0 sec.). (Roman Mysteries Ser.). (ENG., (J). (gr. 7-9). 2005. audio compact disk 24.99 (978-0-7528-6806-6(3)) Pub: OrnChdrns Bks GBR. Dist(s): IPG Chicago

Colostrum, Nature's Antibody Against Cancer. Jack Megason. 1 cass. (Running Time: 30 min.). 6.95 (AC26) Am Media.
Explains how Colostrum, found in mother's milk, contains the antibodies which establish the child's immune system &, when a commercial preparation is taken by adults, may explain the dramatic recovery of many cancer patients.

Colour Blind. unabr. ed. Catherine Cookson. Read by Susan Jameson. 8 cass. (Running Time: 8 hrs.). 1997. 69.95 Set. (978-0-7451-6764-0(0), CAB 1380) AudioGO.
When Bridget McQueen returns to the Fifteen Streets, she knows her life will be anything but easy. She is escaping her possessive brother, but the real battles will have to be fought by her half-white, half-black daughter, Rose-Angela. And when her father is driven away from the family, Rose-Angela is left with nothing but her own courage to face the world.

Colour of Blood. Declan Hughes. 2008. 84.95 (978-0-7531-2940-1(X)); audio compact disk 99.95 (978-0-7531-2941-8(8)) Pub: ISIS Audio GBR. Dist(s): Ulverscroft US

Colour of Blood, unabr. ed. Brian Moore. Narrated by Steven Crossley. 5 cass. (Running Time: 6 hrs.). 1998. 44.00 (978-0-7887-1885-4(1), 95307E7) Recorded Bks.
In a bleak Eastern bloc country, someone is trying to kill the aging Cardinal Bem. It may be the Secret Police or perhaps the assassin is working within the same church the Cardinal serves.

Colour of Magic. Terry Pratchett. 2 cass. (Running Time: 3 hrs.). (Discworld Ser.). 2000. 16.99 (978-0-552-14017-1(1), Corgi RHG) Pub: Transworld GBR. Dist(s): Trafalgar

Colour of Magic. unabr. ed. Terry Pratchett. Read by Nigel Planer. 6 cass. (Running Time: 7 hrs.). (Discworld Ser.). (J). 1997. 54.95 (978-1-85695-800-4(0), 950401) Pub: ISIS Lrg Prnt GBR. Dist(s): Ulverscroft US

Colour of Magic. unabr. ed. Terry Pratchett. Read by Nigel Planer. 6 CDs. (Running Time: 25500 sec.). (Discworld Ser.). 2006. audio compact disk 64.95 (978-0-7531-0708-9(2)) Pub: ISIS Lrg Prnt GBR. Dist(s): Ulverscroft US

Colour Scheme. Ngaio Marsh. Read by Nadia May. 9 CDs. (Running Time: 10 hrs.). 2000. audio compact disk 72.00 (978-0-7861-9837-5(0), 2654) Blckstn Audio.
It was a horrible death, Maurice Questing was lured into a pool of boiling mud & left there to die.

Colour Scheme. unabr. ed. Ngaio Marsh. Read by Nadia May. 7 cass. (Running Time: 10 hrs.). 2000. 49.95 (978-0-7861-1855-7(5), 2654) Blckstn Audio.

Colour Scheme. unabr. ed. Ngaio Marsh. Read by Nadia May. 1 CD. (Running Time: 10 hrs.). 2001. audio compact disk 19.95 (zm2654) Blckstn Audio.
It was a horrible death, Maurice Questing was lured into a pool of boiling mud & left there to die. Chief Inspector Roderick Alleyn, far from home on a wartime quest for German agents, knew that any number of people could have killed him.

Colours of Rajasthan, Vol. 1. Music by Taufiq Qureshi. 1 cass. 1995. (M95021); (CD M95021) Multi-Cultural Bks.
Birth of a Warrior & Lullaby, Valour & Battle, Victorious Return, Royal Court, Love Song, Dunes Night, Without You, Ranthambhor, The Tiger Hunts, Campfire, Mela, Meera.

Colt, unabr. ed. Nancy Springer. Narrated by Ed Sala. 3 pieces. (Running Time: 3 hrs. 15 mins.). (gr. 2 up). 27.00 (978-0-7887-0615-8(2), 94774E7) Recorded Bks.
Colt Vittorio wants nothing more than to be a normal kid; however, spina bifida confines him to a wheelchair. When he learns horseback riding through a handicapped outreach program, he begins to feel tall, strong & powerful, even though any fall, even a hard gallop, may kill him. Available to libraries only.

***Colt-Cure for Woolly Fever.** Peter Dawson. 2009. (978-1-60136-392-3(3)) Audio Holding.

Colt-Cure for Woolly Fever. Peter Dawson. (Running Time: 0 hr. 42 mins.). 1999. 10.95 (978-1-60083-506-3(6)) Iofy Corp.

Colt from Snowy River. unabr. ed. Elyne Mitchell. Read by Caroline Lee. (Running Time: 5 hrs. 25 mins.). (YA). 2009. audio compact disk 63.95 (978-1-74093-979-9(4), 9781740939799) Pub: Bolinda Pubng AUS. Dist(s): Bolinda Pub Inc

Colter's Hell. unabr. ed. Gary McCarthy. Read by Gene Engene. 8 cass. (Running Time: 10 hrs.). 2001. 49.95 (978-1-55686-863-4(4)) Books in Motion.
The goal to reach the land called Yellowstone was a quest young Quinn Wallace would not abandon. Wallace would face hardships, dangers and even love in this mythical land.

Colterville: Saratoga Theater. adpt. ed. Esther Luttrell. Perf. by Al Dunaway et al. 1 cass. Dramatization. 12.95 (978-0-9667485-9-8(X)) Oak Shadow Pr.

Columbella. unabr. ed. Phyllis A. Whitney. Read by Beth Porter. 8 cass. (Running Time: 12 hrs.). 2001. 69.95 (978-0-7540-0688-6(3), CAB 2110) Pub: Chivers Audio Bks GBR. Dist(s): AudioGO
When Jessica Abbott arrived at her Aunt Janet's lovely Carribean hotel, she left nothing of value behind. But wealthy matriarch Maud Hampden had plans for Jessica. Maud saw in Jessica the perfect companion for her granddaughter, Leila, and a perfect antidote to Leila's wild, promiscuous mother, Catherine.

Columbia River. unabr. ed. Jory Sherman. Read by Maynard Villers. 8 cass. (Running Time: 9 hrs. 30 min.). (Rivers West Ser.: Bk. 5). 1996. 49.95 (978-1-55686-719-4(0)) Books in Motion.
Along the banks of the Columbia River bold, strong men sought their fortune. It was a time when the fur trade could make you wealthy or get you killed.

Columbia Workshop: The Day They Gave Babies Away & Rain, Rain Go Away. 1 cass. (Running Time: 1 hr.). 2001. 6.98 (2094) Radio Spirits.

Columbia Workshop Pt. 1 & 2: Moby Dick. 1 cass. (Running Time: 1 hr.). 2001. 6.98 (2155) Radio Spirits.

Columbine. unabr. ed. Dave Cullen. (Running Time: 14 hrs. 0 mins.). 2009. 79.95 (978-1-4332-9042-8(1)) Blckstn Audio.

Columbine. unabr. ed. Dave Cullen. Read by Don Leslie. 11 CDs. (Running Time: 13 hrs.). 2009. audio compact disk 109.00 (978-1-4332-9043-5(X)) Blckstn Audio.

Columbine. unabr. ed. Dave Cullen. Read by Don Leslie. (Running Time: 14 hrs.). 2010. 29.95 (978-1-4332-9046-6(4)) Blckstn Audio.

***Columbine.** unabr. ed. Dave Cullen. Read by Don Leslie. (Running Time: 14 hrs.). 2010. audio compact disk 29.95 (978-1-4332-9045-9(6)) Blckstn Audio.

Columbus see Poetry & Voice of Muriel Rukeyser

Columbus & the Age of Discovery. unabr. ed. William G. Scheller. Read by Sheldon Mirowitz. 1 cass. (Running Time: 75 min.). 1992. pap. bk. 9.98 (978-0-934245-23-4(1)); audio compact disk 10.98 CD Incl. pap. bk. (978-0-934245-22-7(3)) Narada Prodns.
The book examines Columbus, his voyages & the cultural, historical & sociological transformations prompted by his expeditions. The recording presents music from the soundtrack of Columbus & the Age of Discovery, a seven-part television documentary created to commemorate the 500th anniversary of Christopher Columbus' landing in the Americas.

Columbus Day Show: Do Native Americans Have Special Rights? Leonard Peikoff. 1998. 25.95 (LPXXC78) Second Renaissance.

Column Selection in Gas Chromatography: The Critical Step for Efficient Separations. Instructed by Harold M. McNair. 4 cass. (Running Time: 4 hrs. 12 min.). 205.00 incl. 140pp manual. (66) Am Chemical.
The selection of the proper column & column operating parameters determines the effectiveness of gas chromatographic separations. This course emphasizes this selection.

Columns of Light: Thirty Remarkable Saints. Told to John Jay Hughes. (ENG.). 2008. audio compact disk (978-0-9795255-0-6(0)) Now You Know.

Coma. unabr. ed. Robin Cook. Read by Donada Peters. 8 cass. (Running Time: 12 hrs.). 1993. 64.00 (978-0-7366-2465-7(1), 3229) Books on Tape.
Patients in for "minor surgery" get a dose of faulty anesthesia & never wake up, victims of a ghastly plot.

Coma: Awakening Loved Ones with Hypnosis. Contrib. by Salaka Marin. 2000. 19.95 (978-1-893087-16-3(6)) Awaken Vis.

Coma: Program from the Award Winning Public Radio Series. Interview. Hosted by Fred Goodwin. Comment by John Hockenberry. 1 CD. (Running Time: 1 Hour). 2000. audio compact disk 21.99 (978-1-932479-33-1(3), LCM 141) Lichtenstein Creat.
If we're to believe typical depictions on TV and in the movies, when someone wakes up from a coma, they get up, get out of bed and go straight back to their lives without missing a beat. That's not quite accurate. In this hour, we attempt to demystify the condition of coma:-what is it, how it's treated, how patients recover and its impact on the lives of survivors and their families. Guests include: Ian Elliot, coma survivor; Dr. Ronald Cranford of the Hennepin County Medical Center in Minneapolis, Minnesota; Dr. Nancy Childs of the Brown Schools Rehabilitation Center in Austin, Texas; Kay Guynes, whose son Michael is a coma survivor; Dr. Randall Chesnut of the Oregon Health Sciences University in Portland, and Peter Quinn, the executive director of the Brain Trauma Foundation. we also visit the Center for Head Injuries at the JFK Johnson Rehabilitation Center in Edison, New Jersey. Commentary by John Hockenberry.

Coma - Sepsis. Gary Strange & Roger Barkin. (Pediatric Emergencies: The National Conference for Practioners Ser.). 1986. 9.00 (978-0-932491-76-3(6)) Res Appl Inc.

Comanche Captives & The Outcasts. unabr. collector's ed. Will Cook. Read by Christopher Lane. 9 cass. (Running Time: 13 hrs. 30 mins.). 1995. 72.00 (978-0-7366-2935-5(1), 3631) Books on Tape.
From a veteran in the Western genre comes two gritty stories about Indian conflicts in the Old West. Authentic & convincing.

Comanche Code. abr. ed. Matthew S. Hart. Read by Paul Nixon. Abr. by Odin Westgaard. 2 cass. (Running Time: 3 hrs.). (Cody's Law Ser.: No. 12). 2004. 18.00 (978-1-58807-146-0(4)) Am Pubng Inc.
He rides alone for a breed that stands apart. He wears the badge of the Texas Rangers and a pair of silver spurs. He is the servant of a fiercely held code of right and wrong. His name is Cody. The Rangers made Texas a land of law. Men like Cody made the Rangers a legend. When the Governor asks Cody to accompany two prisoners to a federal prison in Florida, Cody knows two things: He can't refuse, and he'll have no shortage of enemies on this assignment. The prisoners, Comanche renegades Red Moon and Twisted Hawk, have reason enough to want Cody dead. The Army escort guarding the Indians is none too happy with interference from the Texas Rangers. Along for the perilous trip east are an oily New York reporter itching for a story, and a lovely do-gooder who wants to set the prisoners free. Add in a raid by a gang of hardcases, and Cody's train ride becomes a one-way trip to hell.

Comanche Dawn. Mike Blakely. Narrated by Jack Garrett. 16 cass. (Running Time: 23 hrs.). 132.00 (978-1-4025-2134-8(0)) Recorded Bks.

Comanche Moon. unabr. ed. Larry McMurtry. Read by Frank Muller. 17 cass. (Running Time: 25 hrs. 30 mins.). (Lonesome Dove Ser.: No. 2). 1998. 136.00 (978-0-7366-4391-7(5)) Books on Tape.
The long-awaited story of how the brash youths of "Dead Man's Walk" grow older & wiser as they fight in the Comanche Wars.

Comanche Moon, Pt. 2. Larry McMurtry. Narrated by Jack Garrett. 21 cass. (Running Time: 30 hrs. 30 mins.). (Lonesome Dove Ser.: No. 2). 169.00 (978-1-4025-2945-0(7)) Recorded Bks.

Comanche Moon, Pt. 2. unabr. ed. Larry McMurtry. Read by Frank Muller. 9 cass. (Running Time: 13 hrs. 30 min.). (Lonesome Dove Ser.: No. 2). 1999. 72.00 (4854-A); 64.00 (4854-B) Books on Tape.
This follows the friendship of Augustus McCrae & Woodrow Call that was tempered in the desperate hardships of "Dead Man's Walk" to the unbreakable bond between the two equally proud, but very different men. Set against the bloody frontier fighting of the Comanche wars, this brings back a whole raft of characters who re-emerge older, if not always wiser, in "Lonesome Dove" & Jake Spoon, Clara, the love of McCrae's life & many others.

Comanche Moon, Py. 2. unabr. ed. Larry McMurtry. Read by Frank Muller. 16 cass. (Lonesome Dove Ser.: No. 2). 1999. 45.00 (FS9-34582) Highsmith.

Comando Tribulacion: El Drama Continuo de los Dejados Atras. Tim LaHaye & Jerry B. Jenkins. 9 cass. (Running Time: 12 hrs. 30 min.). (SPA.). 79.75 (978-1-4025-6310-2(8)) Recorded Bks.

Comatose. Contrib. by Skillet. Prod. by Brian Howes & John L. Cooper. 2007. audio compact disk 17.98 (978-5-557-51581-8(X)) INO Rec.

Combat. unabr. ed. Read by Bruno Oliver. Ed. by Stephen Coonts. 6 cass. (Running Time: 8 hrs.). 2001. 26.95 (978-1-55935-355-7(4)) Soundelux.

Combat Pay. unabr. ed. Curt Messex. Read by Kevin Foley. 12 cass. (Running Time: 11 hrs. 12 min.). 1995. 64.95 (978-1-55686-598-5(8)) Books in Motion.
The author's true story is superbly narrated by Kevin Foley. This is a riveting tale of combat support missions flown in C-130 aircraft over Vietnam by Major Curt Messex, U. S. Air Force.

Combat Support. unabr. ed. Curt Messex. Read by Kevin Foley. 8 cass. (Running Time: 10 hrs. 24 min.). 1995. 49.95 (978-1-55686-600-5(3)) Books in Motion.
Here is the true story of Air Commando Crew 139. Brave airmen who went to war in 1962 in a "Gooney Bird" (C-47) flying combat support missions for the Green Berets in the early days of the Vietnam War.

***Combat Swimmer: Memoirs of a Navy SEAL.** unabr. ed. Captain Robert A., USN(Ret) Gormley. Read by Adams Morgan. (Running Time: 10 hrs.). 2010. 29.95 (978-1-4417-4204-9(2)); audio compact disk 90.00 (978-1-4417-4201-8(8)) Blckstn Audio.

Combat Swimmer: Memoirs of a Navy SEAL. unabr. ed. Robert A. Gormly. Read by Adams Morgan. 7 cass. (Running Time: 10 hrs.). 1998. 49.95 (978-0-7861-1431-3(2), 2317) Blckstn Audio.
Examines war from a strategic point of view as well as from personal experiences. Chronicles SEAL life after Vietnam, including what is perhaps the most graphic description ever of SEAL action in the chaotic invasion of Grenada.

Combating Depression Using Anger Positively, 2. Scripts. 2 cass. (Running Time: 60 mins).Tr. of Como Salir de la Depresion Use el Enojo Positivamente. (SPA.). 2003. 25.00 (978-0-9744786-1-6(X)) A Nogales.
Doctor Nogales is pleased to offer this important series of psychological self-help cassettes. Although they don't replace psychological therapy, they will give you the necessary information to find your own answers and possible solutions to common difficulties and life challenges. They also include practical exercises that can help to guide listeners to a healthier life. "Combating Depression"?Using Anger Positively?.

Combating Principalities Series. unabr. ed. Rick Joyner. 2 cass. (Running Time: 3 hrs.). 2000. 10.00 (RJ09-000) Morning NC.
"Principles of Spiritual Warfare" & "Putting on the Full Armor of God." These tapes highlight practical truths that lead to certain victory in spiritual warfare.

Combating the Darkness: Proceedings of the 45th Annual Conventional Association of Evangelical Buffalo, New York. Read by Jo A. Jankowski. 1 cass. (Running Time: 60 min.). 1987. 4.00 (340) Nat Assn Evan.

Combating the Religious Spirit Series. Rick Joyner. 3 cass. (Running Time: 4 hrs. 30 mins.). 2000. 15.00 (RJ12-000) Morning NC.
"The Nature of a Religious Spirit," "Combating the Spirit of Jezebel" & "Warning Signs of a Religious Spirit." Exposing a deadly enemy of Christianity, this series assaults one of the enemy's most powerful strongholds.

Combating the Spirit of Jezebel. Rick Joyner. 1 cass. (Running Time: 90 mins.). (Combating the Religious Spirit Ser.: Vol. 2). 2000. 5.00 (RJ12-002) Morning NC.

Combatting Depression: Self-Help Techniques. Peter M. Lewisohn. 1 cass. (Running Time: 50 min.). 1989. Guilford Pubns.
Presents very explicit methods that most adults can use to counteract the debilitating symptoms of depression.

Combatting Union Organizing Strategies. 1 cass. (America's Supermarket Showcase '96 Ser.). 1996. 11.00 (NGA96-010) Sound Images.

Combined Full Text Online & Student Resources for Drug Therapy in Nursing. 3rd ed. Diane S. Aschenbrenner. (ENG.). 2008. 59.95 (978-1-60547-870-8(9)) Lppncott W W.

Come All You People. John L. Bell. 1995. 10.95 (355); audio compact disk 15.95 (355) GIA Pubns.

Come Along: The Journey into a More Intimate Faith. Jane Rubietta. (ENG.). 2009. 24.99 (978-1-934384-29-9(1)) Pub: Treasure Pub. Dist(s): STL Dist NA

Come & Be Killed. unabr. ed. E. X. Ferrars. Read by Beverley Dunn. 6 cass. (Running Time: 9 hrs.). (Isis Ser.). (J). 1999. 54.95 (978-0-7531-0407-1(5), 990107) Pub: ISIS Lrg Prnt GBR. Dist(s): Ulverscroft US
Having inherited money, Rachel Gardner had come to Australia to visit her brother, but not only was he not at the airport, he was not at his lodgings either. Then Ian's landlord disappeared. Rachel soon realized that someone wanted her dead. Alone in an alien environment, she needed all her sharp wits, not to mention the support of the young doctor who had a habit of surfacing whenever she need him most.

***Come & Dine.** Perf. by Sammy Pawlak, Jr. & Shannon Pawlak. (ENG.). 2001. audio compact disk 15.00 (978-0-9700513-1-8(X)) Gods Hse Orlan.

Come & Journey. Michael Joncas. Perf. by Marty Haugen & David Haas. 1995. 10.95 (171); audio compact disk 15.95 (171) GIA Pubns.

Come As You Are, Set. Mary J. Leddy. Read by Mary Joe Leddy. 4 cass. (Running Time: 3 hrs. 30 min.). 1993. 34.95 (978-7-900784-19-3(5), AA2670) Credence Commun.
What it means to be a person living fully in grace in the context of a dying culture.

Come Away. Wayne Drain. 2004. audio compact disk 15.99 (978-0-7684-0205-6(0)) Destiny Image Pubs.

Come Away from the Water, Shirley. 2004. 8.95 (978-1-56008-875-2(3)); cass. & flmstrp 30.00 (978-1-56008-653-6(X)) Weston Woods.

Come Away from the Water, Shirley. (J). 2004. pap. bk. 14.95 (978-1-56008-183-8(X)) Weston Woods.

Come Away from the Water, Shirley. John Burningham. (J). 2004. bk. 24.95 (978-1-56008-182-1(1)) Weston Woods.

***Come Back.** unabr. ed. Claire Fontaine & Mia Fontaine. Read by Terra Deva & Anne Twomey. (ENG.). 2008. (978-0-06-176937-5(1), Harper Audio); (978-0-06-176766-1(2), Harper Audio) HarperCollins Pubs.

Come Back, Amelia Bedelia. abr. ed. Peggy Parish & Peggy Parish. Illus. by Wallace Tripp. (Amelia Bedelia Ser.). (J). 2008. 9.99 (978-0-06-133608-9(4), HarperFestival) HarperCollins Pubs.

Come Back, Amelia Bedelia. unabr. abr. ed. Peggy Parish. Illus. by Wallace Tripp. 1 cass. (Amelia Bedelia Ser.). (J). (ps-3). 1990. 8.99 (978-1-55994-225-6(8)) HarperCollins Pubs.

***Come Back, Como.** unabr. ed. Steven Winn. Read by Paul Hemandez. (ENG.). 2009. (978-0-06-196258-5(9), Harper Audio); (978-0-06-184553-6(1), Harper Audio) HarperCollins Pubs.

Come Back Gizmo. unabr. ed. Paul Jennings. 1 cass. (Running Time: 1 hr.). 2002. (978-1-74030-361-3(X)); audio compact disk 18.00 (978-1-74030-751-2(8)) Pub: Bolinda Pubng AUS. Dist(s): Bolinda Pub Inc

Come Before Winter & Share My Hope. Charles R. Swindoll. (Running Time: 60 min.). 1994. 14.99 (978-0-310-41518-3(7)) Zondervan.
Author speaks on preparation, perserverance, & promise.

Come, Bless the Baby. Marietta Renard Roach. 2006. pap. bk. 21.95 (978-0-9768626-0-4(3)) Aaduna.

Come Boldly to the Throne of Grace. Speeches. Creflo A. Dollar. 3 cass. (Running Time: 3 hrs. 30 mins.). 2006. 15.00 (978-1-59944-042-2(3)); audio compact disk 21.00 (978-1-59944-043-9(1)) Creflo Dollar.

Come Celebrate Christmas. Gary Rhodes. 1998. 75.00 (978-0-7673-9239-6(6)); 8.00 (978-0-7673-9053-8(9)); audio compact disk 12.00 (978-0-7673-9241-9(8)); audio compact disk 85.00 (978-0-7673-9240-2(X)); audio compact disk 16.98 (978-0-7673-9238-9(8)) LifeWay Christian.

Come! Celebrate Christmas. Gary Rhodes. 1998. 11.98 (978-0-7673-3562-1(7)) LifeWay Christian.

Come, Christian, Play the Guitar. unabr. ed. Alexa S. Lambert. Perf. by Alexa S. Lambert. 1 cass. (YA). (gr. 4 up). 1996. 8.99 (978-0-9639375-4-4(5)) ASL Music.
Songs from textbook played with a simple pick & strum style for beginners to practice along with tape. Sung & performed by Alexa S. Lambert. Songs selected are old gospel songs familiar to all & new gospel songs written by Alexa S. Lambert, Sharon Daugherty, Carrol Hicks, Gordon Jensen, Alton H. Howard, Don Francisco, & Nancy Honeytree.

Come Christians Join to Sing Clcd. David Lowe. 2000. audio compact disk 16.98 (978-0-633-00758-4(7)) LifeWay Christian.

Come Christians Join to Sing Clcs. David Lowe. 2000. 11.98 (978-0-633-00759-1(5)) LifeWay Christian.

Come Closer: A Call to Life, Love & Breakfast on the Beach. Jane Rubietta. (ENG.). 2009. 24.99 (978-1-934384-28-2(3)) Pub: Treasure Pub. Dist(s): STL Dist NA

Come, Creator Spirit. Derek Prince. 1 cass. 1990. 5.95 (I-4268) Derek Prince.
From Genesis onward, all creation is by the Holy Spirit. His work is consummated in the Church through the new creation.

Come Dance by the Ocean. Ella Jenkins. 1 CD. (Running Time: 1 hr.). (J). 2001. audio compact disk 15.00 (FC 45014CD) Kimbo Educ.

Come Dance by the Ocean. Perf. by Ella Jenkins. 1 cass. (Running Time: 42 min.). (J). (ps-4). 1991. (0-9307-450140-9307-45014-2-9); audio compact disk (0-9307-45014-2-9) Smithsonian Folkways.
Songs dedicated to caring for the environment & appreciating other cultures, languages & places. Includes "You Can't Sing a Rainbow" & "A Solution to Pollution".

Come Dance with Me. Perf. by Joel Chernoff. 2002. audio compact disk Provident Mus Dist.

Come, Emmanuel. 2290th ed. Perf. by Ron Rendek. 1993. 11.00 (978-1-58459-074-3(2)) Wrld Lib Pubns.

Come, Emmanuel. 2292nd ed. Perf. by Rendek Ron. 1 CD. (Running Time: 1 hr. 30 mins.). 1993. audio compact disk 11.00 (978-1-58459-025-5(4)) Wrld Lib Pubns.

Come, Emmanuel: A Christmas Creed. John Chisum. 2000. 75.00 (978-0-633-00786-7(2)); audio compact disk 85.00 (978-0-633-00839-0(7)) LifeWay Christian.

Come, Follow Me! 1985. (0270) Evang Sisterhood Mary.

Come Go with Me to That Land: Black & Red Together: Communism & the Call to the Revolutionary Community see Come Go with Me to That Land: Visions of Community in the Afro-American Freedom Struggle

Come Go with Me to That Land: Can Any Good Thing Come Out of Alabama? - The Southern Freedom Movement & the Beloved Community see Come Go with Me to That Land: Visions of Community in the Afro-American Freedom Struggle

Come Go with Me to That Land: Come Go with Me to That Land: Visions of the New Community, Calls to the Way see Come Go with Me to That Land: Visions of Community in the Afro-American Freedom Struggle

Come Go with Me to That Land: Let My People Go: The Black Struggle Against Slavery As a Quest for a New Community see Come Go with Me to That Land: Visions of Community in the Afro-American Freedom Struggle

Come Go with Me to That Land: Malcolm & Martin & This Great Cloud of Witnesses: Testimonies to the High Cost of Community see Come Go with Me to That Land: Visions of Community in the Afro-American Freedom Struggle

Come Go with Me to That Land: The Long Hard Shadow of Jonestown: Hope, Despair & the Hunger for Community in the Seventies see Come Go with Me to That Land: Visions of Community in the Afro-American Freedom Struggle

Come Go with Me to That Land: The Unfulfilled Promise of the Promised Land: Elusive Hopes & Explosive Struggles in the Urban North see Come Go with Me to That Land: Visions of Community in the Afro-American Freedom Struggle

Come Go with Me to That Land: To Establish Unity, Peace & Brotherhood: Civil War, Black Hope & the Aborted Revolution see Come Go with Me to That Land: Visions of Community in the Afro-American Freedom Struggle

Come Go with Me to That Land: To Lead the Millions up the Heights: Marcus Garvey & the Call to the Ancestral Community see Come Go with Me to That Land: Visions of Community in the Afro-American Freedom Struggle

Come Go with Me to That Land: Visions of Community in the Afro-American Freedom Struggle. Vincent Harding. 10 cass. Incl. Come Go with Me to That Land: Black & Red Together: Communism & the Call to the Revolutionary Community. 1980.; Come Go with Me to That Land: Can Any Good Thing Come Out of Alabama? - The Southern Freedom Movement & the Beloved Community. 1980.; Come Go with Me to That Land: Come Go with Me to That Land: Visions of the New Community, Calls to the Way. 1980.; Come Go with Me to That Land: Let My People Go: The Black Struggle Against Slavery As a Quest for a New Community. 1980.; Come Go with Me to That Land: Malcolm & Martin & This Great Cloud of Witnesses: Testimonies to the High Cost of Community. 1980.; Come Go with Me to That Land: The Long Hard Shadow of Jonestown: Hope, Despair & the Hunger for Community in the Seventies. 1980.; Come Go with Me to That Land: The Unfulfilled Promise of the Promised Land: Elusive Hopes & Explosive Struggles in the Urban North. 1980.; Come Go with Me to That Land: To Establish Unity, Peace & Brotherhood: Civil War, Black Hope & the Aborted Revolution. 1980.; Come Go with Me to That Land: To Lead the Millions up the Heights: Marcus Garvey & the Call to the Ancestral Community. 1980.; Come Go with Me to That Land: What Mean These Stones? - Introduction to a Pilgrimage. 1980.; 1980. 30.00 Set.; 4.50 ea. Pendle Hill.

Come Go with Me to That Land: What Mean These Stones? - Introduction to a Pilgrimage see Come Go with Me to That Land: Visions of Community in the Afro-American Freedom Struggle

Come, Holy Spirit: Contemporary Songs of Faith. Created by World Library Publications. (3 Voices as One Ser.). 2006. audio compact disk 17.00 (978-1-58459-297-6(4)) Wrld Lib Pubns.

Come In see Robert Frost in Recital

Come In see Twentieth-Century Poetry in English, No. 6, Recordings of Poets Reading Their Own Poetry

Come In. Perf. by John P. Kee & New Life Community Choir. 1 cass. 1999. 7.98 Brentwood Music.

Come into the House of God. Eagles' Wings Ministries. 2007. audio compact disk 16.00 (978-0-9665831-7-5(5)) Pub: Kairos Pubg. Dist(s): Destiny Image Pubs

Come Join the Living World. Perf. by Brent Bourgeois. 1 cass. 1994. audio compact disk Brentwood Music.
Former Island recording artist member of Bourgeois/Tagg, this project was co-produced by Dove Award winning producer, Charlie Peacock. Features 4 No. 1 singles: One Love, Restored, A Little More Like Jesus & Blessed be the Name.

***Come Let Us Adore with O Come, All Ye Faithful.** Created by Lillenas Publishing Company. (ENG.). 2008. audio compact disk 24.99 (978-5-557-43541-3(7)) Lillenas.

Come Let Us Be Merry. Perf. by Barolk Folk & Carrie Crompton. 1 cass. (Running Time: 37 min.). (J). (gr. 3 up). 1990. 9.98 (978-1-877737-58-9(5), EB 409); audio compact disk 12.98 (978-1-877737-59-6(3), EB D409) MFLP CA.
Instrumental arrangements of Christmas Carols & dances. Performed on dulcimer, recorder, violin, guitar & piano.

Come Let Us Bow. Perf. by Lori Wilke. 1 cass. (Running Time: 5 min.). 1992. 9.98 Sound track. (978-1-891916-31-1(9)) Spirit To Spirit.

Come Let Us Reason Together, Set. Mac Hammond. 6 cass. (Running Time: 6 hrs.). 1995. Mac Hammond.
If you've ever wanted to explain your faith to a skeptic but didn't feel you had the tools, this series is for you.

Come Let Us Sing for Joy. Marty Haugen. 1 cass. 2000. 10.95 (CS-470); audio compact disk 15.95 (CD-470) GIA Pubns.

Come Let Us Worship. (KOR.). bk. 45.00 (978-0-687-07488-4(6)) Abingdon.

Come, Let's Celebrate - ShowTrax. Music by Rosephanye Powell. 1 CD. (Running Time: 5 mins.). 2000. audio compact disk 19.95 (08703285) H Leonard.
This gospel original is a joyful celebration that is just brimming with rhythmic vitality.

Come Love, Come Hope. unabr. ed. Iris Bromige. Read by Anita Wright. 6 cass. (Running Time: 6 hrs. 15 min.). (Isis Ser.). (J). 2003. 54.95 (978-0-7531-1301-1(5)) Pub: ISIS Lrg Prnt GBR. Dist(s): Ulverscroft US
Garth Melrose was younger than Claire had imagined but just as forbidding. She knew little about him, except that he owned a small business in the country and was a widower with a young daughter. However, in a few weeks, circumstances would make her governess to his daughter, the object of his possessive sister's jealousy, and a pawn in his brother-in-law's game.

Come Love with Me & Be My Life: The Complete Romantic Poetry of Peter McWilliams, Set. Peter McWilliams. 1991. 12.95 (978-0-931580-74-1(9)) Mary Bks.

Come, Now Is the Time to Worship. Contrib. by Phillips Craig & Dean. (Worship Tracks (Word Tracks) Ser.). 2006. audio compact disk 8.98 (978-5-558-26919-2(7), Word Music) Word Enter.

Come Now, Sleep. Contrib. by As Cities Burn. 2007. audio compact disk 17.99 (978-5-557-67160-6(9)) Tooth & Nail.

Come on Everybody, Let's Sing! 4 CDs. Lois Birkenshaw-Fleming. (ENG.). 2002. audio compact disk 29.95 (978-0-7579-8250-7(6), VCD1430A, Warner Bro) Alfred Pub.

Come on in This House. Perf. by Junior Wells. 1 cass., 1 CD. 7.98 (TA 33395); 7.98 (TA 33395); audio compact disk 12.78 CD Jewel box. (TA 83395); audio compact disk 12.78 CD Jewel box. (TA 83395) NewSound.

Come on Out & Play. Bill Harley. (J). 2003. audio compact disk 15.00 (978-1-878126-40-5(7)) Round Riv Prodns.
Stories of fantasy & things that might have happened. Sitting Down to Eat; Sarah's Story; Come on Out & Play; Staying Up; Fox's Sack.

Come on Out & Play. unabr. ed. Bill Harley. Read by Bill Harley. 1 cass. (Running Time: 45 min.). (J). (gr. k-3). 1990. 10.00 (978-1-878126-04-7(0), RRR107) Round Riv Prodns.

Come on over Barneys House. Read by Hinkler Books Staff. (J). 2004. bk. 9.99 (978-1-86515-999-7(9)) Pub: Hinkler AUS. Dist(s): Penton Overseas

Come on Rain! 2004. audio compact disk 12.95 (978-1-55592-891-9(9)) Weston Woods.

Come on Rain. (J). 2004. pap. bk. 14.95 (978-0-7882-0513-2(7)) Weston Woods.

Come on, Rain! 2004. 8.95 (978-1-55592-835-3(8)) Weston Woods.

Come on, Rain! Karen Hesse. (J). 2004. bk. 24.95 (978-1-55592-177-4(9)) Weston Woods.

Come on Seabiscuit! unabr. ed. Ralph Moody. Read by Jim Weiss. 3 cass. (Running Time: 4 hrs.). 2003. 23.95 (978-0-7861-2607-1(8), 3203); audio compact disk 32.00 (978-0-7861-8931-1(2), 3203) Blckstn Audio.

Come Quickly, Lord Jesus: Rev. 22:6-12. Ed Young. 1987. 4.95 (978-0-7417-1587-6(2), 587) Win Walk.

Come Rain or Shine. Susan Sallis. Read by Anne Dover. 13 CDs. (Running Time: 14 hrs. 22 mins.). (Soundings (CDs) Ser.). (J). 2004. audio compact disk 99.95 (978-1-84283-522-7(X)) Pub: ISIS Lrg Prnt GBR. Dist(s): Ulverscroft US

Come Rain or Shine. unabr. ed. Susan Sallis. Read by Anne Dover. 12 cass. (Running Time: 16 hrs.). 1999. 94.95 (978-1-86042-470-0(8), 24708) Pub: Soundings Ltd GBR. Dist(s): Ulverscroft US
There were four of them: young women, dressed decorously in black, employed at an exclusive jewelry store in the 1960s. Close friendships were forged as Natasha, Prudence, Rachel & Maisie worked together. Now, in 1980, Natasha, newly divorced & back from America with a fifteen-year-old daughter, decides there must be a reunion. Pru, always the mysterious one, deeply involved with her commune in Cornwall, unexpectedly offers Prospect House, a property she has inherited in the Malvern Hills where they may all gather. Rachel, married to her former boss, an MP gladly leaves a tangled domestic situation to join the friends she hasn't seen for so long. And Maisie perhaps the most vulnerable of the four, mother of five children, married to the unpredictable Edward, fails to arrive at Prospect House.

Come September. unabr. ed. Arundhati Roy. 1 CD. (Running Time: 1 hr. 30 min.). (AK Press Audio Ser.). 2004. audio compact disk 14.98 (978-1-902593-80-7(4)) Pub: AK Pr GBR. Dist(s): Consort Bk Sales

Come Sing, Jimmy Jo. Katherine Paterson. Read by Linda Stephens. 5 cass. (Running Time: 6 hrs.). (YA). 2000. pap. bk. & stu. ed. 60.24 (978-0-7887-4089-3(X), 41109) Recorded Bks.
In the Johnson family, everybody strums & sings, including 11-year-old James. When the family hires a manager to book their appearances, he quickly gives the boy a stage name & puts him on national TV. Now James has to decide what is most important to him, fame or family.

Come Sing, Jimmy Jo. unabr. ed. Katherine Paterson. Narrated by Linda Stephens. 5 pieces. (Running Time: 6 hrs. 15 mins.). (gr. 5 up). 2000. 47.00 (978-0-7887-4021-3(0), 96142e7) Recorded Bks.

Come Sing, Jimmy Jo. unabr. ed. Katherine Paterson. Narrated by Linda Stephens. 6 CDs. (Running Time: 6 hrs. 15 mins.). (gr. 5 up). 2000. audio compact disk 58.00 (978-0-7887-4650-5(2), C1197E7) Recorded Bks.

Come Sing, Jimmy Jo, Class set. Katherine Paterson. Read by Linda Stephens. 5 cass. (Running Time: 6 hrs.). (YA). 2000. 117.70 (978-0-7887-4090-9(3), 47102) Recorded Bks.

Come Spring. abr. ed. Jill Marie Landis. Read by Jessica Arden. 1 cass. (Running Time: 90 min.). 1995. 5.99 (978-1-57096-025-3(9), RAZ 925) Romance Alive Audio.
Boston-bred Annika Storm is snatched off a train in Wyoming by a rugged mountain man in a case of chaotic mistaken identity. Realizing his mistake too late, the unrefined trapper & the socialite are snowed in together in his cabin. Will the ice thaw inside...& outside...Come Spring?.

Come Sunday. unabr. ed. Isla Morley. Read by Jennifer Wiltsie. (Running Time: 11 hrs. 30 mins. 0 sec.). (ENG.). 2009. audio compact disk 39.95 (978-1-4272-0742-5(9)) Pub: Macmill Audio. Dist(s): Macmillan

Come Test Him & See. Neville Goddard. 1 cass. (Running Time: 62 min.). 1969. 8.00 (78) J & L Pubns.
Neville taught Imagination Creates Reality. He was a powerfully influential teacher of God as Consciousness.

Come the Morning. abr. ed. Shannon Drake. Read by Sandra Burr. 2 cass. 1999. 17.95 (FS9-43366) Highsmith.

Come the Morning. unabr. ed. Shannon Drake. Read by Sandra Burr. (Running Time: 13 hrs.). 2008. 39.25 (978-1-4233-5274-7(2), 9781423352747, BADLE); 24.95 (978-1-4233-5273-0(4), 9781423352730, BAD); audio compact disk 39.25 (978-1-4233-5272-3(6), 9781423352723, Brlnc Audio MP3 Lib); audio compact disk 24.95 (978-1-4233-5271-6(8), 9781423352716, Brilliance MP3) Brilliance Audio.

Come the Spring. Julie Garwood. (Clayborne Brides Ser.: Bk. 5). 2004. 10.95 (978-0-7435-4290-6(8)) Pub: S&S Audio. Dist(s): S and S Inc

Come the Spring. unabr. ed. Julie Garwood. Narrated by Richard Ferrone. 7 cass. (Running Time: 10 hrs. 15 mins.). (Clayborne Brides Ser.: Bk. 5). 1998. 66.00 (978-0-7887-1969-1(6), 95356E7) Recorded Bks.
A federal marshall is trying to capture a gang of murderous bank robbers. But as he questions one lovely witness, she captures his heart.

Come to Bethlehem. Greg Skipper. 1995. 10.98 (978-0-7673-0702-4(X)) LifeWay Christian.

Come to Bethlehem: Based on Old Testament & New Testament Travelers to Bethlehem. Rae Whitney. (Running Time: 40 mins.). (Noel Ser.). 1998. 15.95 (978-1-56212-370-3(X), 416103) FaithAliveChr.

Come to God's Party: Music. Ken Medema. (Firelight Ser.). (gr. 7-9). 2004. audio compact disk 5.99 (978-0-8066-6492-7(4)) Augsburg Fortress.

Come to Grief. Dick Francis. (Sid Halley Adventure Ser.). 2004. 10.95 (978-0-7435-4291-3(6)) Pub: S&S Audio. Dist(s): S and S Inc

Come to Grief. unabr. ed. Dick Francis. Read by David Case. 7 cass. (Running Time: 10 hrs. 30 min.). (Sid Halley Adventure Ser.). 1996. 56.00 (978-0-7366-3274-4(3), 3930) Books on Tape.
He's off! Few things are more thrilling than author Dick Francis at full gallop. Here he returns to the world of racehorses, steeplechase & Sid Halley, the intuitive, one-handed ex-jockey & amateur P.I.

Come to Grief. unabr. ed. Dick Francis. Narrated by Simon Prebble. 8 cass. (Running Time: 10 hrs. 75 min.). (Sid Halley Adventure Ser.). Rental 16.50 Set. (94660) Recorded Bks.

Come to Grief. unabr. ed. Dick Francis. Narrated by Simon Prebble. 8 cass. (Running Time: 10 hrs. 45 mins.). (Sid Halley Adventure Ser.). 2000. 70.00 (978-0-7887-0467-3(2), 94660E7) Recorded Bks.

Come to Me: Conferences on Personal Problems in the Spiritual Life. Benedict J. Groeschel. Read by Benedict J. Groeschel. 7 cass. (Running Time: 6 hrs.). 57.95 incl. vinyl album. (AA1528) Credence Commun.
Outlines ways in which following Christ helps one to cope, grow, & overcome psychological difficulties.

Come to Me: Stories. unabr. collector's ed. Short Stories. Amy Bloom. Read by Tonya Jordan. 4 cass. (Running Time: 6 hrs.). 1998. 32.00 (978-0-7366-4118-0(1), 4622) Books on Tape.
A fresh & stunning collection of short stories explores the lives of ordinary people in extraordinary circumstances, changed by love.

Come to My House. (Greetings Ser.: Vol. 3). (gr. 2-3). 10.00 (978-0-7635-5869-7(9)) Rigby Educ.

Come to the Edge: A Memoir of Romance. unabr. ed. Christina Haag. (Running Time: 9 hrs.). 2008. 39.25 (978-1-4233-3805-5(7), 9781423338055, Brlnc Audio MP3 Lib); 24.95 (978-1-4233-3804-8(9), 9781423338048, Brilliance MP3); 39.25 (978-1-4233-3807-9(3), 9781423338079, BADLE); 87.25 (978-1-4233-3801-7(4), 9781423338017, BrilAudUnabridg); audio compact disk 92.25 (978-1-4233-3803-1(0), 9781423338031, BriAudCD Unabrid) Brilliance Audio.

Come to the Edge: A Memoir of Romance. unabr. ed. Christina Haag. (Running Time: 9 hrs.). 2010. 24.99 (978-1-4233-3806-2(5), 9781423338062, BAD); audio compact disk 29.99 (978-1-4233-3802-4(2), 9781423338024, Bril Audio CD Unabri) Brilliance Audio.

Come to the Manger: Accompaniment/Performance. Composed by Mark Hayes. (ENG.). 2001. audio compact disk 45.00 (978-0-7390-1998-6(8)) Alfred Pub.

Come to the Manger: Preview Pack. Composed by Mark Hayes. (ENG.). 2001. audio compact disk 12.95 (978-0-7390-1997-9(X)) Alfred Pub.

Come to the Table: Music for First Communion Book. Ed. by Robert J. Batastini & Kelly Dobbs Mickus. 2003. spiral bd. 24.95 (978-1-57999-274-3(9), G-6050CD) GIA Pubns.

Come to the Table: The Gospel as Common Ground. Richard Rohr. Read by Richard Rohr. 7 cass. (Running Time: 8 hrs.). 1997. pap. bk. (AA3034) Credence Commun.
The Gospel is an instrument of peace but we need a certain spiritual maturity or else we turn it into arguments about who is right (& self-righteous), & who is liberal-conservative.

Come to the Waters: Ancient Paths. WorldView Group Staff. 2003. audio compact disk 15.00 (978-0-9742778-0-6(0)) STL Dist NA.

***Come to Win.** unabr. ed. Venus Williams. Read by Abby Craden et al. (ENG.). 2010. (978-0-06-201598-3(2), Harper Audio) HarperCollins Pubs.

***Come to Win: Business Leaders, Artists, Doctors, & Other Visionaries on How Sports Can Help You Top Your Profession.** unabr. ed. Venus Williams. Read by Abby Craden et al. (ENG.). 2010. (978-0-06-198881-3(2), Harper Audio) HarperCollins Pubs.

Come Together, Set. abr. ed. Josie Lloyd & Emlyn Rees. 2 cass. (Running Time: 3 hrs.). 1999. 16.85 (978-1-85686-502-9(9)) Ulvrscrft Audio.
Meet Jack: I'm twenty-seven years old, single, & live with my best mate, Matt. Meet Amy: Sometimes in my darker moments I've thought about applying to go on Blind Date. Now find out what happens when they meet each other in the first novel to tell both sides of the story.

Come Together: Insights for women, on Men. Leslie LaMarr. (ENG.). 2007. 7.99 (978-1-934660-03-4(5)) MTW Pub.

Come unto Christ. George Pace. 1 cass. 3.95 (978-1-57734-394-3(8), 34441352) Covenant Comms.

Come unto Christ. George W. Pace. 1 cass. 6.98 (978-1-55503-248-7(6), 06004180) Covenant Comms.
The Gifts of Gifts - Inspiring classic Pace talks.

Come unto Me. Gerald N. Lund. Read by Larry A. McKeever. (Running Time: 71100 sec.). (Kingdom & the Crown Ser.). 2008. audio compact disk 49.95 (978-1-59038-940-9(9), Shadow Mount) Deseret Bk.

Come Up the Mountain. Caryl Krueger. Read by Caryl Krueger. 1 cass. (Running Time: 1 hr. 5 min.). 2001. 9.00 Belleridge.

***Come You on Inside.** Sheila Newberry. 2010. cass. & cass. 24.95 (978-1-84652-605-3(1)); audio compact disk 34.95 (978-1-84652-606-0(X)) Pub: Magna Story GBR. Dist(s): Ulverscroft US

Comeback. abr. ed. Richard Stark, pseud. Read by Jerry Orbach. 2006. 14.98 (978-1-59483-841-5(0)) Pub: Hachet Audio. Dist(s): HachBkGrp

Comeback. collector's unabr. ed. Richard Stark, pseud. Read by Michael Kramer. 4 cass. (Running Time: 6 hrs.). 1999. 32.00 (978-0-7366-4433-4(4), 4692) Books on Tape.
After an absence of decades, master thief Parker returns to steal a flashy televangelist's cash.

Comeback. unabr. ed. Dick Francis. Read by David Case. 7 cass. (Running Time: 10 hrs. 30 min.). 1994. 56.00 (978-0-7366-2669-9(7), 3406) Books on Tape.
It's been over twenty years since the last appearance of Parker, a man who lives for the perfect crime, yet refuses to die committing it. Enjoying retirement with his lady-love, Claire, Parker is lured into one more heist, to steal a cool half million from a flashy televangelist. Unfortunately, whatever can go wrong does: an inside contact wants out, a greedy partner wants more & two teenagers who stumble into murder want anything but what they have. Parker illuminates a gritty world where good can quickly turn bad & vice versa, for example, who's more treacherous, an honest thief like Parker or a larcenous televangelist.

Comeback. unabr. collector's ed. Richard Stark, pseud. Read by Michael Kramer. 4 cass. (Running Time: 6 hrs.). (Parker Ser.). 1998. 32.00 (978-0-7366-4194-4(7), 4692) Books on Tape.
After an absence of decades, master thief Parker returns to steal a flashy televangelist's cash.

Comeback: Conservatism That Can Win Again. David Frum. Read by Lloyd James. (ENG.). 2009. 59.99 (978-1-60775-765-8(6)) Find a World.

Comeback: Conservatism That Can Win Again. unabr. ed. David Frum. Read by Lloyd James. 5 CDs. (Running Time: 5 hrs. 30 mins. 0 sec.). (ENG.). 2008. audio compact disk 29.99 (978-1-4001-0587-8(0)); audio compact disk 59.99 (978-1-4001-3587-5(7)); audio compact disk 19.99 (978-1-4001-5587-3(8)) Pub: Tantor Media. Dist(s): IngramPubServ

Comeback: Overcoming Barrenness, Miscarriage or Stillbirth. Erica Smith. Composed by Kenneth Reese. (ENG.). 2008. per. 12.99 (978-1-933518-81-7(2)) Art Es Pub.

***Comebacks at Work: Using Conversation to Master Confrontation.** unabr. ed. Kathleen Kelley Reardon & Christopher T. Noblet. (ENG.). 2010. (978-0-06-206436-3(3), Harper Audio); (978-0-06-206435-6(5), Harper Audio) HarperCollins Pubs.

Comedian Dies. unabr. ed. Simon Brett. Read by Frederick Davidson. 5 cass. (Running Time: 7 hrs. 30 min.). 1999. 39.95 (1429) Blckstn Audio.
Charles Paris, middle-aged actor & amateur sleuth, visits a small English seaside town, where he witnesses the death of a performer at a local music hall. An accident? The more he inquires about the remaining acts on the bill, the more suspects he uncovers.

Comedian Dies. unabr. ed. Simon Brett. Read by Frederick Davidson. 5 cass. (Running Time: 7 hrs.). 2000. 39.95 (978-0-7861-0477-2(5), 1429) Blckstn Audio.

Comedian Dies. unabr. ed. Simon Brett. (Running Time: 21600 sec.). (Charles Paris Mystery Ser.). 2007. audio compact disk 45.00 (978-0-7861-5922-2(7)) Blckstn Audio.

Comedian Dies. unabr. ed. Simon Brett. Read by Frederick Davidson. (Running Time: 21600 sec.). (Charles Paris Mystery Ser.). 2007. audio compact disk 29.95 (978-0-7861-7300-6(9)) Blckstn Audio.

Comedian Dies. unabr. ed. Simon Brett. Narrated by Simon Prebble. 5 cass. (Running Time: 6 hrs. 15 mins.). (Charles Paris Mystery Ser.: Vol. 5). 1998. 44.00 (978-0-7887-1886-1(X), 95308E7) Recorded Bks.
When Charles Paris visits the Winter Gardens to watch a rising young comedian, he witnesses a murder.

Comedians. unabr. ed. Graham Greene. Read by Joseph Porter. 8 cass. (Running Time: 11 hrs. 30 mins.). 1994. 56.95 (978-0-7861-0459-8(7), 1411) Blckstn Audio.
Set in Haiti, "The Comedians" is a story of love & adventure, hope & disillusion. The Haitian, Doctor Magiot, is committed. His last letter to Brown, the story's narrator, is a statement & an appeal by the committed - by a man whose nature forces him to share the terrible events of his time. But the others - the comedians - have opted out. Brown, a disenchanted part-Englishman from Monaco, a hotel owner; Smith & his wife, an American couple on a good-will mission; Martha, the young German wife of a Latin-American diplomat; Jones, an engaging fool & the solider of fortune on his own mysterious business: all these play their parts in the foreground. They experience love affairs rather than love; they have enthusiasms, but not a faith; & if they die, they die by accident. With alternating comedy, irony, & grim violence, Greene weaves these lives into a pattern of mounting suspense.

***Comedians.** unabr. ed. Graham Greene. Read by Joseph Porter. (Running Time: 11 hrs. 5 mins.). (ENG.). 2011. 29.95 (978-1-4417-0381-1(0)); audio compact disk 29.95 (978-1-4417-0380-4(2)); audio compact disk 100.00 (978-1-4417-0378-1(0)) Blckstn Audio.

Comedians of the Year. Perf. by John Pinette et al. 4 cass. (Running Time: 4 hrs.). (Spoken Word Humor Ser.). 1999. 29.95 Set, clamshell. (978-1-929243-00-6(6), UPR1001) Uproar Ent.
"The Comedians of the Year" featuring RICHARD JENI, MARGARET CHO, JOHN PINETTE & BRIAN REGAN.

Comedies: Ozzie & Harriet, Duffy's Tavern & The Jack Benny Program. Perf. by Jack Benny et al. 2002. bk. 9.98 Radio Spirits.
It's a laugh a minute with TV's favorite comedy episodes.

Comedies Brick Pack. Perf. by Lou Costello et al. 10 cass. (Running Time: 10 hrs.). 2001. 29.98 (7100) Radio Spirits.
20 episodes from Abbott and Costello, Amos 'n' Andy, The Bickersons, Burns and Allen, The Charlie McCarthy Show, Fibber McGee and Molly, The Great Gildersleeve, The Jack Benny Program, The Life of Riley, My Favorite Husband.

Comedy. abr. unabr. ed. Garrison Keillor. 2 CDs. (Running Time: 2 hrs.). (ENG.). 1998. audio compact disk 24.95 (978-1-56511-259-9(8), 1565112598) Pub: HighBridge. Dist(s): Workman Pub

Comedy, Set. 12 cass. (Running Time: 12 hrs.). 1999. 29.98 (AB114) Radio Spirits.

Comedy, Vol. 1. (Running Time: 6 hrs.). 2004. audio compact disk 29.95 (978-1-57816-197-3(5)) Audio File.

Comedy, Vol. 1. Perf. by Jack Benny et al. (Nostalgia Classics Ser.). 19.98 Moonbeam Pubns.

Comedy, Vol. 1, Set. 6 cass. (Running Time: 6 hrs.). 24.95 bookshelf album. (978-1-57816-024-2(3), NC1010) Audio File.
Includes: "Amos 'n' Andy" (10-24-48); "Bob Hope" (3-16-48); "Charlie McCarthy" (9-21-41); Fibber McGee & Molly" (4-6-48); "Fred Allen" (10-21-45); "Great Gildersleeve" (1-8-50); "Jack Benny" (10-20-46); "Jimmy Durante" (12-10-47); "Life with Luigi" (3-4-52); "Our Miss Brooks" (10-24-48); "Adventures of Ozzie & Harriet" (3-27-49); "Red Skelton" (3-19-46).

Comedy, Vol. 2. Perf. by Jack Benny et al. (Nostalgia Classics Ser.). 19.98 Moonbeam Pubns.

Comedy, Vol. 2, Set. 6 cass. (Running Time: 6 hrs.). 24.95 bookshelf album. (978-1-57816-025-9(1), NC2020) Audio File.
Includes: "Amos 'n' Andy" (5-4-45); "Blondie" (1940s); "Bob Hope" (11-9-48); "Charlie McCarthy" (12-7-47); "Eddie Cantor" (1-10-45); "Fibber McGee & Molly" (10-19-48); "Fred Allen" (2-6-49); "Great Gildersleeve" (5-7-52); "Halls of Ivy" (1950); "Jack Benny" (11-9-47); "Life of Riley" (5-17-46); "Mel Blanc Show" (1-28-47).

Comedy... Comin' at Ya! abr. ed. John Caponera. 1 cass. (Running Time: 48 min.). 1997. 6.95; audio compact disk 10.95 Wildstone Media.
Live recording.

Comedy Legends. Radio Spirits Staff. Read by Bob Hope. 12 CDs. (Running Time: 12 hrs.). 2005. audio compact disk 39.98 (978-1-57019-535-8(8), 47052) Radio Spirits.

Comedy Legends. unabr. ed. 8 cass. (Running Time: 12 hrs.). 2002. 39.98 (978-1-57019-536-5(6), 47054) Radio Spirits.
Abbott & Costello, Burns and Allen, Jack Benny, Bob Hope...their names are synonymous with the best of classic comedy. These legendary performers kept radio audiences in stitches more than 50 years ago and still have the same effect today - whether you know their routines by heart or you're hearing them for the first time.

Comedy of Errors. William Shakespeare. 3 cass. 1999. 17.95 Penguin Grp USA.

Comedy of Errors. William Shakespeare. 1 cass. Dramatization. 10.95 (978-0-8045-0888-9(7), SAC 7113) Spoken Arts.
The Folio Theatre Players under the direction of Christopher Casson present the complete play.

***Comedy of Errors.** abr. ed. William Shakespeare. Read by Alec Mccowen & Anna Massey. (ENG.). 2003. (978-0-06-074316-1(6), Caedmon) HarperCollins Pubs.

***Comedy of Errors.** abr. ed. William Shakespeare. Read by Alec Mccowen & Anna Massey. (ENG.). 2004. (978-0-06-081464-9(0), Caedmon) HarperCollins Pubs.

Comedy of Errors. unabr. ed. William Shakespeare. (Running Time: 5280 sec.). (Arkangel Shakespeare Ser.). (ENG.). 2005. audio compact disk 19.95 (978-1-932219-05-0(6)) Pub: AudioGO. Dist(s): Perseus Dist
Mix-ups and mayhem abound in this comedic romp featuring two sets of twins, both separated at birth, all of whom wind up in the same city. This wild and woolly early farce captures the great playwright at the height of his youthful exuberance. Performed by David Tennant, Brendan Coyle, Alan Cox, and the Arkangel cast.

Comedy of Errors. unabr. ed. William Shakespeare. Read by Alec McCowen & Anna Massey. 2 cass. (Running Time: 3 hrs.). Dramatization. 17.95 (H175) Blckstn Audio.
Likely the very first play Shakespeare ever wrote & for that reason alone it deserves a special place in literary history. As accessible & as entertaining as any of the Bard's later comedies.

Comedy of Errors. unabr. ed. William Shakespeare. Read by Audio Partners Staff. 2 cass. (Running Time: 1 hr. 28 mins.). (Arkangel Shakespeare Ser.). 2004. 17.95 (978-1-932219-45-6(5), Atlntc Mnthly) Pub: Grove-Atltc. Dist(s): PerseuPGW
Mix-ups and mayhem abound in this comedic romp featuring two sets of twins, both separated at birth, all of whom wind up in the same city. This wild and woolly early farce captures the great playwright at the height of his youthful exuberance. Performed by David Tennant, Brendan Coyle, Alan Cox, and the Arkangel cast.

Comedy of Errors. unabr. ed. William Shakespeare. 2 cass. 1999. 18.00 (FS9-51072) Highsmith.

Comedy of Errors. unabr. ed. William Shakespeare. Narrated by Flo Gibson. 2 cass. (Running Time: 2 hrs. 30 mins.). 2003. 14.95 (978-1-55685-714-0(4)) Audio Bk Con.
Twin brothers and their twin slaves, separated as infants by a shipwreck, cause much confusion when their paths cross in Ephesus as adults.

Comedy Superstars. unabr. ed. Perf. by Bud Abbott et al. 20 cass. (Running Time: 30 hrs.). (Old-Time Radio Blockbusters Ser.). 2002. pap. bk. 59.98 (978-1-57019-411-5(4), 4481) Radio Spirits.
Ten episodes from each of six of the greatest comedy superstars of the Golden Age of Radio. Includes 60 of the funniest radio broadcasts in history. This special collection also includes a 64 page booklet featuring rare photos and historical commentary. Sit back and laugh along with these classic comedies: The Abbott & Costello Show, Amos 'n' Andy, The burns and Allen Show, The Edgar Bergen and Charlie McCarthy Show, The Jack Benny Program, and The Red Skelton Show.

Comedy Theater. Garrison Keillor. 3 cass., 2 CDs. 15.98 Set, blisterpack. (PHC 51164); audio compact disk 23.98 CD Set, Jewel box. (PHC 51636) NewSound.

Comedy Theater, Vol. 2. abr. unabr. ed. Garrison Keillor. Perf. by Garrison Keillor. Contrib. by Allison Janney et al. 3 CDs. (Running Time: 3 hrs.). (ENG.). 1997. audio compact disk 29.95 (978-1-56511-183-7(4), 1565111834) Pub: HighBridge. Dist(s): Workman Pub

Comedy Through the Ages, Pts. I-II. Instructed by Seth Lerer. 12 cass. (Running Time: 12 hrs.). 2000. 129.95 (978-1-56585-027-9(0)); audio compact disk 179.95 (978-1-56585-286-0(9)) Teaching Co.

Comedy Through the Ages, Vol. 2. Instructed by Seth Lerer. 6 cass. (Running Time: 6 hrs.). 2000. 129.95 (978-1-56585-028-6(9)); audio compact disk 179.95 (978-1-56585-287-7(7)) Teaching Co.

Comedy, Tragedy, History: The Live Drama & Vital Truth of William Shakespeare. Peter Saccio. 4 cass. (Running Time: 12 hrs.). 19.95 Set; 8 lectures; incl. course guide. (263) Teaching Co.
Professor Saccio teaches the course with the perspective Shakespeare shared - that a play is a special form of communication from a playwright, through actors, to an audience.

Come,Emmanuel: A Christmas Creed. John Chisum. 2000. 11.98 (978-0-633-02963-0(7)); audio compact disk 16.98 (978-0-633-02958-6(0)) LifeWay Christian.

Comes the Blind Fury. abr. ed. John Saul. Read by Tanya Eby. 4 cass. Library ed. (Running Time: 6 hrs.). 2003. 62.25 (978-1-59086-860-7(9), 1590868609, BAudLibEd); audio compact disk 74.25 (978-1-59086-862-1(5), 1590868625, BACDLib Ed) Brilliance Audio.
Amanda: A century ago, a gentle blind girl walked the cliffs of Paradise Point. Then the children came-taunting, teasing-until she lost her footing and fell, shrieking her rage to the drowning sea... Michelle: Now Michelle has come from Boston to live in the big house on Paradise Point. She is excited about her new life, ready to make new friends...until a hand reaches out of the swirling mists-the hand of a blind child. She is asking for friendship...seeking revenge...whispering her name.

Comes the Blind Fury. abr. ed. John Saul. Read by Tanya Eby. 5 CDs. (Running Time: 6 hrs.). 2005. audio compact disk 16.99 (978-1-59600-405-4(3), 9781596004054, BCD Value Price) Brilliance Audio.

Comes the Blind Fury. abr. ed. John Saul. Read by Tanya Eby. (Running Time: 6 hrs.). 2007. 39.25 (978-1-4233-0036-6(X), 9781423300366, BADLE); 24.95 (978-1-4233-0035-9(1), 9781423300359, BAD); audio compact disk 39.25 (978-1-4233-0034-2(3), 9781423300342, Brlnc Audio MP3 Lib); audio compact disk 24.95 (978-1-4233-0033-5(5), 9781423300335, Brilliance MP3) Brilliance Audio.

Comet Ikeya-Seki. 1 cass. (Running Time: 20 min.). 14.95 (23348) MMI Corp.
A new comet is discovered. Astronomers discuss comets in detail & this one in particular.

Comet Is Coming, unabr. ed. Nigel Calder. Narrated by Alexander Spencer. 3 cass. (Running Time: 4 hrs. 30 mins.). 1985. 26.00 (978-1-55690-111-9(9), 85460E7) Recorded Bks.
Using the wandering comet as a narrative thread, Calder plots a fantastic course from Newton's fool's quest for gold to a narrowly missed virgin sacrifice in Oklahoma, all in the name of science.

Comets. Compiled by Benchmark Education Staff. 2006. audio compact disk 10.00 (978-1-4108-6697-4(1)) Benchmark Educ.

Comets. Mary Blakely. 1 cass. (978-1-882995-01-1(5)) Azuray Learn.
Self-empowerment educational materials - ages 7-14.

Comets. Franklyn M. Branley. Illus. by Giulio Maestro. 1 cass. (Let's-Read-And-Find-Out-Science Ser.). (J). (ps-3). 1987. bk. 7.95 (JC-211) HarperCollins Pubs.
The first side includes a turn-the-page signal to help young children read along as they listen. Side two is an uninterrupted narration for more experienced readers or for listening enjoyment.

Comets. unabr. ed. Peter M. Spizzirri. Read by Charles Fuller. Ed. by Linda Spizzirri. 1 cass. (Running Time: 15 min.). Dramatization. (Educational Coloring Book & Cassette Ser.). (J). (gr. 1-8). pap. bk. 6.95 (978-0-86545-113-1(3)) Spizzirri.
Find out how comets inspired superstitions & scientific curiosity as you learn about some of the popular & lesser known comets.

Comets, Quasars & Black Holes. Read by Lloyd Motz. 1 cass. (Running Time: 24 min.). 14.95 (35461) MMI Corp.
Discusses recent discoveries in astronomy, how astronomers approach research.

Comfort (Adaigo Classical Music for Yoga) 2005. audio compact disk (978-1-59250-618-7(6)) Gaiam Intl.

Comfort & Joy. abr. ed. Kristin Hannah. Read by Sandra Burr. (Running Time: 2 hrs.). 2006. audio compact disk 9.99 (978-1-4233-1165-2(5), 9781423311652, BCD Value Price) Brilliance Audio.
Joy Candellaro used to love Christmas more than any other time of the year. Now, as the holiday approaches, she finds herself at loose ends. Recently divorced and estranged from her sister, she can't summon the old enthusiasm for celebrating. So without telling anyone, she buys a ticket and boards a plane bound for the rural Northwest. Yet Joy's best-laid plans go terribly awry. The plane crashes deep in the darkness of a forest. Miraculously, Joy walks away from the wreckage as the plane explodes, obliterating all evidence of its passengers. Amid the towering trees, Joy makes a bold and desperate decision to leave her ordinary life behind and embark on an adventure . . . just for the holidays. Daniel O'Shea has returned to the small town of Rain Valley, following the death of his ex-wife. Now he is a single father facing his son's first Christmas without a mother. Six-year-old Bobby isn't making it easy - the boy has closed himself off from the world, surrounding himself with imaginary friends. When Joy and Bobby meet, they form an instant bond. Thrown together by fate, these wounded souls will be touched by the true spirit of Christmas and remember what it means to be a family. Then a dramatic turn of events shows Joy the price of starting over. On a magical Christmas Eve she will come face-to-face with a startling truth. Now she must decide: In a time of impossible dreams and unexpected chances, can she find the faith to reach for the love she has found . . . and the new life only she believes in?.

Comfort & Joy. unabr. ed. Kristin Hannah. Read by Sandra Burr. 4 cass. (Running Time: 21600 sec.). 2005. 62.25 (978-1-59737-904-5(2), 9781597379045, BrilAudUnabridg) Brilliance Audio.

Comfort & Joy. unabr. ed. Kristin Hannah. Read by Sandra Burr. (Running Time: 6 hrs.). 2005. 39.25 (978-1-59737-910-6(7), 9781597379106, BADLE); 24.95 (978-1-59737-909-0(3), 9781597379090, BAD); 24.95 (978-1-59737-903-8(4), 9781597379038, BAU); audio compact disk 24.95 (978-1-59737-907-6(7), 9781597379076, Brilliance MP3); audio compact disk 26.95 (978-1-59737-905-2(0), 9781597379052, Bril Audio CD Unabri); audio compact disk 39.25 (978-1-59737-908-3(5), 9781597379083, Brlnc Audio MP3 Lib); audio compact disk 74.25 (978-1-59737-906-9(9), 9781597379069, BriAudCD Unabrid) Brilliance Audio.

Comfort & Joy. unabr. ed. Kristin Hannah. Read by Sandra Burr. (YA). 2008. 64.99 (978-1-60514-813-7(X)) Find a World.

Comfort During Chemotherapy. Created by Ellen Chernoff Simon. 1 CD. (Running Time: 70 min.). 2004. audio compact disk 18.00 (978-0-9765587-9-8(3)) Imadulation.
This audio CD contains medical hypnosis and guided imagery to provide comfort, peace and inner support during chemotherapy.This program includes affirmations and effective behavioral techniques designed to enhance coping skills during this time.

Comfort Food. unabr. ed. Kate Jacobs. Read by Barbara Rosenblat. 1 MP3-CD. (Running Time: 11 hrs.). 2008. 29.95 (978-1-4332-3480-4(7)); 65.95 (978-1-4332-3476-7(9)); audio compact disk & audio compact disk 90.00 (978-1-4332-3477-4(7)) Blckstn Audio.

Comfort Food. unabr. ed. Kate Jacobs. Read by Barbara Rosenblat. 9 CDs. (Running Time: 11 hrs.). (ENG.). (gr. 8). 2008. audio compact disk 39.95 (978-0-14-314316-1(6), PengAudBks) Penguin Grp USA.

Comfort for Difficult Times. Created by Ellen Chernoff Simon. 1. (Running Time: 70 minutes). 2004. audio compact disk 18.00 (978-0-9765587-3-6(4)) Imadulation.
Comfor for Difficult Times is an audio program that takes you to a state of relaxation, peace, and comfort. You will re-experience the qualitites and characteristics that help you make it through the tough times. You will be introduced to evocative imagery techniques that will give you ease and comfort.

Comfort for the Soul. unabr. ed. Lynne Logan. 3 cass. (Running Time: 3 hrs.). 1997. 28.00 Set. (978-1-890907-06-8(5)) Heaven Only.
Information for treatment on relationships. How to heal from past traumas of life & recovery.

Comfort for Troubled Hearts. 6 cass. 19.95 (20135, HarperThor) HarpC GBR.

Comfort from a Country Quilt. abr. ed. Reba McEntire. Read by Reba McEntire. 2 cass., 3 CDs. (Running Time: 3 hrs.). 1999. (Random AudioBks) Random Audio Pubg.
One of today's most popular country musicians & admired women of our time shares her life experiences.

Comfort Me with Apples: More Adventures at the Table. unabr. ed. Ruth Reichl. Read by Lorelei King. 8 vols. (Running Time: 12 hrs.). 2001. bk. 69.95 (978-0-7927-2512-1(3), CSL 401, Chivers Sound Lib); audio compact disk 79.95 (978-0-7927-9922-1(4), SLD 073, Chivers Sound Lib) AudioGO.
Recounts Reichl's transformation from chef to food writer, a process that led her through restaurants from Bangkok to Paris to Los Angeles and brought lessons in life, love, and food.

Comfort Now My People: The Advent Message from Isaiah. Bert Polman. (Running Time: 40 mins.). (Scripture Alive Ser.). 1998. 15.95 (978-1-56212-369-7(6), 415107) FaithAliveChr.

Comfort of Cats. Doreen Tovey. Read by Mary Lou Conlin. 5 cass. (Running Time: 7 hrs. 30 min.). 2001. 49.95 (2368X) Pub: Soundings Ltd GBR. Dist(s): Ulverscroft US

Comfort of the Holy Spirit. Gloria Copeland. 1 cass. (Walk with God - Obedience Ser.). 1986. 5.00 (978-0-88114-747-6(8)) K Copeland Pubns.
Biblical teaching on the Holy Spirit.

***Comfort to the Enemy & Other Carl Webster Stories.** unabr. ed. Elmore Leonard. 2010. (978-0-06-206195-9(X), Harper Audio) HarperCollins Pubs.

Comfortable Pregnancy. Eldon Taylor. 1 cass. (Running Time: 62 min.). (Inner Talk Ser.). 16.95 (978-1-55978-564-8(0), 5361L) Progress Aware Res.
Soundtrack - Classical with underlying subliminal affirmations.

Comfortable Pregnancy: Music Theme. Eldon Taylor. 1 cass. 16.95 (978-1-55978-142-8(4), 5361D) Progress Aware Res.

Comfortable Pregnancy: Ocean. Eldon Taylor. Read by Eldon Taylor. Ed. by Leslie Brice. 1 cass. (Running Time: 1 hr.). 1992. 16.95 (978-1-56705-298-5(3)) Gateways Inst.
Self improvement.

Comforts of a Muddy Saturday. unabr. ed. Alexander McCall Smith. Read by Davina Porter. 7 cass. (Running Time: 7 hrs. 45 mins.). (Isabel Dalhousie Ser.: No. 5). 2008. 67.75 (978-1-4361-3790-4(X)); audio compact disk 29.99 (978-1-4361-4136-9(2)); audio compact disk 92.75 (978-1-4361-3791-1(8)) Recorded Bks.

Comic Belief. Prod. by Focus on the Family Staff. (Running Time: 6 hrs.). (Adventures in Odyssey Ser.: No. 5). 2000. 24.99 (978-1-56179-848-3(7)) Pub: Focus Family. Dist(s): Nelson
Catch all the excitement of the Adventures In Odyssey(r) radio drama in these action packed volumes, each featuring twelve 30 minute episodes. Available on either cassette or compact disc, these radio shows provide hours of listening fun for children while teaching important values, principles, and truths.

Comic Book Facts. Steck-Vaughn Staff. 2003. (978-0-7398-8423-2(9)) SteckVau.

Comic Books: From Superheroes to Manga. (High Five Reading - Blue Ser.). (ENG.). (gr. 1-2). 2007. audio compact disk 5.95 (978-1-4296-1409-2(9)) CapstoneDig.

Comic Books: From Superheroes to Manga. Joshua Hatch. (High Five Reading Ser.). (ENG., (gr. 4-5). 2005. audio compact disk 5.95 (978-0-7368-5758-1(3)) CapstoneDig.

Comic Relief V. Hosted by Robin Williams et al. 1 CD. (Running Time: 1 hr. 30 mins.). 2001. audio compact disk 9.98 (R2 71165) Rhino Enter.

Comic Relief VII. Hosted by Robin Williams et al. 1 CD. (Running Time: 1 hr. 30 mins.). 1996. audio compact disk 9.98 (R2 72571) Rhino Enter.

Comic Secrets: Writing & Performing Comedy. Mark Mayfield. 1 CASSETTE. 2000. 15.00 (978-0-9700569-0-0(7)) Mayfield Present.
Tips on writing and performing comedy. How to create new bits or funny up existing material.

Comics Come Home. Perf. by Denis Leary & Jay Mohr. 2001. audio compact disk 16.98 (978-1-929243-33-4(2)) Uproar Ent.

Comida Par Llevar/Carry-Out Food. Created by Rigby Staff. (J). 1993. 10.40 (978-0-435-05941-5(6), Rigby PEA) Pearson EdAUS AUS.

Comin' 'Round the Mountain. Perf. by Phil Rosenthal. 1 cass. (Running Time: 40 min.). (J). (gr. k-6). 1993. 9.98 (978-1-879305-16-8(X), AM-C-114) Am Melody.
Lively renditions of traditional & original songs by award-winning folk musician, with vocals & instrumental accompaniment on banjo, guitar, flute, bass, fiddle, mandolin, & harmonica. 1994 ALA Notable Children's Recording.

Comin' up Shouting! Arranged by John A. Ross. 1 CD. (J). 1999. audio compact disk 14.95 (CD1097) Revels Recs.
A recording of African-American Gospel.

Coming Alive. unabr. ed. Robert LeFevre. 1 cass. (Running Time: 1 hr. 14 min.). 12.95 (403) J Norton Pubs.
LeFevre explains the fundamentals of his view of libertarianism, then proceeds to analyze the four necessary components of government: a ruler, sanction of its victims, a point of contact, & a nonproductive elite. He explains how this parasite can be separated from its host.

Coming & Going. Perf. by Mister Rogers. 1 cass. (J). 1998. 10.98 (978-0-945267-68-3(1), YM055-CN); audio compact disk 13.98 (978-0-945267-69-0(X), YM055-CD) Youngheart Mus.
Songs include: "Won't You Be My Neighbor?"; "This Is Just the Day"; "I Like Someone Who Looks Like You"; "It's the Style to Wear a Smile"; "Be Brave, Be Strong"; "Look & Listen"; "I Like to Take My Time" & more.

Coming Apostolic Ministry. abr. ed. Rick Joyner & Jack Deere. (CD Teaching Ser.). 2005. audio compact disk 15.00 (978-1-929371-60-0(8)) Morning NC.

Coming Attractions. 1985. (5091) Am Audio Prose.

Coming Attractions. Robin Jones Gunn. (Running Time: 8 hrs. 5 mins. 38 sec.). (Katie Weldon Ser.). (ENG.). 2009. 14.99 (978-0-310-30246-9(3)) Zondervan.

***Coming Back.** Marcia Muller. Narrated by Deanna Hurst. (Running Time: 7 hrs. 0 mins. 0 sec.). (ENG.). 2010. audio compact disk 29.95 (978-1-60998-104-4(9)) Pub: AudioGO. Dist(s): Perseus Dist

***Coming Back Stronger: Unleashing the Hidden Power of Adversity.** unabr. ed. Drew Brees. Narrated by Drew Brees. Told to Chris Fabry. 2010. audio compact disk 29.99 (978-1-4143-3945-0(3)) Tyndale Hse.

Coming Back to God: Answers to Questions That Keep Men Away. unabr. ed. Patrick M. Morley. 2001. 17.99 (978-0-310-23573-6(1)) Zondervan.

Coming Back to Life. unabr. ed. Poems. Sharon Olds. Read by Sharon Olds. 1 cass. (Running Time: 1 hr.). 12.95 (23656) J Norton Pubs.
Olds explore the conflicts that separate people as well as the ties that bind.

Coming Breed of Ministry. Rick Joyner. 1 cass. (Running Time: 90 mins.). (Call To Leadership Ser.). 2000. 5.00 (RJ01-001) Morning NC.
Rick addresses the qualities required of spiritual leaders in these times.

Coming Conflict. Avi Lipkin. 2 CD's. (Running Time: 2 hrs.). 2006. audio compact disk 19.95 (978-1-57821-361-0(4)) Koinonia Hse.

***Coming Economic Armageddon: What Bible Prophecy Warns about the New Global Economy.** unabr. ed. David Jeremiah. Read by David Jeremiah. Read by Bob Walter. (Running Time: 11 hrs.). (ENG.). 2010. 24.98 (978-1-60788-652-5(9)); audio compact disk 29.98 (978-1-60788-651-8(0)) Pub: Hachet Audio. Dist(s): HachBkGrp

Coming Economic Collapse: How We Can Thrive When Oil Costs $200 a Barrell. unabr. ed. Stephen Leeb. Read by Brian Emerson. Told to Glen C. Strathy. (Running Time: 25200 sec.). 2006. audio compact disk 27.95 (978-0-7861-6548-3(0)) Blckstn Audio.

Coming Economic Collapse: How We Can Thrive When Oil Costs $200 a Barrell. unabr. ed. Stephen Leeb. Read by Brian Emerson. Told to Glen C. Strathy. (Running Time: 25200 sec.). 2006. 25.95 (978-0-7861-4723-6(7)); audio compact disk 29.95 (978-0-7861-7419-5(6)) Blckstn Audio.

Coming Economic Collapse: How You Can Thrive When Oil Costs $200 a Barrel. unabr. ed. Stephen Leeb. Read by Brian Emerson. Told to Glen C. Strathy. (Running Time: 25200 sec.). 2006. 54.95 (978-0-7861-4649-9(4)); audio compact disk 63.00 (978-0-7861-6787-6(4)) Blckstn Audio.

Coming Events in Bible Prophecy. (Running Time: 1 hr). 2005. (978-0-9762892-8-9(8)) Bible Facts.

Coming from Behind. unabr. ed. Howard Jacobson. Read by Raymond Sawyer. 8 cass. (Running Time: 9 hrs. 30 min.). 2001. 69.95 (978-1-85089-732-3(8), 89083) Pub: ISIS Audio GBR. Dist(s): Ulverscroft US
Sefton Goldberg is a thirty-five year old English teacher. He is gnawingly aware of the success of others around him & is therefore determined to make something of himself, so he decides to write a best-selling novel on the subject of urban Jewish life.

Coming Fury. unabr. ed. Bruce Catton. Narrated by Nelson Runger. 14 cass. (Running Time: 20 hrs. 30 mins.). (Centenial History of the Civil War Ser.: Vol. 1). 1989. 112.00 (978-1-55690-112-6(7), 89770E7) Recorded Bks.
First in a comprehensive three-part history of America's Civil War. From the split Democratic Convention in the spring of 1860 to the first battle of Bull Run.

Coming Fury. unabr. ed. Read by Michael Prichard. 14 cass. (Running Time: 1 hr. 30 min. per cass.). (Centennial History of the Civil War Ser.: Pt. I). 98.00 Set. (1202-A); Rental 11.95 (1202-A) Books on Tape.
Fort Sumter & the war beings.

Coming Home. John Betjeman. 2 cass. (Running Time: 2 hrs.). 1998. 16.85 Set. (978-0-563-55734-0(6)) BBC WrldWd GBR.
Britain's best-known & love Poet Laureate.

Coming Home. Composed by David L. Gurnee. (Running Time: 40 mins.). 2000. audio compact disk 17.95 (978-0-9719244-3-7(0), S104) WindTime Pubns.

Coming Home. Rosamunde Pilcher. Read by Donada Peters. 1995. 96.00 (978-0-7366-3194-5(1)) Books on Tape.

Coming Home. Contrib. by Temple. 2007. audio compact disk 17.98 (978-1-59179-584-1(2)) Sounds True.

Coming Home, Pt. A. unabr. ed. Rosamunde Pilcher. Read by Donada Peters. 13 cass. (Running Time: 19 hrs. 30 min.). 1995. 104.00 (978-0-7366-3193-8(3), 3859 A) Books on Tape.
World War II scatters a carefree group of friends & their homecoming is uncertain. Rich & romantic.

Coming Home, Pt. B. unabr. ed. Rosamunde Pilcher. Read by Donada Peters. 12 cass. (Running Time: 18 hrs.). 1995. 96.00 (3859-B) Books on Tape.

Coming Home, Set. Jennie L. Hansen. 2 cass. 12.95 (978-1-57734-281-6(X), 07001827) Covenant Comms.

Coming Home, Vol. 1. unabr. ed. Rosamunde Pilcher. Read by Rowena Cooper. 14 cass. (Running Time: 14 hrs.). 1997. 110.95 Set. (978-0-7451-6638-4(5), CAB 1254) AudioGO.

Coming Home to Freedom. Swami Amar Jyoti. 1 dolby cass. 1985. 9.95 (R-65) Truth Consciousness.
Joy in melting, freedom in Being & stillness. Swanlike, infallible discrimination, choosing the Real. The pure mind of the Son of God. Futility of mental judgements.

Coming Home to Myself. unabr. ed. Wynonna Judd. Told to Patsi Bale Cox. (Running Time: 10 hrs. 0 mins. 0 sec.). (ENG.). 2005. audio compact disk 34.99 (978-1-4001-0187-0(5)) Pub: Tantor Media. Dist(s): IngramPubServ

Coming Home to Myself. unabr. ed. Wynonna Judd. Read by Ellen Archer. Told to Patsi Bale Cox. (Running Time: 10 hrs. 0 mins. 0 sec.). (ENG.). 2005. audio compact disk 69.99 (978-1-4001-3187-7(1)); audio compact disk 22.99 (978-1-4001-5187-5(2)) Pub: Tantor Media. Dist(s): IngramPubServ

Coming Home to our Appetite: Guided Imagery. 2004. audio compact disk 9.95 (978-0-9728883-3-2(0)) R Cooper.

Coming Home to Someplace New Set: Pill Hill Stories, Jay O'Callahan. Perf. by Jay O'Callahan. 2 cass. (Running Time: 1 hr. 40 min.). 1990. 18.00 (978-1-877954-17-7(9)) Artana Prodns.
Three hilarious & poignant stories which reveal the epic drama of growing up.

***Coming Insurrection.** unabr. ed. Invisible Committee Staff. Read by Christopher Lane. (Running Time: 3 hrs.). (Intervention Ser.). 2010. 14.99 (978-1-4418-7549-5(2), 9781441875495, BAD); 39.97 (978-1-4418-7550-1(6), 9781441875501, BADLE); 14.99 (978-1-4418-7547-1(6), 9781441875471, Brilliance MP3); 39.97 (978-1-4418-7548-8(4), 9781441875488, Brlnc Audio MP3 Lib); audio compact disk 14.99 (978-1-4418-7545-7(X), 9781441875457, Bril Audio CD Unabri); audio compact disk 39.97 (978-1-4418-7546-4(8), 9781441875464, BriAudCD Unabrid) Brilliance Audio.

Coming into the Country. unabr. ed. John McPhee. Read by Dan Lazar. 10 cass. (Running Time: 15 hrs.). 1986. 80.00 (978-0-7366-1063-6(4), 1990) Books on Tape.
Alaska & the Alaskans.

Coming into the Country, unabr. ed. John McPhee. Narrated by Nelson Runger. 11 cass. (Running Time: 16 hrs. 30 mins.). 1990. 91.00 (978-1-55690-113-3(5), 90009E7) Recorded Bks.
Those who have traveled into America's only remaining frontier rarely come back out the same. Only in Alaska can we come close to understanding what our forefathers must have felt upon their arrival in the New World.

Coming Mideast War & Business. unabr. ed. Dennis Turner. 1 cass. (Running Time: 57 min.). 12.95 (402) J Norton Pubs.
Discusses counter-economic investments in commodities that should drastically rise in price with the coming of another Mideast War & subsequent governmental interventions.

Coming of Age: Growing up in the Twentieth Century. abr. ed. Studs Terkel. Read by Allen Hamilton & Shirley Venard. 3 CDs. (Running Time: 3 hrs.). (ENG.). 2009. audio compact disk 18.95 (978-1-59887-888-2(3), 1598878883) Pub: HighBridge. Dist(s): Workman Pub

Coming of Age: Growing up in the Twentieth Century. unabr. collector's ed. Studs Terkel. Read by Barrett Whitener. 15 cass. (Running Time: 22 hrs. 30 min.). 1996. 120.00 (978-0-7366-3386-4(3), 4036) Books on Tape.
A collective portrait of our times, woven from the voices of 70 very different people, ages 70 to 99. With surprising vigor, they give us a panorama of American life & work throughout this century & tell us what they think of the changing times.

Coming of Age in America. unabr. ed. Margaret Mead. 1 cass. (Running Time: 1 hr. 20 min.). 12.95 (35010) J Norton Pubs.
Mead contrasts the shoulds & oughts of traditional approaches to childhood & adult development with the realities of our present culture. Of particular interest to persons examining the cultural background of changing, alternative life styles.

Coming of Age in the Milky Way. abr. ed. Timothy Ferris. Read by Timothy Ferris. 2 cass. (Running Time: 3 hrs.). 2004. 18.00 (978-1-931056-15-1(3), N Millennium Audio) New Millenn Enter.
Offers "an exhilarating, wide-ranging journey that takes us from the shores of the Mediterranean, where the second-century astronomer Claudius Ptolemy fashioned his creaky celestial spheres, to modern-day research institutes, where theorists contemplate this & other universes bubbling out of a quantum vacuum".

Coming of Bill. unabr. ed. P. G. Wodehouse. Read by Frederick Davidson. 6 cass. (Running Time: 9 hrs.). 1999. 44.95 (2157) Blckstn Audio.
Kirk & Ruth, recently married, Bill was born. But thereafter all did not go well. Returning from a long & fruitless visit to Columbia, Kirk finds that Ruth is firmly under the thumb of Aunt Lora, whose strong views on the care of children do not accord with Kirk's natural fatherly instincts.

Coming of Bill. unabr. ed. P. G. Wodehouse. Read by Frederick Davidson. 6 cass. (Running Time: 8 hrs. 30 mins.). 2000. 44.95 (978-0-7861-1220-3(4), 2157) Blckstn Audio.

Coming of Christ. Gloriae Dei Cantores Schola. audio compact disk 16.95 (978-1-55725-310-1(2), GDCD033) Paraclete MA.

Coming of Conan the Cimmerian: The Original Adventures of the Greatest Sword & Sorcery Hero of All Time! unabr. ed. Robert E. Howard. Narrated by Todd McLaren. (Running Time: 18 hrs. 30 mins. 0 sec.). (Conan of Cimmeria Ser.). (ENG.). 2009. 29.99 (978-1-4001-6223-9(8)); audio compact disk 79.99 (978-1-4001-4223-1(7)); audio compact disk 39.99 (978-1-4001-1223-4(0)) Pub: Tantor Media. Dist(s): IngramPubServ

***Coming of Hoole.** unabr. ed. Kathryn Lasky. Read by Pamela Garelick. (Running Time: 5 hrs. NaN mins.). (Guardians of Ga'Hoole Ser.). (ENG.). 2011. 19.95 (978-1-4417-8193-2(5)); 34.95 (978-1-4417-8190-1(0)); audio compact disk 19.95 (978-1-4417-8192-5(7)); audio compact disk 49.00 (978-1-4417-8191-8(9)) Blckstn Audio.

***Coming of the Terraphiles.** Michael Moorcock. (Running Time: 10 hrs. 0 mins. 0 sec.). (ENG.). 2011. audio compact disk 39.95 (978-1-4084-6814-2(X)) Pub: AudioGO. Dist(s): Perseus Dist

***Coming of the Third Reich.** unabr. ed. Richard J. Evans. Read by Sean Pratt. (Running Time: 21 hrs.). (ENG.). 2010. 49.98 (978-1-59659-516-3(7), GildAudio) Pub: Gildan Media. Dist(s): HachBkGrp

Coming-Out. Michael P. Marshall. 1 cass. (Running Time: 52 min.). 1995. 9.00 (978-0-912403-06-9(3)) Prod Renaud.
Not just for people who are exploring sexuality. Helps us to understand personal behaviors that have prevented us from reaching our highest development as individuals.

Coming Out. unabr. ed. Danielle Steel. Read by David Garrison. 4 CDs. (Running Time: 4 hrs.). 2006. audio compact disk 63.00 (978-1-4159-3074-8(0)) Books on Tape.

Coming Out. unabr. ed. Danielle Steel. Read by David Garrison. 3 cass. (Running Time: 4 hrs.). 2006. 45.00 (978-1-4159-3073-1(2)) Books on Tape.

Coming Out. unabr. ed. Danielle Steel. Read by David Garrison. (Running Time: 18000 sec.). (ENG.). 2007. audio compact disk 14.99 (978-0-7393-5398-1(5), Random AudioBks) Pub: Random Audio Pubg. Dist(s): Random

Coming Out of Maggie see Favorite Stories by O. Henry

Coming Out of Our Forgetfulness. Swami Amar Jyoti. 1 cass. 1987. 9.95 (M-91) Truth Consciousness.
Forgetfulness, the basic sin. Go beyond the clouds & see the Light. Many Paths, one Goal. If we really open & listen, He does speak to us.

Coming Out of the Ice. unabr. ed. Victor Herman. Read by Christopher Hurt. (Running Time: 50400 sec.). 2007. audio compact disk 24.95 (978-0-7861-9353-0(0), 1899); audio compact disk 99.00 (978-0-7861-6122-5(1)) Blckstn Audio.

Coming Out of the Ice: An Unexpected Life, unabr. ed. Victor Herman. Read by Christopher Hurt. 10 cass. (Running Time: 14 hrs. 30 mins.). 1997. 69.95 (978-0-7861-1134-3(8), 1899) Blckstn Audio.
True story of a young American man who was sent to the Soviet Union with his parents by the Ford Motor Company to set up an auto plant. He was eventually thrown into Soviet prisons & could not return to America until forty-five years later. During his life in & out of Russian prisons, he met & fell in love with a beautiful Russian gymnast who followed him into exile & lived with him & their child for a year in Siberia, in a cave chopped out under the ice.

Coming Out of the Valley. Kenneth E. Hagin. (How to Be an Overcomer Ser.). bk. 17.00 Faith Lib Pubns.

Coming Out Straight CD Series: Understanding & Healing Unwanted Same-Sex Attractiong. Richard Cohen. (ENG.). 2008. 49.95 (978-0-9637058-7-7(3)) Intl Healing.

Coming Plague Pt. 1: Newly Emerging Diseases in a World Out of Balance, unabr. collector's ed. Laurie Garrett. Read by Kimberly Schraf. 11 cass. (Running Time: 16 hrs. 30 min.). 1995. 88.00 (978-0-7366-3076-4(7), 3758-A) Books on Tape.
Minute changes in society's habits can unleash devastating diseases. Do scientists have a handle on them? The answer: probably not.

Coming Plague Pt. 2: Newly Emerging Diseases in a World Out of Balance. unabr. collector's ed. Laurie Garrett. Read by Kimberly Schraf. 13 cass. (Running Time: 19 hrs. 30 min.). 1995. 104.00 (978-0-7366-3077-1(5), 3758-B) Books on Tape.

Coming Revolution. Rick Joyner & Steve Thompson. (Running Time: 2 hrs. 33 mins.). 2007. 13.39 (978-1-4245-0689-7(1)) Tre Med Inc.

Coming Round to Circle Time: The Video Makes It Come Alive! rev. ed. Teresa Bliss & George Robinson. 1995. 59.95 (978-1-873942-38-3(9)) Pub: P Chapman GBR. Dist(s): SAGE

Coming Storm. unabr. ed. Tracie Peterson. Narrated by Ruth Ann Phimister. 10 cass. (Running Time: 14 hrs. 15 mins.). (Heirs of Montana Ser.: Vol. 2). 2004. 89.75 (978-1-4193-1003-4(8), K1118MC) Recorded Bks.

Coming Temple Update. Chuck Missler. 2 cass., notes. (Running Time: 1 hr. 30 min. per cass.). 1994. vinyl bd. 14.95 Set. (978-1-880532-71-3(9)) Koinonia Hse.
Prophetic significance of the Temple & discoveries.

Coming to America: The Story of Immigration. unabr. ed. Betsy Maestro. Illus. by Susannah Ryan. 1 cass. (Running Time: 15 min.). (J). (gr. k-6). 2001. bk. 26.90 (978-0-8045-6853-1(7), 6853) Spoken Arts.
Explores the evolving history of immagration to the United States. It is a fascinating story that explains the richness and diversity of the American people.

Coming to Canada. Ed. by Nivio Ziviani et al. (ENG.). 1992. audio compact disk 18.95 (978-0-88629-305-5(7)) McG-Queens Univ Pr CAN.

Coming to Dispassion. Swami Amar Jyoti. 1 cass. 1982. 9.95 (M-22) Truth Consciousness.
Vairagya, the basic dispassion. Losing identification with false things & games of the mind.

Coming to Ground: A Certain Faith in Uncertain Times. Speeches. Featuring David Whyte. one. 2001. audio compact disk 15.00 (978-1-932887-04-4(0)) Many Rivers Pr.
In the wake of the September attacks, poet David Whyte speaks about coming to ground - a time of silence and gathering in; a time to acknowledge that we are all participants in a greater story - one that brings our private stories into conversation with the larger world. From this time, we can move forward, having opened ourselves to the insights that times of difficulty may spark, standing firmly in our experience and looking to the possibilities of a new era.

Coming to Our Senses: Healing Ourselves & the World Through Mindfulness. abr. ed. Jon Kabat-Zinn. Read by Jon Kabat-Zinn. 3 CDs. (Running Time: 3 hrs. 30 mins.). 2005. audio compact disk 24.98 (978-1-4013-9949-8(5), Hyperion Audio) Pub: Hyperion. Dist(s): HarperCollins Pubs

Coming to School Audio CD see At Home, at School Audio CD: Fiction-to-Fact Kindergarten Theme

Coming to Stillness. Swami Amar Jyoti. 1 cass. 1979. 9.95 (J-31) Truth Consciousness.
Higher knowledge comes after stilling the mind. The real becoming process is unfoldment. The perfect way of meditation. On desires & peace of mind.

Coming to Terms with Sin see Confrontando el Pecado

Coming to Terms with Sin: A Study of Romans 1-5. unabr. ed. Charles R. Swindoll. 6 cass. (Running Time: 5 hrs.). 1998. 30.95 (978-1-57972-258-6(X)) Insight Living.

Coming to Terms with Your Parents. Ray DiGiuseppe. 1 cass. (Running Time: 79 min.). 9.95 (C047) A Ellis Institute.
As people mature & leave home, they frequently experience continued difficulties in getting along with their parents - especially at holidays & family events! This tape helps you to move on & enjoy your relationship with your parents as you progress through life.

Coming to Terms with Your Parents. Ray DiGiuseppe. 1 cass. (Running Time: 79 min.). 9.95 (C047) Inst Rational-Emotive.

Coming to Your Senses Companion: Soaring with Your Soul. Excerpts. Sally M. Veillette. 1 CD. (Running Time: 30 min.). 2004. audio compact disk 11.95 (978-0-9741854-2-2(6)) Pub: Pop Cork Pubng. Dist(s): Hara Pub
30 min companion CD. The author Sally Veillette takes the listener personally through the 8 steps of her book.

Coming Together in Unity. Short Stories. Joel Osteen. 1 Cass. (Running Time: 30 Mins.). 2002. 6.00 (978-1-59349-154-3(9), Ja0154) J Osteen.

Coming Transition. Larry Randolph. 2006. audio compact disk 34.99 (978-1-59933-018-1(0)) Pub: Morning NC. Dist(s): Destiny Image Pubs

Coming Transition. Larry Randolph. (Running Time: 3hrs. 43 mins.). 2007. 34.99 (978-1-4245-0682-8(4)) Tre Med Inc.

***Coming Unglued.** unabr. ed. Rebeca Seitz. Narrated by Brooke Sanford. (Scrapbooker's Ser.). (ENG.). 2008. 19.59 (978-1-60814-743-4(6)) Oasis Audio.

Coming Unglued. unabr. ed. Rebeca Seitz. Narrated by Brooke Sanford. (Sisters Ink Ser.). (ENG.). 2008. audio compact disk 27.99 (978-1-59859-413-3(3)) Oasis Audio.

Coming unto Christ Through the Book of Mormon. Reed A. Benson. 2 cass. 11.98 Set. (978-1-55503-398-9(9), 0700835) Covenant Comms.
How to use the Book of Mormon to draw nearer to the Lord.

Coming up for Air. unabr. ed. George Orwell. Read by Richard Brown. 6 cass. (Running Time: 8 hrs. 30 mins.). (gr. 9-12). 1991. 44.95 (978-0-7861-0269-3(1), 1235) Blckstn Audio.
George Bowling, in middle age, is impelled, as he puts it, to come up for air. "The idea really came to me," he says in the opening sentence, "the day I got my new false teeth." With seventeen pounds he has won at a race, he steals a vacation from his wife & his family & pays a visit to Lower Binfield, the village where he grew up, to fish for carp in a pool he remembers from thirty years before. The pool is gone, Lower Binfield has changed beyond recognition, & the principal event of Bowling's holiday is an accidental bombing by the RAF.

Coming up for Air, unabr. ed. George Orwell. Narrated by Patrick Tull. 6 cass. (Running Time: 7 hrs. 45 mins.). 1988. 51.00 (978-1-55690-114-0(3), 88130E7) Recorded Bks.
George Bowling makes a nostalgic visit to the village of his youth with comic results.

Coming up for Air. unabr. collector's ed. George Orwell. Read by Richard Green. 8 cass. (Running Time: 8 hrs.). 1981. 48.00 (978-0-7366-0566-3(5), 1538) Books on Tape.
George "Tubby" Bowling is a "fat, middle-aged bloke with false teeth & a red face". He sells insurance, a task at which he grimly excels. The father of two ingrates & husband to a slattern, he dutifully makes payments on their dreary home. He regards himself as hostage to his family - with them as wardens, himself as prisoner.

Coming World Civilization. Huston Smith. 1 cass. (Running Time: 1 hr. 30 min.). 1968. 11.00 Big Sur Tapes.

Comision: Cambiando la Historia. Music by Alberto & Aitor. 1 CD.Tr. of Commission: "Changing History". (SPA.). (YA). 2001. audio compact disk 12.99 (978-0-8254-1157-1(2)) Kregel.
Spanish youth inspirational music. The songs combine a praise and worship style with contemporary acoustic melodies.

***Commanche Passport.** Will Henry. 2009. (978-1-60136-446-3(6)) Audio Holding.

Command a King's Ship. Alexander Kent, pseud. Read by Michael Jayston. 10 cass. (Running Time: 15 hrs.). (Richard Bolitho Ser.: Bk. 6). 2002. 84.95 (978-0-7540-0870-5(3), CAB 2292) Pub: Chivers Audio Bks GBR. Dist(s): AudioGO

Command & Control. unabr. ed. Eric Schlosser. (Running Time: 11 hrs.). (ENG.). (gr. 12 up). 2009. audio compact disk 39.95 (978-0-14-314501-1(0), PengAudBks) Penguin Grp USA.

Command Decision. unabr. ed. Elizabeth Moon. Narrated by Cynthia Holloway. (Running Time: 15 hrs. 30 mins. 0 sec.). (Vatta's War Ser.). (ENG.). 2009. audio compact disk 39.99 (978-1-4001-0830-5(6)); audio compact disk 29.99 (978-1-4001-5830-0(3)); audio compact disk 79.99 (978-1-4001-3830-2(2)) Pub: Tantor Media. Dist(s): IngramPubServ

Command, "Do Not Love" Dan Comer. 1 cass. 3.00 (24) Evang Outreach.

Command Performance, Set. unabr. ed. 2 cass. (Running Time: 2 hrs.). 10.95 (978-1-57816-000-6(6), CP2301) Audio File.
Programs from the Armed Forces Radio Service featuring stars from stage, screen & radio.

Command Performance: Bing Crosby & Jack Benny. Perf. by Jack Benny & Bing Crosby. 1 cass. (Running Time: 1 hr.). 2001. 6.98 (2532) Radio Spirits.

***Command Performance, Volume 1.** RadioArchives.com. (Running Time: 600). (ENG.). 2010. audio compact disk 29.98 (978-1-61081-171-2(2)) Radio Arch.

Commander in Chief, Pt. 1. unabr. ed. Eric Larrabee. Read by Grover Gardner. 8 cass. (Running Time: 12 hrs.). 1989. 64.00 (978-0-7366-1633-1(0), 2490-A) Books on Tape.
Few American presidents have exercised the constitutional authority of Commander in Chief with such determination as Franklin D. Roosevelt during WW II. Commander in Chief is the story of FDR's war - a fullsize picture of how he ran it, picked his key military advisors & arranged events so that the Grand Alliance was directed from Washington. Through the stories of FDR's subordinates, Eric Larrabee examines the extent & importance of the President's role in directing America's wartime strategy. He highlights Roosevelt's relationships with Marshall, King, Arnold, MacArthur, Nimitz & others & addresses Roosevelt's responsibility for the war & the degree to which it achieved his purposes.

Commander in Chief, Pt. 2. unabr. ed. Eric Larrabee. Read by Grover Gardner. 7 cass. (Running Time: 10 hrs. 30 min.). 1989. 56.00 (2490-B) Books on Tape.

Commander in Chief, Pt. 3. unabr. ed. Eric Larrabee. Read by Grover Gardner. 9 cass. (Running Time: 13 hrs. 30 min.). 1989. 72.00 (2490-C) Books on Tape.

Commander in Chief: Abraham Lincoln & the Civil War. Albert Marrin. Narrated by John McDonough. 8 cass. (Running Time: 10 hrs.). (YA). 2001. pap. bk. & stu. ed. Recorded Bks.
Lincoln is often considered America's greatest president. He preserved the Union during the Civil War & ended slavery. There is more to this humorous, courageous & complex man who had both strengths & weaknesses.

Commander in Chief: Abraham Lincoln & the Civil War. unabr. ed. Albert Marrin. Narrated by John McDonough. 8 pieces. (Running Time: 10 hrs.). (gr. 6 up). 2001. 72.00 (978-0-7887-4726-7(6), 96400E7) Recorded Bks.

Commander of the Exodus. Yoram Kaniuk. Read by William Sutherland. 2000. 24.95 (978-1-59912-453-7(X)) Iofy Corp.

Commander of the Exodus. unabr. ed. Yoram Kaniuk. Read by William Sutherland. 6 cass. (Running Time: 8 hrs. 30 mins.). 2001. 44.95 (978-0-7861-1937-0(3), 2708) Blckstn Audio.
A modern day Moses defies the blockade of the British Mandate to deliver more than 24,000 displaced Holocaust survivors to Palestine.

Commander of the Exodus. unabr. ed. Yoram Kaniuk. Read by William Sutherland. 7 CDs. (Running Time: 8 hrs. 30 mins.). 2001. audio compact disk 56.00 (978-0-7861-9782-8(X), 2708) Blckstn Audio.

Commander Toad in Space. unabr. ed. Jane Yolen. Read by Lionel Wilson. 1 cass. (Running Time: 22 mins.). (Oliver Pig Ser.). (J). (gr. k-3). 1987. pap. bk. 17.00 (978-0-8072-0120-6(0), FTR117SP, Listening Lib) Random Audio Pubg.
Commander Toad & crew of the spaceship Star Warts go where no spaceship has gone before.

Commanding Heights Pt. 1: The Battle for the World Economy, Daniel Yergin & Joseph Stanislaw. Read by Michael Prichard. 10 cass. (Running Time: 15 hrs.). 1999. 80.00 (5094-A) Books on Tape.
A revealing in-depth investigation of how the upheavals of the last twenty years have radically transformed our world.

Commanding Heights Pt. 2: The Battle Between Government & the Marketplace That Is Remaking the Modern World, Daniel Yergin & Joseph Stanislaw. Read by Michael Prichard. 8 cass. (Running Time: 12 hrs.). 1999. 64.00 (5094-B) Books on Tape.

Commanding Self-Image & Boundless Self-Confidence, Vol. 11. Jonathan Parker. 2 cass. (Running Time: 1 hr. 45 min.). 1992. 17.00 Set. (978-1-58400-010-5(4)) QuantumQuests Intl.

Commandments, Questions & Answers. Michael Wrenn. 1 cass. (National Meeting of the Institute, 1994 Ser.). 4.00 (94N6) IRL Chicago.

Commedia Dell'arte. 1 cass. (Running Time: 50 mins.). (ITA.). pap. bk. 16.95 (SIT245) J Norton Pubs.

Commencement Address. Ram Dass. 1 cass. 9.00 (A0139-89) Sound Photosyn.
With an introduction by Ralph Metzner, this is a warm compassionate boost.

Commencement Address for Humanities at UC Berkeley. Vivienne Verdon-Roe. 1 cass. 9.00 (A0610-90) Sound Photosyn.
Brief, power-packed & inspiring.

Comment ca va? Matt Maxwell. 1 cass. (FRE.). (J). 1988. 20.95 (978-0-8442-1425-2(6), Natl Textbk Co) M-H Contemporary.
Song-based French language program makes imaginative use of music, dance & drama in teaching French to younger students. Basis for program's activities are 12 songs covering everyday topics, performed in rock or folk style.

Commentaries on a Course in Miracles. unabr. ed. Julian Silverman. 8 cass. 1980. 77.00 Vinyl Album Set. (0870) Big Sur Tapes.

Commentary & Spiritual Reflection on the Fourth Gospel. William F. Maestri. 8 cass. 1983. 53.95 incl. shelf-case, outline, & bklet. (TAH099) Alba Hse Comns.
Emphasizes the Gospel challenge to personal growth & maturity.

Commentary of Ruth. 1994. 54.00i (978-1-930918-54-2(2)) Its All About Him.

Commentary on "Spir-Com" Hal Crowther. 1 cass. (138) Natl Humanities.

Commentary on Television & Ethics. O'Connor & Alfred R. Schneider. 1 cass. (286) Natl Humanities.

Comments on Published Autobiography. 1 cass. (Running Time: 1 hr.). 12.00 (L929) MEA A Watts Cass.

Commercial Banks in China: A Strategic Reference 2006. Compiled by Icon Group International, Inc. Staff. 2007. ring bd. 195.00 (978-0-497-35867-9(0)) Icon Grp.

Commercial Drivers License Study Program. pap. bk. & wbk. ed. 138.00 (AVA18243VNB1AIF) Natl Tech Info.

Commercial Insurance Coverage Litigation. 1987. bk. 90.00 incl. book.; 45.00 cass. only.; 45.00 book only. PA Bar Inst.

Commercial Law (Law School Legends Audio Series) 2002. 39.95 (978-0-314-14389-1(0)) West.

Commercial Leases. 1985. bk. 60.00; 35.00 PA Bar Inst.

Commercial Litigation: Evidentiary Issues & Remedies. 1989. 125.00 (AC-523) PA Bar Inst.

Commercial Loan Documentation: Advanced Issues. 4 cass. (Running Time: 5 hrs. 30 min.). 1991. 125.00 Set. (T7-9322) PLI.

Commercial Loan Documents. 1985. bk. 80.00 incl. book.; 60.00 cass. only.; 20.00 book only. PA Bar Inst.

Commercial Paper & Payment Law. Douglas J. Whaley. 3 cass. (Running Time: 4 hrs. 36 mins.). (Outstanding Professors Ser.). 1995. 50.00 (978-0-940366-67-1(3), 28396) Pub: Sum & Substance. Dist(s): West Pub
Lecture given by a prominent American law school professor.

Commercial Paper & Payment Law. 2nd rev. ed. Douglas J. Whaley. 2002. 63.00 (978-0-314-14470-6(6)) Pub: West Pub. Dist(s): West

Commercial Paper, 2005 ed. (Law School Legends Audio Series) 2005. 47.95 (978-0-314-16078-2(7), gilbert) West.

Commercial Paper, 2005 ed. (Law School Legends Audio Series) Michael I. Spak. (Law School Legends Audio Ser.). 2005. 52.00 (978-0-314-16077-5(9), gilbert) West.

Commercial Radio. unabr. ed. Told to Garrison Keillor. (Running Time: 1 hr.). (ENG.). 2004. audio compact disk 14.95 (978-1-56511-896-6(0), 1565118960) Pub: HighBridge. Dist(s): Workman Pub

Commercial Real Estate Leases: Selected Issues in Drafting & Negotiating in Current Markets. 8 cass. (Running Time: 12 hrs.). 1999. 345.00 Set; incl. study guide 592p. (AD73) Am Law Inst.
Advanced course provides an in-depth analysis with a view to existing market conditions.

Commercial Securitization for Real Estate Lawyers: Turmoil in the Capital Markets; Opportunities & Risks for Real Estate Finance. 8 cass. (Running Time: 11 hrs.). 1999. 345.00 Set; incl. study guide 681p. (MD75) Am Law Inst.
New advanced course answers many of the questions commonly asked about securitization, providing valuable tips to borrowers' & lenders' lawyers in the structuring & documenting of a transaction.

Commercial Sponsors: Learn to Find, Please & Keep Them. Dottie Walters & Robin Raymer. 2004. audio compact disk 95.00 (978-0-934344-60-9(4)) Royal Pub.

Commercial Vehicles, Buses, & Heavy Trucks in Australia: A Strategic Reference 2006. Compiled by Icon Group International, Inc. Staff. 2007. ring bd. 195.00 (978-0-497-35808-2(5)) Icon Grp.

Commercialspeak: The New Approach & Changing Techniques for Radio & TV Commercial Voice Performers. unabr. ed. Bettye P. Zoller et al. Read by Bettye P. Zoller et al. Ed. by Dick Orkin. 2 cass. (Running Time: 2 hrs.). (YA). (gr. 6-12). 2003. 25.00 (978-1-884643-14-9(0)) Voicesvoices.
Coaching tips & the latest techniques on winning auditions, interpreting copy, your killer voice over demo, promotional materials, unions, telephone messaging, & more. Dozens of interviews with leading cast directors, talent agents, ad agency creatives, broadcast coaches/educators & voice talents.

Commies: A Journey through the Old Left, the New Left, & the Leftover Left. unabr. ed. Ronald Radosh. Read by Yuri Rasovsky. (Running Time: 7 hrs. 0 mins.). 2008. 44.95 (978-1-4332-3173-5(5)) Blckstn Audio.

Commies: A Journey Through the Old Left, the New Left, & the Leftover Left. unabr. ed. Ronald Radosh. Read by Yuri Rasovsky. (Running Time: 30600 sec.). 2008. audio compact disk 29.95 (978-1-4332-3177-3(8)); audio compact disk & audio compact disk 60.00 (978-1-4332-3174-2(3)) Blckstn Audio.

Commission: The Uncensored History of the 9/11 Investigation. abr. ed. Philip Shenon. Read by Dave Mallow. (Running Time: 6 hrs. 30 mins.). (ENG.). 2008. 14.95 (978-1-60024-067-6(4), Twelve) Pub: GrandCentral. Dist(s): HachBkGrp

Commission: The Uncensored History of the 9/11 Investigation. abr. ed. Philip Shenon. Read by Dave Mallow. 6 CDs. (Running Time: 6 hrs. 30 mins.). (ENG.). 2009. audio compact disk 14.98 (978-1-60024-441-4(6), Twelve) Pub: GrandCentral. Dist(s): HachBkGrp

Commission: "Changing History" see Comision: Cambiando la Historia

Commissioned: The Best of Commissioned. 1 cass., 1 CD. 1999. 10.98; audio compact disk 16.98 CD. Pub: Brentwood Music. Dist(s): Provident Mus Dist
Contemporary Gospel songs.

Commissioned Reunion "Live" Perf. by Commissioned. 2002. audio compact disk Provident Mus Dist.

Commitment: Mark 6:19-24. Ed Young. 1999. 4.95 (978-0-7417-2206-5(2), 1206) Win Walk.

Commitment: The Flame of Focused Passion. Edwene Gaines. Read by Edwene Gaines. (Playaway Adult Nonfiction Ser.). (ENG.). 2009. 39.99 (978-1-60775-717-7(6)) Find a World.

Commitment & Relationships & You Are the Power. Marianne Williamson. Read by Marianne Williamson. 1 cass. (Running Time: 90 mins.). (Lectures on a Course in Miracles). 1999. 10.00 (978-1-56170-308-1(7), M779) Hay House.

Commitment Dialogues: How to Talk Your Way Through the Tough Times & Build a Stronger Relationship. abr. ed. Matthew McKay & Barbara Quick. Read by Lloyd James & Marguerite Gavin. (Running Time: 16200 sec.). 2006. audio compact disk 28.00 (978-1-932378-96-2(0)) Pub: A Media Intl. Dist(s): Natl Bk Netwk

Commitment... the Flame of Focused Passion. unabr. ed. Edwene Gaines. (ENG.). 2006. 14.98 (978-1-59659-107-3(2), GildAudio) Pub: Gildan Media. Dist(s): HachBkGrp

Commitment to Conversion. Thomas Merton. 1 cass. (Running Time: 60 min.). (Conversion Ser.). 8.95 (AA2233) Credence Commun.
Discussions on conversion & the necessity of choosing between the Gospel & the world.

Commitment to Excellence Lombardi Style. Vince Lombardi. 1 cass. 14.95 (15011 PAB) Nightingale-Conant.
Vince Lombardi left behind a legacy of success that includes six divisional titles, five national championships & two Super Bowl victories. He was famous for his ability to motivate players to reach deep down & accomplish the impossible. Now you can use the stirring words of the former Green Bay Packers' coach to help bring out the best in ourself & others.

Commitment to Life & Earthquake Within. Marianne Williamson. Read by Marianne Williamson. 1 cass. (Running Time: 90 mins.). (Lectures on a Course in Miracles). 1999. 10.00 (978-1-56170-179-7(3), M707) Hay House.

Commitments. unabr. ed. Barbara Delinsky. Read by Joyce Bean. 7 cass. (Running Time: 12 hrs.). 2001. 32.95 (978-1-58788-581-5(6), 1587885816, BAU); 78.25 (978-1-58788-582-2(4), 1587885824, Unabridge Lib Edns) Brilliance Audio.
Writer Sabrina Stone had married wealthily and unwisely. Her husband's refusal to love their handicapped son added more strain to an already failing relationship. Yet Sabrina feels a commitment to her marriage - one that she has vowed to honor. Then one day, she encounters an investigative reporter named Derek McGill who is writing a story on parents of special children. They speak for only a few minutes, but it is long enough for the two of them to feel a desire that stuns them . . . a desire they both assume must remain unfulfilled. Eighteen months later, Sabrina's husband is divorcing her and Derek McGill is in prison for murder. Following an impulse, Sabrina travels to Derek's prison to tell him that she believes in his innocence. What started as an act of compassion will turn into a dangerous and passionate test of her courage as she tries to uncover who is responsible for Derek's conviction. And she will discover the meaning of one of the most important

commitments of all - the one a woman makes to herself. The one that will determine the course of her life . . . and the fate of the dreams she has for her child.

Commitments. unabr. ed. Barbara Delinsky. Read by Joyce Bean. (Running Time: 12 hrs.). 2004. 39.25 (978-1-59335-565-4(3), 1593355653, Brlnc Audio MP3 Lib) Brilliance Audio.

Commitments. unabr. ed. Barbara Delinsky. Read by Joyce Bean. (Running Time: 12 hrs.). 2004. 39.25 (978-1-59710-150-9(8), 1597101508, BADLE); 24.95 (978-1-59710-151-6(6), 1597101516, BAD) Brilliance Audio.

***Commitments.** unabr. ed. Barbara Delinsky. Read by Joyce Bean. (Running Time: 13 hrs.). 2010. audio compact disk 29.99 (978-1-4418-4002-8(8), 9781441840028, Bril Audio CD Unabri); audio compact disk 89.97 (978-1-4418-4003-5(6), 9781441840035, BriAudCD Unabrid) Brilliance Audio.

Commitments. unabr. ed. Barbara Delinsky. Read by Joyce Bean. (Running Time: 12 hrs.). 2004. 24.95 (978-1-59335-051-2(1), 1593350511) Soulmate Audio Bks.

Commitments You Can Count On Set: The Key to Becoming Commitment Competent. David Grudermeyer & Rebecca Grudermeyer. 2 cass. 18.95 INCL. HANDOUTS. (T-51) Willingness Wrks.

Committed: A Skeptic Makes Peace with Marriage. unabr. ed. Elizabeth Gilbert. Read by Elizabeth Gilbert. 7 CDs. (Running Time: 9 hrs.). (ENG.). 2010. audio compact disk 29.95 (978-0-14-314575-2(4), PengAudBks) Penguin Grp USA.

***Committed: A Skeptic Makes Peace with Marriage.** unabr. ed. Elizabeth Gilbert. Read by Elizabeth Gilbert. 8 CDs. (Running Time: 10 hrs.). 2009. audio compact disk 100.00 (978-0-307-71535-7(3), BksonTape) Pub: Random Audio Pubg. Dist(s): Random

Commodities Investing Through Managed Accounts Series. 13 cass. Incl. Commodities Investing Through Managed Accounts Series: All about Trading Systems. M. Fishzohn.; Commodities Investing Through Managed Accounts Series: How to Attract Overseas Investors. K. Shewer & M. Goodman.; Commodities Investing Through Managed Accounts Series: Inside Open-Ended Funds. E. Jackson & S. Winn.; Commodities Investing Through Managed Accounts Series: Institutional Investing. R. Nathan & R. Brehm.; Commodities Investing Through Managed Accounts Series: Integrating Commodities into a Balanced Financial Plan. R. Stoker.; Commodities Investing Through Managed Accounts Series: John Linter & Theory of Portfolio Management. A. Orr.; Commodities Investing Through Managed Accounts Series: Managed Accounts vs. Do-It-Yourself Trading. M. Baratz & A. Orr.; Commodities Investing Through Managed Accounts Series: Portfolio Expansion. T. Thomte.; Commodities Investing Through Managed Accounts Series: Stock-Index Futures in a Managed Portfolio. S. Siebens.; Commodities Investing Through Managed Accounts Series: The Role of Commodities in An Investment Portfolio. E. Hargitt.; Commodities Investing Through Managed Accounts Series: Trading & Clearing on Foreign Exchange, Trading in the U. K. D. Anderson & D. Carr.; Commodities Investing Through Managed Accounts Series: Trading Governments in Cash, Forward & Futures Markets. R. Hickey.; Commodities Investing Through Managed Accounts Series: Trading Overseas Futures Markets. J. Tillotson.; 130.00 Set. (Mngd Acct Reprts); 15.00 ea. Futures Pub.

Commodities Investing Through Managed Accounts Series: All about Trading Systems see Commodities Investing Through Managed Accounts Series

Commodities Investing Through Managed Accounts Series: How to Attract Overseas Investors see Commodities Investing Through Managed Accounts Series

Commodities Investing Through Managed Accounts Series: Inside Open-Ended Funds see Commodities Investing Through Managed Accounts Series

Commodities Investing Through Managed Accounts Series: Institutional Investing see Commodities Investing Through Managed Accounts Series

Commodities Investing Through Managed Accounts Series: Integrating Commodities into a Balanced Financial Plan see Commodities Investing Through Managed Accounts Series

Commodities Investing Through Managed Accounts Series: John Linter & Theory of Portfolio Management see Commodities Investing Through Managed Accounts Series

Commodities Investing Through Managed Accounts Series: Managed Accounts vs. Do-It-Yourself Trading see Commodities Investing Through Managed Accounts Series

Commodities Investing Through Managed Accounts Series: Portfolio Expansion see Commodities Investing Through Managed Accounts Series

Commodities Investing Through Managed Accounts Series: Stock-Index Futures in a Managed Portfolio see Commodities Investing Through Managed Accounts Series

Commodities Investing Through Managed Accounts Series: The Role of Commodities in An Investment Portfolio see Commodities Investing Through Managed Accounts Series

Commodities Investing Through Managed Accounts Series: Trading & Clearing on Foreign Exchange, Trading in the U. K. see Commodities Investing Through Managed Accounts Series

Commodities Investing Through Managed Accounts Series: Trading Governments in Cash, Forward & Futures Markets see Commodities Investing Through Managed Accounts Series

Commodities Investing Through Managed Accounts Series: Trading Overseas Futures Markets see Commodities Investing Through Managed Accounts Series

Commodore. C. S. Forester. Read by Geoffrey Howard. 2002. 56.00 (978-0-7366-9118-5(9)); audio compact disk 64.00 (978-0-7366-9119-2(7)) Books on Tape.

Commodore. Patrick O'Brian. Read by David Case. (Aubrey-Maturin Ser.). 1995. audio compact disk 72.00 (978-0-7366-5966-6(8)) Books on Tape.

Commodore. Patrick O'Brian. (Aubrey-Maturin Ser.). 2007. audio compact disk 34.95 (978-1-4281-1182-0(4)) Recorded Bks.

Commodore. abr. ed. Patrick O'Brian. Read by David McCallum. 2 cass. (Running Time: 3 hrs.). (Aubrey-Maturin Ser.). 1998. 17.95 Set. (978-1-55935-165-2(9)) Soundelux.
Captain Jack Aubrey & secret agent Stephen Maturin in their daring service to Her Majesty's Navy.

Commodore. unabr. ed. Patrick O'Brian. Read by David Case. 9 CDs. (Running Time: 10 hrs. 45 mins.). (Aubrey-Maturin Ser.). 2001. audio compact disk 72.00 Books on Tape.
Set in the early 19th century, Aubrey & Maturin take a small fleet of ships to the Gulf of Guinea to put down the slave trade. Their secret mission, however, is to destroy a French fleet that is planning on mounting an invasion of England via Ireland. This mission test Aubrey's seamanship & Maturin's cunning.

Commodore, unabr. ed. Patrick O'Brian. Read by David Case. 8 cass. (Running Time: 11 hrs.). (Aubrey-Maturin Ser.). 2001. 29.95 (978-0-7366-5684-9(7), 3771) Books on Tape.
Set in the early 19th-century. With Stephen Maturin, a medical doctor & agent of the British naval intelligence, Jack Aubrey, now a commodore, takes a small fleet of ships to put down a slave trade in West Africa. But Aubrey's secret mission is to destroy a French fleet mounting an invasion of England via Ireland.

Commodore. unabr. ed. Patrick O'Brian. Narrated by Patrick Tull. 9 cass. (Running Time: 11 hrs. 45 mins.). (Aubrey-Maturin Ser.). 78.00 (978-0-7887-0317-1(X), 94509E7) Recorded Bks.
After a dangerous tour of duty in the Great South Sea, Jack & Stephen finally return to their families in England. For Jack, the return is joyful, but for Stephen, it is heartbreaking. His wife, Diana, has left for parts unknown; his young daughter has all the symptoms of autism. To escape these painful circumstances, Stephen joins Jack on a bizarre decoy mission to the lagoons of the Gulf of Guinea. Available to libraries only.

Commodore. unabr. ed. Patrick O'Brian. Read by Graham Roberts. 10 cass. (Running Time: 15 hrs.). (Aubrey-Maturin Ser.). 2004. 84.95 (978-1-86042-014-6(1), 20141) Pub: UlverLrgPrint GBR. Dist(s): Ulverscroft US

Commodore. unabr. ed. Read by Simon Vance. (Running Time: 36000 sec.). (Aubrey-Maturin Ser.). 2006. 59.95 (978-0-7861-4889-9(6)); audio compact disk 72.00 (978-0-7861-5991-8(X)); audio compact disk 29.95 (978-0-7861-7111-8(1)) Blckstn Audio.

Commodore. unabr. ed. Read by Simon Vance. (Running Time: 36000 sec.). (Aubrey-Maturin Ser.). 2007. 29.95 (978-1-4332-0434-0(7)) Blckstn Audio.

Commodore. unabr. collector's ed. C. S. Forester. Read by Richard Green. 7 cass. (Running Time: 10 hrs. 30 min.). (Hornblower Ser.: No. 8). 1980. 64.00 (978-0-7366-3095-5(3), 1347-A) Books on Tape.
Hornblower returns to to the sea with the rank of Commodore in command of a small but powerful squadron. His mission is so delicate that the fate of Europe hangs on the outcome. Though outgunned & outmanned - but never outfought or outsailed - Hornblower takes his squadron north to win the Czar's resistance against Napoleon.

Commodore, Set. Patrick O'Brian. Read by Graham Roberts. 10 cass. (Aubrey-Maturin Ser.). 1999. 69.95 (20141) Pub: Soundings Ltd GBR. Dist(s): ISIS Pub

Commodore, Set unabr. ed. Read by Christian Rodska. 8 cass. 1999. 69.95 (CAB 1732) AudioGO.

Commodore: Aubrey Maturin Series #17. unabr. ed. Read by Simon Vance. 8 CDs. (Running Time: 36000 sec.). 2007. audio compact disk 29.95 (978-1-4332-0435-7(5)) Blckstn Audio.

Commodore: The Life of Cornelius Vanderbilt. unabr. ed. Edward J. Renehan, Jr. Narrated by John McDonough. (Running Time: 12 hrs. 45 mins.). 2008. 61.75 (978-1-4361-6608-9(X)); audio compact disk 123.75 (978-1-4281-6950-0(4)) Recorded Bks.
Acclaimed historian Edward J. Renehan, Jr. - author of Dark Genius of Wall Street - draws upon previously unreleased documents to deliver the definitive biography of Cornelius Vanderbilt, the 19th-century transportation tycoon who accumulated the largest private fortune in U.S. history.

Common Aberrations in Thinking. unabr. ed. Barbara Branden. 1 cass. (Running Time: 1 hr. 34 min.). (Principles of Efficient Thinking Ser.). 12.95 (708) J Norton Pubs.
Topics include: The fallacy of Equating an abstraction with a concrete; The danger of false axioms; Failures of discrimination in thinking; Intellectual package-dealing; Thinking in a square; Psycho-epistemological "platonism".

Common American Phrases in Everyday Contexts. Spears. audio compact disk 20.00 (978-0-658-00126-0(4)) M-H Contemporary.

Common As Muck: The Autobiography of Roy Chubby Brown. abr. ed. Roy Brown. Read by Roy Brown. (Running Time: 2 hrs. 56 mins.). (ENG., 2007. audio compact disk 24.95 (978-1-4055-0162-0(6)) Pub: Little Bks Ltd GBR. Dist(s): IPG Chicago

***Common Assault Pt. 4: Untold Stories.** Read by Alan Bennett. (Running Time: 2 hrs. 0 mins. 0 sec.). (ENG., 2010. audio compact disk 24.95 (978-1-84607-163-8(1)) Pub: AudioGO. Dist(s): Perseus Dist

Common Birds of Hawaii. Doug Pratt. (JPN.). 2004. audio compact disk 4.95 (978-1-57306-182-7(4)) Bess Pr.

Common Bond: Maintaining the Constancy of Purpose Throughout Your Health Care Organization. Francis L. Ulschak. (Jossey-Bass Health Ser.). 1994. bk. 47.00 (978-1-55542-614-9(X), Jossey-Bass) Wiley US.

Common Courtesy. Emmet L. Robinson. Read by Emmet L. Robinson. 2 cass. (Running Time: 1 hr. 36 min.). 1994. 19.95 set. King Street.
How the little things make the big difference in business.

Common Elements of Different Paths. Swami Amar Jyoti. 1 cass. 1979. 9.95 (M-26) Truth Consciousness.
The door to unbound consciousness. 'Sages call it by many names'. Choosing our path.

Common Fallacies about Capitalism. unabr. ed. Nathaniel Branden. 1 cass. (Running Time: 1 hr. 15 min.). (Basic Principles of Objectivism Ser.). 12.95 (575) J Norton Pubs.
An examination of monopolies & the fact that a free market makes their existance impossible. A discussion of labor unions as a form of monopoly & the economic history of events leading to the depression.

Common Fractures of the Upper Extremities. Paul C. Liu. 1 cass. (Running Time: 54 min.). 1997. bk. 20.00 (978-1-58111-041-8(3)) Contemporary Medical.
Explains diagnosis of upper extremity fractures, emergency & delayed care of fractures, surgical & nonsurgical treatments.

***Common Ground.** unabr. ed. Cal Thomas & Bob Beckel. Read by Cal Thomas & Bob Beckel. Read by Richard Rohan. (ENG.). 2007. (978-0-06-155460-5(X)); (978-0-06-155469-8(3)) HarperCollins Pubs.

Common Ground: How to Stop the Partisan War That Is Destroying America. unabr. ed. Cal Thomas & Bob Beckel. Read by Cal Thomas & Bob Beckel. Read by Richard Rohan. (Running Time: 30600 sec.). 2007. audio compact disk 39.95 (978-0-06-136360-3(X), Harper Audio) HarperCollins Pubs.

Common Ground: The Water, Earth & Air We Share. Molly Garrett Bang. 1 cass. (Running Time: 15 min.). (J). 2001. bk. 23.90 (6856) Spoken Arts.

Common Law. unabr. ed. Oliver W. Holmes, Jr. Read by Robert Morris. 9 cass. (Running Time: 13 hrs.). 1995. 62.95 (978-0-7861-0706-3(5), 1583) Blckstn Audio.
This is one of the true classics in world legal literature. Written by a master of law & language, it is a primary source book for anyone interested either in legal theory or political science. For the laymen, it serves to clarify the very essence of the common law, the cornerstone of our present legal system.

Common Life: The Wedding Story. Jan Karon. Narrated by John McDonough. 5 CDs. (Running Time: 5 hrs.). (Mitford Ser.: Bk. 6). audio compact disk 49.00 (978-0-7887-9620-3(8)) Recorded Bks.

Common Life: The Wedding Story. unabr. ed. Jan Karon. Narrated by John McDonough. 4 cass. (Running Time: 5 hrs.). (Mitford Ser.: Bk. 6). 2001. 42.00 (978-0-7887-4847-9(5), K0062L8) Recorded Bks.
In this heart-warming tale, excitement sweeps the town after Mitford's beloved Episcopal priest announces plans to end his long-time bachelorhood.

Common Loon. Thea M. Holtan. 1 cass. (J). (gr. 1-12). 1994. 10.00 (978-1-887071-12-3(1)) Thea-Thot.
Primary narration is on Side 1; advanced narration is on Side 2. These narrations correspond with the videotape "Loon" by Escape Tapes.

Common Misconceptions about Economics; Historical Definitions. John Robbins. 1 cass. (Introduction to Economics Ser.: No. 1). 5.00 Trinity Found.

Common Mistakes Lawyers Make at Trial. Frank Rothschild. 1 cass. (Running Time: 1 hr. 19 min.). 1995. 29.95 (FAZ170S) Natl Inst Trial Ad.
Discussion of the most common, most predictable, & yet the most avoidable errors trial lawyers make in presenting their cases.

Common Murder. unabr. ed. Val McDermid. Read by Vari Sylvester. 6 cass. (Running Time: 7 hrs. 30 mins.). (Isis Ser.). (J). 2002. 54.95 (978-0-7531-1024-9(5)); audio compact disk 71.95 (978-0-7531-1267-0(1)) Pub: ISIS Lrg Prnt GBR. Dist(s): Ulverscroft US
A protest-group hits the headlines when unrest explodes into murder. Already on the scene, journalist, lindsay Gordon, desperately tries to strike a balance between personal and professional responsibilities. As she peels back the layers of deception surrounding the protest and its opponents, she finds that no one seems wholly above suspicion. Then Lindsay uncovers a truth that even she can hardly believe.

***Common Prayer: A Liturgy for Ordinary Radicals.** unabr. ed. Shane Claiborne et al. (ENG.). 2010. 19.99 (978-0-310-32620-5(6)) Zondervan.

Common Questions & Controversies in Infectious Diseases. Contrib. by Sarah S. Long et al. 1 cass. (American Academy of Pediatrics UPDATE: Vol. 17, No. 8). 1998. 20.00 Am Acad Pediat.

Common Reader, Set unabr. ed. Virginia Woolf. Narrated by Flo Gibson. 6 cass. (Running Time: 8 hrs.). (gr. 10 up). 1999. pap. bk. 24.95 (978-1-55685-622-8(9)) Audio Bk Con.
These essays about the writings of Chaucer, Montaigne, Jane Austen, Charlotte Bronte, George Eliot, Adison & Defoe to name just a few, are a joy for readers of the classics. (four 90's & two 60's).

Common Sense. Thomas Paine. Read by George Vafiadis. (Running Time: 3 hrs.). (C). 2003. 19.95 (978-1-59912-053-9(4), Audiofy Corp) Iofy Corp.

Common Sense. Thomas Paine. Narrated by George Vafiadis. (Running Time: 7200 sec.). (Unabridged Classics in MP3 Ser.). (ENG.). 2008. audio compact disk 24.00 (978-1-58472-663-0(6), In Aud) Sound Room.

Common Sense. unabr. ed. Thomas Paine. Read by George Vafiadis. (YA). 2007. 34.99 (978-1-59895-846-1(1)) Find a World.

Common Sense. unabr. ed. Thomas Paine. Narrated by Adrian Cronauer. 2 cass. (Running Time: 1 hr. 45 mins.). 1986. 18.00 (978-1-55690-115-7(1), 86420E7) Recorded Bks.
One of the most influential pamphlets published prior to the American Revolution on the subject of independence.

Common Sense. unabr. ed. Thomas Paine. Read by George Vafiadis. 3 cds. (Running Time: 2 hrs 45 min). 2002. pap. bk. (978-1-58472-235-9(5), In Aud) Sound Room.
The work that helped spark the Revolutionary War.

Common Sense. unabr. ed. Thomas Paine. Read by George Vafiadis. 3 cds. (Running Time: 2 hrs 45 mins). 2002. audio compact disk 22.95 (978-1-58472-233-5(9), 027, In Aud) Pub: Sound Room. Dist(s): Baker Taylor

Common Sense: The Case Against an Out-of-Control Government, Inspired by Thomas Paine. unabr. ed. Glenn Beck. Read by Glenn Beck. 3 CDs. (Running Time: 3 hrs. 0 mins. 0 sec.). (ENG.). 2009. audio compact disk 19.99 (978-0-7435-9935-1(7)) Pub: S&S Audio. Dist(s): S and S Inc

Common Sense & Declaration of Independence Set: Thomas Paine, Thomas Jefferson, unabr. ed. George H. Smith. Perf. by Bill Middleton. Narrated by Craig Deitschman. 2 cass. (Running Time: 80 mins. per cass.). Dramatization. (Giants of Political Thought Ser.: Vol. 1). 1985. 17.95 (incl. cass. holder & supp. notes. (978-0-938935-01-8(1), 390268) Knowledge Prod.
These works are two of the most enduring documents in American history. Common Sense converted thousands to the idea of independence. Six months later, the Declaration of Independence rallied the people to a new republic. Presentations includes the essential ideas of these classic works, with a narrative explanation of the author's character, his times, the controversies he faced & the opinions of critics & supporters.

Common Sense & the Declaration of Independence. George H. Smith. Read by Craig Deitschman. (Running Time: 9000 sec.). 2006. audio compact disk 25.95 (978-0-7861-6988-7(5)) Pub: Blckstn Audio. Dist(s): NetLibrary CO

Common Sense of Wisdom. Swami Amar Jyoti. 2 cass. 1985. 12.95 (R-67) Truth Consciousness.
Straight, simple, common sense, the challenge of Truth. Does free will exist? The precise descipline of Vedanta.

Common Sense Parenting see Crianza Practica de los Hijos: Audiolibro CD

Common Sense Parenting. abr. ed. Ray Burke & Ronald W. Herron. 2 cass. (Running Time: 3 hrs.). 1997. 14.95 Set. (978-1-889322-01-8(6), 39-424) Boys Town Pr.
How quick are we to criticize our children when they're doing wrong and say nothing when they behave? How often does whining or a temper tantrum make us give in and say "yes" when we meant to say "no?" Common Sense Parenting(r) strengthens families by easing the self-doubt and confusion of parenthood. Proven techniques any mom and dad can use to stay calm and teach children self-control and healthy behaviors, while reducing their acting out are described. Comprehensive in scope, the strategies address problems faced by most parents. Each chapter outlines a parenting skill and gives examples of how to use that skill with children in a variety of situations. Communicating a logical, sensible approach that's easy to understand, Common Sense Parenting enables parents to be teachers, to catch kids being good, and to develop consistent expectations and consequences. All of the strategies, techniques, and advice contained in the book are available in an audio format. The cassette version also includes a wallet-size reminder card for easy reference. Delivering exactly what the title promises, Common Sense Parenting is the definitive guide to parenthood!.

Common Sense Parenting. 2nd abr. ed. Ray Burke & Ron Herron. Narrated by Mike Holland & Moira Mangiameli. 2 CDs. (Running Time: 3 hrs.). (Common Sense Parenting Ser.). 2007. audio compact disk 14.95 (978-1-889322-88-9(1), 39-424-CD) Boys Town Pr.

Common Sense Parenting: Using Your Head as Well as Your Heart to Raise School-Aged Children. 3rd ed. Prod. by Boys Town Press. Narrated by EmJay & James Langdon. 2009. audio compact disk 19.95 (978-1-934490-08-2(3)) Boys Town Pr.

Common Sense Parenting of Toddlers & Preschoolers: Handling the Day-to-Day Challenges of Parenting Young Children, Ages Two to Five. Prod. by Boys Town Press. Narrated by Ozzie Nogg. 2009. audio compact disk 19.95 (978-1-934490-09-9(1)) Boys Town Pr.

Common Sense/the Declaration of Independence. Thomas Paine & Thomas Jefferson. Read by Craig Deitschmann. (Audio Classics (Playaway) Ser.). (ENG.). 2009. 39.99 (978-1-60847-661-9(8)) Find a World.

Common Territory, Different Maps: The Archetypal Underpinnings of Religious Practice. 12 cass. (Running Time: 16 hrs.). 1994. 76.95 set. (978-0-7822-0475-9(9), CTDM) C G Jung IL.
Through careful consideration of various central themes common to religious experience, this course offers the listener an insightful viewing of the ways in which the religious impulse has taken form & shaped culture & individual alike.

Common Wealth: Economics for a Crowded Planet. unabr. ed. Jeffrey D. Sachs. Read by Malcolm Hillgartner. (Running Time: 45000 sec.). 2008. 72.95 (978-1-4332-3333-3(9)); audio compact disk & audio compact disk 29.95 (978-1-4332-3337-1(1)); audio compact disk & audio compact disk 90.00 (978-1-4332-3334-0(7)) Blckstn Audio.

Common Wealth: Economics for a Crowded Planet. unabr. ed. Jeffrey D. Sachs. Contrib. by Malcolm Hilgartner. 10 CDs. (Running Time: 13 hrs.). (ENG.). (gr. 12 up). 2008. audio compact disk 39.95 (978-0-14-314303-1(4), PengAudBks) Penguin Grp USA.

Common Writing Errors. Brenda Wilbee. 1 cass. (Running Time: 45 min.). (Writing for Publication: Fiction that Sells Ser.: No. 3). 1987. 7.95 (978-0-943777-03-0(8)) byBrenda.
Basic common writing errors.

Common Years. unabr. ed. Jilly Cooper. Read by Norma West. 7 cass. (Running Time: 8 hrs.). 2001. 61.95 (978-1-85089-813-9(8), 20691) Pub: ISIS Audio GBR. Dist(s): Ulverscroft US
An affectionate & candid portrait of life on Putney Common. Jilly Cooper lived on the common for ten years, taking daily walks & keeping a diary in which she noted the effects of the changing seasons & wrote about her encounters with dogs & humans.

Commoner. abr. ed. John Burnham Schwartz. Read by Janet K. Song. 5 CDs. (Running Time: 6 hrs. 30 mins.). (ENG.). 2008. audio compact disk 29.95 (978-0-7393-5873-3(1), Random AudioBks) Pub: Random Audio Pubg. Dist(s): Random

Commoner. unabr. ed. John Burnham Schwartz. Read by Janet K. Song. 8 CDs. (Running Time: 9 hrs.). 2008. audio compact disk 100.00 (978-1-4159-4616-9(7), BksonTape) Pub: Random Audio Pubg. Dist(s): Random
It is 1959 when Haruko, a young woman of good family, marries the Crown Prince of Japan, the heir to the Chrysanthemum Throne. She is the first nonaristocratic woman to enter the mysterious, almost hermetically sealed, and longest-running monarchy in the world. Met with cruelty and suspicion by the Empress and her minions, Haruko is controlled at every turn. The only interest the court has in Haruko is her ability to produce an heir. After finally giving birth to a son, she suffers a nervous breakdown and loses her voice. However, determined not to be crushed by the imperial bureaucrats, Haruko perseveres. Thirty years later, now Empress herself, she plays a crucial role in persuading another young woman - a rising star in the foreign ministry - to accept the marriage proposal of her son, the Crown Prince. The consequences are tragic and dramatic. Told from Haruko's perspective, meticulously researched, and superbly imagined, THE COMMONER is the mesmerizing, moving, and surprising story of a brutally rarefied and controlled existence at once hidden and exposed, and of a complex relationship between two isolated women who, despite being visible to all, are truly understood only by each other.

Commonsense MBA. Richard M. Astle. Read by Richard M. Astle. 2 cass. (Running Time: 3 hrs.). 1996. 16.95 Set. (978-1-57511-013-4(X)) Pub Mills.

Commonwealth of Thieves: The Improbable Birth of Australia. Thomas Keneally. Read by Simon Vance. (Playaway Adult Nonfiction Ser.). 2008. 64.99 (978-1-60640-867-4(4)) Find a World.

Commonwealth of Thieves: The Improbable Birth of Australia. unabr. ed. Thomas Keneally. Narrated by Simon Vance. (Running Time: 12 hrs. 30 mins. 0 sec.). (ENG.). 2006. audio compact disk 37.99 (978-1-4001-0291-4(X)); audio compact disk 75.99 (978-1-4001-3291-1(6)); audio compact disk 24.99 (978-1-4001-5291-9(7)) Pub: Tantor Media. Dist(s): IngramPubServ

Commune with Your Angels. Christopher Love. Read by Christopher Love. 1 cass. (Running Time: 30 min.). 1997. 10.95 (978-1-891820-02-1(8)) World Sangha Pubg.
Self-hypnosis meditation for healing, self-improvement & realizing our full & powerful potential as spiritual beings.

Communes, Telepathy, & Dreams. unabr. ed. Stanley Krippner. 1 cass. (Running Time: 90 min.). 1971. 11.00 (03701) Big Sur Tapes.

Communicate in Greek 1. Kleanthis Arvanitakis. 1 cass. (Running Time: 90 mins.). (GRE.). (J). (gr. 1-7). 1997. 11.50 (978-960-8464-09-4(9)) Pub: Deltos Pubns GRC. Dist(s): Cosmos
Audio exercises for beginners level textbook.

Communicate in Greek 2. Kleanthis Arvanitakis. 1 cass. (Running Time: 90 mins.). (GRE.). (J). (gr. 1-7). 1997. 11.50 (978-960-8464-04-9(8)) Pub: Deltos Pubns GRC. Dist(s): Cosmos
Audio exercises for intermediate level.

Communicate in Greek 3. Kleanthis Arvanitakis. 1 cass. (Running Time: 90 mins.). (GRE.). (J). (gr. 1-7). 1997. 11.50 (978-960-8464-07-0(2)) Pub: Deltos Pubns GRC. Dist(s): Cosmos
Audio exercises for advanced level.

***Communicate or Die: Getting Results Through Speaking & Listening.** Thomas Zweifel & Thomas D. Zweifel. (Global Leader Series Ser.). 2009. 9.99 (978-1-59079-195-0(9)) Pub: Select Books. Dist(s): Midpt Trade

Communicate to Get the Response You Want, Set. 6 cass. pap. bk. & wbk. ed. 30.00 (978-0-7612-0497-8(0), 80159) AMACOM.
You'll learn how to: Grab - & keep - your listener's attention; Add punch & power to what you say & what you write; Write memos, letters, & reports that get results; Communicate with a culturally & ethnically diverse workforce; Minimize distractions & disturbances in your communication; Take advantage of the six proven principles of efficient reading; Receive other people's messages more reliably; Improve your basic listening skills & your ability to interpret what you hear.

Communicate to Get the Response You Want, Set 6 cass. pap. bk. & wbk. ed. 155.00 incl. wkbk., 2 multiple choice tests. (978-0-7612-0496-1(2), 80158) AMACOM.

Communicate with Confidence. Tom Kirby. Intro. by A. E. Whyte. 1 cass. (Running Time: 60 min.). (Listen & Learn USA! Ser.). 8.95 (978-0-88684-010-5(4)) Listen USA.
Explains how to communicate with a group of two or more.

Communicate with Confidence. unabr. ed. Claude Farley. Read by Claude Farley. 1 cass. (Running Time: 90 min.). (Self-Help Ser.). 1986. 7.95 (978-0-88749-095-8(6), TDM 0956) HarperCollins Pubs.
Explains why confidence - both in oneself & projected to others - is essential to effective communication & outlines methods for learning how to organize thoughts, peesent oneself in a confident manner & appear more interesting to others.

Communicating: Parents, Teens & Children. John C. Turpin. 1 cass. 1996. 9.98 (978-1-57734-005-8(1), 06005330) Covenant Comms.
Examples, stories & role plays to help families improve their communication.

Communicating Effectively with Hispanic Patients Set: The Complete Guide to Key Vocabulary Words & Essential & Functional Phrases in Spanish for Direct Patient Contact, unabr. ed. Miriam Diaz-Gilbert. Read by Miriam Diaz-Gilbert. Read by Gladys Pollack-Rolon. 4 cass. (Running Time: 5 hrs. 5 min.). (ENG & SPA.). 1991. pap. bk. 175.00 set, incl. audio bookcase. (978-0-9628364-0-4(0)) ICPC.
English to Spanish for medical & health professionals who have direct patient contact with non-English speaking Hispanic patients. Contains over 400 key vocabulary words & over 500 functional & essential phrases in Spanish for direct-patient contact.

***Communicating for Productive & Fulfilling Relationships Cd Rom Study Guide.** rev. ed. Norheim. (ENG.). 2010. audio compact disk 74.58 (978-0-7575-0579-9(1)) Kendall-Hunt.

Communicating for Results. unabr. ed. Michelle F. Poley. Read by Michelle Fairfield Poley. 6 cass. 1994. 59.95 set. (978-1-57294-030-7(1), 11-0612) SkillPath Pubns.
Michelle Poley's message in this presentation is first of all to know what all the communication skills are, understand how to use them to your advantage, & then practice & apply them in your everyday life.

Communicating in Business. 2nd rev. ed. Simon Sweeney. (Running Time: 2 hrs. 30 mins.). (ENG.). 2004. 45.00 (978-0-521-54914-1(0)) Cambridge U Pr.

Communicating in Business, Set. 2nd rev. ed. Simon Sweeney. (Running Time: 2 hrs. 30 mins.). (ENG., 2004. audio compact disk 45.00 (978-0-521-54915-8(9)) Cambridge U Pr.

Communicating in Chinese. Cynthia Ning. (ENG.). 1994. stu. ed., wbk. ed., lab manual ed. 44.95 (978-0-300-10935-1(0)) Yale U Pr.

Communicating in Chinese: Audio Program for Listening & Speaking. Cynthia Ning. 6 cass. (Running Time: 6 hrs.). (Communicating in Chinese Ser.). 1995. bk. 59.95 Set. (978-0-88710-180-9(1)) Yale Far Eastern Pubns.

Communicating in Chinese - Listening & Speaking. Cynthia Ning. (Far Eastern Publications). (ENG.). 1959. audio compact disk 50.00 (978-0-88710-206-6(9)) Yale U Pr.

Communicating Literature: An Introduction to Oral Interpretation. 4th rev. ed. Todd Lewis. (ENG., 2004. audio compact disk 40.83 (978-0-7575-0872-1(3)) Kendall-Hunt.

Communicating Material Noncompliance & Material Internal Control Weaknesses. rev. ed. William A. Broadus, Jr. & Joseph D. Comtois. 2 cass. (Running Time: 10 hrs.). 1995. 125.00 incl. wkbk. set. (749201VC) Am Inst CPA.
The 1994 edition reflects revisions of the following: cases, reporting guidance (including guidance for federal student financial assistance) & HUD audit guidance. It also covers newly revised OMB Circular A-110, on grants to institutions of higher education, hospitals, & other nonprofit organizations. This course considers reporting problems in single audits of state & local governments, nonprofit audits, & individual federal program audits. And it focuses on making sure that enough information is included in the audit report so that corrective action can be taken.

Communicating on Campus: Skills for Academic Speaking. Amy Hemmert & Ged O'Connell. (ENG.). (gr. 10-12). 1998. suppl. ed. 14.95 cass. (978-1-882483-69-3(3)) Alta Bk Ctr Pubs.

Communicating Through the Reins: English Riding. John Lyons. Read by John Lyons. 4 cass. (Running Time: 4 hrs.). 2000. pap. bk. 59.00 (721546) CDH Assocs.
The most comprehensive descriptions ever assembled on how to use the reins to improve any performance horse or to solve any behavioral problems you may encounter with your horse. The principles are easy to understand & will work on all horses, regardless of age, past history, breed or rider's chose style of riding. You can listen to the cassettes in your vehicle or while jogging or riding your horse, then refer to the written version.

Communicating Through the Reins: Western Riding. John Lyons. Read by John Lyons. 4 cass. (Running Time: 4 hrs.). 2000. pap. bk. 59.00 (721447) CDH Assocs.

Communicating with Your Own Soul. unabr. ed. Dean Marshall & Marie Kirkendoll. 3 cass. (Running Time: 3 hrs.). 1986. 29.95 incl. bklet. (978-1-55585-078-4(2)) Quest NW Pub.
Teaches how to begin to contact your own Higher Soul Self or God working within you.

Communicating with your Spirit Guides & Angels. Lexa Finley. (ENG.). 2009. audio compact disk 14.95 (978-0-9822494-4-4(6)) Journey Spirit.

Communication: The Key to Success with the Primary Student. Nechemya Rosen. 1 cass. (Running Time: 90 mins.). 1999. 6.00 (W60FT) Torah Umesorah.

Communication: The Master Key to an Anointed Family. Creflo A. Dollar. 4 cass. (Running Time: 6 hrs.). 2001. 20.00 (978-1-931172-83-7(8), TS45, Kidz Faith) Pub: Creflo Dollar. Dist(s): STL Dist NA

Communication about Freedom, Emotion & Motivation. unabr. ed. Robert LeFevre. 1 cass. (Running Time: 1 hr. 52 min.). 12.95 (1001) J Norton Pubs.
Ways to improve ones ability to communicate & survive.

Communication & Do Animals Have Languages? unabr. ed. David Attenborough. 1 cass. (Running Time: 54 min.). (Animal Language Ser.). 12.95 J Norton Pubs.

Communication & Support. John Novak & Devi Novak. 1 cass. (Ananda Talks about Marriage Ser.). 9.95 (DM-3) Crystal Clarity.
Explains the real meaning of intimacy what to do when your partner is "wrong" how to view your own imperfections; defines attitudes that can destroy a marriage & specific ways to make your marriage more fulfilling.

Communication Audio CD. Adapted by Benchmark Education Company Staff. Based on a work by Katherine Scraper. (Early Explorers Set C Ser.). (J). (gr. 1). 2008. audio compact disk 10.00 (978-1-60437-535-0(3)) Benchmark Educ.

Communication in Workplace. Delmar. 2001. audio compact disk 455.95 (978-0-7668-3987-8(7)) CENGAGE Learn.

Communication Magic. Jonathan Robinson. Read by Jonathan Robinson. 2 cass. (Running Time: 3 hrs.). 1995. 15.95 Set. (978-1-57328-795-1(4)) Focal Pt Calif.
The quality of our relationships is largely due to how effectively we communicate. In this live workshop, Jonathan Robinson explains the most powerful & simplest ways to communicate effectively with anyone. These tools will help you avoid disagreements, understand your intimate partner, & increase the level of Love & connection you consistently experience.

Communication Map. David Alex Steele. (ENG.). 2007. audio compact disk 19.95 (978-0-9755005-8-3(9)) RCN Pr.

Communication Power in an Hour. A. D. Jeary. 1 cass. 9.95 (978-1-883454-03-6(4)) TPG Inc.
How to communicate more effectively. Aimed at both personal & business communication.

Communication Skills. Eric Douglas et al. 1 cass. (Running Time: 2 hrs.). (Personal Growth Ser.). 2000. (978-1-892655-02-8(0), 3-A) Powerplay Audio.
Packed with valuable tips on how to communicate more constructively in all areas in life. Includes 4 book summaries & author interviews.

Communication Skills: Professionals' Effectiveness Training Session - "PETS" (for Men) Eliezer Gewirtz. 1 cass. (Running Time: 90 mins.). 1999. 10.00 (W60F6) Torah Umesorah.

Communication Skills for Cosmetologists. Kathleen Ann Bergant. 1 cass. (SalonOvations Ser.). 1996. 16.95 (978-1-56253-342-7(8), Milady) Delmar.

Communication Skills for Women. Fred Pryor. 6 cass. (Running Time: 6 hrs.). (Fred Pryor Seminars Ser.). 1995. 59.95 Set incl. wkbk. (12350AM) Nightingale-Conant.
Ideal for use as a training or reference tool.

Communication Skills for Women: How to Communicate with Confidence & Power. 6 cass. 59.95 Set incl. wkbk. (12351AS) Pryor Resources.

Communication Then & Now Audio CD. Adapted by Benchmark Education Company Staff. Based on a work by Katherine Scraper. (Early Explorers Set C Ser.). (J). (gr. k-1). 2008. audio compact disk 10.00 (978-1-60437-523-7(X)) Benchmark Educ.

Communication University: Effective Communication in a Difficult Environment. Paul Endress. (ENG., 2009. 295.00 (978-0-9788144-7-2(9)) Maximum Ad.

Communication with Sick Children. Palmer Temple. 1986. 10.80 (0312) Assn Prof Chaplains.

Communication with the Highest. Swami Amar Jyoti. 1 cass. 1990. 9.95 (L-12) Truth Consciousness.
The Great Silence, God, communicate with us by making us in their own image. Relationships with God.

Communications see Comunicacion - Base para un Marketing Exitoso

Communications. Basilio Balli Morales. Read by Basilio Balli Morales. (Running Time: 1 hr.). (C). 2003. 14.95 (978-1-60083-301-4(2), Audiofy Corp) Iofy Corp.

Communicative Value of Intonation in English. David Brazil. (Running Time: hrs. mins.). (ENG., 1997. 26.25 (978-0-521-58588-0(0)) Cambridge U Pr.

Communicator II, Level 2. Steven J. Molinsky & Bill Bliss. 2002. 40.80 (978-0-13-341785-2(9)) Longman.

Communicator 1, Level 1. Steven J. Molinsky & Bill Bliss. 2002. suppl. ed. 40.80 (978-0-13-341777-7(8)) Longman.

Communion. Henry W. Wright. (ENG.). 2008. audio compact disk 24.95 (978-1-934680-49-0(4)) Be in Hlth.

Communion: A True Story. Whitley Strieber. 1 cass. (AA & A Symposium Ser.). 9.00 (A0253-88) Sound Photosyn.

Communion in Its Fullness. Derek Prince. 1 cass. (I-4089) Derek Prince.

Communion of Saints: The Unity of the Family. Jeff Cavins. (ENG.). 2007. audio compact disk 9.95 (978-1-934567-11-1(6)) Excorde Inc.

Communion Series. Mark Hanby. 4 cass. 1992. 29.00 Set. (978-0-938612-65-0(4)) Destiny Image Pubs.

Communion with Christ: Practical Prayer. Featuring Deacon James Keating. Interview with Kris McGregor. Prod. by Kvss. 2008. audio compact disk 25.00 (978-0-9800455-2-9(5)) Pub: IPF Publns. Dist(s): FaithMarket

Communion with God. Neale Donald Walsch. Read by Neale Donald Walsch. Told to Edward Asner & Ellen Burstyn. (Playaway Adult Nonfiction Ser.). (ENG.). 2009. 45.00 (978-1-60775-558-6(0)) Find a World.

Communion with God. unabr. ed. Neale Donald Walsch. Read by Ellyn Burstyn & Edward Asner. 5 CDs. (Running Time: 5 hrs.). (ENG.). 2000. audio compact disk 29.95 (978-1-56511-410-4(8), 1565114108) Pub: HighBridge. Dist(s): Workman Pub

Communion with the Infancy Narratives: A Transforming & Loving Encounter with the Scriptures. Eugene LaVerdiere. Read by Eugene LaVerdiere. 1 cass. (Running Time: 59 min.). 1986. 7.95 (TAH171) Alba Hse Comns.
Utilizes a new literary, rhetorical approach to the bible. This newest approach to the scriptures builds on the classic analyses, ties them together & goes beyond them.

Communism. unabr. ed. Richard Pipes. Narrated by George Wilson. 5 CDs. (Running Time: 5 hrs. 45 min). 2003. audio compact disk 59.00 (978-1-4025-5748-4(5)); 29.95 (978-1-4025-1363-3(1)) Recorded Bks.
An exploration of a promising theory that when put to practice wreaked havoc on the world. An expert on communism, Richard Pipes follows the history of the Soviet Union from the 1917 revolution to the Cold War, and finally, to its deterioration and collapse.

Communism & Freedom Follows the Free Market, Real Danger. unabr. ed. Edmund A. Opitz & Dean Russell. 1 cass. (Running Time: 1 hr. 2 min.). 12.95 (103) J Norton Pubs.

Communism, Fascism, Socialism: Which Is the Worst? Hosted by Leonard Peikoff. 1 cass. (Philosophy: Who Needs It? Ser.). 1998. 12.95 (LPXXC55) Second Renaissance.

Communism vs. Capitalism. Thomas Merton. 1 cass. (Running Time: 60 min.). (Marxism Ser.). 8.95 (AA2235) Credence Commun.
Discussion of what Marx has to offer & why it is so inadequate compared to real Christianity.

Communist Bases in Latin America. unabr. ed. Paul Bethel. 1 cass. (Running Time: 57 min.). 12.95 (144) J Norton Pubs.

Communist Manifesto - The Social Contract Set: Karl Marx, Frederick Engels, Jean Jacques Rousseau, abr. ed. Ralph Raico et al. Perf. by E. R. Davies & Travis Hardison. Narrated by Craig Deitschman. 2 cass. (Running Time: 2 hrs. 50 mins.). Dramatization. (Giants of Political Thought Ser.: Vol. 7). 1986. 17.95 (978-0-938935-07-0(0), 390269) Knowledge Prod.
Two powerful thinkers, Rousseau & Marx, argue that the best interests of the individual consist in merging with the greater social good. These two works were destined to change the course of history. Presentation includes the essential ideas of these classic works, with a narrative explanation of the author's character, his times, the controversies he faced, & the opinions of critics & supporters.

Communist Manifesto/Social Contract. Ralph Raico et al. Read by Craig Deitschman. (Running Time: 10800 sec.). (Giants of Political Thought Ser.). 2006. audio compact disk 25.95 (978-0-7861-7327-3(0)) Pub: Blckstn Audio. Dist(s): NetLibrary CO

Communities Audio CD Theme Set: Set of 6 Set A. Adapted by Benchmark Education Staff. (English Explorers Ser.). (J). (gr. 3-6). 2007. audio compact disk 60.00 (978-1-4108-9839-5(3)) Benchmark Educ.

Communities Then & Now Audio CD. Adapted by Benchmark Education Company Staff. Based on a work by Vickey Herold. (Early Explorers Set C

Ser.). (J). (gr. 2). 2008. audio compact disk 10.00 (978-1-60437-552-7(3)) Benchmark Educ.

Community: Life Giving or Stagnant? John Malich. 2 cass. (Running Time: 2 hrs. 6 min.). 1997. 18.95 Set. (TAH385) St Pauls Alba.
A valuable resource for any community establishment: Religious, fraternal, marital & others. Ideal material for retreat reflections.

Community & the Christian Life. Thomas Merton. 1 cass. 8.95 (AA2456) Credence Commun.

Community & Transformation. Thomas Merton. 1 cass. 8.95 (AA2371) Credence Commun.

***Community Chaplains Audio Theater Empowerment Series.** 2008. audio compact disk 99.99 (978-1-934570-11-1(7)) Lanphier Pr.

Community Experiences: Reading & Communication for Civics. Lynda Terrill. 2004. 23.13 (978-0-07-287077-0(X), 9780072870770, ESL/ELT) Pub: McGrw-H Hghr Educ. Dist(s): McGraw

Community Has Homes Audio CD. Adapted by Benchmark Education Company Staff. Based on a work by Katherine Scraper. (Early Explorers Set C Ser.). (J). (gr. k-1). 2008. audio compact disk 10.00 (978-1-60437-526-8(4)) Benchmark Educ.

Community Helpers Audio CD. Adapted by Benchmark Education Company Staff. Based on a work by Cynthia Swain. (My First Reader's Theater Ser.). (J). (gr. k-1). 2008. audio compact disk 10.00 (978-1-60634-091-2(3)) Benchmark Educ.

Community Involvement Builds Customer Loyalty & Incremental Sales. 1 cass. (America's Supermarket Showcase '96 Ser.). 1996. 11.00 (NGA96-047) Sound Images.

Community Property, Gail Boreman Bird. 4 cass. (Running Time: 6 hrs.). (Audio Tape Ser.). 1998. 57.00 (978-1-57793-042-6(8), 28397, West Lglwrks) West.

Community Property Bar Review: Audio CDs & Outlines. Speeches. Natalia Foley. Voice by Caudle David. 3 CDs. (Running Time: 2 hrs 40 mins). 2005. stu. ed. 25.99 (978-0-9743923-0-1(8), GCC Pubs) Lib Soldiers.

Community Values & Globalization. Benjamin Barber. 2 CDs. (Running Time: 3 hrs.). 2005. audio compact disk 19.95 (978-0-660-18971-0(2)) Pub: Canadian Broadcasting CAN. Dist(s): Georgetown Term

Commute. 3 cass. (Running Time: 3 hrs.). 2001. 19.95 (CREA001) Lodestone Catalog.

Como Agua para Chocolate see Like Water for Chocolate: A Novel in Monthly Installments, with Recipes, Romances & Home Remedies

Como Agua para Chocolate. abr. ed. Laura Esquivel. 4 vols. (SPA.). 2000. 19.95 (978-84-204-9403-6(8)) Alfaguara Ediciones ESP.

Como alcanzar la paz del Corazon. P. Juan Rivas. (SPA.). 2009. audio compact disk 18.95 (978-1-935405-61-0(6)) Hombre Nuevo.

Còmo Alcanzar Sus Metas. unabr. ed. Mario Elnerz. 3 CDs.Tr. of How to Reach Your Goals. (SPA.). 2001. audio compact disk 17.00 (978-958-8161-34-1(7)) YoYoMusic.

Como Comunicarnos en Publico con Poder, Entusiasmo y Efectividad. Camilo Cruz. 2 cass. (Running Time: 2 hrs.).Tr. of How to Speak in Public with Power, Enthusiasm & Effectiveness. (SPA.). 2003. (978-1-931059-26-8(8)) Taller del Exito.
Knowing how to communicate your ideas to others with power and effectiveness is an essential component of your personal and professional success. In a way, our ability to speak with conviction and enthusiasm will determine how far we can get in the game of life. here are several strategies for developing that special charisma that will lead you on your way to becoming a great public speaker.

Cómo confesarse mejor. P. Juan Rivas. (YA). 2006. audio compact disk 16.95 (978-0-9674222-1-3(3)) Hombre Nuevo.

Como Convencer a los Demas. unabr. ed. Mario Elnerz. Read by Pedro Montoya. 3 CDs.Tr. of How to Convince Other People. (SPA.). 2001. audio compact disk 17.00 (978-958-8161-18-1(5)) YoYoMusic.

Como Convertirse en Ciudadano de los Estados Unidos (Amaray Case) Stacey Kammerman. (SPA.). 2007. audio compact disk 9.98 (978-0-9785424-5-0(2)) NPG Music FL.

Como Convertirse en Ciudadano de los Estados Unidos (Jewel Case) Stacey Kammerman. (SPA.). 2007. audio compact disk 9.98 (978-0-9785424-6-7(0)) NPG Music FL.

Como Convertirse en Cuidadano de los Estados Unidos: How to Become A United States Citizen. Created by Kamms. (Running Time: 3600 sec.). (Ingles en el Trabajo Ser.). 2007. audio compact disk 10.98 (978-1-934842-53-9(2)) KAMMS Consult.

Cómo Convertirse en Cuidadano de los Estados Unidos (Digital) Stacey Kammerman. 2007. audio compact disk 15.95 (978-1-934842-06-5(0)) KAMMS Consult.

Como Crear Abundancia en su Vida. Camilo Cruz. 2 cass. (Running Time: 2 hrs.).Tr. of Creating Abundances in Your Life. (SPA.). 2003. 18.00 (978-1-931059-02-2(0)) Taller del Exito.
Helps you evaluate the beliefs and the values that control virtually every financial decision you make to see if they are helping you get ahead or are holding you back from achieving financial freedom. Learn how to develop a mentality of abundance by mastering five powerful habits that will shape the course of you financial life forever.

Como Crear Salud: Mas alla de la Prevencion y Hacia la Perfeccion. Deepak Chopra. 2 cass. (Running Time: 2 hrs.).Tr. of Creating Health, Beyond Prevention, Toward Perfection. (SPA.). 2002. (978-968-5163-00-2(6)) Taller del Exito.
Explores the healing power of the mind for people who are turning to alternative methods of health care as a result of the crisis in traditional care.

Como crear su propio negocio de jardinería - 1 Book + 1 CD: How to start your own landscaping business - Spanish Version. 2nd ed. Excerpts. Maria Peluffo. 1 CD. (Running Time: 60 mins.). (SPA.). 2005. audio compact disk 49.99 (978-0-9758550-4-1(2)) Spanish Audio.
The complete book is read on the CD format.

Como criar ninos emocionalmente Sanos: Satisfaciendo sus cinco necesidades vitales y tambien las de los padres edicion Actualizada. (SPA.). 2009. audio compact disk 29.95 (978-0-932767-17-2(6)) NMI Pubs.

Como Descubrir tus Dones Espiritiuales. Marco Barrientos. 6 cass. (SPA.). 2003. 29.99 (978-0-89985-403-8(6)); audio compact disk 35.00 (978-0-89985-418-2(4)) Christ for the Nations.

Como deshacerse de la Brujeria. Carlos Gonzalez. 1 cd. (Running Time: 32 mins). (SPA.). 2004. audio compact disk 15.00 (978-1-56491-111-7(X)) Imagine Pubs.

Cómo educar hijos Adolescentes. P. Miguel Carmena. (SPA.). (YA). 2007. audio compact disk 16.95 (978-0-9674222-7-5(2)) Hombre Nuevo.

Como Encontrar la Felicidad Ideas y Consejos Sobre la Pareja Ideal see How to Find Happiness Ideas & Advice about Finding the Perfect Partner

Como Encountrar la Pareja Adecuada. 2003. audio compact disk 42.00 (978-1-57972-548-8(1)) Insight Living.

Como Enfrentar Problemas con la Ayuda de Dios. Charles R. Swindoll.Tr. of Facing Life Problems with God's Hope. (SPA.). 2007. audio compact disk 44.00 (978-1-57972-757-4(3)) Insight Living.

Como Escapar de la Prision del Intelecto. Deepak Chopra. 1 cass. (Running Time: 1 hr.).Tr. of Escaping the Prision of the Intellect. (SPA.). 2002. (978-1-931059-16-9(0)) Taller del Exito.
Offers essential guidance for life's journey, demonstrating how to avoid mistaking the images of reality for reality itself.

***Como Evitar Que Te Roban Tus Suenos.** Tr. of How to Keep Your Dreams from Being Stolen. (SPA.). 2009. audio compact disk 18.00 (978-0-944129-35-7(8)) High Praise.

Como Evitar Sentirse Mal: Como Eliminar los Obstaculos que Impiden Amar. unabr. ed. Lilburn S. Barksdale. Tr. by George Teague. 1 cass. (Running Time: 58 min.). (SPA.). 1994. 9.95 (978-0-918588-40-1(5), 119S) NCADD.
Side one reveals the three underlying causes of "feeling bad." Side two declares that love is our natural state, & shows how to avoid the trap of false ideas that are the roadblocks to experiencing it.

Como Expresarse Mejor. Carlos González. Read by Carlos González. Ed. by Dina Gonzalez. 1 cass. (Running Time: 32 min.).Tr. of How to Communicate Better. (SPA.). 1990. 10.00 (978-1-56491-014-1(8)) Imagine Pubs.
In Spanish. Basic information on how to improve personal communication.

Como Ganarse a la Gente: Descubra Principios Que Funcionan Cada Vez. abr. ed. John C. Maxwell. (Running Time: 12600 sec.). (SPA.). 2006. audio compact disk 24.99 (978-0-88113-924-2(6)) Pub: Grupo Nelson. Dist(s): Nelson

Como Hacer Dinero Ya. Sidney A. Friedman.Tr. of How to Make Money Tomorrow Morning. (SPA.). 1998. pap. bk. 19.95 (978-0-7931-2541-8(3)) Kaplan Pubng.

Como Hacer el Amor Toda la Noche: (Y enloquecer a una Mujer) Barbara Keesling. 2 CDs. (Running Time: 2 Hrs). (SPA.). 2005. audio compact disk 24.95 (978-0-9728598-5-1(3)) Fonolibro Inc.
No importando la edad, o la experiencia cualquiera puede alcanzar el nivel de satisfaccion y cumplimiento que nunca penso fuera posible. La sexologa, Dra. Barbara Keesling le dice a los hombres y mujeres el secreto de como alcanzar a?os satisfaccion y placer. Usando las tecnicas de la Dra. Keesling, tu pareja y tu se van a embarcar en una exploracion erotica en el area de los sentidos y disfrutar la intimidad como nunca lo habias experimentado antes. Sus probadas tecnicas y ayudas incluyen:- Como prolongar el hacer el amor hasta donde quieras.- Ejercicios que pueden mejorar el placer.- Aprender como tocar y sentir.- Encender la pasion de tu pareja- Y mucho mas.FonoLibro Inc. te trae en formato de audio libro el Bestseller internacional ?Como Hacer el Amor Toda la Noche? (Y enloquecer a una mujer), donde la Dra. Barbara Keesling revela las tecnicas y ejercicios que ayudan al hombre a prolongar su habilidad de hacer el amor y disfrutar de orgasmos multiples.

Como Hacerle el Amor A una Mujer: Y Que Quede con Ganas de Mas. abr. ed. Barbara Keesling. 3. (Running Time: 12600 sec.). (SPA.). 2007. audio compact disk 24.95 (978-1-933499-13-0(3)) Fonolibro Inc.

Como Iniciar Una Conversacion. abr. ed. Don Gabor. (Running Time: 0 hr. 45 mins. 0 sec.). (ENG.). 2007. audio compact disk 13.00 (978-1-879834-04-0(9)) Pub: Convstn Arts. Dist(s): IPG Chicago

Como Lograr el Éxito: en Ventas, Edicion Empresarial. Javier Madera Camacho.Tr. of How to achieve success in Sales. (SPA.). 2009. DVD & audio compact disk 495.00 (978-0-615-32729-7(X)) JMC Prof Semin.

***Como Lograr el Exito en Ventas.** Javier Madera Camacho. (SPA.). 2008. audio compact disk 59.95 (978-0-9827086-2-0(9)) JMC Prof Semin.

Como lograr las Metas. Carlos González. Read by Carlos González. Ed. by Dina Gonzalez. 1 cass. (Running Time: 32 min.). (SPA.). 2002. 10.00 (978-1-56491-020-2(2)) Imagine Pubs.
In Spanish. Basic know-how to set & achieve goals.

Como Mantenerse Contento. Carlos González. Read by Carlos González. Ed. by Dina Gonzalez. 1 cass. (Running Time: 32 min.).Tr. of How to Remain Happy. (SPA.). 1990. 10.00 (978-1-56491-013-4(X)) Imagine Pubs.
In Spanish. Basic information & mental drills on how to maintain happiness.

Como Nacio el Arco Iris. Alma Flor Ada. (Cuentos Para Todo el Ano Ser.).Tr. of How the Rainbow Came to Be. (SPA., (J). (gr. k-3). 4.95 (978-1-58105-247-3(2)) Santillana.

***Como Olvidar Tu Pasado Y Creer en Tu Futuro.** Tr. of How to Forget Your Past & Believe in Your Future. (SPA.). 2005. audio compact disk 18.00 (978-0-944129-30-2(7)) High Praise.

***Como Pasar Del Rechazo A la Aceptacion.** Tr. of How to Move from Rejection to Acceptance. (SPA.). 2005. audio compact disk 18.00 (978-0-944129-31-9(5)) High Praise.

Como Pelear con sus Seres Queridos. Carlos Cuauhtemoc Sanchez.Tr. of How to Argue with Your Loved Ones. audio compact disk 15.95 (978-968-7277-56-1(4)) Pub: EdSelect MEX. Dist(s): Giron Bks

Como Pronunciar Ingles Correctamente. Kenneth Brown. Contrib. by Kenneth Brown. 1 cass. (Running Time: 060 min.). (How to Pronounce Ser.).Tr. of How to Promote English Correctly. (SPA.). 1995. pap. bk. 16.95 (978-0-8442-0837-4(X), 0837X, Natl Textbk Co) M-H Contemporary.
English as a second language.

Como Salir de la Depresion Use el Enojo Positivamente see Combating Depression Using Anger Positively

Como Salvar, Mantener y Mejorar la Relacion de Pareja. unabr. ed. Mario Elnerz. Read by Hernando Iván Cano.Tr. of How to Save, Maintain & Improve a Couple Relationship. (SPA.). 2002. audio compact disk 13.00 (978-958-43-0146-8(2)) YoYoMusic.

Como Ser Personas de Gracia, Serie en. (SPA.). 2002. audio compact disk 65.50 (978-1-57972-466-5(3)) Insight Living.

¿Como sera el Cielo? Marcos Richards. Created by C. C. Vino Nuevo. 2007. lib. bdg. 1.99 (978-1-933172-45-3(2)) Jayah Producc.

Como Soy Yo? Level 2. 2003. 11.50 (978-0-7652-0986-3(1)) Modern Curr.

Como transmitir educacion sexual Hoy. Lupita Venegas.Tr. of How to talk about sexual education Today. (SPA.). 2009. audio compact disk 15.00 (978-1-935405-36-8(5)) Hombre Nuevo.

Como tratar con gente Dificil. Cesar Lozano.Tr. of How to deal with difficult People. (SPA.). 2009. audio compact disk 17.00 (978-1-935405-44-3(6)) Hombre Nuevo.

***Como un Hombre Piensa.** ed. Tr. by Guillermo DeLaPaz III, 3rd. Narrated by Guillermo DeLaPaz III, 3rd. (Running Time: 58). (SPA.). 2010. audio compact disk 12.95 (978-0-9831142-0-8(X)) AudiBuksInc.

Como un Nino. Zondervan Publishing Staff. (SPA.). 2005. audio compact disk 15.99 (978-0-8297-4775-1(3)) Pub: Vida Pubs. Dist(s): Zondervan

Como Vencer el Insomio. Deepak Chopra. 1 cass. (Running Time: 1 hr. 30 mins.).Tr. of How to Conquer Insomia. (SPA.). 2001. Astran.

Como vender en eBay - 1 Book + 1 CD: How to sell on eBay - Spanish Version. 2nd ed. Excerpts. Maria Peluffo. 1 CD. (Running Time: 60 mins.). (SPA.). 2005. audio compact disk 49.99 (978-0-9758550-5-8(0)) Spanish Audio.
The complete book is read on the CD.

Cómo Vivir Sobre el Nivel de la Mediocridad. 2003. audio compact disk 60.00 (978-1-57972-544-0(9)) Insight Living.

Comodore: And Other Stories Read by the Author. Short Stories. Jon Manchip White. 1 cass. (Running Time: 72 min.). 1997. 10.00 (978-0-916078-14-0(0), Iris) Iris Pub Group.
Four short stories based on Welsh traditional myths read by the author, Jon Manchip White, with brief interludes of Welsh folk music played on the harp.

Compact Disc Jake & the Migration of the Monarch. (SPA.). (J). 2005. audio compact disk 8.95 (978-0-9774038-1-3(5)) Monarch Pubs.

Compact Portuguese (Brazilian) II, Set. unabr. ed. Pimsleur Staff. 5 cass. (POR.). 1997. 95.00 (978-0-671-57962-3(2), Pimsleur) S&S Audio.

Companero: The Life & Death of Che Guevara. collector's ed. Jorge Castaneda. Read by Edward Lewis. 13 cass. (Running Time: 19 hrs. 30 min.). 2000. 104.00 (978-0-7366-5567-5(0)) Books on Tape.
Thirty years ago, in Bolivia, the life of Ernesto Guevara de la Serna came to a sudden, inglorious end - & an unquenchable myth was born.

Companion CD-ROM for Exploring Creation with Physics 2nd Edition. Jay L. Wile. Jon E. Nichols. 2004. audio compact disk 15.00 (978-1-932012-47-7(8)) Apologia Educ.

Companion CD to Frederic Chopin, Son of Poland Early & Later Years. Created by Zeezok Publishing. 1. (J). 2007. 7.95 (978-1-933573-10-6(4), 4719) Zeezok Pubng.

Companion Through Illness. Marilyn Winfield. Read by Marilyn Winfield. 1 cass. (Running Time: 30 mins.). 2000. (978-0-9679210-5-1(8)) Pathwy Heal.
Guided visualizations for those dealing with a life threatening illness.

Companion to the Power of Now: A Guide to Spiritual Enlightenment. unabr. ed. Eckhart Tolle. 2000. 22.95 (978-0-9682364-1-3(3)) Namaste Pub.
The titles of the audio tapes are: "Living the Liberated Life" and "Dealing with the Pain-body." Readers of the book will find these audio tapes to be powerful additions to their understanding of and their ability to live the practices in the book.

Companions: A Windham Hill Sampler. Windham Hill Staff. 1 cass. 1998. 15.00 (978-1-56170-564-1(0)) Hay House.

Company. unabr. ed. Max Barry. Read by William Dufris. (Running Time: 10 hrs. 30 mins. 0 sec.). (ENG.). 2006. audio compact disk 19.99 (978-1-4001-5202-5(X)); audio compact disk 59.99 (978-1-4001-3202-7(9)) Pub: Tantor Media. Dist(s): IngramPubServ

Company. unabr. ed. Robert Littell. Narrated by Scott Brick. 30 cass. (Running Time: 41 hrs. 45 mins.). 2002. 109.75 (978-1-4025-1887-4(0)) Recorded Bks.
The Cold War. A war not fought with guns and ammunition, but by spys, governments and the ever present threat of world domination remains in the minds of most adults living today. Littrell brings to light the events that marked the Cold War in this historical saga chronicalling the interworkings of the CIA from 1950 to 1995.

Company: A Novel. unabr. ed. Max Barry. Read by William Dufris. (Running Time: 10 hrs. 30 mins. 0 sec.). (ENG.). 2006. audio compact disk 29.99 (978-1-4001-0202-0(2)) Pub: Tantor Media. Dist(s): IngramPubServ

Company: A Novel of the CIA. abr. ed. Robert Littell. Read by Scott Brick. 12 cass. (Running Time: 18 hrs.). 2004. 44.95 (978-1-59007-087-1(9)) New Millenn Enter.

Company: A Novel of the CIA. unabr. ed. Robert Littell. Read by Scott Brick. 30 cass. (Running Time: 45 hrs.). 2004. 99.95 (978-1-59007-232-5(4)) New Millenn Enter.

Company: A Novel of the CIA. unabr. ed. Robert Littell. Narrated by Scott Brick. 30 cass. (Running Time: 41 hrs. 45 mins.). 2002. 77.95 (978-1-4025-1891-1(9), RF945) Recorded Bks.

Company: A Novel of the CIA. unabr. abr. ed. Robert Littell. Read by Scott Brick. 16 CDs. (Running Time: 18 hrs.). 2004. audio compact disk 64.95 (978-1-59007-088-8(7)) New Millenn Enter.

Company "Aitch" (H) unabr. ed. Sam R. Watkins. Read by Jim Roberts. 6 cass. (Running Time: 9 hrs.). 1994. 36.00 set in vinyl album. Jimcin Record.
First-person account of the Civil War as seen through the eyes of a Confederate soldier.

Company Aytch (Company H) Sam Watkins. Narrated by Dan Calhoun. (Running Time: 8 hrs. 30 mins.). 2004. 32.95 (978-1-59912-857-3(8)) Iofy Corp.

Company Man. Joseph Finder. Read by Scott Brick. 2005. 26.95 (978-1-59397-699-6(2)) Pub: Macmill Audio. Dist(s): Macmillan

Company Man. abr. ed. Joseph Finder. Read by Scott Sowers. 2005. 17.95 (978-1-59397-698-9(4)) Pub: Macmill Audio. Dist(s): Macmillan

Company Man. abr. ed. Joseph Finder & Scott Brick. Read by Scott Sowers. 5 CDs. (Running Time: 6 hrs. 0 mins. 0 sec.). (ENG.). 2005. audio compact disk 29.95 (978-1-59397-593-7(7)) Pub: Macmill Audio. Dist(s): Macmillan

Company Man. unabr. ed. Joseph Finder. 2 pieces. 2005. 49.95 (978-0-7927-3539-7(0), CMP 780); audio compact disk 110.95 (978-0-7927-3538-0(2), SLD 780) AudioGO.

Company Man. unabr. ed. Joseph Finder. Contrib. by Scott Brick. 9 cass. (Running Time: 064080 sec.). 2005. 79.95 (978-0-7927-3537-3(4), CSL 780) AudioGO.

Company Man. unabr. ed. Joseph Finder. Read by Scott Sowers & Scott Brick. 14 CDs. (Running Time: 18 hrs. 0 mins. 0 sec.). (ENG.). 2005. audio compact disk 49.95 (978-1-59397-595-1(3)) Pub: Macmill Audio. Dist(s): Macmillan

Company of Rebels. unabr. ed. Elizabeth Lord. 7 cass. (Running Time: 9 hrs. 42 mins.). (Isis Cassettes Ser.). (J). 2005. 61.95 (978-0-7531-2166-5(2)) Pub: ISIS Lrg Prnt GBR. Dist(s): Ulverscroft US

Company of Strangers. unabr. ed. Robert Wilson. Read by Sean Barrett. 15 CDs. (Running Time: 16.5 hrs.). 2002. audio compact disk 104.95 (978-0-7531-1571-8(9)) Pub: ISIS Audio GBR. Dist(s): Ulverscroft US
In 1944 the baking summer streets of Lisbon's capital seethe with spies and informers, and the endgame of the intelligence war is silently being fought. The Germans have rocket technology and atomic know-how. The Allies are determined that the ultimate "secret weapon" will not be realised. Into this sophisticated world come Andrea Aspinall, mathematician and spy, and Karl Voss, an embittered and traumatised military attache to the German Legation on a mission to save Germany from annihilation. In this corrupted paradise, Andrea and Voss attempt to find love. After a night of terrible violence Andrea is left with a secret which provokes a lifelong addiction to a clandestine world, from the brutal Portuguese fascist regime to the paranoia of Cold War Germany. And there, in an ice-gripped East Berlin, she discovers that the deepest secrets are held not by governments but by those closest to you.

Company of Strangers. unabr. ed. Robert Wilson. Read by Sean Barrett. 14 cass. (Running Time: 16 hrs. 40 min.). (Isis Ser.). (J). 2002. 99.95 (978-0-7531-1259-5(0)) Pub: ISIS Lrg Prnt GBR. Dist(s): Ulverscroft US
Lisbon 1944. The baking summer streets of the capital seethe with spies and informers, and the endgame of the intelligence war is silently being fought. The Germans have rocket technology and atomic know-how. The Allies are determined that the ultimate "secret weapon" will not be realised.Into this sophisticated world come Andrea Aspinall, mathematician and spy, and Karl Voss, an embittered and traumatised military attache to the German Legation on a mission to save Germany from annihilation.

Company of Swans. unabr. ed. Eva Ibbotson. Narrated by Patricia Conolly. 9 CDs. (Running Time: 10 hrs. 30 mins.). (YA). (gr. 9 up). 2008. audio compact disk 97.75 (978-1-4361-1512-4(4)); 67.75 (978-1-4361-1507-0(8)) Recorded Bks.
Eva Ibbotson, Smarties Prize winner for Journey to the River Sea and finalist for both the Whitbread Award and the Carnegie Medal, sets this compelling story in 1912 England where 19-year-old Harriet Morton leads a dreary existence. Her ballet class is her only joy. When Father won't let her travel on a ballet tour to South America, Harriet creates a clever ruse that covers her escape and triggers an experience far beyond her dreams.

Company She Keeps. abr. ed. Georgia Durante. Read by Georgia Durante. 4 cass. (Running Time: 6 hrs.). 2001. 24.95 (978-1-57511-096-7(2)) Pub Mills.
At 17, Georgia Durante was the dazzling "Kodak girl," the most photographed model in the country. Things took a turn when Durante was raped by her brother-in-law, had a child & a failed marriage before she was 20, & became a Mafia wife, all chronicled in this chilling true story.

***Company We Keep: A Husband-and-Wife True-Life Spy Story.** unabr. ed. Dayna Baer & Robert Baer. Read by Dayna Baer. (ENG.). 2011. audio compact disk 35.00 (978-0-307-87848-9(1), Random AudioBks) Pub: Random Audio Pubg. Dist(s): Random

Company's Coming. Arthur Yorinks. Illus. by David Small. Narrated by Jim Brownold & Dee Hoty. 1 cass. (Running Time: 1 hr.). (J). 2001. bk. (6884) Spoken Arts.
On the day Shirley had invited all of her relatives to dinner and Moe, her husband, was pleasantly tinkering in the yard, a flying saucer quietly landed next to their tool shed. They don't know it yet, but the galaxy is about to get a little bit smaller.

***Compara los números hasta el 100 Audio CD.** April Barth. Adapted by Benchmark Education Co., LLC. (Content Connections Ser.). (SPA.). (J). 2010. audio compact disk 10.00 (978-1-61672-186-2(3)) Benchmark Educ.

Comparative Religion. Instructed by Charles Kimball. 2008. 129.95 (978-1-59803-452-3(9)); audio compact disk 69.95 (978-1-59803-453-0(7)) Teaching Co.

Comparative Religions on File. Facts on File, Inc. Staff. (C). (gr. 6-12). 2001. audio compact disk 149.95 (978-0-8160-4441-2(4)) Facts On File.

Comparative Study of the Gospels. unabr. ed. Samuel Sandmel. 1 cass. (Running Time: 27 min.). 12.95 (31006) J Norton Pubs.
Shows contradictions & repetitions in the Gospels.

Comparing in Nature: Early Explorers Early Set B Audio CD. Jamie A. Schroeder. Adapted by Benchmark Education Staff. (J). 2007. audio compact disk 10.00 (978-1-4108-8238-7(1)) Benchmark Educ.

Comparing Two Cities: Early Explorers Early Set B Audio CD. Anna Lee. Adapted by Benchmark Education Staff. (J). 2007. audio compact disk 10.00 (978-1-4108-8229-5(2)) Benchmark Educ.

Comparsa. Perf. by Eric Mouquet & Michael Sanchez. 1 cass., 1 CD. 8.78 (EPIC 68726); audio compact disk 13.58 CD Jewel box. (EPIC 68726) NewSound.
The musical duo, the musicians behind Deep Forest, have again created a collection of inspired, unique music that bridges the gap between continents & generations.

Compas. Perf. by Gipsy Kings. 1 cass., 1 CD. 8.78 (NONE 79466); audio compact disk 13.58 CD Jewel box. (NONE 79466) NewSound.

Compass. unabr. ed. Tammy Kling & John Spencer Ellis. Read by Dan John Miller. 1 MP3-CD. (Running Time: 4 hrs.). 2009. 24.99 (978-1-4233-9285-9(X), 9781423392859, Brilliance MP3); 39.97 (978-1-4233-9286-6(8), 9781423392866, Brlnc Audio MP3 Lib); 24.99 (978-1-4233-9287-3(6), 9781423392873, BAD); 39.97 (978-1-4233-9288-0(4), 9781423392880, BADLE); audio compact disk 24.99 (978-1-4233-9283-5(3), 9781423392835, Bril Audio CD Unabri); audio compact disk 62.97 (978-1-4233-9284-2(1), 9781423392842, BriAudCD Unabrid) Brilliance Audio.

Compass for Your Heart (A Compilation) Mary M. Morrissey. 4 cass. (Running Time: 4 hrs.). 1998. 29.95 Set. (978-1-886491-20-5(8)) Tiger Mtn Pr.

Compassion. 1 cass. (Running Time: 1 hr.). 12.99 (711) Yoga Res Foun.

Compassion. AIO Team Staff. Prod. by Focus on the Family Staff. (Running Time: 1 hr. 10 mins. 0 sec.). (Adventures in Odyssey Life Lessons Ser.). (ENG.). (J). (gr. 3-7). 2005. audio compact disk 5.99 (978-1-58997-183-7(3)) Pub: Focus Family. Dist(s): Tyndale Hse

Compassion. Osho Oshos. 1 cass. 9.00 (A0650-89) Sound Photosyn.
These tapes are all produced by the Rajneesh Organization, Poona, India. This controversial figure was an intense scholar & articulator of vision.

***Compassion.** unabr. ed. Dalai Lama XIV. Ph.D., Jeffrey Hopkins. (Running Time: 3 hrs. 0 mins. 0 sec.). (ENG.). 2011. audio compact disk 19.99 (978-1-4423-4059-6(2)) Pub: S&S Audio. Dist(s): S and S Inc

Compassion: A Key to Authority. Steve Thompson. 1 cass. (Running Time: 90 mins.). (Understanding Spiritual Authority Ser.: Vol. 3). 2000. 5.00 (ST03-003) Morning NC.
This series reveals the key scriptural foundations & practical applications for moving in true spiritual authority.

Compassion: The Heart of Enlightenment. Dalai Lama XIV. 1 cass. 10.00 (A0734-89) Sound Photosyn.
A deep teaching, in his inimitably melodious voice delivered just after receiving the Nobel Peace Prize. Our powerful personal experiences with him have us hold him in extremely high regard.

Compassion & the Peaceful Mind. Swami Amar Jyoti. 1 cass. 1990. 9.95 (K-127) Truth Consciousness.
Compassion removes tension, makes mind the fit instrument needed for focus & wisdom. Compassion for all creatures.

Compassion & Wisdom in Care for the Dying. Christine Longaker. 1 cass. 1997. 10.95 (978-0-9624884-7-4(X)) Rigpa Pubns.
Motivational.

Compassion, Courage & Regeneration. Jeffrey Mickler. Read by Jeffrey Mickler. 3 cass. (Running Time: 3 hrs.). 1988. 25.95 (TAH201) Alba Hse Comns.
These talks remind priests of God's unfailing love, encourage priests to show compassion towards each other, challenge priests to continue to be compassionate towards their people through living the evangelical counsels & remind priests of basic contemplative techniques that will aid them in drawing strength from nature & creativity from the Creator.

Compassion in Action. Ram Dass & Mirabai Bush. Read by Ram Dass & Mirabai Bush. 2 cass. (Running Time: 3 hrs.). 1992. 15.95 Set. (978-1-879371-16-3(2), 20180) Pub Mills.
Here is the book that will guide people who don't yet know that what is missing from their lives is service to others; it will help them identify their most useful talents & point them in the right direction for meeting specific needs.

Compassion of Our Lord. Kenneth E. Hagin. 6 cass. 24.00 (23H) Faith Lib Pubns.

Compassion of the Miracle. Kenneth Wapnick. 4 CDs. 2006. audio compact disk 24.00 (978-1-59142-245-7(0), CD70) Foun Miracles.

Compassion of the Miracle. Kenneth Wapnick. 2009. 19.00 (978-1-59142-385-0(6)) Foun Miracles.

Compassion Versus Guilt & Other Essays. unabr. ed. Thomas Sowell. Read by Michael Kevin. 5 cass. (Running Time: 7 hrs.). 2000. 39.95 (978-0-7861-0000-2(1), 1001) Blckstn Audio.
Represents a compilation of several of those short essays written for the common reader. Sowell's essays paint some hard truths backed by brilliant scholarship. He discusses many of the extraordinary ideas that preoccupy the Liberal political agenda, exposes the flaws & submits them to reprimand.

Compassionate Communication: With the Memory Impaired. Scripts. Sherril Bover & Nancy Graham. Perf. by Sherril Bover & Nancy Graham. 1. (Running Time: 25 minutes). 2009. audio compact disk (978-0-9771625-4-3(0)) SecondWind.

Compassionate Communion: Trinity in New Language. Michael Downey. 2 cass. (Running Time: 2 hrs.). 2001. vinyl bd. 18.95 (A6230) St Anthony Mess Pr.
Presents the radical consequences for Christian life with the affirmation that God is first and foremost a mystery of persons - Father, Son and Spirit - in loving, compassionate communion.

Compassionate Conservatism: What It Is, What It Does, & How It Can Transform America. unabr. ed. Marvin Olasky. Read by Jeff Riggenbach. 5 cass. (Running Time: 7 hrs.). 2001. 39.95 (978-0-7861-2005-5(3), 2775) Blckstn Audio.
From the "Godfather of compassionate conservatism" & influential advisor to Governor George W. Bush, here is a blueprint of Bush's philosophy of governance.

***Compassionate Conservatism: What It Is, What It Does, & How It Can Transform America.** unabr. ed. Marvin Olasky. Read by Jeff Riggenbach. (Running Time: 7 hrs. NaN mins.). (ENG.). 2011. 29.95 (978-1-4417-8444-5(6)); audio compact disk 69.00 (978-1-4417-8442-1(X)) Blckstn Audio.

Compassionate Correction. Elbert Willis. 1 cass. (Victory of Surrender Ser.: Vol. 2). 4.00 Fill the Gap.

Compassionate Journey. unabr. ed. 2 cass. (Running Time: 2 hrs. 45 min.). (Telepathic Communication Ser.: Vol. 1). 21.95 Set. (978-1-891284-00-7(2)) Critter Cnslt.
Addresses spiritual consciousness of nonhuman animals, telepathic communication with nonhuman animals, compassion among human & nonhuman animals.

Compatibility. Arlene Kramer. 1 cass. 8.95 (769) Am Fed Astrologers.

Compatibility: or The Search for Miss-Mister Right. Lynn Shawver. 1 cass. 8.95 (461) Am Fed Astrologers.
An AFA Convention workshop tape.

Compelling Case, Set. Michael Underwood. Read by Judith Franklyn. 5 cass. 1999. 39.95 (65921) Pub: Soundings Ltd GBR. Dist(s): ISIS Pub

Compelling Interest: Life after Roe V. Wade. unabr. ed. Roger Resler. (ENG.). 2007. 13.99 (978-1-60814-121-0(7)); audio compact disk 19.99 (978-1-59859-232-0(7)) Oasis Audio.

Compelling, Opposing, & Enforcing Discovery in State Courts. Read by Dawn Girard et al. (Running Time: 2 hrs. 30 min.). 1991. 70.00 Incl. 114p. tape materials. (CP-54154) Cont Ed Bar-CA.

Compelling Selling. Linda Cline Chandler. Prod. by Ko Hayashi. (ENG.). 2009. 150.00 (978-0-9639400-6-3(6)) Lrning Two-Thousand.

Compensation for Executives & Broad-Based Employee Groups: Strategy, Design, & Implementation. 9 cass. (Running Time: 13 hrs.). 1999. 345.00 Set; incl. study guide 599p. (AD82) Am Law Inst.
Advanced course presents a wide array of specific compensation topics, covering both design & technical issues, then applies these subjects through the presentation & analysis of a case study.

Compete in the Big Spelling Bee: The Bugville Critters. unabr. ed. Robert Stanek, pseud. Narrated by Ginny Westcott. (Running Time: 29 mins.). (ENG.). (J). 2008. 6.95 (978-1-57545-318-7(5), RP Audio Pubng) Pub: Reagent Press. Dist(s): OverDrive Inc

Competing with the Supercenters. 1 cass. (America's Supermarket Showcase '96 Ser.). 1996. 11.00 (NGA96-003) Sound Images.

Competition. unabr. ed. Stephen E. Heiman. Interview with Diane Sanchez. 2 cass. (Running Time: 1 hr. 36 min.). (Strategic Selling Advanced Ser.: Vol. 3). 1995. Set. (978-0-9619073-7-2(1)); audio compact disk (978-1-889888-02-6(8)) Miller Heiman.
Diane & Steve discuss Miller Heiman's strategy for selling in the highly competitive selling area.

Competition in the Desert - Exotics Versus Natives. Hosted by Nancy Pearlman. 1 cass. (Running Time: 28 min.). 10.00 (224) Educ Comm CA.

Compilation & Review Guide. Nathan M. Bisk & Paul Munter. 4 cass. 199.00 set, incl. textbk. & quizzer. (CPE0120) Bisk Educ.
Presents an understanding of the planning, performance, & reporting requirements that are necessary to complete compilation & review engagements.

Compilation & Review of Financial Statements. rev. ed. Don Pallais. 3 cass. (Running Time: 8 hrs.). 1995. bk. 99.00 set. (743664EZ) Am Inst CPA.
This course provides step-by-step explanations of the provisions & applications of the AICPA's Statements on Standards for Accounting & Review Services. The course offers useful reference tools including a financial statement preparation checklist, inquiry & analysis guidelines, reporting do's & don'ts & alternatives, & engagement letter preparation.

Compilation of Twenty-Fourth Annual Production - Management Seminar Presentations - May 11, 1990: Changes Needed in Manufacturing Men's Clothing in the 90's. 1990. bk. 50.00 (978-0-317-03089-1(2)) Clothing Mfrs.

Compilation 1: Flying Tart. 1 CD. (Running Time: 90 mins.). audio compact disk 15.98 (978-1-57908-298-7(X), 1378) Platinm Enter.

Complaint see Richard Wilbur Readings

Complaint Free Relationships: How to Positively Transform Your Personal, Work, & Love Relationships. unabr. ed. Will Bowen. Read by Will Bowen. (ENG.). 2009. audio compact disk 25.00 (978-0-7393-8320-9(5), Random AudioBks) Pub: Random Audio Pubg. Dist(s): Random

Complaint Free World: How to Stop Complaining & Start Enjoying the Life You Always Wanted. unabr. ed. Will Bowen. Read by Will Bowen. (ENG.). 2007. audio compact disk 21.95 (978-0-7393-5847-4(2), Random AudioBks) Pub: Random Audio Pubg. Dist(s): Random

***Complaints.** unabr. ed. Ian Rankin. (Running Time: 11 hrs.). (ENG.). 2011. 29.98 (978-1-60788-698-3(7)) Pub: Hachet Audio. Dist(s): HachBkGrp

Compleat Angler see Cambridge Treasy Burton

Compleat Angler, unabr. ed. Izaak Walton & Charles Cotton. Narrated by Nelson Runger. 6 cass. (Running Time: 7 hrs. 30 mins.). 1986. 51.00 (978-1-55690-116-4(X), 86920E7) Recorded Bks.
A 17th Century treatise on fishing & its varied delights.

Compleat Angler: Or, the Contemplative Man's Recreation. abr. ed. Izaak Walton. Narrated by Simon Vance. (Running Time: 14400 sec.). 2006. audio compact disk 28.00 (978-1-932378-92-4(8)) Pub: A Media Intl. Dist(s): Natl Bk Netwk

Compleat Cruiser. unabr. collector's ed. L. Francis Herreshoff. Read by Bob Erickson. 8 cass. (Running Time: 12 hrs.). 1984. 64.00 (978-0-7366-0645-5(9), 1606) Books on Tape.
A comprehensive survey of boating that is a joy to all those who love the water. Each chapter is filled with anecdotes & examples that illustrate a wide variety of boating lore.

Compleat Gentleman. Brad Miner. Narrated by Christopher Lane. (Running Time: 8 hrs. 30 mins.). (C). 2004. 27.95 (978-1-59912-644-9(3)) Iofy Corp.

Compleat Gentleman. Brad Miner. Ed. by Christopher Lane. 8 CDs. (Running Time: 8 hrs. 30 mins.). 2004. audio compact disk 64.00 (978-0-7861-8339-5(X), 3368) Blckstn Audio.

Compleat Gentleman. unabr. ed. Brad Miner. Ed. by Christopher Lane. 7 cass. (Running Time: 8 hrs. 30 mins.). 2004. 49.95 (978-0-7861-2836-5(4), 3368) Blckstn Audio.
At a time of astonishing confusion about what it means to be a man, Brad Miner has recovered the oldest and best ideal of manhood: the gentleman. Reviving a thousand-year tradition of chivalry, honor, and heroism, The Compleat Gentleman provides the essential model for twenty-first-century masculinity.

Compleated Autobiography by Benjamin Franklin. Benjamin Franklin. Read by Richard Ferrone. Ed. by Mark Skousen. (Running Time: 50400 sec.). 2006. 79.95 (978-0-7861-4493-8(9)) Blckstn Audio.

Compleated Autobiography by Benjamin Franklin. Mark Skousen. Read by Richard Ferrone. 1 MP3 CD. (Running Time: 16 hrs.). 2006. 29.95 (978-0-7861-7718-9(7)) Blckstn Audio.

Compleated Autobiography by Benjamin Franklin. unabr. ed. Benjamin Franklin. Read by Richard Ferrone. 13 CDs. (Running Time: 50400 sec.). 2005. audio compact disk 32.95 (978-0-7861-7329-7(7)) Blckstn Audio.

Compleated Autobiography by Benjamin Franklin. unabr. ed. Mark Skousen. Read by Richard Ferrone. 11 cass. (Running Time: 16 hrs.). 2005. 32.95 (978-0-7861-4453-2(X)) Blckstn Audio.

Compleated Autobiography by Benjamin Franklin: Covering the Final 33 Years of His Illustrious & Controversial Career - in His Own Words. Benjamin Franklin. Read by Richard Ferrone. Ed. by Mark Skousen. Compiled by Mark Skousen. (Running Time: 50400 sec.). 2006. audio compact disk 99.00 (978-0-7861-7234-4(7)) Blckstn Audio.

Complementary & Alternative Medicine. Contrib. by Ronald A. Chez et al. 1 cass. 1998. 20.00 Am Coll Obstetric.
Obstetrics & Gynecologists update.

Complementary Medicine: Program from the Award Winning Public Radio Series. Interview. Hosted by Fred Goodwin. 1 CD. (Running Time: 1 Hour). 2000. audio compact disk 21.95 (978-1-932479-34-8(1), LCM 98) Lichtenstein Creat.
Herbs, magnets, vitamins,acupuncture....Two out of every five Americans have tried a holistic remedy in increasing number for psychiatric and neurologic conditions. We'll sort through the facts and fictions of complementary medicine and find out which treatments have science to back them up. Plus how music can help repair delicate neural mechanisms in disorders as different as Alzheimer's and stroke.

Complete. Ed. by Justin Gilbert. Contrib. by Lashun Pace et al. 2007. audio compact disk 17.99 (978-5-558-00805-0(9)) Pt of Grace Ent.

***Complete Absolute Beginners Voice Course.** Andres Andrade. (ENG.). 2008. pap. bk. 29.99 (978-0-8256-3669-1(8), 0825636698) Pub: Music Sales. Dist(s): H Leonard

Complete Accompaniment Method for Guitar. Dan Bowden. 2001. per. 22.95 (978-0-7866-4160-4(6), 98688BCD) Mel Bay.

Complete Adventures & Memoirs of Sherlock Holmes. unabr. ed. Arthur Conan Doyle. Read by Ralph Cosham. (YA). 2007. 54.99 (978-1-59895-847-8(X)) Find a World.

Complete Adventures of Sherlock Holmes. Arthur Conan Doyle. Read by Ralph Cosham. (Running Time: 9 hrs. 30 mins.). 2005. 39.95 (978-1-59912-054-6(2), Audiofy Corp) Iofy Corp.

Complete Adventures of Sherlock Holmes. Arthur Conan Doyle. Read by Ralph Cosham. 2005. audio compact disk 67.00 (978-1-58472-694-4(6), In Aud); audio compact disk 34.95 (978-1-58472-693-7(8), In Aud) Sound Room.

Complete & Utter Nonsense, Pt. II. (23326) J Norton Pubs.

Complete Anthology of Elementary Classic Guitar Solos. Joseph Castle. 1997. spiral bd. 22.95 (978-0-7866-2932-9(0), 94641BCD) Mel Bay.

Complete Anthology of Medieval & Renaissance Music. John Renbourn. 1995. pap. bk. 23.95 (978-0-7866-1312-0(2), 95394P) Mel Bay.

Complete Anthology of Medieval & Renaissance Music for Guitar. John Renbourn. 2000. spiral bd. (978-0-7866-5476-5(7), 95394BCD) Mel Bay.

Complete arban Duets: All of the classic Studies. Harold Lieberman. 2004. pap. bk. 34.98 (978-1-59615-424-7(1), 586-017) Pub: Music Minus. Dist(s): Bookworld

Complete Arkangel Shakespeare. unabr. ed. William Shakespeare. Prod. by Tom Treadwell. 98 CDs. (Running Time: 101 hrs. 47 mins.). (ENG.). 2003. audio compact disk 600.00 (978-1-932219-00-5(5)) Pub: AudioGO. Dist(s): Perseus Dist

Complete Arkangel Shakespeare: Fully Dramatized Recordings of 38 Plays. unabr. ed. 98 CDs. (Running Time: 101 hrs. 47 mins.). Dramatization. 2003. audio compact disk 795.00 (978-0-7927-3009-5(7), ARK100) AudioGO.

Complete Audio Holy Bible - King James Version: As read by James Earl Jones & Jon Sherberg. Read by James Earl Jones & Jon Sherberg. (ENG.). 2009. audio compact disk 49.95 (978-1-60077-584-0(5)) TOPICS Ent.

Complete Audio Writing (Nineteen Eighty-Five) Richard Kostelanetz. 9 cass. 75.00 (978-0-932360-71-7(8)) Archae Edns.
Includes Audio Writing, Invocations (with an English opening), Eight Nights/Praying, Openings & Closings, Assdescent/Anacatabasis, Foreshortenings, Seductions/Relationships, Two German Horspiele & Experimental Prose.

Complete Audiobook on Medical Transcription Part I of II: A Step-by-Step Approach. Barbara Cooper. Read by Barbara Cooper. 6 cass. (Running Time: 10 hrs., 30 mins.). 2000. 89.99 (978-0-9703081-0-8(8)) GA Transcript & Med Clms.
Contains over 2000 medical terms, procedures, diagnoses. The words are pronounced & spelled for accuracy & identification purposes.

Complete Audiobook on Medical Transcription Part II of II: A Step-by-Step Approach. Barbara Cooper. Read by Barbara Cooper. 89.99 (978-0-9703081-2-2(4)) GA Transcript & Med Clms.

Complete Audiocassette Package. (Individual Components Ser.). 225.00 (978-0-8092-9462-6(1)) M-H Contemporary.

Complete Automobile Mechanics Refresher Course, Set. rev. ed. Bob Leigh et al. 1981. pap. bk. 70.00 (978-0-88098-073-9(7), H M Gousha) Prntice Hall Bks.

Complete Backstreet Boys. Chrome Dreams. 3 CDs. (Running Time: 5 hrs.). (ENG.). 2001. audio compact disk 29.95 (978-1-84240-090-6(8)) Pub: Chrome Dreams GBR. Dist(s): IPG Chicago

Complete Barchester Chronicles: A BBC Radio Full-Cast Dramatization. Anthony Trollope. (Running Time: 24 hrs. 0 mins. 0 sec.). (ENG.). 2009. audio compact disk 94.95 (978-1-60283-741-6(4)) Pub: AudioGO. Dist(s): Perseus Dist

Complete Bass Guitar by Ear: 2 CD Relative Pitch Ear Training Course. Mark John Sternal. Perf. by Mark John Sternal. 2005. audio compact disk 14.95 (978-0-9762917-4-9(6)) MJS Music.
COMPLETE BASS GUITAR BY EAR2 CD Relative Pitch Ear Training CourseLEARN EVERY NOTE ON YOUR BASS GUITAR BY EAR! No written text or sheet music. Recorded lessons focus on ear training, finger strength, and music theory. So simple a complete beginner can use it. Just pop in the CD and follow the lessons from your very first note to every note - on every fret - on every string of your guitar. Disc 1 the learning disc. Very descriptive showing all you need to play guitar. Disc 2 advanced ear strengthening/training disc. Listen anytime, anywhere to help build your musical ear. Improve pitch recognition, and note relativity Music theory simplified Start with one note and build at your own pace Quickly learn every note on every string by ear No sheet music or sight reading necessary Strengthen your musical ear.

Complete Bible. 61 CDs. (Running Time: 92 hrs.). 1999. audio compact disk 189.99 (978-7-902031-70-7(4)) Chrstn Dup Intl.

Complete Bible. Narrated by E. W. Jeffries. 61 CDs. (Running Time: 92 hrs.). 1999. audio compact disk 199.99 (978-7-902032-12-4(3)) Chrstn Dup Intl.

Complete Bible, Set. Narrated by Stephen Johnson. 42 CDs. 1998. 149.97 (978-1-56563-382-7(2)) Hendrickson MA.

Complete Bible: New International Version. 48 cass. (Running Time: 90 min. per cass.). 1995. 89.99 (978-0-310-20423-7(2)) Zondervan.

Complete Bible-ESV. 2007. audio compact disk 79.99 (978-0-89957-714-2(8)) AMG Pubs.

Complete Bible-ESV. Narrated by Stephen Johnston. 2008. audio compact disk 16.99 (978-0-89957-711-1(3)) AMG Pubs.

Complete Bluegrass Banjo Method. Neil Griffin. 1993. bk. 28.95 (978-0-7866-0915-4(X), 93345P); 9.98 (978-1-56222-587-2(1), 93345) Mel Bay.

Complete Bluegrass Banjo Method. Neil Griffin. 1974. pap. bk. 34.95 (978-0-7866-1620-6(2), 93345CDP) Mel Bay.

Complete Blues Bass. Mike Hiland. 1996. pap. bk. 23.95 (978-0-7866-1317-5(3), 95403P) Mel Bay.

Complete Blues Bass. Mike Hiland. 1996. pap. bk. 29.95 (978-0-7866-1316-8(5), 95403CDP) Mel Bay.

Complete Blues Guitar. Michael Christiansen. 1991. pap. bk. 27.95 (978-0-7866-1396-0(3), 94682CDP) Mel Bay.

Complete Blues Guitar Book. Michael Christiansen. (Complete Book). 1991. bk. 21.95 (978-0-7866-1090-7(5), 94682P); 9.98 (978-1-56222-323-6(2), 94682); audio compact disk 15.98 (978-0-7866-0440-1(9), 94682CD) Mel Bay.

Complete Blues Guitar Method: Beginning Blues Guitar. David Hamburger. (ENG.). 1994. audio compact disk 10.95 (978-0-7390-2517-8(1)) Alfred Pub.

Complete Blues Guitar Method: Intermediate Blues Guitar. M. Smith. (ENG.). 1994. audio compact disk 10.95 (978-0-7390-2523-9(6)) Alfred Pub.

Complete Blues Keyboard Method: Beginning Blues Keyboard. Tricia Woods. (ENG.). 1999. audio compact disk 10.00 (978-0-7390-2518-5(X)) Alfred Pub.

Complete Blues Keyboard Method: Mastering Blues Keyboard. Merrill Clark. (ENG.). 1999. audio compact disk 10.00 (978-0-7390-2525-3(2)) Alfred Pub.

Complete Book DVD - over 7000 Books on one DVD. Ed. by Richard Seltzer. 2004. audio compact disk 149.00 (978-0-931968-93-8(3)) B & R Samizdat.

Complete Book of Blues Guitar Licks & Phrases. Austin Sicard, Jr. (Complete Book). 1992. bk. 23.95 (978-0-7866-1091-4(3), 94687P); 9.98 (978-1-56222-296-3(1), 94687C) Mel Bay.

Complete Book of Blues Guitar Licks & Phrases. Austin Sicard, Jr. 1992. pap. bk. 39.95 (978-0-7866-0606-1(1), 94687CDP) Mel Bay.

Complete Book of Blues Guitar Licks & Phrases. Austin Sicard, Jr. (Complete Book). 1995. audio compact disk 24.98 (978-0-7866-0605-4(3), 94687CD) Mel Bay.

Complete Book of Celtic Music for Appalachian Dulcimer. Mark Nelson. 1996. pap. bk. 34.95 (978-0-7866-0852-2(8), 95530CDP) Mel Bay.

Complete Book of Dragons. E. Nesbit. Narrated by Flo Gibson. 4 CDs. (Running Time: 4 hrs. 23 mins.). (J). 2006. audio compact disk 19.95 (978-1-55685-885-7(X)) Audio Bk Con.
Includes "The Book of Beasts", "Uncle James, or The Purple Stranger", "The Deliverers of Their Country", "The Ice Dragon, or Do As You Are Told", "The Dragon Tamers", "The Fiery Dragon, or The Heart of Stone and the Heart of Gold", "Kind Little Edmond, or The Caves and the Cockatrice, "The Island of Nine Whirlpools" and "The Last of the Dragons".

Complete Book of Dragons, unabr. ed. E. Nesbit. Narrated by Flo Gibson. 3 cass. (Running Time: 4 hrs. 30 min.). (J). 1985. (978-1-55685-049-3(2)) Audio Bk Con.
"The Book of Beasts" & other tales bring us face to face with a variety of dragons & their brave adversaries.

Complete Book of Fiddle Tunes for Acoustic Guitar. Bill Piburn. 2002. per. 29.95 (978-0-7866-6564-8(5), 95471BCD) Mel Bay.

Complete Book of Jazz Guitar Lines & Phrases. Sid Jacobs. 1997. spiral bd. 34.95 (978-0-7866-1794-4(2), 95737CDP) Mel Bay.

Complete Book of Small Business Legal Forms. 3rd ed. Daniel Sitarz. (Small Business Library). 2000. audio compact disk 24.95 (978-0-935755-84-8(5)) Pub: Nova Pub IL. Dist(s): Natl Bk Netwk

Complete Book of Spelling Demons. 2nd ed. Carl W. Salser & C. Theo Yerian. 1983. 158.95 (978-0-89420-210-0(3), 411000) Natl Book.

Complete Business Database of All Companies in Austria. 6th rev. ed. BIA. (J). 2006. audio compact disk 499.00 (978-1-4187-4703-9(3)) Bus Info Agency.

Complete Business Database of Austrian Wholesalers & Retailers. 6th rev. ed. BIA. (J). 2006. audio compact disk 449.00 (978-1-4187-4712-1(2)) Bus Info Agency.

Complete Business Database of Belgian Major Wholesalers & Retailers. 6th rev. ed. BIA. (J). 2006. audio compact disk 519.00 (978-1-4187-4726-8(2)) Bus Info Agency.

Complete Business Database of Belgian Manufacturers. 6th rev. ed. BIA. (J). 2006. audio compact disk 449.00 (978-1-4187-4720-6(3)) Bus Info Agency.

Complete Business Database of Construction Companies of Denmark. 6th rev. ed. BIA. (J). 2006. audio compact disk 479.00 (978-1-4187-4737-4(8)) Bus Info Agency.

Complete Business Database of Construction Companies of the Netherlands. 6th rev. ed. BIA. (J). 2006. audio compact disk 479.00 (978-1-4187-4814-2(5)) Bus Info Agency.

Complete Business Database of Eastern European Wholesalers & Retailers. 6th rev. ed. BIA. (J). 2006. audio compact disk 499.00 (978-1-4187-4597-4(9)) Bus Info Agency.

Complete Business Database of French Construction Companies. 6th rev. ed. BIA. (J). 2006. audio compact disk 449.00 (978-1-4187-4755-8(6)) Bus Info Agency.

Complete Business Database of French Manufacturers. 6th rev. ed. BIA. (J). 2006. audio compact disk 479.00 (978-1-4187-4752-7(1)) Bus Info Agency.

Complete Business Database of French Wholesalers & Retailers. 6th rev. ed. BIA. (J). 2006. audio compact disk 519.00 (978-1-4187-4760-2(2)) Bus Info Agency.

Complete Business Database of German Manufacturers. 6th rev. ed. BIA. (J). 2006. audio compact disk 449.00 (978-1-4187-4768-8(8)) Bus Info Agency.

Complete Business Database of German Wholesalers & Retailers. 6th rev. ed. BIA. (J). 2006. audio compact disk 479.00 (978-1-4187-4776-3(9)) Bus Info Agency.

Complete Business Database of Italian Banking, Financial, & Insurance Companies. 6th rev. ed. BIA. (J). 2006. audio compact disk 249.00 (978-1-4187-4802-9(1)) Bus Info Agency.

Complete Business Database of Italian Manufacturers. 6th rev. ed. BIA. (J). 2006. audio compact disk 599.00 (978-1-4187-4791-6(2)) Bus Info Agency.

Complete Business Database of Italian Wholesalers & Retailers. 6th rev. ed. BIA. (J). 2006. audio compact disk 629.00 (978-1-4187-4799-2(8)) Bus Info Agency.

Complete Business Database of Manufacturers of Denmark. 6th rev. ed. BIA. (J). 2006. audio compact disk 479.00 (978-1-4187-4734-3(3)) Bus Info Agency.

Complete Business Database of Manufacturers of the Netherlands. 6th rev. ed. BIA. (J). 2006. audio compact disk 479.00 (978-1-4187-4811-1(0)) Bus Info Agency.

Complete Business Database of Manufacturers of the United Kingdom. 6th rev. ed. BIA. (J). 2006. audio compact disk 499.00 (978-1-4187-4880-7(3)) Bus Info Agency.

Complete Business Database of Portuguese Manufacturers. 6th rev. ed. BIA. (J). 2006. audio compact disk 449.00 (978-1-4187-4945-3(1)) Bus Info Agency.

Complete Business Database of Spanish Manufacturers. 6th rev. ed. BIA. (J). 2006. audio compact disk 529.00 (978-1-4187-4927-9(3)) Bus Info Agency.

Complete Business Database of Swiss Manufacturers. 6th rev. ed. BIA. (J). 2006. audio compact disk 539.00 (978-1-4187-4896-8(X)) Bus Info Agency.

Complete Business Database of Western Europe Electronic & Electrical Equipment Manufacturers. 6th rev. ed. BIA. (J). 2006. audio compact disk 479.00 (978-1-4187-4679-7(7)) Bus Info Agency.

Complete Business Database of Western European Chemical Manufacturers. 6th rev. ed. BIA. (J). 2006. audio compact disk 439.00 (978-1-4187-4660-5(6)) Bus Info Agency.

Complete Business Database of Western European Clothing Manufacturers. 6th rev. ed. BIA. (J). 2006. audio compact disk 449.00 (978-1-4187-4645-2(2)) Bus Info Agency.

Complete Business Database of Western European Construction Companies. 6th rev. ed. BIA. (J). 2006. audio compact disk 399.00 (978-1-4187-4689-6(4)) Bus Info Agency.

Complete Business Database of Western European Durable Goods Wholesalers. 6th rev. ed. BIA. (J). 2006. audio compact disk 779.00 (978-1-4187-4696-4(7)) Bus Info Agency.

Complete Business Database of Western European Fabricated Metal Manufacturers. 6th rev. ed. BIA. (J). 2006. audio compact disk 519.00 (978-1-4187-4675-9(4)) Bus Info Agency.

Complete Business Database of Western European Food Manufacturers. 6th rev. ed. BIA. (J). 2006. audio compact disk 339.00 (978-1-4187-4639-1(8)) Bus Info Agency.

Complete Business Database of Western European Furniture Manufacturers. 6th rev. ed. BIA. (J). 2006. audio compact disk 389.00 (978-1-4187-4651-3(7)) Bus Info Agency.

Complete Business Database of Western European Industrial Machinery Manufacturers. 6th rev. ed. BIA. (J). 2006. audio compact disk 519.00 (978-1-4187-4678-0(9)) Bus Info Agency.

Complete Business Database of Western European Leather Manufacturers. 6th rev. ed. BIA. (J). 2006. audio compact disk 439.00 (978-1-4187-4666-7(5)) Bus Info Agency.

Complete Business Database of Western European Lumber & Wood Manufacturers. 6th rev. ed. BIA. (J). 2006. audio compact disk 459.00 (978-1-4187-4648-3(7)) Bus Info Agency.

Complete Business Database of Western European Manufacturers. 6th rev. ed. BIA. (J). 2006. audio compact disk 999.00 (978-1-4187-4636-0(3)) Bus Info Agency.

Complete Business Database of Western European Rubber & Plastic Manufacturers. 6th rev. ed. BIA. (J). 2006. audio compact disk 479.00 (978-1-4187-4663-6(0)) Bus Info Agency.

Complete Business Database of Western European Stone & Concrete Manufacturers. 6th rev. ed. BIA. (J). 2006. audio compact disk 489.00 (978-1-4187-4669-8(X)) Bus Info Agency.

Complete Business Database of Western European Transportation Equipment Manufacturers. 6th rev. ed. BIA. (J). 2006. audio compact disk 579.00 (978-1-4187-4682-7(7)) Bus Info Agency.

Complete Business Database of Wholesalers & Retailers of Denmark. 6th rev. ed. BIA. (J). 2006. audio compact disk 479.00 (978-1-4187-4742-8(4)) Bus Info Agency.

Complete Business User's Guide to DOS (CVE) Brian Howard. (Running Time: 6 hrs.). (Micromastery-Systems Management Ser.). 1995. 99.95 incl. study guide & disk. (103439EZ) Am Inst CPA.

Complete Business User's Guide to DOS (MicroMastery) Brian Howard. 1 cass. 99.95 incl. wkbk., disk, reference guide & exam. (103483KQ) Am Inst CPA.
This course will teach you DOS commands & applications dealing with the file & disk management operations.

Complete CAE Class Audio CDs (3) Guy Brook-Hart & Simon Haines. (Running Time: 2 hrs. 43 mins.). (Complete Ser.). (ENG.). 2009. audio compact disk 56.00 (978-0-521-69847-4(2)) Cambridge U Pr.

Complete Cambodian, Set. unabr. ed. University of Iowa, CEEDE Staff. 1 cass. (People & Change Ser.). (CAM.). 1989. 59.00 Incl. tchr's. guide, student text, CAI disk & activity masters. (978-0-7836-0738-2(5), 8934) Triumph Learn.
A problem solving program. Cambodian readings describing episodes in the life of one family.

*__Complete Carmen Browne Series.__ unabr. ed. Stephanie Perry Moore. Narrated by Debora Raell. (Running Time: 13 hrs. 0 mins. 0 sec.). (Carmen Browne Ser.). (ENG.). 2010. audio compact disk 39.98 (978-1-61045-016-4(7), christaudio) christianaud.

Complete Casebook (U) unabr. ed. Arthur Conan Doyle. (Running Time: 10 hrs.). 2009. audio compact disk 54.98 (978-962-634-888-8(7), Naxos AudioBooks) Naxos.

Complete Celtic Fingerstyle Guitar. Stefan Grossman et al. 1995. spiral bd. 29.95 (978-0-7866-1231-4(2), 95217P); spiral bd. 37.95 (978-0-7866-1230-7(4), 95217CDP) Mel Bay.

Complete Celtic Fingerstyle Guitar. Stefan Grossman et al. (ENG.). 2000. spiral bd. 35.00 (978-0-7866-3433-0(2)) Mel Bay.

Complete Chet Atkins Guitar Method. Tommy Flint. 1993. audio compact disk 15.98 (978-0-7866-0729-7(5), 93232CD) Mel Bay.

Complete Chet Atkins Guitar Method. Tommy Flint & Chet Atkins. 1964. pap. bk. 29.95 (978-0-7866-0730-3(0), 93232CDP) Mel Bay.

Complete Chet Atkins Guitar Method. Tommy Flint & Chet Atkins. 1993. 9.98 (978-1-56222-900-9(1), 93232C) Mel Bay.

Complete Chopin Mazurkas: Fifty-One Mazurkas, Newly Arranged for Solo Guitar. Stephen Aron. 2002. spiral bd. 48.95 (978-0-7866-6868-7(7), 98411BCD) Mel Bay.

Complete Chromatic Harmonica Method. Phil Duncan. 1983. spiral bd. 26.95 (978-0-7866-1839-2(6), 93890) Mel Bay.

Complete Chromatic Harmonica Method. Phil Duncan. 1996. audio compact disk 15.98 (978-0-7866-1838-5(8), 93890CD) Mel Bay.

Complete Chronicles of Narnia. unabr. ed. C. S. Lewis. 4 cass. (J). HarperCollins Pubs.

Complete Chronicles of Narnia. unabr. ed. C. S. Lewis. 7 cass. (Running Time: 10 hrs. 30 min.). Incl. Chronicles of Narnia. C. S. Lewis. Read by Claire Bloom. (Chronicles of Narnia Ser.: Bk.2). (J). (gr. 4-8).; Horse & His Boy. Read by Anthony Quayle. Prod. by Paul Scofield. (Chronicles of Narnia Ser.: Bk.5). (J). (gr. 4-8). (CPN 1655); Last Battle. Read by Michael York. (J). (gr. 4-8).; Lion, the Witch & the Wardrobe. C. S. Lewis. Read by Ian Richardson. (Chronicles of Narnia Ser.: Bk.1). (J). (gr. 4-8).; Magician's Nephew. 1 cass. (Running Time: 1 hr. 30 min.). C. S. Lewis. Read by Claire Bloom. (Chronicles of Narnia Ser.). (J). (gr. 4-8). (CPN 1660); (J). 1985. 9.95 HarperCollins Pubs.

*__Complete Cinnamon Bear.__ RadioArchives.com. (Running Time: 420). (ENG.). 2004. audio compact disk 20.98 (978-1-61081-031-9(7)) Radio Arch.

Complete Classic Chicago Blues Harp. David Barrett. (ENG.). 2002. per. 24.95 (978-0-7866-6563-1(7)) Mel Bay.

Complete Clawhammer Banjo. 1994. 9.98 (978-0-7866-0050-2(0), 95153C) Mel Bay.

Complete Clawhammer Banjo Book. Alec Slater & Lisa Schmitz. 1994. bk. 23.95 (978-0-7866-1219-2(3), 95153P) Mel Bay.

Complete Collection of Sonnets. abr. ed. William Shakespeare. Narrated by Ronald Colman. 2 cass. 12.95 (978-0-89926-145-4(0), 833) Audio Bk.

Complete Collection of 431 Faith Library Tapes. Kenneth E. Hagin & Kenneth W. Hagin, Jr. 431 cass. 1393.64 (C8145) Faith Lib Pubns.

Complete Colonial Gentleman: Cultural Legitimacy in Plantation America. Michal J. Rozbicki. (ENG.). 2003. 25.00 (978-0-8139-2236-2(4)) U Pr of Va.

Complete Commercial Database of All Businesses in Belgium. 6th rev. ed. BIA. (J). 2006. audio compact disk 699.00 (978-1-4187-4717-6(3)) Bus Info Agency.

Complete Commercial Database of All Businesses in Denmark. 6th rev. ed. BIA. (J). 2006. audio compact disk 579.00 (978-1-4187-4731-2(9)) Bus Info Agency.

Complete Commercial Database of All Businesses in France. 6th rev. ed. BIA. (J). 2006. audio compact disk 579.00 (978-1-4187-4749-7(1)) Bus Info Agency.

Complete Commercial Database of All Businesses in Germany. 6th rev. ed. BIA. (J). 2006. audio compact disk 579.00 (978-1-4187-4765-7(3)) Bus Info Agency.

Complete Commercial Database of All Businesses in Italy. 6th rev. ed. BIA. (J). 2006. audio compact disk 619.00 (978-1-4187-4789-3(0)) Bus Info Agency.

Complete Commercial Database of All Businesses in Portugal. 6th rev. ed. BIA. (J). 2006. audio compact disk 539.00 (978-1-4187-4941-5(9)) Bus Info Agency.

Complete Commercial Database of All Businesses in Russia. 6th rev. ed. BIA. (J). 2006. audio compact disk 1299.00 (978-1-4187-5298-9(3)) Bus Info Agency.

Complete Commercial Database of All Businesses in Russia & the Former Soviet Republics. 6th rev. ed. BIA. (J). 2006. audio compact disk 1399.00 (978-1-4187-5297-2(5)) Bus Info Agency.

Complete Commercial Database of All Businesses in Spain. 6th rev. ed. BIA. (J). 2006. audio compact disk 599.00 (978-1-4187-4923-1(0)) Bus Info Agency.

Complete Commercial Database of All Businesses in Sweden. 6th rev. ed. BIA. (J). 2006. audio compact disk 549.00 (978-1-4187-4912-5(5)) Bus Info Agency.

Complete Commercial Database of All Businesses in Switzerland. 6th rev. ed. BIA. (J). 2006. audio compact disk 649.00 (978-1-4187-4895-1(1)) Bus Info Agency.

Complete Commercial Database of All Businesses in the Czech Republic. 6th rev. ed. BIA. (J). 2006. audio compact disk 479.00 (978-1-4187-4610-0(X)) Bus Info Agency.

Complete Commercial Database of All Businesses in the Netherlands. 6th rev. ed. BIA. (J). 2006. audio compact disk 639.00 (978-1-4187-4807-4(2)) Bus Info Agency.

Complete Commercial Database of All Businesses in the United Kingdom. 6th rev. ed. BIA. (J). 2006. audio compact disk 579.00 (978-1-4187-4873-9(0)) Bus Info Agency.

Complete Commercial Database of All Businesses in Western Europe. 6th rev. ed. BIA. (J). 2006. audio compact disk 999.00 (978-1-4187-4633-9(9)) Bus Info Agency.

Complete Conan Doyle Sherlock Holmes: Every Sherlock Holmes Novel & Story by Sir Arthur Conan Doyle; Performed by a Full Cast. abr. ed. Arthur Conan Doyle. Clive Merrison & Michael Williams. (ENG.). 2007. audio compact disk 250.00 (978-1-60283-045-5(2)) Pub: AudioGO. Dist(s): Perseus Dist

Complete Country Fiddler. Stacy Phillips. 1992. 9.98 (978-1-56222-438-7(7), 94696C) Mel Bay.

Complete Course. Michael Collings. audio compact disk (978-1-898660-65-1(4)) Fernhurst Bks GBR.

Complete Course to Solve Personal Problems see Curso Completo para Resolver Problemas

Complete CPA Review. 534.60 incl. 4 textbks. with quizzer. (CPA1500) Bisk Educ.

Complete Desktop Guide to Employee Benefits: Includes Coverage of the Americans with Disabilities Act! Nathan M. Bisk & Charles E. Michaels, Jr. 6 cass. 1994. 239.00 set, incl. textbk. & quizzer. (CPE5080); 129.00 extra textbks. & quizzers. (CPE5081); 239.00 software disks, textbk. & quizzer. (CPE5082); 119.00 extra disks & quizzers. (CPE5083) Bisk Educ.
This valuable shelf reference provides more than 600 pages of practical "how to" guidance that will show you how to reduce worker's compensation & unemployment claims, comply with changing regulations, & increase participating in company benefit plans. This informative program also shows you how to set realistic objectives in a cost-conscious environment...how to compare benefit options & coordinate all elements of your plan...how to get both employees & management behind you to maximize participation...how to streamline reporting to regulatory agencies...how to minimize paperwork & your own staff needs...how to cut payroll taxes...how to find cost-effective health insurance alternatives...how to control the rising cost of retiree health benefits...& much more.

Complete Dobro Player. Stacy Phillips. 1996. spiral bd. 48.95 (978-0-7866-1248-2(7), 95271CDP) Mel Bay.

Complete Drumset Rudiments. Contrib. by Peter Magadini. 1998. pap. bk. 14.95 (978-0-7935-8372-0(1), 06620016) H Leonard.

Complete Dulcimer Handbook. Mark Biggs. 1985. 9.98 (978-1-56222-338-0(0), 94047C) Mel Bay.

Complete Electric Blues Guitar. Michael Christiansen. 1993. spiral bd. 23.95 (978-0-7866-1152-2(9), 94846P) Mel Bay.

Complete Electric Blues Guitar. Mike Christiansen. (ENG.). 2004. per. 29.95 (978-0-7866-6867-0(9), 94846SET) Mel Bay.

Complete Electric Blues Guitar Book. Mike Christansen. 1993. 9.98 (978-1-56222-555-1(3), 94846C); audio compact disk 15.98 (978-0-7866-0439-5(5), 94846CD) Mel Bay.

Complete Elegance, No. 5. 1 cass. 10.00 (978-1-885357-89-2(3)) Rational Isl.
Shared experiences of people with physical differences & their allies & about physically different people using re-evaluation counseling.

Complete Elegance, No. 6. 2 cass. 10.00 ea. (978-1-885357-90-8(7)) Rational Isl.
Shared experiences of people with physical differences & their allies, & about physically different people using re-evaluation counseling.

Complete Elegance, No. 7. 2 cass. 10.00 ea. (978-1-885357-91-5(5)) Rational Isl.
Shared experiences of people with physical differences & their allies & about physically different people using re-evaluation counseling.

Complete Elegance, No. 8. 4 cass. 10.00 ea. (978-1-885357-92-2(3)) Rational Isl.

Complete Elegance, Nos. 1, 2, 3 & 4. 1 cass. 10.00 (978-1-885357-88-5(5)) Rational Isl.

Complete English. unabr. ed. University of Iowa, CEEDE Staff. 1 cass. (You & Others Ser.). 1988. 17.00 Incl. tchr's. guide & student text. (978-0-7836-0730-6(X), 8926) Triumph Learn.
English readings of fictional episodes which address common situations. An awareness program for interpersonal relationships & situations.

Complete English, Set. unabr. ed. University of Iowa, CEEDE Staff. 1 cass. (People & Change Ser.). 1989. 59.00 Incl. tchr's. guide, student text, CAI disk & activity masters. (978-0-7836-0739-9(3), 8935) Triumph Learn.
A problem solving program. English readings describing episodes in the life of one family.

Complete Fairy Tales of the Brothers Grimm. Short Stories. Read by Lynn Musgrave. Tr. by Jack D. Zipes. Prod. by Brian Wright. 1 CD. (Running Time: 71 Minutes). Dramatization. 2002. audio compact disk 14.95 (978-0-9720408-0-8(3)) Mercury Media MN.
The timeless wisdom and beauty of fairy tales have provided both children and adults with hours of enjoyment, imagination, and a strong moral compass for countless generations. Now, finally you can hear your favorite classic fairy tales by the Brother?s Grimm in digital audio! Wonderfully read by stage actress Lynn Musgrave, this first volume from a translation by world-renowned scholar of children?s literature, Jack Zipes, includes such favorites as Rapunzel, The Frog King, The Companionship of the Cat and the Mouse, and The Wolf and the Seven Young Kids. Children of all ages will be delighted with this exquisitely produced collection of classic storytelling!.

Complete Fawlty Towers: Radio Dramatization. Connie Booth & John Cleese. 6 CDs. (Running Time: 9 hrs.). 2002. audio compact disk 64.95 (978-0-563-53053-4(7), BBCD 001) BBC Worldwide.

Complete Fifty-Two Lesson Course in the Art of Playing "Chording-Style" Piano. Duane Shinn. 5 cass. bk. 199.99 (CP-11) Duane Shinn.
Includes "How to Play" Professional Position "Chords;" "How to Build Your Own Chords;" "How to Stand a Chord on its Head;" "How to Get Rhythm Into Your Left Hand;" & "How to Form & Play "Far Out" Chords." Includes printed lessons in a binder.

Complete Fingerstyle Guitar. Stefan Grossman. 1996. audio compact disk 24.98 (978-0-7866-0520-0(0), 94561CD) Mel Bay.

Complete Fingerstyle Guitar. Stefan Grossman. 2 CDs. 2000. pap. bk. 29.95 (978-0-7866-1066-2(2), 94561BCD) Mel Bay.

Complete Fingerstyle Jazz Guitar. Alan DeMause. 1996. pap. bk. 37.95 (978-0-7866-1333-5(5), 95434CDP) Mel Bay.

Complete First Certificate Class Audio CDs. Guy Brook-Hart. (Running Time: 3 hrs. 7 mins.). (Complete Ser.). (ENG.). 2008. audio compact disk 43.05 (978-0-521-69830-6(8)) Cambridge U Pr.

Complete Flatpicking Guitar. Steve Kaufman. 1991. pap. bk. 29.95 (978-0-7866-0604-7(5), 94562CDP); spiral bd. 19.95 (978-0-7866-1068-6(9), 94562P); audio compact disk 15.98 (978-0-7866-0603-0(7), 94562CD) Mel Bay.

Complete Flatpicking Guitar Book. Steve Kaufman. (Complete Book). 1991. 9.98 (978-1-56222-178-2(7), 94562C) Mel Bay.

Complete Folkways Recordings. Perf. by Lonnie Johnson. Anno. by Sam Charters. 1 cass. 1993. (0-9307-400670-9307-40067-2-6); audio compact disk (0-9307-40067-2-6) Smithsonian Folkways.
Recorded in 1967, solo studio sessions with superb guitar accompaniment. 24 tales of classic urban blues & popular songs including "C. C. Rider," "Tears Don't Fall No More" & "How Deep Is the Ocean".

Complete Folkways Recordings: The Complete Folkways Recording, 1958. Perf. by Joseph Spence. Contrib. by Sam Charters. 1 cass. or CD. (Running Time: 51 min.). 1992. (0-9307-400660-9307-40066-2-7); audio compact disk (0-9307-40066-2-7) Smithsonian Folkways.

Complete French for Dimwits: Complete Learning Guide & Tapescript. Mark Frobose. 8 cass. (Running Time: 8 hrs.). 1999. stu. ed. 59.00 (978-1-893564-26-8(6)) Macmill Audio.

Complete German for Dimwits: Complete Learning Guide & Tapescript. Mark Frobose. 6 cass. (Running Time: 6 hrs.). (GER.). 1999. stu. ed. 49.00 (978-1-893564-30-5(4)) Macmill Audio.

***Complete Gettysburg Guide: Audio Driving & Walking Tours, Volume 1: the Battlefield.** J. David Petruzzi. 2010. audio compact disk 22.95 (978-1-932714-95-1(2)) Pub: Savas Beatie. Dist(s): Casemate Pubs

Complete Ghost Stories. unabr. collector's ed. Charles Dickens. Read by Jill Masters. Ed. by Peter Haining. 12 cass. (Running Time: 18 hrs.). Incl. Captain Murderer & the Devil's Bargain. 1986. (2000); Christmas Carol. 2 CDs. (Running Time: 2 hrs. 25 mins.). 2001. audio compact disk 16.95 (); Madman's Manuscript. 1986. (2000); Queer Chair. 1986. (2000); Single-Man. 1986. (2000); 1985. 96.00 (978-0-7366-1073-5(1), 2000) Books on Tape.
This collection brings together all Dickens' ghost stories-twenty in all-including several long-lost tales.

Complete Grand Jury Testimony of Monica S. Lewinsky, Set. Perf. by Monica S. Lewinsky. Contrib. by Austin and Nelson Publishers Staff. 2 cass. 1998. 19.95 (978-1-879755-09-3(2)) Recorded Pubns.

Complete Grand Jury Testimony of Monica S. Lewinsky, Set. unabr. ed. Narrated by Judi Barton. 4 cass. (Running Time: 6 hr.). Dramatization. 1998. 19.95 Recorded Pubns.
Live re-enactment.

***Complete GRE Vocabulary.** Verbalearn. 2009. audio compact disk (978-1-61623-653-3(1)) Indep Pub IL.

Complete Guide to Learning the Irish Fiddle. Paul McNevin. (Waltons Irish Folk Music Collection). 1999. pap. bk. 34.95 (978-0-7866-5355-3(8)) Waltons Manu IRL.

Complete Guide to Learning the Irish Tenor Banjo. Gerry O'Connor. 2000. pap. bk. 31.95 (978-1-85720-112-3(4)) Waltons Manu IRL.

Complete Guide to Selling New Cars. Mike Whitty. Ed. by Irene M. McDonald. 1990. pap. bk. 29.95 (978-0-9625079-8-4(9)) Michael Pub.

Complete Guide to Starting or Evaluating a Children's Ministry. Herb Owen. Ed. by Cindy G. Spear. 1993. ring bd. 99.95 (978-0-941005-67-8(4)) Chrch Grwth VA.

Complete Guide to Starting or Evaluating Dynamic Youth Ministry. Larry Maxwell. Ed. by Tamara Johnson & Cindy G. Spear. 1993. bk. 99.95 (978-0-941005-87-6(9)) Chrch Grwth VA.

Complete Guide to the Sea of Cortez. Gerry Cunningham. 1998. cass. & cd-rom 75.00 (978-0-9642450-9-9(4)) Cruising Charts.

Complete Guitar Player, Bk. 1. Russ Shipton. audio compact disk 12.95 (978-0-7119-8183-6(3), AM953161) Music Sales.

Complete Guitar Player, Vol. 2. Russ Shipton. 1 CD. (Running Time: 1 hr. 30 mins.). 2004. bk. 14.95 (978-0-7119-8182-9(5), AM953172) Music Sales.

Complete Guitar Player: Chord Encyclopedia Chordfinder. Contrib. by Arthur Dick. 1996. audio compact disk 16.95 (978-0-7119-3196-1(8), AM 90134) Pub: Music Sales. Dist(s): H Leonard

Complete Guitar Player: Classical Book. Russ Shipton. 1997. audio compact disk 19.95 (978-0-7119-0592-4(4), AM38217) Pub: Music Sales. Dist(s): H Leonard

Complete Harmonica Book. Phil Duncan. 1992. 9.98 (978-1-56222-339-7(9), 94713C) Mel Bay.

Complete Harmonica Player. Stuart Maxwell. 2005. pap. bk. 9.95 (978-0-8256-3406-2(7), AM977438, Amsco Music) Pub: Music Sales. Dist(s): H Leonard

Complete High Five USA Reading Program I. 15 vols. (gr. 4 up). bk. 667.95 (978-0-7368-9580-4(9), High Five) Red Brick Lrning.

Complete High Five USA Reading Program II. 15 vols. (gr. 4 up). bk. 667.95 (978-0-7368-3859-7(7), High Five) Red Brick Lrning.

Complete High Frequency French Course. Mark Frobose. 8 CDs. (Running Time: 8 hrs.). 2004. audio compact disk 49.00 (978-1-893564-03-9(7)) Macmill Audio.

Complete High Frequency Spanish Course. Mark Frobose. 8 CDs. (Running Time: 8 hrs.). 2004. pap. bk. 59.00 (978-1-893564-01-5(0)) Macmill Audio.

Complete Hmong, Set. unabr. ed. University of Iowa, CEEDE Staff. 1 cass. (People & Change Ser.). 1989. 59.00 Incl. tchr's. guide, student text, CAI disk & activity masters. (978-0-7836-0740-5(7), 8936) Triumph Learn.
A problem solving program. Hmong readings describing episodes in the life of one family.

Complete Holy Bible. Read by Andrew Zorsky. 47 vols. (Running Time: 90 mins.). 2004. 64.99 (978-0-89957-424-0(6)); 19.99 (978-0-89957-425-7(4)) Pub: AMG Pubs. Dist(s): STL Dist NA

Complete Idiot's Guide (Chinese) 2006. audio compact disk 45.00 (978-0-7861-7344-0(0)) Blckstn Audio.

Complete Idiot's Guide (German) 2006. audio compact disk 45.00 (978-0-7861-7343-3(2)) Blckstn Audio.

Complete Idiot's Guide (Japanese) 2006. audio compact disk 45.00 (978-0-7861-7345-7(9)) Blckstn Audio.

***Complete Idiot's Guide to Acoustic Guitar Hits: 25 Great Acoustic Guitar Hits.** Created by Alfred Publishing. (Complete Idiot's Guides (Lifestyle Paperback) Ser.). (ENG., 2010. pap. bk. 24.99 (978-0-7390-6705-5(2)) Alfred Pub.

Complete Idiot's Guide to Buying & Selling a Home. abr. ed. Shelley O'Hara & Nancy Lewis. Read by Grover Gardner. (YA). 2007. 34.99 (978-1-60252-747-8(4)) Find a World.

Complete Idiot's Guide to Buying & Selling a Home. abr. ed. Shelley O'Hara & Nancy D. Lewis. Narrated by Grover Gardner. (Complete Idiot's Guides). (ENG.). 2005. 19.59 (978-1-60814-122-7(5)) Oasis Audio.

Complete Idiot's Guide to Closing the Sale. abr. ed. Keith Rosen. Narrated by Rick Plastina. (Complete Idiot's Guides). (ENG.). 2007. 13.99 (978-1-60814-123-4(3)); audio compact disk 19.99 (978-1-59859-224-5(6)) Oasis Audio.

Complete Idiot's Guide to Coping with Difficult People. abr. ed. Arlene Matthews Uhl. Narrated by Kate Burns. (Running Time: 5 hrs. 0 mins. 0 sec.). (Complete Idiot's Guides). (ENG.). 2007. 13.99 (978-1-60814-124-1(1)) Oasis Audio.

Complete Idiot's Guide to Dating. abr. ed. Judy Kuriansky. Read by Judy Kuriansky. 2 cass. (Running Time: 3 hrs.). 2001. 18.00 (978-1-59040-108-8(5), Phoenix Audio) Pub: Amer Intl Pub. Dist(s): PerseuPGW

Complete Idiot's Guide to French: Level I. 4 CDs. (Complete Idiot's Guide Ser.: Level 1). (FRE & ENG.). 2003. audio compact disk 34.99 (978-1-58926-208-9(5), A22M-FR10) Oasis Audio.

Complete Idiot's Guide to French: Level II. 4 cds. (Complete Idiot's Guide Ser.: Level 2). (ENG & FRE.). 2003. audio compact disk 34.99 (978-1-58926-209-6(3), A22M-FR20) Oasis Audio.

Complete Idiot's Guide to French: Level III. 4 cds. (Complete Idiot's Guide Ser.: Level 3). (FRE & ENG.). 2003. audio compact disk 34.99 (978-1-58926-269-0(7), A22M-FR30) Oasis Audio.

Complete Idiot's Guide to French: Level IV. 4 CDs. (Running Time: 5 hrs.). (Complete Idiot's Guide Ser.: Level 4). (FRE & ENG.). 2003. audio compact disk 34.99 (978-1-58926-270-6(0), A22M-FR40) Oasis Audio.

Complete Idiot's Guide to French: Level 1. unabr. ed. Linguistics Team. Narrated by Linguistics Team. (Complete Idiot's Guides). (ENG.). 2005. 6.99 (978-1-60814-125-8(X)) Oasis Audio.

Complete Idiot's Guide to French: Program 1. unabr. ed. Linguistics Team. Narrated by Linguistics Team. (Complete Idiot's Guides). (ENG.). 2005. 13.99 (978-1-60814-127-2(6)) Oasis Audio.

Complete Idiot's Guide to French: Program 2. unabr. ed. Linguistics Team. Narrated by Linguistics Team. (Complete Idiot's Guides). (ENG.). 2005. 27.99 (978-1-60814-126-5(8)) Oasis Audio.

Complete Idiot's Guide to French: Vocabulary. 4 cds. (Complete Idiot's Guide Ser.). (ENG & FRE.). 2003. audio compact disk 34.99 (978-1-58926-271-3(9), A22M-FRVO) Oasis Audio.

Complete Idiot's Guide to German: Level I. 4 CDs. (Running Time: 4 hrs.). (Complete Idiot's Guide Ser.: Level 1). (GER & ENG.). 2003. audio compact disk 34.99 (978-1-58926-210-2(7), A22M-GE10) Oasis Audio.

Complete Idiot's Guide to German: Level II. 4 cds. (Complete Idiot's Guide Ser.: Level 2). (GER & ENG.). 2003. audio compact disk 34.99 (978-1-58926-211-9(5), A22M-GE20) Oasis Audio.

Complete Idiot's Guide to German: Level III. 4 cds. (Complete Idiot's Guide Ser.: Level 3). (GER & ENG.). 2003. audio compact disk 34.99 (978-1-58926-272-0(7), A22M-GE30) Oasis Audio.

Complete Idiot's Guide to German: Level IV. 4 cds. (Complete Idiot's Guide Ser.: Level 4). (GER & ENG.). 2003. audio compact disk 34.99 (978-1-58926-273-7(5), A22M-GE40) Oasis Audio.

Complete Idiot's Guide to German: Level 1. unabr. ed. Linguistics Staff. Narrated by Linguistics Staff. (Complete Idiot's Guides). (ENG.). 2005. 6.99 (978-1-60814-128-9(4)) Oasis Audio.

Complete Idiot's Guide to German: Program 1. unabr. ed. Linguistics Staff. Narrated by Linguistics Staff. (Complete Idiot's Guides). (ENG.). 2005. 13.99 (978-1-60814-129-6(2)) Oasis Audio.

Complete Idiot's Guide to German: Program 2. unabr. ed. Linguistics Staff. Narrated by Linguistics Staff. (Complete Idiot's Guides). (ENG.). 2005. 27.99 (978-1-60814-130-2(6)) Oasis Audio.

Complete Idiot's Guide to German: Vocabulary. 4 CDs. (Running Time: 4 hrs.). (Complete Idiot's Guide Ser.). (GER & ENG.). 2003. audio compact disk 34.99 (978-1-58926-274-4(3), A22M-GEVO) Oasis Audio.

Complete Idiot's Guide to Guerilla Marketing. abr. ed. Susan Drake & Colleen Wells. Narrated by Mark Warner. (Complete Idiot's Guides). (ENG.). 2008. 13.99 (978-1-60814-131-9(4)); audio compact disk 19.99 (978-1-59859-321-1(8)) Oasis Audio.

Complete Idiot's Guide to Italian: Level 1. unabr. ed. Linguistics Staff. Narrated by Linguistics Staff. (Complete Idiot's Guides). (ENG.). 2005. 6.99 (978-1-60814-132-6(2)) Oasis Audio.

Complete Idiot's Guide to Italian: Program 1. unabr. ed. Linguistics Staff. Narrated by Linguistics Staff. (Complete Idiot's Guides). (ENG.). 2005. 13.99 (978-1-60814-133-3(0)) Oasis Audio.

Complete Idiot's Guide to Italian: Program 2. unabr. ed. Linguistics Staff. Narrated by Linguistics Staff. (Complete Idiot's Guides). (ENG.). 2005. 27.99 (978-1-60814-134-0(9)) Oasis Audio.

Complete Idiot's Guide to Japanese: Level I. 2 cds. (Complete Idiot's Guide Ser.: Level 1). (JPN & ENG.). 2004. audio compact disk 34.99 (978-1-58926-214-0(X), A22M-JA10) Oasis Audio.

Complete Idiot's Guide to Japanese: Level II. 4 CDs. (Running Time: 4 hrs.). (Complete Idiot's Guide Ser.: Level 2). (JPN & ENG.). 2004. audio compact disk 34.99 (978-1-58926-215-7(8), A22M-JA20) Oasis Audio.

Complete Idiot's Guide to Japanese: Level 1. unabr. ed. Linguistics Staff. Narrated by Linguistics Staff. (Complete Idiot's Guides). (ENG.). 2005. 6.99 (978-1-60814-135-7(7)) Oasis Audio.

Complete Idiot's Guide to Japanese: Program 1. unabr. ed. Linguistics Staff. Narrated by Linguistics Staff. (Complete Idiot's Guides). (ENG.). 2005. 13.99 (978-1-60814-136-4(5)) Oasis Audio.

Complete Idiot's Guide to Japanese: Program 2. unabr. ed. Linguistics Staff. Narrated by Linguistics Staff. (Complete Idiot's Guides). (ENG.). 2005. 27.99 (978-1-60814-137-1(3)) Oasis Audio.

Complete Idiot's Guide to Japanese: Vocabulary. (Complete Idiot's Guide Ser.). (JPN & ENG.). 2004. audio compact disk (978-1-58926-276-8(X), A22M-JAVO) Oasis Audio.

Complete Idiot's Guide to Jesus. abr. ed. James S. Bell. Narrated by Chris Fabry. (Complete Idiot's Guides). (ENG.). 2004. 19.59 (978-1-60814-138-8(1)) Oasis Audio.

Complete Idiot's Guide to Job Hunting. abr. ed. Marc Dorio. Read by Shauna Zurbrugg. 2 cass. (Running Time: 3 hrs.). 2001. 18.00 (978-1-59040-111-8(5), Phoenix Audio) Pub: Amer Intl Pub. Dist(s): PerseuPGW

Complete Idiot's Guide to Languages (French) Oasis. 2005. audio compact disk 45.00 (978-0-7861-7385-3(8)) Blckstn Audio.

Complete Idiot's Guide to Languages (Italian) Oasis. 2005. audio compact disk 45.00 (978-0-7861-7384-6(X)) Blckstn Audio.

Complete Idiot's Guide to Learning Guitar: CD-ROM. Alfred Publishing Staff. (Complete Idiot's Guide Ser.). (ENG.). 2008. audio compact disk 19.99 (978-0-7390-4952-5(6)) Alfred Pub.

Complete Idiot's Guide to Learning Guitar: Everything You Need to Know to Start Playing Now!, CD-ROM with UV Coating. Alfred Publishing Staff. (Complete Idiot's Guide Ser.). (ENG.). 2009. audio compact disk 19.99 (978-0-7390-5770-4(7)) Alfred Pub.

Complete Idiot's Guide to Learning Piano: CD-ROM. Alfred Publishing Staff. (Complete Idiot's Guide Ser.). (ENG.). 2008. audio compact disk 19.99 (978-0-7390-4953-2(4)) Alfred Pub.

Complete Idiot's Guide to Learning Piano: Everything You Need to Know to Start Playing Now!, CD-ROM with UV Coating. Alfred Publishing Staff. (Complete Idiot's Guide Ser.). (ENG.). 2009. audio compact disk 19.99 (978-0-7390-5771-1(5)) Alfred Pub.

Complete Idiot's Guide to Making Money. abr. ed. Read by Shauna Zurbrugg. 2 cass. (Running Time: 3 hrs.). 2001. 18.00

(978-1-59040-123-1(9), Phoenix Audio) Pub: Amer Intl Pub. Dist(s): PerseuPGW

Complete Idiot's Guide to Managing Money. abr. ed. Christy Heady & Robert K. Heady. 2 cass. (Running Time: 3 hrs.). 2001. 18.00 (978-1-59040-107-1(7), Phoenix Audio) Pub: Amer Intl Pub. Dist(s): PerseuPGW

Complete Idiot's Guide to Managing Your Money. abr. ed. Robert K. Heady & Christy Heady. Narrated by Grover Gardner. (Complete Idiot's Guides). (ENG.). 2004. 19.59 (978-1-60814-139-5(X)) Oasis Audio.

Complete Idiot's Guide to Mandarin Chinese: Level 1. unabr. ed. Linguistics Staff. Narrated by Linguistics Staff. (Complete Idiot's Guides). (ENG.). 2005. 6.99 (978-1-60814-140-1(3)) Oasis Audio.

Complete Idiot's Guide to Mandarin Chinese: Program 1. unabr. ed. Linguistics Staff. Narrated by Linguistics Staff. (Complete Idiot's Guides). (ENG.). 2005. 13.99 (978-1-60814-142-5(X)) Oasis Audio.

Complete Idiot's Guide to Mandarin Chinese: Program 2. unabr. ed. Linguistics Staff. Narrated by Linguistics Staff. (Complete Idiot's Guides). (ENG.). 2005. 27.99 (978-1-60814-141-8(1)) Oasis Audio.

***Complete Idiot's Guide to Rock Guitar Hits: 25 Great Rock Guitar Hits.** Created by Alfred Publishing. (Complete Idiot's Guides (Lifestyle Paperback) Ser.). (ENG., 2010. pap. bk. 24.99 (978-0-7390-6706-2(0)) Alfred Pub.

Complete Idiot's Guide to Sex. abr. ed. Sari Locker. Read by Sari Locker. 2 cass. (Running Time: 3 hrs.). 2001. 18.00 (978-1-59040-112-5(3), Phoenix Audio) Pub: Amer Intl Pub. Dist(s): PerseuPGW

Complete Idiot's Guide to Spanish. abr. ed. Judith A. Stein. Read by Jonuel Pozo. 4 cass. (Running Time: 6 hrs.). 2001. 25.00 (978-1-59040-103-3(4), Phoenix Audio) Pub: Amer Intl Pub. Dist(s): PerseuPGW

Complete Idiot's Guide to Spanish: Level I. 4 cds. (Complete Idiot's Guide Ser.: Level 1). (SPA & ENG.). 2003. audio compact disk 34.99 (978-1-58926-206-5(9), A22M-SP10) Oasis Audio.

Complete Idiot's Guide to Spanish: Level II. 4 cds. (Complete Idiot's Guide Ser.: Level 2). (SPA & ENG.). 2003. audio compact disk 34.99 (978-1-58926-207-2(7), A22M-SP20) Oasis Audio.

Complete Idiot's Guide to Spanish: Level III. 4 cds. (Complete Idiot's Guide Ser.: Level 3). (SPA & ENG.). 2003. audio compact disk 34.99 (978-1-58926-266-9(2), A22M-SP30) Oasis Audio.

Complete Idiot's Guide to Spanish: Level IV. 4 cds. (Complete Idiot's Guide Ser.: Level 4). (SPA & ENG.). 2003. audio compact disk 34.99 (978-1-58926-267-6(0), A22M-SP40) Oasis Audio.

Complete Idiot's Guide to Spanish: Level 1. unabr. ed. Linguistics Staff. Narrated by Linguistics Staff. (Complete Idiot's Guides). (ENG.). 2005. 6.99 (978-1-60814-143-2(8)) Oasis Audio.

Complete Idiot's Guide to Spanish: Program 1. unabr. ed. Linguistics Staff. Narrated by Linguistics Staff. (Complete Idiot's Guides). (ENG.). 2005. 13.99 (978-1-60814-144-9(6)) Oasis Audio.

Complete Idiot's Guide to Spanish: Program 2. unabr. ed. Linguistics Staff. Narrated by Linguistics Staff. (Complete Idiot's Guides). (ENG.). 2005. 27.99 (978-1-60814-145-6(4)) Oasis Audio.

Complete Idiot's Guide to Spanish: Vocabulary. 4 cds. (Complete Idiot's Guide Ser.). (SPA & ENG.). 2003. audio compact disk 34.99 (978-1-58926-268-3(9), A22M-SPVO) Oasis Audio.

Complete Idiot's Guide to Spanish, Level 1: An Oasis Recording. Linguistic Team Staff. Read by Linguistic Team Staff. (Running Time: 5 mins.). 2005. audio compact disk 36.00 (978-0-7861-7685-4(7)) Blckstn Audio.

Complete Idiot's Guide to Starting a Home-Based Business. abr. ed. Barbara Weltman. Narrated by Rebecca Gallagher. (Running Time: 5 hrs. 0 mins. 0 sec.). (Complete Idiot's Guides). (ENG.). 2007. 13.99 (978-1-60814-146-3(2)) Oasis Audio.

Complete Idiot's Guide to Starting an Ebay Business. abr. ed. Barbara Weltman & Malcolm Katt. Narrated by Rebecca Gallagher. (Running Time: 5 hrs. 0 mins. 0 sec.). (Complete Idiot's Guides). (ENG.). 2008. 13.99 (978-1-60814-147-0(0)) Oasis Audio.

Complete Idiot's Guide to String Theory. unabr. ed. George Musser. (Running Time: 11 hrs. 0 mins.). (ENG.). 2009. 29.95 (978-1-4332-7559-3(7)); 65.95 (978-1-4332-7555-5(4)); audio compact disk 29.95 (978-1-4332-7558-6(9)); audio compact disk 90.00 (978-1-4332-7556-2(2)) Blckstn Audio.

Complete Idiot's Guide to the Bible. abr. ed. James S. Bell & Stan Campbell. (Complete Idiot's Guides). (ENG.). 2004. 19.59 (978-1-60814-148-7(9)) Oasis Audio.

Complete Idiot's Guide to the World of Narnia. abr. ed. James S. Bell & Cheryl Dunlop. Narrated by Chris Fabry. (Running Time: 5 hrs. 0 mins. 0 sec.). (Complete Idiot's Guides). (ENG.). 2007. 13.99 (978-1-60814-149-4(7)) Oasis Audio.

Complete in Christ. Theodore H. Epp. Read by Theodore H. Epp. 2 cass. (Running Time: 2 hrs. 30 min.). 1986. 9.95 (978-0-8474-2280-7(1)) Back to Bible.

Features Messages from Colossians, Explaining how spiritual needs are fulfilled in Christ.

Complete Infidel's Guide to the Koran. unabr. ed. Robert Spencer. Narrated by Lloyd James. (Running Time: 8 hrs. 0 mins. 0 sec.). (ENG.). 2009. 19.99 (978-1-4001-6505-6(9)); 15.99 (978-1-4001-8505-4(X)); audio compact disk 29.99 (978-1-4001-1505-1(1)); audio compact disk 59.99 (978-1-4001-4505-8(8)) Pub: Tantor Media. Dist(s): IngramPubServ

Complete Infinity Walk: How-to Companion Audio-Book: the Physical Self. Excerpts. Deborah Sunbeck. 1 cass. (Running Time: 60 min.). 2003. audio compact disk 14.00 (978-0-9705164-2-8(8)) Leonardo Fnd.

A companion abridged Audio-Book CD read by author of The Complete Infinity Walk: The Physical Self, Deborah Sunbeck.

Complete Irish Fiddle Player. Peter Cooper. 1995. pap. bk. 38.95 (978-0-7866-1319-9(X), 95406CDP) Mel Bay.

Complete Irish Fiddle Player Book/2-Cd Set. Pete Cooper. (ENG.). 2002. per. 29.95 (978-0-7866-6557-0(2)) Mel Bay.

Complete Irish Fiddle Player 2-CD Set. Pete Cooper. 1996. audio compact disk 24.98 (978-0-7866-0417-3(4)) Mel Bay.

Complete Irish Flute: Beginning Level. Mizzy McCaskill & Dona Gilliam. 1997. spiral bd. 34.95 (978-0-7866-2930-5(4), 96332CDP) Mel Bay.

Complete Irish Tinwhistle. Mizzy McCaskill & Dona Gilliam. 1996. bk. 32.95 (978-0-7866-2363-1(2), 96191CDP) Mel Bay.

Complete Jazz Guitar Method. Michael Christiansen. 1995. pap. bk. 39.95 (978-0-7866-1307-6(6), 95384CDP) Mel Bay.

Complete Jazz Guitar Method: Mastering Jazz Guitar: Chord/Melody. Jody Fisher. (ENG.). 1995. audio compact disk 10.95 (978-0-7390-2593-2(7)) Alfred Pub.

Complete Jazz Guitar Method: Mastering Jazz Guitar: Improvisation. Jody Fisher. (ENG.). 1995. audio compact disk 10.95 (978-0-7390-2589-5(9)) Alfred Pub.

Complete Jazz Guitarist. Jimmy Stewart. 1994. 9.98 (978-1-56222-989-4(3), 95113C) Mel Bay.

Complete Jazz Keyboard Method: Beginning Jazz Keyboard. Noah Baerman. (ENG.). 1998. audio compact disk 10.95 (978-0-7390-2578-9(3)) Alfred Pub.

Complete Jazz Keyboard Method: Intermediate Jazz Keyboard. Noah Baerman. (ENG.). 1998. audio compact disk 10.95 (978-0-7390-2586-4(4)) Alfred Pub.

Complete Jazz Keyboard Method: Mastering Jazz Keyboard. Noah Baerman. (ENG.). 1998. audio compact disk 10.95 (978-0-7390-2592-5(9)) Alfred Pub.

Complete Jethro Burns Mandolin 2-CD Package. Jethro Burns & Ken Eidson. 1999. pap. bk. 46.95 (978-0-7866-4708-8(6), 94875CDP) Mel Bay.

Complete Jewish Wedding Songbook. Ed. by Joel N. Eglash & Jonathan B. Hall. 2 vols. 2006. pap. bk. 39.95 (978-0-8074-0938-1(3), 993220) URJ Pr.

***Complete Junior Guitarist.** Joe Bennett. 2010. pap. bk. 12.99 (978-1-4234-7518-7(6), 1423475186) Pub: Music Sales. Dist(s): H Leonard

Complete Just So Stories. unabr. ed. Rudyard Kipling. 4 cass. (J). HarperCollins Pubs.

Complete Just So Stories. unabr. ed. Rudyard Kipling. 4 cass. (Running Time: 6 hrs.). Incl. Cat That Walked by Himself: And Other Stories. Rudyard Kipling. (J). (SBC 114); (J). 1978. 29.95 (978-0-89845-038-5(1), SBC 114) HarperCollins Pubs.

Complete Lao, Set. unabr. ed. University of Iowa, CEEDE Staff. 1 cass. (People & Activities Around the World Ser.). (LAO.). 1989. 70.00 Incl. tchr's. guide, student text, filmstrip set & CAI disk. (978-0-7836-0735-1(0), 8931) Triumph Learn.

A cultural awareness program told in Lao for intermediate LEP students, bilingual, ESL, sheltered English, & social studies classes.

Complete Lao Set. unabr. ed. University of Iowa, CEEDE Staff. 1 cass. (People & Change Ser.). (LAO.). 1989. 59.00 Incl. tchr's. guide, student text, CAI disk & activity masters. (978-0-7836-0741-2(5), 8937) Triumph Learn.

A problem solving program. Lao readings describing episodes in the life of one family.

Complete Listening-Speaking Course: Student Centered Teacher Guided. David Christiansen. Ed. by Joan Ashkenas. 4 cass. (C). 2001. 54.95 (978-0-943327-26-6(1)); audio compact disk 63.95 (978-0-943327-27-3(X)) JAG Pubns.

Complete Madonna. Keith Rodway et al. Read by Nancy McClean & Laurel Lyko. 4 CDs. (Running Time: 5 hrs.). (ENG.). 2001. audio compact disk 29.95 (978-1-84240-132-3(7)) Pub: Chrome Dreams GBR. Dist(s): IPG Chicago

Complete Method for Autoharp or Chromaharp. Meg Peterson. 1979. 9.98 (978-1-56222-593-3(6), 93657C) Mel Bay.

Complete Miss Marple Collection: Starring June Whitford as Miss Marple. unabr. ed. Agatha Christie. 24 CDs. audio compact disk 199.95 (978-0-7927-3997-5(3), BBCD148) AudioGO.

***Complete Miss Marple Radio Dramas: Twelve BBC Radio Dramas Starring June Whitfield.** Agatha Christie. Narrated by June Whitfield. (Running Time: 24 hrs. 0 mins. 0 sec.). (ENG.). 2011. audio compact disk 149.95 (978-1-4084-6849-4(2)) Pub: AudioGO. Dist(s): Perseus Dist

Complete Modern Drum, Set. Frank Briggs. 1994. pap. bk. 23.95 (978-0-7866-1289-5(4), 95366P) Mel Bay.

Complete Modern Drum Set. Frank Briggs. 1994. pap. bk. 29.95 (978-0-7866-1288-8(6), 95366CDP) Mel Bay.

Complete Mother Goose. Narrated by Flo Gibson. (ENG.). (J). 2007. audio compact disk 16.95 (978-1-55685-948-9(1)) Audio Bk Con.

Complete Mother Goose, Set. Read by Flo Gibson. 2 cass. (Running Time: 2 hrs. 30 min.). (J). (gr. k up). 1990. 14.95 (978-1-55685-159-9(6)) Audio Bk Con.

All the original rhymes & riddles are here to delight & tickle the imagination.

Complete Music for Fife & Drum. Composed by Walter D. Sweet. 1996. audio compact disk 15.98 (978-0-7866-1850-7(7)) Mel Bay.

Complete Music for the Fife & Drum. Walter D. Seveet. 1996. spiral bd. 32.95 (978-0-7866-1851-4(5), 95483CDP) Mel Bay.

***Complete National Geographic Every Issue Since 1888-2009.** National Geographic Society Staff. 2010. audio compact disk 79.99 (978-1-4263-4011-6(7)) Natl Geog.

Complete Negotiator. abr. ed. Gerard I. Nierenberg. 1992. 17.95 (978-0-7435-4292-0(4)) Pub: S&S Audio. Dist(s): S and S Inc

Complete Negotiator: The Definitive Audio Handbook from the Father of Contemporary Negotiating. abr. ed. Gerard I. Nierenberg. Read by Gerard I. Nierenberg. 3 CDs. (Running Time: 23 hrs. 0 mins. 0 sec.). (ENG.). 2005. audio compact disk 29.95 (978-0-7435-4476-4(5)) Pub: S&S Audio. Dist(s): S and S Inc

Complete New Testament Set: New International Version. Read by Bill Pearce. 39.95 (NT100) Trinity Tapes.

Complete Old Testament Set: New International Version. Read by Bill Pearce. 89.95 (OT100) Trinity Tapes.

Complete Organ Works of Cesar Frank. Cesar Frank. 1996. audio compact disk 27.95 (272) GIA Pubns.

Complete PET Class Audio CDs (2) Emma Heyderman & Peter May. (Running Time: 2 hrs. 38 mins.). (ENG.). 2010. audio compact disk 42.00 (978-0-521-74138-5(6)) Cambridge U Pr.

Complete Postal Exam 473, 473-C, & 473-E Training Program: Featuring 2 Test Prep Audio CDs, Best-Selling Study Guide, & Free Live Support. T. W. Parnell. Illus. by Susie Varner. 2 CD's. 2005. per. 29.95 (978-0-940182-27-1(0)) Pathfinder Dist.

Complete Relaxation. Glenn Harrold. 1 cass. (Running Time: 1 hr. 30 mins.). 2002. 11.95 (978-1-901923-01-8(0)) Pub: Divinit Pubing GBR. Dist(s): Bookworld

Complete Relaxation. Glenn Harrold. 2 CDs. (Running Time: 3 hrs.). 2002. audio compact disk 17.95 (978-1-901923-21-6(5)) Pub: Divinit Pubing GBR. Dist(s): Bookworld

Complete Relaxation. Denise Linn. 2 CDs. (Running Time: 7200 sec.). (ENG.). 2006. audio compact disk 18.95 (978-1-4019-0665-8(6)) Hay House.

Complete Robot, Pt. 1. collector's ed. Isaac Asimov. Read by Larry McKeever. 8 cass. (Running Time: 12 hrs.). 1987. 64.00 (978-0-7366-1171-8(1), 2094-A) Books on Tape.

Though Isaac Asimov coined the world "robotics" his robots are close to human. His metal, plastic & (occasionally) organic mechanical men are very much like people we know, frequently warm, frequently fallible.

Complete Robot, Pt. 2. unabr. collector's ed. Isaac Asimov. Read by Larry McKeever. 9 cass. (Running Time: 13 hrs. 30 min.). 1987. 72.00 (978-0-7366-1172-5(X), 2094-B) Books on Tape.

The complete collection of Asimov's thirty-one robot tales.

Complete Rock Guitar. Michael Christiansen. 1991. pap. bk. 23.95 (978-0-7866-1065-5(4), 94560P) Mel Bay.

Complete Rock Guitar Book. Michael Christiansen. (Complete Book). 1991. 9.98 (978-1-56222-159-1(0), 94560C); audio compact disk 15.98 (978-0-7866-0441-8(7), 94560CD) Mel Bay.

Complete Rock Guitar Book. Mike Christiansen. (ENG.). 2004. per. 29.95 (978-0-7866-6863-2(6), 94560SET) Mel Bay.

Complete Rock Guitar Method: Beginning Rock Guitar. Paul Howard. (ENG.). 1996. audio compact disk 10.95 (978-0-7390-2626-7(7)) Alfred Pub.

Complete Rock Guitar Method: Intermediate Rock Guitar. Paul Howard. (ENG.). 1996. audio compact disk 10.95 (978-0-7390-2639-7(9)) Alfred Pub.

Complete Rock Guitar Method: Mastering Rock Guitar. Erik Halbig. (ENG.). 1997. audio compact disk 10.95 (978-0-7390-2642-7(9)) Alfred Pub.

Complete Rock Keyboard Method: Beginning Rock Keyboard. Joe Bouchard. (ENG.). 1999. audio compact disk 10.00 (978-0-7390-2631-1(3)) Alfred Pub.

Complete Rock Keyboard Method: Intermediate Rock Keyboard. Seth Zowader. (ENG.). 1999. audio compact disk 10.00 (978-0-7390-2640-3(2)) Alfred Pub.

Complete Rock Keyboard Method: Mastering Rock Keyboard. Sheila Romeo. (ENG.). 1999. audio compact disk 10.00 (978-0-7390-2543-7(0)) Alfred Pub.

***Complete Route 66 Audio Collection.** Jimmy Gray. Read by Dennis Stone et al. (Playaway Adult Nonfiction Ser.). (ENG.). 2009. 59.99 (978-1-61545-990-2(1)) Find a World.

Complete Salvation & How to Receive It. Derek Prince. 2 cass. 1990. 5.95 ea. Derek Prince.

Salvation is so much more than "escape from Hell." You can have victory & blessing today! Learn the four steps necessary to enter into complete salvation.

***Complete SAT Vocabulary Course: 500 Key Words, Online Course, iPod MP3's, Audio & Video.** Verbalearn. 2009. audio compact disk (978-1-61623-652-6(3)) Indep Pub IL.

Complete Self-Confidence. Hiary Jones. Read by Hilary Jones. (Running Time: 0 hr. 30 mins.). 2000. 16.95 (978-1-59912-922-8(1)) Iofy Corp.

Complete Sermons of Jean Baptiste Lamy: Fifty Years of Sermons (1837-1886) Thomas J. Steele. 2000. bk. 29.95 (978-1-890689-20-9(3)) LPD Pr.

Complete Shabbat Synagogue Companion. Zalman Goldstein. (Running Time: 54 mins.). 2008. audio compact disk 12.95 (978-1-891293-26-9(5)) Pub: Jewish Lrning. Dist(s): Natl Bk Netwk

Complete Shabbat Table Companion. Zalman Goldstein. (Running Time: 42 mins.). 2008. audio compact disk 12.95 (978-1-891293-27-6(3)) Pub: Jewish Lrning. Dist(s): Natl Bk Netwk

Complete Shakespeare Sonnets. unabr. ed. 2 cass. (Running Time: 2 hrs.). 1999. 18.95 Set. Airplay.

Read by great actors of the American & British stage.

Complete Shakespeare Sonnets. unabr. ed. Perf. by Claire Bloom et al. 2 CDs. (Running Time: 2 hrs.). 2001. audio compact disk 25.00 (978-1-885608-40-6(3)) Airplay.

The truly great voices of contemporary theater come together to read the complete Shakespeare Sonnets.

Complete Shakespeare Sonnets. unabr. ed. Ed. by Charline Spektor. Adapted by Natasha Richardson & Kathleen Turner. 2 cass. (Running Time: 2 hrs.). 1999. 20.00 (978-1-885608-20-8(9)) Airplay.

Complete Sherlock Holmes Collection. unabr. ed. 64 CDs. 2006. audio compact disk 695.00 (978-0-7927-3572-4(2), BBCD087) AudioGO.

Complete Shorter Fiction of Virginia Woolf. unabr. collector's ed. Virginia Woolf. Read by Donada Peters. 9 cass. (Running Time: 13 hrs. 30 min.). 1988. 72.00 (978-0-7366-1260-9(2), 2173) Books on Tape.

Forty-five stories & sketches, dating from 1906 to 1941, including sixteen stories previously unpublished. Among these is "The Water Place", Woolf's last piece of fiction, written shortly before she drowned herself.

Complete Silver Lining. Poems. Ed. by Pent. 1 cass. (Running Time: 1 hr. 30 min.). 19.95 (978-1-888453-07-2(9), BMP Audio) BMP Music.

A collection of 26 of the world's finest actors reading their favorite poems. This expanded 41 poem edition includes 23 award-winning selections.

Complete Sniggles, Squirrels & Chicken Pox. Perf. by Jackie Silberg. 1 cass. (J). (ps-3). 1996. audio compact disk 21.95 CD. Miss Jackie.

Contains many musical styles & includes all songs from both cassette volumes.

Complete Song Box. unabr. ed. 16 cass. (Running Time: 10 min. per cass.). (Song Box Ser.). (J). (gr. k-2). 128.00 Set, incl. song bks. (978-0-7802-1079-0(4), 15269) Wright Group.

A collection of traditional songs & chants designed to be used with accompanying song books.

Complete Sonnets of William Shakespeare. unabr. ed. William Shakespeare. Read by Susan Anspach et al. 5 CDs. (Running Time: 6 hrs.). 2002. audio compact disk 34.95 (978-1-59007-046-8(1), N Millennium Audio) Pub: New Millenn Enter. Dist(s): PerseuPGW

These ever-quoted verses survive the scrutiny and interpretation of scholars through every generation.

Complete Sonnets of William Shakespeare, Set. unabr. ed. William Shakespeare. Read by Vanessa Redgrave et al. 2 cass. (Running Time: 3 hrs.). 2000. 18.00 (978-1-57453-370-5(3)) Audio Lit.

Presents the sonnets in their entirety, allowing a new generation to discover Shakespeare's emotional power, mastery of language & insight into human beings.

Complete Spanish. unabr. ed. University of Iowa, CEEDE Staff. 1 cass. (People & Change Ser.). (SPA.). 1989. 59.00 Incl. tchr's. guide, student text, CAI disk & activity masters. (978-0-7836-0742-9(3), 8938) Triumph Learn.

A problem solving program. Spanish readings describing episodes in the life of one family.

Complete Spanish, Set. unabr. ed. University of Iowa, CEEDE Staff. 1 cass. (People & Activities Around the World Ser.). (SPA.). 1989. 70.00 Incl. tchr's. guide, student text, filmstrip set & CAI disk. (978-0-7836-0736-8(9), 8932) Triumph Learn.

A cultural awareness program told in Spanish for intermediate LEP students, bilingual, ESL, sheltered English, & social studies classes.

Complete Spanish for Dimwits: Complete Learning Guide & Tapescript. Mark Frobose. 8 cass. (Running Time: 8 hrs.). 1999. stu. ed. 59.00 (978-1-893564-25-1(8)) Macmill Audio.

Complete Spanish for Dimwits / 8 CDs / Book. Mark Frobose. 8 cds. (SPA.). 2002. per. 67.50 (978-1-893564-59-6(2)) Macmill Audio.

Complete Spanish for Dimwits/8 Tapes/Booklet. Mark Frobose. 4 CDs. (Running Time: 4 hrs.). 2003. audio compact disk 39.00 (978-1-893564-58-9(4)) Macmill Audio.

Complete Spanish-Language Development Program: Learning System B. National Textbook Company Staff. 5 cass. 2001. 125.00 (978-0-8442-8193-3(X), Natl Textbk Co) M-H Contemporary.

Presents language skills & terminology appropriate to a variety of on-the-job situations. Realistic conversations are accompanied by readings, discussion questions & opportunities to practice written & oral skills.

Complete Spanish-Language Development Program: Learning System C. National Textbook Company Staff. 5 cass. 125.00 (978-0-8442-8260-2(X), Natl Textbk Co) M-H Contemporary.

Complete Spoken Word Bible: The Old Testament. unabr. ed. Read by Theodore Bikel et al. 52 cass. (Running Time: 78 hrs.). 2001. 175.00 (978-1-57453-444-3(0)) Audio Lit.
Rich, evocative and dignified, the King James version of the Bible remains the favorite of millions for both its inspirational and poetic qualities.

Complete Star Wars Trilogy. ltd. unabr. abr. ed. George Lucas & Lucasfilm Ltd. Staff. 15 CDs. (Running Time: 14 hrs. 30 mins.). (ENG.). 1996. audio compact disk 195.00 (978-1-56511-165-3(6), 1565111656) Pub: HighBridge. Dist(s): Workman Pub

Complete Steel. unabr. ed. Catherine Aird. Read by Robin Bailey. 4 cass. (Inspector C. D. Sloan Mystery Ser.). 2001. 34.95 (978-0-7451-5708-5(4), CAB 425) Pub: Chivers Audio Bks GBR. Dist(s): AudioGO
There were two things wrong when someone found Mr. Meredith in the library of Omum House and greeted him with a "Good Morning." For one thing, it was five o'clock in the afternoon; and for another, the greeting was a murderous blow to Mr. Meredith's head. But Inspector Sloan doesn't know any of this until he finds the weapon, a large primitive club, topped with an iron spike. It is hanging in Lord Omum's armory, labeled "Godentag", which taken literally, means good morning.

Complete Still Waters Rosary. Contrib. by Vinny Flynn & Still Waters. 2005. audio compact disk 14.99 (978-1-884479-26-7(X)) Spirit Song.

Complete Stories of Dorothy Parker, unabr. ed. Dorothy Parker. Narrated by Barbara Rosenblat. 16 cass. (Running Time: 21 hrs. 45 mins.). 128.00 (978-0-7887-0443-7(5), 94635E7) Recorded Bks.
Includes 13 previously unpublished stories & a series of sketches. All her best are here: "The Lovely Leave," "Horsie" & "Big Blonde". Available to libraries only.

Complete Stress Relief Program. Created by Israel Maya. 3 CDs. (Running Time: 1 hr. 57 min.). 2005. audio compact disk (978-0-9768945-0-6(5)) Is Maya.
The Complete Stress Relief Program is a unique program to relieve and eliminate stress by the use of explanation techniques and relaxation exercises. This 3-audio CD program was created and produced by certified Master Hypnotherapist Israel Maya.

Complete Tales. Beatrix Potter. Read by Shelly Frasier. (Running Time: 3 hrs. 30 mins.). 2003. 25.95 (978-1-60083-626-8(7), Audiofy Corp) Iofy Corp.

Complete Tales: 1245. unabr. ed. Beatrix Potter. Read by Shelly Frasier. (J). 2006. 39.99 (978-1-59895-675-7(2)) Find a World.

Complete Tales of Beatrix Potter. unabr. ed. Beatrix Potter. Read by Nadia May. 3 cass. (Running Time: 4 hrs.). 2002. 23.95 (978-0-7861-2275-2(7), 2973); audio compact disk 24.00 (978-0-7861-9488-9(X), 2973) Blckstn Audio.
These charming stories about Peter Rabbit, Tom Kitten, Squirrel Nutkin, Mrs. Tittlemouse, and the others have enchanted children for over a hundred years and will surely do so well into the future.

Complete Tales of Peter Rabbit & Friend. unabr. ed. Beatrix Potter. Narrated by Shelly Frasier. (Running Time: 3 hrs. 30 mins. 0 sec.). (ENG.). (J). (gr. k-5). 2008. audio compact disk 35.99 (978-1-4001-3851-7(5)) Pub: Tantor Media. Dist(s): IngramPubServ

Complete Tales of Peter Rabbit & Friends. unabr. ed. Beatrix Potter. Narrated by Shelly Frasier. (Running Time: 3 hrs. 30 mins. 0 sec.). (ENG.). (J). (gr. k-5). 2008. 17.99 (978-1-4001-5851-5(6)); audio compact disk 17.99 (978-1-4001-0851-0(9)) Pub: Tantor Media. Dist(s): IngramPubServ

Complete Teaching of Mahayana. Vajracarya. 3 cass. 1973. 29.50 Vajradhatu.
Six talks: The Reciprocity of Hinayana & Mahayana; Discovering the Potentials; Maitri & the Spiritual Friend; Inviting all Sentient Beings As Your Guest; Skillful Means; Identification with the Teachings.

Complete Teachings of Mahayana. Read by Chogyam Trungpa. 3 cass. 1973. 29.50 (A002) Vajradhatu.
Six talks: An overview of the mahayana path. Topics include: maitri, the spiritual friend, inviting all sentient beings as your guest & skillful means.

Complete Torah Reading Handbook. Ely Simon. 1996. pap. bk. 19.95 (978-1-880582-12-1(0)) Judaica Pr.

Complete Tour of Florence: 10 Spectacular Attractions. Scripts. Created by WhiteHot Productions. 1 CD. (Running Time: 72660 sec.). (Great Discoveries Personal Audio Guides: Florence Ser.). 2006. audio compact disk 19.95 (978-1-59971-118-8(4)) AardGP.
One hour and twelve minutes of playtime provide today's independent traveler with an unparalleled audio tour of the Florentine home to Michelangelo's magnificent statue of David. Professional narrators delight, inform and amuse the listener as they explain the Accademia's great history and discuss the wonderful art contained therein. This 14 track audio tour is in standard CD format, on 1 CD, ready for play on any CD player. Not for use on MP3 players.

Complete Tour of Venice: 9 Spectacular Attractions. Scripts. Created by WhiteHot Productions. 2 CDs. (Running Time: 63600 sec.). (Great Discoveries Personal Audio Guides: Venice Ser.). 2006. audio compact disk 21.95 (978-1-59971-134-8(6)) AardGP.
Two hours and ten minutes of playtime provide today?s independent traveler with an unparalleled audio tour of this majestic but imposing 17th century marble palace that today is a gallery dedicated to 18th century Venetian art. Ca? Rezzonico stands on the right bank of the Grand Canal at its junction with the rio di San Bamaba. It is one of the few palaces in Venice Italy permitting public insight into what lies behind the ornamental, but often secretive, facades of the many exquisite buildings that line the Grand Canal. Ca? Rezzonico was acquired by the City Council of Venice to display its vast collections of 18th century Venetian art. It is one of the finest museums in Venice, largely because of its unique character, where objects designed for great palazzo?s are displayed in a palace, thus the contents and the building harmonize in a way not possible in a purposely built museum. Today the palazzo is furnished with contents more magnificent than at any time in its history. This 23 track audio tour is in standard CD format, on 2 CD?s, ready for play on any CD player. Not for use on MP3 players.

Complete Version of Ye Three Blind Mice. 2004. 8.95 (978-1-56008-876-9(1)); cass. & flmstrp 30.00 (978-1-56008-654-3(8)) Weston Woods.

Complete Vietnamese, Set. unabr. ed. University of Iowa, CEEDE Staff. 1 cass. (People & Activities Around the World Ser.). (VIE.). 1989. 70.00 Incl. tchr's. guide, student text, filmstrip set & CAI disk. (978-0-7836-0737-5(7), 8933) Triumph Learn.
A cultural awareness program told in Vietnamese for intermediate LEP students, bilingual, ESL, sheltered English, & social studies classes.

Complete Vocal Workout. Kain Roger. 2 CDs. 2005. audio compact disk 24.95 (978-1-84492-003-7(8)) Pub: Sanctuary Pubng GBR. Dist(s): H Leonard

Complete War of the Worlds: Mars' Invasion of Earth from H. G. Wells to Orson Welles. H. G. Wells & Howard Koch. Perf. by Orson Welles. 1 CD. (Running Time: 1 hr.). 2001. bk. 39.95 (4416) Radio Spirits.
Tells the story behind the story - how H.G. Wells' tale of Martian invasion captured the imagination of Orson Welles, and how the book and the broadcast went on to inspire hundreds of imitators.

Complete Weight Loss Program (Sublimal & Hypnosis), Vol. 35. Jayne Helle. 4 cass. (Running Time: 56 min. per cass.). 1995. 49.00 Set. (978-1-891826-34-4(4)) Introspect.
Helps develop confidence, let go of negative eating habits, start exercising & establish a life style of good eating habits & wonderful feelings of well being.

***Complete Western Stories of Elmore Leonard.** abr. ed. Elmore Leonard. Read by Henry Rollins. (ENG.). 2004. (978-0-06-081798-5(4), Harper Audio); (978-0-06-081797-8(6), Harper Audio) HarperCollins Pubs.

Complete Western Stories of Elmore Leonard. unabr. abr. ed. Elmore Leonard. Read by David Strathairn. 2004. audio compact disk 29.95 (978-0-06-074992-7(X)) HarperCollins Pubs.

Complete Western Stories of Elmore Leonard. unabr. abr. ed. Elmore Leonard. Read by Henry Rollins. 2004. audio compact disk 9.99 (978-0-06-075765-6(5)) HarperCollins Pubs.

Complete Winnie the Pooh Soundbook. A. A. Milne. Perf. by Carol Channing. 7 cass. (Running Time: 7 hrs.). (J). 50.00 Set. (329) MFLP CA.
One of those lovable, timeless characters who is as charming & entrancing today as he was 65 years ago.

Complete Works. abr. ed. Willie Rushton. Read by Willie Rushton. 1 cass. 1998. 9.35 (978-1-86117-163-4(3)) Ulvrscrft Audio.
He brings his wit to bear upon such topics as fornication, Madame Butterfly & A Merry Xmas to all our Leaders.

Complete WOWs CD Libary, Volume I, English. 4 CDs. 2004. audio compact disk 199.00 (978-0-9779729-4-4(1)) Win Wall Street.

***Complete Yasmin Peace Series.** unabr. ed. Stephanie Perry Moore. Narrated by Robin Miles. (Running Time: 24 hrs. 0 mins. 0 sec.). (Yasmin Peace Ser.). (ENG.). 2010. audio compact disk 49.98 (978-1-61045-010-2(8), christaudio) christianaud.

Complete Yes Minister. Jonathan Lynn & Antony Jay. 2004. audio compact disk 79.95 (978-0-563-52433-5(2)) AudioGO.

Complete 2000 Year Old Man. Carl Reiner & Mel Brooks. 4 cass. (Running Time: 6 hrs.). 1994. 39.98 (978-1-56826-387-8(2), R4 71017); audio compact disk 49.98 (R2 71017) Rhino Enter.

Completely. Contrib. by Ana Laura. (Praise Hymn Soundtracks Ser.). 2006. audio compact disk 8.98 (978-5-558-47747-4(4)) Pt of Grace Ent.

Completely Blessed: Discovering God's Extraordinary Gifts. unabr. ed. Shannon Ethridge. Narrated by Shannon Ethridge. (Running Time: 4 hrs. 0 mins. 0 sec.). (ENG.). 2007. 10.49 (978-1-60814-150-0(0)); audio compact disk 14.99 (978-1-59859-276-4(9)) Oasis Audio.

Completely Forgiven: Responding to God's Transforming Grace. unabr. ed. Shannon Ethridge. Narrated by Shannon Ethridge. (ENG.). 2007. 10.49 (978-1-60814-151-7(9)); audio compact disk 14.99 (978-1-59859-273-3(4)) Oasis Audio.

Completely His: Loving Jesus Without Limits. unabr. ed. Shannon Ethridge. Narrated by Shannon Ethridge. (ENG.). 2007. 13.99 (978-1-60814-152-4(7)); audio compact disk 19.99 (978-1-59859-225-2(4)) Oasis Audio.

Completely Irresistible: Drawing Others Toward God's Extravagant Love. unabr. ed. Shannon Ethridge. Narrated by Shannon Ethridge. (ENG.). 2007. 10.49 (978-1-60814-153-1(5)); audio compact disk 14.99 (978-1-59859-277-1(7)) Oasis Audio.

Completely Loved: Recognizing God's Passionate Pursuit of Us. unabr. ed. Shannon Ethridge. Narrated by Shannon Ethridge. (ENG.). 2007. 10.49 (978-1-60814-154-8(3)); audio compact disk 14.99 (978-1-59859-274-0(2)) Oasis Audio.

Completely Yes. 1 cass., 1 CD. 10.98 (978-1-57908-351-9(X), 5306); audio compact disk 15.98 CD. (978-1-57908-350-2(1)) Platinm Enter.

Completely Yours: A Mother for Choco. Read by Paula Poundstone et al. 1 cass., 1 CD. (Running Time: 18 min.). (J). 1997. 5.95 (978-1-890008-06-2(0)); audio compact disk 7.95 CD. (978-1-890008-07-9(9)) Child Bk of Month.
Includes a collection of spoken word nursery rhymes.

Completing Your Karma. Ariel Kane & Shya Kane. Contrib. by Helene DeLillo. 1 cass. (Running Time: 1 hrs. 23 min.). (Being in the Moment Ser.). 1995. (978-1-888043-07-5(5)) ASK Prodns.
Discover & dissolve "Karma," the lingering ill effects from earlier mechanical ways of relating.

Complex in Biblical Literature. Read by Harmon Bro. 1 cass. (Running Time: 90 min.). 1979. 10.95 (978-0-7822-0027-0(3), 110) C G Jung IL.

Complex Issues in Partnership Taxation. James R. Hamill. 2 cass. 1994. 139.00 incl. wkbk. (741301VC) Am Inst CPA.
Many new developments in partnership taxation have occurred in recent years. Three concepts, in particular, are especially confusing. This course helps you understand them & the morass of rules & regulations that apply to them. They are specifically: 1. The concept of basis in a partner's interest in the partnership. This determines the extent of a partner's gain or loss in many situations. 2. The concept of "substantial economic effect," which governs the taxability of many partner/partnership transactions. 3. The concept of liability sharing among limited & general partners. This can often result in liability where an uninformed partner does not suspect it; but that can sometimes be desirable even for a limited partner.

Complexity & Chaos. unabr. ed. Roger White. Read by Edwin Newman. (Running Time: 9000 sec.). (Audio Classics: Science & Discovery Ser.). 2006. audio compact disk 25.95 (978-0-7861-6495-0(6)) Pub: Blckstn Audio. Dist(s): NetLibrary CO

Complexity & Chaos. unabr. ed. Roger White. Read by Edwin Newman. Ed. by Jack Sommer & Mike Hassell. 2 cass. (Running Time: 2 hrs. 45 min.). Dramatization. (Science & Discovery Ser.). (YA). (gr. 11 up). 1993. 17.95 set. (978-1-56823-004-7(4), 10414) Knowledge Prod.
Newtonian physics described a regular, clock-like world of forces & reactions; randomness was equated with incomplete knowledge. But scientists in the late 20th century have found patterns in things formerly thought to be "chaotic"; their theories help explain the unstable, irregular, yet highly structured features of everyday experience. It now seems likely that randomness & chaos play an essential role in the evolution of the living world - & of intelligence itself.

Compliance Auditing. Harold Monk, Jr. 2 cass. 1993. 119.00 set incl. wkbk. (740200KQ) Am Inst CPA.
This course offers guidance for auditing governmental entities & nonprofit organizations that receive government financial assistance. It also covers government auditing standards officially adopted by several state & local audit organizations.

Compliance Mail: Complicance Training Reminders for the Healthcare Staff. Created by Hcpro. 2006. audio compact disk 149.00 (978-1-57839-897-3(5)) Opus Communs.

Complicated Kindness. abr. ed. Miriam Toews. Read by Cara Pifko. 3 CDs. (Running Time: 4 hrs.). (ENG.). 2005. audio compact disk 24.95 (978-0-86492-327-1(9)) Pub: BTC Audiobks CAN. Dist(s): U Toronto Pr

Complications: A Surgeon's Notes on an Imperfect Science. abr. ed. Atul Gawande. Read by William David Griffith. (Running Time: 7 hrs. 30 mins. 0 sec.). (ENG.). 2007. audio compact disk 19.95 (978-1-4272-0151-5(X)) Pub: Macmill Audio. Dist(s): Macmillan

Complications of Diverticulitis. Moderated by Stanley M. Goldberg. 2 cass. (Colon & Rectal Surgery Ser.: CR-2). 1986. 19.00 (8637) Am Coll Surgeons.

Complications of Laparoscopy & Flexible Endoscopy: Postgraduate Course of the Annual Meeting of the Society of American Gastrointenstinal Endoscopic Surgeons (SAGES) 1994. Ed. by Medical Support Systems Staff. 1994. audio compact disk 170.00 (978-0-387-14219-7(3)) Spri.

Complice. 1 cass. (Running Time: 60 min.). Dramatization. (Maitres du Mystere Ser.). (FRE.). 1996. 11.95 (1375-MA) Olivia & Hill.
Popular radio thriller, interpreted by France's best actors.

Complying with ECRA in Real Estate Sales & Leases. Contrib. by David Farer. (Running Time: 4 hrs.). 1985. 85.00 incl. program handbook. NJ Inst CLE.
Explains how & when to obtain nonapplicability letters, how to avoid ECRA problems, how to draft clauses for leases & sale contracts to protect client from ECRA problems.

Complying with Government Regulations Regarding Data Security: Best Practices for Data Protection, Compliance & Balancing Risks. Michael Callahan. 2009. 250.00 (978-1-59701-485-4(0)) ReedLogic.

Complying with the Labor & Employment Laws of the NAFTA Countries. 1 cass. (Running Time: 12 hrs. 30 min.). 1999. 345.00 Incl. study guide. (AE27) Am Law Inst.

Complying with the New Clean Air Act. 3 cass. (Running Time: 3 hrs. 30 min.). 175.00 (T7-9316) PLI.

Compoint 12. unabr. ed. Robert A. Monroe. Read by Robert A. Monroe. (Running Time: 45 min.). (Gateway Experience - Adventure Ser.). 1983. 14.95 (978-1-56113-273-7(X)) Monroe Institute.
Establish a state of consciousness to utilize when needed.

Components of a Successful Faculty Advising Program: NACADA Webinar Series 03. Featuring Jayne Drake. (ENG.). 2007. audio compact disk 140.00 (978-1-935140-45-0(0)) Nat Acad Adv.

Composed upon Westminster Bridge, September 3, 1802 see Selected Poetry of William Wordsworth

Composer Audio Cassette Set. 41.50 (978-1-59166-094-1(7)) BJUPr.

Composer John Cage see I'm Too Busy to Talk Now

Composers: Pair-It Books. Steck-Vaughn Staff. 1 cass. (Running Time: 90 min.). 2002. 9.00 (978-0-7398-6210-0(3)) SteckVau.

Composers from Our Past: Activity Fun Pack. Sally A. Bonkrude. Ed. by Karla Lange & Steve Bonkrude. Illus. by Terri Bahn. 1 cass. Dramatization. (J). (ps-3). 1988. bk. 24.95 (978-0-924829-07-9(9)); 6.95 (978-0-924829-15-4(X)) Musical Imag.
Information on composers, with songs and reproducible pages for children.

Composers' Letters. Henry Fielding. (Running Time: 2 hrs. 30 mins.). 1999. 22.95 (978-1-60083-712-8(3)) Iofy Corp.

Composers' Letters. abr. ed. Read by Jeremy Nicholas et al. Ed. by Jan Fielden. 2 CDs. (Running Time: 2 hrs. 40 mins.). 1995. audio compact disk 15.98 (978-962-634-030-1(4), NA203012, Naxos AudioBooks) Naxos.
Great composers - Handel, Bach, Mozart, Britten, Stravinsky, Tchaikovsky, Puccini, Berlioz, Elgar, Brahms, Verdi, Mendelssohn, Schubert and others - are brought to life, not only through their music, but also through letters.

Composers' Letters. abr. ed. Read by Jeremy Nicholas et al. Ed. by Jan Fielden. 2 cass. (Running Time: 2 hrs. 40 mins.). 1995. 13.98 (978-962-634-530-6(6), NA203014, Naxos AudioBooks) Naxos.

***Composing a Further Life: The Age of Active Wisdom.** unabr. ed. Mary Catherine Bateson. (Running Time: 8 hrs. 0 mins.). 2010. 15.99 (978-1-4001-8884-0(9)); 19.99 (978-1-4001-6884-2(8)); audio compact disk 71.99 (978-1-4001-4884-4(7)); audio compact disk 29.99 (978-1-4001-1884-7(0)) Pub: Tantor Media. Dist(s): IngramPubServ

Composing Your Masterpiece Self Symphony - Suite No. 1. Melody Ivory. (ENG.). 2009. pap. bk. 29.85 (978-0-9795504-3-0(2)) Melody Ivory.

Composite Charts Using Uranian System. Arlene Kramer. 1 cass. 8.95 (552) Am Fed Astrologers.

Compound. S. A. Bodeen. Read by Christopher Lane. (Playaway Young Adult Ser.). (YA). (gr. 7-12). 2008. 54.99 (978-1-60640-783-7(X)) Find a World.

Compound. unabr. ed. S. A. Bodeen. Read by Christopher Lane. (Running Time: 6 hrs.). 2008. 39.25 (978-1-4233-6562-4(3), 9781423365624, BADLE); 24.95 (978-1-4233-6561-7(5), 9781423365617, BAD) Brilliance Audio.

Compound. unabr. ed. S. A. Bodeen. Read by Christopher Lane. 5 CDs. (Running Time: 6 hrs.). (gr. 7). 2008. audio compact disk 26.95 (978-1-4233-6557-0(7), 9781423365570, Bril Audio CD Unabri) Brilliance Audio.

Compound. unabr. ed. S. A. Bodeen. Read by Christopher Lane. 1 MP3-CD. (Running Time: 21600 sec.). (YA). (gr. 7). 2008. audio compact disk 39.25 (978-1-4233-6560-0(7), 9781423365600, Brlnc Audio MP3 Lib); audio compact disk 24.95 (978-1-4233-6559-4(3), 9781423365594, Brilliance MP3) Brilliance Audio.

Compound. unabr. ed. S. A. Bodeen. Read by Christopher Lane. 5 CDs. (Running Time: 6 hrs.). (YA). (gr. 8 up). 2008. audio compact disk 74.25 (978-1-4233-6558-7(5), 9781423365587, BriAudCD Unabrid) Brilliance Audio.

Comprehension, Set. Edwin T. Cornelius. Illus. by John Odam. (New Technology English Ser.: Vol. 9). 1984. bk. 36.00 (978-0-685-09171-5(6)) Pace Grp Intl.

***Comprehension Skills Assessment Links: Assessment Links Package Level C (grade 3)** Continental Press Staff. 2008. pap. bk. & stu. ed. 294.95 (978-0-8454-5866-2(3)) Continental Pr.

***Comprehension Skills Assessment Links: Assessment Links Package Level D (grade 4)** Continental Press Staff. 2008. pap. bk. & stu. ed. 294.95 (978-0-8454-5867-9(1)) Continental Pr.

***Comprehension Skills Assessment Links: Assessment Links Package Level E (grade 5)** Continental Press Staff. 2008. pap. bk. & stu. ed. 294.95 (978-0-8454-5868-6(X)) Continental Pr.

***Comprehension Skills Assessment Links: Assessment Links Package Level F (grade 6)** Continental Press Staff. 2008. pap. bk. & stu. ed. 294.95 (978-0-8454-5869-3(8)) Continental Pr.

***Comprehension Skills Assessment Links: Assessment Links Package Level G (grade 7)** Continental Press Staff. 2008. pap. bk. & stu. ed. 294.95 (978-0-8454-5870-9(1)) Continental Pr.

***Comprehension Skills Assessment Links: Assessment Links Package Level H (grade 8)** Continental Press Staff. 2008. pap. bk. & stu. ed. 294.95 (978-0-8454-5871-6(X)) Continental Pr.

***Comprehension Skills Assessment Links: Individual CD Level C (grade 3)** Continental Press Staff. 2008. stu. ed. 49.95 (978-0-8454-5800-6(0)) Continental Pr.

***Comprehension Skills Assessment Links: Individual CD Level D (grade 4)** Continental Press Staff. 2008. stu. ed. 49.95 (978-0-8454-5801-3(9)) Continental Pr.

***Comprehension Skills Assessment Links: Individual CD Level E (grade 5)** Continental Press Staff. 2008. stu. ed. 49.95 (978-0-8454-5802-0(7)) Continental Pr.

***Comprehension Skills Assessment Links: Individual CD Level F (grade 6)** Continental Press Staff. 2008. stu. ed. 49.95 (978-0-8454-5803-7(5)) Continental Pr.

***Comprehension Skills Assessment Links: Individual CD Level G (grade 7)** Continental Press Staff. 2008. stu. ed. 49.95 (978-0-8454-5804-4(3)) Continental Pr.

***Comprehension Skills Assessment Links: Individual CD Level H (grade 8)** Continental Press Staff. 2008. stu. ed. 49.95 (978-0-8454-5805-1(1)) Continental Pr.

Comprehension Strategy Assessment. Compiled by Benchmark Education Staff. 2005. audio compact disk 10.00 (978-1-4108-6210-5(0)); audio compact disk 10.00 (978-1-4108-6211-2(9)); audio compact disk 10.00 (978-1-4108-6212-9(7)); audio compact disk 10.00 (978-1-4108-6213-6(5)); audio compact disk 10.00 (978-1-4108-6214-3(3)); audio compact disk 10.00 (978-1-4108-6215-0(1)); audio compact disk 10.00 (978-1-4108-6216-7(X)); audio compact disk 10.00 (978-1-4108-6217-4(8)) Benchmark Educ.

Comprehension Strategy Assessment CD-ROM: Grade 3 (Levels J-K) Benchmark Education Staff. (Bridges Ser.). 2008. audio compact disk (978-1-60437-344-8(X)) Benchmark Educ.

Comprehension Strategy Assessment CD-ROM: Grade 4 (Levels L-M) Benchmark Education Staff. (Bridges Ser.). 2008. audio compact disk (978-1-60437-345-5(8)) Benchmark Educ.

Comprehension Strategy Assessment CD-ROM: Grade 5 (Levels N-P) Benchmark Education Staff. (Bridges Ser.). 2008. audio compact disk (978-1-60437-346-2(6)) Benchmark Educ.

Comprehension Strategy Assessment CD-ROM: Grade 6 (Levels Q-R) Benchmark Education Staff. (Bridges Ser.). 2008. audio compact disk (978-1-60437-347-9(4)) Benchmark Educ.

Comprehensive Audio Program: Elements of Literature. Holt, Rinehart and Winston Staff. 1997. 169.73 (978-0-03-052012-9(6)) Holt McDoug.

Comprehensive Audio Program: Elements of Literature. Holt, Rinehart and Winston Staff. 1997. 169.73 (978-0-03-052009-9(6)) Holt McDoug.

Comprehensive Audio Program: Elements of Literature. Holt, Rinehart and Winston Staff. 20 cass. 1997. 169.73 (978-0-03-052013-6(4)) Holt McDoug.
Features include: Audiocassettes of nearly all selections in Elements of Literature, grades 6-12; Recordings of captivating poems, short stories, and essays written by inspiring classic and contemporary authors; Dramatic readings by professional actors and actresses.

Comprehensive Business Database of Asia. 6th rev. ed. BIA. (J). 2006. audio compact disk 569.00 (978-1-4187-4826-5(9)) Bus Info Agency.

Comprehensive Business Database of Banking, Financial, & Insurance Companies in the United Kingdom. 6th rev. ed. BIA. (J). 2006. audio compact disk 499.00 (978-1-4187-4892-0(7)) Bus Info Agency.

Comprehensive Business Database of Construction Companies in the United Kingdom. 6th rev. ed. BIA. (J). 2006. audio compact disk 479.00 (978-1-4187-4883-8(8)) Bus Info Agency.

Comprehensive Business Database of Construction Companies of Belgium. 6th rev. ed. BIA. (J). 2006. audio compact disk 449.00 (978-1-4187-4721-3(1)) Bus Info Agency.

Comprehensive Business Database of German Construction Companies. 6th rev. ed. BIA. (J). 2006. audio compact disk 449.00 (978-1-4187-4771-8(8)) Bus Info Agency.

Comprehensive Business Database of Health Care Market of Russia. 6th rev. ed. BIA. (J). 2006. audio compact disk 399.00 (978-1-4187-5180-7(4)) Bus Info Agency.

Comprehensive Business Database of Italian Construction Companies. 6th rev. ed. BIA. (J). 2006. audio compact disk 519.00 (978-1-4187-4790-9(4)) Bus Info Agency.

Comprehensive Business Database of Italian Transportation & Communication Companies. 6th rev. ed. BIA. (J). 2006. audio compact disk 449.00 (978-1-4187-4796-1(3)) Bus Info Agency.

Comprehensive Business Database of Key Transportation & Communication Companies in the Netherlands. 6th rev. ed. BIA. (J). 2006. audio compact disk 419.00 (978-1-4187-4817-3(X)) Bus Info Agency.

Comprehensive Business Database of Portuguese Construction Companies. 6th rev. ed. BIA. (J). 2006. audio compact disk 249.00 (978-1-4187-4948-4(6)) Bus Info Agency.

Comprehensive Business Database of Portuguese Wholesalers & Retailers. 6th rev. ed. BIA. (J). 2006. audio compact disk 579.00 (978-1-4187-4953-8(2)) Bus Info Agency.

Comprehensive Business Database of Russian Construction Companies. 6th rev. ed. BIA. (J). 2006. audio compact disk 479.00 (978-1-4187-5187-6(1)) Bus Info Agency.

Comprehensive Business Database of Spanish Banking, Financial, & Insurance Companies. 6th rev. ed. BIA. (J). 2006. audio compact disk 369.00 (978-1-4187-4940-8(0)) Bus Info Agency.

Comprehensive Business Database of Spanish Construction Companies. 6th rev. ed. BIA. (J). 2006. audio compact disk 449.00 (978-1-4187-4932-3(X)) Bus Info Agency.

Comprehensive Business Database of Spanish Wholesalers & Retailers. 6th rev. ed. BIA. (J). 2006. audio compact disk 569.00 (978-1-4187-4937-8(0)) Bus Info Agency.

Comprehensive Business Database of Swedish Wholesalers & Retailers. 6th rev. ed. BIA. (J). 2006. audio compact disk 499.00 (978-1-4187-4920-0(6)) Bus Info Agency.

Comprehensive Business Database of Swiss Banks, Financial, Insurance, & Real Estate Companies. 6th rev. ed. BIA. (J). 2006. audio compact disk 479.00 (978-1-4187-4909-5(5)) Bus Info Agency.

Comprehensive Business Database of Swiss Construction Companies. 6th rev. ed. BIA. (J). 2006. audio compact disk 479.00 (978-1-4187-4897-5(8)) Bus Info Agency.

Comprehensive Business Database of Swiss Transportation & Communication Companies. 6th rev. ed. BIA. (J). 2006. audio compact disk 359.00 (978-1-4187-4905-7(2)) Bus Info Agency.

Comprehensive Business Database of Swiss Wholesalers & Retailers. 6th rev. ed. BIA. (J). 2006. audio compact disk 569.00 (978-1-4187-4906-4(0)) Bus Info Agency.

Comprehensive Business Database of Textile Companies in Western Europe. 6th rev. ed. BIA. (J). 2006. audio compact disk 459.00 (978-1-4187-4642-1(8)) Bus Info Agency.

Comprehensive Business Database of the Netherlands: Banking, Financial, Insurance, & Real Estate Companies. 6th rev. ed. BIA. (J). 2006. audio compact disk 489.00 (978-1-4187-4823-4(4)) Bus Info Agency.

Comprehensive Business Database of Transportation & Communications Companies in the United Kingdom. 6th rev. ed. BIA. (J). 2006. audio compact disk 449.00 (978-1-4187-4886-9(2)) Bus Info Agency.

Comprehensive Business Database of Western European Farms. 6th rev. ed. BIA. (J). 2006. audio compact disk 399.00 (978-1-4187-5196-8(0)) Bus Info Agency.

Comprehensive Business Database of Western European Metallurgical Companies. 6th rev. ed. BIA. (J). 2006. audio compact disk 439.00 (978-1-4187-4672-8(X)) Bus Info Agency.

Comprehensive Business Database of Western European Mining Companies. 6th rev. ed. BIA. (J). 2006. audio compact disk 399.00 (978-1-4187-5296-5(7)) Bus Info Agency.

Comprehensive Business Database of Western European Printing & Publishing Companies. 6th rev. ed. BIA. (J). 2006. audio compact disk 499.00 (978-1-4187-4657-5(6)) Bus Info Agency.

Comprehensive Business Database of Western European Pulp & Paper. 6th rev. ed. BIA. (J). 2006. audio compact disk 399.00 (978-1-4187-4654-4(1)) Bus Info Agency.

Comprehensive Business Database of Western European Transportation Companies. 6th rev. ed. BIA. (J). 2006. audio compact disk 499.00 (978-1-4187-4692-6(4)) Bus Info Agency.

Comprehensive Business Database of Western European Wholesalers of Non-Durable Goods. 6th rev. ed. BIA. (J). 2006. audio compact disk 599.00 (978-1-4187-4695-7(9)) Bus Info Agency.

Comprehensive Business Database of Wholesalers & Retailers in the Netherlands. 6th rev. ed. BIA. (J). 2006. audio compact disk 519.00 (978-1-4187-4820-3(X)) Bus Info Agency.

Comprehensive Classification of Fractures. M. E. Miller. 1994. bk. 159.00 (978-0-387-14150-3(2)) Spri.

Comprehensive Course in Russian. Sarah Smyth & Elena Crosbie. (Running Time: 5 hrs. 28 mins.). (RUS & ENG., (C). 2002. audio compact disk 43.99 (978-0-521-52955-6(7)) Cambridge U Pr.

Comprehensive Database of Manufacturers of Russia. 6th rev. ed. BIA. (J). 2006. audio compact disk 529.00 (978-1-4187-5300-9(9)) Bus Info Agency.

Comprehensive Database of Manufacturers of Russia & the Former Soviet Republics. 6th rev. ed. BIA. (J). 2006. audio compact disk 629.00 (978-1-4187-5299-6(1)) Bus Info Agency.

Comprehensive Exercise Guide: Personal Strategies for Self-Improvement. unabr. ed. Michael J. Mahoney. 3 cass. (Running Time: 2 hrs. 45 min.). 35.00 (29359) J Norton Pubs.
This guide cuts through the welter of contradictory claims & misconceptions about different popular exercises. It provides systematic direction to tailor a program best suited to personal preferences, needs, physical capacity & life style.

Comprehensive Guide to Cassette Ministry: How Ordinary Christians Can Extraordinary Impact For the Kingdom of God. Johnny Berguson. 1997. bk. 19.97 (978-1-883906-12-2(1)) Kingdom Prods.

Comprehensive Index to ASM Handbooks. Christine Kennedy et al. 1994. bk. 225.00 (978-0-614-03403-5(5), 6514U) ASM Intl.

Comprehensive Inquiry of the Psalms: Vision of God & Perfect Christian Prayer. Lawrence Boadt. 5 cass. (Running Time: 8 hrs. 12 min.). 1998. 42.95 Set. (TAH391) Alba Hse Comns.
Fr. Boadt weaves literary, liturgical, & social dimensions into a spirituality of the Psalms that is presented in this course. Material for personal study, parish discussion groups, & Bible study classes.

***Comprehensive Lactation Consultant Exam Review.** 3rd ed. Sandra Smith. 2010. audio compact disk 69.95 (978-1-4496-0346-5(7)) Jones Bartlett.

Comprehensive New User's Guide to DOS. Lewis Robins. 1 cass. 149.95 incl. study guide & disk. (103410KQ) Am Inst CPA.
System requirements: DOS version 5.01.

Comprehensive New User's Guide to DOS (CVE) Lewis Robins. (Running Time: 10 hrs.). (Micromastery-Systems Management Ser.). 1995. 149.95 incl. study guide & disk. (103411EZ) Am Inst CPA.

Comprehensive Sports Medicine CAQ Review, Vol. A108. unabr. ed. 43 cass. (Running Time: 50 hrs.). 1993. 550.00 set. (978-1-57664-354-9(9)) CME Info Svcs.
Continuing medical education home-study. Complete package contains audiotapes, syllabus, self-assessment examination to earn CME Category 1 credit.

Comprehensive Strategy Assessment. Compiled by Benchmark Education Staff. 2005. audio compact disk 10.00 (978-1-4108-6218-1(6)) Benchmark Educ.

Comprehensive Study of Egyptian Arabic, Vol. I & II. Ernest T. Abdel-Massih et al. 9 cass. 1979. 76.26 Set. U MI Lang Res.

Comprehensive Training Set: Relaxation, Feeling & Value Solutions, Russell E. Mason. 18 cass. (Running Time: 17 hrs. 42 min.). 1975. pap. bk. 145.00 (978-0-89533-021-5(0), 69.ST-CT) F I Comm.
Includes all orientation, guides, methods & value considerations noted for other train-ascendance tapes.

Comprenda y Resuelva Sus Miedos Como Manejar la Ansiedad see Understand & Overcome Your Fears Managing Anxiety

***Comprende el valor relativo Audio CD.** April Barth. Adapted by Benchmark Education Co., LLC. (Content Connections Ser.). (SPA.). (J). 2010. audio compact disk 10.00 (978-1-61672-187-9(1)) Benchmark Educ.

Compromise in Egypt. (SWC 1160) HarperCollins Pubs.

Comptines et Fables pour les Tout-Petits. 1 cass. (FRE.). (J). (gr. 3 up). 1991. bk. 19.95 (1AD072) Olivia & Hill.

Compulsion. abr. ed. Jonathan Kellerman. Read by John Rubinstein. (Alex Delaware Ser.: No. 22). (ENG.). 2008. audio compact disk 14.99 (978-0-7393-8237-0(3), Random AudioBks) Pub: Random Audio Pubg. Dist(s): Random

Compulsion. unabr. ed. Jonathan Kellerman. Read by John Rubinstein. 8 CDs. (Alex Delaware Ser.: No. 22). 2008. audio compact disk 100.00 (978-1-4159-4401-1(6), BksonTape) Pub: Random Audio Pubg. Dist(s): Random

Compulsion. unabr. ed. Jonathan Kellerman. Read by John Rubinstein. 8 CDs. (Running Time: 10 hrs.). (Alex Delaware Ser.: No. 22). (ENG.). 2008. audio compact disk 44.95 (978-0-7393-0723-6(1), Random AudioBks) Pub: Random Audio Pubg. Dist(s): Random

Compulsion, Pt. 1. unabr. collector's ed. Meyer Levin. Read by Lloyd James. 9 cass. (Running Time: 13 hrs. 30 min.). 1999. 72.00 (978-0-7366-4387-0(7), 4851-A) Books on Tape.
The mid 1920s introduced Americans to a new type of murder: two immensely wealthy eighteen-year-old university graduates from Chicago randomly kidnapped & murdered a little boy, attempted to obliterate the identity & sex of the body before hiding it & then tried to collect the ransom - simply as an intellectual experiment. The author attempts to discover the psychology of the two young men, to understand how the two of them, Leopold & Loeb, one of them handsome & popular, the other quiet & scholarly, were capable of an act so far beyond rational understanding.

Compulsion, Pt. 2. unabr. collector's ed. Meyer Levin. Read by Lloyd James. 9 cass. (Running Time: 13 hrs. 30 min.). 1999. 72.00 (978-0-7366-4388-7(5), 4851-B) Books on Tape.

Compulsive Gambler: A Profile. unabr. ed. Gerald Fulcher. 1 cass. (Running Time: 50 min.). 1982. 9.95 Newtown Psychological Ctr.
An in-depth interview focusing on the scope of the problem in the U.S., the psychological characteristics of the gambler & the stages of the addictive process.

Compulsory Reading. unabr. ed. Gilbert Highet. 1 cass. (Running Time: 30 min). (Gilbert Highet Ser.). 9.95 (23334) J Norton Pubs.
Tells why we often hate books we are told we must read & how this hatred can be eliminated. The really important books are meant to be read & thought over for many years.

Compulsory Reading & Permanent Books. Gilbert Highet. 1 CD. (Running Time: 27 mins.). (Gilbert Highet Ser.). 2006. audio compact disk 12.95 (978-1-57970-381-3(X), C23334D, Audio-For) J Norton Pubs.
2 superb talks by master monoglist Gilbert Highet. The first is about "compulsory reading": why we often hate books we are told we must read, and how this hatred can be eliminated. The second is on "permanent books": most books can be thrown away after 1 reading, but the really important books are meant to be re-read and thought over for many years.

Computer & High Technology Law. 1990. 75.00 (AC-571) PA Bar Inst.

Computer & Online Games in Germany: A Strategic Reference 2006. Compiled by Icon Group International, Inc. Staff. 2007. ring bd. 195.00 (978-0-497-35969-0(3)) Icon Grp.

Computer-Assisted Software Project for Aural Skills Reinforcement (Caspar) Macintosh & Windows. Leo Kraft & Erik Lund. (C). 1999. (978-0-393-10280-2(7)) Norton.

Computer-Based Training. 1 cass. (America's Supermarket Showcase '96 Ser.). 1996. 11.00 (NGA96-011) Sound Images.

Computer Dictionary Ger-Eng - Eng-Ger. (GER.). 2000. bk. 56.50 (978-3-86063-822-4(X)) Pub: Microsoft GmbH DEU. Dist(s): IBD Ltd

Computer Ethics: Integrating Across the Curriculum. Marion Ben-Jacob. 2009. audio compact disk 16.95 (978-0-7637-7809-5(5)) Jones Bartlett.

Computer Ghost: The Deadly Dare Mysteries, Book 2. Malorie Blackman. Read by Paul Chequer. (Running Time: 13080 sec.). (J). (gr. 6-9). 2007. audio compact disk 21.95 (978-1-4056-5601-6(8), ChiversChildren) AudioGo GBR.

Computer in Business. unabr. ed. Richard Schmidt & William Meyers. 1 cass. (Running Time: 47 min.). 12.95 (13180) J Norton Pubs.
A review of the role of the computer in business management. A discussion of EDP as the focal point of the management information system.

Computer Law: Current Trends & Developments. unabr. ed. Contrib. by Daniel T. Brooks. 4 cass. (Running Time: 5 hrs. 30 min.). 1989. pap. bk. 65.00 (T6-9101) PLI.
This recording of PLI's May 1989 satellite program emphasizes new trends, focusing on: current issues in the copyright area, including screen displays, registration databases & dealing with the Copyright Office Examiners, "look & feel" cases & where the courts are going, dealing with misappropriation & other "unfaithful" acts, system procurement & maintenance agreements, software licenses & support agreements.

Computer Law 1986: Computer & Telecommunications Contracts, Licenses & Litigation. 1986. bk. 100.00 incl. book.; 65.00 cass. only.; 35.00 book only. PA Bar Inst.

Computer Literacy Made Easy...& Fun: Bits, Bytes, Apples & Mice. unabr. ed. James R. Callan. Read by James R. Callan. 2 cass. (Running Time: 2 hrs. 50 min.). 1995. pap. bk. 24.95 Set.; 16.95 Set. (978-0-9646850-4-8(3)) Pennant Pubng.
These cassettes explain & discuss many of the terms & ideas associated with today's computer technology in a non-technical, lighthearted & humorous manner. It is designed to introduce the subject of computers to those unfamiliar or uncomfortable with today's technology, or those who use computers but know little about them.

Computer Numerical Control (CNC) Metal-Cutting Machines in China: A Strategic Reference 2007. Compiled by Icon Group International, Inc. Staff. 2007. ring bd. 195.00 (978-0-497-35868-6(9)) Icon Grp.

Computer Numerical Control (CNC) Metal-Cutting Machines in India: A Strategic Reference 2007. Compiled by Icon Group International, Inc. Staff. 2007. ring bd. 195.00 (978-0-497-36008-5(X)) Icon Grp.

Computer Primer: Hardware-Software-Applications in Legal Practice-Acquisitions & Implementation. 1984. bk. 35.00; 25.00 PA Bar Inst.

Computer Reprints. Ed. by Marco A. V. Bitetto. 1 cass. 2000. (978-1-58578-038-9(3)) Inst of Cybernetics.

Computer Science Handbook. 2nd ed. Miguel J. Bagajewicz. 2004. audio compact disk 162.95 (978-1-58488-468-2(1), C4681) Pub: CRC Pr. Dist(s): Taylor and Fran

Computer Servers & Storage Systems in China: A Strategic Reference 2006. Compiled by Icon Group International, Inc. Staff. 2007. ring bd. 195.00 (978-0-497-35869-3(7)) Icon Grp.

Computer Servers in Germany: A Strategic Reference 2006. Compiled by Icon Group International, Inc. Staff. 2007. ring bd. 195.00 (978-0-497-35970-6(7)) Icon Grp.

Computer Service & Repair a Guide to Upgrading, Configuring, Troubleshooting, & Networking Personal Computers. Richard M. Roberts. (gr. 9-13). tchr. ed. & instr.'s training gde. ed. 220.00 (978-1-59070-338-0(3)) Goodheart.

Computer Software: Protection & Commercial Exploitation. 7 cass. (Running Time: 10 hrs.). 1998. 345.00 Set; incl. study guide 375p. (MD35) Am Law Inst.
Advanced new course provides listeners with an understanding of the latest developments & trends.

Computer Software: Protection & Marketing. unabr. ed. Contrib. by Morton D. Goldberg. 9 cass. (Running Time: 11 hrs.). 1989. 50.00 course handbk. (T7-9222) PLI.
In this recording of PLI's July 1989 seminar, an experienced faculty of practitioners & government officials examine: impact of recent decisions on "SSO" (Structure, Sequence & Organization) & "Look & Feel" in software & database infringement cases, evolving industry practices in the development, protection & marketing of software, developments in Copyright Office procedures for registration & deposit of software, screen displays & databases, patent, trade secret & trademark protection for software, protection of software in foreign countries, agreements for developing, acquisition & marketing of software, contract considerations after recent judicial & statutory developments on work-for-hire, bankruptcy & sovereign immunity, strategy & tactics as to preliminary relief in infringement cases.

Computer Software & Services in Austria: A Strategic Reference 2007. Compiled by Icon Group International, Inc. Staff. 2007. ring bd. 195.00 (978-0-497-35816-7(6)) Icon Grp.

Computer Software & Services in Colombia: A Strategic Reference 2007. Compiled by Icon Group International, Inc. Staff. 2007. ring bd. 195.00 (978-0-497-35898-3(0)) Icon Grp.

Computer Talk Made Easy. Clancy Wells. Illus. by Jim Cherry. 1993. 10.95 (978-0-9633901-1-0(2)) Wells Intl.

Computer Technology: Changes, Challenges, & Choices CD Courses-Full Content Instruction; Text with CD Course. C. Norman Hollingsworth & Mary Carole Hollingsworth. audio compact disk 36.95 (978-0-7638-1076-4(2)) EMC-Paradigm.

Computerized Accounting with Peachtree 2003: Instructor Resources; Instructor's Guide CD. Jim Mazza & Gary Chavez. 2005. audio compact disk 69.00 (978-0-7638-1946-0(8)) EMC-Paradigm.

Computerizing Store Design & the Store Development Department. 1 cass. (America's Supermarket Showcase '96 Ser.). 1996. 11.00 (NGA96-037) Sound Images.

Computers: Exploring Concepts; Instructor Resources. Floyd Fuller. (Tech Edge Ser.). tchr. ed. 69.00 (978-0-7638-1296-6(X)) EMC-Paradigm.

Computers: Navigating Change; Instructor Resources. Floyd Fuller. (Tech Edge Ser.). tchr. ed. 69.00 (978-0-7638-1298-0(6)) EMC-Paradigm.

Computers: Understanding Technology-Brief; Instructor Resources. Floyd Fuller & Brian Larson. (Tech Edge Ser.). 2005. tchr. ed. 69.00 (978-0-7638-2090-9(3)) EMC-Paradigm.

Computers: Understanding Technology-Brief; Instructor Resources; Test Generator CD. Floyd Fuller & Brian Larson. (Tech Edge Ser.). 2005. audio compact disk 78.95 (978-0-7638-2091-6(1)) EMC-Paradigm.

Computers: Understanding Technology; Instructor Resources. Floyd Fuller & Brian Larson. (Tech Edge Ser.). tchr. ed. 69.00 (978-0-7638-1300-0(1)) EMC-Paradigm.

Computers: Understanding Technology; Instructor Resources; Test Generator CD. Floyd Fuller & Brian Larson. (Tech Edge Ser.). audio compact disk 78.95 (978-0-7638-1595-0(0)) EMC-Paradigm.

Computers & Man's Freedom. unabr. ed. Don Myatt. 1 cass. (Running Time: 45 min.). 12.95 (25017) J Norton Pubs.
Man has created mechanical constructs with human qualities. This discussion covers the benefits & problems that arise as more & more of these machines are produced.

Computers & TV: Workshop Four. 2 cass. 1990. 17.00 set. Recorded Res.

Computers Can Help/Big City Life. Steck-Vaughn Staff. 2002. (978-0-7398-5988-9(9)) SteckVau.

Computers from the Inside Out. Richard Phillips Feynman. 1 cass. 9.00 (A0029-85) Sound Photosyn.
The way the Nobel Prize winner describes the internal basics, at Esalen, makes you enjoy the understanding.

Computers in Astrology. ACT Staff. 1 cass. 8.95 (006) Am Fed Astrologers.
Major astrological software companies discuss what's new.

Computers in Small Libraries: Automating with Off-the-Shelf Software. 1 cass. 1990. 8.00 set. Recorded Res.

Computers in Small Libraries: Creative Approaches to Automation. 2 cass. 1990. 16.00 set. Recorded Res.

Comp21 CD-ROM for Mauk/Metz's the Composition of Everyday Life: A Guide to Writing, 2nd. 2nd ed. (C). 2006. audio compact disk 38.95 (978-1-4130-2294-0(4)) Pub: Heinle. Dist(s): CENGAGE Learn

Comrade Charlie. unabr. ed. Brian Freemantle. 10 cass. (Running Time: 13 hrs.). (Soundings Ser.). (J). 2006. 84.95 (978-1-84559-040-6(6)) Pub: ISIS Lrg Prnt GBR. Dist(s): Ulverscroft US

Comrade J: The Untold Secrets of Russia's Master Spy in America after the End of the Cold War. unabr. ed. Pete Earley. Narrated by Michael Prichard. (Running Time: 11 hrs. 0 mins. 0 sec.). (ENG.). 2008. audio compact disk 34.99 (978-1-4001-0552-6(8)); audio compact disk 69.99 (978-1-4001-3552-3(4)) Pub: Tantor Media. Dist(s): IngramPubServ

Comrade J: The Untold Secrets of Russia's Master Spy in America after the End of the Cold War. unabr. ed. Pete Earley. Read by Michael Prichard. (Running Time: 11 hrs. 0 mins. 0 sec.). (ENG.). 2008. audio compact disk 24.99 (978-1-4001-5552-1(5)) Pub: Tantor Media. Dist(s): IngramPubServ

Comrades: Brothers, Fathers, Heroes, Sons, Pals. Stephen E. Ambrose. Narrated by Nelson Runger. 4 CDs. (Running Time: 5 hrs. 30 mins.). audio compact disk 40.00 (978-0-7887-9637-1(2)) Recorded Bks.

Comrades: Brothers, Fathers, Heroes, Sons, Pals. unabr. ed. Stephen E. Ambrose. Narrated by Nelson Runger. 4 cass. (Running Time: 5 hrs. 30 mins.). 2001. 37.00 (978-0-7887-4978-0(1), 96509E7) Recorded Bks.
Examines the bonds formed between men as a result of both family & circumstance. The lasting friendships of various men, from Sioux Indians to Ambrose's own father & brothers. Reaching back through history, Ambrose describes the special relationship between Meriwether Lewis & William Clark, whose faith & trust in one another helped them survive their famous expedition. He pays homage to brothers, such famous pairs as Dwight & Milton Eisenhower & George & Tom Custer. Also a chapter to Richard Nixon, using the late president as an example of why certain men have trouble forming close bonds with other men.

Comrades: Brothers, Fathers, Sons, Pals. Stephen E. Ambrose. 2004. 10.95 (978-0-7435-4525-9(7)) Pub: S&S Audio. Dist(s): S and S Inc

Comstock Camels. unabr. ed. Gary McCarthy. Read by Gene Engene. 6 cass. (Running Time: 6 hrs. 48 min.). (Derby Man Ser.: Bk. 11). 1995. 39.95 (978-1-55686-620-3(8)) Books in Motion.
Darby Buckingham decides to go into the freight business & becomes the owner of twelve dirty & disagreeable camels.

***Comte de Monte-Cristo, Niveau 3.** Alexandre Dumas. (Collection Decouverte Ser.). (FRE.). 2009. audio compact disk 20.95 (978-2-09-032626-0(3)) Cle Intl FRA.

Comtesse de Sancerre. Marquis de Sade. Read by N. Adam. 1 cass. (FRE.). 1995. 17.95 (1753-KFP) Olivia & Hill.
A mother, a daughter & her lover. Will the mother be able to steal her daughter's lover?.

Comunicacion - Base para un Marketing Exitoso. unabr. ed. Basilio Balli Morales.Tr. of Communications. (SPA.). audio compact disk 13.00 (978-958-43-0225-0(6)) YoYoMusic.

Comunicación Creativa. ANISA, Inc. (gr. 4-9). audio compact disk 14.95 (978-1-56835-438-5(X)) Prodns Anisa.

Comunicación creativa (Edad Temprana) ANISA, Inc. audio compact disk 14.95 (978-1-56835-321-0(9)) Prodns Anisa.

Comunication Skills: Professionals' Effectiveness Training Session - "PETS" (for Women) Chaya Newman. 1 cass. (Running Time: 90 mins.). 1999. 10.00 (W60F7) Torah Umesorah.

Comus see Treasury of John Milton

Comus see Dylan Thomas Reading

Comus see Poetry of John Milton

Comus & Samson Agonistes. unabr. ed. John Milton & John Grisham. Read by John Westbrook. 14 cass. (Running Time: 3 hrs. 15 min.). 1994. 34.95 (978-1-85695-746-5(2), 89115) Pub: ISIS Audio GBR. Dist(s): Ulverscroft US
The masque "Comus" was first performed at Ludlow Castle in 1634 & was one of Milton's first works. Over thirty years later in 1672 "Samson Agonistes," his last major work, was published.

Con Brio. 2nd ed. María Concepción Lucas Murillo & Laila M. Dawson. (ENG.). (C). 2010. audio compact disk 25.95 (978-0-470-57388-4(0), JWiley) Wiley US.

Con Brio! Beginning Spanish. 11th ed. Laila M. Dawson & María Concepción Lucas Murillo. (ENG.). (C). 2007. lab manual ed. 21.95 (978-0-471-79801-9(0), JWiley) Wiley US.

Con Ed. abr. ed. Matthew Klein. Read by Norman Dietz. (Running Time: 21600 sec.). 2007. audio compact disk 14.99 (978-1-4233-3139-1(7), 9781423331391, BCD Value Price) Brilliance Audio.

Con Ed. unabr. ed. Matthew Klein. Read by Norman Dietz. (Running Time: 9 hrs.). 2007. 39.25 (978-1-4233-3135-3(4), 9781423331353, Brlnc Audio MP3 Lib); 24.95 (978-1-4233-3134-6(6), 9781423331346, Brilliance MP3); 39.25 (978-1-4233-3137-7(0), 9781423331377, BADLE); 24.95 (978-1-4233-3136-0(2), 9781423331360, BAD); 74.25 (978-1-4233-3131-5(1), 9781423331315, BrilAudUnabridg); audio compact disk 92.25 (978-1-4233-3133-9(8), 9781423331339, BriAudCD Unabrid); audio compact disk 34.95 (978-1-4233-3132-2(X), 9781423331322, Bril Audio CD Unabri) Brilliance Audio.

Con Fantasia. Marcel Danesi. lab manual ed. 32.75 (978-0-8384-5976-8(5)) Heinle.

Con Gozo, Alegria y Paz. Contrib. by Various Artists. (gr. 13). 2008. audio compact disk 11.99 (978-0-8297-5425-4(3)) Pub: CanZion. Dist(s): Zondervan

Con la Biblia en la Mano. P. Juan Rivas. (SPA.). (YA). 2007. audio compact disk 18.95 (978-1-935405-63-4(2)) Hombre Nuevo.

Con Man. unabr. ed. Ed McBain, pseud. Read by Paul Shay. 6 cass. (Running Time: 6 hrs.). (87th Precinct Ser.: Bk. 4). 1990. 36.00 (978-0-7366-1787-1(6), 2624) Books on Tape.
Con man - a trickster taking money from an old woman for his own private charity. Or a cheater fleecing businessmen of their thousands with the oldest gimmick in town. Or a lady-kiler after ladies' dollars with just a little bit of love. Whatever the con, it's a dangerous game. Then there's the boys of the 87th Precinct. After so many years on the beat, you'd think they know every trick in the book. So why are bodies still washing up on the shore? The streetwise cops had better find out quick.

***Con mi familia Audio CD.** Jeffrey B. Fuerst. Adapted by Benchmark Education Company, LLC. (My First Reader's Theater Ser.). (SPA.). (J). 2009. audio compact disk 10.00 (978-1-935470-84-7(1)) Benchmark Educ.

Con Mi Hermano/with My Brother, Audiocassette. Eileen Roe. (Metro Reading Ser.). (J). (gr. k). 2000. 8.46 (978-1-58120-987-7(8)) Metro Teaching.

***Con mi Lengua.** Pellegrino Mariana. Read by Kristine Klanderud. Illus. by Nemitz Mariana.Tr. of With My Tongue. (SPA.). (J). 2010. bk. 17.95 (978-0-9842981-5-0(0)) Lorito Bks.

***Con mi Nariz.** Pellegrino Mariana. Read by Kristine Klanderud. Illus. by Nemitz Mariana.Tr. of With My Nose. (SPA.). (J). 2010. pap. bk. 17.95 (978-0-9842981-4-3(2)) Lorito Bks.

***Con mis Manos.** Pellegrino Mariana. Read by Kristine Klanderud. Illus. by Nemitz Mariana.Tr. of With My Hands. (SPA.). (J). 2010. pap. bk. 1.00 (978-0-9842981-7-4(7)) Lorito Bks.

***Con mis Oídos.** Mariana Pellegrino. Read by Kristine Klanderud. Illus. by Mariana Nemitz. 1 CD. (Running Time: 11 mins.). (SPA.). (J). (ps-2). 2009. pap. bk. 17.95 (978-0-9842981-0-5(X)) Lorito Bks.

***Con mis Ojos.** Pellegrino Mariana. Read by Kristine Klanderud. Illus. by Nemitz Mariana.Tr. of With My Eyes. (SPA.). (J). 2010. pap. bk. 17.95 (978-0-9842981-6-7(9)) Lorito Bks.

Con Mucho Gusto. 4th ed. Jean-Paul Valette. (SPA.). 1995. (978-0-03-010418-3(1)) Harcourt Coll Pubs.

Conc Intr Logic Learn Faci. 7th ed. Patrick Hurley & Joseph P. Demarco. (C). 2000. audio compact disk 23.95 (978-0-534-52013-7(8)) Pub: Wadsworth Pub. Dist(s): CENGAGE Learn

Concannon Sisters Trilogy CD Collection: Born in Fire; Born in Ice; Born in Shame. abr. ed. Nora Roberts. Read by Fiacre Douglas. (Running Time: 18 hrs.). (Concannon Sisters Trilogy: Vols. 1-3). 2007. audio compact disk 34.95 (978-1-4233-3186-5(9), 9781423331865, BACD) Brilliance Audio.

Concentracion. Carlos Gonzalez. 1 CD. (Running Time: 32 mins). (SPA.). 2004. audio compact disk 15.00 (978-1-56491-112-4(8)) Imagine Pubs.

Concentration. 1 cass. 10.00 (978-1-58506-002-3(X), 03) New Life Inst OR.
Learn to concentrate on whatever you want. You can reprogram yourself for intense, powerful, focused concentration.

Concentration. 1 cass. (Running Time: 60 min.). 10.95 (011) Psych Res Inst.
Developing the capacity to quickly learn, retain & recall information.

Concentration. 1 cass. (Running Time: 45 min.). (Educational Ser.). 9.98 (978-1-55909-015-5(4), 28S); 9.98 90 min. extended length stereo music. (978-1-55909-016-2(2), 28X) Randolph Tapes.
Develop your mental ability to focus & be self-disciplined. Subliminal messages are heard 3-5 minutes before becoming ocean sounds or music.

Concentration. 1 cass. (Running Time: 1 hr.). 12.99 (714) Yoga Res Foun.

Concentration. Rick Brown. Read by Rick Brown. Ed. by John Quatro. 1 cass. (Running Time: 30 min.). (Subliminal - Easy Listening Ser.). 1993. 10.95 (978-1-57100-007-1(0), E118); 10.95 (978-1-57100-031-6(3), J118); 10.95 (978-1-57100-065-1(8), N118); 10.95 (978-1-57100-079-8(8), S118); 10.95 (978-1-57100-103-0(4), W118); 10.95 (978-1-57100-127-6(1), H118) Sublime Sftware.
Improves concentration in all students.

Concentration. Swami Amar Jyoti. 1 cass. 1978. 9.95 (P-17) Truth Consciousness.
Practice for pin-pointed focus on the highest Goal. Meditating on God within & without. Why & how we reincarnate.

Concentration. Barrie Konicov. 1 cass. (Running Time: 1 hr. 6 min.). (Video-Audio System Ser.). cass. & video 24.98 (978-0-87082-443-2(0), SYS020); 11.98 (978-0-87082-296-4(9), 020) Potentials.
Provides the key to logical, organized mental ability to concentrate on single thoughts & to keep thinking of them until you are ready to discharge them from your life.

Concentration. Barrie Konicov. 1 CD. 2003. audio compact disk 16.98 (978-0-87082-964-2(5)) Potentials.
If your mind is undisciplined and cluttered, this program teaches you to concentrate on single thoughts.You will find the self-hypnosis on track 1 and the subliminal on track 2. The easy-listening music of the subliminal, together with the self-hypnosis, is the original format which most people love and with which they are most familiar.

Concentration. Barrie Konicov. 2 CDs. 2003. audio compact disk 27.98 (978-1-56001-972-5(7)) Potentials.
The difference in people is not the difference in opportunity, but in the quality of their thoughts. Raise the quality of your thoughts, and you will raise the quality of your life!This 2-CD program from our Super Consciousness series is our newest, most powerful format. On the self-hypnosis CD, SC programs have the Subliminal Persuasion soundtrack added under Barrie?s voice. And the 17th Century Baroque music on the Subliminal CD has the same beat as your body's natural rhythm, thereby allowing the suggestions to enter deeply and effortlessly.

Concentration. Betty L. Randolph. 1 stereo cass. (Running Time: 45 min.). (Self-Hypnosis Ser.). 9.98 (978-1-55909-156-5(8), 901) Randolph Tapes.
Learn how to organize & concentrate fully. Music background & spoken word.

Concentration. Eldon Taylor. 1 cass. (Running Time: 62 min.). (Neurophonics Ser.). 14.95 (978-1-55978-658-4(2), 1009) Progress Aware Res.
Sound patterns for Altered States of Consciousness with underlying subliminal affirmations & frequency response signals. Use with headphones only.

Concentration. abr. ed. Robert A. Monroe. Read by Robert A. Monroe. (Mind Food Ser.). 1981. 14.95 (978-1-56102-403-2(1)) Inter Indus.
Enhance your focus of attention.

Concentration. unabr. ed. Robert A. Monroe. Read by Roland Simon. 1 cass. (Running Time: 30 min.). (Human Plus Ser.). (FRE.). 1992. 14.95 (978-1-56102-055-3(9)) Inter Indus.
Sharply focuses mind & senses on a particular thought, action or event.

Concentration: Hypnotic & Subliminal Learning. David Illig. 2 cass. (Running Time: 2 hrs.). 2000. 14.99 (978-0-86580-022-9(7)) Success World.

Concentration: La Concentracion. Barrie Konicov. 1 cass. (Running Time: 1 hr. 30 min.). (Spanish-Language Audios Ser.). (SPA.). (YA). 1995. 11.98 (978-0-87082-807-2(X), 020) Potentials.
Discipline your mind, bringing thoughts into logical patterns. With this tape learn the key to logical, organized mental ability, how to concentrate on single thoughts until you are ready to discharge them from your mind.

Concentration: Perfect Memory & Recall. Gil Boyne. Read by Gil Boyne. 1 cass. (Running Time: 45 min.). (Hypnosis Motivation Cassettes Ser.). 1977. 9.95 (102) Westwood Pub Co.
The only scientifically-validated memory system known, & it requires no memorization of key words or word associations.

Concentration - Perfect Memory & Recall, 111. 1998. 24.95 (978-1-58557-003-4(6)) Dynamic Growth.

Concentration & Meditation. 1 cass. (Running Time: 1 hr.). 12.99 (603) Yoga Res Foun.

Concentration & Purity of Heart. Swami Amar Jyoti. 1 cass. 1978. 9.95 (K-40) Truth Consciousness.
Purity of heart is the bulk of true religion, concentration is the bulk of Yoga, science. Together they make the impossible possible. On astrology.

Concentration, Contemplation, Meditation. George King. 2005. audio compact disk 12.50 (978-0-937249-23-9(8)) Aetherius Soc.

Concentration is Easy. Eldon Taylor. 1 cass. (Running Time: 62 min.). (Inner Talk Ser.). 16.95 (978-1-55978-360-6(5), 5376A) Progress Aware Res.
Soundtrack - Tropical Lagoon with underlying subliminal affirmations.

Concentration is Easy: Babbling Brook. Eldon Taylor. 1 cass. 16.95 (978-1-55978-496-2(2), 5376F) Progress Aware Res.

Concentration is Easy: Music Theme. Eldon Taylor. 1 cass. 16.95 (978-1-55978-152-7(1), 5376C) Progress Aware Res.

Concentration Made Easy. Norman J. Caldwell. Read by Norman J. Caldwell. Ed. by Achieve Now Institute Staff. 1 cass. (Running Time: 20 min.). (Academic Achievement Ser.). 1988. 9.97 (978-1-56273-079-6(7)) My Mothers Pub.
Be more alert, aware & focused than ever before.

Concentration Power Plus. Dick Sutphen. 1 cass. (Running Time: 1 hr.). (RX17 Ser.). 1986. 14.98 (978-0-87554-317-8(0), RX126) Valley Sun.
Total concentration is yours. You remain alert & focused upon what you are doing. You totally focus your concentration & energy at will. You can do anything you want to do. You block all thoughts but those related to what you are doing. You are a winner who accomplishes your goals.

Concentration vs Remembrance. Swami Amar Jyoti. 2 cass. 1981. 12.95 (M-14) Truth Consciousness.
God is not an object to be concentrated upon. Remembrance opens our heart.

Concept of Corporate Strategy. unabr. ed. Kenneth Andrews. Read by Jordan Rich. 5 cass. (Running Time: 60 min. per cass.). 1990. 50.00 (978-0-942563-02-3(6)); Rental 14.00 (978-0-942563-15-3(8)) CareerTapes.
This book offers an exceptionally clear & lucid description of corporate strategy, from formulation to implementation.

Concept of Energy Medicine in Indigenous Healing. Stanley Krippner. 1 cass. 9.00 (A0213-87) Sound Photosyn.
ICSS '87 with Heinze & Mehl.

Concept of God. unabr. ed. Nathaniel Branden. 1 cass. (Running Time: 1 hr. 28 min.). (Basic Principles of Objectivism Ser.). 12.95 (564) J Norton Pubs.
Topics include: is the concept meaningful? Are the arguments for the existence of God logically defensible? The destructiveness of the concept of God.

Concept of God, Set. ed. Nathaniel Branden. 2 CDs. (Running Time: 88 mins.). (Basic Principles of Objectivism Ser.). 2006. audio compact disk 14.95 (978-1-57970-399-8(2), AF0564D, Audio-For) J Norton Pubs.
Dr. Branden discusses: Is the concept of God meaningful? Are the arguments for the existence of God logically defensible? The destructiveness of the concept of God. (From the series "Basic Principles of Objectivism").

Concept of Marriage. unabr. ed. Nathaniel Branden. 1 cass. (Running Time: 1 hr. 23 min.). 12.95 (616) J Norton Pubs.
Discusses the following: unrealistic expectations concerning marriage; the problems of infidelity; is romantic love for everyone?.

Concept of Organizational Climate. unabr. ed. B. Von Haller Gilmer. 1 cass. (Running Time: 20 min.). 12.95 (13008) J Norton Pubs.
Discusses how individual personalities & job requirements interact to produce a climate that can be significant to both the individual & to the organization.

Conception. Barrie Konicov. 1 cass. 11.98 (978-0-87082-399-2(X), MS 021) Potentials.
Designed for those couples who wish to have a child, but are experiencing difficulty in consummating the pregnancy.

Conception, Perception, & Creation. Swami Amar Jyoti. 1 cass. 1977. 9.95 (O-7) Truth Consciousness.
On the law of nature & free will. The process of creation & purification. The suffering of the Saints.

Concepts for Bass Soloing. Marc Johnson & Chuck Sher. 1993. pap. bk. 26.00 (978-1-883217-00-6(8), 00242100) Pub: Sher Music. Dist(s): H Leonard

Concepts of Athletic Training. 2nd ed. Ronald P. Pfeiffer & Brent C. Mangus. (C). 1998. audio compact disk 395.00 (978-0-7637-0716-3(3), 0716-3) Jones Bartlett.

Concepts of Athletic Training. 3rd ed. Ron Pfeiffer & Brent Mangus. (C). 2001. audio compact disk 99.00 (978-0-7637-1794-0(0), 1794-0) Jones Bartlett.

Concepts of Physical Fitness: Active Lifestyles for Wellness. 10th ed. Charles B. Corbin et al. (C). 2000. pap. bk. 28.75 (978-0-07-242071-5(5), Mc-H Human Soc) McGrw-H Hghr Educ.

Concepts of Revolution. unabr. ed. 1 cass. 12.95 (C19701) J Norton Pubs.

Concepts of the Universe. 1 cass. (Running Time: 27 min.). 14.95 (8362) MMI Corp.
World views of Ptolemy, Newton, Herschel, Hubble, Galileo & Einstein discussed by Thomas Nicholson.

Conceptual Chemistry: Understanding Our World of Atoms & Molecules: Art & Lecture Presentation CD. 2nd rev. ed. Suchocki. audio compact disk 18.97 (978-0-8053-3231-5(6)) Addson-Wesley Educ.

Conceptual Chemistry: Understanding Our World of Atoms & Molecules: Computerized Test Bank. 2nd rev. ed. Suchocki. audio compact disk 49.97 (978-0-8053-3230-8(8)) Addson-Wesley Educ.

Conceptual Housecleaning. SERCON Panel. 1 cass. 9.00 (A0118-87) Sound Photosyn.
Featuring: Pohl Anderson, Nelson, Hartwell, Murphy, Randall & Pournelle.

Conceptual Level of Consciousness, Pt. 1. unabr. ed. Barbara Branden. 1 cass. (Running Time: 1 hr. 34 min.). 12.95 (704) J Norton Pubs.
Concepts as the microfilm of the mind; the destroyers of intelligence; thinking in principles; thinking in essentials; concrete-bound thinking; counterfeit thinking.

Conceptual Level of Consciousness, Pt. 2. unabr. ed. Barbara Branden. 1 cass. (Running Time: 1 hr. 37 min.). 12.95 (705) J Norton Pubs.
The socialized consciousness & the destruction of language; the importance of knowing the source & validation of one's concepts; the role of integration in thinking; evasion as the sabotaging of consciousness.

Conceptualization of Chaplaincy As a Public Ministry. 1 cass. (Care Cassettes Ser.: Vol. 12, No. 1). 1985. 10.80 Assn Prof Chaplains.

Concerning Spiritual Gifts. Tsea. 2006. audio compact disk (978-0-9797500-1-4(6)) TSEA.

Concerns of Women. 5 cass. Incl. Concerns of Women: The Changing Role of Women in the Family. Berit Lakey. 1975.; Concerns of Women: Woman's Place: A Comparison of Women & Other Minority Groups. Demie Kurz. 1975.; Concerns of Women: Women & Nonviolence. Kay Camp. 1975.; Concerns of Women: Women & Religion: Toward a New Humanity Beyond Patriarchy. Judi Breault. 1975.; 1975. 17.50 Set.; 4.50 ea. Pendle Hill.

Concerns of Women: The Changing Role of Women in the Family see Concerns of Women

Concerns of Women: Woman's Place: A Comparison of Women & Other Minority Groups see Concerns of Women

Concerns of Women: Women & Nonviolence see Concerns of Women

Concerns of Women: Women & Religion: Toward a New Humanity Beyond Patriarchy see Concerns of Women

***Concert & Contest Collection for C Flute - Book/CD Pack.** H. Voxman. 2010. pap. bk. 14.99 (978-1-4234-7717-4(0), 1423477170) H Leonard.

Concert Favorites, Vol. 1. (Essential Elements 2000 Band Ser.). 2002. audio compact disk 12.95 (978-0-634-05216-3(0)) H Leonard.

Concert for the King Anthem. Tim Van Brummelen. 1998. 5.00 (978-0-687-08550-7(0)) Abingdon.

Concert Masterworks, Pts. 1-4. Instructed by Robert Greenberg. 16 cass. (Running Time: 24 hrs.). 99.95 (978-1-56585-201-3(X), 710) Teaching Co.

Concert Masterworks, Pts. I-IV. Instructed by Robert Greenberg. 32 CDs. (Running Time: 24 hrs.). 1995. bk. 129.95 (978-1-56585-372-0(5), 710) Teaching Co.

Concert Masterworks Vol. 2: Nationalism & Expressionism in the Late 19th Century: Antonin Dvorak & Richard Strauss. Instructed by Robert Greenberg. 4 cass. (Running Time: 6 hrs.). 1995. 249.95 (978-1-56585-202-0(8)) Teaching Co.

Concert Masterworks Vol. 3: Great 19th-Century Violin Concerti: Beethoven & Brahms. Instructed by Robert Greenberg. 4 cass. (Running Time: 6 hrs.). 1995. 249.95 (978-1-56585-203-7(6)) Teaching Co.

Concert Masterworks Vol. 4: Early Romantic Era Program Music: Felix Mendelssohn's Incidental Music & Overture to a Midsummers Night's Dream & Franz Liszt's Totentanz. Instructed by Robert Greenberg. 4 cass. (Running Time: 6 hrs.). 1995. 249.95 (978-1-56585-204-4(4)) Teaching Co.

Concert of Angels. Asha. 1 cass. 10.95 (LA009); audio compact disk 15.95 (LA009D) Lghtwrks Aud & Vid.
This fully orchestrated music arouses a thrilling & moving sense of spontaneity & adventure, an evocative & spirited pilgrimage to the sublime realm of the soul. Intense & ever expressive, these compositions rejoice in their melodious & superbly inspiring nature. This is the art of the angels, & Asha's greatest skill: embodying the inner world of the soul into a music that can awaken us, change us & enlighten our everyday world.

Concert of Lifetime. Ray Boltz. 1996. video & audio compact disk 29.98 (978-7-01-990560-1(9)) Word Enter.

Concert Performer Collection. 3 CDs. 2004. audio compact disk 21.95 (978-0-8256-1957-1(2), AM974292) Pub: Music Sales. Dist(s): H Leonard

Concert Performer Series: MacDowell - To a Wild Rose. Ed. by Peter Picken. 1 CD. (Running Time: 1 hr.). (Concert Performer Ser.). 2004. audio compact disk 6.95 (978-0-8256-1739-3(1), AM948717) Pub: Music Sales. Dist(s): H Leonard

Concert Performer Series: Shumann - The Happy Farmer. Ed. by Peter Picken. 1 CD. (Running Time: 1 hr.). (Concert Performer Ser.). 2004. audio compact disk 6.95 (978-0-8256-1742-3(1), AM948740) Pub: Music Sales. Dist(s): H Leonard

Concert Pieces for the Serious Violinist: 2-CD Set. Created by Hal Leonard Corporation Staff. 2006. pap. bk. 34.98 (978-1-59615-149-9(8), 1596151498) Pub: Music Minus. Dist(s): H Leonard

Concert Solos: For the Young Player. Created by Hal Leonard Corporation Staff. 2006. pap. bk. 15.95 (978-90-431-2348-8(X), 904312348X); pap. bk. 15.95 (978-90-431-2352-5(8), 9043123528) H Leonard.

Concert Studies for Trumpet: Bb Trumpet - Grade 3-6. Philip Smith. 2001. pap. bk. 17.95 (978-90-431-1269-7(0), 9043112690) H Leonard.

Concertmaster - Solos from Symphonic Works. Created by Hal Leonard Corporation Staff. 2006. pap. bk. 29.98 (978-1-59615-147-5(1), 1596151471) Pub: Music Minus. Dist(s): H Leonard

Concerto. Instructed by Robert Greenberg. 12 cass. (Running Time: 18 hrs). 79.95 (978-1-59803-163-8(5)) Teaching Co.

Concerto. Instructed by Robert Greenberg. 24 CDs. (Running Time: 18 hrs.). 2006. audio compact disk 99.95 (978-1-59803-165-2(1)) Teaching Co.

Concerto According to Manny. Emanuel Ax. Hosted by Eric Friesen. 10 CDs. (Running Time: 10 Hours). 2007. audio compact disk 79.95 (978-0-660-19669-5(7), CBC Audio) Pub: Canadian Broadcasting CAN. Dist(s): Georgetown Term
"Manny" (Emanuel Ax) is a true piano virtuoso and a veteran of 30 years on the international scene. In his performances he combines brilliant technique with poetic lyricism and a probing intellect with a great sense of humour. Join Manny and CBC Radio Two host Eric Friesen for 10 hours of conversation, in-studio demonstrations and recordings about the world of the piano concerto. What better way to experience some of the greatest music ever written and gain insight into some of the most-loved repertoire written for the piano? This collection also contains a booklet with photographs and information on the repertoire.

Concerto According to Pinchas. Interview. Pinchas Zuckerman & Eric Friessen. 10 CDs. (Running Time: 10 hrs.). 2006. audio compact disk 79.95 (978-0-660-19618-3(2), CBC Audio) Canadian Broadcasting CAN.

Concerto in A Major, K. 622: For Clarinet & Orchestra Soloist in Concert Series. Composed by Wolfgang Amadeus Mozart. 2004. pap. bk. 29.95 (978-0-634-07951-1(4), 0634079514) Pub: Casa Ricordi ITA. Dist(s): H Leonard

Concerto in E Minor, Op. 64: For Violin & Orchestra Soloist in Concert Series. Composed by Felix Mendelssohn. 2004. pap. bk. 29.95 (978-0-634-07949-8(2), 0634079492) Pub: Casa Ricordi ITA. Dist(s): H Leonard

Concerto No. 1 in C Major, Op. 15: For Piano & Orchestra Soloist in Concert Series. Composed by Ludwig van Beethoven. 2004. pap. bk. 29.95 (978-0-634-07948-1(4), 0634079484) Pub: Casa Ricordi ITA. Dist(s): H Leonard

Concerto No. 5 in A Major K. 219: For Violin & Orchestra Soloist in Concert Series. Composed by Wolfgang Amadeus Mozart. 2004. pap. bk. 29.95 (978-0-634-07950-4(6), 0634079506) Pub: Casa Ricordi ITA. Dist(s): H Leonard

Conch Bearer. Chitra Banerjee Divakaruni. Read by Alan Cumming. 4 cass. (Running Time: 6 hrs. 31 mins.). (Brotherhood of the Conch Ser.). (J). (gr. 3 up). 2004. 32.00 (978-0-8072-1960-7(6), Listening Lib) Random Audio Pubg.

Concierto Siniestro. Fabiola Franco. 59.95 (978-0-8219-3636-8(0)) EMC-Paradigm.

Concierto Siniestro. unabr. ed. 3 cass. (Running Time: 270 mins.). (Foreign Language Mystery Thrillers Ser.). (SPA.). pap. bk. 49.95 (SSP117) J Norton Pubs.
Recorded by native professional actors, this short-episode thriller on the intermediate level, in a radio-play format, is especially created to develop your listening comprehension skills. Accompanying book provides a transcript of the recording, exercises & vocabulary.

Conciousness & Your Immune System, 1984. Read by Jack Schwarz. Contrib. by Will Noffke. 1984. 12.00 (#N3002) Aletheia Psycho.

Concise Dictionary of Biomedicine & Molecular Biology. Juo. 1999. audio compact disk 199.95 (978-0-8493-2175-7(1), 2175) Pub: CRC Pr. Dist(s): Taylor and Fran

Concise Encyclopaedia. Compiled by Encyclopaedia Britannica, Inc. 2005. audio compact disk (978-1-59339-439-4(X)) Ency Brit Inc.

***Concise History of the Middle East.** unabr. ed. Arthur Goldschmidt, Jr. & Lawrence Davidson. Read by Tom Weiner. (Running Time: 19 hrs. 30 mins.). 2010. 29.95 (978-1-4417-3980-3(7)); 99.95 (978-1-4417-3976-6(9)); audio compact disk 39.95 (978-1-4417-3979-7(3)); audio compact disk 123.00 (978-1-4417-3977-3(7)) Blckstn Audio.

Concise King. abr. ed. Read by Martin Luther King et al. Ed. by Clayborne Carson. (Running Time: 3 hrs.). (ENG.). 2009. 14.98 (978-1-60024-876-4(4)); audio compact disk 19.98 (978-1-60024-874-0(8)) Pub: Hachet Audio. Dist(s): HachBkGrp

Concise Lecture on the Essentials of Creative Writing. Carl Shapiro. 1 cass. (Running Time: 1 hr. 15 min.). 1991. 20.00 (978-0-914937-09-8(X)) Ind Pubns.
Award-winning novelist discusses, in easy to understand language, the most vital aspects of creating stories of vitality & plausibility. He explains the meaning of style, use of dialogue & shows how a writer can imbue his story or novel with insight & stimulation, which will keep readers' interest, etc.

Concise Phoenician-English English-Phoenician Dictionary. Mark A. McMenamin. 1 cass. (Running Time: 90 mins.). 2000. 20.00 (978-1-893882-02-7(0), 112) Meanma Pr.
Dictionary provides pronunciation of phoenician words & translation into English. Phoenician vocabulary for names of places is emphasized.

Conclusion - Logic & Theology: Vantillian Apologetics. John Robbins. 1 cass. (Introduction to Logic Ser.: No. 9). 5.00 Trinity Found.

Conclusion to Illusion: Spiritual vision that touches Reality. Gary Arnold. (ENG.). 2004. audio compact disk 24.95 (978-1-57867-054-3(3)) Pub: Windhorse Corp. Dist(s): New Leaf Dist

Concord Hymn see Poetry of Ralph Waldo Emerson

Concord Hymn see Ralph Waldo Emerson: Poems and Essays

Concord Hymn & Other Poems see Classic American Poetry

Concourse. unabr. ed. S. J. Rozan. Read by Sky Vogel. 8 vols. (Running Time: 8 hrs.). 1998. bk. 69.95 (978-0-7927-2245-8(0), CSL 134, Chivers Sound Lib) AudioGO.
Smith has been hired by an old friend to investigate the brutal killings of a young security guard on the Bronx Home grounds. Going undercover, he wades out into a sea of violence & lies. When a second murder is committed, he knows there's a method to the madness. With the help of a bright, young Chinese-American investigator, he uncovers a web of corruption in the Bronx. Now he has to figure out who will die next.

Concourse. unabr. ed. S. J. Rozan. Read by Sky Vogel. 9 CDs. (Running Time: 12 hrs.). 2004. audio compact disk 89.95 (978-0-7927-3146-7(8), SLD 134, Chivers Sound Lib) AudioGO.

Concrete & Abstract Functions of the Human Mind. Manly P. Hall. 1 cass. 8.95 (978-0-89314-030-4(9), C890521) Philos Res.

Concrete Blonde. abr. ed. Michael Connelly. Read by Dick Hill. 3 CDs. Library ed. (Running Time: 3 hrs.). (Harry Bosch Ser.: No. 3). 2003. audio compact disk 62.25 (978-1-59086-561-3(8), 1590865618, BAU) Brilliance Audio.
The Dollmaker was the name of the serial killer who had stalked Los Angeles ruthlessly, leaving grisly calling cards on the faces of his victims. Now, with a single faultless shot, Harry Bosch thinks he has ended the city's nightmare. But the dead man's widow is suing Harry and the LAPD for killing the wrong man - an accusation that rings terrifyingly true when a new victim is discovered with the Dollmaker's macabre signature. So, for the second time, Harry must hunt down a death-dealer who is very much alive, before he strikes again. It's a blood-tracked quest that will take Harry from the hard edges of the L.A. night to the last place he ever wanted to go - the darkness of his own heart.

Concrete Blonde. abr. ed. Michael Connelly. Read by Sheila Hart. 2 cass. (Running Time: 3 hrs.). (Harry Bosch Ser.: No. 3). 2000. 7.95 (978-1-57815-004-5(3), 1031, Media Bks Audio) Media Bks NJ.
Harry Bosch has only one way to clear his name - find the copycat serial killer.

Concrete Blonde. unabr. ed. Michael Connelly. Read by Dick Hill. (Running Time: 13 hrs.). (Harry Bosch Ser.: No. 3). 2005. 39.25 (978-1-59600-925-7(X), 9781596009257, BADLE); 24.95 (978-1-59600-924-0(1), 9781596009240, BAD); audio compact disk 24.95 (978-1-59600-922-6(5), 9781596009226, Brilliance MP3); 29.95 (978-1-59600-919-6(5), 9781596009196, BAU); audio compact disk 39.25 (978-1-59600-923-3(3), 9781596009233, Brinc Audio MP3 Lib); audio compact disk 112.25 (978-1-59600-921-9(7), 9781596009219, BriAudCD Unabrid); audio compact disk 38.95 (978-1-59600-920-2(9), 9781596009202, Bril Audio CD Unabri) Brilliance Audio.
The Dollmaker was the name of the serial killer who had stalked Los Angeles ruthlessly, leaving grisly calling cards on the faces of his victims. Now, with a single faultless shot, Harry Bosch thinks he has ended the city's nightmare. But the dead man's widow is suing Harry and the LAPD for killing the wrong man - an accusation that rings terrifyingly true when a new victim is discovered with the Dollmaker's macabre signature. So, for the second time, Harry must hunt down a death-dealer who is very much alive, before he strikes again. It's a blood-tracked quest that will take Harry from the hard edges of the L.A. night to the last place he ever wanted to go - the darkness of his own heart.

Concrete Countertops Made Simple. Fu-Tung Cheng. Photos by Matthew Millman. (Made Simple (Taunton Press) Ser.). (ENG., 2008. instr.'s gde. ed. 21.95 (978-1-56158-882-4(2), Taunt) Pub: Taunton. Dist(s): IngramPubServ

Concrete under My Chin. Ave Jeanne. Read by Ave Jeanne. 1 cass. (Running Time: 60 min.). 1985. 5.75 (978-0-932593-17-7(8)) Black Bear.
Performance poetry & jazz.

Concrete under My Chin: Portraits of the City. Ave Jeanne & Jeanne Ave. 1 cass. bk. 5.75 (978-0-932593-04-7(6)) Black Bear.

Concretizing the Principles of Objective Law. Thomas A. Bowden. 4 cass. (Running Time: 4 hrs.). 1997. 39.95 Set. (978-1-56114-328-3(6), PB44D) Second Renaissance.
An explanation of the theoretical framework of objective law.

Concurso de Castillos/Criaturas. Steck-Vaughn Staff. (SPA.). 1999. (978-0-7398-0748-4(X)) SteckVau.

Conde de Monte Cristo. adpt. ed. Scripts. Based on a novel by Alexandre Dumas. Adapted by Severino Puente. 3 CDs. (Running Time: 2 hrs. 40 min). Dramatization.Tr. of Count of Monte Cristo. (SPA.). 2003. audio compact disk 16.95i (978-0-9728598-0-6(2)) Fonolibro Inc.
The Count of Monte Cristo, Audio Book dramatized in Spanish based on the original story by Alexander Dumas, is one of the most popular novels of love and revenge of all times. It is the story of Edmund Dantes, a young sailor (Performed by Luis Jose Santander) that the day that he was named Capitan of the ship the "Faraon" and was planning to marry to his beloved Mercedes, was arrested for treason caused by a planned conspiracy done by people that envied him. After many years in prison in the Chateau D?if, he met a priest, the Abbe Faria, who imparted the knowledge and showed him the way to a great treasure. After escaping from prison and already powerful with a great fortune, Dantes assume the role of the Count of Montecristo to execute his revenge slowly finishing his accusers. (3 CDs - 3 Hour & 20 Minutes).

Conde de Montecristo. abr. ed. Alexandre Dumas. 3 CDs.Tr. of Count of Montecristo. (SPA.). 2002. audio compact disk 17.00 (978-958-9494-79-0(X)) YoYoMusic.

Condemned & Crucified. 6 cass. 19.95 (20142, HarperThor) HarpC GBR.

Condi: The Condoleezza Rice Story. abr. ed. Antonia Felix. 4 cass. (Running Time: 6 hrs.). 2002. 25.99 (978-1-58926-139-6(9), N66L-0110) Oasis Audio.
As National Security Advisor to the President and winner of the NAACP Image Award, Condoleezza Rice has never wasted time getting where she wants to be. For the first time, this biography tells the story of her remarkable life.

Condi: The Condoleezza Rice Story. abr. ed. Antonia Felix. 4 CDs. (Running Time: 6 hrs.). 2003. audio compact disk 27.99 (978-1-58926-140-2(2), N66L-011D) Oasis Audio.

Condi: The Condoleezza Rice Story. abr. ed. Antonia Felix. Narrated by Antonia Felix. (ENG.). 2003. 19.59 (978-1-60814-155-5(1)) Oasis Audio.

Condition. unabr. ed. Jennifer Haigh. Read by Jennifer Van Dyck. 11 CDs. (Running Time: 13 hrs. 30 mins.). 2008. audio compact disk 39.95 (978-0-06-155992-1(X), Harper Audio) HarperCollins Pubs.

***Condition.** unabr. ed. Jennifer Haigh. Read by Jennifer Van Dyck. (ENG.). 2008. (978-0-06-172478-7(5)); (978-0-06-172479-4(3)) HarperCollins Pubs.

Conditioned Relaxation: A Step-by-Step Program for Learning to Relax Instantly. Created by David Bresler. (ENG.). 2007. audio compact disk 19.95 (978-1-887211-00-0(4), Imag Res) AlphaBks CA.

Conditions for Enlightenment. Swami Amar Jyoti. 1 cass. 1976. 9.95 (R-7) Truth Consciousness.
Preparing the instrument for realization. Being with God, fully conscious each moment. The mystery of relativity. What is a true devotee?.

Conditions for Entrance. Elbert Willis. 1 cass. (Understanding the Crucified Life Ser.). 4.00 Fill the Gap.

Conditions for Protection. Elbert Willis. 1 cass. (Angel Protection Guidelines Ser.). 4.00 Fill the Gap.

Condoleezza Rice: An American Life: A Biography. unabr. ed. Elisabeth Bumiller. Read by Kimberly Farr. 11 CDs. (Running Time: 14 hrs.). 2007. audio compact disk 80.00 (978-1-4159-4854-5(2)) Random.

Condominium. unabr. collector's ed. John D. MacDonald. Read by Michael Prichard. 10 cass. (Running Time: 15 hrs.). 1977. 80.00 (978-0-7366-0066-8(3), 1077) Books on Tape.
Set in the Florida Keys, this book centers around the "Condo Culture." Greed & indifference are epitomized by condominium developer Martin Liss, with condo residents being victims.

Condominium Conversion. William M. Ellis et al. 4 cass. (Running Time: 2 hrs.). 25.00 (796-799) J Norton Pubs.

Condominium Transactions from A to Z. Contrib. by Wendell A. Smith & Benjamin D. Lambert, Jr. (Running Time: 6 hrs.). 1985. 150.00 incl. program handbook. NJ Inst CLE.
Provides guidance for condo, co-op & HOA formats, conversions, tenant protection, powers & duties of associations, governing documents, warranties, statutory controls, phasing & sectionalizing.

Condor. Adalbert Stifter. 1 cass. (Running Time: 1 hrs.). (GER.). 1996. pap. bk. 19.50 (978-1-58085-202-9(5)) Interlingua VA.

Condor Canyon. Larry J. Martin. 1 cass. 1994. (978-1-885339-02-7(X)) Wolfpack Pub.
Western fiction.

Condor Magic. Lyn Litlefield Hoopes. Narrated by Tom Chapin. (Humane Society of the United States Animal Tales Ser.). (J). (gr. 1-4). 1997. pap. bk. 19.95 (978-1-882728-99-2(8)) Benefactory.
The true story of the near extinction of the California condor.

Condor Magic. Lyn Litlefield Hoopes. Read by Tom Chapin. (J). (gr. 1-4). 1997. bk. 34.95 (978-1-882728-97-8(1)); pap. bk. 9.95 (978-1-58021-002-7(3)) Benefactory.

Conduct Effective Interviews & Hire the Right People. PUEI. 2007. audio compact disk 199.00 (978-1-934147-67-2(2), Fred Pryor) P Univ E Inc.

Conduct of Major Maxim. unabr. ed. Gavin Lyall. Read by Robin Browne. 8 cass. (Running Time: 9 hrs. 15 min.). 2001. 69.95 (978-1-85089-872-6(3), 92062) Pub: ISIS Audio GBR. Dist(s): Ulverscroft US
When Corporal Ron Blagg killed a German registrar of births & deaths, the Secret Service chose to forget he'd been working for them at the time. Now Blagg is AWOL & running scared. If anyone can help him it will be a soldier who can survive in the world of pinstriped cloak & old school dagger. A soldier like Major Harry Maxim.

Conduct to the Prejudice of Good Order: Final Years of the Vietnam War. Dan Dane. Music by Mike Morningstar. Narrated by Ross Ballard. (ENG.). 2003. audio compact disk 34.95 (978-0-9717801-3-2(7)) Mtn Whispers Pubng.

Conduct Unbecoming: Gays & Lesbians in the U. S. Military, Set. abr. ed. Randy Shilts. Read by Robby Benson. 4 cass. (Running Time: 6 hrs.). 1993. 24.95 (978-1-879371-59-0(6), 692174) Pub Mills.
Celebrated journalist, Randy Shilts interviewed over 1,100 gay & lesbian servicemen & women over a five year period to document the creation of a vast gay subculture within the armed forces & the behind-the-scenes decision making that resulted in the fierce purging of gays in military over the past thirty years.

***Conduct Unbecoming: How Barack Obama Is Destroying the Military & Endangering Our Security.** unabr. ed. Robert Patterson. (Running Time: 8 hrs. 30 mins.). 2010. 29.95 (978-1-4417-6260-3(4)); 54.95 (978-1-4417-6257-3(4)); audio compact disk 76.00 (978-1-4417-6258-0(2)); audio compact disk 29.95 (978-1-4417-6259-7(0)) Blckstn Audio.

Conducting a Successful Interview. unabr. ed. James Richard. 1 cass. (Running Time: 50 min.). 1985. 9.95 Newtown Psychological Ctr.
Covers a number of ways to initiate, maintain, & terminate an interview.

Conducting a Winning Deposition. unabr. ed. Ronald J. Cohen. Read by Ronald Jay Cohen. 6 cass. (Running Time: 6 hrs.). 1996. pap. bk. 165.00 Set. PEG MN.
Explores & builds on the fundamentals of depositions.

Conductor. unabr. ed. Jerry Kennealy. 10 cass. (Running Time: 14 hrs. 30 mins.). 1996. 69.95 (978-0-7861-1046-9(5), 1818) Blckstn Audio.
Mary Ariza, a beautiful, savvy lawyer, knows all the ins & outs of the law & the lawless. Nothing that anyone can do & try to get away with can make her blink. But now, as she stops to help a man having a heart attack on the street, she unknowingly marks herself for death.

Conductor. unabr. ed. Jerry Kennealy. Read by Christopher Lane. (Running Time: 50400 sec.). 2008. audio compact disk 29.95 (978-0-7861-6253-6(8)); audio compact disk & audio compact disk 99.00 (978-0-7861-6252-9(X)) Blckstn Audio.

Conductor & the Orchestra: The Music of Forgiveness. Kenneth Wapnick. 4 CDs. 2006. audio compact disk 23.00 (978-1-59142-228-0(0), CD119) Foun Miracles.

Conductor & the Orchestra: The Music of Forgiveness. Kenneth Wapnick. 2009. 18.00 (978-1-59142-458-1(5)) Foun Miracles.

Cone. unabr. ed. H. G. Wells. Read by Ralph Cosham. 2 cass. (Running Time: 2 hrs. 15 min.). 1994. lib. bdg. 18.95 set incl. vinyl case with notes, author's picture & biography. (978-1-883049-26-3(1)) Sound Room.
A collection of short fiction: "The Cone", "The Diamond Maker", "The Door in the Wall", & "The Country of the Blind".

Cone, Set. unabr. ed. Short Stories. H. G. Wells. Read by Ralph Cosham. 2 cass. (Running Time: 2 hrs. 32 mins.). (H. G. Wells Ser.). 1994. bk. 16.95 Set, trade ed. (978-1-883049-07-2(5), 390207, Commuters Library) Sound Room.
Includes: "The Cone," "The Diamond Maker," "The Door in the Wall" & "The Country of the Blind.".

Conectando con mis Hijos. Marcos Richards. (SPA.). 2003. 3.99 (978-1-885630-72-8(7)) Jayah Producc.

Cones All Around: Early Explorers Emergent Set B Audio CD. Katherine Scraper. Adapted by Benchmark Education Staff. (J). 2007. audio compact disk 10.00 (978-1-4108-8198-4(9)) Benchmark Educ.

Conexion Cuaderno de Ejercicios. Javier Llano et al. (Running Time: 1 hr. 55 mins.). (SPA.). 2001. tchr. ed. 15.00 (978-84-8323-214-9(6)) Cambridge U Pr.

Conexion 2 para el Profesor. Javier Llano et al. (SPA.). 2002. tchr. ed. (978-84-8323-311-5(8)) Cambridge U Pr.

Conexiones: Comunicacion y Cultura. Eduardo Zayas-Bazan. (SPA.). (YA). 2001. stu. ed. 10.97 (978-0-13-920943-7(3), Prentice Hall) P-H.

Conexiones: Comunicacion y Cultura: Audio CD for Student Text. 3rd ed. Eduardo Zayas-Bazan et al. (SPA.). audio compact disk & audio compact disk 10.97 (978-0-13-193523-5(2)) PH School.

Conexiones: Comunicacion y Cultura: Audio CD for Testing Program. 3rd ed. Eduardo Zayas-Bazan et al. (SPA.). audio compact disk 19.97 (978-0-13-193529-7(1)) PH School.

Conexiones: Comunicacion y Cultura: Audio CDs for Student Activities Manual. 3rd ed. Eduardo Zayas-Bazan et al. (SPA.). stu. ed. 47.97 (978-0-13-193534-1(8)); stu. ed. 28.97 (978-0-13-193520-4(8)) PH School.

Conexiones: Comunicacion y Cultura: Instructor's Music CD. 3rd ed. Eduardo Zayas-Bazan et al. (SPA.). audio compact disk (978-0-13-193511-2(9)) PH School.

Confederacy of Dunces. unabr. ed. John Kennedy Toole. Read by Barrett Whitener. 12 CDs. (Running Time: 48600 sec.). 2005. audio compact disk 34.95 (978-0-7861-8246-6(6), ZE1978) Blckstn Audio.

Confederacy of Dunces: A Novel. John Kennedy Toole. Read by Barrett Whitener. 12 CDs. (Running Time: 14 hrs.). 2003. audio compact disk 19.95 (978-0-7861-9214-4(3)); audio compact disk 96.00 (978-0-7861-9879-5(6), 1978) Blckstn Audio.
A green hunting cap squeezed the top of the fleshy balloon of a head. The green earflaps, full of large ears and uncut hair and the fine bristles that grew in the ears themselves, stuck out on either side like turn signals indicating two directions at once. So enters one of the most memorable characters in recent American fiction.This story bursts with wholly original characters, denizens of New Orleans' lower depths, incredibly true-to-life dialogue, and the zaniest series of high and low comic adventures.

Confederacy of Dunces: A Novel. John Kennedy Toole. Read by Barrett Whitener. 12 CDs. (Running Time: 18 hrs.). 2000. audio compact disk 96.00 (z1978) Blckstn Audio.
A huge comic-satiric-tragic one-of-a-kind rendering of the life in New Orleans.

Confederacy of Dunces: A Novel. unabr. ed. John Kennedy Toole. Read by Barrett Whitener. 10 cass. (Running Time: 14 hrs. 30 mins.). 2003. 69.95 (978-0-7861-1232-6(8), 1978) Blckstn Audio.
Comic-satiric-tragic one-of-a-kind rendering of the life in New Orleans.

Confederacy of Dunces: A Novel. unabr. ed. John Kennedy Toole. Read by Raymond Todd. 10 cass. 2004. 39.95 (978-0-7861-2223-3(4)) Blckstn Audio.

Confederacy of Dunces: A Novel. unabr. ed. John Kennedy Toole. Read by Barrett Whitener. 20 cass. (Running Time: 14 hrs. 30 mins.). 2005. reel tape 32.95 (978-0-7861-2916-4(6), E1978); audio compact disk 29.95 (978-0-7861-8310-4(1), ZM1978) Blckstn Audio.

Confederate States of America. abr. ed. Howard Means. Read by Richard Gilliland. 4 cass. (Running Time: 6 hrs.). 2001. 25.00 (978-1-59040-175-0(1), Phoenix Audio) Pub: Amer Intl Pub. Dist(s): PerseuPGW

Confederates in the Attic: Dispatches from the Unfinished Civil War. Read by Arthur Addison. Ed. by Tony Horwitz. 1999. audio compact disk 104.00 (978-0-7366-6064-8(X)) Books on Tape.

Confederates in the Attic: Dispatches from the Unfinished Civil War. unabr. ed. Tony Horwitz. Read by Arthur Addison. 11 cass. (Running Time: 16 hrs. 30 min.). 1999. 88.00 (978-0-7366-4405-1(9), 4866) Books on Tape.
After years of filing dispatches from foreign war zones, the author comes home to the Blue Ridge Mountains only to be awakened by the crackle of musket fire. The author starts filing front line dispatches again - this time from a war close to home & close to his own heart. Propelled by his boyhood passion for the Civil War, the author joins a band of "hardcover" reenactos who crash-diet to achieve the hollow-eyed look of starved Confederates; in Kentucky, he witnesses Klan rallies & calls for race wars & in the book's climax, the author takes a marathon trek from Antietam to Gettysburg to Appomattox.

Confederates in the Attic: Dispatches from the Unfinished Civil War. unabr. ed. Tony Horwitz. Read by Arthur Addison. 13 CDs. (Running Time: 19 hrs. 30 mins.). 2001. audio compact disk 104.00 Books on Tape.
Propelled by his boyhood passion for the Civil War, Tony Horwitz leads us on journey to places and lives held captive by its legacy.

Conference Committees: Capitol Learning Audio Course. Elizabeth Rybicki. Prod. by TheCapitol.Net. (ENG.). 2008. 47.00 (978-1-58733-021-6(0)) TheCapitol.

Conference of Friends in the Americas: Courage for Today - Hope for Tomorrow see Conference of Friends in the Americas: Living in the Spirit

Conference of Friends in the Americas: Go Ye Into All the World see Conference of Friends in the Americas: Living in the Spirit

Conference of Friends in the Americas: God, Christ & World Reconciliation see Conference of Friends in the Americas: Living in the Spirit

Conference of Friends in the Americas: Living in the Spirit. 9 cass. Incl. Conference of Friends in the Americas: Courage for Today - Hope for Tomorrow. Lorton Heusel. 1977.; Conference of Friends in the Americas: Go Ye Into All the World. Harold Smuck. 1977.; Conference of Friends in the Americas: God, Christ & World Reconciliation. Everett Cattell. 1977.; Conference of Friends in the Americas: Quaker Service Without Proclamation. Wallace Collett. 1977.; Conference of Friends in the Americas: Quaker Support for Latin Aspirations. Betty R. Nute. 1977.; Conference of Friends in the Americas: Sacramental Living Without Ritual. Jennifer Haines. 1977.; Conference of Friends in the Americas: The Difference Faith Makes. Mary Autenrieth. 1977.; Conference of Friends in the Americas: Thou Shalt Love the Lord Thy God. Marjorie Sykes. 1977.; Conference of Friends in the Americas: Thou Shalt Love Thy Neighbor. Louis Schneider. 1977.; 1977. 28.00 Set.; 4.50 ea. Pendle Hill.

Conference of Friends in the Americas: Quaker Service Without Proclamation see Conference of Friends in the Americas: Living in the Spirit

Conference of Friends in the Americas: Quaker Support for Latin Aspirations see Conference of Friends in the Americas: Living in the Spirit

Conference of Friends in the Americas: Sacramental Living Without Ritual see Conference of Friends in the Americas: Living in the Spirit

Conference of Friends in the Americas: The Difference Faith Makes see Conference of Friends in the Americas: Living in the Spirit

Conference of Friends in the Americas: Thou Shalt Love the Lord Thy God see Conference of Friends in the Americas: Living in the Spirit

Conference of Friends in the Americas: Thou Shalt Love Thy Neighbor see Conference of Friends in the Americas: Living in the Spirit

Conference on Christianity & Roman Catholicism Series. 9 cass. 45.00 Set. Trinity Found.

Conference on Life Insurance Company Products: Current Securities, Tax, ERISA, & State Regulatory Issues. 8 cass. (Running Time: 11 hrs.). 1997. 275.00 Set; incl. study guide 613p. (MC26) Am Law Inst.
Advanced, concentrated course.

Conference on Life Insurance Litigation. 7 cass. (Running Time: 10 hrs. 30 min.). 1998. 275.00 Set; incl. study guide 295p. (MC72) Am Law Inst.
Advanced course provides a complete overview of recent trends analyzed from both defense & plaintiff's perspectives at company & industry levels.

Confess, Fletch. unabr. ed. Gregory Mcdonald. Read by Gardner Grover. 7 cass. (Running Time: 7 hrs.). (Fletch Ser.: No. 2). 1988. 42.00 (978-0-7366-1323-1(4), 2227) Books on Tape.
Peter Fletcher is back from Europe with another promise of marriage & a fortune in lost paintings behind him. What appears to be a simple apartment swap turns into a web of intrigue when Fletch finds the flat over-decorated with a beautiful corpse. All the evidence points to only one person who could have committed the crime, & Fletch doesn't think that he did it. The police think differently. Fletch figures that if he won't confess, he'll have to find the murderer himself.

Confessing for Money. Peggy M. Fielding. Read by Peggy M. Fielding. 1 cass. (Running Time: 90 mins.). (ENG.). 1990. 12.95 (978-1-880717-20-2(4),) Writers AudioShop.
Inside information on how to write for the largest short story market, the confession magazines. Recorded live at Austin Writers' League workshop.

Confession. Kenneth E. Hagin. 4 cass. 16.00 (26H) Faith Lib Pubns.

Confession. Contrib. by Joshua Williams. 2007. audio compact disk 12.95 (978-5-557-72135-6(5)) WinePress Pub.

Confession. Joshua Williams. 2008. audio compact disk 12.95 (978-82-8857-000-2(3)) WinePress Pub.

***Confession.** abr. ed. John Grisham. Read by Dylan Baker & Scott Sowers. (Running Time: 6 hrs. 30 mins.). (ENG.). 2010. audio compact disk 32.00 (978-0-7393-7617-1(9), Random AudioBks) Pub: Random Audio Pubg. Dist(s): Random

***Confession.** abr. ed. James E. Mcgreevey. Read by James E. Mcgreevey. (ENG.). 2006. (978-0-06-122991-6(1), Harper Audio); (978-0-06-122992-3(X), Harper Audio) HarperCollins Pubs.

***Confession.** unabr. ed. John Grisham. Read by Dylan Baker & Scott Sowers. (ENG.). 2010. audio compact disk 45.00 (978-0-7393-7619-5(5), Random AudioBks) Pub: Random Audio Pubg. Dist(s): Random

Confession. unabr. ed. Beverly Lewis. Read by Marguerite Gavin. 5 cass. (Running Time: 7 hrs.). (Heritage of Lancaster County Ser.: No. 2). 2001. 39.95 (978-0-7861-2592-0(6), 3193); audio compact disk 48.00 (978-0-7861-8947-2(9), 3193) Blckstn Audio.

Confession. unabr. ed. Beverly Lewis. Narrated by Barbara Caruso. 6 cass. (Running Time: 8 hrs. 15 mins.). (Heritage of Lancaster County Ser.: No. 2). 51.00 (978-0-7887-2775-7(3), 95671E7) Recorded Bks.
Katie Lapp has set out to find Laura Mayfield, the birth mother she has never known. But even as she draws near to Laura, evil plans are working to tear away their happiness & their inheritance. Available to libraries only.

Confession. unabr. ed. Len Steinhauer. Read by Robertson Dean. 9 CDs. (Running Time: 11 hrs. 30 mins.). 2003. audio compact disk 72.00 (978-0-7861-8789-8(1), 3218) Blckstn Audio.
With deaths and deceptions snowballing grotesquely.

Confession. unabr. ed. Len Steinhauer. Read by Robertson Dean. 8 cass. (Running Time: 11 hrs. 30 mins.). 2004. 56.95 (978-0-7861-2628-6(0), 3218) Blckstn Audio.

Confession. unabr. ed. Olen Steinhauer. Read by Robertson Dean. 7 pieces. 2004. reel tape 35.95 (978-0-7861-2657-6(4)); audio compact disk 39.95 (978-0-7861-8879-6(0)) Blckstn Audio.

Confession, Set. unabr. ed. Mary Roberts Rinehart. Read by Flo Gibson. 2 cass. (Running Time: 3 hrs.). 1997. 14.95 (978-1-55685-469-9(2), 469-2) Audio Bk Con.
Was that dear little lady Emily Benton guilty of murder or was the written confession trumped up? A suspenseful tale full of caring.

Confession Brings Possession. Bill Winston. 6 cass. (Running Time: 4hr.40min.). (C). 1997. 20.00 (978-1-931289-62-7(X)) Pub: B Winston Min. Dist(s): Anchor Distributors

Confession of Brother Haluin. unabr. ed. Ellis Peters, pseud. Read by Stephen Thorne. 5 cass. (Running Time: 6 hrs. 38 mins.). (Chronicles of Brother Cadfael Ser.: Vol. 15). 2002. 27.95 (978-1-57270-257-8(5)) Pub: Audio Partners. Dist(s): PerseuPGW
The time: 1142. The place: the Benedictine Abbey. Believing himself mortally injured, Brother Haluin makes a shocking confession to Brother Cadfael. When he recovers, the two embark on a pilgrimage to redress the past.

Confession of Brother Haluin. unabr. ed. Ellis Peters, pseud. Read by Stephen Thorne. 6 cass. (Running Time: 6 hrs.). (Chronicles of Brother Cadfael Ser.: Vol. 15). 1995. 54.95 Set. (978-0-7451-4380-4(6), CAB 1064) AudioGO.
The December of 1142 brings a smothering snow that damages a hall at the Benedictine Abbey. As the brothers begin repair, the icy conditions prove near-fatal for Brother Haluin as he slips & has a terrible fall. Apparently on his deathbed, he makes a startling confession to Brother Cadfael. A shocking story of trespass hard for God to forgive emerges. But Haluin does not die. On his recovery, he sets out on a journey of expiation, with Cadfael as his sole companion. An arduous trip, it leads to some shocking discoveries & to murder.

Confession of Brother Haluin. unabr. ed. Ellis Peters, pseud. Read by Stephen Thorne. 6 cass. (Running Time: 9 hrs.). (Chronicles of Brother Cadfael Ser.: Vol. 15). 2000. 49.95 (CAB 1064) Pub: Chivers Audio Bks GBR. Dist(s): AudioGO

Confession of Brother Haluin. unabr. ed. Ellis Peters, pseud. Narrated by Patrick Tull. 6 cass. (Running Time: 7 hrs. 30 mins.). (Chronicles of Brother Cadfael Ser.: Vol. 15). 51.00 (978-0-7887-0322-5(6), 94514E7) Recorded Bks.
Brother Cadfael accompanies a crippled young monk on his journey of penance - a path that will lead them into a web of old jealousy and deceit. Available to libraries only.

***Confessional.** unabr. ed. Jack Higgins. Read by Michael Page. (Running Time: 8 hrs.). (Liam Devlin Ser.: Bk. 3). 2010. 24.99 (978-1-4418-4370-8(1), 9781441843708, Brilliance MP3); 39.97 (978-1-4418-4371-5(X), 9781441843715, Brinc Audio MP3 Lib); 24.99 (978-1-4418-4372-2(8), 9781441843722, BAD); 39.97 (978-1-4418-4373-9(6), 9781441843739, BADLE); audio compact disk 29.99 (978-1-4418-4368-5(X), 9781441843685, Bril Audio CD Unabri); audio compact disk 87.97 (978-1-4418-4369-2(8), 9781441843692, BriAudCD Unabrid) Brilliance Audio.

Confessions see Treasury of French Prose

Confessions. Text by Saint Augustine. 9 cass. (Running Time: 13 hrs.). 1992. 62.95 (978-0-7861-0134-4(2), 1119) Blckstn Audio.

Confessions. Saint Augustine. Narrated by Adam Dudley. (Running Time: 7 hrs. 3 mins.). 2006. audio compact disk 42.95 (978-0-9790364-4-6(5)) A Audiobooks.
Considered by many to be the first autobiography/memoir ever written, Confessions is a retrospective view of a life challenged by uncertainty, doubt, human frailty, and earthly desires. Augustine discovers and cherishes a deeply personal relationship with his God, all while describing the day-to-day dealings of his life in the fading, corrupt days of the Roman Empire.

Confessions. Enid Dame. Ed. by Stanley H. Barkan. (Cross-Cultural Review Chapbook Ser.: No. 12: American Poetry 6). 1980. 10.00 (978-0-89304-836-5(4)) Cross-Cultrl NY.

Confessions. unabr. ed. Kate Brian, pseud. Narrated by Cassandra Campbell. (Running Time: 6 hrs. 0 mins. 0 sec.). (Private Ser.: No. 4). (ENG.). (J). 2010. audio compact disk 59.99 (978-1-4001-4234-7(2)) Pub: Tantor Media. Dist(s): IngramPubServ

Confessions. unabr. ed. Kate Brian, pseud. Narrated by Cassandra Campbell. (Running Time: 6 hrs. 0 mins. 0 sec.). (Private Ser.: No. 4). (ENG.). (YA). (gr. 9-12). 2010. 19.99 (978-1-4001-6234-5(3)); audio compact disk 29.99 (978-1-4001-1234-0(6)) Pub: Tantor Media. Dist(s): IngramPubServ

Confessions. unabr. ed. Read by Bernard Mayes. Text by Saint Augustine. 9 cass. (Running Time: 13 hrs. 30 min.). 1995. 62.95 (978-0-7861-0661-5(1), 1119) Blckstn Audio.
This is an altogether timeless work, completely applicable to everyone who has experienced the struggle between good & evil in his own soul.

Confessions, Pt. 1. unabr. ed. Jean-Jacques Rousseau. Read by Frederick Davidson. 11 cass. (Running Time: 30 hrs. 30 mins.). 1995. 76.95 (978-0-7861-0758-2(8), 1608A,B) Blckstn Audio.
"Confessions" is Rousseau's landmark autobiography. Both brilliant & flawed, it is nonetheless beautifully written & remains one of the most moving human documents in all of literature. In this work, Rousseau "frankly & sincerely" settles accounts with himself in an effort to project his "true" image to the world. In so doing he reveals the details of a man who paid little regard to accepted morality & social conventions.

Confessions, Pt. 2. unabr. ed. Jean-Jacques Rousseau. Read by Frederick Davidson. 10 cass. (Running Time: 30 hrs. 30 mins.). 1995. 69.95 (978-0-7861-0759-9(6), 1608A,B) Blckstn Audio.
Rousseau's landmark autobiography. Both brilliant & flawed, it is nonetheless beautifully written & remains one of the most moving human documents in all of literature. In this work, Rousseau "frankly & sincerely" settles accounts with himself in an effort to project his "true" image to the world. In so doing he reveals the details of a man who paid little regard to accepted morality & social conventions.

Confessions of a Caffeine Addict. (ENG.). 2011. 39.95 (978-0-9747582-0-6(5)) SCR.

Confessions of a Contractor. unabr. ed. Richard Murphy. Read by Dan John Miller. 1 MP3-CD. (Running Time: 8 hrs.). 2009. 24.99 (978-1-4233-8322-2(2), 9781423383222, Brilliance MP3); 39.97 (978-1-4233-8323-9(0), 9781423383239, Brlnc Audio MP3 Lib); 39.97 (978-1-4233-8325-3(7), 9781423383253, BADLE); 24.99 (978-1-4233-8324-6(9), 9781423383246, BAD) Brilliance Audio.

Confessions of a Contractor. unabr. ed. Richard Murphy. Read by Dan john Miller. 7 CDs. (Running Time: 8 hrs.). 2009. audio compact disk 34.99 (978-1-4233-8320-8(6), 9781423383208, Bril Audio CD Unabri) Brilliance Audio.

Confessions of a Contractor. unabr. ed. Richard Murphy. Read by Dan John Miller. 7 CDs. (Running Time: 8 hrs.). 2009. audio compact disk 92.97 (978-1-4233-8321-5(4), 9781423383215, BriAudCD Unabrid) Brilliance Audio.

Confessions of a Dangerous Mind Movie-Tie In: An Unauthorized Autobiography. Chuck Barris. 2004. 15.95 (978-0-7435-4526-6(5)) Pub: S&S Audio. Dist(s): S and S Inc

Confessions of a Divorced Kid. Steve Sullivan. Read by Steve Sullivan. Contrib. by Amy Pecora. 1 cass. (Running Time: 30 min.). (J). (gr. 1-6). cass. & video 12.95 (978-1-890522-02-5(3)) Motivat Resources.
Crisis points of divorce through the eyes of two kids & optimistically concludes that there is life after separation.

Confessions of a Grinder. unabr. collector's ed. Brad A. Lewis. Read by Paul Shay. 8 cass. (Running Time: 8 hrs.). 1989. 48.00 (978-0-7366-1636-2(5), 2491) Books on Tape.
Olympic Gold Medalist Brad Lewis brings to life the glory of an event most sailors only dream about - racing in the America's Cup. Spanning eight months of training & competition from San Francisco to Australia, Confessions of a Grinder bursts with the humor, pain & romance of the race for sailing's most coveted prize. Lewis relives glorious days of sun & surf, rolling waves & squalls, as the USA syndicate turns individuals into one of the world's top sailing teams. You'll get a sailor's mainsail view of the characters who make this life their own, including Dennis Connor, Buddy Melges, Alan Bond & USA's Tom "we don't just want the Cup, we want the whole damned island" Blackaller.

Confessions of a High Roller: Ecc. 9:11-18. Told to Ed Young. 1994. 4.95 (978-0-7417-1999-7(1), 999) Win Walk.

Confessions of a Hollywood P.I. Case File - Babes in Babylon. abr. ed. Don Crutchfield & Mark Hendrickson. 2 cass. (Running Time: 4 hrs.). 1997. 16.95 (978-1-889261-01-0(7)) SOS Beverly Hills.
Inside stories of the effect of fame & fortune on young people raised in Hollywood.

***Confessions of a Jane Austen Addict.** Laurie Viera Rigler. Read by Orlagh Cassidy. (Playaway Adult Fiction Ser.). (ENG.). 2009. 64.99 (978-1-61574-526-5(2)) Find a World.

Confessions of a Knife, unabr. ed. Richard Selzer. Narrated by Sam Gray. 6 cass. (Running Time: 8 hrs. 15 mins.). 51.00 (978-0-7887-0400-0(1), 94592E7) Recorded Bks.
Selzer opens windows on the world of medical oddities in this collection of candid, introspective essays. Selections including "Sarcophagus," "Pages from a Wound-Dresser's Diary" & "Love Sick," reveal Selzer's boundless curiosity about medicine, life & art. Available to libraries only.

Confessions of a Knife. unabr. collector's ed. Richard Selzer. Read by Christopher Hurt. 7 cass. (Running Time: 7 hrs.). 1984. 42.00 (978-0-7366-0615-8(7), 1577) Books on Tape.
Richard Selzer is a poet of surgeons in America who explores not only the human body, but the mind & soul as well. These essays are autobiographical & extend into emotional & medical territory commonly avoided by other writers.

Confessions of a Madwoman: With music by Doll Imago: an Oral Journey. MariJo Moore. Score by Kelly Ward. (ENG.). 2007. (978-0-9767581-4-3(8)) Renegade Planets.

Confessions of a Medical Heretic, unabr. ed. Robert S. Mendelsohn. Narrated by Alan Sklar. 6 cass. (Running Time: 8 hrs. 15 mins.). 1993. 51.00 (978-1-55690-948-1(9), 93430E7) Recorded Bks.
It may be a little disconcerting to hear a medically licensed physician tell you to avoid doctors! avoid hospitals! avoid medication! But that's what this noted patient advocate & nationally syndicated columnist does. If you want to find out how to protect yourself when dealing with doctors, this book is for you. A rejuvenating manual on how to gain control over your own body.

Confessions of a Medical Heretic. unabr. ed. Robert S. Mendelsohn. Read by Alan Sklar. 6 cass. (Running Time: 8 hrs 15 min.). 1993. 49.00 set. (978-1-55690-934-4(9), 93430) Recorded Bks.

Confessions of a Mullah Warrior. unabr. ed. Masood Farivar. Read by Christopher Lane. 1 MP3-CD. (Running Time: 11 hrs.). 2009. 39.97 (978-1-4233-8411-3(3), 9781423384113, Brlnc Audio MP3 Lib) Brilliance Audio.

Confessions of a Mullah Warrior. unabr. ed. Masood Farivar. Read by Christopher A. Lane. 1 MP3-CD. (Running Time: 11 hrs.). 2009. 24.99 (978-1-4233-8410-6(5), 9781423384106, Brilliance MP3) Brilliance Audio.

Confessions of a Mullah Warrior. unabr. ed. Masood Farivar. Read by Christopher Lane. (Running Time: 11 hrs.). 2009. 39.97 (978-1-4233-8413-7(X), 9781423384137, BADLE); audio compact disk 89.97 (978-1-4233-8409-0(1), 9781423384090, BriAudCD Unabrid) Brilliance Audio.

Confessions of a Mullah Warrior. unabr. ed. Masood Farivar. Read by Christopher A. Lane. 9 CDs. (Running Time: 11 hrs.). 2009. audio compact disk 29.99 (978-1-4233-8408-3(3), 9781423384083, Bril Audio CD Unabri) Brilliance Audio.

Confessions of a Mullah Warrior. unabr. ed. Masood Farivar & Masood Farivar. Read by Christopher Lane. (Running Time: 11 hrs.). 2009. 24.99 (978-1-4233-8412-0(1), 9781423384120, BAD) Brilliance Audio.

Confessions of a Nerd. Read by Marco A. V. Bitetto. Read by Marco A. V. Bitetto. 1 cass. 1999. 24.50 (978-1-58578-005-1(7)) Inst of Cybernetics.

Confessions of a Party Animal: Ecc. 2:1-11. Ed Young. 1993. 4.95 (978-0-7417-1978-2(9), 978) Win Walk.

Confessions of a Radical Industrialist: Profits, People, Purpose - Doing Business by Respecting the Earth. unabr. ed. Ray C. Anderson & Robin White. (Running Time: 10 hrs. 0 mins.). (ENG.). 2009. 29.95 (978-1-4417-0683-6(6)); 59.95 (978-1-4417-0679-9(8)); audio compact disk 90.00 (978-1-4417-0680-5(1)); audio compact disk & audio compact disk 29.95 (978-1-4417-0682-9(8)) Blckstn Audio.

Confessions of a Real Estate Entrepreneur: What It Takes to Win in High-Stakes Commercial Real Estate. James A. Randel. 2007. audio compact disk 28.00 (978-1-933309-65-1(2)) Pub: A Media Intl. Dist(s): Natl Bk Netwk

Confessions of a Reformed Dieter. unabr. ed. A. J. Rochester. Read by A. J. Rochester. 6 cass. (Running Time: 9 hrs. 45 mins.). 2003. 48.00 (978-1-74030-985-1(5)) Pub: Bolinda Pubng AUS. Dist(s): Bolinda Pub Inc

Confessions of a Reformed Dieter. unabr. ed. A. J. Rochester. Read by A. J. Rochester. 8 CDs. (Running Time: 9 hrs. 45 mins.). 2003. audio compact disk 87.95 (978-1-74093-082-6(7)) Pub: Bolinda Pubng AUS. Dist(s): Bolinda Pub Inc

Confessions of a Reformed People Pleaser. 1. 2005. audio compact disk 6.00 (978-1-932316-21-6(3)) Great C Pubng.

***Confessions of a Reformission Rev: Hard Lessons from an Emerging Missional Church.** Mark Driscoll. (Running Time: 5 hrs. 29 mins. 0 sec.). (Leadership Network Innovation Ser.). (ENG.). 2009. 16.99 (978-0-310-30469-2(5)) Zondervan.

Confessions of a Serial Novelist. (Running Time: 3600 sec.). 2007. audio compact disk 12.99 (978-1-4281-2935-1(9)) Recorded Bks.

Confessions of a Shopaholic. Sophie Kinsella, pseud. Narrated by Emily Gray. 8 cass. (Running Time: 11 hrs. 45 mins.). (Shopaholic Ser.: Bk. 1). 76.00 (978-1-4025-3392-1(6)) Recorded Bks.

Confessions of a Shopaholic. Sophie Kinsella, pseud. 7 cass. (Running Time: 11 hrs. 45 mins.). (Shopaholic Ser.: Bk. 1). 2004. 29.99 (978-1-4025-3603-8(8), 02504) Recorded Bks.

Confessions of a Shopaholic. unabr. ed. Sophie Kinsella, pseud. Read by Emily Gray. 10 CDs. (Running Time: 11.75 Hrs.). (Shopaholic Ser.: Bk. 1). 2005. audio compact disk 29.99 (978-1-4193-4700-9(4)) Recorded Bks.

***Confessions of a Spam King, vol. 1.** Bill Waggoner. (Running Time: 280). 2010. audio compact disk 14.00 (978-0-9819362-4-6(5)) EW Pubng.

Confessions of a Spy. unabr. ed. Pete Earley. Read by Edward Holland. (Running Time: 15 hrs. 5 mins.). 2008. cass. & audio compact disk 99.00 (978-0-7861-6222-2(8)) Blckstn Audio.

Confessions of a Spy: The Real Story of Aldrich Ames. unabr. ed. Pete Earley. Read by Edward Holland. 11 cass. (Running Time: 16 hrs.). 1998. 76.95 (978-0-7861-1415-3(0), 2291) Blckstn Audio.
Story of the traitor who had been feeding the KGB information for nine years & was responsible for the betrayal that led to the execution of most of the United States' top assets in the Soviet Union. Writer conducted fifty hours of one-on-one interviews; traveled to Moscow to speak to KGB handlers & families of the spies betrayed; & had access to the remarkable CIA mole-hunting team that tracked down the spy through its own detective work.

Confessions of a Spy: The Real Story of Aldrich Ames. unabr. ed. Pete Earley. Read by Edward Holland. (Running Time: 54000 sec.). 2008. audio compact disk 29.95 (978-0-7861-6223-9(6)); audio compact disk & audio compact disk 99.00 (978-0-7861-6220-8(1)) Blckstn Audio.

Confessions of a Video Vixen. unabr. ed. Karrine Steffans & Karen Hunter. Read by Karrine Steffans. 2005. audio compact disk 29.95 (978-0-06-084343-4(8)) HarperCollins Pubs.

***Confessions of a Video Vixen: Wild Times, Rampant 'Roids, Smash Hits,** unabr. ed. Karrine Steffans & Karen Hunter. Read by Karrine Steffans. (ENG.). 2005. (978-0-06-088054-5(6), Harper Audio); (978-0-06-088055-2(4), Harper Audio) HarperCollins Pubs.

Confessions of an Advertising Man. unabr. ed. David Ogilvy. Read by Christopher Godfrey. 6 cass. (Running Time: 1 hr. per cass.). 1990. 60.00 (978-0-942563-04-7(2)); Rental 15.00 (978-0-942563-11-5(5)) CareerTapes.
Tells how to manage an advertising agency from getting & keeping clients to building great ad campaigns. Also explains how to write potent copy, illustrate advertisements & posters, & make good television commercials.

Confessions of an advertising Man. unabr. ed. David Ogilvy. Narrated by Ray Atherton. 3 cass. (Running Time: 4 hrs. 45 mins.). 1989. 26.00 (978-1-55690-117-1(8), 89670E7) Recorded Bks.
The founder of one of the largest advertising agencies, unveils the secrets of his trade.

Confessions of an Alien Hunter: A Scientist's Search for Extraterrestrial Intelligence. unabr. ed. Seth Shostak. Read by Seth Shostak. Read by Patrick G. Lawlor. (Running Time: 10 hrs.). 2010. 39.97 (978-1-4233-7643-9(9), 9781423376439, Brlnc Audio MP3 Lib); 39.97 (978-1-4233-7645-3(5), 9781423376453, BADLE); 24.99 (978-1-4233-7642-2(0), 9781423376422, Brilliance MP3); 24.99 (978-1-4233-7644-6(7), 9781423376446, BAD); audio compact disk 89.97 (978-1-4233-7641-5(2), 9781423376415, BriAudCD Unabrid); audio compact disk 29.99 (978-1-4233-7640-8(4), 9781423376408, Bril Audio CD Unabri) Brilliance Audio.

Confessions of an Eco-Warrior. Dave Foreman. Read by Dave Foreman. 2 cass. (Running Time: 3 hrs.). 1992. 16.95 (978-0-939643-42-4(1), NrthWrd Bks) TandN Child.
Dave Foreman believes that the very fate of the Earth is at stake. With extinctions accelerating and vast habitats disappearing every year, the ability of species to survive and to evolve has been deeply compromised. The ideas and ideals of a modern-day hero are presented - a man with the courage to take action for what he believes in.

Confessions of an Economic Hit Man. John Perkins. Read by Brian Emerson. 7 cass. (Running Time: 9 hrs. 30 mins.). 2005. 29.95 (978-0-7861-3485-4(2)); audio compact disk 29.95 (978-0-7861-7895-7(7)) Blckstn Audio.

Confessions of an Economic Hit Man. John Perkins. Read by Brian Emerson. (Running Time: 9 hrs. 18 mins.). 2005. reel tape 59.95 (978-0-7861-3484-7(4)); audio compact disk 72.00 (978-0-7861-7896-4(5)) Blckstn Audio.

Confessions of an Economic Hit Man. John Perkins. Read by Brian Emerson. 1 MP3. (Running Time: 9 hrs. 30 mins.). 2005. audio compact disk 29.95 (978-0-7861-8103-2(6)) Blckstn Audio.

Confessions of an Economic Hit Man. John Perkins. Narrated by Brian Emerson. (Running Time: 9 hrs. 30 mins.). 2005. 30.95 (978-1-59912-454-4(8)) Iofy Corp.

Confessions of an English Opium-Eater see Cambridge Treasury of English Prose: Austen to Bronte

Confessions of an English Opium-Eater. Thomas de Quincey. Read by Jim Killavey. 4 cass. (Running Time: 4 hrs.). 1987. 24.00 incl. albums. (C-173) Jimcin Record.
An account of opium addiction that is in turns witty, sentimental, & nightmarish.

Confessions of an English Opium-Eater. Thomas de Quincey & Thomas Whitworth. 3 cass. (Running Time: 3 hrs. 30 mins.). 2002. 23.95 (978-0-7861-2709-2(0), 3351) Blckstn Audio.

Confessions of an English Opium-Eater. unabr. ed. Thomas de Quincey. Read by Thomas Whitworth. 3 CDs. (Running Time: 3 hrs. 30 mins.). 2004. audio compact disk 24.00 (978-0-7861-8429-3(9), 3351) Blckstn Audio.

Confessions of an English Opium-Eater. unabr. ed. Thomas de Quincey. Read by Robert L. Halvorson. 2 cass. (Running Time: 180 min.). 14.95 (47) Halvorson Assocs.

Confessions of an English Opium-Eater. unabr. ed. Thomas de Quincey. Perf. by Anthony Quayle. 1 cass. (Running Time: 90 mins.). 1986. 12.95 (SWC 1286) HarperCollins Pubs.
This is an autobiographical account of an upper middle class drop-out who becomes addicted to a mind-distorting drug. Despite his addiction, De Quincey's collected works fill 20 volumes in the definitive American edition.

Confessions of an English Opium-Eater. unabr. collector's ed. Thomas de Quincey. Read by Thomas Whitworth. 4 cass. (Running Time: 4 hrs.). 1987. 24.00 (978-0-7366-2138-0(5), 2937) Books on Tape.
An account of his early life & addiction to opium from the intellectual of the Romantic Age, friend of Wordsworth & Coleridge.

Confessions of an Opium Eater, Set. Thomas de Quincey. Read by Robert L. Halvorson. 2 cass. 14.95 (47) Halvorson Assocs.

Confessions of an Ugly Stepsister. unabr. ed. Gregory Maguire. Narrated by Jenny Sterlin. 10 cass. (Running Time: 11 hrs. 45 mins.). 2000. 81.00 (978-0-7887-4321-4(X), 96227E7) Recorded Bks.
A reincarnation of the Cinderella story, weaving together inner & outer beauty. Iris is a plain but intelligent young girl who is forced to flee England with her mother & older sister. She finds herself swept into a story of love & deception where a ball, a handsome prince & the betrayal of a daughter can lead to everyone living happily ever after.

Confessions of an Unmanager: How "Managing Less" & Employee Teams Saved Our Company. abr. ed. Debra Boggan & Anna VerSteeg. Read by Debra Boggan & Anna VerSteeg. Ed. by Vera Derr. 2 cass. (Running Time: 3 hrs.). 1998. 19.95 Set. (978-0-85013-296-0(7)) Dartnell Corp.
Told with humor & blunt honesty, this business novel is based on real-life experiences of the authors. It's an engaging & enlightening look at how corporate culture can & must change to meet the challenges of an ever more complex & fast-paced business world.

***Confessions of Catherine de Medici.** unabr. ed. C. W. Gortner. (Running Time: 14 hrs. 0 mins.). 2010. 29.95 (978-1-4417-5459-2(8)); 79.95 (978-1-4417-5455-4(5)); audio compact disk 109.00 (978-1-4417-5456-1(3)) Blckstn Audio.

Confessions of Judgement & Deficiency Judgments in Pennsylvania. 1999. bk. 99.00 (ACS-2270) PA Bar Inst.
Examines the procedural & substantive law provisions governing confessions of judgment & deficiency judgments in Pennsylvania. Learn the techniques for attacking a confessed judgment & on how to handle foreign judgments & transferring judgments.

Confessions of Judgment & Deficiency Judgments in Pennsylvania. 1999. bk. 99.00 (ACS-2270) PA Bar Inst.
Examines the procedural & substantive law provisions governing confessions of judgement & deficiency judgments in Pennsylvania. Learn the techniques for attacking a confessed judgment & on how to handle foreign judgments & transferring judgments.

Confessions of Max Tivoli: A Novel. Andrew Sean Greer. Narrated by Brian Keeler. 9 CDs. (Running Time: 11 hrs.). 2004. audio compact disk 29.99 (978-1-4025-7368-2(5), 01482) Recorded Bks.

Confessions of Nat Turner. unabr. collector's ed. William Styron. Read by Wolfram Kandinsky. 12 cass. (Running Time: 18 hrs.). 1985. 96.00 (978-0-7366-0933-3(4), 1877) Books on Tape.
Turner's rebellion took place in the long hot summer of 1831, in the state of Virginia. When it was over, 59 white people were dead; the insurgents were rounded up & either hanged or worse; & Nat Turner, a preacher, confessed to his part in the only effective revolt in the annals of American Negro slavery.

Confessions of Saint Augustine. unabr. ed. Saint Augustine. 10 CDs. (Running Time: 12 hrs. 48 mins. 0 sec.). (ENG.). 2006. audio compact disk 28.98 (978-1-59644-358-7(8), Hovel Audio) christianaud.
Saint Augustine's contributions to Christian theology are second to no other post-apostolic author in the whole sweep of church history. Yet along side his doctrinal treatises, Augustine tells a story of his life devoted to Christ as his only satisfaction. The Confessions is at once the autobiographical account of Augustine's life of Christian faith and at the same time a compelling theology of Christian spirituality for everyone. Among the most important classics in Western literature, it continues to engage modern readers through Augustine's timeless illustrations and beautiful prose. Augustine's Confessions is a book to relish the first time through and then profoundly enjoy over a lifetime of revisiting. This accessible and accurate translation of The Confessions comes alive with Simon Vance's narration. Vance is an award-winning audiobook narrator with hundreds of titles to his credit, including classics by Charles Dickens, H. G. Wells, and Robert Louis Stevenson.

***Confessions of Saint Augustine.** unabr. ed. Saint Augustine. Narrated by Simon Vance. (ENG.). 2006. 16.98 (978-1-59644-359-4(6), Hovel Audio) christianaud.

Confessions of Saint Augustine. unabr. ed. Saint Augustine. Narrated by Simon Vance. 1 MP3CD. (Running Time: 12 hrs. 48 mins. 0 sec.). (ENG.). 2006. lp 19.98 (978-1-59644-360-0(X), Hovel Audio) christianaud.

Confessions of Saint Augustine. unabr. ed. St Aurelius Augustinus. Read by Bernard Mayes. Tr. by Edward Bouverie Pusey. (Running Time: 45000 sec.). 2007. 19.95 (978-0-7861-4914-8(0)); audio compact disk 29.95 (978-0-7861-7058-6(1)); audio compact disk 19.95 (978-0-7861-5932-1(4)) Blckstn Audio.

Confessions of Saint Augustine. unabr. ed. St Aurelius Augustinus. Read by Bernard Mayes. (YA). 2008. 74.99 (978-1-60514-716-1(8)) Find a World.

Confessions of Saint Augustine: Translated by Albert C. Outler. Narrated by Emily Hanna. (ENG.). 2007. 29.00 (978-1-931848-11-4(4)) Christ Class Ethereal.

***Confessions of St. Augustine.** unabr. ed. Saint Augustine. Narrated by Mel Foster. (Running Time: 12 hrs. 0 mins.). 2010. 32.99 (978-1-4001-9612-8(4)); 22.99 (978-1-4001-6612-1(8)); 17.99 (978-1-4001-8612-9(9)); audio compact disk 32.99 (978-1-4001-1612-6(0)); audio compact disk 65.99 (978-1-4001-4612-3(7)) Pub: Tantor Media. Dist(s): IngramPubServ

Confessions of the Reformed Church: The Augsburg & Westminster Confessions & Heidelberg Catechism. unabr. ed. Narrated by David Cochran Heath. (Running Time: 3 hrs. 54 mins. 0 sec.). (ENG.). 2007. audio compact disk 24.98 (978-1-59644-527-7(0), Hovel Audio) christianaud.

***Confessions of the Reformed Church: The Augsburg & Westminster Confessions, & Heidelberg Catechism.** unabr. ed. Narrated by David Cochran Heath. (ENG.). 2007. 14.98 (978-1-59644-528-4(9), Hovel Audio) christianaud.

Confessor. Terry Goodkind. Read by Sam Tsoutsouvas. (Playaway Adult Fiction Ser.). 2008. 139.99 (978-1-60640-589-5(6)) Find a World.

Confessor. Daniel Silva. (Gabriel Allon Ser.: No. 3). 2003. 80.00 (978-0-7366-9043-0(3)); audio compact disk 81.60 (978-0-7366-9280-9(0)) Pub: Books on Tape. Dist(s): NetLibrary CO

Confessor. abr. ed. Terry Goodkind. Read by Sam Tsoutsouvas. (Running Time: 9 hrs.). (Sword of Truth: Bk. 3). 2008. audio compact disk 19.99 (978-1-4233-1665-7(7), 9781423316657, BCD Value Price) Brilliance Audio.

Confessor. abr. ed. Daniel Silva. Read by Arliss Howard. 5 CDs. (Running Time: 21600 sec.). (Gabriel Allon Ser.: No. 3). (ENG.). 2005. audio compact disk 14.99 (978-0-7393-2490-5(X), Random AudioBks) Pub: Random Audio Pubg. Dist(s): Random

Confessor. unabr. ed. John E. Gardner. Read by Michael Tudor Barnes. 10 cass. (Running Time: 12 hr. 30 min.). (Isis Ser.). (J). 1997. 84.95 (978-0-7531-0286-2(2), 971005) Pub: ISIS Lrg Prnt GBR. Dist(s): Ulverscroft US

In intelligence jargon a "confessor" is a specialist in breaking down suspected spies, informants & defectors through relentless interrogation. Gus Keene was one of the best confessors in the business until terrorists blew up his car on a quiet rural road in the middle of the night. Retired Secret Service agent Herbie Kruger, out of shape & out of form, is called back into service to delve into the circumstances of the death of his former colleague.

Confessor. unabr. ed. Terry Goodkind. (Running Time: 24 hrs.). (Sword of Truth: Bk. 3). 2007. 44.25 (978-1-4233-1663-3(0), 9781423316633, BADLE); 29.95 (978-1-4233-1662-6(2), 9781423316626, BAD) Brilliance Audio.

Confessor. unabr. ed. Terry Goodkind. Read by Sam Tsoutsouvas. 22 cass. (Running Time: 24 hrs.). (Sword of Truth: Bk. 3). 2007. 150.25 (978-1-4233-1657-2(6), 9781423316572, BrilAudUnabridg); audio compact disk 49.95 (978-1-4233-1658-9(4), 9781423316589, Bril Audio CD Unabri); audio compact disk 29.95 (978-1-4233-1660-2(6), 9781423316602, Brilliance MP3); audio compact disk 150.25 (978-1-4233-1659-6(2), 9781423316596, BriAudCD Unabrid); audio compact disk 44.25 (978-1-4233-1661-9(4), 9781423316619, Brlnc Audio MP3 Lib) Brilliance Audio.

Confianza en si Mismo. Betty L. Randolph. 1 cass. (Success Ser.). 1989. bk. 9.98 (978-1-55909-187-9(8), 26E) Randolph Tapes.

Presents a program in Spanish. Features male-female voice tracks with the right-left brain.

Confidence. Alan L. McGinnis. 6 cass. (Running Time: 6 hrs.). 1992. 59.95 set. (276A) Nightingale-Conant.

Confidence. Betty L. Randolph. 1 stereo cass. (Running Time: 45 min.). (Self-Hypnosis Ser.). 9.98 (978-1-55909-148-0(7), 808) Randolph Tapes.

Use to produce total change in personal esteem & confidence. Music background & spoken word.

Confidence. Betty L. Randolph. Read by Betty L. Randolph. Read by Leonard Baron. Ed. by Success Education Institute International. 1 cass. (Running Time: 60 min.). (Success Ser.). 1989. bk. 14.98 (978-1-55909-256-2(4), 440P); 9.98 (978-1-55909-011-7(1), 26S); 9.98 90 min. extended length stereo music. (978-1-55909-186-2(X), 26B) Randolph Tapes.

Designed to produce changes in personal esteem & confidence. Subliminal messages are heard for 3-5 minutes before becoming ocean sounds or music.

Confidence. unabr. ed. Henry James. Narrated by Flo Gibson. 5 cass. (Running Time: 7 hrs. 30 mins.). 2003. 20.95 (978-1-55685-731-7(4)) Audio Bk Con.

Bernard and Gordon, two great friends, as they travel to Paris, Baden and beyond, fall in love with the same wise woman.

Confidence: How Winning & Losing Streaks Begin & End. unabr. ed. Rosabeth Moss Kanter. 2004. 63.00 (978-1-4159-0323-0(9)); audio compact disk 81.00 (978-1-4159-0324-7(7)) Books on Tape.

Confidence & Enlightenment. Read by Chogyam Trungpa. 2 cass. 1978. 25.00 (A109) Vajradhatu.

Confidence & enlightenment are not made up; they are a natural state of existence.

Confidence & Positive Thinking. Dick Sutphen. 1 cass. (Running Time: 1 hr.). (Only Subliminals Ser.). 1990. 12.98 (978-0-87554-441-0(X), T201) Valley Sun.

One hour of soothing, digitally mastered stereo music with positive subliminal suggestions phrased for maximum acceptance by your subconscious mind.

Confidence & Self Esteem (Hypnosis) Self Confidence Subliminal, Vol. 4. Jayne Helle. 1 cass. (Running Time: 56 min.). 1996. 15.00 (978-1-891826-03-0(4)) Introspect.

Confidence Building & Goal Setting for Goal Getting. Created by Anne H. Spencer-Beacham. 1. 2003. audio compact disk (978-1-932163-39-1(5)) Infinity Inst.

Confidence Code: A Guide to building self esteem & living Courageously. Christel Nani. (ENG.). 2007. audio compact disk 20.00 (978-0-9741450-5-1(X)) Queens Crt Pr.

Confidence, Composure & Competence for Working Women: How to Build Self-Assurance, Develop Inner Calm & Take Action with Poise & Power. Instructed by Maria Arapakis. 6 cass. (Running Time: 5 hrs. 43 min.). 79.95 Set, incl. wkbk., 26p. (Q10169) CareerTrack Pubns.

Program highlights: 2 ways your confidence can take a nosedive (& what to do about it); How to stop comparing yourself with others; Tips to overcome self-pity & depression; Ways to prevent mental mistakes & "crossed wires"; How to "get it together" when you feel scattered & pulled in all directions; "Attitude adjustments" - ways to improve your outlook.

Confidence Course. abr. ed. Walter Anderson. 1 cass. (Running Time: 3 hrs.). 1999. 18.00 (20467) Courage-to-Change.

Learn how to make anxiety your ally & overcome crippling self-doubt.

***Confidence Course.** abr. ed. Walter Anderson. Read by Walter Anderson. (ENG.). 2005. (978-0-06-112748-9(5), Harper Audio); (978-0-06-112749-6(3), Harper Audio) HarperCollins Pubs.

Confidence Factor: Cosmic Gooses Lay Golden Eggs. Judith Briles. 2001. 40.00 (978-1-885331-06-9(1)) Mile High Pr.

The complete book, The Confidence Factor: Cosmic Gooses Lay Golden Eggs, read by the author. Awarded Best Business Book by the Colorado Independent Publishers' Assn. A Cosmic Goose is an unexpected, sometimes life-changing event. The audio book shows how to learn and grow and thrive when a cosmic goose lands on your doorstep.

Confidence Killer. Speeches. Creflo A. Dollar. 4 cass. (Running Time: 4 hrs. 45 mins.). 2005. 20.00 (978-1-59089-996-0(2)); audio compact disk 28.00 (978-1-59089-997-7(0)) Creflo Dollar.

Confidence Power. Eldon Taylor. 1 cass. (Running Time: 62 min.). (Inner Talk Ser.). 16.95 (978-1-55978-320-0(6), 5378A) Progress Aware Res.

Soundtrack - Tropical Lagoon with underlying subliminal affirmations.

Confidence Power: Babbling Brook. Eldon Taylor. 1 cass. 16.95 (978-1-55978-498-6(9), 5378F) Progress Aware Res.

Confidence Power: Classic. Eldon Taylor. Read by Eldon Taylor. Ed. by Leslie Brice. 1 cass. (Running Time: 1 hr.). 1992. 16.95 (978-1-56705-165-0(0)) Gateways Inst.

Self improvement.

Confidence Power: Easy. Eldon Taylor. Read by Eldon Taylor. Ed. by Leslie Brice. 1 cass. (Running Time: 1 hr.). 1992. 16.95 (978-1-56705-166-7(9)) Gateways Inst.

Confidence Power: Harmonies. Eldon Taylor. Read by Eldon Taylor. Ed. by Leslie Brice. 1 cass. (Running Time: 1 hr.). 1992. 16.95 (978-1-56705-167-4(7)) Gateways Inst.

Confidence Power: Music Theme. Eldon Taylor. 1 cass. 16.95 (978-1-55978-154-1(8), 5378C) Progress Aware Res.

Confidence Power: Ocean. Eldon Taylor. Read by Eldon Taylor. Ed. by Leslie Brice. 1 cass. (Running Time: 1 hr.). 1992. 16.95 (978-1-56705-168-1(5)) Gateways Inst.

Confidence Power: Rhythms. Eldon Taylor. Read by Eldon Taylor. Ed. by Leslie Brice. 1 cass. (Running Time: 1 hr.). 1992. 16.95 (978-1-56705-169-8(3)) Gateways Inst.

Confidence Power: Stream. Eldon Taylor. Read by Eldon Taylor. Ed. by Leslie Brice. 1 cass. (Running Time: 1 hr.). 1992. 16.95 (978-1-56705-170-4(7)) Gateways Inst.

Confidence with the Opposite Sex. Eldon Taylor. 1 cass. (Running Time: 62 min.). (Inner Talk Ser.). 16.95 incl. script. (978-1-55978-522-8(5), 53807F) Progress Aware Res.

Soundtrack - Brook with underlying subliminal affirmations.

Confidence with the Opposite Sex: Pastoral Themes. Eldon Taylor. 1 cass. 16.95 (978-1-55978-583-9(7), 53807M) Progress Aware Res.

Confident Consumer. Sally R. Campbell. (gr. 9-12). tchr. ed. 200.00 (978-1-59070-151-5(8)) Goodheart.

Confident Decision Making. Roger Dawson. 6 cass. bk. 129.00 set. (CPE3155) Bisk Educ.

Get proven techniques on how to define & perfect your personal decision-making style. Then, learn how to improve your ability to making winning choices in any situation.

Confident Decision Making. Roger Dawson. Read by Roger Dawson. 6 cass. 1991. 59.95 set. (864A) Nightingale-Conant.

A series of incisive exercises will help define your decision making style. Learn to improve your career & or life decisions by improving your decision-making abilities.

Confident, Effective, Dynamic Public Speaking. Somers H. White. 4 cass. (Running Time: 60 min. per cass.). 80.00 (C120) S White.

Teaches you methods of organization, style & delivery.

Confident in God's Care: Coping with Fear, Anxiety & Stress. Word Consultants Staff. 1 cass. (Running Time: 60 mins.). 1999. 9.95 (T8298) Liguori Pubns.

Biblical affirmations set to upbeat music. Helps deal with fear, anxiety & stress while also building trust in God. Ideal to use while walking.

***Confident Networking for Career Success.** Stuart Lindenfield. (Running Time: 2 hrs. 8 mins.). (ENG.). 2011. audio compact disk 22.95 (978-1-4055-0903-9(1)) Pub: Little BrownUK GBR. Dist(s): IPG Chicago

Confident Public Speaking. Roko Paskov. 4 cass. 64.95 set. (V10008) CareerTrack Pubns.

This program will help you prepare & deliver your presentations more easily than ever before. It will show you how to: involve your audience, sell your ideas & get the results you want.

Confident Public Speaking Freeway Guide. Susan Leahy. Contrib. by Susan Leahy. (Freeway Guides: Practical Audio for People on the Go Ser.). (ENG.). 2009. 34.99 (978-1-60812-573-9(4)) Find a World.

Confident Speaker: Beat Your Nerves & Communicate at Your Best in Any Situation. Harrison Monarth. 2009. audio compact disk 28.00 (978-1-933309-71-2(7)) Pub: A Media Intl. Dist(s): Natl Bk Netwk

Confident Woman. Marjorie Hansen Shaevitz & Morton H. Shaevitz. Read by Marjorie Hansen Shaevitz & Morton H. Shaevitz. (Running Time: 4 hrs.). (C). 2005. 36.95 (978-1-59912-161-1(1)) Iofy Corp.

Confident Woman: Asserting Yourself at Work, Love & Play. Marjorie H. Shoewitz. 6 cass. 49.95 Set. (696AS) Pryor Resources.

A must for all women wanting to face their world with confidence as they balance all aspects of their ever more complicated lives.

Confident Woman: Start Today Living Boldly & Without Fear. abr. ed. Joyce Meyer. Read by Pat Lentz. 5 CDs. (Running Time: 6 hrs.). (ENG.). 2006. audio compact disk 29.98 (978-1-59483-574-2(8)) Pub: FaithWords. Dist(s): HachBkGrp

Confident Woman: Start Today Living Boldly & Without Fear. abr. ed. Joyce Meyer. Read by Pat Lentz. Told to Todd Hafer. (Running Time: 6 hrs.). (ENG.). 2006. 14.98 (978-1-59483-575-9(6)) Pub: Hachet Audio. Dist(s): HachBkGrp

Confident Woman: Start Today Living Boldly & Without Fear. abr. ed. Joyce Meyer. Read by Pat Lentz. Told to Todd Hafer. (Running Time: 6 hrs.). (ENG.). 2009. 44.98 (978-1-60788-143-8(8)) Pub: Hachet Audio. Dist(s): HachBkGrp

Confidential Agent. unabr. ed. Graham Greene. Read by Patrick Tull. 5 Cass. (Running Time: 7.5 Hrs.). 24.95 (978-1-4025-2824-8(8)) Recorded Bks.

Confidential Agent. unabr. ed. Graham Greene. Narrated by Patrick Tull. 5 cass. (Running Time: 7 hrs. 30 mins.). 1988. 44.00 (978-1-55690-118-8(6), 88790E7) Recorded Bks.

A secret agent is sent to England on a mission, but it seems his identity is known even before the mission begins. As the car he is driving is run down in the fog, a thought strikes him: It isn't probable, not in England, but it seems to be true, nonetheless - They're trying to kill me.

Confidentiality & the Law. rev. ed. 1 cass. (Running Time: 90 min.). (Professional Issues Ser.). 1984. 8.95 (1566G) Hazelden.

Confidentiality Issues. Bruce Hartung & James Gibbons. 1986. 10.80 (0601) Assn Prof Chaplains.

Confining the Inquisition. Lance Auburn Everette. 3 CDs. (Running Time: 3 hrs.). (Michael Ser.: No. 5). 2005. audio compact disk 9.99 (978-1-58943-486-8(2)) Am Pubng Inc.

This is the fifth book in a truly unique series of historical action-adventure novels: Michael. Sometimes, in history, things worked out for the best against all odds. Maybe Somebody intervened on the side of the correct path - even when we didn't know what that path was. But to intervene in the affairs of human beings without disrupting civilization completely is to wield human tools - and human weapons. So when the Archangels arrive to Change Things, watch out! Published for the first time ever by Americana Publishing. Michael: Spirituality - with an edge.

Confirm Thy Soul in Self Control. Ardeth G. Kapp. 1 cass. 5.98 (06003370) Covenant Comms.

Confirmation see Twentieth-Century Poetry in English, No. 23, Recordings of Poets Reading Their Own Poetry

Confirmation. unabr. ed. Thomas Powers. Narrated by George Guidall. 12 cass. (Running Time: 18 hrs.). 2001. 102.00 (978-0-7887-4987-2(0), 96473E7) Recorded Bks.

A routine confirmation hearing for the next Director of Central Intelligence reveals an MIA scandal that plunges Washington into a full-scale media circus & unleashed the wrath of a clandestine militia.

Confirmation: Sacrament of Champions. 2004. 6.95 (978-1-932631-88-3(7)) Ascensn Pr.

Confirmation (CD) Sacrament of Champions. 2004. audio compact disk 7.95 (978-1-932631-89-0(5)) Ascensn Pr.

Confirmation of Crucifixion. Elbert Willis. 1 cass. (Understanding the Crucified Life Ser.). 4.00 Fill the Gap.

Conflict. unabr. ed. Oasis Audio. Read by Kelly Ryan Dolan. Narrated by Jill Shellabarger. (Running Time: 1 hr. 12 mins. 58 sec.). (What the Bible Says Ser.). (ENG.). 2008. audio compact disk 9.99 (978-1-59859-406-5(0)) Oasis Audio.

Conflict: An Aiki Approach. Thomas F. Crum. Read by Thomas F. Crum. 1 cass. (Running Time: 60 min.). 1987. 10.00 (978-1-877803-05-5(7)) Aiki Works.

Basic instruction in the principles of the Aiki Approach to conflict resolution.

Conflict & Gang Violence: Peer Puppet Program. 4 cass. (J). (gr. k-3). 185.00 Set, incl. prevention manual. (257500-SG) Sunburst Comm.

An effective approach to teaching students about critical health issues, based on the premise that kids listen to kids.

***Conflict Contract.** Jonathan Miller. (Rattlesnake Lawyer - Luna Cruz Thriller Ser.). (ENG.). 2010. pap. bk. (978-1-935270-02-7(8)) Cool Titles.

Conflict, Crisis, Climax & Resolution. Brenda Wilbee. 1 cass. (Writing for Publication: Fiction that Sells Ser.: No. 1). 1987. 7.95 (978-0-943777-01-6(1)) byBrenda.

The basic foundation elements of fiction.

Conflict Free Living: How to Build Healthly Relationships for Life. unabr. ed. Joyce Meyer. Read by Sandra McCollum. (Running Time: 4 hrs. 43 mins. 20 sec.). (ENG.). 2008. audio compact disk 22.99 (978-1-59859-420-1(6)) Oasis Audio.

Conflict Free Living: How to Build Healthy Relationships for Life. Joyce Meyer. Read by Sandra McCollom. (Playaway Adult Nonfiction Ser.). (ENG.). 2009. 60.00 (978-1-60775-595-1(5)) Find a World.

Conflict Free Living: How to Build Healthy Relationships for Life. unabr. ed. Joyce Meyer. Narrated by Sandra McCollom. (Running Time: 4 hrs. 43 mins. 20 sec.). (ENG.). 2008. 16.09 (978-1-60814-156-2(X)) Oasis Audio.

***Conflict in the Workplace.** PUEI. 2008. audio compact disk 199.00 (978-1-935041-25-2(8), CareerTrack) P Univ E Inc.

Conflict Management. E. J. Gold. 1 cass. (Running Time: 1 hr. 30 min.). 9.98 (TP119) Union Label.

Talk on the differences between the machine's problems & transformational problems. Life repair, relaxing within tension, & inhibitors of the transformational effect are discussed.

Conflict Management: The Courage to Confront. 2nd ed. Richard J. Mayer. 1997. bk. 49.95 (978-0-614-25851-6(0)) Battelle.

Conflict of Interest. Clair Poulson. 3 cass. 2004. 14.95 (978-1-59156-215-3(5)); audio compact disk 14.95 (978-1-59156-216-0(3)) Covenant Comms.

Conflict of Interest. abr. ed. Nancy Taylor Rosenberg. Narrated by Joyce Bean. 4 CDs. (Running Time: 4 hrs.). 2002. audio compact disk 61.25 (978-1-58788-726-0(6), 1587887266, CD Lib Edit) Brilliance Audio.

While trying three defendants for robbery, Joanne Kuhlman discovers a far more serious crime may be unfolding. One of the defendants is developmentally disabled. His attorney and mother insist he was cruelly exploited by his crime partners. When the young man disappears, Joanne fears he may have been murdered in a ruthless act to silence him. Her sympathies for this defendant lead her to entangle herself with his attractive attorney and compromise her career so the truth may be revealed.

Conflict of Interest. unabr. ed. Nancy Taylor Rosenberg. Read by Joyce Bean. 6 cass. (Running Time: 9 hrs.). 2002. 29.95 (978-1-58788-721-5(5), 1587887215, BAU); 69.25 (978-1-58788-722-2(3), 1587887223, Unabridge Lib Edns) Brilliance Audio.

Conflict of Interest. unabr. ed. Nancy Taylor Rosenberg. Read by Joyce Bean. (Running Time: 9 hrs.). 2004. 39.25 (978-1-59335-436-7(3), 1593354363, Brlnc Audio MP3 Lib) Brilliance Audio.

Conflict of Interest. unabr. ed. Nancy Taylor Rosenberg. Read by Joyce Bean. (Running Time: 9 hrs.). 2004. 39.25 (978-1-59710-153-0(2), 1597101532, BADLE); 24.95 (978-1-59710-152-3(4), 1597101524, BAD) Brilliance Audio.

Conflict of Interest. unabr. ed. Nancy Taylor Rosenberg. Read by Joyce Bean. (Running Time: 9 hrs.). 2004. 24.95 (978-1-59335-072-7(4), 1593350724) Soulmate Audio Bks.

Conflict of Interest: L-Book. Jae. (ENG.). 2008. 18.95 (978-1-934889-24-4(5)) Lbook Pub.

Conflict of Interests. unabr. ed. Clive Egleton. Narrated by Patrick Tull. 6 cass. (Running Time: 8 hrs.). 1988. 51.00 (978-1-55690-119-5(4), 88380E7) Recorded Bks.

When the proprietor of a rather kinky bordello turns up dead in London, the police discover some of her videotapes are missing & on one of those tapes is the face of an Arab terrorist. Suddenly, a squalid little blackmail becomes an international battleground of intrigue.

Conflict of Laws. 2nd ed. Thomas Fischer. 4 cass. (Running Time: 4 hrs. 30 mins.). (Outstanding Professors Ser.). 1996. 50.00 (978-1-57793-015-0(0), 28398) Pub: Sum & Substance. Dist(s): West Pub

Lecture given by a prominent law school professor.

Conflict of Laws. 3rd rev. ed. Patrick J. Borchers. (Law School Legends Audio Ser.). 2008. 52.00 (978-0-314-19879-2(2)) West.

Conflict of Laws. 3rd rev. ed. Thomas Fischer. (Sum & Substance Ser.). 2000. 63.00 (978-0-314-24346-1(1)) Pub: West Pub. Dist(s): West

Conflict of Laws, 2005 ed. (Law School Legends Audio Series) 2005th rev. ed. Patrick J. Borchers. 2005. 47.95 (978-0-314-16079-9(5), gilbert); audio compact disk 47.95 (978-0-314-16080-5(9), gilbert) West.

Conflict of Visions: Ideological Origins of Political Struggles. unabr. ed. Thomas Sowell. Read by Michael Edwards. 5 cass. (Running Time: 7 hrs.). 1988. 39.95 (978-0-7861-0002-6(8), 1003) Blckstn Audio.

Sowell explains that most people have one of two contrasting visions. Those visions are "constrained" & "unconstrained." People holding the constrained vision find nature to be limited in its moral possibility & therefore caution against granting government wide scope of authority. Conversely, those holding the opposing vision deny the existence of a negative element in nature & argue that whole societies can be built by removing environmental impediments such as family, property & custom.

Conflict Resolution. 2001. audio compact disk 25.95 (978-1-889609-15-7(3)) Loving Guidnce.

Conflict Resolution. Becky Bailey. 2 cass. 16.95 Set. (978-1-889609-06-5(4), AT-111) Loving Guidnce.
Learn how to teach your children not only conflict resolution but the keys to happiness. Includes how we unconsciously create conflict, the core cause of all conflict, the seven steps of conflict resolution for children & the three phases of cooperative conflict resolution to use with adults, 1998 Parent's Choice Award.

Conflict Resolution. abr. ed. Marianne Melley. Read by Marianne Melley. 2 cass. (Running Time: 1 hrs. 50 min.). 1998. 19.95 Set; incl. wkbk. (978-1-57294-098-7(0), 11-0222) SkillPath Pubns.
How to deal with disruptive conduct in the workplace? Blunt the effects of gossip? Transform anger into something productive? An insightful, impactful new video tells you how.

Conflict Resolution for Couples. Susan M. Heitler. Perf. by Melissa King & Rob MacMullan. 2 cass. (Running Time: 1 hr. 48 min.). 1994. 19.95 Set. (978-1-884998-07-2(0)) Listen-to-Lrn.
Heitler demonstrates techniques for addressing, & resolving sensitive topics without arguments. Contains easy-to-follow explanations, actors as fight-prone couple, & interactions with live audience.

Conflicting Accounts: The Creation & Crash of the Saatchi & Saatchi Advertising Empire. unabr. ed. Kevin Goldman. Read by Barrett Whitener. 10 cass. (Running Time: 14 hrs. 30 mins.). 1997. 69.95 (978-0-7861-1183-1(6), 1943) Blckstn Audio.
A universal tale of corporate greed & ineffective management. The story of an ugly, publicly fought civil war in an industry that is supposed to know the steep price paid for an image run amok.

Conflicto en el Medio. Nathaniel Price. Narrated by Aaron Olvera et al. (SPA.). 2009. 49.99 (978-1-61545-956-8(1)) Find a World.

Conflicts of Interest under the Rules of Professional Conduct. 1 cass. 1988. 35.00 PA Bar Inst.

Confrontando el Pecado. Orig. Title: Coming to Terms with Sin. 2004. audio compact disk 34.00 (978-1-57972-573-0(2)) Insight Living.

Confrontation. Irving Younger. Read by Irving Younger. 3 cass. (Running Time: 3 hrs.). 1985. pap. bk. 70.00 Set. (978-0-943380-44-5(8)) PEG MN.
Using the confrontation clause.

Confrontation. Perf. by Irving Younger. Created by Irving Younger. 2 CDs. (Running Time: 3 hours). 2004. pap. bk. 199.00 (978-1-932831-06-1(1)) PEG MN.

Confrontation in Group Counseling. 1 cass. (Professional Issues Ser.). 1984. 8.95 (1567G) Hazelden.

Confronting Culture. Joe Wells. (ENG.). (YA). 2007. audio compact disk 10.00 (978-0-9821815-9-1(0)) Focus Pr.

Confronting Hallucinations. Wilson Van Dusen. 2 cass. (Running Time: 2 hrs.). 1968. 18.00 set. (05403) Big Sur Tapes.

Confronting the Troubled Employee. unabr. ed. William Hushion & Thomas Hudson. 1 cass. (Running Time: 50 min.). 1981. 9.95 Newtown Psychological Ctr.
Side 1: Explores signs & myths of alcoholism. Side 2: contains role playing, confrontation & guidelines.

Confucianism & Taoism. unabr. ed. Julia Ching. Read by Ben Kingsley. Ed. by Walter Harrelson & Mike Hassell. Prod. by Pat Childs. (Running Time: 10800 sec.). (Religion, Scriptures, & Spirituality Ser.). 2006. audio compact disk 25.95 (978-0-7861-6480-6(8)) Pub: Blckstn Audio. Dist(s): NetLibrary CO

Confucianism & Taoism. unabr. ed. Julia Ching. Read by Ben Kingsley. Ed. by Walter Harrelson & Mike Hassell. 2 cass. (Running Time: 3 hrs.). Dramatization. (Religion, Scriptures & Spirituality Ser.). 1994. 17.95 (978-1-56823-015-3(X), 10458) Knowledge Prod.
Confucius (6th century B.C.E.) stressed the family, family ethics, & humanistic virtues & values. Taoism has been much more of a religion; yin & yang are seen as fundamental principles of the universe in many religious & philosophical discussions. The I Ching, a collection of maxims, precepts, & religious formulas, also continues to receive much attention.

Confucius. 10.00 Esstee Audios.
The Chinese genius who propounded a way of life based on peace.

Confucius & the Computer. Instructed by Manly P. Hall. 8.95 (978-0-89314-031-1(7), C850922) Philos Res.

***Confucius, Buddha, Jesus, & Muhammad.** Instructed by Mark W. Muesse. 2010. audio compact disk 269.95 (978-1-59803-674-9(2)) Teaching Co.

Confucius in the Boardroom Set: Ancient Wisdom, Modern Lessons for Business, unabr. ed. Read by Blair Underwood & Stephanie Zimbalist. Adapted by Stefan Rudnicki. Compiled by Stefan Rudnicki. 2 cass. (Running Time: 3 hrs.). 1999. 17.95 (978-1-57453-310-1(X)) Audio Lit.
Turning to the ancient wisdom of China for insight into conducting business humanely & effectively, the topics in this program include leadership, strategy, selling, personnel, & ethics. Newly adapted selections from the writings of Confucius, Chuang Tzu, Lao Tzu, & others present a practical vision for the executive.

Confucius in 90 Minutes. unabr. ed. Paul Strathern. Read by Robert Whitfield. (Running Time: 5400 sec.). (Philosophers in 90 Minutes Ser.). 2006. 14.95 (978-0-7861-3682-7(0)) Blckstn Audio.

Confucius, Lao Tzu, & the Chinese Philosophy. unabr. abr. ed. Read by Lynn Redgrave. (Running Time: 9000 sec.). (World of Philosophy Ser.). 2006. audio compact disk 25.95 (978-0-7861-6599-5(5)) Pub: Blckstn Audio. Dist(s): NetLibrary CO

Confusion. Elizabeth Jane Howard. Read by Jill Balcon. 12 vols. (Running Time: 18 hrs.). 2003. audio compact disk 110.95 (978-0-7540-5557-0(4)) Pub: Chivers Audio Bks GBR. Dist(s): AudioGO

Confusion. Elizabeth Jane Howard. 4 cass. (Running Time: 6 hrs.). (ENG., 2001. (978-0-333-67560-1(6)) Macmillan UK GBR.
Story of the Cazalet family in the spring of 1942, and follows them through the war to VE day, 8th May 1945. Polly and Clary have left Home Place for London, Louise has married, and Archie and Polly fall in love.

Confusion. unabr. collector's ed. Elizabeth Jane Howard. Read by Donada Peters. 10 cass. (Running Time: 15 hrs.). (Cazalet Chronicles: Vol. 3). 1997. 80.00 (978-0-7366-4022-0(3), 4520) Books on Tape.
Volume three of the Cazlet Chronicle takes the family through WW II. A masterpiece in the tradition of FORSYTHE SAGA & UPSTAIRS, DOWNSTAIRS.

***Confusion & the Stable Datum.** L. Ron Hubbard. (ENG.). 2002. audio compact disk 15.00 (978-1-4031-1261-3(4)) Bridge Pubns Inc.

Conga Drumming: A Beginner's Guide to Playing with Time. Alan Dworsky & Betsy Sansby. 1994. bk. 24.95 (978-0-9638801-0-9(1)) Pub: Dancing Hands. Dist(s): SCB Distributors

Conga Drumming: A Beginner's Guide to Playing with Time. Alan Dworsky & Betsy Sansby. 1995. pap. bk. 24.95 (978-0-7866-2346-4(2)) Dancing Hands.

Congenital Bilateral Absence of the Vas Deferens - A Bibliography & Dictionary for Physicians, Patients, & Genome Researchers. Compiled by Icon Group International, Inc. Staff. 2007. ring bd. 28.95 (978-0-497-11355-1(4)) Icon Grp.

Congenital Hypothyroidism - A Bibliography & Dictionary for Physicians, Patients, & Genome Researchers. Compiled by Icon Group International, Inc. Staff. 2007. ring bd. 28.95 (978-0-497-11356-8(2)) Icon Grp.

Conger Beasley, Jr. Sundancers & River Demons. Conger Beasley, Jr.. Read by Conger Beasley, Jr. 1 cass. (Running Time: 29 min.). 1990. 10.00 (031690) New Letters.
Author of environmental essays, novels & short stories, reads from a new book, "Sundancers & River Demons: Essays on Landscapes & Rituals".

Congo see Poetry of Vachel Lindsay

***Congratulations ... You're Gifted! Discovering Your God-Given Shape to Make a Difference in the World.** unabr. ed. Doug Fields & Erik Rees. (Running Time: 4 hrs. 0 mins. 0 sec.). (Invert Ser.). (ENG.). 2009. 12.99 (978-0-310-77215-6(X)) Zondervan.

Congregational Health Partnerships. 1 cass. (Care Cassettes Ser.: Vol. 16, No. 1). 1989. 10.80 Assn Prof Chaplains.

Congregations in Health Care. Granger Westburg. 1986. 10.80 (0106B) Assn Prof Chaplains.

Congress & Its Role in Climate Change Policy: Capitol Learning Audio Course. Manik Roy. Prod. by TheCapitol.Net. (ENG.). 2007. 47.00 (978-1-58733-072-8(5)) TheCapitol.

Congress & Its Role in Policymaking: Capitol Learning Audio Course. Chuck Cushman. Prologue by TheCapitol.Net. (ENG.). 2007. 47.00 (978-1-58733-061-2(X)) TheCapitol.

Congress & Its Role in Trade Policy: Capitol Learning Audio Course. Raymond Ahearn. Prod. by TheCapitol.Net. (ENG.). 2007. 47.00 (978-1-58733-071-1(7)) TheCapitol.

Congress, the Legislative Process, & the Fundamentals of Lawmaking Series: Course 1: How the House & Senate Establish Policy, Make Law, & Reconcile Differences. Chris Davis. Prod. by TheCapitol.Net. (ENG.). 2008. 47.00 (978-1-58733-123-7(3)) TheCapitol.

Congress, the Legislative Process, & the Fundamentals of Lawmaking Series: Course 2: How the House & Senate Establish Policy, Make Law, & Reconcile Differences. Chris Davis. Prod. by TheCapitol.Net. (ENG.). 2008. 47.00 (978-1-58733-122-0(5)) TheCapitol.

Congress, the Legislative Process, & the Fundamentals of Lawmaking Series: Course 3: How the House & Senate Establish Policy, Make Law, & Reconcile Differences. Chris Davis. Prod. by TheCapitol.Net. (ENG.). 2008. 47.00 (978-1-58733-121-3(7)) TheCapitol.

Congress, the Legislative Process, & the Fundamentals of Lawmaking Series: Course 4: How the House & Senate Establish Policy, Make Law, & Reconcile Differences. Chris Davis. Prod. by TheCapitol.Net. (ENG.). 2008. 47.00 (978-1-58733-120-6(9)) TheCapitol.

Congress, the Legislative Process, & the Fundamentals of Lawmaking Series: Course 5: How the House & Senate Establish Policy, Make Law, & Reconcile Differences: the Committee of the Whole. Chris Davis. Prologue by TheCapitol.Net. (ENG.). 2008. 47.00 (978-1-58733-119-0(5)) TheCapitol.

Congress, the Legislative Process, & the Fundamentals of Lawmaking Series: Course 6: How the House & Senate Establish Policy, Make Law, & Reconcile Differences. Chris Davis. Prod. by TheCapitol.Net. (ENG.). 2008. 47.00 (978-1-58733-118-3(7)) TheCapitol.

Congress, the Legislative Process, & the Fundamentals of Lawmaking Series: Course 7: How the House & Senate Establish Policy, Make Law, & Reconcile Differences. Chris Davis. Prod. by TheCapitol.Net. (ENG.). 2008. 47.00 (978-1-58733-117-6(9)) TheCapitol.

Congress, the Legislative Process, & the Fundamentals of Lawmaking Series: Course 8: How the House & Senate Establish Policy, Make Law, & Reconcile Differences. Chris Davis. Prod. by TheCapitol.Net. (ENG.). 2008. 47.00 (978-1-58733-116-9(0)) TheCapitol.

Congress, the Legislative Process, & the Fundamentals of Lawmaking Series: Course 9: How the House & Senate Establish Policy, Make Law, & Reconcile Differences. Chris Davis. Prod. by TheCapitol.Net. (ENG.). 2008. 47.00 (978-1-58733-115-2(2)) TheCapitol.

Congressional Appropriations Earmarks for Municipalities: How Local Governments Can Access a Fair Share of Federal Funding. Featuring William LaForge. Prod. by TheCapitol.Net. 2006. 107.00 (978-1-58733-050-6(4)) TheCapitol.

Congressional Committees & Party Leadership: Who Controls the Congressional Agenda. Ed. by TheCapitol.Net. 2005. audio compact disk 107.00 (978-1-58733-031-5(8)) TheCapitol.

Congressional Record see Fourteen American Masterpieces

Congressman Anthony Beilenson Speaks Out on Open Space Needs; Ocelot Research & Whooping Crane Rescues. Hosted by Nancy Pearlman. 1 cass. (Running Time: 28 min.). 10.00 (1207) Educ Comm CA.

Coniunctio: Mystery of Opposites. unabr. ed. Edward Edinger. 2 cass. (Running Time: 1 hr. 36 min.). 1984. 18.00 Set. (12201) Big Sur Tapes.
A clear & exceedingly useful exposition of Carl Jung's final work, "Mysterium Coniunctionus", an anatomy book of the psyche.

Conjoint Family Therapy. Virginia Satir. 10 cass. (Running Time: 14 hrs.). 1968. 90.00 set. (67806) Big Sur Tapes.
Documents a complete Esalen workshop in Big Sur in the 1960s with Virginia Satir. Demonstrates & introduces psychodrama & encounter approaches in family therapy. Includes didactic lectures & discussions, plus experiential group work with Couples, with Men, & with Women.

Conjugacion en Cancion. Frank Bignucolo. Prod. by Sara Jordan. 1 cass. (Running Time: 45 min. 24 secs.). (SPA.). (J). (gr. 1 up). 1998. pap. bk. 14.95 (978-1-895523-94-2(X), JMP S17K) Jordan Music.
Entertaining songs in Spanish teach conjugations of high frequency verbs in the present, preterit and future tenses, including irregular verbs. The accompanying lyrics/activity book includes exciting exercises.

Conjugacion en Cancion. abr. ed. Frank Bignucolo. 1 CD. (Running Time: 30 min.). (Songs that Teach Spanish Ser.). (SPA.). (J). (gr. 4-7). 1998. audio compact disk 13.95 (978-1-895523-96-6(6), JMP S17CD) Pub: S Jordan Publ. Dist(s): CrabtreePubCo

Conjugation Coach: Spanish Home Study. unabr. ed. Steven M. Fedor. 1 CD. 1999. audio compact disk 13.95 (978-0-9668170-1-0(X)) Your Success.
Compact disk helps you master the correct pronunciation for each verb ending in each tense in Spanish.

Conjuguons en Chansons. Frank Bignucolo. Illus. by Alex Filipov. 1 cass. (Running Time: 45 min.). (FRE.). (J). 1998. pap. bk. 14.95 (978-1-895523-85-0(0), JMP F17K) Jordan Music.
Entertaining songs in French teach conjugations of high frequency verbs in the present, passé composé and future tenses including irregular verbs. A complement of "music-only" tracks allows for great karaoke performances and music night productions! The accompanying lyrics/activity book includes very good exercises.

Conjuguons en Chansons. abr. ed. Frank Bignucolo. Lyrics by Blaine Selkirk. Prod. by Sara Jordan. Composed by Sara Jordan. 1 CD. (Running Time: 30 min.). (Songs That Teach French Ser.). (FRE.). (J). (gr. 4-7). 1998. audio compact disk 13.95 (978-1-895523-87-4(7), JMP F17CD) Pub: S Jordan Publ. Dist(s): CrabtreePubCo

Conjunto Bajo Sexto. Contrib. by Joe Torres. (Running Time: 1 hr. 4 mins.). 2005. 14.95 (978-5-558-09001-7(4)) Mel Bay.

Conjure Wife. unabr. ed. Fritz Leiber. Read by Stefan Rudnicki. 4 cass. (Running Time: 6 hrs.). 2002. 25.00 (978-1-59040-555-0(2)) Audio Lit.

Conn Cd-Psych: Concpt/con 9e. 9th ed. Spencer A. Rathus. (C). 2004. audio compact disk 22.95 (978-0-534-46294-9(4)) Pub: Wadsworth Pub. Dist(s): CENGAGE Learn

Conn Kilrea see Classic Ghost Stories, Vol. 3, A Collection

Connect, Vol. 1. Jack C. Richards et al. (Running Time: 2 hrs. 13 mins.). (Secondary Course Ser.). (ENG.). 2004. audio compact disk 43.00 (978-0-521-59488-2(X)) Cambridge U Pr.

Connect: Building Success Through People, Purpose, & Performance. unabr. ed. Keith Harrell & Hattie Hill. Read by Dick Hill. (YA). 2008. 54.99 (978-1-60252-959-5(0)) Find a World.

Connect: Building Success Through People, Purpose, & Performance. unabr. ed. Keith Harrell & Hattie Hill. Read by Dick Hill. (Running Time: 8 hrs. 0 mins. 0 sec.). (ENG.). 2007. audio compact disk 29.99 (978-1-4001-0463-5(7)); audio compact disk 59.99 (978-1-4001-3463-2(3)) Pub: Tantor Media. Dist(s): IngramPubServ

Connect: Building Success Through People, Purpose, & Performance. unabr. ed. Keith Harrell et al. (Running Time: 8 hrs. 0 mins. 0 sec.). (ENG.). 2007. audio compact disk 19.99 (978-1-4001-5463-0(4)) Pub: Tantor Media. Dist(s): IngramPubServ

Connect Class Cassettes 1. Jack C. Richards et al. (Running Time: 2 hrs. 13 mins.). (Secondary Course Ser.). (ENG.). 2004. 43.00 (978-0-521-59491-2(X)) Cambridge U Pr.

Connect Class Cassettes 2. Javk C. Richards et al. (Running Time: 2 hrs. 32 mins.). (ENG.). 2004. 43.00 (978-0-521-59480-6(4)) Cambridge U Pr.

Connect Class Cassettes 3. Jack C. Richards et al. (Running Time: 2 hrs. 32 mins.). (Connect Ser.). (ENG.). 2004. 43.00 (978-0-521-59473-8(1)) Cambridge U Pr.

Connect Class Cassettes 4. Jack C. Richards et al. (Running Time: 2 hrs. 32 mins.). (ENG.). 2004. 43.00 (978-0-521-59467-7(7)) Cambridge U Pr.

Connect Class CD 2. Jack C. Richards et al. (Running Time: 2 hrs. 32 mins.). (ENG.). 2004. audio compact disk 43.00 (978-0-521-59477-6(4)) Cambridge U Pr.

Connect Class CD 3. Jack C. Richards et al. (Running Time: 2 hrs. 32 mins.). (ENG.). 2004. audio compact disk 59.00 (978-0-521-59471-4(5)) Cambridge U Pr.

Connect Class CD 4. Jack C. Richards et al. (Running Time: 2 hrs. 32 mins.). (Secondary Course Ser.). (ENG.). 2004. audio compact disk 59.00 (978-0-521-59464-6(2)) Cambridge U Pr.

Connect Level 1 Class Audio CDs (2) 2nd ed. Jack C. Richards et al. (Running Time: 2 hrs. 13 mins.). (ENG.). 2009. audio compact disk 41.00 (978-0-521-73697-8(8)) Cambridge U Pr.

Connect Level 2 Class Audio CDs (2) 2nd ed. Jack C. Richards et al. (ENG.). 2009. audio compact disk 41.00 (978-0-521-73706-7(0)) Cambridge U Pr.

Connect Level 3 Class Audio CDs (3) 2nd ed. Jack C. Richards et al. (ENG.). 2009. audio compact disk 56.00 (978-0-521-73715-9(X)) Cambridge U Pr.

Connect Level 4 Class Audio CDs (3) 2nd ed. Jack C. Richards et al. (ENG.). 2009. audio compact disk 56.00 (978-0-521-73724-1(9)) Cambridge U Pr.

***Connect the Missing Piece.** Susan Diane Matz. (ENG.). 2010. 15.95 (978-0-9817974-6-5(6)) Abriev Ent.

***Connect to the Quiet.** Jan Barrett. (ENG.). 2009. audio compact disk 19.49 (978-0-615-34401-0(1)) Redbud Yoga.

Connected. unabr. ed. Daniel Altman. Narrated by Alan Sklar. (Running Time: 8 hrs. 30 mins. 0 sec.). (ENG.). 2007. audio compact disk 29.99 (978-1-4001-0429-1(7)) Pub: Tantor Media. Dist(s): IngramPubServ

Connected: The Surprising Power of Our Social Networks & How They Shape Our Lives. abr. unabr. ed. Nicholas A. Christakis & James H. Fowler. Read by Nicholas A. Christakis & James H. Fowler. (Running Time: 11 hrs. 0 mins. 0 sec.). (ENG.). 2009. audio compact disk 39.99 (978-0-7435-7910-0(0)) Pub: S&S Audio. Dist(s): S and S Inc

Connected: 24 Hours in the Global Economy. unabr. ed. Daniel Altman. Narrated by Alan Sklar. (Running Time: 8 hrs. 30 mins. 0 sec.). (ENG.). 2007. audio compact disk 19.99 (978-1-4001-5429-6(4)) Pub: Tantor Media. Dist(s): IngramPubServ

Connected: 24 Hours in the Global Economy. unabr. ed. Daniel Altman. Read by Alan Sklar. (Running Time: 8 hrs. 30 mins. 0 sec.). (ENG.). 2007. audio compact disk 59.99 (978-1-4001-3429-8(3)) Pub: Tantor Media. Dist(s): IngramPubServ

Connected Family: Bridging the Digital Generation Gap. Seymour A. Papert. 1996. audio compact disk 22.95 (978-1-56352-335-9(3)) Pub: Longstreet. Dist(s): Rowman

***Connected Wisdom Audio Recording (en) Living Stories about Living Systems.** Linda Booth Sweeney. Narrated by Courtney Campbell. (ENG.). (J). 2010. audio compact disk 24.95 (978-0-9822480-7-2(5)) SEED.

Connecticut: New London, Mystic, Stonington. 1 cass. (Running Time: 90 min). (Guided Auto Tape Tour). 12.95 (E3) Comp Comms Inc.

Connecticut Building & Residential Code. ICC. 2006. audio compact disk 133.00 (978-1-58001-296-6(5)) Int Code Counc.

Connecticut Yankee. Mark Twain. Narrated by Richard Kiley. (Running Time: 3 hrs.). 2006. 14.95 (978-1-59912-986-0(8)) Iofy Corp.

***Connecticut Yankee in King Arthur's Court.** Mark Twain. Narrated by Flo Gibson. (ENG.). 2010. audio compact disk 36.95 (978-1-60646-181-5(8)) Audio Bk Con.

Connecticut Yankee in King Arthur's Court. Mark Twain. Narrated by Walter Zimmerman. (Running Time: 5 hrs. 30 mins.). 1979. 35.95 (978-1-59912-850-4(0)) Iofy Corp.

Connecticut Yankee in King Arthur's Court. Mark Twain. Read by Kenneth Jay. (Running Time: 2 hrs. 30 mins.). 2005. 20.95 (978-1-60083-713-5(1)) Iofy Corp.

Connecticut Yankee in King Arthur's Court. Mark Twain. Read by Kenneth Jay. 2 cass. (Running Time: 2 hrs. 30 mins.). (Junior Classics Ser.). (J). (gr. 6-12). 2001. 13.98 (978-962-634-718-8(X), NA221814); audio compact disk 17.98 (978-962-634-218-3(8), NA221812) Naxos.
This satirical novel is the tale of Hank Morgan, a 19th century gun factory mechanic from New England, who when knocked unconscious, takes a fascinating journey through time and finds himself in a magical adventure of a lifetime of British chivalry set in England in the year 528.

Connecticut Yankee in King Arthur's Court. Mark Twain. Prod. by Mark Twain. Perf. by Jeff Riches. Adapted by Neil Munro. Directed By Neil Munro. Composed by Jeff Riches. (Running Time: 1 hr.). 2005. audio compact disk 15.95 (978-0-660-19377-9(9)) Canadian Broadcasting CAN.

Connecticut Yankee in King Arthur's Court. abr. ed. Mark Twain. Read by Jack Benson & Walter Zimmerman. 4 cass. (Running Time: 4 hrs. 30 min.). 1989. 21.00 incl. album. (C-3) Jimcin Record.
A Yankee visits "Camelot".

Connecticut Yankee in King Arthur's Court. abr. ed. Mark Twain. Read by Carl Reiner. 2 cass. (Running Time: 3 hrs.). (Ultimate Classics Ser.). 2004. 18.00 (978-1-931056-48-9(X), N Millennium Audio) New Millenn Enter.
The tale begins when the "yankee," a skilled mechanic in a 19th century New England arms factory, is struck on the head during a quarrel & awakens to find himself being taken as a prisoner to the Camelot of 528 A. D. With his 19th century know-how, the "yankee" sets out to modernize the Kingdom, but is opposed by a jealous court magician.

Connecticut Yankee in King Arthur's Court. abr. adpt. ed. Mark Twain. (Bring the Classics to Life: Level 3 Ser.). (ENG.). (gr. 3-16). 2008. audio compact disk 12.95 (978-1-55576-479-1(7)) EDCON Pubng.

Connecticut Yankee in King Arthur's Court. unabr. ed. Mark Twain. Narrated by Flo Gibson. 9 cass. (Running Time: 13 hrs.). 2003. 28.95 (978-1-55685-749-2(7)) Audio Bk Con.
A blow on the head transports an arms factory superintendent from Hartford back to the old world of King Arthur's day. He marries, has a child and another blow returns him to his original time and place. He also makes the sun disappear!.

Connecticut Yankee in King Arthur's Court, unabr. ed. Mark Twain. Read by Stewart Lankton. 8 cass. (Running Time: 11 hrs. 30 mins.). 2000. 56.95 (978-0-7861-1721-5(4), 2525) Blckstn Audio.
An ingenious Yankee mechanic, knocked unconscious in a fight, awakens to find himself at Camelot in AD 528. He is condemned to death, but saves himself by posing as a magician like Merlin, correctly predicting an eclipse & becoming minister to King Arthur. He increases his power by applying 19th-century knowledge of gunpowder & electricity.

Connecticut Yankee in King Arthur's Court. unabr. ed. Mark Twain. 8 cass. (Running Time: 8 hrs.). (Classic Literature Ser.). 1997. pap. bk. 29.95 Set. (978-1-55656-200-6(4)) Dercum Audio.
This time traveling tale captures the imagination of young & old when Hank Morgan finds himself magically transported to 6th century England. Hilarious consequences are intermingled with high adventure as he courageously challenges the infamous knights of the Round Table during this spirited romp into the past.

Connecticut Yankee in King Arthur's Court. unabr. ed. Mark Twain. Narrated by Norman Dietz. 9 cass. (Running Time: 12 hrs. 45 mins.). (gr. 10 up). 1988. 78.00 (978-1-55690-120-1(8), 88997E7) Recorded Bks.
The classic story of a 19th-century New Englander who, after a quarrel, awakens to find himself in sixth-century England.

***Connecticut Yankee in King Arthur's Court.** unabr. ed. Mark Twain. Narrated by William Dufris. (Running Time: 12 hrs. 0 mins. 0 sec.). (ENG.). 2010. 24.99 (978-1-4001-6607-7(1)); 18.99 (978-1-4001-8607-5(2)); audio compact disk 69.99 (978-1-4001-4607-9(0)); audio compact disk 34.99 (978-1-4001-1607-2(4)) Pub: Tantor Media. Dist(s): IngramPubServ

Connecticut Yankee in King Arthur's Court. unabr. ed. Mark Twain & Stuart Langton. (Running Time: 11 hrs. NaN mins.). 2008. 29.95 (978-1-4332-5501-4(4)); audio compact disk 90.00 (978-1-4332-5500-7(6)) Blckstn Audio.

Connecticut Yankee in King Arthur's Court. unabr. abr. ed. Mark Twain. Read by Carl Reiner. (Running Time: 10800 sec.). 2007. audio compact disk 24.00 (978-1-4332-0545-3(9)) Blckstn Audio.

Connecticut Yankee in King Arthur's Court. unabr. abr. ed. Mark Twain. Read by Carl Reiner. (Running Time: 10800 sec.). 2007. audio compact disk 19.95 (978-1-4332-0546-0(7)) Blckstn Audio.

Connecticut Yankee in King Arthur's Court. unabr. collector's ed. Mark Twain. Read by Michael Prichard. 10 cass. (Running Time: 15 hrs.). (J). 1979. 80.00 (978-0-7366-0192-4(9), 1192) Books on Tape.
The tale begins when the "yankee," a skilled mechanic in a 19th century New England arms factory, is struck on the head during a quarrel & awakens to find himself being taken as a prisoner to the Camelot of 528 A. D. With his 19th century know-how, the "yankee" sets out to modernize the Kingdom, but is opposed by a jealous court magician.

***Connecticut Yankee in King Arthurs Court: Bring the Classics to Life.** adpt. ed. Mark Twain. (Bring the Classics to Life Ser.). 2008. pap. bk. 21.95 (978-1-55576-509-5(2)) EDCON Pubng.

Connecticut Yankee in King Arthur's Court: Narrated by Richard Henzel. 2008. 39.99 (978-0-9747237-4-7(6)) R Henzel.

Connecticut Yankee in King Arthur's Court Readalong. Mark Twain. (Illustrated Classics Collection: No. 3). 1994. pap. bk. 14.95 (978-0-7854-0736-2(7), 40449) Am Guidance.

***Connecting Church: Beyond Small Groups to Authentic Community.** Randy Frazee. (Running Time: 5 hrs. 52 mins. 0 sec.). (ENG.). 2008. 16.99 (978-0-310-30437-1(7)) Zondervan.

Connecting Heart to Heart. 2nd ed. 1998. 12.95 (978-1-893027-04-6(X)) Path of Light.

Connecting with God's Master Plan for Your Life: Group Leader's Kit. Gloria Copeland. (ENG.). 2008. DVD & audio compact disk 49.00 (978-1-57562-975-9(5)) K Copeland Pubns.

Connecting with Higher Self, Using Your Intuition. unabr. ed. Kim Falcone & Steven Falcone. Read by Kim Falcone. 1 cass. (Running Time: 53 min.). 1994. 10.95 (978-1-887799-03-4(6), 1-906-456) Creat Aware.
Develop a greater communication with your Higher Self. Learn to trust your intuition.

Connecting with our Children: Guiding Principles for Parents in a Troubled World. Roberta Gilbert. (ENG.). 2006. audio compact disk (978-0-9763455-5-8(2)) Leading Systems.

Connecting with Your Angels. Doreen Virtue. 6 CDs. 2004. audio compact disk 23.95 (978-1-4019-0404-3(1)) Hay House.

Connecting with Your Angels: How to See, Talk & Work with the Angelic Realm. Doreen Virtue. 6 cass. (Running Time: 6 hrs.). 1999. reel tape 59.95 (978-1-56170-713-3(9), 4030) Hay House.
Whether you want to channel angels or just want to clearly hear their divine guidance, Dr. Virtue shows that specifics can be taken to clearly communicate with these heavenly beings. Once anything internal standing in your path is released, divine communications will be received very directly. Again, the angels will help every step of the way.

Connecting with Your Angels: How to See, Talk & Work with the Angelic Realm. abr. ed. Doreen Virtue. 2 cass. (Running Time: 2 hrs.). 2001. reel tape 18.95 (978-1-56170-851-2(8), 4103) Hay House.
Doreen shows how to work with the angelic realm.

Connecting with Your Customers. Bill Bethel. Read by Bill Bethel. 6 cass. (Running Time: 8 hrs.). 1993. 98.00 set, incl. action guide. (2043) Dartnell Corp.
Communication tools that help you tune in better to your customers' mind set.

Connecting with Your Customers. abr. ed. Bill Bethel. Read by Bill Bethel. Ed. by Vera Derr. 2 cass. (Running Time: 3 hrs.). 1996. 15.95 Set. (978-0-85013-246-5(0)) Dartnell Corp.
Will teach you the skills for influencing & persuading others to see your point of view. By knowing how to select the right communication tool at the right time in the sale process, you'll not only get your foot in the door, you'll get the sale.

Connecting with Your Inner Advisor. 2001. 24.95 (978-1-58557-044-7(3)) Dynamic Growth.

Connecting with Your Inner-Teacher & Spirit Guides: Easy Methods for Creating a Bond with Spiritual Helpers. unabr. ed. Angela M. Mattey. Read by Angela M. Mattey. Perf. by Brian Epp. 1 cass. (Running Time: 1 hr. 10 min.). (How to Be an Awakened Human Ser.: Vol. 2). 1998. 9.95 (978-1-882836-03-1(0)) TAM Ent.
Side A is a teaching tape for methods to use for connecting with one's spiritual guidance. Side B is a meditation to establish the connection to one's spiritual guidance.

Connecting with your Spirit Guide. Created by Sunny Dawn Johnston. 2007. audio compact disk 16.00 (978-0-9798119-1-3(0)) Sunlight.

Connections. J. Collins. 2001. (978-0-333-78008-4(6)) Macmillan UK GBR.

Connections of the Heart. Earnie Larsen. 6 cass. (Running Time: 1 hr.). 1995. 45.95 Set. (978-1-56047-064-9(X), A614) E Larsen Enterprises.
This album is about in-depth healing of those parts of our lives that are most wounded. Connections of the heart means we can only heal what we allow ourselves to feel. Feeling can hurt...but beyond that hurt lies the source of profound joy.

***Connectors: How the World's Most Successful Businesspeople Build Relationships & Win Clients for Life.** unabr. ed. Maribeth Kuzmeski. Read by Scott Peterson. (Running Time: 7 hrs.). (ENG.). 2009. 26.98 (978-1-59659-488-3(8), GildAudio) Pub: Gildan Media. Dist(s): HachBkGrp

***Connemara Accordian Vol. 1.** (ENG.). 1990. 11.95 (978-0-8023-7040-2(3)) Pub: Clo Iar-Chonnachta IRL. Dist(s): Dufour

***Connemara Favourites Vol. 2 / Seoda Chonamara 2.** (ENG.). 1990. 11.95 (978-0-8023-7031-0(4)) Pub: Clo Iar-Chonnachta IRL. Dist(s): Dufour

Connersvine. Contrib. by Connersvine. 2007. audio compact disk 13.99 (978-5-557-58538-5(9)) INO Rec.

Connie of Kettle Street. Carol Rivers & Annie Aldington. 2007. 76.95 (978-1-84652-107-2(6)); audio compact disk 89.95 (978-1-84652-108-9(4)) Pub: Magna Story GBR. Dist(s): Ulverscroft US

Connie's Secret. Dwayne Epstein. Narrated by Larry A. McKeever. (Romance Ser.). (J). 2003. 10.95 (978-1-58659-111-3(8)); audio compact disk 14.95 (978-1-58659-340-7(4)) Artesian.

Conocernos. Donna Reseigh Long & Janice Lynn Maclan. bk. 97.65 (978-0-8384-0596-3(7)); bk., wbk. ed., lab manual ed. 148.25 (978-0-8384-0601-4(7)) Heinle.

Conocernos. Donna Reseigh Long & Janice Lynn Maclan. 1992. (978-0-318-69351-4(8)) Heinle.

Conocernos. 2nd ed. Donna Reseigh Long & Janice Lynn Maclan. 42.00 (978-0-8384-6425-0(4)) Heinle.

Conocernos. 2nd ed. Donna Reseigh Long & Janice Lynn Maclan. (C). bk. 83.95 (978-0-8384-8721-1(1)) Heinle.

Conocernos. 2nd ed. Sara Long & Macian. 1 cass. (Running Time: 1 hr.). 1996. stu. ed. 12.50 (978-0-8384-6429-8(7)) Heinle.

Cononcerns. 2nd ed. Sara Long. (C). bk. 124.95 (978-0-8384-8504-0(9)) Heinle.

Conquer Drug/Alcohol Addiction. Bernie Schallen. 1990. audio compact disk 64.50 (978-1-55959-023-5(8)) Taylor and Fran.

Conquer Fear! A Unique Blend of Psychology & Theology to Change Your Beliefs - Thus Your Behavior. Lisa Jimenez. Read by Lisa Jimenez. 5 CDs. (Running Time: 4 hrs 42 min.). 2002. audio compact disk (978-0-9705807-1-9(1)) RX Success.
Face your hidden fears and shatter the limiting beliefs that hold you back. Cultivate your faith and adopt empowering beliefs that will ignite your success in business and in life.

Conquer Fear of Flying, Vol. 123. 2001. 24.95 (978-1-58557-026-3(5)) Dynamic Growth.

Conquer Impotence. 1 cass. (Running Time: 60 min.). 10.95 (029) Psych Res Inst.
Mental conditioning to remove psychological blocks related to the frustrating problems of impotence.

Conquer Male Impotence. Dean A. Montalbano. 6 CDs. (Running Time: 5 hrs. 30 min.). (Hypnotic Sensory Response Audio Ser.). 2004. audio compact disk 89.95 (978-1-932086-13-3(7)) L Lizards Pub Co.

Conquer Male Impotence: An HSR Wellness in Mind Trance-Formation Publication. Excerpts. Dean A. Montalbano. 6 cass. (Running Time: 6 hrs.). (Hypnotic Sensory Response Audio Ser.). 2002. 89.95 (978-1-932086-08-9(0)) L Lizards Pub Co.
Self Hypnotic tape set to help overcome male Impotence.

Conquer Panic Attacks, 2 cass. (Running Time: 2 hrs.). 2000. 24.95 (978-1-58557-031-7(1)) Dynamic Growth.

Conquer Procrastination. Mel Gilley. Ed. by Steven C. Eggleston. 1 cass. (World of Hypnosis Ser.). 1987. 6.95 SCE Prod & List & Lrn.
Self-hypnosis to conquer procrastination habits.

Conquer Stress. unabr. ed. Krs Edstrom. Read by Krs Edstrom. 1 cass. (Running Time: 40 min.). (Inner Mastery Ser.). 1994. 9.95 Norelco size. (978-1-886198-10-4(1)); 12.95 Bk. box size. (978-1-886198-02-9(0), IMS03) Soft Stone Pub.
Helps you permanently alter your relationship to stress as you discover where stress, fear and anxiety lodge in your body and how to release them. Effective guided relaxation and meditation skills that teach you to become aware of how your thoughts and history are stored in your body and how they manifest through states such as stress. Music designed to calm as you cultivate inner awareness and mastery. Provides a new solution to the age-old problem of stress. Too often we "go through the motions" of life, not tuned in to what is happening internally - how our mind and body interrelate and how the outside world and our inside world interrelate. The purpose of these tapes is not only that you feel results after each listen, but that you develop increasingly deeper skills to serve you in all of life's challenges and excursions. Commonly considered negatives such as pain, stress and insomnia are experienced in a new, non-judgmental way that invites insight and is both growth-promoting and freeing. Once perceived enemies turn into welcome teachers. Similarly, positive and everyday events such as watching a bird soar, hitting a ball or conducting business are experienced in a more complete way; a way that enriches your relationship to self and thus the outside world.

Conquer Stress: Meditations to Take You from Tension to Tranquility. unabr. abr. ed. 1 CDs. (Running Time: 2220 sec.). (Inner Mastery Ser.). 2007. audio compact disk 16.95 (978-1-886198-17-3(9)) Pub: Soft Stone Pub. Dist(s): Ingram Bk Co

***Conquer Stress... Auto-matically.** Bob Griswold & Deirdre M. Griswold. (Running Time: 58). 2010. 15.98 (978-1-55848-707-9(7)) EffectiveMN.

Conquer Stress Auto-Matically. Robert E. Griswold & Deirdre Griswold. Read by Robert E. Griswold & Deirdre Griswold. 1 cass. (While-U-Drive Ser.). 1996. 11.98 (978-1-55848-901-1(0)) EffectiveMN.
The process of making positive changes with this program is so enjoyable & effortless that the results achieved may truly seem automatic.

***Conquer the Chaos: How to Grow a Successful Small Business Without Going Crazy.** unabr. ed. Clate Mask et al. Read by Don Hagen. (Running Time: 5 hrs. 30 mins.). (ENG.). 2010. 29.98 (978-1-59659-654-2(6), GildAudio) Pub: Gildan Media. Dist(s): HachBkGrp

Conquer Your Anxiety: With Optimal Thinking. unabr. ed. Rosalene Glickman. (Running Time: 30 mins.). (ENG.). 2009. 6.95 (978-1-59659-479-1(9), GildAudio) Pub: Gildan Media. Dist(s): HachBkGrp

Conquer Your Cosmic Challenges. Elaine Randisi. 1 cass. 8.95 (289) Am Fed Astrologers.
Work with cosmic stresses to evolve into who you want to be.

Conquer Your Depression. Narrated by Dick Lutz. 1 cass. (Running Time: 20 min.). 1981. 7.95 (978-0-931625-04-6(1), 4) DIMI Pr.
Explains different types of depression & what to do about each type. Relaxation narration on reverse side.

Conquer Your Fear, Share Your Faith: An Evangelism Crash Course. unabr. ed. Kirk Cameron & Ray Comfort. (Running Time: 6 hrs. 0 mins. 0 sec.). (ENG.). 2009. audio compact disk 21.98 (978-1-59644-785-1(0), christianSeed) christianaud.

***Conquer Your Fear, Share Your Faith: An Evangelism Crash Course.** unabr. ed. Kirk Cameron & Ray Comfort. Narrated by Erik Synnestvedt. (ENG.). 2009. 12.98 (978-1-59644-786-8(9), christianSeed) christianaud.

Conquer Your Fears. Narrated by Dick Lutz. 1 cass. (Running Time: 24 min.). 1981. 7.95 (978-0-931625-05-3(X), 5) DIMI Pr.
All of us have some fears & if yours keeps you from doing what you want to do, this tape's for you.

Conquer Your Fears. unabr. ed. Read by Richard L. Lutz. 1 cass. 10.95 (AF1961) J Norton Pubs.
Everyone has some fears & for those whose fear keeps them from doing what they want to do this program is ideal. Richard L. Lutz, clinical social worker, provides practical plans for conquering, not just understanding, single, cluster, & general or vague phobias.

Conquer Your Insomnia. Narrated by Dick Lutz. 1 cass. (Running Time: 16 min.). 1981. 7.95 (978-0-931625-06-0(8), 6) DIMI Pr.
Shows several things you can do to start getting a good nights rest. Sleep-inducing narration on reverse side.

Conquer Your Insomnia. unabr. ed. Read by Richard L. Lutz. 1 cass. 10.95 (AF1962) J Norton Pubs.
Learn from Richard L. Lutz, clinical social worker, what you can do to get a good night's rest. His practical techniques & suggestions for determining how much sleep you truly need will help you establish your individual sleep routine. Side 2 of the tape offers guaranteed help.

Conquer Your Shyness. Narrated by Dick Lutz. 1 cass. (Running Time: 19 min.). 1981. 7.95 (978-0-931625-03-9(3), 3) DIMI Pr.
Instructions on Side A tell you exactly what steps to take to become less shy. Relaxation narration for shyness is on reverse side.

Conquered Legacy: A Self-Hypnosis Exercise to Comfort the Inner Child: A Healing Journey. unabr. ed. F. Felicia Ferrara. 1 cass. (Running Time: 1 hrs. 8 min.). (YA). (gr. 9 up). 1998. bk. 14.95 (978-1-892992-02-4(7), 81008); audio compact disk 19.99 CD. (978-1-892992-00-0(0), 81006) CEC Pubs.
Two self-hypnosis exercises: 1) to relax & become familiar with the hypnosis process; 2) to comfort the inner child & strengthen determination to heal.

Conquering Adversity. Chris Novak. 2005. audio compact disk 19.95 (978-0-9772257-0-5(4)) CornerStone Leader.

Conquering Adversity. unabr. ed. Jay R. Jensen. Read by Jay R. Jensen. 1 cass. (Running Time: 60 min.). 1989. 10.00 (978-1-877898-07-5(4)) Pubns Of Worth.
Returned prisoner of war talk.

Conquering an Enemy Called Average. John Mason. 2 cass. 1999. 12.99 Set. (978-1-888103-11-3(6)) Insight Intl.

Conquering Cancer Network: Empowering Teens with Tools, Info. & Inspiring Stories. Degge Group Ltd. Staff. 1 CD. (Running Time: 2 hrs). (YA). 2005. audio compact disk 39.95 (978-0-9632020-3-1(0)) Degge Grp.

Conquering Compulsive Behavior. Gloria Arenson. 2 cass. (Running Time: 60 min. per cass.). 1988. 19.95 (978-0-9621942-1-4(2)) Brockart Bks.
Deals with how to understand compulsive behaviors such as overeating, drinking, drug use, spending, smoking, exercising, cleaning, TV watching, promiscuous sex, computer hacking, or perfectionism as ways people use pleasure to mask pain. Suggests a treatment plan for effectively overcoming compulsive behaviors.

Conquering Computer Fear. abr. ed. Michael Bremer. 1 CD. (Running Time: 55 mins.). (Advice from the Neighborhood Nerd Ser.). 2000. bk. 19.95 (978-0-9669949-3-3(0)) UnTech.
The first step in learning about computers, this audio workshop helps newcomers overcome the fear of computers & technology, & overcome the nervousness of learning.

Conquering Computer Fear. unabr. ed. Michael Bremer. 1 cass. (Running Time: 55 mins.). (Advice from the Neighborhood Nerd Ser.). 2000. pap. bk. 19.99 (978-0-9669949-4-0(9)) UnTech.
The first step in learning about computers, this workshop helps newcomers overcome the fear of computers & technology & overcome the nervousness of learning.

Conquering Conflict Through Character. Francis Frangipane. 1 cass. (Running Time: 90 mins.). (Disciples of the Cross Ser.: Vol. 4). 2000. 5.00 (FF01-004) Morning NC.
In this four-part series, Francis releases important information needed to clearly understand the principles of taking up the cross & following Christ.

Conquering Depression: 11 Cor. 4:7-9; 16. Ed Young. 1983. 4.95 (978-0-7417-1327-8(6), 327) Win Walk.

Conquering Ego's Deception. Read by Chogyam Trungpa & Osel Tendzin. 7 cass. 1981. 75.00 (A076) Vajradhatu.
Five talks. The fact that we do not fundamentally exist produces tremendous panic which causes us to solidify the world.

Conquering Family. unabr. collector's ed. Thomas B. Costain. Read by David Case. 10 cass. (Running Time: 15 hrs.). (History of the Plantaganets Ser.). 1993. 80.00 (978-0-7366-2517-3(8), 3272) Books on Tape.
Story of England from William the Conqueror's arrival in 1066 to the reign of John in 1216. First in series.

Conquering Fear: Living Boldly in an Uncertain World. unabr. ed. Harold S. Kushner. Read by Harold S. Kushner. (ENG.). 2009. audio compact disk 30.00 (978-0-7393-8518-0(6), Random AudioBks) Pub: Random Audio Pubg. Dist(s): Random

Conquering Fears & Anxiety - Peace of Mind. Robert E. Griswold. Read by Robert E. Griswold. 1 cass. (Super Strength Ser.). 1992. 11.98 (978-1-55848-307-1(1)) EffectiveMN.
Two complete non-subliminal programs to help you relax & easily release negative feelings & fears.

Conquering Gotham: A Gilded Age Epic: the Construction of Penn Station & Its Tunnels. unabr. ed. Jill Jonnes. Read by David Drummond. (Running Time: 11 hrs. 30 mins. 0 sec.). (ENG.). 2007. audio compact disk 34.99 (978-1-4001-0436-9(X)); audio compact disk 24.99 (978-1-4001-5436-4(7)); audio compact disk 69.99 (978-1-4001-3436-6(6)) Pub: Tantor Media. Dist(s): IngramPubServ

Conquering Illness. Darrell Franken. 2 cass. (Running Time: 30 min. per cass.). 1986. 12.95 (978-0-934957-15-1(0)) Wellness Pubns.
Gives the reasons for using meditation, imagery, & excercise, to help bring healing.

Conquering Life's Pressures. Elbert Willis. 1 cass. (Growth Series). 4.00 Fill the Gap.

Conquering Low Frustration Tolerance. Albert Ellis. 1 cass. (Running Time: 73 min.). 9.95 (C004) A Ellis Institute.
Practical techniques for avoiding frustration when the world is not the way it "should" be; for overcoming difficult situations; & for getting more of what you want out of life.

Conquering Low Frustration Tolerance. Albert Ellis. 1 cass. (Running Time: 73 min.). 9.95 (C004) Inst Rational-Emotive.
Learn practical techniques for reducing frustration when the world is not the way it "should" be; how to overcome difficult situations; & how to get more of what you want out of life.

Conquering Procrastination: How to Stop Stalling & Start Achieving. Neil Fiore. 6 cass. 1994. 49.95 Set. (10940AX) Nightingale-Conant.
Dr. Fiore's unique approach - which incorporates amusing anecdotes & personal insights - makes it fun & easy to accomplish your goals. His tested methods for conquering procrastination have helped improve the quality of work at Levi Strauss, Safeway Stores, Inc., Union Bank, Bechtel Power Company, Southern Pacific & hundreds of other companies. Includes workbook.

Conquering Procrastination: How to Stop Stalling & Start Achieving! abr. ed. Neil Fiore. Read by Neil Fiore. (Running Time: 2 hrs. 0 mins. 0 sec.). (ENG.). 2008. audio compact disk 19.95 (978-0-7435-7310-8(2), Nightgale) Pub: S&S Audio. Dist(s): S and S Inc

Conquering Stress. Somers H. White. 6 cass. (Running Time: 60 min. per cass.). 100.00 (C115) S White.
Shows what stress is & not, how to evaluate it, respond to it, handle it & how to reduce anixety levels & relax.

Conquering Sword of Conan. unabr. ed. Robert E. Howard. Narrated by Todd McLaren. (Running Time: 18 hrs. 0 mins. 0 sec.). (Conan of Cimmeria Ser.). (ENG.). 2009. audio compact disk 39.99 (978-1-4001-1225-8(7)); audio compact disk 79.99 (978-1-4001-4225-5(3)); audio compact disk 29.99 (978-1-4001-6225-3(4)) Pub: Tantor Media. Dist(s): IngramPubServ

Conquering the Challenges of Life: Coping with Grief & Suffering - the Power of Forgiveness. unabr. ed. Shmuel Irons. 2 cass. (Running Time: 3 hrs.). 19.95 Set. (978-1-889648-01-9(9)) Jwish Her Fdtn.
Rabbi Irons applies the timeless truths found in the Bible & Talmud to gain knowledge, peace of mind, & the practical tools to deal with the difficulties of life.

Conquering the Dire Need for Love. Albert Ellis. 1 cass. (Running Time: 87 min.). 9.95 (C003) A Ellis Institute.
Shows you how to overcome love-slobbism, reduce fears of rejection, & have a more pleasurable relationship with yourself & others.

Conquering the Dire Need for Love. Albert Ellis. 1 cass. (Running Time: 87 min.). 9.95 (C003) Inst Rational-Emotive.

Conquering the Fear of Flight. Contrib. by Wavorly et al. Prod. by Rob Graves. 2007. audio compact disk 13.99 (978-5-557-70348-2(9)) Flicker.

Conquering the Four Maras. Chogyam Trungpa. Read by Chogyam Trungpa. Read by Osel Tendzin. 8 cass. 1980. 79.00 (A075) Vajradhatu.
Nine talks. The four maras are traditional Buddhist categories that describe obstacles to being awake. Conquering the maras is discussed in terms of understanding & mastering reality.

Conquering the Four Maras. Read by Chogyam Trungpa & Osel Tendzin. 6 cass. 1981. 58.50 (A110) Vajradhatu.
Five talks. The four maras are traditional Buddhist categories that describe obstacles to being awake. Conquering the maras is discussed in terms of understanding & mastering reality. The last talk is by Mrs. Lila Rich, Osel Tendzin's wife.

Conquering the Spirit of Jezebel. Francis Frangipane. 1 cass. (Running Time: 90 mins.). (Basics of Spiritual Warfare Ser.: Vol. 6). 2000. 5.00 (FF02-006) Morning NC.
Francis combines years of practical experience with a soundbiblical perspective in this popular & important series.

Conquering Through Conflict: 2 Peter. unabr. ed. Charles R. Swindoll. 5 cass. (Running Time: 4 hrs.). 1998. 25.95 (978-1-57972-274-6(1)) Insight Living.

Conquering Tryouts: For the Male & Female Cheerleader. Jeanne Conner & James Conner. (YA). 2004. reel tape (978-0-9755042-0-8(7)) JC Spirit Co.

Conquering Windows Vista: Self-paced Instructional Training Course. abr. ed. William Stanek. Narrated by Ron Knowles. (Running Time: 4 hrs. 20 mins.). (ENG.). 2008. 29.95 (978-1-57545-319-4(3), RP Audio Pubng) Pub: Reagent Press. Dist(s): OverDrive Inc

Conquering Your Internal Critic So You Can Sing Your Own Song. unabr. ed. Jack N. Singer. 1 cass. (Running Time: 30 mins.). 1998. bk. 9.95 (978-0-9700694-3-6(X)) Psychologically Speak.
Listeners will learn the source of their moods, attitudes & stress. They will learn the 5 "C's" of success in life & how to overcome their own obstacles.

Conquering Your Own Goliaths. Steven A. Cramer. 1 cass. 2004. 9.95 (978-1-55503-241-8(9), 06004164) Covenant Comms.
Six keys to rising above weaknesses, sins & addictions.

Conqueror. Georgette Heyer. Read by Cornelius Garrett. 10 cass. (Running Time: 15 hrs.). 2002. 84.95 (978-0-7540-0924-5(6), CAB 2346) Pub: Chivers Audio Bks GBR. Dist(s): AudioGO

Conquerors: Roosevelt, Truman & the Destruction of Hitler's Germany, 1941-1945. abr. ed. Michael R. Beschloss. Read by Michael R. Beschloss. 2006. 17.95 (978-0-7435-6369-7(7), Audioworks) Pub: S&S Audio. Dist(s): S and S Inc

Conquest. Stephen Coonts. Read by Eric Conger. 6 cass. (Saucer Ser.: No. 2). 54.95 (978-0-7927-3307-2(X), CSL 689); audio compact disk 79.95 (978-0-7927-3308-9(8), SLD 689); audio compact disk 29.95 (978-0-7927-3309-6(6), CMP 689) AudioGO.

Conquest. abr. ed. Stephen Coonts. Read by Dick Hill. (Running Time: 5 hrs.). (Saucer Ser.: No. 2). 2010. audio compact disk 14.99 (978-1-4418-4209-1(8), 9781441842091, BACD) Brilliance Audio.

Conquest. unabr. ed. Stephen Coonts. Read by Dick Hill. (Running Time: 10 hrs.). (Saucer Ser.: No. 2). 2010. 24.99 (978-1-4418-4205-3(5), 9781441842053, Brilliance MP3); audio compact disk 29.99 (978-1-4418-4203-9(9), 9781441842039, Bril Audio CD Unabri) Brilliance Audio.

Conquest of Constantinople - Excerpts. unabr. ed. Excerpts. Geoffrey De Villehardouin. Narrated by John Franklyn-Robbins. 3 cass. (Running Time: 4 hrs. 30 mins.). 1999. 26.00 (978-1-55690-814-9(8), 93131E7) Recorded Bks.
Excerpts from French nobleman Geoffroy de Villehardouin's eyewitness account of the Fourth Crusade, begun in 1202 at the urging of Pope Innocent III, which ultimately disintegrated into a war of conquest against fellow Christians - Frank against Greek, Roman Catholic versus Orthodox.

Conquest of Peru, Set. William Prescott. Read by Flo Gibson. 13 cass. (Running Time: 1 hr. 30 min. per cass.). 1990. 41.95 (978-1-55685-165-0(0)) Audio Bk Con.
In this epic, history is stranger than fiction. The lure of gold & adventure leads to violent conflicts between the Spanish conquistadores & the Incas.

Conquest of the Americas, Pts. I-II. Instructed by Marshall Eakin. 12 CDs. (Running Time: 12 hrs.). 2002. bk. 69.95 (978-1-56585-394-2(6), 888) Teaching Co.

Conquest of the Americas, Pts. I-II. Instructed by Marshall C. Eakin. 12 cass. (Running Time: 12 hrs.). 2002. bk. 54.95 (978-1-56585-268-6(0), 888) Teaching Co.

Conquest of the Americas, Vol. 2. Instructed by Marshall C. Eakin. 6 cass. (Running Time: 6 hrs.). 2002. 129.95 (978-1-56585-269-3(9)) Teaching Co.

***Conquest of the Physical Universe.** L. Ron Hubbard. 2010. audio compact disk 15.00 (978-1-4031-7186-3(6)); audio compact disk 15.00 (978-1-4031-7185-6(8)); audio compact disk 15.00 (978-1-4031-7181-8(5)); audio compact disk 15.00 (978-1-4031-7173-3(4)); audio compact disk 15.00 (978-1-4031-7183-2(1)); audio compact disk 15.00 (978-1-4031-7174-0(2)); audio compact disk 15.00 (978-1-4031-7180-1(7)); audio compact disk 15.00 (978-1-4031-7182-5(3)); audio compact disk 15.00 (978-1-4031-7189-4(0)); audio compact disk 15.00 (978-1-4031-7188-7(2)); audio compact disk 15.00 (978-1-4031-7187-0(4)); audio compact disk 15.00 (978-1-4031-7177-1(7)); audio compact disk 15.00 (978-1-4031-7175-7(0)); audio compact disk 15.00 (978-1-4031-7178-8(5)); audio compact disk 15.00 (978-1-4031-7176-4(9)); audio compact disk 15.00 (978-1-4031-7179-5(3)); audio compact disk 15.00 (978-1-4031-7184-9(X)) Bridge Pubns Inc.

Conquests & Cultures. unabr. collector's ed. Thomas Sowell. Read by Barrett Whitener. 13 cass. (Running Time: 19 hrs. 30 min.). 1999. 104.00 (978-0-7366-4360-3(5), 4832) Books on Tape.
Attempts to understand the meaning of cultural differences including how these differences have influenced the economic & social fates of civilizations, nations, & ethnic groups. This particular installment focuses on how military conquest both destroys & spreads culture by examining the histories of the English, the Africans, the Slavs, & the indigenous people of the New World. The author believes that some cultures - understood as "the working machinery of everyday life" are clearly superior to others.

Conquistador. abr. ed. Barry Sadler. Read by Charlton Griffin. 2 vols. (Casca Ser.: No. 10). 2003. (978-1-58807-539-0(7)) Am Pubng Inc.

Conquistador. abr. ed. Barry Sadler. Read by Charlton Griffin. 2 vols. (Running Time: 3 hrs.). (Casca Ser.: No. 10). 2003. 18.00 (978-1-58807-110-1(3)) Am Pubng Inc.
Sixteenth-century Mexicowhere enemies of Aztec King Moctezuma are sacrificed to his bloodthirsty gods by the thousands. Among the soldiers of Spanish conquistador Hernan Cortes, Casca (alias Carlos Romano) returns to the savage land to seek revenge on the priests who once ripped the very heart from his chest!.

Conquistador. abr. ed. Barry Sadler. Read by Charlton Griffin. 3 vols. (Casca Ser.: No. 10). 2004. audio compact disk (978-1-58807-715-8(2)) Am Pubng Inc.

Conquistador. abr. ed. Barry Sadler. Read by Charlton Griffin. 2 vols. (Casca Ser.: No. 10). 2004. audio compact disk 25.00 (978-1-58807-284-9(3)) Am Pubng Inc.

Conquistador: Bernal Diaz' Preface to His Book see Twentieth-Century Poetry in English: Recordings of Poets Reading Their Own Poetry

Conquistador: Hernan Cortes, King Montezuma, & the Last Stand of the Aztecs. unabr. ed. Buddy Levy. Read by Patrick G. Lawlor. Narrated by Patrick G. Lawlor. (Running Time: 12 hrs. 30 mins. 0 sec.). (ENG.). 2008. audio compact disk 37.99 (978-1-4001-0654-7(0)); audio compact disk 75.99 (978-1-4001-3654-4(7)); audio compact disk 24.99 (978-1-4001-5654-2(8)) Pub: Tantor Media. Dist(s): IngramPubServ

Conquistadors, unabr. ed. Hammond Innes. Narrated by Nelson Runger. 9 cass. (Running Time: 12 hrs. 15 mins.). 1989. 78.00 (978-1-55690-121-8(6), 89140E7) Recorded Bks.
The stories of Cortes & Pizarro & the Spanish conquest of the Aztec & Inca kingdoms.

Conrad Aiken Reading. abr. ed. Conrad Aiken. 1 cass. (Running Time: 90 min.). Incl. Blues of Ruby Matrix. (SWC 1039); Letter from Li Po. (SWC 1039); Time in the Rock: Two Poems. (SWC 1039); 1972. 14.00 (978-0-694-50031-4(3), SWC 1039) HarperCollins Pubs.

Conrad Meander. unabr. collector's ed. Short Stories. Joseph Conrad. Read by Wolfram Kandinsky. 8 cass. (Running Time: 12 hrs.). 1993. 64.00 (978-0-7366-2377-3(9), 3149) Books on Tape.
Accompany Conrad around the world in this collection of six short stories.

Conrad Schnelker: Liberty World: A Floating Free City of The Future. (Running Time: 60 min.). (Freeland II Ser.). 1984. 9.00 (FL10) Freeland Pr.
The author explains his unique idea for new cities.

Conrad's Fate. unabr. ed. Diana Wynne Jones. Narrated by Gerard Doyle. 8 CDs. (Running Time: 8 hrs. 45 mins.). (Chrestomanci Ser.). (YA). (gr. 5-8). 2005. audio compact disk 78.75 (978-1-4193-5618-6(6), C3418); 58.75 (978-1-4193-3549-5(9), 98010) Recorded Bks.
Conrad¿s Fate is part of the clever and humorous Chrestomanci series. Twelve-year-old Conrad Tesdinic is in disguise as a servant-in-training at Stallery Mansion in the town of Stallchester. He wants to figure out what evil he caused in a past life. He and his friend Christopher Chant are trying to repair Conrad¿s very bad karma and to discover what mysterious entity is haunting the town.

Conrad's Fate: Read-Along/Homework Pack. Diana Wynne Jones. Narrated by Gerard Doyle. 6 cass. (Running Time: 8 hrs. 45 mins.). (Chrestomanci Ser.). (YA). (gr. 5-8). 2005. bk. 102.74 (978-1-4193-3551-8(0), 42039) Recorded Bks.

Conscience: Our Guru, Our Friend. Swami Amar Jyoti. 1 dolby cass. 1986. 9.95 (K-84) Truth Consciousness.
Conscience purifies the astral body, makes us eligible for transformation.

Conscience for Change. 40th abr. ed. Martin Luther King, Jr. Prod. by Janet Sommerville & Del MacKenzie. (Running Time: 12600 sec.). (Massey Lectures). (ENG.). 2007. audio compact disk 29.95 (978-0-660-19730-2(8)) Canadian Broadcasting CAN.

Conscience of a Conservative. ed. Interview. Barry Goldwater. 1 CD. (Running Time: 58 mins.). 2005. audio compact disk 9.95 (978-1-57970-346-2(1), C27014D, Audio-For) J Norton Pubs.
Barry Goldwater explains the ideology and problems of the conservative position. He believes that the basic problems of the conservative elements of both parties is that they are disorganized, inarticulate, and not positive.

Conscience of a Conservative. unabr. ed. Barry Goldwater. Read by Robin Lawson. 3 cass. (Running Time: 4 hrs.). 1992. 23.95 (978-0-7861-0375-1(2), 1330) Blckstn Audio.
Written to answer the question of why a conservative nation, such as the United States, was governed by liberal policy-makers. Goldwater believed it was because conservative principles - though predominant among the people - were lacking in eloquent defenders willing to demonstrate their applicability to contemporary problems.

Conscience of a Conservative. unabr. ed. Barry Goldwater. 1 cass. (Running Time: 58 min.). 12.95 (27014) J Norton Pubs.
Goldwater explains the ideology & problems of the conservative position. He believes that the basic problems of the conservative elements of both parties is that they are disorganized, inarticulate & not positive.

Conscience of a Liberal: Reclaiming America from the Right. unabr. ed. Paul Krugman. Read by Jason Culp. (Running Time: 32400 sec.). (ENG.). 2007. audio compact disk 34.95 (978-0-7393-5866-5(9), Random AudioBks) Pub: Random Audio Pubg. Dist(s): Random

Conscience of a Nation; Grades of Virtue. Ann Ree Colton & Jonathan Murro. 1 cass. 7.95 A R Colton Fnd.

Conscience of the Rich. unabr. ed. C. P. Snow. Read by David Case. 7 cass. (Running Time: 10 hrs. 30 min.). (Strangers & Brothers Ser.). 1993. 56.00 (978-0-7366-2563-0(1), 3314) Books on Tape.
The private world of an affluent Anglo-Jewish family. Explores the personal aspects of power: a father's love for his children, their love for him & the opposition of social & personal obligations.

Conscience Speaks in the Darkness. Swami Amar Jyoti. 1 dolby cass. 1983. 9.95 (K-56) Truth Consciousness.
The way out of the darkness. Conscience, symbolic of Guru, awakens the soul. Belief is not knowledge. Patience & perseverance. Millions of miracles in the brain.

Conscientious Objections: Stirring up Trouble about Language, Technology & Education. unabr. ed. Neil Postman. Read by Jeff Riggenbach. 4 cass. (Running Time: 5 hrs. 30 mins.). 1994. 32.95 (978-0-7861-0728-5(6), 1484) Blckstn Audio.
In a series of feisty & ultimately hopeful essays, one of America's sharpest social critics casts a shrewd eye over contemporary culture to reveal the worst - & the best - of our habits of discourse, tendencies in education, & obsessions with technological novelty. Listeners will find themselves rethinking many of their bedrock assumptions: Should education transmit culture or defend us against it? Is technological innovation progress or a peculiarly American addiction? When everyone watches the same television programs - & television producers don't discriminate between the audiences for "Sesame Street" & "Dynasty" - is childhood anything more than a sentimental concept? Writing in the traditions of Orwell & H.L. Mencken, Neil Postman sends shock waves of wit & critical intelligence through the cultural wasteland.

Conscious Aging. Ram Dass. 2006. audio compact disk 19.95 (978-1-59179-497-4(8)) Sounds True.

Conscious Aging, Vol. 2. Deepak Chopra & Elisabeth Kubler-Ross. 1 cass. (Running Time: 1 hr.). (Quest Passion for Life Ser.: Vol. 2). 2001. 12.00 (978-0-7435-0537-6(9), Sound Ideas) S&S Audio.

Conscious & Unconscious Mind. J. Krishnamurti. 1 cass. (Running Time: 1 hr.). (Transformation of Man Ser.: No. 3). 8.50 (ATOM763) Krishnamurti.
This well-liked series between J. Krishnamurti, Professor David Bohm, & psychiatrist, Dr. David Shainberg, explores the conditions of human life & the need to bring about a deep, radical, fundamental change in human consciousness if mankind is to emerge from its misery & conflict.

Conscious Being. Swami Amar Jyoti. 1 cass. 1978. 9.95 (C-15) Truth Consciousness.
We forget Being & are lost in becoming. Surrendering to Him, whatever we are.

Conscious Business: How to Build Value Through Values. Fred Kofman. 12 CDs. (Running Time: 9 hrs 30 min). 2005. audio compact disk 69.95 (978-1-59179-325-0(4), AF00940D) Sounds True.
Conscious business, teaches Fred Kofman, is the capacity to observe, choose, and act in accord with our values at every level of work. For more than ten years, this visionary consultant has helped organizations ranging from small nonprofits to corporations like General Motors, Chrysler, and Microsoft to learn these skills. On Conscious Business, Fred Kofman introduces these proven principles to the public with a complete training program that engages the skills of our higher consciousness - for real world results.

Conscious Business: How to Build Value Through Values. Fred Kofman. 3 CDs. (Running Time: 11700 sec.). 2006. audio compact disk 24.95 (978-1-59179-538-4(9), AW01094D) Sounds True.

Conscious Connectedness. Eldon Taylor. 1 CD. (Running Time: 52 min.). (Whole Brain Innertalk Ser.). 1998. audio compact disk Progress Aware Res.

Conscious Dating for Relationship Success: How to Find the Love of your Life & the Life that You Love. Speeches. Created by David Steele. 1. (Running Time: 72 minutes). 2006. audio compact disk 14.95 (978-0-9755005-6-9(2)) RCN Pr.
Finally! Real-world, practical, effective, comprehensive, do-able advice and information for singles. This Conscious Dating audio program will help you: ?XDecipher dating in today's confusing world?XAvoid the deadly dating traps?XLearn the secrets to finding your perfect partner?XMake a plan to get what you really want in your life and relationships.

Conscious Dying CD Training Program. Bruce Goldberg. (ENG.). 2005. audio compact disk 75.00 (978-1-57968-024-4(0)) Pub: B Goldberg. Dist(s): Baker Taylor

Conscious Dying Training Program, Set. Bruce Goldberg. Read by Bruce Goldberg. 6 cass. (Running Time: 3 hrs.). (ENG.). 2006. 65.00 (978-1-885577-21-4(4)) Pub: B Goldberg. Dist(s): Baker Taylor
Trains the user to ascend and deal with bereavement. Includes self-hypnosis and meditations. Also anger encounters and out-of-body experiences.

Conscious Effort. (Paws & Tales Ser.: Vol. 17). (J). 2001. 3.99 (978-1-57972-418-4(3)); audio compact disk 5.99 (978-1-57972-419-1(1)) Insight Living.

Conscious Evolution. Swami Amar Jyoti. 1 cass. 1994. 9.95 (K-142) Truth Consciousness.
Age of Grace: a new beginning on planet Earth. Conscious participation in God's working. Respecting the evolutionary process in all.

Conscious Expansion. Eldon Taylor. Read by Eldon Taylor. Ed. by Leslie Brice. 1 cass. (Running Time: 1 hr.). 1992. 16.95 (978-1-56705-299-2(1)) Gateways Inst.
Self improvement.

Conscious Expansion. Eldon Taylor. 1 cass. (Running Time: 62 min.). (Inner Talk Ser.). 16.95 incl. script. (978-1-55978-007-0(X), 5407C) Progress Aware Res.
Soundtrack - Musical Themes with underlying subliminal affirmations.

Conscious Expansion: Babbling Brook. Eldon Taylor. 1 cass. 16.95 (978-1-55978-535-8(7), 5407F) Progress Aware Res.

Conscious Living. Swami Amar Jyoti. 1 cass. 1988. 9.95 (A-52) Truth Consciousness.
An enjoyable, interesting life: a totally changed view. The bondage of habit, unconscious, robot-like living. Imbalance, catastrophe & the adaptability of the soul. Peaceful methods of change.

Conscious Loving. Swami Amar Jyoti. 1 cass. (Running Time: 1 hr. 16 min.). 1995. 9.95 (K-144) Truth Consciousness.
Coming out of unconsciousness & limited love allows us to transcend to pure, unconditional love-love for its own sake.

Conscious Meditation. Swami Amar Jyoti. 1 cass. 1988. 9.95 (I-18) Truth Consciousness.
Meditation is not achieving by merging. The secret: letting go of "me". The "how & why" of creation.

Conscious Millionaire Audios Create Profit with Purpose Audio CD: The New Philsophy for Creating Abundant Wealth & Fulfillment. Scripts. J. V. Crum, 3rd. 1 CD. (Running Time: 68 mins). 2005. audio compact disk 24.95 (978-0-9767192-0-5(7)) Consci Wrld.

Conscious Out-of-Body-Experience. Bruce Goldberg. (ENG.). 2005. audio compact disk 17.00 (978-1-57968-040-4(2)) Pub: B Goldberg. Dist(s): Baker Taylor

Conscious Out-of-Body-Experience. Bruce Goldberg. Read by Bruce Goldberg. 1 cass. (Running Time: 25 min.). (ENG.). 2006. 13.00 (978-1-885577-26-9(5)) B Goldberg.
Hypnosis guides one gently out of the body and trains one in the art of conscious dying.

Conscious Passage: Conscious Aging, Conscious Dying. unabr. ed. Liliane Fournier. Read by Liliane Fournier. Read by Liliane Fournier. Ed. by Liliane Fournier. (Running Time: 2 hrs.). (Quest Ser.). 2009. 39.97 (978-1-4233-8050-4(9), 9781423380504, Brlnc Audio MP3 Lib) Brilliance Audio.

Conscious Passage: Conscious Aging, Conscious Dying. unabr. ed. Liliane Fournier. Read by Liliane Fournier. (Running Time: 2 hrs.). (Quest Ser.). 2009. 19.99 (978-1-4233-8049-8(5), 9781423380498, Brilliance MP3) Brilliance Audio.

Conscious Passage: Conscious Aging, Conscious Dying. unabr. ed. Liliane Fournier. Read by Liliane Fournier. Read by Liliane Fournier. Ed. by Liliane Fournier. (Running Time: 2 hrs.). (Quest Ser.). 2009. audio compact disk 55.97 (978-1-4233-8048-1(7), 9781423380481, BriAudCD Unabrid) Brilliance Audio.

Conscious Pregnancy: Enhance Your Physical, Emotional, Mental, & Spiritual Experience of Pregnancy. Mark Bancroft. Read by Mark Bancroft. 1 CD, 1 bklet. (Running Time: 1 hr.). (Pregnancy & Childbirth Ser.). 2006. audio compact disk 20.00 (978-1-58522-059-5(0)) EnSpire Pr.
Two complete sessions plus printed instructionmanual/guidebook. With healing music soundtrack.

Conscious Pregnancy: Enhance Your Physical, Emotional, Mental & Spiritual Experiences. Mark Bancroft. Read by Mark Bancroft. 1 cass., bklet. (Running Time: 1 hr.). (Pregnancy & Childbirth Ser.). 1999. 12.95 (978-1-58522-025-0(6), 505) EnSpire Pr.

Conscious Process. Jacquelyn Small. 1 cass. (Running Time: 90 min.). (Awakening in Time Ser.: Vol. 3). 1990. 10.00 (978-0-939344-06-2(8)) Eupsychian.
Jacquelyn Small teaches the listener how to integrate the contents of our unconscious processes as it emerges into conscious awareness.

Conscious Seeking. Swami Amar Jyoti. 1 dolby cass. 1985. 9.95 (M-53) Truth Consciousness.
Losing ourselves in the mediums, forgetting the Goal. Unconscious life is not living.

Consciously Overcome Mental Illness. Nancy Lynne Harris. 2 CDs. (Running Time: 3 hrs.). Orig. Title: How to Get Rid of Evil Spirits & Restore Yourself to Sanity. 2007. audio compact disk 50.00 (978-0-9636781-7-1(5)) BBCSPub.
Explains what causes mental illness & how to heal it. Shows that it is a completely healable illness through changing your thoughts & attitudes about yourself.

Consciousness: Program from the Award Winning Public Radio Series. Interview. Hosted by Fred Goodwin. Comment by John Hockenberry. 1 CD. (Running Time: 1 Hour). 2001. audio compact disk 21.95 (978-1-932479-35-5(X), LCM 160) Lichtenstein Creat.
This special one-hour program on consciousness explores an issue that has for centuries fascinated the greatest minds in philosophy, theology and the arts, and is now engaging some of the best minds in neuroscience as well. Using the latest technologies, scientists are beginning to unlock some of the hidden secrets of the human experience. But what happens to concepts like free will and the soul? You may be surprised. Guests include: Dr. Andrew Newberg, medical doctor, of the University of Pennsylvania Department of Radiology; Dr. Patricia Churchland, neurophilosopher, of the University of California at San Diego; Dr. Christof Koch, professor of computation and neural systems at the California Institute of Technology; Dr. David Chalmers, professor of philosophy at the University of Arizona and associate director of the university's Center for Consciousness Studies; Sakyong Mipham Rinpoche, leader of the Shambhala tradition of Tibetan Buddhism; with a reading from Descartes' seminal "Discourse on the Method of Rightly Conducting the Reason, and Seeking Truth in the Sciences" by New York actor Bray Poor, and commentary by John Hockenberry.

Consciousness & Energy Medicine. Caroline Myss & Ron Roth. (Consciousness & Energy Medicine). 2001. 55.00 (978-1-893869-50-9(4)) Celbrtng Life.

Consciousness & Its Implications. Instructed by Daniel N. Robinson. 6 cass. (Running Time: 6 hrs.). 2007. 89.95 (978-1-59803-297-0(6)); audio compact disk 39.95 (978-1-59803-298-7(4)) Teaching Co.

Consciousness & New Technology. unabr. ed. Robert A. Monroe. Read by Robert A. Monroe. (Running Time: 45 min.). (Explorer Ser.). 1983. 12.95 (978-1-56113-002-3(8), 3) Monroe Institute.
Explorer discusses the human relationship with higher consciousness.

Consciousness & Reality. unabr. ed. Alyce Green et al. 2 cass. (Running Time: 2 hr. 30 min.). 19.95 (29362-29363) J Norton Pubs.
The different "realities" experienced in altered state of consciousness are changing our notions about human psychology, psychotherapy & even our perception of the universe.

Consciousness & Rhythm. 4 cass. 45.00 set. (5011) MEA A Watts Cass.

Consciousness As Identification: The Nature of Cognition & Concept-Formation. Harry Binswanger. Read by Harry Binswanger. (Running Time: 5 hrs.). 1989. 69.00 (978-1-56114-006-0(6), CB01D) Second Renaissance.
Our anti-conceptual culture, says Dr. Binswanger, stems from mistaken views on the relation of consciousness to existence. This three-lecture series presents the full meaning of Ayn Rand's unique view of consciousness as a process of identification, with emphasis on the mechanics of concept-formation.

Consciousness, Bioenergy & Healing Vol. 2: Self-Healing & Energy Medicine for the 21st Century. Frwd. by C. Norman Shealy. (Healing Research Ser.). (YA). 2004. audio compact disk 24.95 (978-0-9754248-1-0(5)) Pub: WHP. Dist(s): AtlasBooks
This is a life-changing book! Self-healing methods can relieve symptoms and cure illnesses. Complementary and alternative therapies can help with many problems that modern medicine can't cure. Learn how you can use these methods for self-healing and to help others.

Consciousness Expansion. Bruce Goldberg. (ENG.). 2005. audio compact disk 17.00 (978-1-57968-058-9(5)) Pub: B Goldberg. Dist(s): Baker Taylor

Consciousness Expansion. Bruce Goldberg. Read by Bruce Goldberg. 1 cass. (Running Time: 25 min.). (ENG.). 2006. 13.00 (978-1-885577-66-5(4)) Pub: B Goldberg. Dist(s): Baker Taylor
Through self-hypnosis, learn how to expand the levels of awareness & maximize spiritual growth & psychic abilities.

***Consciousness of the Atom: Mp3.** Alice A. Bailey. (ENG.). 2009. audio compact disk 13.00 (978-0-85330-201-8(4)) Lucis Pr GBR.

Consciousness Plague. Paul Levinson. Read by Mark Shanahan. (Running Time: 9 hrs.). 2005. 19.95 (978-1-59912-908-2(6)) Iofy Corp.

Consciousness Plague. Paul Levinson. Read by Mark Shanahan. (Running Time: 30600 sec.). 2005. audio compact disk 29.95 (978-1-59316-038-8(0)) Listen & Live.

Consciousness Plague. unabr. ed. Paul Levinson. Read by Mark Shanahan. (YA). 2008. 39.99 (978-1-60514-689-8(7)) Find a World.

Consecrated to Thee High. Peter B. Allen. 2004. pap. bk. 24.95 (978-5-559-78363-5(3)) Pub: Pt of Grace Ent. Dist(s): STL Dist NA

Consecrated to Thee Medium. Peter B. Allen. 2004. pap. bk. 24.95 (978-5-559-78355-0(2)) Pub: Pt of Grace Ent. Dist(s): STL Dist NA

Consecrating the Priesthood. Francis Frangipane. 1 cass. (Running Time: 90 mins.). (Strategies for our Cities Ser.: Vol. 9). 2000. 5.00 (FF06-009) Morning NC.
This series provides practical, biblical solutions that have been tested & have born fruit for those with a vision for their cities.

Consecration. 1 CD. 1999. audio compact disk 16.98 (978-1-57908-502-5(4), 5345) Platinm Enter.

Consecration Series. Mark Hanby. 4 cass. 1992. 29.00 Set. (978-0-938612-66-7(2)) Destiny Image Pubs.

Consent to God. unabr. ed. Thomas Merton. Read by Thomas Merton. 3 cass. (Running Time: 2 hrs. 19 min.). (Life & Prayer Ser.: No. 2). 1982. 29.95 Elec Paperback.
Discusses the action of God's will as essence of Christian theology & the basis for meditation on the meaning of life.

Consent to Kill: A Thriller. abr. ed. Vince Flynn. Read by Armand Schultz. (Mitch Rapp Ser.: No. 6). 2005. 17.95 (978-0-7435-5221-9(0)) Pub: S&S Audio. Dist(s): S and S Inc

Consent to Kill: A Thriller. abr. ed. Vince Flynn. Read by Stephen Lang. (Running Time: 6 hrs. 0 mins. 0 sec.). No. 6. (ENG.). 2008. audio compact disk 14.99 (978-0-7435-7610-9(1)) Pub: S&S Audio. Dist(s): S and S Inc

Consent to Kill: A Thriller. unabr. ed. Vince Flynn. Read by Stephen Lang. (Mitch Rapp Ser.: No. 6). 2005. 29.95 (978-0-7435-5453-4(1)) Pub: S&S Audio. Dist(s): S and S Inc

Consent to Kill: A Thriller. unabr. ed. Vince Flynn. Read by George Guidall. 15 CDs. (Running Time: 17 hrs. 30 mins. 0 sec.). No. 6. (ENG.). 2005. audio compact disk 49.95 (978-0-7435-5006-2(4)) Pub: S&S Audio. Dist(s): S and S Inc

Consequences. unabr. ed. Penelope Lively. Narrated by Josephine Bailey. (Running Time: 9 hrs. 0 mins. 0 sec.). (ENG.). 2007. audio compact disk 34.99 (978-1-4001-0502-1(1)); audio compact disk 24.99 (978-1-4001-5502-6(9)); audio compact disk 69.99 (978-1-4001-3502-8(8)) Pub: Tantor Media. Dist(s): IngramPubServ

Consequences. unabr. ed. Penelope Lively. Read by Josephine Bailey. (YA). 2007. 59.99 (978-1-60252-827-7(6)) Find a World.

***Consequences of Ideas: Understanding the Concepts that Shaped Our World.** unabr. ed. R. C. Sproul. Narrated by Sean Runnette. (ENG.). 2010. 12.98 (978-1-59644-901-5(2), Hovel Audio) christianaud.

***Consequences of Ideas: Understanding the Concepts that Shaped Our World.** unabr. ed. R. c. Sproul & R. C. Sproul. Narrated by Sean Runnette. (Running Time: 6 hrs. 12 mins. 0 sec.). (ENG.). 2010. audio compact disk 21.98 (978-1-59644-900-8(4), Hovel Audio) christianaud.

Consequences That Work. unabr. ed. Ray Levy & Joe Cates. 1 cass. (Running Time: 1 hr. 30 mins.). 2002. bk. 12.95 (978-0-9701173-1-1(0)) Cates Levy.
Examples and procedures of effective consequences for parents and/or teachers of children/youth 18 years and younger.

Conservation & Property Rights. unabr. ed. Murray Newton Rothbard. 1 cass. (Running Time: 1 hr. 18 min.). (Introduction to Free Market Economics Ser.). 12.95 (312) J Norton Pubs.
Topics discussed include: natural resources; broadcast frequencies; air & water pollution.

Conservationist. unabr. ed. Nadine Gordimer. Read by Nadia May. 6 cass. (Running Time: 9 hrs..). 1992. 44.95 Set. (978-0-7861-0342-3(6), 1299) Blckstn Audio.
Mehring is rich. An industrialist, not yet fifty, he is also attractive to women. He has all the privileges & possessions that South Africa has to offer, but his possessions refuse to remain objects. His wife, son, & mistress leave him; his foreman & workers become increasingly indifferent to his stewardship; even the land rises up, as drought, then flood, destroy his farm.

***Conservationist.** unabr. ed. Nadine Gordimer. Read by Nadia May. (Running Time: 8.5 hrs. NaN mins.). (ENG.). 2011. 29.95 (978-1-4417-7710-2(5)); audio compact disk 76.00 (978-1-4417-7708-9(3)) Blckstn Audio.

Conservatism: An Obituary - Q & A. Ayn Rand. Read by Ayn Rand. 1 cass. (Running Time: 30 min.). 1993. 12.95 (978-1-56114-306-1(5), AR48C) Second Renaissance.

Conservatism: An Obituary (1960) Ayn Rand. Read by Ayn Rand. 1 cass. (Running Time: 60 min.). 12.95 (978-1-56114-070-1(8), AR10C) Second Renaissance.
The appalling spectacle of conservatives trying to evade the meaning & the validation of capitalism - while ostensibly trying to defend it. The urgent need for radicals who will champion capitalism on moral grounds, by rejecting altruism & upholding a code of ethics based on rational self-interest.

Conservatism in the Eighties. Read by M. Stanton Evans. 1 cass. 2.50 (107) ISI Books.

Conservatism vs. Objectivism: The Role of Education. Ayn Rand. 1 cass. (Running Time: 1 hr.). 1993. 12.95 (978-1-56114-273-6(5), AR44C) Second Renaissance.

Conservative Crack-Up. unabr. ed. R. Emmett Tyrell, Jr. Read by William Lavelle. 10 cass. (Running Time: 14 hrs. 30 mins.). 1992. 69.95 (978-0-7861-0377-5(9), 1332) Blckstn Audio.
After a decade of power, is American conservatism coming apart at the seams? With the comic flair & political savvy that have become his trademarks, Tyrell takes a hard look at the long road he & his fellow conservatives have traveled - & arrives at a surprising analysis that will unsettle friends & foes alike. As he did in his earlier autopsy, "The Liberal Crack-Up," he has "journeyed into the fever swamps of American politics & come back with the bugs" - only this time the malaise is on the Right, not the Left.

Conservative Mind: From Burke to Eliot. unabr. ed. Russell Kirk. Read by Phillip Davidson. 15 cass. (Running Time: 22 hrs.). 1989. 95.95 (978-0-7861-0012-5(5), 1011) Blckstn Audio.
Kirk defines what he terms "the conservative mind" by examining the thoughts of many brilliant men starting with Edmund Burke & weaving his way through Macaulay, James Fenimore Cooper, Tocqueville, John Quincy Adams, Nathaniel Hawthorne, Disraeli, Cardinal Newman, Santayana, Babbit & finally to T.S. Eliot.

Conservative Mind: From Burke to Eliot. unabr. ed. Russell Kirk & Frederick Davidson. (Running Time: 20 hrs. 5 mins.). 2008. 44.95 (978-1-4332-5507-6(3)); audio compact disk 125.00 (978-1-4332-5506-9(5)) Blckstn Audio.

Conservative Political Action Conference Banquet, Nineteen Seventy-Five. unabr. ed. Ronald Reagan et al. 1 cass. (Running Time: 1 hr. 7 min.). 12.95 (332) J Norton Pubs.

Conservative Tradition. Instructed by Patrick N. Allitt. (ENG.). 2009. 199.95 (978-1-59803-547-6(9)); audio compact disk 269.95 (978-1-59803-548-3(7)) Teaching Co.

Conservatives Without Conscience. un[illegible]d. John W. Dean. Read by Robertson Dean. 6 cass. (Running Tim[illegible]rs.). 2006. 54.00 (978-1-4159-2998-8(X)); audio compact [illegible] 72.00 (978-1-4159-2999-5(8)) Books on Tape.

***Conservatize Me: How I Tried to Become a Righty with the Help of Richard Nixon, Sean Hannity, Toby Keith, & Beef Jerky.** abr. ed. John Moe. Read by John Moe. (ENG.). 2006. (978-0-06-123056-1(1), Harper Audio); (978-0-06-123055-4(3), Harper Audio) HarperCollins Pubs.

Consider Derivative Houses for Missing Answer. abr. ed. Nance McCullough. Read by Nance McCullough. 1 cass. (Running Time: 58 mins.). 1991. 6.20 (978-0-936916-51-4(6)) NAMAC.
Astrology: Based on how other people in your life is reflected in your astrology chart.

Consider Him: Life Changing Glimpses of the Saviour in the Gospel of Mark. 2001. (978-0-940110-31-1(8)) Life Action Publishing.

Consider Him Conf Audio. Nancy Leigh DeMoss. (ENG.). 2007. audio compact disk 15.99 (978-0-940110-75-5(X)) Life Action Publishing.

Consider Jesus. Kenneth Copeland. 6 cass. 1982. bk. 30.00 Set incl. study guide. (978-0-938458-41-8(8)) K Copeland Pubns.
Learning more of Jesus.

Consider the Elephant: The Life & Death of John Wilkes Booth as Told by his Brother Edwin. Aram Schefrin. prdcast. (Running Time: 12 hrs). 2006. audio compact disk 0.00 (978-1-4276-0040-0(6)) AardGP.
The common wisdom is that John Wilkes Booth was a failed actor and a madman. But the truth is that Wilkes was the matinee idol of his time ? and the attack on Lincoln was not the act of a maniac, but a part of a plan developed at the highest levels of the Confederacy. In ?Consider the Elephant,? the third podcast novel by Aram Schefrin, the story of Wilkes? life and death is told by his brother, Edwin Booth, the greatest Shakespearean actor of his age. The story is soaked in the ambiance of life in the American theater in the mid nineteenth century, and full of rich characters, and it lays out in detail the path Wilkes took to the top of the celebrity heap, his growing involvement with the Southern rebels and the development in Richmond of the plot to kidnap ? later assassinate ? the Union President. The novel can be subscribed to or downloaded chapter by chapter at iTunes and other podcast aggregators, at www.booth.libsyn.com, or from Podiobooks.com.

Consider the End. Neville Goddard. 1 cass. (Running Time: 62 min.). 1965. 8.00 (10) J & L Pubns.
Neville taught Imagination Creates Reality. He was a powerfully influential teacher of God as Consciousness.

Consider the Lobster. abr. ed. David Foster Wallace. Read by David Foster Wallace. 3 CDs. (Running Time: 4 hrs.). (ENG.). 2005. audio compact disk 24.98 (978-1-59483-099-0(1)) Pub: Hachet Audio. Dist(s): HachBkGrp

Consider the Lobster. abr. ed. David Foster Wallace. Read by David Foster Wallace. (Running Time: 1 hr.). (ENG.). 2008. 2.98 (978-1-60024-310-3(X)) Pub: Hachet Audio. Dist(s): HachBkGrp

Consider the Lobster: And Other Essays. abr. ed. David Foster Wallace. (ENG.). 2005. 14.98 (978-1-59483-269-7(2)) Pub: Hachet Audio. Dist(s): HachBkGrp

Consider the Source. Brian Conway. (ENG.). 2008. audio compact disk 25.95 (978-0-8023-8173-6(1)) Pub: Clo Iar-Chonnachta IRL. Dist(s): Dufour

Consider the Source: Surviving the Culture Wars: Genesis 14:1-24. Ed Young. 1994. 4.95 (978-0-7417-2028-3(0), 1028) Win Walk.

Consider This, Senora. unabr. ed. Harriet Doerr. Narrated by Barbara Rosenblat. 5 cass. (Running Time: 6 hrs. 45 mins.). 1993. 44.00 (978-1-55690-927-6(6), 93423E7) Recorded Bks.
Four Americans, each an expatriate for a different reason, settle in an isolated Mexican village & attempt to become a part of the way of life there.

Consider This, Senora. unabr. collector's ed. Harriet Doerr. Read by Frances Cassidy. 6 cass. (Running Time: 6 hrs.). 1994. 36.00 (978-0-7366-2799-3(5), 3514) Books on Tape.
In her first novel since "Stones for Ibarra," Doerr examines the lives of four American expatriates in a Mexican village.

Consider Your Ways: Finding & Removing Your Barriers to Increase. Mac Hammond. 2 cass. (Running Time: 2 hrs.). 1997. 12.00 Set. (978-1-57399-049-3(3)) Mac Hammond.

Considerable Speck see Robert Frost Reads

Considerable Speck see Twentieth-Century Poetry in English, No. 6, Recordings of Poets Reading Their Own Poetry

Considerations - Practicing Astrology. Mary Elness. 1 cass. 8.95 (740) Am Fed Astrologers.

Considere a Jesus, Set. Kenneth Copeland. Tr. by Kenneth Copeland Publications Staff from ENG. 6 cass. (SPA.). 1987. 30.00 (978-0-88114-463-5(0)) K Copeland Pubns.
Biblical study on Jesus ministry.

Considere a Jesus, Vol. 1. Kenneth Copeland. Tr. by Kenneth Copeland Publications Staff from ENG. 1 cass. (SPA.). 1987. 5.00 (978-0-88114-464-2(9)) K Copeland Pubns.
Biblical study on Jesus ministry.

Considere a Jesus, Vol. 2. Kenneth Copeland. Tr. by Kenneth Copeland Publications Staff from ENG. 1 cass. (SPA.). 1987. 5.00 (978-0-88114-465-9(7)) K Copeland Pubns.

Considere a Jesus, Vol. 3. Kenneth Copeland. Tr. by Kenneth Copeland Publications Staff from ENG. 1 cass. (SPA.). 1987. 5.00 (978-0-88114-466-6(5)) K Copeland Pubns.

Considere a Jesus, Vol. 4. Kenneth Copeland. Tr. by Kenneth Copeland Publications Staff from ENG. 1 cass. (SPA.). 1987. 5.00 (978-0-88114-467-3(3)) K Copeland Pubns.

Considere a Jesus, Vol. 5. Kenneth Copeland. Tr. by Kenneth Copeland Publications Staff from ENG. 1 cass. (SPA.). 1987. 5.00 (978-0-88114-468-0(1)) K Copeland Pubns.

Considere a Jesus, Vol. 6. Kenneth Copeland. Tr. by Kenneth Copeland Publications Staff from ENG. 1 cass. (SPA.). 1987. 5.00 (978-0-88114-469-7(X)) K Copeland Pubns.

Consistent Achievement Personal Learning Course: How to Strengthen Follow-Through & Triumph Again & Again, Set. Paul R. Scheele. Read by Paul R. Scheele. 8 cass. (Running Time: 8 hrs.). 2000. pap. bk. 179.95 (978-0-925480-41-5(X), 9CLC) Learn Strategies.

Consistent Ethic: A Philosophical Critique. John C. Finnis & James J. Walter. 1 cass. (Running Time: 20 min.). (Consistent Ethic of Life Symposium Ser.). 1988. 6.00 (978-1-55612-123-4(7), LL7123, SheWard) Rowman.
Two of the keynote speakers at the Consistent Ethic of Life Symposium in Chicago in late 1987.

Consistent Ethic of Life: A Protestant Perspective. James M. Gustafson & Lisa S. Cahill. 1 cass. (Running Time: 20 min.). (Consistent Ethic of Life Symposium Ser.). 1988. 6.00 (978-1-55612-124-1(5), LL7124, SheWard) Rowman.

Consistent Ethic of Life: Public Policy Implications. Read by J. Bryan Hehir & Sidney Callahna. 1 cass. (Running Time: 20 min.). (Consistent Ethic of Life Symposium Ser.). 1988. 6.00 (978-1-55612-125-8(3), LL7125, SheWard) Rowman.

Consistent Ethic of Life in Catholic Moral Theology. unabr. ed. Richard A. McCormick & Frans J. Van Beeck. 1 cass. (Running Time: 20 min.). (Consistent Ethic of Life Symposium Ser.). 1988. 6.00 (978-1-55612-122-7(9), LL7122, SheWard) Rowman.

Consolations of Philosophy. abr. unabr. ed. Alain de Botton. Read by Simon Vance. 7 cass. (Running Time: 21600 sec.). 2006. 27.95 (978-0-7861-4456-3(4)); audio compact disk 27.95 (978-0-7861-7296-2(7)); audio compact disk 29.95 (978-0-7861-7716-5(0)) Blckstn Audio.

Consolations of Philosophy. unabr. ed. Alain de Botton. Read by Simon Vance. (Running Time: 21600 sec.). 2006. 44.95 (978-0-7861-4640-6(0)); audio compact disk 45.00 (978-0-7861-6737-1(8)) Blckstn Audio.

Consolatory Tale see Winter's Tales

Consolidated Tax Return Regulations: Thursday-Friday, September 26-27, 1996, Doubletree Park Terrace Hotel, Washington, D. C. American Law Institute-American Bar Association, Committee on Continuing Professional Education Staff. 8 cass. (Running Time: 11 hrs. 50 min.). 172.50 Incl. course materials. (MB27) Am Law Inst.
Advanced course of study explores the policy & mechanics of these regulations. Leading private practitioners in the field & government officials responsible for drafting the regulations explain these developments. They emphasize the practical implications of these provisions & offer suggestions for sensible planning. Designed to provide guidance both for private practitioners & for corporate tax counsel. Tailored especially to allow substantial periods for responses to questions from registrants.

Consonant Sounds. 1 cass. (RAP-ability Ser.). (J). (ps-2). 1992. 10.95 (RAP1291C) Kimbo Educ.
Kids learn phonics by singing along with wholesome, fun rap music. It's the easiest teaching aid ever. Includes lyric & teaching guide.

Consonant Variations of American English. 4th ed. Lorna D. Sikorski. 5 CDs. (Running Time: 5 hrs., 2 min.). (Mastering Effective English Communication Ser.). 2004. spiral bd. 99.95 (978-1-883574-08-6(0), 5311) LDS & Asocs.

Consonants. Steven Traugh & Susan Traugh. Ed. by Rozanne Lanczak Williams. Illus. by Diane Valko. (Fun Phonics Ser.: Vol. 8025). 1999. pap. bk. & tchr. ed. 13.99 (978-1-57471-639-9(5), 8025) Creat Teach Pr.

***Consonants on Parade, Kit.** EDCON Publishing Group Staff. (ENG.). 2004. 189.00 (978-1-55576-488-3(6)) EDCON Pubng.

Conspicuous Health. 1 cass. (Urban Problems Ser.). 10.00 (UP704) Esstee Audios.
What happens to those people who have income beyond their needs & how & why they spend their money.

Conspiracy. abr. ed. Stephen Coonts & Jim DeFelice. Read by Christopher Lane. (Running Time: 4 hrs.). (Deep Black Ser.: No. 6). 2009. audio compact disk 14.99 (978-1-59737-679-2(5), 9781597376792, BCD Value Price) Brilliance Audio.

Conspiracy. unabr. ed. Stephen Coonts & Jim DeFelice. Read by Christopher Lane. (Running Time: 11 hrs.). (Deep Black Ser.: No. 6). 2008. 39.25 (978-1-59710-845-4(6), 9781597108454, BADLE); 24.95 (978-1-59710-844-7(8), 9781597108447, BAD); audio compact disk 39.25 (978-1-59600-364-4(2), 9781596003644, Brinc Audio MP3 Lib); audio compact disk 36.95 (978-1-4233-3713-3(1), 9781423337133, Bril Audio CD Unabri); audio compact disk 97.25 (978-1-4233-3714-0(X), 9781423337140, BriAudCD Unabrid); audio compact disk 24.95 (978-1-59600-363-7(4), 9781596003637, Brilliance MP3) Brilliance Audio.
Please enter a Synopsis.

Conspiracy. unabr. ed. Harley L. Sachs. 8 cass. (Running Time: 8 hrs.). 2000. 35.00 (978-0-9705390-1-4(0)) I D E V C O.
Tom Godot, co-author of a book about a conspiracy to hijack communication satellites discovers his book is a cover for another conspiracy & he is an unwilling part of it.

Conspiracy. unabr. collector's ed. John Hersey. Read by Dan Lazar. 8 cass. (Running Time: 8 hrs.). 1980. 48.00 (978-0-7366-0318-8(2), 1306) Books on Tape.
Nero's secret police believe they have come on the first hints of a plot against the Emperor's life. Once promising & gifted, Nero has now bloodied himself & grown fat on power. Crass, mediocre men now have his ear & favor. While he & his court give themselves to dreamlike pleasures, the obsessed secret police close in on the conspiracy of the men of letters.

Conspiracy Club. unabr. ed. Jonathan Kellerman. 6 cass. (Running Time: 9 hrs.). 2003. 72.00 (978-0-7366-9432-2(3)) Books on Tape.

Conspiracy in Death. abr. ed. J. D. Robb, pseud. Read by Susan Ericksen. 4 cass. (Running Time: 6 hrs.). (In Death Ser.). 2002. 62.25 (978-1-58788-443-6(7), 1587884437) Brilliance Audio.
#8 in the Bestselling Series At a Time When Human Nature Remains as Predictable as Death, a Killer Plays God - and Puts Innocent Lives in the Palm of his Hand . . . With the precision of a surgeon, a serial killer preys on the most vulnerable souls of the world's city streets. The first victim: a sidewalk sleeper, found dead in New York City. No bruises, no signs of struggle. Just a laser-perfect, fist-sized hole where his heart had once been. Lieutenant Eve Dallas is assigned to investigate. But in the heat of a cat-and-mouse game with the killer, Dallas's job is suddenly on the line. Now her hands are tied. . .between a struggle for justice - and a fight for her career. .

Conspiracy in Death. abr. ed. J. D. Robb, pseud. Read by Susan Ericksen. (Running Time: 6 hrs.). (In Death Ser.). 2007. audio compact disk 14.99 (978-1-4233-1445-5(X), 9781423314455, BCD Value Price) Brilliance Audio.

Conspiracy in Death. unabr. ed. J. D. Robb, pseud. Read by Susan Ericksen. (Running Time: 11 hrs.). (In Death Ser.). 2007. 39.25 (978-1-4233-0040-3(8), 9781423300403, BADLE); 24.95 (978-1-4233-0039-7(4), 9781423300397, BAD); 82.25 (978-1-4233-3717-1(4), 9781423337171, BrilAudUnabridg); audio compact disk 39.25 (978-1-4233-0038-0(6), 9781423300380, Brinc Audio MP3 Lib); audio compact disk 102.25 (978-1-4233-1443-1(3), 9781423314431, BriAudCD Unabrid); audio compact disk 24.95 (978-1-4233-0037-3(8), 9781423300373, Brilliance MP3); audio compact disk 36.95 (978-1-4233-1442-4(5), 9781423314424, Bril Audio CD Unabri) Brilliance Audio.

***Conspiracy in Kiev.** Noel Hynd. (Running Time: 13 hrs. 31 mins. 0 sec.). (Russian Ser.). (ENG.). 2009. 14.99 (978-0-310-77299-6(0)) Zondervan.

Conspiracy Journal - Tales of the Unknown & Unexplained... 22 Dynamic Exposes from Past Issues of the World's Most Controversial Publication. collector's ed. 2005. bk. 20.00 (978-1-892062-89-5(5)) Inner Light.
Includes: Strange Encounter at NATO Base and Engineer Travels Onboard UFO. Also includes articles on Black Triangles, Area 51, Time Travel, Philadelphia Experiment, FEMA, Tesla, Holographic Mind Control.

Conspiracy Number Five. Perf. by Tai Anderson et al. 1 cass. 1997. 10.98 (978-0-7601-1433-9(1), C10006); audio compact disk 16.98 (978-0-7601-1434-6(X), CD10006) Pub: Brentwood Music. Dist(s): Provident Mus Dist
Southern alternative rock.

Conspiracy of Fools: A True Story. abr. ed. Kurt Eichenwald. Read by Stephen Lang. 8 CDs. (Running Time: 36000 sec.). (ENG.). 2005. audio compact disk 19.95 (978-0-7393-2449-3(7), Random AudioBks) Pub: Random Audio Pubg. Dist(s): Random

Conspiracy of Fools: A True Story. unabr. ed. Kurt Eichenwald. 25 CDs. (Running Time: 30 hrs. 30 mins.). 2005. audio compact disk 126.65 (978-1-4159-1666-7(7)); 95.20 (978-1-4159-1581-3(4)) Books on Tape.
With Conspiracy of Fools, Kurt Eichenwald transforms the unbelievable story of the Enron scandal into a rip-roaring narrative of epic proportions, one that is sure to delight readers of thrillers and business books alike, achieving for this new decade what books like Barbarians at the Gate and A Civil Action accomplished in the 1990¿s. Written in the roller-coaster style of a novel, the compelling narrative takes readers behind every closed door - from the Oval Office to the executive suites, from the highest reaches of the Justice Department to the homes and bedrooms of the top officers. It is a tale of global reach - from Houston to Washington, from Bombay to London, from Munich to Sao Paolo - laying out the unbelievable scenes that twisted together to create this shocking true story. Eichenwald reveals never-disclosed details of a story that features a cast including George W. Bush, Dick Cheney, Paul O'Neill, Harvey Pitt, Colin Powell, Gray Davis, Arnold Schwarzenegger, Alan Greenspan, Ken Lay, Andy Fastow, Jeff Skilling, Bill Clinton, Rupert Murdoch and Sumner Redstone. With its you-are-there glimpse into the secretive worlds of corporate power, Conspiracy of Fools is an all-true financial and political thriller of cinematic proportions.

***Conspiracy of Kindness: A Unique Approach to Sharing the Love of Jesus.** unabr. ed. Steve Sjogren. Narrated by Sean Runnette. (ENG.). 2010. 14.98 (978-1-59644-879-7(2)); audio compact disk 24.98 (978-1-59644-878-0(4)) christianaud.

Conspirata. abr. ed. Robert Harris. Read by Oliver Ford Davies. 5 CDs. (Running Time: 6 hrs.). 2010. audio compact disk 29.99 (978-0-7435-6676-6(9)) Pub: S&S Audio. Dist(s): S and S Inc

***Conspirata.** unabr. ed. Robert Harris. Narrated by Simon Jones. 1 Playaway. (Running Time: 14 hrs.). 2010. 64.75 (978-1-4498-1595-0(2)); 98.75 (978-1-4361-5408-6(1)); audio compact disk 123.75 (978-1-4361-5410-9(3)) Recorded Bks.

Conspirata. unabr. ed. Robert Harris. Read by Simon Jones. 12 CDs. (Running Time: 14 hrs.). 2010. audio compact disk 49.99 (978-0-7435-6677-3(7)) Pub: S&S Audio. Dist(s): S and S Inc

***Conspirata.** unabr. collector's ed. Robert Harris. Narrated by Simon Jones. 12 CDs. (Running Time: 14 hrs.). 2010. audio compact disk 56.95 (978-1-4361-5411-6(1)) Recorded Bks.

Constable along the Highway. Nicholas Rhea. Read by Graham Roberts. 8 cass. (Sound Ser.). 2003. 69.95 (978-1-86042-994-1(7)) Pub: UlverLrgPrint GBR. Dist(s): Ulverscroft US

Constable among the Heather. Nicholas Rhea. Read by Christopher Kay. 5 cass. (Running Time: 7 hrs.). 1999. 49.95 (68041) Pub: Soundings Ltd GBR. Dist(s): Ulverscroft US

Constable by the Stream. Nicholas Rhea. Read by Christopher Kay. 6 cass. (Running Time: 9 hrs.). 1999. 54.95 (68432) Pub: Soundings Ltd GBR. Dist(s): Ulverscroft US

Constable Goes to Market. Nicholas Rhea. Read by Christopher Kay. 6 cass. (Sound Ser.). (J). 2002. 54.95 (978-1-84283-195-3(X)) Pub: ISIS Lrg Prnt GBR. Dist(s): Ulverscroft US

Constable on Call. unabr. ed. Nicholas Rhea. Read by Graham Roberts. 7 cass. (Running Time: 9 hrs. 30 mins.). 1999. 61.95 (978-1-85496-903-3(X), 6903X) Pub: Soundings Ltd GBR. Dist(s): Ulverscroft US
Even amidst the rural calm of the North York Moors, the lives of PC Nick Rowan & his doctor wife, Kate, are eventful. Both are always on call, whether from an irate Claude Greengrass, furious that a bigwig has taken a pot shot at him or from a woman about to give birth on a snowbound farm, a woman whose violent ex-convict husband is out to kill her.

Constance Scheerer. Read by Constance Scheerer. 1 cass. (Running Time: 29 min.). 1985. 10.00 New Letters.
Kansas author reads from her book "Writing in Winter".

Constance Urdang & Donald Finkel. Read by Constance Urdang & Donald Finkel. 1 cass. (Running Time: 29 min.). 1986. 10.00 New Letters.
Two poets from St. Louis read on this program.

Constance Urdang & Donald Finkel. unabr. ed. Donald Finkel & Constance Urdang. Read by Donald Finkel & Constance Urdang. 1 cass. (Running Time: 29 min.). 1991. 10.00 (011185) New Letters.

***Constancy of God in a Changing World.** Featuring Ravi Zacharias. 1996. audio compact disk 9.00 (978-1-61256-055-7(5)) Ravi Zach.

Constant Gardener. abr. ed. John le Carré. Read by John le Carré. 2005. 17.95 (978-0-7435-5467-1(1)) Pub: S&S Audio. Dist(s): S and S Inc

Constant Gardener. unabr. ed. John le Carré. Read by Michael Jayston. 14 CDs. (Running Time: 61080 sec.). 2001. audio compact disk 115.95 (978-0-7540-5443-6(8), CCD 134) AudioGO.
This opens with the gruesome murder of the young and beautiful Tessa Quayle near northern Kenya's Lake Turkana, the birthplace of mankind. Her putative African lover and traveling companion, a doctor with one of the aid agencies, has vanished from the scene of the crime. Tessa's much older husband, Justin, a career diplomat at the British High Commission in Nairobi, sets out on a personal odyssey in pursuit of the killers and their motive. What he might know and what he ultimately learns make him suspect among his own colleagues and a target for the profiteers who killed his wife.

Constant Gardener. unabr. ed. John le Carré. Read by Michael Jayston. 14 cass. (Running Time: 21 hrs.). 2001. 110.95 (978-0-7540-0683-1(2), CAB 2105) Pub: Chivers Audio Bks GBR. Dist(s): AudioGO
British diplomat Justin Quale, complacent raiser of freesias and doting husband of the stunning, much younger Tessa, has tended his own garden in Nairobi for too long. Tessa is Justin's opposite, a fiery reformer, "the Princess Diana of the African poor." But now Tessa has turned up naked, raped, and dead on a mysterious visit to remore Lake Turkana in Kenya.

Constant Lover see Palgrave's Golden Treasury of English Poetry

Constant Nymph. unabr. ed. Margaret Kennedy. Read by Judith Porter. 9 cass. (Running Time: 11 hrs. 16 min.). (Isis Ser.). (J). 2003. 76.95 (978-0-7531-1382-0(1)) Pub: ISIS Lrg Prnt GBR. Dist(s): Ulverscroft US
The nymph is Teresa Sanger, the fourteen-year-old ward of Lewis and Florence Dodds. She falls in love with her muscle guardian, and, loving him with no illusions, they run away together. But, inevitably, tragedy intervenes.

Constant Princess. abr. ed. Philippa Gregory. Read by Kate Burton. 2005. 15.95 (978-0-7435-5224-0(5)) Pub: S&S Audio. Dist(s): S and S Inc

Constant Princess. abr. ed. Philippa Gregory. Read by Kate Burton. (Running Time: 6 hrs. 0 mins. 0 sec.). (ENG.). 2007. audio compact disk 14.99 (978-0-7435-6985-9(7)) Pub: S&S Audio. Dist(s): S and S Inc

Constant Tin Soldier see Hans Christian Andersen's Best Known Stories

Constant Tin Soldier. Hans Christian Andersen. Read by Julie Harris. 1 cass. (Running Time: 15 min.). (World of Words Ser.). (J). (gr. k-3). pap. bk. 10.00 (SAC 6500C) Spoken Arts.

Constant Tin Soldier. unabr. ed. Narrated by Julie Harris. 1 cass., 10 bks. (Running Time: 15 min.). (World of Words Ser.). (J). (gr. k-3). 2001. pap. bk. 22.00 (978-0-8045-6703-9(4), 6500-C/10) Spoken Arts.

Constantine to the Middle Ages. Stephen Mansfield. 1 cass. (Running Time: 90 mins.). (Basic Church History Ser.: Vol. 3). 2000. 5.00 (SM01-003) Morning NC.
Stephen does a masterful job of making church history come to life. This is an overview starting from pentecost & continuing through the 20th century.

Constipation: Possible Causes, Testing & Therapies. unabr. ed. Gary S. Ross. Interview with Katheleen S. Ross. 1 cass. (Running Time: 52 min.). (Natural Treatment Ser.). 1994. 15.00 (978-1-891875-00-7(0)) Creat Hlth Wrks.
Explains causes as well as other health problems that can be connected to constipation, how to test for cause, & effective natural therapies.

Constitution. 1 cass. (Running Time: 1 hr.). 9.00 (OP-79-04-27, HarperThor) HarpC GBR.

Constitution. Compiled by Benchmark Education Staff. 2006. audio compact disk 10.00 (978-1-4108-6643-1(2)) Benchmark Educ.

Constitution, Liberty & Government. unabr. ed. Robert LeFevre. 1 cass. (Running Time: 1 hr. 52 min.). 12.95 (1013) J Norton Pubs.
Examination of the Constitution & the "right" amount of government.

Constitution of the United States of America: Pocket edition with audio CD. Narrated by Julian S. Taylor. Julian S. Taylor & Janette K. Taylor. (ENG.). 2008. audio compact disk 15.00 (978-0-9790171-1-7(4)) Boneworthy.

Constitution, the Audio CD Theme Set: Set of 6 Set B. Adapted by Benchmark Education Staff. (English Explorers Ser.). (J). (gr. 3-6). 2007. audio compact disk 60.00 (978-1-4108-9829-6(6)) Benchmark Educ.

Constitutional Convention. George H. Smith. Read by Walter Cronkite. (Running Time: 9000 sec.). (Audio Classics Ser.). 2006. audio compact disk 25.95 (978-0-7861-6978-8(8)) Pub: Blckstn Audio. Dist(s): NetLibrary CO

Constitutional Convention, Set. unabr. ed. George H. Smith. Perf. by E. R. Davies et al. Narrated by Walter Cronkite. 2 cass. (Running Time: 75 min.). Dramatization. (United States Constitution Ser.). 1987. 17.95 (978-0-938935-81-0(X), 390270) Knowledge Prod.
The United States Constitution is the most important document in American history. Its ratification in 1788 created a nation. Its interpretation through centuries has determined the body of law under which we live. But the constitution is not a staid document drafted by legal scholars. It is the vibrant work of American revolutionaries who wished to secure the principles for which they had fought a war & won.

Constitutional Covenant: Spiritual Presuppositions & Practical Applications: Proceedings of the 45th Annual Convention National Association of Evangelicals Buffalo, New York. Read by David Llewellyn. 1 cass. (Running Time: 60 min.). 1987. 4.00 (344) Nat Assn Evan.

Constitutional Factors in Chemical Dependency & Pleasure Factor in Addiction. 1 cass. (Introduction to Chemical Dependency Ser.). 1980. 8.95 (1511G) Hazelden.

Constitutional Journal. unabr. ed. Jeffrey St. John. Read by Jeff Riggenbach. 6 cass. (Running Time: 8 hrs. 30 mins.). 1999. 44.95 (978-0-7861-1666-9(8), 2494) Blckstn Audio.
You are there, in 1787 at America's constitutional convention, with the inside story that reads like a modern-day account of the secret proceedings in Philadelphia. St. John "reports" each day's proceedings, flavoring his dispatches with quotes from private correspondence & notes of the delegates.

Constitutional Journal: A Correspondent's Report from the Convention Of 1787. unabr. ed. Jeffrey St John. Read by Jeff Riggenbach. Frwd. by Warren E. Burger. 8 cass. (Running Time: 27000 sec.). 1989. audio compact disk 29.95 set. (978-0-7861-0121-4(0), 1107) Blckstn Audio.
Here is a crisp examination of the spiritual life of one of the most important figures of 19th century England & Christendom.

Constitutional Journal: A Correspondent's Report from the Convention Of 1787. unabr. ed. Jeffrey St John. Read by Jeff Riggenbach. (Running Time: 27000 sec.). 2007. audio compact disk 55.00 (978-0-7861-0120-7(2)) Blckstn Audio.

Constitutional Law. Steven L. Emanuel. 11 cass. (Emanuel Law Tapes Ser.). 1993. 37.95 set. (978-1-56542-235-3(X), Aspen) WoltersKlu.
For use by law students in the area of Constitutional law.

Constitutional Law. John C. Jeffries, Jr. 1996. 45.95 (978-0-15-901031-0(4)) West.

Constitutional Law. Glenn H. Reynolds. 4 cass. (Blond's Audio Lectures). 1994. 49.99 (978-0-945819-73-8(0)) Sulzburger & Graham Pub.
Audio lectures summarizing the laws of constitutional law for law students.

Constitutional Law, 3rd ed. Mary M. Cheh. 6 cass. (Running Time: 9 hrs.). (Audio Tape Ser.). 1999. 50.00 (978-1-57793-036-5(3)) Pub: Sum & Substance. Dist(s): West Pub

Constitutional Law, 2005 ed. (Law School Legends Audio Series) John C. Jeffries. (Law School Legends Audio Ser.). 2006. 52.00 (978-0-314-16082-9(5), gilbert); 47.95 (978-0-314-16081-2(7), gilbert) West.

Constitutions of the World. Narrated by Blaustein. 1 cass. 1995. 17.95 (978-0-938935-44-5(5), 10229) Knowledge Prod.

Constructing Buildings with Straw Bales. Hosted by Nancy Pearlman. 1 cass. (Running Time: 29 min.). 10.00 (1206) Educ Comm CA.

Construction Contracts: From Concept to Concrete. 1988. 50.00 (AC-460) PA Bar Inst.

Construction Contracts & Litigation 1990. 8 cass. (Running Time: 10 hrs. 30 min.). bk. 75.00 incl. 960-page course handbook. (T6-9156) PLI.

Construction Documents & Services Mock Exam. Ed. by Architectural License Seminars Staff. 2004. audio compact disk 45.00 (978-0-7931-9394-3(X)) Kaplan Pubng.

Construction Drawings 1968-69, Lewis Egerton Smoot Memorial Library. John J. Ballentine, Jr. Ed. by Samuel H. Overman. 2005. audio compact disk (978-0-9635544-1-3(7)) S H Overman.

Construction Equipment & Building Products in Barbados: A Strategic Reference 2006. Compiled by Icon Group International, Inc. Staff. 2007. ring bd. 195.00 (978-0-497-35820-4(4)) Icon Grp.

Construction Equipment & Building Products in China: A Strategic Reference 2006. Compiled by Icon Group International, Inc. Staff. 2007. ring bd. 195.00 (978-0-497-35870-9(0)) Icon Grp.

Construction Equipment & Building Products in Mexico: A Strategic Reference 2006. Compiled by Icon Group International, Inc. Staff. 2007. ring bd. 195.00 (978-0-497-82350-4(0)) Icon Grp.

Construction Equipment & Building Products in Saudi Arabia: A Strategic Reference 2007. Compiled by Icon Group International, Inc. Staff. 2007. ring bd. 195.00 (978-0-497-82405-1(1)) Icon Grp.

Construction Equipment & Machinery in Uruguay: A Strategic Reference 2006. Compiled by Icon Group International, Inc. Staff. 2007. ring bd. 195.00 (978-0-497-82462-4(0)) Icon Grp.

Construction Equipment in Kenya: A Strategic Reference 2006. Compiled by Icon Group International, Inc. Staff. 2007. ring bd. 195.00 (978-0-497-82340-5(3)) Icon Grp.

Construction in Shakespeare. unabr. ed. Ernest Schanzer. 1 cass. (Running Time: 27 min.). (Shakespeare's Critics Speak Ser.). 1965. 12.95 (23108) J Norton Pubs.
An analysis of the nature & function of the two-part structure of four of Shakespeare's plays: "Timon of Athens", "Coriolanus" "Pericles" & "The Winter's Tale".

Construction in Taiwan: A Strategic Reference 2006. Compiled by Icon Group International, Inc. Staff. 2007. ring bd. 195.00 (978-0-497-82427-3(2)) Icon Grp.

Construction Lending: From Deal to Documents. 1987. bk. 115.00 incl. book.; 70.00 cass. only.; 45.00 book only. PA Bar Inst.

Construction Litigation. 1990. 75.00 (AC-586) PA Bar Inst.

Construction Materials in Kazakhstan: A Strategic Reference 2006. Compiled by Icon Group International, Inc. Staff. 2007. ring bd. 195.00 (978-0-497-82338-2(1)) Icon Grp.

Construction Math Program. Dave Buster. 5 cass. 1983. 53.95 set, incl. wkbk. (978-0-935715-02-6(9), 0175) Construct Bkstore.
Covers basic math skills needed in the construction industry. 10 lessons, 5 audio tapes plus workbook with solutions.

Construction Spanish. 2003. ring bd. (978-0-9744783-3-3(4)) Spanish Acad Cu Inst.

Constructional Geometry: Student Syllabus. 2nd ed. Wallace Brunelle & Robert O'Neill. Ed. by Allan W. Gray. (J). 1972. 108.05 (978-0-89420-201-8(4), 350300) Natl Book.

Constructive Adjustments to a World under Stress. Instructed by Manly P. Hall. 8.95 (978-0-89314-032-8(5), C860928) Philos Res.

Constructive Plan for Astro-Counseling. Christopher Gibson. 1 cass. 8.95 (663) Am Fed Astrologers.
An AFA Convention workshop tape.

Constructive Staff Discipline: Management Skills for Directors. Dora C. Fowler. 4 cass. (Running Time: 6 hrs.). 1994. pap. bk. 59.00 Set, incl. 33p. bk. (978-1-57323-002-5(2)) Natl Inst Child Mgmt.
Management training for staff discipline.

***Construye con figuras sólidas Audio CD.** April Barth. Adapted by Benchmark Education Co., LLC. (Content Connections Ser.). (SPA.). (J). 2010. audio compact disk 10.00 (978-1-61672-188-6(X)) Benchmark Educ.

***Construyendo familias Felices.** Javier Madera Camacho. (SPA.). 2007. audio compact disk 39.95 (978-0-9827086-0-6(2)) JMC Prof Semin.

Consuelo, Pt. 2. unabr. ed. George Sand. 8 cass. (Running Time: 1 hr. 30 min. per cass.). 1997. 53.95 Set. Audio Bk Con.

Consuelo, Pt. 2, set. George Sand. 8 cass. (Running Time: 12 hrs.). 1999. 53.95 Audio Bk Con.
This Gothic tale concerns the career & adventures of a rising young Venetian opera singer. Her travels with Haydn & romance with a Bohemian count are some of the highlights.

Consuelo (Part 1), Vol. 11. unabr. ed. George Sand. Read by Flo Gibson. 12 cass. (Running Time: 18 hrs.). 1997. 39.95 (978-1-55685-485-9(4), 485-4) Audio Bk Con.
This gothic tale concerns the career & adventures of a rising young Venetian opera singer. Her travels with Haydn & romance with a Bohemian Count are some of the highlights.

Consuelo (Part 2), Vol. 2. unabr. ed. George Sand. Narrated by Flo Gibson. (Running Time: 11 hrs. 11 mins.). 1997. 26.95 (978-1-55685-800-0(0)) Audio Bk Con.

Consuelo (Parts 1 And 2) unabr. ed. George Sand. Narrated by Flo Gibson. (Running Time: 29 hrs. 3 mins.). 1997. 57.95 (978-1-55685-801-7(9)) Audio Bk Con.

Consul's File. unabr. ed. Paul Theroux. Read by Michael Prichard. 7 cass. (Running Time: 7 hrs.). 1985. 42.00 (978-0-7366-0922-7(9), 1865) Books on Tape.
The consul arrives in Malaysia to examine the "secret" files but finds the insects got there first. What pages remain have little writing & most of them are empty. The consul has to fill in the blanks & this story is how he goes about it.

Consultant's Treasury. Alan Weiss. 4 cass. (Running Time: 4 hrs.). 1997. 120.00 (978-1-928611-02-8(8)) Summit Cons Grp.
Marketing techniques for professional consultants & speakers.

Consultation: A Valuable Resource. Ronald Buch & Frank Moyer. 1986. 10.80 (0805) Assn Prof Chaplains.

Consultative Selling, Set. 4 cass. pap. bk. & wbk. ed. 155.00 INCL. 2 multiple choice tests. (978-0-7612-0508-1(X), 80200NQ1) AMACOM.
This program will show you how to help your customers reduce their costs & increase their revenues. You'll learn how to: Sell as a consultant rather than a vendor; Develop Profit Improvement Proposals (PIP); Sell at high margins; Shorten the sales cycle; Sell to high level customer decision makers & much more.

Consulting in Child Care: Establishing a Successful Practice. Dora C. Fowler. 6 cass. (Running Time: 6 hrs.). 1988. pap. bk. 98.00 Set, incl. 23p. bk. (978-1-57323-003-2(0)) Natl Inst Child Mgmt.

Consulting Skills: Self-Guided Training. Jenny Tucker. (ENG.). 2007. audio compact disk 50.00 (978-1-935321-10-1(2)) OKA Rutledge.

Consumer & Patient Health Information & Medical Library Education Section - The Librarian's Role in Providing Consumer Health Information. 1 cass. (Running Time: 1 hr.). (Medical Library Association 1998 Annual Meeting & Exhibit Ser.). 1998. 12.00 (27) Med Lib Assn.

Consumer & Patient Health Information & Research Sections - Consumer Health Information Services: Do They Make a Difference? 1 cass. (Running Time: 1 hr.). (Medical Library Association 1998 Annual Meeting & Exhibit Ser.). 1998. 12.00 (15) Med Lib Assn.

Consumer Bankruptcy: Debtor - Creditor Perspectives. 1990. 40.00 (AC-587) PA Bar Inst.

Consumer Complaints - Small Claims Court, Side A; Bankruptcy, Side B. Frank L. Natter. 1 cass. (Running Time: 90 min.). (Type Law Tapes Ser.: No. 3). 1989. 10.00 (978-1-878287-58-8(3), ATA-3) Type & Temperament.
Implications & insights to understanding one's own personal legal & financial planning on the given subject.

***Consumer Detox: Less Stuff, More Life.** Mark Powley. (ENG.). 2010. 14.99 (978-0-310-59750-6(1)) Zondervan.

Consumer Economics & Personal Finance: Syllabus. Martha C. Bagby. (J). 1974. bk. 224.55 (978-0-89420-136-3(0)) Natl Book.

Consumer Electronics in China: A Strategic Reference 2006. Compiled by Icon Group International, Inc. Staff. 2007. ring bd. 195.00 (978-0-497-35871-6(9)) Icon Grp.

Consumer Electronics in Philippines: A Strategic Reference 2006. Compiled by Icon Group International, Inc. Staff. 2007. ring bd. 195.00 (978-0-497-82385-6(3)) Icon Grp.

Consumer Electronics in Thailand: A Strategic Reference 2007. Compiled by Icon Group International, Inc. Staff. 2007. ring bd. 195.00 (978-0-497-82439-6(6)) Icon Grp.

Consumer Law. Douglas J. Whaley. 3 cass. (Running Time: 4 hrs. 30 min.). (Outstanding Professor Ser.). 1996. 39.95 Set. (978-1-57793-027-3(4)) Sum & Substance.
Lecture given by a prominent American law school professor.

Consumer Law. 3rd rev. ed. Whaley. 1 cass. (Running Time: 90 mins.). (Audio Tape Ser.). 1999. 63.00 (978-0-314-24280-8(5), 28477, West Lglwrks) West.

Consumer Law for the Non-Specialist. 1997. bk. 99.00 (ACS-1369); bk. 99.00 (ACS-1369) PA Bar Inst.
Basic consumer transactions permeate the lives of your clients. The news is filled with examples of such deals gone awry, from the purchase of and automobile & telemarketing with its potential for abuse to home improvement contracts. All too frequently, lawyers have failed to devote the same attention to consumer cases as more traditional areas of practice. As the nature of consumer commerce & the law evolve, the need for representation in this growing field is greater than ever. Focuses on the law regulations & strategies you must know to be successful.

Consumer Protection Agency?, Do We Need A. unabr. ed. James Buckley & Charles Percy. 1 cass. (Running Time: 1 hr. 4 min.). 12.95 (318) J Norton Pubs.

Consumer Protection for the Mind. Eric Oliver. 4 cass. 1993. set in binder incl. 16p. bklet. (978-1-884605-01-7(X)) Genesis II.
Personal & professional development.

Consumer's Guide to a Brave New World. Wesley J. Smith. Read by Brian Emerson. (Running Time: 30600 sec.). 2006. 54.95 (978-0-7861-4574-4(9)); audio compact disk 63.00 (978-0-7861-7040-1(9)) Blckstn Audio.

Consumer's Guide to a Brave New World. unabr. ed. Wesley J. Smith. Read by Brian Emerson. (Running Time: 30600 sec.). 2006. audio compact disk 29.95 (978-0-7861-7554-3(0)) Blckstn Audio.

Consumer's Guide to Auto Insurance Savings. abr. ed. Michael J. Mattison. Read by E. R. Mattison. Ed. by Betty Daugherty. 1 cass. (Running Time: 33 min.). 1993. 9.95 (978-0-9638559-0-9(5)) Mattison Pubng.
The audio tape tells consumers how to save on their auto insurance & maintain appropriate coverage, & how to be their own best advocate when making claims. With a few changes consumers can save 40 percent or more on some coverages.

Consuming Fantasies: Labor, Leisure, & the London Shopgirl, 1880-1920. Lise Sanders. 2006. audio compact disk 9.95 (978-0-8142-9093-4(0)) Pub: Ohio St U Pr. Dist(s): Chicago Distribution Ctr

Consummation of Something Miraculous. unabr. ed. Charles R. Swindoll. 8 cass. (Running Time: 7 hrs. 30 mins.). 1998. 39.95 (978-1-57972-248-7(2)) Insight Living.

Contact. movie tie-in ed. Carl Sagan. 2004. 14.95 (978-0-7435-4527-3(3)) Pub: S&S Audio. Dist(s): S and S Inc

Contact. unabr. ed. Carl Sagan. Read by Laurel Lefkow. 10 vols. (Running Time: 15 hrs.). 2001. bk. 84.95 (978-0-7927-2434-6(8), CSL 323, Chivers Sound Lib) AudioGO.
December, 1999, the dawn of the millennium. A team of international scientists is poised for the most fantastic adventure in human history. After years of scanning the galaxy for signs of somebody or something else, this team believes they've found a message from an intelligent source & they travel deep into space to meet it.

Contact from the Underworld of Redboy. Perf. by Robbie Robertson. 1 cass., 1 CD. 8.78 (CAP 54243); audio compact disk 13.58 CD Jewel box. (CAP 54243) NewSound.
Includes: "Up on Cripple Creek," "The Night They Drove Old Dixie Down," & "Life is a Carnival".

Contact Has Begun Audio Cass. Phillip H. Krapf. 2000. 16.95 (978-1-57983-015-1(3)) Pub: Origin Pr CA. Dist(s): AtlasBooks

Contact Meditation. Eldon Taylor. 1 CD. (Running Time: 52 min.). (Whole Brain Innertalk Ser.). 1998. audio compact disk (978-1-55978-873-1(9)) Progress Aware Res.

Contact Meditation. Eldon Taylor. 1 CD. (Running Time: 52 min.). (Whole Brain Innertalk Ser.). 1999. audio compact disk (978-1-55978-944-8(1)) Progress Aware Res.

Contact Mr. Delgado. James Pattinson. 5 cass. (Running Time: 6 hrs. 30 mins.). (Soundings Ser.). (J). 2004. 49.95 (978-1-84283-820-4(2)); audio compact disk 64.95 (978-1-84283-858-7(X)) Pub: ISIS Lrg Prnt GBR. Dist(s): Ulverscroft US

Contact of the Forestry Kin. Mark Paul Sebar. (Wyler Scott Ser.: Vol. 1). 2008. (978-1-930246-32-4(3), 1930246323) Sebar Pubng.

Contacting & Inviting Made Easy: Drills Session 1. R. Grant Baker. 2005. audio compact disk (978-1-932583-15-1(7)) digital bates.

Contacting Spiritual Beings. Scripts. Nicholas Whitehead. 1 CD. (Running Time: 30 mins.). Dramatization. 2003. bk. 34.95 (978-1-928754-26-8(0), Magical Ways Pr) Le Brun CAN.
Author reads meditations with original music.

Contacting the Other: Amazing Psychotropic Tales. 1 cass. (Running Time: 1 hr.). 12.95 (WAB1003); audio compact disk 15.95 (WAB1004) Lodestone Catalog.

Contacting the Perfect You. Laurel Elizabeth Keyes. Voice by Laurel Elizabeth Keyes. 1 cass. (Running Time: 90 mins.). 1983. 10.00 (978-0-9791360-5-4(9)) Gentle Living.
Laurel Keyes leads this meditation going deep inside to contact the perfect you. We focus most of our time on our faults and weaknesses and this helps us to know who we truly are.

Contacting Your Guardian Angel. Govinda. Read by Karen Petrella. Ed. by Dietmar R. Rittner. 1 cass. (Running Time: 1 hr. 04 min.). (ViViD-Process Ser.). 1993. 12.95 (978-1-884027-00-0(8)) Magic Sunrise.
A guided visualization to travel with the light body to the realms of the angels, contacting the guardian angel.

Contacting Your Guardian Angel. Joyce Levine. 1 cass. 1995. 11.95 (978-1-885856-08-1(3)) Vizualizations.
Side 1 information. Side 2 guided meditation.

Contacting Your Inner Healer: A Guided Imagery Relaxation Tape (To Help You Access Your Own Inner Source of Wisdom & Divine Guidance in Order to Achieve Greater Health & Healing) Neil F. Neimark. Narrated by Neil F. Neimark. 1 cassette. (Running Time: 50 min). 2002. 12.95 (978-1-893557-08-6(1)) R E P Tech.
Contacting our inner healer places us in touch with a source of wisdom and clarity that can guide us in finding answers to the difficult health problems or emotional traumas we may be facing.

Contacting Your Inner Healer Vol. 2: A Guided Imagery Relaxation Tape with Action Plan, unabr. ed. Neil F. Neimark. 1 cass. (Running Time: 60 min.). 1998. 10.00 Bk. style plastic box. (978-1-893557-01-7(4)) R E P Tech.

***Contae Mhuigheo.** Johnny Mhairtin Learai. (ENG.). 1988. 11.95 (978-0-8023-7013-6(6)) Pub: Clo Iar-Chonnachta IRL. Dist(s): Dufour

Contae Mhuigheo. Contrib. by Johnny Mhairtin Learai. (ENG.). 1993. audio compact disk 21.95 (978-0-8023-8013-5(1)) Pub: Clo Iar-Chonnachta IRL. Dist(s): Dufour

Contagion. unabr. ed. Robin Cook. Read by Arthur Addison. 10 cass. (Running Time: 15 hrs.). (Jack Stapleton Ser.: No. 2). 1996. 80.00 (978-0-7366-3276-8(X), 3932) Books on Tape.
Dr. John Stapleton loses his ophthalmology practice to a giant HMO, then his family in a plane crash. He feels like starting over & he does, in the anonymity of New York City. There he retrains in forensic pathology & buries himself in work. But when a deadly, rare flu wipes out hosts of people, he can't ignore his suspicions. Is that HMO behind a plot to kill off its more costly subscribers.

Contagious. unabr. ed. Scott Sigler. (ENG.). 2008. audio compact disk 34.95 (978-0-7393-7715-4(9), Random AudioBks) Pub: Random Audio Pubg. Dist(s): Random

Contagious Christianity. 2003. 42.00 (978-1-57972-560-0(0)); audio compact disk 42.00 (978-1-57972-559-4(7)) Insight Living.

Contagious Christianity: A Study of 1 Thessalonians. unabr. ed. Charles R. Swindoll. 6 cass. (Running Time: 5 hrs.). 1998. 30.95 (978-1-57972-266-1(0)) Insight Living.

Contagious Confidence: 6 Simple Secrets That Will Help You Stand Proud in a Crowd. Monica Wofford. (ENG.). 2006. audio compact disk 49.95 (978-0-9752722-5-1(X)) Presenters Pubng.

Contagious Leadership: 10 Steps for Turning Managers into Leaders. 2004. audio compact disk 79.95 (978-0-9752722-2-0(5)) Presenters Pubng.

Contaminated or Pure: 11 Kings 17:33-34. Ed Young. 1982. 4.95 (978-0-7417-1269-1(5), 269) Win Walk.

***Contando hasta 10 Audio CD.** Francisco Blane. Adapted by Benchmark Education Company, LLC. (My First Reader's Theater Ser.). (SPA.). (J). 2009. audio compact disk 10.00 (978-1-935470-76-2(0)) Benchmark Educ.

Contatti: A First Course in Italian. Mariolina Freeth & Guiliana Checketts. 2 cass. (Running Time: 3 hrs.). (ITA., 1995. bk. 35.00 (978-0-8120-8236-4(2)) Barron.

Conte see Poetry & Voice of Marilyn Hacker

Contemplation. Robert A. Monroe. Read by Robert A. Monroe. (Running Time: 30 min.). (Human Plus Ser.). 1989. 14.95 (978-1-56102-004-1(4)) Inter Indus.
Facilitates a mentally active state to allow ideas, creativity, intuition & understanding to come from the Higher-self.

Contemplation. unabr. ed. Robert A. Monroe. Read by Roland Simon. 1 cass. (Running Time: 30 min.). (Human Plus Ser.). (FRE.). 1992. 14.95 (978-1-56102-057-7(5)) Inter Indus.

Contemplation, Meditation & Will. Swami Amar Jyoti. 1 dolby cass. 1986. 9.95 (K-83) Truth Consciousness.
Contemplation is not a technique; it arises from the consolidated life.

Contemplative Journey, Vol. 1. Thomas Keating. 12 CDs. (Running Time: 10 hrs 45 Mins). 2005. audio compact disk 99.95 (978-1-59179-335-9(1), AF00942D) Sounds True.
In the darkest hour of the darkest age, Christian monks developed a meditation tradition unique in the Western world. A 14th-century author described their profound mystical experience as entering "the cloud of unknowing." Yet during the 500 years after this great monastic flowering, this precious tradition - and the direct path to union with God it described - was virtually lost. For decades, Father Thomas Keating, together with other monks, examined this great question: could anyone enter "the cloud of unknowing" through a prayer practice specifically created to attain it? A Treasure of "Lost Christianity" Regained On The Contemplative Journey, Father Keating shares the authentic tradition of Christian contemplation that emerged from his spiritual search. This complete 12-CD curriculum teaches every facet of Father Keating's "Centering Prayer" technique, a uniquely Christian meditation technique that is similar to Eastern mystical practices. A Great Masterwork for Lasting Change From infancy, Father Keating begins, we accumulate emotional layers, or "programs," as a result of traumatic experiences. The practice of Centering Prayer engages directly with the unconscious and loosens old traumas that hinder our spiritual development. This form of "divine therapy" has brought profound inner transformation into the lives of thousands of practitioners.

Contemplative Journey, Vol. 2. Thomas Keating. 12 CDs. (Running Time: 10 hrs 30 Mins). 2005. audio compact disk 99.95 (978-1-59179-336-6(X), AF00943D) Sounds True.

Contemplative Life. Swami Amar Jyoti. 1 cass. 1986. 9.95 (A-34) Truth Consciousness.
The birth of the inquistive mind & the contemplative faculty, the door to transformation. Redesigning our life patterns.

Contemplative Prayer. Thomas Keating. 3 CDs. 2004. audio compact disk 24.95 (978-1-59179-306-9(8), AW00263D) Sounds True.
An introduction to "Centering Prayer", Christianity's own meditation tradition for divine union.

Contemplative Prayer. Thomas Merton. Read by Jonathan Montaldo. (Running Time: 16200 sec.). 1993. audio compact disk 4.95 (978-0-86716-826-6(9)) St Anthony Mess Pr.

Contemplative Prayer & Women's Developmental Patterns. Carole Riley. 2 cass. (Running Time: 2 hrs. 55 min.). 1993. 17.95 Set. (TAH298) Alba Hse Comns.
Contemplative prayer is explained by a woman for women taking into consideration feminine developmental patterns. Dr. Riley skillfully blends her religious experience & her competence as a counselor & spiritual director in presenting this direct yet sensitively profound presentation on contemplative prayer.

Contemplative Rosary: Praying the Mysteries with Scripture, Song & Icons. Bob Hurd. 2005. audio compact disk 17.00 (978-5-558-88955-0(1)) OR Catholic.

Contemporary Apologetics: Scientific Creationism: Biblical Apologetics: The Two Temptations. John Robbins. 1 cass. (Introduction to Apologetics Ser.: No. 6). 5.00 Trinity Found.

Contemporary Apologetics: Twentieth Century Confusion. John Robbins. 1 cass. (Introduction to Apologetics Ser.: No. 5). 5.00 Trinity Found.

Contemporary Approaches to Pastoral Counseling. Benedict J. Groeschel. 5 cass. (Running Time: 4 hrs. 14 min.). 1995. 41.95 Set. (TAH339) Alba Hse Comns.
This four part workshop outlines many current issues & offers solutions & practical methodology for dealing with the situations that face the priest in his capacity as counselor, confessor, shepherd & guide.

Contemporary Arabic Readers, Vols. I-II, IV-V. Ernest N. McCarus et al. 28 cass. 171.09 Set. U MI Lang Res.
Includes: Newspaper Arabic; Essays; Short Stories & Plays; & Poetry.

Contemporary Arabic Readers Vol. I: Newspaper Arabic. Ernest N. McCarus & Adil I. Yocoub. 12 cass. 1962. 93.18 Set. U MI Lang Res.

Contemporary Arabic Readers Vol. II: Essays. Ernest N. McCarus et al. 3 cass. 1962. 40.78 Set. U MI Lang Res.

Contemporary Arabic Readers Vol. IV: Short Stories & Plays. Bellamy et al. 7 cass. 1963. 63.30 Set. U MI Lang Res.

Contemporary Arabic Readers Vol. V: Poetry. Bellamy et al. 6 cass. 1962. 57.72 Set. U MI Lang Res.

Contemporary Brush Techniave. Louie Bellson et al. (ENG.). 2000. audio compact disk 10.95 (978-0-7390-1373-1(4), 19625) Alfred Pub.

Contemporary Catholic Problems. Mother Angelica & Father Michael. 1 cass. (Running Time: 60 min.). (Mother Angelica Live Ser.). 1988. 10.00 (978-1-55794-105-3(X), T56) Eternal Wrd TV.
Discusses defining & defending the Faith, how to speak up on controversial issues & misdirected compassion.

Contemporary Christianity, unabr. ed. C. S. Lewis & Thomas Merton. Read by John Cleese & Sidney Lanier. Tr. by Stephen Mitchell. 6 cass. (Running Time: 9 hrs.). 1998. bk. 49.95 (978-1-57453-226-5(X)) Audio Lit.
Includes: "The Screwtape Letters" & "Seven Storey Mountain" & "The Gospel According to Jesus".

Contemporary Church History. Stephen Mansfield. 1 cass. (Running Time: 90 mins.). (Basic Church History Ser.: Vol. 6). 2000. 5.00 (SM01-006) Morning NC.
Stephen does a masterful job of making church history come to life. This is an overview starting from pentecost & continuing through the 20th century.

Contemporary Classic Zen: The Three Pillars of Zen, Zen Mind & Zen Flesh & Zen Bones. abr. ed. Roshi Philip Kapleau & Zen Master Foyan Staff. Read by Mitchell Ryan. 6 cass. (Running Time: 9 hrs.). 1998. bk. 49.95 (978-1-57453-275-3(8)) Audio Lit.
Includes "The Three Pillars of Zen," & "Zen Mind, Beginner's Mind," & "Zen Flesh, Zen Bones".

Contemporary Country: The Early '90s. 1 CD. audio compact disk 9.99 (R9EL08) Time-Life.

Contemporary Country: The Early '90s. 1 cass. 1999. 9.99 (NBFLS7) Time-Life.

Contemporary Czech. unabr. ed. Michael Heim. 3 cass. (Running Time: 3 hrs.). (CZE.). (YA). (gr. 10-12). 1982. pap. bk. 65.00 (978-0-88432-445-4(1), AFCZ10) J Norton Pubs.
Vocabulary & sentences are recorded along with a selection of exercises. Particularly helpful for those who have a command of Russian. Czech-English, English-Cech glossaries are provided.

Contemporary Economic Issues, Pts. 1-4. Instructed by Timothy Taylor. 24 cass. (Running Time: 24 hrs.). 1998. 249.95 (978-1-56585-156-6(0)) Teaching Co.

Contemporary Economic Issues, Pts. I-IV. Instructed by Timothy Taylor. 24 CDs. (Running Time: 24 hrs.). 1998. audio compact disk 359.95 (978-1-56585-359-1(8)) Teaching Co.

Contemporary Economic Issues, Vol. 2. Instructed by Timothy Taylor. 6 cass. (Running Time: 6 hrs.). 1998. 249.95 (978-1-56585-157-3(9)) Teaching Co.

Contemporary Economic Issues, Vol. 3. Instructed by Timothy Taylor. 6 cass. (Running Time: 6 hrs.). 1998. 249.95 (978-1-56585-158-0(7)) Teaching Co.

Contemporary Economic Issues, Vol. 4. Instructed by Timothy Taylor. 6 cass. (Running Time: 6 hrs.). 1998. 249.95 (978-1-56585-159-7(5)) Teaching Co.

Contemporary English Book 2: Units 1-10. Created by McGraw-Hill Staff. 2004. audio compact disk 383.00 (978-0-07-286266-9(1)) McGraw.

Contemporary Guitar Greats. 2007. 24.95 (978-5-557-49799-2(4)) Mel Bay.

Contemporary Guitar Progressions Play Along. Barry Brooksby. 2002. pap. bk. 14.95 (978-0-7866-6456-6(8), 98204CDB) Mel Bay.

Contemporary Intermediate Czech CDs & Text. Michael Heim. 3 CDs. (Running Time: 3 hrs.). (CZE.). 2005. audio compact disk 65.00 (978-1-57970-257-1(0), AFCZ10D, Audio-For) J Norton Pubs.
The text contains a grammar, extensive model sentences, and exercises (Part I) and a series of review lessons (Part II). Vocabulary and sentences are recorded, along with a selection of exercises.
Czech-English/English-Czech glossaries are provided. This intermediate course is particularly useful for those who have a familiarity with Russian.

Contemporary Life: Comments by Andrei Codrescu. Read by Andrei Codrescu. 1 cass. (Running Time: 1 hr.). 10.95 (F0050B090, HarperThor) HarpC GBR.

Contemporary Living. Verdene Ryder & Marjorie B. Harter. (gr. 9-12). tchr. ed. 200.00 (978-1-56637-956-4(3)) Goodheart.

Contemporary Living. ed. Verdene Ryder & Marjorie B. Harter. 2002. audio compact disk 191.20 (978-1-56637-844-4(3)) Goodheart.

Contemporary Living: Individual License. Verdene Ryder & Marjorie B. Harter. (gr. 9-12). tchr. ed. 64.00 (978-1-59070-244-4(1)) Goodheart.

Contemporary Living: Site License. Verdene Ryder & Marjorie B. Harter. (gr. 9-12). tchr. ed. 192.00 (978-1-59070-245-1(X)) Goodheart.

Contemporary Mallet Duets. Karen E. Pershing. 1 CD. (ENG.). 1999. audio compact disk 10.50 (978-0-7390-0379-4(8), 17324) Alfred Pub.

Contemporary Music Education Campaign of the ISCM World New Music Days 2002: Teaching Resource Kit. Editorial Team of the ISCM Contemporary Music Education Campaign. 3 vols. (CHI.). bk. 150.00 (978-962-996-215-9(2)) Pub: Chinese Univ HKG. Dist(s): Col U Pr

Contemporary Praise for Ladies' Voices 2: 14 Arrangements for Ensemble or Choir. Contrib. by Dennis Allen. 2007. audio compact disk 12.00 (978-5-557-58505-7(2)); audio compact disk 90.00 (978-5-557-58507-1(9)); audio compact disk 90.00 (978-5-557-58506-4(0)); audio compact disk 16.99 (978-5-557-58499-9(4)) Lillenas.

Contemporary Reader, Vol. 2. McGraw-Hill Staff. 3 cass. (gr. 4-10). 2004. suppl. ed. 64.00 (978-0-89061-834-9(8)) Pub: Jamestown. Dist(s): McGraw
Audiocassette 1 Selections from Volume 2, Number 1 "Bamboo Can Do!" "Armchair Shopping" "The Pride of Paris" "The Trail of Tears" Selections from Volume 2, Number 2 "Diamonds: Stars from Earth" "Tea: To Your Health" "Cool Customers" "Dogs Who 'Think'" Audiocassette 2 Selections from Volume 2, Number 3 "The Chunnel Under the Sea" "Chicago's Killer Heat Wave" "The Threat of Mount Ranier" "Louis Braille's Magic Dots" Selections from Volume 2, Number 4 "Josephine Baker: The Toast of Paris" "Outfitters of the West" "A Matter of Taste" "The Scoop on Lotteries" Audiocassette 3 Selections from Volume 2, Number 5 "Doomed to Disaster" "The Art of Acupuncture" "Ruins of a People" "Women at War" Selections from Volume 3, Number 6 "The World's Longest Railway" "Habitat for Humanity" "The Birth of the Modern Olympics" "A Tarantula: Big Hairy Deal".

Contemporary Religious Broadcast: Proceedings of 45th Annual Convention National Association of Evangelicals, Buffalo, New York. Read by Sue Bahner. 1 cass. (Running Time: 60 min.). 1987. 4.00 (315) Nat Assn Evan.

Contemporary Slide Guitar. Arvid Smith, Jr. & Barbara Koehler. 1993. bk. 18.95 (978-0-87166-662-8(6), 93373P); 10.98 (978-0-87166-661-1(8), 93373C) Mel Bay.

Contemporary Songs for Worship. Richard Kingsmore. 1999. 75.00 (978-0-633-03956-1(X)) LifeWay Christian.

Contemporary Songs for Worship Ensembles. Richard Kingsmore. 1999. 11.98 (978-0-633-03957-8(8)); audio compact disk 16.98 (978-0-633-03955-4(1)); audio compact disk 85.00 (978-0-633-03954-7(3)) LifeWay Christian.

Contemporary Spoken Persian I, Mehdi Marashi. 8 cass. (Running Time: 8 hrs.). (PER.). (J). (gr. 10-12). 1986. pap. bk. 225.00 (978-0-88432-132-3(0), AFPE01) J Norton Pubs.
Course in modern spoken Persian offers recordings by native speakers & emphasizes practical everyday language. Lesson units include dialogs, vocabulary & in some instances self-tests.

Contemporary Spoken Persian II, Mehdi Marashi. 8 cass. (Running Time: 8 hrs.). (PER.). 1994. pap. bk. 225.00 (978-0-88432-792-9(2), AFPE20) J Norton Pubs.

Contemporary Theatre Songs: Belter/Mezzo-Soprano Collection. 1 CD. (Running Time: 90 mins.). 2000. pap. bk. 22.95 (00740016) H Leonard.
Performances by talented artists & piano accompaniments for practice. Most of these songs have never been recorded apart from the original cast albums. Includes: "Now That I've Seen Her" (Miss Saigon); "Someone Else's Story" (Chess); "Nothing Really Happened" (Is There Life after High School?); "Just a Housewife" (Working); "Tell Me on a Sunday" (Song & Dance); "Sooner or Later" (Dick Tracey; film); "Old Friend" (I'm Getting My Act Together & Taking It on the Road" & more.

Contemporary Theatre Songs: Men's Collection. 1 CD. (Running Time: 90 mins.). 2000. pap. bk. 22.95 (00740017) H Leonard.
Performances by talented artists & piano accompaniments for practice. Most of these songs have never been recorded apart from the original cast albums. Includes: "If I Sing" & "One of the Good Guys" (Closer Than Ever); "The Picture in the Hall" (3 Postcards); "Only with You" (Nine); "What You'd Call a Dream" (Diamonds); "Why God Why?" (Miss Saigon) & more.

Contemporary Theatre Songs: Soprano Collection. 1 CD. (Running Time: 90 mins.). 2000. pap. bk. 22.95 (00740014) H Leonard.
Performances by talented artists & piano accompaniments for practice. Most of these songs have never been recorded apart from the original cast albums. Includes: "In My Life" (Les Miserables); "Not a Day Goes By" (Merrily We Roll Along; "No One Knows Who I Am" (Jekyll & Hyde); "My True Love" & "This Place Is Mine" (Phantom by Yeston); "Simple" & "Unusual Way" (Nine); "Another Suitcase in Another Hall" (Evita); "Green Finch & Linnet Bird" (Sweeney Todd); "Take Me to the World" (Evening Primrose).

Contemporary Tinikling. 1 cass. (Running Time: 1 hr.). (J). 2001. pap. bk. 10.95 (KEA 8095C) Kimbo Educ.
Bamboo pole dancing with 4/4 beat & familiar music for fun, fitness, timing & coordination. Brazilia, The Entertainer, Walk Right In, Put Your Hand in the Hand, You are the Sunshine of My Life & more. Includes manual.

Contemporary Tinkling. 1 LP. (J). stu. ed. 10.95 four 5' bamboo poles. (ACC 8095); stu. ed. 11.95 (KEA 8095) Kimbo Educ.
Modified with 4/4 beat & familiar music. Develops coordination & rhythmic timing.

Contemporary Topics: Advanced Listening Comprehension. David Beglar et al. (Longman Listening Ser.). 1993. 66.00 (978-0-8013-0929-8(8)) Longman.

Contemporary Topics 1: Intermediate Listening & Note-Taking Skills. 2nd ed. Helen Solorzano & Laurie Frazier. (Contemporary Topics Ser.). 2001. 56.00 (978-0-13-094856-4(X)) Longman.

Contemporary Topics 1: Intermediate Listening & Note-Taking Skills. 2nd ed. Helen Solorzano & Laurie Frazier. (Contemporary Topics Ser.). 2001. audio compact disk 56.00 (978-0-13-094857-1(8)) Longman.

Contemporary Topics 2: High Intermediate Listening & Note-Taking Skills. 2nd ed. Ellen Kisslinger. (Contemporary Topics Ser.). 2001. 73.33 (978-0-13-094859-5(4)) Longman.

Contemporary Topics 2: High Intermediate Listening & Note-Taking Skills. 2nd ed. Ellen Kisslinger. (Contemporary Topics Ser.). 2001. audio compact disk 73.33 (978-0-13-094861-8(6)) Longman.

Contemporary Topics 3: Advanced Listening & Note-Taking Skills. 2nd ed. David Beglar & Neil Murray. (Contemporary Topics Ser.). 2001. 73.33 (978-0-13-094864-9(0)); audio compact disk 73.33 (978-0-13-094866-3(7)) Longman.

Contemporary Vietnamese Set: An Intermediate Text. Nguyen B. Thuan. 4 cass. (Southeast Asian Language Ser.). (C). 1997. pap. bk. 12.00 Set. (978-1-877979-40-8(6)) SE Asia.

Contemporary Vocalist Volume 2: The Deva Method Advanced Vocal Exercises. Created by Jeannie Deva. 4 CDs. (Running Time: 3 hrs. 50 mins.). 2003. audio compact disk 59.95 (978-1-882224-22-7(1)) Pub: Jeannie Deva. Dist(s): Baker Taylor
4 Compact Disks in Quad jewel case with short instruction booklet.

Contemporary Vocalist Improvement Course: The Deva Method, a Non-Classical Approach for Singers. Jeannie Deva. Ed. by Julie Lyonn Lieberman. Illus. by Trish Rouelle. Frwd. by Magic Dick. 4 CDs. (Running Time: 3 hrs. 50 mins.). 2001. per. 59.95 (978-1-882224-09-8(4)) Pub: Jeannie Deva. Dist(s): Baker Taylor

Contemporary Woman in Her Middle Years. Kenneth Reed et al. 1986. 10.80 (0202) Assn Prof Chaplains.

Contemporary's Citizenship Now. Aliza Becker & Laurie Edwards. 1997. pap. bk. 23.95 (978-0-8442-0661-5(X), 0661X) M-H Contemporary.
About citizenship.

***Contempt of Congress: Baby Boomers Talk: Sex,Race,Politics,Environment & Revolution.** 2010. audio compact disk 10.00 (978-0-9728416-2-7(8)) Fresh Clean Day.

Contender, unabr. ed. Robert Lipsyte. Narrated by Peter Francis James. 4 pieces. (Running Time: 5 hrs. 15 mins.). (gr. 7 up). 1997. 35.00 (978-0-7887-0732-2(9), 94909E7) Recorded Bks.
Albert Brooks is a high school dropout. His job in a small Harlem grocery store feels like a dead end. Each day Albert's options shrink a little more & his future grows dimmer, until he walks into Donatelli's Gym. Standing before a short, stocky man with a hard face & knowing eyes, Albert dares to dream of becoming a boxer.

Contending for Miracles. As told by Frank Damazio. 6 cass. (Running Time: 4 hrs. 58 mins.). 2003. 59.99 (978-0-914936-49-7(2)) CityChristian.

Contending for Spiritual Gifts. As told by Frank Damazio. 6 cass. (Running Time: 4 hrs. 30 mins.). 2003. 59.99 (978-0-914936-56-5(5)) CityChristian.

Contending for the Gift of Healing. As told by Frank Damazio. 6 cass. 2003. 59.99 (978-1-59383-011-3(4)) CityChristian.

Content Analysis of the Rorschach Test. unabr. ed. Fred Brown. 1 cass. (Running Time: 20 min.). 1952. (29240) J Norton Pubs.
An examination of the symbolic & qualitative aspects of Rorschach responses.

***Content Area Literacy: An Integrated Approach Cd.** 9th rev. ed. Readence. (ENG.). 2010. audio compact disk 74.61 (978-0-7575-4109-4(7)) Kendall-Hunt.

Content Area Readers. Dororthy Kauffman. (Oxford Picture Dictionary for the Content Areas Ser.). 2005. audio compact disk 17.50 (978-0-19-430961-5(4)) OUP.

Content Area Reading Competency Through Modified Cloze, Set 2. Sylvia Van Voorhees & Shirley N. Winters. 3 cass. Incl. Area 1. Content Area Reading Competency Through Modified Cloze: Science. 1 cass. 32.00 incl. 5 bks., 20 activity worksheets & guide. (AKC 350); Area 2. Content Area Reading Competency Through Modified Cloze: Social Studies. 1 cass. 32.00 incl. 5 bks., 20 activity worksheets & guide. (AKC 351); Area 3. Content Area Reading Competency Through Modified Cloze: English. 1 cass. 32.00 incl. 5 bks., 20 activity dittos, guide. (AKC 352); (J). (gr. 6-10). 89.00 set, incl. 15 bks., 60 activity worksheets & guide. (35012) Ed Activities.
Some 60 lessons help students master textual material. Passages of about 250-300 words are written at ascending levels of difficulty for use in three content areas: Science, Social Studies & English. The book in each content area contains 20 cloze passages, with each passage containing seven deletions. An aid in identifying in the five critical components of reading comprehension, Context Clues, Syntactic Clues, Signal Words, Pronoun Referents, Prediction Clues.

Content Area Reading Competency Through Modified Cloze: Elementary, Set 1. Sylvia Van Voorhees & Shirley N. Winters. 3 cass. Incl. . Content Area Reading Competency Through Modified Cloze Set 1: English. 1 cass. (J). 32.00 incl. 5 bks., 20 activity dittos, guide. (978-0-89525-250-0(3), AKC 189); Area 1. Content Area Reading Competency Through Modified Cloze: Science. 1 cass. 32.00 incl. 5 bks., 20 activity worksheets & guide. (AKC 187); Area 2. Content Area Reading Competency Through Modified Cloze: Social Studies. 1 cass. 32.00 incl. 5 bks., 20 activity worksheets & guide. (AKC 188); (J). (gr. 4-8). 89.00 incl. 15 bks., 60 activity worksheets & guide Set. (978-0-89525-169-5(8), 18789) Ed Activities.

Content Area Reading Competency Through Modified Cloze: English see Content Area Reading Competency Through Modified Cloze

Content Area Reading Competency Through Modified Cloze: Science see Content Area Reading Competency Through Modified Cloze: Elementary

Content Area Reading Competency Through Modified Cloze: Science see Content Area Reading Competency Through Modified Cloze

Content Area Reading Competency Through Modified Cloze: Social Studies see Content Area Reading Competency Through Modified Cloze: Elementary

Content Area Reading Competency Through Modified Cloze: Social Studies see Content Area Reading Competency Through Modified Cloze

Content Area Reading Competency Through Modified Cloze, Set 1, English see Content Area Reading Competency Through Modified Cloze: Elementary

Content Areas, Set. Gary Apple & Dorothy Kauffman. 5 CDs. (Oxford Picture Dictionary for the Content Areas Ser.). 2002. audio compact disk 54.95 (978-0-19-438400-1(4)) OUP.

Content of One's Consciousness. J. Krishnamurti. 1 cass. (Running Time: 1 hr.). (Ojai Public Talks - 1982 Ser.: No. 4). 8.50 (AJT824) Krishnamurti.
In the idyllic setting of the oak grove in Ojai, California, Krishnamurti began giving talks in 1922. Over the years, hundreds of thousands of people have heard Krishnamurti explore every aspect of our lives, his language & expression constantly changing, as he strove to communicate to each successive generation those profound truths which he had come upon, & which he maintained were accessible to all.

Contented Cows Give Better Milk: The Plain Truth about Employee Relations & Your Bottom Line. 2001. 30.00 (978-1-890651-08-4(7), Saltillo Press) Williford Communs.

Contentment. (713) Yoga Res Foun.

Contentment. Swami Jyotirmayananda. 1 cass. (Running Time: 1 hr.). 1990. 12.99 Yoga Res Foun.

Contents under Pressure. unabr. collector's ed. Edna Buchanan. Read by Donada Peters. 7 cass. (Running Time: 10 hrs. 30 min.). (Britt Montero Mystery Ser.). 1993. 56.00 (978-0-7366-2378-0(7), 3150) Books on Tape.
Police reporter Britt Montero knows the city's sleaze like her own backyard. When her story about excessive police violence & the death of a black man breaks, so does a truce keeping the city intact.

Contes, Vol. 1. Short Stories. Jacob W. Grimm & Wilhelm K. Grimm. Read by Marianne Epin. 1 cass. (FRE.). 1995. 16.95 (1652-TH) Olivia & Hill.
A collection of classics including "Le Roi Grenouille," "Le Pecheur et sa femme" "Les Trois Cheveux d'or du diable," "Le Petit Poucet," "Peau d'ours" & "Les Gens futes.".

Contes, Vol. 2. Short Stories. Jacob W. Grimm & Wilhelm K. Grimm. Read by Marianne Epin. 1 cass. (FRE.). 1995. 16.95 (1779-TH) Olivia & Hill.
A collection of classics including "Hansel et Gretel," "Le Pauvre Garcon menunier," "La Lumiere bleue," "Les Quatre Freres" & "Lese Musiciens de la ville de Breme.".

Contes a Ninon, Set. Short Stories. Emile Zola. Read by C. Deis & G. Bejean. 2 cass. (FRE.). 1991. 26.95 (1307-VSL) Olivia & Hill.
Zola tells "Ninon" four tales of his native Provence.

Contes Bleus du Chat Perche. Marcel Ayme. Read by Michel Galabru. 1 cass. (FRE.). 1991. bk. 29.95 (1GA053) Olivia & Hill.
Marcel Ayme brings the reader into the world of Delphine & Marinette, two little girls. They play tricks on their parents with the complicity of animals who speak the language of childhood.

Contes Campagnards. unabr. ed. Nicole Foucault Baty. Read by Nicole Foucault Baty. 2007. 69.99 (978-2-35569-045-7(6)) Find a World.

Contes d'Andersen. Read by Philippe Lejour. 1 cass. (FRE.). 1996. 16.95 (1805-LV) Olivia & Hill.
"La Princesse sur un Pois," "Les Habits Neufs de l'Empereur," & "La Petite Sirene.".

Contes de Charles Perrault. unabr. ed. 2 cass. (FRE.). (J). 15.95 Vol. 1. (CFR365); 15.95 Vol. 2. (CFR375) J Norton Pubs.
French fairy tales, beginning level.

Contes de Charles Perrault, Vol. 1. Charles Perrault. Read by Therese Cremieux. 1 cass. (Running Time: 41 min.). (FRE.). (J). 1987. 11.95 (978-0-8045-1173-5(X), SAC 1173) Spoken Arts.
Some of the Best-Loved Fairy Tales. For Any Student of French, or Native French Speaker.

Contes de Charles Perrault, Vol. 2. Charles Perrault. Read by Therese Cremieux. 1 cass. (Running Time: 49 min.). (FRE.). (J). 1987. 11.95 (978-0-8045-1174-2(8), SAC 1174) Spoken Arts.
Certainly No Childhood Is Complete Without Cendrillon (Cinderella), le Chat Botte (Puss in Boots) & le Petit Poucet (Tom Thumb) & French Speaking Youngsters Will Love These Moving Readings.

Contes de la Becasse. Short Stories. Guy de Maupassant. Read by G. Faraoun & C. Deis. 1 cass. (FRE.). 1991. 21.95 (1079-VSL) Olivia & Hill.
The countryside of Normandy, so familiar to Maupassant, is the setting for this collection of tales.

Contes de ma Mere l'Oye. Short Stories. Charles Perrault. Read by Claude Villers. 1 cass. (FRE.). 1992. bk. 29.95 (1GA072) Olivia & Hill.
Famous collection of French fairytales.

Contes de Maupassant, Vol. 2. unabr. ed. Guy de Maupassant. Read by Georges Riquier. 1 cass. (Running Time: 47 min.). Incl. Bapteme. (SAC 48-5); Duel. (SAC 48-5); Parure. (SAC 48-5); (Bibliothèque de la Pléiade Ser.: 253, 275). (FRE.). 11.95 incl. bk. (978-0-8045-0921-3(2), SAC 48-5) Spoken Arts.
Famous artist of the Theatre National Populaire interprets major tales of de Maupassant.

Contes de Maupassant, Vol. II. unabr. ed. Guy de Maupassant. Ed. by Durbin Rowland. Illus. by Helen West Heller. 1 cass. (Running Time: 50 min.). Incl. Mon Oncle Jules. Guy de Maupassant. (SAC 57-3); Parapluie. (SAC 57-3); (University of Chicago Junior College Ser.). 11.95 incl. bk. (978-0-8045-0922-0(0), SAC 57-3) Spoken Arts.
Monsieur Riquier continues with two tales ideal for young & old alike.

Contes de Perrault. unabr. ed. Read by Marcel Weill. 1 cass. Incl. Barbe Bleue (Blue Beard) (SAC 47-6); Cendrillon (Cinderella) (SAC 47-6); Fees (The Fairies) (SAC 47-6); Petit Chaperon Rouge. (SAC 47-6); (FRE.). 11.95 (978-0-8045-0787-5(2), SAC 47-6) Spoken Arts.

Contes de Perrault, 1. Read by Philippe Lejour. 1 cass. (FRE.). 1996. 16.95 (1806-LV) Olivia & Hill.
"La Belle au Bois Dormant," "Le Petit Chaperon Rouge," "Riquet a la Houppe" & "Le Chat Botte.".

Contes de Perrault, 2. Short Stories. Read by Philippe Lejour. 1 cass. (FRE.). 1996. 16.95 (1812-LV) Olivia & Hill.
"Le Petit Poucet," "La Barbe Bleue," "Les Fees," "Cendrillon" & "Peau d'Ane.".

Contes du Jour et de la Nuit. unabr. ed. Guy de Maupassant. Read by Yves Belluardo. (YA). 2007. 69.99 (978-2-35569-033-4(2)) Find a World.

Contes du Lundi. Short Stories. Alphonse Daudet. Read by P. Nehr. 1 cass. (FRE.). 1991. 19.95 (1411-VSL) Olivia & Hill.
Collection of short stories sketching life during the Franco-Prussian War.

Contes d'Une Grand-Mere, Vol. 1. Short Stories. George Sand. 1 cass. (FRE.). 1995. 16.95 (1716-RF) Olivia & Hill.
Short stories set in a rural setting: "Le Chene parlan" et "Le Nuage rose." Told by a cast of radio actors.

Contes d'Une Grand-Mere, Vol. 2. Short Stories. George Sand. 1 cass. (FRE.). 1995. 16.95 (1717-RF) Olivia & Hill.
Les Ailes de courage read by a cast of radio actors.

Contes Fantastiques. Guy de Maupassant. pap. bk. 19.95 (978-88-7754-821-4(5)) Pub: Cideb ITA. Dist(s): Distribks Inc

Contes pour Enfants pas Sages. Jacques Prevert. Read by Luc Alexander et al. 1 cass. 1992. bk. 26.95 (1GA073) Olivia & Hill.
A collection of charming stories written by this famous contemporary poet.

Contes Rouges du Chat Perche, Set. Marcel Ayme. Read by Michel Galabru et al. 2 cass. (FRE.). 1992. bk. 35.95 (1GA066) Olivia & Hill.
More tales by one of France's best known storytellers: "La Patte du Chat," "Le Chien," "Les Boites de Peinture" & "Le Paon.".

Contest. Matthew Reilly. Read by Sean Mangan. (Running Time: 9 hrs.). 2009. 79.99 (978-1-74214-275-3(3), 9781742142753) Pub: Bolinda Pubng AUS. Dist(s): Bolinda Pub Inc

Contest. unabr. ed. Matthew Reilly. Read by Sean Mangan. 8 cass. (Running Time: 9 hrs.). 2001. 64.00 (978-1-74030-563-1(9)) Pub: Bolinda Pubng AUS. Dist(s): Bolinda Pub Inc

Contest. unabr. ed. Matthew Reilly. 8 CDs. (Running Time: 9 hrs.). 2002. audio compact disk 87.95 (978-1-74030-779-6(8)) Pub: Bolinda Pubng AUS. Dist(s): Bolinda Pub Inc

Contest. unabr. ed. Matthew Reilly. Read by Sean Mangan. (Running Time: 32400 sec.). 2007. audio compact disk 43.95 (978-1-921334-48-1(7), 9781921334481) Pub: Bolinda Pubng AUS. Dist(s): Bolinda Pub Inc

Contest & Examination: CM-1. National Shorthand Reporters Association. 1 cass. 9.00 (CT-14) Natl Ct Report.

Contest & Examination: CON-2. National Shorthand Reporters Association. 1 cass. 9.00 (CT-2) Natl Ct Report.
Practice dictation tape covering material from the 1973, 1974, 1975 & 1976. National Shorthand Reporters Association.

Contest & Examination: No. 1. National Shorthand Reporters Association. 1 cass. 9.00 (CT-1) Natl Ct Report.
Contains the full text of four past National Shorthand Reporters Association Speed Contests & part of two others.

Contest & Examination: No. 3. National Shorthand Reporters Association. 1 cass. 9.00 (CT-3) Natl Ct Report.
National Shorthand Reporters Association 1977-1980 National Speed Contests.

Contest & Examination: RPR-1. National Shorthand Reporters Association. 1 cass. 9.00 (CT-13) Natl Ct Report.
Profesionally dictated tests prepared especially for CM testing-by-tapes sites. Includes material from the May 1980 through November 1981 exams.

Contest & Examination: Speed Contest-Legal Opinion. National Shorthand Reporters Association. 1 cass. 9.00 (CT-11) Natl Ct Report.
Twelve legal opinion shorthand dictation selections at 230 wpm.

Contest & Examination: Speed Contest-Literary. National Shorthand Reporters Association. 1 cass. 9.00 (CT-10) Natl Ct Report.
Twelve literary shorthand dictation selections at 220 wpm.

Contest & Examination: Speed Contest-Testimony. National Shorthand Reporters Association. 1 cass. 9.00 (CT-12) Natl Ct Report.
Twelve testimony shorthand dictation selections at 280 wpm.

Contest & Examination: 1981. National Shorthand Reporters Association. 1 cass. 9.00 (CT-4) Natl Ct Report.
Literary shorthand dictation at 220 wpm, legal opinion at 230 wpm & testimony at 280 wpm; side two, literary at 220 wpm, legal opinion at 230 wpm & testimony at 280 wpm.

Contest & Examination: 1982. National Shorthand Reporters Association. 9.00 (CT-5) Natl Ct Report.
Literary dictation at 220 wpm, legal opinion at 230 wpm; side two, literary at 220 wpm, & testimony at 280 wpm, followed by the 1982 National Speed contest.

Contest & Examination No. 1: Speed Contest. National Shorthand Reporters Association. 1 cass. 9.00 (CT-5) Natl Ct Report.

Contest & Examination No. 2: Speed Contest. National Shorthand Reporters Association. 1 cass. 9.00 (CT-7) Natl Ct Report.
Shorthand Reporters Speed Contest Practice Material.

Contest & Examination No. 3: Speed Contest. National Shorthand Reporters Association. 1 cass. 9.00 (CT-8) Natl Ct Report.

Contest & Examination No. 4: Speed Contest. National Shorthand Reporters Association. 1 cass. 9.00 (CT-9) Natl Ct Report.
Literary Shorthand Dictation at 220 wpm, legal opinion at 230 wpm, testimony at 280 wpm.

Contest Fiddling. Stacy Phillips. 1983. 19.95 (978-1-56222-611-4(8), 93940C) Mel Bay.

***Contested Will: Who Wrote Shakespeare?** unabr. ed. James Shapiro. (Running Time: 12 hrs. 30 mins.). 2010. 18.99 (978-1-4001-8648-8(X)); 34.99 (978-1-4001-9648-7(5)) Tantor Media.

***Contested Will: Who Wrote Shakespeare?** unabr. ed. James Shapiro. Narrated by Wanda McCaddon. 1 MP3-CD. (Running Time: 11 hrs. 30 mins. 0 sec.). 2010. 24.99 (978-1-4001-6648-0(9)); audio compact disk 34.99 (978-1-4001-1648-5(1)); audio compact disk 69.99 (978-1-4001-4648-2(8)) Pub: Tantor Media. Dist(s): IngramPubServ

Contesting the Enemy. Elbert Willis. 1 cass. (Understanding the Crucified Life Ser.). 4.00 Fill the Gap.

Contextos. Barbara Freed & Knuts. 1972. 5.00 (978-0-685-59482-7(3)) Heinle.

Contexts in the College Curriculum. Judith Pokras. (Miscellaneous/Catalogs Ser.). 1997. audio compact disk 55.95 (978-0-8384-7262-0(1)) Heinle.

Contextual Knowledge. Peter Schwartz. 1 cass. (Running Time: 1 hr. 30 min.). 1995. 12.95 (978-1-56114-483-9(5), CS06C) Second Renaissance.
An examination of how one's context conditions any piece of knowledge.

Continental Drift. Russell Banks. Read by Russell Banks. 1 cass. (American Audio Prose Library: Series VI). 1986. 13.95 (978-1-55644-147-9(9), 6011) Am Audio Prose.
The author reads two sections, "Pissed Off" & the other from "Vanisse Dorsinville" sections of the book, set in Haiti.

Continental Drifter. Tim Moore. Narrated by Michael Wade. 11 CDs. (Running Time: 13 hrs.). audio compact disk 115.00 (978-1-4025-2923-8(6)) Recorded Bks.

Continental Drifter: Taking the Low Road with the First Grand Tourist. unabr. ed. Tim Moore. 9 cass. (Running Time: 13 hrs.). 2002. 82.00 (978-1-84197-304-3(1), Clipper Audio) Recorded Bks.

Continental Portuguese: Short Course, Set. Paul Pimsleur. 5 cass. (Pimsleur Language Learning Ser.). 1994. pap. bk. & stu. ed. 149.95 (0671-57944-4) SyberVision.

Continually Being Blessed. Elbert Willis. 1 cass. (Growth Series). 4.00 Fill the Gap.

Continually Growing. Elbert Willis. 1 cass. (Growth Series). 4.00 Fill the Gap.

Continuation of Something Great: A Study of Luke 7:1-10:37. unabr. ed. Charles R. Swindoll. 8 cass. (Running Time: 7 hrs.). 1998. 39.95 (978-1-57972-304-0(7)) Insight Living.

Continued Feeling Study for Negative Subtypes: Struggle (Anger, Determination, & Others), Set-HS. Russell E. Mason. 1973. 9.00 (978-0-89533-043-7(1)) F I Comm.

Continuemos! Ana C. Jarvis. (SPA.). (C). 45.96 (978-0-395-91405-2(1)) CENGAGE Learn.

Continuing Chord Piano. Robert Laughlin. Read by Robert Laughlin. 4 cass. (Running Time: 4 hrs.). 77.00 Set, incl. study guide. (978-0-929983-16-5(5)) New Schl Am Music.
Same as our beginning course except geared for those who already understand chord basics.

Continuing Conversations on Customer Loyalty. (Running Time: 21:12). 2005. audio compact disk 17.95 (978-1-930283-03-9(2)) J Brandi.

Continuing Crisis of World Inflation. unabr. ed. William Rees-Mogg. 1 cass. (Running Time: 22 min.). 12.95 (1103) J Norton Pubs.
Rees-Mogg discusses the simple fundamental principles on which gold depends, the link that exists between it & democracy & how hyperinflationary power is a deadly force to democracy.

Continuing Quality Improvement for Rehabilitation Professionals. Dan Mlakar. Interview with Marcia Goodman-Lavey. 1 cass. (Running Time: 57 min.). 1997. bk. 20.00 (978-1-58111-020-3(0)) Contemporary Medical.
Explains the concept of continuing quality improvement; provides a concrete "how to" approach for implementing quality improvement in your work.

Continuing Tradition Vol. 1: A Ballad Sampler. 1 cass. 9.98 (C-75) Folk-Legacy.
Various Folk-Legacy artists contribute.

Continuous Satori-Samadhi. John Lilly. 1 cass. 10.00 (A0067-79) Sound Photosyn.
From Dr. Lilly's personal collection.

Continuous Satori-Samadhi. unabr. ed. John Lilly. 1 cass. (Running Time: 1 hr. 21 min.). 1971. 11.00 (03901) Big Sur Tapes.
Describes the levels of satori, using a numbering system developed by students of Gurdjieff & describes his own experiences of each of these levels. He also discusses the teaching methods of Oscar Ichazo & relates his personal reactions to them.

Continuum of Care for Aphasia: Acute Phase. Richard K. Peach. 1 cass. (Running Time: 1 hr.). 2000. pap. bk. 99.00 (978-1-58041-052-6(9), 0112248) Am Speech Lang Hearing.

Continuum of Care for Aphasia: Long-Term Management Phase. Jon G. Lyon et al. 1 cass. (Running Time: 1 hr.). 2000. pap. bk. 99.00 (978-1-58041-050-2(2), 0112252) Am Speech Lang Hearing.

Contortionist's Handbook. unabr. ed. Craig Clevenger. Read by Craig Clevenger. (Running Time: 7 hrs. 30 mins.). 2009. 29.95 (978-1-4332-9822-6(8)); 54.95 (978-1-4332-9818-9(X)); audio compact disk 69.00 (978-1-4332-9819-6(8)) Blckstn Audio.

Contrabajo y Otros Cuentos Humoristicos. unabr. ed. Anton Chejov. Read by Carlos J. Vega. 3 CDs.Tr. of Double Bass & Other Stories. (SPA.). 2001. audio compact disk 17.00 (978-958-9494-61-5(7)) YoYoMusic.

Contraception - Present & Future. Contrib. by Ronald T. Burkman, Jr. et al. 1 cass. (American College of Obstetrics & Gynecologists UPDATE: Vol. 23, No. 4). 1998. 20.00 Am Coll Obstetric.

Contraception & the Mind of Christ. 1 CD. (Running Time: 1 hr.). 2003. pap. bk. 13.95 (978-1-932631-26-5(7)); 13.95 (978-1-932631-25-8(9)) Ascensn Pr.

Contract. unabr. ed. Gerald Seymour. Read by Dermot Crowley. 10 cass. (Running Time: 10 hrs.). 1993. 84.95 (978-0-7451-6267-6(3)) AudioGO.

Contract on Stone. unabr. ed. David R. Addleman. Read by Rusty Nelson. 4 cass. (Running Time: 4 hrs. 6 min.). (David R. Addleman Mystery Ser.). 2001. 26.95 (978-1-55686-864-1(2)) Books in Motion.
Injured in an attempted street robbery, John Stone is recruited by the same U.S. agency John's late brother served. John finds his assignment may lead to a contract on his life.

Contract with an Angel. unabr. ed. Andrew M. Greeley. Read by Dick Hill. (Running Time: 10 hrs.). 2009. 39.97 (978-1-4233-8639-1(6), 9781423386391, Brlnc Audio MP3 Lib); 39.97 (978-1-4233-8641-4(8), 9781423386414, BADLE); 24.99 (978-1-4233-8638-4(8), 9781423386384, Brilliance MP3); 24.99 (978-1-4233-8640-7(X), 9781423386407, BAD) Brilliance Audio.

Contract with the Earth. unabr. ed. Newt Gingrich & Terry L. Maple. Read by Callista Gingrich. (YA). 2008. 54.99 (978-1-60514-632-4(3)) Find a World.

Contract with the Earth. unabr. ed. Newt Gingrich & Terry L. Maple. Frwd. by E. O. Wilson. 1 MP3-CD. (Running Time: 4 hrs. 30 mins. 0 sec.). (ENG.). 2007. audio compact disk 19.99 (978-1-4001-5462-3(6)) Pub: Tantor Media. Dist(s): IngramPubServ

Contract with the Earth. unabr. ed. Newt Gingrich & Terry L. Maple. Read by Callista Gingrich. Frwd. by E. O. Wilson. 4 CDs. (Running Time: 4 hrs. 30 mins. 0 sec.). (ENG.). 2007. audio compact disk 29.99 (978-1-4001-0462-8(9)); audio compact disk 59.99 (978-1-4001-3462-5(5)) Pub: Tantor Media. Dist(s): IngramPubServ

Contracting Pastoral Services. Ronald Ropp et al. 1986. 10.80 (0904) Assn Prof Chaplains.

Contractor. unabr. ed. Charles Holdefer. Read by Ray Porter. (Running Time: 23400 sec.). 2007. audio compact disk 29.95 (978-1-4332-1104-1(1)) Blckstn Audio.

Contractor. unabr. ed. Charles Holdefer & Ray Porter. (Running Time: 23400 sec.). 2007. 44.95 (978-1-4332-1102-7(5)); audio compact disk 45.00 (978-1-4332-1103-4(3)) Blckstn Audio.

Contractors' Library. Ed. by Socrates Media Editors. 2005. audio compact disk 49.95 (978-1-59546-114-8(0)) Pub: Socrates Med LLC. Dist(s): Midpt Trade

Contracts. Douglas J. Whaley. 4 cass. (Running Time: 6 hrs. 25 mins.). (Outstanding Professors Ser.). 1995. 50.00 (978-0-940366-69-5(X), 28403) Pub: Sum & Substance. Dist(s): West Pub
Lecture given by a prominent American law school professor on the subjects of Civil Procedure, Contracts, Criminal, Real Property, Torts & Exam Skills: Essay Writing.

Contracts. 2nd rev. ed. Douglas J. Whaley. 2002. 63.00 (978-0-314-14469-0(2)) Pub: West Pub. Dist(s): West

Contracts. 2nd rev. ed. Douglas J. Whaley. 2006. audio compact disk 74.00 (978-0-314-14468-3(4)) Pub: West Pub. Dist(s): West

Contracts Bar Review: Audio CDs & Outlines. 2005. audio compact disk (978-0-9743923-3-2(2), GCC Pubs) Lib Soldiers.

Contracts, 2005 ed. (Law School Legends Audio Series) 2005th rev. ed. David Epstein. (Law School Legends Audio Ser.). 2005. 52.00 (978-0-314-16084-3(1), gilbert); 51.95 (978-0-314-16083-6(3), gilbert) West.

Contractual Arbitration. Read by David Greenberg et al. (Running Time: 2 hrs. 30 min.). 1992. 89.00 Incl. 369p. tape materials. (CP-55253) Cont Ed Bar-CA.
Experienced attorneys & an arbitrator explain how to interpret, negotiate, & draft arbitration clauses; how to compel or resist arbitration; how you prepare for the hearing & how it differs from a trial; which rules apply regarding evidence, discovery, & limitations; how the arbitration award differs from a judgment; & what to do about an unfair or illegal award.

***Contrapunto.** abr. ed. Aldous Huxley. Read by Laura Garcia. (SPA.). 2007. audio compact disk 17.00 (978-958-8218-96-0(9)) Pub: Yoyo Music COL. Dist(s): YoYoMusic

Contrarian Effect: Why It Pays (Big) to Take Typical Sales Advice & Do the Opposite. unabr. ed. Michael Port & Elizabeth Marshall. Read by Michael Port. (Running Time: 3 hrs.). (ENG.). 2008. 24.98 (978-1-59659-288-9(5), GildAudio) Pub: Gildan Media. Dist(s): HachBkGrp

Contrastive Syntax & Error Analysis. unabr. ed. J. Nuttall. 1 cass. 1986. 11.95 (E7597) J Norton Pubs.
Reviews contrastive analysis & error analysis for language teachers & students of applied linguistics. Examines the usefulness of contrastive analysis techniques & the accuracy of error analysis as predictive tools.

Control: Morning Talk - KWBI Radio. Interview with Lee Lefebre et al. 1 cass. (Running Time: 1 hr.). 6.00 (978-1-57838-074-9(X)) CrossLife Express.
Christian living.

Control Anger. Mary Lee LaBay. 2006. audio compact disk 5.95 (978-1-934705-18-6(7)) Awareness Engin.

Control Chaos & Clear Out the Clutter. PUEI. 2007. audio compact disk 199.00 (978-1-934147-19-1(2), CareerTrack); audio compact disk 199.00 (978-1-934147-68-9(0), Fred Pryor) P Univ E Inc.

Control Cycle CD. Bruce McNicol & William A. Thrall. 2006. audio compact disk 4.95 (978-0-9770908-6-0(8)) Leadership Cata.

Control Diabetes without Insulin. Read by Kurt W. Donsbach. 1 cass. (Running Time: 45 min.). 10.00 (AC21) Am Media.
How to stimulate the body into producing more of its own insulin by a combination of exercise, supplemental zinc, & a readily available substance

called GTF (Glucose Tolerance Factor). This combination allows many diabetics to reduce their need for artificial insulin or to eliminate it all together.

Control Drinking. 1 cass. (Running Time: 45 min.). (Health Ser.). 9.98 (978-1-55909-029-2(4), 36); 9.98 90 min. extended length stereo music. (978-1-55909-030-8(8), 36X) Randolph Tapes.
Helps you lose the urges, discover self-power & self-discipline. Subliminal messages are heard 3-5 minutes before becoming ocean sounds or music.

Control for Cancer. Read by Ernst T. Krebs, Jr. 1 cass. (Running Time: 60 min.). 10.00 (AC6) Am Media.
The discovery of Laetrile presents a biochemist's view of the origin of cancer & how nature attempts to control it with a substance called amygdalin. When it is purified & concentrated for cancer therapy, it is called Laetrile.

***Control Freaks: 7 Ways Liberals Plan to Ruin Your Life.** unabr. ed. Terence P. Jeffrey. Read by John Pruden. (Running Time: 8 hrs. 30 mins.). 2010. 29.95 (978-1-4417-6055-5(5)); audio compact disk 29.95 (978-1-4417-6054-8(7)) Blckstn Audio.

Control from Within: A Nine-Step Program to Stop Smoking. Wayne W. Dyer. Read by Wayne W. Dyer. 4 cass. 44.95 Set. (852AD) Nightingale-Conant.
Learn what nicotine addiction really is...the real key to stopping (&, in truth, the key to overcoming any obstacle in life)...how to reward yourself...what to do when you slip up...why you shouldn't feel you must be "persistent" or "determined" to quit...how to be growth motivated rather than deficiency motivated...& how to use relaxation & visualization techniques.

***Control of Hysteria.** L. Ron Hubbard. (POR.). 2010. audio compact disk 15.00 (978-1-4031-7311-9(7)); audio compact disk 15.00 (978-1-4031-7308-9(7)); audio compact disk 15.00 (978-1-4031-7316-4(8)); audio compact disk 15.00 (978-1-4031-7301-0(X)); audio compact disk 15.00 (978-1-4031-7303-4(6)); audio compact disk 15.00 (978-1-4031-7315-7(X)); audio compact disk 15.00 (978-1-4031-7312-6(5)); audio compact disk 15.00 (978-1-4031-7305-8(2)); audio compact disk 15.00 (978-1-4031-7302-7(8)); audio compact disk 15.00 (978-1-4031-7304-1(4)); audio compact disk 15.00 (978-1-4031-7314-0(1)); audio compact disk 15.00 (978-1-4031-7306-5(0)); audio compact disk 15.00 (978-1-4031-7307-2(9)); audio compact disk 15.00 (978-1-4031-7309-6(5)); audio compact disk 15.00 (978-1-4031-7310-2(9)); audio compact disk 15.00 (978-1-4031-7313-3(3)) Bridge Pubns Inc.

***Control of Hystermia.** L. Ron Hubbard. (ENG.). 2010. audio compact disk 15.00 (978-1-4031-1601-7(6)) Bridge Pubns Inc.

Control of Mind. 1 cass. (Running Time: 1 hr.). 12.99 (614) Yoga Res Foun.

Control of Nature. unabr. ed. John McPhee. Read by Walter Zimmerman. 8 cass. (Running Time: 8 hrs.). 1991. 48.00 (978-0-7366-1916-5(X), 2740) Books on Tape.
Is "any struggle against natural forces - heroic or venal, rash or well-advised - when human beings conscript themselves to fight against the earth, to take what is not given, to rout the destroying enemy, to surround the base of Mt. Olympus demanding & expecting the surrender of the gods".

Control of Senses. 1 cass. (Running Time: 1 hr.). 12.99 (702) Yoga Res Foun.

Control Spending Habits. 1 cass. (Running Time: 60 min.). 10.95 (032) Psych Res Inst.
Using mental powers to set & keep priority committments & gain financial confidence & control.

Control Stress. 1 cass. (Running Time: 60 min.). 10.95 (005) Psych Res Inst.
Mentally conditions for a stress-free approach to life.

Control the Vital Life Fluid. George King. 2006. audio compact disk (978-0-937249-28-4(9)) Aetherius Soc.

Control your Anger see Controla tu Enojo

Control Your Destiny or Someone Else Will. abr. ed. Noel M. Tichy. Read by Stratford Sherman. 5 vols. (Running Time: 360 min.). 2001. 29.95 (978-0-694-52576-8(6)); 25.95 (978-0-694-52577-5(4)) HarperCollins Pubs.

Control Your Destiny or Someone Else Will: How Jack Welch Has Made General Electric the World's Most Competitive Company. abr. ed. Noel M. Tichy & Stratford Sherman. 2 cass. (Running Time: 3 hrs.). 2001. 16.00 (978-1-55994-986-6(4)) HarperCollins Pubs.

Controla tu Enojo. Grover Bravo.Tr. of Control your Anger. (SPA.). 2009. audio compact disk 15.00 (978-1-935405-52-8(7)) Hombre Nuevo.

Controlled Burn: Stories of Prison, Crime, & Men. unabr. ed. Scott Wolven. Read by William Dufris. (Running Time: 5 hrs. 0 mins. 0 sec.). (ENG.). 2005. audio compact disk 19.99 (978-1-4001-5161-5(9)); audio compact disk 49.99 (978-1-4001-3161-7(8)); audio compact disk 24.99 (978-1-4001-0161-0(1)) Pub: Tantor Media. Dist(s): IngramPubServ

Controlled Chaos. 1 cass. (Running Time: 1 hr.). 2000. 15.95 Prof Pride.
Police radio. 8 unit changing status. Great for beginners.

Controlled Meditative Training: Guided Meditation Technique for Energy Healing & Relaxation. Dmitriy Gushchin. (ENG.). 2007. audio compact disk 19.95 (978-0-9713650-7-0(5)) Inst of Russian Healing.

Controlled Meditative Training: Guided Meditative Technique for Weight Loss & Control. Dmitriy Gushchin. (ENG.). 2007. audio compact disk 29.95 (978-0-9713650-8-7(3)) Inst of Russian Healing.

Controlled Meditative Training: Weight Loss & Control. Dmitriy Gushchin. 1 CD. (Running Time: 61 mins). 2002. audio compact disk 29.99 (978-0-9713650-3-2(2)) Inst of Russian Healing.
Controlled Meditative Training is an age-old Taoist practice rediscovered in Russia by Dmitriy and Victor Kandyba. CMT is not only a great way to balance your energy and achieve good health, but also an amazing way for spiritual development. This intermediate level program will help balance your nervous, digestive and hormonal systems to achieve your best results in weight loss and control.

Controlling ADD/ADHD, 3 cass. (Running Time: 4 hrs. 30 min.). 2001. 24.95 (978-1-58557-033-1(8)) Dynamic Growth.

Controlling Anger. Carol Tavris. 2 cass. (Running Time: 3 hrs.). 1995. 15.95 (978-1-55977-048-4(1)) CareerTrack Pubns.

Controlling Between Meal Snacks. Shad Helmstetter. 1 cass. (Self-Talk Cassettes Ser.). 10.95 (978-0-937065-42-6(0)) Grindle Pr.

Controlling Diver Stress & Panic: Panic Prevention Program. 2 CDs. 2005. audio compact disk 19.95 (978-0-9767750-3-4(4)) ShrtBrstLearn.

Controlling Emotions. Shad Helmstetter. 1 cass. (Self-Talk Ser.). 10.95 (978-0-937065-56-3(0)) Grindle Pr.
Companion Self-Talk Cassettes as mentioned in the book, "What To Say When You Talk To Your Self".

Controlling Fearful Thoughts. Kenneth Copeland. 1 cass. 1988. 5.00 (978-0-88114-804-6(0)) K Copeland Pubns.
Biblical teaching on victory over fear.

***Controlling Interest.** unabr. ed. Elizabeth White. (Running Time: 10 hrs. 6 mins. 0 sec.). (ENG.). 2009. 13.99 (978-0-310-29351-4(0)) Zondervan.

Controlling Interruptions: How to Free an Hour a Day. Verne Harnish. 2 cass. 1995. 15.95 (978-1-55977-109-2(7)) CareerTrack Pubns.

Controlling Interruptions: How to Free up an Hour a Day. Verne Harnish. 2 cass. (Running Time: 2 hrs. 44 min.). 29.95 Set. (V10109) CareerTrack Pubns.
This program shows you tactful & effective ways to prevent people from stealing your time...how to be selective about the phone calls you take...how to guard precious "quiet time"...even how to stick to a schedule.

Controlling Mind. Swami Jyotirmayananda. Read by Swami Jyotirmayananda. 1 cass. (Running Time: 60 min.). 12.99 (725) Yoga Res Foun.

Controlling Retiree & Employee Benefits Costs: Current Trends in Employee Benefits. unabr. ed. Contrib. by Arthur H. Kroll. 4 cass. (Running Time: 5 hrs. 30 min.). 1990. 50.00 course handbk. (T7-9267) PLI.
This recording of PLI's March 1990 satellite program concentrates on methods employers can use to help control the exponential increase in the cost to employers of providing health & welfare benefits to current employees, future retirees & current retirees. The faculty, composed of attorneys & others with extensive experience in plan design, examines the current benefit options available & their advantages & pitfalls. A representative of the Congressional Joint Committee on Taxation discusses pending & potential legislative & regulatory actions.

Controlling Stress & Tension. 6th ed. Daniel A. Girdano. 2000. 6.67 (978-0-205-33437-7(7)) Benjamin-Cummings.

Controlling the Confrontation: Arch Lustberg on Effective Communication Techniques. Arch Lustberg. Read by Arch Lustberg. 1 cass. (Running Time: 46 min.). 1990. 12.00 (978-1-56641-012-0(6)) Library Video.
Media coach Arch Lustberg presents techniques for diffusing confrontation & delivering convincing messages.

Controlling the Flesh. David T. Demola. 11 cass. 1987. 44.00 Faith Fellow Min.

Controlling Weight Problems. Matthew Manning. Music by Mike Rowland. 1 cass. 11.95 (MM-108) White Dove NM.
This tape could aptly be titled "Why Diets Don't Work", as it explores some of the reasons why we overeat. It also explains how self-image affects weight. The second side is a self-help exercise that relaxes as it reinforces positive self-images.

Controlling Your Destiny: How to Change Your Luck - How to Find & Keep Your Soul Mate. unabr. ed. Shmuel Irons. Read by Shmuel Irons. 2 cass. (Running Time: 3 hrs.). 19.95 Set. (978-1-889648-12-5(4)) Jwish Her Fdtn.
Applies the timeless truths found in the Bible & Talmud to gain knowledge, peace of mind, & the practical tools to live a happier life.

Controlling Your Emotions: Scriptual Keys to Dealing with Strife, Stress, & Disappointment. 4 cass. (Running Time: 4 hrs.). (Passing the Test Ser.: 4). 2002. 20.00 (978-1-57399-154-4(6)) Mac Hammond.
God created us to experience emotions-joy, peace, even anger and fear. However, if gone unchecked, emotions can control your life and lead you away from the plans, purposes, and peace of God. In volume five of the Passing the Test series, Mac Hammond gives you keys to help deal with strife, stress, and disappointment.

Controlling Your Mind Guidelines Series, Set. Elbert Willis. 4 cass. 13.00 Fill the Gap.

Controlling Your Money, Vol. 35. Tracy Herrick. 1 cass. (Running Time: 45 min.). (Money Talk Ser.). 1986. 7.95 B & H Comm.
Explains how the management of personal money depends on the use of special internal controls. Gives the four key financial controls & how to properly use them.

Controversial Issues in Surgery. 3 cass. (Spring Meeting Philadelphia, PA Ser.: S87-GS4). 1987. 28.50 (8704) Am Coll Surgeons.
Details total thyroidectomy for carcinoma, preoperative radiation for carcinoma of the rectum & mandatory exploration for penetrating neck wounds.

Controversies & Commanders: Dispatches from the Army of the Potomac. unabr. ed. Stephen W. Sears. Narrated by Nelson Runger. 8 cass. (Running Time: 11 hrs. 30 mins.). 1999. 72.00 (978-0-7887-3493-9(8), 95656E7) Recorded Bks.
Takes a look at some of the most intriguing Union generals & the controversies that swirled around them. Includes analysis of historical documents & personal papers of military officers.

Controversies in Cardiopulmonary Resuscitation. Read by Myron L. Weisfeldt. 1 cass. (Running Time: 90 min.). 1985. 12.00 (C8538) Amer Coll Phys.

Controversy at Ballona Wetlands. Hosted by Nancy Pearlman. 1 cass. 10.00 (101) Educ Comm CA.

Controversy at the Arctic National Wildlife Refuge. Hosted by Nancy Pearlman. 1 cass. (Running Time: 29 min.). 10.00 (502) Educ Comm CA.

Controversy over Using Ward Valley As a Low-Level Radioactive Waste Dump. Hosted by Nancy Pearlman. 1 cass. (Running Time: 28 min.). 10.00 (1035) Educ Comm CA.

Controversy with God. Elbert Willis. 1 cass. (Moving Life's Mountains Ser.). 4.00 Fill the Gap.

Convention 2000. 36 cass. (Running Time: 54 hrs.). 1999. 220.00 (SET60) Torah Umesorah.

Conventional Investments Exposed! Investment Interview & SSA Implosion Discourse. Speeches. Maxwell N. Brandon. 2 Cassettes. (Running Time: 2 hours, 20 min). 2002. (978-0-9717879-8-8(0)) USInvestments.
Two separate & distinct, essential, intense, headline-fresh, late-breaking topical investment Discourses.Approved by and originally broadcast on the Public Broadcasting System (PBS).PROGRAM 1 ... "Conventional Investing Exposed!": The Stock Market is legalized, low-odds gambling - Commodities are a trap - Bonds can't be trusted - Real Estate is overloaded with risk & headaches - Bank instruments and T-Bills return worst of all! Where will an investor GO? What will an investor DO? Listen to this uncut, unedited National Public Radio (NPR) interview of Max Brandon, founder of USInvestments Publishing Corporation of Monument, Colorado as Mr. Brandon objectively compares all investments competing for your investment dollars. Monumental broadcasting!.PROGRAM 2 ... "The Coming Social Security Implosion ... and How to Escape It". For years, the Social Security Administration (SSA) has been in and out of deep financial hot water. The retirement funding of tens of millions of Americans is regularly toyed with, misappropriated, mis-handled and placed at constant grave risk! And - faced with an unpredictable Stock Market and other risky, low-returning investment choices - US citizens feel they have no good alternatives, valid options or even a secure way out of this bureaucratic financial nightmare. But - they DO! There is an EXCELLENT alternative for building retirement income and establishing sure footing for a secure financial future! Treat yourself to Max Brandon's history-making, ground-breaking uncut, unedited address - and know your retirement future NOW!2 Long-Play Cassettes.

Convergence. Charles Sheffield. Read by Geoffrey Howard. 8 CDs. (Running Time: 8 hrs. 30 mins.). (Heritage Universe Ser.: Bk. 4). 2000. audio compact disk 64.00 (978-0-7861-9788-0(9), 2699) Blckstn Audio.
Humans first reached out to the stars traveling at a painfully slow sublight crawl-then they found the Bose network, which allowed ships to jump instantaneously from one node in the galactic arm to another. Once in the Network they found the Artifacts, enigmatic structures, millions of years old, left by a vanished race. Incomprehensible to both human & non-human minds, the Artifacts seemingly defy natural law.

Convergence. Charles Sheffield. Read by Geoffrey Howard. 6 cass. (Running Time: 8 hrs. 30 mins.). (Heritage Universe Ser.: Bk. 4). 2000. 44.95 (978-0-7861-1906-6(3), 2699) Blckstn Audio.
Humans first reached out to the stars traveling at a painfully slow sublight craw. Then they found the Bose network, which allowed ships to jump instantaneously from one node in the galactic arm to another. Once in the network they found the Artifacts, enigmatic structures, millions of years old, left by a vanished race. Incomprehensible to both human & non-human minds, the Artifacts seemingly defy natural law.

Convergence: And Other Stories from Imagination-X. Prod. by Jeffrey Adams. 1 CD. (Running Time: 48 mins). 2004. audio compact disk (978-0-9742012-5-2(1), Imagination X) Bud C Prod.

Convergence of Religions. Bede Griffiths. 2 cass. (Running Time: 1 hr. 44 min.). 1983. 18.00 set. (03304) Big Sur Tapes.

Conversa-Phone's Modern Method Cassette Language Course: Conversational German. abr. ed. 2 cass. (Running Time: 4 hrs.). 1986. 14.95 incl. manual. (978-0-88749-104-7(9), TDM 1049) HarperCollins Pubs.

Conversa-Phone's Modern Method Cassette Language Course: Conversational Spanish. abr. ed. 2 cass. (Running Time: 4 hrs.). 1986. 14.95 incl. manual. (978-0-88749-106-1(5), TDM 1065) HarperCollins Pubs.
An original, short-cut method for learning a foreign language, the program in addition to teaching correct pronounciation, is full of practical, useful everyday expressions to hear, learn & use. Instruction manual helps the student acquire a basic vocabulary which from the beginning is incorporated in useful expressions.

Conversacion y Repaso. 7th ed. Copeland. (C). bk. 195.95 (978-0-8384-7714-4(3)); bk. 154.95 (978-0-8384-8067-0(5)); bk. 166.95 (978-0-8384-8165-3(5)) Heinle.

Conversacion y Repaso: Instructor/Adjunct/TA Toolbox Kit. 7th ed. John G. Copeland et al. (Intermediate Spanish Ser.). (SPA.). 2001. bk. & tchr. ed. (978-0-03-029719-9(2)) Harcourt Coll Pubs.

Conversaciones, Situaciones. Heather Leigh & Salvador Ortiz-Carboneres. (J). (gr. 1-9). 1984. bk. 22.61 (978-0-582-24270-8(3), 70971) Longman.

Conversation Book: English in Everyday Life, Level 1. 3rd ed. Tina K. Carver & Sandra Douglas Fotinos. 2002. 81.60 (978-0-13-792474-5(7)); 43.85 (978-0-13-792466-0(6)); 43.85 (978-0-13-792490-5(9)) Longman.

Conversation Book: English in Everyday Life, Level 2. 3rd ed. Tina K. Carver & Sandra Douglas Fotinos. 2002. 122.35 (978-0-13-792524-7(7)); 66.15 (978-0-13-792516-2(6)); 66.15 (978-0-13-792540-7(9)) Longman.

Conversation Confidence: Talk to Anyone with Confidence Authority & Flair. unabr. ed. Leil Lowndes. Read by Leil Lowndes. 8 CDs. (Running Time: 8 hrs.). 2000. audio compact disk (978-1-931187-29-9(0), CDCC) Word Success.

Conversation Confidence: Talk to Anyone with Confidence, Authority & Flair. unabr. ed. Leil Lowndes. Read by Leil Lowndes. 8 cass. (Running Time: 8 hrs.). 2000. (978-1-931187-10-7(X), CC) Word Success.

Conversation Confidence - Listening to Win. unabr. ed. Charles Harrington Elster. Read by Charles Harrington Elster. 5 cass. (Running Time: 5 hrs.). 2000. (978-1-931187-12-1(6), CCPACK-LW) Word Success.

Conversation Confidence - Listening to Win. unabr. ed. Steve Hays. 4 CDs. (Running Time: 4 hrs.). 2000. audio compact disk (978-1-931187-01-5(0), CDCCPLW) Word Success.

Conversation Confidence - Secrets to Fearless Conversation. unabr. ed. Leil Lowndes. 8 CDs. (Running Time: 8 hrs.). 2000. audio compact disk (978-1-931187-02-2(9), CDCCPACKCC) Word Success.

Conversation Confidence - Secrets to Fearless Conversation. unabr. ed. Leil Lowndes. Read by Leil Lowndes. 8 cass. (Running Time: 8 hrs.). 2000. (978-1-931187-13-8(4), CCPACK-CC) Word Success.

Conversation Confidence - Word Power. 12 CDs. (Running Time: 12 hrs.). 2000. audio compact disk (978-1-931187-03-9(7), CDCCWP) Word Success.

Conversation Confidence - Word Power. unabr. ed. 12 cass. (Running Time: 12 hrs). 2000. (978-1-931187-14-5(2), CCPACK-WP) Word Success.

Conversation Confidence Intro. Leil Lowndes. 2 CDs. (Running Time: 2 hrs.). 2000. audio compact disk 29.95 (978-1-931187-00-8(2), CDCC1) Word Success.

Conversation Confidence Package. unabr. ed. 20 CDs. (Running Time: 20 hrs). 2000. audio compact disk (978-1-931187-28-2(2), CCPACK) Word Success.

Conversation Confidence Package. unabr. ed. Leil Lowndes. 25 cass. (Running Time: 25 hrs.). 2000. (978-1-931187-15-2(0), CCPACK) Word Success.

Conversation of Eiros & Charmion see Cask of Amontillado

Conversation on Trust. unabr. ed. Stephen R. Covey & Stephen M. R. Covey. Read by Stephen R. Covey. (Running Time: 0 hr. 65 mins. 0 sec.). (ENG.). 2009. audio compact disk 15.99 (978-1-933976-83-9(7)) Pub: Franklin Covey. Dist(s): S and S Inc

Conversation Pieces. Susan Mumford. 1 cass. 1983. 12.95; 22.85 incl. student bk., tchr's. bk., cass. Alemany Pr.
Four speakers, two British & two American, discuss a variety of prearranged topics, following a carefully sequenced introduction of elementary structures.

Conversation Power. James K. Van Fleet. 6 CDs. (Running Time: 6 hrs.). 1992. audio compact disk (978-1-55525-034-8(3), 663cd) Nightingale-Conant.
Communicate confidently & effectively.

Conversation Power. James K. Van Fleet. Read by James K. Van Fleet. 6 cass. (Running Time: 6 hrs.). 1992. 59.95 (978-1-55525-033-1(5), 663A) Nightingale-Conant.
A complete course in how to develop the verbal skills you need to be more successful at home, on the job, in social settings or in public gatherings.

Conversation Power: Communication for Business & Personal Success. abr. ed. James K. Van Fleet. Read by James K. Van Fleet. 2 CDs. (Running Time: 20 hrs. 0 mins. 0 sec.). (ENG.). 2002. audio compact disk 19.95 (978-0-7435-2660-9(0), Nightgale) Pub: S&S Audio. Dist(s): S and S Inc
MASTER THE LANGUAGE OF SUCCESS! Whether you're selling, persuading, advising or explaining, you spend most of your dayto-day life in verbal communication with others. The skills you bring to those exchanges will determine whether they go in your favor - or leave you behind as others succeed. If you can't communicate your ideas or intentions, you can't expect others to understand them; on the other hand, the better you can make yourself understood, the higher your chances for climbing to the top. Renowned communications expert James K. Van Fleet guides you through

the most effective verbal communications strategies available today. Whatever the situation, your mastery of these basic communication skills can give you an instant powerful advantage. Imagine yourself: Striking up a conversation with anyone Making lasting friendships from initial meetings Negotiating the services you need from anyone Enhancing crucial communications lines between employees, colleagues, vendors, and supervisors. From business meetings to romantic encounters, artful communication can help make almost any situation go right. With Conversation Power, you'll be able to communicate your way to success!.

Conversation Skills: On the Job & in the Community. 2005. spiral bd. 49.00 (978-1-57861-545-2(3), IEP Res) Attainment.

Conversation with Alan Watts. 1 cass. (Running Time: 1 hr. 2 min.). 12.00 (L820) MEA A Watts Cass.

Conversation with Günter Grass. unabr. ed. Heywood Hale Broun. Interview with Günter Grass. 1 cass. (Running Time: 56 min.). Dramatization. (Broun Radio Ser.). 12.95 (40035) J Norton Pubs.

With the author of "The Tin Drum" & "Diary of a Snail".

Conversation with John Lyons Vol. 1: The Horse That Bites, the Abused Horse. John Lyons. Prod. by Rick Lamb. 1 cass. (Running Time: 1 hr. 30 min.). 2000. 14.95 (978-0-9679487-4-4(6)) Horse Show.

Known as America's Most Trusted Horseman, John Lyons here explains his method for training the horse that bites (side one), and how to bring back a horse that has been abused (side two). Hosted by Rick Lamb.

Conversation with John Lyons Vol. 2: Sensitive Ears, Sensitive Mouth & Feet. John Lyons. Prod. by Rick Lamb. 1 cass. (Running Time: 1 hr. 30 min.). 2000. 14.95 (978-0-9679487-5-1(4)) Horse Show.

Some horses don't like their ears, feet or mouth to be touched. On this tape, John Lyons offers techniques for overcoming these sensitivities. Side one deals with ears, side two with feet and mouth. Hosted by Rick Lamb.

Conversation with John Lyons Vol. 3: Fear in the Rider, Fear in the Horse. John Lyons. Prod. by Rick Lamb. 1 cass. (Running Time: 1 hr. 30 min.). 2000. 14.95 (978-0-9679487-6-8(2)) Horse Show.

Fear, whether in the horse or rider, often leads to undesirable outcomes, but it can be addressed with training. On side one, John Lyons tackles fear in the rider and on side two, fear in the horse. Hosted by Rick Lamb.

Conversation with John Lyons Vol. 4: The Calm down Cue. John Lyons. Prod. by Rick Lamb. 1 cass. (Running Time: 1 hr. 30 min.). 2000. 14.95 (978-0-9679487-8-2(9)) Horse Show.

Any horse can become nervous, excited or fearful, and that poses a danger to the rider. In this tape, John Lyons offers step-by-step instruction for teaching your horse The Calm Down Cue. Hosted by Rick Lamb.

Conversation with John Lyons Vol. 5: A Positive Way of Saying No, Getting Your Horse's Attention. John Lyons. Prod. by Rick Lamb. 1 cass. (Running Time: 1 hr. 30 min.). 2000. 14.95 (978-0-9679487-9-9(7)) Horse Show.

Side one covers the replacement concept, a way of saying "no" to your horse by giving him a positive task to perform. On side two is John's method for getting a horse's attention. Hosted by Rick Lamb.

Conversation with Joseph Heller. unabr. ed. Interview with Heywood Hale Broun & Joseph Heller. 1 cass. (Running Time: 56 min.). (Broun Radio Ser.). 12.95 (40081) J Norton Pubs.

Discussion with the author of "Something Happened" & "Catch 22".

Conversation with Kurt Vonnegut. ed. Interview. Kurt Vonnegut. Interview with Heywood Hale Broun. 1 CD. (Running Time: 55 mins.). (Heywood Hale Broun Ser.). 2007. audio compact disk 12.95 (978-1-57970-453-7(0), C40021D, Audio-For) J Norton Pubs.

Conversation with Kurt Vonnegut. unabr. ed. Interview with Heywood Hale Broun & Kurt Vonnegut. 1 cass. (Running Time: 56 min.). (Broun Radio Ser.). 12.95 (40021) J Norton Pubs.

Discussion with the author of "Breakfast of Champions".

Conversation with Loren Eiseley. Loren Eiseley. Interview with Heywood Hale Broun. 1 CD. (Running Time: 55 mins.). (Heywood Hale Broun Ser.). 2006. audio compact disk 12.95 (978-1-57970-359-2(3), C40218D, Audio-For) J Norton Pubs.

Loren Eiseley discusses his book "All the Strange Hours: The Excavations of a Life.".

Conversation with Loren Eiseley. unabr. ed. Interview with Heywood Hale Broun & Loren C. Eiseley. 1 cass. (Running Time: 56 min). (Broun Radio Ser.). 12.95 J Norton Pubs.

The author talks about "All The Strange Hours" & "The Excavations of a Life".

Conversation with Milton Friedman. Milton Friedman. 2 CDs. (Running Time: 1 hr. 26 mins.). 2006. audio compact disk 12.95 (978-1-57970-384-4(4), AF0161D, Audio-For) J Norton Pubs.

In his answers to questions from libertarians, Friedman criticizes the immorality and ineffectiveness of wage-price controls; finds fault with the makeup of the Price Commission; discusses the gold standard, deflation, devaluation, and the draft; comments on praxeology, his differences with Murray Rothbard and Harry Browne; and explains his role in developing the technique for withholding taxes.

Conversation with Milton Friedman. unabr. ed. Interview with Milton Friedman. 12.95 (161) J Norton Pubs.

Friedman discusses the gold standard, deflation, devaluation & the draft.

Conversation with My Father. Grace Paley. Read by Grace Paley. 1 cass. 1986. 13.95 (978-1-55644-165-3(7), 6101) Am Audio Prose.

Two selections from Paley's 1985 best selling collection, Later the Same Day.

Conversation with Norman Corwin, 1997. Prod. by Midwest Radio Theatre Staff. 1 cass. 1997. 12.95 (978-1-57677-088-7(5), MRTW007) Lodestone Catalog.

Conversation with Norman Corwin, 1998. Prod. by Midwest Radio Theatre Staff. 1 cass. 1998. 12.95 (978-1-57677-100-6(8), MRTW008) Lodestone Catalog.

Conversation with the Heart: The Path to Extreme Freedom. unabr. ed. Lise Janelle. Read by Lise Janelle. (Running Time: 6 hrs. 30 mins.). (ENG.). 2008. 24.98 (978-1-59659-300-8(8), GildAudio) Pub: Gildan Media. Dist(s): HachBkGrp

Conversation with the Mann. John Ridley. Narrated by Dion Graham. 10 cass. (Running Time: 14 hrs.). 2002. 92.00 (978-1-4025-2843-9(4)) Recorded Bks.

Conversation with the Science Fiction Writer at His Home in England. Ian Watson. 1 cass. 9.00 (A0149-86) Sound Photosyn.

We have been left out of this intelligent, thought provoking man's life too long. F & B visit him at his home near Banbury Cross where Faustin interviews.

Conversational Arabic in Nothing Flat - 8, Vol. 2. Mark Frobose. 8 CDs. 2004. audio compact disk 69.00 (978-1-893564-37-4(1)) Macmill Audio.

Conversational Brazilian Portuguese in Nothing Flat, Vol. 1. Mark Frobose. 8 CDs. 2004. audio compact disk 69.00 (978-1-893564-48-0(7)) Macmill Audio.

Conversational Cajun French 1 CD. Randall P. Whatley & Harry Jannise. Narrated by Randall Whatley. (Running Time: 2 hrs.). (FRE & ENG.). 2009. audio compact disk 29.95 (978-1-58980-757-0(X)) Pelican.

Conversational Chinese (Mandarin) in Nothing Flat: 8 One Hour CDs, Vol. 1. Mark Frobose. 8 CDs. 2004. audio compact disk 69.00 (978-1-893564-46-6(0)) Macmill Audio.

Conversational Chinese (Mandarin) in Nothing Flat / Cassette Version: 8 One Hour Cassettes, Vol. 2. Mark Frobose. 8 CDs. 2004. audio compact disk 69.00 (978-1-893564-85-5(1)) Macmill Audio.

Conversational Greek in 7 Days. Howard Middle & Hara G. Middle. 2 cass. (Running Time: 1 hr. 30 min.). (Language in Seven Days Ser.). 1995. bk. 12.95 set. (978-0-8442-4502-7(X), 326228, Passport Bks) McGraw-Hill Trade.

The Language in 7 Days Series is the perfect way for travelers to learn just what they need to know about a language, & the condensed, focused instruction enables them to do so in one short week!.

Conversational Italian in 7 Days. Shirley Baldwin & Sarah Boas. 2 cass. (Running Time: 1 hr. 30 min.). (Language in Seven Days Ser.). 1995. bk. 12.95 set. (978-0-8442-4497-6(X), 326176, Passport Bks) McGraw-Hill Trade.

Conversational Japanese: Learn to Speak & Understand Japanese with Pimsleur Language Programs. 3rd unabr. ed. Pimsleur Staff. 8 CDs. (Running Time: 80 hrs. 0 mins. 0 sec.). (Instant Conversation Ser.). (JPN & ENG.). 2005. audio compact disk 49.95 (978-0-7435-5046-8(3), Pimsleur) Pub: S&S Audio. Dist(s): S and S Inc

Conversational Japanese in 7 Days. Etsuko Tsujita & Colin Lloyd. 2 cass. (Running Time: 1 hr. 30 min.). (Language in Seven Days Ser.). 1995. bk. 12.95 set. (978-0-8442-4516-4(X), 326189, Passport Bks) McGraw-Hill Trade.

Conversational Klingon. Marc Okrand. Read by Marc Okrand. Read by Michael Dorn. (Running Time: 1 hr.). 1996. 19.95 (978-1-60083-439-4(6), Audiofy Corp) Iofy Corp.

Conversational Klingon. Marc Okrand. (Star Trek Ser.). 2004. 7.95 (978-0-7435-4269-2(X)) Pub: S&S Audio. Dist(s): S and S Inc

Conversational Latin for Oral Proficiency. 4th rev. ed. Mark Robert Miner. 2006. audio compact disk 39.00 (978-0-86516-635-6(8)) Bolchazy-Carducci.

Conversational Mandarin Chinese: Learn to Speak & Understand Mandarin with Pimsleur Language Programs. 2nd unabr. ed. Pimsleur. Created by Pimsleur. 8 CDs. (Running Time: 80 hrs. 0 mins. 0 sec.). (Instant Conversation Ser.). (CHI & ENG.). 2005. audio compact disk 49.95 (978-0-7435-5049-9(8), Pimsleur) Pub: S&S Audio. Dist(s): S and S Inc

Conversational Polish. W. Bisko et al. Contrib. by Maria Swiecicka-Ziemianek. 8 cass. (Running Time: 7 hrs.). (YA). (gr. 10-12). 1966. pap. bk. 225.00 (978-0-88432-099-9(5), AFP500) J Norton Pubs.

Beginning-level course contains twenty-six lessons containing three or four brief scenes recorded by actors from the Warsaw stage, with drills & practice exercises.

Conversational Polish: Learn to Speak & Understand Polish with Pimsleur Language Programs. unabr. ed. Pimsleur. 8 CDs. (Running Time: 80 hrs. 0 mins. 0 sec.). (Instant Conversation Ser.). (POL & ENG.). 2006. audio compact disk 49.95 (978-0-7435-5121-2(4)) Pub: S and S. Dist(s): S and S Inc

Conversational Polish CDs & Text. 9 CDs. (Running Time: 7 hrs.). (POL.). 2005. audio compact disk 225.00 (978-1-57970-201-4(5), AFP500D) J Norton Pubs.

Conversational Russian in Seven Days. Shirley Baldwin & Sarah Boas. 2 cass. (Running Time: 1 hr. 30 min.). (Language in Seven Days Ser.). 1995. bk. 12.95 set. (978-0-8442-4533-1(X), 326202, Passport Bks) McGraw-Hill Trade.

The Language in 7 Days Series is the perfect way for travelers to learn just what they need to know about a language, & the condensed, focused instruction enables them to do so in one short week!.

Conversational Spanish. (C). 2003. audio compact disk (978-0-9627755-3-6(3)) B B Saloom.

Conversational Spanish. abr. ed. Stacey Kammerman. (Running Time: 3600 sec.). (Spanish on the Job Ser.). 2008. audio compact disk 15.95 (978-1-934842-65-2(6)) Pub: KAMMS Consult. Dist(s): Natl Bk Netwk

Conversational Spanish: Learn to Speak & Understand Latin American Spanish with Pimsleur Language Programs. 2nd unabr. ed. Pimsleur Staff. 8 CDs. (Running Time: 80 hrs. 0 mins. 0 sec.). (Instant Conversation Ser.). (SPA & ENG.). 2005. audio compact disk 49.95 (978-0-7435-5045-1(5), Pimsleur) Pub: S&S Audio. Dist(s): S and S Inc

Conversational Spanish-Cassette Taoe: Quick & Easy. Barbara B. Saloom. 1 cass. 1996. 9.95 (978-0-9627755-2-9(5)) B B Saloom.

Conversational Spanish in Nothing Flat. Mark Frobose. 8 cds. (SPA., 2002. pap. bk. 68.50 (978-1-893564-56-5(8)) Macmill Audio.

Conversational Spanish in Nothing Flat: Book & Bonus CD. Mark A. Frobose. 8 CDs. (Running Time: 8 hrs.). 2004. audio compact disk 59.00 (978-1-893564-93-0(2)) Macmill Audio.

Conversational Spanish in Nothing Flat 2 / Level 2: 8 One Hour CDs, Vol. 2. Mark Frobose. 8 CDs. 2004. audio compact disk 69.00 (978-1-893564-44-2(4)) Macmill Audio.

Conversational Spanish in 7 Days. Shirley Baldwin & Sarah Boas. 2 cass. (Running Time: 1 hr. 30 min.). (Language in Seven Days Ser.). 1995. bk. 12.95 set. (978-0-8442-4452-5(X), 326137, Passport Bks) McGraw-Hill Trade.

Conversational Thai in 7 Days. Somsong Buasai & David Smyth. 2 cass. (Running Time: 2 hrs.). 1991. 12.95 Set. (Passport Bks) McGraw-Hill Trade.

Conversational Turkish: Learn to Speak & Understand Turkish with Pimsleur Language Programs. unabr. ed. Created by Pimsleur Staff. (Running Time: 80 hrs. 0 mins. 0 sec.). (Instant Conversation Ser.). (TUR & ENG.). 2006. audio compact disk 49.95 (978-0-7435-5146-5(X), Pimsleur) Pub: S&S Audio. Dist(s): S and S Inc

Conversational Vietnamese. unabr. ed. Created by Pimsleur Staff. (Running Time: 80 hrs. 0 mins. 0 sec.). (Instant Conversation Ser.). (ENG.). 2006. audio compact disk 49.95 (978-0-7435-5123-6(0), Pimsleur) Pub: S&S Audio. Dist(s): S and S Inc

Conversational Welsh Course, Bk. 1. Dan L. James. 1 cass. (WEL.). 1970. 59.95 (978-0-8464-4902-7(1)) Beekman Bks.

Conversations at the Edge of Magic. Featuring Terence McKenna. 1994. 9.95 (978-1-59157-020-2(4)) Assn for Cons.

Conversations at the Edge of Magic. Featuring Terence McKenna. 1. 2003. audio compact disk 12.95 (978-1-59157-030-1(1)) Assn for Cons.

Was the taking of mind-altering mushrooms the magical, neurological key that first separated Man from the other primates? Terence offers a spirited and often amusing discussion of the importance of psychedelic plants in the evolution of human psychology, with particular emphasis on the role Psilocybin mushrooms played in the origins of Man's emerging culture and sexuality from prehistory to current times. Ecologist and explorer Terence McKenna was one of the foremost pioneers of ethnopharmacology. He has written several books on human culture & evolution and the importance of the role psychedelic plants have in them. His works include The Archaic Revival, Food of the Gods, True Hallucinations, and The Invisible Landscape, and he made great contributions with his cutting-edge research in the realms of the evolution of mind and spirit.

Conversations I: Questions & Answers. abr. ed. J. Krishnamurti. Read by J. Krishnamurti. 1 cass. (Running Time: 60 min.). (Ojai Talks Ser.). 1988. bk. 9.95 (978-0-06-250479-1(7)) HarperCollins Pubs.

Krishnamurti discusses guilt & ego, racial conditioning, living the peaceful life, the desires of mankind, & the art of conversation as a tennis match.

Conversations II: Questions & Answers. J. Krishnamurti. 1 cass. (Running Time: 60 min.). (Ojai Talks Ser.). 1989. 9.95 HarperCollins Pubs.

Conversations II: Questions & Answers. J. Krishnamurti. Read by J. Krishnamurti. 1 cass. (Running Time: 90 min.). (Ojai Public Talks - 1985 Ser.). 1985. 8.50 (978-0-06-250480-7(0), AJQ852) Krishnamurti.

Conversations in French. unabr. ed. 3 cass. (FRE.). bk. 49.95 Set, incl. 3 bilingual bks. (SFR215) J Norton Pubs.

Conversations of the Heart. bk. 3.89 (978-0-687-76227-9(8)) Abingdon.

Conversations on Population: Dr. M. S. Swaminathen, Father of India's Green Revolution. Hosted by Nancy Pearlman. 1 cass. (Running Time: 30 min.). 10.00 (912) Educ Comm CA.

Conversations on Population - Ann Ehrlich. Hosted by Nancy Pearlman. 1 cass. (Running Time: 29 min.). 10.00 (422) Educ Comm CA.

Conversations on Population - Dr. Garrett Hardin, Pt. 1. Hosted by Nancy Pearlman. 1 cass. (Running Time: 28 min.). 10.00 (802) Educ Comm CA.

Conversations on Population - Dr. Garrett Hardin, Pt. 2. Hosted by Nancy Pearlman. 1 cass. (Running Time: 27 min.). 10.00 (803) Educ Comm CA.

Conversations on Population - Dr. Paul Ehrlich, Pt. 1. Hosted by Nancy Pearlman. 1 cass. (Running Time: 30 min.). 10.00 (418) Educ Comm CA.

Conversations on Population - Dr. Paul Ehrlich, Pt. 2. Hosted by Nancy Pearlman. 1 cass. (Running Time: 30 min.). 10.00 (419) Educ Comm CA.

Conversations on Population - Dr. Paul Ehrlich, Pt. 3. Hosted by Nancy Pearlman. 1 cass. (Running Time: 30 min.). 10.00 (620) Educ Comm CA.

Conversations on Population - Dr. Paul Ehrlich, Pt. 4. Hosted by Nancy Pearlman. 1 cass. (Running Time: 30 min.). 10.00 (621) Educ Comm CA.

Conversations on Population - Dr. Paul Ehrlich (Special) Hosted by Nancy Pearlman. 1 cass. (Running Time: 27 min.). 10.00 (400) Educ Comm CA.

***Conversations on the PMP Exam.** Andy Crowe & Bill Yates. Contrib. by Andy Crowe. Voice by Alderman Louis. (Running Time: 5 hrs. 52 mins. 30 sec.). (ENG.). 2010. audio compact disk 49.95 (978-0-9729673-8-9(9)) Pub: Velociteach. Dist(s): IPG Chicago

Conversations with Corwin. Scripts. Text by Norman Corwin. Directed By Norman Corwin. 2 CDs. (Running Time: 2 hrs. 30 mins.). Dramatization. 2005. audio compact disk 19.95 (978-1-59938-010-0(2)) Lode Cat.

Conversations with Dr. Karl Menninger. Karl Augustus Menninger. Read by Karl Augustus Menninger. Ed. by Stephen Lerner. 1 cass. (Running Time: 47 min.). 1985. 10.00 (978-1-56948-000-7(1)) Menninger Clinic.

Dr. Karl Menninger describes his own beginnings in the mental health field & his career as one of the world's foremost psychiatrists. He outlines his current thinking about the future of the mental health professions & the world we live in.

Conversations with God. 10.00 (RJ123) Esstee Audios.

Conversations with God. Perf. by Yanni et al. 1 cass. 9.98; audio compact disk 16.98 CD. Lifedance.

Inspired by the controversial best-seller. Demo CD or cassette available.

Conversations with God: An audio series on Prayer. Tracy M. Boyd. Created by Influencial Productions. 2008. 25.00 (978-0-9822763-0-3(3)) Influent Prod.

Conversations with God: An Uncommon Dialogue. unabr. ed. Neale Donald Walsch. Read by Neale Donald Walsch. Read by Edward Asner & Ellen Burstyn. (YA). 2008. 54.99 (978-1-60514-764-2(8)) Find a World.

Conversations with God Bk. 1: An Uncommon Dialogue. Neale Donald Walsch. 1998. 16.98 (978-1-56170-483-5(0)); audio compact disk 16.98 (978-1-56170-635-8(3)) Hay House.

Conversations with God Bk. 1: An Uncommon Dialogue. Neale Donald Walsch. 1 cass., 1 CD. (Windham Hill Collection). 1999. 8.78 (WH 11304); 13.58 CD Jewel box. (WH 11304) NewSound.

Featuring Jim Brickman, Will Ackerman, George Winston Yanni, David Arkenstone, new tracks from Ray Lynch & Liz. Story plus book excerpts & spoken word by Ed Asner & Ellen Burstyn.

Conversations with God for Teens. unabr. ed. Neale Donald Walsch. Read by Alanis Morissette & LeVar Burton. 4 cass. (Running Time: 5 hrs. 55 mins.). (J). (gr. 7 up). 2004. 32.00 (978-0-8072-0837-3(X), LYA 368 CX, Listening Lib); pap. bk. 38.00 (978-0-8072-0856-4(6), LYA 368 SP, Listening Lib) Random Audio Pubg.

A look at all the questions that teenagers from every corner of the globe are asking and the answers they have received from God in private meditations.

Conversations with Grandfather: Grandfathers 1st Prophecy, Volume I. Narrated by Tom Brown, Jr. (ENG.). 2007. audio compact disk 22.95 (978-1-60326-006-0(4)) Tracker Pubng.

Conversations with Grandfather: Grandfathers 1st Prophecy, Volume I. Narrated by Tom Brown, Jr. Music by Karl Direske. (ENG.). 2007. 17.95 (978-1-60326-005-3(6)) Tracker Pubng.

Conversations with Grandfather: Grandfathers 2nd Prophecy, Volume II. Narrated by Tom Brown, Jr. Music by Karl Direske. (ENG.). 2008. 17.95 (978-1-60326-007-7(2)); audio compact disk 22.95 (978-1-60326-008-4(0)) Tracker Pubng.

Conversations with Grandfather: Grandfathers 3rd Prophecy, Volume III. Narrated by Tom Brown, Jr. (ENG.). 2008. 17.95 (978-1-60326-009-1(9)) Tracker Pubng.

Conversations with Grandfather: Grandfathers 3rd Prophecy, Volume III. Narrated by Tom Brown, Jr. Music by Karl Direske. (ENG.). 2008. audio compact disk 22.95 (978-1-60326-010-7(2)) Tracker Pubng.

Conversations with Grandfather: Grandfathers 4th Prophecy, Volume IV. Narrated by Tom Brown, Jr. Music by Karl Direske. (ENG.). 2008. 17.95 (978-1-60326-011-4(0)); audio compact disk 22.95 (978-1-60326-012-1(9)) Tracker Pubng.

Conversations with Jesus. Speeches. Glenda Green. 14 cass. (Running Time: 20 hrs, 23 min). 1997. 120.00 (978-0-9666623-6-8(9)) Spiritis Publishing.

Live recordings of the original lectures by Glenda Green about her conversations with Jesus.

Conversations with Jesus. Speeches. Glenda Green. 14 CDs. (Running Time: 19 hrs, 06 min). 2004. audio compact disk 140.00 (978-0-9666623-8-2(5)) Spiritis Publishing.

These are the original live recordings of Glenda Green's lectures: Conversations with Jesus.

Conversations with Mary Evans: For Parents & Teachers of Young Children. Interview. 4 cass. (Running Time: 270 mins.). 2003. 45.00 (978-0-9746674-7-8(1)) Hoberg Stu.

***Conversations with Michael Murphy.** Michael Murphy. (ENG.). 2010. audio compact disk 60.00 (978-1-4507-2461-6(2)) Indep Pub IL.

Conversations with My Dog. unabr. ed. Zig Ziglar. Read by Zig Ziglar. (Running Time: 4 hrs.). 2005. 39.25 (978-1-59600-821-2(0), 9781596008212, BADLE); 24.95 (978-1-59600-820-5(2), 9781596008205, BAD); 39.25 (978-1-59600-819-9(9), 9781596008199, Brlnc Audio MP3 Lib); 24.95 (978-1-59600-818-2(0), 9781596008182, Brilliance MP3); 49.25 (978-1-59600-815-1(6), 9781596008151, BrilAudUnabridg); 19.95 (978-1-59600-814-4(8), 9781596008144, BAU); audio compact disk 69.25 (978-1-59600-817-5(2), 9781596008175, BriAudCD Unabrid); audio compact disk 21.95 (978-1-59600-816-8(4), 9781596008168, Bril Audio CD Unabri) Brilliance Audio.
Most people talk to their pets (some people even talk to their plants), but Zig Ziglar does more than just talk to his dog. He has conversations with her. Taffy is Zig's little Welsh Corgi. Taffy moved into the Ziglar household in early 1995, and it didn't take her long to endear herself to Dad (Zig). Over the years Taffy has been a part of the Ziglar family - including some really painful years of mourning. Dirty Dog (Zig's affectionate nickname for Taffy) and Dad have talked about many facets of life - from faith to health to relationships. They decided (collectively) it was time to write a book. - Themes include communication, humor, consideration, trust, discipline, childrearing, the balanced life, and even the Boy Scouts. - Zig uses this literary device of conversations with Taffy to cleverly and convincingly deliver a poignant and humorous read.

***Conversations with Myself.** unabr. ed. Nelson Mandela. 8 CDs. (Running Time: 9 hrs.). 2010. audio compact disk 39.99 (978-1-4272-1051-7(9)) Pub: Macmill Audio. Dist(s): Macmillan

Conversations with Norman Corwin, 1997. Norman Corwin. 1 cass. (Running Time: 1 hr. 30 mins.). 2001. 12.95 (MRTW007) Lodestone Catalog.

Conversations with Norman Corwin, 1998. Norman Corwin. 1 cass. (Running Time: 1 hr. 30 mins.). 2001. 12.95 (MRTW008) Lodestone Catalog.

Conversations with Nostradamus. Dolores Cannon. 2 cass. (Running Time: 3 hrs.). 1992. reel tape 10.00 set. (978-0-9632776-2-6(6), 28) Ozark Mountn.
Condensed version.

Conversations with Rabbi Small. unabr. ed. Harry Kemelman. Narrated by George Guidall. 6 cass. (Running Time: 7 hrs. 30 mins.). (Rabbi Small Mystery Ser.). 1999. 53.00 (978-0-7887-2943-0(8), 95723E7) Recorded Bks.
Faced with performing a hasty conversion, Rabbi Small delves deep into the fascinating philosophy & history of Judaism.

Conversations with the Countess of Castiglione, Set. Anne Walsh & Chris Kubick. (Running Time: 44 mins. 32 sec.). (Art After Death Ser.). 2001. bk. 15.00 (978-0-9703860-0-7(1)) RAM Publications.

Conversations with the Old World: Ceremonial & Court Music of Turkey. Perf. by Eurasian Ensemble. 1 cass. (Running Time: 48 min.). 9.00 Threshold CA.
Turkish classical music. A gentle combination of ney (flute), tanbur (lute), rebab (a bowed instrument), harp, bendir (drum), & voices.

Conversations with the Spirit World. Lysa Moskowitz-Mateu. Read by Lysa Mateu. 2001. 22.95 (978-0-9707468-7-0(3)) Channeling Spirits.

Conversations with the Spirit World: Souls Who Have Ended Their Lives Speak from Above. Lysa Moskowitz-Mateu & Lysa Mateu. 3 CD'S. (Running Time: 3 hrs.). 2001. pap. bk. & pap. bk. 16.95 (978-0-9707468-6-3(5)) Channeling Spirits.
"What were you thinking right before you killed yourself?" were the words that began my journey, in which I asked questions & received answers from 17 souls, ages 12-51, who had committed suicide.

Converse. Ed. by Robert A. Monroe. 1 cass. (Running Time: 30 min.). (Meta Music Ser.). 1985. 12.95 (978-1-56102-205-2(5)) Inter Indus.
Explore the opposites of your normal perception with musical - Hemi-Sync patterns that may lead you into emotions, visions, & experiences you have never encountered in your conscious waking state.

***Converse with Charisma: How to Talk to Anyone & Enjoy Networking.** unabr. ed. Made For Success. (Running Time: 5 hrs.). (Made for Success Ser.). 2010. audio compact disk 19.95 (978-1-4417-5547-6(0)) Blckstn Audio.

***Converse with Charisma! (Library Edition) How to Talk to Anyone & Enjoy Networking.** unabr. ed. Made for Success. (Running Time: 5 hrs. 0 mins.). (Made for Success Ser.). 2010. audio compact disk 90.00 (978-1-4417-5545-2(4)) Blckstn Audio.

Conversion. Thomas Merton. 1 cass. (Running Time: 60 min.). (Humility Ser.). 4.50 (AA2106) Credence Commun.
Discussions on when humility begins & that trait's growth.

Conversion: From Chaos to Covenant. 1 CD. (Running Time: 60 mins.). 2007. audio compact disk 9.95 (978-0-9717687-3-4(0)) Excorde Inc.

Conversion from Atheism. Mother Angelica & Father Michael. 1 cass. (Running Time: 60 min.). (Mother Angelica Live Ser.). 1988. 10.00 (978-1-55794-109-1(2), T60) Eternal Wrd TV.
The author tells of her philosophical search to find truth, with culminates in her acceptance of the Catholic faith.

Conversion in Christ. Thomas Merton. 1 cass. (Running Time: 60 min.). (Conversion Ser.). 8.95 (AA2229) Credence Commun.
Discussions on conversion & the necessity of choosing between the Gospel & the world.

Conversion of a Baseball Superstar. Dale Murphy. 1 cass. 2004. 3.95 (978-1-57734-393-6(X), 34441344) Covenant Comms.

Conversion of Western Chart into Indian Chart. Barbara Cameron. 1 cass. 8.95 (041) Am Fed Astrologers.
Convert Tropical charts into Sidereal.

Conversion Planning: Designing & Planning Conversion Strategies. 1 cass. 1990. 8.50 Recorded Res.

Converting Engineering Drawings to Optical Disk: Cost-Justification for Converting CAD - CAM Databases. 1 cass. 1990. 8.50 Recorded Res.

Converting Thousands. Grant Von Harrison. Read by Ted Gibbons. (Missionary Success Ser.). 6.95 (978-0-929985-33-6(8)) Jackman Pubng.
Identifies the common denominators found in the scriptures about conversions.

Conviction. Poems. Taylor Mali. 1 CD. (Running Time: 74 mins.). 2003. audio compact disk 15.00 (978-1-893972-06-3(2)) Wrdsmth Pr.
This is Taylor Mali at his best. Includes live recordings from around the country as well as one of his championship efforts at the National Poetry Slam in 2002. Covers, people covering Taylor, group pieces...it's all here.

***Conviction.** unabr. ed. Aaron Allston. (Star Wars Ser.: Bk. 7). (ENG.). 2011. audio compact disk 40.00 (978-0-7393-7673-7(X), Random AudioBks) Pub: Random Audio Pubg. Dist(s): Random

Conviction: A Novel. Richard North Patterson. Read by Patricia Kalember. 10 cass. (Christopher Paget Ser.: Bk. 4). 2005. 90.00 (978-1-4159-1562-2(8)); audio compact disk 95.20 (978-1-4159-1649-0(7)) Pub: Books on Tape. Dist(s): NetLibrary CO

***Convictions That Conquered the World.** Featuring Ravi Zacharias. 2009. audio compact disk 9.00 (978-1-61256-011-3(3)) Ravi Zach.

Convictions vs. Preferences. Contrib. by David Gibbs. 1 cass. (Running Time: 1 hr.). 2002. 9.95 (CLP89525) Christian Liberty.
This classic presentation by attorney contributor provides Christian families with a thought provoking challenge to make their commitment to Christian education a God ordered conviction, instead of a mere preference.

Convicts. unabr. ed. Iain Lawrence. Narrated by John Keating. 5 cass. (Running Time: 6 hrs. 45 mins.). 2005. 45.75 (978-1-4193-6709-0(9), 98241) Recorded Bks.

Convict's Woman. Janet Woods. 2008. 69.95 (978-1-84559-763-4(X)); audio compact disk 84.95 (978-1-84559-764-1(8)) Pub: Soundings Ltd GBR. Dist(s): Ulverscroft US

Convinced. Contrib. by Nicole C. Mullen. (Sound Performance Soundtracks Ser.). 2007. audio compact disk 5.98 (978-5-557-63288-1(3)) Pt of Grace Ent.

Convivial Codfish. Charlotte MacLeod. Read by Mary Peiffer. 2000. 40.00 (978-0-7366-5587-3(5)) Books on Tape.

Convoy of Fear. unabr. ed. Philip McCutchan. Read by Christopher Scott. 6 cass. (Running Time: 9 hrs.). 2000. 54.95 (978-1-86042-491-5(0), 24910) Pub: Soundings Ltd GBR. Dist(s): Ulverscroft US
The east-bound convoy from the Clyde had now reached Malta: a number of ships lost, two crippled & the main body of the convoy yet to be taken through to Alexandria & then the passage of the Suez Canal for Trincomalee.

Cook-a-Doodle-Doo! Janet Stevens & Susan Stevens Crummel. Narrated by Frances Sternhagen. 1 cass. (Running Time: 15 min.). (J). (gr. k-3). 2001. bk. 27.95 (978-0-8045-6865-4(0), 6865) Spoken Arts.
Big Brown Rooster, along with his friends, set out to make the most magnificent strawberry shortcake in the whole world.

Cookbook to Romance: Enticing Ways to Cookup Romantic & Sensual Evenings. Georgette Taylor et al. 1998. 10.00 Aquarius Creat.
Interludes, poetry & recipes.

Cookcamp. unabr. ed. Gary Paulsen. Narrated by C. J. Critt. 2 pieces. (Running Time: 2 hrs. 45 mins.). (gr. 2 up). 1995. 19.00 (978-0-7887-0204-4(1), 94429E7) Recorded Bks.
During World War II, a boy spends a year deep in the woods of Minnesota with his grandmother who is working as a cook for a road crew.

Cooked: My Journey from the Streets to the Stove, from Cocaine to Foie Gras. Jeff Henderson. Read by Jeff Henderson. (Running Time: 28800 sec.). 2007. audio compact disk 34.99 (978-1-4281-4425-5(0)) Recorded Bks.

Cooked: My Journey from the Streets to the Stove, from Cocaine to Foie Gras. unabr. ed. Jeff Henderson. Read by Jeff Henderson. 7 cass. (Running Time: 8 hrs.). 2007. 61.75 (978-1-4281-4426-2(9)); audio compact disk 77.75 (978-1-4281-4428-6(5)) Recorded Bks.

Cookie Girl. unabr. ed. David Novak. Read by David Novak. 1 cass. (Running Time: 56 min.). (American Storytelling Ser.). (J). (ps-5). 1994. 12.00 (978-0-87483-389-8(2)) August Hse.
Stories & songs recorded live with an audience of children.

Cookie Monster's Blue Book. Jane Zion Brauer. 1985. 24.50 (978-0-19-434173-8(9)) OUP.

Cookies & Crutches. unabr. ed. Judy Delton. Narrated by Christina Moore. 1 cass. (Running Time: 45 mins.). (Pee Wee Scouts Ser.: No. 1). (gr. 1 up). 1997. 10.00 (978-0-7887-0636-3(5), 94814E7) Recorded Bks.
This week, at the Pee Wee Scout meeting. Mrs. Peters, the troop leader, shows the first-graders how to make chocolate chip cookies. But when Molly Duff & another scout try to make cookies on their own a few days later, their cookies look like baked frisbees. Next week, the scouts are having a skating party. Will Molly be better at skating than she is at baking cookies?.

Cookin' A Musical Smorgasbord. (Running Time: 40 min.). (J). (ps-4). 1996. 9.98 (9601-4); audio compact disk 13.98 CD. (9601-2) GMR Recs.
Production offers a brief buffet of songs.

Cooking Christmas. 1 cass. 1997. pap. bk. 17.98 (978-0-9654125-1-3(2)) Cooking In Concert.

Cooking in the French Fashion: Recipes in French & English. Stephanie Ovide. 2 cass. (Running Time: 3 hrs.). (ENG.). 2000. 12.95 (978-0-7818-0796-8(4)) Hippocrene Bks.

Cooking up a Country Christmas. 1 cass. 1997. pap. bk. 17.98 (978-0-9654125-2-0(0)) Cooking In Concert.

Cookley Green. Margaret Chappell. Read by Mary Miller. 12 CDs. (Running Time: 13 hrs. 15 mins.). (Story Sound CD Ser.). (J). 2004. audio compact disk 99.95 (978-1-85903-738-6(0)) Pub: Mgna Lrg Print GBR. Dist(s): Ulverscroft US

Cookley Green. unabr. ed. Margaret Chappell. Read by Mary Miller. 10 cass. (Running Time: 13 hrs. 15 mins.). (Story Sound Ser.). (J). 2004. 84.95 (978-1-85903-721-8(6)) Pub: Mgna Lrg Print GBR. Dist(s): Ulverscroft US

Cook's Tour of Ancient Israel. 10.00 (RME104) Esstee Audios.

Cool Aerobics for Kids. Georgiana Stewart. 1 CD. (Running Time: 1 hr.). (J). (ps-4). 2001. pap. bk. 14.95 (KIM 9156CD); pap. bk. 10.95 (KIM 9156C) Kimbo Educ.
Work out to songs such as "The Hokey Pokey" "Shout", "I Heard It Through the Grapevine", "Let's Twist Again", "The Electric Boogie", "The Bunny Hop" & more. Breathing exercises, a warm-up, routines & a cool-down. Includes guide with lyrics and instructions.

Cool & Confident: Be Confident in any Situation. Created by Christine Sherborne. (ENG.). 2007. audio compact disk 19.95 (978-0-9582712-2-6(4)) Pub: Colourstory AUS. Dist(s): APG

Cool Boffin. Pete Johnson. Read by Paul Chequer. (Running Time: 24120 sec.). (J). 2001. audio compact disk 59.95 (978-0-7540-6781-8(5)) AudioGo GBR.

Cool Breeze on the Underground. unabr. ed. Don Winslow & Joe Barrett. (Running Time: 11 hrs. NaN mins.). (Neal Carey Mysteries Ser.). 2008. 29.95 (978-1-4332-2809-4(2)); 65.95 (978-1-4332-2805-6(X)); audio compact disk 90.00 (978-1-4332-2806-3(8)) Blckstn Audio.

Cool Carols for Kids. Don Marsh. 1996. 75.00 (978-0-7673-0820-5(4)); audio compact disk 85.00 (978-0-7673-0821-2(2)) LifeWay Christian.

Cool Creatures Home Connection Kit. Created by Music Movement and Magination. 2009. spiral bd. 19.95 (978-1-935572-10-7(5)) MMnM Bks.

Cool Creatures Home Connection Kit - Bilingual. Created by Music Movement and Magination. (ENG.). 2009. spiral bd. 19.95 (978-1-935572-11-4(3)) MMnM Bks.

Cool Creatures Supplemental Curriculum Kit. 2nd rev. ed. Created by Music Movement and Magination. (ENG.). 2009. spiral bd. 179.95 (978-1-935572-04-6(0)) MMnM Bks.

Cool English Level 1. Herbert Puchta & Günter Gerngross. (Running Time: 1 hr. 7 mins.). (Cool English Ser.). 2005. audio compact disk 23.00 (978-84-8323-457-0(2)) Cambridge U Pr.

Cool English Level 1 Teacher's Guide with Audio CD. Herbert Puchta et al. (Cool English Ser.). 2006. pap. bk. 48.00 (978-84-8323-451-8(3)) Cambridge U Pr.

Cool English Level 2. Herbert Puchta & Günter Gerngross. (Cool English Ser.). 2003. audio compact disk 23.00 (978-84-8323-458-7(0)) Cambridge U Pr.

Cool English Level 3 Teacher's Guide with Audio CDs. Herbert Puchta et al. (Cool English Ser.). 2006. pap. bk. 59.00 (978-84-8323-453-2(X)) Cambridge U Pr.

Cool English Level 4. Herbert Puchta & Günter Gerngross. (Cool English Ser.). 2005. audio compact disk 41.00 (978-84-8323-460-0(2)) Cambridge U Pr.

Cool English Level 5. Herbert Puchta & Günter Gerngross. (Cool English Ser.). 2005. audio compact disk 41.00 (978-84-8323-461-7(0)) Cambridge U Pr.

Cool English Level 6 Audio CD International. Herbert Puchta & Günter Gerngross. (Cool English Ser.). 2005. audio compact disk 41.00 (978-84-8323-462-4(9)) Cambridge U Pr.

Cool Ghoul Halloween Party Mix. 1 cass. 1999. (4045-4); audio compact disk CD. (4045-2) Audioscope.
Includes: Creaks in the Dark (sound effects), "Club Ghoul" by Boys II Ghouls, Hungry Ghouls (sound effects), "Purple People Eater" by Sheb Wooley, Bats in the Belfry (sound effects), "Monster Mash" by Bobby "Boris" Pickett, Heartbeat (sound effects), "Witch Doctor" by Sha-Na-Na, Owl (sound effects), "Spooky Classics IV" featuring Dennis Yost, & more.

Cool Hand Luke. unabr. ed. Donn Pearce. Narrated by Mark Hammer. 6 cass. (Running Time: 9 hrs.). 1991. 51.00 (978-1-55690-641-1(2), 91416E7) Recorded Bks.
Based in part on Pearce's own experiences working on a Florida road gang, this is the classic story of the defiant survivor who refused to be defeated by the forces of corrupt authority.

Cool Hymns for Kids. Don Marsh. 1998. 8.00 (978-0-7673-9977-7(3)); 11.98 (978-0-7673-9950-0(1)); 75.00 (978-0-7673-9928-9(5)); audio compact disk 12.00 (978-0-7673-9972-2(2)); audio compact disk 85.00 (978-0-7673-9936-4(6)); audio compact disk 16.98 (978-0-7673-9934-0(X)) LifeWay Christian.

Cool in School. Bill Harley. (J). 2000. audio compact disk 15.00 (978-1-878126-38-2(5)) Round Riv Prodns.
Cool in School features one of Bill's most popular stories, Zanzibar.

Cool Jazz. Richard Maraday. 1999. pap. bk. 34.98 (978-1-59615-619-7(8), 586-026) Pub: Music Minus. Dist(s): Bookworld

Cool Keyboard Blues. Jeff Hammer. (Fast Forward Ser.). 1997. bk. 15.95 (978-0-7119-5466-3(6)) Pub: Music Sales. Dist(s): H Leonard

Cool Million. unabr. ed. Nathanael West. Read by Peter Joyce. 3 cass. 1996. 34.95 (978-1-86015-438-6(7)) Pub: UlverLrgPrint GBR. Dist(s): Ulverscroft US
Humorous view of the sinking American Dream during the Great Depression.

Cool Repentance. unabr. ed. Antonia Fraser. Read by Joanna Lumley. 6 cass. (Running Time: 9 hrs.). (Jemima Shore Mystery Ser.: Bk. 7). 2000. 49.95 (CSL 064) Pub: Chivers Audio Bks GBR. Dist(s): AudioGO
Having repented of a reckless affair, Christabel Herrick saw no reason she should not return home to her family. She also saw no reason why she should not resume her theatrical career, by starring in two plays at a local festival. Nat Fitzwilliam, the director, was only too happy to have Christabel back. Jemima Shore was delighted to host a TV program about the festival. However, there was one person who was not so content on Christabel's return.

Cool Repentance. unabr. collector's ed. Antonia Fraser. Read by Donada Peters. 5 cass. (Running Time: 7 hrs. 30 min.). 1988. 40.00 (978-0-7366-1303-3(X), 2210) Books on Tape.
A Jemima Shore mystery, from the author of "Quiet as a Nun" & "The Wild Island".

Cool Songs for Cool Kids... in the Classroom: Fun & Interactive Music for Early Childhood. Composed by Franz Moser. Illus. by Robyn Tompkins. Lyrics by Robyn Tompkins. (J). 2003. audio compact disk (978-0-9741647-1-7(2)) NRG Pubns.
Solo/choir performance of music published in Cool Songs for Cool Kids book. Used in classroom, home, car, etc. as sing-along and movement activities.

Cool Songs for Cool Kids... in the Classroom Bk. 1: Fun & Interactive Music & Activities for Early Childhood. Illus. by Robyn Tompkins. Text by Robyn Tompkins. Music by Franz Moser. (J). 2003. audio compact disk (978-0-9741647-0-0(4)) NRG Pubns.

Cool Songs for Cool Kids... in the Classroom Bk. 1: Fun & Interactive Music & Activities for Early Childhood. Robyn Tompkins & Franz Moser. (J). 2003. spiral bd. (978-0-9741647-2-4(0)) NRG Pubns.

Cool Tools & Insects up Close. Steck-Vaughn Staff. (J). 2002. 10.00 (978-0-7398-5901-8(3)) SteckVau.

Cool Women Collect Themselves: 34 Poems. 2007. audio compact disk 10.00 (978-0-9707812-3-9(7)) Cool Women.

Cool Zone with the Pain & the Great One. unabr. ed. Judy Blume. Read by Judy Blume. Read by Kathleen McInerney. 1 CD. (Running Time: 1 hr. 18 mins.). (J). (gr. 1-3). 2008. audio compact disk 20.00 (978-0-7393-6497-0(9), Listening Lib) Pub: Random Audio Pubg. Dist(s): Random
THE PAIN AND the Great One hardly agree on anything. But deep down, they know they can count on each other, especially at school, where it often takes two to figure things out. Like when that first baby tooth falls out on the school bus. Or when an unwanted visitor on Bring Your Pet to School Day needs to be caught. Or worst of all, when a scary bully says you're burnt toast. On days like these it can feel good not to go it alone. (And don't forget Fluzzy the cat, who knows a thing or two himself).

Cool Zone with the Pain & the Great One. unabr. ed. Judy Blume. Read by Judy Blume. Read by Kathleen McInerney. (Running Time: 4680 sec.). (ENG.). (J). (gr. 1-4). 2008. audio compact disk 14.95 (978-0-7393-6495-6(2), Listening Lib) Pub: Random Audio Pubg. Dist(s): Random

Coole & Ballylee see Caedmon Treasury of Modern Poets Reading Their Own Poetry

Cooler King. Dwayne Epstein. Narrated by Larry A. McKeever. (Fantasy Ser.). (J). 2001. 10.95 (978-1-58659-066-6(9)); audio compact disk 14.95 (978-1-58659-330-8(7)) Artesian.

Coolidge Years. (Presidency Ser.). 10.00 (HP518) Esstee Audios.
Provides listeners with a retrospective appraisal of the presidency of Calvin Coolidge. Coolidge is seen as a popular & staunch conservative who was dogmatic in his support of the rich & big business.

Cooperative Education in a New Era: Understanding & Strengthening the Links Between College & the Workplace. Kenneth G. Ryder & James W. Wilson. (Higher Education Ser.). 1987. bk. 53.00 (978-1-55542-072-7(9), Jossey-Bass) Wiley US.

Cooperative Wife's Role. Elbert Willis. 1 cass. (Keys to a Successful Marriage Ser.). 4.00 Fill the Gap.

Cooper's Creek. unabr. ed. Alan Moorehead. Read by Victor Rumbellow. 8 cass. (Running Time: 8 hrs.). 1979. 48.00 (978-0-7366-0178-8(3), 1180) Books on Tape.
In 1860 a small band of men set out to attempt the first transcontinental crossing of Australia. They disappeared into the Australian outback & months later, having completed their trek across a vast desert, returned to their base camp only to find it had been abandoned a few hours earlier & without food or succor, there could be no survivors.

Cooper's Creek: The Opening of Australia. unabr. ed. Alan Moorehead. Narrated by Nelson Runger. 6 cass. (Running Time: 8 hrs. 30 mins.). 1989. 51.00 (978-1-55690-122-5(4), 89394E7) Recorded Bks.
An expedition in 1860, two set off on a dangerous trip across 1,500 miles of unmapped desert wilderness, across unknown Australian desert encounters tragedy & endures terrible odds.

Cootydoo Laklunk Cassette. Stephen Cosgrove. 2004. 5.00 (978-1-58804-427-3(0)) PCI Educ.

Cop & the Anthem see O. Henry Favorites

Cop & the Anthem see Best of O. Henry

Cop & the Anthem see Favorite Stories by O. Henry

Cop Hater. unabr. ed. Ed McBain, pseud. Read by Paul Shay. 6 cass. (Running Time: 6 hrs.). (87th Precinct Ser.: Bk. 1). 1990. 36.00 (978-0-7366-1710-9(8), 2552) Books on Tape.
Someone's eliminating cops. When Detective Reardon is found murdered, with his partner soon following in his footsteps, it looks like the killer is acting on a grudge. But when ace detective number three is murdered, the killer's motives get cloudy. Who's killing the precinct's finest? And why? Detective Steve Carella races to find the answers, & to find the killer before the killer turns him into victim number four.

***Cop Killer.** unabr. ed. Maj Sjöwall & Per Wahlöö. Read by Tom Weiner. (Running Time: 8 hrs. 0 mins.). 2010. 29.95 (978-1-4332-6318-7(1)); 54.95 (978-1-4332-6314-9(9)); audio compact disk 76.00 (978-1-4332-6315-6(7)) Blckstn Audio.

Copains d'Abord. pap. bk. 16.95 (978-88-8148-813-1(2)) Pub: Europ Lang Inst ITA. Dist(s): Distribks Inc

Copenhagen Connection. unabr. ed. Elizabeth Peters, pseud. Read by Grace Conlin. 5 cass. (Running Time: 7 hrs.). 1995. 39.95 (978-0-7861-0760-5(X), 1609) Blckstn Audio.
Elizabeth Jones, vacationing from her New York publishing job, is off to do touristy things in Denmark. The plane ride itself had turned out to be Kismet, introducing Elizabeth to her idol, Nobel Prize-winning historian & famed eccentric Margaret Rosenberg & her long-suffering son Christian. So when Margaret vanishes in Copenhagen, Elizabeth joins the irascible Christian in searching the city from underground crypts to the graves of queens. What they encounter is a baffling ransom demand for a bathrobe, not money. And what they dig up will connect a modern disappearance with an ancient artifact & the oldest of motives for crime.

Copenhagen Connection. unabr. ed. Elizabeth Peters, pseud. Read by Grace Conlin. 6 CDs. (Running Time: 7 hrs.). 2000. audio compact disk 48.00 (978-0-7861-9921-1(0), 1609) Blckstn Audio.

Copenhagen Connection. unabr. ed. Elizabeth Peters, pseud. Read by Grace Conlin. (Running Time: 7 hrs.). 2006. audio compact disk 24.95 (978-0-7861-9604-3(1), 1609) Blckstn Audio.

Coping. unabr. ed. Clayton Barbeau. Read by Clayton Barbeau. Ed. by Cecilia Martinez. 4 cass. (Running Time: 4 hrs.). 1987. 34.95 (9217) Franciscan Comns.
Discussions include: Coping with Self, Coping with Others, Coping with Loss, Coping with Feelings.

Coping Strategies for Burn Survivors & Their Families Vol 1: Welcome & Introduction. Ed. by John Thompson. 1 cass. (Running Time: 60 min.). 1985. 8.00 Phoenix Soc.

Coping Strategies for Burn Survivors & Their Families Vol 2: The Burn Survivor's View. Alan J. Breslau. (Running Time: 60 min.). 1985. 8.00 Phoenix Soc.

Coping Strategies for Burn Survivors & Their Families Vol 3: Emotional Responses. Norman R. Bernstein. 2 cass. (Running Time: 120 min.). 1985. 16.00 Phoenix Soc.

Coping Strategies for Burn Survivors & Their Families Vol 4: Cosmetology & Prostheses. Read by Jean A. Graham. 2 cass. (Running Time: 120 min.). 1985. 16.00 Phoenix Soc.

Coping Strategies for Burn Survivors & Their Families Vol 5: Disfigurement in the Arts. Read by Sandra L. Bertmen. 1 cass. (Running Time: 60 min.). 1985. 8.00 Phoenix Soc.

Coping Strategies for Burn Survivors & Their Families Vol 6: Sexuality. Read by George M. Worthington & Michael Daley. 2 cass. (Running Time: 120 min.). 1985. 16.00 Phoenix Soc.

Coping Strategies for Burn Survivors & Their Families Vol 7: Parents of Burned Children. Read by Sue S. Cahners. 2 cass. (Running Time: 120 min.). 1985. 16.00 Phoenix Soc.

Coping with Anxiety. Frank Minirth & Paul Meier. Read by Frank Minirth & Paul Meier. 1 cass. (Running Time: 70 min.). (Minirth & Meier Home Counseling Audio Library). 1994. 9.95 (978-1-56707-036-1(1)) Dallas Christ Recs.
Controlling anxiety from a psychological, spiritual & physical perspective.

Coping with Anxiety & Depression. unabr. ed. Nathaniel Branden. 1 cass. (Running Time: 35 min.). 12.95 (854) J Norton Pubs.
A skillful evocation of the art of self-hypnosis & self-healing to overcome needless fear & suffering.

Coping with Breaks in Emotional Attachments. Adolph Hansen. 1986. 10.80 (0509) Assn Prof Chaplains.

Coping with Cancer. Prod. by International LLL for Lutheran Hour Ministries Staff. 2 cass. (Running Time: 1 hr. 30 min.). 1993. 12.95 set, incl. bklt. (978-1-877752-26-1(6)) Intl Lutheran.

Coping with Candida: How to Conquer Candida. Sally Rockwell. Perf. by Sally Rockwell. 1986. 10.95 (978-0-916575-04-5(7)) Diet Design.
Dr Sally Rockwell helps you learn to cope. Relax and listen to Sally discuss everything you've wanted to know about candida. Provides how to recognize symptoms, what to eat, 4 steps in getting well.

Coping with Climate Change: National Summit Proceedings. Ed. by Rosina Bierbaum et al. 2008. pap. bk. 29.50 (978-1-59726-556-0(X)) U of Mich Pr.

Coping with Difficult & Negative People - Personal Magnetism. Robert E. Griswold. Read by Robert E. Griswold. 1 cass. (Super Strength Ser.). 1992. 10.95 (978-1-55848-305-7(5)) EffectiveMN.
Two complete non-subliminal programs to help you relax & easily release negative feelings & fears.

Coping with Difficult People: In Business & in Life. abr. ed. Robert Bramson. Read by Robert Bramson. CDs 5. (Running Time: 4 hrs. 0 mins. 0 sec.). (ENG.). 2008. audio compact disk 19.95 (978-0-7435-7304-7(8)) Pub: S&S Audio. Dist(s): S and S Inc

Coping with Difficult People: In Business & in Life. unabr. ed. Read by Robert M. Bramson. 6 cass. 59.95 set, incl. guide. (S02025) J Norton Pubs.
Bramson presents methods for coping with a variety of disagreeable co-workers & family members in specific situations. He shows how to deal with people in order to get a job done; not how to reform them.

Coping with Difficult People in Business & in Life. Robert Bramson. 2004. 7.95 (978-0-7435-1883-3(7)) Pub: S&S Audio. Dist(s): S and S Inc

Coping with Disfigurement. Norman R. Bernstein. 1985. Phoenix Soc.

Coping with Environmental Enforcement & Compliance under the New Administration. unabr. ed. Contrib. by Randy M. Mott. 4 cass. (Running Time: 5 hrs. 30 min.). 1989. 50.00 course handbk. (T7-9227) PLI.
This September 1989 PLI seminar focuses on air, water & waste management, including issues such as acid rain, hazardous waste cleanup & radioactive waste sites. Particular attention is paid to remedies under Superfund, new initiatives for wetlands protection & RCRA enforcement priorities.

Coping with Family & Interpersonal Conflict. Perf. by Gerald T. Rogers. Contrib. by Dennis C. Daley. (Living Sober Ser.: Segment E). 1994. pap. bk. 89.00 NTSC. (978-1-56215-058-7(8), Jossey-Bass) Wiley US.

Coping with Infertility. 1 cass. (Care Cassettes Ser.: Vol. 12, No. 1). 1985. 10.80 Assn Prof Chaplains.

Coping with Loneliness. Edd Anthony. Read by Edd Anthony. 2007. audio compact disk 16.95 (978-1-881586-25-8(1)) Canticle Cass.

Coping with Loss: Psychotherapeutic Use of Leave-Taking Rituals. Ed. by Onno Van der Hart. (C). 1988. reel tape 14.00 (978-0-8290-2304-6(6)) Irvington.

Coping with Male PMS: Parting with Money Syndrome & Other Humorous Conditions; Sunny with a Chance of Tribulation. Joni Hilton. 1 cass. 7.98 (978-1-55503-786-4(0), 06005020) Covenant Comms.
Hilarious tape for both men & women!.

Coping with Mental & Emotional Depression. Instructed by Manly P. Hall. 8.95 (978-0-89314-033-5(3), C820822) Philos Res.

Coping with NLD in the Family - Strategies for Raising a Child with NLD. Kathy Allen. 1 cass. (Running Time: 1 hr. 18 min.). 1998. bk. 20.00 (978-1-58111-061-6(8)) Contemporary Medical.
Challenges & adaptations for raising NLD children, parenting limits, strategies & suggestions & improving family life.

Coping with Parenting. Ray DiGiuseppe. 1 cass. (Running Time: 43 min.). 9.95 (C042) A Ellis Institute.
One of the hardest & most challenging jobs you'll ever have is parenting. If you have children, you know what we mean. Here are practical strategies for dealing with the challenges of handling your reactions to your children's "childish" behavior.

Coping with Relapse Warning Signs. Directed By Gerald T. Rogers. Contrib. by Dennis C. Daley. (Living Sober Ser.: Segment G). 1994. pap. bk. 89.00 NTSC. (978-1-56215-062-4(6), Jossey-Bass) Wiley US.

Coping with Stress. James W. Mills. 1 cass. 10.00 (SP100060) SMI Intl.
Stress is one of the major causes of illnesses in the '90s. Much of it can't be avoided - but it can be confronted & dealt with positively. You encounter stress wherever you are. Learn these positive, practical methods for handling stress & avoid becoming its victim.

Coping with Stress. unabr. ed. Daniel Goleman et al. 4 cass. 36.00 (OC91) Sound Horizons AV.
Life is stress: your job, your boss, your deadlines, your family life. Clinical relaxation is a method of stress reduction, based on Eastern techniques, that allows the attainment of a deeply relaxed state and guards against the accumulation of tension throughout the day.

Coping with Supervisory Nightmares. abr. ed. Michael Singer Dobson & Deborah Singer Dobson. Read by Michael Singer Dobson & Deborah Singer Dobson. 2 cass. (Running Time: 1 hrs. 30 min.). 1998. 19.95 Set; incl. wkbk. (978-1-57294-099-4(9), 11-0220) SkillPath Pubns.
The Dobsons pose "12 Common Nighmares of Leadership & What You Can Do About Them," then apply a unique five-point plan to solve each of the problems.

Coping with Tensions & Anxieties, Set. Arnold Lazarus. 3 CDs. (Running Time: 180 mins.). 2005. audio compact disk 34.50 (978-1-57970-332-5(1), S05096D, Audio-For) J Norton Pubs.
When was the last time you flew off the handle or overreacted to a minor incident? Or were tense and upset when you wanted to be calm and collected? With this program you can learn to cope with stress and avoid these all-too-human responses to the pressures of daily life. Dr. Lazarus developed this program to provide you specific, proven methods of coping. The most meaningful way of dealing with stress is to find effective ways to control emotions. Too often we allow emotions to overrule reason, or think in black and white instead of gray, or overgeneralize from insufficient data. Dr. Lazarus shares proven methods of maintaining perspective as you examine your thoughts and feelings, sexualy outlook, self-worth, and emotional freedom. You will also acquire a set of rational techniques for dealing with emotional disruptions and situations that drain your energies, diminish your perception of self-worth, and lessen your control. (Re-issue on CD of original 3-cassette program.).

Coping with Test Anxiety: Academic Success. Michael S. Prokop. Read by Michael S. Prokop. Ed. by Robert C. Peters. 1 cass. (Running Time: 45 min.). (YA). (gr. 4-12). 1986. 9.95 (978-0-933879-35-5(0), Kaya Books) Alegra Hse Pubs.

***Coping with the Emotional Impact of Cancer: How to Become an Active Patient.** unabr. ed. Neil Fiore. Read by Walter Dixon. (Running Time: 6 hrs.). (ENG.). 2010. 27.98 (978-1-59659-539-2(6), GildAudio) Pub: Gildan Media. Dist(s): HachBkGrp

Coping with the Genuinely Difficult Person. Sean Sammon. 3 cass. 1988. 25.95 (TAH200) Alba Hse Comns.
The purpose of this presentation is to acquire the ability to identify, understand, & cope with difficult people in your life. Brother Sean covers the nature of coping, patterns of difficult behavior & identifying a difficult person.

Coping with Unmanageability. 1 cass. (Recovery - The New Life Ser.). 1979. 8.95 (1591G) Hazelden.

Coping with War: Stress Reduction for Adolescents. Michael S. Prokop. 1 cass. (Running Time: 46 min.). (YA). 9.95 (978-0-933879-40-9(7)) Alegra Hse Pubs.
This tape is designed to improve confidence levels as adolescents learn how to cope & "choose to adjust" to life's problems, including war. Effective stress reduction techniques that will be taught include autogenics, progressive muscle relaxation, & positive imagery.

Copp for Hire. unabr. ed. Don Pendleton. Read by Gene Engene. 6 cass. (Running Time: 6 hrs.). (Joe Copp Ser.: Bk. 1). 1997. 39.95 (978-1-55686-783-5(2)) Books in Motion.
A private investigator is hired by a female stripper, who is suddenly killed in a hit & run accident. Two other victims from the same club are murdered & all the clues lead to a political leader.

Copp in Deep. unabr. ed. Don Pendleton. Read by Gene Engene. 6 cass. (Running Time: 6 hrs. 48 min.). (Joe Copp Ser.: Bk. 3). 2001. 39.95 (978-1-55686-788-0(3)) Books in Motion.
When Joe's buddy Tom Chase is trapped in a defense industry government sting. Joe Copp is asked to help his friend. Joe is drawn into international espionage and murder.

Copp in Shock. unabr. ed. Don Pendleton. Read by Gene Engene. 6 cass. (Running Time: 6 hrs. 48 min.). (Joe Copp Ser.: Bk. 6). 2001. 39.95 (978-1-55686-862-7(6)) Books in Motion.
While recovering from a near fatal wound, Joe faces partial amnesia and a lost three weeks when he married a woman who has since turned up dead.

Copp in the Dark. unabr. ed. Don Pendleton. Read by Gene Engene. 6 cass. (Running Time: 6 hrs. 36 min.). (Joe Copp Ser.: Bk. 4). 2001. 39.95 (978-1-55686-850-4(2)) Books in Motion.
Joe enters the theatre world as the bodyguard of a leading man. Before he knows it, Joe Copp is faced with the murder of four actors and one dead informant.

Copp on Fire. unabr. ed. Don Pendleton. Read by Gene Engene. 4 cass. (Running Time: 5 hrs. 24 min.). (Joe Copp Ser.: Bk. 2). 2001. 26.95 (978-1-55686-786-6(7)) Books in Motion.
The down and dirty world of backlot Hollywood is the setting when a narcotics stake-out proves deadly for those being watched.

Copp on Ice. unabr. ed. Don Pendleton. Read by Gene Engene. 6 cass. (Running Time: 6 hrs. 42 min.). (Joe Copp Ser.: Bk. 5). 2001. 39.95 (978-1-55686-851-1(0)) Books in Motion.
Joe is hired by a city administrator to take over command of the city's police force and to investigate rumors of police and city-wide corruption, high-lighted by the blatant murder of the mayor.

Copper Beech. unabr. ed. Maeve Binchy. Narrated by Barbara Caruso. 9 cass. (Running Time: 12 hrs. 45 mins.). 2000. 78.00 (978-1-55690-865-1(2), 93307K8) Recorded Bks.
The intertwining lives of eight young people, born & raised in a tiny village in the west of Ireland.

Copper Beeches see Adventures of Sherlock Holmes

Copper Bluffs. unabr. ed. Les Savage, Jr. 4 cass. (Running Time: 9 hrs.). (Sagebrush Western Ser.). (J). 2005. 49.95 (978-1-57490-316-4(0)) Pub: ISIS Lrg Prnt GBR. Dist(s): Ulverscroft US

Copper Bracelet. unabr. ed. Jeffery Deaver. Read by Alfred Molina. (Running Time: 10 hrs.). 2010. 39.97 (978-1-4418-3073-9(1), 9781441830739, Brinc Audio MP3 Lib); 39.97 (978-1-4418-3074-6(X), 9781441830746, BADLE); audio compact disk 87.97 (978-1-4418-3071-5(5), 9781441830715, BriAudCD Unabrid); audio compact disk 29.99 (978-1-4418-3070-8(7), 9781441830708) Brilliance Audio.

***Copper Bracelet.** unabr. ed. Jeffery Deaver. Read by Alfred Molina. (Running Time: 10 hrs.). 2010. 24.99 (978-1-4418-3072-2(3), 9781441830722, Brilliance MP3) Brilliance Audio.

Copper Peacock & Other Stories. Ruth Rendell. Read by Penelope Keith. 4 cass. (Running Time: 6 hrs.). 2002. 39.95 (978-0-7540-0731-9(6), CAB 2153) AudioGO.

Copper Peacock & Other Stories. unabr. ed. Ruth Rendell. Read by Penelope Keith. 4 CDs. (Running Time: 6 hrs.). 2002. audio compact disk 49.95 (978-0-7540-5464-1(0), CCD 155) AudioGO.

Copper Peacock & Other Stories. unabr. collector's ed. Ruth Rendell. Read by Donada Peters. 5 cass. (Running Time: 5 hrs.). 1992. 30.00 (978-0-7366-2210-3(1), 3003) Books on Tape.
Eight of suspense & one classic detective story featuring Chief Inspector Reginald Wexford.

Copper Scroll. Joel C. Rosenberg. 2009. audio compact disk 9.99 (978-1-4418-2661-9(0)) Brilliance Audio.

Copper Scroll. abr. ed. Joel C. Rosenberg. Read by Jeff Woodman. (Running Time: 14400 sec.). 2007. audio compact disk 14.99 (978-1-59737-674-7(4), 9781597376747, BCD Value Price) Brilliance Audio.

Copper Scroll. abr. unabr. ed. Joel C. Rosenberg. Read by Jeff Woodman. (Running Time: 36000 sec.). 2006. audio compact disk 97.25 (978-1-59600-315-6(4), 9781596003156, BACDLib Ed) Brilliance Audio.
The second book in a new series of apocalyptic thrillers leading up to the rapture.

Copper Scroll. unabr. ed. Joel C. Rosenberg. Read by Jeff Woodman. (Running Time: 10 hrs.). 2006. 39.25 (978-1-59710-893-5(6), 9781597108935, BADLE); 24.95 (978-1-59710-892-8(8), 9781597108928, BAD); 82.25 (978-1-59600-312-5(X), 9781596003125, BrilAudUnabridg); audio compact disk 24.95 (978-1-59335-999-7(3), 9781593359997, Brilliance MP3); audio compact disk 39.25 (978-1-59600-317-0(0), 9781596003170, Brinc Audio MP3 Lib); audio compact disk 36.95 (978-1-4233-0645-0(7), 9781423306450, Bril Audio CD Unabri) Brilliance Audio.

Copper Sun. unabr. ed. Sharon M. Draper. Read by Myra Lucretia Taylor. 8 CDs. (Running Time: 9 hrs.). (YA). (gr. 8 up). 2006. audio compact disk 84.75 (978-1-4281-2253-6(2)); 65.75 (978-1-4281-2248-2(6)) Recorded Bks.
Fifteen-year-old Amari witnesses the murder of her family and the destruction of her remote African village. She endures countless humiliations as she is beaten, branded, and forced to board a slave ship. The atrocities continue as she struggles through endless days of backbreaking work and daily degradation on a plantation. Somehow, through it all, Amari's hopes and dreams survive because there are moments of kindness from an indentured white girl, Polly and the gentle wife of the plantation owner. Amari and Polly find that by working together freedom could be possible.

Copperhead. Bernard Cornwell. Read by Tom Parker. 14 CDs. (Running Time: 16 hrs.). (Starbuck Chronicles: Vol. 2). 2001. audio compact disk 112.00 (978-0-7861-9754-5(4), 2741) Blckstn Audio.
It is the summer of 1862 & the northern army is threatening to capture Richmond, the Confederate capital. Captain Nathaniel Starbuck, born in Boston but a Confederate hero at Manassas, is again in the thick of Civil War action. Nate suddenly finds himself accused of being a Yankee spy. Proving his innocence & finding the real spy will require courage & endurance rarely seen even in the brutal fog of war. Failure could mean the fall of Richmond & a career-ending defeat for Robert E. Lee.

Copperhead. Bernard Cornwell. Read by Tom Parker. (Starbuck Chronicles: Vol. 2). 2000. 36.95 (978-1-59912-456-8(4)) Iofy Corp.

Copperhead. unabr. ed. Bernard Cornwell. Read by Tom Parker. 11 cass. (Running Time: 16 hrs.). (Starbuck Chronicles: Vol. 2). 2001. 76.95 (978-0-7861-1971-4(3), 2741) Blckstn Audio.

Copperhead. unabr. ed. Bernard Cornwell. Read by David Case. 11 cass. (Running Time: 16 hrs. 30 mins.). (Starbuck Chronicles: Vol. 2). 2001. 88.00 (978-0-7366-6013-6(5)) Books on Tape.
A northerner fighting for the rebel South in America's Civil War. Aided by his spymaster Allan Pinkerton, General McClellan is convinced he can lead the northerners to the gates of the rebel capital of Richmond. Starbuck, expelled

from his regiment by its bombastic founder, Washington Faulconer, must travel a hard road before he can rejoin his comrades.

Copperhead. unabr. ed. Bernard Cornwell. Read by Hayward Morse. 14 CDs. (Running Time: 21 hrs.). (Starbuck Chronicles: Vol. 2). 2001. audio compact disk 99.95 (978-0-7531-1054-6(7), 110547) Pub: ISIS Audio GBR. Dist(s): Ulverscroft US

Copperhead. unabr. ed. Bernard Cornwell. Read by Hayward Morse. 12 cass. (Running Time: 17 hrs.). (Starbuck Chronicles: Vol. 2). (J). 2001. 94.95 (978-1-85695-915-5(5), 950801) Pub: ISIS Lrg Prnt GBR. Dist(s): Ulverscroft US

Copperhead. unabr. ed. Bernard Cornwell. Narrated by Ed Sala. 11 cass. (Running Time: 15 hrs. 30 mins.). (Starbuck Chronicles: Vol. 2). 1994. 91.00 (978-0-7887-3496-0(2), 95778E7) Recorded Bks.
Boston-born Nate Starbuck has turned away from his northern family and is fighting for the Confederate Army. But when he is accused of leaking military information, Nate finds himself labeled a spy by both the North and the South.

Cops & Kids: Policing Juvenile Delinquency in Urban America, 1890-1940. David B. Wolcott. (History of Crime & Criminal Justice Ser.). 2005. audio compact disk 9.95 (978-0-8142-9080-4(9)) Pub: Ohio St U Pr. Dist(s): Chicago Distribution Ctr

Cops & Robbers. unabr. ed. Donald E. Westlake. Read by Dom Alagia. 8 vols. (Running Time: 12 hrs.). 2000. bk. 69.95 (978-0-7927-2206-9(X), CSL 095, Chivers Sound Lib) AudioGO.
Meet Tom and Joe. They've got homes on Long Island and a dream: to pull off the perfect heist. Tom and Joe also have badges, uniforms and guns, just like the rest of the New York City police force! These two shining examples of New York's Finest don't care what they steal or how, as long as it comes out to 2 million dollars. But they get involved with the Mob and find out that robbing Wall Street can be very dangerous.

Coptic Orthodox Liturgy of St. Basil. Ragheb Moftah & Martha Roy. Tr. by Margit Toth. 1998. 12.95 (978-977-424-885-6(6)) Pub: Am Univ Cairo Pr EGY. Dist(s): Intl Pubs Mktg

Copycat. unabr. ed. Gillian White. Read by Jilly Bond. 8 cass. (Running Time: 32400 sec.). (Isis Ser.). 2003. 69.95 (978-0-7531-1777-4(0)) Pub: ISIS Lrg Prnt GBR. Dist(s): Ulverscroft US
Jennie and Martha became friends when Martha moved in next door. Jennie admired everything about Martha - her house, her gorgeous husband, her bohemian clothes and exotic children's names. Martha tolerated Jennie, took her on holiday and helped with the children. As time went on, the roles seemed to reverse. As Jennie became more independent, more successful, Martha's life was falling apart. heir relationship became bitter, twisted - a relationship that only one could survive.

Copyright Considerations for General Practitioners. Read by Franklin A. Miles, Jr. 1 cass. 1990. 20.00 (AL-80) PA Bar Inst.

Copyright Law, 2005 ed. (Law School Legends Audio Series) 2005th rev. ed. Roger E. Schechter. (Law School Legends Audio Ser.). 2005. 52.00 (978-0-314-16086-7(8), gilbert); 47.95 (978-0-314-16085-0(X), gilbert) West.

Copyrights, Leadsheets & All That. Duane Shinn. 1 cass. 19.95 (S-9) Duane Shinn.
Presents a course in the mechanics of getting a song copyrighted, printed in lead-sheet format & ready to go to a publisher.

Coq et le Renard see Fables de La Fontaine

Coquerico. unabr. ed. Read by Lucienne M. Widmer. 1 cass. (Running Time: 45 min.). Incl. Abeille. (SAC 47-5); Moutons. (SAC 47-5); Voici l'Ane. (SAC 47-5); Voici le Chat. (SAC 47-5); Voici le Chien. (SAC 47-5); (FRE.). 11.95 incl. text. (978-0-8045-1063-9(6), SAC 47-5) Spoken Arts.
The stories encourage the learning process by their extreme simplicity. The vocabulary is simple, the grammar is straightforward, the present tense is always used.

Coquette. Hannah Webster Foster. Read by Anais 9000. 2009. 27.95 (978-1-60112-147-9(4)) Babblebooks.

***Coraje: La Fuerza para Enfrentar un Mundo Cambiante.** Tr. of Courage: the Backbone to Face A Changing World. (SPA.). 2009. audio compact disk 12.00 (978-0-944129-39-5(0)) High Praise.

***Coraje de Triunfar.** Ruben Gonzalez. Taller Del Exito Inc. (SPA.). 2009. audio compact disk 24.95 (978-1-60738-006-1(4)) Taller del Exito.

Coral Ember Nails. unabr. ed. Andrew Krya. Read by Ron Varela. 6 cass. (Running Time: 6 hrs. 42 min.). 2001. 39.95 (978-1-55686-767-5(0)) Books in Motion.
When Brad's old girlfriend shows up frightened and rambling about a mysterious box, Brad is drawn deep into a secret criminal operation. Later, the girlfriend turns up missing.

Coral Island. R. M. Ballantyne. 2005. pap. bk. 89.95 (978-1-86015-008-1(X)) Ulverscroft US.

Coral Island. R. M. Ballantyne. Read by Peter Joyce. 7 cass. 2005. 61.95 (978-1-86015-471-3(9)) Ulverscroft US.

Coral Reef Hideaway. 1 cass. (Running Time: 35 min.). (J). (gr. k-4). 2001. 19.95 (SP 4008C) Kimbo Educ.

Coral Reef Hideaway: The Story of a Clown Anemonefish. Doe Boyle. Narrated by Peter Thomas. Illus. by Steven James Petruccio. 1 cass. (Smithsonian Oceanic Collection). (J). (ps-2). 1995. 5.00 (978-1-56899-187-0(8), C4008) Soundprints.
In the lagoon near the island of Papua New Guinea, Percula, a clown anemonefish, hides among the delicate tentacles of her sea anemone home. It's swaying arms sting other fish, but Percula's slimy coating protects her. Soon, a male clown anemonefish joins her & builds a nest for her eggs. One day, rains make the reef murky with mud. Percula rushes to protect her eggs & home from the wrasses & butterflyfish that hunt in the water.

Coral Reefs. Compiled by Benchmark Education Staff. 2005. audio compact disk 10.00 (978-1-4108-5485-8(X)) Benchmark Educ.

Coral Thief. unabr. ed. Rebecca Stott. Narrated by Simon Prebble. 1 MP3-CD. (Running Time: 9 hrs. 0 mins. 0 sec.). (ENG.). 2009. 24.99 (978-1-4001-6338-0(2)); audio compact disk 69.99 (978-1-4001-4338-2(1)); audio compact disk 34.99 (978-1-4001-1338-5(5)) Pub: Tantor Media. Dist(s): IngramPubServ

Coralena. Michael Mail. Narrated by Christopher Kay. 7 cass. (Running Time: 9 hrs. 45 mins.). 2002. 67.00 (978-1-84197-485-9(4)) Recorded Bks.

Coraline. unabr. ed. Neil Gaiman. (J). 2002. audio compact disk 249.90 (978-0-06-050990-3(2)) HarperCollins Pubs.

***Coraline.** unabr. ed. Neil Gaiman. Read by Neil Gaiman. 2003. (978-0-06-073556-2(2)) HarperCollins Pubs.

***Coraline.** unabr. ed. Neil Gaiman. Read by Neil Gaiman. (ENG.). 2005. (978-0-06-112290-3(4)) HarperCollins Pubs.

Coraline. unabr. movie tie-in ed. Neil Gaiman. Read by Neil Gaiman. (J). 2008. audio compact disk 9.95 (978-0-06-166016-0(7), HarperChildAud) HarperCollins Pubs.

Corazón Agradecido. Michael Rodriguez. (SPA.). 2007. audio compact disk 14.99 (978-0-8297-5065-2(7)) Zondervan.

***Corca Dhuibhne.** Diarmuid O. Tuama. (ENG.). 1991. 11.95 (978-0-8023-7061-7(6)) Pub: Clo Iar-Chonnachta IRL. Dist(s): Dufour

Cordelia Underwood. Van Reid. Read by Arthur Addison. 12 cass. (Running Time: 18 hrs.). 1999. 96.00 (5032) Books on Tape.
In the summer of 1896 in Portland, Maine, Cordelia finds the deed to a parcel of land, where something mysterious may be buried.

Corduroy. 9.95 (978-1-59112-180-0(9)) Live Oak Media.

Corduroy. 2004. bk. 24.95 (978-0-7882-0693-1(1)) Weston Woods.

Corduroy. (J). 2004. pap. bk. 32.75 (978-1-55592-210-8(4)); pap. bk. 32.75 (978-1-55592-211-5(2)); pap. bk. 14.95 (978-0-7882-0677-1(X)); pap. bk. 14.95 (978-1-55592-655-7(X)) Weston Woods.

Corduroy. Don Freeman. Read by Linda Terheyden. 1 cass. (Running Time: 30 mins.). (Corduroy Ser.). (J). (gr. k-1). 2000. pap. bk. 19.97 (978-0-7366-9201-4(0)) Books on Tape.
A stuffed teddy bear in a department store, missing a button from his overalls, almost abandons hope of finding a real home until a small girl decides he is the bear for her.

Corduroy. Don Freeman. 1 cass. (Running Time: 35 min.). (Corduroy Ser.). (SPA.). (J). (gr. k-1). 2001. 15.95 (VXS-35C) Kimbo Educ.

Corduroy. Don Freeman. Illus. by Don Freeman. (Running Time: 11 mins.). (J). (ps-1). 1982. audio compact disk 12.95 (978-1-59112-788-8(2)) Live Oak Media.

Corduroy. Don Freeman. 2 cass. (Corduroy Ser.). (SPA.). (J). (gr. k-1). 1999. pap. bk. 29.95 Set. Live Oak Media.

Corduroy. Don Freeman. Illus. by Don Freeman. 14 vols. (Running Time: 11 mins.). 1982. pap. bk. 35.95 (978-1-59112-791-8(2)); 9.95 (978-1-59112-024-7(1)) Live Oak Media.

Corduroy. Don Freeman. (Corduroy Ser.). (J). (gr. k-1). 1983. 32.95 Live Oak Media.

Corduroy. Don Freeman. Illus. by Don Freeman. 14 vols. (Running Time: 10 mins.). 1990. pap. bk. 39.95 (978-1-59519-151-9(8)); 9.95 (978-1-59112-023-0(3)); audio compact disk 12.95 (978-1-59519-149-6(6)) Live Oak Media.

Corduroy. Don Freeman. Illus. by Don Freeman. 11 vols. (Running Time: 10 mins.). (SPA.). (J). 1990. pap. bk. 18.95 (978-1-59519-150-2(X)) Pub: Live Oak Media. Dist(s): AudioGO

Corduroy. Don Freeman. Illus. by Don Freeman. Read by Linda Terheyden. 11 vols. (Running Time: 11 mins.). (J). 2004. pap. bk. 18.95 (978-1-59112-789-5(0)) Pub: Live Oak Media. Dist(s): AudioGO

Corduroy. Don Freeman. (Corduroy Ser.). (J). (gr. k-1). 1989. bk. 53.32 (978-0-676-31871-5(1)) SRA McGraw.

Corduroy. Don Freeman. 1 cass. (Running Time: 30 min.). (Corduroy Ser.). (J). (gr. k-1). bk. 24.95; pap. bk. 32.75; pap. bk. 15.95 (LM1024AC) Weston Woods.
Corduroy is a lovable stuffed bear who waits patiently on a department store shelf for someone to take him home. Lest he be mistaken for "used," he embarks on a storewide search to replace his missing button, risking danger & apprehension. At last he finds his long-sought home with a young, affectionate girl.

Corduroy. Don Freeman. 1 cass. (Running Time: 30 min.). (Corduroy Ser.). (J). (gr. k-1). 2000. pap. bk. 12.95 Weston Woods.
A lovable stuffed bear, who longs for someone to take him home, launches a storewide search for his missing button lest someone mistake him for used.

Corduroy. Don Freeman. (Corduroy Ser.). (J). (gr. k-1). 2004. 8.95 (978-1-56008-445-7(6)) Weston Woods.

Corduroy. unabr. ed. Don Freeman. Illus. by Don Freeman. Read by Linda Terheyden. 14 vols. (Running Time: 11 mins.). (Corduroy Ser.). (J). 1982. pap. bk. & tchr. ed. 33.95 Reading Chest. (978-0-941078-07-8(8)) Live Oak Media.
A stuffed teddy bear in a department store, missing a button from his overalls, almost abandons hope of finding a real home until a small girl decides he is the bear for her.

Corduroy. unabr. ed. Don Freeman. Illus. by Don Freeman. Read by Linda Terheyden. 11 vols. (Running Time: 11 mins.). (Corduroy Ser.). (J). (gr. k-1). 1982. bk. 25.95 (978-0-941078-08-5(6)); pap. bk. 16.95 (978-0-941078-06-1(X)) Pub: Live Oak Media. Dist(s): AudioGO

Corduroy. unabr. ed. Don Freeman. 1 cass. (Running Time: 10 min.). (Corduroy Ser.). (SPA.). (J). (gr. k-1). 1991. 9.95 Live Oak Media.
Readalong of the Spanish translation of Corduroy.

Corduroy. unabr. ed. Don Freeman. Read by Willie Colon. 14 vols. (Running Time: 10 mins.). (Corduroy Ser.). (SPA., (J). (gr. k-1). 1990. pap. bk. & tchr. ed. 37.95 Reading Chest. (978-0-87499-215-1(X)) Live Oak Media.

Corduroy. unabr. ed. Don Freeman. Illus. by Don Freeman. Read by Willie Colon. 11 vols. (Running Time: 10 mins.). (Corduroy Ser.). (SPA.). (J). (gr. k-1). 1990. pap. bk. 16.95 (978-0-87499-213-7(3), LK3796) Pub: Live Oak Media. Dist(s): AudioGO
A stuffed teddy bear longs to exchange his department store home for a real one in this endearing story.

Corduroy, Set. unabr. ed. Don Freeman. Illus. by Don Freeman. 22 vols. (Running Time: 22 mins.). (Corduroy Ser.). (SPA & ENG.). (J). (gr. k-1). 1999. pap. bk. 33.95 (978-0-87499-566-4(3)) Live Oak Media.

Corduroy's Busy Street & Corduroy Goes to the Doctor. Lisa McCue. Characters created by Don Freeman. 1 cass. (Corduroy Ser.). (J). (gr. k-1). 15.95 (VX-78C) Kimbo Educ.
These two board books examine the activities of a typical busy street & help sort out various concerns about going to the doctor.

Corduroy's Busy Street & Corduroy Goes to the Doctor. Lisa McCue. Characters created by Don Freeman. 1 readalong cass. (Running Time: 4 min.). (Corduroy Ser.). (J). (gr. k-1). 1989. pap. bk. 15.95 incl. 2 pap. bks. Live Oak Media.
These two board books introduce Corduroy to pre-schoolers & kindergarteners. In doing so, they examine the activities (& safety considerations) of a typical street environment & dismantle unfounded concerns about going to the doctor.

Corduroy's Busy Street & Corduroy Goes to the Doctor. Lisa McCue. Read by Randye Kaye. Characters created by Don Freeman. 2 vols. (Running Time: 4 hrs.). (Corduroy Ser.). (J). (gr. k-1). 1989. pap. bk. 15.95 (978-0-87499-133-8(1)) Live Oak Media.
Maximizing preschool interest in such wonders as trucks & addressing concerns like a trip to the pediatrician, these appealing look & listen titles, based on Don Freeman's book character, Corduroy, provide an opportunity for small children & adults to share books together.

Corduroy's Day & Corduroy's Party. Read by Barbara Barsky. Characters created by Don Freeman. Illus. by Lisa McCue. 12 cass. (Running Time: 4 mins.). (Corduroy Ser.). (J). (gr. k-1). 1987. bds. 15.95 (978-0-87499-041-6(6)) Live Oak Media.
Artist Lisa McCue introduces the late Don Freeman's Corduroy to preschoolers and kindergartners in these two board books focusing on activities near & dear to the hearts of beginning readers, counting & birthday parties.

Corduroy's Day & Corduroy's Party. Don Freeman. 1 cass. (Corduroy Ser.). (J). (gr. k-1). 15.95 (VX-70C) Kimbo Educ.
Introduce children to Corduroy in these two board focusing on activities dear to beginning readers - counting & birthday parties.

Core Balance Diet: 4 Weeks to Boost Your Metabolism & Lose Weight for Good. Marcelle Pick & Genevieve Morgan. (ENG.). 2009. audio compact disk 23.95 (978-1-4019-2203-0(1)) Hay House.

Core Knowledge Music Collection, Grade 6. (J). 2008. audio compact disk Rental 44.95 (978-1-890517-52-6(6)) Core Knowledge.

Core Knowledge Music Collection, Grade 7. Compiled by Core Knowledge Foundation. (J). 2008. audio compact disk Rental 29.95 (978-1-890517-47-2(X)) Core Knowledge.

Core Knowledge Music Collection, Grade 8. Compiled by Core Knowledge Foundation. (YA). 2008. audio compact disk 29.95 (978-1-890517-46-5(1)) Core Knowledge.

Core Knowledge Music Collection, Grades 1 And 2. (J). 2003. audio compact disk 29.95 (978-1-890517-66-3(6)) Core Knowledge.

Core Knowledge Music Collection, Grades 3, 4, And 5. (J). 2003. audio compact disk 44.95 (978-1-890517-67-0(4)) Core Knowledge.

Core Knowledge Music Collection, Preschool & Kindergarten. (J). 2003. audio compact disk 29.95 (978-1-890517-65-6(8)) Core Knowledge.

Core of Spirituality. John Bradshaw. (Running Time: 7200 sec.). 2008. audio compact disk 70.00 (978-1-57388-014-5(0)) J B Media.

Core of Spirituality. unabr. ed. John Bradshaw. 2 cass. (Running Time: 2 hrs.). 1993. 16.00 Set. (978-1-57388-013-8(2)) J B Media.
John discusses an ancient tradition of spirituality. Using a vast array of philosophical & theological resources, he weaves together a highly practical spirituality.

Core of Zen: The Ordinary Mind Is Tao. Masao Abe. 1 cass. 9.00 (A0702-90) Sound Photosyn.
Dr. Abe is a leading exponent of Zen & Japanese Buddhism in the West.

Core Strength Calm Mind: Meditations for Grounding, Alignment & Pulsation. Swami Shankardev Saraswati & Jayne Stevenson. (ENG.). 2005. audio compact disk 33.00 (978-0-9803496-4-1(8)) Big Shakti AUS.

Core Value Selling: A Contemporary Selling Philosophy for Communicating YOUR Value to YOUR Market. Bill Caskey. 6 CD's. 2005. audio compact disk 199.00 (978-0-9758510-9-8(8)) Caskey Ach Strat.

Coreen sans Peine. 1 cass. (Running Time: 1 hr., 30 min.). (FRE.). 2000. bk. 75.00 (978-2-7005-1367-7(3)) Pub: Assimil FRA. Dist(s): Distribks Inc

Corel WordPerfect 9: Instructor Resources; Test Generator CD. Nita Rutkosky & Ann Miller. (Signature Ser.). audio compact disk 78.95 (978-0-7638-0263-9(8)) EMC-Paradigm.

Corelli: The Man, the Voice. unabr. ed. Marina Boagno. Tr. by Mark Schiavone from ITA. (Great Voices Ser.: No. 5). Orig. Title: Franco Corelli: Un Uomo, Una Voce. 1996. bk. 39.95 (978-1-880909-50-8(2)) Pub: Baskerville. Dist(s): Hushion Hse

***Corelli: Sonata for Descant (Soprano) Recorder & Basso Continuo Op. 5, No. 10 D Major.** Composed by Arcangelo Corelli. (ENG.). 2008. pap. bk. 19.95 (978-3-905477-46-7(7), 3905477467) Pub: Dowani Intl LIE. Dist(s): H Leonard

***Corelli: Sonata for Treble (Alto) Recorder & Basso Continuo Op. 5, No. 7 G Minor.** Composed by Arcangelo Corelli. (ENG.). 2008. pap. bk. 19.95 (978-3-905477-49-8(1), 3905477491) Pub: Dowani Intl LIE. Dist(s): H Leonard

***Corelli: Sonata, Op. 5, No 9 in A Major: For Violin & Basso Continuo.** Ed. by Albrecht Winter. Composed by Arcangelo Corelli. (ENG.). 2008. pap. bk. 19.95 (978-3-905477-76-4(9), 3905477769) Pub: Dowani Intl LIE. Dist(s): H Leonard

Corellian Trilogy Boxed Set: Ambush at Corellia; Assault at Selonia; Showdown at Centerpoint. Roger MacBride Allen. Read by Anthony Heald. 6 cass. (Running Time: 9 hrs.). (Star Wars). (YA). (gr. 5 up). 1999. bk. (893178, Random AudioBks) Random Audio Pubg.
Arriving on the distant planet with Leia, their children & Chewbacca, Hans Solo finds himself part of a deceptive plan whose aim not even he understands.

Coretta Scott King: On Non-Violent Social Change. Narrated by Coretta Scott King. 1 cass. (Running Time: 1 hr.). 10.95 (K0240B090, HarperThor) HarpC GBR.

Corinne ou l'Italie. Madame de Stael. Read by Francoise Fabian. 1 cass. (FRE.). 1991. 24.95 (1127-EF) Olivia & Hill.
The ill-fated love story of a melancholy Englishman, Lord Oswald Nelvil & the passionate, artistic Corinne.

Corinth Revisited: 1 Cor 16:15-24. Ed Young. 1986. 4.95 (978-0-7417-1527-2(9), 527) Win Walk.

Corinthian. unabr. ed. Georgette Heyer. Read by Eve Matheson. 8 cass. (Running Time: 8 hrs.). 1993. 69.95 (978-0-7451-6002-3(6), CAB 595) AudioGO.

Corinthian Columns: Parish Preparation for Lambeth 1998. Phillip McFadyen. 1998. 5.95 (978-1-85311-196-9(1), 6032) Pub: Norwich Bks GBR. Dist(s): Morehouse Pub

Corinthian Strategy: Acts 18:1-28. Ed Young. 1998. 4.95 (978-0-7417-2186-0(4), A1186) Win Walk.

Corinthians I & II Commentary. collector's ed. Chuck Missler. 1 MP3 CD-ROM. (Running Time: 24 hours). (Chuck Missler Commentaries). 2001. cd-rom 44.95 (978-1-57821-148-7(4)) Koinonia Hse.
*Does history repeat itself?The city of Corinth was Hollywood, Las Vegas and New York all rolled into one. Corinth was intellectually alert, materially prosperous, but morally corrupt. Its citizens were devoted to the reckless development of the individual. The church at Corinth is the "carnal church" - spiritual babes, immature and undeveloped. Paul seeks to provide them with the necessary guidance to bring them (and us) to full maturity. * Over 30 hours of Verse-by-Verse audio teaching through the books of I and II Corinthians as MP3 files. * Extensive searchable study notes as PDF files. * A special message from Chuck Missler. * Real? Player and Real? Juke Box. This program will play MP3 audio files. * Adobe Acrobat? Reader.This program will read the PDF notes. * Introduction and I Corinthians 1: Background on the city and church at Corinth. Divisions in the Church. Wisdom is God-given. * I Corinthians 2: Revelation comes from God's Spirit. A look at the "Natural Man" and the "Geometry of Eternity." * I Corinthians 3: We are laborers together with God. What are you building on Christ's foundation? * I Corinthians 4: The ministry of the Apostles, as well as our own stewardship. The Law vs. Grace. Effects of pride. * I Corinthians 5: Background on Jewish feasts. God's Judgment of Immorality. * I Corinthians 6: Going to Law before Unbelievers. The forfeit of the ungodly. God's astonishing Grace. * I Corinthians 7: "now concening marriage..." Was Paul married? The mystical basis of marriage. The cost of broken families. * I Corinthians 8: Food offered to idols. Liberty under Christ vs. love and compassion for the weaker brother. * I Corinthians 9: The rights of those who preach the Gospel. The responsibility of the Church to care for its ministers. * I Corinthians 10: Warnings against idolatry. Jesus as "The Rock." Do all to the glory of God. * I Corinthians 11: Proper decorum necessary for*

*worship. The Lord's Supper; Seven things to ingest. * I Corinthians 12: The spiritual gifts and our relationship with the Holy Spirit. Are the gifts for today? * I Corinthians 13: The Love chapter: Our most urgent essential. * I Corinthians 14: The gifts of tongues. Orderliness and individualism in worship. * I Corinthians 15-A: The Resurrection of the dead. The physics of immortality and the rapture of the Body of Christ.* I Corinthians 15-B & 16: The collection for the saints: The tithe. Paul's plans for travel. Final greetings. * II Corinthians 1: Salutation; Thanksgiving. The postponement of Paul's visit. * II Corinthians 2 & 3: Restoring a sinning saint. Being triumphant in Christ. Being ministers of the New Covenant. * II Corinthians 4: Living by faith. The secret of Endurance. * II Corinthians 5: The ministry of reconciliation. The Judgment Seat of Christ. * II Corinthians 6 & 7: Paul the Evangelist. Paul the example. "Be not unequally yoked." * II Corinthians 8 & 9: The grace of giving. Heaven's law of supply and demand. Stewardship. * II Corinthians 10 & 11: "Secrets" of the ministry. How to wage Spiritual Warfare.* II Corinthians 12 & 13: Paul's defense of his ministry. The thorn in the flesh. Final greetings.*

Corinthians I & II Commentary. deluxe ed. Chuck Missler. 24 cass. (Running Time: 36 hrs.). (Heirloom Edition Ser.). 1996. im. lthr. 89.95 Incls. notes. (978-1-880532-22-5(0)) Koinonia Hse.

***Coriolanus.** abr. ed. William Shakespeare. Read by Richard Burton & Jessica Tandy. (ENG.). 2003. (978-0-06-074324-6(7), Caedmon) HarperCollins Pubs.

***Coriolanus.** abr. ed. William Shakespeare. Read by Richard Burton & Jessica Tandy. (ENG.). 2004. (978-0-06-081466-3(7), Caedmon) HarperCollins Pubs.

Coriolanus. unabr. ed. William Shakespeare. Read by Paul Jesson et al. (Arkangel Shakespeare Ser.). (ENG.). 2006. audio compact disk 24.95 (978-1-932219-06-7(4)) Pub: AudioGO. Dist(s): Perseus Dist

Coriolanus. unabr. ed. William Shakespeare. Read by Audio Partners Staff. 2 cass. (Running Time: 3 hrs. 9 mins.). (Arkangel Shakespeare Ser.). 2004. 17.95 (978-1-932219-46-3(3), Atlntc Mnthly) Pub: Grove-Atltic. Dist(s): PerseuPGW

Coriolanus. unabr. ed. William Shakespeare. Perf. by Richard Burton & Jessica Tandy. 2 cass. Dramatization. 1984. HarperCollins Pubs.
Cast includes: Kenneth Haigh, Michael Hordern, Robert Stephens, Michael Gwynn, Martin Benson, Douglas Wilmer, Dafydd Havard, Llewellyn Rees, John Gayford, Neil Robinson, Eric Corrie, John Magnus, Roland Bartrop, Robert Seagrave, Alan Browning, Kenneth Bromfield, Robert St. Clair, W. F. McCormick, Colin Watson, Tam Bassett, Audrey Fairfax & Lynn Gordon.

Coriolanus. unabr. ed. William Shakespeare. Perf. by Richard Pasco & Fabia Drake. 3 cass. 19.95 (SCN 194) J Norton Pubs.
Set in Ancient Rome, this play derives from Sir Thomas North's translation of Plutarch's Lives. Shakespeare highlights the public & personal dilemma of a military genius who finds himself totally unfitted for peacetime politics.

Coriolanus, Set. unabr. ed. William Shakespeare. Read by Richard Burton & Jessica Tandy. 3 cass. (Running Time: 3 hrs. 30 mins.). Dramatization. 23.95 (H174) Blckstn Audio.
A brooding tragedy that is at once a searing indictment of human frailty & a darkly humorous nod at the absurdities of the political process.

Cork to Shannon. 1 cass. (Running Time: 1 hr. 30 min.). 12.95 (978-1-55606-024-3(6), CCI-457) Comp Comms Inc.
Features a tour through southwestern Ireland.

Cormac: The Tale of a Dog Gone Missing. Sonny Brewer. 2007. audio compact disk 19.99 (978-1-4281-7671-3(3)) Recorded Bks.

Cormac McCarthy Value Collection: All the Pretty Horses; The Crossing; Cities of the Plain. abr. ed. Cormac McCarthy. Read by Brad Pitt. 8 CDs. (Running Time: 8 hrs.). (Border Trilogy). (ENG.). 2005. audio compact disk 34.95 (978-0-7393-2067-9(X)) Pub: Random Audio Pubg. Dist(s): Random

Corn Belt. unabr. ed. Gail Taylor. Read by Gail Taylor. Ed. by James B. Kirgan. 1 cass. (Running Time: 1 hr. 30 min.). (Essence of Nature Ser.: Vol. 8). (J). 1989. 12.99 stereo. (978-1-878362-08-7(9)) Emerald Ent.
On this tape Thumper, the adventure dog, travels eastward across the country. This tape includes the actual sounds one hears while traveling through Illinois, Indiana & Ohio.

Corn (conclusion) see Twentieth-Century Poetry in English, No. 2, Recordings of Poets Reading Their Own Poetry

Corn Woman: Audio Stories & Legends of the Hispanic Southwest. Angel Vigil. 1 cass. (Running Time: 60 min.). (World Folklore Ser.). 1995. 12.00 (978-1-56308-394-5(9), A946) Libs Unl.
Selected tales recorded by the author in a shelf-ready case.

Corn Woman: Audio Stories & Legends of the Hispanic Southwest. Angel Vigil. Tr. by Juan F. Marin & Jennifer A. Lowell. 1 cass. (Running Time: 60 min.). (World Folkore Ser.). (SPA., 1995. 12.50 (978-1-56308-395-2(7), B946) Libs Unl.

Corn Woman: Audio Stories & Legends of the Hispanic Southwest. Angel Vigil. Read by Angel Vigil. Tr. by Juan F. Marin & Jennifer A. Lowell. 2 cass. (Running Time: 60 min. per cass.). (World Folklore Ser.). (ENG & SPA., 1995. 19.50 Set. (978-1-56308-396-9(5), X946) Libs Unl.

Corneilles de Toulonjac. l.t. ed. Alain Gandy. (French Ser.). 2001. bk. 30.99 (978-2-84011-391-1(0)) Pub: UlverLrgPrint GBR. Dist(s): Ulverscroft US

Cornelia de Lange Syndrome - A Bibliography & Dictionary for Physicians, Patients, & Genome Researchers. Compiled by Icon Group International, Inc. Staff. 2007. ring bd. 28.95 (978-0-497-11357-5(0)) Icon Grp.

Cornelius, the Little Dragon Book. Bob Hicks. Illus. by Bob Hicks. (J). 2004. ring bd. (978-0-9722036-5-4(6)) T E Pubng.

Corner Grocery Store. Perf. by Raffi. 1 cass. (Running Time: 1 hr.). (J). 2001. 10.95 (KSR 8107C); lp 10.95 (KSR 8107); audio compact disk 16.95 (KSR8107CD) Kimbo Educ.
You'll Sing a Song & I'll Sing a Song - Frere Jacques - Cluck, Cluck, Red Hen - Boom Boom, Good Night Irene, Popcorn & more.

Corner Grocery Store. Perf. by Raffi. 1 cass., 1 CD. (J). 7.98 (RDR 8053); audio compact disk 12.78 CD Jewel box. (RDR 8053) NewSound.

Corner Grocery Store. Perf. by Raffi. (Running Time: 29 mins.). (J). (978-1-886767-35-5(1)) Rounder Records.
Raffi's third album for children includes traditional songs such as "Frere Jacques" & "Swing Low, Sweet Chariot." Lively, rhythmic, funny, danceable & joyous.

Corner Grocery Store. Perf. by Raffi. (J). 1999. (978-1-886767-61-4(0)); audio compact disk (978-1-886767-34-8(3)); audio compact disk (978-1-886767-60-7(2)) Rounder Records.

Corner of Paradise. unabr. ed. Peter Davies. Read by Tim Davies. 3 cass. (Running Time: 4 hrs.). 2000. 34.95 (978-0-7531-0528-3(4), 990316) Pub: ISIS Audio GBR. Dist(s): Ulverscroft US
Davies recreates the sounds, sights & smells of rural Shropshire after the Second World War, encompassing the poignancy of young love & the tragic death of his father.

Corner of the Universe. unabr. ed. Ann M. Martin. 3 cass. (Running Time: 4 hrs. 30 mins.). (J). (gr. 4-7). 2004. 30.00 (978-0-8072-1671-2(2), Listening Lib); audio compact disk 35.00 (978-0-8072-1776-4(X), Listening Lib) Random Audio Pubg.

***Corner Office: Indispensable Lessons from CEOs on How to Lead & Succeed.** abr. ed. Adam Bryant. (Running Time: 5 hrs. 0 mins. 0 sec.). (ENG.). 2011. audio compact disk 19.99 (978-1-4272-1181-1(7)) Pub: Macmill Audio. Dist(s): Macmillan

Cornerstone: Ephesians 2:19-22. Ed Young. 1986. 4.95 (978-0-7417-1529-6(5), 529) Win Walk.

Cornerstone of Liberty: Property Rights in 21st Century America. unabr. ed. Timothy Sandefur. Read by Jeff Riggenbach. (Running Time: 21600 sec.). 2006. 34.95 (978-0-7861-4878-3(0)); audio compact disk 36.00 (978-0-7861-6042-6(X)); audio compact disk 29.95 (978-0-7861-7120-0(0)) Blckstn Audio.

Cornflakes by Candelight. Stan Crippen. 1 cass. 7.98 (978-1-55503-819-9(0), 06005144) Covenant Comms.
Creative dating ideas.

Cornish Childhood. unabr. ed. A. L. Rowse. Read by Bill Kelsey. 9 cass. (Running Time: 13 hrs. 30 mins.). 1942. 72.00 (978-0-7366-2163-2(6), 2962) Books on Tape.
An affectionate memoir that recalls the sights, sounds & special moments of childhood in Cornwall moments in a bygone era.

Cornish Maid. Rachel Moore. Read by Tanya Myers. 8. 2007. 69.95 (978-1-84652-129-4(7)); audio compact disk 84.95 (978-1-84652-130-0(0)) Pub: ISIS Audio GBR. Dist(s): Ulverscroft US

Cornish Rhapsody. Jean Long. Read by Marjorie Hayward. 4 cass. (Running Time: 6 hrs.). 1999. 44.95 (66952) Pub: Soundings Ltd GBR. Dist(s): Ulverscroft US

Cornishman Abroad. unabr. ed. A. L. Rowse. Read by Stuart Courtney. 10 cass. (Running Time: 15 hrs.). 1986. 80.00 (978-0-7366-0931-9(8), 1875) Books on Tape.
Third volume in the autobiography of A.L. Rowse, Elizabethan historian, poet & man of letters. It depicts Rowse's pilgrimage to France & Weimar Germany where he sought the culture unavailable to him in the working class home of his youth.

Cornishman at Oxford. unabr. ed. A. L. Rowse. Read by Bill Kelsey. 8 cass. (Running Time: 12 hrs.). 64.00 (978-0-7366-1055-1(3), 1982) Books on Tape.
Second part of A.L. Rowse's autobiography deals with his nervous arrival at Oxford on scholarship. He is persuaded to switch from literature to history - a momentous decision for Rowse & his readers.

Cornucopia Kids: Indulged Children Don't Achieve. Bruce A. Baldwin. Read by Bruce A. Baldwin. 1 cass. (Running Time: 40 min.). 1986. 7.95 (978-0-933583-01-6(X), PDC#870) Direction Dynamics.
Book on Tape: Chapter from "Beyond the Cornucopia Kids." Children given too much materially often remain emotionally immature & without achievement motivation, according to the author.

Coromandel Sea Change. unabr. ed. Rumer Godden. Read by Sam Dastor. 6 cass. (Running Time: 9 hrs.). 2000. 54.95 (SAB 027) AudioGO.

Corona de Adoración. Mariana Sá. (SPA.). 2008. audio compact disk 14.99 (978-987-01-0043-0(0)) Pub: Peniel ARG. Dist(s): Zondervan

Coronado. unabr. ed. Dennis Lehane. Read by Stanley Tucci. 3 CDs. (Running Time: 12600 sec.). 2006. audio compact disk 22.95 (978-0-06-114233-8(6), Harper Audio) HarperCollins Pubs.

***Coronado: Unabridged Stories.** unabr. ed. Dennis Lehane. Read by Stanley Tucci. (ENG.). 2006. (978-0-06-122930-5(X), Harper Audio); (978-0-06-122931-2(8), Harper Audio) HarperCollins Pubs.

Coronary Artery Disease: Bypass Angioplasty: Thrombolytic Therapy. 2 cass. (General Sessions Ser.: C84-GS1). 1984. 15.00 (8405) Am Coll Surgeons.

Coronation Street at War. unabr. ed. Daran Little. Read by Jean Alexander. 9 cass. (Running Time: 0.720). (Storysound Ser.). (J). 2001. 76.95 (978-1-85903-404-0(7)) Pub: Mgna Lrg Print GBR. Dist(s): Ulverscroft US

Coronation Summer. unabr. ed. Angela Thirkell. Read by Nadia May. 4 cass. (Running Time: 5 hrs. 30 mins.). 2002. 32.95 (978-0-7861-2194-6(7), 2941) Blckstn Audio.
The seventeen-year-old Fanny journeys from her native Norfolk to London, where she takes up residence with her close friend Emily Dacre (and her father as chaperone) in a Queen Street apartment for the six weeks of festivities surrounding Victoria's coronation.

***Coronilla A la Divina Misericordia.** Prod. by Marian Press Marian Press. (SPA.). 2002. audio compact disk 15.95 (978-1-59614-121-6(2)) Pub: Marian Pr. Dist(s): STL Dist NA

Coronilla a la Divina Misericordia (The Chaplet of Divine Mercy) Perf. by El Coro de San Carlos. 1 cass., 1 CD. (Running Time: 27 min.). (SPA.). 1999. 8.00 (978-1-884479-07-6(3)); audio compact disk 12.00 CD. (978-1-884479-08-3(1)) Spirit Song.
Christian religious songs.

Corporate Anointing: Understanding the Power of a United Body. Mac Hammond. 2009. audio compact disk 6.00 (978-1-57399-417-0(0)) Mac Hammond.

***Corporate Anointing, Vol 1: Activating the Greatest Power Source Available to the Church, Vol 1.** Mac Hammond. 2010. audio compact disk 52.00 (978-1-57399-451-4(0)) Mac Hammond.

***Corporate Anointing, Vol 2: Finding Your Place in the Body of Christ, Vol 2-5 CDs.** Mac Hammond. 2010. audio compact disk 30.00 (978-1-57399-464-4(2)) Mac Hammond.

***Corporate Anointing, Vol 3: How Your Prayer Life Can Affect the World, Vol 3 - 7 CDs.** Mac Hammond. 2010. audio compact disk 38.00 (978-1-57399-465-1(0)) Mac Hammond.

Corporate Athlete: How to Achieve Maximal Performance in Business & Life. Jack Groppel & Bob Andelman. Read by Jack Groppel. 2004. 10.95 (978-0-7435-1960-1(4)) Pub: S&S Audio. Dist(s): S and S Inc

Corporate Bodies. unabr. ed. Simon Brett. Read by Frederick Davidson. 5 cass. (Running Time: 7 hrs.). 1993. 39.95 (978-0-7861-0394-2(9), 1346) Blckstn Audio.
Charles Paris's star gig is as "forklift-driver-for-a-day" in a corporate video. Charles, dressed for the occasion in blue workman's overalls, must position the forklift & then declaim in the trained voice of an actor the wonders of the company & its big, happy family of employees. Charles delivers his lines with his usual aplomb, but he can't help wondering about the "happy family." There's something about the company that is deeply troubling. Mockery, jealousy, lust, envy - they all seem to be pervasive. Still, the work is easy & the pay is good for a couple of hours spouting platitudes. It's even rather fun to learn to manipulate a forklift. But it's a responsibility, too, as Charles learns to his horror: a forklift can be a tool for murder.

Corporate Bodies. unabr. ed. Simon Brett. Narrated by Simon Prebble. 5 cass. (Running Time: 6 hrs. 15 mins.). (Charles Paris Mystery Ser.: Vol. 15). 2000. 44.00 (978-1-55690-654-1(4), 92406E7) Recorded Bks.
Actor Charles Paris investigates a mysterious death on the set of his latest commercial, a corporate video hyping the dubious assets of an all natural snack bar called Delmoleen Green.

Corporate Coaching: Real World Accounts from HR Executives & Executive Coaches. Interview. 6 CDs. (Running Time: 6 hrs. 25 mins.). 2003. audio compact disk 39.50 (978-0-9743973-0-6(X)) HRNow.
This six-CD audio program is a terrific testimony for the POWER OF COACHING in the corporate arena, and an opportunity to eavesdrop on senior executives and corporate coaches as the discuss the real tactical and strategic challenges of coaching. Whether you are a human resources professional, corporate coach or head of your company. this is your chance to learn more about 15 major areas of coaching: current trends, meaningful metrics, effective sponsorship, strategic positioning, business alignment, boundary issues between human resources and coaches and also between coaches and consultants, internal vs. external coaching, technology impacts on coaching, confidentiality and liability issues, coaching fees, coach selection and qualifications, use of coaching pools and coordinated processes, coaching models and the use of assessments.

Corporate Combat. unabr. ed. William E. Peacock. Read by Jeff Riggenbach. 4 cass. (Running Time: 5 hrs. 30 mins.). 1993. 32.95 (978-0-7861-0429-1(5), 1381) Blckstn Audio.
Far from a simple overview of the basics, it details in more than 25 parallel military & corporate case histories many fundamental concepts of strategy. Moreover, the specific obstacles encountered & the strategies & tactics used to overcome them in the case histories are carefully analyzed.

Corporate Conscience. David Freudberg. 3 cass. (Running Time: 3 hrs.). 1984. 19.95 Set. (978-1-886373-03-7(5)) Human Media.
Case studies of creative problem solving for professionals facing questions of human responsibility & ethics on the job & suggestions on how to reduce conflicts, align personal & corporate objectives, increase morale & manage change.

Corporate Cultures: The Rites & Rituals of Corporate Life. Terrence E. Deal & Allan A. Kennedy. Read by Ann Dufresne. 6 cass. (Running Time: 1 hr. per cass.). 1990. 60.00 (978-0-942563-07-8(7)); Rental 15.00 (978-0-942563-08-5(5)) CareerTapes.
The authors find that a company's culture - its inner values, rites, rituals & heroes are more important in determining a firm's long term prosperity than are the rational aspects of management - financial planning, personnel policies, cost control & the like.

Corporate Environmentalism & Other Suicidal Tendencies. Richard M. Salsman. 1 cass. (Running Time: 1 hr. 30 min.). 1994. 12.95 (978-1-56114-399-3(5), HS15C) Second Renaissance.
Condemning the appeasement of environmentalism by business.

Corporate Financial Management: Emerging Trends & Recent Developments. Jonathan B. Schiff. 3 cass. bk. 129.00 set, incl. textbk. & quizzer. (CPE4670) Bisk Educ.
Get practical guidance on major adoption & implementation issues affecting companies today, & a clearer understanding of new developments on the horizon. The program focuses on Activity-Based Cost Management, Total Quality Management, & Internal Controls & Management Accounting.

Corporate Financial Reporting Issues. Paul Munter. 4 cass. 1994. 159.00 set incl. wkbk. & quizzer set, incl. textbk. & quizzer. (CPE1191); 199.00 video, incl. textbk. & quizzer. (CPE1190); 65.00 extra textbks. & quizzers. (CPE1192) Bisk Educ.
Featuring Dr. Paul Munter, the FICPA's 1993 Outstanding Educator, this program pays special attention to the impact of recent accounting & auditing developments on smaller companies, & includes coverage of recently-issued FASB's, SASs, & pronouncements from AcSEC & the EITF.

Corporate Governance: Current & Emerging Issues. 8 cass. (Running Time: 11 hrs. 30 min.). 1998. 275.00 Set; incl. study guide 830p. (MD39) Am Law Inst.
Advanced course examines contemporary issues, with special attention given to developments regarding the activities & responsibilities of institutional investors, executive compensation issues & practices, the effect of recent federal legislation on securities litigation, & important decisions in the Delaware courts.

Corporate Grammar. Margaret M. Bynam. 1 cass. (Running Time: 90 min.). 39.95 incl. ref bk. (1150, Lrn Inc) Oasis Audio.
Practical business-based instruction which can turn just about anyone into a perfect grammarian.

Corporate Grammar. unabr. ed. Eric W. Johnson. 1 cass. 39.95 Incl. assessment test, review-instruction guide, mastery measurement, reference manual. (S1800) J Norton Pubs.
Don't let grammatical errors hold you back in your career. Eliminate embarrassing errors from your speech & writing with this program developed exclusively for business people.

Corporate Income Tax Refresher Course, 1997. Sidney Kess & Barbara Weltman. 4 cass. (Running Time: 4 hrs.). 1996. 125.00 Set. (0912) Toolkit Media.
Provides up-to-date training in the preparation of the 1996 Form 1120. Reviews fundamentals for completing federal corporate tax forms & schedules. Includes study guide & quizzer for CPE credit.

Corporate Mergers & Acquisitions. 1 cass. (Running Time: 12 hrs.). 1999. 345.00 Incl. study guide. (AE12); 95.00 study guide. (SE12) Am Law Inst.

Corporate Practice for the Non-Specialist. 1990. 35.00 (AC-567) PA Bar Inst.

Corporate Records. Ed. by Socrates Media Editors. 2005. audio compact disk 29.95 (978-1-59546-085-1(3)) Pub: Socrates Med LLC. Dist(s): Midpt Trade

Corporate Resource Series. Robert C. Grupe. Read by Robert C. Grupe. 6 cass. (Running Time: 4 hrs. 30 min.). 1994. 49.95 Set. (978-0-9662278-1-9(6)) Grupe & Assocs.
Leadership skills, battling stress, effective meetings, creating a company vision, creating your employment future, understanding violence in the workplace.

Corporate Series. (ENG.). 2008. 137.47 (978-0-9792996-5-0(9)) Summit Dynamics.

Corporate Series. Created by Laura Boynton King. 6 CD's. 2002. audio compact disk 109.95 (978-0-9748885-3-8(2)) Summit Dynamics.
A 6-volume series that guides the user through lessons designed to lead to better public speaking and more motivation and success in both work and personal life.

Corporate Taxation. William L. Raby. 6 cass. 199.00 set, incl. textbk. & quizzer. (CPE0510) Bisk Educ.
Get comprehensive coverage of all key concepts related to federal taxation of corporations & their shareholders, including tax planning alternatives & pitfalls.

Corporate Taxation after the Tax Reform Act of 1986. Bernard D. Wolfman. 1987. 115.00 (978-1-55917-079-6(4)) Natl Prac Inst.

Corporate Training in Philippines: A Strategic Reference 2006. Compiled by Icon Group International, Inc. Staff. 2007. ring bd. 195.00 (978-0-497-82386-3(1)) Icon Grp.

Corporate Transformation: Revitalizing Organizations for a Competitive World. Ralph H. Kilmann et al. (Management Ser.). 1987. bk. 46.95 (978-1-55542-060-4(5), Jossey-Bass) Wiley US.

Corporate Warrior: Beat the Competition. Edward A. Wacks. Read by Edward A. Wacks. 1 cass. (Running Time: 45 min.). 1999. 11.95 (978-1-929843-04-6(6)) Map Pubs.
Based on the Martial Arts principles.

Corporation, Partnership & Other Filings under Title Fifteen. Read by Charles Ottaviano. 1 cass. 1989. 20.00 (AL-70) PA Bar Inst.

Corporations. Instructed by James D. Cox. 5 cass. (Running Time: 7 hrs. 50 min.). (Outstanding Professors Ser.). 1995. 49.95 Set. (978-0-940366-70-1(3)) Sum & Substance.
Lecture given by a prominent American law professor.

Corporations. 2nd ed. James D. Cox. 1999. Sum & Substance.

Corporations. 3rd rev. abr. ed. James D. Cox. (Sum & Substance Ser.). 2007. audio compact disk 74.00 (978-0-314-18819-9(3), West Lglwrks); audio compact disk 74.00 (978-0-314-18820-5(7), West Lglwrks) West.

Corporations 2006. Therese H. Maynard. 57.95 (978-0-314-16087-4(6), gilbert) West.

Corps en Acier. 1 cass. (Running Time: 1 hr.). 2000. 8.99; audio compact disk 12.99 Kidzup Prodns.
Encourages kids to exercise while having fun.

Corpse Had a Familiar Face: Covering Miami, America's Hottest Beat. unabr. collector's ed. Edna Buchanan. Read by Donada Peters. 8 cass. (Running Time: 12 hrs.). 1990. 64.00 (978-0-7366-1678-2(0), 2526) Books on Tape.
Nobody covers love & lunacy, life & death on Miami's mean streets better than Edna Buchanan, the Miami Herald's legendary police reporter. Winner of the Pulitzer Prize, Buchanan has seen it all, including over 5000 corpses. Many of them were people she had known. In The Corpse had a Familiar Face, she introduces us to misfits, the disenchanted, the evil, the wronged & the crazies. Her stories are reflections of a dynamic & troubled city in transition. Counterpoint to the murder & mayhem is the author's own story: a tough New Jersey childhood, her brief marriages, her longtime love affair with Miami & her grueling, fascinating work.

***Corpus Delicti.** Keith McCarthy. 2010. 69.95 (978-1-4450-0035-0(0)) Pub: Isis Pubng Ltd GBR. Dist(s): Ulverscroft US

***Corpus Delicti.** Keith Mccarthy. 2010. audio compact disk 89.95 (978-1-4450-0036-7(9)) Pub: Isis Pubng Ltd GBR. Dist(s): Ulverscroft US

Corpus of Cypriote Antiquities Vol. 25: Ancient Cypriote Art in the T. N. Zintilis Collection. Stella M. Lubsen-Admiraal. (Studies in Mediterranean Archaeology Ser.). (C). 2003. bk. 197.50 (978-91-7081-117-3(2)) Pub: P Astroms SWE. Dist(s): Coronet Bks

Corre a la Gracia. unabr. ed. Claudio Freidzon. (SPA.). 1999. 7.99 (978-0-8297-2489-9(3)) Pub: Vida Pubs. Dist(s): Zondervan

Correction Course. (Paws & Tales Ser.: Vol. 7). (J). 2001. 3.99 (978-1-57972-398-9(5)); audio compact disk 5.99 (978-1-57972-399-6(3)) Insight Living.

Corrections. Jonathan Franzen. Narrated by George Guidall. 19 CDs. (Running Time: 22 hrs.). audio compact disk 154.00 (978-1-4025-3086-9(2)) Recorded Bks.

Corrections. abr. ed. Jonathan Franzen. 2004. 21.95 (978-0-7435-4528-0(1)) Pub: S&S Audio. Dist(s): S and S Inc

Corrections. unabr. ed. Jonathan Franzen. Narrated by George Guidall. 15 cass. (Running Time: 22 hrs.). 2002. 127.00 (978-1-4025-0744-1(5), 96911) Recorded Bks.
Statistically, the Lamberts may be a typical Midwestern family. But in reality, they are far from it. Alfred, the father, is losing his fight to control Parkinson's Disease and dementia. His wife, Enid, no longer in control of her household, feels her choices slipping away. Their three grown children are struggling with their own clashes between dreams and disasters. But for one Christmas, Enid is determined to bring them together for the ideal family holiday.

Correlative Clinic: Case No. 1 - Management of Chronic Pancreatitis & Its Complications. 1 cass. (General Sessions Ser.: C85-SP8-A). 7.50 (8550) Am Coll Surgeons.

Correlative Clinic: Case No. 1 - The Diagnosis & Management of Thelicute Abdomen. Instructed by Isidore Cohn, Jr. 1 cass. (Spring Sessions Ser.: SP-9(A)). 1986. 9.50 (8680) Am Coll Surgeons.

Correlative Clinic: Case No. 2 - Management of the Multiple Injury Patient: Diagnostic & Therapeutic Advances. 1 cass. (General Sessions Ser.: C85-SP8-B). 7.50 (8551) Am Coll Surgeons.

Correlative Clinic: Case No. 2 - Penetrating Cardiac Trauma - Action & Reaction. Moderated by Watts R. Webb. 1 cass. (Spring Sessions Ser.: SP-9(B)). 1986. 9.50 (8681) Am Coll Surgeons.

Corremos. Alma Flor Ada. 1 cass. (Running Time: 33 min.). (SPA.). (J). 1987. 3.93 (978-0-201-16872-3(3)) Pearson ESL.

Correspondance avec Mme du Deffand, Set. Francois Voltaire, pseud. Read by Daniel Mesguich & Sophie Chaveau. 2 cass. (FRE.). 1991. 28.95 (1495-TH) Olivia & Hill.
Mme du Deffand was one of the most celebrated women of the 18th century whose salon was frequented by society & the philosophers.

***Corrido for Billy.** Jane Candia Coleman. 2009. (978-1-60136-429-6(6)) Audio Holding.

Corrido for Billy the Kid. Jane Coleman. (Running Time: 0 hr. 12 mins.). 2000. 10.95 (978-1-60083-519-3(8)) Iofy Corp.

Corridor of Doom see Inner Sanctum: Three Classic Stories

Corridor of Doom & The Lonely Sleep. Perf. by Boris Karloff & Karl Swenson. 1 cass. (Running Time: 60 min.). Dramatization. (Inner Sanctum Mystery Ser.). 6.00 Once Upon Rad.
Mystery & suspense radio broadcasts.

Corridors of Power. unabr. ed. C. P. Snow. Read by John MacDonald. 8 cass. (Running Time: 12 hrs.). (Strangers & Brothers Ser.). 1985. 64.00 (978-0-7366-0444-4(8), 1418) Books on Tape.
Roger Quaife, a tough, adroit & ruthless English politician wants to do something worthwhile with power once he has won it. He decides to take Great Britain out of the nuclear arms race.

Corrie Ten Boom. abr. ed. Sam Wellman. 1 cass. (Running Time: 1 hrs. 30 min.). (Heroes of the Faith Ser.). (C). 4.97 (978-1-57748-091-4(0)) Barbour Pub.

Corriendo para Ganar. Funky. (SPA.). 2007. 17.99 (978-0-8297-5214-4(5)) Zondervan.

Corrugated Carton, Kraft Paper, Kraft Liner Paper, & Corrugated Carton Boxes in Dominican Republic: A Strategic Reference 2006. Compiled by Icon Group International, Inc. Staff. 2007. ring bd. 195.00 (978-0-497-35914-0(6)) Icon Grp.

Corrupting Influences: Achieving Prosperity Through Understanding the Laws of Leaven. Mac Hammond. 1 cass. (LAWS That Govern Prosperity Ser.: Vol. 4). 1997. 42.00 (978-1-57399-042-4(6)) Mac Hammond.
Teaching on how to avoid things that corrupt.

Corrupting Moth: Matthew 6:19-21. Ed Young. (J). 1979. 4.95 (978-0-7417-1043-7(9)) Win Walk.

Corruption of Blood. unabr. ed. Robert K. Tanenbaum. Read by Connor O'Brien. 10 cass. (Running Time: 15 hrs.). (Butch Karp Mystery Ser.). 1998. 80.00 (978-0-7366-4045-9(2), 4544) Books on Tape.
When Congress reopens the JFK case, Manhattan A.D.A. Butch Karp is tapped to head the investigation. But barely has he left home for the nation's capital when he finds himself facing Washington power-plays at their most cynical. The message from above is clear: Rehash the Warren Commission's dubious lone-gunman conclusion & bury any new discoveries. When the going gets tough & the dense fog of conspiracy settles on the case, Butch will need the help of his wife, the former Marlene Ciampi. But key evidence is disappearing without a trace & the husband & wife team will have to work fast.

Corsair. abr. ed. Clive Cussler & Jack Du Brul. (Running Time: 7 hrs.). No. 6. (ENG.). (gr. 12 up). 2009. audio compact disk 29.95 (978-0-14-314416-8(2), PengAudBks) Penguin Grp USA.

Corsair. unabr. ed. Clive Cussler & Jack Du Brul. Read by Scott Brick. 11 CDs. (Running Time: 14 hrs.). No. 6. (ENG.). (gr. 12 up). 2009. audio compact disk 39.95 (978-0-14-314415-1(4), PengAudBks) Penguin Grp USA.

***Corsair.** unabr. ed. Clive Cussler & Jack Du Brul. 11 CDs. (Running Time: 13 hrs. 30 mins.). 2009. audio compact disk 129.00 (978-1-4159-6262-6(6), BksonTape) Pub: Random Audio Pubg. Dist(s): Random

***Corsario Negro.** abr. ed. Emilio Salgari. Read by Daniel Quintero. (SPA.). 2009. audio compact disk 17.00 (978-958-8318-97-4(1)) Pub: Yoyo Music COL. Dist(s): YoYoMusic

Corse sans Peine. (FRE.). 2000. bk. 75.00 (978-2-7005-1344-8(4)) Pub: Assimil FRA. Dist(s): Distribks Inc

Corsican Honor. abr. ed. William Heffernan. Read by Harry Hamlin. 2 cass. (Running Time: 3 hrs.). 1992. 7.95 Set. (978-1-57815-036-6(1), 1003) Media Bks NJ.

Cortina Cassette French. R. D. Cortina. 5 cass. (Running Time: 60 min. per cass.). (FRE.). 1980. 79.95 (978-0-8489-6052-0(1)) Cortina.
Contains exercises centered around situations such as hotel, shopping, etc.

Cortina Traveler's French Course. 2 cass. (Running Time: 60 min. per cass.). bk. 17.95 (978-0-8489-6824-3(7)) Cortina.
Minidialogues followed by pointers on pronunciation, new vocabulary, grammar & idioms.

Coruscation Drain. Poems. John M. Bennett & Ficus Strangulensis. Read by John M. Bennett & Ficus Strangulensis. 1 cass. (Running Time: 1 hr.). 1993. 6.00 (978-0-935350-55-5(1)) Luna Bisonte.
Avant-garde poetry & texts with improvised music.

Corvette, Set. unabr. ed. Richard Woodman. Read by Jeremy Sinden. 6 cass. (Running Time: 8 hrs. 15 min.). (Nathaniel Drinkwater Ser.: Bk. 5). 1992. 49.00 (978-1-55690-679-4(X), 92331) Recorded Bks.
In 1802, the routine convoy duty of a fleet of whaleships leads to treachery, drama & violent action on the Arctic Ocean, as Captain Nathaniel Drinkwater battles with the elements & the enemy.

Cory & the Horned Toad. Blaine Yorgason & Brenton Yorgason. Read by Marvin Payne. 1 cass. (Gospel Power Ser.). 6.95 (978-0-929985-52-7(4)) Jackman Pubng.
A father's letter to his son regarding the concept that Heavenly Father can help us with any problem.

Corza Blanca y la Cruz del Diablo: Beginning Level. (Leer y Aprender Ser.). (SPA.). pap. bk. 15.95 (978-88-7754-511-4(9), CID5119) Pub: Cideb ITA. Dist(s): Continental Bk

Cosas Poderosas. unabr. ed. Coalo Zamorano. 2004. audio compact disk 14.99 (978-0-8297-4592-4(0)) Zondervan.
Song List: Eres fiel, Digno de gloria, Cosas poderosas, Mi vida eres tu, Quien como el Senor?, Con humildad, Solo tu, Mas de Ti, Por quien eres tu, Venimos a adorarte.

Cosecha. Mostaza. 1 CD. (Running Time: 1 hr. 30 min.). 2002. audio compact disk 9.99 (978-0-8297-3762-2(6)) Zondervan.
Latin Christian tunes.

Cosecha. unabr. ed. Mostaza. (SPA.). 2002. 9.99 (978-0-8297-3764-6(2)) Pub: Vida Pubs. Dist(s): Zondervan

Cosi Fan Tutte: An introduction to Mozart's Opera. Thomson Smillie. Read by David Timson. (Opera Explained Ser.). 2003. audio compact disk 8.99 (978-1-84379-087-7(4)) NaxMulti GBR.

Cosi Fan Tutti. unabr. ed. Michael Dibdin. Read by Michael Kitchen. 8 cass. (Running Time: 8 hrs.). (Aurelio Zen Mystery Ser.). 1997. 69.95 (978-0-7540-0026-6(5), CAB 1449) AudioGO.
Aurelio Zen finds himself in Naples, in disgrace - & having the time of his life! Like the rest of Italy, Naples is concerned about its image & is trying to clean up its act. Unfortunately, it seems that someone is taking this too literally; as corrupt politicians, shady businessmen & eminent Mafiosi start disappearing off the streets at an alarming rate.

Cosi Fan Tutti, Set. unabr. ed. Michael Dibdin. Read by Michael Kitchen. 8 cass. (Aurelio Zen Mystery Ser.). 1999. 69.95 (CAB 1449) AudioGO.

Cosmetic & Personal Care Electronic Handbook. Michael Ash & Irene Ash. (Gower Chemical Reference Ser.). 1994. audio compact disk 395.00 (978-0-566-07563-6(6)); audio compact disk 395.00 (978-0-566-07565-0(2)) Ashgate Pub Co.

Cosmetics & Beauty Products in Japan: A Strategic Reference 2007. Compiled by Icon Group International, Inc. Staff. 2007. ring bd. 195.00 (978-0-497-82324-5(1)) Icon Grp.

Cosmetics & Toiletries in China: A Strategic Reference 2006. Compiled by Icon Group International, Inc. Staff. 2007. ring bd. 195.00 (978-0-497-35872-3(7)) Icon Grp.

Cosmetics & Toiletries in France: A Strategic Reference 2006. Compiled by Icon Group International, Inc. Staff. 2007. ring bd. 195.00 (978-0-497-35947-8(2)) Icon Grp.

Cosmetics & Toiletries in Hong Kong: A Strategic Reference 2006. Compiled by Icon Group International, Inc. Staff. 2007. ring bd. 195.00 (978-0-497-35998-0(7)) Icon Grp.

Cosmetics & Toiletries in Mexico: A Strategic Reference 2006. Compiled by Icon Group International, Inc. Staff. 2007. ring bd. 195.00 (978-0-497-82351-1(9)) Icon Grp.

Cosmetics & Toiletries in Panama: A Strategic Reference 2006. Compiled by Icon Group International, Inc. Staff. 2007. ring bd. 195.00 (978-0-497-82379-5(9)) Icon Grp.

***Cosmic.** unabr. ed. Frank Cottrell Boyce. Read by Kirby Heyborne. (ENG.). 2010. (978-0-06-196748-1(3)); (978-0-06-193823-8(8)) HarperCollins Pubs.

Cosmic Banditos: A Contrabandista's Quest for the Meaning of Life. unabr. ed. Weisbecker, Allan C Weisbecker. (Running Time: 1 hr. 0 mins.). (ENG.). 2009. 29.95 (978-1-4417-0028-5(5)); 44.95 (978-1-4417-0024-7(2)); audio compact disk 55.00 (978-1-4417-0025-4(0)) Blckstn Audio.

Cosmic Chants. 1 cass. (Running Time: 1 hr.). 9.95 (CC) Nada Prodns.
Hare Rama; Shree Ram; Jai Sita Ram; Ayodya Vasi; EhiMudam; Sada Shiva; Gouri Suta; Murali Krishna; Shiva Shiva Mahadeva; Shambhu Mahadeva; Jai Shiva Shankar; SambaSada Shiva; Om Bhagavan Jai Om Mata; Hara Hara Mahadeva.

***Cosmic Christmas.** unabr. ed. Max Lucado. Narrated by Tom Dooley. (ENG.). 2007. 6.99 (978-1-60814-742-7(8)) Oasis Audio.

Cosmic City Praise Songs CD. David C. Cook Publishing Company Staff. (Vbs 2008 Ser.). (J). 2007. audio compact disk 12.99 (978-2-608-00985-2(9)) David C Cook.

Cosmic Codes. Chuck Missler. 8 CD set. (Running Time: 8 hours). (Briefing Packages by Chuck Missler). 2004. audio compact disk 49.95 (978-1-57821-267-5(7)) Koinonia Hse.
*Hidden Messages from the Edge of Eternity * Scientists continue to scan the heavens for a message from "out there." * Have we already received a message of extraterrestrial origin?* Why do some scientists believe that the Bible contains such messages?Chuck Missler explores the history of cryptology - the study of secret codes - and the background of proposed interstellar languages. Recent discoveries seem destined to impact each of us in ways that will eclipse all of our other priorities.This collection contains all four Cosmic Codes studies in eight audio CD's, as well as the Automated Multimedia CD-ROM which itself contains the all-new slideshows, downloadable software and the complete set of notes in PDF format. * Volume 1 - Introduction Chuck Missler reviews the history of cryptography - the study of secret codes - and the background of proposed interstellar languages. * Volume Two - Microcodes: An exploration of Microcodes, the unique qualities of Hebrew that make it codeable. * Volume Three - Macrocodes: A study of macrocodes, prophetic messages that God has given through symbolism and types.* Volume Four - Metacodes: A study of metacodes, the codes that God has placed in nature - signals from the tenth dimension and the code of life.Running Time: Approx 8 hours.*

Cosmic Codes Set on CD-ROM MP3: Hidden Messages from the Edge of Eternity. Chuck Missler. 1 MP3 CD-ROM. (Running Time: 8 hours). 2003. 29.95 (978-1-57821-224-8(3)) Koinonia Hse.
*Are we in possession of messages of extraterrestrial origin?If so, what do they mean?What do these messages from the edge of eternity portend for the future?What has the science of cryptology revealed about these ancient texts? Is our universe itself a "digital message"?Do these messages explain the interval between the miracle of our origin and the mystery of our destiny?Read the implications of our finite universe and the shocking discoveries of quantum physics at the very boundaries of reality and learn their significance to our origin and personal destinies!You will grow in excitement as Chuck Missler details astonishing hidden messages within the text of the Torah that could only have been placed there by the Great Author Himself. He explores the impact of information sciences on our understanding of ancient texts...including microcodes, macrocodes, and metacodes...as well as the highly controversial "equidistant letter sequences" discovered in the Bible. You will be able to use this exciting information to discover the hidden messages yourself because many of them do not require a computer to decipher.This CD-ROM contains all four Cosmic Codes audio studies as 8 individual MP3 files, comprehensive study notes and the all-new eight session Multimedia Slideshow Presentations . * Volume 1 - Introduction Chuck Missler reviews the history of cryptography - the study of secret codes - and the background of proposed interstellar languages. * Volume Two - Microcodes: An exploration of Microcodes, the unique qualities of Hebrew that make it codeable. * Volume Three - Macrocodes: A study of macrocodes, prophetic messages that God has given through symbolism and types.* Volume Four - Metacodes: A study of metacodes, the codes that God has placed in nature - signals from the tenth dimension and the code of life.*

***Cosmic Cow Pie... Connecting the Dots.** (ENG.). 2009. audio compact disk 24.95 (978-0-9841999-1-4(8)) CR Pr AZ.

Cosmic Creation Story. unabr. ed. Brian Swimme. 2 cass. 1986. 18.00 set. (978-1-56964-816-2(6), A0140-86) Sound Photosyn.
Smart & entertaining.

Cosmic Dream CD. Music by ThunderBeat ThunderVision Records. 2008. (978-0-9814651-8-0(8)) ThunderVision.

Cosmic Mandala. unabr. ed. Adi Da Avatar. Read by Adi Da Avatar. 1 cass. (Running Time: 70 min.). 1998. 11.95 (978-1-57097-000-9(9)) Dawn Horse Pr.
A discourse on the near death or after death process.

Cosmic Mind & the Submanifest Order of Being. abr. ed. Deepak Chopra. 1 CD. 2005. audio compact disk 10.95 (978-1-4019-0450-0(5)) Hay House.

Cosmic Music of the Harmonic Choir. 1 cass. (Running Time: 30 min.). 9.95 (C0650B090, HarperThor) HarpC GBR.

Cosmic Plan. George King. 1. (Running Time: 2 hrs.). 2005. audio compact disk 12.50 (978-0-937249-20-8(3)) Aetherius Soc.

Cosmic Power of the Elohim of the Violet Ray. Sai Maa Lakshmi Devi. 2002. audio compact disk 22.00 (978-1-933488-13-4(1)) HIU Pr.
This special, limited edition CD was created by Sai Maa Lakshmi Devi as a gift for those who seek Mastery. Sai Maa gives profound teachings on the use of the Violet Ray, "the most powerful transmuting shakti," which releases one from human creation and develops Ascended Master Consciousness.Recorded in Bordeaux, France May 2003"Anyone who has been around Maa for more than 4 minutes should own this CD." Aaron Anderson, D.C., Redding, CA, Humanity in Unity2 Versions on this CD: Spoken & Spoken with Music.

Cosmic Voices Audio Set; A Guided Meditation for Vibrational Medicine Cards & Gaia Matrix Oracle. Rowena P. Kryder. 3 cass. 1997. 30.00 Set. (978-0-9624716-4-3(X)) Golden Point Prod.

Cosmic Voyage: A Scientific Discovery of Extraterrestrials Visiting Earth. unabr. ed. Courtney Brown. Read by Connor O'Brien. 7 cass. (Running Time: 10 hrs. 30 mins.). 1997. 56.00 (978-0-913369-48-7(9), 4252) Books on Tape.
He reveals surprising new data about alien visitors & discusses the essence of the human soul.

Cosmobiology & Uranian Astrology. Edward Kluska. 1 cass. 7.95 (198) Am Fed Astrologers.
Enhance ability to interpret & forecast with 90 degree dial.

Cosmobiology in Contrast with the Uranian System. Steve Pincus. 1 cass. 8.95 (279) Am Fed Astrologers.
Compare methods underlying dial-oriented schools of Astrology.

Cosmogenesis & Anthropogeny: The Creation of the Universe & Man. Louise Fimlaid. (YA). 1999. pap. bk. & wbk. ed. 80.00 (978-0-9630409-5-4(2)) Galaxy Pub.

Cosmology & Mythic Imagination: The Inner Reaches of Outer Space. unabr. ed. Joseph Campbell. 1 cass. (Joseph Campbell Collection). 1983. 11.00 (00426) Big Sur Tapes.
Campbell delves into the mysteries of our modern scientific cosmologies - the Big Bang, the expansion of space, relativity. His astonishment & awe of the cosmos lead him to see that "this is the secret of all myth: the imagery of myth is supplied from the out-of-the-world, outer world, outer space. It comes by way of the senses to the mind. But the image does not become mythologized until it meets the message from the heart".

Cosmology of Inner Space: The Gnostic Vision in Jung's Psychology & the World Today. 5 cass. (Running Time: 6 hrs. 15 min.). 1993. 39.95 set. (978-0-7822-0430-8(9), GNOSTIC) C G Jung IL.
Symposium.

Cosmopolite in a Cafe see Favorite Stories by O. Henry

Cosmos. Contrib. by Send. Prod. by Aaron Sprinkle & Steve Wilson. 2007. audio compact disk 13.99 (978-5-557-67273-3(7)) Tooth & Nail.

Cosmos As Myth & Human Possibility. Robert Moore. Read by Robert Moore. 5 cass. (Running Time: 6 hrs. 25 min.). 1992. 38.95 set. (978-0-7822-0398-1(1), 497) C G Jung IL.
Jungian analyst & author Robert Moore (King, Warrior, Magician, Lover) leads a workshop examining the cross-cultural mythology of the struggle for Cosmos, for a just & peaceful world order, a struggle that has fascinated our forebears for thousands of years.

Cosmos Reprints. Ed. by Marco A. V. Bitetto. 1 cass. 2000. (978-1-58578-041-9(3)) Inst of Cybernetics.

Cossacks. 2006. 44.95 (978-0-7861-4433-4(5)); audio compact disk 55.00 (978-0-7861-7377-8(7)) Blckstn Audio.

Cossacks. unabr. ed. Leo Tolstoy. Read by David Thorn. 2006. 29.95 (978-0-7861-7752-3(7)) Blckstn Audio.

Cossacks. unabr. ed. Leo Tolstoy. Read by Walter Zimmerman. 6 cass. (Running Time: 8 hrs.). 1984. 34.00 incl. album. (C-105) Jimcin Record.
One of the finest portrayals of the Russian people in all Russian literature. It is Tolstoy's best typical novel - the song of his youth.

Cossacks. unabr. collector's ed. Leo Tolstoy. Read by Walter Zimmerman. 8 cass. (Running Time: 8 hrs.). 1982. 48.00 (978-0-7366-3879-1(2), 9103) Books on Tape.
The young hero, Olenin, an educated aristocrat, comes to the Caucasus to find himself. He falls in love with a young Cossack girl, Maryanka. She shreds his cherished control & refinement & the desires she awakes in him take his emotions by storm.

Cost & Managerial Accounting. Melvin B. Seiden & Robert L. Monette. 6 cass. 199.00 set, incl. textbk. & quizzer. (CPE0100) Bisk Educ.
Provides a basic overview of cost & managerial accounting. Includes manufacturing cost elements, job order costing, allocation of service costs, ABC, standard costing, cost-volume-profit analysis & more. Includes numerous examples & illustrations.

Cost-Benefit & Cost-Effectiveness. Read by John M. Eisenberg. 1 cass. (Running Time: 90 min.). 1986. 12.00 (C8649) Amer Coll Phys.

Cost Engineering. Instructed by Forrest D. Clark. Prod. by American Chemical Society Staff. 5 cass. (Running Time: 6 hrs. 40 min.). 27.00 manual. Am Chemical.
Explains the intricates of project planning, budgeting, & control. Listeners will learn how management teams are organized & how to participate & contribute to these teams. Other topics include types of estimates & estimate accuracy; estimating methods, coding, escalation, & contingency; & cost control during conceptual engineering, detailed engineering, & construction.

Cost of Collusion. Created by Louise LeBrun. (Women & Power Ser.: Vol. 6). 1999. 10.95 (978-0-9685566-5-8(5)) Par3tners Renewal CAN.

Cost of Dinner: Early Explorers Fluent Set B Audio CD. Danielle S. Hammelef. Adapted by Benchmark Education Staff. (J). 2007. audio compact disk 10.00 (978-1-4108-8252-3(7)) Benchmark Educ.

Cost of Discipleship. Peter Kreeft et al. Read by Peter Kreeft et al. 6 cass. 29.95 Set. (150-C) Ignatius Pr.
Outlines what it means to live as a Catholic in today's world & explains what is at stake when Christians profess their Faith.

Cost of Discipleship. unabr. ed. Dietrich Bonhhoeffer. Narrated by Paul Michael. (Running Time: 9 hrs. 0 mins. 0 sec.). (ENG.). 2009. lp 19.98 (978-1-59644-669-4(2), Hovel Audio) christianaud.

Cost of Discipleship. unabr. ed. Dietrich Bonhhoeffer. Read by Paul Michael. (Running Time: 9 hrs. 0 mins. 0 sec.). (ENG.). 2009. audio compact disk 28.98 (978-1-59644-668-7(4), Hovel Audio) christianaud.

***Cost of Discipleship.** unabr. ed. Dietrich Bonhoeffer. Narrated by Paul Michael. (ENG.). 2009. 16.98 (978-1-59644-670-0(6), Hovel Audio) christianaud.

Cost of Faithfulness: Hebrews 11:33-40. 1992. 4.95 (978-0-7417-1933-1(9), 933) Win Walk.

Cost of the Firm. unabr. ed. Murray Newton Rothbard. 1 cass. (Running Time: 1 hr. 28 min.). (Introduction to Free Market Economics Ser.). 12.95 (306) J Norton Pubs.
Topics discussed include: revenue, cost & profit; "cost-plus;" the science of welfare economics.

Cost, Quality & Access in Health Care: New Roles for Health Planning in a Competitive Environment. Frank A. Sloan. Ed. by James F. Blumstein & James M. Perrin. (Health Management Ser.). 1988. bk. 47.00 (978-1-55542-094-9(X), Jossey-Bass) Wiley US.

Cost to Be Wise. Maureen McHugh. Read by Vanessa Hart. (ENG.). 2007. audio compact disk 17.99 (978-1-884612-75-6(X)) AudioText.

Costa Rican Rainforest Artist Rosita Gottlieb & Kenya's "Rhino Man" Michael Werikhe. Hosted by Nancy Pearlman. 1 cass. (Running Time: 29 min.). 10.00 (1012) Educ Comm CA.

Costello Syndrome - A Bibliography & Dictionary for Physicians, Patients, & Genome Researchers. Compiled by Icon Group International, Inc. Staff. 2007. ring bd. 28.95 (978-0-497-11358-2(9)) Icon Grp.

Costly Anointing. unabr. ed. Lori Wilke. Read by Tom Wilke. 2 cass. (Running Time: 3 hrs.). 1998. 12.98 Set. (978-1-891916-03-8(3)) Spirit To Spirit.
An in-depth study of God's anointing.

Costume de L'empereur. (Plaisir de Lire Ser.). 5.95 (978-88-8148-704-2(7)) EMC-Paradigm.

Cotillion. abr. ed. Georgette Heyer. Read by Clare Wille. (Running Time: 5 hrs.). 2009. audio compact disk 28.98 (978-962-634-897-0(6), Naxos AudioBooks) Naxos.

Cotillion. unabr. ed. Georgette Heyer. Read by Phyllida Nash. 10 cass. (Running Time: 12 hrs. 45 mins.). 2000. 84.95 (978-0-7540-0454-7(6), CAB 1877) Pub: Chivers Audio Bks GBR. Dist(s): AudioGO
The three great nephews of Mr. Penicuik know better than to ignore his summons, especially when it concerns the bestowal of his fortune. The wily old gentleman has hatched a freakish plan for his stepdaughter's future: his fortune will by Kitty's dowry. But while the nephews are scrambling for her hand, Kitty has other ideas.

Cotswold Killing. unabr. abr. ed. Rebecca Tope. Read by Caroline Lennon. 8 cass. (Running Time: 37800 sec.). (Soundings Ser.). 2006. 69.95 (978-1-84559-106-9(2)) Pub: ISIS Lrg Prnt GBR. Dist(s): Ulverscroft US

Cotswold Mystery. Rebecca Tope. 2009. 69.95 (978-1-4079-0016-2(1)); audio compact disk 84.95 (978-1-4079-0017-9(X)) Pub: Soundings Ltd GBR. Dist(s): Ulverscroft US

Cotswold Ordeal. unabr. ed. Rebecca Tope. Read by Caroline Lennon. 8 cass. (Soundings Ser.). 2007. 69.95 (978-1-84559-396-4(0)) Pub: ISIS Lrg Prnt GBR. Dist(s): Ulverscroft US

Cottage. unabr. ed. Danielle Steel. Read by David Garrison. 6 cass. (Running Time: 9 hrs.). 2002. 44.95 (978-0-7366-8439-2(5)) Books on Tape.
Cooper Winslow is a movie star on the decline who finds that, out of economic necessity, he has to rent out rooms in his enormous Bel Air estate called The Cottage. Unforeseen events change people's lives in unexpected ways, and this proves to be the case with his new tenants. Mark's wife has walked out, and Jimmy's wife has died of a devastating illness. When Mark brings his teenagers to stay, they bring their loud music and careening skateboards, which do not mix with the daily parade of starlets to see Coop. Unforeseeably, the three men become friends, and a new woman lodger may have long-term potential for Coop. The rental may well change Coop's life in...unexpected ways.

Cottage in Portugal. unabr. collector's ed. Richard Hewitt. Read by Michael Russotto. 7 cass. (Running Time: 10 hrs. 30 mins.). 1997. 56.00 (978-0-7366-3560-8(2), 4205) Books on Tape.
The dream of a place of their own, far removed from the rigors of urban New England, prompts Richard & Barbara Hewitt to buy a 300-year-old cottage in a Portuguese village. Their adventures in renovating the cottage take on a surreality that is both funny & moving.

Cottontail at Clover Crescent. C. Drew Lamm. Illus. by Allen Davis. Narrated by Alexi Komisar. 1 cass. (Smithsonian's Backyard Ser.). (J). (ps-2). 1995. 5.00 (978-1-56899-113-9(4), C5005) Soundprints.
In a soft, safe nest behind the green house on Clover Crescent, Cottontail covers her bunnies with a blanket of leaves. Then she is off to eat, always watching for dangerous nighttime predators! But soon, she encounters another cottontail. Together they leap & twist as if dancing under the spring moon. What can all this frolic be?.

Cottontale Christmas & the Cottontail Farm. deluxe unabr. ed. Patricia H. Wallace. 1 cass. (Running Time: 1 hr.). (J). 2000. lib. bdg. 12.00 (978-0-932079-03-9(2)) TimeFare AudioBks.

Could Anything Be Worse? 2004. 8.95 (978-1-56008-877-6(X)); cass. & flmstrp 30.00 (978-1-56008-655-0(6)) Weston Woods.

Could Anything Be Worse? (J). 2004. pap. bk. 14.95 (978-1-56008-184-5(8)) Weston Woods.

Could I Forget. unabr. ed. Denise Robins. Read by Elizabeth Henry. 7 cass. (Running Time: 10 hrs. 30 min.). 1993. 61.95 (978-1-85496-806-7(8), 68068) Pub: UlverLrgPrint GBR. Dist(s): Ulverscroft US
Laura had never liked young Dr. Marsh, for when he came to the Yorkshire moors, her father's medical practice suffered. After her father died, loyalty & pride stood between them until the rising tide of Philip Marsh's love began to weaken her defenses.

Could I Forget, Set. Denise Robins. Read by Elizabeth Henry. 7 cass. 1999. 61.95 (68068) Pub: Soundings Ltd GBR. Dist(s): ISIS Pub

Could It Be Verse?, Pt. B. (23321) J Norton Pubs.

***Council of Dads.** unabr. ed. Bruce Feiler. Read by Bruce Feiler. (ENG.). 2010. (978-0-06-199296-4(8), Harper Audio) HarperCollins Pubs.

***Council of Dads: My Daughters, My Illness, & the Men Who Could Be Me.** unabr. ed. Bruce Feiler. Read by Bruce Feiler. (ENG.). 2010. (978-0-06-199295-7(X), Harper Audio) HarperCollins Pubs.

Council of Dads: My Daughters, My Illness, & the Men Who Could Be Me. unabr. ed. Bruce S. Feiler. Read by Bruce S. Feiler. 2010. audio compact disk 29.99 (978-0-06-198849-3(9), Harper Audio) HarperCollins Pubs.

Counseling: Visualizing & Guiding Energy Expression. Doris C. Doane. 1 cass. 8.95 (610) Am Fed Astrologers.
An AFA Convention workshop tape.

Counseling & Psychotherapy with Adolescents, Set. unabr. ed. 6 cass. (Running Time: 80 min.). 49.50 (SO6006) J Norton Pubs.
Program to help adults develop or improve their skills to give away every adolescent special consideration.

Counseling Business Clients on Insurance Issues. 1989. 45.00 (AC-498) PA Bar Inst.

Counseling Clients in the Entertainment Industry: Music, Personal & Business Management-Development of an Entertainment Law Practice, Film & Television. unabr. ed. Contrib. by Martin E. Silfen. 12 cass. 50.00 course handbk. (T6-9087) PLI.

Counseling Demonstration with Preadolescents. unabr. ed. Rudolf Dreikurs. 1 cass. (Running Time: 53 min.). 10.95 (29137) J Norton Pubs.
Demonstration of group counseling with 4 boys & 4 girls, ages 11-12.

Counseling Distressed Hospitals. 1989. 85.00 (AC-536) PA Bar Inst.

Counseling for Nutrition Therapists: Frequently Asked Questions. Interview. 1 CD. (Running Time: 1 hr.). 2006. 15.00 (978-1-933944-01-2(3)) Kg Pr.

Counseling Medical Professionals & Their Practices. (Running Time: 9 hrs. 30 min.). 1995. 175.00 Incl. 428p. coursebk. (2074) NYS Bar.
This series of presentations addresses many of the current legal, regulatory, financial & operational issues on which attorneys & accountants are asked for advice & guidance by their health care practitioners/providers-clients. Half of the recording is devoted to "formation & retirement" issues & the second half concentrates on recent statutory & regulatory developments in the health care field that affect how the medical practitioner guides & delivers care & service to his or her patients.

Counseling Small Businesses. 1999. bk. 99.00 (ACS-2163) PA Bar Inst.
This two-volume set of books serves as an introduction for new lawyers & a review & update for general practitioners. It addresses in a "nuts & bolts," practical fashion every major issue that can arise in counseling a small business, from formation to dissolution.

Counseling Techniques. Jessie L. Nagle. 1 cass. 1992. 8.95 (1074) Am Fed Astrologers.

Counseling the Biblical Way: 2007 CCEF Annual Conference. Featuring CCEF Faculty. 2007. audio compact disk 11.99 (978-1-934885-21-5(5)) New Growth Pr.

Counseling the Elderly. Contrib. by Paul W. Armstrong et al. (Running Time: 4 hrs.). 1983. 85.00 incl. program handbook. NJ Inst CLE.
Covering such topics as public entitlements, pension & senior citizen care, health care benefits & health facilities, home equity, age discrimination.

Counseling the Fiduciary. 1999. bk. 99.00 (ACS-1365) PA Bar Inst.
Unique issues face lawyers who represent trustees, executors & guardians. Ethical dilemmas often arise in representing a fiduciary. Who is the client? Does the fiduciary's lawyer have any duty to the beneficiary?.

Counseling the Older Client on Trusts & Nursing Home Issues. Contrib. by Clifton B. Kruse, Jr. 6 cass. (Running Time: 6 hrs.). 1997. 75.00 Set; incl. study outlines. (M208/M209/M210) Am Law Inst.
Series of advanced programs consists of three titles "Special Needs Trusts: Administering, Advising, & Representing the Trustee;" "Advising Your Client on Nursing Home Issues;" & "Creating Supplemental Care, Self-Settled, Pooled Account, or Revocable Trusts for Elderly Clients." The series planning chair & moderator was Clifton B. Kruse, Jr. of Colorado Springs. Recorded from live teleseminar presentations.

Counselling the Poor Performer, Incl. tape. Hugh Fitzwilliams. 1991. audio compact disk 65.95 (978-0-566-02967-7(7), Gower Pubng) Pub: Ashgate Pub GBR. Dist(s): Ashgate Pub

***Counselor.** abr. ed. Ted Sorensen. Read by Ted Sorensen. (ENG.). 2008. (978-0-06-163060-6(8)); (978-0-06-163061-3(6)) HarperCollins Pubs.

Counselor: A Life at the Edge of History. abr. ed. Ted Sorensen. Read by Ted Sorensen. 10 CDs. (Running Time: 12 hrs.). 2008. audio compact disk 39.95 (978-0-06-155754-5(4), Harper Audio) HarperCollins Pubs.

Counselor Training Program CD Series: Assisting Those with Same-Sex Attraction & Their Loved Ones. Richard Cohen. (ENG.). 2008. 350.00 (978-0-9637058-6-0(5)) Intl Healing.

Count Belisarius, Pt. A. unabr. collector's ed. Robert Graves. Read by Bill Kelsey. 7 cass. (Running Time: 10 hrs. 30 min.). 1988. 56.00 (978-0-7366-1437-5(0), 2321A) Books on Tape.
This is the story of Emperor Justinian's greatest general, who led the Imperial armies to the Eastern Frontier on the Euphrates, across the Mediterranean to Carthage & to Rome.

Count Belisarius, Pt. B. unabr. collector's ed. Robert Graves. Read by Bill Kelsey. 6 cass. (Running Time: 9 hrs.). 1988. 48.00 (978-0-7366-1438-2(9), 2321B) Books on Tape.

Count It All Joy. Contrib. by Susie Luchsinger. Prod. by Darrin Vincent. Contrib. by Ken Harding & Gaylea McDougal. 2005. audio compact disk 16.98 (978-5-559-07876-2(X)) Pt of Grace Ent.

Count Karlstein. unabr. ed. Philip Pullman. 5 CDs. (Running Time: 5 hrs. 32 mins.). (J). (gr. 4-7). 2006. audio compact disk 45.00 (978-0-307-28600-0(2), Listening Lib); 35.00 (978-0-307-28599-7(5), Listening Lib) Pub: Random Audio Pubg. Dist(s): Random
Can you hear the distant howling of hounds and the thunder of ghostly hooves? It's All Souls' Eve and Zamiel the Demon Huntsman has come to claim his prey! He's headed straight for Castle Karlstein, where the evil count has hatched an evil plan; he'll sacrifice his two young nieces to save himself. Can Lucy and Charlotte outwit their uncle and his oily henchmen to escape their dreadful fate?.

Count Karlstein. unabr. ed. Philip Pullman. (Running Time: 4 hrs.). (ENG.). (J). 2006. 17.50 (978-0-307-28400-6(X), Listening Lib) Pub: Random Audio Pubg. Dist(s): Random

Count Karlstein. unabr. ed. Philip Pullman. Read by Full Cast Production Staff & Jo Thurley. 5 CDs. (Running Time: 5 hrs. 32 mins.). (ENG.). (J). (gr. 3-7). 2006. audio compact disk 35.00 (978-0-307-28399-3(2), Listening Lib) Pub: Random Audio Pubg. Dist(s): Random

Count Magnus. unabr. ed. M. R. James. Read by Walter Covell. 1 cass. (Running Time: 52 min.). Dramatization. 1981. 7.95 (S-18) Jimcin Record.
Evil forces in strange forms.

Count of Monte Cristo see Conde de Monte Cristo

Count of Monte Cristo. Alexandre Dumas. Read by Richard Matthews. 2002. 240.00 (978-0-7366-8954-0(0)) Books on Tape.

Count of Monte Cristo. Alexandre Dumas. Read by Bill Homewood. (Running Time: 2 hrs. 30 mins.). 1999. 20.95 (978-1-60083-714-2(X)) Iofy Corp.

Count of Monte Cristo. Alexandre Dumas. Read by Bill Homewood. 2 CDs. (Running Time: 2 hrs. 30 mins.). (Works of Alexandre Dumas). 1995. audio compact disk 17.98 (978-962-634-039-4(8), NA203912, Naxos AudioBooks) Naxos.
Edmond Dante, a young, energetic sailor is falsely accused of treason on his wedding day and incarcerated. Tells of his escape and ultimate revenge on those who wronged him.

Count of Monte Cristo. Alexandre Dumas. Read by Bill Homewood. 2 cass. (Running Time: 2 hrs. 30 mins.). (Works of Alexandre Dumas). 1996. 13.98 (978-962-634-539-9(X), NA203914, Naxos AudioBooks) Naxos.
Edmond Dante, a young energetic sailor is falsely accused of treason on his wedding day and incarcerated. Tells of his escape and ultimate revenge on those who wronged him.

Count of Monte Cristo. Alexandre Dumas. 1 cass. (Running Time: 1 hr.). (Radiobook Ser.). 1987. 4.98 (978-0-929541-18-1(9)) Radiola Co.

Count of Monte Cristo. Alexandre Dumas. Read by David Case. (Running Time: 63000 sec.). (ENG.). 2006. audio compact disk 99.99 (978-1-4001-3210-2(X)) Pub: Tantor Media. Dist(s): IngramPubServ

Count of Monte Cristo. Alexandre Dumas. Retold by Alan Venable. 2007. pap. bk. 69.00 (978-1-4105-0803-4(X)); audio compact disk 18.95 (978-1-4105-0801-0(3)) D Johnston Inc.

Count of Monte Cristo. abr. ed. Alexandre Dumas. 1 cass. (Running Time: 50 min.). Dramatization. (Classics Illustrated Bks.). (J). 5.95; Audio Bk.
Full cast.

Count of Monte Cristo. abr. ed. Alexandre Dumas. 3 CDs. (Running Time: 4 Hrs. 30 Mins.). 2004. audio compact disk 9.99 (978-1-57050-041-1(X)) Multilingua.

Count of Monte Cristo. abr. ed. Alexandre Dumas. Read by David Case. (YA). 2006. 84.99 (978-1-59895-682-5(5)) Find a World.

Count of Monte Cristo. abr. unabr. ed. Alexandre Dumas. Narrated by David Case. (Running Time: 17 hrs. 30 mins. 0 sec.). (ENG.). 2008. audio compact disk 35.99 (978-1-4001-0862-6(4)) Pub: Tantor Media. Dist(s): IngramPubServ

***Count of Monte Cristo.** adpt. ed. Alexandre Dumas. (Bring the Classics to Life Ser.). (ENG.). 2008. audio compact disk 12.95 (978-1-55576-586-6(6)) EDCON Pubng.

Count of Monte Cristo. unabr. ed. Alexandre Dumas. Read by John Lee. (Running Time: 47 hrs. 50 mins.). 2008. 69.95 (978-1-4332-1583-4(7)) Blckstn Audio.

Count of Monte Cristo. unabr. ed. Alexandre Dumas. Narrated by David Case. (Running Time: 17 hrs. 30 mins. 0 sec.). (ENG.). 2008. 27.99 (978-1-4001-5862-1(1)); audio compact disk 72.99 (978-1-4001-3862-3(0)) Pub: Tantor Media. Dist(s): IngramPubServ

Count of Monte Cristo. unabr. collector's ed. Alexandre Dumas. Read by David Case. 12 cass. (Running Time: 18 hrs.). 1989. 96.00 (978-0-7366-1471-9(0), 2350) Books on Tape.
The Alexandre Dumas story of long, intolerate years in captivity, a miraculous escape & a carefully wrought revenge creates a dramatic tale of mystery & intrigue & paints a vision of France.

Count of Monte Cristo, Level 2. Alexandre Dumas & Clare West. (Dominoes Ser.). 2006. 14.25 (978-0-19-424383-4(4)) OUP.

Count of Monte Cristo, Pt. 1. unabr. ed. Alexandre Dumas. Read by Frederick Davidson. 12 cass. (Running Time: 51 hrs.). (gr. 9-12). 2003. 83.95 (978-0-7861-1077-3(5), 1847A, B, C) Blckstn Audio.
Edmond Dantes, a man on the threshold of a bright career & a happy marriage, is imprisoned on a false political charge. After escaping, he becomes wealthy & plots revenge against his old enemies.

Count of Monte Cristo, Pt. 2. unabr. ed. Alexandre Dumas. Read by Frederick Davidson. 12 cass. (Running Time: 51 hrs.). 2003. 83.95 (978-0-7861-1105-3(4), 1847A, B, C) Blckstn Audio.

Count of Monte Cristo, Pt. 3. unabr. ed. Alexandre Dumas. Read by Frederick Davidson. 11 cass. (Running Time: 51 hrs.). 2003. 76.95 (978-0-7861-1106-0(2), 1847A, B, C) Blckstn Audio.

***Count of Monte Cristo: Bring the Classics to Life.** adpt. ed. Alexandre Dumas. (Bring the Classics to Life Ser.). 2008. pap. bk. 21.95 (978-1-55576-656-6(0)) EDCON Pubng.

Count of Monte Cristo: Classic Collection. unabr. ed. Alexandre Dumas. (Running Time: 50 hrs. 50 mins.). 2009. audio compact disk 59.95 (978-1-4332-1579-7(9)) Blckstn Audio.

Count of Monte Cristo- Part A. unabr. ed. Alexandre Dumas. Read by John Lee. (Running Time: 15 hrs. 50 mins.). (ENG.). 2008. 85.95 (978-1-4332-1580-3(2)); audio compact disk 130.00 (978-1-4332-1577-3(2)) Blckstn Audio.

Count of Monte Cristo- Part B. unabr. ed. Alexandre Dumas. Read by John Lee. (ENG.). 2008. 85.95 (978-1-4332-1581-0(0)); audio compact disk 130.00 (978-1-4332-1578-0(0)) Blckstn Audio.

Count of Monte Cristo- Part C. unabr. ed. Alexandre Dumas. Read by John Lee. (Running Time: 16 hrs. 0 mins.). (ENG.). 2008. 89.95 (978-1-4332-1582-7(9)) Blckstn Audio.

Count of Montecristo see Conde de Montecristo

Count of Montecristo. Alexandre Dumas. Read by Guillermo Piedrahita. (Running Time: 3 hrs.). 2002. 16.95 (978-1-60083-210-9(5), Audiofy Corp) Iofy Corp.

Count the Cost: Luke 14:25:33. Ed Young. (J). 1982. 4.95 (978-0-7417-1220-2(2), 220) Win Walk.

Count Your Blessings: Matthew 15:36, 637. Ed Young. 1987. 4.95 (978-0-7417-1637-8(2), 637) Win Walk.

***Count Zero.** unabr. ed. William Gibson. Read by Jonathan Davis. (Running Time: 12 hrs.). (Sprawl Trilogy). 2011. 39.97 (978-1-61106-213-7(6), 9781611062137, BADLE); 39.97 (978-1-61106-212-0(8), 9781611062120, Brlnc Audio MP3 Lib); 24.99 (978-1-61106-211-3(X), 9781611062113, Brilliance MP3); audio compact disk 79.97 (978-1-61106-210-6(1), 9781611062106, BriAudCD Unabrid); audio compact disk 29.99 (978-1-61106-209-0(8), 9781611062090, Bril Audio CD Unabri) Brilliance Audio.

Countdown. Based on a novel by Greg Cox. 2010. audio compact disk 19.99 (978-1-59950-629-6(7)) GraphicAudio.

Countdown. Iris Johansen. (Eve Duncan Ser.). 2005. 81.00 (978-1-4159-1584-4(9)); audio compact disk 84.15 (978-1-4159-1669-8(1)) Pub: Books on Tape. Dist(s): NetLibrary CO

Countdown. Ben Mikaelsen. Read by George Guidall. 5 cass. (Running Time: 6 hrs. 45 mins.). (YA). 1999. pap. bk. & stu. ed. 60.20 (978-0-7887-3793-0(7), 41037) Recorded Bks.
Living worlds apart, 14-year-olds Elliot & Vincent meet by short wave radio. Elliot is NASA's first Junior Astronaut. Vincent is an African Masai warrior. At first their communications are fraught with misunderstanding. But as they learn about each other's culture, their friendship captures the world's attention.

Countdown. abr. ed. David Hagberg. Read by Bruce Watson. 4 vols. (Kirk McGarvey Ser.). 2003. (978-1-58807-676-2(8)) Am Pubng Inc.

Countdown. unabr. ed. Keith Douglass. Read by David Hilder. 8 cass. (Running Time: 12 hrs.). (Carrier Ser.: No. 6). 2001. 29.95 (978-0-7366-6792-0(X)) Books on Tape.
Tombstone Magruder & the Jefferson head of Russian submarines outfitted with nuclear warheads to prevent total mayhem.

Countdown, unabr. ed. Ben Mikaelsen. Narrated by George Guidall. 5 pieces. (Running Time: 6 hrs. 45 mins.). (gr. 7 up). 2000. 46.00 (978-0-7887-3822-7(4), 96063E7) Recorded Bks.
Living worlds apart, 14-year-olds Elliot & Vincent meet by short wave radio. Elliot is NASA's first Junior Astronaut. Vincent is an African Masai warrior. At first their communications are fraught with misunderstanding. But as they learn about each other's culture, their friendship captures the world's attention.

***Countdown.** unabr. ed. Deborah Wiles. (ENG.). (J). 2011. audio compact disk 40.00 (978-0-307-87965-3(8), Listening Lib) Pub: Random Audio Pubg. Dist(s): Random

Countdown. unabr. collector's ed. Keith Douglass. Read by David Hilder. 8 cass. (Running Time: 12 hrs.). (Carrier Ser.: No. 6). 1996. 64.00 (978-0-7366-3250-8(6), 3908) Books on Tape.
Russia's Commonwealth of Independent States crumbles as civil war erupts & the threat of nukes looms large. U.S. intelligence reveals that one of the feuding factions plans to deploy Russian Typhoons off the country's northwest coast. They're the largest submarines in the world...& probably armed with nuclear weapons.

Countdown, Class set. Ben Mikaelsen. Read by George Guidall. 5 cass. (Running Time: 6 hrs. 45 mins.). (YA). 1999. 126.30 (978-0-7887-3864-7(X), 47029) Recorded Bks.
Living worlds apart, 14-year-olds Elliot & Vincent meet by short wave radio. Elliot is NASA's first Junior Astronaut. Vincent is an African Masai warrior. At first their communications are fraught with misunderstanding. But as they learn about each other's culture, their friendship captures the world's attention.

***Countdown in Cairo.** Noel Hynd. (Running Time: 12 hrs. 56 mins. 0 sec.). (Russian Ser.). (ENG.). 2010. 14.99 (978-0-310-77300-9(8)) Zondervan.

Countdown to Christmas. Scripts. Dale VonSeggen. Prod. by One Way Street Staff. (Running Time: 27 minutes). 2002. audio compact disk 18.00 (978-1-58302-220-7(1)) One Way St.
This fun Christmas musical stars Cameron, a crazy camel DJ coming to you on METV in the Middle East. His witty newscasts, weather report, and sprots highlights are interspersed with five great songs for the season. Songs include: Little Packages; We Three Camels; What Can I Give to the King?; Wise Men Still adore Him; My Gift is Me. In the midst of the fun, Cameron Camel will help you discover that YOU are the only gift Jesus wants this Christmas.

Countdown to Kindergarten. Alison McGhee. Illus. by Harry Bliss. 14 vols. pap. bk. (978-1-59112-469-6(7)); pap. bk. (978-1-59112-929-5(X)) Live Oak Media.

Countdown to Kindergarten. Alison McGhee. Illus. by Harry Bliss. (Running Time: 12 mins.). (J). (ps-2). 2004. audio compact disk 12.95 (978-1-59112-926-4(5)) Live Oak Media.

Countdown to Kindergarten. Alison McGhee. Illus. by Harry Bliss. 11 vols. (Running Time: 12 mins.). (J). 2004. bk. 25.95 (978-1-59112-468-9(9)); bk. 28.95 (978-1-59112-928-8(1)); 9.95 (978-1-59112-466-5(2)) Live Oak Media.

Countdown to Relaxation. D.A. Tubesing. 1 cass. (Running Time: 38 min.). (Sensational Relaxation Ser.: No. 5). 11.95 (978-0-938586-82-1(3), CD) Whole Person.
Do you occasionally (or often!) suffer from stress overload? Do you find it difficult to unwind or fall asleep? Learn two powerful autohypnotic relaxation techniques that can help you feel in control of the stress that plageus you. Side A: Countdown. When your nervous system is hot-wired, reset it to a healthy self-renewing pace with this ten-step deep relaxation process. The narrator leads you through an unusual autogenic sequence to a state of integration & wholeness. Side B: Staircase. Step by step, the narrator guides you through a breathing & visualization process that will bring you to a meditative state of profound relaxation.

Counted Clockwise. Jacques Dorsan. 1 cass. 8.95 (101) Am Fed Astrologers.
Explanation of why houses must be counted clockwise.

Counter Attach: Acts 14:1-28. Ed Young. 1998. Rental 4.95 (978-0-7417-2181-5(3), A1181) Win Walk.

Counter-Tenor's Daughter. unabr. ed. Elizabeth Falconer. Read by Anita Wright. 8 cass. (Running Time: 10 hrs.). 1999. 69.95 (978-0-7531-0376-0(1), 980409) Pub: ISIS Audio GBR. Dist(s): Ulverscroft US
Dido Patridge leads a bohemian existence in an old houseboat on the Thames, shared with Jacob, a film director & her erratic but long-term partner. When she discovers that he has been entertaining another woman on the houseboat she books the first flight out of Heathrow & ends up in Corfu. There Dido becomes aware of Guy, a lawyer who left London for the solitude of the island when his disability, the result of a childhood accident, became too much for him to bear. As Dido and Guy start to heal the wounds which each of them has acquired through the years they both begin to see how their lives can change.

Counterattack. unabr. collector's ed. W. E. B. Griffin. Read by Michael Russotto. 13 cass. (Running Time: 19 hrs. 30 min.). (Corps Ser.: Bk. 3). 1992. 104.00 (978-0-7366-2211-0(X), 3004) Books on Tape.
Highlights counterstrike against the Japanese at Guadalcanal. Novel takes you to the front lines of victory & into the heart of courage.

Counterclockwise: Mindful Health & the Power of Possibility. unabr. ed. Ellen J. Langer. Read by Sandra Burr. (Running Time: 7 hrs.). 2009. 24.99 (978-1-4233-9770-0(3), 9781423397700, Brilliance MP3); 24.99 (978-1-4233-9772-4(X), 9781423397724, BAD); 39.97 (978-1-4233-9771-7(1), 9781423397717, Brlnc Audio MP3 Lib); 39.97 (978-1-4233-9773-1(8), 9781423397731, BADLE); audio compact disk 24.99 (978-1-4233-9768-7(1), 9781423397687, Bril Audio CD Unabri); audio compact disk 82.97 (978-1-4233-9769-4(X), 9781423397694, BriAudCD Unabrid) Brilliance Audio.

Countercoup: Struggle for Control of Iran. unabr. collector's ed. Kermit Roosevelt. Read by Justin Hecht. 7 cass. (Running Time: 7 hrs.). 1982. 42.00 (978-0-7366-0290-7(9), 1278) Books on Tape.
It was typical June weather in Washington: hot & humid. Kermit Roosevelt, grandson of Theodore Roosevelt & a veteran of the OSS, was hurrying to a meeting with John Foster Dulles at the State Department. That meeting in 1953 was to lead to one of the greatest triumphs in America's covert operations in foreign affairs. For at that time it was believed that Iran, under the leadership of Prime Minister Mossadegh, was slipping under Russian domination. At the meeting in Dulles' office, Kermit Roosevelt was given the go-ahead to mastermind the overthrow of Mossadegh & return the Shah to the Peacock Throne.

Countercultural Woman CD: A Fresh Look at Proverbs 31. Nancy Leigh DeMoss. (ENG.). 2007. audio compact disk 43.99 (978-0-940110-81-6(4)) Life Action Publishing.

Counterfeit Conversion. Steve Hill. 1 cass. 1996. 7.00 (978-0-7684-0016-8(3)) Destiny Image Pubs.

Counterfeit Gods: The Empty Promises of Money, Sex, & Power, & the Only Hope That Matters. unabr. ed. Timothy Keller. Read by Timothy Keller. Read by Tom Parks. (Running Time: 6 hrs.). 2009. 19.99 (978-1-4418-3047-0(2), 9781441830470, Brilliance MP3); 19.99 (978-1-4418-3049-4(9), 9781441830494, BAD); 39.97 (978-1-4418-3048-7(0), 9781441830487, Brlnc Audio MP3 Lib); 39.97 (978-1-4418-3050-0(2), 9781441830500, BADLE); audio compact disk 19.99 (978-1-4418-3045-6(6), 9781441830456, Bril Audio CD Unabri); audio compact disk 69.97 (978-1-4418-3046-3(4), 9781441830463, BriAudCD Unabrid) Brilliance Audio.

Counterfeit Grace: Logos June 21, 1998. Ben Young. 1998. 4.95 (978-0-7417-6087-6(8), B0087) Win Walk.

Counterfeit Killers. unabr. ed. Bill Knox. Read by James Bryce. 6 cass. (Running Time: 9 hrs.). 1999. 54.95 (978-0-7531-0200-8(5), 970908) Pub: ISIS Audio GBR. Dist(s): Ulverscroft US
A multi-million pound counterfeit fashion operation with money-making international connections has moved into the Scottish crime scene, & Colin Thane of the elite Scottish Crime Squad is given the task of smashing it.

***Counterfeit Magic.** unabr. ed. Kelley Armstrong. (Running Time: 5 hrs. 0 mins.). 2010. 24.99 (978-1-4001-9975-4(1)); 13.99 (978-1-4001-8975-5(6)); 19.99 (978-1-4001-6975-7(5)); audio compact disk 59.99 (978-1-4001-4975-9(4)); audio compact disk 24.99 (978-1-4001-1975-2(8)) Pub: Tantor Media. Dist(s): IngramPubServ

Counterfeit Revival: A Critical Look at the "Laughing Renewal" Hank Hanegraaff. 1 cass. 1997. 15.99 (978-0-8499-6202-8(1)) Nelson.
Revival is spreading across the world like wildfire...but that's not necessarily good news according to Hank Hanegraaff, author & noted expert on cults & the Bible. Hanegraaff investigates & reveals the real energy source behind the "laughing renewal." Those who attend these extraordinary events experience "holy laughter," as well as other "miraculous" manifestations including drunkenness, animal noises, & violent seizures - supposedly the result of divine encounter. The author clearly points out that while this "renewal" is circling the globe its origin may be more demonic than divine. Employing his popular teaching style provides a solid test for truth so readers can distinguish a counterfeit revival from a true revival.

Counterfeit Wife. unabr. ed. Tom E. Neet. Read by Lynda Evans. 6 cass. (Running Time: 6 hrs. 30 min.). (Mel Tippett Detective Ser.: Bk. 5). 1996. 39.95 (978-1-55686-680-7(1)) Books in Motion.
A British aristocrat in the U. S. on business becomes a target for murder. Mel Tippett is hired to investigate the case & keep him alive.

Counterforce. unabr. ed. Loren Robinson. Read by Cameron Beierle. 8 cass. (Running Time: 9 hrs. 48 min.). (Hawk Adventure Ser.: Bk. 1). 2001. 49.95 (978-1-58116-024-6(0)) Books in Motion.
International operative Lane Palmer discovers a conspiracy to overthrow several major governments, including the United States. And now he is the target of an assassin named Omega, a ruthless agent leading a group of killer robots.

Countering the Dark Side of Spiritual Gifts. Bill Hybels. (Defining Moments Ser.: Vol. 24). 2001. 9.99 (978-0-310-20446-6(1)) Zondervan.

Counterlife. unabr. ed. Philip Roth. Narrated by George Guidall. 9 cass. (Running Time: 13 hrs.). 2005. 89.75 (978-1-4025-0762-5(3), 96904) Recorded Bks.
Time calls Philip Roth "the uncontested master of comic irony." He is a best-seller and the winner of the National Book Critics Circle Award, the National Book Award, and the Pulitzer Prize in fiction. The Counterlife brings back Roth's most notorious character, the novelist Nathan Zuckerman. Now Nathan's married brother, Henry the dentist, is suffering from impotence as a result of taking heart medication - and he's willing to risk his life in a dangerous operation just to regain his sexual prowess in order to satisfy the needs of his office assistant.

Countermarch! the American Civil War. Short Stories. Gary C. Martin. Narrated by Luke Behan. 4 CDs. (Running Time: 4 hours). Dramatization. 2002. audio compact disk Rental 9.95 (978-0-9721444-5-2(5)) Audio History.
The 40 plus unknown Battles that took place during the last 2 weeks of March, 1862 as told in the words of the participants.

Countermoves. AIO Team Staff. Compiled by Focus on the Family Staff. 4 CDs. (Running Time: 6 hrs.). (Adventures in Odyssey Ser.: No. 37). (ENG.). (J). (gr. 3 up). 2004. audio compact disk 24.99 (978-1-58997-028-1(4)) Pub: Focus Family. Dist(s): Tyndale Hse

Counterpane Fairy, unabr. ed. Katharine Pyle. Read by Flo Gibson. 2 cass. (Running Time: 2 hrs. 40 min.). (J). (gr. 1-3). 1992. 14.95 (978-1-55685-247-3(9)) Audio Bk Con.
Travel with Teddy & the Counterpane Fairy to visit a princess in a golden palace, a circus, ice floes with mermen & polar bears, a land of dreams, the Rainbow Children & a rat hole. Katharine Pyle was as skilled, prolific & imaginative a writer as her brother Howard & she illustrated many books, including his "The Wonder Clock.".

Counterpoint/Clawhammer Banjo. Michael Miles. 1996. pap. bk. 17.95 (978-0-7866-0549-1(9), 95550BCD) Mel Bay.

Countess. Catherine Coulter. Read by Mary Peiffer. 1999. audio compact disk 72.00 (978-0-7366-5202-5(7)) Books on Tape.

Countess. Catherine Coulter. Read by Mary Peiffer. 9 CDs. (Running Time: 10 hrs. 36 mins.). 2001. audio compact disk 72.00 Books on Tape.
The fourth book in the Bride Quest series, the Bride Quest moves to 1176 Scotland where Countess Eglantine loses her second husband & vows to find husbands for her two daughters.

Countess. collector's unabr. ed. Catherine Coulter. Read by Mary Peiffer. 8 cass. (Running Time: 12 hrs.). 1999. 64.00 (978-0-7366-4738-0(4), 5076) Books on Tape.
With The Countess, the Bride Quest moves to 1176 Scotland where Countess Eglantine loses her second husband & vows to find husbands for her two daughters.

Countess below Stairs. unabr. ed. Eva Ibbotson. Narrated by Davina Porter. 8 cass. (Running Time: 9 hrs. 30 mins.). (YA). (gr. 8 up). 2007. 61.75 (978-1-4281-6457-4(X)); audio compact disk 87.75 (978-1-4281-6461-1(8)) Recorded Bks.
In this thrilling novel, young Russian countess Anna must flee to England after the Russian Revolution. She hides her identity and becomes a servant for an important family. But will she be able to suppress her attraction to Rupert, the dashing Earl of Westerholme?.

Counting: Meditation for Well-Being. Voice by Catheirne Sheen. 2005. audio compact disk 22.95 (978-0-9773381-1-5(8)) Reach In.

Counting & Coloring Dinosaurs. 1 cass. Dramatization. (J). pap. bk. 6.95 (978-0-86545-097-4(8)) Spizzirri.
Dinosaurs & reptiles of the prehistoric world are used to teach simple addition & subtraction.

Counting & Coloring Dinosaurs. Ed. by Linda Spizzirri. 1 cass. Dramatization. (J). (gr. 1-8). pap. bk. 4.98 incl. educational coloring bk. (978-0-86545-044-8(7)) Spizzirri.

Counting Games & Rhythms for Little Ones. Ella Jenkins. 1 CD. (Running Time: 1 hr.). (J). 2001. audio compact disk 15.00 (FC 45029CD) Kimbo Educ.

Counting Games & Rhythms for the Little Ones. Perf. by Ella Jenkins. 1 cass. (J). (ps). 1990. (0-9307-450290-9307-45029-2-1); audio compact disk (0-9307-45029-2-1) Smithsonian Folkways.
Teaches basic number skills & math in an easy-to-follow style. Ella's voice animates 9 classic counting & game songs like "One Potato, Two Potato," "One, Two, Buckle My Shoe" & "Ten Little Indians".

Counting Kittens & Other Math Songs & Activities. John Archambault & David Plummer. Ed. by Kim Cernek. (Happy Song Sing-Alongs Ser.: Vol. 2356). 1999. pap. bk. & tchr. ed. 13.99 (978-1-57471-637-5(9), 2356) Creat Teach Pr.

Counting Kittens & Other Math Songs & Activities, Grades Preschool-2. John Archambault & David Plummer. Ed. by Kim Cernek. Des. by Marek Janci. Illus. by Darcy Tom. 1 cass. (Happy Song Sing-Alongs Ser.). 1999. pap. bk. & tchr. ed. 13.99 (978-1-57471-550-7(X), 2361) Creat Teach Pr.

Counting on Grace. unabr. ed. Elizabeth Winthrop. Read by Lili Gamache. 5 CDs. (Running Time: 5 hrs. 46 mins.). (J). (gr. 4-7). 2006. audio compact disk 45.00 (978-0-7393-4864-2(7), Listening Lib) Pub: Random Audio Pubg. Dist(s): Random

Counting Pencils: Early Explorers Emergent Set B Audio CD. Katherine Scraper. Adapted by Benchmark Education Staff. (J). 2007. audio compact disk 10.00 (978-1-4108-8193-9(8)) Benchmark Educ.

Counting Sheep. Perf. by Collin Raye. Music by Karen Taylor-Good & Robert Ellis Orrall. 1 cass. (J). 1999. 9.98 (Sony Wonder); audio compact disk 16.98 (Sony Wonder) Sony Music Ent.
Songs include: "Counting Sheep," "I'm Gonna Love You," "Blackbird," "A Mother & Father's Prayer" (Duet with Melissa Manchester), "When You Wish upon a Star," "Cool Cat," "Too Ra Loo Ta Loo Ral," "Hearts Are for When You Want to Love Someone," "The Dream Song," "When You Say Your Prayers" & "Stay Awake.".

Counting Sleepy Sheep. Rory Zuckerman. Illus. by Maryn Roos. 1 CD. (Running Time: 18 mins.). (Sleepy Sheep Ser.). (J). (ps). 2007. bds. 7.95 (978-0-9796393-3-3(6)) Little Lion Pr.

Counting Songs. (J). (ps-3). 2000. 2.99 (978-1-85781-213-8(1)) Cimino Pub Grp.

Counting the Cost. Neville Goddard. 1 cass. (Running Time: 62 min.). 1964. 8.00 (74) J & L Pubns.
Neville taught Imagination Creates Reality. He was a powerfully influential teacher of God as Consciousness.

Counting the Ways. unabr. ed. Jennifer Curry. Read by Trudy Harris. 6 cass. (Running Time: 8 hrs.). 1998. 69.95 (978-1-85903-243-5(5)) Pub: Magna Story GBR. Dist(s): Ulverscroft US
Lewis and Maureen set out on separate journeys to the past, each counting the ways that they loved and were loved so long ago.

Counting Theme Audio CD. ed. (J). 2004. audio compact disk (978-1-4108-1756-3(3)) Benchmark Educ.

Counting to 10 Audio CD. Adapted by Benchmark Education Company Staff. Based on a work by Francisco Blane. (My First Reader's Theater Ser.). (J). (gr. k-1). 2008. audio compact disk 10.00 (978-1-60634-103-2(0)) Benchmark Educ.

Countries of Europe Series: World Events over Time Collection. Eugene Lieber. (ENG.). 2006. audio compact disk 220.00 (978-1-935069-21-8(7)) IAB Inc.

Country: Bass Play-along Volume 11. Created by Hal Leonard Corporation Staff. 2006. pap. bk. 12.95 (978-1-4234-1423-0(3), 1423414233) H Leonard.

Country Baby Story CD (Babytown Storybook) Short Stories. Created by Queen Lane. Illus. by Queen Lane. Voice by Jaina Lane. 1 CD. (Running Time: 22 mins). Dramatization. (BABYTOWN Ser.: Bk. 3). (J). 2005. audio compact disk 10.00 (978-0-9772738-5-0(7)) Quebla.
Can you imagine what life would be like if you were born able to talk? Well, Baby can! Considered the town?s most ambitious under-one-nager, Baby is proud to be like-a-girl as she ventures through life dissecting the who, what, and whys of everything in sight. Baby is the littlest prodigy with the biggest imagination, always ready to save the day. Children of all ages will be delighted to just see how silly things can be through the eyes of an infant.It?s Country Baby?s birthday and everyone is excited, everyone except Baby. She is afraid of meeting her new family, as well as, everything else around her. Baby has to learn to be a big girl and not be so scared.

Country Back-Up Guitar. Fred Sokolow. 1996. pap. bk. 17.95 (978-0-7866-0847-8(1), 95533BCD) Mel Bay.

Country Balladeers. 2006. audio compact disk 5.95 (978-1-59987-527-9(6)) Braun Media.

Country Bass Method. Stephan Richter. (Progressive Ser.). 2004. pap. bk. 19.95 (978-1-86469-083-5(6), 256-042) Kolala Music SGP.

Country Beyond. unabr. ed. James Oliver Curwood. Read by Ric Benson. 8 cass. (Running Time: 8 hrs. 30 min.). 2001. 49.95; audio compact disk 45.50 (978-1-58116-114-4(X)) Books in Motion.
"Jolly" Roger McKay has fled into the Northern wilderness with the Royal Canadian Mounted Police hot on his trail. It has been a gentlemen's game of cat and mouse with McKay always one step ahead, until he met Nada.

Country Blues Guitar. Tommy Flint. 1997. bk. 17.95 (978-0-7866-2780-6(8), 93346BCD) Mel Bay.

Country Blues Guitar Basics. (ENG.). 2009. pap. bk. 19.99 (978-1-890490-95-9(4)) Pub: String Letter. Dist(s): H Leonard

Country Bouquet. unabr. ed. Phyllis Nicholson. Read by Tracey Lord. 3 cass. (Running Time: 4 hrs. 30 min.). (Isis Ser.). (J). 2001. 34.95 (978-0-7531-0372-2(9), 980617) Pub: ISIS Lrg Prnt GBR. Dist(s): Ulverscroft US
A unique yearly companion with a chapter for every month, originally published just after the Second World War, it evokes the essence of what each month meant to the author.

Country Burial see Twentieth-Century Poetry in English, No. 12, Recordings of Poets Reading Their Own Poetry

Country Calendar. unabr. ed. Flora Thompson. Read by Anita Wright. 3 cass. (Running Time: 4 hrs.). (Isis Ser.). (J). 2004. 34.95 (978-0-7531-0417-0(2), 980917) Pub: ISIS Lrg Prnt GBR. Dist(s): Ulverscroft US
A collection of the articles she wrote for a small magazine, the Catholic Fireside, between 1916 & 1928, when she lived in Liphook in Hampshire as the postmaster's wife. Her interest was captured by many things, including a kestrel hunting in the January skies, the return of migrant birds in april, the skies of the elder tree & the solitary life of the plowman.

Country Characters. Read by Jackie Torrence. 1 cass. (J). (gr. 2 up). 1989. 10.00 (978-1-886929-03-6(3), EWC4909) Earwig.
Jackie Torrence takes her listeners off into a world full of eccentric characters - preachers, fiddlers, geezers, grumpy blacksmiths, even a sly & rather fetching devil. Their country ways & doings provide the backdrop for these ghost stories which often tell of scotching death in return for living out some eerie ritual forever. We hear of the dead playing prodigious music at a fiddling contest, & we see a dead brakeman glooming up & down the tracks searching for his severed head. Jackie, a well-known storyteller, uses her extraordinary deep voice to wrap us into a deep spell punctuated with thrilling jolts of surprise.

Country Cheating & Leaving Songs. 2006. audio compact disk 5.95 (978-1-59987-525-5(X)) Braun Media.

Country Christmas. 2007. audio compact disk 32.98 (978-5-557-58299-5(1)) Madacy Ent Grp CAN.

Country Days. unabr. ed. Alice Taylor. Narrated by Gerri Halligan. 4 CDs. (Running Time: 4 hrs. 15 mins.). 2000. audio compact disk 43.00 (978-1-84197-138-4(3), C1248E7) Recorded Bks.
Accounts of the easy-going, anecdotal life in rural Ireland.

Country Days. unabr. ed. Alice Taylor. Narrated by Gerri Halligan. 3 cass. (Running Time: 4 hrs. 15 mins.). 2001. 30.00 (978-1-84197-030-1(1), H1030E7) Recorded Bks.

Country Doctor. Sarah Orne Jewett & Kate Reading. 2002. 44.95 (978-0-7861-2858-7(5)); 24.95 (978-0-7861-8415-6(9)); 56.00 (978-0-7861-8431-6(0)) Blckstn Audio.

Country Doctor, Set. unabr. ed. Sarah Orne Jewett. Read by Flo Gibson. 6 cass. (Running Time: 8 hrs. 30 min.). 1992. 24.95 (978-1-55685-233-6(9)) Audio Bk Con.
Written in 1884 this surprisingly modern novel concerns a woman's independence as she chooses between marriage & commitment to her vocation as a country doctor in Maine.

Country Drumming. Craig Lauritsen. (Progressive Ser.). 2004. pap. bk. 19.95 (978-1-86469-084-2(4), 256-043) Kolala Music SGP.

Country Electric Guitar Ear Training. Brad Davis. 2002. audio compact disk (99896CD) Mel Bay.

Country Fingerpicking Guitar: For Beginners. Brett Duncan. 2008. pap. bk. 24.95 (978-1-86469-374-4(6)) Kolala Music SGP.

Country Full of Guns. unabr. ed. E. R. Slade. Read by Gene Engene. 4 cass. (Running Time: 5 hrs. 12 min.). 1994. 26.95 (978-1-55686-496-4(5)) Books in Motion.
When gun-slingers backshot Tom Dodge & jumped his gold claim, Tom's old side-kick Hank Brandeen vowed to track down the killers & nail their hides to the wall.

Country Goes Raffi: A Tribute Album. Perf. by Raffi et al. 1 cass. (Running Time: 0.40). (J). 2001. 11.98 (978-1-57940-076-7(0)); audio compact disk 17.98 Rounder Records.

Country Gospel Piano Solos. Gail Smith. 1996. pap. bk. 17.95 (978-0-7866-2529-1(5), 95992P) Mel Bay.

Country Guitar Method. Brett Duncan. (Progressive Ser.). 2004. pap. bk. 19.95 (978-1-86469-077-4(1), 256-044) Kolala Music SGP.

Country Guitar Songs: Hal Leonard Guitar Method. Created by Hal Leonard Corporation Staff. 2009. pap. bk. 14.99 (978-1-4234-8442-4(8), 1423484428) H Leonard.

Country Guitar Tech. Brett Duncan. (Progressive Ser.). 2004. pap. bk. 19.95 (978-1-86469-089-7(5), 256-045) Kolala Music SGP.

Country Jubilee. 1 cass. 6.98 (978-1-57908-462-2(1)); audio compact disk 9.98 (978-1-57908-461-5(3)) Platinm Enter.

Country Jukebox Classics. (Running Time: 24 mins.). 2006. audio compact disk 5.95 (978-1-59987-524-8(1)) Braun Media.

Country Keyboard Method. Peter Gelling. (Progressive Ser.). 2004. pap. bk. 19.95 (978-1-86469-081-1(X), 256-047) Kolala Music SGP.

Country Kid. Kidzup Productions Staff. 1 cass. (Running Time: 90 mins.). (Kidzup Toddler Ser.). (J). 1999. 8.99 (978-1-894281-17-1(9)); audio compact disk 12.99 (978-1-894281-18-8(7)) Pub: Kidzup CAN. Dist(s): Penton Overseas
A great way to introduce your toddlers to country music. The perfect balance between our lively & fun original tunes & the nursery songs we all know & love.

Country Life. unabr. ed. Charlotte Bingham. 6 cass. (Running Time: 9 hrs.). 2001. 54.95 (978-0-7531-1139-0(X)) Pub: ISIS Audio GBR. Dist(s): Ulverscroft US

Country Life: A Novel. unabr. ed. Rachel Cusk. Narrated by Jenny Sterlin. 9 cass. (Running Time: 13 hrs. 15 mins.). 1997. 78.00 (978-0-7887-3754-1(6), 95444E7) Recorded Bks.
When Stella leaves London for a small village, she hopes that country life will lead her to self-discovery. But, as an au pair for a dispiriting family, she finds misfortune from weather, wildlife & unwelcome suitors.

Country Mouse & the Town Mouse see Pony Engine & Other Stories for Children

Country of the Blind see Tales of Terror & the Supernatural: A Collection

Country of the Blind. unabr. ed. Christopher Brookmyre. 12 cass. (Isis Cassettes Ser.). (J). 2006. 94.95 (978-0-7531-1900-6(5)); audio compact disk 99.95 (978-0-7531-2266-2(9)) Pub: ISIS Lrg Prnt GBR. Dist(s): Ulverscroft US

Country of the Blind. unabr. ed. H. G. Wells. Read by Walter Zimmerman. (Running Time: 75 min.). Dramatization. 1979. 7.95 (N-27) Jimcin Record.
Would the one-eyed man really be king? This story provides a surprising answer.

Country of the Blind - Classic Unabridged Audio Book: Unabridged HG Wells the Country of the Blind. H. G. Wells. Read by Martyn Tott. Hosted by Tom Mitchell. Prod. by Troy / Rulon Thayne. Illus. by James Hildebrandt. (YA). 2007. audio compact disk 15.00 (978-1-4276-1672-2(8)) AardGP.

Country of the Pointed Firs. unabr. ed. Sarah Orne Jewett. Read by Tracy Lord. 4 cass. (Running Time: 3 hrs. 30 min.). (Voices Ser.: Vol. 1). 1993. 24.95 (978-1-883332-00-6(1), 391959) Audio Bkshelf.
Classic regional fiction that remains timeless 100 years later. Jewett's "Jewel" of 19th century coastal Maine during the era of its decay from the grandeur of West Indian trading days.

Country of the Pointed Firs. unabr. ed. Sarah Orne Jewett. Read by Cindy Hardin. 3 cass. (Running Time: 4 hrs. 30 min.). 1992. 23.95 (978-0-7861-0631-8(X), 2121) Blckstn Audio.
Depicts the close personal & family relationships in a Maine seaport town during the era of its decay from the grandeur of West Indian trading days. Jewett's precise, alluringly subdued sketches of the gently perishing glory of the Maine countryside & ports have placed her at the top of the class among the school of writers who count local-color as a chief literary objective.

Country of the Pointed Firs. unabr. ed. Sarah Orne Jewett. Read by Shaela Connor. 3 cass. (Running Time: 4 hrs. 15 min.). Dramatization. 1993. 21.95 (978-1-55686-449-0(3), 449) Books in Motion.
A visitor from a more urban environment, finds herself drawn irresistably into the deep currents of life within the small north coastal community of Dunnet Landing, Maine.

Country of the Pointed Firs. unabr. ed. Sarah Orne Jewett. Read by Cindy Hardin. 4 cass. (Running Time: 5 hrs. 30 min.). 1981. 24.00 incl. album. (C-77) Jimcin Record.
Charming story of life in the village of Dunnet, Maine.

Country of the Pointed Firs. unabr. collector's ed. Sarah Orne Jewett. Read by Cindy Hardin. 5 cass. (Running Time: 5 hrs.). 1982. 30.00 (978-0-7366-3869-2(5), 9077) Books on Tape.
Depicts the close personal & family relationships in a small New England village.

Country of the Pointed Firs, Set. Sarah Orne Jewett. Narrated by Flo Gibson. 4 cass. (Running Time: 6 hrs..). 1986. 19.95 (978-1-55685-001-1(8)) Audio Bk Con.
Portrays with humor & compassion the world of the inhabitants of a small seacoast village & the remote islands of Maine, where courage & caring are so well exemplified.

***Country of Vast Designs: James K. Polk, the Mexican War & the Conquest of the American Continent.** unabr. ed. Robert W. Merry. Narrated by Michael Prichard. (Running Time: 20 hrs. 0 mins.). 2010. 23.99 (978-1-4001-8495-8(9)); 49.99 (978-1-4001-9495-7(4)) Tantor Media.

***Country of Vast Designs: James K. Polk, the Mexican War & the Conquest of the American Continent.** unabr. ed. Robert W. Merry. Narrated by Michael Prichard. (Running Time: 19 hrs. 0 mins. 0 sec.). (ENG.). 2010. 34.99 (978-1-4001-6495-0(8)); audio compact disk 99.99 (978-1-4001-4495-2(7)); audio compact disk 49.99 (978-1-4001-1495-5(0)) Pub: Tantor Media. Dist(s): IngramPubServ

Country Piano Method. Peter Gelling. (Progressive Ser.). 2004. pap. bk. 19.95 (978-1-86469-212-9(X), 256-049) Kolala Music SGP.

Country Pickin' for Autoharp. Meg Peterson. 1993. 9.98 (978-1-56222-621-3(5), 94060C) Mel Bay.

Country Pop Hits. 2006. audio compact disk 5.95 (978-1-59987-519-4(5)) Braun Media.

Country Rock: Easy Rhythm Guitar Series Volume 7. Created by Hal Leonard Corporation Staff. 2007. pap. bk. 14.99 (978-1-4234-1941-9(3), 1423419413) H Leonard.

Country Songs, Old & New. Perf. by Country Gentlemen. Anno. by John Duffey & Dick Spottswood. Contrib. by Mike Seeger. 1 CD. (Running Time: 44 min.). 1990. audio compact disk (0-9307-40004-2-7) Smithsonian Folkways.
Demonstrates how the original Country Gentlemen helped define modern bluegrass. Recorded in 1959.

Country Songs, Old & New. Perf. by Country Gentlemen et al. Anno. by John Duffey & Dick Spottswood. Contrib. by Mike Seeger. 1 cass. (Running Time: 44 min.). 1990. (0-9307-400040-9307-40004-2-7) Smithsonian Folkways.

Country Summer see Twentieth-Century Poetry in English, No. 12, Recordings of Poets Reading Their Own Poetry

Country Tot. 1 cass., 1 CD. (Kidzup Ser.). (J). audio compact disk 7.98 CD Jewel box. (KPI 119720) NewSound.
Includes: "Head & Shoulders," "The Wheels on the Bus," "Smile, Smile, Smile," "I'm a Big Kid Now" & more.

Country Tot. Kidzup Productions Staff. 1 cass. (Running Time: 90 mins.). (Kidzup Toddler Ser.). (J). 1999. 8.99 (978-1-894281-21-8(7)); audio compact disk 12.99 (978-1-894281-22-5(5)) Pub: Kidzup CAN. Dist(s): Penton Overseas
A great way to introduce your toddlers to country music. The perfect balance between our lively & fun original tunes & the nursery songs we all know & love.

Country Tot Song Book. 1 cass., 1 CD. (Running Time: 1 hr.). (Kidzup Ser.). (J). 2001. pap. bk. 12.99 (978-1-894281-81-2(0)) Pub: Kidzup CAN. Dist(s): Penton Overseas
Contains the perfect balance between our lively & fun original tunes & toddler favorites we all know & love.

Country Walking: Beginner. 1 cass. 1994. 9.95 (978-1-55569-674-0(0)) Great Am Audio.

Country Western CD Counter Display 32 Units. 2007. audio compact disk 255.00 (978-1-59987-591-0(8)) Braun Media.

***Country Wife: Classic Radio Theatre Series.** William Wycherley. Told to Maggie Smith & Jonathan Pryce. (Running Time: 2 hrs. 0 mins. 0 sec.). (ENG.). 2010. audio compact disk 24.95 (978-1-4084-2785-9(0)) Pub: AudioGO. Dist(s): Perseus Dist

Country Wives. unabr. ed. Rebecca Shaw. Read by Gordon Griffin. 8 cass. (Running Time: 9 hrs.). (Sound Ser.). 2002. 69.95 (978-1-84283-166-3(6)) Pub: UlverLrgPrint GBR. Dist(s): Ulverscroft US

Country Year. Sue Hubbell. Read by Alexandra O'Karma. 4 Cass. (Running Time: 6 Hrs). 19.95 (978-1-4025-5595-4(4)) Recorded Bks.

Country Year. Sue Hubbell. 2 cass. (Running Time: 3 hrs.). 1993. pap. bk. 16.95 (978-0-939643-51-6(0), NrthWrd Bks) TandN Child.
Essays.

Country Year, unabr. ed. Sue Hubbell. Narrated by Alexandra O'Karma. 4 cass. (Running Time: 6 hrs.). 1989. 35.00 (978-1-55690-123-2(2), 89680E7) Recorded Bks.
Hubbel, a self-taught naturalist. took refuge in the Missouri Ozarks & turned to commercial beekeeping to make a living.

***Countryside Birds: The Bird Songs of the British Countryside.** George Baker et al. (ENG.). 2010. audio compact disk 15.00 (978-0-7123-0590-7(4)) Pub: Britis Library GBR. Dist(s): Chicago Distribution Ctr

Count's Countdown. 1 cass. (J). 1997. 9.98 (Sony Wonder); audio compact disk 13.98 CD. (Sony Wonder) Sony Music Ent.
The Count's passion for counting knows no bounds, & he goes all out with his friends, Zoe, Ftatateeta & the Bats & Elmo. Includes: Little Miss Count Along, Count up to Nine, One Potato, The Count's Countdown, The Song of the Count & more.

County Fair. unabr. ed. Katherine Valentine. Read by John McDonough. 8 cass. (Running Time: 9 hrs.). 2007. 67.75 (978-1-4281-6588-5(6)); audio compact disk 92.75 (978-1-4281-6590-8(8)) Recorded Bks.

Coup. unabr. ed. John Updike. Read by Marvin Miller. 8 cass. 47.60 (A-102) Audio Bk.
This novel describes events in the imaginary African nation of Kush.

Coup. unabr. collector's ed. John Updike. Read by Wolfram Kandinsky. 8 cass. (Running Time: 12 hrs.). 1979. 64.00 (978-0-7366-0294-5(1), 1282) Books on Tape.
Narrated by its exiled president, Colonel Felix Ellellou, this story is about a modern African state called Kush.

Coup De Coeur! audio compact disk 6.95 (978-88-8148-804-9(3)) EMC-Paradigm.

Coup de Grace see Great American Short Stories, Vol. II, A Collection

Couple Next Door, Vol. 1, Set. Peggy Lynch. 6 cass. (Running Time: 6 hrs.). 1999. 19.98 (AB212) Radio Spirits.

Couple Next Door, Vol. 2, Set. Peggy Lynch. 6 cass. (Running Time: 6 hrs.). 1999. 19.98 (AB213) Radio Spirits.

Couplehood. unabr. ed. Paul Reiser. 3 cass. 1996. 16.95 set. (51899) Books on Tape.
Comedian Reiser comments on "the stuff that's good & bad about being part of a couple." Also says Reiser: "It's pretty funny. My wife laughed".

Couples. unabr. collector's ed. John Updike. Read by John MacDonald. 12 cass. (Running Time: 18 hrs.). 1983. 96.00 (978-0-7366-0374-4(3), 1353) Books on Tape.
Explores the psychosexual natures of a group of young middle-class marrieds of 1963 in Tarbox, Massachusetts.

Couples: How to Stop Arguing & Solve Your Problems. Bob Lancer. (Running Time: 60 mins.). 9.95 (978-0-9628666-9-2(5)) Parent Sol.

Couples Course: Rev up Your Relationship. Barry Neil Kaufman. (ENG.). 2007. audio compact disk 34.50 (978-0-9798105-7-2(4)) Option Inst.

Couples Facing Infertility. abr. ed. Byron Calhoun et al. 2 cass. (Running Time: 2 hrs.). 1995. 9.95 Set. (978-1-57229-024-2(2)) FamilyLife.
How to deal with infertility.

Couples in Crime: Radio Detectives & Their Ladies. Perf. by Joseph Curtin & Alice Frost. 2008. audio compact disk 26.95 (978-0-9789973-2-8(8)) Radio Spirits.

Coupon Treasure Hunt Dialogue. Alfreda C. Doyle. Read by Frieda Carrol. 1 cass. (Running Time: 15 min.). 1991. 9.00 (S.O.R. 4005) Sell Out Recordings.
Possibilities for hunting coupons.

Coupons, Refunding: Your Guide to Ideas & Possibilities. 1 cass. (Running Time: 23 min.). 12.95 (CFSS/CS29) Ctr Self Suff.

Courage. AIO Team Staff. Prod. by Focus on the Family Staff. (Running Time: 1 hr. 10 mins. 0 sec.). (Adventures in Odyssey Life Lessons Ser.). (ENG.). (J). (gr. 3-7). 2005. audio compact disk 5.99 (978-1-58997-180-6(9)) Pub: Focus Family. Dist(s): Tyndale Hse

Courage. Linda Eyre & Richard Eyre. 2 cass. (Running Time: 3 hrs.). (Teaching Your Children Values Ser.). (J). (ps-7). 2000. bk. 16.95 (978-1-56015-784-7(4)) Penton Overseas.
Tape 1: a coaching, "how-to" program for parents; Tape 2: "Alexander's Amazing Adventures" program featuring stories, songs, sound effects & background music, that helps children ages 4-12 to develop social skills, communication skills & life skills. Includes activity cards.

Courage: I Can Do Anything. Stuart Wilde. 1 cass. 11.95 (978-0-930603-49-6(4)) White Dove NM.
Fly like an eagle to the upper limits of your life! Dare to believe in your own power & watch the magic happen! Use this excellent subliminal tape to channel the rivers of power & energy already within you & make your dreams come true.

Courage: Program from the award winning public radio Series. Interview. Hosted by Fred Goodwin. Comment by John Hockenberry. 1 CD. (Running Time: 1 Hour). 2000. audio compact disk 21.95 (978-1-932479-36-2(8), LCM 130) Lichtenstein Creat.
What separates the ordinary neighbor from the heroic life-saver? The bystander from the holocaust rescuer? We?ll look at the science and spectacle of courage.Guests on this show include sociologist Samuel Oliner, writer and lawyer, Harriet Johnson, psychologist Marvin Zuckerman, Carnegie medalist James Stack, and Tony Tedeschi, Ed Mislynski, and

George Healy from the New York City Fire Department?s Rescue Company One. Commentary by John Hockenberry.

Courage & Boldness. Swami Amar Jyoti. 1 cass. 1976. 9.95 (K-2) Truth Consciousness.
Courage & Boldness, truth & justice, The science of cultivating & applying virtues. Persisting in virtue, starting by seeing ourselves.

Courage & Confidence: Egar & the Land of the Twoids. unabr. ed. Trenna Daniells. Read by Trenna Daniells. 12 cass. (Running Time: 30 min.). (One to Grow On Ser.). (J). 1982. 9.95 (978-0-918519-04-7(7), 12003) Trenna Prods.
Helps children learn the values of taking risks the safe & the secure for the better & how sometimes one must risk in order to gain.

Courage & Confidence- Egar & the Land of the Twoids. Trenna Daniells. Narrated by Trenna Daniells. (ENG.). (J). 2009. (978-0-918519-29-0(2)) Trenna Prods.

***Courage & Consequence: My Life as a Conservative in the Fight.** abr. ed. Karl Rove. Read by Karl Rove. 7 CDs. (Running Time: 8 hrs.). 2010. audio compact disk 29.99 (978-1-4423-3406-9(1)) Pub: S&S Audio. Dist(s): S and S Inc

Courage & Honor. Norman Corwin. Perf. by Frederic March. 2 cass. (Running Time: 2 hrs.). (Best of Corwin Ser.: Vol. 1). 1996. 16.95 Set. (978-1-57677-047-4(8)) Lodestone Catalog.
Includes a powerful & poetic drama inspired by the deliberate bombing of innocent people during the Spanish Civil War, a piece that dramatizes the courage & fortitude of the Czechoslovakian people under Nazi occupation; a documentation of life in a typical English village, under constant threat of enemy attack; & a poignant review of the life of a young American soldier killed in battle.

Courage of a Mother: 11 Samuel 21:6. Ed Young. 1982. 4.95 (978-0-7417-1229-5(6), 229) Win Walk.

Courage of Commitment. Helen Caldicott. 1 cass. 9.00 (A0247-87) Sound Photosyn.
A stirring speech from the well informed activist.

Courage of Sanctity: After Dinner Address. Mother Angelica. 1 cass. (National Meeting of the Institute, 1995 Ser.). 4.00 (95N5) IRL Chicago.

Courage of Sarah Noble. Alice Dalgliesh. (J). 1991. 21.75 (978-0-394-76910-3(4)) SRA McGraw.
During pioneer times, eight year-old Sarah Noble and her father, journey into the wild to build a house.

Courage of Sarah Noble. unabr. ed. Alice Dalgliesh. Narrated by Barbara Caruso. 1 cass. (Running Time: 60 min.). (J). 1954. bk. 24.20 (978-0-7887-2658-3(7), 40818) Recorded Bks.
In 1707, an eight-year-old girl travels with her father to build a new home in the Connecticut wilderness. She is afraid when she is left with their Indian neighbors, while her father goes to get the rest of the family. But she remembers her mother's parting words "Keep up your courage, Sarah Noble" & learns to be brave.

Courage of Sarah Noble. unabr. ed. Alice Dalgliesh. Narrated by Barbara Caruso. 1 cass. (Running Time: 1 hr.). (gr. 1 up). 1954. 11.00 (978-0-7887-2629-3(3), 95633E7); audio compact disk 12.00 (978-1-4025-1492-0(1), C1617) Recorded Bks.

Courage of the Heart. 1984. Comn Studies.

Courage: the Backbone to Face A Changing World see Coraje: La Fuerza para Enfrentar un Mundo Cambiante

Courage to Be a Success. Speeches. Mervin L. Evans. 1 cd. (Running Time: 60M). 2002. audio compact disk 19.99 (978-0-914391-31-9(3)) Comm People Pr.

***Courage to Be Free: Discover Your Original Fearless Self.** unabr. ed. Guy Finley. Narrated by Sean Runnette. (Running Time: 2 hrs. 30 mins. 0 sec.). 2010. 19.99 (978-1-4526-5036-4(5)); 11.99 (978-1-4526-7036-2(6)); audio compact disk 19.99 (978-1-4526-0036-9(8)) Pub: Tantor Media. Dist(s): IngramPubServ

***Courage to Be Free (Library Edition) Discover Your Original Fearless Self.** unabr. ed. Guy Finley. Narrated by Sean Runnette. (Running Time: 2 hrs. 30 mins.). 2010. 19.99 (978-1-4526-2036-7(9)); audio compact disk 47.99 (978-1-4526-3036-6(4)) Pub: Tantor Media. Dist(s): IngramPubServ

Courage to Be Rich: The Financial & Emotional Pathways to Material & Spiritual Abundance. abr. ed. Suze Orman. Read by Suze Orman. 5 CDs. (Running Time: 6 hrs.). (ENG., 1999. audio compact disk 29.95 (978-0-553-45641-7(5)) Pub: Random Audio Pubg. Dist(s): Random

Courage to Care: Goodness. Elbert Willis. 1 cass. (Gentleness & Goodness Ser.). 4.00 Fill the Gap.

Courage to Create. 5 cass. Incl. Courage to Create: Fairy Tales. David Hart. 1974.; Courage to Create: Illustrating the Classics. Fritz Eichenberg. 1974.; Courage to Create: The Courage to Create. Edith Wallace. 1974.; Courage to Create: The Courage to Create. Silas Warner. 1974.; Courage to Create: The Courage to Create. M. C. Richards. 1974.; 1974. 17.50 Set.; 4.50 ea. Pendle Hill.

Courage to Create. Interview with Jeanne Moreau et al. 2 cass. (Running Time: 2 hrs.). 20.50 set. (SP-78-04-29, HarperThor) HarpC GBR.

Courage to Create: Fairy Tales see Courage to Create

Courage to Create: Illustrating the Classics see Courage to Create

Courage to Create: The Courage to Create see Courage to Create

Courage to Heal. abr. ed. Ellen Bass & Laura Davis. 1 cass. (Running Time: 3 hrs.). 1999. pap. bk. 40.50 (15303) Courage-to-Change.
Offers hope & encouragement for every woman who was sexually abused as a child.

Courage to Live Your Dreams. Les Brown. 6 cass. 69.95 set. (769PAX) Nightingale-Conant.
One of America's most uplifting & inspiring speakers presents a warm, touching & humorous program of practical usefulness. With wit & wisdom, Les Brown reveals rare insights & deeply moving stories from his personal life & successful career as a disc jockey, politician, public speaker & television personality. Gain The Courage to Live Your Dreams with his powerful message.

Courage to Say No. John L. Bell. Perf. by Wild Goose Worship Group. 1996. 10.95 (369); audio compact disk 15.95 (369) GIA Pubns.

Courage to See Clearly: Living More Fully by Living the Truth. Roger Mellott. 1995. 9.95 (978-1-55977-252-5(2)) CareerTrack Pubns.

***Courage to Stand.** unabr. ed. Tim Pawlenty. (ENG.). 2011. audio compact disk 29.99 (978-1-4143-4574-1(7)) Tyndale Hse.

Courage to Teach: Exploring the Inner Landscape of a Teacher's Life. unabr. ed. Parker J. Palmer. (Running Time: 7 hrs. 0 mins.). (ENG.). 2009. 59.95 (978-1-4417-0000-1(5)); audio compact disk 90.00 (978-1-4417-0001-8(3)) Blckstn Audio.

Courage to Teach: Exploring the Inner Landscape of a Teacher's Life. unabr. ed. Parker J. Palmer. Read by Stefan Rudnicki. (Running Time: 8 hrs. 30 mins.). 2010. audio compact disk 29.95 (978-1-4417-0003-2(X)) Blckstn Audio.

Courage to Teach: Exploring the Inner Landscape of a Teacher's Life. unabr. anniv. ed. Parker J. Palmer. Read by Stefan Rudnicki. (Running Time: 8 hrs. 30 mins.). (ENG.). 2010. 29.95 (978-1-4417-0004-9(8)) Blckstn Audio.

Courage to Think. Shelley Pinz. 2000. (978-0-9700251-2-8(2)) S Pinz Music.

Courage to Think. Shelley Pinz. 1 cass. (Running Time: 1 hr.). 2001.; audio compact disk (978-0-9700251-1-1(4)) S Pinz Music.
A spoken word collection by Chele.

Courageous. unabr. ed. Jack Campbell. Read by Christian Rummel. (Running Time: 10 hrs.). (Lost Fleet Ser.). 2010. 24.99 (978-1-4418-0656-7(3), 9781441806567, Brilliance MP3); 39.97 (978-1-4418-0657-4(1), 9781441806574, Brlnc Audio MP3 Lib); audio compact disk 29.99 (978-1-4418-0654-3(7), 9781441806543, Bril Audio CD Unabri); audio compact disk 97.97 (978-1-4418-0655-0(5), 9781441806550, BriAudCD Unabrid) Brilliance Audio.

***Courageous.** unabr. ed. Jack Campbell. Read by Christian Rummel. (Running Time: 10 hrs.). (Lost Fleet Ser.). 2010. 39.97 (978-1-4418-0658-1(X), 9781441806581, BADLE) Brilliance Audio.

Courageous Customer Care, Vol. 1. unabr. ed. 1 cass. (978-1-891076-08-4(6)) Gemini Press.

Courageous Leadership. unabr. ed. Bill Hybels. (Running Time: 8 hrs. 23 mins. 0 sec.). 2002. audio compact disk 34.99 (978-0-310-24790-6(X)) Zondervan.

Courageous Leadership. unabr. ed. Bill Hybels. (Running Time: 8 hrs. 23 mins. 0 sec.). (ENG.). 2003. 16.99 (978-0-310-26146-9(5)) Zondervan.

Courageous Parenting. Jack Graham & Deb Graham. Read by Wayne Shepherd. (Running Time: 5 hrs. 4 mins.). 2007. audio compact disk 22.99 (978-1-58134-925-2(4)) CrosswayIL.

Course CBT: MCSD Guide to Solution Architectures. Course Technology Staff. 2000. audio compact disk 60.95 (978-0-619-01629-6(9)) Course Tech.

Course CBT: Microsoft NT Workstation 4.0 for End-Users. Joan Carey & Steven M. Johnson. 2000. audio compact disk 26.95 (978-0-619-01384-4(2)) Course Tech.

Course CBT: Microsoft Office 2000 Certified with Windows 98 - Expert. David W. Beskeen et al. 2000. audio compact disk 56.95 (978-0-619-00134-6(8)) Course Tech.

Course CBT: Microsoft PowerPoint 2000 Certified. David W. Beskeen. 2000. audio compact disk 26.95 (978-0-619-00126-1(7)) Course Tech.

Course CBT: Visual Basic 6.0. Course Technology Staff. 2000. audio compact disk 53.95 (978-0-619-03404-7(1)) Course Tech.

Course I. 24. 1992. 100.00 (978-1-878114-29-7(8)) Biblical Counseling.
The audio tapes reflect the teaching in the regular 24-weekSelf-Confrontation course. Each of the 24 tapes is 90 minutesin length, about the amount of teaching time that is available in the two-hour lessons of the course.

Course ILT: A+ CertBlaster (2003 Objectives) 2nd rev. ed. Course Technology Ilt Staff. 2003. audio compact disk 9.94 (978-0-619-25747-7(4)) Course Tech.

Course in Catalan for Foreigners. unabr. ed. 8 cass. (Running Time: 6 hrs.). (CAT.). 1993. pap. bk. & stu. ed. 245.00 (978-0-88432-818-6(X), AFCT10) J Norton Pubs.

Course in Catalan for Foreigners CDs & Text. 5 CDs. (Running Time: 6 hrs.). (CAT.). 2005. audio compact disk 245.00 (978-1-57970-109-3(4), AFCT10D) J Norton Pubs.

Course in Enlightenment. Gary N. Arnold. (ENG.). 2006. audio compact disk 24.95 (978-1-57867-019-2(5)) Windhorse Corp.

Course in Human Design Vol. 2: The Definitive & Complete Reference for the Human Design System. Ed. by Chaitanyo .. Illus. by Chaitanyo . Des. by ZC Design Staff. Prod. by ZC Design Staff. Comment by Zeno . Text by Zeno . 2007. per. 200.00 (978-1-931164-71-9(1)) zc design.

Course in Miracles. Sue Apitz-Upwall. Read by Sue Apitz-Upwall. 1 cass. (Running Time: 90 min.). 1994. 8.95 (1127) Am Fed Astrologers.

Course in Miracles. Jack Boland. 4 cass. 1981. 34.95 (978-0-88152-007-1(1)) Master Mind.
Miracles are natural. When they do not occur, something is wrong. Break the failure pattern that separates you from the source of your good.

Course in Miracles. Foundation for Inner Peace Staff. 42 cass. (Running Time: 42 hrs.). (978-1-55525-027-0(0), 9001A) Nightingale-Conant.
Transcend all limitations & find true contentment & inner peace.

Course in Miracles. unabr. ed. Diane B. Gusic. 9.00 Introduction; 1 cass. (OC117); 54.00 Beginners Program; 6 cass. (OC118); 45.00 Advanced Program; 5 cass. (OC119) Sound Horizons AV.
These are clear, inspired presentation of basic ACIM concepts, & are an excellent learning aid for anyone new to the course - or for anyone studying the course without a teacher.

Course in Miracles, Set. Foundation for Inner Peace Staff. 42 cass. 140.00 (900AX) Nightingale-Conant.
This is an internationally recognized day-by-day self-study program. In this enlightening program, you'll discover: Why love depends on your willingness to give, rather than your desire to get; Why changing the way you see the world works better than trying to change the world itself; Why only God's plan for salvation will work, & why teaching love is the best way to learn it. Includes guidebook.

Course in Miracles: A Collection of Favorite Passages. abr. rev. ed. Richard Thomas et al. 3 cass. (Running Time: 4 hrs. 30 mins. 0 sec.). (ENG.). 1992. 24.95 (978-1-55927-212-4(0)) Pub: Macmill Audio. Dist(s): Macmillan

Course in Miracles: Contains Accept This Gift, a Gift of Healing, & a Gift of Peace. abr. rev. ed. Frances Vaughn & Roger Walsh. Read by Richard Thomas. 4 CDs. (Running Time: 4 hrs. 30 mins. 0 sec.). (ENG.). 2001. audio compact disk 24.95 (978-1-55927-638-2(X)) Pub: Macmill Audio. Dist(s): Macmillan

Course in Miracles: What It Says. Kenneth Wapnick. 1 cass. (Running Time: 1 hr.). 1980. 10.00 (978-1-883360-11-5(0), F-7) Found Inner Peace.

Course in Miracles, a Book for All & None. Kenneth Wapnick. 3 CDs. 2005. audio compact disk 16.00 (978-1-59142-222-8(1), CD118) Foun Miracles.

Course in Miracles, a Book for All & None. Kenneth Wapnick. 2009. 13.00 (978-1-59142-463-5(1)) Foun Miracles.

Course in Miracles & Everyday Life, Set. unabr. ed. Diane B. Gusic. 2 cass. 1994. 16.95 (978-1-879323-20-9(6)) Sound Horizons AV.
For those who have found inspiration & courage from A Course in Miracles, these programs by Diane provide a new & deeper dimension of experience. Here is a firm but gentle voice, leading the way through emotional tangles into a healthier state of mind.

Course in Miracles, Basic & Only the Love Is Real. Marianne Williamson. Read by Marianne Williamson. 1 cass. (Running Time: 90 mins.). (Lectures on a Course in Miracles). 1999. 10.00 (978-1-56170-176-6(9), M704) Hay House.

Course in Miracles on Tape. 42 cass. (Running Time: 63 hrs.). 1985. 140.00 (978-1-883360-08-5(0), F-12) Found Inner Peace.

Course in Miracles Overview (6 CD Set) Speeches. Jerry F. Stefaniak. 6 CD's. (Running Time: 8 Hours total). 2006. audio compact disk 36.00 (978-0-9778706-0-8(X)) J Stefaniak.
If you are interested in learning more about A Course in Miracles, there is no better way of understanding the concepts than by attending Jerry Stefaniak's classes. The next best thing is listening to his talks. This six CD series is an excellent resource for new and seasoned students of the Course. It covers the basic concepts, how they apply to your life and practical support in using these ideas in your daily life. This series also includes his powerful meditations.Reverend Stefaniak uses humor, real down-to-earth, day-to-day examples, and his own life to help the listener understand these wonderful and powerful lessons. Altogether these talks total over 8 hours of spiritual and practical support. Topics covered are:- What are Miracles- What is the Ego- Love and Fear- Releasing Judgments- Healing Relationships- Forgiveness.

Course in Miracles": What It Says see Was "Ein Kurs in Wundern": Besagt

Course in Spoken Tamazight: Berber Dialects of the Middle Atlas. Ernest T. Abdel-Massih. 7 cass. 1971. 63.58 Set. U MI Lang Res.

Course in Weight Loss: 21 Spiritual Lessons for Surrendering Your Weight Forever. unabr. ed. Marianne Williamson. (ENG.). 2010. audio compact disk 29.95 (978-1-4019-2154-5(X)) Hay House.

Course in Winning. Denis Waitley. 20 cass. 159.95 Set incl. flascards & slipcase. (1073AB) Nightingale-Conant.
You can master the 10 qualities of a total winner. This step-by-step instruction course will show you all the new ideas & technologies available in the field of peak performance.

Course of Honor. Lindsey Davis. Read by Diana Bishop. 2000. audio compact disk 115.00 Recorded Bks.

Course of Honour. unabr. ed. Lindsey Davis. Narrated by Diana Bishop. 9 cass. (Running Time: 12 hrs. 45 mins.). 2000. 82.00 (978-1-84197-127-8(8), H1125E7) Recorded Bks.
In AD 31, The Roman Empire was controlled by the Emperor Tiberius. This fact has very little to do with the palace slave Caenis, except that she's as relieved as everyone else that he's generally absent. As Caenis takes a break it is interrupted by a senator & his brother.

Course of Honour. unabr. ed. Lindsey Davis. Narrated by Diana Bishop. 11 CDs. (Running Time: 12 hrs. 45 mins.). 2001. audio compact disk 115.00 (978-1-84197-168-1(5), C1286E7) Recorded Bks.
One morning in 31 A.D., as Caenis, a Roman palace slave, eats breakfast, she is interrupted by a senator & his brother Vespasian, who are destined not only to share her meal, but the rest of her life as well.

Course of Human Events. unabr. ed. David McCullough. Read by David McCullough. 2005. 8.95 (978-0-7435-5201-1(6)); audio compact disk 14.00 (978-0-7435-5038-3(2)) Pub: S&S Audio. Dist(s): S and S Inc

Course of My Life: The Autobiography of Edward Heath. abr. ed. Edward Heath. Read by Edward Heath. 2 cass. (Running Time: 3 hrs.). 1998. 16.85 Set. (978-1-85998-978-4(0)) Ulvrscrft Audio.
Valuable & entertaining insights into the events of the past sixty years.

Course TBT: Database Technologies. Course Technology. 2003. audio compact disk 26.95 (978-0-619-15974-0(X)) Pub: Course Tech. Dist(s): CENGAGE Learn

Course TBT: E-Commerce Curriculum. Course Technology. 2003. audio compact disk 26.95 (978-0-619-15973-3(1)) Pub: Course Tech. Dist(s): CENGAGE Learn

Court Approved Special Advocate (CASA) A Basic Introduction. 2005. 29.95 (978-1-59808-026-1(1)); audio compact disk 24.95 (978-1-59808-025-4(3)) Whsprng Pine.

Court-Martial of Charlie Newell. Gerard Shirar. Narrated by Allen Hite. 2009. audio compact disk 33.95 (978-1-60031-064-5(8)) Spoken Books.

Court of Appeal see Twentieth-Century Poetry in English, No. 26, Recordings of Poets Reading Their Own Poetry

***Courtesan's Scandal.** unabr. ed. Julia London. (Running Time: 11 hrs.). (Scandalous Ser.). 2011. 24.99 (978-1-4418-5168-0(2), 9781441851680, Brilliance MP3); 39.97 (978-1-4418-5169-7(0), 9781441851697, Brlnc Audio MP3 Lib); 24.99 (978-1-4418-5170-3(4), 9781441851703, BAD); 39.97 (978-1-4418-5171-0(2), 9781441851710, BADLE); audio compact disk 19.99 (978-1-4418-5166-6(6), 9781441851666, Bril Audio CD Unabri); audio compact disk 79.97 (978-1-4418-5167-3(4), 9781441851673, BriAudCD Unabrid) Brilliance Audio.

Courting Disaster. Pat Robertson. Ed. by Pat Robertson. Ed. by Terry Meeuwsen. 5 cass. (Running Time: 6 hrs.). 2004. 40.00 (978-0-7861-8378-4(0), 3363) Blckstn Audio.

***Courting Disaster.** unabr. ed. Marc A. Thiessen. Read by Bronson Pinchot. (Running Time: 12 hrs. 15 mins.). 2010. 29.95 (978-1-4417-5633-6(7)); audio compact disk 32.95 (978-1-4417-5632-9(9)) Blckstn Audio.

Courting Disaster: How the Supreme Court Is Usurping the Power of Congress & the People. unabr. ed. Pat Robertson. Narrated by Terry Meeuwsen. 5 CDs. (Running Time: 6 hrs.). (ENG.). 2004. audio compact disk 27.99 (978-1-58926-716-9(8), 6716) Oasis Audio.

Courting Disaster: How the Supreme Court Is Usurping the Power of Congress & the People. unabr. ed. Pat Robertson. Narrated by Terry Meeuwsen. (ENG.). 2004. 19.59 (978-1-60814-157-9(8)) Oasis Audio.

Courting of Sister Wisby see Great American Short Stories, Vol. III, A Collection

Courting of Sister Wisby. Sarah Orne Jewett. 1986. (S-62) Jimcin Record.

Courting Trouble. Lisa Scottoline. Read by Barbara Rosenblat. 1975. 14.95 (978-0-06-074374-1(3)) HarperCollins Pubs.

Courting Trouble. Lisa Scottoline. Read by Kate Burton. 1975. 9.99 (978-0-06-074376-5(X)); audio compact disk 9.99 (978-0-06-074375-8(1)) HarperCollins Pubs.

Courting Trouble. abr. ed. Deeanna Gist. Narrated by Brooke Sanford. (ENG.). 2007. 13.99 (978-1-60814-158-6(6)) Oasis Audio.

Courting Trouble. abr. ed. Deeanna Gist. Narrated by Brooke Sanford. (Running Time: 21600 sec.). (ENG.). 2007. audio compact disk 19.99 (978-1-59859-244-3(0)) Oasis Audio.

***Courting Trouble.** abr. ed. Lisa Scottoline. Read by Kate Burton. (ENG.). 2004. (978-0-06-081425-0(X), Harper Audio); (978-0-06-079793-5(2), Harper Audio) HarperCollins Pubs.

Courting Trouble. abr. ed. Lisa Scottoline. Read by Kate Burton. 2008. audio compact disk 14.99 (978-0-06-167363-4(3), Harper Audio) HarperCollins Pubs.

***Courting Trouble.** unabr. ed. Lisa Scottoline. Read by Barbara Rosenblat. (ENG.). 2004. (978-0-06-078548-2(9), Harper Audio) HarperCollins Pubs.

***Courting Trouble.** unabr. ed. Lisa Scottoline. Read by Barbara Rosenblat. (ENG.). 2004. (978-0-06-081414-4(4), Harper Audio) HarperCollins Pubs.

Courting Trouble. unabr. ed. Lisa Scottoline. Narrated by Barbara Rosenblat. 8 cass. (Running Time: 11 hrs.). 2002. 76.00 (978-0-7887-5163-9(8)) Recorded Bks.

Courting Trouble. unabr. ed. Lisa Scottoline. Narrated by Barbara Rosenblat. 8 cass. (Running Time: 11 hrs.). 2002. 39.95 (978-1-4025-2397-7(1), RG089) Recorded Bks.
Attorney Anne Murphy joins a Philadelphia-based law firm coming across the country to escape her past. Over a holiday weekend she is shocked to read of her own death in the morning paper. Determined to flush out the murderer before he finds that he killed the wrong woman, Anne reluctantly enlists the help of her new colleagues. Their hesitance to become involved however, can cost all of them their lives.

Courting Trouble. unabr. ed. Lisa Scottoline. Narrated by Barbara Rosenblat. 9 CDs. (Running Time: 11 hrs.). 2002. audio compact disk 89.00 (978-1-4025-2967-2(8), C1856) Recorded Bks.

Courtroom Conduct: Tactics, Ethics, Contempt, & Common Sense. Read by Maxine M. Chesney et al. (Running Time: 2 hrs. 30 min.). 1991. 70.00 Incl. 115p. tape materials. (CP-54157) Cont Ed Bar-CA.
Learn what conduct is unproductive & improper; proper zealous representation, voir dire, argument, trial objection, motion, or opening statement; what matters should be heard outside the jury's presence; handling a lying witness; how to avoid pitfalls in representing multiple defendants; balancing duty of confidentiality with duties as officer of the court.

Courtroom Procedures for Court Reporters: Syllabus. Robert E. Bennett. 1977. 42.30 (978-0-89420-137-0(9), 456000) Natl Book.

Courts of Chaos. Roger Zelazny. Read by Roger Zelazny. 2 vols. (Chronicles of Amber: Bk. 5). 2002. (978-1-58807-518-5(4)) Am Pubng Inc.

Courts of Chaos. Roger Zelazny. Read by Roger Zelazny. 2 vols. (Chronicles of Amber: Bk. 5). 2003. audio compact disk 25.00 (978-1-58807-257-3(6)); audio compact disk (978-1-58807-688-5(1)) Am Pubng Inc.

Courts of Chaos. abr. ed. Roger Zelazny. Read by Roger Zelazny. 2 vols. (Running Time: 3 hrs.). (Chronicles of Amber: Bk. 5). 2002. 18.00 (978-1-58807-130-9(8)) Am Pubng Inc.
Amber, the one real world of which all others - including our own Earth - are but Shadows For untold millennia, the cosmic Pattern sustained order in Amber and all the known worlds. But now the forces of Chaos have succeeded in disrupting the Pattern, unleashing destructive forces beyond measure...forces meant to reshape the universe. To save Amber, Corwin, prince of the blood, champion of the perfect realm, must undertake the most perilous journey of his life. A journey that will take him through all the terrors of Shadows to the enemy's last stonghold. A journey beyond the very edge of existence...to the Courts of Chaos.

Courts of Love. unabr. collector's ed. Ellen Gilchrist. Read by Mary Peiffer. 7 cass. (Running Time: 10 hrs. 30 min.). 1997. 56.00 (978-0-7366-3701-5(X), 4386) Books on Tape.
Probes the intricate, sometimes fragile bonds between friends, family & lovers.

Courts of Love: The Story of Eleanor of Aquitaine. unabr. ed. Jean Plaidy. Read by Lindsay Sandison. 16 cass. (Running Time: 24 hrs.). (Isis Ser.). (J). 1996. 104.95 (978-1-85695-222-4(3), 960209) Pub: ISIS Lrg Prnt GBR. Dist(s): Ulverscroft US

***Courtship.** Zondervan. (Running Time: 10 hrs. 3 mins. 36 sec.). (Singing River Ser.). (ENG.). 2010. 9.99 (978-0-310-86978-8(1)) Zondervan.

Courtship. abr. ed. Catherine Coulter. Read by Anne Flosnik. (Running Time: 21600 sec.). (Bride Ser.). 2007. audio compact disk 14.99 (978-1-59737-828-4(3), 9781597378284, BCD Value Price) Brilliance Audio.

Courtship. unabr. ed. Catherine Coulter. Read by Anne Flosnik. (Running Time: 10 hrs.). (Bride Ser.). 2006. 39.25 (978-1-59737-826-0(7), 9781597378260, BADLE); 24.95 (978-1-59737-825-3(9), 9781597378253, BAD); 82.25 (978-1-59737-820-8(8), 9781597378208, BrilAudUnabridg); audio compact disk 97.25 (978-1-59737-822-2(4), 9781597378222, BriAudCD Unabrid); audio compact disk 39.25 (978-1-59737-824-6(0), 9781597378246, Brinc Audio MP3 Lib); audio compact disk 36.95 (978-1-59737-821-5(6), 9781597378215, Bril Audio CD Unabri); audio compact disk 24.95 (978-1-59737-823-9(2), 9781597378239, Brilliance MP3) Brilliance Audio.
Dear Reader: You met Heatherington in The Sherbrooke Bride and Helen Mayberry in Mad Jack. Now the two get together to track down a mystical treasure that Helen calls King Edward's Lamp. Helen is a big girl - only two inches shorter than Heatherington - a resolute taskmistress, owner of her own inn. She adores her father, Lord Prith, and wants to find the lamp more than anything. It is her only passion - until she meets Heatherington. Spenser Heatherington, Lord Beecham, enjoys Helen's pursuit of him. He is a renowned womanizer, a resolute bachelor, and really enjoys his life. When she throws him to the ground and sits on him, and he finally admits that he will succumb to her, she informs him, to his chagrin, that she doesn't want a lover, she wants a partner. But things work out a bit differently than either of them expect. Indeed, Heatherington, unused to being thwarted, takes drastic steps to change his "big girl's" mind. Do they find Helen's lamp? Is there more to this treasure than either of them knows? Listen and find out . . . I hope you enjoy visiting the Sherbrookes when they stick their oars into the treasure hunt. Write me and tell me how you liked The Courtship at P.O. Box 17, Mill Valley, CA 94942 or email me at ReadMoi@aol.com. Catherine Coulter.

Courtship after Marriage: Romance Can Last a Lifetime. Zig Ziglar. Read by Zig Ziglar. 1 cass. (Zig Ziglar Presents Ser.). 1990. 9.95 (978-1-56207-004-5(5)) Zig Ziglar Corp.
Remember the feelings you had when you were courting? Zig will convince you it's possible to recapture those feelings & rekindle the spark of romance. Zig shares practical & specific action steps that help you "start over" & "court" your spouse just as you did before you were married.

Courtship after Marriage: Romance Can Last a Lifetime. Zig Ziglar. Read by Zig Ziglar. 6 cass. 1991. bk. 64.95 set.; 59.95 set. (978-1-56207-208-7(0)) Zig Ziglar Corp.

Courtship Gift. unabr. ed. Julie Parsons. Narrated by Gerri Halligan. 8 cass. (Running Time: 11 hrs.). 2000. 72.00 (978-1-84197-208-4(8), H1207L8) Recorded Bks.
David Neale & his wife, Anna, are being watched. When David is found dead under mysterious circumstances, Anna is suddenly on her own - defenseless & vulnerable. But this is just what a man who calls himself Matthew has always wanted. He is watching & waiting in anticipation. When he is ready, he will bring her his gift - a courtship gift of death & betrayal, woven together in a shroud of silk.

***Courtship of Carol Sommars: A Selection from Right Next Door.** unabr. ed. Debbie Macomber. Read by Angela Dawe. (Running Time: 5 hrs.). 2010. 14.99 (978-1-4418-6312-6(5), 9781441863126, BAD); 14.99 (978-1-4418-6311-9(7), 9781441863119, Brilliance MP3); audio compact disk 14.99 (978-1-4418-6310-2(9), 9781441863102, Bril Audio CD Unabri) Brilliance Audio.

Courtship of Miles Standish: The Lover's Errand see Best Loved Poems of Longfellow

Courtship of Miles Standish & Evangeline. Henry Wadsworth Longfellow. 1 cass. (Running Time: 1 hr.). (Radiobook Ser.). 1987. 4.98 (978-0-929541-13-6(8)) Radiola Co.
Two complete stories.

Courtship Through the Ages see My World & Welcome to It

Cousin Bette. Honoré de Balzac. Read by Juan Carlos J. Vega. (Running Time: 3 hrs.). 2002. 16.95 (978-1-60083-253-6(9), Audiofy Corp) Iofy Corp.

Cousin Bette. unabr. ed. Honoré de Balzac. Read by Johanna Ward. 12 cass. (Running Time: 17 hrs. 30 mins.). 2000. 83.95 (978-0-7861-1820-5(2), 2619) Blckstn Audio.
Bette is Lisbeth Fischer, an excruciatingly cunning poor relative who both depends upon & nurses a grudge against the family of her beautiful cousin, Adeline. That family is slowly being ruined by the uncontrollable sexual appetites of Adeline's husband, Baron Hulot - appetites that will give Cousin Bette opportunity to extract her vengeance.

Cousin Bette. unabr. ed. Read by Johanna Ward. (Running Time: 59400 sec.). 2007. audio compact disk 44.95 (978-0-7861-5914-7(6)); audio compact disk 108.00 (978-0-7861-5913-0(8)) Blckstn Audio.

Cousin Henry. Anthony Trollope. Read by Anais 9000. 2009. 27.95 (978-1-60112-229-2(2)) Babblebooks.

Cousin Henry, Set. unabr. ed. Anthony Trollope. Read by Flo Gibson. 5 cass. (Running Time: 7 hrs. 30 mins.). (gr. 8 up). 1991. 20.95 (978-1-55685-215-2(0)) Audio Bk Con.
The timid & cowardly Henry Jones alone knows the whereabouts of a second will which disinherits him from his uncle's property. During his guilt throes he arouses the suspicion of all around him.

Cousin Jacks: The Cornish in America. unabr. ed. A. L. Rowse. Read by Bill Kelsey. 10 cass. (Running Time: 15 hrs.). 1988. 80.00 (978-0-7366-1373-6(0), 2268) Books on Tape.
Cornwall is the southwestern-most country of England. The people of this country, the Cornish, had their own Celtic language & were great resistors against the Saxons. It was the last part of England to be settled. The land was too confining to hold them, so in the 18th century they set off to make fortunes abroad.

Cousin Jess Motor Tour of Orange County, California: A Self-Guided Audio Tour. Short Stories. Charla Spence. Concept by Charla Spence. Ed. by Florence Dann. Prod. by Tortuga Enterprises. Contrib. by Florence Dann. Illus. by Nancy Redd. Engineer Bill Trousdale. 1 CD. (Running Time: 75 min 21 sec.). 2003. audio compact disk 19.95 (978-0-9744643-0-5(9)) Tortuga Enterp.
A self-guided audio CD tour from a "local's perspective" of things to see and do in Orange County California including sightseeing, restaurants, major attactions, sporting activities, and nearby side trips. Little known treasures of the area.

Cousin Kate. unabr. ed. Georgette Heyer. Read by Sian Phillips. 10 cass. (Running Time: 12 hrs. 30 min.). 1990. 84.95 set. (978-0-7451-6008-5(5), CAB 501) AudioGO.
Lady Minerva brings her orphaned niece Kate to live at her secluded estate & treats the young woman like royalty. So at first, Kate doesn't notice that nobody ever leaves Staplewood's grounds. But when she sees her last tie to the outside world gently severed & then discovers Minerva's sinister plans, Kate realizes she must escape - if there's still time.

Cousin Phillis. Elizabeth Gaskell. 2005. pap. bk. 51.95 (978-1-86015-007-4(1)); pap. bk. 34.95 (978-1-86015-475-1(1)) Ulverscroft US.

Cousin Phyllis. Elizabeth Gaskell. Read by Kenneth Branagh. 3 cass. (Running Time: 3 hrs 55 min.). 19.95 (CC/027) C to C Cassettes.
Against a background of new commercial ideas confronting traditional pastoral themes is a story of unfulfilled love.

Cousin Phyllis. unabr. ed. Elizabeth Gaskell. Narrated by Flo Gibson. 3 cass. (Running Time: 4 hrs.). 2003. 16.95 (978-1-55685-737-9(3)) Audio Bk Con.
With a young love thwarted, a sympathetic cousin tries his best to ease the pain.

Cousin Pons. unabr. ed. Honoré de Balzac. Narrated by Flo Gibson. 7 cass. (Running Time: 10 hrs.). (gr. 10 up). 2000. 25.95 (978-1-55685-637-2(7)) Audio Bk Con.
Purest friendship is pitted against callousness & greed over a dying art collector's treasures.

Cousins. Excerpts. Paulette Jiles. Read by Paulette Jiles. 1 cass. (Running Time: 60 min.). 1993. 13.95 (978-1-55644-382-4(X), 13011) Am Audio Prose.
Novel excerpts.

Cousins. unabr. ed. Elizabeth Spencer. Read by Elizabeth Spencer. 2 cass. (Running Time: 1 hr. 47 min.). 1993. 13.95 set. (978-1-55644-388-6(9), 13031) Am Audio Prose.
Novella.

Cousin's Challenge. unabr. ed. Wanda E. Brunstetter. Narrated by Jill Shellabarger. (Running Time: 7 hrs. 49 mins. 53 sec.). (Indiana Cousins Ser.: Bk. 3). (ENG.). 2010. 20.99 (978-1-60814-616-1(2)); audio compact disk 29.99 (978-1-59859-670-0(5)) Oasis Audio.

Cousins in the Castle. unabr. ed. Barbara Brooks Wallace. Narrated by Steven Crossley. 4 cass. (Running Time: 5 hrs. 15 mins.). (J). 2001. pap. bk. & stu. ed. 55.24 Recorded Bks.
When 11-year-old Amelia loses her father in a hotel fire, she must leave her London home & live in America with a relative she has never seen. But when her ship arrives in New York City, Amelia is left alone on the pier.

Cousins in the Castle. unabr. ed. Barbara Brooks Wallace. Narrated by Steven Crossley. 4 pieces. (Running Time: 5 hrs. 15 mins.). (gr. 3 up). 2001. 42.00 (978-0-7887-4659-8(6), 96186E7) Recorded Bks.

Cousin's Prayer. unabr. ed. Wanda E. Brunstetter. Narrated by Jill Shellabarger. (Running Time: 8 hrs. 12 mins. 46 sec.). (Indiana Cousins Ser.: Bk. 2). (ENG.). 2009. 20.99 (978-1-60814-571-3(9)); audio compact disk 29.99 (978-1-59859-618-2(7)) Oasis Audio.

Cousin's Promise. unabr. ed. Wanda E. Brunstetter. Narrated by Jill Shellabarger. (Running Time: 7 hrs. 44 mins. 57 sec.). (Indiana Cousins Ser.: Bk. 1). (ENG.). 2009. audio compact disk 27.99 (978-1-59859-551-2(2)) Oasis Audio.

Cousin's Promise. unabr. ed. Wanda E. Brunstetter. Narrated by Jill Shellabarger. (Running Time: 7 hrs. 44 mins. 57 sec.). (Indiana Cousins Ser.: Bk. 1). (ENG.). 2009. 19.59 (978-1-60814-468-6(2)) Oasis Audio.

Cove. abr. ed. Catherine Coulter. Read by Sandra Burr. (Running Time: 21600 sec.). (FBI Thriller Ser.: No. 1). 2006. audio compact disk 16.99 (978-1-4233-1825-5(0), 9781423318255, BCD Value Price) Brilliance Audio.
The Cove is a quaint little postcard town made up only of old folk who sell the World's Greatest Ice Cream - a secret recipe that brings lots of tourists into town. Into The Cove comes Sally Brainerd, daughter of murdered Amory St. John of Washington, D.C., seeking sanctuary, and FBI Special Agent James Quinlan who's undercover and after her. He's got a murder to solve, and he believes she's the key. But is she really?.

Cove. abr. unabr. ed. Catherine Coulter. Read by Sandra Burr. (Running Time: 39600 sec.). (FBI Thriller Ser.: No. 1). 2006. audio compact disk 39.25 (978-1-4233-0042-7(4), 9781423300427, Brinc Audio MP3 Lib); audio compact disk 24.95 (978-1-4233-0041-0(6), 9781423300410, Brilliance MP3) Brilliance Audio.

Cove. unabr. ed. Catherine Coulter. Read by Mary Peiffer. 8 cass. (Running Time: 12 hrs.). (FBI Thriller Ser.: No. 1). 1997. 64.00 (978-0-913369-49-4(7), 4253) Books on Tape.
An FBI agent goes undercover, tracks a female murder suspect to a seaside town. He doesn't expect to fall in love with her.

Cove. unabr. ed. Catherine Coulter. Read by Mary Peiffer. 8 cass. (Running Time: 12 hrs.). (FBI Thriller Ser.: No. 1). 1996. 104.00 (978-0-7366-2564-7(X), 4253) Books on Tape.
The Cove is a postcard town, world-famous for ice cream & its endless supply of peace & quiet. To this charming retreat comes Sally Brainerd, daughter of Amory St. John, recently murdered - & on Sally's heels, James Quinlan, an undercover FBI agent.

Cove. unabr. ed. Catherine Coulter. Read by Sandra Burr. (Running Time: 11 hrs.). (FBI Thriller Ser.: No. 1). 2006. 39.25 (978-1-4233-0044-1(0), 9781423300441, BADLE); 82.25 (978-1-4233-1824-8(2), 9781423318248, BrilAudUnabridg); audio compact disk 97.25 (978-1-4233-1823-1(4), 9781423318231, BriAudCD Unabrid); audio compact disk 36.95 (978-1-4233-1822-4(6), 9781423318224) Brilliance Audio.
The Cove is a quaint little postcard town made up only of old folk who sell the World's Greatest Ice Cream - a secret recipe that brings lots of tourists into town. Into The Cove comes Sally Brainerd, daughter of murdered Amory St. John of Washington, D.C., seeking sanctuary, and FBI Special Agent James Quinlan who's undercover and after her. He's got a murder to solve, and he believes she's the key. But is she really?.

Coven of Witches' Tales. unabr. ed. Read by Vincent Price. 1 cass. (Running Time: 90 min.). Incl. Bewitched Court. Dorothy Gladys Spicer. (J). (CPN 1338); Coven of Witches' Tales: To Cause a Witch to Die. (J). (CPN 1338); Coven of Witches' Tales: To Make a Witch Pockmarked. (J). (CPN 1338); Coven of Witches' Tales: To Summon Another Witch. (J). (CPN 1338); Stone King. Dorothy G. Spicer. (J). (CPN 1338); Thirteen Witches: Old Sal's Curse. Dorothy G. Spicer. (J). (CPN 1338); (J). 1988. 9.95 (978-0-89845-800-8(5), CPN 1338) HarperCollins Pubs.
These tales are gathered from England, Wales & Russia.

Coven of Witches' Tales: To Cause a Witch to Die see Coven of Witches' Tales

Coven of Witches' Tales: To Make a Witch Pockmarked see Coven of Witches' Tales

Coven of Witches' Tales: To Summon Another Witch see Coven of Witches' Tales

Covenant. 2006. audio compact disk 17.98 (978-5-558-18339-9(X), Verity) Brentwood Music.

Covenant. Beverly Lewis. Narrated by Christina Moore. 6 cass. (Running Time: 8 hrs. 30 mins.). (Abram's Daughters Ser.: No. 1). 54.00 (978-1-4025-3703-5(4)) Recorded Bks.

Covenant. James A. Michener. Read by Larry McKeever. 1993. 104.00 (978-0-7366-2565-4(8)); 112.00 (978-0-7366-2566-1(6)) Books on Tape.

***Covenant.** abr. ed. Beverly Lewis. Narrated by Aimee Lilly. (ENG.). 2010. 5.98 (978-1-59644-138-5(0), christaudio); audio compact disk 5.98 (978-1-59644-918-3(7), christaudio) christianaud.

Covenant, Pt. 1. unabr. ed. James A. Michener. Read by Larry McKeever. 13 cass. (Running Time: 6 hrs. 30 min.). 1993. 104.00 (3315A) Books on Tape.
Black & white immigrants carve an empire out of the vast wilderness that becomes South Africa.

Covenant, Pt. 2. unabr. ed. James A. Michener. Read by Larry McKeever. 13 cass. (Running Time: 6 hrs. 30 min.). 1993. 104.00 (3315B) Books on Tape.

Covenant, Pt. 3. unabr. ed. James A. Michener. Read by Larry McKeever. 14 cass. (Running Time: 21 hrs.). 1993. 112.00 (3315C) Books on Tape.

Covenant Brothers. Perf. by Lonnie Brown. 1 cass., 1 CD. 9.98 (978-1-57908-363-2(3), 1432); audio compact disk 15.98 CD. (978-1-57908-362-5(5), 1432) Platinm Enter.

Covenant CD #30431;#32004; CD: #23567;#32650;#21109;#20316;#35433;#27468;#38598; 2. (CHI.). 2001. audio compact disk 15.00 (978-0-9721862-4-7(7)) Lamb Music & Min.

Covenant Christmas Sampler. 1 cass. 2.37 (10001123); audio compact disk 8.95 (2800837) Covenant Comms.
Destined to become a favorite each Christmas season.

Covenant Household. Read by Douglas Wilson. 8 cass. 1997. 10.00 (978-1-59128-322-5(1)) Canon Pr ID.

Covenant Made by Blood. Kenneth Copeland. 6 cass. 1988. 30.00 Set incl. study guide. (978-0-88114-790-2(7)) K Copeland Pubns.
Blessings of the blood covenant.

Covenant Music Sampler. 1 cass. 5.95 (10001077); audio compact disk 9.95 (2800705) Covenant Comms.

Covenant of Blessing: Viewing Life Through the Larger Context of God's Covenant. Mac Hammond. 5 CDs. 2006. audio compact disk 25.00 (978-1-57399-301-2(8)) Mac Hammond.
You don't have to be confused in the midst of turmoil! As Mac Hammond shares in this series, you can position your life for increase amid tough circumstances by understanding your covenant of blessing with the Lord.

Covenant of Blood. 2001. 39.95 (978-0-9706661-0-9(1)) Heart Min.

Covenant of Favor. Creflo A. Dollar. 2008. audio compact disk 14.00 (978-1-59944-705-6(3)) Creflo Dollar.

***Covenant of Genesis.** unabr. ed. Andy McDermott. Narrated by Gildart Jackson. (Running Time: 17 hrs. 30 mins. 0 sec.). (Nina Wilde/Eddie Chase Ser.). 2011. audio compact disk 95.99 (978-1-4526-3019-9(4)) Pub: Tantor Media. Dist(s): IngramPubServ

***Covenant of Genesis: A Novel.** unabr. ed. Andy McDermott. Narrated by Gildart Jackson. (Running Time: 17 hrs. 30 mins.). (Nina Wilde/Eddie Chase Ser.). 2011. 21.99 (978-1-4526-7019-5(6)); 29.99 (978-1-4526-5019-7(5)); audio compact disk 39.99 (978-1-4526-0019-2(8)) Pub: Tantor Media. Dist(s): IngramPubServ

***Covenant of Genesis (Library Edition) A Novel.** unabr. ed. Andy McDermott. Narrated by Gildart Jackson. (Running Time: 17 hrs. 30 mins.). (Nina Wilde/Eddie Chase Ser.). 2011. 39.99 (978-1-4526-2019-0(9)) Tantor Media.

Covenant of Increase. Creflo A. Dollar. 2008. audio compact disk 14.00 (978-1-59944-699-8(5)) Creflo Dollar.

Covenant of Love. unabr. ed. Gilbert Morris. Read by Maynard Villers. 12 cass. (Running Time: 12 hrs. 24 min.). (Appomattox Ser.: Bk. 1). 1998. 64.95 Set. (978-1-55686-832-0(4)) Books in Motion.
Two cousins vie for the hand of beautiful Melanie Benton & her final decision sparks a spiralling descent for the rejected suitor. Set against the backdrop of the Civil War, the Rocklin family, like the nation, has been ripped apart.

Covenant of Marriage: Eternal Truths for a Lifetime of Happiness. Mac Hammond. 1 cass. 1996. 18.00 (978-1-57399-028-8(0)) Mac Hammond.
Teaching on marriage relationship.

Covenant of Surrender. Swami Amar Jyoti. 1 cass. 1975. 9.95 (E-28) Truth Consciousness.
The first virtue of a disciple. Taking refuge unto silence.

Covenant of the Flame. unabr. ed. David Morrell. Read by David Regal. (Running Time: 15 hrs.). 2006. 39.25 (978-1-59737-778-2(3), 9781597377782, BADLE); 24.95 (978-1-59737-777-5(5), 9781597377775, BAD); 39.25 (978-1-59737-776-8(7), 9781597377768, Brinc Audio MP3 Lib); audio compact disk 117.25 (978-1-59737-774-4(0), 9781597377744, BriAudCD Unabrid); audio compact disk 29.95 (978-1-59737-773-7(2), 9781597377737, Bril Audio CD Unabri); audio compact disk 24.95 (978-1-59737-775-1(9), 9781597377751, Brilliance MP3) Brilliance Audio.
For two thousand years a hidden conflict has been waged. Now it is bursting into the open - in a pitched battle over the very future of the planet... In the Amazon and in Africa, from oil spills to animal slaughters, the earth is being defiled, and two covert armies are locked in mortal conflict - with a woman reporter caught in the middle. Drawn into the mysterious disappearance of a gray-eyed stranger and his horrific murder by fire, Tess Drake and a veteran New York City police officer follow the trail of blood from Manhattan to Washington to the ancient caverns of Europe. Hunted by both sides, fighting for her life, Tess races toward the dark heart of a secret that will rock the world.

Covenant of Wealth & Exchange. Creflo A. Dollar. 3 cass. (Running Time: 4 hrs. 30 mins.). 2000. 15.00 (978-1-931172-76-9(5), TS279, Kidz Faith) Pub: Creflo Dollar. Dist(s): STL Dist NA

Covenant Purpose for Angels. Creflo A. Dollar. 2008. audio compact disk 21.00 (978-1-59944-709-4(6)) Creflo Dollar.

Covenant to Prosper. Creflo A. Dollar. cass. & video 25.00 (978-1-59089-122-3(8)) Pub: Creflo Dollar. Dist(s): STL Dist NA

Covenant World. Speeches. 6 CDs. (Running Time: 6 hrs. 30 mins.). 2004. audio compact disk 40.00 (978-1-59089-876-5(1)) Creflo Dollar.

Covenant World. Speeches. Creflo A. Dollar. 6 cassettes. (Running Time: 6 hrs. 30 minutes). 2003. 29.00 (978-1-59089-875-8(3)) Creflo Dollar.

Covenants of God. Lester Sumrall. 8 cass. (Running Time: 12 hrs.). 1999. 32.00 (978-1-58568-022-1(2)) Sumrall Pubng.

Covenants of Prayer. Stephen Mansfield. 1 cass. (Running Time: 90 mins.). (Studies in Church History Ser.: Vol. 6). 2000. 5.00 (SM02-006) Morning NC.
An in-depth look at different philosophies that have influenced church history, this series provides excellent keys for understanding how to effectively confront the important issues of our times.

Coventry Carol. Perf. by Point of Grace Staff. 1 cass. 1999. Provident Music.

Cover Girls. abr. ed. T. D. Jakes. Read by Pamala Tyson. (ENG.). 2005. 14.98 (978-1-59483-287-1(0)) Pub: Hachet Audio. Dist(s): HachBkGrp

Cover Her Face. P. D. James. 2 CDs. (Running Time: 2 hrs. 0 mins. 0 sec.). (Adam Dalgliesh Mystery Ser.). (ENG.). 2002. audio compact disk 24.95 (978-0-563-52827-2(3)) Pub: AudioGO. Dist(s): Perseus Dist

Cover Her Face. P. D. James. Contrib. by Robin Ellis. 2 CDs. (Running Time: 1 hr. 55 mins.). (Adam Dalgliesh Mystery Ser.). 2006. audio compact disk 29.95 (978-0-7927-3983-8(3), BBCD 134) AudioGO.

Cover Her Face. unabr. ed. P. D. James. Read by Penelope Dellaporta. 7 cass. (Running Time: 10 hrs. 30 min.). (Adam Dalgliesh Mystery Ser.). 1993. 56.00 (978-0-7366-2330-8(2), 3110) Books on Tape.
Chief Inspector Adam Dalgliesh investigates the murder of a social climber, her climb abruptly ended by a strangler's fingers.

Cover Her Face. unabr. ed. P. D. James. Read by John Franklyn-Robbins. 5 Cass. (Running Time: 8.25 Hrs). (Adam Dalgliesh Mystery Ser.). 24.95 (978-1-4025-2358-8(0)) Recorded Bks.

Cover Her Face. unabr. ed. P. D. James. Narrated by John Franklyn-Robbins. 6 cass. (Running Time: 8 hrs.). (Adam Dalgliesh Mystery Ser.). 1992. 51.00 (978-1-55690-676-3(5), 92329E7) Recorded Bks.
Inspector Dalgliesh of Scotland Yard is called upon to solve the murder of the young master of a manor house's fiance.

Cover of Night. abr. ed. Linda Howard. Read by Joyce Bean & Dick Hill. (Running Time: 21600 sec.). 2007. audio compact disk 14.99 (978-1-4233-1008-2(X), 9781423310082, BCD Value Price) Brilliance Audio.

Cover of Night. unabr. ed. Linda Howard. Read by Joyce Bean & Dick Hill. (Running Time: 12 hrs.). 2006. 39.25 (978-1-4233-1006-8(3), 9781423310068, BADLE); 24.95 (978-1-4233-1005-1(5), 9781423310051, BAD) Brilliance Audio.

Cover of Night. unabr. ed. Linda Howard. Read by Dick Hill & Joyce Bean. (Running Time: 43200 sec.). 2006. 82.25 (978-1-4233-1000-6(4), 9781423310006, BriAudUnabridg); 32.95 (978-1-4233-0999-4(5), 9781423309994, BAU); audio compact disk 97.25 (978-1-4233-1002-0(0), 9781423310020, BriAudCD Unabrid); audio compact disk 39.25 (978-1-4233-1004-4(7), 9781423310044, Brinc Audio MP3 Lib); audio compact disk 36.95 (978-1-4233-1001-3(2), 9781423310013, Bril Audio CD Unabri) Brilliance Audio.
Please enter a Synopsis.

Cover of Night. unabr. ed. Linda Howard. Read by Susan Ericksen et al. (Running Time: 43200 sec.). 2006. audio compact disk 24.95 (978-1-4233-1003-7(9), 9781423310037, Brilliance MP3) Brilliance Audio.

Cover Story. unabr. ed. Colin Forbes. Read by David Rintoul. 10 cass. (Running Time: 13 hrs. 45 min.). 2001. 84.95 (978-1-85089-616-6(X), 91051) Pub: ISIS Audio GBR. Dist(s): Ulverscroft US
"Adam Procane has to be stopped..." It was the last message Bob Newman's wife ever sent, & even as he read it, he knew she was dead. Bob Newman is out for revenge.

Cover the Bible. Ralph W. Neighbour, Jr. 9 cass. (Running Time: 26 hrs.). 2001. 129.95 (CTB4); 169.95 (CTB3) Touch Pubns.
End confusion & gain clarity & understanding about what the Bible teaches with detailed one hour lectures.

Cover the Earth. Contrib. by Integrity Music. 2006. audio compact disk 17.98 (978-5-558-11362-4(6)) Integrity Music.

Cover to Cover, No. 2. Ed. by Oxford Staff. (Cover to Cover Ser.). 2007. audio compact disk 39.95 (978-0-19-475817-8(6)) OUP.

***Cover-up.** unabr. ed. Michele Martinez. Read by Nanette Savard. (ENG.). 2007. (978-0-06-144756-3(0), Harper Audio); (978-0-06-145121-8(5), Harper Audio) HarperCollins Pubs.

Cover-Up: Mystery at the Super Bowl. John Feinstein. Read by John Feinstein. 5 CDs. (Running Time: 6 hrs. 4 mins.). (YA). (gr. 5-8). 2007. audio compact disk 50.00 (978-0-7393-6235-8(6), Listening Lib) Pub: Random Audio Pubg. Dist(s): Random
The Super Bowl. America's biggest sports spectacle. More than ninety-five million fans will be watching. But Steve Thomas and Susan Carol Anderson know that what they'll be watching is a lie. They know that the entire offensive line of the California Dreams have failed their doping tests and shouldn't be allowed to play. They know that the Dreams' owner is trying to cover up the test results until after the game. They know that they are sitting on the biggest sports scandal of the decade. What they don't know - yet - is how to prove it. These two fourteen-year-old reporters have broken big stories before. In fact, their past successes have made them a little bit famous. But nothing prepares you for the sheer size of the Super Bowl. The players are huge. The hype is overwhelming. The egos are gigantic. And the money? Astronomical. So a Super Bowl scandal is by far the biggest story Steve and Susan Carol have tried to tackle - with the biggest opponents lining up to take them down.

Cover-up: Mystery at the Super Bowl. unabr. ed. John Feinstein. Read by John Feinstein. (Running Time: 21840 sec.). (ENG.). (J). (gr. 5-9). 2008. audio compact disk 30.00 (978-0-7393-6233-4(X), Listening Lib) Pub: Random Audio Pubg. Dist(s): Random

Cover Us Daddy So the Wrong Fires Won't Start. Rita Twiggs. 1 cass. (Running Time: 60 mins.). 2001. 5.99 (978-0-88368-263-0(X), 77263X) Pub: Whitaker Hse. Dist(s): Anchor Distributors

Cover Your Assets. 2005. cd-rom & audio compact disk 99.00 (978-0-9746844-4-4(9)) SuccessDNA.

Covered or Uncovered: 1 Cor. 11:1-17. Ed Young. 1986. Rental 4.95 (978-0-7417-1505-0(8), 505) Win Walk.

Covered Wagon Women Vol. 2: Diaries & Letters from the Western Trails, 1850. unabr. ed. Selected by Beverly Benson Van Horn. 2 cass. (Running Time: 3 hrs.). (Living Voices of the Past Ser.: Vol. 1). 1999. 18.00 Set. (978-0-9671885-0-8(4)) Beverlys Ltd.
The personal diary of a woman crossing America in a covered wagon. Tales of courage, bravery, fear, boredom, & danger encountered.

Covering Your Household with the Blood. Lynne Hammond. 1 cass. (Running Time: 1 hr.). 2005. 5.00 (978-1-57399-214-5(3)) Mac Hammond.

Covet. Tara Moss. Read by Tara Moss. (Running Time: 9 hrs. 45 mins.). 2009. 89.99 (978-1-74214-269-2(9), 9781742142692) Pub: Bolinda Pubng AUS. Dist(s): Bolinda Pub Inc

Covet. unabr. ed. Tara Moss. Read by Tara Moss. (Running Time: 9 hrs. 45 mins.). 2006. audio compact disk 98.95 (978-1-74093-601-9(9)) Pub: Bolinda Pubng AUS. Dist(s): Bolinda Pub Inc

***Covet.** unabr. ed. Tara Moss. Read by Tara Moss. (Running Time: 9 hrs. 45 mins.). 2010. 43.95 (978-1-74214-580-8(9), 9781742145808) Pub: Bolinda Pubng AUS. Dist(s): Bolinda Pub Inc

Covet: A Novel of the Fallen Angels. unabr. ed. J. R. Ward, pseud. Read by Eric Dove. (Running Time: 15 hrs.). (Fallen Angels Ser.). 2009. 24.99 (978-1-4418-3026-5(X), 9781441830265, Brilliance MP3) Brilliance Audio.

Covet: A Novel of the Fallen Angels. unabr. ed. J. R. Ward, pseud. Read by Eric G. Dove. (Running Time: 15 hrs.). (Fallen Angels Ser.). 2009. 24.99 (978-1-4418-3028-9(6), 9781441830289, BAD) Brilliance Audio.

Covet: A Novel of the Fallen Angels. unabr. ed. J. R. Ward, pseud. Read by Eric Dove. (Running Time: 15 hrs.). (Fallen Angels Ser.). 2009. 39.97 (978-1-4418-3027-2(8), 9781441830272, Brinc Audio MP3 Lib) Brilliance Audio.

Covet: A Novel of the Fallen Angels. unabr. ed. J. R. Ward, pseud. Read by Eric G. Dove. (Running Time: 15 hrs.). (Fallen Angels Ser.). 2009. 39.97 (978-1-4418-3029-6(4), 9781441830296, BADLE) Brilliance Audio.

Covet: A Novel of the Fallen Angels. unabr. ed. J. R. Ward, pseud. Read by Eric Dove. (Running Time: 15 hrs.). (Fallen Angels Ser.). 2009. audio compact disk 29.99 (978-1-4418-3030-2(8), 9781441830302, Bril Audio CD Unabri); audio compact disk 99.97 (978-1-4418-3025-8(1), 9781441830258, BriAudCD Unabrid) Brilliance Audio.

Cow Country. unabr. collector's ed. Short Stories. Will James. Read by Connor O'Brien. 4 cass. (Running Time: 6 hrs.). (Tumbleweed Ser.). 1999. 32.00 (978-0-7366-4401-3(6), 4862) Books on Tape.
Imagine round-up wagons, saddle horses, riders, branding irons & the wide open range, a place where "there's not a fence as far as you can see, nothin' but the blue grass ripplin' in the sun." James delivers all of that & more in these eight stories.

Cow County Law. unabr. ed. M. Lehman. Read by Tim Behrens. 6 cass. (Running Time: 6 hrs.). Dramatization. 1991. 39.95 (978-1-55686-371-4(3), 371) Books in Motion.
A tenderfoot New York attorney gets an unwanted transplant to 1930 Montana & learns that the West is still just about as unsettled as he is.

***Cow in the Parking Lot: A Zen Approach to Overcoming Anger.** unabr. ed. Susan Edmiston & Leonard Scheff. (ENG.). 2010. audio compact disk 19.95 (978-1-61573-114-5(8), 1615731148) Pub: HighBridge. Dist(s): Workman Pub

Cow Who Clucked. Denise Fleming. 1 CD. (Running Time: 10 mins.). (J). (ps-1). 2007. bk. 29.95 (978-0-8045-4174-9(4)); bk. 27.95 (978-0-8045-6951-4(7)) Spoken Arts.
What's a cow to do when she's lost her moo? Go out and find it, of course! Join Cow and her friends as they conduct their barnyard search. Cow searches right into the starry night until she can go no farther. But, in the end, Cow and her moo are reunited and all is well. Caldecott Honor winner Denise Fleming has created a character that will appeal directly to a child's sense of humor. The simple repetition will have children chanting right along with Cow!.

Cow Who Fell in the Canal. 2004. bk. 24.95 (978-1-56008-241-5(0)); pap. bk. 14.95 (978-1-56008-185-2(6)); 8.95 (978-1-56008-878-3(8)); cass. & flmstrp 30.00 (978-1-56008-656-7(4)) Weston Woods.

Coward. Guy de Maupassant. (J). 1984. Multi Media TX.

Coward Readalong. Helen McCann. 1 cass. (Running Time: 1 hr.). (Ten-Minute Mysteries Ser.). (YA). (gr. 6-12). 1994. pap. bk. 12.95 (978-0-7854-1050-8(3), 40756) Am Guidance.

Coward's Guide to Conflict. Timothy Ursiny. Read by Rolland Lopez. (Running Time: 3 hrs.). (C). 2005. 19.95 (978-1-59912-894-8(2)) Iofy Corp.

Coward's Guide to Conflict: Empowering Solutions for Those Who Would Rather Run Than Fight. abr. ed. Tim Ursiny. 2 cass. (Running Time: 3 hrs. 30 mins.). 2003. 17.95 (978-1-59316-001-2(1)); audio compact disk 23.95 (978-1-59316-002-9(X)) Listen & Live.

Cowboy. 1 cass. (Running Time: 1 hr.). 11.50 (G0460B090, HarperThor) HarpC GBR.

Cowboy. unabr. ed. Larry Goodman. Read by Charlie O'Dowd. (Running Time: 015 min.). (J). 2000. pap. bk. 18.00 (978-1-58807-038-8(7)) Am Pubng Inc.

Cowboy: In Song & Story. unabr. ed. Jimmy Gray. Perf. by Wayne Salveson. Narrated by Rick Schulman. Prod. by Joe Loesch. 1 cass. (Running Time: 1 hr.). (Wild West Ser.). (YA). 1999. 12.95 (978-1-887729-66-6(6)) Toy Box Prods.
Learn about the life of a cowboy through song & story. The old west comes to life in this tale of life on the range. Songs include: "Home on the Range," "Red River Valley," "The Zebra Dun," "The Strawberry Roan," "Punchin' Dough," "Cowboy Jack," "Chisholm Trail," "Utah Carroll," "When the Work's All Done This Fall," "My Home's in Montana," "The Trail to Mexico," "Old Paint," "Billy Venero," "Patanio," "The Cowboy's Dream" & "Little Joe the Wrangler.".

Cowboy: Texas Night Before Christmas. Pelican Publishing Staff. (Night Before Christm Ser.). 1998. 9.95 (978-1-56554-385-0(8)) Pelican.

Cowboy Album. 1 cass. (Running Time: 30 min.). (J). 1992. 7.99 (978-0-930589-64-6(5)); audio compact disk 11.99 CD. (978-0-930589-79-0(3)) Rhino Enter.
In nostalgic selections such as Gene Autry's "Back in the Saddle Again" & Roy Rogers's "Happy Trails," this album happily recalls - in a listenable, eminently singable form - an American era for today's youngsters. Enthusiastic choruses of "Yi-pi-yi-yay, yi-pi-yi-o" & other prairie refrains will echo forth when kids (& no doubt many grownups) give a listen to these Western ditties.

Cowboy Alphabet/Cowboy Rodeo. Narrated by Harvey Derrick. 1 cass. (Running Time: 26 min.). (ENG.). (J). (gr. k-3). 2000. 9.95 (978-1-56554-757-5(8)) Pelican.

Cowboy & Wills: A Remarkable Little Boy & the Puppy That Changed His Life. unabr. ed. Monica Holloway. Read by Monica Holloway. 7 CDs. (Running Time: 8 hrs. 0 mins. 0 sec.). (ENG.). 2009. audio compact disk 29.99 (978-1-4423-0065-1(5)) Pub: S&S Audio. Dist(s): S and S Inc

Cowboy Celtic Collection. 2000. audio compact disk (978-1-55105-170-3(2)) Lone Pine Publ CAN.

Cowboy Christmas. Scripts. Tawnya Albright. Prod. by One Way Street Staff. (Running Time: 25 minutes). 2002. audio compact disk 18.00 (978-1-58302-217-7(1)) One Way St.
This 25 minute musical has plenty of country flavor with a strong Christmas message for all ages. Main characters include: Jeb, a cowboy who uses a lasso th share God's love; Sal, chief cook at the ranch; and Flint, a cowpoke who figures he knows how to run his own life without God. the script has five speaking parts plus extra voices needed for the songs. Songs include: Joyful Joyful; King of Jing-Aling; Born in a Barn; Come on Ring Those Bells.

Cowboy Cuisine. Poems. Phil Kennington. Read by Phil Kennington. 1 cass. 1999. 8.00 (978-1-890672-18-8(1)) Phil Don.
Selected poems from "Trail Dust II".

Cowboy Detective. abr. ed. Charles A. Siringo. Read by Michael Martin Murphey. 2 cass. (Running Time: 3 hrs.). 1996. 17.95 (978-1-57453-056-8(9)) Audio Lit.
After years of cowboying, Charles Siringo becomes a Pinkerton detective in the wilder parts of the West. Living more by his wits than deductive reasoning, he sees action in labor riots, hunts moonshiners & chases Butch Cassidy's Wild Bunch through the Southwest.

Cowboy Ghost. Robert Newton Peck. Read by Johnny Heller. 3 cass. (Running Time: 4 hrs. 15 mins.). (YA). 1999. pap. bk. & stu. ed. 52.95 (978-0-7887-3189-1(0), 40924) Recorded Bks.
Story of a boy becoming a man on the frontier. Tee, at sixteen, can rope a wild mustang & round up cattle on his family's ranch. To really prove himself though, he must go on a risky cattle drive through the Florida wilderness. When real tragedy strikes, will his courage hold?.

Cowboy Ghost, Class set. Robert Newton Peck. Read by Johnny Heller. 3 cass. (Running Time: 4 hrs. 15 mins.). (YA). 1999. 197.80 (978-0-7887-3235-5(8), 46891) Recorded Bks.

Cowboy Ghost, Class Set unabr. ed. Robert Newton Peck. Narrated by Johnny Heller. 3 pieces. (Running Time: 4 hrs. 15 mins.). (gr. 5 up). 1999. 30.00 (978-0-7887-3208-9(0), 95795E7) Recorded Bks.

Cowboy Granola. Poems. Phil Kennington. Read by Phil Kennington. 1 cass. 1992. 8.00 (978-1-890672-11-9(4)) Phil Don.
Selected poems from "Trail Dust I" & "Trail Dust II".

Cowboy... in Song & Story. unabr. ed. Jimmy Gray. Read by Rick Schulman. Perf. by Wayne Salveson. Ed. by James E. Gray. 1 cass. (Running Time: 60 min.). (Americana Ser.). 1959. 9.95 (978-1-887262-00-2(8), AudioMagazine) Natl Tape & Disc.
The story of the American cowboy told with narrative & 16 old-time cowboy songs, with background music.

Cowboy Mentality & the Big One That Got Away. abr. ed. Baxter Black. 2 CDs. 2001. audio compact disk 24.95 (978-0-939343-34-8(7)) Coyote Cowboy.

Cowboy Poetry: A Gathering. unabr. ed. Poems. Ed. by Hal Cannon. 2 cass. (Running Time: 3 hrs.). 1997. 18.95 (978-1-57453-206-7(5)) Audio Lit.
In these selections from some of today's & yesterday's finest practitioners, Canon has corralled the best of the genre. How good is it? The poems have the smell of sagebrush & campfire in them. You can't get any higher praise.

Cowboy Smarts by Dancing Beetle. Perf. by Eugene Ely. 1 cass. (Running Time: 77 min.). (J). 1991. 10.00 Erthviibz.
Cowboy poetry & nature sounds come together when Ms. Prarie Dog & the spunky musicians read & sing with Dancing Beetle.

Cowboy Songs: With Historical Narration. Keith McNeil & Rusty McNeil. Read by Keith McNeil & Rusty McNeil. 2 cass. (Running Time: 3 hrs.). (American History Through Folksong Ser.). (J). (gr. 4 up). 1992. 19.95 Set, Stereo. (978-1-878360-05-2(1)) WEM Records.
Fifty songs which chronicle the story of America's favorite folk hero, the cowboy. The songs document the cowboy's Spanish & Mexican roots, the trail drives, the cowtowns & the building of the huge cattle empires in the West.

Cowboy Songs: With Historical Narration. Keith McNeil & Rusty McNeil. Read by Keith McNeil & Rusty McNeil. (American History Through Folksong Ser.). (YA). (gr. 4 up). 1996. audio compact disk 26.95 (978-1-878360-12-0(4)) WEM Records.

Cowboy Songs, Jokes, Lingo & Lore. Wayne Eribson. 1997. pap. bk. 19.95 (978-0-7866-2522-2(8)) Mel Bay.

Cowboy Songs of the Wild Frontier. Perf. by Wayne Erbsen. 1 cass. (Running Time: 52 min.). 9.95 (978-1-883206-07-9(3), NG400); audio compact disk 14.95 CD. (978-1-883206-08-6(1), NG-CD-400) Native Ground.
Classic songs of the cowboys with vocals, played on old-time instruments.

Cowboy Songs on Folkways. Perf. by Harry Jackson et al. Anno. by Guy Logsdon. 1 cass. (Running Time: 1 hr.). 1991. (0-9307-400430-9307-40043-2-6) Smithsonian Folkways.
Fifteen performers sing, boast & recite poetry on 26 tracks. Through music they describe the life of honest & hard-working cowboys.

Cowboy Songs on Folkways. Perf. by Harry Jackson et al. Anno. by Guy Logsdon. Selected by Guy Logsdon. 1 CD. (Running Time: 1 hr. 3 mins.). 1991. audio compact disk Smithsonian Folkways.

Cowboy Trailmix. Poems. Phil Kennington. Read by Phil Kennington. 1 cass. 1995. 8.00 (978-1-890672-10-2(6)) Phil Don.
Selected poems from "Trail Dust III" & "Trail Dust IV".

Cowboys. Rick Steber. Illus. by Don Gray. 1 cass. (Tales of the Wild West Ser.: Vol. 4). (J). 1988. pap. bk. 9.95 (978-0-945134-54-1(1)) Bonanza Pub.

Cowboys. unabr. ed. Ed. by Linda Spizzirri. 48 cass. (Running Time: 15 min.). Dramatization. (Educational Coloring Book & Cassette Package Ser.). (J). (gr. k-8). 1989. pap. bk. 6.95 (978-0-86545-152-0(4)) Spizzirri.
From the Early "Vaqueros" to the Cowboys of today-how they worked, lived, their clothes & equipment.

Cowboys Are My Weakness. abr. ed. Pam Houston. Read by Pam Houston. 2 cass.. (Running Time: 3 hrs.). 2000. 7.95 (978-1-57815-151-6(1), 1110, Media Bks Audio) Media Bks NJ.
A real cowboy is hard to find these days, even in the West. This is a collection of strong, shrewd & funny stories, about the smart women who are looking for the love of a good man & men who are wild & hard to pin down.

Cowboys Are My Weakness, Set. unabr. ed. Short Stories. Pam Houston. Read by Pam Houston. 2 cass. (Running Time: 3 hrs.). 1993. 15.95 (978-1-879371-31-6(6), 390568) Pub Mills.
Set in the West & sometimes in Alaska, these stories are about women who are smart & susceptible to love & men who are wild & hard to pin down. Our heroines are daredevils, philosophers & acute observers of the nuances of modern romance.

Cowboys, Critters, & a Little Bit of Love. unabr. ed. Poems. Don Germain. Read by Don Germain. Read by Julie Nichols. 1 cass. (Running Time: 54 min.). 1995. 7.50 (978-1-887804-01-1(3)) Cent Mont Pubng.
Collection of cowboy poetry.

Cowboys Full. abr. ed. James McManus. (Running Time: 7 hrs. 0 mins. 0 sec.). (ENG.). 2009. audio compact disk 29.99 (978-1-4272-0799-9(2)) Pub: Macmill Audio. Dist(s): Macmillan

Cowboys North & South. unabr. collector's ed. Short Stories. Will James. Read by Connor O'Brien. 3 cass. (Running Time: 4 hrs. 30 mins.). 1999. 24.00 (978-0-7366-4399-3(0), 4860) Books on Tape.
A classic collection of eight cowboy stories. Captures the lifestyle & picturesque vernacular of the American cowboy.

Cowboys on Mount Everest. (Running Time: 90 min.). 1989. 23.00 (B0020B090, HarperThor) HarpC GBR.

Cowboys, Sisters, Rascals & Dirt. Waylon Jennings. 1 cass. (J). 1993. 7.69 BMG Distribution.

Cowboys, Sisters, Rascals & Dirt. Waylon Jennings. 1 cass., 1 CD. (J). 7.98 (SME 63450); audio compact disk 11.18 CD Jewel box. (SME 63450) NewSound.
Includes: "I'm Little," "Just Can't Wait," "When I Get Big," "All of My Sisters Are Girls" & more.

Cowboys, Sisters, Rascals & Dirt. Waylon Jennings. 1 cass., 1 CD. (J). 1998. 9.98 (Sony Wonder); audio compact disk 13.98 CD. Sony Music Ent.
Songs deal with kids whose concerns are thoroughly modern yet completely timeless. Whether he's singing about dirt & mischief or saving the whales & dolphins, it captures the affection & affinity between "outlaws" & the children.

Cowboys, Sisters, Rascals, & Dirt. Waylon Jennings. (J). (ps-3). 1993. 10.98 (978-1-56668-604-4(0)) BMG Distribution.

Cowden Syndrome - A Bibliography & Dictionary for Physicians, Patients, & Genome Researchers. Compiled by Icon Group International, Inc. Staff. 2007. ring bd. 28.95 (978-0-497-11359-9(7)) Icon Grp.

Cowgirl Kate & Cocoa: Rain or Shine. unabr. ed. Erica Silverman. Narrated by Liz Morton. 1 cass. (Running Time: 1 hr. 15 mins.). (J). 2008. 15.75 (978-1-4281-5812-2(X)); audio compact disk 15.75 (978-1-4361-0461-6(0)) Recorded Bks.

Cowgirls Dream (Kooky Kountry) Sandi Johnson. Perf. by Dora Saad. 1 cass. (Kooky Kountry Ser.). (J). 2000. 8.99 (978-1-929063-57-4(1), 156); audio compact disk 12.99 (978-1-929063-58-1(X), 157) Moons & Stars.
A little girl spends a lot of time on the porch of her dude ranch with her friends, dreaming of being a country singer. Cowgirls single & country favorites included.

Cowgirls of the Wild West: A Skilled & Independent Breed. 1 cass. (Running Time: 30 min.). 8.00 (HO-82-06-30, HarperThor) HarpC GBR.

Coyote. unabr. ed. Linda Barnes. Narrated by C. J. Critt. 5 cass. (Running Time: 7 hrs. 30 mins.). (Carlotta Carlyle Mystery Ser.). 1994. 44.00 (978-0-7887-0036-1(7), 94235E7) Recorded Bks.
Carlotta Carlyle stumbles across a scam artist who preys upon illegal immigrants desparate for green cards.

Coyote. unabr. ed. Linda Barnes. Read by C. J. Critt. 5 cass. (Running Time: 7 hrs. 30 min.). (Carlotta Carlyle Mystery Ser.). 1994. Rental 13.50 Set. (94235) Recorded Bks.

Coyote. unabr. ed. Bill Harley. Read by Bill Harley. 1 cass. (Running Time: 34 min.). (C). 1987. 10.00 (978-1-878126-05-4(9), RRR201) Round Riv Prodns.
A collection of original songs about the earth, the stars, music, friends, coyotes & hope. Turn to Each Other; Northern Hills; In His Eyes; Over the Bay; Keep It Up; Coyote; Leave Them Alone; The Piper's Chair; One More Story; For the Earth.

Coyote: Native American Folk Tales. abr. ed. Joe Hayes. Read by Joe Hayes. 1 cass. (Running Time: 57 min.). (J). (gr. 1-6). 1986. 10.95 (978-0-939729-12-8(1)) Trails West Pub.
Eight Native American coyote stories.

Coyote: Stories. Short Stories. Nancy K. Duncan et al. As told by Nancy K. Duncan. Music by Michael Fitzsimmons. 1. (Running Time: 55 mins). (J). 2002. audio compact disk 15.00 (978-0-9719007-1-4(X)) STORY PERFORM.
Storyteller Nancy Duncan tells stories about the coyote as critter and character. Three are family stories, three are adapations of traditional Native American folktales, and two are literary: Ursula LeGuin's "Dried Mice" and "The Coyotes are Coming Back by Jim Heynen. The Second Story Review says: If I hadn't heard boyotes before, I would feel certain that I had after listening to Nancy Duncan's barked and howled conversation between her son and a young coyote at the zoo. What amazing sounds!...In addition to a couple of of Duncan family stories, Coyote contains stories from Ursula LeGuin, Joe Bruchac, and others. All are told with truth and skill. Duncan creates characters with her voice, and balances those beautifully with her own narrative voice. Also well balanced is the use of music, supplied by Michael Fitzsimmons. Sometimes it ssets the mood for a story, often it accents parts of the story as Duncan tells....the music was the perfect accent to the words.".

Coyote & Rock: And Other Lushootseed Stories. abr. ed. Perf. by Vi Hilbert. Music by Ken Cooper & Wolf James. 1 cass. (Running Time: 1 hr.). (Native American Storytime Ser.). (J). (ps-5). 2001. 11.95 Parabola Bks.
Nine stories from the people of the Puget Sound. Includes "Lady Louse Cleans House," "Skunk's Important Information" and "Owl and His Wife, Frog," with traditional flute music.

Coyote & Rock: And Other Lushootseed Stories. unabr. ed. Ron Evans. 1 cass. (Running Time: 60 min.). (J). (ps-5). 1992. 11.00 (978-1-55994-586-8(9), HarperChildAud) HarperCollins Pubs.
Ron Evans is of Chippewa-Cree & Assiniboin descent, tribes located in Montana & Western Canada respectively. Now, for the first time, he tells stories that were passed down to him as "the keeper of the talking sticks" - the one responsible for learning the oral traditions of the tribe.

Coyote Crossing. unabr. ed. Frank Roderus. Read by Kevin Foley. 4 cass. (Running Time: 5 hrs. 30 min.). (Heller Ser.). 1995. 26.95 (978-1-55686-581-7(3)) Books in Motion.
Carl Heller goes undercover south of the border to investigate the disappearance of a young Mexican last seen trying to buy his way into Texas from a notorious local "coyote".

Coyote Frontier: A Novel of Interstellar Colonization. Allen Steele. Narrated by Allen Steele. Narrated by Therese Plummer & Peter Ganim. (Playaway Adult Fiction Ser.). (ENG.). 2009. 69.99 (978-1-60847-681-7(2)) Find a World.

Coyote Soup for the Grownup Soul. Duncan Sings-Alone. 1 cass. (Running Time: 51 mins.). 2000. 11.95 (978-1-929590-01-8(6)); audio compact disk 16.95 (978-1-929590-00-1(8)) Two Canoes.
Traditional & contemporary Native American trickster tales told by Cherokee grandfather Duncan Sings-Alone. Most of the contemporary tales are autobiographical.

Coyote Steals the Summer. Scripts. 1 cass. or 1 CD. (Running Time: 15 mins.). (J). (gr. k-3). 2000. pap. bk. & tchr. ed. 29.95 Bad Wolf Pr.
Summer was trapped in a bag inside a tipi at the snow's edge (a very, very long long way from here). This Native American tale tells how Coyote brings summer to the world & earns his famous gift of trickery as a reward. Sheet music available.

Coyote Tails. Rondal Snodgrass. Read by Rondal Snodgrass. 1 cass. (J). (gr. k up). 1988. 6.98 tape-norelco pkg. (978-1-877737-11-4(9), MLP-305) MFLP CA.
Features a collection of children's stories.

Coyote Waits. Tony Hillerman. Read by Tony Hillerman. 1 cass. (Running Time: 29 min.). 1990. 10.00 (060190) New Letters.
Hillerman reads from a new mystery, "Coyote Waits," & talks about growing up among native Americans in Oklahoma.

Coyote Waits. unabr. ed. Tony Hillerman. Read by John MacDonald. 7 cass. (Running Time: 7 hrs.). (Joe Leaphorn & Jim Chee Novel Ser.). 1990. 56.00 (978-0-7366-1788-8(4), 2625) Books on Tape.
Into the close-knit society of Navajo religious & political leaders, murder intrudes. An elderly shaman is charged with killing a police officer. Lt. Joe Leaphorn, hero of earlier Tony Hillerman tales, a competent & cool operator with roots in Anglo as well as Navajo culture, enters the investigation. He & fellow officer Joe Chee track leads faint as moccasin prints on a rock ledge...but track them they do, & to a conclusion unexpected, unique & satisfying.

Coyote Wind. Peter Bowen. (Running Time: 5 hrs. 0 mins.). 2005. 34.95 (978-0-7861-3488-5(7)) Blckstn Audio.

Coyote Wind. Peter Bowen. Read by Christopher Lane. (Running Time: 18000 sec.). (Gabriel du Pre Mystery Ser.). 2005. audio compact disk 36.00 (978-0-7861-7892-6(2)) Blckstn Audio.

Coyote Wind -Lib. Peter Bowen & Christopher Lane. (Running Time: 5 hrs. 0 mins.). 2005. 29.95 (978-0-7861-8100-1(1)) Blckstn Audio.

Coyote Winter. unabr. ed. J. D. Kincaid. Read by John Chancer. 3 cass. (Running Time: 4 hrs. 30 min.). (Audio Books Ser.). 1992. 34.95 (978-1-85496-684-1(7)) Pub: UlverLrgPrint GBR. Dist(s): Ulverscroft US
Major Joe Daly & his gang of killers, the Wyoming Phantoms, terrorize the entire territory with a series of stagecoach hold-ups. And to ensure that no one can identify them, they murder all their victims. When Amy Scarlett survives one of their hold-ups, Daly is determined to track her down. But Daly hadn't reckoned on the intervention of Kentuckian gunfighter Jack Stone & soon finds out, they don't come any more dangerous or deadly than Stone.

Coyote's Canyon: A Collection of Stories, Set. Terry T. Williams. Read by Terry Tempest Williams. 2 cass. (Running Time: 3 hrs.). 1994. 16.95 (978-0-939643-26-4(X), 3528, NrthWrd Bks) TandN Child.
Four Corners region of Utah, Arizona, New Mexico, & Colorado. Set in this land of myth, legend, & magic, each story uses legend as an avenue for understanding some aspect of the natural world.

***Coyote's in the House.** unabr. ed. Elmore Leonard. Read by Neil Patrick Harris. (ENG.). 2004. (978-0-06-081369-7(5), Harper Audio) HarperCollins Pubs.

Coyote's in the House. unabr. ed. Elmore Leonard. Read by Neil Patrick Harris. 3 CDs. (Running Time: 4 hrs. 30 mins.). 2004. audio compact disk 22.00 (978-0-06-072882-3(5)) HarperCollins Pubs.

***Coyote's in the House.** unabr. ed. Elmore Leonard. Read by Neil Patrick Harris. (ENG.). 2004. (978-0-06-077855-2(5), Harper Audio) HarperCollins Pubs.

CPA Exam AudioLearn. Created by Ellen Singer. 6 CDs. 2003. audio compact disk 239.00 (978-0-9704199-7-2(X)) AudioLearn.

CPA Exam Review: Financial Accounting & Reporting. 3rd ed. Anita L. Feller. (ENG.). 2008. audio compact disk 85.00 (978-0-470-32333-5(7), JWiley) Wiley US.

CPA Exam Review Set: Auditing & Attestation. 3rd ed. Anita L. Feller. (ENG.). 2008. audio compact disk 85.00 (978-0-470-32336-6(1), JWiley) Wiley US.

CPA Exam Review Set: Regulation. 3rd ed. Anita L. Feller. (ENG.). 2008. audio compact disk 85.00 (978-0-470-32338-0(8), JWiley) Wiley US.

CPA Ready Financial Accounting & Reporting. 35th ed. Created by Bisk CPA Review. (Running Time: 46800 sec.). 2006. audio compact disk 129.95 (978-1-57961-481-2(7)) Bisk Educ.

CPA Review Auditing Audio Lectures: 2001-2002. 9th ed. Irvin N. Gleim & William A. Hillison. 2001. 79.95 (978-1-58194-157-9(9)) Gleim Pubns.

CPA Review Business Law Audio Lectures: 2001-2002. 9th ed. Irvin N. Gleim & Jordan B. Ray. 2001. 79.95 (978-1-58194-158-6(7)) Gleim Pubns.

CPA Review Financial Audio Lectures: 2001-2002. 9th ed. Irvin N. Gleim. 2001. 79.95 (978-1-58194-159-3(5)) Gleim Pubns.

CPA Review TAX-MAN-GOV Audio Lectures. 9th ed. Irvin N. Gleim. 2001. 79.95 (978-1-58194-160-9(9)) Gleim Pubns.

CPA's Guide to Calculating Economic Damages. Jeff Litvak. 6 cass. bk. 159.00 set. (CPE3190) Bisk Educ.
Discusses the roles of a CPA as an expert witness & litigation support consultant, plus provides proven strategies to help you effectively determine & present the extent of economic damages sustained by an injured party.

Cpcu Bus & Fin Anal Ppt Cd. Ed. by Kaplan Publishing Staff. 2005. (978-1-4195-1911-6(5)) Dearborn Financial.

Cpcu Bus & Fin Anal Terms Cd. Ed. by Kaplan Publishing Staff. 2005. (978-1-4195-1920-8(4)) Dearborn Financial.

Cpcu Cmr Lbl Rsk Mgt Ppt Cd. Ed. by Kaplan Publishing Staff. 2005. (978-1-4195-1983-3(2)) Dearborn Financial.

Cpcu Cmr Lbl Rsk Mgt Terms Cd. Ed. by Kaplan Publishing Staff. 2005. (978-1-4195-1996-3(4)) Dearborn Financial.

Cpcu Cmr Prp Rsk Mgt Ppt Cd. Ed. by Kaplan Publishing Staff. 2005. (978-1-4195-1907-9(7)) Dearborn Financial.

Cpcu Cmr Prp Rsk Mgt Terms Cd. Ed. by Kaplan Publishing Staff. 2005. (978-1-4195-1908-6(5)) Dearborn Financial.

Cpcu Fin Srvcs Inst Ppt Cd. Ed. by Kaplan Publishing Staff. 2005. (978-1-4195-1883-6(6)) Dearborn Financial.

Cpcu Fin Srvcs Inst Trms Cd. Ed. by Kaplan Publishing Staff. 2005. (978-1-4195-1885-0(2)) Dearborn Financial.

Cpcu Fndns Rsk Mgt Ppt Cd. Ed. by Kaplan Publishing Staff. 2005. (978-1-4195-1991-8(3)) Dearborn Financial.

Cpcu Fndns Rsk Mgt Terms Cd. Ed. by Kaplan Publishing Staff. 2005. (978-1-4195-2057-0(1)) Dearborn Financial.

Cpcu Ins Oper & Reg Ppt Cd. Ed. by Kaplan Publishing Staff. 2005. (978-1-4195-2058-7(X)) Dearborn Financial.

Cpcu Ins Oper & Reg Terms Cd. Ed. by Kaplan Publishing Staff. 2005. (978-1-4195-1999-4(9)) Dearborn Financial.

Cpcu Lgl Env Rsk Mgt Ppt Cd. Ed. by Kaplan Publishing Staff. 2005. (978-1-4195-1916-1(6)) Dearborn Financial.

Cpcu Lgl Env Rsk Mgt Terms Cd. Ed. by Kaplan Publishing Staff. 2005. (978-1-4195-1917-8(4)) Dearborn Financial.

Cpcu Prsnl Rsk Mgt Ppt Cd. Ed. by Kaplan Publishing Staff. 2005. (978-1-4195-1859-1(3)) Dearborn Financial.

Cpcu Prsnl Rsk Mgt Terms Cd. Ed. by Kaplan Publishing Staff. 2005. (978-1-4195-1835-5(6)) Dearborn Financial.

CPR for Business Success. Silvana Clark. 1 cass. (Running Time: 60 min.). 9.95 (5013) Natl Inst Child Mgmt.
Managing a business requires having CPR, or Creativity, Passion & Research. To gain the competitive edge in any business, you need to think beyond the traditional way of solving problems. Develop your own style of creativity, which in turn gives you new ideas. Then see how spending time on research can make you stand out from others in your field.

Crab Nebula. (Running Time: 23 min.). 14.95 (23352) MMI Corp.
Hayden planetarium astronomers discuss characteristics of this important system.

Crack at Edge of World. Simon Winchester. 2005. 39.99 (978-1-59895-034-2(7)) Find a World.

***Crack Cocaine Diet.** unabr. ed. Laura Lippman. Read by Linda Emond & Francois Battiste. (ENG.). 2008. (978-0-06-176294-9(6), Harper Audio); (978-0-06-176293-2(8), Harper Audio) HarperCollins Pubs.

***Crack in the Edge of the World.** abr. ed. Simon Winchester. Read by Simon Winchester. (ENG.). 2005. (978-0-06-089422-1(9), Harper Audio); (978-0-06-089423-8(7), Harper Audio) HarperCollins Pubs.

***Crack in the Edge of the World.** unabr. ed. Simon Winchester. Read by Simon Winchester. (ENG.). 2005. (978-0-06-089420-7(2), Harper Audio); (978-0-06-089421-4(0), Harper Audio) HarperCollins Pubs.

Crack in the Edge of the World: America & the Great California Earthquake of 1906. abr. ed. Simon Winchester. Read by Simon Winchester. 2005. audio compact disk 29.95 (978-0-06-082386-3(0)) HarperCollins Pubs.

Crack in the Edge of the World: America & the Great California Earthquake of 1906. unabr. ed. 13 CDs. (Running Time: 45360 sec.). 2005. audio compact disk 112.95 (978-0-7927-3765-0(2), SLD 848, Chivers Sound Lib) AudioGO.

Crack in the Edge of the World: America & the Great California Earthquake of 1906. unabr. ed. Simon Winchester. 10 cass. 2005. 84.95 (978-0-7927-3764-3(4), CSL 848, Chivers Sound Lib); audio compact disk 49.95 (978-0-7927-3837-4(3), CMP 848, Chivers Sound Lib) AudioGO.

Crack in the Edge of the World: America & the Great California Earthquake of 1906. unabr. ed. Simon Winchester. Read by Simon Winchester. 2005. audio compact disk 39.95 (978-0-06-082387-0(9)) HarperCollins Pubs.

Crack in the Lens. unabr. ed. Steve Hockensmith. Narrated by William Dufris. (Running Time: 10 hrs. 0 mins. 0 sec.). (Holmes on the Range Ser.). (ENG.). 2009. audio compact disk 69.99 (978-1-4001-4282-8(2)); audio compact disk 24.99 (978-1-4001-6282-6(3)) Pub: Tantor Media. Dist(s): IngramPubServ

Crack in the Lens. unabr. ed. Steve Hockensmith. Read by William Dufris. 8 CDs. (Running Time: 10 hrs. 0 mins. 0 sec.). (Holmes on the Range Ser.). (ENG.). 2009. audio compact disk 34.99 (978-1-4001-1282-1(6)) Pub: Tantor Media. Dist(s): IngramPubServ

Crackdown. collector's ed. Bernard Cornwell. Read by David Case. 8 cass. (Running Time: 12 hrs.). 2000. 64.00 (978-0-7366-5513-2(1), 5353) Books on Tape.
Drug pirates stalk their victims in the treacherous waters of the Bahamas, then return to their fortress island of Murder Cay like primal sharks after a kill.

Crackdown. unabr. ed. Bernard Cornwell. Read by Terrence Hardiman. 8 cass. (Running Time: 8 hrs.). 1992. bk. 69.95 set. (978-0-7451-5873-0(0), CAB 565) AudioGO.
Nick Breakspear wants nothing to do with the brittle theatrical world inhabited by his father, so he joins the Royal Navy. But his dreams of paradise are shattered when he is swept up into a deadly corner of the war against drug runners who infest the Bahamian waters. His only defense - to draw upon the despised skills of his father's world & pray that his performance is believable.

Cracker! The Best Dog in Vietnam. unabr. ed. Cynthia Kadohata. Read by Kimberly Farr. 6 CDs. (Running Time: 7 hrs.). (YA). (gr. 5-8). 2007. audio compact disk 45.00 (978-0-7393-4856-7(6), Listening Lib) Pub: Random Audio Pubg. Dist(s): Random

Cracker! The Best Dog in Vietnam. unabr. ed. Cynthia Kadohata. Read by Kimberly Farr. 6 CDs. (Running Time: 27120 sec.). (ENG.). (J). (gr. 5 up). 2007. audio compact disk 39.00 (978-0-7393-3888-9(9), Listening Lib) Pub: Random Audio Pubg. Dist(s): Random

Cracker Legacy Subdivide This. Gordon A. Stevens. 6 CDs. (Running Time: 6 hours 30 minutes). 2006. audio compact disk 35.00 (978-1-56142-201-2(0)) Intl Video Projects.
Unabridged version read by the author, Gordon A. Stevens.

Cracker Sees the World/World of Wonders. Steck-Vaughn Staff. (J). 1999. (978-0-7398-0934-1(2)) SteckVau.

Crackerjill - Crackerjack: How to Approach, Greet & Win over Strangers in Droves, Groups, Twos & Ones. unabr. ed. Heather Latimer. Read by Heather Latimer. 1 cass. (Running Time: 2 hrs. 45 min.). 1999. 16.00 (978-0-943698-25-0(1)) Papyrus Letterbox.
Vital information for employees/volunteers who need rapid, surefire communication skills for dealing with tourists & other strangers.

Crackers. Roy Blount, Jr.. Read by Roy Blount, Jr. 1 cass. (Running Time: 1 hr.). 1983. 13.95 (978-1-55644-066-3(9), 3031) Am Audio Prose.
Blount reads his popular essays.

Crackers. abr. ed. 1 cass. (Running Time: 12 mins.). (J). (gr. k-3). 2002. bk. 26.90 (978-0-8045-6886-9(3)) Pub: Spoken Arts. Dist(s): Follett Med Dist
Crackers can't find a job because he likes mice and employers expect cats to chase mice. Fortunately for Crackers, the manager of the Squeak & Company Cheese Shop is a different kind of mouse.

Cracking Da Vinci's Code. unabr. ed. James L. Garlow & Peter Jones. Read by Joyce Bean & Bill Richards. (Running Time: 6 hrs.). 2004. 62.25 (978-1-59355-995-3(X), 159355995X, BriAudUnabridg); audio compact disk 74.25 (978-1-59355-997-7(6), 1593559976, BriAudCD Unabrid) Brilliance Audio.

The controversy grows with every sale of the bestselling novel. Throughout the contemporary fictional storyline of The Da Vinci Code, author Dan Brown skillfully weaves "historical" assertions intended to shake the very foundations of Christianity: • Was Jesus merely human and not divine? • Did Jesus and Mary Magdalene marry and have children? • Is there a Holy Grail? If so, what is it and where can it be found? CRACKING DA VINCI'S CODE is the long-awaited answer to these and other questions. Authors James L. Garlow and Peter Jones present compelling evidence that Brown's assertions are not only historically inaccurate, but may also contain a hidden agenda.

Cracking Da Vinci's Code. unabr. ed. James L. Garlow & Peter Jones. Read by Joyce Bean & Bill Richards. 5 CDs. (Running Time: 6 hrs.). 2004. 24.95 (978-1-59335-317-9(0), 1593353170, Brilliance MP3) Brilliance Audio.

Cracking Da Vinci's Code: You've Read the Book, Now Hear the Truth. unabr. ed. James L. Garlow & Peter Jones. Read by Joyce Bean & Bill Richards. (Running Time: 6 hrs.). 2004. 39.25 (978-1-59335-477-0(0), 1593354770, Brinc Audio MP3 Lib) Brilliance Audio.

Cracking Da Vinci's Code: You've Read the Book, Now Hear the Truth. unabr. ed. James L. Garlow & Peter Jones. Read by Joyce Bean & Bill Richards. (Running Time: 6 hrs.). 2005. 39.25 (978-1-59710-777-8(8), 9781597107778, BADLE); 24.95 (978-1-59710-609-2(7), 9781597106092, BAD) Brilliance Audio.

Cracking the Code of Experience. abr. ed. Adi Da Samraj. (Running Time: 4675 sec.). (Adidam Revelation Discourses Ser.). 2006. audio compact disk 16.95 (978-1-57097-190-7(0)) Dawn Horse Pr.

Cracking the Communication Code: The Secret to Speaking Your Mate's Language. unabr. ed. Emerson Eggerichs. (Running Time: 21000 sec.). 2007. audio compact disk 34.99 (978-1-59145-583-7(9)) Nelson.

Cracking the Millionaire Code: What Rich People Know That You Don't. unabr. ed. Robert G. Allen & Mark Victor Hansen. 7 CDs. (Running Time: 9 hrs.). 2004. audio compact disk 63.00 (978-1-4159-1679-7(9)) Books on Tape.

Cracking the Millionaire Code: What Rich People Know That You Don't. unabr. ed. Robert G. Allen & Mark Victor Hansen. 6 cass. (Running Time: 9 hrs.). 2005. 54.00 (978-1-4159-1595-0(4)) Books on Tape.

Cracking the Millionaire Code: Your Key to Enlightened Wealth. abr. ed. Robert G. Allen & Mark Victor Hansen. Read by Robert G. Allen & Mark Victor Hansen. (Running Time: 3 hrs.). (ENG.). 2005. audio compact disk 23.95 (978-0-7393-1777-8(6), Random AudioBks) Pub: Random Audio Pubg. Dist(s): Random

Cracking the Wall. Eileen Lucas. Illus. by Mark Anthony. Narrated by Charles Turner. (J). (gr. k-4). 2007. 9.95 (978-1-59519-936-2(5)); audio compact disk 12.95 (978-1-59519-940-9(3)) Live Oak Media.

Cracking the Wall: The Struggles of the Little Rock Nine. Eileen Lucas. Illus. by Mark Anthony. (Running Time: 18 mins.). 2007. pap. bk. 16.95 (978-1-59519-937-9(3)); pap. bk. 39.95 (978-1-59519-943-0(8)) Live Oak Media.

Cracking Your Retirement Nest Egg. Margaret A. Malaspina. Read by Celeste Lawson. (Running Time: 6 hrs. 30 mins.). 2003. 27.95 (978-1-59912-457-5(2)) Iofy Corp.

Cracking Your Retirement Nest Egg. unabr. ed. Margaret A. Malaspina. Read by Celeste Lawson. 6 CDs. (Running Time: 7 hrs.). 2003. audio compact disk 48.00 (978-0-7861-9138-4(3), 3152); 39.95 (978-0-7861-2519-7(5), 3152) Blckstn Audio.

Whatever you have-or haven't-put away, if you are getting serious about retirement, this book can show you the right moves to make and the pitfalls to avoid.

Cradle & All. James Patterson. 2001. (978-1-57042-996-5(0)); audio compact disk 29.98 (978-1-58621-014-4(9)) Hachet Audio.

Cradle & All. abr. ed. James Patterson. Read by Ally Sheedy & Len Cariou. (ENG.). 2005. 14.98 (978-1-59483-464-6(4)) Pub: Hachet Audio. Dist(s): HachBkGrp

Cradle & All. unabr. ed. James Patterson. 2001. (978-1-58621-013-7(0)) Hachet Audio.

Cradle & All. unabr. ed. James Patterson. Read by Barbara Caruso. (ENG.). 2005. 16.98 (978-1-59483-463-9(6)) Pub: Hachet Audio. Dist(s): HachBkGrp

Cradle & All. unabr. collector's ed. James Patterson. Read by Barbara Caruso. 7 cass. (Running Time: 10 hrs. 30 min.). 2000. 44.95 (978-0-7366-5073-1(3), 5287) Books on Tape.

An ex-nun & a priest must investigate two apparent virgin pregnancies in a world suffering from apocalyptic plagues.

Cradle of Thorns. unabr. ed. Josephine Cox. Read by Carole Boyd. 10 cass. (Running Time: 10 hrs.). 1998. 84.95 Set. (978-0-7540-0083-9(4), CAB1506) AudioGO.

Nell Reece has never known her mother, & her father's burden of guilt about his wife has kept him working as a laborer on his sister's farm. For all her aunt's attempts to break Nell's independent spirit, she has never succeeded. Now pregnant & alone, Nell is forced to leave on a journey full of hazards for a vulnerable young woman.

Cradle Song see Gathering of Great Poetry for Children

Cradle That Rocked the World. Contrib. by Geron Davis. Created by Geron Davis & Christopher Phillips. Created by Christopher Phillips & Jukka Palonen. 2008. audio compact disk 16.98 (978-5-557-40901-8(7), Brentwood-Benson Music); audio compact disk 10.00 (978-5-557-40899-8(1), Brentwood-Benson Music) Brentwood Music.

Cradle That Rocked the World: Alto. Contrib. by Luke Gambill et al. Prod. by Geron Davis & Christopher Phillips. Prod. by Jukka Palonen. 2008. audio compact disk 5.00 (978-5-557-40897-4(5), Brentwood-Benson Music) Brentwood Music.

Cradle That Rocked the World: Baritone. Contrib. by Geron Davis & Christopher Phillips. 2008. audio compact disk 5.00 (978-5-557-40896-7(7), Brentwood-Benson Music) Brentwood Music.

Cradle That Rocked the World: Sab. Contrib. by Geron Davis. Created by Geron Davis & Christopher Phillips. Created by Christopher Phillips & Jukka Palonen. 2008. audio compact disk 90.00 (978-5-557-40900-1(9), Brentwood-Benson Music) Brentwood Music.

Cradle That Rocked the World: Soprano. Contrib. by Luke Gambill et al. Prod. by Geron Davis & Christopher Phillips. Prod. by Jukka Palonen. 2008. audio compact disk 5.00 (978-5-557-40898-1(3), Brentwood-Benson Music) Brentwood Music.

Cradle to Cradle: Remaking the Way We Make Things. unabr. ed. William McDonough & Michael Braungart. Read by Stephen Hoye. Narrated by Stephen Hoye. (Running Time: 5 hrs. 30 mins. 0 sec.). (ENG.). 2008. audio compact disk 49.99 (978-1-4001-3761-9(6)); audio compact disk 24.99 (978-1-4001-0761-2(X)); audio compact disk 19.99 (978-1-4001-5761-7(7)) Pub: Tantor Media. Dist(s): IngramPubServ

Cradle Will Rock, Regina & No for an Answer. Marc Blitzstein & Roddy McDowell Company. 10.95 (978-0-8045-0717-2(1), SAC 717) Spoken Arts.

Craft & its Symbols. Allen E. Roberts. 2 cass. 2004. (978-1-887560-05-4(X)) M Poll Pub.

Craft for a Dry Lake. unabr. ed. Kim Mahood. Read by Kate Hood. 5 cass. (Running Time: 8 hrs.). 2004. 40.00 (978-1-74030-591-4(4)) Pub: Bolinda Pubng AUS. Dist(s): Lndmrk Audiobks

Craft of Investing. unabr. ed. John Train. Read by Jonathan Reese. 5 cass. (Running Time: 7 hrs. 30 min.). 1995. 40.00 (978-0-7366-3130-3(5), 3805) Books on Tape.

A master of finance, John Train founded a highly respected investment firm in New York, authored a number of successful books on money & investing & has written hundreds of articles for the "Wall Street Journal," the "New York Times," "Forbes" magazine & "Harvard" magazine. He explains growth investing, timing purchases & sales, spotting emerging markets & saving on taxes.

Craft of Investing. unabr. ed. John Train. Narrated by Nelson Runger. 6 cass. (Running Time: 8 hrs. 15 mins.). 1998. 53.00 (978-0-7887-2480-0(0), 95555K8) Recorded Bks.

Key information about investing in today's complex financial world. With his clear explanations, you'll understand the psychology of the market & most importantly, how to achieve financial independence.

***Craft of Ka-Yip.** Dan Cushman. 2009. (978-1-60136-471-5(7)) Audio Holding.

Craft of Ka-Yip. Dan Cushman. (Running Time: 0 hr. 30 mins.). 1999. 10.95 (978-1-60083-493-6(0)) Iofy Corp.

Craft of the Mystery Story. P. D. James. 1 cass. (Running Time: 56 mins.). 2001. 12.95 Smithson Assocs.

Crafting Your Vision: 12 Industry Giants share their Insights on Vision, How you craft one & then how to achieve it! Richard Brooke & Richard Brooke. 12 CD's. 2002. audio compact disk 97.00 (978-0-9744363-3-3(X)) Prime Concepts Grp.

Cranberry Birthday. unabr. ed. Wende Devlin & Harry Devlin. 1 cass. (Running Time: 11 min.). (J). (ps-3). 1992. bk. 24.90 (978-0-8045-6557-8(0), 6557) Spoken Arts.

Cranberry Christmas. unabr. ed. Wende Devlin & Harry Devlin. 1 cass. (Running Time: 11 min.). (J). (ps-3). 1991. pap. bk. 16.95 (978-0-8045-6659-9(3), 6552-C) Spoken Arts.

Cranberry Easter. unabr. ed. Wende Devlin & Harry Devlin. 1 cass. (Running Time: 11 min.). (J). (ps-3). 1992. pap. bk. 16.95 (978-0-8045-6583-7(X), 6583) Spoken Arts.

Easter is coming to Cranberryport, but when Mr. Whiskers reminds his friend Seth about the annual Easter Egg hunt, he gets a terrible shock.

Cranberry Halloween. unabr. ed. Wende Devlin & Harry Devlin. 1 cass. (Running Time: 12 min.). (J). (ps-3). 1990. bk. 23.90 (978-0-8045-6552-3(X), 6552-A) Spoken Arts.

Cranberry Halloween. unabr. ed. Wende Devlin & Harry Devlin. 1 cass. (Running Time: 15 min.). (J). (gr. k-3). 2001. pap. bk. 16.95 (978-0-8045-6657-5(7), 6552-A) Spoken Arts.

On Halloween night the people of Cranberryport almost lose all the money they have raised to build a new dock.

Cranberry Mystery. unabr. ed. Wende Devlin & Harry Devlin. 1 cass. (Running Time: 11 min.). (J). (ps-3). 1992. bk. 23.90 (978-0-8045-6553-0(8), 6553) Spoken Arts.

Cranberry Summer. unabr. ed. Wende Devlin & Harry Devlin. 1 cass. (Running Time: 10 min.). (J). (ps-3). 1992. bk. 24.90 (978-0-8045-6700-8(X), 6700) Spoken Arts.

Cranberry Thanksgiving. unabr. ed. Wende Devlin & Harry Devlin. 1 cass. (Running Time: 12 min.). (J). (ps-3). 1991. bk. 23.90 (6552-B) Spoken Arts.

Cranberry Thanksgiving. unabr. ed. Wende Devlin & Harry Devlin. 1 cass. (Running Time: 15 min.). (J). (gr. k-3). 2001. pap. bk. 16.95 (978-0-8045-6658-2(5), 6552-B) Spoken Arts.

Grandmother almost loses her secret recipe for Cranberry bread to one of her Thanksgiving dinner guests.

Cranberry Valentine. unabr. ed. Wende Devlin & Harry Devlin. 1 cass. (Running Time: 9 min.). (J). (ps-3). 1991. pap. bk. 16.95 (6552-D) Spoken Arts.

Maggie, her grandmother and the sewing circle make Cranberryport a brighter place for Mr. Whiskers when they send him secret valentines.

Crane. unabr. ed. Jeff Stone. Read by Kiki Barrera. 5 CDs. (Running Time: 6 hrs 1 min.). (Five Ancestors Ser.: Bk. 4). (J). (gr. 4-7). 2007. audio compact disk 36.00 (978-0-7393-4855-0(8)) Books on Tape.

Crane. unabr. ed. Jeff Stone. Read by Kiki Barrera. (Running Time: 21600 sec.). (Five Ancestors Ser.: Bk. 4). (ENG.). (J). (gr. 5-9). 2007. audio compact disk 35.00 (978-0-7393-3864-3(1), Listening Lib) Pub: Random Audio Pubg. Dist(s): Random

Crane Wife. Created by Steck-Vaughn Staff. (Running Time: 29100 sec.). (Pair-It Bks.). (J). (gr. 2-6). 1997. (978-0-8172-7368-2(9)) SteckVau.

Cranefly Orchid Murders. Cynthia Riggs. Read by Davina Porter. (Running Time: 30600 sec.). (Martha's Vineyard Mystery Ser.). 2006. 59.95 (978-0-7861-4595-9(1)); audio compact disk 63.00 (978-0-7861-6993-1(1)) Blckstn Audio.

Cranefly Orchid Murders. unabr. ed. Cynthia Riggs. Read by Davina Porter. (Running Time: 30600 sec.). (Martha's Vineyard Mystery Ser.). 2006. audio compact disk 29.95 (978-0-7861-7509-3(5)) Blckstn Audio.

Crane's Story - Tales of Love from Japan: Musical Adventures with Elizabeth Falconer Volume III. Perf. by Elizabeth Falconer. 1 CD. (Running Time: 54:06). (YA). 2002. audio compact disk 15.00 (978-0-9770499-4-3(9)) Koto World.

"Unique and inviting..."Elizabeth Falconer artfully blends original koto music and finely crafted storytelling in this excellent production. While these three traditional stories may be familiar to some listeners, her inventive use of her the 13-stringed instrument makes this a unique and inviting recording. The title story, told from the crane's point of view, recounts the bird's transformation into a young woman and her relationship with an elderly, childless couple. "The Tanabata Legend" explains the sad tale of the Weaver Star and the Cowherd Star separated because the night sky is in disarray. "The Golden Arrow" is a classic quest with the prince required to perform three tasks in order to win the hand of a koto-playing princess. Throughout the recording, Falconer accentuates the story's action and emotion with well-placed koto music. There are also two musical solos on the disc that add to the pleasing qualities of the presentation. Useful liner notes and an attractive cover add to the recording's overall quality. This excellent production would be a valuable asset to collections seeking fresh multicultural titles. - School Library Journal.

***Cranford.** unabr. ed. Elizabeth Gaskell. Narrated by Prunella Scales. 6 CDs. (Running Time: 6 hrs. 50 mins.). 2010. audio compact disk 49.95 (978-0-7927-7002-2(1), SLD1921, Chivers Sound Lib) AudioGO.

***Cranford.** unabr. ed. Elizabeth Gaskell. Narrated by Wanda McCaddon. (Running Time: 8 hrs. 0 mins.). 2010. 15.99 (978-1-4001-8945-8(4)); 19.99 (978-1-4001-6945-0(3)); audio compact disk 66.99 (978-1-4001-4945-2(2)); audio compact disk 27.99 (978-1-4001-1945-5(6)) Pub: Tantor Media. Dist(s): IngramPubServ

Cranford; the Cage at Cranford; the Moorland Cottage, Set. unabr. ed. Elizabeth Gaskell. Read by Flo Gibson. 8 cass. (Running Time: 11 hrs. 30 min.). 1987. 26.95 (978-1-55685-073-8(5)) Audio Bk Con.

This intimate glimpse of life in a small English country town in the early 19th century is full of humor, pathos & the warmth of true friendship.

Cranford 1851. Elizabeth Gaskell. Narrated by Prunella Scales. (Running Time: 6 hrs. 50 mins. 0 sec.). (ENG.). 2010. audio compact disk 29.95 (978-1-60283-861-1(5)) Pub: AudioGO. Dist(s): Perseus Dist

Cranford 1851. Elizabeth Gaskell. Read by Anais 9000. 2008. 27.95 (978-1-60112-179-0(2)) Babblebooks.

Cranford 1851. Elizabeth Gaskell. Read by Nadia May. (Running Time: 7 hrs.). 2002. 27.95 (978-1-59912-458-2(0)) Iofy Corp.

Cranford 1851. Read by Clare Wille. (Complete Classics Ser.). 2008. audio compact disk 34.98 (978-962-634-850-5(X), Naxos AudioBooks) Naxos.

Cranford 1851. unabr. ed. Elizabeth Gaskell. Read by Nadia May. 5 cass. (Running Time: 7 hrs.). 2002. 39.95 (978-0-7861-2203-5(X), 2953); audio compact disk 48.00 (978-0-7861-9540-4(1), 2953) Blckstn Audio.

A comic portrait of early Victorian life in a country town that describes with poignant wit the uneventful lives of its lady-like inhabitants, offering an ironic commentary on the separate spheres and diverse experiences of men and women. As the external world necessarily impinges even on Cranford, the unlikely juxtapositions of old and new brought about by the pace of change are also explored: the effects of Victorian commerce and imperial expansion co-exist with the survival of customs and habits of thought from much earlier times.

Cranford 1851. unabr. ed. Elizabeth Gaskell. Read by Nadia May. (Running Time: 7 hrs. 0 mins.). 2009. 29.95 (978-1-4332-7084-0(6)); audio compact disk 19.95 (978-1-4332-7083-3(8)) Blckstn Audio.

Cranford 1851. unabr. ed. Elizabeth Gaskell. Read by Clare Wille. (YA). 2008. 54.99 (978-1-60514-701-7(X)) Find a World.

Crank. unabr. ed. Ellen Hopkins. Read by Laura M. Flanagan. 4 CDs. (Running Time: 4 hrs. 30 mins.). (ENG., 2008. audio compact disk 24.95 (978-1-59887-752-6(6), 1598877526) Pub: HighBridge. Dist(s): Workman Pub

Crank Calls. Jonathan Winters. 1 cass. (Running Time: 50 min.). 10.95 Pub Mills.

When Jonathan Winters, the elder statesman of surreal improvisational comedy, "Leaves a message at the tone" the result is comic genius. It seems that Jonathan's peripatetic buddy Jim Smith is quite the elusive fellow. Regardless of season or time of day, Jonathan can never reach Mr. Smith by phone...but that's a stroke of luck for the fans of Winters brand of inventive off-the-cuff antics. "Crank Calls" captures for posterity actual phone message left by Winters on Smith's answering machine. The result is uninhibitied, unscripted, & uniquely Winters.

Crank Calls. Jonathan Winters. 1 cass. (Running Time: 50 min.). 1995. audio compact disk 12.98 CD. (978-1-879371-87-3(1), 40370) Pub Mills.

Cranks & Shadows. unabr. ed. K. C. Constantine. Read by Lloyd James. 9 cass. (Running Time: 13 hrs. 30 min.). (Mario Balzic Ser.). 1997. 72.00 (978-0-7366-3692-6(7), 4371) Books on Tape.

Mario Balzic has to deal with a slashed municipal budget & a mayor who has privatized everything from the sanitation department to the town plumber.

Crank(y) Calls. Perf. by Jonathan Winters. 2000. audio compact disk 16.98 (978-1-929243-20-4(0)) Uproar Ent.

Craps Made Simple. Thomas B. Gallagher. Read by Thomas B. Gallagher. 1 cass. (Running Time: 1 hr.). 1987. 14.95 (978-0-938706-03-8(9)) Thomas Compny.

A seminar on Craps. Includes advise on how to play, place proper bets & manage money.

Crash. Contrib. by Decyfer Down. Prod. by Paul Ebersold. (ENG.). 2009. audio compact disk 13.62 (978-5-557-36786-8(1)) INO Rec.

Crash. Jerry Spinelli. Read by Jeff Woodman. 3 cass. (Running Time: 4 hr.). (J). (gr. 6). 1995. pap. bk. 40.24 HOMEWORK SET. (978-0-7887-0976-0(3), 40315); pap. bk. 97.70 CLASS SET. (978-0-7887-1952-3(1), 46009) Record Bks.

Seventh-grader Crash Coogan is a jock. Crashing through life as long as he can remember, he runs over anyone & anything that stand in his way. When a geeky pacifist moves onto his block, Crash doesn't know whether he wants this odd boy's friendship. Crash struggles to develop ways to deal with life other than brute force.

Crash. unabr. ed. Jerry Spinelli. Narrated by Jeff Woodman. 3 pieces. (Running Time: 4 hrs.). (gr. 6 up). 1997. 27.00 (978-0-7887-0717-9(5), 94893E7) Recorded Bks.

Crash. unabr. collector's ed. J. G. Ballard. Read by David Case. 7 cass. (Running Time: 7 hrs.). 1997. 42.00 (978-0-913369-80-7(2), 4351) Books on Tape.

The thrill of speed & destruction - a cultural death drive - is the force that moves this surreal novel.

Crash! Bang! Boom! The Best of WB Sound FX. 1 CD. (Running Time: 1 hr.). (J). 2002. audio compact disk 17.99 (978-0-7379-0139-9(X), 79866) Rhino Enter.

It's the ultimate WB sound effects album with over 100 digitally restored classic world-famous cartoon sound effects interspersed with ACME commercials, Looney Tunes answering-machine messages, fun cartoon dialogue and music. Great effects to add to home videos, computers, parties and more.

Crash Course: The American Automobile Industry's Road to Bankruptcy & Bailout-and Beyond. unabr. ed. Paul Ingrassia. (Running Time: 12 hrs. 30 mins. 0 sec.). (ENG.). 2010. 24.99 (978-1-4001-6510-0(5)) Pub: Tantor Media. Dist(s): IngramPubServ

Crash Course: The American Automobile Industry's Road to Bankruptcy & Bailout-and Beyond. unabr. ed. Paul Ingrassia. Narrated by Patrick G. Lawlor. (Running Time: 12 hrs. 30 mins.). 2010. 18.99 (978-1-4001-8510-8(6)); audio compact disk 69.99 (978-1-4001-4510-2(4)); audio compact disk 34.99 (978-1-4001-1510-5(8)) Pub: Tantor Media. Dist(s): IngramPubServ

Crash Course Acoustic Guitar. Mead David. 2005. audio compact disk 16.95 (978-1-84492-031-0(3)) Pub: Sanctuary Pubng GBR. Dist(s): H Leonard

Crash Course: Bass. Clayton Stuart. 2005. audio compact disk 14.95 (978-1-84492-015-0(1)) Pub: Sanctuary Pubng GBR. Dist(s): H Leonard

Crash Course: Djing. Ron Cowan & Tom Frederikse. 2005. audio compact disk 14.95 (978-1-84492-020-4(8)) Pub: Sanctuary Pubng GBR. Dist(s): H Leonard

Crash Course: Drums. Pete Riley. 2006. audio compact disk 14.95 (978-1-84492-014-3(3), 1844920143) H Leonard.

Crash Course Electric Guitar. Humphries Jamie. 2 CDs. 2006. audio compact disk 16.95 (978-1-84492-068-6(2), 1844920682) H Leonard.

Crash Course in Christian Coaching. Christopher McCluskey. 2001. 19.99 (978-0-9707934-5-4(6)) Coachng for Chrstn Living.

Crash Course in Forces & Motion with Max Axiom, Super Scientist. Emily Sohn & Charles Barnett III. Illus. by Steve Erwin. (Graphic Science Ser.). (ENG.). (gr. 3-4). 2007. audio compact disk 6.95 (978-1-4296-1122-0(7)) CapstoneDig.

Crash Course on Getting Things Done: 17 Proven Principles for Overcoming Procrastination. unabr. ed. Larry J. Koenig. Narrated by Jon Gauger. (Crash Course Ser.). (ENG.). 2007. 9.09 (978-1-60814-159-3(4)); audio compact disk 12.99 (978-1-59859-301-3(3)) Oasis Audio.

Crash Course on Losing Weight: 21 Practical Ways to Look & Feel Better. unabr. ed. Larry J. Koenig. Narrated by Jon Gauger. (Crash Course Ser.). (ENG.). 2007. 9.09 (978-1-60814-160-9(8)); audio compact disk 12.99 (978-1-59859-302-0(1)) Oasis Audio.

Crash Course on Successful Parenting: 13 Dynamics of Raising Great Kids. unabr. ed. Larry J. Koenig. Narrated by Jon Gauger. (Crash Course Ser.). (ENG.). 2007. 9.09 (978-1-60814-161-6(6)); audio compact disk 12.99 (978-1-59859-255-9(6)) Oasis Audio.

***Crash of the Titans: How the Decline & Fall of Merrill Lynch Crippled Bank of America & Nearly Destroyed America's Financial System.** unabr. ed. Greg Farrell. Read by Dan Woren. (ENG.). 2010. audio compact disk 45.00 (978-0-307-75116-4(3), Random AudioBks) Pub: Random Audio Pubg. Dist(s): Random

Crash Proof: How to Profit from the Coming Economic Collapse. unabr. ed. Peter D. Schiff & John Downes. Read by Sean Pratt. (Running Time: 9 hrs.). (ENG.). 2008. 24.98 (978-1-59659-249-0(4), GildAudio) Pub: Gildan Media. Dist(s): HachBkGrp

Crash Proof: How to Profit from the Coming Economic Collapse. unabr. ed. Peter D. Schiff & John Downes. Read by Sean Pratt. (Running Time: 8 hrs. 30 mins.). (ENG.). 2009. audio compact disk 29.98 (978-1-59659-277-3(X)) Pub: Gildan Media. Dist(s): HachBkGrp

Crash Proof 2.0: How to Profit from the Economic Collapse. unabr. ed. Peter D. Schiff. Read by Sean Pratt. (Running Time: 12 hrs.). (ENG.). 2009. 29.98 (978-1-59659-465-4(9), GildAudio) Pub: Gildan Media. Dist(s): HachBkGrp

Crashed. Robin Wasserman. Read by Kate Reinders. (Playaway Young Adult Ser.). (ENG.). (YA). 2009. 54.99 (978-1-4418-1001-4(3)) Find a World.

Crashed. unabr. ed. Robin Wasserman. Read by Kate Reinders. (Running Time: 9 hrs.). 2009. 24.99 (978-1-4233-7496-1(7), 9781423374961, Brilliance MP3); 24.99 (978-1-4233-7498-5(3), 9781423374985, BAD); 39.97 (978-1-4233-7497-8(5), 9781423374978, Brinc Audio MP3 Lib); 39.97 (978-1-4233-7499-2(1), 9781423374992, BADLE); audio compact disk 29.99 (978-1-4233-7494-7(0), 9781423374947, Bril Audio CD Unabri) Brilliance Audio.

Crashed. unabr. ed. Robin Wasserman. Read by Kate Reinders. 9 CDs. (Running Time: 11 hrs.). (YA). (gr. 9 up). 2009. audio compact disk 72.97 (978-1-4233-7495-4(9), 9781423374954, BriAudCD Unabrid) Brilliance Audio.

Crashed Flying Saucers. Stanton Friedman. 2 cass. (Running Time: 2 hrs.). 1994. 15.95 set. (978-1-57124-013-2(6)) Creat Seminars.
Research on UFO's.

Crasher. unabr. ed. Shirley Lord. Narrated by Suzanne Toren. 11 cass. (Running Time: 15 hrs. 45 mins.). 1998. 93.00 (978-0-7887-3492-2(X), 95499E7) Recorded Bks.
All Ginny Walker has ever wanted to do is design clothes. But breaking into the high fashion world in New York City is easier said than done. Trying to be noticed, she crashes galas wearing her creations - -until one terrible night, her game turns deadly.

***Crashers.** unabr. ed. Dana Haynes. (Running Time: 11 hrs. 30 mins. 0 sec.). (ENG.). 2010. audio compact disk 39.99 (978-1-4272-1215-3(5)) Pub: Macmill Audio. Dist(s): Macmillan

Crashes, Booms, Panics, & Government Regulation. Narrated by Louis Rukeyser. Contrib. by Robert Sobel & Roger Lowenstein. 2 cass. (Running Time: 2 hrs. 30 mins.). (Secrets of the Great Investors Ser.: Vol. 2). 17.95 (978-1-56823-054-2(0)) Pub: Knowledge Prod. Dist(s): APG
Financial markets have an impressive history of gains & progress for prudent & judicious investors - but these advances are often interrupted by powerful & sudden setbacks or forward lurches. What is it about investment psychology (& the structure of financial markets) that causes this? How should we react to short term gyrations that can excite or frighten? And what is the role of government regulation in stabilizing financial markets?.

Crashes, Booms, Panics & Government Regulation. unabr. abr. ed. Roger Lowenstein. Read by Louis Rukeyser. (Running Time: 9000 sec.). (Secrets of the Great Investors Ser.). 2006. audio compact disk 25.95 (978-0-7861-6489-9(1)) Pub: Blckstn Audio. Dist(s): NetLibrary CO

Crashing down of My Divine Grace. Da Avabhasa. 1 cass. 1993. 11.95 (978-0-918801-82-1(6)) Dawn Horse Pr.

Crashing Through: A Story of Risk, Adventure, & the Man Who Dared to See. unabr. ed. Robert Kurson. Read by Doug Ordunio. 9 CDs. (Running Time: 10 hrs. 30 mins.). 2007. audio compact disk 90.00 (978-1-4159-3871-3(7)); 90.00 (978-1-4159-4046-4(0)) Books on Tape.
Blinded at age three, Mike May defied expectations by breaking world records in downhill speed skiing, joining the CIA, and becoming a successful inventor, entrepreneur, and family man. He had never yearned for vision. Then, in 1999, a chance encounter brought startling news: a revolutionary stem cell transplant surgery could restore May's vision. The procedure was filled with risks, some of them deadly, others beyond May's wildest dreams. There were countless reasons for May to refuse vision. He could think of only a single reason to go forward. Whatever his decision, he knew it would change his life.

Crashlander. unabr. collector's ed. Larry Niven. Read by Connor O'Brien. 7 cass. (Running Time: 10 hrs. 30 min.). 1998. 56.00 (978-0-7366-4083-1(5), 4592) Books on Tape.
This collection of stories features Crashlander Beowulf Shaeffer, an irresistible anti-hero who can't avoid trouble.

***Crave.** unabr. ed. J. R. Ward, pseud. Read by Eric G. Dove. (Running Time: 13 hrs.). (Fallen Angels Ser.). 2010. 24.99 (978-1-4418-3091-3(X), 9781441830913, Brilliance MP3); 39.97 (978-1-4418-3092-0(8), 9781441830920, Brinc Audio MP3 Lib); 24.99 (978-1-4418-3093-7(6), 9781441830937, BAD); 39.97 (978-1-4418-3094-4(4), 9781441830944, BADLE); audio compact disk 29.99 (978-1-4418-3089-0(8), 9781441830890, Bril Audio CD Unabri); audio compact disk 89.97 (978-1-4418-3090-6(1), 9781441830906, BriAudCD Unabrid) Brilliance Audio.

Craven Street. Perf. by Elizabeth Montgomery et al. Prod. by Yuri Rasovsky. 5 cass. (Running Time: 5 hrs.). 34.95 (978-1-57677-142-6(3), HTOE001) Lodestone Catalog.

Craven Street: Ben Franklin in London. Yuri Rasovsky. Directed By Yuri Rasovsky. (Running Time: 14400 sec.). 2006. audio compact disk 45.00 (978-0-7861-7192-7(8)) Blckstn Audio.

Craven Street: Ben Franklin in London. Yuri Rasovsky. Prod. by Yuri Rasovsky. (Running Time: 14400 sec.). 2006. 44.95 (978-0-7861-4512-6(9)) Blckstn Audio.

Craven Street: Ben Franklin in London. unabr. ed. Yuri Rasovsky. Directed By Yuri Rasovsky. (Running Time: 14400 sec.). 2006. audio compact disk 29.95 (978-0-7861-7651-9(2)) Blckstn Audio.

Crawdads, Doodlebugs & Creasy Greens: Songs, Stories & Lore Celebrating the Natural World. Doug Elliot. 1997. pap. bk. 23.95 (978-0-7866-1683-1(0), 95708CDP) Mel Bay.

Crawdads, Doodlebugs & Creasy Greens: Songs, Stories & Lore Celebrating the Natural World. Doug Elliot. 1997. pap. bk. 18.95 (978-0-7866-1684-8(9), 95708P) Mel Bay.

Crawdads, Doodlebugs & Creasy Greens: Songs, Stories & Lore Celebrating the Natural World. Doug Elliott. Read by Doug Elliott. 1 cass. (Running Time: 60 min.). (J). 1995. 9.95 (978-1-883206-10-9(3), NG600); audio compact disk 14.95 CD. (978-1-883206-15-4(4), NG-CD-600) Native Ground.

Crawfish Mountain. unabr. ed. Ken Wells. Read by Dick Hill. (Running Time: 57600 sec.). 2007. 59.95 (978-1-4332-0511-8(4)); audio compact disk 29.95 (978-1-4332-0515-6(7)); audio compact disk 72.00 (978-1-4332-0512-5(2)) Blckstn Audio.

Crawfish Mountain. unabr. ed. Ken Wells. Read by Dick Hill. (Running Time: 57600 sec.). 2007. 24.95 (978-1-4332-0513-2(0)); audio compact disk 24.95 (978-1-4332-0514-9(9)) Blckstn Audio.

Crazed. Ha Jin. Narrated by Norm Lee. 7 cass. (Running Time: 10 hrs.). 67.00 (978-1-4025-3034-0(X)) Recorded Bks.

Crazed: A Novel. unabr. ed. Ha Jin. 6 cass. (Running Time: 10 hrs.). 2004. 29.99 (978-1-4025-2498-1(6), 01794) Recorded Bks.
Professor Yang, a respected literature scholar, suffers a stroke and is confined to a hospital bed. Now Jian Wan, Yang's brightest student and future son-in-law, must suspend his rigorous studies to care for his mentor. Jian dutifully keeps watch as Yang begins raving madly, often pleading with unseen tormentors. Has Yang lost his grip on sanity, or is he no longer capable of hiding deeply buried, painful secrets?.

Crazed Moon see Poetry of William Butler Yeats

***Crazies to the Left of Me Wimps to the Right.** unabr. ed. Bernard Goldberg. Read by Bernard Goldberg. (ENG.). 2007. (978-0-06-144950-5(4), Harper Audio); (978-0-06-144949-9(0), Harper Audio) HarperCollins Pubs.

Crazies to the Left of Me, Wimps to the Right: How One Side Lost Its Mind & the Other Lost Its Nerve. unabr. ed. Bernard Goldberg. Read by Bernard Goldberg. (Running Time: 25200 sec.). 2007. audio compact disk 29.95 (978-0-06-143561-4(9), Harper Audio) HarperCollins Pubs.

***Crazy.** unabr. ed. William Peter Blatty. (Running Time: 4 hrs. 30 mins.). 2010. 24.99 (978-1-4001-9868-9(2)); 12.99 (978-1-4001-8868-0(7)); 19.99 (978-1-4001-6868-2(6)); audio compact disk 24.99 (978-1-4001-1868-7(9)); audio compact disk 59.99 (978-1-4001-4868-4(5)) Pub: Tantor Media. Dist(s): IngramPubServ

Crazy: A Father's Search Through America's Mental Health Madness. Pete Earley. Read by Michael Prichard. (Playaway Adult Nonfiction Ser.). 2008. 64.99 (978-1-60640-854-4(2)) Find a World.

Crazy: A Father's Search Through America's Mental Health Madness. unabr. ed. Pete Earley. Narrated by Michael Prichard. 10 CDs. (Running Time: 12 hrs. 0 mins. 0 sec.). (ENG.). 2006. audio compact disk 34.99 (978-1-4001-0256-3(1)) Pub: Tantor Media. Dist(s): IngramPubServ
Pete Earley had no idea. He'd been a journalist for over thirty years, and the author of several award-winning - -even bestselling - -nonfiction books about crime and punishment and society. Yet he'd always been on the outside looking in. He had no idea what it was like to be on the inside looking out until his son, Mike, was declared mentally ill, and Earley was thrown headlong into the maze of contradictions, disparities, and catch-22s that is America's mental health system. The more Earley dug, the more he uncovered the bigger picture: Our nation's prisons have become our new mental hospitals. Crazy tells two stories. The first is his son's. The second describes what Earley learned during a yearlong investigation inside the Miami-Dade County jail, where he was given complete, unrestricted access. There, and in the surrounding community, he shadowed inmates and patients; interviewed correctional officers, public defenders, prosecutors, judges, mental-health professionals, and the police; talked with parents, siblings, and spouses; consulted historians, civil rights lawyers, and legislators.

Crazy: A Father's Search Through America's Mental Health Madness. unabr. ed. Pete Earley. Read by Michael Prichard. (Running Time: 12 hrs. 0 mins. 0 sec.). (ENG.). 2006. audio compact disk 24.99 (978-1-4001-5256-8(9)); audio compact disk 69.99 (978-1-4001-3256-0(8)) Pub: Tantor Media. Dist(s): IngramPubServ

Crazy Bosses & Sun Tzu. abr. ed. Stanley Bing. Read by Stanley Bing. 5 CDs. (Running Time: 21600 sec.). 2007. audio compact disk 29.95 (978-0-06-123551-1(2)) HarperCollins Pubs.

***Crazy Bosses & Sun Tzu.** abr. ed. Stanley Bing. Read by Stanley Bing. (ENG.). 2007. (978-0-06-144989-5(X), Harper Audio); (978-0-06-144988-8(1), Harper Audio) HarperCollins Pubs.

Crazy Cats - Los Gatos Locos: Colors - Los Colores. Clamshell. 1 cass. (Running Time: 1 hr. 30 min.). (SPA & ENG., (J). (ps-1). 2000. pap. bk. 9.95 (978-1-886972-30-8(3)) Pub: Emaginit. Dist(s): Penton Overseas
Bilingual program features a cast of Crazy Cats, original music and sound effects. English is on one side; Spanish is on the other! Book is filled with large illustrations for children to follow along and learn words in either language.

Crazy Cats - Los Gatos Locos: Colors, Numbers & Positions. 3 cass. (Running Time: 4 hrs. 30 min.). (ENG & SPA., (J). (ps-1). 2000. pap. bk. 25.95 (978-1-886972-40-7(0)) Pub: Emaginit. Dist(s): Penton Overseas

Crazy Cats - Los Gatos Locos: Numbers - Los Numeros. Clamshell. 1 cass. (Running Time: 1 hr. 30 min.). (ENG & SPA., (J). (ps-1). 2000. pap. bk. 9.95 (978-1-886972-31-5(1)) Pub: Emaginit. Dist(s): Penton Overseas

Crazy Cats - Los Gatos Locos: Positions - Las Posiciones. Clamshell. 1 cass. (Running Time: 1 hrs. 30 min.). (ENG & SPA., (J). (ps-1). 2000. pap. bk. 9.95 (978-1-886972-32-2(X)) Pub: Emaginit. Dist(s): Penton Overseas

***Crazy Crow.** Ger Horgan. Steve Mcsweeney. (ENG.). 1994. 11.95 (978-0-8023-7097-6(7)) Pub: Clo Iar-Chonnachta IRL. Dist(s): Dufour

Crazy for Cornelia. unabr. ed. Chris Gilson. Read by Nick Sullivan. 8 vols. (Running Time: 12 hrs.). 2000. bk. 69.95 (978-0-7927-2382-0(1), CSL 271, Chivers Sound Lib) AudioGO.
Once upon a time, a gorgeous debutante found her knight in shining armor as he held the door to her luxury co-op - so goes the legend passed through generations of New York's top doormen. Kevin Doyle, struggling artist-turned doorman, dismisses the fairy tale until the lovely Cornelia Lord steps into his life. As Cornelia runs away from a lineage of wealth & privilege, she is trust into the midst of a grab at the Lord fortune. Together, she & Kevin must stop this plot before they can sort their feelings for each other.

***Crazy for God: How I Grew up as One of the Elect, Helped Found the Religious Right, & Lived to Take All (or Almost All) of It Back.** unabr. ed. Frank Schaeffer. (Running Time: 10 hrs.). (ENG.). 2010. 34.98 (978-1-59659-674-0(0), GildAudio) Pub: Gildan Media. Dist(s): HachBkGrp

***Crazy for the Storm.** unabr. ed. Norman Ollestad. Read by Norman Ollestad. (ENG.). 2009. (978-0-06-190192-8(X), Harper Audio); (978-0-06-190193-5(8), Harper Audio) HarperCollins Pubs.

Crazy for the Storm: A Memoir of Survival. unabr. ed. Norman Ollestad. (Running Time: 8.5 hrs. 0 mins.). 2009. 29.95 (978-1-4332-9093-0(6)); 59.95 (978-1-4332-9089-3(8)); audio compact disk 70.00 (978-1-4332-9090-9(1)) Blckstn Audio.

Crazy for the Storm: A Memoir of Survival. unabr. ed. Norman Ollestad. Read by Norman Ollestad. 6 CDs. (Running Time: 7 hrs. 45 mins.). 2009. audio compact disk 39.99 (978-0-06-177445-4(6), Harper Audio) HarperCollins Pubs.

Crazy for You. abr. ed. Jennifer Crusie, pseud. Read by Sandra Burr. (Running Time: 6 hrs.). 2004. 62.25 (978-1-59355-358-6(7), 1593553587, BAudLibEd); audio compact disk 74.25 (978-1-59355-925-0(9), 1593559259, BACDLib Ed) Brilliance Audio.
Quinn McKenzie has always lived what she calls a "beige" life. She's dating the world's nicest guy, she has a good job as a high school art teacher, she's surrounded by family and friends who rely on her, and she's bored to the point of insanity. But when Quinn decides to change her life by adopting a stray dog over everyone's objections, everything begins to spiral out of control. Now she's coping with dog-napping, breaking and entering, seduction, sabotage, stalking, more secrets than she really wants to know, and two men who are suddenly crazy...for her. "The story comes together with just the right touches of humor and some pretty sexy dialogue. Crusie hasn't yet achieved the name recognition of Sandra Brown or Nora Roberts, but this effort proves she is every bit as good." - Library Journal "Crazy for You is witty, wicked and wonderful reality." - The Courier-Herald (Atlanta, GA) "Engaging...Fun and a little wild." - Pittsburgh Post-Gazette.

Crazy for You. abr. ed. Jennifer Crusie, pseud. Read by Sandra Burr. (Running Time: 6 hrs.). 2005. audio compact disk 16.99 (978-1-59600-411-5(8), 9781596004115, BCD Value Price) Brilliance Audio.

Crazy for You. abr. ed. Jennifer Crusie, pseud. Read by Sandra Burr. (Running Time: 6 hrs.). 2006. 39.25 (978-1-4233-0048-9(3), 9781423300489, BADLE); 24.95 (978-1-4233-0047-2(5), 9781423300472, BAD); 39.25 (978-1-4233-0046-5(7), 9781423300465, Brinc Audio MP3 Lib); audio compact disk 24.95 (978-1-4233-0045-8(9), 9781423300458, Brilliance MP3) Brilliance Audio.

Crazy for You. abr. ed. Jennifer Crusie, pseud. Read by Sandra Burr. (Running Time: 6 hrs.). 2009. audio compact disk 9.99 (978-1-4418-2646-6(7), 9781441826466, BCD Value Price) Brilliance Audio.

***Crazy Good Sex: Putting to Bed the Myths Men Have about Sex.** unabr. ed. Les Parrott III. (Running Time: 3 hrs. 9 mins. 0 sec.). (ENG.). 2009. 19.99 (978-0-310-29883-0(0)) Zondervan.

***Crazy Hair.** unabr. ed. Neil Gaiman. Read by Neil Gaiman. (ENG.). 2009. (978-0-06-198735-9(2)) HarperCollins Pubs.

***Crazy Hair Day.** Barney Saltzberg. 1 CD. (Running Time: 10 mins.). (J). (gr. k-3). 2009. audio compact disk 12.95 (978-0-545-13442-2(0)) Weston Woods.

Crazy Hair Day. Barney Saltzberg. Narrated by Zach Braff. 1 CD. (Running Time: 10 mins.). (J). (gr. k-3). 2009. audio compact disk 12.95 Weston Woods.

Crazy Hair Day. Barney Saltzberg. Illus. by Barney Saltzberg. Narrated by Zach Braff. 1 CD. (Running Time: 10 mins.). (J). (gr. k-3). 2009. bk. 29.95 (978-0-545-13450-7(1)) Weston Woods.

Crazy Hair Day, Set. Barney Saltzberg. Narrated by Zach Braff. 1 CD. (Running Time: 10 mins.). (J). (gr. k-3). 2009. pap. bk. 38.75 (978-0-545-15157-3(0)) Weston Woods.

***Crazy Heart.** unabr. ed. Thomas Cobb. Read by Thomas Cobb. (ENG.). 2010. (978-0-06-201520-4(6), Harper Audio) HarperCollins Pubs.

Crazy Heart. unabr. ed. Thomas Cobb. Narrated by Jerry Farden. 6 cass. (Running Time: 9 hrs.). 1989. 51.00 (978-1-55690-124-9(0), 89110E7) Recorded Bks.
A country & western singer tries to make a final comeback.

***Crazy Heart: A Novel.** unabr. ed. Thomas Cobb. Read by Thomas Cobb. (ENG.). 2010. (978-0-06-200622-6(3), Harper Audio) HarperCollins Pubs.

Crazy Horse. Larry McMurtry. Read by Scott Brick. 1999. audio compact disk 28.00 (978-0-7366-5190-5(X)) Books on Tape.

Crazy Horse. abr. ed. Larry McMurtry. 1999. 19.95 (PengAudBks) Penguin Grp USA.
Documentation on the life & times of the great Sioux warrior.

Crazy Horse. unabr. ed. Larry McMurtry. Read by Scott Brick. 3 CDs. (Running Time: 3 hrs. 36 mins.). 2001. audio compact disk 15.95 Books on Tape.
Looking back across more than one hundred & twenty years at the life & death of the great Sioux warrio.

Crazy Horse. unabr. ed. Larry McMurtry. 2 cass. (Running Time: 3 hrs.). 1999. 17.95 (978-0-7366-4693-2(0)) Books on Tape.

Crazy Horse. unabr. collector's ed. Larry McMurtry. Read by Scott Brick. 3 cass. (Running Time: 4 hrs 30 min.). 1999. 28.00 (978-0-7366-4607-9(8), 4993) Books on Tape.
Biography looks back across more than one hundred & twenty years at the life & death of this great Sioux Warrior who became a reluctant leader at the Battle of the Little Bighorn. The betrayal by representatives of the U.S. government was a tragic turning point in the history of the west.

Crazy Horse. unabr. collector's ed. Mari Sandoz. Read by John MacDonald. 10 cass. (Running Time: 15 hrs.). 1992. 80.00 (978-0-7366-2139-7(3), 2938) Books on Tape.
Crazy Horse was one of the last Indian chiefs to war against the settlers. He was charismatic, known for his valor & bravery, openly admired by his opponents. In 1876 he led the Sioux nation out of its reservation & into the wilderness. He held off pursuing armies for months. In the end, dressed in fine regalia, he surrendered, later to be treacherously stabbed & killed.

Crazy Horse's Vision. 11 vols. pap. bk. 16.95 (978-1-59112-451-1(4)); pap. bk. (978-1-59112-453-5(0)); pap. bk. 18.95 (978-1-59112-911-0(7)); pap. bk. (978-1-59112-913-4(3)); 9.95 (978-1-59112-450-4(6)); audio compact disk 12.95 (978-1-59112-910-3(9)) Live Oak Media.

Crazy Horse's Vision. Joseph Bruchac. Read by Curtis Zunigha. 11 vols. (J). 2005. bk. 25.95 (978-1-59112-452-8(2)); bk. 28.95 (978-1-59112-912-7(5)) Pub: Live Oak Media. Dist(s): AudioGO

Crazy Hunter. Kay Boyle. Read by Kay Boyle. 1 cass. (Running Time: 56 min.). (American Audio Prose Library: Series V). 1985. 13.95 (978-1-55644-122-6(3), 5011) Am Audio Prose.
The author reads excerpts from "The Crazy Hunter" & "A Declaration for 1955".

Crazy in Alabama. Mark Childress. Narrated by Tom Stechschulte. 15 CDs. (Running Time: 16 hrs. 15 mins.). audio compact disk 134.00 (978-0-7887-8967-0(8)) Recorded Bks.

Crazy in Alabama. unabr. ed. Mark Childress. Narrated by Tom Stechschulte. 11 cass. (Running Time: 16 hrs. 15 mins.). 2001. 97.00 (978-0-7887-4034-3(2), 96157E7) Recorded Bks.
The continuing life of 12-year-old Peejoe & his Aunt Lucille in 1965. After decapitating her oppressive husband, Lucille heads for Hollywood & stardom. Peejoe remains home & witnesses the explosive civil rights struggle.

Crazy in Alabama, Set. abr. ed. Mark Childress. Read by Mark Childress. 2 cass. 1999. 18.00 (FS9-51017) Highsmith.

Crazy in Berlin. unabr. collector's ed. Thomas Berger. Read by Michael Russotto. 12 cass. (Running Time: 18 hrs.). (Reinhart Ser.). 1991. 96.00 (978-0-7366-1974-5(7), 2792) Books on Tape.
The first novel in the saga of Carlo Reinhart. Reinhart is a young army medic, stationed in Germany during the early days of the Allied occupation. Large, generous, kind-hearted, he caretakes a shattered civilization. Wartime stereotypes dissolve in the wash of individuals.

Crazy in Love. Chris Manby. 2009. 61.95 (978-0-7531-4268-4(6)); audio compact disk 79.95 (978-0-7531-4269-1(4)) Pub: Isis Pubng Ltd GBR. Dist(s): Ulverscroft US

Crazy in the Cockpit. unabr. ed. Randy Blume. Narrated by C. J. Critt. 6 cass. (Running Time: 8 hrs.). 1999. 51.00 (978-0-7887-4059-6(8), 96099E7) Recorded Bks.
College student Kendra Davis timidly answers an ad claiming "Anyone Can Be a Pilot for $20." Within minutes of takeoff, she is handling the controls of the Cessna while dealing with the advances of the young male instructor. With this witty tale, pilot & novelist Randy Blume reveals what is really going on in the cockpit while the plane soars above the clouds.

Crazy Jack. Donna Jo Napoli. Read by Robert Ramirez. 3 cass. (Running Time: 3 hrs. 45 mins.). (YA). 2000. pap. bk. & stu. ed. 51.95 (978-0-7887-4159-3(4), 41099) Recorded Bks.
This imaginative retelling of "Jack & the Beanstalk" will enchant listeners of all ages with its fascinating psychological spin on a well-known fairy tale. Captures the magic of the story & the courage of the determined Jack.

Crazy Jack. unabr. ed. Donna Jo Napoli. Narrated by Robert Ramirez. 3 pieces. (Running Time: 3 hrs. 45 mins.). (gr. 7 up). 2000. 29.00 (978-0-7887-4010-7(5), 96084E7) Recorded Bks.

Crazy Jack, Class set. Donna Jo Napoli. Read by Robert Ramirez. 3 cass. (Running Time: 3 hrs. 45 mins.). (YA). 2000. 196.80 (978-0-7887-4160-9(8), 47092) Recorded Bks.

Crazy Jane & Jack the Journeyman see Poetry of William Butler Yeats

Crazy Jane & the Bishop see Poetry of William Butler Yeats

Crazy Jane Grown Old Looks at the Dancers see Poetry of William Butler Yeats

Crazy Jane on God see Poetry of William Butler Yeats

Crazy Jane on the Day of Judgement see Poetry of William Butler Yeats

Crazy Jane Reproved see Poetry of William Butler Yeats

Crazy Jane Talks with the Bishop see Poetry of William Butler Yeats

***Crazy Ladies.** abr. ed. Michael Lee West. Read by Michael Lee West. (ENG.). 2006. (978-0-06-113544-6(5), Harper Audio); (978-0-06-113545-3(3), Harper Audio) HarperCollins Pubs.

Crazy Lady! Jane Leslie Conly. Read by Ed Begley, Jr. 2 cass. (Running Time: 217 mins.). (J). 2000. 18.00 (978-0-7366-9028-7(X)) Books on Tape.
Vernon & his friends call Maxine "the crazy lady" & poke fun at her special needs son Ronald. But, as Vernon gets to know them & learns what their life is really like, he begins to understand this mother's fierce love for her son, his own loss & the unexpected strengths within this odd little family.

Crazy Little Thing Called Love - ShowTrax. Arranged by Mark Brymer. 1 CD. (Running Time: 5 mins.). 2000. audio compact disk 19.95 (08201162) H Leonard.
Dwight Yoakum topped the country charts with his remake of the 1980 #1 song by Queen.

Crazy Love: A Memoir. unabr. ed. Leslie Morgan Steiner. Read by Tanya Eby Sirois. 1 MP3-CD. (Running Time: 9 hrs.). 2009. 24.99 (978-1-4233-8328-4(1), 9781423383284, Brilliance MP3); 39.97 (978-1-4233-8329-1(X), 9781423383291, Brinc Audio MP3 Lib); 39.97 (978-1-4233-8331-4(1), 9781423383314, BADLE); 24.99 (978-1-4233-8330-7(3), 9781423383307, BAD); audio compact disk 92.97 (978-1-4233-8327-7(3), 9781423383277, BriAudCD Unabrid); audio compact disk 34.99 (978-1-4233-8326-0(5), 9781423383260, Bril Audio CD Unabri) Brilliance Audio.

Crazy Love: Overwhelmed by a Relentless God. unabr. ed. Francis Chan. Narrated by Francis Chan. Told to Danae Yankoski. (ENG.). 2008. 13.99 (978-1-60814-163-0(2)) Oasis Audio.

Crazy Love: Overwhelmed by a Relentless God. unabr. ed. Francis Chan. Narrated by Francis Chan. Told to Danae Yankoski. Frwd. by Chris Tomlin. (Running Time: 4 hrs. 18 mins. 0 sec.). 2008. audio compact disk 19.99 (978-1-59859-396-9(X)) Oasis Audio.

Crazy Makers. Arynne Simon. 1 cass. 1995. 14.95 (978-1-882389-16-2(6)) Wilarvi Communs.
Handling manipulative, aggressive tactics that cause anger & anxiety. Learn how to keep out of people traps.

Crazy Praise. Contrib. by Dice Gamble. 2007. audio compact disk 13.99 (978-5-557-62804-4(5)) Pt of Grace Ent.

Crazy Praise: Vol. 1 & Vol. 2. Created by Brentwood-Benson Music Publishing Staff. (J). (gr. 4-7). 2003. 9.99 (978-5-559-94935-2(3)) BB Music.

Crazy Praise, Volume 4: Songs from the Lighter Side: Demonstration. Contrib. by Ed Kee. Created by Ed Kee. Created by Gary Forsythe. (ENG.). (J). 2008. 19.99 (978-5-557-38263-2(1)) BB Music.

***Crazy Rhythm.** Max Brand. 2009. (978-1-60136-430-2(X)) Audio Holding.

Crazy Rythmn. Max Brand. (Running Time: 0 hr. 30 mins.). 1999. 10.95 (978-1-60083-509-4(0)) Iofy Corp.

Crazy School: A Madeline Dare Mystery. unabr. ed. Cornelia Read. Read by Hilary Huber. (Running Time: 30600 sec.). 2008. 29.95 (978-1-4332-0819-5(9)) Blckstn Audio.

Crazy School: A Madeline Dare Mystery. unabr. ed. Cornelia Read. Read by Hillary Huber. (Running Time: 30600 sec.). 2008. 65.95 (978-1-4332-0822-5(9)) Blckstn Audio.

Crazy School: A Madeline Dare Mystery. unabr. ed. Cornelia Read. Read by Hilary Huber. 7 CDs. (Running Time: 8 hrs. 30 mins.). 2008. audio compact disk 29.95 (978-1-4332-0820-1(2)) Blckstn Audio.

Crazy School: A Madeline Dare Mystery. unabr. ed. Cornelia Read. Read by Hillary Huber. (Running Time: 30600 sec.). 2008. audio compact disk 29.95 (978-1-4332-0821-8(0)); audio compact disk & audio compact disk 72.00 (978-1-4332-0823-2(7)) Blckstn Audio.

Crazy Wisdom, abr. ed. Wes Nicker. Read by Wes Nicker. 2 cass. (Running Time: 3 hrs.). 1995. 15.95 (978-0-944993-58-3(3)) Audio Lit.
An ebullient collection of wisdom from the ages in a form that makes us laugh, while providing deep insight into the meaning of the spiritual search.

Crazy Wisdom I. Vajracarya. Read by Chogyam Trungpa. 6 cass. 1972. 54.00 (A031) Vajradhatu.
Includes: Padmasambhava & Buddhist Spirituality; The Tantric Path; Sudden Enlightenment; Tantric Aspects of Padmasambhava's Life.

Crazy Wisdom II. Vajracarya. Read by Chogyam Trungpa. 7 cass. 1972. 65.50 (A032) Vajradhatu.
Includes: Principle of Padmasambhava, Hopelessness & Crazy Wisdom, The Eight Aspects.

Crazy Wisdom Lineage. Vajracarya. Read by Chogyam Trungpa. 7 cass. 1975. 70.00 (A033) Vajradhatu.
Includes: Wisdom; Nowness; Warmth; Emptiness; Padmasambhava; Crazy Wisdom Lineage; Crazy Wisdom.

Crazybone. unabr. ed. Bill Pronzini. Read by Norman Dietz. 6 vols. (Running Time: 9 hrs.). (Nameless Detective Mystery Ser.). 2001. bk. 54.95 (978-0-7927-2418-6(6), CSL 307, Chivers Sound Lib) AudioGO.
Behind the stuccoed facades of the Spanish-style houses in the affluent community of Greenwood, a murderous maze of deceit, adultery, fraud & betrayal lurks. The investigator's darker suspicions have been aroused, for why would Sheila Hunter no matter how much money & beautiful & bereaved, refuse to claim fifty thousand dollars due to her in life insurance?.

Crazybusy: Overstretched, Overbooked, & about to Snap! Strategies for Coping in a World Gone ADD. abr. ed. Edward M. Hallowell. Read by Edward M. Hallowell. (Running Time: 10800 sec.). (ENG.). 2006. audio compact disk 22.95 (978-0-7393-3473-7(5), Random AudioBks) Pub: Random Audio Pubg. Dist(s): Random

CRC Concise Encyclopedia of Mathematics. 2nd rev. ed. Ed. by Eric W. Weisstein. 2002. audio compact disk 125.95 (978-0-8493-1946-4(3), 1946, Chap & Hall CRC) Pub: CRC Pr. Dist(s): Taylor and Fran

Creacion de Empresas. unabr. ed. Basilio Balli Morales et al.Tr. of Start of a New Business. (SPA.). audio compact disk 13.00 (978-958-43-0226-7(4)) YoYoMusic.

Creaking Door: Morgue. 6 cass. (Running Time: 6 hrs.). 1999. 19.98 (AB107) Radio Spirits.

Creaking Porch Stories. Short Stories. 1 CD. Dramatization. (YA). 2003. audio compact disk 15.00 (978-0-9741935-0-2(X)) Roberta Brown.

Cream Puff Murder. unabr. ed. Joanne Fluke. Narrated by Suzanne Toren. 8 CDs. (Running Time: 9 hrs. 45 mins.). (Hannah Swensen Mystery Ser.: No. 11). 2009. audio compact disk 34.99 (978-1-4361-9839-4(9)) Recorded Bks.

Cream Puff Murder. unabr. ed. Joanne Fluke. Narrated by Suzanne Toren. 8 cass. (Running Time: 9 hrs. 45 mins.). (Hannah Swensen Mystery Ser.: No. 11). 2009. 67.75 (978-1-4361-7462-6(7)); audio compact disk 92.75 (978-1-4361-7463-3(5)) Recorded Bks.

Cream Puff Murder. unabr. ed. Joanne Fluke. Narrated by Suzanne Toren. (Running Time: 9 hrs. 45 mins.). (Hannah Swensen Mystery Ser.: No. 11). 2009. 56.75 (978-1-4361-9254-5(4)) Recorded Bks.

Create a Joyful Life. Eldon Taylor. Read by Eldon Taylor. Ed. by Leslie Brice. 8 cass. (Running Time: 8 hrs.). 1992. 89.95 set. (978-1-56705-366-1(1)) Gateways Inst.
Self improvement.

Create an Abundant Life. Cheryl Richardson. 1 CD. 2002. audio compact disk 10.95 (978-1-4019-0167-7(0), 1670) Hay House.

Create Miracles & Heal Your Life: Powerful Psychological Discovery on How to Utilize the Mind Body Connection to Achieve True Healing. 3rd rev. ed. Michele Blood & Russell Feingold. Illus. by Musivation International Staff & Copy Print LID Staff. 2 cass. (Running Time: 2 hrs.). 2000. 19.95 (978-1-890679-09-5(7)) Micheles.

Create Money. Lexa Finley. Tammy Chi. 2009. audio compact disk 14.95 (978-0-9822494-2-0(X)) Journey Spirit.

Create Powerful Self-Confidence with Mind Power, Vol. 33, set. Jonathan Parker. Read by Jonathan Parker. 2 CDs. (Running Time: 2 hrs.). (Success Ser.: Vol. 3). 1999. audio compact disk (978-1-58400-032-7(5)) QuantumQuests Intl.
Disc 1 contains several guided visualizations. Disc 2 contains audible & subliminal positive affirmations.

Create Prosperity with Mind Power, Vol. 30, set. Jonathan Parker. Read by Jonathan Parker. 2 CDs. (Running Time: 2 hrs.). (Success Ser.: Vol. 3). 1999. audio compact disk (978-1-58400-030-3(9)) QuantumQuests Intl.
Disc 1 contains several guided visualizations. Disc 2 contains audible & subliminal positive affirmations with music.

Create Success: Activate your internal tools for Success. Kelly Howell. 1 cass. (Running Time: 1 hr.). (Brain Wave Subliminal Ser.). 1996. 9.95 (978-1-881451-30-3(5)) Brain Sync.
Activate the formula for success. Inspiration floods your mind and body while creativity comes alive to help you make your dreams come true.

Create Success: Tap into the Power of Your Subconscious Mind. Kelly Howell. 1 CD. (Running Time: 60 mins.). (ENG.). 2004. audio compact disk 14.95 (978-1-881451-82-2(8)) Brain Sync.
You already possess everything you need to succeed in making your dreams a reality. The subconscious holds untold power to draw in people, ideas and opportunities that support you in manifesting your vision. The trick is tapping into this power and making it work for you. This Brain Wave Subliminal activates the power of your subconscious because it incorporates brain wave frequencies that induce sates of hyper-receptivity to subliminal messages. Here, a new set of self-empowering beliefs are firmly imprinted in the unconscious. You'll notice a remarkable change in attitude that dramatically increases your personal magnetism. And it might even feel as though the universe is conspiring with you to make your dreams a reality. The results are life transforming.

Create Unlimited Financial Abundance. Glenn Harrold. 1 cass. (Running Time: 1 hr. 30 mins.). 2002. 11.95 (978-1-901923-07-0(X)) Pub: Divinit Pubing GBR. Dist(s): Bookworld

Create Unlimited Financial Abundance. Glenn Harrold. 2 CDs. (Running Time: 3 hrs.). 2003. audio compact disk 17.95 (978-1-901923-27-8(4)) Pub: Divinit Pubing GBR. Dist(s): Bookworld

Create Wealth While You're Young Enough to Enjoy it. unabr. ed. Jerry Gillies. Read by Jerry Gillies. 1 cass. (Running Time: 90 min.). (Self-Help Ser.). 1986. 9.95 (978-0-07-023377-5(2), TDM 1170) HarperCollins Pubs.
Gillies shares his methods & techniques for both acquiring wealth & learning how to enjoy it immediately by rethinking attitudes towards money, earning, spending & investing.

Create Your Digital Portfolio Instructor's Resources: The Fast Track to Career Success. Susan Amirian & Eleanor Flanigan. audio compact disk 29.95 (978-1-59357-255-6(7), J2557) JIST Pubng.

Create Your Future. Willis Harman. 1 cass. (Running Time: 60 min.). 1989. 9.95 (978-0-945093-10-7(1)) Enhanced Aud Systs.

Create Your Own Economy: The Path to Prosperity in a Disordered World. unabr. ed. Tyler Cowen. Narrated by Patrick G. Lawlor. (Running Time: 8 hrs. 0 mins. 0 sec.). (ENG.). 2009. 19.99 (978-1-4001-6219-2(X)); audio compact disk 29.99 (978-1-4001-1219-7(2)); audio compact disk 59.99 (978-1-4001-4219-4(9)) Pub: Tantor Media. Dist(s): IngramPubServ

Created & Redeemed. 2004. 49.95 (978-1-932927-01-6(8)); audio compact disk 49.95 (978-1-932927-00-9(X)) Ascensn Pr.

Created for Love. Thomas Merton. 1 cass. (Running Time: 44 min.). 1993. 8.95 (AA2619) Credence Commun.
Bernard & Merton's mystical theology. Lyrical.

Created in Christ Jesus. Kenneth Copeland. 1 cass. 1992. 5.00 (978-0-88114-840-4(7)) K Copeland Pubns.
Biblical teaching on giving.

Created to Be God's Friend: Lessons from the Life of Abraham. abr. unabr. ed. Henry T. Blackaby. 4 cass. (Running Time: 6 hrs.). 2003. 24.99 (978-1-58926-258-4(1)) Oasis Audio.
Abraham learned to recognize the all-compelling voice that led him away to a strange land. What an honor to have God call him his intimate friend! Yet, we know God desires all of us to have such a close relationship with him that we learn to hear and respond to his voice.

Created to Be God's Friend: Lessons from the Life of Abraham. abr. unabr. ed. Henry T. Blackaby. Narrated by Wayne Shepherd. 5 CDs. (Running Time: 6 hrs.). (Christian Perspective Ser.). (ENG.). 2004. audio compact disk 26.99 (978-1-58926-259-1(X)) Oasis Audio.

Created to Be God's Friend: Lessons from the Life of Abraham. unabr. ed. Henry T. Blackaby. Narrated by Wayne Shepherd. (Christian Perspective Ser.). (ENG.). 2004. 18.89 (978-1-60814-164-7(0)) Oasis Audio.

Created to Be His Help Meet: Discover How God Can Make Your Marriage Glorious. Debi Pearl. Read by Rebekah Anast. 9 cds. (Running Time: 10 hrs 30 mins). 2006. audio compact disk (978-1-892112-86-6(8)) No Greater Joy.

Created to Be His Help Meet: Discover How God Can Make Your Marriage Glorious. Debi Pearl. 1 MP3 cd. (Running Time: 10 hrs. 30 mins). (ENG.). 2009. 12.95 (978-1-892112-85-9(X)) Pub: No Greater Joy. Dist(s): AtlasBooks

Created to Believe. 4.95 (C11) Carothers.

Created/God's Friend. Henry Blackaby. 2000. 9.99 (978-0-7852-9722-2(7)) Nelson.

Creating. 6 cass. (Running Time: 6 hrs.). 2004. 49.95 (978-0-9725536-1-2(4)); audio compact disk 49.95 (978-0-9725536-2-9(2)) R Fritz.
The book Creating on audio, read by Rosalind Fritz.

Creating a Brilliant Book Outline. Jeff Davidson. 1995. 9.95 (978-1-60729-361-3(7)) Breath Space Inst.

Creating a CD-ROM Product: The Process from Start to Finish. 2 cass. 1990. 16.00 set. Recorded Res.

Creating a Legacy see Dejando un Legado

Creating A Legacy. 2005. 21.00 (978-1-57972-677-5(1)); audio compact disk 21.00 (978-1-57972-676-8(3)) Insight Living.

Creating a Life of Joy: A Meditative Guide. unabr. ed. Salle Merrill Redfield. (Running Time: 3 hrs.). (ENG.). 2006. 14.98 (978-1-59483-768-5(6)) Pub: Hachet Audio. Dist(s): HachBkGrp

Creating a Message That Resonates with Your Audience: Capitol Learning Audio Course. Michael Shannon. Prod. by TheCapitol.Net. (ENG.). 2008. 47.00 (978-1-58733-079-7(2)) TheCapitol.

Creating a Million Dollar Image for Your Business. abr. ed. Bobbie Gee. Read by Bobbie Gee. Prod. by Brad Fregger. 2 cass. (Running Time: 3 hrs.). 1995. 17.50 Set. (978-1-886392-05-2(6), Parrot Bks) Walberg Pubng.
As an internationally renowned consultant on image for major corporations & organizations, Bobbie Gee introduces you to each element that is essential for building a positive business image.

Creating a More Romantic Marriage. abr. ed. Dennis Rainey & Barbara Rainey. Ed. by Keith Lynch. 6 cass. (Running Time: 6 hrs.). 1995. 29.95 Set. (978-1-57229-009-9(9)) FamilyLife.

***Creating a New Earth: Teachings to Awaken Consciousness - the Best of Eckhart Tolle TV - Season One.** Eckhart Tolle. 2010. audio compact disk 99.00 (978-1-60407-094-1(3)) Sounds True.

Creating a New Sense of Home. Malidoma P. Some. Read by Malidoma P. Some. Ed. by Richard Chelew. 1 cass. (Running Time: 90 min.). (Wisdom of Africa Ser.). 1993. 10.95 (978-1-880155-08-0(7), OTA9301) Oral Trad Arch.
Some, PhD, an initiated Dagara tribesman & graduate of the Sorbonne & Brandeis University, describes the growing sense of loss of meaning & purpose among people in the modern world. He addresses the deep desire in us to recover our "inner indigenous" - being at home in our bodies, the natural world & our communities. He describes the right use of ritual, importance of expressing grief & working in same-gender groups.

Creating a New Sense of Home: The Tribal Community of the Heart. Malidoma P. Some. Read by Malidoma P. Some. Ed. by Richard Chelew. 1 cass. (Running Time: 1 hr. 30 min.). (Wisdom of Africa Ser.). 1994. bk. 10.95 Bookpack. (978-1-880155-14-1(1)) Oral Trad Arch.
Initiated tribesman, M. Some, addresses the loss of meaning & purpose in modern life & how to re-connect with one's "inner indigenous" - being at home in our bodies, the natural world, & air communities using ritual, expression of grief, working in same gender groups, etc.

Creating A New You: Become the Person you want to Be. Created by Christine Sherborne. (ENG.). 2007. audio compact disk 19.95 (978-0-9804155-0-6(0)) Pub: Colourstory AUS. Dist(s): APG

Creating a Powerful Presence. Bert Decker. 6 cass. (Running Time: 6 hrs.). 1996. 59.95 Set, incl. fold out card. (14390A) Nightingale-Conant.

Creating a Prosperity Mindset: In 30 minutes a day or less - Step-by-step. Mike Hayden. Voice by Mike Hayden. Voice by Rick Itzkowich & Lindon Crow. (ENG., 2009. 24.95 (978-0-9723725-5-8(5)) Documn Express.

Creating a Social Media Policy for Your Company: Sharing with Employees What They Can & Can Not do on Twitter, Facebook, LinkedIn & Other Social Media Sites. Steve Helland. 2009. 250.00 (978-1-59701-491-5(5)) ReedLogic.

Creating a Stress-Less Life. unabr. ed. Dorothy Campbell. Read by Dorothy Campbell. 1 cass. (Running Time: 1 hr. 30 mins.). (Self-Power Tape Ser.). 1998. (978-0-9658996-3-5(2)) Positive Pr MA.
Basic skill & tools to reduce & handle stress in everyday life.

Creating a Successful & Sustainable Practice: Practical Guide for Psychologists, Counsellors & Life Coaches. Clare Mann et al. (ENG.). 2008. audio compact disk 297.00 (978-0-9775026-3-9(5)) koromiko AUS.

Creating A Successful Holistic Health Practice: Meditations for Success. Dawn Fleming. (ENG.). 2007. audio compact disk 16.00 (978-0-9797795-3-4(7)) Infinite Wisdom.

Creating a World Without Poverty: How Social Business Can Transform Our Lives. unabr. ed. Muhammad Yunus. Told to Karl Weber. (Running Time: 37800 sec.). 2008. audio compact disk 29.95 (978-1-4332-0836-2(9)) Blckstn Audio.

Creating a World Without Poverty: How Social Business Can Transform Our Lives. unabr. ed. Muhammad Yunus. Read by Patrick G. Lawlor. Told to Karl Weber. (Running Time: 37800 sec.). 2008. 29.95 (978-1-4332-0834-8(2)); 54.95 (978-1-4332-0837-9(7)); audio compact disk 29.95 (978-1-4332-0835-5(0)); audio compact disk & audio compact disk 63.00 (978-1-4332-0838-6(5)) Blckstn Audio.

Creating Abundances in Your Life see Como Crear Abundancia en su Vida

Creating Abundant Health & Wellbeing: Focused Visualizations. Heraty Eugenie. (ENG.). 2007. 16.98 (978-1-934332-04-7(6), Heal Voice) Inter Med Pub.

Creating Affluence: The A to Z Steps to a Richer Life. Deepak Chopra. Read by Deepak Chopra. (Playaway Adult Nonfiction Ser.). 2009. 40.00 (978-1-60775-589-0(0)) Find a World.

Creating Affluence: The A to Z Steps to a Richer Life. unabr. ed. Deepak Chopra. Read by Deepak Chopra. Frwd. by Richard Carlson. 2 CDs. (Running Time: 1 hr.). (Chopra, Deepak Ser.). (ENG.). 2003. audio compact disk 12.95 (978-1-878424-76-1(9)) Amber-Allen Pub.

Creating America: a History of the United States: America's Music. (gr. 6-12). 2005. audio compact disk (978-0-618-03721-6(7), 2-81169) Holt McDoug.

Creating America: a History of the United States: Reading Study Guide. (gr. 6-12). 2005. audio compact disk (978-0-618-40730-9(8), 2-00585); audio compact disk (978-0-618-41093-4(7), 2-00674) Holt McDoug.

Creating America: Beginnings Through Reconstruction: Reading Study Guide. (gr. 6-12). 2005. audio compact disk (978-0-618-03711-7(X), 2-81167); audio compact disk (978-0-618-41091-0(0), 2-00672) Holt McDoug.

Creating America: 1877 to the 21st Century: Reading Study Guide. (gr. 6-12). 2005. audio compact disk (978-0-618-40736-1(7), 2-00589); audio compact disk (978-0-618-41092-7(9), 2-00673) Holt McDoug.

Creating an Intimate Marriage: Rekindle Romance Through Affection, Warmth & Encouragement. unabr. abr. ed. Jim Burns. Read by Jim Burns. (Running Time: 5 hrs.). 2006. audio compact disk 19.99 (978-0-7642-0260-5(X)) Pub: Bethany Hse. Dist(s): Baker Pub Grp

Creating an Open Heaven. Mark Crow. 4 cass. (Running Time: 4 hrs.). 2001. (978-1-931537-09-4(7)) Vision Comm Creat.

Creating & Implementing a Successful Discovery Plan. (Running Time: 3 hrs.). 1993. 89.00 Incl. tape materials. (CP-56081) Cont Ed Bar-CA.
Learn how to set your discovery objectives & utilize techniques to get the most out of each case.

Creating & Sustaining Fulfilling Relationships. Galexis. 2 cass. (Running Time: 3 hrs.). 1994. 17.95 Set. (978-1-56089-028-7(2)) Visionary FL.
Heal & reDream your relationship fantasy, moving it into a free & loving reality. Includes meditation on Side 4.

Creating Breastfeeding Friendly Environments, Module 1. Sally Page Goertz & Sarah McCamman. (Breastfeeding Management Ser.). (C). 2000. audio compact disk 29.95 (978-0-7637-1132-0(2), 0763711322) Jones Bartlett.

Creating Caring Customers, Vol. 1. unabr. ed. 1 cass. (978-1-891076-10-7(8)) Gemini Press.

Creating Celebrity for Experts & Authors. 1 CD. (Running Time: 70 minutes). 2004. audio compact disk 59.00 (978-0-9748906-0-9(X)) LeadThink.
In this entertaining and instructional audio CD, you will learn the tactics that master publicist Judy Safern uses to position and promote her clients from obscurity to celebrity, from celebrity to ubiquity - and how all of that translates into millions of dollars in sales! You will learn how she designs each campaign with built-in crisis preparation to "bullet-proof" an expert's authority and reputation.

Creating Character Voices. Patrick Fraley. 2 cass. (Running Time: 2 hrs.). 21.90 (978-0-8045-3041-5(6), PCC 3041) Spoken Arts.

Creating Christian Community. Richard Rohr. 5 cass. (Running Time: 8 hrs.). 39.95 Set in vinyl album. (AA2784) Credence Commun.
In one of his most passionate programs, Father Rohr talks about the labor of creating community: community that is real, that makes a difference, & that lasts. In the process of discussing community Richard models a powerful four-stage method of approaching scripture. If you are in any kind of small group, this program will be pointedly practical. If you aren't, it will only be inspiring.

Creating, Coaching, & Collecting Coaching Groups. Interview. 3 CDs. (Running Time: 2 hrs.). 2002. audio compact disk (978-0-9743239-0-9(X)) Conical Pr.

Creating Common Purpose. Innovation Groups Staff. Contrib. by Peter Block & Joel Henning. 1 cass. (Transforming Local Government Ser.: Vol. 2). 1999. 10.00 (978-1-882403-58-5(4), IG9902) Alliance Innov.

Creating Community, Evolving Humanity. Sai Maa Lakshmi Devi. 2004. audio compact disk 16.00 (978-1-933488-04-2(2)) HIU Pr.
During this live teleconference recording, Sai Maa places the following powerful questions before all who are seeking to co-create a community for the betterment of the planet. She asks, "Are we ready for the great quantum leap of togetherness? Are we ready to be in that place where we all feel included, where we diminish the illusion of separation? A place where human consciousness evolves into divine consciousness? A place of reconciliation with divinity (the Buddha or Christ in us)? A place of forgiveness?....And at the same time engage ourselves at the deeper level where the unconscious is stirred, is awakened to be able to enlighten the darker chambers in the humanhood? A place of trust in the brother/sisterhood consciousness?"With grace and beauty, Sai Maa shares the vision of a community focused on evolving into Oneness and creating a civilization of love, light, respect, compassion, maturity, loyalty, balance and freedom...a community that allows individual healing to move and expand to planetary healing...a community that lives in the great vibration of Love and a collective higher consciousness which is for the betterment of the world. This CD is a heart-stirring invitation by Sai Maa to those who choose, to come and create this community where she will show us how to love ourselves, each other and the world.

***Creating Competitive Advantage: Give Customers a Reason to Choose You over Your Competitors.** Jaynie L. Smith. (ENG.). 2009. audio compact disk 29.95 (978-0-692-00828-7(4)) Smart Advant.

Creating Connections: A Course in Communication. Speeches. Perf. by Dennis Deaton. 1 CD. (Running Time: 1 hr. 8 mins.). 2006. audio compact disk 29.95 (978-1-881840-19-0(0)) Quma Learning.

Creating Connections & Building Trust. Innovation Groups Staff. Contrib. by Joel Henning. 1 cass. (Transforming Local Government Ser.: Vol. 4). 1999. 10.00 (978-1-882403-60-8(6), IG9904) Alliance Innov.

Creating Constellations. 1 cass. (Running Time: 31 min.). 14.95 (13564) MMI Corp.
How constellations are named- covers Orion & Aurora Borealis, discussed by American Museum of Natural History group.

Creating Context for the Sacred & Quantum Easter. Marianne Williamson. Read by Marianne Williamson. 1 cass. (Running Time: 90 mins.). (Lectures on a Course in Miracles). 1999. 10.00 (978-1-56170-180-3(7), M708) Hay House.

Creating Courage. Created by Plain Solomon. 1 cd. (Running Time: 1hr). 2006. audio compact disk 24.95 (978-1-59971-844-6(8)) AardGP.
As companies are demanding that employees take more risks, do more with less, and try to anticipate the future, courage has become a critical and often overlooked element of a leader's skill set. What it takes to build a strong, effective and thriving organization depends on our ability to make difficult decisions confidently and quickly... and with less information than ever before. Learn how to "build" your courage and create organizations that thrive on change.

***Creating Creativity: Embodying the Creative Process.** Created by Uncommon Sensing LLC. (ENG.). 2002. audio compact disk 60.00 (978-0-9826724-4-0(6)) Uncommon Sens.

Creating Crusaders. Lance Auburn Everette. Read by Marguerite Gavin. 2 cass. (Running Time: 3 hrs.). 2005. 15.99 (978-1-58943-270-3(3)) Am Pubng Inc.
This is the second book in a truly unique series of historical action-adventure novels: Michael. Sometimes, in history, things worked out for the best against all odds. Maybe Somebody intervened on the side of the correct path - even when we didn't know what that path was. But to intervene in the affairs of human beings without disrupting civilization completely is to wield human tools - and human weapons. So when the Archangels arrive to Change Things, watch out! The Pope needs an army of men-at-arms to free the Holy Land from the Saracens, but where will he find troops when they are busy battling each other and slaughtering defenseless peasants? Thousands stopped their low-level chaos and took the cross for the First Crusade. Did Somebody help? Published for the first time ever by Americana Publishing. Michael: Spirituality - with an edge.

Creating Crusaders. Lance Auburn Everette. Read by Marguerite Gavin. 3 CDs. (Running Time: 3 hrs.). 2005. audio compact disk 9.99 (978-1-58943-483-7(8)) Am Pubng Inc.

Creating Customer Evangelists (Audio) How Loyal Customers Become a Volunteer Sales Force. Ben McConnell & Jackie Huba. Frwd. by Seth Godin. 6 CDs. 2003. audio compact disk 29.95 (978-0-9726852-1-4(9)) North Clark.
When customers are thrilled about their experience with your product or service, they can become outspoken ?evangelists? for your company. With traditional marketing tactics declining in their effectiveness, passionate customer-driven referrals are the valuable new currency.Based on seven case-study companies, including Krispy Kreme and Southwest Airlines, Creating Customer Evangelists identifies six solid strategies for creating your own customer evangelism plan. This recording is read by the authors.

Creating Demos & Products That Sell: Previews, Promos & Products for Profit. Featuring Sommer Rob. Interview with Rebecca L. Morgan. 1 cass. (Running Time: 1 hr. 30 mins.). 2000. 25.00 (978-1-930039-02-5(6)) Morgan Seminar.

Creating Eden: The Garden As a Healing Space. Marilyn Barrett. Read by Marilyn Barrett. Contrib. by Peter Muni. 3 cass. (Running Time: 4 hrs. 30 min.). 1997. 24.95 Set. (978-0-9661023-0-7(4)) EdenArt.

Creating Equal. unabr. ed. Ward Connerly. Read by Ward Connerly. 7 cass. (Running Time: 10 hrs.). 2001. 49.95 (978-0-7861-2040-6(1), 2849) Blckstn Audio.
Part memoir, part history lesson, and part road map, this story tells how a black man fought against affirmative action in California and Washington.

***Creating Equal: My Fight against Race Preferences.** unabr. ed. Ward Connerly. Read by Ward Connely. (Running Time: 9 hrs.). 2010. 29.95 (978-1-4417-6748-6(7)); audio compact disk 76.00 (978-1-4417-6746-2(0)) Blckstn Audio.

Creating Faith. Shad Helmstetter. 1 cass. (Self-Talk Ser.). 10.95 Grindle Pr.
Companion Self-Talk Cassettes as mentioned in the book, "What To Say When You Talk To Your Self".

Creating Family. unabr. ed. Clayton Barbeau. Read by Clayton Barbeau. 5 cass. (Running Time: 4 hrs. 10 min.). 1983. 49.95 (9399) Franciscan Comns.
Discussion include Husband/Wife Relationship, Creating Family, Teens, Singles & Love vs Sex, The Male/Female Crisis, Parents as Role Models.

Creating Financial Security in Unstable Economic Times: Philantro-Nomics the Economic Alternative. Charles Moore. 2 Cass. (Running Time: 120 Minutes). 2002. 39.99 (978-0-914391-85-2(2)) Comm People Pr.

Creating from the Spirit: Living Each Day As a Creative Act. abr. ed. Dan Wakefield. Read by Dan Wakefield. 2 cass. (Running Time: 3 hrs.). 1996. 17.95 (978-1-57453-043-8(7)) Audio Lit.
Drawing on examples from religion, philosophy and literature, this program teaches that the key to creation is clarity of body, mind and spirit.

Creating Godly Male Leaders. Alfred D. Harvey, Jr. 4 Cass. 2003. 20.00 (978-1-932508-27-7(9)) Doers Pub.

Creating Happiness. 1985. 14.99 (978-0-86580-040-3(5)) Success World.

Creating Harmony in Your Center. Janet Hauter. 2 cass. (Running Time: 2 hrs. 30 min.). 25.00 Set. (5006) Natl Inst Child Mgmt.
Addresses the fact that some level of disharmony indicates that a center may be evolving, growing, & changing to meet needs. Examines: issues that create disharmony (root causes); solutions to the root causes, & the development of a team to resolve issues themselves; team effectiveness; the "problem employee" as a root cause of disharmony, & how to deal with him-her; & tips on building a healthy, positive, productive, profitable center.

Creating Health: Honoring Women's Wisdom. Christiane Northrup. 1 cass. 49.95 Aquarius Prods.
This five-part series will help women learn more about their bodies, nutrition & total wellness. Chris is a physician, author & the founder of the first all-women's health clinic.

Creating Health, Beyond Prevention, Toward Perfection see Como Crear Salud: Mas alla de la Prevencion y Hacia la Perfeccion

Creating Heaven on Earth. unabr. ed. Perf. by Eknath Easwaran. 1 cass. (Running Time: 1 hr.). 1986. 7.95 (978-1-58638-516-3(X)) Nilgiri Pr.

Creating Hope. Shad Helmstetter. 1 cass. (Self-Talk Ser.). 10.95 (978-0-937065-57-0(9)) Grindle Pr.
Companion Self-Talk Cassettes as mentioned in the book, "What To Say When You Talk To Your Self".

Creating Inner Peace & Calm. Glenn Harrold. 1 cass. (Running Time: 1 hr. 30 mins.). 2002. 11.95 (978-1-901923-13-1(4)); audio compact disk 17.95 (978-1-901923-33-9(9)) Pub: Divinit Pubing GBR. Dist(s): Bookworld

Creating Jack & the Bean Tree: Tradition & Technique. 2004. 8.95 (978-1-56008-879-0(6)); cass. & flmstrp 30.00 (978-0-89719-589-8(2)) Weston Woods.

Creating Jack & the Bean Tree: Tradition & Technique; Jack & the Bean Tree. 2004. cass. & flmstrp 30.00 (978-1-56008-806-6(0)) Weston Woods.

Creating Keepsakes Fresh Fonts. Prod. by Primedia Staff. 2002. audio compact disk 24.95 (978-1-929180-37-0(3)) Creating Keepsakes.

Creating Keepsakes Fresh Fonts 2, Vol. 2. Prod. by Primedia Staff. 2004. audio compact disk 24.95 (978-1-929180-71-4(3)) Creating Keepsakes.

Creating Love Workshop. John E. Bradshaw. (Running Time: 14400 sec.). 2008. audio compact disk 100.00 (978-1-57388-115-9(5)) J B Media.

Creating Miracles Every Day: How to Turn Ordinary Moments into Extraordinary Experiences. unabr. ed. Richard Carlson. 6 cass. (Running Time: 6 hrs.). 1998. wbk. ed. 59.95 (978-1-55525-003-4(3), 19110A); audio compact disk 69.95 (978-1-55525-020-1(3), 19110CD) Nightingale-Conant.
Richard Carlson, author of the runaway best sellers Don't Sweat The Small Stuff & Don't Worry, Make Money, has brought his acclaimed brand of simple yet remarkable wisdom.

Creating More Love. Steve Halpern. 1 cass. 1993. 9.98 (978-1-878625-21-2(7)) Inner Peace Mus.

Creating Music: Hearing Music (Home Version), CD-ROM. Alfred Publishing Staff. (Creating Music Ser.). (ENG.). 2009. audio compact disk 9.95 (978-0-7390-6502-0(5)) Alfred Pub.

Creating Music: Making More Music, CD-ROM. Morton Subotnick. (Creating Music Ser.). (ENG.). 2008. audio compact disk 39.95 (978-0-7390-5493-2(7)) Alfred Pub.

Creating Music: Making More Music (Home Version), CD-ROM. Alfred Publishing Staff. (Creating Music Ser.). (ENG.). 2009. audio compact disk 9.95 (978-0-7390-6504-4(1)) Alfred Pub.

Creating Music: Making Music. Morton Subotnick. (Creating Music Ser.). (ENG.). 2008. audio compact disk 39.95 (978-0-7390-5391-1(4)) Alfred Pub.

Creating Music: Making Music (Home Version), CD-ROM. Alfred Publishing Staff. (Creating Music Ser.). (ENG.). 2009. audio compact disk 9.95 (978-0-7390-6503-7(3)) Alfred Pub.

Creating Music: Playing Music. Morton Subotnick. (Creating Music Ser.). (ENG.). 2008. audio compact disk 39.95 (978-1-933413-37-2(9)) Alfred Pub.

Creating Music: Playing Music (Home Version), CD-ROM. Alfred Publishing Staff. (Creating Music Ser.). (ENG.). 2009. audio compact disk 9.95 (978-0-7390-6501-3(7)) Alfred Pub.

Creating Music: World of Music (Beginner), CD-ROM. Morton Subotnick. (Creating Music Ser.). (ENG.). 2008. audio compact disk 39.95 (978-0-7390-5386-7(8)) Alfred Pub.

Creating Music: World of Music (Beginner) (Home Version), CD-ROM. Morton Subotnick. (Creating Music Ser.). (ENG.). 2009. audio compact disk 9.95 (978-0-7390-5387-4(6)) Alfred Pub.

Creating Music: World of Music (Intermediate), CD-ROM. Morton Subotnick. (Creating Music Ser.). (ENG.). 2008. audio compact disk 39.95 (978-0-7390-5388-1(4)) Alfred Pub.

Creating Music: World of Music (Intermediate) (Home Version), CD-ROM. Alfred Publishing Staff. (Creating Music Ser.). (ENG.). 2009. audio compact disk 9.95 (978-0-7390-6500-6(9)) Alfred Pub.

Creating New Energy & Enthusiasm. Shad Helmstetter. 1 cass. (Self-Talk Cassettes Ser.). 10.95 (978-0-937065-22-8(6)) Grindle Pr.

Creating New Futures: Art of Destiny. unabr. ed. Galexis. 2 cass. (Running Time: 3 hrs.). (Fortress Ser.: Vol. 2). 1996. 19.95 Set. (978-1-56089-048-5(7), G126) Visionary FL.
How to leave the Fortress & create a sustaining resonance/anchor to your visions/dreams. Meditation included.

Creating Personal & Professional Visions. unabr. ed. Jennifer James. Read by Jennifer James. 1 cass. (Running Time: 1 hr.). 9.95 (978-0-915423-51-4(0)) Jennifer J.

Creating Powerteams. G. Michael Durst. Read by G. Michael Durst. 1 cass. (Running Time: 45 min.). 12.00 Train Sys.

Creating Professional Drum Loo. Ed Roscetti. 2005. pap. bk. 14.95 (978-0-8256-2836-8(9), AM978615, Amsco Music) Pub: Music Sales. Dist(s): H Leonard

Creating Prosperity: Creative Visualizations for Creating a New Reality. Created by Stanley Haluska. 1 CD. (Running Time: 70 mins). 2004. audio compact disk 15.00 (978-0-9668872-6-6(3), AP111) Awakening Pubns Inc.

Creating Prosperity: Creative Visualizations into Self Empowerment & Spiritual Identity. (ENG.). 2009. 15.95 (978-0-9758866-6-3(5)) Awakening Pubns Inc.

Creating Prosperity & Abundance: Classic. Eldon Taylor. Read by Eldon Taylor. Ed. by Leslie Brice. 1 cass. (Running Time: 1 hr.). 1992. 16.95 (978-1-56705-047-9(6)) Gateways Inst.
Self improvement.

Creating Prosperity & Abundance: Easy. Eldon Taylor. Read by Eldon Taylor. Ed. by Leslie Brice. 1 cass. (Running Time: 1 hr.). 1992. 16.95 (978-1-56705-048-6(4)) Gateways Inst.

Creating Prosperity & Abundance: Ocean. Eldon Taylor. Read by Eldon Taylor. Ed. by Leslie Brice. 1 cass. (Running Time: 1 hr.). 1992. 15.95 (978-1-56705-049-3(2)) Gateways Inst.

Creating Prosperity & Abundance: Rhythms. Eldon Taylor. Read by Eldon Taylor. Ed. by Leslie Brice. 1 cass. (Running Time: 1 hr.). 1992. 16.95 (978-1-56705-050-9(6)) Gateways Inst.

Creating Prosperity & Abundance: Stream. Eldon Taylor. Read by Eldon Taylor. Ed. by Leslie Brice. 1 cass. (Running Time: 1 hr.). 1992. 16.95 (978-1-56705-051-6(4)) Gateways Inst.

Creating Prosperity with the Law of Attraction: A Practical Guide to Attracting Abundance & Wealth. Christine Sherborne. (ENG.). 2009. audio compact disk 19.95 (978-0-9804386-2-8(4)) Pub: Colourstory AUS. Dist(s): APG

Creating Protection: Protecting Yourself with the Power of Your Own Mind. Elena Bussolino. Illus. by Albert Bussolino. Music by Rizwan Ahmad. Engineer Khalid Muhammad. Orig. Title: Original. 2000. 12.95 (978-0-9706743-3-3(3)) Bagatto.

Creating Protection: Protecting yourself with the power of your own Mind. Anna Florentis. 2001. 12.95 (978-0-9720314-5-5(6)) Bagatto.

Creating Sales Success. Scripts. Rebecca L. Morgan. Read by Rebecca L. Morgan. 1 cass. (Running Time: 46 min.). 1993. 12.95 (978-0-9660740-3-1(3)) Morgan Seminar.
Interviews with top perfomers & what they said made them successful; commitment, listening skills, perspective, positive self confidence.

Creating Sales Velocity (Audio Book 3 CD's) Matthew Ferry. As told by Matthew Ferry. 3 CDs. 2005. audio compact disk (978-0-9761929-1-6(8)) Spirit Pub CA.

Creating Serendipity Set: How to Benefit from Everything That Happens. David Grudermeyer & Rebecca Grudermeyer. 2 cass. 18.95 INCL. HANDOUTS. (T-28) Willingness Wrks.

Creating Supplemental Care, Self-Settled, Pooled Account, or Revocable Trusts for Elderly Clients. 2 cass. (Running Time: 2 hrs.). 1997. 25.00 Set; incl. study outline. (M210) Am Law Inst.
Advanced program explores the uses of, & requirements for, a variety of trusts commonly created for older clients, including supplemental care trusts created by these parties; self-settled trusts created for the benefit of the disabled settlor-beneficiary; pooled account trusts created for disabled persons but ultimately benefiting charities; & revocable trusts, including their effect on Medicaid eligibility. Will help the elder law practitioner decide the kind of trust that is appropriate for the client.

Creating Teamwork. Lee Shelton. (Running Time: 4 hrs.). 49.95 CareerTrack Pubns.
Presents strategies for getting the most & best from employees & creating that "Mission Impossible" team.

Creating the Future in Partnership. Riane Eisler. 1 cass. 9.00 (A0339-88) Sound Photosyn.
Exploring the vision toward which we can aspire which may be the only solution to the overall imbalance in the human situation. From the "Spiritual in the Art of the Future Symposium".

Creating the Work You Love: Courage, Commitment & Career. unabr. ed. Rick Jarow. 2 cass. 1993. 18.00 set. (OC332-70) Sound Horizons AV.

Creating True Peace: Ending Violence in Yourself, Your Family, Your Community, & the World. abr. ed. Thich Nhat Hanh. Read by Michael York. 2003. 15.95 (978-0-7435-4529-7(X)) Pub: S&S Audio. Dist(s): S and S Inc

Creating True Prosperity. unabr. ed. Shakti Gawain. Read by Shakti Gawain. 2 cass. (Running Time: 3 hrs.). 1997. 17.95 (978-1-57731-055-6(1)) Pub: New Wrld Lib. Dist(s): PerseuPGW
Shows how people, regardless of their wealth, eventually become dissatisfied with material accomplishments. Shows how money can reflect where we need more balance in our lives.

Creating Trust & Spontaneity in Your Life. Ron Hofsess. Voice by Ron Hofsess. Des. by Christine Malloy. (Running Time: 18 mins.). 2001. (978-0-9727001-3-9(7)) Choose2Trust.
A relaxing, guided journey. This journey invites you to gently travel to further depths of yourself and encourages you to allow more trust and spontaneity in your life.

Creating Trust & Spontaneity in Your Life. Ron Hofsess. Voice by Ron Hofsess. Des. by Christiine Malloy. (Running Time: 18 mins.). 2001. audio compact disk 12.50 (978-0-9727001-2-2(9)) Choose2Trust.

Creating Visual Aids That 'Wow' Your Audience. 2000. 25.00 (978-1-930039-10-0(7)) Morgan Seminar.

Creating Wealth: Retire in Ten Years Using Allen's Seven Principles of Wealth. Robert G. Allen. Intro. by A. E. Whyte. 1 cass. (Running Time: 77 min.). (Listen & Learn USA! Ser.). 8.95 (978-0-88684-000-6(7)) Listen USA.
Provides practical principles & techniques for working towards personal growth.

Creating Wealth: Retire in Ten Years Using Allen's Seven Principles of Wealth. abr. ed. Robert G. Allen. Read by Robert G. Allen. 2006. 17.95 (978-0-7435-6212-6(7)) Pub: S&S Audio. Dist(s): S and S Inc

Creating Your Heart's Desire. Sonia Choquette. 6 cass. (Running Time: 6 hrs.). 1998. suppl. ed. & wbk. ed. (18790A) Nightingale-Conant.
Fulfill your heart's desire.

Creating Your Invisible Armor. Thomas A. Hensel. 2001. audio compact disk 14.95 (978-1-890405-04-5(3)) Pub: LightLines. Dist(s): New Leaf Dist

Creating Your Invisible Armor. Speeches. Thomas A. Hensel. 1. (Running Time: 56mins). 2000. audio compact disk 14.95 (978-1-890035-42-6(4)) New Centry Pr.
Do you ever feel drained after being around a certain person or in a particular place? Is there someone in your life who has decided that you are their personal doormat? Ever feel ?just plain bad? for no discernible reason?If the answer to any of these questions was "YES," then you are in need of "Invisible Armor." Both alone and in conjunction with the book, Invisible Armor: Protecting Your Personal Energy these powerful visualizations teach you how to create sacred space in your meditations, how to cleanse your personal energy and how to protect that energy from unwanted intrusion.

Creating Your Own Miracles. Patricia O'Malley. Perf. by Barry Weiss. 1 cass. (Running Time: 50 min.). 1998. 11.95 (978-1-892450-08-1(9), 150) Pub: Promo Music. Dist(s): Penton Overseas
Set your own intention to the miracle you want to happen & then focus the energy to create it.

Creating Your Personal Vision. abr. ed. Samuel A. Berne. Read by Samuel A. Berne. Read by Charly Drobeck. (Running Time: 3 hrs.). 1994. 18.95 (978-0-9641599-7-6(X)) Color Stone.
Tape on natural vision improvement exercises.

Creating Your Reality. unabr. ed. Dorothy Campbell. Read by Dorothy Campbell. 1 cass. (Running Time: 1 hr.). (Self-Power Tape Ser.). 1998. (978-0-9658996-4-2(0)) Positive Pr MA.
Step-by-step method of achieving goals through affirmations & visualization.

Creating Your World the Way You Really Want It to Be. Wayne W. Dyer & Deepak Chopra. 6 CDs. (Running Time: 9 hrs.). 2002. audio compact disk 59.95 (978-1-4019-0035-9(6)) Hay House.

Creating Your World the Way You Really Want It to Be. unabr. ed. Wayne W. Dyer & Deepak Chopra. Read by Wayne W. Dyer & Deepak Chopra. (YA). 2007. 64.99 (978-1-60252-748-5(2)) Find a World.

Creation. SF Study Ctr.

Creation. Neville Goddard. 1 cass. (Running Time: 62 min.). 1965. 8.00 (55) J & L Pubns.
Neville taught Imagination Creates Reality. He was a powerfully influential teacher of God as Consciousness.

Creation. Glenn Hass. 1 cass. 1993. 6.95 (978-1-55523-608-3(1)) Life & Peace.

Creation, Pt. 1. 1 cass. (Running Time: 60 min.). (Mother Angelica Live Ser.). 10.00 (978-1-55794-083-4(5), T34) Eternal Wrd TV.

Creation & Biblical Prayer. Jose Hobday & Carroll Stuhlmueller. 3 cass. (Running Time: 1 hr. 30 min.). 1991. 26.95 set. (TAH243) Alba Hse Comns.
A delightful & serious talk on creator & scripture.

Creation & the Heartbeat of the Earth As Told by Patrick Gorlick Through the Ancient Art of Storytelling. Hosted by Nancy Pearlman. 1 cass. (Running Time: 29 min.). 10.00 (1031) Educ Comm CA.

Creation Comes Out of Meditation. J. Krishnamurti. 1 cass. (Running Time: 80 min.). (Krishnamurti at Los Alamos Laboratory Ser.: Q-A No. 1). 8.50 (ALA842) Krishnamurti.
On March 20 & 21, 1984, Krishnamurti spoke to a large group of nuclear scientists at the Los Alamos National Laboratories in New Mexico, the main USA government center for atomic research. Krishnamurti explores creativity & science, accumulating knowledge, meditation, inquiry, violence, attention, & scepticism.

Creation Evangelism for the New Millennium. 1 cass. (Running Time: 1 hr.). 12.99 (978-0-89051-288-3(4)) Master Bks.

Creation-Evolution Controversy. John Schoenheit. Read by John Schoenheit. 4 cass. (Running Time: 6 hrs.). 1992. 10.00 set. Chris Ed Ser.
Examines the evidence (or lack thereof) for the theory of evolution from a scientific standpoint. Arrives at the conclusion that the earth & mankind were created, & shows that this conclusion is supported not only from a biblical standpoint, but from a scientific standpoint as well.

Creation in Death. J. D. Robb, pseud. Read by Susan Ericksen. (In Death Ser.). 2008. 74.99 (978-1-60640-590-1(X)) Find a World.

Creation in Death. abr. ed. Read by Susan Ericksen. (Running Time: 21600 sec.). (In Death Ser.). 2008. audio compact disk 14.99 (978-1-4233-3746-1(8), 9781423337461, BCD Value Price) Brilliance Audio.

Creation in Death. unabr. ed. J. D. Robb, pseud. Read by Susan Ericksen. 1 MP3-CD. (Running Time: 12 hrs.). (In Death Ser.). 2007. 24.95 (978-1-4233-3741-6(7), 9781423337416, Brilliance MP3); 39.25 (978-1-4233-3744-7(1), 9781423337447, BADLE); 24.95 (978-1-4233-3743-0(3), 9781423337430, BAD); 97.25 (978-1-4233-3738-6(7), 9781423337386, BrilAudUnabridg); audio compact disk 39.25 (978-1-4233-3742-3(5), 9781423337423, Brlnc Audio MP3 Lib); audio compact disk 102.25 (978-1-4233-3740-9(9), 9781423337409, BriAudCD Unabrid); audio compact disk 38.95 (978-1-4233-3739-3(5), 9781423337393, Bril Audio CD Unabri) Brilliance Audio.

Creation, Little People & Rabbit's Short Tail (Choctaw) unabr. ed. 1 cass. (Running Time: 30 mins.). 14.95 (C19201) J Norton Pubs.
Authentic Indian legends.

Creation Spirituality. unabr. ed. Matthew Fox. 3 cass. 27.00 (OC89W) Sound Horizons AV.

Creation Stories. Megan McKenna. 1 cass. (Running Time: 1 hr. 05 min.). 1993. 9.95 (978-7-900785-04-6(3), AA2667) Credence Commun.
All religious traditions have creation stories. McKenna talks about what most have in common.

Creation Stories of the Native American Tradition. Jose Hobday. 1 cass. (Running Time: 55 min.). 8.95 (AA2510) Credence Commun.
Native American creation stories don't pretend to scientifically explain the origins of the universe. But they say a great deal about what it means to be a human in that universe. They are entertaining but not entertainment. They are oral wisdom literature. And nobody tells a story better than Jose.

Creation Story. Voice by Steve de C. Cook. (ENG.). 2009. audio compact disk (978-0-9821616-1-6(1)) Five Talents.

Creation Story & The Monkey & the Turtle: From Mga Kuwentong Bayan: Folk Stories from the Philippines. Read by Alex Torres. Perf. by Mahal. Ed. by Alice Lucas. 2 cass. (ENG & TAG.). (J). (gr. k-12). 1995. 15.00 set. SF Study Ctr.
Dramatic reading in Tagalog & English of two stories from Mga Kuwentong Bayan, with music played on indigenous instruments.

Creation Story Verbatim. E. J. Gold. Read by Grace K. Rivera & Robbert Trice. 2 cass. (Running Time: 2 hrs.). Dramatization. 18.98 set. (TP157) Union Label.
Live performance of comic play dialogue between The Lord & The Archangel Gabriel, addressing heavenly & earthly topics.

Creation Versus Evolution Tape Pack. 2001. (978-1-931713-07-8(3)) Calvar ChalPub.

Creation's Gentleness Is All I See. Tara Singh. 1 cass. (Running Time: 1 hr.). (Exploring a Course in Miracles Ser.). 9.95 (978-1-55531-205-3(5), #A162) Life Action Pr.
A session at the school for training teachers to bring A COURSE IN MIRACLES into application.

Creation's Journey: Native American Music Presented by the National Museum of the American Indian. Anno. by Charlotte Heth. 1 cass. (Running Time: 64 min.). 1994. Incl. bklet. (0-9307-404100-9307-40410-2-4); audio compact disk (0-9307-40410-2-4) Smithsonian Folkways.
From powwow music to Christian songs in Cherokee to Irish reels, Native peoples from the U. S., Canada, Mexico & Bolivia present living traditions & crossovers to Euro-American musics.

Creative Abundance: Keys to Spiritual & Material Prosperity. unabr. ed. Elizabeth Clare Prophet. 1 cass. (Running Time: 1 hr. 30 mins.). 2002. 10.95 (978-0-922729-71-5(9), 942-058) Pub: Summit Univ. Dist(s): Natl Bk Netwk

Creative Beginnings: Compact Disk. Scott D. Reeves. (C). 1996. 21.80 (978-0-13-573098-0(8), Macmillan Coll) P-H.

Creative Brainstorming. Thomas R. Condon. 1 cass. (Creativity Unlimited Training Ser.). 12.95 (978-1-884305-82-5(2)) Changeworks.
This tape will help open your thinking to creative possibilities & inventive solutions. Hypnotic exercises to generate productive results & make creative connections between unrelated facts & ideas.

Creative Child for Happy Dreams. Read by Mary Richards. 1 cass. (Running Time: 45 min.). (J). 2007. audio compact disk 19.95 (978-1-56136-171-7(2)) Master Your Mind.

Creative Choice in Hypnosis, Vol. 4. Milton H. Erickson. Ed. by Ernest L. Rossi & Margaret O. Ryan. (Seminars, Workshops & Lectures of Milton H. Erickson Ser.: Vol. IV). 1992. bk. 42.50 (978-0-8290-2418-0(2)) Irvington.

Creative Church Solutions for Non-Mega Churches. Edwin F. Hill. Read by Edwin F. Hill. 2 cass. (Running Time: 3 hrs.). (Church Builder Ser.). 1995. 21.95 Set. (978-1-57052-047-1(X)) Chrch Grwth VA.
Proven ideas, creative examples of how the non-mega church can maximize its ministry using the money, manpower, & materials already available.

Creative Clips & Fonts for Boys. Prod. by Primedia Staff. 2003. audio compact disk 29.95 (978-1-929180-47-9(0)) Creating Keepsakes.

Creative Clips & Fonts for Everyday Celebrations. Prod. by Primedia Staff. 2004. audio compact disk 29.95 (978-1-929180-52-3(7)) Creating Keepsakes.

Creative Clips & Fonts for Girls. Prod. by Primedia Staff. 2003. audio compact disk 29.95 (978-1-929180-46-2(2)) Creating Keepsakes.

Creative Clips & Fonts for Home, Family & Pets. Prod. by Primedia Staff. 2005. audio compact disk 19.95 (978-1-929180-82-0(9)) Creating Keepsakes.

Creative Clips & Fonts for Winter Memories. Prod. by Primedia Staff. 2004. audio compact disk 29.95 (978-1-929180-73-8(X)) Creating Keepsakes.

Creative Companion: How to Free Your Creative Spirit. S. A. R. K. 1 cass. (Running Time: 1 hr.). 2001. 10.95 Audio Lit.

Creative Composer. Roy Tuckman. 2 cass. 18.00 set. (A0733-90) Sound Photosyn.
A vibrant talk & musical performance on synthesizer.

Creative Divorce. unabr. collector's ed. Mel Krantzler. Read by Paul Shay. 8 cass. (Running Time: 8 hrs.). 1985. 48.00 (978-0-7366-0426-0(X), 1398) Books on Tape.
This deals with the gut feelings of men & women facing the need to build new lives in the wake of loneliness, guilt, anger, rejection & a sense of failure. Krantzler takes a positive approach to this painful period, perceiving it as a time of transition that can lead to growth.

Creative Fire. Clarissa Pinkola Estes. 3 CDs. (Running Time: 2 hrs 45 mins). 2005. audio compact disk 24.95 (978-1-59179-387-8(4)) Sounds True.
This recording was produced specifically for people who create for a living - writers, artists, thinkers, teachers - anyone who must depend on their creative powers every day. Through the seamless retelling of myths and tales gathered from many world cultures, Dr. Clarissa Pinkola Estes examines the inner fires of creativity: what she calls "the nutritive mother of the soul." These timeless stories will familiarize you with the fundamental forces which inspire humans to achieve artistic greatness. Dr. Estes - best known as the author of the national bestseller Women Who Run With the Wolves - concludes with a demonstration of a powerful Jungian technique called "active imagination," which analysts look upon as a dependable tool for finding inspiration and loosening psychic log-jams. The Creative Fire is a wellspring of poetic stories, each one a useful illustration of how creativity illuminates our lives. Additional Contents: The cycles of creativity; incubation; remaining true to your personal vision; the necessity of descent; the myth of Mother Earth; myth of Calaban; the Medial Woman; the archetypal world; what kills creativity; raising creative children; much more.

Creative Force of Words. Creflo A. Dollar. 2006. 8.00 (978-1-59944-060-6(1)); audio compact disk 11.00 (978-1-59944-031-6(8)) Creflo Dollar.

Creative Guitar Mastery: Modal Improvisation 101. Chris Miller. Ed. by Chris Miller. 2003. audio compact disk 9.99 (978-0-9743571-1-9(1), 31201, CreativeGuitar) DoublePlanet.

Creative Guitar 1: Cutting-Edge Techniques. Guthrie Govan. 2005. audio compact disk 24.95 (978-1-86074-462-4(1)) Pub: Sanctuary Pubng GBR. Dist(s): H Leonard

Creative Guitar 2: Advanced Techniques. Guthrie Govan. 2005. audio compact disk 24.95 (978-1-86074-467-9(2)) Pub: Sanctuary Pubng GBR. Dist(s): H Leonard

Creative Guitar 3: Recording & Effects. Phil Hilborne. audio compact disk 24.95 (978-1-84492-011-2(9), 1844920119) Pub: Sanctuary Pubng GBR. Dist(s): H Leonard

Creative Harmonics. Rowena Pattee. 1 cass. 9.00 (A0099-86) Sound Photosyn.
At the Art of Healing Conference.

Creative Imagination; The Nature of the Higher Self. Jonathan Murro & Ann Ree Colton. 1 cass. 7.95 A R Colton Fnd.

Creative Inspiration. Thomas R. Condon. 1 cass. (Creativity Unlimited Training Ser.). 12.95 (978-1-884305-78-8(4)) Changeworks.
This tape will provide a refuge from the hectic pace of modern life. It offers a chance to relax & renew, consider priorities, or listen to "the still, small voice of the heart.".

Creative Job Search. Brian S. Tracy. 1 cass. 79.95 (1070PVX) Nightingale-Conant.
In this program, Brian Tracy shows you methods that have worked for job changers, career switchers & anyone looking to advance. You'll learn how to identify the "hidden" job market (where nearly 85 percent of all jobs are)...find out about networking...how to make a favorable first impression...how to negotiate a salary 20 percent higher than the one you're first offered. You'll even learn how to benefit by "turning the tables" & becoming the interviewer. Includes videocassete plus workbook.

Creative Journal for Children. Read by Lucia Capacchione. 2 cass. (Running Time: 2 hrs.). 1989. 16.95 Set. (978-0-7822-0031-7(1), 398) C G Jung IL.

Creative Kid Tunes for Relaxation & Imagination. unabr. ed. Phyllis U. Hiller. 1 cass. (Running Time: 30 min.). (J). (ps-2). 1992. 10.95 Incl. shell & case. (978-1-884877-10-0(9), 199216CKC) Creat Mats Lib.
Songs & narration to encourage relaxation for young children; effective for kids who tend to be hyperactive.

Creative Kids: Fantastic Fall. Arranged by Creative Kids. 1 CD. (Running Time: 40min 48sec). (J). 2005. audio compact disk 9.95 (978-1-932226-44-7(3)) Wizard Acdmy.

Creative Kids: Sensational Spring. Created by Creative Kids. 1 CD. (Running Time: 37min 32sec). (J). 2005. audio compact disk 9.95 (978-1-932226-46-1(X)) Wizard Acdmy.

Creative Kids: Wonderful Winter. Created by Creative Kids. 1 CD. (Running Time: 32min 44sec). (J). 2005. audio compact disk 9.95 (978-1-932226-45-4(1)) Wizard Acdmy.

Creative Law of Assumption. Neville Goddard. 1 cass. (Running Time: 62 min.). 1965. 8.00 (61) J & L Pubns.
Neville taught Imagination Creates Reality. He was a powerfully influential teacher of God as Consciousness.

Creative Leadership. PUEI. audio compact disk 89.95 (978-1-933328-92-8(4), Fred Pryor) P Univ E Inc.

Creative Magic Vol. 14: Unleash Your Creative Powers. Jonathan Parker. 2 cass. (Running Time: 1 hr. 45 min.). 1992. 17.00 Set. (978-1-58400-013-6(9)) QuantumQuests Intl.

Creative Manager. Brian S. Tracy. Read by Brian S. Tracy. 2 cass. (Effective Manager Seminar Ser.: No. 14). 95.00 Set, incl. 1-hr. videotape & 2 wkbks., program notes & study guide. (755VD) Nightingale-Conant.
Solving problems with creative thinking. Innovation: "busting loose.".

Creative Marriage. unabr. collector's ed. Mel Krantzler & Pat Krantzler. Read by Paul Shay. 11 cass. (Running Time: 16 hrs. 30 min.). 1986. 88.00 (978-0-7366-0569-4(X), 1541) Books on Tape.
Identifies six natural "passages" or marriages-within-a-marriage that every wedded couple experiences. At each stage both husband & wife have different needs, expectations & even behavior. In recognizing these mini-marriages lies the secret of happiness rather than discontent thoughout a lifetime of living together.

Creative Memories: The 10 Timeless Principles Behind the Company That Pioneered the Scrapbooking Industry. Cheryl Lightle. 2005. audio compact disk 28.00 (978-1-932378-68-9(5)) Pub: A Media Intl. Dist(s): Natl Bk Netwk

Creative Mind. Oscar Janiger. 1 cass. (Running Time: 20 min.). 7.00 (A0047-87) Sound Photosyn.
An intense 20 minute videod rant.

Creative Mind System. abr. ed. Jeffrey Thompson. (Running Time: 1:00:00). 2004. audio compact disk 19.98 (978-1-55961-767-3(5)) Sounds True.

Creative Mothering: A Rainbow Journey - To Sleep-To Dream. Diana Keck. 1 cass. 1985. 17.95 (978-0-929653-19-8(X), TAPE 702) Mntn Spirit Tapes.

Creative Mothering: Child of Love - Seeing Through Your Child's Eyes. Diana Keck. Read by Diana Keck. 1 cass. 1985. 9.95 (978-0-929653-18-1(1), TAPE 701) Mntn Spirit Tapes.

Creative Mothering: The Child Within - Preparing for Birth. Diana Keck. 1 cass. 1985. 9.95 (978-0-929653-17-4(3), TAPE 700) Mntn Spirit Tapes.

Creative Movement & Rhythmic Exploration. Perf. by Hap Palmer. 1 LP. (J). pupil's gde. ed. 11.95 (EA 533); 11.95 (EA 533C) Kimbo Educ.
The Moving Game - Grandpa Builds a Table - Fast & Slow March - How Many Ways & more.

Creative Myths & Monsters. abr. ed. Julia Cameron. 2 cass. 1993. 18.00 set. (OC350-73) Sound Horizons AV.

Creative Parenting: Helping Children Learn to Be Happy Adults. C. Eugene Walker. 2 cass. 21.95 Self-Control Sys.
Overviewing & general philosophy of child rearing. Focuses on typical childhood problems & how to deal with them.

Creative Personal Power. Thomas R. Condon. 1 cass. (Creativity Unlimited Training Ser.). 12.95 (978-1-884305-79-5(2)) Changeworks.
Hypnotic exercises to help you find creative intelligence for your daily life & actions. This tape will also evoke the parts of you involved in good decision making & peak performance.

Creative Priority. Jerry Hirshberg. 1997. 18.00 Basic.

Creative Problem Solving. 4 cass. (Running Time: 4 hrs.). Incl. Creative Problem Solving: Clearing the Way to Creativity. (80218); Creative Problem Solving: Creative Problem Solving Is Based on Facts. (80218); Creative Problem Solving: Expanding Your Creativity. (80218); Creative Problem Solving: Group Creativity & Problem Solving. (80218); Creative Problem Solving: More Techniques of Creative Problem Solving. (80218); Creative Problem Solving: Overturning Roadblocks to Creativity. (80218); Creative Problem Solving: Putting Your Creative Ideas to Work. (80218); Creative Problem Solving: Techniques of Creative Problem Solving. (80218); Creative Problem Solving: The Problem in Creative Problem Solving. (80218); Creative Problem Solving: What's the Big Idea? (80218); Creative Problem Solving: Zeroing in on the Answer. (80218); Expanding Your Creativity. (80218); Techniques of Creative Problem Solving. (80218); Creative Problem Solving. (80218); 155.00 (80218); 30.00 wkbk. (80219) AMACOM.
Learn to: generate new & innovative ideas with clockwork regularity; select the most useful solution from the many you generate; translate this solution into practical terms & specific strategies & win support for your ideas & put them into action.

Creative Problem Solving. Thomas R. Condon. 1 cass. (Creativity Unlimited Training Ser.). 12.95 (978-1-884305-81-8(4)) Changeworks.
This tape will "give you ideas" & ways to carry them out in the world. It is designed to assist you with all kinds of problems, projects, questions & challenges. Takes place on a tropical island getaway.

Creative Problem Solving. Mary Lee LaBay. 2006. audio compact disk 9.95 (978-1-934705-10-0(1)) Awareness Engin.

Creative Problem Solving: Clearing the Way to Creativity see Creative Problem Solving

Creative Problem Solving: Creative Problem Solving Is Based on Facts see Creative Problem Solving

Creative Problem Solving: Expanding Your Creativity see Creative Problem Solving

Creative Problem Solving: Group Creativity & Problem Solving see Creative Problem Solving

Creative Problem Solving: More Techniques of Creative Problem Solving see Creative Problem Solving

Creative Problem Solving: Overturning Roadblocks to Creativity see Creative Problem Solving

Creative Problem Solving: Putting Your Creative Ideas to Work see Creative Problem Solving

Creative Problem Solving: Techniques of Creative Problem Solving see Creative Problem Solving

Creative Problem Solving: The Problem in Creative Problem Solving see Creative Problem Solving

Creative Problem Solving: What's the Big Idea? see Creative Problem Solving

Creative Problem Solving: Zeroing in on the Answer see Creative Problem Solving

Creative Relaxation. unabr. ed. John Sears. 1 cass. (Running Time: 57 min.). 10.95 (769) J Norton Pubs.
The best cure for tension & stress is deep, natural relaxation. This tape will help you achieve that state.

Creative Self-Expression, the Lost Art: Release the Individuality in Your Own Soul. Instructed by Manly P. Hall. 8.95 (978-0-89314-034-2(1), C610203) Philos Res.

Creative Solutions-Series 3000. Read by Mary Richards. 1 cass. (Running Time: 60 min.). (Series Two Thousand). 2007. audio compact disk 19.95 (978-1-56136-100-7(3)) Master Your Mind.

Creative Storytelling. Marsh Cassady. 3 cass. (Running Time: 3 hrs.). 29.95 set. ResPubnsCA.
Audio program which demonstrates some of the dramatic techniques used in storytelling.

Creative Tax Planning for Real Estate Transactions. 1 cass. (Running Time: 17 hrs.). 1999. 395.00 Incl. study guide. (AE30) Am Law Inst.

Creative Tax Planning for Real Estate Transactions: Thursday-Saturday, October 22-24, 1998, U.S. Grant Hotel, San Diego. 11 cass. (Running Time: 16 hrs. 50 min.). 395.00 Incl. course materials. (MD31) Am Law Inst.
Concentrates on the development of strategic & state-of-the-art planning techniques for dealing with the Federal income tax consequences of real estate investments & transactions.

Creative Thinking. 1 cass. (Running Time: 45 min.). (Educational Ser.). 1989. bk. 14.98 (978-1-55909-048-3(0)); 9.98 (46S) Randolph Tapes.
Use new ways of thinking to solve problems quickly. Subliminal messages are heard 3-5 minutes before becoming ocean sounds or music.

Creative Thinking. Barrie Konicov. 1 cass. (Video-Audio System Ser.). cass. & video 24.98 (978-0-87082-444-9(9), SYS023); 11.98 (978-0-87082-426-5(0), 023) Potentials.
A creative idea can raise your opportunities, propel you to unlimited prosperity, happiness & fulfillment.

Creative Thinking. Barrie Konicov. Read by Barrie Konicov. 4 cass. 16.98 (978-1-56001-317-4(6), SC-II 023) Potentials.

Creative Thinking. Barrie Konicov. 2 CDs. 2003. audio compact disk 27.98 (978-1-56001-973-2(5)) Potentials.
The difference in people is not the difference in opportunity, but in the quality of their thoughts. Raise the quality of your thoughts, and you will raise the quality of your life! This 2-CD program from our Super Consciousness series is our newest, most powerful format. On the self-hypnosis CD, SC programs have the Subliminal Persuasion soundtrack added under Barrie?s voice. And the 17th Century Baroque music on the Subliminal CD has the same beat as your body's natural rhythm, thereby allowing the suggestions to enter deeply and effortlessly.

Creative Thinking. Barrie Konicov. 1 CD. 2004. audio compact disk 19.98 (978-1-56001-679-3(5)) Potentials.
The difference in people is not the difference in opportunity, but in the quality pf their thoughts. Raise the quality of your thoughts, and you will raise the quality of your life!You will find the self-hypnosis on track 1 and the subliminal on track 2. The easy-listening music of the subliminal, together with the self-hypnosis, is the original format which most people love and with which they are most familiar.

Creative Thinking. Betty L. Randolph. Read by Betty L. Randolph. Read by Leonard Baron. Ed. by Success Education Institute International Staff. 1 cass. (Running Time: 60 min.). 1990. bk. 9.98 (978-1-55909-274-6(2), 46B) Randolph Tapes.
Sixty thousand messages left-right brain; Male-female voice tracks. Messages subliminally parallel music. Orchestrated specially arranged Baroque classical music with 60 beats for accelerated learning. Exclusively recorded for Success Education Institute by a world class symphony orchestra. All messages heard audibly for 3-5 minutes before covered by music.

Creative Thinking, Vol. 2-A. abr. ed. Don Hahn et al. 1 cass. (Personal Growth Ser.). 2000. (978-1-892655-01-1(2)) Powerplay Audio.
This program proves that creativity is within everyone's reach. It's just a matter of tapping into it & having the courage to follow your dreams.

Creative Thinking & Problem-Solving. 1 cass. 10.00 (978-1-58506-031-3(3), 63) New Life Inst OR.
You can transform yourself into a pulsating dynamo of creative power. Produce a flood of breakthrough ideas on any subject, whenever you wish.

Creative Use of Memory. Manly P. Hall. 8.95 (978-0-89314-035-9(X), C880911) Philos Res.
Deals with psychology & self-help.

Creative Visualization. Matthew Manning. 1 cass. 11.95 (MM-103) White Dove NM.
Matthew's biggest selling title. Side One describes the differences in the left & right hemispheres of the brain & how we use them. Side Two contains an excellent meditation to help both sides of the brain communicate more freely.

Creative Visualization. Dick Sutphen. 1 cass. (Running Time: 1 hr.). (RX17 Digital-Holophonic Ser.). 14.98 (978-0-87554-386-4(3), RX150) Valley Sun.
Teaches & programs to use creative visualization to program the subconscious mind in attaining desires.

Creative Visualization. abr. ed. Shakti Gawain. 6 cass. 54.00 (OC24W) Sound Horizons AV.

Creative Visualization: Create Your Life the Way You Want It to Be. Joyce Levine. Read by Joyce Levine. 1 cass. (Running Time: 55 min.). 1994. 11.95 (978-1-885856-01-2(6)) Vizualizations.
Side 1 - How visualization works; Side 2 - Visualization, guided meditation.

Creative Visualization: Create Your Own Reality! (ENG., 2009. audio compact disk 19.95 (978-0-9766735-5-2(X)) R Seals.

Creative Visualization: The Complete Book on Tape. unabr. ed. Shakti Gawain. 1 cass. (Running Time: 3 hrs.). 16.95 (AN5105) Lghtwrks Aud & Vid.
Shakti Gawain's classic guide to using the power of your imagination to create whatever you want in life. Includes techniques like Deep Relaxation, Asking for Guidance, Visualizing Goals & Affirmations on Self, Love & Abundance.

Creative Visualization: Use the Power of Your Imagination to Create What You Want in Your Life. 25th unabr. anniv. rev. ed. Shakti Gawain. Read by Shakti Gawain. 3 CDs. (Running Time: 3 hrs. 0 mins. 0 sec.). (Gawain, Shakti Ser.). (ENG.). 2002. audio compact disk 21.95 (978-1-57731-239-0(2)) Pub: New Wrld Lib. Dist(s): PerseuPGW
In this complete compact disc audio version of her popular book, Shakti Gawain guides listeners through meditations, exercises, and easy-to-use techniques that use mental imagery and affirmation to produce positive changes ? in health, business, sports, personal relationships, and the creative arts. These techniques include: deep relaxation, asking for guidance, visualizing goals, creating an inner sanctuary, opening up the natural energy centers, and affirmation of self, love, and abundance.

Creative Visualization: Visualizing & Achieving Your Goal. Melita Denning & Osborne Phillips. Featuring Melita Denning & Osborne Phillips. 1988. 9.95 (978-1-59157-018-9(2)) Assn for Cons.

Creative Visualization Meditations. 2nd rev. unabr. ed. Shakti Gawain. Read by Shakti Gawain. Intro. by Marc Allen. 1 CD. (Running Time: 1 hr. 0 mins. 0 sec.). (Gawain, Shakti Ser.). (ENG.). 2002. audio compact disk 14.95 (978-1-57731-240-6(6)) Pub: New Wrld Lib. Dist(s): PerseuPGW
The meditations on this one-hour compact disc detail the practical techniques of using mental imagery and affirmation to produce prositive change in one's life. In each meditiation, Shakti Gawain describes specific images and directs listeners as they go though the meditation process. Meditations include Meditation Journey; Deep Relaxation; Visualizing a Goal; Running Energy; and much more.

Creative Visualizations for Children: A First Step Towards Meditation. Michael N. Deranja. 1 cass. (Running Time: 60 min.). (Spiritual Child-Raising Ser.). 9.95 (AT-33) Crystal Clarity.
A variety of imaginative adventures draw children into relaxed stillness & calm concentration & leads them into meditative awareness.

Creative Ways of Teaching. unabr. ed. E. Paul Torrance. 1 cass. (Running Time: 26 min.). 12.95 (17021) J Norton Pubs.
A presentation & discussion of important ways by which teachers can establish a positive classroom atmosphere for creative thinking.

***Creative Ways to Cut & Control Costs.** PUEI. 2009. audio compact disk 199.00 (978-1-935041-48-1(7), CareerTrack) P Univ E Inc.

***Creative Ways to Reward & Motivate Employees.** PUEI. 2008. audio compact disk 199.00 (978-1-935041-01-6(0), CareerTrack) P Univ E Inc.

Creative World. Bunny Hull. Illus. by Synthia Saint-James. 1 cass. (Running Time: 35 mins.). (J). (ps-5). 2003. pap. bk. 10.95 (978-0-9673762-6-4(2), BH102CA, Kids Creative Classics) BrassHeart.
Creative development through music. A collection of fourteen original, classic songs.

Creative World. Bunny Hull & Synthia Saint-James. 1 CD. (Running Time: 35 mins.). (J). (ps-5). 2003. pap. bk. 15.95 (978-0-9673762-7-1(0), BH102CD, Kids Creative Classics) BrassHeart.

Creative Writing. 1 cass. (Running Time: 60 min.). 10.95 (043) Psych Res Inst.
Gain assurance that creativity & imagination can be effective through the written word.

Creative Writing. Barrie Konicov. 1 cass. 11.98 (978-0-87082-297-1(7), 024) Potentials.
Certain mental techniques that, once learned, will allow you to write as easily & effortlessly as you read, are revealed in this program.

Creative Writing. Barrie Konicov. 1 CD. 2003. audio compact disk 16.98 (978-0-87082-977-2(7)) Potentials.
Did you know there are certain mental techniques that, once learned, will allow you to write as easily and effortlessly as you read? Barrie used these techniques in creating scripts for over 180 self-hypnosis programs and you, too, can make use of them in any area where you need to use your writing skills. You will find the self-hypnosis on track 1 and the subliminal on track 2. The easy-listening music of the subliminal, together with the self-hypnosis, is the original format which most people love and with which they are most familiar.

Creative Writing. Barrie Konicov. 2 CDs. 2003. audio compact disk 27.98 (978-1-56001-974-9(3)) Potentials.

Creative Writing Level 1. A. J. Spencer, 1st. 2008. audio compact disk 5.99 (978-0-9755851-2-2(6)) A Eanes.

Creative Writing Level 2. A. J. Spencer, 1st. (ENG.). 2008. audio compact disk 5.99 (978-0-9755851-3-9(4)) A Eanes.

Creative Writing Level 3. A. J. Spencer, 1st. (ENG.). 2008. audio compact disk 5.99 (978-0-9755851-4-6(2)) A Eanes.

Creatively Managing Stress. Robert Conroy. Read by Robert Conroy. Ed. by Ellen Harkins & Patricia Magerkurth. 1 cass. (Running Time: 1 hr.). (Life Stages Ser.). 1991. 10.00 (978-1-56948-015-1(X)) Menninger Clinic.
When executives effectively manages stress, they are more productive, healthier, & are more adept leaders. Stress is a factor that can create health problems & can significantly undermine productivity in the workplace. Robert Conroy, MD, of the Menninger Management Institute, discusses the factors that create stress & offers a formula for coping constructively with stress.

Creativity. 5 cass. 10.00 ea. (978-1-885357-93-9(1)) Rational Isl.
Shared experiences of all kinds: of artists, about art & about using re-evaluation counseling.

Creativity. Osho Oshos. 1 cass. 9.00 (A0651-89) Sound Photosyn.

Creativity. Barry Tesar. 1 cass. (Running Time: 1 hr.). (Subliminal Inspiration Ser.). 1992. 9.98 (978-1-56470-000-1(3)) Success Cass.
Subliminal program.

Creativity, Pt. 1. Michael P. Marshall. Read by Michael P. Marshall. Ed. by Jonathan C. Renaud. Music by Ted Crook. 1 cass. (Running Time: 52 min.). 1995. 9.00 (978-0-912403-14-4(4)) Prod Renaud.
To date, our most powerful tape. Includes a 20 minute, guided meditation that will reveal the source of all personal creativity.

Creativity, Pt. 2. Michael P. Marshall. Read by Michael P. Marshall. Ed. by Jonathan C. Renaud. Music by Ted Crook. 1 cass. (Running Time: 52 min.). 1995. 9.00 (978-0-912403-15-1(2)) Prod Renaud.
Once activated, what do you do with your creative energy & ideas? Here's how to harness & direct this fabulous energy.

Creativity: Classic. Eldon Taylor. Read by Eldon Taylor. Ed. by Leslie Brice. 1 cass. (Running Time: 1 hr.). 1992. 16.95 (978-1-56705-174-2(X)) Gateways Inst.
Self improvement.

Creativity: Harnessing Your Competitive Edge. Miriam Rheinstein. 1986. 9.75 (978-0-932491-42-8(1)) Res Appl Inc.
Helps to unleash your inner potential for creative genius.

Creativity: Manifesting Your Creativity. Stuart Wilde. 1 cass. (Running Time: 1 hr.). (978-0-930603-40-3(0)) White Dove NM.
Pure creativity is not learned. It is a matter of having the courage to develop it from within you & committing to belief in yourself. Reprogram your mind with this subliminal tape to manifest the tangible successes that your creative splendor deserves.

Creativity: Ocean. Eldon Taylor. Read by Eldon Taylor. Ed. by Leslie Brice. 1 cass. (Running Time: 1 hr.). 1992. 16.95 (978-1-56705-175-9(8)) Gateways Inst.
Self improvement.

Creativity: Program from the Award Winning Public Radio Series. Hosted by Fred Goodwin. Comment by John Hockenberry. Contrib. by Dean Simonton et al. 1 cass. (Running Time: 1 hr.). (Infinite Mind Ser.). 1999. audio compact disk 21.95 (978-1-888064-19-3(6), LCM 52) Lichtenstein Creat.
Creativity can be mysterious - even to those who earn their livelihood by practicing it. This week, we shed some [illegible] on the creative process and talk to leading researchers about artistic, s[illegible], and corporate creativity. We also hear from a chef, a poet, and singe[illegible]ngwriter Suzanne Vega. Plus, creativity and mental illness, and John Hockenberry explains why "creative" is not always a compliment.

Creativity: Stream. Eldon Taylor. Read by Eldon Taylor. Ed. by Leslie Brice. 1 cass. (Running Time: 1 hr.). 1992. 16.95 (978-1-56705-176-6(6)) Gateways Inst.
Self improvement.

Creativity: The Wisdom Bearer Passes Through the Portals of Our Hearts. Stephen R. Schwartz. 3 cass. 28.00 Set. Riverrun Piermont.

Creativity & Individuation: The Insights of Egyptian Creation Myths. Read by Beverley Zabriskie. 1 cass. (Running Time: 2 hrs.). 1990. 16.95 (978-0-7822-0340-0(X), 405) C G Jung IL.

Creativity & Initiative. 2 cass. (Running Time: 2 hrs.). 14.95 (ST-4) Crystal Clarity.
Discusses three ingredients for maximum creative satisfaction: independent thinking; joyful tenacity; living in the moment.

Creativity & Self-Confidence & Being in a Loving Place. Marianne Williamson. Read by Marianne Williamson. 1 cass. (Running Time: 90 mins.). (Lectures on a Course in Miracles). 1999. 10.00 (978-1-56170-181-0(5), M709) Hay House.

***Creativity & Spirit in History & Today.** Ira Progoff. 2010. audio compact disk 15.00 (978-1-935859-05-5(6)) Dialogue Assoc.

Creativity & Spirituality. unabr. ed. Ram Dass. 2 cass. (Running Time: 1 hr. 56 min.). 1987. 18.00 Big Sur Tapes.

Creativity & the Chakras. Asha Praver. 1 cass. 9.95 (ST-67) Crystal Clarity.
Topics include: How the chakras affect your magnetism; magnetism & creativity; pitfalls of ego-centeredness; the importance of inwardness & enjoyment.

Creativity & the Daimonic. unabr. ed. Rollo May. 2 cass. (Running Time: 2 hrs. 23 min.). 1968. 18.00 Set. (00601) Big Sur Tapes.
In psychotherapy & the creative process, May considers it necessary to confront & wrestle with the daimonic. He defines the daimonic as any natural function which has the power of taking over the personality - sex & eros, anger & rage, & the craving of power - & discusses the curious phenomenon that a creative person always lives with, & produces partly by virtue of the daimonic.

Creativity & the Spiritual Path. Asha Praver. 1 cass. 9.95 (AT-17) Crystal Clarity.
Includes: How creativity affects personal development; the role of consciousness; what blocks our creativity?; specific ways to increase it; creativity as a receptive, yet active, process.

Creativity Factor. 2 CDs. 2004. audio compact disk 19.95 (978-1-57734-893-1(1)) Covenant Comms.

Creativity Is Natural. Eldon Taylor. Read by Eldon Taylor. Interview with XProgress Aware Staff & Progress Aware Staff. 1 cass. (Running Time: 1 hr. 30 min.). (Power Imaging Ser.). 16.95 incl. script. (978-1-55978-176-3(9), 8007) Progress Aware Res.
Hypnosis & soundtrack with underlying subliminal affirmations.

Creativity Is Natural: Power Imaging. Eldon Taylor. Read by Eldon Taylor. Ed. by Leslie Brice. 1 cass. (Running Time: 1 hr.). 1992. 12.95 (978-1-56705-025-7(5)) Gateways Inst.
Self improvement.

Creativity Plus. Read by Mary Richards. (Subliminal Impact Ser.). 12.95 Master Your Mind.
Explains how to celebrate life with creativity.

Creativity Unlimited Training Series. Thomas R. Condon. 6 cass. 69.95 set. (978-1-884305-84-9(9)) Changeworks.
This new tape series will give you dependable access to your creative resources. It will open you up to your creative potential & help you apply creativity to practical problems, daily situations, long range goals, etc.

Creator & Creation. Swami Amar Jyoti. 1 cass. 1979. 9.95 (R-28) Truth Consciousness.
What is Number One for us? Going to the Source, starting from the right assumption, "Me & my God are One, let me realize it.".

Creator Beyond Time & Space. Chuck Missler & Mark Eastman. 2 CD's. (Running Time: 120 min. aprox.). (Briefing Packages by Chuck Missler). 1996. audio compact disk 19.95 (978-1-57821-311-5(8)) Koinonia Hse.
What are the implications of the current upheavals in traditional cosmology, astronomy, and physics? What is the significance of the recent discovery that the Universe is finite? Has science unlocked the mystery of our origins? Chance or Design - What are the odds? As scientists begin to understand the interactions of basic forces, they discover an unending series of incredible interdependencies, delicately balanced. It appears that the universe has been uniquely designed to support humanity - from the Earth's distance from the Sun, down to the stability of the proton.As part of their recent Creator series, Chuck Missler and Dr. Mark Eastman explore the recent scientific evidences revealing the Infinite Designer of a finite universe - the Creator who lives outside of time and space.

Creator Beyond Time & Space: Twentieth Century Evidence for a Transcendent Creator. Chuck Missler & Mark Eastman. 2 cass. (Running Time: 2.5 hours). (Creator Ser.). 1996. vinyl bd. 14.95 Set, incl. study notes. (978-1-880532-38-6(7)) Koinonia Hse.
** What are the implications of the current upheavals in traditional cosmology, astronomy, and physics? * What is the significance of the recent discovery that the Universe is finite? * Has science unlocked the mystery of our origins? * Chance or Design - What are the odds?As scientists begin to understand the interactions of basic forces, they discover an unending series of incredible interdependencies, delicately balanced. It appears that the universe has been uniquely designed to support humanity - from the Earth's distance from the Sun, down to the stability of the proton.As part of their recent Creator series, Chuck Missler and Dr. Mark Eastman explore the recent scientific evidences revealing the Infinite Designer of a finite universe - the Creator who lives outside of time and space.*

***Creator Series.** Chuck Missler & Mark Eastman. 2009. audio compact disk 49.95 (978-1-57821-444-0(0)) Koinonia Hse.

Creator Series. collector's ed. Chuck Missler & Mark Eastman. 1 MP3 CD-Rom. (Running Time: 8 hours). (Creator Ser.). 2001. cd-rom 29.95 (978-1-57821-147-0(6)) Koinonia Hse.
*Astonishing discoveries have surfaced which point to the existence of a transcendent extra-dimensional Creator. Furthermore, numerous recent discoveries now confirm the incredible scientific and historical accuracy of the Bible, as well as the supernatural origin of its texts.The entire Creator Series is now available in this one, self-contained CD-ROM (compatible with both Windows and Macintosh operating systems). This CD-ROM includes all of these great studies:The Creator Beyond Time and Space: * What are the implications of the current upheavals in traditional cosmology, astronomy, and physics? What is the significance of the recent discovery that the Universe is finite? * As scientists begin to understand the interactions of basic forces, they discover an unending series of incredible interdependencies, delicately balanced. * As part of their recent series on the Creator Beyond Time and Space, Chuck Missler and Dr. Mark Eastman explore the recent scientific evidences revealing the Infinite Designer and a finite universe.The Bible: An Extraterrestrial Message: * In the 20th century we have witnessed one of the most remarkable discoveries in recorded history: the universe is finite. The implications of this discovery are indeed staggering. * Because a transcendent Creator possesses the sufficient means to act in our space-time domain, He also has the capability to get a message to us. The Bible claims to be that message.* Based on scientific accuracy and foreknowledge, design of the text, and the predictive prophecy of the Bible, Chuck Missler and Dr. Mark Eastman explore the absolute uniqueness of the Biblical message in light of recent discoveries.Immanuel: The Deity of Messiah: * Was there really a visitor to our Planet Earth from outside time and space? Why do we believe that Jesus was the Messiah? * Chuck Missler and Dr. Mark Eastman explore the historical evidence, claims, attributes, and authentication of the Messiah.The Divine Watchmaker:* What does molecular biology, the information sciences, and the design of advanced machines tell us about our origins? Why is "Evolution" the biggest hoax of the century?Review Neo-Darwinian concepts and how modern discoveries have rendered them obsolete.Modern Microbiology has revealed that even the simplest organisms are complex machines beyond our imagining.*

Creators: A History of Heroes of the Imagination. Daniel J. Boorstin. Read by Michael Jackson. 4 cass. (Running Time: 6 hrs.). 1992. 24.95 Set. (978-1-879371-40-8(5), 60010) Pub Mills.
A companion volume to Dr. Boorstin's best-selling "The Discoveries," "The Creators" is a history of what man has added to the world, a history of man's heritage - from the builders of the pyramids to the author of "Ulysses.".

Creators: A History of Heroes of the Imagination. abr. ed. Scripts. Daniel J. Boorstin. Read by Michael Jackson. 4 cass. (Running Time: 6 hrs.). 2004. 24.95 (978-1-59007-359-9(2)) Pub: New Millenn Enter. Dist(s): PerseuPGW

Creators Pt. 1: A History of Heroes of the Imagination. unabr. ed. Daniel J. Boorstin. Read by Michael Prichard. 14 cass. (Running Time: 21 hrs.). 1993. 112.00 (3151-A) Books on Tape.
Boorstin puts flesh on the great figures & gives dimension to the great events in our cultural heritage. He celebrates Confucius & Picasso, Mozart & James Joyce, Isadora Duncan & Virginia Woolf, Chinese art & modern photography, Stonehenge & skyscrapers.

Creators Pt. 2: A History of Heroes of the Imagination. unabr. ed. Daniel J. Boorstin. Read by Michael Prichard. 27 cass. (Running Time: 20 hrs. 30 min.). 1993. 104.00 (978-0-7366-2379-7(5), 3151-B) Books on Tape.

Creator's Lap of Golden Energy. unabr. ed. Carolyn Ann O'Riley. 1 cass. (Running Time: 45 mins.). 2000. audio compact disk 12.50 (978-1-891870-15-6(7)) Archangels Pen.
Archangel Michael inspired Meditation Tape. Side A: "The Creator's Lap of Golden Energy"; Side B: "The Gift of Manifesting Tools.".

Creator's Map. unabr. ed. Emilio Calderón. Read by Tony Chiroldes. 7 CDs. (Running Time: 8 hrs. 30 mins.).Tr. of Mapa del Creador. (ENG., 2008. audio compact disk 32.95 (978-1-59887-650-5(3), 1598876503) Pub: HighBridge. Dist(s): Workman Pub

Creature Features. abr. ed. Engle & Barnes. Directed By Sandra Bovee. (Running Time: 7200 sec.). (Strange Matter Ser.). (J). 2007. audio compact disk 25.25 (978-1-4233-0895-9(6), 9781423308959, BACDLib Ed) Brilliance Audio.

Creature Features. abr. ed. Engle & Barnes. Read by Full Cast Production Staff. 2. (Running Time: 7200 sec.). (Strange Matter Ser.). (J). 2007. audio compact disk 9.95 (978-1-4233-0894-2(8), 9781423308942, BACD) Brilliance Audio.

Creature Features. abr. ed. Engle & Barnes. (Running Time: 2 hrs.). (Strange Matter Ser.). 2007. 9.95 (978-1-4233-0896-6(4), 9781423308966, BAD) Brilliance Audio.

Creature Features. abr. ed. Engle & Julian Barnes. Read by Multivoice Production Staff. (Running Time: 2 hrs.). (Strange Matter Ser.). 2007. 25.25 (978-1-4233-0897-3(2), 9781423308973, BADLE) Brilliance Audio.

Creature Features: Comprehension Development. Eunice Insel & Ann Edson. 5 cass. (J). (gr. 3-6). 89.00 set, incl. 10 activity bks. & guide. (978-0-89525-222-7(8), AMC 84) Ed Activities.
Includes finding the main idea, recalling details following sequence, following directions, locating answers, reading in context, drawing conclusions, inferring, indentifying cause & effect, predicting outcomes.

Creature Features: Structural Analysis. Eunice Insel & Ann Edson. 5 cass. (J). (gr. 3-6). 89.00 set, incl. 10 activity bks., & guide. (978-0-89525-220-3(1), AMC 70) Ed Activities.
Includes forming compound words, forming plurals, identifying root words, adding 'ing' & 'ed' endings to words, identifying prefixes & suffixes, identifying singular & plural possessive, counting vowel sounds & syllables & dividing words into syllable patterns.

Creature Features: Study & Research Skills. Eunice Insel & Ann Edson. 5 cass. (J). (gr. 3-6). 89.00 set, incl. 10 activity bks. & guide. (978-0-89525-223-4(6), AMC 72) Ed Activities.
Includes using the dictionary, reference materials such as an encyclopedia, atlas, almanac, interpreting maps, charts & graphs, working with newspapers & magazines, using the library, identifying parts of a book, selecting the topic, outlining & writing a report.

Creature Features: Vocabulary Development. Eunice Insel & Ann Edson. 5 cass. (J). (gr. 3-6). 89.00 set, incl. 10 activity bks. & guide. (978-0-89525-221-0(X), AMC 71) Ed Activities.
Includes using nouns, recognizing verbs, identifying adjectives, introducing adverbs, detecting pronouns, using negatives, discriminating synonyms & antonyms & recognizing homonyms.

Creature from Jekyll Island. G Edward Griffin. Read by G Edward Griffin. 1 cass. 1998. 10.00 (978-0-912986-22-7(0)) Am Media.

***Creature in the Dark.** unabr. ed. Robert Westall. (Running Time: 1 hr. 40 mins.). 2003. audio compact disk 24.00 (978-1-74093-122-9(X)) Pub: Bolinda Pubng AUS. Dist(s): Bolinda Pub Inc

Creature to Tell the Time by see Brian Patten Reading His Poetry

CREC Exam of Douglas Wilson-mp3. 4. 2004. 9.50 (978-1-59128-410-9(4)) Canon Pr ID.

CREC Exam of Douglas Wilson-tape. 4 cass. 2004. 12.00 (978-1-59128-412-3(0)) Canon Pr ID.

Crecian Urn. (Paws & Tales Ser.: Vol. 26). (J). 2002. audio compact disk 5.99 (978-1-57972-435-1(3)) Insight Living.

Creciendo por medio de las Experiencias Dolorosas. 2006. audio compact disk 34.00 (978-1-57972-726-0(3)) Insight Living.

Credeaux Canvas. Keith Bunin. Contrib. by Chad Lowe et al. 2 CDs. (Running Time: 5940 sec.). (L. A. Theatre Works). 2003. audio compact disk 25.95 (978-1-58081-265-8(1), CDTPT178) Pub: L A Theatre. Dist(s): NetLibrary CO

Credenda/Agenda: Against Gravity (Vol. 18, Issue 4) Read by Douglas Wilson. (ENG.). 2007. audio compact disk 12.00 (978-1-59128-320-1(5)) Canon Pr ID.

***Credibility: How Leaders Gain & Lose It, Why People Demand It, Revised Edition.** unabr. ed. James M. Kouzes & Barry Z. Posner. Read by Erik Synnestvedt. (Running Time: 10 hrs.). (ENG.). 2010. 39.98 (978-1-59659-580-4(9), GildAudio) Pub: Gildan Media. Dist(s): HachBkGrp

Credibility & Cross-Examination. Irving Younger. Read by Irving Younger. 3 cass. (Running Time: 3 hrs.). 1985. pap. bk. 70.00 Set. (978-0-943380-39-1(1)) PEG MN.
Controlling witnesses responses for effective testimony.

Credibility & Cross Examination. Read by Irving Younger. (Running Time: 6 hrs.). 125.00 incl. study guide. (154) Natl Prac Inst.
What to ask & how to ask it.

Credibility & Cross Examination. Irving Younger. 1981. 125.00 (978-1-55917-085-7(9)) Natl Prac Inst.

Credibility & Cross Examination. Speeches. Perf. by Irving Younger. Created by Irving Younger. 2 CDs. (Running Time: 3 hours). 2004. pap. bk. 199.00 (978-1-932831-00-9(2)) PEG MN.

Credible Witnesses. John Arnott. 1 cass. 1996. 7.00 (978-0-7684-0001-4(5)) Destiny Image Pubs.

Credit after Bankruptcy: A step-by-step action plan to quick & lasting recovery after personal Bankruptcy. (ENG.). 1999. (978-1-891945-01-4(7)) Chapter Twenty.

Credit Builders CD. Compiled by Grace Forms. (ENG.). 2009. audio compact disk 9.95 (978-0-9819801-2-6(0)) Grace Forms.

Credit Card Services in Brazil: A Strategic Reference 2006. Compiled by Icon Group International, Inc. Staff. 2007. ring bd. 195.00 (978-0-497-35834-1(4)) Icon Grp.

Credit Repair. Ed. by Socrates Media Editors. 2005. audio compact disk 29.95 (978-1-59546-096-7(9)) Pub: Socrates Med LLC. Dist(s): Midpt Trade

Credit Repair, Kit. 2nd abr. ed. Steve Bucci. Read by Brett Barry. 2008. audio compact disk 14.95 (978-0-06-167279-8(3), Harper Audio) HarperCollins Pubs.

***Credit Repair Kit for Dummies.** abr. ed. Steve Bucci. Read by Brett Barry. (ENG.). 2008. (978-0-06-170729-2(5)); (978-0-06-170733-9(3)) HarperCollins Pubs.

Credit Repair Kit for Dummies. 2nd abr. ed. Steve Bucci. Read by Brett Barry. (Playaway Adult Nonfiction Ser.). (ENG.). 2009. 59.99 (978-1-60812-579-1(3)) Find a World.

Credit Repair Made Easy: Six Steps to Good Credit. Credifix Corporation Staff. Read by Peter Thomas. 1 cass. (Running Time: 40 min.). 1994. 10.95 (978-0-9649174-0-8(8)) Credifix.
An easy to understand six step program, that shows people with bad credit, how to get their good credit back.

Credit Repair Made Easy for Small Business Owners. Speeches. Mervin L. Evans. 3 Audio CD. (Running Time: 4H 30 M). 2003. 49.99 (978-0-914391-48-7(8)) Comm People Pr.
Credit Repair Made Easy for Small Business Owners is a audiotape set for business ownerswho have credit problems, be are looking for investoment capital.

Credit Repair Made Easy for Women. Mervin Evans. 2 CDs. (Running Time: 1 hr. 50 min.). 2004. audio compact disk 29.99 (978-0-914391-92-0(5)) Comm People Pr.

Credit, Sales & Other Consumer Transactions. 1988. 45.00 (AC-472) PA Bar Inst.

***Credit 911: Secrets & Strategies to Saving Your Financial Life.** unabr. ed. Rodney Anderson. Read by Don Hagen. (Running Time: 7 hrs.). (ENG.). 2010. 27.98 (978-1-59659-677-1(5), GildAudio) Pub: Gildan Media. Dist(s): HachBkGrp

CreditBooster PRO. Created by holoMaXx technologies Staff. (ENG.). 2006. audio compact disk 49.95 (978-0-615-15250-9(3)) holoMaXx Tech.

Creditor Protection: Offered by Alaska & Delaware Statutes & Other Current Issues in Asset Protection Planning. 1 cass. (Running Time: 2 hrs.). 1999. bk. 59.00 (ACS-2251) PA Bar Inst.
Recent legislation in Delaware & Alaska has drawn attention to new techniques for protecting your client's assets from creditors & their impact on estate planning.

Credo. (J). 1995. 39.95 (978-1-886412-08-8(1)) Preserv Press.

Credo: The Drama of Belief. Franklyn McAfee. 1 cass. (Inspiring Presentations from the National Rosary Congress Ser.). 2.50 (978-1-56036-086-5(0)) AMI Pr.

Credo of a Modern Kabbalist. unabr. ed. Zalman Schachter-Shalomi. Read by Zalman Schachter-Shalomi. 6 cass. (Running Time: 10 hr. 15 min.). 1995. 56.00 Set. (31004) Big Sur Tapes.
Faced with the task of conveying traditional wisdom to future generations, Reb Zalman considers which basic beliefs, practices & texts are most crucial to maintain.

Cree en ti Mismo see Believe in Yourself Audio Story in Spanish

Cree en ti Mismo see Believe in Yourself Audio Story with Finger Puppet in Spanish

Cree, Language of the Plains (tapes/CD) Jean L. Okimasis. (University of Regina Publications(UR) Ser.). (ENG.). 2005. audio compact disk 39.95 (978-0-88977-212-0(6)) Pub: Can Plains Res CAN. Dist(s): U Toronto Pr

Creed. unabr. ed. James Herbert. Read by William Hope. 11 CDs. (Running Time: 12 hrs.). (Isis Ser.). (J). 2002. audio compact disk 99.95 (978-0-7531-1572-5(7)) Pub: ISIS Lrg Prnt GBR. Dist(s): Ulverscroft US
Joseph Creed is a paparazzo, a sleaze of the first order, but good at his job. After the funeral of a major Hollywood actress, he photographs a man of ravaged appearance desecrating the grave. The person he has photographed bears a remarkable resemblance to a man hanged in the 1930s for murder and the mutilation of children. Creed himself is observed and there follows a series of horrific events designed to intimidate him into handing over the film.

Creed. unabr. ed. James Herbert. Read by William Hope. 8 cass. (Running Time: 12 hrs.). (Isis Ser.). (J). 2004. 69.95 (978-0-7531-0442-2(3), 981105) Pub: ISIS Lrg Prnt GBR. Dist(s): Ulverscroft US
Joseph Creed is a paparazzo, & after the funeral ceremony of a major Hollywood actress, he photographs a man of ravaged appearance desecrating the grave. The person he photographed bears a remarkable resemblance to a man hanged in the 1930s for murder & mutilation of children. But Creed has been noticed & a series of horrific events unfold designed to intimidate him into handing over the film.

Creed & the Christian: A Twelve-Part Study of the Apostles' Creed. unabr. ed. Marni Shideler McKenzie. Intro. by Dave Lange. 6 cass. (Running Time: 48 min. per cass.). 1993. bk. 24.95 set incl. student guide & leader's guide. (978-1-882630-01-1(7)) Mercy Pr.
Each cassette is a teaching explanation of a chosen phrase from the Apostles' Creed.

Creed for the Third Millennium. unabr. ed. Colleen McCullough. Read by Penelope Dellaporta. 12 cass. (Running Time: 18 hrs.). 1986. 96.00 (978-0-7366-0647-9(5), 1608) Books on Tape.
A warm & caring doctor clashes with Health Depart bureaucrat.

Creed of the Mountain Man. abr. ed. William W. Johnstone. Read by Doug van Liew. 4 cass. (Running Time: 6 hrs.). (Mountain Man Ser.: No. 23). 2002. 24.95 (978-1-890990-86-2(8), 99086) Otis Audio.
Western with sound effects.

Creed; Questions & Answers; Award to Arch. A. Cacciavillan. John Myers. 1 cass. (National Meeting of the Institute, 1994 Ser.). 4.00 (94N3) IRL Chicago.

Creek Walk & Other Stories, unabr. ed. Molly Giles. Read by Molly Giles. 2 cass. (Running Time: 3 hrs.). 1997. 17.95 (978-1-57453-207-4(3)) Audio Lit.
Vivid, funny stories about what goes on in women's minds. Brings a fresh look at both the comedy & tragedy of life & the extraordinary persistence of the human spirit.

Creele a Dios: Como Vivir Por Fe en Su Palabra. unabr. abr. ed. Beth Moore. Read by Yolanda Lopez. Tr. by Carolina Galan Caballero. (Running Time: 14400 sec.). 2007. audio compact disk 27.00 (978-1-4332-1138-6(6)) Blckstn Audio.

Creep from the Deep. R. L. Stine. Narrated by Jeff Woodman. (Goosebumps HorrorLand Ser.: No. 2). (ENG.). (J). (gr. 4-7). 2008. audio compact disk 9.95 (978-0-545-08848-0(8)) Scholastic Inc.

Creep from the Deep. unabr. ed. R. L. Stine. Read by Jeff Woodman. (Goosebumps HorrorLand Ser.: No. 2). (J). 2008. 34.99 (978-1-60514-778-9(8)) Find a World.

Creep from the Deep. unabr. ed. R. L. Stine. Narrated by Jeff Woodman. 2 CDs. (Running Time: 2 hrs. 28 mins.). (Goosebumps HorrorLand Ser.: No. 2). (ENG.). (J). (gr. 2-4). 2008. audio compact disk 29.95 (978-0-545-08849-7(6)) Scholastic Inc.

Creeper. unabr. ed. Morris Gleitzman & Paul Jennings. Read by Stig Wemyss & Kate Hosking. 2 CDs. (Running Time: 1 hr. 15 mins.). (Wicked! Ser.: Bk. 5). (J). audio compact disk 24.00 (978-1-74093-427-5(X)) Bolinda Pubng AUS.

Creeper. unabr. ed. Morris Gleitzman & Paul Jennings. (Running Time: 1 hr. 15 mins.). (Wicked! Ser.: Bk. 5). (YA). 2001. 18.00 (978-1-74030-470-2(5)) Pub: Bolinda Pubng AUS. Dist(s): Bolinda Pub Inc

Creepers. abr. ed. David Morrell. Read by Patrick G. Lawlor. (Running Time: 14400 sec.). 2006. audio compact disk 14.99 (978-1-4233-0611-5(2), 9781423306115, BCD Value Price) Brilliance Audio.
On a cold October night, five people gather in a run-down motel on the Jersey shore and begin preparations to break into the Paragon Hotel. Built in the glory days of Asbury Park by a reclusive millionaire, the magnificent structure - which foreshadowed the beauties of art deco architecture - is now boarded up and marked for demolition. The five people are "creepers," the slang term for urban explorers: city archeologists with a passion for investigating abandoned buildings and their dying secrets. On this evening, they are joined by a reporter who wants to profile them - anonymously, as this is highly illegal activity - for a New York Times article. Frank Balenger, a sandy-haired, broad-shouldered reporter with a decided air of mystery about him, isn't looking for just a story, however. And after the group enters the rat-infested tunnel leading to the hotel, it becomes clear that he will get much more than he bargained for. Danger, terror, and death await the creepers in a place ravaged by time and redolent of evil.

Creepers. unabr. ed. David Morrell. Read by Patrick G. Lawlor. (Running Time: 8 hrs.). 2005. 39.25 (978-1-59737-471-2(7), 9781597374712, BADLE); 24.95 (978-1-59737-470-5(9), 9781597374705, BAD); 39.25 (978-1-59737-469-9(5), 9781597374699, Brlnc Audio MP3 Lib); 74.25

(978-1-59737-465-1(2), 9781597374651, BrilAudUnabridg); audio compact disk 87.25 (978-1-59737-467-5(9), 9781597374675, BriAudCD Unabrid); audio compact disk 24.95 (978-1-59737-468-2(7), 9781597374682, Brilliance MP3); audio compact disk 32.95 (978-1-59737-466-8(0), 9781597374668, Bril Audio CD Unabri) Brilliance Audio.

Creepers: Haunted Cattle Drive. Connie Kingrey. Read by Gerald Drake et al. 1998. 6.98 (978-1-57375-622-8(9), 4090) Audioscope.

Creepy Campfire Chillers #1. Johnathan Rand. (YA). 2003. audio compact disk 9.99 (978-1-893699-60-1(9)) Pub: AudioCraft. Dist(s): Partners Bk Dist

Creepy CD Collection Display. Perf. by Daniel Sjerven. Created by Daniel Sjerven. Prod. by Braun Media. (ENG.). 2008. (978-1-59987-673-3(6)) Braun Media.

Creepy Company: Ten Tales of Terror. unabr. ed. Joan Aiken. Read by Eve Karpf. 4 cass. (Running Time: 6 hrs.). (J). (gr. 1-8). 1999. 32.95 (CCA 3384, Chivers Child Audio) AudioGO.

Creepy Stories. 1 CD. (Running Time: 30 min.). (Halloween Party Ser.). (J). (gr. k-5). 2001. pap. bk. 5.98 (9685-2) Peter Pan.
Spooky songs, sounds and stories with holiday spirit. Includes Halloween Party Tip Guide.

Creerle a Dios: Cómo Vivir Por Fe en Su Palabra. abr. ed. Beth Moore. Narrated by Yolanda Lopez. (Running Time: 3 hrs. 52 mins. 5 sec.). (SPA.). 2006. audio compact disk 14.99 (978-1-59859-036-4(7)) Oasis Audio.

Creerle A Dios (Believing God) Como Vivir Por Fe en Su Palabra. abr. ed. Beth Moore. Narrated by Yolanda Lopez. (SPA.). 2006. 10.49 (978-1-60814-165-4(9)) Oasis Audio.

Cremation of Sam McGee see Poetry of Robert W. Service

Cremcimiento de una Mision que se Expande. Charles R. Swindoll.Tr. of Growth of an Expanding Mission. (SPA.). 2007. audio compact disk 46.00 (978-1-57972-756-7(5)) Insight Living.

Creole sans Peine. (FRE.). 2000. bk. 75.00 (978-2-7005-1323-3(1)) Pub: Assimil FRA. Dist(s): Distribks Inc

Crepe Suzette. 1 cass. (Running Time: 60 min.). Dramatization. (Maitres du Mystere Ser.). (FRE.). 1996. 11.95 (1838-MA) Olivia & Hill.
Popular radio thriller, interpreted by France's best actors.

***Crescendo.** unabr. ed. Becca Fitzpatrick. Read by Caitlin Greer. (Running Time: 9 hrs. 30 mins. 0 sec.). (ENG.). (YA). 2010. audio compact disk 34.99 (978-1-4423-3419-9(3)) Pub: S&S Audio. Dist(s): S and S Inc

Crescendo 2e-Lab Audio Cds(7) 2nd ed. Italiano & Nick Jones. (C). 2007. audio compact disk 44.95 (978-1-4130-1136-4(5)) Pub: Heinle. Dist(s): CENGAGE Learn

Crescendo 2e-Text Audio Cd (Stand Alone Version) 2nd ed. Francesca Italiano & Irene Marchegiani Jones. (ITA & ENG., 2007. audio compact disk (978-1-4130-2924-6(8)) Heinle.

***Crescent Dawn.** Clive Cussler. Read by Scott Brick. (Running Time: 14 hrs.). (Dirk Pitt Adventure Ser.). (ENG.). 2010. audio compact disk 39.95 (978-0-14-242873-3(6), PengAudBks) Penguin Grp USA.

***Crescent Dawn.** abr. ed. Clive Cussler. Read by Richard Ferrone. (Running Time: 6 hrs.). (Dirk Pitt Adventure Ser.). (ENG.). 2010. audio compact disk 29.95 (978-0-14-242874-0(4)) Penguin Grp USA.

Crescent Moon. Rabindranath Tagore. Read by Deepak Chopra. Ed. by Deepak Chopra. Music by G. S. Sachdev. 1 cass. (Running Time: 45 min.). (ENG.). 1996. reel tape 11.95 (978-1-878424-20-4(3)) Amber-Allen Pub.

***Crescent Moon Audio-mp3.** Sherry J. Campbell. 2010. 18.95 (978-1-4507-1284-2(3)) Indep Pub IL.

Cress Delahanty. unabr. ed. Jessamyn West. Read by Roses Prichard. 6 cass. (Running Time: 9 hrs.). (J). 1980. 48.00 (978-0-7366-0205-1(4), 1203) Books on Tape.
A child of the West grows up.

Creswell Photographic Archive: Architecture of the Islamic World. K. A. C. Creswell. cass. & cd-rom 85.00 (978-1-85444-090-7(X)) Pub: Ashmolean Mus GBR. Dist(s): Weatherhill

Cretaceous Paradox. unabr. ed. Frank J. Carradine. Read by Jerry Sciarrio. 6 cass. (Running Time: 7 hrs. 42 min.). 2001. 39.95 (978-1-58116-073-4(9)); audio compact disk 45.50 (978-1-58116-113-7(1)) Books in Motion.
1047 A.D., the Earth's pollution has rendered the drug Zamite useless against a hybrid cancer. Scientists must travel back in time to the Cretaceous Period to harvest a genetically superior Zamite to avert an international disaster.

Crewel Yule. Monica Ferris. Read by Melissa Hughes. 5 cass. (Needlecraft Mystery Ser.). 49.95 (978-0-7927-3774-2(1), CSL 853); audio compact disk 64.95 (978-0-7927-3775-9(X), SLD 853) AudioGO.

Cri-du-Chat Syndrome - A Bibliography & Dictionary for Physicians, Patients, & Genome Researchers. Compiled by Icon Group International, Inc. Staff. 2007. ring bd. 28.95 (978-0-497-11360-5(0)) Icon Grp.

***Crianza de los Hijos: De Sobrevivir a Prosperar.** Charles R. Swindoll.Tr. of Parenting: from Surviving to Thriving. 2009. audio compact disk 34.00 (978-1-57972-850-2(2)) Insight Living.

Crianza Practica de los Hijos: Audiolibro. abr. ed. Ray Burke & Ronald W. Herron. 2 cass. (Running Time: 2 hrs. 30 mins.). 1997. 14.95 Set, Spanish version. (978-1-889322-30-8(X), 39-425) Boys Town Pr.
La Crianza Practica De Los Hijos contains all of the winning strategies and successful teaching techniques that made Common Sense Parenting popular. The book describes methods that enable parents to develop meaningful relationships with their children. Each chapter focuses on a particular skill that encourages, among other things, honesty, open communication, positive behaviors, and problem solving. Examples on how to use each skill during various circumstances are shared. The book also expands to include practical tips for parents on helping children succeed in school, resist peer pressure, and understand the sometimes negative influences of media and pop culture. La Crianza Practica De Los Hijos is also available as an audiobook. The cassette version communicates the same logical, practical approach to parenthood and includes a wallet-size reminder card for easy reference.

Crianza Practica de los Hijos: Audiolibro CD. 2nd abr. ed. 2. (Running Time: 2 hrs. 30 mins.). (Common Sense Parenting Ser.).Tr. of Common Sense Parenting. (SPA.). 2006. audio compact disk 14.95 (978-1-889322-89-6(X), 39-425-CD) Boys Town Pr.

Cricket Clicket Cassette. Stephen Cosgrove. 2004. 5.00 (978-1-58804-396-2(7)) PCI Educ.

Cricket in Times Square. George Selden. Read by Rene Auberjonois. 2 cass. (Running Time: 2 hrs. 50 mins). (Chester Cricket Ser.). (J). (gr. 3-6). 2000. 32.00 (978-0-7366-9062-1(X)) Books on Tape.
A Connecticut cricket named Chester hops a ride in a picnic basket & ends up in a near-bankrupt newsstand in Times Square. He teams up with the son of the newsstand's owners, a fast-talking mouse & a local cat to rescue the business.

Cricket in Times Square. George Selden. Read by Rene Auberjonois. 3 CDs. (Running Time: 2 hrs. 39 mins.). (Chester Cricket Ser.). (J). (gr. 3-7). 2004. audio compact disk 25.50 (978-0-8072-0503-7(6), Listening Lib) Pub: Random Audio Pubg. Dist(s): NetLibrary CO

Cricket in Times Square. George Selden. (Chester Cricket Ser.). (J). (gr. 3-6). 1986. 21.33 (978-0-394-76814-4(0)) SRA McGraw.

Cricket in Times Square. unabr. ed. George Selden. Read by Tony Shalhoub. Illus. by Garth Williams. 2 CDs. (Running Time: 2 hrs. 30 mins. 0 sec.). (Chester Cricket & His Friends Ser.). (ENG.). (J). (gr. 3-6). 2008. audio compact disk 14.95 (978-1-4272-0445-5(4)) Pub: Macmill Audio. Dist(s): Macmillan

Cricket in Times Square. unabr. ed. George Selden. Read by Rene Auberjonois. 2 vols. (Running Time: 2 hrs. 39 mins.). (Chester Cricket Ser.). (J). (gr. 3-7). 2004. pap. bk. 29.00 (978-0-8072-8310-3(X), S YA 158 SP, Listening Lib); 23.00 (978-0-8072-8309-7(6), LL0178, Listening Lib) Random Audio Pubg.

Cricket in Times Square. unabr. ed. George Selden. Narrated by Barbara Caruso. 3 pieces. (Running Time: 3 hrs. 15 mins.). (Chester Cricket Ser.). (gr. 4 up). 1995. 27.00 (978-0-7887-0142-9(8), 94367E7) Recorded Bks.
Chester Cricket is carried away in a picnic basket & is stranded in New York's Times Square subway station, where he befriends a mouse, a cat & a little boy.

Cricket in Times Square. unabr. ed. George Selden. Narrated by Barbara Caruso. 3 CDs. (Running Time: 3 hrs. 15 mins.). (Chester Cricket Ser.). (gr. 4 up). 2000. audio compact disk 27.00 (978-0-7887-3451-9(2), C1057E7) Recorded Bks.

Cricket in Times Square. unabr. ed. George Selden. Narrated by Rene Auberjonois. 2 cass. (Running Time: 2 hrs.). (Chester Cricket Ser.). (J). (gr. 3-6). pap. bk. 23.00 (LL1030AC) Weston Woods.
Chester Cricket's beautiful music (as managed by Tucker Mouse) brings fame to Chester and fortune to the subway-station newspaper stand where they live.

Cricket on the Hearth & the Signalman, Set. unabr. ed. Charles Dickens. Narrated by Flo Gibson. 3 cass. (Running Time: 4 hrs. 30 mins.). (J). 1984. 16.95 (978-1-55685-050-9(6)) Audio Bk Con.
John & Dot Perrybingle, Caleb Plummer & his blind daughter, Bertha & a cricket on the hearth find truth, beauty & the true spirit of Christmas together.

Crickets see George Seferis

Crickwing. Janell Cannon. Narrated by Kevin R. Free. (Running Time: 15 mins.). (J). 2000. audio compact disk 12.75 (978-1-4193-1737-8(7)) Recorded Bks.

Crictor. 2004. 8.95 (978-0-89719-908-7(1)); 8.95 (978-1-56008-126-5(0)); cass. & flmstrp 30.00 (978-0-89719-508-9(6)) Weston Woods.

Crictor. (J). 2004. bk. 24.95 (978-0-89719-867-7(0)); pap. bk. 32.75 (978-1-55592-188-0(4)); pap. bk. 14.95 (978-1-56008-020-6(5)) Weston Woods.

Crictor. Tomi Ungerer. 1 cass. (Running Time: 6 min.). (J). bk. 24.95; pap. bk. 12.95 (PRA263); pap. bk. 32.75 Weston Woods.
One side with page turn signals, one side without.

Crictor. Tomi Ungerer. 1 cass. (Running Time: 6 min.). (J). (ps-3). pap. bk. 12.95 (RAC263) Weston Woods.
An affectionate & quick-thinking boa constrictor saves the day during a burglary & receives a medal.

Cries & Whiskers. unabr. ed. Clea Simon. Read by Tavia Gilbert. (Running Time: 36000 sec.). (Theda Krakow Mysteries Ser.). 2007. audio compact disk 29.95 (978-1-4332-1278-9(1)); audio compact disk & audio compact disk 63.00 (978-1-4332-1277-2(3)) Blckstn Audio.

Cries & Whiskers: A Theda Krakow Mystery. unabr. ed. Clea Simon. Read by Tavia Gilbert. (Running Time: 36000 sec.). (Theda Krakow Mysteries Ser.). 2007. 54.95 (978-1-4332-1276-5(5)) Blckstn Audio.

Cries of the Damned. Dan Corner. 1 cass. 3.00 (25) Evang Outreach.

Crime & Astrology I. Pat Bouder. 1 cass. 8.95 (030) Am Fed Astrologers.
Analysis of crime from Bouder's work with police.

Crime & Astrology II. Pat Bouder. 1 cass. 8.95 (031) Am Fed Astrologers.
Procure data from dead crime victim's chart.

Crime & Consequences. Contrib. by Phanatik. 2007. audio compact disk 13.99 (978-5-557-57368-9(2)) C Mason Res.

Crime & Punishment see Crimen y Castigo

Crime & Punishment. Fyodor Dostoyevsky. Read by Graeme Malcolm. 18 cds. 2005. audio compact disk 29.95 (978-1-59803-001-3(9)) Teaching Co.

Crime & Punishment. Fyodor Dostoyevsky. Narrated by Flo Gibson. 15 cass. (Running Time: 10 hrs. 40 mins.). (Classic Books on Cassette). 2005. 43.95 (978-1-55685-852-9(3)) Audio Bk Con.

Crime & Punishment. Fyodor Dostoyevsky. Read by Nigel Anthony. 2002. pap. bk. (978-1-901768-77-0(5)) CSA Telltapes GBR.

Crime & Punishment. Fyodor Dostoyevsky. Read by Michael Sheen. (Running Time: 3 hrs. 45 mins.). 1998. 24.95 (978-1-60083-715-9(8)) Iofy Corp.

Crime & Punishment. Fyodor Dostoyevsky. Read by Fabio Camero. (Running Time: 3 hrs.). 2001. 16.95 (978-1-60083-163-8(X), Audiofy Corp) Iofy Corp.

Crime & Punishment. Fyodor Dostoyevsky. Narrated by Walter Zimmerman. (Running Time: 22 hrs. 30 mins.). 2006. 25.95 (978-1-59912-375-2(4)) Iofy Corp.

Crime & Punishment. Fyodor Dostoyevsky. Read by Walter Zimmerman. 17 cass. (Running Time: 25 hrs.). 1989. 94.00 (C-120) Jimcin Record.
Psychological study of crime.

Crime & Punishment. Fyodor Dostoyevsky. Read by Michael Sheen. 3 cass. (Running Time: 3 hrs. 45 mins.). (Classic Fiction Ser.). 1996. 17.98 (978-962-634-509-2(8), NA300914, Naxos AudioBooks) Naxos.
The most terrible crimes of the twentieth century have undoubtedly been the result of such idealistic theories - in which dubious means justify the ends - as ensnared Dostoyevsky in his youth & Raskonikov in this novel.

Crime & Punishment. Fyodor Dostoyevsky. Read by George Guidall. 14 Cass. (Running Time: 25.5 Hrs.). 34.95 (978-1-4025-3323-5(3)) Recorded Bks.

Crime & Punishment. Fyodor Dostoyevsky. 2006. audio compact disk 49.95 (978-1-4281-0114-2(4)) Recorded Bks.

Crime & Punishment. abr. ed. Fyodor Dostoyevsky. Read by Michael Sheen. 3 CDs. (Running Time: 3 hrs. 45 min.). 1995. audio compact disk 22.98 (978-962-634-009-7(6), NA300912, Naxos AudioBooks) Naxos.

Crime & Punishment. abr. ed. Fyodor Dostoyevsky & Alex Jennings. (Running Time: 5 hrs.). (ENG.). (gr. 12 up). 2005. audio compact disk 16.95 (978-0-14-305814-4(2), PengAudBks) Penguin Grp USA.

Crime & Punishment. unabr. ed. Fyodor Dostoyevsky. Read by Anthony Heald. (Running Time: 20 hrs. 5 mins.). 2007. 105.95 (978-1-4332-0974-1(8)) Blckstn Audio.

Crime & Punishment, unabr. ed. Fyodor Dostoyevsky. Tr. by Constance Garnett. Narrated by George Guidall. 18 cass. (Running Time: 25 hrs. 30 mins.). 1991. 144.00 (978-1-55690-125-6(9), 91317E7) Recorded Bks.
A young man murders a pawn broker & undergoes an intellectual & spiritual crisis.

***Crime & Punishment.** unabr. ed. Fyodor Dostoyevsky. Narrated by Dick Hill. (Running Time: 23 hrs. 30 mins. 0 sec.). (ENG.). 2010. 34.99 (978-1-4001-6603-9(9)); 26.99 (978-1-4001-8603-7(X)); audio compact disk 45.99 (978-1-4001-1603-4(1)); audio compact disk 91.99 (978-1-4001-4603-1(8)) Pub: Tantor Media. Dist(s): IngramPubServ

Crime & Punishment. unabr. ed. Fyodor Dostoyevsky. Read by Anthony Heald. (Running Time: 73800 sec.). (Classic Collection (Blackstone Audio) Ser.). 2009. audio compact disk 29.95 (978-1-4332-0977-2(2)) Blckstn Audio.

Crime & Punishment. unabr. ed. Fyodor Dostoyevsky. Read by Anthony Heald. (Running Time: 73800 sec.). (Classic Collection (Blackstone Audio) Ser.). 2007. audio compact disk 44.95 (978-1-4332-0976-5(4)); audio compact disk & audio compact disk 120.00 (978-1-4332-0975-8(6)) Blckstn Audio.

Crime & Punishment, Pt. A. unabr. collector's ed. Fyodor Dostoyevsky. Read by Walter Zimmerman. 9 cass. (Running Time: 13 hrs. 30 min.). 1983. 72.00 (978-0-7366-3891-3(1), 9120A) Books on Tape.
A student's experimental rebellion includes a senseless murder which teaches him that happiness can only be earned through suffering.

Crime & Punishment, Pt. B. collector's unabr. ed. Fyodor Dostoyevsky. Read by Walter Zimmerman. 8 cass. (Running Time: 12 hrs.). 1983. 64.00 (978-0-7366-3892-0(X), 9120-B) Books on Tape.

Crime & the Crystal. unabr. ed. E. X. Ferrars. Read by Graham Roberts. 5 cass. (Running Time: 7 hrs. 30 mins.). 2001. 49.95 (22926) Pub: Soundings Ltd GBR. Dist(s): Ulverscroft US

Crime Beat: A Decade of Covering Cops & Killers. abr. ed. Michael Connelly. Read by Len Cariou et al. (Running Time: 6 hrs.). (ENG.). 2006. 14.98 (978-1-59483-515-5(2)) Pub: Hachet Audio. Dist(s): HachBkGrp

Crime Beat: A Decade of Covering Cops & Killers. abr. ed. Michael Connelly. Read by Len Cariou et al. (Running Time: 6 hrs.). (ENG.). 2009. 49.98 (978-1-60788-123-0(3)) Pub: Hachet Audio. Dist(s): HachBkGrp

Crime Beat: A Decade of Covering Cops & Killers. unabr. ed. Michael Connelly. 9 cass. (Running Time: 9 hrs.). 2006. 81.00 (978-1-4159-3002-1(3)); audio compact disk 99.00 (978-1-4159-3003-8(1)) Books on Tape.

Crime Classics, collector's ed. Perf. by Lou Merrill. 6 cass. (Running Time: 9 hrs.). 1998. bk. 17.49 (4389) Radio Spirits.
"True crime stories from the records and newspapers of every land from every time." 18 never-before-released episodes.

Crime de Lord Saville. 1 cass. (Running Time: 60 min.). Dramatization. (Maitres du Mystere Ser.). (FRE.). 1996. 11.95 (1835-MA) Olivia & Hill.
Popular radio thriller, interpreted by France's best actors.

Crime de Sylvestre Bonnard, Set. abr. ed. Anatole France. Read by Bernard Merle. 2 cass. (FRE.). 1995. 26.95 (1752-KFP) Olivia & Hill.
An action-packed novel set during the French Revolution.

Crime in America. 1 cass. 10.00 (HV213) Esstee Audios.
What causes fear in the streets & Americans living behind locked doors.

Crime in the Neighborhood. unabr. ed. Suzanne Berne. Narrated by Alyssa Bresnahan. 6 cass. (Running Time: 8 hrs.). 2000. 58.00 (978-0-7887-4456-3(9), 96277E7) Recorded Bks.
In the summer of 1973 Marsha is nine years old. Looking back as an adult, it is a time when her father's abandonment of his family becomes entwined with the arrival of a new neighbor & the death of a boy who lives down the street.

Crime in the Neighborhood. unabr. ed. Suzanne Berne. Read by Alyssa Bresnahan. 6 cass. (Running Time: 8 hrs.). 2000. 81.00 (95958) Recorded Bks.
In the summer of 1973 Marsha is nine. Looking back as an adult, it is a time when her father's abandonment of his family becomes entwined with the arrival of a new neighbor & a death.

Crime in Toronto, Canadian Racism, & Free Trade with the United States. Raymond Samuels. 2006. video 69.00 (978-1-897036-25-9(6)) Agora Pub Consort CAN.

Crime of Galileo. Steve Kellmeyer. 2005. 11.95 (978-0-9767368-6-8(1)) Bridegroom.

Crime Printanier. l.t. ed. J. B. Livingstone. (French Ser.). 1994. bk. 30.99 (978-2-84011-094-1(6)) Pub: UlverLrgPrint GBR. Dist(s): Ulverscroft US

Crime Wave: Reportage & Fiction from the Underside of L. A. James Ellroy. Read by Michael Prichard. 1999. audio compact disk 80.00 (978-0-7366-8043-1(8)) Books on Tape.

Crime Wave: Reportage & Fiction from the Underside of L. A. collector's ed. James Ellroy. Read by Michael Prichard. 8 cass. (Running Time: 12 hrs.). 1999. 64.00 (978-0-7366-4584-3(5), 4963) Books on Tape.
From the scandal sheets of the 1950's to this morning's police blotter, & from his mother's unsolved murder to the slaying of Nicole Brown Simpson, Ellroy investigates true crimes & restores humanity to their victims.

Crime Wave: Reportage & Fiction from the Underside of L. A. unabr. ed. James Ellroy. Read by Michael Prichard. 8 cass. (Running Time: 12 hrs.). 1999. 29.95 (978-0-7366-4479-2(2), 4963) Books on Tape.

***Crime Writer: Unabridged Value-Priced Edition.** Gregg Hurwitz. Narrated by Scott Brick. (Running Time: 10 hrs. 50 mins. 0 sec.). (ENG.). 2010. audio compact disk 14.95 (978-1-60283-995-3(6)) Pub: AudioGO. Dist(s): Perseus Dist

Crime Zero. unabr. ed. Michael Cordy. 10 cass. (Isis Ser.). (J). 2002. 84.95 (978-0-7531-1344-8(9)) Pub: ISIS Lrg Prnt GBR. Dist(s): Ulverscroft US

Crime Zero. unabr. ed. Michael Cordy. Narrated by Paul Hecht. 8 cass. (Running Time: 11 hrs. 45 mins.). 2000. 71.00 (978-1-84197-075-2(1), H1066E7) Recorded Bks.
Criminal psychologist Luke Decker is about to resign from the FBI when he learns about Project Conscience, an attempt to treat criminals by using gene therapy. Thrust together with Kathy Kerr, his old flame & ideological adversary, he finds himself in the midst of a perilous search to uncover the ruthless secrets beneath an even darker project: Crime Zero. Kathy & Luke must put aside their differences to fight a scheme so vast & ruthless that it could change the very evolution of mankind.

Crimen y Castigo. abr. ed. Read by Fabio Camero. Ed. by Fyodor Dostoyevsky. 3 CDs.Tr. of Crime & Punishment. (SPA.). 2001. audio compact disk 17.00 (978-958-9494-49-3(8)) YoYoMusic.

Crimenes Imperceptibles see Oxford Murders

***Crimes Against Liberty: An Indictment of President Barack Obama.** David Limbaugh. Read by Don Leslie. 1 Playaway. 2010. 59.99 (978-1-4417-6207-8(8)) Blckstn Audio.

***Crimes Against Liberty: An Indictment of President Barack Obama.** unabr. ed. David Limbaugh. (Running Time: 8 hrs. 30 mins.). 2010. audio compact disk 76.00 (978-1-4417-6202-3(7)) Blckstn Audio.

***Crimes Against Liberty: An Indictment of President Barack Obama.** unabr. ed. David Limbaugh. Read by Don Leslie. 1 MP3-CD. (Running Time: 8 hrs. 30 mins.). 2010. 29.95 (978-1-4417-6204-7(3)); 54.95 (978-1-4417-6201-6(9)); audio compact disk 29.95 (978-1-4417-6203-0(5)) Blckstn Audio.

***Crimes by Moonlight: Mysteries from the Dark Side.** unabr. ed. Charlaine Harris, Editor. (Running Time: 12 hrs.). 2011. 39.97 (978-1-4558-0437-5(1), 9781455804375, Brinc Audio MP3 Lib); 39.97 (978-1-4558-0439-9(8),

9781455804399, BADLE); 24.99 (978-1-4558-0436-8(3), 9781455804368, Brilliance MP3); 24.99 (978-1-4558-0438-2(X), 9781455804382, BAD); audio compact disk 79.97 (978-1-4558-0435-1(5), 9781455804351, BriAudCD Unabrid); audio compact disk 29.99 (978-1-4558-0434-4(7), 9781455804344, Bril Audio CD Unabri) Brilliance Audio.

Crimes of Jordan Wise. Bill Pronzini. Narrated by Richard Ferrone. 5 cass. (Running Time: 27060 sec.). 2006. 49.95 (978-0-7927-4233-3(8), CSL 961); audio compact disk 64.95 (978-0-7927-4055-1(6), SLD 961) AudioGO.

Crimes of the Heart. unabr. ed. Beth Henley. Perf. by Ray Baker et al. 2 cass. (Running Time: 1 hr. 56 mins.). Dramatization. 1996. 23.95 (978-1-58081-061-6(6), RDP23) L A Theatre.
A deeply touching comedy about three eccentric sisters from a small southern town, which is rocked by scandal when Babe, the youngest, shoots her husband. Babe's "crime of the heart" is the catalyst that draws her sister Meg, an unsuccessful lounge singer, back to Hazelhurst. Mississippi where Babe has taken refuge with spinster sister, Lenny, in the family home. Humor & pathos abound as the sisters unite with an intense young lawyer to save Babe from a murder charge, & overcome their family's painful past.

Criminal Conversation. unabr. ed. Evan Hunter. Read by Michael Kramer. 9 cass. (Running Time: 13 hrs. 30 min.). 1994. 72.00 (978-0-7366-2809-9(6), 3523) Books on Tape.
When a young DA meets a mobster's sensual mistress, his glands start to work on his brain. What do you think wins?.

Criminal Conversations: Victorian Crimes, Social Panic, & Moral Outrage. Judith Rowbotham & Kim Stevenson. 2005. audio compact disk 9.95 (978-0-8142-9043-9(4)) Pub: Ohio St U Pr. Dist(s): Chicago Distribution Ctr

Criminal Damage. unabr. ed. Margaret Yorke. Read by June Barrie. 8 cass. (Running Time: 12 hrs.). 2002. 69.95 (978-0-7540-0759-3(6), CAB 2182) AudioGO.
Daniel and Jennifer had bought a house together and their friends assumed they would eventually marry. Then everything changed. Stephanie stole Daniel from Jennifer. Confused, humiliated, and increasingly angry, Jennifer took to following Stephanie around London. Her obsessive love prompted her towards violent revenge. It would also lead her coming under suspicion by the police, for a crime she did not commit.

Criminal Enforcement in Environmental Laws. 1 cass. 1990. bk. 45.00 (AC-577) PA Bar Inst.

Criminal Enforcement of Environmental Laws. 9 cass. (Running Time: 12 hrs. 30 min.). 1995. 172.50 Set; incl. study guide. (MA05) Am Law Inst.
Advanced course covers the full panoply of policy issues & practical pointers that are important to prosecutors, representatives from the business community, & defense counsel.

Criminal Intentions. unabr. ed. David Williams. Read by Kenneth Knowles. 8 cass. (Running Time: 10 hrs. 35 min.). (Storysound Ser.). (J). 2003. 69.95 (978-1-85903-618-1(X)) Pub: Mgna Lrg Print GBR. Dist(s): Ulverscroft US

Criminal Justice after the O. J. Simpson Case. Alan M. Dershowitz. 1 cass. (Running Time: 1 hr. 18 mins.). 2001. 12.95 Smithson Assocs.

Criminal Justice Today: an Introductory Text for the 21st Century: Standalone CD-ROM. 8th ed. Frank M. Schmalleger. audio compact disk 14.97 (978-0-13-119511-0(5)) PH School.

Criminal Law, 2nd ed. J. Dressler. 5 cass. (Running Time: 7 hr. 12 mins.). (Audio Tape Ser.). 1998. 50.00 (978-1-57793-038-9(X), 28407) Pub: Sum & Substance. Dist(s): West Pub

Criminal Law & Procedure: The Counter Revolution. Charles H. Whitebread. 1987. 115.00 (978-1-55917-088-8(3)) Natl Prac Inst.

Criminal Law Conference, 3rd Annual, The Big Not so Easy (2006) 2006. audio compact disk 130.00 (978-1-56986-344-2(X)) Federal Bar.

Criminal Law Practice: Recent Developments (1992) Read by William McKinstry et al. (Running Time: 3 hrs. 30 min.). 1992. 70.00 Incl. 473p. tape materials. (CR-55238) Cont Ed Bar-CA.
A respected jurist, public defender, district attorney, & defense counsel review the past year's criminal law developments including search & seizure; preliminary examinations; hearsay; discovery; probation revocation; sentencing; defenses; juvenile detention; DUI; evidence; & interpretations of Propositions 8 & 115.

Criminal Law Practice after Proposition One Hundred Fifteen. Read by William McKinstry et al. (Running Time: 3 hrs. 30 min.). 1990. 69.00 Incl. 448p. tape materials. (CR-54172) Cont Ed Bar-CA.

Criminal Law, 2005 ed. (Law School Legends Audio Series) 2005th rev. ed. Charles H. Whitebread, II. (Law School Legends Audio Ser.). 2005. 52.00 (978-0-314-16090-4(6), gilbert); 47.95 (978-0-314-16089-8(2), gilbert) West.

Criminal Mind: Program from the Award Winning Public Radio Series. Hosted by Fred Goodwin. Comment by John Hockenberry. Contrib. by Gary Wells et al. 1 cass. (Running Time: 1 hr.). (Infinite Mind Ser.). 1998. audio compact disk 21.95 (978-1-888064-40-7(4), LCM 15) Lichtenstein Creat.
Murderers, stalkers, child abusers and people who shoot up their workplace - what makes these people act the way they do? With top experts including criminal psychiatrist Dr. Park Dietz, consultant on cases ranging from the Unabomber to Jeffery Dahmer to the Menendez brothers.

Criminal Paradise. unabr. ed. Steven M. Thomas. Read by Patrick G. Lawlor. (Running Time: 32400 sec.). 2008. 29.95 (978-1-4332-0950-5(0)); audio compact disk 29.95 (978-1-4332-0951-2(9)) Blckstn Audio.

Criminal Paradise. unabr. ed. Steven M. Thomas. Read by Patrick G. Lawlor. (Running Time: 32400 sec.). 2008. 59.95 (978-1-4332-0948-2(9)); audio compact disk & audio compact disk 29.95 (978-1-4332-0952-9(7)); audio compact disk & audio compact disk 55.00 (978-1-4332-0949-9(7)) Blckstn Audio.

Criminal Procedure, 2nd ed. Joshua Dressler. 5 cass. (Running Time: 7 hrs. 30 min.). (Audio Tape Ser.). 50.00 (978-1-57793-039-6(8), 28409) Pub: Sum & Substance. Dist(s): West Pub

***Criminal Procedure.** 5th rev. ed. Joshua Dressler. (Sum & Substance Ser.). 2010. audio compact disk 74.00 (978-0-314-26692-7(5), West Lglwrks); audio compact disk 74.00 (978-0-314-26693-4(3), West Lglwrks) West.

Criminal Procedure, 2005 ed. (Law School Legends Audio Series) 2005th rev. ed. Charles H. Whitebread, II. (Law School Legends Audio Ser.). 2005. 52.00 (978-0-314-16092-8(2), gilbert); 47.95 (978-0-314-16091-1(4), gilbert) West.

Criminal Trial Evidence. 1997. bk. 99.00 (ACS-1305) PA Bar Inst.
In the courtroom, you must react quickly & confidently. In order to do so, a good grasp of the rules of evidence is needed. This is specially designed for anyone who practices criminal law. Learn how to handle key points of Pennsylvania evidence arising in criminal cases.

Criminal Trial Practice. Contrib. by Richard L. Friedman et al. (Running Time: 4 hrs.). 1985. 70.00 incl. program handbook. NJ Inst CLE.
Analysis including significant recent developments, initial meeting with client, retainer agreement & fees, pre-indictment & grand jury procedures, pre-trial motions, voir dire.

Criminalization of Christianity: Listen to This Before it Becomes Illegal! Janet L. Folger. 2005. audio compact disk 27.99 (978-1-58926-926-2(8)) Oasis Audio.

Criminalization of Christianity: Listen to This Before it Becomes Illegal! unabr. ed. Janet L. Folger. Narrated by Janet L. Folger. (ENG.). 2005. 19.59 (978-1-60814-166-1(7)) Oasis Audio.

Criminology Lecture Series. Terance D. Miethe. (C). 2009. audio compact disk (978-1-61623-936-7(0)) Indep Pub IL.

Crimson Cavalier. Mary Andrea Clarke. 2009. 61.95 (978-1-4079-0358-3(6)); audio compact disk 79.95 (978-1-4079-0359-0(4)) Pub: Soundings Ltd GBR. Dist(s): Ulverscroft US

Crimson Empire I. abr. unabr. ed. Mike Richardson et al. 2 CDs. (Running Time: 2 hrs.). Dramatization. (ENG.). 1999. audio compact disk 25.95 (978-1-56511-309-1(8), 1565113098) Pub: HighBridge. Dist(s): Workman Pub

Crimson Joy. unabr. collector's ed. Robert B. Parker. Read by Michael Prichard. 5 cass. (Running Time: 5 hrs.). (Spenser Ser.). 1990. 40.00 (978-0-7366-1758-1(2), 2597) Books on Tape.
A serial killer is on the loose in Beantown & the cops can't catch him. But when the killer leaves his red rose calling card for Spenser's own Susan Silverman, he gets all the attention he & Hawk can give. Spenser plays against time while he tracks the Red Rose Killer from Boston's "combat zone" to the suburbs. His trap is both daring & brave, & gives the story a satisfying climax.

Crimson Masquerade. unabr. ed. Loretta Jackson & Vickie Britton. Read by Stephanie Brush. 8 cass. (Running Time: 9 hrs. 30 min.). (Ardis Cole Ser.). 2001. 49.95 (978-1-55686-941-9(X)) Books in Motion.
Archaeologist Ardis Cole is called to China in search of a Han dynasty cave tomb. But the past meets present when a centuries old "crime of passion" is eerily replayed on the research team.

Crimson Portrait. unabr. ed. Jody Shields. Narrated by Josephine Bailey. (Running Time: 9 hrs. 0 mins. 0 sec.). (ENG.). 2007. audio compact disk 34.99 (978-1-4001-0338-6(X)); audio compact disk 69.99 (978-1-4001-3338-3(6)); audio compact disk 24.99 (978-1-4001-5338-1(7)) Pub: Tantor Media. Dist(s): IngramPubServ

Crimson Ramblers of the World, Farewell. unabr. ed. Jessamyn West. Read by Roses Prichard. 6 cass. (Running Time: 9 hrs.). Incl. Child of the Century. 1945. (1210); Day of the Hawk. 1945. (1210); Hunting for Hoot Owls. 1945. (1210); Night Piece for Julia. 1945. (1210); 1980. 48.00 (978-0-7366-0212-9(7), 1210) Books on Tape.
Tragedy, joy, suspense & romance in this fine collection of short stories.

***Crimson Rooms: A Novel.** unabr. ed. Katharine McMahon. Narrated by Josephine Bailey. 2 MP3-CDs. (Running Time: 14 hrs. 30 mins. 0 sec.). 2010. 29.99 (978-1-4001-6657-2(8)); 20.99 (978-1-4001-8657-0(9)); audio compact disk 39.99 (978-1-4001-1657-7(0)); audio compact disk 79.99 (978-1-4001-4657-4(7)) Pub: Tantor Media. Dist(s): IngramPubServ

Crimson Tide, Set. abr. ed. Richard P. Henrick. Read by George Dzundza. Contrib. by Michael Schiffer. 2 cass. (Running Time: 3 hrs.). 1995. 17.00 (978-1-56876-038-4(8), 392968) Soundlines Ent.
The cold war has ended but the weapons remain & the unthinkable is once again a reality when a mad man in Russia takes control of a nuclear command post & prepares to fire on the U.S. The USS Alabama is commissioned to the front line, this tactical fully equipped nuclear submarine is the last defense. Headed by a forty year veteran & his new XO, Hunter, when the Alabama receives orders to release its nuclear weapons, the crew scrambles to action. When they are attacked by another sub, & lose contact with command Hunter questions the orders & the crew takes sides, with a rebellion under water.

Crimsoned Prairie. unabr. collector's ed. S. L. A. Marshall. Read by Michael Prichard. 6 cass. (Running Time: 9 hrs.). 1979. 48.00 (978-0-7366-0175-7(9), 1177) Books on Tape.
Story of the Indian wars on the Great Plains told by one of America's foremost writers on military affairs. The long war between America's neglected post-Civil War army and the Sioux, Cheyenne and other Plains Indians has been covered in many books, but this is the first to provide a thorough-going analysis of military tactics.

Cringe: The Stories of Opie & Anthony. abr. ed. Opie and Anthony. Read by Opie and Anthony. 2010. 17.95 (978-0-7435-6095-5(7)) Pub: S&S Audio. Dist(s): S and S Inc

Cripple Creek Dulcimer. 1999. audio compact disk 15.98 (978-0-7866-5225-9(X)) Mel Bay.

Crisantemo. Kevin Henkes. 1 cass. (Running Time: 10 min.).Tr. of Chrysanthemum. (SPA.). (J). pap. bk. 12.95; pap. bk. 32.75 Weston Woods.
A little mouse thinks her name is absolutely perfect until she starts school & all the kids make fun of her - except for Mrs. Twinkle, the music teacher, who thinks Chrysanthemum's name is absolutely perfect, too!.

Crisantemo. unabr. ed. Narrated by Meryl Streep. 1 cass. (SPA.). (J). (ps-2). 1998. 8.95 Spanish. (978-0-7882-0125-7(5), RAC369SP) Weston Woods.
A little mouse thinks her name is perfect until kids make fun - except for Mrs. Twinkle, music teacher, who thinks Chrysanthemum's name is perfect too.

Crises & Renewal in Clergy. Canice Connors. 2 cass. (Running Time: 2 hrs. 11 min.). 1997. 18.95 Set. (TAH378) St Pauls Alba.
Fr. Connors, identifies some of the contemporary issues facing the priesthood & offers his suffestions toward dealing with them in a pastoral way. Excellent material for a personal retreat or reflection.

Crisis. 1 cass. 12.95 Aquarius Prods.
A crisis can be like a baby's cry, coming at inconvenient times & often in the middle of the night. Offers comfort & reassurance at those times when outside help is not available, serving as an adjunct to therapy.

Crisis. Robin Cook. Read by George Guidall. (Running Time: 14 hrs.). No. 6. (ENG.). (gr. 8). 2007. audio compact disk 24.95 (978-0-14-314224-9(0), PengAudBks) Penguin Grp USA.

Crisis. Janalea Hoffman. 1 cass. (Running Time: 45 min.). 1984. 9.95 (978-1-886051-00-3(3)) Rhythmic Med.
Guided imagery & music used for therapeutic purposes.

Crisis. unabr. ed. Robin Cook. Read by George Guidall. 12 cass. (Running Time: 14 hrs. 15 mins.). (Jack Stapleton Ser.: No. 6). 2006. 82.75 (978-1-4281-0197-5(7)); audio compact disk 119.75 (978-1-4281-0199-9(3)) Recorded Bks.
In Crisis, Cook delivers a taut thriller that doesn't let up until its breathtaking conclusion. When medical examiner Jack Stapleton suggests the body at the heart of a malpractice suit be exhumed, startling evidence comes to light - and there are those who will stop at nothing to keep this information buried.

Crisis, Set. Winston Churchill. Read by Flo Gibson. 11 cass. (Running Time: 1 hr. 30 min. per cass.). (gr. 10 up). 1988. 34.95 (978-1-55685-127-8(8)) Audio Bk Con.
The American author's historical novel depicts the Civil War & romance between Stephen Brice, a New Englander, & Virginia Carvel the daughter of a Southern Colonel.

Crisis & Hope: Theirs & Ours. Noam Chomsky. (Running Time: 1 hr. 0 mins. 0 sec.). (PM Audio Ser.). (ENG.). 2010. audio compact disk 14.95 (978-1-60486-211-9(4)) Pub: Pm Pre. Dist(s): IPG Chicago

Crisis & Leviathan. Robert Higgs. 1 cass. (Running Time: 60 min.). 1988. 9.95 (978-0-945999-09-6(7)) Independent Inst.
Government's Explosive Growth During the 20th Century Has Resulted Not from Necessity but As the Result of Special Interests' Use of Alleged National Emergencies to Extend Government Power over Society. Such Periods Have Predominantly Involved Wars & Panics.

Crisis at the Bar. unabr. ed. Jethro Leiberman & Herman B. Glaser. 1 cass. (Running Time: 56 min.). 12.95 (40340) J Norton Pubs.

Crisis Communications: Capitol Learning Audio Course. Bill Noxon. Prod. by TheCapitol.Net. (ENG.). 2008. 47.00 (978-1-58733-052-0(0)) TheCapitol.

Crisis Communications: Hoping That It Will Never Happen, but Glad You Planned for It. Ed. by TheCapitol.Net. 2005. audio compact disk 107.00 (978-1-58733-024-7(5)) TheCapitol.

Crisis Counselor. abr. ed. Jeffrey R. Caponigro. 4 cass. (Running Time: 5 hrs.). 1999. 24.95 (978-0-9659606-1-8(7)) Barker Business Bks.
All businesses must learn to protect themselves from situations that can turn into crises.

***Crisis Economics: A Crash Course in the Future of Finance.** unabr. ed. Nouriel Roubini & Stephen Mihm. Contrib. by L. J. Ganser. (Running Time: 14 hrs.). (ENG.). 2010. audio compact disk 39.95 (978-0-14-242771-2(3), PengAudBks) Penguin Grp USA.

Crisis Four. Andy McNab. Narrated by Steven Crossley. 11 cass. (Running Time: 15 hrs. 45 mins.). 2001. 99.00 (978-0-7887-4351-1(1), 96304E7); audio compact disk 124.00 (978-0-7887-5160-8(3), C1323E7) Recorded Bks.
Andy Stone, highly trained by SAS to be methodical & ruthless, now works as a secret agent in "deniable" operations. His current assignment is to hunt down & kill Sarah, the only woman he has ever cared for. In order to fulfill his mission he first has to help her escape. Fleeing with Sarah, Nick is headed for a confrontation beyond anything he could have imagined.

Crisis Four. unabr. ed. Andy McNab. Read by Clive Mantle. 12 cass. (Running Time: 18 hrs.). 2000. 96.95 (978-0-7540-0528-5(3), CAB 1951) Pub: Chivers Audio Bks GBR. Dist(s): AudioGO
Nick Stone, ex-SAS, now working for British Intelligence, is tough, resourceful & ruthless. Sarah is beautiful, intelligent, cunning - the only woman that Stone has ever let under his guard. And now he's been sent to hunt her down.

Crisis in Contemporary Catechetics. Michael Wrenn. 1 cass. 1992. 2.50 (978-1-56036-047-6(X)) AMI Pr.

Crisis in Culture. George Rutler. Read by George Rutler. 6 cass. 29.95 Set. (5506-C) Ignatius Pr.
Thirteen-part series on how the present day crisis in the Church & the crisis in society are actually one in the same. Shows how the answer to the present crisis in our culture can only be found if man returns to God.

Crisis in Education: Stress & Burnout in the American Teacher. Barry A. Farber. Frwd. by P. Michael Timpane. (Education-Higher Education Ser.). 1991. bk. 38.45 (978-1-55542-271-4(3), Jossey-Bass) Wiley US.

Crisis in Ministry. Carroll Wise. 1986. 10.80 (0104A) Assn Prof Chaplains.

Crisis in Ourselves. J. Krishnamurti. 1 cass. (Running Time: 1 hr.). (Ojai Public Talks - 1982 Ser.: No. 2). 8.50 (AJT822) Krishnamurti.
In the idyllic setting of the oak grove in Ojai, California, Krishnamurti began giving talks in 1922. Over the years, hundreds of thousands of people have heard Krishnamurti explore every aspect of our lives, his language & expression constantly changing, as he strove to communicate to each successive generation those profound truths which he had come upon, & which he maintained were accessible to all.

Crisis Intervention Techniques for Spontaneous Psi Experiences. Cynthea Siegel. 1 cass. 9.00 (A0352-88) Sound Photosyn.
From the 1986 ICSS, with Brala, Waller, & Palmer.

Crisis Management: Be Prepared. 1 cass. (America's Supermarket Showcase '96 Ser.). 1996. 11.00 (NGA96-031) Sound Images.

Crisis of Action in Nineteenth-Century English Literature. Stefanie Markovits. 2006. audio compact disk 9.95 (978-0-8142-9118-4(X)) Pub: Ohio St U Pr. Dist(s): Chicago Distribution Ctr

Crisis of Democracy. Bill Moyers. 1 cass. (World of Ideas Ser.: Vol. 2). 1990. 10.95 (978-1-56176-146-3(X)) Mystic Fire.
Conversations with noted Americans examining Americans' political & economic ideals (from the PBS series).

Crisis of Islam: Holy War & Unholy Terror. unabr. ed. Bernard Lewis. Read by Bernard Lewis. 3 cass. (Running Time: 3 hrs. 30 mins.). (J). 2003. 24.00 (978-0-7366-9068-3(9)) Books on Tape.

Crisis of Perception. Fritjof Capra. 1 cass. 9.00 (A0490-89) Sound Photosyn.
The best, most inspiring talk we have heard from Fritjof. A must for friends of the earth.

Crisis of Religion. unabr. ed. Frederic Spiegelberg. 3 cass. (Running Time: 3 hrs. 52 min.). 1981. 26.00 Set. (08802) Big Sur Tapes.
Throughout his extensive travels, Spiegelberg tells us that he found the "spirit of religion is alive" but everything else about religion "is only talking in the realm of shadow".

Crisis on Doona. Anne McCaffrey. Contrib. by Jody Lynn Nye. 3 CDs. (Running Time: 3 hrs.). (Doona Ser.). audio compact disk 11.99 (978-1-57815-553-8(3), 1197CD3, Media Bks Audio) Media Bks NJ.
The futuristic planet of Doona is the setting of this novel about cohabitation between species and what some will do to destroy it.

Crisis on Doona. abr. ed. Anne McCaffrey. Contrib. by Jody Lynn Nye. 2 cass. (Running Time: 3 hrs.). (Doona Ser.). 2002. 7.95 (978-1-57815-297-1(6), 1197, Media Bks Audio) Media Bks NJ.

Crisis on Infinite Earths, Pt. 1. unabr. ed. Marv Wolfman. Read by Christopher Graybill & Richard Rohan. 6 CDs. (Running Time: 7 hrs.). 2009. audio compact disk 19.99 (978-1-59950-597-8(5)) GraphicAudio.

Crisis Preparation & Management Essentials: HR Executive Answers. (ENG.). 2009. audio compact disk 497.00 (978-1-60029-000-8(0)) M Lee Smith.

Crispin: At the Edge of the World. Avi. Read by Ron Keith. 5. (Running Time: 6 hrs.). 2006. 39.75 (978-1-4281-1792-1(X)); audio compact disk 51.75 (978-1-4281-1797-6(0)) Recorded Bks.

Crispin: The Cross of Lead. Avi. Read by Ron Keith. 6 CDs. (J). (gr. 3-6). 2003. audio compact disk 58.00 (978-1-4025-4553-5(3)) Recorded Bks.

Crispin: The Cross of Lead. unabr. ed. Avi. Narrated by Ron Keith. 5 pieces. (Running Time: 6 hrs. 15 mins.). (gr. 5 up). 2002. 47.00 (978-1-4025-2202-4(9)) Recorded Bks.

***Criss Cross.** unabr. ed. Lynne Rae Perkins. Read by Danielle Ferland. (ENG.). 2006. (978-0-06-123214-5(9), Harper Audio); (978-0-06-123215-2(7), Harper Audio) HarperCollins Pubs.

Criss Cross. unabr. ed. Lynne Rae Perkins. Read by Danielle Ferland. 5 CDs. (Running Time: 19800 sec.). (J). (gr. 5-9). 2006. audio compact disk 25.95 (978-0-06-116119-3(5), HarperChildAud) HarperCollins Pubs.

Criss Cross. unabr. ed. Lynne Rae Perkins. Read by Danielle Ferland. 5 CDs. (Running Time: 5 hrs. 30 mins.). 2006. audio compact disk 84.75

(978-1-4193-9450-8(9), C3731); 59.75 (978-1-4193-9445-4(2), 98376) Recorded Bks.

Fourteen year-old Debbie wishes on her necklace that something will happen to her - something exciting, and soon. At the same time, in another area of town, Hector stares at his reflection in the mirror and wonders about his potential. As she waits, Debbie spends her summer helping elderly Mrs. Bruning maintain her house. Hector learns how to play the guitar. And the two, along with their close friends feel the subtle push and pull of blooming love, new opportunities and changes in the order of the universe as the necklace tries to work its magic. Lynne Rae Perkins has earned a Newbery Medal and starred reviews from both School Library Journal and Booklist for this poignant and humorous story about the barely perceptible changes involved in the beginning of young adulthood. Young listeners will feel spellbound by Danielle Ferland's eloquent narration.

Cristianismo Contagioso. 2003. audio compact disk 32.50 (978-1-57972-525-9(2)) Insight Living.

Cristianismo Firme. 2006. audio compact disk 34.00 (978-1-57972-707-9(7)) Insight Living.

***Cristianismo Firme: Steadfast Christianity.** Charles R. Swindoll. 2009. audio compact disk 27.00 (978-1-57972-860-1(X)) Insight Living.

Cristo Frente a Las Encrucijadas. 2004. audio compact disk 48.00 (978-1-57972-596-9(1)) Insight Living.

***Cristo salva, sana y libera a la Familia.** Hombre Nuevo.Tr. of Christ saves, heals & frees the Family. (SPA.). 2010. 24.95 (978-0-9825744-5-4(2)) Hombre Nuevo.

Criticism & Discipline Skills for Managers. PUEI. 2008. audio compact disk 199.00 (978-1-934147-84-9(2), CareerTrack) P Univ E Inc.

Critic: The Second of Enzo Files. unabr. ed. Peter May. Read by James Adams. (Running Time: 37800 sec.). 2007. 54.95 (978-1-4332-1132-4(7)); audio compact disk 29.95 (978-1-4332-1134-8(3)); audio compact disk 55.00 (978-1-4332-1133-1(5)) Blckstn Audio.

Critical. Robin Cook. Read by George Guidall. (Running Time: 13 hrs.). No. 7. (ENG.). (gr. 8). 2007. audio compact disk 39.95 (978-0-14-314199-0(6), PengAudBks) Penguin Grp USA.

Critical. unabr. ed. Robin Cook. Read by George Guidall. 12 CDs. (Running Time: 14 hrs.). (Jack Stapleton Ser.: No. 7). 2007. audio compact disk 123.75 (978-1-4281-5327-1(6)); 98.75 (978-1-4281-5325-7(X)) Recorded Bks.

In Critical, successful doctor and entrepreneur Angela Dawson has a controlling stake in Angels Healthcare, the highly successful medical company she founded. But something unexpected and deeply troubling is happening at her three New York specialty hospitals - drug-resistant staph infections are on the rise, killing patients.

Critical & Historical Essays see Cambridge Treasury of English Prose: Austen to Bronte

Critical Care. collector's ed. Richard Dooling. Read by John Edwardson. 7 cass. (Running Time: 10 hrs. 30 min.). 2000. 56.00 (978-0-7366-5443-2(7)) Books on Tape.

When Dr. Ernst stands in the center of the ICU unit, surrounded on all sides by computer terminals & cardiac monitors, he imagines he is on the bridge of the starship Enterprise, a guardian of unknown galaxies. But by 3:00 a.m. the space fantasy has dissipated into the air like so much ether, leaving behind only a profound & desperate desire for sleep. But the needs of Ernst's patients are as endless as his round of duty. Their lives are mere blips on the VDT console, their last bids for fading life sound as alarm bells in the night.

Critical Care. unabr. ed. Richard Dooling. Narrated by Richard Ferrone. 8 cass. (Running Time: 11 hrs. 30 mins.). 1994. 70.00 (978-1-55690-665-7(X), 92135E7) Recorded Bks.

Critical Communication: Correcting Without Conflict. Bruce A. Baldwin. Read by Bruce A. Baldwin. (Running Time: 60 min.). 1983. 8.95 (978-0-933583-08-5(7), PDC836) Direction Dynamics.

Discusses how to develop skills to give negative feedback with positive results.

Critical Conditions. Stephen White. Read by Michael Kramer. (Dr. Alan Gregory Ser.). 1998. audio compact disk 80.00 (978-0-7366-8039-4(X)) Books on Tape.

Critical Conditions. abr. ed. Stephen White. Read by Dick Hill. (Running Time: 6 hrs.). (Dr. Alan Gregory Ser.). 2009. audio compact disk 26.99 (978-1-4233-9467-9(4), 9781423394679, BACD) Brilliance Audio.

Critical Conditions. abr. ed. Stephen White. Read by Dick Hill. (Running Time: 6 hrs.). (Dr. Alan Gregory Ser.). 2010. audio compact disk 14.99 (978-1-4233-9468-6(2), 9781423394686, BCD Value Price) Brilliance Audio.

Critical Conditions. unabr. ed. Stephen White. Read by Michael Kramer. 8 cass. (Running Time: 12 hrs.). (Dr. Alan Gregory Ser.). 1998. 64.00 (978-0-7366-4184-5(X), 4682) Books on Tape.

Merritt Strait, a beautiful fifteen-year-old, lies in a hospital, survivor of a suicide attempt. Gregory, clinical psychologist & amateur sleuth, befriends the girl. He learns that Merritt's stepsister has a potentially fatal heart condition that might be cured by an experimental treatment, a treatment denied by the Straits' health care system. When an executive of that very HMO is murdered & a gun & bloody clothes are found in Merritt's bedroom, she becomes a prime suspect. But Gregory discovers other individuals with motives for murder & learns just how far people will go for revenge & love.

Critical Conditions. unabr. ed. Stephen White. Read by Dick Hill. (Running Time: 12 hrs.). (Dr. Alan Gregory Ser.). 2009. 24.99 (978-1-4233-9463-1(1), 9781423394631, Brilliance MP3); 39.97 (978-1-4233-9464-8(X), 9781423394648, Brlnc Audio MP3 Lib); 24.99 (978-1-4233-9465-5(8), 9781423394655, BAD); 39.97 (978-1-4233-9466-2(6), 9781423394662, BADLE); audio compact disk 36.99 (978-1-4233-9461-7(5), 9781423394617, Bril Audio CD Unabri); audio compact disk 97.97 (978-1-4233-9462-4(3), 9781423394624, BriAudCD Unabrid) Brilliance Audio.

Critical Decisions in Trauma Care. Moderated by David S. Mulder. (Postgraduate Courses Ser.). 1986. 115.00 (8615(C86-PG5)) Am Coll Surgeons.

Provides knowledge on several controversial issues in the care of the patient with multi-system injuries. 12 hours CME credit.

Critical Family Issues. Larry Burkett. 1988. 5.00 (978-1-56427-087-0(4)) Crown Fin Min Inc.

Critical Incident Stress: What, Why, & How for Pastoral Involvement. 1 cass. (Care Cassettes Ser.: Vol. 22, No. 7). 1995. 10.80 Assn Prof Chaplains.

Critical Incidents: Compassion in Crisis. 2007. audio compact disk 17.99 (978-1-934570-07-4(9)) Lanphier Pr.

Critical Issues in American Philanthropy: Strengthening Theory & Practice. Jon Van Til et al. (Nonprofit Sector-Public Administration Ser.). 1990. bk. 45.00 (978-1-55542-278-3(0), Jossey-Bass) Wiley US.

Critical Issues in Educating African American Youths. Jawanza Kunjufu. 1 cass. (Running Time: 60 mins.). 1999. 5.95 (AT23) African Am Imag.

Critical Judgment. unabr. ed. Michael Palmer. Read by Michael Kramer. 10 cass. (Running Time: 15 hrs.). 1997. 80.00 (978-0-913369-35-7(7), 4206) Books on Tape.

A mysterious set of symptoms has a young medical star making dangerous inquiries into Colstar manufacturing. Tense emergency room drama.

Critical Mass. abr. ed. David Hagberg. Read by Bruce Watson. 4 vols. (Kirk McGarvey Ser.). 2003. (978-1-58807-678-6(4)) Am Pubng Inc.

Critical Mass, unabr. ed. Steve Martini. Narrated by Frank Muller. 9 cass. (Running Time: 12 hrs. 30 mins.). 1999. 80.00 (978-0-7887-2481-7(9), 95556E7) Recorded Bks.

When arms inspector Gideon Van Ry discovers two Russian nuclear devices are missing, his investigation points to a renegade militia group. Suddenly he finds himself in a frantic struggle to prevent a horrifying disaster.

Critical Mass. unabr. ed. Whitley Strieber. Narrated by Alan Sklar. (Running Time: 12 hrs. 30 mins. 0 sec.). (ENG.). 2009. audio compact disk 34.99 (978-1-4001-1157-2(9)); audio compact disk 24.99 (978-1-4001-6157-7(6)); audio compact disk 69.99 (978-1-4001-4157-9(5)) Pub: Tantor Media. Dist(s): IngramPubServ

Critical Path. R. Buckminster Fuller. 2 cass. (Running Time: 2 hrs. 54 min.). 1982. 18.00 (00701) Big Sur Tapes.

The opening address at a conference on health & wellness & a workable world, on the Island of Maui in 1982.

Critical Response to Private Revelation. Benedict J. Groeschel. 1 cass. (Running Time: 1 hr. 17 min.). 1995. 8.95 (TAH338) Alba Hse Comns.

Crucial pastoral information for priests or other clergy who may be in a position to receive reports of private revelation, or for anyone who wishes to reach informed conclusions in light of faith & church teachings.

Critically Ashamed. Contrib. by FM Static. 2006. audio compact disk 16.99 (978-5-558-33301-5(4)) Tooth & Nail.

Criticism. unabr. ed. Jennifer James. Read by Jennifer James. 1 cass. (Running Time: 40 min.). 1985. 9.95 (978-0-915423-23-1(5)) Jennifer J.

We all get criticism. When someone puts you down, it can ruin a day or a lifetime. Learn who is most likely to criticize & how to make them stop.

Criticism & Discipline for Managers & Supervisors. PUEI. 2007. audio compact disk 199.00 (978-1-934147-11-5(7), CareerTrack); audio compact disk 199.00 (978-1-934147-52-8(4), CareerTrack) P Univ E Inc.

Criticism & Reviewing. SERCON Panel. 1 cass. 9.00 (A0122-87) Sound Photosyn.

At the SF writers convention featuring Norman Spinrad, Keller, Murphy, Preuss, & Chow.

Criticism & You Are Not Your Drama. Marianne Williamson. Read by Marianne Williamson. 1 cass. (Running Time: 90 mins.). (Lectures on a Course in Miracles). 1999. 10.00 (978-1-56170-182-7(3), M710) Hay House.

Criticoses, Pt. B. (23333) J Norton Pubs.

Critique of Modern Youth Ministry AudioBook. Christopher Schlect. Read by Aaron Wells. 7 CDs. (ENG.). 2007. audio compact disk 10.00 (978-1-59128-243-3(8)) Canon Pr ID.

Critique of Pure Reason see Postive Philosophy

Crito see Apology for Socrates

Critter County: Celebrating the Dream. Paula Bussard & Christine Wyrtzen. 1 cass. (50-Day Spiritual Adventure Ser.). (J). (ps-2). 1993. 4.99 (978-1-879050-37-2(4)) Chapel of Air.

26 Bible verses set to music.

Critter County Clubhouse: Scripture Memory Tape. Christine Wyrtzen & Paula Bussard. Read by Christine Wyrtzen. 1 cass. (50-Day Spiritual Adventure Ser.). (J). (gr. k-2). 1996. 6.00 (978-1-57849-004-2(9)) Chapel of Air.

Children's scripture memory verses put to music.

Critter County Power Buddies: Scripture Memory Tape. Christine Wyrtzen & Paula Bussard. Read by Christine Wyrtzen. 1 cass. (Nineteen Ninety-Eight Fifty-Day Spiritual Adventure Ser.). (J). (gr. k-2). 1997. 6.00 (978-1-57849-043-1(X)) Mainstay Church.

Critter County Scripture Memory Tape. Paula Bussard. 1 cass. (Running Time: 60 min.). (Fifty Day Spiritual Adventure 1999 Ser.). (J). 1998. 7.00 (978-1-57849-110-0(X)) Mainstay Church.

Critters & Company. 1 CD. (Running Time: 30 min.). (J). 2005. audio compact disk 14.95 (978-0-9765887-1-9(4)) S Edu Res LLC.

CRM, Sales & Marketing Leadership Conference - the World's Top CEOs on Best Practices & Strategies for Success. ReedLogic. 1. (Running Time: 4 hrs). 2005. audio compact disk 299.95 (978-1-59701-051-1(0)) Aspatore Bks.

*The CRM, Sales & Marketing Leadership Conference features ten speeches totaling approximately four hours of authoritative, insider?s perspectives on the best practices of the world?s top CRM, sales & marketing software providers. Featuring executives representing some of the industry?s most successful companies, this conference provides a broad yet comprehensive overview of implementing dynamic strategies to provide clients with superior CRM, sales and marketing solutions. Each speaker shares their insight for successful strategies and industry expertise in a format similar to a radio address, with graphics displayed in the background - a speech within a presentation. Simply insert the CD-ROM into your computer, sit back, and watch and learn from the top professionals in the field as they discuss their specific processes for working with clients and best practices for ensuring success. The breadth of perspectives presented enable attendees to get inside some of the great minds of the CRM world without leaving the office. The Conference has been produced on CD-ROM and can be viewed in PowerPoint by any PC-based computer.The conference features presentations and speeches by:*Mike Adams, President and CEO: Arial Software - ?Authenticity?*Gene Austin, CEO: Convio, Inc. - ?Elevate the Internet?*John Bailye, CEO: Dendrite, Inc. - ?Know Your Customer?*Arturo Coto, CEO: Inquisite, Inc. - ?Listen and Understand?*Scott Dorsey, Co-Founder and President: ExactTarget - ?On-Demand Software?*Keith Eades, Chairman and Senior Managing Partner: SPI - ?The Six Factors?*Stephen Gold, President and CEO: Azerity - ?Be Proactive?*Lauren Goldstein, Director of Account Services and Denise Barnes, COO: Babcock And Jenkins - ?One To One?*Robert LoCascio, CEO and Chairman: LivePerson - ?Not Just Content?*Robert Rappaport, President and CEO: Conversive, Inc. - ?Listen to the Customer?.In This CD You Will Learn: *How to generate growing profits and revenues for your company*The 5 most important things to know about CRM, sales and marketing software*The most useful resources for achieving success in the industry*Where the industry is heading in the next five to ten years and how to prepare for the changes*Due diligence items necessary for choosing the right software provider for your company.*

***Cro-Magnon: How the Ice Age Gave Birth to the First Modern Humans.** unabr. ed. Brian Fagan. Narrated by James Langton. (Running Time: 10 hrs. 0 mins.). 2010. 34.99 (978-1-4001-9594-7(2)); 24.99 (978-1-4001-6594-0(6)); 16.99 (978-1-4001-8594-8(7)); audio compact disk 69.99 (978-1-4001-4594-2(5)); audio compact disk 34.99 (978-1-4001-1594-5(9)) Pub: Tantor Media. Dist(s): IngramPubServ

Croaked. unabr. ed. Morris Gleitzman & Paul Jennings. Read by Stig Wemyss & Kate Hosking. 2 CDs. (Running Time: 1 hr. 23 mins.). (Wicked! Ser.: Bk. 3). (J). audio compact disk 24.00 (978-1-74093-425-1(3)) Bolinda Pubng AUS.

Croaked. unabr. ed. Morris Gleitzman & Paul Jennings. (Running Time: 1 hr. 23 mins.). (Wicked! Ser.: Bk. 3). (J). 2001. 18.00 (978-1-74030-465-8(9)) Pub: Bolinda Pubng AUS. Dist(s): Bolinda Pub Inc

Croatian. Ed. by Berlitz Publishing. (In 60 MINUTES Ser.). 2008. audio compact disk 9.95 (978-981-268-398-4(4)) Pub: APA Pubns Serv SGP. Dist(s): Langenscheidt

Croatian: Learn to Speak & Understand Croatian with Pimsleur Language Programs. Pimsleur Staff. 5 cass. (Running Time: 500 hrs. 0 mins. NaN sec.). (Pimsleur Language Program Ser.). (ENG.). 1999. 95.00 (978-0-671-58189-3(9), Pimsleur) Pub: S&S Audio. Dist(s): S and S Inc

SPEAK CROATIAN TO LEARN CROATIAN The Pimsleur Method will have you speaking Croatian in just a few short, easy-to-use lessons. Learn at your own pace, comfortably and conveniently. No books to study. No memorization drills. LEARN CROATIAN AS YOU LEARNED ENGLISH You learned English by listening. With Pimsleur, you listen to learn Croatian. This Language Program was developed by renowned memory expert, Dr. Paul Pimsleur. His research led him to the realization that the most important use of memory is in language learning. Based on this, Dr. Pimsleur designed a learning program that works for any language. The Pimsleur Language Program is an integrated system which immerses you in the language, encouraging you to hear, understand and use the language all at the same time. Now you can take advantage of Dr. Pimsleur's research. At the completion of these eight lessons you will comfortably understand and speak at a beginner level.

Croatian: Learn to Speak & Understand Croatian with Pimsleur Language Programs. Pimsleur Staff. . (Running Time: 500 hrs. 0 mins. NaN sec.). (Compact Ser.). (KOR & ENG.). 2003. audio compact disk 115.00 (978-0-7435-2871-9(9), Pimsleur) Pub: S&S Audio. Dist(s): S and S Inc

Listen to learn Croatian. The Pimsleur Language Program is an integrated system which immerses you in the language, encouraging you to hear, understand and use the language all at the same timeigned program that works for any language.

Croatian: Learn to Speak & Understand Croatian with Pimsleur Language Programs. abr. ed. Pimsleur. Created by Pimsleur. 5 CDs. (Running Time: 50 hrs. 0 mins. 0 sec.). (Compact Ser.). (CRO & ENG.). 2005. audio compact disk 49.95 (978-0-7435-5054-3(4), Audioworks) Pub: S&S Audio. Dist(s): S and S Inc

Croatian: Learn to Speak & Understand Croatian with Pimsleur Language Programs. unabr. ed. Pimsleur. (Running Time: 5 hrs. 0 mins. 0 sec.). (Basic Ser.). (ENG.). 2009. audio compact disk 24.95 (978-0-7435-6206-5(2), Pimsleur); audio compact disk 49.95 (978-0-7435-6205-8(4), Pimsleur); audio compact disk 345.00 (978-0-7435-6204-1(6), Pimsleur) Pub: S&S Audio. Dist(s): S and S Inc

Croatian: World Citizen Edition. unabr. ed. 10 CDs. (Running Time: 10 hrs.). 2003. audio compact disk 115.00 (978-0-7887-9770-5(0)); 95.00 (978-0-7887-9703-3(4)) Recorded Bks.

Dr. Paul Pimsleur's original and unique method enables you to acquire another language as easily as you learned English-by listening. With the Pimsleur program, you'll learn vocabulary and grammar correctly and easily in conversation without mindless repetition.

Croatian Phrase Book. Berlitz Publishing Staff. (Berlitz Phrase Books & CD Ser.). (SER & ENG., 2007. audio compact disk 14.95 (978-981-268-187-4(6)) Pub: Berlitz Pubng. Dist(s): Langenscheidt

Croc-Blanc, Set. Jack London. Read by G. Bejean & B. Roza. 4 cass.Tr. of White Fang. (FRE.). 34.95 (1580-VSL) Olivia & Hill.

The adventures of White-Fang, a dog born from a wolf & a sled dog, who must face two enemies: man & other dogs, in the frozen north.

***Croc Called Capone.** Barry Jonsberg. Read by Stig Wemyss. (Running Time: 3 hrs. 40 mins.). (J). 2010. 54.99 (978-1-74214-616-4(3), 9781742146164) Pub: Bolinda Pubng AUS. Dist(s): Bolinda Pub Inc

Croc Called Capone. unabr. ed. Barry Jonsberg. Read by Stig Wemyss. (Running Time: 3 hrs. 40 mins.). (J). 2009. audio compact disk 54.95 (978-1-74214-143-5(9), 9781742141435) Pub: Bolinda Pubng AUS. Dist(s): Bolinda Pub Inc

***Croch Suas E Arist!** (ENG.). 11.95 (978-0-8023-7010-5(1)) Pub: Clo Iar-Chonnachta IRL. Dist(s): Dufour

***Croch Suas E Arist Eile!** (ENG.). 11.95 (978-0-8023-7011-2(X)) Pub: Clo Iar-Chonnachta IRL. Dist(s): Dufour

Crock of Gold. unabr. ed. James Stephens. Narrated by Donal Donnelly. 5 cass. (Running Time: 7 hrs. 30 mins.). 1990. 44.00 (978-1-55690-126-3(7), 90094E7) Recorded Bks.

Two philosophers inhabit the heart of a dark pine wood & help a farmer discover a pot of gold.

***Crocodile & Hen.** unabr. ed. Joan M. Lexau. (ENG.). 2008. (978-0-06-169398-4(7)); (978-0-06-172140-3(9)) HarperCollins Pubs.

Crocodile Bird. Ruth Rendell. Read by Donada Peters. 7 cass. (Running Time: 10 hrs.). 2001. 29.95 (978-0-7366-6800-2(4)) Books on Tape.

A mother & daughter's obsessive love is linked to a series of mysterious deaths near a remote English manor.

Crocodile Bird. unabr. ed. Ruth Rendell. Read by Juliet Stevenson. 10 cass. (Running Time: 15 hrs.). 2000. 69.95 (978-0-7451-4303-3(2), CAB 986) Pub: Chivers Audio Bks GBR. Dist(s): AudioGO

When Eve tells her daughter that she must leave their remote country home, Liza is terrified. Although seventeen years old, Liza has almost no knowledge of the outside world, a world described by her mother as destructive and evil. But now their strange, enclosed life is over, because Liza's mother has killed a man, and he is not the first.

Crocodile Bird, unabr. ed. Ruth Rendell. Narrated by Jill Tanner. 9 cass. (Running Time: 12 hrs. 15 mins.). 1994. 78.00 (978-1-55690-944-3(6), 93440E7) Recorded Bks.

Young Liza Beck is raised in a remote rural hamlet over which towers Shrove House, a magnificent manor perched atop a high hill. In full view of the manor, Liza lives alone with her mother in the gatekeeper's cottage, sheltered completely from the outside world. One evening, for reasons not fully clear, Liza's mother orders her to leave her home forever. Paralyzed at having to fend for herself, Liza finds refuge with Sean, an aimless drifter with whom she begins to share the bizarre story of her life.

Crocodile Bird. unabr. collector's ed. Ruth Rendell. Read by Donada Peters. 7 cass. (Running Time: 10 hrs 30 min.). 1994. 56.00 (978-0-7366-2670-5(0), 3407) Books on Tape.

Mother & daughter's obsessive love linked to a series of mysterious deaths near a remote English manor.

***Crocodile Charlie & the holy Grail.** unabr. ed. John Kolm & Peter Ring. Read by John Kolm. (Running Time: 5 hrs.). 2010. 43.95 (978-1-74214-647-8(3), 9781742146478) Pub: Bolinda Pubng AUS. Dist(s): Bolinda Pub Inc

Crocodile on the Sandbank. Elizabeth Peters, pseud. Narrated by Susan O'Malley. (Running Time: 9 hrs.). (Amelia Peabody Ser.: No. 1). 2000. 27.95 (978-1-59912-459-9(9)) Iofy Corp.

Crocodile on the Sandbank. Elizabeth Peters, pseud. Narrated by Barbara Rosenblat. 6 cass. (Running Time: 10 hrs.). (Amelia Peabody Ser.: No. 1). 29.95 (978-1-4025-6282-2(9)) Recorded Bks.

Crocodile on the Sandbank. Elizabeth Peters, pseud. (Amelia Peabody Ser.: No. 1). 2004. audio compact disk 99.75 (978-1-4025-6687-5(5)) Recorded Bks.

Crocodile on the Sandbank. unabr. ed. Elizabeth Peters, pseud. Read by Susan O'Malley. 1 CD MP3. (Running Time: 8 hrs. 30 mins.). (Amelia Peabody Ser.: No. 1). 2000. audio compact disk 24.95 (978-0-7861-9354-7(9), 2696) Blckstn Audio.
Amelia Peabody, that indomitable product of the Victorian age, embarks on her first Egyptian adventure armed with unshakable self-confidence, a journal to record her thoughts & of course, a sturdy umbrella.

Crocodile on the Sandbank. unabr. ed. Elizabeth Peters, pseud. Read by Susan O'Malley. 6 cass. (Running Time: 8 hrs. 30 mins.). (Amelia Peabody Ser.: No. 1). 2000. 44.95 (978-0-7861-1903-5(9), 2696); audio compact disk 64.00 (978-0-7861-9791-0(9), 2696) Blckstn Audio.

Crocodile on the Sandbank. unabr. ed. Elizabeth Peters, pseud. Read by Susan O'Malley. 6 pieces. (Amelia Peabody Ser.: No. 1). 2004. 29.95 (978-0-7861-2228-8(5)) Blckstn Audio.

Crocodile on the Sandbank. unabr. ed. Elizabeth Peters, pseud. Read by Susan O'Malley. (Running Time: 32400 sec.). (Amelia Peabody Ser.: No. 1). 2007. audio compact disk 26.95 (978-1-4332-0485-2(1)) Blckstn Audio.

Crocodile on the Sandbank. unabr. ed. Elizabeth Peters, pseud. Narrated by Barbara Rosenblat. 7 cass. (Running Time: 10 hrs.). (Amelia Peabody Ser.: No. 1). 1990. 69.75 (978-1-55690-127-0(5), 90085E7) Recorded Bks.
Amelia Peabody, Egyptologist & inquirer, never takes no for an answer as her mere staid Victorian colleagues soon discover.

***Crocodile Tears.** unabr. ed. Anthony Horowitz. Narrated by Simon Prebble. 1 Playaway. (Running Time: 9 hrs. 45 mins.). (Alex Rider Ser.: Bk. 8). (YA). (gr. 5-9). 2010. 59.75 (978-1-4407-5460-9(8)); 67.75 (978-1-4407-5450-0(0)); audio compact disk 97.75 (978-1-4407-5454-8(3)) Recorded Bks.

***Crocodile Tears.** unabr. collector's ed. Anthony Horowitz. Narrated by Simon Prebble. 9 CDs. (Running Time: 9 hrs. 45 mins.). (Alex Rider Ser.: Bk. 8). (YA). (gr. 5-9). 2010. audio compact disk 51.95 (978-1-4407-5455-5(1)) Recorded Bks.

Crofter & the Laird. unabr. ed. John McPhee. Read by David Case. 4 cass. (Running Time: 4 hrs.). 1991. 24.00 (978-0-7366-1975-2(5), 2793) Books on Tape.
McPhee traces his roots to a small Scottish island still practicing the feudal system today.

Crohn Disease - A Bibliography & Dictionary for Physicians, Patients, & Genome Researchers. Compiled by Icon Group International, Inc. Staff. 2007. ring bd. 28.95 (978-0-497-11361-2(9)) Icon Grp.

Crome Yellow. Aldous Huxley. Read by Anais 9000. 2008. 27.95 (978-1-60112-170-7(9)) Babblebooks.

Crome Yellow. Aldous Huxley. Read by Robert Whitfield. 5 cass. (Running Time: 7 hrs. 30 mins.). 1998. 39.95 (978-0-7861-1356-9(1), 2265) Blckstn Audio.
Aldous Huxley introduces us to a deligtfully cynical, comic & severe group of artists & intellectuals engaged in the most free thinking & modern kind of talk imaginable. Poetry, occultism, ancestral history, & Italian primitive painting are just a few of the subjects competing for discussion among the amiable cast of eccentrics drawn together at Crome - an intensely English country manor.

Cromwell, Pt. 1. collector's ed. Antonia Fraser. Read by Donada Peters. 9 cass. (Running Time: 13 hrs. 30 mins.). 1985. 72.00 (978-0-7366-0881-7(8), 1827-A) Books on Tape.
Englands Puritan protector displaced the Monarch in 1650's Civil War. Like others, he was corrupted by abolute power.

Cromwell, Pt. 2. collector's ed. Antonia Fraser. Read by Donada Peters. 8 cass. (Running Time: 12 hrs.). 1985. 64.00 (978-0-7366-0882-4(6), 1827-B) Books on Tape.

Cromwell, Pt. C. unabr. collector's ed. Antonia Fraser. Read by Donada Peters. 9 cass. (Running Time: 13 hrs. 30 min.). 1985. 72.00 (978-0-7366-0883-1(4), 1827C) Books on Tape.

Cronkite Remembers. Walter Cronkite. 2002. audio compact disk 14.00 (978-0-7435-2838-2(7), Audioworks) S&S Audio.

Cronkite Remembers. abr. ed. Walter Cronkite. 2004. 10.95 (978-0-7435-4774-1(8)) Pub: S&S Audio. Dist(s): S and S Inc

Crooked Creek Cricket. Louie Swift. Read by Barry McAlister. 2 cass. (Running Time: 30 min.). Dramatization. (Froggie's Tales: Vol. 2). (J). (ps-3). 2001. 12.95 (978-0-9675577-4-8(7)) Puddleduck Pubg.
Thirteen songs, stories & poems for children with music, character voices & sound effects. Includes "The Crooked Creek Cricket", "The Puppy Dog", "I'm Just a Little Lamb" & more. With character voices, music & sound effects.

Crooked Gun. unabr. ed. Orville D. Johnson. Read by Kevin Foley. 6 cass. (Running Time: 7 hrs.). 1994. 39.95 (978-1-55686-538-1(4)) Books in Motion.
Badly wounded in the Civil War, Whit Stewart takes his crooked body home to fight land grabbers that are attempting to steal the family ranch in Colorado.

Crooked Hearts. 1 cass. (Running Time: 1 hr.). 2001. 11.95 (LTYH001) Lodestone Catalog.
Augustine has a clever disguise, but can't hide from love.

Crooked House. Agatha Christie. Read by Hugh Fraser. 2007. 27.95 (978-1-57270-736-8(4)) Pub: Audio Partners. Dist(s): PerseuPGW

Crooked House. Agatha Christie. Narrated by Hugh Fraser. (Running Time: 20700 sec.). (Mystery Masters Ser.). (ENG., 2007. audio compact disk 27.95 (978-1-57270-735-1(6)) Pub: AudioGO. Dist(s): Perseus Dist

Crooked House: A BBC Radio Full-Cast Dramatization. Agatha Christie. (Running Time: 2 hrs. 0 mins. 0 sec.). (ENG.). 2009. audio compact disk 24.95 (978-1-60283-729-4(5)) Pub: AudioGO. Dist(s): Perseus Dist

Crooked Island. unabr. ed. Victoria McKernan. Read by Francis Cassidy. 6 cass. (Running Time: 9 hrs.). 1994. 48.00 (978-0-7366-2860-0(6), 3567) Books on Tape.
Sabotage, blackmail, kidnapping & romance make this suspense tale of underwater adventure a story to remember.

Crooked Kind of Perfect. unabr. ed. Linda Urban. Read by Tai Alexandra Ricci. 3 CDs. (Running Time: 3 hrs. 17 mins.). (J). (gr. 4-6). 2007. audio compact disk 30.00 (978-0-7393-6144-3(9)) Pub: Random Audio Pubg. Dist(s): Random

Crooked Kind of Perfect. unabr. ed. Linda Urban. Read by Tai Alexandra Ricci. 3 CDs. (Running Time: 4 hrs.). (ENG.). (J). (gr. 4). 2007. audio compact disk 25.00 (978-0-7393-5961-7(4), Listening Lib) Pub: Random Audio Pubg. Dist(s): Random

***Crooked Letter, Crooked Letter.** unabr. ed. Tom Franklin. (Running Time: 11 hrs.). 2010. 29.95 (978-1-4417-6344-0(9)); 65.95 (978-1-4417-6341-9(4)); audio compact disk 29.95 (978-1-4417-6343-3(0)); audio compact disk 100.00 (978-1-4417-6342-6(2)) Blckstn Audio.

Crooked Little Vein. unabr. ed. Warren Ellis. Read by Todd McLaren. (YA). 2008. 54.99 (978-1-60514-566-2(1)) Find a World.

Crooked Little Vein. unabr. ed. Warren Ellis. Narrated by Todd McLaren. (Running Time: 5 hrs. 30 mins. 0 sec.). (ENG.). 2007. audio compact disk 29.99 (978-1-4001-0561-8(7)); audio compact disk 19.99 (978-1-4001-5561-3(4)); audio compact disk 59.99 (978-1-4001-3561-5(3)) Pub: Tantor Media. Dist(s): IngramPubServ

Crooked Man see Memoirs of Sherlock Holmes

Crooked Man. Arthur Conan Doyle. 1 cass. 1989. 7.95 (S-77) Jimcin Record.
Strange apparition leads to murder.

Crooked Man: A Sherlock Holmes Adventure. (ENG.). 2007. (978-1-60339-073-6(1)); cd-rom & audio compact disk (978-1-60339-074-3(X)) Listenr Digest.

Crooked Pieces. Sarah Grazebrook. 2008. 84.95 (978-1-4079-0204-3(0)); audio compact disk 99.95 (978-1-4079-0205-0(9)) Pub: Soundings Ltd GBR. Dist(s): Ulverscroft US

Crooked Wood. Michael Underwood. Read by Christopher Kay. 5 cass. (Running Time: 7 hrs. 30 min.). 1999. 49.95 (66529) Pub: Soundings Ltd GBR. Dist(s): Ulverscroft US

Crop Circles. unabr. ed. George Wingfield. 2 cass. 1992. 18.00 set. (OC320-69) Sound Horizons AV.

Cross. Ken Bruen. (Jack Taylor Ser.: Bk. 6). 2008. 49.95 (978-0-7531-3789-5(5)); audio compact disk 64.95 (978-0-7531-2770-4(9)) Pub: ISIS Audio GBR. Dist(s): Ulverscroft US

Cross. abr. ed. James Patterson. Read by Peter Jay Fernandez & Jay O. Sanders. (Running Time: 6 hrs.). (Alex Cross Ser.: No. 12). (ENG.). 2006. 14.98 (978-1-59483-600-8(0)) Pub: Hachet Audio. Dist(s): HachBkGrp

Cross. abr. ed. James Patterson. Read by Jay O. Sanders & Peter Jay Fernandez. 5 CDs. (Running Time: 6 hrs.). (Alex Cross Ser.: No. 12). (ENG.). 2008. audio compact disk 14.98 (978-1-60024-419-3(X)) Pub: Hachet Audio. Dist(s): HachBkGrp

Cross. unabr. ed. Arthur Blessitt. Narrated by Wayne Shepherd. (Running Time: 5 hrs. 11 mins. 58 sec.). (ENG.). 2009. audio compact disk 22.99 (978-1-59859-498-0(2)) Oasis Audio.

Cross. unabr. ed. Arthur Blessitt. Narrated by Wayne Shepherd. (Running Time: 5 hrs. 11 mins. 58 sec.). (ENG.). 2009. 16.09 (978-1-60814-486-0(0)) Oasis Audio.

Cross. unabr. ed. James Patterson. 5 cass. (Running Time: 7 hrs.). (Alex Cross Ser.: No. 12). 2006. 45.00 (978-1-4159-3466-1(5)); audio compact disk 63.00 (978-1-4159-3467-8(3)) Books on Tape.

Cross. unabr. ed. James Patterson. Read by Peter Jay Fernandez & Jay O. Sanders. (Alex Cross Ser.: No. 12). (YA). 2006. 59.99 (978-1-59895-443-2(1)) Find a World.

Cross. unabr. ed. James Patterson. Read by Peter Jay Fernandez & Jay O. Sanders. (Running Time: 8 hrs.). (Alex Cross Ser.: No. 12). (ENG.). 2006. 16.98 (978-1-59483-602-2(7)); audio compact disk 39.98 (978-1-59483-603-9(5)) Pub: Hachet Audio. Dist(s): HachBkGrp

Cross. unabr. ed. James Patterson. Read by Peter Jay Fernandez & Jay O. Sanders. (Running Time: 8 hrs.). (Alex Cross Ser.: No. 12). (ENG.). 2009. 59.98 (978-1-60788-283-1(3)) Pub: Hachet Audio. Dist(s): HachBkGrp

Cross: Victory over Death. Thomas Merton. 1 cass. 8.95 (AA2455) Credence Commun.

Cross: Word & Sacrament. unabr. ed. Adrienne Von Speyr. Read by Andrea Pruseau. Tr. by Graham Harrison. 2 cass. Orig. Title: Kreuzeswort und Sakrament. 9.95 set. (949) Ignatius Pr.
A profound contemplation on the seven last words of Our Lord on the cross, with specific application to the seven sacraments instituted by Christ. Striking for doctrinal penetration & originality, flashing with bright insights into the suffering of the God-Man on the cross.

Cross & the Resurrection. Jack Deere. 1 cass. (Running Time: 90 mins.). (Cross Ser.: Vol. 2). 2000. 5.00 (JD01-002) Morning NC.
These are outstanding messages on the work & power of the most important truths of our faith.

Cross & the Switch Blade. unabr. ed. David Wilkerson et al. Read by Paul Michael. (Running Time: 7 hrs. 30 mins. 0 sec.). (ENG.). 2007. audio compact disk 24.98 (978-1-59644-535-2(1)) christianaud.

Cross & the Switchblade. abr. ed. David Wilkerson. 4 cass. (Running Time: 6 hrs. 30 min.). (Life of Glory Ser.). 2003. 25.99; audio compact disk 25.99 Oasis Audio.

Cross & the Switchblade. unabr. ed. David Wilkerson. Contrib. by John Sherrill & Elizabeth Sherrill. Narrated by Raymond Todd. 5 cass. (Running Time: 7 hrs. 30 mins.). 2002. 39.95 (978-0-7861-2165-6(3), P2915); audio compact disk 48.00 (978-0-7861-9549-7(5), ZP2915) Blckstn Audio.
Led by incredible faith, David Wilkerson took a seemingly bizarre step from his country pulpit in 1958 to the streets of New York City, where a murder trial of seven teenage boys intensified society's antipathy toward them. Even Wilkerson was bewildered by his sense of compassion but, in spite of doubt, he followed the Spirit's prompting to help the boys.

***Cross & the Switchblade.** unabr. ed. David Wilkerson & John Sherill. Narrated by Paul Michael. (ENG.). 2007. 14.98 (978-1-59644-536-9(X), Hovel Audio) christianaud.

Cross & the Switchblade; God's Smuggler. abr. ed. David Wilkerson & Brother Andrew. (Life of Glory Ser.). 2004. 25.99 (978-1-58926-226-3(3)); audio compact disk 25.99 (978-1-58926-227-0(1)) Oasis Audio.

Cross-Aspect Comparison. Annie Hershey. 1 cass. 8.95 (154) Am Fed Astrologers.
An AFA Convention workshop tape.

Cross at the Center. Derek Prince. 2 cass. 1990. 5.95 ea. Derek Prince.
The Cross distinguishes Christianity from all other religions. Learn to see that it is the source of all grace; the basis of Satan's defeat; the door to God's secret wisdom; the ultimate demonstration of God's love.

Cross Bearing. Perf. by Lil' Raskull. 1 cass. 1997. audio compact disk 15.99 CD. (D7523) Diamante Music Grp.
Lil' Raskull is called to reach back into the dark sinful world that he is well familiar with, & to lead many of our nation's young people to Christ with God-given lyrics that relate directly to everyday situations that they are faced with.

Cross Between. Perf. by Cross Between Staff. Prod. by Regie Hamm. 1 cass., 1 CD. 1998. 10.98 (978-0-7601-2457-4(4)) Provident Mus Dist.

Cross Between. Regie Hamm. Prod. by Regie Hamm. Perf. by Cross Between Staff. 1 cass., 1 CD. 1998. audio compact disk 16.98 CD. (978-0-7601-2458-1(2)) Provident Mus Dist.

Cross Bones. abr. ed. Kathy Reichs. Read by Michele Pawk. (Temperance Brennan Ser.: No. 8). 2005. 17.95 (978-0-7435-5161-8(3)) Pub: S&S Audio. Dist(s): S and S Inc

Cross Bones. abr. ed. Kathy Reichs. Read by Michele Pawk. (Running Time: 50 hrs. 0 mins. 0 sec.). No. 8. (ENG.). 2007. audio compact disk 14.99 (978-0-7435-6977-4(6)) Pub: S&S Audio. Dist(s): S and S Inc

Cross Bones. unabr. ed. Kathy Reichs. Narrated by Michele Pawk. 8 cass. (Running Time: 11 hrs.). (Temperance Brennan Ser.: No. 8). 2005. 109.75 (978-1-4193-4929-4(5), 98097) Recorded Bks.
When an orthodox Jew is found shot to death in Montreal, Temperance Brennan is called in to examine the body and to figure out the puzzling damage to the corpse. Before she knows it, Tempe is involved in an international mystery.

Cross Bones. unabr. ed. Kathy Reichs. Read by Michele Pawk. (Temperance Brennan Ser.: No. 8). 2005. 23.95 (978-0-7435-5239-4(3)); audio compact disk 39.95 (978-0-7435-4436-8(6), Audioworks) Pub: S&S Audio. Dist(s): S and S Inc

Cross Country. abr. ed. James Patterson. Read by Peter Jay Fernandez & Dion Graham. (Running Time: 6 hrs. 30 mins.). (Alex Cross Ser.: No. 14). (ENG.). 2008. 19.98 (978-1-60024-386-8(X)); audio compact disk 29.98 (978-1-60024-385-1(1)) Pub: Hachet Audio. Dist(s): HachBkGrp

Cross Country. unabr. ed. James Patterson. Read by Peter Jay Fernandez & Dion Graham. (Running Time: 8 hrs.). (Alex Cross Ser.: No. 14). (ENG.). 2008. 26.98 (978-1-60024-388-2(6)) Pub: Hachet Audio. Dist(s): HachBkGrp

Cross Country. unabr. ed. James Patterson. Read by Peter Jay Fernandez & Dion Graham. (Running Time: 8 hrs.). (Alex Cross Ser.: No. 14). (ENG.). 2009. audio compact disk 19.98 (978-1-60024-824-5(1)) Pub: Hachet Audio. Dist(s): HachBkGrp

Cross Country. unabr. ed. James Patterson. Read by Peter Jay Fernandez & Dion Graham. 5 cass. (Alex Cross Ser.: No. 14). 2008. 90.00 (978-1-4159-6101-8(8), BksonTape); audio compact disk 90.00 (978-1-4159-5429-4(1), BksonTape) Pub: Random Audio Pubg. Dist(s): Random

Cross-Country Cat. Mary Calhoun. Read by Christina Moore. 1 cass. (Running Time: 15 mins.). (J). (gr. 1 up). 1999. pap. bk. & stu. ed. 23.20 (978-0-7887-3638-4(8), 41003) Recorded Bks.
Who would believe that a cat could ski? You will when you hear the delightful tale of Henry, the sassy hind-leg walking Siamese. When Henry gets trapped at a mountain cabin, he decides to try the tiny skis & poles that were made for him. But will his skills & courage be enough to save him from a hungry coyote?.

Cross-Country Cat. unabr. ed. Mary Calhoun. Narrated by Christina Moore. 1 cass. (Running Time: 15 mins.). (gr. 1 up). 2000. 10.00 (978-0-7887-3539-4(X), 95928E7) Recorded Bks.

Cross Country Cat. unabr. ed. Mary Calhoun. Read by Peter Thomas. Illus. by Erick Ingraham. 1 cass. (Running Time: 15 mins.). (J). (gr. k-3). 1992. pap. bk. 17.00 (978-0-8072-6025-8(8), MR 21 SP, Listening Lib) Random Audio Pubg.
What kind of cat would go sliding off on skis? When the family accidentally leaves Henry behind at a ski lodge, he takes matters into his own paws.

Cross-Country Cat, Class set. unabr. ed. Mary Calhoun. Read by Christina Moore. 1 cass. (Running Time: 15 mins.). (J). (gr. 1 up). 1999. 80.30 (978-0-7887-3667-4(1), 46970) Recorded Bks.
Who would believe that a cat could ski? You will when you hear the delightful tale of Henry, the sassy hind-leg walking Siamese. When Henry gets trapped at a mountain cabin, he decides to try the tiny skis & poles that were made for him. But will his skills & courage be enough to save him from a hungry coyote?.

Cross-Country Skiing. Jeff Nowak. 4 cass. 39.95 incl. video, training guide. (1218) SyberVision.

Cross Cultural Healing Processes. Stanley Krippner. 1 cass. 7.00 (A0058-86) Sound Photosyn.
ICSS '86.

Cross-Cultural Shamanic Practice. Angeles Arrien. 2 cass. (Running Time: 2 hrs. 58 min.). 1991. 18.00 set. (00204) Big Sur Tapes.

Cross-Cultural Visions in African American Modernism: From Spatial Narrative to Jazz Haiku. Yoshinobu Hakutani. 2006. audio compact disk 9.95 (978-0-8142-9107-8(4)) Pub: Ohio St U Pr. Dist(s): Chicago Distribution Ctr

Cross Examination of the Defendant's Financial Expert. James W. Jeans, Sr. et al. 1 cass. (Running Time: 45 min.). (Using Financial Experts in Business Litigation Ser.). 1988. 20.00 (FAZ0408) Natl Inst Trial Ad.

Cross-examining the Child Witness. Irving Younger. 1 cass. (Running Time: 39 min.). (Mastering the Art of Cross Examination Ser.). 1987. 20.00 (FAMAC06) Natl Inst Trial Ad.

Cross-examining the Expert Accountant Witness. Irving Younger. 1 cass. (Running Time: 51 min.). (Mastering the Art of Cross Examination Ser.). 1987. 20.00 (FAMAC10) Natl Inst Trial Ad.

Cross-examining the Expert Attorney Witness. Irving Younger. 1 cass. (Running Time: 54 min.). (Mastering the Art of Cross Examination Ser.). 1987. 20.00 (FAMAC11) Natl Inst Trial Ad.

Cross-examining the Expert Medical Witness. Irving Younger. 1 cass. (Running Time: 35 min.). (Mastering the Art of Cross Examination Ser.). 1987. 20.00 (FAMAC09) Natl Inst Trial Ad.

Cross-examining the Eyewitness. Irving Younger. 1 cass. (Running Time: 52 min.). (Mastering the Art of Cross Examination Ser.). 1987. 20.00 (FAMAC05) Natl Inst Trial Ad.

Cross-examining the Hostile Witness. Irving Younger. 1 cass. (Running Time: 51 min.). (Mastering the Art of Cross Examination Ser.). 1987. 20.00 (FAMAC03) Natl Inst Trial Ad.

Cross-examining the Law Enforcement Witness. Irving Younger. 1 cass. (Running Time: 41 min.). (Mastering the Art of Cross Examination Ser.). 1987. 20.00 (FAMAC08) Natl Inst Trial Ad.

Cross-examining the Well-Prepared Witness. Irving Younger. 1 cass. (Running Time: 47 min.). (Mastering the Art of Cross Examination Ser.). 1987. 20.00 (FAMAC02) Natl Inst Trial Ad.
Cross examining the sympathetic witness.

Cross-examining the Witness of the Opposite Sex. Irving Younger. 1 cass. (Running Time: 45 min.). (Mastering the Art of Cross Examination Ser.). 1987. 20.00 (FAMAC07) Natl Inst Trial Ad.

Cross Fire. abr. ed. James Patterson. Read by Tim Cain & Michael Cerveris. (Running Time: 5 hrs.). (Alex Cross Ser.: No. 16). (ENG.). 2009. 14.98 (978-1-60024-767-5(9)) Pub: Hachet Audio. Dist(s): HachBkGrp

***Cross Fire.** abr. ed. James Patterson. Read by Tim Cain & Michael Cerveris. (Running Time: 5 hrs.). 2010. audio compact disk 14.98 (978-1-60788-653-2(7)) Pub: Hachet Audio. Dist(s): HachBkGrp

***Cross Fire.** abr. ed. James Patterson. Read by Andre Braugher & Jay O. Sanders. (Running Time: 6 hrs.). (ENG.). 2010. 19.98 (978-1-60788-664-8(2)); audio compact disk 24.98 (978-1-60788-663-1(4)) Pub: Hachet Audio. Dist(s): HachBkGrp

***Cross Fire.** unabr. ed. James Patterson. Read by Tim Cain & Michael Cerveris. 1 MP3-CD. (Running Time: 7 hrs.). 2009. 49.99

(978-1-60788-001-1(6)); audio compact disk 79.99 (978-1-60788-000-4(8), SLD1847) Pub: Hachet Audio. Dist(s): HachBkGrp

Cross Fire. unabr. ed. James Patterson. Read by Tim Cain & Michael Cerveris. (Running Time: 7 hrs.). (Alex Cross Ser.: No. 16). (ENG.). 2009. 26.98 (978-1-60024-769-9(5)); audio compact disk 39.98 (978-1-60024-768-2(7)) Pub: Hachet Audio. Dist(s): HachBkGrp

*__Cross Fire.__ unabr. ed. James Patterson. Read by Andre Braugher & Jay O. Sanders. (Running Time: 8 hrs.). 2010. 26.98 (978-1-60788-666-2(9)); audio compact disk 39.98 (978-1-60788-665-5(0)) Pub: Hachet Audio. Dist(s): HachBkGrp

Cross Gardener. unabr. ed. Jason F. Wright. (Running Time: 6 hrs.). (ENG.). 2010. audio compact disk 29.95 (978-0-14-314564-6(9)) Penguin Grp USA.

Cross Image. Ben Young. 2000. 4.95 (978-0-7417-6186-6(6), B0186) Win Walk.

Cross in My Life. Derek Prince. 2 cass. 1990. 5.95 ea. Derek Prince.
The Cross applied to our own life provides a fivefold deliverance: from this present evil age; from the law; from self; from the flesh; from the world.

Cross in the Road. Steve Amerson. (ENG.). 2002. audio compact disk 15.98 (978-5-550-12357-7(6)) Pub: Amerson Mus Min. Dist(s): STL Dist NA

Cross in the Road Tracks. Steve Amerson. (ENG.). 2007. audio compact disk 29.95 (978-5-550-12358-4(4)) Pub: Amerson Mus Min. Dist(s): STL Dist NA

Cross is the Power of God. Rick Joyner. 1 cass. (Running Time: 90 mins.). (Foundation Ser.: Vol. 9). 2000. 5.00 (RJ05-009) Morning NC.
As an overview of God's plan for His church, this series contains essential truths for everyone who wants to see the church become all that she is called to be.

Cross My Heart. abr. ed. Carly Phillips. Read by Marie Caliendo. (Running Time: 14400 sec.). 2007. audio compact disk 14.99 (978-1-4233-1240-6(6), 9781423312406, BCD Value Price) Brilliance Audio.

Cross My Heart. unabr. ed. Maureen McCarthy. Read by Kate Hood. 6 cass. (Running Time: 9 hrs. 55 mins.). 2002. (978-1-74030-704-8(6)) Bolinda Pubng AUS.

Cross My Heart. unabr. ed. Carly Phillips. Read by Marie Caliendo. (Running Time: 8 hrs.). 2006. 39.25 (978-1-59737-196-4(3), 9781597371964, BADLE); 24.95 (978-1-59737-195-7(5), 9781597371957, BAD); 74.25 (978-1-59737-190-2(4), 9781597371902, BrilAudUnabridg); audio compact disk 87.25 (978-1-59737-192-6(0), 9781597371926, BriAudCD Unabrid); audio compact disk 39.25 (978-1-59737-194-0(7), 9781597371940, Brinc Audio MP3 Lib); audio compact disk 34.95 (978-1-59737-191-9(2), 9781597371919, Bril Audio CD Unabri); audio compact disk 24.95 (978-1-59737-193-3(9), 9781597371933, Brilliance MP3) Brilliance Audio.
Please enter a Synopsis.

Cross My Heart & Hope to Spy. unabr. ed. Ally Carter. Read by Renée Raudman. (Running Time: 7 hrs.). (Gallagher Girls Ser.: No. 2). 2007. 39.25 (978-1-4233-4037-9(X), 9781423340379, BADLE); 24.95 (978-1-4233-4036-2(1), 9781423340362, BAD) Brilliance Audio.

Cross My Heart & Hope to Spy. unabr. ed. Ally Carter. Read by Renée Raudman. 6 CDs. (Running Time: 7 hrs.). (Gallagher Girls Ser.: No. 2). (YA). (gr. 8-12). 2007. audio compact disk 82.25 (978-1-4233-4033-1(7), 9781423340331, BriAudCD Unabrid); audio compact disk 39.25 (978-1-4233-4035-5(3), 9781423340355, Brinc Audio MP3 Lib); audio compact disk 29.95 (978-1-4233-4032-4(9), 9781423340324, Bril Audio CD Unabri); audio compact disk 24.95 (978-1-4233-4034-8(5), 9781423340348, Brilliance MP3) Brilliance Audio.

Cross My Heart & Hope to Spy. unabr. ed. Ally Carter & Renée Raudman. 5 cass. (Running Time: 25200 sec.). (Gallagher Girls Ser.: No. 2). (YA). (gr. 8-12). 2007. 69.25 (978-1-4233-4031-7(0), 9781423340317, BrilAudUnabridg) Brilliance Audio.

Cross of Christ. 20th unabr. ed. John Stott. (Running Time: 14 hrs. 0 mins. 0 sec.). (ENG.). 2007. audio compact disk 28.98 (978-1-59644-549-9(1), Hovel Audio) christianaud.

*__Cross of Christ: 20th Anniversary Edition.__ unabr. ed. John Stott. Narrated by Simon Vance. (ENG.). 2007. 16.98 (978-1-59644-550-5(5), Hovel Audio) christianaud.

Cross of Fire. unabr. ed. Colin Forbes & Peter Wickham. 12 cass. (Isis Ser.). (J). 2000. 94.95 (978-0-7531-0725-6(2)) Pub: ISIS Lrg Prnt GBR. Dist(s): Ulverscroft US

Cross of Jesus Christ. Ord L. Morrow. Read by Ord L. Morrow. 1 cass. (Running Time: 1 hr. 30 min.). 1988. 4.95 (978-0-8474-2321-7(2)) Back to Bible.
Features four messages to help understand the importance of the cross & its meaning in one's life.

Cross of Joy. Read by Basilea Schlink. 1 cass. (Running Time: 30 min.). 1985. (0275) Evang Sisterhood Mary.
Topics are: How sorrow can lose its sting in our lives; an offer to experience the all-transforming power of God.

Cross Outstreached: John 1:29. Ed Young. (J). 1981. 4.95 (978-0-7417-1171-7(0), A0171) Win Walk.

Cross Pull: James 4:1-10, 627. Ed Young. 1987. 4.95 (978-0-7417-1627-9(5), 627) Win Walk.

Cross Purposes: Discovering the Great Love of God for You. unabr. ed. D. James Kennedy. Narrated by D. James Kennedy. (ENG.). 2007. 13.99 (978-1-60814-167-8(5)) Oasis Audio.

Cross Purposes: Discovering the Great Love of God for You. unabr. ed. D. James Kennedy. Narrated by D. James Kennedy. Read by Jerry Newcombe. (Running Time: 18000 sec.). (ENG.). 2007. audio compact disk 19.99 (978-1-59859-190-3(8)) Oasis Audio.

*__Cross Roads.__ abr. ed. Fern Michaels. Read by Laural Merlington. (Running Time: 5 hrs.). (Sisterhood Ser.). 2010. 9.99 (978-1-4418-9394-9(6), 9781441893949, BAD); audio compact disk 14.99 (978-1-4418-1888-1(X), 9781441818881, BACD) Brilliance Audio.

*__Cross Roads.__ unabr. ed. Fern Michaels. Read by Laural Merlington. (Running Time: 9 hrs.). (Sisterhood Ser.). 2010. 24.99 (978-1-4418-1884-3(7), 9781441818843, Brilliance MP3); 24.99 (978-1-4418-1886-7(3), 9781441818867, BAD); 39.97 (978-1-4418-1885-0(5), 9781441818850, Brinc Audio MP3 Lib); 39.97 (978-1-4418-1887-4(1), 9781441818874, BADLE); audio compact disk 29.99 (978-1-4418-1882-9(0), 9781441818829, Bril Audio CD Unabri); audio compact disk 87.97 (978-1-4418-1883-6(9), 9781441818836, BriAudCD Unabrid) Brilliance Audio.

Cross Roads: Matthew 7:12-14. Ed Young. (J). 1979. 4.95 (978-0-7417-1090-1(0), A0090) Win Walk.

Cross-Sectional Anatomy Tutor: 1.0 IBM. Duke University Staff. (C). 1997. audio compact disk 74.95 (978-0-7637-0534-3(9), 0534-9) Jones Bartlett.

Cross Series. Jack Deere. 4 cass. (Running Time: 6 hrs.). 2000. 20.00 (JD01-000) Morning NC.
These are outstanding messages on the work & power of the most important truths of our faith.

Cross the Border into Spanish Fluency: Answer Keys & Tapescript. Mark Frobose. 8 cds. (SPA.). 2002. per. 69.00 (978-1-893564-98-5(3)) Macmill Audio.

Cross the Border into Spanish Fluency: Answer Keys & Tapescript. Mark Frobose. (SPA., 2002. per. 24.99 (978-1-893564-96-1(7)) Macmill Audio.

Cross-the Key to Heaven. 1985. (0207) Evang Sisterhood Mary.

Cross Through the Open Tomb. Ed Young. 1995. 4.95 (978-0-7417-2055-9(8), 1055) Win Walk.

Cross Tuning Your Fiddle. William Shull. 1996. bk. 17.95 (978-0-7866-2641-0(0), 95238BCD) Mel Bay.

Crossbow Killer. (Start-to-Finish Books). (J). (gr. 2-3). (978-1-58702-423-8(3)) D Johnston Inc.

Crossbow Killer. (Start-to-Finish Books). (J). (gr. 2-3). 2002. 100.00 (978-1-58702-980-6(4)) D Johnston Inc.

Crossbow Killer. unabr. ed. (Start-to-Finish Books). (J). (gr. 2-3). (978-1-893376-07-6(9), F02K2) D Johnston Inc.

Crossbow Mystery at Yellowstone Park. Jerry Stemach. (Nick Ford Mysteries Ser.). 1999. audio compact disk 18.95 (978-1-4105-0129-5(9)) D Johnston Inc.

Crossbow Mystery at Yellowstone Park, Vol. 2. Jerry Stemach. Ed. by Jerry Stemach. Ed. by Gail Portnuff Venable & Dorothy Tyack. Illus. by Phillip Dizick. Narrated by Ed Smaron. Contrib. by Ted S. Hasselbring. (Start-to-Finish Books). (J). (gr. 2-3). 2001. 35.00 (978-1-58702-726-0(7)) D Johnston Inc.

Crossbow Mystery at Yellowstone Park, Vol. 2. unabr. ed. Jerry Stemach. Ed. by Jerry Stemach. Ed. by Gail Portnuff Venable & Dorothy Tyack. Illus. by Phillip Dizick. Narrated by Ed Smaron. Contrib. by Ted S. Hasselbring. 1 cass.. (Running Time: 1 hr.). (Start-to-Finish Books). (J). (gr. 2-3). 2001. 7.00 (978-1-58702-710-9(0), F02) D Johnston Inc.

Crosscurrents: A Fly Fisher's Progress. James Babb. 2008. audio compact disk 28.00 (978-1-933309-33-0(4)) Pub: A Media Intl. Dist(s): Natl Bk Netwk

Crosscut. Meg Gardiner. Read by Tanya Eby Sirois. (Playaway Adult Fiction Ser.). (ENG.). 2009. 74.99 (978-1-60775-881-5(4)) Find a World.

Crosscut. unabr. ed. Meg Gardiner. Read by Tanya Eby Sirois. (Running Time: 12 hrs.). (Evan Delaney Ser.). 2008. 39.25 (978-1-4233-6141-1(5), 9781423361411, Brinc Audio MP3 Lib); 39.25 (978-1-4233-6143-5(1), 9781423361435, BADLE); 24.95 (978-1-4233-6142-8(3), 9781423361428, BAD); 24.95 (978-1-4233-6140-4(7), 9781423361404, Brilliance MP3); audio compact disk 102.25 (978-1-4233-6139-8(3), 9781423361398, BriAudCD Unabrid); audio compact disk 36.95 (978-1-4233-6138-1(5), 9781423361381, Bril Audio CD Unabri) Brilliance Audio.

Crosse at Ninety Miles an Hour see Richard Eberhart Reading His Poetry

Crosse en l'Air. Jacques Prevert. Read by Michel Boy. 1 cass. (FRE.). 1995. 21.95 (1663-LQP) Olivia & Hill.
A drunken bishop staggering through the streets of Paris launches Prevert into a bizarre tale revealing his anticlericalism & concern with the rise of facism.

Crossed Numbers see Carl Sandburg's Poems for Children

Crossers. unabr. ed. Philip Caputo. Narrated by Paul Boehmer. 2 MP3-CDs. (Running Time: 22 hrs. 0 mins. 0 sec.). 2009. 34.99 (978-1-4001-6426-4(5)); audio compact disk 99.99 (978-1-4001-4426-6(4)); audio compact disk 49.99 (978-1-4001-1426-9(8)) Pub: Tantor Media. Dist(s): IngramPubServ

*__Crossers: A Novel.__ unabr. ed. Philip Caputo. Narrated by Paul Boehmer. (Running Time: 22 hrs. 0 mins.). 2009. 24.99 (978-1-4001-8426-2(6)) Tantor Media.

*__Crossfire.__ Dick Francis & Felix Francis. Contrib. by Martin Jarvis. (Running Time: 10 hrs.). 2010. audio compact disk 39.95 (978-0-14-242847-4(7), PengAudBks) Penguin Grp USA.

Crossfire. abr. ed. David Hagberg. Read by Bruce Watson. 4 vols. (Kirk McGarvey Ser.). 2003. (978-1-58807-677-9(6)) Am Pubng Inc.

Crossfire. unabr. ed. B. J. Green. Read by Stephanie Brush. 12 cass. (Running Time: 9 hrs. 54 min.). 2001. 64.95 (978-1-55686-916-7(9)) Books in Motion.
Alex Ramsey's wedding plans end when she finds that her fiance is a miltia group leader, with a plot so daring he kidnaps Alex's eight-year-old daughter to prevent the plan's detection.

Crossfire Killings, Set. unabr. ed. Bill Knox. 6 cass. 1998. 69.95 (978-1-85903-126-1(9)) Pub: Magna Story GBR. Dist(s): Ulverscroft US

Crossing. Cormac McCarthy. Read by Alexander Adams. (Border Trilogy: No. 2). 2002. 80.00 (978-0-7366-8804-8(8)) Books on Tape.

Crossing. unabr. ed. Howard Fast. Narrated by Norman Dietz. 4 cass. (Running Time: 6 hrs.). 1988. 35.00 (978-1-55690-128-7(3), 88690E7) Recorded Bks.
The unforgettable novelistic recreation of the night before Christmas when General Washington & a rag-tag army slipped across the Delaware to surprise the Hessians & forge a nation.

Crossing, unabr. ed. Gary Paulsen. Narrated by Mark Hammer. 2 pieces. (Running Time: 2 hrs. 45 mins.). (gr. 7 up). 19.00 (978-1-55690-951-1(9), 93443E7) Recorded Bks.
A young Mexican boy, who must struggle every day just to survive, dreams of finding a way to cross the border into the United States. Available to libraries only.

Crossing Boundaries: Knowledge, Disciplinarities, & Interdisciplinarities. Julie T. Klein. (ENG.). 1996. 19.50 (978-0-8139-1679-8(8)) U Pr of Va.

Crossing by Night. unabr. ed. David Aaron. Read by Multivoice Production Staff. (Running Time: 14 hrs.). 2008. 39.25 (978-1-4233-5798-8(1), 9781423357988, BADLE) Brilliance Audio.

Crossing by Night. unabr. ed. David Aaron. Read by Sandra Burr & Bill Weideman. (Running Time: 14 hrs.). 2008. 39.25 (978-1-4233-5796-4(5), 9781423357964, Brinc Audio MP3 Lib) Brilliance Audio.

Crossing by Night. unabr. ed. David Aaron. Read by Multivoice Production Staff et al. (Running Time: 14 hrs.). 2008. 24.95 (978-1-4233-5795-7(7), 9781423357957, Brilliance MP3) Brilliance Audio.

Crossing by Night. unabr. ed. David Aaron. Read by Multivoice Production Staff et al. (Running Time: 14 hrs.). 2008. 24.95 (978-1-4233-5797-1(3), 9781423357971, BAD) Brilliance Audio.

Crossing Guard. unabr. ed. David Rabe. Read by Dick Hill. (Running Time: 13 hrs.). 2009. 39.97 (978-1-4233-8591-2(8), 9781423385912, Brinc Audio MP3 Lib); 24.99 (978-1-4233-8590-5(X), 9781423385905, Brilliance MP3); 39.97 (978-1-4233-8593-6(4), 9781423385936, BADLE); 24.99 (978-1-4233-8592-9(6), 9781423385929, BAD) Brilliance Audio.

Crossing Hoffa: A Teamster's Story. Steven Harper. Narrated by Mort Crim. (ENG.). 2008. audio compact disk 29.95 (978-1-60031-039-3(7)) Spoken Books.

Crossing Jordan. Adrian Fogelin. Read by Adrian Fogelin. 5 CDs. (Running Time: 5 hrs. 20 mins.). (J). (gr. 4-8). 2009. audio compact disk 42.00 (978-1-934180-88-4(2)) Full Cast Audio.

Crossing Open Ground. abr. ed. Barry Lopez. Read by Barry Lopez. 2 cass. (Running Time: 3 hrs.). Dramatization. 1994. 16.95 (978-0-939643-57-8(X), 3502, NrthWrd Bks) TandN Child.
In a distinguished collection of essays, Barry Lopez reveals the bond between mankind and the land and man's heartbreaking betrayal of that bond.

*__Crossing Over.__ unabr. ed. Anna Kendall. (Running Time: 12 hrs. 30 mins.). 2010. 29.95 (978-1-4417-6649-6(9)); 72.95 (978-1-4417-6646-5(4)); audio compact disk 105.00 (978-1-4417-6647-2(2)); audio compact disk 32.95 (978-1-4417-6648-9(0)) Blckstn Audio.

Crossing the Border. unabr. ed. Gail Taylor. Read by Gail Taylor. Ed. by James B. Kirgan. 1 cass. (Running Time: 1 hr. 30 min.). (Essence of Nature Ser.: Vol. 4). (J). 1989. 12.99 stereo. (978-1-878362-04-9(6)) Emerald Ent.
On this tape Thumper, the adventure dog, crosses the U. S.-Canadian border from Waterton National Park (Canada) into Glacier National Park (United States). This tape includes the actual sounds of nature in both of these National Parks.

Crossing the Boulevard: Strangers, Neighbors, Aliens in a New America. unabr. ed. Warren Lehrer & Judith Sloan. 1 CD. (Running Time: 1 hr. 30 mins.). 2003. audio compact disk 15.00 (978-0-393-10588-9(1)) Norton.

Crossing the Continent 1527-1540: The Story of the First African American Explorer of the American South. unabr. ed. Robert Goodwin. (Running Time: 12 hrs. 0 mins. 0 sec.). (ENG.). 2008. audio compact disk 69.99 (978-1-4001-3972-9(4)); audio compact disk 34.99 (978-1-4001-0972-2(8)); audio compact disk 24.99 (978-1-4001-5972-7(5)) Pub: Tantor Media. Dist(s): IngramPubServ

Crossing the Craton: From Annals of the Former World. unabr. ed. John McPhee. Narrated by Nelson Runger. 2 cass. (Running Time: 1 hr. 30 mins.). 2000. 19.00 (978-0-7887-4393-1(7), 96023E7) Recorded Bks.
Reveals what's going on beneath your feet in the basement of the continent, the mostly flat land masses forming Illinois, Iowa, Nebraska & thereabouts.

Crossing the Great Void. Short Stories. (4011) Am Audio Prose.

Crossing the Line: A Year in the Land of Apartheid. unabr. collector's ed. William Finnegan. Read by Grover Gardner. 12 cass. (Running Time: 18 hrs.). 1990. 96.00 (978-0-7366-1759-8(0), 2598) Books on Tape.
In 1980, a young white Californian landed a job teaching in a high school of "colored" students on the Cape flats, outside Cape Town, in South Africa. So began William Finnegan's odyssey of discovery as he crossed the South African color line & encountered at first hand the daily nightmare of life under apartheid. On the first day, Finnegan is put on the spot by a politically astute older student who asks "Sir" what exactly he is doing in South Africa, anyway. Some of his pupils amuse themselves by "playing the fool" with him, until Finnegan catches on to the age-old game favored by South African blacks when dealing with whites. We feel affection for these children & are sympathetic when they join a boycott that grows into a massive protest against apartheid in education.

Crossing the Line: Discovering Your True Fitness Potential. Nancy Georges. 2 CDs. (Running Time: 90). 2006. audio compact disk 39.95 (978-0-9778132-1-6(5)) Ins Pub Co.
Crossing The Line is a unique audio program that delivers the results you have been looking for. Join Fitness Champion, Nancy Georges as she powers you through this motivational audio program. You will learn the techniques and strategies for crossing that mental line over to the world where all your physical dreams are not only a possibility, but a reality. Nancy will share with you her key to mental focus and mental discipline. Here is what you will learn:-Mental strategies for Crossing The Line-How to successfully achieve goals-Secrets to increasing your metabolism-Overcoming feelings of guilt-Foods that eliminate cravings-How to get and stay motivated-Healthy eating strategies-Resolving internal conflict-Plus mental exercises to help you integrate your new way of thinking.Plus, as a special bonus, Nancy will talk about her favorite supplements, and what makes them so important. If you are ready to take fitness to the next level, and discover your true fitness potential, then you are ready for Crossing The Line.

Crossing the River of Love: Music of the Bauls of Bengal. Sanatan Das Baul. 1 cass. (Running Time: 90 min.). 1992. 11.95 (978-0-934252-38-6(6)) Hohm Pr.
Music of the Bauls of India recorded while on tour in America 1991.

Crossing the Threshold: A Shift in Consciousness. unabr. ed. Kim Falcone & Steven Falcone. Read by Kim Falcone & Steven Falcone. 1 cass. (Running Time: 69 min.). 1995. 10.95 (978-1-887799-08-9(7), 2-006-584) Creat Aware.
A guided journey through time & space travel the corridors of your mind.

Crossing the Threshold: Beholding Your New Self. unabr. ed. Galexis. 2 cass. (Running Time: 3 hrs.). 1998. 19.95 Set. (978-1-56089-058-4(4), G141) Visionary FL.
In the growth process of Self, one must change self image, release the limits of the past, & step through to the new level to dream again - anew. Details are given on how to do this & what happens along the way. Includes questions & answers, & meditation.

Crossing the Threshold of Hope with the Flame of the Catholic Faith. Assumpta Long. 1 cass. 4.00 (96C3) IRL Chicago.

Crossing the Tracks for Love: What to Do When You & Your Partner Grew up in Different Worlds. Ruby K. Payne. 2005. audio compact disk 30.00 (978-1-929229-59-8(3)) aha Process.

Crossing the Wire. unabr. ed. Will Hobbs. Read by Ramon de Ocampo. 5 CDs. (Running Time: 6 hrs.). (YA). 2006. audio compact disk 49.75 (978-1-4281-1133-2(6), C3847); 39.75 (978-1-4281-1128-8(X), 98480) Recorded Bks.
With nothing but dogged determination, 15year-old Victor leaves his Mexican village to illegally enter the U.S. and help his starving family. Soon he must outwit gangs, drug-runners, and border agents as he endures shivering nights, blistering days, and gnawing hunger. But can his longing for the beckoning opportunity of El Norte carry him through such impossible obstacles?.

Crossing to Avalon Set: A Woman's Mid-Life Pilgrimage. Jean S. Bolen. Read by Jean Shinoda Bolen. 2 cass. (Running Time: 2 hrs.). 1994. 16.95 (978-0-7822-0468-1(6), 545) C G Jung IL.

Crossover. Michael Jan Friedman. Read by Jonathan Frakes. (Star Trek). 2004. 10.95 (978-0-7435-4626-3(1)) Pub: S&S Audio. Dist(s): S and S Inc

Crossover Dribble Audio Book. Pam P. J. Farris. (ENG.). (YA). 2009. audio compact disk 19.95 (978-1-932278-48-4(6)) Pub: Mayhaven Pub. Dist(s): Baker Taylor

*__Crossroad.__ abr. ed. Beverly Lewis. Narrated by Aimee Lilly. (Amish Country Crossroads Ser.). (ENG.). 2010. 12.98 (978-1-59644-923-7(3), christaudio) christianaud.

Crossroad. unabr. ed. C. K. Crigger. Read by Stephanie Brush. 8 cass. (Running Time: 9 hrs. 48 min.). (Time Travel Gunsmith Ser.: Bk. 3). 2001. 49.95 (978-1-58116-093-2(3)) Books in Motion.
The mysterious Teagun Dill appears at Boothenay's Gunshop to have a Weatherby pistol repaired. But the repair is only half the request. Boothenay

finds herself propelled foward in time as Dill's partner, when he faces a band of outlaws in a very futuristic earth setting.

Crossroad. unabr. ed. Beverly Lewis. Narrated by Barbara Caruso. 6 cass. (Running Time: 7 hrs. 45 mins.). 2000. 57.00 (978-0-7887-4955-1(2), K0010E7) Recorded Bks.
Journalist Philip Bradley can't forget Rachel Yoder, the blind Amish woman he met while on assignment in Pennsylvania. He is determined to find a cure for her & to get to know her better but before Rachel can move on in her life, she must confront traumatic memories. Can their growing love survive the gulf between their two worlds & Rachel's agonizing road to recovery?.

Crossroad. unabr. ed. Beverly Lewis. Narrated by Barbara Caruso. 6 cass. (Running Time: 8 hrs. 15 mins.). 2000. 57.00 (978-0-7887-4843-1(2), K0005E7) Recorded Bks.
Set in rural Pennsylvania, this poignant & inspiring work is filled with scenes from life in the Amish community. In a terrible moment, Rachel Yoder loses her husband, her son & her unborn child. Now, Rachel leads a reclusive life with her young daughter but the discovery of an old postcard, hidden for years, is about to change Rachel's world & renew her faith.

Crossroads. Shirley Brod & Irene Frankel. Told to Earl Stevick. (Crossroads Ser.). 1992. 39.95 (978-0-19-434384-8(7)) OUP.

Crossroads. La Resa Darrington. 3 cass. 2004. 14.95 (978-1-59156-185-9(X)) Covenant Comms.

Crossroads. Irene Frankel. (Crossroads Ser.). 1995. 24.50 (978-0-19-434686-3(2)) OUP.

Crossroads. abr. ed. Belva Plain. Read by Ann Marie Lee. 4 CDs. (Running Time: 5 hrs.). (ENG.). 2008. audio compact disk 27.95 (978-0-7393-0920-9(X)) Pub: Random Audio Pubg. Dist(s): Random

Crossroads. unabr. ed. Chris Grabenstein. Read by J. J. Myers. 5 CDs. (Running Time: 5 hrs. 47 mins.). (J). (gr. 4-7). 2008. audio compact disk 38.00 (978-0-7393-6704-9(8), Listening Lib) Pub: Random Audio Pubg. Dist(s): Random

Crossroads. unabr. ed. Chris Grabenstein. Read by J. J. Myers. (Running Time: 20820 sec.). (ENG.). (J). (gr. 4-7). 2008. audio compact disk 35.00 (978-0-7393-6702-5(1), Listening Lib) Pub: Random Audio Pubg. Dist(s): Random

***Crossroads.** unabr. ed. L. Ron Hubbard. Read by Edoardo Ballerini et al. Narrated by R. F. Daley. 2 CDs. (Running Time: 2 hrs.). (YA). 2010. audio compact disk 9.95 (978-1-59212-241-7(8)) Gala Pr LLC.

Crossroads, Level 4. Irene Frankel. Told to Earl W. Stevick. (Crossroads Ser.). 1994. 39.95 (978-0-19-434392-3(8)) OUP.

Crossroads, Pt. 1. Irene Frankel & Cliff Meyers. Told to Earl W. Stevick. (Crossroads Ser.). 1991. 39.95 (978-0-19-434380-0(4)) OUP.

Crossroads: Popular Music in America. Elizabeth F. Barkley. 2002. audio compact disk 28.00 (978-0-13-097147-0(2), P-H) Pearson Educ CAN CAN.

Crossroads: The Multicultural Roots of America's Popular Music. 2nd ed. Elizabeth F. Barkley. 2007. pap. bk. 72.07 (978-0-13-175590-1(0)) Pearson Educ CAN CAN.

***Crossroads: The Teenage Girl's Guide to Emotional Wounds.** Stephanie Smith & Suzy Weibel. (Running Time: 3 hrs. 19 mins. 0 sec.). (Invert Ser.). (ENG.). (YA). 2009. 9.99 (978-0-310-77240-8(0)) Zondervan.

Crossroads: 3 Keys to Making Better Decisions More Easily. Speeches. Stephanie deLuse'. 1 CD. (Running Time: 1 hour, 5 minutes). 2003. audio compact disk 24.95 (978-0-9746711-0-9(X)) Bast Cat.
Every decision is a crossroad of sorts and we each struggle to one degree or another with certain decisions at home or at work. Sometimes they truly are big decisions while other times we make mountains out of molehills. Either way, you can reduce the confusion, the worry, and the fear as you step on to the road. Come reflect on the process and leave with some insights that, should you decide to use them, will bring structure and focus to your decision-making. Can't decide whether to invest in this CD? Then you definitely need to!.

Crossroads Cafe: Assessment Tape A. Savage. 1 cass. 1.00 (978-0-8384-8088-5(8)) Heinle.

Crossroads: Caught in the ACT, Orange Level. Created by Steck-Vaughn Company. (Running Time: 2145 sec.). (J). 2007. audio compact disk 13.93 (978-1-4189-5020-0(3)) Heinemann Rai.

Crossroads of Faith. Richard Rohr. 2 cass. (Running Time: 2 hrs. 42 min.). 1994. 17.95 Set. (TAH317) Alba Hse Comns.
Fr. Rohr shows us how to recognize & accept our woundedness, & through contemplative exercises how to recognize & let go of those things that cloud our vision of God & self. He shows us how pain can often force us to give up control & how we can act out of the presence of God & Christ at our center.

Crossroads of Freedom: Antietam: The Battle That Changed the Course of the Civil War. unabr. ed. James M. McPherson. Narrated by Nelson Runger. 4 cass. (Running Time: 5 hrs. 45 mins.). 2002. 48.00 (978-1-4025-2877-4(9)) Recorded Bks.
Reconstructs the gripping Battle of Antietam-the single bloodiest day in the history of American combat. The South, after a series of setbacks in the spring of 1862, had reversed the war's momentum during the summer, and was on not only on the "brink of military victory" but about to achieve diplomatic recognition by European nations, most notably England and France.

Crossroads of Freedom: Antietam: The Battle That Changed the Course of the Civil War. unabr. ed. James M. McPherson. Narrated by Nelson Runger. 4 cass. (Running Time: 5 hrs. 45 mins.). 2004. 19.99 (978-1-4025-2805-7(1), 02064); audio compact disk 24.99 (978-1-4025-3070-8(6), 00582) Recorded Bks.
In this powerful book, he reconstructs the gripping Battle of Antietam-the single bloodiest day in the history of American combat. In stunning detail and with remarkable insight, McPherson makes a convincing case that Antietam was the battle that changed the course of the war.

Crossroads of Praise. Steven Warner. (Running Time: 49 mins.). 1999. audio compact disk 17.00 (978-1-58459-013-2(0), 7258) Wrld Lib Pubns.

Crossroads of Praise. Steven C. Warner. 1 cass. 1999. 11.00 (978-1-58459-012-5(2)) Wrld Lib Pubns.
Religous text & music.

Crossroads of Twilight. unabr. ed. Robert Jordan. 18 cass. (Running Time: 27 hrs.). (Wheel of Time Ser.: Bk. 10). 2003. 144.00 (978-0-7366-9250-2(9)) Books on Tape.
Fleeing from Ebou Dar, Mat Cauthon learns that he can neither keep his betrothed nor let her go. Perrin Aybara seeks to free his wife, Faile, a captive of the Shaido, but his only hope may be an alliance with the enemy. At Tar Valon, Egwene al'Vere, the young Amyrlin of the rebel Aes Sedai, lays siege to the heart of Aes Sedai power, but she must win quickly. In Andor, Elayne Trakland fights for the Lion Throne that is hers by right, but enemies and Darkfriends plot her destruction.

Crossroads of Twilight. unabr. ed. Robert Jordan. Read by Michael Kramer & Kate Reading. (Wheel of Time Ser.: Bk. 10). 2003. audio compact disk 160.00 (978-0-7366-9252-6(5)) Books on Tape.

Crossroads of Twilight. unabr. rev. ed. Robert Jordan. Read by Michael Kramer & Kate Reading. 21 CDs. (Running Time: 27 hrs. 0 mins. 0 sec.). (Wheel of Time Ser.: Bk. 10). (ENG., 2003. audio compact disk 75.00 (978-1-55927-806-5(4)) Pub: Macmill Audio. Dist(s): Macmillan

Crossroads, U. S. A. Discovering American Culture & Language with the Daily Newspaper. Robert S. Hughes. 3 cass. (Running Time: 3 hrs.). 2000. pap. bk., tchr. ed., stu. ed. 47.95 (P0451-X); 49.32 (P0434-X) M-H Contemporary.
Gain insight into American culture & life with this collection of recent articles from the "Chicago Tribune," the paper that has been taking the pulse of America for 150 years.

Crossroads, U. S. A. Discovering American Culture & Language with the Daily Newspaper. Robert S. Hughes. 2001. 47.95 (978-0-8442-0448-2(X), 0448x) M-H Contemporary.

Crossroads 3. Irene Frankel. Told to Earl Stevick. (Crossroads Ser.). 1992. 39.95 (978-0-19-434388-6(X)) OUP.

Crosswind. abr. ed. M. Warwick. 2 cass. (Running Time: 180 min.). 1999. 11.95 (978-1-894188-01-2(2)) APG.

Crossword Deluxe. (Timesaving Software Tools for Teachers Ser.). 2004. audio compact disk 19.99 (978-0-7439-3805-1(4)) Tchr Create Ma.

Crouzon Syndrome - A Bibliography & Dictionary for Physicians, Patients, & Genome Researchers. Compiled by Icon Group International, Inc. Staff. 2007. ring bd. 28.95 (978-0-497-11362-9(7)) Icon Grp.

Crouzonodermoskeletal Syndrome - A Bibliography & Dictionary for Physicians, Patients, & Genome Researchers. Compiled by Icon Group International, Inc. Staff. 2007. ring bd. 28.95 (978-0-497-11363-6(5)) Icon Grp.

Crow Biddy. unabr. ed. Gillian White. Read by Jilly Bond. 6 cass. (Running Time: 6 hrs. 48 mins.). (Isis Cassettes Ser.). (J). 2004. 54.95 (978-0-7531-1928-0(5)) Pub: ISIS Lrg Prnt GBR. Dist(s): Ulverscroft US

Crow Biddy. unabr. ed. Gillian White. 6 CDs. (Running Time: 7 hrs. 42 mins.). (Isis (CDs) Ser.). (J). 2004. audio compact disk 64.95 (978-0-7531-2305-8(3)) Pub: ISIS Lrg Prnt GBR. Dist(s): Ulverscroft US

Crow Boy. 2004. 8.95 (978-1-56008-880-6(X)); cass. & flmstrp 30.00 (978-0-89719-625-3(2)) Weston Woods.

Crow Boy. (J). 2004. bk. 24.95 (978-0-89719-868-4(9)); pap. bk. 32.75 (978-1-55592-190-3(6)); pap. bk. 14.95 (978-1-56008-050-3(7)) Weston Woods.

Crow Boy. Taro Yashima. Read by Jerry Terheyden. 1 cass. (J). 2000. pap. bk. 19.97 (978-0-7366-9208-3(8)) Books on Tape.
A shy mountain boy in Japan is ridiculed by his schoolmates, until they understand why he is different.

Crow Boy. Taro Yashima. Illus. by Taro Yashima. 14 vols. (Running Time: 11 mins.). pap. bk. 35.95 (978-1-59112-803-8(X)) Live Oak Media.

Crow Boy. Taro Yashima. Illus. by Taro Yashima. (Running Time: 11 mins.). (J). (gr. k-3). 1982. 9.95 (978-1-59112-025-4(X)) Live Oak Media.

Crow Boy. Taro Yashima. Illus. by Taro Yashima. (Running Time: 11 mins.). 1982. audio compact disk 12.95 (978-1-59112-800-7(5)) Live Oak Media.

Crow Boy. Taro Yashima. Read by Jerry Terheyden. 11 vols. (Running Time: 11 mins.). (J). 2005. pap. bk. 18.95 (978-1-59112-801-4(3)) Pub: Live Oak Media. Dist(s): AudioGO

Crow Boy. Taro Yashima. 1 cass., 5 bks. (Running Time: 30 min.). (J). pap. bk. 32.75 Weston Woods.
A small boy who is different is finally accepted by the other children when he shows off his talent of imitating the voices of the crows. From the book by Taro Yashima.

Crow Boy. Taro Yashima. 1 cass. (J). (ps-4). pap. bk. 12.95 (PRA042); 8.00 (RAC042) Weston Woods.

Crow Boy. Taro Yashima. 1 cass. (Running Time: 30 min.). (J). (ps-4). 2000. pap. bk. 12.95 Weston Woods.

Crow Boy. Taro Yashima. Tr. by Maria A. Fiot. (J). (gr. 7-8). 2004. 8.95 (978-1-56008-127-2(9)) Weston Woods.

Crow Boy. unabr. ed. Taro Yashima. Read by Jerry Terheyden. 11 vols. (Running Time: 11 mins.). (J). (gr. k-3). 1975. bk. 25.95 (978-0-670-24936-7(X)); pap. bk. 16.95 (978-0-670-24939-8(4)); pap. bk. & tchr. ed. 33.95 Reading Chest. (978-0-670-24933-6(5)) Live Oak Media.
A shy mountain boy in Japan is ridiculed by his schoolmates. This stops when they understand why he is different.

Crow Boy cassette LC-753CS. Taro Yashima. Illus. by Taro Yashima. 9.95 (978-1-59112-502-0(2)) Live Oak Media.

Crow Boy; Petunia; Little Tim & the Brave Sea Captain; Three Billy Goats Gruff. 2004. (978-0-89719-810-3(7)); cass. & flmstrp (978-0-89719-719-9(4)) Weston Woods.

Crow Dog: Four Generations of Sioux Medicine Men, Set. abr. ed. Leonard Crow Dog & Richard Erdoes. Read by Machiste. 2 cass. (Running Time: 3 hrs.). 1995. 17.00 (978-0-694-51489-2(6), 390582) HarperCollins Pubs.
A multi-generational oral history of the Sioux clan.

Crow Dreaming. Poems. Edward Hanson. (Running Time: 30 minutes). 2004. audio compact disk 10.00 (978-0-9769593-1-1(3)) Bear Tracks.

Crow Feather. abr. ed. Paul A. Hawkins. Read by Ben Hall. 4 cass. (Running Time: 6 hrs.). 2001. 24.95 (978-1-890990-58-9(2), 99058) Otis Audio.
Tyson Garth came to the Montana Territory with one thought: to find & kill a traitor. Yet thoughts of vengeance are soon pushed aside by the adventure & beauty of the wild Western frontier & by the love he finds with the lovely half-Indian woman called Bird.

Crow-Girl. unabr. ed. Bodil Bredsdorff. Narrated by Felice Yeh. 3 CDs. (Running Time: 3 hrs. 45 mins.). (J). 2005. audio compact disk 39.75 (978-1-4193-3824-3(2), C3271); 32.75 (978-1-4193-3611-9(8), 98020) Recorded Bks.
Beloved Danish author Bodil Bredsdorff, a Mildred L. Batchelder Award winner, has written many wonderful books for children. This touching story of a girl who lives with her grandmother by the sea is Bredsdorff ¿s first novel to be translated into English. Crow-Girl and grandmother live a peaceful, solitary life together. But grandmother is very old, and warns her granddaughter that one day soon she may die. Before that day comes, she imparts important lessons about the kinds of people Crow-Girl will encounter on her journey toward finding a new family.

Crow in the House, Wolf at the Door. Frances Nail. Read by Frances Nail. Music by Carrie Rodriguez. 2006. audio compact disk 15.00 (978-0-9657883-8-0(5)) F Nail.

Crow Road, Set. unabr. ed. Iain Banks, pseud. Read by Ewan Stewart. 12 cass. 1999. 96.95 (978-0-7540-0024-2(9), CAB1447) AudioGO.
Prentice McHoan returns home to his complex but enduring Scottish family. Relations with his father are strained & the woman of his dreams is simply out of reach. He is also deeply preoccupied with death, sex, God, drink & illegal substances. But his greatest preoccupation is with Uncle Rory, a traveler & some-times magician, whose most successful act had been his own disappearance.

Crowd see Fantastic Tales of Ray Bradbury

Crowded Land of Liberty. unabr. ed. Chase Eldredge Dirk. Read by Jeff Riggenbach. 3 cass. (Running Time: 4 hrs.). 2004. 23.95 (978-0-7861-2794-8(5), 3321); audio compact disk 32.00 (978-0-7861-8482-8(5), 3321) Blckstn Audio.

***Crowded Shadows.** unabr. ed. Celine Kiernan. Read by Ellen Grafton & Kate Rudd. (Running Time: 14 hrs.). (Moorehawke Trilogy). 2010. 24.99 (978-1-4418-9183-9(8), 9781441891839, BAD); 39.97 (978-1-4418-9184-6(6), 9781441891846, BADLE); 24.99 (978-1-4418-9181-5(1), 9781441891815, Brilliance MP3); 39.97 (978-1-4418-9182-2(X), 9781441891822, Brlnc Audio MP3 Lib) Brilliance Audio.

***Crowded Shadows.** unabr. ed. Celine Kiernan. Read by Ellen Grafton. (Running Time: 16 hrs.). (Moorehawke Trilogy). 2010. audio compact disk 34.99 (978-1-4418-9179-2(X), 9781441891792, Bril Audio CD Unabri) Brilliance Audio.

***Crowded Shadows.** unabr. ed. Celine Kiernan. Read by Ellen Grafton & Kate Rudd. (Running Time: 16 hrs.). (Moorehawke Trilogy). 2010. audio compact disk 89.97 (978-1-4418-9180-8(3), 9781441891808, BriAudCD Unabrid) Brilliance Audio.

Crowdsourcing: Why the Power of the Crowd Is Driving the Future of Business. unabr. ed. Jeff Howe. Read by Kirby Heyborne. 8 CDs. (Running Time: 10 hrs. 15 mins.). 2008. audio compact disk 100.00 (978-1-4159-4957-3(3), BksonTape) Pub: Random Audio Pubg. Dist(s): Random

Crowdsourcing: Why the Power of the Crowd Is Driving the Future of Business. unabr. ed. Jeff Howe. Read by Kirby Heyborne. (Running Time: 5 hrs.). (ENG.). 2008. 20.00 (978-0-7393-6659-2(9)); audio compact disk 34.95 (978-0-7393-6658-5(0), Random AudioBks) Pub: Random Audio Pubg. Dist(s): Random

Crown Chakra Workshop. Jackie Woods. 2003. audio compact disk 49.95 (978-0-9659665-8-0(5)) Adawehi Pr.

Crown Him King Cassette Kit. Marty Parks. 1999. 54.95 (978-0-633-00511-5(8)) LifeWay Christian.

Crown Him King Cd Kit. Marty Parks. 1999. audio compact disk 59.95 (978-0-633-00512-2(6)) LifeWay Christian.

Crown Him King Cd Promo Pak. Marty Parks. 1999. audio compact disk 12.00 (978-0-633-00513-9(4)) LifeWay Christian.

Crown Him King Choral Cassette. Marty Parks. 1999. 11.98 (978-0-633-00529-0(0)) LifeWay Christian.

Crown Him King Choral Cd. Marty Parks. 1999. audio compact disk 16.98 (978-0-633-00521-4(5)) LifeWay Christian.

Crown Him King Split Acc Cd. Marty Parks. 1999. audio compact disk 50.00 (978-0-633-00525-2(8)) LifeWay Christian.

Crown Him King Stereo/Split Acc Cassette. Marty Parks. 1999. 40.00 (978-0-633-00533-7(9)) LifeWay Christian.

Crown in Darkness. unabr. ed. Paul C. Doherty. Narrated by Paul Matthews. 5 cass. (Running Time: 7 hrs.). 2001. 47.00 (978-1-84197-186-5(3), H1170E7) Recorded Bks.
Alexander III, King of Scotland, perishes suddenly on a murky, rainy night. Since he has no heir, the Scottish throne immediately becomes a hotly contested prize. However, there are some who believe that the king's death was no accident. Hugh Corbett, clerk to the English Chancellor Bishop Burnell, is sent north to investigate.

Crown Jewel. abr. ed. Fern Michaels. Read by John Dossett. 2004. 15.95 (978-0-7435-4530-3(3)) Pub: S&S Audio. Dist(s): S and S Inc

Crown Jewel. abr. ed. Fern Michaels. Read by John Dossett. (Running Time: 4 hrs. 30 mins. 0 sec.). (ENG.). 2007. audio compact disk 14.95 (978-0-7435-6108-2(5)) Pub: S&S Audio. Dist(s): S and S Inc

Crown Living Language Plus. 1 cass. (Running Time: 90 min.). 10.00 incl. script. (LivingLang) Random Info Grp.
Dialogues featuring an American & a Frenchman in a particular setting.

Crown of Age. Marion K. Woodward. 2 CDs. 2005. audio compact disk 19.95 (978-1-59179-269-7(X), AW00528D) Sounds True.

Crown of Lights. Phil Rickman. 2009. 99.95 (978-0-7531-3371-2(7)); audio compact disk 104.95 (978-0-7531-3372-9(5)) Pub: Isis Pubng Ltd GBR. Dist(s): Ulverscroft US

Crown of Swords. abr. ed. Scripts. Robert Jordan. Perf. by Mark Rolston. 4 cass. (Running Time: 6 hrs.). (Wheel of Time Ser.: Bk. 7). 2003. 24.95 (978-1-59007-328-5(2), N Millennium Audio); 34.95 (978-1-59007-329-2(0), N Millennium Audio) Pub: New Millenn Enter. Dist(s): PerseuPGW

Crown of Swords. abr. ed. Robert Jordan. Read by Mark Rolston. 4 cass. (Running Time: 6 hrs.). (Wheel of Time Ser.: Bk. 7). 1996. 24.95 (978-1-879371-96-5(0)) Pub Mills.

Crown of Swords. unabr. ed. Robert Jordan. Read by Kate Reading & Michael Kramer. 27 CDs. (Running Time: 31 hrs. 0 mins. 0 sec.). (Wheel of Time Ser.: Bk. 7). (ENG.). 2006. audio compact disk 69.95 (978-1-59397-976-8(2)) Pub: Macmill Audio. Dist(s): Macmillan

Crown of Swords. unabr. ed. Scripts. Robert Jordan. Perf. by Michael Kramer & Kate Reading. 22 CDs. (Running Time: 26 hrs.). (Wheel of Time Ser.: Bk. 7). 2003. audio compact disk 69.95 (978-1-59007-397-1(5), N Millennium Audio); 49.95 (978-1-59007-396-4(7), N Millennium Audio) Pub: New Millenn Enter. Dist(s): PerseuPGW
As the disastrous heat wave continues to damage the world, Rand ever developing powers are put to the test as he must travel through the land of the blood-hungry Mashadar to confront Sammael, a Forsaken one.

Crown of Swords, Pt. 1. unabr. ed. Robert Jordan. Read by Kate Reading & Michael Kramer. 11 cass. (Running Time: 16 hrs. 30 min.). (Wheel of Time Ser.: Bk. 7). 1998. 88.00 (978-0-7366-4173-9(4), 4673-A) Books on Tape.
The tale is set in a mythic land torn between the forces of Light & Darkness. A young man from a small farming village, Rand al'Thor is destined to become the Dragon Reborn, the champion who will confront the ultimate evil known as the Dark One.

Crown of Swords, Pt. 2. unabr. ed. Robert Jordan. Read by Kate Reading & Michael Kramer. 11 cass. (Running Time: 16 hrs. 30 min.). (Wheel of Time Ser.: Bk. 7). 1998. 88.00 (978-0-7366-4174-6(2), 4673-B) Books on Tape.

Crown on Life: Rev. 2:8-10. Ed Young. 1986. 4.95 (978-0-7417-1551-7(1), 551) Win Walk.

Crowned Heads. unabr. collector's ed. Thomas Tryon. Read by Dan Lazar. 10 cass. (Running Time: 15 hrs.). 1977. 80.00 (978-0-7366-0094-1(9), 1102) Books on Tape.
Takes us into the lives of four film stars.

Crowned with Glory. Ed Young. 1991. 4.95 (978-0-7417-1877-8(4)) Win Walk.

***Crowning Glory of Calla Lily Ponder.** Rebecca Wells. Read by Judith Ivey. 10 CDs. (Running Time: 12 hrs. 30 mins.). 2009. audio compact disk 100.00 (978-1-4159-6613-6(3), BksonTape) Pub: Random Audio Pubg. Dist(s): Random

Crowning Glory of Calla Lily Ponder. unabr. ed. Rebecca Wells. Read by Judith Ivey. 2009. audio compact disk 39.99 (978-0-06-180376-5(6), Harper Audio) HarperCollins Pubs.

***Crowning Glory of Calla Lily Ponder.** unabr. ed. Rebecca Wells. Read by Judith Ivey. (ENG.). 2009. (978-0-06-196149-6(3), Harper Audio); (978-0-06-196150-2(7), Harper Audio) HarperCollins Pubs.

Crows & Cards. unabr. ed. Joseph Helgerson. Read by MacLeod Andrews. 1 MP3-CD. (Running Time: 7 hrs.). 2009. 24.99 (978-1-4233-9176-0(4), 9781423391760, Brilliance MP3); 24.99 (978-1-4233-9178-4(0), 9781423391784, BAD); 39.97 (978-1-4233-9177-7(2), 9781423391777, Brinc Audio MP3 Lib); 39.97 (978-1-4233-9179-1(9), 9781423391791, BADLE); audio compact disk 24.99 (978-1-4233-9174-6(8), 9781423391746) Brilliance Audio.

Crows & Cards. unabr. ed. Joseph Helgerson. Read by MacLeod Andrews. 6 CDs. (Running Time: 7 hrs.). (J). (gr. 4-8). 2009. audio compact disk 69.97 (978-1-4233-9175-3(6), 9781423391753, BriAudCD Unabrid) Brilliance Audio.

Crows & the Serpent - The Monkey & the Crocodile. Naseeruddin Shah. 1 cass. (Running Time: 048 min.). (Karadi Tales Ser.). (YA). (gr. 1-4). 1998. bk. 15.99 (978-81-86838-04-4(X)) APG.
Asian fairy tales & folklore.

CRS (Computer-Related Syndrome) The Prevention & Treatment of Computer-Related Injuries. Richard Dean Smith & Steven T. Garske. (ENG., 1997. 23.98 (978-1-57392-145-9(9)) Prometheus Bks.

***Cruach Na Caoile.** Michael Ghabha. (ENG.). 1988. 11.95 (978-0-8023-7007-5(1)) Pub: Clo Iar-Chonnachta IRL. Dist(s): Dufour

Crucial Confrontations. abr. ed. Kerry Patterson et al. Read by Barrett Whitener. (Running Time: 16200 sec.). 2005. audio compact disk 28.00 (978-1-932378-82-5(0)) Pub: A Media Intl. Dist(s): Natl Bk Netwk

Crucial Conversations: Tools for Talking When Stakes Are High. abr. ed. Kerry Pattersom et al. 3 cass. (Running Time: 4 hrs. 30 mins.). (McGraw Hill Audiobks.). 2003. 24.00 (978-0-9724462-2-8(2)) Pub: A Media Intl. Dist(s): Natl Bk Netwk
Crucial Conversaions gives people the tools to handle life's most difficult and important conversations.

Crucial Conversations: Tools for Talking When Stakes Are High. abr. ed. Kerry Patterson et al. 4 CDs. (Running Time: 4 hrs. 30 mins.). (McGraw Hill Audiobks.). 2003. audio compact disk 28.00 (978-0-9724889-0-7(1)) Pub: A Media Intl. Dist(s): Natl Bk Netwk
This book gives people the tools to handle life's most difficult and important conversations.

Crucial Years, 1938-45. 1 cass. 10.00 Esstee Audios.
A collection of vital newscasts from the Hitlerian era to post World War II giving an overview of a exciting period.

Crucible. unabr. ed. Arthur Miller. Perf. by Richard Dreyfuss & Stacy Keach. 2 CDs. (Running Time: 7140 sec.). Dramatization. (L. A. Theatre Works). 2001. audio compact disk 25.95 (978-1-58081-219-1(8), CDRDP5) Pub: L A Theatre. Dist(s): NetLibrary CO
Based on the witch trials in Salem Village.

Crucible. unabr. ed. Arthur Miller. Read by Richard Dreyfuss & Stacy Keach. (YA). 2008. 34.99 (978-1-60514-881-6(4)) Find a World.

Crucible: A Play in Four Acts. Arthur Miller. 1994. pap. bk. & tchr. ed. 64.95 (978-0-14-024277-5(5)) Penguin Elect.

Crucible: A Play in Four Acts. unabr. ed. Arthur Miller. Perf. by Jerome Dempsey & Alexandra Stoddart. 4 cass. (Running Time: 6 hrs.). Dramatization. 1984. 35.95 (978-0-694-50914-0(0), SWC 356) HarperCollins Pubs.
Cast includes: Theresa Merritt, Pamela Payton-Wright, Crickett Coan, Pauline Flanagan, Ben Hammer, Kathleen Doyle, Nora Heflin, Robert Foxworth, Aline MacMahon, Sydney Walker, Robert Phelan, Martha Henry, Wendell Phillips, John Newton, Richard Kline, Robert Symonds, Stephen Elliott, Doris Rich & Stuart Pankin.

Crucible: A Play in Four Acts. unabr. ed. Arthur Miller. Perf. by Richard Dreyfuss & Stacy Keach. 2 cass. (Running Time: 1 hr. 59 mins.). Dramatization. 2001. 23.95 (978-1-58081-204-7(X), RDP5) L A Theatre.
Based on the witch trials in Salem Village.

Crucible Soundtrack. Prod. by Myattic Studio. (YA). 2000. audio compact disk 89.95 (978-0-7365-3270-9(6)) Films Media Grp.

Crucificado Contigo. unabr. ed. 1 CD. 2001. audio compact disk 11.99 (978-0-8297-3492-8(9)) Zondervan.

Crucificado Contigo. unabr. ed. Paul Rodriguez & Zondervan Publishing Staff. (SPA.). 2001. 7.99 (978-0-8297-3494-2(5)) Zondervan.

Crucified with Christ. Contrib. by Dale Mathews & Michael Frazier. 1996. 24.95 (978-0-7601-1180-2(4), 75600280) Pub: Brentwood Music. Dist(s): H Leonard

Crucified with Christ. Elbert Willis. 1 cass. (Understanding the Crucified Life Ser.). 4.00 Fill the Gap.

Crucifixion & Resurrection: Images of Death & Rebirth. Read by David Dalrymple. 1 cass. (Running Time: 90 min.). (Patterns of Divinity Ser.: No. 3). 1988. 10.95 (978-0-7822-0051-5(6), 303) C G Jung IL.

***Crucifixion, Death & Resurrection of Jesus.** unabr. ed. Zondervan. (Running Time: 0 hr. 14 mins. 52 sec.). (Best-Loved Stories of the Bible, NIrV Ser.). (ENG.). (J). 2010. 1.99 (978-0-310-86534-6(4)) Pub: Zondkidz. Dist(s): Zondervan

Cruel & Unusual. Patricia Cornwell. Narrated by C. J. Critt. 10 CDs. (Running Time: 11 hrs. 45 mins.). (Kay Scarpetta Ser.: No. 4). 2001. audio compact disk 97.00 (978-0-7887-5177-6(8), C1339E7) Recorded Bks.
When an executed murderer's fingerprints turn up at a new crime scene, Kay Scarpetta investigates.

Cruel & Unusual. unabr. ed. Patricia Cornwell. Narrated by C. J. Critt. 8 cass. (Running Time: 11 hrs. 45 mins.). (Kay Scarpetta Ser.: No. 4). 2000. 70.00 (978-1-55690-849-1(0), 93217E7) Recorded Bks.
The Richmond police & Virginia's chief medical examiner are stumped when a convicted murderer dies in the Virginia electric chair, only to reappear as a possible suspect in a similar case later.

Cruel & Unusual. unabr. collector's ed. Patricia Cornwell. Read by Donada Peters. 8 cass. (Running Time: 12 hrs.). (Kay Scarpetta Ser.: No. 4). 1993. 64.00 (978-0-7366-2518-0(6), 3273) Books on Tape.
The state executes Ronnie Joe Waddell, a convicted killer, but it can't kill his legacy. Some papers he stole are still missing, papers the governor would do just about anything to retrieve. Then Waddell's fingerprints turn up at the scene of a new murder, after his death? Kay Scarpetta becomes a suspect herself in a case that threatens her life & career. Somewhere in the state's corridors of power, perhaps in her own office, lurks an enemy who will destroy her unless she can clear her name.

Cruel as the Grave: A Sheriff Bramlett Mystery. unabr. ed. John Armistead. Narrated by Mark Hammer. 9 cass. (Running Time: 12 hrs. 30 mins.). (Sheriff Bramlett Mystery Ser.). 1966. 78.00 (978-0-7887-4053-4(9), 96004E7) Recorded Bks.

Cruel Death. unabr. ed. M. William Phelps. Read by J. Charles. (Running Time: 11 hrs.). 2009. 39.97 (978-1-4233-8335-2(4), 9781423383352, Brinc Audio MP3 Lib); 24.99 (978-1-4233-8334-5(6), 9781423383345, Brilliance MP3); 39.97 (978-1-4233-8337-6(0), 9781423383376, BADLE); 24.99 (978-1-4233-8336-9(2), 9781423383369, BAD); audio compact disk 36.99 (978-1-4233-8332-1(X), 9781423383321, Bril Audio CD Unabri); audio compact disk 97.97 (978-1-4233-8333-8(8), 9781423383338, BriAudCD Unabrid) Brilliance Audio.

Cruel Intent. abr. ed. J. A. Jance. Read by Karen Ziemba. 5 CDs. (Running Time: 6 hrs. 0 mins. 0 sec.). No. 4. (ENG.). 2008. audio compact disk 29.99 (978-0-7435-7487-7(7)) Pub: S&S Audio. Dist(s): S and S Inc

***Cruel Intent.** abr. ed. J. A. Jance. Read by Karen Ziemba. (Running Time: 6 hrs. 0 mins. 0 sec.). (ENG.). 2010. audio compact disk 14.99 (978-1-4423-3554-7(8)) Pub: S&S Audio. Dist(s): S and S Inc

Cruel Intent. unabr. ed. J. A. Jance. Read by Karen Ziemba. 9 CDs. (Running Time: 9 hrs. 30 mins.). (Ali Reynolds Ser.: No. 4). 2009. audio compact disk 39.99 (978-1-4361-7823-5(1)) Recorded Bks.

Cruel Intent. unabr. ed. J. A. Jance. Read by Karen Ziemba. (Running Time: 10 hrs. 0 mins. 0 sec.). No. 4. (ENG.). 2008. audio compact disk 39.99 (978-0-7435-7489-1(3)) Pub: S&S Audio. Dist(s): S and S Inc

Cruel Justice. unabr. ed. William Bernhardt. Read by Jonathan Marosz. 9 cass. (Running Time: 13 hrs. 30 min.). (Ben Kincaid Ser.: No. 5). 1998. 72.00 (978-0-7366-4180-7(7), 4678) Books on Tape.
Ten years ago, a black caddy at a prestigious golf club was charged with murdering a white woman. With delays in the legal system, the caddy is only now being brought to trial. Oklahoma lawyer, Ben Kincaid, enrolls as defense attorney. Meanwhile, a young boy falls prey to a pedophile, then vanishes without a trace. Could a missing boy & an old golf murder be linked.

Cruel Sanctuary. unabr. ed. Brad Reynolds. Read by Kevin Foley. 12 cass. (Running Time: 12 hrs. 30 min.). (Father Mark Townsend Mystery Ser.). 2001. 64.95 (978-1-58116-181-6(6)); audio compact disk 71.50 (978-1-58116-189-2(1)) Books in Motion.
An act of charity backfires on Father Mark when he becomes a suspect in a murder case.

Cruel Sea. abr. ed. Nicholas Monsarrat. Perf. by Jack Hawkins & Laurence Payne. 1 cass. (Running Time: 90 min.). Dramatization. 1984. 9.95 (978-0-89845-803-9(X), CDL5 1604) HarperCollins Pubs.
Cast includes: Martin Starke, Russell Napier, Andrew Crawford, Deryck Guyler, Victor Maddern, Jeffrey Segal, Jack Allen, Derek Birch, Peter Howell, Michael Turner & Edgar Norfolk.

Cruel Sea. unabr. ed. Nicholas Monsarrat. Read by Chris Winfield. 11 cass. (Running Time: 16 hrs. 30 mins.). 1977. 88.00 (978-0-7366-0044-6(2), 1055) Books on Tape.
The Cruel Sea draws upon Monsarrat's experiences during World War II & centers around two British ships: Compass Rose, a corvette & Saltesh, a frigate. Monsarrat describes the naval war in the North Atlantic through a series of often gruesome, powerful episodes.

Cruel Venus. unabr. ed. Susan Lewis. 14 cass. (Isis Ser.). (J). 2002. 99.95 (978-0-7531-1363-9(5)) Pub: ISIS Lrg Prnt GBR. Dist(s): Ulverscroft US

Cruelest Miles: The Heroic Story of Dogs & Men in a Race Against an Epidemic. abr. ed. Gay Salisbury. (Running Time: 6 hrs.). (ENG.). 2003. 14.95 (978-0-375-41939-3(X)) Random.

Cruelest Month. unabr. ed. Louise Penny. Read by Ralph Cosham. (Running Time: 11 hrs. 30 mins.). (Chief Inspector Armand Gamache Ser.: Bk. 3). 2010. audio compact disk 32.95 (978-1-4332-3379-1(7)) Blckstn Audio.

Cruellest Month. unabr. ed. Louise Penny. Read by Ralph Cosham. (Running Time: 43200 sec.). (Chief Inspector Armand Gamache Ser.: Bk. 3). 2008. 65.95 (978-1-4332-3376-0(2)); audio compact disk & audio compact disk 90.00 (978-1-4332-3377-7(0)); audio compact disk & audio compact disk 29.95 (978-1-4332-3380-7(0)) Blckstn Audio.

Cruelty: Ancient & Modern: Exodus 1. Ed Young. 1984. 4.95 (978-0-7417-1410-7(8), 410) Win Walk.

Cruise. unabr. ed. Brendan Guy Alimo. 9 CDs. (Running Time: 9 hrs. 38 min.). 2003. audio compact disk 49.95 (978-0-9724806-5-9(X)) BGA Stories.
A unique Cruise missile, painted like a shark, vanishes after being test-launched in the distant Pacific. Solitary, Amazon anthropologist, Ignatius Tapp, sees it land intact by parachute while he is recording a Xingaru boy exploring the Earth Mother, sacred lair of the flesh-eating spirit of the forest. Drugged by the Shaiman's potions, Karkamo believes Cruise is the dreaded Curupira.

Cruise. unabr. ed. Brendan Guy Alimo. Read by Brendan Guy Alimo. 7 cass. (Running Time: 9 hrs. 30 min.). 2003. 44.95 (978-0-9724806-6-6(8)) BGA Stories.

Cruise Connection. Peter Kerr. 2009. 76.95 (978-1-4079-0644-7(5)); audio compact disk 89.95 (978-1-4079-0645-4(3)) Pub: Soundings Ltd GBR. Dist(s): Ulverscroft US

Cruise Control. unabr. ed. Terry Trueman. Narrated by Andy Paris. 3 cass. (Running Time: 3 hrs. 30 mins.). (YA). 2005. 31.75 (978-1-4193-3109-1(4), 97996) Recorded Bks.
Paul McDaniel is an A student, an exceptional athlete and a high school senior planning a promising future at Georgetown University. He is also incredibly angry. He is the "other" son: the healthy, gifted, normal one. His 14-year-old brother Shawn is a "veg" confined to a wheelchair with cerebral palsy and no way of communicating with the family. Their father recently moved out of the house, leaving Paul and his mother to deal with Shawn. Angry that his father abandoned the family, Paul expresses his rage with extreme violence. Basketball offers him an escape from the pain; but, with fighting he senses a "weird relief." Controlling his anger is crucial before Paul can take control of his life. Stuck in Neutral (RB# 96932), a Printz Honor Book, gives a different perspective on this struggling family.

Cruise of the Commissioner. Richard Woodman. 7 CDs. (Sound Ser.). (J). 2003. audio compact disk 71.95 (978-1-84283-518-0(1)) Pub: ISIS Lrg Prnt GBR. Dist(s): Ulverscroft US

Cruise of the Commissioner. unabr. ed. Richard Woodman. Read by Gordon Griffin. 7 cass. (Running Time: 7 hrs.). 2001. 61.95 (978-1-86042-705-3(7)) Pub: Soundings Ltd GBR. Dist(s): Ulverscroft US
Captain James St. John Stanier, formerly Porth Ardur's ambitious Harbor Master, has now been elected a commissioner of Celtic Lighthouses. And from this elevated position he is determined to get even with Septimus Macready, captain of the lighthouse tender, Caryatid. So when Macready's ship steam-rollers Bishop Island's bakery, Stanier sees a heaven-sent opportunity to ruin his old rival.

Cruise of the Dazzler. Jack London. Read by Jim Killavey. 3 cass. (Running Time: 3 hrs.). 1987. 21.00 incl. albums. (C-170) Jimcin Record.
A teenager runs away from the restrictions of home only to be captured by bay pirates.

***Cruisers.** unabr. ed. Walter Dean Myers. (Running Time: 2 hrs.). (Cruisers Ser.). 2010. 19.99 (978-1-4418-6331-7(1), 9781441863317, BAD); 14.99 (978-1-4418-6329-4(X), 9781441863294, Brilliance MP3); 39.97 (978-1-4418-6332-4(X), 9781441863324, BADLE) Brilliance Audio.

***Cruisers.** unabr. ed. Walter Dean Myers. Read by Kevin R. Free. (Running Time: 2 hrs.). (Cruisers Ser.). 2010. 39.97 (978-1-4418-6330-0(3), 9781441863300, Brinc Audio MP3 Lib); audio compact disk 49.97 (978-1-4418-6328-7(1), 9781441863287, BriAudCD Unabrid) Brilliance Audio.

***Cruisers.** unabr. ed. Walter Dean Myers. Read by Kevin Free. (Running Time: 2 hrs.). (Cruisers Ser.). (YA). 2010. audio compact disk 19.99 (978-1-4418-6327-0(3), 9781441863270, Bril Audio CD Unabri) Brilliance Audio.

Cruisin' Route 66: America's Main Street. unabr. ed. Joe Loesch & Readio Theatre Staff. Read by Joe Loesch. 3 CDs. (Running Time: 3 hrs. 0 mins. 0 sec.). (ENG.). 2009. audio compact disk 19.99 (978-1-59859-475-1(3), SpringWater) Oasis Audio.

Cruising Home. unabr. ed. Gail Taylor. Read by Gail Taylor. Ed. by James B. Kirgan. 1 cass. (Running Time: 1 hr. 30 min.). (Essence of Nature Ser.: Vol. 15). (J). 1989. 12.99 stereo. (978-1-878362-15-5(1)) Emerald Ent.
On this tape Thumper, the adventure dog, sails on a cruise from Washington State to Alaska to rejoin the pack of Samoyeds. This tape includes actual sounds from both a Pacific cruise & the Mount McKinley National Park.

Cruising Life. unabr. collector's ed. Ross Norgrove. Read by Bob Erickson. 7 cass. (Running Time: 10 hrs. 30 mins.). 1983. 56.00 (978-0-7366-0549-6(5), 1523) Books on Tape.
If you yeam to abandon your landlocked existence & sail off into the sunset, whether you are just daydreaming or seriously considering it, "The Cruising Life" provides answers to such questions as: How do I do this? What does it cost? Have those who've relinquished steady jobs been able to eam enough to continue this life?.

Crummy Mummy & Me. unabr. ed. Anne Fine. Read by Brenda Blethyn. 2 cass. (Running Time: 2 hrs. 30 mins.). 2002. (978-1-85549-746-7(8)) Cover To Cover GBR.
How would you feel if your mother had royal-blue hair and wore lavender fishnet tights? It is not easy for Minna being the only sensible one in the family.

Crumpet, the Cat: Audiocassette. Jill Eggleton. Illus. by Kelvin Hawley. (Sails Literacy Ser.). (gr. 1 up). 10.00 (978-0-7578-4043-2(4)) Rigby Educ.

Crunch: Why Do I Feel So Squeezed? (and Other Unsolved Economic Mysteries) unabr. ed. Jared Bernstein. Read by Erik Synnestvedt. (Running Time: 6 hrs.). (ENG.). 2008. 24.98 (978-1-59659-234-6(6), GildAudio) Pub: Gildan Media. Dist(s): HachBkGrp

***Crunch Point: The 21 Secrets to Succeeding When It Matters Most.** unabr. ed. Brian Tracy. (Running Time: 3 hrs.). (ENG.). 2010. 19.98 (978-1-59659-588-0(4), GildAudio) Pub: Gildan Media. Dist(s): HachBkGrp

Crunk Fest II. Prod. by Arrow Records. 1 CD. (YA). 2005. audio compact disk 12.00 (978-1-59089-961-8(X)) Creflo Dollar.
A collection of songs produced by Arrow Records.

Crusade. unabr. ed. Taylor Anderson. Narrated by William Dufris. (Running Time: 16 hrs. 0 mins. 0 sec.). (Destroyermen Ser.). (ENG.). 2008. audio compact disk 39.99 (978-1-4001-0807-7(1)); audio compact disk 79.99 (978-1-4001-3807-4(8)) Pub: Tantor Media. Dist(s): IngramPubServ

***Crusade.** unabr. ed. Read by Nicola Barber. (Running Time: 11 hrs.). (YA). 2010. audio compact disk 24.99 (978-1-4418-8860-0(8), 9781441888600, Bril Audio CD Unabri) Brilliance Audio.

***Crusade.** unabr. ed. Nancy Holder & Debbie Viguié. (Running Time: 11 hrs.). (Crusade Ser.: Bk. 1). 2010. 24.99 (978-1-4418-8862-4(4), 9781441888624, Brilliance MP3); 39.97 (978-1-4418-8863-1(2), 9781441888631, Brinc Audio MP3 Lib); audio compact disk 54.97 (978-1-4418-8861-7(6), 9781441888617, BriAudCD Unabrid) Brilliance Audio.

***Crusade.** unabr. ed. Nancy Holder & Debbie Viguié. (Running Time: 11 hrs.). (Crusade Ser.: Bk. 2). 2010. 39.97 (978-1-4418-8864-8(0), 9781441888648, BADLE) Brilliance Audio.

Crusade: Destroyermen. unabr. ed. Taylor Anderson. Narrated by William Dufris. (Running Time: 16 hrs. 0 mins. 0 sec.). (Destroyermen Ser.). (ENG.). 2008. audio compact disk 29.99 (978-1-4001-5807-2(9)) Pub: Tantor Media. Dist(s): IngramPubServ

Crusade Pt. 1: The Untold Story of the Persian Gulf War. unabr. ed. Rick Atkinson. Read by Jeff Riggenbach. 10 cass. (Running Time: 26 hrs.). 1996. 69.95 Set. (978-0-7861-0924-1(6), 1680A,B) Blckstn Audio.
Throughout the Gulf War of 1991, the allied governments & the Pentagon combined to impose unprecedented restrictions on the media's access to the battlefield. As a result, the true story of that brief brutal conflict has remained untold. Now, after two years of intensive research, Rick Atkinson has written what will surely come to be recognized as the definitive chronicle of the war. "Crusade" follows the unfolding battle from the first night to the final day, providing vivid accounts of bombing runs & White House strategy sessions, fire-fights & bitter interservice conflicts.

Crusade Pt. 2: The Untold Story of the Persian Gulf War. unabr. ed. Rick Atkinson. Read by Jeff Riggenbach. 8 cass. (Running Time: 26 hrs.). 1996. 56.95 Set. (978-0-7861-0925-8(4), 1680A,B) Blckstn Audio.

Crusade in Europe. Dwight D. Eisenhower. Read by Michael Prichard. 15 cass. (Running Time: 22 hrs. 30 mins.). 2001. 120.00 (978-0-7366-8077-6(2)) Books on Tape.
General Dwight D. Eisenhower was one of the most important military figures of World War II. This is his personal story of the conduct of the war, from his summons by General George Marshall to plan the defense of the Philippines to his appointment as Supreme Allied Commander, with all the responsibilities and burdens that that entailed. There is no one like him for describing the events of the war from a leader's point of view. We are with him in the tense moments after he has unleashed the forces of Operation Overlord, and, as elsewhere in this great book, he reveals what counts.

Crusade in Europe. unabr. ed. Dwight D. Eisenhower. Read by Michael Pritchard. 15 cass. (Running Time: 22 hrs. 30 mins.). 2001. 90.00 Books on Tape.
General Dwight D. Eisenhower gives his own personal account of the conduct of World War II.

Crusader. Max Brand & Patrick G. Lawlor. 6 cass. (Running Time: 8 hrs.). 2002. 49.95 (978-0-7861-2867-9(4), 3258) Blckstn Audio.

Crusader: A Western Story. unabr. ed. Max Brand. Read by Patrick G. Lawlor. 6 pieces. (Running Time: 8 hrs.). 2004. reel tape 29.95 (978-0-7861-2679-8(5)); audio compact disk 29.95 (978-0-7861-8696-9(8)) Blckstn Audio.
Throughout the Gulf War of 1991, the allied governments and the Pentagon combined to impose unprecedented restrictions on the media's access to the battlefield. As a result, the true story of that brief, brutal conflict has remained untold. Now, after two years of intensive research, Rick Atkinson has written what will surely come to be recognized as the definitive chronicle of the war.

Crusader's Cross. abr. ed. James Lee Burke. Read by Will Patton. (Dave Robicheaux Ser.). 2005. 17.95 (978-0-7435-5162-5(1)) Pub: S&S Audio. Dist(s): S and S Inc

Crusader's Cross. abr. ed. James Lee Burke. Read by Will Patton. CDs 5. (Running Time: 60 hrs. 0 mins. 0 sec.). (Dave Robicheaux Ser.). 2008. audio compact disk 14.99 (978-0-7435-7206-4(8)) Pub: S&S Audio. Dist(s): S and S Inc

Crusader's Cross. abr. unabr. ed. James Lee Burke. Read by Will Patton. 10 CDs. (Running Time: 120 hrs. 0 mins. 0 sec.). (Dave Robicheaux Ser.). 2005. audio compact disk 49.95 (978-0-7435-5000-0(5)) Pub: S&S Audio. Dist(s): S and S Inc

Crusader's Cross. unabr. ed. James Lee Burke. Narrated by Will Patton. 10 CDs. (Running Time: 10 hrs.). (Dave Robicheaux Ser.). 2005. audio compact disk 119.75 (978-1-4193-4867-9(1), C3359); 89.75 (978-1-4193-4865-5(5), 98084) Recorded Bks.
With two Edgar Awards and more than a dozen New York Times best-sellers to his credit, James Lee Burke is among the most celebrated mystery writers in the world. Crusader's Cross earned starred reviews from Publishers Weekly and Booklist. Dave Robicheaux has his hands full. But in between searching for a prostitute his brother loved nearly 50 years ago and tracking down a serial killer, he just might find some time for romance.

Crusader's Cross. unabr. ed. James Lee Burke. Read by Will Patton. (Dave Robicheaux Ser.). 2005. 29.95 (978-0-7435-5237-0(7)) Pub: S&S Audio. Dist(s): S and S Inc

Crusades. unabr. ed. Antony Bridge. Read by David Case. 8 cass. (Running Time: 12 hrs.). 1990. 64.00 (978-0-7366-1711-6(6), 2553) Books on Tape.
The Crusades is the brutal drama of 200 years of struggle for the Holy Land. It is a bloody tale of Turk & Greek, Arab & English, Egyptian & Frank, Moslem & Christian slaughtering each other for the love of God. The era was peopled by men larger than life - Richard the Lion Heart, Saladin, Barbarossa, Jenghiz Khan. It was characterized by simple Crusaders who relished the luxuries of their enemies - carpets, baths, spices, oranges - & made magnificent by construction of the finest castles in the world.

Crusades. unabr. ed. Zoe Oldenbourg. Read by Nadia May. Tr. by Anne Carter. (Running Time: 97200 sec.). 2008. audio compact disk 44.95 (978-1-4332-4594-7(9)); audio compact disk & audio compact disk 140.00 (978-1-4332-4593-0(0)) Blckstn Audio.

Crusades, Pt. 1. unabr. ed. Zoë Oldenbourg. Read by Nadia May. 10 cass. (Running Time: 29 hrs.). 1997. 69.95 (978-0-7861-1156-5(9), 1926A,B) Blckstn Audio.

Crusades, Pt. 2. unabr. ed. Zoë Oldenbourg. Read by Nadia May. 10 cass. (Running Time: 29 hrs.). 1997. 69.95 (978-0-7861-1168-8(2), 1926A,B) Blckstn Audio.

Crusades Through Arab Eyes. unabr. collector's ed. Amin Maalouf. Read by David Case. 8 cass. (Running Time: 8 hrs.). 1990. 48.00 (978-0-7366-1760-4(4), 2599) Books on Tape.
European & Arab versions of the Crusades have little in common. For the Arabs, the 12th & 13th centuries were not a time of glorious conquest, rather they were years of sacrifice & deprivation spent in repelling a brutal & destructive invasion by hordes of Western barbarians. Then too, the conflict was fought on their lands. When, under Saladin, a powerful Muslim army - inspired by prophets & poets - succeeded in destroying Crusader kingdoms, it was the greatest victory ever won by a non-European society against the West. The memory of it still lives in the minds of Arabs today.

Crush. Sandra Brown. Narrated by Tom Wopat. 9 cass. (Running Time: 12 hrs. 15 mins.). 83.00 (978-1-4025-1610-8(X)); audio compact disk 99.00 (978-1-4025-3478-2(7)) Recorded Bks.

***Crush.** Alan Jacobson. Read by Tish Hicks. (Playaway Adult Fiction Ser.). (ENG.). 2010. 59.99 (978-1-61587-652-5(9)) Find a World.

Crush. abr. ed. Sandra Brown. Read by Tom Wopat. (Running Time: 5 hrs. 0 mins. 0 sec.). 2006. audio compact disk 14.95 (978-0-7435-5521-0(X), S&S Encore) Pub: S&S Audio. Dist(s): S and S Inc

Crush. unabr. ed. Sandra Brown. Narrated by Tom Wopat. 4 cass. (Running Time: 5 hrs. 15 mins.). 2002. 29.95 (978-1-4025-3385-3(3), RG256) Recorded Bks.
Unnerved by an accused murderer, Dr. Rennie Newton finds herself defending his rights when she serves as a juror during his trial. After his acquittal, Rennie is caught between a bitter cop and the man whom she has learned to believe in, quickly discovering that in this ferocious game of cat and mouse, no one can win. Packed with electrifying suspense, this tale is one not to miss.

***Crush It!** unabr. ed. Gary Vaynerchuk. Read by Gary Vaynerchuk. (ENG.). 2010. (978-0-06-198163-0(X), Harper Audio) HarperCollins Pubs.

***Crush It! Why NOW Is the Time to Cash in on Your Passion.** unabr. ed. Gary Vaynerchuk. Read by Gary Vaynerchuk. (ENG.). 2010. (978-0-06-198162-3(1), Harper Audio) HarperCollins Pubs.

Crush Price Objections: Hold the Line on Prices!, Set. unabr. ed. Tom Reilly. Read by Tom Reilly. 2 cass. 1999. 20.00 (978-0-944448-16-8(X)) Motivation Pr.

Crush the Cell: How to Defeat Terror Without Terrorizing Ourselves. unabr. ed. Michael A. Sheehan. Narrated by David Drummond. (Running Time: 10 hrs. 30 mins. 0 sec.). (ENG.). 2008. audio compact disk 24.99 (978-1-4001-5641-2(6)); audio compact disk 69.99 (978-1-4001-3641-4(5)) Pub: Tantor Media. Dist(s): IngramPubServ

Crush the Cell: How to Defeat Terrorism Without Terrorizing Ourselves. Michael A. Sheehan. Read by David Drummond. (Playaway Adult Nonfiction Ser.). 2008. 59.99 (978-1-60640-553-6(5)) Find a World.

Crush the Cell: How to Defeat Terrorism Without Terrorizing Ourselves. unabr. ed. Michael A. Sheehan. Read by David A. Drummond. (Running Time: 10 hrs. 30 mins. 0 sec.). (ENG.). 2008. audio compact disk 34.99 (978-1-4001-0641-7(9)) Pub: Tantor Media. Dist(s): IngramPubServ

Crushed: The Perilous Journey Called Ministry. Gary L. Pinion. Read by Gary L. Pinion. (ENG.). 2006. audio compact disk 19.99 (978-1-930034-69-3(5)) Casscomm.

Crux. unabr. ed. Richard Aellen. Read by David Colacci. (Running Time: 9 hrs.). 2008. 39.25 (978-1-4233-5852-7(X), 9781423358527, Brlnc Audio MP3 Lib); 39.25 (978-1-4233-5854-1(6), 9781423358541, BADLE); 24.95 (978-1-4233-5853-4(8), 9781423358534, BAD); 24.95 (978-1-4233-5851-0(1), 9781423358510, Brilliance MP3) Brilliance Audio.

Cruzatte & Maria. Peter Bowen & Christopher Lane. 5 cass. (Running Time: 6 hrs. 30 mins.). 2002. 39.95 (978-0-7861-2856-3(9), 3347) Blckstn Audio.

Cry: The Beloved Country. Alan Paton. audio compact disk (978-1-4025-4845-1(1)) Recorded Bks.

Cry Dance. unabr. ed. Mitchell, Kirk Mitchell. Read by Stefan Rudnicki. (Running Time: 1 hr. 0 mins.). (ENG.). 2009. 29.95 (978-1-4417-0081-0(1)); 65.95 (978-1-4417-0077-3(3)); audio compact disk 100.00 (978-1-4417-0078-0(1)) Blckstn Audio.

Cry for the Spiritual Fath Aud. Kreider Larry. 2004. 29.00 (978-1-886973-53-4(9)) Hse2HsePubns.

Cry for the Strangers. abr. ed. John Saul. Read by Mel Foster. 4 cass. Library ed. (Running Time: 6 hrs.). 2003. 62.25 (978-1-59086-847-8(1), 1590868471, BAudLibEd); audio compact disk 74.25 (978-1-59086-849-2(8), 1590868498, BACDLib Ed) Brilliance Audio.
Clark's Harbor was the perfect coastal haven, jealously guarded against outsiders. But now strangers have come to settle there. And a small boy is suddenly free of a frenzy that had gripped him since birth... His sister is haunted by fearful visions... And one by one, in violent, mysterious ways the strangers are dying. Never the townspeople. Only the strangers. Has a dark bargain been struck between the people of Clark's Harbor and some supernatural force? Or is it the sea itself calling out for human sacrifice? A howling, deadly...Cry for the Strangers.

Cry for the Strangers. abr. ed. John Saul. Read by Mel Foster. (Running Time: 6 hrs.). 2005. audio compact disk 16.99 (978-1-59600-415-3(0), 9781596004153, BCD Value Price) Brilliance Audio.

Cry for the Strangers. abr. ed. John Saul. Read by Mel Foster. (Running Time: 6 hrs.). 2006. 39.25 (978-1-4233-0052-6(1), 9781423300526, BADLE); 24.95 (978-1-4233-0051-9(3), 9781423300519, BAD); 39.25 (978-1-4233-0050-2(5), 9781423300502, Brlnc Audio MP3 Lib); audio compact disk 24.95 (978-1-4233-0049-6(1), 9781423300496, Brilliance MP3) Brilliance Audio.

***Cry for the Strangers.** abr. ed. John Saul. 2010. audio compact disk 9.99 (978-1-4418-5630-2(7)) Brilliance Audio.

Cry for the Strangers, Comes the Blind Fury, the Unloved. abr. ed. John Saul. Read by Sandra Burr. (Running Time: 18 hrs.). 2005. audio compact disk 34.95 (978-1-59737-708-9(2), 9781597377089, BACD) Brilliance Audio.
Cry for the Strangers: Clark's Harbor was the perfect coastal haven, jealously guarded against outsiders. But now strangers have come to settle there. And a small boy is suddenly free of a frenzy that had gripped him since birth... His sister is haunted by fearful visions... And one by one, in violent, mysterious ways the strangers are dying. Never the townspeople. Only the strangers. Comes the Blind Fury: A century ago, a gentle blind girl walked the cliffs of Paradise Point. Then the children came - taunting, teasing - until she lost her footing and fell, shrieking her rage to the drowning sea... Now Michelle has come from Boston to live in the big house on Paradise Point. She is excited about her new life, ready to make new friends...until a hand reaches out of the swirling mists - the hand of a blind child. She is asking for friendship...seeking revenge...whispering her name... The Unloved: On a lush island off the South Carolina coast stands the Devereaux mansion, a once-great plantation house now crumbling. Here, Marguerite Devereaux has cast off her dreams to care for her aged, demanding mother. Now, for the first time in twenty years, Kevin Devereaux has returned home to visit his mother - hated, frightening Mother. Suddenly, horribly, Mother dies inside the locked nursery. All the secrets of this once-proud southern family emerge like tortured spirits from the sinister past to wrap their evil around the unsuspecting children.

Cry Havoc! The Crooked Road to Civil War 1861. Nelson D. Lankford. Read by Michael Prichard. (Playaway Adult Nonfiction Ser.). (ENG.). 2008. 59.99 (978-1-60640-976-3(X)) Find a World.

Cry Havoc! The Crooked Road to Civil War 1861. unabr. ed. Nelson D. Lankford. Narrated by Michael Prichard. (Running Time: 10 hrs. 0 mins. 0 sec.). (ENG.). 2007. audio compact disk 59.99 (978-1-4001-3330-7(0)); audio compact disk 19.99 (978-1-4001-5330-5(1)) Pub: Tantor Media. Dist(s): IngramPubServ

Cry Havoc! The Crooked Road to Civil War 1861. unabr. ed. Nelson D. Lankford. Read by Michael Prichard. 7 CDs. (Running Time: 10 hrs. 0 mins. 0 sec.). (ENG.). 2007. audio compact disk 29.99 (978-1-4001-0330-0(4)) Pub: Tantor Media. Dist(s): IngramPubServ

Cry in the Corridor see Secret Garden: A Young Reader's Edition of the Classic Story

Cry Me a River. Ernest Hill. Narrated by Peter Jay Fernandez. 8 cass. (Running Time: 11 hrs.). 2003. 74.00 (978-1-4025-3957-2(6)) Recorded Bks.

Cry Me a River. unabr. ed. T. R. Pearson. Narrated by Tom Stechschulte. 8 cass. (Running Time: 10 hrs.). 1995. Rental 16.50 Set. (94331) Recorded Bks.
A cop investigates the murder of one of his fellow officers in a small Southern town full of unusual characters.

Cry Me a River. unabr. ed. T. R. Pearson. Narrated by Tom Stechschulte. 8 cass. (Running Time: 10 hrs.). 1995. 70.00 (978-0-7887-0053-8(7), 94331E7) Recorded Bks.

Cry Mercy. abr. ed. Mariah Stewart. Read by Joyce Bean. (Running Time: 6 hrs.). (Mercy Street Ser.: No. 2). 2010. audio compact disk 14.99 (978-1-4233-7231-8(X), 9781423372318, BCD Value Price) Brilliance Audio.

Cry Mercy. unabr. ed. Mariah Stewart. Read by Joyce Bean. 1 MP3-CD. (Running Time: 11 hrs.). (Mercy Street Ser.: No. 2). 2009. 39.97 (978-1-4233-7227-1(1), 9781423372271, Brlnc Audio MP3 Lib); 39.97 (978-1-4233-7229-5(8), 9781423372295, BADLE); 24.99 (978-1-4233-7122-9(4), 9781423371229, Brilliance MP3); 24.99 (978-1-4233-7228-8(X), 9781423372288, BAD); audio compact disk 92.97 (978-1-4233-7121-2(6), 9781423371212, BriAudCD Unabrid); audio compact disk 34.99 (978-1-4233-7120-5(8), 9781423371205) Brilliance Audio.

Cry No More. Linda Howard. Read by Joyce Bean. (Playaway Adult Fiction Ser.). 2008. 69.99 (978-1-60640-905-3(0)) Find a World.

Cry No More. Created by Wendy Leigh. 1 cass. (Running Time: 60 min.). (Smart Baby Ser.). 1997. 9.99 (978-1-890680-01-5(X)) Smart Baby.
Quality recordings of white noise to calm babies, featuring bathtub filling & air conditioner.

Cry No More. abr. ed. Linda Howard. Read by Joyce Bean. (Running Time: 6 hrs.). 2007. audio compact disk 14.99 (978-1-4233-3359-3(4), 9781423333593, BCD Value Price) Brilliance Audio.

Cry No More. unabr. ed. Linda Howard. Read by Joyce Bean. 9 CDs. (Running Time: 10 hrs.). 2003. audio compact disk 36.95 (978-1-59086-169-1(8), 1590861698, CD); audio compact disk 97.25 (978-1-59086-170-7(1), 1590861701, CD Unabridged); 32.95 (978-1-59086-166-0(3), 1590861663, BAU); 82.25 (978-1-59086-167-7(1), 1590861671, CD Unabrid Lib Ed) Brilliance Audio.
Count your blessings; they can be snatched away in an instant. It is a sentiment Milla Edge knows too well. With an astonishing blend of savvy, instinct, and passion, Milla displays an uncanny gift for finding lost children. When all seems helpless, desperate souls from across the country come to her for hope and results. Driven by an obsessive desire to fill the void in other people's lives, Milla throws herself into every case - all the while trying to outrun the brutal emotions stemming from a horrific tragedy in her past. Traveling to a small village in Mexico on a reliable tip, Milla begins to uncover the dire fate of countless children who have disappeared over the years in the labyrinth of a sinister baby-smuggling ring. The key to nailing down the organization may rest with an elusive one-eyed man. To find him, Milla joins forces with James Diaz, a suspicious stranger known as the Tracker who conceals his own sinister agenda. As the search intensifies, the mission becomes more treacherous. For the ring is part of something far larger and more dangerous, reaching the highest echelons of power and influence. Caught between growing passion and imminent peril, Milla suddenly finds herself the hunted - in the crosshairs of an invisible, lethal assassin who aims to silence her permanently.

Cry No More. unabr. ed. Linda Howard. Read by Joyce Bean. (Running Time: 10 hrs.). 2004. 39.25 (978-1-59335-518-0(1), 1593355181, Brlnc Audio MP3 Lib) Brilliance Audio.

Cry No More. unabr. ed. Linda Howard. Read by Joyce Bean. (Running Time: 10 hrs.). 2004. 39.25 (978-1-59710-157-8(5), 1597101575, BADLE); 24.95 (978-1-59710-156-1(7), 1597101567, BAD) Brilliance Audio.

Cry No More. unabr. ed. Linda Howard. Read by Joyce Bean. (Running Time: 10 hrs.). 2004. 24.95 (978-1-59335-252-3(2), 1593352522) Soulmate Audio Bks.

Cry No More - Kiss Me While I Sleep - Cover of Night. abr. ed. Linda Howard. Directed By Susie Breck & Laural Merlington. Narrated by Joyce Bean & Dick Hill. (Running Time: 18 hrs.). 2007. audio compact disk 34.95 (978-1-4233-3423-1(X), 9781423334231, BACD) Brilliance Audio.

Cry of Humanity, Poetry & Prose: Love, Peace & Paradise. 2006. pap. bk. 30.00 (978-0-9656467-1-0(8)) FreedJml.

Cry of the Cat. unabr. ed. Emily Rodda. Read by Rebecca Macauley. (Running Time: 10800 sec.). (Raven Hill Mysteries). (J). 2006. audio compact disk 54.95 (978-1-74093-781-8(3)) Pub: Bolinda Pubng AUS. Dist(s): Bolinda Pub Inc

Cry of the Halidon. abr. unabr. ed. Robert Ludlum. Read by Robert Foxworth. 4 cass. (Running Time: 6 hrs.). 2004. 25.00 (978-1-59007-200-4(6)) Pub: New Millenn Enter. Dist(s): PerseuPGW
It's an offer Alex McAuliff just can't refuse: two million dollars for a geological survey of Jamaica's dark interior. All Dunstone, Limited, asks for in return is his time, his expertise, and above all his absolute secrecy. No one is to know of Dunstone's involvement, not even McAuliff's handpicked team.

Cry of the Halidon. unabr. collector's ed. Robert Ludlum. Read by Michael Prichard. 12 CDs. (Running Time: 14 hrs.). 2000. audio compact disk 96.00 (978-0-7366-6055-6(0)) Books on Tape.
A geologist runs for his life in Jamaica when he finds he's a pawn. Can he trust British Intelligence?.

Cry of the Halidon. unabr. collector's ed. Robert Ludlum. Read by Michael Prichard. 10 cass. (Running Time: 15 hrs.). 1996. 96.00 (978-0-913369-25-8(X), 4176) Books on Tape.
When Dunstone, Ltd. offers Alex McAuliff, a geologist, $2 million to survey Jamaica's dark interior, there's a catch: no one can know Dunstone's involved. But British Intelligence finds out & warns Alex that the last survey team Dunstone dispatched vanished without a trace.

Cry of the Heart. William McNamara. 2 cass. (Running Time: 1 hr. 35 min.). 1995. 17.95 Set. (TAH349) Alba Hse Comns.
In this two part presentation delivered as a conference for priests, Fr. McNamara uncovers the realities of what it takes to maintain one's effectiveness as a priest. If the priest is available to God, then God will be able to send him forth to the people. Reliable & inspiring material for priests or other ministers desiring a spiritual uplift.

Cry of the Heart: Psalms of Lament & Longing. Narrated by Max E. McLean. 2002. audio compact disk 9.95 (978-1-931047-23-4(5)) Fellow Perform Arts.

Cry of the Kalahari. unabr. ed. Delia Owens. Read by Michael Prichard & Roses Prichard. Ed. by Mark James Owens. 10 cass. (Running Time: 15 hrs.). 1988. 80.00 (978-0-7366-1439-9(7), 2322) Books on Tape.
In 1974, carrying little more than a change of clothes & a pair of binoculars, two young Americans, Mark & Delia Owens caught a plane to Africa, bought a third-hand Land Rover & drove into the Kalahari Desert.

Cry of the Manatee. unabr. ed. Perf. by Ray Dretske & Larry David. Ed. by Charles Beres. 1 cass. (Running Time: 48 min.). 1996. 9.98 (978-1-883152-10-9(0), AD106); audio compact disk 14.98 CD. (978-1-883152-11-6(9)) Amirra Pr.
Actual manatee sounds introduce each instrumental piece of music. Gentle piano & synthesizer orchestra.

Cry of the Panther. unabr. collector's ed. James P. McMullen. Read by Grover Gardner. 10 cass. (Running Time: 15 hrs.). 1987. 80.00 (978-0-7366-1130-5(4), 2053) Books on Tape.
After Vietnam, with shrapnel in his back & the jungle on his mind, James McMullen got into his car & headed as far south as he could go-the Everglades-the one place in America most like Nam.

Cry of the Sandhill Crane. 1 cass. (Running Time: 60 min.). 1994. audio compact disk 15.95 CD. (2711, Creativ Pub) Quayside.
Cranes vocalizations range from soothing murmurs to dramatic gar-ooo-a-as. Tens of thousands of cranes.

Cry of the Sandhill Crane. 1 cass. (Running Time: 60 min.). 1994. 9.95 (2710, NrthWrd Bks) TandN Child.

Cry Out to Jesus. Contrib. by Third Day. (Mastertrax Ser.). 2005. audio compact disk 9.98 (978-5-558-63150-0(3)) Pt of Grace Ent.

Cry Revenge! abr. ed. Carolyn Anderson. Read by Carolyn Anderson. 3 cass. (Running Time: 5 hrs.). Dramatization. (Audio Play Ser.). 1994. 21.95 set. (978-1-883778-02-6(6)) Starlite Prods.
Spicy love murder mystery about one woman out to kill another because she has the job & man she wants.

Cry, the Beloved Country. Alan Paton. Read by Maggie Soboil. 9 CDs. (Running Time: 10.25 Hrs). audio compact disk 29.95 (978-1-4025-7462-7(2)) Recorded Bks.

Cry, the Beloved Country. unabr. ed. Alan Paton. Read by Frederick Davidson. 8 CDs. (Running Time: 10 hrs.). 2004. audio compact disk 64.00 (978-0-7861-8883-3(9), 1378) Blckstn Audio.
Beyond the intense and insoluble personal tragedy, it is the story of the beautiful and tragic land of South Africa, its landscape, its people, its bitter racial ferment and unrest.

Cry, the Beloved Country. unabr. ed. Alan Paton. Read by Frederick Davidson. 7 cass. (Running Time: 10 hrs.). 1994. 49.95 SET. (978-0-7861-0426-0(0), 1378) Blckstn Audio.
An indictment of a social system which drives the native races into resentment & crime; it is a story of Fate, as inevitable, as relentless, as anything of Thomas Hardy's. Beautifully wrought with high poetic compassion, this book is more than just a story - it is a profound experience of the human spirit. And beyond the intense & insoluble personal tragedy, it is the story of the beautiful & tragic land of South Africa, its landscape, its people, its bitter racial ferment & unrest.

Cry, the Beloved Country. unabr. ed. Alan Paton. Read by Frederick Davidson. (Running Time: 10 hrs.). 2000. audio compact disk 24.95 (978-0-7861-8718-8(2), 1378) Blckstn Audio.

Cry, the Beloved Country. unabr. ed. Alan Paton. Read by Frederick Davidson. 8 CDs. 2004. audio compact disk 39.95 (978-0-7861-8898-7(7)); reel tape 35.95 (978-0-7861-2615-6(9)) Blckstn Audio.
Cry, the Beloved Country is in some ways a sad book; it is an indictment of a social system that drives the native races into resentment and crime; it is a story of Fate, as inevitable, as relentless, as anything of Thomas Hardy's. Beautifully wrought with high poetic compassion, Cry, the Beloved Country is more than just a story-it is a profound experience of the human spirit. And beyond the intense and insoluble personal tragedy, it is the story of the beautiful and tragic land of South Africa, its landscape, its people, its bitter racial ferment and unrest.

Cry, the Beloved Country. unabr. ed. Alan Paton. Read by Michael York. 8 CDs. (Running Time: 10 hrs.). 2008. audio compact disk & audio compact disk 19.95 (978-1-4332-1369-4(9)) Blckstn Audio.

Cry, the Beloved Country. unabr. ed. Alan Paton. Narrated by Maggie Soboil. 7 cass. (Running Time: 10 hrs.). 62.00 (978-1-55690-650-3(1), 92345E7) Recorded Bks.
Stephen Kumalo, a Zulu pastor, takes the train to Johannesburg in search of his son Absalom, of whom he has heard nothing for many months. Unfaltering courage & simple faith lead him through a country now alien to him, past people to whom he is invisible, in search of a son & in search of answers to the questions that haunt him. What is justice? Where is hope? Available to libraries only.

Cry, the Beloved Country. unabr. ed. Alan Paton. Narrated by Maggie Soboil. 7 cass. (Running Time: 10 hrs.). 2003. 37.95 (978-0-7887-6963-4(4)) Recorded Bks.

Cry, the Beloved Country. unabr. ed. Alan Paton. Read by Frederick Davidson. (YA). 2007. 49.99 (978-1-60252-497-2(1)) Find a World.

Cry, the Beloved Country. unabr. ed. Alan Paton & Alan Paton. Read by Michael York. (Running Time: 36000 sec.). 2008. 59.95 (978-1-4332-1366-3(4)); audio compact disk 29.95 (978-1-4332-1368-7(0)); audio compact disk & audio compact disk 80.00 (978-1-4332-1367-0(2)) Blckstn Audio.

Cry, the Beloved Country. unabr. collector's ed. Alan Paton. Read by Richard Green. 6 cass. (Running Time: 9 hrs.). 1982. 48.00 (978-0-7366-0345-4(X), 1331) Books on Tape.
An old & humble Zulu parson, from the hills above Ixopo, sets out for Johannesburg in search of his only son. He finds him in prison, charged with the murder of a white man.

Cry, the Beloved Country: Abridged. (ENG.). 2007. (978-1-60339-041-5(3)); cd-rom & audio compact disk (978-1-60339-042-2(1)) Listenr Digest.

Cry Wolf. abr. ed. Tami Hoag. Read by Joyce Bean. 4 cass. Library ed. (Running Time: 6 hrs.). 2001. 53.25 (978-1-58788-632-4(4), 1587886324, Lib Edit) Brilliance Audio.
In the rural parishes of Louisiana's French Triangle, young women are disappearing one by one, only to turn up on the banks of the bayou, strangled and cast aside where they are sure to be found. But there is one trophy the killer prizes above all others, one woman who must be silenced forever . . . Attorney Laurel Chandler did not come back to Bayou Breaux to seek justice. That once-burning obsession had destroyed her credibility, her career, her marriage - and nearly her sanity. But when a ruthless predator strikes too close to home, she's lured into a perverse game from which there may be no escape. Once before, Laurel's cries against a monstrous evil went unanswered. Who will listen now?.

Cry Wolf. abr. ed. Tami Hoag. Read by Joyce Bean. (Running Time: 6 hrs.). 2006. 39.25 (978-1-4233-0056-4(4), 9781423300564, BADLE); 24.95 (978-1-4233-0055-7(6), 9781423300557, BAD); 39.25 (978-1-4233-0054-0(8), 9781423300540, Brinc Audio MP3 Lib); audio compact disk 24.95 (978-1-4233-0053-3(X), 9781423300533, Brilliance MP3) Brilliance Audio.

Cry Wolf. abr. ed. Tami Hoag. Read by Joyce Bean. (Running Time: 6 hrs.). 2007. audio compact disk 14.99 (978-1-4233-1935-1(4), 9781423319351, BCD Value Price) Brilliance Audio.

Cry Wolf. unabr. ed. Susan Gates. Read by PH.D., Daniel Hill. 2 CDs. (Running Time: 7800 sec.). (J). (gr. 4-7). 2002. audio compact disk 21.95 (978-0-7540-6549-4(9), CHCD 049) AudioGO.

Cry Wolf. unabr. ed. Wilbur Smith. Read by Nigel Davenport. 12 cass. (Running Time: 13 hrs. 20 min.). (Audio Bks.). 1991. 96.95 Set. (978-0-7451-6290-4(8), CAB 560) AudioGO.
In the winter of 1935 the 'Wolf of Rome' - the modern army of Mussolini's Italy - threatens to annihilate the people of Ethiopia. Two lone adventurers strike a deal to deliver a consignment of ancient weapons. Travelling with them is a beautiful young American journalist who has pledged her life to the people's cause.

Cry Wolf. unabr. collector's ed. Wilbur Smith. Read by Richard Brown. 11 cass. (Running Time: 16 hrs. 30 min.). (Ballantyne Novels Ser.). 1988. 88.00 (978-0-7366-1396-5(X), 2285) Books on Tape.
The wolf of Rome-the army of Italy-threatens defenseless Ethopia with annihilation.

***Cryer's Cross.** unabr. ed. Lisa McMann. (Running Time: 5 hrs. 30 mins. 0 sec.). (ENG.). (YA). 2011. audio compact disk 24.99 (978-1-4423-3738-1(9)) Pub: S&S Audio. Dist(s): S and S Inc

***Crying Blood.** unabr. ed. Donis Casey. Read by Pam Ward. (Running Time: 8.5 hrs. NaN mins.). (Alafair Tucker Mysteries Ser.). 2011. 29.95 (978-1-4417-7588-7(9)); 54.95 (978-1-4417-7585-6(4)); audio compact disk 76.00 (978-1-4417-7586-3(2)) Blckstn Audio.

Crying Game. unabr. collector's ed. John Braine. Read by Stuart Courtney. 8 cass. (Running Time: 12 hrs.). 1984. 64.00 (978-0-7366-0493-2(6), 1467) Books on Tape.
Frank Batcombe, a conservative North country journalist newly arrived in London, works as a reporter for a national newspaper. A chance encounter changes his life.

Crying in the Dark: Psalm 107. Ed Young. 1989. 4.95 (978-0-7417-1765-8(4), 765) Win Walk.

Crying Mountain: Audiocassette. (Greetings Ser.: Vol. 1). (gr. 3-5). 10.00 (978-0-7635-1842-4(5)) Rigby Educ.

Crying Wolf. unabr. ed. Peter Abrahams. Read by James Daniels. (Running Time: 9 hrs.). 2008. 49.97 (978-1-4233-4429-2(4), 9781423344292, BADLE); 39.25 (978-1-4233-4427-8(8), 9781423344278, Brinc Audio MP3 Lib); 24.95 (978-1-4233-4428-5(6), 9781423344285, BAD); 24.95 (978-1-4233-4426-1(X), 9781423344261, Brilliance MP3) Brilliance Audio.

***Crying Wolf.** unabr. ed. Peter Abrahams. (Running Time: 9 hrs.). 2010. audio compact disk 29.99 (978-1-4418-4119-3(9), 9781441841193) Brilliance Audio.

***Crying Wolf.** unabr. ed. Peter Abrahams. Read by James Daniels. (Running Time: 9 hrs.). 2010. audio compact disk 89.97 (978-1-4418-4120-9(2), 9781441841209, BriAudCD Unabrid) Brilliance Audio.

***Cryoburn.** unabr. ed. Lois McMaster Bujold. Read by Grover Gardner. (Running Time: 18 hrs. 30 mins.). 2010. 29.95 (978-1-4417-4747-1(8)); 65.95 (978-1-4417-4743-3(5)); audio compact disk 100.00 (978-1-4417-4744-0(3)); audio compact disk 29.95 (978-1-4417-4746-4(X)) Blckstn Audio.

Cryonics, Life Extension, Cloning, & Other Realities. Paul Segall. 1 cass. 9.00 (A0114-87) Sound Photosyn.
Cryonics is the science of freezing a creature before or after it dies, in anticipation of it coming back to life at a later date. During this talk, an apparently happy dog was brought out to the audience that had successfully undergone this process.

Crystal. unabr. ed. V. C. Andrews. Read by Laurel Lefkow. 3 cass. (Running Time: 4 hrs. 30 min.). (Orphan Ser.: Vol. 2). 2001. 34.95 (978-0-7531-0632-7(9), 990901) Pub: ISIS Audio GBR. Dist(s): ISIS Pub
The Morrises have chosen Crystal as their new daughter & as wonderful as it is at first, Crystal realizes that sadness isn't far away as unexpected tragedy shakes their lives.

Crystal. unabr. ed. V. C. Andrews. 4 CDs. (Running Time: 3 hrs. 31 min.). (Orphans Ser.: No. 2). (J). 2001. audio compact disk 51.95 (978-0-7531-1320-2(1)) Pub: ISIS Lrg Prnt GBR. Dist(s): Ulverscroft US
When the Morris's choose Crystal from all the boys and girls in the orphanage, she is full of optimism. Karl Morris, her new dad, likes math as much as she likes science, and he's already proud of her being a good student. Thelma, her new mother, makes her feel truly wanted for the first time. Crystal is especially pleased when the Morris's approve of her first boyfriend. But no one is prepared when a shocking tragedy comes rattling to the door.

Crystal & Sound: Enjoy the Subtle Effects of Rock Crystal Combined with Crystal Singing Bowls. Dick de Ruiter & Tosca Tetteroo. (Running Time: 1 hr. 13 mins.). 2004. bk. 21.95 (978-90-74597-70-8(X)) Pub: Binkey Kok NLD. Dist(s): Red Wheel Weiser

Crystal Apple. 2004. 8.95 (978-1-56008-881-3(8)); cass. & flmstrp 30.00 (978-1-56008-657-4(2)) Weston Woods.

Crystal Bowl & Tibetan Bowl Meditation. River Guerguerian. 2008. audio compact disk 19.98 (978-1-55961-975-2(9)) Pub: Relaxtn Co. Dist(s): S and S Inc

Crystal Bowl & Tibetan Bowl Meditation. abr. ed. River Guerguerian. (Running Time: 2:00:00). 2008. audio compact disk 19.98 (978-1-55961-974-5(0)) Sounds True.

Crystal Castle Journey. unabr. ed. Marci Archambeault. Read by Marci Archambeault. 1 cass. (Running Time: 1 hr.). (J). 1994. pap. bk. 14.95 (978-1-888861-03-7(7)) Quest MA.
Meditation designed for children to help them to relax & visualize, to be more creative, to feel free to express themselves, & to live healthier, happier lives.

Crystal Cave. unabr. ed. Mary Stewart. Read by Stephen Thorne. 12 cass. (Running Time: 18 hrs.). (Merlin Ser.: Bk. 1). 2000. 79.95 (978-0-7451-6305-5(X), CAB 676) Pub: Chivers Audio Bks GBR. Dist(s): AudioGO
Plunges deep into 5th-century Britain, a country in chaos and division. This is Merlin's world. The illegitimate son of a South Wales princess, he possesses a great natural gift, The Sight. Against a background of wars and conquest, we see his emergence into manhood, and his dramatic role in the coming of King Arthur.

Crystal City. Orson Scott Card. Read by Stefan Rudnicki & M. E. Willis. 10 CDs. (Running Time: 41460 sec.). (Sound Library). 2004. audio compact disk 94.95 (978-0-7927-3413-0(0), SLD 731); audio compact disk 29.95 (978-0-7927-3414-7(9), CMP 731) AudioGO.

Crystal City: A Tale of Alvin Maker. Orson Scott Card. Read by Stefan Rudnicki & M. E. Willis. 7 cass. (Running Time: 41460 sec.). (Sound Library). 2004. 59.95 (978-0-7927-3412-3(2), CSL 731) AudioGO.

Crystal City: Guided Meditation. Yana L. Freeman. 1 CD. (Running Time: 36:43 mins). (ENG.). 2007. audio compact disk 15.00 (978-0-9768728-6-3(2)) Sacred Path.

Crystal City No. 6. unabr. rev. ed. Orson Scott Card. Read by M. E. Willis & Stefan Rudnicki. 10 CDs. (Running Time: 11 hrs. 30 mins. 0 sec.). (Alvin Maker Ser.). (ENG.). 2004. audio compact disk 44.95 (978-1-59397-486-2(8)) Pub: Macmill Audio. Dist(s): Macmillan

Crystal Clear Picture Of God's Will: Knowing God's Will Series, Sept. Ben Young. 2000. 4.95 (978-0-7417-6198-9(X), B0198) Win Walk.

Crystal Egg see Star & Other Stories

Crystal Egg: The Star see Tales of Space & Time

Crystal Elohim Meditation. Maureen J. St. Germain. Ed. by Maureen J. St. Germain. 2 CDs. (Running Time: 3 hrs.). 2002. audio compact disk 15.95 (978-0-9721799-3-5(3)) M StGermain.
Spoken meditation to the Elohim based on the Ancient Hebrew/Christian tradition. The author has used crystals and matalics to describe and tune in to the Elohim.

Crystal Eye. abr. ed. Deborah Chester. 1 CD. (Running Time: 2 Hours). (Lucasfilm's Alien Chronicles: Bk. 3). 1999. audio compact disk 24.95 (978-1-56511-316-9(0)) HighBridge.

Crystal Fire: The Birth of the Information Age. Michael Riordan & Lillian Hoddeson. Read by Dennis McKee. 9 cass. (Running Time: 10 hrs.). 1999. 62.95 (978-0-7861-1375-0(8), 2259) Blckstn Audio.
A tale of the human factors in technology - the pride & jealousies coupled with scientific & economic aspiration that led to the creation of modern microelectronics & ignited the greatest technological explosion in history.

Crystal Harp. unabr. ed. Virginia Kron. Read by Virginia Kron. 1 cass. (Running Time: 48 min.). (J). (gr. 1-6). 1992. 9.95 (978-0-9636376-0-4(6), 92A) Silkstone Recs.
Emery pulls on his adventuring boots & journeys to find the stolen crystal harp. Ultimately he finds the harp & love. Fully underscored with harp & cello music. Irony, humor, love, drama.

***Crystal Harp: Divinely Inspired Music of Harp & Crystal Bowls.** Carol J. Spears. (Playaway Adult Nonfiction Ser.). (ENG.). 2010. 39.99 (978-1-61587-632-7(4)) Find a World.

Crystal Line. Anne McCaffrey. 2 cass. (Running Time: 3 hrs.). (Crystal Singer Ser.). 7.95 (978-1-57815-298-8(4), Media Bks Audio); audio compact disk 11.99 (978-1-57815-554-5(1), 1198CD3, Media Bks Audio) Media Bks NJ.
Crystal had destroyed Killashandra's memory, and only Crystal could restore it - if she dared!.

Crystal MacLean-Field. Read by Crystal MacLean-Field. 1 cass. (Running Time: 29 min.). 1985. 10.00 New Letters.
Kansas City poet Crystal MacLean-Field reads from "My Sister's Leather Bag".

Crystal Meditation Journey: Awaken Your Higher Self. unabr. ed. Johnny Rockit & Catherine Benejet. Read by Johnny Rockit & Catherine Benejet. 1 cass. (Running Time: 60 min.). 1997. 9.99 (978-1-892654-07-6(5), BET080) FutureLife.
Guided meditation program drawing on crystals to focus concentration & promote mental clarity.

Crystal Palace: A Tale from the Gold Country. Paula Bonnier Anawalt. Narrated by Paula Bonnier Anawalt. 1 cass. (Running Time: 16 mins.). (J). (gr. k-4). 1999. 4.95 (978-0-9668414-3-5(3)) Abongold.

Crystal Path. unabr. ed. Uma Silbey & Ramana D. Silbey. Read by Uma Silbey & Ramana D. Silbey. 1 cass. (Running Time: 40 min.). 1986. 9.95 (978-0-938925-01-9(6), U-103) U-Music.
Details getting into the crystal's core & healing with crystals.

Crystal Prison. unabr. ed. Robin Jarvis. Read by Roe Kendall. (Running Time: 30600 sec.). (Deptford Mice Ser.). (J). 2007. 54.95 (978-1-4332-0260-5(3)); audio compact disk 29.95 (978-1-4332-0262-9(X)); audio compact disk 63.00 (978-1-4332-0261-2(1)) Blckstn Audio.

Crystal Serpent & Other Mexican Legends: Plays for Beginning Spanish Students. Nancy Humbach. (SPA.). (YA). (gr. 6-10). 1995. suppl. ed. 17.47 (978-0-8013-1530-5(1), 76883) Longman.

Crystal Singer. Jan Tober. Read by Jan Tober. 1 cass. (Running Time: 17 min.). (Kryon Tapes Ser.). 1995. 12.00 (978-0-9636304-1-4(5)) Kryon Writings.
Musical meditation tape - vocal.

Crystal Skull. abr. ed. Manda Scott. Read by Susan Duerden. (Running Time: 23400 sec.). (ENG.). 2008. audio compact disk 29.95 (978-0-7393-2903-0(0), Random AudioBks) Pub: Random Audio Pubg. Dist(s): Random

Crystal Sounds. 74th ed. Selected by Rainer Tillman. (Running Time: 1 hr. 3 mins.). 2000. audio compact disk 16.95 (978-1-57863-070-7(3), Red) Red Wheel Weiser.

Crystal Sounds: Deva - Crystal Singing Bowls for Meditation & Healing. Rainer Tillman. 1 cass. (Running Time: 74 min.). 10.00 (978-1-57863-071-4(1), Red) Red Wheel Weiser.
The singing bowls on this album are crystal, with their mysterious contemplative sounds, incomparable to any other musical instrument. This wonderful recording takes you on a journey through an enchanting wonderland of the elements of Mother Earth.

Crystal Stair. Scripts. Grace Chetwin. Narrated by Grace Chetwin. Prod. by Feral Press Staff. 8 CDs. (Running Time: 8 hrs. 31 mins.). Dramatization. (Tales of Gom in the Legends of Ulm Ser.: Vol. 3). 2002. audio compact disk 60.00 (978-1-930094-10-9(8)) Feral Press.
A revised, unabridged edition of The Crystal Stair narrated by the author with notes on the music, graphics from the book, and a navigational aid comprising complete list of tracks with times.

Crystal Suite. Music by Steven Halpern. 1 cass. 9.95 (LA128); audio compact disk 14.95 (LA128D) Lghtwrks Aud & Vid.
You'll enjoy the benefits of this music almost immediately as the soft blanket of sound envelops you in its warm embrace. The unique sequence of ascending musical keynotes resonates with your chakras & literally "tunes your human instrument" - your body, mind & spirit - with electric piano, celestial choir & gently sustained strings.

***Crystal Technology in Atlantis.** Diana Cooper. Andrew Brel. (Running Time: 1 hr. 6 mins. 0 sec.). (Information & Meditation Ser.). (ENG.). 2010. audio compact disk 14.95 (978-1-84409-523-0(1)) Pub: Findhorn Pr GBR. Dist(s): IPG Chicago

Crystal Vision. Gilbert Sorrentino. Read by Gilbert Sorrentino. 1 cass. (Running Time: 30 min.). 1982. 8.95 (AMF-15) Am Audio Prose.
Sorrentino reads from "Crystal Vision" & talks about literature as abstract art.

Crystalline Experience. Karen L. Simmons. 1. (Running Time: 52 mins). audio compact disk 16.95 (978-0-9724682-1-3(8)) Except Resource.

Crystallize Creativity. 1 cass. (Running Time: 60 min.). 10.95 (004) Psych Res Inst.
Designed to energize imagination & let the creative powers flow naturally.

Crystals & Astrology. unabr. ed. Randall Leonard. Read by Randall Leonard. (Running Time: 90 min.). 1988. 8.95 (731) Am Fed Astrologers.
Explains how to take care of crystals, their use & impact on ones lives.

Crystals, Chakras, Color & Sound. Ramana D. Silbey & Uma Silbey. 1 cass. (Running Time: 40 min.). (Crystal Visualizations-Meditations Ser.). 1987. 9.95 (978-0-938925-02-6(4), U-104) U-Music.
Using Crystals, the listener experiences two different ways to, get in touch with, & balance, the main energy centers of the body, & then connect with earth & sky. Great for relieving stress & tension.

Crystal's Chance. Susannah Brin. Narrated by Larry A. McKeever. (Romance Ser.). (J). 2003. 10.95 (978-1-58659-112-0(6)); audio compact disk 14.95 (978-1-58659-341-4(2)) Artesian.

Cryus: The Storytelling Encyclopedia, Vol. 1. Carmen Marois. 1 cass. (Running Time: 50 mins.). (J). (ps-2). 2000. audio compact disk 12.95 (978-2-89517-026-6(6)) Pub: Coffragants CAN. Dist(s): Penton Overseas
Cyrus gathers the most pertinent questions asked by children from the popular CBC radio show 275-Allo.

CSA, OSCE: Absolutely Simple & Easy. Ljubo Skebie. (Running Time: 10 hrs.). 2003. 150.00 (978-1-932622-09-6(8)) Postgraduate Med Rev Ed.

CSIRO total wellbeing Diet: Audio companion to Australia's no 1 diet Book. unabr. ed. Peter Clifton & Manny Noakes. Read by Humphrey Bower & Odette Joannidis. (Running Time: 4 hrs. 45 mins.). 2007. audio compact disk 57.95 (978-1-74093-881-5(X)) Pub: Bolinda Pubng AUS. Dist(s): Bolinda Pub Inc

CSM...Clinically Standardized Meditation. unabr. ed. Patricia Carrington. Read by Patricia Carrington. 3 cass. (Running Time: 3 hrs.). 49.50 set, incl. 98p. wkbk. (AF1961) J Norton Pubs.
CSM is taught by its originator, leading psychologist Dr. Patricia Carrington of Princeton University, in a step-by-step method using tapes & a workbook. After just one instruction session, you will be successfully meditating on your own.

CST 2 Aw Kids, Level 2. M. Walker. 1990. bk. 19.03 (978-0-201-52128-3(8)) Longman.

***Cuado se Atraviesa Tiempos Dificiles.** Charles R. Swindoll.Tr. of Getting Through the Tough Stuff. 2010. audio compact disk 38.00 (978-1-57972-881-6(2)) Insight Living.

Cuan Grande Es Nuestro Dios. Contrib. by Chris Tomlin. (Soundtraks Ser.). 2006. audio compact disk 8.99 (978-5-558-04357-0(1)) Christian Wrld.

Cuando Dios Manifiesta Su Nombre. Tita Bremer. 6 cass. (SPA.). 2003. 29.99 (978-0-89985-401-4(X)); audio compact disk 35.00 (978-0-89985-420-5(6)) Christ for the Nations.

Cuando Era Puertorriquena: Casi una Mujer. unabr. ed. Esmeralda Santiago. 7 cass. (Running Time: 9 hrs.). 2005. 69.75 (978-1-4025-9545-5(X), E1080) Recorded Bks.
From a rippled zinc shack in rural Puerto Rico to "the better life" in a decaying Brooklyn tenement, Esmeralda Santiago's Puerto Rican childhood is one of sorcery, smoldering war between the sexes, and high comedy. Hers is a portrait of a harsh but enchanted world that can never be reclaimed. Selling over 16,000 copies in hardcover, this triumphant coming-of-age memoir is now available in paperback editions in both English and Spanish. In the tradition of Black Ice, Santiago writes lyrically of her childhood on her native island and of her bewildering years of transition in New York City.

Cuando Hace Frio. Created by Rigby Staff. 1993. 10.40 (978-0-435-05935-4(1), Rigby PEA) Pearson EdAUS AUS.

Cuando Laura Estuvo Ausente. Created by Rigby Staff. 1993. 10.40 (978-0-435-05955-2(6), Rigby PEA) Pearson EdAUS AUS.

Cuando Seamos Grandes, EDL Level 12. (Fonolibros Ser.: Vol. 4). (SPA.). 2003. 11.50 (978-0-7652-1025-8(8)) Modern Curr.

Cuando una mujer ora por sus Hijos. Gloria Richards. 2006. audio compact disk 4.99 (978-1-933172-24-8(X)) Jayah Producc.

***¿Cuántos en total? Audio CD.** April Barth. Adapted by Benchmark Education Co., LLC. (Content Connections Ser.). (SPA.). (J). 2010. audio compact disk 10.00 (978-1-61672-189-3(8)) Benchmark Educ.

Cuatro Acuerdos: Una Guia Practica para la Libertad Personal. abr. ed. Miguel Ruiz & Don Miguel Ruiz. Read by Ruben Moya. 2 CDs. (SPA &

ENG.). 2005. audio compact disk 18.95 (978-1-878424-97-6(1)) Amber-Allen Pub.

Every action, says don Miguel Ruiz, is based on agreements people make - with other people, with God, with life. But the most important agreements are those people make with themselves. In these agreements they tell themselves who they are, how to behave, what is possible, what is impossible. One single agreement is not such a problem, but so many agreements come from fear, deplete energy, and diminish self-worth. In The Four Agreements, don Miguel reveals the source of self-limiting agreements that take away joy and create needless suffering. For those ready to change these agreements, there are four deceptively simple, yet powerful agreements that can be adopted as guiding principles: be impeccable with your word; don't take anything personally; don't make assumptions; and always do your best. These tenets can rapidly transform anyone's life to a new experience of freedom, true happiness, and love.

Cuatro Jinetes del Apocalipsis. abr. ed. Vicente Blasco Ibanez. 3 CDs.Tr. of Four Riders of the Apocalypse. (SPA.). 2002. audio compact disk 17.00 (978-958-43-0181-9(0)) YoYoMusic.

Cub see Your Own World

Cuba. Stephen Coonts. Read by Michael Prichard. (Jake Grafton Novel Ser.: Vol. 7). 1999. 96.00 (978-0-7366-4645-1(0)); audio compact disk 112.00 (978-0-7366-7127-9(7)) Books on Tape.

Cuba. Stephen Coonts. Read by Richard Gilliland. 4 CDs. (Running Time: 6 hrs.). (Jake Grafton Novel Ser.: Vol. 7). 2002. audio compact disk 14.99 (978-1-57815-550-7(9), 4439CD5, Media Bks Audio) Media Bks NJ.

Grafton becomes a key player in an action-filled power struggle that could explode at any second.

Cuba. abr. ed. Stephen Coonts. Perf. by Richard Gilliland. 4 cass. (Running Time: 6 hrs.). (Jake Grafton Novel Ser.: Vol. 7). 2001. 25.00 (978-1-59040-052-4(6), Phoenix Audio) Pub: Amer Intl Pub. Dist(s): PerseuPGW

Rear Admiral Jake Grafton returns as the United States and Cuba engage in a terrifying, high-risk game of brinkmanship. When America's president secretly installs weapons in Cuba, Grafton finds himself the key player in a tense, action-filled power struggle that could explode at any second.

Cuba. abr. ed. Stephen Coonts. Read by Richard Gilliland. 4 cass. (Running Time: 6 hrs.). (Jake Grafton Novel Ser.: Vol. 7). 2002. 12.99 (978-1-57815-293-3(3), 4439, Media Bks Audio) Media Bks NJ.

Grafton becomes a key player in an action-filled power struggle that could explode at any second.

Cuba. unabr. ed. Stephen Coonts. Read by Michael Prichard. 12 cass. (Running Time: 18 hrs.). (Jake Grafton Novel Ser.: Vol. 7). 1999. 96.00 (5026) Books on Tape.

The hero of five New York Times bestsellers returns as the United States & Cuba engage in a terrifying game of brinksmanship, a gamble that could break the last military taboo & destroy both countries.

Cuba. unabr. ed. Joseph Stromberg. Read by Harry Reasoner. Ed. by Wendy McElroy. (Running Time: 9000 sec.). (World's Political Hot Spots Ser.). 2006. audio compact disk 25.95 (978-0-7861-6694-7(0)) Pub: Blckstn Audio. Dist(s): NetLibrary CO

Cuba, Set. abr. ed. Stephen Coonts. Read by Richard Gilliland. 4 cass. (Jake Grafton Novel Ser.: Vol. 7). 1999. 25.00 (FS9-51001) Highsmith.

Cuba, Set. abr. ed. Joseph Stromberg. Read by Harry Reasoner et al. 2 cass. (Running Time: 3 hrs.). (World's Political Hot Spots Ser.). 1991. 17.95 (978-0-938935-91-9(7), 390271) Knowledge Prod.

This island was once a clearing house for importing slaves into the New World. It became one of the world's bastions of Marxism, proclaiming socio-economic equality.

Cuba & the Night. unabr. collector's ed. Pico Iyer. Read by John Edwardson. 6 cass. (Running Time: 9 hrs.). 1995. 48.00 (978-0-7366-3169-3(0), 3839) Books on Tape.

Two misplaced souls meet in Cuba. Richard an American news photographer in Havana, plans to move on. Lourdes, a young cubana who might be looking fo a way out, gets his attention.

Cuba in the American Imagination: Metaphor & the Imperial Ethos. Louis A. Pérez, Jr. (ENG., 2008. 18.00 (978-0-8078-8698-4(X)); audio compact disk 18.00 (978-0-8078-8700-4(5)) U of NC Pr.

Cuba Libre. abr. ed. Elmore Leonard. 4 cass. (Running Time: 6 hrs.). 1998. 23.95 (978-0-553-47847-1(8), Random AudioBks) Random Audio Pubg.

Three days after the battleship Maine is sunk in Havana harbor, cow boy Ben Tyler arrives with a cargo of horses to sell-cover for running guns to Cubans fighting Spanish occupation. Ben agrees to sell the horses to Roland Boudreaux, an American plantation owner. Boudreaux cheats Ben & gets him jailed. But Amelia Brown, Boudreaux's mistress, falls in love with the young cowboy & hatches a plot with a Cuban revolutionary to break Ben out of jail.

Cuba Libre. unabr. ed. Elmore Leonard. Read by Alexander Adams. 6 cass. (Running Time: 9 hrs.). 1998. 48.00 (978-0-7366-4124-1(6), 896025) Books on Tape.

A spellbinding journey into the heart & soul of the Cuban Revolution of a hundred years ago. An explosive mix of high adventure, history brought to life & a honey of a love story.

***Cuba Libre.** unabr. ed. Elmore Leonard. Read by George Guidall. (ENG.). 2010. (978-0-06-199382-4(4), Harper Audio); (978-0-06-199749-5(8), Harper Audio) HarperCollins Pubs.

Cuba Libre, unabr. ed. Elmore Leonard. Narrated by George Guidall. 7 cass. (Running Time: 9 hrs. 30 mins.). 1998. 60.00 (978-0-7887-1866-3(5), 95288E7) Recorded Bks.

In the turmoil of the impending Spanish-American War, three rouges are set on a collision course. The result is an explosive story of power & romance.

Cuba Libre. unabr. ed. Elmore Leonard. Narrated by George Guidall. 8 CDs. (Running Time: 9 hrs. 30 mins.). 2000. audio compact disk 78.00 (978-0-7887-4466-2(6), C1163E7) Recorded Bks.

Cuba Strait. abr. ed. Carsten Stroud. Read by Armand Schultz. 2004. 15.95 (978-0-7435-4531-0(1)) Pub: S&S Audio. Dist(s): S and S Inc

Cuban Life under Castro. (Running Time: 67 min.). 1989. 11.95 (K0910B090, HarperThor) HarpC GBR.

Cuban Missile Crisis, Pts. I & II. Kenneth Bruce. 2 cass. (Running Time: 2 hrs.). Dramatization. (Excursions in History Ser.). 12.50 Set. Alpha Tape.

Cuban Missile Crisis: A Retrospective. Read by Maxwell Taylor & Theodore Sorenson. 1 cass. (Running Time: 1 hr.). 10.95 (K0800B090, HarperThor) HarpC GBR.

Cucamonga. Rudy VanderLans. 2004. bk. 35.00 (978-0-9669409-1-6(1)) Pub: Emig. Dist(s): Gingko Press

Cuchulain Comforted see Poetry of William Butler Yeats

Cucina Italiana: La Pasta. 2 cass. (Running Time: 1 hr.). (ITA.). pap. bk. 34.95 (SIT215) J Norton Pubs.

Intermediate-level readings with accompanying cassettes can improve both reading & listening comprehension. 2 16p. texts include exercises & answer key.

Cuckoo Child. unabr. ed. Dick King-Smith. Read by Nigel Anthony. 2 cass. (Running Time: 2 hrs.). (J). 1997. 18.95 (CTC 117, Chivers Child Audio) AudioGO.

Cuckoo Clock, Set. unabr. ed. Mary L. Molesworth. Read by Flo Gibson. 3 cass. (Running Time: 4 hrs.). (J). 1988. 16.95 (978-1-55685-121-6(9)) Audio Bk Con.

A cuckoo fills the life of a lonely little girl with excitement & friendship.

Cuckoo in June. unabr. ed. David Atkins. 5 cass. 1998. 63.95 Set. (978-1-85903-073-8(4)) Pub: Magna Story GBR. Dist(s): Ulverscroft US

Cuckoo Marans in the Taproom, unabr. ed. Derek Brock. Read by Gareth Armstrong. 5 cass. (Running Time: 6 hrs. 30 min.). (Isis Ser.). (J). 2004. 49.95 (978-0-7531-0330-2(3), 971217) Pub: ISIS Lrg Prnt GBR. Dist(s): Ulverscroft US

Derek Brock's father-in-law was an irascible & legendary country publican at the 16th century Six Bells Inn at Penmark, who expected his son-in-law to follow in his footsteps. Despite his inexperience of the bar trade, young Brock rather liked the idea of dispensing pints to the locals. He hadn't bargained, though, for the three dozen Cuckoo Maran hens, six store cattle, three sows & litters & a varied assortment of other livestock that went with the job. Little wonder, perhaps, that his father-in-law had retired early with heart trouble!.

Cuckoo's Child. Suzanne Freeman. 4 cass. (J). 23.98 Set, blisterpack. (BYA 941) NewSound.

Living in Beirut in 1962 is difficult for Mia Veery. Her non-traditional parents have picked up the family & moved them from Ohio to Lebanon. She longs to return to America. She gets her wish of returning, but not the way she had hoped; her parents have vanished while on a sailing vacation. A group of friends & family help Mia to accept the inevitable about her parents, & to accept herself as well.

Cuckoo's Child. unabr. ed. Suzanne Freeman. Read by Christy Carlson Romano. 4 cass. (YA). 1999. 29.98 (FS9-34539) Highsmith.

Cuckoo's Child. unabr. ed. Suzanne Freeman. Read by Christy Carlson Romano. 4 cass. (Running Time: 6 hrs. 18 min.). (J). 1998. pap. bk. 34.98 (978-0-8072-7882-6(3), YA941SP, Listening Lib); 32.00 (978-0-8072-7881-9(5), LL0109, Listening Lib) Random Audio Pubg.

This audio is about a girl who must adjust to a new life when her parents are lost at sea. She learns the true essence of family & discovers the joy in following her heart.

Culian Trilogy. Standish O'Grady. Read by Ralph Cosham. (Running Time: 10 hrs.). 2003. 29.95 (978-1-59912-056-0(9), Audiofy Corp) Iofy Corp.

Cuculian Trilogy. Standish O'Grady. Narrated by Ralph Cosham. (Running Time: 36600 sec.). (Unabridged Classics in MP3 Ser.). (ENG.). 2008. audio compact disk 26.00 (978-1-58472-478-0(1), In Aud) Sound Room.

Cuculian Trilogy. unabr. ed. Standish O'Grady. Read by Ralph Cosham. 9 cds. 2002. audio compact disk 49.95 (978-1-58472-236-6(3), In Aud) Pub: Sound Room. Dist(s): Baker Taylor

Cuculian Trilogy. unabr. ed. Standish O'Grady. Read by Ralph Cosham. 1 cd. 2002. audio compact disk 18.95 (978-1-58472-384-4(X), In Aud) Pub: Sound Room. Dist(s): Baker Taylor

MP3 format.

Cucullin & the Legend of Knockmany see Irish Fairy Tales

Cuenta Regresiva A Jerusalen. John Hagee. Read by Juan Ovalle. (SPA.). 2007. audio compact disk 29.99 (978-1-930034-45-7(8)) Casscomm.

Cuentitos Simpaticos. 2 cass. (SPA.). 2001. 25.00 (978-0-8442-7058-6(X), NT0483) Glencoe.

Helps build listening comprehension, model correct pronunciation & expose students to real-life interactions that demonstrate Spanish at work.

cuento de Dona Chila. (Saludos Ser.: Vol. 3). (SPA.). (gr. 3-5). 10.00 (978-0-7635-1781-6(X)) Rigby Educ.

Cuento de Ferdinando. 1 cass. (Running Time: 35 min.).Tr. of Story of Ferdinand. (SPA.). (J). 2001. 15.95 (VXS-34C) Kimbo Educ.

Cuento de Ferdinando. Tr. of Story of Ferdinand. 9.95 (978-1-59112-183-1(3)) Live Oak Media.

Cuento de Ferdinando. Munro Leaf. Illus. by Robert Lawson. 14 vols. (Running Time: 11 mins.). 1990. pap. bk. 39.95 (978-1-59519-154-0(2)); 9.95 (978-1-59112-026-1(8)); audio compact disk 12.95 (978-1-59519-152-6(6)) Live Oak Media.

Cuento de Ferdinando. Munro Leaf. Illus. by Robert Lawson. 11 vols. (Running Time: 11 mins.). (SPA.). (J). 1990. pap. bk. 18.95 (978-1-59519-153-3(4)) Pub: Live Oak Media. Dist(s): AudioGO

Cuento de Ferdinando. unabr. ed. Munro Leaf. Read by Angel Pineda. Illus. by Robert Lawson. 11 vols. (Running Time: 11 mins.). (J). (gr. 1-3). 1990. pap. bk. 16.95 (978-0-87499-216-8(8), LK3799) Pub: Live Oak Media. Dist(s): AudioGO

In this enduring tale, a gentle bull prefers to sit and smell flowers than fight in the bullring.

Cuento de Ferdinando, Grades K-3. unabr. ed. Munro Leaf. Read by Angel Pineda. Illus. by Robert Lawson. 14 vols. (Running Time: 11 mins.).Tr. of Story of Ferdinand. (SPA.). (J). 1990. pap. bk. & tchr. ed. 37.95 Reading Chest. (978-0-87499-218-2(4)) Live Oak Media.

Cuento Del Rey Pancho y el Primer Reloj. Norbert Lopez. (J). (gr. 2-7). 1970. pap. bk. 7.94 (978-0-685-03700-3(2)) Oddo.

Cuento, Dos Cuentos, Tres Cuentos. Gloria Fuentes. (SPA.). 1996. 8.76 (978-84-305-7996-9(6), SU4863) Lectorum Pubns.

Cuentos de Andersen. unabr. ed. Hans Christian Andersen. Read by Yadira Sánchez. 3 CDs.Tr. of Stories from Han Andersen. (SPA.). 2001. audio compact disk 17.00 (978-958-9494-42-4(0)) YoYoMusic.

Cuentos de Grimm. unabr. ed. Jacob W. Grimm. 4 cass. (Running Time: 2 hrs. 40 mins.).Tr. of Stories by Grimm. (SPA.). (J). 1999. (978-1-55935-202-4(7), 394106) Soundelux.

Spanish language adaptation of "Snow White & the Seven Dwarves," "Hansel & Gretel," "Rumpelstiltskin" & "The Fisherman & His Wife.".

Cuentos de la Luna, EDL Level 20. (Fonolibros Ser.: Vol. 12). (SPA.). 2003. 11.50 (978-0-7652-1033-3(9)) Modern Curr.

Cuentos de las 1001 Noches. unabr. ed. Read by Laura Garcia. 3 CDs.Tr. of Tales from the Arabian Nights. (SPA.). 2001. audio compact disk 17.00 (978-958-9494-46-2(3)) YoYoMusic.

Cuentos de los Hermanos Grimm. unabr. ed. Jacob W. Grimm & Wilhelm K. Grimm. 3 CDs. (SPA.). 2001. audio compact disk 17.00 (978-958-9494-23-3(4)) YoYoMusic.

Cuentos de Los Hermanos Grimm: Tales by the Brothers Grimm. unabr. ed. Jacob W. Grimm & William Grimm. Read by Laura Garcia. (J). 2007. 34.99 (978-1-60252-523-8(4)) Find a World.

Cuentos Eroticos. unabr. ed. Zweig et al. 3 CDs.Tr. of Erotic Tales. (SPA.). 2001. audio compact disk 17.00 (978-958-9494-35-6(8)) YoYoMusic.

Cuentos Faciles Vol. 1: El Tiempo es Oro y 15 Cuentos Mas. Interlingua Staff. 1 cass. (Running Time: 1 hrs.).Tr. of Easy Spanish Stories: Time is Money & 15 Other Stories. (SPA.). 1996. pap. bk. 19.50 (978-1-58085-256-2(4)) Interlingua VA.

Cuentos Faciles Vol. 2: La Casilla del Perro y Otros Cuentos. Interlingua Staff. 1 cass. (Running Time: 1 hrs.).Tr. of Easy Spanish Stories: The Dog House & Other Stories. (SPA.). 1996. pap. bk. 19.50 (978-1-58085-257-9(2)) Interlingua VA.

Cuentos Faciles Vol. 3: El Asno Robado y Otros Cuentos. Interlingua Staff. 1 cass. (Running Time: 1 hr.).Tr. of Easy Spanish Stories: The Stolen Ass & Other Stories. (SPA.). 1996. pap. bk. 19.50 (978-1-58085-258-6(0)) Interlingua VA.

Cuentos Faciles Vol. 4: La Cuerda y Otros Cuentos. Interlingua Staff. 1 cass. (Running Time: 1 hrs.).Tr. of Easy Spanish Stories: The Rope & Other Stories. (SPA.). 1996. pap. bk. 19.50 (978-1-58085-259-3(9)) Interlingua VA.

Cuentos Insolitos. Short Stories. 2 cass. (Running Time: 3 hrs.). (SPA.). 2001. 22.95 (SSP135) J Norton Pubs.

A collection of 9 "Twilight Zone" type stories with unexpected & surprising endings by Argentinean author.

***Cuentos para celebrar (English Audio)** Alma Flor Ada & F. Isabel Campoy.Tr. of Stories to Celebrate (English Audio). (ENG.). (J). 2008. audio compact disk 34.95 (978-1-59820-906-8(X), Alfaguara) Santillana.

***Cuentos para Celebrar /Stories to Celebrate.** Alma Flor Ada & F. Isabel Campoy.Tr. of Stories to Celebrate (Spanish Audio). (SPA.). (J). 2008. audio compact disk 34.95 (978-1-59820-905-1(1), Alfaguara) Santillana.

Cuentos para Pensar. Jorge Bucay. (SPA.). 2000. bk. 18.95 (978-970-651-360-1(4), 1260) Pub: Edit Oceano De Mex MEX. Dist(s): Libros Fronteras

Cuentos para Todo el Ano. abr. ed. Alma Flor Ada. (Cuentos para Todo el Ano / Stories the Year Round Ser.). (SPA.). (J). (ps-3). 2008. audio compact disk 24.95 (978-1-60396-348-0(0), Alfaguara) Santillana.

Cuentos Simpaticos. 2 cass. (SPA.). 2001. 25.00 (978-0-8442-7092-0(X), NT0493) Glencoe.

Helps build listening comprehension, model correct pronunciation & expose students to real-life interactions that demonstrate Spanish at work.

Cuervo y la Zorra y Muchos Cuentos Mas. abr. ed.Tr. of Raven & the Fox, Little Thumb & Many More Tales. (SPA.). 2001. audio compact disk 13.00 (978-958-9494-28-8(5)) YoYoMusic.

***Cugel's Saga.** unabr. ed. Jack Vance. Read by Arthur Morey. (Running Time: 13 hrs.). (Tales of the Dying Earth Ser.). 2010. 24.99 (978-1-4418-1469-2(8), 9781441814692, Brilliance MP3); 39.97 (978-1-4418-1470-8(1), 9781441814708, Brlnc Audio MP3 Lib); 39.97 (978-1-4418-1472-2(8), 9781441814722, BADLE); 24.99 (978-1-4418-1471-5(X), 9781441814715, BAD); audio compact disk 29.99 (978-1-4418-1467-8(1), 9781441814678); audio compact disk 79.97 (978-1-4418-1468-5(X), 9781441814685, BriAudCD Unabrid) Brilliance Audio.

Cuidado con las Mujeres Astutas see Watch Out for Clever Women!

***Cuimhni Ceoil.** Aine Bean Ui Laoi. (ENG.). 1992. 11.95 (978-0-8023-7077-8(2)) Pub: Clo Iar-Chonnachta IRL. Dist(s): Dufour

Cuisine Bourgeoise. 1 cass. (Running Time: 60 mins.). Dramatization. (Maitres du Mystere Ser.). (FRE.). 1996. 11.95 (1827-MA) Olivia & Hill.

Popular radio thriller, interpreted by France's best actors.

***Cujo.** unabr. ed. Stephen King. (Running Time: 11 hrs. 30 mins.). 2010. 29.95 (978-1-4417-3287-3(X)); 65.95 (978-1-4417-3283-5(7)); audio compact disk 60.00 (978-1-4417-3284-2(5)) Blckstn Audio.

Cujo. unabr. ed. Stephen King. 12 CDs. (Running Time: 14 hrs.). (ENG.). 2010. audio compact disk 39.95 (978-0-14-242785-9(3), PengAudBks) Penguin Grp USA.

Culebra. unabr. ed. James C. Glass. Read by Cameron Beierle. 12 cass. (Running Time: 12 hrs. 24 min.). 2001. 64.95 (978-1-55686-995-2(9)) Books in Motion.

In the elite Zed Force of Nova Brasilia, Culebra led his charges and fought with vengeance for his cause. Now leading a different life, Culebra must return in order to save the lives of innocents caught in a hopeless new war.

Culhwch & Olwen: A Tale of King Arthur & his Warriors. As told by David Lee Summers. Music by Kevin Schramm & Nancy McCallion. 2001. audio compact disk 12.00 (978-1-885093-21-9(7)) Hadrosaur Pr.

Culhwch & Olwen: A Tale of King Arthur & His Warriors. unabr. ed. Dave L. Summers & Kevin Schramm. Read by Dave L. Summers. Music by Nancy McCallion & Kevin Schrann. 1 cass. (Running Time: 1 hr. 10 min.). 1995. 7.95 (978-1-885093-07-3(1), HP07) Hadrosaur Pr.

A modern re-telling of the tale of Culwch & Olwen, Arthurian Legend's oldest story. The tale is enhanced with music by Kevin Schramm.

Culinary Kid: A Nutrition Guide & Cookbook for Parents & Kids. St. Joseph Hospital Staff et al. Ed. by Mecca B. Carpenter. Illus. by Barbara Cummings. 1986. 19.95 (978-0-9616857-1-3(9)) St Joseph Hosp.

Culinary Knives Vol. 2: Knife Skills. Food & Bev Inst USA Staff. (Culinary Knives Ser.). 2004. reel tape (978-1-58315-315-4(2)) Food & Bev Inst.

Culinary Writer M. F. K. Fisher see I'm Too Busy to Talk Now

Culloden: The Last Jacobite Rising. unabr. ed. John Prebble. Narrated by Davina Porter. 8 cass. (Running Time: 11 hrs. 30 mins.). 1986. 70.00 (978-1-55690-129-4(1), 86840E7) Recorded Bks.

An account of the Battle of Culloden on April 16, 1746 when English troops faced the rebellious forces of Bonnie Prince Charlie for the last time.

Cully Cully & the Bear. Wilson Gage. Illus. by James Stevenson. (Running Time: 10 min.). (J). (ps-6). 1988. pap. bk. 7.95 HarperCollins Pubs.

Culpepper's Cannon; Dunc Gets Tweaked. unabr. ed. Gary Paulsen. Read by Bill Fantini. 2 pieces. (Culpepper Adventures Ser.: Nos. 3-4). (gr. 3-5). lib. bdg. 16.95 set. (978-1-55656-185-6(7), DAB 076) Pub: Dercum Audio. Dist(s): APG

Culpepper's Cannon; Dunc Gets Tweaked. unabr. ed. Gary Paulsen. Read by Bill Fantini. 2 vols. (Running Time: 3 hrs.). (Culpepper Adventures Ser.: Nos. 3-4). (gr. 3-5). 1993. pap. bk. 9.95 (978-1-55656-184-9(9)) Pub: Dercum Audio. Dist(s): APG

Culpepper's Cannon & Dunc Gets Tweaked. The two best friends investigate a time portal & try to find a "copped" skateboard.

Culprit & the Cure: Why Lifestyle Is the Culprit Behind America's Poor Health & How Tranforming That Lifestyle Can Be the Cure. Steven G. Aldana. 2006. audio compact disk 29.95 (978-0-9758828-2-5(1)) Pub: Maple Mountn. Dist(s): Natl Bk Netwk

Cult Insanity: A Memoir of Polygamy, Prophets, & Blood Atonement. unabr. ed. Irene Spencer. (Running Time: 10 hrs. 30 mins. 0 sec.). (ENG.). 2009. 24.99 (978-1-4001-6326-7(9)); audio compact disk 34.99 (978-1-4001-1326-2(1)); audio compact disk 69.99 (978-1-4001-4326-9(8)) Pub: Tantor Media. Dist(s): IngramPubServ

***Cultivate Contentment CD Set: Using Ancient Wisdom to Thrive in Today's World.** Johanna Mosca. (ENG.). 2010. 19.95 (978-0-9679567-8-7(1)) Sedona Spirit.

Cultivate Merit & Virtue Without Marks. Contrib. by Hua. (978-0-88139-601-0(X)) Buddhist Text.

Cultivated Life: A Year in a California Vineyard. unabr. ed. Joy Sterling. Narrated by Barbara Caruso. 6 cass. (Running Time: 8 hrs.). 1994. 51.00 (978-0-7887-0097-2(9), 94338E7) Recorded Bks.

A year in the life of California's Iron Horse winery as told by the wine maker's wife, who is also sales, marketing & public relations manager for the vineyard.

Cultivating a Desire for God. Francis Frangipane. 1 cass. (Running Time: 90 mins.). (Time to Seek God Ser.: Vol. 1). 2000. 5.00 (FF04-001) Morning NC.

This mini-series challenges believers with the important issue of intimacy with God.

Cultivating a Hearing Ear. Steve Thompson. 1 cass. (Running Time: 90 mins.). (Prophetic Ministry Ser.: Vol. 2). 2000. 5.00 (ST01-002) Morning NC.

Now updated & expanded, this popular series combines insights from the Scriptures & personal experience to explain how we can more effectively hear from God & minister prophetically.

Cultivating an Abundant Mentality. Steve Clark. Read by Steve Clark. 1 CD. (Running Time: 44min 21sec). 2004. pap. bk. 12.95 (978-1-932226-29-4(X)) Wizard Acdmy.

?If you want to change your life, you have to begin by changing the way you think. If you change the way you think, you'll change your beliefs. Sow a thought, reap an action; sow an action, reap a habit; sow a habit and reap a destiny. It all starts with the thought process. That's how you create habits that produce results.? Steve Clark Join us for a powerful lesson that will teach you why the current circumstances you are experiencing in your life are the result of your thoughts and beliefs. By listening and applying the principles on this CD you will learn how to harness your thoughts and Cultivate Abundance in your business, family, personal, and spiritual life.As a master teacher, Steve will help you understand and apply the timeless principle that ?you will see it when you believe it.? Get ready for one of the most thought provoking lessons you have ever heard.?Learning and applying the principles and concepts that Steve teaches on this CD has helped me to earn over $1,000,000 per year in personal sales commissions.?Kevin Campbell-President, Campbell Agency?This CD is awesome. The message is so powerful that I keep listening to it over and over again. It is so inspiring that I have ordered copies for my staff and friends.?Teresa Dos Santos -President, Contract Resources, Inc.?Super Achievers have an Abundant Mentality. Steve's classic presentation on this CD will help you develop that mentality. Steve's ability to help our producers develop and maintain this attitude is one of the reasons that he continues to be one of the most influential outside consultants that we use at First Protective.?Andy Martin, CLU, ChFC-President, First Protective, CEO, Top Producers TalksIncludes:44min 21sec Audio CD39 page booklet.

Cultivating an Unshakable Character: How to Walk Your Talk All the Way to the Top. Jim Rohn. 6 cass. (Running Time: 6 hrs.). 1996. bk. 59.95 (13750AC) Nightingale-Conant.

Mr. Rohn mixes concrete examples with powerful insights & anecdotes, uncovering the 12 pillars of character that form the indestructible foundation for personal & professional success.

Cultivating Awareness. unabr. ed. Rama Berch. 1 cass. (Running Time: 50 min.). (Relaxations Ser.: Vol. 1). 1992. (978-1-930559-00-4(3)); audio compact disk (978-1-930559-01-1(1)) STC Inc.

A guided relaxation to give you a deep, restful & profoundly peaceful experience.

Cultivating Dynamic Spirituality, Set. James J. Bacik. 2 cass. (Running Time: 2 hrs. 27 min.). 1999. 19.95 (TAH421) Alba Hse Comns.

Calling heavily on the experiential theology of Karl Rahner, moves through our limitations into a blossoming realization of God & ourselves in dynamic transition.

Cultivating Heart of Compassion. Ram Dass. 2 cass. 18.00 Set. (A0658-87) Sound Photosyn.

Cultivating Initiative in Your Staff: How to Get Your People to Act with More Gumption & Confidence. Cathy Shaughnessy. 4 cass. (Running Time: 3 hrs. 1 min.). 59.95 Set incl. 32p. wkbk. (V10152) CareerTrack Pubns.

This program will help you discover ways to get your people to work more on their own...to think for themselves...to buy into the goals of the organization. How? By learning to share your authority without sacrificing control. And that takes the kinds of skills you'll gain from this program.

Cultivating Purity in an Impure World. 2005. audio compact disk 12.00 (978-1-57972-591-4(0)) Insight Living.

Cultivating the Heart to Hear. Rick Joyner. 1 cass. (Running Time: 90 mins.). (Hearing God Ser.: Vol. 6). 2000. 5.00 (RJ10-006) Morning NC.

"Principles of Spiritual Warfare" & "Putting on the Full Armor of God." These tapes highlight practical truths that lead to certain victory in spirtual warfare.

Cultivation of Subtle Feelings. (ENG.). 2008. 15.00 (978-0-9708648-2-6(5)) Self Enquiry.

Cultura with L. C. Audio CD. 6th ed. Mary Lee Bretz et al. (C). 2006. pap. bk. 46.25 (978-0-07-310574-1(0), Mc-H Human Soc) Pub: McGrw-H Hghr Educ. Dist(s): McGraw

Cultural & Emotional Formation. Assumpta Long. 1 cass. (National Meeting of the Institute, 1990 Ser.). 4.00 (90N3) IRL Chicago.

Cultural & Natural Wonders of the Santa Monica Mountains & Rim of the Valley Corridor. Hosted by Nancy Pearlman. 1 cass. (Running Time: 28 min.). 10.00 (402) Educ Comm CA.

Cultural & Personal Implications of Typology in Integrated Masculinity. Read by John Giannini. 1 cass. (Running Time: 2 hrs.). 1988. 12.95 (978-0-7822-0071-3(0), 329) C G Jung IL.

Cultural Crosswords. 1 cass. pap. bk. 19.95 (SFR310) J Norton Pubs.

A multi-faceted approach to French language & culture. History, music, sports, business, literature & locale are the subjects of brief descriptive sketches that can be used in any order. Embedded in these descriptive sketches (20) are the answers to the clues for the accompanying crossword puzzles.

Cultural Exchange see Poetry & Reflections

Cultural Heritage of Tibet. unabr. ed. Lama A. Govinda. 1 cass. (Running Time: 1 hr.). 1976. 11.00 (06301) Big Sur Tapes.

Traces the cultural heritage of Tibet which, more than the heritage of just one country, is the combined heritage of Buddhism in India & its development in Tibet.

Cultural Influences. unabr. ed. Milton Diamond. 1 cass. (Running Time: 1 hr.). (Human Sexuality Ser.). 12.95 (34008) J Norton Pubs.

Cultural Landscape: An Introduction to Human Geography. 9th ed. James M. Rubenstein. 2007. bk. 115.33 (978-0-13-234426-5(2)) Pearson Educ CAN CAN.

Cultural Literacy: What Every American Needs to Know. unabr. ed. E. D. Hirsch, Jr. Read by Barrett Whitener. 7 cass. (Running Time: 10 hrs.). 1996. 49.95 (978-0-7861-0938-8(6), 1691) Blckstn Audio.

In this forceful manifesto, Professor Hirsch argues that children in the United States are being deprived of the basic knowledge that would enable them to function in contemporary society. They lack cultural literacy: a grasp of background information that writers & speakers assume their audience already has.

Cultural Literacy: What Every American Needs to Know. unabr. ed. E. D. Hirsch, Jr. Read by Barrett Whitener. (Running Time: 36000 sec.). 2007. audio compact disk 72.00 (978-0-7861-6228-4(7)) Blckstn Audio.

Cultural Literacy: What Every American Needs to Know. unabr. ed. E. D. Hirsch, Jr. Read by Barrett Whitener. (Running Time: 36000 sec.). 2007. audio compact disk 29.95 (978-0-7861-5923-9(5)) Blckstn Audio.

Cultural Relativity & Belief Systems. unabr. ed. Gregory Bateson. 1 cass. (Running Time: 1 hr. 26 min.). 1976. 11.00 (02801) Big Sur Tapes.

Relates value systems to cultural function & discusses the role of logic in belief systems.

Cultural Unconscious. Read by Joseph Henderson. 1 cass. (Running Time: 1 hr.). 1987. 9.95 (978-0-7822-0089-8(3), 276) C G Jung IL.

Cultural Update. Ayn Rand. Read by Ayn Rand. 1 cass. (Running Time: 90 min.). 12.95 (978-1-56114-072-5(4), AR12C) Second Renaissance.

Ayn Rand reviews the themes of all the Ford Hall Forum lectures she had previously delivered, & asks: "Have things changed since then, &, if so, in what direction?".

Culturally Speaking. Marion Forrest. Read by Marion Forrest. Read by Jennifer Forrest. 2 cass. (Running Time: 1 hr. 30 min.). (Success Express Ser.). (YID.). 1986. 14.95 Set, incl. expression bklt. (978-0-9618523-0-6(5)) Forrest Prodns.

Expressions for all occasions, enhance everyday English conversation with the world's most savvy expressions, in French, Italian, Latin, German & Yiddish.

Culturally Speaking. Read by Forrest Jennifer Forrest & Bruce Hollihan. Created by Marion Forrest. (ENG.). 2009. audio compact disk 18.95 (978-0-9618523-1-3(3)) Forrest Prodns.

Culturally Speaking: A Conversation & Culture Text. 2nd ed. Rhona B. Genzel & Martha G. Cummings. (J). 1994. 18.00 (978-0-8384-4212-8(9)) Heinle.

Culture & Anarchy Set: Landmarks in the History of Education. unabr. ed. Matthew Arnold. Read by Robert L. Halvorson. 4 cass. (Running Time: 360 min.). 28.95 (13) Halvorson Assocs.

Culture & Counterculture. unabr. ed. Ralph Metzner et al. 2 cass. (Running Time: 2 hrs. 30 min.). 19.95 (29364-29365) J Norton Pubs.

The new values which emerged in the sixties have contributed to the formation of a new "social paradigm" which has consequences for our society & for our relations with the Third World.

Culture & International Trade. Jorge W. Garcia. 1 cass. (Running Time: 60 min.). 1984. 6.99 (978-0-911727-01-2(9)) PAE Pubns.

Helps bridge the international corporate barriers. Deals with vital role that cultural & social factors play in international dealings. Gives hints on how to choose good translators.

***Culture & Irony: Studies in Joseph Conrad's Major Novels.** Anthony Winner. (Victorian Literature & Culture Ser.). (ENG.). 27.50 (978-0-8139-2946-0(6)) U Pr of Va.

Culture Capsules in Spanish. Janis M. Yates. (ENG.). 2005. audio compact disk 12.95 (978-1-57970-322-6(4), Audio-For) J Norton Pubs.

***Culture Clash: Managing the Global High-Performance Team.** Thomas D. Zweifel. (Global Leader Series Ser.). 2009. 14.95 (978-1-59079-194-3(0)) Pub: Select Books. Dist(s): Midpt Trade

Culture Code: Ingenious Way to Understand Why People Around the World Live & Buy as They Do. rev. unabr. ed. Clotaire Rapaille. Read by Barrett Whitener. (Running Time: 6 hrs. 30 mins.). (ENG.). 2007. audio compact disk 29.98 (978-1-59659-126-4(9), GildAudio) Pub: Gildan Media. Dist(s): HachBkGrp

***Culture Making: Recovering Our Creative Calling.** unabr. ed. Andy Crouch. Narrated by Sean Runnette. (ENG.). 2010. 14.98 (978-1-59644-871-1(7)); audio compact disk 24.98 (978-1-59644-870-4(9)) christianaud.

Culture of Corruption: Obama & His Team of Tax Cheats, Crooks, & Cronies. unabr. ed. Michelle Malkin. Narrated by Johnny Heller. 1 MP3-CD. (Running Time: 8 hrs. 30 mins. 0 sec.). (ENG.). 2009. 24.99 (978-1-4001-6324-3(2)); audio compact disk 34.99 (978-1-4001-1324-8(5)); audio compact disk 69.99 (978-1-4001-4324-5(1)) Pub: Tantor Media. Dist(s): IngramPubServ

Culture of Death: A Threat to Religious Communities. William Coulson. 1 cass. 4.00 (96A2) IRL Chicago.

Culture of Fear: Why Americans Are Afraid of the Wrong Things. abr. ed. Barry Glassner. Read by Barry Glassner. 4 cass. (Running Time: 5 hrs.). 2003. 24.95 (978-1-57270-353-7(9), 490496); audio compact disk 24.95 (978-1-57270-354-4(7), 590426) Pub: Audio Partners. Dist(s): PerseuPGW

Exposes the people and organizations that manipulate our perceptions and profit from our anxieties. These peddlers of fear - politicians, advocacy groups, and TV newsmagazines, among others - cost Americans dearly, weighing us down with needless worries and causing us to squander billions of dollars on fixing fanciful problems. Glassner points out that scare topics like political terrorism, child-care sadists, and fire on the operating table get major play, even though statistically speaking, an American is far more likely to be killed by lightning than to experience these problems. Ultimately, national scares prevent us from correcting the true cause of a problem.

***Culture of War.** unabr. ed. Martin van Creveld. Narrated by Arthur Morey. (Running Time: 18 hrs. 30 mins. 0 sec.). (ENG.). 2010. audio compact disk 119.99 (978-1-4001-4862-2(6)) Pub: Tantor Media. Dist(s): IngramPubServ

***Culture of War.** unabr. ed. Martin van Creveld. Narrated by Arthur Morey. (Running Time: 18 hrs. 30 mins. 0 sec.). (ENG.). 2010. 34.99 (978-1-4001-6862-0(7)); 22.99 (978-1-4001-8862-8(8)); audio compact disk 49.99 (978-1-4001-1862-5(X)) Pub: Tantor Media. Dist(s): IngramPubServ

***Culture Shift: Engaging Current Issues with Timeless Truth.** unabr. ed. Albert Mohler. (ENG.). 2008. 12.98 (978-1-59644-538-3(6), Hovel Audio) christianaud.

Culture Shift: Engaging Current Issues with Timeless Truth. unabr. ed. R. Albert Mohler & R. Albert Mohler, Jr. Read by R. Albert Mohler, Jr. (Running Time: 3 hrs. 12 mins. 0 sec.). (ENG.). 2008. audio compact disk 21.98 (978-1-59644-537-6(8)) christianaud.

Culture, Universals & the Particulars of Affective Expression. Read by William Willeford. 1 cass. (Running Time: 1 hr.). 1987. 9.95 (978-0-7822-0326-4(4), 283) C G Jung IL.

Culture Warrior. unabr. ed. Bill O'Reilly. Read by Bill O'Reilly. 6 cass. (Running Time: 9 hrs.). 2006. 54.00 (978-1-4159-3333-6(2)); audio compact disk 61.20 (978-1-4159-3334-3(0)) Pub: Books on Tape. Dist(s): NetLibrary CO

Culture Warrior. unabr. ed. Bill O'Reilly. Read by Bill O'Reilly. (YA). 2006. 49.99 (978-0-7393-7463-4(X)) Find a World.

Culture Warrior. unabr. ed. Bill O'Reilly. Read by Bill O'Reilly. (Running Time: 21600 sec.). (ENG.). 2007. audio compact disk 14.99 (978-0-7393-5869-6(3), Random AudioBks) Pub: Random Audio Pubg. Dist(s): Random

Culture Wars Series. 5. 2001. 24.95 (978-0-7417-0036-0(0)) Win Walk.

Cultured Handmaiden. unabr. ed. Catherine Cookson. Read by Susan Jameson. 8 cass. (Running Time: 8 hrs.). 1993. 69.95 (978-0-7451-5858-7(7), CAB 336) AudioGO.

Cultures As a Social Spectacle. unabr. ed. R. Andrews. 1 cass. 1986. 12.95 (I7959) J Norton Pubs.

Examines the criteria on which a new form of drama, based on Latin & Greek models, was constructed in Italian theatre in 1500-1520. Discusses how Italian Humanist scholars were working to replace medieval forms of drama & spectacle with this new, Neo-Classical form of drama. Describes how audiences responded to the new dramatic pieces & new translations of classical comedies.

***Cultures of War: Pearl Harbor / Hiroshima / 9-11 / Iraq.** unabr. ed. John W. Dower. Narrated by Kevin Foley. (Running Time: 18 hrs. 0 mins. 0 sec.). 2010. 29.99 (978-1-4001-6958-0(5)); 21.99 (978-1-4001-8958-8(6)); audio compact disk 95.99 (978-1-4001-4958-2(4)); audio compact disk 39.99 (978-1-4001-1958-5(8)) Pub: Tantor Media. Dist(s): IngramPubServ

***Cum Laude WMA.** Cecily Von Ziegesar. (ENG.). 2010. 24.99 (978-1-4013-9427-1(2)) Pub: Hyperion. Dist(s): HarperCollins Pubs

Cumar. Contrib. by Mary et. al. Bergin. (ENG.). 2000. 13.95 (978-0-8023-7141-6(8)) Pub: Clo Iar-Chonnachta IRL. Dist(s): Dufour

***Cumar.** Mary Et. El. Bergin. (ENG.). 2000. audio compact disk 21.95 (978-0-8023-8141-5(3)) Pub: Clo Iar-Chonnachta IRL. Dist(s): Dufour

Cumberland Vendetta & Others. John Fox, Jr. Read by Maynard Villers. 6 cass. (Running Time: 7 hrs. 12 min.). 1994. 39.95 (978-1-55686-543-5(0)) Books in Motion.

Includes "A Mountain Europa" & "The Last Stetson". Set in the Kentucky hills of the Cumberland Mountains this trio of stories reveal a way of life long forgotten.

Cumbre Level 2: Curso de Espanol para Extranjeros. Aquilino Sánchez et al. 2 cass. (Running Time: 3 hrs.). (SPA, ENG & ITA., (978-84-7143-632-0(9)) Sociedad General ESP.

Cumbre Level 3: Curso de Espanol para Extranjeros. Aquilino Sánchez et al. 2 cass. (Running Time: 3 hrs.). (SPA, ENG & ITA., (978-84-7143-633-7(7)) Sociedad General ESP.

Cumbres Borrascosas. Emily Brontë. 2 CDs. (Running Time: 2 hrs.).Tr. of Wuthering Heights. (SPA.). 2006. audio compact disk 16.95 (978-1-933499-03-1(6)) Fonolibro Inc.

Cumbres Borrascosas. abr. ed. Emily Brontë. Read by Laura Garcia. 3 CDs.Tr. of Wuthering Heights. (SPA.). 2002. audio compact disk 17.00 (978-958-8161-10-5(X)) YoYoMusic.

Cumpleanos de Minina Timida. Tr. of Jenny's Birthday Book. (SPA.). 2004. 8.95 (978-0-7882-0265-0(0)) Weston Woods.

Cumpleanos en la Granja. (Cuenta y Canta una Historia Ser.). 18.95 (978-88-536-0223-7(6)) EMC-Paradigm.

Cunning Man. unabr. ed. Robertson Davies. Read by Frederick Davidson. 11 cass. (Running Time: 16 hrs.). 1996. 76.95 (978-0-7861-1060-5(0), 1831) Blckstn Audio.

"Should I have taken the false teeth?" This is what Dr. Jonathan Hullah, a former police surgeon, thinks after he watches Father Hobbes die in front of the High Altar at Toronto's St. Aidan's on the morning of Good Friday. How did the good father die? We do not learn the answer until the last pages of this "Case Book" of a man's rich & highly observant life. But we learn much more about many things, & especially about Dr. Hullah.

Cunning Man. unabr. ed. Robertson Davies. Narrated by George Guidall. 12 cass. (Running Time: 17 hrs.). 1996. 97.00 (978-0-7887-0294-5(7), 94487E7) Recorded Bks.

Dr. Jonathan Hullah, a former police surgeon with "a high degree of cunning," is shocked when St. Aidan's Father Hobbes drops dead during church services. What made the good & perfectly healthy clergyman die so suddenly? To solve the mystery, Dr. Hullah whisks us on a tour of his own rich & highly observant life.

cunning Man. unabr. ed. Celia Rees. Read by Shirley Barthelmie. (Running Time: 4 hrs. 20 mins.). (YA). 2007. audio compact disk 57.95 (978-1-74093-896-9(8)) Pub: Bolinda Pubng AUS. Dist(s): Bolinda Pub Inc

Cunning of the Mountain Man. abr. ed. William W. Johnstone. Read by Doug van Liew. 4 cass. (Running Time: 6 hrs.). (Mountain Man Ser.: No. 14). 2001. 24.95 (978-1-890990-63-3(9), 99[illegible]) Otis Audio.

Framed for the murder of a rancher, S[illegible]Jensen must escape the angry lynch mob out for his blood, win the tru[illegible]he widow of his supposed victim & clear his name by exposing the land-hungry killers responsible for the crime.

Cup of Cheer. Read by Rosalyn Landor & Tony Jay. 1 cass. (Running Time: 40 min.). (978-1-883446-03-1(1)) Poet Tree CA.

"Cup of Cheer" includes Poet Tree's "Joys of Christmas Past" cassette, a ceramic coffee or tea mug, & a packet of spiced cider. "Joys of Christmas Past" includes a collection of 31 Christmas-themed poems performed by professional actors & accompanied by music. "A Visit from St. Nicholas" is among the selections.

Cup of Christmas Tea, A & Memory of Christmas Tea. unabr. ed. Tom Hegg. Read by Tom Hegg. (YA). 2007. 34.99 (978-1-60252-678-5(8)) Find a World.

***Cup of Friendship: A Novel.** unabr. ed. Deborah Rodriguez. (ENG.). 2011. audio compact disk 35.00 (978-0-307-87917-2(8), Random AudioBks) Pub: Random Audio Pubg. Dist(s): Random

Cup of Gold: A Life of Sir Henry Morgan, Buccaneer, with Occasional Reference to History. unabr. collector's ed. John Steinbeck. Read by Michael Keenan. 7 cass. (Running Time: 7 hrs.). (J). 1991. 42.00 (978-0-7366-2042-0(7), 2856) Books on Tape.

In the 1670s Henry Morgan, a pirate & outlaw of legendary viciousness, ruled the Spanish Main. He ravaged the coasts of Cuba & America, striking terror wherever he went. Morgan was obsessive. He had two driving ambitions: one, to possess the beautiful woman called La Santa Roja; the other, to conquer Panama, the "cup of gold".

Cup of the World. John Dickinson. Narrated by Alyssa Bresnahan. 9 cass. (Running Time: 13 hrs. 15 mins.). (YA). 2004. 81.75 (978-1-4193-0872-7(6)) Recorded Bks.

Cup of Turkish Coffee. Buket Uzuner. 2 cass. (Running Time: 2 hrs.). (YA). 2001. bk. 11.95 (978-1-84059-309-9(1)); bk. 11.95 (978-1-84059-308-2(3)) Pub: Milet Pub. Dist(s): Tuttle Pubng

Cupboard Door: A Collection of Poetry. Karen Jean Matsko Hood. (Running Time: 2 hours 30 minutes). 2006. 24.95 (978-1-59210-127-6(5)); audio compact disk 29.95 (978-1-59210-156-6(9)) Whsprng Pine.

Cupid: A Tale of Love & Desire. unabr. ed. Julius Lester. Read by Stephen McKinley Henderson. 5 CDs. (Running Time: 5 hrs. 37 mins.). (YA). (gr. 7 up). 2007. audio compact disk 36.00 (978-0-7393-4850-5(7)) Books on Tape.

Cupid: A Tale of Love & Desire. unabr. ed. Julius Lester. Read by Stephen McKinley Henderson. (Running Time: 20220 sec.). (ENG.). (J). (gr. 7-12). 2007. audio compact disk 35.00 (978-0-7393-3878-0(1), Listening Lib) Pub: Random Audio Pubg. Dist(s): Random

Cupid & Campaspe see Palgrave's Golden Treasury of English Poetry

Cupid Delivers. unabr. ed. Contrib. by Susan Musleh. 1 cass. (Running Time: 3 min.). (Susan's Romantic Adventures - A Secret Admirer's Kit Ser.). (C). 1998. 24.95 (978-1-893494-00-8(4), CD-200) Susans Romantic Adv.

Cupid's Revenge. Leta N. Childers. Read by Leta N. Childers. 1 cass. (Running Time: 1 hr. 50 min.). 1999. bk. 6.50 (978-1-58495-003-5(X)) DiskUs Publishing.
Romantic Comedy.

Cupid's Valentine. Phyllis Dolgin. 1 cass. (Running Time: 7 min.). (Holidays Are Fun Ser.). (J). (ps-2). 1985. 23.95 incl. 8 paperback bks. & 1 activity card. Jan Prods.
Cupid, the Persian cat, struggles to declare his love to Valentine, the new pet cat across the hall.

Cura biblica para el DDA y la hiperactividad, La see Bible Cure for ADD & Hyperactivity: Ancient Truths, Natural Remedies & the Latest Findings for Your Health Today

Cura biblica para la presion alta, La see High Blood Pressure: Ancient Truths, Natural Remedies & the Latest Findings for Your Health Today

cura para todos los Males. Pescao Vivo. 2008. audio compact disk 14.99 (978-0-8297-5452-0(0)) Pub: Vida Pubs. Dist(s): Zondervan

***Curable Romantic.** unabr. ed. Joseph Skibell. Read by Jeff Woodman. 18 CDs. (Running Time: 22 hrs. 30 mins.). 2010. audio compact disk 49.95 (978-1-61573-530-3(5), 1615735305) Pub: HighBridge. Dist(s): Workman Pub

Curacion por el Pensamiento. Angel Escudero. 1 cass. (Running Time: 1 hr. 30 mins.).Tr. of Healing Through the Mind. (SPA.). 2001. Astran.

Curb TV Snacking. 1 cass. (Running Time: 60 min.). 10.95 (031) Psych Res Inst.
Supplement to weight loss program directed at binge snacking.

Curbing the Epidemic in IV Drug Users. Harold Ginzburg. (AIDS: The National Conference for Practitioners). 1986. 9.00 (978-0-932491-52-7(9)) Res Appl Inc.

Cure. Jack D. Hunter. Narrated by William Dufris. (Running Time: 11 hrs. 30 mins.). 2003. 34.95 (978-1-59912-645-6(1)) Iofy Corp.

Cure. unabr. ed. Robin Cook. (Running Time: 12 hrs.). (ENG.). 2010. audio compact disk 39.95 (978-0-14-242810-8(8), PengAudBks) Penguin Grp USA.

Cure. unabr. ed. Sarah Gorham & Sonia Levitin. Narrated by Suzanne Toren. 5 pieces. (Running Time: 7 hrs. 15 mins.). (gr. 8 up). 2001. 48.00 (978-0-7887-7241-2(4)) Recorded Bks.

Cure. unabr. ed. Jack D. Hunter. Read by William Dufris. 9 CDs. (Running Time: 11 hrs. 30 mins.). 2003. audio compact disk 72.00 (978-0-7861-9182-6(1), 3142); audio compact disk 24.95 (978-0-7861-8917-5(7), 3142); 56.95 (978-0-7861-2509-8(8), 3142) Blckstn Audio.
A gripping tale of cutting-edge medicine and international intrigue, exposing the dark underside of the modern medical establishment.

Cure. unabr. ed. Jack D. Hunter. Read by William Dufris. 8 pieces. 2004. reel tape 39.95 (978-0-7861-2616-3(7)); audio compact disk 44.95 (978-0-7861-8897-0(9)) Blckstn Audio.

Cure: The Hero's Journey with Cancer. G. Frank Lawlis. Read by G. Frank Lawlis. 2 cass. (Running Time: 2 hrs.). 1993. 39.95 Set, incl. 2 trade pap. bks. ResPubnsCA.
Relaxation Techniques, Imagery, Vision Quest, Introduction to Storytelling.

Cure by Crying. Thomas A. Stone. 12 cass. (Running Time: 12 hr.). 1995. 75.00 (978-0-9647674-2-3(2)) Lightell-Stone.

Cure D'Ars. George Rutler. Read by George Rutler. 6 cass. 1995. 24.95 Set. (770-C) Ignatius Pr.
Fr. Rutler reads his own book in which he gives new & inspiring insights about the life of the Cure (St. John Vianney) & his message for today's Church.

Cure d'Ars Today. George Rutler. Read by George Rutler. 6 cass. 24.95 Set. (770-C) Ignatius Pr.
Gives new & inspiring insights about the life of the Cure (St. John Vianney) & his message for today's Church.

Cure de Tours, Set. Honoré de Balzac. Read by Bernard Merle. 2 cass. (FRE.). 1995. 26.95 (1758-KFP) Olivia & Hill.
In Tours, under the Restauration, Father Birotteau has one ambition: to succeed his friend Father Chapeloud upon the latter's death. He will encounter his rival Father Troubert & the vengeful Mlle. Gamard, a devout spinster.

Cure for All Diseases: An Interview with Dr. Hulda R. Clark. Interview. Hulda Regehr Clark. 2 cass. 1998. 19.95 (978-1-890035-99-0(8)) New Centry Pr.

Cure for Modern Life. abr. ed. Lisa Tucker. Read by Scott Brick. (Running Time: 6 hrs.). 2009. audio compact disk 14.99 (978-1-4233-4889-4(3), 9781423348894, BCD Value Price) Brilliance Audio.

Cure for Modern Life. unabr. ed. Lisa Tucker. Read by Scott Brick. 1 MP3-CD. (Running Time: 11 hrs.). 2008. 24.95 (978-1-4233-4885-6(0), 9781423348856, Brilliance MP3); 24.95 (978-1-4233-4887-0(7), 9781423348870, BAD); audio compact disk 97.25 (978-1-4233-4884-9(2), 9781423348849, BriAudCD Unabrid); audio compact disk 39.25 (978-1-4233-4886-3(9), 9781423348863, Brinc Audio MP3 Lib); audio compact disk 36.95 (978-1-4233-4883-2(4), 9781423348832, Bril Audio CD Unabri) Brilliance Audio.

Cure for Modern Life. unabr. ed. Lisa Tucker. Read by Scott Brick. (Running Time: 11 hrs.). 2009. 39.97 (978-1-4418-5035-5(X), 9781441850355, BADLE) Brilliance Audio.

***Cure for the Chronic Life: Overcoming the Hopelessness That Holds You Back.** unabr. ed. Deanna Favre & Shane Stanford. (Running Time: 7 hrs. 0 mins. 0 sec.). (ENG.). 2011. audio compact disk 25.99 (978-1-59859-844-5(9)) Oasis Audio.

Cure for the Common Life: Living in Your Sweet Spot. abr. ed. Max Lucado. Read by Mike Flynn. (Running Time: 12600 sec.). 2006. audio compact disk 24.99 (978-0-8499-6381-0(8)) Nelson.

***Cure of Ars.** Bartholomew O'Brien. Read by Emily Bissonnette. Patrick Reis. (ENG.). 2009. audio compact disk 16.95 (978-1-936231-01-0(8)) Cath Audio.

Cure of Souls. Phil Rickman. 2009. 99.95 (978-0-7531-3374-3(1)); audio compact disk 104.95 (978-0-7531-3375-0(X)) Pub: Isis Pubng Ltd GBR. Dist(s): Ulverscroft US

Cure Su Vida. Carlos González. Read by Carlos González. Ed. by Dina Gonzalez. 1 cass. (Running Time: 32 min.).Tr. of Heal Your Life. (SPA.). 1991. 10.00 (978-1-56491-026-4(1)) Imagine Pubs.
In Spanish. Positive suggestions that helps the person to improve mental attitude towards their body and health.

Cure Your Cravings. abr. ed. Yefim Shubentsov & Barbara Gordon. Read by Bill Morelock. (Running Time: 3 hrs. 15 mins.). (ENG.). 2005. audio compact disk 24.95 (978-1-59887-084-8(X), 159887084X) Pub: HighBridge. Dist(s): Workman Pub

Curese con el Poder del Pensamiento. unabr. ed. Carlos González. Ed. by Dina Gonzalez. 4 cass. (Running Time: 2 hrs. 8 min.). (SPA.). 1993. 49.00 (978-1-56491-061-5(X)) Imagine Pubs.
A perfect way to help yourself to anul illnesses.

Curing the Cause & Preventing Disease: A New approach to the Diagnosis & Treatment of Illness & Aging with Functional Diagnostic Medicine. Curing The Cause & Preventing Disease. (ENG.). 2007. audio compact disk (978-0-9796135-1-7(5)) Curing the Cause.

Curing the Cause & Preventing Disease: A New Approach to the Diagnosis & Treatment of Illness & Aging with Functional Diagnostic Medicine. Steven Ross. (ENG.). 2007. audio compact disk (978-0-9796135-3-1(1)) Curing the Cause.

Curiosity Shop. Stephanie K. Burton. 1998. 9.95 (978-1-889163-09-3(0)); audio compact disk 13.95 (978-1-889163-08-6(2)) Panda Bear Pub.

Curiosity Shop. Stephanie K. Burton & Phyllis Campbell. 2000. pap. bk. 17.95 (978-1-889163-07-9(4)) Panda Bear Pub.

Curiosity Shop Book. Stephanie K. Burton & Phyllis Campbell. 2000. pap. bk. 21.95 (978-1-889163-06-2(6)) Panda Bear Pub.

***Curious?** abr. ed. Todd Kashdan. Read by Todd Kashdan. (ENG.). 2009. (978-0-06-180590-5(4), Harper Audio); (978-0-06-180591-2(2), Harper Audio) HarperCollins Pubs.

Curious Adventures of Jimmy Mcgee. Eleanor Estes. Read by Jane Jacobs. (Running Time: 5 hrs.). 2005. 21.95 (978-1-60083-349-6(7)) Iofy Corp.

Curious Adventures of Jimmy Mcgee. Eleanor Estes. Read by Jane Jacobs. (Running Time: 18000 sec.). (J). (ps-7). 2005. audio compact disk 27.95 (978-1-59316-067-8(4)) Listen & Live.

Curious Affair of the Third Dog. unabr. ed. Patricia Moyes. Read by Nadia May. 6 cass. (Running Time: 8 hrs. 30 mins.). (Henry Tibbett Mystery Ser.). 1993. 44.95 (978-0-7861-0428-4(7), 1380) Blckstn Audio.
In a fast-moving & intricate plot, Patricia Moyes weaves together the contrasting strands of English village life & London's underworld, until the two collide with an explosion of violence at their one point of contact - a greyhound racing stadium.

Curious Case of Benjamin Button: And Other Jazz Age Tales. F. Scott Fitzgerald. Read by Grover Gardner. (Running Time: 14400 sec.). (ENG.). 2006. audio compact disk 19.99 (978-1-4001-5235-3(6)); audio compact disk 49.99 (978-1-4001-3235-5(5)) Pub: Tantor Media. Dist(s): IngramPubServ

Curious Case of Benjamin Button: And Other Stories. F. Scott Fitzgerald. Read by Scott Brick & Grover Gardner. (Running Time: 10800 sec.). 2007. 22.95 (978-0-7861-4987-2(6)) Blckstn Audio.

Curious Case of Benjamin Button: And Other Stories. unabr. ed. F. Scott Fitzgerald. Read by Scott Brick & Grover Gardner. 3 CDs. (Running Time: 10800 sec.). 2007. audio compact disk 19.95 (978-0-7861-6045-7(4)); audio compact disk 29.95 (978-0-7861-7151-4(0)) Blckstn Audio.

Curious Case of Benjamin Button: And Other Stories. unabr. ed. F. Scott Fitzgerald. Read by Grover Gardner. 3 CDs. (Running Time: 10800 sec.). 2007. audio compact disk 27.00 (978-0-7861-5776-1(3)) Blckstn Audio.

Curious Case of Benjamin Button: And Other Stories. unabr. ed. F. Scott Fitzgerald. Read by Scott Brick et al. (Running Time: 10800 sec.). 2007. 19.95 (978-0-7861-4859-2(4)) Blckstn Audio.

Curious Case of Benjamin Button & Other Jazz Age Tales. unabr. ed. F. Scott Fitzgerald. Read by Grover Gardner. (YA). 2007. 39.99 (978-1-60252-524-5(2)) Find a World.

Curious Case of Benjamin Button & Other Jazz Age Tales. unabr. ed. F. Scott Fitzgerald. Read by Grover Gardner. 8 CDs. (Running Time: 8 hrs.). (ENG.). 2006. audio compact disk 24.99 (978-1-4001-0235-8(9)) Pub: Tantor Media. Dist(s): IngramPubServ
F. Scott Fitzgerald, one of the greatest American writers, is best known for The Great Gatsby, considered by many to be the most important novel of the 20th century. But Fitzgerald also made his living as a short story writer, and The Curious Case of Benjamin Button and Other Jazz Age Tales collects nine of his best. The title story is soon to be a major motion picture starring Brad Pitt and directed by David Fincher - -the same team that made Seven and Fight Club. It is fantasy story about a man who is in his 70s at birth and progressively ages backwards. All of the stories were written before The Great Gatsby and represent a clear movement in theme and character that Fitzgerald would develop with Gatsby.

Curious Case of Benjamin Button & Other Jazz Age Tales. unabr. ed. F. Scott Fitzgerald. Narrated by Grover Gardner. 1 MP3-CD. (Running Time: 4 hrs. 0 mins. 0 sec.). (ENG.). 2008. 17.99 (978-1-4001-5977-2(6)); audio compact disk 17.99 (978-1-4001-0977-7(9)); audio compact disk 35.99 (978-1-4001-3977-4(5)) Pub: Tantor Media. Dist(s): IngramPubServ

Curious Case of Benjamin Button, Apt. 3W. unabr. ed. Gabriel Brownstein. Read by Scott Brick. 6 CDs. (Running Time: 7 hrs. 30 mins.). 2007. audio compact disk 55.00 (978-1-4332-1055-6(X)) Blckstn Audio.

Curious Case of Benjamin Button, Apt 3W. unabr. ed. Gabriel Brownstein. Read by Scott Brick. (Running Time: 27000 sec.). 2007. 54.95 (978-1-4332-1054-9(1)) Blckstn Audio.

Curious Case of Benjamin Button, Apt 3W. unabr. ed. Gabriel Brownstein & Scott Brick. (Running Time: 27000 sec.). 2007. audio compact disk 29.95 (978-1-4332-1056-3(6)) Blckstn Audio.

Curious Curate & the Buried Treasure: A BBC Radio Full-Cast Dramatization. M. C. Beaton, pseud. (Running Time: 1 hr. 45 mins. 0 sec.). (Agatha Raisin Mystery Ser.: Bk. 13). (ENG.). 2009. audio compact disk 24.95 (978-1-60283-734-8(1)) Pub: AudioGO. Dist(s): Perseus Dist

Curious George. H. A. Rey. (Curious George Ser.). (J). (ps-2). 2000. pap. bk. 9.95 (4-94351) HM Schl Div.

Curious George. unabr. ed. H. A. Rey. Read by Julie Harris. 1 cass. (Running Time: 90 min.). Incl. Curious George Gets a Medal. H. A. Rey. (Curious George Ser.). (J). (ps-2). (CPN 1420); Curious George Rides a Bike. H. A. Rey. (Curious George Ser.). (J). (ps-2). (CPN 1420); Curious George Takes a Job. H. A. Rey. (Curious George Ser.). (J). (ps-2). (CPN 1420); (Curious George Ser.). (J). (ps-2). 1984. 9.95 (978-0-89845-109-2(4), CPN 1420) HarperCollins Pubs.

***Curious George: And Other Stories.** H. A. Rey. Read by Don Wescott. (Playaway Children Ser.). (ENG.). (J). 2009. 39.99 (978-1-61587-687-7(1)) Find a World.

Curious George Flies a Kite see Curious George Learns the Alphabet

***Curious George Flies a Kite & More Adventures: For Beginning Readers.** Margret Rey & H. A. Rey. Read by Cheryl McMahon et al. (Playaway Children Ser.). (ENG.). (J). 2009. 39.99 (978-1-61587-690-7(1)) Find a World.

Curious George Gets a Medal see Curious George

Curious George Goes to the Hospital see Curious George Learns the Alphabet

Curious George Learns the Alphabet. abr. ed. H. A. Rey. Read by Julie Harris. 1 cass. (Running Time: 90 min.). Incl. Curious George Flies a Kite. Margret Rey & H. A. Rey. (Curious George Ser.). (J). (ps-2). (CPN 1421); Curious George Goes to the Hospital. Margret Rey & H. A. Rey. (Curious George Ser.). (J). (ps-2). (CPN 1421); (Curious George Ser.). (J). (ps-2). 1984. 9.95 (978-0-89845-812-1(9), CPN 1421) HarperCollins Pubs.

Curious George Rides a Bike see Curious George

Curious George Rides a Bike see Jorge, el Monito Ciclista

Curious George Rides a Bike. 2004. 8.95 (978-1-56008-882-0(6)); cass. & flmstrp 30.00 (978-0-89719-556-0(6)); audio compact disk 12.95 (978-1-55592-869-8(2)) Weston Woods.

Curious George Rides a Bike. (J). 2004. pap. bk. 18.95 (978-1-55592-802-5(1)); pap. bk. 18.95 (978-1-55592-770-7(X)); pap. bk. 38.75 (978-1-55592-819-3(6)); pap. bk. 38.75 (978-1-55592-785-1(8)); pap. bk. 32.75 (978-1-55592-213-9(9)); pap. bk. 32.75 (978-1-55592-214-6(7)); pap. bk. 14.95 (978-1-56008-096-1(5)); pap. bk. 14.95 (978-1-55592-721-9(1)) Weston Woods.

Curious George Rides a Bike. H. A. Rey. 1 cass. (Running Time: 10 min.). (Curious George Ser.). (J). (ps-2). bk. 24.95; pap. bk. 32.75 Weston Woods.
The curious monkey embarks on a wild series of adventures in a traveling circus.

Curious George Rides a Bike. H. A. Rey. 1 cass. (Running Time: 10 min.). (Curious George Ser.). (J). (ps-2). 1993. pap. bk. 8.95 (978-1-56008-116-6(3), RAC017); pap. bk. 14.95 (978-1-56008-097-8(3), PRA017) Weston Woods.
From the book by H. A. Rey. The curious monkey embarks on a wild series of adventures in a traveling circus.

Curious George Rides a Bike: And Other Storybook Classics. H. A. Rey et al. Narrated by Bruce Johnson & Ian Thomson. (Playaway Children Ser.). (ENG.). (J). (ps-3). 2009. 44.99 (978-1-60812-563-0(7)) Find a World.

Curious George Rides a Bike; Five Chinese Brothers, the; In the Forest; Jenny's Birthday Book. 2004. (978-0-89719-804-2(2)) Weston Woods.

Curious George Rides a Bike; Five Chinese Brthers, the; In the Forest; Jenny's Birthday Book. 2004. cass. & flmstrp (978-0-89719-713-7(5)) Weston Woods.

Curious George Takes a Job see Curious George

Curious Glimpse of Michigan. Kammeraad Hipp. 2007. audio compact disk 14.95 (978-0-9669504-4-1(5)) Pub: EDCO Pubng Inc. Dist(s): Partners Bk Dist

Curious Incident of the Dog in the Night-Time. unabr. ed. Mark Haddon. 4 cass. Library ed. (Running Time: 6 hrs. 25 min.). 2003. 45.00 (978-1-4025-5978-5(X)) Recorded Bks.

Curious Incident of the Dog in the Night-Time. unabr. ed. Mark Haddon. Narrated by Jeff Woodman. 5 CDs Library ed. (Running Time: 6 hrs. 25 min.). 2003. audio compact disk 45.00 (978-1-4025-5980-8(1), C2320) Recorded Bks.

Curious Incident of the Dog in the Night-Time. unabr. ed. Mark Haddon. Narrated by Jeff Woodman. 4 cass. (Running Time: 6 hrs. 15 mins.). 2004. 19.99 (978-1-4025-5598-5(9), 03294); audio compact disk 24.99 (978-1-4025-6885-5(1), 01302) Recorded Bks.
From award-winning author Mark Haddon comes a story like no other. Featuring a 15-year-old boy with a condition similar to autism as the narrator, The Curious Incident of the Dog in the Night-time is a spectacularly unique achievement. Christopher has Asperger's Syndrome. A math whiz, he loves lists, patterns and the truth. But he doesn't know much about people, and he hates being touched. Never in his lifetime has he gone further, on his own, than the end of his road. But when a neighbor's dog is murdered, he assumes the role of detective and embarks on a funny, yet terrifying adventure.

Curlew Island. unabr. ed. Sally Stewart. Read by Maragret Sircom. 4 cass. (Running Time: 5 hrs. 15 min.). 1999. 57.95 (978-1-85903-251-0(6)) Pub: Magna Story GBR. Dist(s): Ulverscroft US
Helping author Tod Harriman trace his family roots, Londoner Frances Campbell finds more than she bargained for in the remote Hebridean Island of Cullin.

Curly Tale. Vayu Naidu. 1 cass. (Running Time: 022 min.). (Under the Banyan Ser.). (YA). (gr. 2 up). 1998. bk. 11.99 (978-81-86838-33-4(3)) APG.
Fairy tales & folklore.

Curran vs. Catholic University. unabr. ed. Larry Witham. Read by Robin Lawson. 9 cass. (Running Time: 13 hrs.). 1992. 62.95 (978-0-7861-0338-6(8), 1295) Blckstn Audio.
Through biography, history, theology & courtroom drama, this book recounts the quintessential conflict between an American theologian & the Vatican. The Curran case framed an era, from 1965 to 1990, & left behind unresolved questions about authority & freedom in the Catholic Church today.

Currency Trading Manual. Thomas Worthington. 2002. pap. bk. 39.95 (978-1-884350-82-5(8)) Alpha Pubng.

Current & the Cure: Logos September 20, 1998. Ben Young. 1998. 4.95 (978-0-7417-6099-9(1), B0099) Win Walk.

Current Anti-Tax Movement. Read by Jack Matonis et al. 2 cass. (Running Time: 2 hrs.). (Cal State Univ., Long Beach Ser.). 1981. 18.00 (F128A & B) Freeland Pr.
Each panelist shares their experiences in tax avoidance & run-ins with the IRS. Panel discussion.

Current, Best Instructional Strategies for Your Gifted & Highly Capable Students. unabr. ed. Contrib. by Roger Taylor. 6 cass. (Running Time: 5 hrs. 33 mins.). 2002. 89.00 (978-1-886397-48-4(1)) Bureau of Educ.

Current Best Strategies for Enhancing Your First Grade Reading & Writing Instruction, Judy Lynch. Read by Judy Lynch. 6 cass. (Running Time: 4 hr. 32 min.). 1996. 75.00 Incl. handbk. (978-1-886397-09-5(0)) Bureau of Educ.
Live audio seminar.

Current Best Strategies for Helping Your Emergent, Early & Fluent Readers, Set. Cheryl Sweeney. 6 cass. (Running Time: 4 hr. 4 min.). (J). (gr. 1-2). 1997. 75.00 Incl. handbk. (978-1-886397-13-2(9)) Bureau of Educ.

Current Best Strategies for Strengthening Your Second Grade Program. abr. ed. Narrated by Cheryl Sweeney. 6 cass. (Running Time: 4 hrs. 20 mins.). 2001. 85.00 (978-1-886397-38-5(4)) Bureau of Educ.
Live audio workshop & a comprehensive resource handbook.

Current Concepts in Cancer Chemotherapy. Read by Paul Calabresi. 1 cass. (Running Time: 90 min.). 1986. 12.00 (C8666) Amer Coll Phys.

Current Concepts in Management of Vitreo-Retinal Diseases: Interdisciplinary Symposium. Moderated by James G. Diamond. 3 cass. (Ophthalmic Surgery Ser.: OP-1). 1986. 28.50 (8650) Am Coll Surgeons.

Current Concepts of Breast Cancer. 3 cass. (Spring Meeting Philadelphia, PA Ser.: S87-GS5). 1987. 28.50 (8705) Am Coll Surgeons.
Details conservative surgery, adjuvant chemotherapy, hormonal treatment for primary & metastatic carcinoma, humoral & cellular markers of prognostic significance, patient management & early & late reconstruction.

Current Developments in Bankruptcy & Reorganization. unabr. ed. Contrib. by Arnold M. Quittner. 8 cass. (Running Time: 11 hrs.). 1989. 50.00 course handbk. (T7-9204) PLI.

Current Developments in Cooperative & Condominium Practice: Beyond the Basics. unabr. ed. Contrib. by Jay A. Neveloff. 4 cass. (Running Time: 5 hrs.). 1989. 50.00 course handbk. (T7-9249) PLI.
This recording of PLI's November 1989 program goes beyond the basics in its examination of cooperative & condominium practice. An experienced faculty of attorneys & consultants explores recent developments in such areas as: market conditions, case law, unusual offerings, transfer & gains tax & alteration issues. A special feature of the program is hypothetical transactions presented for analysis by both the faculty & registrants.

Current Developments in Employment Law. 11 cass. (Running Time: 15 hrs. 50 min.). 1998. 315.00 Set, incl. course materials. (MD06) Am Law Inst.

Current Developments in Patent Law & Litigation. 8 cass. (Running Time: 12 hrs.). 1995. 345.00 Set; incl. Studyguide 490p. (MA15) Am Law Inst.
Advanced course includs seeping statutory changes mandated by GATT, & discusses how best to apply the new developments to serve clients' interests.

Current Developments in Public Employee Labor Law. 1998. bk. 149.00 (ACS-2097) PA Bar Inst.
From Act 195 to Act 111, from school districts to municipalities, the substance & procedure of labor law continues to change. You will read about the latest decisions & learn savvy insights on how they impact your clients & cases.

Current Directions in Computer Music Research: Sound Examples. Ed. by Max V. Mathews. (ENG.). 1989. audio compact disk 42.00 (978-0-262-63121-1(0)) MIT Pr.

Current Eclipse Patterns. Buz Myers. 1 cass. 8.95 (734) Am Fed Astrologers.

Current Indications for Hysterectomy. 2 cass. (Gynecology & Obstetrics Ser.: C85-GO7). 15.00 (8565) Am Coll Surgeons.

Current Issues in Managed Care. Contrib. by Larry P. Griffin et al. 1 cass. (American College of Obstetrics & Gynecologists UPDATE: Vol. 22, No. 1). 1998. 20.00 Am Coll Obstetric.

Current Issues in Public Contracting. 1987. bk. 120.00 incl. book.; 70.00 cass. only.; 50.00 book only. PA Bar Inst.

Current Issues in the Diagnosis & Management of Vasculitis. Moderated by Sheldon M. Wolff. Contrib. by Charles L. Christian & Anthony S. Fauci. 1 cass. (Running Time: 90 min.). 1986. 12.00 (A8629) Amer Coll Phys.
This topic is discussed by a moderator & experts who offer differing opinions.

Current Management of Acute Pancreatitis. 2 cass. (General Sessions Ser.). 15.00 (8538 (C85-GS3)) Am Coll Surgeons.

Current Management of Bleeding Esophageal Varices. Moderated by Bernard Langer. 2 cass. (General Sessions Ser.: Spring 1986). 1986. 15.00 (8607) Am Coll Surgeons.
Definition of the problem & management of the whole patient, non-surgical therapy for control of bleeding - balloons, drug, & sclerotherapy, the place of devascularization procedures & portosystemic shunting.

Current Management of Chronic Hepatitis. Moderated by Telfer B. Reynolds. Contrib. by Jay H. Hoofnagle et al. 1 cass. (Running Time: 90 min.). 1985. 12.00 (A8509) Amer Coll Phys.
This topic is discussed by a moderator & experts who offer differing opinions.

Current Management of Tubes & Drains in Gynecological Surgery: Interdisciplinary Panel Discussion. Moderated by Edgardo L. Yordan. 3 cass. (Gynecology & Obstetrics Ser.: GO-3). 1986. 28.50 (8642) Am Coll Surgeons.

Current Perspectives in Professional Liability. 2 cass. (General Sessions Ser.: C84-GS2). 1984. 15.00 (8406) Am Coll Surgeons.

Current Problems in Federal Practice. 1989. 55.00 (AC-497) PA Bar Inst.

Current Status of Transplantation Surgery. 2 cass. (General Sessions Ser.: C84-GS6). 1984. 15.00 (8410) Am Coll Surgeons.

Current Topics in Pennsylvania Securities Law. 1990. 75.00 (AC-582) PA Bar Inst.

***Currents of Space.** unabr. ed. Isaac Asimov. Narrated by Kevin T. Collins. 1 MP3-CD. (Running Time: 7 hrs. 30 mins.). 2009. 44.95 (978-0-7927-6477-9(3)); audio compact disk 74.95 (978-0-7927-6057-3(3)) AudioGO.

Curriculum Cd-Firefighter. (C). 2004. audio compact disk 259.95 (978-1-4018-7175-8(5)) Pub: Delmar. Dist(s): CENGAGE Learn

Curriculum for the Eighties: Science Fiction, Science Fact. Isaac Asimov et al. Read by Isaac Asimov et al. 1 cass. (Running Time: 30 min.). 8.00 (NJ-81-02-16, HarperThor) HarpC GBR.

Curse see Poetry of Edna St. Vincent Millay

Curse see Love Poems of John Donne

Curse. unabr. ed. Nancy Holder & Debbie Viguié. Read by Cassandra Morris. (Running Time: 7 hrs.). (Wicked Ser.). 2010. audio compact disk 24.99 (978-1-4418-3533-8(4), 9781441835338, Bril Audio CD Unabri) Brilliance Audio.

***Curse.** unabr. ed. Nancy Holder & Debbie Viguié. Read by Cassandra Morris. (Running Time: 7 hrs.). (Wicked Ser.). 2010. 24.99 (978-1-4418-3535-2(0), 9781441835352, Brilliance MP3); 39.97 (978-1-4418-3536-9(9), 9781441835369, Brinc Audio MP3 Lib); 39.97 (978-1-4418-3537-6(7), 9781441835376, BADLE); audio compact disk 54.97 (978-1-4418-3534-5(2), 9781441835345, BriAudCD Unabrid) Brilliance Audio.

Curse Breaker/Being Made by God. rev. ed. Scripts. T. B. Williams. 1 cd. (Running Time: 1 hr 20mins). 2006. per. 20.00 (978-0-9793339-0-3(3)) FBT.

***Curse Dark As Gold.** Elizabeth Bunce. Contrib. by Scholastic, Inc. Staff. (ENG.). 2010. audio compact disk 79.99 (978-0-545-24959-1(7)) Scholastic Inc.

Curse of Chalion. Lois McMaster Bujold. Read by Lloyd James. (Running Time: 19 hrs.). 2004. 50.95 (978-1-59912-646-3(X)) Iofy Corp.

Curse of Chalion. unabr. ed. Lois McMaster Bujold. Read by Lloyd James. 13 cass. (Running Time: 17 hrs. 30 mins.). 2002. 85.95 (978-0-7861-2770-2(8)) Blckstn Audio.
Lord Cazaril has been, in turn, courtier, castle-warder, and captain; now he is but a crippled ex-galley slave seeking nothing more than a menial job in the kitchens of the Dowager Provincara, the noble patroness of his youth. But Cazaril finds himself promoted to the exalted and dangerous position of tutor to Iselle, the beautiful, fiery sister of the heir to Chalion¿s throne.

Curse of Chalion. unabr. ed. Lois McMaster Bujold. Read by Lloyd James. 12 pieces. (Running Time: 17 hrs. 30 mins.). 2004. reel tape 34.95 (978-0-7861-2685-9(X)); audio compact disk 49.95 (978-0-7861-8692-1(5)) Blckstn Audio.

Curse of Chalion. unabr. ed. Lois McMaster Bujold. Read by Lloyd James. 15 CDs. (Running Time: 17 hrs. 30 mins.). 2004. audio compact disk 120.00 (978-0-7861-8598-6(8)) Blckstn Audio.

Curse of Chalion. unabr. ed. Lois McMaster Bujold. Read by Lloyd James. 2 CDs. (Running Time: 17 hrs. 30 mins.). 2004. audio compact disk 39.95 (978-0-7861-8559-7(7)) Blckstn Audio.

Curse of Dracula. 1 CD. (Running Time: 1 hr.). 2001. audio compact disk 12.95 (SOMT002) Lodestone Catalog.

Curse of Five Eighty-Nine. Scripts. Text by Norman Corwin. Directed By Norman Corwin. 1 CD. (Running Time: 58 mins.). Dramatization. 2005. audio compact disk 15.95 (978-1-59938-004-9(8)) Lode Cat.

Curse of Five Eighty-Nine. Norman Corwin. Perf. by Carl Reiner et al. Prod. by Mary Beth Kirchner. 1 cass. (Running Time: 1 hr.). 12.95 (978-1-57677-072-6(9), CORW012) Lodestone Catalog.
A scientist is confronted by a leprechaun who wants to put a curst on science. Production Script available.

Curse of Five Eighty-Nine. Norman Corwin. Perf. by William Shatner et al. 1 CD. (Running Time: 1 hr.). 2001. audio compact disk 15.95 (CORW024) Lodestone Catalog.
A scientist is confronted by a leprechaun who wants to put a curse on science. Production Script available.

Curse of Senmut. unabr. ed. Loretta Jackson & Vickie Britton. Read by Stephanie Brush. 8 cass. (Running Time: 10 hrs. 24 min.). (Ardis Cole Ser.: Bk. 1). 2001. 49.95 (978-1-55686-936-5(3)) Books in Motion.
Archaeologist Ardis Cole travels to Egypt to search for the crypt of Senmut, advisor to the last Queen of Egypt. But recovery is hampered by unknown killers.

Curse of the Bane. unabr. ed. Joseph Delaney. Read by Christopher Evan Welch. 7 CDs. (Running Time: 8 hrs.). (Last Apprentice Ser.: Bk. 2). (J). (gr. 5-8). 2006. audio compact disk 29.95 (978-0-06-114042-6(2), HarperChildAud) HarperCollins Pubs.

Curse of the Bane. unabr. ed. Joseph Delaney. Read by Christopher Evan Welch. 7 cass. (Running Time: 8 hrs.). (Last Apprentice Ser.: Bk. 2). (YA). (gr. 5-8). 2006. 49.75 (978-1-4281-1704-4(0)); audio compact disk 74.75 (978-1-4281-1709-9(1)) Recorded Bks.

Curse of the Blue Tattoo: Being an Account of the Misadventures of Jacky Faber, Midshipman & Fine Lady. L. A. Meyer. Read by Katherine Kellgren. (Bloody Jack Adventures Ser.: Bk. 2). (J). 2008. 39.99 (978-1-60640-633-5(7)) Find a World.

Curse of the Blue Tattoo: Being an Account of the Misadventures of Jacky Faber, Midshipman & Fine Lady. unabr. ed. L. A. Meyer. Read by Katherine Kellgren. 11 CDs. (Running Time: 14 hrs.). (Bloody Jack Adventures Ser.: Bk. 2). (YA). (gr. 8 up). 2008. audio compact disk 29.95 (978-1-59316-134-7(4)) Listen & Live.

Curse of the Campfire Weenies: And Other Warped & Creepy Tales. unabr. ed. David Lubar. Read by Paul Michael Garcia. (Running Time: 4.5 hrs. 0 mins.). (ENG.). 2009. 19.95 (978-1-4332-9175-3(4)); 34.95 (978-1-4332-9171-5(1)); audio compact disk 49.00 (978-1-4332-9172-2(X)) Blckstn Audio.

Curse of the Cockers. unabr. ed. Gerald Hammond. Read by Donald Douglas. 4 cass. (Running Time: 6 hrs.). 1999. 44.95 (978-0-7531-0479-8(2), 981009) Pub: ISIS Audio GBR. Dist(s): Ulverscroft US
John & Beth Cunningham are called to the scene of a fatal accident at which a terrified cocker spaniel has been found. The victim was killed by a hit & run driver of a Land Rover, but further clues are scarce. Angus Todd is a close friend of the Cunninghams & protest his innocence when traces of blood are found on his Land Rover bumper. Angus asks the Cunninghams to help him clear his name, but what starts as a favor for a friend develops into a hunt for a double killer, when a vital clue is discovered linking two deaths. Cunningham follows the killers trail straight into a nightmarish encounter with a ruthless psychopath.

Curse of the Cockers. unabr. ed. Gerald Hammond. Read by Donald Douglas. 5 CDs. (Running Time: 7 hrs. 30 min.). 2001. audio compact disk 59.95 (978-0-7531-1243-4(4), 1243-4) Pub: ISIS Audio GBR. Dist(s): ISIS Pub

Curse of the Golden Trough. Nicholas Rhea. Read by Graham Padden. 7 cass. (Running Time: 9 hrs. 15 mins.). (Story Sound Ser.). (J). 2005. 61.95 (978-1-85903-832-1(8)); audio compact disk 79.95 (978-1-85903-881-9(6)) Pub: Mgna Lrg Print GBR. Dist(s): Ulverscroft US

Curse of the Incredible Priceless Corncob. John R. Erickson. 2 cass. (Running Time: 3 hrs.). (Hank the Cowdog Ser.: No. 7). 2001. 24.00 (978-0-7366-6133-1(6)) Books on Tape.
A bizarre little monkey named Pasha of Shizzam arrives at the ranch willing to answer to Hank's beck & call. Or is he?.

Curse of the Incredible Priceless Corncob. collector's ed. John R. Erickson. 3 CDs. (Running Time: 4 hrs. 30 mins.). (Hank the Cowdog Ser.: No. 7). (J). (gr. 2-5). 2001. audio compact disk 28.00 Books on Tape.
Convinced by Pete the Barncat that an old corncob is worth a fortune, Hank quits his job as Head of Ranch Security & hits the road.

Curse of the Incredible Priceless Corncob. unabr. ed. John R. Erickson. Read by John R. Erickson. 2 cass. (Running Time: 3 hrs.). (Hank the Cowdog Ser.: No. 7). (J). 2001. 16.95 (978-0-7366-6903-0(5)) Books on Tape.
A bizarre little monkey named Pasha of Shizzam arrives at the ranch willing to answer to Hank's beck & call. Or is he?.

Curse of the Incredible Priceless Corncob. unabr. ed. John R. Erickson. Read by John R. Erickson. 2 cass. (Running Time: 3 hrs.). (Hank the Cowdog Ser.: No. 7). (J). (gr. 2-5). 2001. 16.95 (978-0-7366-6896-5(9)) Books on Tape.
Convinced by Pete the Barncat that an old corncob is worth a fortune, Hank quits his job as Head of Ranch Security & hits the road.

Curse of the Incredible Priceless Corncob. unabr. ed. John R. Erickson. Read by John R. Erickson. Illus. by Gerald L. Holmes. 2 cass. (Hank the Cowdog Ser.: No. 7). (J). (gr. 2-5). 1986. bk. 13.95 (978-0-916941-23-9(X)) Maverick Bks.

Curse of the Incredible Priceless Corncob. unabr. ed. John R. Erickson. Read by John R. Erickson. 2 cassettes. (Running Time: approx 3 hours). (Hank the Cowdog Ser.: No. 7). (J). 2002. Rental 17.99 (978-1-59188-307-4(5)) Maverick Bks.

Curse of the Incredible Priceless Corncob. unabr. ed. John R. Erickson. Read by John R. Erickson. 3 CDs. (Running Time: Approx. 3 hours). (Hank the Cowdog Ser.: No. 7). (J). 2002. audio compact disk 19.99 (978-1-59188-607-5(4)) Maverick Bks.
When Pete the Barncat offers to trade good, juicy steak scraps for a couple of old corncobs, Hank the Cowdog smells a rat. Why would Pete want to trade?unless the corncobs are worth a fortune? So, armed with his Incredible Priceless Corncobs, Hank sets out to plan his Early Retirement. But retirement and the life of luxury don?t come as easily as Hank expects. It seems as though everyone is after his treasure?even his faithful sidekick, Drover! Can Hank save his fortune without losing his friends, or will he have to give up his riches for the sake of the ranch? You?ll hear two great new songs: ?I?m Rich!? and ?My Heart Goes Wild For You? in this hilarious adventure for the entire family.

Curse of the Incredible Priceless Corncob. unabr. collector's ed. John R. Erickson. 3 CDs. (Running Time: 4 hrs. 30 mins.). (Hank the Cowdog Ser.: No. 14). (J). (gr. 2-5). 2001. audio compact disk 28.00 Books on Tape.
A bizarre little monkey named Pasha of Shizzam arrives at the ranch willing to answer to Hank's beck & call. Or is he?.

Curse of the Incredible Priceless Corncob. unabr. collector's ed. John R. Erickson. 2 cass. (Running Time: 3 hrs.). (Hank the Cowdog Ser.: No. 7). (J). (gr. 2-5). 2001. (978-0-7366-6140-9(9)) Books on Tape.
Convinced by Pete the Barncat that an old corncob is worth a fortune, Hank quits his job as Head of Ranch Security & hits the road.

Curse of the Incredible Priceless Corncob, No. 7. unabr. ed. John R. Erickson. 2 cass. (Running Time: 3 hrs.). (Hank the Cowdog Ser.: No. 7). 2001. (978-0-7366-6142-3(5)) Books on Tape.
What happens when an honest, hard working ranch dog falls heir to a fortune? How is it Hank, a steak loving dog, changed so that he would say, "We'd be fools to trade priceless corncobs for a miserable pile of steak scraps?" Hank and Drover fight over "money," put on airs, even quit their jobs and leave the ranch.

Curse of the Incredible Priceless Corncob, Set. unabr. ed. John R. Erickson. 2 cass. (Hank the Cowdog Ser.: No. 7). (J). (gr. 2-5). 1998. 17.00 (21649) Recorded Bks.

Curse of the Incredible Priceless Corncob & the Case of the One-Eyed Killer Stud Horse. unabr. ed. John R. Erickson. Read by John R. Erickson. 4 cass. (Running Time: 6 hrs.). (Hank the Cowdog Ser.: Nos. 7-8). (J). 2002. 26.99 (978-0-916941-64-2(7)); audio compact disk 31.99 (978-0-916941-84-0(1)) Maverick Bks.
When Pete the Barncat offers to trade good, juicy steak scraps for a couple of old corncobs, Hank the Cowdog smells a rat. Why would Pete want to trade unless the corncobs are worth a fortune. So, armed with his incredible priceless corncobs, Hank sets out to plan his early retirement. But retirement and the life of luxury don't come as easily as Hank expects.

Curse of the Kings. unabr. ed. Victoria Holt. Read by Janet Dale. 8 cass. (Running Time: 8 hrs.). 1998. 69.95 (978-0-7540-0211-6(X), CAB 1634) AudioGO.
Judith Osmond's dream of marrying Tybalt Travers, a brilliant archeologist has finally come true, & when he asks her to be his wife & travel to Egypt in search of Pharaoh's burial chambers, her happiness is assured. Her joy is however, short-lived, as Tybalt becomes a silent, menacing stranger.

Curse of the Kings. unabr. ed. Victoria Holt. Narrated by Virginia Leishman. 8 cass. (Running Time: 10 hrs. 45 mins.). 1997. 70.00 (978-0-7887-1748-2(0), 9522675) Recorded Bks.
Beautiful Judith Osmond is happily traveling through Egypt with her archeologist husband. But her joy soon dissolves in the deadly shadow of an ancient curse.

Curse of the Kings. unabr. collector's ed. Victoria Holt. Read by Donada Peters. 7 cass. (Running Time: 10 hrs. 30 mins.). 1994. 56.00 (978-0-7366-2768-9(5), 3489) Books on Tape.
Whoever disturbs the tombs of the kings dies. For centuries this curse has haunted the tombs of the pharaohs. Thus when two eminent archaeologist mysteriously croak, Judith Osmond is certain the curse killed them, yet, or so she things, it has nothing to do with her. then, overnight, everything in her life changes. First, an unexpected inheritance, then Tybalt, a young archaeologist, asks her to marry him but Tybalt plans to explore the tombs during their honeymoon, so the curse of the kings comes to haunt Judith.

Curse of the Painted Cats. Heather Latimer. Read by Heather Latimer. 2 cass. (Running Time: 2 hrs. 45 min.). 1989. 15.95 (978-0-943698-06-9(5)) Papyrus Letterbox.

Curse of the Pharaohs. unabr. ed. Elizabeth Peters, pseud. Read by Susan O'Malley. 7 cass. (Running Time: 10 hrs.). (Amelia Peabody Ser.: No. 2). 2000. 49.95 (978-0-7861-1799-4(0), 2598); audio compact disk 72.00 (978-0-7861-9865-8(6), 2598) Blckstn Audio.
The joys of home & hearth are about to drive Victorian gentlewoman Amelia Peabody Emerson mad. While she & her husband, the renowned archaeologist Radcliffe Emerson, dutifully go about raising their son Ramses, she dreams only of the dust & detritus of ancient civilizations.

Curse of the Pharaohs. unabr. ed. Elizabeth Peters, pseud. Read by Susan O'Malley. (Running Time: 10 hrs.). 2009. audio compact disk 29.95 (978-1-4417-1178-6(3)) Blckstn Audio.

Curse of the Pharaohs. unabr. ed. Elizabeth Peters, pseud. Narrated by Barbara Rosenblat. 8 cass. (Running Time: 11 hrs. 15 mins.). (Amelia Peabody Ser.: No. 2). (gr. 10). 1990. 70.00 (978-1-55690-130-0(5), 90095E7) Recorded Bks.
The tomb was sealed; Sir Henry Baskerville was the first to break in. Was it the curse or something more sinister - like murder.

Curse of the Pharaohs. unabr. ed. Elizabeth Peters, pseud. 7 cass. (Running Time: 630 min.). (Amelia Peabody Ser.: No. 2). 1999. (90095) Recorded Bks.

Curse of the Ruby Rood. rev. ed. Gina Beth Clark. 1 CD. (Running Time: 1 hr. 30 mins.). 2002. audio compact disk (978-0-9712681-6-6(9)) G B C Audio Bk.

Curse of the Ruby Rood. rev. ed. Gina Beth Clark. Read by Gina Beth Clark. 4 cass. (Running Time: 6 hrs.). 2002. (978-0-9712681-4-2(2)) G B C Audio Bk.

Curse of the Spider King. unabr. ed. Wayne Thomas Batson & Christopher Hopper. Narrated by Greg Whalen. (Running Time: 9 hrs. 30 mins. 0 sec.). (Berinfell Prophecies Ser.). (ENG.). 2009. 20.99 (978-1-60814-605-5(7)) Oasis Audio.

Curse of the Spider King. unabr. ed. Wayne Thomas Batson & Christopher Hopper. Narrated by Greg Whalen. 10 CDs. (Running Time: 11 hrs. 44 mins. 13 sec.). (Berinfell Prophecies Ser.). (ENG.). (YA). (gr. 6-9). 2009. audio compact disk 29.99 (978-1-59859-657-1(8)) Oasis Audio.

Curse of the Swift Short Stop. George Khoury. (J). 1983. 17.99 Jan Prods.

Curse of the Swift Short-Stop. unabr. ed. George Khoury. 1 cass. (Running Time: 20 min.). (J). (gr. 4-8). 1983. bk. 16.99 (978-0-934898-48-5(0)); pap. bk. 9.95 (978-0-934898-16-4(2)) Jan Prods.
Lucius Watson joins a champion minor league baseball team only to find foul play - & not only on the field.

Curse of the Werewolf. 1 cass. (Running Time: 1 hr. 30 mins.). (SmartReader Ser.). (J). 1999. pap. bk. & tchr. ed. 19.95 (978-0-7887-1152-7(0), 79412T3) Recorded Bks.
When your best friend turns into a werewolf, what do you do? Do you run, or fight until it eats you alive?.

***Curse the Dawn.** unabr. ed. Karen Chance. Narrated by Cynthia Holloway. (Running Time: 15 hrs. 0 mins.). (Cassandra Palmer Ser.). 2010. 20.99 (978-1-4001-8737-9(0)); 29.99 (978-1-4001-6737-1(X)); audio compact disk 39.99 (978-1-4001-1737-6(2)); audio compact disk 95.99 (978-1-4001-4737-3(9)) Pub: Tantor Media. Dist(s): IngramPubServ

Cursed. Barry Sadler. Read by Charlton Griffin. Abr. by Odin Westgaard. 2 vols. (Casca Ser.: No. 18). 2004. 18.00 (978-1-58807-118-7(9)); (978-1-58807-558-1(3)); audio compact disk (978-1-58807-723-3(3)) Am Pubng Inc.

Cursed. abr. ed. Barry Sadler. Read by Charlton Griffin. Abr. by Odin Westgaard. 2 vols. (Casca Ser.: No. 18). 2004. audio compact disk 25.00 (978-1-58807-292-4(4)) Am Pubng Inc.

Cursed. unabr. ed. Carol Higgins Clark. Read by Carol Higgins Clark. 5 CDs. (Running Time: 6 hrs. 0 mins. 0 sec.). (ENG.). 2009. audio compact disk 29.99 (978-0-7435-7966-7(6)) Pub: S&S Audio. Dist(s): S and S Inc

***Cursed.** unabr. ed. Carol Higgins Clark. Read by Carol Higgins Clark. (Running Time: 6 hrs. 0 mins. 0 sec.). (ENG.). 2011. audio compact disk 14.99 (978-1-4423-3767-1(2)) Pub: S&S Audio. Dist(s): S and S Inc

Cursed in the Blood. collector's ed. Sharan Newman. Read by Donada Peters. 9 cass. (Running Time: 13 hrs. 30 min.). 2000. 72.00 (978-0-7366-5534-7(4)) Books on Tape.
Catherine LeVendeur & her husband, Edgar, are living in Paris with their new son when Edgar receives news from his family: his two older brothers have been murdered & he must return to Scotland to help avenge their deaths. At first, Edgar refuses to go, knowing what may await them in his war-torn homeland, but Catherine believes in family loyalty & insists upon accompanying him with their baby. In Scotland, Edgar's father, Waldeve, is a cold tyrant & his remaining siblings are distant & secretive. Separated from Edgar & cast out of his family's home, Catherine searches for her husband while also seeking to learn who among Waldeve's enemies hates him enough to destroy his whole family - including her son.

Curses: Cause & Cure. Derek Prince. 3 cass. 14.95 (I-CC1) Derek Prince.

Cursillo Spiritual Directors' Talks. Chester P. Michael. 1985. 20.00 (978-0-940136-19-9(8)) Open Door Inc.

Curso Completo para Resolver Problemas. unabr. ed. Carlos González. Ed. by Dina Gonzalez & Imagine Publishers Staff. 12 cass. (Running Time: 11 hrs. 30 min.).Tr. of Complete Course to Solve Personal Problems. (SPA.). 1993. 120.00 set. (978-1-56491-056-1(3)) Imagine Pubs.
Lectures given in Guadalajara, Mexico - regarding several techniques to solve problems.

Curso de Autohipnosis para ser un Buen Estudiante. Carlos Diaz Lastra. 1 cass. (Running Time: 1 hr. 30 mins.). (SPA.). 2001. Astran.

Curso de Introducción, Selected Readings with Program Notes. Holt, Rinehart and Winston Staff. (SPA.). 1997. 34.20 (978-0-03-095168-8(2)) Holt McDoug.

Cursor's Fury. unabr. ed. Jim Butcher. (Running Time: 21 hrs.). Bk. 3. (ENG.). (gr. 8). 2008. audio compact disk 49.95 (978-0-14-314378-9(6), PengAudBks) Penguin Grp USA.

Curtain. Korda. 2004. 10.95 (978-0-7435-4532-7(X)) Pub: S&S Audio. Dist(s): S and S Inc

Curtain Up! Mormon Tabernacle Choir. 1 cass. 4.98 (1500546); audio compact disk 8.98 (1500554) Covenant Comms.
Stage & screen show-stoppers such as "Oklahoma" & "Sunrise, Sunset".

Curtains for Three. unabr. collector's ed. Rex Stout. Read by Michael Prichard. 7 cass. (Running Time: 7 hrs.). (Nero Wolfe Ser.). 1997. 56.00 (978-0-7366-3747-3(8), 4422) Books on Tape.
In theses three baffling mysteries of motive & murder, even the great Nero Wolfe finds himself stumped. First there is the case of the two passionate lovebirds who want to make sure that neither is a cold-blooded killer. Then it's off to the races, where Wolfe must choose from a stable of five likely suspects to corral a killer on horseback. And finally the detective finds himself the confidant of a distraught, self-described grifter who claims a murderer is stalking Wolfe's own brownstone.

Curve of Binding Energy. unabr. ed. John McPhee. Read by Dan Lazar. 6 cass. (Running Time: 6 hrs.). 1986. 36.00 (978-0-7366-1064-3(2), 1991) Books on Tape.
"Binding Energy" may be described loosely as the force that holds things together. In physics the term applies to atomic structuring & resultant weaponry. With his customary skill & accuracy, McPhee walks us through atom-land in an easy & uncomplicated stroll.

Curzon Case. Francis Durbridge. 2007. 44.95 (978-0-7531-3797-0(6)); audio compact disk 51.95 (978-0-7531-2778-0(4)) Pub: ISIS Audio GBR. Dist(s): Ulverscroft US

Custard the Dragon. 2004. 8.95 (978-1-56008-883-7(4)); cass. & flmstrp 30.00 (978-1-56008-658-1(0)) Weston Woods.

Custard the Dragon. (J). 2004. bk. 24.95 (978-1-56008-186-9(4)) Weston Woods.

Custard the Dragon & the Wicked Knight. Ogden Nash. Read by John McDonough. 1 cass. (Running Time: 15 mins.). (J). (gr. k up). 1999. pap. bk. & stu. ed. 25.20 (978-0-7887-2986-7(1), 40868) Recorded Bks.
Belinda lives in a little white house with her courageous pets & cowardly Custard, a "realio trulio" dragon. All is well until an evil, evil knight bursts through the door. The whimsical illustrations will captivate youngsters as they follow along with the print book included.

Custard the Dragon & the Wicked Knight. unabr. ed. Ogden Nash. Narrated by John McDonough. 1 cass. (Running Time: 15 mins.). (gr. k up). 1999. 11.00 (978-0-7887-2956-0(X), 95731E7) Recorded Bks.

Custard the Dragon & the Wicked Knight, Class set. Ogden Nash. Read by John McDonough. 1 cass. (Running Time: 15 mins.). (J). (gr. k up). 1999. pap. bk. 91.30 (978-0-7887-3016-0(9), 46833) Recorded Bks.

Custer: The Controversial Life of George Armstrong Custer. unabr. ed. Jeffry D. Wert. Read by Dick Estell. 10 cass. (Running Time: 15 hrs.). 1997. 80.00 (978-0-913369-50-0(0), 4254) Books on Tape.
What led George Custer, an experienced Civil War officer, into the death trap at Little Big Horn?.

Custer Wolf. unabr. ed. Roger A. Caras. Narrated by Sam Gray. 4 cass. (Running Time: 5 hrs. 15 mins.). (gr. 10). 1992. 35.00 (978-1-55690-626-8(9), 92323E7) Recorded Bks.
The story of Lobo, a rare white wolf born near Custer, South Dakota whose exploits from 1915 to 1920 triggered a sixteen state war on predators. Drawn in part from factual documentation on the Wolf, this is his extraordinary story, from the moment of birth to his violent death.

Custom, Set. unabr. ed. Michel de Montaigne. Read by Robert L. Halvorson. 2 cass. (Running Time: 180 min.). Incl. Cannibals. (32); Friendship. Running Press Staff. (32); Moderation. (32); 14.95 (32) Halvorson Assocs.

Custom Design Your Own Destiny. Bruce Goldberg. (ENG.). 2005. audio compact disk 17.00 (978-1-57968-089-3(5)) Pub: B Goldberg. Dist(s): Baker Taylor

Custom Design Your Own Destiny. Bruce Goldberg. Read by Bruce Goldberg. 1 cass. (Running Time: 25 min.). (ENG.). 2007. 13.00 (978-1-885577-30-6(3)) Pub: B Goldberg. Dist(s): Baker Taylor
Self-hypnosis exercise to lay out an empowered & highly desirable future.

Custom Design Your Own Destiny Cassette Album, Set. Scripts. Bruce Goldberg. Read by Bruce Goldberg. 6 cass. (Running Time: 3 hrs.). (ENG.). 2006. 65.00 (978-1-885577-73-3(7)) Pub: B Goldberg. Dist(s): Baker Taylor
Self-hypnosis program training to see into the future and select the ideal path.

Custom Design Your Own Destiny CD Album. Bruce Goldberg. (ENG.). 2005. audio compact disk 75.00 (978-1-57968-026-8(7)) Pub: B Goldberg. Dist(s): Baker Taylor

Custom of the Country. unabr. ed. Edith Wharton. Read by Flo Gibson. 10 cass. (Running Time: 1 hr. 30 min. per cass.). (Classic Books on Cassettes Coll.). 1998. 80.00 Set. Audio Bk Con.
In a culture dominated by men who refuse to take women seriously, excluding them from the real business of life, Undine Spragg strikes out to find how far beauty & daring can carry her. She is the small-town girl made good, the rustic who outsmarts New York society & moves on to continental princelings. There seems to be no limit to her conquests, but happiness evades her. We can predict her fall, but are powerless to intervene.

Custom of the Country. unabr. ed. Edith Wharton. Read by Grace Conlin. 10 cass. (Running Time: 14 hrs. 30 mins.). 1995. 69.95 (978-0-7861-0751-3(0), 1519) Blckstn Audio.
First published in 1913, "The Custom of the Country" is a trenchant novel which illustrates the dangers of excessive ambition. Its heroine, Undine Spragg, is one of the most ruthless characters in all of literature. She is as selfishly unscrupulous as she is fiercely beautiful. Her rise to the top of New York's society elite from the nouveau riche provides a poignant & provocative commentary on the excessive aspirations of the upwardly mobile in their quest to climb the class ladder. One of Edith Wharton's most acclaimed works, "The Custom of the Country" is a blistering indictment of materialism, power & misplaced values.

Custom of the Country. unabr. collector's ed. Edith Wharton. Read by Flo Gibson. 10 cass. (Running Time: 15 hrs.). 1983. 80.00 (978-0-7366-0407-9(3), 1383) Books on Tape.
In a culture dominated by men who refuse to take women seriously, excluding them from the real business of life, Undine Spragg strikes out to find how far beauty & daring can carry her. She is the small-town girl made good, the rustic who outsmarts New York society & moves on to continental princelings. There seems to be no limit to her conquests, but happiness evades her. We can predict her fall, but are powerless to intervene.

Custom of the Country, Set. Edith Wharton. 10 cass. (Running Time: 12 hrs. 30 min.). 1999. 80.00 Audio Bk Con.

Customer & Patient Care: With Practical Techniques for Improving Customer Care & Patient Relationships in Healthcare, for All Levels Such As Office Manager, Doctor, Nurse, Practice Administrator, Dentist, & Executives, Who Want to Implement Total Quality Management in Their Organization. Daniel Farb. 2004. audio compact disk 49.95 (978-1-932634-51-8(7)) Pub: UnivofHealth. Dist(s): AtlasBooks

Customer Care in Healthcare Certificate Program: For All Members of a Healthcare Organization, Including Office Staff, Executives, Receptionists, Managers, Doctors, Nurses, Therapists, & Other Healthcare Workers, with Hundreds of Techniques to Improve Customer Care in Any Organization & Implement Total Quality Management in Customer Service. Daniel Farb. 2004. audio compact disk 199.95 (978-0-9743674-6-0(X)) Pub: UnivofHealth. Dist(s): AtlasBooks

Customer Care in Healthcare 10 Users. Daniel Farb. 2005. audio compact disk 499.95 (978-1-59491-166-8(5)) Pub: UnivofHealth. Dist(s): AtlasBooks

Customer Care in Healthcare 100 Users. Daniel Farb. 2005. audio compact disk 2999.95 (978-1-59491-205-4(X)) Pub: UnivofHealth. Dist(s): AtlasBooks

Customer Care in Healthcare 25 Users. Daniel Farb. 2005. audio compact disk 999.95 (978-1-59491-203-0(3)) Pub: UnivofHealth. Dist(s): AtlasBooks

Customer Care in Healthcare 5 Users: For All Members of a Healthcare Organization, Including Office Staff, Executives, Receptionists, Managers, Doctors, Nurses, Therapists, & other Healthcare Workers, with Hundreds of Techniques to Improve Customer Care in Any Organization & Implement Total Quality Management in Customer Service. Daniel Farb. 2005. audio compact disk 399.95 (978-1-59491-131-6(2)) Pub: UnivofHealth. Dist(s): AtlasBooks

Customer Care in Healthcare 50 Users. Daniel Farb. 2005. audio compact disk 1699.95 (978-1-59491-204-7(1)) Pub: UnivofHealth. Dist(s): AtlasBooks

Customer Complaints. PUEI. 2007. audio compact disk 199.00 (978-1-934147-66-5(4), Fred Pryor) P Univ E Inc.

Customer Intimacy: Build the Customer Relationships That Ensure Your Company's Success. Fred Wiersema. 1 cass. (Running Time: 90 min.). 1996. 14.00 (978-1-888232-01-1(3)) Pub: Spurge ink. Dist(s): Natl Bk Netwk

Customer Mania! It's Never Too Late to Build a Customer-Focused Company. unabr. ed. Ken Blanchard et al. 2004. 17.95 (978-0-7435-4496-2(X)) Pub: S&S Audio. Dist(s): S and S Inc

Customer Relationship Management (CRM) Software in Germany: A Strategic Reference 2006. Compiled by Icon Group International, Inc. Staff. 2007. ring bd. 195.00 (978-0-497-35971-3(5)) Icon Grp.

Customer Service see Servicio al cliente conexion al Exito

Customer Service Is Not the Thing: It's the Only Thing! Somers H. White. 8 cass. (Running Time: 8 hrs.). 1992. 200.00 set. S White.

CustomerCentric Sellling. Michael Bosworth. 3 cass. 2004. 24.00 (978-1-932378-52-8(9)) Pub: A Media Intl. Dist(s): Natl Bk Netwk

CustomerCentric Sellling. Michael Bosworth. 4 CDs. 2004. audio compact disk 28.00 (978-1-932378-53-5(7)) Pub: A Media Intl. Dist(s): Natl Bk Netwk

Customers Count. National Examining Board For Supervisory Management Staff. 1997. (978-0-7506-3710-7(2)) Sci Tech Bks.

Cut. unabr. ed. Patricia McCormick. Read by Clea Lewis. 3 vols. (Running Time: 4 hrs.). (J). (gr. 7 up). 2004. pap. bk. 36.00 (978-0-8072-0868-7(X), LYA 320 SP, Listening Lib); 25.50 (978-0-8072-0523-5(0), Listening Lib) Pub: Random Audio Pubg. Dist(s): NetLibrary CO
While confined to a mental hospital, thirteen-year-old Callie slowly comes to understand some of the reasons behind her self-mutilation, and gradually starts to get better.

***Cut.** unabr. ed. George P. Pelecanos. (Running Time: 9 hrs.). (ENG.). 2011. 24.98 (978-1-60941-792-5(5)); audio compact disk & audio compact disk 29.98 (978-1-60941-791-8(7)) Pub: Hachet Audio. Dist(s): HachBkGrp

Cut & Run. abr. ed. Ridley Pearson. Read by Dick Hill. (Running Time: 21600 sec.). 2006. audio compact disk 16.99 (978-1-59600-836-6(9), 9781596008366, BCD Value Price) Brilliance Audio.
Six years ago, witness protection marshal Roland Larson did the unthinkable: he fell in love with a protected witness, Hope Stevens, whose testimony was to put away prominent members of the Romero crime family. When Hope's plan to "cut and run" is interrupted by both the government and the mob, she disappears into a new identity, taking with her not only her testimony but a secret never shared with Larson. Larson, who has been looking for her ever since, is put back on her trail when the Romeros intercept the master WITSEC list from the Justice Department and Hope is believed among the first protected witnesses to be targeted for execution. In a series of terrifying encounters, Larson matches wits with a brutally ingenious killer whose sole target is Hope Stevens. For Larson, the stakes couldn't be higher - he must find Hope in order to protect her, and simultaneously prevent the mob from auctioning off the master witness protection list - an act that will put seven thousand innocent, and not-so-innocent, lives in jeopardy. Taut and edge-of-the-seat compelling, Cut and Run is a unique thriller that skillfully blends romance and suspense - Ridley Pearson at his heart-pounding best.

Cut & Run. abr. ed. Ridley Pearson. Read by Dick Hill. (Running Time: 6 hrs.). 2009. audio compact disk 9.99 (978-1-4418-2647-3(5), 9781441826473, BCD Value Price) Brilliance Audio.

Cut & Run. unabr. ed. Ridley Pearson. Read by Dick Hill. (Running Time: 10 hrs.). 2005. 39.25 (978-1-59710-159-2(1), 9781597101592, BADLE); 24.95 (978-1-59710-158-5(3), 9781597101585, BAD); 24.95 (978-1-59335-956-0(X), 9781593359560, Brilliance MP3); 39.25 (978-1-59335-957-7(8), 9781593359577, Brlnc Audio MP3 Lib); 82.25 (978-1-59600-176-3(3), 9781596001763, BrilAudUnabridg); 32.95 (978-1-59600-175-6(5), 9781596001756, BAU); audio compact disk 34.95 (978-1-59600-178-7(X), 9781596001787, Bril Audio CD Unabri); audio compact disk 92.25 (978-1-59600-179-4(8), 9781596001794, BriAudCD Unabrid) Brilliance Audio.
Please enter a Synopsis.

Cut Bird. 1 cass. (Bilingual Fables). 12.00 (Natl Textbk Co) M-H Contemporary.
Presents a story in Spanish & English.

Cut by Stars: No. 5 in the River Road Poetry Series. Judith Beveridge. Read by Judith Beveridge. Executive Producer Carol Jenkins. (ENG.). 2008. audio compact disk 18.00 (978-0-9804148-4-4(9)) RivRoad AUS.

Cut of the Action Readalong. Janet Lorimer. 1 cass. (Running Time: 1 hr.). (Ten-Minute Thrillers Ser.). (YA). (gr. 6-12). 1995. pap. bk. 12.95 (978-0-7854-1074-4(0), 40801) Am Guidance.

Cut Throat. Lyndon Stacey. Read by David Rintoul. 12 vols. (Running Time: 46980 sec.). 2003. 96.95 (978-0-7540-0965-8(3)) Pub: Chivers Audio Bks GBR. Dist(s): AudioGO

Cut to Black. Graham Hurley. 12 cass. (Isis Cassettes Ser.). (J). 2005. 94.95 (978-0-7531-2122-1(0)) Pub: ISIS Lrg Prnt GBR. Dist(s): Ulverscroft US

Cut to the Chase: And 99 Other Rules to Liberate Yourself & Gain Back the Gift of Time. unabr. ed. Stuart Levine. Narrated by Alan Sklar. (Running Time: 3 hrs. 0 mins. 0 sec.). (ENG.). 2007. audio compact disk 19.99 (978-1-4001-0301-0(0)); audio compact disk 39.99 (978-1-4001-3301-7(7)); audio compact disk 19.99 (978-1-4001-5301-5(8)) Pub: Tantor Media. Dist(s): IngramPubServ

Cut to the Chase: 3 Short Stories of Murder, Mystery, & Mayhem. Joyce Caddell. 2007. audio compact disk 19.99 (978-1-60247-632-5(2)) Tate Pubng.

***Cut Your Grocery Bill in Half with America's Cheapest Family: Includes So Many Innovative Strategies You Won't Have to Cut Coupons.** unabr. ed. Steve Economides & Annette Economides. 2010. audio compact disk 24.99 (978-1-4002-0312-3(0)) Nelson.

Cut Your Trading Taxes in Half. Instructed by Ted Tesser. (Running Time: 60 mins.). 2000. 19.95 (978-1-883272-77-7(7)) Marketplace Bks.
There are two tax systems in this country, one for the knowledgable and one for the ignorant, and this audio will ensure you are knowledgeable about the tax system. You watch your trades tick-by-tick and this tool tells you how to avoid giving it away in taxes. In 1997, the tax code was changed and provided a number of opportunities specifically for traders, but you can bet the IRS isn't going to call you to tell you about them. In fact, your accountant may not even be aware of them. But in this audio, Ted Tesser shares the strategies that he uses himself to significantly reduce his taxes. You'll find out how to pay less taxes by understanding:- How to reduce your declared income- What deductibles traders are entitled to- Which expenses traders can deduct that other people may not be able to- What tax programs give you the most advantage as a traderThere are advantages to being recognized as a trader as opposed to an investor by the IRS and this audio tells you what you need to do to achieve trader status. Tesser also oulines his Triple Crown Tax Strategy that will cut your taxes in half! Proven strategies and vital information about the tax advantages unique to traders make this a must-have audio for any investor or trader.

Cut Your Trading Taxes in Half. Instructed by Ted Tesser. (Running Time: 64 mins.). 2005. audio compact disk 19.95 (978-1-59280-160-2(9)) Marketplace Bks.

Cute Kids & Stuff Clip Art for Family Fun. (Timesaving Software Tools for Teachers Ser.). 2004. audio compact disk 21.99 (978-0-7439-3455-8(5)) Tchr Create Ma.

Cute Kids & Stuff Clip Art for School. (Timesaving Software Tools for Teachers Ser.). 2004. audio compact disk 21.99 (978-0-7439-3454-1(7)) Tchr Create Ma.

Cutter's Run. unabr. ed. William G. Tapply. Read by John Michalski. 8 vols. (Running Time: 8 hrs.). (Brady Coyne Ser.). 1999. bk. 69.95 (978-0-7927-2317-2(1), CSL 206, Chivers Sound Lib) AudioGO.
One morning while driving the back roads of Garrison, Maine, Brady Coyne meets Charlotte Gillespie, a middle-aged African American woman who is carrying a sick dog. Brady drives her to the veterinarian & back home again, where he sees that someone has painted a large swastika on a "No Trespassing" sign. When the dog later dies, probably of poisoning, Charlotte hints at something larger at play that she can't discuss. The following weekend, Brady receives a letter from Charlotte asking for help. But when he goes to visit her, he finds her house empty.

Cutthroat Island, Set. abr. ed. John Gregory Betancourt. 2 cass. 1995. 17.00 (978-1-56876-043-8(4)) Soundlines Ent.

Cutting Blades. unabr. ed. Victoria Blake. Contrib. by Julie Maisey. 9 cass. (Story Sound Ser.). 2006. 76.95 (978-1-85903-965-6(0)) Pub: Mgna Lrg Print GBR. Dist(s): Ulverscroft US

Cutting Blades. unabr. ed. Victoria Blake & Julie Maisey. Contrib. by Julie Maisey. 10 CDs. (Story Sound CD Ser.). 2006. audio compact disk 89.95 (978-1-84652-040-2(1)) Pub: Mgna Lrg Print GBR. Dist(s): Ulverscroft US

Cutting Edge. unabr. ed. John Harvey. Narrated by Ron Keith. 10 CDs. (Running Time: 11 hrs.). (Charlie Resnick Mystery Ser.). 2005. audio compact disk 119.75 (978-1-4193-4423-7(4), CP332) Recorded Bks.

Cutting Edge. unabr. ed. John Harvey. Narrated by Ron Keith. 8 cass. (Running Time: 11 hrs.). (Charlie Resnick Mystery Ser.). 2005. 79.75 (978-1-84197-144-5(8), H1138, Clipper Audio) Recorded Bks.
Dr. Tim Fletcher had found hospital rotas inconvenient; it didn't occur to him they could be dangerous. Finishing work at 2 am, he didn't notice the figure behind him, dressed in black and armed with a scalpel. Charlie Resnick doesn't like what he sees. Tim's muscles were deliberately injured to cause long term damage - damage that will prevent him from becoming a surgeon. Evidence points to a personal grudge, until a spate of similar attacks leaves Resnick looking for a killer.

Cutting Edge: Blues Guitar. Mark Dziuba. (Cutting Edge Ser.). (ENG.). 1998. audio compact disk 9.95 (978-0-7390-2537-6(6)) Alfred Pub.

Cutting Edge: Jury Psychology & Advanced Courtroom Skills. Paul M. Lisnek. Read by Paul M. Lisnek. Ed. by Robert L. Sandidge. 5 cass. 1993. 179.95 SET. (978-1-57654-206-4(8), CPAB501) Creat Core.
Presents the many teachings of the science of NLP as they apply in the courtroom.

Cutting Edge: Rock Guitar. Mark Dziuba. (Cutting Edge Ser.). (ENG.). 1998. audio compact disk 9.95 (978-0-7390-2538-3(4)) Alfred Pub.

Cutting for Stone. unabr. ed. Abraham Verghese. Read by Sunil Malhotra. 19 CDs. (Running Time: 24 hrs.). (ENG.). 2009. audio compact disk 44.95 (978-0-7393-8285-1(3), Random AudioBks) Pub: Random Audio Pubg. Dist(s): Random

Cutting Forests Selectively or by Clearcut & Backyard Composting. Hosted by Nancy Pearlman. 1 cass. (Running Time: 29 min.). 10.00 (1038) Educ Comm CA.

Cutting Room. unabr. ed. Laurence Klavan. Read by Nick Sullivan. 2005. 29.95 (978-0-7927-3453-6(X), CMP 747); 49.95 (978-0-7927-3451-2(3), CSL 747); audio compact disk 64.95 (978-0-7927-3452-9(1), SLD 747) AudioGO.

Cutting the Cords, with Archangel Michael. Elisabeth Constantine. (Running Time: 57 mins.). (Light Meditations Series I Ser.). (ENG.). 2004. audio compact disk 17.99 (978-1-84409-040-2(X)) Pub: Findhorn Pr GBR. Dist(s): IPG Chicago

Cutting the Sweetness, Set. unabr. ed. Peta Taylor. 9 cass. 1998. 90.95 (978-1-85903-151-3(X)) Pub: Magna Story GBR. Dist(s): Ulverscroft US

Cutting Through Fear. Tsultrim Allione. 3 CDs. (Running Time: 3 Hrs). 2005. audio compact disk 24.95 (978-1-59179-403-5(X)) Sounds True.

Women who are interested in Buddhism have few models to draw inspiration from. Yet, within the oldest teachings of Tibetan Buddhism lies a rich but hidden legacy of a teacher who was a powerful woman and legendary spiritual leader. On her first ever audio publication, Tsultrim Allione - one of contemporary Buddhism's most experienced teachers - draws from the spiritual transmissions of an 11th century Tibetan yogini that holds a special promise for anyone who has experienced difficult and even paralyzing emotions. Based on the traditional Tibetan visualization technique ch'd (literally "to cut"), this approach is adapted specifically for our times. This four-step solution for encountering, nurturing, and dissolving the delusion of difficult emotions is a timeless teaching - which is still used in Tibet to treat mental and physical illness and as a path to enlightenment. We all encounter the "monsters" of fear, anger, and other difficult emotions in our lives, too often as a daily event. Now we have a rare and useful tool to stop fighting against them, and instead liberate them on the spot, with Cutting through Fear.

Cutty Sark see Poetry of Hart Crane

Cutty Wren. Contrib. by Parson's Hat. (ENG.). 1994. 13.95 (978-0-8023-7101-0(9)); audio compact disk 21.95 (978-0-8023-8101-9(4)) Pub: Clo Iar-Chonnachta IRL. Dist(s): Dufour

CW2. unabr. ed. Layne Heath. Read by Walter Lawrence. 9 cass. (Running Time: 13 hrs. 30 mins.). 1990. 72.00 (978-0-7366-1853-3(8), 2686) Books on Tape.

One tour in Vietnam didn't do it for Billy Roark, so after a year stateside he returned. This time, with new choppers to fly & new missions to run, Billy was going to do it right - he was going to make a difference. But war if ambiguous robs a soldier of purpose. Billy falters...until he confronts an unsettled score from his first tour & finds a bloody destiny flying at his side.

Cyanide in My Shoe. unabr. ed. Josephine Butler. Read by Diana Bishop. 8 cass. (Running Time: 12 hrs.). 2001. 69.95 (978-1-85695-859-2(0), 950512) Pub: ISIS Audio GBR. Dist(s): Ulverscroft US

Cyanide Wells. abr. ed. Marcia Muller. Read by J. Charles & Sandra Burr. (Running Time: 4 hrs.). 2004. audio compact disk 69.25 (978-1-59355-804-8(X), 159355804X, BACDLib Ed) Brilliance Audio.

A hard, four-hour drive north of San Francisco leads to sparsely populated Soledad County, a combination of spectacular seashore, inland forests, and small towns steeped in gold-mining history. One of those towns is Cyanide Wells, now an artsy community, whose name comes from the miners' use of cyanide to refine ore and the time the area's water supply was tragically poisoned. To Matthew Lindstrom, that sinister legacy is ironically appropriate for the place he finally expects to find his ex-wife, Gwen. Fourteen years earlier, her baffling disappearance branded him a murderer and destroyed his reputation and career as a photographer. Suddenly, after all this time, an anonymous phone caller tells him that Gwen is alive - and well aware of what she has done. Matt comes to Cyanide Wells looking for answers...and revenge. Here, where the surrounding thick forest conceals twisted paths and old sins, Matt works to uncover the details of Gwen's new life. But before he can confront her, his ex vanishes once more. With his future again threatened by suspicion, Matt must join forces with Carly McGuire - a local woman with secrets of her own - and begin a hunt through Soledad's untamed landscape and an interior geography of betrayal and darkness. There perhaps lies the truth about past crimes and Gwen's fate...as well as Matt's own.

Cyanide Wells. unabr. ed. Marcia Muller. Read by Sandra Burr & J. Charles. 5 cass. (Running Time: 7 hrs.). 2003. 27.95 (978-1-59086-823-2(4), 1590868234, BAU); 69.25 (978-1-59086-824-9(2), 1590868242, Unabridge Lib Edns) Brilliance Audio.

Cyanide Wells. unabr. ed. Marcia Muller. Read by J. Charles & Sandra Burr. (Running Time: 7 hrs.). 2004. 39.25 (978-1-59335-622-4(6), 1593356226, Brlnc Audio MP3 Lib) Brilliance Audio.

Cyanide Wells. unabr. ed. Marcia Muller. Read by Sandra Burr & J. Charles. (Running Time: 7 hrs.). 2004. 39.25 (978-1-59710-160-8(5), 1597101605, BADLE); 24.95 (978-1-59710-161-5(3), 1597101613, BAD) Brilliance Audio.

Cyanide Wells. unabr. ed. Marcia Muller. Read by Sandra Burr J. Charles. (Running Time: 7 hrs.). 2004. 24.95 (978-1-59335-212-7(3), 1593352123) Soulmate Audio Bks.

Cybele's Secret. unabr. ed. Juliet Marillier. Read by Justine Eyre. 11 CDs. (Running Time: 13 hrs. 51 mins.). (YA). (gr. 8 up). 2008. audio compact disk 70.00 (978-0-7393-7936-3(4), Listening Lib) Pub: Random Audio Pubg. Dist(s): Random

Cybele's Secret. unabr. ed. Juliet Marillier. Read by Justine Eyre. (ENG.). (J). (gr. 7). 2008. audio compact disk 50.00 (978-0-7393-7934-9(8), Listening Lib) Pub: Random Audio Pubg. Dist(s): Random

Cyber Art & the Mandala System. Vincent J. Vincent & Susan Wyshyski. 1 cass. 9.00 (A0701-90) Sound Photosyn.

Meet the developers of creative innovations that allow you to dance & play in the Cyber world.

Cyber-Prince or Cyborg Punk? Norman Spinrad. 1 cass. 9.00 (A0268-88) Sound Photosyn.

Faustin questions the feisty science fiction author as Brian records.

Cyber Psych: Program from the Award Winning Public Radio Series. Interview. Hosted by Fred Goodwin. 1 CD. (Running Time: 1 Hour). 2000. audio compact disk 21.95 (978-1-932479-37-9(6), LCM 140) Lichtenstein Creat.

In this age of cyber-everything, it's hard to imagine anything that can't be gotten on-line, and that includes mental health information and services. In this hour, we discuss Internet mental health in terms of treatment, ethics, privacy, law and money. Guests include: psychologist and researcher John Grohol of HelpHorizons.com; clinical psychologist and attorney Dr. Russ Newman, executive director for the professional practice for the American Psychological Association; attorney and psychiatrist Dr. Gregg Bloche, professor and co-director of the Georgetown/Johns Hopkins Joint Program in Law and Public Health; and Internet psychotherapist Dr. Richard Sansbury, who has also practiced traditional therapy for more than 20 years. Web consultant Martha Ainsworth reads excerpts from her own on-line therapy.

Cyberbuch. Chun. 1 cass. 1997. pap. bk. 22.95 (978-0-312-18255-7(4)) Pub: St Martin. Dist(s): Macmillan

Cyberclass for EMT-B. 7th ed. AAOS Staff. (C). 1999. audio compact disk 46.95 (978-0-7637-1102-3(0), 1102-0) Jones Bartlett.

Cyberclass for Health & Wellness. 6th ed. Gordon Edlin et al. (C). 1999. audio compact disk 46.95 (978-0-7637-1103-0(9), 1103 - 9) Jones Bartlett.

Cyberclass for Human Biology. 3rd ed. Daniel D. Chiras. 1999. audio compact disk 37.50 (978-0-7637-1136-8(5), 1136-5) Jones Bartlett.

***Cyberdeterrence & Cyberwar.** unabr. ed. Martin C. Libicki. (Running Time: 8 hrs. NaN mins.). (ENG.). 2010. 29.95 (978-1-4417-7690-7(7)); audio compact disk 29.95 (978-1-4417-7689-1(3)) Blckstn Audio.

***Cyberdeterrence & Cyberwar.** unabr. ed. Martin C. Libicki. Read by To be Announced. (Running Time: 8 hrs. NaN mins.). (ENG.). 2010. 54.95 (978-1-4417-7687-7(7)); audio compact disk 76.00 (978-1-4417-7688-4(5)) Blckstn Audio.

Cybermen. unabr. ed. Gerry Davis. Narrated by Anneke Wills & Nicholas Briggs. (Running Time: 5 hrs. 0 mins. 0 sec.). (Doctor Who Ser.). (ENG.). 2010. audio compact disk 34.95 (978-1-60283-824-6(0)) Pub: AudioGO. Dist(s): Perseus Dist

CyberNation. abr. ed. Steve Perry & Netco Partners Staff. Read by Sam Freed. Created by Tom Clancy & Steve Pieczenik. 6 hrs. (Running Time: 4 cass.). (Tom Clancy's Net Force Ser.: Bk. 6). 2001. 25.95 (978-0-06-000067-7(8)) HarperCollins Pubs.

Cybernetic Ghosts: Literature in the Age of Science & Technology. Ed. by Dorothy Figueira. 2004. 24.95 (978-0-8425-2591-6(2), BYU Press) Brigham.

Literature's once dominant status among communications media and cultural practices faces serious challenges from recent technological advances. Rejected as the socially distinguished genre of discourse, literature has lost its primacy to image and sound. It is not longer an essential embodiment of language but one version among several others. As such, it plays a smaller and smaller part in education and socialization. Will there be a time or have we already reached an epoch when cultural productions seek to do what literature can do within the framework or using the methods of computer technology? Can we envision something along the lines of programming a computer with the narrative devices and aesthetic techniques of various authors. There is a mania among computer-trained people to take everything and redo it via a computer. From Washington to our suburban classrooms, "technophile reformers" are promoting belief that the technologization of learning provides the solution to a gamut of education and societal ills. The underlying assumption is that everything in the world is translated into computer representation and, implicitly, that computer technology will do it better. With this project in mind, the Executive Board of the International Comparative Literature Associate (ICLA) organized a conferent in June 2002 on the topic of the status of literature in the age of theory and technology. This volume presents the fruits of this conference.

Cybernetics Laboratory. Marco A. V. Bitetto. Read by Marco A. V. Bitetto. 2000. (978-1-58578-026-6(X)) Inst of Cybernetics.

Cybernetics Reprints. Ed. by Marco A. V. Bitetto. 1 cass. 2000. (978-1-58578-044-0(8)) Inst of Cybernetics.

Cyberorgasm. Prod. by Lisa Palac. (Running Time: 60 min.). 2001. 11.95 (978-1-886238-15-2(4)); audio compact disk 16.95 (978-1-886238-13-8(8)) Passion Press.

Cyberorgasm 2. Ed. by Lisa Palac. (Running Time: 60 min.). 2001. 11.95 (978-1-886238-14-5(6)) Passion Press.

Cyberorgasm 2. Prod. by Lisa Palac. (Running Time: 60 min.). 2001. audio compact disk 16.95 (978-1-886238-16-9(2)) Passion Press.

Cyberspace: Essay from MIT Press. Contrib. by Michael Benedikt et al. 1 cass. (Running Time: 2 hrs. 30 min.). 1995. 17.95 (978-1-879557-33-8(9)) Audio Scholar.

Cyberspace: Essays from MIT Press. Grover Gardner. 2 cass. (Running Time: 2 hrs. 30 min.). 1995. 17.95 Audio Scholar.

Cyberthon. Jaron Lanier et al. 5 cass. 45.00 set. (A0721-90) Sound Photosyn.

Based on this exceptional San Francisco event, with its emphasis on "Virtual Reality".

Cybertutor CD-ROM for Intermediate MacRoeconomics. Roger LeRoy Miller & David D. VanHoose. (C). 1998. audio compact disk 42.95 (978-0-538-88087-9(2)) Pub: South-West. Dist(s): CENGAGE Learn

Cycle see Twentieth-Century Poetry in English, No. 29, Recordings of Poets Reading Their Own Poetry

Cycle of Action in the Brain. Frank Barr. 2 cass. 18.00 set. (A0005-83) Sound Photosyn.

Another elaborate & worthwhile excursion.

Cycle of the Phoenix: A New Approach to the Philosophy of History. Instructed by Manly P. Hall. 5 cass. 8.50 ea. o.p. Pt. 1: 600 B.C.- Era of the Ancient Teachers. (800167-A) Philos Res.

Cycle of the Phoenix: A New Approach to the Philosophy of History. Instructed by Manly P. Hall. 5 cass. (Running Time: 150 min.). 1999. 40.00 Set. incl. album. (978-0-89314-038-0(4)) Philos Res.

Cycle of the Phoenix in World History. Instructed by Manly P. Hall. 8.95 (978-0-89314-037-3(6), C851215) Philos Res.

Cycle of the West & Other Poems. unabr. ed. Poems. John Neihardt. 1 cass. 1984. 12.95 (978-0-694-50346-9(0), SWC 1665) HarperCollins Pubs.

Cycles: Their Practical Application. D. Modin. 1 cass. 8.95 (236) Am Fed Astrologers.

Improve personality, work harmoniously & productively.

Cycles of American Political Thought. Instructed by Joseph F. Kobylka. 18 cass. (Running Time: 18 hrs.). 2006. 199.95 (978-1-59803-262-8(3)); audio compact disk 99.95 (978-1-59803-263-5(1)) Teaching Co.

Cycles of Discipleship: A Stewardship Program for the Local Church. Jack Phillips. 2007. 300.00 (978-0-88177-497-9(9)) Upper Room Bks.

Cycles of the Maya. Emma B. Donath. 1 cass. (Running Time: 90 min.). 1990. 8.95 (812) Am Fed Astrologers.

***Cycles of Time: An Extraordinary New View of the Universe.** unabr. ed. Roger Penrose. (ENG.). 2011. audio compact disk 35.00 (978-0-307-93317-1(2), Random AudioBks) Pub: Random Audio Pubg. Dist(s): Random

Cycles of Transformation. Reed Hayes. 1 cass. 8.95 (148) Am Fed Astrologers.

Planetary cycles as growth stimulators.

Cyclodextrin: From Basic Research to Market. Contrib. by Al Star Co. Staff. 2000. audio compact disk 29.50 (978-0-9721582-0-6(0)) Wacker Biochem.

Cyclops see Poetry & Voice of Margaret Atwood

Cyclops. Clive Cussler. Read by Michael Prichard. (Dirk Pitt Ser.). 1993. audio compact disk 120.00 (978-0-7366-8282-4(1)) Books on Tape.

Cyclops. unabr. ed. Clive Cussler. Read by Michael Prichard. 12 cass. (Running Time: 18 hrs.). (Dirk Pitt Ser.). 1993. 96.00 (978-0-7366-2567-8(4), 3316) Books on Tape.

A wealthy American financier disappears aboard an antique blimp while hunting for a ship lost in the Bermuda Triangle in 1918. The blimp drifts toward Florida with a crew of dead men, Soviet cosmonauts. Meanwhile, Dirk Pitt discovers that a group of U.S. industrialists has put a colony on the moon, a secret base they will defend at any cost. Threatened in space, the Russians plan a savage retaliation & only Dirk Pitt can stop them. From Cuban torture chamber to the cold ocean depths, Pitt races to defuse an international conspiracy that threatens to shatter world stability.

Cylce of Leadership: How Great Leaders Teach Their Companies to Win. unabr. abr. ed. Noel M. Tichy. Read by Nancy Cardwell & Ron McClarty. 5 CDs. (Running Time: 6 hrs.). 2002. audio compact disk 29.95 (978-0-06-009261-0(0)) HarperCollins Pubs.

Cylinder 137k. (Paws & Tales Ser.: No. 34). 2002. 3.99 (978-1-57972-486-3(8)); audio compact disk 5.99 (978-1-57972-487-0(6)) Insight Living.

Cymbeline. abr. ed. William Shakespeare. 3 CDs. 1997. audio compact disk 21.00 (978-0-694-51810-4(7)) HarperCollins Pubs.

***Cymbeline.** abr. ed. William Shakespeare. Read by Claire Bloom & Boris Karloff. (ENG.). 2003. (978-0-06-074333-8(6), Caedmon) HarperCollins Pubs.

***Cymbeline.** abr. ed. William Shakespeare. Read by Claire Bloom & Boris Karloff. (ENG.). 2004. (978-0-06-082424-2(7), Caedmon) HarperCollins Pubs.

Cymbeline. unabr. ed. William Shakespeare. Read by Arkangel Cast. Narrated by Jack Shepherd et al. (Arkangel Shakespeare Ser.). (ENG.). 2005. audio compact disk 24.95 (978-1-932219-07-4(2)) Pub: AudioGO. Dist(s): Perseus Dist

Not only is Imogen, King Cymbeline's daughter, persecuted by her evil stepmother, but her husband Posthumus has bet his roguish friend Iachimo that Imogen will remain faithful no matter what. After the queen banishes Posthumus, Iachimo is determined to prove his friend wrong. Performed by Jack Sheperd, Sophie Thompson, and the Arkangel cast.

Cymbeline. unabr. ed. William Shakespeare. Read by Audio Partners Staff. 2 cass. (Running Time: 3 hrs. 19 mins.). (Arkangel Shakespeare Ser.). 2004. 17.95 (978-1-932219-47-0(1), Atlntc Mnthly) Pub: Grove-Atltc. Dist(s): PerseuPGW

Cymbeline. unabr. ed. William Shakespeare. 2 cass. (Running Time: 3 hrs.). (Arkangel Complete Shakespeare Ser.). 2001. 17.95 (PengAudBks) Penguin Grp USA.

Cymbeline, Set. unabr. ed. William Shakespeare. Perf. by Claire Bloom & Boris Karloff. 3 cass. (Running Time: 4 hrs. 30min.). Dramatization. 1984. 27.95 (978-0-694-50758-0(X), SWC 236) HarperCollins Pubs.

Cast includes: Pamela Brown, John Fraser, Alan Dobie, Walter Hudd, John Dane, Paul Daneman, Robin Palmer, Wallas Eaton, James Caimcross, Stephen Moore, Harold Lang, Eric House, Eric Jones, Douglas Muir, Richard Dare, Derek Godfrey & Judith South.

Cynthia Macdonald. Read by Cynthia Macdonald. 1 cass. (Running Time: 29 min.). 1985. 10.00 New Letters.

Former opera singer Cynthia Macdonald reads from "Wholes & Transplants".

Cynthia Ozick: Interview with Cynthia Ozick & Kay Bonetti. Interview. Cynthia Ozick. Interview with Cynthia Ozick. Interview with Kay Bonetti. 1 cass. 1986. 13.95 (978-1-55644-164-6(9), 6092) Am Audio Prose.

Discusses the writer's concept of the Sacral Imagination, her commitment to writing out of her Jewishness, the Jewish tradition, feminism & her development as a writer.

Cypress Creek Tour Travel Guide: Driving Trip in the Texas Hill Couuntry by way of Cypress Creek Road. 2nd exp. enl. ed. 2008. pap. bk. 20.00 (978-0-9676931-8-7(7)) Skyline Ranch.

Cypress Grove. Rose Boucheron & Margaret Sircom. 2008. 54.95 (978-1-84652-137-9(8)); audio compact disk 64.95 (978-1-84652-138-6(6)) Pub: Magna Story GBR. Dist(s): Ulverscroft US

***Cypress House.** unabr. ed. Michael Koryta. Read by Robert Petkoff. (Running Time: 10 hrs.). (ENG.). 2011. 24.98 (978-1-60788-681-5(2)) Pub: Hachet Audio. Dist(s): HachBkGrp

***Cyrano.** Read by Cynthia Bishop. Retold by Geraldine McCaughrean. (ENG.). (J). 2010. audio compact disk 34.00 (978-1-936223-15-2(5)) Full Cast Audio.

Cyrano. Perf. by José Ferrer. 1 cass. 10.00 (MC1014) Esstee Audios.

Radio drama.

Cyrano de Bergerac. abr. ed. Edmond Rostand. Perf. by St. Charles Players. 2 cass. (Running Time: 1 hr. 30 min.). Dramatization. (Adventure Theatre Ser.). 1999. 16.95 Set. (978-1-56994-515-5(2), 309914, Monterey SoundWorks) Monterey Media Inc.

A swashbucking swordsman extraordinaire, a wordsmith of unparalleled flair, action & romance follow him everywhere, as he of the pronounced protuberance beyond compare, seeks the favor of his beloved Roxanne, by waxing poetic...for another man.

Cyrano de Bergerac: A Heroic Comedy in Five Acts. Edmond Rostand. Narrated by Grover Gardner. 2007. audio compact disk 19.95 (978-1-55685-895-6(7)) Audio Bk Con.

Cyrano de Bergerac: A Heroic Comedy in Five Acts. As told by Edmond Rostand. Edmond Rostand. 2 CDs. (Running Time: 2 hrs.). 2005. audio compact disk 19.95 (978-0-660-19389-2(2)) Canadian Broadcasting CAN.

Cyrano de Bergerac: A Heroic Comedy in Five Acts, Set. Read by Philippe Noiret. As told by Edmond Rostand. Edmond Rostand. 2 cass. (FRE.). 1995. 28.95 (1728-LQP) Olivia & Hill.

Cyrano, the soldier-poet with a large nose, who declares his love to Roxane through his goodlooking friend, Christian. The most popular French play of the 19th century.

Cyrano de Bergerac: A Heroic Comedy in Five Acts, Set. abr. ed. Perf. by St. Charles Players. As told by Edmond Rostand. Edmond Rostand. 2 cass. Dramatization. 1999. 16.95 (FS9-51429) Highsmith.

Cyrano de Bergerac: A Heroic Comedy in Five Acts, Set. unabr. ed. As told by Edmond Rostand. Edmond Rostand. Narrated by Grover Gardner. 3 cass. (Running Time: 4 hrs. 51 min.). 1984. (978-1-55685-002-8(6)) Audio Bk Con.

The Story of Cyrano, his famous nose & his undying love for the beautiful Roxanne is told in ravishing verse & evokes the wit & panache of 17th century France.

Cyrano de Bergerac: A Shadow Too Long. Music by Lee Kweller. Text by Joshua Brown & John Esposito. 1 cass. (Running Time: 7 min.). (Educational Song Ser.: Vol. 2). (YA). (gr. 7-12). 1998. 19.98 cass. & study guide. (978-1-57649-002-0(5), 76002) Arkadia Ent.

Based on Edmond Rostand's Cyrano de Bergerac, a play about pride, poetry & an oversized nose.

Cyrano de Bergerac: Abridged. 2007. (978-1-60339-005-7(7)); cd-rom & audio compact disk (978-1-60339-006-4(5)) Listenr Digest.

Cyrus Vol. 1: The Storytelling Encyclopedia. 1 CD. (Running Time: 50 mins.). (J). (ps-2). 2000. 16.95 (978-2-89517-027-3(4)) Pub: Coffragants CAN. Dist(s): Penton Overseas
Cyrus gathers the most pertinent questions asked by children from the popular CBC radio show 275-Allo.

Cyrus Vol. 2: The Storytelling Encyclopedia. 1 CD. (Running Time: 50 mins.). (J). (gr. k-6). 2000. 16.95 (978-2-89517-033-4(9)) Coffragants CAN.

Cyrus Vol. 2: The Storytelling Encyclopedia. Carmen Marois. 1 cass. (Running Time: 50 mins.). (J). (gr. k-6). audio compact disk 12.95 (978-2-89517-032-7(0)) Coffragants CAN.

Cyrus Vol. 3: The Storytelling Encyclopedia. 1 CD. (Running Time: 50 mins.). (J). (gr. k-12). 2000. 16.95 (978-2-89517-036-5(3)) Coffragants CAN.
Cyrus will brighten the days of curious children, tired parents & desperate babysitters!.

Cyrus Vol. 3: The Storytelling Encyclopedia. Carmen Marois. 1 cass. (Running Time: 50 mins.). (J). (gr. k-6). 2000. audio compact disk 12.95 (978-2-89517-037-2(1)) Coffragants CAN.
Cyrus gathers the most pertinent questions asked by children from the popular CBC radio show 275-Allo.

Cyrus Colter: "Chance Meeting" Cyrus Colter. Read by Cyrus Colter. 1 cass. (Running Time: 29 min.). 1984. 10.00 (122280) New Letters.
The black Chicago writer reads his story about two men who worked for the same white woman, but who held differing opinions about her.

Cyrus, l'Encyclopedie Racontee, Vol. 1. Marina Orsini. 1 cass. (Running Time: 50 mins.). (Children's French Ser.).Tr. of Cyrus, the Storytelling Encyclopedia. (FRE.). (J). (ps-2). 2000. audio compact disk 12.95 (978-2-89517-024-2(X)) Pub: Coffragants CAN. Dist(s): Penton Overseas

Cyrus, l'Encyclopedie Racontee, Vol. 1. Narrated by Marina Orsini. 1 CD. (Running Time: 50 mins.). (Children's French Ser.).Tr. of Cyrus, the Storytelling Encyclopedia. (FRE.). (J). (ps-2). 2000. 16.95 (978-2-89517-025-9(8)) Pub: Coffragants CAN. Dist(s): Penton Overseas

Cyrus, l'Encyclopedie Racontee, Vol. 2. Christiane Duchesne & Carmen Marois. 1 cass. (Running Time: 50 mins.). (Children's French Ser.).Tr. of Cyrus, the Storytelling Encyclopedia. (FRE., (J). (gr. k-12). 2000. audio compact disk 12.95 (978-2-89517-034-1(7)) Pub: Coffragants CAN. Dist(s): Penton Overseas

Cyrus, l'Encyclopedie Racontee, Vol. 2. Christiane Duchesne & Carmen Marois. 1 cass. (Running Time: 50 mins.). (Children's French Ser.).Tr. of Cyrus, the Storytelling Encyclopedia. (FRE., (J). (gr. k up). 2000. pap. bk. 12.95 (978-2-89517-030-3(4)) Pub: Coffragants CAN. Dist(s): Penton Overseas

Cyrus, l'Encyclopedie Racontee, Vol. 3. Christiane Duchesne & Carmen Marois. 1 CD. (Running Time: 50 mins.). (Children's French Ser.).Tr. of Cyrus, the Storytelling Encyclopedia. (FRE.). (J). (gr. k-12). 2000. 16.95 (978-2-89517-035-8(5)) Pub: Coffragants CAN. Dist(s): Penton Overseas

Cyrus McCormick, Inventor of the Reaper. abr. ed. Christopher Crennen. Read by Christopher Crennen. 1 cass. (Running Time: 38 min.). 1995. 9.95 incl. script. (978-0-9629733-1-4(9)) Rainbow Audio.
A biography of the American inventor, Cyrus McCormick (1809-1884), his parents, his struggle to perfect his reaper, the manufacturing & marketing of the McCormick reaper, McCormick's habits & family & the significance of his invention in increasing the world food supply.

Cyrus, the Storytelling Encyclopedia see Cyrus, l'Encyclopedie Racontee

Cystic Fibrosis - A Bibliography & Dictionary for Physicians, Patients, & Genome Researchers. Compiled by Icon Group International, Inc. Staff. 2007. ring bd. 28.95 (978-0-497-11364-3(3)) Icon Grp.

Cystinosis - A Bibliography & Dictionary for Physicians, Patients, & Genome Researchers. Compiled by Icon Group International, Inc. Staff. 2007. ring bd. 28.95 (978-0-497-11365-0(1)) Icon Grp.

Cystinuria - A Bibliography & Dictionary for Physicians, Patients, & Genome Researchers. Compiled by Icon Group International, Inc. Staff. 2007. ring bd. 28.95 (978-0-497-11366-7(X)) Icon Grp.

CZ-7 CD (Audio CD) unabr. ed. 1 CD. (Running Time: 90 min.). 2001. 14.99 (978-0-8297-3612-0(3)) Zondervan.
The international group Zona 7 together with the Spanish group Comision, in a musical production with the objective to raise the praise and worship to God in a style which the youth can identify with.

Czarist Russia. 10.00 (HE804) Esstee Audios.
A picture of the unappealing life which was prevalent in Russia under the Czars.

Czech. Ed. by Berlitz Publishing. (In 60 MINUTES Ser.). 2008. audio compact disk 9.95 (978-981-268-399-1(2)) Pub: APA Pubns Serv SGP. Dist(s): Langenscheidt

Czech. Berlitz Publishing Staff. (Running Time: 1 hr. 14 mins.). (Berlitz Travel Pack CD Ser.). (CZE & ENG., 2004. audio compact disk 21.95 (978-981-246-589-4(8), 465898) Pub: Berlitz Pubng. Dist(s): Langenscheidt

Czech. Collins. (CZE & ENG., 2005. 15.00 (978-0-00-720118-1(4)) Pub: HarpC GBR. Dist(s): Trafalgar

Czech. Penton Overseas, Inc. Staff. 2 cass. (Running Time: 80 min.). (Language - Thirty Library). bk. 16.95 set in vinyl album. Moonbeam Pubns.
Using the proven method based on the famous U.S. Military accelerated language learning program, Language/30 courses stress conversationally useful words & phrases.

Czech. Alena Walter. Tr. by Karen Von Kunes from GER. 1 cass. (Running Time: 1 hrs. 30 min.). (TravelWise Ser.). (ENG & CZE., 1998. pap. bk. 16.95 (978-0-7641-7109-3(7)) Barron.
Designed especially for international travelers, provides introductions to foreign destinations.

Czech. unabr. ed. Ed. by Charles Berlitz. 2 cass. (Running Time: 1 hr. 30 mins.). (Language/30 Brief Course Ser.). pap. bk. 21.95 (AF1061) J Norton Pubs.
Quick, highly condensed introduction to the words & phrases you'll need to communicate effectively in the country you're visiting. Cassettes & phrase guide book are in a vinyl album.

Czech. unabr. ed. Pimsleur Staff. (Running Time: 160 hrs. 0 mins. 0 sec.). (Comprehensive Ser.). (ENG.). 2005. audio compact disk 345.00 (978-0-7435-4481-8(1), Pimsleur) Pub: S&S Audio. Dist(s): S and S Inc

Czech: Language/30. rev. ed. Educational Services Corporation Staff. Intro. by Charles Berlitz. 2 cass. (CZE.). 1995. pap. bk. 21.95 (978-0-910542-81-4(3)) Educ Svcs DC.
Czech self-teaching language course.

Czech: Learn to Speak & Understand Czech with Pimsleur Language Programs. unabr. ed. Pimsleur Staff. 5 CDs. (Running Time: 5 hrs. 0 mins. 0 sec.). (Basic Ser.). (CZE & ENG.). 2005. audio compact disk 24.95 (978-0-7435-5125-0(7), Pimsleur); audio compact disk 49.95 (978-0-7435-5117-5(6), Pimsleur) Pub: S&S Audio. Dist(s): S and S Inc

Czech: Short Course. Paul Pimsleur. 5 cass. (Pimsleur Language Learning Ser.). 1993. pap. bk. & stu. ed. 149.95 (0671-57912-6) SyberVision.

Czech: The Complete Course for Beginners. James Naughton. 1 cass. (Running Time: 60 min.). (Colloquials Ser.). (CZE & ENG.). 1988. pap. bk. 15.95 (978-0-7102-1104-0(X), 1104x, Routledge Thoemms) Routledge.

Czech: The Complete Course for Beginners. 2nd rev. ed. James Naughton. (Colloquial Ser.). 2002. audio compact disk 34.95 (978-0-415-30137-4(8)) Pub: Routledge. Dist(s): Taylor and Fran

***Czech: The Complete Course for Beginners.** 3rd rev. ed. James Naughton. (Colloquial Ser.). 2010. audio compact disk 34.95 (978-0-415-49633-9(0), Rout) Pub: Tay Francis Ltd GBR. Dist(s): Taylor and Fran

Czech: World Citizen Edition. unabr. ed. 10 cass. (Running Time: 10 hrs.). 2003. 95.00 (978-0-7887-9704-0(2)); audio compact disk 115.00 (978-0-7887-9771-2(9)) Recorded Bks.

Czech Christmas Carols: Koledy. unabr. ed. Perf. by Lonsdale, MN Koledy Choir. Ed. by Anita Smisek. 1 cass. (Running Time: 45 min.). 1994. 10.00 (978-1-57193-090-3(6), AP-001) Alliance Pubns.
Ethnic Czech Christmas carols (Koledy) sung by a mixed choir of residents from Czech-speaking rural communities in Southern Minnesota; a testimony to a legacy which has survived for over 125 years.

Czech for Speakers of English, Compact. unabr. ed. 5 cass. (Running Time: 5 hrs.). (Pimsleur Tapes Ser.). (CZE.). 1993. 129.00 set. (18443, Pimsleur) S&S Audio.
A ten-lesson-unit program based upon the Pimsleur Spoken Language Programmed Instructional Method, providing basic beginning language training to the ACTFL Novice Level.

Czech Indispensables. unabr. ed. 1 cass. (Running Time: 23 min.). 1996. 11.95 (978-0-88432-951-0(8), CCZ104) J Norton Pubs.
Useful phrases for foreign travel.

Czech Indispensables Vocabulary Builder. 1 CD. (Running Time: 25 mins.). (CZE.). 2005. audio compact disk 9.95 (978-1-57970-281-6(3), CCZ104, Audio-For) J Norton Pubs.
A basic vocabulary of 50 words and phrases, recorded by native speakers, that will help you deal with most common situations.

Czech Trombone Treasures: A Collection of 33 Musical Gems. Perf. by St. Olaf College Trombone Choir. Ed. by Joel Blahnik. Contrib. by Paul Niemisto. 1 cass. (Running Time: 45 min.). 1990. 10.00 (978-1-878158-01-7(5), AP-003) Alliance Pubns.
A collection of 33 musical gems from various sources.

Czechoslovakian Folk Music. unabr. ed. 1 cass. 1994. 12.95 (978-0-88432-354-9(4), C11147) J Norton Pubs.

Czechoslovakian with Ease see Tchechisch Ohne Muhe

D

D-Boy Set: Plantin' a Seed - Lyrical Strength. 2 CDs. 1999. audio compact disk 12.99 (KMGD8664) Provident Mus Dist.

D-Day: Airbourne Assault, Hit the Beach, U. S. Rangers, Glider Attack. unabr. ed. 4 CDs. (Running Time: 4 hrs.). (In Their Own Words Ser.: Vol. 1). 2002. audio compact disk 19.95 (978-0-9715690-0-3(2)) First Person.

D-Day: June 6, 1944 - The Climactic Battle of WWII. Stephen E. Ambrose. Read by Stephen E. Ambrose. 2004. 15.95 (978-0-7435-1875-8(6)) Pub: S&S Audio. Dist(s): S and S Inc

D-Day: The Battle for Normandy. Antony Beevor. Contrib. by Cameron Stewart. (Running Time: 20 hrs.). (ENG.). (gr. 12 up). 2009. audio compact disk 39.95 (978-0-14-314491-5(X), PengAudBks) Penguin Grp USA.

D-Day Pt. 1: June 6, 1944 - The Climactic Battle of World War II. unabr. ed. Stephen E. Ambrose. Read by Barrett Whitener. 10 cass. (Running Time: 15 hrs.). 1995. 80.00 (978-0-7366-3154-9(2), 3827-A) Books on Tape.
Some call it the most important day in the 20th century: D-Day. The largest naval armada ever assembled transported 175,000 men & 50,000 vehicles across more than 60 miles of open water to land in Normandy & confront what had been the strongest, most feared army Europe had ever seen. It began the battle that ended World War II. Stephen Ambrose, military historian & Eisenhower biographer, focuses brilliantly on 24 hours of fierce ground combat. He draws on new government documents & interviews with more than 1,200 participants from Allied & German forces. D-Day was filled with chaos, he says. But individual acts of incredible heroism made the difference.

D-Day Pt. 2: June 6, 1944 - The Climactic Battle of World War II. unabr. ed. Stephen E. Ambrose. Read by Barrett Whitener. 8 cass. (Running Time: 12 hrs.). 1995. 64.00 (978-0-7366-3155-6(0), 3827-B) Books on Tape.
Some call it the most important day in the 20th century: D-Day. The largest naval armada ever assembled transported 175,000 men and 50,000 vehicles across more than 60 miles of open water to land in Normandy and confront what had been the strongest, most feared army Europe had ever seen. It began the battle that ended World War II.

D-Day Dispatches: Original Recordings from the BBC Sound Archives, June 1944. unabr. ed. Compiled by British Broadcasting Corporation Staff. (Running Time: 1 hr. 0 mins. 0 sec.). (ENG.). 2010. audio compact disk 24.95 (978-1-60283-807-9(0)) Pub: AudioGO. Dist(s): Perseus Dist

D-Day on the Normandy Beaches: A Narrated Auto Tour of the Normandy Beaches. Brian N. Morton. 2 cass. (Running Time: 90 min. per cass.). (Touring France with Brian Morton Ser.). 1993. 19.95 set. (978-0-934034-25-8(7)) Olivia & Hill.
While driving on the autoroute from Paris to Normandy, you'll listen to a brief background to the invasion: preparations in England, disputes between the allied officers, secret missions to the French coast, & the assembling of the vast invasion armada. Then you'll follow your personal guide Brian Morton, as he visits each landing site. Drawing on biographies, military reports, & personal accounts of infantry & paratroopers, he transports you from the peaceful beaches of today to the turmoil of Normandy, June 6, 1944.

D-E-D Dead! unabr. ed. Geoffrey McGeachin. Read by Peter Hosking. (Running Time: 6 hrs.). 2007. audio compact disk 63.95 (978-1-74093-879-2(8)) Pub: Bolinda Pubng AUS. Dist(s): Bolinda Pub Inc

D. H. Lawrence. unabr. ed. Stephen Spender. 1 cass. (Running Time: 58 min.). 1953. 12.95 (23015) J Norton Pubs.
Lawrence protested against man's preoccupation with a cerebral life that inhibits the forces of instinct. His vision was of man as a three-dimensional object moving & attaining equilibrium among other objects, relating himself to them with forces of life deeper than intelligence.

D. H. Lawrence: The Mysteries of Life's Dynamism. Stephan Hoeller. 1 cass. 1999. 11.00 (40028) Big Sur Tapes.
1983 Los Angeles.

D. H. Lawrence Pt. 1: The Story of a Marriage. unabr. collector's ed. Brenda Maddox. Read by Donada Peters. 9 cass. (Running Time: 13 hrs. 30 min.). 1996. 72.00 (978-0-7366-3252-2(2), 3910 A) Books on Tape.
D. H. Lawrence lived like the heroes he created: passionate & often out of bounds. Nowhere was this truer than in his marriage to Frieda von Richthofen Weekley, who was the wife of his college professor & the mother of three when they met.

D. H. Lawrence Pt. 2: The Story of a Marriage. unabr. collector's ed. Brenda Maddox. Read by Donada Peters. 8 cass. (Running Time: 12 hrs.). 1996. 64.00 (978-0-7366-3253-9(0), 3910-B) Books on Tape.

D. H. Lawrence - A Collection of Short Stories Set. unabr. ed. Short Stories. D. h. Lawrence. 4 cass. (Running Time: 5 hrs. 30 min.). 1997. 19.95 (978-1-55685-490-3(0), 490-0) Audio Bk Con.
The first World War impacts on the emotions & reactions in such stories as "England, My England", "You Touched Me", & "Tickets, Please". There is erotica in parts of this collection.

D. H. Lawrence in 90 Minutes. unabr. ed. Paul Strathern. Read by Robert Whitfield. (Running Time: 2 hrs. NaN mins.). 2009. audio compact disk 22.95 (978-1-4332-1757-9(0)); audio compact disk 27.00 (978-1-4332-1758-6(9)) Blckstn Audio.

D Is for Deadbeat. unabr. collector's ed. Sue Grafton. Read by Mary Peiffer. 7 cass. (Running Time: 7 hrs.). (Kinsey Millhone Mystery Ser.). 1993. 56.00 (978-0-7366-2568-5(2), 3317) Books on Tape.
Stiffed for retainer, Kinsey finds out her client's real name is John Daggett, ex-con, ex-liar, ex-alchy, currently dead. The cops called it an accident but Kinsey differs. A lot of people hated him: abused ex-wives, drug dealers, the families of five people he killed driving drunk. In short, he wasn't popular.

D. M. Turner. Interview with Elizabeth Gips. 1 cass. 1999. 11.00 (32008) Big Sur Tapes.
Turner is the author of The Essential Psychedelic Explorer - 1995 Santa Cruz.

D Tales of Dan: Guardian Angel Doll. Carol Gilchrist & Dan Thomason. Read by Dan Thomason. 1 cass. (Running Time: 3 hrs. 30 min.). T Gilchrist.
Told from the point of view from the Guardian Angel Doll, who describes its feelings about being a gift to the child & is intended to convey an angelic comfort to needy children.

D. Van der Merr: Good Game Better. Read by D. Van der Merr. 1 cass. 9.95 (978-0-89811-107-1(2), 7158) Lets Talk Assocs.
D. Van der Merr talks about the people & events which influenced his career & his own approach to his speciality.

D. Van der Merr: Screwed up Strokes. Read by D. Van der Merr. 1 cass. 9.95 (978-0-89811-137-8(4), 7181) Lets Talk Assocs.

D. Van der Merr: Tennis Basics. Read by D. Van der Merr. 1 cass. 9.95 (978-0-89811-105-7(6), 7156) Lets Talk Assocs.

Da Capo. 5th ed. Lazzarino. (C). bk. 80.95 (978-0-8384-8002-1(0)) Heinle.

Da Capo: An Italian Review Grammar. 4th ed. Graziana Lazzarino & Annamaria Moneti. (ITA.). 1996. lab manual ed. (978-0-03-016182-7(7)) Harcourt Coll Pubs.

Da Capo: An Italian Review Grammar Kit. 4th ed. Graziana Lazzarino & Annamaria Moneti. (ITA., 1995. pap. bk. 64.95 (978-0-03-016273-2(4)) Heinle.

Da Nataraj. unabr. ed. Perf. by Free Daist and Chanting Guild. 1 cass. (Running Time: 1 hr. 10 min.). 1993. 11.95 Dawn Horse Pr.
New choral chants inspired by Hindu Bajans & other Eastern chants.

***Da un Regalo Util.** Tr. of Give A Gift Worth Giving. (SPA.). 2007. audio compact disk 6.00 (978-0-944129-43-2(9)) High Praise.

Da Vinci Code see Codigo Da Vinci

Da Vinci Code. Dan Brown. 2005. 44.99 (978-1-59895-015-1(0)) Find a World.

Da Vinci Code. Dan Brown. 2006. cd-rom 49.99 (978-1-59895-476-0(8)) Find a World.

Da Vinci Code. movie tie-in abr. ed. Dan Brown. Read by Paul Michael. (Running Time: 21600 sec.). (ENG.). 2006. audio compact disk 29.95 (978-0-7393-3978-7(8), Random AudioBks) Pub: Random Audio Pubg. Dist(s): Random

Da Vinci Code. movie tie-in unabr. ed. Dan Brown. Read by Paul Michael. (Running Time: 57600 sec.). (ENG.). 2006. audio compact disk 45.00 (978-0-7393-3979-4(6), Random AudioBks) Pub: Random Audio Pubg. Dist(s): Random

Da Vinci Code. unabr. ed. Dan Brown. Read by Paul Michael. 11 cass. (Running Time: 16 hrs. 30 mins.). 2003. 80.00 (978-0-7366-8970-0(2)); audio compact disk 99.45 (978-0-7366-9648-7(2)) Pub: Books on Tape. Dist(s): NetLibrary CO

Da Vinci Code. unabr. ed. Dan Brown. Read by Paul Michael. (YA). 2005. 64.99 (978-0-7393-7465-8(6)) Find a World.

***Da Vinci Code: A Novel.** abr. ed. Dan Brown. Read by Paul Michael. (ENG.). 2010. audio compact disk 14.99 (978-0-307-87925-7(9), Random AudioBks) Pub: Random Audio Pubg. Dist(s): Random

Da Vinci Code & the Bible: Separating Fact from Fiction. Ted Sri. 2006. audio compact disk 9.95 (978-1-932927-68-9(9)) Ascensn Pr.

Da Vinci Code Decoded. Martin Lunn. 2 CDs. (ENG.). 2005. audio compact disk 14.95 (978-1-932857-14-6(1)) Pub: Disinform Co. Dist(s): Consort Bk Sales

Da Vinci Hoax: Exposing the Errors in the Da Vinci Code. Carl E. Olson & Sandra Miesel. 2006. audio compact disk 39.95 (978-5-558-34244-4(7)) Ignatius Pr.

Daboteau. Dean Hughes. 2006. audio compact disk 39.95 (978-1-59038-697-2(3)) Desert Bks.

Dad, Dames, Demons & a Dwarf: My Trip down Freedom Road. abr. ed. Mancow Muller. Read by Mancow Muller. 2003. audio compact disk 29.95 (978-0-06-055684-6(6), ReganBooks) HarperCollins Pubs.

Dad, You're Not Funny: And Other Poems. unabr. ed. Steve Turner. Read by Steve Turner. 1 CD. (Running Time: 54 mins.). (J). (gr. 3-6). 2006. audio compact disk 9.95 (978-1-4056-5563-7(1), Chivers Child Audio) AudioGO.

Daddy. unabr. ed. Chasen Gaver. Read by Chasen Gaver. 1 cass. (Watershed Tapes of Contemporary Poetry). 1978. 12.95 (23623) J Norton Pubs.

Daddy & the Bon. Alexander McCall Smith. (No. 1 Ladies' Detective Agency Ser.: No. 1). 2009. audio compact disk 19.95 (978-1-60283-634-1(5)) AudioGO.

Daddy & the Bon. Alexander McCall Smith. 7 CDs. (No. 1 Ladies' Detective Agency Ser.: No. 1). 2004. audio compact disk 69.75 (978-1-4025-4594-8(0)) Recorded Bks.

Daddy & the Bon. Alexander McCall Smith. 7 CDs. (Running Time: 8 hrs. 25 mins.). (No. 1 Ladies' Detective Agency Ser.: No. 1). 2004. audio compact disk 29.99 (978-1-4025-4535-1(5), 01102) Recorded Bks.

Daddy & the Bon. unabr. ed. Alexander McCall Smith. 6 cass. (Running Time: 8 hrs. 15 min.). (No. 1 Ladies' Detective Agency Ser.: No. 1). 2003. 59.75 (978-1-4025-4738-6(2)) Recorded Bks.

Daddy & the Bon. unabr. ed. Alexander McCall Smith. Read by Lisette Lecat. 5 cass. (Running Time: 8 hrs. 25 mins.). (No. 1 Ladies' Detective Agency Ser.: No. 1). 2004. 24.99 (978-1-4025-4180-3(5), 02994) Recorded Bks.
Mma "Precious" Ramotswe sets up a detective agency in Botswana on the edge of the Kalahari Desert, making her the only female detective in the country. At first, cases are hard to come by. But eventually, troubled people come to Precious with a variety of concerns. Potentially philandering husbands, seemingly schizophrenic doctors, and a missing boy who may have been killed by witch doctors all compel Precious to roam about in her tiny van, searching for clues.

Daddy Clock. unabr. ed. Judy Markey. Read by Multivoice Production Staff. (Running Time: 8 hrs.). 2009. 39.97 (978-1-4233-8559-2(4), 9781423385592, Brlnc Audio MP3 Lib); 39.97 (978-1-4233-8561-5(6), 9781423385615, BADLE); 24.99 (978-1-4233-8558-5(6), 9781423385585, Brilliance MP3); 24.99 (978-1-4233-8560-8(8), 9781423385608, BAD) Brilliance Audio.

Daddy Cut My Hair. Perf. by Gary Chapman. 1 cass. 1999. 8.98 (978-0-7601-3156-5(2)) Provident Music.

Daddy Goose Collection. Vivian French. Read by Daniel Hill. 2 CDs. (Running Time: 1 hr. 1 min.). (J). (gr. k-2). 2008. audio compact disk 21.95 (978-1-4056-5982-6(3), Chivers Sound Lib) AudioGO.

Daddy-Long-Legs. Jean Webster. Narrated by Flo Gibson. (ENG.). (J). 2008. audio compact disk 19.95 (978-1-55685-942-7(2)) Audio Bk Con.

Daddy-Long-Legs. Jean Webster. Read by Kate Forbes. 3 cass. (Running Time: 4 hrs.). (YA). 2000. pap. bk. & stu. ed. 42.24 (978-0-7887-4327-6(9), 41122) Recorded Bks.
Jerusha Abbott is the oldest orphan in the John Grier Home. Soon she will graduate from high school & be on her own. When an anonymous wealthy donor sends her to college, Jerusha can hardly believe her good fortune. All she must do in return is send him a letter once a month.

Daddy-Long-Legs, unabr. ed. Jean Webster. Read by Flo Gibson. 3 cass. (Running Time: 4 hrs. 30 min.). (Classic Books on Cassette). (J). 1988. (978-1-55685-112-4(X)) Audio Bk Con.
Mischievous Jerusha Abbott corresponds with her unknown benefactor after she leaves the orphan asylym for college, expanding horizons & romance.

Daddy-Long-Legs. unabr. ed. Jean Webster. Narrated by Kate Forbes. 3 pieces. (Running Time: 4 hrs.). (gr. 7 up). 2000. 29.00 (978-0-7887-4243-9(4), 96211E7) Recorded Bks.
Jerusha Abbott is the oldest orphan in the John Grier Home. Soon she will graduate from high school & be on her own. When an anonymous wealthy donor sends her to college, Jerusha can hardly believe her good fortune. All she must do in return is send him a letter once a month.

Daddy-Long-Legs. unabr. ed. Jean Webster. Narrated by Kate Forbes. 4 CDs. (Running Time: 4 hrs.). (gr. 7 up). 2000. audio compact disk 39.00 (978-0-7887-4736-6(3), C1219E7) Recorded Bks.

Daddy-Long-Legs, Class set. unabr. ed. Jean Webster. Read by Kate Forbes. 3 cass. (Running Time: 4 hrs.). (YA). 2000. pap. bk. 99.70 (978-0-7887-4428-0(3), 47119) Recorded Bks.

Daddy Longlegs at Birch Lane. Beverley Brenna. Narrated by Alexi Komisar. Illus. by Sandra Blair. 1 cass. (Smithsonian's Backyard Ser.). (J). (ps-2). 1996. 5.00 (978-1-56899-326-3(9), C5012) Soundprints.
On a warm spring day Harvester, a daddy longlegs, hatches from her tiny egg. She seems vulnerable, the perfect snack for a hungry bird or bug. But they won't find her so easy to catch; her natural defenses protect her from predators. She is not so well prepared when the threat is a pail of water. One day, while drinking - Splash! - she tumbles in!.

Daddy Longlegs at Birch Lane. Beverley Brenna. Illus. by Sandra Blair. Narrated by Alexi Komisar. 1 cass. (Smithsonian's Backyard Ser.). (J). (ps-2). 1996. bk. 19.95 (978-1-56899-325-6(0), BC5012) Soundprints.

Daddy-O Daddy! Rare Family Songs of Woody Guthrie. Read by Woody Guthrie. Lyrics by Woody Guthrie. Perf. by Kim Wilson et al. 1 cass. (J). 2001. 10.98; audio compact disk 15.98 Rounder Records.

Daddy Saved the Day. (Greetings Ser.: Vol. 3). (gr. 2-3). 10.00 (978-0-7635-5868-0(0)) Rigby Educ.

Daddyji. unabr. collector's ed. Ved Mehta. Read by David Case. 5 cass. (Running Time: 5 hrs.). 1989. 30.00 (978-0-7366-1539-6(3), 2409) Books on Tape.
Daddyji is that portion of Ved Mehta's autobiography dealing primarily with his father, Amolak Ram Mehta, senior member of the clan & a British-trained physican.

Daddy's Girl. 2001. 6.00 (978-1-58602-084-2(6)); audio compact disk 9.99 (978-1-58602-093-4(5)) E L Long.

***Daddy's Girl.** abr. ed. Lisa Scottoline. Read by Kate Burton. (ENG.). 2007. (978-0-06-126248-7(X), Harper Audio); (978-0-06-126247-0(1), Harper Audio) HarperCollins Pubs.

Daddy's Girl. abr. ed. Lisa Scottoline. Read by Kate Burton. (Running Time: 21600 sec.). 2008. audio compact disk 14.95 (978-0-06-157122-0(9), Harper Audio) HarperCollins Pubs.

Daddy's Girl. unabr. ed. Lisa Scottoline. Read by Barbara Rosenblat. 8 CDs. (Running Time: 10 hrs.). 2007. audio compact disk 39.95 (978-0-06-122715-8(3)) HarperCollins Pubs.

***Daddy's Girl.** unabr. ed. Lisa Scottoline. Read by Barbara Rosenblat. (ENG.). 2007. (978-0-06-126250-0(1), Harper Audio); (978-0-06-126249-4(8), Harper Audio) HarperCollins Pubs.

Daddy's Girl. unabr. ed. Lisa Scottoline. Read by Barbara Rosenblat. 8 cass. (Running Time: 10 hrs.). 2007. 72.75 (978-1-4281-5290-8(3)); audio compact disk 92.75 (978-1-4281-5292-2(X)) Recorded Bks.

***Daddy's Little Helper.** unabr. ed. Debbie Macomber. Read by Dan John Miller. (Running Time: 5 hrs.). (Midnight Sons Ser.: Bk. 3). 2010. 14.99 (978-1-4418-5331-8(6), 9781441853318, Brilliance MP3); 14.99 (978-1-4418-5332-5(4), 9781441853325, BAD); audio compact disk 14.99 (978-1-4418-5329-5(4), 9781441853295, Bril Audio CD Unabri) Brilliance Audio.

Daddy's Little Helper; Because of the Baby. unabr. ed. Debbie Macomber. Read by Dan John Miller. (Running Time: 10 hrs.). (Midnight Sons Ser.: Bks. 3-4). 2010. 24.99 (978-1-4418-1649-8(6), 9781441816498, Brilliance MP3); 24.99 (978-1-4418-1651-1(8), 9781441816511, BAD); 39.97 (978-1-4418-1652-8(6), 9781441816528, BADLE); audio compact disk 29.99 (978-1-4418-1647-4(X), 9781441816474) Brilliance Audio.

Daddy's Little Helper; Because of the Baby, Vol. 2. unabr. ed. Debbie Macomber. Read by Dan John Miller. (Running Time: 10 hrs.). (Midnight Sons Ser.: Bks. 3 -4). 2010. audio compact disk 87.97 (978-1-4418-1648-1(8), 9781441816481, BriAudCD Unabrid) Brilliance Audio.

Daddy's Little Helper; Because of the Baby, Vol. 2. unabr. ed. Debbie Macomber. Read by Dan John Miller. (Running Time: 10 hrs.). (Midnight Sons Ser.: Bks. 3-4). 2010. 39.97 (978-1-4418-1650-4(X), 9781441816504, Brlnc Audio MP3 Lib) Brilliance Audio.

Daddy's Lullabies. Twin Sisters Productions Staff. 1 CD. (Running Time: 54 mins). (Growing Minds with Music Ser.: TW 3054CD). (J). 2004. audio compact disk 12.99 (978-1-57583-721-5(8)) Twin Sisters.
Twelve traditional and original lullabies for a new Dad to sing to his little one. Tracks 1-12 feature great male vocalist to help Dad learn the lullabies; tracks 13-24 are instrumental so that baby can hear only daddy!.

Daddysongs. Kevin Roth. Perf. by Kevin Roth. 1 cass. (Running Time: 30 min.). (J). 1992. 8.98 (978-1-56406-547-6(2)); 8.98 Incl. sleeve pack. (978-1-56406-576-6(6)); audio compact disk 13.98 CD. (978-1-56406-563-6(4)) Sony Music Ent.
Twelve songs from Daddy's special point of view.

Daddy@Work: Loving Your Family, Loving Your Job ... Being Your Best in Both Worlds. abr. ed. Robert Wolgemuth. (Running Time: 2 hrs. 0 mins. 0 sec.). (ENG.). 2003. 10.99 (978-0-310-26026-4(4)) Zondervan.

Daddy@Work: Loving Your Family, Loving Your Job... Being Your Best in Both Worlds. abr. ed. Robert Wolgemuth. 1999. 17.99 (978-0-310-23332-9(1)) Zondervan.

Dad's Always Right; The Swineherd; The Emperor's New Clothes. unabr. ed. Hans Christian Andersen. Narrated by Aurora Wetzel. 1 cass. (J). (ps up). 1995. 9.95 (978-1-887393-07-2(2)) Aurora Audio.
Three stories that will appeal to all.

Dads & Daughters - Fathers & Sons. unabr. ed. John Lee. 2 cass. (Running Time: 2 hrs.). 1994. pap. bk. 16.95 set. (978-1-879323-12-4(5)) Sound Horizons AV.
John discusses the impact of the "Father Wound." He says any woman or man whose father was abusive or "absent" must heal this wound before they can maintain healthy relationships.

Dad's Army No. 9: A Man of Action. David Croft et al. 2 cass. (Running Time: 2 hrs.). 1999. 16.85 Set. (978-0-563-55887-3(3)) BBC WrldWd GBR.

Dad's Army: Very Best Episodes: A BBC Radio Series. Created by Broadcasting Corp. British. (Running Time: 2 hrs. 0 mins. 0 sec.). (ENG.). 2009. audio compact disk 24.95 (978-1-60283-746-1(5)) Pub: AudioGO. Dist(s): Perseus Dist

Dad's Guide to the First Year. Armin A. Brott. Read by Armin A. Brott. 9 CDs. (Running Time: 10 hrs.). (New Father Ser.). (ENG.). 2008. audio compact disk 36.95 (978-0-7892-0968-9(3)) Pub: Abbeville Pr. Dist(s): Perseus Dist

Dad's Who Win: Selected Scriptures. Ed Young. 1993. 4.95 (978-0-7417-1973-7(8), 973) Win Walk.

Daemon see Twentieth-Century Poetry in English, No. 2, Recordings of Poets Reading Their Own Poetry

***Daemon.** Daniel Suarez. Read by Jeff Gurner & Garet Scott. (Playaway Adult Fiction Ser.). (ENG.). 2009. 69.99 (978-1-61587-752-2(5)) Find a World.

Daemon. unabr. ed. Daniel Suarez. Narrated by Jeff Gurner. 13 CDs. (Running Time: 16 hrs.). (ENG.). (gr. 8 up). 2009. audio compact disk 44.95 (978-0-14-314444-1(8), PengAudBks) Penguin Grp USA.

Daffodil Sea. unabr. ed. Emma Blair. Read by Eve Karpf. 14 cass. (Running Time: 14 hrs.). 1996. 110.95 (978-0-7451-4374-3(1), CAB1062) AudioGO.

Daffodils see Treasury of William Wordsworth

Daffodils of Newent. unabr. ed. Susan Sallis. Read by Jacqueline King. 9 cass. (Running Time: 13 hrs. 30 min.). 2001. 79.95 (978-1-85496-865-4(3), 68653) Pub: Soundings Ltd GBR. Dist(s): Ulverscroft US
They were called the Daffodil Girls, spirited & bright, enduring, loving & dancing their way through the gay & desperate twenties.

Dahara Upasana. (715) Yoga Res Foun.

Dahara Upasana. Swami Jyotirmayananda. 1 cass. (Running Time: 1 hr.). 1990. 12.99 Yoga Res Foun.

Dahn Yoga Energy Breathing. Prod. by Best Life Media. (ENG.). 2007. audio compact disk 17.95 (978-0-9799388-2-5(1)) Pub: BEST Life. Dist(s): SCB Distributors

Dahomean. unabr. ed. Frank Yerby. Read by Dan Lazar. 11 cass. (Running Time: 16 hrs. 30 min.). 1981. 88.00 (978-0-7366-0429-1(4), 1401) Books on Tape.
Examines the culture of the West African kingdom of Dahomean in the early 19th century. The principal character is Nyasany, who becomes a powerful chieftan in his own country until he falls victim to the slave trade.

Daily Chop-Builders for Bass. Josquin Des Pres. 1999. pap. bk. 17.95 (978-0-7866-4477-3(X), 97774BCD) Mel Bay.

Daily Confessions. Speeches. Creflo A. Dollar. 1 CD. (Running Time: 1 hr. 20 mins.). 1999. audio compact disk 7.00 (978-1-59089-132-2(5)) Creflo Dollar.

Daily Confessions for the Family. Speeches. Creflo A. Dollar. 1 CD. (Running Time: 1 hr). 2006. audio compact disk 10.00 (978-1-59944-072-9(5)) Creflo Dollar.

Daily Conscious Chart. Glenda Tomosovich. 1 cass. 8.95 (593) Am Fed Astrologers.
Chart the time you awaken for transits' impact.

Daily Coyote: A Story of Love, Survival, & Trust in the Wilds of Wyoming. Shreve Stockton. Read by Cassandra Campbell. (Playaway Adult Nonfiction Ser.). (ENG.). 2009. 59.99 (978-1-60812-536-4(X)) Find a World.

Daily Coyote: A Year with Charlie. unabr. ed. Shreve Stockton. Narrated by Cassandra Campbell. (Running Time: 8 hrs. 0 mins. 0 sec.). (ENG.). 2008. audio compact disk 59.99 (978-1-4001-3997-2(X)); audio compact disk 29.99 (978-1-4001-0997-5(3)); audio compact disk 19.99 (978-1-4001-5997-0(0)) Pub: Tantor Media. Dist(s): IngramPubServ

Daily Dexterity Studies for the Guitarist: 24 Week. Jay Weik. 1998. pap. bk. 19.95 (978-0-7866-0791-4(2), 95606BCD) Mel Bay.

Daily Disciples. David Wardell & Jeffrey Leever. 2008. audio compact disk 13.95 (978-0-615-22172-4(6)) Sapphire Dig.

Daily Faith Confessions. Speeches. Creflo A. Dollar. 1 cass. (Running Time: 1 hr. 20 mins.). (ENG.). 2002. 5.00 (978-1-59089-131-5(7)) Pub: Creflo Dollar. Dist(s): STL Dist NA

Daily Gifts of Love. Eknath Easwaran. 1 cass. (Running Time: 52 min.). 1989. 7.95 (978-1-58638-517-0(8), DGL) Nilgiri Pr.
The difference between divine love & temporal love; how devotion gives us endurance.

Daily Grace: Logos July 26. 1998. Ben Young. 1998. 4.95 (978-0-7417-6090-6(8), B0090) Win Walk.

Daily Growth for Broader Experiences or Awareness, Achievements, Purposeful Relaxation & Comfort, Set-DG. rev. ed. Russell E. Mason. 1975. pap. bk. 60.00 (978-0-89533-011-6(3)) F I Comm.

Daily Habits for Overcoming in Life see Habitos Diarios para Vencer en la Vida

Daily Life in Russia. unabr. ed. Henri Troyat. Read by Wolfram Kandinsky. 7 cass. (Running Time: 10 hrs. 30 min.). 1986. 56.00 (978-0-7366-0889-3(3), 1833) Books on Tape.
Henri Troyat tells his story through the eyes of a fictional young Englishman visiting a prosperous Russian merchant family. He sees Moscow as it was, from public entertainments to private, from family gatherings to the devotions of the Orthodox.

Daily Meditation: To Listen to the Small Voice Within! (ENG., 2009. audio compact disk 19.95 (978-0-9766735-0-7(9)) R Seals.

Daily Meditations for Self-Empowerment. unabr. ed. Mercedes Leidlich. Read by Mercedes Leidlich. 1 cass. (Running Time: 1 hr.). 1992. 10.95 in Norelco box. (978-1-882174-08-9(9), MLL-009) UFD Pub.
The soothing, relaxation tape guides the listener through a series of gentle meditations designed to enhance self-esteem, assertiveness, & self-empowerment. A valuable recovery tool. Also excellent for every day use to help retain a sense of calm in these hectic times.

Daily Message: Complete Message Bible. unabr. ed. Eugene H. Peterson. Narrated by Kelly Ryan Dolan. (Running Time: 80 hrs. 0 mins. 0 sec.). (ENG.). 2006. 29.99 (978-1-60814-168-5(3)) Oasis Audio.

Daily Planet. Perf. by Hero. 2002. audio compact disk Provident Mus Dist.

Daily Prayer. 1 CD. 2005. audio compact disk 9.00 (978-1-933207-09-4(4)) Ransomed Heart.

Daily Prayers: A Collection of 365 Prayers with Bible Verses. Karen Jean Matsko Hood. 2008. audio compact disk 24.95 (978-1-59434-528-9(7)) Whsprng Pine.

Daily Prayers & Akathist to the Mother of God. Perf. by Jane M. deVyver. 1 cass. (Running Time: 1 hrs.). (Treasury of Orthodox Christian Prayers Ser.: Vol. 1). 1993. 6.95 (978-1-881211-12-9(6)) Firebird Videos.
Side 1: Morning, Mid-Day & Evening Daily Prayers. Side 2: Annunciation Akathist to the Mother of God.

Daily Prayers During Times of Financial Stress. Karen Jean Matsko Hood. 2006. 29.95 (978-1-59434-427-5(2)); audio compact disk 24.95 (978-1-59434-428-2(0)) Whsprng Pine.

Daily Prayers for Children: A Collection of Prayers & Bible Verses to Encourage Children in Daily Prayer. Karen Jean Matsko Hood. (J). 2005. 24.95 (978-1-59210-041-5(4)); 29.95 (978-1-59210-178-8(X)) Whsprng Pine.

Daily Prayers for Foster Children. Karen Jean Matsko Hood. (J). 2007. 29.95 (978-1-59649-527-2(8)); audio compact disk 24.95 (978-1-59649-526-5(X)) Whsprng Pine.

Daily Prayers for Mothers. 2005. audio compact disk 24.95 (978-1-59808-645-4(6)) Whsprng Pine.

Daily Prayers to God & Roman Catholic Saints. 2005. 29.95 (978-1-59808-627-0(8)); audio compact disk 24.95 (978-1-59808-626-3(X)) Whsprng Pine.

Daily Rate. unabr. ed. Grace Livingston Hill. Narrated by Susan O'Malley. 5 cass. (Running Time: 7 hrs.). 2001. 39.95 (978-0-7861-2121-2(1), 2881); audio compact disk 56.00 (978-0-7861-9635-7(1), 2881) Blckstn Audio.
Life holds little joy for Celia Murray. Forced by poverty to leave her aunt, who has been her only source of love and warmth, Celia goes to the city to find a job. There she tries to make the best of her new home: a dreary boarding house. Then everything changes! Celia receives an unexpected inheritance and sets about making her dreams come true. She sends for her Aunt Hannah, and together they work a miraculous transformation on the old boarding house, turning it into a place of warmth and laughter. Yet Celia struggles with a sense that there is something, or someone, missing. Enter handsome Horace Stafford, minister of the mission chapel. At first Celia believes this is a man whose faith and compassion match her own. But when a terrible misunderstanding comes between them, will Celia ever be able to confess, even to Horace, the deepest desire of her heart.

Daily Rate. unabr. ed. Grace Livingston Hill. Read by Susan O'Malley. (Running Time: 1 hr. 0 mins.). (ENG.). 2009. 29.95 (978-1-4332-9998-8(4)) Blckstn Audio.

Daily Readings from Become a Better You: Devotions for Improving Your Life Every Day. abr. ed. Joel Osteen. Read by Joel Osteen. (Running Time: 3 hrs. 0 mins. 0 sec.). (ENG.). 2008. audio compact disk 19.99 (978-0-7435-7871-4(6)) Pub: S&S Audio. Dist(s): S and S Inc

Daily Readings from Your Best Life Now: 90 Devotions for Living at Your Full Potential. abr. ed. Joel Osteen. (ENG.). 2006. 14.98 (978-1-59483-259-8(5)) Pub: Hachet Audio. Dist(s): HachBkGrp

Daily Readings from Your Best Life Now: 90 Devotions for Living at Your Full Potential. abr. ed. Joel Osteen. (Running Time: 3 hrs.). (ENG.). 2009. 19.98 (978-1-60788-280-0(9)) Pub: Hachet Audio. Dist(s): HachBkGrp

Daily Readings from Your Best Life Now: 90 Devotions for Living at Your Full Potential. abr. ed. Joel Osteen. (Running Time: 3 hrs.). (ENG.). 2009. audio compact disk 14.98 (978-1-60024-827-6(6)) Pub: Hachet Audio. Dist(s): HachBkGrp

Daily Reflections for Highly Effective People: Living the Seven Habits of Highly Effective People Every Day. Stephen R. Covey. Read by Stephen R. Covey. 2 cass. 1999. 16.85 (978-0-671-01110-9(3)) UlverLrgPrint GBR.
A pathway for living with fairness, integrity, honesty & human dignity.

Daily Relaxer Audio Companion: Soothing Guided Meditations for Deep Relaxation for Anytime, Anywhere. Matthew McKay & Patrick Fanning. 2 CDs. (Running Time: 75 mins). (Relaxation Skills CD Ser.). (ENG.). 2008. audio compact disk 19.95 (978-1-57224-636-2(7)) New Harbinger.

***Daily Show: A Visitor's Guide to the Human Race.** unabr. ed. Jon Stewart. 3 CDs. (Running Time: 3 hrs. 30 mins.). 2010. audio compact disk 24.98 (978-1-60788-615-0(4)) Pub: Hachet Audio. Dist(s): HachBkGrp

Daily Show with Jon Stewart Presents America (the Audiobook) A Citizen's Guide to Democracy Inaction. abr. ed. Jon Stewart. Read by Jon Stewart. Read by Daily Show Staff. (ENG.). 2005. 14.98 (978-1-59483-151-5(3)) Pub: Hachet Audio. Dist(s): HachBkGrp

Daily Show with Jon Stewart Presents America (the Book) A Citizen's Guide to Democracy Inaction. abr. ed. Jon Stewart & Daily Show Writers Staff. Read by Jon Stewart. 3 CDs. (Running Time: 3 hrs. 30 mins.). (ENG.). 2004. audio compact disk 24.98 (978-1-58621-701-3(1)) Pub: Hachet Audio. Dist(s): HachBkGrp

Daily Show with Jon Stewart Presents America (the Book) A Citizen's Guide to Democracy Inaction. abr. ed. Jon Stewart & Daily Show Writers Staff. (Running Time: 3 hrs. 30 mins.). (ENG.). 2009. 39.98 (978-1-60024-641-8(9)) Pub: Hachet Audio. Dist(s): HachBkGrp

***Daily Show with Jon Stewart Presents Earth: A Visitor's Guide to the Human Race.** unabr. ed. Jon Stewart. (Running Time: 3 hrs. 30 mins.). (ENG.). 2010. 19.98 (978-1-60788-616-7(2)) Pub: Hachet Audio. Dist(s): HachBkGrp

Daily Steps Toward Peaceful Planet. unabr. ed. Perf. by Eknath Easwaran. 1 cass. (Running Time: 1 hr.). 1991. 7.95 (978-1-58638-518-7(6)) Nilgiri Pr.

Daily Trends with Diurnal Charts. Sophia Mason. 1 cass. (Running Time: 90 min.). 1986. 8.95 (560B) Am Fed Astrologers.

Dain Curse. unabr. ed. Dashiell Hammett. Read by Michael Prichard. 7 cass. (Running Time: 7 hrs.). 1980. 42.00 (978-0-7366-0264-8(X), 1259) Books on Tape.
This is the story of Gabriella Leggett, a young woman who appears to suffer from the curse of the mad Dains. She has all the signs - stigma, neuroses, rages...& a pistol. Beginning with a robbery, the plot moves quickly to drugs, obscene rituals & murder, all connected with the temple of a sinister cult.

Dain Curse. unabr. ed. Dashiell Hammett. Read by William Dufris. 6 CDs. (Running Time: 9 hrs.). 2001. audio compact disk 64.95 (978-0-7531-1082-9(2)) Pub: ISIS Audio GBR. Dist(s): Ulverscroft US

Dain Curse. unabr. ed. Dashiell Hammett. Read by William Dufris. 6 cass. (Running Time: 7 hrs.). 1996. 54.95 (978-1-85695-717-5(9), 941101) Pub: ISIS Audio GBR. Dist(s): Ulverscroft US
A young woman believed to be suffering from the curse of the mad Dains has all the signs - stigmata, neuroses, rages & a pistol. Beginning with a robbery, the plot moves to drugs, obscene rituals & murder.

Dairy Processing Equipment in Ukraine: A Strategic Reference 2006. Compiled by Icon Group International, Inc. Staff. 2007. ring bd. 195.00 (978-0-497-82446-4(9)) Icon Grp.

Dairy Queen. unabr. ed. Catherine Gilbert Murdock. Read by Natalie Moore. 5 CDs. (Running Time: 22140 sec.). (ENG.). (J). (gr. 5). 2006. audio compact disk 30.00 (978-0-7393-3547-5(2), Listening Lib) Pub: Random Audio Pubg. Dist(s): Random

Dairy Queen: A Novel. unabr. ed. Catherine Gilbert Murdock. Read by Natalie Y. Moore. 5 CDs. (Running Time: 6 hrs. 9 mins.). (YA). (gr. 7-10). 2006. audio compact disk 38.25 (978-0-7393-3612-0(6), Listening Lib); 35.00 (978-0-7393-3611-3(8), Listening Lib) Pub: Random Audio Pubg. Dist(s): Random
When you don't talk, there's a lot of stuff that ends up not getting said. Harsh words indeed, from Brian Nelson of all people. But, D.J. can't help admitting, maybe he's right. When you don't talk, there's a lot of stuff that ends up not getting said. Stuff like why her best friend, Amber, isn't so friendly anymore. Or why her little brother, Curtis, never opens his mouth. Why her mom has two jobs and a big secret. Why her college-football-star brothers won't even call home. Why her dad would go ballistic if she tried out for the high school football team herself. And why Brian is so, so out of her league. When you don't talk, there's a lot of stuff that ends up not getting said. Welcome to the summer that fifteen-year-old D.J. Schwenk of Red Bend, Wisconsin, learns to talk, and ends up having an awful lot of stuff to say.

Daisies & Ducklings. Fran Avni. Read by Fran Avni. 1 cass. (J). (ps-3). 1992. 9.98 (978-1-877737-86-2(0), MLP 280) MFLP CA.
Cheerful songs composed to gently connect children with issues of ecology.

Daisy see Tusenskonan

Daisy see Prestekragen

Daisy Aldan Reads Mallarme. Poems. Stephane Mallarme. Read by Daisy Aldan. 1 cass. (Running Time: 40 min.). 1999. 11.95 (978-0-9652364-4-7(7)) Sky Blue Pr.
Daisy Aldan, poet, reads a selection of her translations from her book "To Purify the Words of the Tribe: the Major Verse Poems of Stephane Mallarme'.

Daisy Chain. Sally Stewart. 7 cass. (Running Time: 9 hrs. 15 mins.). (Story Sound Ser.). (J). 2004. 61.95 (978-1-85903-674-7(0)) Pub: Mgna Lrg Print GBR. Dist(s): Ulverscroft US

***Daisy Chain: A Novel.** Mary E. DeMuth. (Running Time: 10 hrs. 35 mins. 0 sec.). (Defiance Texas Ser.). (ENG.). 2009. 14.99 (978-0-310-30233-9(1)) Zondervan.

Daisy Miller. Henry James. Narrated by Flo Gibson. 2008. audio compact disk 16.95 (978-1-60646-067-2(6)) Audio Bk Con.

Daisy Miller. Henry James. Narrated by Jim Killavey. (Running Time: 2 hrs. 30 mins.). 2006. 20.95 (978-1-59912-805-4(5)) Iofy Corp.

Daisy Miller. abr. ed. Henry James. Read by Margaret Robertson. Contrib. by Michael Voysey. 1 cass. 12.95 (ECN 079) J Norton Pubs.
The story's dominant theme is the clash between American & European cultures.

Daisy Miller. abr. ed. Henry James. Read by Jim Killavey. 2 cass. (Running Time: 2 hrs. 50 min.). (YA). (gr. 10-12). 1991. 14.95 set. (T-1) Jimcin Record.
Daisy was "a child of nature & freedom." She defied European conventions & made herself & her author famous.

Daisy Miller. unabr. ed. Henry James. Read by Susan O'Malley. 2 cass. (Running Time: 3 hrs.). 2001. 17.95 (978-0-7861-2082-6(7), P2849) Blckstn Audio.
Frederick Winterbourne, an American expatiate visiting at Vevey, Switzerland, meets commonplace, newly rich Mrs. Miller from Schenectady, NY, her mischievous small son, Randolph and her daughter, Daisy, an "inscrutable combination of audacity and innocence." The Millers have no perception of the complex code that underlies behavior in European society, the complex code that underlies behavior in European society and Winterbourne is astonished at the girl's innocence and her mother's unconcern when Daisy accompanies him to Castle of Chillon.

Daisy Miller. unabr. ed. Henry James. Read by Jean DeBarbieris. 2 cass. (Running Time: 2 hrs. 15 min.). 16.95 (978-1-55686-137-6(0), 137) Books in Motion.
An emotional drama of love and desperation with Daisy caught in the fast lane of Europe's international set and victimized by them.

Daisy Miller, unabr. ed. Henry James. Narrated by Flo Gibson. 2 cass. (Running Time: 2 hrs.). 1999. 18.00 (978-1-55690-131-7(3), 81130E7) Recorded Bks.
Daisy is free as air, an American abroad with Europe at her feet.

***Daisy Miller.** unabr. ed. Henry James. Read by Susan O'Malley. (Running Time: 2.5 hrs. NaN mins.). (ENG.). 2011. 19.95 (978-1-4417-8391-2(1)); audio compact disk 28.00 (978-1-4417-8389-9(X)) Blckstn Audio.

Daisy Miller, Set. unabr. ed. Henry James. Narrated by Flo Gibson. 2 cass. (Running Time: 2 hr. 30 min.). 1984. 14.95 (978-1-55685-003-5(4)) Audio Bk Con.
The innocent Daisy Miller confronts youth, love & tradition in her European travels that lead to a tragic end.

Daisy Miller & The Real Thing. unabr. collector's ed. Henry James. Read by Walter Zimmerman. 4 cass. (Running Time: 4 hrs.). 1983. 24.00 (978-0-7366-3974-3(8), 9520) Books on Tape.
Daisy is a "child of nature & freedom." She deliberately defies European conventions & for her troubles became the literary toast of two continents. Not incidentally, she made her creator instantly famous; "The Real Thing" is a fable of the reality of the imagination & the insubstantiality of the "real".

Daja's Book. unabr. ed. Tamora Pierce. Read by Full Cast Production Staff. (Circle of Magic Ser.: No. 3). (YA). 2006. 39.99 (978-1-59895-505-7(5)) Find a World.

Dakota! abr. ed. Dana Fuller Ross, pseud. Read by Charlie O'Dowd. 4 vols. (Wagons West Ser.: No. 11). 2003. (978-1-58807-546-8(X)) Am Pubng Inc.

Dakota! abr. ed. Dana Fuller Ross, pseud. Read by Charlie O'Dowd. 4 cass. (Running Time: 6 hrs.). (Wagon West Ser.: No. 11). 2003. 25.00 (978-1-58807-016-6(6)) Am Pubng Inc.
Toby Holt is forced to quell the northern tier from Ma Hastings and Red Cloud, such as he had to in Montana. Meanwhile, Beth Blake undergoes captivity and the duress of a homicide trial.

Dakota! abr. ed. Dana Fuller Ross, pseud. Read by Charlie O'Dowd. 5 vols. (Wagons West Ser.: No. 11). 2004. audio compact disk 30.00 (978-1-58807-378-5(5)); audio compact disk (978-1-58807-857-5(4)) Am Pubng Inc.

Dakota. unabr. ed. Martha Grimes. Read by Renée Raudman. 11 CDs. (Running Time: 14 hrs.). (ENG.). (gr. 12 up). 2008. audio compact disk 39.95 (978-0-14-314301-7(8), PengAudBks) Penguin Grp USA.

Dakota. unabr. ed. Martha Grimes. Read by Renée Raudman. 8 cass. (Running Time: 14 hrs.). 2008. 110.00 (978-1-4159-2613-0(1), BksonTape); audio compact disk 110.00 (978-1-4159-2614-7(X), BksonTape) Pub: Random Audio Pubg. Dist(s): Random
In this stunning sequel to Grimes's Biting the Moon, Andi Oliver, amnesiac and drifter, is still running from the memory - her only memory - of an occurrence in a Santa Fe bed-and-breakfast. Forced to invent details of her past as she manages to hang on to a precarious present ("Lying," says one co-worker, "it's what the girl does."), Andi moves from one small-town job to another across Idaho, across Montana, and into North Dakota. In Dakota she gets herself hired at Klavan's, a massive pig farming facility that specializes in the dark art of modern livestock management. As Andi begins to uncover the truth about Klavan¿s and its sister facility, Big Sun, a stranger out of her past, who has been stalking her for more than a year, appears at her door demanding information of which she has no memory. DAKOTA signals the return of one of Martha Grimes's most intrepid heroines, a young woman who invents her life step-by-step as she moves through a landscape that throws up one danger after another. Set against the breathtakingly expansive backdrop of the plains, DAKOTA will reward Grimes's legion of fans, and fans of western literature as a whole.

Dakota: A Spiritual Geography. unabr. ed. Kathleen Norris. Read by Mary Peiffer. 7 cass. (Running Time: 7 hrs.). 1995. 42.00 (978-0-7366-3118-1(6), 3794) Books on Tape.
Kathleen Norris, a New Yorker, planned a brief stay on a South Dakota farm. But it lasted 20 years. Away from the city where people busily (read: neurotically) stave off emptiness, the vast space opened a door into a simple, more spiritual condition.

***Dakota Cipher.** unabr. ed. William Dietrich. Read by William Dufris. (ENG.). 2009. (978-0-06-180552-3(1), Harper Audio); (978-0-06-180550-9(5), Harper Audio) HarperCollins Pubs.

Dakota Cipher. unabr. ed. William Dietrich. Read by William Dufris. 2009. audio compact disk 39.99 (978-0-06-171950-9(1), Harper Audio) HarperCollins Pubs.

Dakota of the White Flats. unabr. ed. Philip Ridley. Read by Josie Lawrence. 3 cass. (Running Time: 4 hrs., 30 min.). (J). (gr. 1-8). 1999. 24.95 (CCA 3495, Chivers Child Audio) AudioGO.

Dakota Trail. abr. ed. Robert Vaughn. Read by Jim Gough. 4 cass. (Running Time: 6 hrs.). (Trail Drive Ser.: Vol. 14). 2002. 24.95 (978-1-890990-91-6(4), 99091) Otis Audio.
Western with sound effects.

Dalai Lama: Man, monk, Mystic. Mayank Chhaya. Read by Paul English. (Running Time: 10 hrs.). 2009. 84.99 (978-1-74214-201-2(X), 9781742142012) Pub: Bolinda Pubng AUS. Dist(s): Bolinda Pub Inc

Dalai Lama: Man, Monk, Mystic. unabr. ed. Mayank Chhaya. Read by Paul English. (Running Time: 36600 sec.). 2008. audio compact disk 118.95 (978-1-921415-47-0(9), 9781921415470) Pub: Bolinda Pubng AUS. Dist(s): Bolinda Pub Inc

Dalai Lama: Man, monk, Mystic. unabr. ed. Mayank Chhaya. Read by Paul English. (Running Time: 10 hrs.). 2009. 43.95 (978-1-74214-147-3(1), 9781742141473) Pub: Bolinda Pubng AUS. Dist(s): Bolinda Pub Inc

Dalai Lama in America: Central Park Lecture. Dalai Lama XIV. 2004. 8.95 (978-0-7435-4533-4(8)) Pub: S&S Audio. Dist(s): S and S Inc

Dalai Lama in America: Cultivating Compassion. Dalai Lama XIV. 2004. 15.95 (978-0-7435-4567-9(2)) Pub: S&S Audio. Dist(s): S and S Inc

Dalai Lama in America: Mindful Enlightenment. Dalai Lama XIV. 2004. 15.95 (978-0-7435-4569-3(9)) Pub: S&S Audio. Dist(s): S and S Inc

Dalai Lama in America: Training the Mind. Dalai Lama XIV. 2004. 15.95 (978-0-7435-4571-6(0)) Pub: S&S Audio. Dist(s): S and S Inc

Dalai Lama My Son. unabr. ed. Diki Tsering. Read by Arabella Hong. 2004. 15.95 (978-0-7435-4573-0(7)) Pub: S&S Audio. Dist(s): S and S Inc

Dale Brown CD Collection: Flight of the Old Dog, Silver Tower. abr. ed. Dale Brown. Read by Richard Allen. (Running Time: 12 hrs.). 2005. audio compact disk 29.95 (978-1-59737-702-7(3), 9781597377027, BACD) Brilliance Audio.
Flight of the Old Dog (Director: Jim Bond): Flight of the Old Dog is the runaway bestseller that launched the phenomenal career of Dale Brown. It is the riveting story of America's military superiority being surpassed as our greatest enemy masters space-to-Earth weapons technology - neutralizing the U.S. arsenal of nuclear missiles. America's only hope: The Old Dog Zero One, a battle-scarred bomber fully renovated with modern hardware - and equipped with the deadliest state-of-the-art armaments known to man... Silver Tower (Director: Patrick Lawlor): Iran has been invaded. And America responds in a grueling counterattack by air, by sea - and by a brave new technology that will redefine war. The most sophisticated laser defense system ever. It is called Silver Tower. And it will change the balance of world power forever.

Dale Brown CD Collection 2: Silver Tower, Strike Force, Shadow Command. abr. ed. Dale Brown. (Running Time: 18 hrs.). 2009. audio compact disk 34.99 (978-1-4418-0149-4(9), 9781441801494, BACD) Brilliance Audio.

***Dale Brown's Dreamland.** abr. ed. Dale Brown. Read by J. K. Simmons. (ENG.). 2005. (978-0-06-085678-6(5), Harper Audio); (978-0-06-085679-3(3), Harper Audio) HarperCollins Pubs.

***Dale Brown's Dreamland CD Collection: Dale Brown's Dreamland: Retribution, Dale Brown's Dreamland: Revolution.** abr. ed. Dale Brown. (Running Time: 12 hrs.). (Dreamland Ser.). 2010. audio compact disk 19.99 (978-1-4418-6158-0(0), 9781441861580, BACD) Brilliance Audio.

***Dale Brown's Dreamland: Razor's Edge.** abr. ed. Dale Brown. Read by David Mccallum. (ENG.). 2005. (978-0-06-085683-0(1), Harper Audio); (978-0-06-085682-3(3), Harper Audio) HarperCollins Pubs.

***Dale Brown's Dreamland: Satan's Tail.** abr. ed. Dale Brown. Read by Larry Pressman. (ENG.). 2005. (978-0-06-087668-5(9), Harper Audio); (978-0-06-087670-8(0), Harper Audio) HarperCollins Pubs.

***Dale Brown's Dreamland: Strike Zone.** abr. ed. Dale Brown. Read by J. K. Simmons. (ENG.). 2005. (978-0-06-085681-6(5), Harper Audio); (978-0-06-085680-9(7), Harper Audio) HarperCollins Pubs.

Dale Carnegie Leadership Mastery Course: How to Challenge Yourself & Others to Greatness. abr. ed. Dale Carnegie. 6 CDs. (Running Time: 60 hrs. 0 mins. 0 sec.). (ENG.). 2001. audio compact disk 34.95 (978-0-7435-0937-4(4), Nightgale) Pub: S&S Audio. Dist(s): S and S Inc

Dale Miller/Country, Blues & Ragtime Guitar Styles. Dale Miller. 1996. pap. bk. 17.95 (978-0-7866-2711-0(5), 96557BCD) Mel Bay.

Dalek Conquests. unabr. ed. Narrated by Nicholas Briggs. (Running Time: 9300 sec.). (Doctor Who Ser.). (ENG.). 2007. audio compact disk 19.95 (978-1-60283-313-5(3)) Pub: AudioGO. Dist(s): Perseus Dist

***Daleks: Mission to the Unknown.** unabr. ed. John Peel. 5 CDs. (Running Time: 4 hrs. 0 mins. 0 sec.). (Doctor Who Ser.). (ENG.). 2010. audio compact disk 39.95 (978-1-4084-0998-5(4)) Pub: AudioGO. Dist(s): Perseus Dist

Daleks' Master Plan. Dennis Spooner & Terry Nation. Perf. by William Hartnell. 2004. audio compact disk 59.95 (978-0-563-52610-0(6)) AudioGO.

Dali & I: The Surreal Story. unabr. ed. Stan Lauryssens. Read by William Dufris. Narrated by William Dufris. (Running Time: 8 hrs. 0 mins. 0 sec.). (ENG.). 2008. audio compact disk 29.99 (978-1-4001-0739-1(3)); audio compact disk 59.99 (978-1-4001-3739-8(X)); audio compact disk 19.99 (978-1-4001-5739-6(0)) Pub: Tantor Media. Dist(s): IngramPubServ

Dali Code: A Parody. unabr. ed. Cathy Crimmins. 2004. 24.95 (978-1-59007-613-2(3), New Millenn Pr); audio compact disk 29.95 (978-1-59007-612-5(5), New Millenn Pr) New Millenn Enter.

Dallas: Hosea 3:1-3. Ed Young. 1991. 4.95 (978-0-7417-1866-2(9), 866) Win Walk.

Dallas Partner Conference 2004. 2005. (978-1-59024-192-9(4)); audio compact disk (978-1-59024-193-6(2)) B Hinn Min.

Dalva. unabr. ed. Jim Harrison. Narrated by Alyssa Bresnahan & Frank Muller. 10 cass. (Running Time: 14 hrs. 15 mins.). 1994. 85.00 (978-0-7887-0094-1(4), 94335E7) Recorded Bks.
A young woman returns home to search for her identity & the baby she gave up as a teenager.

Dalva. unabr. ed. Jim Harrison. Read by Alyssa Bresnahan & Frank Muller. 10 cass. (Running Time: 14 hrs. 15 min.). 1994. Rental 17.50 Set. (94335) Recorded Bks.

Daly Life. abr. ed. Chuck Daly & Joe Falls. Read by Joe Burke. Ed. by Steven Alpert & Greg Nielson. 2 cass. (Running Time: 3 hrs.). Dramatization. 1992. bk. 15.95 Set. (978-1-56703-001-3(7)) High-Top Sports.

Dam see Poetry & Voice of Muriel Rukeyser

Dam Neck, Virginia see Twentieth-Century Poetry in English, No. 1, Recordings of Poets Reading Their Own Poetry

Dama de las Camelias. Scripts. Ed. by Alejandro Dumas & Alejandro Dumas. Adapted by Ligia Lezama. 3 CDs. (Running Time: 3 Hrs. 20 Mins). Dramatization. (SPA.). 2003. audio compact disk 18.95 (978-0-9728598-3-7(7)) Fonolibro Inc.
The Lady of the Camellias, audio book dramatized in Spanish based on the original story of Alexander Dumas Fils. It is the story of a beautiful courtesan, Marguerite Gautier (Performed by Mayra Alejandra Rodriguez), who falls in love for a handsome young nobleman, Armand Duval (Performed by Arquimedes Rivero). Her love for Armand makes her decide to leave the comfortable lifestyle provided by a Duke. Their romance raises conflicts, and to prove her love, she sacrifices her own happiness. Based on a true story written by the son of the recognized author of adventures (The Count of Monte Cristo, The Three Musketeers, The Man with the Iron Mask, etc), this masterpiece in audio book format would make you live one of the most beautiful love stories ever told. (3 CDs - 3 Hours 20 Minutes).

Dama de las Camelias. abr. ed. Read by Laura García. Ed. by Alejandro Dumas & Alejandro Dumas. 3 CDs. (SPA.). 2001. audio compact disk 17.00 (978-958-9494-44-8(7)) YoYoMusic.

Dama S Sobachkoy. Anton Chekhov. 1 cass. (Running Time: 1 hr.). (RUS.). 1996. pap. bk. 19.50 (978-1-58085-564-8(4)) Interlingua VA.
Includes Russian text. The combination of written text & clarity & pace of diction will open the door for intermediate & advanced students to genuine comprehension & the use of literary texts for advancement in rapid understanding of written & oral language materials. The audio text plus written text concept makes foreign languages accessible to a much wider range of students than books alone.

***Damage.** abr. ed. John Lescroart. (Running Time: 6 hrs.). 2011. 9.99 (978-1-4418-9405-2(5), 9781441894052, BAD) Brilliance Audio.

***Damage.** abr. ed. John Lescroart. Read by David Colacci. (Running Time: 6 hrs.). 2011. audio compact disk 24.99 (978-1-4418-0262-0(2), 9781441802620, BACD) Brilliance Audio.

Damage. unabr. ed. Josephine Hart. Narrated by Simon Prebble. 4 cass. (Running Time: 6 hrs.). 1994. 35.00 (978-1-55690-659-6(5), 92134E7) Recorded Bks.
When she turned to face him at a crowded party, for a glimmering moment he seemed to break out of the self-imposed exile that was his life. And as he watched her tall, black-suited figure move away from him, cutting through the insensible crowd, he knew he would never be free again.

***Damage.** unabr. ed. John Lescroart. (Running Time: 13 hrs.). 2011. 24.99 (978-1-4418-0260-6(6), 9781441802606, BAD); 39.97 (978-1-4418-0261-3(4), 9781441802613, BADLE) Brilliance Audio.

***Damage.** unabr. ed. John Lescroart. Read by David Colacci. (Running Time: 13 hrs.). 2011. 24.99 (978-1-4418-0258-3(4), 9781441802583, Brilliance MP3); 39.97 (978-1-4418-0259-0(2), 9781441802590, Brlnc Audio MP3 Lib); audio compact disk 36.99 (978-1-4418-0256-9(8), 9781441802569, Bril Audio CD Unabri); audio compact disk 89.97 (978-1-4418-0257-6(6), 9781441802576, BriAudCD Unabrid) Brilliance Audio.

Damage Control. abr. ed. Robert Dugoni. Read by Christopher Lane. (Running Time: 21600 sec.). 2008. audio compact disk 14.99 (978-1-4233-2659-5(8), 9781423326595, BCD Value Price) Brilliance Audio.

Damage Control. unabr. ed. Robert Dugoni. (Running Time: 39600 sec.). 2007. audio compact disk 24.95 (978-1-4233-2654-0(7), 9781423326540, Brilliance MP3) Brilliance Audio.

Damage Control. unabr. ed. Robert Dugoni. Read by Christopher Lane. (Running Time: 11 hrs.). 2007. 39.25 (978-1-4233-2657-1(1), 9781423326571, BADLE); 24.95 (978-1-4233-2656-4(3), 9781423326564, BAD); 87.25 (978-1-4233-2651-9(2), 9781423326519, BrilAudUnabridg); audio compact disk 102.25 (978-1-4233-2653-3(9), 9781423326533, BriAudCD Unabrid); audio compact disk 39.25 (978-1-4233-2655-7(5), 9781423326557, Brlnc Audio MP3 Lib); audio compact disk 38.95 (978-1-4233-2652-6(0), 9781423326526, Bril Audio CD Unabri) Brilliance Audio.

***Damage Control.** unabr. ed. J. A. Jance. Read by Johanna Parker. (ENG.). 2008. (978-0-06-170233-4(1)); (978-0-06-170235-8(8)) HarperCollins Pubs.

Damage Control. unabr. ed. J. A. Jance. Read by Johanna Parker. (Joanna Brady Mystery Ser.). 2008. audio compact disk 39.95 (978-0-06-168435-7(X), Harper Audio) HarperCollins Pubs.

Damage Profiling & Physical Evidence: A Tutorial. Wiley L. Howell. 2002. audio compact disk 15.95 (978-1-884566-46-2(4)) Inst Police Tech.

Damage You Have Done see Poems from Black Africa

***Damaged.** abr. ed. Alex Kava. Read by Tanya Eby. (Running Time: 3 hrs.). (Maggie O'Dell Ser.: Bk. 8). 2010. audio compact disk 14.99 (978-1-4418-1000-7(5), 9781441810007, BACD) Brilliance Audio.

***Damaged.** unabr. ed. Alex Kava. Read by Tanya Eby. (Running Time: 6 hrs.). (Maggie O'Dell Ser.). 2010. 24.99 (978-1-4418-1288-9(1), 9781441812889, BAD) Brilliance Audio.

***Damaged.** unabr. ed. Alex Kava. Read by Tanya Eby. (Running Time: 6 hrs.). (Maggie O'Dell Ser.: Bk. 8). 2010. 24.99 (978-1-4418-1286-5(5), 9781441812865, Brilliance MP3); 39.97 (978-1-4418-1287-2(3), 9781441812872, Brlnc Audio MP3 Lib); 39.97 (978-1-4418-1289-6(X), 9781441812896, BADLE); audio compact disk 29.99

(978-1-4418-1284-1(9), 9781441812841, Bril Audio CD Unabri); audio compact disk 79.97 (978-1-4418-1285-8(7), 9781441812858, BriAudCD Unabrid) Brilliance Audio.

Damaged Goods. June Hampson. 2008. 69.95 (978-0-7531-3219-7(2)); audio compact disk 84.95 (978-0-7531-3220-3(6)) Pub: Isis Pubng Ltd GBR. Dist(s): Ulverscroft US

Damages in Commercial Litigation. 1986. bk. 70.00 incl. book.; 35.00 cass. only.; 35.00 book only. PA Bar Inst.

Damages in Commercial Litigation - Proof & Recovery. 1997. bk. 99.00 (ACS-1218); bk. 99.00 (ACS-1218) PA Bar Inst.
Offers practical trial strategies & techniques for proving & recovering commercial litigation damages. It is designed to reveal how jurors look at damages, how to use visual aids effectively, how to optimize the testimony of expert witnesses, how to apply the law & economic principles of damages, & how to become more successful in your next trial.

Damascened Blade. Barbara Cleverly. Read by Terry Wale. 8 cass. (Running Time: 10 hrs.). (Detective Joe Sandilands Ser.). (J). 2004. 69.95 (978-1-84283-684-2(6)) Pub: ISIS Lrg Prnt GBR. Dist(s): Ulverscroft US

Damascened Blade. Barbara Cleverly. (Detective Joe Sandilands Ser.). (J). 2005. audio compact disk 84.95 (978-1-84559-085-7(6)) Pub: ISIS Lrg Prnt GBR. Dist(s): Ulverscroft US

Damascus Gate. unabr. ed. Robert Stone. Narrated by George Guidall. 14 cass. (Running Time: 19 hrs. 30 mins.). 1998. 117.00 (978-0-7887-2208-0(5), 95451E7) Recorded Bks.
Set in modern day Jerusalem, a disillusioned American journalist is adrift in the supercharged atmosphere at the end of the millennium.

Damascus Gate, Set. abr. ed. Robert Stone. Read by Frank Muller. 6 cass. (Running Time: 9 hr.). 1999. 29.95 (978-1-57511-058-5(X)) Pub Mills.
On the cusp of the new millennium, Jerusalem becomes a battleground filled with religious fanatics.

Dame. collector's ed. Richard Stark, pseud. Read by Michael Kramer. 4 cass. (Running Time: 6 hrs.). 2000. 32.00 (978-0-7366-5535-4(2)) Books on Tape.
Alan Grofield is a part-time actor & part-time thief. When working on a heist with a guy named Parker, he's all business. On his own, he's ready for anything at all, especially if it involves a woman. The first time Grofield sees Belle Danemato at her villa in the Puerto Rican jungle, she makes him an offer he can readily refuse. The next time he sees her, she's dead. And her husband, mob boss B. G. Danemato, can't get it out of his head Grofield is responsible. To get out of this alive, Grofield can take his chances against the mobster's men in the perilous depths of the rain forest or find the real killer without delay.

Dame. unabr. ed. R. A. Salvatore. Read by Erik Singer. (Running Time: 12 hrs. 0 mins. 0 sec.). Bk. 3. 2009. audio compact disk 49.95 (978-1-4272-0683-1(X)) Pub: Macmill Audio. Dist(s): Macmillan

dame à la Forêt. unabr. ed. Henri Loevenbruck. Read by Emmanuel Michalon. (YA). 2007. 69.99 (978-2-35569-081-5(2)) Find a World.

Dame aux Camelias, Pt. 2, Set. Alexandre Dumas. Read by G. Bejean et al. 3 cass. (FRE.). 1995. 31.95 (1563-VSL) Olivia & Hill.
The story of the ill-fated love of a courtesan, Marguerite Gautier, "la dame aux camelias," & Armand Durval.

Dame aux Camelias, Set. Alexandre Dumas. Read by G. Bejean et al. 6 cass. (FRE.). 1995. 56.95 (1562/63) Olivia & Hill.

Dame du Lac. 1 cass. (Running Time: 60 mins.). Dramatization. (Maitres du Mystere Ser.). (FRE.). 1996. 11.95 (1830-MA) Olivia & Hill.
Popular radio thriller, interpreted by France's best actors.

Damia. unabr. ed. Anne McCaffrey. Read by Jean Reed-Bahle. (Running Time: 12 hrs.). (Rowan/Damia Ser.). 2004. 39.25 (978-1-59335-437-4(1), 1593354371, Brlnc Audio MP3 Lib) Brilliance Audio.
The Rowan was one of the greatest telepaths ever born, treasured by the people she saved from alien invasion - and loved by a young man who never hoped to win her heart. In spite of his feelings, Afra remained loyal to the Rowan. He stayed by her side and helped to raise her Talented daughter, Damia. Now years later, Damia is a full-grown Talent of great power. Terrible alien voices echo within her mind. And a wondrous new feeling for Afra is growing within her heart... In a universe under seige, only one thing can defeat the power of fear: the power of love.

Damia. unabr. ed. Anne McCaffrey. Read by Jean Reed-Bahle. (Running Time: 12 hrs.). (Rowan/Damia Ser.). 2004. 49.97 (978-1-59710-163-9(X), 159710163X, BADLE) Brilliance Audio.

Damia. unabr. ed. Anne McCaffrey. Read by Jean Reed Bahle. (Running Time: 12 hrs.). (Rowan/Damia Ser.). 2004. 24.95 (978-1-59710-162-2(1), 1597101621, BAD) Brilliance Audio.

Damia. unabr. ed. Anne McCaffrey. Read by Jean Reed-Bahle. (Running Time: 12 hrs.). (Rowan/Damia Ser.). 2004. 24.95 (978-1-59335-073-4(2), 1593350732) Soulmate Audio Bks.

***Damia.** unabr. ed. Anne McCaffrey. Read by Jean Reed Bahle. (Running Time: 12 hrs.). (Rowan/Damia Ser.). 2010. audio compact disk 29.99 (978-1-4418-4063-9(X), 9781441840639, Bril Audio CD Unabri); audio compact disk 89.97 (978-1-4418-4064-6(8), 9781441840646, BriAudCD Unabrid) Brilliance Audio.

Damian Marley: Mr. Marley. Perf. by Damian Marley et al. 1 cass. 1996. 9.98 (978-1-56896-153-8(7), 54177-4); audio compact disk 15.98 CD. (978-1-56896-152-1(9), 54177-2) Lightyear Entrtnmnt.
Noted for his talent as a DJ, he formed his own group "The Shepards" with Shiah (son of third world guitarist Cat Coore.) The Marley family celebrated the Natural Mystic with over 10,000 people in Central Park, which they were a major success.

Damia's Children. unabr. ed. Anne McCaffrey. Read by Jean Reed-Bahle. (Running Time: 8 hrs.). (Rowan/Damia Ser.). 2005. 39.25 (978-1-59737-698-3(1), 9781597376983, BADLE) Brilliance Audio.

Damia's Children. unabr. ed. Anne McCaffrey. Read by Jean Reed Bahle. (Running Time: 8 hrs.). (Rowan/Damia Ser.). 2005. 24.95 (978-1-59737-697-6(3), 9781597376976, BAD) Brilliance Audio.

Damia's Children. unabr. ed. Anne McCaffrey. Read by Jean Reed-Bahle. (Running Time: 28800 sec.). (Rowan/Damia Ser.). 2005. audio compact disk 39.25 (978-1-59737-696-9(5), 9781597376969, Brlnc Audio MP3 Lib); audio compact disk 24.95 (978-1-59737-695-2(7), 9781597376952, Brilliance MP3) Brilliance Audio.

***Damia's Children.** unabr. ed. Anne McCaffrey. Read by Jean Reed Bahle. (Running Time: 9 hrs.). (Rowan/Damia Ser.). 2010. audio compact disk 29.99 (978-1-4418-4065-3(6), 9781441840653) Brilliance Audio.

***Damia's Children.** unabr. ed. Anne McCaffrey. Read by Jean Reed Bahle. (Running Time: 9 hrs.). (Rowan/Damia Ser.). 2010. audio compact disk 89.97 (978-1-4418-4066-0(4), 9781441840660, BriAudCD Unabrid) Brilliance Audio.

Damming the Narmada. unabr. ed. Julian C. Hollick. 1 cass. (Running Time: 60 min.). 1989. 15.00 (978-1-56709-031-4(1), 1063) Indep Broadcast.
Plans to harness the waters of the Narmada River in western India may bring vital irrigation waters to drought-prone regions but the environmental & human costs may outweigh the benefits. This three-part series examines these issues & the role of the U.S. Congress & the World Bank in one of the environmental "cause celebres" of the 1990s.

Damming Wild Rivers. Hosted by Nancy Pearlman. 1 cass. (Running Time: 29 min.). 10.00 (302) Educ Comm CA.

Damnation of Theron Ware. Harold Frederic. Read by Anais 9000. 2008. 27.95 (978-1-60112-188-2(1)) Babblebooks.

Damnation of Theron Ware. Harold Frederic. Read by John Chatty. 9 cass. (Running Time: 12 hrs.). 1987. 39.00 incl. albums. (C-180) Jimcin Record.
A minister is brought to ruin through earthly desires.

Damnation of Theron Ware. unabr. ed. Harold Frederic. Read by Flo Gibson. 8 cass. (Running Time: 12 hrs.). 1993. 26.95 (978-1-55685-272-5(X)) Audio Bk Con.
A small town Methodist minister's emotional conflicts, confusion & disenchantment are dramatically revealed through his involvement with three women.

Damnation Street. abr. ed. Andrew Klavan. Read by Andrew Klavan. (Running Time: 21600 sec.). (Weiss & Bishop Ser.). 2007. audio compact disk 14.99 (978-1-4233-1287-1(2), 9781423312871, BCD Value Price) Brilliance Audio.

Damnation Street. unabr. ed. Andrew Klavan. Read by Andrew Klavan. (Running Time: 10 hrs.). (Weiss & Bishop Ser.). 2006. 39.25 (978-1-4233-1285-7(6), 9781423312857, BADLE); 24.95 (978-1-4233-1284-0(8), 9781423312840, BAD); 82.25 (978-1-4233-1279-6(1), 9781423312796, BrilAudUnabridg); audio compact disk 97.25 (978-1-4233-1281-9(3), 9781423312819, BriAudCD Unabrid); audio compact disk 39.25 (978-1-4233-1283-3(X), 9781423312833, Brlnc Audio MP3 Lib); audio compact disk 34.95 (978-1-4233-1280-2(5), 9781423312802, Bril Audio CD Unabri); audio compact disk 24.95 (978-1-4233-1282-6(1), 9781423312826, Brilliance MP3) Brilliance Audio.
Please enter a Synopsis.

Damned. abr. ed. Barry Sadler. Read by Charlton Griffin. 2 vols. (Casca Ser.: No. 7). 2003. (978-1-58807-527-7(3)); audio compact disk 25.00 (978-1-58807-281-8(9)); audio compact disk (978-1-58807-712-7(8)) Am Pubng Inc.

Damned. abr. ed. Barry Sadler. Read by Charlton Griffin. 2 cass. (Running Time: 3 hrs.). (Casca Ser.: No. 7). 2003. 18.00 (978-1-58807-107-1(3)) Am Pubng Inc.
With Ching Lis military intelligence and his secret weapon, a scroll bearing the writings titled, The Art of War, Attila the Hun is confident of his battle plan to overtake Europe. Shadowing the lands with death by barbaric rule, smaller territories quickly forfeit their lands to Attila, securing his army with food and passage towards his long-awaited prize: the siege of Rome. But, with every great leader who craves tyrannical power, a tragic flaw follows closely behind. For Attila, that flaw is unadulterated, blinding greed. Unbeknownst to Attila, his vicious style of rule breeds adversaries inside of his camp, leaving many to lust for his death. With so many enemies, who will hold the glory of bringing down one of the most formidable foes of all time? Surrounded by predators, Attila blindly forges towards his spectacular, final battle, where he pits his Huns against the legendary, military leadership of the unforgiving and eternal mercenary known as CASCA: THE DAMNED.

Damned Good Show. Derek Robinson. 2007. 89.95 (978-1-84559-861-7(X)); audio compact disk 99.95 (978-1-84559-862-4(8)) Pub: Soundings Ltd GBR. Dist(s): Ulverscroft US

Damned in Paradise. unabr. ed. Max Allan Collins. Narrated by Jeff Woodman. 8 cass. (Running Time: 11 hrs. 45 mins.). 1997. 70.00 (978-0-7887-0855-8(4), 95001E7) Recorded Bks.
A group of native Hawaiian men have been convicted of raping an American woman. Now her family is charged with murdering one of these men during a botched attempt to force a confession.

Damned Thing see Great American Short Stories, Vol. III, A Collection

Damned Thing see Tales of Terror

Damned Thing. (SWC 1345) HarperCollins Pubs.

Damned Thing. Short Stories. 1981. (S-58) Jimcin Record.

Damocles Sword. unabr. collector's ed. Elleston Trevor. Read by David Case. 8 cass. (Running Time: 12 hrs.). 1990. 64.00 (978-0-7366-1761-1(2), 2600) Books on Tape.
In the darkest days of WW II British Intelligence concocted a plan that would stymie the Germans. But it required a very brave man to carry it out, one who could infiltrate the elite SS corps. Martin Benedict was the man, & all went well until his cover got blown. Remarkably, success was still possible - but at increased risk. Could he bring it off? The answer reveals itself in an agony of suspense, which is no surprise, for Elleston Trevor is a master of the genre. His first bestseller was Flight of the Phoenix, made into a memorable & durable film.

Damon Runyon Stories. unabr. ed. Damon Runyon. Read by Nathan Lane. 2 cass. (Running Time: 4 hrs.). 2001. 25.00; audio compact disk 25.00 Airplay.

Damon Runyon Theatre. 1 cass. (Running Time: 60 min.). Incl. Damon Runyon Theatre: Broadway Financier. (CC-5050); Damon Runyon Theatre: The Brain Goes Home. (CC-5050); 7.95 (CC-5050) Natl Recrd Co.
In the story "The Brain Goes Home," the Brain, a wealthy but shady character discusses a personal problem with his friend, Broadway, also a shady character. The solution to the Brain's problem is unique, & complicated by a few of his "good & trusted friends." In the story "Broadway Financier," Satan Clark, a con-artist about to die, wants Broadway to look after his daughter Silk, a 17-year-old doll. Silk learned from her father how to become a con-artist, & she scores $3,000,000 big ones. Broadway discovers something Silk didn't learn from her father.

Damon Runyon Theatre, Vol. 1. collector's unabr. ed. Perf. by John Brown. 6 cass. (Running Time: 9 hrs.). 1999. bk. 34.98 (978-1-57019-127-5(1), 4005) Radio Spirits.
Enter the world of Damon Runyon through the eyes of "Broadway" the lovable hood in 18 episodes.

Damon Runyon Theatre, Vol. 2. collector's ed. Perf. by John Brown. 6 cass. (Running Time: 9 hrs.). 2001. bk. 34.98 (4435) Radio Spirits.
Celebrate Old Manhattan and the world of chorus girls, racetrack touts, bookies and underworld thugs. Eighteen classic radio programs.

Damon Runyon Theatre: Broadway Financier see Damon Runyon Theatre

Damon Runyon Theatre: Cemetery Bait & The Brakeman's Daugher. Hosted by John Brown. 1 cass. (Running Time: 1 hr.). 2001. 6.98 (1926) Radio Spirits.

Damon Runyon Theatre: Joe Terrace & Tight Shoes. Hosted by John Brown. 1 cass. (Running Time: 1 hr.). 2001. 6.98 (1847) Radio Spirits.

Damon Runyon Theatre: Palm Beach Santa Claus & Neat Strip. Hosted by John Brown. 1 cass. (Running Time: 1 hr.). 2001. 6.98 (1945) Radio Spirits.

Damon Runyon Theatre: The Brain Goes Home see Damon Runyon Theatre

Damsel. collector's ed. Richard Stark, pseud. Read by Michael Kramer. 4 cass. (Running Time: 6 hrs.). 2000. 32.00 (978-0-7366-4996-4(4)) Books on Tape.

Damsel in Distress. unabr. ed. P. G. Wodehouse. Read by Frederick Davidson. 6 cass. (Running Time: 8 hrs. 30 mins.). 1995. 44.95 (978-0-7861-0480-2(5), 1432) Blckstn Audio.
Strange things are happening at Belpher Castle. For starters, the Earl's sister is intent on pairing off her stepson, Reggie, & niece, Lady Patricia (known as Maud). Maud, however, is in hot pursuit of Geoffrey Raymond, & she is also being pursued by the unacceptable composer, George Bevan. "Reggie was a troubled spirit these days. He was in love, & he had developed a bad slice with his mid-iron. He was practically a soul in torment".

Damsel in Distress. unabr. ed. P. G. Wodehouse. Read by Jonathan Cecil. 6 cass. (Running Time: 9 hrs.). 2003. 54.95 (978-0-7540-8312-2(8), CAB 2434); audio compact disk 64.95 (978-0-7540-5584-6(1), CCD 275) Pub: Chivers Audio Bks GBR. Dist(s): AudioGO

Damsel in Distress, Set. P. G. Wodehouse. Read by Flo Gibson. 5 cass. (Running Time: 7 hrs. 30 min.). 1996. 20.95 (978-1-55685-426-2(9)) Audio Bk Con.
Comedy reigns supreme as the Earl of Marshmoreton's sister's plans for marrying off her relatives to landed gentry go awry.

Dan & Louie Vol. 1: The Greatest Stories Ever Told, deluxe ed. Short Stories. Perf. by Dan Betzer. Created by Dan Betzer. Des. by Robison Gamble Creative. Photos by Robison Gamble Creative. 10 CDs. Dramatization. (J). 2005. bk. 89.95 (978-1-933497-00-6(9)) Robison Gamble.
A collection of Bible Stories for children presented with humor and creativity by Dan Betzer and his witty little sidekick, Louie. These audio recordings fire the imagination and leave kids of all ages asking for more.

Dan & Louie Vol. 2: The Greatest Stories Ever Told. enl. ed. Short Stories. Dan Betzer. As told by Dan Betzer. Des. by Robison Gamble Creative. Engineer Robison Gamble Creative. 10 CDs. Dramatization. (J). 2005. bk. 89.00 (978-1-933497-01-3(7)) Robison Gamble.

Dan & Louie - CD 1. Short Stories. Dan Betzer. Perf. by Dan Betzer. Des. by Robison Gamble Creative. Engineer Robison Gamble Creative. 1 CD. (J). 2005. audio compact disk 14.95 (978-1-933497-02-0(5)) Robison Gamble.

Dan & Louie - CD 10. Short Stories. Dan Betzer. Perf. by Dan Betzer. Des. by Robison Gamble Creative. Engineer Robison Gamble Creative. 1 CD. (J). 2005. audio compact disk 14.95 (978-1-933497-11-2(4)) Robison Gamble.

Dan & Louie - CD 11. Short Stories. Dan Betzer. Perf. by Dan Betzer. Des. by Robison Gamble Creative. Engineer Robison Gamble Creative. 1 CD. (J). 2005. audio compact disk 14.95 (978-1-933497-12-9(2)) Robison Gamble.

Dan & Louie - CD 12. Short Stories. Dan Betzer. Perf. by Dan Betzer. Des. by Robison Gamble Creative. Engineer Robison Gamble Creative. 1 CD. (J). 2005. audio compact disk 14.95 (978-1-933497-13-6(0)) Robison Gamble.

Dan & Louie - CD 13. Short Stories. Dan Betzer. Perf. by Dan Betzer. Des. by Robison Gamble Creative. Engineer Robison Gamble Creative. 1 CD. (J). 2005. audio compact disk 14.95 (978-1-933497-14-3(9)) Robison Gamble.

Dan & Louie - CD 14. Short Stories. Dan Betzer. Perf. by Dan Betzer. Des. by Robison Gamble Creative. Engineer Robison Gamble Creative. 1 CD. (J). 2005. audio compact disk 14.95 (978-1-933497-15-0(7)) Robison Gamble.

Dan & Louie - CD 15. Short Stories. Dan Betzer. Perf. by Dan Betzer. Des. by Robison Gamble Creative. Engineer Robison Gamble Creative. 1 CD. (J). 2005. audio compact disk 14.95 (978-1-933497-16-7(5)) Robison Gamble.

Dan & Louie - CD 16. Short Stories. Dan Betzer. Perf. by Dan Betzer. Des. by Robison Gamble Creative. Engineer Robison Gamble Creative. 1 CD. (J). 2005. audio compact disk 14.95 (978-1-933497-17-4(3)) Robison Gamble.

Dan & Louie - CD 17. Short Stories. Dan Betzer. Perf. by Dan Betzer. Des. by Robison Gamble Creative. Engineer Robison Gamble Creative. 1 CD. (J). 2005. audio compact disk 14.95 (978-1-933497-18-1(1)) Robison Gamble.

Dan & Louie - CD 18. Short Stories. Dan Betzer. Perf. by Dan Betzer. Des. by Robison Gamble Creative. Engineer Robison Gamble Creative. 1 CD. (J). 2005. audio compact disk 14.95 (978-1-933497-19-8(X)) Robison Gamble.

Dan & Louie - CD 19. Short Stories. Dan Betzer. Perf. by Dan Betzer. Des. by Robison Gamble Creative. Engineer Robison Gamble Creative. 1 CD. (J). 2005. audio compact disk 14.95 (978-1-933497-20-4(3)) Robison Gamble.

Dan & Louie - CD 2: The Greatest Stories Ever Told. Dan Betzer. Perf. by Dan Betzer. Des. by Robison Gamble Creative. Engineer Robison Gamble Creative. 1 CD. (J). 2005. audio compact disk 14.95 (978-1-933497-03-7(3)) Robison Gamble.

Dan & Louie - CD 20: All New Stories! Short Stories. Dan Betzer. Perf. by Dan Betzer. Des. by Robison Gamble Creative. Engineer Robison Gamble Creative. 1 CD. (J). 2005. audio compact disk 14.95 (978-1-933497-21-1(1)) Robison Gamble.

Dan & Louie - CD 3. Short Stories. Dan Betzer. Perf. by Dan Betzer. Des. by Robison Gamble Creative. Engineer Robison Gamble Creative. 1 CD. (J). 2005. audio compact disk 14.95 (978-1-933497-04-4(1)) Robison Gamble.

Dan & Louie - CD 4. Short Stories. Dan Betzer. Perf. by Dan Betzer. Des. by Robison Gamble Creative. Engineer Robison Gamble Creative. 1 CD. (J). 2005. audio compact disk 14.95 (978-1-933497-05-1(X)) Robison Gamble.

Dan & Louie - CD 5. Dan Betzer. Perf. by Dan Betzer. Des. by Robison Gamble Creative. Engineer Robison Gamble Creative. 1 CD. (J). 2005. audio compact disk 14.95 (978-1-933497-06-8(8)) Robison Gamble.

Dan & Louie - CD 7. Short Stories. Dan Betzer. Perf. by Dan Betzer. Des. by Robison Gamble Creative. Engineer Robison Gamble Creative. 1 CD. (J). 2005. audio compact disk 14.95 (978-1-933497-07-5(6)); audio compact disk 14.95 (978-1-933497-08-2(4)) Robison Gamble.

Dan & Louie - CD 8. Short Stories. Dan Betzer. Perf. by Dan Betzer. Des. by Robison Gamble Creative. Engineer Robison Gamble Creative. 1 CD. (J). 2005. audio compact disk 14.95 (978-1-933497-09-9(2)) Robison Gamble.

Dan & Louie - CD 9. Short Stories. Dan Betzer. Perf. by Dan Betzer. Des. by Robison Gamble Creative. Engineer Robison Gamble Creative. 1 CD. (J). 2005. audio compact disk 14.95 (978-1-933497-10-5(6)) Robison Gamble.

Dan Barry's Daughter. unabr. collector's ed. Max Brand. Read by Jonathan Marosz. 7 cass. (Running Time: 7 hrs.). 1995. 42.00 (978-0-7366-3010-8(4), 3696) Books on Tape.
A young woman hits the adventure trail when she sets out to clear her father's name in a murder he didn't commit. Classic Brand.

Dan Brown Gift Set: Angels & Demons; Deception Point. abr. ed. Dan Brown. (ENG.). 2004. audio compact disk 59.95 (978-0-7435-3691-2(6), Audioworks) Pub: S&S Audio. Dist(s): S and S Inc
TWO EDGE -OF-YOUR SEAT AUDIOBOOKS FROM THE #1 BESTSELLING AUTHOR OF THE DA VINCI CODE ANGELS & DEMONS Read by Richard Poe World-renowned Harvard symbologist Robert Langdon is summoned to a Swiss research facility to analyze a cryptic symbol seared into the chest of a murdered physicist. What he discovers is unimaginable: a deadly vendetta against the Catholic Church by a centuries-old underground organization - the Illuminati. Desperate to save the Vatican from a powerful time bomb, Langdon joins forces in Rome with the beautiful and mysterious scientist Vittoria Vetra. Together they embark on a frantic hunt through sealed crypts, dangerous catacombs, deserted cathedrals, and the most secretive vault on earth...the long-forgotten Illuminati lair. DECEPTION POINT Read by Boyd Gaines When a NASA

satellite discovers an astonishingly rare object buried deep in the Arctic ice, the floundering space agency proclaims a much-needed victory - a victory with profound implications for NASA policy and the impending presidential election. To verify the authenticity of the find, the White House calls upon the skills of intelligence analyst Rachel Sexton. Accompanied by a team of experts, including the charismatic scholar Michael Tolland, Rachel travels to the Arctic and uncovers the unthinkable: evidence of scientific trickery - a bold deception that threatens to plunge the world into controversy. But before she can warn the President, Rachel and Michael are ambushed by a deadly team of assassins. Fleeing for their lives across a desolate and lethal landscape, their only hope for survival is to discover who is behind this masterful plot. The truth, they will learn, is the most shocking deception of all.

***Dan Fesperman: The Prisoner of Guantánamo, Amateur Spy.** unabr. ed. Dan Fesperman. (Running Time: 26 hrs.). 2010. audio compact disk 29.99 (978-1-4418-7143-5(8), 9781441871435, Bril Audio CD Unabri) Brilliance Audio.

Dan Gerber. Dan Gerber. Read by Dan Gerber. 1 cass. (Running Time: 29 min.). 1986. 10.00 New Letters.
Michigan poet reads from "Snow on the Backs of Animals".

Dan Inosanto, Vol. 3. 1 cass. (Running Time: 40 min.). (From the Source Ser.). 1987. 9.95 (978-0-944831-14-4(1)) Health Life.

Dan Jaffe. Read by Dan Jaffe. 1 cass. (Running Time: 29 min.). 1985. 10.00 New Letters.
In addition to a reading by the Kansas City poet, the program features Jaffe's poems set to music for choral works.

Dan Jaffe Two. unabr. ed. Dan Jaffe. Read by Dan Jaffe. 1 cass. (Running Time: 29 min.). 1988. 10.00 (060388) New Letters.
Jaffe reads from two of his collections: The poems from "Round for One Voice" & "In Seasons of the River".

Dan O'Brien. unabr. ed. Dan O'Brien. 1 cass. (Running Time: 29 min.). (New Letters on the Air Ser.). 1992. 10.00 (092791) New Letters.
In his novel, "In the Center of the Nation," O'Brien presents an ecological tale in the form of a fight between cattle ranchers & developers.

Dan Oxley Praise Band. 1997. 10.98 (978-0-7601-1027-0(1), C50028); audio compact disk 15.98 CD. (978-0-7601-1028-7(X), CD50028) Brentwood Music.
With a unique blend of an inspiring praise team & exciting instrumental group, the Dan Oxley Praise Band creates a dynamic praise & worship experience. Featuring the powerful performance of trumpeter & leader Dan Oxley, this recording will lift your eyes & heart to Father. With special guest, First Call.

Dan Quayle: Reality & the Press. (Running Time: 60 min.). 1989. 11.95 (K0510B090, HarperThor) HarpC GBR.

***Dan Quixote: Boy of Nuevo Jersey.** unabr. ed. Shevi Arnold. Read by Shevi Arnold. 3 CDs. (Running Time: 3 hrs.). (J). (gr. 3-8). 2010. audio compact disk 18.95 (978-1-936242-01-6(X)) Play Along.

Dan Rattiner's Hamptons Fables. Short Stories. Dan Rattiner. 1 CD. (Running Time: 1 hr., 8 mins.). 2003. audio compact disk 13.00 (978-0-9740201-4-3(1)) Harbor Electronic.
Award-winning writer, publisher, cartoonist, cartographer, and raconteur Dan Rattiner is the proprietor of Dan's Papers where he has chronicled the fables and foibles of the Hamptons for more than forty years. On this CD Dan reads some of his favorite stories from issues of the past few years. Most document the local lore of Long Island's famous Hamptons, some range as far as New Zealand and Mars. All will remind you of classic American humorists, from Mark Twain to Ambrose Beirce, from Jean Shepard to Garrison Keilor. You'll hear about the refugee chickens from Survivor enjoying their last days at Tate King's North Sea Farms, how an East End whale got buried on Staten Island, why North Dakota is like Shinnecock Hills, the plan for New Zealand's sheep-gas defense, and much, much more.

Dan Rostenkowski: How to Lower the Deficit. (Running Time: 60 min.). 1989. 11.95 (K0540B090, HarperThor) HarpC GBR.

Dan Tanna Ain't Dead. Jack Bates. 2008. audio compact disk 5.49 (978-0-9821192-3-5(2)) Mind Wings Aud.

***Dan Tanna Ain't Dead: A Harry Landers Episode.** Jack Bates. Read by Erik Parker. (Running Time: 55). (ENG.). 2008. 2.99 (978-1-61114-002-6(1)) Mind Wings Aud.

***Dan Winkler - the Mountains & Valleys of the Christian Life.** Arranged by Polishing the Pulpit. 2010. audio compact disk 25.00 (978-1-60644-120-6(5)) Heart Heart.

Dana Gioia. unabr. ed. Ed. by Jim McKinley. Prod. by Rebekah Presson. 1 cass. (Running Time: 29 min.). (New Letters on the Air Ser.). 1994. 10.00 (050994) New Letters.
In his highly controversial book of essays, "Can Poetry Matter," Gioia - a poet himself - takes on such topics as the Poet as Businessman, the New Formalism & the effect Howard Moss, long the poetry editor of "The New Yorker," has had on contemporary poetry.

Dana's Best Rock & Roll Fairy Tales. Perf. by Dana Cohenour. Prod. by Clay Mills. 1 cass. (Running Time: 46 mins.). (J). 1999. 9.95 (978-1-889449-08-1(3)); audio compact disk 14.95 (978-1-889449-09-8(1)) Real Music Kidz.
Dana re-spins familiar tales, setting them to her original upbeat tunes. Includes: "Once Upon a Time (Never Rocked This Way!)," "The Goldilocks Rock," "The Gingerbread Man," "Twisted Rapunzel," "Three Billy Goats Groove," "The Frog & the Valley Girl Princess," "Jack & the Beanstalk," "Happy Ever After".

Dana's Best Sing & Play-A-Long Tunes!, RMFK 102. Dana Cohenour. 1 cass. (Running Time: 40 min.). (Dana's Best Ser.: RMFK 300). 1995. 9.95 UPC 706891010 240. (978-1-889449-01-2(6), RMFK 102C); audio compact disk 14.95 CD UPC 706891010 226. (978-1-889449-04-3(0), RMFK 102J) Real Music Kidz.
1995 National Parenting Publications Gold Award. Dana's 12 original songs & adaptations of old favorites stimulate imaginations & inspire participation, hand clapping & foot stomping.

Dana's Best Sing & Swing-A-Long Tunes! Dana. Contrib. by Clay Mills. 1 cass. (Running Time: 40 min.). (J). 1997. 9.95 (RMFK104); audio compact disk 14.95 CD. Real Music Kidz.

Dana's Best Travelin' Tunes! Songs to Shorten the Ride, RMFK 103. Dana Cohenour. 1 cass. (Running Time: 40 min.). (Dana's Best Ser.: RMFK 300). (J). 1995. 9.95 UPC 706891010 349. (978-1-889449-02-9(4), RMFK 103E); audio compact disk 14.95 CD UPC 706891010 325. (978-1-889449-05-0(9), RMFK 103J) Real Music Kidz.
Dana's 12 "Travelin' Tunes" shorten the ride for the entire family! Country, rock, jazz & island beats make learning about counting colors, traffic safety friendship & sharing a joy ride for all. A blend of original songs & new versions of old classics.

Dance. Jay O'Callahan. Perf. by Jay O'Callahan. (ENG.). (YA). 2007. audio compact disk 22.95 (978-1-877954-55-9(1)) Pub: Artana Prodns. Dist(s): High Windy Audio

***Dance.** abr. ed. Oriah. Read by Oriah. (ENG.). 2006. (978-0-06-113054-0(0), Harper Audio); (978-0-06-113053-3(2), Harper Audio) HarperCollins Pubs.

Dance. unabr. ed. Jay O'Callahan. Perf. by Jay O'Callahan. 2 cass. (Running Time: 1 hr. 33 min.). Dramatization. (J). (gr. 9 up). 1992. 18.00 (978-1-877954-35-1(7)) Pub: Artana Prodns. Dist(s): Yellow Moon
The boiling inner world of a boy coming to manhood. A two-cassette sequel to "Coming Home to Someplace New" Studio Recording.

Dance: Moving to the Rhythms of Your True Self. unabr. abr. ed. Oriah Mountain Dreamer Staff. Read by Oriah Mountain Dreamer Staff. 3 cass. (Running Time: 5 hrs.). 2001. 24.00 (978-0-694-52641-3(X)) HarperCollins Pubs.

Dance a Little Longer, Vol. 3. unabr. ed. Jane Roberts Wood. Narrated by C. J. Critt. 6 cass. (Running Time: 7 hrs. 45 mins.). 1995. 51.00 (978-0-7887-0396-6(X), 94588E7) Recorded Bks.
With her husband & four-year-old son, Lucy moves to a small farm on the drought-stricken prairie of West Texas. Here she meets a colorful cast of local characters who will help her find meaning in life when a terrible tragedy strikes the farm.

Dance-Along. 1 cass., 1 CD. (Sing-Along Ser.). (J). bk. 11.99 (978-0-7634-0273-0(7)) W Disney Records.

Dance Along. unabr. ed. (J). 1997. 15.98 W Disney Records.
A Collection of dance tunes for kids, complete with an instruction booklet for learning popular moves.

Dance-Along, Vol. 1. 1 cass., 1 CD. (Sing-Along Ser.). (J). (ps-3). 1997. audio compact disk 12.99 CD Incl. bk. (978-0-7634-0308-9(3)) W Disney Records.

Dance at a Glance: Being a Quick Musical Guide. Perf. by Katherine Westine & Phebe Craig. Text by Katherine Westine & Phebe Craig. 2005. audio compact disk 39.95 (978-0-9769698-0-8(7)) KATastroPHE.

Dance Dance Dance. unabr. ed. Haruki Murakami & Rupert Degas. 11.Tr. of Dansu Dansu Dansu. 2007. audio compact disk 67.98 (978-962-634-435-4(0), Naxos AudioBooks) Naxos.

Dance: Dream: A World Dance-Groove Odyssey Set in the Key of D (for Dreamtime) Shaman's Dream. (Running Time: 1 hr. 12 m). 2007. audio compact disk 17.98 (978-1-59179-533-9(8), M1089D) Sounds True.

Dance for Me When I Die: Death As a Rite of Passage. Alla R. Bozarth. Read by Alla R. Bozarth. 1 cass. (Running Time: 1 hr. 30 min.). 1995. 9.95 Wisdom House.
Explores the meaning & mystery of physical death as a transformation, not an end, of relationship: poetry, meditation, stories - talk given to terminal care givers.

Dance for Rain see Twentieth-Century Poetry in English, No. 10, Recordings of Poets Reading Their Own Poetry

Dance for the Dead. unabr. ed. Thomas Perry. Narrated by Joyce Bean. (Running Time: 12 hrs. 0 mins. 0 sec.). (Jane Whitefield Ser.). (ENG.). 2009. audio compact disk 69.99 (978-1-4001-4021-3(8)) Pub: Tantor Media. Dist(s): IngramPubServ

Dance for the Dead. unabr. abr. ed. Thomas Perry. Narrated by Joyce Bean. (Running Time: 12 hrs. 0 mins. 0 sec.). (Jane Whitefield Ser.). (ENG.). 2009. 24.99 (978-1-4001-6021-1(9)); audio compact disk 34.99 (978-1-4001-1021-6(1)) Pub: Tantor Media. Dist(s): IngramPubServ

Dance Hall of the Dead. Tony Hillerman. Read by Walter Hawn. 3 cass. (Running Time: 4 hrs. 30 min.). (Joe Leaphorn & Jim Chee Novel Ser.). 1993. 37.20 Set. (978-1-56544-025-8(0), 250021); Rental 6.70 30 day rental Set. (250021) Literate Ear.
Strange laws of Zuni religious rites complicate Lieutenant Joe Leaphorn's investigation of the disappearance of two young boys.

Dance Hall of the Dead. Tony Hillerman & George Guidall. 6 CDs. (Running Time: 6.25 Hrs). (Joe Leaphorn & Jim Chee Novel Ser.). audio compact disk 29.95 (978-1-4025-5847-4(3)) Recorded Bks.

Dance Hall of the Dead. abr. ed. Tony Hillerman. Read by Michael Ansara. 2 cass. (Running Time: 2 hrs. 45 min.). (Joe Leaphorn & Jim Chee Novel Ser.). 2004. 15.95 (978-0-88690-127-1(8), N20024) Pub: Audio Partners. Dist(s): PerseuPGW
Winner of the Edgar Allan Poe award for best mystery novel, this story ranges from the ancient secrets of the Zunis to the hidden crimes of white men.

Dance Hall of the Dead. unabr. ed. Tony Hillerman. Read by Jonathan Marosz. 6 cass. (Running Time: 6 hrs.). (Joe Leaphorn & Jim Chee Novel Ser.). 1994. 48.00 (978-0-7366-2610-1(7), 3352) Books on Tape.
Lt. Joe Leaphorn scours the reservation for a missing Navajo boy. They've found his friend, a Zuni, murdered. Who would want to do in a couple of kids? Leaphorn intends to find out. It takes all his tracker skills to connect the few clues & unravel the mystery. Hillerman's second novel, Dance Hall of the Dead won the Edgar Allan Poe Award for Best Novel in 1974.

Dance Hall of the Dead. unabr. ed. Tony Hillerman. Read by George Guidall. 1 CD. (Running Time: 1 hr. 30 min.). (Joe Leaphorn & Jim Chee Novel Ser.). 2005. audio compact disk 14.95 (978-0-06-081511-0(6)) HarperCollins Pubs.

Dance Hall of the Dead. unabr. ed. Tony Hillerman. Read by George Guidall. 4 Cass. (Running Time: 6.25 Hrs). (Joe Leaphorn & Jim Chee Novel Ser.). 19.95 (978-1-4025-5846-7(5)) Recorded Bks.

Dance Hall of the Dead. unabr. ed. Tony Hillerman. Narrated by George Guidall. 5 cass. (Running Time: 6 hrs. 15 mins.). (Joe Leaphorn & Jim Chee Novel Ser.). (gr. 10). 1991. 44.00 (978-1-55690-134-8(8), 91122E7) Recorded Bks.
Lt. Leaphorn must unravel a skein of mysteries to uncover the truth in this Navaho crime thriller.

Dance Hall of the Dead. unabr. ed. Tony Hillerman. Read by George Guidall. (Running Time: 6 hrs. 15 mins.). 2008. 56.75 (978-1-4361-6524-2(5)); audio compact disk 56.75 (978-1-4361-4932-7(0)) Recorded Bks.

Dance in the Breeze: Stories, Songs & Poems in Honor of the Beloved. unabr. ed. Mary Lloyd Dugan & Daniel Ladinsky. Perf. by Bobbi Bernstein. 1 CD. (Running Time: 58 mins.). Dramatization. 2000. audio compact disk 14.98 (978-0-9709751-1-9(2)) Dancing Pony Prod.

Dance in Your Pants. David S. Jack. 1 cass. (J). 8.78 (KE 2005) NewSound.

Dance in Your Pants: Great New Songs for Little Kids to Dance To. Perf. by David S. Jack & Susan J. Cooper. 1 cass. (Running Time: 25 min.). (J). (ps-3). 1988. pap. bk. 9.98; 9.98 (978-0-942181-04-3(2), TD 2005) Ta-Dum Prodns.
Designed to encourage active participation & develop movement skills for all children. A favorite of parents & teachers alike - this cassette is widely used in schools across the country.

Dance Like This. Perf. by Mr. AL. Prod. by Mr. AL. 1 cass. (J). (ps-2). 2001. 10.95; audio compact disk 13.95 Child Like.

Dance Little Lady. Lilian Harry. 12 cass. (Running Time: 15 hrs.). (Soundings Ser.). (J). 2005. 94.95 (978-1-84283-977-5(2)); audio compact disk 104.95 (978-1-84559-004-8(X)) Pub: ISIS Lrg Prnt GBR. Dist(s): Ulverscroft US

Dance of a Child's Dreams. David Levine. 1998. pap. bk. 23.95 (978-0-7866-3088-2(4), 96790CDP) Mel Bay.

Dance of Anger. 2 cass. (Twelve Step Living Discussion Tape Ser.). 15.95 (6954) Hazelden.

***Dance of Anger.** abr. ed. Harriet Lerner. Read by Harriet Lerner. (ENG.). 2004. (978-0-06-081365-9(2), Harper Audio); (978-0-06-077413-4(4), Harper Audio) HarperCollins Pubs.

Dance of Anger. abr. ed. Harriet G. Lerner. 1 cass. (Running Time: 3 hrs.). 1999. 18.00 (70207) Courage-to-Change.
Helps women change relationships rather than remain stuck in patterns of emotional distancing or fighting or blaming.

Dance of Anger: A Woman's Guide to Changing the Pattern of Intimate Relationships. abr. ed. Harriet Lerner. Read by Harriet Lerner. 2004. audio compact disk 22.00 (978-0-06-072650-8(4)) HarperCollins Pubs.

Dance of Anger: A Woman's Guide to Changing the Pattern of Intimate Relationships, unabr. ed. Harriet G. Lerner. Narrated by Barbara Caruso. 5 cass. (Running Time: 7 hrs.). 1999. 46.00 (978-0-7887-2924-9(1), 95538E7) Recorded Bks.
Anger can be a painful & difficult emotion, but the author shows you how to use it as a powerful tool for change. Anyone interested in creating healthier, more satisfying relationships can benefit from Lerner's transformational message.

***Dance of Connection.** abr. ed. Harriet Lerner. Read by Harriet Lerner. (ENG.). 2005. (978-0-06-085304-4(2), Harper Audio); (978-0-06-085303-7(4), Harper Audio) HarperCollins Pubs.

Dance of Connection: How to Talk to Someone When You're Mad, Hurt, Scared, Frustrated, Insulted, Betrayed, or Desperate. unabr. ed. Harriet G. Lerner. Narrated by Barbara Caruso. 6 cass. (Running Time: 8 hrs.). 2002. 54.00 (978-1-4025-1332-9(1)) Recorded Bks.
Broaches the difficult task of communicating with people even when they have caused us pain.

Dance of Death see Danse Macabre

***Dance of Death.** Kate Sedley. 2010. 69.95 (978-1-4079-1304-9(2)); audio compact disk 84.95 (978-1-4079-1305-6(0)) Pub: Soundings Ltd GBR. Dist(s): Ulverscroft US

Dance of Death. abr. ed. Douglas Preston & Lincoln Child. Read by Rene Auberjonois. (Pendergast Ser.: No. 6). (ENG.). 2005. 14.98 (978-1-59483-241-3(2)) Pub: Hachet Audio. Dist(s): HachBkGrp

Dance of Death. abr. ed. Douglas Preston & Lincoln Child. Read by Rene Auberjonois. (Running Time: 6 hrs.). (ENG.). 2009. 49.98 (978-1-60788-049-3(0)) Pub: Hachet Audio. Dist(s): HachBkGrp

***Dance of Deception.** abr. ed. Harriet Lerner. Read by Harriet Lerner. (ENG.). 2004. (978-0-06-081363-5(6), Harper Audio); (978-0-06-077415-8(0), Harper Audio) HarperCollins Pubs.

Dance of Deception: Pretending & Truth-Telling in Women's Lives. abr. ed. Harriet Lerner. Read by Harriet Lerner. 2004. audio compact disk 22.00 (978-0-06-072664-5(4)) HarperCollins Pubs.

***Dance of Dreams.** unabr. ed. Nora Roberts. Read by Angela Dawe. (Running Time: 5 hrs.). 2011. 24.99 (978-1-4418-5725-5(7), 9781441857255, Brilliance MP3); 39.97 (978-1-4418-5726-2(5), 9781441857262, Brlnc Audio MP3 Lib); 39.97 (978-1-4418-5727-9(3), 9781441857279, BADLE); audio compact disk 24.99 (978-1-4418-5723-1(0), 9781441857231, Bril Audio CD Unabri); audio compact disk 69.97 (978-1-4418-5724-8(9), 9781441857248, BriAudCD Unabrid) Brilliance Audio.

***Dance of Intimacy.** abr. ed. Harriet Lerner. Read by Harriet Lerner. (ENG.). 2004. (978-0-06-077414-1(2), Harper Audio); (978-0-06-081362-8(8), Harper Audio) HarperCollins Pubs.

Dance of Intimacy. abr. ed. Harriet G. Lerner. Read by Harriet G. Lerner. 2 cass. (Running Time: 4 hrs.). 1997. 18.95 (978-1-55994-147-1(2), CPN 2144, Harper Audio) HarperCollins Pubs.

Dance of Life. Swami Amar Jyoti. 1 dolby cass. 1986. 9.95 (A-32) Truth Consciousness.
Flowing in rhythm & tune, life is free, joyful & creative.

Dance of Life. unabr. ed. Jennifer James. Read by Jennifer James. 2 cass. (Running Time: 2 hrs.). 14.95 set. (978-0-915423-57-6(X)) Jennifer J.

Dance of the Dollars: Psalm 112:5. Ed Young. 1991. 4.95 (978-0-7417-1857-0(X), 857) Win Walk.

Dance of the Dolphin. Ed. by Charles Beres & Randy Beres. 1 cass. (Running Time: 40 min.). 1991. 9.95 (978-1-883152-00-0(3)); 15.95 compact disc. (978-1-883152-01-7(1)) Amirra Pr.
Recording of dolphins in their natural habitat.

Dance of the Gods. Nora Roberts. Read by Dick Hill. (Circle Trilogy: Bk. 2). 2009. 69.99 (978-1-60775-689-7(7)) Find a World.

Dance of the Gods. abr. ed. Nora Roberts. Read by Dick Hill. (Running Time: 21600 sec.). (Circle Trilogy: Bk. 2). 2007. audio compact disk 14.99 (978-1-4233-0917-8(0), 9781423309178, BCD Value Price) Brilliance Audio.

Dance of the Gods. unabr. ed. Nora Roberts. Read by Dick Hill. (Running Time: 10 hrs.). (Circle Trilogy: Bk. 2). 2006. 39.25 (978-1-4233-0915-4(4), 9781423309154, BADLE); 24.95 (978-1-4233-0914-7(6), 9781423309147, BAD); 39.25 (978-1-4233-0913-0(8), 9781423309130, Brlnc Audio MP3 Lib); 82.25 (978-1-4233-0909-3(X), 9781423309093, BrilAudUnabridg); audio compact disk 97.25 (978-1-4233-0911-6(1), 9781423309116, BriAudCD Unabrid); audio compact disk 36.95 (978-1-4233-0910-9(3), 9781423309109, Bril Audio CD Unabri); audio compact disk 24.95 (978-1-4233-0912-3(X), 9781423309123, Brilliance MP3) Brilliance Audio.
Raised in a family of demon hunters, Blair Murphy has her own personal demons to fight - the father who trained, then abandoned her, and the fiancé who walked out on her after learning what she is. Now she finds herself training a sorcerer from 12th century Ireland, a witch from modern day New York, a scholar and a shape changer from the mythical land of Gaell, while trying to keep herself from staking the sixth of their circle and host: a vampire sired by Lilith, the vampire queen they've been charged with defeating on Samhain. No stranger to butt-kicking, Blair finds herself taking a good whipping when it comes to that handsome and flirtatious Geallian, Larkin. And a couple of run-ins with Lilith's right-hand gal gives Blair more than she reckoned for, mentally and physically. But will she be able to stay afloat long enough to defeat Lilith's loyal in pre-battle bouts? Or will she find herself falling for the one thing she vowed never to give in to again? If the vampires don't do her in, Larkin is certainly up to the task.

Dance of the Kora. Perf. by Moussa Kanoute. 1 cass.; 1 CD. 1998. 10.98 (978-1-56628-094-5(X), 72536); audio compact disk 15.98 CD. (978-1-56628-093-8(1), 71536D) MFLP CA.

Dance of the Light/ Rivers of Life. James Asher. 1 CD. (Running Time: 2 hrs. 17 min.). 2003. audio compact disk (978-1-891319-78-5(7)) Spring Hill CO.

Dance of the Money Bees: A Professional Speaks Frankly about Investing, unabr. ed. John Train. Narrated by James Hamilton. 5 cass. (Running Time: 7 hrs. 30 mins.). 1982. 44.00 (978-1-55690-132-4(1), 82010E7) Recorded Bks.
No dire predictions, no easy routes to instant riches. Instead a common-sense evaluation of unpredictable markets & advice on how to really put those money bees to work.

Dance of the Renaissance. Richard Searles & Gilbert Yslas. 1 cass. (J). (gr. k up). 9.98 (2256); audio compact disk 16.98 (D2256) MFLP CA.
The most popular dance tunes of 400 years ago come alive in these sparkling arrangements for guitars, recorders, oboe, harpsichord & more.

Dance of the Selves in Relationship. Hal Stone & Sidra Stone. 1 cass. (Mendocino Ser.). 1990. 10.95 (978-1-56557-006-1(5), T02) Delos Inc.
Will introduce you to the concept of "bonding patterns" & the Stones' revolutionary "no fault" approach to relationship. It explains how you can make each of your relationships an exciting & positive experience, using relationship itself, as a teacher, a healer & a guide.

Dance of the Thunder Dogs. unabr. ed. Kirk Mitchell. Read by Stefan Rudnicki. (Running Time: 13 hrs. 0 mins.). 2010. 29.95 (978-1-4417-1444-2(8)); 72.95 (978-1-4417-1440-4(5)); audio compact disk 105.00 (978-1-4417-1441-1(3)) Blckstn Audio.

Dance of the Thunderbolts. 2004. audio compact disk 14.95 (978-0-8258-5350-0(8)) Fischer Inc NY.

Dance of the Tiger. unabr. ed. Bjorn Kurten. Narrated by Jamie Hanes. 6 cass. (Running Time: 9 hrs.). (gr. 10 up). 1988. 51.00 (978-1-55690-133-1(X), 88610E7) Recorded Bks.
A recreation of the meeting 30,000 years ago between Neanderthal & Cro-Magnon man in Scandinavia.

Dance of the Tumblers. 2004. audio compact disk 14.95 (978-0-8258-5353-1(2)) Fischer Inc NY.

Dance of the Universe. Swami Amar Jyoti. 1 cass. 1978. 9.95 (R-11) Truth Consciousness.
The rhythmic movement of all creation. God's ecstatic dance. Coming in tune, dancing with the Lord.

Dance Party Fun. 1 CD. (Running Time: 36 min.). (ps up). 2001. audio compact disk 14.95 Kimbo Educ.
Popular music and easy-to-follow choreography for young listeners.

Dance Party Fun. 1 cass. (Running Time: 36 min.). (J). (ps up). 2001. 10.95 Kimbo Educ.

Dance Real Slow. unabr. ed. Michael Grant Jaffe. Read by Barrett Whitener. 6 cass. (Running Time: 6 hrs.). 1996. 36.00 (978-0-913369-61-6(6), 4293) Books on Tape.
Introduces Gordon Nash, a young lawyer whose wife abandons him & their four year-old son, Calvin.

Dance Sing & Listen. Esther Nelson & Bruce Haack. 1 cass. (Running Time: 45 min.). (J). (ps-3). 1987. 9.95 (978-0-945110-03-3(0), D701) Granny Pr.
Instructs children to follow directions given to music, with the goal of intensifying the listener's imagination & creativity through body movement.

Dance Sing & Listen Again. Esther Nelson & Bruce Haack. 1 cass. (Running Time: 45 min.). (J). (ps-3). 1987. 9.95 (978-0-945110-04-0(9), D702) Granny Pr.
Instructs children to follow directions given to music, with the goal of intensifying the listeners imagination & creativity through body movement.

Dance Sing & Listen Again & Again. Esther Nelson & Bruce Haack. 1 cass. (Running Time: 45 min.). (J). (ps-3). 1987. 9.95 (978-0-945110-05-7(7), D703) Granny Pr.

Dance, Sing, & Listen Series. Esther Nelson & Bruce Haack. 6 cass. (Running Time: 9 hrs.). (J). (ps-3). 59.70 (978-0-945110-12-5(X)) Granny Pr.
The highly lauded series, now on cassette, integrates music & movement with the spellbinding tales of Esther Nelson & Bruce Haack's magical synthesized sounds.

Dance the Spiral. Danielle Jackson. 6 cass. (Running Time: 4 hrs. 40 mins.). (Meditation Tapes Ser.: Vol. 1). 1995. pap. bk. & wbk. ed. 79.95 (978-0-9700763-0-4(4), 2256) Dance The Spiral.
Address many areas of spirituality.

Dance to the Music. Esther Nelson & Bruce Haack. Read by Esther Nelson & Bruce Haack. 1 cass. (Running Time: 43 min.). (Dance Sing & Listen Ser.). (J). (ps-3). 1989. 9.95 (978-0-945110-10-1(3)) Granny Pr.
Guides listeners through a new set of wacky activities set to their wonderful electomic music: A square dance for fingers, a kissing, nose-sniffing, tongue-clicking "New Macdonald's Farm," an utterly original version of Musical Chairs, & more.

Dance to the Music of Time, Vol. 1. unabr. collector's ed. Anthony Powell. Read by David Case. 11 cass. (Running Time: 16 hrs. 30 min.). 1996. 88.00 (978-0-7366-3458-6(4), 4102) Books on Tape.
This wonderful saga, recently re-issued in its entirety by the University of Chicago Press, combines 12 intricate notably detailed novels in one beautifully realized chronicle. Powell's remarkable re-creation of English upper-middle class life from the First World War through the sixties flows through the vision of his appealing narrator.

Dance to the Music of Time, Vol. 2. unabr. collector's ed. Anthony Powell. Read by David Case. 10 cass. (Running Time: 15 hrs.). 1996. 80.00 (978-0-7366-3459-5(2), 4103) Books on Tape.
Re-creation of English upper-middle class life from the First World War through the Sixties.

Dance to the Music of Time, Vol. 3. unabr. collector's ed. Anthony Powell. Read by David Case. 11 cass. (Running Time: 16 hrs. 30 min. per cass.). 1996. 88.00 (978-0-7366-3460-1(6), 4104) Books on Tape.
Includes: Casanova's Chinese Restaurant; The Kindly Ones.

Dance to the Music of Time, Vol. 4. unabr. collector's ed. Anthony Powell. Read by David Case. 10 cass. (Running Time: 15 hrs.). 1996. 80.00 (978-0-7366-3461-8(4), 4105) Books on Tape.
Includes: The Valley of Bones; The Soldier's Art.

Dance to the Music of Time, Vol. 5. unabr. collector's ed. Anthony Powell. Read by David Case. 11 cass. (Running Time: 16 hrs. 30 min.). 1996. 88.00 (978-0-7366-3462-5(2), 4106) Books on Tape.
Includes: The Military Philosophers; Books Do Furnish a Room.

Dance to the Music of Time, Vol. 6. unabr. collector's ed. Anthony Powell. Read by David Case. 12 cass. (Running Time: 18 hrs.). 1996. 96.00 (978-0-7366-3463-2(0), 4107) Books on Tape.
Includes: Temporary Kings; Hearing Secret Harmonies.

Dance to the Piper. unabr. ed. Nora Roberts. Read by Marie Caliendo. (Running Time: 7 hrs.). (O'Hurleys Ser.). 2010. 14.99 (978-1-4418-3021-0(9), 9781441830210, Brilliance MP3); 39.97 (978-1-4418-3022-7(7), 9781441830227, Brlnc Audio MP3 Lib); 39.97 (978-1-4418-3023-4(5), 9781441830234, BADLE); audio compact disk 24.99 (978-1-4418-3019-7(7), 9781441830197, Bril Audio CD Unabri); audio compact disk 79.97 (978-1-4418-3020-3(0), 9781441830203, BriAudCD Unabrid) Brilliance Audio.

***Dance to the Piper.** unabr. ed. Nora Roberts. Read by Marie Caliendo. (Running Time: 7 hrs.). (O'Hurleys Ser.). 2010. audio compact disk 14.99 (978-1-61106-124-6(5), 9781611061246, BCD Value Price) Brilliance Audio.

Dance upon the Air. abr. ed. Nora Roberts. Read by Sandra Burr. 4 CDs. (Running Time: 4 hrs.). (Three Sisters Island Trilogy: Vol. 1). 2004. audio compact disk 14.99 (978-1-59355-321-0(8), 1593553218, BCD Value Price) Brilliance Audio.

Dance upon the Air. unabr. ed. Nora Roberts. Read by Sandra Burr. 1 MP3-CD. (Running Time: 9 hrs.). (Three Sisters Island Trilogy: Vol. 1). 2004. 39.25 (978-1-59335-564-7(5), 1593355645, Brlnc Audio MP3 Lib) Brilliance Audio.
Steeped in history, romance, and legend, Dance Upon the Air is an unforgettable tale of friendship, fate and the mysterious ways of the heart . . . When Nell Channing arrives on charming Three Sisters Island, she believes that she's finally found refuge from her abusive husband - and from the terrifying life she fled so desperately eight months ago . . . But even in this quiet, peaceful place, Nell never feels entirely at ease. Careful to conceal her true identity, she takes a job as a cook at the island bookstore café - and begins to explore her feelings for the island sheriff, Zack Todd. But there is a part of herself she can never reveal to him - for she must continue to guard her secrets if she wants to keep the past at bay. One careless word, one misplaced confidence, and the new life she's so carefully created could shatter completely. Just as Nell starts to wonder if she'll ever be able to break free of her fear, she realizes that the island suffers from a terrible curse - one that can only be broken by the descendants of the Three Sisters, the witches who settled the island back in 1692. And now, with the help of two other strong, gifted women - and the nightmares of the past haunting her every step - she must find the power to save her home, her love . . . and herself . .

Dance upon the Air. unabr. ed. Nora Roberts. Read by Sandra Burr. (Running Time: 9 hrs.). (Three Sisters Island Trilogy: Vol. 1). 2004. 39.25 (978-1-59710-164-6(8), 1597101648, BADLE); 24.95 (978-1-59710-165-3(6), 1597101656, BAD) Brilliance Audio.

Dance upon the Air. unabr. ed. Nora Roberts. Read by Sandra Burr. 8 CDs. (Running Time: 32400 sec.). (Three Sisters Island Trilogy: Vol. 1). 2007. audio compact disk 92.25 (978-1-4233-3410-1(8), 9781423334101, BriAudCD Unabrid); audio compact disk 34.95 (978-1-4233-3409-5(4), 9781423334095, Bril Audio CD Unabri) Brilliance Audio.

Dance upon the Air. unabr. ed. Nora Roberts. Read by Sandra Burr. 1 MP3-CD. (Running Time: 9 hrs.). (Three Sisters Island Trilogy: Vol. 1). 2004. 24.95 (978-1-59335-050-5(3), 1593350503) Soulmate Audio Bks.

Dance While You Can. unabr. ed. Susan Lewis. Narrated by Barbara Rosenblat & Simon Prebble. 9 cass. (Running Time: 12 hrs. 45 mins.). 1991. 78.00 (978-1-55690-135-5(6), 91305E7) Recorded Bks.
For Elizabeth Sorrill, the job at the private school for boys was planned as an escape: from her past, from London, from loneliness. It became the discovery of Alexander. But she knew their passionate, consuming affair was impossible.

Dance with Dragons. unabr. ed. George R. R. Martin. (Song of Ice & Fire Ser.: Bk. 5). (ENG.). 2012. audio compact disk 50.00 (978-0-7393-7597-6(0), Random AudioBks) Pub: Random Audio Pubg. Dist(s): Random

Dance with Me. abr. ed. Luanne Rice. Read by Karen Ziemba. 2004. 15.95 (978-0-7435-3927-2(3)) Pub: S&S Audio. Dist(s): S and S Inc

Dance with Rosie. unabr. ed. Patricia Reilly Giff. Narrated by C. J. Critt. 1 cass. (Running Time: 1 hr.). (Ballet Slippers Ser.). (gr. 1 up). 1998. 10.00 (978-0-7887-2059-8(7), 95412E7) Recorded Bks.
When Rosie goes to enroll in Miss Deirdre's ballet class, the class is full! How can she join the ballet lessons?.

Dance with the Ego. Stephen R. Schwartz. 3 cass. 28.00 Set. Riverrun Piermont.

Dance Without End. abr. ed. Laura Simms. Read by Laura Simms. 2 cass. (Running Time: 2 hrs.). Dramatization. (Myth & the Natural World Ser.). 1994. pap. bk. 16.95 (978-0-939643-59-2(6), 3594, NrthWrd Bks) TandN Child.
A collection of early tales and ancient sacred myths about the origins of existence from Aztec, Inuit, Scandinavian, African, New Zealand and the Native American cultures.

Dance Writing for Classical Ballet: Read & Write Ballet in Sutton Dancewriting. Valerie J. Sutton. 8 Audio Cassettes. (Running Time: 8 hrs.). (C). 1978. ring bd. 120.00 (978-0-914336-05-1(3)) Ctr Sutton Movement.

Danceland. 1 cass. (Running Time: 50 min.). (Jumpstart Ser.). (J). (ps-2). 1999. 20.00 (978-1-893601-51-2(X), JSDPP-2) Sensory Res.
Creative music & song games introduce children to an imaginary world filled with dance rhythms & activites for every mood & all ability levels.

Danceland: Fun Songs & Activities to Improve Sensory Skills. 2nd ed. Kristen Fitz Taylor & Cheryl McDonald. Contrib. by Aubrey Lande. (ps-k). 2008. 19.95 (978-1-931615-04-4(7)) Sensory Res.

***Danceland: Songames & Activities to Improve Sensory Skills.** Kristen Fitz Taylor et al. (ENG.). 2010. audio compact disk 21.95 (978-1-935567-10-3(1)) Pub: Sensory Res. Dist(s): IngramPubServ

Dancer: A Novel. Colum McCann. 9 vols. 2004. 79.95 (978-0-7927-3144-3(1), CSL 634, Chivers Sound Lib); audio compact disk 99.95 (978-0-7927-3145-0(X), SLD 634, Chivers Sound Lib) AudioGO.

Dancer: A Novel. unabr. ed. Colum McCann. Read by Moira Driscoll et al. 9 cass. (Running Time: 13 hrs.). 2004. 36.95 (978-1-57270-373-5(3)); audio compact disk 44.95 (978-1-57270-374-2(1)) Pub: Audio Partners. Dist(s): PerseuPGW

Dancers in Mourning. unabr. ed. Margery Allingham. Read by Francis Matthews. 8 cass. (Running Time: 12 hrs.). (Albert Campion Ser.: Bk. 9). 2000. 59.95 (978-0-7451-4011-7(4), CAB 708) Pub: Chivers Audio Bks GBR. Dist(s): AudioGO
When Albert Campion is called to investigate practical jokes being played on performer Jimmy Sutane, it's no laughing matter when people start turing up dead. As the death toll rises and tension mounts, the imperturbable Campion loses his heart when he falls in love with Jimmy Sutane's wife.

Dancers in the Sunset Sky: The Musings of a Bird Hunter. abr. ed. Robert F. Jones. Narrated by Michael Kramer. (Running Time: 16200 sec.). 2006. audio compact disk 28.00 (978-1-933309-13-2(X)) Pub: A Media Intl. Dist(s): Natl Bk Netwk

Dances for Little People. 1 cass. (Running Time: 1 hr.). (J). 2001. pap. bk. 10.95 (KIM 0860C); 11.95 (KIM 0860) Kimbo Educ.
Simple folk dances & patterns. Going to Boston, Bow, Bow, Belinda, Dance to the Rhythm of your Name, Move the Circle 'Round & more. Includes guide.

Dances in a Line. Instructed by Rudy Franklin. 1 cass . (Running Time: 1 hr.). (J). 2001. pap. bk. 10.95 (KEA 1147C); pap. bk. & pupil's gde. ed. 14.95 (KEA 1147CD) Kimbo Educ.
The line forms here for fun! Easy to do dances without partners is great for co-ed classes & a hit with seniors too! Includes The Bus Stop, Amos Moses, Bad, Walk & the 12th Street Rag. Includes dance instructional guide.

Dances of Indonesia w/Audio CD & Dance Demo DVD. Vicki Corona. Created by Vicki Corona. Merelika Shamash. (Celebrate the Cultures Ser.: 6-12C). 1989. pap. bk. 32.95 (978-1-58513-155-6(5)) Dance Fantasy.

Dances of Indonesia w/Music CD, 6-12A. 2nd ed. Vicki Corona. Queenie Bayantagahi. (Celebrate the Cultures Ser.: 6-12A). 2004. pap. bk. 24.95 (978-1-58513-124-2(5)) Dance Fantasy.

Dances of Kuwait w/Music CD. Vicki Corona. (ENG.). 2000. audio compact disk 24.95 (978-1-58513-106-8(7)) Dance Fantasy.

Dances of Melanesia Booklet w/Music CD. Vicki Corona. Prod. by Vicki Corona. (Celebrate the Cultures Ser.: 2-35A). 2004. pap. bk. 24.95 (978-1-58513-113-6(X)) Dance Fantasy.

Dances of Switzerland w/Music CD. Vicki Corona. (Celebrate the Cultures Ser.: 8-12A). 2004. 24.95 (978-1-58513-123-5(7)) Dance Fantasy.

Dances of Three Centuries: Recorder Play-along Pack. Created by Hal Leonard Corporation Staff. 2006. pap. bk. 24.98 (978-1-59615-336-3(9), 1596153369) Pub: Music Minus. Dist(s): H Leonard

Dances with Trout. John Gierach. Read by John Gierach. 2 cass. (Running Time: 2 hrs. 45 min.). 1994. 16.95 (978-0-939643-55-4(3), 3582, NrthWrd Bks) TandN Child.
From Texas to Scotland and back to Alaska. Sporting adventures in the natural world.

Dances with Wolves. unabr. ed. Michael Blake. Read by Michael Blake. (Running Time: 7 hrs. 40 min.). 29.95 (978-0-9627387-2-2(7)) Seven Wolves.
This is the story of John J. Dunbar, a young cavalry lieutenant who finds himself at the edge of the American Frontier in the year 1863. Though circumstance has left him completely alone at one of the Army's most isolated outposts, Dunbar is entranced by the wild, open country surrounding him. The Comanches have returned as they always have to their favorite summer hunting grounds. Thus the stage is set for one man's classic adventure with the free people of the plains in a time long past...the time of Dances with Wolves.

Dances with Wolves: An American Metaphor. Fred Gustafson. Read by Fred Gustafson. 2 cass. (Running Time: 1 hr. 40 min.). 1993. 16.95 set. (978-0-7822-0424-7(4), 507) C G Jung IL.
This book & film Dances with Wolves has touched the hearts & imaginations of many North American peoples - Indian & non-Indian alike. The soul's passion to reconnect to the earth & to one's indigenous roots is not only the core of our collective grief but also the hope of renewal for this earth & for ourselves as part of it. Using the film's story as a reference, Jungian analyst Fred Gustafson explores our vital need to connect Western forms of spirituality with the earth in an attempt to find the balance so desperately needed in both the inner & outer ecosystems. Includes an insightful discussion of many contemporary Native American issues.

Dancin' in the Spirit II. 1 cass., 1 CD. 10.98 (978-1-57908-329-8(3), 14054); audio compact disk 15.98 CD. (978-1-57908-328-1(5)) Platinm Enter.

Dancin' Magic. Read by Joanie Bartels. Prod. by David Wohlstadter & Ellen Wohlstadter. 1 cass. (Magic Ser.). (J). (gr. k-4). 1991. pap. bk. 9.95 (978-1-881225-08-9(9)) Discov Music.
Get ready to dance up a storm to rock 'n' roll hits, classic dance tunes...even the polka! Children will enjoy hopping, skipping, twisting, & singin' along with this swingin' & swayin' collection!.

Dancin' Magic. Read by Joanie Bartels. 1 cass. (J). (ps-7). 9.98 (2113); audio compact disk 17.98 CD. (D2113) MFLP CA.
With a bop-bop-shoo-bop, Joanie Bartels' newest recording starts off with a "Peppermint Twist" that inspires young ones to roll up the rugs & rock 'n' roll all over the living room.

Dancin' Magic. Joanie Bartels. 1 cass., 1 CD. (J). 7.98 (DIS 4408); 7.98 (DIS 4408); audio compact disk 12.98 CD. (DIS 4408) NewSound.
The Peppermint Twist; Rocking Robin; Limbo Rock; La Bamba; The Loco-Motion; Dance, Dance, Dance; The Polka Dot Polka; Dancin' on the Ceiling; The Martian Hop; Barefootin'; Hokey Pokey; Dinosaur Rock'n Roll; & Happy Feet.

Dancin' with Vicki Jo Boyer. Instructed by Vicki Jo Boyer. 1 cass., 1 CD. 15.00 (KIM 4065C); audio compact disk 18.00 CD Incl. manual. (KIM4065CD) Kimbo Educ.
All new original jazz & tap routines with a big band sound. Show-stopping routines set to Hard Hearted Hanna, Shuffle off to Buffalo, Blues in the Night, 42nd Street, Hurray for Hollywood, Sing, Sing, Sing & more.

Dancing at the Harvest. Ray Makeever. 2004. audio compact disk 16.98 (978-0-8006-5595-2(8)) Augsburg Fortress.
Written in a variety of popular musical styles, these songs can be used in worship and on other occasions. The collection is arranged according to the seasons of the church and themes of Christian life.

Dancing at the Holiday Ball. Chaitania Hein. Read by Chaitania Hein. Read by Bob Kechley. 1 cass. (Running Time: 60 min.). (Dance Impulse with Chaitania Ser.). (J). (ps-2). 1988. 9.99 (978-0-929676-02-9(5)) Alim Azim Prodns.
Storytelling with music & creative dance instruction.

Dancing at the Rascal Fair. unabr. collector's ed. Ivan Doig. Read by Paul Shay. 13 cass. (Running Time: 19 hrs. 30 min.). 1989. 104.00 (978-0-7366-1490-0(7), 2366) Books on Tape.
A tale of the uncertainties of friendship, of brutal winters & battles of will & of two loves: one delightful & heartbreaking in its intensity, the other born of sadness, equally moving in its stoical devotion.

Dancing Bear. unabr. ed. James Crumley. Read by Rob McQuay. 8 cass. (Running Time: 8 hrs.). 1997. 48.00 (978-0-7366-3819-7(9), 4487) Books on Tape.
Sarah Weddington is stirring painful memories in Milo. She offers him his first case since he abandoned his private practice.

Dancing Child: Pre-Ballet (Ages 5-7) Instructed by Constance Reynolds. 1 cass. (J). (gr. k-2). 15.00 incl. guide. (KIM 1019C) Kimbo Educ.
Constance Reynolds presents simple barre & centre work, adagio, allegro, & movements on the diagonal.

Dancing Cowboy. John R. Erickson. Read by John R. Erickson. (Running Time: 4560 sec.). (Hank the Cowdog Ser.). (ENG.). (J). 2009. audio compact disk 12.99 (978-1-59188-686-0(4)) Maverick Bks.

Dancing Floor see Dancing Floor

***Dancing Floor.** abr. ed. Barbara Michaels, pseud. Read by Barbara Rosenblat.Tr. of Dancing Floor. (ENG.). 2005. (978-0-06-088893-0(8), Harper Audio); (978-0-06-088894-7(6), Harper Audio) HarperCollins Pubs.

Dancing Floor. unabr. ed. Barbara Michaels, pseud. Narrated by Barbara Rosenblat. 8 cass. (Running Time: 11 hrs.).Tr. of Dancing Floor. 1998. 75.00 (978-0-7887-0806-0(6), 94955E7) Recorded Bks.
Discovering her ancestral ties to 17th-century Troytan House, a modern American tourist is compelled to discover the mysterious connection between a bewitching maze, a missing child & a house fire.

***Dancing from the Heart Cd.** 2nd rev. ed. Cross. (ENG.). 2010. audio compact disk 67.50 (978-0-7575-7629-4(X)) Kendall-Hunt.

Dancing Granny: And Other African Folktales. unabr. ed. Ashley Bryan. Read by Ashley Bryan. 1 cass. (Running Time: 90 min.). (J). 1985. 9.95 (978-1-55994-046-7(8), CPN 1765) HarperCollins Pubs.
Ashley Bryan performs his retellings of African folktales.

Dancing Healer: A Doctor's Journey of Healing with Native Americans. abr. ed. Carl A. Hammerschlag. Read by Lisa J. Cohen. 2 cass. (Running Time: 1 hr. 57 min.). 1995. bk. 29.95 Set. (978-1-889166-00-1(6)) Turtle Isl Pr.
In Carl's unique storytelling style he tells of his journey with Native Americans.

Dancing Healer Vol. 1: A Doctor's Journey of Healing with Native Americans. abr. ed. Carl A. Hammerschlag. Read by Lisa J. Cohen. 1 cass. (Running Time: 55 min.). 1995. 29.95 (978-1-889166-01-8(4)) Turtle Isl Pr.

Dancing Healer Vol. 2: A Doctor's Journey of Healing with Native Americans. abr. ed. Carl A. Hammerschlag. Read by Lisa J. Cohen. 1 cass. (Running Time: 62 min.). 1995. 29.95 (978-1-889166-02-5(2)) Turtle Isl Pr.

Dancing in Cadillac Light. Kimberly Willis Holt. Read by Kimberly J. Brown. 3 vols. (Running Time: 4 hrs. 16 mins.). (J). (gr. 4-7). 2004. pap. bk. 36.00 (978-0-8072-2095-5(7), Listening Lib) Random Audio Pubg.

Dancing in Cadillac Light. unabr. ed. Kimberly Willis Holt. Read by Kimberly J. Brown. 3 cass. (Running Time: 4 hrs. 16 mins.). (J). (gr. 4-7). 2004. 30.00 (978-0-8072-8872-6(1), Listening Lib) Random Audio Pubg.

***Dancing in My Nightgown: The Rhythms of Widowhood.** Betty Auchard. Read by Betty Auchard. (ENG.). 2010. audio compact disk 14.95 (978-1-935043-24-9(2)) Pub: Stephens Press. Dist(s): Midpt Trade

Dancing in My Nuddy-Pants. Louise Rennison & Stina Nielsen. 3 cass. (Running Time: 4 hrs. 45 min.). (Confessions of Georgia Nicolson Ser.: No. 4). 2003. (978-1-4025-4586-3(X)) Recorded Bks.
New York Times best-selling author Louise Rennison delivers another uproarious chapter from the life of teenaged British wondergirl Georgia Nicolson, the irrepressible star of Angus, Thongs and Full-Frontal Snogging (RB# 96771). Georgia has chosen Robbie the Sex God over Dave the Laugh as her permanent snogging partner. But has she made the right choice.

Dancing in My Nuddy-Pants. unabr. ed. Louise Rennison & Louise Rennison. 3 cass. (Running Time: 4 hrs. 45 mins.). (Confessions of Georgia Nicolson Ser.: No. 4). 2004. 14.99 (978-1-4025-4602-0(5), 70094) Recorded Bks.
From the life of teenaged British wondergirl Georgia Nicolson, the irrepressible star of Angus, Thongs and Full-Frontal Snogging (RB# 96771). Georgia has chosen Robbie the Sex God over Dave the Laugh as her permanent snogging partner. But has she made the right choice?.

Dancing in Stillness see Sister Bernetta Quinn & W. R. Moses

Dancing in the Arms of God: Finding Intimacy & Fulfillment by Following His Lead. Connie Neal. 2 cass. (Running Time: 60 min. per cass.). 1995. 14.99 (978-0-310-20419-0(4)) Zondervan.
A woman's true fulfillment cannot come from a man, a career, or even from within. It comes from a dynamic relationship with God who makes dreams come true: her dreams for life & God's dreams for her.

Dancing in the Dark. Mary Jane Clark. Read by Eliza Foss. (KEY News Ser.: Bk. 8). 2005. 17.95 (978-1-59397-720-7(4)) Pub: Macmill Audio. Dist(s): Macmillan

Dancing in the Dark. unabr. ed. Mary Jane Clark. 6 cass. (Running Time: 25140 sec.). (KEY News Ser.: Bk. 8). 2005. 54.95 (978-0-7927-3672-1(9), CSL 816); audio compact disk 79.95 (978-0-7927-3673-8(7), SLD 816) AudioGO.

Dancing in the Dark. unabr. ed. Stuart M. Kaminsky. Narrated by Mark Hammer. 5 cass. (Running Time: 6 hrs. 75 min.). (Toby Peters Mystery Ser.: No. 19). Rental 13.50 Set. (94795) Recorded Bks.

Dancing in the Dark. unabr. ed. Stuart M. Kaminsky. Narrated by Mark Hammer. 5 cass. (Running Time: 6 hrs. 45 mins.). (Toby Peters Mystery Ser.: No. 19). 1996. 44.00 (978-0-7887-0621-9(7), 94795E7) Recorded Bks.
Private eye Toby finds himself dancing with Betty Grable & Rita Hayworth as he desperately tries to unmask a fast-stepping killer.

Dancing in the Dark. unabr. ed. Maureen Lee. Read by Clare Higgins. 10 cass. (Running Time: 15 hrs.). 2000. 84.95 (978-0-7540-0467-7(8), CAB 1890) Pub: Chivers Audio Bks GBR. Dist(s): AudioGO
Millie Cameron dreads sorting through the belongings of her aunt Flo, who has recently died. But when she arrives in Flo's basement flat, Millie's interest is awakened. As Millie begins sorting through her aunt's collection of photographs, letters & newspaper clippings, Millie makes a startling discovery about herself.

***Dancing in the Dark: A Cultural History of the Great Depression.** unabr. ed. Morris Dickstein. (Running Time: 21 hrs.). 2010. audio compact disk 39.95 (978-1-4417-6252-8(3)) Blckstn Audio.

***Dancing in the Dark: A Cultural History of the Great Depression.** unabr. ed. Morris Dickstein. Read by Malcolm Hillgartner. (Running Time: 21 hrs.). 2010. 44.95 (978-1-4417-6253-5(1)); audio compact disk 123.00 (978-1-4417-6251-1(5)) Blckstn Audio.

***Dancing in the Dark (Part 1 Of 2) A Cultural History of the Great Depression.** unabr. ed. Morris Dickstein. Read by Malcolm Hillgartner. (Running Time: 21 hrs.). 2010. 59.95 (978-1-4417-6250-4(7)) Blckstn Audio.

Dancing in the Streets: A History of Collective Joy. unabr. ed. Barbara Ehrenreich. Read by Pam Ward. (Running Time: 34200 sec.). 2007. 27.95 (978-0-7861-4794-6(6)); 72.95 (978-0-7861-4797-7(0)); audio compact disk 27.95 (978-0-7861-6245-1(7)); audio compact disk 29.95 (978-0-7861-7203-0(7)); audio compact disk 90.00 (978-0-7861-6240-6(6)) Blckstn Audio.

Dancing in Tune with the Lord. unabr. ed. Swami Amar Jyoti. 1 cass. (Satsangs of Swami Amar Jyoti Ser.). (C). 1997. 9.95 (M-104) Truth Consciousness.
Coming in tune with the Lord for transformation & freedom. Merging, surrender to the Lord. Our loving, open acceptance is needed.

Dancing Men see Return of Sherlock Holmes

Dancing on Snowflakes, Set. unabr. ed. Malcolm Ross. Read by Marie McCarthy. 10 cass. (Running Time: 13 hrs. 15 mins.). 1999. 98.95 (978-1-85903-269-5(9)) Pub: Magna Story GBR. Dist(s): Ulverscroft US
Hoping to put Katya O'Barry beyond reach of an unsuitable young man, her parents pack her off to Stockholm in the spring of 1899. Instead, they have given a repressed & chaperoned Victorian miss her first taste of freedom. Befriended by a young man of mischievous intentions & a Russian Grand Duchess, Katya is soon the proud possession of a real job at one of Stockholm's best hotel. Setting out to experience the whole of life, Katya learns about independence, responsibility & about love.

Dancing on the Brink of the World: A Star Waltz in the Keys of Canvas, Music, & Myth. Sven Eberlein. Illus. by Evelyn Terranova. Frwd. by Steven Forrest. 2009. pap. bk. 25.00 (978-0-9794598-0-1(X)) Tuber Creations.

Dancing on the Head of a Pin. unabr. ed. Thomas E. Sniegoski. Read by Luke Daniels. (Running Time: 8 hrs.). (Remy Chandler Ser.). 2010. 24.99 (978-1-4418-1760-0(3), 9781441817600, Brilliance MP3); 24.99 (978-1-4418-1762-4(X), 9781441817624, BAD); 39.97 (978-1-4418-1761-7(1), 9781441817617, Brlnc Audio MP3 Lib); 39.97 (978-1-4418-1763-1(8), 9781441817631, BADLE); audio compact disk 29.99 (978-1-4418-1758-7(1), 9781441817587, Bril Audio CD Unabri); audio compact disk 89.97 (978-1-4418-1759-4(X), 9781441817594, BriAudCD Unabrid) Brilliance Audio.

Dancing on the Moon: Out of This World Fun! Tr. by John Archambault & David Plummer. 1 cass. (Running Time: 1 hr.). (J). (ps-4). 2000. 10.98 (978-1-57471-754-9(5), YM129 CN); audio compact disk 13.98 (978-1-57471-755-6(3)) Youngheart Mus.
Children's educational music.

Dancing on the Sand. Kathleen M. Hollenbeck. (J). (ps-2). 2001. bk. 19.95 (SP 4017C) Kimbo Educ.
A sensational story of an Atlantic blue crab. Includes book.

Dancing on Your Destiny. Don Nori. 1 cass. 1996. 10.99 (978-1-56043-711-6(1)); 14.99 (978-1-56043-724-6(3)) Destiny Image Pubs.

Dancing on Your Destiny. Don Nori. (Running Time: 51 minutes, 58 seconds). 2007. 14.99 (978-1-4245-0700-9(6)) Tre Med Inc.

Dancing Outside the Box: Consciously Creating Your Destiny. abr. ed. Marlene Chism. Read by Marlene Chism. 1 cass. (Running Time: 1 hr. 7 mins.). 2000. 14.95 (978-0-9679411-0-3(5)) ICARE.
Play the "why-not" game & say your ABC's to discover patterns that keep you straddling the fence or tucked in your box. Use the power of conscious choice to get F.A.T. out of your life so you can consciously create your destiny.

Dancing Princesses. (J). (CDL5 1331) HarperCollins Pubs.

Dancing 'Round the World: Songs for Movement & Dance! Pamela Ott. 1 cass. 14.95 (978-1-886655-11-9(1), 85080) Corwin Pr.

Dancing 'Round the World: Songs for Movement & Dance! Pamela Ott. 1 CD. (Teaching Tunes Ser.). 2000. audio compact disk 14.95 (978-0-8039-6874-5(4), 85079) Corwin Pr.

Dancing Seagull: Stories for the Young at Heart. Mitchell Reese. Perf. by Mitchell Reese. 1 cass. (Running Time: 42 mins.). (YA). 1999. audio compact disk 14.98 (978-1-893967-13-7(1), EK5011) Emphasis Ent.
Accomplished Australian storyteller serves up a collection of original & adapted tales. Recorded at Baulkham Hill Studies in Australia.

Dancing Shoes. Colin Granger. (J). 1989. 14.95 (978-0-435-27819-9(3), DeltPubng) Delta Systems.

Dancing with Fire. Short Stories. Jay O'Callahan. 1 CD. (Running Time: 1 hr. 1 min.). Dramatization. (Jay O'Callahan's Short Stories Collection). 1998. audio compact disk 15.00 (978-1-877954-27-6(6)) Pub: Artana Prodns. Dist(s): Yellow Moon
Includes: "My Wild Beauty," "Max," "What Laura Couldn't Say," "Head First," "Night Fire," "Fallin," & NPR Versions of "Father Joe," & "The Dance".

Dancing with Fire. Short Stories. Jay O'Callahan. Perf. by Jay O'Callahan. 1 cass. (Running Time: 1 hr. 10 min.). Dramatization. (Jay O'Callahan's Short Stories Collection). 1998. 10.00 (978-1-877954-26-9(8)) Pub: Artana Prodns. Dist(s): Yellow Moon

***Dancing with Max: A Mother & Son Who Broke Free.** Zondervan Publishing Staff & Emily Colson. Told to Charles Colson. (Running Time: 6 hrs. 35 mins. 24 sec.). (ENG.). 2010. 16.99 (978-0-310-41249-6(8)) Zondervan.

Dancing with the Dragon. unabr. ed. Joe Weber. Read by Dick Hill. 7 cass. (Running Time: 10 hrs.). 2002. 32.95 (978-1-58788-954-7(4), 1587889544, BAU); 78.25 (978-1-58788-955-4(2), 1587889552, Unabridge Lib Edns) Brilliance Audio.
Scott Dalton and Jackie Sullivan, intelligence specialists and former military pilots, are called in to investigate the mysterious mid-air destruction of two American fighter planes. As they proceed, they are surprised to learn that the loss of two navy jets is just the latest in a series of seemingly unrelated, and previously unexplained losses of American combat aircraft. It soon becomes clear that the culprit is China, using a ship-mounted laser to target American aircraft. Relations between the two global powers deteriorate, ultimately to the point of armed conflict. As the United States begins to achieve decisive battlefield success, the finger of the Chinese president is poised over the nuclear button.

Dancing with the Dragon. unabr. ed. Joe Weber. Read by Dick Hill. (Running Time: 10 hrs.). 2005. 39.25 (978-1-59600-787-1(7), 9781596007871, BADLE); 24.95 (978-1-59600-786-4(9), 9781596007864, BAD); audio compact disk 24.95 (978-1-59600-784-0(2), 9781596007840, Brilliance MP3); audio compact disk 39.25 (978-1-59600-785-7(0), 9781596007857, Brlnc Audio MP3 Lib) Brilliance Audio.

Dancing with the Ghosts of the Dead. Tony Moffeit. Read by Tony Moffeit. Ed. by A. Jeanne Ronzettlemoyer. 1 cass. (Running Time: 60 min.). 1988. 4.50 (978-0-932593-14-6(3)) Black Bear.
Poetry from live readings.

Dancing with the Indians. Angela Shelf Medearis. Illus. by Samuel Byrd. 11 vols. (Running Time: 5 mins.). 2000. pap. bk. 18.95 (978-1-59519-248-6(4)); pap. bk. 39.95 (978-1-59519-249-3(2)); 9.95 (978-1-59112-027-8(6)); audio compact disk 12.95 (978-1-59519-247-9(6)) Live Oak Media.

Dancing with the Indians. Angela Shelf Medearis. Read by Constance Marshall. Illus. by Samuel Byrd. 1 cass. (Running Time: 5 mins.). (J). (gr. 1-6). 2000. bk. 24.95 (978-0-87499-333-2(4)); pap. bk. 16.95 (978-0-87499-332-5(6)) Pub: Live Oak Media. Dist(s): AudioGO
A young black girl recounts her family's annual participation in the ceremonies of the Seminole tribe that during the Civil War, some seventy years earlier, had given sanctuary to her grandfather, an escaped slave.

Dancing with the Indians, Grades 1-6. unabr. ed. Angela Shelf Medearis. Read by Constance Marshall. Illus. by Samuel Byrd. 14 vols. (Running Time: 5 mins.). (J). 2000. pap. bk. & tchr. ed. 37.95 Reading Chest. (978-0-87499-334-9(2)) Live Oak Media.
A recounting by a young black girl of her family's annual visit to & participation in the ceremonies of the Seminole tribe that during the Civil War, some seventy years earlier, had given sanctuary to her grandfather, an escaped slave.

Dancing with the Moon; Merging Worlds. Jonathan Murro & Ann Ree Colton. 1 cass. 7.95 A R Colton Fnd.

Dancing with the Two-Headed Tigress. Tina Biswas. Read by Aileen Gonsalves. 7 cass. (Running Time: 9 hrs. 20 mins.). (Isis Cassettes Ser.). 2006. 61.95 (978-0-7531-3663-8(5)) Pub: ISIS Lrg Prnt GBR. Dist(s): Ulverscroft US

Dancing with the Virgins. Stephen Booth. Read by Terry Wale. 12 cass. (Sound Ser.). (J). 2002. 94.95 (978-1-84283-183-0(6)) Pub: ISIS Lrg Prnt GBR. Dist(s): Ulverscroft US

Dancing with Tigers Program. Created by Janet E. Lapp. 6 cass. 2002. 39.95 (978-1-885365-40-8(3)) Demeter Pr.

Dancing with Your Shadow. Laurie Brady. Read by Laurie Brady. 1 cass. (Running Time: 90 min.). 1994. 8.95 (1150) Am Fed Astrologers.

Dancing Wu Li Masters. unabr. ed. Gary Zukav. Read by Grover Gardner. 8 cass. (Running Time: 11 hrs.). 2001. 29.95 (978-0-7366-5679-5(0)) Books on Tape.
The bible for those who are curious about the mind-expanding discoveries of advanced physics, but who have no scientific background.

Dancing Wu Li Masters. unabr. collector's ed. Gary Zukav. Read by Grover Gardner. 8 cass. (Running Time: 12 hrs.). 1992. 64.00 (978-0-7366-2169-4(5), 2968) Books on Tape.

Dancing/the King Who Loved to Dance. Created by Steck-Vaughn Staff. (Running Time: 357 sec.). (Primary Take-Me-Home Books Level A Ser.). 1998. 9.80 (978-0-8172-8661-3(6)) SteckVau.

Dandelion. Don Freeman. Illus. by Don Freeman. (Running Time: 14 mins.). (J). (ps-2). 1982. 9.95 (978-1-59112-028-5(4)) Live Oak Media.

Dandelion. Don Freeman. Illus. by Don Freeman. 14 vols. (Running Time: 14 mins.). 1982. pap. bk. 35.95 (978-1-59519-024-6(4)); audio compact disk 12.95 (978-1-59519-022-2(8)) Live Oak Media.

Dandelion. Don Freeman. Illus. by Don Freeman. 11 vols. (Running Time: 14 mins.). (J). 1982. pap. bk. 18.95 (978-1-59519-023-9(6)) Pub: Live Oak Media. Dist(s): AudioGO

Dandelion. Don Freeman. Illus. by Don Freeman. (J). (gr. k-3). 1982. bk. 22.95 (978-0-941078-11-5(6)) Live Oak Media.

Dandelion. Don Freeman. Illus. by Don Freeman. Read by Jerry Terheyden. 14 vols. (Running Time: 14 mins.). (J). 1982. pap. bk. & tchr. ed. 33.95 Reading Chest. (978-0-941078-10-8(8)) Live Oak Media.
A lion overreacts to an invitation to a come-as-you-are party & turns himself into an overdressed fop.

Dandelion. Don Freeman. Illus. by Don Freeman. Read by Jerry Terheyden. 11 vols. (Running Time: 14 mins.). (J). (gr. k-3). 1982. pap. bk. 16.95 (978-0-941078-09-2(4)) Pub: Live Oak Media. Dist(s): AudioGO

Dandelion Fire. unabr. ed. N. D. Wilson. Read by Russell Horton. 10 CDs. (Running Time: 12 hrs. 31 mins.). (100 Cupboards Ser.: Bk. 2). (YA). (gr. 5-8). 2009. audio compact disk 65.00 (978-0-7393-7859-5(7), Listening Lib) Pub: Random Audio Pubg. Dist(s): Random

Dandelion Fire. unabr. ed. N. D. Wilson. Read by Russell Horton. (100 Cupboards Ser.: Bk. 2). (ENG.). (J). (gr. 3). 2009. audio compact disk 44.00 (978-0-7393-7857-1(0), Listening Lib) Pub: Random Audio Pubg. Dist(s): Random

Dandelion Wine. unabr. ed. Ray Bradbury. (Running Time: 2 mins.). (YA). 2007. audio compact disk 24.00 (978-0-7861-5849-2(2)) Blckstn Audio.

Dandelion Wine. unabr. ed. Ray Bradbury. Read by Jerry Robbins & Colonial Radio Players. (Running Time: 7200 sec.). 2007. 17.95 (978-0-7861-4714-4(8)); 22.95 (978-0-7861-4946-9(9)); audio compact disk 17.95 (978-0-7861-6582-7(0)) Blckstn Audio.

***Dandelion Wine.** unabr. ed. Ray Bradbury. Narrated by Stephen Hoye. (Running Time: 8 hrs. 0 mins.). 2010. 15.99 (978-1-4001-8823-9(7)); 19.99 (978-1-4001-6823-1(6)); audio compact disk 29.99 (978-1-4001-1823-6(9)) Pub: Tantor Media. Dist(s): IngramPubServ

Dandelion Wine. unabr. collector's ed. Ray Bradbury. Read by Michael Prichard. 8 cass. (Running Time: 8 hrs.). 1987. 48.00 (978-0-7366-0500-7(2), 1474) Books on Tape.
The place is Green Town, Illinois, the year 1928. Douglas Spaulding is twelve. The people parading through his life that summer belong to an America of trolley cars & electric runabouts & of dandelion wine bottled in the summer for the winter's sipping. It is during this summer when the magic of childhood just begins to be perceived by the child growing up.

***Dandelion Wine: A Novel.** unabr. ed. Ray Bradbury. Read by Paul Michael Garcia. (Running Time: 10 hrs. NaN mins.). (ENG.). 2011. 29.95 (978-1-4417-7483-5(1)); 59.95 (978-1-4417-7480-4(7)); audio compact disk 29.95 (978-1-4417-7482-8(3)); audio compact disk 90.00 (978-1-4417-7481-1(5)) Blckstn Audio.

Dandelion Wine (dramatized) Colonial Radio Theatre on the Air Production. unabr. ed. Ray Bradbury. (Running Time: 2 mins.). (YA). 2007. audio compact disk 29.95 (978-0-7861-7350-1(5)) Blckstn Audio.

***Dandelion Wine (Library Edition)** unabr. ed. Ray Bradbury. Narrated by Stephen Hoye. (Running Time: 8 hrs. 0 mins.). 2010. 29.99 (978-1-4001-9823-8(2)); audio compact disk 71.99 (978-1-4001-4823-3(5)) Pub: Tantor Media. Dist(s): IngramPubServ

Dando Todo lo Que Tenemos Y un Poquito Más. (SPA.). 2008. audio compact disk 19.99 (978-0-9767943-2-5(2)) Edit Arc.

Danger. unabr. ed. Dick Francis. Read by Tony Britton. 8 cass. (Running Time: 10 hrs.). 2000. 34.95 (978-1-57270-128-1(5), N81128u) Pub: Audio Partners. Dist(s): PerseuPGW
One of the top women jockeys in the world has been kidnapped & Detective Andrew Douglas is sent to negotiate her release. As more kidnappings follow, the Italian police bungle the case & the victims' families begin to worry about their loved ones' safety.

Danger. unabr. ed. Dick Francis. Narrated by Tony Britton. (Running Time: 36000 sec.). (Mystery Masters Ser.). (ENG.). 2007. audio compact disk 37.95 (978-1-57270-856-3(5)) Pub: AudioGO. Dist(s): Perseus Dist

Danger. unabr. ed. Dick Francis. Read by Tony Britton. 8 cass. (Running Time: 12 hrs.). 2000. 59.95 (978-0-7451-5959-1(1), CAB 303) Pub: Chivers Audio Bks GBR. Dist(s): AudioGO
Liberty Market Ltd. advises people at risk on how not to be kidnapped, or if a kidnapping has occurred, they help with the negotiations. And when Alessia Cenci, a champion woman jockey, is grabbed in Bologna, Liberty Market sends agent Andrew Douglas to secure her release. For Andrew, an encounter with the Italian police is only the first in a chain of catastrophic events.

Danger - High Voltage: Exodus 20:7. Ed Young. 1985. 4.95 (978-0-7417-1430-5(2), 430) Win Walk.

Danger at 20 Fathoms. Created by Saddleback Educational Publishing. (Barclay Family Adventure Ser.). (J). 2003. audio compact disk (978-1-56254-978-7(2)) Saddleback Edu.

***Danger Box.** Blue Balliett. Contrib. by Scholastic, Inc. Staff. (ENG.). 2010. audio compact disk 64.99 (978-0-545-24956-0(2)) Scholastic Inc.

***Danger Box.** Blue Balliett. Read by Alex Wyse et al. (J). 2010. audio compact disk 34.99 (978-0-545-24953-9(8)) Scholastic Inc.

***Danger in a Red Dress.** unabr. ed. Christina Dodd. (Running Time: 9 hrs.). (Fortune Hunter Ser.). 2010. 24.99 (978-1-4418-2578-0(9), 9781441825780, BAD); 39.97 (978-1-4418-2579-7(7), 9781441825797, BADLE) Brilliance Audio.

***Danger in a Red Dress.** unabr. ed. Christina Dodd. Read by Angela Dawe. (Running Time: 9 hrs.). (Fortune Hunter Ser.). 2010. 24.99 (978-1-4418-2576-6(2), 9781441825766, Brilliance MP3); 39.97 (978-1-4418-2577-3(0), 9781441825773, Brlnc Audio MP3 Lib); audio compact disk 29.99 (978-1-4418-2574-2(6), 9781441825742, Bril Audio CD Unabri); audio compact disk 89.97 (978-1-4418-2575-9(4), 9781441825759, BriAudCD Unabrid) Brilliance Audio.

Danger in the Canyon. 1 cass. (Running Time: 1 hr. 30 mins.). (SmartReader Ser.). (J). 1999. pap. bk. & tchr. ed. 19.95 (978-0-7887-0128-3(2), 79316T3) Recorded Bks.
It's a beautiful day as Joe & Steve set out on a hike in Thunder Canyon. But when the weather changes suddenly, Joe desperately tries to remember the survival skills he has learned.

Danger in the Church. Warren W. Wiersbe. Read by Warren W. Wiersbe. 1 cass. (Running Time: 1 hr. 30 min.). 1986. 4.95 (978-0-8474-2285-2(2)) Back to Bible.

Presents messages on apostasy & false teaching, as expressed in the Book of Jude.

Danger in the Dark. unabr. ed. L. Ron Hubbard. Read by Karen Black. Narrated by Jim Meskimen. 2 CDs. (Running Time: 2 hrs.). (Stories from the Golden Age Ser.). (ENG.). (gr. 6). 2009. audio compact disk 9.95 (978-1-59212-240-0(X)) Gala Pr LLC.

Danger of Apathy: Rev. 3:14-22. Ed Young. 1986. 4.95 (978-0-7417-1557-9(0), 557) Win Walk.

Danger on Ice Level 1. (J). 2002. (978-0-7398-5088-6(1)); audio compact disk (978-0-7398-5319-1(8)) SteckVau.

Danger on Midnight River. unabr. ed. Gary Paulsen. Narrated by Jeff Woodman. 1 cass. (Running Time: 1 hr.). (Gary Paulsen's World of Adventure Ser.: Bk. 6). (gr. 4 up). 1997. 10.00 (978-0-7887-0879-4(1), 95017E7) Recorded Bks.

Instead of spending the summer with his uncle, Daniel is going to camp. But on the way, the camp van plunges through a bridge into a raging river.

Danger Signals, Vol. 36. Focus on the Family Staff & AIO Team Staff. 4 CDs. (Running Time: 6 hrs.). (Adventures in Odyssey Ser.: Vol. #36). (ENG.). (J). (gr. 3 up). 2004. audio compact disk 24.99 (978-1-56179-960-2(2)) Pub: Focus Family. Dist(s): Tyndale Hse

Danger to Windward. unabr. collector's ed. Armstrong Sperry. Read by Paul Shay. 6 cass. (Running Time: 9 hrs.). (J). 1988. 48.00 (978-0-7366-1440-5(0), 2323) Books on Tape.

Hugh Dewar turned anxiously toward the house on the moor. Well he might, for had he known that he would find his uncle & cousin thieves, as well as near murderers, he might never have entered that house of mistrust.

Danger Trail, Set. Boyd C. Richardson. 2 cass. 11.98 (978-1-55503-801-4(8), 07001061) Covenant Comms.

Knife Thrower's journey west.

Danger Zone. unabr. ed. Howard Goldsmith. Read by Rusty Nelson. 4 cass. (Running Time: 5 hrs.). 2001. 26.95 (978-1-58116-029-1(1)) Books in Motion.

College Junior Andrew Norris, an African-American junior at Summit University, is on the staff of the college paper. When investigating a tip about a Nazi organization based in a nearby town, Andrew becomes harassed by local law enforcement, and involved in Nazi activity.

Dangerous. abr. ed. Diana Palmer. Read by Phil Gigante. (Running Time: 5 hrs.). (Long, Tall Texans Ser.). 2010. audio compact disk 19.99 (978-1-4233-8270-6(6), 9781423382706, BACD) Brilliance Audio.

Dangerous. abr. ed. Diana Palmer. (Running Time: 5 hrs.). 2011. audio compact disk 14.99 (978-1-4233-8271-3(4), 9781423382713, BCD Value Price) Brilliance Audio.

Dangerous. unabr. ed. Diana Palmer. Read by Phil Gigante. (Running Time: 9 hrs.). (Long, Tall Texans Ser.). 2010. 24.99 (978-1-4233-8266-9(8), 9781423382669, Brilliance MP3); 39.97 (978-1-4233-8267-6(6), 9781423382676, Brinc Audio MP3 Lib); 39.97 (978-1-4233-8269-0(2), 9781423382690, BADLE); 24.99 (978-1-4233-8268-3(4), 9781423382683, BAD); audio compact disk 87.97 (978-1-4233-8265-2(X), 9781423382652, BriAudCD Unabrid); audio compact disk 34.99 (978-1-4233-8264-5(1), 9781423382645, Bril Audio CD Unabri) Brilliance Audio.

Dangerous. unabr. ed. Amanda Quick, pseud. Read by Anne Flosnik. (Running Time: 11 hrs.). 2010. 39.97 (978-1-4233-8793-0(7), 9781423387930, Brinc Audio MP3 Lib); 39.97 (978-1-4233-8795-4(3), 9781423387954, BADLE); 24.99 (978-1-4233-8792-3(9), 9781423387923, Brilliance MP3); 24.99 (978-1-4233-8794-7(5), 9781423387947, BAD); audio compact disk 82.97 (978-1-4233-8791-6(0), 9781423387916, BriAudCD Unabrid); audio compact disk 29.99 (978-1-4233-8790-9(2), 9781423387909, Bril Audio CD Unabri) Brilliance Audio.

Dangerous Assignment. Contrib. by Brian Donlevy. (Running Time: 10800 sec.). 2004. audio compact disk 9.98 (978-1-57019-564-8(1)) Radio Spirits.

Dangerous Assignment. Contrib. by Steve Mitchell & Brian Donlevy. (Running Time: 10800 sec.). 2004. 9.98 (978-1-57019-563-1(3)) Radio Spirits.

Dangerous Assignment: Assignment in the Islands & Road to Mandalay. Perf. by Brian Donlevy. 1 cass. (Running Time: 1 hr.). 2001. 6.98 (2414) Radio Spirits.

Dangerous Assignment: Blackmail Letter & Desert Sheik Controls Uranium. Perf. by Brian Donlevy. 1 cass. (Running Time: 1 hr.). 2001. 6.98 (1631) Radio Spirits.

Dangerous Assignment: File & Murdered Correspondent in Burma. Perf. by Brian Donlevy. 1 cass. (Running Time: 1 hr.). 2001. 6.98 (1628) Radio Spirits.

Dangerous Assignment: Mine Disaster & Latin American Party Leader Murdered. Perf. by Brian Donlevy. 1 cass. (Running Time: 1 hr.). 2001. 6.98 (2275) Radio Spirits.

Dangerous Assignment: Missing Arabian Oil & Lecturing Professors. Perf. by Brian Donlevy. 1 cass. (Running Time: 1 hr.). 2001. 6.98 (1633) Radio Spirits.

Dangerous Assignment: Missing Japanese Weapons & Captain Rock. Perf. by Brian Donlevy. 1 cass. (Running Time: 1 hr.). 2001. 6.98 (1629) Radio Spirits.

Dangerous Assignment: Mysterious Oriental Guerilla Leader & The Trained Seal. Perf. by Brian Donlevy. 1 cass. (Running Time: 1 hr.). 2001. 6.98 (1634) Radio Spirits.

Dangerous Assignment: Portuguese Alien Smuggling & Paris Murders. Perf. by Brian Donlevy. 1 cass. (Running Time: 1 hr.). 2001. 6.98 (1627) Radio Spirits.

Dangerous Assignment: Stolen Radar Plans & Wire Recording. Perf. by Brian Donlevy. 1 cass. (Running Time: 1 hr.). 2001. 6.98 (1630) Radio Spirits.

Dangerous Assignment: Sunken Ships & Nigeria. Perf. by Brian Donlevy. 1 cass. (Running Time: 1 hr.). 2001. 6.98 (1626) Radio Spirits.

Dangerous Assignment: Sunken Treasure & Flying Saucer Terrorizes an Airliner. Perf. by Brian Donlevy. 1 cass. (Running Time: 1 hr.). 2001. 6.98 (1632) Radio Spirits.

Dangerous Assignment: The Australia Adventure & The Smuggling Ring. Perf. by Brian Donlevy. 1 cass. (Running Time: 1 hr.). 2001. 6.98 (1636) Radio Spirits.

Dangerous Assignment: Thief Spotted in Indonesia & The Underground Press. Perf. by Brian Donlevy. 1 cass. (Running Time: 1 hr.). 2001. 6.98 (1637) Radio Spirits.

Dangerous Assignment: Troop Movement Papers & Drugged Diplomat. Perf. by Brian Donlevy. 1 cass. (Running Time: 1 hr.). 2001. 6.98 (1635) Radio Spirits.

Dangerous Book for Boys. abr. ed. Conn Iggulden & Hal Iggulden. Read by Oliver Wyman. 3 CDs. (Running Time: 10800 sec.). (gr. 5 up). 2007. audio compact disk 24.95 (978-0-06-146910-7(6), Harper Audio) HarperCollins Pubs.

***Dangerous Book for Boys.** unabr. ed. Conn Iggulden & Hal Iggulden. Read by Oliver Wyman. (ENG.). 2007. (978-0-06-147589-4(0), Harper Audio); (978-0-06-147591-7(2), Harper Audio) HarperCollins Pubs.

Dangerous Business. Michael Underwood. Read by Julia Franklin. 5 cass. (Sound Ser.). (J). 2002. 49.95 (978-1-84283-209-7(3)) Pub: ISIS Lrg Prnt GBR. Dist(s): Ulverscroft US

***Dangerous Church: Risking Everything to Reach Everyone.** unabr. ed. John Bishop. (Leadership Network Innovation Ser.). (ENG.). 2011. 18.99 (978-0-310-40238-1(7)) Zondervan.

Dangerous Connections see Las Relaciones Peligrosas

Dangerous Curves. unabr. ed. Peter Cheyney. Read by Nigel Stranger. 5 cass. (Running Time: 7 hrs. 30 mins.). (Sound Ser.). 2004. 49.95 (978-1-85496-237-9(X)) Pub: UlverLrgPrint GBR. Dist(s): Ulverscroft US

Dangerous Davies: The Last Detective. unabr. ed. Leslie Thomas. Read by Alexander John. 8 cass. (Running Time: 10 hrs.). 1999. 69.95 (978-0-7531-0214-5(5), 970912) Pub: ISIS Audio GBR. Dist(s): Ulverscroft US

In the seedier sprawl of London's northwest frontier, he's the copper who gets all the scruffy jobs & manages to make them scruffier. He's Dangerous Daivies, the Last Detective. When Dangerous is allocated a murder case, it proves to be a twenty-five year old sex crime. His witnesses range from a veteran of the Zulu Wars to a bloke who thinks he's Peter the Great & the mightily endowed Ena Lind, cat-suit wearer & creme-de-menthe drinker. Exhibit A is the pair of pale green knickers that the victim wasn't wearing.

Dangerous Davies: The Last Detective. unabr. ed. Leslie Thomas. Read by Alexander John. 8 CDs. (Running Time: 8 hrs. 59 mins.). (Isis Ser.). (J). 2002. audio compact disk 79.95 (978-0-7531-1397-4(X)) Pub: ISIS Lrg Prnt GBR. Dist(s): Ulverscroft US

Dangerous Davies & the Lonely Heart. unabr. ed. Leslie Thomas. Read by Gregory York. 8 cass. (Running Time: 10 hrs.). (Isis Ser.). (J). 2001. 69.95 (978-0-7531-0570-2(5), 990506) Pub: ISIS Lrg Prnt GBR. Dist(s): Ulverscroft US

Dangerous Davies has retired from the Metropolitan Police & is now working as a private eye in Northwest London. Suddenly he is thrown into two mysteries, the murders of women answering to lonely hearts adverts & the disappearance of a young girl student. Davies's world is peopled by eccentric & dangerous characters old & new, including a philosopher sidekick & a Harley Davidson rider. Can Davies solve these mysteries, or is his career as a private detective over before it has even begun? This highly original detective story is as ingenious as it is touching & funny.

Dangerous Days. unabr. ed. James Patterson. Read by Milo Ventimiglia. Contrib. by Michael Ledwidge. (Running Time: 4 hrs.). (Daniel X Ser.). (ENG.). 2009. audio compact disk 14.98 (978-1-60024-615-9(X)) Pub: Hachet Audio. Dist(s): HachBkGrp

Dangerous Days. unabr. ed. James Patterson. Read by Milo Ventimiglia. Contrib. by Michael Ledwidge. (Running Time: 4 hrs.). (Daniel X Ser.). (ENG.). 2008. 15.98 (978-1-60024-201-4(4)) Pub: Little Brn Bks. Dist(s): HachBkGrp

Dangerous Days. unabr. ed. James Patterson & Michael Ledwidge. Read by Milo Ventimiglia. 4 CDs. (Running Time: 4 hrs. 15 mins.). (Daniel X Ser.). 2008. audio compact disk 40.00 (978-1-4159-5423-2(2), BksonTape) Pub: Random Audio Pubg. Dist(s): Random

He was born with great power. The greatest superpower of all isn't to be part spider, part man, or to cast magic spells - the greatest power is the power to create. Daniel X has that power. And a Deadly Secret. Daniel's secret abilities - like being able to manipulate objects and animals with his mind or to re-create himself in any shape he chooses - have helped him survive. But Daniel doesn't have a normal life. He is the protector of Earth, the Alien Hunter, with a mission beyond anyone's imagining. Now the fate of the world rests on Daniel X. From the day that his parents were brutally murdered before his very eyes, Daniel has used his unique gifts to hunt down their assassin. Finally, with the help of The List, bequeathed to him in his parents' dying breath, he is closing in on the killer.

Dangerous Days. unabr. ed. Mary Roberts Rinehart. Read by Flo Gibson. 8 cass. (Running Time: 11 hrs.). 1997. 26.95 (978-1-55685-494-1(3), 494-3) Audio Bk Con.

This romantic novel concerns World War I & the growing commitment of Americans before & after U.S. involvement. A divided family & an attack on a munitions plant add to this stirring tale.

Dangerous Dream. unabr. ed. Felice Buckner. Read by Lynda Evans. 4 cass. (Running Time: 4 hrs. 54 min.). 2001. 26.95 (978-1-55686-925-9(8)) Books in Motion.

World War II has ended and 13-year-old Hella Weiss has survived the Nazi's Jewish extermination plan. When she is united with her father, whom she barely remembers, she suspects he is an imposter and one of the soldier's from the Nazi death camps trying to escape the war criminal investigations.

***Dangerous Duty of Delight: The Glorified God & the Satisfied Soul.** unabr. ed. John Piper. Narrated by David Cochran Heath. (ENG.). 2007. 9.98 (978-1-59644-510-9(6), Hovel Audio) christianaud.

Dangerous Duty of Delight: The Glorified God & the Satisfied Soul. unabr. ed. John Piper. (Running Time: 2 hrs. 0 mins. 0 sec.). (ENG.). 2007. audio compact disk 15.98 (978-1-59644-509-3(2), Hovel Audio) christianaud.

Dangerous Edge, Ted Allbeury. Read by Gordon Griffin. 6 cass. 1999. 54.95 (66251) Pub: Soundings Ltd GBR. Dist(s): Ulverscroft US

***Dangerous Edge of Things.** unabr. ed. Tina Whittle. (Running Time: 8.5 hrs. NaN mins.). 2011. 29.95 (978-1-4417-7581-8(1)); 54.95 (978-1-4417-7578-8(1)); audio compact disk 76.00 (978-1-4417-7579-5(X)) Blckstn Audio.

Dangerous Faith. unabr. ed. James Lund & Peb Jackson. (ENG.). 2008. 16.09 (978-1-60814-169-2(1)) Oasis Audio.

Dangerous Faith: True Stories of Answering the Call to Adventure. unabr. ed. James Lund & Peb Jackson. Read by Jon Gauger. (Running Time: 7 hrs. 30 mins. 0 sec.). (ENG.). 2008. audio compact disk 22.99 (978-1-59859-370-9(6)) Oasis Audio.

Dangerous Fortune. unabr. ed. Ken Follett. Read by Michael Page. 12 cass. (Running Time: 17 hrs.). 2002. 29.95 (978-1-59086-574-3(X), 159086574X, BAU) Brilliance Audio.

In 1866 tragedy strikes at the exclusive Windfield School when a mysterious accident takes the life of a student. Among the student's circle of friends are Hugh Pilaster; Hugh's older cousin Edward, dissolute heir to the Pilaster banking fortune; and Micky Miranda, the handsome son of a brutal South American oligarchy. The death and its aftermath begin the spiraling circle of treachery that will span three decades and entwine many lives. From the exclusive men's clubs that cater to every dark desire of England's upper classes to the luxurious ballrooms of the manipulators of the world's wealth, Follett conjures up a stunning panorama of intrigue. "A Dangerous Fortune" brings us characters swept toward a perilous climax where greed, fed by the shocking truth of a young man's death, must be stopped - or the dreams of a nation will die.

Dangerous Fortune. unabr. ed. Ken Follett. Read by Michael Page. (Running Time: 17 hrs.). 2004. 39.25 (978-1-59335-528-9(9), 1593355289, Brinc Audio MP3 Lib) Brilliance Audio.

Dangerous Fortune. unabr. ed. Ken Follett. Read by Michael Page. (Running Time: 17 hrs.). 2004. 39.25 (978-1-59710-167-7(2), 1597101672, BADLE); 24.95 (978-1-59710-166-0(4), 1597101664, BAD) Brilliance Audio.

Dangerous Fortune. unabr. ed. Ken Follett. Read by Michael Page. (Running Time: 17 hrs.). 2007. audio compact disk 38.95 (978-1-4233-2859-9(0), 9781423328599, Bril Audio CD Unabri); audio compact disk 122.25 (978-1-4233-2860-5(4), 9781423328605, BriAudCD Unabrid) Brilliance Audio.

Dangerous Fortune, unabr. ed. Ken Follett. Narrated by John Franklyn-Robbins. 14 cass. (Running Time: 18 hrs. 30 mins.). 1994. 112.00 (978-1-55690-965-8(9), 94108E7) Recorded Bks.

The deception began with a drowning incident at Windfield School, an exclusive boys' school in Victorian England. Several young men, all from wealthy families & all witnesses to the unfortunate moment are irrevocably bound by fear & distrust. For Micky Miranda, the blackmailing son of a South American political powerhouse & Edward Pilaster, heir to the mighty Pilaster banking empire, the incident solidifies a friendship based on deceit & depravity that lasts for decades.

Dangerous Fortune. unabr. ed. Ken Follett. Read by Michael Page. (Running Time: 17 hrs.). 2004. 24.95 (978-1-59335-181-6(X), 159335181X) Soulmate Audio Bks.

In 1866 tragedy strikes at the exclusive Windfield School when a mysterious accident takes the life of a student. Among the student's circle of friends are Hugh Pilaster; Hugh's older cousin Edward, dissolute heir to the Pilaster banking fortune; and Micky Miranda, the handsome son of a brutal South American oligarchy. The death and its aftermath begin the spiraling circle of treachery that will span three decades and entwine many lives. From the exclusive men's clubs that cater to every dark desire of England's upper classes to the luxurious ballrooms of the manipulators of the world's wealth, Follett conjures up a stunning panorama of intrigue. "A Dangerous Fortune" brings us characters swept toward a perilous climax where greed, fed by the shocking truth of a young man's death, must be stopped - or the dreams of a nation will die.

Dangerous Fortune, Set. unabr. ed. Ken Follett. Narrated by Simon Prebble. 10 cass. (Running Time: 14 hrs. 30 min.). 1999. 85.00 (94985) Recorded Bks.

The lavish tale of Mack McAsh & Lizzie Hallim's passionate search for freedom.

Dangerous Friend. abr. ed. Ward Just. 4 cass. (Running Time: 6 hrs.). 2001. 25.00 (978-1-59040-119-4(0), Phoenix Audio) Pub: Amer Intl Pub. Dist(s): PerseuPGW

***Dangerous Games.** unabr. ed. Keri Arthur. Narrated by Angela Dawe. (Running Time: 10 hrs. 30 mins.). (Riley Jenson Guardian Ser.). 2010. 24.99 (978-1-4526-5004-3(7)); 34.99 (978-1-4526-0004-8(X)); 16.99 (978-1-4526-7004-1(8)) Tantor Media.

Dangerous Games. unabr. ed. Lesley Grant-Adamson. Read by Edmund Dehn. 7 cass. (Running Time: 9 hr. 30 min.). (Isis Ser.). (J). 1995. 61.95 (978-1-85695-944-5(9), 950502) Pub: ISIS Lrg Prnt GBR. Dist(s): Ulverscroft US

Dangerous Games. unabr. ed. Lesley Grant-Adamson. Read by Edmund Dehn. 9 CDs. (Running Time: 9 hrs. 31 mins.). (Isis Ser.). (J). 2002. audio compact disk 84.95 (978-0-7531-1489-6(5)) Pub: ISIS Lrg Prnt GBR. Dist(s): Ulverscroft US

Jim is a liar and a charmer. Escaping charges of murder and fraud, his Caribbean hideaway becomes a trap. But he can't resist playing a game of his own with a couple of hustlers who claim to have found a Spanish treasure galleon. Soon the edges of truth and fantasy blur and the result is murder.

Dangerous Games. unabr. ed. Julian Rathbone. 8 cass. (Isis Ser.). (J). 2004. 69.95 (978-1-85695-412-9(9)) Pub: ISIS Lrg Prnt GBR. Dist(s): Ulverscroft US

***Dangerous Games (Library Edition)** unabr. ed. Keri Arthur. Narrated by Angela Dawe. (Running Time: 10 hrs. 30 mins.). (Riley Jenson Guardian Ser.). 2010. 34.99 (978-1-4526-2004-6(0)); 83.99 (978-1-4526-3004-5(6)) Tantor Media.

Dangerous Ground. abr. ed. Larry Bond. Read by Dick Hill. (Running Time: 21600 sec.). 2006. audio compact disk 16.99 (978-1-59737-355-5(9), 9781597373555) Brilliance Audio.

The USS Memphis, a dilapidated submarine that should have been mothballed decades ago, has been given one last mission by the newly elected president. The task: To sneak illegally into Russia's coastal waters and recon the leaking nuclear fuel containers hidden on the floor of the Arctic Ocean. More than just an environmental nightmare, this radioactive burial ground houses enough nuclear capability to destroy most of America's major cities. The Memphis's commander, Lowell Hardy, had been looking forward to flag rank and pleasantly upon the sub's decommissioning. Now he is trapped in inconceivably dangerous and illegal mission that could easily end his career, if not his life and the lives of his crew. And it's the crew who feel Hardy's tension as he tyrannizes over everyone onboard in an effort to ensure they'll be ready for anything: Jerry Mitchell: A former naval pilot with political connections, he is a novice submariner, unprepared for his demanding job as a weapons officer. Central to the Memphis's mission, Mitchell may be its greatest liability...or its ultimate salvation. Dr. Joanna Patterson: The senior civilian scientist, appointed by and reporting to the president, she is a world-class expert on nuclear fuel contamination - and every bit as demanding as Hardy. Patterson and her partner, Dr. Emily Davis, soon find themselves battling flaring tempers, faulty machinery, lethal radioactivity, and the raging Arctic seas. The submariners: Seething with rage at their Captain Bligh-like commander and the equally domineering Joanna Patterson, they are also at war with Jerry Mitchell and one another. Like the captain, they feel they deserve better, not this antiquated relic of a sub, not this hostile scientist, not this novice weapons officer, and definitely not this disastrously dangerous mission. Nor is the mission what it seems. Lurking beneath the frigid, black, radioactive waters is a secret far more deadly than anything naval command could imagine - a secret so menacing the Russian fleet is hell-bent on destroying the Memphis and all who sail in her.

Dangerous Ground. unabr. ed. Larry Bond. Read by Dick Hill. (Running Time: 15 hrs.). 2005. 39.25 (978-1-59710-169-1(9), 9781597101691, BADLE); 24.95 (978-1-59710-168-4(0), 9781597101684, BAD); 39.25 (978-1-59335-996-6(9), 9781593359966, Brinc Audio MP3 Lib); 24.95 (978-1-59335-995-9(0), 9781593359959, Brilliance MP3); 102.25 (978-1-59600-300-2(6), 9781596003002, BrilAudUnabridg); 34.95 (978-1-59600-299-9(9), 9781596002999, BAU); audio compact disk 117.25 (978-1-59600-303-3(0), 9781596003033, BriAudCD Unabrid); audio compact disk 38.95 (978-1-59600-871-7(7), 9781596008717, Bril Audio CD Unabri) Brilliance Audio.

Dangerous Hour. unabr. ed. Marcia Muller. Read by Susan Ericksen. 6 CDs. (Running Time: 7 hrs.). (Sharon McCone Mystery Ser.: No. 22). 2004. 24.95

(978-1-59335-765-8(6), 1593357656, Brilliance MP3); 39.25 (978-1-59335-899-0(7), 1593358997, Brinc Audio MP3 Lib) Brilliance Audio.
Complacency can make a person careless, and Sharon McCone, who makes crime her business, should know that better than most. One minute she's riding high with her detective agency expanding, her bank account growing, and her only "problem" a marriage proposal from her lover, Hy Ripinsky, that's kicking up her longtime fears of commitment. The next minute, in the time it takes for a single phone call to bring bad news, she stands to lose everything. McCone is stunned to learn that a favorite employee, streetwise and savvy Julia Rafael, has been charged with credit-card fraud. She thinks there must be a mistake - until she finds the goods charged to the stolen credit card in the firm's mailroom. As she starts to dig into the facts of the case, McCone realizes that someone is out to ruin her business, blacken her reputation, and harm those close to her... Reaching back into her past to look for answers, she must come to grips with the violent twists and turns of her career, the choices she's faced, and the enemies she's made. How does the formerly trustworthy Julia fit into the big picture? And how does this new crisis tie into the recent murder of a popular Mission District fund-raiser? But when someone breaks into her car, invades her home, and upsets every aspect of her life, McCone knows one thing for sure: Now it's her turn to prove how tough she really is, and how far she'll go to get justice...and some payback of her own.

Dangerous Hour. unabr. ed. Marcia Muller. Read by Susan Eriksen. 5 cass. (Running Time: 7 hrs.). (Sharon McCone Mystery Ser.: No. 22). 2004. 27.95 (978-1-59355-877-2(5), 1593558775, BAU) Brilliance Audio.

Dangerous Hour. unabr. ed. Marcia Muller. Read by Susan Ericksen. (Running Time: 7 hrs.). (Sharon McCone Mystery Ser.: No. 22). 2004. 69.25 (978-1-59355-878-9(3), 1593558783, BrilAudUnabridg) Brilliance Audio.

Dangerous Hour. unabr. ed. Marcia Muller. Read by Susan Eriksen. 6 CDs. (Running Time: 7 hrs.). (Sharon McCone Mystery Ser.: No. 22). 2004. audio compact disk 29.95 (978-1-59355-879-6(1), 1593558791, Bril Audio CD Unabri) Brilliance Audio.

Dangerous Hour. unabr. ed. Marcia Muller. Read by Susan Ericksen. (Running Time: 7 hrs.). (Sharon McCone Mystery Ser.: No. 22). 2004. audio compact disk 82.25 (978-1-59355-880-2(5), 1593558805, BriAudCD Unabrid) Brilliance Audio.

Dangerous Hour. unabr. ed. Marcia Muller. Read by Susan Ericksen. (Running Time: 7 hrs.). (Sharon McCone Mystery Ser.: No. 22). 2004. 39.25 (978-1-59710-171-4(0), 1597101710, BADLE); 24.95 (978-1-59710-170-7(2), 1597101702, BAD) Brilliance Audio.

Dangerous Kiss. Jackie Collins. (Lucky Santangelo Ser.: Bk. 5). 2001. (978-0-333-78160-9(0)) Macmillan UK GBR.

Dangerous Kiss. Jackie Collins. Narrated by Barbara Rosenblat. 13 CDs. (Running Time: 15 hrs.). (Lucky Santangelo Ser.: Bk. 5). audio compact disk 124.00 (978-0-7887-9857-3(X)) Recorded Bks.

Dangerous Kiss. abr. ed. Jackie Collins. Read by Jackie Collins. 4 cass. (Lucky Santangelo Ser.: Bk. 5). 1999. 25.00 (FS9-50894) Highsmith.

Dangerous Kiss. abr. ed. Jackie Collins. (Lucky Santangelo Ser.: Bk. 5). 2004. 15.95 (978-0-7435-4579-2(6)) Pub: S&S Audio. Dist(s): S and S Inc

Dangerous Kiss. unabr. ed. Jackie Collins. Narrated by Barbara Rosenblat. 11 cass. (Running Time: 15 hrs.). (Lucky Santangelo Ser.: Bk. 5). 2001. 96.00 (978-0-7887-4979-7(X), 96486L8) Recorded Bks.
A survivor who has fought for everything she has: a happy marriage & loads of power in her position as a Hollywood studio chief. So when a senseless random holdup leaves a member of her family dead & places her own marriage in trouble, we find Lucky striking back & determined to do everything she can to bring the killer to justice.

Dangerous Liaisons. Choderlos De Laclos. Read by Sarah Woodward et al. 3 cass. (Running Time: 4 hrs.). (Classic Literature with Classical Music Ser.). 1996. 17.98 (978-962-634-532-0(2), NA303214, Naxos AudioBooks) Naxos.
Tale of passion, treachery & cruelty.

Dangerous Liaisons. Choderlos De laclos. (Running Time: 3 hrs. 45 mins.). 2006. 24.95 (978-1-60083-717-3(4)) Iofy Corp.

Dangerous Liaisons. Choderlos de Laclos & Polly Hayes. Read by Michael Sheen & Sarah Woodward. 3 CDs. 2004. audio compact disk 22.98 (978-962-634-312-8(5)) Naxos.

Dangerous Love. Sabrina Jeffries. Narrated by Vanessa Maroney. 9 cass. (Running Time: 13 hrs.). 81.00 (978-1-4025-0369-6(5)) Recorded Bks.

Dangerous Love. Katrina Wright. Read by Vivien Young. 2 cass. (Running Time: 3 hrs.). 1999. 24.95 (62094) Pub: Soundings Ltd GBR. Dist(s): Ulverscroft US

Dangerous Love. unabr. collector's ed. Catherine Lanigan. Read by Anna Fields. 7 cass. (Running Time: 10 hrs. 30 mins.). 1996. 56.00 (978-0-7366-3464-9(9), 4108) Books on Tape.
Richard Bartlow betrayed the women in his life: Mary, his first wife, abandoned with their two children; Alicia, dumped after stabilizing his career; & Michelle, duped into thinking she was his one & only. When Richard dies, why do all three appear at the funeral & why in mourning?.

Dangerous Love, Set. unabr. ed. Cynthia Harrod-Eagles. Read by Julia Franklin. 5 cass. (Running Time: 6 hrs. 35 min.). 1999. 63.95 (978-1-85903-275-6(3)) Pub: Magna Story GBR. Dist(s): Ulverscroft US

Dangerous Lover: Gothic Villains, Byronism, & the Nineteenth-Century Seduction Narrative. Deborah Lutz. 2006. audio compact disk 9.95 (978-0-8142-9111-5(2)) Pub: Ohio St U Pr. Dist(s): Chicago Distribution Ctr

Dangerous Mourning. unabr. ed. Anne Perry. Narrated by Davina Porter. 11 cass. (Running Time: 15 hrs.). (William Monk Novel Ser.). 1995. 91.00 (978-0-7887-0417-8(6), 94609E7) Recorded Bks.
When the daughter of Sir Basil Moidore is stabbed to death in her bed, Inspector Monk & Nurse Latterly uncover a tale of shame & scandal.

Dangerous Odyssey. unabr. ed. Jane Edwards. Read by Laurie Klein. 4 cass. (Running Time: 4 hrs. 54 min.). Dramatization. 1993. 26.95 (978-1-55686-467-4(1), 467) Books in Motion.
Kelsey Anderson is assigned to care for Zoe whose parents have disappeared while searching for gold artifacts in Greece. Kelsey & Zoe fly to Greece & are followed by a strange man from the airport to their hotel room.

Dangerous Pursuits. Alanna Knight. 2008. 61.95 (978-1-84559-916-4(0)); audio compact disk 71.95 (978-1-84559-917-1(9)) Pub: Soundings Ltd GBR. Dist(s): Ulverscroft US

Dangerous Relations. Choderlos De Laclos. Read by Yadira Sánchez - Santiago Munevar. (Running Time: 3 hrs.). 2002. 16.95 (978-1-60083-271-0(7), Audiofy Corp) Iofy Corp.

Dangerous Shores. Jessica Blair & Anne Dover. 2009. 89.95 (978-1-84652-321-2(4)); audio compact disk 99.95 (978-1-84652-320-5(6)) Pub: Magna Story GBR. Dist(s): Ulverscroft US

Dangerous Skies. Suzanne Fisher Staples. Read by Peter MacNicol. 4 cass. (Running Time: 5 hrs. 30 mins.). (J). 2000. 30.00 (978-0-7366-9064-5(6)) Books on Tape.
A gripping tale of the friendship between Buck Smith, descended from the farmers who settle this Virginian shore & Tunes Smith, whose forebears where the slaves brought from Africa to work the farm.

Dangerous Skies. unabr. ed. Suzanne Fisher Staples. Narrated by Tom Stechschulte. 5 pieces. (Running Time: 6 hrs.). (gr. 5 up). 44.00 (978-0-7887-0893-0(7), 95031E7) Recorded Bks.
One horrifying spring afternoon changes the lives of two innocent children forever. An authentic portrait, both beautiful & grim, of contemporary life on the Chesapeake Bay. This story about racial prejudice & injustice faces some difficult issues that have haunted our country since its birth. Available to libraries only.

Dangerous Summer. unabr. ed. Ernest Hemingway. Read by Alexander Adams. 8 cass. (Running Time: 9 hrs.). 2001. 29.95 (978-0-7366-5672-6(3)) Books on Tape.
In 1959 Life magazine hired Ernest Hemingway to report an extraordinary event, a series of bull-fights that pitted two of Spain's greatest matadors, Manolette & Antonio Ordonez, against each other in a series of matches, mano-a-mano. It was a classic plot: a legendary champion coming out of retirement to face a young challenger. Hemingway traveled with the contenders, as a member of their circle. His report became this book, one of the finest he ever wrote.

Dangerous Summer. unabr. collector's ed. Ernest Hemingway. Read by Wolfram Kandinsky. 8 cass. (Running Time: 8 hrs.). 1990. 48.00 (978-0-7366-1789-5(2), 2626) Books on Tape.

Dangerous Surrender: What It Takes to Change Your World. unabr. ed. Kay Warren. (Running Time: 5 hrs. 30 mins. 0 sec.). (ENG.). 2007. 12.99 (978-0-310-28175-7(X)) Zondervan.

Dangerous to Know. Jane Adams. 7 cass. (Running Time: 9 hrs. 15 mins.). (Story Sound Ser.). (J). 2005. 61.95 (978-1-85903-766-9(6)) Pub: Mgna Lrg Print GBR. Dist(s): Ulverscroft US

Dangerous to Know. unabr. ed. Barbara Taylor Bradford. Read by Kate Reading. 7 cass. (Running Time: 10 hrs. 30 mins.). 1996. 56.00 (978-0-7366-3209-6(3), 3872) Books on Tape.
Sebastian Locke, the 56-year-old patriarch of a powerful American family, is handsome, charismatic, charming & very intelligent. He's also a philanthropist who travels the globe to give millions to those in need. That's why the police are baffled when he's found dead, apparently murdered. But who would want to kill him? Could such an upstanding man have had enemies? Vivienne Trent, an American journalist,who was once married to Locke, uncovers startling revelations that turn her life around.

Dangerous Woman. Debra Lee. audio compact disk 8.00 (978-0-7443-0245-5(5)) SynergEbks.

Dangerous Woman. collector's ed. Mary McGarry Morris. Read by Kimberly Schraf. 10 cass. (Running Time: 15 hrs.). 2000. 80.00 (978-0-7366-4981-0(6)) Books on Tape.
Martha Horgan is not like other women. She stares. She has violent crushes on people. She can't stop telling the truth. Martha craves love, independence, & companionship, but her relentless honesty makes her painfully vulnerable to those around her: Frances, her wealthy aunt & begrudging guardian; Birdy who befriends her, then cruelly rejects her; & Colin Mackey, the seductive man who preys on her desires. Confused & bitter, distrusting even those with her best interests at heart, Martha is propelled into a desperate attempt to gain control over her own life.

Dangerous Woman. unabr. ed. Mary McGarry Morris. Read by Mary McGarry Morris. Interview with Rebekah Presson. 1 cass. (Running Time: 29 min.). 1991. 10.00 (032291) New Letters.
Morris' first novel, "Vanished", was a critical success & a bestseller. She talks about this & her second novel, A Dangerous Woman, in this interview.

Dangerous Woman. unabr. ed. Mary McGarry Morris. Narrated by Ruth Ann Phimister. 10 cass. (Running Time: 14 hrs. 15 mins.). 1998. 85.00 (978-0-7887-1874-8(6), 95296E7) Recorded Bks.
Powerful heartbreaking story of a woman who is dangerous to herself. The reader will take you into Martha's world of pain, hope & honesty.

Dangerous Women: Original Stories from Today's Greatest Suspense Writers. abr. unabr. ed. Otto Penzler. 3 CDs. (Running Time: 11 hrs. 30 mins. 0 sec.). (ENG.). 2005. audio compact disk 34.99 (978-1-4001-0145-0(X)) Pub: Tantor Media. Dist(s): IngramPubServ

Dangerous Women: Original Stories from Today's Greatest Suspense Writers. unabr. ed. Lorenzo Carcaterra et al. Narrated by Ellen Archer et al. (Running Time: 11 hrs. 30 mins. 0 sec.). (ENG.). 2005. audio compact disk 69.99 (978-1-4001-3145-7(5)) Pub: Tantor Media. Dist(s): IngramPubServ

Dangerous Women: Original Stories from Today's Greatest Suspense Writers. unabr. ed. Otto Penzler et al. Narrated by Ellen Archer et al. (Running Time: 11 hrs. 30 mins. 0 sec.). (ENG.). 2005. audio compact disk 22.99 (978-1-4001-5145-5(7)) Pub: Tantor Media. Dist(s): IngramPubServ

***Dangerously Funny: The Uncensored Story of the Smothers Brothers Comedy Hour.** unabr. ed. David Bianculli. Narrated by Johnny Heller. (Running Time: 11 hrs. 30 mins.). (ENG.). 2010. 17.99 (978-1-4001-8570-2(X)) Tantor Media.

***Dangerously Funny: The Uncensored Story of the Smothers Brothers Comedy Hour.** unabr. ed. David Bianculli. Narrated by Johnny Heller. (Running Time: 11 hrs. 30 mins. 0 sec.). (ENG.). 2010. 24.99 (978-1-4001-6570-4(9)); audio compact disk 37.99 (978-1-4001-1570-9(1)); audio compact disk 75.99 (978-1-4001-4570-6(8)) Pub: Tantor Media. Dist(s): IngramPubServ

Danger's Hour: The Story of the USS Bunker Hill & the Kamikaze Pilot Who Crippled Her. unabr. ed. Maxwell Taylor Kennedy. Narrated by Michael Prichard. (Running Time: 17 hrs. 30 mins. 0 sec.). (ENG.). 2008. audio compact disk 49.99 (978-1-4001-0832-9(2)); audio compact disk 99.99 (978-1-4001-3832-6(9)) Pub: Tantor Media. Dist(s): IngramPubServ

Danger's Hour: The Story of the USS Bunker Hill & the Kamikaze Pilot Who Crippled Her. unabr. ed. Maxwell Taylor Kennedy. Read by Michael Prichard. (Running Time: 17 hrs. 30 mins. 0 sec.). (ENG.). 2008. audio compact disk 34.99 (978-1-4001-5832-4(X)) Pub: Tantor Media. Dist(s): IngramPubServ

Dangers of Psychic Self Deception. Instructed by Manly P. Hall. 8.95 (978-0-89314-039-7(2), C821024) Philos Res.

Dangers of Strife. Short Stories. Joel Osteen. 1 Cass. (Running Time: 30 Mins.). 2002. 6.00 (978-1-59349-156-7(5), JA0156) J Osteen.

Dangers of Strife. Speeches. Joel Osteen. 4 audio cass. (J). 2002. 16.00 (978-1-931877-21-3(1), JAS017); audio compact disk 16.00 (978-1-931877-38-1(6), JCS017) J Osteen.

Dangling in the Tournefortia. Charles Bukowski. 1 cass. (Running Time: 30 min.). 8.95 (AMF-3) Am Audio Prose.
Besides reading the poem, the author talks about horses, women, writing, & Los Angeles.

Daniel see Poetry of Vachel Lindsay

Daniel. (LifeLight Bible Studies: Course 24). 13.95 Set. (20-2752) Concordia.

Daniel. 1993. audio compact disk 22.95 (978-0-634-09196-4(4)) H Leonard.

Daniel. Charles R. Swindoll.Tr. of Daniel. 2006. audio compact disk 43.00 (978-1-57972-733-8(6)) Insight Living.

Daniel: God's Pattern for the Future. Charles R. Swindoll. 9 cass. (Running Time: 14 hrs.). 1996. 44.95 (978-1-57972-026-1(9)) Insight Living.
Bible study on the life of Daniel & prophecies about the future kingdoms on the earth.

Daniel Amos: Our Personal Favorite Famous Hits. Perf. by Daniel Amos. 1 CD. 1999. audio compact disk 16.98 (KMGD8684) Provident Mus Dist.

Daniel & Nephi. Chris Heimerdinger. 5 cass. (J). 2004. 19.95 (978-1-57734-822-1(2)) Covenant Comms.

Daniel & Nephi, Set. abr. ed. Chris Heimerdinger. Read by Chris Heimerdinger. 2 cass. (YA). (gr. 6-12). 1993. 11.98 (978-1-55503-594-5(9), 0700916) Covenant Comms.
Fiction.

Daniel Boone see Poetry of Benet

Daniel Boone. unabr. ed. John Mack Faragher. Read by Tom Parker. 9 cass. (Running Time: 13 hrs.). 1993. 62.95 (978-0-7861-0444-4(9), 1396) Blckstn Audio.
Drawing from popular narrative, the public record, scraps of documentation from Boone's own hand, & a treasure of reminiscence & recollection gathered by nineteenth-century antiquarians, Faragher employs the methods of new social history to produce a portrait that defines the man & the times he helped shape. Blending these themes from a much-vitalized western & frontier history with the words & ideas of ordinary people, Faragher has produced a book that will stand as the definitive life of Daniel Boone for the next century.

Daniel Boone. unabr. ed. Robert Hogrogian. 1 cass. (Running Time: 20 min.). (People to Remember Ser.: Set II). (J). (gr. 4-7). 1979. bk. 16.99 (978-0-934898-86-7(3)); pap. bk. 9.95 (978-0-934898-12-6(X)) Jan Prods.
The adventure-filled tale of the man who led the way to the Western Frontier.

Daniel Boone: The Life & Legend of an American Pioneer. unabr. ed. John Mack Faragher. Read by Tom Parker. (Running Time: 46800 sec.). 2007. audio compact disk & audio compact disk 90.00 (978-0-7861-6197-3(3)) Blckstn Audio.

Daniel Boone: The Life & Legend of an American Pioneer. unabr. ed. John Mack Faragher. Narrated by Richard Poe. 11 cass. (Running Time: 15 hrs. 45 mins.). 1994. 91.00 (978-0-7887-0055-2(3), 94254E7) Recorded Bks.
In the first biography of Daniel Boone in more than fifty years, award-winning historian John Mack Faragher portrays both the hero himself & the uniquely American process of heromaking.

Daniel Boone: The Life & Legend of an American Pioneer. unabr. ed. John Mack Faragher. Read by Tom Parker. (Running Time: 46800 sec.). 2007. audio compact disk 29.95 (978-0-7861-6204-8(X)) Blckstn Audio.

Daniel Boone: Wilderness Scout. unabr. ed. Stewart Edward White. 5 cass. (Running Time: 7 hrs.). 2000. 39.95 (978-0-7861-1759-8(1), 2562) Blckstn Audio.
Daniel Boone (1734-1820) is one of the most famous pioneers in United States history. He spent most of his life exploring & settling the American frontier. Boone had little formal education, but he did learn the skills of a woodsman early in life. By age 12 his sharp hunter's eye & skill with a rifle helped keep his family well provided with wild game. In 1756 Boone married Rebecca Bryan & spent most of the next ten years hunting & farming to feed his family. In 1769 Boone, & old friend, John Findley & five men traveled along wilderness trails & through the Cumberland gap in the Appalachian mountains into Kentucky. They found a "hunter's paradise." In 1799 Boone moved west again, leading hundreds of settlers to new homes in Missouri.

Daniel Boone: Young Hunter & Tracker. unabr. ed. Augusta Stevenson. Read by Lloyd James. 4 cass. (Running Time: 5 hrs. 30 mins.). (Childhood of Famous Americans Ser.). (gr. 1-3). 2001. pap. bk. 35.95 (978-0-7861-2063-5(0), K2824) Blckstn Audio.
From the opening scene describing a standoff with an enraged cinnamon bear, children will be enthralled with this account of the childhood of the boy who would become a frontier hero, who blazed a trail through the Cumberland Gap & led the first settlers to Kentucky. Daniel's early lessons in tracking & forestry, his upbringing in a Quaker family & his encounters with various Indian tribes vividly illustrates life in the wilderness.

Daniel Commentary. Chuck Missler. 16 audio CD's. (Running Time: 16 hours). (Chuck Missler Commentaries). 2004. audio compact disk 69.95 (978-1-57821-276-7(6)) Koinonia Hse.
*The Book of Daniel contains the most amazing prophecies of the Bible, and is one of the most authenticated books of the Old Testament. The numerous detailed prophecies of the period of Gentile dominion make this one of the most important foundational studies for anyone who takes the Bible seriously.THis Audio CD set covers: * Daniel 1; Dare to be a Daniel - Introduction to the Book. Background, authentication, etc. * Daniel 2; Nebuchadnezzar's Dream - The poly-metallic image; an overview of all the Gentile dominion on the Planet Earth. Daniel and his three friends avoid death penalty and get promoted. * Daniel 3; Bow or Burn - Nebuchadnezzar's ego trip; the worship of his image. * Daniel 4; Nebachadnezzar's lesson in pride - The only chapter in the Bible written by a Gentile king. * Daniel 5; The Fall of Babylon - The "handwriting on the wall" and the fall of Babylon to the Persians. * The Mystery of Babylon - Babylon in Bible prophecy; it's ultimate destruction; an update on current events; the "Mystery Babylon" of Revelation. * Daniel 6; Daniel in the Lion's Den - How Daniel avoided the "mark of the beast." * Daniel 7; The Times of the Gentiles - The four empires which climax Gentile dominion on the Earth. * Daniel 8; The Ram and the Goat - The succession of the Persian and Greek Empires and the rise of Alexander the Great. * Daniel 9A; The 69 Weeks - The Angel Gabriel predicts the precise day on which Jesus presented Himself as the "Meshiach Nagid" (The Messiah the King). * Daniel 9B; The 70th Week of Daniel - The mysterious interval between the 69th and 70th "weeks" of Daniel and the final seven years of world history. * Daniel 10; The Dark Side - The spooky glimpse of the spiritual warfare that lies behind world events. * Daniel 11; The Silent Years- The amazing prediction of the conflicts between the Ptolemaic and Seleucid Empires and the emergence of the final World Leader. * Daniel 12 - The Climax of All History * Europa Rising Part I - Biblical Background* Europa Rising Part II - The European Union Today.*

Daniel Commentary. deluxe ed. Chuck Missler. 16 cass. (Running Time: 24 hrs.). (Heirloom Edition Ser.). 1996. im. lthr. 69.95 Incl. notes. (978-1-880532-20-1(4)) Koinonia Hse.
The Book of Daniel contains the most amazing prophecies of the Bible, and is one of the most authenticating books of the Old Testament. The numerous detailed prophecies of the period of Gentile dominion make this one of the most important foundational studies for anyone who takes the Bible seriously.

Daniel Commentary: Verse-by-Verse with Chuck Missler. Chuck Missler. 1 CD-ROM. (Running Time: 16 hours aprox). (Chuck Missler Commentaries). 2000. cd-rom 39.95 (978-1-57821-092-3(5)) Koinonia Hse.

Daniel Curley. unabr. ed. Read by Daniel Curley. 1 cass. (Running Time: 29 min.). 1985. 10.00 New Letters.
Daniel Curley reads a story, "Trinity" & exerpts from a second story, "The Contrivance".

Daniel Deronda. George Eliot. Contrib. by Anna Chancellor. 3 CDs. (Running Time: 2 hrs. 50 mins.). 2006. audio compact disk 39.95 (978-0-7927-4344-6(X), BBCD 171) AudioGO.

Daniel Deronda. George Eliot. 2 cass. (Running Time: 3 hrs.). 1998. 16.85 Set. (978-0-563-55708-1(7)) BBC WrldWd GBR.
Young Daniel Deronda & his fateful relationship with Gwendolen Harleth.

Daniel Deronda. George Eliot. Read by Amy von Lecteur. 2009. 33.95 (978-1-60112-998-7(X)) Babblebooks.

Daniel Deronda. unabr. ed. George Eliot. (Running Time: 108000 sec.). 2007. audio compact disk 44.95 (978-0-7861-5820-1(4)) Blckstn Audio.

Daniel Deronda. unabr. ed. George Eliot. Read by Nadia May. (Running Time: 108000 sec.). 2007. audio compact disk 160.00 (978-0-7861-5819-5(0)) Blckstn Audio.

Daniel Deronda. unabr. ed. George Eliot. Read by Nadia May. (YA). 2008. 144.99 (978-1-60514-882-3(2)) Find a World.

Daniel Deronda, Pt. 1. unabr. ed. George Eliot. Read by Nadia May. 11 cass. (Running Time: 32 hrs.). 1997. 76.95 (978-0-7861-1327-9(8), 2224A,B) Blckstn Audio.
Considered by many to be the best work of English fiction ever written, it is the story about the truth of one's nature.

Daniel Deronda, Pt. 2. unabr. ed. George Eliot. 9 cass. (Running Time: 1 hr. 30 min. per cass.). 1992. 59.95 Set. Audio Bk Con.

Daniel Deronda, Pt. 2. unabr. ed. George Eliot. Read by Nadia May. 11 cass. (Running Time: 32 hrs.). 1997. 76.95 (978-0-7861-1328-6(6), 2224A,B) Blckstn Audio.
Two tales in one: that of the hero Daniel Deronda & of the heroine Gwendolen Harleth. Daniel is the adopted son of an aristocratic English-man & a young man of gracious personality & positive values; he discovers that he is of Jewish parentage & ends by marrying a Jewish girl, Mirah & devoting himself to the cause of establishing a Jewish homeland. Gwendolen belongs to an impoverished upper-class family & marries (under pressure from her clergyman uncle) a rich & entirely self-centered aristocrat, Henleigh Grandcourt, to redeem their fortunes.

Daniel Deronda, Pt. 2, Set. George Eliot. 9 cass. (Running Time: 13 hrs. 30 min.). 1999. 59.95 Audio Bk Con.
The frivolous, beautiful Gwendolen Harleth finds in Deronda a man indifferent to her charms. In trying to win his regard, she develops her finer qualities. Deronda, kind & idealistic, is raised by a wealthy Christian guardian & later learns of his Jewish parentage. He falls in love with the lovely Mirah Cohen, whose invalid brother inspires him with the cause of Jewish nationalism.

Daniel Deronda (Part 1), Vol. 1. unabr. ed. George Eliot. Read by Flo Gibson. 12 cass. (Running Time: 1 hr. 30 min. per cass.). 1992. 39.95 (978-1-55685-244-2(4)) Audio Bk Con.
The frivolous, beautiful Gwendolen Harleth finds in Deronda a man indifferent to her charms. In trying to win his regard, she develops her finer qualities. Deronda, kind & idealistic, is raised by a wealthy Christian guardian & later learns of his Jewish parentage. He falls in love with the lovely Mirah Cohen, whose invalid brother inspires him with the cause of Jewish nationalism.

Daniel Deronda (Part 2), Vol. 2. unabr. ed. George Eliot. Narrated by Flo Gibson. (Running Time: 12 hrs. 32 mins.). 1992. 28.95 (978-1-55685-802-4(7)) Audio Bk Con.

Daniel Deronda (Parts 1 And 2) unabr. ed. George Eliot. Narrated by Flo Gibson. (Running Time: 30 hrs. 20 mins.). 1992. 59.95 (978-1-55685-803-1(5)) Audio Bk Con.

Daniel Halpern. Interview with Daniel Halpern. 1 cass. (Running Time: 25 min.). 1978. 11.95 (L032) TFR.
Halpern talks about emerging from a series of personal difficulties to write a new kind of poetry. He describes the birth & death of his highly regarded literary magazine, "Antaeus".

Daniel Halpern. unabr. ed. Read by Daniel Halpern. 1 cass. (Running Time: 29 min.). 1985. 10.00 New Letters.
The well known editor of "Antaeus" was recorded at a public reading of his poetry.

Daniel Pinkwater: Portrait of the Artist. (Running Time: 36 min.). 1989. 11.95 (A0170B090, HarperThor) HarpC GBR.

Daniel Stern: The Liberal Imagination by Lionel Trilling. unabr. ed. Short Stories. Daniel Stern. Read by Daniel Stern. 1 cass. (Running Time: 29 min.). 1987. 10.00 (112787) New Letters.
Stern is an advertising executive & the author of ten books, the best known of which is his 1968 novel "The Suicide Academy". He reads from "The Liberal Imagination by Lionel Trilling (A Story)," an account of the New York literary scene in the 1950's.

Daniel Volume 1: God's Man for the Moment. Charles R. Swindoll. 2008. audio compact disk 38.00 (978-1-57972-826-7(X)) Insight Living.

Daniel Volume 2: God's Plan for the Future. Charles R. Swindoll. 2008. audio compact disk 38.00 (978-1-57972-827-4(8)) Insight Living.

Daniel Wolff. unabr. ed. Read by Daniel Wolff. 1 cass. (Running Time: 29 min.). 1985. 10.00 New Letters.
Daniel Wolff reads "subway poems" & work sonnets about a house painter.

Daniel Woodrell. unabr. ed. Read by Daniel Woodrell & Rebekah Presson. Ed. by James McKinley. 1 cass. (Running Time: 29 min.). (New Letters on the Air Ser.). 1992. 10.00 (110692); 18.00 2-sided cass. New Letters.
Woodrell is interviewed by Rebekah Presson & reads from The Ones You Do.

Daniel 2005. unabr. ed. 2005. 9.99 (978-0-8297-4654-9(4)) Zondervan.

Daniel 2005. unabr. ed. Daniel Calvetti. 2005. audio compact disk 14.99 (978-0-8297-4652-5(8)) Zondervan.
After " Solo tu Gracia" (Just Your Grace), Daniel Calveti presents "Vivo para Ti" (I Live For You), a project of impactfull music. Recorded in concert in Puerto Rico where Daniel Calveti presented a devotional model divided into three principle points:How to get close to Him with gratitude, recognizing who He is,Presenting our needs,andMinistering to the heart of God.Each of these stages is represented with specific themes, such as "Tu eres la luz" (You Are The Light), "La niña de tus ojos" (The Child of Your Eyes) and "La ultima palabra" (The Last Word). These will lead you by the hand into a deep worship experience, in your personal time of worship as well as with your congregations.

Danielito Y el Dinosaurio. Tr. of Danny & the Dinosaur. (SPA.). 2004. 8.95 (978-0-7882-0275-9(8)) Weston Woods.

Danielito y el Dinosaurio. Syd Hoff. 1 cass. (Running Time: 10 min.). (SPA.). (J). bk. 24.95 Weston Woods.

Danielito y el Dinosaurio. Syd Hoff. Tr. by Teresa Mlawer. (SPA.). (J). (gr. k-2). 2004. 8.95 (978-0-7882-0129-5(8), WW0751) Weston Woods.

Danielle Steel CD Collection: Amazing Grace, Honor Thyself, Rogue. abr. ed. Danielle Steel. (Running Time: 17 hrs.). 2009. audio compact disk 34.99 (978-1-4418-1197-4(4), 9781441811974, BACD) Brilliance Audio.

Danielle Steel CD Collection 2: A Good Woman, One Day at a Time. abr. ed. Danielle Steel. (Running Time: 11 hrs.). 2010. audio compact disk 19.99 (978-1-4418-4962-5(9), 9781441849625, BACD) Brilliance Audio.

Danielle Steel Collection: Fine Things, Jewels, & Vanished. abr. ed. Danielle Steel. Read by Richard Thomas et al. 9 CDs. (Running Time: 9 hrs.). (Danielle Steel Ser.). (ENG.). 2004. audio compact disk 35.00 (978-0-7393-1262-9(6)) Pub: Random Audio Pubg. Dist(s): Random

Daniel's Duck. unabr. ed. Clyde Robert Bulla. Narrated by Jeff Woodman. 1 cass. (Running Time: 15 mins.). (I Can Read Bks.). (gr. 1 up). 1998. 10.00 (978-0-7887-2058-1(9), 95411E7) Recorded Bks.
Every evening in the long Tennessee winter, young Daniel sits by the fire with a block of wood. He is carving a duck that he plans to sell at the spring fair. But when he displays his finished sculpture, everyone laughs!.

Daniel's Story. Carol Matas. Read by Daniel Carpenter-Gold. 3 CDs. (Running Time: 3 hrs. 30 mins.). (YA). (gr. 7). 2008. audio compact disk 39.95 (978-0-9814890-2-5(8)) Audio Bkshelf.

Daniel's Story. unabr. ed. Carol Matas. Read by Daniel Carpenter-Gold. (YA). 2008. 59.99 (978-1-60514-765-9(6)) Find a World.

Daniel's 70 Weeks see Las 70 Semanas de Daniel

Daniel's 70 Weeks. Chuck Missler. 2 CD's. (Running Time: 120 min. aprox.). (Briefing Packages by Chuck Missler). 2000. audio compact disk 19.95 (978-1-57821-112-8(3)) Koinonia Hse.
Do you know the Most Amazing Passage in the entire Bible? In this study of Daniel's 70 Weeks, you will discover this amazing prophecy in the Old Testament predicted the very day that Jesus presented Himself as the Meschiach Nagid, the Messiah the King, to Jerusalem. The Seventy Week Prophecy of Daniel 9 includes the most incredible validation of Jesus Christ as the Messiah, which He held them accountable to have known. In a confidential briefing to His disciples, Jesus also highlights this passage as the key to understanding all other prophecies concerning His return. It is essential to understanding the Book of Revelation and other related passages.

Danish. 2 cass. (Running Time: 80 min.). (Language - Thirty Library). bk. 16.95 set in vinyl album. Moonbeam Pubns.
Using the proven method based on the famous U.S. Military accelerated language learning program, Language/30 courses stress conversationally useful words & phrases.

Danish. Ed. by Berlitz Publishing. (In 60 MINUTES Ser.). 2008. audio compact disk 9.95 (978-981-268-507-0(3)) Pub: APA Pubns Serv SGP. Dist(s): Langenscheidt

Danish. unabr. ed. Ed. by Charles Berlitz. 2 cass. (Running Time: 1 hr. 30 mins.). (Language/30 Brief Course Ser.). pap. bk. 21.95 (AF1033) J Norton Pubs.
Quick, highly condensed introduction to the words & phrases you'll need to communicate effectively in the country you're visiting. Cassettes & phrase guide book are in a vinyl album.

Danish: Language/30. rev. ed. Educational Services Corporation Staff. Intro. by Charles Berlitz. 2 cass. (DAN.). 1995. pap. bk. 21.95 (978-0-910542-76-0(7)) Educ Svcs DC.
Danish self-teaching language course.

Danish: Learn to Speak & Understand Danish with Pimsleur Language Programs. Pimsleur Staff & Pimsleur. 5 cass. (Running Time: 500 hrs. 0 mins. NaN sec.). (Pimsleur Language Program Ser.). (ENG.). 1999. 95.00 (978-0-671-04397-1(8), Pimsleur) Pub: S&S Audio. Dist(s): S and S Inc
SPEAK DANISH TO LEARN DANISH The Pimsleur Method will have you speaking Danish in just a few short, easy-to-use lessons. Learn at your own pace, comfortably and conveniently. No books to study. No memorization drills. LEARN DANISH AS YOU LEARNED ENGLISH You learned English by listening. With Pimsleur, you listen to learn Danish. This Language Program was developed by renowned memory expert, Dr. Paul Pimsleur. His research led him to the realization that the most important use of memory is in language learning. Based on this, Dr. Pimsleur designed a learning program that works for any language. The Pimsleur Language Program is an integrated system which immerses you in the language, encouraging you to hear, understand and use the language all at the same time. Now you can take advantage of Dr. Pimsleur's research. At the completion of these eight lessons you will comfortably understand and speak at a beginner level.

Danish: Learn to Speak & Understand Danish with Pimsleur Language Programs. Pimsleur Staff & Pimsleur. (Running Time: 500 hrs. 0 mins. NaN sec.). (Compact Ser.). (KOR & ENG.). 2003. audio compact disk 115.00 (978-0-671-79123-0(0), Pimsleur) Pub: S&S Audio. Dist(s): S and S Inc

Danish: Learn to Speak & Understand Danish with Pimsleur Language Programs. unabr. ed. Pimsleur Staff & Pimsleur. 5 CDs. (Running Time: 50 hrs. 0 mins. 0 sec.). (Compact Ser.). (DAN & ENG.). 2006. audio compact disk 49.95 (978-0-7435-5062-8(5), Pimsleur) Pub: S&S Audio. Dist(s): S and S Inc

Danmarks Dyreliv 9: De danske graeshopper. (Orthoptera.) (the Danish Grasshoppers.) O. Fogh Nielsen.Tr. of Animal Life of Denmark. (DAN.). 2000. bk. 60.00 (978-87-88757-50-7(1)) Pub: Apollo Books DNK. Dist(s): Intl Spec Bk

Danny & the Boys. unabr. collector's ed. Robert Traver. Read by Wolfram Kandinsky. 7 cass. (Running Time: 10 hrs. 30 min.). 1990. 56.00 (978-0-7366-1679-9(9), 2527) Books on Tape.
Rugged is the word for Danny McGinnis - & his "boys." It is the Depression, they all live together, refugees from the outside world, in a little logging shack in Hungry Hollow, on Michigan's Upper Peninsula. The Hollow is long logged out & now the main activities center on fishing, hunting, shooting the breeze, moonshine & periodic rampages through town. They turn a dollar any way they can, play pranks on each other & the townspeople, practice their rugged democracy in a traditional American way, which includes respecting individual eccentricities. Robert Traver is the pen name of John Voelker, author of Anatomy of a Murder & lifelong resident of Michigan's "U. P." This collection of stories is based on characters he has known there, & is clearly a labor of love.

Danny & the Dinosaur see Danielito Y el Dinosaurio

Danny & the Dinosaur. (SPA.). 2004. bk. 24.95 (978-0-7882-0130-1(1)); bk. 24.95 (978-0-89719-869-1(7)); pap. bk. 18.95 (978-1-55592-803-2(X)); pap. bk. 18.95 (978-1-55592-771-4(8)); pap. bk. 38.75 (978-1-55592-820-9(X)); pap. bk. 38.75 (978-1-55592-786-8(6)); pap. bk. 32.75 (978-1-55592-215-3(5)); pap. bk. 32.75 (978-1-55592-216-0(3)); pap. bk. 14.95 (978-1-56008-051-0(5)); pap. bk. 14.95 (978-1-55592-847-6(1)); cass. & flmstrp 30.00 (978-1-56008-659-8(9)); audio compact disk 12.95 (978-1-55592-870-4(6)); 8.95 (978-1-56008-884-4(2)) Weston Woods.
This is the story of a boy's friendship with a dinosaur and how they spend one happy day together.

Danny & the Dinosaur. Syd Hoff. 1 read-along cass. (Running Time: 15 min.). (I Can Read Bks.). (J). (ps-1). HarperCollins Pubs.
One side has a turn-the-page beep signal & the other side is uninterrupted narration for more experienced readers.

Danny & the Dinosaur. Syd Hoff. 1 read-along cass. (Running Time: 10 min.). (I Can Read Bks.). (ENG & SPA.). (J). bk. 8.95 Spanish. (RAC067SP); bk. 24.95 Spanish. (HRA367SP); pap. bk. 32.75; 8.95 (RAC067); pap. bk. 12.95 (PRA067) Weston Woods.
This is the story of a boy's friendship with a dinosaur & how they spend one happy day together.

Danny & the Dinosaur. Syd Hoff. (J). 2004. 8.95 (978-1-56008-128-9(7)) Weston Woods.

Danny & the Dinosaur. abr. ed. Syd Hoff. Illus. by Syd Hoff. 1 cass. (I Can Read Bks.). (J). (ps-3). 1990. 8.99 (978-1-55994-226-3(6)) HarperCollins Pubs.

Danny & the Dinosaur. abr. ed. Syd Hoff. Illus. by Syd Hoff. (I Can Read Bks.). (J). (gr. k-3). 2005. 9.99 (978-0-06-078687-8(6), HarperFestival) HarperCollins Pubs.

Danny & the Dinosaur. unabr. ed. Syd Hoff. 1 cass. (Running Time: 1 hr. 30 mins.). 2003. 7.99 (978-0-06-058460-3(2)) HarperCollins Pubs.

Danny & the Dinosaur Go to Camp. abr. ed. Syd Hoff. Illus. by Syd Hoff. (I Can Read Bks.). (J). (ps-3). 2002. 8.99 (978-0-694-70110-0(6)) HarperCollins Pubs.

Danny & the Dinosaur Go to Camp. abr. ed. Syd Hoff. Illus. by Syd Hoff. (I Can Read Bks.). (J). (gr. k-3). 2005. 9.99 (978-0-06-078688-5(4), HarperFestival) HarperCollins Pubs.

Danny & the Fiery Dragon. Gretchen L. Randolph & Wanda H. Appleton. Composed by Peter A. Appleton. 1 cass. (Running Time: 12 min.).Tr. of Danny y el Dragon Fogoso. (J). (gr. k-6). 1996. pap. bk. 26.95 Incl. bk. (978-1-890239-76-3(3)) Healthy Assn.
Danny gets angry because his little sister has taken his soccer ball. He is about to hit her, when something remarkable happens, he stops! He listens to the fiery dragon & takes positive action to change things. Educational materials help children work with their feelings.

Danny & the Fiery Dragon. Gretchen L. Randolph & Wanda H. Appleton. Composed by Peter A. Appleton. 1 cass. (Running Time: 12 min.).Tr. of Danny y el Dragon Fogoso. (J). (gr. k-6). 1997. pap. bk. 26.95 Incl. bk. (978-1-890239-77-0(1)) Healthy Assn.

Danny Boy. unabr. ed. Anne Bennett. Contrib. by Caroline Lennon. 11 cass. (Story Sound Ser.). (J). 2006. 89.95 (978-1-85903-920-5(0)) Pub: Mgna Lrg Print GBR. Dist(s): Ulverscroft US

Danny Boy. unabr. ed. Anne Bennett & Caroline Lennon. Contrib. by Caroline Lennon. 13 vols. (Story Sound CD Ser.). (J). 2006. audio compact disk 99.95 (978-1-85903-952-6(9)) Pub: Mgna Lrg Print GBR. Dist(s): Ulverscroft US

***Danny Boy.** unabr. ed. Henry Hack. Narrated by Joe O'Shaughnessy. 1 MP3-CD. (Running Time: 8 hrs. 15 mins.). 2009. 24.95 (978-1-60548-340-5(0)); audio compact disk 47.95 (978-1-60548-339-9(7)) Books in Motion.

Danny Kaye Show. unabr. ed. Perf. by Eve Arden et al. 1 cass. (Running Time: 60 min.). Dramatization. 1944. 7.95 Norelco box. (CC-9801) Natl Recrd Co.
First show: Comedian Danny Kaye presents a program of comedy & variety. Danny performs his "Russian Composers" routine, sings "Minnie the Moocher," & does a sketch in which he plays all the characters. Pabst Blue Ribbon Beer. Second show: Danny, along with the regulars, present the "Life Story of Danny Kaye," with Eve Arden featured as his childhood schoolteacher. Danny sings the "Lobby Number" from his hit film, "Up in Arms." Pabst Blue Ribbon Beer.

Danny Kaye Show. unabr. ed. Perf. by Eve Arden & Eddie Cantor. 1 cass. (Running Time: 1 hr.). 4.95 (978-1-57816-096-9(0), DK136) Audio File.
Two radio shows, on 1/16/45 & 1/13/45.

Danny the Dragon Book & CD Set. (ENG., (J). 2009. pap. bk. 14.95 (978-0-9800721-6-7(6)) Imag Pub Group.

Danny y el Dragon Fogoso see Danny & the Fiery Dragon

Danois sans Peine. 1 cass. (Running Time: 1 hr., 30 min.). (DAN & FRE.). 2000. bk. 75.00 (978-2-7005-1041-6(0)) Pub: Assimil FRA. Dist(s): Distribks Inc

Dan's Greatest Hits! Read by Dan Rattiner. (Running Time: 68 min.). 2004. audio compact disk 9.95 (978-0-9740201-5-0(X)) Harbor Electronic.

Danse. David Hamilton. 2006. pap. bk. 49.95 (978-3-937406-18-3(2)) Pub: edel CLASS DEU. Dist(s): Natl Bk Netwk

Danse Ce Soir - Fiddle & Accordion Music of Quebec. Laurie Hart & Greg Sandell. 2001. audio compact disk 15.98 Mel Bay.

Danse Macabre see Osbert Sitwell Reading His Poetry

Danse Macabre. abr. ed. Laurell K. Hamilton. Read by Cynthia Holloway. (Running Time: 7 hrs.). (Anita Blake, Vampire Hunter Ser.: No. 14). 2007. audio compact disk 19.99 (978-1-59737-670-9(1), 9781597376709, BCD Value Price) Brilliance Audio.

Danse Macabre. unabr. ed. Laurell K. Hamilton. Read by Cynthia Holloway. (Running Time: 21 hrs.). (Anita Blake, Vampire Hunter Ser.: No. 14). 2006. 44.25 (978-1-59710-829-4(4), 9781597108294, BADLE); 29.95 (978-1-59710-828-7(6), 9781597108287, BAD); 117.25 (978-1-59600-039-1(2), 9781596000391, BrilAudUnabridg); audio compact disk 142.25 (978-1-59600-042-1(2), 9781596000421, BACDLib Ed); audio compact disk 49.95 (978-1-59600-868-7(7), 9781596008687, Bril Audio CD Unabri); audio compact disk 29.95 (978-1-59335-786-3(9), 9781593357863, Brilliance MP3); audio compact disk 44.25 (978-1-59335-920-1(9), 9781593359201, Brlnc Audio MP3 Lib) Brilliance Audio.
Please enter a Synopsis.

Danse Macabre. unabr. ed. Stephen King. Read by William Dufris. (Running Time: 18 hrs.).Tr. of Dance of Death. 2010. 24.99 (978-1-4418-3109-5(6), 9781441831095, BAD); 39.97 (978-1-4418-3108-8(8), 9781441831088, Brlnc Audio MP3 Lib); 39.97 (978-1-4418-3110-1(X), 9781441831101, BADLE); 24.99 (978-1-4418-3107-1(X), 9781441831071, Brilliance MP3); audio compact disk 99.97 (978-1-4418-3106-4(1), 9781441831064, BriAudCD Unabrid); audio compact disk 29.99 (978-1-4418-3105-7(3), 9781441831057) Brilliance Audio.

Dansing Star. unabr. ed. Kirby Jonas. Read by James Drury. 12 cass. (Running Time: 12 hrs. 6 min.). 2001. 64.95 (978-1-55686-977-8(0)) Books in Motion.
Mort Dansing was a white man raised by Apaches. His return to white society was vengeance laden and the star he now wore on his vest was his badge of honor, or possibly... dishonor.

Dansu Dansu Dansu see Dance Dance Dance

***Danta / Poems.** Pearse Hutchinson. (ENG.). 1998. 11.95 (978-0-8023-0030-0(8)) Pub: Clo Iar-Chonnachta IRL. Dist(s): Dufour

Dante. R. W. B. Lewis. Read by Grover Gardner. 2001. audio compact disk 40.00 (978-0-7366-7142-2(0)) Books on Tape.

Dante. unabr. ed. R. W. B. Lewis. 4 cass. (Running Time: 6 hrs.). 2001. 32.00 (978-0-7366-7036-4(X)) Books on Tape.
In Dante he traces the life and complex development-emotional, artistic, philosophical-of this supreme poet-historian, from his wanderings through Tuscan hills and splendid churches to his days as a young soldier fighting for democracy, and to his civic leadership and years of embittered exile from the city that would fiercely reclaim him a century later.

Dante. unabr. ed. R. W. B. Lewis. 4 cass. (Running Time: 6 hrs.). 2001. 24.95 (978-0-7366-6810-1(1)) Books on Tape.
Traces the life & complex development of this supreme poet-historian - whose monumental search for ultimate truth surfaces in "The Divine Comedy".

Dante: Poet of the Impossible. Greg Kelly. 4 CDs. (Running Time: 6 hrs.). 2005. audio compact disk 24.95 (978-0-660-18913-0(5)) Pub: Canadian Broadcasting CAN. Dist(s): Georgetown Term

Dante Club. abr. ed. Matthew Pearl. 2004. 15.95 (978-0-7435-4895-3(7)) Pub: S&S Audio. Dist(s): S and S Inc

Dante Club. unabr. ed. Matthew Pearl. Read by John Seidman. 2006. 29.95 (978-0-7435-6392-5(1), Audioworks) Pub: S&S Audio. Dist(s): S and S Inc

Dante Gebel la Coleccion Pack 3: Serie Motivacional. unabr. ed. Dante Gebel. (SPA.). 2006. audio compact disk 19.99 (978-0-8297-4759-1(1)) Pub: Vida Pubs. Dist(s): Zondervan

Dante, Introduction To. unabr. ed. Gilbert Highet. Read by Gilbert Highet. 1 cass. (Running Time: 30 min.). 9.95 (23315-A) J Norton Pubs.

***Dante Valentine.** unabr. ed. Lilith Saintcrow. (Running Time: 9 hrs.). 2011. 24.99 (978-1-4418-8296-7(0), 9781441882967, Brilliance MP3); 39.97 (978-1-4418-8297-4(9), 9781441882974, Brlnc Audio MP3 Lib); 39.97 (978-1-4418-8299-8(5), 9781441882998, BADLE); 24.99 (978-1-4418-8298-1(7), 9781441882981, BAD); audio compact disk 29.99 (978-1-4418-8293-6(6), 9781441882936, Bril Audio CD Unabri); audio compact disk 79.97 (978-1-4418-8294-3(4), 9781441882943, BriAudCD Unabrid) Brilliance Audio.

Dante's Divine Comedy, Pts. I-II. Instructed by William Cook & Ronald Herzman. 12 CDs. (Running Time: 12 hrs.). 2001. bk. 69.95 (978-1-56585-312-6(1), 287) Teaching Co.

Dante's Divine Comedy, Pts I-II, Vol. 1. Instructed by Ronald Herzman & William Cook. 12 cass. (Running Time: 12 hrs.). 2001. 54.95 (978-1-56585-058-3(0), 287) Teaching Co.

Dante's Divine Comedy, Vol. 2. Instructed by William Cook & Ronald Herzman. 6 CDs. (Running Time: 6 hrs.). 2001. audio compact disk 179.95 (978-1-56585-313-3(X)) Teaching Co.

Dante's Divine Comedy, Vol. 2. Instructed by Ronald Herzman & William Cook. 6 cass. (Running Time: 6 hrs.). 2001. 129.95 (978-1-56585-059-0(9)) Teaching Co.

Dante's Inferno. Lynette Rohrer Shirk et al. Narrated by Colin Redgrave. Composed by Robin Rimbaud. Retold by Arthur Brown. Narrated by Laurie Anderson. (Running Time: 1 hr. 10 mins. 5 sec.). (ENG.). 2009. audio compact disk 15.00 (978-1-934997-37-6(4)) Pub: CSAWord. Dist(s): PerseuPGW

Dantes' Inferno. unabr. ed. Sarah Lovett. Read by Joyce Bean. 7 cass. (Running Time: 10 hrs.). (Dr. Sylvia Strange Ser.: Vol. 4). 2001. 32.95 (978-1-58788-396-5(1), 1587883961, BAU); 78.25 (978-1-58788-397-2(X), 158788397X) Brilliance Audio.
When a massive explosion blasts through the J. Paul Getty Museum in Malibu and kills innocent visitors - including children on a class trip - the police peg mysterious loner John Dantes as the killer. But there's something about him that puzzles Dr. Sylvia Strange, who is called in to perform a psychiatric evaluation. She's not convinced that he's the key to understanding - and finding - the bomber. Can Dr. Strange unravel Dantes' madness and bring the real killer to justice?.

Dantes' Inferno. unabr. ed. Sarah Lovett. Read by Joyce Bean. (Running Time: 10 hrs.). (Dr. Sylvia Strange Ser.: Vol. 4). 2004. 39.25 (978-1-59335-440-4(1), 1593354401, Brlnc Audio MP3 Lib) Brilliance Audio.

Dantes' Inferno. unabr. ed. Sarah Lovett. Read by Joyce Bean. (Running Time: 10 hrs.). 2004. 39.25 (978-1-59710-172-1(9), 1597101729, BADLE) Brilliance Audio.

Dantes' Inferno. unabr. ed. Sarah Lovett. Read by Joyce Bean. (Running Time: 10 hrs.). (Dr. Sylvia Strange Ser.: Vol. 4). 2004. 24.95 (978-1-59335-074-1(0), 1593350740) Soulmate Audio Bks.

Dantes' Inferno. unabr. ed. Sarah Lovett. Read by Joyce Bean. (Running Time: 10 hrs.). 2004. 24.95 (978-1-59710-173-8(7), 1597101737, BAD) Brilliance Audio.

Dante's La Vita Nuova: Mystical Meanings of the Mystical Experience. Dante Alighieri. Instructed by Manly P. Hall. 8.95 (978-0-89314-040-3(6), C8109271) Philos Res.

***Dante's Numbers.** unabr. ed. David Hewson. Narrated by Saul Reichlin. 12 CDs. (Running Time: 14 hrs.). 2009. audio compact disk 123.75 (978-1-4074-1992-3(7)) Pub: Howes Ltd GBR. Dist(s): Recorded Bks

Dante's Way to the Stars. unabr. ed. Claudio Naranjo. 1 cass. (Running Time: 55 min.). 1968. 11.00 (04202) Big Sur Tapes.
"Midway in our life's journey I went astray from the straight road & woke to find myself alone in a dark wood." Thus Dante begins his journey, which may lead to one's full spiritual goal after knowledge of hell. Naranjo relates Dante's "way" to mystical schools, religions & modern psychology.

Danza y Paz. unabr. ed. Jonathan Settel. (SPA.). 2000. 7.99 (978-0-8297-3104-0(0)) Pub: Vida Pubs. Dist(s): Zondervan

Danza y Paz. unabr. ed. Jonathan Settel. 2000. audio compact disk 11.99 (978-0-8297-3105-7(9)) Zondervan.

Danzig Passage. abr. ed. Bodie Thoene & Brock Thoene. (Zion Covenant Ser.: Bk. 5). 2003. audio compact disk 27.99 (978-1-58926-160-0(7)) Oasis Audio.

Danzig Passage. unabr. ed. Bodie Thoene & Brock Thoene. Read by Susan O'Malley. 13 cass. (Running Time: 19 hrs.). (Zion Covenant Ser.: Bk. 5). 2002. 85.95 (978-0-7861-2236-3(6), 2960); audio compact disk 128.00 (978-0-7861-9525-1(8), 2960) Blckstn Audio.
A boarded-up church, a dressmaker's shop, a "borrowed" apartment, a Vienna pawnshop, a locked train compartment-are these places of safety leading to the Danzig Passage or way stations to betrayal and destruction?.

Dao de Jing. Scripts. Perf. by Albert A. Anderson. Tr. by Keping Wang. 2 CDs. (Running Time: 1.5 hours). 2004. audio compact disk 25.00 (978-1-887250-39-9(5)) Agora Pubns.

Dao de Jing: A Philosophical Translation. abr. ed. Roger T. Ames & David Hall. 3 cass. (Running Time: 3 hrs. 30 mins.). 2003. 22.95 (978-1-57270-308-7(3)); audio compact disk 24.95 (978-1-57270-309-4(1)) Pub: Audio Partners. Dist(s): PerseuPGW

Dapfere Schneiderlein. Jacob W. Grimm & Wilhelm K. Grimm. 1 cass. (Running Time: 60 min.). (Bruder Grimm Kinder & Hausmarchen Ser.). (GER.). 1996. pap. bk. 19.50 (978-1-58085-206-7(8), GR-01) Interlingua VA.
Includes German language transcript & literal English translation. Includes title story, Das Totenhemdchen, Das Eigen sinnige kind, Marchen von Einem, der Auszog, & Das Furchten zu Lernen.

Dara Wier. unabr. ed. Dara Wier. Read by Dara Wier. 1 cass. (Running Time: 29 min.). 1988. 10.00 (031188) New Letters.
Wier reads from her latest just released by Carnegie-Mellon, "The Book of Knowledge".

Darcy's Utopia. unabr. ed. Fay Weldon. Read by Tamara Ustinov. 7 cass. (Running Time: 7 hrs. 50 min.). 2001. 61.95 (978-1-85089-673-9(9), 91112) Pub: ISIS Audio GBR. Dist(s): Ulverscroft US
"Weldon is a gifted tease of a writer...Darcy's Utopia is among the most frolicsome of her novels, but it still manages to display her quiet, grave insistence that we change our ways." - Sunday Times.

Dare, unabr. ed. R. L. Stine. Narrated by Christina Moore. 3 pieces. (Running Time: 3 hrs. 30 mins.). (Fear Street Ser.). (gr. 7 up). 1994. 27.00 (978-0-7887-0134-4(7), 94359E7) Recorded Bks.
A girl considers murdering her teacher when dared by a boy she admires.

Dare to be a Daniel 13-Session Training CD-ROM. Billy Graham Evangelistic Association. 2007. audio compact disk (978-1-59328-130-4(7)) Billy Graham Evangelistic Association.

Dare to Be A Man. David Evans. (ENG.). (YA). (gr. 8). 2008. audio compact disk 29.95 (978-0-14-314341-3(7), PengAudBks) Penguin Grp USA.

Dare to Be a Man: The Truth Every Man Must Know... & Every Woman Needs to Know about Him. David G. Evans. Read by David G. Evans. (Playaway Top Adult Picks B Ser.). (ENG.). 2009. 69.99 (978-1-4418-1016-8(1)) Find a World.

Dare to Be a Man: The Truth Every Man Must Know... & Every Woman Needs to Know about Him. unabr. ed. Bishop David G. Evans. Read by Bishop David G. Evans. (Running Time: 9 hrs.). 2009. 14.99 (978-1-4418-0156-2(1), 9781441801562, Brilliance MP3); 39.97 (978-1-4418-0157-9(X), 9781441801579, Brlnc Audio MP3 Lib); 14.99 (978-1-4418-0158-6(8), 9781441801586, BAD); 39.97 (978-1-4418-0159-3(6), 9781441801593, BADLE); audio compact disk 29.99 (978-1-4418-0154-8(5), 9781441801548, Bril Audio CD Unabri); audio compact disk 69.97 (978-1-4418-0155-5(3), 9781441801555, BriAudCD Unabrid) Brilliance Audio.

***Dare to Be a Man: The Truth Every Man Must Know... & Every Woman Needs to Know about Him.** unabr. ed. Bishop David G. Evans. Read by Bishop David G. Evans. (Running Time: 9 hrs.). 2010. audio compact disk 14.99 (978-1-4418-8723-8(7), 9781441887238, BCD Value Price) Brilliance Audio.

Dare to Be an Inner Winner. Dave Johnson. (Dave Johnson Educational Library). 65.00 D Johnson.
Identifies those attitudes which defeat & then reveals how to turn them around to become more of an Inner Winner.

Dare to Be Different. Troy Dunn. 1 CD. audio compact disk 10.98 (978-1-57734-118-5(X), 2500760) Covenant Comms.
A dynamic young man motivates youth to live their beliefs.

Dare to Be Different. Troy Dunn. 1 cass. 2004. 7.98 (978-1-55503-321-7(0), 069101) Covenant Comms.
A lively, funny, dynamic young man motivates youth to live their beliefs.

Dare to Be Free. Lynne Hammond. 1 cass. (Running Time: 1 hr.). 2005. 5.00 (978-1-57399-215-2(1)); audio compact disk 5.00 (978-1-57399-267-1(4)) Mac Hammond.

Dare to Connect: Reaching Out in Romance, Friendship, & the Workplace. unabr. ed. Susan Jeffers. Read by Susan Jeffers. 4 cass. (Running Time: 6 hrs. 48 min.). 1992. 25.00 (978-1-56170-040-0(1), 309) Hay House.
Susan Jeffers presents listeners with the tools to gain the confidence, courage & self-love they need to start connecting with all those around - mates, friends, & colleagues. A powerful tape for those who feel unsure, alone & unable to reach out.

Dare to Dream. Christine Wyrtzen et al. 1 cass. (50-Day Spiritual Adventure Ser.). 1993. 9.99 (978-1-879050-23-5(4)) Chapel of Air.
Religious songs for adult listeners.

Dare to Dream: Creative Stories & Poems for Kids. Ruth Degman-Reed. Narrated by Amanda Williamson & Dave Giorgio. (ENG.). (J). 2007. audio compact disk 9.95 (978-1-60031-013-3(3)) Spoken Books.

Dare to Dream: Solo Track. Christine Wyrtzen. 1 cass. (50-Day Spiritual Adventure Ser.). 1993. 9.99 (978-1-879050-25-9(0)) Chapel of Air.
Accompaniment track for solo singer.

Dare to Live Daily. abr. ed. Ruth Lycke. 8 cass. (Running Time: 8 hrs.). 1999. 39.95 Set. (DTLD9901) Edgemont Inc.

Dare to Prepare: How to Win Before You Begin! Ronald M. Shapiro. Read by Ronald M. Shapiro. Told to Gregory Jordan. (Playaway Adult Nonfiction Ser.). 2008. 54.99 (978-1-60640-751-6(1)) Find a World.

Dare to Prepare: How to Win Before You Begin! unabr. ed. Ronald M. Shapiro. Read by Ronald M. Shapiro. (Running Time: 27000 sec.). 2008. 44.95 (978-1-4332-0896-6(2)); audio compact disk & audio compact disk 29.95 (978-1-4332-0900-0(4)); audio compact disk & audio compact disk 55.00 (978-1-4332-0897-3(0)) Blckstn Audio.

Dare to Prepare: How to Win Before You Begin! unabr. ed. Ronald M. Shapiro. Read by Ronald M. Shapiro. Told to Gregory Jordan. (Running Time: 27000 sec.). 2008. 19.95 (978-1-4332-0898-0(9)); audio compact disk 19.95 (978-1-4332-0899-7(7)) Blckstn Audio.

Dare to Run. Compiled by Ken Bible. 1989. 19.99 (978-0-685-68413-9(X), TA-9108S) Lillenas.

Dare to Succeed: Survive & Thrive in the Game of Life. abr. ed. Mark Burnett. Read by Alan Shearman. 2 cass. (Running Time: 3 hrs.). 2001. 17.98 (Hyperion Audio) Hyperion.

Darell Weist Promotes Responsible Tourism; Butterfly Tagging; Bighorn Sheep Relocation; Nature Tourism in Texas; Civilian Conservation Corps Reunion. Hosted by Nancy Pearlman. 1 cass. (Running Time: 28 min.). 10.00 (1304) Educ Comm CA.

Dari, Basic: Learn to Speak & Understand Dari with Pimsleur Language Programs. Pimsleur. (Running Time: 5 hrs. 0 mins. 0 sec.). (Basic Ser.). (ENG.). 2009. audio compact disk 24.95 (978-0-7435-7155-5(X), Pimsleur) Pub: S&S Audio. Dist(s): S and S Inc

Dari, Comprehensive: Learn to Speak & Understand Dari with Pimsleur Language Programs. Pimsleur. (Running Time: 16 hrs. 0 mins. 0 sec.). (Comprehensive Ser.). (ENG.). 2009. audio compact disk 345.00 (978-0-7435-7154-8(1), Pimsleur) Pub: S&S Audio. Dist(s): S and S Inc

Dari, Conversational: Learn to Speak & Understand Dari with Pimsleur Language Programs. Pimsleur. (Running Time: 8 hrs. 0 mins. 0 sec.). (Conversational Ser.). (ENG.). 2009. audio compact disk 49.95 (978-0-7435-7156-2(8), Pimsleur) Pub: S&S Audio. Dist(s): S and S Inc

Darien's Rise. Paul McCusker & AIO Team Staff. (Adventures in Odyssey Passages Ser.). (ENG.). (J). 2009. audio compact disk 19.99 (978-1-58997-590-3(1)) Pub: Focus Family. Dist(s): Tyndale Hse

***Daring Book for Girls.** abr. ed. Andrea J. Buchanan & Miriam Peskowitz. Read by Ilyana Kadushin. (ENG.). 2007. (978-0-06-155576-3(2)); (978-0-06-155577-0(0)) HarperCollins Pubs.

Daring Book for Girls. abr. ed. Miriam Peskowitz & Andrea J. Buchanan. Read by Ilyana Kadushin. 3 CDs. (Running Time: 4 hrs.). 2007. audio compact disk 22.95 (978-0-06-147788-1(5), Harper Audio) HarperCollins Pubs.

***Daring Chloe.** unabr. ed. Laura Jensen Walker. (Running Time: 9 hrs. 45 mins. 0 sec.). (Getaway Girls Ser.). (ENG.). 2009. 14.99 (978-0-310-77209-5(5)) Zondervan.

Daring Deeds: And Sinister Schemes. unabr. ed. Focus on the Family Staff & AIO Team Staff. 4 CDs. (Running Time: 6 hrs.). (Adventures in Odyssey Ser.: Vol. 5). (ENG.). (J). 2005. audio compact disk 24.99 (978-1-58997-074-8(8)) Pub: Focus Family. Dist(s): Tyndale Hse

Daring Dewey. unabr. ed. Dave Kinnoin. 1 cass., 1 CD. (Running Time: 38 min.). (J). (gr. 1-6). 1990. 9.98 (978-1-881304-01-2(9), SW102-4); audio compact disk 12.98 CD. (978-1-881304-11-1(6), SW102-2) Song Wizard Recs.
Fun & inspiring original songs, sung by Dave Kinnoin.

Daring to Dream. abr. ed. Nora Roberts. Read by Sandra Burr. (Running Time: 3 hrs.). (Dream Trilogy: Bk. 1). 2009. audio compact disk 14.99 (978-1-4233-7903-4(9), 9781423379034) Brilliance Audio.

Daring to Dream. unabr. ed. Nora Roberts. Read by Sandra Burr. (Running Time: 11 hrs.). (Dream Trilogy: Bk. 1). 2008. 39.25 (978-1-4233-7875-4(X), 9781423378754, Brlnc Audio MP3 Lib); 39.25 (978-1-4233-7877-8(6), 9781423378778, BADLE); 24.95 (978-1-4233-7876-1(8), 9781423378761, BAD); 24.95 (978-1-4233-7874-7(1), 9781423378747, Brilliance MP3); audio compact disk 102.25 (978-1-4233-7873-0(3), 9781423378730, BriAudCD Unabrid); audio compact disk 34.95 (978-1-4233-7872-3(5), 9781423378723, Bril Audio CD Unabri) Brilliance Audio.

Daring Young Men: The Heroism & Triumph of the Berlin Airlift, June 1948-May 1949. unabr. ed. Richard Reeves. Narrated by Johnny Heller. (Running Time: 8 hrs. 30 mins. 0 sec.). (ENG.). 2010. 24.99 (978-1-4001-6402-8(8)); audio compact disk 34.99 (978-1-4001-1402-3(0)); audio compact disk 69.99 (978-1-4001-4402-0(7)) Pub: Tantor Media. Dist(s): IngramPubServ

***Daring Young Men: The Heroism & Triumph of the Berlin Airlift, June 1948-May 1949.** unabr. ed. Richard Reeves. Narrated by Johnny Heller. (Running Time: 8 hrs. 30 mins.). 2010. 34.99 (978-1-4001-9402-5(4)); 15.99 (978-1-4001-8402-6(9)) Tantor Media.

***Darius Jones.** unabr. ed. Mary B. Morrison. (Running Time: 10 hrs. 0 mins.). 2010. 29.95 (978-1-4417-5475-2(X)); 59.95 (978-1-4417-5471-4(7)); audio compact disk 29.95 (978-1-4417-5474-5(1)); audio compact disk 100.00 (978-1-4417-5472-1(5)) Blckstn Audio.

Dark. Read by Sean Barrett. 2 cass. (Running Time: 3 hrs.). (ENG.). 2001. 16.99 (978-0-333-78238-5(0)) Pub: Macmillan UK GBR. Dist(s): Trafalgar

Dark: Stories of Madness, Murder & the Supernatural. unabr. ed. Edgar Allan Poe et al. Ed. by Clint Willis. Narrated by Grover Gardner & Graeme Malcolm. 4 cass. (Running Time: 6 hrs.). (Adrenaline Ser.). (YA). 2000. 24.95 (978-1-885408-54-9(4), LL047) Listen & Live.
Dark contains the best writing from fiction masters about the things that scare us the most: murder, ghosts, insanity & our own vulnerability.

Dark-Adapted Eye. abr. ed. Barbara Vine, pseud. Read by Sophie Ward. 2 cass. (Running Time: 3 hrs.). 1994. 16.95 (978-0-945353-93-5(6), N20393) Pub: Audio Partners. Dist(s): PerseuPGW
When Vera Hillyard was hanged for murder, the reason was hidden by a genteelly respectable veneer. England in the fifties was not kind to women who erred, so something was done about it behind closed curtains.

Dark-Adapted Eye. abr. ed. Barbara Vine, pseud. Read by Sophie Ward. 2 cass. (Running Time: 3 hrs.). 2000. 7.95 (978-1-57815-185-1(6), 1125, Media Bks Audio) Media Bks NJ.
Faith Severn's family hid the truth for thirty years about why her aunt was hanged for murder, the reason behind her dark deed died with her.

Dark-Adapted Eye. unabr. ed. Barbara Vine, pseud. Read by Harriet Walter. 10 cass. (Running Time: 10 hrs.). 1993. bk. 84.95 (978-0-7451-6340-6(8), CAB 456) AudioGO.

***dark Age.** unabr. ed. Traci Harding. Read by Edwina Wren. (Running Time: 19 hrs. 46 mins.). (Ancient Future Ser.). 2010. audio compact disk 123.95 (978-1-74214-722-2(4), 9781742147222) Pub: Bolinda Pubng AUS. Dist(s): Bolinda Pub Inc

Dark Alchemy. unabr. ed. Sarah Lovett. Read by Joyce Bean. 5 cass. (Running Time: 7 hrs.). (Dr. Sylvia Strange Ser.: Vol. 5). 2003. 27.95 (978-1-59086-622-1(3), 1590866223, BAU); 69.25 (978-1-59086-623-8(1), 1590866231, CD Unabrid Lib Ed) Brilliance Audio.
Dr. Sylvia Strange - forensic psychiatrist and expert on criminal sexuality - returns in a thrilling new suspense novel and comes head-to-head with a terrifying serial killer whose weapon of choice is a poison nearly impossible to trace and, when ingested, nearly impossible to counteract. A baffling series of deaths have occurred over the span of a decade in some of the most prestigious research laboratories around the world. Now Dr. Sylvia Strange, forensic expert, and criminal profiler Edmund Sweetheart, FBI consultant, are called in to investigate what is looking like murder. Their prime suspect is Dr. Christine Palmer, a brilliant scientist whose work with scientific think tanks around the world made her one of three scientists knowledgeable about exotic neurotoxins and their antidotes. What follows is a taut and terrifying investigation, in which Sylvia finds herself able to trust no one - but herself.

Dark Alchemy. unabr. ed. Sarah Lovett. Read by Joyce Bean. (Running Time: 7 hrs.). (Dr. Sylvia Strange Ser.: Vol. 5). 2004. 39.25 (978-1-59335-438-1(X), 159335438X, Brlnc Audio MP3 Lib) Brilliance Audio.

Dark Alchemy. unabr. ed. Sarah Lovett. Read by Joyce Bean. (Running Time: 7 hrs.). (Dr. Sylvia Strange Ser.). 2004. 39.25 (978-1-59710-175-2(3), 1597101753, BADLE) Brilliance Audio.

Dark Alchemy. unabr. ed. Sarah Lovett. Read by Joyce Bean. (Running Time: 7 hrs.). (Dr. Sylvia Strange Ser.: Vol. 5). 2004. 24.95 (978-1-59335-075-8(9), 1593350759) Soulmate Audio Bks.

Dark Alchemy. unabr. ed. Sarah Lovett. Read by Joyce Bean. (Running Time: 7 hrs.). (Dr. Sylvia Strange Ser.). 2004. 24.95 (978-1-59710-174-5(5), 1597101745, BAD) Brilliance Audio.

***Dark & Hollow Places.** unabr. ed. Carrie Ryan. (ENG.). (J). 2011. audio compact disk 48.00 (978-0-307-74724-2(7), Listening Lib) Pub: Random Audio Pubg. Dist(s): Random

Dark & Sinful Death. unabr. ed. Alison Joseph. Read by Phyllida Nash. 10 cass. (Running Time: 10 hrs.). 1998. 84.95 Set, Dolby Sound. (978-0-7540-0155-3(5), CAB 1578) AudioGO.
Agnes Bourdillon isn't the kind of woman you would expect to be a nun. She's attractive, stylish, & not naturally saintly. She is sent to a girls' boarding school in West Yorkshire to teach. It's hardly a place that one would expect to find a woman as disturbed as Joanna Baines. When the gardener is murdered the day after Joanna goes missing, it seems only Agnes can discover who is lying & why.

Dark & Sinful Death, Set unabr. ed. Alison Joseph. Read by Phyllida Nash. 10 cass. 1999. 84.95 (CAB 1578) AudioGO.

Dark Is Rising. unabr. ed. Susan Cooper. Read by Alex Jennings. 6 cass. (Running Time: 9 hrs.). (J). (gr. 1-8). 1999. 40.00 (LL 0139, Chivers Child Audio) AudioGO.

Dark Is Rising. unabr. ed. Susan Cooper. Read by Alex Jennings. 6 cass. (Running Time: 8 hrs. 40 mins.). (Dark Is Rising Sequence Ser.). (J). (gr. 4-7). 1999. 40.00 (978-0-8072-8059-1(3), YA990CX, Listening Lib); 46.00 (978-0-8072-8060-7(7), YA990SP, Listening Lib) Random Audio Pubg.
On his eleventh birthday Will Stanton discovers he is the last of The Old Ones, dedicated to fighting the forces of evil. Will's journey to search for six magical signs needed for the battle between dark & light.

Dark Is Rising. unabr. ed. Susan Cooper. Narrated by Alex Jennings. 6 cass. (Running Time: 6 hrs.). (YA). 44.00 (LL1031AC) Weston Woods.

Dark Is Rising. unabr. ed. Susan Cooper & Susan Cooper. Read by Alex Jennings. (Running Time: 31320 sec.). (Dark Is Rising Sequence Ser.). (ENG.). (J). (gr. 5-7). 2007. audio compact disk 37.00 (978-0-7393-5973-0(8), Listening Lib) Pub: Random Audio Pubg. Dist(s): Random

Dark Is Rising, Set. unabr. ed. Susan Cooper. Read by Alex Jennings. 6 cass. (YA). 1999. 37.98 (FS9-43380) Highsmith.

***Dark Is the Moon.** unabr. ed. Ian Irvine. Read by Grant Cartwright. (Running Time: 23 hrs. 56 mins.). (View from the Mirror Ser.). 2010. audio compact disk 123.95 (978-1-74214-721-5(6), 9781742147215) Pub: Bolinda Pubng AUS. Dist(s): Bolinda Pub Inc

Dark Is the Sun. unabr. ed. Philip Jose Farmer. Read by Rebecca Rogers. (Running Time: 14 hrs. 30 mins.). 2010. 29.95 (978-1-4417-2349-9(8)); 85.95 (978-1-4417-2345-1(5)); audio compact disk 118.00 (978-1-4417-2346-8(3)) Blckstn Audio.

***Dark Jenny.** unabr. ed. Alex Bledsoe. Read by To be Announced. (Running Time: 10 hrs. 5 mins.). (Eddie Lacrosse Mysteries Ser.). (ENG.). 2011. 29.95 (978-1-4417-8249-6(4)); 65.95 (978-1-4417-8246-5(X)); audio compact disk 100.00 (978-1-4417-8247-2(8)) Blckstn Audio.

Dark Justice. collector's ed. William Bernhardt. Read by Jonathan Marosz. 9 cass. (Running Time: 13 hrs. 30 min.). (Ben Kincaid Ser.: No. 8). 2000. 72.00 (978-0-7366-5081-6(4), 5295) Books on Tape.
Years ago, Ben Kincaid successfully defended professional activist George Zakin against a charge of murder. Now, accused of killing a lumberjack, Zakin is counting on Ben to save him a second time. Ben knows that his client is innocent, but in a town where logging is a way of life & environmentalists are branded "echo-terrorists," winning the case will be an uphill fight. With the odds stacked against him, Ben walks into a courtroom war zone & potential killing field in the streets & woods of Magic Valley, an explosive place in the Pacific Northwest where allies & enemies are hard to tell apart & digging for the truth is as good as digging your grave.

Dark Justice. unabr. ed. Jack Higgins. Read by Michael Page. (Running Time: 6 hrs.). (Sean Dillon Ser.). 2004. 39.25 (978-1-59335-904-1(7), 1593359047, Brlnc Audio MP3 Lib); 24.95 (978-1-59335-770-2(2), 1593357702, Brilliance MP3); 29.95 (978-1-59355-873-4(2), 1593558732, BAU); audio compact disk 74.25 (978-1-59355-876-5(7), 1593558767, BriAudCD Unabrid) Brilliance Audio.
It is night in Manhattan. The President of the United States is scheduled to have dinner with an old friend, but in the building across the street, a man has disabled the security and stands at a window, a rifle in his hand. Fortunately, his attempt is not successful - but this is only the beginning. Someone is recruiting a shadowy network of agents with the intention of creating terror. Their range is broad, their identities masked, their methods subtle. White House operative Blake Johnson and his opposite number in British intelligence, Sean Dillon, set out to trace the source of the havoc, but behind the first man they find another, and behind him another still. And that man is not pleased by the interference. Soon he will target them all: Johnson, Dillon, Dillon's colleagues. And one of them will fall.

Dark Justice. unabr. ed. Jack Higgins. Read by Michael Page. (Running Time: 6 hrs.). (Sean Dillon Ser.). 2004. 39.25 (978-1-59710-176-9(1), 1597101761, BADLE); 24.95 (978-1-59710-177-6(X), 159710177X, BAD) Brilliance Audio.

Dark Justice. unabr. ed. Jack Higgins. Read by Michael Page. (Running Time: 21600 sec.). (Sean Dillon Ser.). 2006. audio compact disk 16.99 (978-1-4233-1567-4(7), 9781423315674) Brilliance Audio.

Dark Justice-UAB. Jack Higgins. 2010. audio compact disk 9.99 (978-1-4418-4180-3(6)) Brilliance Audio.

***Dark King & Lightning Tower.** Dan Abnett & Graham McNeill. (ENG.). 2010. 17.00 (978-1-84416-359-5(8), Black Library) Pub: BL Pubng GBR. Dist(s): S and S Inc

Dark Lady. Richard North Patterson. Read by Anne Twomey. 9 cass. (Running Time: 13 hrs. 30 min.). 1999. 72.00 (978-0-7366-4674-1(4), 5056) Books on Tape.
Stella Marz, a driven county prosecutor, pursues criminals infesting a struggling Midwestern city.

Dark Lady. unabr. ed. Louis Auchincloss. Read by Dan Lazar. 8 cass. (Running Time: 8 hrs.). 1977. 48.00 (978-0-7366-0104-7(X), 1112) Books on Tape.
The story of Ivy, a fashion editor & social arbiter & Elesina, a beauty with "good" background, who ally themselves in a successful assault on fame, wealth & political power.

Dark Lady. unabr. ed. Richard North Patterson. Read by Anne Twomey. 9 cass. (Running Time: 14 hrs. 30 min.). 1999. 39.95 (N120, Random AudioBks) Random Audio Pubg.
In Steelton, a struggling Midwestern city on the verge of an economic turnaround, two prominent men are found dead within days of each other. In each case, homicide is suspected, but not immediately provable. Stella Marz, Assistant County Prosecutor, head of the homicide division of the prosecutor's office is about to discover that these deaths are connected in less obvious, more insidious ways.

Dark Lady, Set. abr. ed. Richard North Patterson. Read by Patricia Kalember. 4 cass. 1999. 25.95 (FS9-51005) Highsmith.

Dark Lady, Set. unabr. ed. Richard North Patterson. 11 cass. 1999. 39.95 (FS9-51014) Highsmith.

Dark Lantern. unabr. ed. Gerri Brightwell. Read by Anne Flosnik. (Running Time: 39600 sec.). 2008. 65.95 (978-1-4332-3400-2(9)); audio compact disk & audio compact disk 90.00 (978-1-4332-3401-9(7)); audio compact disk & audio compact disk 29.95 (978-1-4332-3404-0(1)) Blckstn Audio.

Dark Life. Kat Falls. (Running Time: 7 hrs.). (ENG.). (J). 2010. audio compact disk 34.99 (978-0-545-20705-8(3)) Scholastic Inc.

Dark Life. Kat Falls. Read by Keith Nobbs. (ENG.). (J). 2010. audio compact disk 64.99 (978-0-545-22613-4(9)) Scholastic Inc.

Dark Light. Jayne Castle, pseud. Read by Joyce Bean. (Harmony Ser.: No. 6). 2009. 64.99 (978-1-60775-678-1(1)) Find a World.

Dark Light. abr. ed. Jayne Castle, pseud. Read by Joyce Bean. (Running Time: 5 hrs.). (Harmony Ser.: No. 6). 2009. audio compact disk 14.99 (978-1-4233-6257-9(8), 9781423362579) Brilliance Audio.

Dark Light. unabr. ed. Jayne Castle, pseud. Read by Joyce Bean. (Running Time: 9 hrs.). (Harmony Ser.: No. 6). 2008. 24.95 (978-1-4233-6252-4(7), 9781423362524, Brilliance MP3); 39.25 (978-1-4233-6255-5(1), 9781423362555, BADLE); 39.25 (978-1-4233-6253-1(5), 9781423362531, Brlnc Audio MP3 Lib); 24.95 (978-1-4233-6254-8(3), 9781423362548, BAD); audio compact disk 34.95 (978-1-4233-6250-0(0), 9781423362500, Bril Audio CD Unabri); audio compact disk 92.25 (978-1-4233-6251-7(9), 9781423362517, BriAudCD Unabrid) Brilliance Audio.

Dark Light. unabr. ed. Randy Wayne White. Read by Henry Strozier. (Running Time: 13 hrs.). No. 13. (ENG.). (gr. 8). 2007. audio compact disk 24.95 (978-0-14-314198-3(8), PengAudBks) Penguin Grp USA.

Dark Lord. unabr. ed. Ed Greenwood. Read by Christopher Lane. (Running Time: 14 hrs.). (Falconfar Saga Ser.). 2007. 39.25 (978-1-4233-4896-2(6), 9781423348962, BADLE); 24.95 (978-1-4233-4895-5(8), 9781423348955, BAD); 107.25 (978-1-4233-4890-0(7), 9781423348900, BrilAudUnabridg); audio compact disk 39.25 (978-1-4233-4894-8(X), 9781423348948, Brlnc Audio MP3 Lib); audio compact disk 112.25 (978-1-4233-4892-4(3), 9781423348924, BriAudCD Unabrid); audio compact disk 38.95 (978-1-4233-4891-7(5), 9781423348917, Bril Audio CD Unabri); audio compact disk 24.95 (978-1-4233-4893-1(1), 9781423348931, Brilliance MP3) Brilliance Audio.

Dark Lord: The Rise of Darth Vader. abr. ed. James Luceno. Read by Jonathan Davis. (Running Time: 21600 sec.). (Star Wars (Random House Audio) Ser.). (ENG.). 2005. audio compact disk 29.95 (978-0-7393-2394-6(6), Random AudioBks) Pub: Random Audio Pubg. Dist(s): Random

Dark Lords of the Sith. abr. unabr. ed. Kevin J. Anderson & Tom Veitch. (Running Time: 2 hrs. 15 mins.). No. II. (ENG.). 2005. audio compact disk 22.95 (978-1-56511-974-1(6), 1565119746) Pub: HighBridge. Dist(s): Workman Pub

Dark Matter. unabr. ed. Philip Kerr. 7 cass. (Running Time: 10 hrs.). 2002. 72.00 (978-0-7366-8926-7(5)) Books on Tape.

Dark Matter. unabr. ed. Peter Straub. Read by Robertson Dean. 2010. 45.00 (978-0-7393-2241-3(9), Random AudioBks) Pub: Random Audio Pubg. Dist(s): Random

Dark Mirror. abr. ed. Juliet Marillier. Read by Michael Page. (Running Time: 28800 sec.). (Bridei Chronicles: Bk. 1). 2005. audio compact disk 92.25 (978-1-59600-296-8(4), 9781596002968, BACDLib Ed) Brilliance Audio.
Please enter a Synopsis.

Dark Mirror. abr. ed. Juliet Marillier. Read by Michael Page. (Running Time: 8 hrs.). (Bridei Chronicles: Bk. 1). 2006. audio compact disk 19.99 (978-1-59737-342-5(7), 9781597373425, BCD Value Price) Brilliance Audio.
Bridei is a young nobleman fostered at the home of Broichan, one of the most powerful druids in the land. His earliest memories are not of hearth and kin but of this dark stranger who, while not unkind, is mysterious in his ways. The tasks that he sets for Bridei appear to have one goal - to make him a vessel for some distant purpose. What that purpose is Bridei cannot fathom but he trusts the man and is content to learn all he can about the ways of the world. But something happens that will change Bridei's world forever, and possibly wreck all of Broichan's plans: Bridei finds a child on their doorstep on a bitter MidWinter Eve, a child seemingly abandoned by the fairie folk. It is uncommonly bad luck to have truck with the Fair Folk and all counsel the babe's death. But Bridei sees an old and precious magic at work here and, heedless of the danger, fights to save the child. Broichan relents but is wary. The two grow up together and as Bridei comes to manhood, he sees the shy girl Tuala blossom into a beautiful woman. Broichan sees the same process and feels only danger; Tuala could be a key part in Bridei's future...or could spell his doom.

Dark Mirror. unabr. ed. Juliet Marillier. Read by Michael Page. (Running Time: 22 hrs.). (Bridei Chronicles: Bk. 1). 2005. 44.25 (978-1-59710-179-0(6), 9781597101790, BADLE); 29.95 (978-1-59710-178-3(8), 9781597101783, BAD); 117.25 (978-1-59600-294-4(8), 9781596002944, BrilAudUnabridg); 46.95 (978-1-59600-293-7(X), 9781596002937, BAU); audio compact disk 44.25 (978-1-59335-990-4(X), 9781593359904, Brlnc Audio MP3 Lib); audio compact disk 29.95 (978-1-59335-989-8(6), 9781593359898, Brilliance MP3) Brilliance Audio.
Please enter a Synopsis.

Dark Nantucket Noon. unabr. ed. Jane Langton. Read by Michael Prichard. 8 cass. (Running Time: 8 hrs.). 1982. 48.00 (978-0-7366-0630-1(0), 1591) Books on Tape.
The brilliant but exceptionally vulnerable young poet, Kitty Clark, goes to Nantucket to view an eclipse of the sun. At the foot of a deserted lighthouse, as the day plunges into darkness, she stumbles over the bloody body of the wife of her ex-lover, the well-known novelist Joe Green.

Dark Night of the Soul. Swami Amar Jyoti. 1 cass. 1979. 9.95 (C-20) Truth Consciousness.
What is the dark night of the soul? Intense longing & deliverance.

Dark Night of the Soul. Candace Long. Arranged by Candace Long. Composed by Robert Stearns. 2006. audio compact disk 8.95 (978-0-9788322-5-4(6)) auDEO Media.

***Dark Night of the Soul.** St. John of the Cross. Patrick Reis. (ENG.). 2009. audio compact disk 18.95 (978-1-936231-02-7(6)) Cath Audio.

***Dark Night of the Soul.** unabr. ed. St John of the Cross. Narrated by Michael Kramer. (ENG.). 2007. 14.98 (978-1-59644-482-9(7), Hovel Audio) christianaud.

Dark Night of the Soul. unabr. ed. Saint John of the Cross. Read by Michael Kramer. 6 CDs. (Running Time: 5 hrs. 0 mins. 0 sec.). (ENG.). 2007. audio compact disk 24.98 (978-1-59644-481-2(9), Hovel Audio) christianaud.

Dark Night of the Soul: A Sacred Journey to Joy & Enlightenment. Ron Roth. 4 cass. (Running Time: 4 hrs.). 1999. 25.00 (978-1-56170-634-1(5), 651) Hay House.
How to get through tough times & find joy.

Dark Night of the Soul: And Other Great Works. Saint John of the Cross. (Pure Gold Classics Ser.). 2007. pap. bk. 14.99 (978-0-88270-402-9(8)) Bridge-Logos.

Dark Night of the Soul: Genesis 15. Ed Young. 1994. 4.95 (978-0-7417-2029-0(9), 1029) Win Walk.

Dark Night's Work, Set. unabr. ed. Elizabeth Gaskell. Read by Flo Gibson. 5 cass. (Running Time: 6 hrs. 30 min.). 1994. 20.95 (978-1-55685-326-5(2)) Audio Bk Con.
The gripping plot concerns a hidden crime, a jilting, & a false accusation of murder.

Dark of Day. unabr. ed. Barbara Parker. Narrated by Elisabeth S. Rodgers. 10 CDs. (Running Time: 12 hrs.). 2008. audio compact disk 99.95 (978-0-7927-5465-7(4)) AudioGO.
C.J. Dunn is an expert at spinning her clients' image in the media and the perfect lawyer to deflect police interest in Rick Slater, head of security for a U.S. Congressman from Miami. Slater was seen at a South Beach party with the recently vanished Alana Martin, but in election season, any hint of scandal could doom the Congressman's chances. If she succeeds, friends of the Congressman have assured her they will arrange a spot for her as a legal commentator on a national media outlet. For a woman living alone, with few close friends, a celebrity life has its appeal. When Alana Martin is found dead and C.J.'s investigator implicates Rick Slater, C.J. is slammed between the media and the need to defend a client she no longer trusts. Then he delivers a bombshell: C.J.'s daughter, Traci Willis, the child she gave up for adoption seventeen years ago, was a friend of Alana Martin's. Traci has information that could save Rick Slater, but at the same time reveal a devastating secret that would put C.J.'s career, and even her life, on the line.

Dark of Day. unabr. ed. Barbara Parker. Narrated by Elisabeth S. Rodgers. 10 CDs. (Running Time: 12 hrs.). (ENG.). 2008. audio compact disk 29.95 (978-1-60283-418-7(0)) Pub: AudioGO. Dist(s): Perseus Dist

Dark of Mind. Jenniffer Dawn. Engineer Daniel Ringquist. Illus. by Marc Nordstrom. Narrated by Marc Nordstrom. Directed By Darryl Gregory. (YA). 2009. audio compact disk 29.99 (978-1-935582-05-2(4)) FST PULP.

Dark of Night. abr. ed. Suzanne Brockmann. (Running Time: 6 hrs.). (Troubleshooter Ser.: No. 14). 2009. audio compact disk 26.99 (978-1-4233-4272-4(0), 9781423342724, BACD) Brilliance Audio.

Dark of Night. abr. ed. Suzanne Brockmann. Read by Patrick G. Lawlor & Renée Raudman. (Running Time: 6 hrs.). (Troubleshooter Ser.: No. 14). 2009. audio compact disk 14.99 (978-1-4233-4273-1(9), 9781423342731, BCD Value Price) Brilliance Audio.

Dark of Night. unabr. ed. Suzanne Brockmann. (Running Time: 18 hrs.). (Troubleshooter Ser.: No. 14). 2009. 44.97 (978-1-4233-4269-4(0), 9781423342694, Brlnc Audio MP3 Lib) Brilliance Audio.

Dark of Night. unabr. ed. Suzanne Brockmann. Read by Patrick G. Lawlor & Renée Raudman. (Running Time: 18 hrs.). (Troubleshooter Ser.: No. 14). 2009. 44.97 (978-1-4233-4271-7(2), 9781423342717, BADLE); 29.99 (978-1-4233-4270-0(4), 9781423342700, BAD) Brilliance Audio.

Dark of Night. unabr. ed. Suzanne Brockmann. Read by Lawlor Patrick G. & Raudman Renée. (Running Time: 18 hrs.). (Troubleshooter Ser.: No. 14). 2009. 29.99 (978-1-4233-4268-7(2), 9781423342687, Brilliance MP3) Brilliance Audio.

Dark of Night. unabr. ed. Suzanne Brockmann. Read by Patrick G. Lawlor & Raudman Renée. (Running Time: 18 hrs.). (Troubleshooter Ser.: No. 14). 2009. audio compact disk 117.97 (978-1-4233-4267-0(4), 9781423342670, BriAudCD Unabrid) Brilliance Audio.

Dark of Night. unabr. ed. Suzanne Brockmann. Read by Lawlor Patrick G. & Raudman Renée. (Running Time: 18 hrs.). (Troubleshooter Ser.: No. 14). 2009. audio compact disk 38.99 (978-1-4233-4266-3(6), 9781423342663, Bril Audio CD Unabri) Brilliance Audio.

Dark of the Moon. John Sandford, pseud. (Running Time: 6 hrs.). No. 1. (ENG., (gr. 8). 2008. audio compact disk 14.95 (978-0-14-314383-3(2), PengAudBks) Penguin Grp USA.

Dark of the Moon. unabr. ed. John Sandford, pseud. Read by Eric Conger. 9 CDs. (Running Time: 11 hrs.). No. 1. (ENG.). (gr. 8). 2007. audio compact disk 39.95 (978-0-14-314250-8(X), PengAudBks) Penguin Grp USA.

Dark of the Sun. Wilbur Smith. 2 cass. (Running Time: 4 hrs.). (ENG., 2001. 16.99 (978-0-333-78246-0(1)) Pub: Macmillan UK GBR. Dist(s): Trafalgar
They hunt diamonds. They hunt cannibals. They hunt each other. They're mercenaries in the Congo, a battlefield torn apart like a vast, wide-open wound. For mercenary leader Bruce Curry, the mission means hunting the thing he hates most and savoring every shameless minute. For beyond hate, beyond revenge, is the thrill of hunting the most dangerous and cunning game of all - man.

Dark of the Sun. unabr. collector's ed. Wilbur Smith. Read by Richard Brown. 7 cass. (Running Time: 10 hrs. 30 min.). (Ballantyne Novels Ser.). 1988. 56.00 (978-0-7366-1324-8(2), 2228) Books on Tape.
Bruce Curry sets out with a trainload of mercenaries to relieve a minning town besieged by rebels in the heart of the African jungle. The journey turns into a nightmare, softened only by Shermaine, a Belgain girl he meets & with whom he falls in love.

Dark Paradise. Tami Hoag. 2010. audio compact disk 9.99 (978-1-4418-4181-0(4)) Brilliance Audio.

Dark Paradise. abr. ed. Tami Hoag. Read by Joyce Bean. 4 cass. (Running Time: 6 hrs.). 2001. 53.25 (978-1-58788-635-5(9), 1587886359, Nova Audio Bks) Brilliance Audio.
New Eden, Montana, is a piece of heaven on earth where one woman died in her own private hell. Now it's up to ex-court reporter Marilee Jennings to decipher the puzzle of her best friend's death. But someone has a stake in silencing her suspicion. Someone with secrets worth killing for - and the power to turn this beautiful haven into a . . .Dark Paradise. And as Mari digs deeper beneath New Eden's picture-perfect exterior, finding the truth is suddenly no longer a matter of justice.

Dark Paradise. abr. ed. Tami Hoag. Read by Joyce Bean. (Running Time: 6 hrs.). 2006. 39.25 (978-1-4233-0060-1(2), 9781423300601, BADLE); 24.95 (978-1-4233-0059-5(9), 9781423300595, BAD); audio compact disk 39.25 (978-1-4233-0058-8(0), 9781423300588, Brlnc Audio MP3 Lib); audio compact disk 24.95 (978-1-4233-0057-1(2), 9781423300571, Brilliance MP3) Brilliance Audio.

Dark Pasture. unabr. ed. Jessica Stirling. Read by Vivien Heilbron. 12 cass. (Running Time: 12 hrs.). 1998. 96.95 Set, Dolby Sound. (978-0-7540-0190-4(3), CAB 1613) AudioGO.
Seventeen years have passed since the close events described in "The Hiring Fair." In Blacklaw, the depression has brought poverty to the town. In Edinburgh, Drew Stalker has fulfilled his promise, climbing high in Edinburgh society. Only scandal can bring him down now, which threatens to happen when Neil Stalker is accused of murder.

***Dark Peril: A Carpathian Novel.** abr. ed. Christine Feehan. Read by Natalie Ross and Phil Gigante. (Running Time: 6 hrs.). (Dark Ser.). 2010. 9.99 (978-1-4418-9390-1(3), 9781441893901, BAD) Brilliance Audio.

Dark Planet. Patrick Carman. Narrated by Jonathan Davis. (Running Time: 7 hrs. 30 mins.). (Atherton Ser.: No. 3). (J). (gr. 4-7). 2009. 64.99 (978-1-60775-986-7(1)) Find a World.

Dark Planet. Patrick Carman. Narrated by Jonathan Davis. (Atherton Ser.: No. 3). 2008. audio compact disk 39.95 (978-0-545-07625-8(0)) Scholastic Inc.

Dark Planet. unabr. ed. Patrick Carman. Narrated by Jonathan Davis. 6 CDs. (Running Time: 7 hrs. 30 mins.). (Atherton Ser.: No. 3). (ENG.). (J). (gr. 4-7). 2009. audio compact disk 84.95 (978-0-545-07685-2(4)) Scholastic Inc.

Dark Pond. unabr. ed. Joseph Bruchac. Narrated by Ramon de Ocampo. 2 cass. (Running Time: 2 hrs. 45 mins.). (J). 2005. 19.75 (978-1-4193-3103-9(5), 97995) Recorded Bks.
Critically acclaimed author of the thrilling ALA Notable Children's Book and School Library Journal Best Book Skeleton Man (RB# 97772), Joseph Bruchac draws from his knowledge of Native American myths to craft his suspenseful tales. When Armie arrives at the North Mountains School, he is immediately drawn to an eerie, dark pond in the woods nearby. It seems to be calling to him. In the past, Armie has turned to the legends of his Shawnee ancestors for guidance in matters of the supernatural. This time he'll need all the help he can get!.

Dark Portal. unabr. ed. Robin Jarvis. Read by Roe Kendall. 6 cass. (Running Time: 8 hrs. 80 mins.). 2002. 44.95 (978-0-7861-2331-5(1), 3039); audio compact disk 56.00 (978-0-7861-9347-9(6), 3039) Blckstn Audio.
On the other side of the Grill lie the sewers, where bloodthirsty gangs of rats roam the tunnels. It is in the depths of this blackness that the mysterious god Jupiter has his lair.

Dark Possession. Christine Feehan. Read by Phil Gigante & Jane Brown. (Playaway Adult Fiction Ser.). 2008. 89.99 (978-1-60640-906-0(9)) Find a World.

Dark Possession. abr. ed. Christine Feehan. Read by Phil Gigante & Jane Brown. (Running Time: 6 hrs.). (Dark Ser.: Bk. 18). 2008. audio compact disk 14.99 (978-1-4233-4021-8(3), 9781423340218, BCD Value Price) Brilliance Audio.

Dark Possession. unabr. ed. Christine Feehan. Read by Phil Gigante & Jane Brown. (Running Time: 13 hrs.). (Dark Ser.: Bk. 18). 2007. 39.25 (978-1-4233-4019-5(1), 9781423340195, BADLE); 24.95 (978-1-4233-4018-8(3), 9781423340188, BAD); 82.25 (978-1-4233-4013-3(2), 9781423340133, BrilAudUnabridg); audio compact disk 39.25 (978-1-4233-4017-1(5), 9781423340171, Brinc Audio MP3 Lib); audio compact disk 97.25 (978-1-4233-4015-7(9), 9781423340157, BriAudCD Unabrid); audio compact disk 36.95 (978-1-4233-4014-0(0), 9781423340140, Bril Audio CD Unabri); audio compact disk 24.95 (978-1-4233-4016-4(7), 9781423340164, Brilliance MP3) Brilliance Audio.

Dark Power Collection. Bill Myers. (Running Time: 2 hrs. 35 mins. 0 sec.). (Forbidden Doors Ser.). (ENG.). (YA). 2009. 4.99 (978-0-310-77260-6(5)) Zondervan.

***Dark Power Collection.** unabr. ed. Bill Myers. (Running Time: 8 hrs. 15 mins. 46 sec.). (Forbidden Doors Ser.). (ENG.). (YA). 2010. 12.99 (978-0-310-42633-2(2)) Zondervan.

***Dark Power Collection: the Deceived.** Bill Myers. (Running Time: 2 hrs. 57 mins. 0 sec.). (Forbidden Doors Ser.). (ENG.). (YA). 2009. 4.99 (978-0-310-72029-4(X)) Zondervan.

***Dark Power Collection: the Spell.** Bill Myers. (Running Time: 2 hrs. 44 mins. 0 sec.). (Forbidden Doors Ser.). (ENG.). (YA). 2009. 4.99 (978-0-310-72030-0(3)) Zondervan.

***Dark Pursuit.** Brandilyn Collins. (Running Time: 7 hrs. 32 mins. 0 sec.). (ENG.). 2009. 14.99 (978-0-310-77291-0(5)) Zondervan.

***Dark Riders of Doom.** Peter Dawson. 2009. (978-1-60136-393-0(1)) Audio Holding.

Dark Riders of Doom. Peter Dawson. (Running Time: 1 hr. 24 mins.). 2000. 10.95 (978-1-60083-538-4(4)) Iofy Corp.

Dark River Legacy. unabr. ed. B. J. Hoff. Read by Jean DeBarbieris. 6 cass. (Running Time: 5 hrs. 54 min.). (Daybreak Mystery Ser.: Bk. 5). 1999. 39.95 (978-1-55686-859-7(6)) Books in Motion.
A struggling college professor is thrilled when the woman he loves reenters his life, but is shaken an intimidating stranger follows.

Dark Rivers of the Heart. unabr. ed. Dean Koontz. Read by Anthony Heald. (Running Time: 70200 sec.). (Dean Koontz Ser.). (ENG.). 2007. audio compact disk 39.95 (978-0-7393-4144-5(8), Random AudioBks) Pub: Random Audio Pubg. Dist(s): Random

Dark Rivers of the Heart, Set. unabr. ed. Dean Koontz. Read by Anthony Heald. 12 cass. 1999. 49.95 (FS9-34496) Highsmith.

Dark Romance of Dian Fossey. unabr. collector's ed. Harold T. Hayes. Read by Grover Gardner. 7 cass. (Running Time: 10 hrs. 30 mins.). 1991. 56.00 (978-0-7366-2043-7(5), 2857) Books on Tape.
Without scientific training, but with abundant determination, Dian Fossey persuaded the eminent Louis Leakey to send her to Africa to study the last remaining mountain gorillas. Fossey, always extreme, was what you call "hands on." She virtually lived with the gorillas, slowly earning their trust. However, the closer to anthropoids, the farther from humans. More militant each year, she antagonized even her friends. Enemies she had plenty. In the end they killed her.

Dark Room. abr. ed. Minette Walters. Read by Laural Merlington. 2 cass. (Running Time: 3 hrs.). 2000. 7.95 (978-1-57815-169-1(4), 1112, Media Bks Audio) Media Bks NJ.

Dark Room. abr. ed. Minette Walters. Read by Laural Merlington. 3 CDs. (Running Time: 3 hrs.). (YA). 2000. audio compact disk 11.99 (978-1-57815-504-0(5), 1112 CD3, Media Bks Audio) Media Bks NJ.
Something so terrible, that was to frightening to search her memory. She seeks the help of a doctor who begins to unlock her nightmares.

Dark Room. unabr. ed. Minette Walters. Read by Laural Merlington. (Running Time: 13 hrs.). 2009. 39.97 (978-1-4233-7162-5(3), 9781423371625, BADLE); 39.97 (978-1-4233-7160-1(7), 9781423371601, Brinc Audio MP3 Lib); 24.99 (978-1-4233-7161-8(5), 9781423371618, BAD); 24.99 (978-1-4233-7159-5(3), 9781423371595, Brilliance MP3) Brilliance Audio.

Dark Rose, unabr. ed. Cynthia Harrod-Eagles. Read by Nigel Graham. 14 cass. (Running Time: 20 hr. 45 min.). (Morland Dynasty Ser.: No. 2). (J). 2001. 99.95 (978-0-7531-0399-9(0), 980611) Pub: ISIS Lrg Prnt GBR. Dist(s): Ulverscroft US
Paul, the inheritor of the Morland estates, has two sons-Amyas, from his arranged marriage & Adrian, illegitimate but much loved. Conflict between the two sparks a bitter jealousy, a conflict which carries with it the seeds of destruction & death. At court, Nanette has become maid-in-waiting to the King's new favorite, Anne Boleyn. Nanette adores her vivacious young mistress, one of the most romantic figures in British history & is witness to her poignant development from beautiful, pleasure seeking young girl into a woman capable of dying a noble death. In this powerful saga of birth & death, love & hatred, personal triumph & heartbreak, the might of a proud Dynasty increases as, against the rich backcloth of a tumultuous era, the Morlands aspire to still greater wealth & prestige.

Dark Safari. unabr. ed. John Bierman. Read by Frederick Davidson. 11 cass. (Running Time: 16 hrs.). 1991. 76.95 (978-0-7861-0168-9(7), 1150) Blckstn Audio.
Henry Morton Stanley is often referred to as "the toughest man who ever lived." Best remembered for the classically fatuous phrase with which he greeted David Livingstone on the shore of Lake Tanganyika ("Dr. Livingstone, I presume"), he was the most celebrated explorer of an age that worshipped explorers as ours reveres movie stars & rock musicians.

Dark Shadows Memories. abr. ed. Kathryn Leigh Scott. 2 CDs. (Running Time: 1 hr. 42 mins. 0 sec.). (ENG.). 2005. audio compact disk 19.95 (978-0-938817-85-7(X)) Pub: Pomegranate Pr. Dist(s): PerseuPGW

Dark Shadows of Depression: Reaching the Light. unabr. ed. Lynne Logan. Read by Lynne Logan. 1 cass. (Running Time: 1 hrs.). 1995. 11.00 (978-1-890907-04-4(9), 0005) Heaven Only.
Kinds of depression, symptoms of depression, & treatment of depression.

Dark Shadows 1. 1 the House of Despair. Stuart Manning. 2009. audio compact disk 15.95 (978-1-84435-243-2(9)) Pub: Big Finish GBR. Dist(s): Natl Bk Netwk

Dark Shadows 1. 2 the Book of Temptation. Scott Handcock. 2009. audio compact disk 15.95 (978-1-84435-244-9(7)) Pub: Big Finish GBR. Dist(s): Natl Bk Netwk

Dark Shadows 1. 3 the Christmas Presence. Scott Handcock. 2009. audio compact disk 15.95 (978-1-84435-245-6(5)) Pub: Big Finish GBR. Dist(s): Natl Bk Netwk

Dark Shadows 1. 4 the Rage Beneath. Scott Alan Woodard. 2009. audio compact disk 15.95 (978-1-84435-246-3(3)) Pub: Big Finish GBR. Dist(s): Natl Bk Netwk

Dark Side: The Inside Story of How the War on Terror Turned into a War on American Ideals. unabr. ed. Jane Mayer. Read by Richard McGonagle. 13 CDs. (Running Time: 16 hrs. 30 mins.). 2008. audio compact disk 100.00 (978-1-4159-5799-8(1), BksonTape) Pub: Random Audio Pubg. Dist(s): Random
In the days immediately following September 11th, the most powerful people in the country were panic-stricken. The radical decisions about how to combat terrorists and strengthen national security were made in a state of utter chaos and fear, but the key players, Vice President Dick Cheney and his powerful, secretive adviser David Addington, used the crisis to further a long held agenda to enhance Presidential powers to a degree never known in U.S. history, and obliterate Constitutional protections that define the very essence of the American experiment. THE DARK SIDE is a dramatic, riveting, and definitive narrative account of how the United States made terrible decisions in the pursuit of terrorists around the world - decisions that not only violated the Constitution to which White House officials took an oath to uphold, but also hampered the pursuit of Al Qaeda. In gripping detail, acclaimed New Yorker writer and bestselling author, Jane Mayer, relates the impact of these decisions - U.S.-held prisoners, some of them completely innocent, were subjected to treatment more reminiscent of the Spanish Inquisition than the twenty-first century. THE DARK SIDE will chronicle real, specific cases, shown in real time against the larger tableau of what was happening in Washington, looking at the intelligence gained - or not - and the price paid. In some instances, torture worked. In many more, it led to false information, sometimes with devastating results. For instance, there is the stunning admission of one of the detainees, Sheikh Ibn al-Libi, that the confession he gave under duress - which provided a key piece of evidence buttressing congressional support of going to war against Iraq - was in fact fabricated, to make the torture stop. In all cases, whatever the short term gains, there were incalculable losses in terms of moral standing, and our country's place in the world, and its sense of itself. THE DARK SIDE chronicles one of the most disturbing chapters in American history, one that will serve as the lasting legacy of the George W. Bush presidency.

Dark Side: The Inside Story of How the War on Terror Turned into a War on American Ideals. unabr. ed. Jane Mayer. Read by Richard McGonagle. (Running Time: 16 hrs. 30 mins.). (ENG.). 2008. 25.00 (978-0-7393-7593-8(8), Random AudioBks) Pub: Random Audio Pubg. Dist(s): Random

Dark Side: The Inside Story of How the War on Terror Turned into a War on American Ideals. unabr. ed. Jane Mayer. Read by Richard McGonagle. 13 CDs. (Running Time: 16 hrs. 30 mins.). (ENG.). 2008. audio compact disk 34.95 (978-0-7393-7592-1(X), Random AudioBks) Pub: Random Audio Pubg. Dist(s): Random

Dark Side of Change. unabr. ed. Innovation Groups Staff. 1 cass. (Running Time: 1 hrs. 15 min.). (Transforming Local Government Ser.: Vol. 21). 1999. 10.00 (978-1-882403-77-6(0), IG9922) Alliance Innov.

Dark Side of Genius: The Life of Alfred Hitchcock, Pt. I. unabr. ed. Donald Spoto. Read by Jeff Riggenbach. 10 cass. (Running Time: 24 hrs. 30 mins.). 1999. 69.95 (978-0-7861-1618-8(8), 2446A, B) Blckstn Audio.
Explores the roots of Alfred Hitchcock's obsessions & traces the origins of his incomparable, bizarre genius, from his childhood & education to the golden years of his career in America.

Dark Side of Genius: The Life of Alfred Hitchcock, Pt. II. unabr. ed. Donald Spoto. Read by Jeff Riggenbach. 7 cass. (Running Time: 24 hrs. 30 mins.). 1999. 49.95 (978-0-7861-1682-9(X), 2446A, B) Blckstn Audio.
His subject matter ranges from he dark drama of Cary Grant possibly trying to kill his wife, Joan Fontaine in "Suspicion," to the humorous problem of disposing of a body faced by Shirley MacLaine & John Forsythe in "The Trouble with Harry.".

Dark Side of God. unabr. ed. Ernest Bel. 1 cass. (Running Time: 1 hr. 34 min.). 1981. 11.00 (11501) Big Sur Tapes.
With a great sense of humor, which he considers necessary to address the subject of the shadow, Bel represents the Jungian view that God is an archetype, & that all archetypes have a dark side.

Dark Side of Moon. Susan Britting. Read by Susan Britting. 1 cass. (Running Time: 90 min.). 1994. 8.95 (1171) Am Fed Astrologers.

Dark Side of Nowhere. unabr. ed. Neal Shusterman. Read by Jason Harris. 3 cass. (Running Time: 4 hrs. 42 mins.). (J). (gr. 4-7). 2004. 30.00 (978-0-8072-8756-9(3), YA258CX, Listening Lib); pap. bk. 36.00 (978-0-8072-8757-6(1), YA258SP, Listening Lib) Random Audio Pubg.
Jason Miller feels trapped in the small town of Billington, where nothing ever happens. But when his friend Ethan dies of what the doctor calls a burst appendix, Jason's life changes forever. First he is given a mysterious glove that can shoot pellets with deadly force. Then he learns that the monthly shots he gets from the friendly town doctor are not for his health but for a far more sinister purpose.

Dark Side of the Game: My Life in the NFL. abr. ed. Tim Green. (Running Time: 1 hr. 30 mins.). (ENG.). 2006. 14.98 (978-1-59483-698-5(1)) Pub: Hachet Audio. Dist(s): HachBkGrp

Dark Side of the Game: My Life in the NFL, unabr. ed. Tim Green. Narrated by Richard Poe. 5 cass. (Running Time: 7 hrs. 15 mins.). 1997. 44.00 (978-0-7887-0807-7(4), 94956E7) Recorded Bks.
Sportscaster & former National Football League defensive end Tim Green reveals what it's really like to play in the NFL. Packed with hard-hitting inside information, ranging from the perfect partnership between the mob & the NFL to what it takes to win the Super Bowl.

Dark Side of the Island. unabr. collector's ed. Jack Higgins. Read by Mark Howell. 5 cass. (Running Time: 5 hrs.). 1983. 30.00 (978-0-7366-0480-2(4), 1455) Books on Tape.
Hugh Lomax is sent by the British to aid the Greeks in their struggle. They succeed brilliantly, but, on leaving for another assignment, are betrayed. Those who collaborated with him are executed, & the survivors hold Lomax, who has disappeared, responsible for the carnage. With a price on his head, he returns, nevertheless, to clear his name.

Dark Side of the Moon. abr. ed. Sherrilyn Kenyon. Read by Maggi-Meg Reed. 4 CDs. (Running Time: 5 hrs. 0 mins. 0 sec.). (Dark-Hunter Ser.: Bk. 10). (ENG.). 2006. audio compact disk 19.95 (978-1-59397-901-0(0)) Pub: Macmill Audio. Dist(s): Macmillan

Dark Side of the Moon. abr. ed. Sherrilyn Kenyon. (Dark-Hunter Ser.: Bk. 10). 2006. 14.95 (978-1-59397-914-0(2)) Pub: Macmill Audio. Dist(s): Macmillan

Dark Side of the Moon. unabr. ed. Sherrilyn Kenyon. Narrated by Carrington MacDuffie. 10 CDs. (Running Time: 41820 sec.). (Dark-Hunter Ser.: Bk. 10). 2006. audio compact disk 94.95 (978-0-7927-4058-2(0), Chivers Sound Lib); audio compact disk 29.95 (978-0-7927-4236-4(2), Chivers Sound Lib) AudioGO.

***Dark Side of the Street.** unabr. ed. Jack Higgins. (Running Time: 5 hrs.). (Simon Vaughn Bk #1, Paul Chevasse Bk #5 Ser.). 2010. 24.99 (978-1-4418-4436-1(8), 9781441844361, Brilliance MP3); 24.99 (978-1-4418-4438-5(4), 9781441844385, BAD); 39.97 (978-1-4418-4440-8(6), 9781441844408, BADLE) Brilliance Audio.

***Dark Side of the Street.** unabr. ed. Jack Higgins. Read by Michael Page. (Running Time: 5 hrs.). (Simon Vaughn Bk #1, Paul Chevasse Bk #5 Ser.). 2010. 39.97 (978-1-4418-4437-8(6), 9781441844378, Brinc Audio MP3 Lib); audio compact disk 29.99 (978-1-4418-4433-0(3), 9781441844330, Bril Audio CD Unabri); audio compact disk 87.97 (978-1-4418-4435-4(X), 9781441844354, BriAudCD Unabrid) Brilliance Audio.

Dark Side of the Street. unabr. collector's ed. Jack Higgins. Read by Rupert Keenlyside. 6 cass. (Running Time: 6 hrs.). 1984. 36.00 (978-0-7366-0984-5(9), 1924) Books on Tape.
With commando-like precision, someone was breaking Britain's most notorious prisoners out of jail, & delivering convicted spies back to the Communists.

Dark Side of the Sun. Terry Pratchett. Read by Stephen Briggs. (Running Time: 18900 sec.). (Isis Cassettes Ser.). 2007. 44.95 (978-0-7531-3693-5(7)); audio compact disk 59.95 (978-0-7531-2655-4(9)) Pub: ISIS Lrg Prnt GBR. Dist(s): Ulverscroft US

Dark Side of the Sun. unabr. ed. Elizabeth Palmer. Read by Kelly Hunter. 8 cass. (Running Time: 11 hrs.). (Isis Ser.). (J). 2002. 69.95 (978-0-7531-0856-7(9)) Pub: ISIS Lrg Prnt GBR. Dist(s): Ulverscroft US

Dark Slayer. abr. ed. Christine Feehan. Read by Phil Gigante & Jane Brown. (Running Time: 6 hrs.). (Dark Ser.: Bk. 20). 2009. audio compact disk 26.99 (978-1-4233-6932-5(7), 9781423369325, BACD) Brilliance Audio.

Dark Slayer. abr. ed. Christine Feehan. Read by Phil Gigante & Jane Brown. (Running Time: 6 hrs.). (Dark Ser.: Bk. 20). 2010. audio compact disk 14.99 (978-1-4233-6933-2(5), 9781423369332, BCD Value Price) Brilliance Audio.

Dark Slayer. unabr. ed. Christine Feehan. Read by Phil Gigante & Jane Brown. (Running Time: 14 hrs.). (Dark Ser.: Bk. 20). 2009. 39.97 (978-1-4233-6929-5(7), 9781423369295, Brinc Audio MP3 Lib); 24.99 (978-1-4233-6930-1(0), 9781423369301, BAD) Brilliance Audio.

Dark Slayer. unabr. ed. Christine Feehan. Read by Jane Brown & Phil Gigante. (Running Time: 14 hrs.). (Dark Ser.: Bk. 20). 2009. 24.99 (978-1-4233-6928-8(9), 9781423369288, Brilliance MP3) Brilliance Audio.

Dark Slayer. unabr. ed. Christine Feehan. Read by Phil Gigante & Jane Brown. (Running Time: 15 hrs.). (Dark Ser.: Bk. 20). 2009. audio compact disk 99.97 (978-1-4233-6927-1(0), 9781423369271, BriAudCD Unabrid) Brilliance Audio.

Dark Slayer. unabr. ed. Christine Feehan. Read by Jane Brown & Phil Gigante. (Running Time: 15 hrs.). (Dark Ser.: Bk. 20). 2009. audio compact disk 38.99 (978-1-4233-6926-4(2), 9781423369264, Bril Audio CD Unabri) Brilliance Audio.

Dark Slayer. unabr. ed. Christine Feehan & Jane Brown. Read by Phil Gigante. (Running Time: 15 hrs.). (Dark Ser.: Bk. 20). 2009. 39.97 (978-1-4233-6931-8(9), 9781423369318, BADLE) Brilliance Audio.

***Dark Sons.** Nikki Grimes. (Running Time: 1 hr. 38 mins. 37 sec.). (ENG.). (YA). 2010. 8.99 (978-0-310-55571-1(X)) Zondervan.

Dark Stairs. unabr. ed. Betsy Byars. Read by Blain Fairman. 2 cass. (Running Time: 3 hrs.). (Herculeah Jones Mystery Ser.). (YA). 1999. 16.98 (FS9-26767) Highsmith.

Dark Stairs. unabr. ed. Betsy Byars. Read by Blain Fairman. 2 cass. (Running Time: 2 hrs. 38 mins.). (Herculeah Jones Mystery Ser.). (J). (gr. 3-5). 1995. pap. bk. 28.00 (978-0-8072-7572-6(7), YA883SP, Listening Lib); 23.00 (978-0-8072-7571-9(9), YA883CX, Listening Lib) Random Audio Pubg.
It all started on Friday the 13th, & it spiraled into a terrifying & complex mystery for Herculeah Jones. But mysteries were right up her sleeve, for her father was on the police force, & her mother was a private eye. But the case of Dead Oaks, a derelict estate full of murder, insanity & an unsolved disappearance, soon turns out to be more than Herculeah bargained for.

Dark Star. collector's ed. Alan Furst. Read by Stuart Langton. 10 cass. (Running Time: 15 hrs.). 1999. 80.00 (978-0-7366-4886-8(0)) Books on Tape.
In the back alleys & glittering salons of Europe, war is already underway as Soviet intelligence & the Nazi Gestapo confront each other in an intricate duel of espionage. On the front line is Szara, a survivor - of the Polish pogroms, the Stalinist purges & the Russian civil wars. As deputy director of one of the red Orchestra spy networks in Paris, he recruits an agent from Berlin who can supply information on German aircraft production & finds himself caught in a crisis of conscience. His only goal is to keep going, but slowly, inextricably, he is drawn into the dark intrigues of pre-war Europe where life is a gray uncertainty of cheap hotel rooms, short love affairs & friends who have ceased to exit.

Dark Star Safari: Overland from Cairo to Cape Town. unabr. ed. Paul Theroux. Narrated by Norman Dietz. 16 cass. Library ed. (Running Time: 23 hrs.). 2004. 99.75 (978-1-84197-761-4(6), H1531); audio compact disk 109.75 (978-1-4025-7283-8(2), CP029) Recorded Bks.

Dark Star Safari: Overland from Cairo to Cape Town. unabr. collector's ed. Paul Theroux. Narrated by Norman Dietz. 19 CDs. (Running Time: 23 hrs.). 2004. audio compact disk 64.95 (978-1-4025-7766-6(4), CC062) Recorded Bks.
Forty years ago, Paul Theroux first went to Africa as a teacher in the Malawi bush. Now, nearing 60, he returns to travel by train, canoe, bus, and cattle truck from one end of Africa to the other. From Cairo to Cape Town, what he finds is recorded in the style that has stamped Theroux as a master of the travelogue. His curiosity and intelligent observations help create an unforgettable portrait of the varied land that is Africa today.

Dark Summer. abr. ed. Iris Johansen. Read by Joyce Bean. (Running Time: 6 hrs.). 2009. audio compact disk 14.99 (978-1-4233-2922-0(8), 9781423329220, BCD Value Price) Brilliance Audio.

Dark Summer. unabr. ed. Iris Johansen. 1 MP3-CD. (Running Time: 11 hrs.). 2008. 39.25 (978-1-4233-2918-3(X), 9781423329183, Brinc Audio MP3 Lib) Brilliance Audio.

Dark Summer. unabr. ed. Iris Johansen. Read by Joyce Bean. 1 MP3-CD. (Running Time: 11 hrs.). 2008. 24.95 (978-1-4233-2917-6(1), 9781423329176, Brilliance MP3); 39.25 (978-1-4233-2920-6(1), 9781423329206, BADLE); 24.95 (978-1-4233-2919-0(8), 9781423329190, BAD); audio compact disk 36.99 (978-1-4233-2915-2(5), 9781423329152, Bril Audio CD Unabri); audio compact disk 97.25 (978-1-4233-2916-9(3), 9781423329169, BriAudCD Unabrid) Brilliance Audio.

Dark Summit: The True Story of Everest's Most Controversial Season. unabr. ed. Nick Heil. Narrated by David Drummond & Karen White. (Running Time: 8 hrs. 30 mins. 0 sec.). (ENG.). 2008. audio compact disk 69.99 (978-1-4001-3770-1(5)) Pub: Tantor Media. Dist(s): IngramPubServ

Dark Summit: The True Story of Everest's Most Controversial Season. unabr. ed. Nick Heil. Read by David A. Drummond. Narrated by Karen White. (Running Time: 8 hrs. 30 mins. 0 sec.). (ENG.). 2008. audio compact disk 24.99 (978-1-4001-5770-9(6)); audio compact disk 34.99 (978-1-4001-0770-4(9)) Pub: Tantor Media. Dist(s): IngramPubServ

Dark Sun Pt. 1: The Making of the Hydrogen Bomb. unabr. ed. Richard Rhodes. Read by Alexander Adams. 9 cass. (Running Time: 13 hrs. 30 min.). 1996. 72.00 (978-0-7366-3339-0(1), 3989-A) Books on Tape.
Richard Rhodes, who won a Pulitzer Prize for "The Making of the Atomic Bomb," picks up where he left off. He gives the dramatic account of how we learned to make an H-bomb & just how close we came to nuclear Armageddon.

Dark Sun Pt. 2: The Making of the Hydrogen Bomb. Richard Rhodes. Read by Grover Gardner. 10 cass. (Running Time: 15 hrs.). 1996. 80.00 (3989-B) Books on Tape.

Dark Sun Rises. Denise Williamson. Narrated by Peter Jay Fernandez. 15 cass. (Running Time: 22 hrs.). 1998. 122.00 (978-0-7887-9600-5(3)) Recorded Bks.

Dark sun the making of the hydrogen Bomb. Richard Rhodes. 2004. 15.95 (978-0-7435-4580-8(X)) Pub: S&S Audio. Dist(s): S and S Inc

Dark Tales of the Supernatural. unabr. ed. Odds Bodkin Storytelling Library Staff. 1 cass. (Running Time: 1 hr. 20 mins.). Dramatization. (Odds Bodkin Musical Story Collection). (gr. 3 up). 2003. 9.95 (978-1-882412-04-4(4)) Pub: Rivertree. Dist(s): Penton Overseas
Includes: "Treasure Trove," a Tale of Russia's serfs; "The Phantom Train of Marshall's Pass," a Rocky Mountain Legend; "The Panther Boys," a Chinese Tale & "The Storm Breeder," a New England Ghost Story. Performed on six & twleve-string guitar & alto recorder.

Dark Things. unabr. ed. Joseph F. Brown. Read by Ric Benson. 4 cass. (Running Time: 5 hrs. 36 min.). 2001. 26.95 (978-1-58116-038-3(0)) Books in Motion.
Young Jarrod Blackwell is able to read minds and create things out of his imagination that become real. One more thing: Jarrod has used the "green crystal root" to move 100 years into the future.

***Dark Tide.** unabr. ed. Andrew Gross. Read by Melissa Leo. (ENG.). 2008. (978-0-06-163017-0(9)); (978-0-06-163019-4(5)) HarperCollins Pubs.

Dark Tide. unabr. ed. Andrew Gross. Read by Melissa Leo. 2009. audio compact disk 19.99 (978-0-06-172757-3(1), Harper Audio) HarperCollins Pubs.

Dark Tort. Diane Mott Davidson. Read by Elizabeth Marvel. (Goldy Schulz Culinary Mysteries Ser.: No. 13). 2007. audio compact disk 14.95 (978-0-06-128455-7(6), Harper Audio) HarperCollins Pubs.

***Dark Tort.** abr. ed. Diane Mott Davidson. Read by Elizabeth Marvel. (ENG.). 2006. (978-0-06-115435-5(0), Harper Audio); (978-0-06-115436-2(9), Harper Audio) HarperCollins Pubs.

Dark Tort. abr. ed. Diane Mott Davidson. Read by Elizabeth Marvel. (Running Time: 21600 sec.). (Goldy Schulz Culinary Mysteries Ser.: No. 13). 2006. audio compact disk 29.95 (978-0-06-089830-4(5)) HarperCollins Pubs.

***Dark Tort.** unabr. ed. Diane Mott Davidson. Read by Barbara Rosenblat. (ENG.). 2006. (978-0-06-115438-6(5), Harper Audio); (978-0-06-115437-9(7), Harper Audio) HarperCollins Pubs.

Dark Tort. unabr. ed. Diane Mott Davidson. Read by Barbara Rosenblat. (Running Time: 37800 sec.). (Goldy Schulz Culinary Mysteries Ser.: No. 13). 2006. audio compact disk 39.95 (978-0-06-089832-8(1), Harper Audio) HarperCollins Pubs.

Dark Tower. unabr. ed. Stephen King. 2003. 481.85 (978-0-7435-2262-5(1), Audioworks) Pub: S&S Audio. Dist(s): S and S Inc

Dark Tower. unabr. ed. Stephen King. Read by George Guidall. (Running Time: 270 hrs. 0 mins. 0 sec.). Bk. 7. (ENG.). 2004. audio compact disk 75.00 (978-0-7435-3811-4(0), Audioworks) Pub: S&S Audio. Dist(s): S and S Inc

Dark Tower. unabr. ed. Stephen King. Read by George Guidall. (Dark Tower Ser.: Bk. 7). 2006. 44.95 (978-0-7435-6171-6(6)) Pub: S&S Audio. Dist(s): S and S Inc

Dark Truth. abr. unabr. ed. Mariah Stewart. Read by Anna Fields. 7 pieces. (Running Time: 23400 sec.). 2006. 29.95 (978-0-7861-4479-2(3)); audio compact disk 29.95 (978-0-7861-7275-7(4)) Blckstn Audio.

Dark Truth. abr. ed. Mariah Stewart. Read by Anna Fields. (Running Time: 23400 sec.). 2006. audio compact disk 29.95 (978-0-7861-7702-8(0)) Blckstn Audio.

Dark Truth. unabr. ed. Mariah Stewart. Read by Anna Fields. (Running Time: 23400 sec.). 2006. 44.95 (978-0-7861-4641-3(9)); audio compact disk 55.00 (978-0-7861-6789-0(0)) Blckstn Audio.

Dark Tunnel. Kenneth Millar. Read by Tom Parker. 6 CDs. (Running Time: 7 hrs.). 1996. audio compact disk 48.00 (978-0-7861-9786-6(2), 2700) Blckstn Audio.
Doctor Robert Branch is a university professor, not a secret agent, but his best friend is dead & Branch knows that it can't have been suicide. He is also certain that the murder has been arranged by a Nazi espionage group operating on campus. The only trouble is, no one will believe him. He's even narrowed his choice of executioner down to three, a psychotic homosexual, a respected educator & the women he loves.

Dark Tunnel. Kenneth Millar. Read by Tom Parker. 5 cass. (Running Time: 7 hrs.). 2000. 39.95 (978-0-7861-1907-3(1), 2700) Blckstn Audio.

Dark Twin see Poetry & Voice of Marilyn Hacker

Dark Venture: Pursuit & Eclipse. 1 cass. (Running Time: 1 hr.). 2001. 6.98 (2095) Radio Spirits.

Dark Victory. William Shatner. Read by William Shatner. 2004. 10.95 (978-0-7435-1955-7(8)) Pub: S&S Audio. Dist(s): S and S Inc

Dark Volume. unabr. ed. Gordon Dahlquist. Read by John Lee. 15 CDs. (Running Time: 19 hrs. 0 mins. 0 sec.). (ENG.). 2009. audio compact disk 49.99 (978-1-4001-1009-4(2)); audio compact disk 34.99 (978-1-4001-6009-9(X)); audio compact disk 99.99 (978-1-4001-4009-1(9)) Pub: Tantor Media. Dist(s): IngramPubServ

Dark Voyage. Alan Furst. Read by Graeme Malcolm. 2004. 15.95 (978-0-7435-3995-1(8)) Pub: S&S Audio. Dist(s): S and S Inc

Dark Voyage. unabr. ed. Alan Furst. Read by George Guidall. 7 cass. (Running Time: 9 hrs. 30 mins.). 2004. 69.75 (978-1-4193-0772-0(X), 97873MC) Recorded Bks.

Dark Watch. unabr. ed. Clive Cussler & Jack Du Brul. Read by Scott Brick. 11 CDs. (Running Time: 13 hrs.). (Oregon Files Ser.: No. 3). 2005. audio compact disk 99.00 (978-1-4159-1856-2(2)); 81.00 (978-1-4159-1855-5(4)) Books on Tape.
The author of the bestselling NUMA and Dirk Pitt series returns with an all-new novel of adventure and intrigue featuring his unbeatable hero of the high seas-Juan Cabrillo. Cabrillo and his motley crew aboard the clandestine spy ship Oregon have made a very comfortable and very dangerous living working for high-powered Western interests. But their newest clients have come from the Far East to ask for Cabrillo's special brand of assistance: a consortium of Japanese shipping magnates whose fortunes are being threatened by brutal pirates trolling the waters of Southeast Asia. Normally, such attacks on the high seas are limited to smaller ships and foreign-owned yachts-easy targets on the open ocean. Now, however, giant commercial freighters are disappearing. But when Cabrillo confronts the enemy, he learns that the pirates' predations hide a deadly international conspiracy-a scheme of death and slavery that Juan Cabrillo is going to blow out of the water.

Dark Watch. unabr. ed. Clive Cussler & Jack Du Brul. 9 CDs. (Running Time: 11 hrs.). No. 3. (gr. 12 up). 2005. audio compact disk 39.95 (978-0-14-305804-5(5), PengAudBks) Penguin Grp USA.

Dark Water Rising. unabr. ed. Marian Hale. Read by Stephen Hoye. 5 CDs. (Running Time: 5 hrs. 19 mins.). (YA). (gr. 6 up). 2007. audio compact disk 45.00 (978-0-7393-6169-6(4), Listening Lib) Pub: Random Audio Pubg. Dist(s): Random
You'd think every dang person from Lampasas to Houston wanted to go to Galveston this hot August day. Everyone but Seth. Galveston, Texas, may be the booming city of the brand-new twentieth century, filled with opportunites for all, but to Seth it is the end of a dream. He longs to be a carpenter like his father, yet Papa has moved the family to Galveston so that Seth can become a doctor. Still, the last few weeks of summer might not be so bad. Seth has landed his first real job as a builder, and there's that girl across the street, the one with the sun-bright hair. Things seem to be looking up . . . until a storm warning is raised one sweltering afternoon. They say a north wind always brings change, but no one could ever have imagined this. Set during the Galveston Storm of 1900, this is an unforgettable story of survival in the face of natural disaster.

Dark Whispers. Bruce Coville. Read by Bruce Coville. Read by Mark Austin et al. (Unicorn Chronicles Ser.). (J). (gr. 5). 2008. 59.99 (978-1-60640-930-5(1)) Find a World.

Dark Whispers. unabr. ed. Bruce Coville. Narrated by Bruce Coville. 10 CDs. (Running Time: 10 hrs. 15 mins.). (Unicorn Chronicles: Bk. 3). (YA). (gr. 5-8). 2008. audio compact disk 65.00 (978-1-934180-28-0(9)) Full Cast Audio.

Dark Wind. Tony Hillerman. Read by Nelson Runger. 4 cass. (Running Time: 5 hrs. 30 min.). 1993. 39.80 Set. (250023); Rental 7.30 30 day rental Set. (250023) Literate Ear.
Hopi braves discover the Navajo body. They know the meaning of the gruesome sight - the victim's hands & feet have been "scalped." Bad blood runs between the tribes. Soon, Sgt. Jim Chee of the Navajo Tribal Police has more than one body on his roster.

Dark Wind. Tony Hillerman. Narrated by George Guidall. 7 CDs. (Running Time: 8 hrs). 1982. audio compact disk 34.95 (978-1-4025-3926-8(6)) Recorded Bks.

Dark Wind. abr. ed. Tony Hillerman. Read by Gil Silverbird. (Joe Leaphorn & Jim Chee Novel Ser.). 2005. audio compact disk 14.95 (978-0-06-081509-7(4)) HarperCollins Pubs.

Dark Wind. unabr. ed. Tony Hillerman. Read by Jonathan Marosz. 7 cass. (Running Time: 7 hrs.). (Joe Leaphorn & Jim Chee Novel Ser.). 1994. 56.00 (978-0-7366-2689-7(1), 3424) Books on Tape.
Murder draws Navajo police investigator Jim Chee into rituals of Indian sorcery. Mysterious & compelling.

Dark Wind. unabr. ed. Tony Hillerman. Narrated by George Guidall. 6 cass. (Running Time: 8 hrs.). (Joe Leaphorn & Jim Chee Novel Ser.). (gr. 10 up). 1990. 51.00 (978-1-55690-136-2(4), 91101E7) Recorded Bks.
What appears to be a ritual murder sets Sergeant Jim Chee on the trail of some unpredictable killers.

Dark Winds. unabr. ed. Graham Watkins. Read by Michael Hanson. 9 cass. (Running Time: 13 hrs. 23 min.). 1989. 54.00 Set. (978-0-9624010-0-8(5)) Readers Chair.
Sometimes, desire is the deadliest terror of all. For Elliot Collins, such a desire has a name: Nikki, his dead father's mistress. She lives in his wildest dreams, where dangerously erotic, she is calling to him, luring him to a fate beyond his control. Beyond his imagination. Beyond his own death.

***Dark Worlds Lovecraft V1.** H. P. Lovecraft. (Running Time: 4 mins.). 2009. 19.95 (978-1-897331-02-6(9), AudioRealms) Dorch Pub Co.

***Dark Worlds Lovecraft V2.** H. P. Lovecraft. (Running Time: 3 mins.). 2009. 19.95 (978-1-897331-03-3(7), AudioRealms) Dorch Pub Co.

***Dark Worlds Lovecraft V4.** H. P. Lovecraft. (Running Time: 4 mins.). 2009. 19.95 (978-1-897331-04-0(5), AudioRealms) Dorch Pub Co.

***Dark Worlds Lovecraft V6.** H. P. Lovecraft. (Running Time: 5 mins.). 2009. 19.95 (978-1-897331-07-1(X), AudioRealms) Dorch Pub Co.

Dark Worlds of H. P. Lovecraft. H. P. Lovecraft. (Running Time: 4 mins.). 2009. audio compact disk 25.95 (978-1-897304-24-2(2)); audio compact disk 25.95 (978-1-897304-00-6(5)); audio compact disk 25.95 (978-1-897304-04-4(8)); audio compact disk 25.95 (978-1-897304-01-3(3)) Dorch Pub Co.

Dark Worlds of H. P. Lovecraft, Vol. 3. H. P. Lovecraft. 2007. audio compact disk 25.95 (978-0-8095-7185-7(4)) Diamond Book Dists.

Dark Worlds of H. P. Lovecraft, Vol. 4. H. P. Lovecraft. 2007. audio compact disk 25.95 (978-0-8095-7187-1(0)) Diamond Book Dists.

***Dark Worlds of H. P. Lovecraft, Vol. 5.** H. P. Lovecraft. Read by Wayne June. 1 MP3-CD. (Running Time: 4 mins.). 2009. 19.95 (978-1-897331-06-4(1), AudioRealms) Dorch Pub Co.

Dark Worlds of H. P. Lovecraft, Vol. 5. unabr. ed. H. P. Lovecraft. Read by Wayne June. 3 CDs. (Running Time: 3 hrs. 30 mins.). 2007. audio compact disk 25.95 (978-0-8095-7189-5(7)) Diamond Book Dists.

Dark Worlds of H. P. Lovecraft, Vol. 5. unabr. ed. H. P. Lovecraft. Read by Wayne June. 3 CDs. (Running Time: 4 mins.). 2009. audio compact disk 25.95 (978-1-897304-25-9(0)) Dorch Pub Co.

Dark Worlds of H. P. Lovecraft, Vol. 6. H. P. Lovecraft. 2007. audio compact disk 27.95 (978-0-8095-7190-1(0)) Diamond Book Dists.

Dark Worlds of H. P. Lovecraft, Vol. 6. H. P. Lovecraft. (Running Time: 5 mins.). 2009. audio compact disk 27.95 (978-1-897304-26-6(9)) Dorch Pub Co.

Dark Worlds of H. P. Lovecraft, Vol. 7. H. P. Lovecraft. 2007. audio compact disk 25.95 (978-0-8095-7199-4(4)) Diamond Book Dists.

Dark Worlds of H. P. Lovecraft, Vol. 8. H. P. Lovecraft. 2007. audio compact disk 25.95 (978-0-8095-7217-5(6)) Diamond Book Dists.

***Dark Worlds of H. P. Lovecraft, Volume Four.** H. p. Lovecraft. Read by Wayne June. (Running Time: 9660 sec.). (Dark Worlds of H. P. Lovecraft Ser.). (ENG.). 2009. audio compact disk (978-1-897331-05-7(3), AudioRealms) Dorch Pub Co.

Dark Zone. abr. ed. Stephen Coonts & Jim DeFelice. Read by J. Charles. 4 CDs. (Running Time: 4 hrs.). (Deep Black Ser.: No. 3). 2004. audio compact disk 69.25 (978-1-59600-051-3(1), 1596000511, BACDLib Ed) Brilliance Audio.
The mission seems routine: go to London, meet someone in a park, obtain a list of computers that are being used secretly by terrorists to pass messages. But just as Deep Black operatives Charlie Dean and Tommy Karr are about to meet their contact, a sniper guns the stranger down. A Deep Black investigation begins. Former Delta Force trooper Lia DeFrancesca, a sexy ass-kicking woman and Dean's only weakness, gets called in to help. The three operatives start cracking some leads, but the investigation doesn't kick in to high gear until the murder is discovered to be connected to the disappearance of a French atomic warhead built in the 1960s. Soon it becomes apparent that what was thought to be an elaborate plan by terrorists to blow up the Eiffel Tower is only a diversionary plan for the real target: the Chunnel. A nuclear warhead going off in the Chunnel will create an earthquake and thus a tsunami that will wipe out the coasts of France and England, killing hundreds of thousands. It is up to Deep Black to expose the plot and thwart the terrorists' plans. This is Deep Black's most dangerous mission yet. It will require all their talents and all their teamwork to make sure that things go right and that justice is served.

Dark Zone. abr. ed. Stephen Coonts & Jim DeFelice. Read by J. Charles. (Running Time: 14400 sec.). (Deep Black Ser.: No. 3). 2005. audio compact disk 14.99 (978-1-59600-430-6(4), 9781596004306, BCD Value Price) Brilliance Audio.

Dark Zone. unabr. ed. Stephen Coonts & Jim DeFelice. Read by J. Charles. (Running Time: 10 hrs.). (Deep Black Ser.: No. 3). 2004. 39.25 (978-1-59710-199-8(0), 1597101990, BADLE); 24.95 (978-1-59710-198-1(2), 1597101982, BAD); 24.95 (978-1-59335-675-0(7), 1593356757, Brilliance MP3); 39.25 (978-1-59335-809-9(1), 1593358091, Brlnc Audio MP3 Lib); 29.95 (978-1-59086-703-7(3), 1590867033); 82.25 (978-1-59086-704-4(1), 1590867041, BrilAudUnabridg) Brilliance Audio.

Darkening Leaf, Set. unabr. ed. Caroline Stickland. 7 cass. 1998. 76.95 (978-1-85903-134-6(X)) Pub: Magna Story GBR. Dist(s): Ulverscroft US

Darkening of the Light: The Relationship Between Physical Pain, Illness, & Individuation. Arthur Colman. Read by Arthur Colman. 4 cass. (Running Time: 6 hrs.). 1993. 31.95 set. (978-0-7822-0436-0(8), 515) C G Jung IL.
In this workshop, San Francisco analyst Arthur Colman creates a fascinating collage from analytic work, personal story, myth (the Finnish epic The Kalevala), philosopher Michel Foucault, & contemporary practices of body manipulation. The discussion of this raw material attempts to provoke a deeper appreciation of the role of suffering in individuation.

Darkening Sea. unabr. ed. Alexander Kent, pseud. Read by Michael Jayston. 10 cass. (Running Time: 10 hrs.). (Richard Bolitho Ser.: Bk. 20). 1998. 84.95 (978-0-7540-0222-2(5), CAB 1645) AudioGO.
France's alliance with America threatens the British trade routes, & Vice-Admiral Bolitho is ordered to report to the Indian Ocean immediately. He, however, has mixed feelings about the newest Admiral.

Darkening Sky. Alison Joseph. Read by Julia Franklin. 8 cass. (Running Time: 10 hrs. 35 mins.). (Story Sound Ser.). (J). 2005. 69.95 (978-1-85903-775-1(5)); audio compact disk 84.95 (978-1-85903-886-4(7)) Pub: Magna Lrg Print GBR. Dist(s): Ulverscroft US

Darker Place. abr. ed. Jack Higgins. Read by Michael Page. (Running Time: 5 hrs.). (Sean Dillon Ser.). 2010. audio compact disk 14.99 (978-1-4418-3418-8(4), 9781441834188, BACD) Brilliance Audio.

Darker Place. abr. ed. Jack Higgins. Read by Michael Page. (Running Time: 5 hrs.). (Sean Dillon Ser.). 2011. audio compact disk 9.99 (978-1-4418-3419-5(2), 9781441834195, BCD Value Price) Brilliance Audio.

***Darker Place.** abr. ed. Jack Higgins. Read by Michael Page. (Running Time: 5 hrs.). (Sean Dillon Ser.). 2010. 9.99 (978-1-4418-9352-9(0), 9781441893529, BAD) Brilliance Audio.

Darker Place. unabr. ed. Jack Higgins. Read by Michael Page. (Running Time: 9 hrs.). (Sean Dillon Ser.). 2009. 39.97 (978-1-4233-7615-6(3), 9781423376156, BADLE); 39.97 (978-1-4233-7613-2(7), 9781423376132, Brlnc Audio MP3 Lib); 24.99 (978-1-4233-7614-9(5), 9781423376149, BAD); 24.99 (978-1-4233-7612-5(9), 9781423376125, Brilliance MP3); audio compact disk 87.97 (978-1-4233-7611-8(0), 9781423376118, BriAudCD Unabrid); audio compact disk 34.99 (978-1-4233-7610-1(2), 9781423376101) Brilliance Audio.

Darker Place. unabr. ed. Laurie R. King. Narrated by Alyssa Bresnahan. 10 cass. (Running Time: 14 hrs. 45 mins.). 1999. 87.00 (978-0-7887-3121-1(1), 95648 E7) Recorded Bks.
Professor Anne Waverly teaches religious studies at a respected university. But occasionally she works for the FBI. As Ana Wakefield, an eager seeker of higher truths, she infiltrates cults. Now leaving the security of academia, she is on her way to Arizona to investigate a group called Change.

Darker Side. Shirley Wells. 2009. 54.95 (978-1-84652-445-5(8)) Pub: Magna Story GBR. Dist(s): Ulverscroft US

Darker Side. Shirley Wells & Margaret Sircom. 2009. audio compact disk 71.95 (978-1-84652-446-2(6)) Pub: Magna Story GBR. Dist(s): Ulverscroft US

Darker Side. unabr. ed. Cody McFadyen. Read by Joyce Bean. 1 MP3-CD. (Running Time: 12 hrs.). (Smoky Barrett Ser.: No. 3). 2008. 39.25 (978-1-4233-7005-5(8), 9781423370055, Brlnc Audio MP3 Lib); 39.25 (978-1-4233-7007-9(4), 9781423370079, BADLE); 24.95 (978-1-4233-7006-2(6), 9781423370062, BAD); 24.95 (978-1-4233-7004-8(X), 9781423370048, Brilliance MP3); audio compact disk 117.25 (978-1-4233-7003-1(1), 9781423370031, BriAudCD Unabrid); audio compact disk 38.95 (978-1-4233-7002-4(3), 9781423370024, Bril Audio CD Unabri) Brilliance Audio.

Darker Than Amber. unabr. collector's ed. John D. MacDonald. Read by Michael Prichard. 7 cass. (Running Time: 7 hrs.). (Travis McGee Ser.: Vol. 7). 1978. 42.00 (978-0-7366-0216-7(X), 1214) Books on Tape.
Travis McGee & his philosophical cohort Meyer rescue a beautiful Eurasian woman from her "friends". Her eyes, just a little "darker than amber", pull them into a crisis that nearly finishes our hero. As the mystery unfolds, McGee follows to its end the trail of a band of murderous profiteers.

Darkest Before Dawn. unabr. ed. Katie Flynn. Read by Anne Dover. 14 CDs. (Running Time: 15 hrs.). (Soundings (CDs) Ser.). (J). 2006. audio compact disk 104.95 (978-1-84559-315-5(4)) Pub: ISIS Lrg Prnt GBR. Dist(s): Ulverscroft US

Darkest Before Dawn. unabr. ed. Katie Flynn. Read by Anne Dover. 12 cass. (Soundings Ser.). (J). 2006. 94.95 (978-1-84559-247-9(6)) Pub: ISIS Lrg Prnt GBR. Dist(s): Ulverscroft US

Darkest Child. unabr. ed. Delores Phillips. Narrated by Cherise Boothe. (Running Time: 14 hrs.). 2008. 61.75 (978-1-4361-7769-6(3)); 98.75 (978-1-4281-8355-1(8)); audio compact disk 123.75 (978-1-4281-8357-5(4)) Recorded Bks.

Darkest Child. unabr. collector's ed. Delores Phillips. Narrated by Cherise Boothe. 12 CDs. (Running Time: 14 hrs.). 2008. audio compact disk 56.95 (978-1-4281-8358-2(2)) Recorded Bks.

Darkest Evening of the Year. unabr. ed. Dean Koontz. Read by Kirsten Kairos. 8 CDs. (Running Time: 9 hrs.). 2007. audio compact disk 100.00 (978-1-4159-4325-0(7), BksonTape) Pub: Random Audio Pubg. Dist(s): Random
Amy Redwing has dedicated her life to the southern California organization she founded to rescue abandoned and endangered golden retrievers. Among dog lovers, she's a legend for the risks she'll take to save an animal from abuse. Among her friends, Amy's heedless devotion is often cause for concern. To widower Brian McCarthy, whose commitment she can't allow herself to return, Amy's behavior is far more puzzling and hides a shattering secret. No one is surprised when Amy risks her life to save Nickie, nor when she takes the female golden into her home. The bond between Amy and Nickie is immediate and uncanny. Even her two other goldens, Fred and Ethel, recognize Nickie as special, a natural alpha. But the instant joy Nickie brings is shadowed by a series of eerie incidents. An ominous stranger. A mysterious home invasion. And the unmistakable sense that someone is

watching Amy's every move and that, whoever it is, he's not alone. Someone has come back to turn Amy into the desperate, hunted creature she's always been there to save. But now there's no one to save Amy and those she loves.

Darkest Evening of the Year. unabr. ed. Dean Koontz. Read by Kirsten Kairos. 8 CDs. (Running Time: 9 hrs.). (ENG.). 2007. audio compact disk 44.95 (978-0-7393-3296-2(1), Random AudioBks) Pub: Random Audio Pubg. Dist(s): Random

Darkest Fear. Harlan Coben. Read by Jonathan Marosz. (Myron Bolitar Ser.: No. 7). 2000. audio compact disk 56.00 (978-0-7366-6171-3(9)) Books on Tape.

Darkest Fear. collector's unabr. ed. Harlan Coben. Read by Jonathan Marosz. 6 cass. (Running Time: 9 hrs.). (Myron Bolitar Ser.: No. 7). 2001. 29.95 (978-0-7366-5668-9(5)) Books on Tape.
Myron Bolitar must battle a serial killer in order to save the life of a son he just discovered he has.

Darkest Fear. unabr. ed. Harlan Coben. Read by Jonathan Marosz. 6 cass. (Running Time: 9 hrs.). (Myron Bolitar Ser.: No. 7). 2000. 48.00 (978-0-7366-5468-5(2), 5339) Books on Tape.
Though the plot is dark and the theme serious, Coben leavens it with his characteristic humor. Myron's first love, who dumped him years ago for a more successful basketball player, drops back into his life. Her 13-year old son needs a bone marrow transplant. The only suitable registered donor has disappeared. Can Myron find him? Oh, by the way, she informs Myron, he's the boy's father. Myron rallies to the call and on the way to saving his son takes on a killer other than cancer.

Darkest Fear. unabr. ed. Harlan Coben. Read by Jonathan Marosz. 7 CDs. (Running Time: 10 hrs. 30 mins.). (Myron Bolitar Ser.: No. 7). 2001. audio compact disk 56.00 Books on Tape.
Myron Bolitar must battle a serial killer in order to save the life of a son he just discovered he has.

Darkest Fear. unabr. ed. Harlan Coben. Read by Jonathan Marosz. (Running Time: 27000 sec.). (Myron Bolitar Ser.: No. 7). 2008. audio compact disk 19.99 (978-0-7393-4119-3(7), Random AudioBks) Pub: Random Audio Pubg. Dist(s): Random

Darkest Hour. unabr. ed. V. C. Andrews. 9 cass. (Running Time: 11 hrs. 27 mins.). (Isis Cassettes Ser.). (J). 2004. 76.95 (978-0-7531-1776-7(2)) Pub: ISIS Lrg Prnt GBR. Dist(s): Ulverscroft US

***Darkest Kiss.** unabr. ed. Keri Arthur. Narrated by Angela Dawe. (Running Time: 10 hrs. 30 mins.). (Riley Jenson Guardian Ser.). 2010. 24.99 (978-1-4526-5006-7(3)); 16.99 (978-1-4526-7006-5(4)); 34.99 (978-1-4526-0006-2(6)) Tantor Media.

***Darkest Kiss (Library Edition)** unabr. ed. Keri Arthur. Narrated by Angela Dawe. (Running Time: 10 hrs. 30 mins.). (Riley Jenson Guardian Ser.). 2010. 83.99 (978-1-4526-3006-9(2)); 34.99 (978-1-4526-2006-0(7)) Tantor Media.

***Darkest Mercy.** unabr. ed. Melissa Marr. (ENG.). 2011. (978-0-06-206200-0(X)); (978-0-06-206201-7(8)) HarperCollins Pubs.

Darkest Midnight. unabr. ed. Perf. by Noirin Ni Riain. 1 CD. (Running Time: 41 mins.). (GAE.). 1996. audio compact disk 16.98 (978-1-56455-454-3(6), MM00322D) Sounds True.
Celebrate Christmas in the Irish tradition with a treasury of rare & authentic Irish Christmas music performed along with the monks of Glenstal Abbey.

Darkest Place. abr. ed. Daniel Judson. Read by Dick Hill. (Running Time: 21600 sec.). 2007. audio compact disk 14.99 (978-1-4233-0424-1(1), 9781423304241, BCD Value Price) Brilliance Audio.

Darkest Place. unabr. ed. Daniel Judson. Read by Dick Hill. (Running Time: 12 hrs.). 2006. 39.25 (978-1-4233-0422-7(5), 9781423304227, BADLE); 24.95 (978-1-4233-0421-0(7), 9781423304210, BAD); 87.25 (978-1-4233-0535-4(3), 9781423305354, BrilAudUnabridg); audio compact disk 102.25 (978-1-4233-0418-0(7), 9781423304180, BriAudCD Unabrid); audio compact disk 39.25 (978-1-4233-0420-3(9), 9781423304203, Brinc Audio MP3 Lib); audio compact disk 36.95 (978-1-4233-0417-3(9), 9781423304173); audio compact disk 24.95 (978-1-4233-0419-7(5), 9781423304197, Brilliance MP3) Brilliance Audio.
On a night of record cold, a powerfully built man drives his white van to the edge of Long Island's Shinnecock Bay and sets adrift a dead body. An hour later, wanna-be PI Tommy Miller hears over his police scanner that the body of a young man has been discovered - it is the third body to be found in as many months - and rushes to the scene. The next morning, failed-writer-turned-college-instructor Deacon Kane is met at his office by two detectives investigating the apparent suicide-by-drowning of one of his students. And later that afternoon, Reggie Clay, a burned out PI discovers a clue that calls into question the official account not only of this boy's death, but the deaths of two other boys as well. Police suspicions quickly fall on Kane, who forms an uneasy alliance with Miller and Clay - and their mysterious boss, a man known only as Mac. Together these four race to unmask a killer who seems somehow to know Kane's mind better than Kane himself knows it, and in the process are drawn deeper and deeper into the underside of the Hamptons.

***Darkest Summer: Pusan & Inchon 1950 - The Battles That Saved South Korea - - And the Marines - - From Extinction.** unabr. ed. Bill Sloan. Narrated by Michael Prichard. (Running Time: 14 hrs. 30 mins.). 2009. 19.99 (978-1-4001-8328-9(6)) Tantor Media.

Darkest Summer: Pusan & Inchon 1950 - The Battles That Saved South Korea - - And the Marines - - From Extinction. unabr. ed. Bill Sloan. Narrated by Michael Prichard. (Running Time: 14 hrs. 30 mins. 0 sec.). (ENG.). 2010. 29.99 (978-1-4001-6328-1(5)); audio compact disk 79.99 (978-1-4001-4328-3(4)); audio compact disk 39.99 (978-1-4001-1328-6(8)) Pub: Tantor Media. Dist(s): IngramPubServ

Darkfall. unabr. ed. Dean Koontz. Read by Christopher Lane. (Running Time: 10 hrs.). 2008. 39.25 (978-1-4233-3945-8(2), 9781423339458, BADLE); 24.95 (978-1-4233-3944-1(4), 9781423339441, BAD); audio compact disk 39.25 (978-1-4233-3943-4(6), 9781423339434, Brinc Audio MP3 Lib); audio compact disk 97.25 (978-1-4233-3941-0(X), 9781423339410, BriAudCD Unabrid); audio compact disk 24.95 (978-1-4233-3942-7(8), 9781423339427, Brilliance MP3); audio compact disk 36.95 (978-1-4233-3940-3(1), 9781423339403, Bril Audio CD Unabri) Brilliance Audio.

Darkfever. abr. ed. Karen Marie Moning. Read by Joyce Bean. (Running Time: 21600 sec.). (Fever Ser.: No. 1). 2007. audio compact disk 14.99 (978-1-4233-1978-8(8), 9781423319788, BCD Value Price) Brilliance Audio.

***Darkfever.** abr. ed. Karen Marie Moning. 2010. audio compact disk 9.99 (978-1-4418-5631-9(5)) Brilliance Audio.

Darkfever. unabr. ed. Karen Marie Moning. Read by Joyce Bean. (Running Time: 9 hrs.). (Fever Ser.: No. 1). 2006. 39.25 (978-1-4233-1976-4(1), 9781423319764, BADLE); 24.95 (978-1-4233-1975-7(3), 9781423319757, BAD); 74.25 (978-1-4233-1970-2(2), 9781423319702, BrilAudUnabridg); audio compact disk 92.25 (978-1-4233-1972-6(9), 9781423319726, BriAudCD Unabrid); audio compact disk 39.25 (978-1-4233-1974-0(5), 9781423319740, Brinc Audio MP3 Lib); audio compact disk 24.95 (978-1-4233-1973-3(7), 9781423319733, Brilliance MP3); audio compact disk 34.95 (978-1-4233-1971-9(0), 9781423319719, Bril Audio CD Unabri) Brilliance Audio.
With her New York Times bestseller Spell of the Highlander, Karen Marie Moning brought a world of ancient magic and timeless love to life. Now, Moning embarks on a fantastic new series about a woman drawn into a seductive other-worldly realm-only to be caught up in a universe-altering battle. A sizzling spin-off from the popular "Highlander" series, Darkfever is filled with captivating characters, paranormal elements, and unparalleled sensuality and heat. Darkfever opens approximately three and a half years after Spell of the Highlander ends. MacKayla O'Connor's life is good. Or so she thinks until something extraordinary happens... When her sister is murdered, leaving a single clue to her death - a cryptic message on Mac's cell phone - Mac journeys to Ireland in search of answers. The quest to find her sister's killer draws her into a shadowy realm where nothing is as it seems, where good and evil wear the same treacherously seductive mask. She soon is faced with an even greater challenge - staying alive long enough to learn how to handle a power she had no idea she possessed - a gift that allows her to see beyond the world of man, into the dangerous realm of the Fae. As Mac delves deeper into the mystery of her sister's death, the ruthless Vlane - an alpha Fae who makes sex an addiction for human women - closes in on her. And as the boundary between worlds begins to crumble, Mac's true mission becomes clear: find the elusive Sinsar Dubh before someone else claims the all-powerful Dark Book... because whoever gets to it first holds nothing less than complete control of the very fabric of both worlds in their hands.

***Darklight.** unabr. ed. Lesley Livingston. Read by Lesley Livingston. (ENG.). 2009. (978-0-06-193827-6(0)); (978-0-06-196749-8(1)) HarperCollins Pubs.

Darkling. unabr. ed. Yasmine Galenorn. Narrated by Cassandra Campbell. (Running Time: 11 hrs. 0 mins. 0 sec.). (Sisters of the Moon Ser.). (ENG.). 2009. audio compact disk 34.99 (978-1-4001-1001-8(7)); audio compact disk 24.99 (978-1-4001-6001-3(4)); audio compact disk 69.99 (978-1-4001-4001-5(3)) Pub: Tantor Media. Dist(s): IngramPubServ

Darkling I Listen. Katherine Sutcliffe. Read by Alyssa Bresnahan. 12 cass. (Running Time: 18 hrs.). 2001. 96.00 (978-0-7366-8080-6(2)); audio compact disk 120.00 (978-0-7366-8260-2(0)) Books on Tape.
At the end of three long years in the penitentiary, movie star Brandon Carlyle's bad boy career is on the skids. He seeks sanctuary with his beloved aunt and uncle, who live in the tiny, eccentric town of Ticky Creek, Texas. But there's nothing about Ticky Creek that's truly peaceful. The local corrupt sheriff, who put him away the first time, is going for him again; the sheriff's horny sister is going for him, too. What's more, a crazed anonymous fan has been writing him a series of threatening letters that could mean harm for him and his family. As the stalker closes in, beautiful tabloid journalist Alyson James appears; she seems like the right woman for Carlyle, but could she be the stalker.

Darkling I Listen. unabr. ed. Katherine Sutcliffe. Read by Alyssa Bresnahan. 12 cass. (Running Time: 18 hrs.). 2001. 72.00; audio compact disk 90.00 Books on Tape.
When a movie star with a tarnished past moves to small-town Texas, a stalker and a beautiful tabloid journalist close in on him.

Darklore Manor. Nox Arcana. Illus. by Joseph Vargo. Composed by Joseph Vargo. Engineer William Piotrowski. Music by William Piotrowski. 1 CD. (Running Time: 52 min.). (ENG.). 2003. audio compact disk 13.99 (978-0-9675756-4-3(8)) Monolith.
Enter Darklore Manor, where creatures of the night lurk in shadows and ghostly sounds echo through the halls. Nox Arcana invites you to embark on a musical journey throughout a legendary haunted house with a dark and sinister history. This gothic soundscape contains 21 tracks of haunting melodies, eerie voices, Latin chants, and foreboding orchestrations to set the mood for your darkest nightmare.

Darkly Dreaming Dexter. unabr. ed. Jeff Lindsay. Read by Nick Landrum. 6 cass. (Running Time: 8 hrs. 30 mins.). 2004. 59.75 (978-1-4025-9630-8(8)); audio compact disk 74.75 (978-1-4025-9632-2(4)) Recorded Bks.

Darkly Dreaming Dexter. unabr. ed. Jeff Lindsay. Narrated by Nick Landrum. 8 CDs. (Running Time: 11 hrs. 30 mins.). 2004. audio compact disk 24.99 (978-1-4025-8138-0(6), 01632) Recorded Bks.
Dexter Morgan appears to be the perfect gentleman. He is handsome and polite, and has been in a relationship for nearly a year and a half. Then again, he does have one little secret. He has killed a few dozen people. But only bad people! When another, much more visible serial killer emerges, Dexter notices the new guy's style is similar to his own. Could this possibly be a challenge to come out and play?.

Darkness & the Dawn. 2002. audio compact disk 62.00 (978-1-57972-438-2(8)) Insight Living.

Darkness & the Dawn: Cassette Series. 2002. 48.00 (978-1-57972-391-0(8)) Insight Living.

Darkness at Noon. unabr. ed. Arthur Koestler. Narrated by Frank Muller. 7 CDs. (Running Time: 8 hrs. 15 mins.). 1999. audio compact disk 66.00 (978-0-7887-3722-0(8), C1079E7) Recorded Bks.
A portrayal of an aging revolutionary, this is a commentary on nightmare politics. Imprisoned by the Party to which he has dedicated his life, the hero reveals his tempestuous career.

Darkness at Noon. unabr. ed. Arthur Koestler. Narrated by Frank Muller. 6 cass. (Running Time: 8 hrs. 15 mins.). 2000. 51.00 (978-0-7887-3103-7(3), 95814E7) Recorded Bks.

Darkness, Be My Friend. John Marsden. Read by Suzi Dougherty. (Running Time: 7 hrs.). (Tomorrow Ser.). (YA). 2009. 69.99 (978-1-74214-335-4(0), 9781742143354) Pub: Bolinda Pubng AUS. Dist(s): Bolinda Pub Inc

Darkness, Be My Friend. unabr. ed. John Marsden. Read by Suzi Dougherty. 6 CDs. (Running Time: 7 hrs.). (Tomorow Ser.). (YA). 2001. audio compact disk 77.95 (978-1-74030-400-9(4)) Pub: Bolinda Pubng AUS. Dist(s): Bolinda Pub Inc

Darkness, Be My Friend. unabr. ed. John Marsden. Read by Suzi Dougherty. (Running Time: 25200 sec.). (Tomorrow Ser.). 2008. audio compact disk 43.95 (978-1-921334-91-7(6), 9781921334917) Pub: Bolinda Pubng AUS. Dist(s): Bolinda Pub Inc

Darkness Before Dawn. Sharon M. Draper. Narrated by Sisi Aisha Johnson. 6 pieces. (Running Time: 8 hrs.). (Hazelwood High Trilogy: Bk. 3). (YA). 2001. 54.00 (978-1-4025-0927-8(8)) Recorded Bks.

Darkness Before Dawn. Paul McCusker & AIO Team Staff. Prod. by Focus on the Family Staff. 4 CDs. (Running Time: 6 hrs.). (Adventures in Odyssey Ser.: Vol. 25). (ENG.). (J). (gr. 3-7). 1996. audio compact disk 24.99 (978-1-56179-449-2(X)) Pub: Focus Family. Dist(s): Tyndale Hse

Darkness Falls. unabr. ed. Kyle Mills. Narrated by Erik Steele. (Running Time: 30600 sec.). (ENG.). 2007. audio compact disk 29.95 (978-1-60283-311-1(7)) Pub: AudioGO. Dist(s): Perseus Dist

Darkness Falls. unabr. ed. Kyle Mills. Read by Erik Steele. (YA). 2008. 64.99 (978-1-60514-567-9(X)) Find a World.

Darkness Forged in Fire. unabr. ed. Chris Evans. Narrated by Michael Kramer. 2 MP3-CDs. (Running Time: 15 hrs. 30 mins. 0 sec.). (Iron Elves Ser.). (ENG.). 2008. audio compact disk 34.99 (978-1-4001-5836-2(2)); audio compact disk 99.99 (978-1-4001-3836-4(1)) Pub: Tantor Media. Dist(s): IngramPubServ

Darkness Forged in Fire. unabr. ed. Chris Evans. Read by Michael Kramer. 12 CDs. (Running Time: 15 hrs. 30 mins. 0 sec.). (Iron Elves Ser.). (ENG.). 2008. audio compact disk 49.99 (978-1-4001-0836-7(5)) Pub: Tantor Media. Dist(s): IngramPubServ

Darkness in Him: A Novel. unabr. ed. Andrew Lyons. Read by Christopher Lane. 6 cass. (Running Time: 8 hrs. 30 mins.). 2003. 44.95 (978-0-7861-2397-1(4), 3074); audio compact disk 56.00 (978-0-7861-9298-4(4), 3074) Blckstn Audio.
Jake Conason goes to a party at his Jefferson University fraternity house, and he's sitting on top of the world. He's got great grades, a gorgeous girlfriend named Jordan, and an almost certain acceptance to his dream law school. He's golden, set to ride a wave of opportunity and advantage far into his adulthood. Little does he know that the moment he walks into the party, his life will change forever.

Darkness More Than Night. abr. ed. Michael Connelly. (Harry Bosch Ser.: No. 7). 2002. 25.98 (978-1-58621-105-9(6)) Hachet Audio.

Darkness More Than Night. abr. ed. Michael Connelly. Read by Michael Beck. (Harry Bosch Ser.: No. 7). (ENG.). 2005. 14.98 (978-1-59483-427-1(X)) Pub: Hachet Audio. Dist(s): HachBkGrp

Darkness More Than Night. unabr. ed. Michael Connelly. (Harry Bosch Ser.: No. 7). 2002. 25.98 (978-1-58621-106-6(4)) Hachet Audio.

Darkness More Than Night. unabr. ed. Michael Connelly. Read by Richard Davidson. (Harry Bosch Ser.: No. 7). (ENG.). 2005. 16.98 (978-1-59483-428-8(8)) Pub: Hachet Audio. Dist(s): HachBkGrp

Darkness More Than Night. unabr. ed. Michael Connelly. Read by Richard Davidson. (Running Time: 12 hrs. 30 mins.). (Harry Bosch Ser.: No. 7). (ENG.). 2009. 59.98 (978-1-60788-074-5(1)) Pub: Hachet Audio. Dist(s): HachBkGrp

***Darkness More Than Night.** unabr. ed. Michael Connelly. Read by Richard Davidson. (Running Time: 12 hrs. 30 mins.). (ENG.). 2010. audio compact disk 24.98 (978-1-60788-650-1(2)) Pub: Hachet Audio. Dist(s): HachBkGrp

Darkness More Than Night. unabr. collector's ed. Michael Connelly. Read by Richard M. Davidson. 8 cass. (Running Time: 12 hrs.). (Harry Bosch Ser.: No. 7). 2000. 35.95 (978-0-7366-5932-1(3)) Books on Tape.
A retired FBI agent is asked by the LAPD to help them investigate a murder. The prime suspect is an LAPD detective.

Darkness of Divine Persecution: Individuation & Psychopathology. Robert Moore. Read by Robert Moore. 3 cass. (Running Time: 3 hrs. 45 min.). 1991. 24.95 set. (978-0-7822-0353-0(1), 450) C G Jung IL.

Darkness Peering. unabr. ed. Alice Blanchard. Narrated by Alyssa Bresnahan. 9 cass. (Running Time: 12 hrs.). 1999. 80.00 (978-0-7887-4075-6(X), 96161E7) Recorded Bks.
Peers into the dark corners of the human heart. When Detective Rachel Storrow gets pulled into the unsolved murder case that drove her daddy to suicide 17 years ago, a cunning psychopath forces her to question her own motives.

Darkness Peering, Set. abr. ed. Alice Blanchard. Read by Patricia Kalember. 4 cass. 1999. 25.00 (FS9-51007) Highsmith.

Darkness to Light see Expanding in Light

Darkness Will Not Prevail. John Corapi. 3 cass. 19.95 set. (7000-C) Ignatius Pr.
Father John Corapi's conversion story & journey to the priesthood is riveting audiences all across America. Hear his powerful testimony of how, after being a Green Beret soldier, a Las Vegas CPA, multimillionaire businessman, cocaine addict & a homeless destitute, he had a stunning conversion to Catholicism. Since his ordination by Pope John Paul II, who told him "go back to America where I need you!", Father Corapi has been a powerful Catholic preacher in his mission to help John Paul II re-evangelize the Church.

Darkside. Tom Becker. Read by Colin Moody. (Running Time: 6 hrs.). (YA). 2009. 69.99 (978-1-74214-298-2(2), 9781742142982) Pub: Bolinda Pubng AUS. Dist(s): Bolinda Pub Inc

Darkside. unabr. ed. Tom Becker. Read by Colin Moody. 6 CDs. (Running Time: 6 hrs.). (YA). (gr. 7). 2008. audio compact disk 77.95 (978-1-921415-34-0(7), 9781921415340) Pub: Bolinda Pubng AUS. Dist(s): Bolinda Pub Inc

Darkside. unabr. ed. P. T. Deutermann. Read by Dick Hill. 11 cass. (Running Time: 16 hrs.). 2002. 34.95 (978-1-59086-110-3(8), 1590861108, BAU); 102.25 (978-1-59086-111-0(6), 1590861116, Unabridge Lib Edns) Brilliance Audio.
When a midshipman plunges six stories to his death, the U.S. Naval Academy begins investigating an apparent suicide. But there's a bizarre twist: the young man's body is found wearing undergarments belonging to Midshipman Julie Markham, a senior at the academy. Julie's father Ev, an Annapolis graduate who is now a professor there, fears his daughter will be blamed by the "Darkside" - the bureaucracy that wants to protect the academy at all costs from scandal. Then there's another death, and the beautiful grounds and impregnable traditions of Annapolis are revealed as the hiding place for a relentless predator who can no longer control an impulse to kill.

Darkside. unabr. ed. P. T. Deutermann. Read by Dick Hill. (Running Time: 16 hrs.). 2004. 39.25 (978-1-59335-563-0(7), 1593355637, Brinc Audio MP3 Lib) Brilliance Audio.

Darkside. unabr. ed. P. T. Deutermann. Read by Dick Hill. (Running Time: 16 hrs.). 2004. 39.25 (978-1-59710-181-3(8), 1597101818, BADLE); 24.95 (978-1-59710-180-6(X), 159710180X, BAD) Brilliance Audio.

Darkside. unabr. ed. P. T. Deutermann. Read by Dick Hill. (Running Time: 16 hrs.). 2004. 24.95 (978-1-59335-049-9(X), 159335049X) Soulmate Audio Bks.

Darktown Strutters. L. A. Wilson, Jr. Read by Aaron Tucker & Melissa Exelberth. (ENG.). 2009. audio compact disk 5.49 (978-0-9821192-7-3(5)) Mind Wings Aud.

***Darktown Strutters.** L. A. Wilson, Jr. Read by Aaron Tucker & Melissa Exelberth. (Running Time: 51). 2009. 2.99 (978-1-61114-007-1(2)) Mind Wings Aud.

Darkwing Duck. 1 cass. (Running Time: 15 min.). (Disney Afternoon Read-Along Ser.). (J). bk. 5.98 Disney Prod.

Darlene Mccoy. Contrib. by Darlene McCoy et al. 2007. audio compact disk 17.99 (978-5-558-77438-2(X)) Pt of Grace Ent.

Darling. unabr. ed. Russell Banks. Read by Mary Beth Hurt. 2004. audio compact disk 39.95 (978-0-694-52423-5(9)) HarperCollins Pubs.

***Darling.** unabr. ed. Russell Banks. Read by Mary Beth Hurt. (ENG.). 2004. (978-0-06-082470-9(0), Harper Audio); (978-0-06-082471-6(9), Harper Audio) HarperCollins Pubs.

Darling. unabr. ed. Read by Mary Beth Hurt. 2 pieces. 49.95 (978-0-7927-3338-6(X)); 79.95 (978-0-7927-3336-2(3)); audio compact disk 110.95 (978-0-7927-3337-9(1)) AudioGO.

Darling Buds of May, Set. unabr. ed. H. E. Bates. Read by Bruce Montague. 4 cass. (Running Time: 6 hrs.). (Larkin Family Ser.: Bk. 1). 2001. 34.95 (978-0-7451-5780-1(7), CAB 178) Pub: Chivers Audio Bks GBR. Dist(s): AudioGO
Here they come, the immortal Larkins: thirsty, hungry, lusty, happy, and irrepressible! Crashing their way through the English countryside in the wake of Pop, the quick-eyed junk dealer, and Ma, who had a laugh like a jelly, in their first hilarious adventure.

Darling Corey & Goofing-Off Suite. Perf. by Pete Seeger. Anno. by Pete Seeger. Anno. by Anthony Seeger et al. 1 cass. 1993. (0-9307-400180-9307-40018-2-0); audio compact disk (0-9307-40018-2-0) Smithsonian Folkways.
Combines two early 1950s LPs. In "Darling Corey" Pete paid homage to the mountain musicians whose banjo styles he adopted; in "Goofing-Off Suite" he took the banjo into new musical territory & blazed a trail many have followed.

Darling, It's Death. unabr. ed. Richard S. Prather. Read by Maynard Villers. 6 cass. (Running Time: 6 hrs. 6 min.). (Shell Scott Ser.: Bk. 7). 2001. 39.95 (978-1-55686-911-2(8)) Books in Motion.
While working on a case of blackmail involving a beautiful woman, Scott is told to "leave town or die." Shell soon uncovers a larger plot involving the unions and the defense industry.

Darling Jim. unabr. ed. Christian Moerk. Narrated by Stephen Hoye & Justine Eyre. (Running Time: 11 hrs. 0 mins. 0 sec.). 2009. audio compact disk 69.99 (978-1-4001-4198-2(2)); audio compact disk 24.99 (978-1-4001-6198-0(3)) Pub: Tantor Media. Dist(s): IngramPubServ

Darling Jim. unabr. ed. Christian Moerk. Read by Stephen Hoye & Justine Eyre. (Running Time: 11 hrs. 0 mins. 0 sec.). (ENG.). 2009. audio compact disk 34.99 (978-1-4001-1198-5(6)) Pub: Tantor Media. Dist(s): IngramPubServ

Darnell Rock Reporting. unabr. ed. Walter Dean Myers. Narrated by Peter Francis James. 3 pieces. (Running Time: 3 hrs. 30 mins.). (gr. 2 up). 1995. 27.00 (978-0-7887-0205-1(X), 94430E7) Recorded Bks.
Thirteen year old Darnell Rock discovers the power & responsibility that comes with being a reporter for the school paper & how he can use his position to make the world a better place. Darnell is an especially meaningful hero for African American boys who confront many of the same pressures that Darnell faces.

Darryl. Darryl Strawberry & Art Rust, Jr. Read by Art Rust, Jr. 2 cass. (Running Time: 3 hrs.). Dramatization. 15.95 set. (978-1-56703-007-5(6)) High-Top Sports.
A no-holds-barred autobiography of Darryl Strawberry, his alcoholic, violent confrontations with his wife, & playing a sport still tainted by racism.

Dartmouth Conspiracy. James Stevenson. 2008. 69.95 (978-1-4079-0251-7(2)); audio compact disk 84.95 (978-1-4079-0252-4(0)) Pub: Soundings Ltd GBR. Dist(s): Ulverscroft US

Darwin & Evolution. unabr. ed. Michael T. Ghiselin. Read by Edwin Newman. (Running Time: 10800 sec.). (Audio Classics Ser.). 2006. audio compact disk 25.95 (978-0-7861-6497-4(2)) Pub: Blckstn Audio. Dist(s): NetLibrary CO

Darwin & Evolution. unabr. ed. Michael T. Ghiselin. Read by Edwin Newman. Ed. by Jack Sommer & Mike Hassell. 2 cass. (Running Time: 2 hrs. 45 min.). Dramatization. (Science & Discovery Ser.). (YA). (gr. 11 up). 1993. 17.95 set. (978-0-938935-74-2(7), 10409) Knowledge Prod.
For centuries man was seen as a created species, distinct from any other animal. Then, Darwin persuasively argued that mankind & other species are descended from common ancestors; most scientists soon agreed. Darwin also said that "natural selection" (often called "survival of the fittest") explains how life evolved through strictly natural processes. This upset many who believed that life was created by a supernatural God, & it sparked a debate that continues today.

Darwin & the Beagle. unabr. collector's ed. Alan Moorehead. Read by Michael Prichard. 6 cass. (Running Time: 6 hrs.). 1985. 36.00 (978-0-7366-0640-0(8), 1599) Books on Tape.
When the H.M.S Beagle sailed in 1831, she carried young naturalist, Charles Darwin. Destined for the church, Darwin was at ease with his belief in Genesis. But everything he encountered on the voyage - from the primitive people of Tierra del Fuego to the finches of the Galapagos Islands-challenged bibical assumption & led finally to "The Origin of Species".

Darwin Awards: Evolution in Action. abr. ed. Wendy Northcutt. Read by John Ritter. Narrated by Jason Harris. 2 cass. (Running Time: 3 hrs.). (From Hit Websites Ser.). (YA). 2001. 16.95 (978-1-885408-71-6(4), LL063); audio compact disk 22.95 (978-1-885408-72-3(2), LL064) Listen & Live.
Commemorates those who improve our gene pool by removing themselves from it, showing us just how uncommon common sense can be. Tales of trial & awe-inspiring error illustrates the ongoing daga of survival of the fittest in all its selective glory!.

Darwin Awards: Evolution in Action: Evolution in Action. Wendy Northcutt. Read by Jason Harris. (Running Time: 3 hrs. 30 mins.). (C). 2005. 21.95 (978-1-60083-346-5(2)) Iofy Corp.

Darwin Awards II Vol. 2: Unnatural Selection. abr. ed. Wendy Northcutt. Narrated by Jason Harris. 2 cass. (Running Time: 3 hrs.). (From Hit Websites Ser.). (YA). 2001. 16.95 (978-1-885408-75-4(7)); audio compact disk 22.95 (978-1-885408-76-1(5)) Listen & Live.

Darwin Awards III Vol. 3: Survival of the Fittest. abr. ed. Wendy Northcutt. 2 cass. (Running Time: 3 hrs.). (From Hit Websites Ser.). (YA). 2003. 17.95 (978-1-59316-013-5(5), 392621); audio compact disk 23.95 (978-1-59316-014-2(3), 490369) Listen & Live.
A third helping of satisfies the appetite of fans of smart humor with a fresh collection of stories honoring those who continue to improve our gene pool by removing themselves from it in a sublimely idiotic fashion! Included are over one hundred stories of award-winners, honorable mentions, and (debunked) urban legends verified by the author and endorsed by website readers together with a few returning all-time favorites, and exclusive material never before seen.

Darwin Awards 3: Survival of the Fittest: Survival of the Fittest. Wendy Northcutt. Read by Julie Schaller et al. (Running Time: 3 hrs. 30 mins.). (C). 2005. 21.95 (978-1-60083-347-2(0)) Iofy Corp.

Darwin Awards 4: Intelligent Design. Wendy Northcutt. 2006. cd-rom 23.95 (978-1-59316-085-2(2)) Listen & Live.

Darwin Awards 5. Wendy Northcutt. 2008. audio compact disk 23.95 (978-1-59316-135-4(2)) Listen & Live.

Darwin Conspiracy. John Darnton. 2005. 39.25 (978-1-59710-521-7(X)) Brilliance Audio.

Darwin Conspiracy. abr. ed. John Darnton. Read by Bernadette Quigley et al. (Running Time: 21600 sec.). 2006. audio compact disk 16.99 (978-1-59737-351-7(6), 9781597373517, BCD Value Price) Brilliance Audio.
Please enter a Synopsis.

Darwin Conspiracy. abr. unabr. ed. John Darnton. Read by Bernadette Quigley et al. 5 CDs. (Running Time: 43200 sec.). 2005. audio compact disk 97.25 (978-1-59355-005-9(7), 9781593550059, BACDLib Ed) Brilliance Audio.

Darwin Conspiracy. unabr. ed. John Darnton. (Running Time: 12 hrs.). 2005. 24.95 (978-1-59710-520-0(1), 9781597105200, BAD); audio compact disk 38.95 (978-1-4233-0612-2(0), 9781423306122, Bril Audio CD Unabri) Brilliance Audio.
In this riveting new novel, bestselling author John Darnton transports us to Victorian England and around the world to reveal the secrets of a legendary nineteenth-century figure. Darnton elegantly blends the power of fact and the insights of fiction to explore the many mysteries attached to the life and work of Charles Darwin. What led Darwin to the theory of evolution? Why did he wait twenty-two years to write On the Origin of Species? Why was he incapacitated by mysterious illnesses and frightened of travel? Who was his secret rival? These are some of the questions driving Darnton's richly dramatic narrative, which unfolds through three vivid points of view: Darwin's own as he sails around the world aboard the Beagle; his daughter Lizzie's as she strives to understand the guilt and fear that struck her father at the height of his fame; and that of present-day anthropologist Hugh Kellem and Darwin scholar Beth Dulcimer, whose obsession with Darwin (and with each other) drives them beyond the accepted boundaries of scholarly research. What Hugh and Beth discover - Lizzie's diaries and letters lead them to a hidden chapter of Darwin's autobiography - is a maze of bitter rivalries, petty deceptions, and jealously guarded secrets, at the heart of which lies the birth of the theory of evolution.

Darwin Conspiracy. unabr. ed. John Darnton. Read by Bernadette Quigley et al. 8 cass. (Running Time: 43200 sec.). 2005. 87.25 (978-1-59355-002-8(2), 9781593550028, BrilAudUnabridg); audio compact disk 24.95 (978-1-59335-696-5(X), 9781593356965, Brilliance MP3); audio compact disk 39.25 (978-1-59335-830-3(X), 9781593358303, Brlnc Audio MP3 Lib) Brilliance Audio.
Please enter a Synopsis.

Darwin in a Nutshell. unabr. ed. Peter Whitfield. (Running Time: 1 hr. 20 mins.). 2009. audio compact disk 14.98 (978-962-634-944-1(1), Naxos AudioBooks) Naxos.

Darwin Myth: The Life & Lies of Charles Darwin. unabr. ed. Benjamin Wiker. (Running Time: 4 hrs. 30 mins.). 2010. 19.95 (978-1-4417-1683-5(1)); 34.95 (978-1-4417-1679-8(3)); audio compact disk 49.00 (978-1-4417-1680-4(7)) Blckstn Audio.

Darwin on Trial. unabr. ed. Phillip E. Johnson. Read by Frederick Davidson. 5 cass. (Running Time: 7 hrs.). 1992. 39.95 (978-0-7861-0355-3(8), 1312) Blckstn Audio.
Berkeley law professor, Phillip Johnson, looks at the evidence for Darwinistic evolution the way a lawyer would, with a cold dispassionate eye for logic & proof. His discovery is that scientists have put the cart before the horse. They prematurely accepted Darwin's theory as fact & have been scrambling to find evidence for it, mostly unsuccessfully. As the evidentiary difficulties have piled up, scientists have clung to the theory out of fear of encouraging religious fundamentalism & in the process turned belief in Darwinism into their own religion.

***Darwin Selection.** Charles Darwin. Read by Richard Dawkins. Adapted by Richard Dawkins. (Running Time: 13 hrs. 0 mins. 0 sec.). (ENG.). 2011. audio compact disk 40.95 (978-1-934997-66-6(8)) Pub: CSAWord. Dist(s): PerseuPGW

Darwinian Revolution. Instructed by Frederick Gregory. 2008. 129.95 (978-1-59803-501-8(0)); audio compact disk 69.95 (978-1-59803-502-5(9)) Teaching Co.

Darwinism & the Constitutionality of God-mp3. Read by Phillip Johnson. 4. 2004. 10.00 (978-1-59128-488-8(0)) Canon Pr ID.

Darwinism & the Constitutionality of God-tape. Read by Phillip Johnson. 4 cass. 2004. 12.50 (978-1-59128-490-1(2)) Canon Pr ID.

Darwin's Children. unabr. ed. Greg Bear. 12 cass. (Running Time: 18 hrs.). 2003. 72.00 (978-0-7366-8967-0(2)) Books on Tape.

Darwin's Origin of Species: A Biography. unabr. ed. Janet Browne. Narrated by Josephine Bailey. (Running Time: 4 hrs. 30 mins. 0 sec.). (Books That Changed the World Ser.). (ENG.). 2007. audio compact disk 24.99 (978-1-4001-0388-1(6)); audio compact disk 49.99 (978-1-4001-3388-8(2)) Pub: Tantor Media. Dist(s): IngramPubServ

Darwin's Origin of Species: A Biography. unabr. ed. Janet Browne. Narrated by Josephine Bailey. (Running Time: 4 hrs. 30 mins. 0 sec.). (Books That Changed the World Ser.). (ENG.). 2007. audio compact disk 19.99 (978-1-4001-5388-6(3)) Pub: Tantor Media. Dist(s): IngramPubServ

Darwin's Radio: In the Next Stage of Evolution, Humans Are History. Greg Bear. Narrated by George Guidall. 15 CDs. (Running Time: 17 hrs. 30 mins.). 2000. audio compact disk 119.75 (978-0-7887-4748-9(7), C1234E7) Recorded Bks.
It has won multiple Hugo & Nebula Awards & choruses of critical acclaim. Now, Bear creates a non-stop thriller swirling with provocative ideas about the next step of human evolution. When a virus that has slept in our DNA for millions of years wakes up, will the human race survive?.

Darwin's Radio: In the Next Stage of Evolution, Humans Are History. unabr. ed. Greg Bear. Narrated by George Guidall. 12 cass. (Running Time: 17 hrs. 30 mins.). 1999. 109.75 (978-0-7887-4087-9(3), 96168E7) Recorded Bks.

Daryl Coley: Live in Oakland. 1997. 10.98 (978-0-7601-1720-0(9)); audio compact disk 15.98 CD. (978-0-7601-1721-7(7)) Brentwood Music.
Gospel vocals including "Yes, Jesus Loves Me," "I Will Bless Your Name," & more.

Dasavatara. 1 cass.; 1 CD. 4.95 (CD-8); audio compact disk 14.95 CD. Bhaktivedanta.

Dash. 2003. audio compact disk 39.95 (978-0-9742493-2-2(7)) Dash Systems.

Dashing Through the Snow. unabr. ed. Mary Higgins Clark & Carol Higgins Clark. Read by Carol Higgins Clark. 5 CDs. (Running Time: 6 hrs. 0 mins. 0 sec.). (ENG.). 2008. audio compact disk 29.99 (978-0-7435-8212-4(8)) Pub: S&S Audio. Dist(s): S and S Inc

Dasi: Prayers by Women. 2004. audio compact disk 15.95 (978-1-932771-54-1(9)) Mandala Pub.

DAT Audiolearn: Dental Admission Test AudioLearn. 3rd ed. Scripts. Shahrad Yazdani. 5 CDs & a CD-Rom. (Running Time: Over 3 Hours). (C). 2003. audio compact disk 79.00 (978-0-9704199-9-6(6)) AudioLearn.
DAT AudioLearn is available on tape cassette or CD, with high-quality narration and comprehensive coverage of the entire syllabus for the DAT. This easy-listening, user-friendly revision course provides the ideal supplement to your more conventional methods of study by offering an opportunity to continue your revision as easily at home as on the move, while traveling to work or driving in the car.

Dat tennessee 'possum Hollor. David W. Lewis, Sr. Illus. by Paul L. Hart, Sr. (ENG.). (YA). 1978. audio compact disk (978-0-9822457-0-5(X)) DLewis ID.

Data Abstraction & Structures Using C++ 2nd ed. Mark Headington & David Riley. (C). 2001. audio compact disk 101.00 (978-0-7637-1539-7(5), 1539-5) Jones Bartlett.

Data Model Resource Book Vol. 2: A Library of Data Models for Specific Industries. rev. ed. Len Silverston. 2001. audio compact disk 400.00 (978-0-471-38841-8(6)) Wiley US.

Data Structures in Java. Nell Dale et al. (C). 2001. audio compact disk 101.00 (978-0-7637-1541-0(7), 1541-7) Jones Bartlett.

Date Rape: The Crime of Ordinary Men. (Running Time: 30 min.). 10.95 (HO 881206, HarperThor) HarpC GBR.

Date with Dad & Other Calamities. AIO Team Staff. Read by Paul Herlinger et al. (Running Time: 4 hrs. 0 sec.). (Adventures in Odyssey Ser.). (ENG.). (J). (gr. 1-7). 2006. audio compact disk 24.99 (978-1-58997-346-6(1), Tyndale Ent) Tyndale Hse.

***Date You Can't Refuse.** unabr. ed. Harley Jane Kozak. Read by Deanna Hurst. 11 CDs. (Running Time: 14 hrs. 30 mins.). 2009. audio compact disk 99.95 (978-0-7927-6053-5(0)) AudioGO.

Dates, Double Dates & Big, Big Trouble. Karen McCombie. Read by Daniela Denby-Ashe. 3 CDs. (J). 2004. audio compact disk 29.95 (978-0-7540-6650-7(9), Chivers Child Audio) AudioGO.

Dating: No Guts, No Glory, Set. abr. ed. Joni Hilton. 2 cass. 11.98 (978-1-55503-411-5(X), 0700851) Covenant Comms.

Dating: Tips, Trips & Traps & Shouldn't Life Be Happy? Victor Harris. Read by Victor Harris. 1 cass. (YA). (gr. 10-12). 1993. 7.98 (978-1-55503-588-4(4), 06004814) Covenant Comms.

Dating a Stripper Is a Recipe for Perspective (an Essay from Things I've Learned from Women Who've Dumped Me) abr. ed. Patton Oswalt. Read by Patton Oswalt. Ed. by Ben Karlin. (Running Time: 15 mins.). (ENG.). 2008. 1.98 (978-1-60024-349-3(5)) Pub: Hachet Audio. Dist(s): HachBkGrp

Dating & Courtship. Joshua Harris. 1 cass. (Running Time: 4 min.). 1994. 8.00 (978-1-56857-014-3(7)) Noble Pub Assocs.
A new attitude towards dating & courtship, given by a dynamic 19 year old, to challenge teens to pursue God's best in their relationships.

Dating & Social Comfort. Steven Gurgevich. (ENG.). 2004. audio compact disk 19.95 (978-1-932170-30-6(8), HWH) Tranceformation.

Dating as an Adult. unabr. ed. Howard B. Lyman. 1 cass. (Running Time: 25 min.). (Single Again Ser.). 12.95 (35020) J Norton Pubs.

Dating Big Bird. Laura Zigman. Read by Laura Hicks. 6 vols. (Running Time: 9 hrs.). 2000. bk. 54.95 (978-0-7927-2357-8(0), CSL 246, Chivers Sound Lib) AudioGO.
Ellen has a life many people dream about, a glamorous fashion industry job, an apartment in Greenwich Village, good friends & yet Ellen feels herself at sixes & sevens, filled with a vague longing for, what? Then the sight of her newborn niece makes her realize what she's been missing: a child. But the man she loves is too scarred by the long-ago death of his young son to ever consider fatherhood again.

Dating Big Bird. unabr. ed. Laura Zigman. Read by Laura Hicks. 8 CDs. (Running Time: 12 hrs.). 2000. audio compact disk 79.95 (978-0-7927-9950-4(X), SLD 001, Chivers Sound Lib) AudioGO.
Ellen is consumed by a powerful longing to have a baby. There's just one problem. Malcolm, the man she loves is too scarred by the long ago death of his to ever consider fatherhood again.

Dating Big Bird. unabr. ed. Laura Zigman. 4 cass. (Running Time: 6 hrs.). 2001. 24.95 (978-1-57511-068-4(7)) Pub Mills.
A woman's fractured love life turns out some humorous yet humanistic goings on.

Dating Dead Men. unabr. ed. Harley Jane Kozak. Read by Deanna Hurst. (YA). 2008. 74.99 (978-1-60514-633-1(1)) Find a World.

Dating Game. Danielle Steel. 2003. audio compact disk 72.00 (978-0-7366-9281-6(9)) Books on Tape.

Dating in the Kingdom: Biblically Rich, Practical, Helpful & Just Plain Fun! unabr. ed. Jim Brown & Teresa Brown. 3 cass. (Running Time: 3 hrs.). 1997. 16.99 Set. (978-1-57782-025-3(8)) Discipleshp.
The Browns present material on Christian dating that is biblically rich, practically helpful & just plain fun. Tape 3 includes a special session for men & a special session for women. Not just for steady dating couples.

Dating Is Murder. unabr. ed. Harley Jane Kozak. Read by Bernadette Dunne. 8 cass. (Running Time: 11 hrs.). 2005. 81.00 (978-1-4159-1852-4(X)); audio compact disk 99.00 (978-1-4159-1853-1(8)) Books on Tape.

Dating Tips to Prepare for the Temple. Victor Harris. 1 cass. 9.95 (978-1-57734-247-2(X), 06005799) Covenant Comms.
Help teens get the most out of dating & preparing for the temple.

Dating Your Money: How to Build a Long-Lasting Relationship with Your Money in 8 Easy Steps. Jennifer S. Wilkov. Read by Jennifer S. Wilkov. (Dating Your Money Ser.). 2010. audio compact disk 34.95 (978-0-9777347-1-9(4)) Pub: Beaufort Bks NY. Dist(s): Midpt Trade

Dau Gi Bach. Flach. 2005. audio compact disk 8.99 (978-88-88029-86-3(9)) De Falco ITA.

Dau Gi Bach. Flach. 2005. 4.99 (978-0-00-067982-6(8)) Zondervan.

Daufuskie Island. 1 cass. (Running Time: 30 min.). 8.00 (HO-83-05-11, HarperThor) HarpC GBR.

***Daughter of Darkness.** unabr. ed. V. C. Andrews. Narrated by Marguerite Gavin. (Running Time: 11 hrs. 30 mins.). 2010. 17.99 (978-1-4526-7034-8(X)); 24.99 (978-1-4526-5034-0(9)); 34.99 (978-1-4526-2034-3(2)); audio compact disk 34.99 (978-1-4526-0034-5(1)); audio compact disk 83.99 (978-1-4526-3034-2(8)) Pub: Tantor Media. Dist(s): IngramPubServ

Daughter of Deceit. unabr. ed. Victoria Holt. Read by Judy Bennett. 10 cass. (Running Time: 15 hrs.). 2000. 69.95 (978-0-7451-4341-5(5), CAB 1024) Pub: Chivers Audio Bks GBR. Dist(s): AudioGO
Born into the theatrical world of Victorian London, Noelle Tremanston's childhood was unusual, but happy. At the center of it was her fascinating and wildly unconventional mother, Desiree. However, the entry into their lives of Lisa Fennell changes things for Noelle. And when tragedy strikes, Noelle is left devastated.

Daughter of Deceit, Set. unabr. ed. Victoria Holt. Read by Judy Bennett. 10 cass. 2000. 84.95 (CAB 1024) Pub: Chivers Audio Bks GBR. Dist(s): AudioGO

Daughter of Fortune. unabr. ed. Isabel Allende. Read by Blair Brown. 10 cass. (Running Time: 15 hrs.).Tr. of Hija de la Fortuna. 1999. 44.95 (978-0-7366-4811-0(9), 5127) Books on Tape.
Portrays a violent era with compassion. Orphaned at birth, Eliza Sommers is raised in the British colony of Valparaiso, Chile, by prosperous pair of Victorian siblings. In 1849, the pregnant young woman follows her lover to the California gold mines. With the help of her good friend, the Chinese doctor Tao Chien, California opens the door to a new life of freedom.

Daughter of Fortune. unabr. ed. Isabel Allende. Read by Blair Brown. 11 CDs. (Running Time: 13 hrs.).Tr. of Hija de la Fortuna. 2008. audio compact disk 19.95 (978-0-06-157557-0(7), Harper Audio) HarperCollins Pubs.

Daughter of Mine. Anne Bennett & Caroline Lennon. 2007. 94.95 (978-1-84652-131-7(9)); audio compact disk 104.95 (978-1-84652-132-4(7)) Pub: Magna Story GBR. Dist(s): Ulverscroft US

***Daughter of Silk.** unabr. ed. Linda Lee Chaikin. (Running Time: 12 hrs. 39 mins. 0 sec.). (Silk House Ser.). (ENG.). 2008. 14.99 (978-0-310-30520-0(9)) Zondervan.

Daughter of the Elm. Granville Davisson Hall. Music by Leonard Carpenter. Narrated by Ross Ballard. (ENG.). 2002. audio compact disk 26.95 (978-0-9717801-1-8(0)) Mtn Whispers Pubng.

Daughter of the Forest. unabr. ed. Vella Munn. Read by Laurie Klein. 12 cass. (Running Time: 11 hrs. 42 min.). (Women of the West Ser.). 1995. 64.95 (978-1-55686-606-7(2)) Books in Motion.
Twana, a Nisqually Indian maiden is endowed with the unusual mental power to commune with animals. Her power is of great importance when a grizzly bear stalks her Tillamook village.

Daughter of the Mountain. unabr. ed. Vella Munn. Read by Stephanie Brush. 8 cass. (Running Time: 11 hrs. 30 min.). (Women of the West Ser.). 1996. 49.95 (978-1-55686-636-4(4)) Books in Motion.
Jessie Speer prayed for a miracle. Snow-cloaked mountains held them prisoner. Blizzard after blizzard left them aching with cold, one step away from starvation.

Daughter of the Nile-57 B. C. unabr. ed. Kristiana Gregory. Narrated by Josephine Bailey. (Running Time: 3 hrs. 30 mins. 0 sec.). (ENG.). (J). 2006. audio compact disk 19.99 (978-1-4001-5243-8(7)) Pub: Tantor Media. Dist(s): IngramPubServ

Daughter of the Nile-57 B. C. unabr. ed. Kristiana Gregory. Narrated by Josephine Bailey. 4 CDs. (Running Time: 3 hrs. 30 mins. 0 sec.). (ENG.). (J). (gr. 4-8). 2006. audio compact disk 24.99 (978-1-4001-0243-3(X)) Pub: Tantor Media. Dist(s): IngramPubServ

Daughter of the Nile-57 B. C. unabr. ed. Kristiana Gregory. Read by Josephine Bailey. (Running Time: 3 hrs. 30 mins. 0 sec.). (ENG.). (J). (gr. 4-8). 2006. audio compact disk 49.99 (978-1-4001-3243-0(6)) Pub: Tantor Media. Dist(s): IngramPubServ

Daughter of the Stars. unabr. ed. Phyllis A. Whitney. Read by Anna Fields. 5 cass. (Running Time: 7 hrs.). 1997. 39.95 (978-0-7861-1221-0(2), 2162) Blckstn Audio.
Lacey Elliot has been a woman without a past since the day her mother whisked her off to Charlottesville, refusing for thirty years to speak of her father, her family or her history. When Lacey intercepts a desperate letter from an aunt in Harpers Ferry, West Virginia, Lacey sees her chance to confront the past that has terrified her mother & to fill in the gaps in her own life.

***Daughter of the Stars.** unabr. ed. Phyllis A. Whitney. Read by Anna Fields. (Running Time: 7 hrs. 0 mins.). 2010. 29.95 (978-1-4417-6224-5(8)); audio compact disk 69.00 (978-1-4417-6222-1(1)) Blckstn Audio.

Daughter of Time. Josephine Tey. Read by Derek Jacobi. 2005. audio compact disk 29.95 (978-1-57270-466-4(7)) Pub: Audio Partners. Dist(s): PerseuPGW
When Scotland Yard Inspector Alan Grant is confined to a hospital bed, a friend brings him an assortment of pictures of famous historical figures. Grant is engrossed with the portrait of King Richard III and wonders how such an apparently sensitive soul could have murdered his own nephews to secure the British crown for himself. With the help of the British Museum and an American scholar who agrees to be Grant's research assistant, Inspector Grant reconsiders 500-year-old evidence pertaining to one of the most intriguing murder mysteries of all time. Who really killed the two princes in the Tower of London? Tey's answer to this question has provoked controversy among historians and will captivate listeners. A key piece of evidence for Inspector Grant's analysis, the portrait of Richard III - which actually resides at the National Portrait Gallery in London - is featured on the CD cover for listeners' reference. Read by Derek Jacobi.

Daughter of Time. unabr. ed. Josephine Tey. Read by Derek Jacobi. 4 cass. (Running Time: 5 hrs. 20 mins.). 2000. 24.95 (978-1-57270-138-0(2), N41138u) Pub: Audio Partners. Dist(s): PerseuPGW
Who really killed the two princes in the Tower of London? Was it the so-called Wicked Uncle, Richard III? Tey's answer to this question sparked major controversy.

Daughter of Time. unabr. ed. Josephine Tey. Read by Derek Jacobi. 6 cass. (Running Time: 9 hrs.). (Inspector Grant Mystery Ser.: Bk. 5). 2000. 49.95 (978-0-7451-6323-9(8), CAB 092) Pub: Chivers Audio Bks GBR. Dist(s): AudioGO
Inspector Grant begins the job of unravelling the centuries-old mystery of Richard III. Was he really the monster that history books made him out to be? Did he murder the two Princes in the Tower? Inspector Grant was ready to investigate the scandal.

Daughter of Time. unabr. ed. Josephine Tey. Read by Derek Jacobi. 6 CDs. (Inspector Grant Mystery Ser.). 2000. audio compact disk 64.95 (978-0-7540-5369-9(5), CCD 060) Pub: Chivers Audio Bks GBR. Dist(s): AudioGO
Inspector Grant begins the job of unraveling the centuries-old mystery of Richard III. Was he really the monster that history books made him out to be? Did he murder the two Princes in the Tower? Inspector Grant was ready to find the truth.

Daughter of Time. unabr. ed. Josephine Tey. Read by Derek Jacobi. 6 CDs. (Running Time: 5 hrs. 30 mins.). (ENG.). 2009. audio compact disk 24.95 (978-1-60283-644-0(2)) AudioGO.

***Daughter of Winter.** unabr. ed. Pat Lowery Collins. (Running Time: 7 hrs.). 2010. 19.99 (978-1-4418-8992-8(2), 9781441889928, Candlewick Bril); 39.97 (978-1-4418-8993-5(0), 9781441889935, Candlewick Bril) Brilliance Audio.

***Daughter of Winter.** unabr. ed. Pat Lowery Collins. Read by Kate Rudd. (Running Time: 6 hrs.). 2010. audio compact disk 39.97 (978-1-4418-8991-1(4), 9781441889911, Candlewick Bril) Brilliance Audio.

***Daughter of Winter.** unabr. ed. Pat Lowery Collins. Read by Kate Rudd. (Running Time: 6 hrs.). 2010. audio compact disk 24.99 (978-1-4418-8988-1(4), 9781441889881, Candlewick Bril) Brilliance Audio.

***Daughter of Winter.** unabr. ed. Pat Lowry Collins. Read by Kate Rudd. (Running Time: 6 hrs.). 2010. audio compact disk 19.99 (978-1-4418-8990-4(6), 9781441889904, Candlewick Bril); audio compact disk 54.97 (978-1-4418-8989-8(2), 9781441889898, Candlewick Bril) Brilliance Audio.

Daughter of York. unabr. ed. Anne Easter Smith. 19 CDs. (Running Time: 23 hrs. 15 mins.). 2008. audio compact disk 129.00 (978-1-4159-4921-4(2), BksonTape) Pub: Random Audio Pubg. Dist(s): Random
It is 1461. Edward, son of Richard of York, ascends to the throne, and his willful sister, Margaret, immediately becomes a pawn in European politics as Edward negotiates her marriage. The young Margaret falls deeply in love with Anthony Woodville, the married brother of Edward's queen, Elizabeth. But Edward has arranged for his sister to wed Charles, son of the Duke of Burgundy, and soon Margaret is setting sail for her new life. Her official escort: Anthony Woodville. Margaret of York eventually commanded the respect and admiration of much of Europe, but it appears to history that she had no emotional intimate. Anne Easter Smith's rare gift for storytelling and her extensive research reveal the love that burned at the center of Margaret's life, adding a new dimension to the story of one of the fifteenth century's most powerful women.

Daughter of Zion. Bodie Thoene. Contrib. by Brock Thoene. Narrated by Suzanne Toren. 7 cass. (Running Time: 10 hrs. 15 mins.). (Zion Chronicles: Bk. 2). 2000. 62.00 (978-0-7887-4954-4(4), K0009E6) Recorded Bks.
Transports you to Jerusalem in 1948 as the Jews battle to establish a homeland. Rachel survived the Holocaust at great personal cost. Now she hopes to begin her life again in the besieged Jewish Quarter. But the secrets of the past alienate her from her own people & plunge her into a life & death struggle for survival.

Daughter of Zion. unabr. ed. Bodie Thoene & Brock Thoene. Read by Susan O'Malley. 7 cass. (Running Time: 10 hrs.). (Zion Chronicles: Bk. 2). 2001. 49.95 (978-0-7861-1962-2(4), 2733); audio compact disk 72.00 (978-0-7861-9761-3(7), 2733) Blckstn Audio.
Rachel Lebowitz has survived the Holocaust, but only at a great personal cost. Joining the thousands of Jewish people streaming into Israel after the Nazi desolation, she is smuggled into the besieged Jewish Quarter of Jerusalem, where she discovers members of her long-lost family. Rachel decides she cannot leave the Old City or the people who stand as one thin line holding onto its survival. When secrets of her past are uncovered, she is discredited before those she wants so desperately to help. Alienated from her own people & left in despair, she is not aware of the enemy forces that threaten her very life.

Daughters. unabr. ed. Joanna Philbin. Read by Michal Friedman. (Running Time: 8 hrs.). 2010. 19.98 (978-1-60788-300-5(7)); audio compact disk 22.98 (978-1-60788-299-2(X)) Pub: Hachet Audio. Dist(s): HachBkGrp

***Daughters Break the Rules.** unabr. ed. Joanna Philbin. Read by Michal Friedman. (Running Time: 7 hrs.). (ENG.). (J). 2010. 16.98 (978-1-60788-719-5(3)) Pub: Hachet Audio. Dist(s): HachBkGrp

Daughter's Inheritance. abr. ed. Tracie Peterson & Judith Miller. (Broadmoor Legacy Ser.: Bk. 1). 2008. 16.09 (978-1-60814-079-4(2)) Oasis Audio.

Daughter's Inheritance. abr. ed. Tracie Peterson & Judith Miller. Read by Aimee Lilly. (Running Time: 21600 sec.). (Broadmoor Legacy Ser.: Bk. 1). 2008. audio compact disk 22.99 (978-1-59859-317-4(X)) Oasis Audio.

Daughters of Cain. unabr. ed. Colin Dexter. Read by Frederick Davidson. 7 cass. (Running Time: 10 hrs.). 1995. 49.95 (978-0-7861-0714-8(6), 1591) Blckstn Audio.
Chief Inspector Morse & Detective Sergeant Lewis uncover startling new information about the life & death of Dr. Felix McClure, late of Wolsey College, Oxford. Soon another body is discovered & suddenly Morse finds himself with too many suspects.

Daughters of Cain. unabr. ed. Colin Dexter. Read by Terrence Hardiman. 8 cass. (Running Time: 12 hrs.). (Inspector Morse Mystery Ser.: Bk. 11). 1995. 59.95 (978-0-7451-6555-4(9), CAB 1171) Pub: Chivers Audio Bks GBR. Dist(s): AudioGO
So little progress had been made on the recent discovery of a corpse in North Oxford that Chief Inspector Morse was contemplating retirement. The victim, Dr. Felix McClure, had been killed by a single stab to the stomach. Yet the police had no weapon, no suspect & no motive. Then another body is soon uncovered, & suddenly suspects abound.

Daughters of Cain. unabr. ed. Colin Dexter. Narrated by Patrick Tull. 8 cass. (Running Time: 10 hrs. 45 mins.). (Inspector Morse Mystery Ser.: Vol. 11). 2000. 70.00 (978-0-7887-0297-6(1), 94490E7) Recorded Bks.

***Daughters of Darkness.** L. J. Smith. Contrib. by Emily Durante. (Night World Ser.: Vol. 2). (J). 2009. 44.99 (978-1-4418-2727-2(7)) Find a World.

Daughters of Darkness. unabr. ed. L. J. Smith. Read by Emily Durante. (Running Time: 6 hrs.). (Night World Ser.: Vol. 2). 2009. 19.99 (978-1-4418-0443-3(9), 9781441804433, Brilliance MP3); 39.97 (978-1-4418-0444-0(7), 9781441804440, Brinc Audio MP3 Lib); 19.99 (978-1-4418-0445-7(5), 9781441804457, BAD); 39.97 (978-1-4418-0446-4(3), 9781441804464, BADLE); audio compact disk 19.99 (978-1-4418-0441-9(2), 9781441804419, Bril Audio CD Unabri); audio compact disk 59.97 (978-1-4418-0442-6(0), 9781441804426, BriAudCD Unabrid) Brilliance Audio.

Daughters of England. unabr. ed. Philippa Carr. Read by Lindsay Sandison. 10 cass. (Running Time: 13 hrs.). 2001. 84.95 (960102) Pub: ISIS Audio GBR. Dist(s): Ulverscroft US
Sarah Standish has dreams of being a famous actress. Only fifteen, she runs away to London where she meets the charming Lord Rosslyn, who lures her away to love & marriage. But it is not long before Sarah learns that she has been cruelly deceived, & she is on the run again - until tragedy strikes & Lord Rosslyn comes to claim his young daughter, Kate. Then Charles II dies, & England is thrown into chaos. Kate discovers the sacrifice her father has made for her, giving her the chance to let go of the past & look towards the future.

Daughters of England. unabr. ed. Philippa Carr. 10 cass. (Isis Ser.). (J). 2004. 84.95 (978-1-85695-293-4(2)) Pub: ISIS Lrg Prnt GBR. Dist(s): Ulverscroft US

Daughters of Fire. unabr. ed. Barbara Erskine. Narrated by Judith Boyd. 20 cass. (Running Time: 26 hrs.). 2007. 113.75 (978-1-84632-626-4(5), Clipper Audio) Recorded Bks.

Daughters of Ishi-Shini: Ancient Tales of the Americas. Barb Stevens-Newcomb. Read by Barb Stevens-Newcomb. 1 cass. (Running Time: 63 min.). 10.00; audio compact disk 15.00 CD. Black Cricket.
Depicts collected stories from the native peoples of North & South America.

Daughters of Ishi-Shini: Ancient Tales of the Americas. Read by Barb Stevens-Newcomb. (Running Time: 63 min.). 1997. 10.00 CD. Black Cricket.
Collected stories of Native American people from both North & South America.

Daughters of Ishi-Shini: Ancient Tales of the Americas. Barb Stevens-Newcomb. Read by Barb Stevens-Newcomb. Music by Nina Spiro et al. 1 cass. (Running Time: 63 min.). 1996. pap. bk. 10.00 (978-0-9657667-4-6(8), 74334-4); audio compact disk 15.00 CD. (978-0-9657667-2-2(1)) Black Cricket.
Five ancient tales of transformation, adapted & performed by award-winning storyteller Barb Stevens-Newcomb. Includes flute, cello, guitar, drums.

Daughters of the Celtic Moon. Perf. by Lisa Lynne. 1 cass., 1 CD. 8.78 (WH 11293); audio compact disk 13.58 CD Jewel box. (WH 11293) NewSound.

Daughters of the Grail. Elizabeth Chadwick. 2008. 94.95 (978-1-84559-868-6(7)); audio compact disk 99.95 (978-1-84559-869-3(5)) Pub: Soundings Ltd GBR. Dist(s): Ulverscroft US

Daughters of the Late Colonel see Garden Party

Daughters of the Moon. Susan Sallis. Read by Carole Boyd. 12 cass. (Running Time: 18 hrs.). 2001. 94.95 (29625) Pub: Soundings Ltd GBR. Dist(s): Ulverscroft US

Daughter's Sacrifice, the Maiden's Transformation. Read by Rachel Hillel. 1 cass. (Running Time: 90 min.). 1991. 10.95 (978-0-7822-0091-1(5), 436) C G Jung IL.
In the biblical myth of Jephtha, as in the Greek myth of Iphigenia, the daughter is sacrificed by the father. Through an exploration of Jewish legend & the mythic drama of Euripedes, the symbolic meanings of this motif & of the maiden/priestess archetypes are uncovered, & are shown to give meaning to the autonomous future directedness of the feminine principle which is alive in women today. Hillel is a Jungian analyst in Amherst, MA & New York City.

D'Aulaires' Book of Greek Myths. unabr. ed. Ingri Parin D'Aulaire & Edgar Parin D'Aulaire. Read by Paul Newman et al. 4 cass. (Running Time: 4 hrs.). 1996. 18.95 (978-1-885608-14-7(4), 496010) Airplay.
An enchanting narration of the D'Aulaires' classic. Here are the gods, goddesses of Ancient Greece; mighty Zeus, vengeful Hera, wise Athena, powerful Hercules & many others brought to life in a wonderful reading by four outstanding artists. An audiobook for listeners of all ages.

D'Aulaires' Book of Greek Myths. unabr. ed. Ingri Parin D'Aulaires & Edgar Parin D'Aulaires. Read by Paul Newman et al. 4 CDs. (Running Time: 4 hrs.). 2001. audio compact disk 25.00 (978-1-885608-15-4(2)) Airplay.
An enchanting narration of the D'Aulaires' classic. Here are the gods & goddesses of Ancient Greece; mighty Zeus, vengeful Hera, wise Athena, powerful Hercules & many others brought to life in a wonderful reading by four outstanding artists. An audiobook for listeners of all ages.

Daumesdick. Jacob W. Grimm & Wilhelm K. Grimm. 1 cass. (Running Time: 60 min.). (Bruder Grimm Kinder & Hausmarchen Ser.). (GER.). pap. bk. 19.50 (978-1-58085-214-2(9), GR-09) Interlingua VA.
Includes German transcription. Includes title story, Die zertanzten Schuhe, Der Eisenhans, Lieb und Leid teilen. The combination of written text & clarity & pace of diction will open the door for intermediate & advanced students to genuine comprehension & the use of literary texts for advancement in rapid understanding of written & oral language materials. The audio text plus written text concept makes foreign languages accessible to a much wider range of students than books alone.

Dauphin County Arbitration Procedures. P. Daniel Altland. 1 cass. 1988. 20.00 PA Bar Inst.

Dauphin County Motion Practice. Read by Warren G. Morgan & J. Stephen Feinour. 1 cass. 20.00 (AL-59) PA Bar Inst.

Dauphin County Rules - The Role of the Court Administrator. Read by John E. Minnich & Carolyn C. Thompson. 1 cass. 1991. 20.00 (AL-109) PA Bar Inst.

Davalliaceae: A Family of Old World (Sub-)Tropical Ferns. H. P. Nooteboom. (World Biodiversity Database Ser.). 2000. audio compact disk 59.95 (978-3-540-14818-0(3)) Spri.

Dave Anderson's 15 Commandments for Peak Performance in Sales, Vol. 3, Set. Dave Anderson. Read by Dave Anderson. 2 cass. (Running Time: 2 hrs. 56 mins.). 1999. D Anderson Corp.

Dave at Night. Gail Levine. Narrated by Johnny Heller. 6 CDs. (Running Time: 6 hrs. 15 mins.). (gr. 4 up). audio compact disk 58.00 (978-0-7887-6161-4(7)) Recorded Bks.

Dave at Night. Gail Carson Levine. Read by Johnny Heller. 5 cass. (Running Time: 6 hrs. 15 mins.). (YA). 1999. pap. bk. & stu. ed. 69.95 (978-0-7887-3794-7(5), 41038); 214.80 (978-0-7887-3865-4(8), 47030) Recorded Bks.
No one wants an 11-year-old "rascal," so Dave is shuffled off to the Hebrew Home for Boys. When he sneaks out of the orphanage at night, he meets an old "gonif" who becomes his guide to the jazz-filled nightlife of the Harlem Renaissance.

Dave at Night. unabr. ed. Gail Carson Levine. Read by Jason Harris. 4 vols. (Running Time: 5 hrs. 31 mins.). (J). (gr. 4-7). 2004. pap. bk. 38.00 (978-0-8072-8379-0(7), YA174SP, Listening Lib); 32.00 (978-0-8072-8378-3(9), YA174CX, Listening Lib) Random Audio Pubg.
The year is 1926. Dave's beloved father is dead & his stepmother doesn't want him. Only the Hebrew Home for Boys will take him in. But Dave is tough & a troublemaker. He can take care of himself. If he doesn't like the Home, he'll run away & find a better place. Only it's not that simple.

***Dave at Night.** unabr. ed. Gail Carson Levine. Read by Joshua Harris. (Running Time: 5 hrs. 31 mins.). (ENG.). (J). 2011. audio compact disk 30.00 (978-0-307-91655-6(3), Listening Lib) Pub: Random Audio Pubg. Dist(s): Random

Dave at Night. unabr. ed. Gail Carson Levine. Narrated by Johnny Heller. 5 pieces. (Running Time: 6 hrs. 15 mins.). (gr. 4 up). 2000. 47.00 (978-0-7887-3824-1(0), 96046E7) Recorded Bks.

Dave at Night. unabr. ed. Gail Carson Levine. Narrated by Johnny Heller. 5 CDs. (Running Time: 6 hrs. 15 min.). (YA). (gr. 5-8). 2001. audio compact disk 58.00 (C1385) Recorded Bks.
No one wants an 11-year-old "rascal," so Dave is shuffled off to the Hebrew Home for Boys. When he sneaks out of the orphanage at night, he meets an old "gonif" who becomes his guide to the jazz-filled nightlife of the Harlem Renaissance.

Dave Barry: A Lighter Side to Journalism. Dave Barry. Read by Dave Barry. 1 cass. (Running Time: 1 hr.). 10.95 (NP-88-07-01, HarperThor) HarpC GBR.

Dave Barry: Dave Barry Is Not Taking This Sitting Down, Dave Barry Hits below the Beltway, Boogers Are My Beat. unabr. ed. Dave Barry. Read by Dick Hill. (Running Time: 18 hrs.). 2005. audio compact disk 34.95 (978-1-59737-707-2(4), 9781597377072, Bril Audio CD Unabri) Brilliance Audio.
Dave Barry Is Not Taking This Sitting Down: What's been getting Dave Barry all worked up lately? What can possibly induce him to rise up - yes, actually out of his chair - in indignation? Well, lots of things, including the real skinny on the IRS, Donald Trump, the airlines, and so much more... Dave Barry Hits Below the Beltway: Below the Beltway includes Barry's stirring account of how the United States was born, including his version of a properly written Declaration (When in the course of human events it behooves us, the people, not to ask "What can our country do for us, anyway?" but rather whether we have anything to fear except fear itself) and a revised Constitution (Section II: The House of Representatives shall be composed of people who own at least two dark suits and have not been indicted recently). Boogers Are My Beat: Dave Barry gives us the real scoop on: • The scientific search for the world's funniest joke • RV camping in the Wal-Mart parking lot • Outwitting "smart" kitchen appliances and service contracts • Elections in Florida • The Olympics, where people from all over the world come together to accuse each other of cheating • The truth about the Dakotas, the Lone Ranger, and feng shui • The choice between death and taxes And much, much more - including some truths about journalism and serious thoughts about 9/11.

Dave Barry Collection: Dave Barry Is Not Taking This Sitting Down;Dave Barry Hits below the Beltway; Tricky Business. abr. ed. Dave Barry. Read by Dick Hill. (Running Time: 16 hrs.). 2004. 29.95 (978-1-59355-639-6(X), 159355639X) Brilliance Audio.
Dave Barry Is Not Taking This Sitting Down (Susie Breck, Melissa Coates): What's been getting Dave Barry all worked up lately? What can possibly induce him to rise up - yes, actually out of his chair - in indignation? Well, lots of things, including the real skinny on the IRS, Donald Trump, the airlines, and so much more... Dave Barry Hits Below the Beltway (Laura

Grafton, Melissa Coates): Below the Beltway includes Barry's stirring account of how the United States was born, including his version of a properly written Declaration (When in the course of human events it behooves us, the people, not to ask "What can our country do for us, anyway?" but rather whether we have anything to fear except fear itself) and a revised Constitution (Section II: The House of Representatives shall be composed of people who own at least two dark suits and have not been indicted recently). Tricky Business (Susie Breck, Mike Council): The Extravaganza of the Seas is a five-thousand-ton cash cow, a top-heavy tub whose sole function is to carry gamblers three miles from the Florida coast, take their money, then bring them back so they can find more money. What happens to its passengers and crew in the midst of the fiercest storm in years will change their lives and send them ricocheting off each other like a giant game of pinball.

Dave Barry Does Japan. unabr. ed. Dave Barry. Read by Arte Johnson. 4 cass. (Running Time: 6 hrs.). 2001. 25.00 (978-1-59040-154-5(9), Phoenix Audio) Pub: Amer Intl Pub. Dist(s): PerseuPGW

Dave Barry Hits below the Beltway. unabr. ed. Dave Barry. Read by Dick Hill. (Running Time: 6 hrs.). 2004. 39.25 (978-1-59335-552-4(1), 1593355521, Brlnc Audio MP3 Lib) Brilliance Audio.
Understanding the urgent need for a deeply thoughtful, balanced book to explain our national political process, Dave Barry has not even come close. Though he himself has covered many campaigns, run for president several times, and run for cover at the rainy inauguration of George W. Bush (the man will spare nothing for his art), Barry has instead outdone himself. Below the Beltway includes Barry's stirring account of how the United States was born, including his version of a properly written Declaration (When in the course of human events it behooves us, the people, not to ask "What can our country do for us, anyway?" but rather whether we have anything to fear except fear itself) and a revised Constitution (Section II: The House of Representatives shall be composed of people who own at least two dark suits and have not been indicted recently). Dave also cracks the income-tax code and explains the growth(s) of government, congressional hearing difficulties, and the persistent rumors of the influence of capital in the Capitol. Among other civic contributions, his tour of Washington D.C. should end school class trips forever.

Dave Barry Hits below the Beltway. unabr. ed. Dave Barry. Read by Dick Hill. (Running Time: 6 hrs.). 2004. 39.25 (978-1-59710-183-7(4), 1597101834, BADLE); 24.95 (978-1-59710-182-0(6), 1597101826, BAD) Brilliance Audio.

***Dave Barry Hits below the Beltway.** unabr. ed. Dave Barry. 2010. audio compact disk 9.99 (978-1-4418-5659-3(5)) Brilliance Audio.

Dave Barry Hits below the Beltway: A Vicious & Unprovoked Attack on Our Most Cherished Political Institutions. unabr. ed. Dave Barry. Read by Dick Hill. 4 cass. (Running Time: 6 hrs.). 2001. 53.25 (978-1-58788-847-2(5), 1587888475, Unabridge Lib Edns); audio compact disk 69.25 (978-1-58788-849-6(1), 1587888491, CD Unabrid Lib Ed) Brilliance Audio.

Dave Barry Hits Below the Beltway: A Vicious & Unprovoked Attack on Our Most Cherished Political Institutions. unabr. ed. Dave Barry. Read by Dick Hill. (Running Time: 6 hrs.). 2004. audio compact disk 16.99 (978-1-59355-684-6(5), 1593556845, BCD Value Price) Brilliance Audio.

Dave Barry Hits Below the Beltway: A Vicious & Unprovoked Attack on Our Most Cherished Political Institutions. unabr. ed. Dave Barry. Read by Dick Hill. (Running Time: 6 hrs.). 2004. 24.95 (978-1-59335-048-2(1), 1593350481) Soulmate Audio Bks.

Dave Barry in Cyberspace. abr. ed. Perf. by Shadoe Stevens. 4 cass. (Running Time: 3 hrs.). 2001. 25.00 (978-1-59040-031-9(3), Phoenix Audio) Pub: Amer Intl Pub. Dist(s): PerseuPGW
Now here's a matchup, sports fans: Dave Barry vs. the information superhighway, "mano a mano." Hang onto your hats and head for the last frontier.

Dave Barry Is from Mars & Venus. abr. ed. Read by Shadoe Stevens. 4 cass. (Running Time: 6 hrs.). 2001. 25.00 (978-1-59040-029-6(1), Phoenix Audio) Pub: Amer Intl Pub. Dist(s): PerseuPGW
Dave Barry reveals the shocking secret of his biplanetary androgyny in a transparent attempt to get on some afternoon talk shows and sell this collection of his syndicated columns.

Dave Barry Is Not Making This Up. Dave Barry. Narrated by Johnny Heller. 4 cass. (Running Time: 5 hrs. 45 mins.). 43.00 (978-1-4025-2565-0(6)) Recorded Bks.

Dave Barry Is Not Making This Up, Vol. 2. unabr. ed. Dave Barry. Read by Arte Johnson. 2 cass. (Running Time: 3 hrs.). 2004. 18.00 (978-1-59007-162-5(X)) Pub: New Millenn Enter. Dist(s): PerseuPGW
Dave Barry wouldn't lie - and here are the real life, laughout-loud stories from across America to prove it: a U.S. Supreme Court justice shares his remedy for preventing gas ("I had not realized that this was a matter of concern in the highest levels of government"); a newspaper headline in Ohio announces the combustibility of strawberry Pop-Tarts ("A story that can really help you gain a better understanding of how you can be killed by breakfast snack food"); the frightening fact that snakes have mastered the pipelines leading directly to your toilet - and they're not shy ("Many women might view this as a fair punishment for all the billions of times that guys have left the seat up".

Dave Barry Is Not Taking This Sitting Down! unabr. ed. Dave Barry. Read by Dick Hill. 4 cass. (Running Time: 6 hrs.). 2000. 44.25 (978-1-58788-270-8(1), 1587882701, Unabridge Lib Edns); audio compact disk 57.25 (978-1-58788-268-5(X), 158788268X, Unabridge Lib Edns) Brilliance Audio.
Following the bestselling success of Dave's novel, Big Trouble, here is a hilarious new collection of columns from the writer critics have called "the funniest man in America." What's been getting Dave Barry all worked up lately? What can possibly induce him to rise up - yes, actually out of his chair - in indignation? Well, lots of things. For instance . . . The plague of low-flow toilets Day trading and other careers that never require you to take off your bathrobe The parent-misery quotient of school science fairs Pine-sap transfusions for tired Christmas trees The real skinny on the IRS, Donald Trump, the airlines, and so much more.

Dave Barry Is Not Taking This Sitting Down! unabr. ed. Dave Barry. Read by Dick Hill. (Running Time: 6 hrs.). 2005. audio compact disk 16.99 (978-1-59355-701-0(9), 9781593557010, BCD Value Price) Brilliance Audio.

Dave Barry Is Not Taking This Sitting Down. unabr. ed. Dave Barry. Read by Dick Hill. (Running Time: 6 hrs.). 2004. 39.25 (978-1-59600-488-7(6), 1596004886, Brlnc Audio MP3 Lib); 39.25 (978-1-59600-490-0(8), 1596004908, BADLE); 24.95 (978-1-59600-489-4(4), 1596004894, BAD); 24.95 (978-1-59600-487-0(8), 1596004878, Brilliance MP3) Brilliance Audio.

Dave Barry Talks Back. Dave Barry. Narrated by Johnny Heller. 4 cass. (Running Time: 5 hrs. 30 mins.). 1991. 44.00 (978-1-4025-3854-4(5)) Recorded Bks.

Dave Barry Talks Back. abr. ed. Dave Barry. Read by Arte Johnson. 2 cass. (Running Time: 3 hrs.). 2004. 18.00 (978-1-59007-163-2(8)) Pub: New Millenn Enter. Dist(s): PerseuPGW
This is a tough one, because caring about sports is, let's face it, silly. I mean, suppose you have a friend who, for no apparent reason, suddenly becomes obsessed with the Amtrak Corporation. He babbles about Amtrak constantly, citing obscure railroad statistics from 1978; he puts Amtrak bumper stickers on his car; and when something bad happens to Amtrak, such as a train crashes and investigators find that the engineer was drinking and wearing a bunny suit, your friend becomes depressed for weeks. You'd think he was crazy, right? "Bob," you'd say to him, as a loving and caring friend, "you're a moron. The Amtrak Corporation has nothing to do with you.

Dave Barry's Complete Guide to Guys. abr. ed. Dave Barry. Read by John Ritter. 2 cass. (Running Time: 3 hrs.). 2004. 18.00 (978-1-59007-164-9(6)) Pub: New Millenn Enter. Dist(s): PerseuPGW
In this wholly original book - except for one classic column on testosterone - Pulitzer Prize-winning journalist Dave Barry explains why the American guy is not to be confused with a husband, father, hunk, or intellectual, and provides tips for women who want to better understand the species.

Dave Barry's Funniest Stuff. abr. ed. Dave Barry. Read by Arte Johnson. 4 cass. (Running Time: 6 hrs.). 2001. 25.00 (978-1-59040-030-2(5), Phoenix Audio) Pub: Amer Intl Pub. Dist(s): PerseuPGW
Here is the absolute best of Dave Barry; selections from four of his most popular books, including the hilarious Guide to Guys. There's no such thing as too many laughs! Dave Barry is on the loose and no one is safe!.

Dave Barry's Greatest Hits & Dave Barry's Complete Guide to Guys. unabr. ed. Dave Barry. Read by Dave Barry. Read by John Ritter. (YA). 2008. 54.99 (978-1-60514-766-6(4)) Find a World.

Dave Barry's History of the Millennium (So Far) unabr. ed. Dave Barry. Read by Patrick Frederic. (Running Time: 16200 sec.). (ENG.). (gr. 8). 2007. audio compact disk 25.95 (978-0-14-314242-3(9), PengAudBks) Penguin Grp USA.

Dave Barry's Money Secrets: Like: Why Is There a Giant Eyeball on the Dollar? unabr. ed. Dave Barry. Read by Dick Hill. (Running Time: 5 hrs.). 2006. 39.25 (978-1-59737-170-4(X), 9781597371704, BADLE); 24.95 (978-1-59737-169-8(6), 9781597371698, BAD); 62.25 (978-1-59737-164-3(5), 9781597371643, BrilAudUnabridg); 24.95 (978-1-59737-163-6(7), 9781597371636, BAU); audio compact disk 39.25 (978-1-59737-168-1(8), 9781597371681, Brlnc Audio MP3 Lib); audio compact disk 24.95 (978-1-59737-167-4(X), 9781597371674, Brilliance MP3); audio compact disk 74.25 (978-1-59737-166-7(1), 9781597371667, BriAudCD Unabrid); audio compact disk 26.95 (978-1-59737-165-0(3), 9781597371650, Bril Audio CD Unabri) Brilliance Audio.
Did you ever wish that you really understood money? Well, Dave Barry wishes that he did, too. But that hasn't stopped him from writing a book about how to understand money. In it, Dave explores (as only he can) such topics as: · How the U.S. economy works, including the often-overlooked role of Adam Sandler. · Why it is not a good idea to use squirrels for money. · Strategies that will give you the confidence you need to try for a good job, even though you are, let's be honest, a no-talent loser. · Why corporate executives, simply by walking into their offices, immediately become much stupider. · An absolutely foolproof system for making money in the stock market, requiring only a little effort (and access to time travel). · Surefire tips for buying and selling real estate, the key one being: Never buy, or for that matter sell, real estate. · How to minimize your federal taxes, safely and legally, by cheating. · Why good colleges cost so much, and how to make sure your child does not get into one. · How to reduce the cost of your medical care by basically not getting any. · Estate planning, especially the often-overlooked financial benefits of early death. But that's only the beginning! Dave has also included in this book all of the important points in a book written by Donald Trump, so you don't have to read it yourself. Plus he explains how to tip; how to negotiate for everything, including bridge tolls; how to argue with your spouse about money; and how much allowance to give your children (three dollars is plenty). He also presents, for the first time in print anywhere, the Car Dealership Code of Ethics ("Ethic Seven: The customer is an idiot"). Also there are many gratuitous references to Angelina Jolie naked. You can't afford NOT to buy this book! Probably you need several.

Dave Barry's Worst Songs & Other Hits. abr. ed. Dave Barry. Perf. by Arte Johnson & John Ritter. 2 cass. (Running Time: 3 hrs.). 2004. 18.00 (978-1-59007-165-6(4)) Pub: New Millenn Enter. Dist(s): PerseuPGW
Did you know Dave can sing? Well, he can't. But, the words to these songs will make you smile, and even laugh. His humor, sense of irony, and poignant touches will keep you thinking and humming? A long time.

Dave Benoit Answers Your Most Often Asked Questions. David Benoit. Read by David Benoit. 1 cass. (Running Time: 1 hr. 30 min.). 1987. 6.00 (978-0-923105-04-4(2)) Glory Ministries.
Answers questions such as "Is contemporary Christian music an alternative to rock?" "What about country music?" "What's wrong with those fantasy cartoons?" "What about the 'We Are The World" and Aid to Africa Programs?" and more.

Dave Brubeck - Improvisationen und Kompositionen: Die Idee der Kulturellen Wechselbeziehungen. Ilse Storb & Klaus-Gotthard Fischer. (Europaische Hochschulschriften: Bd. 57). (GER., 1990. pap. bk. 48.80 (978-3-631-43114-6(7)) P Lang Pubng.

Dave Etter. unabr. ed. Read by Dave Etter. 1 cass. (Running Time: 29 min.). 1985. 10.00 New Letters.
Dave Etter's poems depict, with wit & humor, characters from Midwestern small towns.

Dave Grusin. Read by Dave Grusin. 1 cass. (Running Time: 60 min.). (Marian McPartland's Piano Jazz Ser.). 13.95 (MM-87-05-14, HarperThor) HarpC GBR.

Dave Harris Anthology. Perf. by Dave Harris. cass. & video 69.95 Hiline Videoworks CAN.

Dave Henderson's Dog Stories: A Collection. 2006. 24.95 (978-0-7861-4431-0(9)); audio compact disk 36.00 (978-0-7861-7379-2(3)) Blckstn Audio.

Dave Henderson's Dog Stories: A Collection. unabr. ed. Dave Henderson. Read by Alan Sklar. 2006. 19.95 (978-0-7861-7754-7(3)) Blckstn Audio.

***Dave Lieber's Watchdog Nation: Bite Back When Businesses & Scammers Do You Wrong.** Read by Dave Lieber. (ENG.). 2010. audio compact disk 20.00 (978-0-9708530-7-3(6)) Yankee Cowboy.

Dave Marash: No Free Speech Equals Bad Press. Dave Marash. Read by Dave Marash. 1 cass. (Running Time: 1 hr.). 10.95 (NP-88-09-14, HarperThor) HarpC GBR.

Dave Marr: His Game is Golf. Read by Dave Marr. 1 cass. 9.95 (978-0-89811-104-0(8), 7155) Lets Talk Assocs.
Dave Marr talks about the people & events which influenced his career, & his own approach to his speciality.

***Dave Niehaus, Voice of the Mariners: Baseball Voices, the Hall of Fame Series.** 2009. audio compact disk 16.00 (978-0-9818365-7-7(7)) Baseball Voice.

Dave of True Hallucinations. Miguelito Lasky. 1 cass. 7.00 (A0060-77) Sound Photosyn.
Recorded casually by Faustin & Brian in South America in 1977 hear of the Experiment at La Chorera as told by Miguelito, portrayed by Terence as "Dave".

Dave Oliphant. unabr. ed. Read by Dave Oliphant. 1 cass. (Running Time: 29 min.). 1985. 10.00 New Letters.
Texas poet Dave Oliphant reads from "Lines & Mounds," & "Footprints".

Dave Robicheaux Audio Collection. abr. gif. ed. James Lee Burke. Read by Will Patton. 15 CDs. (Running Time: 15 hrs. 30 mins. 0 sec.). (Dave Robicheaux Ser.). 2006. audio compact disk 39.95 (978-0-7435-5524-1(4), Audioworks) Pub: S&S Audio. Dist(s): S and S Inc

Dave Smith. unabr. ed. Read by Dave Smith. 1 cass. (Running Time: 29 min.). 1985. 10.00 New Letters.
Widely published poet Dave Smith includes work from "Goshawk Antelope".

Dave Smith Two: The Roundhouse Voices. unabr. ed. Dave Smith. Read by Dave Smith. 1 cass. (Running Time: 29 min.). 1988. 10.00 (090988) New Letters.
Smith, a Virginian reads from his ninth book of verse, "The Roundhouse Voices".

Dave Weckl: Contemporary Drummer Plus One. Dave Weckl. Ed. by Emily A. Frankewicz. 1 cass. (Running Time: 78 min.). pap. bk. 32.95 incl. 9 studio charts. DCI Music Video.
Contemporary Drummer Plus One is an innovative teaching system for the intermediate to advanced player which combines three elements: 78 minute listening/play along audio cassette, nine separate studio charts & a comprehensive book.

Davening with the Rebbe. Jewish Educational Media. 1 CD. (Running Time: 50 mins.). 2004. audio compact disk 15.00 (978-0-8266-9981-7(2)) Kehot Pubn Soc.

Davening with the Rebbe. unabr. ed. Jewish Educational Media. 1 cass. (Running Time: 50 mins.). 2004. 9.00 (978-0-8266-9982-4(0)) Kehot Pubn Soc.
"This close-up view is a rare opportunity to see and hear the Lubavitcher Rebbe pray. Excerpted from various films and videotapes, the program includes Shacharit, aliyot, Sukkot prayers with lulav and etrog and visits to the Ohel. We see and hear the Rebbe leading the morning prayers on the yahrzeit of his mother. Original music by Yitzchak Perlman, Yaron Gershovsky, Andy Statman and Susan Stolovy complement the presentation.".

David. 2003. 79.00 (978-1-57972-547-1(3)); audio compact disk 79.00 (978-1-57972-563-1(5)) Insight Living.

David: A Man of Passion & Destiny Part 1. Charles R. Swindoll. 2009. audio compact disk 12.99 (978-1-57972-843-4(X)) Insight Living.

***David: A Man of Passion & Destiny Radio Theater, Part 2.** Charles R. Swindoll. 2009. audio compact disk 12.99 (978-1-57972-864-9(2)) Insight Living.

David & Dog. 2004. 8.95 (978-0-89719-900-1(6)); 8.95 (978-1-56008-129-6(5)); cass. & flmstrp 30.00 (978-0-89719-500-3(0)) Weston Woods.

David & Dog. (J). 2004. bk. 24.95 (978-0-89719-871-4(9)); pap. bk. 14.95 (978-0-7882-0657-3(5)) Weston Woods.

David & Goliath. 1 cass. (J). (978-0-944391-72-3(9)) DonWise Prodns.
Narrates biblical story designed especially for children.

David & Goliath. Dalmatian Press Staff. (J). (ps-3). 2000. pap. bk. 4.97 (978-1-888567-35-9(X)) Dalmatian Pr.

David & Goliath - Saul Chases David. abr. ed. Laura Williams. 1 cass. (Running Time: 1 hr.). Dramatization. (Best Loved Bible Stories Ser.). (J). (ps-3). 1995. 9.99 (978-0-8423-6076-0(X)) Tyndale Hse.
Fully dramatized Bible stories for kids with original music & songs. Two stories & a 48-page activity booklet.

David & Goliath Read Along. 1 cass. (Running Time: 60 mins.). (Sunday Morning Ser.). (J). (ps-3). 1999. pap. bk. 6.98 (978-0-7634-0577-9(9)) W Disney Records.

David & the Phoenix. unabr. ed. Edward Ormondroyd. Read by Full Cast Production Staff. (J). 2007. 34.99 (978-1-60252-525-2(0)) Find a World.

***David Attenborough Life Stories.** Fabrice Moireau. Read by David Attenborough. (Running Time: 4 hrs. 0 mins. 0 sec.). (ENG.). 2010. audio compact disk 29.95 (978-1-4084-2744-6(3)) Pub: AudioGO. Dist(s): Perseus Dist

***David Attenborough: the Early Years.** Read by David Attenborough. (Running Time: 9 hrs. 0 mins. 0 sec.). (ENG.). 2011. audio compact disk 79.95 (978-1-4084-6850-0(6)) Pub: AudioGO. Dist(s): Perseus Dist

David Baker. unabr. ed. Poems. David Baker. Ed. by James McKinley. Prod. by Rebeah Presson. 1 cass. (Running Time: 29 min.). (On the Air Ser.). 1992. 10.00 New Letters.
Baker reads from his poetry collection Sweet Home Saturday Night & interview.

David Balfour see Catriona

David Benoit, 'Live on KGO Radio' & Dave Benoit on 'Open Line' on the Moody Broadcasting Network. David Benoit. Read by David Benoit. 1 cass. (Running Time: 2 hrs.). 1987. 6.00 (978-0-923105-05-1(0)) Glory Ministries.
Discusses rock music, satanism, and contemporary Christian music.

David Bergland: The Future of Non-Interventionism. (Running Time: 60 min.). (Cypress College). 1980. 9.00 (F112) Freeland Pr.
Covers such topics as international free trade vs. protectionism, self-determination, defense, & the relationship between domestic & foreign policies.

David Bradley. unabr. ed. Read by David Bradley. 1 cass. (Running Time: 29 min.). Incl. Chaneysville Incident; 1987. 10.00 New Letters.
Author reads excerpts from his novel about a black historian's search for truth among slave legends.

David Brower - Pioneer Environmentalist. Hosted by Nancy Pearlman. 1 cass. (Running Time: 29 min.). 10.00 (514) Educ Comm CA.

David Coppefield. Charles Dickens. Gary Cady et al. 2009. audio compact disk 29.95 (978-1-60283-632-7(9)) Pub: AudioGO. Dist(s): Perseus Dist

David Copperfield. Charles Dickens. Read by Anton Lesser. (Running Time: 5 hrs. 15 mins.). 2002. 28.95 (978-1-60083-718-0(2)) Iofy Corp.

David Copperfield. Charles Dickens. Read by Guillermo Piedrahita. (Running Time: 3 hrs.). 2002. 16.95 (978-1-60083-196-6(6), Audiofy Corp) Iofy Corp.

David Copperfield. Charles Dickens. Read by Anton Lesser. 4 cass. (Running Time: 5 hr. 15 mins.). (Works of Charles Dickens). 1998. 22.98 (978-962-634-651-8(5), NA415114, Naxos AudioBooks) Naxos.
The story of a young man and his misadventures that scales the heights and plumbs the troughs of the emotions and captures the evil of Uriah Heep

as convincingly as it does Agnes' tender, patient love and Uncle Dick's harmless ravings.

David Copperfield. Charles Dickens. 1 cass. (Running Time: 1 hr.). (Radiobook Ser.). 1987. 4.98 (978-0-929541-43-3(X)) Radiola Co.

David Copperfield. Charles Dickens & Martin Jarvis. (Running Time: 124200 sec.). (Cover to Cover Classics Ser.). (ENG.). 2006. audio compact disk 39.95 (978-1-57270-719-1(4)) Pub: AudioGO. Dist(s): Perseus Dist

David Copperfield. abr. ed. Charles Dickens. Read by Roger Rees. 1 cass. (Running Time: 90 min.). (J). 1984. 9.95 (978-1-55994-082-5(4), CDL5 1706) HarperCollins Pubs.

David Copperfield. abr. ed. Charles Dickens. Read by Ben Kingsley. 2 cass. (Running Time: 3 hrs.). 2000. 7.95 (978-1-57815-114-1(7), 1076, Media Bks Audio) Media Bks NJ.
Copperfield runs away from home, is adopted by his aunt & discovers himself at Canturbury School.

David Copperfield. abr. ed. Charles Dickens. Read by Anton Lesser. 4 CDs. (Running Time: 5 hrs. 15 mins.). (Works of Charles Dickens). 1998. audio compact disk 28.98 (978-962-634-151-3(3), NA415112, Naxos AudioBooks) Naxos.
The story of a young man and his misadventures that scales the heights and plumbs the troughs of the emotions and captures the evil of Uriah Heep as convincingly as it does Agnes' tender, patient love and Uncle Dick's harmless ravings.

David Copperfield. abr. ed. Charles Dickens. Read by Paul Scofield. 3 CDs. (Running Time: 3 hrs.). 2004. audio compact disk 24.95 (978-1-59007-571-5(4)); 18.00 (978-1-931056-57-1(9), N Millennium Audio) New Millenn Enter.
"I am born". However, this is a birth which is blighted by its timing: 12 o'clock on a Friday night at precisely the time the clock began to strike. Such untimeliness meant that David was destined to be unlucky in life and would be privileged to see ghosts and spirits. A dubious privilege.

David Copperfield. abr. ed. Charles Dickens. Read by Guillermo Piedrahita. 3 CDs. (SPA.). 2002. audio compact disk 17.00 (978-958-9494-71-4(4)) YoYoMusic.

David Copperfield. adpt. ed. Charles Dickens. (Bring the Classics to Life: Level 4 Ser.). (ENG.). 2008. audio compact disk 12.95 (978-1-55576-576-7(9)) EDCON Pubng.

David Copperfield. unabr. ed. Charles Dickens. Read by Martin Jarvis. 26 cass. (Running Time: 34 hrs.). 2002. 99.95 (978-1-57270-253-0(2), F91253) Pub: Audio Partners. Dist(s): PerseuPGW
The fatherless David is continually beset by personal difficulties. He rises from a poverty-stricken, abusive childhood to a world of fame and fortune. David is no simple innocent like Oliver Twist; David is more like Pip in Great Expectations, who struggles through initial difficulties to cherish and covet the world of prosperity and success, giving depth and a darker cast to his character.

David Copperfield. unabr. ed. Charles Dickens. Read by Frederick Davidson. (Running Time: 129600 sec.). 2007. audio compact disk 54.95 (978-0-7861-8962-5(2)) Blckstn Audio.

David Copperfield. unabr. ed. Charles Dickens. Read by Frederick Davidson. (YA). 2008. 164.99 (978-1-60514-717-8(6)) Find a World.

David Copperfield. unabr. ed. Charles Dickens. Read by Nathaniel Parker. (Running Time: 5 hrs. 45 mins. 0 sec.). (ENG., (gr. 12 up). 2004. 23.00 (978-0-14-180525-2(0), PenGlobal) Penguin Grp USA.

David Copperfield. unabr. ed. Charles Dickens. Narrated by Patrick Tull. 27 cass. (Running Time: 38 hrs. 30 mins.). 2001. 186.00 (978-0-7887-2173-1(9), 95469E7) Recorded Bks.
Follows the experiences of David Copperfield as he becomes a successful novelist & endeavors to become the hero of his own life.

David Copperfield. unabr. ed. Charles Dickens. Narrated by Simon Vance. 3 MP3-CDs. (Running Time: 34 hrs. 0 mins. 0 sec.). (Tantor Unabridged Classics Ser.). (ENG.). 2009. audio compact disk 44.99 (978-1-4001-6174-4(6)); audio compact disk 64.99 (978-1-4001-1174-9(9)); audio compact disk 129.99 (978-1-4001-4174-6(5)) Pub: Tantor Media. Dist(s): IngramPubServ

David Copperfield, Pt. 1. unabr. ed. Charles Dickens. Read by Frederick Davidson. 13 cass. (Running Time: 38 hrs.). 2003. 85.95 (978-0-7861-0381-2(7), 1335A,B) Blckstn Audio.
Of all Charles Dickens' novels, this is perhaps the most revealing, both of Dickens himself & of the society of his time. "David Copperfield" firmly embraces the eternal freshness, the comic delights, the tender warmth, & the ghastly horrors of childhood. It is a timeless tale of growing up, an enchanting story of a thoughtful orphan discovering how to live & love in a cutthroat adult world.

David Copperfield, Pt. 1, set. unabr. ed. Charles Dickens. Read by Frederick Davidson. 13 cass. 1999. 85.95 (FS9-51110) Highsmith.

David Copperfield, Pt. 2. unabr. ed. Charles Dickens. Read by Frederick Davidson. 13 cass. (Running Time: 38 hrs.). 2003. 85.95 (978-0-7861-0382-9(5), 1335A,B) Blckstn Audio.

David Copperfield, Pt. 2, set. Charles Dickens. 10 cass. (Running Time: 12 hrs.). 2000. 65.95 Audio Bk Con.
Through young David's trials with the Murdstones & Uriah Heep, his experiences with the Peggoty family & the Micawbers & his love for emily, dora & agnes, we watch him grow to maturity. A heartwarming story told with humor & great compassion.

David Copperfield, Pt. 2, Set. unabr. ed. Charles Dickens. Read by Flo Gibson. 10 cass. (Running Time: 13 hrs. 8 min.). 1999. bk. 65.95 Audio Bk Con.

David Copperfield, Pt. 2, set. unabr. ed. Charles Dickens. Read by Frederick Davidson. 13 cass. 1999. 85.95 (FS9-51136) Highsmith.

David Copperfield, Pt. A. unabr. collector's ed. Charles Dickens. Read by Angela Cheyne. 10 cass. (Running Time: 15 hrs.). (J). 1977. 80.00 (978-0-7366-0064-4(7), 1076-A) Books on Tape.
His exploits from youth to manhood; surrounded by a parade of famous & unforgettable fictional characters.

David Copperfield, Pt. B. collector's unabr. ed. Charles Dickens. Read by Angela Cheyne. 12 cass. (Running Time: 18 hrs.). (J). 1977. 96.00 (978-0-7366-0065-1(5), 1076-B) Books on Tape.

David Copperfield, Set. Charles Dickens. Read by Marianne Epin. 4 cass. (FRE.). 1995. 39.95 (1778-TH) Olivia & Hill.

David Copperfield, Set. unabr. ed. Charles Dickens. Narrated by Patrick Tull. 27 cass. (Running Time: 38 hrs. 30 min.). 1999. 186.00 (95469) Recorded Bks.
Listen as David recounts the experiences of his rise to successful novelist & endeavors to become the hero of his own life.

David Copperfield, Vol. 2. unabr. ed. Charles Dickens. Narrated by Flo Gibson. (Running Time: 13 hrs. 46 mins.). 44.95 (978-1-55685-804-8(3)) Audio Bk Con.

***David Copperfield: Bring the Classics to Life.** adpt. ed. Charles Dickens. (Bring the Classics to Life Ser.). 2008. pap. bk. 21.95 (978-1-55576-617-7(X)) EDCON Pubng.

David Copperfield: Radio Dramatization. Charles Dickens. 2 cass. (Running Time: 2 hrs.). 2003. 79.95 (978-0-563-52415-1(4)) AudioGO.

David Copperfield - Part 1. Charles Dickens. Narrated by Flo Gibson. 2008. audio compact disk 44.95 (978-1-55685-993-9(7)) Audio Bk Con.

***David Copperfield & Oliver Twist.** abr. ed. Charles Dickens. Compiled by James Baldwin. Narrated by James Adams. (ENG.). 2010. 9.98 (978-1-59644-961-9(6), MissionAud); audio compact disk 15.98 (978-1-59644-960-2(8), MissionAud) christianaud.

David Copperfield, Part 1. unabr. ed. Charles Dickens. Read by Frederick Davidson. (Running Time: 64800 sec.). 2007. audio compact disk 120.00 (978-0-7861-6052-5(7)) Blckstn Audio.

David Copperfield (Part 1), Vol. 11. unabr. ed. Charles Dickens. Read by Flo Gibson. 12 cass. (Running Time: 17 hrs. 55 min.). 1999. 39.95 (978-1-55685-565-8(6)) Audio Bk Con.
Through young David's trials with the Murdstones & Uriah Heep, his experiences with the Peggoty family & the Micawbers & his love for Emily, Dora & Agnes, we watch him grow to maturity. A heartwarming story told with humor & great compassion.

David Copperfield (Part 2) Charles Dickens. Narrated by Flo Gibson. (ENG.). 2008. audio compact disk 39.95 (978-1-55685-994-6(5)) Audio Bk Con.

David Copperfield Part 2. unabr. ed. Charles Dickens. Read by Frederick Davidson. (Running Time: 64800 sec.). 2007. audio compact disk 120.00 (978-0-7861-6053-2(5)) Blckstn Audio.

David Copperfield (Parts 1 And 2) unabr. ed. Charles Dickens. Narrated by Flo Gibson. (Running Time: 31 hrs. 19 mins.). 1999. 61.95 (978-1-55685-805-5(1)) Audio Bk Con.

David Crockett Frontiersman, Soldier & Man for the Ages. abr. ed. 3 cass. (Running Time: 4 hrs. 18 min.). (History As It Happens Ser.: Vol. 1). 2000. 19.95 (978-1-889252-06-3(9)) Photosensitive.

David Faces Goliath: Showdown in the Desert. unabr. ed. 1 cass. (Bible Stories for Kids Ser.). (J). (gr. k-6). 1999. 6.98 (978-1-887729-32-1(1)) Toy Box Prods.
The Babbling Bullfrogs from Bethlehem give a dramatic blow-by-blow account of how David defeats Goliath.

David Faces Goliath: Showdown in the Desert. unabr. ed. Joe Loesch. Ed. by Cheryl J. Hutchinson. Illus. by Brian T. Cox. 1 CD. (Bible Stories for Kids Ser.). (J). (ps-3). 1999. pap. bk. 16.95 (978-1-887729-22-2(4)) Toy Box Prods.

David Faces Goliath: Showdown in the Desert. unabr. ed. Joe Loesch. Ed. by Cheryl J. Hutchinson. Illus. by Brian T. Cox. 1 cass. (Bible Stories for Kids Ser.). (J). (ps-3). 1999. pap. bk. 14.95 (978-1-887729-21-5(6)) Toy Box Prods.

David Grier-Freewheeling. David Grier. 1999. pap. bk. 29.95 (978-0-7866-4108-6(8), 97751CDP) Mel Bay.

David Halberstam. Interview with David Halberstam. 1 cass. (Running Time: 30 min.). 13.95 (L030) TFR.
Halberstam talks about "The Best & The Brightest," his book on how the U. S. became involved in Vietman & his responses to criticism that he failed to interview many of the most important people in the book. In a separate interview he discusses his book, "Ho," the story of the North Vietnamese leader, Ho Chi Min.

David Halberstam: Journalist, Author. Interview. Interview with David Halberstam. 1 cass. (Running Time: 30 min.). 9.95 (A0360B090, HarperThor) HarpC GBR.

David Harding, Counterspy: Case of the Hot Car Killer & Case of the Flatbush Fagan. Perf. by Don MacLaughlin. 1 cass. (Running Time: 1 hr.). 2001. 6.98 (1638) Radio Spirits.

David Harding, Counterspy: Kleptomaniac Clues & Captured Contact. Perf. by Don MacLaughlin. 1 cass. (Running Time: 1 hr.). 2001. 6.98 (2533) Radio Spirits.

David Harding, Counterspy: Magic Murder & Mile High Murders. Perf. by Don MacLaughlin. 1 cass. (Running Time: 1 hr.). 2001. 6.98 (2513) Radio Spirits.

David Harding, Counterspy Pt. 1& 2: The Case of the Cold-blooded Professor. Perf. by Don MacLaughlin. 1 cass. (Running Time: 1 hr.). 2001. 6.98 (1559) Radio Spirits.

David Holmgren: Collected Writings 1978-2000. David Holmgren. 2003. audio compact disk 30.00 (978-0-646-41846-9(7)) Pub: HolmgrenDS AUS. Dist(s): Chelsea Green Pub

David Holt: The Hairyman & Other Wild Tales. 2004. 8.95 (978-0-89719-939-1(1)) Weston Woods.

David Holt Live & Kickin' at the National Storytelling Festival. David Holt. 1 CD. (Running Time: 1 hr. 4 mins.). 2004. audio compact disk 15.00 (978-0-942303-18-6(0)) Pub: August Hse. Dist(s): Natl Bk Netwk

David Hume: Scotland (1711-1776) Nicholas Capaldi. Read by Charlton Heston. (Running Time: 7200 sec.). (Audio Classics: the Giants of Philosophy Ser.). 2006. audio compact disk 25.95 (978-0-7861-6938-2(9)) Pub: Blckstn Audio. Dist(s): NetLibrary CO

David Hume: Scotland (1711-1776), Set. unabr. ed. Read by Charlton Heston. 2 cass. (Giants of Philosophy Ser.). 17.95 (K122) Blckstn Audio.
See how one of the world's most important philosophers created a complete system of thought, including his views on ethics, metaphysics, politics & aesthetics. Learn about his epistemology - how we know what we know.

David Hume, Biography, Set. unabr. ed. Thomas Henry Huxley. Read by Robert L. Halvorson. 4 cass. (Running Time: 360 min.). 28.95 (24) Halvorson Assocs.

David Ignatow. unabr. ed. Read by David Ignatow. 1 cass. (Running Time: 29 min.). 1985. 10.00 New Letters.
New York poet David Ignatow includes work from "Tread the Dark" & "Facing the Tree".

David Ignatow II. unabr. ed. David Ignatow. 1 cass. (Running Time: 29 min.). (New Letters on the Air Ser.). 1992. 10.00 (112291) New Letters.
This program includes poems about dying from "Shadowing the Ground" & an interview about moving away from urban poetry.

David Jones: Songs of Exquisite Taste. 1 cass. 9.98 (C-564) Folk-Legacy.
Wonderful songs, many from the English Music Hall.

David Jones: Widdecombe Fair. 1 cass., 1 CD. 9.98 (C-507); audio compact disk 14.98 CD. (CD-507) Folk-Legacy.
Traditional songs for all ages, from a fine English singer.

David Kherdian. unabr. ed. David Kherdian. Read by David Kherdian. Interview with Rebekah Presson. 1 cass. (Running Time: 29 min.). 1991. 10.00 (011191) New Letters.
Poet Kherdian is an Armenian-American who has been a prominent figure in the confessional mode of poetry writing for more than 20 years.

David Lee. David Lee. (Listener's Guide to Poetry Ser.). (ENG.). 1999. audio compact disk 12.00 (978-1-55659-137-2(3)) Pub: Copper Canyon. Dist(s): Consort Bk Sales

David Levine. Interview with David Levine. 1 cass. (Running Time: 45 min.). 1978. 13.95 (L045) TFR.
Levine, the cartoonist who has established a new & much imitated stlye of drawing literary figures, talks about his work. Saul Steinberg, the New Yorker cartoonist, talks about his life, Washington as a Heraldic City & baseball.

David Lewis. Interview with David Lewis. 1 cass. (Running Time: 20 min.). 1970. 9.95 (L044) TFR.
On King: A Critical Biography, the first book to assess Martin Luther King Jr. as a whole man. Lewis talks of the mistakes as well as the achievements to place him in historical perspective.

David Livingstone. unabr. ed. Thomas Hughes. Read by Frederick Davidson. 6 cass. (Running Time: 8 hrs. 30 mins.). 1997. 44.95 (978-0-7861-1080-3(5), 1850) Blckstn Audio.
In 1841 Livingstone left for Africa as a medical missionary & stayed there for 30 years, returning to Scotland for a total of two years. His accomplishments are legendary: Missionary geographer, ethnologist, chemist, botanist, astronomer, anthropologist, discoverer of Victoria Falls & the source of the Congo, & the first to cross the continent.

David Livingstone: A Concise Biography. unabr. ed. C. Nichols. Read by Nigel Graham. 2 cass. (Running Time: 3 hrs.). (Isis Ser.). (J). 2004. 24.95 (978-0-7531-0501-6(2), 981116) Pub: ISIS Lrg Prnt GBR. Dist(s): Ulverscroft US
A missionary & explorer, a traveller of talents, enterprise & excellent constitution. Tales of his discovery of Victoria Falls & being able to map much of central Africa's waterways, but how his later journeys appeared to be failures, although they provided the water world with vivid descriptions of the hitherto unknown interior of Africa. The book provides an account of his life, from his humble beginnings in Scotland & his struggle to gain medical qualifications to his employment with the London Missionary Society & his search for the source of the Nile.

***David Livingstone: Man of Prayer & Action.** unabr. ed. C. Silvester Horne. Read by Ralph Cosham. (Running Time: 4 hrs. 30 mins.). 2010. 19.95 (978-1-4332-2249-8(3)); 34.95 (978-1-4332-2245-0(0)); audio compact disk 49.00 (978-1-4332-2246-7(9)) Blckstn Audio.

David Madden I: "Bijou" unabr. ed. Read by David Madden. 1 cass. (Running Time: 29 min.). 1986. 10.00 New Letters.
Louisiana novelist juxtaposes the fantasy world of movies with the world of a teenage theatre usher in this excerpt from "Bijou".

David Madden II: "Cassandra Singing" unabr. ed. Read by David Madden. 1 cass. (Running Time: 29 min.). 1986. 10.00 New Letters.
Madden recreates the excitement of a bicycle race.

David Madden III: "In the Bag" unabr. ed. Read by David Madden. 1 cass. (Running Time: 29 min.). 1986. 10.00 New Letters.
A story about the adventure of a man abducted at a railway station.

David Malouf. unabr. ed. Read by David Maloug & Rebekah Presson. Ed. by James McKinley. 1 cass. (Running Time: 29 min.). (New Letters on the Air Ser.). 1994. 10.00 (122694); 18.00 2-sided cass. New Letters.
Malouf is interviewed by Rebekah Presson & reads from Remembering Babylon.

David McCullough. unabr. ed. Ed. by Jim McKinley. Prod. by Rebekah Presson. 1 cass. (Running Time: 29 min.). (New Letters on the Air Ser.). 1994. 10.00 (040293) New Letters.
McCullough reads from his Pulitzer Prize winning presidential biography, "Truman" & talks about the president he calls an "uncommon common man".

David Merrick: American Theatre see Buckley's Firing Line

David Paton: Music from the Mountain. 1 cass., 1 CD. 9.98 (C-120); audio compact disk 14.98 CD. (CD-120) Folk-Legacy.
Celtic tunes featuring the English concertina.

David Ray I: "The Tramp's Cup" unabr. ed. Read by David Ray et al. 1 cass. (Running Time: 29 min.). 1986. 10.00 New Letters.
"The Tramp's Cup" won the 1979 William Carlos Williams award from the Poetry Society of America.

David Ray II: "Enough of Flying" unabr. ed. Read by David Ray. 1 cass. (Running Time: 29 min.). 1986. 10.00 New Letters.
David Ray reads from his book of poetry - "Poems Inspired By the Ghazals of Ghalib".

David Ray III: "Live from the Levee" unabr. ed. Read by David Ray. 1 cass. (Running Time: 29 min.). 1986. 10.00 New Letters.
A live recording of David Ray from the Levee, a bar in Kansas City.

David Ray IV: "The Touched Life" unabr. ed. Read by David Ray. 1 cass. (Running Time: 29 min.). 1986. 10.00 New Letters.
David reads from his book of poetry & talks about the writing process.

David Ray V: "Images of India" unabr. ed. Read by David Ray. 1 cass. (Running Time: 29 min.). 1986. 10.00 New Letters.
David Ray reads poems inspired by his year-long stay in India.

David Ray VI: "On Wednesday I Cleaned Out My Wallet" unabr. ed. Read by David Ray. 1 cass. (Running Time: 29 min.). 1986. 10.00 New Letters.

David Ray VII: Sam's Book. unabr. ed. Poems. David Ray. Read by David Ray. 1 cass. (Running Time: 29 min.). 1987. 10.00 (103087) New Letters.
The founder of "New Letters on the Air" reads from his new book of poems, "Sam's Book".

David Romtvedt. unabr. ed. Read by David Rontvedt & Rebekah Presson. Ed. by James McKinley. 1 cass. (Running Time: 29 min.). (New Letters on the Air Ser.). 1992. 10.00 (092592); 18.00 2-sided cass. New Letters.
Romtvedt is interviewed by Rebekah P[illegible]on & reads from his poems.

David Sedaris, Set. unabr. ed. David Se[illegible] Running Time: 14 hrs.). (ENG.). 2007. 51.98 (978-1-60024-004[illegible] Pub: Hachet Audio. Dist(s): HachBkGrp

David Sedaris: Live at Carnegie Hall. unabr. ed. David Sedaris. (Running Time: 1 hr. 10 mins.). (ENG.). 2009. 24.98 (978-1-60024-983-9(3)) Pub: Hachet Audio. Dist(s): HachBkGrp

David Sedaris: Live for Your Listening Pleasure. unabr. ed. David Sedaris. Read by David Sedaris. (Running Time: 1 hr.). (ENG.). 2009. 17.98 (978-1-60024-719-4(9)); audio compact disk 17.98 (978-1-60024-718-7(0)) Pub: Hachet Audio. Dist(s): HachBkGrp

David Sedaris: Live for Your Listening Pleasure. unabr. abr. ed. David Sedaris. Read by David Sedaris. (Running Time: 1 hr.). (ENG.). 2010. 24.98 (978-1-60788-447-7(X)) Pub: Hachet Audio. Dist(s): HachBkGrp

David Sedaris - 14 CD Boxed Set. abr. ed. David Sedaris. (Running Time: 15 hrs.). (ENG.). 2009. 119.98 (978-1-60788-157-5(8)) Pub: Hachet Audio. Dist(s): HachBkGrp

David Sedaris Box Set. David Sedaris. 2002. 59.98 (978-1-58621-211-7(7)) Hachet Audio.

David Sedaris Box Set, Set. unabr. abr. ed. David Sedaris. Read by David Sedaris. 14 CDs. (Running Time: 15 hrs.). (ENG.). 2002. audio compact disk 79.98 (978-1-58621-434-0(9)) Pub: Hachet Audio. Dist(s): HachBkGrp

David Shields. unabr. ed. Ed. by Jim McKinley. Prod. by Rebekah Presson. 1 cass. (Running Time: 29 min.). (New Letters on the Air Ser.). 1994. 10.00 (042393) New Letters.
The author of two acclaimed novels, "Dead Languages" & "Heros," Shields reads from his new book of related short stories, "Handbook for Drowning;" & talks about minimalist writing. He also relates how growing up a stutterer in a highly articulate family led him to become a writer.

David Shrigley. David Shrigley. (ENG., 2008. audio compact disk 49.95 (978-3-86560-315-9(7)) Pub: Verlag der Buchhandlung DEU. Dist(s): Dist Art Pubs

David Susskind: Media Blues see Buckley's Firing Line

David Swanger. unabr. ed. Read by David Swanger. 1 cass. (Running Time: 29 min.). 1985. 10.00 New Letters.
This California poet reads from "The Shape of Water," & "Inside The Horse".

David the Best Model Maker in the World. unabr. ed. James Moloney. Read by Stig Wemyss. 1 CD. (Aussie Bites Ser.). (J). 2002. audio compact disk 39.95 (978-1-74030-849-6(2)) Pub: Bolinda Pubng AUS. Dist(s): Bolinda Pub Inc

David the King: A Psychological Perspective. Robert Moore. Read by Robert Moore. 3 cass. (Running Time: 3 hrs. 20 min.). 1992. 22.95 set. (978-0-7822-0394-3(9), 487) C G Jung IL.
The problems & promise of the masculine soul are powerfully imaged in the story of Israel's beloved David - warrior, lover, poet, & king. This workshop examines the significance of David's life & legend for contemporary psychology & spirituality.

David Thompson: Basketball. Read by David Thompson. 1 cass. 9.95 (978-0-89811-101-9(3), 7152) Lets Talk Assocs.
David Thompson talks about the people & events which influenced his career, & his own approach to his speciality.

David Wagoner. Interview. Interview with David Wagoner & Kay Bonetti. 1 cass. (Running Time: 1 hr. 20 min.). 13.95 (978-1-55644-028-1(6), 1152) Am Audio Prose.
Wagoner discusses this novel as metaphor for the creative process, the relationship between his poetry & his novels, his writing methods, his mentor Theodore Roethke, & the making of his novel into film.

David Young. unabr. ed. Read by David Young. 1 cass. (Running Time: 29 min.). 1985. 10.00 New Letters.
Ohio poet David Young's books include "Boxcar" & "The Names of A Hare in English".

David's Harp: Setting the Captives Free, Vol. I. Deanne Day. 1 cass. (Running Time: 37 min.). 1995. audio compact disk 15.98 CD. (978-0-9652154-1-1(5)) Mending Hrts Music.
Music & lyrics that bring healing to the brokenhearted.

David's Harp Vol. I: Setting the Captives Free. Deanne Day. 1 cass. (Running Time: 37 min.). 1995. 10.98 (978-0-9652154-0-4(7)) Mending Hrts Music.

David's Heart. Rick Joyner. 1 cass. (Running Time: 90 mins.). (Apostolic Calling & Ministry Ser.: Vol. 3). 2000. 5.00 (RJ07-003) Morning NC.
This series gives a foundational understanding of the true apostolic authority that is being restored to the church.

David's Spiritual Secret: Overcoming Life's Unending Struggles. 2006. 15.00 (978-1-933561-17-2(3)) BFM Books.

David's Spiritual Secret - Overcoming Life's Unending Struggles. 2005. 15.00 (978-1-933561-12-7(2)) BFM Books.

Davidson, Jim Interviewed by Mark Tier. unabr. ed. Jim Davidson. 1 cass. (Running Time: 53 min.). 12.95 (943) J Norton Pubs.
A discussion of the political forces behind rising taxes, inflation, regulation & government waste - & how his organization is fighting back.

Davies Memorial Address. unabr. ed. Adlai Stevenson. 1 cass. (Running Time: 55 min.). 12.95 (27006) J Norton Pubs.

DaVinci Deception. Erwin W. Lutzer. 2004. 24.99 (978-0-8423-8432-2(4)) Tyndale Hse.

DaVinci Deception. Chuck Missler. 2 CD's. (Running Time: 120 mins.). (Briefing Packages by Chuck Missler). 2004. audio compact disk 19.95 (978-1-57821-260-6(X)) Koinonia Hse.
Dan Brown's bestselling book, The DaVinci Code is a real page-turner but constitutes an intentional and very malicious attack on the person of Jesus Christ and Christianity. It has caused much confusion among those inadequately informed about the origins of the Gospels and the history of the early church.While it is admittedly a work of fiction, it presents, in advance, a series of statements which Brown declares are true and accurate that are not . Brown's deliberate twisting and distortion of facts throughout the book are cleverly crafted to mislead the uninformed.The many questions deriving from the outrageous heresies promoted by the book will be answered in this briefing. Chuck includes insights - and hidden codes - which appear to have been missed in the deluge of critiques the book has stimulated.

Davy Crockett see American Tall Tales

Davy Crockett. As told by Nicolas Cage. Music by David Bomberg. Illus. by Steven Brodner. 1 cass. (Running Time: 1 hr.). 9.95 Weston Woods.
Half-alligator & half-snapping turtle, with a touch of earthquake thrown in, Davy Crockett is the ultimate American legend. These adventures include the Battle of the Alamo.

Davy Crockett. unabr. ed. 1 cass. (Running Time: 20 min.). (People to Remember Ser.: Set II). (J). (gr. 4-7). 1979. bk. 16.99 (978-0-934898-56-0(1)); pap. bk. 9.95 (978-0-934898-11-9(1)) Jan Prods.
The Story of a man who was as quick with a tall take as the was to stand up for what was right.

Davy Crockett: An American Hero. Gina D. B. Clemen. (Green Apple Step One Ser.). (J). (gr. 4-7). 2005. pap. bk. 21.95 (978-88-530-0109-2(7)) Cideb ITA.

Davy Crockett: My Own Story. unabr. ed. David Crockett. Narrated by Jonathan Reese. (Running Time: 4 hrs. 30 mins. 0 sec.). (ENG.). 2008. audio compact disk 19.99 (978-1-4001-0793-3(8)); audio compact disk 39.99 (978-1-4001-3793-0(4)); audio compact disk 19.99 (978-1-4001-5793-8(5)) Pub: Tantor Media. Dist(s): IngramPubServ

Davy Crockett: My Own Story. unabr. collector's ed. David Crockett. Read by Jonathan Reese. 4 cass. (Running Time: 4 hrs.). 1995. 24.00 (978-0-7366-2936-2(X), 492819) Books on Tape.
Famous as a hunter & soldier, the "King of the World Frontier" was also a formidable politician who fought to ensure free land for settlers, relief for debtors & an expanded banking system for Tennessee.

Davy Crockett: The Legend of the Wild Frontier. unabr. ed. Richard Bruce Winders. (Running Time: 2 hrs.). (Library of American Lives & Times Ser.). 2009. 19.99 (978-1-4233-9447-1(X), 9781423394471, Brilliance MP3); 39.97 (978-1-4233-9448-8(8), 9781423394488, Brinc Audio MP3 Lib); 39.97 (978-1-4233-9449-5(6), 9781423394495, BADLE); audio compact disk 39.97 (978-1-4233-9446-4(1), 9781423394464, BriAudCD Unabrid) Brilliance Audio.

Davy Crockett: The Legend of the Wild Frontier. unabr. ed. Richard Bruce Winders. Read by Benjamin Becker. (Running Time: 2 hrs.). (Library of American Lives & Times Ser.). 2009. audio compact disk 19.99 (978-1-4233-9445-7(3), 9781423394457, Bril Audio CD Unabri) Brilliance Audio.

Davy Crockett: Young Rifleman. unabr. ed. Aileen Wells Parks. Read by Lloyd James. 4 cass. (Running Time: 5 hrs. 30 mins.). (Childhood of Famous Americans Ser.). (gr. 1-3). 2001. pap. bk. 35.95 (978-0-7861-2064-2(9), K2825) Blckstn Audio.
Davy grew up listening to his father's frontier tales of the settlers in the Smokey Mountains of 1775, including skirmishes with Indians & wild bears. A narrow escape with a brown bear begins his own adventures as the famous frontiersman who would eventually become a Congressman.

Davy Crockett & Pecos Bill. abr. ed. Adrien Stoutenburg. Read by Ed Begley. 1 cass. (Running Time: 90 min.). (J). 1984. 8.98 (978-0-89845-522-9(7), CDL5 1319) HarperCollins Pubs.

Davy D's Dog. Jill Eggleton. Illus. by Dave Gibson. (Sails Literacy Ser.). (gr. k up). 10.00 (978-0-7578-4038-8(8)) Rigby Educ.

Dawn. 2004. 8.95 (978-1-56008-885-1(0)); cass. & flmstrp 30.00 (978-1-56008-660-4(2)) Weston Woods.

Dawn. Elie Wiesel. Narrated by George Guidall. (Running Time: 10800 sec.). 2006. audio compact disk 14.99 (978-1-4193-9672-4(2)) Recorded Bks.

Dawn. unabr. ed. V. C. Andrews. Read by Donada Peters. 8 cass. (Running Time: 12 hrs.). (Cutler Ser.). 1991. 64.00 (978-0-7366-1944-8(5), 2765) Books on Tape.
In her new Virginia school Dawn Longchamp feels happy & safe. At last Dawn & her brother Jimmy have a change for a respectable life & Dawn's dream to study singing can come true. Then Dawn's mother suddenly dies & their world crumbles. After a terrible new shock, Dawn is thrust into another family & an evil web of unspoken sins. Humiliated & scorned, Dawn tries desperately to strip away the lies that surround her.

Dawn. unabr. ed. V. C. Andrews. Read by Laurel Lefkow. 9 cass. (Isis Ser.). (J). 2003. 76.95 (978-0-7531-1772-9(X)); audio compact disk 89.95 (978-0-7531-2231-0(6)) Pub: ISIS Lrg Prnt GBR. Dist(s): Ulverscroft US
In hew new school, Dawn Longchamp feels happy and safe. Her hope to study singing can finally come true. Then Dawn's mother dies suddenly and her entire world crumbles.

Dawn. unabr. ed. Elie Wiesel. Narrated by George Guidall. 2 cass. (Running Time: 2 hrs. 45 mins.). 1999. 18.00 (978-1-55690-805-7(9), 93114E7) Recorded Bks.
An Israeli soldier spends the night guarding a British prisoner-of-war who is due to be executed in the morning.

Dawn at Trout Lake. Bernie Krause. 1 cass. (Running Time: 60 min.). (Wild Sanctuary Ser.). 1994. audio compact disk 15.95 CD. (2326, Creativ Pub) Quayside.
Special lake nestled in the mountains of Washington. Sounds of the natural world as it wakes: the voices of blackbirds, ravens, sparrows, jays, robins, & leaping trout.

Dawn at Trout Lake. Bernie Krause. 1 cass. (Running Time: 60 min.). (Wild Sanctuary Ser.). 1994. 9.95 (2325, NrthWrd Bks) TandN Child.

***Dawn Chorus: A Sound Portrait of a British Woodland at Sunrise.** British Library Staff. (Running Time: 1 hr. 12 mins.). (ENG.). 2010. audio compact disk 15.00 (978-0-7123-0520-4(3)) Pub: Britis Library GBR. Dist(s): Chicago Distribution Ctr

Dawn Escapes. Contrib. by Falling Up. Prod. by Michael Baskette. 2005. audio compact disk 16.98 (978-5-558-77742-0(7)) BEC Recordings.

Dawn in Eclipse Bay. abr. ed. Jayne Ann Krentz. Read by Joyce Bean. 4 cass. (Running Time: 6 hrs.). (Eclipse Bay Ser.: Vol. 2). 2001. 53.25 (978-1-58788-258-6(2), 1587882582, Lib Edit) Brilliance Audio.
The second novel in a dramatic trilogy set in breathtaking Eclipse Bay, a town filled with rivalries as fierce and compelling as the rugged Oregon coast. . . Nothing was ever simple between a Madison and a Harte. The feud that had divided their families still simmered. Now, only months after their siblings' wedding, Lillian Harte and Gabe Madison are at each other's throats. Successful CEO Gabe had insisted on becoming a client of Lillian's matchmaking service. And after five disastrous dates, Lillian is at her wit's end. If she hadn't already decided to close her business and move home to Eclipse Bay, Gabe would have been the final straw. But when she finds Gabe at her door demanding she fulfill their business contract, the sparks between them suddenly turn personal. Once again, Eclipse Bay will witness a showdown - between a relentless Madison and irresistible Harte . . . Eclipse Bay is "Krentz at her best." - The Detroit Free Press.

Dawn in Eclipse Bay. abr. ed. Jayne Ann Krentz. Read by Joyce Bean. (Running Time: 6 hrs.). (Eclipse Bay Ser.: Vol. 2). 2006. 39.25 (978-1-4233-0064-9(5), 9781423300649, BADLE); 24.95 (978-1-4233-0063-2(7), 9781423300632, BAD); audio compact disk 39.25 (978-1-4233-0062-5(9), 9781423300625, Brinc Audio MP3 Lib); audio compact disk 24.95 (978-1-4233-0061-8(0), 9781423300618, Brilliance MP3) Brilliance Audio.

Dawn in Eclipse Bay. abr. ed. Jayne Ann Krentz. Read by Joyce Bean. (Running Time: 6 hrs.). (Eclipse Bay Ser.: Vol. 2). 2008. audio compact disk 14.99 (978-1-4233-6232-6(2), 9781423362326, BCD Value Price) Brilliance Audio.

Dawn in Eclipse Bay. unabr. ed. Jayne Ann Krentz. 7 cass. (Running Time: 10 hrs. 30 mins.). (Eclipse Bay Ser.: Vol. 2). 2001. 56.00 (978-0-7366-6838-5(1)) Books on Tape.
When Gabe Madison insists that Lillian Harte fulfill their business contract, the sparks between them turn personal.

Dawn in Eclipse Bay. unabr. ed. Jayne Ann Krentz. Read by Joyce Bean. (Running Time: 9 hrs.). (Eclipse Bay Ser.: Vol. 1). 2009. audio compact disk 29.99 (978-1-4233-8675-9(2), 9781423386759) Brilliance Audio.

Dawn in Eclipse Bay. unabr. ed. Jayne Ann Krentz. Read by Joyce Bean. (Running Time: 9 hrs.). (Eclipse Bay Ser.: Vol. 2). 2009. 39.97 (978-1-4233-8678-0(7), 9781423386780, Brinc Audio MP3 Lib); 24.99 (978-1-4233-8677-3(9), 9781423386773, Brilliance MP3); 39.97 (978-1-4233-8680-3(9), 9781423386803, BADLE); 24.99 (978-1-4233-8679-7(5), 9781423386797, BAD); audio compact disk 87.97 (978-1-4233-8676-6(0), 9781423386766, BriAudCD Unabrid) Brilliance Audio.

Dawn Land. abr. ed. Joseph Brucac & Joseph Bruchac III. Read by Joseph Brucac. 2 cass. (Running Time: 3 hrs.). (ENG.). (gr. 4). 1998. audio compact disk 16.95 (978-1-55591-149-2(8)) Pub: Fulcrum Pub. Dist(s): Consort Bk Sales

Dawn Light: Dancing with Cranes & Other Ways to Start the Day. unabr. ed. Diane Ackerman. Narrated by Laural Merlington. 1 MP3-CD. (Running Time: 7 hrs. 0 mins. 0 sec.). (ENG.). 2009. 19.99 (978-1-4001-6314-4(5)); audio compact disk 29.99 (978-1-4001-1314-9(8)); audio compact disk 59.99 (978-1-4001-4314-6(4)) Pub: Tantor Media. Dist(s): IngramPubServ

***Dawn Light: Dancing with Cranes & Other Ways to Start the Day.** unabr. ed. Diane Ackerman. Narrated by Laural Merlington. (Running Time: 7 hrs. 0 mins.). 2009. 14.99 (978-1-4001-8314-2(6)) Tantor Media.

Dawn Like Thunder: The True Story of Torpedo Squadron Eight. unabr. ed. Robert Mrazek. Narrated by Dick Hill. (Running Time: 15 hrs. 30 mins. 0 sec.). (ENG.). 2008. audio compact disk 39.99 (978-1-4001-0879-4(9)) Pub: Tantor Media. Dist(s): IngramPubServ

Dawn Like Thunder: The True Story of Torpedo Squadron Eight. unabr. ed. Robert J. Mrazek. Narrated by Dick Hill. (Running Time: 15 hrs. 30 mins. 0 sec.). (ENG.). 2008. audio compact disk 79.99 (978-1-4001-3879-1(5)) Pub: Tantor Media. Dist(s): IngramPubServ

Dawn Like Thunder: The True Story of Torpedo Squadron Eight. unabr. ed. Robert J. Mrazek. Read by Dick Hill. (Running Time: 15 hrs. 30 mins. 0 sec.). (ENG.). 2008. audio compact disk 29.99 (978-1-4001-5879-9(6)) Pub: Tantor Media. Dist(s): IngramPubServ

Dawn Melodies. Perf. by Leonardo Rubinstein. Created by Matthew Manning. Prod. by Stuart Wilde. 1 cass. 10.95 (CN614) White Dove NM.
Music for meditation which draws its inspiration from an enchanting combination of both classical music & Leonardo Rubinstein's own South American roots. With beautiful soaring melodies, this delightfully inspired music creates a warm, comfortable state of being which will lift you into realms of tranquility & peace.

Dawn of A New Day-Music. 2007. audio compact disk Rental 16.95 (978-1-56136-430-5(4)) Master Your Mind.

Dawn of Fury. abr. ed. Ralph Compton. Read by Jim Gough. 4 cass. (Running Time: 6 hrs.). (Gun Ser.). 2000. 24.95 (978-1-890990-39-8(6), 99039) Otis Audio.
Nathan Stone, driven to avenge the murder of his family, becomes the greatest gunfighter on the untamed frontier, matching wits & skill against the likes of Wild Bill Hichkok, John Wesley Hardin & Ben Thompson.

Dawn of Redemption. Don Marsh. 1999. 75.00 (978-0-7673-9720-9(7)); 11.98 (978-0-7673-9710-0(X)); audio compact disk 16.98 (978-0-7673-9701-8(0)); audio compact disk 85.00 (978-0-7673-9694-3(4)); audio compact disk 12.00 (978-0-7673-9652-3(9)) LifeWay Christian.

Dawn of Redemption Cassette Promo Pack. Don Marsh. 1999. 8.00 (978-0-7673-9642-4(1)) LifeWay Christian.

***Dawn of the Dreadfuls.** unabr. ed. Steve Hockensmith. Read by Katherine Kellgren. Characters created by Jane Austen. 1 MP3 CD. (Running Time: 11 hrs.). 2010. 24.99 (978-1-4418-5045-4(7), 9781441850454, Brilliance MP3); 39.97 (978-1-4418-5046-1(5), 9781441850461, Brinc Audio MP3 Lib); 39.97 (978-1-4418-5047-8(3), 9781441850478, BADLE); audio compact disk 29.99 (978-1-4418-5043-0(0), 9781441850430, Bril Audio CD Unabri); audio compact disk 92.97 (978-1-4418-5044-7(9), 9781441850447, BriAudCD Unabrid) Brilliance Audio.

Dawn on a Distant Shore. Sara Donati. 14 cass. (Running Time: 21 hrs.). (Wilderness Ser.: No. 2). 2001. 112.00 (978-0-7366-6836-1(5)) Books on Tape.

Dawn on a Distant Shore. unabr. ed. Sara Donati. Read by Kate Reading. 14 cass. (Running Time: 21 hrs.). (Wilderness Ser.: No. 2). 2001. 44.95 (978-0-7366-6745-6(8)) Books on Tape.
A sweeping epic novel of romance, adventure & history that travels from the New York frontier to Scotland.

Dawn on the Desert. unabr. ed. 1 cass. (Solitudes Ser.). 9.95 (C11205) J Norton Pubs.
This tape tunes in the sounds & experiences of the natural environment.

Dawn Palace. unabr. ed. Helen M. Hoover. Narrated by Alyssa Bresnahan. 6 cass. (Running Time: 8 hrs. 15 mins.). (gr. 6 up). 1994. 51.00 (978-0-7887-0129-0(0), 94354E7) Recorded Bks.
Medea, princess of Colchis, falls in love with Jason, leader of the Argonauts & uses her magical powers to advance him, only to be betrayed.

Dawn Patrol. unabr. ed. Don Winslow. (Running Time: 10 hrs. 5 mins.). 2008. 29.95 (978-1-4332-1488-2(1)); cass. & audio compact disk 29.95 (978-1-4332-1489-9(X)) Blckstn Audio.

Dawn Patrol. unabr. ed. Don Winslow. Read by Ray Porter. (Running Time: 11 hrs. 0 mins.). 2008. 29.95 (978-1-4332-1490-5(3)); 65.95 (978-1-4332-1486-8(5)); audio compact disk 90.00 (978-1-4332-1487-5(3)) Blckstn Audio.

Dawn Raid see Dylan Thomas Reading His Poetry

Dawning. 1 cass. (Running Time: 60 min.). 1994. audio compact disk 15.95 CD. (2524, Creativ Pub) Quayside.
Ken Davis combines the pan flute & synthesized harmonies with gentle sounds of nature.

Dawning. 1 cass. (Running Time: 60 min.). 1994. 9.95 (2522, NrthWrd Bks) TandN Child.

Dawning of Aquarian Age II. Norman N. Arens. 1 cass. 1992. 8.95 (1006) Am Fed Astrologers.

Dawn's Light. unabr. ed. Terri Blackstock. (Running Time: 10 hrs. 30 mins. 0 sec.). (Restoration Ser.: No. 4). (ENG.). 2008. audio compact disk 29.99 (978-0-310-26923-6(7)) Zondervan.

Dawn's Light. unabr. ed. Terri Blackstock. (Running Time: 10 hrs. 30 mins. 0 sec.). (Restoration Ser.: No. 4). (ENG.). 2008. 14.99 (978-0-310-26949-6(0)) Zondervan.

Dawn's Prelude. abr. ed. Tracie Peterson. Narrated by Sherri Berger. (Running Time: 7 hrs. 17 mins. 28 sec.). (Song of Alaska Ser.). (ENG.). 2009. 18.19 (978-1-60814-573-7(5)); audio compact disk 25.99 (978-1-59859-620-5(9)) Oasis Audio.

Day see Twentieth-Century Poetry in English, No. 5, Recordings of Poets Reading Their Own Poetry

Day. Elie Wiesel. Narrated by George Guidall. (Running Time: 14400 sec.). 2006. audio compact disk 14.99 (978-1-4193-9671-7(4)) Recorded Bks.

***Day after Night.** unabr. ed. Anita Diamant. Narrated by Dagmara Dominczyk. 7 CDs. (Running Time: 8 hrs.). 2009. audio compact disk 102.75 (978-1-4407-5023-6(8)) Recorded Bks.

***Day after Night.** unabr. ed. Anita Diamant. Read by Dagmara Dominczyk. 1 Playaway. (Running Time: 8 hrs.). 2009. 59.75 (978-1-4407-5025-0(4)); 61.75 (978-1-4407-5022-9(X)) Recorded Bks.

Day after Night. unabr. ed. Anita Diamant. Read by Dagmara Dominczyk. 7 CDs. (Running Time: 8 hrs. 0 mins. 0 sec.). (ENG.). 2009. audio compact disk 29.99 (978-0-7435-9839-2(3)) Pub: S&S Audio. Dist(s): S and S Inc

***Day after Night.** unabr. collector's ed. Anita Diamant. Read by Dagmara Dominczyk. 7 CDs. (Running Time: 8 hrs.). 2009. audio compact disk 39.99 (978-1-4407-5024-3(6)) Recorded Bks.

Day after Sunday see Twentieth-Century Poetry in English, No. 29, Recordings of Poets Reading Their Own Poetry

Day after Tomorrow. unabr. ed. Allan Folsom. Read by Michael Kramer. 16 cass. (Running Time: 24 hrs.). 1994. 120.00 (978-0-7366-2769-6(3), 3490A/B) Books on Tape.
An American surgeon on a heart-pounding chase across Europe stops an international conspiracy of apocalyptic proportions.

Day after Tomorrow. unabr. ed. Allan Folsom. Narrated by George Guidall. 17 cass. (Running Time: 24 hrs.). 1994. 136.00 (978-0-7887-0063-7(4), 94319E7) Recorded Bks.
An American cop & a French detective pursue a mysterious killer & a secret society with a shocking agenda.

Day after Tomorrow, Pt. 1. unabr. ed. Allan Folsom. Read by Michael Kramer. 8 cass. (Running Time: 12 hrs.). 1994. 64.00 (3490-A) Books on Tape.
In Paris, an American surgeon named Paul Osborn sees a man he believes murdered his father years ago & tries to kill him. In London, an L.A. homocide detective on assignment to Interpol investigates a baffling series of decapitations. In Geneva, a beautiful medical student begins a love affair that will change her life forever. In New Mexico, a physical therapist is invited to accompany a very special patient back to Switzerland. And in Germany, a select group of industrialists prepares for a momentous celebration. Weaving together these disparate events, Folsom reveals an international conspiracy of apocalyptic proportions, a sinister cable that sends Osborn on a heart-pounding chase across Europe.

Day after Tomorrow, Pt. 2. Allan Folsom. Read by Michael Kramer. 8 cass. (Running Time: 12 hrs.). 1994. 64.00 (3490-B) Books on Tape.

Day Ambrosia Stood Still. Prod. by Focus on the Family Staff. 2 CDs. (Last Chance Detectives Ser.). (ENG.). (YA). 2004. audio compact disk 14.97 (978-1-58997-269-8(4)) Pub: Focus Family. Dist(s): Tyndale Hse

Day & Night. Eddie Tucker. 2005. 14.99 (978-0-88368-803-8(4)) Whitaker Hse.
What do you get when you weave spiritual lyrics with a modern urban R&B flavor? You get Day and Night, Eddie Tucker's refreshingly energetic debut album. Eddie's smooth, Rich voice lifts praises to the Lord, accompanied by infectious beats and hip-hop inspiration. Day and Night offers a variety of musical styles, ranging from the victorious pop hit "Our God" to the meditative ballad "Teach Me.".

Day at Old MacDonald's Farm. 1 cass., 1 CD. (Kidsongs Ser.). (J). 7.98 (SME 63461); audio compact disk 11.18 CD Jewel box. (SME 63459) NewSound.
Includes: "Old MacDonald Had a Farm," "Skip to My Lou," "Mary Had a Little Lamb" & more.

Day at the Races. Frances Paige. 6 cass. (Running Time: 8 hrs.). (Story Sound Ser.). (J). 2004. 54.95 (978-1-85903-705-8(4)) Pub: Mgna Lrg Print GBR. Dist(s): Ulverscroft US

Day at the Spa. unabr. ed. Twin Sisters Productions. Read by Twin Sisters. (YA). 2007. 44.99 (978-1-60252-828-4(4)) Find a World.

Day at the Zoo. Richard Flint. 5 cass. Incl. Day at the Zoo: Some Observations from Watching the Animals. 1985.; Day at the Zoo: Stroll Through the Zoo. 1985.; Day at the Zoo: Zoo Notes. 1985.; Day at the Zoo: Zoo's & Don'ts. 1985.; Day at the Zoo. Richard Flint. 1985.; Day at the Zoo. Richard Flint. 1985.; 1985. 70.00 (978-0-937851-03-6(5)) Pendelton Lane.
This cassette album is a look at those unique animals within the corporate zoo that frustrate management & organizations. It is based on the philosophy that personalities, not people, cause frustrations.

Day at the Zoo: Some Observations from Watching the Animals see Day at the Zoo

Day at the Zoo: Stroll Through the Zoo see Day at the Zoo

Day at the Zoo: Zoo Notes see Day at the Zoo

Day at the Zoo: Zoo's & Don'ts see Day at the Zoo

Day Boy & the Night Girl. George MacDonald. As told by Daniel Koehn. 2005. audio compact disk 15.00 (978-1-59975-227-3(1)) Indep Pub IL.

Day Boy & the Night Girl. unabr. ed. George MacDonald. 2 CDs. (Running Time: 1 hr. 30 mins. 0 sec.). (Fairy Tale (Hovel Audio) Ser.). (ENG.). (J). (gr. 4-7). 2004. audio compact disk 15.98 (978-1-59644-016-6(3), Hovel Audio) christianaud.

***Day Boy & the Night Girl.** unabr. ed. George MacDonald. Narrated by Paul Eggington. (Running Time: 1 hr. 30 mins. 0 sec.). (ENG.). 2004. 9.98 (978-1-59644-014-2(7), Hovel Audio) christianaud.

Day by Day. Sandra Steffen. Narrated by Alexandra O'Karma. 10 cass. (Running Time: 13 hrs. 30 mins.). 88.00 (978-1-4025-2256-7(8)) Recorded Bks.

Day by Day. ldr.'s ed. (J). (gr. 1-6). 2000. audio compact disk 69.95 (978-0-633-00445-3(6)) LifeWay Christian.

Day by Day: English for Employment Communication. Steven J. Molinsky & Bill Bliss. 2002. 20.40 (978-0-13-339045-2(4)) Longman.

***Day by Day: Loving God More Dearly.** Frederick Borsch. 2009. audio compact disk 20.00 (978-0-8192-2405-7(7), MoreHse Pubng) Church Pub Inc.

***Day by Day Armageddon.** unabr. ed. J. L. Bourne. Read by Jay Snyder. (Running Time: 7 hrs.). (Day by Day Armageddon Ser.). 2010. 39.97 (978-1-4418-7495-5(X), 9781441874955, BADLE); 24.99 (978-1-4418-7493-1(3), 9781441874931, Brilliance MP3); 39.97 (978-1-4418-7494-8(1), 9781441874948, Brlnc Audio MP3 Lib); audio compact disk 24.99 (978-1-4418-7491-7(7), 9781441874917, Bril Audio CD Unabri); audio compact disk 74.97 (978-1-4418-7492-4(5), 9781441874924, BriAudCD Unabrid) Brilliance Audio.

Day Care: How to Choose the Right Person to Take Care of Your Child. unabr. ed. Thomas Amshay & Christina Clement. Read by Thomas Amshay. Intro. by Donald Grass. 1 cass. (Running Time: 1 hr.). 1987. 5.00 (978-0-939401-06-2(1)) RFTS Prod.
Discusses choosing day care that will enhance a child's emotional & intellectual growth.

Day Care for Children. 1 cass. (Running Time: 1 hr.). 10.95 (ME-84-09-07, HarperThor) HarpC GBR.

Day Diana Died, Set. abr. ed. Christopher Andersen. Read by Dandy Dutch. 2 cass. (Running Time: 3 hr.). 1998. 17.95 (978-1-55935-285-7(X), 396202) Soundelux.
This account of Princess Diana's life & tragic death details background information about her relationship with Dodi.

Day Donny Herbert Woke Up: A True Story. unabr. ed. Rich Blake. Read by Kimberly Farr. 5 CDs. (Running Time: 6 hrs.). 2007. audio compact disk 80.00 (978-1-4159-4215-4(3), BksonTape) Pub: Random Audio Pubg. Dist(s): Random
Donny Herbert was a hardworking Buffalo city firefighter who, in December 1995, was searching the attic of a burning house when the snow-laden roof collapsed. For six minutes he was without oxygen. A beloved husband, a father of four boys, Donny fell into a vegetative state that lasted nearly a decade. He was, for all practical purposes, gone. Until one day, in April 2005, when he woke up and spoke almost nonstop to his family and loved ones for nearly eighteen hours. ere is the story of this remarkable moment, which was covered by the press worldwide. For his wife, Linda, it was a miracle. For his doctors and nurses, it was a medical mystery. For his sons - including his youngest, with whom he had never before had a conversation - it was a blessing. After his remarkable day, Donny Herbert fell into a deep sleep and never experienced a comparable moment of clarity. He died, in February 2006, from pneumonia. Written by Linda's cousin, THE DAY DONNY HERBERT WOKE UP makes the listener wonder: What brought Donny back? More than anything, Linda credits Donny himself - a man with the strength to will himself back into his family's lives, if only to remind them one last time of how very much he loved them. This is as much Linda's story - one of perseverance and faith - as it is of a remarkable husband, father, and firefighter.

***Day for Night: A Novel.** unabr. ed. Frederick Reiken. Narrated by Laural Merlington & George K. Wilson. (Running Time: 11 hrs. 0 mins.). 2010. 17.99 (978-1-4001-8749-2(4)); 24.99 (978-1-4001-6749-4(3)); 34.99 (978-1-4001-9749-1(X)); audio compact disk 83.99 (978-1-4001-4749-6(2)); audio compact disk 34.99 (978-1-4001-1749-9(6)) Pub: Tantor Media. Dist(s): IngramPubServ

Day Freedom Died: The Colfax Massacre, the Supreme Court, & the Betrayal of Reconstruction. unabr. ed. Charles Lane. Read by Jim Bond. (Running Time: 13 hrs.). 2008. 39.25 (978-1-4233-6076-6(1), 9781423360766, BADLE); 39.25 (978-1-4233-6074-2(5), 9781423360742, Brlnc Audio MP3 Lib); 24.95 (978-1-4233-6075-9(3), 9781423360759, BAD); 102.25 (978-1-4233-6070-4(2), 9781423360704, BrilAudUnabridg); audio compact disk 107.25 (978-1-4233-6072-8(9), 9781423360728, BriAudCD Unabrid); audio compact disk 24.95 (978-1-4233-6073-5(7), 9781423360735, Brilliance MP3); audio compact disk 38.95 (978-1-4233-6071-1(0), 9781423360711, Bril Audio CD Unabri) Brilliance Audio.

Day God's Word Went on Trial. 1 cass. 7.95 (22-7, HarperThor) HarpC GBR.

Day Gogo Went to Vote. Elinor Batezat Sisulu. Read by Lisette Lecat. 1 cass. (Running Time: 15 mins.). (YA). 2000. pap. bk. 24.20 (978-0-7887-4161-6(6), 41106); 90.30 (978-0-7887-4162-3(4), 47099) Recorded Bks.
In their Soweto homeland, little Thembi's great grandmother, Gogo, tells her stories of the olden days. When Gogo learns that black South Africans will soon be allowed to vote, the old woman surprises Thembi. Gogo intends to vote, even though she will have to travel a great distance to the polls.

Day Gogo Went to Vote. unabr. ed. Elinor Batezat Sisulu. Narrated by Lisette Lecat. 1 cass. (Running Time: 15 mins.). (J). (gr. 2 up). 2000. 10.00 (978-0-7887-4018-3(0), 96139E7) Recorded Bks.

Day He Wore My Crown. Contrib. by David T. Clydesdale. 1982. 90.00 (978-0-00-691423-5(3), 75609268) Pub: Brentwood Music. Dist(s): H Leonard

Day He Wore My Crown. Contrib. by David T. Clydesdale. 1988. 11.98 (978-0-00-519592-5(6), 75609267) Pub: Brentwood Music. Dist(s): H Leonard

Day I Ate Whatever I Wanted: And Other Small Acts of Liberation. unabr. ed. Elizabeth Berg. Read by Elizabeth Berg. 7 CDs. (Running Time: 8 hrs.). 2008. audio compact disk 50.00 (978-1-4159-4393-9(1), BksonTape) Pub: Random Audio Pubg. Dist(s): Random

Day I Ate Whatever I Wanted: And Other Small Acts of Liberation. unabr. ed. Elizabeth Berg. Read by Elizabeth Berg. (Running Time: 28800 sec.). (ENG.). 2008. audio compact disk 34.95 (978-0-7393-3190-3(6), Random AudioBks) Pub: Random Audio Pubg. Dist(s): Random

Day I Carried the King. 2006. audio compact disk 10.99 (978-1-59886-894-4(2)) Tate Pubng.

Day I Fell down the Toilet & Other Poems. Steve Turner. 2006. audio compact disk 9.95 (978-0-7540-6723-8(8), Chivers Child Audio) AudioGO.

Day I Had to Play with My Sister. Crosby N. Bonsall. Read by Jeff Woodman. 1 cass. (Running Time: 15 mins.). (J). (ps up). 2000. stu. ed. 22.20 (41107) Recorded Bks.
Big brother is trying to teach little sister to play hide-&-seek, but she won't cooperate.

***Day I Had to Play with My Sister.** unabr. ed. Crosby Bonsall. (ENG.). 2008. (978-0-06-169402-8(9)); (978-0-06-171003-2(2)) HarperCollins Pubs.

Day I Had to Play with My Sister, Class set. Crosby N. Bonsall. Read by Jeff Woodman. 1 cass. (Running Time: 15 mins.). (J). (ps up). 2000. 70.30 (978-0-7887-4164-7(0), 47100) Recorded Bks.

Day I Had to Play with My Sister: A My First I Can Read Book. unabr. ed. Crosby N. Bonsall. Narrated by Jeff Woodman. 1 cass. (Running Time: 15 mins.). (ps up). 2000. 10.00 (978-0-7887-4019-0(9), 96140E7) Recorded Bks.

***Day I Shot Cupid: Hello, My Name Is Jennifer Love Hewitt & I'm a Love-Aholic.** unabr. ed. Jennifer Love Hewitt. Narrated by Jennifer Love Hewitt. 1 MP3-CD. (Running Time: 2 hrs. 0 mins. 0 sec.). 2010. 19.99 (978-1-4001-6683-1(7)); 11.99 (978-1-4001-8683-9(8)); audio compact disk 19.99 (978-1-4001-1683-6(X)); audio compact disk 39.99 (978-1-4001-4683-3(6)) Pub: Tantor Media. Dist(s): IngramPubServ

***Day I Swapped My Dad for Two Goldfish.** abr. ed. Neil Gaiman. Read by Neil Gaiman. (ENG.). 2006. (978-0-06-123234-3(3)) HarperCollins Pubs.

***Day I Swapped My Dad for Two Goldfish.** unabr. ed. Neil Gaiman. Read by Neil Gaiman. (ENG.). 2009. (978-0-06-198736-6(0)) HarperCollins Pubs.

Day in a Life. Karen Johns. 1 cass. 7.95 (177) Am Fed Astrologers.
Which techniques are most valid - progressions, horary, returns?.

Day in Marin. 2006. audio compact disk 15.00 (978-1-890246-37-2(9)) B Katie Int Inc.

Day in the Life. Capital Radio. (Running Time: 1 hr.). 2005. 16.95 (978-1-59912-923-5(X)) Iofy Corp.

Day in the Life of Dennis Day: Asks Mr. Willoughby for a Raise & Selling to a Railroad President. Perf. by Dennis Day. 1 cass. (Running Time: 1 hr.). 2001. 6.98 (1585) Radio Spirits.

Day in the Life of Dennis Day: Betting on Baby & Room for Rent. Perf. by Dennis Day. 1 cass. (Running Time: 1 hr.). 2001. 6.98 (2322) Radio Spirits.

Day in the Life of Dennis Day: Dennis's Inheritance & Dennis's Radio Show. Perf. by Dennis Day. 1 cass. (Running Time: 1 hr.). 2001. 6.98 (1599) Radio Spirits.

Day in the Life of Dennis Day: Multiple Personalities & Football Fiasco. Perf. by Dennis Day. 1 cass. (Running Time: 1 hr.). 2001. 6.98 (2323) Radio Spirits.

Day in the Life of Dennis Day: Sales Success & Surprise Wedding. Perf. by Dennis Day. 1 cass. (Running Time: 1hr.). 2001. 6.98 (2320) Radio Spirits.

Day in the Life of Dennis Day: Stable Boy & City Manager. Perf. by Dennis Day. 1 cass. (Running Time: 1 hr.). 2001. 6.98 (2318) Radio Spirits.

Day in the Life of Dennis Day: Temptation & The Great Gambini. Perf. by Dennis Day. 1 cass. (Running Time: 1 hr.). 2001. 6.98 (2321) Radio Spirits.

Day in the Life of Dennis Day: Unemployed Again! & Love Letter to Lily. Perf. by Dennis Day. 1 cass. (Running Time: 1 hr.). 2001. 6.98 (2324) Radio Spirits.

Day in the Life of Dennis Day: Weaverville, U. S. A. & Neither Rain Nor Snow. Perf. by Dennis Day. 1 cass. (Running Time: 1 hr.). 2001. 6.98 (2319) Radio Spirits.

Day in the Season of the LA Dodgers. Tom Zimmerman. Read by Jaime Jarrin. 1 cass. (Running Time: 3 hrs.). (SPA.). bk. 15.99 (978-1-56703-021-1(1)) High-Top Sports.
Take a rare, historic look at the stadium life of one of the most successful & beloved franchises in sports: the Los Angeles Dodgers.

Day in the Season of the LA Dodgers. abr. ed. Tom Zimmerman. Read by Tom Zimmerman. Ed. by Donald V. Allen. 2 cass. (Running Time: 2 hrs. 40 min.). 1992. bk. 15.95 set. (978-1-56703-002-0(5), 003) High-Top Sports.
A day with the Los Angeles Dodgers, starting at 6 AM with the arrival of the grounds crew & ending when the players leave the parking lot after the game.

Day in Tim's Garden. Tim Cain. Read by Tim Cain. 1 cass. (Running Time: 1 hr. 04 min.). (J). (ps-3). 1995. 9.98 double-sided. (978-1-884115-02-8(0)); audio compact disk 14.98 CD. (978-1-884115-03-5(9)) Tims Tunes.
Sing-along songs for children 3-8 years old.

Day Is Done see Treasury of Henry Wadsworth Longfellow

Day It Snowed Tortillas: Tales from Spanish New Mexico. abr. ed. Joe Hayes. Read by Joe Hayes. 1 cass. (Running Time: 55 min.). (J). (gr. 2-8). 1986. 10.95 (978-0-939729-11-1(3), CPP9113) Pub: Trails West Pub. Dist(s): Cinco Puntos
Features a selection of traditional Hispanic tales.

Day Jimmy's Boa Ate the Wash. 2004. bk. 24.95 (978-0-89719-870-7(0)); pap. bk. 18.95 (978-1-55592-400-3(X)); pap. bk. 18.95 (978-1-55592-403-4(4)); pap. bk. 38.75 (978-1-55592-402-7(6)); pap. bk. 38.75 (978-1-55592-404-1(2)); pap. bk. 32.75 (978-1-55592-217-7(1)); pap. bk. 32.75 (978-1-55592-218-4(X)); pap. bk. 14.95 (978-1-55592-670-0(3)); 8.95 (978-0-89719-950-6(2)); cass. & flmstrp 30.00 (978-0-89719-562-1(0)); audio compact disk 12.95 (978-1-55592-906-0(0)) Weston Woods.

Day Jimmy's Boa Ate the Wash. Trinka Hakes Noble. 1 cass. (Running Time: 5 min.). (J). (ps-4). 8.95 (RAC303) Weston Woods.
Jimmy's boa constrictor turns an ordinary class trip to a farm into an uproarious outing.

Day Jimmy's Boa Ate the Wash. Trinka Hakes Noble. Illus. by Steven Kellogg. 1 cass., 5 bks. (Running Time: 30 min.). (J). pap. bk. 32.75 Weston Woods.

Day Jimmy's Boa Ate the Wash. Trinka Hakes Noble. Illus. by Steven Kellogg. 1 cass. (Running Time: 5 min.). (J). (ps-4). bk. 24.95 Weston Woods.

Day Jimmy's Boa Ate the Wash. Trinka Hakes Noble. Illus. by Steven Kellogg. 1 cass. (Running Time: 5 min.). (J). (ps-4). 2000. pap. bk. 12.95 (PRA303) Weston Woods.

Day Jimmy's Boa Ate the Wash. Trinka Hakes Noble. (J). 2004. 8.95 (978-1-56008-108-1(2)) Weston Woods.

Day Jimmy's Boa Ate the Wash. unabr. ed. Trinka Hakes Noble. Read by Sandy Duncan. 1 cass. (Running Time: 90 min.). (J). 1985. 9.95 (978-0-89845-898-5(6), CPN 1778) HarperCollins Pubs.
A funny & convoluted explanation of why Jimmy's Boa ate the wash.

Day Jimmy's Boa Ate the Wash, the; Picnic; Napping House, the; Very Worst Monster. 2004. (978-1-56008-822-6(2)); cass. & flmstrp (978-0-89719-759-5(3)) Weston Woods.

Day John Died. abr. ed. Christopher Andersen. Read by Bob Loza. 2 cass. (Running Time: 3 hrs.). 2000. 18.00 (978-1-55935-351-9(1)) Soundelux.
About the Kennedy's.

Day John Met Paul: An Hour-by-Hour Account of How the Beatles Began. abr. ed. James O'Donnell. Read by Rod Davis. 2 cass. (Running Time: 3 hrs.). 1997. 16.00 Set. (978-0-9636905-8-6(2), 31554) Hall Fame Bks.
Rod Davis, who played in John Lennon's band, The Quarry men, relates the true story of the day Lennon met Paul McCartney in 1957 in Liverpool.

Day Late & a Dollar Short. Terry McMillan. Read by Desiree Coleman & M. E. Willis. 2001. 88.00 (978-0-7366-6033-4(X)); audio compact disk 104.00 (978-0-7366-6180-5(8)) Books on Tape.

Day Late & a Dollar Short. unabr. ed. Terry McMillan. Read by Desiree Coleman & M. E. Willis. 11 cass. (Running Time: 16 hrs. 30 mins.). 2001. 88.00; audio compact disk 104.00 Books on Tape.
The members of the Pierce family see life & one another through thick & thin & entirely on their own terms.

Day Lincoln Was Shot. unabr. ed. Jim Bishop. Read by Allen Cornell. 6 cass. (Running Time: 9 hrs.). 1987. 48.00 (978-0-7366-1118-3(5), 2041) Books on Tape.
Minute-by-minute account of the last 24 hours of the President's life.

Day Lincoln Was Shot. unabr. ed. Jim Bishop. Narrated by Nelson Runger. 10 CDs. (Running Time: 11 hrs. 15 mins.). 1999. audio compact disk 87.00 (978-0-7887-3420-5(2), C1026E7) Recorded Bks.
Crowds celebrate in the streets day & night, during the final days of the Civil War, while President Lincoln's enemies furtively plot his destruction.

Day Lincoln Was Shot. unabr. ed. Jim Bishop. Narrated by Nelson Runger. 8 cass. (Running Time: 11 hrs. 15 mins.). 1997. 70.00 (978-0-7887-0934-0(8), 95074E7) Recorded Bks.

***Day My Bum Went Psycho.** unabr. ed. Andy Griffiths. Read by Stig Wemyss. (Running Time: 5 hrs. 32 mins.). (J). 2004. audio compact disk 40.00 (978-1-74093-307-0(9)) Pub: Bolinda Pubng AUS. Dist(s): Bolinda Pub Inc

Day My Mother Left. unabr. ed. James Prosek. Read by Joel Johnstone. 4 CDs. (Running Time: 4 hrs. 31 mins.). (YA). (gr. 5-8). 2007. audio compact disk 45.00 (978-0-7393-4866-6(3), Listening Lib) Pub: Random Audio Pubg. Dist(s): Random

Day No Pigs Would Die. Robert Newton Peck. Contrib. by Robert Sevra. 3 cass. (J). (gr. 4-7). 1989. (978-0-8072-8529-9(3)) Chivers Audio Bks GBR.

Day No Pigs Would Die. unabr. ed. Robert Newton Peck. Read by Terry Bregy. 3 CDs. (Running Time: 3 hrs.). (YA). 1993. audio compact disk 29.95 (978-1-883332-59-4(1)) Audio Bkshelf.

Day No Pigs Would Die. unabr. ed. Robert Newton Peck. Read by Terry Bregy. 2 cass. (Running Time: 3 hrs.). (YA). (gr. 7 up). 1993. 21.95 (978-1-883332-05-1(2), 390616) Audio Bkshelf.
A heartwarming, soul-wrenching story of a young boy coming of age & the love he shares with his father. When conditions on the farm force him to butcher his pet pig, he learns a thing or two about life itself.

Day No Pigs Would Die. unabr. ed. Robert Newton Peck. 3 CDs. (Running Time: 3 hrs.). 2001. audio compact disk 29.95 Audio Bkshelf.

Day No Pigs Would Die. unabr. ed. Robert Newton Peck. Read by Terry Bregy. (J). 2008. 34.99 (978-1-60514-767-3(2)) Find a World.

Day No Pigs Would Die. unabr. ed. Robert Newton Peck. 1 read-along cass. (Running Time: 56 min.). (Young Adult Cliffhangers Ser.). (J). (gr. 7 up). 1985. 15.98 (978-0-8072-1802-0(2), JRH 101 SP, Listening Lib); (Listening Lib) Random Audio Pubg.
Boyhood on a Vermont farm, the love between a father & son, & a coming to manhood are told in this story.

Day No Pigs Would Die. unabr. ed. Robert Newton Peck. Read by Robert Sevra. 3 vols. (Running Time: 3 hrs. 35 mins.). (J). (gr. 7 up). 1989. pap. bk. 36.00 (978-0-8072-8533-6(1), LL0015, Listening Lib); 30.00 (978-0-8072-8507-7(2), LB3CX, Listening Lib) Random Audio Pubg.
Filled with raw emotion, & packed with humor & wisdom, "A Day No Pigs Would Die" is a heartwarming, soul-wrenching story of a young boy coming of age & the love he shares with his father. When conditions on the farm force him to butcher his pet pig, he learns a thing or two about life itself.

Day No Pigs Would Die. unabr. ed. Robert Newton Peck. Read by Lincoln Hoppe. (ENG.). (J). (gr. 5). 2010. 28.00 (978-0-307-24585-4(3), Listening Lib) Pub: Random Audio Pubg. Dist(s): Random

Day No Pigs Would Die, unabr. ed. Robert Newton Peck. Narrated by Johnny Heller. 3 pieces. (Running Time: 3 hrs. 15 mins.). (gr. 5 up). 1995. 27.00 (978-0-7887-0363-8(3), 94555E7) Recorded Bks.
The timeless story of one Shaker boy, his beloved pet pig & the joys & hardships that mark his passage into manhood.

Day No Pigs Would Die, Set. unabr. ed. Robert Newton Peck. Read by Robert Sevra. 3 cass. (YA). 1999. 23.98 (FS9-25228) Highsmith.

Day of Absolution. unabr. ed. John E. Gardner. Read by Frederick Davidson. 10 cass. (Running Time: 14 hrs. 30 mins.). 2001. 69.95 (978-0-7861-2071-0(1), 2832); audio compact disk 88.00 (978-0-7861-9696-8(3), 2832) Blckstn Audio.
Charlie Gauntlet, a retired lawyer who was "something dodgy for the Foreign Office," is recently married to the much younger Rebecca "Bex" Olesker, a Detective Sergeant in the London Metropolitan Police's Anti-Terrorist Branch. Charlie has more or less come to terms with Bex's demanding and dangerous job, though its hard for him to stay home when his young wife is on the front lines. Especially when she's facing Alchemist, an unidentified hired assassin who strikes high-profile targets and demands a big payoff. Now Bex may be the one to find him, but will she survive the encounter.

Day of Atonement. unabr. ed. Faye Kellerman. Read by Mitchell Greenberg. 6 CDs. (Running Time: 7 hrs.). 2009. audio compact disk 19.99 (978-0-06-144179-0(1), Harper Audio) HarperCollins Pubs.

***Day of Atonement.** unabr. ed. Faye Kellerman. Read by Mitchell Greenberg. (ENG.). 2009. (978-0-06-172480-0(7)); (978-0-06-172481-7(5)) HarperCollins Pubs.

***Day of Awakening: A Book of Revelation & Self-discovery.** Tony Titshall. (ENG.). 2010. 110.00 (978-0-9817547-3-4(2), RevwayPubns) T Titshall.

***Day of Awakening: A Book of Revelation & Self-discovery.** Tony Titshall. Read by Tony Titshall. (ENG.). (YA). 2010. audio compact disk 110.00 (978-0-9817547-4-1(0), RevwayPubns) T Titshall.

***Day of Awakening: A Book of Revelation & Self-discovery.** Read by Tony Titshall. (ENG.). 2010. 75.00 (978-0-9817547-6-5(7), RevwayPubns) T Titshall.

Day of Battle: The War in Sicily & Italy, 1943-1944. abr. ed. Rick Atkinson. Read by Rick Atkinson. (Running Time: 9 hrs. 30 mins. 0 sec.). (ENG.). 2007. audio compact disk 39.95 (978-0-7435-2797-2(6)) Pub: S&S Audio. Dist(s): S and S Inc

Day of Battle: The War in Sicily & Italy, 1943-1944. unabr. ed. Rick Atkinson. Narrated by Jonathan Davis. 28 CDs. (Running Time: 32 hrs. 45 mins.). 2007. audio compact disk 123.75 (978-1-4281-6930-2(X)) Recorded Bks.
New York Times best-selling author Rick Atkinson won the Pulitzer Prize for his riveting WWII chronicle An Army at Dawn. In The Day of Battle, he shifts his focus from northern Africa to the southern European front. Beginning with the invasion of Sicily, Allied forces worked their way through fierce fighting, cutting a swath through enemy lines on their way to Rome and victory.

Day of Battle: The War in Sicily & Italy, 1943-1944. unabr. ed. Rick Atkinson. Narrated by Jonathan Davis. 28 cass. (Running Time: 32 hrs. 45 mins.). 2008. 113.75 (978-1-4281-6928-9(8)) Recorded Bks.

***Day of Change: A Groundbreaking Workshop for Parents of Children with Autism & Other Neurodevelopmental Disorders.** Instructed by Nicole Beurkens & Michelle VanderHeide. (ENG.). 2010. audio compact disk 47.00 (978-0-9794787-7-2(4)) Horizons DRC.

Day of Confession. Allan Folsom. 1999. (978-1-57042-783-1(6)) Hachet Audio.

Day of Confession. abr. ed. Allan Folsom. 1999. (978-1-57042-740-4(2)); (978-1-57042-782-4(8)) Hachet Audio.

Day of Confession. abr. ed. Allan Folsom. (Running Time: 4 hrs.). (ENG.). 2006. 14.98 (978-1-59483-699-2(X)) Pub: Hachet Audio. Dist(s): HachBkGrp

Day of Confession. unabr. ed. Allan Folsom. Read by Michael Kramer. 12 cass. (Running Time: 18 hrs.). 1998. 96.00 (978-0-7366-4532-4(2), 4707) Books on Tape.
A cardinal of the Catholic Church is assassinated in Rome & the prime suspect is a Vatican priest, an American named Danny Addison, believed killed in a bus explosion.

Day of Days: Luke 24:1-3. Ed Young. 1990. 4.95 (978-0-7417-1795-5(6), 795) Win Walk.

Day of Grace. 2001. 29.95 (978-1-888992-22-9(0)) Catholic Answers.

Day of Grace. 2003. audio compact disk 34.95 (978-1-888992-42-7(5)) Catholic Answers.

Day of Infamy. Kenneth Bruce. 1 cass. (Running Time: 1 hr.). Dramatization. (Excursions in History Ser.). 12.50 Alpha Tape.

Day of Infamy. unabr. ed. Walter Lord. Read by Tom Parker. 5 cass. (Running Time: 7 hrs.). 1995. 39.95 (978-0-7861-0912-8(2), 1711) Blckstn Audio.
Vivid re-creation of the Japanese attack on Pearl Harbor on Sunday, December 7, 1941. The reader accompanies Admiral Nagumo's task force as it sweeps toward Hawaii; looks on while warning after warning is ignored on Oahu; is enmeshed in the panic, confusion, courage & heroism of the final attack.

Day of Infamy. unabr. ed. Walter Lord. Read by Tom Parker. 6 CDs. (Running Time: 7 hrs.). 2000. audio compact disk 48.00 (978-0-7861-9919-8(9), 1711) Blckstn Audio.

Day of Infamy. unabr. ed. Walter Lord. Narrated by Richard Poe. 6 cass. (Running Time: 8 hrs. 30 mins.). 1999. 51.00 (978-1-55690-672-5(2), 92319E7) Recorded Bks.
The story of December 7, 1942 the Japanese attack on Pearl Harbor, as seen through the eyes of the men on both sides who participated. Accompany Admiral Nagumo's task force as it sweeps toward Hawaii; watch as warnings are ignored on Oahu; & witness the confusion, panic & courage of the U.S. Armed Forces response to Admiral Yamamoto's planned sneak attack against a nation that thought it was at peace.

Day of Infamy. unabr. ed. Walter Lord. Narrated by Richard Poe. 6 cass. (Running Time: 8 hrs. 30 mins.). 2002. 34.95 (978-0-7887-6450-9(0), RC999) Recorded Bks.
This re-creation of the Japanese attack on Pearl Harbor will make you feel like you're in the middle of the attack. You'll accompany Admiral Nagumo's task force as it sweeps toward Hawaii; watch as warnings are ignored on Oahu; and witness the confusion, panic, and courage of the U.S. Armed Forces' response to Admiral Yamamoto's planned sneak attack against a nation that thought it was at peace.

Day of Infamy. unabr. ed. Walter Lord & Hatsuho Naito. 10 cass. (Running Time: 15 hrs.). (Battles, Ships & Glory Ser.). (YA). 2001. 39.95 (978-1-56015-922-3(7)) Penton Overseas.
Includes "Day of Infamy" which traces the human drama of the great attack on Pearl Harbor. "Thunder Gods" is a compelling first-hand account of the Kamikaze pilots who pledged themselves to die for their emperor.

***Day of Judgement.** unabr. ed. Jack Higgins. (Running Time: 9 hrs.). (Simon Vaughn Ser.). 2010. 24.99 (978-1-4418-4447-7(3), 9781441844477, BAD) Brilliance Audio.

***Day of Judgement.** unabr. ed. Jack Higgins. Read by Michael Page. (Running Time: 9 hrs.). (Simon Vaughn Ser.). 2010. 24.99 (978-1-4418-4445-3(7), 9781441844453, Brilliance MP3); 39.97 (978-1-4418-4446-0(5), 9781441844460, Brlnc Audio MP3 Lib); 39.97 (978-1-4418-4448-4(1), 9781441844484, BADLE); audio compact disk 29.99 (978-1-4418-4443-9(0), 9781441844439, Bril Audio CD Unabri); audio compact disk 87.97 (978-1-4418-4444-6(9), 9781441844446, BriAudCD Unabrid) Brilliance Audio.

Day of Judgement. unabr. ed. Scripts. Jack Higgins. Perf. by Aden Gillett. 6 cass. (Running Time: 9 hrs.). 2004. 29.95 (978-1-59007-380-3(0)) Pub: New Millenn Enter. Dist(s): PerseuPGW

Day of Judgment. abr. ed. Jack Higgins. Read by Edward Woodward. 2 cass. (Running Time: 3 hrs.). 2004. 18.00 (978-1-59007-188-5(3)) Pub: New Millenn Enter. Dist(s): PerseuPGW
In May 1963, President John F. Kennedy prepares to make his historic visit to West Berlin, and in East Berlin a covert group of killers prepares its final plan for the destruction of the West. The one man with the power to oppose them is Father Sean Conlin, hero of the West German resistance. In a dungeon far from the border, he is being held by the most brutal man in East Germany, and they have already begun to break him. His only hope: a desperate rescue attempt by a ragtag team of fighter who operate outside official channels. But even as they attempt the impossible, the enemy is lying in the shadows, waiting for the opportunity to destroy the resistance once and for all.

Day of Our Own: Music for a Wedding Liturgy. Liam Lawton. (ENG.). 2004. audio compact disk 26.95 (978-1-85390-875-0(4)) Pub: Veritas Pubns IRL. Dist(s): Dufour

Day of Peace & Rest. Robert C. Bowden. 1 cass. 9.95 (10001344); audio compact disk 14.95 (2800950) Covenant Comms.
Sacred music for the Sabbath day.

Day of Pleasure: Stories of a Boy Growing up in Warsaw. unabr. ed. Isaac Bashevis Singer. Read by Peter MacDonald. 4 cass. (Running Time: 4 hrs.). 1987. 24.00 (978-0-7366-0388-1(3), 1365) Books on Tape.
Contains stories about growing up in a pre-World War I ghetto in Warsaw. These stories explore the boyhood mysteries of urban life. Rich in depictions of religious faith, close family ties & recollection of lost innocence in times irretrievably gone by.

Day of Reckoning. unabr. ed. Jack Higgins. Narrated by Frank Muller. 6 CDs. (Running Time: 6 hrs. 15 mins.). (Sean Dillon Ser.). audio compact disk 58.00 (978-0-7887-4894-3(7), C1269E7) Recorded Bks.
In this layered story of revenge & suspense, a brutal death in Brooklyn sends shock repercussions around the world. When journalist Katherine Johnson learns to much about crime boss Jack Fox, he silences her once & for all. But he does not reckon with her ex-husband Blake Johnson, a former FBI agent with formidable British connections. Intent on hitting Fox where it hurts most, Blake unleashes his own deadly brand of vengeance - destroying Fox's illegal holdings from New York to the Middle East. Available to libraries only.

Day of Reckoning. unabr. ed. Jack Higgins. Narrated by Frank Muller. 5 cass. (Running Time: 6 hrs. 15 mins.). (Sean Dillon Ser.). 2000. 50.00 (978-0-7887-4301-6(5), 96218E7) Recorded Bks.
When journalist Katherine Johnson learns too much about crime boss Jack Fox, he silences her once & for all. But he doesn't reckon with her ex-husband Blake Johnson, a former FBI agent with formidable British connections.

Day of Reckoning. unabr. collector's ed. Jack Higgins. Read by Patrick Macnee. 4 cass. (Running Time: 6 hrs.). (Sean Dillon Ser.). 2000. 29.95 (978-0-7366-5068-7(7), 5282) Books on Tape.
With the president's permission, former FBI agent Blake Johnson sets out to kill the mob boss who murdered his ex-wife.

Day of Tears. unabr. rev. ed. Julius Lester. 3 CDs. (Running Time: 3 hrs.). (YA). (gr. 6-9). 2006. audio compact disk 29.75 (978-1-4193-6811-0(7), C3514); 19.75 (978-1-4193-6806-6(0), 98243) Recorded Bks.
As did his father before him, Pierce Butler treats his plantation slaves like family. But massive gambling debts force him to sell 429 "family" members. When the auction begins, torrential rain falls - not stopping until the final slave is sold the next day. The ominous rainfall prompts these words: "This ain't rain. This is God's tears." Based on the largest slave auction in U.S. history, this poignant montage is the fictionalized account of that 1859 Georgia tragedy. All the shrieks and groans, the betrayal and fury, the sorrow and regret are here in the stark, vivid monologues that pour from the souls of master and slave, auctioneer and observer during this "Weeping Time".

Day of the Archer. Louis Tridico. Abr. by Louis Tridico. Read by Charlie O'Dowd. 3 CDs. (Running Time: 3 hrs.). (Delta Code Ser.: No. 3). 2004. audio compact disk 25.00 (978-1-58807-322-8(X)) Am Pubng Inc.
An American executive's daughter is kidnapped in Colombia and Special Forces veteran Doug Malone and his High Ground security firm are called in to arrange for ransom or rescue. But Colombian politics and a stubborn reporter are in the way. Malone will need to turn lemons into lemonade to save his client's daughter, but he is not the only member of his firm with friends in strange places.

Day of the Archer. abr. ed. Louis Tridico. Abr. by Louis Tridico. Read by Carol Eason. 2 cass. (Running Time: 180 mins.). (Delta Code Ser.: No. 3). 2004. 18.00 (978-1-58807-371-6(8)) Am Pubng Inc.

Day of the Archer: Delta Code #3. abr. ed. Louis Tridico. Abr. by Louis Tridico. Read by Carol Eason. 2 cass. (Running Time: 180 mins.). No. 3. 2004. (978-1-58807-639-7(3)) Am Pubng Inc.

Day of the Dead. John Creed. 7 CDs. (Running Time: 8 hrs.). (Isis (CDs) Ser.). (J). 2004. audio compact disk 71.95 (978-0-7531-2350-8(9)) Pub: ISIS Lrg Prnt GBR. Dist(s): Ulverscroft US

***Day of the Dead.** abr. ed. J. A. Jance. Read by J. R. Horne. (ENG.). 2004. (978-0-06-078265-8(X), Harper Audio); (978-0-06-081376-5(8), Harper Audio) HarperCollins Pubs.

Day of the Dead. abr. ed. J. A. Jance & J. R. Horne. 4 CDs. (Running Time: 6 hrs.). (Brandon Walker Ser.: Bk. 3). 2004. audio compact disk 29.95 (978-0-06-072359-0(9)) HarperCollins Pubs.

Day of the Dead. unabr. ed. John Creed. Read by Sean Barrett. 7 cass. (Running Time: 8 hrs.). (Isis Cassettes Ser.). (J). 2004. 61.95 (978-0-7531-1807-8(6)) Pub: ISIS Lrg Prnt GBR. Dist(s): Ulverscroft US

Day of the Dead. unabr. ed. J. A. Jance. Read by Tim Jerome. 8 cass. (Brandon Walker Ser.: Bk. 3). 2005. bk. 69.95 (978-0-7927-3279-2(0), CSL 678); bk. 94.95 (978-0-7927-3280-8(4), SLD 678); audio compact disk 29.95 (978-0-7927-3281-5(2), CMP 678) AudioGO.

Day of the Dead. unabr. ed. J. A. Jance. Read by Tim Jerome. (Brandon Walker Ser.: Bk. 3). (YA). 2007. 79.99 (978-1-60252-807-9(1)) Find a World.

***Day of the Dead.** unabr. ed. J. A. Jance. Read by Tim Jerome. (ENG.). 2004. (978-0-06-081378-9(4), Harper Audio); (978-0-06-078266-5(8), Harper Audio) HarperCollins Pubs.

Day of the Djinn Warriors. P. B. Kerr. Narrated by Ron Keith. 9 CDs. (Running Time: 11 hrs. 13 mins.). (Children of the Lamp Ser.: No. 4). (ENG.). (J). (gr. 4-7). 2009. audio compact disk 84.95 (978-0-545-11527-8(2)) Scholastic Inc.

Day of the Djinn Warriors. Philip Kerr. Read by Ron Keith. (Running Time: 11 hrs. 13 mins.). (Children of the Lamp Ser.: No. 4). (J). (gr. 4-7). 2009. 75.00 (978-1-60775-490-9(8)) Find a World.

Day of the Dragon King. unabr. ed. Mary Pope Osborne. Read by Mary Pope Osborne. (Running Time: 41 mins.). (Magic Tree House Ser.: No. 14). (J). (gr. k-3). 2004. pap. bk. 17.00 (978-0-8072-0783-3(7), S FTR 242 SP, Listening Lib) Random Audio Pubg.

Day of the Field Trip Zombies. Scott Nickel. 1 CD. (School Zombies Ser.). (J). (gr. 1-4). 2008. audio compact disk 14.60 (978-1-4342-0599-5(1)) CapstoneDig.
The evil scientist Dr. Brainium is up to something fishy. When Trevor and his class take a field trip to an aquarium, Dr. B. turns the students into radio-controlled zombies.

Day of the Hawk **see Crimson Ramblers of the World, Farewell**

Day of the Iguana. Henry Winkler & Lin Oliver. Read by Henry Winkler. 2 vols. (Running Time: 3 hrs.). (Hank Zipzer Ser.: No. 3). (J). (gr. 2-6). 2004. pap. bk. 29.00 (978-1-4000-9008-2(3), Listening Lib) Random Audio Pubg.

Day of the Iguana. unabr. ed. Henry Winkler & Lin Oliver. Read by Henry Winkler. 2 cass. (Running Time: 3 hrs.). (Hank Zipzer Ser.: No. 3). (J). (gr. 2-6). 2004. 23.00 (978-0-8072-2352-9(2), Listening Lib) Random Audio Pubg.
Hank is a fourth grade self-professed "idea man" who has a magic act with his best friends Frankie (the magician) and Ashley (the money person). He talks them into entertaining at his bratty twin cousins' birthday party on Long Island by promising Frankie that he will tape the television broadcast of a rarely shown horror flick. When the taping goes awry, Frankie no longer speaks to Hank. Hank's learning disabilities make it difficult for him to concentrate at school and on homework at the best of times.

***Day of the Jackal.** Frederick Forsyth. Read by Simon Prebble. (Playaway Adult Fiction Ser.). (ENG.). 2010. 69.99 (978-1-4417-1168-7(6)) Find a World.

Day of the Jackal. unabr. ed. Frederick Forsyth. Read by David Rintoul. 10 cass. (Running Time: 10 hrs.). 1995. 84.95 Set. (978-0-7451-6827-2(2), CAB 328) AudioGO.
In 1963, General de Gaulle is not only the President of France, but also the most closely & skillfully guarded figure in the Western World. The Jackal's assignment is to assassinate de Gaulle. Coldly, & with calculated efficiency, he makes his arrangements.

Day of the Jackal, unabr. ed. Frederick Forsyth. Read by Richard Brown. 11 cass. (Running Time: 16 hrs.). 1992. 76.95 (978-0-7861-0283-9(7), 1249) Blckstn Audio.
France, infuriated by Charles de Gaulle's withdrawal from Algeria, had failed in six known attempts to assassinate the General. This book assumes that the seventh, most deadly attempt involved a professional killer-for-hire who would be unknown to the French police. The code name of this killer: Jackal. His price: half a million dollars. His demand: total secrecy, even from his employers.

Day of the Jackal. unabr. ed. Frederick Forsyth. Read by Richard Brown. 13 CDs. (Running Time: 16 hrs.). 2006. audio compact disk 104.00 (978-0-7861-8992-2(4), 1249) Blckstn Audio.

Day of the Jackal. unabr. ed. Frederick Forsyth. (Running Time: 15 hrs.). 2009. audio compact disk 34.95 (978-1-4417-1164-9(3)) Blckstn Audio.

Day of the Jackal. unabr. ed. Frederick Forsyth. Read by Simon Prebble. (Running Time: 15 hrs. 0 mins.). 2009. 29.95 (978-1-4417-1165-6(1)); 85.95 (978-1-4417-1161-8(9)); audio compact disk 104.00 (978-1-4417-1162-5(7)) Blckstn Audio.

Day of the Jackal. unabr. ed. Frederick Forsyth. Read by David Case. 9 cass. (Running Time: 13 hrs. 30 min.). 1989. 72.00 (978-0-7366-1481-8(8), 2357) Books on Tape.
It is a fact that Charles de Gaulle's enemies launched six major assassination attempts. All failed. This book assumes that a seventh, more deadly attempt was organized in 1963 & that it employed an outsider, a professional: the Jackal.

Day of the Jackal. unabr. ed. Frederick Forsyth. Read by David Rintoul. 10 cass. (Running Time: 15 hrs.). 2000. 49.95 (SAB 032) Pub: Chivers Audio Bks GBR. Dist(s): AudioGO
In 1963, General de Gaulle is not only the President of France, but also the most closely guarded figure in the Western World. The Jackal's assignment is to assassinate de Gaulle. Coldly, and with calculated efficiency, he makes his arrangements.

Day of the Pelican. unabr. ed. Katherine Paterson. Read by Tavia Gilbert. (Running Time: 4 hrs.). 2009. 39.97 (978-1-4418-0209-5(6), 9781441802095, Brlnc Audio MP3 Lib); 19.99 (978-1-4418-0210-1(X), 9781441802101, BAD); 39.97 (978-1-4418-0211-8(8), 9781441802118, BADLE); audio compact disk 24.99 (978-1-4418-0206-4(1), 9781441802064, Bril Audio CD Unabri) Brilliance Audio.

Day of the Pelican. unabr. ed. Katherine Paterson. Read by Tavia Gilbert. 1 MP3-CD. (Running Time: 4 hrs.). (YA). 2009. 19.99 (978-1-4418-0208-8(8), 9781441802088, Brilliance MP3) Brilliance Audio.

Day of the Pelican. unabr. ed. Katherine Paterson. Read by Tavia Gilbert. 4 CDs. (Running Time: 4 hrs.). (YA). (gr. 5-8). 2009. audio compact disk 69.97 (978-1-4418-0207-1(X), 9781441802071, BriAudCD Unabrid) Brilliance Audio.

Day of the Scorpion. unabr. ed. Paul Scott. Read by Garard Green. 16 cass. (Running Time: 21 hrs. 30 mins.). (Raj Quartet: No. 2). (J). 1999. 104.95 (978-0-7531-0340-1(0), 980505) Pub: ISIS Lrg Prnt GBR. Dist(s): Ulverscroft US
Ex-Chief Minister Mohammed Ali Kasim's detainment by police officers at his home in Ranpur is the first of the wholesale arrests of influential Indians suspected of sympathizing with the Congress Committee's call on the British to quit India. For families such as the Laytons, who have livid & served in India for generations, the social & political realities are both disturbing & tragic. While they are forced to confront the violent years that lie ahead of them the shadow of Daphne Manner's death & the inhumane treatment of her young Indian lover, Hari Kumar, continues to cast a shadow over Imperial India.

Day of the Scorpion. unabr. collector's ed. Paul Scott. Read by Richard Brown. 8 cass. (Running Time: 12 hrs.). (Raj Quartet: No. 2). 1992. 64.00 (978-0-7366-2099-4(0), 2905A); 72.00 (978-0-7366-2100-7(8), 2905B) Books on Tape.
Change becomes the only constant for those caught up in the turmoil of British India during WW II.

Day of the Storm. unabr. ed. Rosamunde Pilcher. Read by Kelly Hunter. 6 cass. (Running Time: 6 hrs.). 1996. 54.95 Set. (978-0-7451-4315-6(6), CAB 998) AudioGO.
When Rebecca Bayliss rushes to the bedside of her dying mother, she is confronted by more than grief when her mother reveals the existence of a family her daughter knows nothing about. Rebecca is determined to find this family, & her destination is a Cornwall mansion that reveals her grandfather's explosive secret & Joss Gardner, a sensual craftsmen with an intriguing past. Rebecca realizes that her family's mystery may hold the key to her future.

Day of the Storm. unabr. ed. Rosamunde Pilcher. Read by Donada Peters. 6 cass. (Running Time: 6 hrs.). 1992. 48.00 (978-0-7366-2170-0(9), 2969) Books on Tape.
On her deathbed, Rebecca's mother reveals a hidden family. Determined to find her family, Rebecca journeys to a Cornwall mansion & into relationships torn by passion & greed.

***Day of the Triffids.** abr. ed. John Wyndham. Narrated by Alex Jennings. 4 CDs. (Running Time: 5 hrs. 0 mins. 0 sec.). (ENG.). 2010. audio compact disk 26.95 (978-1-934997-60-4(9)) Pub: CSAWord. Dist(s): PerseuPGW

Day of the Triffids. unabr. ed. John Wyndham. Read by Samuel West. 8 cass. (Running Time: 12 hrs.). 1996. 59.95 (978-0-7451-6587-5(7), CAB 1203) Pub: Chivers Audio Bks GBR. Dist(s): AudioGO
The Triffids are a monstrous species of stinging plants: they walk, they talk, they dominate the world.The end of the old world had come & a new & terrifying world was on the horizon. Any survivors had to contend with its fantastic, yet horrific & thoroughly plausible truth. A razor-edge balance between wry satire & stark tragedy.

Day of the Triffids: Classic Radio Sci-Fi. John Wyndham. (Running Time: 2 hrs. 55 mins. 0 sec.). (ENG.). 2009. audio compact disk 29.95 (978-1-60283-778-2(3)) Pub: AudioGO. Dist(s): Perseus Dist

Day of Wrath. unabr. ed. Larry Bond. Read by Michael Prichard. 12 cass. (Running Time: 18 hrs.). 1998. 96.00 (978-0-7366-4187-6(4), 4685) Books on Tape.
A plane carrying an American arms inspection team mysteriously crashes in Russia. Not long afterward, a senior American diplomat is assassinated. The warning shots have been fired. A bold gambit to destroy America as a world power is well under way.

Day on Trial: Advocacy for the New Millenniem. Thomas A. Mauet & Dominic J. Gianna. Instructed by Thomas A. Mauet & Dominic J. Gianna. 6 cass. (Running Time: 6 hrs.). 2001. pap. bk. 185.00 (978-0-943380-93-3(6)) PEG MN.

Day on Trial! Advocacy for the New Millennium. Thomas A. Mauet & Dominic J. Gianna. 6 CDs. (Running Time: 6 hrs.). 2002. pap. bk. 205.00 (978-0-943380-66-7(9)) PEG MN.

Day the Birds Sang. Kit Watson. (J). 2007. audio compact disk 9.99 (978-1-60247-186-3(X)) Tate Pubng.

Day the Cowboys Quit. abr. ed. Elmer Kelton. Read by Ronald Wilcox. Ed. by Stephen Holland. 4 cass. (Running Time: 6 hrs.). (Texas Tradition Ser.: No. 7). 1993. 24.95 set. (978-1-883268-03-9(6)) Spellbinders.
A novel built around the true event of a cowboy strike in 1883.

Day the Earth Stood Still. Read by Michael Rennie. Based on a story by Harry Bates. 1 cass. (Running Time: 1 hr.). 7.95 (SF-8020) Natl Recrd Co.
In the first presentation a visitor from another planet & his robot, Gork, land in Washington D. C. & request to meet all of the great leaders of the world, before Earth is destroyed. "Exploring Tomorrow" is an exciting science fiction story of an interplanetary space liner, "The Martian Queen", hurtling toward Earth on a collision course of 216,000 miles per second.

Day the Falls Stood Still. unabr. ed. Cathy Marie Buchanan. Narrated by Karen White. 1 MP3-CD. (Running Time: 11 hrs. 30 mins. 0 sec.). (ENG.). 2009. 24.99 (978-1-4001-6481-3(8)); audio compact disk 69.99 (978-1-4001-4481-5(7)); audio compact disk 34.99 (978-1-4001-1481-8(0)) Pub: Tantor Media. Dist(s): IngramPubServ

***Day the Falls Stood Still.** unabr. ed. Cathy Marie Buchanan. Narrated by Karen White. (Running Time: 11 hrs. 30 mins.). 2009. 17.99 (978-1-4001-8481-1(9)) Tantor Media.

Day the Lights Went Out: On Going Blind. 1 cass. (Running Time: 30 min.). 9.95 (HO-85-06-19, HarperThor) HarpC GBR.

Day the Rabbi Resigned. unabr. ed. Harry Kemelman. Narrated by George Guidall. 5 cass. (Running Time: 7 hrs. 15 mins.). (Rabbi Small Mystery Ser.). 1992. 48.00 (978-0-7887-4631-4(6), 96341E7) Recorded Bks.
For nearly 25 years, Rabbi Small has maintained an uneasy relationship with his congregation. Now, just as they are set to reward him for his long service, the rabbi has decided to explore new options with his life. To make things more complicated, the recent murder of a college professor has the Barnard's Crossing police baffled. Can the rabbi's quiet introspection offer insights the police may have overlooked?.

Day the Thames Caught Fire. unabr. ed. Peter Chambers. Read by Terry Wale. 8 cass. (Running Time: 12 hrs.). (Sound Ser.). 2004. 69.95 (978-1-85496-800-5(9), 68009) Pub: UlverLrgPrint GBR. Dist(s): Ulverscroft US
Mercenary Philip Baxter's mission entails the theft of 10 million pounds in gold bullion from a Thameside warehouse. Of his reward he is uncertain - does anyone intend to pay him his money, or is he being double-crossed?.

Day the TV Broke. unabr. ed. Roni S. Denholtz. Illus. by Nelsy Fontalvo. (Running Time: 7 min.). (Friends & Neighbors Ser.). (J). (gr. k-2). 1986. lib. bdg. 16.99 incl. hardcover. (978-0-87386-016-1(0)) Jan Prods.
The TV in Jose's house is broken. It's too cold & snowy to play outside so he puts on his own TV show with his friends.

Day the Universe Changed. abr. ed. James Burke. Read by James Burke. 3 CDs. (Running Time: 10800 sec.). (ENG.). 2006. audio compact disk 19.95 (978-1-59397-979-9(7)) Pub: Macmill Audio. Dist(s): Macmillan

Day the War Ended: May 8, 1945 - Victory in Europe. unabr. collector's ed. Martin Gilbert. Read by David Case. 15 cass. (Running Time: 22 hrs. 30 min.). 1996. 120.00 (978-0-7366-3210-2(7), 3873) Books on Tape.
The lights come on, church bells ring, couples embrace, the bereaved mourn their loved ones. It's May 8, 1945, the last day of a war that has lasted five years & eight months. German forces have already capitulated, & at 30 minutes before midnight, the German High Command signs the final instrument of surrender. The world rejoices & asks, "What now?" Here are the stories of that wonderful, long-awaited day, a half century ago: the stories of the front-line troops & civilians; of the statesmen & the war criminals, the victors & the vanquished. It is VE Day, & although Japan fights on, May 8, 1945 marks the start of a new era for all nations.

Day the World Ended at Little Big Horn: A Lakota History. unabr. ed. Joseph M. Marshall, III. Read by Joseph M. Marshall, III. (Running Time: 30600 sec.). 2007. 59.95 (978-1-4332-0598-9(X)); audio compact disk 29.95 (978-1-4332-0600-9(5)) Blckstn Audio.

Day the World Ended at Little Bighorn: A Lakota History. unabr. ed. Joseph M. Marshall, III. Read by Joseph M. Marshall, III. (Running Time: 30600 sec.). 2007. audio compact disk 72.00 (978-1-4332-0599-6(8)) Blckstn Audio.

Day Trader. unabr. ed. Stephen Frey. Read by Grover Gardner. 7 CDs. (Running Time: 10 hrs. 30 mins.). 2001. audio compact disk 56.00 (978-0-7366-8497-2(2)) Books on Tape.
Augustus McKnight, nearly broke, is losing the love of his wife Melanie. His only respite is day trading, where a sudden windfall gives him some of his dignity back. It is too late for his marriage, though. His wife admits an affair and requests a divorce. A day later, she is found with her throat slit on the streets of New York. Augustus is the beneficiary of her million-dollar life insurance policy. To ease his pain, he goes into day trading full time, and is remarkably successful. But he is being pursued by a relentless insurance investigator and by a relentless cop, both intending to prove he murdered Melanie for the money. He discovers he is the pawn in a dark conspiracy, and the target of revenge.

Day Trading Smart Right from the Start. Instructed by David Nassar. (Trade Secrets Audio Ser.). 2000. 19.95 (978-1-883272-70-8(X)) Marketplace Bks.

Day Trading Tools: Finding the Right Combination of Data & Software. Instructed by Robert Deel. (Trade Secrets Audio Ser.). 2000. 19.95 (978-1-883272-73-9(4)) Marketplace Bks.

Day Trading Wizard. Instructed by Tony Oz. (Trade Secrets Audio Ser.). 2000. 19.95 (978-1-883272-71-5(8)) Marketplace Bks.

Day We Found the Universe. unabr. ed. Marcia Bartusiak. Read by Erik Synnestvedt. (Running Time: 10 hrs. 30 mins.). (ENG.). 2009. 29.98 (978-1-59659-396-1(2), GildAudio) Pub: Gildan Media. Dist(s): HachBkGrp

Day Will Come. unabr. ed. Audrey Howard. Read by Kelly Hunter. 16 cass. (Running Time: 16 hrs.). 1997. 124.95 Set. (978-0-7540-0043-3(5), CAB 1466) AudioGO.
Daisy Brindle is hired by a brutal master for stone picking in Lancashire. Miles Thornley, heir to a great estate, seduces her & then casually casts her aside. Driven to the streets, Daisy is rescued by Sam Lassiter, & as his wife & business partner, Daisy comes to enjoy the better things in life. But her drive for revenge on Miles threatens the destruction of her marriage.

Day with a Perfect Stranger. unabr. ed. David Gregory. Read by Ellen Reilly. (Running Time: 7200 sec.). (ENG.). 2006. audio compact disk 12.95 (978-0-7393-3331-0(3), Random AudioBks) Pub: Random Audio Pubg. Dist(s): Random

Day with Dr. Bernie Siegel. 3 cass. 27.00 (BS3) Sound Horizons AV.
Siegel shares some amazingly heart-warming stories about his experiences and techniques treating cancer patients.

Day with Mother Teresa. Mother Teresa of Calcutta. Read by Mother Teresa of Calcutta. Ed. by James Downey. 2 cass. (Running Time: 3 hrs.). 1981. 8.00 Set. (8 IP) IRL Chicago.
Speaks on a variety of topics - family life, life as a nun, loving God & serving people, etc.

Day with Two Scientific Consciousness Explorers. John Lilly & Claudio Naranjo. 3 cass. 27.00 set. (A0065-87) Sound Photosyn.
These two great adventurers inspire us & each other with stories, reminiscences, & speculations at satisfying length. Perhaps never appearing together again, Lilly & Naranjo trace their illustrious histories, individually & together, each a seeker & a sought.

***Day with Wilbur Robinson.** unabr. ed. William Joyce. Read by Jim Dale. (ENG.). 2007. (978-0-06-145215-4(7)); (978-0-06-147290-9(5)) HarperCollins Pubs.

Daybreak. Ed. by Robert A. Monroe. 1 cass. (Running Time: 30 min.). (Meta Music Artist Ser.). 1989. 14.95 (978-1-56102-206-9(3)) Inter Indus.
A full orchestral treatment of the change from one state of awareness to another, as darkness becomes light, then the explosive brilliance of sun rays onto a mental countryside - & into the day itself.

Daybreak. unabr. ed. Belva Plain. Read by Kate Harper. 10 cass. (Running Time: 10 hrs.). 1995. 84.95 set. (978-0-7451-6562-2(1), CAB 1178) AudioGO.
When blood tests reveal that the Crawfield's dying son is not theirs, they discover a hospital mix-up after his birth, & that their biological son still lives. Meanwhile, in the Rice family, Laura & her husband are virtual strangers to one another, while their elder son is caught up in the town's violent political upheaval. Against this background of newly discovered truths, the story draws to a jolting, soul-shattering conclusion.

Daybreak - Sundown. D.A. Tubesing. 1 cass. (Running Time: 44 min.). (Sensational Relaxation Ser.: No. 6). 11.95 (978-0-938586-83-8(1), DS) Whole Person.
When modern life puts you out of touch with your natural rhythms, this tape can help restore the balance. Use it at your bedside for a wonderful drug-free way to wake up in the morning & wind down at night. Side A: Daybreak. Experience a new beginning any time of the day with visions of a sunrise that put you at peace, yet full of energy. Side B: Sundown. Sunset images help you let go of the day's stress & strain & drift into a peaceful natural state.

Daybreakers. unabr. ed. Louis L'Amour. Read by David Strathairn. 5 CDs. (Running Time: 21600 sec.). (Sacketts Ser.: No. 6). (ENG.). 2006. audio compact disk 25.95 (978-0-7393-1904-8(3)) Pub: Random Audio Pubg. Dist(s): Random

Daycare As a Business. 1 cass. (Running Time: 21 min.). 10.95 (D0200B090, HarperThor) HarpC GBR.

Daydream Believers: How a Few Grand Ideas Wrecked American Power. unabr. ed. Fred Kaplan. Read by Stefan Rudnicki. (Running Time: 28800 sec.). 2008. 24.95 (978-1-4332-0961-1(6)); 54.95 (978-1-4332-0959-8(4)); audio compact disk 24.95 (978-1-4332-0962-8(4)); audio compact disk & audio compact disk 29.95 (978-1-4332-0963-5(2)); audio compact disk & audio compact disk 55.00 (978-1-4332-0960-4(8)) Blckstn Audio.

Daydreamer. Perf. by Priscilla Herdman. 1 cass. (J). 1993. 9.98 (978-1-56628-011-2(7), 42591); audio compact disk 15.98 (978-1-56628-010-5(9), 42591D) MFLP CA.
This album is dedicated to daydreamers of all ages & comes with the wish that no matter how old you grow, you'll never forget how to dream with your eyes & your heart wide open.

Daydreamer. unabr. ed. 4 cass. (Running Time: 3 hrs.). 2005. 19.75 (978-1-4025-3986-2(X)) Recorded Bks.

Daydreams & Lullabies. Susan Hammond. 1 cass., 1. 1993. audio compact disk 18.98 (978-1-895404-68-5(1)) Consort Bk Sales.

Daydreams & Lullabies. Susan Hammond. 1 cass. (J). 1993. 18.98; 10.98 (978-1-895404-66-1(5)) Consort Bk Sales.

Daydreams Three: Relaxing Retreats. Andrew Schwartz & Nancy L. Tubesing. 1 cass. (Running Time: 44 min.). 1995. 11.95 (978-1-57025-069-9(3)) Whole Person.
Relaxation cassette: Six opportunities for letting go of tension & creating inner peace - all through the power of your imagination.

Daylight Saving & God. 1 cass. (Running Time: 29 min.). 12.00 (L330) MEA A Watts Cass.

Days see Poetry of Ralph Waldo Emerson

Days Between. Allen M. Steele. Narrated by Tom Dheere. (ENG.). 2008. audio compact disk 10.99 (978-1-884612-81-7(4)) AudioText.

Days Gone By. 1 cass. (Running Time: 60 min.). 2001. 9.98 (978-1-56628-244-4(6)); audio compact disk 15.98 (978-1-56628-243-7(8)) MFLP CA.
Includes 11 original songs based on the poetry of well-known nineteenth-century American poets.

Days Gone By Vol. 1: Songs of the American Poets. James Whitcomb Riley et al. Perf. by Ted Jacobs. 1 cass. (Running Time: 90 mins.). (J). 2000. 9.98 MFLP CA.
An introduction to the world of 19th century poetry through music.

Days Gone By Vol. 1: Songs of the American Poets. James Whitcomb Riley et al. Perf. by Ted Jacobs. 1 CD. (Running Time: 90 mins.). (J). 2000. audio compact disk 15.98 MFLP CA.

Days in the Life: The Lost Beatles Archives. 2001. 7.99 (978-0-9711870-2-3(9)) Thane Intl Inc.

Days Jimmy's Boa Ate the Wash. 2004. pap. bk. 14.95 (978-1-56008-044-2(2)) Weston Woods.

Days of Defiance. Maury Klein. 15 cass. (Running Time: 12 hrs. 30 mins.). 2001. 120.00 (978-0-7366-6355-7(X)) Books on Tape.
Abraham Lincoln's November 1860 election set in motion one of the most extraordinary series of events in American history. The secession of South Carolina in December exposed the essential weakness of the federal government. Meanwhile, a thrilling siege in Charleston harbor gripped the attention of Northerners & Southerners alike.

Days of drums: A Novel. Philip Selby. 2004. 10.95 (978-0-7435-4582-2(6)) Pub: S&S Audio. Dist(s): S and S Inc

Days of Gold. (Running Time: 60 mins.). 2002. audio compact disk 15.99 (978-1-904972-64-8(0)) Global Jmy GBR GBR.

Days of Gold. abr. ed. Jude Deveraux. Read by Gabra Zackman. (Running Time: 6 hrs. 0 mins. 0 sec.). (Edilean Ser.: Bk. 2). 2009. audio compact disk 29.99 (978-0-7435-9893-4(8)) Pub: S&S Audio. Dist(s): S and S Inc

***Days of Gold.** abr. ed. Jude Deveraux. Read by Gabra Zackman. (Running Time: 6 hrs. 0 mins. 0 sec.). Bk. 2. (ENG.). 2010. audio compact disk 14.99 (978-1-4423-3641-4(2)) Pub: S&S Audio. Dist(s): S and S Inc

***Days of Grace: A Novel.** unabr. ed. Catherine Hall. Narrated by Josephine Bailey. (Running Time: 10 hrs. 30 mins. 0 sec.). (ENG.). 2010. 24.99 (978-1-4001-6740-1(X)); 15.99 (978-1-4001-8740-9(0)); audio compact disk 34.99 (978-1-4001-1740-6(2)); audio compact disk 83.99 (978-1-4001-4740-3(9)) Pub: Tantor Media. Dist(s): IngramPubServ

Days of Grace: Meditations & Practices for Living with Illness. Mary C. Earle. Read by Mary C. Earle. Music by Ben T. King. Explorefaith.org. (ENG.). 2008. (978-0-9798958-8-3(X)) Mat Media.

Days of Grace: Meditations & Practices for Living with Illness. Mary C. Earle. Read by Mary C. Earle. Music by Ben T. King. Concept by Explorefaith.org. (ENG.). 2008. audio compact disk (978-0-9798958-9-0(8)) Mat Media.

Days of Infamy. Walter Lord. 6 CDs. (Running Time: 9 hrs.). 2000. audio compact disk 59.99 (z1711) Blckstn Audio.

Days of Infamy. unabr. ed. Newt Gingrich & William R. Forstchen. Read by William Dufris. 10 CDs. (Running Time: 12 hrs. 30 mins. 0 sec.). (ENG.). 2008. audio compact disk 39.95 (978-1-4272-0427-1(6)) Pub: Macmill Audio. Dist(s): Macmillan

***Days of Infamy.** unabr. ed. Harry Turtledove. Narrated by John Allen Nelson. (Running Time: 20 hrs. 0 mins. 0 sec.). (Days of Infamy Ser.). (ENG.). 2010. audio compact disk 99.99 (978-1-4001-4392-4(6)) Pub: Tantor Media. Dist(s): IngramPubServ

***Days of Infamy: A Novel of Alternate History.** unabr. ed. Harry Turtledove. Narrated by John Allen Nelson. (Running Time: 20 hrs. 0 mins.). (Days of Infamy Ser.). 2010. 23.99 (978-1-4001-8392-0(8)) Tantor Media.

***Days of Infamy: A Novel of Alternate History.** unabr. ed. Harry Turtledove. Narrated by John Allen Nelson. (Running Time: 20 hrs. 0 mins. 0 sec.). (Days of Infamy Ser.). (ENG.). 2010. 34.99 (978-1-4001-6392-2(7)); audio compact disk 49.99 (978-1-4001-1392-7(X)) Pub: Tantor Media. Dist(s): IngramPubServ

Days of Infamy: Military Blunders of the 20th Century. collector's unabr. ed. Michael Coffey. Read by Robert Abia. 8 CDs. (Running Time: 9 hrs. 25 mins.). 2000. audio compact disk 34.95 (978-0-7366-5214-8(0)) Books on Tape.
A concise review of modern military blunders from the trivial to the monumental that underscores the expected nature of war.

Days of Infamy: Military Blunders of the 20th Century. unabr. ed. Michael Coffey. Read by Robert Abia. 8 CDs. (Running Time: 12 hrs.). 2000. audio compact disk 32.00 (978-0-7366-5048-9(2)) Books on Tape.

Days of Infamy: Military Blunders of the 20th Century. unabr. ed. Michael Coffey. Read by Robert Abia. 6 cass. (Running Time: 9 hrs.). 2001. 29.95 (978-0-7366-4933-9(6)) Books on Tape.

Days of Infamy: Military Blunders of the 20th Century. unabr. collector's ed. Michael Coffey. Read by Robert Abia. 6 cass. (Running Time: 9 hrs.). 1999. 29.95 (978-0-7366-4835-6(6), 5182) Books on Tape.

Days of Little Texas. unabr. ed. R. A. Nelson. Read by Luke Daniels. 7 CDs. (Running Time: 8 hrs.). (YA). (gr. 9 up). 2009. audio compact disk 69.97 (978-1-4233-9482-2(8), 9781423394822, BriAudCD Unabrid) Brilliance Audio.

Days of Little Texas. unabr. ed. R. A. Nelson. Read by Luke Daniels. (Running Time: 8 hrs.). 2009. 24.99 (978-1-4233-9483-9(6), 9781423394839, Brilliance MP3); 39.97 (978-1-4233-9484-6(4), 9781423394846, Brinc Audio MP3 Lib); 24.99 (978-1-4233-9485-3(2), 9781423394853, BAD); 39.97 (978-1-4233-9486-0(0), 9781423394860, BADLE); audio compact disk 29.99 (978-1-4233-9481-5(X), 9781423394815, Bril Audio CD Unabri) Brilliance Audio.

Days of Magic, Nights of War. Clive Barker. Narrated by Richard Ferrone. 11 cass. (Running Time: 14 hrs. 30 mins.). (YA). 2004. 94.75 (978-1-4193-0577-1(8)); audio compact disk 116.75 (978-1-4193-1821-4(7)) Recorded Bks.

Days of Magic, Nights of War. unabr. ed. Clive Barker. Read by Richard Ferrone. 10 cass. (Running Time: 15 hrs.). (J). 2004. audio compact disk 39.95 (978-0-06-073589-0(9), HarperChildAud) HarperCollins Pubs.

Days of My Life. Contrib. by Antonio Neal et al. Prod. by Tedd T. 2005. audio compact disk 16.98 (978-5-558-97843-8(0)) Pt of Grace Ent.

Days of Oaks, Years of Salt. Lucienne Bloch. 1 cass. (Running Time: 30 min.). 10.95 (AO-110, HarperThor) HarpC GBR.

Days of Obligation. unabr. ed. Richard Rodriguez. Read by Michael Anthony. 6 cass. (Running Time: 8 hrs 30 mins.). 1994. 44.95 (978-0-7861-0787-2(1), 1512) Blckstn Audio.
Mexico & the United States are portrayed as moral rivals upon the landscape of Mr. Rodriguez's beloved California. Mexico wears the mask of tragedy, the United States wears the mask of comedy. By the end of the book the reader recognizes an historical irony: the United States is becoming a culture of tragedy; Mexico, meanwhile, revels in youthful optimism. Mexico & the United States have changed roles.

Days of Obligation: An Argument with My Mexican Father. unabr. ed. Richard Rodriguez & Michael Anthony. (Running Time: 8 hrs. NaN mins.).

2008. 29.95 (978-1-4332-5475-8(1)); audio compact disk 70.00 (978-1-4332-5474-1(3)) Blckstn Audio.

Days of Rondo. abr. ed. Evelyn Fairbanks. Read by Evelyn Fairbanks. 2 cass. (Running Time: 2 hrs. 35 min.). (Borealis Ser.). 1993. reel tape 16.95 set. (978-0-87351-289-3(8), Borealis Book) Minn Hist.
Evelyn reads from her book, "The Days of Rondo", about growing up during the 1930s & 1940s in St. Paul's largest black community.

Days of the French Revolution. collector's ed. Christopher Hibbert. Read by David Case. 8 cass. (Running Time: 12 hrs.). 2000. 64.00 (978-0-7366-5581-1(6)) Books on Tape.
This is a fresh, original & vibrant retelling of the French Revolution, the epochal events of which have had so much influence on our own times. Hibbert highlights the events of the most momentous days, the storming of the Bastille, the Declaration of the Rights of Man, the king's attempt to flee, the Bloody Terror, the betrayals of Thermidor & Napoleon's coup. Brought to life are the unforgettable men & women who influenced the course of the Revolution.

Days of Wine & Roses/Sensual Sax - the Bob Wilber All-Stars: Alto Sax Play-along Book/CD Pack. Bob Wilber. 2007. pap. bk. 24.98 (978-1-59615-599-2(X), 159615599X) Pub: Music Minus. Dist(s): H Leonard

Days of '49. unabr. ed. Wyman Windsor. Narrated by Donnie Blanz. Prod. by Joe Loesch. 2 cass. (Running Time: 2 hrs.). (Americana Ser.). 1999. 16.95 (978-1-887729-70-3(4)) Toy Box Prods.
On January 24th, 1848, a carpenter found a small bit of gold in the American River of California. Gold Fever swept the country. By the end of 1849, more than 80,000 miners & prospectors were at work digging.

Days of '49 - the California Gold Rush. Jimmy Gray. Read by Donnie Blanz et al. (Running Time: 3 hrs.). 2005. 20.95 (978-1-60083-565-0(1), Audiofy Corp) Iofy Corp.

Days to Remember, Vol. 31. Focus on the Family Staff & AIO Team Staff. 4 CDs. (Running Time: 6 hrs.). (Adventures in Odyssey Ser.: Vol. 31). (J). (gr. 3-7). 1998. audio compact disk 24.99 (978-1-56179-684-7(0)) Pub: Focus Family. Dist(s): Tyndale Hse

Days with Frog & Toad. Arnold Lobel. Read by Arnold Lobel. 1 read-along cass. (Running Time: 15 min.). (I Can Read Bks.). (J). (gr. 1-3). 1979. HarperCollins Pubs.
One side has a turn-the-page beep signal & other is uninterrupted narration for more experienced readers.

Days with Frog & Toad. Arnold Lobel. (J). 1982. 18.66 (978-0-394-69359-0(0)) SRA McGraw.

***Days with Frog & Toad.** abr. ed. Arnold Lobel. Read by Arnold Lobel. (ENG.). 2006. (978-0-06-123224-4(6)) HarperCollins Pubs.

***Days with Frog & Toad.** unabr. ed. Arnold Lobel. Read by Arnold Lobel. (ENG.). 2008. (978-0-06-171237-1(X)) HarperCollins Pubs.

Days with Frog & Toad. unabr. abr. ed. Arnold Lobel. Illus. by Arnold Lobel. 1 cass. (I Can Read Bks.). (J). (ps-3). 1990. 8.99 (978-1-55994-227-0(4)) HarperCollins Pubs.

Days with Henry & Mudge. Cynthia Rylant. Illus. by Suçie Stevenson. 44 vols. (Running Time: 40 mins.). (Henry & Mudge Ser.). 2000. pap. bk. 68.95 (978-1-59112-853-3(6)) Live Oak Media.

Days with Henry & Mudge. Cynthia Rylant. Read by John Beach. Illus. by Suçie Stevenson. 44 vols. (Running Time: 40 mins.). (Henry & Mudge Ser.). (J). (gr. k-3). 2000. pap. bk. 61.95 (978-0-87499-705-7(4)) Live Oak Media.
Includes: "Henry & Mudge & the Careful Cousin," "Henry & Mudge & the Long Weekend," "Henry & Mudge Get the Cold Shivers" & "Henry & Mudge & the Forever Sea.".

DayStarters Vol. 1: Becoming Intimate with God. Narrated by Ron Jenson. Prod. by Randy Ray. 3 cass. (Running Time: 90 min.). 1993. 17.98 (978-1-57919-006-4(5)) Randolf Prod.
Praise, Bible teaching & prayer.

DayStarters Vol. 2: Discovering the Secrets of Encouragement. Narrated by Ron Jenson. Prod. by Randy Ray. 3 cass. (Running Time: 3 hrs.). 1995. 17.98 (978-1-57919-007-1(3)) Randolf Prod.

Dayton & Daughter. unabr. ed. Tessa Barclay. Read by Marie McCarthy. 14 cass. (Running Time: 18 hrs. 45 mins.). 2000. 99.95 (978-1-86042-642-1(5), 26425) Pub: Soundings Ltd GBR. Dist(s): Ulverscroft US

Dayton & Daughter. unabr. ed. Tessa Barclay. Read by Marie McCarthy. 14 CDs. (Running Time: 14.5 hrs.). (Sound Ser.). 2002. audio compact disk 104.95 (978-1-86042-911-8(4)) Pub: UlverLrgPrint GBR. Dist(s): Ulverscroft US
Beth Dayton has spent several years in Denmark where her architectural designs have won many awards. Reaching her thirtieth birthday, her father, also an architect, offers her a place in the family firm and the opportunity to return home to York. It isn't long before Beth's modern approach and interest in conservation finds her in the midst of controversy, especially when she discovers her father has been doing some 'wheeling and dealing' with the local demolition firm in connection with a contract that they have won to redevelop a local town centre.

Daytrading 101: Myths vs. Reality. Instructed by David Nassar. (Running Time: 60 mins.). 2000. 19.95 (978-1-883272-67-8(X)) Marketplace Bks.
t?s the greatest bull market ever and you want to get your share of the profits, but you know you need to eliminate as many risks as possible. Now you can get step-by-step instructions for getting started in day trading from this leading expert in the field. David Nassar shares his knowledge and allows you to take advantage of his 14-plus years of trading experience to reduce your errors. You?ll learn the most common mistakes new day traders make and how to understand and avoid them. Your motivation is the key to continuously improving your returns and this audio tells you exactly what you need to realize about yourself to ensure your success.The basics are all here:- How orders flow- What market makers do and how they make money- What makes day trading possible- What kind of support you will need- What to look for in your trading firmWith so much information out there on day trading what do you believe? In this powerful audio Nassar shares with you the Seven Myths of Day Trading. These misconceptions could be costly, but by understanding them and how they impact your trading, you can find the winning strategies quicker. You get clear definitions of crucial concepts like the difference between online trading and direct access trading. Learn the different trading disciplines; day trading, swing trading, and trend trading so you can decide which best fits you and which will make you the most money. The tools are here as well, even information on how to use Level II screens to set your trades up to win. From what day trading is to specific techniques you can use, this is the best place to start.

Daytripping to Bath. unabr. ed. Ronald Hutton. Read by Ronald Hutton. Ed. by Craig Mayes. 2 cass. (Running Time: 2 hrs.). (Personal Courier Ser.). 1991. 19.95 Set. (978-1-878877-05-5(4)) Educ Excursions.
An audio excursion to the historic city of Bath, famous since Roman times. Designed for travelers & armchair listeners alike. The narration weaves its way through the history of Bath & through its legends. Also includes the prehistoric sites of Silbury Hill & Avebury Temple.

Daytripping to Oxford & Stratford-upon-Avon. unabr. ed. Ronald Hutton. Read by Ronald Hutton. Ed. by Craig Mayes. 2 cass. (Running Time: 2 hrs.). (Personal Courier Ser.). 1991. 19.95 Set. (978-1-878877-04-8(6)) Educ Excursions.
For travelers & armchair listeners, the history of Oxford & Stratford, including local legends, folk tales, & a fascinating look at the man behind the plays - William Shakespeare.

Daytripping to Stonehenge, Salisbury & Winchester. Ronald Hutton. Read by Ronald Hutton. Ed. by Craig Mayes. 2 cass. (Running Time: 1 hr. 40 min.). (Personal Courier Ser.). 1990. 19.95 (978-1-878877-03-1(8), 03-8) Educ Excursions.
A spellbinding excursion from London to the Salisbury Plain with British historian Dr. Ronald Hutton, as he relates the facts & theories behind the 5000 years of Stonehenge's mysterious existence...then continues to Salisbury & tales of Old Sarum...& finally, on to the ancient capital of Winchester & its rich history.

Daze on the Plains: A New Yorker on the Level. Pat Staten. (ENG.). (gr. 4). 1992. audio compact disk 19.95 (978-1-55591-085-3(8)) Pub: Fulcrum Pub. Dist(s): Consort Bk Sales

Dazhan - Lecture on Tape. Douglas Dunn. 1 cass. (Running Time: 90 min.). 1989. 6.95 (978-0-944363-05-8(9)) Word Wizards.
Step-by-step program of interpersonal relations. Skills & techniques based on enjoying happiness through compassion & goodwill.

Dazzle. abr. ed. Judith Gould. Read by Theresa Saldana. 2 cass. (Running Time: 3 hrs.). 2000. 7.95 (978-1-57815-059-5(0), 1016, Media Bks Audio) Media Bks NJ.
Three generations of fire & fame, they were born to star, born to dazzle! Three lives burning with power & passion.

Dazzle. abr. ed. Judith Gould. Read by Theresa Saldana. 3 vols. (YA). 2001. audio compact disk 11.99 (978-1-57815-519-4(3), Media Bks Audio) Media Bks NJ.

Dazzle. abr. ed. Judith Gould. Read by Theresa Saldana. 2 cass. (Running Time: 3 hrs.). 1991. 15.95 (978-1-879371-02-6(2), 390623) Pub Mills.
Three generations of fire & fame, they were born to star, born to dazzle! Senda, Tamara, & Daliah: Three women as fiery as priceless diamonds. Three lives burning with power & passion.

Dazzling Darkness. Swami Amar Jyoti. 1 cass. 1978. 9.95 (R-17) Truth Consciousness.
On "nothingness." The ultimate expression of Perfection. What is darkness? "Because That shines, everything shines." Divine space, the Invisible Unmanifested.

DC Comics: Infinite Crisis - Part 2. 2007. 19.99 (978-1-59950-364-6(6)) GraphicAudio.

DC Comics: 52 Part I. Based on a novel by Greg Cox. (ENG.). 2007. (978-1-59950-370-7(0)) GraphicAudio.

Dctalk. Contrib. by dcTalk & Steve Blair. (Early Years (EMI-Cmg) Ser.). 2006. audio compact disk 7.99 (978-5-558-24624-7(3)) FF Rcds.

Dd Ibm-Stat Tool Soc Res 7e. 7th ed. (C). 2004. audio compact disk 34.95 (978-0-534-62799-7(4)) Pub: Wadsworth Pub. Dist(s): CENGAGE Learn

DD795 Matter & Energy Overhead. Lakeshore Learning Materials Staff. (J). 2008. 19.95 (978-1-60666-758-3(0)) Lkeshore Learn Mats.

DD796 Force & Motion Overhead. Lakeshore Learning Materials Staff. (J). 2008. audio compact disk 19.95 (978-1-60666-759-0(9)) Lkeshore Learn Mats.

De Abajo: Novela de la Revolucion Mexicana. unabr. ed. Mariano Azuela. Read by Patrick Treadway. 4 cass. (Running Time: 4 hrs. 30 min.). 1989. 26.95 (978-1-55686-299-1(7), 299) Books in Motion.
Demetrio Macias, a peace-loving Indian, is forced to join Villa's army to save his family. He becomes disillusioned as the rebel cause suffers defeat after defeat.

de Canciones a Viva Voz 2. (SPA.). (YA). 2004. audio compact disk (978-1-932507-47-8(7)) Untd Bible Amrcas Svce.

De-Conditioning the Mind. Swami Amar Jyoti. 1 cass. 1982. 9.95 (M-20) Truth Consciousness.
Coming out of our self-created dungeons. Liberation is de-conditioning of consciousness.

De-Discomfort. abr. ed. Robert A. Monroe. Read by Robert A. Monroe. (Human Plus Ser.). 1989. 14.95 (978-1-56102-005-8(2)) Inter Indus.
Enables turning down the volume of chronic pain signals.

De Donde Salen los Pantalones Vaqueros?, EDL Level 24. (Fonolibros Ser.: Vol. 17). (SPA.). 2003. 11.50 (978-0-7652-1039-5(8)) Modern Curr.

De Gaulle et l'appel du 18 Juin. Henri Amouroux. (Francais sous l'occupation Ser.). (FRE.). 1991. 26.95 (1224-RF) Olivia & Hill.
Paris is an open city.

De-Hab. abr. ed. Robert A. Monroe. Read by Robert A. Monroe. (Running Time: 30 min.). (Human Plus Ser.). 1989. 14.95 (978-1-56102-006-5(0)) Inter Indus.
Diminish & released detrimental physical, mental & emotional patterns or habits.

De-Hab Smoking. abr. ed. Robert A. Monroe. Read by Robert A. Monroe. (Mind Food Ser.). 1985. 14.95 (978-1-56102-405-6(8)) Inter Indus.
Help break the smoking habit with this exercise.

De Imitatio Christi see Imitation of Christ

De Jar de Usar Drogas. Betty L. Randolph. 1 cass. (I Can Ser.). (SPA.). 1989. bk. 9.98 (978-1-55909-272-2(6), 62E) Randolph Tapes.
Presents a program in spanish. Features male-female voice tracks with the right-left brain.

De Kooning's Bicycle: Artists & Writers in the Hamptons. Robert Long. Read by Grover Gardner. (Running Time: 19800 sec.). 2006. 54.95 (978-0-7861-4496-9(3)); audio compact disk 63.00 (978-0-7861-7232-0(0)) Blckstn Audio.

De Kooning's Bicycle: Artists & Writers in the Hamptons. unabr. ed. Robert Long. Read by Grover Gardner. (Running Time: 19800 sec.). 2006. audio compact disk 29.95 (978-0-7861-7666-3(0)) Blckstn Audio.

De la Seleccion. (Scott Foresman Lectura Ser.). (SPA.). (gr. 1 up). 2000. 48.99 (978-0-673-64881-5(8)) Addson-Wesley Educ.
Readings of every Pupil Edition selection are presented at a pace that children can follow as they read along.

De la Seleccion. 1 cass. (Running Time: 1 hr.). (Scott Foresman Lectura Ser.). (SPA.). (gr. 2 up). 2000. 48.99 (978-0-673-64882-2(6)) Addson-Wesley Educ.

De la Seleccion. 1 cass. (Running Time: 1 hr.). (SPA.). (gr. 3 up). 2000. 76.10 (978-0-673-64883-9(4)) Addson-Wesley Educ.

De la Seleccion. (Scott Foresman Lectura Ser.). (SPA.). (gr. 4 up). 2000. audio compact disk 110.34 (978-0-673-64877-8(X)); 76.10 (978-0-673-64884-6(2)) Addson-Wesley Educ.

De la Seleccion. (Scott Foresman Lectura Ser.). (SPA.). (gr. 5 up). 2000. audio compact disk 110.34 (978-0-673-64878-5(8)); 76.10 (978-0-673-64885-3(0)) Addson-Wesley Educ.

De L'Amitie see Treasury of French Prose

De Maupassant Short Stories. Guy de Maupassant. Read by Edward Blake. 2 cass. (Running Time: 1 hr. 43 min.). 1995. 15.95 set. (8628Q) Filmic Archives.
Includes "The Diamond Necklace", "In the Moonlight", "The Englishman", "A Piece of String", "The Signal", "The Devil", "My Uncle Sosthenes", & "Was It a Dream?".

De Maupassant Short Stories, Set. unabr. ed. Guy de Maupassant. Read by Edward Blake. 2 cass. (Running Time: 1 hr. 43 min.). Incl. Devil. 1973. (CB 118 CXR); Diamond Necklace. 1973. (CB 118 CXR); Englishman. 1973. (CB 118 CXR); In the Moonlight. 1973. (CB 118 CXR); My Uncle Sosthenes. 1973. (CB 118 CXR); Piece of String. 1973. (CB 118 CXR); Signal. 1973. (CB 118 CXR); Was It a Dream? 1973. (CB 118 CXR); 1973. 15.95 (978-0-8072-3536-2(9), CB 118 CXR, Listening Lib) Random Audio Pubg.
Edward Blake reads better known short stories by this French author.Includes "The Diamond Necklace," "In the Moonlight," "The Englishman," "a Piece of String," "The Signal," "The Devil," "My Uncle Sosthenes," & "Was It a Dream.".

De Niro. unabr. collector's ed. John Parker. Read by Michael Prichard. 8 cass. (Running Time: 12 hrs.). 1997. 64.00 (978-0-7366-3632-2(3), 4294) Books on Tape.
In the current pantheon of American screen actors, Robert De Niro reigns supreme.

De Orbe Novo see Twentieth-Century Poetry in English, No. 10, Recordings of Poets Reading Their Own Poetry

De padre a Hijo: Audiocassette. (Saludos Ser.: Vol. 1). (SPA.). (gr. 3-5). 10.00 (978-0-7635-1756-4(9)) Rigby Educ.

De Paseo. 2nd ed. Sara Long. 1 cass. stu. ed. 6.50 (978-0-8384-8098-4(5)) Heinle.

De Paseo. 2nd ed. Sara Long. (C). bk. & wbk. ed. 37.95 (978-0-8384-7751-9(8)) Heinle.

***De Paseo: Curso Intermedio de Espanol.** 3rd ed. Janice L. Macian & Donna Reseigh Long. (ENG.). (C). 2004. 38.95 (978-1-4130-0206-5(4)) Pub: Heinle. Dist(s): CENGAGE Learn

De Profundis. Perf. by Daughters of Mary. 1 cass. (Running Time: 60 mins.). 1999. 9.95 (T8410); audio compact disk 14.95 (K1130) Liguori Pubns.
Songs include: "De Profundis," "Soul of My Savior," "Ave Verum," "Immaculate Mary" & many more.

De Profundis. Oscar Wilde. Read by Corin Redgrave & Merlin Holland. (Running Time: 1 hr.). 2005. 16.95 (978-1-59912-924-2(8)) Iofy Corp.

De-Sensitization by Systematic Steps with Relaxation, Set-D. Russell E. Mason. 1975. pap. bk. 35.00 (978-0-89533-005-5(9)) F I Comm.

De-Tox: Body. abr. ed. Robert A. Monroe. Read by Robert A. Monroe. (Running Time: 30 min.). (Human Plus Ser.). 1989. 14.95 (978-1-56102-007-2(9)) Inter Indus.
Enhance the body's ability to cleanse chemicals & other destructive substances.

De-Valuing of America: The Fight for Our Culture & Our Children. unabr. ed. William J. Bennett. Read by Robert Morris. 9 cass. (Running Time: 13 hrs.). 1995. 62.95 Set. (978-0-7861-0654-7(9), 1554) Blckstn Audio.
In this remarkably candid personal account of the making & unmaking of education, drug control, & cultural policy, William J. Bennett reveals what he saw & what he learned - & the people he came across & was crossed by - during his controversial years as Chairman of the National Endowment of the Humanities, Secretary of Education, & Director of the Office of National Drug Control Policy.

Deacon's Masterpiece, or The Wonderful "One-Hoss Shay" see Classic American Poetry

Deacons Partners Kit. Jim Henry. 2006. 249.99 (978-1-933376-11-0(2)) Sampson Res.

Dead. unabr. ed. James Joyce. Read by Jim Killavey. 2 cass. (Running Time: 1 hr. 45 min.). (YA). (gr. 11-12). 1991. 12.95 set. (T-2) Jimcin Record.
Joyce's starkly realistic portrait of social conventions & the birth & death of hope.

Dead. unabr. ed. James Joyce. Read by Richard Setlok. 2 cass. (Running Time: 2 hrs.). 1993. lib. bdg. 18.95 set incl. vinyl case, notes, author's picture & biography. (978-1-883049-21-8(0)) Sound Room.
Two stories from "Dubliners." "Ivy Day in the Committee Room" & "The Dead." "Audio Best of the Year" - Publishers Weekly.

Dead, Set. unabr. ed. Short Stories. James Joyce. Read by Richard Setlok. 2 cass. (Running Time: 2 hrs.). 1993. bk. 16.95 (978-1-883049-02-7(4), 390165, Commuters Library) Sound Room.
Two stories from "Dubliners." "Ivy Day in the Committee Room," a story of comradery, politics & Irish history. "The Dead," a beautiful story, one of the greatest pieces of short fiction.

Dead Again. unabr. ed. Jennie Melville. Read by Norma West. 6 cass. (Running Time: 9 hrs.). 2001. 54.95 (978-0-7540-0669-5(7), CAB 2091) Pub: Chivers Audio Bks GBR. Dist(s): AudioGO
Three former partners in crime plan to reunite with a fourth who is getting out of prison. But before she can be released, murders start happening, with corpses bearing the same marking as those of her victims years before.

***Dead Aim.** unabr. ed. Thomas Perry. Narrated by Michael Kramer. (Running Time: 12 hrs. 0 mins.). 2010. 34.99 (978-1-4001-9026-3(6)); 17.99 (978-1-4001-8026-4(0)) Tantor Media.

***Dead Aim.** unabr. ed. Thomas Perry. Narrated by Michael Kramer. (Running Time: 12 hrs. 30 mins. 0 sec.). (ENG.). 2010. 24.99 (978-1-4001-6026-6(X)); audio compact disk 69.99 (978-1-4001-4026-8(9)); audio compact disk 34.99 (978-1-4001-1026-1(2)) Pub: Tantor Media. Dist(s): IngramPubServ

Dead Aim. unabr. ed. Collin Wilcox. Read by Larry McKeever. 8 cass. (Running Time: 8 hrs.). (Frank Hastings Ser.). 1996. 48.00 (978-0-7366-3373-4(1), 4023) Books on Tape.
Hastings agonizes over his commitment to another case. Two nights earlier, someone mugged & killed a housewife, which destroyed a family. Duty & politics force him to work around the clock on both cases, chasing leads in elegant drawing rooms & dark, dank alleyways. In a few violent hours, he brings both killers to bay.

Dead Air. abr. ed. Charles Jaco. Read by Charles Jaco. 1 cass. 1998. (978-1-56876-074-2(4)) Soundlines Ent.

Dead Air. unabr. ed. Iain Banks, pseud. Read by Kenny Blyth. 12 cass. (Running Time: 11 hrs. 51 mins.). (Isis Cassettes Ser.). (J). 2005. 94.95 (978-0-7531-1751-4(7)); audio compact disk 99.95 (978-0-7531-2211-2(1)) Pub: ISIS Lrg Prnt GBR. Dist(s): Ulverscroft US

Dead Alive. Contrib. by Soul Embraced. Prod. by Barry Poynter. 2008. audio compact disk 13.99 (978-5-557-43697-7(9)) Solid State MO.

Dead & Alive. unabr. ed. Dean Koontz & Ed Gorman. Read by John Bedford Lloyd. (Dean Koontz's Frankenstein Ser.: Bk. 3). (ENG.). 2009. audio compact disk 30.00 (978-0-7393-1717-4(2), Random AudioBks) Pub: Random Audio Pubg. Dist(s): Random

Dead & Buried. Quintin Jardine. Read by James Bryce. (Running Time: 43800 sec.). (Isis (CDs) Ser.). 2007. audio compact disk 99.95 (978-0-7531-2629-5(X)) Pub: ISIS Lrg Prnt GBR. Dist(s): Ulverscroft US

Dead & Buried: Would You Kill a Best Friend to Save a Life? Quintin Jardine. Read by James Bryce. 9 cass. (Running Time: 12 hrs. 10 mins.). (Isis Cassettes Ser.). 2007. 76.95 (978-0-7531-3642-3(2)) Pub: ISIS Lrg Prnt GBR. Dist(s): Ulverscroft US

Dead & Gone. unabr. ed. Charlaine Harris. Read by Johanna Parker. (Running Time: 9 hrs.). (Sookie Stackhouse Ser.: Bk. 9). 2009. 61.75 (978-1-4407-0366-9(3)); 67.75 (978-1-4407-0363-8(9)); audio compact disk 123.75 (978-1-4407-0364-5(7)) Recorded Bks.

Dead & Gone. unabr. ed. Charlaine Harris. Read by Joanna Parker. 8 CDs. (Running Time: 9 hrs.). (Sookie Stackhouse Ser.: Bk. 9). 2009. audio compact disk 39.99 (978-1-4407-1718-5(4)) Recorded Bks.

Dead & Gone. unabr. ed. Andrew Vachss. Read by Phil Gigante. (Running Time: 11 hrs.). (Burke Ser.). 2010. audio compact disk 29.99 (978-1-4418-2404-2(9), 9781441824042, Bril Audio CD Unabri) Brilliance Audio.

***Dead & Gone.** unabr. ed. Andrew Vachss. Read by Phil Gigante. (Running Time: 11 hrs.). (Burke Ser.). 2010. 24.99 (978-1-4418-2408-0(1), 9781441824080, BAD); 24.99 (978-1-4418-2406-6(5), 9781441824066, Brilliance MP3); 39.97 (978-1-4418-2409-7(X), 9781441824097, BADLE); 39.97 (978-1-4418-2407-3(3), 9781441824073, Brlnc Audio MP3 Lib); audio compact disk 79.97 (978-1-4418-2405-9(7), 9781441824059, BriAudCD Unabrid) Brilliance Audio.

Dead & Gone, Set. unabr. ed. Dorothy Simpson. Read by Terrence Hardiman. 8 cass. (Running Time: 12 hr.). 1999. 69.95 (978-0-7540-0386-1(8), CAB1809) AudioGO.

Dead & Kicking. unabr. ed. Geoffrey McGeachin. Read by Peter Hosking. (Running Time: 6 hrs.). 2009. audio compact disk 63.95 (978-1-74214-421-4(7), 9781742144214) Pub: Bolinda Pubng AUS. Dist(s): Bolinda Pub Inc

Dead & Other Stories. unabr. ed. James Joyce. Read by Ralph Cosham. 2 CDs. (Running Time: 2 hrs. 30 mins.). 2000. audio compact disk 18.95 (Commuters Library) Sound Room.

Dead & the Gone. unabr. ed. Susan Beth Pfeffer. Read by Robertson Dean. 7 CDs. (Running Time: 8 hrs. 51 mins.). (YA). (gr. 7 up). 2008. audio compact disk 55.00 (978-0-7393-6368-3(9), Listening Lib) Pub: Random Audio Pubg. Dist(s): Random

When life as Alex Morales had known it changed forever, he was working behind the counter at Joey's Pizza. He was worried about getting elected as senior class president and making the grades to land him in a good college. He never expected that an asteroid would hit the moon, knocking it closer in orbit to the earth and catastrophically altering the earth's climate. He never expected to be fighting just to stay alive.

Dead & the Gone. unabr. ed. Susan Beth Pfeffer. Read by Robertson Dean. (J). (gr. 7). 2010. 45.00 (978-0-7393-6366-9(2), Listening Lib) Pub: Random Audio Pubg. Dist(s): Random

***Dead Are Talking (Audio CD Book)** Ross Hemsworth. (ENG.). 2008. cd-rom & audio compact disk 25.95 (978-1-61033-077-0(3), TGSPubng) T G S.

Dead As a Dodo: A Homer Kelly Mystery. unabr. ed. Jane Langton. Read by Michael Prichard. 7 cass. (Running Time: 10 hrs. 30 min.). 1997. 56.00 (978-0-913369-62-3(4), 4295) Books on Tape.

The murder of a watchman at the University Museum shatters the tranquillity of ancient Oxford. Enter visiting lecturer Homer Kelly, who puts aside his studies in natural history to investigate the crime. Assisted by his charming wife, Mary, Homer is drawn into a deadly academic jigsaw puzzle.

Dead As a Doornail. unabr. ed. Charlaine Harris. (Sookie Stackhouse Ser.: Bk. 5). 2005. audio compact disk 34.99 (978-1-4193-3730-7(0)) Recorded Bks.

Dead Beat. unabr. ed. Jim Butcher. (Running Time: 15 hrs.). Bk. 7. (ENG.). 2010. audio compact disk 49.95 (978-0-14-242807-8(8), PengAudBks) Penguin Grp USA.

***Dead Beat.** unabr. ed. Marilyn Johnson. Read by Marilyn Johnson. (ENG.). 2010. (978-0-06-206211-6(5), Harper Audio); (978-0-06-204711-3(6), Harper Audio) HarperCollins Pubs.

***Dead Beautiful.** unabr. ed. Yvonne Woon. Read by Caitlin Davies. (Running Time: 12 hrs.). 2010. 39.97 (978-1-4418-8838-9(1), 9781441888389, BADLE) Brilliance Audio.

***Dead Beautiful.** unabr. ed. Yvonne Woon. Read by Caitlin Davies. (Running Time: 13 hrs.). (YA). 2010. 24.99 (978-1-4418-8836-5(5), 9781441888365, Brilliance MP3); 39.97 (978-1-4418-8837-2(3), 9781441888372, Brlnc Audio MP3 Lib); audio compact disk 29.99 (978-1-4418-8834-1(9), 9781441888341, Bril Audio CD Unabri); audio compact disk 74.97 (978-1-4418-8835-8(7), 9781441888358, BriAudCD Unabrid) Brilliance Audio.

Dead by Sunset: Perfect Husband, Perfect Killer? Ann Rule. 2004. 10.95 (978-0-7435-4585-3(0)) Pub: S&S Audio. Dist(s): S and S Inc

Dead by Sunset: Perfect Husband, Perfect Killer? unabr. ed. Ann Rule. Read by Kate Reading. 13 cass. (Running Time: 19 hrs. 30 min.). 1996. 104.00 (978-0-7366-3316-1(2), 3968) Books on Tape.

Brad Cunningham, charismatic & handsome, married five bright, beautiful women - & left each one. But not before fathering six children with three of them & draining the fortunes of two. Wife No. 4 wasn't as lucky: Brad killed her. Why did these women let one man destroy them?.

Dead by Sunset: Perfect Husband, Perfect Killer?, Set. abr. ed. Ann Rule. Read by Sharon Gless. 2 cass. (Running Time: 3 hrs.). 1999. (393080) S&S Audio.

Who is Brad Cunningham? How could five intelligent & successful women believe he was their dream man? This is the researched study of destructive relationships, multiple marriages, financial manipulations & monstrous acts of harrassment & revenge that surround Brad & his wives.

Dead Calm. unabr. collector's ed. Charles Williams. Read by Michael Russotto. 8 cass. (Running Time: 8 hrs.). 1993. 48.00 (978-0-7366-2466-4(X), 3230) Books on Tape.

An idyllic honeymoon cruise becomes a fight for survival when couple rescues survivor of sinking ship.

Dead Center. David Rosenfelt. Read by Grover Gardner. (Running Time: 8 hrs.). 2006. 23.95 (978-1-60083-329-8(2)) Iofy Corp.

Dead Center. unabr. ed. David Rosenfelt. Read by Grover Gardner. 6 CDs. (Running Time: 28800 sec.). 2006. audio compact disk 29.95 (978-1-59316-079-1(8), LL171) Listen & Live.

Dead Center. unabr. ed. Collin Wilcox. Read by Michael Kramer. 8 cass. (Running Time: 8 hrs.). (Frank Hastings Ser.). 1993. 48.00 (978-0-7366-2519-7(4), 3274) Books on Tape.

Lt. Frank Hastings hunts a serial killer preying on wealthy & famous men.

Dead Cert. Dick Francis. 2 cass. (Running Time: 90 min. per cass.). 1990. 15.95 HarperCollins Pubs.

Dead Cert. Dick Francis. Narrated by Simon Prebble. 6 cass. (Running Time: 9 hrs.). 51.00 (978-0-7887-0293-8(9)) Recorded Bks.

Dead Cert. Dick Francis. Narrated by Peter Jay Fernandez & Simon Prebble. 8 CDs. (Running Time: 9 hrs.). 2001. audio compact disk 78.00 (978-0-7887-5181-3(6), C1343E7) Recorded Bks.

Amateur jockey Alan York wins the steeplechase, but it's a hollow victory. The champion horse & rider in the lead fails to clear a fence & the professional jockey dies of his injuries. Curious about how this could happen, Alan begins an investigation that points to corruption transcending the racing circuit.

Dead Cert. abr. ed. Dick Francis. Read by James Fox. 2008. audio compact disk 14.95 (978-0-06-149821-3(1), Harper Audio) HarperCollins Pubs.

Dead Cert. unabr. ed. Dick Francis. Read by David Case. 6 cass. (Running Time: 9 hrs.). 1994. 48.00 (978-0-7366-2721-4(9), 3451) Books on Tape.

Alan York knows that racing is a dangerous sport. Horses fall & jockeys get hurt. But he also knows the death of champion Bill Davidson was no accident. Searching for the killer, York runs a race for his own life.

Dead Cert. unabr. ed. Dick Francis. Read by Tony Britton. 6 cass. (Running Time: 9 hrs.). 2000. 49.95 (978-0-7451-6828-9(0), CAB 437) Pub: Chivers Audio Bks GBR. Dist(s): AudioGO

Bill Davidson is riding a dead cert, a horse that is certain to win easily, but instead the horse falls at a fence and crushes Bill. The next rider sees Bill go down and notices something odd on the ground. When he returns later to verify what he saw, it is gone. Was the fall an accident or murder?.

Dead Cert. unabr. ed. Dick Francis. Narrated by Simon Prebble. 6 cass. (Running Time: 9 hrs.). 1996. 51.00 (94486E7) Recorded Bks.

Amateur jockey Alan York wins the steeplechase, but it's a hollow victory. The champion horse & rider in the lead fails to clear a fence & the professional jockey dies of his injuries. Curious about how this could happen, Alan begins an investigation that points to corruption transcending the racing circuit.

Dead Connection. abr. ed. Alafair Burke. Read by Christopher Lane. (Running Time: 6 hrs.). 2008. audio compact disk 14.99 (978-1-4233-4387-5(5), 9781423343875, BCD Value Price) Brilliance Audio.

Dead Connection. unabr. ed. Alafair Burke. Read by Christopher Lane. (Running Time: 11 hrs.). 2007. 39.25 (978-1-4233-4342-4(5), 9781423343424, BADLE); 24.95 (978-1-4233-4341-7(7), 9781423343417, BAD); 82.25 (978-1-4233-4336-3(0), 9781423343363, BrilAudUnabridg); audio compact disk 39.25 (978-1-4233-4340-0(9), 9781423343400, Brlnc Audio MP3 Lib); audio compact disk 97.25 (978-1-4233-4338-7(7), 9781423343387, BriAudCD Unabrid); audio compact disk 24.95 (978-1-4233-4339-4(5), 9781423343394, Brilliance MP3); audio compact disk 36.95 (978-1-4233-4337-0(9), 9781423343370, Bril Audio CD Unabri) Brilliance Audio.

Dead Connection. unabr. ed. Charlie Price. Read by Robert Ramirez. 6 CDs. (Running Time: 7 hrs.). (YA). (gr. 8 up). 2006. audio compact disk 64.75 (978-1-4281-2233-8(8)); 49.75 (978-1-4281-2228-4(1)) Recorded Bks.

Teenager Murray Keifer just doesn't fit in at school. And it doesn't help that his mother is too busy entertaining male friends to be involved in his life. His only friends are "Dearly" and "Beloved" - dead people buried in the local cemetery. That's right, Murray talks to the dead. But Murray's peaceful and unusual world is torn asunder when he hears the voice of missing teen Nikki Parker, buried in someone else's grave. Daughter of the groundskeeper and Murray's one living friend, Pearl believes in his special gift and is determined to give Nikki justice. Meanwhile Deputy Roman Gates draws closer to solving the mystery behind Nikki's disappearance.

Dead Doctors Don't Lie. Joel Wallach. 1 cass. (Running Time: 2 hrs.). 1994. 4.00 (978-1-889502-03-8(0)) Adv Wrks & Prodn.

This positive lecture centers on good health, disease reversal, & longevity in our day. Dr. Wallach reveals the hidden keys to how five modern cultures around the globe consistently enjoy active lives of 120 to 140 years. Dr. Wallach discusses case treatment of, & recovery from, over 800 diseases. These diseases include diabetes, hypoglycemia, high blood pressure, heart attack, arthritis, ulcers, osteoporosis, cancer, Alzheimer's, cystic fibrosis, attention deficit disorder (ADD), infertility, migraines, Shogun's disease, spasmodic torticollis, mononucleosis, emphysema, hemachromatosis, adrenal gland problems, macular degeneration, Parkinson's, multiple sclerosis, Lou Gehrig's disease, Grave's disease, tic douloureux, baldness, elephantman disease, gout, & more.

Dead Dog Cafe, Vol. 2. Tom King. Prod. by Tom King. 3 CDs. (Running Time: 3 hrs.). 2005. audio compact disk 24.95 (978-0-660-19375-5(2)) Canadian Broadcasting CAN.

Dead Dog Cafe: Volume 3, Vol. 3. abr. ed. Tom King. Contrib. by Don Ross. 3 CDs. (Running Time: 10800 sec.). (Dead Dog Cafe Comedy Hour Ser.). 2005. audio compact disk 24.95 (978-0-660-19466-0(X)) Canadian Broadcasting CAN.

Dead Dog Cafe: Volume 4, Vol. 4. abr. ed. Short Stories. Tom King. Read by Tom King. Read by Floyd Favel & Edna Rain. 3 CDs. (Running Time: 10800 sec.). (Dead Dog Cafe Comedy Hour Ser.). 2006. audio compact disk 24.95 (978-0-660-19543-8(7), CBC Audio) Pub: Canadian Broadcasting CAN. Dist(s): Georgetown Term

Dead Dog Cafe Comedy Hour. Tom King. 2005. audio compact disk 24.95 (978-0-660-19320-5(5)) Canadian Broadcasting CAN.

Dead Dog in the City: Volume 1. Thomas King. Prod. by Kathleen Flaherty. 3 CDs. (Running Time: 10800 sec.). Dramatization. 2007. audio compact disk 24.95 (978-0-660-19672-5(7), CBC Audio) Pub: Canadian Broadcasting CAN. Dist(s): Georgetown Term

There have been some major changes at the Dead Dog Cafe, and we?re not talking about renovations. The place has been sold, and Gracie has packed up everything and moved to Toronto to star in a cooking show. Tom agrees to drive Jasper to Toronto. After all, he has a pickup truck and someone has to pay for the coffee. And Jasper has his pirate radio news for 3 minutes each week on random days so the CRTC can?t triangulate the location. Dead Dog in the City is a new show with familiar voices. Where the satire is hard. Where anything can happen. Where anyone can show up. And where we still don?t know exactly what ?Stay Calm, Be Brave, Wait for the Signs? really means.

Dead End. unabr. ed. Cynthia Harrod-Eagles. Read by Terry Wale. 9 cass. (Running Time: 12 hrs.). (Bill Slider Mystery Ser.: No. 4). 2000. 79.95 (978-1-86042-433-5(3), 24333) Pub: Soundings Ltd GBR. Dist(s): Ulverscroft US

***Dead End Gene Pool: A Memoir.** unabr. ed. Wendy Burden. Narrated by Coleen Marlo. (Running Time: 10 hrs. 0 mins.). 2010. 34.99 (978-1-4001-9569-5(1)); 24.99 (978-1-4001-6569-8(5)); 16.99 (978-1-4001-8569-6(6)); audio compact disk 34.99 (978-1-4001-1569-3(8)); audio compact disk 69.99 (978-1-4001-4569-0(4)) Pub: Tantor Media. Dist(s): IngramPubServ

Dead Ends. Nicholas Rhea. 8 cass. (Running Time: 10 hrs. 35 mins.). (Story Sound Ser.). (J). 2004. 69.95 (978-1-85903-756-0(9)); audio compact disk 79.95 (978-1-85903-772-0(0)) Pub: Mgna Lrg Print GBR. Dist(s): Ulverscroft US

Dead Even. abr. ed. Brad Meltzer. Contrib. by Kate Burton. (Running Time: 21600 sec.). 2007. audio compact disk 14.95 (978-0-06-128456-4(4), Harper Audio) HarperCollins Pubs.

Dead Even. unabr. ed. Brad Meltzer. Read by Alexander Adams. 9 cass. (Running Time: 13 hrs. 30 min.). 1998. 72.00 (978-0-7366-4258-3(7), 4734) Books on Tape.

Sara Tate takes a job as a New York City prosecutor just as massive layoffs are announced. Her best hope is to find a high-profile case & win it.

Dead Even. unabr. ed. Brad Meltzer. Read by Scott Brick. (Running Time: 14 hrs.). (ENG.). 2008. 16.98 (978-1-60024-480-3(7)); audio compact disk 24.98 (978-1-60024-477-3(7)) Pub: Hachet Audio. Dist(s): HachBkGrp

Dead Eyes. Stuart Woods. Narrated by Richard Ferrone. 8 CDs. (Running Time: 9 hrs. 15 mins.). audio compact disk 78.00 (978-1-4025-2936-8(8)) Recorded Bks.

***Dead Eyes.** abr. ed. Stuart Woods. Read by Joan Allen. (ENG.). 2005. (978-0-06-084192-8(3), Harper Audio); (978-0-06-084193-5(1), Harper Audio) HarperCollins Pubs.

Dead Eyes, unabr. ed. Stuart Woods. Narrated by Richard Ferrone. 7 cass. (Running Time: 9 hrs. 15 mins.). 1995. 60.00 (978-0-7887-0161-0(4), 94386E7) Recorded Bks.

A stalker who calls himself "Admirer," threatens the life of a Hollywood starlet. As Police Detective Jon Larsen begins the hunt for Admirer, he knows he faces a stalker more cunning & meticulous than any he has ever tracked.

Dead Famous. unabr. ed. Ben Elton. Read by David Thorpe. 10 cass. (Running Time: 12 hrs.). (Isis Ser.). (J). 2002. 84.95 (978-0-7531-1456-8(9)) Pub: ISIS Lrg Prnt GBR. Dist(s): Ulverscroft US

One House. Ten Contestants. Thirty cameras. Forty microphones, Yet again the public gorges its voyeuristic appetite as another group of unknown and unremarkable people submit themselves to the brutal exposure of the televised real-life soap opera. House Arrest. Who will crack first? Who will have sex and with whom? All the usual questions. And then, suddenly, some new ones. Who is the murderer? How did he or she manage to kill under the constant gaze of the thirty television cameras? Why did they do it? And who will be next.

Dead Famous. unabr. ed. Ben Elton. Read by David Thorpe. 9 CDs. (Running Time: 11 hrs. 15 mins.). (Isis (CDs) Ser.). (J). 2004. audio compact disk 84.95 (978-0-7531-2285-3(5)) Pub: ISIS Lrg Prnt GBR. Dist(s): Ulverscroft US

Dead Famous: A Mallory Novel. O'Connell. Read by Alyssa Bresnahan. 2009. audio compact disk 29.95 (978-1-59316-450-8(5)) Listen & Live.

Dead Famous: A Mallory Novel. unabr. ed. Carol O'Connell. Read by Alyssa Bresnahan. (YA). 2006. 49.99 (978-1-59895-201-8(3)) Find a World.

Dead Famous: A Mallory Novel. unabr. ed. Carol O'Connell. Read by Alyssa Bresnahan. 7 cass. (Running Time: 12 hrs.). (Mysteries Ser.). 2003. 32.95 (978-1-59316-017-3(8), 100385) Listen & Live.

Night had fallen, and the woman looked down at the crumpled letter, as if, in absolute darkness, she could read the postscript: Only a monster can play this game. In Chicago, an FBI agent is killed in a psychiatrist's waiting room. In New York, the jurors from a controversial trial are murdered one by one. The only connections between the two: a flamboyant shock-jock, whose on-air comments seem to be taking him dangerously close to the edge, and a woman, her body misshapen since childhood, whose job it is to clean up crime scenes and maybe create them as well.

Dead Father. unabr. ed. Donald Barthelme. Read by Dennis Holland. (Running Time: 5 hrs.). 2010. 24.99 (978-1-4233-9575-1(1), 9781423395751, Brilliance MP3); 39.97 (978-1-4233-9576-8(X), 9781423395768, Brlnc Audio MP3 Lib); 39.97 (978-1-4233-9577-5(8), 9781423395775, BADLE); audio compact disk 24.99 (978-1-4233-9573-7(5), 9781423395737, Bril Audio CD Unabri); audio compact disk 74.97 (978-1-4233-9574-4(3), 9781423395744, BriAudCD Unabrid) Brilliance Audio.

Dead Father's Club. unabr. ed. Matt Haig. 6 CDs. (Running Time: 24300 sec.). (ENG.). 2007. audio compact disk 32.95 (978-1-59887-087-9(4), 1598870874) Pub: HighBridge. Dist(s): Workman Pub

Dead Fathers Club. unabr. ed. Matt Haig. Read by Andrew Dennis. (YA). 2007. 39.99 (978-1-59895-848-5(8)) Find a World.

Dead Folks' Blues. abr. ed. Steven Womack. Read by Bernard Bridges. Ed. by Richard Haywood. 2 cass. (Harry Denton Ser.). 1995. 17.00 Set. (978-1-883268-25-1(7)) Spellbinders.

Conrad Fletcher's murder leads private investigator, Harry James Denton, into parts of Nashville that no one ever sings about...unless they're singing the dead folk's blues.

Dead Folks' Blues. unabr. ed. Steven Womack. Read by Ron Varela. 8 cass. (Running Time: 8 hrs. 12 min.). (Harry Denton Ser.). 2001. 49.95; audio compact disk 45.50 (978-1-58116-166-3(2)) Books in Motion.

Reporter turned-P.I. Harry James Denton has a case to solve when the doctor husband of his client turns up dead. Being a suspect himself, Denton searches for the killer in parts of Nashville that no one ever sings about.

Dead Folks Blues. unabr. ed. Steven Womack. Read by Ron Varela. 8 cass,. (Running Time: 8 hrs.). 2000. 44.95 (978-1-55686-996-9(7)) Books in Motion.

Dead Girls' Dance. unabr. ed. Rachel Caine. Narrated by Cynthia Holloway. (Running Time: 9 hrs. 0 mins. 0 sec.). (Morganville Vampires Ser.: Bk. 2). (ENG.). (YA). (gr. 8-12). 2009. 24.99 (978-1-4001-6191-1(6)); audio compact disk 69.99 (978-1-4001-4191-3(5)); audio compact disk 34.99 (978-1-4001-1191-6(9)) Pub: Tantor Media. Dist(s): IngramPubServ

Dead Giveaway. unabr. ed. Simon Brett. Read by Simon Brett. 6 cass. (Running Time: 9 hrs.). (Charles Paris Mystery Ser.: Bk. 11). 2000. 49.95 (978-0-7451-4210-4(9), CAB 893) Pub: Chivers Audio Bks GBR. Dist(s): AudioGO

Charles Paris knows his career as an actor is failing when he is awarded a role simply because he is an unknown face. But when murder occurs in the studio, Paris launches into his role as amateur sleuth.

Dead Giveaway. unabr. ed. Simon Brett. Narrated by Simon Prebble. 4 cass. (Running Time: 5 hrs.). 1993. 40.00 (978-0-7887-8987-8(2), H1223L8) Recorded Bks.

Veteran British character actor Charles Paris is usually thankful for any work. But appearing on the game show If the Cap Fits as someone whose occupation must be guessed (the producers wanted an actor no one would recognize) is a new low, even for him. When the show's sleazy, skirt-chasing host drops dead of cyanide poisoning, however, Paris gets to use his greatest talent: amateur sleuthing.

Dead Ground. unabr. ed. Gerald Seymour. Read by Robert Whitfield. 9 cass. (Running Time: 13 hrs.). 2003. 62.95 (978-0-7861-1729-1(X), 2534) Blckstn Audio.

A mission of revenge, a haunting love story & a chilling tale, in the definitive novel of the end of the Cold War era. One frozen night Tracy Barnes witnesses the killing of her lover by the secret police. Years later, when the Wall has crumbled & old enemies are new friends, Tracy encounters the murderer & plans to make him pay.

Dead Ground. unabr. ed. Gerald Seymour. (Running Time: 46800 sec.). 2007. audio compact disk 99.00 (978-0-7861-0109-2(1)); audio compact disk 29.95 (978-0-7861-0110-8(5)) Blckstn Audio.

Dead Hand: The Untold Story of the Cold War Arms Race & Its Dangerous Legacy. unabr. abr. ed. David Hoffman. Read by Bob Walter. (ENG.). 2009. audio compact disk 40.00 (978-0-7393-8485-5(6), Random AudioBks) Pub: Random Audio Pubg. Dist(s): Random

Dead Heat. Joel C. Rosenberg. 2009. audio compact disk 9.99 (978-1-4418-2664-0(5)) Brilliance Audio.

Dead Heat. abr. ed. Joel C. Rosenberg. Read by Phil Gigante. (Running Time: 6 hrs.). 2008. audio compact disk 14.99 (978-1-4233-3094-3(3), 9781423330943, BCD Value Price) Brilliance Audio.

Dead Heat. unabr. ed. Dick Francis & Felix Francis. Read by Martin Jarvis. 9 CDs. (Running Time: 11 hrs.). (ENG.). (gr. 8). 2007. audio compact disk 34.95 (978-0-14-314279-9(8), PengAudBks) Penguin Grp USA.

Dead Heat. unabr. ed. Dick Francis & Felix Francis. Read by Martin Jarvis. 9 CDs. 2007. audio compact disk 90.00 (978-1-4159-4521-6(7), BksonTape) Pub: Random Audio Pubg. Dist(s): Random
Max Moreton is a rising culinary star, and his Newmarket restaurant, the Hay Net, has brought him great acclaim and a widening circle of admirers. But when nearly all the guests who enjoyed one of his meals at a private catered affair fall victim to severe food poisoning, his kitchen is shuttered and his reputation takes a hit. Scrambling to meet his next obligation, an exclusive luncheon for forty in the glass-fronted private boxes at the 2,000 Guineas, Max must overcome the previous evening's disaster and provide the new American sponsors of the year's first Classic race with a day to remember. Then a bomb blast rips through the private boxes, killing some of Max's trusted staff and many of the guests. As survivors are rushed to the hospital, he is left to survey the ruins of the grandstand - and of his career. Two close calls are too close for comfort, and Max vows to protect his name, and himself, before it's too late.

Dead Heat. unabr. ed. Frank Roderus. Read by Kevin Foley. 6 cass. (Running Time: 6 hrs.). (Heller Ser.: Bk. 6). 1995. 36.95 (978-1-55686-584-8(8)) Books in Motion.
Carl Heller agrees to protect a valuable race horse for a friend & a fat fee. If it involves taking on the New Mexico faction of organized crime - well, Heller never takes the easy way out.

Dead Heat. unabr. ed. Joel C. Rosenberg. Read by Phil Gigante. (Running Time: 10 hrs.). 2008. 39.25 (978-1-4233-3092-9(7), 9781423330929, BADLE); 24.95 (978-1-4233-3091-2(9), 9781423330912, BAD); 92.25 (978-1-4233-3086-8(2), 9781423330868, BrilAudUnabridg); audio compact disk 24.95 (978-1-4233-3089-9(7), 9781423330899, Brilliance MP3); audio compact disk 36.95 (978-1-4233-3087-5(0), 9781423330875, Bril Audio CD Unabri); audio compact disk 97.25 (978-1-4233-3088-2(9), 9781423330882, BriAudCD Unabrid); audio compact disk 39.25 (978-1-4233-3090-5(0), 9781423330905, Brlnc Audio MP3 Lib) Brilliance Audio.

Dead Hour. abr. ed. Denise Mina. Read by Heather O'Neill. (YA). 2007. 44.99 (978-1-60252-498-9(X)) Find a World.

Dead I Well May Be. Adrian McKinty. Read by Gerard Doyle. 8 cass. (Running Time: 11 hrs. 30 mins.). 2004. 65.95 (978-0-7861-2882-2(8), 3384); audio compact disk 81.00 (978-0-7861-8294-7(6), 3384) Blckstn Audio.

Dead I Well May Be. unabr. ed. Adrian McKinty. Read by Gerard Doyle. 8 cass. (Running Time: 11 hrs.). (YA). 2006. 29.95 (978-0-7861-4421-1(1)); audio compact disk 29.95 (978-0-7861-7390-7(4)) Blckstn Audio.

Dead I Well May Be. unabr. ed. Adrian McKinty. Read by Gerard Doyle. (YA). 2007. 64.99 (978-1-60252-605-1(2)) Find a World.

***Dead in the Family.** unabr. ed. Charlaine Harris. Narrated by Johanna Parker. 9 CDs. (Running Time: 10 hrs. 45 mins.). (Sookie Stackhouse Ser.: Bk. 10). 2010. audio compact disk 34.99 (978-1-4498-0614-9(7)) Recorded Bks.

***Dead in the Family.** unabr. ed. Charlaine Harris. Narrated by Johanna Parker. 1 Playaway. (Running Time: 9 hrs. 45 mins.). (Sookie Stackhouse Ser.: No. 10). 2010. 59.75 (978-1-4407-9354-7(9)); 72.75 (978-1-4407-9351-6(4)); audio compact disk 92.75 (978-1-4407-9352-3(2)) Recorded Bks.

Dead in the Water. Dana Stabenow. Read by Marguerite Gavin. 4 cass. (Running Time: 6 hrs.). (Kate Shugak Ser.). 1999. 32.00 (978-0-7366-4694-9(9), 5019) Books on Tape.
Stone barrington, ex-cop & Manhattan attorney, has arrived on St. Marks in the Caribbean for a sailing vacation when he is called to defend Allison Manning, accused of murdering her husband at sea. Did she really kill her husband, or is she being framed.

***Dead in the Water.** abr. ed. Stuart Woods. Read by Tony Roberts. (ENG.). 2005. (978-0-06-084184-3(2), Harper Audio); (978-0-06-084183-6(4), Harper Audio) HarperCollins Pubs.

Dead in the Water. collector's ed. Dana Stabenow. Read by Marguerite Gavin. 4 cass. (Running Time: 6 hrs.). (Kate Shugak Ser.). 1999. 32.00 (978-0-7366-4621-5(3), 5019) Books on Tape.
Stone Barrington, ex-cop & Manhattan attorney, has arrived on St. Marks in the Caribbean for a sailing vacation when he is called to defend Allison Manning, accused of murdering her husband at sea. Did she really kill her husband, or is she being framed.

Dead in the Water, unabr. ed. Stuart Woods. Read by Jonathan Marosz. 7 cass. (Running Time: 10 hrs. 30 min.). (Stone Barrington Ser.: No. 3). 1997. 56.00 (978-0-7366-3753-4(2), 4428) Books on Tape.
Stone barrington, ex-cop & Manhattan attorney, has arrived on St. Marks in the Caribbean for a sailing vacation when he is called to defend Allison Manning, accused of murdering her husband at sea. Did she really kill her husband, or is she being framed.

Dead in the Water, unabr. ed. Stuart Woods. Narrated by Richard Ferrone. 8 cass. (Running Time: 10 hrs. 45 mins.). (Stone Barrington Ser.: No. 3). 1997. 70.00 (978-0-7887-1776-5(6), 95250E7) Recorded Bks.
Ex-cop, Manhattan attorney Stone Barrington, has taken a January vacation in the Caribbean. There he meets blonde, beautiful Allison Manning, who must explain how her husband has disappeared. Stone attempts to rescue her from the hangman's noose.

Dead in the Water. unabr. ed. Stuart Woods. Narrated by Richard Ferrone. 9 CDs. (Running Time: 10 hrs. 45 mins.). (Stone Barrington Ser.: No. 3). 1999. audio compact disk 79.00 (978-0-7887-3423-6(7), C1029E7) Recorded Bks.

Dead in There see Poetry of Langston Hughes

Dead Irish. abr. ed. John Lescroart. Read by David Colacci. (Running Time: 21600 sec.). (Dismas Hardy Ser.: No. 1). 2008. audio compact disk 14.99 (978-1-4233-2300-6(9), 9781423323006, BCD Value Price) Brilliance Audio.

Dead Irish. unabr. ed. John Lescroart. Read by David Colacci. (Running Time: 10 hrs.). (Dismas Hardy Ser.: No. 1). 2007. 39.25 (978-1-4233-2296-2(7), 9781423322962, Brlnc Audio MP3 Lib); 24.95 (978-1-4233-2295-5(9), 9781423322955, Brilliance MP3); 39.25 (978-1-4233-2298-6(3), 9781423322986, BADLE); 24.95 (978-1-4233-2297-9(5), 9781423322979, BAD); audio compact disk 97.25 (978-1-4233-2294-8(0), 9781423322948, BriAudCD Unabrid); audio compact disk 36.95 (978-1-4233-2293-1(2), 9781423322931, Bril Audio CD Unabri) Brilliance Audio.

***Dead Is a State of Mind.** unabr. ed. Marlene Perez. Read by Suzyn Jackson. (Running Time: 5 hrs.). (Dead Is Ser.). 2010. 39.97 (978-1-4418-7174-9(8), 9781441871749, BADLE); 19.99 (978-1-4418-7172-5(1), 9781441871725, Brilliance MP3); 39.97 (978-1-4418-7173-2(X), 9781441871732, Brlnc Audio MP3 Lib); audio compact disk 54.97 (978-1-4418-7171-8(3), 9781441871718, BriAudCD Unabrid) Brilliance Audio.

***Dead Is a State of Mind.** unabr. ed. Marlene Perez. Read by Suzyn Jackson. (Running Time: 4 hrs.). (Dead Is Ser.). (YA). 2010. audio compact disk 19.99 (978-1-4418-7170-1(5), 9781441871701, Bril Audio CD Unabri) Brilliance Audio.

***Dead Is Just a Rumor.** unabr. ed. Marlene Perez. Read by Suzyn Jackson. (Running Time: 6 hrs.). (Dead Is Ser.). 2010. 39.97 (978-1-4418-7164-0(0), 9781441871640, BADLE); 19.99 (978-1-4418-7162-6(4), 9781441871626, Brilliance MP3); 39.97 (978-1-4418-7163-3(2), 9781441871633, Brlnc Audio MP3 Lib); audio compact disk 19.99 (978-1-4418-7160-2(8), 9781441871602, Bril Audio CD Unabri); audio compact disk 54.97 (978-1-4418-7161-9(6), 9781441871619, BriAudCD Unabrid) Brilliance Audio.

***Dead Is So Last Year.** unabr. ed. Marlene Perez. Read by Suzyn Jackson. (Running Time: 5 hrs.). (Dead Is Ser.). 2010. 39.97 (978-1-4418-7179-4(9), 9781441871794, BADLE) Brilliance Audio.

***Dead Is So Last Year.** unabr. ed. Marlene Perez. Read by Suzyn Jackson. (Running Time: 5 hrs.). (Dead Is Ser.). (YA). 2010. 19.99 (978-1-4418-7177-0(2), 9781441871770, Brilliance MP3); 39.97 (978-1-4418-7178-7(0), 9781441871787, Brlnc Audio MP3 Lib); audio compact disk 19.99 (978-1-4418-7175-6(6), 9781441871756, Bril Audio CD Unabri); audio compact disk 54.97 (978-1-4418-7176-3(4), 9781441871763, BriAudCD Unabrid) Brilliance Audio.

***Dead Is the New Black.** unabr. ed. Marlene Perez. Read by Suzyn Jackson. (Running Time: 6 hrs.). (Dead Is Ser.). 2010. 39.97 (978-1-4418-7169-5(1), 9781441871695, BADLE); 19.99 (978-1-4418-7167-1(5), 9781441871671, Brilliance MP3); 39.97 (978-1-4418-7168-8(3), 9781441871688, Brlnc Audio MP3 Lib); audio compact disk 19.99 (978-1-4418-7165-7(9), 9781441871657, Bril Audio CD Unabri); audio compact disk 54.97 (978-1-4418-7166-4(7), 9781441871664, BriAudCD Unabrid) Brilliance Audio.

Dead Lagoon. unabr. ed. Michael Dibdin. Read by Michael Tudor Barnes. 8 cass. (Running Time: 11 hrs. 45 min.). (Aurelio Zen Mystery Ser.). (J). 2001. 69.95 (978-1-85695-898-1(1), 950302) Pub: ISIS Lrg Prnt GBR. Dist(s): Ulverscroft US

Dead Liberty, Set. unabr. ed. Catherine Aird. Read by Robin Bailey. 6 cass. (Running Time: 9 hrs.). (Inspector C. D. Sloan Mystery Ser.). 2001. 49.95 (978-0-7451-5705-4(X), CAB 234) Pub: Chivers Audio Bks GBR. Dist(s): AudioGO
Lucy Durmast, arraigned on the charge of murder, remained silent. This was no help to those investigating the death of Kenneth Carline, an employee at her father's firm. The involvement of Lucy's father with the African kingdom of Dlasa, coupled with the disappearance of the King's son, complicated the matter further. Detective-Inspector C. D. Sloan came to the case just in time to see justice done.

***Dead Lift: An Emily Locke Mystery.** unabr. ed. Rachel Brady. Read by Carrington MacDuffie. (Running Time: 8 hrs. 30 mins.). (Botswana Mysteries Ser.). 2010. 29.95 (978-1-4417-6453-9(4)); 59.95 (978-1-4417-6450-8(X)); audio compact disk 76.00 (978-1-4417-6451-5(8)) Blckstn Audio.

Dead Lines: A Novel of Life ... after Death. Greg Bear. Read by Jason Culp. 2004. 29.95 (978-0-7927-3270-9(7), CMP 674, Chivers Sound Lib); bk. 89.95 (978-0-7927-3269-3(3), SLD 674, Chivers Sound Lib) AudioGO.

Dead Lines: A Novel of Life ... after Death. unabr. ed. Greg Bear. Read by Jason Culp. 7 vols. 2004. bk. 59.95 (978-0-7927-3268-6(5), CSL 674, Chivers Sound Lib) AudioGO.

Dead Man, set. unabr. ed. Joe Gores. Read by Lloyd Battista. 8 cass. (Running Time: 12 hrs.). 1995. 69.95 (978-0-7862-9974-4(6), CSL 083) AudioGO.
Life had been good to Eddie Dain. He had a wife, a beautiful 3-year-old son, & a good job. But when Eddie decides that a seemingly accidental death was no accident, it blows up in his face. Two thugs with shotguns are sent after Eddie. And when they are through with him, Eddie has to be reborn, this time as a dead man. He's now dead to this past, dead to his family, & dead to love. With the "Tibetan Book of the Dead" as his guide, Dain sets out to find the two killers that destroyed his life.

Dead Man in Istanbul. unabr. ed. Michael Pearce. Narrated by Bill Wallis. 5 cass. 2006. 54.95 (978-0-7927-4534-1(5), CSL 1010) AudioGO.

Dead Man in Istanbul. unabr. ed. Michael Pearce. Narrated by Bill Wallis. 6 CDs. (Running Time: 23340 sec.). 2006. audio compact disk 64.95 (978-0-7927-4480-1(2), SLD 1010) AudioGO.

Dead Man in Trieste. Michael Pearce. Read by Clive Mantle. 5 cass. 2005. 49.95 (978-0-7927-3758-2(X), CSL 845, Chivers Sound Lib); audio compact disk 64.95 (978-0-7927-3759-9(8), SLD 845, Chivers Sound Lib) AudioGO.

Dead Man Lies see Poetry & Voice of Ted Hughes

Dead Man Running. Roy Lewis. 5 cass. (Running Time: 6 hrs. 35 mins.). (Story Sound Ser.). (J). 2004. 49.95 (978-1-85903-745-4(3)) Pub: Mgna Lrg Print GBR. Dist(s): Ulverscroft US

Dead Man Talking. Richard Woodman. 10 CDs. (Running Time: 11 hrs. 30 mins.). (Soundings (CDs) Ser.). (J). 2004. audio compact disk 89.95 (978-1-84283-937-9(3)) Pub: ISIS Lrg Prnt GBR. Dist(s): Ulverscroft US

Dead Man Talking. Richard Woodman. Read by Michael Tudor Barnes. 8 cass. (Running Time: 11 hrs. 30 mins.). (Soundings Ser.). (J). 2004. 69.95 (978-1-84283-712-2(5)) Pub: ISIS Lrg Prnt GBR. Dist(s): Ulverscroft US

Dead Man Walking, unabr. ed. Helen Prejean. Narrated by Barbara Caruso. 8 cass. (Running Time: 11 hrs. 15 mins.). 70.00 (978-0-7887-0587-8(3), 94764E7) Recorded Bks.
This best-selling novel is the inspiration for the Academy Award-winning movie. Measures the devastating costs of the death penalty. Available to libraries only.

Dead Man Walking: An Eyewitness Account of the Death Penalty in the United States. Helen Prejean. 1 cass. (Running Time: 1 hr.). 1995. 29.95 (AA8376) Credence Commun.
Sister Prejean gave this talk to a spellbound group of lawyers at the Notre Dame Law School. She told the stories of her dealing with the men on death row: what she saw, what she was told & what she believes. Prejean has been lecturing on this topic extensively ever since her book on the topic was nominated for a Pulitzer Prize.

Dead Man Walking: An Eyewitness Account of the Death Penalty in the United States. Helen Prejean. Read by Barbara Caruso. 7 Cass. (Running Time: 11.25 Hrs). 29.95 (978-1-4025-2798-2(5)) Recorded Bks.

Dead Man's Chest. Roger L. Johnson. Read by Geoffrey Howard. (Running Time: 17 hrs. 30 mins.). 2002. 48.95 (978-1-59912-460-5(2)) Iofy Corp.

***Dead man's Chest.** unabr. ed. Kerry Greenwood. (Running Time: 8 hrs. 33 mins.). (Phryne Fisher Mystery Ser.). 2010. audio compact disk 83.95 (978-1-74214-895-3(6), 9781742148953) Pub: Bolinda Pubng AUS. Dist(s): Bolinda Pub Inc

Dead Man's Chest. unabr. ed. Roger L. Johnson. Read by Geoffrey Howard. 14 CDs. (Running Time: 17 hrs. 30 mins.). 2002. audio compact disk 112.00 (978-0-7861-9385-1(9), 3026); 83.95 (978-0-7861-2367-4(2), 3026) Blckstn Audio.
Begins with Long John Silver's escape from the merchantman Hispaniola at Puerta Plata and culminates with the American Revolution more than a decade later. It describes in rich detail the unholy alliance between this softhearted cutthroat, his teenage nephew, David Noble, and Captain John Paul Jones. Together they work to retrieve a king's ransom of Spanish gold and jewels from a dead man's chest.

Dead Man's Folly. unabr. ed. Agatha Christie. Read by David Suchet. 4 cass. (Running Time: 6 hrs. 6 min.). 2001. 25.95 (978-1-57270-236-3(2), N61236u) Pub: Audio Partners. Dist(s): PerseuPGW
Mystery writer Ariadne Oliver suspects that something isn't quite right at her Murder Hunt & calls old friend Hercule Poirot for help. The game is to be the central event at the village fete. And Hercule Poirot is to present the prize to the player who finds the body. Only this time, the make-believe clues lead to a genuine corpse!.

Dead Man's Folly. unabr. ed. Agatha Christie. Read by David Suchet. (Running Time: 21780 sec.). (Mystery Masters Ser.). (ENG.). 2006. audio compact disk 27.95 (978-1-57270-547-0(7)) Pub: AudioGO. Dist(s): Perseus Dist

***Dead Man's Folly: A BBC Full-Cast Radio Drama.** Agatha Christie. Narrated by Full Cast Production Staff & John Moffatt. (Running Time: 2 hrs. 0 mins. 0 sec.). (ENG., 2010. audio compact disk 24.95 (978-1-4056-7720-2(1)) Pub: AudioGO. Dist(s): Perseus Dist

Dead Man's Island. unabr. ed. Carolyn G. Hart. Read by Kate Reading. 6 cass. (Running Time: 9 hrs.). (Henrie O Mystery Ser.). 1997. 48.00 (978-0-7366-3837-1(7), 4557) Books on Tape.
Chase Prescott, media magnate, is nearly killed by a box of cyanide candy. Fearing for his life, he calls his former lover, retired reporter Henrietta O'Dwyer Collins. His request is simple: He'll assemble all the suspects if she will kindly point out the would-be murderer. On Chase's private island off the South Carolina coast, Henrie O meets the players in this deadly drama. Henrie O meets the players in this deadly drama. Henrie O has her work cut out for her. As she unearths a will & new evidence, a killer hurricane sweeps up from Cuba, threatening to maroon them. But in this luxurious vacation spot, the storm's fury is less dangerous than the murderous greed of one of Prescott's guests.

Dead Man's Mine. unabr. ed. Orville D. Johnson. Read by David Sharp. 4 cass. (Running Time: 4 hrs. 42 min.). 1994. 26.95 (978-1-55686-516-9(3)) Books in Motion.
An Army Sergeant returns to his home town to sell his dead father's played out gold mine. He changes his mind when the buyers appear too eager & a dead body shows up.

Dead Man's Mirror. unabr. ed. Agatha Christie. Read by Hugh Fraser. 2002. 18.95 (978-1-57270-295-0(8)) Pub: Audio Partners. Dist(s): PerseuPGW

Dead Man's Mirror. unabr. ed. Agatha Christie. Narrated by Hugh Fraser. (Mystery Masters Ser.). (ENG.). 2002. audio compact disk 19.95 (978-1-57270-296-7(6)) Pub: AudioGO. Dist(s): Perseus Dist

Dead Man's Ransom. Ellis Peters, pseud. Read by Derek Jacobi. 2 cass. (Running Time: 3 hrs.). (Chronicles of Brother Cadfael Ser.: Vol. 9). 1998. (978-1-84032-155-5(5), HoddrStoughton) Hodder General GBR.
An exchange of valuable prisoners is arranged & the sheriff is to be recovered in place of a young Welsh lordling who had been captured in the course of a misguided assault on a convent. But before the exchange can be completed, one captive is murdered. To Brother Cadfael, who first notices the evidence of unatural death, falls the task of gathering enough clues to prove it.

Dead Man's Ransom. unabr. ed. Ellis Peters. Read by Roe Kendall. 6 cass. (Running Time: 8 hrs. 30 mins.). (Chronicles of Brother Cadfael Ser.: Vol. 9). 2000. 44.95 (978-0-7861-1825-0(3), 2624); audio compact disk 56.00 (978-0-7861-9848-1(6), 2624) Blckstn Audio.
It is early in the twelfth century & the civil war between King Stephen & the Empress Maud rages with renewed vigor. In the battle of Lincoln, the sheriff of Shropshire is captured & the king himself is detained by his enemies. An exchange of prisoners is arranged: the sheriff will be bartered for a young Welsh lordling who has been captured during a misguided assault on a convent. All seems to be going according to plan until one of the prisoners dies under mysterious circumstances before the exchange is completed. Canny as ever, Brother Cadfael suspects that more than a little evil is afoot.

Dead Man's Ransom. unabr. ed. Ellis Peters, pseud. Read by Roe Kendall. 1 CD. (Running Time: 8 hrs.). (Chronicles of Brother Cadfael Ser.: Vol. 9). 2001. audio compact disk 19.95 (zm2624) Blckstn Audio.

Dead Man's Ransom. unabr. ed. Ellis Peters, pseud. Read by Stephen Thorne. 6 cass. (Running Time: 9 hrs.). (Chronicles of Brother Cadfael Ser.: Vol. 9). 2000. 49.95 (978-0-7451-4039-1(4), CAB 736) Pub: Chivers Audio Bks GBR. Dist(s): AudioGO
Civil war rages and after the sheriff to Shropshire is captured at the battle of Lincoln, the king himself is taken prisoner. Though an exchange of prisoners is agreed, with the sheriff to be recovered in place of a young Welsh lord, it is soon halted: one captive is dead! Brother Cadfael recognized unnatural death but he must find enough clues to prove it.

Dead Man's Ransom. unabr. ed. Ellis Peters, pseud. Narrated by Patrick Tull. 6 cass. (Running Time: 8 hrs. 15 mins.). (Chronicles of Brother Cadfael Ser.: Vol. 9). 1993. 51.00 (978-1-55690-931-3(4), 93427E7) Recorded Bks.
When Shrewsbury's sheriff, Gilbert Prestcote, is taken prisoner by the Empress Maud's forces, its citizens are prepared to exchange him for a man of equal value they have within their possession. But soon after Prestcote arrives for the prisoner exchange, he dies. Was it death by natural causes or a most unnatural murder?.

Dead Man's River. Elizabeth Laird. 1 cass. (Running Time: 1 hr. 30 mins.). (J). (978-0-582-05858-3(9), PutnaJuv) Penguin Grp USA.

Dead Man's Rule. 1 cass. 1989. bk. 35.00 (AC-504) PA Bar Inst.

***Dead Man's Shoes.** 2010. audio compact disk (978-1-59171-227-5(0)) Falcon Picture.

Dead Man's Walk: A Novel. Larry McMurtry. Narrated by Jack Garrett. 14 cass. (Running Time: 19 hrs. 15 mins.). (Lonesome Dove Ser.: No. 1). 119.00 (978-1-4025-2472-1(2)) Recorded Bks.

Dead Man's Walk: A Novel. unabr. ed. Larry McMurtry. Read by Will Patton. 10 cass. (Running Time: 15 hrs.). (Lonesome Dove Ser.: No. 1). 1996. 80.00 (978-0-7366-3211-9(5), 3874) Books on Tape.
The first adventures of Gus & Call, the heroes of "Lonesome Dove," hover perilously close to being their last in this prequel to the novel. The author takes us back in time. Gus & Call are Texas Rangers, but still in their teens. Led by ex-pirate Caleb Cobb, they try to capture Santa Fe. After falling, they must cross the perilous Jornada del Muerto - the "Dead Man's Walk" - in a chapter so vivid you can feel the heat. And that's just the beginning of their adventures.

Dead Man's Walk: A Novel. unabr. ed. Larry McMurtry. Read by Will Patton. 10 cass. (Running Time: 140 hrs. 0 mins. 0 sec.). No. 1. (ENG.). 1995. 45.00 (978-0-671-55169-8(8), 113285, Audioworks) Pub: S&S Audio. Dist(s): S and S Inc

Dead March: A Civil War Mystery. unabr. ed. Ann McMillan. Read by Kimberly Schraf. 7 cass. (Running Time: 10 hrs. 30 min.). 1999. 56.00 (978-0-7366-4417-4(2), 4878) Books on Tape.
In the gilded Virginia spring of 1861, Narcissa Powers, a well-to-do young white widow, is thrown together with Judah Daniel, a free black herbalist, to solve the murder of a slave girl whose cadaver is dug up by anatomists & their grave robbers. Aided by a fledging British news correspondent, these two women risk their lives as they infiltrate the worlds of men, medicine & war that are about to collide in the bloody battle of First Manassas.

Dead Men. Stephen Leather. 2008. 89.95 (978-0-7531-3100-8(5)); audio compact disk 99.95 (978-0-7531-3101-5(3)) Pub: Isis Pubng Ltd GBR. Dist(s): Ulverscroft US

***Dead Men Kill.** unabr. ed. L. Ron Hubbard. Read by Jennifer Aspen et al. Narrated by R. F. Daley. 2 CDs. (Running Time: 2 hrs.). (Stories from the Golden Age Ser.). (YA). (gr. 7 up). 2010. audio compact disk 9.95 (978-1-59212-350-6(3)) Gala Pr LLC.

Dead Men Prowl. 6 episodes on 3 cas. (Running Time: 60 min. per cass.). (Adventures by Morse Collection). 1998. 19.98 Boxed set. (4304) Radio Spirits.
The two wealthiest residents of a small vacation island are dead. A young man is shot through the heart. Why won't their bodies stay in the morgue.

Dead Men Tell No Tales. Perf. by Chynna Pozzessere. Compiled by Heather Pozzessere. 2007. audio compact disk 9.99 (978-1-4276-2422-2(4)) AardGP.

Dead Men Walking. Nathaniel Holcomb. 3 cass. (Running Time: 4 hrs. 30 mins.). 1999. (978-1-930918-24-5(0)) Its All About Him.

Dead Men's Boots. unabr. ed. Mike Carey. Narrated by Michael Kramer. (Running Time: 16 hrs. 0 mins. 0 sec.). (Felix Castor Ser.). (ENG.). 2009. 29.99 (978-1-4001-6163-8(0)); 39.99 (978-1-4001-9163-5(7)); 20.99 (978-1-4001-8163-6(1)); audio compact disk 39.99 (978-1-4001-1163-3(3)) Pub: Tantor Media. Dist(s): IngramPubServ

Dead Men's Boots. unabr. ed. Mike Carey. Narrated by Michael Kramer. (Running Time: 16 hrs. 0 mins. 0 sec.). (Felix Castor Ser.). (ENG.). 2009. audio compact disk 79.99 (978-1-4001-4163-0(X)) Pub: Tantor Media. Dist(s): IngramPubServ

***Dead Moon Epilogue.** Illus. by Luis Royo. (ENG.). 2010. bk. (978-1-935351-27-6(3)) Heavy Metal Magazine.

Dead North. Sue Henry. (Jessie Arnold Mystery Ser.). audio compact disk 17.99 (978-0-7366-7651-9(1)) Books on Tape.

Dead North. Sue Henry. (Jessie Arnold Mystery Ser.). 2001. 48.00 (978-0-7366-7153-8(6)); audio compact disk 56.00 (978-0-7366-7907-7(3)) Books on Tape.

Dead North. unabr. ed. Sue Henry. Read by Mary Peiffer. 6 cass. (Running Time: 9 hrs.). (Jessie Arnold Mystery Ser.). 2001. 29.95 (978-0-7366-5697-9(9)) Books on Tape.
After fire levels her home in the Alaskan bush, dogsledder Jesse Arnold is homeless. When a friend asks her to drive a motor home north from Idaho, she jumps at the chance. On the long, scenic ride, she meets a teenage runaway and ends up in danger from the boy's shadowy pursuer.

Dead of Jericho. abr. ed. Colin Dexter. 2 cass. (Running Time: 3 hrs.). (ENG., 2001. (978-0-333-90662-0(4)) Macmillan UK GBR.

Dead of Jericho. unabr. ed. Colin Dexter. Read by Colin Dexter. 6 cass. (Running Time: 9 hrs.). (Inspector Morse Mystery Ser.: Bk. 5). 2000. 49.95 (978-0-7451-5894-5(3), CAB 442) Pub: Chivers Audio Bks GBR. Dist(s): AudioGO
They were neighbors in Oxford's run-down Jericho district. The shapely divorcee had been hanged by the neck, the seedy odd-job man murdered amongst his home library of pornography. Inspector Morse might have taken a more coolly professional interest if he had not been at the point of accepting the lady's open invitation only minutes after the murder squad began their investigation into her death.

Dead of Night. John Marsden. Read by Suzi Dougherty. (Running Time: 7 hrs.). (Tomorrow Ser.). (YA). 2009. 69.99 (978-1-74214-337-8(7), 9781742143378) Pub: Bolinda Pubng AUS. Dist(s): Bolinda Pub Inc

Dead of Night. abr. ed. Randy Wayne White. Read by Dick Hill. (Running Time: 6 hrs.). (Doc Ford Ser.: No. 12). 2005. audio compact disk 74.25 (978-1-59737-426-2(1), 9781597374262, BACDLib Ed) Brilliance Audio.
Later, my conscience would play the inevitable game of "What if . . ." What if I had stopped by Jobe's home on Friday morning instead of Sunday night? What if I hadn't interrupted the two people who were alternately interrogating and beating him? Would he have lived? Or would he have died? And what would have happened then? It started when Doc Ford got the call from his old friend Frieda Matthews - her reclusive biologist brother Jobe wasn't answering the phone. Could Doc check on him? Ford can't think of a reason not to, but soon he will think of a hundred. Not only will it be one of the worst scenes he has ever encountered, but the consequences of that visit will draw him into the heart of a nightmare. A catastrophe is coming to Florida, and just maybe there is something Ford can do about it - but he doesn't know how or where or when . . . or even if he is already too late. Filled with the remarkable prose and rich atmosphere that have won White so many fans, and featuring some of the best suspense characters in fiction, Dead of Night is White's biggest thriller yet - "like strapping yourself onto the exposed bow of a South Florida airboat" (The Miami Herald).

Dead of Night. abr. ed. Randy Wayne White. Read by Dick Hill. (Running Time: 21600 sec.). (Doc Ford Ser.: No. 12). 2006. audio compact disk 16.99 (978-1-59600-849-6(0), 9781596008496, BCD Value Price) Brilliance Audio.
Later, my conscience would play the inevitable game of "What if . . ." What if I had stopped by Jobe's home on Friday morning instead of Sunday night? What if I hadn't interrupted the two people who were alternately interrogating and beating him? Would he have lived? Or would he have died? And what would have happened then? It started when Doc Ford got the call from his old friend Frieda Matthews - her reclusive biologist brother Jobe wasn't answering the phone. Could Doc check on him? Ford can't think of a reason not to, but soon he will think of a hundred. Not only will it be one of the worst scenes he has ever encountered, but the consequences of that visit will draw him into the heart of a nightmare. A catastrophe is coming to Florida, and just maybe there is something Ford can do about it - but he doesn't know how or where or when . . . or even if he is already too late. Filled with the remarkable prose and rich atmosphere that have won White so many fans, and featuring some of the best suspense characters in fiction, Dead of Night is White's biggest thriller yet - "like strapping yourself onto the exposed bow of a South Florida airboat" (The Miami Herald).

Dead of Night. unabr. ed. John Marsden. Read by Suzi Dougherty. 4 cass. (Running Time: 6 hrs.). 2001. (590908) Bolinda Pubng AUS.

Dead of Night. unabr. ed. John Marsden. 6 CDs. (Running Time: 7 hrs.). (Tomorow Ser.). (YA). 2001. audio compact disk 77.95 (978-1-74030-397-2(0)) Pub: Bolinda Pubng AUS. Dist(s): Bolinda Pub Inc

Dead of Night. unabr. ed. John Marsden. Read by Suzi Dougherty. 4 cass. (Running Time: 7 hrs.). (Tomorrow Ser.). (YA). 2004. 32.00 (978-1-876584-91-7(2), 590908) Bolinda Pubng AUS.
John Marsden has sold over two million books world-wide. John has won every major writing award in Australia for young people's fiction, as well as numerous awards both in the USA and Europe. John has three titles in the top ten list of all Australian books sold.

Dead of Night. unabr. ed. John Marsden. Read by Suzi Dougherty. (Running Time: 25200 sec.). (Tomorrow Ser.). 2008. audio compact disk 43.95 (978-1-921334-53-5(3), 9781921334535) Pub: Bolinda Pubng AUS. Dist(s): Bolinda Pub Inc

Dead of Night. unabr. ed. Randy Wayne White. Read by Dick Hill. (Running Time: 11 hrs.). (Doc Ford Ser.: No. 12). 2005. 39.25 (978-1-59710-184-4(2), 9781597101844, BADLE); 24.95 (978-1-59710-185-1(0), 9781597101851, BAD); 24.95 (978-1-59335-693-4(5), 9781593356934, Brilliance MP3); 34.95 (978-1-59086-966-6(4), 9781590869666, BAU); 87.25 (978-1-59086-967-3(2), 9781590869673, BrilAudUnabridg); DVD 39.25 (978-1-59335-827-3(X), 9781593358273, Brinc Audio MP3 Lib) Brilliance Audio.
Later, my conscience would play the inevitable game of "What if . . ." What if I had stopped by Jobe's home on Friday morning instead of Sunday night? What if I hadn't interrupted the two people who were alternately interrogating and beating him? Would he have lived? Or would he have died? And what would have happened then? It started when Doc Ford got the call from his old friend Frieda Matthews - her reclusive biologist brother Jobe wasn't answering the phone. Could Doc check on him? Ford can't think of a reason not to, but soon he will think of a hundred. Not only will it be one of the worst scenes he has ever encountered, but the consequences of that visit will draw him into the heart of a nightmare. A catastrophe is coming to Florida, and just maybe there is something Ford can do about it - but he doesn't know how or where or when . . . or even if he is already too late. Filled with the remarkable prose and rich atmosphere that have won White so many fans, and featuring some of the best suspense characters in fiction, Dead of Night is White's biggest thriller yet - "like strapping yourself onto the exposed bow of a South Florida airboat" (The Miami Herald).

Dead on Its Tracks. abr. ed. Johnny Ray Barnes, Jr. & Marion Engle. Read by Multivoice Production Staff. (Running Time: 7200 sec.). (Strange Matter Ser.). (J). (gr. 4-7). 2006. audio compact disk 25.25 (978-1-4233-0891-1(3), 9781423308911, BACDLib Ed) Brilliance Audio.

Dead on Its Tracks. abr. ed. Engle & Barnes. Read by Full Cast Production Staff. (Running Time: 7200 sec.). (Strange Matter Ser.). (J). (gr. 4-7). 2006. audio compact disk 9.95 (978-1-4233-0890-4(5), 9781423308904, BACD) Brilliance Audio.

Dead on Its Tracks. abr. ed. Engle & Barnes. (Running Time: 2 hrs.). (Strange Matter Ser.). 2006. 9.95 (978-1-4233-0892-8(1), 9781423308928, BAD) Brilliance Audio.

Dead on Its Tracks. abr. ed. Engle & Julian Barnes. Read by Multivoice Production Staff. (Running Time: 2 hrs.). (Strange Matter Ser.). 2006. 25.25 (978-1-4233-0893-5(X), 9781423308935, BADLE) Brilliance Audio.

Dead on the Island. unabr. ed. Bill Crider. Read by Jim Kille. 2 cass. (Running Time: 3 hrs.). 1995. 17.00 Set. (978-1-883268-19-0(2)) Spellbinders.
Galveston P.I. Truman Smith is asked by a friend to find his missing daughter. Having picked up a lead, Tru finds the trail gets uncomfortably close to those he knows best.

***Dead or Alive.** abr. ed. Tom Clancy & Grant Blackwood. (Running Time: 9 hrs.). (Jack Ryan Ser.). 2010. audio compact disk 27.99 (978-1-4418-8813-6(6), 9781441888136) Brilliance Audio.

***Dead or Alive.** abr. ed. Tom Clancy & Grant Blackwood. Read by Lou Diamond Phillips. (Running Time: 9 hrs.). (Jack Ryan Ser.). 2010. audio compact disk 44.97 (978-1-4418-8815-0(2), 9781441888150, BACDLib Ed) Brilliance Audio.

***Dead or Alive.** unabr. ed. Tom Clancy & Grant Blackwood. Read by Lou Diamond Phillips. (Running Time: 21 hrs.). (Jack Ryan Ser.). 2010. 29.99 (978-1-4418-8809-9(8), 9781441888099, Brilliance MP3); 49.97 (978-1-4418-8810-5(1), 9781441888105, Brinc Audio MP3 Lib); audio compact disk 39.99 (978-1-4418-8806-8(3), 9781441888068, Bril Audio CD Unabri); audio compact disk 99.97 (978-1-4418-8807-5(1), 9781441888075, BriAudCD Unabrid) Brilliance Audio.

***Dead or Alive (Plus Bonus Digital Copy of Dead or Alive)** unabr. ed. Tom Clancy & Grant Blackwood. Read by Lou Diamond Phillips. (Running Time: 21 hrs.). (Jack Ryan Ser.). 2010. audio compact disk 44.99 (978-1-4558-0043-8(0), 9781455800438, Bril Audio CD Unabri) Brilliance Audio.

Dead Past see Best of Isaac Asimov

***Dead Path.** unabr. ed. Stephen M. Irwin. Read by Michael Carman. (Running Time: 14 hrs. 18 mins.). 2010. audio compact disk 108.95 (978-1-74214-678-2(3), 9781742146782) Pub: Bolinda Pubng AUS. Dist(s): Bolinda Pub Inc

***dead Path.** unabr. ed. Stephen M. Irwin. Read by Michael Carman. (Running Time: 14 hrs. 18 mins.). 2010. 43.95 (978-1-74214-766-6(6), 9781742147666) Pub: Bolinda Pubng AUS. Dist(s): Bolinda Pub Inc

***Dead Point.** Peter Temple. Read by Michael Carman. (Running Time: 8 hrs.). 2010. 59.99 (978-1-74214-287-6(7), 9781742142876) Pub: Bolinda Pubng AUS. Dist(s): Bolinda Pub Inc

Dead Point. unabr. ed. Peter Temple. Read by Michael Carmen. 6 cass. (Running Time: 8 hrs.). 2001. 48.00 (978-1-74030-479-5(9)) Pub: Bolinda Pubng AUS. Dist(s): Bolinda Pub Inc

Dead Point. unabr. ed. Peter Temple. Read by Michael Carman. 7 CDs. (Running Time: 8 hrs.). (Jack Irish Ser.). 2008. audio compact disk 83.95 (978-1-921334-21-4(5), 9781921334214) Pub: Bolinda Pubng AUS. Dist(s): Bolinda Pub Inc

***Dead Point.** unabr. ed. Peter Temple. Read by Michael Carman. (Running Time: 8 hrs.). 2010. 43.95 (978-1-74214-646-1(5), 9781742146461) Pub: Bolinda Pubng AUS. Dist(s): Bolinda Pub Inc

Dead Question. Gerald Hammond & Cathleen McCarron. 2008. 49.95 (978-1-84652-225-3(0)); audio compact disk 59.95 (978-1-84652-226-0(9)) Pub: Magna Story GBR. Dist(s): Ulverscroft US

Dead Reckoning. Clive Egleton. Read by Christopher Kay. 12 CDs. (Sound Ser.). 2003. audio compact disk 99.95 (978-1-86042-919-4(X)) Pub: UlverLrgPrint GBR. Dist(s): Ulverscroft US

Dead Reckoning. Patricia Hall. Read by Michael Tudor Barnes. 7 cass. (Soundings Ser.). (J). 2005. 61.95 (978-1-84283-674-3(9)) Pub: ISIS Lrg Prnt GBR. Dist(s): Ulverscroft US

Dead Reckoning. unabr. ed. Clive Egleton. Read by Christopher Kay. 12 cass. (Running Time: 16 hrs.). (Sound Ser.). 2001. 94.95 (978-1-86042-666-7(2), 26662) Pub: UlverLrgPrint GBR. Dist(s): Ulverscroft US

***Dead Ringer.** abr. ed. Lisa Scottoline. Read by Kate Burton. (ENG.). 2004. (978-0-06-075232-3(7), Harper Audio); (978-0-06-081312-3(1), Harper Audio) HarperCollins Pubs.

Dead Ringer. abr. ed. Lisa Scottoline. Read by Kate Burton. 2004. audio compact disk 14.95 (978-0-06-077508-7(4)) HarperCollins Pubs.

Dead Ringer. unabr. ed. Morris Gleitzman & Paul Jennings. (Running Time: 1 hr. 17 mins.). (Wicked! Ser.: Bk. 4). (J). 2001. 18.00 (978-1-74030-466-5(7)) Pub: Bolinda Pubng AUS. Dist(s): Bolinda Pub Inc

Dead Ringer. unabr. ed. Paul Jennings & Morris Gleitzman. Read by Kate Hosking & Stig Wemyss. 2 CDs. (Running Time: 1 hr. 17 mins.). (Wicked! Ser.: Bk. 4). (J). audio compact disk 24.00 (978-1-74093-426-8(1)) Bolinda Pubng AUS.

***Dead Ringer.** unabr. ed. Lisa Scottoline. Read by Kate Burton. (ENG.). 2003. (978-0-06-073559-3(7), Harper Audio) HarperCollins Pubs.

***Dead Ringer.** unabr. ed. Lisa Scottoline. Read by Kate Burton. (ENG.). 2004. (978-0-06-081496-0(9), Harper Audio) HarperCollins Pubs.

Dead Ringer. unabr. ed. Lisa Scottoline. 8 cass. (Running Time: 11 hrs.). 2003. 78.00 (978-1-4025-4828-4(1)) Recorded Bks.

Dead Romantic. unabr. ed. Simon Brett. Read by Simon Brett. 6 cass. (Running Time: 5 hrs. 30 mins.). 2000. 54.95 (978-0-7540-0520-9(8), CAB 1943) Pub: Chivers Audio Bks GBR. Dist(s): AudioGO
Madeleine Severn is a woman, beautifully groomed & sublimely self-confident, a glorious love object who has yet to surrender to lust. But now she is in danger from those who thought she could control. As one affair reaches new heights of passion, Madeleine doesn't realize that she has another admirer, someone who is obsessively tracking every move.

***Dead Room.** Chris Mooney. 2010. 69.95 (978-1-4450-0004-6(0)); audio compact disk 84.95 (978-1-4450-0005-3(9)) Pub: Isis Pubng Ltd GBR. Dist(s): Ulverscroft US

Dead Room. abr. ed. Heather Graham. Read by Joyce Bean. (Running Time: 21600 sec.). 2008. audio compact disk 14.99 (978-1-4233-3171-1(0), 9781423331711, BCD Value Price) Brilliance Audio.

Dead Room. unabr. ed. Heather Graham. Read by Joyce Bean. (Running Time: 10 hrs.). 2007. 39.25 (978-1-4233-3169-8(9), 9781423331698, BADLE); 24.95 (978-1-4233-3168-1(0), 9781423331681, BAD); 82.25 (978-1-4233-3163-6(X), 9781423331636, BrilAudUnabridg); audio compact disk 39.25 (978-1-4233-3167-4(2), 9781423331674, Brinc Audio MP3 Lib); audio compact disk 97.25 (978-1-4233-3165-0(6), 9781423331650, BriAudCD Unabrid); audio compact disk 24.95 (978-1-4233-3166-7(4), 9781423331667, Brilliance MP3); audio compact disk 36.95 (978-1-4233-3164-3(8), 9781423331643, Bril Audio CD Unabri) Brilliance Audio.

Dead Room Farce. unabr. ed. Simon Brett. Read by Simon Brett. 6 cass. (Running Time: 6 hrs.). 1998. 54.95 Set, Dolby Sound. (978-0-7540-0150-8(4), CAB 1573) AudioGO.
Charles Paris has taken a part in the new farce, "Not On Your Wife!" which may make a West End run. Rehearsals have gone well, the laughs are plenty, & there's the attraction of Cookie Stone. But it's not long before a darker mood sets in: Charles' old friend Mark has a drinking problem that amounts to a death wish. And it's not the drink that kills Mark, it's someone in the cast.

Dead Room Farce. unabr. ed. Simon Brett. Read by Frederick Davidson. 5 cass. (Running Time: 7 hrs.). 2003. 39.95 (978-0-7861-1642-3(0), 2470) Blckstn Audio.
It's not Beckett exactly, but a three-month run of "Not on Your Wife!" - a new farce by the prolific British farceur, Bill Blunden - is not to be sniffed at by a jobbing actor. Especially when the presence in the cast of Bernard Walton makes a West End run a distinct possibility. But somebody in the cast has a dirty little secret that must not be revealed.

Dead Run. abr. ed. Read by Buck Schimer. (Running Time: 21600 sec.). (Monkeewrench Ser.). 2006. audio compact disk 16.99 (978-1-59737-341-8(9), 9781597373418, BCD Value Price) Brilliance Audio.
Monkeewrench founders Grace McBride and Annie Belinsky, along with Deputy Sharon Mueller, are driving from Minneapolis to Green Bay, Wisconsin, where they believe a new serial killer is just warming up, when their car breaks down, deep in the northern woods, far away from civilization and cell towers. A walk through the forest leads them to the crossroads town of Four Corners, where they had hoped to find a landline and a mechanic, but instead find...absolutely nothing. Something terrible has happened in Four Corners, and the complete absence of life and severed phone lines in every building make it impossible to get help. Grace, her senses honed by a lifetime of justifiable paranoia, sees the sinister in every detail, and her intuition barely saves all three of them when they witness a horrifying double murder. Grace, Annie, and Sharon are suddenly running for their lives, while the rest of the Monkeewrench crew, along with Minneapolis cops Leo Magozzi and Gino Rolseth, strike out on a blind search to find them.

Dead Run. abr. ed. P. J. Tracy. Read by Buck Schimer. (Running Time: 6 hrs.). (Monkeewrench Ser.). 2005. audio compact disk 74.25 (978-1-59600-131-2(3), 9781596001312, BACDLib Ed) Brilliance Audio.
Please enter a Synopsis.

Dead Run. unabr. ed. P. J. Tracy. Read by Buck Schimer. (Running Time: 10 hrs.). (Monkeewrench Ser.). 2005. 39.25 (978-1-59710-187-5(7), 9781597101875, BADLE); 24.95 (978-1-59710-186-8(9), 9781597101868, BAD); 24.95 (978-1-59335-938-6(1), 9781593359386, Brilliance MP3); 39.25 (978-1-59335-939-3(X), 9781593359393, Brinc Audio MP3 Lib); 32.95 (978-1-59600-128-2(3), 9781596001282, BAU); 82.25 (978-1-59600-129-9(1), 9781596001299, BrilAudUnabridg) Brilliance Audio.

Dead Sea Cipher. Elizabeth Peters, pseud. Narrated by Grace Conlin. (Running Time: 8 hrs. 30 mins.). 1996. 27.95 (978-1-59912-647-0(8)) Iofy Corp.

Dead Sea Cipher. unabr. ed. Elizabeth Peters, pseud. Read by Grace Conlin. 6 cass. (Running Time: 8 hrs. 30 mins.). 1998. 44.95 (978-0-7861-1357-6(X), 2266) Blckstn Audio.
An odyssey of terror that takes Dinah Van der Lyn to the fabled cities of Sidon, Tyro, Damascus...and then Jerusalem, racing through the twisting streets, not knowing if the man she is following will lead her to safety...or into a deadly trap.

Dead Sea Cipher. unabr. ed. Elizabeth Peters, pseud. Read by Grace Conlin. (Running Time: 8 hrs. 30 mins.). 1998. 24.95 (978-0-7861-8708-9(5)); audio compact disk 56.00 (978-0-7861-8835-2(9)) Blckstn Audio.

Dead Sea Cipher, Set. unabr. ed. Elizabeth Peters, pseud. Read by Grace Conlin. 6 cass. 1999. 44.95 (FS9-43270) Highsmith.

Dead Sea Cypher. unabr. ed. Elizabeth Peters, pseud. Read by Grace Conlin. 7 CDs. (Running Time: 8 hrs. 30 mins.). 2000. audio compact disk 56.00 (978-0-7861-8779-9(4), 2266) Blckstn Audio.

***Dead Sea Scrolls.** Instructed by Gary A. Rendsburg. 2010. 129.95 (978-1-59803-629-9(7)); audio compact disk 179.95 (978-1-59803-630-5(0)) Teaching Co.

Dead Sea Scrolls: Foundations of Christian Scriptural Tradition. Joseph Fitzmyer. 3 cass. (Running Time: 4 hrs. 21 min.). 1998. 29.95 Set. (TAH399) Alba Hse Comns.
Fr. Fitzmyer helps to direct the listener toward a comprehensive view of the essence of God's Word revealed through the Dead Sea Scrolls of Qumran.

Dead Sea Scrolls after Forty Years, Set. Moderated by Hershel Shanks et al. 4 cass. 1991. 29.95 (978-1-880317-29-7(X), 7HC1) Biblical Arch Soc.
Biblical archaeology & biblical studies.

Dead Secret. abr. ed. Wilkie Collins. Read by David March. Contrib. by Neville Teller. 3 cass. 19.95 (SCN 181) J Norton Pubs.
Rosamond & her husband try to uncover the secret contained in a hidden letter. First published in 1857.

Dead Secret. unabr. ed. Roy H. Lewis. Read by Robbie MacNab. 5 CDs. (Running Time: 6 hrs. 35 mins.). (Story Sound CD Ser.). (J). 2002. audio compact disk 59.95 (978-1-85903-553-5(1)) Pub: Mgna Lrg Print GBR. Dist(s): Ulverscroft US

Dead Secret, Set. unabr. ed. Wilkie Collins. Read by Flo Gibson. 9 cass. (Running Time: 12 hrs.). 1994. 28.95 (978-1-55685-307-4(6)) Audio Bk Con.
The terrible secret hidden in Porthgenna Tower all but ruins the life of Sarah Leeson, a young servant girl, & comes back to haunt Rosamond, the heiress to the mansion, fifteen years later. Vivid & eccentric characters such as Arthur Treverton, the irascible hermit, Schrowl, his bullying servant, & Uncle Joseph, a kindly bumbler, add to the dimensions of this detective thriller.

Dead Shall Be Raised Incorruptible see Poetry & Voice of Galway Kinnell

Dead Shot. abr. ed. Jack Coughlin & Donald A. Davis. Read by Scott Sowers. 5 CDs. (Running Time: 6 hrs. 0 mins. 0 sec.). (ENG.). 2009. audio compact disk 29.95 (978-1-4272-0619-0(8)) Pub: Macmill Audio. Dist(s): Macmillan

Dead Side of the Mike. unabr. ed. Simon Brett. Read by Frederick Davidson. 5 cass. (Running Time: 7 hrs.). 1992. 39.95 (978-0-7861-0340-9(X), 1297) Blckstn Audio.
Charles Paris tackles his sixth case when, between acting jobs (what else is new?), he's hired by BBC radio to research & write a program on Swinburne for a new series called "Who Reads Them Now?" Paris hasn't glanced at Swinburne since leaving Oxford nearly thirty years ago, but the pay is good & the surroundings congenial. Then a young studio manager is found dead, her wrists slashed. When Charles learns that she was involved with a shady American record producer who also has turned up dead - another apparent suicide - he begins an investigation. On his first trip to the United States, he picks up information about the American connection. A complicated murder plot is eventually uncovered, but Charles exhausts a list of possible suspects before stumbling onto the solution.

Dead Side of the Mike. unabr. ed. Simon Brett. Narrated by Simon Prebble. 5 cass. (Running Time: 7 hrs.). (Charles Paris Mystery Ser.: No. 6). 1998. 44.00 (978-0-7887-2520-3(3), 95593E7) Recorded Bks.
Charles Paris has started a new career as a radio actor for the BBC. But after an attractive producer commits suicide in front of her microphone, curiosity lures Charles into an investigation.

Dead Silence. unabr. ed. David Harris. Read by Peter Hardy. 2 cass. (Running Time: 2 hrs. 30 mins.). 2002. 24.00 (978-1-74030-357-6(1)) Pub: Bolinda Pubng AUS. Dist(s): Lndmrk Audiobks

Dead Silence. unabr. ed. Randy Wayne White. Read by George Guidall. 10 CDs. (Running Time: 12 hrs.). No. 16. (ENG.). (gr. 12 up). 2009. audio compact disk 39.95 (978-0-14-314417-5(0), PengAudBks) Penguin Grp USA.

Dead Sleep. Greg Iles. 2009. audio compact disk 9.99 (978-1-4418-2649-7(1)) Brilliance Audio.

Dead Sleep. abr. ed. Greg Iles. Read by Susie Breck. (Running Time: 6 hrs.). 2004. audio compact disk 16.99 (978-1-59355-678-5(0), 1593556780, BCD Value Price) Brilliance Audio.
An intricate and emotionally resonant story from one of the most versatile thriller writers at work today. Jordan Glass, a photojournalist on a well-earned vacation, wanders into a Hong Kong art museum and is puzzled to find fellow patrons eying her with curiosity. Minutes later, she stumbles upon a gallery containing a one-artist exhibition called "The Sleeping Women," a mysterious series of paintings that has caused a sensation in the world of modern art. Collectors have come to believe that the canvases depict female nudes not in sleep but in death, and they command millions at auction. When Jordan approaches the last work in the series, she freezes. The face in the painting seems to be her own. This unsettling event hurls her back into a nightmare she has fought desperately to put behind her - for, in fact, the face in the painting belongs not to Jordan but to her twin sister, murdered one year ago. At the urging of the FBI, Jordan becomes both hunter and hunted in a duel with the anonymous artist, a gifted murderer who knows the secret history of Jordan's family, and truths that even she has never had the courage to face.

Dead Sleep. unabr. ed. Greg Iles. Read by Susie Breck. 9 cass. (Running Time: 13 hrs.). 2001. 34.95 (978-1-58788-524-2(7), 1587885247, BAU); 96.25 (978-1-58788-475-7(5), 1587884755, Unabridge Lib Edns) Brilliance Audio.

Dead Sleep. unabr. ed. Greg Iles. Read by Susie Breck. (Running Time: 13 hrs.). 2005. 39.25 (978-1-59600-699-7(4), 9781596006997, BADLE); 24.95 (978-1-59600-698-0(6), 9781596006980, BAD); audio compact disk 39.25 (978-1-59600-697-3(8), 9781596006973, Brinc Audio MP3 Lib); audio compact disk 24.95 (978-1-59600-696-6(X), 9781596006966, Brilliance MP3) Brilliance Audio.

Dead Sleep. unabr. ed. Greg Iles. Read by Susie Breck. (Running Time: 46800 sec.). 2007. audio compact disk 107.25 (978-1-4233-3402-6(7), 9781423334026, BriAudCD Unabrid); audio compact disk 38.95 (978-1-4233-3401-9(9), 9781423334019, Bril Audio CD Unabri) Brilliance Audio.

Dead Souls see Las Almas Muertas

Dead Souls. Nikolai Gogol. Read by Gordon Griffin. (Running Time: 5 hrs.). 2003. 28.95 (978-1-60083-719-7(0)) Iofy Corp.

Dead Souls. Nikolai Gogol. Read by Gordon Griffin. 4 CDs. (Running Time: 5 hrs.). 2003. audio compact disk 28.98 (978-962-634-284-8(6), Naxos AudioBooks) Naxos.

Dead Souls. Nikolai Gogol. Read by Santiago Munévar. (Running Time: 3 hrs.). 2002. 16.95 (978-1-60083-232-1(6), Audiofy Corp) Iofy Corp.

Dead Souls. abr. ed. Nikolai Gogol. 5 cass. (Running Time: 5 hrs.). Dramatization. (Globe Audiodramas Ser.). 1987. bk. 39.95 (978-0-295-75540-3(7)) U of Wash Pr.
Adapted for radio theatre, brings together a cast of 34 performers & a narrator. More thn 40 characters drawn from the story enact the major events of the novel. The final half-hour tape is a rendition of the original music composed for the series.

Dead Souls. unabr. ed. Nikolai Gogol. Read by Tom Weiner. (Running Time: 18 hrs. 0 mins.). (ENG.). 2009. 44.95 (978-1-4332-9518-8(0)); 95.95 (978-1-4332-9514-0(8)); audio compact disk 123.00 (978-1-4332-9515-7(6)) Blckstn Audio.

Dead Souls. unabr. ed. Ian Rankin. 9 cass. (Running Time: 13 hrs. 30 mins.). 2001. 72.00 (978-0-7366-6209-3(X)) Books on Tape.
A colleague's suicide. Pedophiles. A missing child. A serial killer. You never know your luck, muses Rebus. Driven by instinct & experience, he searches for connections, against official skepticism. But at night, unsoothed by whiskey, Rebus faces his ghosts - & the prospect of his daughter's possibly permanent paralysis.

Dead Souls. unabr. ed. Ian Rankin. Read by Geoffrey Howard. 9 cass. (Running Time: 12 hrs.). 2002. 34.95 (978-0-7366-6749-4(0)) Books on Tape.
Rebus has a plate full of unsavory cases that only intensify his own personal crisis.

Dead Souls, Set. unabr. ed. Nikolai Gogol. Read by Flo Gibson. 10 cass. (Running Time: 14 hrs.). 1997. 29.95 (978-1-55685-476-7(5), 476-5) Audio Bk Con.
Chichikov, an arch swindler, buys the certificates of serfs who have died since the last census with the intention of mortgaging them to acquire an estate. This was acclaimed one of Russia's greatest novels for its humor, style & characterizations, despite the fact that it was unfinished.

Dead Street. unabr. ed. Mickey Spillane. Read by Richard Ferrone. (YA). 2008. 54.99 (978-1-60514-568-6(8)) Find a World.

Dead Sure: John 3:16 & Romans 3:21-30. Ed Young. 2000. 4.95 (978-0-7417-2259-1(3), 1259) Win Walk.

Dead Time. abr. ed. Stephen White. Read by Dick Hill. 5 CDs. (Running Time: 6 hrs.). (Dr. Alan Gregory Ser.). 2008. audio compact disk 26.95 (978-1-4233-2894-0(9), 9781423328940, BACD) Brilliance Audio.

Dead Time. abr. ed. Stephen White. Read by Dick Hill. (Running Time: 6 hrs.). (Dr. Alan Gregory Ser.). 2009. audio compact disk 14.99 (978-1-4233-2895-7(7), 9781423328957, BCD Value Price) Brilliance Audio.

Dead Time. unabr. ed. Stephen White. Read by Dick Hill. (Running Time: 13 hrs.). (Dr. Alan Gregory Ser.). 2008. 39.25 (978-1-4233-2893-3(0), 9781423328933, BADLE); 39.25 (978-1-4233-2891-9(4), 9781423328919, Brinc Audio MP3 Lib); 24.95 (978-1-4233-2892-6(2), 9781423328926, BAD); 102.25 (978-1-4233-2887-2(6), 9781423328872, BriAudUnabridg); audio compact disk 38.95 (978-1-4233-2888-9(4), 9781423328889, Bril Audio CD Unabri); audio compact disk 24.95 (978-1-4233-2890-2(6), 9781423328902, Brilliance MP3); audio compact disk 107.25 (978-1-4233-2889-6(2), 9781423328896, BriAudCD Unabrid) Brilliance Audio.

Dead to Rights. unabr. ed. J. A. Jance. Read by Nancy Lee Painter. 8 cass. (Running Time: 10 hrs. 36 min.). (Joanna Brady Mystery Ser.). 1999. 49.95 (978-1-55686-831-3(6)) Books in Motion.
A grieving husband is accused of murdering the drunk driver who killed his wife.

***Dead to Rights.** unabr. ed. J. A. Jance. Read by C. J. Critt. (ENG.). 2010. (978-0-06-196750-4(5), Harper Audio); (978-0-06-195386-6(5), Harper Audio) HarperCollins Pubs.

Dead to Sin: Romans 6:1-14. Ed Young. 1984. Rental 4.95 (978-0-7417-1367-4(5), 367) Win Walk.

Dead-Tossed Waves. unabr. ed. Carrie Ryan. Read by Tara Sands. (J). (gr. 9). 2010. audio compact disk 48.00 (978-0-307-71030-7(0), Listening Lib) Pub: Random Audio Pubg. Dist(s): Random

Dead Trouble. Margaret Duffy. (Story Sound Ser.). (J). 2005. 54.95 (978-1-85903-767-6(4)) Pub: Mgna Lrg Print GBR. Dist(s): Ulverscroft US

Dead until Dark. Charlaine Harris. Narrated by Christine Marshall & William Dufris. 1 CD. (Running Time: 10 hrs. 31 mins.). (Sookie Stackhouse Ser.: Bk. 1). 2004. audio compact disk 18.45 (978-1-58439-001-5(8)) Pbk Dig Inc.

Dead Watch. John Sandford, pseud. Read by Richard Ferrone. (Running Time: 36000 sec.). (ENG.). (gr. 8). 2007. audio compact disk 24.95 (978-0-14-314222-5(4), PengAudBks) Penguin Grp USA.

Dead Watch. abr. ed. John Sandford, pseud. Ed. by Eric Conger. (Running Time: 21600 sec.). (ENG.). (gr. 8). 2007. audio compact disk 14.95 (978-0-14-314223-2(2), PengAudBks) Penguin Grp USA.

Dead Watch. unabr. ed. John Sandford, pseud. Read by Richard Ferrone. 9 CDs. (Running Time: 10 hrs.). 2006. audio compact disk 89.75 (978-1-4193-8999-3(8), C3707); 69.75 (978-1-4193-8997-9(1), 98353) Recorded Bks.
John Sandford is renowned for his crime novels. He tackles the political thriller with Dead Watch. At the request of the White House, Jake Winter investigates the disappearance of former Senator Lincoln Bowe. But the trail of clues leads Jake into the heart of a scandal that could cost him his life and topple the federal government.

Dead Water. unabr. ed. Ngaio Marsh. Read by James Saxon. 6 cass. (Running Time: 9 hrs.). (Inspector Alleyn Mystery Ser.). 2000. 49.95 (978-0-7451-6139-6(1), CAB 280) Pub: Chivers Audio Bks GBR. Dist(s): AudioGO
Times are good in the Cornish village of Portcarrow, as hundreds of unfortunates flock to taste the miraculous waters of Pixie Falls. Then Emily pride inherits Portcarrow, and puts an end to the thriving village trade in miracle cures. So one of them determines to put an end to Miss Pride which presents a pretty puzzle for her old friend, Detective Roderick Alleyn of the Yard.

Dead Witch Walking. unabr. ed. Kim Harrison. Read by Marguerite Gavin. (Hollows Ser.: Bk. 1). (YA). 2007. 59.99 (978-1-60252-893-2(4)) Find a World.

Dead Witch Walking. unabr. ed. Kim Harrison. Read by Marguerite Gavin. (Running Time: 13 hrs. 30 mins. 0 sec.). (Hollows Ser.: Bk. 1). (ENG.). 2007. audio compact disk 39.99 (978-1-4001-0471-0(8)); audio compact disk 29.99 (978-1-4001-5471-5(5)); audio compact disk 79.99 (978-1-4001-3471-7(4)) Pub: Tantor Media. Dist(s): IngramPubServ

Dead Woman's Photograph see Classic Ghost Stories, Vol. 3, A Collection

***Dead-Wood.** unabr. ed. Joe Hill. (ENG.). 2007. (978-0-06-155223-6(2)) HarperCollins Pubs.

***Dead Wrong.** abr. ed. J. A. Jance. Read by Debra Monk. (ENG.). 2006. (978-0-06-122914-5(8), Harper Audio); (978-0-06-122911-4(3), Harper Audio) HarperCollins Pubs.

Dead Wrong. abr. ed. J. A. Jance. Read by Debra Monk. (Running Time: 21600 sec.). (Joanna Brady Mystery Ser.). 2006. audio compact disk 25.95 (978-0-06-089795-6(3)) HarperCollins Pubs.

Dead Wrong. unabr. ed. Narrated by Susan Ericksen. 7 cass. (Running Time: 39420 sec.). (Joanna Brady Mystery Ser.). 2006. 59.95 (978-0-7927-4250-0(8), CSL 952); audio compact disk 79.95 (978-0-7927-4046-9(7), SLD 952); audio compact disk & audio compact disk 29.95 (978-0-7927-4251-7(6), CMP 952) AudioGO.

***Dead Wrong.** unabr. ed. J. A. Jance. Read by Susan Ericksen. (ENG.). 2006. (978-0-06-122913-8(X), Harper Audio); (978-0-06-122912-1(1), Harper Audio) HarperCollins Pubs.

Dead Wrong. unabr. ed. J. A. Jance. Read by Susan Ericksen. 9 CDs. (Running Time: 39600 sec.). (Joanna Brady Mystery Ser.). 2006. audio compact disk 39.95 (978-0-06-089794-9(5), Harper Audio) HarperCollins Pubs.

Dead Wrong. unabr. ed. William X. Kienzle. Read by Edward Holland. 8 cass. (Running Time: 12 hrs.). (Father Koesler Mystery Ser.: No. 15). 2001. 48.00 Books on Tape.
Father Koesler is forced to investigate a thirty-year-old murder when scandal threatens to affect his family.

Dead Wrong. unabr. ed. William X. Kienzle. Read by Edward Holland. 8 cass. (Running Time: 12 hrs.). (Father Koesler Mystery Ser.: No. 15). 2001. 64.00 (978-0-7366-8086-8(1)) Books on Tape.
In 1960, Agnes Ventimiglia believes, after a whirlwind courtship, that a proposal of marriage is imminent. Instead, she is killed. Thirty years later, Father Robert Koesler is forced to look into the unsolved case, and, in doing so, he must look into the secrets of his own family. The situation is precipitated by a real estate magnate on his deathbed, who urges Father Koesler to stop an affair between his son and Koesler's foster cousin. The affair could mean scandal for both the Church and the real estate company, but solving that problem will only send Father Koesler on a further twisting path that will intersect with that of Agnes Ventimiglia.

Dead Yard. Adrian McKinty. Read by Gerard Doyle. (Running Time: 37800 sec.). 2006. 65.95 (978-0-7861-4451-8(3)) Blckstn Audio.

Dead Yard. unabr. ed. Adrian McKinty. Read by Gerard Doyle. 8 cass. (Running Time: 43200 sec.). 2006. 29.95 (978-0-7861-4395-5(9)); audio compact disk 29.95 (978-0-7861-7443-0(9)); audio compact disk 29.95 (978-0-7861-7774-5(8)); audio compact disk 81.00 (978-0-7861-7332-7(7)) Blckstn Audio.

***Dead Zero.** abr. ed. Stephen Hunter. Read by Buck Schimer. (Running Time: 6 hrs.). (Bob Lee Swagger Ser.). 2010. audio compact disk 24.99 (978-1-4418-5387-5(1), 9781441853875) Brilliance Audio.

***Dead Zero.** unabr. ed. Stephen Hunter. Read by Buck Schimer. (Running Time: 13 hrs.). (Bob Lee Swagger Ser.). 2010. 24.99 (978-1-4418-5383-7(9), 9781441853837, Brilliance MP3); 39.97 (978-1-4418-5384-4(7), 9781441853844, Brinc Audio MP3 Lib); audio compact disk 36.99 (978-1-4418-5381-3(2), 9781441853813, Bril Audio CD Unabri); audio compact disk 92.97 (978-1-4418-5382-0(0), 9781441853820, BriAudCD Unabrid) Brilliance Audio.

Deadfall. Cynthia Harrod-Eagles. Read by Marie McCarthy. 5 cass. (Running Time: 5 hrs. 30 mins.). (Soundings Ser.). (J). 2004. 49.95 (978-1-84283-644-6(7)) Pub: ISIS Lrg Prnt GBR. Dist(s): Ulverscroft US

Deadfall. Sue Henry. (Jessie Arnold Mystery Ser.). audio compact disk 57.60 (978-0-7366-5198-1(5)); audio compact disk 17.99 (978-0-7366-7811-7(5)) Books on Tape.

Deadfall. Sue Henry. Read by Mary Peiffer. (Jessie Arnold Mystery Ser.). 1999. audio compact disk 64.00 (978-0-7366-5156-1(X)) Books on Tape.

Deadfall. unabr. ed. Sue Henry. Read by Mary Peiffer. 8 CDs. (Running Time: 9 hrs. 25 mins.). (Jessie Arnold Mystery Ser.). 2001. audio compact disk 64.00 Books on Tape.
Someone is stalking musher Jessie Arnold: someone who makes ominous phone calls, leaves threatening messages, & then raises the stakes immeasurably by setting traps to injure, perhaps kill, her beloved sled dogs.

Deadfall. unabr. ed. Sue Henry. Read by Mary Peiffer. 6 cass. (Running Time: 9 hrs.). (Jessie Arnold Mystery Ser.). 2000. 29.95 (978-0-7366-4428-0(8)) Books on Tape.

Deadfall. unabr. ed. Robert Liparulo. (Running Time: 13 hrs.). 2007. 39.25 (978-1-4233-4349-3(2), 9781423343493, BADLE); 24.95 (978-1-4233-4348-6(4), 9781423343486, BAD) Brilliance Audio.

Deadfall. unabr. ed. Robert Liparulo. Read by Phil Gigante. 1 MP3-CD. (Running Time: 13 hrs.). 2007. 39.25 (978-1-4233-4347-9(6), 9781423343479, Brinc Audio MP3 Lib); 107.25 (978-1-4233-4343-1(3), 9781423343431, BrilAudUnabridg); audio compact disk 112.25 (978-1-4233-4345-5(X), 9781423343455, BriAudCD Unabrid); audio compact disk 34.95 (978-1-4233-4344-8(1), 9781423343448, Bril Audio CD Unabri) Brilliance Audio.

Deadfall. unabr. collector's ed. Sue Henry. Read by Mary Peiffer. 6 cass. (Running Time: 9 hrs.). (Jessie Arnold Mystery Ser.). 1998. 48.00 (978-0-7366-4375-7(3)) Books on Tape.
To avoid a stalker, Jessie Arnold journeys to a remote island but winds up playing a terrifying game of hide & seek with the killer.

Deadfall: A Thriller. unabr. ed. Robert Liparulo. Read by Phil Gigante. 1 MP3-CD. (Running Time: 46800 sec.). 2007. audio compact disk 24.95 (978-1-4233-4346-2(8), 9781423343462, Brilliance MP3) Brilliance Audio.

Deadheads. Reginald Hill. Read by Colin Buchanan. (Running Time: 30000 sec.). (Dalziel & Pascoe Ser.). 2003. audio compact disk 79.95 (978-0-7540-8756-4(5)) Pub: Chivers Audio Bks GBR. Dist(s): AudioGO

Deadheads. unabr. ed. Reginald Hill. Read by Colin Buchanan. 8 cass. (Dalziel & Pascoe Ser.). 1999. 69.95 (978-0-7540-0286-4(1), CAB 1709) AudioGO.

Deadheads, Set unabr. ed. Reginald Hill. Read by Colin Buchanan. 8 cass. (Dalziel & Pascoe Ser.). 1999. 69.95 (CAB 1709) AudioGO.

Deadhouse. abr. ed. Linda Fairstein. (Alexandra Cooper Mysteries Ser.). 2004. 15.95 (978-0-7435-4586-0(9)) Pub: S&S Audio. Dist(s): S and S Inc

Deadlier Than the Sword. Jean Rowden & Geoffrey Annis. 2009. 54.95 (978-1-84652-546-9(2)); audio compact disk 71.95 (978-1-84652-547-6(0)) Pub: Magna Story GBR. Dist(s): Ulverscroft US

Deadlight. unabr. ed. Graham Hurley. Read by Tim Pepper. 10 cass. (Running Time: 14 hrs. 16 mins.). (Isis Cassettes Ser.). (J). 2004. 84.95 (978-0-7531-1893-1(9)) Pub: ISIS Lrg Prnt GBR. Dist(s): Ulverscroft US

Deadline. abr. ed. Randy C. Alcorn. Narrated by Frank Muller. (Ollie Chandler Ser.). (ENG.). 2006. 16.09 (978-1-60814-170-8(5)); audio compact disk 22.99 (978-1-59859-147-7(9)) Oasis Audio.

Deadline. unabr. ed. Chris Crutcher. Narrated by Steven Boyer. 8 CDs. (Running Time: 9 hrs.). (YA). (gr. 9 up). 2008. audio compact disk 87.75 (978-1-4281-8821-1(5)) Recorded Bks.

Deadline. unabr. ed. Chris Crutcher. Read by Steven Boyer. 8 cass. (Running Time: 9 hrs.). (YA). (gr. 9 up). 2008. 61.75 (978-1-4281-8816-7(9)) Pub: Recorded Bks. Dist(s): NetLibrary CO

Deadline. unabr. ed. John Dunning. Narrated by Ed Sala. 7 CDs. (Running Time: 8 hrs.). audio compact disk 69.00 (978-0-7887-4908-7(0), C1289E7) Recorded Bks.
A suspensful tale that begins in a dusty newsroom, spins out into a dark world of conspiracy & murder. Although Dalton Walker is an award-winning journalist, his attempt to write fiction has one nowhere. He hires on at a small New Jersey newspaper, the Tribune, hungry again for the excitement of headlines & hard hitting features. His job begins with covering a child's death in a fire & a showgirl's Amish background. But these routine assignments soon lead the reporter in unexpected directions, deep into disturbing new emotions & back into his own turbulent past. As Walker tries to obey his reporter's instinct, the risks mount with each piece of information he gathers. These deadlines could be a death sentence. Available to libraries only.

Deadline, unabr. ed. John Dunning. Narrated by Ed Sala. 6 cass. (Running Time: 8 hrs.). 2000. 57.00 (978-0-7887-4413-6(5), 96130E7) Recorded Bks.
A tale that begins in a dusty newsroom, but spins out into a dark work of conspiracy & murder. After Dalton Walker, award-winning journalist, hires on at a small New Jersey newspaper, two routine assignments demand deadlines that could prove fatal for Walker.

***Deadline.** unabr. ed. Mira Grant. (Running Time: 16 hrs.). (Newsflesh Ser.). 2011. 26.98 (978-1-60941-235-7(4)) Pub: Hachet Audio. Dist(s): HachBkGrp

Deadline. unabr. ed. Jennifer Rowe. Read by Tracey Callander. 8 cass. (Running Time: 8 hrs. 30 mins.). 2004. 64.00 (978-1-86442-341-9(2), 590166) Pub: Bolinda Pubng AUS. Dist(s): Lndmrk Audiobks
A series of bizarre & mystifying murders plunges Tessa Vance into a hunt for an obsessive killer while a terrifying shadow from the past threatens to overwhelm her. In her first case with her new homicide division, Tessa has to prove herself, especially to her new partner, Steve Hayden. She knows there won't be any second chances & the killer is clever, ruthless & implacable. The grotesque clues left at the crime scenes lead nowhere. The murderer's victims seem to have nothing in common but Tessa knows that deaths form a pattern. Her discovery of just what that pattern is shocks & surprises her but even more shocking is the twist that turns the investigation on its head.

Deadline Affairs. unabr. ed. Julie Titone. Read by Marilyn Langbehn. 8 cass. (Running Time: 9 hrs.). Dramatization. 1992. 44.95 set. (978-1-55686-413-1(2), 413) Books in Motion.
Reporter Josie Antonelli faces danger when she stumbles onto a trail of murder, vengeance & corruption while investigating the North Idaho White supremacist movement.

Deadline for a Critic. unabr. ed. William X. Kienzle. Read by Edward Holland. 8 cass. (Running Time: 12 hrs.). (Father Koesler Mystery Ser.: No. 9). 2001. 64.00 (978-0-7366-6019-8(4)) Books on Tape.
A critic who killed careers has himself been killed & Father Koesler must find out who did it.

Deadline for a Dream. unabr. ed. Bill Knox. Read by James Bryce. 6 cass. (Running Time: 7 hr. 30 min.). 1998. 54.95 (978-0-7531-0367-8(2), 980308) Pub: ISIS Audio GBR. Dist(s): Ulverscroft US
In this first introduction of the notorious Chief Inspector Thane & Inspector Moss, a crime reporter, a gun, a money-worshipping girlfriend & inside knowledge of a factory payroll car's movements are a recipe for disaster.

***Deadline Man.** unabr. ed. Jon Talton. (Running Time: 8 hrs. 0 mins.). 2010. 29.95 (978-1-4417-3917-9(3)); 54.95 (978-1-4417-3913-1(0)); audio compact disk 76.00 (978-1-4417-3914-8(9)) Blckstn Audio.

Deadline Y2K. collector's ed. Mark Joseph. Read by Michael Kramer. 7 cass. (Running Time: 10 hrs. 30 min.). 1999. 56.00 (978-0-7366-4776-2(7)) Books on Tape.
On New Year's Eve 1999, a chain reaction of computer meltdowns turns what was to be a global gala into a catastrophe. As the "Millennium Bug" passes through each time zone it moves inexorably toward the epicenter of the global economy, New York City. At 10:30 AM on December 31, a safeway in New York is hit by the Bug. All systems freeze & what begins as a simple malfunction snowballs into looting & rioting. Pandemonium reigns on the streets of Manhattan & as the day progresses, the blaze of fear increases to the point of insanity. Only a group of cyberpunks, straight from central casting, can save the city from total annihilation.

Deadlines. unabr. ed. C. S. Fuqua. Read by Kevin Foley. 8 cass. (Running Time: 8 hrs. 6 min.). (Deadlines Ser.: Bk. 2). 1996. 49.95 (978-1-55686-708-8(5)) Books in Motion.
Investigative reporter Dean Moore involves himself in uncovering information about political payoffs, illegal contracts & possibly murder, behind the scenes at a local utility company.

Deadlines & Datelines: Essays at the Turn of the Century. unabr. ed. Dan Rather. Read by David Ackroyd. 4 cass. (Running Time: 6 hrs.). 2001. 25.00 (978-1-59040-011-1(9), Phoenix Audio) Pub: Amer Intl Pub. Dist(s): PerseuPGW
With his distinctive blend of frontline determination and a journalist's knack for a good story, Dan Rather looks at the awesome struggles and everyday accomplishments he's witnessed at home and around the globe... and shows yet again the skill and intelligence that have made him an important part of our world for more than four decades.

Deadlock. Iris Johansen. Read by Jennifer Van Dyck. (Playaway Adult Fiction Ser.). 2009. 69.99 (978-1-60812-678-1(1)) Find a World.

Deadlock. Sara Paretsky. Read by Donada Peters. (V. I. Warshawski Novel Ser.). 1993. audio compact disk 56.00 (978-0-7366-7496-6(9)) Books on Tape.

Deadlock. abr. ed. Iris Johansen. Read by Jennifer Van Dyck. (Running Time: 6 hrs.). 2009. audio compact disk 14.99 (978-1-4233-2931-2(7), 9781423329312, BCD Value Price) Brilliance Audio.

Deadlock. abr. ed. Sara Paretsky. Read by Jean Smart. 4 cass. (Running Time: 6 hrs.). (V. I. Warshawski Novel Ser.). 2001. 25.00 (978-1-59040-109-5(3), Phoenix Audio) Pub: Amer Intl Pub. Dist(s): PerseuPGW

***Deadlock.** unabr. ed. James Scott Bell. (Running Time: 10 hrs. 12 mins. 0 sec.). (ENG.). 2009. 12.90 (978-0-310-29348-4(0)) Zondervan.

Deadlock. unabr. ed. Iris Johansen. Read by Jennifer Van Dyck. 1 MP3-CD. (Running Time: 13 hrs.). 2009. 24.99 (978-1-4233-2926-8(0), 9781423329268, Brilliance MP3); 39.97 (978-1-4233-2927-5(9), 9781423329275, Brlnc Audio MP3 Lib); 39.97 (978-1-4233-2929-9(5), 9781423329299, BADLE); 24.99 (978-1-4233-2928-2(7), 9781423329282, BAD); audio compact disk 36.99 (978-1-4233-2924-4(4), 9781423329244, Bril Audio CD Unabri); audio compact disk 97.97 (978-1-4233-2925-1(2), 9781423329251, BriAudCD Unabrid) Brilliance Audio.

Deadlock. unabr. collector's ed. Sara Paretsky. Read by Donada Peters. 6 cass. (Running Time: 9 hrs.). (V. I. Warshawski Novel Ser.). 1993. 48.00 (978-0-7366-2382-7(5), 3153) Books on Tape.
V. I. Warshawski looks for answers about cousin's death that lie at the center of Chicago's shipping industry.

Deadly! unabr. ed. Morris Gleitzman & Paul Jennings. 6 cass. (Running Time: 10 hrs.). (Deadly! Ser.). (J). 2004. 48.00 (978-1-74030-760-4(7)) Bolinda Pubng AUS.

Deadly Amber Chase. unabr. ed. Howard H. Hilton. Read by Gene Engene. 8 cass. (Running Time: 10 hrs.). (Howard H. Hilton International Mystery Ser.). 2001. 49.95 (978-1-55686-942-6(8)) Books in Motion.
Two competing groups attempt to secure extraordinary art stolen by the Germans during WWII. The frantic race to locate the treasures takes both the Germans, and a French couple, on a life and death struggle from the Baltic to the Austrian Alps.

Deadly Audio Collection. abr. ed. Kathy Reichs. (Running Time: 140 hrs. 0 mins. 0 sec.). (ENG.). 2008. audio compact disk 19.99 (978-0-7435-8155-4(5)) Pub: S&S Audio. Dist(s): S and S Inc

Deadly Campaign. unabr. ed. Michael Bracken. Read by Jack Labbe. 4 cass. (Running Time: 4 hrs. 42 min.). 1994. 26.95 (978-1-55686-521-3(X)) Books in Motion.
Reporter Dan Fox finds himself deeply immersed in a mystery that involves underworld ganglords, political intrigue & blackmail.

Deadly Canyon. unabr. ed. Jake Page. Read by Buck Schirner. (Running Time: 8 hrs.). 2008. 39.25 (978-1-4233-7130-4(5), 9781423371304, BADLE); 24.95 (978-1-4233-7127-4(5), 9781423371274, Brilliance MP3); 24.95 (978-1-4233-7129-8(1), 9781423371298, BAD); 39.25 (978-1-4233-7128-1(3), 9781423371281, Brlnc Audio MP3 Lib) Brilliance Audio.

Deadly Care. abr. ed. Leonard S. Goldberg. Perf. by Nancy Allen. 2 cass. 1996. 17.00 Set. (978-1-56876-055-1(8)) Soundlines Ent.

Deadly Climate. unabr. ed. Richard Barth. Narrated by Roslyn Alexander. 5 cass. (Running Time: 7 hrs. 15 mins.). (Margaret Binton Mysteries Ser.). 2000. 44.00 (978-1-55690-844-6(X), 93211E7) Recorded Bks.
Miami's friendly marinas are turning deadly to tourists until a gang of New York senior citizens take things into their own hands.

Deadly Dance. unabr. ed. M. C. Beaton, pseud. Read by Donada Peters. 4 cass. (Running Time: 6 hrs.). (Agatha Raisin Mystery Ser.: Bk. 15). 2004. 45.00 (978-1-4159-0795-5(1)); audio compact disk 54.00 (978-1-4159-0796-2(X)) Books on Tape.
Agatha Raisin has finally opened her own detective agency. But when it seems like that all she's doing is looking for missing cats while being outclassed by her sixty-seven year-old secretary, she wonders has she finally bitten off more than she can chew.

Deadly Dare: The Deadly Dare Mysteries Book One. unabr. ed. Malorie Blackman. Read by Paul Chequer & Syan Blake. 3 CDs. (Running Time: 13860 sec.). (J). (gr. 6-9). 2007. audio compact disk 29.95 (978-1-4056-5602-3(6)) Pub: AudioGo GBR. Dist(s): AudioGO

Deadly Dark. unabr. ed. Howard L. Peterson. Read by Maynard Villers. 4 cass. (Running Time: 6 hrs.). (Sheriff Burley Grantham Ser.). 1995. 26.95 (978-1-55686-613-5(5)) Books in Motion.
Sheriff Burley Grantham returns in this story to solve a bizarre murder case that takes the life of town councilman Oren Gentry while participating in a seance.

***Deadly Deals.** abr. ed. Fern Michaels. Read by Laural Merlington. (Running Time: 3 hrs.). (Sisterhood Ser.). 2010. audio compact disk 14.99 (978-1-4418-1690-0(9), 9781441816900) Brilliance Audio.

***Deadly Deals.** abr. ed. Fern Michaels. Read by Laural Merlington. (Running Time: 3 hrs.). (Sisterhood Ser.). 2010. 9.99 (978-1-4418-9350-5(4), 9781441893505, BAD) Brilliance Audio.

***Deadly Deals.** unabr. ed. Fern Michaels. Read by Laural Merlington. (Running Time: 7 hrs.). (Sisterhood Ser.). 2010. 24.99 (978-1-4233-7992-8(6), 9781423379928, Brilliance MP3); 39.97 (978-1-4233-7993-5(4), 9781423379935, Brlnc Audio MP3 Lib); 39.97 (978-1-4233-7995-9(0), 9781423379959, BADLE); 24.99 (978-1-4233-7994-2(2), 9781423379942, BAD); audio compact disk 29.99 (978-1-4233-7990-4(X), 9781423379904); audio compact disk 87.97 (978-1-4233-7991-1(8), 9781423379911, BriAudCD Unabrid) Brilliance Audio.

Deadly Deceit. unabr. ed. Marian Babson. Read by Diana Bishop. 4 cass. (Running Time: 6 hrs.). 2002. 34.95 (978-0-7540-0765-4(0), CAB 2187, Chivers Sound Lib) AudioGO.

Deadly Decisions. Kathy Reichs. Read by Katherine Borowitz. (Temperance Brennan Ser.: No. 3). 2004. 15.95 (978-0-7435-2011-9(4)) Pub: S&S Audio. Dist(s): S and S Inc

Deadly Decisions. unabr. ed. Kathy Reichs. Read by Lorelei King. 8 vols. (Running Time: 12 hrs.). (Temperance Brennan Ser.: No. 3). 2001. bk. 69.95 (978-0-7927-2393-6(7), CSL 282, Chivers Sound Lib) AudioGO.
A beautiful spring day, at FBI's headquarters at Quantico, finds Dr. Temperance Brennan, a forensic anthropologist, teaching a body recovery course when she is urgently called back to Quebec. A biker war is raging & two of the foot soldiers have blown themselves up.

Deadly Decisions. unabr. ed. Kathy Reichs. Read by Lorelei King. 10 CDs. (Running Time: 15 hrs.). (Temperance Brennan Ser.: No. 3). 2002. audio compact disk 94.95 (978-0-7927-9944-3(5), SLD 095, Chivers Sound Lib) AudioGO.
Forensic anthropologist Dr. Temperance Brennan is teaching a body recovery course at Quantico when she is called back to Quebec. A biker war is raging and two of the foot soldiers have blown themselves up. The only person qualified to make sense of what remains is Tempe. When the body of a nine-year-old girl is wheeled into the morgue, she vows to lend her skills to help fight this evil.

Deadly Delivery. abr. ed. Engle & Barnes. (Running Time: 2 hrs.). (Strange Matter Ser.). 2006. 9.95 (978-1-4233-0888-1(3), 9781423308881, BAD) Brilliance Audio.

Deadly Delivery. abr. ed. Engle & Julian Barnes. Read by Multivoice Production Staff. (Running Time: 2 hrs.). (Strange Matter Ser.). 2006. 25.25 (978-1-4233-0889-8(1), 9781423308898, BADLE); audio compact disk 25.25 (978-1-4233-0887-4(5), 9781423308874, BACDLib Ed); audio compact disk 9.95 (978-1-4233-0886-7(7), 9781423308867, BACD) Brilliance Audio.
How could things get worse? First the frantic call from Mom saying that she and Dad would be late getting home, and that the clueless sitter would be over soon to watch us. Then the worst storm in Fairfield history pounds our house, knocking out our power, lights, and phone. And now a hideous man is lurking at our door and won't go away! He is frantically peering in the windows and ringing the doorbell over and over. . . It's a special, late night delivery for Simon and Sarah White. A deadly delivery. A package of disaster that sends them screaming through the wildest, scariest, most dangerous night of their lives. . . in their very own house. At least, it was their house. Then they opened the box, flipped the latches and peeked under the lid. Now it's loose and planning on a little. . . redecorating. And once it's out, getting it back in is murder.

***Deadly Descent.** unabr. ed. Charlotte Hinger. (Running Time: 9 hrs. 30 mins.). 2010. 29.95 (978-1-4417-4590-3(4)); 59.95 (978-1-4417-4587-3(4)); audio compact disk 90.00 (978-1-4417-4588-0(2)) Blckstn Audio.

Deadly Diamond. unabr. ed. Dorothy R. Kliewer. Read by Denise S. Utter. 6 cass. (Running Time: 5 hrs. 54 min.). 1996. 39.95 (978-1-55686-730-9(1)) Books in Motion.
Rory Frayne attends a Jeweler's Convention where a famous diamond figures in a murder & Rory becomes a suspect. She desperately hunts the real killer to clear her name.

Deadly Edge. unabr. ed. Richard Stark, pseud. 4 cass. (Running Time: 6 hrs.). 2001. 32.00 (978-0-7366-7639-7(2)) Books on Tape.
Parker and three cohorts crash a rock concert and split the proceeds. That should have been the end, but, of course, it wasn't.

Deadly Embrace. abr. ed. Jackie Collins. 2004. 15.95 (978-0-7435-4596-9(6)) Pub: S&S Audio. Dist(s): S and S Inc

Deadly Embrace Pt. 2: Hitler, Stalin & the Nazi-Soviet Pact 1939-1941. collector's ed. Anthony Read & David Fisher. Read by Walter Zimmerman. 12 cass. (Running Time: 18 hrs.). 1990. 96.00 (978-0-7366-1713-0(2), 2554-B) Books on Tape.
The unholy alliance between Hitler & Stalin enabled Germany to strike Poland without interference. In turn, Russia absorbed vast tracts of eastern Europe. This would cost 20 million Russian lives & end in a deadly reversal which helped destroy the Third Reich. The Deadly Embrace reconstructs the scenery of those years - the pacifism of Neville Chamberlain, Britain's failure to shore up its alliances, the cold-blooded trading between Molotov & Ribintrop, the Russian & German foreign ministers. When the non-aggression pact was signed in 1939, Poland's fate was sealed.

Deadly Embrace Pt. 2: Hitler, Stalin & the Nazi-Soviet Pact 1939-1941. unabr. collector's ed. Anthony Read & David Fisher. Read by Walter Zimmerman. 12 cass. (Running Time: 18 hrs.). 1990. 96.00 (978-0-7366-1712-3(4), 2554-A) Books on Tape.

Deadly Emotions: Understand the Mind-Body-Spirit Connection That Can Heal or Destroy You. Don Colbert. Read by Greg Wheatley. 6 CDs. (Running Time: 5 hrs. 30 mins.). 2004. audio compact disk 48.00 (978-0-7861-8740-9(9), 3249); 32.95 (978-0-7861-2643-9(4), 3249) Blckstn Audio.
Did you know that negative emotions can adversely affect your health? Depression, anger, guilt, condemnation, low self-esteem these are only a few of the lethal toxins that threaten the body and spirit. Dr. Colbert offers hope in the form of God's power to deliver listeners from these toxins, focusing on the power of forgiveness and repentance, the value of a merry heart, and the joy of the Lord.

Deadly Emotions: Understand the Mind-Body-Spirit Connection That Can Heal or Destroy You. abr. ed. Don Colbert. 4 cass. (Running Time: 6 hrs.). 2003. 27.00 (978-1-58926-250-8(6), 690948) Oasis Audio.
Explores the deadly effect of negative emotions on the body, mind and spirit, and offers techniques for releasing these toxic catalysts.

Deadly Emotions: Understand the Mind-Body-Spirit Connection That Can Heal or Destroy You. abr. ed. Don Colbert. Narrated by Greg Wheatley. (ENG.). 2003. 19.59 (978-1-60814-171-5(3)) Oasis Audio.

Deadly Emotions: Understand the Mind-Body-Spirit Connection That Can Heal or Destroy You. abr. unabr. ed. Don Colbert. Narrated by Greg Wheatley. 6 CDs. (Running Time: 6 hrs.). (ENG.). 2003. audio compact disk 22.99 (978-1-58926-251-5(4), 750636) Oasis Audio.

Deadly Evolution: The Virulence of Viruses. Paul Ewald & Alan Herre. Read by Paul Ewald & Alan Herre. 1 cass. (Running Time: 30 min.). 1996. 10.95 (978-1-57511-010-3(5)) Pub Mills.
A radio documentary of the Smithsonian Institution & Soundprint. A flu suddenly becomes deadly & kills more than 20 million people. Malaria, once easily treated, has become one of the most persistent diseases of our time. Smithsonian biologists Paul Ewald & Alan Herre believe a critical influence on the spread & deadliness of disease - evolution - has been overlooked. Their studies may provide critical information on how viruses become more virulent, including such complex ones as HIV. Probe the theories of evolution that could lead to changes in the treatment of infectious disease.

Deadly Faith. unabr. ed. John S. Morgan. Read by Kevin Foley. 8 cass. (Running Time: 8 hrs. 30 min.). 2001. 49.95 (978-1-55686-976-1(2)) Books in Motion.
Tristan Apthorp and Hillary Jane Daniels attempt to solve a trio of murders that may include collusion within a union. or could the killers be linked to a union busting trade association?.

Deadly Feasts: The Prion Controversy & the Public's Health. Richard Rhodes. Narrated by George Wilson. 6 cass. (Running Time: 9 hrs.). 59.00 (978-1-4025-2836-1(1)) Recorded Bks.

Deadly Feasts: Tracking the Secrets of a Terrifying New Plague. Richard Rhodes. 2004. 10.95 (978-0-7435-4608-9(3)) Pub: S&S Audio. Dist(s): S and S Inc

Deadly Feasts: Tracking the Secrets of a Terrifying New Plague. unabr. ed. Richard Rhodes. Read by Barrett Whitener. 8 cass. (Running Time: 8 hrs.). 1997. 48.00 (978-0-7366-3758-9(3), 4433) Books on Tape.
Follows the daring explorations of maverick scientists as they track the emergence of the deadly "stealth" maladies, such as Mad Cow disease - strange new disease agents unlike any others known on earth.

Deadly Friends. Stuart Pawson & Jonathan Keeble. 2009. 61.95 (978-1-84652-379-3(6)); audio compact disk 71.95 (978-1-84652-380-9(X)) Pub: Magna Story GBR. Dist(s): Ulverscroft US

Deadly Gamble. unabr. ed. Connie Shelton. Read by Lynda Evans. 6 cass. (Running Time: 6 hrs. 54 min.). (Charlie Parker Mystery Ser.: No. 1). 1996. 39.95 (978-1-55686-653-1(4)) Books in Motion.
Introducing Charlie Parker, female detective. Devout in her dedication for the underdog, Charlie gets drawn into perilous predicaments while sticking her neck out for friends & clients.

***Deadly Game.** unabr. ed. Christine Feehan. Narrated by Tom Stechschulte. 2 MP3-CDs. (Running Time: 13 hrs. 21 mins.). (GhostWalkers Ser.: No. 5). 2009. 69.95 (978-0-7927-6837-1(X), Chivers Sound Lib); audio compact disk 110.95 (978-0-7927-6028-3(X), Chivers Sound Lib) AudioGO.

Deadly Game: PageTurner Spy. Janet Lorimer. 1 cass. (Running Time: 62 mins 15 secs). (PageTurner Spy Ser.). (YA). 2002. 10.95 (978-1-56254-491-1(8), SP 4918) Saddleback Edu.
Word-for-word read-along of A Deadly Game.

Deadly Gift. unabr. ed. Heather Graham. Read by Phil Gigante. (Running Time: 10 hrs.). (Flynn Brothers Trilogy: No. 3). 2010. 39.97 (978-1-4233-9868-4(8), 9781423398684, Brlnc Audio MP3 Lib); 24.99 (978-1-4233-9867-7(X), 9781423398677, Brilliance MP3); 24.99 (978-1-4233-9869-1(6), 9781423398691, BAD); 39.97 (978-1-4233-9870-7(X), 9781423398707, BADLE); audio compact disk 29.99 (978-1-4233-9865-3(3), 9781423398653); audio compact disk 97.97 (978-1-4233-9866-0(1), 9781423398660, BriAudCD Unabrid) Brilliance Audio.

Deadly Gift. unabr. ed. Heather Graham. Read by Phil Gigante. (Running Time: 10 hrs.). (Flynn Brothers Trilogy: No. 3). 2011. audio compact disk 14.99 (978-1-4418-2600-8(9), 9781441826008, BCD Value Price) Brilliance Audio.

Deadly Harvest. unabr. ed. Heather Graham. Read by Phil Gigante. (Running Time: 10 hrs.). (Flynn Brothers Trilogy: No. 2). 2010. 39.97 (978-1-4233-9862-2(9), 9781423398622, Brlnc Audio MP3 Lib); 24.99 (978-1-4233-9861-5(0), 9781423398615, Brilliance MP3); 24.99 (978-1-4233-9863-9(7), 9781423398639, BAD); 39.97 (978-1-4233-9864-6(5), 9781423398646, BADLE); audio compact disk 29.99 (978-1-4233-9859-2(9), 9781423398592); audio compact disk 97.97 (978-1-4233-9860-8(2), 9781423398608, BriAudCD Unabrid) Brilliance Audio.

Deadly Harvest. unabr. ed. Heather Graham. Read by Phil Gigante. (Running Time: 10 hrs.). (Flynn Brothers Trilogy: No. 2). 2011. audio compact disk 14.99 (978-1-4418-2620-6(3), 9781441826206, BCD Value Price) Brilliance Audio.

Deadly Harvest. unabr. ed. Brad Reynolds. Read by Kevin Foley. 8 cass. (Running Time: 10 hrs. 30 min.). (Father Mark Townsend Mystery Ser.). 2001. 49.95 (978-1-58116-182-3(4)) Books in Motion.
A mysterious end-of-the-world preacher may be involved in murder and a scam. Father Mark investigates.

Deadly Harvest, Set, Level 6. Carolyn Walker. Contrib. by Philip Prowse. (Running Time: 3 hrs. 7 mins.). (Cambridge English Readers Ser.). (ENG., 2000. 17.85 (978-0-521-77696-7(1)) Cambridge U Pr.

Deadly Housewives. unabr. ed. Nevada Barr et al. Read by Shannon Engemann & Henrietta Tiefenthaler. (YA). 2008. 54.99 (978-1-60514-836-6(9)) Find a World.

Deadly Illusions: The KGB Orlov Dossier Reveals Stalin's Master Spy. unabr. collector's ed. John Costello & Oleg Tsarev. Read by Richard Brown. 15 cass. (Running Time: 22 hrs. 30 min.). 1994. 120.00 (978-0-7366-2611-8(5), 3353) Books on Tape.
Until now, Alexander Orlov has been regarded in the West as the highest-ranking Soviet intelligence defector. But Deadly Illusions challenges that conclusion. After he surfaced in 1953, Orlov sustained the illusion of his defection for 21 years. But the secrets contained in his 17-volume dossier, recently retrieved from the newly-opened Soviet archives, indicate that he remained a dedicated communist until his death in 1973 - taking a multitude of secrets to the grave.

Deadly Innocence - The Kimberly Bergalis Case: Solving the Greatest Murder Mystery in the History of American Medicine. abr. ed. Leonard G. Horowitz. 2 cass. (Running Time: 3 hrs.). 1997. pap. bk. 19.95 (978-0-923550-13-4(5)) Tetrahedron Pub.
Dr. Horowitz reads this critically acclaimed investigation into the Florida dental AIDS tragedy that concludes the dentist-Dr. Acer was a serial killer who injected his patients with HIV tainted anesthetics & government officials covered up the evidence of his deadly deeds.

Deadly Judgement. unabr. ed. Jessica Fletcher & Donald Bain. Read by Beth Porter. 6 vols. (Running Time: 6 hrs.). (Murder, She Wrote Ser.). 1999. bk. 54.95 (978-0-7927-2310-3(4), CSL 199, Chivers Sound Lib) AudioGO.
Jessica Fletcher is off to Boston to help her eccentric lawyer friend, Malcolm McLeon, defend a tycoon accused of fratricide. Her uncanny sleuthing talents will come in handy when the two old acquaintances dive into the case with their characteristic vigor. But when the defendant's girlfriend & his only alibi, is found dead in her apartment, the case takes a murderous turn for the worse. Is someone out to make sure the accused gets convicted? Jessica has her suspicions & when the jurors become victims of deadly accidents, she must find the real culprit-before the killer finds her.

Deadly Judgment. unabr. ed. Jessica Fletcher & Donald Bain. Read by Beth Porter. 6 cass. (Running Time: 6 hrs.). (Murder, She Wrote Ser.). 2000. 29.95 (978-1-57270-172-4(2), N61172u) Pub: Audio Partners. Dist(s): PerseuPGW
Jessica Fletcher is in Boston, helping her eccentric lawyer friend defend a tycoon accused of fratricide. The defendant's only "alibi" is unfortunately found dead. Is someone out to make sure the accused gets convicted.

Deadly Justice. unabr. ed. William Bernhardt. Read by Jonathan Marosz. 6 cass. (Running Time: 9 hrs.). (Ben Kincaid Ser.: No. 3). 1998. 48.00 (978-0-7366-4107-4(6), 4612) Books on Tape.
Tulsa is gripped by a mystifying series of murders & Ben Kincaid contends with the most elusive opponent yet. On the seedy side of town, a van cruises the streets under the cover of night. It stops beside a prostitute who is understandably uneasy. One of her colleagues has recently been murdered. But she needs the cash. Throwing caution to the wind, she gets inside, never noticing a black garbage bag & a whit e silken cord in the back. Prostitutes are dying on the streets of Tulsa & Ben Kincaid must keep himself & his clients alive long enough to see that justice is served. The question is: Does he have the resources to do it.

Deadly Legacy. unabr. ed. Betty Rowlands. Read by Phyllida Nash. 6 cass. (Running Time: 6 hrs.). 1998. 54.95 (978-0-7540-0218-5(7), CAB 1641) AudioGO.
Crime writer Melissa Craig must deal with recent plague of a sex strangler, a series of burglaries, & most recently the death of novelist Leonora Jewell. While completing her unfinished novel, she discovers that her death was not accidental.

***Deadly Loyalty Collection.** unabr. ed. Bill Myers. (Running Time: 8 hrs. 34 mins. 39 sec.). (Forbidden Doors Ser.). (ENG.). (YA). 2010. 12.99 (978-0-310-42635-6(9)) Zondervan.

***Deadly Loyalty Collection: the Curse.** Bill Myers. (Running Time: 2 hrs. 44 mins. 0 sec.). (Forbidden Doors Ser.). (ENG.). (YA). 2009. 4.99 (978-0-310-77262-0(1)) Zondervan.

***Deadly Loyalty Collection: the Scream.** Bill Myers. (Running Time: 2 hrs. 57 mins. 0 sec.). (Forbidden Doors Ser.). (ENG.). (YA). 2009. 4.99 (978-0-310-72034-8(6)) Zondervan.

***Deadly Loyalty Collection: the Undead.** Bill Myers. (Running Time: 2 hrs. 55 mins. 0 sec.). (Forbidden Doors Ser.). (ENG.). (YA). 2009. 4.99 (978-0-310-72033-1(8)) Zondervan.

Deadly Night. unabr. ed. Heather Graham. Read by Phil Gigante. (Running Time: 10 hrs.). (Flynn Brothers Trilogy: No. 1). 2010. 39.97 (978-1-4233-9856-1(4), 9781423398561, Brinc Audio MP3 Lib); 24.99 (978-1-4233-9855-4(6), 9781423398554, Brilliance MP3); 24.99 (978-1-4233-9857-8(2), 9781423398578, BAD); 39.97 (978-1-4233-9858-5(0), 9781423398585, BADLE); audio compact disk 29.99 (978-1-4233-9853-0(X), 9781423398530); audio compact disk 97.97 (978-1-4233-9854-7(8), 9781423398547, BriAudCD Unabrid) Brilliance Audio.

Deadly Night. unabr. ed. Heather Graham. Read by Phil Gigante. (Running Time: 11 hrs.). (Flynn Brothers Trilogy: No. 1). 2011. audio compact disk 14.99 (978-1-4418-2621-3(1), 9781441826213, BCD Value Price) Brilliance Audio.

Deadly Nightshade. Elizabeth Daly. Read by Ray Verna. 5 cass. (Running Time: 6 hrs. 15 min.). 1993. Rental 8.80 30 day rental Set. (250013) Literate Ear.
It began with the children poisoned by the wild berry, deadly nightshade. A young state trooper died that same night, but it appeared to be a motorcycle accident. A little girl & her cat are missing. A local official calls on Henry Gamadge, a New York City amateur detective - the best detective he knows.

Deadly Nightshade. Elizabeth Daly. Read by Ray Verna. 5 cass. (Running Time: 6 hrs. 15 min.). 1993. 44.20 Set. (978-1-56544-034-0(X), 250013) Literate Ear.

Deadly Nightshade. Cynthia Riggs. Read by Davina Porter. (Running Time: 32400 sec.). (Martha's Vineyard Mystery Ser.). 2006. 59.95 (978-0-7861-4519-5(6)); audio compact disk 72.00 (978-0-7861-7185-9(5)) Blckstn Audio.

Deadly Nightshade. unabr. ed. Cynthia Riggs. Read by Davina Porter. (Running Time: 32400 sec.). (Martha's Vineyard Mystery Ser.). 2006. audio compact disk 29.95 (978-0-7861-7619-9(9)) Blckstn Audio.

Deadly Petard. unabr. ed. Roderic Jeffries. Read by Steven Crossley. 4 cass. (Running Time: 5 hrs. 30 min.). 2000. 44.95 (978-1-86042-650-6(6), 26506) Pub: Soundings Ltd GBR. Dist(s): Ulverscroft US

Deadly Pursuit. abr. ed. Theodore V. Olsen. Read by Dick Hill. (Running Time: 3 hrs.). (Five Star Westerns Ser.). 2007. 39.25 (978-1-4233-3546-7(5), 9781423335467, BADLE); 24.95 (978-1-4233-3545-0(7), 9781423335450, BAD) Brilliance Audio.

Deadly Pursuit. abr. ed. Theodore V. Olsen. Read by Dick Hill. (Running Time: 10800 sec.). (Five Star Westerns Ser.). 2007. audio compact disk 24.95 (978-1-4233-3543-6(0), 9781423335436, Brilliance MP3); audio compact disk 39.25 (978-1-4233-3544-3(9), 9781423335443, Brinc Audio MP3 Lib) Brilliance Audio.

Deadly Pursuit. unabr. ed. Theodore V. Olsen. Read by Arthur Addison. 7 cass. (Running Time: 7 hrs.). 1996. 42.00 sale to libraries only. (978-0-7366-3387-1(1), 4037) Books on Tape.
Beggars can't be choosers & now Silas & Noah will have to hash things out as they lead a posse on the trail of a deadly foe. Will Silas make it to old age?.

Deadly Revenge. unabr. ed. Howard Peterson. Read by David Sharp. 4 cass. (Running Time: 4 hrs. 30 min.). (Sheriff Burley Grantham Ser.). 1995. 26.95 (978-1-55686-574-9(0)) Books in Motion.
Hanna & Blade Bauer's marriage was on the rocks, but until Hanna's murder, no one in the small town of Summit knew how completely.

Deadly Secrets: It Began as a Sordid Affair. It Ended in Bloody Murder. unabr. ed. M. William Phelps. Read by J. Charles. 1 MP3-CD. (Running Time: 10 hrs.). 2009. 39.97 (978-1-4233-6818-2(5), 9781423368182, Brinc Audio MP3 Lib); 39.97 (978-1-4233-6820-5(7), 9781423368205, BADLE); 24.99 (978-1-4233-6817-5(7), 9781423368175, Brilliance MP3); 24.99 (978-1-4233-6819-9(3), 9781423368199, BAD); audio compact disk 97.97 (978-1-4233-6816-8(9), 9781423368168, BriAudCD Unabrid); audio compact disk 36.99 (978-1-4233-6815-1(0), 9781423368151, Bril Audio CD Unabri) Brilliance Audio.

***Deadly! Series.** Paul Jennings & Morris Gleitzman. Read by Francis Greenslade & Melissa Eccleston. (Running Time: 10 hrs.). (J). 2010. 84.99 (978-1-74214-615-7(5), 9781742146157) Pub: Bolinda Pubng AUS. Dist(s): Bolinda Pub Inc

Deadly! Series. unabr. ed. Morris Gleitzman & Paul Jennings. Read by Melissa Eccleston & Francis Greenslade. (Running Time: 10 hrs.). (J). 2009. audio compact disk 87.95 (978-1-74214-574-7(4), 9781742145747) Pub: Bolinda Pubng AUS. Dist(s): Bolinda Pub Inc

Deadly Shade of Gold. unabr. ed. John D. MacDonald. Read by Michael Prichard. 8 cass. (Running Time: 12 hrs.). (Travis McGee Ser.: Vol. 5). 2001. 29.95 (978-0-7366-6783-8(0)) Books on Tape.
An Aztec icon, solid gold, lures Travis McGee into mortal peril.

Deadly Shade of Gold. unabr. collector's ed. John D. MacDonald. Read by Michael Prichard. 8 cass. (Running Time: 12 hrs.). (Travis McGee Ser.: Vol. 5). 1978. 64.00 (978-0-7366-0106-1(6), 1114) Books on Tape.
Travis McGee's buddy, Sam Taggart, shows up for an impromptu visit. Sam shows Travis a gold figurine of an Aztec deity & tells Travis that he plans to regain possession of 27 additional idols which once belonged to him. A few hours later Sam Taggart is a corpse with a slit in his throat.

***Deadly Spin: An Insurance Company Insider Speaks Out on How Corporate PR Is Killing Health Care & Deceiving Americans.** unabr. ed. Wendell Potter. (Running Time: 8 hrs. 30 mins. 0 sec.). (ENG.). 2010. 19.99 (978-1-4001-6925-2(9)); 15.99 (978-1-4001-8925-0(X)); audio compact disk 29.99 (978-1-4001-1925-7(1)) Pub: Tantor Media. Dist(s): IngramPubServ

***Deadly Spin (Library Edition) An Insurance Company Insider Speaks Out on How Corporate PR Is Killing Health Care & Deceiving Americans.** unabr. ed. Wendell Potter. (Running Time: 8 hrs. 30 mins.). 2010. 29.99 (978-1-4001-9925-9(5)); audio compact disk 71.99 (978-1-4001-4925-4(8)) Pub: Tantor Media. Dist(s): IngramPubServ

Deadly Trust. unabr. ed. John S. Morgan. Read by Kevin Foley. 8 cass. (Running Time: 9 hrs.). 2001. 49.95 (978-1-55686-785-9(9)) Books in Motion.
A posh law firm is turned upside down when the founder's grandson is accused of murdering one of his clients. Tristan Apthorp takes on his son's case, his first defense in capital crime.

Deadly Valentine. unabr. ed. Carolyn G. Hart. Read by Kate Reading. 6 cass. (Running Time: 9 hrs.). (Death on Demand Mystery Ser.: No. 6). 1996. 48.00 (978-0-7366-3407-6(X), 4053) Books on Tape.
A mother-in-law is no joke if she meddles in your marriage. Laurel Laurance doesn't see it that way: she's "helping" Annie, her son's wife.

Deadly Waters. Pauline Rowson. 2009. 54.95 (978-1-4079-0383-5(7)); audio compact disk 71.95 (978-1-4079-0384-2(5)) Pub: Soundings Ltd GBR. Dist(s): Ulverscroft US

Deadman's Bluff. unabr. ed. James Swain. Narrated by Alan Sklar. 8 CDs. (Running Time: 32520 sec.). (Tony Valentine Novel Ser.). 2006. audio compact disk 79.95 (978-0-7927-4346-0(6), SLD 988) AudioGO.

Deadman's Poker. James Swain. Narrated by Alan Sklar. 8 CDs. (Running Time: 33420 sec.). (Tony Valentine Novel Ser.). 2006. audio compact disk 79.95 (978-0-7927-4059-9(9), SLD 966) AudioGO.

Deadwood. Hank Mitchum. Read by Charlie O'Dowd. 4 vols. 2004. 25.00 (978-1-58807-194-1(4)) Am Pubng Inc.

Deadwood. Hank Mitchum. Read by Charlie O'Dowd. 4 vols. No. 11. 2004. (978-1-58807-595-6(8)) Am Pubng Inc.

Deadwood. unabr. ed. Matt Braun. Narrated by Richard Ferrone. 5 cass. (Running Time: 6 hrs. 45 mins.). 2000. 48.00 (978-0-7887-3889-0(5), 95765E7) Recorded Bks.
Based on historical records of Butch Cassidy & the Hole-in-the-Wall gang. Against them the author pits Luke Starbuck, a manhunter determined to catch his prey.

Deadwood Beetle. unabr. ed. Mylene Dressler. Read by David Darlow. 4 cass. (Running Time: 6 hrs.). 2001. 53.25 (978-1-58788-815-1(7), 1587888157, Unabridge Lib Edns) Brilliance Audio.
Tristan Martens, a retired entomologist, is shaken by the discovery of his mother's sewing table in a New York antique shop. He hasn't seen it since he was a boy in Holland, but he vividly remembers the last time he did. Only Tristan knows the painful truth behind the scrawled - and misunderstood - inscription on the bottom of the table, and he embarks on a scheme to acquire it from the shop's owner, Cora Lowenstein, who insists it's not for sale. But as their lives become entangled, Tristan must make a choice. Can he tell Cora the truth? Begun in deceit, their relationship and Tristan's salvation hinge on his willingness to confront and finally confess the terrible secrets of his family's past. In startlingly beautiful prose resonant with dramatic tension, Mylene Dressler tells the heartrending story of an old man taking his last chance and struggling toward an elusive redemption and the even more distant hope of love.

Deadwood Beetle: A Novel. unabr. ed. Mylene Dressler. Read by David Darlow. (Running Time: 6 hrs.). 2004. 39.25 (978-1-59335-413-8(4), 1593354134, Brinc Audio MP3 Lib) Brilliance Audio.

Deadwood Beetle: A Novel. unabr. ed. Mylene Dressler. Read by David Darlow. (Running Time: 6 hrs.). 2004. 39.25 (978-1-59710-189-9(3), 1597101893, BADLE); 24.95 (978-1-59710-188-2(5), 1597101885, BAD) Brilliance Audio.

Deadwood Beetle: A Novel. unabr. ed. Mylene Dressler. Read by David Darlow. (Running Time: 6 hrs.). 2004. 24.95 (978-1-59335-047-5(3), 1593350473) Soulmate Audio Bks.

Deadwood Trail. abr. ed. Ralph Compton. Read by Jim Gough. 4 cass. (Running Time: 6 hr.). (Trail Drive Ser.: Vol. 12). 1999. Rental 24.95 (978-1-890990-26-8(4)) Otis Audio.
The only riches Texans had left after the Civil War were five million maverick longhorns & the brains, brawn & boldness to drive them north to where the money was.

Deafening. unabr. ed. Frances Itani. Read by Lorraine Hamelin. 8 cass. (Running Time: 12 hrs.). 2003. 34.95 (978-1-59086-912-3(5), 1590869125, BAU); 87.25 (978-1-59086-913-0(3), 1590869133, Unabridge Lib Edns) Brilliance Audio.

Deafening. unabr. ed. Frances Itani. Read by Lorraine Hamelin. (Running Time: 12 hrs.). 2004. 39.25 (978-1-59335-503-6(3), 1593355033, Brinc Audio MP3 Lib) Brilliance Audio.
Set on the eve of the Great War, Deafening is a novel of remarkable virtuosity and power spanning two continents and the life and loves of a young deaf woman in Canada named Grania O'Neill. As a result of a childhood illness, Grania's is a world without sound, a world bounded by a powerful family love that tries to insulate her from undue suffering. When it becomes clear that Grania can no longer thrive in the world of the hearing, her family sends her to live at the Ontario School for the Deaf where, protected from the often unforgiving hearing world outside, she learns sign language and speech. Then she meets Jim Lloyd, a hearing man, and the two, in wonderment, begin to create a new emotional vocabulary that encompasses both sound and silence. But as history would have it, Jim must leave home only two weeks after their wedding to serve as a stretcher-bearer on the blood-soaked battlefields of Flanders. During this long and brutal war of attrition, Jim and Grania are pulled to the center of cataclysmic events that will alter civilization forever.

Deafening. unabr. ed. Frances Itani. Read by Lorraine Hamelin. (Running Time: 12 hrs.). 2004. 39.25 (978-1-59710-190-5(7), 1597101907, BADLE); 24.95 (978-1-59710-191-2(5), 1597101915, BAD) Brilliance Audio.

Deafening. unabr. ed. Frances Itani. Read by Lorraine Hamelin. (Running Time: 12 hrs.). 2004. 24.95 (978-1-59335-231-8(X), 159335231X) Soulmate Audio Bks.

Deal. abr. ed. Joe Hutsko. Read by Jim Bond. 2 cass. 1999. 17.95 (FS9-43322) Highsmith.

Deal. unabr. ed. Joe Hutsko. Read by Jim Bond. (Running Time: 9 hrs.). 2009. 39.97 (978-1-4233-8579-0(9), 9781423385790, Brinc Audio MP3 Lib); 39.97 (978-1-4233-8581-3(0), 9781423385813, BADLE); 24.99 (978-1-4233-8578-3(0), 9781423385783, Brilliance MP3); 24.99 (978-1-4233-8580-6(2), 9781423385806, BAD) Brilliance Audio.

Deal: A Novel of Hollywood. unabr. ed. Peter Lefcourt. Read by William H. Macy. (Running Time: 32400 sec.). 2008. 19.95 (978-1-4332-0695-5(1)); 44.95 (978-1-4332-0693-1(5)); audio compact disk 19.95 (978-1-4332-0696-2(X)); audio compact disk & audio compact disk 55.00 (978-1-4332-0694-8(3)) Blckstn Audio.

Deal: A Novel of Hollywood. unabr. ed. Peter Lefcourt & William H. Macy. (Running Time: 32400 sec.). 2008. audio compact disk 29.95 (978-1-4332-0697-9(8)) Blckstn Audio.

***Deal & Heal: 4 steps for healing from all types of Abuse.** (ENG.). 2010. 7.00 (978-0-9801251-3-9(8)) Rochel Roc.

Deal Breaker. Harlan Coben. Read by Jonathan Marosz. 6 cass. (Running Time: 9 hrs.). (Myron Bolitar Ser.: No. 1). 1999. 48.00 (4977) Books on Tape.
Defending a rookie quarterback accused of murder, Myron Bolitar uncovers a series of leads that suggest the victim is still alive.

Deal Breaker. unabr. ed. Harlan Coben. Read by Jonathan Marosz. 6 cass. (Running Time: 9 hrs.). (Myron Bolitar Ser.: No. 1). 1999. 48.00 (978-0-7366-4570-6(5), 4977) Books on Tape.
Sports agent Myron Bolitar's prized client, rookie quarterback Christian Steele, is poised on the edge of the big-time. But when Christian gets a phone call from a former girlfriend, a woman who everyone, including the police, believed was dead the deal starts to go sour. Suddenly Myron is plunged into a mystery of sex and blackmail. Trying to unravel the truth about a family's tragedy, a woman's secret, and a man's lies, Myron is up against the dark side of his business, where image and talent make you rich, but the truth can get you killed.

Deal Breaker. unabr. ed. Harlan Coben. Read by Jonathan Marosz. (Myron Bolitar Ser.: No. 1). (YA). 2007. 49.99 (978-0-7393-7467-2(2)) Find a World.

Deal Breaker. unabr. ed. Harlan Coben. Read by Jonathan Marosz. (Running Time: 32400 sec.). (Myron Bolitar Ser.: No. 1). (ENG.). 2006. audio compact disk 19.99 (978-0-7393-4094-3(8), Random AudioBks) Pub: Random Audio Pubg. Dist(s): Random

Deal Breakers: When to Work on a Relationship & When to Walk Away. unabr. ed. Bethany Marshall. Narrated by Renée Raudman. (Running Time: 5 hrs. 30 mins. 0 sec.). 2007. audio compact disk 24.99 (978-1-4001-0435-2(1)) Pub: Tantor Media. Dist(s): IngramPubServ

Deal Breakers: When to Work on a Relationship & When to Walk Away. unabr. ed. Bethany Marshall. Read by Renée Raudman. (Running Time: 5 hrs. 30 mins. 0 sec.). (ENG.). 2007. audio compact disk 49.99 (978-1-4001-3435-9(8)); audio compact disk 19.99 (978-1-4001-5435-7(9)) Pub: Tantor Media. Dist(s): IngramPubServ

***Deal in Wheat & Other Stories.** Frank Norris. Read by Anais 9000. 2009. 27.95 (978-1-60112-237-7(3)) Babblebooks.

Deal Maker: How William C. Durant Made General Motors. Axel Madsen. Narrated by Nelson Runger. 9 CDs. (Running Time: 10 hrs.). 2001. audio compact disk 89.00 (978-0-7887-5174-5(3), C1336E7) Recorded Bks.
Chronicles the people who shaped the 20th century. Sheds light on a man whose tireless optimism led to the formation of the first supercorporation. Durant's creation of General Motors essentially invented modern-day corporate America, gaining & losing him three fortunes in the process. Highlights the uneasy relationship between inventors & those who control the capital to exploit invention.

Deal Maker: How William C. Durant Made General Motors. unabr. ed. Axel Madsen. Narrated by Nelson Runger. 7 cass. (Running Time: 10 hrs.). 1999. 65.00 (978-0-7887-4392-4(9), 96195E7) Recorded Bks.
Chronicles the people who shaped the 20th-century. Sheds light on a man whose tireless optimism led to the formation of the first super-corporation. Durant's creation of General Motors essentially invented modern-day corporate America, gaining & losing him three fortunes in the process. Highlights the uneasy relationship between inventors & those who control the capital to exploit invention.

Deal Makers, Brokers, & Bankers. unabr. ed. Austin Lynas & Henry R. Hecht. Read by Louis Rukeyser. (Running Time: 10800 sec.). (Secrets of the Great Investors Ser.). 2006. audio compact disk 25.95 (978-0-7861-6499-8(9)) Pub: Blckstn Audio. Dist(s): NetLibrary CO

Deal of a Lifetime: Matt. 13:44-47. Ed Young. 1993. 4.95 (978-0-7417-1959-1(2), 959) Win Walk.

Deal on Ice. unabr. ed. Les Standiford. Narrated by Ron McLarty. 7 cass. (Running Time: 10 hrs. 15 mins.). 2001. 64.00 (978-0-7887-5513-2(7)) Recorded Bks.
As John Deal tries to salvage his relationship with his estranged wife, a string of murders rocks Miami.

Deal to Die For. unabr. ed. Les Standiford. Narrated by Ron McLarty. 9 cass. (Running Time: 12 hrs. 45 mins.). 2000. 80.00 (978-0-7887-3111-2(4), 95822E7) Recorded Bks.
Contractor John Deal is shocked to learn that his closest friend, Barbara, is dead. Although the police tag it as suicide, Deal is suspicious. And when Barbara's sister, a beautiful film star, disappears, he is driven to find the connection between the two cases.

Deal with the Dead. Les Standiford. Narrated by Ron McLarty. 8 cass. (Running Time: 11 hrs. 30 mins.). 74.00 (978-1-4025-1882-9(X)); audio compact disk 97.00 (978-1-4025-3498-0(1)) Recorded Bks.

***Dealer's Choice.** Sara Paretsky. 2009. (978-1-60136-540-8(3)) Audio Holding.

Dealer's Choice-4. Thomas Henry Kelly. 2004. audio compact disk 35.00 (978-1-56142-186-2(3)) T Kelly Inc.

***Dealers of Lightning.** abr. ed. Michael A. Hiltzik. Read by Forrest Sawyer. (ENG.). 2005. (978-0-06-112745-8(0), Harper Audio); (978-0-06-112744-1(2), Harper Audio) HarperCollins Pubs.

Dealin with Life: Dealing. unabr. ed. Chief Little Summer. Interview with Warm Night Rain. 1 CD. (Dealing With Life). (J). (gr. 6-12). 1999. audio compact disk 14.95 CD. (978-1-880440-10-0(5)) Piqua Pr.
American Indian philosophy historical - nature teaching with humor psycology of teen age girls. All about girls of today.

Dealing Productively with Sexual Distress. Ann Seagrave & Faison Covington. Read by Ann Seagrave & Faison Covington. 2 cass. (Anxiety Treatment Ser.). 25.00 CHAANGE.
Part 1 - An Overview of Human Sexuality; Part 2 - Anxiety & Sexual Distress.

Dealing with a Religious Spirit. Jack Deere. 1 cass. (Running Time: 90 mins.). (Exposing the Religious Spirit Ser.: Vol. 2). 2000. 5.00 (JD11-002) Morning NC.
This series exposes one of the greatest enemies of every move of God.

Dealing with & Getting Past Loss/Separation. 1998. 24.95 (978-1-58557-017-1(6)) Dynamic Growth.

***Dealing with Anger II: Helping Your Child Deal with Explosions.** Sleep'n Sync. (ENG.). 2010. 17.99 (978-1-935887-03-4(3)) Sleep n Syn.

Dealing with Angry Customers. (Running Time: 25 min.). 12.95 (202) Salenger.
Suggests a method for dealing with angry customers.

Dealing with Angry Debtors. Jane K. Cleland. 1 cass. (Running Time: 60 min.). (Improving Accounts Receivable Collections: Tape 2). 1991. 39.50 (978-1-877680-08-3(7)) Tiger Pr.
Tape 2 helps collectors calm angry debtors, preserve a good relationship & collect the money. Lots of word-for-word examples are given.

Dealing with Arbitration & with Insurance Companies. Contrib. by Harvey Halberstadter et al. (Running Time: 4 hrs.). 1984. 70.00 incl. program handbook. NJ Inst CLE.
Eight experts in insurance matters discuss New Jersey Supreme Court rules regarding arbitration, practical considerations when presenting a case in arbitration, dealing effectively with the American Arbitration Association.

Dealing with Back Pain. 1 cass. (Running Time: 94 min.). (Intelligent Body Ser.). 1986. 15.00 (978-1-889618-57-9(8)) Feldenkrais Move.
Movement education - Feldenkrais awareness through movement lessons.

Dealing with Conflict & Confrontation. PUEI. 2002. audio compact disk 89.95 (978-1-933328-38-6(X), CareerTrack) P Univ E Inc.

Dealing with Conflict & Confrontation. Helga A. Rhode. 2 cass. (Running Time: 114 min.). 1996. 15.95 (978-1-55977-487-1(8)) CareerTrack Pubns.

Dealing with Conflict & Confrontation: How to Keep Your Cool, Stand Your Ground & Reach a Positive Resolution. Helga Rhode. 4 cass. (Running Time: 3 hrs. 42 min.). 59.95 Set incl. 40p. wkbk. (V10145) CareerTrack Pubns.
Conflicts are inevitable. Anger, grudges, hurt & blame are not. In fact, most of your conflicts can be resolved fairly easily. Even better, you can do it in a way that actually benefits all concerned. This insight-packed program will show you how.

Dealing with Dad. unabr. ed. Susan Besze Wallace & Monica Reed. Narrated by Christian Taylor. (Running Time: 1 hr. 21 mins. 53 sec.). (New Moms' Guides). (ENG.). 2009. 9.09 (978-1-60814-488-4(7)) Oasis Audio.

Dealing with Dad. unabr. ed. Susan Wallace & Monica Reed. Narrated by Christian Taylor. (Running Time: 1 hr. 21 mins. 53 sec.). (New Moms' Guides). (ENG.). 2009. audio compact disk 12.99 (978-1-59859-484-3(2)) Oasis Audio.

Dealing with Difficult Depression. Paschal Preston. 1998. 70.00 (978-0-8002-4429-3(X)) Taylor and Fran.

Dealing with Difficult Patients & Family Members. PUEI. 2007. audio compact disk 199.00 (978-1-934147-08-5(7), CareerTrack) P Univ E Inc.

Dealing with Difficult Patients & Their Families. PUEI. 2008. audio compact disk 199.00 (978-1-934147-86-3(9), CareerTrack) P Univ E Inc.

Dealing with Difficult People. 1 cass. (Running Time: 1 hr.). 9.95 (PS-88-03-05, HarperThor) HarpC GBR.

Dealing with Difficult People. Ben Bissell. 3 cass. (Running Time: 4 hrs.). 49.00 Set. C Bissell.
This presentation was recorded live & includes the five characteristics of difficult people, the four pitfalls to avoid & the positive steps to take in dealing with difficult people.

Dealing with Difficult Students & Their Parents. Ben Bissell. 1 cass. (Running Time: 23 min.). 15.00 C Bissell.
This is a version of Ben's popular seminar, "Dealing with Difficult People," & is designed to help teachers deal with difficult students & their parents.

Dealing with Disabilities in the Workplace. 2 cass. (Running Time: 2 hrs.). 1998. 25.00 Set; incl. study outline. (M214) Am Law Inst.
Includes examination of the U.S. Supreme Court ruling on asymptomatic HIV & the definition of a disability under the Americans with Disabilities Act. Considers whether the statutory definition is broadened as a result & how the EEOC's recent policy on mental disabilities affects employers & employees. Live recording from the three-part Employment Law Update telephone seminars series.

Dealing with Divorce. 1 cass. (Care Cassettes Ser.: Vol. 9, No. 10). 1982. 10.80 Assn Prof Chaplains.

Dealing with Doubts: Matt. 14:28. Ed Young. 1988. 4.95 (978-0-7417-1692-7(5), 692) Win Walk.

Dealing with Dragons. unabr. ed. Patricia C. Wrede. Read by Words Take Wing Repertory Company Staff. 4 cass. (Running Time: 5 hrs. 12 mins.). (Enchanted Forest Chronicles: Bk. 1). (J). (gr. 6 up). 1996. 32.00 (978-0-8072-7634-1(0), YA906CX, Listening Lib) Random Audio Pubg.
Independent-minded Cimorene volunteers to be a dragon's princess, where she learns to fireproof herself, consort with witches, read magic tomes, outwit djinns, & at the same time solve the murder of the King of the Dragons.

Dealing with Dragons. unabr. ed. Patricia C. Wrede. Read by Words Take Wing Repertory Company Staff. 4 vols. (Running Time: 5 hrs. 12 mins.). (Enchanted Forest Chronicles: Bk. 1). (J). (gr. 6 up). 1996. pap. bk. 38.00 (978-0-8072-7635-8(9), YA906SP, Listening Lib) Random Audio Pubg.

Dealing with Dragons, Set. unabr. ed. Patricia C. Wrede. 4 cass. (Enchanted Forest Chronicles: Bk. 1). (YA). 1999. 29.98 (FS9-34147) Highsmith.

Dealing with Emotional Repression in Marriage. unabr. ed. Nathaniel Branden. 1 cass. (Running Time: 1 hr. 12 min.). 12.95 (612) J Norton Pubs.
Discusses: repression & communication; repression & sexual problems; breaking through repressive block.

Dealing with Evil: Matt. 13:34-30, 36-43. Ed Young. 1993. 4.95 (978-0-7417-1950-8(9), 950) Win Walk.

Dealing with Life's Delemmas: Ecc. 8:1-17. Ed Young. 1994. 4.95 (978-0-7417-1994-2(0), 994) Win Walk.

Dealing with Manipulators. unabr. ed. Read by Gayle D. Erwin. 1 cass. (Running Time: 1 hr.). 1992. 4.95 (978-1-56599-507-9(4), C-7) Yahshua Pub.
Servant by choice.

Dealing with Our Grief. John Thomas. 1986. 10.80 (0209B) Assn Prof Chaplains.

Dealing with People. (Running Time: 44 min.). 12.95 (204) Salenger.
Provides advice on developing interpersonal skills.

Dealing with People. Swami Amar Jyoti. 1 cass. 1976. 9.95 (L-1) Truth Consciousness.
The difference between interest & desire, love & attachment. The spiritual way to deal with employees, co-workers & worldly problems. Eliminating tensions.

***Dealing with People You Can't Stand.** unabr. ed. Rick Brinkman & Rick Kirschner. (Running Time: 8 hrs. 30 mins. 0 sec.). (ENG.). 2011. audio compact disk 29.99 (978-1-4272-1174-3(4)) Pub: Macmill Audio. Dist(s): Macmillan

Dealing with Problems. Shad Helmstetter. 1 cass. (Self-Talk Cassettes Ser.). 10.95 (978-0-937065-36-5(6)) Grindle Pr.

Dealing with Rage: Fear, Guilt, Resentment. D. Modin. 1 cass. 8.95 (237) Am Fed Astrologers.

Dealing with Relational Stress. Mark Crow. 2 cass. (Running Time: 3 hrs.). 2001. (978-1-931537-28-5(3)) Vision Comm Creat.

Dealing with the Age of Rage. Mark Crow. 2 cass. (Running Time: 2 hrs.). 2001. (978-1-931537-16-2(X)) Vision Comm Creat.

Dealing with the Gifted Child. unabr. ed. Hosted by Nathaniel Branden. 1 cass. (Famous Authorities Talk about Children Ser.). 12.95 (AF0555) J Norton Pubs.
A selection of audio cassettes for parents & caring adults.

Dealing with the IRS Appeals Division. Stephen T. Galloway & Cris Van den Branden. 3 cass. bk. 159.00 set. (CPE4370) Bisk Educ.
Demonstrates the "how-to's" of working with the Appeals Division of the IRS, plus provides tips on securing information from the IRS regarding your client's case.

Dealing with the IRS Collection Division. Nathan M. Bisk. 3 cass. bk. 159.00 set. (CPE4360) Bisk Educ.
Learn how to correspond with the IRS, obtain IRS records, make offers in compromise, present payment arguments, use legal remedies, & more.

Dealing with the Reorganizing Debtor: Transactions, Negotiations & Litigation. 8 cass. (Running Time: 10 hrs. 30 min.). 1990. bk. 95.00 incl. 1471-page course handbook. (T6-9159) PLI.

Dealing with the Resolution Trust Corporation (RTC) Read by Neil Van Winkle et al. (Running Time: 3 hrs. 15 min.). 1991. 115.00 Incl. 245p. tape materials. (RE-55230) Cont Ed Bar-CA.

Dealing with Uncle, Income Tax, Social Security & Government Relations. Kermit Smith et al. 1986. 10.80 (0802) Assn Prof Chaplains.

Dealing with Your Client's Physician - Are You in Control? Read by Lee C. Swartz. 1 cass. 1988. 20.00 (AL-55) PA Bar Inst.

Dealmaker: All the Business Negotiating Skills & Secrets You Need. Robert L. Kuhn. Read by Robert L. Kuhn. 6 cass. 69.95 Set, incl. wkbk. (743AD) Nightingale-Conant.
Knowing how to get what you want, at the price you want to pay, is probably the single most important set of skills you need for building your career & creating the lifestyle you desire. You'll learn the ploys & tricks of the world's greatest deal makers, because most of them have sat across the table from Robert Lawrence Kuhn. Dr. Kuhn gives you step-by-step guidelines for setting your deal-making goals & keeping those goals focused throughout the negotiating process.

Deals on Wheels. Tana Reiff. (That's Life Ser.: Bk. 5). 1994. 10.95 (978-0-7854-1099-7(6), 40715) Am Guidance.

Deals on Wheels Home Study Course: How to Buy, Sell & Finance Used Mobile Homes for Big Profits & Cash Flow. Lonnie Scruggs. (ENG.). 2008. ring bd. 189.00 (978-1-933553-04-7(9)) Atomic Sound.

Dean Acheson. Interview with Dean Acheson. 1 cass. (Running Time: 30 min.). 1968. 13.95 (L000) TFR.
Acheson talks about his autobiography "Present at the Creation" & details his friendship with President Truman & his hostility toward Senator Joseph McCarthy.

Dean Duffy, unabr. ed. Randy Powell. Narrated by Jeff Woodman. 4 pieces. (Running Time: 4 hrs. 45 mins.). (gr. 8 up). 2001. 35.00 (978-0-7887-0602-8(0), 94781E7) Recorded Bks.
Although he's only just graduated from high school, 18-year-old Dean thinks of himself as a has-been. Mired in an inexplicable & frustrating two-year batting slump, he helplessly watches as a once-promising baseball career fizzles. But when a longtime mentor arranges a baseball scholarship, he finds himself daring to dream.

Dean Martin & Jerry Lewis Show, collector's ed. 6 cass. (Running Time: 9 hrs.). 1999. bk. 17.49 (4109); bk. 19.99 (4110) Radio Spirits.
Eighteen never-before-released programs.

Dean Martin & Jerry Lewis Show: Christmas Show & Mrs. Roy Rogers & Dale Evans. Perf. by Roy Rogers et al. Hosted by Dean Martin et al. 1 cass. (Running Time: 1 hr.). 2001. 6.98 (2096) Radio Spirits.

Dean Martin & Jerry Lewis Show: Debbie Reynolds & Jeff Chandler. Perf. by Debbie Reynolds & Jeff Chandler. Hosted by Jerry Lewis & Dean Martin. 1 cass. (Running Time: 1 hr.). 2001. 6.98 (2542) Radio Spirits.

Dean Martin & Jerry Lewis Show: Joanne Dru & Fred MacMurray. Perf. by Joanne Dru & Fred MacMurray. Hosted by Dean Martin & Jerry Lewis. 1 cass. (Running Time: 1 hr.). 2001. 6.98 (2523) Radio Spirits.

Dean Martin & Jerry Lewis Show: Laraine Day & Anne Baxter. Perf. by Anne Baxter & Loraine Day. Hosted by Dean Martin & Jerry Lewis. 1 cass. (Running Time: 1 hr.). 2001. 6.98 (2500) Radio Spirits.

Dean Martin & Jerry Lewis Show: New Nightclub & Dorothy Kristen. Perf. by Dorothy Kirsten. Hosted by Jerry Lewis & Dean Martin. 1 cass. (Running Time: 1 hr.). 2001. 6.98 (2087) Radio Spirits.

Dean Martin & Jerry Lewis Show: Sheldon Leonard & Jane Russell. Perf. by Sheldon Leonard & Jane Russell. 1 cass. (Running Time: 1 hr.). 2001. 6.98 (2227) Radio Spirits.

Dean Martin & Jerry Lewis Show: Spoof: You Bet Your Life & Spoof: A Spot in the Shade. Perf. by Sheldon Leonard & Jane Russell. Hosted by Jerry Lewis et al. 1 cass. (Running Time: 1 hr.). 2001. 6.98 (2124) Radio Spirits.

Dear American Airlines. unabr. ed. Jonathan Miles. (Running Time: 6.3 hrs. NaN mins.). 2008. 24.95 (978-1-4332-1473-8(3)) Blckstn Audio.

Dear American Airlines. unabr. ed. Jonathan Miles. Read by Mark Bramhall. (Running Time: 8 hrs. 0 mins.). 2008. 44.95 (978-1-4332-1471-4(7)); audio compact disk 29.95 (978-1-4332-1475-2(X)); audio compact disk 50.00 (978-1-4332-1472-1(5)); audio compact disk & audio compact disk 24.95 (978-1-4332-1474-5(1)) Blckstn Audio.

Dear & Glorious Physician. unabr. ed. Taylor Caldwell. Narrated by John McDonough. 23 cass. (Running Time: 32 hrs. 45 mins.). 2001. 177.00 (978-0-7887-5016-8(X), 96521E7) Recorded Bks.
The spellbinding life story of Luke, the physician of the New Testament. As Lucanus watches loved ones suffer & die, he turns his back on the Unknown God who would allow this, until he learns more about an amazing rabbi.

Dear Bill: A Memoir. 2nd abr. ed. W. F. Deedes. Read by W. F. Deedes. (Running Time: 3 hrs. 0 mins. 0 sec.). (ENG., 2006. audio compact disk 21.95 (978-1-4050-9233-3(5)) Pub: Macmillan UK GBR. Dist(s): IPG Chicago

Dear Bunny. Michaela Morgan. (ENG.). (J). (ps-k). 2009. audio compact disk 18.95 (978-0-545-13858-1(2)) Scholastic Inc.

Dear Daughter, I Forgot Some Things. David F. Salter. 1 CD. (Running Time: 79min 30sec). (J). (gr. 3-7). 2004. audio compact disk 12.95 (978-1-932226-30-0(3)) Wizard Acdmy.
Your daughter?s just turned 13 and, in her eyes, you?ve become as smart as a box of hammers. Talking to your teenage daughter can raise more emotions than helping your wife select draperies for the guest bathroom. But it?s got to be done.A recent study shows nearly half of teenagers have had intercourse before age 18. An estimated 10 million girls and women in America suffer from an eating disorder.In a series of letters to his teenage daughter, Salter discusses a number of critical thoughts that fathers need to share with their teenage girls. This is not a ?how-to? primer from a child psychologist. It?s a candid conversation from a regular Dad who wakes up every morning with three girls fighting for the bathroom, the hair dryer and the ?good? hairbrush."David Salter speaks eloquently, and - thankfully at times - humorously about how impossible it is today to raise daughters. I have two, both of legal age, and sometimes I have no idea how they got there without me totally screwing them up. This is well worth several evenings of your time."-Peter King, Sports Illustrated"Hey Dads, if you think you've told your daughter everything she'll need to know for life, love and success, then great! But if you're like most of us, there's far too much stuff we don't pass on and expect them to pick up on their own. David Salter's "Dear Daughter, I Forgot Some Things" gives us the perfect tool to ease the passage from girlhood to womanhood. You might even learn a few things yourself!"-Steve Rae, President, Raedio Inc. (Ontario, Canada)Author, Exercising Your Imagination"As the father of four daughters, I've often been disappointed that they did not come with instruction manuals. Listening to the advice that David Salter is giving to his own daughter renews my faith that we'll all come through this growing-up ordeal in fine shape. If you have daughters of your own, you owe it to yourself to use every resource you can find to make sure you're giving them the best fatherly advice possible."-David Young, Wizard of Ads partner (Sidney, NE.)Author, Why We Blog.

Dear Deer: A Book of Homophones. Gene Barretta. 1 cass. (Running Time: 9 mins.). (J). (gr. k-3). 2007. bk. 27.95 (978-0-8045-6958-3(4)); bk. 29.95 (978-0-8045-4181-7(7)) Spoken Arts.

Dear Emily. unabr. ed. Fern Michaels. Read by Melissa Hughes. 8 vols. (Running Time: 12 hrs.). 2000. bk. 69.95 (978-0-7927-2381-3(3), CSL 270, Chivers Sound Lib) AudioGO.
At forty, all Emily Thorn has to show for twenty years of marriage is a Federal Express letter from her doctor husband that begins "Dear Emily" & ends their life together. After putting her own life on hold to pay for his medical school, she believed him when he told her that some day she would have everything she ever wanted. Emily slims down & starts over, starting a chain of fitness centers. Finding herself now involved with two men, one kind & compassionate, the other unpredictable & alarmingly sensual, all she has to do is choose the right one.

Dear Emily. unabr. ed. Fern Michaels. Read by Melissa Hughes. 10 CDs. (Running Time: 15 hrs.). 2002. audio compact disk 94.95 (978-0-7927-2753-8(3), SLD 270, Chivers Sound Lib) AudioGO.
At 40, all Emily has to show for 20 years of marriage is a FedEx letter from her doctor husband that begins "Dear Emily" - and ends their life together. Overweight, out of shape, and dumped, she slims down and starts over with her own successful chain of fitness centers. Soon she's involved with two men, one compassionate, the other unpredictable and sensual. Now all she has to do is choose the right one.

Dear Emma. unabr. ed. Johanna Hurwitz. Narrated by Barbara McCulloh. 2 pieces. (Running Time: 3 hrs.). 2002. 19.00 (978-1-4025-4130-8(9)) Recorded Bks.
When 12-year-old Dossi Rabinowitz returns home to bustling 1910 New York City after spending a quiet summer with a Vermont farm family, nearly everything in her life has changed. In a series of letters to her new friends in Vermont, Dossi relates all the joys and sorrows of a year in New York. From the excitement of a new niece to the terror of a factory fire, Dossi learns that to accept and appreciate all life has to offer, she must look inside herself for strength and understanding.

Dear Enemy, Set. unabr. ed. Jean Webster. Read by Flo Gibson. 5 cass. (Running Time: 7 hrs.). 1992. 20.95 (978-1-55685-237-4(1)) Audio Bk Con.
In this sequel to "Daddy-Long-Legs" Judy & Jervis Pendleton appoint lively, red-headed Sallie McBride as Superintendent of the John Grier Orphan Asylum. Her clashes with Dr. Sandy MacRae (the "dear enemy" of this epistolary novel) over the children's freedom & welfare are hilarious & appealing.

Dear Heart. unabr. ed. Jenny Davis. Read [illegible] Rebecca Davis & Stuart Halusz. 2 cass. (Running Time: 2 hrs.). 1999. ([illegible]876584-04-7(1), 590686) Bolinda Pubng AUS.
Between 1941 & 1945 Wynne Brooks waited for her young soldier husband Mickey to return to her. In all the time he was away she wrote to him, first daily, then weekly, never knowing his whereabouts. In 1945, at the end of the war, her letters were returned, their messages of comfort & love unread, bearing the War Office stamp 'No Trace'. Wynne's letters, discovered by her niece Jenny Davis in 1988, offer a valuable glimpse into the hearts & minds of the women waiting at home, facing each day without news. This book is an exquisite, true-life account of an exceptional love that knows no boundaries of time & place.

Dear Heart, Come Home: The Path of Midlife Spirituality. Joyce Rupp. 1 cass. 1996. 18.00 (978-0-8245-3013-6(6), Crossroad Classic) Pub: Crossroad NY. Dist(s): IPG Chicago
An ideal companion to Joyce Rupp's newest bestseller on the path of midlife spirituality, these chants & visualizations can also be listened to with great peace & insight apart from the book.

***Dear Husband.** unabr. ed. Joyce Carol Oates. Narrated by Arthur Morey et al. 11 CDs. (Running Time: 14 hrs.). 2009. audio compact disk 90.00 (978-1-4159-6421-7(1), BksonTape) Pub: Random Audio Pubg. Dist(s): Random

Dear Irene. unabr. ed. Jan Burke. Narrated by Eliza Foss. (Running Time: 9 hrs. 30 mins.). 2008. 56.75 (978-1-4361-7686-6(7)); audio compact disk 92.75 (978-1-4361-1365-6(2)) Pub: Recorded Bks. Dist(s): NetLibrary CO

Dear John. unabr. ed. Nicholas Sparks. Read by Holter Graham. 6 cass. 2006. 63.00 (978-1-4159-3483-8(5)); audio compact disk 81.00 (978-1-4159-3484-5(3)) Books on Tape.

Dear John. unabr. ed. Nicholas Sparks. Read by Holter Graham. (YA). 2007. 59.99 (978-1-60252-894-9(2)) Find a World.

Dear John. unabr. ed. Nicholas Sparks. Read by Holter Graham. (Running Time: 9 hrs.). (ENG.). 2006. 14.98 (978-1-59483-795-1(3)) Pub: Hachet Audio. Dist(s): HachBkGrp

Dear John. unabr. ed. Nicholas Sparks. Read by Holter Graham. (Running Time: 9 hrs.). (ENG.). 2008. audio compact disk 14.98 (978-1-60024-277-9(4)) Pub: Hachet Audio. Dist(s): HachBkGrp

Dear John. unabr. ed. Nicholas Sparks. Read by Holter Graham. (Running Time: 9 hrs.). (ENG.). 2009. 19.98 (978-1-60788-279-4(5)) Pub: Hachet Audio. Dist(s): HachBkGrp

Dear John. unabr. ed. Nicholas Sparks. Read by Holter Graham. 8 CDs. (Running Time: 9 hrs.). (ENG.). 2009. audio compact disk 17.98 (978-1-60024-931-0(0)) Pub: Hachet Audio. Dist(s): HachBkGrp

Dear Kilroy - Audio Edition: A Dog to Guide Us. Nora Vitz Harrison. Read by Nora Vitz Harrison. Music by Rebecca Kragnes. 3 CDs. (Running Time: 3 hours). 2006. audio compact disk 24.95 (978-0-9785484-0-7(X)) Echo Pubns OR.
DEAR KILROY reminds us that some of the best teachers in this world have four legs and bark. Nora Vitz Harrison weaves the tender and wise humor of Kilroy and Riley, two canine correspondents, among heart-tugging essays on the magical relationship between people and dogs. Even if you have never been owned by a dog, you will be moved by this joyful yet bittersweet guide to life.

Dear Mae R, Nineteen Ninety-Three. Mae R. Wilson-Ludlam. 1 cass. 1992. 8.95 (1097) Am Fed Astrologers.

Dear Ming, Love, Mei-Ling. unabr. ed. Joy B. Conrad-Rice. 3 cass. (Running Time: 3 hrs.). (J). 1989. pap. bk. 39.50 Set, ESL. (978-0-88432-261-0(0), SEN100) J Norton Pubs.
Provide students with an opportunity to share experiences with someone in situations similar to their own, with similar problems, through a series of letters written by Mei-Ling to her friend Ming back home.

***Dear Money.** unabr. ed. Martha McPhee. (Running Time: 12 hrs. 0 mins.). 2010. 29.95 (978-1-4417-4260-5(3)); 72.95 (978-1-4417-4256-8(5)); audio compact disk 29.95 (978-1-4417-4259-9(X)); audio compact disk 105.00 (978-1-4417-4257-5(3)) Blckstn Audio.

Dear Mr. Henshaw. Beverly Cleary. (J). 1984. 21.33 (978-0-676-30833-4(3)) SRA McGraw.

***Dear Mr. Henshaw.** unabr. ed. Beverly Cleary. Read by Pedro Pascal. (ENG.). 2009. (978-0-06-176266-6(0)); (978-0-06-180554-7(8)) HarperCollins Pubs.

Dear Mr. Henshaw. unabr. ed. Beverly Cleary. Narrated by George Guidall. 2 pieces. (Running Time: 2 hrs.). (gr. 4 up). 1992. 19.00 (978-1-55690-594-0(7), 92130E7) Recorded Bks.
Story of a sixth grade boy who learns to cope with his parents' divorce when he begins exchanging letters with a famous author.

Dear Mr. Henshaw. unabr. ed. Beverly Cleary. Narrated by George Guidall. 2 CDs. (Running Time: 2 hrs.). (gr. 4 up). 2000. audio compact disk 19.00 (978-0-7887-3740-4(6), C1111E7) Recorded Bks.

Dear Mr. Jefferson: Letters from a Nantucket Gardener. Laura Simon. 1999. 42.00 (95935R4) Recorded Bks.

Dear Mr. Jefferson: Letters from a Nantucket Gardener. unabr. ed. Laura Simon. Narrated by Suzanne Toren. 5 cass. (Running Time: 7 hrs. 15 mins.). 1999. 44.00 (978-0-7887-3757-2(0), 95935E7) Recorded Bks.
As novelist Laura Simon lovingly tilled the land around her home, she longed to share her gardening passion with a kindred soul. Choosing the avid 18th century gardener, Thomas Jefferson, she wrote him insightful letters reflecting on the joys of leading a well-cultivated life.

Dear Mr President Abraham Lincoln. Andrea Davis Pinkney. Illus. by Andrea Davis Pinkney. 2002. 9.95 (978-0-87499-979-2(0)); 9.95 (978-0-87499-980-8(4)) Live Oak Media.

Dear Mr President Series. Elizabeth Winthrop et al. Illus. by Elizabeth Winthrop et al. 6 cass. (Running Time: 6 hrs. 20 mins.). 2004. 51.95 (978-0-87499-995-2(2)) Live Oak Media.

Dear Mr President Thomas Jefferson. Jennifer Armstrong. Illus. by Jennifer Armstrong. 2002. 9.95 (978-0-87499-985-3(5)); 9.95 (978-0-87499-986-0(3)) Live Oak Media.

***Dear Penthouse Forum (A First Draft)** unabr. ed. Laura Lippman. Read by Linda Emond & Francois Battiste. (ENG.). 2008. (978-0-06-176296-3(2), Harper Audio); (978-0-06-176295-6(4), Harper Audio) HarperCollins Pubs.

Dear Santa - Letters & Songs to the North Pole (A Merry Mini-Musical for Unison Voices) SoundTrax. Composed by Sally K. Albrecht & Jay Althouse. (ENG.). 2006. audio compact disk 44.95 (978-0-7390-4020-1(0)) Alfred Pub.

Dear Santa Letter Collection, Vol. 1. Perf. by Brian Cummings. 1 cass. (Running Time: 30 min.). (J). 1996. Dear Santa Pub.
A musical journey inside Santa's workshop as he reads letters from children. Full audio production with the voices of children's wishes & dreams.

Dear Sir. George Bernard Shaw. 1 CD. (Running Time: 1 hr. 30 mins.). 2005. audio compact disk 15.95 (978-0-660-18918-5(6)) Canadian Broadcasting CAN.

Dear Sister. unabr. ed. Judith Summers. Read by Melissa Sinden. 7 cass. (Running Time: 10 hrs. 30 mins). (Sound Ser.). 2004. 61.95 (978-1-85496-305-5(8), 63058) Pub: UlverLrgPrint GBR. Dist(s): Ulverscroft US

Dear Stranger Extant in Memory by the Blue Juniata see Poetry & Voice of Galway Kinnell

Dearest Dorothy, Help! I've Lost Myself! 3: Welcome to Partonville. unabr. ed. Charlene Ann Baumbich. Narrated by Cynthia Darlow. 6 cass. (Running Time: 9 hrs.). 2004. 59.75 (978-1-4025-6557-1(7), K1066MC) Recorded Bks.

Dearest Friend. unabr. ed. Lynne Withey. 11 CDs. (Running Time: 13 hrs. 30 mins.). 2002. audio compact disk 88.00 (978-0-7366-8736-2(X)) Books on Tape.
Abigail Adams, wife of President John Adams, was a formidable intellectual force who aided her husband with wise counsel.

Dearest Friend. unabr. ed. Lynne Withey. Read by Anna Fields. 9 cass. (Running Time: 13 hrs. 30 mins.). 2002. 72.00 (978-0-7366-8607-5(X)) Books on Tape.
Abigail Adams, the wife of President John Adams, was a woman of prodigious intellect and pronounced moral views. As a girl, she read voraciously, everything from Shakespeare to Locke, and was encouraged by her father to do so in an age when women were taught that sewing and decorum were sufficient. It was well that John Adams married her, as she became his most trusted advisor and confidante. Abigail held advanced views, such as the necessity of separation from England, emancipation of the slaves, and the need for a strong federal government. Yet she was also subject to her emotions, keenly feeling John's absence as he went about his commissions in Europe even while she sagely managed his domestic affairs. Abigail Adams was a remarkable woman, for her or any time.

Dearly Departed. unabr. ed. Elinor Lipman. Read by Jen Taylor. 4 vols. (Running Time: 6 hrs.). 2001. bk. 39.95 (978-0-7927-2495-7(X), CSL 384, Chivers Sound Lib); audio compact disk 64.95 (978-0-7927-9931-3(3), SLD 082, Chivers Sound Lib) AudioGO.
Everyone in King George, New Hampshire, loved Margaret Batten, part-time actress, full-time wallflower, and single mother to a now-distant daughter, Sunny. Her death brings Sunny back to the scene of her unhappy adolescence, to the community that remembers her solely as "the girl who golfed.".

Dearly Devoted Dexter. unabr. ed. Jeff Lindsay. Read by Nick Landrum. 8 cds. (Running Time: 34200 sec.). 2005. audio compact disk 29.99 (978-1-4193-3517-4(0)) Recorded Bks.

Death. 1 cass. (Running Time: 38 min.). 12.00 (L936) MEA A Watts Cass.

Death. J. Krishnamurti. 1 cass. (Running Time: 1 hr.). (Krishnamurti with Dr. Allan W. Anderson Ser.: No. 14). 8.50 (APA7414) Krishnamurti.
These 1974 dialogues cover the entire spectrum of Krishnamurti's teaching in a series highly regarded for its depth of inquiry into each particular subject.

Death. J. Krishnamurti. 1 cass. (Discussions with a Buddhist Scholar Ser.: No. 2). 8.50 (ABS792) Krishnamurti.
This is a systematic inquiry into the nature of truth & death with J. Krishnamurti, Dr. Rahula, a Buddhist scholar, Feroz Mehta, G. Narayan, Dr. Parchure & four members of the Brockwood Park staff in 1979.

Death. Osho Oshos. 1 cass. 9.00 (A0648-89) Sound Photosyn.

Death: Before & after the Fact. Robert Donath. 1 cass. (Running Time: 90 min.). 1988. 8.95 (654) Am Fed Astrologers.

Death: Just Like the Open Sky. unabr. ed. Osho Oshos. Read by Osho Oshos. 1 cass. (Running Time: 1 hr. 30 min.). 1993. 10.95 (DRG-022687B) Oshos.
On helping the dying: if one can transform a death into a moment of celebration, one has given the dying person the greatest gift that is possible in existence.

Death: The Last Taboo. 5 cass. (AA & A Symposium Ser.). 45.00 set. (A0353-90) Sound Photosyn.
The Foundation for Human Development, in cooperation with the Institute of Noetic Sciences, & Home Hospice of Sonoma County present an all-day affair aimed at bringing us a better understanding of death.

Death: The Zen Attitude. unabr. ed. Osho Oshos. Read by Osho Oshos. 1 cass. (Running Time: 1 hr. 30 min.). 1993. 10.95 (DVB-0008) Oshos.
An exploration of the authentic Zen attitude toward death: laughter, joy, celebration.

Death: Tragedy or Destiny. Spencer W. Kimball. 1 cass. 2004. 4.98 (978-1-55503-077-3(7), 06003559) Covenant Comms.
Essential understanding of death.

Death - Coping & Understanding the Reality. Norman J. Caldwell. Read by Norman J. Caldwell. Ed. by Achieve Now Institute Staff. 1 cass. (Running Time: 20 min.). (Fear No More Ser.). 1988. 9.97 (978-1-56273-102-1(5)) My Mothers Pub.
Develop your ability to view death as something natural that everyone will experience.

Death along the Cimarron. abr. ed. Ralph Compton Novel. (ENG.). 2003. audio compact disk 22.95 (978-1-56511-805-8(7), 1565118057) Pub: HighBridge. Dist(s): Workman Pub

Death & Dying. Barrie Konicov. 1 cass. 11.98 (978-0-87082-316-9(7), 025) Potentials.
Discover why it is necessary to understand the dying process & how it opens new worlds & new lives. You will learn how to prepare for death's arrival.

Death & Dying. Gay Luce. 2 cass. 18.00 set. (A0451-89) Sound Photosyn.
Participants were comforted, strengthened, & guided in a calm, reassuring way. With references to Tibetan & other traditions.

Death & Dying: Basic Assumptions & Pastoral Perspectives. Carl Nighswonger. 1986. 10.80 (0105B) Assn Prof Chaplains.

Death & Grieving: Music, Meditation & Prayer. Marianne Williamson. 1 cass. (Running Time: 45 min.). 1998. 10.95 (978-1-56170-438-5(5), M821) Hay House.
Helps ease the pain of a loved one's death.

Death & Honor. W. E. B. Griffin. Read by Scott Brick. (Running Time: 19 hrs.). Bk. 4. (ENG.). (gr. 8). 2008. audio compact disk 39.95 (978-0-14-314310-9(7), PengAudBks) Penguin Grp USA.

Death & Judgement. unabr. ed. Donna Leon. Read by Anna Fields. 6 cass. (Running Time: 1 hr. 30 min. per cass.). (Commissario Guido Brunetti Mystery Ser.: Bk. 4). 1998. 44.95 Set. (1983) Blckstn Audio.
Someone is killing Italy's prominent businessmen - but why? Venice's most charming & tenacious detective, Vice-Commissario Guido Brunetti, suspects a fatal link. What he uncovers in his unorthodox investigation, is a disturbing international web of exploitation run by Venice's most influential citizens, & an outsider's insatiable lust for retribution.

Death & Judgment. unabr. ed. Donna Leon. Read by Anna Fields. 6 cass. (Running Time: 8 hrs. 30 mins.). (Commissario Guido Brunetti Mystery Ser.: Bk. 4). 1997. 44.95 (978-0-7861-1236-4(0), 1983) Blckstn Audio.
Someone is killing Italy's prominent businessmen - but why? At first glance the murders appear unrelated. However, Venice's most charming & tenacious detective, Vice Commissario Guido Brunetti, suspects a fatal link. Unraveling the city's complexities & nuances as no one else can, Brunetti mounts an unorthodox investigation.

Death & Judgment. unabr. collector's ed. Donna Leon. Read by Anna Fields. 6 cass. (Running Time: 9 hrs.). (Commissario Guido Brunetti Mystery Ser.: Bk. 4). 1999. 48.00 (978-0-7366-4293-4(5), 4786) Books on Tape.
Commissario Guido Brunetti mounts an investigation into the killing of Italy's prominent businessmen. At first glance the murders appear unrelated but Brunetti begins to suspect a fatal link. What he uncovers is an international web of exploitation run by some of Venice's most influential citizens & an outsider's insatiable quest for retribution.

Death & Other Lovers. unabr. ed. Jo Bannister. 6 cass. 1998. 69.95 Set. (978-1-85903-005-9(X)) Pub: Magna Story GBR. Dist(s): Ulverscroft US

Death & Rebirth: The Bardo Teachings. Ole Nydahl. 2 cass. 18.00 set. (A0624-90) Sound Photosyn.
Hear the Yogi with direct blessing of the Karmapa, at Shared Visions, offer a detailed scenario of the continuum of existance from form to form in the context of open clear limitless space.

Death & Shadows. unabr. ed. Paula Gosling. Read by Liza Ross. 12 cass. (Running Time: 16 hrs.). 1999. 94.95 (978-1-86042-648-3(4), 26484) Pub: Soundings Ltd GBR. Dist(s): Ulverscroft US
Laura Brandon didn't want to work for her uncle because she valued her independence. So she recommended her friend Julie for the job of physiotherapist at the exclusive Mountview Clinic. A few months later Julie is brutally murdered in the woods that surround the clinic. Laura, tinged with guilt, wants to find out why - so she offers herself as Julie's replacement. It isn't long before she begins to regret her impulsive move. Confronted by tight-lipped nurses, inter-staff feuds & strange tales about a shadowy evil that lurks in the woods, she realizes that Mountview & the town of Black water itself may have something to hide. But playing detective is rather awkward when the clinics owner/manager is your very own uncle & you don't even know where to begin.

Death & the Cornish Fiddler. Deryn Lake. Read by Michael Tudor Barnes. 8 cass. 2007. 69.95 (978-1-84559-562-3(9)) Pub: ISIS Audio GBR. Dist(s): Ulverscroft US

Death & the Dancing Footman. Ngaio Marsh. Read by James Saxon. 10 cass. (Running Time: 15 hrs.). 2002. 84.95 (978-0-7540-0697-8(2), CAB 2119) AudioGO.

***Death & the Dancing Footman.** Ngaio Marsh. Read by Anton Lesser. (Running Time: 2 hrs. 56 mins.). (ENG.). 2011. audio compact disk 24.95 (978-1-4055-0802-5(7)) Pub: Little BrownUK GBR. Dist(s): IPG Chicago

Death & the Dancing Footman. unabr. ed. Ngaio Marsh. Read by James Saxon. 10 CDs. (Running Time: 15 hrs.). 2002. audio compact disk 94.95 (978-0-7540-5456-6(X), CCD 147) AudioGO.
It began as entertainments: eight people, many of them enemies, gathered for a winter weekend by a host with a love for theater. They would be the characters in a drama that he would devise. It ended in snowbound disaster. Everyone had an alibi, and most a motive as well. But Chief Detective Inspector Alleyn cast his suspicions upon Thomas, the dancing footman.

Death & the Dancing Footman. unabr. ed. Ngaio Marsh. Read by James Saxon. 10 cass. (Running Time: 15 hrs.). 2002. 69.95 (CAB 2119) AudioGO.

Death & the Hero-Meditation Death & Rebirth. unabr. ed. Roger Woolger. 2 cass. 18.00 (OC14L) Sound Horizons AV.

Death & the Joyful Woman. unabr. ed. Ellis Peters, pseud. Narrated by Simon Prebble. 5 cass. (Running Time: 7 hrs. 30 mins.). (Inspector George Felse Mystery Ser.: Vol. 2). 1992. 44.00 (978-1-55690-657-2(9), 92227E7) Recorded Bks.
Alfred Armiger was like a bull in the ring, belligerent & sure of himself. But Armiger was mortal after all. There was no stronger proof of it than the blood that oozed from his skull, mingling with the red wine he'd spilled on the floor at the moment of impact.

Death & the Jubilee. David Dickinson. 12 cass. (Running Time: 14 hrs.). (Soundings Ser.). (J). 2005. 94.95 (978-1-84559-026-0(0)) Pub: ISIS Lrg Prnt GBR. Dist(s): Ulverscroft US

Death & the Language of Happiness: A Cecil Younger Mystery. unabr. ed. John Straley. Read by Tim Jerome. 6 vols. (Running Time: 9 hrs.). 2000. bk. 54.95 (978-0-7927-2222-9(1), CSL 111, Chivers Sound Lib) AudioGO.
97-year-old William Flynn wants Cecil Younger, a P.I. in a rough Alaskan town, to kill a man! Cecil decides to meet with his potential client. Flynn is not too clear about what happened this week, but he's razor-sharp on the events of eight decades past. Angela Rameriez, who used to visit Flynn at his nursing home has been murdered. Flynn wants Cecil to find and kill the man he believes is responsible for Angela's death: her husband, Simon Delaney. Delaney's trail leads Cecil to a decades-old murder that is still reaching into the present.

Death & the Maiden. unabr. ed. Ariel Dorfman. Perf. by John Kapelos et al. 1 cass. (Running Time: 1 hr. 23 min.). 1994. 19.95 (978-1-58081-004-3(7)) L A Theatre.
A democratic new age is dawning in a Latin American country, but Paulina is haunted by the past. Once a political prisoner, she is still captive to terrifying memories. Suspense mounts when she & her husband offer hospitality to a stranger & Paulina thinks she recognizes, in their guest, the man who tortured her in prison & used Shubert's chamber music to drown out her screams.

Death & the Pregnant Virgin. unabr. ed. S. T. Haymon. Read by Patrick Romer. 7 cass. (Running Time: 8 hrs. 45 min.). 1993. 61.95 (978-1-85089-848-1(0), 40791) Pub: ISIS Audio GBR. Dist(s): Ulverscroft US
Inspector Benjamin Jurnet, confronted by murder, love, guilt & fear, finds the past & present merging strangely in his quest for a killer.

Death & What to Do about It. Jack Boland. 1 cass. 8.00 (BW07) Master Mind.

Death Angel. Linda Howard. Read by Joyce Bean. (Playaway Adult Fiction Ser.). 2009. 70.00 (978-1-60775-525-8(4)) Find a World.

Death Angel. abr. ed. Linda Howard. (Running Time: 6 hrs.). 2009. audio compact disk 14.99 (978-1-4233-1028-0(4), 9781423310280) Brilliance Audio.

Death Angel. unabr. ed. Linda Howard. Read by Joyce Bean. 1 MP3-CD. (Running Time: 11 hrs.). 2008. 24.95 (978-1-4233-1023-5(3), 9781423310235, Brilliance MP3); 39.25 (978-1-4233-1026-6(8), 9781423310266, BADLE); 39.25 (978-1-4233-1024-2(1), 9781423310242, Brinc Audio MP3 Lib); 24.95 (978-1-4233-1025-9(X), 9781423310259, BAD); audio compact disk 36.95 (978-1-4233-1021-1(7), 9781423310211, Bril Audio CD Unabri); audio compact disk 97.25 (978-1-4233-1022-8(5), 9781423310228, BriAudCD Unabrid) Brilliance Audio.

Death As an Affirmation of Life. Kriyananda, pseud. 1 cass. (Running Time: 90 min.). 9.95 (ST-39) Crystal Clarity.
Topics include: how to measure the success of a life; being prepared for death as the source of true detachment; the process of dying; making the transition to the astral world; how to assist departed souls; the importance of dying without bitterness or regrets.

Death As an Ally Vol. 2: Meeting at Holocaust Museum. 2nd ed. Excerpts. Prod. by Eli Jaxon-Bear. 1 CD. (Running Time: 60 mins).Tr. of English. 2001. audio compact disk 14.95 (978-1-893840-03-4(4)) Leela Found.

Death at Apothecaries' Hall. Deryn Lake. 8 cass. (Running Time: 10 hrs. 30 mins.). (Soundings Ser.). (J). 2004. 69.95 (978-1-84283-898-3(9)) Pub: ISIS Lrg Prnt GBR. Dist(s): Ulverscroft US

Death at Apothecaries' Hall. Deryn Lake. Read by Michael Tudor Barnes. 9 CDs. (Running Time: 37800 sec.). (Soundings (CDs) Ser.). 2004. audio compact disk 84.95 (978-1-84283-928-7(4)) Pub: ISIS Lrg Prnt GBR. Dist(s): Ulverscroft US

Death at Jamestown. Noe Venable. (Step into History Ser.). 2002. audio compact disk 18.95 (978-1-4105-0186-8(8)) D Johnston Inc.

Death at Jamestown. Noe Venable. Ed. by Jerry Stemach et al. Illus. by Rick Clubb. Narrated by Joe Sikora. Contrib. by Ted S. Hasselbring. (Start-to-Finish Books). 2002. 35.00 (978-1-58702-782-6(8)) D Johnston Inc.

Death at Jamestown. Noe Venable. Ed. by Jerry Stemach et al. Illus. by Rick Clubb. Narrated by Joe Sikora. Contrib. by Ted S. Hasselbring. (Start-to-Finish Books). (J). (gr. 2-3). 2002. 100.00 (978-1-58702-998-1(7)) D Johnston Inc.

Death at Jamestown. unabr. ed. Noe Venable. Ed. by Jerry Stemach et al. Illus. by Rick Clubb. Narrated by Joe Sikora. Contrib. by Ted S. Hasselbring. 1 cass. (Running Time: 1 hr.). (Start-to-Finish Books). 2002. 7.00 (978-1-58702-767-3(4)) D Johnston Inc.
The romance of John Smith and Pocahontas is one of the most famous legends in American history and the most commonly known in the history of Jamestown. However, historians now know that the romance never happened at all! So what is the real story of Jamestown? It is the story of a group of men and boys who come to America with dreams, but wind up trying desperately to survive in tidewater Virginia. These men faced sickness, starvation, mutiny, and attacks by the natives.

Death at la Fenice. unabr. collector's ed. Donna Leon. Read by Anna Fields. 6 cass. (Running Time: 9 hrs.). (Commissario Guido Brunetti Mystery Ser.: Bk. 1). 1998. 48.00 (978-0-7366-4217-0(X), 4715) Books on Tape.
A Venetian policeman's investigation into the murder of a famed conductor reveals chilling discoveries.

Death at St Jame's Palace. unabr. ed. Deryn Lake. Read by Michael Tudor Barnes. 8 cass. (Running Time: 9 hrs.). (Sound Ser.). (J). 2003. 69.95 (978-1-84283-535-7(1)) Pub: ISIS Lrg Prnt GBR. Dist(s): Ulverscroft US

Death at St James's Palace. unabr. ed. Deryn Lake. Read by Michael Tudor Barnes. 9 CDs. (Running Time: 9 hrs.). (Sound Ser.). (J). 2003. audio compact disk 84.95 (978-1-84283-696-5(X)) Pub: ISIS Lrg Prnt GBR. Dist(s): Ulverscroft US

Death at the Bar. Ngaio Marsh. Narrated by Nadia May. (Running Time: 8 hrs. 30 mins.). 1996. 27.95 (978-1-59912-461-2(0)) Iofy Corp.

Death at the Bar. unabr. ed. Ngaio Marsh. Read by Nadia May. 6 cass. (Running Time: 8 hrs. 30 mins.). 1997. 44.95 (978-0-7861-1075-9(9), 1845) Blckstn Audio.
After an evening of friendly darts and vintage brandy, a distinguished, although amorous, barrister expires - leaving one less lawyer in the world. Everyone in the cozy pub swears that the untimely death was caused by a dart that punctured the victim's finger. But to Inspector Roderick Alleyn, the "accident" was really a case of murder.

Death at the Crossroads: A Samurai Mystery. Dale Furutani. Read by Jonathan Marosz. 5 cass. (Running Time: 7 hrs. 30 min.). 1999. 24.95 (978-0-7366-4703-8(1)) Books on Tape.
Matsuyama Kaze is a "ronin," a Japanese knight-errant. Kaze must travel across Japan until he fulfills a promise made to his dying Lord & Lady to find their nine-year-old daughter. As this masterless samurai searches the countryside, he is caught up in a series of mysteries that test his strength & skills as well as his Confucian training. Kaze stumbles upon a corpse shot with an arrow at the crossroads leading to a small town. He becomes embroiled with an unlikely & untrustworthy cast of characters, who are as colorful as they are crafty. Each has secrets to keep & axes to grind & it will take all of Kaze's subtlety, stealth & Samurai skills to unravel the mystery & unmask the killer. Richly atmospheric, filled with historically accurate detail & evokes the world of long-ago Japan & the often-lonely life of an honor-bound warrior.

Death at the Crossroads: A Samurai Mystery. collector's ed. Dale Furutani. Read by Jonathan Marosz. 5 cass. (Running Time: 7 hrs. 30 min.). 1999. 40.00 (978-0-7366-4619-2(1), 5005) Books on Tape.

Death at the Dolphin. unabr. ed. Ngaio Marsh. Read by James Saxon. 8 cass. (Running Time: 12 hrs.). (Inspector Alleyn Mystery Ser.). 2000. 59.95 (978-0-7451-6681-0(4), CAB 1297) Pub: Chivers Audio Bks GBR. Dist(s): AudioGO
When the Dolphin Theater is given to Peregrine Jay by a mysterious patron, he is overjoyed. Then he's given a glove that belonged to Shakespeare, and he puts it on display at the theater and writes a play about it that becomes an enormous success. But a murder takes place, a boy is attacked, and the glove is stolen. Then Inspector Alleyn is called in.

Death at the Dutch House. unabr. ed. Barbara Whitehead. Read by Trudy Harris. 7 cass. (Running Time: 9 hrs. 15 min.). 1998. 76.95 (978-1-85903-200-8(1)) Pub: Magna Story GBR. Dist(s): Ulverscroft US
One of the Dutch House community is murdered. Detective Chief Inspector thinks the murderer must be someone from outside, but changes his mind as he discovers that not all is as it seems in the lives of the flat-dwellers.

Death at the Excelsior. Based on a story by P. G. Wodehouse. (ENG.). 2007. 5.00 (978-1-60339-111-5(8)); audio compact disk 5.00 (978-1-60339-112-2(6)) Listenr Digest.

***Death at Victoria Dock.** unabr. ed. Kerry Greenwood. Read by Stephanie Daniel. (Running Time: 5 hrs. 30 mins.). (Phryne Fisher Mystery: Ser.). 2009. audio compact disk 63.95 (978-1-921415-81-4(9), 9781921415814) Pub: Bolinda Pubng AUS. Dist(s): Bolinda Pub Inc

Death at Wentwater Court. Carola Dunn. Narrated by Bernadette Dunne. (Running Time: 6 hrs. 30 mins.). (Daisy Dalrymple Mystery Ser.). 2005. 25.95 (978-1-59912-462-9(9)) Iofy Corp.

Death at Wentwater Court. Carola Dunn & Bernadette Dunne. (Running Time: 6 hrs. 18 mins.). (Daisy Dalrymple Mystery Ser.). 2005. 29.95 (978-0-7861-8102-5(8)); reel tape 44.95 (978-0-7861-3486-1(0)); audio compact disk 55.00 (978-0-7861-7894-0(9)) Blckstn Audio.

Death Be Not Proud see Treasury of John Donne

Death Be Not Proud & The Bait see Hearing Great Poetry: From Chaucer to Milton

Death Before Dying. unabr. ed. Collin Wilcox. Read by Larry McKeever. 7 cass. (Running Time: 10 hrs. 30 min.). (Frank Hastings Ser.). 1992. 56.00 (978-0-7366-2212-7(8), 3005) Books on Tape.
A chance meeting reunites Detective Frank Hastings with an old school friend. Meredith seems to have everything...beauty, wealth, success. Over lunch, 25 years dissolve in nostalgia & they develop an unexpected intimacy.

Death before Wicket. Kerry Greenwood. Read by Stephanie Daniel. (Running Time: 8 hrs. 10 mins.). (Phryne Fisher Mystery: Ser.). 2009. 74.99 (978-1-74214-232-6(X), 9781742142326) Pub: Bolinda Pubng AUS. Dist(s): Bolinda Pub Inc

Death Before Wicket. unabr. ed. Kerry Greenwood. Read by Stephanie Daniel. (Running Time: 8 hrs. 10 mins.). (Phryne Fisher Ser.). 2007. audio compact disk 83.95 (978-1-74093-891-4(7)) Pub: Bolinda Pubng AUS. Dist(s): Bolinda Pub Inc

Death Begins at Fifty. unabr. ed. John S. Morgan. Read by Kevin Foley. 6 cass. (Running Time: 7 hrs. 48 min.). 1996. 39.95 (978-1-55686-684-5(4)) Books in Motion.
A mass layoff at a Pittsburg plant results in the murder of the company president. Successors attempt to salvage the company, save their jobs & help find the murderer.

Death Benefits. unabr. ed. Thomas Perry. Narrated by Michael Kramer. (Running Time: 13 hrs. 0 mins. 0 sec.). (ENG.). 2009. 29.99 (978-1-4001-6027-3(8)); audio compact disk 39.99 (978-1-4001-1027-8(0)); audio compact disk 79.99 (978-1-4001-4027-5(7)) Pub: Tantor Media. Dist(s): IngramPubServ

Death Beyond the Nile. unabr. ed. Jessica Mann. Read by Frances Jeater. 4 cass. (Running Time: 5 hrs. 40 min.). 2001. 44.95 (978-1-85089-637-1(2), 10591) Pub: ISIS Audio GBR. Dist(s): Ulverscroft US
Tamara Hoyland is an undercover agent. When a scientist goes slightly off the rails & books herself on a tour of Egypt, Tamara is the ideal person to keep an eye on her.

Death-Bringers: A Lieutenant Luis Mendoza Mystery. unabr. ed. Dell Shannon. Read by Alan Sklar. 6 cass. (Running Time: 9 hrs.). 2000. 49.95 (978-0-7451-2205-2(1), CSL 094) Pub: Chivers Audio Bks GBR. Dist(s): AudioGO
Lieutenant Mendoza of the Los Angeles Homicide Squad is up to his eyes in work. With three murder cases and a series of bank robberies by a lone thug whose latest victim is Sergeant Bert Dwyer, Mendoza's friend and colleague, work is very chaotic. Dwyer struggled to speak as he died: "Two-" was all he managed to say. It's not a great lead, but Mendoza doesn't have anything else to go by.

Death by Black Hole: And Other Cosmic Quandaries. unabr. ed. Neil deGrasse Tyson. Read by Dion Graham. (Running Time: 43200 sec.). 2007. 72.95 (978-1-4332-0210-0(7)) Blckstn Audio.

Death by Black Hole: And Other Cosmic Quandaries. unabr. ed. Neil deGrasse Tyson. Read by Dion Graham. (Running Time: 43200 sec.). 2007. 29.95 (978-1-4332-0020-5(1)); audio compact disk 29.95 (978-1-4332-0021-2(X)) Blckstn Audio.

Death by Black Hole: And Other Cosmic Quandaries. unabr. ed. Neil deGrasse Tyson. Read by Dion Graham. (Running Time: 43200 sec.). 2007. audio compact disk 29.95 (978-1-4332-0022-9(8)); audio compact disk 90.00 (978-1-4332-0211-7(5)) Blckstn Audio.

Death by Dentistry: Holistic Dentistry Panel, LA Health Expo, October, 17, 1998. Ed. by S. H. Shakman. 1 cass. 1998. 14.95 (978-1-892506-12-2(2)) Inst of Science.

Death by Love: Letters from the Cross. Gerry Breshears. Read by Mark Driscoll. Wayne Shepherd. (Running Time: 10 hrs. 15 mins.). (Re:Lit: Vintage Jesus Ser.). 2008. audio compact disk 34.99 (978-1-4335-0578-2(9)) CrosswayIL.

Death by Meeting: A Leadership Fable... about Solving the Most Painful Problem in Business. unabr. rev. ed. Patrick Lencioni. Read by Jack Arthur. 4 CDs. (Running Time: 5 hrs. 15 mins. 0 sec.). (ENG.). 2004. audio compact disk 22.95 (978-1-59397-441-1(8)) Pub: Macmill Audio. Dist(s): Macmillan

Death by Proxy. unabr. ed. W. Bartow Wright. Read by Rusty Nelson. 6 cass. (Running Time: 6 hrs. 42 min.). (Bucky Dolan Ser.: Bk. 4). 2001. 39.95 (978-1-55686-968-6(1)) Books in Motion.
Abe Foster, a newly retired CEO of a hi-tech company, has rented a house in Albuquerque, posing as his fictitious brother. On Christmas eve, he receives an e-mail reporting his own suicide and cremation in Santa Monica. He calls on Bucky for help.

Death by Water. Kerry Greenwood. Read by Stephanie Daniel. (Running Time: 8 hrs. 10 mins.). (Phryne Fisher Mystery: Ser.). 2009. 74.99 (978-1-74214-235-7(4), 9781742142357) Pub: Bolinda Pubng AUS. Dist(s): Bolinda Pub Inc

Death by Water. unabr. ed. Kerry Greenwood. Read by Stephanie Daniel. (Running Time: 29400 sec.). (Phryne Fisher Ser.). 2007. audio compact disk 83.95 (978-1-921334-38-2(X), 9781921334382) Pub: Bolinda Pubng AUS. Dist(s): Bolinda Pub Inc

Death Bytes. unabr. ed. Bill Knox. Read by James Bryce. 6 cass. (Running Time: 8 hrs. 46 min.). (Isis Ser.). (J). 2001. 54.95 (978-0-7531-0627-3(2)) Pub: ISIS Lrg Prnt GBR. Dist(s): Ulverscroft US
In the midst of a move to new headquarters, an unusual murder arrives on Thane's lap. Unusual because it took place in broad daylight beneath the windows of Glasgow High Court with judges looking on. Unusual because the victim had links with a high-tech world - where memory power is measured in bytes and megabytes. A new super-chip can be worth a fortune to anyone who can supply it and dangerous criminals are moving in fast.

Death Camps. Ernest Yaniger. Read by Tim O'Connor. 1 cass. (Running Time: 29 min. per cass.). 1980. 10.00 (HE831) Esstee Audios.
A detailed report about how the annihilation of six million people was initiated, planned, carried out, & rationalized.

Death Camps Proved Him Real. Maria Winowska. 6 cass. 24.95 (704) Ignatius Pr.
Life of St. Maximilian Kolbe, who gave his life for a fellow prisoner.

***Death Cloud.** Andrew Lane. Read by Dan Stevens. (Running Time: 3 hrs.). 2010. audio compact disk 19.95 (978-0-230-74512-4(1)) Pub: Pan Macmillan GBR. Dist(s): Trans-Atl Phila

***Death Cloud.** unabr. ed. Andrew Lane. (Running Time: 8 hrs. 0 mins. 0 sec.). (Young Sherlock Holmes Ser.). (ENG.). (YA). 2011. audio compact disk 29.99 (978-1-4272-1122-4(1)) Pub: Macmill Audio. Dist(s): Macmillan

Death Collector. unabr. ed. Justin Richards. Read by Steven Pacey. 6 CDs. (Running Time: 7 hrs. 29 mins.). (J). (gr. 4-7). 2006. audio compact disk 50.00 (978-0-7393-3564-2(2), Listening Lib); 40.00 (978-0-7393-3572-7(3), Listening Lib) Pub: Random Audio Pubg. Dist(s): Random
The foggy streets of Victorian London are thick with thieves. But when Eddie "Dipper" Hopkins steals George Archer's wallet, he has no idea that he is entering a dark world of grave robbers, assassins, and zombies. Because George Archer is no ordinary citizen. He is the newest and youngest member of the Department of Unclassified Artifacts at the British Museum, a department that investigates the bizarre and the unexplained. And in George's wallet is a clue to one of the biggest mysteries of all time, a secret as old as the dinosaurs - and one that certain people would kill for. Suddenly on the run for their lives, Eddie and George join forces with budding actress Elizabeth Oldfield to escape the clutches of a depraved genius - a man who needs the secret to carry out a terrifying plan. In this heart-stopping race against time, Eddie, George, and Elizabeth have only one chance to unravel the secret they possess before London is overrun by creatures from the dead... one of which is already prowling the streets.

Death Collector. unabr. ed. Justin Richards. Read by Steven Pacey. 7 CDs. (Running Time: 26940 sec.). (ENG.). (J). (gr. 5). 2006. audio compact disk 34.00 (978-0-7393-3539-0(1), Listening Lib) Pub: Random Audio Pubg. Dist(s): Random

Death Collectors. abr. ed. Read by Dick Hill. Notes by Jack Kerley. Jack Kerley. (Running Time: 14400 sec.). (Carson Ryder/Harry Nautilus Ser.). 2005. DVD, audio compact disk, audio compact disk 69.25 (978-1-59355-588-7(1), 9781593555887, BACDLib Ed) Brilliance Audio.
Please enter a Synopsis.

Death Collectors. abr. ed. Read by Dick Hill. Notes by Jack Kerley. Jack Kerley. (Running Time: 14400 sec.). (Carson Ryder/Harry Nautilus Ser.). 2006. audio compact disk 14.99 (978-1-59737-347-0(8), 9781597373470) Brilliance Audio.
In 1972, on the day of his sentencing, renowned artist and serial killer Marden Hexcamp is shot dead in the courtroom. Members of his Mansonesque band of followers are imprisoned or simply disappear. Fast-forward more than thirty years: A suspected prostitute is found murdered in a candlelit motel room, the first in a series of horrors suggesting Hexcamp's art remains alive and treacherous. Following a trail of beautiful - and profoundly disturbing - artwork, homicide detectives Carson Ryder and Harry Nautilus descend into the shocking world of the Death Collectors, people who spend vast sums to collect serial-killer memorabilia. As Ryder and Nautilus race to solve a thirty-year conspiracy, it becomes sadly evident that at the intersection of art and madness, death is beauty, tragedy a memento, and suffering suitable for framing.

Death Collectors. unabr. ed. Read by Dick Hill. Notes by Jack Kerley. Jack Kerley. (Running Time: 9 hrs.). (Carson Ryder/Harry Nautilus Ser.). 2005. 39.25 (978-1-59710-885-0(5), 9781597108850, BADLE); 24.95 (978-1-59710-884-3(7), 9781597108843, BAD); 29.95 (978-1-59355-584-9(9), 9781593555849, BAU); 74.25 (978-1-59355-585-6(7), 9781593555856, BriAudUnabridg); DVD & audio compact disk 24.95 (978-1-59335-741-2(9), 9781593357412, Brilliance MP3); audio compact disk 39.25 (978-1-59335-875-4(X), 9781593358754, Brinc Audio MP3 Lib) Brilliance Audio.

Death Comes As Epiphany. unabr. collector's ed. Sharan Newman. Read by Donada Peters. 6 cass. (Running Time: 9 hrs.). 1999. 48.00 (978-0-7366-4359-7(1), 4831) Books on Tape.
Catherine LeVendeur has taken service in the Convent of the Paraclete of conquer her sin of pride. But service can come in many forms..a manuscript that the convent produced for the great Abbe Suger has disappeared, & rumors have surfaced that the book contains sacrilegious passages that may harm the convent itself. To save her Order, Catherine will risk much; disgrace, the wrath of family & Church, even the loss of her immortal soul.

Death Comes as the End. unabr. ed. Agatha Christie. Read by Emilia Fox. (Running Time: 25920 sec.). (Audio Editions Mystery Masters Ser.). 2006. 29.95 (978-1-57270-519-7(1)) Pub: Audio Partners. Dist(s): PerseuPGW

Death Comes as the End. unabr. ed. Agatha Christie. Narrated by Emilia Fox. (Running Time: 25920 sec.). (Audio Editions Mystery Masters Ser.). (ENG.). 2006. audio compact disk 29.95 (978-1-57270-518-0(3)) Pub: AudioGO. Dist(s): Perseus Dist

Death Comes for the Archbishop. unabr. ed. Willa Cather. Narrated by Flo Gibson. 5 cass. (Running Time: 7 hrs.). 2002. 35.95 (978-1-55685-689-1(X),) Audio Bk Con.
Two French missionaries, Fathers Latour & Vaillant, go to New Mexico in hopes of reviving religious interest there among the Mexicans & Indians.

Death Cycle Machine. unabr. ed. Charlotte Mayerson. Read by Ellen Burstyn. 1 cass. (Running Time: 45 min.). 1996. 10.95 (978-1-57453-022-3(4), 330109) Audio Lit.
A mother's poems about the death of her son from AIDS evoke the grandeur of death as well as its pain.

Death Dance. abr. ed. Linda Fairstein. Read by Blair Brown. (Alexandra Cooper Mysteries Ser.). 2006. 15.95 (978-0-7435-6466-3(9)) Pub: S&S Audio. Dist(s): S and S Inc

Death Dance. abr. ed. Linda Fairstein. Read by Blair Brown. (Running Time: 60 hrs. 0 mins. 0 sec.). (Alexandra Cooper Mysteries Ser.). 2008. audio compact disk 14.99 (978-0-7435-7137-1(1)) Pub: S&S Audio. Dist(s): S and S Inc

Death Dance. unabr. ed. Linda Fairstein. Read by Barbara Rosenblat. 10 CDs. (Running Time: 11 hrs.). (Alexandra Cooper Mysteries Ser.). 2006. audio compact disk 119.75 (978-1-4193-6901-8(6), C3517); 79.75 (978-1-4193-6899-8(0), 98244) Recorded Bks.
Alexandra Cooper is an assistant DA in the New York sex crimes division. Her vivid cases have made every book in this mystery series a best-seller. Death Dance plunges Cooper into an increasingly dangerous investigation. A world-renowned Russian ballerina has been murdered at the Met shortly after one of her performances. Cooper soon discovers that the clues to the crime are as complex as the corridors that run throughout the great opera house.

Death Dealer. abr. ed. Heather Graham. Read by Fred Stella and Natalie Ross & Natalie Ross. (Running Time: 5 hrs.). 2010. audio compact disk 14.99 (978-1-4418-2561-2(4), 9781441825612, BACD) Brilliance Audio.

Death Dealer. unabr. ed. Heather Graham. (Running Time: 9 hrs.). 2009. 39.97 (978-1-4233-9743-4(6), 9781423397434, BADLE) Brilliance Audio.

Death Dealer. unabr. ed. Heather Graham. Read by Fred Stella. (Running Time: 9 hrs.). 2009. 24.99 (978-1-4233-9742-7(8), 9781423397427, BAD) Brilliance Audio.

Death Dealer. unabr. ed. Heather Graham. Read by Fred Stella & Natalie Ross. (Running Time: 9 hrs.). 2009. 39.97 (978-1-4233-9741-0(X), 9781423397410, Brlnc Audio MP3 Lib); audio compact disk 97.97 (978-1-4233-9739-7(8), 9781423397397, BriAudCD Unabrid) Brilliance Audio.

Death Dealer. unabr. ed. Heather Graham. Read by Fred Stella et al. (Running Time: 9 hrs.). 2009. 24.99 (978-1-4233-9740-3(1), 9781423397403, Brilliance MP3) Brilliance Audio.

Death Dealer. unabr. ed. Heather Graham. Read by Fred Stella et al. (Running Time: 9 hrs.). 2009. audio compact disk 29.99 (978-1-4233-9738-0(X), 9781423397380, Bril Audio CD Unabri) Brilliance Audio.

Death Department. unabr. ed. Bill Knox. Read by James Bryce. 6 cass. (Running Time: 9 hrs.). (Isis Ser.). (J). 2004. 54.95 (978-0-7531-0388-3(5), 980603) Pub: ISIS Lrg Prnt GBR. Dist(s): Ulverscroft US

Death Divided. unabr. ed. Clare Francis. Read by Alex Jennings. 10 CDs. (Running Time: 39900 sec.). 2001. audio compact disk 94.95 (978-0-7540-5526-6(4), CCD 217) Pub: Chivers Audio Bks GBR. Dist(s): AudioGO

Death Divided. unabr. ed. Clare Francis. Read by Alex Jennings. 10 cass. (Running Time: 15 hrs.). 2002. 84.95 (978-0-7540-0853-8(3), CAB 2275) Pub: Chivers Pr GBR. Dist(s): AudioGO

Death Does Not Exist/Finding the Kingdom Within. Marianne Williamson. Read by Marianne Williamson. 1 cass. (Running Time: 90 mins.). (Lectures on a Course in Miracles). 1999. 10.00 (978-1-56170-183-4(1), M711) Hay House.

Death du Jour. Kathy Reichs. 4 cass. (Running Time: 6 hrs.). (Temperance Brennan Ser.: No. 2). 1999. 24.35 Set. (978-1-85686-522-7(3)) Ulvrscrft Audio.

Death du Jour. abr. ed. Kathy Reichs. (Temperance Brennan Ser.: No. 2). 2004. 14.95 (978-0-7435-4610-2(5)) Pub: S&S Audio. Dist(s): S and S Inc

Death du Jour. unabr. ed. Kathy Reichs. Read by Bonnie Hurren. 12 CDs. (Running Time: 18 hrs.). (Temperance Brennan Ser.: No. 2). 2002. audio compact disk 110.95 (SLD 095) AudioGO.
From the crime scene to the morgue & to the lab, Tempe Brennan uses her considerable forensic skills to probe a mystery that begins with horrifying deaths in a fire in Quebec, leads her to the Carolinas & then to Montreal. Now, during a bitter Montreal winter & in a convent graveyard, Tempe is digging for a corpse buried more than a hundred years ago & she's headed for a startling showdown.

Death du Jour. unabr. ed. Kathy Reichs. Read by Bonnie Hurren. 12 vols. (Temperance Brennan Ser.: No. 2). 2000. bk. 96.95 (978-0-7927-2346-2(5), CSL 235, Chivers Sound Lib) AudioGO.

Death du Jour. unabr. ed. Kathy Reichs. Read by Bonnie Hurren. 12 CDs. (Running Time: 12 hrs.). (Temperance Brennan Ser.: No. 2). 2000. audio compact disk 110.95 (978-0-7540-5330-9(X), CCD 021) Pub: Chivers Audio Bks GBR. Dist(s): AudioGO
Tempe Brennan uses her forensic skills to probe a mystery that begins with horrifying deaths in a fire in Quebec, leads her to the Carolinas & then to Montreal. Now, in a Montreal graveyard, Tempe is digging for a 100-year-old corpse & she's headed for a startling showdown.

Death, Dying & Rebirth. unabr. ed. Stanislov Grof. 4 cass. 1993. 36.00 set. (OC337-71) Sound Horizons AV.

Death, Dying & the Afterlife. John E. Bradshaw. (Running Time: 14400 sec.). 2008. audio compact disk 100.00 (978-1-57388-119-7(8)) J B Media.

Death Echo. unabr. ed. Elizabeth Lowell. Read by Beth McDonald. 2010. audio compact disk 39.99 (978-0-06-198852-3(9), Harper Audio) HarperCollins Pubs.

***Death Echo.** unabr. ed. Elizabeth Lowell. Read by Beth Mcdonald. (ENG.). 2010. (978-0-06-200874-9(9), Harper Audio); (978-0-06-201599-0(0), Harper Audio) HarperCollins Pubs.

Death Ethics. Richard Dayringer. 1986. 10.80 (0709B) Assn Prof Chaplains.

Death for Sale see Inner Sanctum: Three Classic Stories

Death Goes on Retreat. Sister Carol Anne O'Marie. Narrated by Marguerite Gavin. (Running Time: 7 hrs. 30 mins.). 2000. 27.95 (978-1-59912-463-6(7)) Iofy Corp.

Death Goes on Retreat. unabr. ed. Carol Anne O'Marie. Read by Vera Rosewalker. 6 cass. (Running Time: 8 hrs. 22 min.). (Sister Mary Helen Mystery Ser.). 2001. 29.95 (978-1-57270-187-8(0), N61187u) Pub: Audio Partners. Dist(s): PerseuPGW

Death Goes on Retreat. unabr. ed. Carol Anne O'Marie. Read by Marguerite Gavin. 6 CDs. (Running Time: 7 hrs.). 2001. audio compact disk 48.00 (978-0-7861-9784-2(6), 2705) Blckstn Audio.
Sister Mary Helen still spry at seventy-something arrives at St. Colette's Retreat a week early.Unfortunately so have a convention of San Francisco priests. Instead of a few tranquil days of spiritual renewal she encounters a boisterous group of hard-drinking pastors, a crotcherty cook & a dead body. Also someone has killed a former seminary student & left his corpse under the mountain pines.

Death Goes on Retreat. unabr. ed. Carol Anne O'Marie. Read by Marguerite Gavin. 5 cass. (Running Time: 7 hrs.). 2001. 39.95 (978-0-7861-1933-2(0), 2705) Blckstn Audio.
Sister Mary Helen arrives at St. Colette's Retreat a week early & also a convention of San Francisco priests. Instead of a few tranquil days of spiritual renewal she encounters a boisterous group of hard-drinking pastors. Also someone has killed a former seminary student & left his corpse under the mountain pines.

Death Goes on Retreat: A Sister Mary Helen Mystery. unabr. ed. Sister Carol Anne O'Marie. Read by Marguerite Gavin. (Running Time: 7 hrs. 0 mins.). (ENG.). 2009. 29.95 (978-1-4332-9424-2(9)) Blckstn Audio.

Death Grip. abr. ed. Jerry Ahern. Read by Alan Zimmerman. 4 vols. (Running Time: 6 hrs.). (Defender Ser.: No. 9). 2003. 25.00 (978-1-58807-029-6(8)) Am Pubng Inc.
A death grip is strangling our precious liberty as martial law marches across the land. The President has been murdered, and the Big Lie told the American people-that David Holden and his Patriots are guilty! But there is one hope: evidence exists in the form of videotape that exposes the terrorists' FLNA and the new president as the real assassins. Now David and his crack commando troops must load their Uzis for one final mission: to get the truth to the nation or all is lost.

Death Grip. unabr. ed. Jerry Ahern. Read by Alan Zimmerman. 2 vols. No. 9. 2003. (978-1-58807-533-8(8)) Am Pubng Inc.

Death Grip. unabr. ed. Jerry Ahern. Read by Alan Zimmerman. 4 vols. No. 9. 2004. audio compact disk 30.00 (978-1-58807-271-9(1)); audio compact disk (978-1-58807-702-8(0)) Am Pubng Inc.

Death Has a Thirst & The Letter. 1 cass. (Running Time: 60 min.). Dramatization. (Whistler Ser.). 6.00 Once Upon Rad.
Radio broadcasts - mystery & suspense.

Death in a Cold Hard Light. unabr. collector's ed. Francine Mathews. Read by Bernadette Dunne. 8 cass. (Running Time: 12 hrs.). (Merry Folger Ser.). 1998. 64.00 (978-0-7366-4262-0(5), 4761) Books on Tape.
A young man's corpse is found in the storm-churned waters off Nantucket.

Death in a Mood Indigo. unabr. collector's ed. Francine Mathews. Read by Bernadette Dunne. 8 cass. (Running Time: 12 hrs.). (Merry Folger Ser.). 1997. 64.00 (978-0-7366-4006-0(1), 4504) Books on Tape.
A skeleton washed up on a beach raises questions about a serial killer & the disappearance of a sculptor.

Death in a Prairie House: Frank Lloyd Wright & the Taliesin Murders. William R. Drennan. Read by Jim Fleming. (ENG.). 2009. audio compact disk 27.95 (978-0-299-23230-6(1)) Pub: U of Wis Pr. Dist(s): Chicago Distribution Ctr

Death in a Strange Country. unabr. collector's ed. Donna Leon. Read by Anna Fields. 6 cass. (Running Time: 9 hrs.). (Commissario Guido Brunetti Mystery Ser.: Bk. 2). 1998. 48.00 (978-0-7366-4218-7(8), 4716) Books on Tape.
Venetian Detective Brunett's murder investigation reveals a massive conspiracy involving Mafia, government, the U.S. Army & toxic waste.

***Death in A White Tie.** Ngaio Marsh. 2010. 76.95 (978-0-7531-4446-6(8)); audio compact disk 89.95 (978-0-7531-4447-3(6)) Pub: Isis Pubng Ltd GBR. Dist(s): Ulverscroft US

Death in a White Tie. abr. ed. Ngaio Marsh. Read by Benedict Cumberbatch. (Running Time: 3 hrs. 44 mins. 0 sec.). (ENG.). 2008. audio compact disk 28.95 (978-1-4055-0506-2(0)) Pub: Little BrownUK GBR. Dist(s): IPG Chicago

Death in Belmont. Sebastian Junger. 6 cass. (Running Time: 29880 sec.). (Sound Library). 2006. 54.95 (978-0-7927-4220-3(6), CSL 974) AudioGO.

Death in Belmont. Sebastian Junger. Narrated by Kevin Conway. 7 CDs. 2006. audio compact disk 74.95 (978-0-7927-4067-4(X), SLD 974) AudioGO.

Death in Belmont. Sebastian Junger. Narrated by Kevin Conway. (Running Time: 29880 sec.). 2006. audio compact disk 29.95 (978-0-7927-4221-0(4), CMP 974) AudioGO.

***Death in Belmont.** abr. ed. Sebastian Junger. Read by Kevin Conway. (ENG.). 2006. (978-0-06-113507-1(0), Harper Audio); (978-0-06-113506-4(2), Harper Audio) HarperCollins Pubs.

Death in Belmont. unabr. ed. Sebastian Junger. Read by Kevin Conway. 7 CDs. (Running Time: 28800 sec.). 2006. audio compact disk 34.95 (978-0-06-082995-7(8), Harper Audio) HarperCollins Pubs.

***Death in Belmont.** unabr. ed. Sebastian Junger. Read by Kevin Conway. (ENG.). 2006. (978-0-06-113501-9(1), Harper Audio); (978-0-06-113500-2(3), Harper Audio) HarperCollins Pubs.

Death in Dark Waters. unabr. ed. Patricia Hall. Read by Michael Tudor Barnes. 6 cass. (Running Time: 30600 sec.). (Sound Ser.). 2003. 54.95 (978-1-84283-458-9(4)) Pub: ISIS Lrg Prnt GBR. Dist(s): Ulverscroft US

Death in Dark Waters. unabr. ed. Maeve Haran & Patricia Hall. Read by Jacqueline King. 9 CDs. (Running Time: 8 hrs. 30 min.). (Sound Ser.). (J). 2003. audio compact disk 84.95 (978-1-84283-693-4(5)) Pub: ISIS Lrg Prnt GBR. Dist(s): Ulverscroft US

Death in Disguise. Caroline Graham. Read by Hugh Ross. 10 cass. (Chief Inspector Barnaby Ser.: Bk. 3). 1999. 84.95 (978-0-7540-0310-6(8), CAB1733) AudioGO.

Death in Disguise. unabr. ed. Caroline Graham. Read by Hugh Ross. 10 cass. (Running Time: 15 hrs.). (Chief Inspector Barnaby Ser.: Bk. 3). 2000. 69.95 (CAB 1733) Pub: Chivers Audio Bks GBR. Dist(s): AudioGO
When a death at the Elizabethan Manor House is announced to the village, few are surprised. The house is home to an unlikely bunch of oddballs and it was only a matter of time before one of them came to a bad end. This time it was an accident. However, the next death is murder. To Inspector Barnaby, it's soon apparent that the case includes the most bizarre suspects he has ever encountered.

Death in Ecstasy. unabr. ed. Ngaio Marsh. Read by James Saxon. 8 cass. (Running Time: 12 hrs.). (Inspector Alleyn Mystery Ser.). 2000. 59.95 (978-0-7451-6140-2(5), CAB 597) Pub: Chivers Audio Bks GBR. Dist(s): AudioGO
The poison was cyanide, slipped into the sacred wine of ecstasy just before it was presented to Miss Cara Quayne at the House of the Sacred Flame. The victim was a deeply religious Initiate who had trained for a month for her last ceremony. The suspects were the other Initiates and the High Priest. All claimed they were above earthly passions. But Cara Quayne had provoked lust, jealousy and murder. Roderick Alleyn suspected that more evil still lurked behind the Sign of the Sacred Flame.

Death in Ecstasy. unabr. ed. Ngaio Marsh. Read by James Saxon. 8 CDs. (Inspector Roderick Alleyn Mysteries Ser.). 2000. audio compact disk 79.95 (978-0-7540-5360-6(1), CCD 051) Pub: Chivers Audio Bks GBR. Dist(s): AudioGO
Cara Quayne was poisoned at the House of the Sacred Flame. She was a deeply religious Initiate who had trained for a month for her last ceremony. The suspects were the other Initiates & the High Priest. All claimed they were above earthly passions. Inspector Alleyn knew better.

Death in Everyday Life. Read by Chogyam Trungpa. 1 cass. 1975. 10.00 (#A086) Vajradhatu.
A seminar by the scholar & meditation master trained in the philosophical & meditative traditions of Buddhism in Tibet.

Death in Hellfire. Deryn Lake. 2009. 69.95 (978-1-4079-0498-6(1)); audio compact disk 79.95 (978-1-4079-0499-3(X)) Pub: Soundings Ltd GBR. Dist(s): Ulverscroft US

Death in Holy Orders. unabr. ed. P. D. James. Read by Charles Keating. 12 cass. (Running Time: 18 hrs.). (Adam Dalgliesh Mystery Ser.). 2001. 49.95 (PH822) Blckstn Audio.
The body of a student at a theological college is found on the shore, suffocated by a fall of sand. Adam Dalgliesh is called upon to reexamine the verdict of accidental death (which the student's father would not accept). Having visited the College of St. Anselm in his boyhood, he finds the investigation has a strong nostalgic aspect for him. But that is soon overtaken by the realization that he has encountered the most horrific case of his career and another visitor to the college dies a horrible death.

Death in Holy Orders. unabr. ed. P. D. James. 10 cass. (Running Time: 10 hrs.). (Adam Dalgliesh Mystery Ser.). 2001. 80.00 (978-0-7366-6854-5(3)) Books on Tape.
On the bleak coast of East Anglia, atop a sweep of low cliffs, stands the small theological college of St. Anselm's. On the shore not far away, smothered beneath a fall of sand, lies the body of one of the school's young ordinands. He is the son of Sir Alred Treves, a hugely successful businessman who is accustomed to getting what he wants - and in this case what he wants is for Commander Adam Dalgliesh to investigate his son's death.

Death in Kashmir. unabr. ed. M. M. Kaye. Read by Virginia McKenna. 8 cass. (Running Time: 8 hrs.). 1993. bk. 69.95 (978-0-7451-6082-5(4), CAB 367) AudioGO.

Death in Lacquer Red. Jeanne M. Dams. Read by Kate Reading. (Hilda Johansson Mystery Ser.: Bk. 1). 2000. audio compact disk 48.00 (978-0-7366-8014-1(4)) Books on Tape.

Death in Lacquer Red. collector's ed. Jeanne M. Dams. Read by Kate Reading. 5 cass. (Running Time: 7 hrs. 30 min.). (Hilda Johansson Mystery Ser.: Bk. 1). 2000. 40.00 (978-0-7366-5465-4(8)) Books on Tape.
The year is 1900 & Hilda Johansson is a young Swedish woman working in the South Bend, Indiana, home of the Studebaker family. She faces the typical problems of an immigrant & the demands of a job that is both exhausting & exhilarating. Her struggle to be a good servant is compounded when discovers, on the Studebaker estate, the body of a woman just returned from missionary work in China.

Death in Little Tokyo. unabr. collector's ed. Dale Furutani. Read by Jonathan Marosz. 4 cass. (Running Time: 6 hrs.). (Ken Tanaka Ser.). 1999. 32.00 (978-0-7366-4414-3(8), 4875) Books on Tape.
It's Ken Tanaka's turn to stage a mock mystery for the Los Angeles Mystery Club & the forty-year-old amateur sleuth is determined to do it right. Tanaka sets himself up as a fake P.I., office & all, only to be hired by a passing blond bombshell. Taking the case on a whim, Ken's detecting leads him to a mutilated corpse. Now a suspect & out to clear his name, Tanaka becomes caught up in a mystery involving the Japanese Mafia & an international smuggling scheme.

Death in Lovers' Lane. unabr. ed. Carolyn G. Hart. Read by Kate Reading. 6 cass. (Running Time: 9 hrs.). (Henrie O Mystery Ser.). 1998. 48.00 (978-0-7366-4168-5(8), 4670) Books on Tape.
Henrietta "Henrie O" Collins, an ex-reporter turned sleuth, is teaching journalism at Thorndyke University, where she encourages an ambitious student to pursue an investigative series about three unrelated & hitherto unsolved local crimes. But the student's study habits get her killed. The police & the powers-that-be at Thorndyke are rabidly against Henrie O's involvement in the case. But the stubborn, sixtysomething investigator is committed to dredging up a past everyone wants to keep buried, even if it means placing herself firmly in the killer's path.

Death in Paradise. Carolyn G. Hart. Read by Kate Reading. 6 cass. (Running Time: 9 hrs.). (Henrie O Mystery Ser.). 2000. 29.95 (978-0-7366-4434-1(2)) Books on Tape.
Henrie O, receiving a tip that her husband's tragic fall six years ago was not an accident, is lured back to the scene of the crime.

Death in Paradise. Robert B. Parker. Contrib. by Robert Forster. (Playaway Adult Fiction Ser.). 2008. 59.99 (978-1-60640-658-8(2)) Find a World.

Death in Paradise. Robert B. Parker. 6 CDs. (Running Time: 6 hrs.). (Jesse Stone Ser.: No. 3). 2001. audio compact disk 34.95 (N Millennium Audio) New Millenn Enter.

Death in Paradise. Robert B. Parker. Narrated by Robert Forster. 5 CDs. (Running Time: 5 hrs.). (Jesse Stone Ser.: No. 3). audio compact disk 48.00 (978-1-4025-1587-3(1)) Recorded Bks.

Death in Paradise. abr. ed. Carolyn G. Hart. Read by Penny Fuller. 2 cass. (Running Time: 3 hrs.). (Henrie O Mystery Ser.). 2001. 18.00 (978-1-59040-157-6(3), Phoenix Audio) Pub: Amer Intl Pub. Dist(s): PerseuPGW

Death in Paradise. unabr. ed. Carolyn G. Hart. Read by Kate Reading. 6 cass. (Running Time: 9 hrs.). (Henrie O Mystery Ser.). 1998. 48.00 (978-0-7366-4263-7(3), 4762) Books on Tape.
Henrietta O'Dwyer Collins finds out her husband's death may not have been an accident.

Death in Paradise. unabr. ed. Carolyn G. Hart. Read by Kate Reading. 8 CDs. (Running Time: 12 hrs.). (Henrie O Mystery Ser.). 2002. audio compact disk 64.00 (978-0-7366-8537-5(5)) Books on Tape.
Henrietta O'Dwyer Collins, better known as "Henrie O", has experienced much sadness and loss in her life, yet nothing more tragic than the sudden death six years ago of her husband, Richard, on Kauai. Then, on a brisk March morning, a package arrives by courier that shatters her fragile peace of mind, a chilling message that claims Richard's fatal fall from a towering island cliff was no accident. It was murder. It is news that enrages the normally self-contained Henrie O, and creates a summons she cannot ignore. She follows cryptic clues and her infallible instincts to a secret-shrouded tropic Eden, a lush and verdant Pacific paradise where giant palm fronds hide evil deeds from inquisitive eyes and the soft, salt-scented ocean breeze whispers of treachery and death.

Death in Paradise. unabr. ed. Robert B. Parker. 4 cass. (Running Time: 6 hrs.). (Jesse Stone Ser.: No. 3). 2001. 25.00 (N Millennium Audio) New Millenn Enter.

Death in Paradise. unabr. ed. Robert B. Parker. Perf. by Robert Forster. 5 cass. (Running Time: 9 hrs.). (Jesse Stone Ser.). 2004. 29.95 (978-1-59007-071-0(2)) Pub: New Millenn Enter. Dist(s): PerseuPGW
Former L.A. homicide detective Jesse Stone is now Chief of Police in Paradise, Massachusetts after alcohol ruined both his detective job and his marriage. When the body of a young girl is found in a lake during one of Jesse's softball games, Chief Stone must use his well-honed investigative skills to find the killer.

Death in Paradise. unabr. ed. Robert B. Parker. Perf. by Robert Forster. 6 CDs. (Running Time: 9 hrs.). (Jesse Stone Ser.: No. 3). 2004. audio compact disk 34.95 (978-1-59007-072-7(0)) New Millenn Enter.

Death in Paradise. unabr. ed. Robert B. Parker. Narrated by Robert Forster. 4 cass. (Running Time: 5 hrs.). (Jesse Stone Ser.: No. 3). 2002. 46.00 (978-1-4025-0732-8(1), 96890) Recorded Bks.
Jesse Stone, Chief of Police in the quiet New England town of Paradise, is enjoying a beer with his softball buddies when he hears a call for help. The body of a teenage girl has been found...shot in the head and floating in a nearby lake. As Jesse investigates, he discovers the girl had quite a reputation for sleeping around. Her own parents won't even admit she was their daughter. But why would anyone want to kill her? Adding depth and realism to the tale, Jesse fights to keep his personal life in order, as he deals with alcoholism and strong feelings for his ex-wife.

Death in Rough Water. unabr. collector's ed. Francine Mathews. Read by Bernadette Dunne. 7 cass. (Running Time: 10 hrs. 30 min.). (Merry Folger Ser.: Vol. 2). 1997. 56.00 (978-0-7366-3631-5(5), 4292) Books on Tape.
Del Duarte's father, an experienced fisherman, falls overboard. The police rule the death an accident, but Del suspects murder & goes to her friend Merry Folger. Defying her father, the chief of police, Merry conducts her own investigation & finds a disturbing mix of fraud & revenge.

Death in Service. unabr. ed. C. S. Fuqua. Read by Kevin Foley. 8 cass. (Running Time: 8 hrs. 30 min.). (Deadlines Ser.: Bk. 1). 1996. 49.95 (978-1-55686-704-0(2)) Books in Motion.
Investigative reporter Dean Moore investigates the murder of a high level government bureaucrat & his lead suspect is a state senator.

Death in Summer. unabr. ed. William Trevor. Narrated by Simon Prebble. 5 cass. (Running Time: 6 hrs. 30 mins.). 1998. 48.00 (978-0-7887-4630-7(8), 96247E7) Recorded Bks.
Thaddeus Davenant, haunted by his wife's sudden death, seeks a nanny for his infant. Although she doesn't get the job, one young woman forms an immediate, secret attachment to Thaddeus & the baby, an attachment that will eventually become dangerous.

Death in the Afternoon. unabr. ed. Ernest Hemingway. Read by Alexander Adams. 8 cass. (Running Time: 11 hrs.). 2001. 29.95 (978-0-7366-5673-3(1)) Books on Tape.
Ernest Hemingway's classic work on the art of bullfighting. It tells of the bullfighters & the bulls, the bravery & cowardice, the pageantry & the history - enlivened by Hemingway's pungent comments on life & literature.

Death in the Afternoon. unabr. ed. Ernest Hemingway. 2007. 23.95 (978-0-7435-6353-6(0), Audioworks) Pub: S&S Audio. Dist(s): S and S Inc

Death in the Afternoon. unabr. ed. Ernest Hemingway. Read by Boyd Gaines. 8 CDs. (Running Time: 10 hrs. 0 mins. 0 sec.). (ENG.). 2007. audio compact disk 39.95 (978-0-7435-6445-8(6)) Pub: S&S Audio. Dist(s): S and S Inc

Death in the Afternoon. unabr. collector's ed. Ernest Hemingway. Read by Wolfram Kandinsky. 8 cass. (Running Time: 12 hrs.). 1990. 64.00 (978-0-7366-1680-5(2), 2528) Books on Tape.
Death in the Afternoon is Ernest Hemingway's classic work on the art of bullfighting. It tells of the bullfighters & the bulls, the bravery & cowardice, the pageantry & the history - enlivened by Hemingway's pungent comments on life & literature.

Death in the Air see Death in the Clouds

Death in the Clouds. Agatha Christie. 2 CDs. (Running Time: 1 hr. 25 mins.). Orig. Title: Death in the Air. 2005. audio compact disk 29.95 (978-0-7927-3599-1(4), BBCD 114) AudioGO.

Death in the Clouds: A Hercule Poirot Mystery. unabr. ed. Agatha Christie. Read by Hugh Fraser. 2005. 27.95 (978-1-57270-452-7(7)) Pub: Audio Partners. Dist(s): PerseuPGW
Aboard a plane, a woman dies in her seat, apparently the victim of a wasp sting. Then, a venom-tipped dart from a South American blowgun is found in the aisle. Everyone is suspect, including Hercule Poirot, who was sitting a mere fifteen feet from the victim. Poirot finds closer ties between some of

the passengers on the plane than they would admit, but who could have wanted the woman dead? He must find the real murderer and the truth of the case, if only to clear his own name. Read by Hugh Fraser.

Death in the Clouds: A Hercule Poirot Mystery. unabr. ed. Agatha Christie. Narrated by Hugh Fraser. (Mystery Masters Ser.). (ENG.). 2005. audio compact disk 29.95 (978-1-57270-453-4(5)) Pub: AudioGO. Dist(s): Perseus Dist

Death in the Dark Continent. unabr. collector's ed. Peter H. Capstick. Read by Ron Shoop. 5 cass. (Running Time: 7 hrs. 30 mins.). 1986. 40.00 (978-0-7366-1078-0(2), 2005) Books on Tape.
Capstick has written accounts of hunting the five most dangerous killers on the African continent - lion, leopard, elephant, Cape buffalo & rhinoceros.

Death in the Desert see Troll Garden

Death in the Devil's Acre. unabr. ed. Anne Perry. Narrated by Davina Porter. 6 cass. (Running Time: 8 hrs. 30 min.). (Thomas Pitt Ser.). 2003. 57.00 (978-1-4025-6633-2(6)) Recorded Bks.
Two dead bodies have been discovered, both similarly mutilated. As Inspector Thomas Pitt examines one body, he recognizes the man from a previous case. With the help of his perceptive wife, Charlotte, Thomas intends to solve this gruesome crime.

Death in the Devil's Acre, Set. unabr. ed. Anne Perry. 6 cass. (Thomas Pitt Ser.). 1998. 69.95 (978-1-85903-208-4(7)) Pub: Magna Story GBR. Dist(s): Ulverscroft US

Death in the Dojo: Level 5. Sue Leather. Contrib. by Philip Prowse. (Running Time: 2 hrs. 20 mins.). (Cambridge English Readers Ser.). (ENG.). 1999. 15.75 (978-0-521-65620-7(6)) Cambridge U Pr.

Death in the Family. unabr. ed. James Agee. Narrated by Mark Hammer. 9 cass. (Running Time: 13 hrs.). 2000. 81.00 (978-0-7887-4401-3(1), 96226E7) Recorded Bks.
Jay Follet is healthy, robust & in the prime of life when he sets out from home one hot summer night to tend to his sick father. He leaves behind a wife & two small children, promising to return the next evening if at all possible. A story of the complex ways that people deal with life, love & loss.

Death in the Family. unabr. ed. James Agee. Narrated by Mark Hammer. 11 CDs. (Running Time: 13 hrs.). 2001. audio compact disk 111.00 (978-0-7887-7164-4(7), C1417) Recorded Bks.

Death in the Off-Season. unabr. collector's ed. Francine Mathews. Read by Bernadette Dunne. 8 cass. (Running Time: 12 hrs.). (Merry Folger Ser.: Vol. 1). 1997. 64.00 (978-0-7366-3600-1(5), 4255) Books on Tape.
The scion of Nantucket's oldest & wealthiest family is found dead one foggy night in a cranberry bog. But what brought Rusty Mason home in the first place.

Death in the Redwoods. deluxe unabr. ed. Barbara Wrede. 6 cass. (Running Time: 7 hrs). 2001. lib. bdg. 35.00 (978-0-932079-13-8(X), 7913X) TimeFare AudioBks.
Politics, murder, and a tangled love story play out amid the towering redwoods on California's far north coast.

Death in the Setting Sun. unabr. ed. Deryn Lake. 7 cass. 2007. 61.95 (978-1-84559-133-5(X)) Pub: Soundings Ltd GBR. Dist(s): Ulverscroft US

Death in the Silent Places. unabr. collector's ed. Peter H. Capstick. Read by Paul Shay. 7 cass. (Running Time: 10 hrs. 30 mins.). 1988. 56.00 (978-0-7366-1261-6(0), 2174) Books on Tape.
True stories from the lives of famous big-game hunters, including Col. H.J. Patterson, Col. Jim Corbett, & Karamojo Bell.

Death in the Stocks. unabr. ed. Georgette Heyer. Read by Robbie MacNab. 8 cass. (Running Time: 12 hrs.). 1996. 69.95 (978-1-85695-258-3(4), 960112) Pub: ISIS Audio GBR. Dist(s): Ulverscroft US
A moonlit night, a sleepy village & a corpse dressed in formal attire locked into the old stocks on the village common. The superintendent is on the trail of a killer so cunning that even his phenomenal powers of deduction are tested to the full.

Death in the Stocks. unabr. ed. Georgette Heyer. Read by Robbie MacNab. 8 CDs. (Running Time: 12 hrs.). 2001. audio compact disk 79.95 (978-0-7531-1133-8(0), 111330) Pub: ISIS Audio GBR. Dist(s): Ulverscroft US

Death in the Valley of Shadows. Deryn Lake. Read by Michael Tudor Barnes. 8 cass. (Soundings Ser.). (J). 2005. 69.95 (978-1-84283-760-3(5)) Pub: ISIS Lrg Prnt GBR. Dist(s): Ulverscroft US

Death in the Valley of Shadows. unabr. ed. Deryn Lake. Read by Michael Tudor Barnes. 8 CDs. (Running Time: 10 hrs.). (Soundings (CDs) Ser.). 2005. audio compact disk 79.95 (978-1-84559-268-4(9)) Pub: Soundings Ltd GBR. Dist(s): Ulverscroft US

Death in Venice. unabr. ed. Thomas Mann. 1 cass. (Running Time: 1 hr. 30 mins.).Tr. of Tod in Venedig. 2004. 18.95 (978-0-06-072434-4(X)) HarperCollins Pubs.

***Death in Venice.** unabr. ed. Thomas Mann. Read by Simon Callow & Michael Cunningham.Tr. of Tod in Venedig. 2004. (978-0-06-077905-4(5), Harper Audio); (978-0-06-081372-7(5), Harper Audio) HarperCollins Pubs.

Death in Venice & Other Tales. unabr. ed. Short Stories. Thomas Mann. Tr. by Joachim Neugroschel. Narrated by Paul Hecht. 10 cass. (Running Time: 13 hrs.). 2000. 85.00 (978-0-7887-2482-4(7), 95557E7) Recorded Bks.
Using striking, contemporary language reinterprets the celebrated short works for modern readers.

Death in Vienna. Daniel Silva. (Gabriel Allon Ser.: No. 4). 2005. audio compact disk 96.00 (978-0-7366-9743-9(8)) Books on Tape.

Death in Vienna. abr. ed. Daniel Silva. Read by Tony Goldwyn. 5 CDs. (Running Time: 6 hrs.). (Gabriel Allon Ser.: No. 4). (ENG.). 2005. audio compact disk 14.99 (978-0-7393-1814-0(4)) Pub: Random Audio Pubg. Dist(s): Random

Death in Vienna. unabr. ed. Daniel Silva. 7 cassettes. (Running Time: 10.5 hrs). (Gabriel Allon Ser.: No. 4). 2004. 90.00 (978-0-7366-9742-2(X)) Books on Tape.

Death in Zanzibar & Death in Kenya. unabr. collector's ed. M. M. Kaye. Read by Kate Reading. 12 cass. (Running Time: 18 hrs.). 1994. 96.00 (978-0-7366-2861-7(4), 3568) Books on Tape.
Murders in Africa, told with chilling precision by one of this century's great narrative authors.

***Death Is a Lonely Business.** unabr. ed. Ray Bradbury. (Running Time: 9 hrs. 0 mins.). 2010. 15.99 (978-1-4001-8822-2(9)); audio compact disk 34.99 (978-1-4001-1822-9(0)) Pub: Tantor Media. Dist(s): IngramPubServ

***Death Is a Lonely Business.** unabr. ed. Ray Bradbury. Narrated by Peter Berkrot. (Running Time: 8 hrs. 30 mins. 0 sec.). (ENG.). 2010. 24.99 (978-1-4001-6822-4(8)) Pub: Tantor Media. Dist(s): IngramPubServ

Death Is a Lonely Business. unabr. collector's ed. Ray Bradbury. Read by Michael Prichard. 6 cass. (Running Time: 9 hrs.). 1990. 48.00 (978-0-7366-1790-1(6), 2627) Books on Tape.
In Death is a Lonely Business, Ray Bradbury, a master of the modern supernatural, works his magic in a new way, giving us a novel that is a loving tribute to the hard-boiled detective genre & a nostalgic evocation of time & place. It is 1949 in Venice, California & the last great amusement pier is coming down. Amid this death there are four others - all seeming accidental or natural. But two people are not so sure. One is detective Elmo Crumley. The other a young man who sits all day pounding out stories for True Detectives. They both believe these deaths are murders & suddenly the killer is stalking them.

***Death Is a Lonely Business (Library Edition)** unabr. ed. Ray Bradbury. Narrated by Peter Berkrot. (Running Time: 8 hrs. 30 mins. 0 sec.). (ENG.). 2010. audio compact disk 83.99 (978-1-4001-4822-6(7)) Pub: Tantor Media. Dist(s): IngramPubServ

Death Is a Red Rose. Dorothy Eden. Read by Delia Corrie. 4 cass. (Running Time: 6 hrs.). 1999. 44.95 (60857) Pub: Soundings Ltd GBR. Dist(s): Ulverscroft US

Death Is a Red Rose. abr. ed. Dorothy Eden. Read by Delia Corrie. 4 cass. (Running Time: 6 hrs.). (Sound Ser.). 2004. 44.95 (978-1-85496-085-6(7), 60857) Pub: UlverLrgPrint GBR. Dist(s): Ulverscroft US

Death is Dead: Luke:13-15 & John 19:38-41. Ed Young. (J). 1979. 4.95 (978-0-7417-1050-5(1), A0051) Win Walk.

Death Is Not at the Far End of Life. J. Krishnamurti. 1 cass. (Running Time: 75 min.). (Madras, India Talks 1985 Ser.: No. 4). 1999. 8.50 (AMT854) Krishnamurti.
Krishnamurti addresses the timeless questions which mankind has always asked & he invites each one of us to suspend our beliefs & theories, to observe together, to walk together with the speakers as we inquire into the human condition.

Death Is Not the End. unabr. ed. Ian Rankin. Read by Joe Dunlop. 2 cass. (Running Time: 2 hrs.). (Isis Cassettes Ser.). 2000. 24.95 (978-0-7531-0752-1(2X), 991218) Pub: ISIS Audio GBR. Dist(s): Ulverscroft US

Death Is Not the End. unabr. ed. Ian Rankin. Read by Joe Dunlop. 2 CDs. (Running Time: 2 hrs.). (Isis Ser.). (J). 2001. audio compact disk 34.95 (978-0-7531-0900-7(X), 10900X) Pub: ISIS Lrg Prnt GBR. Dist(s): Ulverscroft US
Damon Mee was last seen in a blurred security video on the dance floor of a Kirkcaldy night club. It was a routine missing-persons case & wasn't even on his patch, but Inspector John Rebus said he'd look into it as a favor to the boy's father, a friend from his school days.

Death Is Not the End of Anything. Adi Da Love-Ananda Samiraj. 1 cass. 1995. 11.95 (978-1-57097-022-1(X)) Dawn Horse Pr.

Death Is Now My Neighbor: An Inspector Morse Novel. unabr. ed. Colin Dexter. Read by Terrence Hardiman. 8 cass. (Running Time: 12 hrs.). (Inspector Morse Mystery Ser.: Bk. 13). 1998. 59.95 (978-0-7451-6775-6(6), CAB 1391) Pub: Chivers Audio Bks GBR. Dist(s): AudioGO
Summoned to 17 Bloxham Drive, Chief Inspector Morse discovers the body of Rachel James. She was shot at point-blank range. Unfortunately, few of the residents can be helpful about what they saw or heard on that fateful morning. The discovery of a love poem & a photograph of Rachel with a mystery man is enough to send Morse on the trail. But then Morse faces a far more personal crisis.

Death Is Now My Neighbor: An Inspector Morse Novel. unabr. ed. Colin Dexter. Read by Terrence Hardiman. 8 CDs. (Running Time: 8 hrs.). (Inspector Morse Mystery Ser.). 2000. audio compact disk 79.95 (978-0-7540-5349-1(0), CCD 040) Pub: Chivers Audio Bks GBR. Dist(s): AudioGO
Inspector Morse has discovered the body of Rachel James, who was shot at point blank range. Unfortunately, none of her neighbors saw or heard anything on that fateful morning. But the discovery of a love poem & a photograph of Rachel with a mystery man is enough to send Morse on the trail.

Death Is Now My Neighbour. 3rd rev. abr. ed. Colin Dexter. Read by Kevin Whately. 3 CDs. (Running Time: 3 hrs.). (ENG., 2001. audio compact disk (978-0-333-90351-3(X)) Macmillan UK GBR.

Death Is Swallowed up in Victory (Easter) 1 Cor. 15:1-58, 719. Ed Young. 1989. 4.95 (978-0-7417-1719-1(0), 719) Win Walk.

Death List. Paul Johnston & Andrew Wincott. 2009. 76.95 (978-1-84652-330-4(3)); audio compact disk 89.95 (978-1-84652-331-1(1)) Pub: Magna Story GBR. Dist(s): Ulverscroft US

Death Lust! Carol Eason. Read by Carol Eason. 3 CDs. (Running Time: 3 hrs.). (Mercenary Ser.: No. 11). 2005. audio compact disk (978-1-58807-968-8(6)); audio compact disk 25.00 (978-1-58807-335-8(1)) Am Pubng Inc.
Hank Frost, the one-eyed merc captain, is trailing the black market arms buys of Eva Chapmann, "The Deathwitch". From the high seas of the Mediterranean, to Sicily, to the Greek islands and the Pillars of Hercules, Frost, with a force of Cosa Nostra hitmen for his commando team, battles time and superior odds to put a bullet through the heart of The Deathwitch before she plunges the world into nuclear war. And then there's the exquisite Constanza, who handles a ship or a submachine gun as well as a man - and she's with Hank Frost all the way.

Death Lust. Axel Kilgore. Read by Carol Eason. Abr. by Odin Westgaard. 2 vols. No. 11. 2004. 18.00 (978-1-58807-167-5(7)); (978-1-58807-658-8(X)) Am Pubng Inc.

***Death Marks Time in Trampas: A Western Quintet.** T. T. Flynn. 2009. (978-1-60136-523-1(3)) Audio Holding.

Death Mask. unabr. ed. Ellis Peters, pseud. Read by Richard Owens. 7 cass. (Running Time: 7 hrs. 12 min.). 1993. 61.95 (978-1-85089-462-9(0), 92041) Pub: ISIS Audio GBR. Dist(s): Ulverscroft US
When Crispen's father is killed in Greece, he has reason to believe it was no accident. Crispen baits a trap to lure the murderer out of hiding, fully realizing how dangerous a game he is playing.

Death Masks. unabr. ed. Jim Butcher. Read by James Marsters. (Running Time: 12 hrs.). Bk. 5. (ENG.). (gr. 12). 2009. audio compact disk 49.95 (978-0-14-314519-6(3), PengAudBks) Penguin Grp USA.

Death Match. Lincoln Child. Read by Barrett Whitener. (Running Time: 14 hrs.). 2004. 38.95 (978-1-59912-464-3(5)) Iofy Corp.

Death Match. unabr. ed. Lincoln Child. Read by Barrett Whitener. 10 cass. (Running Time: 14 hrs. 30 mins.). 2004. 69.95 (978-0-7861-2811-2(9), 3270); audio compact disk 80.00 (978-0-7861-8485-9(X), 3270) Blckstn Audio.

Death Match. unabr. ed. Lincoln Child. Read by Barret Whitener. 8 pieces. (Running Time: 13 hrs.). 2004. reel tape 29.95 (978-0-7861-2695-8(7)); audio compact disk 39.95 (978-0-7861-8681-5(X)) Blckstn Audio.
The Thorpes were the perfect couple, young, attractive, and ideally matched. But when the Thorpes are found dead-a double suicide-alarms go off in the offices of Eden, Incorporated, the worldwide matchmaking phenomenon that had originally brought the two people together. Christopher Lash, forensic psychologist, is brought in by Eden to perform a quick and quiet investigation. As Lash begins his "psychological autopsy," another ideal couple commits double suicide, and Lash's investigation refocuses on Eden, Inc., and the labyrinthine world of technology and psychology.

Death May Surprise Us. Ted Willis. Read by Christopher Scott. 9 cass. (Running Time: 13 hrs. 30 mins.). 1999. 79.95 (67274) Pub: Soundings Ltd GBR. Dist(s): Ulverscroft US

Death Notes, unabr. ed. Ruth Rendell. Narrated by Davina Porter. 6 cass. (Running Time: 7 hrs. 45 mins.). (Inspector Wexford Mystery Ser.: Vol. 11). (gr. 10). 1991. 51.00 (978-1-55690-137-9(2), 91117E7) Recorded Bks.
Inspector Wexford & his assistant Burden unravel the threads connecting the drowning of an elderly, world-renowned flautist & the murder of a woman whose identity confounds them.

Death of a Bore. unabr. ed. M. C. Beaton, pseud. Read by Graeme Malcolm. (Hamish Macbeth Mystery Ser.). 2005. 24.95 (978-1-57270-447-3(0)) Pub: Audio Partners. Dist(s): PerseuPGW
Minor writer John Heppel has a problem - he's by all accounts a consummate bore. When he's found dead in his cottage, there are plenty of suspects. But surely boredom shouldn't be cause for murder, or so thinks local bobby and sleuth Hamish Macbeth, whose investigation of Heppel's soap opera script uncovers much more than melodrama. Popular reader and actor Graeme Malcolm makes this intricate whodunit set in Beaton's beloved Scottish village a memorable audio experience. This is the newest title in the popular Hamish Macbeth series.

Death of a Bore. unabr. ed. M. C. Beaton, pseud. Narrated by Graeme Malcolm. (Hamish Macbeth Mystery Ser.). (ENG.). 2005. audio compact disk 27.95 (978-1-57270-448-0(9)) Pub: AudioGO. Dist(s): Perseus Dist

Death of a Bore. unabr. ed. M. C. Beaton, pseud. Read by Graeme Malcolm. (Hamish Macbeth Mystery Ser.). 2005. 39.95 (978-0-7927-3477-2(7), CSL 749); audio compact disk 59.95 (978-0-7927-3478-9(5), SLD 749) AudioGO.

Death of a Cad. unabr. ed. M. C. Beaton, pseud. Narrated by Davina Porter. 5 cass. (Running Time: 6 hrs.). (Hamish Macbeth Mystery Ser.). 1999. 46.00 (978-0-7887-4080-0(6), H1074E7) Recorded Bks.
When beautiful Priscilla Halburton-Smythe brings home her fiance, a famous playwright, all of Lochdubh clamors to meet the London celebrity - except for her long-time friend Hamish. But the fiance is pushed aside when one of the guests, a widely-hated hunter, is found shot to death. Everyone is quick to point out it could only be a tragic accident, but Hamish proves otherwise.

Death of a Cad. unabr. ed. M. C. Beaton, pseud. Narrated by Davina Porter. 5 CDs. (Running Time: 6 hrs.). (Hamish Macbeth Mystery Ser.). 2000. audio compact disk 52.00 (978-0-7887-4479-2(8), C1176E7) Recorded Bks.

Death of a Celebrity. unabr. ed. M. C. Beaton, pseud. Read by Graeme Malcolm. 6 CDs. (Running Time: 9 hrs.). (Hamish Macbeth Mystery Ser.). 2003. audio compact disk 64.95 (978-0-7927-2784-2(3), CCD 287); 49.95 (978-0-7927-2783-5(5), CAB 2486) AudioGO.
Blonde, glamorous BBC reporter Crystal French has blown into Lochdubh with Highland Life, a hard-hitting TV show that has more than just the heather shaking. Roaring into town in her bright yellow Porsche, her arrival is heralded by a speeding ticket from Constable Hamish Macbeth, in spite of her attempts at bribery and seduction. Out of revenge, her show first bumps off Felicity Pearson's Countryside program, then insults the shopkeepers to the outrage of the entire village, and finally targets Hamish Macbeth for public humiliation. But when Crystal turns up dead, an apparent suicide that turns out to be murder, the entire village becomes suspect.

Death of a Charming Man. unabr. ed. M. C. Beaton, pseud. Narrated by Davina Porter. 5 cass. (Running Time: 6 hrs. 30 mins.). (Hamish Macbeth Mystery Ser.). 1997. 44.00 (978-0-7887-1084-1(2), 95088E7) Recorded Bks.
When the dashing Peter Hynd arrives in the backwater village of Drim, he causes quite a stir, & Macbeth, the one-man police force of Scotland's Lochdubh, isn't surprised when he is soon missing.

***Death of a Chimney Sweep.** M. C. Beaton, pseud. Narrated by Graeme Malcom. (Running Time: 5 hrs. 30 mins. 0 sec.). (Hamish Macbeth Mystery Ser.). (ENG.). 2011. audio compact disk 29.95 (978-1-60283-931-1(X)) Pub: AudioGO. Dist(s): Perseus Dist

Death of a Colonial. Bruce Alexander. Read by Stuart Langton. 2000. 56.00 (978-0-7366-5466-1(6)) Books on Tape.

Death of a Dancer, Program 3. Read by Hector Elizondo. (F007BB090) Natl Public Radio.

Death of a Dean. Hazel Holt & Hazel Holt. Read by Patricia Gallimore. (Running Time: 23400 sec.). (Sheila Malory Mystery Ser.: No. 7). 2007. audio compact disk 64.95 (978-1-84559-854-9(7)) Pub: ISIS Audio GBR. Dist(s): Ulverscroft US

Death of a Dean. Hazel Holt & Hazel Holt. Read by Patricia Gallimore. (Running Time: 23400 sec.). (Sheila Malory Mystery Ser.: No. 7). 2007. 49.95 (978-1-84559-491-6(6)) Pub: Soundings Ltd GBR. Dist(s): Ulverscroft US

Death of a Dentist. unabr. ed. M. C. Beaton, pseud. Narrated by Davina Porter. 5 cass. (Running Time: 6 hrs. 30 mins.). (Hamish Macbeth Mystery Ser.). 1998. 44.00 (978-0-7887-2044-4(9), 95408E7) Recorded Bks.
Fast-paced action & delightfully quirky characters transport you to the Scottish Highlands.

Death of a Dissident. unabr. ed. Stuart M. Kaminsky. Narrated by Mark Hammer. 6 cass. (Running Time: 7 hrs. 45 mins.). (Inspector Porfiry Rostnikov Mystery Ser.: No. 1). 1993. 51.00 (978-1-55690-898-9(9), 93340E7) Recorded Bks.
A dissident soon to be on trial for crimes against the state is murdered right under the noses of the KGB: Inspector Rostnikov investigates.

Death of a Division. unabr. collector's ed. Charles Whiting. Read by Christopher Hurt. 5 cass. (Running Time: 5 hrs.). 1984. 30.00 (978-0-7366-0695-0(5), 1658) Books on Tape.
Story of how the U.S. 106th infantry division, fondly nicknamed "The Golden Lions," was routed on the night of December 16, 1944.

Death of a DJ. unabr. ed. Jane Rubino. Read by Christine Clayburg. 6 cass. (Running Time: 7 hrs. 48 min.). 2001. 39.95 (978-1-58116-055-0(0)) Books in Motion.
The murder of a controversial shock jock leads reporter-turned-detective Cat Austin on a search to unravel the twisted story of the radioman's life. It seems the killer believes Dudek told Cat his secrets, and is determined to tie up loose ends.

Death of a Don. unabr. ed. Howard Shaw. Read by Graham Roberts. 6 cass. (Running Time: 7 hrs.). (Sound Ser.). 2002. 54.95 (978-1-86042-622-3(0)) Pub: UlverLrgPrint GBR. Dist(s): Ulverscroft US
Sinister things are afoot at Beaufort College, Oxford. The Beaufort Letter, a priceless part of the College's library is stolen. Next, one of the most respected dons in the College is found propped up at his desk with a large dent in his head. As if this is not enough, another murder is to follow, even more gruesome than the last. To add insult to fatal injury, the deed has been done with a Beaufort tie. Inspector Barnaby of the local police is called to investigate, but the case is not solved before several other unsavory events are brought to light.

Death of a Dormouse. Reginald Hill. 2009. 69.95 (978-0-7531-3917-2(0)); audio compact disk 84.95 (978-0-7531-3918-9(9)) Pub: Isis Pubng Ltd GBR. Dist(s): Ulverscroft US

Death of a Doxy. unabr. ed. Rex Stout. Read by Michael Prichard. 4 cass. (Running Time: 6 hrs.). (Nero Wolfe Ser.). 2002. 24.95 (978-1-57270-269-1(9)) Pub: Audio Partners. Dist(s): PerseuPGW
A doxy, a prostitute or paramour, is found dead and one of Nero Wolfe's longtime acquaintances stands accused. Wolfe reluctantly lays out bait in the form of a showgirl, whose talents may equal his own.

Death of a Doxy. unabr. collector's ed. Rex Stout. Read by Michael Prichard. 6 cass. (Running Time: 6 hrs.). (Nero Wolfe Ser.). 1998. 48.00 (978-0-7366-4044-2(4), 4543) Books on Tape.
Blackmail is such an ugly world. But then again. so is murder. Unfortunately, both terms have been laid at the feet of one of Nero Wolfe's oldest Acquaintances, a fellow P.I. with a knack for finding trouble & now Nero's on the case.

Death of a Doxy: A Nero Wolfe Mystery. Rex Stout. Narrated by Michael Prichard. (Running Time: 5 hrs. 0 mins. 0 sec.). (Nero Wolfe Mystery Ser.). (ENG.). 2010. audio compact disk 29.95 (978-1-60283-904-5(2)) Pub: AudioGO. Dist(s): Perseus Dist

Death of a Dreamer. M. C. Beaton, pseud. 6 CDs. (Running Time: 19620 sec.). (Hamish Macbeth Mystery Ser.). 2006. audio compact disk 59.95 (978-0-7927-3951-7(5), SLD 927) AudioGO.

Death of a Dreamer. M. C. Beaton, pseud. Read by Graeme Malcolm. 4 cass. (Running Time: 19620 sec.). (Hamish Macbeth Mystery Ser.). 2006. 39.95 (978-0-7927-3950-0(7), CSL 927) AudioGO.

Death of a Dreamer. Read by Graeme Malcolm. Ed. by M. C. Beaton. (Hamish Macbeth Mystery Ser.). 2006. audio compact disk 29.95 (978-0-7927-3976-0(0), CMP 927) AudioGO.

Death of a Dreamer. unabr. ed. M. C. Beaton, pseud. Read by Graeme Malcolm. (Hamish Macbeth Mystery Ser.). 2006. 27.95 (978-1-57270-515-9(9)) Pub: Audio Partners. Dist(s): PerseuPGW

Death of a Dreamer. unabr. ed. M. C. Beaton, pseud. Read by M. C. Beaton, pseud. Narrated by Graeme Malcolm. (Running Time: 19800 sec.). (Hamish Macbeth Mystery Ser.). (ENG.). 2006. audio compact disk 27.95 (978-1-57270-514-2(0)) Pub: AudioGO. Dist(s): Perseus Dist

Death of a Dude. collector's ed. Rex Stout. Read by Michael Prichard. 5 cass. (Running Time: 7 hrs. 30 min.). (Nero Wolfe Ser.). 2000. 40.00 (978-0-7366-5084-7(9)) Books on Tape.
The great detective Nero Wolfe travels to Montana, eats canned soup, makes his own bed & assists Archie, his assistant, to solve a very messy rifle-shot murder.

Death of a Dustman. unabr. ed. M. C. Beaton, pseud. Read by Graeme Malcolm. 5 CDs. (Running Time: 7 hrs. 30 mins.). (Hamish Macbeth Mystery Ser.). 2003. audio compact disk 59.95 (978-0-7927-2781-1(9), CCD 286); 39.95 (978-0-7927-2780-4(0), CAB 2485) AudioGO.
When Fergus Macleod, an abusive drunk, is put in charge of a recycling center and dubbed the "environment officer," Constable Hamish Macbeth smells trouble piling up. Sure enough, Fergus becomes a bullying tyrant with his new power, issuing unwarranted fines and blackmailing residents. And when his body is found stuffed in a recycling bin, no one's sorry including his long-suffering family. But the lawman's inquiries hit a wall when he finds that many wronged residents are strangely reluctant to spread the dirt on the nefarious dustman. And when violence strikes again, Hamish must quickly sift through the litter of lies and dark secrets, before a killer's grime overruns the town.

Death of a Fool. Ngaio Marsh. Narrated by Nadia May. (Running Time: 10 hrs.). 2001. 30.95 (978-1-59912-465-0(3)) Iofy Corp.

Death of a Fool. unabr. ed. Ngaio Marsh. Narrated by Nadia May. 7 cass. (Running Time: 10 hrs.). 2001. 49.95 (978-0-7861-2139-7(4), 2890); audio compact disk 64.00 (978-0-7861-9595-4(9), 2890) Blckstn Audio.
At the winter solstice, South Mardian's swordsmen weave their blades in an ancient ritual dance. But for one of them, the excitement proves too heady, and his decapitation turns the fertility rite into a pageant of death. Now Inspector Roderick Alleyn must penetrate not only the mysteries of folklore but also the secrets and sins of an eccentric group, including a surly blacksmith, a domineering dowager, and a not-so-simple village idiot.

Death of a Garden Pest. unabr. ed. Ann Ripley. Read by Lynda Evans. 6 cass. (Running Time: 7 hrs.). (Gardening Mystery Ser.: Bk. 2). 2001. 39.95 (978-1-55686-872-6(3)) Books in Motion.
Organic gardener and new television host Louise Eldridge has a nasty confrontation with the former host. And when the woman is found poisoned, Louise is suspect number one.

Death of a Gentle Lady. unabr. ed. M. C. Beaton, pseud. Narrated by Graeme Malcolm. 1 MP3-CD. (Running Time: 6 hrs.). (Hamish Macbeth Mystery Ser.). 2008. 39.95 (978-0-7927-5325-4(9)); audio compact disk 59.95 (978-0-7927-5243-1(0)) AudioGO.
Gentle by name, gentle by nature. Everyone in the sleepy Scottish town of Lochdubh adores elderly Mrs. Gentle - everyone but Hamish Macbeth, that is. Hamish thinks the gentle lady is quite sly and vicious, and the citizens of Lochdubh think he is overly cranky. Perhaps it's time for him to get married, they say. But who has time for marriage when there's a murder to be solved? When Mrs. Gentle dies under mysterious circumstances, the town is shocked and outraged. Chief Detective Inspector Blair suspects members of her family, but Hamish Macbeth thinks there's more to the story, and begins investigating the truth behind this lady's gentle exterior.

Death of a Gentle Lady. unabr. ed. M. C. Beaton, pseud. Narrated by Graeme Malcolm. (Running Time: 19800 sec.). (Hamish Macbeth Mystery Ser.). (ENG.). 2008. audio compact disk 29.95 (978-1-60283-345-6(1)) Pub: AudioGO. Dist(s): Perseus Dist

Death of a Gentle Lady. unabr. ed. M. C. Beaton, pseud. Read by Graeme Malcolm. (Hamish Macbeth Mystery Ser.). (YA). 2008. 54.99 (978-1-60514-956-1(X)) Find a World.

Death of a Ghost. unabr. ed. Margery Allingham. Read by Francis Matthews. 8 cass. (Running Time: 12 hrs.). (Albert Campion Ser.: Bk. 6). 2001. 59.95 (978-0-7451-5724-5(6), CAB 228) Pub: Chivers Audio Bks GBR. Dist(s): AudioGO
John Sebastian Lafadio, probably the greatest painter since Rembrandt (according to himself), is dead. But his influence is not. He wanted lasting fame, so he left instructions to his wife, Belle, for one painting to be exhibited every year after his death. Eight years later, in Little Venice, a select group of friends and family gather to view the eighth painting. They are treated instead to a murder, when a young man is stabbed to death. Albert Campion is one of the guests, and in his deceptively calm way he begins searching for the murderer.

Death of a Go-Between. James Pattinson & James Pattinson. (Soundings (CDs) Ser.). 2006. audio compact disk 59.95 (978-1-84559-303-2(0)) Pub: ISIS Lrg Prnt GBR. Dist(s): Ulverscroft US

Death of a Go-Between. James Pattinson & James Pattinson. Read by Gordon Griffin. 4 cass. (Soundings Ser.). 2006. 44.95 (978-1-84559-119-9(4)) Pub: ISIS Lrg Prnt GBR. Dist(s): Ulverscroft US

Death of a Gossip. unabr. ed. M. C. Beaton, pseud. Narrated by Davina Porter. 4 cass. (Running Time: 4 hrs. 45 mins.). (Hamish Macbeth Mystery Ser.). 1999. 35.00 (978-0-7887-3127-3(0), 95696E7) Recorded Bks.
Lady Jane Hamilton, one of the guests at the Lochdubh School of Casting, is positively ruining everyone's holiday with her knack for digging up nasty secrets. But who would actually kill her? Whether you're wading through trout-filled streams or fishing for clues at Constable Macbeth's side, your trip to the Highlands is sure to delight.

Death of a Hired Man see Robert Frost Reads

Death of a Hollow Man. unabr. ed. Caroline Graham. Read by Hugh Ross. 8 cass. (Running Time: 12 hrs.). (Chief Inspector Barnaby Ser.: Bk. 2). 2000. 59.95 (CAB 1546) Pub: Chivers Audio Bks GBR. Dist(s): AudioGO
For Detective Chief Inspector Barnaby, a visit to Causton Amateur Dramatic Society's production of Amadeus with his wife is not an ideal evening of entertainment. The leading man, Essalyn Carmichael, suspects his wife of having an affair. In the final act, the scene takes a gruesome turn and Barnaby has a new case on his hands.

Death of a Holy Murderer. Madelaine Duke. Read by Hazel Temperley. 3 cass. (Running Time: 4 hrs. 30 mins.). 1999. 34.95 (62388) Pub: Soundings Ltd GBR. Dist(s): Ulverscroft US

Death of a Hussy. M. C. Beaton, pseud. Narrated by Davina Porter. 4 cass. (Running Time: 5 hrs. 15 mins.). (Hamish Macbeth Mystery Ser.). 2002. 29.95 (H1181) Recorded Bks.
Internationally acclaimed series features red-haired constable Hamish Macbeth, who keeps order in Scotland's Lochdubh with his wry humor and stubborn determination. In this baffling mystery, he has his hands full when a wealthy, middle-aged woman burns to death in her own car, and it was no accident.

Death of a Hussy. unabr. ed. M. C. Beaton, pseud. Narrated by Davina Porter. 4 cass. (Running Time: 5 hrs. 15 mins.). (Hamish Macbeth Mystery Ser.). 2001. 40.00 (978-0-7887-5958-1(2), H1181E7) Recorded Bks.
Hamish Macbeth has his hands full when a wealthy, middle-aged woman burns to death in her own car - & it was no accident.

Death of a Literary Widow. unabr. ed. Robert Barnard. Read by Jay Fitts. 6 cass. (Running Time: 6 hrs.). 1984. 36.00 (978-0-7366-0899-2(0), 1843) Books on Tape.
The story of Walter Machin, novelist & ardent supporter of working class aspirations. His meager literary output, although spirited, has failed to raise the pulse of England's demanding connoisseurs. After his death, however, his reputation begins to flower. But when one of the widows from his two marriages also dies, Greg Hocking begins to investigate.

Death of a Macho Man. unabr. ed. M. C. Beaton, pseud. Narrated by Davina Porter. 5 cass. (Running Time: 6 hrs. 45 mins.). (Hamish Macbeth Mystery Ser.). 1997. 44.00 (978-0-7887-1749-9(9), 95227E7) Recorded Bks.
Hamish Macbeth - Lochdubh's one-man police force - has suddenly become a prime murder suspect.

Death of a Maid. unabr. ed. M. C. Beaton, pseud. Narrated by Graeme Malcolm. (Running Time: 20160 sec.). (Hamish Macbeth Mystery Ser.). (ENG.). 2007. audio compact disk 29.95 (978-1-60283-021-9(5)) Pub: AudioGO. Dist(s): Perseus Dist

Death of a Nag. unabr. ed. M. C. Beaton, pseud. Narrated by Davina Porter. 5 cass. (Running Time: 6 hrs. 15 mins.). (Hamish Macbeth Mystery Ser.). 1997. 44.00 (978-0-7887-1285-2(3), 95147E7) Recorded Bks.
Updates the classic British Manor House mystery. Police constable Hamish Macbeth-Lochdubh's one-man police force - is in a foul mood. He's lost his promotion & his fiancee, &, instead of solitude, his vacation at "Friendly House" yields a freshly murdered corpse & an inn full of suspects who each longed to commit the crime.

Death of a Nation: Hos. 13:14. Ed Young. 1988. 4.95 (978-0-7417-1663-7(1), 663) Win Walk.

Death of a Perfect Wife. unabr. ed. M. C. Beaton, pseud. Narrated by Davina Porter. 4 cass. (Running Time: 5 hrs.). (Hamish Macbeth Mystery Ser.). 2000. 39.00 (978-0-7887-4495-2(X), H1084E7) Recorded Bks.
Village newcomers Paul & Trixie Thomas don't seem to fit in with Lochdubh's locals, after all, they're British & unemployed. But Trixie doesn't let that stop her. When she isn't pushing her Anti-Smoking League, vegetarian cooking & birdwatching society, she is wheedling belongings from her new neighbours. In fact, her influence affects the whole community until the day someone silences her forever.

Death of a Poison Pen. M. C. Beaton, pseud. Read by Graeme Malcolm. 4 Audiocassettes. (Hamish Macbeth Mystery Ser.). 2004. 39.95 (978-0-7927-3162-7(X)); audio compact disk 59.95 (978-0-7927-3163-4(8)) AudioGO.

Death of a Poison Pen. unabr. ed. M. C. Beaton, pseud. Read by Graeme Malcom. 4 cass. (Running Time: 6 hrs.). (Hamish Macbeth Mystery Ser.). 2004. 24.95 (978-1-57270-377-3(6)) Pub: Audio Partners. Dist(s): PerseuPGW

Death of a Poison Pen. unabr. ed. M. C. Beaton, pseud. Read by Graeme Malcom. 5 vols. (Hamish Macbeth Mystery Ser.). (ENG.). 2004. audio compact disk 27.95 (978-1-57270-378-0(4)) Pub: AudioGO. Dist(s): Perseus Dist

Death of a Political Plant. unabr. ed. Ann Ripley. Read by Lynda Evans. 6 cass. (Running Time: 7 hrs. 30 min.). (Gardening Mystery Ser.: Bk. 3). 2001. 39.95 (978-1-55686-875-7(8)) Books in Motion.
Organic Gardener Louise Eldridge welcomes old friend and journalist J. McCormick to D.C... When McCormick ends up dead, Louise finds a plot that includes Washington's power brokers.

Death of a Prankster. unabr. ed. M. C. Beaton, pseud. Narrated by Davina Porter. 4 cass. (Running Time: 5 hrs.). (Hamish Macbeth Mystery Ser.). 1992. 39.75 (978-1-4193-2681-3(3), 95701MC) Recorded Bks.

Death of a Princess. Nicholas Rhea. Read by Graham Padden. 7 cass. (Storysound Ser.). (J). 2001. 61.95 (978-1-85903-422-4(5)) Pub: Mgna Lrg Print GBR. Dist(s): Ulverscroft US

Death of a Russian Priest. unabr. ed. Stuart M. Kaminsky. Narrated by Mark Hammer. 6 cass. (Running Time: 8 hrs. 30 mins.). (Inspector Porfiry Rostnikov Mystery Ser.: No. 8). 1995. 51.00 (978-0-7887-0104-7(5), 94345E7) Recorded Bks.
Inspector Rostnikov investigates two cases: the death of a dissident priest outside his rural church, & the disappearance of a Syrian Oil Minister's daughter in Moscow.

Death of a Salesman see Theatre Highlights

Death of a Salesman see Sound of Modern Drama: The Crucible

Death of a Salesman: The Audio BookNotes Guide. (Audio BookNotes Guide). (C). 2002. audio compact disk 9.95 (978-1-929011-02-5(4)) Scholarly Audio.

Death of a Scriptwriter. unabr. ed. M. C. Beaton, pseud. Narrated by Davina Porter. 5 cass. (Running Time: 6 hrs. 45 mins.). (Hamish Macbeth Mystery Ser.). 1998. 44.00 (978-0-7887-2175-5(5), 95471E7) Recorded Bks.
Spirited Constable Hamish Macbeth - Lochdubh's one-man police force - has his hands full after a glitzy TV company arrives in search of higher ratings at any cost.

Death of a Snob. M. C. Beaton, pseud. Narrated by Davina Porter. 4 CDs. (Running Time: 4 hrs. 45 mins.). (Hamish Macbeth Mystery Ser.). 1991. audio compact disk 52.00 (978-1-4025-4049-3(3)) Recorded Bks.

Death of a Snob. unabr. ed. M. C. Beaton, pseud. Narrated by Davina Porter. 4 cass. (Running Time: 4 hrs. 45 mins.). (Hamish Macbeth Mystery Ser.). 2002. 40.00 (978-1-4025-2489-9(7)) Recorded Bks.
Hamish Macbeth is miserable. It's Christmas, and he is alone with a terrible head cold. So when the beautiful Jane Weatherby asks him to spend the holiday at her Scottish island retreat, Hamish is glad to accept. But something is very wrong at this colorful resort-something that will soon claim the life of one of the guests. Now it's up to Hamish to find out who did it.

Death of a Stranger. unabr. ed. Anne Perry. Read by David Colacci. 8 cass. (Running Time: 11 hrs.). (William Monk Novel Ser.). 2002. 34.95 (978-1-59086-233-9(3), 1590862333, BAU); 87.25 (978-1-59086-234-6(1), 1590862341, Unabridge Lib Edns) Brilliance Audio.
For the prostitutes of Leather Lane, nurse Hester Monk's clinic is a lifeline, providing medicine, food, and a modicum of peace - especially since lately their ailments have escalated from bruises and fevers to broken bones and knife wounds. At the moment, however, the mysterious death of railway magnate Nolan Baltimore in a sleazy neighborhood brothel overshadows all else. Whether he fell or was pushed, the shocking question in everyone's mind is: What was such a pillar of respectability doing in a seedy place of sin? Meanwhile, brilliant private investigator William Monk acquires a new client, a mysterious beauty who asks him to ascertain beyond a shadow of a doubt whether or not her fiance, an executive in Nolan Baltimore's thriving railway firm, has become enmeshed in fraudulent practices that could ruin him. As Hester ventures into violent streets to learn who is responsible for the brutal abuse of her patients, Monk embarks upon a journey into the English countryside, where the last rails are being laid for a new line. But the sight of the tracks stretching into the distance revives memories once stripped from his consciousness by amnesia - as a past almost impossible to bear returns, eerily paralleling a fresh tragedy that has already begun its inexorable unfolding.

Death of a Stranger. unabr. ed. Anne Perry. Read by David Colacci. (Running Time: 11 hrs.). (William Monk Novel Ser.). 2004. 39.25 (978-1-59335-562-3(9), 1593355629, Brinc Audio MP3 Lib) Brilliance Audio.

Death of a Stranger. unabr. ed. Anne Perry. Read by David Colacci. (Running Time: 11 hrs.). (William Monk Novel Ser.). 2004. 39.25 (978-1-59710-193-6(1), 1597101931, BADLE); 24.95 (978-1-59710-192-9(3), 1597101923, BAD) Brilliance Audio.

Death of a Stranger. unabr. ed. Anne Perry. Read by David Colacci. (Running Time: 12 hrs.). (William Monk Ser.). 2010. audio compact disk 29.99 (978-1-4418-3578-9(4), 9781441835789, Bril Audio CD Unabri); audio compact disk 89.97 (978-1-4418-3579-6(2), 9781441835796, BriAudCD Unabrid) Brilliance Audio.

Death of a Stranger. unabr. ed. Anne Perry. Read by David Colacci. (Running Time: 11 hrs.). (William Monk Novel Ser.). 2004. 24.95 (978-1-59335-046-8(5), 1593350465) Soulmate Audio Bks.

Death of a Supertanker. Antony Trew. 7 cass. (Soundings Ser.). (J). 2005. 61.95 (978-1-84283-951-5(9)) Pub: ISIS Lrg Prnt GBR. Dist(s): Ulverscroft US

Death of a Swagman. unabr. ed. Arthur W. Upfield. Read by Peter Hosking. 6 cass. (Running Time: 9 hrs.). (Inspector Napoleon Bonaparte Mysteries). 2004. 48.00 (978-1-86442-385-3(4), 590372) Pub: Bolinda Pubng AUS. Dist(s): Lndmrk Audiobks
In an isolated hut not far from the sleepy country town of Merino, stockman George Kendall is found dead & it looks very much like murder. Six weeks later when the murderer is still at large, another stockman turns up in the township & as a first move provokes the local sergeant to lock him up. This particular stockman is Detective-Inspector Napoleon Bonaparte & there's method in his seeming madness. While serving a semi-detention sentence & being made to paint the police station, he wears the best of all possible disguises for a policeman on the trail of a ruthless & single-minded killer.

Death of a Swagman. unabr. ed. Arthur W. Upfield. Read by Peter Hosking. (Running Time: 7 hrs. 30 mins.). (Inspector Napoleon Bonaparte Mysteries). 2009. audio compact disk 77.95 (978-1-74214-050-6(5), 9781742140506) Pub: Bolinda Pubng AUS. Dist(s): Bolinda Pub Inc

Death of a Travelling Man. unabr. ed. M. C. Beaton, pseud. Narrated by Davina Porter. 4 cass. (Running Time: 4 hrs. 45 mins.). (Hamish Macbeth Mystery Ser.). 2005. 39.75 (978-1-4025-6481-9(3), H1536); audio compact disk 49.75 (978-1-4025-7543-3(2), C2538) Recorded Bks.
When a suspicious gypsy and his girlfriend park their van in the midst of Lochdubh, it's not long before the crime rate begins to soar. Although none of the villagers wants to give him any information, Police Constable Hamish Macbeth must solve a case that is truly bizarre. This series enjoys enduring popularity in the U.K. and the U.S. for its local color, eccentric characters, and intriguing mysteries.

Death of a Valentine. unabr. ed. M. C. Beaton, pseud. Narrated by Graeme Malcolm. 5 CDs. (Running Time: 5 hrs. 30 mins. 0 sec.). (Hamish Macbeth Mystery Ser.). (ENG.). 2010. audio compact disk 29.95 (978-1-60283-855-0(0)) Pub: AudioGO. Dist(s): Perseus Dist

***Death of a Valentine.** unabr. ed. M. C. Beaton, pseud. Narrated by Graeme Malcolm. 1 Playaway. (Running Time: 6 hrs. 8 mins.). 2010. 59.95 (978-0-7927-6879-1(5), Chivers Sound Lib); 29.95 (978-0-7927-6878-4(7), Chivers Sound Lib); audio compact disk 44.95 (978-0-7927-5956-0(7), Chivers Sound Lib) AudioGO.

Death of a Witch. unabr. ed. M. C. Beaton, pseud. Narrated by Graeme Malcolm. (Hamish Macbeth Mystery Ser.). (ENG.). 2009. audio compact disk 29.95 (978-1-60283-609-9(4)) Pub: AudioGO. Dist(s): Perseus Dist

Death of a Witch. unabr. ed. M. C. Beaton, pseud. Read by Graeme Malcolm. (Running Time: 5 hrs. 37 mins.). (Hamish Macbeth Mystery Ser.). 2009. 64.95 (978-0-7927-6177-8(4), Chivers Sound Lib) AudioGO.

Death of a Witch. unabr. ed. M. C. Beaton, pseud. Read by Graeme Malcom. 1 MP3-CD. (Running Time: 5 hrs. 37 mins.). (Hamish Macbeth Mystery Ser.). 2009. 39.95 (978-0-7927-6176-1(6), Chivers Sound Lib) AudioGO.

Death of a Witch. unabr. ed. M. C. Beaton, pseud. Read by Graeme Malcolm. 5 CDs. (Running Time: 5 hrs. 37 mins.). (Hamish Macbeth Mystery Ser.). 2009. audio compact disk 59.95 (978-0-7927-5955-3(9), Chivers Sound Lib) AudioGO.

Death of Abbe Didier. Richard Grayson. Read by Gordon Griffin. 5 cass. (Running Time: 7 hrs. 30 mins.). 1999. 49.95 (65700) Pub: Soundings Ltd GBR. Dist(s): Ulverscroft US

Death of Achilles. unabr. ed. Boris Akunin. Read by Paul Michael. 8 cass. (Running Time: 12 hrs.). 2006. 72.00 (978-1-4159-2970-4(X)); audio compact disk 90.00 (978-1-4159-2971-1(8)) Books on Tape.
In 1882, after six years of foreign travel and adventure, renowned diplomat and detective Erast Fandorin returns to Moscow in the heart of Mother Russia. His Moscow homecoming is anything but peaceful. In the hotel where he and his loyal if impertinent manservant Masa are staying, Fandorin's old war-hero friend General Michel Sobolev ("Achilles" to the crowd) has been found dead, felled in his armchair by an apparent heart

attack. But Fandorin suspects an unnatural cause. His suspicions lead him to the boudoir of the beautiful singer - "not exactly a courtesan" - known as Wanda. Apparently, in Wanda's bed, the general secretly breathed his last.

Death of Amy Parris. unabr. ed. T. R. Bowen. Narrated by Paul Matthews. 8 cass. (Running Time: 10 hrs. 30 mins.). 1999. 71.00 (978-1-84197-034-9(4), H1034E7) Recorded Bks.
Shortly before he is called in to give an opinion on Amy Parris' death, John Bewick happens to be talking to eye-opening scientist Sally Vernon. Her knowledge of DNA throws a whole new light on the suspect, overturning the case which Bewick's rival, DCI Jones, put together so confidently. Nevertheless, things are far from easy for Bewick; unknown to him, only two people smelt an undetected rat in the facts revealed, & one of them has been violently murdered. Probing into the case, he unearths all sorts of aggressive tensions amongst those involved. All at once, the whole affair spirals out of control in a burst of violence from which none of them seem safe.

Death of an Addict. unabr. ed. Roy Moxham. Narrated by Davina Porter. 5 cass. (Running Time: 6 hrs. 15 mins.). (Hamish Macbeth Mystery Ser.). 1999. 46.00 (978-0-7887-3486-1(5), 95690E7) Recorded Bks.
When a recovering addict is murdered, our red-headed hero must leave his idyllic Scottish village & travel to Amsterdam to match wits with big-time drug dealers. Will see tougher side of Constable Macbeth as he dons smart suits & falls in love with is gorgeous superior officer.

Death of an Angel: A Sister Mary Helen Mystery. unabr. ed. Carol Anne O'Marie. Read by Grace Conlin. 5 cass. (Running Time: 7 hrs.). 1998. 39.95 (978-0-7861-1452-8(5), 2314) Blckstn Audio.
In this seventh outing for Sister Mary Helen & her coconspirator, Sister Eileen, the two nuns take time out from their duties when a wealthy widow, a benefactor of the college & dear friend, is the second victim of a local rapist-murderer.

***Death of an Angel: A Sister Mary Helen Mystery.** unabr. ed. Sister Carol Anne O'Marie. Read by Grace Conlin. 5 cass. (Running Time: 7 hrs.). 2010. 29.95 (978-1-4417-4134-9(8)); audio compact disk 69.00 (978-1-4417-4131-8(3)) Blckstn Audio.

Death of an Eagle. unabr. ed. Kirby Jonas. Read by James Drury. 8 cass. (Running Time: 9 hrs. 42 min.). 2001. 49.95 (978-1-55686-978-5(9)) Books in Motion.
Mauled by a giant grizzly and left to die, 16-year-old Jose Olano's chances for life were remote. Then, like a guardian angel, came "Gray Eagle" McAllister to bring Jose back from the brink of death and train him as a mountain man.

Death of an Effendi. Michael Pearce. Read by Nigel Carrington. 4 cass. (Running Time: 6 hrs.). 2002. 39.95 (978-0-7540-0699-2(9), CAB 2121) AudioGO.

Death of an Expert Witness. P. D. James. Narrated by John Franklyn-Robbins. 7 cas. (Running Time: 11.5 hrs.). (Adam Dalgliesh Mystery Ser.). 29.95 (978-1-4025-3927-5(4)) Recorded Bks.

Death of an Expert Witness. unabr. ed. P. D. James. Read by Penelope Dellaporta. 9 cass. (Running Time: 13 hrs. 30 min.). (Adam Dalgliesh Mystery Ser.). 1993. 72.00 (978-0-7366-2569-2(0), 3318) Books on Tape.
Adam Dalgliesh searches for a scientist's killer. It's about appearance versus reality.

Death of an Expert Witness. unabr. ed. P. D. James. Narrated by John Franklyn-Robbins. 8 cass. (Running Time: 11 hrs. 30 mins.). (Adam Dalgliesh Mystery Ser.). 1993. 70.00 (978-1-55690-884-2(9), 93326E7) Recorded Bks.
A group of forensic scientists are taken by surprise when a member of their team is found murdered; Inspector Dalglieh investigates.

Death of an Old Master. unabr. ed. David Dickinson. 10 cass. (Soundings Ser.). (J). 2005. 84.95 (978-1-84559-027-7(9)) Pub: ISIS Lrg Prnt GBR. Dist(s): Ulverscroft US

Death of an Outsider. unabr. ed. M. C. Beaton, pseud. Narrated by Gregor Hunt. 4 cass. (Running Time: 5 hrs. 15 mins.). (Hamish Macbeth Mystery Ser.). 1999. 38.00 (978-1-84197-009-7(3), H1009E7) Recorded Bks.
Nobody in the Scottish town of Cnothan had liked the abrasive Englishman & now that he has been murdered, in a most original fashion, nobody much minds. Constable Hamish Macbeth's hard luck is that he happens to be on temporary duty in this cloistered Highlands village when the killer strikes. And he has his work cut out for him, dragging from Mainwaring's close-mouthed neighbours enough facts to start solving this peculiar case. But Hamish is crafty & with practiced aplomb he slowly extracts from the locals a scandalous tale of illicit romance, secret vices, real estate wheeling & dealing, even witchcraft, all so unbelievable that it can only be true.

Death of an Outsider, Set. unabr. ed. M. C. Beaton, pseud. Narrated by Gregor Hunt. 4 cass. (Hamish Macbeth Mystery Ser.). 1999. 38.00 (H1009K4, Clipper Audio) Recorded Bks.

Death of Arthur. Thomas Malory. Read by Philip Madoc. (Running Time: 4 hrs.). 1998. 24.95 (978-1-60083-720-3(4)) Iofy Corp.

Death of Arthur. abr. ed. Thomas Malory. Read by Philip Madoc. 3 CDs. (Running Time: 4 hrs.). 1995. audio compact disk 22.98 (978-962-634-001-1(0), NA300112, Naxos AudioBooks) Naxos.
Brings together most of the great stories & themes of the Arthurian legend.

Death of Bunny Munro. unabr. ed. Nick Cave. Read by Nick Cave. (Running Time: 8 hrs. 0 mins. 0 sec.). (ENG.). 2009. audio compact disk 34.99 (978-1-4272-0803-3(4)) Pub: Macmill Audio. Dist(s): Macmillan

***Death of Capital: How New Policy Can Restore Stability.** unabr. ed. Michael E. Lewitt. Read by Erik Synnestvedt. (Running Time: 10 hrs.). (ENG.). 2010. 29.98 (978-1-59659-591-0(4), GildAudio) Pub: Gildan Media. Dist(s): HachBkGrp

Death of Christ & His Descent into the Underworld. Read by Marvin Acklin. 1 cass. (Running Time: 1 hr.). 1987. 9.95 (978-0-7822-0008-9(7), 255) C G Jung IL.

Death of Common Sense: How Law Is Suffocating America. unabr. ed. Philip K. Howard. Narrated by Richard Poe. 5 cass. (Running Time: 6 hrs. 25 min.). Rental 13.50 Set. (94638) Recorded Bks.

Death of Common Sense: How Law Is Suffocating America, unabr. ed. Philip K. Howard. Narrated by Richard Poe. 5 cass. (Running Time: 6 hrs. 45 mins.). 44.00 (978-0-7887-0445-1(1), 94638E7) Recorded Bks.
Howard, a lawyer & civic leader, has carefully gathered the evidence of our frustration with governmental laws & the paperwork of a legal system that is suffocating America. Howard's goal: a shift of focus that promises a better way for the system to work. Available to libraries only.

Death of Common Sense Set: How Law Is Suffocating America. abr. ed. Philip K. Howard. Read by Philip K. Howard. 4 cass. (Running Time: 6 hrs.). 1996. 24.95 (978-1-57511-007-3(5), 593927) Pub Mills.

Death of Competition: Leadership & Strategy in the Age of Business Ecosystems. unabr. ed. James F. Moore. Read by Jonathan Reese. 7 cass. (Running Time: 10 hrs. 30 min.). 1996. 56.00 (978-0-7366-3465-6(7), 4109) Books on Tape.
James Moore demonstrates that today's great enterprises no longer compete for product superiority or even industry dominance. What matters now is total system leadership.

Death of Conservatism. unabr. ed. Sam Tanenhaus. Narrated by Alan Sklar. 1 MP3-CD. (Running Time: 4 hrs. 0 mins. 0 sec.). (ENG.). 2009. 19.99 (978-1-4001-6365-6(X)); audio compact disk 19.99 (978-1-4001-1365-1(2)); audio compact disk 39.99 (978-1-4001-4365-8(9)) Pub: Tantor Media. Dist(s): IngramPubServ

Death of Corinne. R. T. Raichev. 2008. 61.95 (978-1-4079-0202-9(4)); audio compact disk 71.95 (978-1-4079-0203-6(2)) Pub: Soundings Ltd GBR. Dist(s): Ulverscroft US

***Death of Evolution: Restoring Faith & Wonder in a World of Doubt.** Zondervan. (Running Time: 4 hrs. 9 mins. 44 sec.). (ENG.). 2010. 16.99 (978-0-310-42764-3(9)) Zondervan.

Death of Halpern Frayser see Eyes of the Panther & Other Stories

Death of Ivan Ilyich & Master & Man. unabr. ed. Leo Tolstoy. Read by Walter Zimmerman. 5 cass. (Running Time: 7 hrs.). 1981. 39.95 (978-0-7861-0593-9(3), 2082) Blckstn Audio.
Tolstoy asks how an unreflective man confronts the moment of truth when he comes face to face with his own mortality. The result is a strong testament to the possibility of finding spiritual salvation. "Master & Man" is a captivating story which keeps us in suspense to the end. Whether or not his motives are right, the merchant Brekhunov attempts, in a most business-like fashion, to save his servant's life.

Death of Ivan Ilyich & Master & Man. unabr. ed. Leo Tolstoy. Read by Walter Zimmerman. 5 cass. (Running Time: 5 hrs.). 1981. 35.00 (C-59) Jimcin Record.
Relates the experiences of a very human, sympathetic individual coming to see, in its most profound sense, the meaning of life & death. In the Master & Man, a merchant named Brekhnov attempts to save his servant, a task he approaches as if it were a business deal-what benefits his servant will also benefit him. The story takes on a larger significance: do we help others to help them, to help the world, or to help ourselves?.

Death of Ivan Ilyich & Other Stories. unabr. ed. Leo Tolstoy. Read by Oliver Ford Davies. (YA). 2008. 34.99 (978-1-60514-702-4(8)) Find a World.

Death of Ivan Ilyich & Other Stories. unabr. ed. Leo Tolstoy. Read by Oliver Ford Davies. 3 CDs. (Running Time: 3 hrs.). (Complete Classics Ser.). 2008. audio compact disk 22.98 (978-962-634-851-2(8), Naxos AudioBooks) Naxos.

Death of Ivan Ilyich & other Stories. unabr. ed. Leo Tolstoy. Narrated by George K. Wilson. (Running Time: 8 hrs. 0 mins. 0 sec.). (ENG.). 2009. audio compact disk 27.99 (978-1-4001-1077-3(7)); audio compact disk 19.99 (978-1-4001-6077-8(4)); audio compact disk 55.99 (978-1-4001-4077-0(3)) Pub: Tantor Media. Dist(s): IngramPubServ

Death of Ivan Ilyich & Other Stories. unabr. collector's ed. Leo Tolstoy. Read by Walter Zimmerman. 5 cass. (Running Time: 5 hrs.). 1981. 30.00 (978-0-7366-3859-3(8), 9059) Books on Tape.
Tortured into truth, this utters "what joy!" at his death; "Master and Man" also embraces life, sacrifice & redemption.

Death of Jim Lonely. (5071) Am Audio Prose.

***Death of Justina.** abr. ed. John Cheever. Read by Meryl Streep et al. (ENG.). 2009. (978-0-06-125287-7(5), Caedmon) HarperCollins Pubs.

***Death of Justina.** unabr. ed. John Cheever. Read by Meryl Streep et al. (ENG.). 2009. (978-0-06-196861-7(7), Caedmon) HarperCollins Pubs.

Death of Karen Silkwood. Ed. by Oxford University Press Staff. 2008. audio compact disk 11.95 (978-0-19-478980-6(2)) OUP.

***Death of Kings: Book II of the Emperor Series.** Conn Iggulden. (Running Time: 12 hrs. 0 mins. 0 sec.). (ENG.). 2011. audio compact disk 29.95 (978-1-60998-169-3(3)) Pub: AudioGO. Dist(s): Perseus Dist

Death of Oedipus: The Decline of Analysis. James Hillman. Read by James Hillman. 2 cass. (Running Time: 2 hrs. 30 min.). 1992. pap. bk. 19.95 (978-1-879816-05-3(9)) Pub: Spring Audio. Dist(s): Daimon Verlag
Hillman takes on the Oedipal ideas of psychoanalysis and its father, Freud. He exposes analysis and its myth of the search for identity which is still with us, is still binding us, is still trying to turn people into Oedipus on both sides of the analytical couch.

Death of Oliver Becaille see Three by Zola

Death of Oliver Becaille. unabr. ed. Emile Zola. Read by Walter Covell. 1 cass. (Running Time: 56 min.). Dramatization. 7.95 (N-51) Jimcin Record.
A man thought dead is buried alive.

Death of Outrage: Bill Clinton & the Assault on American Ideals. William J. Bennett. Read by Charlton Heston. 2004. 10.95 (978-0-7435-4614-0(8)) Pub: S&S Audio. Dist(s): S and S Inc

Death of Persuasion: Essential Strategies to Solve the Most Painful Problems in Sales. Bill Caskey. 1CD. (Running Time: 74 mins). 2004. audio compact disk 29.95 (978-0-9758510-7-4(1)) Caskey Ach Strat.
So I know what happened - you looked at the title of this and silently said to yourself?COME ON?PERSUASION?S NOT DEAD. In fact, what I need is MORE persuasion not less. And people persuade all the time. WHAT ABOUT POLITICIANS?WHAT ABOUT ADVERTISERS?WHAT ABOUT THE BEST SALES PEOPLE I KNOW? THEY ALL PERSUADE!!!!?M ASSUMING THAT the reason this CD ended up in your player is because you are involved in some way?in professional sales ?perhaps a front line sales person or sales manager?or the President of a small company that also sells and negotiates? or maybe you?re a service professional who suddenly has awakened to find that you are responsible for bringing in business.Regardless, I?m here to tell you that MOST of what you?ve heard about how to sell ? the PERSUASION model is wrong and doesn?t work. Now before you get angry at me for saying that, let me share with you that this CD is designed to walk you through how it has come to be that the old concept of PERSUASION doesn?t work in professional sales?. and what to do about it.And if you?re like most?when you look at your results, you get a bit frustrated because you can?t understand how you work SO hard and achieve so little. I know you feel you?re doing OK?keeping just ahead of the debt monsters?but there is a little voice inside you that says?. I?m still underperforming. And I know there?s that same voice that says ?work harder.?And you probably think persuasion is at the heart of the problem. Well it is. But maybe not in the same way you might think. I?m here to tell you, ?WORKING HARDER IS NOT THE ANSWER.? I?m also here to tell you not to beat yourself up too badly when your results don?t meet your expectations. I wouldn?t go so far as to say its not your fault?. because you do have personal responsibility for your future?but I would go so far as to say? there?s a high likelihood that you?ve been taught wrong strategies and weak techniques to get you where you want to go. There is another way to communicate your value as a company - -and as a person? a strategy that is profoundly more effective at getting your point across and getting higher market results. And it has NOTHING TO DO WITH traditional PERSUASIONtactics.On this CD, you will learn what the solution is and how to get access to it. I will walk you step by step through some proven strategies that offer an alternative to the old persuasion skills that someone may have taught you?or you have read in some book. give you some quick sales strategies that you can go out and apply in your marketplace today ? AND SEE RESULTSWhen I watch traditional sales trainers teach persuasion skills, I?m offended. The way persuasion is taught does NOT WORK! And it?s time for me to do something about it.____This is the exact CD that we give to all of our constituents when we startdevelopment work. So in a way, by you listening to this, you?ve already begun work on yourself.You have enormous value as a person and a company. It?s time you used strategies that help you communicate that value and get paid for it. Listen to this CD again and again and again?and make notes?take some of these principles into your business in the next 48 hours ? so you can see for yourself the power of a new perspective on persuasion.

Death of Pessimism: Neh. 12:27-47. Ed Young. 1990. 4.95 (978-0-7417-1820-4(0), 820) Win Walk.

Death of Stonewall Jackson see Poetry of Benet

Death of Stonewall Jackson see Twentieth-Century Poetry in English, No. 23, Recordings of Poets Reading Their Own Poetry

Death of the Dream: Farmhouses in the Heartland. Prod. by John Whitehead. Narrated by Linda Kelsey. Contrib. by Steve Heitzeg. 1 CD. (Running Time: 40 mins.). 2004. audio compact disk 15.95 (978-1-890434-34-2(5)) Afton Hist Soc.

Death of the Fox. George P. Garrett. Read by George P. Garrett. 1 cass. (Running Time: 55 min.). 13.95 (978-1-55644-101-1(0), 4061) Am Audio Prose.
Reading excerpts from these best-selling historical novels.

Death of the Good Guy. unabr. ed. J. R. Chabot. Read by Maynard Villers. 6 cass. (Running Time: 8 hrs. 30 min.). 1995. 39.95 (978-1-55686-646-3(1)) Books in Motion.
One murder, followed by another twenty years later, are primary elements in this mystery that becomes even more complicated when the Will of the currently deceased revealed.

***Death of the Liberal Class.** Chris Hedges. Narrated by Arthur Morey. (ENG.). 2010. 29.99 (978-1-61120-019-5(9)) Dreamscap OH.

***Death of the Liberal Class.** Chris Hedges. Narrated by Arther Morey. (ENG.). 2010. 39.99 (978-1-61120-000-3(8)) Dreamscap OH.

Death of the Office Witch. unabr. ed. Marlys Millhiser. Read by Lynda Evans. 8 cass. (Running Time: 9 hrs. 30 min.). (Charlie Greene Mystery Ser.: Bk. 2). 2001. 49.95 (978-1-55686-764-4(6)) Books in Motion.
Literary Agent Charlie Greene admits to police that she has spoken with unpopular office receptionist, Gloria, after Gloria's murder.

Death of the Panther. unabr. ed. Howard Peterson. Read by David Sharp. 6 cass. (Running Time: 6 hrs.). (Sheriff Burley Grantham Ser.). 1995. 39.95 (978-1-55686-588-6(0)) Books in Motion.
In the small town of Summit, Sheriff Burley Grantham is stumped by a conflict of identities in a murder case until he learns that spies are involved using the code name "Panther".

Death of the Sheriff (Part 1) see Twentieth-Century Poetry in English: Recordings of Poets Reading Their Own Poetry

Death of Tsotsi see Tales from a Troubled Land

Death of Vishnu. unabr. ed. Manil Suri. Read by John Lee. 7 cass. (Running Time: 10 hrs. 30 mins.). 2001. 56.00 (978-0-7366-6034-1(8)) Books on Tape.
Metaphorical story of contemporary India & the soul's progress through the various stages of existence.

Death of Vishnu. unabr. abr. ed. Manil Suri. Read by John Lee. 8 cass. (Running Time: 10 hrs.). 2001. 39.95 (978-0-694-52442-6(5)) HarperCollins Pubs.

Death of William Posters. unabr. ed. Alan Sillitoe. Read by Richard Green. 7 cass. (Running Time: 10 hrs. 30 min.). 1977. 56.00 (978-0-7366-0054-5(X), 1066) Books on Tape.
Frank Dauley, a 27-year-old factory worker who finds himself looking ahead to a life at the lathe, breaks away to search for new beginnings.

Death on Demand. Carolyn G. Hart. Read by Kate Reading. (Death on Demand Mystery Ser.: No. 1). 2000. 40.00 (978-0-7366-4838-7(0)); audio compact disk 48.00 (978-0-7366-7500-0(0)) Books on Tape.

Death on Demand. unabr. ed. Carolyn G. Hart. Read by Kate Reading. 5 cass. (Running Time: 90 mins. per cass.). (Death on Demand Mystery Ser.: No. 1). 2000. 30.00 (5185) Books on Tape.
Annie Laurance is a prime suspect in an murder investigation, when an author is murdered at her bookstore.

Death on the Air & Other Stories. Ngaio Marsh. Narrated by Nadia May. (Running Time: 7 hrs.). 2000. 27.95 (978-1-59912-466-7(1)) Iofy Corp.

Death on the Air & Other Stories. unabr. ed. Ngaio Marsh. Read by Nadia May. 5 cass. (Running Time: 7 hrs.). 2002. 39.95 (978-0-7861-2318-6(4), 3003); audio compact disk 48.00 (978-0-7861-9431-5(6), 3003) Blckstn Audio.
A man dies with his hand on a radio dial. A disguised aristocrat finds murder at the opening night of a play. A cryptogram produces death in an English churchyard.

Death on the Cards. l.t. ed. Richard Grayson. (Ulverscroft Large Print Ser.). 1990. bk. 32.50 (978-0-7089-2190-6(6)) Pub: UlverLrgPrint GBR. Dist(s): Ulverscroft US

***Death on the D-List WMA.** Nancy Grace. (ENG.). 2010. 21.99 (978-1-4013-9519-3(8)) Pub: Hyperion. Dist(s): HarperCollins Pubs

Death on the Downs. unabr. ed. Simon Brett. Read by Geoffrey Howard. 1 MP3 CD. (Running Time: 8 hrs. 30 mins.). 2002. audio compact disk 24.95 (978-0-7861-9250-2(X), 2925); 44.95 (978-0-7861-2174-8(2), 2925); audio compact disk 56.00 (978-0-7861-9545-9(2), 2925) Blckstn Audio.
It isn't the rain that upsets Carole Seddon during her walk on the West Sussex Downs. It isn't the dilapidated barn in which she is forced to seek shelter. No, what upsets her is the human skeleton she discovers there, neatly packed into two blue fertilizer bags.... So begins the second investigation for strait-laced Carole and her more laid-back neighbor Jude. This time their inquiries take them away from their seaside village of Fethering to the small downland hamlet of Weldisham.

Death on the Downs. unabr. ed. Simon Brett. Read by Geoffrey Howard. 7 CDs. 2004. audio compact disk 35.95 (978-0-7861-8690-7(9)); reel tape 29.95 (978-0-7861-2210-3(2)) Blckstn Audio.

Death on the Downs. unabr. ed. Simon Brett. Read by Simon Brett. 6 cass. (Running Time: 8 hrs. 25 min.). (Isis Ser.). (J). 2001. 54.95 (978-0-7531-1166-6(7)); audio compact disk 71.95 (978-0-7531-1213-7(2)) Pub: ISIS Lrg Prnt GBR. Dist(s): Ulverscroft US
It wasn't the rain that upset Carole Seddon during her walk on the West Sussex Downs. No, it was her discovery of a human skeleton. So begins the second investigation for Carole and her unconventional neighbor Jude. The

focus for their enquiries this time is the small downland hamlet of Weldisham, where the locals rather too readily identify the corpse.

Death on the Highway & I Walk in the Night. 1 cass. (Running Time: 60 min.). Dramatization. (Inner Sanctum Mystery Ser.). 1949. 6.00 Once Upon Rad.
Mystery & suspense radio broadcasts.

Death on the Nile. unabr. ed. Agatha Christie. Read by David Suchet. (Running Time: 30720 sec.). (Hercule Poirot Mystery Ser.). (ENG.). 2005. audio compact disk 31.95 (978-1-57270-475-6(6)) Pub: AudioGO. Dist(s): Perseus Dist
Aboard a Nile steamer, Hercule Poirot meets Linnet Doyle, a woman who appears to have everything: youth, beauty, wealth, and a loving husband. But the husband was stolen from her friend Jacqueline de Bellefort, who has been haunting the newlyweds' path, showing up to wreak havoc in their plans. They've secretly booked passage on the steamer to escape, but still, tragedy strikes: Linnet is shot through the head. As the complications multiply, Poirot and his little grey cells are faced with nothing but airtight alibis.

Death on the Nile. unabr. ed. Agatha Christie. Read by David Suchet. 6 cass. (Running Time: 8 hrs. 32 min.). 2001. 29.95 (978-1-57270-203-5(6), N61203u) Pub: Audio Partners. Dist(s): PerseuPGW
This classic Christie takes place aboard a Nile steamer,where the famous Belgian detective Hercule Poirot meets an alluring woman. Young, beautiful, stylish, rich, she even has a loving husband. Then tragedy strikes when she is shot through the head. With customary panache, Poirot probes the airtight alibis until he brilliantly bursts open the case.

Death on the Nile: A BBC Radio Full-Cast Dramatization. Agatha Christie. (Running Time: 2 hrs. 20 mins. 0 sec.). (ENG.). 2009. audio compact disk 24.95 (978-1-60283-731-7(7)) Pub: AudioGO. Dist(s): Perseus Dist

Death on the River Walk. Carolyn G. Hart. Read by Kate Reading. (Henrie O Mystery Ser.). 1999. audio compact disk 64.00 (978-0-7366-5197-4(7)) Books on Tape.

Death on the River Walk. collector's ed. Carolyn G. Hart. Read by Kate Reading. 7 cass. (Running Time: 10 hrs. 30 min.). (Henrie O Mystery Ser.). 1999. 56.00 (978-0-7366-4662-8(0), 5044) Books on Tape.
A frantic phone call from an old & dear friend on the other side of the world sends Henrie O to San Antonio, Texas, in search of her friend's granddaughter, Iris Chavez. Iris had been working at the family owned Tesoros Gallery, a shop renowned for the priceless treasures it hunts for its rich & famous patrons. Iris has disappeared without a word, her apartment has been ransacked, yet nothing is missing & nobody at Tesoros seems to care. Why? Somewhere in the gallery or among the family members who run the business is a secret, a secret Henrie O must uncover if she is to find Iris.

Death on the River Walk. unabr. ed. Carolyn G. Hart. Read by Kate Reading. 8 CDs. (Running Time: 9 hrs. 25 mins.). (Henrie O Mystery Ser.). 2001. audio compact disk 64.00 Books on Tape.

Death on the River Walk. unabr. ed. Carolyn G. Hart. Read by Kate Reading. 7 cass. (Running Time: 10 hrs.). (Henrie O Mystery Ser.). 2000. 29.95 (978-0-7366-4701-4(5)) Books on Tape.

Death Orbit. abr. ed. Mack Maloney. 2 cass. (Running Time: 3 hrs.). (Wingman Ser.: Vol. 13). 2002. 9.95 (978-1-931953-05-4(8)) Listen & Live.

Death Penalty: A Catholic Viewpoint. Helen Prejean. 2 cass. (Running Time: 2 hrs.). 2001. 17.95 (A7000) St Anthony Mess Pr.
The woman behind the Academy Award winning movie "Dead Man Walking" speaks of people on death row, their victims, the families involved and a complex legal system that distorts justice.

Death Poems for the Grieving Heart Audio Cassette: Spiritual, Healing Poetry. D. N. Sutton. Read by D. N. Sutton. (ENG.). 2001. 6.00 (978-0-940361-31-7(0)) Sherwood-Spencer Pub.

Death Poems for the Grieving Heart CD: Spiritual, Healing Poetry. D. N. Sutton. Read by D. N. Sutton. (ENG.). 2001. audio compact disk 12.00 (978-0-940361-41-6(8)) Sherwood-Spencer Pub.

Death Poems for the Grieving Heart CD & Book: Spiritual, Healing Poetry. D. N. Sutton. Read by D. N. Sutton. (ENG.). 2001. per. 20.00 (978-0-940361-51-5(5)) Sherwood-Spencer Pub.

Death Qualified. unabr. ed. Kate Wilhelm. Read by Anna Fields. 13 CDs. (Running Time: 16 hrs.). 2003. audio compact disk 104.00 (978-0-7861-9339-4(5), 3047); 76.95 (978-0-7861-2345-2(1), 3047) Blckstn Audio.
Barbara Halloway is determined to quit the practice of law. But when she receives a call from her father imploring her help with a tough case, she finds herself sucked into a vortex of murder, high-tech mystery, and the maelstrom within herself.

Death Qualified. unabr. ed. Kate Wilhelm. Read by Anna Fields. 1 CD. (Running Time: 54000 sec.). 2003. audio compact disk 24.95 (978-0-7861-9065-2(5), 3047) Blckstn Audio.

Death Quest. abr. ed. L. Ron Hubbard. 2 cass. (Running Time: 3 hrs.). (Mission Earth Ser.: Vol. 6). 2002. 15.95 (978-1-59212-062-8(8)) Gala Pr LLC.
Alien assassin Soltan Gris will stop at nothing to destroy Fleet Officer Jettero Heller and sabotage his mission to save Earth from drowning in its own environmental problems, while, at the same time, he's forced to play husband to two wives and keep up with a teenage nymphomaniac.

Death Rides a Chestnut Mare. abr. ed. Ralph Compton. Read by Jim Gough. 4 cass. (Running Time: 6 hrs.). (Gun Ser.: No. 6). 2001. 24.95 (978-1-890990-66-4(3)) Otis Audio.
After the Civil War, a blacksmith from Missouri decides to travel to Texas to purchase a cattle herd. He hopes to sell the herd up north & turn a profit for his family to live on. However, the blacksmith had not reckoned on the dangers of the lawless plains & is killed by a band of outlaws. When news of his death reaches his family, his eldest daughter straps on her father's guns & rides off on her father's chestnut mare, using her father's name in a personal campaign for revenge!.

Death Rides This Trail. Steve Frazee. Read by Richard Rohan. (Running Time: 1 hr. 42 mins.). 1998. 10.95 (978-1-60083-460-8(4)) Iofy Corp.

Death Room see Robert Graves Reads from His Poetry & the White Goddess

Death Shall Have No Dominion see Dylan Thomas

***Death Ship.** (ENG.). 2010. audio compact disk (978-1-59171-270-1(X)) Falcon Picture.

***Death Song on the Singing Wires.** Frank Bonham. 2009. (978-1-60136-431-9(8)) Audio Holding.

Death Song on the Singing Wires. Frank Bonham. (Running Time: 0 hr. 48 mins.). 1999. 10.95 (978-1-60083-512-4(0)) Iofy Corp.

Death Squad. Roy Lewis & Martyn Waites. 2008. 54.95 (978-1-84652-223-9(4)); audio compact disk 64.95 (978-1-84652-224-6(2)) Pub: Magna Story GBR. Dist(s): Ulverscroft US

Death Switch. unabr. ed. David Pettigrew. Read by Ellen Travolta. 4 cass. (Running Time: 5 hrs. 12 min.). 1995. 26.95 (978-1-55686-596-1(1)) Books in Motion.
Maggie Broderick, a street-smart, New Jersey private eye, is hired to solve a million dollar murder case that has unusual implications for her ex-husband, police-detective Broderick.

Death Takes Passage. unabr. ed. Sue Henry. Read by Mary Pfeiffer. 7 cass. (Running Time: 10 hrs.). (Jessie Arnold Mystery Ser.). 2000. 56.00 (978-0-7366-4352-8(4)) Books on Tape.
In July of 1897, the S.S. PORTLAND sailed from Alaska to Seattle carrying two tons of Yukon gold, setting off the famed Klondike Gold Rush. Now, the SPIRIT OF '98 is recreating that historic voyage and Alex Jensen is assigned to watch the gold. With his lady love, the famous "musher" Jessie Arnold, at his side, he is looking forward to the leisurely trip, until an unexplained rash of shipboard robberies and a probable death jolts him into action.

Death Takes up a Collection. unabr. ed. Carol Anne O'Marie. Read by Barbara Rosenblat. 5 cass. (Running Time: 7 hrs.). (Sister Mary Helen Mystery Ser.). 2001. 39.95 (978-0-7861-1949-3(7), 2720); audio compact disk 48.00 (978-0-7861-9770-5(6), 2720) Blckstn Audio.
Holiday festivities are dampened by the murder of a pastor of the nearby St. Agatha's Church on St. Patrick's Day. Merry mayhem ensues as the nosy pair of nuns delve into the much-disliked Monsignor's dirty past to uncover the killer.

Death Takes up a Collection: A Sister Mary Helen Mystery. unabr. ed. Carol Anne O'Marie. Read by Agnes Herrmann. 6 vols. (Running Time: 9 hrs.). 2000. bk. 54.95 (978-0-7927-2258-8(2), CSL 147, Chivers Sound Lib) AudioGO.
Sister Mary Helen and Sister Eileen are delivering loaves of Irish soda bread on St. Patrick's day to all of the Mount St. Francis College benefactors. Eager to finish, they make their last stop at St. Agatha's Church, where they interrupt a meeting of several prominent community members. Invited to stay for tea by Monsignor Joseph Higgins, the nuns agree, but sensing tension, they hurry out shortly thereafter. The next day they learn that the monsignor is dead and that he was poisoned. It's up to Sister Mary Helen and Sister Eileen to find out who killed the Monsignor and why.

Death, The Greatest Fiction. Osho Oshos. Read by Osho Oshos. 6 cass. (Running Time: 9 hrs.). 49.95 (DCM-0013) Oshos.
Offers insight on the art of living & dying, death, reincarnation & euthanasia.

Death Times Three. collector's ed. Rex Stout. Read by Michael Prichard. 5 cass. (Running Time: 7 hrs. 30 min.). (Nero Wolfe Ser.). 2000. 40.00 (978-0-7366-5638-2(3)) Books on Tape.
A collection of three novellas: "Assault on a Brownstone," "Frame-Up for Murder," & "Bitter End." "Assault on a Brownstone" is a novella featuring Nero Wolfe in his most shocking confrontation with the law when his Thirty-fifth Street brownstone is invaded by Treasury officials. "Frame-Up for Murder" concerns a famous fashion designer & a neatly stitched plot that weaves a deadly pattern of death. And "Bitter End" is a suspenseful story containing one of the nastiest incidents ever to occur at Wolfe's dinner table.

Death to All Sacred Cows: How Successful Businesses Put the Old Rules Out to Pasture. unabr. ed. Beau Fraser et al. Read by Johnny Heller. (Running Time: 4 hrs. 0 mins. 0 sec.). (ENG.). 2008. audio compact disk 49.99 (978-1-4001-3584-4(2)); audio compact disk 19.99 (978-1-4001-5584-2(3)) Pub: Tantor Media. Dist(s): IngramPubServ

Death to All Sacred Cows: How Successful Businesses Put the Old Rules Out to Pasture. unabr. ed. Beau Fraser et al. Read by Johnny Heller. (Running Time: 4 hrs. 0 mins. 0 sec.). (ENG.). 2008. audio compact disk 24.99 (978-1-4001-0584-7(6)) Pub: Tantor Media. Dist(s): IngramPubServ

***Death to the Dictator! A Young Man Casts a Vote in Iran's 2009 Election & Pays a Devastating Price.** unabr. ed. Afsaneh Moqadam. Narrated by Johnny Heller. (Running Time: 4 hrs. 30 mins. 0 sec.). 2010. 19.99 (978-1-4001-6772-2(8)); 13.99 (978-1-4001-8772-0(9)); audio compact disk 24.99 (978-1-4001-1772-7(0)); audio compact disk 59.99 (978-1-4001-4772-4(7)) Pub: Tantor Media. Dist(s): IngramPubServ

Death to the Landlords. unabr. ed. Ellis Peters, pseud. Read by Derek Hutchinson. 6 CDs. (Running Time: 7 hrs.). (Inspector George Felse Mystery Ser.: Vol. 11). 2000. audio compact disk 64.95 (978-0-7531-0905-2(0), 109050) Pub: ISIS Audio GBR. Dist(s): Ulverscroft US
Landlords the world over are not the most popular people & there is little mourning when the greedy, ruthless Mahandralal Bakhle is blown up on his boat. Suspicion rests on the boat-boy who died in the explosion, but Dominic Felse, one of a party of tourists who are accidentally involved in the fatality, is not convinced of the boy's guilt. When they move on, it seems that the terror is still pursuing them. Violence & death erupt again in the home of a different landowner in which Dominic & his friends are guests. Dominic & his friend the Swami must unravel a deadly puzzle of hatred & murder.

Death to the Landlords. unabr. ed. Ellis Peters, pseud. Read by Derek Hutchinson. 6 cass. (Running Time: 9 hrs.). (Inspector George Felse Mystery Ser.: Vol. 11). (J). 2001. 54.95 (978-1-85695-994-0(5), 960309) Pub: ISIS Lrg Prnt GBR. Dist(s): Ulverscroft US

Death Train to Boston. Dianne Day. 6 cass. (Running Time: 9 hrs.). 2001. 48.00 (978-0-7366-6210-9(3)) Books on Tape.
Fremont Jones & her "partner in love & work," Michael Archer, have been hired to look into a series of petty vandalisms plaguing the Southern Pacific Railroad. They are riding a train incognito when it is blown to smithereens just east of Salt Lake City. Michael suffers only a broken collarbone, but Fremont disappears. Believing that Fremont is still alive, Michael sets out to find her.

Death Troopers. unabr. ed. Joe Schreiber. Read by Sean Kenin. (ENG.). 2009. audio compact disk 30.00 (978-0-307-57826-6(7), Random AudioBks) Pub: Random Audio Pubg. Dist(s): Random

Death Trust. abr. ed. David A. Rollins. Read by Mel Foster. (Running Time: 6 hrs.). (Vin Cooper Ser.). 2008. audio compact disk 14.99 (978-1-4233-3251-0(2), 9781423332510, BCD Value Price) Brilliance Audio.

Death Trust. unabr. ed. David Rollins. Read by Mel Foster. (Running Time: 13 hrs.). (Vin Cooper Ser.). 2007. 39.25 (978-1-4233-3249-7(0), 9781423332497, BADLE); 24.95 (978-1-4233-3248-0(2), 9781423332480, BAD); 92.25 (978-1-4233-3243-5(1), 9781423332435, BriAudUnabridg); audio compact disk 38.95 (978-1-4233-3244-2(X), 9781423332442, Bril Audio CD Unabri); audio compact disk 24.95 (978-1-4233-3246-6(6), 9781423332466, Brilliance MP3); audio compact disk 107.25 (978-1-4233-3245-9(8), 9781423332459, BriAudCD Unabrid); audio compact disk 39.25 (978-1-4233-3247-3(4), 9781423332473, Brlnc Audio MP3 Lib) Brilliance Audio.

Death under Sail. unabr. ed. C. P. Snow. Read by Ian Whitcomb. 6 cass. (Running Time: 9 hrs.). 1984. 48.00 (978-0-7366-0447-5(2), 1421) Books on Tape.
Murder mystery of imposing tension, not only an ingenious who-dunnit, but also a superb study of human motivation.

Death under the Dryer. Simon Brett. 2007. 61.95 (978-0-7531-3652-2(X)); audio compact disk 84.95 (978-0-7531-2747-6(4)) Pub: ISIS Audio GBR. Dist(s): Ulverscroft US

***Death Vows.** Richard Stevenson. Read by Richard Stevenson. Music by Tyler Gasek. (ENG.). 2009. audio compact disk 25.00 (978-0-9818091-4-4(6)) BMA Studios.

Death Was the Other Woman. Linda L. Richards. Read by Joyce Bean. (Playaway Adult Fiction Ser.). 2008. 64.99 (978-1-60640-784-4(8)) Find a World.

Death Was the Other Woman. unabr. ed. Linda L. Richards. (Running Time: 7 hrs.). 2008. 39.25 (978-1-4233-4974-7(1), 9781423349747, BADLE); 24.95 (978-1-4233-4973-0(3), 9781423349730, BAD) Brilliance Audio.

Death Was the Other Woman. unabr. ed. Linda L. Richards. Read by Joyce Bean. 6 cass. (Running Time: 25200 sec.). 2008. 82.25 (978-1-4233-4968-6(7), 9781423349686, BrilAudUnabridg); audio compact disk 39.25 (978-1-4233-4972-3(5), 9781423349723, Brlnc Audio MP3 Lib); audio compact disk 87.25 (978-1-4233-4970-9(9), 9781423349709, BriAudCD Unabrid); audio compact disk 29.95 (978-1-4233-4969-3(5), 9781423349693, Bril Audio CD Unabri) Brilliance Audio.

Death Was the Other Woman: A Mystery. unabr. ed. Linda L. Richards. Read by Joyce Bean. 1 MP3-CD. (Running Time: 25200 sec.). 2008. audio compact disk 24.95 (978-1-4233-4971-6(7), 9781423349716, Brilliance MP3) Brilliance Audio.

Death Wears a Red Hat. unabr. collector's ed. William X. Kienzle. Read by Edward Holland. 7 cass. (Running Time: 10 hrs. 30 min.). (Father Koesler Mystery Ser.: No. 2). 1997. 56.00 (978-0-7366-4063-3(0), 4574) Books on Tape.
Father Koesler investigates the serial murders of Detroit's criminal masterminds, whose heads are rolling.

Death with Honors, Pt. 3. unabr. ed. Ron Nessen & Johanna Neuman. Read by Lloyd James. 6 cass. (Running Time: 8 hrs. 30 mins.). (Knight & Day Mystery Ser.). 1999. 44.95 (978-0-7861-1484-9(3), 2336) Blckstn Audio.
An opinionated right-wing talk show host - & his partner, a liberal reporter for "The Washington Post," are caught in the cross-fire between power-concious Washington & media-mad Hollywood. The results are murder.

Death without Tenure. unabr. ed. Joanne Dobson. (Running Time: 12 hrs. 30 mins.). 2010. 29.95 (978-1-4417-1667-5(X)); 72.95 (978-1-4417-1663-7(7)); audio compact disk 105.00 (978-1-4417-1664-4(5)) Blckstn Audio.

Deathalnds 45: Starfall. Based on a novel by Axler James. 2007. audio compact disk 19.99 (978-1-59950-391-2(3)) GraphicAudio.

Deathbed. collector's ed. William X. Kienzle. Read by Edward Holland. 8 cass. (Running Time: 12 hrs.). (Father Koesler Mystery Ser.: No. 8). 1999. 64.00 (978-0-7366-4617-8(5), 5003) Books on Tape.

Deathlands 0: Encounter. James Axler. 2008. audio compact disk 19.99 (978-1-59950-507-7(X)) GraphicAudio.

Deathlands 1: Pilgrimage to Hell. James Axler. (Running Time: 28800 sec.). 2005. audio compact disk 19.99 (978-1-59950-000-3(0)) GraphicAudio.

Deathlands #1 - 10 MP3 Special Boxed Set. 2006. audio compact disk 110.49 (978-1-59950-307-3(7)) GraphicAudio.

Deathlands #1 - 5 Special Boxed Set. 2006. audio compact disk 84.95 (978-1-59950-305-9(0)) GraphicAudio.

Deathlands 10: Northstar Rising. 2005. audio compact disk 19.99 (978-1-59950-032-4(9)) GraphicAudio.

Deathlands 11: Time Nomads. 2006. audio compact disk 19.99 (978-1-59950-086-7(8)) GraphicAudio.

Deathlands 12: Latitude Zero. 2006. audio compact disk 19.99 (978-1-59950-088-1(4)) GraphicAudio.

Deathlands 13: Seedling. 2006. audio compact disk 19.99 (978-1-59950-107-9(4)) GraphicAudio.

Deathlands 14: Dark Carnival. 2006. audio compact disk 19.99 (978-1-59950-108-6(2)) GraphicAudio.

Deathlands 15: Chill Factor. 2006. audio compact disk 19.99 (978-1-59950-087-4(6)) GraphicAudio.

Deathlands 16: Moon Fate. 2006. audio compact disk 19.99 (978-1-59950-103-1(1)) GraphicAudio.

Deathlands 17: Fury's Pilgrims. 2006. audio compact disk 19.99 (978-1-59950-130-7(9)) GraphicAudio.

Deathlands 18: Shockscape. 2006. audio compact disk 19.99 (978-1-59950-138-3(4)) GraphicAudio.

Deathlands 19: Deep Empire. 2006. audio compact disk 19.99 (978-1-59950-139-0(2)) GraphicAudio.

Deathlands 2: Red Holocaust. 2005. audio compact disk 19.99 (978-1-59950-007-2(8)) GraphicAudio.

Deathlands 20: Cold Asylum. 2006. audio compact disk 19.99 (978-1-59950-176-5(7)) GraphicAudio.

Deathlands 21: Twilight Children. 2006. audio compact disk 19.99 (978-1-59950-178-9(3)) GraphicAudio.

Deathlands 22: Rider, Reaper. 2006. audio compact disk 19.99 (978-1-59950-187-1(2)) GraphicAudio.

Deathlands 23: Road Wars. 2007. audio compact disk 19.99 (978-1-59950-319-6(0)) GraphicAudio.

Deathlands 24: Trader Redux. 2007. audio compact disk 19.99 (978-1-59950-336-3(0)) GraphicAudio.

Deathlands 25: Genesis Echo. James Axler. 2007. audio compact disk 19.99 (978-1-59950-354-7(9)) GraphicAudio.

Deathlands 26: Shadowfall. Based on a book by James Axler. 2007. audio compact disk 19.99 (978-1-59950-372-1(7)) GraphicAudio.

Deathlands 27: Ground Zero. Based on a novel by James Axler. 2007. audio compact disk 19.99 (978-1-59950-381-3(6)) GraphicAudio.

Deathlands 28: Emerald Fire. Based on a novel by James Axler. 2008. audio compact disk 19.99 (978-1-59950-399-8(9)) GraphicAudio.

Deathlands 29: Bloodlines. Based on a novel by James Axler. 2008. audio compact disk 19.99 (978-1-59950-407-0(3)) GraphicAudio.

Deathlands 3: Neutron Solstice. 2005. audio compact disk 19.99 (978-1-59950-009-6(4)) GraphicAudio.

Deathlands 30: Crossways. Directed By Bob Supan. Contrib. by Richard Rohan et al. (Running Time: 21600 sec.). (Deathlands Ser.). 2008. audio compact disk 19.99 (978-1-59950-435-3(9)) GraphicAudio.

Deathlands 31: Keepers of the Sun. Based on a novel by James Axler. 2008. audio compact disk 19.99 (978-1-59950-443-8(X)) GraphicAudio.

Deathlands 32: Circle Thrice. Based on a novel by James Axler. 2008. audio compact disk 19.99 (978-1-59950-449-0(9)) GraphicAudio.

Deathlands 33: Eclipse at Noon. Based on a novel by James Axler. 2008. audio compact disk 19.99 (978-1-59950-457-5(X)) GraphicAudio.

Deathlands 34: Stoneface. Based on a novel by James Axler. 2008. audio compact disk 19.99 (978-1-59950-472-8(3)) GraphicAudio.

Deathlands 35: Bitter Fruit. James Axler. 2008. audio compact disk 19.99 (978-1-59950-491-9(X)) GraphicAudio.

Deathlands 36: Skydark. James Axler. 2009. audio compact disk 19.99 (978-1-59950-515-2(0)) GraphicAudio.

Deathlands 37: Demons of Eden. James Axler. 2009. audio compact disk 19.99 (978-1-59950-523-7(1)) GraphicAudio.

Deathlands 38: The Mars Arena. James Axler. 2009. audio compact disk 19.99 (978-1-59950-596-1(7)) GraphicAudio.

Deathlands 39: Watersleep. James Axler. 2009. audio compact disk 19.99 (978-1-59950-573-2(8)) GraphicAudio.

Deathlands 4: Crater Lake. 2005. audio compact disk 19.99 (978-1-59950-013-3(2)) GraphicAudio.

Deathlands 40: Nightmare Passage. Based on a novel by James Axler. 2009. audio compact disk 19.99 (978-1-59950-616-6(5)) GraphicAudio.

***Deathlands 41: Freedom Lost.** James Axler. 2010. audio compact disk 19.99 (978-1-59950-649-4(1)) GraphicAudio.

***Deathlands 42: Way of the Wolf.** James Axler. 2010. audio compact disk 19.99 (978-1-59950-657-9(2)) GraphicAudio.

Deathlands 43: Dark Emblem. James Axler. (Running Time: 25200 sec.). (Deathlands Ser.). 2005. audio compact disk 19.99 (978-1-59950-004-1(3)) GraphicAudio.

Deathlands 44: Crucible of Time. 2006. audio compact disk 19.99 (978-1-59950-071-3(X)) GraphicAudio.

Deathlands 44: Crucible of Time. 2006. audio compact disk 19.99 (978-1-59950-188-8(0)) GraphicAudio.

Deathlands 46: Gemini Rising. James Axler. 2004. audio compact disk 19.99 (978-1-933059-50-1(8)) GraphicAudio.

Deathlands 47: Gaia's Demise. James Axler. 2004. audio compact disk 19.99 (978-1-933059-51-8(6)) GraphicAudio.

Deathlands 48: Dark Reckoning. James Axler. 2004. audio compact disk 19.99 (978-1-933059-52-5(4)) GraphicAudio.

Deathlands 49: Shadow World. James Axler. 2004. audio compact disk 19.99 (978-1-933059-56-3(7)) GraphicAudio.

Deathlands 5: Homeward Bound. 2005. audio compact disk 19.99 (978-1-59950-015-7(9)) GraphicAudio.

Deathlands 50: Pandora's Redoubt. James Axler. 2004. audio compact disk 19.99 (978-1-933059-57-0(5)) GraphicAudio.

Deathlands 51: Rat King. James Axler. 2004. audio compact disk 19.99 (978-1-933059-60-0(5)) GraphicAudio.

Deathlands 52: Zero City. James Axler. 2004. audio compact disk 19.99 (978-1-933059-61-7(3)) GraphicAudio.

Deathlands 53: Savage Armada. James Axler. 2005. audio compact disk 19.99 (978-1-933059-64-8(8)) GraphicAudio.

Deathlands 54: Judas Strike. James Axler. 2005. audio compact disk 19.99 (978-1-933059-65-5(6)) GraphicAudio.

Deathlands 55: Shadow Fortress. James Axler. 2005. audio compact disk 19.99 (978-1-933059-68-6(0)) GraphicAudio.

Deathlands 56: Sunchild. James Axler. 2005. audio compact disk 19.99 (978-1-933059-69-3(9)) GraphicAudio.

Deathlands 57: Breakthrough. James Axler. 2005. audio compact disk 19.99 (978-1-933059-72-3(9)) GraphicAudio.

Deathlands 58: Salvation Road. James Axler. 2005. audio compact disk 19.99 (978-1-933059-73-0(7)) GraphicAudio.

Deathlands 59: Amazon Gate. James Axler. 2005. audio compact disk 19.99 (978-1-933059-76-1(1)) GraphicAudio.

Deathlands 6: Pony Soldiers. 2006. audio compact disk 19.99 (978-1-59950-019-5(1)) GraphicAudio.

Deathlands #6 - 10 Special Boxed Set. 2006. audio compact disk 84.95 (978-1-59950-306-6(9)) GraphicAudio.

Deathlands 60: Destiny's Truth. James Axler. 2005. audio compact disk 19.99 (978-1-933059-77-8(X)) GraphicAudio.

Deathlands 61: Skydark Spawn. James Axler. 2005. audio compact disk 19.99 (978-1-933059-80-8(X)) GraphicAudio.

Deathlands 62: Damnation Road Show. James Axler. 2005. audio compact disk 19.99 (978-1-933059-81-5(8)) GraphicAudio.

Deathlands 63: Devil Riders. James Axler. 2006. audio compact disk 19.99 (978-1-933059-84-6(2)) GraphicAudio.

Deathlands 64: Bloodfire. James Axler. 2005. audio compact disk 19.99 (978-1-933059-85-3(0)) GraphicAudio.

Deathlands 65: Hellbenders. James Axler. 2005. audio compact disk 19.99 (978-1-933059-88-4(5)) GraphicAudio.

Deathlands 66: Separation. James Axler. 2005. audio compact disk 19.99 (978-1-933059-89-1(3)) GraphicAudio.

Deathlands 67: Death Hunt. James Axler. 2005. audio compact disk 19.99 (978-1-933059-92-1(3)) GraphicAudio.

Deathlands 68: Shaking Earth. James Axler. 2005. audio compact disk 19.99 (978-1-933059-93-8(1)) GraphicAudio.

Deathlands 69: Black Harvest. James Axler. 2005. audio compact disk 19.99 (978-1-933059-96-9(6)) GraphicAudio.

Deathlands 7: Dectra Chain. 2006. audio compact disk 19.99 (978-1-59950-025-6(6)) GraphicAudio.

Deathlands 70: Vengeance Trail. James Axler. 2005. audio compact disk 19.99 (978-1-933059-97-6(4)) GraphicAudio.

Deathlands 71: Ritual Chill. 2005. audio compact disk 19.99 (978-1-59950-002-7(7)) GraphicAudio.

Deathlands 72: Atlantis Reprise. 2006. audio compact disk 19.99 (978-1-59950-021-8(3)) GraphicAudio.

Deathlands 73: Labyrinth. 2006. audio compact disk 19.99 (978-1-59950-072-0(8)) GraphicAudio.

Deathlands 74: Strontium Swamp. 2006. audio compact disk 19.99 (978-1-59950-131-4(7)) GraphicAudio.

Deathlands 75: Shatter Zone. 2006. audio compact disk Rental 19.99 (978-1-59950-168-0(6)) GraphicAudio.

Deathlands 76: Perdition Valley. 2007. audio compact disk 19.99 (978-1-59950-197-0(X)) GraphicAudio.

Deathlands 77: Cannibal Moon. 2007. audio compact disk 19.99 (978-1-59950-310-3(7)) GraphicAudio.

Deathlands 78: Sky Raider. James Axler. 2007. audio compact disk 19.99 (978-1-59950-327-1(1)) GraphicAudio.

Deathlands 79: Remember Tomorrow. James Axler. 2007. audio compact disk 19.99 (978-1-59950-345-5(X)) GraphicAudio.

Deathlands 8: Ice & Fire. 2006. audio compact disk 19.99 (978-1-59950-027-0(2)) GraphicAudio.

Deathlands 80: Sunspot. Based on a novel by James Axler. 2008. audio compact disk 19.99 (978-1-59950-416-2(2)) GraphicAudio.

Deathlands 81: Desert Kings. Based on a novel by James Axler. 2008. audio compact disk 19.99 (978-1-59950-464-3(2)) GraphicAudio.

Deathlands 82: Apocalypse Unborn. James Axler. 2008. audio compact disk 19.99 (978-1-59950-499-5(5)) GraphicAudio.

Deathlands 83: Thunder Road. James Axler. 2009. audio compact disk 19.99 (978-1-59950-531-2(2)) GraphicAudio.

Deathlands 84: Plague Lords. James Axler. 2009. audio compact disk 19.99 (978-1-59950-567-1(3)) GraphicAudio.

Deathlands 85: Dark Resurrection. James Axler. 2009. audio compact disk 19.99 (978-1-59950-588-6(6)) GraphicAudio.

Deathlands 86: Eden's Twilight. Based on a book by James Axler. (ENG.). 2009. audio compact disk 19.99 (978-1-59950-600-5(9)) GraphicAudio.

Deathlands 87: Desolation Crossing. Based on a novel by James Axler. 2010. audio compact disk 19.99 (978-1-59950-624-1(6)) GraphicAudio.

Deathlands 88: Alpha Wave. Based on a novel by James Axler. 2010. audio compact disk 19.99 (978-1-59950-632-6(7)) GraphicAudio.

***Deathlands 89: Time Castaways.** James Axler. 2010. audio compact disk 19.99 (978-1-59950-713-2(7)) GraphicAudio.

Deathlands 9: Red Equinox. 2006. audio compact disk 19.99 (978-1-59950-030-0(2)) GraphicAudio.

***Deathlands 90: Prophecy.** James Axler. 2010. audio compact disk 19.99 (978-1-59950-716-3(1)) GraphicAudio.

***Deathlands 91: Blood Harvest.** James Axler. 2011. audio compact disk 19.99 (978-1-59950-730-9(7)) GraphicAudio.

***Deathlands 92: Arcadian's Asylum.** James Axler. 2011. audio compact disk 19.99 (978-1-59950-738-5(2)) GraphicAudio.

***Deathride: Hitler vs. Stalin - -the Eastern Front, 1941-1945.** unabr. ed. John Mosier. (Running Time: 18 hrs. 0 mins.). 2010. 22.99 (978-1-4001-8736-2(2)); 49.99 (978-1-4001-9736-1(8)) Tantor Media.

***Deathride: Hitler vs. Stalin - -the Eastern Front, 1941-1945.** unabr. ed. John Mosier. Narrated by Michael Prichard. (Running Time: 13 hrs. 0 mins. 0 sec.). (ENG.). 2010. 24.99 (978-1-4001-6736-4(1)); audio compact disk 83.99 (978-1-4001-4736-6(0)); audio compact disk 34.99 (978-1-4001-1736-9(4)) Pub: Tantor Media. Dist(s): IngramPubServ

Death's Acre: Inside the Legendary Forensics Lab - the Body Farm - Where the Dead Do Tell Tales. abr. ed. Bill Bass. Read by George Grizzard. Based on a work by Jon Jefferson. 2004. 15.95 (978-0-7435-4615-7(6)) Pub: S&S Audio. Dist(s): S and S Inc

Death's Door. Quintin Jardine. 2008. 89.95 (978-0-7531-3810-6(7)); audio compact disk 99.95 (978-0-7531-2791-9(1)) Pub: ISIS Audio GBR. Dist(s): Ulverscroft US

***Death's Excellent Vacation.** unabr. ed. Read by Christopher Lane & Amanda Ronconi. Ed. by Charlaine Harris & Toni L. P. Kelner. (Running Time: 13 hrs.). 2010. 24.99 (978-1-4418-6252-5(8), 9781441862525, Brilliance MP3); 39.97 (978-1-4418-6253-2(6), 9781441862532, Brinc Audio MP3 Lib); 24.99 (978-1-4418-6254-9(4), 9781441862549, BAD); audio compact disk 29.99 (978-1-4418-6250-1(1), 9781441862501, Bril Audio CD Unabri); audio compact disk 79.97 (978-1-4418-6251-8(X), 9781441862518, BriAudCD Unabrid) Brilliance Audio.

***Death's Excellent Vacation.** unabr. ed. Read by Amanda Ronconi & Christopher Lane. Ed. by Charlaine Harris & Toni L. P. Kelner. (Running Time: 13 hrs.). 2010. 39.97 (978-1-4418-6255-6(2), 9781441862556, BADLE) Brilliance Audio.

***Death's Head Revisited.** 2010. audio compact disk (978-1-59171-229-9(7)) Falcon Picture.

Death's Little Helpers. unabr. ed. Peter Spiegelman. 10 cass. (Running Time: 51780 sec.). (John March Mysteries Ser.). 2005. 79.95 (978-0-7927-3692-9(3), CSL 823); audio compact disk 110.95 (978-0-7927-3693-6(1), SLD 823) AudioGO.

***Death's Mistress.** unabr. ed. Karen Chance. Narrated by Joyce Bean. (Running Time: 15 hrs. 30 mins.). (Dorina Basarab Ser.). 2010. 20.99 (978-1-4001-8739-3(7)) Tantor Media.

***Death's Mistress.** unabr. ed. Karen Chance. Narrated by Joyce Bean. (Running Time: 14 hrs. 0 mins. 0 sec.). (Dorina Basarab Ser.). (ENG.). 2010. 29.99 (978-1-4001-6739-5(6)); audio compact disk 95.99 (978-1-4001-4739-7(5)); audio compact disk 39.99 (978-1-4001-1739-0(9)) Pub: Tantor Media. Dist(s): IngramPubServ

Death's Own Door. Andrew Taylor. Read by Peter Wickham. 10 cass. (Running Time: 11 hrs. 30 mins.). (Soundings Ser.). (J). 2004. 84.95 (978-1-84283-295-0(6)) Pub: ISIS Lrg Prnt GBR. Dist(s): Ulverscroft US

Death's Own Door. Andrew Taylor. 2009. audio compact disk 89.95 (978-1-4079-0485-6(X)) Pub: Soundings Ltd GBR. Dist(s): Ulverscroft US

Deathstalker Episode 4: Hostile Takeover. abr. ed. Simon R. Green. Narrated by Richard Rohan & Nanette Savard. 2 cass. (Running Time: 3 hrs.). (Deathstalker Ser.). 2002. 9.95 (978-1-931953-21-4(X)) Listen & Live.
The imperial Majesty Lionstone XIV ruled the human Empire with fear. When Owen Deathstalker, unwilling head of his clan, sought to avoid the perils of the Empire's warring factions, he unexpectedly found a price on his head. He fled to Mistworld, where he began to build an unlikely force to topple the thrown. With the help of his crew, Deathstalker took the first step on a far more dangerous journey to claim the role for which he'd been destined since before his birth.

Deathstalker Episode 5: The Darkvoid Device. unabr. abr. ed. Simon R. Green. Narrated by Richard Rohan & Nanette Savard. 2 cass. (Running Time: 3 hrs.). (Deathstalker Ser.). 2002. 9.95 (978-1-931953-22-1(8)) Listen & Live.

Deathstalker Coda 1 1: Armies & Forces Gathering Srength. Based on a novel by Simon R. Green. (Deathstalker Legacy Ser.: Bk. 3). 2008. audio compact disk 19.99 (978-1-59950-450-6(2)) GraphicAudio.

Deathstalker Coda 2 2: Here Be Monsters. Based on a novel by Simon R. Green. (Deathstalker Legacy Ser.: Bk. 3). 2008. audio compact disk 19.99 (978-1-59950-465-0(0)) GraphicAudio.

Deathstalker Coda 3 3: Journey's End. Simon R. Green. (Deathstalker Legacy Ser.: Bk. 3). 2008. audio compact disk 19.99 (978-1-59950-497-1(9)) GraphicAudio.

Deathstalker Destiny. Based on a book by Simon R. Green. (Life & Times of Owen Deathstalker Ser.: Bk. 5). 2007. 49.99 (978-1-59950-481-0(2)) GraphicAudio.

Deathstalker Destiny Box Set. Based on a novel by Simon R. Green. (Life & Times of Owen Deathstalker Ser.). 2007. audio compact disk 74.99 (978-1-59950-366-0(2)) GraphicAudio.

Deathstalker Destiny 1: Blood Debt. Simon R. Green. (Running Time: 10800 sec.). (Deathstalker Ser.). 2007. audio compact disk 19.99 (978-1-59950-129-1(5)) GraphicAudio.

Deathstalker Destiny 2: Burning Bridges. 2006. audio compact disk 19.99 (978-1-59950-137-6(6)) GraphicAudio.

Deathstalker Destiny 3: Even Legends Die. 2006. audio compact disk 19.99 (978-1-59950-170-3(8)) GraphicAudio.

Deathstalker Destiny 4: Royal Wedding. 2006. audio compact disk 19.99 (978-1-59950-181-9(3)) GraphicAudio.

Deathstalker Destiny 5: The Last Deathstalker. 2006. audio compact disk 19.99 (978-1-59950-191-8(0)) GraphicAudio.

Deathstalker Honor. Based on a book by Simon R. Green. (Life & Times of Owen Deathstalker Ser.: Bk. 4). 2007. 49.99 (978-1-59950-480-3(4)) GraphicAudio.

Deathstalker Honor Box Set. Based on a novel by Simon R. Green. (Life & Times of Owen Deathstalker Ser.: Bk. 4). 2007. audio compact disk 74.99 (978-1-59950-365-3(4)) GraphicAudio.

Deathstalker Honor 1: Charnel House. 2005. audio compact disk 19.99 (978-1-59950-012-6(4)) GraphicAudio.

Deathstalker Honor 2: Enemies of Humanity. 2005. audio compact disk 19.99 (978-1-59950-018-8(3)) GraphicAudio.

Deathstalker Honor 3: Welcome to New Haden. 2005. audio compact disk 19.99 (978-1-59950-006-5(X)) GraphicAudio.

Deathstalker Honor 4: No More Secrets. 2005. audio compact disk 19.99 (978-1-59950-075-1(2)) GraphicAudio.

Deathstalker Honor 5: Cry Havoc. 2006. audio compact disk 19.99 (978-1-59950-091-1(4)) GraphicAudio.

Deathstalker Honor 6: The Red Brain. Simon R. Green. Narrated by Richard Rohan. (Running Time: 14400 sec.). (Deathstalker Ser.). 2006. audio compact disk 19.99 (978-1-59950-111-6(2)) GraphicAudio.

Deathstalker Legacy: MP3 CD Long Haul Boxset. Based on a book by Simon R. Green. (Deathstalker Legacy Ser.). 2007. 49.99 (978-1-59950-482-7(0)) GraphicAudio.

Deathstalker Legacy 2. Simon R. Green. (Deathstalker Legacy Ser.: Bk. 1). 2007. 19.99 (978-1-59950-295-3(X)) GraphicAudio.

Deathstalker Legacy Box Set. Based on a novel by Simon R. Green. (Deathstalker Legacy Ser.). 2007. audio compact disk 74.99 (978-1-59950-367-7(0)) GraphicAudio.

Deathstalker Legacy 1: The Ceremony of Innocence. 2007. audio compact disk 19.99 (978-1-59950-291-5(7)) GraphicAudio.

Deathstalker Legacy 2: Winning Friends & Influencing People. 2007. audio compact disk 19.99 (978-1-59950-292-2(5)) GraphicAudio.

Deathstalker Legacy 3: All Kinds of Betrayal. 2007. (978-1-59950-309-7(3)); audio compact disk 19.99 (978-1-59950-293-9(3)) GraphicAudio.

Deathstalker Legacy 4: Questionable Choices. 2007. audio compact disk 19.99 (978-1-59950-312-7(3)) GraphicAudio.

Deathstalker Legacy 5: Terror in the Night. 2007. audio compact disk 19.99 (978-1-59950-321-9(2)) GraphicAudio.

Deathstalker Legacy 6: The Better Part of Valor. 2007. audio compact disk 19.99 (978-1-59950-329-5(8)) GraphicAudio.

Deathstalker Rebellion Episode 1: Opening Gambit. abr. ed. Simon R. Green. Narrated by Nanette Savard. 2 cass. (Running Time: 3 hrs.). (Life & Times of Owen Deathstalker Ser.: Bk. 2). 2003. 9.95 (978-1-931953-23-8(6)) Listen & Live.
Only Owen Deathstalker-outlawed, with a price on his head and a mighty warrior lineage in his veins-had the courage to take up sword and energy gun against Queen Lionstone XIV. Now as he gathers his unlikely force-the legendary washed-up hero Jack Random, the beautiful pirate Hazel d'Arc, the original Deathstalker long since presumed dead, and the alien Hadenmen-the eyes of the downtrodden are upon his, while the freedom of a galaxy awaits!.

Deathstalker Rebellion Episode 3: Meeting of Minds. abr. ed. Simon R. Green. Narrated by Richard Rohan & Nanette Savard. 2 cass. (Running Time: 3 hrs.). (Life & Times of Owen Deathstalker Ser.: Bk. 2). 2003. 9.95 (978-1-931953-25-2(2)) Listen & Live.

Deathstalker Rebellion Episode 4: Voices in the Dark. abr. ed. Simon R. Green. Narrated by Richard Rohan & Nanette Savard. 2 cass. (Running Time: 3 hrs.). (Life & Times of Owen Deathstalker Ser.: Bk. 2). 2003. 9.95 (978-1-931953-26-9(0)) Listen & Live.

Deathstalker Rebellion Episode 5: The Circles of Hell. abr. ed. Simon R. Green. Narrated by Richard Rohan & Nanette Savard. 2 cass. (Running Time: 3 hrs.). (Life & Times of Owen Deathstalker Ser.: Bk. 2). 2003. 9.95 (978-1-931953-24-5(4)) Listen & Live.
Only Owen Deathstalker-outlawed, with a price on his head and a mighty warrior lineage in his veins-had the courage to take up sword and energy gun against Queen Lionstone XIV. Now as he gathers his unlikely force-the legendary washed-up hero Jack Random, the beautiful pirate Hazel d'Arc, the original Deathstalker long since presumed dead, and the alien Hadenmen-the eyes of the downtrodden are upon him?while the freedom of a galaxy awaits!.

Deathstalker Rebellion Episode 5: The Circles of Hell. abr. ed. Simon R. Green. Narrated by Richard Rohan & Nanette Savard. 2 cass. (Running Time: 3 hrs.). (Life & Times of Owen Deathstalker Ser.: Bk. 2). 2003. 9.95 (978-1-931953-27-6(9)) Listen & Live.
Only Owen Deathstalker-outlawed, with a price on his head and a mighty warrior lineage in his veins-had the courage to take up sword and energy gun against Queen Lionstone XIV. Now as he gathers his unlikely force-the legendary washed-up hero Jack Random, the beautiful pirate Hazel d'Arc, the original Deathstalker long since presumed dead, and the alien Hadenmen-the eyes of the downtrodden are upon him while the freedom of a galaxy awaits.

Deathstalker Return 1: In the Footsteps of Legends. 2007. audio compact disk 19.99 (978-1-59950-338-7(7)) GraphicAudio.

Deathstalker Return 2: Brotherly Love & My Red Heaven. 2007. audio compact disk 19.99 (978-1-59950-347-9(6)) GraphicAudio.

Deathstalker Return 3: Changing Tides. 2007. audio compact disk 19.99 (978-1-59950-356-1(5)) GraphicAudio.

Deathstalker Return 4 4: Predators & Victims. Based on a novel by Simon R. Green. (Deathstalker Legacy Ser.: Bk. 2). 2007. audio compact disk 19.99 (978-1-59950-374-5(3)) GraphicAudio.

Deathstalker Return 5 5: The Terrible Truth. Based on a novel by Simon R. Green. (Deathstalker Legacy Ser.: Bk. 2). 2007. audio compact disk 19.99 (978-1-59950-389-9(1)) GraphicAudio.

Deathstalker War Episode 1. abr. ed. 2 cass. (Running Time: 3 hrs.). (Deathstalker War Ser.). 2003. 9.95 (978-1-931953-49-8(X)) Listen & Live.

Deathstalker War Episode 2. abr. ed. 2 cass. (Running Time: 3 hrs.). (Deathstalker War Ser.). 2003. 9.95 (978-1-931953-50-4(3)) Listen & Live.

Deathstalker War Episode 3. abr. ed. 2 cass. (Running Time: 3 hrs.). (Deathstalker War Ser.). 2003. 9.95 (978-1-931953-51-1(1)) Listen & Live.

Deathstalker War Episode 4. abr. ed. 2 cass. (Running Time: 3 hrs.). (Deathstalker War Ser.). 2003. 9.95 (978-1-931953-52-8(X)) Listen & Live.

Deathstalker War Episode 5. abr. ed. 2 cass. (Running Time: 3 hrs.). (Deathstalker War Ser.). 2003. 9.95 (978-1-931953-53-5(8)) Listen & Live.

Deathwatch. Robb White. Read by Ed Sala. 4 cass. (Running Time: 5 hrs. 15 mins.). (YA). (gr. 9 up). 1999. pap. bk. & stu. ed. 48.24 (978-0-7887-3082-5(7), 40896) Recorded Bks.
Because Ben will earn enough to pay next year's expenses for college, he reluctantly guides a rich businessman, Madec, into the mountains to hunt for bighorn sheep. Now they are miles from nowhere, Madec is armed with a .358 Magnum & Ben is his prey.

Deathwatch. unabr. ed. Robb White. Narrated by Ed Sala. 4 pieces. (Running Time: 5 hrs. 15 mins.). (gr. 9 up). 1999. 35.00 (978-0-7887-3081-8(9), 95796E7) Recorded Bks.

Deathwatch. unabr. collector's ed. Adam Hall. Read by Carl Schmidt. 7 cass. (Running Time: 7 hrs.). 1987. 42.00 (978-0-7366-1057-5(X), 1984) Books on Tape.
Political & technological spy thriller concerning the development of secret weapons by the U. S. S. R. & the U. S. (Originally recorded for radio; slightly abridged).

Deathwatch, Class set. Robb White. Read by Ed Sala. 4 cass. (Running Time: 5 hrs. 15 mins.). (YA). (gr. 9 up). 1999. 105.70 (978-0-7887-3083-2(5), 46859) Recorded Bks.
Because Ben will earn enough to pay next year's expenses for college, he reluctantly guides a rich businessman, Madec, into the mountains to hunt for bighorn sheep. Now they are miles from nowhere, Madec is armed with a .358 Magnum & Ben is his prey.

Deathwind. unabr. ed. G. M. Farley. Read by Jack Sondericker. 3 cass. (Running Time: 3 hrs.). Dramatization. 1992. 21.95 (978-1-55686-420-9(5), 420) Books in Motion.
The Indians of the Ohio frontier called him Le Vent de la Morte, the Wind of Death. The white settlers called him Lewis Wetzel. He was the most feared of all the bordermen from Ft. Dearborn to the Kentucky settlements. But now he lay bound & helpless in Walking Bear's village.

***Deb Nelson Gourley Presents: Kings of Norway.** Anders Kvåle Rue. Illus. by Anders Kvåle Rue. Tr. by Skurdall Jim. Kari Grønningsæter. (ENG & NOB.). (YA). 2006. bk. 39.95 (978-0-9760541-2-2(4)) Astri My Astri.

Debarquement en Normandie. 1 cass. (FRE.). 1995. 16.95 (1785-MU) Olivia & Hill.
Dedicated to General Eisenhower, this cassette groups a series of oral documents on D-Day: the preparations, the landings & victory. Many participants recall the day.

Debate Between Luce & William Kunstler. unabr. ed. Phillip A. Luce. 1 cass. (Running Time: 1 hr. 47 min.). 12.95 (169) J Norton Pubs.

Debate: Eric Garris vs. Prof. Kent: Pros & Cons- Sen. John Briggs Initiative. (Running Time: 90 min.). (Remanent Tapes). 1978. 10.00 (R304) Freeland Pr.

Debate: George Smith vs. Jeffrey Johnson: Libertarianism vs. Conservatism: The Future of Victimless Crimes & Religion. (Running Time: 60 min.). (Cypress College). 1980. 9.00 (F103) Freeland Pr.
Smith, an atheist, advocates voluntaryism, in contrast to Johnson who would enforce moral obligation & an instilled sense of duty (Johnson is a theist).

Debate: George Smith vs. Les Antman: Libertarianism vs. Electoral Politics. 2 cass. (Running Time: 2 hrs.). (Remanent Tapes). 1983. 18.00 (R305A & B) Freeland Pr.
Smith argues that all political action leads to violation of individual rights & invasive acts. Antman rebuts Smith by saying that political libertarianism is the only way to educate the public.

Debate: George Smith vs. Thomas Bartman: Should Public Education Be Abolished? (Running Time: 2 hrs. 30 min.). (Cal State Univ., Long Beach). 1982. 19.00 (F139A & B) Freeland Pr.
Smith presents himself as a thorough researcher while Bartman comes across as a smooth politician who never does address the issue. Controversial, especially with the audience.

Debate: Jeffrey Rogers Hummel & Dr. David Friedman: Should America Have a Military Force for Defense? 2 cass. (Running Time: 2 hrs.). (Cal State Univ., Long Beach). 1982. 18.00 (F141A & B) Freeland Pr.

Debate: Lowell Ponte vs. Prof. John Wiener: Libertarianism or Marxism: Which Direction for the Future? (Running Time: 60 min.). (Cypress College). 1980. 9.00 (F102) Freeland Pr.
Shows the deep chasm between the two philosophies. Wiener contends that there are no isolated individuals, only classes & social structures. Ponte, a free-lance writer, argues that theoretical Marxism leads only to dictatorship.

Debate: Samuel E. Konkin III vs. Manuel Klausner: Counter-Economics or Political Action: Which Direction for the Future? (Running Time: 60 min.). (Cypress College). 1980. 7.00 (F110) Freeland Pr.
Konkin, an advocate of counter-economics, proposes a "do nothing" approach when it comes to registering for anything; Klausner counters with a defense for political action.

Debate: Wendy McElroy vs. Jeff Hummel: Non-Voting vs. Electoral Politics. 2 cass. (Running Time: 2 hrs.). (Remanent Tapes). 1983. 18.00 (R306A & B) Freeland Pr.
Hummel states that political voting or running for office is not unlibertarian for strategic reasons, & that not all members of the state are liable for their governments' actions. McElroy Belives that government & its members (bureacrats, soldiers, elected officials, etc.) can be held responsible, even if they did not engage in aggressive acts.

Debate with the Social Workers Party. unabr. ed. Roy Childs & John Hospers. 2 cass. (Running Time: 2 hrs. 12 min.). 19.90 (186) J Norton Pubs.

Debbie Friedman at Carnegie Hall, Set. abr. ed. Perf. by Debbie Friedman. Interview with Donna Lander. 2 cass. (Running Time: 1 hr., 27 min.). (YA). 1996. 19.95 (978-1-890161-23-1(3), SWP612C); audio compact disk 24.95 (978-1-890161-24-8(1), SWP612CD) Sounds Write.
Twenty-two selections from Debbie's 25th Anniversary Concert recorded live on January 7, 1996.

Debbie Friedman Live at the Del. abr. ed. Perf. by Debbie Friedman. Interview with Donna Lander. 1 cass., 1 CD. (Running Time: 1 hr. 03 min.). 1990. audio compact disk 15.95 CD. (978-1-890161-12-5(8), SWP607CD) Sounds Write.
Concert performance recorded live at the Hotel Del Coronado, San Diego, CA on June 3, 1990. Debbie at her best - performing, teaching & interacting with a dynamic audience.

Debbie Friedman Live at the Del. abr. ed. Perf. by Debbie Friedman. Interview with Donna Lander. 1 cass., 1 CD. (Running Time: 1 hr. 03 min.). (J). 1990. 12.95 (978-1-890161-11-8(X), SWP607C) Sounds Write.

Debbie Go Home see Tales from a Troubled Land

Debbie Macomber: Susannah's Garden, Back on Blossom Street, Twenty Wishes. abr. ed. Debbie Macomber. (Running Time: 17 hrs.). 2009. audio compact disk 34.99 (978-1-4418-0148-7(0), 9781441801487, BACD) Brilliance Audio.

***Debbie's dishes on Disc.** Debbie Briske. 2010. audio compact disk 24.99 (978-0-578-05408-7(6)) Debbies Dishes.

Debbie's Ditties Vol. 4: Come Dance S'More. Prod. by Rainbows within Reach Staff. 1 CD. (Running Time: 1 hr.). (J). 2004. audio compact disk 15.95 (978-0-9705987-3-8(4)) Rainbows.

Debbie's Ditties 3: At the Library. unabr. ed. 1 CD. (Running Time: 45 mins.). 2002. audio compact disk 15.95 (978-0-9705987-2-1(6)) Rainbows.

Debbie's Ditties 5: Jump, Jam, Jive. Debbie Clement. 1 CD. (Running Time: 55 mins.). (J). (ps-3). 2007. audio compact disk 15.95 (978-0-9705987-6-9(9)) Rainbows.

Debbie's Ditties 6: The Handwriting Mix. Debbie Clement. 1 CD. (Running Time: 40 mins.). (J). (ps-1). 2008. audio compact disk 15.95 (978-0-9705987-7-6(7)) Rainbows.

Debido a Jesus see Because of Jesus

Debora: Una Mujer Admirable: Serie Heroes de la Fe. 2000. (978-1-57697-842-9(7)) Untd Bible Amrcas Svce.

Deborah Digges. unabr. ed. Deborah Digges. 1 cass. (Running Time: 29 min.). (New Letters on the Air Ser.). 1992. 10.00 (032092) New Letters.
Digges talks about her book, "Fugitive Spring," a memoir of life in a midwestern immigrant family.

Deborah Fatow: Submerged. Perf. by Deborah Fatow. 1 cass., 1 Cd. 1998. 10.98 (978-0-7601-2149-8(4)); audio compact disk 15.98 CD. (978-0-7601-2150-4(8)) Provident Mus Dist.
Songs with passion about the issues affecting her generation, like trust, forgivemess, & spiritual emptiness.

***Deborah Whitney of Shady Flat.** Katie Willmarth Green. Based on a novel by Katie Willmarth Green. Read by Colleen Madden. Prod. by Pineneedle Press. Engineer Mike Schmidt. Des. by Kristin Mitchell Design. (Running Time: 504 minutes). (ENG.). (YA). 2010. audio compact disk 39.95 (978-0-9828023-1-1(5)) MYID_Q_KRISTIN.

Debra Beckers Meditation CD: Meditation CD. Debra Becker. 2008. audio compact disk 14.99 (978-1-4276-2982-1(X)) AardGP.

Debra's Dog: Audiocassette. (gr. k-3). 10.00 (978-0-7635-6363-9(3)) Rigby Educ.

Debriefing: A Novel of Deception. unabr. ed. Robert Littell. 2004. 29.95 (978-1-59007-598-2(6)); audio compact disk 49.95 (978-1-59007-599-9(4)) Pub: New Millenn Enter. Dist(s): PerseuPGW

***Debt.** Roberta Kray. 2010. cass. & cass. 89.95 (978-1-84652-824-8(0)); audio compact disk & audio compact disk 99.95 (978-1-84652-825-5(9)) Pub: Magna Story GBR. Dist(s): Ulverscroft US

***Debt Crisis Of 2012: How to Prepare & Prosper.** unabr. ed. Harry S. Dent, Jr. (Running Time: 2 hrs. 11 mins. 0 sec.). (ENG.). 2011. audio compact disk 24.95 (978-1-59859-914-5(3)) Oasis Audio.

Debt Cures: They Don't Want You to Know About. unabr. ed. Kevin Trudeau. Narrated by Kevin Trudeau. (Running Time: 36600 sec.). (ENG.). 2008. audio compact disk 29.95 (978-1-60283-470-5(9)) Pub: AudioGO. Dist(s): Perseus Dist

***Debt-Free for Life: The Finish Rich Plan for Financial Independence.** unabr. ed. David Bach. (ENG.). 2010. audio compact disk & audio compact disk 30.00 (978-0-7393-6887-9(7), Random AudioBks) Pub: Random Audio Pubg. Dist(s): Random

Debt-Free In 2003. Bill Winston. 4 cass. (Running Time: 3hr.08min.). (C). 2003. 20.00 (978-1-931289-20-7(4)) Pub: B Winston Min. Dist(s): Anchor Distributors

***Debt-Free Living: Eliminating Debt in a New Economy.** unabr. ed. Larry Burkett. Narrated by Wayne Shepherd. (Running Time: 5 hrs. 6 mins. 14 sec.). (ENG.). 2010. 16.09 (978-1-60814-669-7(3)); audio compact disk 22.99 (978-1-59859-718-9(3)) Oasis Audio.

***Debt of Bones.** unabr. ed. Terry Goodkind. Read by Sam Tsoutsouvas. (Running Time: 3 hrs.). (Sword of Truth Ser.). 2010. 19.99 (978-1-4418-8671-2(0), 9781441886712, Brilliance MP3); 39.97 (978-1-4418-8672-9(9), 9781441886729, Brlnc Audio MP3 Lib); 19.99 (978-1-4418-8673-6(7), 9781441886736, BAD); 39.97 (978-1-4418-8674-3(5), 9781441886743, BADLE); audio compact disk 74.97 (978-1-4418-8670-5(2), 9781441886705, BriAudCD Unabrid); audio compact disk 19.99 (978-1-4418-8669-9(9), 9781441886699, Bril Audio CD Unabri) Brilliance Audio.

Debt of Dishonour. unabr. ed. Robert Goddard. Read by Frederick Davidson. 13 cass. (Running Time: 19 hrs. 30 mins.). 1995. 85.95 (978-0-7861-0820-6(7), 1643) Blckstn Audio.
The estate at Clouds Frome was architect Geoffrey Staddon's greatest achievement. It was also the site of his greatest dishonour - for it was there he met Consuela Caswell, the beautiful Brazilian wife of Clouds Frome's proprietor. He loved Consuela immediately, fiercely, recklessly. In retum, she risked everything for him - until he betrayed her for his own ambitious dreams of glory.

***Debt of Honor.** Ray Hogan. 2009. (978-1-60136-432-6(6)) Audio Holding.

Debt of Honor. Ray Hogan. (Running Time: 0 hr. 36 mins.). 1998. 10.95 (978-1-60083-482-0(5)) Iofy Corp.

Debt of Honor. abr. ed. Tom Clancy. Read by John Rubinstein. 4 CDs. (Running Time: 6 hrs.). (Tom Clancy Ser.). (ENG.). 1999. audio compact disk 30.00 (978-0-375-40700-0(6)) Pub: Random Audio Pubg. Dist(s): Random

Debt of Honor, Pt. 1. unabr. ed. Tom Clancy. Read by John MacDonald. 13 cass. (Running Time: 19 hrs. 30 min.). 1994. 104.00 (978-0-7366-2862-4(2), 3569-A) Books on Tape.
Jack Ryan, the new president's National Security Adviser, sees the problems of peace fully as complex as those of war. Enemies have become friends, friends enemies & even the form of conflict has changed. And when one of the new enemies prepares to strike American territory, Ryan must prepare an untested president to meet the challenge.

Debt of Honor, Pt. 2. unabr. ed. Tom Clancy. Read by John MacDonald. 13 cass. (Running Time: 19 hrs. 30 mins.). 1994. 104.00 (978-0-7366-2863-1(0), 3569-B) Books on Tape.

Debt of Honor, Set. abr. ed. Tom Clancy. Read by John Rubinstein. 4 cass. (Running Time: 6 hrs.). 1994. 29.95 (Random AudioBks) Random Audio Pubg.

Debt of Love: Romans 13:1-7. Ed Young. 1997. 4.95 (978-0-7417-2140-2(6), 1140) Win Walk.

Debt-Proof Your Kids. abr. ed. Mary Hunt. Read by Mary Hunt. 2 cass. (Running Time: 3 hrs.). 15.99 Set. (978-0-8054-1825-5(3)) BH Pubng Grp.
Shares how parents can help children become responsible money managers. It's a simple plan that will give children the financial confidence they need to live debt-free in the real world.

Debt to Pleasure. abr. ed. John Lanchester. Read by Nick Ullett. 2 cass. (Running Time: 3 hrs.). 1996. 17.95 (978-1-57453-025-4(9), 330093) Audio Lit.

Debt to Pleasure. unabr. collector's ed. John Lanchester. Read by David Case. 8 cass. (Running Time: 8 hrs.). 1997. 48.00 (978-0-7366-3724-4(9), 4405) Books on Tape.
Tarquin Winot, an Englishman of indeterminate age & very determined tastes of food.

***Debunkery.** unabr. ed. Ken Fisher. (ENG.). 2010. (978-0-06-206936-8(5)) HarperCollins Pubs.

Debunkery: Learn It, Do It, & Profit from It - Seeing Through Wall Street's Money-Killing Myths. abr. unabr. ed. Kenneth L. Fisher. (ENG.). 2010. (978-0-06-167257-6(2), Harper Audio) HarperCollins Pubs.

Debunking Defenders of the State. unabr. ed. Frank Chodorov. 1 cass. (Running Time: 57 min.). 12.95 (197) J Norton Pubs.

Debussey: "Palleas et Melisande" Read by David Timson. audio compact disk 8.99 (978-1-84379-099-0(8), 8.558172) NaxMulti GBR.

Debutante Divorcee. abr. unabr. ed. Plum Sykes. Read by Sonya Walger. (Running Time: 25200 sec.). 2007. audio compact disk 14.95 (978-1-4013-8735-8(7), Hyperion Audio) Pub: Hyperion. Dist(s): HarperCollins Pubs

Debutantes. Charlotte Bingham. (Isis Cassettes Ser.). (J). 1995. 104.95 (978-0-7531-0053-0(3)) Pub: ISIS Lrg Prnt GBR. Dist(s): Ulverscroft US

Débuts Pt. 1: An Introduction to French. H. Jay Siskin et al. (C). 2002. stu. ed. 24.38 (978-0-07-249930-8(3), 9780072499308, Mc-H Human Soc) Pub: McGrw-H Hghr Educ. Dist(s): McGraw

Decada. unabr. ed. René González. (SPA.). 1998. 9.99 (978-0-8297-2783-8(3)) Pub: Vida Pubs. Dist(s): Zondervan

Decada. unabr. ed. Rene Gonzalez. 1 CD. 1998. 14.99 (978-0-8297-2784-5(1)) Zondervan.

Decameron. abr. ed. Giovanni Boccaccio. Read by Stephen Thorne et al. 4 CDs. (Running Time: 16873 sec.). (Classic Literature with Classical Music Ser.). 2006. audio compact disk 28.98 (978-962-634-380-7(X), Naxos AudioBooks) Naxos.

Decameron, Bk. I. Giovanni Boccaccio. Read by Flo Gibson. 10 cass. (Running Time: 12 hrs. 30 min.). 1996. 44.95 (978-1-55685-425-5(0)) Audio Bk Con.
This Middle-English flavored translation contains fifty stories told by seven ladies & three young gentlemen who leave Florence during the plague to reside on a palatial estate near Fiesole. The tales are mainly concerned with love affairs, unfaithfulness & lust, often involving members of the clergy, which may amuse or raise the eyebrows.

Decameron, Pt. 1. unabr. ed. Giovanni Boccaccio. Read by Frederick Davidson. 11 cass. (Running Time: 20 hrs. 30 mins.). 1999. 76.95 (978-0-7861-1657-7(9), 2485A,B) Blckstn Audio.
This collection of tales is set in 1348, the year of the Black Death. Florence is a dying, corrupt city, described plainly in all of its horrors. Seven ladies & three gentlemen meet in a church & decide to escape from the charnel house of reality.

Decameron, Pt. 2. unabr. ed. Giovanni Boccaccio. Read by Frederick Davidson. 10 cass. (Running Time: 20 hrs. 30 mins.). 1999. 69.95 (978-0-7861-1708-6(7), 2485A,B) Blckstn Audio.

Decameron: Or Ten Days' Entertainment. unabr. ed. Giovanni Boccaccio. Read by Frederick Davidson. (Running Time: 30 hrs. 0 mins.). (ENG.). 2009. 44.95 (978-1-4332-9963-6(1)); audio compact disk 160.00 (978-1-4332-9960-5(7)) Blckstn Audio.

Decameron - Selecciones. unabr. ed. Giovanni Boccaccio. 3 CDs.Tr. of Decameron - Selections. (SPA.). 2002. audio compact disk 17.00 (978-958-9494-77-6(3)) YoYoMusic.

Decameron - Selections see Decameron - Selecciones

Decameron - Selections. Giovanni Boccaccio. Read by Laura García. (Running Time: 3 hrs.). 2002. 16.95 (978-1-60083-205-5(9), Audiofy Corp) Iofy Corp.

Decamerone - Ferondo in Purgatorio, Il Canto dell'Usignuolo. Giovanni Boccaccio. Read by Francesco Noli. 1 cass. (Running Time: 1 hr.). (ITA.). 1996. bk. 17.50 (978-1-58085-456-6(7)) Interlingua VA.
Includes dual Italian-English transcription. The combination of written text & clarity & pace of diction will open the door for intermediate & advanced students to genuine comprehension & the use of literary texts for advancement in rapid understanding of written & oral language materials. The audio text plus written text concept makes foreign languages accessible to a much wider range of students than books alone.

Decapodos de Chile: Hybrid Version. M. A. Retamal. (World Biodiversity Database Ser.). (SPA.). 2000. audio compact disk 160.00 (978-3-540-14672-8(5)) Spri.

***Deceit.** Brandilyn Collins. (Running Time: 8 hrs. 18 mins. 38 sec.). (ENG.). 2010. 14.99 (978-0-310-77292-7(3)) Zondervan.

Deceit. abr. ed. James Siegel. Read by Dylan Baker. (Running Time: 6 hrs.). (ENG.). 2006. 14.98 (978-1-59483-529-2(2)) Pub: Hachet Audio. Dist(s): HachBkGrp

Deceit. abr. ed. James Siegel. Read by Dylan Baker. (Running Time: 6 hrs.). (ENG.). 2009. 44.98 (978-1-60788-137-7(3)) Pub: Hachet Audio. Dist(s): HachBkGrp

Deceit. unabr. ed. Clare Francis. Read by Frances Tomelty. 12 cass. (Running Time: 12 hrs.). 1994. 96.95 Set. (978-0-7451-4298-2(2), CAB 981) AudioGO.
Ellen's husband Harry has been missing at sea, presumed dead. It's at his memorial service that she learns of the scandals surrounding his life. As Ellen struggles to salvage memories of Harry, Moreland, an old colleague of Harry's, enters her life & tries to uncover the truth about his death. But it's a truth that Ellen would soon prefer to be left undisturbed.

Deceit: Hos. 10:1-5. Ed Young. 1988. 4.95 (978-0-7417-1660-6(7), 660) Win Walk.

***Deceived.** James Scott Bell. (Running Time: 9 hrs. 33 mins. 13 sec.). (ENG.). 2009. 14.99 (978-0-310-30283-4(8)) Zondervan.

Deceived by Flight. Perf. by John Thaw. 2 cass. (Running Time: 1 hr. 50 min.). (Inspector Morse Mystery Ser.). 1998. 14.95 enhanced audiotrack. (978-1-56938-257-8(3), AMP-2573) Acorn Inc.
When an alumni cricket team gathers for an annual match, one member meets his untimely death before the first ball is even bowled. Inspector Morse proves that the players have more than cricket on their minds.

Deceiver. unabr. ed. Frederick Forsyth. Read by David Case. 13 cass. (Running Time: 19 hrs. 30 min.). 1991. 104.00 (978-0-7366-2044-4(3), 2858) Books on Tape.
Sam McCready serves Britain as Chief of Covert Operations for the Secret Intelligence Service. He's competent, dedicated, in his prime. Why then this push to get him out.

Deceivers. unabr. ed. John Masters. Narrated by Patrick Tull. 8 cass. (Running Time: 11 hrs.). 1990. 70.00 (978-1-55690-138-6(0), 90084E7) Recorded Bks.
William Savage, British representative in Bhadora, India in 1825, faces the mysterious & deadly sect of thugs in trying to impose order on the community.

December Gifts: SoundTrax. Jay Althouse. Composed by Sally K. Albrecht. (ENG.). 2003. audio compact disk 39.95 (978-0-7390-3119-3(8)) Alfred Pub.

December Holidays in the United States, Set. unabr. ed. Maria Latona. Ed. by Marybeth Hageman. 3 cass. (English for You! Ser.). 1998. pap. bk. & stu. ed. 39.95 (48002) Recorded Bks.
ESL students will understand & enjoy celebrations along with their native speaker friends. Student texts contain key vocabulary & a wide range of exercises including: conversation practice, comprehension, discussion, writing, grammar, & critical thinking.

December Nights, December Lights, Listening. Jay Althouse & Lois Brownsey. Composed by Sally K. Albrecht. 1 CD. (Running Time: 1 hr. 30 mins.). (ENG.). 2000. audio compact disk 16.95 (978-0-7390-0459-3(X), 19241) Alfred Pub.

December Nights, December Lights, SoundTrax. Jay Althouse & Lois Brownsey. Composed by Sally K. Albrecht. 1 CD. (Running Time: 1 hr. 30

mins.). (ENG.). 2000. audio compact disk 59.95 (978-0-7390-0458-6(1), 19240) Alfred Pub.

December Secrets. unabr. ed. Patricia Reilly Giff. 1 cass. (Running Time: 1 hr. 14 mins.). (Follow the Reader Ser.). (J). (gr. 1-2). 1984. pap. bk. 17.00 incl. bk. & guide. (978-0-8072-0096-4(4), FTR103SP, Listening Lib) Random Audio Pubg.
Follow the kids in Ms. Rooney's second-grade class as they learn & grow through an entire school year filled with fun & surprises.

December Stillness. unabr. ed. Mary Downing Hahn. Narrated by Julie Dretzin. 4 pieces. (Running Time: 4 hrs. 45 mins.). (gr. 6 up). 1998. 37.00 (978-0-7887-2134-2(8), 95443E7) Recorded Bks.
Fifteen-year-old Kelly McAllister decides to interview Mr. Weems, a homeless Vietnam vet, for a social studies paper. But getting to know him isn't so easy.

December Stillness, Class Set. unabr. ed. Mary Downing Hahn. Read by Julie Dretzin. 4 cass., 10 bks. (Running Time: 4 hrs. 45 min.). (YA). 1998. bk. 102.80 (978-0-7887-2561-6(0), 46731) Recorded Bks.

December Stillness, Homework Set. unabr. ed. Mary Downing Hahn. Read by Julie Dretzin. 4 cass. (Running Time: 4 hrs. 45 min.). (YA). (gr. 7). 1998. bk. 49.75 (978-0-7887-2136-6(4), 40710) Recorded Bks.

December 6. abr. ed. Martin Cruz Smith. Read by John Slattery. (Running Time: 60 hrs. 0 mins. 0 sec.). (ENG.). 2008. audio compact disk 14.99 (978-0-7435-7614-7(4)) Pub: S&S Audio. Dist(s): S and S Inc

December 6. unabr. ed. Martin Cruz Smith. Read by L. J. Ganser. 8 vols. (Running Time: 12 hrs.). 2002. bk. 69.95 (978-0-7927-2714-9(2), CSL 500, Chivers Sound Lib); audio compact disk 94.95 (978-0-7927-2740-8(1), SLD 500, Chivers Sound Lib); audio compact disk 49.95 (978-0-7927-2765-1(7), CMP 500, Chivers Child Audio) AudioGO.
As seen through the eyes of a U.S. spy hours before the Japanese sneak attack, December 6. With an exotic locale and colorful, complex characters, it is a taut and suspenseful tale about a young American agent who infiltrates Japanese Intelligence, and uncovers knowledge about the imminent strike. Working against time, he must warn Washington and escape with his family before it's too late.

***Decenas y unidades Audio CD.** April Barth. Adapted by Benchmark Education Co., LLC. (Content Connections Ser.). (SPA.). (J). 2010. audio compact disk 10.00 (978-1-61672-190-9(1)) Benchmark Educ.

Decently & in Order. John Arnott. 1 cass. 1996. 7.00 (978-0-7684-0004-5(X)) Destiny Image Pubs.

Deception. Marion Chesney. Narrated by Jill Tanner. 4 cass. (Running Time: 6 hrs.). (Daughters of Mannerling Ser.: Vol. 3). 39.00 (978-1-4025-0970-4(7)) Recorded Bks.

Deception. Marion Chesney. Narrated by Jill Tanner. 5 CDs. (Running Time: 6 hrs. 15 mins.). (Daughters of Mannerling Ser.: Vol. 3). 1997. audio compact disk 48.00 (978-1-4025-3817-9(0)) Recorded Bks.

Deception. abr. ed. Randy C. Alcorn. Narrated by Roger Mueller. (Ollie Chandler Ser.). (ENG.). 2007. 20.99 (978-1-60814-172-2(1)); audio compact disk 29.99 (978-1-59859-148-4(7)) Oasis Audio.

Deception. abr. ed. Jonathan Kellerman. Read by John Rubinstein. (ENG.). 2010. audio compact disk 32.00 (978-0-7393-6893-0(1), Random AudioBks) Pub: Random Audio Pubg. Dist(s): Random

Deception. unabr. ed. Catherine Coulter. Read by Denica Fairman. 10 vols. (Running Time: 15 hrs.). 2000. bk. 84.95 (978-0-7927-2259-5(0), CSL 148, Chivers Sound Lib) AudioGO.
The Duke of Portsmouth offers an impecunious relative a job as his young son's nanny. What he quickly discovers is that he wants her, badly. But, Evangeline de Beauchamp is in way over her head. She has far more to cope with than a 19-year-old should, for she must play the role of an experienced widow with a man who knows women all too well.

***Deception.** unabr. ed. Jonathan Kellerman. Read by John Rubinstein. 9 CDs. 2010. audio compact disk 100.00 (978-0-307-70481-8(5), BksonTape) Pub: Random Audio Pubg. Dist(s): Random

Deception. unabr. ed. Jonathan Kellerman. Read by John Rubinstein. (ENG.). 2010. audio compact disk 45.00 (978-0-7393-6895-4(8), Random AudioBks) Pub: Random Audio Pubg. Dist(s): Random

Deception. unabr. ed. Amanda Quick, pseud. Read by Anne Flosnik. (Running Time: 12 hrs.). 2010. 39.97 (978-1-4233-8799-2(6), 9781423387992, Brlnc Audio MP3 Lib); 39.97 (978-1-4233-8801-2(1), 9781423388012, BADLE); 24.99 (978-1-4233-8798-5(8), 9781423387985, Brilliance MP3); 24.99 (978-1-4233-8800-5(3), 9781423388005, BAD); audio compact disk 82.97 (978-1-4233-8797-8(X), 9781423387978, BriAudCD Unabrid); audio compact disk 29.99 (978-1-4233-8796-1(1), 9781423387961, Bril Audio CD Unabri) Brilliance Audio.

Deception. unabr. ed. Philip Roth. Read by Susan Ericksen & David Colacci. (Running Time: 4 hrs.). 2009. 24.99 (978-1-4418-0107-4(3), 9781441801074, Brilliance MP3); 39.97 (978-1-4418-0108-1(1), 9781441801081, Brlnc Audio MP3 Lib); 24.99 (978-1-4418-0109-8(X), 9781441801098, BAD); 39.97 (978-1-4418-0110-4(3), 9781441801104, BADLE); audio compact disk 24.99 (978-1-4418-0105-0(7), 9781441801050, Bril Audio CD Unabri); audio compact disk 82.97 (978-1-4418-0106-7(5), 9781441801067, BriAudCD Unabrid) Brilliance Audio.

Deception. unabr. ed. Terry Teykl. 6 cass. 1996. 25.00 Set. (978-1-57892-031-0(0)) Prayer Pt Pr.
Sermon/teaching on deception.

Deception: Joshua 9:3-27. Ed Young. 1985. 4.95 (978-0-7417-1454-1(X), 454) Win Walk.

Deception of the Emerald Ring. unabr. ed. Lauren Willig. Read by Kate Reading. 11 CDs. (Running Time: 13 hrs. 45 mins.). (Pink Carnation Ser.: Bk. 3). 2006. audio compact disk 79.20 (978-1-4159-3439-5(8)) Books on Tape.

Deception on His Mind, Pt. A. unabr. ed. Elizabeth George. Read by Donada Peters. 8 cass. (Running Time: 12 hrs.). (Inspector Lynley Ser.). 1997. 64.00 (978-0-7366-3827-2(X), 4495-A) Books on Tape.
Balford-le-Nez is a dying seaside town on the coast of Essex. But, when a member of the town's small but growing Asian community is found dead, the sleepy town ignites.

Deception on His Mind, Pt. B. Elizabeth George. Read by Donada Peters. 8 cass. (Running Time: 12 hrs.). (Inspector Lynley Ser.). 1997. 64.00 (978-0-7366-3828-9(8), 4495-B) Books on Tape.

Deception Point. abr. ed. Dan Brown. Read by Boyd Gaines. 5 CDs. (Running Time: 60 hrs. 0 mins. 0 sec.). (ENG.). 2003. audio compact disk 30.00 (978-0-7435-3575-5(8), Audioworks) Pub: S&S Audio. Dist(s): S and S Inc
A shocking scientific discovery. A conspiracy of staggering brilliance. A thriller unlike any you've ever heard... When a NASA satellite discovers an astonishingly rare object buried deep in the Arctic ice, the floundering space agency proclaims a much-needed victory - a victory with profound implications for NASA policy and the impending presidential election. To verify the authenticity of the find, the White House calls upon the skills of intelligence analyst Rachel Sexton. Accompanied by a team of experts, including the charismatic scholar Michael Tolland, Rachel travels to the Arctic and uncovers the unthinkable: evidence of scientific trickery - a bold deception that threatens to plunge the world into controversy. But before she can warn the President, Rachel and Michael are ambushed by a deadly team of assassins. Fleeing for their lives across a desolate and lethal landscape, their only hope for survival is to discover who is behind this masterful plot. The truth, they will learn, is the most shocking deception of all.

Deception Point. abr. ed. Dan Brown. Read by Boyd Gaines. 2004. 15.95 (978-0-7435-5021-5(8)) Pub: S&S Audio. Dist(s): S and S Inc

Deception Point. abr. ed. Dan Brown. Read by Boyd Gaines. (Running Time: 60 hrs. 0 mins. 0 sec.). (ENG.). 2010. audio compact disk 14.99 (978-0-7435-9910-8(1)) Pub: S&S Audio. Dist(s): S and S Inc

Deception Point. unabr. ed. Dan Brown. Narrated by Richard Poe. 15 CDs. (Running Time: 17 hrs.). 2004. audio compact disk 119.75 (978-1-4025-7544-0(0), C2539) Recorded Bks.
In Deception Point, NASA discovers a strange meteorite buried deep in an Arctic ice field. Intelligence agent Rachel Sexton is sent to investigate this miracle find one that could change the way humans think about the universe, and put her in mortal danger.

Deception Point. unabr. ed. Dan Brown. Narrated by Richard Poe. 12 cass. Library Ed. (Running Time: 17 hrs. 15 min.). 2004. 109.75 (978-1-4025-6775-9(8), 97597) Recorded Bks.

Deception Point. unabr. ed. Dan Brown. Read by Richard Poe. 7 CDs. (Running Time: 140 hrs. 0 mins. 0 sec.). (ENG.). 2004. audio compact disk 49.95 (978-0-7435-3947-0(8), Audioworks) Pub: S&S Audio. Dist(s): S and S Inc
A shocking scientific discovery. A conspiracy of staggering brilliance. A thriller unlike any you've ever heard... When a NASA satellite discovers an astonishingly rare object buried deep in the Arctic ice, the floundering space agency proclaims a much-needed victory - a victory with profound implications for NASA policy and the impending presidential election. To verify the authenticity of the find, the White House calls upon the skills of intelligence analyst Rachel Sexton. Accompanied by a team of experts, including the charismatic scholar Michael Tolland, Rachel travels to the Arctic and uncovers the unthinkable: evidence of scientific trickery - a bold deception that threatens to plunge the world into controversy. But before she can warn the President, Rachel and Michael are ambushed by a deadly team of assassins. Fleeing for their lives across a desolate and lethal landscape, their only hope for survival is to discover who is behind this masterful plot. The truth, they will learn, is the most shocking deception of all.

Deception Point. unabr. ed. Dan Brown. Read by Richard Poe. 2004. 29.95 (978-0-7435-4018-6(2)) Pub: S&S Audio. Dist(s): S and S Inc

Deception Point. unabr. collector's ed. Dan Brown. Narrated by Richard Poe. 12 cass. (Running Time: 17 hrs. 15 min.). 2004. 44.95 (978-1-4025-6776-6(6), RG897) Recorded Bks.
NASA discovers a strange meteorite buried deep in an Arctic ice field. Intelligence agent Rachel Sexton is sent to investigate this miracle find?one that could change the way humans think about the universe, and put her in mortal danger.

Deceptions. abr. ed. Michael Weaver. Read by Joe Mantegna. 2 cass. (Running Time: 3 hrs.). 2000. 17.00 (978-1-57042-175-4(7), 4-521757) Hachet Audio.
Old demons surface when the United States Attorney General learns that the woman whose murder he had arranged through the Mafia, is, in fact, still alive. Should the woman surface & reveal what she knows about a perverse episode that turned murderous, his career - and possibly his life - are in dire jeopardy.

Deceptions. abr. ed. Michael Weaver. (ENG.). 2006. 14.98 (978-1-59483-827-9(5)) Pub: Hachet Audio. Dist(s): HachBkGrp

Deceptive Relations. unabr. ed. Annette Roome. Narrated by Juanita McMahon. 9 cass. (Running Time: 11 hrs. 30 mins.). 2000. 80.00 (978-1-84197-049-3(2), H1082E7) Recorded Bks.
Chris Martin, reporter for "The Tipping Herald" is busy investigating two apparently unconnected deaths: a suicide & a murder. But as Chris digs deeper into the evidence, connections between the two crimes become clearer & more disturbing. Now the reporter is determined to uncover the true stories behind the deaths, no matter how dangerous the quest may be.

Decide ~ Believe ~ Dream: 3 Simple Steps for Producing Life-Altering Results. Denise Hedges & Denise Hedges. 2006. audio compact disk 24.95 (978-0-9778813-0-7(X)) LifeWork Coach.

Decide Ganar. David Gonzalez.Tr. of Decide to Win. (SPA.). 2005. act. bk. ed. 15.00 (978-0-9767782-1-9(1)) Buzon del Exito.

Decide Hoy. unabr. ed. 2000. audio compact disk 11.99 (978-0-8297-3341-9(8)) Zondervan.

Decide Hoy. unabr. ed. Maranatha Singers & Zondervan Publishing Staff. (SPA.). 2000. 7.99 (978-0-8297-3340-2(X)) Pub: Vida Pubs. Dist(s): Zondervan

Decide to Win see Decide Ganar

Decider. Dick Francis. Narrated by Simon Prebble. 9 CDs. (Running Time: 10 hrs.). audio compact disk 89.00 (978-0-7887-9867-2(7)) Recorded Bks.

Decider. Dick Francis. Read by Simon Prebble. 6. (Running Time: 10 Hours). 29.95 (978-1-4025-4524-5(X)); audio compact disk 39.95 (978-1-4025-4525-2(8)) Recorded Bks.

Decider. abr. ed. Dick Francis. 2004. 10.95 (978-0-7435-4616-4(4)) Pub: S&S Audio. Dist(s): S and S Inc

Decider. unabr. ed. Dick Francis. Read by David Case. 7 cass. (Running Time: 10 hrs. 30 min.). 1994. 56.00 (978-0-7366-2771-9(5), 3491) Books on Tape.
With millions on the line, an architect-engineer-builder faces his own ruin, even death.

Decider. unabr. ed. Dick Francis. Narrated by Simon Prebble. 7 cass. (Running Time: 10 hrs.). 1994. 60.00 (978-0-7887-0022-4(7), 94221E7) Recorded Bks.
Lee Morris, architect, engineer, & part-time builder, is surprised by his special invitation to the shareholders' meeting at Stratton Park racecourse. Although he inherited his mother's eight shares in the park, he never really had the desire to be involved in racecourse politics. Now that all sides are involved in a bitter & deadly feud, it may take his influence to swing the vote - he may be the decider.

Deciding Factor: The Power of Analytics to Make Every Decision a Winner. unabr. ed. Josh Larry & Nash E. Rosenberger. Read by Scott Peterson. (Running Time: 5 hrs.). (ENG.). 2009. 24.98 (978-1-59659-417-3(9), GildAudio) Pub: Gildan Media. Dist(s): HachBkGrp

Deciding for God. Kenneth Wapnick. 2 CDs. (Running Time: 2 hrs.). 2003. audio compact disk 15.00 (978-1-59142-113-9(6), CD89) Foun Miracles.
This seminar focuses on what is entailed in deciding for God. Central to this process is the recognition that we first decided for the ego and therefore for a self embedded in a dualistic universe. To decide for God thus means deciding against this self. All difficulty in understanding and applying "A Course in Miracles" is rooted in this recognition. Jesus teaches us how to use this ego identity to decide against itself, encouraging us not to deny our bodily experience but rather to accept his forgiving interpretation of it. Thus will our misguided decisions be corrected as we follow him beyond all thought of separation to the oneness of our Identity with our loving Creator and Source.

***Deciding for God.** Kenneth Wapnick. 2010. 12.00 (978-1-59142-481-9(X)) Foun Miracles.

Decimals at Sea Audio CD: Set B. Benchmark Education Co. (Math Explorers Ser.). (J). (gr. 3-8). 2009. audio compact disk 10.00 (978-1-935441-51-9(5)) Benchmark Educ.

Decimals at the Bank Audio CD: Set B. Benchmark Education Co. (Math Explorers Ser.). (J). (gr. 3-8). 2009. audio compact disk 10.00 (978-1-935441-56-4(6)) Benchmark Educ.

Decimals at the Beach Audio CD: Set B. Benchmark Education Co. (Math Explorers Ser.). (J). (gr. 3-8). 2009. audio compact disk 10.00 (978-1-935441-54-0(X)) Benchmark Educ.

Decimals at the Farmer's Market Audio CD: Set B. Benchmark Education Co. (Math Explorers Ser.). (J). (gr. 3-8). 2009. audio compact disk 10.00 (978-1-935441-55-7(8)) Benchmark Educ.

Decimals at the Pizzeria Audio CD: Set B. Benchmark Education Co. (Math Explorers Ser.). (J). (gr. 3-8). 2009. audio compact disk 10.00 (978-1-935441-52-6(3)) Benchmark Educ.

Decimals Audio CD Set. Adapted by Benchmark Education Company Staff. (Math Explorers Ser.). (J). (gr. 3-8). 2008. audio compact disk 75.00 (978-1-60634-141-4(3)) Benchmark Educ.

Decimals in the News Audio CD: Set B. Benchmark Education Co. (Math Explorers Ser.). (J). (gr. 3-8). 2009. audio compact disk 10.00 (978-1-935441-50-2(7)) Benchmark Educ.

Decimals with Desi- Additon & Subtraction. 2000. pap. bk. (978-0-9709083-0-8(X)) Smiling Butterfly.

Deciphering Race: White Anxiety, Racial Conflict, & the Turn to Fiction in Mid-Victorian English Prose. Laura Callanan. 2005. audio compact disk 9.95 (978-0-8142-9089-7(2)) Pub: Ohio St U Pr. Dist(s): Chicago Distribution Ctr

Decision at Sundown. Barry Cord. (Running Time: 0 hr. 42 mins.). 1999. 10.95 (978-1-60083-497-4(3)) Iofy Corp.

***Decision in Sundown.** Kane Cord. 2009. (978-1-60136-433-3(4)) Audio Holding.

Decision Is Yours. Kenneth Copeland. 1 cass. 1991. 5.00 (978-0-88114-818-3(0)) K Copeland Pubns.
How to make quality decisions.

Decision Is Yours. Derek Prince. 2 cass. 11.90 Set. (127-128) Derek Prince.
True spirituality is based on decision, not emotion. Eight specific decisions we need to make.

Decision Maker. unabr. ed. John D. Arnold. Read by John D. Arnold. 1 cass. (Running Time: 90 min.). 1986. 9.95 (978-0-07-002398-7(0), TDM 0735) HarperCollins Pubs.
Offers a system for sorting things out so that innate intelligence can go to work making better decisions in everyday life, both the seemingly trivial ones that take up so much time & the important often paralyzing ones. Arnold helps the listener formulate objectives, discover alternatives & find out how to anticipate problems before they become overwhelming.

Decision Maker: "Throned Above Fate" Kenneth Wapnick. 2008. audio compact disk 15.00 (978-1-59142-341-6(4)) Foun Miracles.

Decision Maker: Throned above Fate. Kenneth Wapnick. 2008. 12.00 (978-1-59142-342-3(2)) Foun Miracles.

Decision Makers Top 10: A Leaders Legacy; Blink; The Leader of the Future 2; The Starfish & the Spider; 360 Degree Leader; Blueprint to a Billion; Break from the Pack; Creating & Dominating New Markets; The Definitive Drucker; Green to Gold. unabr. ed. James Kouzes et al. Read by Malcolm Gladwell et al. (YA). 2008. 54.99 (978-1-60514-768-0(0)) Find a World.

Decision-Making - Life Styles (T-F & J-P), Pt. I. Frank L. Natter. 1 cass. (Improving Your Personal Problem-Solving Ser.). 1989. 10.00 (978-1-878287-63-2(X), ATA-7) Type & Temperament.
Basics of Psychological Type as related to Problem-Solving; Focus on Decision-Making styles (Feeling & Thinking) & Lifestyles (Judging & Perceiving).

Decision Making & the Will of God, Set. Gregory Koukl. Featuring Garry Friesen. 4 cass. 1999. 16.95 (978-0-9673584-6-8(9)) Stand to Reason.
Greg will question much of what you understand about the "leading" of the Holy Spirit.

Decision, Not Emotion. Derek Prince. 1 cass. (B-4017) Derek Prince.

***Decision Points.** abr. ed. George W. Bush. Read by George W. Bush. 2010. audio compact disk 35.00 (978-0-307-74864-5(2), Random AudioBks) Pub: Random Audio Pubg. Dist(s): Random

Decision Time. unabr. ed. Jerry Ahern. Read by Alan Zimmerman. 4 vols. No. 4. 2002. (978-1-58807-513-0(3)) Am Pubng Inc.

Decision Time. unabr. ed. Jerry Ahern. Read by Alan Zimmerman. 3 vols. (Running Time: 4 hrs. 30 mins.). (Defender Ser.: No. 4). 2002. 22.00 (978-1-58807-024-1(7)) Am Pubng Inc.
In the streets of Americas most violent city, the radical FLNA continues a ruthless campaign against freedom. Their law and order candidate for mayor is backed by an international syndicate doing a billion dollar business in drugs and guns. Only David Holden and his Patriots have the guts and the grit to stand in their way. When the FLNA savagely attacks a member of the Special Task Force and kidnaps another, their actions are meant as a deadly warning. But for Holden and his freedom fighters, theres no turning back.

Decision Time. unabr. ed. Jerry Ahern. Read by Alan Zimmerman. 4 vols. No. 4. 2003. audio compact disk 28.00 (978-1-58807-266-5(5)); audio compact disk (978-1-58807-697-7(0)) Am Pubng Inc.

Decision to Love. unabr. ed. Perf. by Eknath Easwaran. 1 cass. (Running Time: 1 hr.). 1983. 7.95 (978-1-58638-519-4(4)) Nilgiri Pr.

Decisions. T. D. Jakes. 1 cass. 1999. 15.00 (978-1-57855-405-8(5)) T D Jakes.

Decisions. Winans, The. 1 cass., 1 CD. 7.98 (25510-4); audio compact disk 11.98 CD. (25510-2) Warner Christian.

Decisions for Health: Guide to Reading: Blue Edition. 4th ed. Holt, Rinehart and Winston Staff. 2003. audio compact disk 235.66 (978-0-03-066876-0(X)) Holt McDoug.

Decisions for Health: Guide to Reading: Blue Edition. 4th ed. Holt, Rinehart and Winston Staff. (SPA.). 2004. audio compact disk 228.80 (978-0-03-066879-1(4)) Holt McDoug.

Decisions for Health: Guide to Reading: Green Edition. 4th ed. Holt, Rinehart and Winston Staff. 2003. audio compact disk 235.66 (978-0-03-066873-9(5)) Holt McDoug.

Decisions for Health: Guide to Reading: Green Edition. 4th ed. Holt, Rinehart and Winston Staff. (SPA.). 2004. audio compact disk 228.80 (978-0-03-066877-7(8)) Holt McDoug.

Decisions for Health: Guide to Reading: Red Edition. 4th ed. Holt, Rinehart and Winston Staff. 2003. audio compact disk 235.66 (978-0-03-066874-6(3)) Holt McDoug.

Decisions for Health: Guide to Reading: Red Edition. 4th ed. Holt, Rinehart and Winston Staff. (SPA.). 2004. audio compact disk 228.80 (978-0-03-066878-4(6)) Holt McDoug.

Decisions for Health: Guided Reading Program. 5th ed. Holt, Rinehart and Winston Staff. (SPA.). 2005. audio compact disk 240.40 (978-0-03-039409-6(0)); audio compact disk 240.40 (978-0-03-039412-6(0)); audio compact disk 240.40 (978-0-03-039417-1(1)) Holt McDoug.

Decisive Action Personal Learning Course Set: How to Break Free & Leap Forward to Success. Paul R. Scheele. Read by Paul R. Scheele. 8 cass. (Running Time: 8 hrs.). 1999. pap. bk. 179.95 (978-0-925480-40-8(1), 9DCC) Learn Strategies.

Deck Discussion at Brooktree, Vol. II. Timothy Leary. 2 cass. 18.00 set. (A0064-87) Sound Photosyn.
A small relaxed gathering of psychologists & researchers allow Tim to express thoughts which answer candid questions rarely ventured in more public situations.

Deck Discussion at Brooktree Vol. 1: Psychology & Cyber-Punk. Timothy Leary. 1 cass. 9.00 (A0063-87) Sound Photosyn.
A lovely afternoon gathering.

Deck the Halls. 1 cd. audio compact disk 10.98 (978-1-57908-393-9(5), 1666) Platinm Enter.

Deck the Halls. abr. ed. Mary Higgins Clark & Carol Higgins Clark. (Regan Reilly Mystery Ser.). 2004. 15.95 (978-0-7435-4522-8(2)) Pub: S&S Audio. Dist(s): S and S Inc

Deck the Halls. unabr. ed. Mary Higgins Clark & Carol Higgins Clark. Read by Carol Higgins Clark. Intro. by Mary Higgins Clark. 4 vols. (Running Time: 6 hrs.). (Regan Reilly Mystery Ser.). 2000. bk. 39.95 (978-0-7927-2446-9(1), CSL 335, Chivers Sound Lib) AudioGO.
Regan Reilly, a dynamic young sleuth, meets Alvirah Meehan, the famous lottery winner & amatuer detective. Regan is in hopes of reconnecting with her busy father, who is scheduled for a routine dentist visit. When it becomes apparent that her father is not going to make the appointment, Alvirah offers Regan a ride home. A disturbing call comes through on Regan's cell phone telling her that her father & his driver are being held for $1,000,000 ransom.

Deck the Halls. unabr. ed. Mary Higgins Clark & Carol Higgins Clark. Read by Carol Higgins Clark. Intro. by Mary Higgins Clark. 6 CDs. (Running Time: 9 hrs.). (Regan Reilly Mystery Ser.). 2001. audio compact disk 64.95 (978-0-7927-9945-0(3), SLD 096, Chivers Sound Lib) AudioGO.

Deck the Halls. unabr. ed. Mary Higgins Clark & Carol Higgins Clark. (Regan Reilly Mystery Ser.). 2004. 15.95 (978-0-7435-4617-1(2)) Pub: S&S Audio. Dist(s): S and S Inc

Declaration. unabr. ed. Gemma Malley. Read by Charlotte Parry. 7 cass. (Running Time: 10 hrs. 30 mins.). (YA). (gr. 9 up). 2007. 67.75 (978-1-4281-7276-0(9)); audio compact disk 97.75 (978-1-4281-7281-4(5)) Recorded Bks.

Declaration of Dependance: Understanding Your Attack. Voice by Eddie Long. 2007. audio compact disk 32.00 (978-1-58602-364-5(0)) Pub: E L Long. Dist(s): Anchor Distributors

Declaration of Independence. John Ridpath. 1 cass. (Running Time: 1 hr. 30 min.). 1997. 12.95 (978-1-56114-329-0(4), ER44C) Second Renaissance.
A stirring historical & philosophical discussion of this crucial document.

Declaration of Independence: A Reading. Thomas Jefferson et al. Read by Susan Stamberg et al. 1 cass. (Running Time: 9 min.). 9.95 (K0860B090, HarperThor) HarpC GBR.

Declaration of Independence! A Statement of Truth! Black Power! Reuben Beckles. Read by Reuben Beckles. Contrib. by Gregory R. Beckles. 6 cass. (Running Time: 9 hrs.). 1997. 59.95 Set, Background Music Version, incl. pap. textbk. (978-0-9657004-1-2(0)); 39.95 Set, Voice Only Version, incl. pap. textbk. (978-0-9657004-2-9(9)) Aquarian Pub Co.
Story of a young black man who came into his own during the turmoil of the sixties & found the destiny of himself & his nation! Based on a true story.

Declaration of Independence & the Constituion of the United States. unabr. ed. Read by Frank Langella & Boyd Gaines. (Running Time: 3600 sec.). (ENG.). 2007. audio compact disk 12.00 (978-0-7393-4368-5(8), Random AudioBks) Pub: Random Audio Pubg. Dist(s): Random

Declaration of Independence & the Constitution of the United States. unabr. ed. Read by Geoffrey G. Forward & Elisabeth Howard. 1 cass. (Running Time: 1 hrs. 16 min.). (J). 1987. 12.95 (978-0-944200-06-3(0)) Perfom Arts Global.
Readings of the documents.

Declaration of Independence in Translation: What It Really Means. Amie J. Leavitt. Contrib. by Miles Tagmeyer & Scott Combs. (Kids' Translations Ser.). (ENG.). (gr. 3-4). 2008. audio compact disk 17.32 (978-1-4296-3222-5(4)) CapstoneDig.

Declaration of Peace & War. unabr. ed. Warren W. Wiersbe. Read by Warren W. Wiersbe. 1 cass. (Running Time: 22 min.). 1989. 4.95 (978-0-8474-2335-4(2)) Back to Bible.
Three truths concerning the declaration of Christ's birth & their meaning in the believer's life.

Declaration of Something Mysterious: A Study of Luke 10:38-16:18. unabr. ed. Charles R. Swindoll. 9 cass. (Running Time: 8 hrs.). 1998. 44.95 (978-1-57972-309-5(8)) Insight Living.

Declarations of Faith. As told by Scarlett Bishop. 2 cass. (Running Time: 1 hr. 30 min.). 2000. 10.00 (978-0-9628301-7-4(8)) M Bishop Minis.

***Declare.** unabr. ed. Tim Powers. (Running Time: 20 hrs. 30 mins.). 2011. 44.95 (978-1-4417-5713-5(9)); 105.95 (978-1-4417-5709-8(0)); audio compact disk 34.95 (978-1-4417-5712-8(0)); audio compact disk 123.00 (978-1-4417-5710-4(4)) Blckstn Audio.

***Declaring His Power.** Muyiwa and Riversongz. (ENG.). 2007. audio compact disk 15.99 (978-5-557-90594-7(4)) Pub: Kingsway Pubns GBR. Dist(s): STL Dist NA

Declaring the Mysteries of God Vol. 4: Understanding the Gifts of Tongues & Interpretation & Prophecy. Mac Hammond. 2 cass. (Running Time: 1 hr.). (Annointing Ser.: Vol. 4). 1998. 12.00 Set. (978-1-57399-068-4(X)) Mac Hammond.

Declinations. James Garrett & Helen Garrett. 1 cass. 8.95 (125) Am Fed Astrologers.
Explanation and interpretation.

Declinations in Chart Interpretation. Dorothy Moore. 1 cass. (Running Time: 90 min.). 1984. 8.95 (239) Am Fed Astrologers.

Decline & Fall. unabr. collector's ed. Evelyn Waugh. Read by David Case. 7 cass. (Running Time: 7 hrs.). 1991. 42.00 (978-0-7366-1976-9(3), 2794) Books on Tape.
Waugh's famous first novel. Paul Pennyfeather, innocent victim of a drunken orgy, is expelled from Oxford College, which costs him a career in the church. He turns to teaching, frequently the last resort of failures, & at Llanabba Castle meets a friend, Beste-Chetwynde. But Margot, her mother, introduces him to the questionable delights of high society. Suddenly, & improbably, he is engaged to marry Margot. Just as they are about to say "I do", Scotland Yard arrives & arrests him for his involvement in Margot's white-slave trading ring.

Decline & Fall of American Language. unabr. ed. Read by Heywood Hale Broun et al. 1 cass. (Running Time: 56 min.). (Broun Radio Ser.). 12.95 (40083) J Norton Pubs.
With Edwin Newman ("Strictly Speaking") & William Morris ("American Heritage Dictionary").

Decline & Fall of Rome. Thomas F. Madden. 2008. audio compact disk 29.99 (978-1-4361-7436-7(8)) Recorded Bks.

Decline & Fall of the Roman Empire Vol. 2: The History of the Empire from A. D. 180 to A. D. 395. Edward Gibbon. Read by Philip Madoc & Neville Jason. 6 cass. (Running Time: 7 hrs. 54 mins.). (C). 1995. 32.98 (978-962-634-571-9(3), NA607114, Naxos AudioBooks) Naxos.
Charts the gradual collapse of the Roman rule from Augustus (23 BC- AD 14) to the first of the barbarian kings, Odoacer (476-490 AD).

Decline & Fall of the Roman Empire Vol. 2: The History of the Empire from A. D. 180 to A. D. 395. abr. ed. Edward Gibbon. Read by Philip Madoc & Neville Jason. 6 CDs. (Running Time: 7 hrs. 54 mins.). 1995. audio compact disk 41.98 (978-962-634-071-4(1), NA607112, Naxos AudioBooks) Naxos.
Charts the gradual collapse of the Roman rule from Augustus (23 BC-AD 14) to the first of the barbarian kings, Odoacer (476-490 AD).

Decline & Fall of the Roman Empire Vol. 2: The History of the Empire from A. D. 180 to A. D. 395. unabr. collector's ed. Edward Gibbon. Read by David Case. 15 cass. (Running Time: 22 hrs. 30 mins.). 1992. 120.00 (978-0-7366-2213-4(6), 3006) Books on Tape.
No other book has portrayed with such clarity the march of Rome's empire into anarchy & ruin & no other historian has given his readers so much to ponder in their own situations. Concentrating on the centuries form the rule of Antoniinus Pius (138-161 AD) to the fall of the Empire in the West, this abridged volume chronicles "the triumph of barbarism & religion" in the disruption of the unified Empire, the rise of christianity, the progress of the Asiatic Huns & the revolt of the Goths.

Decline & Fall of the Roman Empire Vol. 2: The History of the Empire from A. D. 180 to A. D. 395, Vol. 1, Pt. 1. unabr. ed. Edward Gibbon. Read by Bernard Mayes. 16 cass. (Running Time: 42 hrs. 30 mins.). 1992. 99.95 (978-0-7861-0312-6(4), 1274A,B) Blckstn Audio.
Undeniably the greatest historical work in the English language. "The Decline & Fall of the Roman Empire" proves that brilliance of style & accuracy of statement are perfectly compatible in an historian. Gibbon traces the history of more than 13 centuries & covers the great events as well as the general historical progression. He thoroughly examines the movement & settlements of the Teutonic tribes that eventually held the Western empire in fee, the rise of Islam, & the Crusades. This first volume covers 180 A. D. to 395 A. D., which includes the establishment of Christianity.

Decline & Fall of the Roman Empire Vol. 2: The History of the Empire from A. D. 180 to A. D. 395, Vol. 1, Pt. 2. unabr. ed. Edward Gibbon. Read by Bernard Mayes. 13 cass. (Running Time: 42 hrs. 30 mins.). 1992. 85.95 (978-0-7861-0313-3(2), 1274A,B) Blckstn Audio.

Decline & Fall of the Roman Empire Vol. 2: The History of the Empire from A. D. 180 to A. D. 395, Vol. 2. Edward Gibbon. Read by Philip Madoc & Neville Jason. 6 cass. (Running Time: 7 hrs. 42 mins.). 1997. 32.98 (978-962-634-622-8(1), NA612214, Naxos AudioBooks) Naxos.
A continuation of the gradual collapse of the Roman rule. Looks East to the weakness of the Byzantine state, the spread of Islam and the crusades.

Decline & Fall of the Roman Empire Vol. 2: The History of the Empire from A. D. 180 to A. D. 395, Vol. 2. abr. ed. Edward Gibbon. Read by Philip Madoc & Neville Jason. 6 CDs. (Running Time: 8 hrs.). 1997. audio compact disk 41.98 (978-962-634-122-3(X), NA612212, Naxos AudioBooks) Naxos.
A continuation of the gradual collapse of the Roman rule looking East, to the weakness of the Byzantine state, the spread of Islam and the crusades.

Decline & Fall of the Roman Empire Vol. 2: The History of the Empire from A. D. 180 to A. D. 395, Vol. 2. unabr. ed. Edward Gibbon. Read by Bernard Mayes. 14 cass. (Running Time: 42 hrs. 30 mins.). 1992. 89.95 (978-0-7861-0326-3(4), 1287A,B); 95.95 (978-0-7861-0327-0(2), 1287A,B) Blckstn Audio.
Gibbon's masterpiece remains the most celebrated history in English literature. There is no work like it in all of modern western European letters & virtually no work from any period comparable to it. This second volume covers 395 A.D. to 1185 A.D., from the reign of Justinian in the East to the establishment of the German empire of the West. It recounts the desperate attempts to hold off the barbarians, palace revolutions & assassinations, theological controversy, lecheries & betrayals, all in a setting of phenomenal magnificence.

Decline & Fall of the Roman Empire Vol. 2: The History of the Empire from A. D. 180 to A. D. 395, Vol. 3. unabr. ed. Edward Gibbon. Read by Bernard Mayes. 16 cass. (Running Time: 47 hrs.). 1992. 99.95 (978-0-7861-0330-0(2), 1290A,B); 83.95 (978-0-7861-0331-7(0), 1290A,B) Blckstn Audio.
This final volume of Gibbon's historical masterpiece covers 1185 A.D. - 1453 A.D. & explores the rise of Islam, the Crusades, the invention of gunpowder, Genghis Khan & the Mongol invasions, the Turkish conquests, & the beginning of the Renaissance. The publication of this work in 1788 ended 20 years of Gibbon's contemplation & vast research on his subject & made this virtually self-educated man the most famous historian of his time.

Decline & Fall of the Roman Empire, Volume One: The History of the Empire from A. D. 180 to A. D.. 395. unabr. ed. Edward Gibbon & Bernard Mayes. (Running Time: 149400 sec.). 2007. audio compact disk 59.95 (978-0-7861-6103-4(5)) Blckstn Audio.

Decline & Fall of the Roman Empire, Volume 1, Part 1. unabr. ed. Edward Gibbon. Read by Bernard Mayes. (Running Time: 82800 sec.). 2007. audio compact disk 130.00 (978-0-7861-6074-7(8)) Blckstn Audio.

Decline & Fall of the Roman Empire, Volume 1, Part 2. unabr. ed. Edward Gibbon. Read by Bernard Mayes. (Running Time: 66600 sec.). 2007. audio compact disk 120.00 (978-0-7861-6102-7(7)) Blckstn Audio.

Decline & Fall of the Roman Empire, Volume 2. unabr. ed. Edward Gibbon. Read by Bernard Mayes. (Running Time: 145800 sec.). 2007. audio compact disk 59.95 (978-0-7861-6106-5(X)) Blckstn Audio.

Decline & Fall of the Roman Empire, Volume 2, Part 1. unabr. ed. Edward Gibbon. Read by Bernard Mayes. (Running Time: 70200 sec.). 2007. audio compact disk 120.00 (978-0-7861-6104-1(3)) Blckstn Audio.

Decline & Fall of the Roman Empire, Volume 2, Part 2. unabr. ed. Edward Gibbon. Read by Bernard Mayes. (Running Time: 75600 sec.). 2007. audio compact disk 120.00 (978-0-7861-6105-8(1)) Blckstn Audio.

Decline & Fall of the Roman Empire, Volume 3. unabr. ed. Edward Gibbon. Read by Bernard Mayes. (Running Time: 140400 sec.). 2007. audio compact disk 59.95 (978-0-7861-6109-6(4)) Blckstn Audio.

Decline & Fall of the Roman Empire, Volume 3, Part 1. unabr. ed. Edward Gibbon. Read by Bernard Mayes. (Running Time: 72000 sec.). 2007. audio compact disk 120.00 (978-0-7861-6107-2(8)) Blckstn Audio.

Decline & Fall of the Roman Empire, Volume 3, Part 2. unabr. ed. Edward Gibbon. Read by Bernard Mayes. (Running Time: 68400 sec.). 2007. audio compact disk 99.00 (978-0-7861-6108-9(6)) Blckstn Audio.

Decline of Culture in Pursuit of Eternal Adolescence. Read by Jeffrey Burke Satinover. 1 cass. (Running Time: 90 min.). 1984. 10.95 (978-0-7822-0246-5(2), 142) C G Jung IL.

Decline of Theology in America. Gordon Clark. 1 cass. (Miscellaneous Lectures: No. 2). 5.00 Trinity Found.

Decoding Your Dreams. Hal Stone & Sidra Stone. 1 cass. 1990. 10.95 (978-1-56557-010-8(3), T31) Delos Inc.
A general guide for making sense of your dreams - those magical messages from the deepest parts of yourself which can provide you with amazingly accurate practical information as well as profound spiritual teachings. Hal Stone's Jungian background gives an added depth to the lifetime of experience with dreams that is summarized & clearly presented by the Drs. Stone.

***Deconstructing Sammy.** abr. ed. Matt Birkbeck. Read by Peter Jay Fernandez. (ENG.). 2008. (978-0-06-170249-5(8)); (978-0-06-170250-1(1)) HarperCollins Pubs.

Deconstructing Sammy: Music, Money, Madness, & the Mob. abr. ed. Matt Birkbeck. Read by Peter Jay Fernandez. 5 CDs. (Running Time: 6 hrs.). 2008. audio compact disk 29.95 (978-0-06-166453-3(7), Harper Audio) HarperCollins Pubs.

Decontaminate Your Leisure: Don't "Work" at Play. Bruce A. Baldwin. Read by Bruce A. Baldwin. (Running Time: 60 min.). (Personal Development Ser.). 1983. 8.95 (978-0-933583-13-9(3), PDC838) Direction Dynamics.
Book on Tape: Chapter from "It's All in Your Head." Teaches techniques to emotionally separate from work & experience relaxation.

Decoration of Houses, unabr. ed. Edith Wharton & Ogden Codman, Jr. Read by Grace Conlin. 4 cass. (Running Time: 5 hrs. 30 mins.). 1995. 32.95 (978-0-7861-0907-4(6), 1714) Blckstn Audio.
In addition to charm, Wharton provides us with numerous keen & practical axioms for house design, giving the listener a rule of thumb for making any interior or exterior as appealing to the eye as possible.

Decoration of Houses, Set. unabr. ed. Edith Wharton & Ogden Codman, Jr. Read by Flo Gibson. 4 cass. (Running Time: 6 hrs.). 1997. 19.95 (978-1-55685-478-1(1), 478-1) Audio Bk Con.
European 18th & 19th century architecture & decoration are discussed & contrasted with modern concepts in this detailed study which is full of "do's" & "don'ts".

Decorative Painting 1-2-3 (Dvd) Meredith Books Staff. 2008. 14.95 (978-0-696-24105-5(6), Home Depot) Meredith Bks.

Decouverte et Creation: Les Bases du Francais Moderne. 5th ed. Gerard Jian & Ralph Hester. (C). 1990. 38.36 (978-0-395-52938-6(7)) CENGAGE Learn.

Decouverte et Creation: Les Bases du Francais Moderne. 5th ed. Gerard Jian & Ralph Hester. (C). 1990. 38.36 (978-0-395-52937-9(9)) CENGAGE Learn.

Decrease to Increase CD Series. 4 CDs. 2006. audio compact disk (978-0-9787128-5-3(4)) Palm Tree.

***Decreed Time: The Difference Between God¿s Time Clock & Yours.** Lynne Hammond. 2010. audio compact disk 6.00 (978-1-57399-467-5(7)) Mac Hammond.

Dedicated. Tru Vine Records Staff & Sharrond King. 2005. audio compact disk 15.98 (978-5-558-85947-8(4)) Pub: Pt of Grace Ent. Dist(s): STL Dist NA

***Dedicated Man.** unabr. ed. Peter Robinson. Narrated by Mark Honan. (Running Time: 8 hrs. 30 mins.). (Inspector Banks Mystery Ser.). 2010. 15.99 (978-1-4001-8268-8(9)); 34.99 (978-1-4001-9268-7(4)) Tantor Media.

***Dedicated Man.** unabr. ed. Peter Robinson. Narrated by Mark Honan & James Langton. (Running Time: 8 hrs. 0 mins. 0 sec.). (Inspector Banks Mystery Ser.). (ENG.). 2010. 24.99 (978-1-4001-6268-0(8)); audio compact disk 69.99 (978-1-4001-4268-2(7)); audio compact disk 34.99 (978-1-4001-1268-5(0)) Pub: Tantor Media. Dist(s): IngramPubServ

Dedicated to Diz: Live at the Village Vanguard. Perf. by Slide Hampton. 1 cass., 1 CD. 7.98 (TA 33323); audio compact disk 12.78 CD Jewel box. (TA 83323) NewSound.

Dedicated unto God. Swami Amar Jyoti. 1 cass. 1976. 9.95 (M-57) Truth Consciousness.
Genuine dedication from within rather than cultivated virtues.

Dedication. (Paws & Tales Ser.: No. 30). 2002. 3.99 (978-1-57972-478-8(7)); audio compact disk 5.99 (978-1-57972-479-5(5)) Insight Living.

Dedication. abr. ed. Emma McLaughlin & Nicola Kraus. Read by Ashley West. (Running Time: 6 hrs.). 2008. audio compact disk 14.99 (978-1-4233-4030-0(2), 9781423340300, BCD Value Price) Brilliance Audio.

Dedication. unabr. ed. Emma McLaughlin & Nicola Kraus. (Running Time: 32400 sec.). 2007. audio compact disk 34.95 (978-1-4233-4023-2(X), 9781423340232, Bril Audio CD Unabri) Brilliance Audio.

Dedication. unabr. ed. Emma McLaughlin & Nicola Kraus. Read by Ashley West. (Running Time: 9 hrs.). 2007. 39.25 (978-1-4233-4028-7(0), 9781423340287, BADLE); 24.95 (978-1-4233-4027-0(2), 9781423340270, BAD); 74.25 (978-1-4233-4022-5(1), 9781423340225, BrilAudUnabridg); audio compact disk 92.25 (978-1-4233-4024-9(8), 9781423340249, BriAudCD Unabrid); audio compact disk 39.25 (978-1-4233-4026-3(4), 9781423340263, Brinc Audio MP3 Lib); audio compact disk 24.95 (978-1-4233-4025-6(6), 9781423340256, Brilliance MP3) Brilliance Audio.

Dedications & Inspirations. Perf. by Jim Hall. 1 cass., 1 CD. 7.98 (TA 33365); audio compact disk 12.78 CD Jewel box. (TA 83365) NewSound.

Dedos Arriba, Dedos Abajo see Toes Up, Toes Down

Deductions: A Road Map for the Small Business. Kimberly Colgate. 2 cass. 1995. 109.00 Set. (0928) Toolkit Media.
Covers the basic business deductions, including definitions & in-depth coverage of Code Sections 162 & 212, plus discussions on levels of business activity, amortization of start-up expenditures, & more.

Dee Brown. unabr. ed. Interview with Dee Brown. 1 cass. (Running Time: 29 min.). 1987. 10.00 New Letters.
Author reads & talks about his research & writing.

Deed of Trust. unabr. ed. Claudia K. Allen. Perf. by Tyne Daly et al. 1 cass. (Running Time: 1 hr. 17 min.). 1994. 19.95 (978-1-58081-077-7(2)) L A Theatre.
Issues of inheritance have splintered a family for twenty years before an enterprising sister begins a crusade for change. Universal story with characteristic warmth & eccentric humor.

Deedo & Dido. Robert Lardinois et al. Illus. by Robert Lardinois. (Our Feathered & Furry Friends Ser.). (J). (ps-2). 1992. 7.95 (978-0-9629715-3-2(7)) Jewel Publishing.

***Deeds of My Fathers: How My Grandfather & Father Built New York & Created the Tabloid World of Today.** unabr. ed. Paul David Pope. (Running Time: 14 hrs. 30 mins.). 2010. 29.95 (978-1-4417-6892-6(0)); 85.95 (978-1-4417-6889-6(0)); audio compact disk 32.95 (978-1-4417-6891-9(2)); audio compact disk 118.00 (978-1-4417-6890-2(4)) Blckstn Audio.

Deeds of the Disturber. Elizabeth Peters, pseud. Read by Susan O'Malley. 11 CDs. (Running Time: 13 hrs.). (Amelia Peabody Ser.: No. 5). 2000. audio compact disk 88.00 (978-0-7861-9886-3(9), 2572) Blckstn Audio.
When the body of a night watchman is found sprawled in the shadow of a rare Nineteenth-Dynasty mummy case, panic ensues. For no one doubts that the guard's untimely demise is the work of an ancient Egyptian curse. No one, that is, except that tart-tongued Victorian Egyptologist, Amelia Peabody, whose remarkable talent for criminal investigation has frustrated villains from London to Cairo. Now fresh from her daring exploits in Egypt, Amelia, her sexy archaeologist husband, Emerson & their catastrophically precocious son, Ramses, have returned to their native England just in time to get wrapped up in the intrigue.

Deeds of the Disturber. unabr. ed. Elizabeth Peters, pseud. Read by Susan O'Malley. 9 cass. (Running Time: 13 hrs.). (Amelia Peabody Ser.: No. 5). 2000. 62.95 (978-0-7861-1769-7(9), 2572) Blckstn Audio.
When the body of a night watchman is found sprawled in the shadow of a rare Nineteenth-Dyantsy mummy case, panic ensures. No one doubts that the guard's untimely demise is the work of an ancient Egyptian curse. No, one, that is, except Victorian Egyptologist Amelia Peabody, whose remarkable talent for criminal investigation has frustrated villains from London to Cairo.

***Deeds of the Disturber.** unabr. ed. Elizabeth Peters, pseud. Read by Susan O'Malley. (Running Time: 13 hrs.). 2010. audio compact disk 29.95 (978-1-4417-4755-6(9)) Blckstn Audio.

***Deeds of the Disturber.** unabr. ed. Elizabeth Peters, pseud. Read by Susan O'Malley. (Running Time: 12 hrs.). 2010. 29.95 (978-1-4417-4756-3(7)) Blckstn Audio.

Deeds of the Disturber. unabr. ed. Elizabeth Peters, pseud. Narrated by Barbara Rosenblat. 10 cass. (Running Time: 14 hrs.). (Amelia Peabody Ser.: No. 5). 1993. 85.00 (978-1-55690-942-9(X), 93438E7) Recorded Bks.
Amelia & Emerson investigate a series of mysterious murders in London surrounding valuable Egyptian antiquities.

Deena Metzger. unabr. ed. Read by Deena Metzger. 1 cass. (Running Time: 29 min.). 1985. 10.00 New Letters.
This California poet reads from "The Woman Who Slept with Men to Take The War out of The M" & "Tree".

Deena Sings - Fire Safety. Deena Carr. Ed. by Joan D. Dorony. 1 cass. (Running Time: 30 min.). (Deena Sings Ser.). (J). 1993. pap. bk. 9.95 (978-1-882797-00-4(0), DJ10) DJ Pub OH.
Fire Safety Guidelines taught through music & song.

Deenie. unabr. ed. Judy Blume. 1 read-along cass. (Running Time: 66 min.). (Young Adult Cliffhangers Ser.). (J). (gr. 7 up). 1985. 15.98 (978-0-8072-1810-5(3), JRH 105 SP, Listening Lib); (Listening Lib) Random Audio Pubg.
Deenie isn't exactly against being a model, but her mother's nagging about her posture is a bore. Then the doctors discover a problem that will keep Deenie in a brace from neck to hips for years.

***Deenie.** unabr. ed. Judy Blume. Read by Kim Mai Guest. (ENG.). (J). 2011. audio compact disk 28.00 (978-0-307-74772-3(7), Listening Lib) Pub: Random Audio Pubg. Dist(s): Random

Deep see Best of Isaac Asimov

***Deep.** Peter Benchley. Narrated by Mark Feuerstein. (Running Time: 8 hrs. 24 mins. 0 sec.). (ENG.). 2010. audio compact disk 29.95 (978-1-60998-135-8(9)) Pub: AudioGO. Dist(s): Perseus Dist

***Deep Black.** Stephen Coonts. 2010. audio compact disk 29.99 (978-1-4418-4129-2(6)) Brilliance Audio.

Deep Black. abr. ed. Stephen Coonts & Jim DeFelice. Read by J. Charles. 5 CDs, Library ed. (Running Time: 4 hrs.). (Deep Black Ser.: No. 1). 2003. audio compact disk 69.25 (978-1-59086-838-6(2), 1590868382, BACDLib Ed) Brilliance Audio.
A spy plane gathering data on a new Russian weapon is blown out of the sky by a mysterious MiG. Is it an accident or the start of the next world war? One U.S. agency has what it takes to find out-the National Security Agency and its covert operations team: DEEP BLACK. Working for the NSA, ex-Marine sniper Charlie Dean is dispatched to Russia, hooking up with former Delta Force trooper Lia DeFrancesca to find out what happened to the plane. The Deep Black team stumbles across an even more alarming secret-a plot to assassinate the Russian president and overthrow the democratic government by force. The coup could have dire consequences for Russia and the world. With no clearance from the government it's called on to protect, the National Security Agency goes to war. But before Lia and Dean can unravel the conspiracy, they learn that one of the spy plane's passengers-an NSA techie-survived the crash. Critical information could fall into enemy hands. And that enemy is playing to the death. "Coonts knows how to write and build suspense." - The New York Times Book Review.

Deep Black. abr. ed. Stephen Coonts & Jim DeFelice. Read by J. Charles. (Running Time: 4 hrs.). (Deep Black Ser.: No. 1). 2004. audio compact disk 14.99 (978-1-59355-693-8(4), 1593556934, BCD Value Price) Brilliance Audio.

Deep Black. unabr. ed. Stephen Coonts & Jim DeFelice. Read by J. Charles. 6 cass. (Running Time: 10 hrs.). (Deep Black Ser.: No. 1). 2003. 82.25 (978-1-59086-696-2(7), 1590866967, Unabridge Lib Edns); 29.95 (978-1-59086-695-5(9), 1590866959, BAU) Brilliance Audio.

Deep Black. unabr. ed. Stephen Coonts & Jim DeFelice. Read by J. Charles. (Running Time: 10 hrs.). (Deep Black Ser.: No. 1). 2004. 39.25 (978-1-59335-584-5(X), 159335584X, Brlnc Audio MP3 Lib) Brilliance Audio.

Deep Black. unabr. ed. Stephen Coonts & Jim DeFelice. Read by J. Charles. (Running Time: 10 hrs.). (Deep Black Ser.: No. 1). 2004. 39.25 (978-1-59710-194-3(X), 159710194X, BADLE); 24.95 (978-1-59710-195-0(8), 1597101958, BAD) Brilliance Audio.

Deep Black. unabr. ed. Stephen Coonts & Jim DeFelice. Read by J. Charles. (Running Time: 10 hrs.). (Deep Black Ser.: No. 1). 2004. 24.95 (978-1-59335-076-5(7), 1593350767) Soulmate Audio Bks.

***Deep Black: Biowar.** abr. ed. Stephen Coonts & Jim DeFelice. Read by J. Charles. (Running Time: 11 hrs.). 2010. audio compact disk 29.99 (978-1-4418-4133-9(4), 9781441841339, Bril Audio CD Unabri) Brilliance Audio.

Deep Black: Biowar, Deep Black Dark Zone. abr. ed. Stephen Coonts & Jim DeFelice. Read by J. Charles. (Running Time: 12 hrs.). (Deep Black Ser.: Nos. 1-3). 2006. audio compact disk 29.95 (978-1-59737-723-2(6), 9781597377232) Brilliance Audio.
Deep Black: A spy plane gathering data on a new Russian weapon is blown out of the sky by a mysterious MiG. Is it an accident or the start of the next world war? One U.S. agency has what it takes to find out - the National Security Agency and its covert operations team: DEEP BLACK. Ex-Marine sniper Charlie Dean is dispatched to Russia, hooking up with former Delta Force trooper Lia DeFrancesca to find out what happened to the plane. Deep Black: Biowar: Dr. James Kegan, a world-renowned scientist specializing in germ warfare, has vanished from his upstate New York home. With time running out NSA operative Charlie Dean and Delta Force trooper Lia Francesca must find Kegan, uncover his secrets, cut a terrorist threat to the quick, and stop the unimaginable outbreak of a new biological nightmare. Deep Black Dark Zone: In a secluded headquarters on the other side of the globe, a terrorist mission is underway - a plan to set off an underwater explosion so great, and with such hellish force, that it could shift the very foundation of the earth's surface, causing untold calamity and world-wide disaster. When Charlie Dean's suspicions of a traitor in his shadow become frighteningly true, Dean's race against time could mean the end of the free world.

***Deep Black: Payback.** Stephen Coonts. 2010. audio compact disk 9.99 (978-1-4418-5632-6(3)) Brilliance Audio.

***Deep Black: Sea of Terror.** abr. ed. Stephen Coonts & William H. Keith. 2011. audio compact disk 9.99 (978-1-4233-4421-6(9)) Brilliance Audio.

***Deep Black: Sea of Terror.** unabr. ed. Stephen Coonts & William H. Keith. Read by Phil Gigante. (Running Time: 15 hrs.). (Nsa Ser.). 2010. 24.99 (978-1-4233-4418-6(9), 9781423344186, BAD); 39.97 (978-1-4233-4417-9(0), 9781423344179, Brlnc Audio MP3 Lib); 39.97 (978-1-4233-4419-3(7), 9781423344193, BADLE); audio compact disk 97.97 (978-1-4233-4415-5(4), 9781423344155, BriAudCD Unabrid) Brilliance Audio.

***Deep Black: Biowar: Biowar.** unabr. ed. Stephen Coonts & Jim DeFelice. Read by J. Charles. (Running Time: 11 hrs.). 2010. audio compact disk 89.97 (978-1-4418-4134-6(2), 9781441841346, BriAudCD Unabrid) Brilliance Audio.

***Deep Black Dark Zone.** unabr. ed. Stephen Coonts & Jim DeFelice. Read by J. Charles. (Running Time: 11 hrs.). (Nsa Ser.). 2010. audio compact disk 29.99 (978-1-4418-4131-5(8), 9781441841315, Bril Audio CD Unabri); audio compact disk 89.97 (978-1-4418-4132-2(6), 9781441841322, BriAudCD Unabrid) Brilliance Audio.

***Deep Black: Death Wave: Death Wave.** abr. ed. Stephen Coonts & William H. Keith. (Running Time: 6 hrs.). (Nsa Ser.). 2011. 9.99 (978-1-4418-8598-2(6), 9781441885982, BAD) Brilliance Audio.

***Deep Black: Death Wave: Death Wave.** abr. ed. Stephen Coonts & William H. Keith. Read by Phil Gigante. (Running Time: 6 hrs.). (Nsa Ser.). 2011. audio compact disk 24.99 (978-1-4418-8597-5(8), 9781441885975, BACD) Brilliance Audio.

***Deep Black: Death Wave: Death Wave.** unabr. ed. Stephen Coonts & William H. Keith. (Running Time: 13 hrs.). (Nsa Ser.). 2011. audio compact disk 89.97 (978-1-4418-8592-0(7), 9781441885920, BriAudCD Unabrid); audio compact disk 34.99 (978-1-4418-8591-3(9), 9781441885913, Bril Audio CD Unabri) Brilliance Audio.

***Deep Black: Death Wave: Death Wave.** unabr. ed. Stephen Coonts & William H. Keith. Read by Phil Gigante. (Running Time: 13 hrs.). (Nsa Ser.). 2011. 39.97 (978-1-4418-8594-4(3), 9781441885944, Brlnc Audio MP3 Lib); 24.99 (978-1-4418-8593-7(5), 9781441885937, Brilliance MP3) Brilliance Audio.

***Deep Black: Sea of Terror: Sea of Terror.** abr. ed. Stephen Coonts & William H. Keith. Read by Phil Gigante. (Running Time: 6 hrs.). (Nsa Ser.). 2010. audio compact disk 14.99 (978-1-4233-4420-9(0), 9781423344209, BACD) Brilliance Audio.

***Deep Black: Sea of Terror: Sea of Terror.** unabr. ed. Stephen Coonts & William H. Keith. Read by Phil Gigante. (Running Time: 15 hrs.). (Nsa Ser.). 2010. 24.99 (978-1-4233-4416-2(2), 9781423344162, Brilliance MP3); audio compact disk 36.99 (978-1-4233-4414-8(6), 9781423344148, Bril Audio CD Unabri) Brilliance Audio.

***Deep Blue.** Tom Morrisey. (Running Time: 10 hrs. 57 mins. 0 sec.). (Beck Easton Adventure Ser.). (ENG.). 2009. 14.99 (978-0-310-30423-4(7)) Zondervan.

Deep Blue: Stories of Shipwreck, Sunken Treasure & Survival. unabr. ed. Ed. by Clint Willis. 4 cass. (Running Time: 6 hrs.). (Adrenaline Ser.). 2001. 24.95 (978-1-885408-63-1(3), LL055) Listen & Live.
Offers compelling tales of shipwrecks & salvage, submarine adventure & free diving, nautical survival & cannibalism.

Deep Blue Alibi. unabr. ed. Paul Levine. Read by William Dufris. (Running Time: 41400 sec.). (Solomon vs. Lord Novels Ser.). 2007. 59.95 (978-1-4332-1126-3(2)); audio compact disk 72.00 (978-1-4332-1127-0(0)) Blckstn Audio.

Deep Blue Alibi: A Solomon vs. Lord Novel. unabr. ed. Paul Levine. Read by William Dufris. (Running Time: 41400 sec.). (Solomon vs. Lord Novels Ser.). 2007. audio compact disk 29.95 (978-1-4332-1128-7(9)) Blckstn Audio.

Deep Blue Goodbye. unabr. ed. John D. MacDonald. Read by Michael Prichard. 6 cass. (Running Time: 9 hrs.). (Travis McGee Ser.: Vol. 1). 2001. 29.95 (978-0-7366-6784-5(9)) Books on Tape.
Travis McGee comes to the aid of a lady tarnished by gems.

Deep Blue Goodbye. unabr. collector's ed. John D. MacDonald. Read by Michael Prichard. 6 cass. (Running Time: 6 hrs.). (Travis McGee Ser.: Vol. 1). 1983. 36.00 (978-0-7366-0699-8(8), 1662) Books on Tape.
Introduces John D. McDonald's alter-ego, the rugged & articulate Travis McGee, who has romped, muscled & moralized his way through a 20-book series of thrillers to date. In this initial story, McGee comes to the aid of a lovely lady who has been dragged through so much mud that she may never feel clean again. The plot concerns some precious stones liberated by McGee's client's father in India during World War II.

Deep Blue Rhapsody. (Running Time: 60 mins.). 2002. audio compact disk 15.99 (978-1-904972-33-4(0)) Global Jrny GBR GBR.

Deep Blue Sea for Beginners. abr. ed. Luanne Rice. Read by Blair Brown. (ENG.). 2009. audio compact disk 29.95 (978-0-7393-4366-1(1), Random AudioBks) Pub: Random Audio Pubg. Dist(s): Random

Deep Calls to Deep. Perf. by Lori Wilke. 1 cass. (Running Time: 5 min.). 1988. 9.98 Sound track. (978-1-891916-19-9(X)) Spirit To Spirit.

***Deep Church: A Third Way Beyond Emerging & Traditional.** unabr. ed. Jim Belcher. Narrated by Sean Runnette. (ENG.). 2009. 14.98 (978-1-59644-836-0(9), Hovel Audio); audio compact disk 24.98 (978-1-59644-835-3(0), Hovel Audio) christianaud.

Deep Comedy. Read by Peter J. Leithart. 4. 2007. 16.00 (978-1-59128-494-9(5)) Canon Pr ID.

Deep Comedy AudioBook: Trinity, Tragedy, & Hope in Western Literature. unabr. ed. Peter J. Leithart. Read by Aaron Wells. 4 CDs. (ENG.). 2007. audio compact disk 20.00 (978-1-59128-495-6(3)) Canon Pr ID.

Deep Comedy-AudioBook-tape. Read by Peter J. Leithart. 4 cass. 2007. 20.00 (978-1-59128-496-3(1)) Canon Pr ID.

Deep Dark: Disaster & Redemption in America's Richest Silver Mine. Gregg Olsen. 2005. audio compact disk 39.99 (978-1-4193-3692-8(4)) Recorded Bks.

Deep Dark: Disaster & Redemption in America's Richest Silver Mine. unabr. ed. Gregg Olsen. Narrated by L. J. Ganser. 11 CDs. (Running Time: 13 hrs.). 2005. audio compact disk 119.75 (978-1-4193-2066-8(1), C2929); 89.75 (978-1-4193-2068-2(8), 97943) Recorded Bks.
In 1972, fire broke out in Idaho's Sunshine Mine. When the first whisps of smoke appeared, the miners thought little of it. But soon, 91 workers were dead from smoke inhalation or carbon monoxide poisoning. New York Times best-selling author Gregg Olsen delivers the shocking true story of this disaster, which led to much-needed improvements in mine safety.

***Deep Dark Secret.** unabr. ed. Kimberla Lawson Roby. Narrated by Cherise Boothe. 4 CDs. (Running Time: 4 hrs. 45 mins.). 2009. audio compact disk 72.75 (978-1-4407-2890-7(9)) Recorded Bks.

Deep Daydreams. 1 cass. 14.95 Aquarius Prods.
Inspired by nature's own soothing sounds of water in a gentle brook, Hoffman wrote this metered music to lower heart rate & blood pressure. One side is exactly 50 beats a minute & the other side is exactly 60 beats a minute.

Deep Daydreams. Janalea Hoffman. 1 cass. (Running Time: 45 min.). 1988. 12.95 (978-1-886051-04-1(6)) Rhythmic Med.
Therapeutic music composed for deep relaxation, one side exactly 50-beats-a-minute, one side exactly 60-beats-a-minute. Aids in lowering heart rate & blood pressure.

***Deep Dish.** abr. ed. Mary Kay Andrews. Read by Isabel Keating. (ENG.). 2008. (978-0-06-162973-0(1)); (978-0-06-162974-7(X)) HarperCollins Pubs.

Deep Dish. abr. ed. Mary Kay Andrews & Mary K. Andrews. Read by Isabel Keating. 2009. audio compact disk 14.99 (978-0-06-172754-2(7), Harper Audio) HarperCollins Pubs.

Deep Dish. unabr. ed. Mary Kay Andrews. Read by Julia Gibson. 12 cass. (Running Time: 13 hrs. 45 mins.). 2008. 92.75 (978-1-4281-8107-6(5)); audio compact disk 123.75 (978-1-4281-8109-0(1)) Recorded Bks.

Deep End of the Ocean. Jacquelyn Mitchard. Read by Frances Cassidy. 1996. audio compact disk 112.00 (978-0-7366-6167-6(0)) Books on Tape.

Deep End of the Ocean. unabr. ed. Jacquelyn Mitchard. Read by Frances Cassidy. 14 CDs. (Running Time: 21 hrs.). 2001. audio compact disk 112.00 Books on Tape.
A three-year-old boy's family falls apart when he's kidnapped. Nine years later, he shows up. How will the family react?.

Deep End of the Ocean. unabr. ed. Jacquelyn Mitchard. Read by Frances Cassidy. 11 cass. (Running Time: 16 hrs. 30 mins.). 1999. 88.00 (978-0-7366-4366-3(5), 4110) Books on Tape.
"Watch your brother," says Beth Cappadora to her seven year-old son, Vincent, as she checks into a hotel. Five minutes later, three year-old Ben has disappeared. A police search yields no clues & no Ben. In the nine years that follow the kidnapping, Beth, overwhelmed with grief, neglects her two other children & her husband. The family disintegrates. Then one day a 12-year-old boy knocks at the door of the Cappadora house, looking for yardwork. Can Ben's return revitalize the family.

Deep Enough for Ivorybills. unabr. collector's ed. James Kilgo. Read by Wolfram Kandinsky. 5 cass. (Running Time: 7 hrs. 30 mins.). 1990. 40.00 (978-0-7366-1714-7(0), 2555) Books on Tape.
Jim Kilgo was born & raised not far from the bottomlands of the Great Pee Dee River in South Carolina, but it was not until he was grown that he began to respond to the powerful lure of the forests, fields & swamps of the South. For Kilgo, reentry into the wilderness becomes a window on the life that men can lead in nature. His discoveries illuminate the truth that the lives of human beings are an integral part of the larger rhythms of nature & the seasons.

***Deep Fathom.** unabr. ed. James Rollins. Read by John Meagher. (ENG.). 2010. (978-0-06-196700-9(9), Harper Audio); (978-0-06-195858-8(1), Harper Audio) HarperCollins Pubs.

Deep Fire Rising. unabr. ed. Jack Du Brul. Read by J. Charles. 11 cass. (Running Time: 15 hrs.). (Philip Mercer Ser.: Vol. 0). 2003. 97.25 (978-1-59086-801-0(3), 1590868013, CD Unabrid Lib Ed) Brilliance Audio.
Hired to lead the excavation of caverns deep beneath Area 51, Philip Mercer finds himself drilling straight into the epicenter of an age-old conspiracy. A reclusive order of Himalayan monks, through special knowledge of the earth's tectonic movement, has predicted the end of the world - and is determined to see the prediction unfold accordingly. Now, with icebergs floating through the South Pacific and a thermonuclear bomb set to destroy an island paradise, the stage is set for Armageddon - and it is up to Philip Mercer and the beautiful, mysterious Tisa Nguyan to prevent a cataclysm beyond imagination.

Deep Fire Rising. unabr. ed. Jack Du Brul. Read by J. Charles. 11 cass. (Running Time: 15 hrs.). (Philip Mercer Ser.: Vol. 0). 2003. 34.95 (978-1-59086-800-3(5), 1590868005, BAU) Brilliance Audio.

Deep Fire Rising. unabr. ed. Jack Du Brul. Read by J. Charles. (Running Time: 15 hrs.). (Philip Mercer Ser.). 2004. 39.25 (978-1-59335-458-9(4), 1593354584, Brlnc Audio MP3 Lib) Brilliance Audio.

Deep Fire Rising. unabr. ed. Jack Du Brul. Read by J. Charles. (Running Time: 15 hrs.). (Philip Mercer Ser.). 2004. 39.25 (978-1-59710-200-1(8), 1597102008, BADLE); 24.95 (978-1-59710-201-8(6), 1597102016, BAD) Brilliance Audio.

Deep Fire Rising. unabr. ed. Jack Du Brul. Read by J. Charles. (Running Time: 15 hrs.). (Philip Mercer Ser.). 2004. 24.95 (978-1-59335-256-1(5), 1593352565) Soulmate Audio Bks.

Deep Freeze. unabr. ed. Patricia Hall. Read by Michael Tudor Barnes. 8 cass. (Running Time: 9 hrs.). (Yorkshire Mystery Ser.). (J). 2002. 69.95 (978-1-84283-190-8(9)) Pub: ISIS Lrg Prnt GBR. Dist(s): Ulverscroft US

Deep, Healing Sleep: Relax into Healing Series (Spoken Audio CD & Booklet) Nancy Hopps. (Relax Into Healing Ser.). 2001. pap. bk. 19.95 (978-0-9663069-6-5(1), Relas into Healing) Pub: Syner Systs. Dist(s): Baker Taylor

Deep in the Heart of Trouble. abr. ed. Deeanna Gist. Narrated by Brooke Sanford. (ENG.). 2008. 16.09 (978-1-60814-173-9(X)) Oasis Audio.

Deep in the Heart of Trouble. abr. ed. Deeanne Gist. Narrated by Brooke Sanford. (ENG.). 2008. audio compact disk 22.99 (978-1-59859-400-3(1)) Oasis Audio.

Deep in the Jungle. Dan Yaccarino. 1 cass. (Running Time: 36 min.). (J). (ps-4). 1987. 9.95 (978-0-916123-08-6(1)) Ed Graphics Pr.

Deep in the Jungle: Jumpin' Jungle Rhythms for Kids. Joe Scruggs. 1 cass. (J). (ps-3). 1997. 9.98 (978-1-57064-181-7(1)); audio compact disk 14.98 (978-1-57064-182-4(X)) Lyrick Studios.

Deep in the Jungle: Jumpin' Jungle Rhythms for Kids. Joe Scruggs. (J). 1998. 9.98 (978-1-57064-183-1(8)) Lyrick Studios.
Music - Popular.

Deep Insight: Expand Awareness. unabr. ed. Kelly Howell. 1 cass. (Running Time: 1 hr.). 1991. 11.95 (978-1-881451-04-4(6)) Brain Sync.
The heightened awareness & hyper-suggestibility this program induces makes it ideal for learning, problem solving & exploring the contents of your subconscious.

Deep Insight: Sound waves that move your Mind. unabr. ed. Kelly Howell. 1 CD. (Running Time: 60 min.). (ENG.). 2005. audio compact disk 14.95 (978-1-881451-48-8(8)) Brain Sync.

***Deep Justice in a Broken World: Helping Your Kids Serve Others & Right the Wrongs around Them.** Zondervan. (Running Time: 8 hrs. 58 mins. 0 sec.). (ENG.). 2010. 18.99 (978-0-310-86917-7(X)) Zondervan.

Deep Learning. Kelly Howell. 1 cass., 1 CD. audio compact disk 14.95 CD. Brain Sync.
Memory receptors & neural pathways are gently stimulated as the frequencies balance & relaax your mind.

Deep Learning: Enhance Memory & Concentration. unabr. ed. Kelly Howell. 1 cass., 1 CD. 1992. 11.95 (978-1-881451-17-4(8)) Brain Sync.
Memory receptors & neural pathways are gently stimulated as the frequencies balance & relax your mind.

Deep Learning: Strengthen your memory & Concentration. unabr. ed. Brain Sync. 1 CD. (Running Time: 60 min.). 1997. audio compact disk 14.95 (978-1-881451-92-1(5)) Brain Sync.

Deep Lie. unabr. ed. Stuart Woods. Read by James Daniels. 7 cass. (Running Time: 10 hrs.). (Will Lee Ser.: No. 3). 2001. 32.95 (978-1-58788-152-7(7), 1587881527, BAU); 78.25 (978-1-58788-153-4(5), 1587881535, Unabridge Lib Edns) Brilliance Audio.
The classic techno-thriller of superpower espionage from New York Times bestselling master of suspense Stuart Woods! Sifting through reams of seemingly unrelated intelligence, CIA analyst Katherine Rule discovers a chilling pattern: an ultrasecret Baltic submarine base...a crafty Russian spy-master in command...a carefully planned invasion about to be launched from dark waters. Her suspicions, however, are dismissed by those higher up; her theory, they say, is too crazy to be true. But to Katherine, it's just crazy enough to succeed - unless she can stop it. If she's right, an attack sub has already penetrated friendly waters. Worse yet, the enemy has penetrated deep into her own life, so deep she can touch him. And in this game, one wrong touch can mean Armageddon.

Deep Lie. unabr. ed. Stuart Woods. Read by James Daniels. (Running Time: 10 hrs.). (Will Lee Ser.: No. 3). 2004. 39.25 (978-1-59335-645-3(5), 1593356455, Brinc Audio MP3 Lib); 24.95 (978-1-59335-293-6(X), 159335293X, Brilliance MP3) Brilliance Audio.

Deep Lie. unabr. ed. Stuart Woods. Read by James Daniels. (Running Time: 10 hrs.). (Will Lee Ser.). 2004. 24.95 (978-1-59710-203-2(2), 1597102032, BAD) Brilliance Audio.

Deep Lie. unabr. ed. Stuart Woods. Read by James Daniels. (Running Time: 10 hrs.). (Will Lee Ser.: No. 3). 2004. 39.25 (978-1-59710-202-5(4), 1597102024, BADLE) Brilliance Audio.

Deep Lie. unabr. ed. Stuart Woods. Read by James Daniels. (Running Time: 10 hrs.). (Will Lee Ser.: No. 3). 2008. audio compact disk 97.25 (978-1-4233-3664-8(X), 9781423336648, BriAudCD Unabrid); audio compact disk 36.95 (978-1-4233-3663-1(1), 9781423336631, Bril Audio CD Unabri) Brilliance Audio.

Deep Meditation: Ascend to Higher Levels. unabr. ed. Kelly Howell. 1 cass. (Running Time: 1 hr.). 1987. 11.95 (978-1-881451-06-8(2)) Brain Sync.
Quickly reach depths of meditation that would otherwise take years of practice to attain.

Deep Meditation: Ascend to higher Levels. unabr. ed. Kelly Howell. 1 CD. (Running Time: 60 min.). 1997. audio compact disk 14.95 (978-1-881451-90-7(9)) Brain Sync.

***Deep Ministry in a Shallow World: Not-So-Secret Findings about Youth Ministry.** Zondervan. (Running Time: 6 hrs. 58 mins. 20 sec.). (ENG.). 2010. 9.99 (978-0-310-86909-2(9)) Zondervan.

Deep Play. abr. ed. Diane Ackerman. 4 cass. (Running Time: 6 hrs.). 1999. 24.95 (978-1-57453-331-6(2)) Audio Lit.
Described as the state of full engagement in life that makes possible a person's finest accomplishments & most deeply felt experiences. It is a quality of life, a feeling of balance, inspiration & a sense of being at peace with the world, that everyone has experienced & longs to repeat.

Deep Range. unabr. collector's ed. Arthur C. Clarke. Read by Dan Lazar. 8 cass. (Running Time: 8 hrs.). 1980. 48.00 (978-0-7366-0257-0(7), 1252) Books on Tape.
This story takes place about 100 years in the future, when the Earth's population is fed principally from the sea - on whale products or from plankton farms. Its hero is Walter Franklin, a grounded space engineer now assigned to a submarine patrol tending the whale herds.

Deep Relaxation. Bob Griswold. 1 CD. (Running Time: 4560 sec.). (Love Tapes Ser.). 2005. audio compact disk 15.98 (978-1-55848-150-3(8), Love Tapes) EffectiveMN.
Knowing how to relax is a key to enjoying life. This program will make it easy for you to enjoy complete physical and mental relaxation.This CD contains 3 programs. The first is a guided meditation with powerful imagery and techniques for achieving total relaxation. It also includes two excellent subliminal programs, one with the sound of ocean waves and the other with relaxing original music.

Deep Relaxation. Robert E. Griswold. Read by Robert E. Griswold. 1 cass. 1992. 10.95 (978-1-55848-007-0(2)) EffectiveMN.
Teaches progressive relaxation, which is a method that has been used by some doctors for over fifty years.

Deep Relaxation. Paul R. Scheele. 1 cass. (Running Time: 34 min.). (Paraliminal Tapes Ser.). 1989. 14.95 (978-0-925480-08-8(8)) Learn Strategies.
Guides to enter the deepest state of mind & body relaxation.

Deep Relaxation. unabr. ed. Daniel Goleman. 1 cass. 12.95 (29297) J Norton Pubs.
Goleman leads you through a deep relaxation procedure that you can learn & do on your own.

Deep Relaxation. unabr. ed. Sirah Vettese. Read by Sirah Vettese. 1 cass. (Running Time: 90 min.). (Self-Help Ser.). 1986. 9.95 (978-0-07-067300-7(4), TDM 0948) HarperCollins Pubs.
Incorprates imagery & visualization techniques to reduce stress & stressful influences. Experience deep relaxation & increase energy levels for a fuller enjoyment of life.

Deep Relaxation & Restful Slumber. Gil Boyne. Read by Gil Boyne. 1 cass. (Running Time: 45 min.). (Hypnosis Motivation Cassettes Ser.). 1977. 9.95 (103) Westwood Pub Co.
Describes a totally new way of going to sleep.

Deep Relaxation for Beginners. unabr. ed. Mercedes Leidlich. Read by Mercedes Leidlich. 1 cass. (Running Time: 1 hr.). 1992. 10.95 in Norelco box. (978-1-882174-02-7(X), MLL-003) UFD Pub.
Deep relaxation has been proven to be physiologically healing. While in a state of deep relaxation a person experiences alpha brain waves, which calm the body & quiet the mind. This tape teaches how relaxation can lower blood pressure & reduce anxiety symptoms, as well as teaching how to cope with daily stressors. Side B presents a deep relaxation exercise with guided imagery, set to soothing sounds of harp music. A perfect exercise for beginning meditators.

Deep Relaxation (Hypnosis), Vol. 18. Jayne Helle. 1 cass. (Running Time: 28 min.). (Stress Management Ser.). 1995. 15.00 (978-1-891826-17-7(4)) Introspect.
Being deeply relaxed helps one to overcome stress, sleep better & feel happier.

Deep Relaxations for Pregnancy. Created by Patty Slote. Prod. by The Movement Center. 1 CD. (Running Time: 30 mins.). 2005. audio compact disk 10.00 (978-0-915801-99-2(X)) Rudra Pr.
Three 10-minute guided relaxations to help a pregnant woman connect with her growing baby and experience a state of total well being. Perfect after yoga or whenever she needs a break. Relaxations also appear in the DVD "Prenatal Yoga: A Complete Home Practice for a Healthy Mother and Baby.".

Deep River. Contrib. by Meredith. 2007. audio compact disk 17.00 (978-1-58459-367-6(9)) Wrld Lib Pubns.

***Deep River.** unabr. ed. Shusaku Endo. Narrated by David Holt. (Running Time: 8 hrs. 38 mins. 48 sec.). (ENG.). 2010. audio compact disk 29.99 (978-1-59859-742-4(6), SpringWater) Oasis Audio.

Deep River: The Performance Encores of Robert Fountain. 2007. audio compact disk 15.00 (978-1-931569-09-5(6)) Pub: U of Wis Pr. Dist(s): Chicago Distribution Ctr

Deep-Sea Fish. unabr. ed. Peter M. Spizzirri. Read by Charles Fuller. Ed. by Linda Spizzirri. 1 cass. (Running Time: 15 min.). Dramatization. (Educational Coloring Book & Cassette Ser.). (J). (gr. 1-8). pap. bk. 6.95 (978-0-86545-107-0(9)) Spizzirri.
See huge mouths, stretching stomachs & dagger-like teeth, as you learn about life in the dark ocean depths.

Deep Shadow. unabr. ed. Randy Wayne White. Read by George Guidall. 10 CDs. (Running Time: 11 hrs.). (gr. 12 up). 2010. audio compact disk 39.95 (978-0-14-314542-4(8), PengAudBks) Penguin Grp USA.

***Deep Shadow.** unabr. ed. Randy Wayne White. Narrated by George Guidall. 9 cass. (Running Time: 11 hrs.). 2010. 72.75 (978-1-4407-8663-1(1)); audio compact disk 102.75 (978-1-4407-8664-8(X)) Recorded Bks.

***Deep Shadow.** unabr. ed. Randy Wayne White. Narrated by George Guidall. 1 Playaway. (Running Time: 11 hrs.). 2010. 59.75 (978-1-4407-8666-2(6)) Recorded Bks.

***Deep Shadow.** unabr. collector's ed. Randy Wayne White. Narrated by George Guidall. 9 CDs. (Running Time: 11 hrs.). 2010. audio compact disk 51.95 (978-1-4407-8665-5(8)) Recorded Bks.

Deep Six. Clive Cussler. Read by Michael Prichard. (Dirk Pitt Ser.). 1992. audio compact disk 88.00 (978-0-7366-5965-9(X)) Books on Tape.

Deep Six. unabr. ed. Clive Cussler. Read by Michael Prichard. 9 cass. (Running Time: 13 hrs. 30 min.). (Dirk Pitt Ser.). 1992. 72.00 (978-0-7366-2275-2(6), 3063) Books on Tape.
A deadly tide poisons ocean waters, a ghost ship drifts empty in the calm open sea, a Soviet luxury liner explodes into flames & the U.S. President disappears without a trace. As the fate of the U.S. government hangs in the balance, Dirk Pitt must face down a vicious Asian shipping cartel.

Deep Six. unabr. ed. Clive Cussler. Read by Michael Prichard. 11 CDs. (Running Time: 16 hrs. 30 mins.). (Dirk Pitt Ser.). 2001. audio compact disk 88.00 Books on Tape.

Deep Six, Set. abr. ed. Clive Cussler. Read by Tom Wopat. 2 cass. (Running Time: 3 hrs.). (Dirk Pitt Ser.). 1999. (978-0-671-57762-9(X), 390640, Audioworks) S&S Audio.
A deadly tide poisons ocean waters, a ghost ship drifts empty in calm seas, a Soviet luxury liner explodes into flames, & the U.S. President disappears without a trace. As the fate of the U.S. government hangs in the balance, Dirk Pitt faces down a vicious Asian shipping cartel.

Deep Sleep. unabr. ed. Frances Fyfield. Read by Julian Glover. 6 cass. (Running Time: 6 hrs.). (Prosecutor Helen West Mysteries Ser.). 1996. 54.95 (978-0-7451-4144-2(7), CAB827) AudioGO.

Deep Sleep: Experience peace & Tranquility. Kelly Howell. 1 cass. (Running Time: 1 hr.). (Brain Wave Subliminal Ser.). 1996. 9.95 (978-1-881451-31-0(3)) Brain Sync.
Your subconscious mind is nurtured with thoughts and images of peace and tranquility, where you can experience the wonderfully regenerative rest you desire.

Deep Sleep: Sweet Dreams. Stuart Wilde. 1 cass. 11.95 (978-0-930603-29-8(X)) White Dove NM.
This subliminal tape will help you get the rest you need. It also works while you are asleep, reinforcing the idea that you are in control of your sleeping patterns. It will help you be more receptive to your other subliminal programs. Accompanied by a soothing background of new age music with no talking or introduction.

Deep Sleep: Tap into the Power of Your Subconscious Mind. Kelly Howell. (ENG.). 2004. audio compact disk 14.95 (978-1-881451-83-9(6)) Brain Sync.
Slip on your headphones, close your eyes and turn out the lights. Within minutes you'll feel like your brain is being massaged. Soothing Delta frequencies, associated with deep restorative sleep, and subliminal messages are masterfully woven into gentle music. As your brain cells resonate with Delta waves, you start to slowly swirl and drift. Pestering concerns are washed away - allowing you to fall into deep sleep states that bring the refreshing slumber your body and mind need for optimum performance.

Deep Sleep & Sweet Dreams. 1 cass. 12.95 (978-1-884305-63-4(6)) Changeworks.
On the one hand this tape is designed to help with chronic insomnia as well as times when you just can't sleep. Once you are asleep, the tape will also enrich your dreams in especially enjoyable ways.

Deep Sleep Every Night. Glenn Harrold. 1 cass. (Running Time: 1 hr. 30 mins.). 2002. 11.95 (978-1-901923-00-1(2)); audio compact disk 17.95 (978-1-901923-20-9(7)) Pub: Divinit Pubing GBR. Dist(s): Bookworld

Deep Sleep; Sweet Dreams. Christopher Love. Read by Christopher Love. 1 cass. (Running Time: 30 min.). 1997. 10.95 (978-1-891820-14-4(1)) World Sangha Pubg.
Self-hypnosis meditation for healing, self-improvement & realizing our full & powerful potential as spiritual beings.

Deep Sleep with Medical Self-Hypnosis. unabr. ed. Steven Gurgevich. (Running Time: 2:19:56). 2009. audio compact disk 19.95 (978-1-59179-714-2(4)) Sounds True.

Deep Sound Sleep. Michael P. Bovines. Read by Michael P. Bovines. Ed. by Christian Flint. 1 cass. (Running Time: 30 min.). (Healing Ser.). 1993. pap. bk. 9.98 (978-1-885768-01-8(X), M403) Circle of Light.

Deep South. unabr. ed. Nevada Barr. Narrated by Barbara Rosenblat. 11 CDs. (Running Time: 12 hrs. 15 mins.). (Anna Pigeon Ser.: No. 8). audio compact disk 111.00 (978-0-7887-4895-0(5), C1270E7) Recorded Bks.
Anna leaves behind her beloved Mesa Verde to take on a position as district park ranger of the Mississippi Natchez Trace Parkway. Once there she faces an angry staff that refuses to work with a woman supervisor but she pushes that difficulty aside when she stumbles over the body of a teenage girl, shrouded in a hood reminiscent of the KKK. As Anna searches for the truth amidst lies & evasions, she discovers the overgrown woods, that hold dark secrets that can only lead to violence. Available to libraries only.

Deep South. unabr. ed. Nevada Barr. Narrated by Barbara Rosenblat. 9 cass. (Running Time: 12 hrs. 15 mins.). (Anna Pigeon Ser.: No. 8). 2000. 83.00 (978-0-7887-4307-8(4), 96111E7) Recorded Bks.
Anna Pigeon accepts a promotion as district park ranger of the Mississippi Natchez Trace Parkway. There she stumbles over the body of a teenage girl, shrouded in a hood reminiscent of the KKK. As Anna searches for the truth amidst evasions, she discovers the overgrown woods hold dark secrets that lead to violence.

Deep Space Nine Fallen Heroes. Dafydd ab Hugh. (Star Trek Ser.). 2004. 10.95 (978-0-7435-4623-2(7)) Pub: S&S Audio. Dist(s): S and S Inc

Deep Still: Authentic Celtic Hymns & Songs of Praise. Featuring Ron Davis et al. 1 CD. (Running Time: 45 mins.). 2000. (978-1-58229-136-9(5)) Brentwood Music.
Songs include: "Because We Believe," "The River Is Here," "Celebration Jig," "Lamb of God," "Deep Peace" & more.

Deep Storm. abr. ed. Lincoln Child. Read by Scott Brick. (Running Time: 27000 sec.). (ENG.). 2008. audio compact disk 14.99 (978-0-7393-6570-0(3), Random AudioBks) Pub: Random Audio Pubg. Dist(s): Random

Deep Storm. unabr. ed. Lincoln Child. 9 cass. (Running Time: 13 hrs.). 2007. 90.00 (978-1-4159-3707-5(9)); audio compact disk 110.00 (978-1-4159-3554-5(8)) Books on Tape.

Deep Stress Relief: When You Need a Long Vacation, but Only Have a Short Time: Total Relaxation & Guided Relaxation. Kelly Howell. (Running Time: 7200 sec.). 2006. audio compact disk 16.95 (978-1-881451-51-8(8)) Brain Sync.

Deep Survival: Who Lives, Who Dies, & Why. unabr. ed. Laurence Gonzales. Read by Stefan Rudnicki. 8 cass. (Running Time: 37800 sec.). 2006. 19.95 (978-0-7861-4603-1(6)); audio compact disk 19.95 (978-0-7861-6896-5(X)); audio compact disk 29.95 (978-0-7861-7502-4(8)) Blckstn Audio.

Deep Survival: Who Lives, Who Dies, & Why: True Stories of Miraculous Endurance & Sudden Death. unabr. ed. Laurence Gonzales. Read by Stefan Rudnicki. (Running Time: 37800 sec.). 2006. 65.95 (978-0-7861-4749-6(0)); audio compact disk 72.00 (978-0-7861-6397-7(6)) Blckstn Audio.

Deep Ten Relaxation. abr. ed. Robert A. Monroe. Read by Robert A. Monroe. (Mind Food Ser.). 1985. 14.95 (978-1-56102-404-9(X)) Inter Indus.
Designed to guide into states of relaxation.

Deep Ten Relaxation. unabr. ed. Robert A. Monroe. Read by Robert A. Monroe. 1 cass. (Running Time: 30 min.). (TimeOut Ser.). 1991. 14.95 (978-1-56102-805-4(3)) Inter Indus.
Leads you into profound relaxation & leaves you in normal sleep.

Deep Time, Deep Ecology. Joanna Macy. 2 cass. 18.00 set. (A0613-90) Sound Photosyn.
One of the most impassioned spokespersons of the great wheel of life.

Deep Trance Music. Nick Kemp. (Running Time: 42 mins.). audio compact disk 24.95 (978-0-9545993-5-5(7)) Pub: Human Alchemy GBR. Dist(s): Crown Hse

Deep Trance Shamanic Journey Vol. 1: Pachamama's Child. Jessie E. Ayani & Richard Shulman. 1 CD. (Running Time: 65 mins.). 2000. audio compact disk 16.00 (978-0-9648763-6-1(1)) Pub: Hrt of the Sun. Dist(s): New Leaf Dist
Recorded journeys for healing.

Deep Trance Shamanic Journey: Volume III: Reclaiming Power. Narrated by Jessie E. Ayani. Music by Richard Shulman. (ENG.). 2008. audio compact disk 16.00 (978-0-9648763-8-5(8)) Pub: Hrt of the Sun. Dist(s): New Leaf Dist

Deep Trance Shamanic Journeys Volume II: Right Relationship. Composed by Richard Shulman. Voice by Jessie Ayani. (ENG.). 2003. audio compact disk 16.00 (978-0-9648763-7-8(X)) Pub: Hrt of the Sun. Dist(s): New Leaf Dist

Deep Trouble. Walt Morey. (J). 1996. 7.98 (978-0-7634-0088-0(2)) W Disney Records.

Deep Trouble. Lesley Thompson. (Dominoes Ser.). 2004. 14.25 (978-0-19-424417-6(2)) OUP.

Deep Waters. 2004. audio compact disk 16.99 (978-7-5124-0086-3(1)) Destiny Image Pubs.

Deep Waters. Thomas Eno. 2002. audio compact disk 14.95 (978-1-59156-037-1(3)) Covenant Comms.

Deep Waters. Jayne Ann Krentz. Read by Moira Kelly. 2004. 10.95 (978-0-7435-4618-8(0)) Pub: S&S Audio. Dist(s): S and S Inc

Deep Waters. Barbara Nadel. Read by Sean Barrett. 10 vols. (Running Time: 15 hrs.). 2003. 84.95 (978-0-7540-8323-8(3)) Pub: Chivers Audio Bks GBR. Dist(s): AudioGO

Deep Waters. unabr. ed. Jayne Ann Krentz. Read by Stephanie Diaz. 8 vols. (Running Time: 12 hrs.). 2001. bk. 69.95 (978-0-7927-2473-5(9), CSL 362, Chivers Sound Lib) AudioGO.
Charity Truitt & Elia Winter, two of the Pacific Northwest's most powerful corporate figures, are both facing crises of career & the heart. Fate has brought them together in Washington's tiny Whispering Waters Cove, each eager to downsize & simplify. Elias is a novice at relationships: a formidable former CEO, Charity is starting in the mail room when it comes to love. But when the town is rocked by two shocking murders, Charity & Elias realize that they must join forces to catch a killer.

Deep Waters. unabr. ed. Jayne Ann Krentz. Read by Stephanie Diaz. 10 CDs. (Running Time: 15 hrs.). 2001. audio compact disk 94.95 (978-0-7927-9941-2(0), SLD 092, Chivers Sound Lib) AudioGO.
Charity Truitt and Elias Winter, two of the Pacific Northwest's most powerful corporate figures, are both facing crises of career and the heart. Fate has brought them together in Washington's tiny Whispering Waters Cove, each eager to downsize and simplify. When the town is rocked by two shocking murders, Charity and Elias realize they must join forces to catch a killer.

Deep Well at Noon. unabr. ed. Jessica Stirling. Read by Sheila Steafel. 16 cass. (Running Time: 16 hrs.). (Beckman Trilogy: Vol. 1). 1996. 124.95 set. (978-0-7451-6603-2(2), CAB1219) AudioGO.
When World War I ended in 1918, Holly Beckman couldn't wait to leave the gray streets of Lambeth & return to work in Mr. Aspinall's antique shop. But she is soon drawn into conflict with Aspinall's undutiful heirs: one a shrew, the other a dissolute charmer. Holly must draw on her inner strength in order to combat them, her drunken father's rages, & her brother's criminal intentions.

Deep Well Tapes Audio Book: Samples from the Deep Well Tapes Book Series. Marc Bregman. Read by Christa Lancaster et al. Ed. by Sue Scavo. Prod. by Sue Scavo & Bill St.Cyr. (ENG.). 2008. 20.00 (978-0-9792415-3-6(7)) North of Eden.

Deep Wizardry. Diane Duane. Narrated by Christina Moore. 7 CDs. (Running Time: 8 hrs. 30 mins.). (gr. 5 up). 2001. audio compact disk 69.00 (978-0-7887-5379-4(7), C1375E7) Recorded Bks.
Young wizards Nita & Kit have sworn to help S'ree fight the evil Lone Power. But although S'ree is a wizard, she is also a whale & the final confrontation will take place 16,000 feet below the surface of the Atlantic Ocean. Available to libraries only.

Deep Wizardry, unabr. ed. Diane Duane. Narrated by Christina Moore. 6 pieces. (Running Time: 8 hrs. 30 mins.). (gr. 5 up). 51.00 (978-0-7887-2638-5(2), 95639E7) Recorded Bks.

Deep Wood. unabr. collector's ed. Elleston Trevor. Read by Gary Martin. 6 cass. (Running Time: 9 hrs.). (Woodlander Ser.). (J). 1992. 48.00 (978-0-7366-2089-5(3), 2895) Books on Tape.
Elleston Trevor is a former RAF pilot whose first books were about flying & warfare. The classic children's stories written in the 1940s & 1950s about the inhabitants of Deep Wood, Old Stripe the Badger, Potter-the-Otter, Woo Owl & Digger Mole.

Deepe Coffyn, Set. Janet Laurence. Read by Diana Bishop. 5 cass. 1999. 49.95 (67797) Pub: Soundings Ltd GBR. Dist(s): ISIS Pub

Deeper. Riverview Staff. 1 CD. (Running Time: 45 min.). 2003. audio compact disk 14.95 (978-5-550-29494-9(X)) STL Dist NA.

***Deeper.** unabr. ed. Roderick Gordon & Brian Williams. Narrated by Steven Crossley. 1 Playaway. (Running Time: 19 hrs.). (YA). (gr. 5-9). 2009. 64.75 (978-1-4407-0367-6(1)); 102.75 (978-1-4361-3715-7(2)); audio compact disk 108.75 (978-1-4361-3720-1(9)) Recorded Bks.

***Deeper.** unabr. collector's ed. Roderick Gordon & Brian Williams. Narrated by Steven Crossley. 15 CDs. (Running Time: 19 hrs.). (YA). (gr. 5-9). 2009. audio compact disk 72.95 (978-1-4361-3774-4(8)) Recorded Bks.

Deeper Foundation. Rick Joyner. 1 cass. (Running Time: 90 mins.). (Walking in Truth Ser.: Vol. 2). 2000. 5.00 (RJ02-002) Morning NC.
Rick reinforces our calling to walk in truth & integrity while pursuing God's perfect will for our lives.

Deeper Level. Created by Integrity Music. (Worshiptools Ser.). 2007. pap. bk. 29.95 (978-5-557-60491-8(X)) Integrity Music.

Deeper Level. Contrib. by Israel & New Breed et al. 2007. pap. bk. 19.95 (978-5-557-59908-5(8)) Integrity Music.

Deeper Level. Contrib. by Israel and New Breed. Prod. by Israel Houghton & Aaron W. Lindsey. 2007. audio compact disk 16.98 (978-5-557-60950-0(4)) Integrity Music.

Deeper Magic: Logos 10/18/98. Ben Young. 1998. 4.95 (978-0-7417-6102-6(5), B0052) Win Walk.

Deeper Metaphysics. Michele Blood & Lawrence T. Bond. (Musivation Ser.). 2003. audio compact disk 29.95 (978-1-890679-47-7(X)) Micheles.

Deeper Relationship with God. Swami Amar Jyoti. 1 cass. 1987. 9.95 (C-43) Truth Consciousness.
Going beyond the shallows of thank-fulness. At the Feet of the Lord, a living, conscious connection. Abiding, stable peace. Training the mind. A humble, simple prayer.

Deeper Relationship with the Holy Spirit: Exploring the Personality & Voice of the Holy Spirit. Speeches. Tim N. Enloe. 2005. audio compact disk 17.99 (978-0-9749739-8-2(X)) E M Pubns.

***Deeper Relaxation Hypnosis: Enjoy the Benefits of Deeper Relaxation.** Paul Dale Anderson. Perf. by Paul Dale Anderson. (ENG.). 2010. audio compact disk 21.00 (978-0-937491-10-2(1)) TwoAM Pubns.

***Deeper, Richer, Fuller: Discover the Spiritual Life You Long For.** unabr. ed. Tom Paterson. Narrated by Maurice England. (Running Time: 8 hrs. 39 mins. 46 sec.). (ENG.). 2010. 19.59 (978-1-60814-713-7(4)); audio compact disk 27.99 (978-1-59859-758-5(2)) Oasis Audio.

Deeper Sleep. unabr. ed. Dana Stabenow. 6 cass. (Running Time: 9 hrs.). (Kate Shugak Ser.). 2007. 60.00 (978-1-4159-3710-5(9)); audio compact disk 80.00 (978-1-4159-3520-0(3)) Books on Tape.

Deeper Than Desire. unabr. ed. 1 cass. (Running Time: 1 hr.). 1985. 7.95 (978-1-58638-520-0(8)) Nilgiri Pr.
Discusses how to arm one's self & young people against compulsive desires.

Deeper Than the Dead. abr. ed. Tami Hoag. Read by Kirsten Potter. (ENG.). 2009. audio compact disk 30.00 (978-0-7393-6577-9(0), Random AudioBks) Pub: Random Audio Pubg. Dist(s): Random

***Deeper Than the Dead.** abr. ed. Tami Hoag. Read by Kirsten Potter. (ENG.). 2010. audio compact disk 14.99 (978-0-307-91424-8(0), Random AudioBks) Pub: Random Audio Pubg. Dist(s): Random

Deeper Than the Dead. unabr. ed. Tami Hoag. Read by Kirsten Potter. (ENG.). 2009. audio compact disk 40.00 (978-0-7393-6580-9(0), Random AudioBks) Pub: Random Audio Pubg. Dist(s): Random

***Deeper Than the Dead.** unabr. ed. Tami Hoag. Read by Kirsten Potter. 11 CDs. (Running Time: 13 hrs. 45 mins.). 2009. audio compact disk 80.00 (978-1-4159-5661-8(8), BksonTape) Pub: Random Audio Pubg. Dist(s): Random

Deeper Wells, Sweeter Waters Set: Keeping Love Flowing Throughout Marriage. unabr. ed. Ed Y. Susskind. Read by Ed Y. Susskind. Adapted by Zalman Goldstein. 4 cass. (Running Time: 3 hrs.). 1999. bk. 39.95 (978-1-891293-25-2(7), JLG-A01) Jewish Lrning.
Culled from over 25 years of professional experience as a marital therapist, Dr. Susskind presents practical, understandable, time-proven counsel.

***Deepest Cut.** unabr. ed. Dianne Emley. Read by Carrington MacDuffie. 11 CDs. (Running Time: 13 hrs. 30 mins.). 2009. audio compact disk 120.00 (978-1-4159-6452-1(1), BksonTape) Pub: Random Audio Pubg. Dist(s): Random

Deepest Water. unabr. ed. Kate Wilhelm. Narrated by Marguerite Gavin. 7 cass. (Running Time: 10 hrs.). 2002. 49.95 (978-0-7861-2149-6(1), 2899); audio compact disk 64.00 (978-0-7861-9592-3(4), 2899) Blckstn Audio.
When Jud Connors, a successful writer, is found murdered in his isolated cabin in the woods of Oregon, his daughter Abby's world starts to fall apart. Who wanted her father dead and why? More puzzling is how anyone could have gotten to the cabin undetected. Was the murderer someone Jud knew? As Abby embarks on her own investigation, she soon realizes that the clue to the murderer's identity is buried in her father's latest novel, finished just weeks before his death.

Deepest Water. unabr. ed. Kate Wilhelm. Read by Marguerite Gavin. (Running Time: 9 hrs.). 2009. audio compact disk 29.95 (978-1-4417-1184-7(8)) Blckstn Audio.

Deephaven. unabr. ed. Sarah Orne Jewett. Read by Flo Gibson. 4 cass. (Running Time: 5 hrs. 30 min.). (gr. 8 up). 1991. 19.95 (978-1-55685-212-1(6)) Audio Bk Con.
Two aristocratic young ladies from Boston share their experiences & their delight in a small harbour village in Maine, as well as the salty yarns of several sea captains & gentlewomen.

Deeply Etched Forever. Dawn Pate. 2000. audio compact disk 13.99 (978-0-615-11505-4(5)) Dawn Prod.

Deepwater. unabr. ed. Matthew F. Jones. Narrated by Richard Ferrone. 7 cass. (Running Time: 9 hrs. 30 mins.). 2002. 68.00 (978-1-4025-1342-8(9), 96408) Recorded Bks.
An erotic psychological thriller begins on a desolate, mountain road. There a relationship begins that will ultimately change the lives of the players involved forever.

Deepwater. unabr. ed. Matthew F. Jones. Narrated by Richard Ferrone. 8 CDs. (Running Time: 9 hrs. 30 mins.). 2002. audio compact disk 78.00 (978-1-4025-1562-0(6)) Recorded Bks.

Deer Mouse at Old Farm Road. Laura Gates Galvin. (J). (ps-2). 2001. bk. 19.95 (SP 5015C) Kimbo Educ.
Deer mouse readies her nest for the birth of her babies. Includes book.

Deer Mouse at Old Farm Road. Laura Gates Galvin. Illus. by Katy Bratun. Narrated by Alexi Komisar. (Smithsonian's Backyard Ser.). (J). (ps-2). 1998. 5.00 (978-1-56899-524-3(5)) Soundprints.

Deerslayer. James Fenimore Cooper. Read by Raymond Todd. 2 CDs. (Running Time: 20 hrs. 30 mins.). 2001. audio compact disk 29.95 (978-0-7861-9402-5(2), 2887) Blckstn Audio.
We meet Natty Bumppo as a young man living in upstate New York in the early 1740s. The action begins as Bumppo, called "Deerslayer," and his friend Hurry Harry approach Lake Glimmerglass, or Oswego, where the trapper Thomas Hutter lives with his daughters, the beautiful Judith and the feeble-minded Hetty. Hutter's floating log fort is attacked by Iroquois Indians, and the two frontiersmen join in the fight.

Deerslayer. James Fenimore Cooper. Narrated by Raymond Todd. (Running Time: 20 hrs. 30 mins.). 2001. 50.95 (978-1-59912-648-7(6)) Iofy Corp.

Deerslayer. unabr. ed. James Fenimore Cooper. Read by Raymond Todd. 14 cass. (Running Time: 21 hrs.). 2001. 89.95 (978-0-7861-2127-4(0), P2887); audio compact disk 144.00 (978-0-7861-9626-5(2), ZP2887) Blckstn Audio.

Deerslayer, Pt. A. unabr. collector's ed. James Fenimore Cooper. Read by Walter Zimmerman. 8 cass. (Running Time: 12 hrs.). (J). 1983. 64.00 (978-0-7366-3981-1(0), 9529A) Books on Tape.
Set in the wilds of colonial New York, a 20-year-old frontiersman, Natty Bumppo, brought up among the Delaware Indians & known as Leather Stocking, helps defend a settler's family during the warfare between the Delawares & the Hurons.

Deerslayer, Pt. B. collector's ed. James Fenimore Cooper. Read by Walter Zimmerman. 8 cass. (Running Time: 12 hrs.). 1983. 64.00 (978-0-7366-3982-8(9), 9529-B) Books on Tape.

Defeat Depression. 2000. 24.95 (978-1-58557-030-0(3)) Dynamic Growth.

Defeat Pain. unabr. ed. Krs Edstrom. Read by Krs Edstrom. 1 cass. (Running Time: 40 min.). (Inner Mastery Ser.). 1994. 9.95 Norelco size. (978-1-886198-09-8(8)); 12.95 Bk. Box size. (978-1-886198-01-2(2), IMS02) Soft Stone Pub.
The perfect tape to "keep in the medicine cabinet" and reach for before resorting to pills. From headaches to the dying process, it teaches you how to free yourself from pain's imprisonment with powerful techniques that you will use forever. She teaches people to become aware of how their thoughts and history are stored in the body and how they manifest through physical and/or psychological pain. The "body-talk" techniques she uses include meditation, imagery and energy releasing work. Specially composed music helps facilitate your journey.Too often we "go through the motions" of life, not tuned in to what is happening internally - how our mind and body interrelate and how the outside world and our inside world interrelate. The purpose of these tapes is not only that you feel results after each listen, but that you develop increasingly deeper skills to serve you in all of life's challenges and excursions. Commonly considered negatives such as pain, stress and insomnia are experienced in a new, non-judgmental way that invites insight and is both growth-promoting and freeing. Once perceived enemies turn into welcome teachers. Similarly, positive and everyday events such as watching a bird soar, hitting a ball or conducting business are experienced in a more complete way; a way that enriches your relationship to self and thus the outside world.

Defeat Pain: Meditations to Transform Pain to Peace. unabr. ed. Krs Edstrom. 1 CD. (Running Time: 40 mins.). 2006. audio compact disk 16.95 (978-1-886198-16-6(0)) Soft Stone Pub.
Free yourself from pain¿s imprisonment. Powerful guided mindfulness meditations and soothing music dissolve your physical and emotional pain at their source. You will be able to apply your new skills to any pain forevermore. Learn to become aware of how your thoughts and history are stored in the body and how they manifest through physical and/or psychological pain. Transform the stuck energy of pain into a liberating journey of self-discovery.

Defeating Discouragement: Neh. 4:10-23. Ed Young. 1990. 4.95 (978-0-7417-1809-9(X), 809) Win Walk.

Defeating the Four Thieves of Prosperity. Speeches. 2cass. (Running Time: 90 min). 2002. 10.00 (978-1-931996-02-0(4)) M Bishop Minis.

Defeating the Jezebel Spirit. Francis Frangipane. 1 cass. (Running Time: 90 mins.). (Three Battlegrounds Ser.: Vol. 2). 2000. 5.00 (FF03-002) Morning NC.
This two-tape series is brief, but foundational.

Defeating the 8 Demons of Distraction: Proven Strategies to Increase Productivity & Decrease Stress. Geraldine Markel. 2007. audio compact disk 18.95 (978-0-9791279-6-0(3)) Managing Mind.

Defection of A. J. Lewinter: A Novel of Duplicity. unabr. ed. Robert Littell. Read by Scott Brick. 6 cass. (Running Time: 8 hrs.). 2004. 32.95 (978-1-59007-286-8(3)); audio compact disk 45.00 (978-1-59007-285-1(5)) Pub: New Millenn Enter. Dist(s): PerseuPGW
Political provacateur Bill Maher tells it like it is in a useful and hilarious guide for the many Americans who want to do more here at home to help in the war effort, but are at a loss as to how. 33 dynamic new posters and several classics from our government's archive, accompanied by text from one of our leading pundits and cutting-edge comedians make this the perfect book for this time in our nation's history, the zeitgeist of one-year-past-9/11 America. This will help Americans make the connection between what we can do and how it will help our troops to victory.

Defector. abr. ed. Daniel Silva. Read by Phil Gigante. (Running Time: 6 hrs.). (Gabriel Allon Ser.: No. 9). 2009. audio compact disk 26.99 (978-1-4233-2812-4(4), 9781423328124, BACD) Brilliance Audio.

Defector. abr. ed. Daniel Silva. Read by Phil Gigante. (Running Time: 6 hrs.). (Gabriel Allon Ser.: No. 9). 2010. audio compact disk 14.99 (978-1-4233-2813-1(2), 9781423328131, BCD Value Price) Brilliance Audio.

Defector. unabr. ed. Evelyn Anthony. Read by Carolyn Pickles. 10 cass. (Running Time: 10 hrs.). 1996. 84.95 (978-0-7451-6605-6(9), CAB1221) AudioGO.
Ivan Sasanove was a top KGB agent & potentially important defector. Davina Graham was his debriefer: a dedicated British operative who made her work her life. She had to get him out of Russia. And although she was falling in love with him, he would only cooperate if his wife & daughter were also brought out. The mission was lined with treachery & deceit, & even if she succeeded, she would have lost the only thing she really wanted.

Defector. unabr. ed. Daniel Silva. Read by Phil Gigante. (Running Time: 11 hrs.). (Gabriel Allon Ser.: No. 9). 2009. 24.99 (978-1-4233-2808-7(6), 9781423328087, Brilliance MP3); 39.97 (978-1-4233-2809-4(4), 9781423328094, Brlnc Audio MP3 Lib); 39.97 (978-1-4233-2811-7(6), 9781423328117, BADLE); 24.99 (978-1-4233-2810-0(8), 9781423328100, BAD); audio compact disk 36.99 (978-1-4233-2806-3(X), 9781423328063, Bril Audio CD Unabri); audio compact disk 97.97 (978-1-4233-2807-0(8), 9781423328070, BriAudCD Unabrid) Brilliance Audio.

***Defector.** unabr. ed. Daniel Silva. Narrated by Phil Gigante. 1 Playaway. (Running Time: 11 hrs.). (Gabriel Allon Ser.: No. 9). 2009. 69.99 (978-1-61545-525-6(6)) Find a World.

Defend & Betray. unabr. ed. Anne Perry. Narrated by Davina Porter. 12 cass. (Running Time: 16 hrs. 30 mins.). (William Monk Novel Ser.). 2000. 97.00 (978-0-7887-0403-1(6), 94595E7) Recorded Bks.
Ten people gather together for an elegant London dinner party. By the end of the party, only nine are alive. Sometime after dinner, General Thaddeus Carylon is brutally murdered in the hallway. Who had strength - and motive - to murder the distinguished military hero? Nurse Latterly and Inspector Monk find the answers in a nightmarish legacy of evil.

Defend on Something's Happening! Daniel Duchaine. 1 cass. (Roy Tuckman Interview Ser.). 9.00 (A0690-90) Sound Photosyn.
An interview with Daniel Duchaine of Power Distributors on the problems of drug testing & the uses of Defend, a product which can nullify those tests.

Defender see X Minus One

***Defenders & Other Stories.** Phillip K. Dick. Narrated by William Coon. (Running Time: 219). (ENG.). 2010. 10.95 (978-0-9844138-7-4(1)) Pub: Eloq Voice. Dist(s): OverDrive Inc

Defending Antitrust Violations. Douglas S. Eakeley. 2006. audio compact disk 99.95 (978-1-59701-093-1(6)) Aspatore Bks.

Defending Baltimore Against Enemy Attack: A Boyhood Year During World War II. unabr. ed. Charles Osgood. Read by Charles Osgood. (Running Time: 3 hrs.). 2004. 49.25 (978-1-59355-483-5(4), 1593554834, BrilAudUnabridg); audio compact disk 62.25 (978-1-59355-485-9(0), 1593554850, BriAudCD Unabrid) Brilliance Audio.
The year is 1942. Charles Osgood is a nine-year-old living in Baltimore. His idols are Franklin Roosevelt and Babe Ruth, a hometown hero. Charlie spends his days delivering newspapers on his daily route, riding the trolley to the local amusement park, going to Orioles' baseball games, and playing with his younger sister, Mary Ann. With great attention to detail, Osgood captures the texture of life in a very different era, before anyone had heard of penicillin or the atomic bomb. In his neighborhood of Liberty Heights, gas lights glowed on every corner, milkmen delivered bottles of milk, and a loaf of bread cost nine cents. Although Osgood had many interests as a child, what captivated him more than anything else was the radio. He would listen huddled under the covers, after his parents had turned off the lights, to Spiderman, Superman, The Lone Ranger, the Shadow - and of course baseball.

Defending Baltimore Against Enemy Attack: A Boyhood Year During World War II. unabr. abr. ed. Charles Osgood. Read by Charles Osgood. (Running Time: 10800 sec.). 2006. audio compact disk 14.99 (978-1-4233-1561-2(8), 9781423315612, BCD Value Price) Brilliance Audio.

Defending Baltimore Against Enemy Attack: A Boyhood Year During WWII. unabr. ed. Charles Osgood. Read by Charles Osgood. 2 CDs. (Running Time: 3 hrs.). 2004. 24.95 (978-1-59335-313-1(8), 1593353138, Brilliance MP3); 39.25 (978-1-59335-473-2(8), 1593354738, Brlnc Audio MP3 Lib) Brilliance Audio.

Defending Baltimore Against Enemy Attack: A Boyhood Year During WWII. unabr. ed. Charles Osgood. Read by Charles Osgood. (Running Time: 3 hrs.). 2004. 39.25 (978-1-59710-205-6(9), 1597102059, BADLE); 24.95 (978-1-59710-204-9(0), 1597102040, BAD) Brilliance Audio.

Defending Billy Ryan. unabr. ed. George V. Higgins. Read by Adams Morgan. 5 cass. (Running Time: 7 hrs.). 1997. 39.95 Set. (978-0-7861-1234-0(4), 1980) Blckstn Audio.
In this electrifying legal thriller, Jerry Kennedy is the guy his ex-wife calls the classiest, sleazy criminal lawyer.

Defending Billy Ryan. unabr. ed. George V. Higgins. (Running Time: 27000 sec.). 2007. audio compact disk 29.95 (978-0-7861-0488-8(0)); audio compact disk 55.00 (978-0-7861-0484-0(8)) Blckstn Audio.

Defending Identity: Its Indispensable Role in Protecting Democracy. unabr. ed. Natan Sharansky. Read by Stefan Rudnicki. Told to Shira Weiss Wolosky. (Running Time: 25200 sec.). 2008. 29.95 (978-1-4332-1206-2(4)) Blckstn Audio.

Defending Identity: Its Indispensable Role in Protecting Democracy. unabr. ed. Natan Sharansky. Read by Stefan Rudinicki. Told to Shira Weiss Wolosky. 6 CDs. (Running Time: 7 hrs.). 2008. audio compact disk 29.95 (978-1-4332-1207-9(2)) Blckstn Audio.

Defending Identity: Its Indispensable Role in Protecting Democracy. unabr. ed. Natan Sharansky & Shira Weiss Wolosky. (Running Time: 7.5 hrs. 0 mins.). 2008. 29.95 (978-1-4332-1208-6(0)) Blckstn Audio.

Defending Identity: Its Indispensable Role in Protecting Democracy. unabr. ed. Natan Sharansky & Shira Wolosky Weiss. Read by Stefan Rudnicki. (Running Time: 7.5 hrs. 0 mins.). 2008. 59.95 (978-1-4332-1204-8(8)); audio compact disk 72.00 (978-1-4332-1205-5(6)) Blckstn Audio.

Defending the Faith. 2002. (978-1-931713-42-9(1)) Word For Today.

Defending the Faith. 2003. audio compact disk (978-1-931713-83-2(9)); audio compact disk (978-1-931713-84-9(7)) Word For Today.

Defending the Fatherless. Douglas W. Phillips. 1 cass. (Running Time: 56 mins.). 2000. 7.00 (978-1-929241-13-2(5)) Pub: Vsn Forum. Dist(s): STL Dist NA

Defending the Fatherless. Douglas W. Phillips. 1 CD. (Running Time: 56 mins.). 2000. audio compact disk 10.00 (978-1-929241-74-3(7)) Pub: Vsn Forum. Dist(s): STL Dist NA
The most neglected group in the Church is children of single-mother homes. It is a biblical obligation to help such mothers stay off welfare and out of the

workforce, and to enable them to home educate their children. This is true religion.

Defending the Undefendable. 1 cass. (Running Time: 60 min.). 1988. 9.95 (978-0-945999-10-2(0)) Independent Inst.
A Provocative & Hilarious Defense of the Economic & Social Benefits of a Host of Traditionally Unpopular Social Figures, Such As the Slumlord, Prostitute, Blackmailer, etc.

Defending the Undefendables. unabr. ed. Walter Block. 1 cass. (Running Time: 51 min.). 12.95 (745) J Norton Pubs.

***Defending Your Faith: An Introduction to Apologetics.** unabr. ed. R. C. Sproul. Narrated by Robertson Dean. (ENG.). 2008. 14.98 (978-1-59644-459-1(2), Hovel Audio) christianaud.

Defending Your Faith: An Introduction to Apologetics. unabr. ed. Robert C. Sproul. Read by Robertson Dean. (Running Time: 6 hrs. 0 mins. 0 sec.). (ENG.). 2008. audio compact disk 24.98 (978-1-59644-458-4(4)) christianaud.

Defense Against Alzheimer's Disease: A Rational Blueprint for Prevention. unabr. ed. H. J. Roberts. Read by H. J. Roberts. 4 cass. (Running Time: 5 hrs.). 1995. 39.95 Set. (978-1-884243-03-5(7)) Sunshine Sentinel.
An unprecedented & original clarification of the nature & evolution of AD, its early warning signs & risk factors prior to dementia, & a panoramic program of prevention efforts before extensive & irreversible brain damage has occurred. These measures encompass nutrition, the avoidance or minimizing of exposure to neurotoxic influences, & suggestions about living in contemporary society.

Defense Agencies, Pts. 1 & 2. unabr. ed. Murray Newton Rothbard. 2 cass. (Running Time: 1 hr. 55 min.). 19.95 (184) J Norton Pubs.

Defense Equipment in India: A Strategic Reference 2007. Compiled by Icon Group International, Inc. Staff. 2007. ring bd. 195.00 (978-0-497-36009-2(8)) Icon Grp.

Defense Equipment in Philippines: A Strategic Reference 2006. Compiled by Icon Group International, Inc. Staff. 2007. ring bd. 195.00 (978-0-497-82387-0(X)) Icon Grp.

Defense for the Devil. unabr. ed. Read by Anna Fields & Carrington MacDuffie. (Running Time: 46800 sec.). (Barbara Holloway Novels Ser.). 2007. audio compact disk 90.00 (978-0-7861-6730-2(0)) Blckstn Audio.

Defense for the Devil. unabr. ed. Kate Wilhelm. Afterword by Carrington MacDuffie. (Running Time: 46800 sec.). (Barbara Holloway Novels Ser.). 2007. audio compact disk 29.95 (978-0-7861-7064-7(6)) Blckstn Audio.

Defense for the Devil. unabr. ed. Kate Wilhelm. Read by Carrington MacDuffie. (Running Time: 46800 sec.). (Barbara Holloway Novels Ser.). 2007. 72.95 (978-0-7861-4676-5(1)) Blckstn Audio.

Defense in Mexico: A Strategic Reference 2006. Compiled by Icon Group International, Inc. Staff. 2007. ring bd. 195.00 (978-0-497-82363-4(2)) Icon Grp.

Defense is Ready: Life in the Trenches of Criminal Law. Leslie Abramson. 2004. 10.95 (978-0-7435-4619-5(9)) Pub: S&S Audio. Dist(s): S and S Inc

Defense Is the First Act of War. 2006. audio compact disk 15.00 (978-1-890246-43-3(3)) B Katie Int Inc.

Defense Mechanisms. Robert Stone. 1 cass. 1983. 10.00 (978-0-938137-01-6(8)) Listen & Learn.
Topics include: The Origin of Defense Mechanisms; Compensation; Disassociation; Denial; Introjection; Rationalization; Displacement; Sublimation; Conversion; Projection; Regression; Repression; Suppression; Reaction Formation; Symbolization; Undoing.

Defense of the West. unabr. collector's ed. Basil H. Liddell-Hart. Read by Bill Kelsey. 9 cass. (Running Time: 13 hrs. 30 min.). 1988. 72.00 (978-0-7366-1413-9(3), 2300) Books on Tape.
Hart presents a series of "riddles of war & peace" & his considered answers. He sorts his riddles into yesterday, today & tomorrow.

Defense Spending: Who Benefits? 1 cass. (Running Time: 30 min.). 9.95 (AT-85-07-08, HarperThor) HarpC GBR.

Defensive Investing. unabr. ed. Steve Buckstein. 1 cass. (Running Time: 49 min.). 12.95 (416) J Norton Pubs.

Deferred see Poetry of Langston Hughes

Deferred Compensation Arrangements. Read by Raymond Hedger. 1 cass. 1990. 20.00 (AL-97) PA Bar Inst.

Defi d'Olga, Set. Henri Troyat. 3 cass. (FRE.). 1996. 38.95 (1802-LQP) Olivia & Hill.
The story of an exiled Russian novelist in Paris who attains fame at the end of her life. Based on the life of Nina Berberova.

***Defiance.** unabr. ed. Don Brown. (Running Time: 11 hrs. 19 mins. 0 sec.). (Navy Justice Ser.). (ENG.). 2008. 12.99 (978-0-310-30058-8(4)) Zondervan.

Defiance: The Bielski Partisans. unabr. ed. Nechama Tec. Read by Stefan Rudnicki. (Running Time: 13 hrs. 0 mins.). 2008. 29.95 (978-1-4332-6593-8(1)); audio compact disk 24.95 (978-1-4332-6592-1(3)); audio compact disk 99.00 (978-1-4332-6590-7(7)); audio compact disk 72.95 (978-1-4332-6589-1(3)) Blckstn Audio.

Defiant. Paul Dengelegi. Read by Charlton Griffin. Characters created by Barry Sadler. 2 vols. (Casca Ser.). 2004. 18.00 (978-1-58807-124-8(3)); (978-1-58807-573-4(7)) Am Pubng Inc.

Defiant Hero. unabr. ed. Suzanne Brockmann. Read by Carrington MacDuffie. 10 cass. (Running Time: 14 hrs.). (Troubleshooter Ser.: No. 2). 2004. 84.95 (978-0-7927-3223-5(5), CSL 657, Chivers Sound Lib); audio compact disk 110.95 (978-0-7927-3224-2(3), SLD 657, Chivers Sound Lib) AudioGO.
There are eight words Meg Moore has never been able to forget: "The United States refuses to negotiate with terrorists." But what was merely a chilling warning when she worked as a translator in a European embassy, now spells out a potential death sentence for her daughter and grandmother who have been kidnapped by a lethal group called the Extremists. Meg has to act-and quickly. Going against everything she was taught, she will now do anything to meet their unspeakable demands; anything-even kill-to save her child. When Navy SEAL Lieutenant, junior grade, John Nilsson is summoned to Washington, D.C. by the FBI to help negotiate a hostage situation, the last person he expects to see holding a foreign ambassador at gunpoint is Meg. He hasn't seen her in years, but he's never forgotten how it feels to hold her in his arms. John could lose his career if he helps her escape. She will lose her life if he doesn't.

Defining Beauty. Perf. by Danielle Skorich. 1 CD. (Running Time: 1 hr. 30 mins.). 2001. audio compact disk 16.00 (978-1-58459-089-7(0)) Wrld Lib Pubns.

Defining Dulcie. unabr. ed. Paul Acampora. Read by Jennifer Ikeda. 4 CDs. (Running Time: 3 hrs. 45 mins.). (YA). 2006. audio compact disk 44.75 (978-1-4281-1739-6(3), C3897); 28.75 (978-1-4281-1734-1(2), 98522) Recorded Bks.
Paul Acampora makes his exciting debut in young adult fiction with this poignant tale of a girl coping with the recent death of her father. When her mother moves the family to California, Dulcie decides to drive her father¿s pickup truck back to Connecticut on her own.

Defining from Your Heart Workshop. Jackie Woods. 2003. audio compact disk 49.95 (978-0-9659665-9-7(3)) Adawehi Pr.

Defining Moment: FDR's Hundred Days & the Triumph of Hope. Jonathan Alter. Read by Grover Gardner. (Running Time: 45300 sec.). (Audio Editions Mystery Masters Ser.). 2006. 39.95 (978-1-57270-554-8(X)) Pub: Audio Partners. Dist(s): PerseuPGW

Defining Moment: FDR's Hundred Days & the Triumph of Hope. unabr. ed. Jonathan Alter. Narrated by Grover Gardner. 10 CDs. (Running Time: 12 hrs..). (ENG.). 2006. audio compact disk 19.95 (978-1-57270-553-1(1)) Pub: AudioGO. Dist(s): Perseus Dist

Defining Moments: How to Seize Life's Little Opportunities & Turn Them into Something Big. unabr. ed. Stephen Perrine. Read by Stephen Perrine. Told to Mike Zimmerman. (Running Time: 8 hrs.). (ENG.). 2010. audio compact disk 39.98 (978-1-59659-380-0(6), GildAudio) Pub: Gildan Media. Dist(s): HachBkGrp

Defining Your Destiny: A Spiritual Guide to Wholeness, Vol. 1. Aletha B. Ray. 1996. 13.95 (978-0-9655114-1-4(3)) Defining Your Destiny.

Definitely above Average: Stories & Comedy for You & Your Poor Old Parents. abr. ed. Garrison Keillor. Read by Garrison Keillor. 2 CDs. (Running Time: 2 hrs. 30 mins.). (ENG.). 2000. audio compact disk 24.95 (978-1-56511-412-8(4), 1565114124) Pub: HighBridge. Dist(s): Workman Pub

Definitely Dead. Charlaine Harris. Narrated by Johanna Parker. (Running Time: 37800 sec.). (Sookie Stackhouse Ser.: Bk. 6). 2006. audio compact disk 34.99 (978-1-4193-9326-6(X)) Recorded Bks.

Definition of Family: John 19:26-27. Ed Young. 1999. 4.95 (978-0-7417-2209-6(7), 1209) Win Walk.

Definitions - Formal Logic. John Robbins. 1 cass. (Introduction to Logic Ser.: No. 4). 5.00 Trinity Found.

Definitive Collection. Contrib. by Michael Knott & LSU. (Running Time: 3600 sec.). 1999. audio compact disk 16.99 (978-5-551-88433-0(3)) Pamplin.

Definitive Collection. Contrib. by David Meece. 2007. audio compact disk 7.97 (978-5-558-14540-3(4), Word Records) Word Enter.

Definitive Collection. Contrib. by Leslie Phillips. 2007. audio compact disk 7.97 (978-5-558-14538-0(2), Word Records) Word Enter.

Definitive Collection. unabr. ed. Rhino. Read by Rhino. (YA). 2008. 34.99 (978-1-60514-548-8(3)) Find a World.

Definitive Hospital Management of Life Threatening Emergencies. (Postgraduate Programs Ser.: C85-PG5). 85.00 (8515) Am Coll Surgeons.
Provides the latest controversies related to the evaluation & management of severe multisystem injury. 12 hours CME Category 1 credit.

Deflating Fear Barriers. Virgil B. Smith. Read by Virgil B. Smith. 1 cass. (Running Time: 11 min.). 1979. 5.95 (978-1-878507-08-2(7), 28C) Human Grwth Services.
Guided imagery for getting rid of listener's doubts about his/her ability to reach possible goals for behavior change; includes music & sound effects.

Deflation Reconsidered. unabr. ed. Murray Newton Rothbard. 1 cass. (Running Time: 22 min.). (Symposium on the Geographical Aspects of Inflation: Tape 4 of 5). 12.95 (464) J Norton Pubs.

Defrosting Telephone Cold Calls. Rebecca L. Morgan. Read by Rebecca L. Morgan. 1 cass. (Running Time: 33 min.). 1993. 12.95 incl. script. (978-0-9660740-4-8(1)) Morgan Seminar.
How to get through the "rejectionists" (receptionists); How to qualify, closing for the appointment, following up easily.

Deftones: The Unauthorized Biography of the Deftones. Martin Harper. 1 CD. (Running Time: 1 hr.). (Maximum Ser.). (ENG.). 2001. audio compact disk 14.95 (978-1-84240-092-0(4)) Pub: Chrome Dreams GBR. Dist(s): IPG Chicago

Defy Aging: Develop the Mental & Emotional Vitality to Live Longer, Healthier, & Happier. Excerpts. Michael Brickey. 9 cass. (Running Time: 13 hours). 2003. 79.95 (978-0-9701555-1-1(4)) New Resour.
Book on tape read by the author: Research, theory, and how to for living longer, healthier, and happier. Emphasis is on Attitudes, Beliefs, and Coping Skills. Featured on Oprah and CNN.

Defy Gravity: Healing Beyond the Bounds of Reason. Caroline Myss. 2009. audio compact disk 23.95 (978-1-4019-2293-1(7)) Hay House.

Defying Hitler. unabr. ed. Sebastian Haffner. Read by Robert Whitfield. 7 CDs. (Running Time: 8 hrs. 30 mins.). 2003. audio compact disk 56.00 (978-0-7861-9141-3(4), 3149); 44.95 (978-0-7861-2516-6(0), 3149) Blckstn Audio.
Spanning the period from 1907 to 1933, this book offers a unique perspective on how the average educated German grappled with the rise of Hitler, the growing influence of Nazism and a rapidly changing society.

DeGaulle: 22 Aout 1962 - l'Attentat du Petit-Clamart. 1 cass. (FRE.). 1995. 16.95 (1737-RF) Olivia & Hill.
The General escapes from the most serious attempt made on his life. Recordings of the time.

DeGaulle: 27 Avril 1969 - le Referendum. 1 cass. (FRE.). 1995. 16.95 (1740-RF) Olivia & Hill.
On 27 April 1969, the General decides to retire to Colombey-les-Deux-Eglises when the French voted against his reforms. Recordings of the time.

Degree of Guilt. unabr. collector's ed. Richard North Patterson. Read by Alexander Adams. 13 cass. (Running Time: 19 hrs. 30 min.). (Christopher Paget Ser.: Bk. 2). 1994. 104.00 (978-0-7366-2612-5(3), 3354) Books on Tape.
Christopher Paget is a trial lawyer with a famous past. As a young investigator he brought down a president. It cost him his relationship with Mary Carelli. Fifteen years have passed while Paget raises their son, seeking privacy. Then a murder changes everything.

Degree Symbols. William Whisenant. 1 cass. 8.95 (361) Am Fed Astrologers.
Sabian symb. of Jones & Wheeler replicated.

Degrees of Connection. Jon Cleary. 6 cass. (Running Time: 8 hrs.). (Story Sound Ser.). (J). 2005. 54.95 (978-1-85903-816-1(6)); audio compact disk 71.95 (978-1-85903-821-5(2)) Pub: Mgna Lrg Print GBR. Dist(s): Ulverscroft US

Degrees of Spiritual Awareness. Doug Curnayn. (Running Time: 24540 sec.). 2008. audio compact disk 29.99 (978-1-60604-202-1(5)) Tate Pubng.

Deidre of the Sorrows. Perf. by Patrick Cassidy. 1 cass., 1 CD. 8.78 (WH 11247); audio compact disk 13.58 CD Jewel box. (WH 11247) NewSound.

Deirdre of the Sorrows. Short Stories. Perf. by Diane Edgecomb & Margot Chamberlain. Adapted by Diane Edgecomb. Score by Tom Megan. Arranged by Margot Chamberlain. 1 CD. (Running Time: 43 mins). Dramatization. 2004. audio compact disk 15.99 (978-0-9651669-2-8(9)) Living Myth Audio.
Deirdre is Ireland's most beloved romance; a haunting legend of love and betrayal set in the turbulent world of the pre-Christian Celts. Diane Edgecomb's powerful re-telling is underscored by composer Tom Megan using both original and traditional melodies. Long-time collaborator, Margot Chamberlain accompanies the spoken word performance on Celtic harp.

Deitch: Animating Picture Books; Animating Strega Nonna. 2004. cass. & flmstrp 30.00 (978-1-56008-649-9(1)) Weston Woods.

Deity Formerly Known as God. Jarrett Stevens. (Running Time: 3 hrs. 46 mins. 0 sec.). (ENG.). 2009. 14.99 (978-0-310-30438-8(5)) Zondervan.

Déjà Dead. abr. ed. Kathy Reichs. (Temperance Brennan Ser.: No. 1). 2004. 14.95 (978-0-7435-4620-1(2)) Pub: S&S Audio. Dist(s): S and S Inc

Déjà Dead. unabr. ed. Kathy Reichs. Narrated by Barbara Rosenblat. 11 cass. (Running Time: 16 hrs.). (Temperance Brennan Ser.: No. 1). 1998. 96.00 (978-0-7887-1750-5(2), 95228E7) Recorded Bks.
A forensic anthropologist pursues a serial killer when the police would not follow the clues.

***Deja Vu.** abr. ed. Fern Michaels. Read by Laural Merlington. (Running Time: 3 hrs.). (Sisterhood Ser.). 2011. 9.99 (978-1-4418-9401-4(2), 9781441894014, BAD); audio compact disk 14.99 (978-1-4418-1896-6(0), 9781441818966, BACD) Brilliance Audio.

***Deja Vu.** unabr. ed. Fern Michaels. Read by Laural Merlington. (Running Time: 9 hrs.). (Sisterhood Ser.). 2011. 39.97 (978-1-4418-1893-5(6), 9781441818935, Brinc Audio MP3 Lib); 24.99 (978-1-4418-1894-2(4), 9781441818942, BAD); 39.97 (978-1-4418-1895-9(2), 9781441818959, BADLE); 24.99 (978-1-4418-1892-8(8), 9781441818928, Brilliance MP3); audio compact disk 29.99 (978-1-4418-1890-4(1), 9781441818904, Bril Audio CD Unabri); audio compact disk 79.97 (978-1-4418-1891-1(X), 9781441818911, BriAudCD Unabrid) Brilliance Audio.

Dejalos Ir con Amor see Letting Go with Love: The Grieving Process

Déjame Que Te Alabe. unabr. ed. Jaime Murrell, Sr. (SPA.). 1997. 9.99 (978-0-8297-2355-7(2)) Zondervan.

***Dejando un Legado.** Charles R. Swindoll.Tr. of Creating a Legacy. 2010. audio compact disk 15.00 (978-1-57972-895-3(2)) Insight Living.

Deje de Fumar. Betty L. Randolph. 1 cass. (Health Ser.). 1989. bk. 12.98 (978-1-55909-191-6(6), 30E) Randolph Tapes.
Presents a program in spanish. Features male-female voice tracks with the right-left brain.

Dejection: An Ode see Poetry of Coleridge

Del Llanto a la Sonrisa. Alex Campos. (Especialidades Juveniles Ser.). (YA). (gr. 7-12). 2008. pap. bk. 10.99 (978-0-8297-5290-8(0)) Pub: Vida Pubs. Dist(s): Zondervan

Del Llanto a Sonrisa / From Sadness to Happiness. unabr. ed. Alex Campos. (Especialidades Juveniles Ser.). (SPA.). 2009. audio compact disk 11.99 (978-0-8297-5748-4(1)) Pub: Vida Pubs. Dist(s): Zondervan

Delaware Corporation Laws Annotated. Ed. by Lexis Editorial Staff. pap. bk. 32.00 (978-0-8205-8183-5(6)) LEXIS Pub.

Delay Damages - New Rule 238. Read by Ronald L. Wolf. 1 cass. 1990. 20.00 (AL-100) PA Bar Inst.

Delegating & Supervising. Brian S. Tracy. Read by Brian S. Tracy. 2 cass. (Effective Manager Seminar Ser.: No. 6). 95.00 Set, incl. 1-hr. videotape & 2 wkbks., program notes & study guide. (748VD) Nightingale-Conant.
How to "multiply yourself" - how to "let go." Monitoring & controlling.

Delegation Secrets of Tom Sawyer: Neh. 3:1-32. Ed Young. 1990. 4.95 (978-0-7417-1807-5(3), 807) Win Walk.

Delete, Vol. 10. unabr. ed. Jon McCormick. Read by Randy Nyborg. 5 cass. (Running Time: 5 hrs.). 1999. 19.95 (978-1-57002-113-8(9)) U P H.
Secrets of success by a million dollar club auto salesman.

***Delf B1 200 Activities.** Isabelle Normand & Richard Lescure. (FRE., 2008. pap. bk. & pap. bk. (978-2-09-035230-6(2)) Cle Intl FRA.

***DELF Junior Scolaire A1 Nouveau Diplome: 150 Activites.** Created by CLE International. (FRE.). (YA). 2007. audio compact disk (978-2-09-032844-8(4)) Cle Intl FRA.

***DELF Junior Scolaire A2: 200 Activites.** Cecile Jouhanne & Stephanie Boussat. (FRE., 2005. pap. bk. & pap. bk. (978-2-09-035248-1(5)) Cle Intl FRA.

***Delf Junior Scolaire B1: 200 Activites.** Alain Rausch et al. (FRE., (YA). 2006. pap. bk. (978-2-09-035236-8(1)) Cle Intl FRA.

***Delf Junior Scolaire B2: 200 Activites.** Alain Rausch et al. (FRE., (YA). 2002. pap. bk. (978-2-09-035258-0(2)) Cle Intl FRA.

Delft Thunderclap. 2001. audio compact disk 9.95 (978-1-930805-15-6(2)) XC Pubng.

***Deliberate Church.** unabr. ed. Mark Dever. Narrated by Cris Obryon. (ENG.). 2007. 14.98 (978-1-59644-461-4(4), Hovel Audio) christianaud.

Deliberate Church: Building Your Ministry on the Gospel. unabr. ed. Mark Dever & Paul Alexander. Read by Cris O'Bryon. Frwd. by D. A. Carson. (Running Time: 6 hrs. 0 mins. 0 sec.). (ENG.). 2007. audio compact disk 23.98 (978-1-59644-460-7(6)) christianaud.

Delicate Edible Birds: And Other Stories. unabr. ed. Lauren Groff. Read by Susan Ericksen. 1 MP3-CD. (Running Time: 10 hrs. 0 mins. 0 sec.). (ENG.). 2009. audio compact disk 19.99 (978-1-4001-6070-9(7)); audio compact disk 29.99 (978-1-4001-1070-4(X)); audio compact disk 59.99 (978-1-4001-4070-1(6)) Pub: Tantor Media. Dist(s): IngramPubServ

Delicate Fade: Common Children. Perf. by Common Children. 1 cass., 1 CD. 1997. 16.98 Cd. Provident Mus Dist.
The love & redemption of God through honest & poetic lyrics.

Delicate Line. Valerie Green. 1 cass. (Running Time: 070 min.). 1999. 7.95 (978-1-894188-02-9(0)) APG.

Delicate Prey. abr. ed. Read by Paul Bowles. 1 cass. (Running Time: 50 min.). 10.95 (978-0-8045-0855-1(0), SAC 43-6) Spoken Arts.
The author reads from two of his most memorable & disturbing works.

***Delicious.** unabr. ed. Susan Mallery. Read by Therese Plummer. (Running Time: 9 hrs.). (Buchanan Saga Ser.). 2011. 39.97 (978-1-4418-7615-7(4), 9781441876157, BADLE); 19.99 (978-1-4418-7613-3(8), 9781441876133, Brilliance MP3); 39.97 (978-1-4418-7614-0(6), 9781441876140, Brinc Audio MP3 Lib); audio compact disk 19.99 (978-1-4418-7611-9(1), 9781441876119, Bril Audio CD Unabri); audio compact disk 79.97 (978-1-4418-7612-6(X), 9781441876126, BriAudCD Unabrid) Brilliance Audio.

Delicious Holiday Chocolate & Cookies. Compiled by Evelyn L. Beilenson. Illus. by Joanna Roy. 1 CD. (Running Time: 1 hr.). (BookNotes Ser.). 1998. bk. 14.99 (978-0-88088-408-2(8)) Peter Pauper.

Delight see J. B. Priestley

Delightful Recreation: The Music of Thomas Jefferson. 1 CD. (Running Time: 1 hr.). 2003. audio compact disk (978-1-931592-02-4(0)) Colonial Williamsburg.
Thomas Jefferson loved music. He amassed a huge collection of sheet music from which these selections are taken. The songs were recorded in Colonial Williamsburg at the Governor?s Palace with instruments of the period. Jefferson played the violin at the Palace during his student days and during his tenure as Virginia governor.

Delights of a Word Filled Marriage - Living out Marriage God's Way. 2005. 15.00 (978-1-933561-13-4(0)) BFM Books.

Delineating a Business Chart. Weiss Kelly. 1 cass. 8.95 (544) Am Fed Astrologers.
Interpret charts of current firms.

Delineating Ray-Centered Chart. Joan Titsworth. Read by Joan Titsworth. 1 cass. (Running Time: 90 min.). 1994. 8.95 (1103) Am Fed Astrologers.
Ray-centered astrology.

Delineation. Beverly J. Farrell. 1 cass. 8.95 (611) Am Fed Astrologers.
An AFA Convention workshop tape.

Delineation of Progressions. Joan Titsworth. 1 cass. 8.95 (467) Am Fed Astrologers.
Predict events with progressions.

***Delirious.** unabr. ed. Daniel Palmer. (Running Time: 13 hrs.). 2011. 39.97 (978-1-61106-349-3(3), 9781611063493, BADLE); 24.99 (978-1-61106-348-6(5), 9781611063486, BAD) Brilliance Audio.

***Delirious.** unabr. ed. Daniel Palmer. Read by Peter Berkrot. (Running Time: 13 hrs.). 2011. 39.97 (978-1-61106-347-9(7), 9781611063479, Brinc Audio MP3 Lib); 24.99 (978-1-61106-345-5(0), 9781611063455, Brilliance MP3); audio compact disk 79.97 (978-1-61106-344-8(2), 9781611063448, BriAudCD Unabrid); audio compact disk 29.99 (978-1-61106-343-1(4), 9781611063431, Bril Audio CD Unabri) Brilliance Audio.

Delirious Summer. abr. ed. Ray Blackston. 2004. audio compact disk 34.99 (978-1-58926-649-0(8)) Oasis Audio.

Delirious Summer. unabr. ed. Ray Blackston. Narrated by Andrew Peterson. 9 CDs. (Running Time: 9 hrs.). (ENG.). 2004. audio compact disk 34.99 (978-1-58926-633-9(1), Oasis Kids) Oasis Audio.

Delirious Summer. unabr. ed. Ray Blackston. Narrated by Andrew Peterson. (ENG.). 2004. 24.49 (978-1-60814-080-0(6)) Oasis Audio.

Delirious Summer. unabr. ed. Read by Andrew Peterson. 6 cass. (Running Time: 9 hrs.). 29.99 (978-1-58926-632-2(3), Oasis Kids) Oasis Audio.

***Delirium.** unabr. ed. Lauren Oliver. (ENG.). 2011. (978-0-06-201252-4(5)) HarperCollins Pubs.

Delitos Economicos y Financieros en la Empresa Publica y Privada. unabr. ed. Danilo Lugo.Tr. of Economic & Financial Crimes. (SPA.). audio compact disk 13.00 (978-958-43-0230-4(2)) YoYoMusic.

Deliver Me from Adam. 2003. 19.99 (978-1-58602-134-4(6)); audio compact disk 24.99 (978-1-58602-135-1(4)) E L Long.

Deliver Me from Adam, Vol. 2. 2003. 20.00 (978-1-58602-144-3(3)); audio compact disk 25.00 (978-1-58602-145-0(1)) E L Long.

Deliver Me from Evil. unabr. ed. Mary Monroe. Narrated by Patricia R. Floyd. 1 CD (digital). (Running Time: 11 hrs. 15 mins.). 2008. 56.75 (978-1-4361-3228-2(2)); 82.75 (978-1-4281-7501-3(6)); audio compact disk 123.75 (978-1-4281-7503-7(2)) Recorded Bks.
Hot, edgy, and undeniably addictive, New York Times best-selling author Mary Monroe's contemporary dramas entice readers. Demonstrating the same verve for storytelling that rocketed her previous novels onto the best-seller lists, Deliver Me from Evil introduces Christine Thurman, a vivacious 31-year-old about to enter a dangerous new phase in her life.

Deliver the Message. unabr. ed. M. Lewis Peterson. Read by M. Lewis Peterson. 1 cass. (Running Time: 1 hr.). Dramatization. (J). (gr. 7-12). 1994. 11.00 (978-1-885721-01-3(3)) L P Prods.
Motivational free verse poems that focus on African American culture, male/female relationships & self determination through character development.

Deliver the Message. unabr. rev. ed. M. Lewis Peterson. Read by M. Lewis Peterson. 1 cass. (Running Time: 1 hr.). Dramatization. (J). (ps-12). 1994. pap. bk. 27.00 (978-1-885721-00-6(5)) L P Prods.

Deliver Us from Evil. abr. ed. David Baldacci. Read by Ron McLarty. (Running Time: 6 hrs.). (ENG.). 2010. audio compact disk 29.98 (978-1-60024-966-2(3)) Pub: Hachet Audio. Dist(s): HachBkGrp

***Deliver Us from Evil.** abr. ed. David Baldacci. Read by Ron McLarty. (Running Time: 6 hrs.). (ENG.). 2010. 19.98 (978-1-60788-167-4(5)) Pub: Hachet Audio. Dist(s): HachBkGrp

***Deliver Us from Evil.** abr. ed. David Baldacci. Read by Ron McLarty. 5 CDs. (Running Time: 6 hrs.). (ENG.). 2011. audio compact disk 14.98 (978-1-60788-700-3(2)) Pub: Hachet Audio. Dist(s): HachBkGrp

***Deliver Us from Evil.** abr. ed. Sean Hannity. Read by Sean Hannity. (ENG.). 2004. (978-0-06-076413-5(9), Harper Audio); (978-0-06-081357-4(1), Harper Audio) HarperCollins Pubs.

Deliver Us from Evil. unabr. ed. David Baldacci. Read by Ron McLarty. (Running Time: 14 hrs. 30 mins.). (ENG.). 2010. audio compact disk 39.98 (978-1-60024-964-8(7)) Pub: Hachet Audio. Dist(s): HachBkGrp

***Deliver Us from Evil.** unabr. ed. David Baldacci. Read by Ron McLarty. (Running Time: 14 hrs. 30 mins.). (ENG.). 2010. 26.98 (978-1-60024-963-1(9)) Pub: Hachet Audio. Dist(s): HachBkGrp

***Deliver Us from Evil: Defeating Terrorism, Despotism, & Liberalism.** abr. ed. Sean Hannity. Read by Sean Hannity. 2010. audio compact disk 14.99 (978-0-06-202042-0(0), Harper Audio) HarperCollins Pubs.

Deliver Us from Evil - Audiobook: True Cases of Haunted Houses & Demonic Attacks. J. F. Sawyer. Read by Sharon Brogden. As told by Ed Warren & Lorraine Warren. 2009. audio compact disk 9.99 (978-0-9819624-2-9(4)) OmniMedia.

Deliver Us from Normal. unabr. ed. Kate Klise. Narrated by Johnny Heller. 4 cass. (Running Time: 4 hrs. 45 mins.). 2005. 29.95 (978-1-4193-3618-8(5)) Recorded Bks.
Author Kate Klise is known for her quirky graphic mysteries she created with her sister and illustrator, M. Sarah Klise . This, her first solo effort, is a story of self-acceptance. Everyone knows sixth-grader Charles Harrisong is so not normal! At least, this is what Charles thinks. He lives with his large family in Normal, Illinois and attends Normal Junior High where he is embarrassed by everything. Charles is headed towards a major meltdown. Then, he and his family pack up one night and mysteriously move away. This could be their new beginning as a "normal" family. But, then again.

Deliver Us from Normal. unabr. ed. Kate Klise. Narrated by Johnny Heller. 4 CDs. (Running Time: 4 hrs. 45 mins.). (YA). (gr. 5-8). 2005. audio compact disk 39.95 (978-1-4193-3820-5(X), C3270); 29.95 (978-1-4193-3617-1(7), 98021) Recorded Bks.

Deliver Us from Normal: Read-Along/Homework Pack. unabr. ed. Kate Klise. Narrated by Johnny Heller. 4 cass. (Running Time: 4 hrs. 45 mins.). (YA). (gr. 5-8). 2005. bk. 65.70 (978-1-4193-3619-5(3), 42050) Recorded Bks.

Deliverance see James Dickey Reads His Poetry & Prose

Deliverance. Instrumental Voices of Praise. (Running Time: 50 min.). 2004. audio compact disk 17.98 (978-5-559-77291-2(7)) Pub: Pt of Grace Ent. Dist(s): STL Dist NA

Deliverance. Swami Amar Jyoti. 1 cass. 1975. 9.95 (R-68) Truth Consciousness.
Emancipation, merging in timelessness & spacelessness. The inward gaze; gathering up the senses, going within to know "who am I?".

Deliverance: A Decade of Deliverance. 1 CD. (Running Time: 1 hr. 8 mi). 1999. audio compact disk 16.98 (KMGD9495) Provident Mus Dist.

Deliverance: Camelot in Smithereens. 1 CD. 1999. audio compact disk 16.98 (KMGD9543) Provident Mus Dist.

Deliverance: Learn. 1 CD. 1999. audio compact disk 16.98 (KMGD9454) Provident Mus Dist.

Deliverance Set: Weapons of Our Warfare. 2 CDs. 1999. audio compact disk 12.99 (KMGD8650) Provident Mus Dist.

Deliverance & Demonology. Derek Prince. 6 cass. 29.95 (B-DD1) Derek Prince.

Deliverance from Anxiety. Francis Frangipane. 1 cass. (Running Time: 90 mins.). (Pulling down Strongholds Ser.: Vol. 6). 2000. 5.00 (FF05-006) Morning NC.
Some of Francis' most famous life-changing messages are contained in this comprehensive 10-tape series.

Deliverance from Control. Francis Frangipane. 1 cass. (Running Time: 90 mins.). (Pulling down Strongholds Ser.: Vol. 8). 2000. 5.00 (FF05-008) Morning NC.

Deliverance from Demonic Influence. Kenneth E. Hagin. 4 cass. 16.00 (25H); 24.00 (65H) Faith Lib Pubns.

Deliverance from Demonic Influence Series. Kenneth E. Hagin. 4 cass. 1982. 16.00 Set. (71H) Faith Lib Pubns.

Deliverance from Fear. Francis Frangipane. 1 cass. (Running Time: 90 mins.). (Pulling down Strongholds Ser.: Vol. 5). 2000. 5.00 (FF05-005) Morning NC.

Deliverance from Self-Pity, No. 1. Francis Frangipane. 1 cass. (Running Time: 90 mins.). (Pulling down Strongholds Ser.: Vol. 3). 2000. 5.00 (FF05-003) Morning NC.

Deliverance from Self-Pity, No. 2. Francis Frangipane. 1 cass. (Running Time: 90 mins.). (Pulling down Strongholds Ser.: Vol. 4). 2000. 5.00 (FF05-004) Morning NC.

Deliverance from the Fear of Man. Rick Joyner. 1 cass. (Running Time: 90 mins.). (Prophetic Ministry & Gifts Ser.: Vol. 8). 2000. 5.00 (RJ06-008) Morning NC.
These messages contain advanced teaching on the prophetic ministry, including discussion of strongholds & hindrances.

Deliverance in Shanghai. unabr. collector's ed. Jerome Agel & Eugene Boe. Read by Rupert Keenlyside. 9 cass. (Running Time: 13 hrs. 30 min.). 1985. 72.00 (978-0-7366-0282-2(8), 1272) Books on Tape.
The winds of war blew twenty thousand frantic European Jews to the far East to the wickedest city on earth - Shanghai. The refugees had no choice. Nobody else wanted them. This is the story of the men, women & children who traded German subjugation for Japanese.

Delivered see Bible in Living Sound: Life and Times of the Old Testament; Life and Times of Jesus; Life and Times of Paul

Delivered from Distraction: Getting the Most out of Life with Attention Deficit Disorder. abr. ed. Edward M. Hallowell & John J. Ratey. Read by Edward M. Hallowell. (Running Time: 3 hrs.). (ENG.). 2005. audio compact disk 22.95 (978-0-7393-1762-4(8), Random AudioBks) Pub: Random Audio Pubg. Dist(s): Random

Delivered to Satan. 2 cass. 7.95 (22-13) Grace You.

Delivered to Serve. Rick Joyner. 1 cass. (Running Time: 90 mins.). (Foundation Ser.: Vol. 8). 2000. 5.00 (RJ04-008) Morning NC.
Firmly establishing basic Christian principles, these messages also illuminate some of the primary enemies of truth, such as legalism & the control spirit.

***Delivering Happiness: A Path to Profits, Passion, & Purpose.** Tony Hsieh. Read by Author. (Running Time: 9 hrs.). (ENG.). 2011. audio compact disk & audio compact disk 19.98 (978-1-60941-280-7(X)) Pub: Hachet Audio. Dist(s): HachBkGrp

Delivering Happiness: A Path to Profits, Passion, & Purpose. unabr. ed. Tony Hsieh. 8 CDs. (Running Time: 9 hrs.). (ENG.). 2010. audio compact disk 29.98 (978-1-60788-230-5(2)) Pub: Hachet Audio. Dist(s): HachBkGrp

Delivering Happiness: A Path to Profits, Passion, & Purpose. unabr. ed. Read by Tony Hsieh. (Running Time: 9 hrs.). 2010. 24.98 (978-1-60788-231-2(0)) Pub: Hachet Audio. Dist(s): HachBkGrp

Delivering Knock Your Socks off Service. 4th unabr. ed. Performance Research Associates Staff. Read by Lloyd James & Sean Pratt. (Running Time: 5 hrs.). (ENG.). 2008. 24.98 (978-1-59659-177-6(3), GildAudio); audio compact disk 29.98 (978-1-59659-173-8(0), GildAudio) Pub: Gildan Media. Dist(s): HachBkGrp

Delivering Rome: The Adventures of a Young Roman Courier. unabr. ed. Donna Getzinger. Read by Terence Aselford. (J). 2007. 34.99 (978-1-60252-555-9(2)) Find a World.

Delivering Rome: The Adventures of a Young Roman Courier. unabr. ed. Donna Getzinger. 1 cd. (Running Time: 45 mins). (J). 2002. pap. bk. 35.00 (978-1-58472-240-3(1), In Aud) Pub: Sound Room. Dist(s): Baker Taylor

Delivering Rome: The Adventures of a Young Roman Courier. unabr. ed. Donna Getzinger. 1 cd. (Running Time: 45 mins). (J). 2002. audio compact disk 16.95 (978-1-58472-238-0(X), In Aud) Pub: Sound Room. Dist(s): Baker Taylor

Delivering Rome: the Advertures of a Young Roman Courier: The Advertures of a Young Roman Courier. Donna Getzinger. Read by Terence Asleford. (Running Time: 0 hr. 45 mins.). 2002. 14.95 (978-1-59912-057-7(7), Audiofy Corp) Iofy Corp.

Delivering the Buddha into Your Palm. Read by Chogyam Trungpa & Osel Tendzin. 3 cass. 1976. 29.50 (A107) Vajradhatu.
Five talks: 1) Willingness to Practice; 2) Back to Square One; 3) The Uncompromising Teacher; 4) Good Morning; 5) The Open Palm. The last talk is by The Vajra Regent Osel Tendzin.

Delivering Value & Life Planning Strategies for Clients in Turbulent Times. Instructed by Robert Barry. (Running Time: 90 mins.). 2004. audio compact disk 19.95 (978-1-59280-116-9(1)) Marketplace Bks.
Financial service firms must start thinking of financial planning as a tool for achieving the end - not as an end itself - if they hope to survive the turbulence of volatile markets, corporate scandals, terrorism and all life's uncertainties, according to expert Robert Barry. He effectively argues for creative ?life planning? strategies as a viable alternative to ?financial planning" in his entertaining new workshop for building solid, successful practices. The result of innovative thinking, Barry contends, is a practice firmly rooted in assisting clients through a lifetime of transitions that deepen, rather than strain, a client's reliance on you - their trusted financial professional.Barry's powerful new presentation helps advisors learn to think creatively "outside the box" when developing long-term client relationships. With a keen wit and a critical eye, he presents:- The 3 key ways to break into a market-Vital ingredients for break-through relationships with clients-Essential steps for setting-up well defined systems & processesPlus, -Methods for identifying the most important "drivers" that influence people's decisions-Fees for life planning versus financial planning, and much more. With so many challenges facing financial service firms these days - from theincreasing commoditization of the asset management industry and disinclination of clients to implement what planners recommend, to general market uncertainty - advisors need an arsenal of innovative new techniques to rely on. Now - find a wealth of refreshing new strategies from a proven industry pro.

Delivery Media Pt. 1: Track One. 3 cass. 1990. 25.50 set. Recorded Res.
Topics covered include networks, cable MSO's, & testing.

Delivery Media Pt. 2: Track One. 2 cass. 1990. 17.00 set. Recorded Res.
Topics covered include VCR/video disc & software, telephone, & standards.

Delmar's Automotive ASE Test Prep: Advance Engine Performance, Set 1. Delmar Publishers Staff. (C). 2000. audio compact disk 633.95 (978-0-7668-2489-8(6)) Pub: Delmar. Dist(s): CENGAGE Learn

Delmar's Automotive ASE Test Prep: Advance Engine Performance, Set 3. Delmar Publishers Staff. 4 cass. (C). 2000. audio compact disk 633.95 (978-0-7668-2503-1(5)) Pub: Delmar. Dist(s): CENGAGE Learn

Delmars Community Health Nursing Case Study. 2nd ed. Hitchcock. (C). 2002. audio compact disk 47.95 (978-0-7668-3499-6(9)) Pub: Delmar. Dist(s): CENGAGE Learn

Delmar's Comprehensive Medical Terminology: A Competency Based Approach. Betty Davis Jones. 2 cass. (Running Time: 3 hrs.). 1999. 136.95 (978-0-7668-0496-8(8)) Delmar.

Delmar's Electronic Care Plan Maker. Susan Sheehy. 1997. audio compact disk 42.95 (978-0-7668-0291-9(4)) Delmar.

Delmar's Medical Terminology. Delmar Publishers Staff. 8 cass. (Running Time: 12 hrs.). 1998. 372.95 (978-0-7668-0491-3(7)) Pub: Delmar. Dist(s): CENGAGE Learn
As an added bonus for purchasing this product there this is an Online CompanionTM that provides Portable Document Format (PDF) files for the audiotape scripts. The scripts can be printed to use while listening to each tape. When you receive the Audiotapes, there will be special instructions on how to obtain these free audio scripts for Delmar's Audiotape Set for Medical Terminology. A great supplement to any medical terminology course or library that can be used to supplement any book. These eight 70-minute audiotapes include the term, word parts, definition of the word parts and term, examples of terms used in context and then the word again. Not only will the user hear the term to understand correct pronunciation; they will also hear the word parts pronounced and defined. (medical terminology, med term, audio, pronunciation).

Delmar's Medium/Heavy Duty Truck Ase Test Prep: Preventive. Delmar Publishers Staff. (C). 2001. audio compact disk 633.95 (978-0-7668-2464-5(0)) Pub: Delmar. Dist(s): CENGAGE Learn

Delmar's Medium/Heavy Duty Truck ASE Test Prep: Preventive, Set 2. Delmar Publishers Staff. 4 CDs. (C). 2001. audio compact disk 633.95 (978-0-7668-2474-4(8)) Pub: Delmar. Dist(s): CENGAGE Learn

Delmar's Medium/Heavy Duty Truck ASE Test Prep: Preventive, Set 3. Delmar Publishers Staff. 4 CDs. (C). 2001. audio compact disk 633.95 (978-0-7668-2482-9(9)) Pub: Delmar. Dist(s): CENGAGE Learn

Delphi & Olympia, Lecture 7. 2000. Teaching Co.

Delphinium Blues. unabr. ed. Stevie Morgan. Read by Stevie Morgan. 9 cass. (Running Time: 12 hrs.). 2001. 69.95 (978-0-7531-0625-9(6)) Pub: ISIS Audio GBR. Dist(s): Ulverscroft US

Delphinus Chronicles. R. G. Roane. Read by Helen Lisanti. 6 CDs. (Running Time: 7 hrs). 2003. audio compact disk 29.95 (978-0-9723298-1-1(1)) Pub: Cherry Hill Pubng. Dist(s): Baker Taylor
6-CD audiobook, unabridged.

Delphinus Chronicles. R. G. Roane. Read by Helen Lisanti. Prod. by Cherry Hill Publishing. Music by Kennedy Smith. 8 cass. (Running Time: 7 hrs. 30 mins). Dramatization. 2003. 29.95 (978-0-9723298-3-5(8), 0-9723298-3-8); audio compact disk 29.95 (978-0-9723298-4-2(6)) Pub: Cherry Hill Pubng. Dist(s): Baker Taylor
Students at a small college in Southern California program their supercomputer to learnlanguages on its own, but the school is adjacent to an aquatic amusement park and thecomputer mistakenly learns to communicate with the world's dolphin population. The dolphinsultimately reveal explosive information about the true origins of mankind, which falls intothe wrong hands and sets off a chain of events that threatens to unravel society as we know it.

Delta Blues. Fruteland Jackson. (Guitar Roots Ser.). 1999. pap. bk. 14.95 (978-0-7390-0072-4(1), 18486) Alfred Pub.

Delta ESL Phonics: Double Letter Consonants. Marilyn Rosenthal & Patrick Hwang. (Delta ESL Phonics: Double Letter Consonants Ser.). (ENG.). (J). 2004. audio compact disk 13.95 (978-1-932748-03-1(2), DeltPubng) Delta Systems.

Delta ESL Phonics: Double Letter Vowels. Marilyn Rosenthal & Patrick Hwang. (Delta ESL Phonics: Double Letter Vowels Ser.). (ENG.). (J). 2004. audio compact disk 13.95 (978-1-932748-04-8(0), DeltPubng) Delta Systems.

Delta ESL Phonics: Long Vowels. Marilyn Rosenthal & Patrick Hwang. (Delta ESL Phonics: Long Vowels Ser.). (ENG.). (J). 2004. audio compact disk 13.95 (978-1-932748-02-4(4), DeltPubng) Delta Systems.

Delta ESL Phonics: Short Vowels. Marilyn Rosenthal & Patrick Hwang. (Delta ESL Phonics: Short Vowels Ser.). (ENG.). (J). 2004. audio compact disk 13.95 (978-1-932748-01-7(6), DeltPubng) Delta Systems.

Delta ESL Phonics: Single Letter Sounds. Patrick Hwang. (Delta ESL Phonics: Single Letter Sounds Ser.). (ENG.). (J). 2004. audio compact disk 13.95 (978-1-932748-00-0(8), DeltPubng) Delta Systems.

Delta of Venus. abr. ed. Anais Nin. Narrated by Ann Mavrolean. 2 cass. (Running Time: 2 hrs. 4 min.). 12.95 (978-0-89926-178-2(7), 866) Audio Bk.
This collection of stories is from the diary of Anais Nin & presents unexpurgated selections of erotica that were written for a private collector.

Delta of Venus. unabr. collector's ed. Anais Nin. Read by Violet Cielo. 7 cass. (Running Time: 10 hrs. 30 min.). 1979. 56.00 (978-0-7366-0122-1(8), 1129) Books on Tape.
Triple X for sex & language. A combination of poetry & pornography.

Delta of Venus, Erotica. unabr. ed. Anais Nin. Read by Amy Judd. 6 cass. 35.70 (C-125) Audio Bk.

Delta One. abr. ed. Louis Tridico. Abr. by Louis Tridico. Read by Carol Eason. 2 cass. (Running Time: 180 mins.). (Delta Code Ser.: No. 5). 2004. 18.00 (978-1-58807-373-0(4)) Am Pubng Inc.
While attending the funeral of ex-Delta-Force trooper and friend Frank Higdon, Doug Malone meets Higdon's girlfriend, Nina Grasso. She believes the CIA paramilitary officer didn't die in an ambush in Afghanistan - that he might still be alive. She enlists Malone's help in finding the truth and, together with a resourceful Afghan teenager, they uncover a deadly al-Qaeda scheme involving opium, illegal arms and the Russian mob. As they unravel the terrorists' latest plans to obtain new weapons, they also get closer to the truth about Higdon's fate. But that truth may cost them their lives.

Delta One. abr. ed. Louis Tridico. Abr. by Louis Tridico. Read by Charlie O'Dowd. 3 CDs. (Running Time: 3 hrs.). (Delta Code Ser.: No. 5). 2004. audio compact disk 25.00 (978-1-58807-324-2(6)) Am Pubng Inc.
While attending the funeral of an ex-Delta-Force trooper and friend, corporate security expert and former Special Forces officer Doug Malone meets Higdon's fiancee. She believes the CIA paramilitary officer didn't die in an ambush in Afghanistan - that he might still be alive. She enlists Malone's help in finding the truth and, together with a resourceful Afghan

teenager, they uncover a deadly al-Qaeda scheme involving opium, illegal arms, and the Russian mob. As they unravel the terrorists' latest plans to obtain new weapons, they also get closer to the truth about Higdon's fate. But that truth may cost them their lives. Abridged by the author.

Delta One: Delta Code #5. abr. ed. Louis Tridico. Abr. by Louis Tridico. Read by Carol Eason. 2 cass. (Running Time: 180 mins.). No. 5. 2004. (978-1-58807-641-0(5)) Am Pubng Inc.

Delta Return see Charles Bell 1 & 2

Delta Sleep CD - Single. 2004. audio compact disk (978-1-59250-366-7(7)) Gaiam Intl.

Delta Sleep System. Jeffrey Thompson. 2 CDs. (Running Time: 2 hrs.). 2001. audio compact disk 20.00 (82-0048) Relaxtn Co.

The clinically proven audio technology works with the body's brainwave frequencies to provide a natural and inexpensive treatment for sleeping disorders.

Delta Sleep System. Jeffrey Thompson. 2 CDs. (Running Time: 2 hrs.). 1999. audio compact disk 19.95 (978-1-55961-520-4(6)) Relaxtn Co.

Delta Sleep System. abr. ed. Jeffrey Thompson. (Running Time: 2:00:00). 1997. audio compact disk 19.98 (978-1-55961-724-6(1)) Sounds True.

There are several stages of sleep which people pass through in the course of a good restful night. In each stage our sleep gets deeper, our bodies get more relaxed and our brainwave patterns slow down. The deepest and most rejuvenating levels of sleep are associated with Delta brainwave patterns.

Delta Style: Eve Wasn't a Size 6 & Neither Am I. abr. ed. Delta Burke. Read by Delta Burke. 2 cass. (Running Time: 3 hrs.). 1998. 17.95 (978-1-55935-300-7(7)) Soundelux.

Tips on how positive thinking can transform your state of mind & give you confidence to succeed.

Delta Wedding. unabr. ed. Eudora Welty. Read by Sally Darling. 7 Cass. (Running Time: 12 Hrs). 29.95 (978-1-4025-2362-5(9)) Recorded Bks.

Delta Wedding. unabr. ed. Eudora Welty. Narrated by Sally Darling. 8 cass. (Running Time: 12 hrs.). 1994. 70.00 (978-1-55690-998-6(5), 94137E7) Recorded Bks.

Set on the Mississippi Delta in 1923, this story captures the mind & manners of the Fairchilds, a large aristocratic family, self-contained & elusive. The vagaries of the Fairchilds are keenly observed & sometimes harshly judged, by nine-year-old Laura McRaven, in town for Dabney Fairchild's wedding.

Delta's Key to the Next Generation Toefl CD's. Nancy Gallagher. 2005. audio compact disk 59.95 (978-1-887744-95-9(9), DeltPubng) Delta Systems.

Delta's Key to the Next Generation Toefl Practice Test CDs. Nancy Gallagher. 2006. audio compact disk 41.95 (978-1-932748-55-0(5), DeltPubng) Delta Systems.

Delta's Key to the Next Generation Toefl Practice Test Package. Nancy Gallagher. 2006. audio compact disk 59.95 (978-1-934960-37-0(3), DeltPubng) Delta Systems.

Delta's Key to the Next Generation Toefl Test Package. Nancy Gallagher. 2005. audio compact disk 84.95 (978-1-934960-36-3(5), DeltPubng) Delta Systems.

Deltoid Pumpkin Seed. unabr. ed. John McPhee. Read by Wolfram Kandinsky. 7 cass. (Running Time: 7 hrs.). 1992. 42.00 (978-0-7366-2214-1(4), 3007) Books on Tape.

True story of a dream to build a completely different type of aircraft.

Deluge. Contrib. by Bethany Live. Prod. by Brent Milligan. 2008. audio compact disk 13.99 (978-5-557-47915-8(5)) Integrity Music.

Deluxe Anthology of Fiddle Styles. David Reiner. 1979. 9.98 (978-0-87166-498-3(4), 93647C) Mel Bay.

Deluxe Bluegrass Mandolin Method. Ray Valla. 1993. bk. 18.95 (978-0-7866-0914-7(1), 93340P); 10.98 (978-0-87166-755-7(X), 93340C) Mel Bay.

Deluxe Business Library. Ed. by Socrates Media Editors. 2005. audio compact disk 49.95 (978-1-59546-116-2(7)) Pub: Socrates Med LLC. Dist(s): Midpt Trade

Deluxe Fiddling Method. Craig Duncan. 1981. bk. 18.95 (978-0-87166-627-7(8), 93742P) Mel Bay.

Deluxe Fiddling Method. Craig Duncan. 1981. spiral bd. 24.95 (978-0-7866-1660-2(1), 93742CDP); 9.98 (978-0-87166-626-0(X), 93742C) Mel Bay.

Deluxe Fiddling Method. Craig Duncan. 1995. audio compact disk 15.98 (978-0-7866-1646-6(6), 93742CD) Mel Bay.

Deluxe Fiddling Method. Craig Duncan. (ENG.). 2002. spiral bd. 19.95 (978-0-7866-6524-2(6)) Mel Bay.

Deluxe Finger Style Guitar Method, Vol. 1. Tommy Flint. 1983. pap. bk. 24.95 (978-0-7866-1698-5(9), 93967CDP) Mel Bay.

Deluxe Fingerstyle Guitar Method. Tommy Flint. 1995. audio compact disk 15.98 (978-0-7866-1697-8(0), 93967CD) Mel Bay.

Deluxe Harmonica Method. Phil Duncan. 1993. bk. 17.95 (978-0-87166-384-9(8), 93737P); audio compact disk 15.98 (978-0-7866-0601-6(0), 93737CD) Mel Bay.

Deluxe Harmonica Method. Phil Duncan. 1981. pap. bk. 24.95 (978-0-7866-0602-3(9), 93737CDP); 9.98 (978-0-87166-383-2(X), 93737C) Mel Bay.

Deluxe Jazz & Rock Bass Method. Vincent Bredice. 1993. bk. 21.95 (978-0-7866-0932-1(X), 93766P) Mel Bay.

Deluxe Jazz & Rock Bass Method. Vincent Bredice. 1986. 9.98 (978-1-56222-600-8(2), 93766C) Mel Bay.

Deluxe Math (Multiplication - Addition) 2 cass. (Twin Sisters Ser.). (J). bk. 23.98 Set, blisterpack, incl. 55 multiplication flashcards, poster, 8 pk. crayons, & Windows CD-Rom prog. (TWIN 951) NewSound.

Deluxe Pedal Steel Guitar Method. Dewitt Scott. 1982. spiral bd. 39.95 (978-0-7866-0610-8(X), 93849CDP); audio compact disk 15.98 (978-0-7866-0609-2(6), 93849CD) Mel Bay.

Deluxe Phonics Kit, Set. Kim Mitzo Thompson & Karen Mitzo Hilderbrand. 2 cass. (Twin Sisters Ser.). (J). bk. 23.98 Set, blisterpack, incl. 55 phonic flashcards, poster, 8 pk. crayons & Windows CD Rom prog. (TWIN 950) NewSound.

Includes Phonics 1 & 2, Phonetic skills including: consonants, vowels, blends, diagraphs, rhyming words, compound words, synonyms, antonyms & homonyms.

Deluxe 1960 Bible. Narrated by Samuel Montoya. 48 cass. (Running Time: 72 hrs.). (SPA.). 1999. 134.98 (978-7-902031-91-2(7)) Chrstn Dup Intl.

Dem Bones. 1 cass. (Running Time: 1 hr. 30 min.). 2004. bk. 24.95 (978-1-55592-692-2(4)); audio compact disk 12.95 (978-1-55592-551-2(0)); 8.95 (978-1-55592-544-4(8)) Weston Woods.

A skeleton band supplies words and music to the well-known song based on the African-American spiritual. Children will enjoy learning about the human body and having their funny bones tickled at the same time. Music and vocals by Raul Malo, narration and additional vocals by Chris Thomas King.

Dem Bones & Other Sing-along Stories: Dem Bones; Antarctic Antics; Waiting for Wings; Joseph Had a Little Overcoat. unabr. ed. Bob Barner et al. Read by Chris Thomas King et al. (J). 2008. 44.99 (978-1-60514-942-4(X)) Find a World.

Demelza: A Novel of Cornwall, 1788-1790. unabr. ed. Winston Graham. Read by Tony Britton. 12 cass. (Running Time: 12 hrs.). (Poldark Ser.: Vol. 2). 1995. 96.95 Set. (978-0-7451-6469-4(2), CAB 1086) AudioGO.

The second Poldark novel finds Demelza, daughter of a Cornish miner, married to Ross Poldark. Ross has great sympathy for the poor, but with her background of squalor, Demelza finds she has much to learn of the ways of society, men, & her husband. Is their love strong enough to survive? The fascinating 18th century mining background adds an authentic flavor to this absorbing love story.

Demelza: A Novel of Cornwall, 1788-1790. unabr. ed. Winston Graham. Read by Tony Britton. 12 cass. (Running Time: 18 hrs.). (Poldark Ser.: Bk. 2). 2000. 79.95 (CAB 1086) Pub: Chivers Audio Bks GBR. Dist(s): AudioGO

Dementia Nursing: A Guide to Practice (Book & Audio CDs Package) Ed. by Rosalie Hudson. 2 vols. (Running Time: 2 hours). (Guide to Practice Ser.). 2004. pap. bk. 59.95 (978-0-9750445-6-8(7)) Pub: Ausmed AUS. Dist(s): MPHC

Demeter & Kore. Read by Lucille Klein. 1 cass. (Running Time: 90 min.). (Facing the Gods Ser.: No. 4). 1987. 10.95 (978-0-7822-0127-7(X), 288) C G Jung IL.

Demian. unabr. ed. Hermann Hesse. Narrated by Jeff Woodman. (ENG.). 2008. audio compact disk 29.95 (978-1-60283-424-8(5)) Pub: AudioGO. Dist(s): Perseus Dist

Demian: The Story of Emil Sinclair's Youth. unabr. ed. Hermann Hesse. Read by Jeff Woodman. (Running Time: 5 hrs. 45 mins.). 2008. 44.95 (978-0-7927-5596-8(0), Chivers Sound Lib); audio compact disk 64.95 (978-0-7927-5472-5(7), Chivers Sound Lib) AudioGO.

A brilliant psychological portrait of a troubled young man's quest for self-awareness, this coming-of-age novel achieved instant critical and popular acclaim upon its 1919 publication. A landmark in the history of 20th-century literature, it reflects the author's preoccupation with the duality of human nature and the pursuit of spiritual fulfillment.

***Demigod Files.** unabr. ed. Rick Riordan. Read by Jesse Bernstein. 3 CDs. (Running Time: 3 hrs. 7 mins.). (Percy Jackson & the Olympians Ser.). (YA). (gr. 5-8). 2009. audio compact disk 30.00 (978-0-7393-8125-0(3), Listening Lib) Pub: Random Audio Pubg. Dist(s): Random

Demigod Files. unabr. ed. Rick Riordan. Read by Jesse Bernstein. (ENG.). (J). (gr. 5). 2009. audio compact disk 19.95 (978-0-7393-8123-6(7), Listening Lib) Pub: Random Audio Pubg. Dist(s): Random

Democracy Set: An American Novel. unabr. ed. Henry Adams. Read by Flo Gibson. 5 cass. (Running Time: 7 hrs.30 mins.). 1992. 20.95 (978-1-55685-255-8(X)) Audio Bk Con.

A Roman a clef caricature of political & social intrigue in the 1870's. When wealthy widow, Mrs. Lightfoot Lee comes to the capitol idealizing the government, she is disillusioned by vote buying, slander, graft, & the preposterous tactics of political boss Senator Ratcliffe.

Democracy in America. Cerebellum Academic Team. (Running Time: 30 mins.). (Just the Facts Ser.). 2001. 24.95 (978-1-59163-289-4(7)) Cerebellum.

Democracy in America. Wendy, Ralph and McElroy Raico. Read by Craig with a. supporting cast Deitschman. (Running Time: 180 hrs. NaN mins.). 2006. audio compact disk 25.95 (978-0-7861-6979-5(6)) Pub: Blckstn Audio. Dist(s): NetLibrary CO

***Democracy in America.** unabr. ed. Alexis de Tocqueville. Read by Frederick Davidson. Tr. by George Lawrence. (Running Time: 19 hrs.). 2010. 44.95 (978-1-4417-4197-4(6)); audio compact disk 160.00 (978-1-4417-4194-3(1)) Blckstn Audio.

***Democracy in America.** unabr. ed. Alexis de Tocqueville. Narrated by John Pruden. (Running Time: 34 hrs. 30 mins. 0 sec.). (ENG.). 2010. 44.99 (978-1-4001-6811-8(2)); 36.99 (978-1-4001-8811-6(3)); 64.99 (978-1-4001-9811-5(9)); audio compact disk 64.99 (978-1-4001-1811-3(5)); audio compact disk 155.99 (978-1-4001-4811-0(1)) Pub: Tantor Media. Dist(s): IngramPubServ

Democracy in America, Set. abr. ed. Alexis de Tocqueville. Read by Robert L. Halvorson. 4 cass. (Running Time: 360 min.). 28.95 (48) Halvorson Assocs.

Democracy in America: Origins of the United States. Alexis de Tocqueville. Read by Ray Smith. 2 cass. (Running Time: 2 hrs.). (ENG & ACE.). 1997. 19.50 Set. (978-1-58085-651-5(9)) Interlingua VA.

Democracy in America: Part 1 Of 2, Vol. 1. unabr. ed. Alexis de Tocqueville. Read by Frederick Davidson. Tr. by George Lawrence. 13 cass. (Running Time: 19 hrs.). 1989. 85.95 (978-0-7861-0073-6(7), 1068-A,B) Blckstn Audio.

A canonical text in the curriculum of college history & political theory courses in the United States. More than 150 years after its publication, it continues to command the attention of scholars.

Democracy in America: Part 2 Of 2, Vol. 2. unabr. ed. Alexis de Tocqueville. Read by Frederick Davidson. Tr. by George Lawrence. 9 cass. (Running Time: 19 hrs.). 1989. 62.95 (978-0-7861-0074-3(5), 1068-A,B) Blckstn Audio.

Democracy in America: The Blacks in the United States. Alexis de Tocqueville. Read by Ray Smith. 1 cass. (Running Time: 1 hrs. 30 min.). 1997. 14.50 (978-1-58085-652-2(7)) Interlingua VA.

Democracy in America Set: Alexis de Tocqueville. unabr. ed. Ralph Raico. Narrated by Craig Deitschmann. 2 cass. (Running Time: 2 hrs. 50 mins.). Dramatization. (Giants of Political Thought Ser.: Vol. 12). 1987. 17.95 (978-0-938935-12-4(7), 390272) Knowledge Prod.

Alexis de Tocqueville considered American democracy to be the greatest political experiment of modern times. In the 1830's he wrote what remains the best portrait ever of the American character. The presentation includes the essential ideas of this classic work, with a narrative explanation of the author's character, his times, the controversies he faced & the opinions of critics & supporters.

Democracy in America - Excerpts. unabr. ed. Excerpts. Alexis de Tocqueville. Narrated by George Guidall. 3 cass. (Running Time: 4 hrs. 30 mins.). 1999. 26.00 (978-1-55690-673-2(0), 92320E7) Recorded Bks.

Excerpts from the diaries kept by explorers Meriwether Lewis & William Clark on their expedition across the American continent following President Thomas Jefferson's purchase of the Louisiana territory.

Democracy Matters: Winning the Fight Against Imperialism. unabr. ed. Cornel West. 6 CDs. (Running Time: 7 hrs.). (ENG.). (gr. 12 up). 2004. audio compact disk 29.95 (978-0-14-305703-1(0), PengAudBks) Penguin Grp USA.

Democratic Schooling: What Harvard Won't Teach You. unabr. ed. Speeches. Mimsy Sadofsky. 1 cass. (Running Time: 1 hr 15 mins.). 2000. 10.00 (978-1-888947-60-1(8)) Sudbury Valley.

Talk given at Harvard Graduate School of Education by Mimsy Sadofsky, with Anna Rossetti.

Democratic Vistas of Walt Whitman. unabr. ed. Louis Untermeyer. 1 cass. (Running Time: 22 min.). (Makers of the Modern World Ser.). 1968. 12.95 (23037) J Norton Pubs.

A discussion of "Leaves of Grass".

Democratization of Clothing in America: Student Syllabus. Barbara H. Salser. (YA). (gr. 10-12). 1979. 89.10 (978-0-89420-204-9(9), 165000) Natl Book.

Demoiselle aux Yeux Verts, Set. Maurice Leblanc. 4 cass. (FRE.). 1991. 36.95 (1417-LV) Olivia & Hill.

A group of actors interpret one of the many exciting mysteries starring the "gentleman crook," Arsene Lupin, the French answer to Sherlock Holmes.

Demolition Angel. unabr. ed. Robert Crais. Narrated by Paul Hecht. 8 cass. (Running Time: 11 hrs.). 2000. 76.00 (978-0-7887-4853-0(X), 96346E7) Recorded Bks.

Looking at the life-on-the-edge world of the Los Angeles bomb squad.Three years ago Carol Starkey was one of L. A.'s best bomb squad technicians.The freak accident while disarming a bomb left her scarred inside & out. Now a Detective-2 with the LAPD's Criminal Conspiracy Section, she is struggling to rebuild her shattered world. When an explosion claims the life of a technician who was a colleague & friend, Carol is assigned to head up the investigation. With the help of an ATF agent, she discovers that a brilliant madman is designing bombs intended to kill the people whose job it is to disarm them.

Demolition Angel. unabr. ed. Robert Crais. Narrated by Paul Hecht. 9 CDs. (Running Time: 11 hrs.). 2001. audio compact disk 89.00 (978-0-7887-6170-6(6), C1394) Recorded Bks.

Three years ago, Carol Starkey was one of L.A.'s best bomb squad technicians. Then a freak accident while disarming a bomb left her scarred inside & out. Now a Detective-2 with the LAPD's Criminal Conspiracy Section, she is struggling to rebuild her shattered world. When an explosion claims the life of a technician who was a colleague & friend, Carol is assigned to head up the investigation. With the help of an ATF agent, she discovers that a brilliant madman is designing bombs intended to kill the people whose job it is to disarm them. But as they begin their chase of the man known as Mr. Red, Carol finds that nothing about the case is as it appears. All she knows for certain is that she is the next target.

Demon. Mikhail Lermontov. 1 cass. (Running Time: 60 min.). (RUS.). 1996. pap. bk. 19.50 (978-1-58085-576-1(8)) Interlingua VA.

Includes text, notes, vocabulary. The combination of written text & clarity & pace of diction will open the door for intermediate & advanced students to genuine comprehension & the use of literary texts for advancement in rapid understanding of written & oral language materials. The audio text plus written text concept makes foreign languages accessible to a much wider range of students than books alone.

Demon & Exorcism. Jack Van Impe. 1977. 7.00 (978-0-934803-29-8(3)) J Van Impe.

Sermon cassette that discusses questions about demons, such as "Where did Satan originate?" & "What part do demons play in future events?".

Demon Bike Rider. unabr. ed. Robert Leeson. Read by Kenneth Shanley. 2 cass. (Running Time: 3 hrs.). (J). (gr. 1-8). 1999. 18.95 (CCA 3078, Chivers Child Audio) AudioGO.

Demon-Haunted World: Science As a Candle in the Dark. abr. ed. Carl Sagan. Read by Michael Page. 2 cass. (Running Time: 3 hrs.). 2000. 7.95 (978-1-57815-170-7(8), 1113, Media Bks Audio) Media Bks NJ.

The respected scientist and author shows how scientific thinking is necessary to safeguard our democratic institutions in our high-tech world.

Demon Headmaster. unabr. ed. Gillian Cross. Read by Judy Bennett. 3 CDs. (Running Time: 12120 sec.). (J). 2001. audio compact disk 29.95 (978-0-7540-6507-4(3), CHCD 007, Chivers Child Audio) AudioGO.

Demon Headmaster Strikes Again. unabr. ed. Gillian Cross. Read by Judy Bennett. 3 cass. (Running Time: 4 hrs., 30 min.). (J). (gr. 1-8). 1999. 24.95 (CCA 3471, Chivers Child Audio) AudioGO.

Demon Headmaster Strikes Again. unabr. ed. Gillian Cross. Read by Judy Bennett. 3 CDs. (Running Time: 13620 sec.). (J). 2001. audio compact disk 29.95 (978-0-7540-6508-1(1), CHCD 008, Chivers Child Audio) AudioGO.

Demon in the Freezer: A True Story. Richard Preston. Read by Paul Boehmer. 2002. 63.00 (978-0-7366-8680-8(0)); audio compact disk 68.85 (978-0-7366-8783-6(1)) Pub: Books on Tape. Dist(s): NetLibrary CO

***Demon King.** unabr. ed. Cinda Williams Chima. Read by Carol Monda. 1 Playaway. (Running Time: 15 hrs. 15 mins.). (YA). (gr. 7 up). 2010. 64.75 (978-1-4407-3694-0(4)); 102.75 (978-1-4407-3684-1(7)); audio compact disk 108.75 (978-1-4407-3688-9(X)) Recorded Bks.

***Demon King.** unabr. collector's ed. Cinda Williams Chima. Narrated by Carol Monda. 13 CDs. (Running Time: 15 hrs. 15 mins.). (YA). (gr. 7 up). 2010. audio compact disk 61.95 (978-1-4407-3692-6(8)) Recorded Bks.

Demon Lover. unabr. collector's ed. Victoria Holt. Read by Donada Peters. 8 cass. (Running Time: 12 hrs.). 1994. 64.00 (978-0-7366-2684-2(0), 3420) Books on Tape.

Like all the Collisons before her, Kate paints miniatures. When her father's eyesight falls, she agrees to complete his most important commission. Portraits of the powerful Baron de Centeville & his fiancee but what begins as a small deception turns into a nightmare of passion & terror. No blushing bridegroom, the man kate depicts is a complex creature, cruel & graceful, ruthless & charming.

Demon Lover, Set unabr. ed. Victoria Holt. Read by Leonie Mellinger. 10 cass. 1999. 84.95 (CAB 1477) AudioGO.

***Demon Mistress.** unabr. ed. Yasmine Galenorn. Narrated by Cassandra Campbell. (Running Time: 10 hrs. 30 mins.). (Sisters of the Moon Ser.). 2010. 16.99 (978-1-4001-8619-8(6)) Tantor Media.

***Demon Mistress.** unabr. ed. Yasmine Galenorn. Narrated by Cassandra Campbell. (Running Time: 11 hrs. 30 mins. 0 sec.). (Sisters of the Moon Ser.). (ENG.). 2010. 24.99 (978-1-4001-6619-0(5)); audio compact disk 69.99 (978-1-4001-4619-2(4)); audio compact disk 34.99 (978-1-4001-1619-5(8)) Pub: Tantor Media. Dist(s): IngramPubServ

Demon of the Waters: The True Story of the Mutiny on the Whaleship Globe. Gregory Gibson. Narrated by Richard M. Davidson. 8 cass. (Running Time: 9 hrs. 15 mins.). 85.00 (978-1-4025-2563-6(X)) Recorded Bks.

***Demon Quest.** Paul Magrs & British Broadcasting Corporation Staff. (Running Time: 5 hrs. 0 mins. 0 sec.). (Doctor Who Ser.). (ENG.). 2011. audio compact disk 74.95 (978-1-60283-958-8(1)) Pub: AudioGO. Dist(s): Perseus Dist

Demon Rumm. unabr. ed. Sandra Brown. 3 cass. (Running Time: 5 hrs.). 2004. 28.00 (978-1-4159-0798-6(6)); audio compact disk 30.60 (978-1-4159-0799-3(4)) Pub: Books on Tape. Dist(s): NetLibrary CO

Demon Rumm. unabr. ed. Sandra Brown. Read by Staci Snell. 4 CDs. (Running Time: 6 hrs.). (ENG.). 2004. audio compact disk 29.95 (978-0-7393-1823-2(3)) Pub: Random Audio Pubg. Dist(s): Random

***Demon Seed.** unabr. ed. Dean Koontz. (Running Time: 5 hrs.). 2010. 24.99 (978-1-4418-1732-7(8), 9781441817327, BAD); 39.97 (978-1-4418-1733-4(6), 9781441817334, BADLE) Brilliance Audio.

***Demon Seed.** unabr. ed. Dean Koontz. Read by Christopher Lane. (Running Time: 6 hrs.). 2010. 39.97 (978-1-4418-1731-0(X), 9781441817310, Brinc Audio MP3 Lib); 24.99 (978-1-4418-1730-3(1), 9781441817303, Brilliance MP3); audio compact disk 97.97 (978-1-4418-1729-7(8), 9781441817297, BriAudCD Unabrid); audio compact disk 34.99 (978-1-4418-1728-0(X), 9781441817280, Bril Audio CD Unabri) Brilliance Audio.

Demon under the Microscope: From Battlefield Hospitals to Nazi Labs, One Doctor's Heroic Search for the World's First Miracle Drug. Thomas Hager. Read by Stephen Hoye. (Playaway Adult Nonfiction Ser.). 2008. 64.99 (978-1-60640-868-1(2)) Find a World.

Demon under the Microscope: From Battlefield Hospitals to Nazis Labs, One Doctor's Heroic Search for the World's First Miracle Drug. unabr. ed. Thomas Hager. Read by Stephen Hoye. (Running Time: 12 hrs. 30 mins. 0 sec.). (ENG.). 2006. audio compact disk 37.99 (978-1-4001-0306-5(1)); audio compact disk 24.99 (978-1-4001-5306-0(9)); audio compact disk 75.99 (978-1-4001-3306-2(8)) Pub: Tantor Media. Dist(s): IngramPubServ

Demon Wars Saga (Book 1) The Demon Awakens (Part 1) Based on a novel by R. A. Salvatore. (Running Time: 6 hrs.). (Demon Wars Ser.: Bk. 1). 2009. audio compact disk 19.99 (978-1-59950-551-0(7)) GraphicAudio.

Demon Wars Saga (Book 1) The Demon Awakens (Part 2), Vol. 2. Based on a novel by R. A. Salvatore. (Demon Wars Ser.: Bk. 1). 2009. audio compact disk 19.99 (978-1-59950-553-4(3)) GraphicAudio.

Demon Wars Saga (Book 1) The Demon Awakens (Part 3), Vol. 3. R. A. Salvatore. (Demon Wars Ser.: Bk. 1). 2009. audio compact disk 19.99 (978-1-59950-566-4(5)) GraphicAudio.

Demon Wars Saga (Book 2) The Demon Spirit (Part 1), Vol. 1. R. A. Salvatore. (Demon Wars Ser.: Bk. 2). 2009. audio compact disk 19.99 (978-1-59950-577-0(0)) GraphicAudio.

Demon Wars Saga (Book 2) The Demon Spirit (Part 2), Vol. 2. R. A. Salvatore. (Demon Wars Ser.: Bk. 2). 2009. audio compact disk 19.99 (978-1-59950-586-2(X)) GraphicAudio.

Demon Wars Saga (Book 2) The Demon Spirit (Part 3), Vol. 3. R. A. Salvatore. (Demon Wars Ser.: Bk. 2). 2009. audio compact disk 19.99 (978-1-59950-592-3(4)) GraphicAudio.

Demon Wars Saga (Book 3) The Demon Apostle (Part 1 Of 3), Vol. 1. Based on a novel by R. A. Salvatore. (Demon Wars Ser.: Bk. 3). 2009. audio compact disk 19.99 (978-1-59950-605-0(X)) GraphicAudio.

Demon Wars Saga (Book 3) The Demon Apostle (Part 2 Of 3), Vol. 2. Based on a novel by R. A. Salvatore. (Demon Wars Ser.: Bk. 3). 2009. audio compact disk 19.99 (978-1-59950-613-5(0)) GraphicAudio.

Demon Wars Saga (Book 3) The Demon Apostle (Part 3 Of 3), Vol. 3. Based on a novel by R. A. Salvatore. (Demon Wars Ser.: Bk. 3). 2009. audio compact disk 19.99 (978-1-59950-621-0(1)) GraphicAudio.

Demon Wars Saga (Book 4) Mortalis (Part 1 Of 3), Vol. 1. Based on a novel by R. A. Salvatore. (Demon Wars Ser.: Bk. 4). 2010. audio compact disk 19.99 (978-1-59950-628-9(9)) GraphicAudio.

Demon Wars Saga (Book 4) Mortalis (Part 2 Of 3), Vol. 2. Based on a novel by R. A. Salvatore. (Demon Wars Ser.: Bk. 4). 2010. audio compact disk 19.99 (978-1-59950-637-1(8)) GraphicAudio.

Demon Wars Saga (Book 4) Mortalis (Part 3 Of 3) Based on a novel by R. A. Salvatore. (Demon Wars Ser.: Bk. 4). 2010. audio compact disk 19.99 (978-1-59950-644-9(0)) GraphicAudio.

***Demon Wars Saga (Book 7) Immortalis (1 Of 3)** R. A. Salvator. 2010. audio compact disk 19.99 (978-1-59950-691-3(2)) GraphicAudio.

***Demon Wars Saga (Book 7) Immortalis (2 Of 3)** R. A. Salvatore. 2010. audio compact disk 19.99 (978-1-59950-697-5(1)) GraphicAudio.

***Demon Wars Saga (Book 7) Immortalis (3 Of 3)** R. A. Salvatore. 2010. audio compact disk 19.99 (978-1-59950-707-1(2)) GraphicAudio.

Demonic Inroads. Jack Deere. 5 cass. (Running Time: 7 hrs. 30 mins.). 2000. 25.00 (JD02-000) Morning NC.

First laying a foundation of insight into Satan's overall strategy, Jack then builds upon it with practical knowledge of the Christian's authority over demonic forces.

Demonic Toys. 1 cass. 1991. (978-0-7921-2258-6(5)); audio compact disk (978-0-7921-2257-9(7)) Paramount Pictures.

Demonology & Deliverance I. Lester Sumrall. 12 cass. (Running Time: 18 hrs.). 1999. 48.00 (978-1-58568-028-3(1)) Sumrall Pubng.

Demonology & Deliverance II. Lester Sumrall. 16 cass. (Running Time: 24 hrs). 1999. 64.00 (978-1-58568-030-6(3)) Sumrall Pubng.

Demons. Bill Pronzini. Read by Nick Sullivan. 5 cass. (Nameless Detective Mystery Ser.). 2004. 49.95 (978-0-7927-3169-6(7), CSL 636, Chivers Sound Lib); audio compact disk 64.95 (978-0-7927-3170-2(0), SLD 636, Chivers Sound Lib); audio compact disk 29.95 (978-0-7927-3171-9(9), CMP 636, Chivers Sound Lib) AudioGO.

Demons. unabr. ed. Bill Pronzini. Read by Jerry Longe. 8 cass. (Running Time: 12 hrs.). (Nameless Detective Mystery Ser.). 2000. Rental 11.50 (GKT) Chivers Audio Bks GBR.

Nameless sets out to find the "other woman" to help save a friends marriage on the rocks. What he uncovers is a modern-day Circe who has bewitched legions of lovers and whose mysterious disappearance may lead to an even greater tragedy.

Demons, According to the Bible. Dan Corner. 1 cass. 3.00 (26) Evang Outreach.

***Demons & Druids.** James Patterson & Adam Sadler. Read by Milo Ventimiglia. (Running Time: 5 hrs.). (ENG.). 2011. audio compact disk & audio compact disk 9.98 (978-1-60941-274-6(5)) Pub: Hachet Audio. Dist(s): HachBkGrp

Demons & Druids. unabr. ed. James Patterson & Adam Sadler. Read by Milo Ventimiglia. (Running Time: 6 hrs.). (Daniel X Ser.). (ENG.). 2010. 15.98 (978-1-60788-245-9(0)); audio compact disk 22.98 (978-1-60788-244-2(2)) Pub: Hachet Audio. Dist(s): HachBkGrp

Demon's Covenant. unabr. ed. Sarah Rees Brennan. (Running Time: 10 hrs. 0 mins. 0 sec.). (Demon's Lexicon Trilogy). (ENG.). (YA). 2010. audio compact disk 34.99 (978-1-4423-0460-4(X)) Pub: S&S Audio. Dist(s): S and S Inc

Demon's Lexicon. unabr. ed. Sarah Rees Brennan. Read by James Langton. (Running Time: 10 hrs. 0 mins. 0 sec.). (ENG.). (YA). 2009. audio compact disk 34.99 (978-0-7435-8198-1(9)) Pub: S&S Audio. Dist(s): S and S Inc

Demons of the Ocean. unabr. ed. Justin Somper. Read by John Curless. 6 CDs. (Running Time: 7 hrs.). (Vampirates Ser.). (YA). (gr. 6-9). 2006. audio compact disk 94.75 (978-1-4281-1083-0(6)); 65.75 (978-1-4281-1078-6(X)) Recorded Bks.

Vampirates is a colorful extravaganza with a wildly eccentric cast and lashings of swashbuckling adventure, punctuated with horror and old-school romance. Conor and Grace are twins, recently orphaned after their widowed father's death. Rather than being adopted by the town's busy-bodies, they decide to set sail for new pastures in their father's last single possession, his sailing boat. But a vicious storm sees their boat capsize and the twins are separated. Two mysterious ships sail to their rescue - each picking up one twin before disappearing into the mist. Conor wakes to find himself on a pirate ship and is soon being trained up with a cutlass. Meanwhile Grace finds herself locked in a darkened room, as the vampirates wait for night to fall and their feasting to begin...Determined to find each other, yet intrigued by their new shipmates, the twins are about to embark on the biggest adventure of their life.

Demon's Pass. abr. ed. Ralph Compton. 4 cass. (Running Time: 6 hrs.). 2001. 24.95 (978-1-890990-75-6(2)) Otis Audio.

Begins with the brutal attack of a family at the hands of the Cheyenne. His sister kidnapped & loved ones slaughtered, young Parker Stanley has nowhere to turn. But a smooth-talking entrepreneur may be his salvation, if they can make it to Utah in one piece.

Demonstrating Satan's Defeat, Pt. 2. Speeches. Joel Osteen. 1 Cass. (Running Time: 30 Mins.). (J). 2000. 6.00 (978-1-59349-064-5(X), JA0064) J Osteen.

Demonstrating Satan's Defeat, Pt. 3. Speeches. Joel Osteen. 1 Cass. (Running Time: 30 Mins.). (J). 2000. 6.00 (978-1-59349-065-2(8), JA0065) J Osteen.

Demonstration of Power. Steve Hill. (ENG.). 2007. audio compact disk 15.00 (978-1-892853-82-0(5)) Togthr Hrvest.

Demonstrations of Auditory Scene Analysis: The Perceptual Organization of Sound. Albert S. Bregman & Pierre A. Ahad. 1 cass. (ENG.). 1996. audio compact disk 47.00 (978-0-262-52221-2(7)) MIT Pr.

Demonstrative Evidence. Mark A. Dombroff. 1983. 125.00 (978-1-55917-113-7(8)) Natl Prac Inst.

Den of Thieves. unabr. ed. James B. Stewart. Read by Grover Gardner. 13 cass. (Running Time: 19 hrs. 30 min.). 1992. 104.00 (978-0-7366-2215-8(2), 3008) Books on Tape.

The 1980s belonged to Wall Street but its core was rotten. A portrait of human nature & big business - also of white collar crime of staggering proportions.

Den stille pige see Quiet Girl

Den Vita Lejoninnan see White Lioness

Deniable Man. Sol Stein. Read by Patrick Cullen. (Running Time: 32400 sec.). 2007. 59.95 (978-1-4332-0116-5(X)); audio compact disk 72.00 (978-1-4332-0117-2(8)); audio compact disk 29.95 (978-1-4332-0118-9(6)) Blckstn Audio.

Denial. unabr. ed. Stuart M. Kaminsky. Read by Scott Brick. 6 cass. (Running Time: 8 hrs.). (Lew Fonesca Mystery Ser.: Vol. 4). 2005. 50.40 (978-1-4159-2186-9(5)) Books on Tape.

Lew Fonesca is living a self-imposed exile in Sarasota, FL, following the death of his wife in a Chicago hit-and-run accident. He earns money by serving warrants at $75 a pop and does a little private investigating on the side. Clearly, Lew is miserable, morose, and living day by day, but he still has a soft spot for helping people. One day, he receives two requests for help in solving two different murders. The first one apparently took place in an assisted-living facility and was witnessed by an elderly woman, but none of the residents are missing. The second case involves the intentional murder of a teenager by an unknown driver.

Denial. unabr. ed. Peter Sagal. Perf. by Stephanie Zimbalist et al. 2 cass. (Running Time: 1 hr. 58 min.). 1999. 22.95 (978-1-58081-138-5(8), TPT132) L A Theatre.

A tenacious civil liberties attorney defends a right-wing Holocaust denier, arguing her case against a young, committed Jewish federal prosecutor.

Denial of Death. Ernest Becker. Read by Raymond Todd. (Running Time: 12 mins.). 2005. 72.95 (978-0-7861-3699-5(5)); audio compact disk 63.00 (978-0-7861-7686-1(5)) Blckstn Audio.

Denial of Death. unabr. ed. Ernest Becker. Read by Raymond Todd. (Running Time: 12 mins.). 2005. 29.95 (978-0-7861-7924-4(4)) Blckstn Audio.

Denier du Reve, Set. Marguerite Yourcenar. Read by Dominique Sandra. 4 cass. (FRE.). 1991. 34.95 (1306-AV) Olivia & Hill.

The first version of this novel about fascist Italy appeared in 1934 & Yourcenar reworked it in the late 1950s. The characters, who seem to come straight out of the Tragedia dell' Arte, live & die in a heavy atmosphere announcing the impending war.

***Denim & Diamonds.** unabr. ed. Debbie Macomber. Read by Tanya Eby. (Running Time: 6 hrs.). (Wyoming Ser.: Bk. 1). 2010. audio compact disk 9.99 (978-1-4418-6133-7(5), 9781441861337, Bril Audio CD Unabri) Brilliance Audio.

***Denim & Diamonds: A Selection from Wyoming Brides.** unabr. ed. Debbie Macomber. Read by Tanya Eby. (Running Time: 5 hrs.). 2010. 9.99 (978-1-4418-6134-4(3), 9781441861344, Brilliance MP3); 9.99 (978-1-4418-6135-1(1), 9781441861351, BAD) Brilliance Audio.

Denis Waitley Live on Winning. Denis Waitley. 6 cass. 79.95 set. (V10114) CareerTrack Pubns.

Develop a new vision of yourself, your profession & your personal world. It's all possible with the insights you'll gain in this program. They're simple, subtle - yet they have the power to make every day more positive for you.

Denise Levertov. unabr. ed. Read by Denise Levertov. 1 cass. (Running Time: 29 min.). 1985. 10.00 New Letters.

Author reads poems & discusses political activism & the responsibility of a writer.

Dennis Finnell. unabr. ed. Read by Dennis Finnell. 1 cass. (Running Time: 29 min.). 1985. 10.00 New Letters.

One of a weekly half-hour radio program with authors talking & presenting their own works.

Dennis Hysom Sings "The Wooleycats Favorite Nursery Rhymes" Dennis Hysom & Christine Walker. Perf. by Dennis Hysom. 1 cass. (Running Time: 33 min.). (Once upon a Tune Ser.). (J). 1992. 8.95 (978-1-881225-00-3(3)) Discov Music.

Dennis Hysom & his friend the Wooleycat introduce children to favorite nursery rhymes through story & songs.

Denny Zeitlin. Read by Denny Zeitlin. 1 cass. (Running Time: 1 hr.). (Marian McPartland's Piano Jazz Ser.). 13.95 (MM-87-04-30, HarperThor) HarpC GBR.

Denominational Women's Ministries Leaders: National Association of Evangelicals, 47th Annual Convention, Columbus, Ohio, March 7-9, 1989. Fran Wolfley. 1 cass. (Workshops Ser.: No. 34-Thursda). 1989. 4.25 ea. 1-8 tapes.; 4.00 ea. 9 tapes or more. Nat Assn Evan.

Density of Souls. unabr. ed. Christopher Rice. Read by James Daniels. 6 cass. (Running Time: 9 hrs.). 2000. 29.95 (978-1-56740-475-3(8), 1567404758, BAU) Brilliance Audio.

Density of Souls. unabr. ed. Christopher Rice. Read by James Daniels. (Running Time: 9 hrs.). 2004. 39.25 (978-1-59600-506-8(8), 1596005068, BADLE); 24.95 (978-1-59600-505-1(X), 159600505X, BAD); 39.25 (978-1-59600-504-4(1), 1596005041, Brinc Audio MP3 Lib); 24.95 (978-1-59600-503-7(3), 1596005033, Brilliance MP3) Brilliance Audio.

Four high school students in present-day New Orleans are torn apart by envy, passion, and tragedy. Meredith, Brandon, Greg, and Stephen quickly discover the fragile boundaries between friendship and betrayal as they enter high school and form new alliances. Brandon and Greg gain popularity as football jocks and Meredith joins the bulimic in-crowd, while Stephen becomes the target of homophobia in a school that viciously mocks him. Then two violent deaths disrupt the core of what they once shared. Five years later, the friends are drawn back together as new facts about their mutual history are revealed, and what was held to be a tragic accident is discovered to be murder. As the true story emerges, other secrets begin to unravel and the casual cruelties of high school develop into acts of violence that threaten an entire city. A Density of Souls is a stunning debut novel that lays bare the darker side of the teenage experience in modern-day America.

Dental Anxiety & Pain Control: Reduce Dental Anxiety & Effectively Detach from Pain. Mark Bancroft. Read by Mark Bancroft. 1 CD, bklet. (Running Time: 1 hr.). (Alternative Health & Healing Ser.). 2006. audio compact disk 20.00 (978-1-58522-063-2(9)) EnSpire Pr.

Two complete sessions plus printed instructionmanual/guidebook. With healing music soundtrack.

Dental Anxiety & Pain Control: Release Dental Anxiety & Effectively Detach from Pain. Mark Bancroft. Read by Mark Bancroft. 1 cass., bklet. (Running Time: 1 hr.). (Alternative Health & Healing Ser.). 1999. 12.95 (978-1-58522-039-7(6), 205) EnSpire Pr.

Dental Assistant: Syllabus. E. A. Jacobson & Alma Jacobson. (J). 1978. bk. 228.60 (978-0-89420-139-4(5)) Natl Book.

Dental Equipment & Supplies in Croatia: A Strategic Reference 2007. Compiled by Icon Group International, Inc. Staff. 2007. ring bd. 195.00 (978-0-497-35900-3(6)) Icon Grp.

Dental Equipment & Supplies in Ecuador: A Strategic Reference 2006. Compiled by Icon Group International, Inc. Staff. 2007. ring bd. 195.00 (978-0-497-35918-8(9)) Icon Grp.

Dental Equipment & Supplies in Sweden: A Strategic Reference 2007. Compiled by Icon Group International, Inc. Staff. 2007. ring bd. 195.00 (978-0-497-82421-1(3)) Icon Grp.

Dental Equipment, Supplies, & Services in Bulgaria: A Strategic Reference 2007. Compiled by Icon Group International, Inc. Staff. 2007. ring bd. 195.00 (978-0-497-35848-8(4)) Icon Grp.

Dental Fear. Bruce Goldberg. 1 cass. (Running Time: 20 min.). (ENG.). 2006. 13.00 (978-1-885577-08-5(7)) Pub: B Goldberg. Dist(s): Baker Taylor

This tape removes the anxiety concerning dental visits & trains the listener in pain control through self hypnosis.

Dental Health. (Running Time: 45 min.). (Health Ser.). 9.98 (978-1-55909-132-9(0), 108) Randolph Tapes.

Feeling confident at the dentist's.

Dental Industry in Mexico: A Strategic Reference 2006. Compiled by Icon Group International, Inc. Staff. 2007. ring bd. 195.00 (978-0-497-82362-7(4)) Icon Grp.

Dental-Nutrition & B-17 Link. unabr. ed. Edward Arana. 1 cass. (Running Time: 35 min.). 12.95 (938) J Norton Pubs.

Dental Office Design Audio Course: 5 Hours of Expert Inside Knowledge on How to Create an Attractive, Ergonomic Dental Office. adpt. ed. Narrated by Harry Demaree. Anno. by 4WebResults Staff. 1 CD. (Running Time: 5 hours - MP3 format). 2003. audio compact disk 349.00 (978-0-9748370-0-0(8)) Four Web Results.

Dental Persuasion, Set. Planned Marketing Staff. 12 cass. 1994. 195.00 (978-1-882306-04-6(X)) Planned Mktg.

Training.

Dental Tele-Pro. Perf. by Planned Marketing Staff. 3 cass. (Dental Pro Audiotape Ser.: No. 1). 75.00 Set. (978-1-882306-02-2(3)) Planned Mktg.

Telephone skills that go beyond the basic, to maximize the use of the No. 1 practice building tool in your office...you & the phone.

Dentinogenesis Imperfecta - A Bibliography & Dictionary for Physicians, Patients, & Genome Researchers. Compiled by Icon Group International, Inc. Staff. 2007. ring bd. 28.95 (978-0-497-11367-4(8)) Icon Grp.

Dentist, I Am All Smiles: Overcome Detal Fears, an HSR Trance Formation Tape. Dean A. Montalbano. 2 cass. (Running Time: 2 Hours). 2002. 39.95 (978-1-932086-06-5(4)) L Lizards Pub Co.

Dentist, I Am All Smiles on CD: Overcome Detal Fears, an HSR Trance Formation Tape. Dean A. Montalbano. 2 cds. (Running Time: 2.25 hrs). 2004. audio compact disk 39.95 (978-1-932086-14-0(5)) L Lizards Pub Co.

Denver History As Told by Annie Oakley. Cynthia L. Schoeppel. 9.95 (978-1-887608-01-5(X)) HRC Pub.

History.

Denzel Principle: Why Black Women Can't Find Good Black Men. unabr. ed. Jimi Izrael. (Running Time: 10 hrs. 30 mins.). 2010. 29.95 (978-1-4417-2922-4(4)); audio compact disk 32.95 (978-1-4417-2921-7(6)) Blckstn Audio.

Denzel Principle: Why Black Women Can't Find Good Black Men. unabr. ed. Jimi Izrael. (Running Time: 10 hrs. 30 mins.). 2010. 65.95 (978-1-4417-2918-7(6)); audio compact disk 100.00 (978-1-4417-2919-4(4)) Blckstn Audio.

Depardieu. unabr. ed. Paul Chutkow. Read by Frederick Davidson. 11 cass. (Running Time: 16 hrs.). 1995. 76.95 (978-0-7861-0650-9(6), 1562) Blckstn Audio.

Gerard Depardieu's own extraordinary candor underlies the unique resonance of this full-scale biography, the first to be written with the great French film star's total cooperation. We see his rise from impossible beginnings in extreme poverty to mischief, petty crime & even violence; yet at the same time, escaping into - falling in love with - American movies.

Departing Spirits. George Bloomer. audio compact disk Whitaker Hse.

Departing Spirits. George Bloomer. 2003. audio compact disk 14.99 (978-0-88368-969-1(3)) Whitaker Hse.

Department Audio CDs for use with Ear Training. 7th ed. Bruce Benward & J. Timothy Kolosick. (C). 2004. audio compact disk 320.31 (978-0-07-293678-0(9), 9780072936780, Mc-H Human Soc) Pub: McGrw-H Hghr Educ. Dist(s): McGraw

Department of Education. 1 cass. (Running Time: 1 hr.). (Advocacy Before Administrative Agencies Ser.). 1984. 20.00 PA Bar Inst.

Department of Insurance. 1 cass. (Running Time: 1 hr.). (Advocacy Before Administrative Agencies Ser.). 1986. 20.00 PA Bar Inst.

Department of Revenue Board of Appeals. 1 cass. (Running Time: 1 hr.). (Advocacy Before Administrative Agencies Ser.). 1985. 20.00 PA Bar Inst.

Departmental see Robert Frost Reads

Departmental see Twentieth-Century Poetry in English, No. 6, Recordings of Poets Reading Their Own Poetry

Departures & Arrivals. unabr. ed. Eric Newby. Read by Andrew Sachs. 6 cass. (Running Time: 22140 sec.). (Rumpole Crime Ser.). 2000. 54.95 (978-0-7540-0488-2(0), CAB1911) AudioGO.

Highly observant & always entertaining, this is a recollection of highlights from an eventful life. You will be transported around the world, from Newby's earliest childhood adventures in darkest Barnes, to an elephant fair in India; from the faded glamour of days & nights on the Orient Express, to a trogodytic settlement of opal miners in Australia. Listeners will enjoy the exuberance & humor that distinguished Newby's best work.

Dependence on the Holy Spirit. Steve Thompson. 1 cass. (Running Time: 90 mins.). (Baptism of Power Ser.: Vol. 2). 2000. 5.00 (ST02-002) Morning NC.
This discussion of the baptism of power that Jesus referred to will help you discover the spiritual power available to every Christian.

Deposing an Expert. James McElhaney et al. 1 cass. (Running Time: 49 min.). (Training the Advocate: The Pretrial Stage Ser.). 1985. 20.00 (FAPTA10) Natl Inst Trial Ad.

Deposing the Financial Expert. James W. Jeans, Sr. et al. 1 cass. (Running Time: 59 min.). (Using Financial Experts in Business Litigation Ser.). 1988. 20.00 (FAZ0403) Natl Inst Trial Ad.

Deposing the Lay Witness. James McElhaney et al. 1 cass. (Running Time: 57 min.). (Training the Advocate: The Pretrial Stage Ser.). 1985. 20.00 (FAPTA07) Natl Inst Trial Ad.

Deposition Practice & Practicalities in State & Federal Court. (Running Time: 5 hrs.). 1995. 92.00 Incl. 310p. coursebk. (20541) NYS Bar.
All aspects of deposition practice are covered in this program: the initial preparation, the conduct of a deposition & using the deposition at the trial. The presentations offer practical pointers in making strategic & tactical decisions in conducting & defending depositions.

Deposition Preparation. Paul M. Lisnek. Read by Paul M. Lisnek. 1 cass. (Running Time: 50 min.). 1993. 22.95 (978-1-57654-203-3(3), CPAB105) Creat Core.
A review of the most important keys to effective testimony.

Deposition Rules: A Guide to Who, What, When, Where, Why, & How. David Malone. 1 cass. 1995. 21.95 (AUDZ260S) NITA.
Reference to the rules, procedures, & practices which govern depositions.

Deposition Strategies & Techniques. James McElhaney et al. 1 cass. (Running Time: 45 min.). (Training the Advocate: The Pretrial Stage Ser.). 1985. 20.00 (FAPTA05) Natl Inst Trial Ad.

Deposition Techniques. Read by Marshall Bernstein. 1 cass. 1990. 20.00 (AL-82) PA Bar Inst.

Deposition Techniques in Commercial Litigation. unabr. ed. Contrib. by Henry L. Hecht. 4 cass. (Running Time: 5 hrs. 30 min.). 1987. pap. bk. 75.00 cass. & pap. bk. (T6-9099) PLI.
Experienced litigators & trial lawyers use a hypothetical case to discuss deposition tactics, techniques & strategies for both the examining & defending attorney. Subjects covered in this recording of PLI's June 1987 satellite program include: planning the examination, preparing a witness to testify, dealing with the difficult witness, questioning a witness about conversations & documents, deposing corporate officers, making objections, handling the aggressive opponent, using depositions at trial, ethical behavior & improper practice.

Depositions for P.I. Litigators. 1991. bk. 98.00 (ACS-664) PA Bar Inst.

Depraved: Romans 1:17-23. Ed Young. 1983. 4.95 (978-0-7417-1347-6(0), 347) Win Walk.

Depreciation: A Practical Guide. Jonathan S. Ingber. 6 cass. bk. 159.00 set. (CPE4100) Bisk Educ.
This program clarifies complex depreciation rules & shows you how to apply the proper alternative for your clients.

Depression. 1 cass. (Running Time: 40 min.). 10.95 (SM-81-10-03, HarperThor) HarpC GBR.

Depression. 1 cass. (Running Time: 60 min.). 10.95 (009) Psych Res Inst.
Designed to eliminate depression by introducing positive attitudes.

Depression. Contrib. by Robert A. Bashford et al. 1 cass. (American College of Obstetrics & Gynecologists UPDATE: Vol. 22, No. 6). 1998. 20.00 Am Coll Obstetric.

Depression. Read by Robert S. Friedman & Kelly Howell. 1 cass. (Running Time: 60 min.). (Sound Techniques for Healing Ser.). 11.95 (978-1-881451-19-8(4)) Brain Sync.
Positive energy is created to break through blocked channels to release negativity, stress & mental turmoil. Spirits feel lifted & a new outlook becomes possible.

Depression. Bruce Goldberg. (ENG.). 2005. audio compact disk 17.00 (978-1-57968-086-2(0)) Pub: B Goldberg. Dist(s): Baker Taylor

Depression. Bruce Goldberg. Read by Bruce Goldberg. 1 cass. (Running Time: 25 min.). (ENG.). 2006. 13.00 (978-1-885577-51-1(6)) Pub: B Goldberg. Dist(s): Baker Taylor
Through self-hypnosis, elevate mood without medication, and increase both energy and enjoyment of life.

Depression. Eldon Taylor. 2 cass. (Running Time: 62 min. per cass.). (Omniphonics Ser.). 29.95 incl. script Set. (978-1-55978-813-7(5), 4014) Progress Aware Res.
3-D soundtrack with underlying subliminal affirmations, night & day versions.

Depression. unabr. ed. Peter M. Lewinsohn. 1 cass. (Running Time: 49 min.). 12.95 (29351) J Norton Pubs.
Makes clear both the origins & the signs of depression, as well as methods one may use to counteract its debilitating symptoms.

Depression: A Disorder of Power. Susan M. Heitler. 1 cass. (Running Time: 45 min.). 1995. bk. 14.95 (978-1-884998-09-6(7)) Listen-to-Lrn.
Lecture format recorded live demonstrates examples of depression & what makes it go away. Includes audience participation & offers a uniquely uplifting perspective on depression's causes & cures.

Depression: A Stubborn Darkness - Light for the Path. Edward T. Welch. (ENG.). 2004. audio compact disk 35.95 (978-1-934885-65-9(7)) New Growth Pr.

Depression: A Stubborn Darkness - Light for the Path. unabr. ed. Edward T. Welch. 3 cass. (Running Time: 3 hrs.). 2003. 35.95 (978-1-930921-02-3(0)) Resources.

Depression: Chemical Imbalance. William Wait. 1 cass. 7.98 (978-1-55503-058-2(0), 06003397) Covenant Comms.
A personal survival story.

Depression: Mood Booster. Steven Gurgevich. (ENG.). 2005. audio compact disk 19.95 (978-1-932170-23-8(5), HWH) Tranceformation.

Depression: Positive Strategies for Change. Allan G. Hedberg. 2 cass. 21.95 Self-Control Sys.
Teaches a basic understanding of the nature of depression & how to prevent stress.

Depression: The Stubborn Darkness. unabr. ed. Edward T. Welcn. 3 CDs. (Running Time: 3 hrs.). 2003. audio compact disk 35.95 (978-1-930921-27-6(6)) Resources.

Depression: Treating to Remission, Vol. 3. Interview. Interview with Stephen M. Stahl. Featuring Charles DeBattista. 1 CD. 2004. audio compact disk (978-1-4225-0009-5(8)) NEI Pr.

Depression: Voices of an Illness. Lichtenstein Creative Media, Inc. Staff. Narrated by Rod Steiger. 1 cass. (Running Time: 1 hr.). 1996. 29.00 incl. script Lib. & inst. Lichtenstein Creat.
Features a Harvard professor, an engineer, a high school student, among others, telling their stories of struggle & triumph over this common, yet often unrecognized & untreated brain disorder that affects one out of every ten Americans. Mental health experts, from the National Institute of Mental Health & elsewhere, highlight groundbreaking new medications & talk therapies helping people with clinical depression return to healthy lives. Academy Award-winner Rod Steiger adds his own voice, sharing his personal battle with clinical depression. Has won top awards from the American Psychiatric Association, The National Easter Seals Society & the National Mental Health Association among others. Includes transcript & educational material written in conjunction with the National Institute of Mental Health.

Depression: Voices of an Illness. P.e.r. 1942. 95.00 (978-0-8002-4402-6(8)) Taylor and Fran.

Depression: 11 Cor. 7:2-16. Ed Young. 1990. 4.95 (978-0-7417-1790-0(5), 790) Win Walk.

Depression - The Cause: 1 Kings 19:1-21. Ed Young. 1987. 4.95 (978-0-7417-1600-2(3), 600) Win Walk.

Depression - The Cause & Cure: Numbers 10-14. Ed Young. 1985. 4.95 (978-0-7417-1440-4(X), 440) Win Walk.

Depression & Anxiety: Ancient Truths, Natural Remedies & the Latest Findings for Your Health Today. unabr. ed. Don Colbert. Narrated by Steve Hiller. (Running Time: 1 hr. 30 mins.). (Bible Cure Ser.). (ENG.). 2002. audio compact disk 9.99 (978-1-58926-117-4(8)) Oasis Audio.

Depression & Anxiety Management: Cognitive Techniques for Managing Emotional Problems. John D. Preston. Read by John D. Preston. 1 cass. (Running Time: 1 hr. 30 min.). (Unassigned Ser.). 1993. 11.95 (978-1-879237-46-9(6)) New Harbinger.

Depression: Characteristics That Differentiate from Feeling "Bad" A Reasonable Response to Christmas. George Benson. 1986. 10.80 (0611) Assn Prof Chaplains.

Depression from a Spiritual Point of View. 1 cass. (Care Cassettes Ser.: Vol. 15, No. 1). 1988. 10.80 Assn Prof Chaplains.

Depression in the Brain: Program from the Award Winning Public Radio Series. Interview. Hosted by Fred Goodwin. 1 CD. (Running Time: 1 hr). (Infinite Mind Ser.). 2003. audio compact disk 21.95 (978-1-932479-02-7(3), LCM 263) Lichtenstein Creat.
We examine new research on the biology of depression - including new findings showing depression is not only a disease that affects the balance of chemicals in the brain, but the anatomy of the brain, as well. This is the latest scientific evidence confirming that clinical depression is a physical, medical illness which causes changes in the brain. Guests include: Virginia Heffernan,the television critic for the online magazine Slate and a contributor to the anthology Unholy Ghost: Writers on Depression; Dr. Robert Sapolsky, professor of biology and neurology at Stanford University and the author of both popular and academic books related to stress and its effects; Dr. Yvette Sheline, associate professor of psychiatry and radiology at Washington University in St. Louis; Dr. Ronald Duman, a neuroscientist and professor of psychiatry and pharmacology at Yale University; and singer-songwriter Dar Williams.

Depression/It's OK to Cry. Marianne Williamson. Read by Marianne Williamson. 1 cass. (Running Time: 90 mins.). (Lectures on a Course in Miracles). 1999. 10.00 (978-1-56170-184-1(X), M712) Hay House.

Deprivers. Steven-Elliot Altman & Christopher Lane. 2002. 44.95 (978-0-7861-2611-8(6)) Blckstn Audio.

Deprivers. unabr. ed. Steven-Elliot Altman. Read by Christopher Lane. (Running Time: 8 hrs. 30 mins.). 2003. 24.95 (978-0-7861-8770-6(0)); audio compact disk 56.00 (978-0-7861-8939-7(8)) Blckstn Audio.

Depth Healing & Renewal Through Christ: Guided Meditations for Inner Healing. (Running Time: 090 min.). 1998. 9.95 (978-0-8358-0664-0(2)) Upper Room Bks.

Depth Healing, Wholistic Spirituality for the 21st Century. Jeffrey Mickler. 1 cass. 1981. 7.95 (TAH090) Alba Hse Comns.
Presents a summary of the Christian journey out of sin & weakness & toward perfection in Christ.

Depth Psychology & Politics: Reflections on the Mythopoetic Men's Movement. Andrew Samuels. Read by Andrew Samuels. 1 cass. (Running Time: 90 min.). 1991. 10.95 (978-0-7822-0369-1(8), 468) C G Jung IL.
In this provocative two-pronged presentation, British analyst Andrew Samuels calls for a greater recognition by all depth psychologists of the "political development of the person." He also offers a timely critique of the mythopoetic men's movement, by pointing out the shadow elements & political implications of its ideas. Part of the conference set Gold in Dark Places: Shadow Work in the Struggle for Selfhood.

Depths of Glory: A Biographical Novel of Camille Pissarro. unabr. ed. Irving Stone. Read by Larry McKeever. 10 cass. (Running Time: 15 hrs.). 1988. 80.00 (2175-B) Books on Tape.
Biographical novel of the life of French Impressionist painter Camille Pissaro & his fight against the critics & the public in 19th century Paris.

Depths of Glory Pt. 1: A Biographical Novel of Camille Pissarro. unabr. ed. Irving Stone. Read by Larry McKeever. 10 cass. (Running Time: 15 hrs.). 1988. 80.00 (978-0-7366-1262-3(9), 2175-A) Books on Tape.

Derailed. James Siegel. 2003. 81.00 (978-0-7366-9162-8(6)); audio compact disk 99.00 (978-0-7366-9165-9(0)) Books on Tape.

Derailed. abr. ed. James Siegel. (ENG.). 2005. 14.98 (978-1-59483-263-5(3)) Pub: Hachet Audio. Dist(s): HachBkGrp

Derailed. abr. ed. James Siegel. Read by Gregory Harrison. (Running Time: 6 hrs.). (ENG.). 2009. 49.98 (978-1-60788-058-5(X)) Pub: Hachet Audio. Dist(s): HachBkGrp

Deraindamaged. unabr. ed. Vince Valenzuela. Perf. by Vince Valenzuela. 1 cass., 1 CD. (Running Time: 50 min.). 1996. 7.98; audio compact disk 10.98 CD. Pub Mills.
A laugh out loud performance by one of the country's fast rising stand-up comedy talents.

Derby Man. unabr. ed. Gary McCarthy. Read by Gene Engene. 4 cass. (Running Time: 6 hrs.). (Derby Man Ser.: Bk. 1). 1994. 26.95 (978-1-55686-506-0(6)) Books in Motion.
Darby Buckingham became wealthy writing pulp westerns. His rugged nature is revealed when he goes west to do research & learns firsthand about frontier justice & frontier heroism.

Derek the Knitting Dinosaur. unabr. ed. Mary Blackwood. Read by Larry Robinson. Illus. by Kerry Argent. 1 cass. (Running Time: 5 mins.). (J). (gr. k-3). 1997. bk. 24.95 (978-0-87499-391-2(1)) Live Oak Media.
A little green dinosaur stays home knitting while his larger relatives are out fierce-filling his cozy house with garments that prove wonderfully useful when the Ice Age arrives.

Derek the Knitting Dinosaur, Grades K-3. Mary Blackwood. 14 vols. (Running Time: 5 mins.). 1997. pap. bk. & tchr. ed. 33.95 (978-0-87499-392-9(X)) Live Oak Media.
A little green dinosaur stays home knitting while his larger relatives are out fierce-filling his cozy house with garments that prove wonderfully useful when the Ice Age arrives.

Derivative Instruments: A Guide to Theory & Practice. Moorad Choudhry & Brian Anthony Eales. (Quantitative Finance Ser.). (ENG., 2003. 112.00 (978-0-7506-5419-7(8), Butter Sci Hein) Sci Tech Bks.

Derivative Products: Current Accounting & Control Considerations. Michael S. Joseph & Stephen R. Howe. 3 cass. 1995. bk. 129.00 set. (CPE0080) Bisk Educ.
Get current pronouncements affecting accounting for derivative transactions. You also get an in-depth look at the control environment surrounding derivative products.

Derivative Products: Pricing & Valuation of Options & Swaps. Christopher Ito & Jerome L. Raffaldini, II. 3 cass. 1995. bk. 129.00 set. (CPE0086) Bisk Educ.
Learn how to price & value options, how to compare & contract exchange & over-the-counter options & how to properly analyze the pricing & valuation process for swaps. Also included in info on foreign exchange-linked derivatives.

Dermaphoria. unabr. ed. Craig Clevenger. Read by Craig Clevenger. (Running Time: 6 hrs. 0 mins.). 2010. 29.95 (978-1-4332-9814-1(7)); 44.95 (978-1-4332-9810-3(4)); audio compact disk 55.00 (978-1-4332-9811-0(2)) Blckstn Audio.

Dermatology, Plastic Surgery & Cosmetics for More Youthful Skin, Set. Erlinda Fang & Elliott Lavey. 2 cass. (Running Time: 1 hr. 28 min.). 1998. bk. 20.00 (978-1-58111-070-8(7)) Contemporary Medical.
Discussion of skin rejuvenation techniques by plastic surgeons & dermatologists includes skin care products.

Dernier Jour d'un Condamne, Set. Victor Hugo. 2 cass. (FRE.). 1991. 27.95 (1361-LV) Olivia & Hill.
Hugo describes the last hours of a man condemned to death & makes a moving plea against the death penalty.

Dernier Mot. 1 cass. (Running Time: 60 mins.). Dramatization. (Maitres du Mystere Ser.). (FRE.). 1996. 11.95 (1829-MA) Olivia & Hill.
Popular radio thriller, interpreted by France's best actors.

Derrama de tu Gloria. Read by Mario Rodriguez. 2007. audio compact disk 14.99 (978-0-8297-5498-8(9)) Pub: Vida Pubs. Dist(s): Zondervan

Derribemos Fortalezas. Hector Torres. 2 cass. (SPA.). 1999. 10.99 (978-0-88113-275-5(6)) Grupo Nelson.

Dersu the Trapper. unabr. collector's ed. V. K. Arseniev. Read by Daniel Grace. 8 cass. (Running Time: 12 hrs.). 1976. 64.00 (978-0-7366-0034-7(5), 1046) Books on Tape.
In "Dersu the Trapper," Arseniev gives an account of his travels in the Ussuri Region of far eastern Siberia in the early 1900's. This region is a wilderness filled with creatures & tribes that make our wild west look tame. Much of the narrative is woven around the character of Dersu Uzala, a native of the region.

Dervish Drum & Chant. unabr. ed. Adnan M. El-Sarhan. 1 cass. (Running Time: 1 hr. 26 min.). 1970. 11.00 (10301) Big Sur Tapes.
El-Sarhan demonstrates chanting & drumming as practiced by Dervishes. Not just for casual listening, this is intended for those disciplined in high-energy meditation, chant, & dance.

Deryni Checkmate. unabr. ed. Katherine Kurtz. Read by Jeff Woodman. (Running Time: 10 hrs.). (Chronicles of the Deryni Ser.). 2010. audio compact disk 29.99 (978-1-4418-1591-0(0), 9781441815910) Brilliance Audio.

***Deryni Checkmate.** unabr. ed. Katherine Kurtz. Read by Jeff Woodman. (Running Time: 10 hrs.). (Chronicles of the Deryni Ser.). 2010. 39.97 (978-1-4418-1594-1(5), 9781441815941, Brinc Audio MP3 Lib); 39.97 (978-1-4418-1595-8(3), 9781441815958, BADLE); 24.99 (978-1-4418-1593-4(7), 9781441815934, Brilliance MP3); audio compact disk 87.97 (978-1-4418-1592-7(9), 9781441815927, BriAudCD Unabrid) Brilliance Audio.

Deryni Rising. unabr. ed. Katherine Kurtz. Read by Jeff Woodman. (Running Time: 8 hrs.). (Chronicles of the Deryni Ser.). 2010. 24.99 (978-1-4418-1588-0(0), 9781441815880, Brilliance MP3); 39.97 (978-1-4418-1589-7(9), 9781441815897, Brinc Audio MP3 Lib); 39.97 (978-1-4418-1590-3(2), 9781441815903, BADLE); audio compact disk 29.99 (978-1-4418-1586-6(4), 9781441815866, Bril Audio CD Unabri); audio compact disk 87.97 (978-1-4418-1587-3(2), 9781441815873, BriAudCD Unabrid) Brilliance Audio.

Des airs de Grammaire. Mariana Toader. Prod. by Sara Jordan. Composed by Sara Jordan. Engineer Mark Shannon. Illus. by Glen Wyand. Rev. by Martin Lacasse. 1 cass. (Running Time: 51 min. 6 secs.). (FRE.). (J). 1995. pap. bk. 14.95 (978-1-895523-60-7(5), JMP F09K) Jordan Music.
Ten upbeat French grammar songs that teach basic grammar: nouns and pronouns (masculine, feminine, singular and plural), adjectives and how they vary, sentence structures including questions and the conjugation of verbs in present and past tenses. Activities and crossword puzzles, which may be reproduced by the classroom teacher, are included in the lyrics book. A complement of "music-only" tracks allows for great karaoke performances and music night productions! Good for all ages!.

Des Airs de Grammaire. abr. ed. Mariana Toader. Prod. by Sara Jordan. Composed by Sara Jordan. 1 CD. (Running Time: 30 min.). (Songs That Teach French Ser.). (FRE.). (J). (gr. 4-7). 1995. audio compact disk 13.95 (978-1-894262-09-5(3), JMP F09CD) Pub: S Jordan Publ. Dist(s): CrabtreePubCo

Des Moines Register Democratic Candidates Debate, 15 Jan. 1988. 2 cass. (Running Time: 2 hrs.). 21.90 Set. (NI-88-01-15, HarperThor) HarpC GBR.

Des Moines Register Republican Candidates Debate, 8 January 1988. 2 cass. (Running Time: 2 hrs.). 21.90 Set. (NI-88-01-08, HarperThor) HarpC GBR.

Des Parfums et Des Jours, Set. Short Stories. 3 cass. (FRE.). 1995. 32.95 (1744-RF) Olivia & Hill.
How to make perfume speak on the radio? Twelve leading actors, including Fanny Ardant & Anny Duperey, read stories about the mystery of perfumes.

Desacralization of the West, Pt. 1. Read by James Hitchcock. (138) ISI Books.

Desacralization of the West, Pt. 2. Read by James Hitchcock. 1 cass. 3.00 (139) ISI Books.

Desafinado - ShowTrax. Arranged by Paris Rutherford. 1 CD. (Running Time: 5 mins.). 2000. audio compact disk 19.95 (08742297) H Leonard.
Listeners will dig the great Latin groove.

Desarrolle el Líder que está en Usted. John C. Maxwell. (SPA.). 2009. audio compact disk 24.99 (978-1-60255-246-3(0)) Nelson.

***Desarrollo Trilateral.** Juan G. Ruelas. 2010. audio compact disk 12.00 (978-0-9825883-4-5(8)) Editorial Equipov.

Desastre Monumental Vol. 12: Level 4. (Fonolibros Ser.). 2003. 11.50 (978-0-7652-0999-3(3)) Modern Curr.

Descartes, Bacon, & Modern Philosophy. unabr. ed. Jeffrey Tlumak. Read by Lynn Redgrave. (Running Time: 10800 sec.). (World of Philosophy Ser.). 2006. audio compact disk 25.95 (978-0-7861-6389-2(5)) Pub: Blckstn Audio. Dist(s): NetLibrary CO

Descartes' Bones: A Skeletal History of the Conflict Between Faith & Reason. Russell Shorto. 2008. audio compact disk 34.99 (978-1-4361-3910-6(4)) Recorded Bks.

Descartes' Error: Emotion, Reason, & the Human Brain. abr. ed. Antonio Damasio. 2 cass. (Running Time: 3 hrs.). 1995. 16.95 Set. (978-1-879371-89-7(8), 20380) Pub Mills.
"Descartes' Error" is a journey of discovery, from the story of Phineas Gage, the famous nineteenth-century case of behavioral change that followed brain damage, to the contemporary re-creation of Gage's brain; & from the doubts of a young neurologist to a testable hypothesis concerning the emotions & their fundamental role in rational human behavior.

Descartes in 90 Minutes. Paul Strathern. Narrated by Robert Whitfield. (Running Time: 1 hr. 30 mins.). 2003. 17.95 (978-1-59912-468-1(8)) Iofy Corp.

Descartes in 90 Minutes. unabr. ed. Paul Strathern. Read by Robert Whitfield. (Running Time: 1 hr 30 mins.). 2000. 14.95 (978-0-7861-2435-0(0), 3114); reel tape 14.95 (978-0-7861-2531-9(4)); audio compact disk 14.95 (978-0-7861-9044-7(2)) Blckstn Audio.

Descartes in 90 Minutes. unabr. ed. Paul Strathern. Read by Robert Whitfield. 2 CDs. (Running Time: 1 hr. 30 mins.). 2001. audio compact disk 16.00 (978-0-7861-9229-8(1), 3114) Blckstn Audio.

***Descendants.** Kaui Hart Hemmings. Narrated by Jonathan Davis. (Running Time: 9 hrs. 11 mins. 0 sec.). (ENG.). 2010. audio compact disk 29.95 (978-1-60998-108-2(1)) Pub: AudioGO. Dist(s): Perseus Dist

Descending into Greatness. Bill Hybels & Wilkins. 1 cass. 1993. 14.99 (978-0-310-54478-4(5)) Zondervan.

Descent see William Carlos Williams Reads His Poetry

Descent. Jeff Long. Read by Boyd Gaines. 2004. 14.95 (978-0-7435-4646-1(6)) Pub: S&S Audio. Dist(s): S and S Inc

Descent, Set. abr. ed. Jeff Long. Read by Boyd Gaines. 4 cass. 1999. 24.00 (FS9-50948) Highsmith.

Descent into Chaos: The U. S. & the Disaster in Pakistan, Afghanistan, & Central Asia. unabr. ed. Ahmed Rashid. Read by Arthur Morey. (Running Time: 19 hrs.). 2008. 44.25 (978-1-4233-6811-3(8), 9781423368113, BADLE); 29.95 (978-1-4233-6810-6(X), 9781423368106, BAD); audio compact disk 132.25 (978-1-4233-6807-6(X), 9781423368076, BriAudCD Unabrid); audio compact disk 29.95 (978-1-4233-6808-3(8), 9781423368083, Brilliance MP3); audio compact disk 49.95 (978-1-4233-6806-9(1), 9781423368069, Bril Audio CD Unabri) Brilliance Audio.

Descent into Chaos: The U. S. & the Disaster in Pakistan, Afghanistan, & Central Asia. unabr. ed. Ahmed Rashid. Read by Arthur Morey. Directed By Laura Grafton. Contrib. by Kristopher Kessel. (Running Time: 68400 sec.). 2008. audio compact disk 44.25 (978-1-4233-6809-0(6), 9781423368090, Brlnc Audio MP3 Lib) Brilliance Audio.

Descent into Europa: A David Foster Starman Adventure. abr. ed. Michael D. Cooper. Abr. by Michael D. Cooper. Read by Charlie O'Dowd. 2 cass. (Running Time: 180 mins.). No. 4. 2004. (978-1-58807-794-3(2)); 18.00 (978-1-58807-477-5(3)) Am Pubng Inc.
The Starmen have learned that a mysterious alien race visited our Solar System thousands of years ago. In the third Starman book, Journey to the Tenth Planet, Zip Foster called them "The Benefactors" because of the kindness these people showed the diminutive people who live on Titan. While they were on the tenth planet, the Starmen discovered that the Benefactors have a vicious implacable enemy - the Xenobots, a violent race that is searching for its "ancient enemy," and will demolish Earth if necessary to further the search. In Descent Into Europa, Zip Foster organizes a desperate search to find the Benefactors before the enemy does. Without their help, Earth stands no chance against the technologically superior Xenobots. With impeccable logic, the Starman leader has determined that if the Benefactors had a central base in the Solar System, it had to be on Europa, one of the moons of Jupiter. What the Starmen do not even suspect is that there is also a powerful enemy close to home.

Descent into Hell: 1 Peter 3:24-4:6. Ed Young. (J). 1983. 4.95 (978-0-7417-1281-3(4), 281) Win Walk.

Descent into the Maelstrom see Mind of Poe

Descent of Man see Great American Short Stories, Vol. II, A Collection

Descent of Man. unabr. ed. Edith Wharton. Read by Cindy Hardin. 1 cass. (Running Time: 52 min.). Dramatization. 1983. 7.95 (S-57) Jimcin Record.
One of the best of Warton's early short stories.

Descent of the Gods. Read by Norman Corwin. 1 cass. 10.00 (MC1016) Esstee Audios.
Radio drama.

Deschooled Society. unabr. ed. Ivan Illich. 1 cass. (Running Time: 33 min.). 12.95 (729) J Norton Pubs.
Illich argues that the function of modern education is simply to produce consumers & workers for an industrial society. In the process, individual autonomy is sacrificed.

Describing the Indescribable. Swami Amar Jyoti. 1 cass. 1982. 9.95 (R-40) Truth Consciousness.
Beyond thought, throbbing Oneness communicates. Going within our own soul. Love, the nearest door. The vacuum of golden silence.

Descriptions de Dessins: French Picture Descriptions. Carmen Waggoner. Ed. by Frederique Parr. Intro. by Harris Winitz. Illus. by Sydney M. Baker.Tr. of Picture Descriptions. (FRE.). (YA). (gr. 7 up). 1989. pap. bk. 35.00 (978-0-939990-77-1(6)) Intl Linguistics.

Descriptions Practice. 1 cass. (Running Time: 1 hr.). 2000. 15.95 Prof Pride.
Practice taking vehicle & subject descriptions. Valuable skill builder. Specify Adam Boy Practice or alpha Bravo.

Descubriendo el Poder para Bendecir a Mil Generaciones. Hugo Martinez. 6 cass. (SPA.). 2003. 29.99 (978-0-89985-417-5(6)); audio compact disk 35.00 (978-0-89985-416-8(8)) Christ for the Nations.

Descubrir Nuevas Oportunidades. Scripts. David J. Bowman. 1 cass, 1 CD. (Running Time: 40 mins). (SPA.). 2002. pap. bk. 24.99 (978-0-9742258-1-4(9)) TTG Consultants.
Contiene una Cassette de 40 minutos de la Audiofrecuencia y un CD de la Audiofrecuencia. Proporciona de manera facil a un mejor y el trabajo mas alto que paga. El vestigio rapido a la calidad extra en la vida. Esto ?el seguro de la carrera? es una inversion permanente en su futuro. Esta audiofrecuencia le mostrara la manera a una carrera remuneradora que aumentara su seguridad financiera. (Contains a 40 minute Audio Cassette and an Audio CD. It provides the easy way to a better, higher paying job. The fast track to extra quality in life. This ?career insurance? is a permanent investment in your future. This audio will show you the way to a rewarding career that will increase your financial security.).

Desde la Eternidad. Osvaldo Carnival. (SPA.). 2009. audio compact disk 14.99 (978-0-8297-6124-5(1)) Pub: Vida Pubs. Dist(s): Zondervan

Desde la soledad y la Esperanza: Antonio, Fernando, Ramón, René, Gerardo. Tr. of Hoping in Solitude. (SPA., 2008. pap. bk. 25.00 (978-959-211-308-4(4)) Pathfinder NY.

Desde otro Lugar. (SPA.). 2008. audio compact disk 11.99 (978-0-8297-6105-4(5)) Pub: Vida Pubs. Dist(s): Zondervan

Desecration: Antichrist Takes the Throne. Tim LaHaye & Jerry B. Jenkins. Narrated by Frank Muller. 8 CDs. (Running Time: 9 hrs. 45 mins.). (Left Behind Ser.: Bk. 9). audio compact disk 78.00 (978-1-4025-0478-5(0)) Recorded Bks.

Desecration: Antichrist Takes the Throne. Tim LaHaye & Jerry B. Jenkins. Narrated by Frank Muller. 7 cass. (Running Time: 9 hrs. 45 mins.). (Left Behind Ser.: Bk. 9). 2001. 67.00 (978-1-4025-1162-2(0), 96479) Recorded Bks.
Continues the sweeping, apocalyptic saga of the end times on planet earth. Mixing biblical prophecy and current events with an engaging storyline. It takes you into the horrifying world after the Rapture, where evil reigns under Antichrist Nicolae Carpathia.

Desecration: Antichrist Takes the Throne. Tim LaHaye & Jerry B. Jenkins. 8 CDs. (Running Time: 9 hrs. 45 mins.). (Left Behind Ser.: Bk. 9). 2004. audio compact disk 39.95 (978-0-7887-8965-6(1), 00202) Recorded Bks.
The end times on earth and the horrifying world of Rapture, blending Biblical prophecy and current events.

Desecration: Antichrist Takes the Throne. abr. ed. Tim LaHaye & Jerry B. Jenkins. Read by Frank Muller. 3 CDs. (Left Behind Ser.: Bk. 9). (ENG.). 2001. audio compact disk 19.99 (978-0-8423-3969-8(8)) Tyndale Hse.

Desecration: Antichrist Takes the Throne. unabr. ed. Tim LaHaye & Jerry B. Jenkins. 6 cass. (Running Time: 9 hrs. 45 mins.). (Left Behind Ser.: Bk. 9). 2004. 29.95 (978-0-7887-8964-9(3), 00484) Recorded Bks.
The horror and suffering of the Great Tribulation persist as the Antichrist Nicolae Carpathia, now the complete and total embodiment of evil, desecrates the temple in Jerusalem by entering and declaring himself god.

Deseos y Su Sombra. unabr. ed. Ana Clavel. Narrated by Adriana Sananes. 7 cass. (Running Time: 9 hrs.). (SPA.). 2003. 62.00 (978-1-4025-1630-6(4)) Recorded Bks.
A troubled woman, contemplating suicide, encounters a spirit who may help her through an emotional crisis.

Desert. Dorling Kindersley Publishing Staff. (Eyewitness Videos Ser.). (ENG.). (J). 2010. 12.99 (978-0-7566-6297-4(4)) DK Pub Inc.

Desert Contract. unabr. ed. John Lathrop. Narrated by David Drummond. (Running Time: 11 hrs. 0 mins. 0 sec.). (ENG.). 2008. audio compact disk 69.99 (978-1-4001-3756-5(X)); audio compact disk 24.99 (978-1-4001-5756-3(0)) Pub: Tantor Media. Dist(s): IngramPubServ

Desert Contract. unabr. ed. John Lathrop. Read by David A. Drummond. (Running Time: 11 hrs. 0 mins. 0 sec.). (ENG.). 2008. audio compact disk 34.99 (978-1-4001-0756-8(3)) Pub: Tantor Media. Dist(s): IngramPubServ

Desert Crop. unabr. ed. Catherine Cookson. Read by Susan Jameson. 8 cass. (Running Time: 8 hrs.). 1998. 69.95 Set, Dolby Sound. (978-0-7540-0151-5(2), CAB 1574) AudioGO.

Desert Crucible. Zane Grey & Jim Gough. 8 cass. (Running Time: 11 hrs. 30 mins.). 2002. 56.95 (978-0-7861-2599-9(3), 3172); audio compact disk 72.00 (978-0-7861-8940-3(1), 3172) Blckstn Audio.

Desert Crucible. unabr. ed. Zane Grey. Read by Jim Gough. 8 cass. 2001. 39.95 (978-0-7861-4407-5(6)); audio compact disk 39.95 (978-0-7861-7429-4(3)) Blckstn Audio.

Desert Crucible. unabr. ed. Zane Grey. Read by Jim Gough. 8 pieces. 2004. reel tape 39.95 (978-0-7861-2526-5(8)); audio compact disk 39.95 (978-0-7861-9077-5(9)) Blckstn Audio.
Young John Shefford, a tenderfoot from Illinois who?s escaping from his troubled past, heads west to follow up the curious legend of three people who live imprisoned in isolated Surprise Valley, one of whom is a beautiful young girl named Fay Larkin. Shefford, half in love with the girl he?s never met, is determined to find the valley and free her?if she?s still alive.

Desert Crucible. unabr. ed. Zane Grey & Jim Gough. (Running Time: 11 hrs. 30 mins.). 2002. audio compact disk 24.95 (978-0-7861-8771-3(9), 3172) Blckstn Audio.

Desert Cut. unabr. ed. Betty Webb. Read by Marguerite Gavin. (Running Time: 28800 sec.). (Lena Jones Mystery Ser.). 2008. 54.95 (978-1-4332-1145-4(9)) Blckstn Audio.

Desert Cut: A Lena Jones Mystery. unabr. ed. Betty Webb. Read by Marguerite Gavin. (Running Time: 28800 sec.). (Lena Jones Mystery Ser.). 2008. audio compact disk & audio compact disk 70.00 (978-1-4332-1146-1(7)); audio compact disk & audio compact disk 29.95 (978-1-4332-1147-8(5)) Blckstn Audio.

Desert Danger, unabr. ed. Peg Kehret. Narrated by Carine Montbertrand. 2 pieces. (Running Time: 2 hrs. 45 mins.). (Frightmares Ser.: No. 4). (gr. 5 up). 1997. 19.00 (978-0-7887-0741-4(8), 94918E7) Recorded Bks.
Rosie Saunders & Kayo Benton are enjoying a perfect vacation in Arizona. But when kidnappers looking for the daughter of a wealthy businessman grab Kayo by mistake, Rosie must desperately search for a way to rescue her.

Desert Death Song. unabr. ed. Louis L'Amour. Read by John Malloy & Stan Winiarski. 1 cass. (Running Time: 1 hr.). Dramatization. 1993. 7.95 (978-1-882071-26-5(3), 028) B-B Audio.
Desert Death SongPete Daly had never liked Nat Bodine. Nat married the girl Pete wanted. And now Pete is trying to hang Nat. Yet, to hang a man, he must be caught, and Bodine has lost himself in that broken rugged country known as Powder Basin.Tr.

Desert Dwellers Fiesta! Patty Horn. 1 cass. (J). (gr. k-6). 1998. 8.95 incl. songbook.; audio compact disk 15.95 CD incl. songbook. Two Geckos Mus.

***Desert Fire.** David Hagberg. 2009. (978-1-60136-498-2(9)) Audio Holding.

Desert Gold. Zane Grey. Contrib. by John Bolen. (Unabridged Classics (Playaway) Ser.). (ENG.). 2009. 79.99 (978-1-60775-792-4(3)) Find a World.

Desert Gold. Zane Grey. Read by John Bolen. (ENG.). 2005. audio compact disk 90.00 (978-1-4001-3033-7(6)) Pub: Tantor Media. Dist(s): IngramPubServ

Desert Gold. unabr. ed. Zane Grey. Read by Gene Engene. 8 cass. (Running Time: 11 hrs. 30 mins.). 1985. 49.95 (978-1-55686-215-1(6), 102581) Books in Motion.
Beautiful Mercedes Castaneda has attracted the eye of the ruthless bandit, Rojas & the Texas Ranger, Thorne. Thorne & Mercedes escape to the desert with Rojas & his bandits in hot pursuit.

Desert Gold. unabr. ed. Zane Grey. Narrated by John Bolen. (Running Time: 10 hrs. 30 mins. 0 sec.). (Tantor Unabridged Classics Ser.). (ENG.). 2009. 22.99 (978-1-4001-5936-9(9)); audio compact disk 65.99 (978-1-4001-3936-1(8)) Pub: Tantor Media. Dist(s): IngramPubServ

Desert Heat. unabr. ed. J. A. Jance. Read by Ellen Travolta. 6 cass. (Running Time: 8 hrs. 20 mins.). (Joanna Brady Mystery Ser.). 1995. 39.95 (978-1-55686-637-1(2)) Books in Motion.
Joanna Brady is the wife of a Cochise County deputy who's mysteriously killed. She suspects the sheriff & tries to prove it.

Desert Heat. unabr. ed. J. A. Jance. Read by Jean DeBarbieris. 6 cass. (Running Time: 8 hrs. 40 mins.). (Joanna Brady Mystery Ser.). 1994. 36.95 (978-1-55686-490-2(6), 752470) Books in Motion.
Joanna Brady is the wife of a Cochise County deputy who is mysteriously killed. She suspects the sheriff & sets out to prove it.

***Desert Heat.** unabr. ed. J. A. Jance. Read by Hillary Huber. (ENG.). 2009. (978-0-06-196927-0(3), Harper Audio); (978-0-06-195387-3(3), Harper Audio) HarperCollins Pubs.

Desert Hell, abr. ed. Dalton Walker. Read by Dick Wilkinson. 2 cass. (Running Time: 3 hr.). (Shiloh: Bk. 2). 1999. Rental 16.95 (978-1-890990-25-1(6)) Otis Audio.

Desert Is Theirs. unabr. ed. Byrd Baylor. Narrated by Will Rogers. 1 cass. (Running Time: 10 min.). (Byrd Baylor Ser.). (J). (gr. k-6). 1988. 5.95 (978-0-929937-12-0(0)) SW Series.
Describes the Tohono O'ohdam people and their relationship to the land.

Desert Junk Food Vol. 26: Banish Junk Food & Sugar Addiction. Jonathan Parker. 2 cass. (Running Time: 1 hr. 45 min.). 1992. 17.00 Set. (978-1-58400-025-9(2)) QuantumQuests Intl.

Desert Lost: A Lena Jones Mystery. unabr. ed. Betty Webb. (Running Time: 8 hrs. 0 mins.). 2009. 29.95 (978-1-4417-1412-1(X)); 54.95 (978-1-4417-1408-4(1)); audio compact disk 76.00 (978-1-4417-1409-1(X)) Blckstn Audio.

Desert Mercenary. abr. ed. Barry Sadler. Read by Charlton Griffin. Abr. by Odin Westgaard. 2 vols. (Casca Ser.: No. 16). 2003. 18.00 (978-1-58807-116-3(2)); (978-1-58807-556-7(7)) Am Pubng Inc.

Desert Mercenary. abr. ed. Barry Sadler. Read by Charlton Griffin. Abr. by Odin Westgaard. 2 vols. (Casca Ser.: No. 16). 2004. audio compact disk 25.00 (978-1-58807-290-0(8)); audio compact disk (978-1-58807-721-9(7)) Am Pubng Inc.

Desert Mothers: Spiritual Practices from the Women of the Wilderness. Mary C. Earle. 2008. audio compact disk 25.00 (978-0-8192-2333-3(6), MoreHse Pubng) Church Pub Inc.

Desert Mothers Spiritual Practices from the Women of the Wilderness: Unabridged Audio Book. Mary C. Earle. (ENG.). 2007. audio compact disk (978-0-9798958-3-8(9)) Mat Media.

Desert of Wheat. Read by Jim Gough. Ed. by Zane Grey. 11 CDs. (Running Time: 14 hrs.). 2004. audio compact disk 99.00 (978-0-7861-8146-9(X)) Blckstn Audio.

Desert of Wheat. unabr. ed. Zane Grey. Narrated by Jim Gough. 10 cass. (Running Time: 14 hrs. 30 mins.). 2002. 69.95 (978-0-7861-2166-3(1), 2916) Blckstn Audio.
Young farmer Kurt Dorn is torn between going to France to fight the German or staying in America to be with the woman he loves and protecting his wheat crop against saboteurs who question his loyalties. He struggles to come to terms with his deepest belief.

Desert of Wheat. unabr. ed. Zane Grey. Read by Jim Gough. 11 CDs. (Running Time: 14 hrs. 30 mins.). 2003. audio compact disk 88.00 (978-0-7861-9195-6(3), 2916) Blckstn Audio.

Desert Ordeal. Created by Saddleback Educational Publishing. (Barclay Family Adventure Ser.). (YA). 2003. audio compact disk 10.95 (978-1-56254-979-4(0)) Saddleback Edu.

Desert Places see Robert Frost in Recital

***Desert Queen.** unabr. ed. Susanna De Vries. Read by Beverley Dunn. (Running Time: 8 hrs. 40 mins.). 2010. audio compact disk 93.95 (978-1-74214-156-5(0), 9781742141565) Pub: Bolinda Pubng AUS. Dist(s): Bolinda Pub Inc

Desert Rain. abr. ed. Elizabeth Lowell. Read by Laural Merlington. (Running Time: 21600 sec.). 2007. audio compact disk 14.99 (978-1-4233-2380-8(7), 9781423323808, BCD Value Price) Brilliance Audio.

Desert Rain. unabr. ed. Elizabeth Lowell. Read by Laural Merlington. (Running Time: 8 hrs.). 2006. 39.25 (978-1-4233-2378-5(5), 9781423323785, BADLE); 24.95 (978-1-4233-2377-8(7), 9781423323778, BAD); 69.25 (978-1-4233-2372-3(6), 9781423323723, BrilAudUnabridg); audio compact disk 39.25 (978-1-4233-2376-1(9), 9781423323761, Brlnc Audio MP3 Lib); audio compact disk 87.25 (978-1-4233-2374-7(2), 9781423323747, BriAudCD Unabrid); audio compact disk 32.95 (978-1-4233-2373-0(4), 9781423323730, Bril Audio CD Unabri); audio compact disk 24.95 (978-1-4233-2375-4(0), 9781423323754, Brilliance MP3) Brilliance Audio.
Holly She is a fragile innocent haunted by memories of her past and by dreams of the man who once shared her secrets...the only man she can ever truly love. Shannon One of the world's great beauties, her face and figure grace the fashion pages of the most elegant magazines. Though many desire her, only one may have her. Holly Shannon North She is a contradiction: assured yet vulnerable, irresistible yet untouched. Destiny has brought her back to Hidden Springs, where she can be one person, where romance once touched her tender young heart - back to Lincoln McKenzie, the proud California rancher, long since hardened by life's tragedies. Now, in the icy chill of a desert storm, they must find the way back to love together - to rekindle the fire whose healing warmth has drawn them home.

Desert Rose: A Novel. unabr. collector's ed. Larry McMurtry. Read by Roses Prichard. 8 cass. (Running Time: 8 hrs.). 1985. 48.00 (978-0-7366-1007-0(3), 1940) Books on Tape.
Harmony is a fading flower. When she arrived in Vegas 20 years ago she had "the best legs in town" but now she's 39 & has only memories. But in falling down in life, Harmony is a triumph - an unabashed romantic who sees the silver lining in every cloud. She finds life a joy, thus brings joy into the lives she touches.

Desert Shall Rejoice see Christmas Stories

Desert Smells Like Rain. Gary P. Nabhan. Read by Gary P. Nabhan. 2 cass. (Running Time: 2 hrs. 30 min.). 1990. 16.95 set. (978-0-939643-30-1(8)) Audio Pr.
A portrait of centuries old agricultural traditions in the desert southwest. From the author's books, Gathering the Desert & The Desert Smells Like Rain.

Desert Solitaire, unabr. collector's ed. Edward Abbey. Read by Paul Shay. 8 cass. (Running Time: 12 hrs.). 1988. 64.00 (978-0-7366-1282-1(3), 2191) Books on Tape.
Philosophical reflections & personal experiences from three seasons the author spent as a ranger in a Utah preserve.

Desert Solitudes. Bernie Krause. 1 cass. (Running Time: 60 min.). (Wild Sanctuary Ser.). 1994. audio compact disk 15.95 CD. (2333, Creativ Pub) Quayside.
Natural wonders of southern New Mexico with two unique desert songs. In Dawn at Juniper Wells, coyotes, desert birds, & great horned owls blend with hot desert winds rustling dry grasses. Desert Serenade begins with haunting winds accented by ravens, meadowlarks, & mockingbirds; as evening descends choruses of toads, frogs, & crickets sing from a nearby marsh.

Desert Solitudes. Bernie Krause. 1 cass. (Running Time: 60 min.). (Wild Sanctuary Ser.). 1994. 9.95 (2331, NrthWrd Bks) TandN Child.

Desert Song, Set. Marilyn Arnold. 2 cass. 1999. 11.95 (978-1-57734-273-1(9), 07001703) Covenant Comms.
Novel about a rebellious soul who finds her way home.

Desert Spirituality & Contemporary Ministry. abr. ed. 3 CDs. (Running Time: 10680 sec.). 2006. audio compact disk 34.95 (978-1-59471-081-0(3)) Ave Maria Pr.
Nouwen offers both ideas and disciplines to people who minister in the Church that they might remain vital and enthusiastic witnesses to Christ in years of temptations to despair or the desire to live a comfortable life.

Desert Treasure/Life in the Desert. Steck-Vaughn Staff. 1997. (978-0-8172-7388-0(3)) SteckVau.

Desert Wife. abr. ed. Prod. by Beverly Benson Van Horn. 2 cass. (Running Time: 3 hrs. 10 mins.). (Living Voices of the Past Ser.: Vol. 3). 2000. 17.95 (978-0-9671885-2-2(0)) Beverlys Ltd.

Deserted Village see Treasury of Oliver Goldsmith, Thomas Gray & William Collins

Deserter. unabr. ed. John D. Heisner. Read by Maynard Villers. 6 cass. (Running Time: 5 hrs. 54 min.). (Chinook Ser.: Bk. 4). 2001. 39.95 (978-1-55686-856-6(1)) Books in Motion.
U.S. Marshall turned cattleman Jackson Kane fights to protect his herd, while helping a new friend in his battle against those who know the friend's past.

Deserter: Murder at Gettysburg. unabr. ed. Jane Langton. 6 cass. (Running Time: 9 hrs.). 2003. 56.00 (978-0-7366-9477-3(3)) Books on Tape.

Deserving Capacity. Swami Amar Jyoti. 1 cass. 1976. 9.95 (E-3) Truth Consciousness.
The grace of deserving & rightly using what we are given. The seven chakras.

Deserving to Succeed. Shad Helmstetter. 1 cass. (Self-Talk Ser.). 10.95 (978-0-937065-61-7(7)) Grindle Pr.
Companion Self-Talk Cassettes as mentioned in the book, "What To Say When You Talk To Your Self".

Deshi. John J. Donohue. Read by Barrett Whitener. (Running Time: 37800 sec.). 2005. audio compact disk 81.00 (978-0-7861-8278-7(4)) Blckstn Audio.

Deshi - Cancelled: A Martial Arts Thriller. unabr. ed. John Donohue. 20 cass. (Running Time: 11 hrs. 30 mins.). 2005. reel tape 29.95 (978-0-7861-2897-6(6), E3392); audio compact disk 32.95 (978-0-7861-8279-4(2), ZE3392); audio compact disk 29.95 (978-0-7861-8320-3(9), ZM3392) Blckstn Audio.

Deshi -Lib. (Running Time: 11 hrs. 30 mins.). 2005. 65.95 (978-0-7861-2898-3(4)) Blckstn Audio.

Design for Living. Noel Coward. Perf. by Claire Forlani et al. 2 CDs. (Running Time: 1 hr. 44 mins.). 2005. audio compact disk 25.95 (978-1-58081-284-9(8), CDTPT199) Pub: L A Theatre. Dist(s): NetLibrary CO

Design for Murder, unabr. ed. Carolyn G. Hart. Read by Kate Reading. 6 cass. (Running Time: 9 hrs.). (Death on Demand Mystery Ser.: No. 2). 1999. 48.00 (978-0-7366-4457-0(1), 4902) Books on Tape.
Invited to stage a murder for the annual spring house tour sponsored by the Historical Society of Chastain, South Carolina, Annie Laurance instead finds herself the leading lady in a flesh-&-blood drama. When the curtain falls on mean-spirited grande dame Corinne Webster, Annie is accused of the murder. With her fiance, Max Darling, Annie pieces together evidence to clear her name - until her chief witness is murdered. Now it will take all her sleuthing skills to discover the evil in the heart of Chastain's Beautiful People.

Design for Murder, Set. unabr. ed. Erica Quest. 6 cass. 1998. 69.95 (978-1-872672-26-7(4)) Pub: Magna Story GBR. Dist(s): Ulverscroft US

Design It! Build It! Sundance/Newbridge, LLC Staff. (Early Science Ser.). (gr. k-3). 2007. audio compact disk 12.00 (978-1-4007-6606-2(0)); audio compact disk 12.00 (978-1-4007-6607-9(9)); audio compact disk 12.00 (978-1-4007-6605-5(2)) Sund Newbridge.

Design of a Brain. Ed. by Marco A. V. Bitetto. 1 cass. 2000. (978-1-58578-092-1(8)) Inst of Cybernetics.

Design of Plants: An Introduction. Ra Uru Hu. Ed. by Chaitanyo. 1 cass. (Running Time: 58 mins.). 2000. audio compact disk 15.00 (978-0-9671115-2-0(8)) zc design.
The interaction between plants & humans in the light of the Human Design System.

***Design Revolution: Answering the Toughest Questions about Intelligent Design.** unabr. ed. William Dembski. Narrated by Grover Gardner. (ENG.). 2006. 19.98 (978-1-59644-289-4(1), Hovel Audio) christianaud.

Design Revolution: Answering the Toughest Questions about Intelligent Design. unabr. ed. William A. Dembski. Frwd. by Charles W. Colson. 11 CDs. (Running Time: 14 hrs. 0 mins. 0 sec.). (ENG.). 2006. audio compact disk 30.98 (978-1-59644-288-7(3), Hovel Audio) christianaud.
Is it science? Is it religion? What exactly is the Design Revolution? This book answers the toughest questions about Intelligent Design. As the Intelligent Design movement has gained momentum over recent years, questions have naturally arisen to challenge its provocative claims. With clarity and concision, William Dembski responds to the most vexing questions and objections raised by experts and non-experts.

Design Revolution: Answering the Toughest Questions about Intelligent Design. unabr. ed. William A. Dembski. Frwd. by Charles W. Colson. Narrated by Grover Gardner. 2 MP3CDs. (Running Time: 14 hrs. 0 mins. 0 sec.). (ENG.). 2006. lp 24.98 (978-1-59644-287-0(5), Hovel Audio) christianaud.

Design Solutions: Tessellations Unit. Jonathan Schneider. (YA). 2007. audio compact disk 79.99 (978-1-4276-1546-6(2)) AardGP.

Design Your Life: Using Self-Talk to Create Your Life One Day at a Time. Michael Russ. Read by Michael Russ. (ENG.). 2005. audio compact disk Rental 13.95 (978-0-9747064-7-4(7), ABridge) Russ Invis.

Designation Gold. abr. ed. Richard Marcinko. Based on a work by John Weisman. (Rogue Warrior Ser.). 2004. 10.95 (978-0-7435-4584-6(2)) Pub: S&S Audio. Dist(s): S and S Inc

Designed for Health. 4.95 (C4) Carothers.

Designing & Planning Foodservice Programs That Work. 1 cass. (America's Supermarket Showcase '96 Ser.). 1996. 11.00 (NGA96-049) Sound Images.

Designing, Constructing, & Maintaining Today's Airport Projects. Ed. by William J. Sproule & Stacy Jansen. 2002. audio compact disk 76.00 (978-0-7844-0646-5(4), 40646) Am Soc Civil Eng.

Designing Environments. unabr. ed. R. Buckminster Fuller. 2 cass. (Running Time: 1 hr. 57 min.). 1967. 18.00 Set. (00703) Big Sur Tapes.

Designing for a New Age. Ralph Alan Dale. Read by Ralph Alan Dale. 1 cass. (Running Time: 90 min.). 1982. 9.00 (2) Dialectic Pubng.
The origins & future of design.

Designing God's Woman. Kay Kuzma. 6 cass. (Running Time: 6 hrs.). (978-0-910529-07-5(8)) Family Mtrs.
Self-help & motivational seminar for women.

Designing Quality. unabr. ed. Accreditation Council on Services for People with Disabilities Staff. Read by Robert L. Sandidge. Des. by Robert Sandidge. 2 cass. (Running Time: 1 hr. 45 min.). 1996. 27.50 SET. (978-1-57654-222-4(X)) Creat Core.
Provides an introduction & orientation to using outcome measures of quality in services & supports for people with disabilities.

Designing the Life of Your Dreams: A Guided Visualization for Creating the Life You Desire. Mitch Meyerson & Laurie Ashner. Read by Mitch Meyerson. 1 cass. (Running Time: 50 min.). (Unassigned Ser.). 1999. 11.95 (978-1-57224-155-8(1), 71) New Harbinger.

Designing Woman. unabr. ed. Vera Cowie. Read by Tanya Myers. 5 cass. (Storysound Ser.). (J). 2000. 49.95 (978-1-85903-372-2(5)) Pub: Mgna Lrg Print GBR. Dist(s): Ulverscroft US

Desintoxification. unabr. ed. Robert A. Monroe. Read by Roland Simon. 1 cass. (Running Time: 30 min.). (Human Plus Ser.). (FRE.). 1993. 14.95 (978-1-56102-062-1(1)) Inter Indus.
Enhance the body's ability to cleanse chemicals & other destructive substances.

***Desirable Residence: A Novel of Love, Family, Adultery, & Real Estate.** unabr. ed. Madeleine Wickham. Read by Katherine Kellgren. 7 CDs. (Running Time: 8 hrs. 30 mins. 0 sec.). (ENG.). 2010. audio compact disk 29.99 (978-1-4272-1006-7(3)) Pub: Macmill Audio. Dist(s): Macmillan

Desire. J. Krishnamurti. 1 cass. (Running Time: 1 hr.). (Krishnamurti with Dr. Allan W. Anderson Ser.: No. 7). 8.50 (APA747) Krishnamurti.
These 1974 dialogues cover the entire spectrum of Krishnamurti's teaching in a series highly regarded for its depth of inquiry into each particular subject.

Desire. unabr. ed. Amanda Quick, pseud. Read by Anne Flosnik. (Running Time: 11 hrs.). 2010. 39.97 (978-1-4233-8805-0(4), 9781423388050, Brinc Audio MP3 Lib); 39.97 (978-1-4233-8807-4(0), 9781423388074, BADLE); 24.99 (978-1-4233-8804-3(6), 9781423388043, Brilliance MP3); 24.99 (978-1-4233-8806-7(2), 9781423388067, BAD); audio compact disk 82.97 (978-1-4233-8803-6(8), 9781423388036, BriAudCD Unabrid); audio compact disk 29.99 (978-1-4233-8802-9(X), 9781423388029, Bril Audio CD Unabri) Brilliance Audio.

Desire: Attract What You Need & Desire. Kelly Howell. 2000. audio compact disk 14.95 (978-1-881451-73-0(9)) Brain Sync.

Desire: Live with Passion. Kelly Howell. 1 cass. (Running Time: 60 min.). 1998. 11.95 (978-1-881451-59-4(3)) Brain Sync.
Desire is the fire of life - the driving force of creation. When this sacred energy is embodied fully it creates an irresistible inner magnetism that attracts the very things we long for. In this life-transforming meditation, Kelly Howell guides you to experience the fulfillment of your deepest desires at a core cellular level. In states of blissful reverie you are exalted empowered to manifest your dreams.

Desire: The Journey We Must Take to Find the Life God Offers. John Eldredge. 2005. audio compact disk 19.99 (978-1-59859-097-5(9)) Oasis Audio.

Desire: The Journey We Must Take to Find the Life God Offers. unabr. ed. John Eldredge. Read by Kelly Ryan Dolan. 6 cass. (Running Time: 8 hrs.). 2004. 27.99 (978-1-58926-626-1(9)) Oasis Audio.

Desire: The Journey We Must Take to Find the Life God Offers. unabr. ed. John Eldredge. Narrated by Kelly Ryan Dolan. (ENG.). 2004. 23.09 (978-1-60814-263-7(9)) Oasis Audio.

Desire: The Journey We Must Take to Find the Life God Offers. unabr. ed. John Eldredge. Read by Kelly Ryan Dolan. 7 CDs. (Running Time: 8 hrs.). (ENG.). 2004. audio compact disk 32.99 (978-1-58926-627-8(7)) Oasis Audio.

Desire & Deceit: The Real Cost of the New Sexual Tolerance. R. Albert Mohler, Jr. (ENG.). 2009. 19.99 (978-1-934384-25-1(9)) Pub: Treasure Pub. Dist(s): STL Dist NA

Desire & the Soul. unabr. ed. Gilbert Highet. Read by Gilbert Highet. 1 cass. (Running Time: 30 min.). 9.95 (23310-A,B) J Norton Pubs.
The author discusses the meaning of the myth of Psyche & Cupid with references to modern treatments.

Desire & Will. Eknath Easwaran. 1 cass. (Running Time: 1 hr.). (Easwaran on Tape Ser.). 1989. 7.95 (978-1-58638-521-7(6)) Nilgiri Pr.

Desire, Envy, Competition, Ambition. Douglas Wilson. (ENG.). 2008. audio compact disk 16.00 (978-1-59128-367-6(1)) Canon Pr ID.

Desire Lines. unabr. collector's ed. Christina Baker Kline. Read by Mary Peiffer. 8 cass. (Running Time: 12 hrs.). 2000. 64.00 (978-0-7366-4903-2(4)) Books on Tape.
When Kathryn Campbell comes back to her hometown, she delves into the disappearance of her friend Jennifer, who vanished ten years ago.

Desire of Ages. Ellen G. White. 2004. audio compact disk (978-1-883012-09-0(0)) Remnant Pubns.

Desire of Ages. unabr. ed. Ellen G. White. 27 CDs. (Running Time: 27 hrs.). 2002. audio compact disk (978-1-883012-99-1(6)) Remnant Pubns.

Desire of Heaven: Audio Book on CD. unabr. ed. Sheila Walsh. 2010. audio compact disk 29.99 (978-1-4003-1632-8(4)) Nelson.

Desire of the Everlasting Hills: The World Before & after Jesus. unabr. ed. Thomas Cahill. Read by Brian O'Bryne. 8 CDs. (Running Time: 9 hrs. 30 min.). (Hinges of History Ser.: Vol. 3). 2000. audio compact disk 34.95 (Random AudioBks) Random Audio Pubg.

Desire to Take Hold. 9 cass. Incl. Desire to Take Hold: A World Citizen's Agenda for the Next Decade. Steve Thiermann. 1984.; Desire to Take Hold: Aging in a Changing World. Phyllis Sanders. 1984.; Desire to Take Hold: Criminal Justice: A Little Bit on the Ailment & a Lot More on the Cure. Phil Mullen. 1984.; Desire to Take Hold: Lord, When Did We See You? Domenic Rossi. 1984.; Desire to Take Hold: National Politics: The Agenda Before Us. Alison Oldham. 1984.; Desire to Take Hold: Racism Is... John Churchville. 1984.; Desire to Take Hold: Say Only What You Know: Friends' Testimonies & an Introduction to the Series. Steve Stalonas. 1984.; Desire to Take Hold: Science & Ethics. Stanley Cherim. 1984.; Desire to Take Hold: Women & Families in the Twenty-First Century. Demie Kurz. 1984.; 1984. 28.00 Set.; 4.50 ea. Pendle Hill.

Desire to Take Hold: A World Citizen's Agenda for the Next Decade see Desire to Take Hold

Desire to Take Hold: Aging in a Changing World see Desire to Take Hold

Desire to Take Hold: Criminal Justice: A Little Bit on the Ailment & a Lot More on the Cure see Desire to Take Hold

Desire to Take Hold: Lord, When Did We See You? see Desire to Take Hold

Desire to Take Hold: National Politics: The Agenda Before Us see Desire to Take Hold

Desire to Take Hold: Racism Is... see Desire to Take Hold

Desire to Take Hold: Say Only What You Know: Friends' Testimonies & an Introduction to the Series see Desire to Take Hold

Desire to Take Hold: Science & Ethics see Desire to Take Hold

Desire to Take Hold: Women & Families in the Twenty-First Century see Desire to Take Hold

***Desire Unchained: A Demonica Novel.** unabr. ed. Larissa Ione. (Running Time: 12 hrs.). (Demonica Ser.). (ENG.). 2011. 24.98 (978-1-60941-477-1(2)) Pub: Hachet Audio. Dist(s): HachBkGrp

Desire under the Elms. Eugene O'Neill. Contrib. by Amy Brenneman et al. (Playaway Adult Fiction Ser.). (ENG.). 2009. 39.99 (978-1-60775-738-2(9)) Find a World.

Desired. unabr. ed. Carter Brown. 3 cass. (Running Time: 4 hrs.). 2004. 28.00 (978-1-74030-700-0(3)) Pub: Bolinda Pubng AUS. Dist(s): Lndmrk Audiobks

Desiree's Baby see Women in Literature, the Short Story: A Collection

Desiree's Baby. Kate Chopin. 1 cass. (Running Time: 57 min.). Dramatization. Incl. Mortal Immortal. Mary Wollstonecraft Shelley. 1977. (D-6); Winter Courtship. Sarah Orne Jewett. 1977. (D-6); 1977. 7.95 (D-6) Jimcin Record.
Best stories of three famous women, dramatized by a cast of characters.

Desiree's Baby. unabr. ed. Kate Chopin. Read by Jacqueline Kinlow. 2 cass. (Running Time: 2 hrs. 23 min.). 1994. lib. bdg. 18.95 Set, incl. vinyl case with notes, author's picture & biography, library ed. (978-1-883049-33-1(4)) Sound Room.
A collection of Louisiana stories including: "Desiree's Baby," "Love on the Bon-Dieu," "A Lady of Bayou St. John," "The Unexpected Fedora" & "At the Cadian Ball".

Desiree's Baby, Set. unabr. ed. Short Stories. Kate Chopin. Read by Jacqueline Kinlow. 2 cass. (Running Time: 2 hrs. 30 mins). (Kate Chopin Ser.). 1994. bk. 16.95 (978-1-883049-13-3(X), 390227) Sound Room.
Stories of love & adventure with the Creoles & the Cajuns. Includes: "Desiree's Baby," "A Lady of Bayou St. John," "The Unexpected Fedora," "God Mother," "At the Cadian Ball" & "The Story of an Hour.".

Desirelessness. Swami Amar Jyoti. 1 cass. 1977. 9.95 (B-13) Truth Consciousness.
No desire brings perpetual happiness. Do we follow our desires or God's Will?.

Desires & Our Will. Swami Amar Jyoti. 1 cass. 1978. 9.95 (B-4) Truth Consciousness.
A fresh outlook on desires & how to exhaust them.

Desiring God: Meditations of a Christian Hedonist. John Piper. Read by Grover Gardner. (Running Time: 45000 sec.). 2006. audio compact disk 90.00 (978-0-7861-7190-3(1)) Blckstn Audio.

Desiring God: Meditations of a Christian Hedonist. unabr. ed. John Piper. Read by Grover Gardener. 10 CDs. (Running Time: 12 hrs. 18 mins. 0 sec.). (ENG.). 2005. audio compact disk 28.98 (978-1-59644-104-0(6), Hovel Audio); lp 19.98 (978-1-59644-105-7(4), Hovel Audio) christianaud.
In this paradigm-shattering classic, John Piper reveals that the debate between duty and delight doesn't truly exist: delight is our duty. Join him as he unveils stunning, life-impacting truths from the Bible that you've heard, but never dared to believe.

***Desiring God: Meditations of A Christian Hedonist.** unabr. ed. John Piper. Narrated by Grover Gardner. (ENG.). 2005. 16.98 (978-1-59644-106-4(2), Hovel Audio) christianaud.

Desiring Rome: Male Subjectivity & Reading Ovid's Fasti. Richard Jackson King. 2006. audio compact disk 9.95 (978-0-8142-9097-2(3)) Pub: Ohio St U Pr. Dist(s): Chicago Distribution Ctr

Desk Kicks: Desk. Natalie R. Manor. 1 cass. (Running Time: 50 min.). (Kicks Ser.). 1993. 14.95 (978-1-881680-01-7(0)) Events Extraord.
Fitness/stress relief in your office, at your desk or chair.

Desmitificacion de una Diva: La Verdad Sobre la Lupe. Juan A. Moreno-Velazquez. Tr. by Carlos Jose Restrepo. (SPA., (J). 2003. bk. 24.95 (978-958-04-7429-6(X)) Pub: Norma S A COL. Dist(s): Distr Norma

Desmond Tutu: A Scourge As Bad As Hitler's. Desmond Tutu. Read by Desmond Tutu. 1 cass. (Running Time: 63 min.). 11.95 (K0390B090, HarperThor) HarpC GBR.

Desolation Island. Patrick O'Brian. Narrated by Simon Vance. (Running Time: 10 hrs. 30 mins.). (Aubrey-Maturin Ser.). 2005. 30.95 (978-1-59912-469-8(6)) Iofy Corp.

Desolation Island. Patrick O'Brian. Narrated by Patrick Tull. 11 CDs. (Running Time: 13 hrs.). (Aubrey-Maturin Ser.: Vol. 5). audio compact disk 111.00 (978-0-7887-9868-9(5)) Recorded Bks.
Jack?s prize money has set the household accounts aright, but if he continues frittering it on naive extravagances, it will be gone in a fortnight. Fortunately he gets a commission aboard the Leopard, bound for Australia to rescue the hated and captive Captain Bligh.

Desolation Island. Patrick O'Brian & Simon Vance. 8 cass. (Running Time: 10 hrs. 30 mins.). (Aubrey-Maturin Ser.). 2002. 56.95 (978-0-7861-2865-5(8), 3356); audio compact disk 72.00 (978-0-7861-8399-9(3), 3356) Blckstn Audio.

Desolation Island. unabr. ed. Patrick O'Brian. Read by Simon Vance. 8 cass. (Running Time: 10 hrs. 30 mins.). (Aubrey-Maturin Ser.). 2005. 29.95 (978-0-7861-2922-5(0)); audio compact disk 24.95 (978-0-7861-8408-8(6), 3356) Blckstn Audio.

Desolation Island. unabr. ed. Patrick O'Brian. Read by Simon Vance. 9 CDs. (Running Time: 37800 sec.). (Aubrey-Maturin Ser.). 2005. audio compact disk 29.95 (978-0-7861-8227-5(X)) Blckstn Audio.

Desolation Island. unabr. ed. Patrick O'Brian. Read by Richard Brown. 9 cass. (Running Time: 13 hrs. 30 min.). (Aubrey-Maturin Ser.). 1992. 72.00 (978-0-7366-2249-3(7), 3038) Books on Tape.
Bound for Australia, Aubrey & Maturin encounter a Dutch man of war in action "...that for sheer descriptive power can match anything in sea fiction." (The Guardian).

Desolation Island. unabr. ed. Patrick O'Brian. Narrated by Patrick Tull. 9 cass. (Running Time: 13 hrs.). (Aubrey-Maturin Ser.: No. 5). 78.00 (978-1-55690-839-2(3), 93207E7) Recorded Bks.
Jack's prize money has set the household accounts aright, but if he continues frittering it on naive extravagances, it will be gone in a fortnight. Fortunately he gets a commission aboard the "Leopard," bound for Australia to rescue the hated & captive Capt. William Bligh. Available to libraries only.

Desolation Island. unabr. ed. Patrick O'Brian. Read by Patrick Tull. 8 Cass. (Running Time: 13.25 Hrs.). (Aubrey-Maturin Ser.). 34.95 (978-1-4025-3929-9(0)) Recorded Bks.

Desorden de Tu Nombre. Juan Jose Millas. (Coleccion Leer en Espanol: Nivel 3 Ser.). (SPA., 2008. pap. bk. 13.99 (978-84-9713-064-6(2)) Santillana Univ de Salamanca ESP.

Despegue con Ellen Ochoa! Audiocassette. (Saludos Ser.: Vol. 3). (SPA.). (gr. 2-3). 10.00 (978-0-7635-5887-1(7)) Rigby Educ.

Despegue en Ingles. 1 cass. (Running Time: 1 hr. 30 mins.).Tr. of Lift off in English. (SPA.). 2001. (978-970-607-289-4(6)) Larousse Eds MEX.

***Desperado Who Stole Baseball.** unabr. ed. John H. Ritter. Narrated by Robert Ramirez. 1 Playaway. (Running Time: 7 hrs. 30 mins.). (YA). (gr. 5-8). 2009. 59.75 (978-1-4407-3009-2(1)); 61.75 (978-1-4407-2999-7(9)); audio compact disk 87.75 (978-1-4407-3003-0(2)) Recorded Bks.

***Desperado Who Stole Baseball.** unabr. collector's ed. John H. Ritter. Narrated by Robert Ramirez. 7 CDs. (Running Time: 7 hrs. 30 mins.). (YA).

(gr. 5-8). 2009. audio compact disk 41.95 (978-1-4407-3007-8(5)) Recorded Bks.

Desperate Acts. unabr. ed. Jane Candia Coleman. Read by Mary Peiffer. 7 cass. (Running Time: 10 hrs. 30 mins.). 2001. 56.00 (978-0-7366-8320-3(8)) Books on Tape.
Jake, a cruel and abusive husband, inexplicably sends Nan and her son to a Western dude ranch. There, they recover from their mistreatment, and meet Ben, the ranch owner. Ben is a Western man schooled by his faithless ex-wife in the ways of human unhappiness. Nan and Ben realize that they have much in common, and that they share a mutual attraction. However, Nan still has hopes that Jake can reform. But when Nan and her son return home, Jake's hostility drives the boy to attempt suicide. Nan gets the message that it's time to leave Jake and find a new life.

Desperate Deception. unabr. ed. Thomas E. Mahl. Read by William Sutherland. 6 cass. (Running Time: 8 hrs. 30 mins.). 2000. 44.95 (978-0-7861-1610-2(2), 2438) Blckstn Audio.

Desperate Deception: British Covert Operations in the United States, 1939-44. unabr. ed. Thomas E. Mahl. Read by William Sutherland. 6 cass. (Running Time: 9 hrs.). 1999. 44.95 (2438) Blckstn Audio.
Faced with the growing prospect of war with Germany in 1939, the British government mounted a massive secret political campaign in the United States to weaken the isolationists, bring America into World War II, & then influence U.S. war policy in England's favor. Reveals Britain's widespread use of front groups, agents, & collaborators & shows how its agents manipulated polling data & influenced election campaigns.

***Desperate Duchesses.** unabr. ed. Eloisa James. Read by Rosalyn Landor. (ENG.). 2010. (978-0-06-202542-5(2), Harper Audio); (978-0-06-204075-6(8), Harper Audio) HarperCollins Pubs.

Desperate for God Series. Reuven Doron. 3 cass. (Running Time: 4 hrs. 30 mins.). 2000. 15.00 (RD03-000) Morning NC.
Includes "The Presence of God," "The Value of Suffering" & "A True Cry for God." In this series, Reuven stresses the importance of developing true dependency on God.

Desperate Journeys, Abandoned Souls: True Stories of Castaways & Other Survivors. unabr. ed. Short Stories. Edward E. Leslie. Read by Patrick Cullen. 15 cass. (Running Time: 22 hrs.). 1999. 95.95 (978-0-7861-1481-8(9), 2333) Blckstn Audio.
The most remarkable stories imaginable of maroons, castaways & other survivors from the 1500s to the present, their moral dilemmas & their influence on society, literature & art. Included are accounts of shipwrecks & descriptions of being marooned in isolated corners of the globe.

Desperate Journeys, Abandoned Souls: True Stories of Castaways & Other Survivors. unabr. ed. Edward E. Leslie. (Running Time: 77400 sec.). 2007. audio compact disk 120.00 (978-0-7861-5971-0(5)); audio compact disk 44.95 (978-0-7861-5972-7(3)) Blckstn Audio.

Desperate Marriages: Moving Toward Hope & Healing in Your Relationship. unabr. ed. Gary Chapman. Narrated by Chris Fabry. (Running Time: 6 hrs. 17 mins. 45 sec.). (ENG.). 2009. 18.19 (978-1-60814-503-4(4)) Oasis Audio.

Desperate Marriages: Moving Toward Hope & Healing in Your Relationship. unabr. ed. Gary Chapman. Read by Gary Chapman. Narrated by Chris Fabry. 6 CDs. (Running Time: 6 hrs. 17 mins. 45 sec.). (ENG.). 2009. audio compact disk 25.99 (978-1-59859-483-6(4)) Oasis Audio.

Desperate Measures. unabr. ed. Kate Wilhelm. Narrated by Marguerite Gavin. 9 cass. (Running Time: 13 hrs.). 2002. 62.95 (978-0-7861-2161-8(0), 2911); audio compact disk 88.00 (978-0-7861-9578-7(9), 2911) Blckstn Audio.
Barbara Holloway has a reputation for taking on the toughest cases in the Pacific Northwest and winning them. But this time it looks as though she's up against an unbeatable opponent. The trial involves the murder of Gus Marchand, a hard-working, God-fearing man who was found dead on his kitchen floor. Without any real evidence, the locals cast their suspicions toward Alex Feldman, Marchand's hideously deformed neighbor. At the request of a fellow attorney, Barbara agrees to defend him. But another suspect is the high-school principal, Hilde Franz, who'd had a contretemps with the dead man earlier that week. He had threatened to have her investigated and Hilde was seen near Marchand's property around the time of his death, giving police both a motive and an opportunity for murder. Hilde also happens to be an old friend of Barbara's father, Frank, so naturally he's going to defend her. Will Barbara have to square off against the man who taught her all she knows.

Desperate Measures. unabr. ed. Kate Wilhelm. Read by Marguerite Gavin. 9 pieces. 2004. reel tape 39.95 (978-0-7861-2212-7(9)) Blckstn Audio.

Desperate to Live above the Natural. Creflo A. Dollar. 4 cass. (Running Time: 6 hrs.). 2001. 20.00 (978-1-931172-91-2(9), TS69, Kidz Faith) Pub: Creflo Dollar. Dist(s): STL Dist NA

Desperately Seeking Sushi. Jerrilyn Farmer. Read by Carrington MacDuffie. 7 cass. (Madeline Bean Catering Mystery Ser.). 2006. 59.95 (978-0-7927-3920-3(5), CSL 912); audio compact disk 89.95 (978-0-7927-3921-0(3), SLD 912) AudioGO.

Desperation. abr. ed. Stephen King. Contrib. by Kathy Bates. 8 CDs. (Running Time: 9 hrs.). (ENG.). (gr. 12 up). 2009. audio compact disk 39.95 (978-0-14-314389-5(1), PengAudBks) Penguin Grp USA.

Desperation, unabr. ed. Stephen King. Narrated by Stephen King. 15 cass. (Running Time: 21 hrs. 30 mins.). 1997. 125.00 (978-0-7887-0950-0(X), 95010E7) Recorded Bks.
Tells of a desparate group of highway travelers who find themselves trapped in a deserted Nevada town by a supernatural menace.

Desperation Band. Contrib. by Desperation Band. 2007. audio compact disk 21.95 (978-5-557-57366-5(6)) Integrity Music.

Desperation Valley. unabr. ed. John Hunter. Narrated by Frank Muller. 4 cass. (Running Time: 5 hrs.). 1979. 35.00 (978-1-55690-139-3(9), 79060E7) Recorded Bks.
Shawn McCord rides herd on a cattle-drive until a Cherokee blood feud changes his course.

Despertar CD. Composed by Mabel Katz, X. (SPA.). 2006. audio compact disk 29.95 (978-0-9748820-7-9(0)) Your Business.

Despertar de la Gracia. 2006. audio compact disk 46.00 (978-1-57972-729-1(8)) Insight Living.

Despicable Me. unabr. ed. Read by Tim Curry. Text by Annie Auerbach. (Running Time: 2 hrs.). 2010. 12.98 (978-1-60788-371-5(6)); audio compact disk 12.98 (978-1-60788-370-8(8)) Pub: Hachet Audio. Dist(s): HachBkGrp

Despisals see Poetry & Voice of Muriel Rukeyser

Despues de la Tormenta. Alma Flor Ada. (Cuentos Para Todo el Ano Ser.). (SPA., (J). (gr. k-3). 4.95 (978-1-58105-254-1(5)) Santillana.

Dessa Rose. abr. ed. Sherley Anne Williams. Read by Ruby Dee. 2 cass. (Running Time: 3 hrs.). 2000. 7.95 (978-1-57815-148-6(1), 1107, Media Bks Audio) Media Bks NJ.
Story of an extraordinary friendship between two remarkable women, both caught in the shadow of slavery in the nineteenth-century South.

Destinae: (des-Tin-Ay): A City That Exists in Vertical Time. Roy H. Williams. 3 CDs. (Running Time: 3hrs. 25mins.). Dramatization. 2003. audio compact disk 23.95 (978-1-932226-07-2(9)) Wizard Acdmy.
Three, one-hour CDs relate the story of a lawyer named Intellect and a beagle named Intuition on the road to self-discovery. What will they find? Featuring 19 professional character voices, music, and sound effects, the narrative arc is that of a straightforward and delightful children's story. But the sophisticated reader will see complexities revealed beyond their wildest expectation. The companion hardback available from Wizard Academy Press includes the verbatim transcript of all you will hear on these CDs, as well as dozens of interchaptoral comments and quotes not included here - "keys" to unlocking the multiple hidden mysteries this powerful story contains. Also included in the hardback version are a series of three lengthy discussions about the book involving 10 leading experts in their fields. The author's recommendation is that you hear the story in it's pure narrative form - listen to these CDs - then read the trilogy in hardback to embark on a journey you'll never forget.

Destination German: Language Instructional. 2 cass. 1995. 15.95 accompanying bk. M-H Contemporary.

Destination Karminia. audio compact disk 6.95 (978-88-8148-589-5(3)) EMC-Paradigm.

Destination Spanish. Brian Young et al. 2 cass. (Running Time: 3 hrs.). (Destination Ser.). 1995. pap. bk. 15.95 (978-0-8442-9399-8(7)) M-H Contemporary.

Destination Unknown. unabr. ed. Agatha Christie. Read by Emilia Fox. 5 cass. (Running Time: 7 hrs. 30 mins.). 2004. 27.95 (978-1-57270-399-5(7)) Pub: Audio Partners. Dist(s): PerseuPGW
Tom Betterton, a young nuclear physicist, has disappeared, with no clues as to his fate. And he is just the latest British scientist to do so. His associates and wife are questioned but know nothing. When his wife dies in Morocco, the investigator on the case enlists the help of a woman on the verge of suicide to impersonate Mrs. Betterton and travel in her place. Can she pull it off? Will she find the missing scientists at the end of her journey? This story is based on the real-life espionage case in the 1950s of two scientists who turned against their countries to work for Communist Russia.

Destination Unknown. unabr. ed. Agatha Christie. Narrated by Emilia Fox. 6 CDs. (Running Time: 9 hrs.). (Mystery Masters Ser.). (ENG.). 2004. audio compact disk 29.95 (978-1-57270-400-8(4)) Pub: AudioGO. Dist(s): Perseus Dist

***Destined for an Early Grave: A Night Huntress Novel.** unabr. ed. Jeaniene Frost. (Running Time: 13 hrs. 30 mins.). (Night Huntress Ser.). 2011. 29.95 (978-1-4417-7123-0(9)); 79.95 (978-1-4417-7120-9(4)); audio compact disk 29.95 (978-1-4417-7122-3(0)); audio compact disk 109.00 (978-1-4417-7121-6(2)) Blckstn Audio.

Destined for Destiny: The Unauthorized Autobiography of George W. Bush. unabr. ed. Scott Dikkers & Peter Hilleren. Read by Scott Dikkers. 2006. 17.95 (978-0-7435-6558-5(4), Audioworks) Pub: S&S Audio. Dist(s): S and S Inc

Destined for Greatness: Judges 13:1-25. Ed Young. 1998. 4.95 (978-0-7417-2171-6(6), A1171) Win Walk.

Destined for Second. Contrib. by Jeff Myers et al. 1 CD. 2003. cass. & DVD 19.95 (SWV10003) MVD Ent.

Destined to Witness: Growing up Black in Nazi Germany. Hans J. Massaquoi. Narrated by Peter Jay Fernandez. 14 cass. (Running Time: 20 hrs.). 114.00 (978-0-7887-5119-6(0)) Recorded Bks.

Destino Karminia. audio compact disk 6.95 (978-88-8148-608-3(3)) EMC-Paradigm.

Destinos. unabr. ed. Bill Van Patten. 6 cass. (Running Time: 9 hrs.). 1997. 36.60 (978-0-07-913077-8(1), Mc-H Human Soc) McGrw-H Hghr Educ.

Destinos. unabr. ed. Bill Van Patten. 8 cass. (Running Time: 12 hrs.). 1999. 42.60 (978-0-07-913076-1(3), Mc-H Human Soc) McGrw-H Hghr Educ.

Destinos, Pt. 1. 2nd ed. Vanpatten. (SPA & ENG.). (C). 2002. stu. ed. 74.38 (978-0-07-250440-8(4), 0072504404, Mc-H Human Soc) Pub: McGrw-H Hghr Educ. Dist(s): McGraw

Destinos, Pt. 2. 2nd ed. Vanpatten. (SPA & ENG.). (C). 2002. stu. ed. 74.38 (978-0-07-250439-2(0), 0072504390, Mc-H Human Soc) Pub: McGrw-H Hghr Educ. Dist(s): McGraw

Destiny. unabr. ed. Susan Ferrier. Narrated by Flo Gibson. 15 cass. (Running Time: 22 hrs.). 2003. 43.95 (978-1-55685-746-1(2)) Audio Bk Con.
Set in the Scottish Highlands, Edith, the chief's daughter, mourns the loss of a beloved cousin and being jilted by her adored lover. She survives many trials and finds tribulations.

Destiny. unabr. ed. Tim Parks. Read by Michael Kitchen. 8 cass. (Running Time: 12 hrs.). 2000. 69.95 (978-0-7540-0529-2(1), CAB 1952) AudioGO.

Destiny: Embrace the Ultimate Dream. Kelly Howell. 1 cass. (Running Time: 60 min.). 1998. 11.95 (978-1-881451-60-0(7)) Brain Sync.
Everyday we shape our destiny by what we think and do. With only a subtle shift in perception we can manifest a destiny that fulfills our deepest intent. In this breakthrough audio, Kelly Howell guides you to stretch far beyond your present boundaries to create the future of your dreams. As you embrace all that you long for, the blueprint for your life unfolds. The universe conspires with you to manifest the destiny held deep in your most sacred dreams.

Destiny: Live Your Vision. Kelly Howell. 2000. audio compact disk 14.95 (978-1-881451-74-7(7)) Brain Sync.

Destiny... Choosing Your Eternal Partner. Spencer W. Kimball. 1 cass. 9.95 (978-1-57734-486-5(3), 06006043) Covenant Comms.
Understanding the importance of eternal marriage.

Destiny Disrupted: A History of the World Through Islamic Eyes. unabr. ed. Tamim Ansary. (Running Time: 11 hrs. 0 mins.). (ENG.). 2009. 29.95 (978-1-4332-7227-1(X)); audio compact disk 29.95 (978-1-4332-7226-4(1)) Blckstn Audio.

Destiny Disrupted: A History of the World through Islamic Eyes. unabr. ed. Tamim Ansary. (Running Time: 11 hrs. 0 mins.). (ENG.). 2009. 65.95 (978-1-4332-7223-3(7)); audio compact disk 90.00 (978-1-4332-7224-0(5)) Blckstn Audio.

Destiny Kills. unabr. ed. Keri Arthur. Narrated by Cassandra Campbell. (Running Time: 9 hrs. 30 mins. 0 sec.). (Myth & Magic Ser.: No. 1). (ENG.). 2009. audio compact disk 24.99 (978-1-4001-6148-5(7)); audio compact disk 69.99 (978-1-4001-4148-7(6)) Pub: Tantor Media. Dist(s): IngramPubServ

Destiny Kills. unabr. ed. Keri Arthur. Read by Cassandra Campbell. Narrated by Cassandra Campbell. (Running Time: 9 hrs. 30 mins. 0 sec.). (Myth & Magic Ser.: No. 1). (ENG.). 2009. audio compact disk 34.99 (978-1-4001-1148-0(X)) Pub: Tantor Media. Dist(s): IngramPubServ

Destiny of Souls Set: New Case Studies of Life Between Lives. abr. ed. Michael Newton. 4 cass. (Running Time: 6 hrs.). 2000. 25.00 (978-1-57453-375-0(4)) Audio Lit.
The author explores what happens to the soul after death. Among other topics of enduring mystery, he addresses angels, ghosts, reincarnation, why certain people are drawn together & what lessons the soul is intended to learn, casting new light on life's events & relationships.

Destiny/Guiltless Love. Marianne Williamson. Read by Marianne Williamson. 1 cass. (Running Time: 90 mins.). (Lectures on a Course in Miracles). 1999. 10.00 (978-1-56170-186-5(6), M714) Hay House.

Destiny's Child Collector's Box. Keith Rodway. As told by Zoe-Anne Phillips & Nancy McClean. 3 CDs. 2005. audio compact disk (978-1-84240-325-9(7)) Chrome Dreams GBR.
Destiny?s Child are the most successful R n? B girl group in the world. Shaking their booty at any given opportunity, they have topped the charts with each new album and single release. Consistently going from strength to strength there appears to be no stopping these Independent Women . This 3 CD box set tells the full story of Destiny?s Child through spoken word biographies, interviews with the band members and rarely seen photographs. With postcards, booklets, posters and many other features it is sure to become a collector?s item of the first order.

***Destiny's Drum.** L. Ron Hubbard. Read by Michelle Stafford et al. Narrated by R. F. Daley. 2 CDs. (Running Time: 2 hrs.). (YA). 2010. audio compact disk 9.95 (978-1-59212-293-6(0)) Gala Pr LLC.

***Destrezas para Mapas Audio Cd.** Matthew Frank. Adapted by Benchmark Education Company, LLC. (Content Connections Ser.). (SPA.). (J). 2009. audio compact disk 10.00 (978-1-935472-60-5(7)) Benchmark Educ.

Destroy All Monsters. 1 CD. 2003. audio compact disk 14.98 (978-1-57813-380-2(7), CD/004, ADV Music) A D Vision.

Destroy All Monsters. 2004. DVD & audio compact disk 19.98 (978-1-57813-916-3(3), DDAM/002) ADV.

Destroyer of Worlds. unabr. ed. Larry Niven. (Running Time: 12 hrs. 30 mins.). 2009. 72.95 (978-1-4417-1727-6(7)); audio compact disk 105.00 (978-1-4417-1728-3(5)) Blckstn Audio.

Destroyer of Worlds. unabr. ed. Larry Niven. Read by Tom Weiner. (Running Time: 12 hrs. 30 mins.). 2009. 29.95 (978-1-4417-1731-3(5)); audio compact disk 39.95 (978-1-4417-1730-6(7)) Blckstn Audio.

Destroyer 100: Last Rites. 2006. audio compact disk 19.99 (978-1-59950-185-7(6)) GraphicAudio.

Destroyer 101: Bidding War. 2006. audio compact disk 19.99 (978-1-59950-195-6(3)) GraphicAudio.

Destroyer 102: Unite & Conquer. 2007. audio compact disk 19.99 (978-1-59950-203-8(8)) GraphicAudio.

Destroyer 103: Engines of Destruction. 2007. audio compact disk 19.99 (978-1-59950-214-4(3)) GraphicAudio.

Destroyer 104: Angry White Mailmen. 2007. audio compact disk 19.99 (978-1-59950-225-0(9)) GraphicAudio.

Destroyer 105: Scorched Earth. 2007. audio compact disk 19.99 (978-1-59950-315-8(8)) GraphicAudio.

Destroyer 106: White Water. 2007. audio compact disk 19.99 (978-1-59950-324-0(7)) GraphicAudio.

Destroyer 107: Feast or Famine. 2007. audio compact disk 19.99 (978-1-59950-332-5(8)) GraphicAudio.

Destroyer 108: Bamboo Dragon. 2007. audio compact disk 19.99 (978-1-59950-341-7(7)) GraphicAudio.

Destroyer 109: American Obsession. 2007. audio compact disk 19.99 (978-1-59950-350-9(6)) GraphicAudio.

Destroyer 110: Never Say Die. 2007. audio compact disk 19.99 (978-1-59950-359-2(X)) GraphicAudio.

Destroyer 111: Prophet of Doom. Warren Murphy & Richard Sapir. (Destroyer Ser.: No. 111). 2007. audio compact disk 19.99 (978-1-59950-377-6(8)) GraphicAudio.

Destroyer 112: Brain Storm. Warren Murphy & Richard Sapir. (Destroyer Ser.: No. 112). 2007. audio compact disk 19.99 (978-1-59950-383-7(2)) GraphicAudio.

Destroyer 113: The Empire Dreams. Warren Murphy & Richard Sapir. (Destroyer Ser.: No. 113). 2007. audio compact disk 19.99 (978-1-59950-398-1(0)) GraphicAudio.

Destroyer 114: Failing Marks. Warren Murphy. 2009. audio compact disk 19.99 (978-1-59950-428-5(6)) GraphicAudio.

Destroyer 115: Misfortune Teller. Warren Murphy. 2008. audio compact disk 19.99 (978-1-59950-405-6(7)) GraphicAudio.

Destroyer 116: The Final Reel. Warren Murphy & Richard Sapir. (Running Time: 21600 sec.). (Destroyer Ser.: No. 116). 2008. audio compact disk 19.99 (978-1-59950-439-1(1)) GraphicAudio.

Destroyer 117: Deadly Genes. Based on a novel by Warren Murphy & Richard Sapir. (Destroyer Ser.: No. 117). 2008. audio compact disk 19.99 (978-1-59950-453-7(7)) GraphicAudio.

Destroyer 118: Killer Watts. Based on a novel by Warren Murphy & Richard Sapir. 2008. audio compact disk 19.99 (978-1-59950-468-1(5)) GraphicAudio.

Destroyer 119: Fade to Black. Warren Murphy. 2008. audio compact disk 19.99 (978-1-59950-498-8(7)) GraphicAudio.

Destroyer 120: The Last Monarch. Alex Archer. 2008. audio compact disk 19.99 (978-1-59950-504-6(5)) GraphicAudio.

Destroyer 121: A Pound of Prevention. Warren Murphy. 2009. audio compact disk 19.99 (978-1-59950-530-5(4)) GraphicAudio.

Destroyer 122: Syndication Rites. Warren Murphy & Richard Sapir. 2009. audio compact disk 19.99 (978-1-59950-578-7(9)) GraphicAudio.

Destroyer 95: High Priestess. Created by Warren Murphy & Richard Sapir. (Running Time: 28800 sec.). (Destroyer Ser.). 2005. audio compact disk 19.99 (978-1-59950-005-8(1)) GraphicAudio.

Destroyer 95-104: MP3 CD Long Haul Boxset. Based on a book by Warren Murphy & Richard Sapir. (ENG.). 2007. 110.00 (978-1-59950-483-4(9)) GraphicAudio.

Destroyer 96: Infernal Revenue. 2006. audio compact disk 19.99 (978-1-59950-023-2(X)) GraphicAudio.

Destroyer 97: Identity Crisis. Warren Murphy. 2006. audio compact disk 19.99 (978-1-59950-115-4(5)) GraphicAudio.

Destroyer 98: Target of Opportunity. 2006. audio compact disk 19.99 (978-1-59950-136-9(8)) GraphicAudio.

Destroyer 99: The Color of Fear. 2006. audio compact disk 19.99 (978-1-59950-174-1(0)) GraphicAudio.

***Destroyermen: Distant Thunders.** unabr. ed. Taylor Anderson. (Running Time: 16 hrs. 0 mins.). (Destroyermen Ser.). 2010. 20.99 (978-1-4001-8502-3(5)); 39.99 (978-1-4001-9502-2(0)) Tantor Media.

***Destroyermen: Distant Thunders.** unabr. ed. Taylor Anderson. Narrated by William Dufris. (Running Time: 17 hrs. 0 mins. 0 sec.). (Destroyermen Ser.). (ENG.). 2010. 29.99 (978-1-4001-6502-5(4)); audio compact disk 39.99 (978-1-4001-1502-0(7)) Pub: Tantor Media. Dist(s): IngramPubServ

***Destroyermen: Rising Tides.** unabr. ed. Taylor Anderson. (Running Time: 17 hrs. 0 mins.). (Destroyermen Ser.). 2011. 29.99 (978-1-4001-6503-2(2)); 39.99 (978-1-4001-1503-7(5)); 21.99 (978-1-4001-8503-0(3)) Tantor Media.

***Destroyermen: Rising Tides (Library Edition)** unabr. ed. Taylor Anderson. (Running Time: 17 hrs. 0 mins.). (Destroyermen Ser.). 2011. 95.99 (978-1-4001-4503-4(1)); 39.99 (978-1-4001-9503-9(9)) Tantor Media.

Destroying Angel. Alanna Knight. 2009. 54.95 (978-1-4079-0054-4(4)); audio compact disk 71.95 (978-1-4079-0055-1(2)) Pub: Soundings Ltd GBR. Dist(s): Ulverscroft US

Destroying Myths about Spiritual Gifts. Jack Deere. 1 cass. (Running Time: 90 mins.). (Receiving Spiritual Gifts Ser.: Vol. 1). 2000. 5.00 (JD03-001) Morning NC.
This is a powerful debunking of aguments against the use of spiritual gifts & reveals major hindrances to believers walking in the power of God.

Destroying the Fear of Lack. Creflo A. Dollar. 2009. audio compact disk 14.00 (978-1-59944-774-2(6)) Creflo Dollar.

Destruction of Jerusalem - Excerpts. unabr. ed. Excerpts. Josephus. Narrated by Norman Dietz. 3 cass. (Running Time: 4 hrs. 30 mins.). 1999. 26.00 (978-1-55690-749-4(4), 92118E7) Recorded Bks.
Excerpts from the writings of the first century A.D. historian. Contains one of the few historical accounts we have of the wars of the Jews & the first destruction of Jerusalem by Titus during the Roman occupation of Palestine in 70 A.D.

Destruction of Kamsa. Swami Jyotirmayananda. 1 cass. (Running Time: 45 min.). 1990. 10.00 Yoga Res Foun.

Destruction of Neva. unabr. ed. Vickie Britton & Loretta Jackson. Read by Stephanie Brush. 8 cass. (Running Time: 9 hrs.). (Ardis Cole Ser.: Bk. 5). 2001. 49.95 (978-1-55686-991-4(6)) Books in Motion.
The expertise of Ardis Cole is summoned to Russia to locate the priceless statue of Neva. Did the creator destroy his own masterpiece prior to his suicide, or are there others involved in a plot for possession of the missing sculpture?.

Destruction of Sennacherib see Treasury of George Gordon, Lord Byron

Destruction of the Family Due to Radical Feminism. Frank Bertels. 1 cass. (Running Time: 1 hrs.). 1985. 10.00 Brun Pr.
Male rights broadcast interview, censored & feminist management & never broadcast. Bertels saved a copy of this interview. Also side 2 did get on the air, as it was a live broadcast. The last, as the female management heard this broadcast coming to work, & Bertels was forever banned from the station.

Destruction of the World's System: Ren. 18:1-24. Ed Young. 1987. 4.95 (978-0-7417-1579-1(1), 579) Win Walk.

Destructive Emotions - How Can We Overcome Them? A Scientific Dialogue with the Dalai Lama. abr. rev. ed. Daniel Goleman & Dalai Lama XIV. Read by Ed Levin. 4 CDs. (Running Time: 5 hrs. 30 mins. 0 sec.). (ENG., 2003. audio compact disk 29.95 (978-1-55927-819-5(6)) Pub: Macmill Audio. Dist(s): Macmillan

Destructive Generation. unabr. ed. Peter Collier & David Horowitz. Read by Robert Morris. 9 cass. (Running Time: 13 hrs.). 1989. 62.95 (978-0-7861-0090-3(7), 1083) Blckstn Audio.
Included are discussions of the Weather Underground, the impact of one feminist-lesbian lawyer named Fay Stender, life in Berkeley & the formidable strategy of the radical political machine, along with snapshots showing the involvement of several notables including Huey Newton, George Jackson, Bernadine Dohrn, Tom Hayden, Jane Fonda & several others.

Destruir Influencias Negativas, Set. 3rd ed. Carlos González. Read by Carlos González. Ed. by Dina Gonzalez. 3 CDs. (Running Time: 1hr 40 mins). (Habilidades Ser.).Tr. of How to Destroy Negative Influences. (SPA.). 2005. audio compact disk 29.00 (978-1-56491-030-1(X)) Imagine Pubs.
In Spanish. A program that helps people improve their ability to handle people who are negative towards them.

Destry Rides Again. Max Brand. (Isis Cassettes Ser.). 1995. 54.95 (978-1-85695-656-7(3)) Pub: ISIS Lrg Prnt GBR. Dist(s): Ulverscroft US

Destry Rides Again. unabr. ed. Max Brand. Narrated by John Randolph Jones. 6 cass. (Running Time: 8 hrs. 45 mins.). 1992. 51.00 (978-1-55690-692-3(7), 92348E7) Recorded Bks.
Harry Destry spends six years in jail for a crime he didn't commit. He returns to the western town of Wham a beaten man. But in fact it's a ruse. And soon he takes revenge on the cowards who framed him.

Destry Rides Again. unabr. collector's ed. Max Brand. Read by Wolfram Kandinsky. 7 cass. (Running Time: 10 hrs. 30 min.). 1991. 56.00 (978-0-7366-2079-6(6), 2884) Books on Tape.
Destry, young & reckless but no criminal, sat stunned as the judge pronounced him guilty. But he was innocent! He eyed the 12-man jury, then responded with words that would become legend in the little frontier town of Wham.

Detaching with Love & Why Didn't We Do This Before? 1 cass. (Overcoming Roadblocks in Recovery Ser.). 1984. 8.95 (1525G) Hazelden.

Detachment. Rick Brown. Read by Rick Brown. Ed. by John Quatro. 1 cass. (Running Time: 30 min.). (Subliminal - Easy Listening Ser.). 1993. 10.95 (978-1-57100-020-0(8), E148); 10.95 (978-1-57100-044-6(5), J148); 10.95 (978-1-57100-068-2(2), N148); 10.95 (978-1-57100-092-7(5), S148); 10.95 (978-1-57100-116-0(6), W148); 10.95 (978-1-57100-140-5(9), H148) Sublime Sftware.
Detachment turns down over-empathetic emotions.

Detachment Bravo. Richard Marcinko. Read by Richard Marcinko. (Rogue Warrior Ser.). 2004. 10.95 (978-0-7435-1939-7(6)) Pub: S&S Audio. Dist(s): S and S Inc

Detachment Makes Love Possible. 1 cass. 1981. 7.95 (978-1-58638-522-4(4)) Nilgiri Pr.
Explains developing detachment from one's self.

Detailing for Building Construction. GLC. 1997. audio compact disk (978-0-7506-2658-3(5), Arch Sci Pr) Sci Tech Bks.

Details at 10. unabr. ed. Ardella Garland. Narrated by Patricia R. Floyd. 5 cass. (Running Time: 6 hrs. 30 mins.). 2000. 45.00 (978-0-7887-8944-1(9), F0050L8) Recorded Bks.
Georgia Barnett is a daring television news reporter. When a girl witnesses a drive-by shooting & reports it to Georgia on live TV, the girl soon turns up missing. Feeling responsible, Georgia works her way through a terrifying world of gang violence in an effort to crack the case.

Details Do Make a Difference. Constance Mayer. 1 cass. 8.95 (224) Am Fed Astrologers.
Three-way system to extract important chart information.

Details Make the Story. unabr. ed. Elizabeth R. Bills. 1 cass. (Running Time: 29 min.). (Secrets of Successful Writers Ser.). 1963. 12.95 (23026) J Norton Pubs.
Story-telling is the art of working an abundance of definite, well-choosen details into a pattern. How does the writer go about doing this?.

Details on Cyprus see George Seferis

Detecting Faith's Destroyer. Elbert Willis. 1 cass. (Faith School Ser.; Vol. 1). 4.00 Fill the Gap.

Detecting Sir Arthur Conan Doyle: A Light & Enlightening Lecture, Featuring Elliot Engel. 2000. bk. 15.00 (978-1-890123-30-7(7)) Media Cnslts.

Detecting with the Rorschach Suicide Risks. unabr. ed. Marguerite Hertz. 1 cass. (Running Time: 30 min.). 1966. (29241) J Norton Pubs.
Assessment of suicidal danger through clinical analysis of personality structures & dynamics, including evaluation of related current research with Rorschach.

Detection & Management of Cervical Dysplasia. Contrib. by Arthur L. Herbst et al. 1 cass. (American College of Obstetrics & Gynecologists UPDATE: Vol. 22, No. 3). 1998. 20.00 Am Coll Obstetric.

Detections of Dr. Sam Johnson. unabr. ed. Lillian De La Torre. Narrated by Alexander Spencer. 5 cass. (Running Time: 7 hrs. 30 mins.). 1990. 44.00 (978-1-55690-140-9(2), 90007E7) Recorded Bks.
Period mysteries featuring the literary giant & his faithful biographer.

Detective at Death's Door. unabr. ed. Read by Sheila Mitchell. 5 CDs. (Running Time: 26760 sec.). 2005. audio compact disk 59.95 (978-0-7927-3723-0(7), SLD 833) AudioGO.

Detective at Death's Door. unabr. abr. ed. Read by Sheila Mitchell. 4 cass. (Running Time: 26760 sec.). 2005. 39.95 (978-0-7927-3722-3(9), CSL 833) AudioGO.

***Detective Dinosaur.** unabr. ed. James Skofield. (ENG.). 2008. (978-0-06-169407-3(X)); (978-0-06-172141-0(7)) HarperCollins Pubs.

Detective in Love. unabr. ed. H. R. F. Keating. Read by Sheila Mitchell. 6 cass. (Running Time: 9 hrs.). 2002. 54.95 (978-0-7540-0856-9(6), CAB 2278) Pub: Chivers Pr GBR. Dist(s): AudioGO

Detective Stories of the Nineteenth Century, Set. Geoffrey Wood et al. Read by Flo Gibson. 4 cass. (Running Time: 6 hrs.). 1996. 19.95 (978-1-55685-443-9(9)) Audio Bk Con.
"Murder under the Microscope," "Waters," "Going Through the Tunnel", "Dr. Varvill's Prescription"l, "The Great Ruby Robbery", "The Wedding Guest", "The Story of Baelbrow", "The Black Bag Left on the Doorstep" & "The Sheriff of Gullmore" are full of mystery & suspense.

Detective under Fire. H. R. F. Keating. Read by Sheila Mitchell. 6 vols. (Running Time: 9 hrs.). 2003. 54.95 (978-0-7540-8355-9(1)) Pub: Chivers Audio Bks GBR. Dist(s): AudioGO

Detectives, Vol. 1. (Running Time: 6 hrs.). 2004. audio compact disk 29.95 (978-1-57816-198-0(3)) Audio File.

Detectives Salvajes see Savage Detectives

Detente. unabr. ed. Robert A. Monroe. Read by Roland Simon. 1 cass. (Running Time: 30 min.). (Human Plus Ser.). (FRE.). 1992. 14.95 (978-1-56102-056-0(7)) Inter Indus.
Gain instant relief from tensions while staying alert.

Detente Exposed. unabr. ed. Stefan Possony. 1 cass. (Running Time: 34 min.). 12.95 (437) J Norton Pubs.

***Deterioration of Liberty.** L. Ron Hubbard. (ENG.). 2010. audio compact disk 15.00 (978-1-4031-1105-0(7)) Bridge Pubns Inc.

***Deterioration of Liberty.** L. Ron Hubbard. (POR.). 2010. audio compact disk 15.00 (978-1-4031-7327-0(3)); audio compact disk 15.00 (978-1-4031-7325-6(7)); audio compact disk 15.00 (978-1-4031-7329-4(X)); audio compact disk 15.00 (978-1-4031-7318-8(4)); audio compact disk 15.00 (978-1-4031-7330-0(3)); audio compact disk 15.00 (978-1-4031-7332-4(X)); audio compact disk 15.00 (978-1-4031-7317-1(6)); audio compact disk 15.00 (978-1-4031-7323-2(0)); audio compact disk 15.00 (978-1-4031-7319-5(2)); audio compact disk 15.00 (978-1-4031-7328-7(1)); audio compact disk 15.00 (978-1-4031-7331-7(1)); audio compact disk 15.00 (978-1-4031-7326-3(5)); audio compact disk 15.00 (978-1-4031-7321-8(4)); audio compact disk 15.00 (978-1-4031-7320-1(6)); audio compact disk 15.00 (978-1-4031-7324-9(9)); audio compact disk 15.00 (978-1-4031-7322-5(2)) Bridge Pubns Inc.

Determination & Willpower. Shad Helmstetter. 1 cass. (Self-Talk Cassettes Ser.). 10.95 (978-0-937065-18-1(8)) Grindle Pr.

Determined. Eldon Taylor. Read by Eldon Taylor. Interview with XProgress Aware Staff. 2 cass. (Running Time: 62 min. per cass.). (Omniphonics Ser.). 29.95 incl. script Set. (978-1-55978-819-9(4), 4020) Progress Aware Res.
3-D soundtrack with underlying subliminal affirmations, night & day versions.

Deth Interrupts Th Dansing / a Strangr Space. Bill Bissett. Prod. by Pete Danko. (GER & ENG.). 2007. audio compact disk 12.95 (978-0-88995-328-4(7)) Pub: Red Deer CAN. Dist(s): IngramPubServ

Detonators: The Secret Plot to Destroy America & an Epic Hunt for Justice. unabr. ed. Chad Millman. Read by Lloyd James. (Running Time: 10 hrs. 0 mins. 0 sec.). (ENG.). 2006. audio compact disk 24.99 (978-1-4001-5282-7(8)); audio compact disk 34.99 (978-1-4001-0282-2(0)); audio compact disk 69.99 (978-1-4001-3282-9(7)) Pub: Tantor Media. Dist(s): IngramPubServ

Detour. abr. ed. James Siegel. Read by Holter Graham. (ENG.). 2005. 14.98 (978-1-59483-130-0(0)) Pub: Hachet Audio. Dist(s): HachBkGrp

Detour. abr. ed. James Siegel. Read by Holter Graham. (Running Time: 6 hrs.). (ENG.). 2009. 44.98 (978-1-60788-027-1(X)) Pub: Hachet Audio. Dist(s): HachBkGrp

Detox Box. Mark Hyman. 2 CDs. (Running Time: 2 hrs.). 2006. audio compact disk 24.95 (978-1-59179-100-3(6), W826D) Sounds True.

Detox Flow Yoga. unabr. ed. Seane Corn. (Running Time: 3:51:50). 2009. audio compact disk 24.95 (978-1-59179-712-8(8)) Sounds True.

Detox Strategy: Vibrant Health in 5 Easy Steps. unabr. ed. Brenda Watson. Read by Susan Ericksen. Told to Leonard Smith. (Running Time: 11 hrs. 30 mins. 0 sec.). (ENG.). 2008. audio compact disk 34.99 (978-1-4001-0712-4(1)) Pub: Tantor Media. Dist(s): IngramPubServ

Detox Strategy: Vibrant Health in 5 Easy Steps. unabr. ed. Brenda Watson & Leonard Smith. Narrated by Susan Ericksen. (Running Time: 11 hrs. 30 mins. 0 sec.). (ENG.). 2008. audio compact disk 69.99 (978-1-4001-3712-1(8)); audio compact disk 24.99 (978-1-4001-5712-9(9)) Pub: Tantor Media. Dist(s): IngramPubServ

Deus lo Volt! A Chronicle of the Crusades, abr. ed. Evan S. Connell. 4 cass. (Running Time: 6 hrs.). 2000. 24.95 (978-1-55935-335-9(X)) Soundelux.
From the bestselling author of "Son of the Morning Star," comes a magisterial work of historical imagination.

Deuteronomy Commentary. Chuck Missler. 1 CD. (Hierloom Edition). 2003. 29.95 (978-1-57821-242-2(1)) Koinonia Hse.
Whose sermons are quoted most in the Bible? The answer may surprise you. Deuteronomy is essentially a series of sermons by the greatest Old Testament prophet. Jesus Himself quoted more from Deuteronomy than from any other portion of the Old Testament. Just as the New Testament epistles are our primary interpretive commentary on the historical narratives (The Gospels and Acts), the most venerated portion of the Old Testament - the Torah - has, within it, its primary commentary in the form of three sermons by Moses.

Deutsch Aktiv Neu 1A. Gerd Neuner et al. 2 cass. (GER.). 2005. bk. 23.95 (978-3-468-84550-5(2)); 36.50 (978-3-468-84551-2(0)) Langenscheidt.

Deutsch Aktiv Neu 1B. Gerd Neuner et al. 2 cass. (GER.). 2005. 23.00 (978-3-468-84555-0(3)); 36.50 (978-3-468-84556-7(1)) Langenscheidt.

Deutsch Aktiv Neu 1C. Gerd Neuner et al. 2 cass. (GER.). 2005. 23.95 (978-3-468-84560-4(X)) Langenscheidt.

Deutsch Aktuell 1: Audio CD Program. 5th ed. Wolfgang S. Kraft et al. (GER.). audio compact disk 299.95 (978-0-8219-2550-8(4)) EMC-Paradigm.

Deutsch Aktuell 1: Audio CD Program Manual. 5th ed. Wolfgang S. Kraft et al. (GER.). audio compact disk (978-0-8219-2551-5(2)) EMC-Paradigm.

Deutsch Aktuell 1: Listening Activities. 5th ed. Wolfgang S. Kraft et al. (GER.). audio compact disk 99.95 (978-0-8219-2543-0(1)) EMC-Paradigm.

Deutsch Aktuell 1: Test Generator CD, IBM/Mac. 5th ed. Wolfgang S. Kraft et al. (GER.). audio compact disk 92.00 (978-0-8219-2549-2(0)) EMC-Paradigm.

Deutsch Aktuell 1: Testing/Assessment Program. 5th ed. Wolfgang S. Kraft et al. (GER.). audio compact disk 149.00 (978-0-8219-2545-4(8)) EMC-Paradigm.

Deutsch Aktuell 2: Audio CD Program. 5th ed. Wolfgang S. Kraft et al. (GER.). audio compact disk 309.95 (978-0-8219-2573-7(3)) EMC-Paradigm.

Deutsch Aktuell 2: Audio CD Program Manual. 5th ed. Wolfgang S. Kraft et al. (GER.). audio compact disk (978-0-8219-2574-4(1)) EMC-Paradigm.

Deutsch Aktuell 2: Listening Activities. 5th ed. Wolfgang S. Kraft et al. (GER.). audio compact disk 99.95 (978-0-8219-2566-9(0)) EMC-Paradigm.

Deutsch Aktuell 2: Test Generator CD, IBM/Mac. 5th ed. Wolfgang S. Kraft et al. (GER.). audio compact disk 95.00 (978-0-8219-2572-0(5)) EMC-Paradigm.

Deutsch Aktuell 2: Testing/Assessment Program. 5th ed. Wolfgang S. Kraft et al. (GER.). audio compact disk 159.00 (978-0-8219-2568-3(7)) EMC-Paradigm.

Deutsch Aktuell 3: Audio CD Program. 5th ed. Wolfgang S. Kraft et al. (GER.). audio compact disk 319.95 (978-0-8219-2613-0(6)) EMC-Paradigm.

Deutsch Aktuell 3: Audio CD Program Manual. 5th ed. Wolfgang S. Kraft et al. (GER.). audio compact disk (978-0-8219-2614-7(4)) EMC-Paradigm.

Deutsch Aktuell 3: Testing/Assessment Program. 5th ed. Wolfgang S. Kraft et al. (GER.). audio compact disk 169.00 (978-0-8219-2610-9(1)) EMC-Paradigm.

Deutsch Heute: Introductory German. 3rd ed. Jack R. Moeller & Helmut Liedloff. (GER.). 1984. 2.75 (978-0-685-08252-2(0)) HM.

Deutsch im Krankenhaus. Ulrike Firnhaber-Sensen & Gabriele Schmidt. 1 cass. (GER.). 1994. 39.95 (978-3-468-49428-4(9)) Langenscheidt.

Deutsch in 30 Tagen. Angelika G. Beck.Tr. of German in 30 Days/Deutsch in 30 Tagen. (GER & ENG.). 2005. bk. 34.95 (978-3-468-29916-2(8)) Langenscheidt.

Deutsch in 30 Tagen. Read by Angelika G. Beck.Tr. of German in 30 Days/Deutsch in 30 Tagen. (DUT, GER & TAG.). 2005. bk. 34.95 (978-3-468-29917-9(6)) Langenscheidt.

Deutsch Konkret 1. Gerd Neuner et al. 2 cass. Incl. Deutsch Konkret 1 No. 1A: Dialogue & Ear-Training Exercises. 1 cass. Gerd Neuner. (GER.). 2005. 23.95 (978-3-468-84430-0(1)); 26.25 Langenscheidt.
Cassettes designed to accompany "Deutsch konkret 1." A course for the 12-16 year old with no prior knowledge of German.

Deutsch Konkret 1, No. 1A, Dialogue & Ear-Training Exercises see Deutsch Konkret 1

Deutsch: Na Klar Part 1: An Intoductory German Course. unabr. ed. 1999. (978-0-07-229223-7(7), Mc-H Human Soc) McGrw-H Hghr Educ.
Students using Deutsch: Na Klar! practice all 4 skills, but work more on the receptive skills of listening and reading than in a traditional German text. A classroom listening comprehension program and the very engaging authentic readings provide this additional skill practice.

Deutsch: Na Klar Part 2: An Introductory German Course. unabr. ed. Didonato. 1 cass. (Running Time: 90 min.). 1998. (978-0-07-229225-1(3), Mc-H Human Soc) McGrw-H Hghr Educ.
Students using Deutsch: Na Klar! practice all 4 skills, but work more on the receptive skills of listening and reading than in a traditional German text. A classroom listening comprehension program and the very engaging authentic readings provide this additional skill practice.

Deutsch: Na klar! Vol. 2: An Introductory German Course. 4th ed. Lida Daves-Schneider. (GER.). (J). (gr. 6-12). 2003. stu. ed. 20.00 (978-0-07-284985-1(1), 9780072849851) Pub: Glencoe. Dist(s): McGraw

Deutsch: Na Klar! Audio Program. 5th ed. Di Donato et al. (ENG.). (C). 2007. audio compact disk 34.38 (978-0-07-327801-8(7), 0073278017, Mc-H Human Soc) Pub: McGrw-H Hghr Educ. Dist(s): McGraw

Deutsche Juristen im Gesprach: Textbuch. Gisela Shaw. (GER.). (C). 1994. 45.00 (978-3-12-675182-7(2)) Pub: Klett Ernst Verlag DEU. Dist(s): Intl Bk Import

Deutsche Literatur in Text und Darstellung Set: Lesebuch und Literaturgeschichte in Einem. O. F. Best & H. J. Schmitt. (GER.). 2000. (978-3-15-030022-0(3)) P Reclam DEU.

Deutsche Phonetik für Ausländer. Roland Rausch & Ilka Rausch. (GER.). 2005. 22.50 (978-3-324-00701-6(1)) Langenscheidt.

Deutsche Wirtschaftssprache für Amerikaner. 3rd ed. Merrifield. (GER & ENG.). (C). 1994. 46.95 (978-0-471-00868-2(0)) Wiley US.

Deutschmobil Level 2: Lehrerhandbuch. J. Douvitsas-Gamst et al. (GER.). (J). 1991. 33.50 (978-3-12-675053-0(2)) Pub: Klett Ernst Verlag DEU. Dist(s): Intl Bk Import

Deutschmobil. Deutsch als Fremdsprache fuer Kinder Level 1: Lehrbuch. J. Douvitsas-Gamst et al. (GER.). (J). 1990. 30.75 (978-3-12-675043-1(5)) Pub: Klett Ernst Verlag DEU. Dist(s): Intl Bk Import

Deutsch:Na klar! An Introductory German Course: Listening Comprehension (Component) 4th ed. Robert Di Donato & Monica D. Clyde. (C). 2003. audio compact disk 18.75 (978-0-07-249238-5(4), 9780072492385, Mc-H Human Soc) Pub: McGrw-H Hghr Educ. Dist(s): McGraw

Deutschvergnugen: Deutsch Lernen mit Rap und Liedem. Uwe Kind & Erika Broschek. 2 cass. (Running Time: 1 hr.). (GER.). 2005. tchr. ed. 33.00 (978-3-468-49558-8(7)) Langenscheidt.

Deux Amis - Le Père Milon. unabr. ed. Guy de Maupassant. (Guy de Maupassant Ser.: Vol. 5). (FRE.). bk. 16.95 (SFR455) J Norton Pubs.

Deux ans de Vacances. Jules Verne. pap. bk. 19.95 (978-88-7754-836-8(3)) Pub: Cideb ITA. Dist(s): Distribks Inc

Deuxième Sexe see Second Sex

Deva Method Advanced Vocal Exercises, Set. Jeannie Deva. 4 cass. (Running Time: 3 hrs. 45 min.). 1996. 39.95 (978-1-882224-20-3(5)) Jeannie Deva.
Advanced exercises to complement "The Contemporary Vocalist Improvement Course.".

Deva Method Vocal Warm-Ups & Cool-Downs: For Singers & Professional Speakers. Created by Jeannie Deva. 1 CD. (Running Time: 1 hr.). 2001. audio compact disk 14.95 (978-1-882224-21-0(3), Voice Studio Pr) Jeannie Deva.

Devas & Nature Spirits. unabr. ed. William Bloom. 2 cass. 18.00 (OC115) Sound Horizons AV.

Devastating Circumstances. Candace Long. Composed by Candace Long. 2006. audio compact disk 8.95 (978-0-9788322-3-0(X)) auDEO Media.

Devayani: Sukracarya's Daughter. 1 cass. (Spiritual Stories Ser.). 5.00 Bhaktivedanta.

Develop a Great Sense of Humor: Easy. Eldon Taylor. Read by Eldon Taylor. Ed. by Leslie Brice. 1 cass. (Running Time: 1 hr.). 1992. 16.95 (978-1-56705-221-3(5)) Gateways Inst.
Self improvement.

Develop a Great Sense of Humor: Ocean. Eldon Taylor. Read by Eldon Taylor. Ed. by Leslie Brice. 1 cass. (Running Time: 1 hr.). 1992. 16.95 (978-1-56705-222-0(3)) Gateways Inst.

Develop a Great Sense of Humor: Stream. Eldon Taylor. Read by Eldon Taylor. Ed. by Leslie Brice. 1 cass. (Running Time: 1 hr.). 1992. 16.95 (978-1-56705-223-7(1)) Gateways Inst.

Develop a Powerful Memory. Glenn Harrold. 1 cass. (Running Time: 1 hr. 30 mins.). 2002. 11.95 (978-1-901923-11-7(8)) Pub: Divinit Pubing GBR. Dist(s): Bookworld
Utilising skilled Hypnotherapy techniques to help the listener improve their memory and concentration skills. Also gives practical advice and techniques for storing and recalling information.

Develop a Powerful Memory. Glenn Harrold. 2 CDs. (Running Time: 3 hrs.). 2003. audio compact disk 17.95 (978-1-901923-31-5(2)) Pub: Divinit Pubing GBR. Dist(s): Bookworld

Develop a Powerful Memory & Concentration with Mind Power, Vol. 42, set. Jonathan Parker. Read by Jonathan Parker. 2 CDs. (Running Time: 2 hrs.). (Success Ser.: Vol. 3). 1999. audio compact disk (978-1-58400-041-9(4)) QuantumQuests Intl.
Disc 1 contains several guided visualizations. Disc 2 contains both audible & subliminal positive affirmations with music.

Develop a Powerful Speaking Voice. Karen Oleson. 1 cass. (Running Time: 45 min.). (Speakease Ser.). 1991. bk. 11.95 (978-1-886789-01-2(0), 0506-74) VoiceTech WA.
Sound like you mean business. This tape will help you improve presentations & everyday conversations. Control pitch, rate of speech, volume, nasality & breathing. Popular with business people, professional speakers, actors & community volunteers. Speakease is perfect for anyone who wants to sound even better & be taken seriously. Instruction booklet included.

Develop a Super Memory Auto-Matically. Robert E. Griswold & Deirdre Griswold. Read by Robert E. Griswold & Deirdre Griswold. 1 cass. (Running Time: 60 min.). (While-U-Drive Ser.). 1996. 11.98 (978-1-55848-902-8(9)) EffectiveMN.
Learn how to reprogram the mind so memory can function at its best.

Develop & Abundance of Positivity & Optimism. 1998. 24.95 (978-1-58557-004-1(4)) Dynamic Growth.

Develop Confidence with the Opposite Sex: Easy. Eldon Taylor. Read by Eldon Taylor. Ed. by Leslie Brice. 1 cass. (Running Time: 1 hr.). 1992. 16.95 (978-1-56705-300-5(9)) Gateways Inst.
Self improvement.

Develop Confidence with the Opposite Sex: Ocean. Eldon Taylor. Read by Eldon Taylor. Ed. by Leslie Brice. 1 cass. (Running Time: 1 hr.). 1992. 16.95 (978-1-56705-301-2(7)) Gateways Inst.

Develop E. S. P. 1 cass. (Running Time: 45 min.). (Relationship Ser.). 12.98 (978-1-55909-039-1(1), 41) Randolph Tapes.
Addresses creativity & capabilities as boundless. Subliminal messages are heard 3-5 minutes before becoming ocean sounds or music.

Develop Enthusiasm. Barrie Konicov. 1 cass. (Video-Audio System Ser.). cass. & video 24.98 (978-0-87082-445-6(7), SYS026); 11.98 (978-0-87082-427-2(9), 026) Potentials.
Explores how to approach everything you do with enthusiasm & then how you will always do it better.

Develop Enthusiasm. Barrie Konicov. 1 CD. 2004. audio compact disk 19.98 (978-1-56001-674-8(4)) Potentials.
Start an inner fire! Approach everything you do with enthusiasm and you will always do it better!You will find the self-hypnosis on track 1 and the subliminal on track 2. The easy-listening music of the subliminal, together with the self-hypnosis, is the original format which most people love and with which they are most familiar.

Develop Faith: Element of God's Love, Vol. 5 Pt 1. Speeches. Creflo A. Dollar. 4 cass. (Running Time: 5 hrs.). 2002. 20.00 (978-1-59089-736-2(6)) Creflo Dollar.

Develop Faith: Element of God's Love, Vol. 5 Pt 3. Speeches. Creflo A. Dollar. 5 cass. (Running Time: 6 hrs.). 2002. 25.00 (978-1-59089-741-6(2)) Creflo Dollar.

Develop Faith Vol. 5, Pt. 1: Element of God's Love. Speeches. Creflo A. Dollar. 4 CDs. (Running Time: 5 hrs.). 2002. audio compact disk 20.00 (978-1-59089-738-6(2)) Creflo Dollar.

Develop Faith Vol. 5, Pt. 2: Element of God's Love. Speeches. Creflo A. Dollar. 5 cass. (Running Time: 6 hrs.). 2002. 25.00 (978-1-59089-746-1(3)) Creflo Dollar.

Develop Faith Vol. 5, Pt. 3: Element of God's Love. Speeches. Creflo A. Dollar. 5 CDs. (Running Time: 6 hrs.). 2002. audio compact disk 34.00 (978-1-59089-742-3(0)) Creflo Dollar.

Develop Faith Vol. 5,Pt. 2: Element of God's Love. Speeches. Creflo A. Dollar. 5 CDs. (Running Time: 6 hrs.). 2002. audio compact disk 34.00 (978-1-59089-739-3(0)) Creflo Dollar.

Develop Goodness & Gentleness Vol. 4: An Element of Love. Speeches. 3 cass. (Running Time: 4 hrs.). 2003. 15.00 (978-1-59089-734-8(X)) Creflo Dollar.

Develop Goodness & Gentleness Vol. 4: An Element of Love. Speeches. Creflo A. Dollar. 3 CDs. (Running Time: 4 hrs.). 2003. audio compact disk 21.00 (978-1-59089-735-5(8)) Creflo Dollar.

Develop Joy Vol. 6: An Element of Love. Speeches. Creflo A. Dollar. 5 cass. (Running Time: 6 hrs.). 2003. 25.00 (978-1-59089-763-8(3)); audio compact disk 34.00 (978-1-59089-765-2(X)) Creflo Dollar.

Develop Longsuffering Vol. 2: An Element of Love. Speeches. Creflo A. Dollar. 5 cass. (Running Time: 6 hrs.). 2002. 25.00 (978-1-59089-731-7(5)); audio compact disk 34.00 (978-1-59089-727-0(7)) Creflo Dollar.

Develop Mediumship with Gordon Smith. Gordon Smith. 2007. audio compact disk (978-1-4019-1170-6(6), 418) Hay Hse GBR.

Develop Meekness: An Element of Love, Vol. 1. Speeches. Creflo A. Dollar. 3 cass. (Running Time: 4 hrs.). 2002. 15.00 (978-1-59089-730-0(7)) Creflo Dollar.

Develop Meekness Vol. 1: An Element of Love. Short Stories. Creflo A. Dollar. 3 CDs. (Running Time: 4 hrs.). 2002. audio compact disk 21.00 (978-1-59089-726-3(9)) Creflo Dollar.

Develop Peace Vol. 7: An Element of Love. Speeches. Creflo A. Dollar. 4 cass. (Running Time: 5 hrs.). 2003. 20.00 (978-1-59089-760-7(9)); audio compact disk 28.00 (978-1-59089-762-1(5)) Creflo Dollar.

Develop Psychic Abilities. Barrie Konicov. 2 CDs. 2003. audio compact disk 27.98 (978-1-56001-975-6(1)) Potentials.
Each of us possesses some degree of E.S.P. You can develop it far beyond your present capabilities.This 2-CD program from our Super Consciousness series is our newest, most powerful format. On the self-hypnosis CD, SC programs have the Subliminal Persuasion soundtrack added under Barrie?s voice. And the 17th Century Baroque music on the Subliminal CD has the same beat as your body's natural rhythm, thereby allowing the suggestions to enter deeply and effortlessly.

Develop Psychic Intuition. unabr. ed. Dick Sutphen. Read by Dick Sutphen. 1 cass. (Running Time: 1 hr.). (Spirit Guide Meditations). 1999. 14.98 (978-0-87554-632-2(3), SG105) Valley Sun.
With a spirit guide's help, rapidly develop extra-sensory & precognitive talents.

Develop Sattwa (Purity) Swami Jyotirmayananda. 1 cass. (Running Time: 1 hr.). 1990. 12.99 Yoga Res Foun.

Develop Successful Relationships. Glenn Harrold. 1 cass. (Running Time: 1 hr. 30 mins.). 2002. 11.95 (978-1-901923-08-7(8)) Pub: Divinit Pubing GBR. Dist(s): Bookworld

Develop Successful Relationships. Glenn Harrold. 2 CDs. (Running Time: 3 hrs.). 2003. audio compact disk 17.95 (978-1-901923-28-5(2)) Pub: Divinit Pubing GBR. Dist(s): Bookworld

Develop Temperance Vol. 3, Pt. 1: An Element of Love. Speeches. Creflo A. Dollar. 4 cass. (Running Time: 5 hrs.). 2002. 20.00 (978-1-59089-732-4(3)) Creflo Dollar.

Develop Temperance Vol. 3. Pt 2: An Element of Love. Speeches. Creflo A. Dollar. 3 CDs. (Running Time: 4 hrs.). 2002. audio compact disk 21.00 (978-1-59089-729-4(3)) Creflo Dollar.

Develop Temperance Vol. 3, Pt. 2: An Element of Love. Speeches. Creflo A. Dollar. 3 cass. (Running Time: 4 hrs.). 2002. 15.00 (978-1-59089-733-1(1)) Creflo Dollar.

Develop Winning Willpower. unabr. ed. Bruce Bowman. Read by Bruce Bowman. 1 cass. (Running Time: 90 min.). (Self-Help Ser.). 1986. 7.95 (978-0-88749-115-3(4), TDM 1154) HarperCollins Pubs.
Bowman explores the concept of willpower & explains what it is, why willpower is important & how to benefit by improving self-discipline. His systematic program will help the listener visualize how easy succeeding can be.

Develop Your Psychic Abilities. Barrie Konicov. 1 cass. 11.98 (978-0-87082-400-5(7), 027) Potentials.
The author, says that each of us possesses some degree of ESP, that you can develop far beyond your present capability &, in doing so, enrich your life greatly.

Develop Your Psychic Abilities. Barrie Konicov. 1 CD. 2003. audio compact disk 16.98 (978-0-87082-961-1(0)) Potentials.
Each of us possesses some degree of E.S.P. You can develop it far beyond your present capabilities.You will find the self-hypnosis on track 1 and the subliminal on track 2. The easy-listening music of the subliminal, together with the self-hypnosis, is the original format which most people love and with which they are most familiar.

Develop Your Psychic Abilities (Desarrolle Sus Habilidades Psiquicas) Barrie Konicov. 1 cass. (Running Time: 1 hr. 30 min.). (Spanish-Language Audios Ser.). (SPA.). 1995. 11.98 (978-0-87082-774-7(X), 027) Potentials.
Each of us possesses some degree of ESP that can be developed far beyond its present capacity to enrich your life & help it run smoothly.

Develop Your Psychic Powers. Bruce Goldberg. (ENG.). 2005. audio compact disk 17.00 (978-1-57968-104-3(2)) Pub: B Goldberg. Dist(s): Baker Taylor

Develop Your Psychic Powers. Bruce Goldberg. Read by Bruce Goldberg. 1 cass. (Running Time: 25 min.). (ENG.). 2006. 13.00 (978-1-885577-64-1(8)) Pub: B Goldberg. Dist(s): Baker Taylor
Through self-hypnosis learn how to harness intuition & natural ESP abilities.

Develop Your Self Confidence. Glenn Harrold. 1 cass. (Running Time: 1 hr. 30 mins.). 2002. 11.95 (978-1-901923-02-5(9)); audio compact disk 17.95 (978-1-901923-22-3(3)) Pub: Divinit Pubing GBR. Dist(s): Bookworld

***Developing a Biblically Healthy View of God.** Gordon Ferguson. 2009. 10.00 (978-0-9842006-7-2(3)) Illumination MA.

Developing a Conscience. Thomas Merton. 1 cass. 8.95 (AA2458) Credence Commun.

Developing a Conversational Intimacy with God. Short Stories. Featuring John Eldredge et al. 2 CDs. (Running Time: 2 hrs., 20 mins.). 2005. audio compact disk 21.00 (978-1-933207-02-5(7)) Ransomed Heart.
We are created for intimacy with God. Its what our hearts long for. And that intimacy includes a conversational relationship with him.All of those wonderful stories we read about in Scripture, where ?The Lord said to Moses? and ?Moses said to the Lord,? where King David ?inquired of the Lord? ? those are examples of what a normal relationship with God looks like. This is available for every Believer. For as Jesus said, ?his sheep follow him because they know his voice?I am the good shepherd; I know my sheep and my sheep know me?They too will listen to my voice? (John 10:4, 14, 16). In this conversation, John Eldredge, Craig McConnell and Gary Barkalow discuss how to develop a conversational intimacy with God. They explain the centrality of the Word of God, but also how to learn to discern the voice of the Lord when he speaks to us personally. Both are essential for the Christian life. Both are vital as we navigate through this dangerous world.Developing a conversational intimacy with God will revolutionize your life!.

Developing a Covenant Attitude for Covenant Prosperity. Creflo A. Dollar. 3 cass. (Running Time: 3 hrs.). 2000. 15.00 (978-1-931172-32-5(3), TS272, Kidz Faith) Pub: Creflo Dollar. Dist(s): STL Dist NA

Developing a Customer Retention Program: How to Increase Repeat Business & Build Customer Loyalty. Lisa Ford. 4 cass. (Running Time: 3 hrs. 53 min.). 1994. 59.95 Set incl. 40p. wkbk. (Q10176) CareerTrack Pubns.
A commitment to customer retention must start at the top. That's why this program was developed with key decision makers in mind. It is particularly important for management personnel in customer service centers, operations, telecommunications, retail sales, order processing...& anyone who trains them. With the step-by-step approach this program teaches, all your managers will have a solid plan - & concrete skills - get your organization committed to retaining more customers.

Developing a Godly Self-Image. Speeches. Joel Osteen. 6 audio cass. (J). 2001. 24.00 (978-1-931877-13-8(0), JAS009) J Osteen.

Developing a Godly Self-Image. Short Stories. Ed. by Joel Osteen. 1 Cass. (Running Time: 30 Mins.). 2001. 6.00 (978-1-59349-098-0(4), JA0098) J Osteen.

Developing a Godly Self-Image. Speeches. Ed. by Joel Osteen. 3 CDs. (J). 2001. audio compact disk 24.00 (978-1-931877-30-5(0), JCS009) J Osteen.

Developing a Godly Self-Image, Pt. 2. Speeches. Joel Osteen. 1 Cass. (Running Time: 30 Mins.). 2001. Rental 6.00 (978-1-59349-100-0(X), JA0100) J Osteen.

Developing a Godly Self-Image, Pt. 4. Speeches. Joel Osteen. 1 Cass. (Running Time: 30 Mins.). 2001. 6.00 (978-1-59349-102-4(6), JA0102) J Osteen.

Developing a Godly Self-Image, Pt. 5. Speeches. Joel Osteen. 1 Cass. (Running Time: 30 Mins.). 2001. Rental 6.00 (978-1-59349-103-1(4), JA0103) J Osteen.

Developing a Godly Self-Image, Pt. 6. Speeches. Joel Osteen. 1 Cass. (Running Time: 30 Mins.). 2001. 6.00 (978-1-59349-104-8(2), JA0104) J Osteen.

Developing a Hunger & Thirst for the Anointed One & His Anointing. Creflo A. Dollar. 2 cass. (Running Time: 3 hrs.). 2001. 10.00 (978-1-931172-94-3(3), TS129, Kidz Faith) Pub: Creflo Dollar. Dist(s): STL Dist NA

Developing a Learning Community. Contrib. by Jerry Fox et al. 1 cass. (Transforming Local Government Ser.). Alliance Innov.

Developing a Relationship with Yourself - Red Collection: Developing the Values of Self Knowledge. Trenna Daniells. Narrated by Trenna Daniells. 2 CDs. (J). (ps-6). 2009. audio compact disk 19.95 (978-0-918519-64-1(0)) Trenna Prods.

Developing a Restoration Mentality. Speeches. Joel Osteen. 1 Cass. (Running Time: 30 Mins.). 2001. 6.00 (978-1-59349-108-6(5), JA0108) J Osteen.

Developing a Strategy for the City: Proceedings of the 45th Annual Convention National Association of Evangelicals Buffalo, New York. Read by Paul McKaughan. 1 cass. (Running Time: 60 min.). 1987. 4.00 (314) Nat Assn Evan.

Developing a Supernatural Lifestyle Audio Book. Kris Vallotton. 2008. audio compact disk 34.99 (978-0-7684-2709-7(6)) Destiny Image Pubs.

Developing a Warrior Mentality. Speeches. Joel Osteen. 1 Cass. (Running Time: 30 Mins.). 2002. 6.00 (978-1-59349-147-5(6), JA0147) J Osteen.

Developing a Winning Personal Injury Case. 1986. bk. 75.00 incl. book.; 45.00 cass. only.; 30.00 book only. PA Bar Inst.

Developing a Winning Personality. Shad Helmstetter. 1 cass. (Self-Talk Cassettes Ser.). 10.95 (978-0-937065-37-2(4)) Grindle Pr.

Developing a Winning System for Trading High-Performance. Instructed by Tim Cho. 1. (Running Time: 90 mins). (Trade Secrets Audio Ser.). 2002. 19.95 (978-1-931611-59-6(9)) Marketplace Bks.
Tim Cho's thorough, 90 min. workshop covers the basic criteria he uses to select stocks ready to rally - and those on the verge of collapse, detailing the characteristics he examines to find stocks capable of producing triple-digit returns in all market climates. You'll learn: 16 key conditions for identifying high-performance stocks - before they take off; 10 key points for selecting which stocks to sell short; and a strategy for - Switching sides - - trading both up & down moves in a volatile stock. This hard-hitting, high-powered presentation gives you the 3 basic perspectives you need to prosper big - no matter which way the market turns.

Developing Ability to Love Series, Set. Elbert Willis. 4 cass. 13.00 Fill the Gap.

Developing Agape Love. Elbert Willis. 1 cass. (Keys to a Successful Marriage Ser.). 4.00 Fill the Gap.

Developing an Employee Orientation & Training Program, Set. 6 cass. 1993. pap. bk. & wbk. ed. 155.00 (978-0-7612-0525-8(X), 80160) AMACOM.
You'll learn how to: Determine the true cost of recruiting, hiring, & orienting employees in your company; Reduce employee turnover because of poor orientation or training; Evaluate your current orientation program & identify areas that need improvement; Design an employee handbook that new hirees will really use; Pinpoint your company's training needs; Use a proven four-step training method that multiplies the effectiveness of your training.

Developing an Interceding Life Series, Set. Elbert Willis. 4 cass. 13.00 Set. Fill the Gap.

Developing & Conducting Training for Foodservice Employees: A Guide for Trainers. Karen Eich Drummond. 1 cass. 1992. bk. & stu. ed. 25.00 (978-0-88091-102-3(6)) Am Dietetic Assn.
Contains step-by-step guidelines for developing & conducting new employee orientation, & job & inservice training. Includes sample orientation & training checklists & class outlines.

Developing & Maintaining Empowered Teams. abr. ed. Cliff Kirk. Read by Cliff Kirk. 2 cass. (Running Time: 2 hrs. 31 min.). 1998. 19.95 Set; incl. wkbk. (978-1-57294-101-4(4), 11-0214) SkillPath Pubns.
Real-life, action-based solution providing innovative ways to spark your group to achieving goals, the framework that allows them to make a smooth, easy transition into teams.

Developing Big Vision. Mark Crow. 2000. (978-1-931537-23-0(2)) Vision Comm Creat.

Developing Bridge Between Science & Shamanism. William C. Gough. 1 cass. 9.00 (A0336-89) Sound Photosyn.
Bill Gough was responsible as Director of the Stanford Site Office for the Stanford Linear Accelerator Center, & the basic science research at the Stanford Synchrotron Radiation Laboratory. His published works appear in "Scientific American," & other professional journals. The presentation given here is a clear, concise, informative, & elegant approach, making difficult concepts understandable even to the non-scientific mind. Sound Photosynthesis is pleased to have the opportunity to offer the transcript of this talk (from the 6th ICSS). Both the video & the audio demonstrate Bill's recent concentration on futuristic studies & the development of a bridge between science & the ancient wisdoms of inner knowing.

Developing Capable Young People CD's. (ENG.). 2006. audio compact disk 49.95 (978-0-9816250-5-8(3)) EmpoweringUT.

Developing Career & Living Skills Instructor's CD-ROM. Mary Sue Burkhardt. (YA). audio compact disk 39.95 (978-1-59357-114-6(3), J1143) JIST Pubng.

Developing Character in Teens with Love & Logic: Kids Who Look Good on Paper vs. Kids with Character. unabr. ed. Jim Fay. Read by Jim Fay. 1 cass. (Running Time: 1hr. 25 mins.). 2000. 11.95 (978-1-930429-06-2(1)); audio compact disk 13.95 (978-1-930429-09-3(6)) Pub: Love Logic. Dist(s): Penton Overseas
How do we teach teens to do the "right thing?" It's every parents' dream to send their child into the world prepared to make a positive contribution & raise kids who are honest, caring, & ethical with the "right" qualities. Jim Fay helps make this a reality with warmth & humor.

Developing Character Voices. unabr. ed. Liz VonSeggen. 2 cass. (Running Time: 2 hrs.l). 2001. audio compact disk 15.00 (978-1-58302-201-6(5)) One Way St.
Features demonstrations and explanations on how you can produce many different character voices. You'll discover all the basic elements of voice and how to apply those basics to create your own character voices. You'll be

surprised how many voices you'll be taught, from Grandpa to a duck to a Martian. The CD gives instructions for pitch, volume, diction, and accents.

Developing Common Interest Ownership Projects: Condominiums, Community Associations, Cooperatives, Air Space Regimes. 1985. bk. 65.00; 40.00 PA Bar Inst.

Developing Compassion. Eldon Taylor. 1 CD. (Running Time: 52 min.). (Whole Brain Innertalk Ser.). 1998. audio compact disk (978-1-55978-851-9(8)) Progress Aware Res.

Developing Compassion. Eldon Taylor. 1 CD. (Running Time: 52 min.). (Whole Brain Innertalk Ser.). 1999. audio compact disk (978-1-55978-921-9(2)) Progress Aware Res.

Developing Concentration. Swami Amar Jyoti. 2 cass. 1980. 12.95 (K-39) Truth Consciousness.
Concentration & communication of the highest truth. Purity of heart as the starting point. Selfishness versus legitimate needs on individual & social levels.

Developing Critical Thinking. Eunice Insel & Ann Edson. 4 cass. (Running Time: 2 hrs. 40 min.). (YA). (gr. 7-12). 1988. 39.95 ea. incl. 8 activity bks. & guide. Ed Activities.
Series develops & improves students' analytical reasoning skills.

Developing Discrimination. unabr. ed. Perf. by Eknath Easwaran. 1 cass. (Running Time: 1 hr.). 1988. 7.95 (978-1-58638-523-1(2)) Nilgiri Pr.

Developing Dispassion. Swami Jyotirmayananda. Read by Swami Jyotirmayananda. 1 cass. (Running Time: 45 min.). 10.00 (828) Yoga Res Foun.

Developing Foresight & Perspective. Shad Helmstetter. 1 cass. (Self-Talk Cassettes Ser.). 10.95 (978-0-937065-08-2(0)) Grindle Pr.

Developing Friendship with God. Kenneth Copeland. 4 cass. 1987. 20.00 Set. (978-0-88114-908-1(X)) K Copeland Pubns.
Biblical teaching on relationship with God.

Developing Goals That Work, Not Frustrate. Richard Flint. 5 cass. Incl. Developing Goals That Work, Not Frustrate: Dream versus Fantasy. 1985.; Developing Goals That Work, Not Frustrate: The Crystalization Process. 1985.; Developing Goals That Work, Not Frustrate: The Frustration Explained. 1985.; Developing Goals That Work, Not Frustrate: The Survivor Mentality. 1985.; Developing Goals That Work, Not Frustrate: Three Dimensions of Your Life. 1985.; 1985. 70.00 (978-0-937851-20-3(5)) Pendelton Lane.
The result of two years of research, this cassette explores the concept of goal-setting. It explains what goals are & deals with the major reasons why goals can become a frustration instead of the defined direction they are meant to be.

Developing Goals That Work, Not Frustrate: Dream versus Fantasy see Developing Goals That Work, Not Frustrate

Developing Goals That Work, Not Frustrate: The Crystalization Process see Developing Goals That Work, Not Frustrate

Developing Goals That Work, Not Frustrate: The Frustration Explained see Developing Goals That Work, Not Frustrate

Developing Goals That Work, Not Frustrate: The Survivor Mentality see Developing Goals That Work, Not Frustrate

Developing Goals That Work, Not Frustrate: Three Dimensions of Your Life see Developing Goals That Work, Not Frustrate

Developing Intuition. Shakti Gawain. 1 cass. (Running Time: 1 hr.). 1995. 11.95 (978-1-882591-09-1(7), 950) Nataraj Pub.
Shakti explains what intuition is, how to connect with it, & why it's important to develop it.

Developing Intuition: Practical Guidance for Daily Life. Shakti Gawain. Read by Shakti Gawain. (Running Time: 2 hrs. 35 mins. 0 sec.). (ENG.). 2007. audio compact disk 21.95 (978-1-57731-565-0(0)) Pub: New Wrld Lib. Dist(s): PerseuPGW

Developing Jobs for Persons with Disabilities. Richard Pimentel. (Running Time: 6 hrs.). 1987. 59.95 M Wright & Assocs.
Provides tools & techniques for job developers in time management, applicant assessment & counseling, dispelling job market myths, job market research, marketing, telephone & in-person contact with employers, applicant-employer interview, & placement follow-up.

Developing Leadership Power. Ben Bissell. 1 cass. (Running Time: 30 min.). 15.00 C Bissell.
Dr. Bissell deals with how to identify power in groups & how to lead them to higher levels of productivity.

Developing More Self-Confidence. Stuart Wilde. 2 cass. (Self-Help Tape Ser.). 1992. 21.95 Set. (978-0-930603-53-3(2)) White Dove NM.
Stuart shows you how to arrange your thinking to develop a sense of positive expectancy. Learn how to dominate the reality around you so the circumstances of your life become an affirmation of your ever-expanding self-confidence.

Developing Organizational Policies Regarding AIDS: National Association of Evangelicals, 47th Annual Convention, Columbus, Ohio, March 7-9, 1989. Richard Crespo. 1 cass. (Workshops Ser.: No. 27-Thursda). 1989. 4.25 ea. 1-8 tapes.; 4.00 ea. 9 tapes or more. Nat Assn Evan.

Developing Our Health & Wholeness before God. William Hulme. 1986. 10.80 (0609B) Assn Prof Chaplains.

Developing Person Through Childhood & Adolescence: Instructor's Resources. 6th ed. Kathleen Stassen Berger & Ross A. Thompson. audio compact disk 52.50 (978-0-7167-5285-1(9)) Pub: W H Freeman. Dist(s): Macmillan

Developing Positive Assertiven. Crisp Learning Staff. 2001. audio compact disk 99.00 (978-1-56052-624-7(6)) Crisp Pubns.

Developing Positive Self-Images & Discipline in Black Children. Jawanza Kunjufu. 1 cass. (Running Time: 60 mins.). 1999. 29.95 (AT2) African Am Imag.
What is the relationship between self-esteem & student achievement? Find the answers to this & other questions.

Developing Relationships with Kids Who are Hard to Love. unabr. ed. Ray Levy & Joe Cates. 1 cass. (Running Time: 1 hr. 30 mins.). 2002. bk. 12.95 (978-0-9701173-3-5(7)) Cates Levy.
Strategies for parents and teachers who parent/teach children who are difficult to form "loving" or friendly relationships with.

Developing Responsibility in Your Child: Five Essential Steps. Bettie B. Youngs. 6 cass. 29.95 (5014) SyberVision.
A five step program for parents that helps children aged two to 10 become responsible, caring members of the family team.

Developing Self-Esteem. 2nd ed. Connie Palladino. 1993. pap. bk. 249.00 (978-1-56052-372-7(7)) Pub: Crisp Pubns. Dist(s): CENGAGE Learn

Developing Self-Esteem in Your Child. Bettie B. Youngs. 6 cass. (Child Development Ser.). 1991. 29.95 set. SyberVision.

Developing Speaking Skills. Geraldine Chapey. 1988. (978-0-07-087528-9(6)) McGraw.

Developing Stability, Set. Elbert Willis. 4 cass. 13.00 Set. Fill the Gap.

Developing Staff for the New Millennium. Janet Hauter. 4 cass. (Running Time: 4 hrs.). bk. 49.00 Set. (5009) Natl Inst Child Mgmt.
In-service resource includes: Tape 1: "The Center's Leadership Perspective," Tape 2: "Shining the Light Within," Tape 3: "Awakening the Spirit Within," Tape 4: "Building a Covenant Center, Developing a Covenant Team".

Developing Successful Study Habits. unabr. ed. John Rosella. 1 cass. (Running Time: 50 min.). 1981. 9.95 Newtown Psychological Ctr.
Provides lecture presentation dealing with organization skills, efficient time management & various study techniques. Gives a relaxation-imagery exercise designed to reduce study & classroom anxiety.

Developing Talents & Abilities: Discovering Your Path in Life. Eldon Taylor. 1 CD. (Running Time: 52 min.). (Whole Brain Innertalk Ser.). 1998. audio compact disk (978-1-55978-879-3(8)) Progress Aware Res.

Developing the Christ Life. Elbert Willis. 1 cass. (Resurrection Living Ser.). 4.00 Fill the Gap.

Developing the Difference-Maker in You. Jeff Conley. Read by Jeff Conley. 6 cass. 1991. 59.95 set. (978-1-56207-219-3(6)) Zig Ziglar Corp.
Every day you carry within yourself enough to be a "difference-maker." You may not yet fully understand how to use what you have, but it is there. The only difference between you & other "difference-makers" is that you have yet to give yourself permission to be just like them, & Jeff Conley will show you how.

Developing the Human Spirit. Kenneth E. Hagin. 5 cass. 20.00 (20H) Faith Lib Pubns.

Developing the Innate Musical Creativity of Children. unabr. ed. Irving Cheyette. 1 cass. (Running Time: 20 min.). 1969. 12.95 (29153) J Norton Pubs.
Philosophical & psychological nature of creativity applied to helping children discover musical elements in their environment.

Developing the Leader Within You. John C. Maxwell. 1993. 16.99 (978-0-7852-7303-5(4)) Nelson.

Developing the Leader Within You. abr. ed. John C. Maxwell. (Running Time: 2 hrs. 40 mins.). 2004. audio compact disk 24.99 (978-0-7852-6033-2(1)) Nelson.

Developing the Leaders Around You: How to Help Others Reach Their Full Potential. abr. ed. John C. Maxwell. (Running Time: 3 hrs.). 2003. audio compact disk 21.99 (978-0-7852-6240-4(7)) Nelson.
Dr. John C. Maxwell is committed to more than just being a leader_he_s also committed to nurturing and mentoring thousands of potential leaders around him. This passion is what caused him to found INJOY and EQUIP, and it is the driving force in his ministry. Both practical and inspirational, Developing the Leaders Around You is crammed with strategies that help you effectively transform your goals into reality by building leadership in the people around you. Emphasizing that an organization can't grow until its members grow, Dr. Maxwell encourages readers to foster a productive team spirit, make difficult decisions, handle confrontation, and to nurture, encourage, and equip people to be leaders.

Developing the Sixth Sense. Instructed by Stuart Wilde. 4 cass. (Self-Help Tape Ser.). 29.95 set. (978-0-930603-11-3(7)) White Dove NM.
We are all special beings who possess an ability to perceive beyond the physical plane. Too often, through lack of direction or perhaps lack of commitment, people fail to achieve mastery of that elusive extrasensory power that is really a part of every individual's potential.

Developing the Whole Person from Childhood to Maturity. Kriyananda, pseud. 1 cass. 9.95 (ST-73) Crystal Clarity.
Includes: maturity from a spiritual perspective; fallacies of Darwin's theory of evolution; how to inspire children & help them mature; the need to balance discipline & control with openness & receptivity.

Developing winner Habits. Denis Waitley. 2004. 7.95 (978-0-7435-4647-8(4)) Pub: S&S Audio. Dist(s): S and S Inc

Developing Your Intuition (Hypnosis), Vol. 19. Jayne Helle. 1 cass. (Running Time: 28 min.). 1997. 15.00 (978-1-891826-18-4(2)) Introspect.
Everyone is intuitive. Removes all blocks & helps one to listen to that inner voice & receive psychic guidance.

Developing Your Law Practice. 1 cass. 1985. 10.00 PA Bar Inst.

Developing Your Magnificent Mind. Zig Ziglar. Read by Zig Ziglar. 1 cass. (Zig Ziglar Classics Ser.). 1990. 9.95 (978-1-56207-006-9(1)) Zig Ziglar Corp.
Zig Ziglar will help you understand why what you put into your mind affects your performance, & how to put the information into your mental computer that will help you to succeed.

Developing Your Potential. Speeches. Joel Osteen. 1 Cass. (Running Time: 30 Mins). 2001. 6.00 (978-1-59349-087-4(9), JA0087) J Osteen.

Developing Your Psychic Energy. Jean Munzer. 2 cass. (Running Time: 2 hrs. 30 min.). 1992. 19.95 set. Creat Seminars.
Explore the nature of psychic experiences.

Developing Your Senses. Trenna Daniells. Read by Trenna Daniells. 1 cass. (Running Time: 30 min.). (One to Grow On! Ser.). (J). (gr. 4 up). 9.95 (12009) Trenna Prods.

Developing Your Sixth Sense. Stuart Wilde. 6 cass. (Running Time: 6 hrs.). 1999. 59.95 Set. (83-0030) Explorations.
Learn seven levels of supersensory communication, how to control your etheric body, how to open your chakras for healing, how to protect yourself from negative energy & techniques for communicating with other realms of existence.

Developing Your Sixth Sense: Master Your Awareness for Greater Clarity, Wisdom & Power. Stuart Wilde. 6 cass. (Running Time: 6 hrs.). 1997. pap. bk. (15880A) Nightingale-Conant.
Open yourself to higher awareness.

Developing Your Talents & Abilities: Discovering Your Path in Life. Eldon Taylor. 1 CD. (Running Time: 52 min.). (Whole Brain Innertalk Ser.). 1999. audio compact disk (978-1-55978-941-7(7)) Progress Aware Res.

Development & Applications of Empirically Based Assessment. Thomas M. Achenbach. 1 cass. (Running Time: 45 mins.). 1999. 26.50 (9-23168) Riverside Pub Co.

Development Life Cycle of a Digital Imaging System. 2 cass. 1990. 17.00 set. Recorded Res.

Development of Prajna. Vajracarya. Read by Chogyam Trungpa. 1 cass. 1976. 12.50 (A083) Vajradhatu.
A seminar by the scholar & meditation master trained in the philosophical & meditative traditions of Buddhism in Tibet.

Development of Quaker Education: A Historical Assessment. Helen G. Hole. 5 cass. Incl. Development of Quaker Education: Friends, Schools & College in the Twentieth Century. 1974.; Development of Quaker Education: Quaker Education: Has It a Future? 1974.; Development of Quaker Education: The Closed Garden, 1850-1900. 1974.; Development of Quaker Education: The Idea of a Community: The Beginning of Quaker Education. 1974.; Development of Quaker Education: The Quaker Concept of Authority: A Basis of Institutional Governance. 1974.; 1974. 17.50 Set.; 4.50 ea. Pendle Hill.

Development of Quaker Education: Friends, Schools & College in the Twentieth Century see Development of Quaker Education: A Historical Assessment

Development of Quaker Education: Quaker Education: Has It a Future? see Development of Quaker Education: A Historical Assessment

Development of Quaker Education: The Closed Garden, 1850-1900 see Development of Quaker Education: A Historical Assessment

Development of Quaker Education: The Idea of a Community: The Beginning of Quaker Education see Development of Quaker Education: A Historical Assessment

Development of Quaker Education: The Quaker Concept of Authority: A Basis of Institutional Governance see Development of Quaker Education: A Historical Assessment

Development of Samadhi. Read by Chogyam Trungpa. 6 cass. 1974. 63.00 (A122) Vajradhatu.
Six talks. Samadhi refers to the state of meditative absorption.

Development of Standards for Pastoral Care Departments: A History. 1 cass. (Care Cassettes Ser.: Vol. 10, No. 6). 1983. 10.80 Assn Prof Chaplains.

Development of the Whole Man: Spirit, Soul, & Body. Kenneth Copeland. 12 cass. 1983. bk. 60.00 Set incl. study guide. (978-0-938458-35-7(3)) K Copeland Pubns.
Becoming what God desires.

Development of Western Music Vol. I, Vol. 1. 3rd rev. ed. K. Marie Stolba. (ENG.). (C). 1998. audio compact disk 119.69 (978-0-697-32872-4(4), 0697328724, Mc-H Human Soc) Pub: McGrw-H Hghr Educ. Dist(s): McGraw

Development Report Card for the States, 1993: Economic Benchmarks for State & Corporate Decision-Makers. 7th rev. ed. Corporation for Enterprise Development Staff. 1 cass. 1993. pap. bk. 45.00 (978-1-883187-00-2(1)) Corp Ent Dev.
Economic development.

Developmental Model of Recovery. Terence T. Gorski. 4 cass. Incl. Developmental Model of Recovery: Developmental Model of Recovery, An Overview. 8.95 (A-171); 32.95 Set. Grt Lks Training.
Presentation detailing the CENAPS model of treatment. Describes specific tasks each person must accomplish, consciously or unconsciously during recovery from addictive disease.

Developmental Model of Recovery: Developmental Model of Recovery, An Overview see Developmental Model of Recovery

Developments in Directors' & Officers' Liability. Donald A. Tortorice. 1 cass. 1987. 20.00 PA Bar Inst.

Developments in Federal & State Tax Laws for Tax-Exempt Organizations. 1 cass. 1988. 35.00 PA Bar Inst.

Developments in Health Law. 1988. bk. 180.00; 85.00 PA Bar Inst.

Developments in Health Law, 1991. 1991. 85.00 (AC-621) PA Bar Inst.

Develping Faith. unabr. ed. Perf. by Eknath Easwaran. 1 cass. (Running Time: 1 hr.). 1992. 7.95 (978-1-58638-524-8(0)) Nilgiri Pr.

Deviant Moth. Gwen Moffat. Read by Maggie Mash. 6 cass. (Running Time: 6 hrs. 30 min.). 2001. (978-1-84283-100-7(3)) Soundings Ltd GBR.
Ruth Stanton is a famous crime novelist who has just returned from another foreign research trip. Her husband had stayed at work as usual and whilst she has been away, two women from the village have disappeared. One is Olive, the landlord Bill Lynch?s wife, and the other is Judy, his lover. If they are dead, where have the bodies been hidden? There would be plenty of hiding places around in the countryside. If the murderer or murderers are within the small Derbyshire community a very close one which of the locals are closing ranks.

Deviant Ways. unabr. ed. Chris Mooney. Narrated by Richard Ferrone. 11 cass. (Running Time: 15 hrs.). 2001. 94.00 (978-0-7887-5988-8(4), 96639x7) Recorded Bks.
Jack Casey was the FBI's best profiler until a madman forced him to watch the brutal murder of his pregnant wife. After six years of rehab, he's pursuing another killer through a deadly world of secret experiments, hidden cameras & devastating explosions. Shocking violence & astonishing unpredictability blend to create a gripping study of psychological terror.

Devic Kingdom. 2007. audio compact disk (978-0-937249-36-9(X)) Aetherius Soc.

Devices & Desires. P. D. James. Contrib. by Robin Ellis. 3 CDs. (Running Time: 2 hrs. 50 mins.). (Adam Dalgliesh Mystery Ser.). 2006. audio compact disk 39.95 (978-0-7927-3989-0(2), BBCD 140) AudioGO.

Devices & Desires. P. D. James & E. M. Delafield. Narrated by Robin Ellis. 3 CDs. (Running Time: 3 hrs. 0 mins. 0 sec.). (Adam Dalgliesh Mystery Ser.). (ENG.). 2002. audio compact disk 29.95 (978-0-563-52828-9(1)) Pub: AudioGO. Dist(s): Perseus Dist

Devices & Desires. unabr. ed. P. D. James. Read by Michael Jayston. 12 cass. (Running Time: 18 hrs.). (Adam Dalgliesh Mystery Ser.). 2000. 79.95 (978-0-7451-6067-2(0), CAB 663) Pub: Chivers Audio Bks GBR. Dist(s): AudioGO
Inspector Dalgliesh of Scotland Yard has just published a new book of poems, and has taken a brief vacation on the Norfolk Coast. But a psychopathic strangler of young women is at large in Norfolk. It's not long before Dalgliesh is involved in the tangled emotions and motives of the suspects.

Devices & Desires. unabr. ed. P. D. James. Read by Barbara Rosenblat. 10. (Running Time: 17.5 Hours). (Adam Dalgliesh Mystery Ser.). 39.95 (978-1-4025-4526-9(6)) Recorded Bks.

Devices & Desires. unabr. ed. P. D. James. Narrated by Barbara Rosenblat. 12 cass. (Running Time: 17 hrs. 30 mins.). (Adam Dalgliesh Mystery Ser.). 1990. 97.00 (978-1-55690-141-6(0), 90089E7) Recorded Bks.
A strangler is loose in the quiet lanes of Norfolk. Inspector Dalgliesh forsakes a well-earned vacation to track a murderer.

Devices & Desires. unabr. collector's ed. P. D. James. Read by Penelope Dellaporta. 12 cass. (Running Time: 18 hrs.). (Adam Dalgliesh Mystery Ser.). 1990. 96.00 (978-0-7366-1819-9(8), 2655) Books on Tape.
After publication of his latest book of poetry, Adam Dalgliesch escapes from the hubbub of London for a remote Norfolk headland & the converted windmill his aunt left him. But Dalgliesch cannot so easily escape from murder. In Norfolk, a deranged killer prowls the countryside, holding tranquility hostage. Murders proliferate. Is there a connection with the nuclear power station? Not far from it, the killer has left his victims, all women, strangled. Dalgliesch suspects his own neck is very exposed.

Devil see De Maupassant Short Stories

Devil: A Biography. unabr. ed. Peter Stanford. Read by Arthur Addison. 7 cass. (Running Time: 10 hrs. 30 mins.). 1999. 56.00 (978-0-7366-4440-2(7), 4885) Books on Tape.
Survey brings the Devil to the forefront focusing on the Church, literature, folklore, psychology & history.

***Devil Amongst the Lawyers: A Ballad Novel.** unabr. ed. Sharyn McCrumb. (Running Time: 10 hrs.). (Ballad Ser.). 2010. 24.99 (978-1-4418-6772-8(4), 9781441867728, Brilliance MP3); 39.97 (978-1-4418-6773-5(2), 9781441867735, Brlnc Audio MP3 Lib); 24.99 (978-1-4418-6774-2(0), 9781441867742, BAD); 39.97 (978-1-4418-6775-9(9), 9781441867759, BADLE) Brilliance Audio.

***Devil Amongst the Lawyers: A Ballad Novel.** unabr. ed. Sharyn McCrumb. Read by MacLeod Andrews. (Running Time: 10 hrs.). (Ballad Ser.). 2010. audio compact disk 99.97 (978-1-4418-6771-1(6), 9781441867711, BriAudCD Unabrid); audio compact disk 29.99 (978-1-4418-6770-4(8), 9781441867704, Bril Audio CD Unabri) Brilliance Audio.

Devil & Daniel Webster. Stephen Vincent Benet. 10.00 (LSS1128) Esstee Audios.

Devil & Daniel Webster. abr. ed. Stephen Vincent Benet. Perf. by Pat Hingle. 1 cass. (Running Time: 90 mins.). 1984. 12.95 (978-0-694-50318-6(5), SWC 1591) HarperCollins Pubs.

Devil & Daniel Webster, Daniel Webster & the Sea Serpent. Stephen Vincent Benet. 1 cass. (Running Time: 1 hr.). (Radiobook Ser.). 1987. 4.98 (978-0-929541-31-0(6)) Radiola Co.
Two complete stories.

***Devil & Miss Prym.** abr. ed. Paulo Coelho. Read by Linda Emond. (ENG.). 2006. (978-0-06-113475-3(9), Harper Audio); (978-0-06-113476-0(7), Harper Audio) HarperCollins Pubs.

Devil & Miss Prym: A Novel of Temptation. unabr. ed. Paulo Coelho. Read by Linda Emond. (Running Time: 16200 sec.). 2006. audio compact disk 29.95 (978-0-06-111771-8(4)) HarperCollins Pubs.

Devil & Sherlock Holmes: Tales of Murder, Madness, & Obsession. unabr. ed. David Grann. Read by Mark Deakins. (ENG.). 2010. audio compact disk 40.00 (978-0-307-73457-0(9), Random AudioBks) Pub: Random Audio Pubg. Dist(s): Random

Devil & Tom Walker. Washington Irving. 10.00 (LSS1124) Esstee Audios.

Devil & Your Thoughts. C. S. Lovett. 1 cass. (Running Time: 50 min.). 6.95 (7034) Prsnl Christianity.
Expands on truths of the "Dealing with the Devil" book.

Devil As the Shadow of God. unabr. ed. Stephan Hoeller. 1 cass. (Running Time: 1 hr. 30 min.). 1982. 11.00 (40004) Big Sur Tapes.
Traces historically the many views & definitions of evil, from the most ancient people & their matter-of-fact attitude, to today's attitude of evil as a great & awesome metaphysical concern & mystery.

Devil Behind Me. unabr. ed. Frederick E. Smith. Read by Jack Paulin. 7 CDs. (Running Time: 8 hrs.). (Story Sound CD Ser.). 2007. audio compact disk 71.95 (978-1-84652-092-1(4)) Pub: Mgna Lrg Print GBR. Dist(s): Ulverscroft US

Devil Behind Me. unabr. ed. Frederick E. Smith. Read by Jack Paulin. 6 cass. (Running Time: 28800 sec.). (Story Sound Ser.). 2007. 54.95 (978-1-85903-963-2(4)) Pub: Mgna Lrg Print GBR. Dist(s): Ulverscroft US

Devil Bones. abr. ed. Kathy Reichs. Read by Linda Emond. (Running Time: 6 hrs. 0 mins. 0 sec.). No. 11. (ENG.). 2008. audio compact disk 29.95 (978-0-7435-7189-0(4)) Pub: S&S Audio. Dist(s): S and S Inc

Devil Bones. unabr. ed. Kathy Reichs. Read by Linda Emond. 8 CDs. (Running Time: 10 hrs. 0 mins. 0 sec.). No. 11. (ENG.). 2008. audio compact disk 39.95 (978-0-7435-7191-3(6)) Pub: S&S Audio. Dist(s): S and S Inc

***Devil Brand.** T. T. Flynn. 2009. (978-1-60136-395-4(8)) Audio Holding.

Devil Brand. T. T. Flynn. (Running Time: 1 hr. 24 mins.). 1999. 10.95 (978-1-60083-504-9(X)) Iofy Corp.

Devil Came on Horseback: Bearing Witness to the Genocide in Darfur. unabr. ed. Brian Steidle & Gretchen Steidle Wallace. Read by Jeff Cummings. (Running Time: 28800 sec.). 2007. 19.95 (978-1-4332-0002-1(3)); 54.95 (978-1-4332-0000-7(7)); audio compact disk 19.95 (978-1-4332-0003-8(1)); audio compact disk 63.00 (978-1-4332-0001-4(5)); audio compact disk 29.95 (978-1-4332-0004-5(X)) Blckstn Audio.

***Devil Colony.** unabr. ed. James Rollins. 2011. audio compact disk 39.99 (978-0-06-200852-7(8), Harper Audio) HarperCollins Pubs.

Devil Drives: A Life of Sir Richard Burton. unabr. collector's ed. Fawn Brodie. Read by Penelope Dellaporta. 12 cass. (Running Time: 18 hrs.). 1992. 96.00 (978-0-7366-2171-7(7), 2970) Books on Tape.
Burton's own published works, Fawn Brodie creates a fascinating portrait of this intrepid explorer.

***Devil in a Blue Dress.** unabr. ed. Walter Mosley. Read by Michael Boatman. (Running Time: 5 hours and 35 mins.). (Easy Rawlins Mystery Ser.). 2009. 21.95 Audible.

Devil in a Blue Dress. unabr. ed. Walter Mosley. Read by G. C. Simms. 6 cass. (Running Time: 6 hrs.). (Easy Rawlins Mystery Ser.). 1994. 48.00 (978-0-7366-2810-5(X), 3524) Books on Tape.
It's 1948. Easy Rawlins just got fired from his job. He thinks it's good money to find a blond beauty who frequents L.A.'s black jazz clubs. But behind the dollars lurks a grim killer.

***Devil in Pew Number Seven: A True Story.** unabr. ed. Rebecca Nichols Alonzo & Bob DeMoss. (ENG.). 2010. 14.98 (978-1-61045-100-0(7)); audio compact disk 24.98 (978-1-61045-099-7(X)) christianaud.

Devil in Texas & Other Cowboy Tales. adpt. ed. John R. Erickson. Read by John R. Erickson. Illus. by Gerald L. Holmes. 2 cass. (J). (gr. k up). 1983. bk. 13.95 (978-0-916941-24-6(8)) Maverick Bks.
Presents humorous tales of contemporary cowboy life.

Devil in the Details: Scenes from an Obsessive Girlhood. Jennifer Traig. Read by Melinda Wade. (Playaway Adult Nonfiction Ser.). (ENG.). 2008. 44.99 (978-1-60640-626-7(4)) Find a World.

Devil in the Junior League. abr. ed. Linda Francis Lee. Read by Jenna Lamia. (Running Time: 14400 sec.). 2007. audio compact disk 14.99 (978-1-4233-2425-6(0), 9781423324256, BCD Value Price) Brilliance Audio.

Devil in the Junior League. unabr. ed. Linda Francis Lee. Read by Jenna Lamia. (Running Time: 12 hrs.). 2006. 39.25 (978-1-4233-2423-2(4), 9781423324232, BADLE); 24.95 (978-1-4233-2422-5(6), 9781423324225, BAD); 87.25 (978-1-4233-2417-1(X), 9781423324171, BrilAudUnabridg); audio compact disk 97.25 (978-1-4233-2419-5(6), 9781423324195, BriAudCD Unabrid); audio compact disk 39.25 (978-1-4233-2421-8(8), 9781423324218, Brlnc Audio MP3 Lib); audio compact disk 36.95 (978-1-4233-2418-8(8), 9781423324188, Bril Audio CD Unabri); audio compact disk 24.95 (978-1-4233-2420-1(X), 9781423324201, Brilliance MP3) Brilliance Audio.
The Junior League of Willow Creek, Texas, is tres exclusive, and its members work hard to keep it that way. Undesirables need not apply. Fredericka Mercedes Hildebrand Ware (Frede to her friends) is a member beyond reproach...until her life begins to unravel. When her husband Gordon betrays her, steals her money, and runs off to places unknown, it's something she'd rather keep under wraps. The last thing she needs is to become fodder for the JLWC gossip mill. And to make matters worse, the only lawyer in town who stands a chance at helping Frede get revenge is Howard Grout, an ambulance-chasing, gold-chain-wearing sleaze who has bought his way into Frede's exclusive neighborhood. With no money to her name, Frede is forced to hire Howard in exchange for a favor: get his tacky, four-inch-stiletto-and-pink-spandex-wearing wife into the Junior League. Linda Francis Lee has written a hysterical novel about the lengths to which one woman goes to bring her cheating husband to justice.

Devil in the White City: Murder, Magic, & Madness at the Fair That Changed America. Erik Larson. Read by Scott Brick. 12 cds. 2005. audio compact disk 74.50 (978-0-7366-9230-4(4)) Pub: Books on Tape. Dist(s): NetLibrary CO

Devil in the White City: Murder, Magic, & Madness at the Fair That Changed America. abr. ed. Erik Larson. Read by Tony Goldwyn. 5 CDs. (Running Time: 6 hrs.). (ENG.). 2005. audio compact disk 19.95 (978-0-7393-2359-5(8), Random AudioBks) Pub: Random Audio Pubg. Dist(s): Random

Devil in the White City: Murder, Magic, & Madness at the Fair That Changed America. collector's ed. Erik Larson. Read by Scott Brick. 10 cass. (J). 2000. 72.00 (978-0-7366-9004-1(2), 5157) Books on Tape.
Poems set to music. Includes: "Rat for Lunch!" "I Met a Dozen Duhduhs," & "We're Loudies!".

Devil in the White City: Murder, Magic, & Madness at the Fair That Changed America. unabr. ed. Erik Larson. Read by Scott Brick. (Running Time: 52200 sec.). (ENG.). 2007. audio compact disk 34.95 (978-0-7393-4381-4(5), Random AudioBks) Pub: Random Audio Pubg. Dist(s): Random

***Devil in Winter.** unabr. ed. Lisa Kleypas. Read by Rosalyn Landor. (Running Time: 10 hrs.). (Wallflower Ser.: Bk. 3). 2010. 24.99 (978-1-4418-5191-8(7), 9781441851918, Brilliance MP3); 39.97 (978-1-4418-5192-5(5), 9781441851925, Brlnc Audio MP3 Lib); 24.99 (978-1-4418-5193-2(3), 9781441851932, BAD); 39.97 (978-1-4418-5194-9(1), 9781441851949, BADLE); audio compact disk 29.99 (978-1-4418-5189-5(5), 9781441851895, Bril Audio CD Unabri); audio compact disk 79.97 (978-1-4418-5190-1(9), 9781441851901, BriAudCD Unabrid) Brilliance Audio.

Devil Is Your Slave. Perf. by Rose Leibundguth. 2 cass. (Running Time: 2 hrs.). 2001. 8.00 (978-1-931262-08-8(X)) Rose Leibund.

Devil Knows How to Ride. unabr. ed. Edward E. Leslie. Read by Patrick Cullen. 13 cass. (Running Time: 19 hrs.). 1998. 35.95 (978-0-7861-1329-3(4), 2217) Blckstn Audio.
William Clarke Quantrill was a quiet Ohio schoolteacher & Confederate soldier who became the most feared & notorious guerrilla of the Civil War. A brilliant tactician, Quantrill was a brave & charismatic man who, throughout the war, attracted hundreds to his side, notably the teenaged Frank James, Jesse James & Cole Younger. The peak of Quantrill's career came when he led 450 men in the dawn raid that became known as the Lawrence Massacre, considered to be the greatest atrocity of the Civil War.

***Devil Knows How to Ride: The True Story of William Clarke Quantrill & His Confederate Raiders.** unabr. ed. Edward E. Leslie. Read by Patrick Cullen. (Running Time: 18 hrs. 30 mins.). 2010. 44.95 (978-1-4417-1915-7(6)); audio compact disk 123.00 (978-1-4417-1912-6(1)) Blckstn Audio.

Devil Latch. unabr. ed. Sonya Hartnett. Read by Caroline Lee. (Running Time: 19080 sec.). 2007. audio compact disk 63.95 (978-1-74093-400-8(8)) Pub: Bolinda Pubng AUS. Dist(s): Bolinda Pub Inc

***Devil Made Me Do It: And Five Other Lies That Satan Tries to Trap Us with.** Anthony Sweat. 2011. audio compact disk 14.99 (978-1-60908-005-1(X)) Deseret.

***Devil Made Me Do It Again: Comtemporary Tales of Subtle Horror.** Paul Dale Anderson. Read by Paul Dale Anderson. (ENG.). 2010. audio compact disk 21.00 (978-0-937491-08-9(X)) TwoAM Pubns.

Devil May Care. abr. ed. Sebastian Faulks. Read by Tristan Layton. 5 CDs. (Running Time: 6 hrs.). (ENG.). 2008. audio compact disk 29.95 (978-0-7393-6621-9(1), Random AudioBks) Pub: Random Audio Pubg. Dist(s): Random

Devil May Care. unabr. ed. Sebastian Faulks. Read by John Lee. 5 cass. 2008. 90.00 (978-1-4159-5502-4(6), BksonTape); audio compact disk 90.00 (978-1-4159-4887-3(9), BksonTape) Pub: Random Audio Pubg. Dist(s): Random
An Algerian drug runner is savagely executed in the desolate outskirts of Paris. This seemingly isolated event leads to the recall of Agent 007 from his sabbatical in Rome and his return to the world of intrigue and danger where he is most at home. The head of MI6, M, assigns him to shadow the mysterious Dr. Julius Gorner, a power-crazed pharmaceutical magnate, whose wealth is exceeded only by his greed. Gorner has lately taken a disquieting interest in opiate derivatives, both legal and illegal, and this urgently bears looking into. Bond finds a willing accomplice in the shape of a glamorous Parisian named Scarlett Papava. He will need her help in a life-and-death struggle with his most dangerous adversary yet, as a chain of events threaten to lead to global catastrophe. A British airliner goes missing over Iraq. The thunder of a coming war echoes in the Middle East. And a tide of lethal narcotics threatens to engulf a Great Britain in the throes of the social upheavals of the late sixties. Picking up where Fleming left off, Sebastian Faulks takes Bond back to the height of the Cold War in a story of almost unbearable pace and tension. Devil May Care not only captures the very essence of Fleming's original novels but also shows Bond facing dangers with a powerful relevance to our own times.

Devil May Care. unabr. ed. Elizabeth Peters, pseud. Read by Grace Conlin. 6 cass. (Running Time: 8 hrs. 30 mins.). 1998. 44.95 (978-0-7861-1441-2(X), 2303) Blckstn Audio.
Ellie & Henry, young, happy & in love are ready to spend two weeks house-sitting her Aunt Kate's Virginia mansion. Everything was in front of them & they laughed in the sunlight & then Ellie screamed. The book she had found in the antiquarian shop was to be a special gift for Aunt Kate, a story of the town's aristocracy. Every aristocracy has its secrets, though & Burton, Virginia wanted theirs kept that way. And so, it seemed, did their ancestors.

Devil-May-Care. unabr. ed. Elizabeth Peters, pseud. Read by Grace Conlin. (Running Time: 27000 sec.). 2007. audio compact disk 55.00 (978-0-7861-5853-9(0)); audio compact disk 29.95 (978-0-7861-5854-6(9)) Blckstn Audio.

Devil May Cry. unabr. ed. Sherrilyn Kenyon. Read by Holter Graham. 1 MP3-CD. (Running Time: 11 hrs. 13 mins.). (Dark-Hunter Ser.: Bk. 11). 2007. 59.95 (978-0-7927-4918-9(9)); audio compact disk 94.95 (978-0-7927-4871-7(9)); 64.95 (978-0-7927-4936-3(7)) AudioGO.
Sin was born a Sumerian god, until he was tricked into Artemis' service as a Dark-Hunter. This immortal has dreamed only of regaining his godhood and seeking revenge on the goddess who betrayed him. But when a beautiful woman, in perilous danger from those he now hunts, suddenly appears in his life, Sin knows that his world will never be the same again. Filled with sexy humor, sparkling with imagination, Devil May Cry is the next great thrill ride of the year.

Devil May Cry. unabr. ed. Sherrilyn Kenyon. Read by Holter Graham. (Running Time: 11 hrs. 0 mins. 0 sec.). (Dark-Hunter Ser.: Bk. 11). (ENG.). 2007. audio compact disk 39.95 (978-1-4272-0139-3(0)) Pub: Macmill Audio. Dist(s): Macmillan

Devil Met a Lady. unabr. ed. Stuart M. Kaminsky. Read by Christopher Lane. 5 cass. (Running Time: 7 hrs.). (Toby Peters Mystery Ser.: No. 17). 1995. 39.95 (978-0-7861-0881-7(9), 1536) Blckstn Audio.
Why has fabulous Bette Davis - the best known face in the world behind Roosevelt & Hitler - been kidnapped not once, not twice, but three times? What in the world does this star abduction have to do with Third Reich designs on America's plans for a top-secret superbomber? And who else but Hollywood private eye Toby Peters to plunge into this hair-raising adventure in pursuit of the answers.

Devil of a Dream. Robin Williams & Linda Williams. 1 cass., 1 CD. 7.98 (SUH 1059); audio compact disk 12.78 CD Jewel box. (SUH 1059) NewSound.

Devil of Nanking. unabr. ed. Mo Hayder. Narrated by Josephine Bailey & Simon Vance. (Running Time: 12 hrs. 30 mins. 0 sec.). (ENG.). 2005. audio compact disk 69.99 (978-1-4001-3162-4(6)); audio compact disk 34.99 (978-1-4001-0162-7(X)) Pub: Tantor Media. Dist(s): IngramPubServ

Devil of Nanking. unabr. ed. Mo Hayder. Read by Josephine Bailey & Simon Vance. (Running Time: 12 hrs. 30 mins. 0 sec.). (ENG.). 2005. audio compact disk 22.99 (978-1-4001-5162-2(7)) Pub: Tantor Media. Dist(s): IngramPubServ

***Devil of the Highlands.** unabr. ed. Lynsay Sands. Read by Marianna Palk. (ENG.). 2010. (978-0-06-195866-3(2), Harper Audio); (978-0-06-196701-6(7), Harper Audio) HarperCollins Pubs.

Devil on Horseback. unabr. ed. Victoria Holt. Narrated by Davina Porter. 9 cass. (Running Time: 13 hrs. 30 mins.). 1997. 78.00 (978-0-7887-0923-4(2), 95063E7) Recorded Bks.
Enamored by a handsome & arrogant French aristocrat, eighteen-year-old Minella is drawn into a complicated world of danger, betrayal & murder. Against the backdrop of the incipient French Revolution, she struggles with her fascination for the seductive & mysterious count.

Devil on My Doorstep. unabr. ed. Stuart M. Kaminsky. Read by Nick Sullivan. 6 vols. (Running Time: 9 hrs.). (Rockford Files Ser.). 2000. bk. 54.95 (978-0-7927-2313-4(9), CSL 202, Chivers Sound Lib) AudioGO.
Jim Rockford is in one hell of a mess: the credit companies are after his stuff, and his buddy Angel has cooked up another scheme that is a sure thing (sure to get them killed). When a young girl shows up at his door claiming to be the daughter of an old flame, he's dubious. When she claims that she's his daughter, all the bells go off! She's on the run, scared, and tells Jim that she thinks someone has killed her mother: her stepfather.

Devil Soldier: The American Soldier of Fortune Who Became a God in China. unabr. ed. Caleb Carr. Narrated by George Wilson. 11 cass. (Running Time: 15 hrs. 45 mins.). 1999. 91.00 (978-0-7887-0222-8(X), 94447E7) Recorded Bks.
It is the astonishing true tale of Frederick Townsend Ward, an American soldier of fortune who changed the course of Chinese history by leading one of the most extraordinary military campaigns the world has ever seen. Generations of anti Americanism & political turmoil in China have erased nearly all traces of Ward's legacy.

Devil under the Skin. James Pattinson. 2009. 44.95 (978-1-4079-0025-4(0)); audio compact disk 59.95 (978-1-4079-0026-1(9)) Pub: Soundings Ltd GBR. Dist(s): Ulverscroft US

Devil Water, Pt. 1. unabr. ed. Anya Seton. Read by Penelope Dellaporta. 8 cass. (Running Time: 12 hrs.). Incl. Pt. 2. Devil Water. 10 cass. (Running Time: 15 hrs.). Anya Seton. Read by Penelope Dellaporta. 1981. 80.00 (1221-B); 1981. 64.00 (978-0-7366-0223-5(2), 1221-A) Books on Tape.
The true story of Charles Radcliffe, who escaped from Newgate Prison in 1715 after his brother's execution & of his daughter Jenny. The themes of this book are loyalty & courage. It is a story of the old world & the new & it combines thoroughly documented history with storytelling.

Devil We Know: Dealing with the New Iranian Superpower. abr. unabr. ed. Robert Baer. Read by Ted Barker. (ENG.). 2008. audio compact disk 34.95 (978-0-7393-7604-1(7), Random AudioBks) Pub: Random Audio Pubg. Dist(s): Random

Devil Wears Prada. abr. ed. Lauren Weisberger. Read by Rachel Leigh Cook. 5 CDs. (Running Time: 6 hrs.). (ENG.). 2004. audio compact disk 14.99 (978-0-7393-1772-3(5)) Pub: Random Audio Pubg. Dist(s): Random

Devil Went down to Austin. Rick Riordan. Narrated by Tom Stechschulte. 9 cass. (Running Time: 12 hrs.). (Tres Navarre Ser.: No. 4). 83.00 (978-1-4025-1617-7(7)) Recorded Bks.

Devil Who Tamed Her. Johanna Lindsey. Read by Laural Merlington. (Reid Family Ser.). 2009. 64.99 (978-1-60775-679-8(X)) Find a World.

Devil Who Tamed Her. abr. ed. Johanna Lindsey. Read by Laural Merlington. (Running Time: 6 hrs.). (Reid Family Ser.). 2008. audio compact disk 14.99 (978-1-4233-2786-8(1), 9781423327868, BCD Value Price) Brilliance Audio.

Devil Who Tamed Her. unabr. ed. Johanna Lindsey. Read by Laural Merlington. (Running Time: 9 hrs.). (Reid Family Ser.). 2007. 39.25 (978-1-4233-2784-4(5), 9781423327844, BADLE); 24.95 (978-1-4233-2783-7(7), 9781423327837, BAD); 74.25 (978-1-4233-2778-3(0), 9781423327783, BrilAudUnabridg); audio compact disk 24.95 (978-1-4233-2781-3(0), 9781423327813, Brilliance MP3); audio compact disk 36.95 (978-1-4233-2779-0(9), 9781423327790, Bril Audio CD Unabri); audio compact disk 92.25 (978-1-4233-2780-6(2), 9781423327806, BriAudCD Unabrid); audio compact disk 39.25 (978-1-4233-2782-0(9), 9781423327820, Brlnc Audio MP3 Lib) Brilliance Audio.

Devil You Know. unabr. ed. Mike Carey. Read by Michael Kramer. (Running Time: 14 hrs. 0 mins. 0 sec.). (Felix Castor Ser.). (ENG.). 2007. audio compact disk 39.99 (978-1-4001-0515-1(3)); audio compact disk 29.99 (978-1-4001-5515-6(0)); audio compact disk 79.99 (978-1-4001-3515-8(X)) Pub: Tantor Media. Dist(s): IngramPubServ

Devil You Know. unabr. ed. Josephine Cox. Read by Carole Boyd. 8 cass. (Running Time: 8 hrs.). 1997. 69.95 Set. (978-0-7451-6750-3(0), CAB 1366) AudioGO.
Sonny Fareham's lover & boss is Tony Bridgeman; a ruthless man who gets what he wants. But upon hearing a private conversation between Tony & his wife one night, Sonny flees north, realizing her life is in great danger. There, she meets a mysterious man who is drawn to her, & Sonny believes she just might be happy again. But never far away is the one person who wants to destroy her life.

Devil You Know: A fully produced radio suspense Mystery. Prod. by AudioMovieStudio.com. 2007. cd-rom 19.95 (978-0-9786133-0-3(9)) Audio Movie.

Devil's Advocate. Morris West. Narrated by George Guidall. 8 cass. (Running Time: 10 hrs. 45 mins.). 76.00 (978-0-7887-5472-2(6)); audio compact disk 89.00 (978-1-4025-1552-1(9)) Recorded Bks.

Devil's Advocates: Greatest Closing Arguments in Criminal Law. unabr. ed. Michael S. Lief. Read by Gabrielle De Cuir & Stephen Hoye. (Running Time: 77400 sec.). 2006. audio compact disk 29.95 (978-0-7861-7503-1(6)) Blckstn Audio.

Devil's Advocates: Greatest Closing Arguments in Criminal Law. unabr. ed. Michael S. Lief. Read by Gabrielle De Cuir et al. 14 CDs. (Running

Time: 77400 sec.). 2006. audio compact disk 29.95 (978-0-7861-6898-9(6)) Blckstn Audio.

Devil's Advocates: Greatest Closing Arguments in Criminal Law. unabr. ed. Michael S. Lief & H. Mitchell Caldwell. Read by Gabrielle De Cuir & Stephen Hoye. (Running Time: 77400 sec.). 2006. 24.95 (978-0-7861-4738-0(5)) Blckstn Audio.

Devil's Advocates: Greatest Closing Arguments in Criminal Law. unabr. ed. Michael S. Lief & H. Mitchell Caldwell. Read by Gabrielle De Cuir et al. (Running Time: 77400 sec.). 2006. audio compact disk 36.00 (978-0-7861-6426-4(3)) Blckstn Audio.

Devil's Advocates: Greatest Closing Arguments in Criminal Law. unabr. ed. Michael S. Lief & Mitchell Caldwell. Read by Gabrielle De Cuir. 12 cass. (Running Time: 77400 sec.). 2006. 29.95 (978-0-7861-4602-4(8)) Blckstn Audio.

Devil's Alternative. unabr. ed. Frederick Forsyth. Read by David Rintoul. 12 cass. (Running Time: 18 hrs.). 2000. 79.95 (978-0-7451-4168-8(4), CAB 851) Pub: Chivers Audio Bks GBR. Dist(s): AudioGO
"Whichever option I choose, people are going to die." This is the devil's alternative, an appalling choice. It must be confronted by the President of the United States and other world leaders. In a gripping story that spans from Moscow to London and Washington, to a house in Ireland and an oil tanker in the North Sea, the devil's alternative is realized in one of the most exciting stories ever told.

Devil's Alternative. unabr. collector's ed. Frederick Forsyth. Read by Ken Ohst. 10 cass. (Running Time: 15 hrs.). 1984. 80.00 (978-0-7366-0900-5(8), 1844) Books on Tape.
A man is found unconscious & near death in the Black Sea off the coast of Turkey. He is party to international terror & intrigue & is marked as a high priority target.

Devil's Arithmetic, unabr. ed. Jane Yolen. Narrated by Barbara Rosenblat. 4 pieces. (Running Time: 5 hrs.). (gr. 6 up). 2001. 35.00 (978-0-7887-0541-0(5), 94736E7) Recorded Bks.
Plunges the listener into the terrible realities of the Nazi concentration camps. A celebration of the strength of the human spirit & a dramatic introduction to the darkest period of modern history.

Devil's Backbone. abr. ed. Terry C. Johnston. Read by Dick Wilkinson. 4 cass. (Running Time: 6 hrs.). 2002. 24.95 (978-1-890990-98-5(1), 99098) Otis Audio.
Western with sound effects.

Devil's Bargain. Gail Mallin. 2009. 61.95 (978-1-4079-0395-8(0)); audio compact disk 79.95 (978-1-4079-0396-5(9)) Pub: Soundings Ltd GBR. Dist(s): Ulverscroft US

Devil's Bones. abr. ed. Jefferson Bass. Read by Tom McKeon. (Running Time: 21600 sec.). (Body Farm Ser.). 2008. audio compact disk 29.95 (978-0-06-146847-6(9), Harper Audio) HarperCollins Pubs.

***Devil's Bones.** abr. ed. Jefferson Bass. Read by Tom Mckeon. (ENG.). 2008. (978-0-06-162971-6(5)); (978-0-06-162972-3(3)) HarperCollins Pubs.

Devil's Breath. unabr. ed. David Gilman. Read by David Thorn. 9 CDs. (Running Time: 11 hrs. 28 mins.). (YA). (gr. 6-9). 2008. audio compact disk 55.00 (978-0-7393-7272-2(6), Listening Lib) Pub: Random Audio Pubg. Dist(s): Random

Devil's Breath. unabr. ed. David Gilman. Read by David Thorn. (ENG.). (J). (gr. 6). 2008. audio compact disk 44.00 (978-0-7393-7270-8(X), Listening Lib) Pub: Random Audio Pubg. Dist(s): Random

Devil's Bride. Stephanie Laurens. Narrated by Simon Prebble. 11 cass. (Running Time: 15 hrs. 30 mins.). (Cynster Family Ser.: Bk. 1). 94.00 (978-0-7887-9644-9(5)) Recorded Bks.

Devil's Bride, Set. unabr. ed. Penelope Stratton, pseud. Read by Tanya Myers. 6 cass. (Running Time: 8 hrs.). 1999. 69.95 (978-1-85903-304-3(0)) Pub: Magna Story GBR. Dist(s): Ulverscroft US
Black rumours swirled around Lord Rupert Glennister; now an outraged society made him an outcast until he could redeem himself by marrying a woman of virtue. Calvina Bracewell was a parson's daughter, but was bullied into servitude by her "benefactors." Rescued by Lord Rupert, she found herself agreeing to his shocking demand that they marry that very night. For a while she was happy, but then attempts on her life began. Only one man could want her dead & that was the husband she'd grown to love.

Devil's Canyon. Scripts. Hank Mitchum. 5 CDs. (Running Time: 6 hrs.). (Stagecoach Ser.: 22). 2005. 14.99 (978-1-58807-800-1(0)) Am Pubng Inc.
At nineteen, Billy Starbuck is the most feared outlaw in Arizona. Then top stage driver Simon Tyree made a fool of Billy by sneaking a big payroll right past his nose. So Billy is determined to steal a big shipment of gold from Tyree's stage. Tyree is just as determined to deliver his cargo. But the passengers and a freak storm in Devil's Canyon upset both their plans.

Devil's Canyon, abr. ed. Ralph Compton. Read by Jim Gough. 4 cass. (Running Time: 6 hrs.). (Sundown Riders Ser.). 2000. 24.95 (978-1-890990-37-4(X), 99037) Otis Audio.
Four soldiers of fortune take the biggest gamble of their lives when they deliver an expensive cargo to Devil's Canyon in Southern Utah.

Devil's Claw. unabr. ed. J. A. Jance. Read by Stephanie Brush. 12 cass. (Running Time: 12 hrs. 30 min.). (Joanna Brady Mystery Ser.). 2000. 64.95 (978-1-58116-075-8(5)) Books in Motion.
Arizona sheriff Joanna Brady's wedding plans are disrupted by the death of a neighbor who leaves his ranch to her, much to his daughter's chagrin and by the murder of Sandra Ridder, a recently paroled convict. Sandra, once a militant Native American college student, was convicted of murdering her husband and now her 15-year-old daughter, Lucy, runs away to evade her mothers' killer.

Devil's Claw. unabr. ed. J. A. Jance. Read by Stephanie Brush. 11 CDs. (Running Time: 12 hrs. 30 min.). (Joanna Brady Mystery Ser.). 2001. audio compact disk 71.50 (978-1-58116-115-1(8)) Books in Motion.
The homicide victim at Cochise Stronghold in the Dragoon Mountains is an Indian woman recently released for the manslaughter killing of her husband.

***Devil's Claw.** unabr. ed. J. A. Jance. Read by C. J. Critt. (ENG.). 2010. (978-0-06-195388-0(1), Harper Audio); (978-0-06-196702-3(5), Harper Audio) HarperCollins Pubs.

Devil's Code. unabr. ed. John Sandford, pseud. Narrated by Richard Ferrone. 6 cass. (Running Time: 9 hrs.). 2000. 59.00 (978-0-7887-4946-9(3), 96464E7) Recorded Bks.
A twisted run through the enigmatic world of high-tech computer security & the hackers who live beyond the fringes of both law & identity. Kidd is an artist & computer specialist who makes most of his money in less-than-legal pursuits. When a programmer friend dies under mysterious circumstances, Kidd sees no reason to get involved until his hacker code name starts showing up on government most-wanted lists. Reluctantly, Kidd realizes he'd better get to the bottom of the murder quickly if he wants to keep his profitable anonymity.

Devil's Code. unabr. ed. John Sandford, pseud. Narrated by Richard Ferrone. 8 CDs. (Running Time: 9 hrs.). 2001. audio compact disk 78.00 (978-0-7887-6171-3(4), C1395) Recorded Bks.
Kidd is an artist & computer specialist who makes most of his money in less-than-legal pursuits. When a programmer friend dies under mysterious circumstances, Kidd sees no reason to get involved until his hacker code name starts showing up on government most-wanted lists.

Devil's Company. unabr. ed. David Liss. Read by Simon Vance. (Running Time: 15 hrs.). (Benjamin Weaver Ser.). 2009. 24.99 (978-1-4233-2705-9(5), 9781423327059, Brilliance MP3); 39.97 (978-1-4233-2706-6(3), 9781423327066, Brinc Audio MP3 Lib); 39.97 (978-1-4233-2708-0(X), 9781423327080, BADLE); 24.99 (978-1-4233-2707-3(1), 9781423327073, BAD); audio compact disk 38.99 (978-1-4233-2703-5(9), 9781423327035, Bril Audio CD Unabri); audio compact disk 99.97 (978-1-4233-2704-2(7), 9781423327042, BriAudCD Unabrid) Brilliance Audio.

***Devil's Corner.** abr. ed. Lisa Scottoline. Read by Kate Burton. (ENG.). 2005. (978-0-06-085459-1(6), Harper Audio); (978-0-06-085460-7(X), Harper Audio) HarperCollins Pubs.

Devil's Corner. abr. ed. Lisa Scottoline. Read by Kate Burton. (Running Time: 21600 sec.). 2008. audio compact disk 14.95 (978-0-06-157124-4(5), Harper Audio) HarperCollins Pubs.

***Devil's Corner.** unabr. ed. Lisa Scottoline. Read by Barbara Rosenblat. (ENG.). 2005. (978-0-06-085458-4(8), Harper Audio); (978-0-06-085457-7(X), Harper Audio) HarperCollins Pubs.

Devil's Corner. unabr. ed. Lisa Scottoline. Read by Barbara Rosenblat. Contrib. by Barbara Rosenblat. 2005. audio compact disk 39.95 (978-0-06-078576-5(4)) HarperCollins Pubs.

Devil's Cub. unabr. ed. Georgette Heyer. Read by Michael Drew. 8 cass. (Running Time: 9 hrs. 30 mins.). 2002. 69.95 (978-0-7540-0740-1(5), CAB 2162) AudioGO.
The excesses of the young Marquis of Vidal are even wilder than his father's before him. Not for nothing is the reckless duelist and gamester called the Devil's Cub. But when he is forced to leave the country, Mary Challoner discovers his fiendish plan to abduct her sister. And only by daring to impersonate her can Mary save her from certain ruin.

Devil's Den. unabr. ed. Concho Bradley. Read by Steven Crossley. 3 cass. (Running Time: 4 hrs.). 2000. 34.95 (978-1-86042-518-9(6), 25186) Pub: Soundings Ltd GBR. Dist(s): Ulverscroft US

Devil's Disciple. George Bernard Shaw. Perf. by Richard Dreyfuss et al. 1 cass. (Running Time: 1 hr. 32 min.). 1998. 19.95 (978-1-58081-105-7(1), WTA3) L A Theatre.
Never has the Revolutionary War been so entertaining. Shaw stands "do or die" melodrama on its head, with a cast of unforgettable characters, including the Devil's Disciple himself, a young hero who disdains heroism, even as he makes the ultimate sacrifice for honor & country.

Devil's Door. collector's ed. Sharan Newman. Read by Donada Peters. 9 cass. (Running Time: 13 hrs. 30 min.). 1999. 72.00 (978-0-7366-4663-5(9), 5045) Books on Tape.
A wealthy countess, brutally beaten, lies dying at the convent of the Paraclete. Despite entreaties, she refuses to name her killer. Catherine LeVendeur, the Paraclete's most learned young novice-scholar, vows to find out the indentity of the woman's assailant, but Catherine is torn between her quest for justice & the pledge made to her beloved Edgar, who has come to lead her from the convent to a life of the flesh. If Catherine abandoned her crusade for the truth, others will die, & the convent she loves might be destroyed.

Devil's Dream, unabr. ed. Lee Smith. Narrated by Linda Stephens et al. 10 cass. (Running Time: 13 hrs. 30 mins.). 1998. 85.00 (978-0-7887-0842-8(2), 94988E7) Recorded Bks.
As the 150-year saga of a musical Southern family unfolds, generations of a musical Southern family unfolds, generations of down-home mountain folk spring to life, colorful dialects & all.

Devil's Feather. unabr. ed. Minette Walters. Narrated by Josephine Bailey. (Running Time: 11 hrs. 0 mins. 0 sec.). (ENG.). 2006. audio compact disk 34.99 (978-1-4001-0314-0(2)); audio compact disk 69.99 (978-1-4001-3314-7(9)); audio compact disk 24.99 (978-1-4001-5314-5(X)) Pub: Tantor Media. Dist(s): IngramPubServ

Devil's Food. Kerry Greenwood. Read by Louise Siversen. (Running Time: 8 hrs. 20 mins.). (Corinna Chapman Mystery: Ser.). 2009. 74.99 (978-1-74214-241-8(9), 9781742142418) Pub: Bolinda Pubng AUS. Dist(s): Bolinda Pub Inc

Devil's Food. unabr. ed. Kerry Greenwood. Read by Louise Siversen. (Running Time: 8 hrs. 20 mins.). (Corinna Chapman Ser.). 2008. audio compact disk 87.95 (978-1-921415-60-9(6), 9781921415609) Pub: Bolinda Pubng AUS. Dist(s): Bolinda Pub Inc

Devil's Garden. unabr. ed. Ace Atkins. Read by Dick Hill. 1 MP3-CD. (Running Time: 13 hrs.). 2009. 24.99 (978-1-4233-4996-9(2), 9781423349969, Brilliance MP3); 39.97 (978-1-4233-4997-6(0), 9781423349976, Brinc Audio MP3 Lib); 39.97 (978-1-4233-4999-0(7), 9781423349990, BADLE); 24.99 (978-1-4233-4998-3(9), 9781423349983, BAD); audio compact disk 36.99 (978-1-4233-4994-5(6), 9781423349945, Bril Audio CD Unabri); audio compact disk 97.97 (978-1-4233-4995-2(4), 9781423349952, BriAudCD Unabrid) Brilliance Audio.

Devil's Garden. unabr. ed. Ralph Peters. Read by Edward Lewis. 9 cass. (Running Time: 13 hrs.). 1998. 62.95 (978-0-7861-1448-1(7), 2310) Blckstn Audio.
Powerful & provocative, rich in authentic detail & breathtaking in suspense, an unforgettable novel in which the fate of nations comes down to the fate of two human beings. One strand in a spider's web of fraud & intrigue.

Devil's Garden. unabr. ed. Ralph Peters. Read by Edward Lewis. (Running Time: 45000 sec.). 2007. audio compact disk 29.95 (978-0-7861-6260-4(0)); audio compact disk & audio compact disk 90.00 (978-0-7861-6259-8(7)) Blckstn Audio.

Devil's Garden. unabr. ed. Allan Zullo. Read by John Ratzenberger. 2008. 1.37 (978-1-4233-8063-4(0), 9781423380634, BAD) Brilliance Audio.

Devil's Half Acre Pt. 2: Mysteries of Winterthurn. unabr. ed. Joyce Carol Oates. Narrated by John McDonough. 8 cass. (Running Time: 11 hrs. 30 mins.). 2000. 70.00 (978-0-7887-0563-2(6), 94752E7) Recorded Bks.
Five young women have been found in a desolate plot of land aptly-named Devil's Half Acre - all mutilated and murdered. Can amateur detective Xavier Kilgarvan discover the identity of "the Gentleman Suitor" who wooed each victim to the area's massive rocks?.

Devil's Heiress. Jo Beverley. Narrated by Simon Prebble. 9 cass. (Running Time: 12 hrs. 15 mins.). 81.00 (978-1-4025-2146-1(4)) Recorded Bks.

Devil's Heiress. unabr. ed. Jo Beverley. Narrated by Simon Prebble. 9 cass. (Running Time: 12 hrs. 15 mins.). 2002. 42.95 (978-1-4025-2147-8(2), RF993) Recorded Bks.

Devil's Horsemen: The Mongol Invasion of Europe. unabr. ed. James Chambers. Narrated by Alexander Spencer. 5 cass. (Running Time: 7 hrs.). 1983. 44.00 (978-1-55690-142-3(9), 83058E7) Recorded Bks.
The Mongol invasion of Europe in the Thirteenth Century changed the face of a continent. It nearly changed the world. Chronicle reveals how Khan transformed the art of war using massed firepower, mobility, communication, unity of command & speed & how his success inspired World War II leaders such as General Patton & Kommandant Rommel.

Devils in the Mirror. unabr. ed. Lesley Horton. Contrib. by Maggie Mash. 11 cass. (Story Sound Ser.). 2006. 89.95 (978-1-85903-975-5(8)) Pub: Mgna Lrg Print GBR. Dist(s): Ulverscroft US

Devils in the Mirror. unabr. ed. Lesley Horton & Maggie Mash. Contrib. by Maggie Mash. 13 CDs. (Story Sound CD Ser.). 2006. audio compact disk 99.95 (978-1-84652-031-0(2)) Pub: Mgna Lrg Print GBR. Dist(s): Ulverscroft US

Devil's Island. unabr. ed. David Harris. Read by Peter Hardy. 2 cass. (Running Time: 2 hrs. 30 mins.). (Cliffhangers: Ser.). (YA). 2001. 24.00 (978-1-74030-355-2(5)) Pub: Bolinda Pubng AUS. Dist(s): Bolinda Pub Inc

Devil's Kiss. Sarwat Chadda. Read by Anne Flosnik. (Playaway Top Young Adult Picks Ser.). (ENG.). (J). 2009. 39.99 (978-1-4418-0995-7(3)) Find a World.

Devil's Kiss. unabr. ed. Sarwat Chadda. Read by Anne Flosnik. (Running Time: 6 hrs.). 2009. 24.99 (978-1-4418-0166-1(9), 9781441801661, Brilliance MP3); 39.97 (978-1-4418-0167-8(7), 9781441801678, Brinc Audio MP3 Lib); 24.99 (978-1-4418-0168-5(5), 9781441801685, BAD); 39.97 (978-1-4418-0169-2(3), 9781441801692, BADLE); audio compact disk 24.99 (978-1-4418-0164-7(2), 9781441801647, Bril Audio CD Unabri) Brilliance Audio.

Devil's Kiss. unabr. ed. Sarwat Chadda. Read by Anne Flosnik. 7 CDs. (Running Time: 8 hrs.). (YA). (gr. 9 up). 2009. audio compact disk 54.97 (978-1-4418-0165-4(0), 9781441801654, BriAudCD Unabrid) Brilliance Audio.

Devil's Labyrinth. John Saul. Read by Jim Bond. (Playaway Adult Fiction Ser.). (ENG.). 2009. 70.00 (978-1-60775-526-5(2)) Find a World.

Devil's Labyrinth. abr. ed. John Saul. Read by Jim Bond. (Running Time: 6 hrs.). 2008. audio compact disk 14.99 (978-1-4233-0452-4(7), 9781423304524, BCD Value Price) Brilliance Audio.

Devil's Labyrinth. unabr. ed. John Saul. Read by Jim Bond. (Running Time: 11 hrs.). 2007. 39.25 (978-1-4233-0450-0(0), 9781423304500, BADLE); 24.95 (978-1-4233-0449-4(7), 9781423304494, BAD); 82.25 (978-1-4233-0444-9(6), 9781423304449, BrilAudUnabridg); audio compact disk 36.95 (978-1-4233-0445-6(4), 9781423304456, Bril Audio CD Unabri); audio compact disk 24.95 (978-1-4233-0447-0(0), 9781423304470, Brilliance MP3); audio compact disk 97.25 (978-1-4233-0446-3(2), 9781423304463, BriAudCD Unabrid); audio compact disk 39.25 (978-1-4233-0448-7(9), 9781423304487, Brinc Audio MP3 Lib) Brilliance Audio.

***Devil's Light.** unabr. ed. Richard North Patterson. (Running Time: 11 hrs. 0 mins. 0 sec.). (ENG.). 2011. audio compact disk 39.99 (978-1-4423-4018-3(5)) Pub: S&S Audio. Dist(s): S and S Inc

Devil's Novice. unabr. ed. Ellis Peters. Read by Vanessa Benjamin. 6 cass. (Running Time: 8 hrs. 30 mins.). 2003. 44.95 (978-0-7861-1307-1(3), 2222) Blckstn Audio.

Devil's Novice. unabr. ed. Ellis Peters, pseud. Read by Vanessa Benjamin. 6 cass. (Running Time: 9 hrs.). (Chronicles of Brother Cadfael Ser.: Vol. 8). 1999. 44.95 (2222) Blckstn Audio.
Outside the pale of the Abbey of Saint Peters & Saint Paul, in September of the year of our Lord 1140, a priestly emissary for King Stephen has been reported missing. But inside the pale, what troubles Brother Cadfael is a proud, secretive nineteen-year-old novice.

Devil's Novice. unabr. ed. Ellis Peters, pseud. Narrated by Patrick Tull. 6 cass. (Running Time: 8 hrs. 45 mins.). (Chronicles of Brother Cadfael Ser.: Vol. 8). 1993. 51.00 (978-1-55690-885-9(7), 93327E7) Recorded Bks.
Meriet Aspley, a new novice at the Abbey of Saint Peter & Saint Paul causes quite a disturbance with his bizarre behavior. His violent nightmares cause him to scream his anguish in the dead of night, earning him the nickname, Devil's Novice.

Devil's Oasis. unabr. ed. Bartle Bull. Read by Fred Williams. (Running Time: 59400 sec.). 2007. 89.95 (978-1-4332-0263-6(8)); audio compact disk 120.00 (978-1-4332-0264-3(6)); audio compact disk 44.95 (978-1-4332-0265-0(4)) Blckstn Audio.

Devil's Own. Olwen Edwards. Read by Tracey Shaw. 3 cass. (Running Time: 4 hrs. 30 mins.). 1999. 34.95 (60865) Pub: Soundings Ltd GBR. Dist(s): Ulverscroft US

Devil's Own. unabr. ed. Garry Douglas. Read by Cornelius Garrett. 8 cass. (Running Time: 12 hrs.). 2000. 59.95 (978-0-7540-0109-6(1), CAB 1532) Pub: Chivers Audio Bks GBR. Dist(s): AudioGO
It is Crimean War, and the British and their allies are facing hard times. Sergeant Jack Crossman is part of the 88th regiment, also know as the Devil's Own. Nick-named Fancy Jack by the troops for his aristocratic background, Crossman must lead a series of suicide missions against the Cossacks, where success or failure could determine the outcome of the war.

Devil's Own Luck. David Donachie. 2008. 84.95 (978-1-84559-904-1(7)); audio compact disk 89.95 (978-1-84559-905-8(5)) Pub: Soundings Ltd GBR. Dist(s): Ulverscroft US

Devil's Priest. Kate Ellis. 2008. 61.95 (978-1-4079-0290-6(3)); audio compact disk 79.95 (978-1-4079-0291-3(1)) Pub: Soundings Ltd GBR. Dist(s): Ulverscroft US

Devil's Punchbowl. abr. ed. Greg Iles. Read by Dick Hill. 5 CDs. (Running Time: 6 hrs.). 2009. audio compact disk 14.99 (978-1-4233-1820-0(X), 9781423318200, BCD Value Price) Brilliance Audio.

Devil's Punchbowl. unabr. ed. Greg Iles. Read by Dick Hill. 2 MP3-CDs. (Running Time: 24 hrs.). 2009. 29.99 (978-1-4233-1815-6(3), 9781423318156, Brilliance MP3); 44.97 (978-1-4233-1816-3(1), 9781423318163, Brinc Audio MP3 Lib); 44.97 (978-1-4233-1818-7(8), 9781423318187, BADLE); 29.99 (978-1-4233-1817-0(X), 9781423318170, BAD); audio compact disk 38.99 (978-1-4233-1813-2(7), 9781423318132, Bril Audio CD Unabri); audio compact disk 99.97 (978-1-4233-1814-9(5), 9781423318149, BriAudCD Unabrid) Brilliance Audio.

***Devil's Queen.** unabr. ed. Jeanne Kalogridis. Narrated by Kate Reading. 14 CDs. (Running Time: 16 hrs. 30 mins.). 2009. audio compact disk 115.95 (978-0-7927-6384-0(X)) AudioGO.

Devil's Queen. unabr. ed. Jeanne Kalogridis. Read by Kate Reading. (Running Time: 5 hrs. 30 mins. 0 sec.). (ENG.). 2009. audio compact disk 29.95 (978-1-4272-0712-8(7)) Pub: Macmill Audio. Dist(s): Macmillan

Devil's Steps. unabr. ed. Arthur W. Upfield. Read by Peter Hosking. 7 cass. (Running Time: 10 hrs. 30 mins.). (Inspector Napoleon Bonaparte Mysteries). 1999. (978-1-876584-28-3(9), 590788) Bolinda Pubng AUS.
Detective-Inspector Napoleon Bonaparte leaves his familiar outback environment for Melbourne & a nearby mountain resort on a special assignment for Military Intelligence. Although out of his element among city

people, Bony displays his characteristic skills to interpret some puzzling clues & catch a murderer.

Devil's Steps. unabr. ed. Arthur W. Upfield. Read by Peter Hosking. (Running Time: 7 hrs. 30 mins.). (Inspector Napoleon Bonaparte Mysteries). 2009. audio compact disk 77.95 (978-1-74214-123-7(4), 9781742141237) Pub: Bolinda Pubng AUS. Dist(s): Bolinda Pub Inc

Devil's Storybook. 2004. bk. 24.95 (978-1-56008-187-6(2)); pap. bk. 14.95 (978-1-56008-188-3(0)); 8.95 (978-1-56008-886-8(9)) Weston Woods.

Devil's Teardrop. abr. ed. Jeffery Deaver. Read by Jay Patterson. 2004. 14.95 (978-0-7435-4648-5(2)) Pub: S&S Audio. Dist(s): S and S Inc

Devil's Teardrop. abr. ed. Jeffery Deaver. Read by Jay Patterson. (Running Time: 4 hrs. 30 mins. 0 sec.). (ENG.). 2007. audio compact disk 14.95 (978-0-7435-6103-7(1)) Pub: S&S Audio. Dist(s): S and S Inc

Devil's Teardrop. unabr. ed. Jeffery Deaver. Read by William Dufris. 10 vols. (Running Time: 12 hrs.). 2000. bk. 84.95 (978-0-7927-2421-6(6), CSL 310, Chivers Sound Lib) AudioGO.
New Year's Eve, 1999. An early morning machine gun attackby the Digger, an emotionless, robot-like madman, leaves dozens dead in the Washington, D.C., subway system. In a message to the mayor's office, a criminal mastermind demands twenty million dollars by midnight or the culprit will again be at the mercy of his accomplice. However, the extortionist, is killed in a freak accident.

Devil's Teardrop. unabr. ed. Jeffery Deaver. Read by William Dufris. 12 CDs. (Running Time: 18 hrs.). 2001. audio compact disk 110.95 (978-0-7927-9983-2(6), SLD 034, Chivers Sound Lib) AudioGO.
New Year's Eve, 1999. An early morning machine gun attack by the Digger, an emotionless, robot-like madman, leaves dozens dead in the Washington, D.C., subway system. A message sent to the mayor's office, a criminal mastermind demanding twenty million dollars by midnight or the capital will again be at the mercy of his accomplice. Special Agent Margaret Lukas & Peter Kincaid must track down the Digger by midnight or the first moments of the new century will be their last on earth.

Devil's Toenail. unabr. ed. Sally Prue. Read by Robert Glenister. 3 CDs. (Running Time: 4 hrs. 30 min.). (J). 2004. audio compact disk 29.95 (978-0-7540-6652-1(5), Chivers Child Audio) AudioGO.

Devil's Waltz. unabr. ed. Jonathan Kellerman. Read by Alexander Adams. 9 cass. (Running Time: 13 hrs. 30 min.). (Alex Delaware Ser.: No. 7). 1993. 72.00 (978-0-7366-2424-4(4), 3189) Books on Tape.
Twenty-one-month-old Cassie Jones is bright & energetic. But over the past 18 months Cassie has been rushed to Western Pediatric Medical Center with alarming frequency. Each time her pediatrician fails to come up with a diagnosis & finally calls in Dr. Alex Delaware. Instinct tells him that someone is deliberately making Cassie ill & the prime suspects are the parents. But Alex also realizes that something disturbing is going on in the hospital itself. Then a staff physician is murdered & Alex rushes to identify the link between the shadowy machinations at Western Peds & the fate of a child before another innocent life is lost.

Devil's Workshop, Set. abr. ed. Stephen J. Cannell. Read by Stephen J. Cannell. 3 cass. 1999. 25.00 (FS9-51015) Highsmith.

Devilweed, Set. unabr. ed. Bill Knox. 5 cass. 1998. 63.95 (978-1-85903-152-0(8)) Pub: Magna Story GBR. Dist(s): Ulverscroft US

***Devious.** abr. ed. Lisa Jackson. (Running Time: 6 hrs.). 2011. 9.99 (978-1-4558-0195-4(X), 9781455801954, BAD); audio compact disk 26.99 (978-1-4418-1334-3(9), 9781441813343, BACD) Brilliance Audio.

***Devious.** unabr. ed. Lisa Jackson. (Running Time: 16 hrs.). 2011. 24.99 (978-1-4418-1332-9(2), 9781441813329, BAD); 39.97 (978-1-4418-1333-6(0), 9781441813336, BADLE); 24.99 (978-1-4418-1330-5(6), 9781441813305, Brilliance MP3); 39.97 (978-1-4418-1331-2(4), 9781441813312, Brlnc Audio MP3 Lib); audio compact disk 36.99 (978-1-4418-1328-2(4), 9781441813282, Bril Audio CD Unabri); audio compact disk 97.97 (978-1-4418-1329-9(2), 9781441813299, BriAudCD Unabrid) Brilliance Audio.

***Devolver al Remitente.** unabr. ed. Julia Alvarez.Tr. of Return to Sender. (ENG.). (J). 2010. audio compact disk 39.00 (978-0-307-70766-6(0), Listening Lib) Pub: Random Audio Pubg. Dist(s): Random

***Devolver al Remitente.** unabr. ed. Julia Alvarez. Narrated by Ozzie Rodriguez & Olivia Preciado. 6 CDs.Tr. of Return to Sender. (SPA.). (J). (gr. 3-6). 2010. audio compact disk 39.00 (978-0-307-70768-0(7), Listening Lib) Pub: Random Audio Pubg. Dist(s): Random

***Devoted.** Geraldine Latty. (ENG.). 2006. audio compact disk 17.99 (978-92-822-4392-3(3)) Pub: Kingsway Pubns GBR. Dist(s): STL Dist NA

***Devoted to God & Each Other.** Deane Schuessler. 2010. audio compact disk (978-1-4507-0461-8(1)) Indep Pub IL.

***Devoted to God & Each Other.** Deane Schuessler. (ENG.). 2010. pap. bk. (978-1-60615-053-5(7)) WinePress Pub.

Devoted to God & Each Other. abr. ed. Deane Schuessler. 2006. audio compact disk 15.00 (978-1-57921-870-6(9)) Pub: WinePress Pub. Dist(s): Spring Arbor Dist

Devotion. 1 CD. 1999. audio compact disk 16.98 (978-1-57908-503-2(2), 5346) Platinm Enter.

Devotion. Sai Maa Lakshmi Devi. 2002. audio compact disk 16.00 (978-1-933488-05-9(0)) HIU Pr.
Discourses with Chalanda Sai Maa Lakshmi Devi1. The Mantra 2. The Nature of the Mind 3. The Grace of the Guru.

Devotion. unabr. collector's ed. Katherine Sutcliffe. Read by Kate Reading. 7 cass. (Running Time: 10 hrs. 30 min.). 1996. 56.00 (978-0-7366-3467-0(3), 4111) Books on Tape.
When autumn comes, Trey Hawthorne, a Duke, hasn't fortified his estate & it costs him dearly. Highwaymen not only rob him, they leave him a cripple. Tale is set in 19th century England.

Devotion: Understanding Its Deeper Aspects in The Search for God. Brother Anandamoy. 1984. 8.50 (2508) Self Realization.
The author explains: why we need to cultivate desire for God; surrender - what it is, & how it helps us to become receptive to the presence, guidance & blessings of God & Guru; the liberating power of selfless love; how God's nearness is found by a trusting, personal approach.

***Devotion of Suspect X.** unabr. ed. Keigo Higashino. Read by David Pittu. Tr. by Alexander O. Smith. (Running Time: 9 hrs. 0 mins. 0 sec.). (ENG.). 2011. audio compact disk 39.99 (978-1-4272-1195-8(7)) Pub: Macmill Audio. Dist(s): Macmillan

Devotion Series. 7 cass. 52.00 incl. vinyl storage album. Crystal Clarity.
Focuses on: How to Develop Devotion; How to Live a Divine Life; How to Please God; Keeping the Consciousness of God; Self-honesty & the Flow of Grace.

Devotion to Sadhana. Swami Amar Jyoti. 1 cass. 1991. 9.95 (P-54) Truth Consciousness.
A living, loving attitude in spiritual practices. Purifying ourselves. Defusing disturbances.

Devotion to the Supreme. Swami Amar Jyoti. 1 cass. 1978. 9.95 (C-12) Truth Consciousness.
Unconditional linking with our Supreme Self. Pure devotion to That.

***Devotions for a Sacred Marriage: A Year of Weekly Devotions for Couples.** unabr. ed. (ENG.). 2010. 14.99 (978-0-310-41580-0(2)) Zondervan.

***Devotions for Sacred Parenting: A Year of Weekly Devotions for Parents.** (ENG.). 2010. 14.99 (978-0-310-41582-4(9)) Zondervan.

Devotions in Honor of Our Mother of Perpetual Help. Perpetual Help Confraternity Staff. 1 cass. (Running Time: 0 hr. 45 min.). 1994. 8.95 (309) ACTA Pubns.

Devouring Mother. Read by Catharine Jones. 1 cass. (Running Time: 70 min.). 1988. 10.95 (978-0-7822-0104-8(0), 337) C G Jung IL.

Dew Breaker. Narrated by Edwidge Danticat. 5 cass. (Running Time: 6 hrs. 45 mins.). 2004. 24.99 (978-1-4025-7201-2(8), 03944) Recorded Bks.

Dewey. unabr. ed. Vicki Myron. Read by Suzanne Toren. (Running Time: 4 hrs. 30 mins.). 2009. 59.99 (978-1-60775-656-9(0)) Find a World.

Dewey: The Small-Town Library Cat Who Touched the World. abr. ed. Vicki Myron. Read by Suzanne Toren. Told to Bret Witter. (Running Time: 4 hrs. 30 mins.). (ENG.). 2008. 16.98 (978-1-60024-383-7(5)); audio compact disk 22.98 (978-1-60024-382-0(7)) Pub: Hachet Audio. Dist(s): HachBkGrp

***Dewey: The Small-Town Library Cat Who Touched the World.** unabr. ed. Vicki Myron. Read by Susan McInerny. Told to Bret Witter. (Running Time: 8 hrs.). (ENG.). 2010. 18.98 (978-1-60788-622-8(7)); audio compact disk 18.98 (978-1-60788-621-1(9)) Pub: Hachet Audio. Dist(s): HachBkGrp

Dewey Defeats Truman: Matthew 13:24-30. Ed Young. (J). 1981. 4.95 (978-0-7417-1190-8(7), A0190) Win Walk.

***Dewey the Library Cat: A True Story.** unabr. ed. Vicki Myron. (Running Time: 4 hrs.). (YA). 2010. audio compact disk 24.99 (978-1-4418-8547-0(1), 9781441885470, Bril Audio CD Unabri) Brilliance Audio.

***Dewey the Library Cat: A True Story.** unabr. ed. Vicki Myron & Bret Witter. (Running Time: 4 hrs.). (YA). 2010. 24.99 (978-1-4418-8551-7(X), 9781441885517, BAD); 39.97 (978-1-4418-8552-4(8), 9781441885524, BADLE) Brilliance Audio.

***Dewey the Library Cat: A True Story.** unabr. ed. Vicki Myron & Bret Witter. Read by Laura Hamilton. (Running Time: 4 hrs.). (YA). 2010. 24.99 (978-1-4418-8549-4(8), 9781441885494, Brilliance MP3); 39.97 (978-1-4418-8550-0(1), 9781441885500, Brlnc Audio MP3 Lib); audio compact disk 44.97 (978-1-4418-8548-7(X), 9781441885487, BriAudCD Unabrid) Brilliance Audio.

***Dewey's Nine Lives: The Magic of a Small-Town Library Cat Who Touched Millions.** Vicki Myron. (Running Time: 13 hrs.). (ENG.). 2010. audio compact disk 29.95 (978-0-14-242859-7(0), PengAudBks) Penguin Grp USA.

Dewsweepers: Seasons of Golf & Friendship. unabr. ed. James Dodson. Read by Michael Kramer. 7 cass. (Running Time: 10 hrs. 30 mins.). 2001. 56.00 (978-0-7366-8093-6(4)) Books on Tape.
A sufferer from a golf "mid-life crisis" recovers his happiness and his game with the help of a group of golfers called the Dewsweepers. These takers of the earliest weekend tee times are a bunch of "rich white Republicans" from Syracuse who have their own crusty, often off-color brand of golf and wisdom, and this is what they impart to Dodson. As a result, Dodson's game and outlook improve; he makes friends, bonds with the Dewsweepers, and eventually recovers his love of golf.

Dexter by Design. unabr. ed. Jeff Lindsay. Read by Nick Landrum. 9 CDs. (Running Time: 10 hrs. 30 mins.). (Dexter Morgan Ser.: Bk. 4). 2009. audio compact disk 39.99 (978-1-4407-1720-8(6)) Recorded Bks.

***Dexter by Design.** unabr. ed. Jeff Lindsay. Read by Nick Landrum. 1 Playaway. (Running Time: 10 hrs. 30 mins.). (Dexter Morgan Ser.: Bk. 4). 2009. 64.75 (978-1-4407-1801-4(6)); 72.75 (978-1-4407-1798-7(2)); audio compact disk 102.75 (978-1-4407-1799-4(0)) Recorded Bks.

Dexter in the Dark. unabr. ed. Jeff Lindsay. (Running Time: 45000 sec.). 2007. audio compact disk 34.99 (978-1-4281-5663-0(1)) Recorded Bks.

Dexter in the Dark. unabr. ed. Jeff Lindsay. Read by Nick Landrum. 11 CDs. (Running Time: 13 hrs.). 2007. audio compact disk 123.75 (978-1-4281-3240-5(6)); 92.75 (978-1-4281-3238-2(4)) Recorded Bks.
Macabre yet hugely entertaining, Dexter in the Dark takes America's most endearing murderer - star of a hit Showtime series - to places even he isn't comfortable exploring. A blood spatter analyst for the Miami police,Dexter has seen his share of gruesome deeds - and committed a few himself. But when he investigates a particularly terrible crime scene at a local university, everything changes.

***Dexter Is Delicious.** unabr. ed. Jeff Lindsay. Read by Jeff Lindsay. 2010. audio compact disk 40.00 (978-0-307-57754-2(6), Random AudioBks) Pub: Random Audio Pubg. Dist(s): Random

Dexter's Laboratory: Home Boy Genius. Perf. by De La Soul & Prince Paul. 1 CD. (Running Time: 1 hr.). (J). 2002. audio compact disk 7.98 Rhino Enter.
A new compilation of music inspired by the hit Cartoon Network show. Features new songs by hip hop stars along with the Dexter's Theme Song and other science-related favorites.

Dexter's Laboratory: The Musical Time Machine. Rhino Records Staff. 1 CD. (Running Time: 30 mins.). (J). (ps-3). 1998. audio compact disk 11.98 (978-1-56826-901-6(3), R2 75277) Rhino Enter.
A new compilation of music inspired by this hit show. Featuring new songs by hip-hop stars De La Soul, Prince Paul, and more, along with the Dexter's Theme Song and other science-related favorites.

Dexter's Laboratory: The Musical Time Machine. Rhino Records Staff. 1 cass. (Running Time: 030 min.). (J). (ps-3). 1998. 9.98 (978-1-56826-900-9(5)) Rhino Enter.

DeYoung Educational Productions. Garry De Young. Read by Garry De Young. 4 cass. (Running Time: 30 min.). (Environmental Cassettes). 1989. 5.00 De Young Pr.
Explains how to enlarge on physical envieonment to include social and psychological environmental impacts.

DE22 Work Safely with Electricity. Bergwall Productions Staff. 1998. audio compact disk 510.00 (978-0-8064-0919-1(3), DelLearn) Delmar.

DE70 Electronic Communications Cd Rom Win 95/3.1. Bergwall Productions Staff. 1998. audio compact disk 510.00 (978-0-8064-0982-5(7), DelLearn) Delmar.

***Dfree: Breaking Free from Financial Slavery.** DeForest B. Soaries. (ENG.). 2011. 14.99 (978-0-310-33316-6(4)) Zondervan.

Dhamma Verses: Poems of a Modern Day Master of Vipassana Meditation. unabr. ed. S. N. Goenka. 1 cass. (Running Time: 1 hr. 32 min.). 2000. bk. & pap. bk. 12.00 (978-0-9649484-4-0(3)) Pariyatti Pubng.
A recorded collection of inspiring Hindi dohas.

Dhammapada Talk. E. J. Gold. 2 cass. (Running Time: 2 hrs.). 18.98 set. (TP070) Union Label.
A talk on death, transit, & rebirth; difference between the psychotic & the mystic; "Be-ing" in nonexistence; experiencing the between-lives state. Given at Dhammapada Bookstore in Los Angeles.

Dharma Bums. Jack Kerouac. Read by Tom Parker. 6 CDs. (Running Time: 7 hrs.). 2005. audio compact disk 48.00 (978-0-7861-8388-3(8), 1309) Blckstn Audio.

Dharma Bums. Jack Kerouac. Read by Tom Parker. (Running Time: 7 hrs.). 1992. 27.95 (978-1-59912-649-4(4)) Iofy Corp.

Dharma Bums. unabr. ed. Jack Kerouac. Read by Tom Parker. 5 cass. (Running Time: 7 hrs.). 1992. 39.95 (978-0-7861-0352-2(3), 1309) Blckstn Audio.
Two ebullient young men are engaged in a passionate search for Dharma, or Truth. Their major adventure is the pursuit of the Zen way, which takes them climbing into the high Sierras to seek the lesson of solitude - a lesson that has a hard time surviving their forays into the pagan groves of San Francisco's Bohemia with its marathon wine-drinking bouts, poetry jam sessions, experiments in "yabyum," & similar nonascetic pastimes.

Dharma Bums. unabr. ed. Jack Kerouac. Read by Tom Parker. 13 vols. (Running Time: 7 hrs.). 2005. audio compact disk 24.95 (978-0-7861-9302-8(6), 1309); audio compact disk 19.95 (978-0-7861-8579-5(1), ZE3324); reel tape 19.95 (978-0-7861-2683-5(3), E1309) Blckstn Audio.

Dharma, Ego, & Liberation. Swami Amar Jyoti. 1 cass. 1989. 9.95 (K-111) Truth Consciousness.
Dharma brings well being but its goal is Liberation. On Lord Ganesha.

Dharma, the Law of Existence. Swami Amar Jyoti. 1 dolby cass. 1983. 9.95 (K-58) Truth Consciousness.
We exist because of Dharma; where Dharma is violated, disintegration follows. How to know one's Dharma. The deeper justice.

Dharma, The Law of Love. unabr. ed. Perf. by Eknath Easwaran. 1 cass. (Running Time: 1 hr.). 1992. 7.95 (978-1-58638-525-5(9)) Nilgiri Pr.

Dharma, the Liberating Force. Swami Amar Jyoti. 1 cass. 1989. 9.95 (K-108) Truth Consciousness.
Living according to Dharma, the highest stage of life, gateway from illusion to Reality. Man & the natural forces.

Dharmic Lifestyle. Swami Amar Jyoti. 1 cass. 1990. 9.95 (A-46) Truth Consciousness.
Reintroducing Dharma in its thousand details, for wellness, balance & harmony. Fundamental, individual & collective Dharma. Results of violating Dharma.

Dhola Maru. Perf. by Musafir. 1 CD. (Running Time: 1 hr. 9 mins.). 1999. audio compact disk 16.98 (978-1-56455-727-8(8), MM00114D) Sounds True.
A whirlwind of masterful rhythms & spiraling polyphonies from Rajasthan, electrifying Muslim qawwali chant, soaring North Indian raga & authentic songs from the dawn of Gypsy culture.

Dhrupad: Rudra Veena. Music by Baha-Ud-Din Dagar. 1 cass. 1997. (A97016) Multi-Cultural Bks.

Dhrupad: Vocal. Music by F. Wasif-Ud-Din Dagar. 1 cass. 1997. (A97015) Multi-Cultural Bks.

Dhyana (Meditation) & Samadhi - The Ishta or Chosen Ideal. unabr. ed. Vivekananda. Read by Robert Adjemian & Alan Arkin. 1 cass. (Running Time: 43 min.). 1990. 7.95 (978-1-882915-12-5(7)) Vedanta Ctr Atlanta.
The nature of meditation & its ultimate state - Samadhi; The role of a person's chosen ideal (incarnation, prophet) in spiritual life & practice.

Dia de Nieve. 1 cass. (Running Time: 35 min.).Tr. of Snowy Day. (SPA.). (J). 2001. 15.95 (XVS-37C) Kimbo Educ.

Dia de Nieve. Ezra Jack Keats. Illus. by Ezra Jack Keats. 14 vols. (Running Time: 6 mins.). 1991. pap. bk. 39.95 (978-1-59519-158-8(5)); 9.95 (978-1-59112-029-2(2)); audio compact disk 12.95 (978-1-59519-156-4(9)) Live Oak Media.

Dia de Nieve. Ezra Jack Keats. Illus. by Ezra Jack Keats. 11 vols. (Running Time: 6 mins.). (SPA.). (J). 1991. pap. bk. 18.95 (978-1-59519-157-1(7)) Pub: Live Oak Media. Dist(s): AudioGO

Dia de Nieve. Ezra Jack Keats. 1 cass. (Running Time: 10 min.). (SPA.). (J). bk. 24.95; pap. bk. 15.95 Weston Woods.

Dia de Nieve. unabr. ed. Ezra Jack Keats. Illus. by Ezra Jack Keats. Read by Marilyn Sanabria. 14 vols. (Running Time: 6 mins.). (SPA.). (J). 1991. pap. bk. & tchr. ed. 37.95 Reading Chest. (978-0-87499-247-2(8)) Live Oak Media.
Readalong of the Spanish translation of The Snowy Day.

Dia de Nieve. unabr. ed. Ezra Jack Keats. Illus. by Ezra Jack Keats. Read by Marilyn Sanabria. 11 vols. (Running Time: 6 mins.). (SPA.). (J). (gr. k-3). 1991. bk. 25.95 (978-0-87499-246-5(X)); pap. bk. 16.95 (978-0-87499-245-8(1)) Pub: Live Oak Media. Dist(s): AudioGO
This Caldecott Medal-winning tale tells of a young boy's adventures when a storm blankets the city in snow.

día Más. Daniel Calveti. Contrib. by Uncion Tropical. (SPA.). 2007. audio compact disk 14.99 (978-0-8297-5213-7(7)) Zondervan.

Dia Nevado. Tr. of Snowy Day, the. (SPA.). 2004. 8.95 (978-0-7882-0272-8(3)) Weston Woods.

Diabetes. Lilly B. Gardner. Contrib. by Ann J. Gardner. 1 cass. (Running Time: 30 min.). 1997. 20.00 Boxed kit, incl. bklet, recipe cards, sample nutrition labels, & exchange lists. (978-0-9659500-2-2(6)) Precepts.

Diabetes: Ancient Truths, Natural Remedies & the Latest Findings for Your Health Today. unabr. ed. Don Colbert. Narrated by Steve Hiller. (Running Time: 1 hr. 30 mins.). (Bible Cure Ser.). 2003. audio compact disk 9.99 (978-1-58926-118-1(6)) Oasis Audio.

Diabetes? Good Food to the Rescue. Michael Klaper. 1 cass. (Running Time: 30 min.). (Help Yourself to Health Ser.). 7.00 (978-0-929274-05-8(9)) Gentle World.
One of a series of tapes discussing the relationship between a diet free of animal products & improving one's health or a particular disease.

Diabetes Care: FactCheck. Facts and Comparisons Staff. (ENG.). 2005. 29.95 (978-1-01-475032-7(6)) Lppncott W W.

***Diabetes for Dummies.** abr. ed. Alan Rubin. Read by Brett Barry. (ENG.). 2008. (978-0-06-176488-2(4), Harper Audio); (978-0-06-176489-9(2), Harper Audio) HarperCollins Pubs.

Diabetes for Dummies. 3rd abr. ed. Alan Rubin. Read by Brett Barry. (Playaway Adult Nonfiction Ser.). (ENG.). 2009. 59.99 (978-1-60812-580-7(7)) Find a World.

Diabetes Mellitus see James Dickey Reads His Poetry & Prose

Diable: A Dog. 1980. (N-35) Jimcin Record.

Diable-a Dog. Jack London. (J). 1991. 17.98 (978-0-89061-307-8(9)) Jamestown.

Diable a Quatre. l.t. ed. Pierre Jakez Helias. (French Ser.). 1994. bk. 30.99 (978-2-84011-088-0(1)) Pub: UlverLrgPrint GBR. Dist(s): Ulverscroft US

Diable au Coin du Feu. 1 cass. (Running Time: 60 mins.). Dramatization. (Maitres du Mystere Ser.). (FRE.). 1996. 11.95 (1840-MA) Olivia & Hill.
Popular radio thriller, interpreted by France's best actors.

Diable au Corps, Set. Raymond Radiguet. Read by Jacques Perrin. 4 CDs. (FRE.). 1991. audio compact disk 36.95 (1110-AV) Olivia & Hill.
Radiguet was part of the entourage of the avant-garde literary group of Apollinaire. A 16-year-old boy seduces Marthe while her husband is away at war.

Diablerie. abr. unabr. ed. Walter Mosley. Read by Richard Allen. (Running Time: 6 hrs. 0 mins. 0 sec.). (ENG.). 2008. audio compact disk 49.99 (978-1-4001-3638-4(5)); audio compact disk 19.99 (978-1-4001-5638-2(6)) Pub: Tantor Media. Dist(s): IngramPubServ

Diablerie. unabr. ed. Walter Mosley. Read by Richard Allen. (YA). 2008. 39.99 (978-1-60514-770-3(2)) Find a World.

Diablerie. unabr. ed. Walter Mosley. Read by Richard Allen. 5 CDs. (Running Time: 6 hrs. 0 mins. 0 sec.). (ENG.). 2008. audio compact disk 24.99 (978-1-4001-0638-7(9)) Pub: Tantor Media. Dist(s): IngramPubServ

Diaboliques: Le Rideau Cramoisi, Set. Barbey D'Aurevilly. Read by G. Bejean et al. 2 cass. (FRE.). 1995. 26.95 (1680-VSL) Olivia & Hill.
Under the first Empire a young officer, Vicomte de Brassard, finds himself in a small sleepy town in the French countryside where he meets a beautiful young woman who incarnates evil.

Diagnosing Through Acupuncture. Ralph Alan Dale. Read by Ralph Alan Dale. 1 cass. (Running Time: 90 min.). 1980. 9.00 (14) Dialectic Pubng.
Methods of diagnosing disorders used in acupuncture.

Diagnosis. Alan Lightman. Read by Scott Brick. 2000. audio compact disk 80.00 (978-0-7366-6075-4(5)) Books on Tape.

Diagnosis. unabr. ed. Alan Lightman. Read by Scott Brick. 9 cass. (Running Time: 13 hrs. 30 mins.). 2001. 36.00 (978-0-7366-5923-9(4)) Books on Tape.
On his way to work one morning, Bill Chalmers suddenly discovers that he cannot remember where he is going, what he is meant to be doing or, indeed, who he is. He remembers only one thing, "The Maximum Information in the minimum Time", his company's motto but when his memory returns, it is accompanied by a numbness that gradually affects his entire body. As Chalmers chases down the elusive diagnosis of his illness, he descends into a Kafkaesque nightmare in which the more he discovers, the more he realizes what he has already lost.

Diagnosis. unabr. collector's ed. Alan Lightman. Read by Scott Brick. 9 cass. (Running Time: 12 hrs.). 2000. 34.95 (978-0-7366-5903-1(X)); audio compact disk 34.95 (978-0-7366-5904-8(8)) Books on Tape.

Diagnosis & Management in Pediatric Dermatology. Contrib. by Walter W. Tunnesen, Jr. et al. 1 cass. (American Academy of Pediatrics UPDATE: Vol. 16, No. 3). 1998. 20.00 Am Acad Pediat.

Diagnosis & Management of Chronic Active Hepatitis. Read by Willis C. Maddrey. 1 cass. (Running Time: 90 min.). 1986. 12.00 (C8643) Amer Coll Phys.

Diagnosis & Therapy of Gastroesophageal Reflux. Read by Donald O. Castell. 1 cass. (Running Time: 90 min.). 1986. 12.00 (C8636) Amer Coll Phys.

Diagnosis & Treatment of Sexual Issues. unabr. ed. Marty Klein. 3 cass. (Running Time: 5 hrs. 10 mins.). 1997. (978-0-9704526-0-3(8)) CA Sex Ed Assocs.
Whether through desire conflicts, chronic dissatisfaction or affairs, sexual issues are part of every therapist's practice. This compelling, positive model of sexuality challenges clients' self-disempowerment; sees society's sex-negativity as a source of psycho-sexual pathology; confronts ways in which psychotherapy & medicine misunderstand or even demonize sexuality.

Diagnosis, Staging & Therapy of Interstitial Lung Disease. Read by Ronald G. Crystal. 1 cass. (Running Time: 90 min.). 1985. 12.00 (C8547) Amer Coll Phys.

Diagnostic: And how to fix it: Why Your Writing Isn't Working. Speeches. 1 CD. (Running Time: 1 hour). 2002. 17.95 (978-0-9656309-8-6(6)) A Cappela Pub.
Learn the seven most common problems that keep your works from being published - and how to fix them for publishing success. By Patrika Vaughn, Publisher and Author's Advocate.

Diagnostic & Therapeutic Radiologic Procedures for the Intensive Care Patient: Pre- & Postoperative Care Panel Discussion. Moderated by Frank R. Lewis, Jr. 2 cass. (Spring Sessions Ser.: SP-7). 1986. 19.00 (8678) Am Coll Surgeons.

Diagnostic Modalities in Extracranial Vascular Disease. 3 cass. (Neurological Surgery Ser.: C85-NS1). 1985. 15.00 (8566) Am Coll Surgeons.

Diagnostic Testing. Steve Alexander, Jr. & Richard Leavitt. (AIDS: The National Conference for Practitioners). 1986. 9.00 (978-0-932491-57-2(X)) Res Appl Inc.

Diagnostic Utilization of MRI & CT in Orthopaedic Surgery. Moderated by James A. Nunley, 2nd. 3 cass. (Orthopaedic Surgery Ser.: OR-3). 1986. 28.50 (8653) Am Coll Surgeons.

Diagnostic Wisdom & Therapeutic Skills. unabr. ed. Yeshi Donden. 7 cass. 56.00 (OC12W) Sound Horizons AV.

Dial M for Mantra. Contrib. by Rara Avis & Shaman's Dream. (Running Time: 3600 sec.). 2007. audio compact disk 17.98 (978-1-59179-610-7(5)) Sounds True.

Dialectics of Flight see Twentieth-Century Poetry in English, No. 25, Records of Poets Reading Their Own Poetry

Dialoghi Simpatici. Carlo Graziano. 1 cass. (ITA.). (J). (gr. 7-10). 15.00 (978-0-8442-8034-9(8), Natl Textbk Co) M-H Contemporary.
For beginning students. Brief, humorous dialogues. 30 dialogues are presented in Italian, with a vocabulary of high-frequency words & expressions, tailored to meet the needs of beginners.

Dialogos Simpaticos. Anthony J. DeNapoli. 1 cass. (SPA.). 15.00 (978-0-8442-7563-5(8), Natl Textbk Co) M-H Contemporary.
Helps build listening comprehension, model correct pronunciation & expose students to real-life interactions that demonstrate Spanish at work.

Dialogs in French. ed. 3 CDs. (Running Time: 2 hrs. 25 mins.). (FRE.). 2005. audio compact disk 49.95 (978-1-57970-348-6(8), SFR260D, Audio-For) J Norton Pubs.
Short conversations recorded live in France in their natural background - a market, a park, a study, wherever the native speakers happen to be. Speakers vary in accent, age, social class, and profession. A wide range of topics is discussed, including daily life in Paris. These dialogs help learners assimilate intonation patterns, vocabulary, and idiomatic expressions. Intermediate/advanced level. Accompanying booklets provide bilingual notes. Reissue in CD format of original audio cassette version.

Dialogs in French: (Intermediate - Advance Level), unabr. ed. 3 cass. (Running Time: 3 hrs.). 1994. 49.95 (978-0-88432-523-9(7), SFR260) J Norton Pubs.
Short conversations recorded live in France in their natural background: a market, a park, a study, wherever the native speakers happen to be. A wide range of topics is discussed. Includes bilingual notes.

Dialogue. unabr. ed. J. Krishnamurti & Swami Venkatesananda. 1 cass. (Running Time: 1 hr. 18 min.). 1969. 11.00 (09501) Big Sur Tapes.
Posed are answers to questions such as: Can a guru dispel the darkness in others? How do I know when I've "found it" or that "it" is the truth? Can practice bring enlightenment? How can the individual realize he is the collective.

Dialogue among Young Drug Offenders. unabr. ed. William Schweiker. 1 cass. (Running Time: 55 min.). 12.95 (35008) J Norton Pubs.
A dialogue among seven imprisoned users aged 17 to 22. Relates their personal opinions as the antecedents of drug abuse, increasing involvement & consequences for both the individual & society.

Dialogue for Human Survival. Comment by Ram Dass & Daniel Ellsberg. (Running Time: 58 min.). 1987. Original Face.
Addresses such questions as these: Who are the war-makers? What motivates them? What can change them?.

***Dialogue House Concept.** Ira Progoff. 2010. audio compact disk 15.00 (978-1-935859-13-0(7)) Dialogue Assoc.

***Dialogue House Experience.** Ira Progoff. 2010. audio compact disk 15.00 (978-1-935859-03-1(X)) Dialogue Assoc.

Dialogue of Self & Soul see Dylan Thomas Reads the Poetry of W. B. Yeats & Others

Dialogue of Self & Soul see Poetry of William Butler Yeats

Dialogue of St. Catherine of Sienna. 10 cass. 39.95 (911) Ignatius Pr.
Dictated by St. Catherine while in ecstasy.

Dialogue on the Control of Human Behavior. unabr. ed. Carl Ransom Rogers & B. F. Skinner. Ed. by Gerald Gladstein. 6 cass. pap. bk. 49.50 (978-0-88432-028-9(6), S29244) J Norton Pubs.
The full version of the famous two-day confrontation between Rogers & Skinner.

Dialogue on Thinking, Feeling & Learning. Carl Ransom Rogers & Gregory Bateson. 1 cass. (Running Time: 1 hr. 23 min.). 1975. 11.00 (02204) Big Sur Tapes.

Dialogue with Jack Kerouac & Afterthoughts. Interview. Interview with Jack Kerouac. 1 cass. (Running Time: 1 hr.). 9.95 Ithaca Pr MA.
Writer, Jack Kerouac, is interviewed by his biographer Professor Charles Jarvis as well as James Curtis. The interview is followed by a commentary by Jarvis, a Professor of English at the University of Massachusetts.

Dialogue with Jack Kerouac & Afterthoughts. Perf. by Jack Kerouac. Interview with Charles E. Jarvis & James T. Curtis. 1 cass. (Running Time: 1 hr.). 1986. pap. bk. 14.95; 9.95 Ithaca Pr MA.
An Interview with Jack Kerouac, Famous Writer of the Beat Generation. Also, a Critical Commentary by Professor Charles E. Jarvis of the University of Massachusetts.

Dialogue with Marxism. Thomas Merton. 1 cass. (Running Time: 60 min.). (Marxism Ser.). 8.95 (AA2234) Credence Commun.
Discussion of what Marxism has to offer & why it is so inadequate compared to real Christianity.

Dialogue with Oneself. J. Krishnamurti. Read by J. Krishnamurti. 1 cass. (Running Time: 90 min.). 8.50 (ABQ771) Krishnamurti.
At the Brockwood Park gathering in 1977, Krishnamurti "discusses" with himself what a human being sees in the mirror of daily relationship.

Dialogues. unabr. ed. Vivekananda. Read by John Batiste & Alan Arkin. 1 cass. (Running Time: 42 min.). 1990. 7.95 (978-1-882915-10-1(0)) Vedanta Ctr Atlanta.
Selections on various religious topics discussed by Vivekananda with one of his disciples.

Dialogues & Idioms Vol. 1: For Korean Students Learning English. Ronald J. Seiber. 2000. pap. bk. 8.99 (978-0-615-11634-1(5)) Goliard.

Dialogues & Idioms Vol. 1: For Korean Students Learning English. Ronald J. Seiber. 2001. pap. bk. 8.99 (978-0-615-11635-8(3)) Goliard.

Dialogues de Betes. Sidonie-Gabrielle Colette. Read by C. Sauvage. 1 cass. (FRE.). 1995. 16.95 (1647-DI) Olivia & Hill.
Dialogues between Toby, the dog & Kiki, the cat. They talk with humor & tenderness about their masters on "two legs.".

Dialogues in Dermatology: The Monthly Audiojournal of Dermatology. 1 cass. per month. 130.00 1 yr. subscription. Am Acad Dermatology.
Yearly subscriptions beginning either April or October provide you with monthly information for clinical dermatologists. New diagnostic, therapeutic approaches & practice issues are discussed in an interview format. Three to five different topics are discussed each month.

Dialogues of Plato. unabr. ed. Plato. Read by Pat Bottino. Tr. by Benjamin Jowett. 4 cass. (Running Time: 5 hrs. 30 mins.). 1995. 32.95 (978-0-7861-0857-2(6), 1655) Blckstn Audio.
Plato's Dialogues (427-347 B.C.) rank with the writings of Aristotle as the most important & influential philosophical works in Western thought. In them Plato cast his teacher Socrates as the central disputant in colloquies that brilliantly probe a vast spectrum of philosophical ideas & issues.

Diamant du Rio Verde. unabr. ed. Dan Dastier. Read by Sebastian Lazennec. 2007. 69.99 (978-2-35569-051-8(0)) Find a World.

Diamond. 2005. 72.95 (978-0-7861-4354-2(1)) Blckstn Audio.

Diamond. Julie Baumgold. Read by Simon Vance. (Running Time: 48600 sec.). 2005. audio compact disk 90.00 (978-0-7861-7493-5(5)) Blckstn Audio.

Diamond. unabr. ed. Julie Baumgold. Read by Simon Vance. 9 cass. (Running Time: 48600 sec.). 2005. 29.95 (978-0-7861-3537-0(9), E3509); audio compact disk 29.95 (978-0-7861-7787-5(X), ZE3509); audio compact disk 29.95 (978-0-7861-8008-0(0), ZM3509) Blckstn Audio.

Diamond & Other New Carbon Materials IV. Ed. by P. Vincenzini & E. Cappelli. (Advances in Science & Technology Ser.: Vol. 48). audio compact disk 113.00 (978-3-908158-04-2(4)) Trans T Pub CHE.

Diamond Approach: A Path of Inner Discovery. A. H. Almaas. 2009. audio compact disk 69.95 (978-1-59179-733-3(0)) Sounds True.

Diamond As Big As the Ritz & Other Stories: Bernice Bobs Her Hair; the Ice Palace; May Day; the Bowl. unabr. ed. F. Scott Fitzgerald. Read by Vincent Marzello. 6 cass. (Running Time: 9 hrs.). 2000. 49.95 (CAB 106) Pub: Chivers Audio Bks GBR. Dist(s): AudioGO
John T. Unger attends St. Midas's School, the most exclusive boy's preparatory school in the world. He likes rich people and is fascinated with wealth. Then Percy Washington joins the school, and John finds that he has never known real wealth. For Percy's father owns a diamond that is literally bigger than the Ritz-Carlton Hotel!.

Diamond Cat. unabr. ed. Marian Babson. Narrated by Juanita McMahon. 5 cass. (Running Time: 6 hrs. 45 mins.). 2000. 46.00 (978-1-84197-067-7(0), H1064E7) Recorded Bks.
Life with her mother is never ideal, but this particular weekend, Bettina finds it far worse than usual. When her mother, enraged, lets the cats out, Bettina finds them near a dead carrier pigeon, which is carrying a wealth of diamonds in its messenger tube. A newspaper article about local police thefts has Bettina vacillating about what to do, completely forgetting the owner may want to find the gems. Further problems arise when some shady characters do appear & one of the cats swallowed a diamond.

Diamond Dogs. unabr. ed. Alan Watt. Read by Matthew Powell. 4 cass. (Running Time: 5 hrs.). 2000. 24.95 (978-1-58788-071-1(7), 1587880717, BAU) Brilliance Audio.

Diamond Dogs. unabr. ed. Alan Watt. Read by Matthew Powell. (Running Time: 5 hrs.). 2004. 39.25 (978-1-59600-510-5(6), 1596005106, BADLE); 24.95 (978-1-59600-509-9(2), 1596005092, BAD); 39.25 (978-1-59600-508-2(4), 1596005084, Brinc Audio MP3 Lib); 24.95 (978-1-59600-507-5(6), 1596005076, Brilliance MP3) Brilliance Audio.
Neil Garvin is a seventeen year old living in a small town outside Las Vegas; abandoned by his mother when he was three, he blames his abusive father - who is the local sheriff - for driving her away. The quarterback of the high school football team, Neil is good looking, popular, and as cruel to his peers as his father is to him. He plans to get out of town on his "million dollar arm," until the night he accidentally commits a terrible crime, which his father, unasked, covers up for him. As the FBI arrives and begins to circle, Neil and his father become locked in a confrontation that will break them apart - and set them free.

Diamond Dust. unabr. ed. Peter Lovesey. Read by Steve Hodson. 10 cass. (Running Time: 15 hrs.). (Peter Diamond Mystery Ser.). 2002. 84.95 (978-0-7540-0877-4(0)) Pub: Chivers Audio Bks GBR. Dist(s): AudioGO

Diamond Eyes Readalong. Prescott Hill. 1 cass. (Running Time: 1 hr.). (Ten-Minute Thrillers Ser.). (YA). (gr. 6-12). 1995. pap. bk. 12.95 (978-0-7854-1076-8(7), 40807) Am Guidance.

Diamond Hunters. unabr. ed. Wilbur Smith. Read by Roy Marsden. 6 cass. (Running Time: 9 hrs.). (Ballantyne Novel Ser.). 2000. 49.95 (978-0-7451-6294-2(0), CAB 053) Pub: Chivers Audio Bks GBR. Dist(s): AudioGO
"Benedict will hound you and bring the company down!" In an unreasoning passion of hatred, old man Van Der Byl lashed out at Johnny. Dying, he rasped out his bitterness that his son Benedict could never equal Johnny's brilliance and success in the Van Der Byl Diamond Company. And now, by the terms in his Will, he sets the stage for a struggle that can only resolve in destruction for one of them.

Diamond Hunters. unabr. collector's ed. Wilbur Smith. Read by Richard Brown. 6 cass. (Running Time: 9 hrs.). (Ballantyne Novels Ser.). 1989. 48.00 (978-0-7366-1569-3(5), 2436) Books on Tape.
What power remains to a dying man? What act can he commission that will live on after him? There is an obvious answer: his will. When we meet Van der Byl, he is so consumed with hatred & bitterness that we think he is dying of those two complaints. But no matter the cause, the illness is fatal. And at stake is more than his life...there is the Van der Byl Diamond Company & two contestants for it, Van der Byl's son Benedict or his rival, Johnny Lance. But between them is Tracey, Benedict's sister, whose childhood devotion to Johnny is growing into love; & Ruby, Johnny's wife, whose personal ambition is a deadly force.

Diamond in the Rough - With the Hug Bug. Perf. by Charlotte Diamond. 1 cass. (J). (C0318) NewSound.

Diamond in the Ruff. Emily Carmichael. Narrated by Barbara Rosenblat. 8 cass. (Running Time: 11 hrs. 45 mins.). 74.00 (978-1-4025-0952-0(9)) Recorded Bks.

Diamond in Your Pocket: Discovering Your True Radiance. Gangaji. 5 CDs. (Running Time: 23100 sec.). 2007. audio compact disk 29.95 (978-1-59179-553-7(2), AW01114D) Sounds True.

Diamond Lens. Fitz James O'Brien. 1 cass. 11.95 (978-1-56268-003-9(X)); 14.95 CD. Spencer Library.
Fitz-James O'Brien, considered heir apparent to the Poe legacy of strange storytelling, was able to publish only a few works before a Civil War bullet cut short his life & robbed us all of stories from a fantastic mind. A tale of science, murder & obsessive love, "The Diamond Lens" is considered his best writing.

Diamond Necklace see De Maupassant Short Stories

Diamond Necklace. 2 cass. (Running Time: 3 hrs.). (SmartReader Ser.). (J). 1999. pap. bk. & tchr. ed. 19.95 (978-0-7887-2853-2(9), 79670T3) Recorded Bks.
When Matilda's husband comes home with an invitation to a wonderful party, she cries. She is ashamed to be seen in her old dress. Step back to 1800s France & discover how she solves her problem.

Diamond Necklace. Guy de Maupassant. 10.00 (LSS1127) Esstee Audios.

Diamond Necklace & Other Stories. unabr. ed. Short Stories. Guy de Maupassant. Narrated by George Guidall. 3 cass. (Running Time: 4 hrs. 30 mins.). 1995. 26.00 (978-0-7887-0162-7(2), 94387E7) Recorded Bks.
Includes: "Boule de Suif"; "The Piece of String"; "Beside Schopenhauer's Corpse"; "Mademoiselle Fifi"; "Miss Harriet" & "The Legend of Mont St. Michel".

Diamond of Darkhold. unabr. ed. Jeanne DuPrau. Read by Katherine Kellgren. (Books of Ember Ser.: Bk. 4). (ENG.). (J). (gr. 5). 2008. audio compact disk 34.00 (978-0-7393-6818-3(4), Listening Lib) Pub: Random Audio Pubg. Dist(s): Random

Diamond of Darkhold: The Fourth Book of Ember. unabr. ed. Jeanne DuPrau. Read by Katherine Kellgren. 6 CDs. (Running Time: 6 hrs. 30 mins.). (J). (gr. 4-7). 2008. audio compact disk 50.00 (978-0-7393-6812-1(5), Listening Lib) Pub: Random Audio Pubg. Dist(s): Random

***Diamond Ruby: A Novel.** unabr. ed. Joseph Wallace. Read by Lorna Raver. (Running Time: 16 hrs.). 2010. 29.95 (978-1-4417-6316-7(3)); 89.95 (978-1-4417-6313-6(9)); audio compact disk 118.00 (978-1-4417-6314-3(7)); audio compact disk 32.95 (978-1-4417-6315-0(5)) Blckstn Audio.

Diamond Way. unabr. ed. Alan Watts. 1 cass. (Running Time: 1hr.). 1969. 11.00 (02506) Big Sur Tapes.
Speaks of the relationship of certain Buddhist principles to contemporary problems & explores what the Tibetan Lamas have to offer us in the West.

***Diamond Willow.** unabr. ed. Helen Frost. 2 cass. (Running Time: 2 hrs.). (YA). (gr. 5-8). 2009. 25.75 (978-1-4361-9613-0(2)); 25.75 (978-1-4361-9617-8(5)) Recorded Bks.

Diamonds & Danger, Set. Lynn Gardner. 2 cass. 1997. 11.98 Set. (978-1-57734-109-3(0), 07001509) Covenant Comms.
A nail-biting romantic sequel to "Pearls & Peril".

Diamonds & Daydreams. Perf. by Charlotte Diamond. 1 cass., 1 CD. (J). (C0324) NewSound.
Eighteen thoughtful & singable songs. Includes: "Roots & Wings," "Momingtown Ride," "The Carousel," "My Favourite Things" & An Eriskay Love Lilt".

Diamonds & Dragons. Perf. by Charlotte Diamond. 1 cass., 1 CD. (J). (C0320) NewSound.

Diamonds Are A Girl's Best Friend. Jenny Colgan. 2009. 54.95 (978-0-7531-4166-3(3)); audio compact disk 79.95 (978-0-7531-4167-0(1)) Pub: Isis Pubng Ltd GBR. Dist(s): Ulverscroft US

Diamonds Are Forever. Ian Fleming. Read by Robert Whitfield. (Running Time: 6 hrs. 30 mins.). 2000. 27.95 (978-1-59912-470-4(X)) Iofy Corp.

Diamonds Are Forever. unabr. ed. Ian Fleming. Read by David Rintoul. 6 cass. (Running Time: 7 hrs. 10 min.). (James Bond Ser.). 1990. 54.95 set. (978-0-7451-5928-7(1), CAB 511) AudioGO.
A major diamond-smuggling network runs from Sierra Leone to England to New York State, & its James Bond's mission to eliminate it. The Spangled Mob throws numerous lethal obstacles in his way, & Bond has his work cut out for him. Luckily, he also has the indispensable assistance of Tiffany Case.

Diamonds Are Forever. unabr. ed. Ian Fleming. Read by Robert Whitfield. 5 cass. (Running Time: 7 hrs.). (James Bond Ser.). 2001. 39.95 (978-0-7861-1941-7(1), 2712); audio compact disk 48.00 (978-0-7861-9779-8(X), 2712) Blckstn Audio.
African diamonds are being smuggled into the United States via London & it's up to the British Secret Service to infiltrate the organized crime families in America & destroy the smugglers.

Diamonds Are Forever. unabr. ed. Ian Fleming. Read by Simon Vance. (Running Time: 7 hrs. 0 mins.). 2009. audio compact disk 19.95 (978-1-4332-5855-8(2)) Blckstn Audio.

Diamonds in Danby Walk. Pamela Evans. (Soundings (CDs) Ser.). (J). 2006. audio compact disk 99.95 (978-1-84559-365-0(0)) Pub: ISIS Lrg Prnt GBR. Dist(s): Ulverscroft US

Diamonds in Danby Walk. unabr. ed. Pamela Evans. Read by Annie Aldington. 12 cass. (Running Time: 16 hrs.). 2000. 94.95 (978-1-86042-766-4(9), 27669) Pub: Soundings Ltd GBR. Dist(s): Ulverscroft US

Diamonds in the Dust: 365 Sparkling Devotions. abr. ed. Joni Eareckson Tada. 2 cass. (Running Time: 60 min.). 1993. 14.99 (978-0-310-37958-4(X)) Zondervan.
Condensed version of the book.

Diamonds in the Dust: 6 Sparkling Devotions. abr. ed. Joni Eareckson Tada. (Running Time: 2 hrs. 30 mins. 0 sec.). (ENG.). 2003. 16.99 (978-0-310-26028-8(0)) Zondervan.

Dian & the Gorillas: 1,000 Headwords. Norma Shapiro. (Dominoes Ser.). 2003. 19.50 (978-0-19-424421-3(0)) OUP.

Diana: A Dedication in Seven Ages. unabr. ed. Poems. Ed. by David Owen. 2 CDs. (Running Time: 2 hrs. 34 min.). (YA). 1998. audio compact disk 15.98 (978-962-634-157-5(2), 215712, Naxos AudioBooks) Naxos.
Tribute to Diana, Princess of Wales is an anthology of 120 poems read by 40 leading actors, enhanced with music. Works by Kipling, Lear, Hood, Blake, Coleridge, Eliot, Shakespeare & many others are included.

Diana Chronicles. abr. ed. Tina Brown. Read by Tina Brown. 5 CDs. (Running Time: 19800 sec.). (ENG.). 2007. audio compact disk 29.95 (978-0-7393-4347-0(5), Random AudioBks) Pub: Random Audio Pubg. Dist(s): Random

Diana Chronicles. unabr. ed. Tina Brown. Read by Rosalyn Landor. 17 CDs. (Running Time: 21 hrs.). 2007. audio compact disk 110.00 (978-1-4159-3890-4(3)) Books on Tape.

Diana her new Life. Andrew Morton. Read by Lynn Redgrave. 2004. 7.95 (978-0-7435-4649-2(0)) Pub: S&S Audio. Dist(s): S and S Inc

Diana; her true Story: Her True Story. Andrew Morton. Read by Stephanie Beacham. 2004. 7.95 (978-0-7435-4650-8(4)) Pub: S&S Audio. Dist(s): S and S Inc

Diana of the Crossways. George Meredith. Read by Anais 9000. 2008. 33.95 (978-1-60112-063-2(X)) Babblebooks.

Diana of the Crossways, Set. unabr. ed. George Meredith. Read by Flo Gibson. 10 cass. (Running Time: 13 hrs.). 1998. bk. 44.95 (978-1-55685-541-2(9)) Audio Bk Con.
After an unhappy marriage, watch the beautiful & witty Diana, as she is pursued by a trail of suitors. Her sparkling repartee & occasional passages of the author's intellectualized philosophy give this novel unusual depth.

Diana O'Hehir: Interview with Diana O'Hehir & Kay Bonetti. 1 cass. (Running Time: 47 min.). 13.95 (978-1-55644-352-7(8), 10022) Am Audio Prose.
The author discusses how her personal experiences influence her writing.

***Diana Palmer CD Collection: Fearless, Heartless.** abr. ed. Diana Palmer. Read by Phil Gigante. (Running Time: 10 hrs.). 2010. audio compact disk 19.99 (978-1-4418-6162-7(9), 9781441861627, BACD) Brilliance Audio.

Diana, Princess of Wales Tribute. 2 cass., 2 CD. 15.98 Blisterpack, double. (CBS 69012); audio compact disk 19.98 CD Jewel box, double. (CBS 69012) NewSound.

Diana's Boys: William & Harry & the Mother They Loved. abr. ed. Christopher Andersen. Read by Derek Partridge. 2 cass. (Running Time: 3 hrs.). 2001. 18.95 HighBridge.

Diane Ferlatte Favorite Stories. Short Stories. 1 cassette. (Running Time: 57 minutes). (J). 1991. 10.00 (978-0-9760432-1-8(1)) D Ferlatte.

Diane Glancy. unabr. ed. Ed. by Jim McKinley. Prod. by Rebekah Presson. 1 cass. (Running Time: 29 min.). (New Letters on the Air Ser.). 1994. 10.00 (121393) New Letters.
Glancy's recent book of "essays" (which are really prose poems) won the American Book Award, given by the Before Columbus Foundation & the first North American Indian Prose Award. Glancy reads from the book, "Claiming Breath" & from other books of poetry & talks about drawing inspiration from her mixed-blood heritage.

Diane Johnson. Interview. Interview with Diane Johnson. 1 cass. (Running Time: 1 hr.). 13.95 (978-1-55644-017-5(0), 1092) Am Audio Prose.
Johnson discusses her use of the "thriller" form, the state of the American novel, & the varied aspects of sexism in publishing & criticism.

Diane Johnson. unabr. ed. Diane Johnson. Read by Diane Johnson. 1 cass. (Running Time: 29 min.). 1989. 10.00 New Letters.
Johnson reads from the novel Health & Happiness & is interviewed.

Diane Schuur. Read by Diane Schuur. 1 cass. (Running Time: 60 min.). (Marian McPartland's Piano Jazz Ser.). 13.95 (MM-87-04-16, HarperThor) HarpC GBR.

Diane Wakoski, Pts. 1 & 11. unabr. ed. Read by Diane Wakoski. 2 cass. (Running Time: 29 min. per cass.). 1985. 10.00 ea. One-sided cass.; 18.00 Two-sided cass. New Letters.
In one reading Diane Wakoski includes poems from "Motorcycle Betrayal Poems." The second program presents work from "The Magician's Feast Letter" & "The Rings of Saturn".

Diane's Point of View Vol. 1: A Doggerel Life Poem. Poems. Read by Sylvia Lackore. Perf. by Mogul Sound staff. 2 cass. (Running Time: 1 hrs. 30 min.). 1997. bk. 19.95 Set. (978-1-891421-01-3(8), DCLP) Diagnostic Ctr.
Based on 20 years of research & hundreds of self-help books (& textbooks) on the subject of identity read by the outhor in the process of forming the poem in a humorous doggeral format. Presented in the female perspective.

Dianetica: La Ciencia Moderna de la Salud Mental. L. Ron Hubbard. (Running Time: 20 hrs. 40 mins. 0 sec.).Tr. of Dianetics: The Modern Science of Mental Health. (SPA.). 2007. audio compact disk 35.00 (978-1-4031-5688-4(3)) Bridge Pubns Inc.

Dianetica: La Evolucion de una Ciencia. L. Ron Hubbard. (Running Time: 2 hrs. 32 mins. 0 sec.). (SPA.). 2007. audio compact disk 20.00 (978-1-4031-5538-2(0)) Bridge Pubns Inc.

Dianetica: La Tesis Original. L. Ron Hubbard. (Running Time: 3 hrs. 57 mins. 0 sec.). (SPA.). 2007. audio compact disk 20.00 (978-1-4031-5673-0(5)) Bridge Pubns Inc.

Dianetics: An Education in Yourself. L. Ron Hubbard. 1992. 10.99 (978-0-88404-683-7(4)) Bridge Pubns Inc.

Dianetics: Lectures & Demonstrations. unabr. ed. Narrated by L. Ron Hubbard. 4 cass. (Running Time: 4 hrs. 21 mins.). 24.99 (978-1-4031-0908-8(7)); audio compact disk 29.95 (978-1-4031-0892-0(7)) Bridge Pubns Inc.

***Dianetics: The Evolution of a Science.** L. Ron Hubbard. (HUN.). 2007. audio compact disk 20.00 (978-1-4031-5531-3(3)); audio compact disk 20.00 (978-1-4031-5525-2(9)); audio compact disk 20.00 (978-1-4031-5533-7(X)); audio compact disk 20.00 (978-1-4031-5534-4(8)); audio compact disk 20.00 (978-1-4031-5527-6(5)); audio compact disk 20.00 (978-1-4031-5536-8(4)); audio compact disk 20.00 (978-1-4031-5526-9(7)); audio compact disk 20.00 (978-1-4031-5539-9(9)); audio compact disk 20.00 (978-1-4031-5535-1(6)); audio compact disk 20.00 (978-1-4031-5692-1(1)); audio compact disk 20.00 (978-1-4031-5537-5(2)); audio compact disk 20.00 (978-1-4031-5530-6(5)); audio compact disk 20.00 (978-1-4031-5532-0(1)); audio compact disk 20.00 (978-1-4031-5529-0(1)); audio compact disk 20.00 (978-1-4031-5528-3(3)) Bridge Pubns Inc.

***Dianetics: The Evolution of a Science.** L. Ron Hubbard. (GER.). 2008. 14.00 (978-1-4031-5875-8(4)); 14.00 (978-1-4031-5877-2(0)); 14.00 (978-1-4031-5873-4(8)); 14.00 (978-1-4031-5872-7(X)); 14.00 (978-1-4031-5876-5(2)); 14.00 (978-1-4031-5874-1(6)) Bridge Pubns Inc.

***Dianetics: The Evolution of a Science.** L. Ron Hubbard. 2010. audio compact disk 20.00 (978-1-4031-6885-6(7)); audio compact disk 35.00 (978-1-4031-6880-1(6)); audio compact disk 20.00 (978-1-4031-6873-3(3)); audio compact disk 20.00 (978-1-4031-6879-5(2)); audio compact disk 20.00 (978-1-4031-6882-5(2)); audio compact disk 20.00 (978-1-4031-6865-8(2)); audio compact disk 20.00 (978-1-4031-6886-3(5)); audio compact disk 20.00 (978-1-4031-6872-6(5)); audio compact disk 20.00 (978-1-4031-6875-7(X)); audio compact disk 20.00 (978-1-4031-6878-8(4)); audio compact disk 20.00 (978-1-4031-6881-8(4)); audio compact disk 20.00 (978-1-4031-6883-2(0)); audio compact disk 20.00 (978-1-4031-6877-1(6)); audio compact disk 20.00 (978-1-4031-6884-9(9)); audio compact disk 20.00 (978-1-4031-6876-4(8)); audio compact disk 20.00 (978-1-4031-6874-0(1)) Bridge Pubns Inc.

Dianetics: The Evolution of a Science. abr. ed. L. Ron Hubbard. Read by Lloyd Sherr. (Running Time: 3 hrs. 58 mins. 0 sec.). (ENG.). 2007. audio compact disk 20.00 (978-1-4031-5524-5(0)) Bridge Pubns Inc.

Dianetics: The Evolution of a Science. unabr. ed. L. Ron Hubbard. Read by Lloyd Sherr. 2 cass. (Running Time: 2 hrs.). 2002. 17.95 (978-1-4031-0545-5(6)) Bridge Pubns Inc.

***Dianetics: The Modern Science of Mental Health.** L. Ron Hubbard. (DAN.). 2007. audio compact disk 35.00 (978-1-4031-5675-4(1)); audio compact disk 35.00 (978-1-4031-5681-5(6)); audio compact disk 35.00 (978-1-4031-5684-6(0)); audio compact disk 35.00 (978-1-4031-5683-9(2)); audio compact disk 35.00 (978-1-4031-5690-7(5)); audio compact disk 35.00 (978-1-4031-5689-1(1)); audio compact disk 35.00 (978-1-4031-5680-8(8)); audio compact disk 35.00 (978-1-4031-5682-2(4)); audio compact disk 35.00 (978-1-4031-5677-8(8)); audio compact disk 35.00 (978-1-4031-5687-7(5)); audio compact disk 35.00 (978-1-4031-5679-2(4)); audio compact disk 35.00 (978-1-4031-5685-3(9)); audio compact disk 35.00 (978-1-4031-5676-1(X)); audio compact disk 35.00 (978-1-4031-5686-0(7)); audio compact disk 35.00 (978-1-4031-5678-5(6)) Bridge Pubns Inc.

***Dianetics: The Modern Science of Mental Health.** L. Ron Hubbard. (ITA.). 2008. 21.00 (978-1-4031-5846-8(0)); 21.00 (978-1-4031-5847-5(9)); 21.00 (978-1-4031-5845-1(2)); 21.00 (978-1-4031-5843-7(6)); 21.00 (978-1-4031-5844-4(4)); 21.00 (978-1-4031-5842-0(8)) Bridge Pubns Inc.

***Dianetics: The Modern Science of Mental Health.** L. Ron Hubbard. 2010. audio compact disk 35.00 (978-1-4031-6915-0(2)); audio compact disk 35.00 (978-1-4031-6904-4(7)); audio compact disk 35.00 (978-1-4031-6907-5(1)); audio compact disk 35.00 (978-1-4031-6912-9(8)); audio compact disk 35.00 (978-1-4031-6906-8(3)); audio compact disk 35.00 (978-1-4031-6903-7(9)); audio compact disk 35.00 (978-1-4031-6917-4(9)); audio compact disk 35.00 (978-1-4031-6914-3(4)); audio compact disk 35.00 (978-1-4031-6911-2(X)); audio compact disk 35.00 (978-1-4031-6905-1(5)); audio compact disk 35.00 (978-1-4031-6909-9(8)); audio compact disk 35.00 (978-1-4031-6913-6(6)); audio compact disk 35.00 (978-1-4031-6910-5(1)); audio compact disk 35.00 (978-1-4031-6916-7(0)); audio compact disk 35.00 (978-1-4031-6867-2(9)); audio compact disk 35.00 (978-1-4031-6908-2(X)) Bridge Pubns Inc.

Dianetics: The Modern Science of Mental Health. L. Ron Hubbard. (Running Time: 17 hrs. 30 mins. 0 sec.). (ENG.). 2007. audio compact disk 35.00 (978-1-4031-5542-9(9)) Bridge Pubns Inc.

Dianetics: The Modern Science of Mental Health. abr. ed. L. Ron Hubbard. Read by Lloyd Sherr. 5 cass. (Running Time: 7 hrs. 15 mins.). 2002. 29.95 (978-1-4031-0539-4(1)) Bridge Pubns Inc.

***Dianetics: The Original Thesis.** L. Ron Hubbard. (ITA.). 2007. audio compact disk 20.00 (978-1-4031-5667-9(0)); audio compact disk 20.00 (978-1-4031-5691-4(3)); audio compact disk 20.00 (978-1-4031-5660-0(3)); audio compact disk 20.00 (978-1-4031-5663-1(8)); audio compact disk 20.00 (978-1-4031-5664-8(6)); audio compact disk 20.00 (978-1-4031-5661-7(1)); audio compact disk 20.00 (978-1-4031-5669-3(7)); audio compact disk 20.00 (978-1-4031-5665-5(4)); audio compact disk 20.00 (978-1-4031-5672-3(7)); audio compact disk 20.00 (978-1-4031-5666-2(2)); audio compact disk 20.00 (978-1-4031-5668-6(9)); audio compact disk 20.00 (978-1-4031-5671-6(9)); audio compact disk 20.00 (978-1-4031-5662-4(X)); audio compact disk 20.00 (978-1-4031-5674-7(3)); audio compact disk 20.00 (978-1-4031-5670-9(0)) Bridge Pubns Inc.

***Dianetics: The Original Thesis.** L. Ron Hubbard. (JPN.). 2008. 14.00 (978-1-4031-5883-3(5)); 14.00 (978-1-4031-5878-9(9)); 14.00 (978-1-4031-5879-6(7)); 14.00 (978-1-4031-5880-2(0)); 14.00 (978-1-4031-5882-6(7)); 14.00 (978-1-4031-5881-9(9)) Bridge Pubns Inc.

***Dianetics: The Original Thesis.** L. Ron Hubbard. (HUN.). 2010. audio compact disk 35.00 (978-1-4031-6894-8(6)); audio compact disk 20.00 (978-1-4031-6888-7(1)); audio compact disk 20.00 (978-1-4031-6891-7(1)); audio compact disk 20.00 (978-1-4031-6887-0(3)); audio compact disk 20.00 (978-1-4031-6899-3(7)); audio compact disk 20.00 (978-1-4031-6901-3(2)); audio compact disk 20.00 (978-1-4031-6889-4(X)); audio compact disk 20.00 (978-1-4031-6902-0(0)); audio compact disk 20.00 (978-1-4031-6892-4(X)); audio compact disk 20.00 (978-1-4031-6898-6(9)); audio compact disk 20.00 (978-1-4031-6895-5(4)); audio compact disk 20.00 (978-1-4031-6897-9(0)); audio compact disk 20.00 (978-1-4031-6866-5(0)); audio compact disk 20.00 (978-1-4031-6896-2(2)); audio compact disk 20.00 (978-1-4031-6900-6(4)); audio compact disk 20.00 (978-1-4031-6890-0(3)) Bridge Pubns Inc.

Dianetics: The Original Thesis. L. Ron Hubbard. Read by Lloyd Sherr. (Running Time: 2 hrs. 4 mins. 0 sec.). (ENG.). 2007. audio compact disk 20.00 (978-1-4031-5543-6(7)) Bridge Pubns Inc.

Dianetics: The Modern Science of Mental Health see Dianetica: La Ciencia Moderna de la Salud Mental

Diaper Gym. 1 cass. (Running Time: 1 hr.). (J). (ps). 2001. pap. bk. 10.95 (KIM 9096C); pap. bk. 14.95 (KIM 9096CD); pap. bk. & pupil's gde. ed. 11.95 (KIM 9096) Kimbo Educ.
Fun-filled songs & nursery rhymes encourage the development of a baby's sitting, crawling, pulling up & walking skills. Wiggles & Giggles, Ten Little Indians, How Big Is Baby?, Farmer in the Dell, Pat a Cake & more. Includes guide.

Diaries of Adam & Eve. Mark Twain. 1 cass. (Running Time: 1 hr. 10 mins.). 1999. (978-0-7588-0005-3(3)); audio compact disk (978-0-7588-0006-0(1)) Goss Commns.

Diaries of Adam & Eve. unabr. ed. Mark Twain. Read by Mandy Patinkin & Betty Buckley. Narrated by Walter Cronkite. 2 cass. (Running Time: 2 hrs. 5 min.). 1999. 18.00 (978-0-9658811-7-3(2)); audio compact disk 20.00 (978-0-9658811-6-6(4)) Pub: Fairoaks Pr. Dist(s): SCB Distributors
Twain's good humor & lyrical tendencies bring forth his imagined diaries of Adam & Eve.

Diaries, 1915-1918. unabr. ed. Siegfried Sassoon. Read by John Westbrook. 12 cass. (Running Time: 12 hrs.). 1995. 94.95 (978-1-85089-741-5(7), 89091) Pub: ISIS Audio GBR. Dist(s): Ulverscroft US
Siegfried Sassoon was almost twenty-eight when he enlisted in August of 1914. It was the terrible impact of the Western Front that turned him from a versifier into a poet. These diaries, written in tiny notebooks, sometimes in pencil, often by the light of a solitary candle in dug-out, provided the material for his first three prose books, which, along with his war poems, established his fame. They form an unforgettable picture of an appalling time by one of its greatest recorders.

Diaries 1969-1979: The Python Years. abr. ed. Michael Palin. Read by Michael Palin. 4 CDs. (Running Time: 5 hrs. 0 mins. 0 sec.). (ENG.). 2007. audio compact disk 24.95 (978-1-4272-0226-0(5)) Pub: Macmill Audio. Dist(s): Macmillan

Diario de Aurora: Vivencias de una Joven en la Revolucion. unabr. ed. Alejandro Rosas. Narrated by Irma Bello. 4 cass. (Running Time: 5 hrs.).Tr. of Aurora's Diary: A Girl's Memories of the Revolution. (SPA.). 2002. 38.00 (978-1-4025-1671-9(1)) Recorded Bks.

Diario de Clara Eugenia. Jose Manuel Villalpando Cesar. Narrated by Adriana Sananes. 4 cass. (Running Time: 5 hrs. 30 mins.). 38.00 (978-1-4025-1635-1(5)) Recorded Bks.

***Diario de un Seductor.** abr. ed. Soren Kierkegaard. Read by Santiago Munevar & Adelia Espinosa. (SPA.). 2008. audio compact disk 17.00 (978-958-8318-42-4(4)) Pub: Yoyo Music COL. Dist(s): YoYoMusic

Diary see Cambridge Treasy Burton

Diary. unabr. ed. Eileen Goudge. Read by Susan Ericksen. 5 CDs. (Running Time: 6 hrs.). (ENG.). 2009. audio compact disk 24.95 (978-1-60283-572-6(1)) Pub: AudioGO. Dist(s): Perseus Dist

Diary of a Country Priest. unabr. ed. Georges Bemanos. Read by Al Covaia. 8 cass. 32.95 set. (327) Ignatius Pr.
The New York Book Review called this novel "A book of the utmost sensitiveness & compassion ... a strange & sad, yet a beautiful & triumphant story ... a work of deep, subtle & singularly encompassing art.".

Diary of a Dirty Little War. unabr. ed. Harvey Rosenfield. Read by Ian Esmo. 10 cass. (Running Time: 14 hrs. 30 mins.). 1998. 69.95 (978-0-7861-1271-5(9), 2206) Blckstn Audio.
Diary tells of the many Americans who have not received their proper recognition for service in this conflict. Their heroism merits attention, as does the war that provided the setting for their deeds.

Diary of a Fairy Godmother. unabr. collector's ed. Esme Raji Codell. Read by Rachael Lillis & Rachael Lillis. Illus. by Rachael Lillis. 2 cass. (Running Time: 3 hrs. 26 mins.). (J). (gr. 4-7). 2005. 23.00 (978-0-8072-2367-3(0), BksonTape) Random Audio Pubg.

Diary of a Fairy Godmother. unabr. collector's ed. Read by Rachael Lillis & Rachel Lillis. Illus. by Rachael Lillis. 3 CDs. (Running Time: 3 hrs. 26 mins.). (J). (gr. 4-7). 2005. audio compact disk 30.00 (978-0-307-24540-3(3), BksonTape) Random Audio Pubg.
Hunky Dory's mother always told her, "You'll be the wickedest witch wherever the four winds blow." And why not? She's at the top of her class in charm school. She can make flowers wilt like wet spaghetti. And she can turn any prince into a frog - but she always changes him back. That's when she knows she has a problem. Hunky Dory's interest in wishcraft over witchcraft gets her kicked out of charm school. Now she's determined to follow her heart and become a fairy godmother. But how to go about doing it? She gives a woodsman a new mustache, and grants Wolf his strange wish for a grandmother costume. Finally, motivated by jealousy over her friend Rumpelstiltskin's crush on the girl in the roomful of straw, she meets the ticket to realizing her career dream - Cinderella. This fresh, funny twist on fairy tales is just right for girls who have not quite outgrown the magic of classic stories - and who are open to unconventional happily-ever-afters!.

Diary of a Fly. Doreen Cronin. Read by Harry Bliss. Illus. by Harry Bliss. 1 cass. (Running Time: 13 mins.). (J). (ps-3). 2008. bk. 25.95 (978-1-4301-0404-9(X)); bk. 28.95 (978-1-4301-0407-0(4)) Live Oak Media.

Diary of a Fly. Doreen Cronin. Narrated by Abigail Breslin. 1 CD. (Running Time: 10 mins.). (J). (ps-3). 2008. audio compact disk 12.95 (978-0-545-09447-4(X)); bk. 29.95 (978-0-545-09454-2(2)) Weston Woods.
The day-to-day existence of a little fly that wants to be a superhero and who is not afraid to dream big, really big!.

Diary of a Mad Housewife: A Novel. unabr. ed. Sue Kaufman. Read by Nancy Dannevik. 7 cass. (Running Time: 10 hrs. 30 mins.). 56.00 (978-0-7366-0277-8(1), 1267) Books on Tape.
The story of an American housewife caught in our male-oriented society. She is 36-year-old Tina Balser, mother of two lovely children, wife & helpmate of a handsome & successful husband, doyenne of a bright apartment on Central Park West. But she's not content. On the contrary, she's on the verge of madness & hysteria. She has completely lost sight of her purpose in life, & believes that only by writing a diary - her personal form of self-therapy - can she regain her sanity.

Diary of a Madhouse. abr. ed. Family Osbourne. Read by Family Osbourne. (Running Time: 43 hrs. 0 mins. 0 sec.). (ENG.). 2003. audio compact disk 30.00 (978-0-7435-2824-5(7), Audioworks) Pub: S&S Audio. Dist(s): S and S Inc

Diary of a Madhouse. abr. ed. Family Osbourne & Family Osbourne. Read by Family Osbourne. 1 cass. (Running Time: 43 hrs. 0 mins. 0 sec.). (ENG.). 2003. 25.00 (978-0-7435-2823-8(9), Audioworks) Pub: S&S Audio. Dist(s): S and S Inc

Diary of a Madman. Perf. by John Dehner. 1 cass. 10.00 (MC1017) Esstee Audios.
Radio drama.

Diary of a Madman. Nikolai Gogol. Contrib. by Stephen Ouimette. Adapted by Elliot Hayes. (Running Time: 3600 sec.). (Bank of Montreal Stratford Festival Ser.). 2007. audio compact disk 15.95 (978-0-660-19733-3(2)) Canadian Broadcasting CAN.

Diary of a Medical Intuitive: The Talk that Inspired the Book! Christel Nani. Read by Christel Nani. 1 CD. (Running Time: 78 minutes). 2003. audio compact disk 18.95 (978-0-9741450-0-6(9)) Queens Crt Pr.
In this sold-out talk in San Diego, Medical Intuitive Christel Nani recounts the story of how she discovered her profound clairvoyant gifts for identifying and healing illness, her discoveries of how the human energy system works, and the poignant and emotional journey of her own healing from a Shaman in Peru. Teaching about energetic illness, she shows the listener how to begin ending energy leaks. Her escorting of people to the other side when they die is movingly and passionately described; her description of the other side leaves no doubt in the listener?s mind about the powerful and loving presence of God.An authentic and compassionate spiritual teacher, her pinpoint accuracy in locating the traumas, decisions and emotional patterns contributing to a patient?s illness and gift for identifying the ?Priority Task? that will reverse these patterns, makes Christel widely known as ?the real thing.? [TRACKS]Introduction The Power of Tribal Beliefs Crossing Over Energetic Illness Lessons of Peru.

Diary of a Mistress. unabr. ed. Miasha. Read by Claudia Aleck. (Running Time: 8 hrs. 30 mins.). 2010. 29.95 (978-1-4417-2732-9(9)); 54.95 (978-1-4417-2728-2(0)); audio compact disk 76.00 (978-1-4417-2729-9(9)) Blckstn Audio.

Diary of a Napoleonic Foot Soldier. unabr. ed. Jakob Walter. Narrated by Patrick Tull. 3 cass. (Running Time: 4 hrs. 30 mins.). 1992. 26.00 (978-1-55690-666-4(8), 92136E7) Recorded Bks.
A survivor of Napoleon's disastrous March on Moscow recounts the invasion & retreat.

Diary of a Nobody. George Grossmith. Read by Martin Jarvis. (Running Time: 5 hrs.). 2001. 28.95 (978-1-60083-716-6(6)) Iofy Corp.

Diary of a Nobody. George Grossmith & Weedon Grossmith. Read by Alfred von Lecteur. 2009. 27.95 (978-1-60112-978-9(5)) Babblebooks.

Diary of a Nobody. unabr. ed. George Grossmith & Weedon Grossmith. Read by Frederick Davidson. 4 cass. (Running Time: 5 hrs. 30 mins.). 1992. 32.95 (978-0-7861-0309-6(4), 1271) Blckstn Audio.
This is a delightful social comedy, & listeners are certain to learn why Hilaire Belloc asserted that Pooter was "an immortal achievement".

Diary of a Nobody. unabr. ed. George Grossmith & Weedon Grossmith. Read by Martin Jarvis. 4 CDs. (Classic Literature with Classical Music Ser.). 2006. audio compact disk 28.98 (978-962-634-403-3(2), Naxos AudioBooks) Naxos.

Diary of a Nobody. unabr. ed. George Grossmith & Weedon. Read by Frederick Davidson. (Running Time: 4.5 hrs. 0 mins.). (ENG.). 2009. 19.95 (978-1-4417-0581-5(3)); audio compact disk 49.00 (978-1-4417-0578-5(3)) Blckstn Audio.

Diary of a Pilgrimage. unabr. ed. Jerome K. Jerome. Read by Peter Joyce. 3 cass. 2000. 34.95 (978-1-86015-467-6(0)) Ulverscroft US.

Diary of a Pioneer Boy/The Pioneer Way. Steck-Vaughn Staff. 1 cass. (Running Time: 90 min.). (J). 1999. (978-0-7398-0932-7(6)) SteckVau.

Diary of a Provincial Lady. unabr. ed. E. M. Delafield. Read by Judith Franklin. 5 cass. (Running Time: 4 hrs. 40 min.). 2001. 49.95 (978-1-85089-568-8(6), 91095) Pub: ISIS Audio GBR. Dist(s): Ulverscroft US
A delightful, witty & shrewd account of daily life in a Devonshire village between the wars by a provincial lady.

Diary of a Rebellious Teen: 1 Samuel 15-19. Ed Young. 1982. 4.95 (978-0-7417-1242-4(3), 242) Win Walk.

Diary of a Spider. unabr. ed. Doreen Cronin. Narrated by Angus T. Jones. Illus. by Harry Bliss. 1 CD. (Running Time: 9 mins.). (J). (ps-3). 2006. bk. 29.95 (978-0-439-90579-4(6)); bk. 24.95 (978-0-439-90573-2(7)) Weston Woods.
This is the diary of a spider who's a lot like you! He goes to school, but he also spins sticky webs and takes wind-catching lessons. From the creators of the best-selling Diary of a Worm, this portrait of an upside-down web will have kids wishing they could be spiders too!.

***Diary of a Wimpy Kid: The Ugly Truth.** Jeffrey T. Kenney. 2010. audio compact disk 19.99 (978-1-4498-4285-7(2)) Recorded Bks.

Diary of a Worm. 2004. 8.95 (978-0-7882-0542-2(0)); audio compact disk 12.95 (978-0-7882-0543-9(9)) Weston Woods.

Diary of a Worm. (J). 2004. bk. 24.95 (978-0-7882-0536-1(6)) Weston Woods.

Diary of a Worm. Doreen Cronin. Illus. by Harry Bliss. 11 vols. (Running Time: 11 mins.). pap. bk. 16.95 (978-1-59112-867-0(6)); pap. bk. (978-1-59112-869-4(2)); pap. bk. 18.95 (978-1-59112-871-7(4)); pap. bk. (978-1-59112-873-1(0)) Live Oak Media.

Diary of a Worm. Doreen Cronin. Illus. by Harry Bliss. (Running Time: 11 mins.). 2004. 9.95 (978-1-59112-866-3(8)); audio compact disk 12.95 (978-1-59112-870-0(6)) Live Oak Media.

Diary of a Worm. Doreen Cronin. Read by Harry Bliss. 11 vols. (Running Time: 11 mins.). (J). 2004. bk. 25.95 (978-1-59112-868-7(4)); bk. 28.95 (978-1-59112-872-4(2)) Pub: Live Oak Media. Dist(s): AudioGO

Diary of an Unfit Mother. abr. ed. Anne Robinson. Read by Anne Robinson. 5 CDs. (Running Time: 7.5 hrs.). 2004. audio compact disk 34.95 (978-1-59007-069-7(0)) Pub: New Millenn Enter. Dist(s): PerseuPGW

Diary of an Unfit Mother. unabr. ed. Anne Robinson. Read by Anne Robinson. 8 cass. (Running Time: 12 hrs.). 2004. 34.95 (978-1-59007-068-0(2)) Pub: New Millenn Enter. Dist(s): PerseuPGW

Diary of Anais Nin, Pts. 1 & 2. abr. ed. Anais Nin. 2 cass. (Running Time: 1 hr. 36 min.). 21.90 (978-0-8045-3043-9(2), SAC 995, SACSAC 995); 10.95 (978-0-8045-0995-4(6), SAC 995); 10.95 (978-0-8045-0996-1(4), SAC 996) Spoken Arts.
Anais Nin reads from her famous diary - events in the years 1931-1934.

Diary of Ellen Rimbauer: My Life at Rose Red. Joyce Reardon. Narrated by Alexandra O'Karma. 7 cass. (Running Time: 9 hrs. 45 mins.). 69.00 (978-1-4025-2381-6(5)); audio compact disk 78.00 (978-1-4025-2905-4(8)) Recorded Bks.

Diary of Ellen Rimbauer: My Life at Rose Red. unabr. ed. Joyce Reardon. Narrated by Alexandra O'Karma. 7 cass. (Running Time: 9 hrs. 30 min.). 2002. 37.95 (978-1-4025-2382-3(3)) Recorded Bks.
When Ellen Rimbauer's oil baron husband builds Rose Red in early 1900s Seattle, he stubbornly does so directly atop an Indian burial ground. The house itself may be a living spirit. For at Rose Red, women tend to disappear without a trace - while men have a habit of dying. Allegedly culled from Ellen's personal writings by a supposed professor of paranormal studies, The Diary of Ellen Rimbauer has become a national phenomenon.

Diary of J. G. Reeder. unabr. ed. Edgar Wallace. 4 cass. (Running Time: 5 hrs.). lib. bdg. 26.95 (978-1-55656-074-3(5)) Pub: Dercum Audio. Dist(s): APG
Edgar Wallace was one of the most prolific authors of the 20th century. In 1920s England, one out of every four books sold was written by him. The Diary of J. G. Reeder features one of Wallace's most famous investigators as he looks at the seamy side of life.

Diary of J. G. Reeder. unabr. ed. Edgar Wallace. 4 cass. (Running Time: 5 hrs.). (Mystery Library). 1997. pap. bk. 21.95 (978-1-55656-220-4(9)) Pub: Dercum Audio. Dist(s): APG
Edgar Wallace was one of the most prolific authors of the twentieth centur. He wrote nearly 200 novels, hundreds of short stories and newspaper articles, 40 plays, and directed some 25 fim versions of his books. In 1920s England, one out of every four books sold was written by Edgar Wallace. He would sit in his study for days on end, without sleep, dictating an average of 3,000 words per hour, while drinking fresh pots of heavily sweetened tea every half hour, and chain smoking cigarettes.

Diary of Samuel Marchbanks. Robertson Davies. 1 CD. (Running Time: 1 hr. 30 mins.). 2005. audio compact disk 12.95 (978-0-660-18919-2(4)) Pub: Canadian Broadcasting CAN. Dist(s): Georgetown Term

Diary of Samuel Pepys. Samuel Peys. Read by Michael Maloney. (Running Time: 4 hrs.). 2005. 28.95 (978-1-60083-724-1(7)) Iofy Corp.

Diary of Samuel Pepys. abr. ed. Samuel Pepys. 1 cass. (Running Time: 53 min.). Incl. Charles II, the Merry Monarch. (SAC 1028); Great Fire of London. (SAC 1028); 10.95 (978-0-8045-1028-8(8), SAC 1028) Spoken Arts.
John Franklyn characterizes the famous chronicles.

Diary of Samuel Pepys - Excerpts. unabr. ed. Samuel Pepys. Narrated by Alexander Spencer. 3 cass. (Running Time: 4 hrs. 15 mins.). 1991. 26.00 (978-1-55690-143-0(7), 91326E7) Recorded Bks.
Samuel Pepys was born in 1633 & lived through some of London's most momentous events, including the great plague & fire of 1665 & 1666.

Diary of Vaslav Nijinsky. unabr. ed. Vaslav Nijinsky. 6 cass. (Running Time: 9 hrs.). 2001. 32.00 (978-1-59040-102-6(6), Phoenix Audio) Pub: Amer Intl Pub. Dist(s): PerseuPGW

Diastole - Hospital Hill. unabr. ed. E. Grey Dimond. Read by E. Grey Dimond. 9 cass. (Running Time: 1 hr.). 100.00 Diastole-Hospital Hill.
Covers many phases of medicine; the current social scene, clinical pearls, historical; humor & satire.

Diastrophic Dysplasia - A Bibliography & Dictionary for Physicians, Patients, & Genome Researchers. Compiled by Icon Group International, Inc. Staff. 2007. ring bd. 28.95 (978-0-497-11368-1(6)) Icon Grp.

Diccionario Abreviado del Espanol Actual. Manuel Seco. (SPA., (J). (gr. 6-12). audio compact disk 39.95 (978-84-294-6628-7(2)) Pub: Aguilar MEX. Dist(s): Santillana

Diccionario de uso del español. Edición Electrónica. Maria Moliner. 2008. reel tape 119.99 (978-84-249-3584-9(5)) Pub: RBA Libros ESP. Dist(s): Santillana

Diccionario del Espanol Actual, Set. Manuel Seco et al. (SPA., 1999. audio compact disk 124.95 (978-84-294-6472-6(7)) Pub: Aguilar MEX. Dist(s): Santillana

Dicey's Song. Cynthia Voigt. Read by Jodi Benson. 4 cass. (Running Time: 6 hrs. 20 mins.). (Tillerman Cycle Ser.: Bk. 2). (J). 2000. 30.00 (978-0-7366-9066-9(2)) Books on Tape.
Young Dicey Tillerman struggles to cope with her mother's mental illness. When she brings her abandoned family to the home of their eccentric grandmother, she learns how to trust & when to let go.

Dicey's Song. Cynthia Voigt. Narrated by Barbara Caruso. 8 CDs. (Running Time: 9 hrs.). (Tillerman Cycle Ser.: Bk. 2). (gr. 8 up). audio compact disk 78.00 (978-0-7887-9518-3(X)) Recorded Bks.

Dicey's Song. unabr. ed. Cynthia Voigt. Narrated by Barbara Caruso. 6 pieces. (Running Time: 9 hrs.). (Tillerman Cycle Ser.: Bk. 2). (gr. 8 up). 1992. 51.00 (978-1-55690-619-0(6), 92312E7) Recorded Bks.
In this sequel to "Homecoming," Dicey Tillerman has brought her brothers & sisters safely to their grandmother's house on the Chesapeake Bay. Now Dicey's problem is Dicey herself.

Dicho y Hecho Set: With Intrroduction to Spanish & Student Survey. 5th ed. Michael Dawson. (SPA.). 1998. bk. & wbk. ed. 82.00 (978-0-471-31679-4(2)) Wiley US.

Dicho y hecho, Lab Audio CD: Beginning Spanish. 7th rev. ed. Laila M. Dawson & Albert C. Dawson. (ENG.). (C). 2004. audio compact disk 39.95 (978-0-471-59420-8(2)) Wiley US.

Dicho y hecho, Laboratory Audio Program: Beginning Spanish. 8th ed. Kim Potowski et al. (ENG.). (C). 2008. audio compact disk 43.95 (978-0-470-17331-2(9), JWiley) Wiley US.

Diciembre en Mexico. Donna Pena. 1994. 10.95 (322); audio compact disk 15.95 (322) GIA Pubns.

Dicision-Making & God's Will: Knowing God Will Series, Sept. Ben Young. 2000. 4.95 (978-0-7417-6199-6(8), B0199) Win Walk.

Dick Axelrod Pt. 1: Engaging the Organization in Change. unabr. ed. Innovation Groups Staff. 1 cass. (Running Time: 1 hrs. 30 min.). (Transforming Local Government Ser.: Vol. 15). 1999. 10.00 (978-1-882403-71-4(1), IG9915) Alliance Innov.

Dick Bakken. unabr. ed. Dick Bakken. Read by Dick Bakken. Interview with Rebekah Presson. 1 cass. (Running Time: 29 min.). 1990. 10.00 (101990) New Letters.
Performance poet talks about & performs some of his work.

***Dick Barton: The Mystery of the Missing Formula.** Mike Dorrell. Narrated by Toby Stephens. (Running Time: 2 hrs. 0 mins. 0 sec.). (ENG.). 2010. audio compact disk 24.95 (978-1-4084-1052-3(4)) Pub: AudioGO. Dist(s): Perseus Dist

Dick Barton: Special Agent! A BBC Radio Full-Cast Dramatization. Edward J. Mason. (Running Time: 2 hrs. 0 mins. 0 sec.). (ENG.). 2009. audio compact disk 24.95 (978-1-60283-749-2(X)) Pub: AudioGO. Dist(s): Perseus Dist

Dick Cavett: TV Talk Show Host. Interview. Interview with Dick Cavett. 1 cass. (Running Time: 30 min.). 9.95 (A0200B090, HarperThor) HarpC GBR.

Dick Francis: A Racing Life. unabr. ed. Graham Lord. Narrated by Christopher Kay. 10 cass. (Running Time: 12 hrs.). 2001. 92.00 (978-1-84197-154-4(5)) Recorded Bks.

Dick Gibson Show. unabr. ed. Stanley Elkin. Narrated by George Guidall. 10 cass. (Running Time: 14 hrs. 15 mins.). 1998. 85.00 (978-0-7887-1994-3(7), 95381E7) Recorded Bks.
One night, a young technician stands in front of a microphone. As his voice fills the airways, the radio personality of Dick Gibson is born.

Dick Katz. 1 cass. (Running Time: 1 hr.). (Marian McPartland's Piano Jazz Ser.). 13.95 (MM-88-06-25, HarperThor) HarpC GBR.

Dick Morris Syndrome: Judges 16:1-12. Ed Young. 1998. 4.95 (978-0-7417-2174-7(0), A1174) Win Walk.

Dick Stockton: Serve, Volley & Overhead. Read by Dick Stockton. 1 cass. 9.95 (978-0-89811-148-4(X), 7188) Lets Talk Assocs.
Dick Stockton talks about the people & events which influenced his career & his own approach to his speciality.

Dick Sutphen's Master of Life Wisdom Book. Dick Sutphen. Read by Dick Sutphen. 2 cass. (Running Time: 3 hrs.). (New Age Nonfiction Ser.). 1991. 14.95 set. (978-0-87554-466-3(5), N111) Valley Sun.
A collection of concepts, dialogues & philosophy to serve as steppingstones of awareness to help you cast away your delusions - the way to end suffering & achieve enlightenment.

Dick Tracy: Broadcasts & Broadcasts. Perf. by Ned Weaver. 1 cass. (Running Time: 1 hr.). (J). 2001. 6.98 (1639) Radio Spirits.

Dick Tracy Pt. 2: Broadcasts & Broadcasts. Perf. by Ned Weaver. 1 cass. (Running Time: 1 hr.). (J). 2001. 6.98 (1640) Radio Spirits.

Dick Whittington & His Cat see Favorite Children's Stories: A Collection

Dick Whittington & His Cat & Other English Fairy Tales. unabr. ed. Read by Claire Bloom. Ed. by James Reeves. 1 cass. (Running Time: 90 mins.). Incl. Simpleton Peter. (J). (CDL5 1265); Tattercoats. (J). (CDL5 1265); Tom Tit Tot. (J). (CDL5 1265); (J). 1984. 9.95 (978-0-89845-513-7(8), CDL5 1265) HarperCollins Pubs.

Dickens, Pt. C. unabr. ed. Peter Ackroyd. Read by David Case. 11 cass. (Running Time: 16 hrs. 30 mins.). 1992. 88.00 (2971C) Books on Tape.
Peter Ackroyd creates Dickens as the consummate artist & entertainer, a man whose public persona gave little hint of the darkness of his private life.

Dickens, Pt. A. unabr. ed. Peter Ackroyd. Read by David Case. 13 cass. (Running Time: 19 hrs. 30 mins.). 1992. 104.00 (978-0-7366-2172-4(5), 2971A) Books on Tape.

Dickens, Pt. B. unabr. ed. Peter Ackroyd. Read by David Case. 13 cass. (Running Time: 19 hrs. 30 mins.). 1992. 104.00 (2971B) Books on Tape.

Dickens: A Light & Enlightening Lecture, 2nd ed. 2000. bk. 15.00 (978-1-890123-34-5(X)) Media Cnslts.

Dickens: A Light & Enlightening Lecture: the Third Edition, 3rd ed. Featuring Elliot Engel. 2000. bk. 15.00 (978-1-890123-35-2(8)) Media Cnslts.

Dickens' A Christmas Carol. unabr. ed. Charles Dickens. Read by Patrick Horgan. 2 cass. (Running Time: 2 hrs. 54 min.). 1987. 15.98 (978-0-8072-3442-6(7), CB114CX, Listening Lib) Random Audio Pubg.
The classic Christmas ghost story that is a cherished favorite of the past, present & future. Join Ebenezer Scrooge, whose name has become synonymous with miserliness, as he learns the true meaning of Christmas.

Dickens Duets. abr. ed. Charles Dickens. Read by Frank Pettingell. 1 cass. (Running Time: 49 min.). 10.95 (978-0-8045-0741-7(4), SAC 7127) Spoken Arts.
Scenes from "Oliver Twist," "David Copperfield," "Great Expectations," "Martin Chuzzlewit" & "The Pickwick Papers".

Dickens for Our Time. Tom Wolfe. 1 cass. (Running Time: 1 hr. 15 mins.). 2001. 12.95 Smithson Assocs.

Dickens Ghost Stories. Charles Dickens. Narrated by Flo Gibson. 2007. audio compact disk 24.95 (978-1-55685-924-3(4)) Audio Bk Con.

Dickens' Ghost Stories. unabr. ed. Short Stories. Charles Dickens. Read by Flo Gibson. 4 cass. (Running Time: 6 hrs.). (gr. 5-12). 1997. 19.95 (978-1-55685-445-3(5), 445-5) Audio Bk Con.
A macabre collection including: "The Lawyer & the Ghost", "The Queer Chair", "The Haunted Man & the Ghosts Bargain", "Christmas Ghosts", "The Ghost Chamber", & "Four Ghost Stories".

Dickens Nobody Knows Vol. 1: A Light & Enlightening Lecture. Featuring Elliot Engel. 2000. bk. 15.00 (978-1-890123-16-1(1), CD1) Media Cnslts.

Dickens Trilogy I: David Copperfield, Great Expectations, & Oliver Twist. abr. ed. Charles Dickens. Read by Martin Jarvis. (Running Time: 7 hrs. 30 mins. 0 sec.). (Dickens Trilogies Ser.). (ENG.). 2008. audio compact disk 31.95 (978-1-934997-09-3(9)) Pub: CSAWord. Dist(s): PerseuPGW

Dickens Trilogy II. abr. ed. Charles Dickens. Narrated by Martin Jarvis. (Running Time: 7 hrs. 30 mins. 0 sec.). (Dickens Trilogies Ser.). (ENG.). 2010. audio compact disk 31.95 (978-1-934997-51-2(X)) Pub: CSAWord. Dist(s): PerseuPGW

Dickens' Women. abr. ed. Miriam Margolyes & Sonia Fraser. Read by Miriam Margolyes. 1 cass. (Running Time: 1 hr. 25 mins.). 2004. 12.95 (978-1-57270-091-8(2), D11091a) Pub: Audio Partners. Dist(s): PerseuPGW
Traces the startling similarity of the women in Dickens' work & in his life.

Dickinson by Dancing Beetle. Perf. by Eugene Ely. 1 cass. (Running Time: 90 min.). (J). 1995. 10.00 Erthviibz.
Emily Dickinson nature sounds & parody come together when Ms. Bumblebee & the spunky humans read & sing with Dancing Beetle.

Dickon see Secret Garden: A Young Reader's Edition of the Classic Story

Dictados en Espanol, Vol. I. unabr. ed. 1 cass. (Running Time: 90 mins.). (SPA.). 1999. bk. 16.95 (SSP381) J Norton Pubs.
These dictations test proficiency in comprehension, pronunciation, & spelling for intermediate level. Includes selections from works of Galdos, Rueda, de Moratin, de Alarcon & Becquer.

Dictados en Espanol, Vol. II. 1 cass. 1999. 16.95 (SSP382) J Norton Pubs.

Dictados en Espanol Vol. I: Tipos Paisajes de Espana. Read by Eva Llorens & Manuel Duran. 1 cass. (Running Time: 27 min.). (SPA.). 11.95 (978-0-8045-0852-0(6), SAC 49-2) Spoken Arts.
Tests proficiency on comprehension, pronunciation & spelling. Selections from Galdos, Rueda, de Moratin & Gustavo Adolfo Becquer are included.

Dictados en Espanol Vol. II: Ejercicios Especiales. unabr. ed. Read by Eva Llorens & Manuel Duran. 1 cass. (Running Time: 30 min.). (SPA.). 11.95 (978-0-8045-0853-7(4), SAC 50-2) Spoken Arts.
Help improve spelling with respect to such difficult letters as c, s, & z. Includes selections by de Pereda, de Aarcon, & Vincente de la Fuente.

Dictados en Español Vol. 1 CD & Booklet. ed. Salvador Rueda et al. Read by Manuel Duran & Eva Llorens. 1 CD. (Running Time: 60 mins.). (SPA.).

2006. audio compact disk 16.95 (978-1-57970-392-9(5), SSP381D, Audio-For) J Norton Pubs.

These dictations test proficiency in comprehension, pronunciation, and spelling for intermediate-level learners of Spanish. (No translations are provided.).

Dictados en Español Vol. 2: CD & Booklet. ed. José María de Pereda et al. Read by Manuel Duran & Eva Llorens. 1 CD. (Running Time: 60 mins.). (SPA.). 2006. audio compact disk 16.95 (978-1-57970-393-6(3), SSP382D, Audio-For) J Norton Pubs.

Thes dictations test proficiency in comprehension, pronunciation, and spelling for intermediate-level Spanish learners. Readings are from the works of de Pereda, de Alarcón, de la Fuente, and Bécquer. (No English translations are provided.).

Dictation at Fifty to Eighty WPM. unabr. ed. Conversa-Phone Institute Staff. 1 cass. (Running Time: 55 min.). (Secretarial Courses Ser.). 1992. 9.95 (978-1-56752-050-7(2)) Conversa-phone.

Dictation of letters given at different speeds. Manual for correcting work.

Dictation at Fifty to Sixty WPM. unabr. ed. Conversa-Phone Institute Staff. 1 cass. (Running Time: 55 min.). (Secretarial Courses Ser.). 1992. 9.95 (978-1-56752-052-1(9)) Conversa-phone.

Dictation at Ninety - One Hundred Thirty WPM. unabr. ed. Conversa-Phone Institute Staff. 1 cass. (Running Time: 55 min.). (Secretarial Courses Ser.). 1992. 9.95 (978-1-56752-051-4(0)) Conversa-phone.

Dictation at One Hundred Forty - One Hundred Eighty WPM. unabr. ed. Conversa-Phone Institute Staff. 1 cass. (Running Time: 55 min.). (Secretarial Courses Ser.). 1992. 9.95 (978-1-56752-107-8(X)) Conversa-phone.

Dictation at Thirty to Forty WPM. unabr. ed. Conversa-Phone Institute Staff. 1 cass. (Running Time: 55 min.). (Secretarial Courses Ser.). 1992. 9.95 (978-1-56752-053-8(7)) Conversa-phone.

Dictations for Discussion: A Listening / Speaking Text. Judy DeFilippo & Catherine Sadow. (gr. 9-12). 2003. audio compact disk 20.00 (978-0-86647-171-8(5)) Pro Lingua.

Dictees Elementaires et Moyennes. Jean-Philippe Gaussens. 1 cass. (Running Time: 45 min.). (FRE.). 11.95 (978-0-8045-0879-7(8), SAC 47-3) Spoken Arts.

Dictations written by a twelve-year-old French student. Tests proficiency of comprehension, pronunciation & spelling.

Dictees Francaises: French Sans Tears. Read by Lucienne M. Widmer. 1 cass. (Running Time: 45 min.). (FRE.). 11.95 (978-0-8045-1020-2(2), SAC 47-2) Spoken Arts.

Basic rules of French Pronunciation. All technicalities are explained in English, & all French words are translated to avoid confusing the beginner. Side two is for the more advanced student . It lists 150 current every-day French expressions & idioms.

Dictees Moyennes. unabr. ed. 1 cass. (FRE.). bk. 16.95 (SFR475) J Norton Pubs.

Dictionary of Biographical Quotations. unabr. ed. Read by Heywood Hale Broun. Ed. by Richard Kenin. (Running Time: 56 min). (Broun Radio Ser.). 12.95 (40368) J Norton Pubs.

Dictionary of Commonly Cited Compounds. 2001. audio compact disk 119.95 (978-1-58488-251-0(4), DCC1099, Chap & Hall CRC) Pub: CRC Pr. Dist(s): Taylor and Fran

Dictionary of Minor Planet Names. 4th ed. Lutz D. Schmadel. 2000. audio compact disk 59.95 (978-3-540-14814-2(0)) Spri.

Dictionnaire des Idees Recues, Set. Gustave Flaubert. Read by G. Bejean & C. Deis. 2 cass. 1992. 26.95 (1565-VSL) Olivia & Hill.

Collection of trite remarks which Flaubert took pleasure in compiling all through his life.

Did Adam & Eve Have Belly Buttons? Matt Pinto. 5 CDs. (Running Time: 5 hrs.). 2002. audio compact disk 30.95 (978-1-57058-437-4(0), rc09-cd) St Joseph Communs.

There's no doubt about it, teenagers are full of questions! "If God cares for people, how come He lets people kill each other?" "If God knows everything we do, then how come we have to go to Confession?" "How could there be a place like hell if Jesus loves people unconditionally?" "How do you prove that Catholicism is the correct religion to believe in?" Yes, teenagers have lots of questions and Matt Pinto has compiled lots of solid Catholic answers in his best-selling book for Catholic Teens, Did Adam and Eve Have Belly Buttons? available now for the first time on 5 CDs, exclusively from St. Joseph Communications!Clear, Concise Answers Read by the author, this new audio version of his popular work offers today's Catholic, young and old alike, a collection of clear and concise answers to questions about the Catholic Faith. Best of all, the 200 questions addressed by Mr. Pinto came from real Catholic teenagers from all over the United States. A well-known apologist and co-founder of the popular apologetics journal Envoy Magazine, Matt Pinto has an extensive personal background working with Catholic youth. Working for the Archdiocese of San Diego in both youth and young adult ministry, Matt developed a program of evangelization that has become a national model for success. Popular Catholic speaker and host of EWTN's youth oriented TV show Life on the Rock, Jeff Cavins says of Matt Pinto, "Those who know the author are impressed with his energy and enthusiasm in his work with young people. He knows how they think and the social and spiritual situations they face. As a popular youth speaker, Matt Pinto is a master at applying the truths of the Church to the ever-changing moral and social landscape. And now he brings his energy, enthusiasm, and skills to the written page." And now St. Joseph Communications has put his work into a format that can meet teens where they are: at home, in the car, on the beach, or wherever they listen to CDs!Clear Catholic Truth Through his involvement in Catholic youth and young adult ministry, Matt Pinto has personally witnessed hundreds of teens and "Generation Xers" experience genuine conversion and surety of faith after being effectively introduced to the powerful life-changing teachings of Jesus Christ and the Catholic Church. What's the secret? According to Matt, teens want clear Catholic truth, and respond most enthusiastically when the faith isn't "watered down." He relates that, contrary to popular opinion among some DREs and other Catholic educators, teens don't run from the "tough teachings" when Catholic truth is taught with conviction. Teens are looking for a firm foundation in a changing world. The Catholic Church provides that foundation and Did Adam and Eve Have Belly Buttons? provides the kind of uncompromising answers that teens are hungry for. Matt Pinto insists that "Without a firm understanding of Catholic truth, young Catholics will flounder. They will be unsure of who they are and what they stand for." But with the answers in this timely presentation, young Catholics will be equipped to embrace, explain, share and defend their faith. Did Adam and Eve Have Belly Buttons? is perfect for Confirmation class, RCIA, youth group or other religious education classes. Order today!Questions Asked:How do I know that God loves me? What is the meaning of life? If we were created by God, why do scientists have such strong evidence that we evolved from apes? Are the stories in the Bible true? Why are religion and church so boring? How do we know Jesus even existed? Is the Catholic religion the only correct religion? Why is the Catholic Church so close-minded? Are Catholics allowed to have an abortion for any reason? And much more!.

Did Christ Give Us Priests? The Priesthood Debate. 2005. 16.95 (978-1-888992-67-0(0)); audio compact disk 21.95 (978-1-888992-68-7(9)) Catholic Answers.

Did Lincoln Own Slaves? And Other Frequently Asked Questions about Abraham Lincoln. unabr. ed. Gerald J. Prokopowicz. Read by Norman Dietz. 9 CDs. (Running Time: 10 hrs. 30 mins. 0 sec.). (ENG.). 2008. audio compact disk 34.99 (978-1-4001-0616-5(8)); audio compact disk 24.99 (978-1-4001-5616-0(5)); audio compact disk 69.99 (978-1-4001-3616-2(4)) Pub: Tantor Media. Dist(s): IngramPubServ

Did No One Condemn You? John 8:1-12, 714. Ed Young. 1989. 4.95 (978-0-7417-1714-6(X), 714) Win Walk.

***Did Not Survive.** unabr. ed. Ann Littlewood. (Running Time: 8 hrs. 30 mins.). 2010. 29.95 (978-1-4417-4968-0(3)); 54.95 (978-1-4417-4964-2(0)); audio compact disk 76.00 (978-1-4417-4965-9(9)) Blckstn Audio.

Did the Father Go to the Far Country? Luke 15. Ed Young. (C). 1985. 4.95 (978-0-7417-1459-6(0), 459) Win Walk.

Didgeridoo: Music for Meditation - Didgeridoo with Bells, Bowls, Gongs & Chimes. Perf. by Barramundi. 1 cass. (Running Time: 48 mins.). reel tape 10.00 (978-1-57863-051-6(7), Red); audio compact disk 16.95 (978-1-57863-050-9(9), Red) Red Wheel Weiser.

Derk Mulder, Rene Stahn & Klaas Bil of Barramundi bring an earthy, grounding, meditative experience. This is a richly varied musical treatment with didgeridoos, Chinese & Balinese gongs, Tibetan singing bowls, Burmese temple bells, wind chimes, Indian drum & occasional birds.

Didgeridoo Package. Schellberg Barramundi. 1998. bk. 29.95 (978-90-74597-08-1(4)) Pub: Binkey Kok NLD. Dist(s): Red Wheel Weiser

Didn't I Tell You to Take Out the Trash?! Techniques for Getting Kids to Do Chores Without Hassles. 1 CD. (Running Time: 60 mins.). 2002. audio compact disk 13.95 (978-1-930429-27-7(4)) Pub: Love Logic. Dist(s): Penton Overseas

Didn't I Tell You to Take Out the Trash? Techniques for Getting Kids to Do Chores Without Hassles. Jim Fay & Foster W. Cline. Read by Jim Fay & Foster W. Cline. Ed. by Bert Gurule Mizke. 1 cass. (Running Time: 60 mins.). 1996. 11.95 (978-0-944634-34-9(6)) Pub: Love Logic. Dist(s): Penton Overseas

Dido: The Unauthorized Biography in Words & Pictures. Darren Brooks. 1 CD. (Running Time: 1 hr.). (Maximum Ser.). (ENG.). 2001. audio compact disk 14.95 (978-1-84240-174-3(2)) Pub: Chrome Dreams GBR. Dist(s): IPG Chicago

Dido: The Unauthorized Biography of Dido. Sally Wilford. (Maximum Ser.). (ENG., 2001. audio compact disk 14.95 (978-1-84240-153-8(X)) Pub: Chrome Dreams GBR. Dist(s): IPG Chicago

Die a Little. unabr. ed. Megan Abbott. Read by Ellen Archer. 6 CDs. (Running Time: 7 hrs. 30 mins. 0 sec.). (ENG.). 2005. audio compact disk 29.99 (978-1-4001-0151-1(4)) Pub: Tantor Media. Dist(s): IngramPubServ

Die a Little. unabr. ed. Megan E. Abbott. Read by Ellen Archer. (Running Time: 7 hrs. 30 mins. 0 sec.). (ENG.). 2005. audio compact disk 19.99 (978-1-4001-5151-6(1)); audio compact disk 59.99 (978-1-4001-3151-8(0)) Pub: Tantor Media. Dist(s): IngramPubServ

Die Another Day. Raymond Benson. Read by Robert Whitfield. 2 cass. 2002. 17.95 (978-0-7861-2371-1(0)); audio compact disk 19.95 (978-0-7861-9381-3(6)) Blckstn Audio.

Die Another Day. abr. ed. Raymond Benson. Read by Robert Whitfield. 3 CDs. (Running Time: 4 hrs.). 2002. audio compact disk 24.00 (978-0-7861-9392-9(1), 3018); 23.95 (978-0-7861-2359-9(1), 3018) Blckstn Audio.

After months of torture in a North Korean prison, Bond is released, only to find that M has deactivated him. On his own, 007 follows the trail of a megalomaniac menace through seedy streets in Shanghai and Havana hideaways to exclusive London haunts. Finally, in a magnificent crystalline ice palace, he encounters two fiery femmes fatales and a master plot to destroy the planet with a demonic weapon of mass destruction.

Die Another Day. unabr. ed. Raymond Benson. Read by Michael Page. 5 CDs. (Running Time: 6 hrs.). (James Bond Ser.). 2002. audio compact disk 74.25 (978-1-59086-515-6(4), 1590865154, CD Unabrid Lib Ed); 62.25 (978-1-59086-513-2(8), 1590865138, Unabridge Lib Edns) Brilliance Audio.

From North Korea to Iceland, Bond circles the world in his quest to unmask a traitor and prevent a war of catastrophic proportions. Crossing paths with beautiful allies and deadly assassins in a high-octane, action adventure of intrigue, revenge and betrayal. Never has Bond been so vulnerable, nor so dangerous.... additional copyright information: (actual DAD logo) (c)2002 Danjaq, LLC and United Artists Corporation. All Rights Reserved. (actual DAD logo) is a trademark of Danjaq, LLC licensed by Eon Productions Ltd. "Die Another Day" and cover artwork (c) 2002 Danjaq, LLC and United Artists Corporation. All Rights Reserved. (actual gun symbol logo) (c)1962 Danjaq, LLC and United Artists Corporation. All Rights Reserved. (actual gun symbol logo) is a Trademark of Danjaq, LLC, licensed by Eon Productions Ltd. (actual DAD logo) (c)2002 Danjaq, LLC and United Artists Corporation. All Rights Reserved. (actual DAD logo) is a Trademark of Danjaq, LLC, licensed by Eon Productions Ltd.

Die Another Day. unabr. ed. Raymond Benson. Read by Michael Page. (Running Time: 6 hrs.). (James Bond Ser.). 2004. 39.25 (978-1-59335-334-6(0), 1593353340, Brlnc Audio MP3 Lib) Brilliance Audio.

Die Another Day. unabr. ed. Raymond Benson. Read by Michael Page. (Running Time: 6 hrs.). (James Bond Ser.). 2004. 39.25 (978-1-59710-206-3(7), 1597102067, BADLE); 24.95 (978-1-59710-207-0(5), 1597102075, BAD) Brilliance Audio.

Die Another Day. unabr. ed. Raymond Benson. Read by Michael Page. (Running Time: 6 hrs.). (James Bond Ser.). 2004. audio compact disk 16.99 (978-1-59355-690-7(X), 159355690X, BCD Value Price) Brilliance Audio.

Die Another Day. unabr. ed. Raymond Benson. Read by Michael Page. (Running Time: 6 hrs.). (James Bond Ser.). 2004. 24.95 (978-1-59335-000-0(7), 1593350007) Soulmate Audio Bks.

Die Dancing. unabr. ed. Jonathan Gash. 8 cass. (Running Time: 11 hrs.). 2001. 72.00 (978-1-84197-178-0(2)) Recorded Bks.

Die Dancing. unabr. ed. Jonathan Gash. Narrated by Richard Greenwood. 8 cass. (Running Time: 11 hrs.). 2001. 72.00 (978-1-84197-085-1(9), H1162) Recorded Bks.

One more danger invades the life of Dr. Claire Burtonall. While she is busy thinking of ways to monopolize her lover, Bonn, her name is linked to a bizarre murder case. Soon Claire is unwittingly pulled into Manchester's criminal underworld by Bonn & the agency for which he works.

Die Faile des KommissarWagner. U. Plasger. (Running Time: 30 mins.). 2005. audio compact disk 19.85 (978-3-468-49490-1(4)) Langenscheidt.

Die Fledermaus: An Introduction to J. Strauss Jr.'s Opera. Thomson Smillie. Read by David Timson. 1 CD. (Running Time: 1 hr. 30 min.). (Opera Explained Ser.). 2003. audio compact disk 8.99 (978-1-84379-086-0(6)) NaxMulti GBR.

Die for Love. unabr. ed. Elizabeth Peters, pseud. Read by Grace Conlin. 7 cass. (Running Time: 10 hrs.). 1999. 49.95 (978-0-7861-1476-4(2), 2328) Blckstn Audio.

Jacqueline Kirby, assistant head librarian at Coldwater College in Nebraska, attends the convention of the Historical Romance Writers of the World in New York. First, Dubretta Duberstein, the scandal columnist, dies under mysterious circumstances. Then, one of the most popular of the writers at the convention asks Jacqueline for help. Someone, it seems is threatening to kill the novelist.

Die for Love. unabr. ed. Elizabeth Peters, pseud. Read by Liza Ross. 9 CDs. (Running Time: 9 hrs. 30 min.). 2000. audio compact disk 89.95 (978-0-7531-0694-5(9), 106949) Pub: ISIS Audio GBR. Dist(s): ISIS Pub

Die for Love, Set. unabr. ed. Elizabeth Peters, pseud. Read by Grace Conlin. 7 cass. 1999. 49.95 (FS9-43388) Highsmith.

Die for Love: A Jacqueline Kirby Mystery. unabr. ed. Elizabeth Peters, pseud. Read by Grace Conlin. (Running Time: 9.5 hrs. NaN mins.). 2009. 29.95 (978-1-4332-6725-3(X)); audio compact disk 80.00 (978-1-4332-6722-2(5)) Blckstn Audio.

***Die for Me.** unabr. ed. Karen Rose. Read by Tavia Gilbert. (Running Time: 16 hrs. 45 mins.). 2010. audio compact disk 32.95 (978-1-4417-5918-4(2)) Blckstn Audio.

Die for Me. unabr. ed. Karen Rose & Tavia Gilbert. (Running Time: 21 hrs. NaN mins.). 2008. 105.95 (978-1-4332-5263-1(5)); audio compact disk 125.00 (978-1-4332-5264-8(3)) Blckstn Audio.

Die for Me. unabr. ed. Karen Rose & Tavia Gilbert. (Running Time: 16 hrs. 45 mins.). 2010. 44.95 (978-1-4332-5265-5(1)) Blckstn Audio.

Die Happy, Vol. 2, Set. 2 CDs. 1999. audio compact disk 12.99 (KMGD8662) Provident Mus Dist.

Die in Plain Sight. Elizabeth Lowell. Read by Maria Tucci. 1975. 9.99 (978-0-06-074366-6(2)) HarperCollins Pubs.

***Die in Plain Sight.** abr. ed. Elizabeth Lowell. Read by Maria Tucci. (ENG.). 2004. (978-0-06-078325-9(7), Harper Audio) HarperCollins Pubs.

***Die in Plain Sight.** abr. ed. Elizabeth Lowell. Read by Maria Tucci. (ENG.). 2004. (978-0-06-081486-1(1), Harper Audio) HarperCollins Pubs.

Die in Plain Sight. unabr. ed. Elizabeth Lowell. 10 cass. (Running Time: 13 hrs. 45 min.). 2003. 93.00 (978-1-4025-4820-8(6)) Recorded Bks.

Lacey Quinn inherits striking landscape paintings done by her late, much-loved grandfather. But they are more than the works of a talented master. They are anguished voices from the grave¿crying murder!.

Die Like a Dog, Set. unabr. ed. Gwen Moffat. 5 cass. 1998. 63.95 (978-1-85903-143-8(9)) Pub: Magna Story GBR. Dist(s): Ulverscroft US

Die Lonesome. abr. ed. Matthew S. Hart. Read by Charlton Griffin. 2 vols. 2003. 18.00 (978-1-58807-244-3(4)) Am Pubng Inc.

Die Lonesome. abr. ed. Matthew S. Hart. Read by Charlton Griffin. 2 vols. No. 2. 2003. (978-1-58807-739-4(X)) Am Pubng Inc.

Die, My Darling, Die. unabr. ed. Alf Harris. Read by Rusty Nelson. 6 cass. (Running Time: 6 hrs. 24 min.). 2001. 39.95 (978-1-55686-932-7(0)) Books in Motion.

Two "working" he/she assassins find the attraction to each other too irresistible to pass up. But it doesn't stand in the way when the time comes to assassinate each other.

Die Ödipale Kultur: Wege aus der Verstrickung. Pierre F. Walter. (GER., 2010. 12.00 (978-0-9760433-1-7(9), IPUBLICA_PAA) Sirius C Media.

Die Prapositiverganzung im Deutschen und im Spanischen: Zur Semantik der Prapositionen. Maria Jose Dominguez Vazquez. Contrib. by Gerd Wotjak. Vol. 20. (GER., 2005. bk. 57.95 (978-3-631-53312-3(8)) P Lang Pubng.

Die Rache Des Computers. Bottcher et al. audio compact disk 12.95 (978-0-8219-3805-8(3)) EMC-Paradigm.

Die Spur Fuhrt Nach Bayern. Hans J. Konig. 59.95 (978-0-8219-3631-3(X)) EMC-Paradigm.

Die to Live. unabr. ed. John S. Morgan. Read by Nancy Lee Painter. 6 cass. (Running Time: 7 hrs. 30 min.). 2001. 39.95 (978-1-55686-778-1(6)) Books in Motion.

Desperately waiting for a needed kidney transplant, Maxine Marshall enters the frightening world of a medical black market in body parts. Maxine learns of a complicated scheme that has already cost three people their lives.

Die Trying. unabr. ed. Lee Child. (Running Time: 14 hrs.). (Jack Reacher Ser.). 2004. 24.95 (978-1-59335-737-5(0), 1593357370, Brilliance MP3) Brilliance Audio.

Die Trying. unabr. ed. Lee Child. Read by Dick Hill. (Running Time: 14 hrs.). (Jack Reacher Ser.). 2004. 39.25 (978-1-59335-871-6(7), 1593358717, Brlnc Audio MP3 Lib); 29.95 (978-1-59355-559-7(8), 1593555598, BAU) Brilliance Audio.

In a Chicago suburb, a dentist is met in his office parking lot by three men and ordered into the trunk of his Lexus. On a downtown sidewalk, Jack Reacher and an unknown woman are abducted in broad daylight by two men - practiced and confident - who stop them at gunpoint and hustle them into the same sedan. Then Reacher and the woman are switched into a second vehicle and hauled away, leaving the dentist bound and gagged inside his car with the woman's abandoned possessions, two gallons of gasoline. . . and a burning match. The FBI is desperate to rescue the woman, a Special Agent from the Chicago office, because the FBI always - always - takes care of its own, and because this woman is not just another agent. Reacher and the woman join forces, against seemingly hopeless odds, to outwit their captors and escape. But the FBI thinks Jack is one of the kidnappers - and when they close in, the Bureau snipers will be shooting to kill.

Die Trying. unabr. ed. Lee Child. Read by Dick Hill. (Running Time: 14 hrs.). (Jack Reacher Ser.). 2004. 39.25 (978-1-59710-208-7(3), 1597102083, BADLE); 24.95 (978-1-59710-209-4(1), 1597102091, BAD) Brilliance Audio.

Die Trying. unabr. ed. Lee Child. Read by Dick Hill. (Running Time: 50400 sec.). (Jack Reacher Ser.). 2007. audio compact disk 112.25 (978-1-4233-3398-2(5), 9781423333982, BriAudCD Unabrid); audio compact disk 38.95 (978-1-4233-3397-5(7), 9781423333975, Bril Audio CD Unabri) Brilliance Audio.

***Die Twice: A David Trevellyan Novel.** unabr. ed. Andrew Grant. (Running Time: 12 hrs.). 2010. audio compact disk 29.95 (978-1-4417-3737-3(5)) Blckstn Audio.

***Die Twice: A David Trevellyan Novel.** unabr. ed. Andrew Grant. Read by John Lee. (Running Time: 12 hrs. 0 mins.). 2010. 29.95 (978-1-4417-3738-0(3)); 72.95 (978-1-4417-3734-2(0)); audio compact disk 105.00 (978-1-4417-3735-9(9)) Blckstn Audio.

Die Umwelt und ich CD. Kinder Lernen Deutsch Task Force.Tr. of Environment & I CD. (GER.). (YA). 2004. audio compact disk 25.00 (978-1-932737-05-9(7)) Amer Assn Teach German.

Died in the Wool. unabr. ed. Ngaio Marsh. Read by Nadia May. 6 cass. (Running Time: 8 hrs. 30 mins.). 1996. 44.95 (978-0-7861-0999-9(8), 1776) Blckstn Audio.

A missing Member of Parliament is found dead, pressed in a bale of wool - & a year later Inspector Roderick Alleyn receives a desperate plea involving

him in a gruesome war of espionage where he becomes as much the "quarry" as the hunter.

Diego Rivera Speaking. abr. ed. Diego Rivera. 1 cass. (Running Time: 90 min.). (SPA.). 1984. 12.95 (978-0-694-50052-9(6), SWC 1065) HarperCollins Pubs.

Dies the Fire. unabr. ed. S. M. Stirling. Narrated by Todd McLaren. (Running Time: 23 hrs. 0 mins. 0 sec.). (Emberverse Ser.). (ENG.). 2008. audio compact disk 49.99 (978-1-4001-0676-9(1)); audio compact disk 34.99 (978-1-4001-5676-4(9)) Pub: Tantor Media. Dist(s): IngramPubServ

Dies the Fire. unabr. ed. S. M. Stirling. Read by Todd McLaren. Narrated by Todd McLaren. (Running Time: 23 hrs. 0 mins. 0 sec.). (Emberverse Ser.). (ENG.). 2008. audio compact disk 99.99 (978-1-4001-3676-6(8)) Pub: Tantor Media. Dist(s): IngramPubServ

Diesel. unabr. ed. Donald V. Allen. Read by Diesel. 1 cass. (Running Time: 30 min.). Dramatization. (Official Audio Biography Series of the World Wrestling Federation). 5.99 (978-1-56703-041-9(6)) High-Top Sports.

Diet Analysis Plus 5.1 for Windows. 5th ed. Esha Research Staff. 2001. audio compact disk 23.95 (978-0-534-59414-5(X)) Wadsworth Pub.

Diet Analysis Plus 7. 1 Windows/Mac CD-ROM. 7th ed. Wadsworth. (C). 2005. audio compact disk 26.95 (978-0-495-10618-0(6)) Pub: Brooks-Cole. Dist(s): CENGAGE Learn

Diet Code: Revolutionary Weight Loss Secrets from Da Vinci & the Golden Ratio. abr. ed. Stephen Lanzalotta. (Running Time: 3 hrs.). (ENG.). 2006. 14.98 (978-1-59483-506-3(3)) Pub: Hachet Audio. Dist(s): HachBkGrp

Diet Enforcer. unabr. ed. Dick Sutphen. Read by Dick Sutphen. (Running Time: 30 min.). (Quick Fix Meditations Ser.). 1998. 10.98 (978-0-87554-620-9(X), QF102) Valley Sun.
Teaches listener to take control of weight & find the willpower to support an intelligent diet. Eat healthy foods & smaller portions at meals.

Diet for a New America. John Robbins. Read by John Robbins. 1 cass. (Running Time: 2 hrs.). 1990. 15.95 (978-0-945093-03-9(9)) Enhanced Aud Systs.
The story of how John Robbins, heir to the Baskin-Robbins ice cream fortune, left a life of luxury to rebond with nature. Reveals how our eating habits are having a devastating effect on the ecology. Features radio personality, Casey Kasem.

Diet of Treacle. unabr. ed. Lawrence Block. Narrated by Christian Conn. 4 CDs. (Running Time: 4 hrs. 30 mins.). 2008. audio compact disk 49.95 (978-0-7927-5234-9(1)) AudioGO.
Anita Carbone was a good girl - and it bored her. That's why she took the long subway ride down to Greenwich Village, home of the Beats and the stoners, home to every kind of misfit and dropout and free spirit you could imagine. It was where she met Joe Milani, the troubled young war veteran with the gentle touch. But it was also where she met his drug-dealing roommate - a man whose unnatural appetites led to murder.

Diet to Lose & Win. rev. ed. Merilyn Cummings. 1987. 24.95 (978-0-9617195-1-7(6)); 19.95 (978-0-9617195-9-3(1)) Abrahamson Pub.

Dieta South Beach: El Delicioso Plan Disenado Por un Medico para Asegurar el Adelgazamiento Rapido y Saludable Ahora en Audio Libro. abr. ed. Scripts. Arthur Agatston. 6 Cds. (Running Time: 25200 sec.). (SPA.). 2006. audio compact disk 29.95 (978-1-933499-22-2(2)) Fonolibro Inc.
La dieta que todos estan comentando !Ahora en audiolibro en espa?ol! Escuche de una manera amena, facil de aprender y de seguir, las indicaciones y las recetas de la dieta mas popular de los ultimos tiempos en un audiolibro con la calidad de FonoLibro.Durante a?os, el cardiologo Arthur Agatston urgia a sus pacientes a perder peso por el bien de sus corazones, pero las dietas resultaron demasiado dificiles de seguir o muy severas. Algunas eran hasta peligrosas. Aparentemente nadie podia seguir los regimenes bajos en grasa durante mucho tiempo. Y una dieta no sirve para nada si uno no la puede seguir.Por lo tanto, el Dr. Agatston invento su propia dieta. La dieta South Beach no es complicada y tampoco requiere que se pase hambre. Disfrutara porciones normales de carne, aves y pescado. Tambien disfrutara huevos, queso, frutos secos y verduras. Las meriendas (refrigerios, tentempies) tambien son de rigor en esta dieta. Aprendera a evitar los carbohidratos malos como harina blanca, azucar blanca y papas al horno. Lo mejor de todo es que a medida que adelgace, !perdera esa terca grasa abdominal primero!La dieta del Dr. Agatston ha producido resultados que han sido constantemente impactantes (!un perdida de entre 8 y 13 libras durante las primeras 2 semanas!) y ha creado un furor en el sur de la Florida e internacionalmente. FonoLibro ahora les trae en formato de audiolibro la maravillosa dieta que le permitira unirse a las filas de los que ahora ostentan figuras fabulosas, gracias a la dieta South Beach.

Dietary Management of Early Renal Insufficiency. Moderated by Rex L. Jamison. Contrib. by Kevin J. Martin et al. 1 cass. (Running Time: 90 min.). 1985. 12.00 (A8510) Amer Coll Phys.
This topic is discussed by a moderator & experts who offer differing opinions.

Dietary Supplements in Mexico: A Strategic Reference 2007. Compiled by Icon Group International, Inc. Staff. 2007. ring bd. 195.00 (978-0-497-82352-8(7)) Icon Grp.

Dietrich Bonhoeffer. unabr. ed. Susan Martins Miller. Read by Patrick Cullen. (Running Time: 14400 sec.). (Men of Faith (Blackstone) Ser.). 2007. 23.95 (978-0-7861-2481-7(4)); audio compact disk 32.00 (978-0-7861-9125-3(2)) Blckstn Audio.

***Dietrich Bonhoeffer's Meditations on Psalms.** Zondervan. (Running Time: 3 hrs. 1 mins. 38 sec.). (ENG.). 2010. 9.99 (978-0-310-86918-4(8)) Zondervan.

Diets Don't Work(r) System Introduction. 1998. 19.95 (978-0-9728883-1-8(4)) R Cooper.

Diety of Christ: Logos October 19, 1997. Ben Young. 1997. 4.95 (978-0-7417-6052-4(5), B0052) Win Walk.

Dieux Ont Soif. Anatole France. 9 cass. (Running Time: 9 hrs.). (FRE.). 1996. pap. bk. 99.50 set. (978-1-58085-356-9(0)) Interlingua VA.
Includes French language text with notes. The combination of written text & clarity & pace of diction will open the door for intermediate & advanced students to genuine comprehension & the use of literary texts for advancement in rapid understanding of written & oral language materials. The audio text plus written text concept makes foreign languages accessible to a much wider range of students than books alone.

Difference see Poetry of Benet

Difference: How Anyone Can Prosper in Even the Toughest Times. abr. ed. Jean Chatzky. (ENG.). 2009. audio compact disk 27.95 (978-0-7393-8215-8(2), Random AudioBks) Pub: Random Audio Pubg. Dist(s): Random

***Difference: How Anyone Can Prosper in Even the Toughest Times.** unabr. ed. Jean Chatzky. Narrated by Susan Denaker. 8 CDs. (Running Time: 9 hrs. 45 mins.). 2009. audio compact disk 50.00 (978-1-4159-6172-8(7), BksonTape) Pub: Random Audio Pubg. Dist(s): Random

Difference A Father Makes: Calling Out the Magnificent Destiny in Your Children. unabr. ed. Ed McGlasson. Narrated by Erik Synnestvedt. (Running Time: 2 hrs. 24 mins. 0 sec.). (ENG.). 2009. audio compact disk 15.98 (978-1-59644-675-5(7), christianSeed) christianaud.

***Difference a Father Makes: Calling Out the Magnificent Destiny in Your Children.** unabr. ed. Ed McGlasson. Narrated by Erik Synnestvedt. (ENG.). 2009. 9.98 (978-1-59644-676-2(5), Hovel Audio) christianaud.

Difference Between a Test & a Temptation. David T. Demola. 1 cass. 4.00 (S-1079-9); 8.00 (S-1082) Faith Fellow Min.

***Difference Between Scientology & Other Philosophies.** L. Ron Hubbard. (ENG.). 2010. audio compact disk 15.00 (978-1-4031-1380-1(7)) Bridge Pubns Inc.

***Difference Engine.** unabr. ed. William Gibson & Bruce Sterling. (Running Time: 15 hrs.). 2010. 29.99 (978-1-4418-9077-1(7), 9781441890771, BAD); 44.97 (978-1-4418-9078-8(5), 9781441890788, BADLE) Brilliance Audio.

***Difference Engine.** unabr. ed. William Gibson & Bruce Sterling. Read by Simon Vance. 1 MP3-CD. (Running Time: 14 hrs.). 2010. 29.99 (978-1-4418-9075-7(0), 9781441890757, Brilliance MP3); 44.97 (978-1-4418-9076-4(9), 9781441890764, Brinc Audio MP3 Lib); audio compact disk 34.99 (978-1-4418-9073-3(4), 9781441890733, Bril Audio CD Unabri); audio compact disk 89.97 (978-1-4418-9074-0(2), 9781441890740, BriAudCD Unabrid) Brilliance Audio.

Difference in Magnitude: The World's First Nuclear Attacks as Chronicled by 1945 & 1946 Documents & Recording. Read by Ralph Cosham. Created by Pocket University. (Running Time: 10800 sec.). 2005. audio compact disk 30.00 (978-1-58472-817-7(5)); audio compact disk 19.95 (978-1-58472-818-4(3)) Sound Room.

Difference in Magnitude: The World's First Nuclear Attacks as Chronicled by 1945 & 1946 Documents & Recordings. Pocket University. Read by Ralph Cosham. (Playaway Adult Nonfiction Ser.). 2008. 39.99 (978-1-60640-819-3(4)) Find a World.

Difference in Magnitude: the World's First Nuclear Attacks as Chronicled by 1945 & 1946 Documents & Recordings: The World's First Nuclear Attacks as Chronicled by 1945 & 1946 Documents & Recordings. Read by Ralph Cosham. (Running Time: 3 hrs.). 2005. 19.95 (978-1-59912-058-4(5), Audiofy Corp) Iofy Corp.

Difference Maker: Making Your Attitude Your Greatest Asset. abr. ed. John C. Maxwell. Read by Wayne Shepherd. (Running Time: 10800 sec.). 2006. audio compact disk 17.99 (978-0-7852-6099-8(4)) Nelson.

Difference One Can Make. Larry Johnson. 1 CD. audio compact disk 10.95 (978-1-57734-453-7(7), 2500825) Covenant Comms.
The absorbing story of the life & death of Kent Williams.

Difference One Can Make. Larry Johnson. 1 cass. 2004. 9.95 (978-1-55503-107-7(2), 06003591) Covenant Comms.

Differences Between Natural Healing & Conventional Medicine. David Christopher. 1 cass. (Running Time: 44 min.). 1988. 4.95 (978-1-879436-12-1(4), AHY102) Christopher Pubns.
Describes differences in theory & practice between natural healing & conventional medicine.

***Differences Between Scientology & Other Philosophies.** L. Ron Hubbard. (CHI.). 2010. audio compact disk 15.00 (978-1-4031-7348-5(6)); audio compact disk 15.00 (978-1-4031-7347-8(8)); audio compact disk 15.00 (978-1-4031-7343-0(5)); audio compact disk 15.00 (978-1-4031-7346-1(X)); audio compact disk 15.00 (978-1-4031-7333-1(8)); audio compact disk 15.00 (978-1-4031-7334-8(6)); audio compact disk 15.00 (978-1-4031-7345-4(1)); audio compact disk 15.00 (978-1-4031-7337-9(0)); audio compact disk 15.00 (978-1-4031-7344-7(3)); audio compact disk 15.00 (978-1-4031-7338-6(9)); audio compact disk 15.00 (978-1-4031-7168-9(8)); audio compact disk 15.00 (978-1-4031-7335-5(4)); audio compact disk 15.00 (978-1-4031-7340-9(0)); audio compact disk 15.00 (978-1-4031-7336-2(2)); audio compact disk 15.00 (978-1-4031-7342-3(7)); audio compact disk 15.00 (978-1-4031-7341-6(9)); audio compact disk 15.00 (978-1-4031-7339-3(7)) Bridge Pubns Inc.

Differences Between Scientology & Other Studies. unabr. ed. L. Ron Hubbard. 1 cass. (Running Time: 1 hr.). 2001. 20.00 Bridge Pubns Inc.

Differences in the Way Men & Women Perceive Love. Earnie Larsen. 1 cass. (Running Time: 1 hr.). 1986. 10.95 (978-1-56047-000-7(3), A101) E Larsen Enterprises.
Discusses how the Opposite sexes understand love, themselves, & life can greatly reduce stress in a relationship.

Different Drum. M. Scott Peck. 2004. 9.95 (978-0-7435-4651-5(2)) Pub: S&S Audio. Dist(s): S and S Inc

***Different Drummer.** abr. ed. Michael K. Deaver. Read by Michael K. Deaver. (ENG.). 2005. (978-0-06-088462-8(2), Harper Audio); (978-0-06-088463-5(0), Harper Audio) HarperCollins Pubs.

Different Drummer, unabr. ed. Clive Egleton. Narrated by Simon Prebble. 6 cass. (Running Time: 8 hrs. 30 mins.). 1991. 51.00 (978-1-55690-144-7(5), 91322E7) Recorded Bks.
A group of terrorists breaks into British Intelligence's Central Data Reserve.

Different Drummer: My Thirty Years with Ronald Reagan. Michael K. Deaver. Narrated by Michael K. Deaver. 4 cass. (Running Time: 6 hrs.). 2001. 37.00 (978-0-7887-5290-2(1), 96557) Recorded Bks.
Michael Deaver, deputy chief of staff and longtime friend to Ronald Reagan, gives the inside scoop on his relationship with the former president. Deaver's unprecedented access allows him to shed light on little-known aspects of Reagan's life and personality. Commendably, Deaver does not shy away from the tough subjects, including the assassination attempt and Mr. Reagan's fight with Alzeimer's disease. Also included is a foreword by former first lady, Nancy Reagan.

Different Drummer: My Thirty Years with Ronald Reagan. Michael K. Deaver. Narrated by Michael K. Deaver. 5 CDs. (Running Time: 6 hrs.). 2002. audio compact disk 48.00 (978-1-4025-1536-1(7)) Recorded Bks.
A longtime friend to Ronald Reagan, Michael K. Deaver gives the inside scoop on his relationship with the former president. While governor of California and president of the United States, Reagan could count on Deaver, who steadfastly remained at his side. Despite his tremendous political popularity and acting success, Reagan remains a mystery to many.

Different Drummer: My Thirty Years with Ronald Reagan. unabr. ed. Michael K. Deaver. Narrated by Michael K. Deaver. 4 cass. (Running Time: 6 hrs.). 2004. 29.95 (978-1-4025-1032-8(2)) Recorded Bks.

Different Drummer: Thirty Years with Ronald Reagan. unabr. abr. ed. Michael K. Deaver. Read by Michael K. Deaver. 5 CDs. (Running Time: 6 hrs.). 2001. audio compact disk 29.95 (978-0-694-52458-7(1)) HarperCollins Pubs.

***Different Eyes: The Art of Living Beautifully.** unabr. ed. Steve Chalke & Alan Mann. (Running Time: 5 hrs. 10 mins. 20 sec.). (ENG.). 2010. 14.99 (978-0-310-57203-9(7)) Zondervan.

Different Just Like Me. abr. ed. Lori Mitchell. Narrated by Julia Gibson. 1 cass. (Running Time: 30 mins.). (gr. k up). 2002. 10.00 (978-0-7887-9030-0(7)) Recorded Bks.
In a week, April and her mother will take a train to her grandmother's house. As the days go by, April encounters people who are different sizes and shapes, and have different needs. At her, grandmother's, April will see many flowers, each one as different as the people she has seen during the week.

Different Kind of Christmas. unabr. ed. Naomi Fox. Narrated by Robert Guillaume. Music by Neal Fox. 1 cass. (Running Time: 15 min.). Dramatization. (J). 1993. pap. bk. 9.95 (978-1-882179-18-3(8)) Confetti Ent.
The Confetti Company, a cast of multi-ethnic children, enact an original fairytale with a modern upbeat tempo & message.

Different Kind of Pluto. Connie Grippo. 1 cass. 8.95 (410) Am Fed Astrologers.

Different Levels of Faith. Chester P. Michael. 1985. 12.00 (978-0-940136-15-1(5)) Open Door Inc.

Different Life: Growing up Learning Disabled & Other Adventures. Quinn Bradlee. Told to Jeff Himmelman. (ENG.). 2009. 24.95 (978-1-58648-755-3(8)) Pub: PublicAffairs NY. Dist(s): Perseus Bks Grp

Different Paths. unabr. ed. Judy Clemens. (Running Time: 8 hrs. NaN mins.). 2008. 29.95 (978-1-4332-5226-6(0)); 54.95 (978-1-4332-5224-2(4)); audio compact disk 70.00 (978-1-4332-5225-9(2)) Blckstn Audio.

Different Road. Perf. by Kathy Troccoli. 1 cass. 1999. 8.98 (978-0-7601-2727-8(1)) Brentwood Music.

Different Spirit. 2001. 15.00 (978-1-58602-078-1(1)) E L Long.

Different Turf. unabr. ed. Jon Cleary. Read by David Tredinnick. 8 cass. (Running Time: 12 hrs.). 2004. 64.00 (978-1-86340-796-0(0), 580336) Pub: Bolinda Pubng AUS. Dist(s): Lndmrk Audiobks
Homicide detective, Scobie Malone, tackles one of his toughest cases yet: in the gay community of Sydney, where "gay bashings" are a daily occurrence, someone has taken the law into their own hands & is eliminating the culprits. to make matters more confusing, each shooting appears to have been done by a different person.

Different View of Mental Illness. unabr. ed. Thomas Szasz. 1 cass. (Running Time: 34 min.). 12.95 (760) J Norton Pubs.
Concerns involuntary psychiatric commitment & treatment. Szasz outlines his controversial view that mental illness is a myth, tells why he advocates the complete abolition of coercive psychotherapy, & rebuts several criticisms of his views.

Different View of the Planets. Emma B. Donath. 1 cass. 8.95 (400) Am Fed Astrologers.

Different War. unabr. ed. Craig Thomas. Read by Stephen Thorne. 12 cass. (Running Time: 18 hrs.). 2000. 79.95 (978-0-7540-0075-4(3), CAB 1498) Pub: Chivers Audio Bks GBR. Dist(s): AudioGO
On its final test flight, a new American airliner crashes mysteriously in the Arizona desert, and Mitchell Gant is sent in to investigate. Meanwhile in England, Marian Pyott, MP, finds evidence of a massive fraud involving millions of dollars. Then a second airliner crashes taking Gant and Pyott on a race across the globe to uncover the truth.

Different Way of Life. J. Krishnamurti. 1 cass. (Running Time: 1 hr.). (Krishnamurti with Dr. Allan W. Anderson Ser.: No. 13). 8.50 (APA7413) Krishnamurti.
These 1974 dialogues cover the entire spectrum of Krishnamurti's teaching in a series highly regarded for its depth of inquiry into each particular subject.

Different Women Dancing. unabr. ed. Jonathan Gash. Narrated by Paul Martin. 8 cass. (Running Time: 11 hrs.). 2000. 72.00 (978-1-84197-081-3(6), H1113E7) Recorded Bks.
Dr. Clare Burtonall is having a bad day. In addition, Clare's husband is acting most suspiciously. Newly alert, Clare decides to investigate. Only one person can help.

Different Worlds Audio Cassette. Margaret Johnson. As told by Caroline Faber. Contrib. by Philip Prowse. (Running Time: 1 hr. 14 mins.). (Cambridge English Readers Ser.). (ENG.). 2003. 9.00 (978-0-521-53656-1(1)) Cambridge U Pr.

Different yet the Same. 2008. audio compact disk 3.99 (978-0-9802359-4-4(4)) Abena Pub.

Differentiate or Die. unabr. ed. Jack Trout. Read by Patrick Cullen. Contrib. by Steve Rivkin. 5 cass. (Running Time: 7 hrs.). 2001. 39.95 (978-0-7861-2085-7(1), 2846); audio compact disk 48.00 (978-0-7861-9686-9(6), 2846) Blckstn Audio.
Takes marketers to task for taking the easy route too often, employing high-tech razzle-dazzle and sleight of hand when they should be working to discover and market their product's uniquely valuable qualities. He examines successful differentiation initiatives?from giants like Dell Computer, Southwest Airlines, and Wal-Mart to smaller success stories like Streit's Matzoh and Connecticut's tiny Trinity College?to determine why some marketers succeed at differentiating themselves while others fail.

Differentiating Instruction Tape 2: Instructional & Management Strategies. 1997. cass. & video 347.00 (978-0-87120-698-5(6)) ASCD.

Differentiating the Pastoral Function. Calvert Brand. 1986. 10.80 (0108A) Assn Prof Chaplains.

Difficult Conversations. abr. ed. Douglas Stone et al. Read by Douglas Stone et al. 5 CDs. (Running Time: 6 hrs.). (ENG., 1999. audio compact disk 29.95 (978-0-553-45612-7(1)) Pub: Random Audio Pubg. Dist(s): Random

Difficult Decisions in Vascular Surgery. Moderated by John R. Gutelius. 2 cass. (General Sessions Ser.: Spring 1986). 1986. 15.00 (8609) Am Coll Surgeons.
Discusses carotid artery surgery, abdominal aortic aneurysms, aortoiliac occlusive disease, femoro - popliteal - tibial disease.

Difficult Saint. Sharan Newman. Read by Celeste Lawson. (Running Time: 11 hrs. 30 mins.). 2003. 34.95 (978-1-59912-650-0(8)) Iofy Corp.

Difficult Saint. unabr. ed. Sharan Newman. Read by Celeste Lawson. 8 cass. (Running Time: 11 hrs. 30 mins.). 2004. 56.95 (978-0-7861-2652-1(3), 3216); audio compact disk 80.00 (978-0-7861-8887-1(1), 3216) Blckstn Audio.
Catherine, wife of one-handed Edgar, daughter of a Jewish merchant, and mother of two small children, is a Christian convert. Agnes, her estranged sister, has returned to Paris with the news that she is to marry a German lord. She wants no part of her Jewish family, except the sizable dowry her father can provide. After Agnes departs for Germany, her family receives terrible news: Agnes?s husband has been murdered by poison and Agnes herself is the prime suspect. Catherine, putting their differences aside, goes undercover in the dangerous anti-Semitic climate of twelfth century Germany to save her sister?s life and possibly lose her own in the effort.

Difficult woman, complicated Woman see Mujeres dificiles, hombres Complicados

Difficulties with Girls, unabr. collector's ed. Kingsley Amis. Read by David Case. 8 cass. (Running Time: 12 hrs.). 1990. 64.00 (978-0-7366-1820-5(1), 2656) Books on Tape.
Twenty-five years ago, Kingsley Amis wrote Take a Girl Like You, a comedy about a lusty young couple, Patrick & Jenny, each engaged with equal ardor in gaining an opposite goal - he with getting her into bed, she with staying out of it. They both win. In Difficulties with Girls Jenny & Patrick are back with us. They're older, though not much wiser - Jenny, devoted but aggrieved; Patrick, boozing & unfaithful. Each lives in a fantasyland projecting life through lenses not calibrated in this world.

Difficulty in Poetry: Obscure Beauty. unabr. ed. I. A. Richards. 1 cass. (Running Time: 58 min.). 1970. 12.95 (23155) J Norton Pubs.
A discussion of complicacy in poetry - a pro & con presentation.

Difficulty of Grown Children Relating to Their Parents: Genesis 2:24. Ed Young. 1994. 4.95 (978-0-7417-2021-4(3), 1021) Win Walk.

Difficulty of Thinking Together. 1 cass. (Running Time: 55 min.). 8.50 (ABWD82) Krishnamurti.
Dr. David Bohm & Nobel Prize winner Dr. Maurice Wilkins met with Krishnamurti on February 12, 1982, to discuss the problems of thinking & co-operating together. This conversation explores love, fear, grief, loss & attachment.

DIFS Makes the Difference in Student Motivation: NACADA Webinar Series 23. Featuring Ken Kiewra. (ENG.). 2009. audio compact disk 140.00 (978-1-935140-65-8(5)) Nat Acad Adv.

Dig. Alan Dean Foster. 1997. (978-1-57042-523-3(X)) Hachet Audio.

Dig. abr. ed. Alan Dean Foster. Read by John Shea. 2 cass. 2001. 7.95 (978-1-57815-198-1(8), Media Bks Audio) Media Bks NJ.

Dig for the Light. Michael Lewis. 1 CD. audio compact disk 16.98 (978-1-57908-444-8(3)) Platinm Enter.

Digby. unabr. ed. Pamela Hill. Read by Brian Rapkin. 5 cass. (Running Time: 7 hrs. 30 min.). (Audio Books Ser.). 1989. 49.95 (978-1-85496-270-6(1)) Pub: UlverLrgPrint GBR. Dist(s): Ulverscroft US
Kenelm Digby was the son of one of the infamous Gunpowder Plotters, & his father's disgrace & execution affected his whole life. A restless & active man, he was, at various stages in his life, scientist, philosopher, pirate & poet. Welcomed at courts throughout Europe, he was the particular favorite of the Queen of France who wanted him to be her lover. But Kenelm Digby loved another: the beautiful Venetia.

Digby & Kate. unabr. ed. Barbara Baker. Narrated by Barbara Caruso. 1 cass. (Running Time: 15 mins.). (gr. 1 up). 1998. 10.00 (978-0-7887-1907-3(6), 95328E7) Recorded Bks.
Story of two inseparable best friends, even though they are dog & cat.

Digby & Kate. unabr. ed. Barbara Baker. Read by Barbara Caruso. 1 cass. (Running Time: 15 min.). (J). (gr. 4). 1998. 22.24 HMWK SET . (978-0-7887-1935-6(1), 40642) Recorded Bks.
Digby & Kate are best friends even though Digby is a dog, & Kate is a cat.

Digest of the Early Connecticut Probate Records, 1635-1750, Vols. 1-3. Charles William Manwaring. 2002. audio compact disk 32.00 (978-0-7884-2174-7(3)) Heritage Bk.

Digestive Wellness. 3rd abr. ed. Elizabeth Lipski. Narrated by Beth Richmond. 2006. audio compact disk 22.95 (978-1-933310-06-0(5)) A Media Intl.

Digestive Wellness: How to Strengthen the Immune System & Prevent Disease Through Healthy Digestion. 3rd ed. Elizabeth Lipski. (Running Time: 4 hrs. 30 min.). 2005. audio compact disk 28.00 (978-1-932378-85-6(5)) A Media Intl.

Digger Dave & Backhoe Joe. l.t. ed. Dennis Frogberg. 1 cass. (Running Time: 20 mins.). (J). (ps-4). 2001. 10.95 (978-1-928632-54-2(8)) Writers Mrktpl.
Spend a day learning about construction from Digger Dave and Backhoe Joe. Includes a laminated book.

Digger Doug's Underground: Episode 3: Dinosaurs & Artifacts, Episode 4: Dinosaurs & Natural History. Created by Apologetics Press. (Running Time: 3360 sec.). (Digger Doug's Underground Ser.). (ENG.). 2007. 12.95 (978-0-932859-96-9(8)) Pub: Apologetic Pr. Dist(s): STL Dist NA

Diggers. Terry Pratchett. 2 cass. (Running Time: 3 hrs.). (ENG.). (YA). 2003. 16.99 (978-0-552-14006-5(6)) Pub: Random GBR. Dist(s): Trafalgar

Diggin the New Breed: The Beat Generation & Postwar America. Keith Rodway & Robin Clifford. (Enlightenment Ser.). (ENG., 2000. audio compact disk 15.95 (978-1-84240-004-3(5)) Pub: Chrome Dreams GBR. Dist(s): IPG Chicago

Digging Deeper into the Beginnings: Genesis. abr. ed. Narrated by Kailey Bell. (Kidz Rock Ser.). (ENG.). (J). 2008. 6.29 (978-1-60814-006-0(7)) Oasis Audio.

Digging for the Truth: One Man's Epic Adventure Exploring the World's Greatest Archaeological Mysteries. unabr. ed. Josh Bernstein. Read by William Dufris. (Running Time: 7 hrs. 30 mins. 0 sec.). (History Channel Audiobook Ser.). (ENG.). 2006. audio compact disk 59.99 (978-1-4001-3344-4(0)); audio compact disk 19.99 (978-1-4001-5344-2(1)); audio compact disk 29.99 (978-1-4001-0344-7(4)) Pub: Tantor Media. Dist(s): IngramPubServ

Digging to America. unabr. ed. Anne Tyler. Read by William Hope. (YA). 2006. 49.99 (978-0-7393-7469-6(9)) Find a World.

Digging to America. unabr. ed. Anne Tyler. Read by Blair Brown. 7 cass. (Running Time: 8 hrs. 30 mins.). 2006. 63.00 (978-1-4159-3031-1(7), BksonTape); audio compact disk 81.00 (978-1-4159-3032-8(5), BksonTape) Pub: Random Audio Pubg. Dist(s): Random

Digging to America. unabr. ed. Anne Tyler. Read by Blair Brown. 7 CDs. (Running Time: 30600 sec.). (ENG.). 2006. audio compact disk 34.95 (978-0-7393-3310-5(0), Random AudioBks) Pub: Random Audio Pubg. Dist(s): Random

Digging up Dinosaurs. unabr. ed. Aliki. Read by Jerry Terheyden. 1 cass. (Running Time: 11 mins.). (Follow the Reader Ser.). (J). (gr. 1-3). 1987. pap. bk. 17.00 (978-0-8072-0048-3(4), FTR79SP, Listening Lib) Random Audio Pubg.
Explains the jobs of the scientists & workers, specialists & shippers who reconstruct dinosaurs for the education & enjoyment of all who see them in museums.

Digging up Dinosaurs Book & Tape. abr. ed. Aliki. Illus. by Aliki. 1 cass. (Let's-Read-And-Find-Out-Science Ser.). (J). (gr. k-4). 1991. 8.99 (978-1-55994-302-4(5)) HarperCollins Pubs.

Digging up the Past. Alasdair Blair & Wolfe. 3 cass. 2004. 14.95 (978-1-59156-302-0(X)); audio compact disk 15.95 (978-1-59156-319-8(4)) Covenant Comms.

Digging up the Truth: Biblical Archaeology. Chuck Missler & Bob Cornuke. 1 CD. (Running Time: 3 hrs.). (Briefing Packages by Chuck Missler). 2001. audio compact disk 14.95 (978-1-57821-137-1(9)) Koinonia Hse.
Skeptics ridicule, and historians mock, but each time the archaeologist's spade penetrates the soil of history they are silenced. Join Chuck Missler and the real-life Indiana Jones, Bob Cornuke, as they take you on an overview of the archaeological proof for the Bible. Bob and Chuck will also talk about the modern world of archaeology. This briefing is an incredible tool that will strengthen and equip you in your defense of the Faith.

Digilabs: Digital workflow Software. 2004. spiral bd. 400.00 (978-0-9754991-1-5(4)); spiral bd. 400.00 (978-0-9754991-2-2(2)) Digilabs.

Digital Aboriginal. abr. ed. Mikela Tarlow & Philip Tarlow. (ENG.). 2005. 14.98 (978-1-59483-389-2(3)) Pub: Hachet Audio. Dist(s): HachBkGrp

Digital Atlas of Indonesian History. Robert Cribb. 2005. bk. 45.00 (978-87-91114-66-3(7)) Pub: Nordic Institute DNK. Dist(s): UH Pr

***Digital Barbarism.** unabr. ed. Mark Helprin. Read by David Colacci. (ENG.). 2009. (978-0-06-180593-6(9), Harper Audio); (978-0-06-178015-8(4), Harper Audio) HarperCollins Pubs.

Digital Entertainment Services in Taiwan: A Strategic Reference 2006. Compiled by Icon Group International, Inc. Staff. 2007. ring bd. 195.00 (978-0-497-82428-0(0)) Icon Grp.

Digital Equipment for Movie Exhibition in Brazil: A Strategic Reference 2006. Compiled by Icon Group International, Inc. Staff. 2007. ring bd. 195.00 (978-0-497-35835-8(2)) Icon Grp.

Digital Fortess see Fortaleza Digital

Digital Fortress. Dan Brown. Read by Paul Michael. 8 cass. 2005. 81.00 (978-0-7366-9689-0(X)); audio compact disk 99.00 (978-0-7366-9695-1(4)) Books on Tape.

Digital Fortress. abr. rev. ed. Dan Brown. Read by Bruce Sabath. 5 CDs. (Running Time: 6 hrs. 0 mins. 0 sec.). (ENG.). 2004. audio compact disk 29.95 (978-1-59397-359-9(4)) Pub: Macmill Audio. Dist(s): Macmillan

Digital Fortress, unabr. ed. Dan Brown. Read by Patrick Cullen. 9 cass. (Running Time: 13 hrs. 30 mins.). 1998. 62.95 (978-0-7861-1372-9(3), 2279) Blckstn Audio.
When the National Security Agency's invincible code-breaking machine encounters a mysterious code it cannot break, the agency calls in its head cryptographer, Susan Fletcher. What she uncovers sends shock waves through the corridors of power. The NSA is being held hostage by a code so complex that if released, it would cripple U.S. intelligence. Fletcher battles to save the agency. Betrayed on all sides, she finds herself fighting not only for her country but for her life, & the life of the man she loves.

Digital Fortress. unabr. rev. ed. Dan Brown. Read by Paul Michael. 10 CDs. (Running Time: 12 hrs. 0 mins. 0 sec.). (ENG.). 2004. audio compact disk 44.95 (978-1-59397-563-0(5)) Pub: Macmill Audio. Dist(s): Macmillan

***Digital Handshake: Seven Proven Strategies to Grow Your Business Using Social Media.** unabr. ed. Paul Chaney. Read by Scott Peterson. (Running Time: 6 hrs. 30 mins.). (ENG.). 2010. 27.98 (978-1-59659-549-1(3), GildAudio) Pub: Gildan Media. Dist(s): HachBkGrp

Digital Music in United Kingdom: A Strategic Reference 2006. Compiled by Icon Group International, Inc. Staff. 2007. ring bd. 195.00 (978-0-497-82452-5(3)) Icon Grp.

Digital Paper Trail. Oliver E. Frascona & Katherine E. Reece. 2003. bk. Rental 159.90 (978-0-941937-05-4(4)) Real Law Bks.

Digital Paranoia Codex CC Assortment. 2004. audio compact disk 359.40 (978-1-59397-509-8(0)) Pub: Macmill Audio. Dist(s): Macmillan

Digital Paranoia Codex Sam Assortment. 2004. audio compact disk 359.40 (978-1-59397-506-7(6)) Pub: Macmill Audio. Dist(s): Macmillan

***Digital Plague.** unabr. ed. Jeff Somers. Narrated by Todd McLaren. (Running Time: 10 hrs. 30 mins.). (Avery Cates Ser.). 2010. 16.99 (978-1-4001-8675-4(7)); 34.99 (978-1-4001-9675-3(2)); 24.99 (978-1-4001-6675-6(6)); audio compact disk 69.99 (978-1-4001-4675-8(5)); audio compact disk 34.99 (978-1-4001-1675-1(9)) Pub: Tantor Media. Dist(s): IngramPubServ

Digital Signal Processing Handbook: CRCnetBASE 1999. Ed. by Vijay K. Madisetti & Douglas B. Williams. 1999. audio compact disk 199.95 (978-0-8493-2135-1(2), 2135) Pub: CRC Pr. Dist(s): Taylor and Fran

Dignity of Woman - God's Masterpiece. 2004. audio compact disk 7.95 (978-1-932631-92-0(5)) Ascensn Pr.

Dignity of Woman - God's Masterpiece (AC) 2004. 6.95 (978-1-932631-91-3(7)) Ascensn Pr.

Digory the Dragon Slayer. unabr. ed. Angela McAllister. Read by Richard Mitchley. 2 CDs. (Running Time: 1 hr. 39 mins.). (J). (gr. 3-5). 2006. audio compact disk 21.95 (978-1-4056-5538-5(0), Chivers Sound Lib) AudioGO.
Nothing much ever happened to Digory when he was in the forest, until one day when he found something that changed his life for ever-a dragon's tooth. Soon the village gossips spread the word that Digory had killed a dragon, and single-handedly saved the entire village from extinction. How wrong could they be? Digory is an ordinary boy who does not want to do brave deeds and save maidens. Even talking about it makes him feel a bit frightened. So when the villagers send him off to face another evil dragon, can Digory keep himself out of harm's way, as well as maintain his new and wonderful reputation?.

Dilbert, Set. unabr. gif. abr. ed. Scott Adams. Read by Scott Adams. 3 cass. (Running Time: 5 hrs.). 1997. 29.95 (978-0-694-51893-7(X)) HarperCollins Pubs.

Dilbert & the Way of the Weasel. Scott Adams. Narrated by Norman Dietz. 7 CDs. (Running Time: 8 hrs.). audio compact disk 69.00 (978-1-4025-3794-3(8)) Recorded Bks.

Dilbert & the Way of the Weasel. Scott Adams. Narrated by Norman Dietz. 6 cass. (Running Time: 8 hrs.). 2002. 59.00 (978-1-4025-4024-0(8)) Recorded Bks.

***Dilbert & the Way of the Weasel.** abr. ed. Scott Adams. Read by Scott Adams. (ENG.). 2005. (978-0-06-089808-3(9), Harper Audio); (978-0-06-089809-0(7), Harper Audio) HarperCollins Pubs.

***Dilbert Future.** abr. ed. Scott Adams. Read by Scott Adams. (ENG.). 2005. (978-0-06-089806-9(2), Harper Audio); (978-0-06-089807-6(0), Harper Audio) HarperCollins Pubs.

Dilbert Future: Thriving on Stupidity in the 21st Century. abr. ed. Scott Adams. 1 cass. (Running Time: 60 min.). 2001. (978-0-333-73220-5(0)) Macmillan UK GBR.
Featuring a mix of essays and cartoons. Offers humorous predictions on business, technology, society and government and how human greed and stupidity will shape the future.

***Dilbert Principle.** abr. ed. Scott Adams. Read by Scott Adams. (ENG.). 2005. (978-0-06-089803-8(8), Harper Audio); (978-0-06-089805-2(4), Harper Audio) HarperCollins Pubs.

Dilbert Principle: A Cubicle's-Eye View of Bosses, Meetings, Management Fads & Other Workplace Afflictions. Scott Adams. 1 cass. (Running Time: 60 min.). 2001. (978-0-333-72218-3(3)) Macmillan UK GBR.

Dilbert Principle: A Cubicle's-Eye View of Bosses, Meetings, Management Fads & Other Workplace Afflictions. abr. ed. Scott Adams. 1 cass. 9.95 (69453) Books on Tape.
Dilbert is the cartoon hero for the nineties who takes on bizarre bosses, buzzword management & hapless co-workers. His creator brings us this funny collection of moronic office capers, drawing on Dilbert's attempts to survive the absurdities of corporate America.

Dilbert Principle: A Cubicle's-Eye View of Bosses, Meetings, Management Fads & Other Workplace Afflictions. unabr. ed. Scott Adams. Narrated by Norman Dietz. 6 CDs. (Running Time: 6 hrs. 30 mins.). 1999. audio compact disk 49.00 (978-0-7887-3419-9(9), C1025E7) Recorded Bks.
Demonstrates how even the lowliest cubicle-dwelling workers can learn the dirty little secret that have kept them from empowering their careers: the most ineffective workers will be systematically moved to the place where they can do the least damage - management.

Dilbert Principle: A Cubicle's-Eye View of Bosses, Meetings, Management Fads & Other Workplace Afflictions, unabr. ed. Scott Adams. Narrated by Norman Dietz. 5 cass. (Running Time: 6 hrs. 30 mins.). 1997. 49.00 (978-0-7887-1162-6(8), 95047E7) Recorded Bks.

Dildine Family: Classic Children's Songs Loved for Generations. Perf. by Dildine Family Staff. 1 cass. (Running Time: 40 min.). (J). (gr. k up). 1982. 9.95 (978-0-939065-17-2(7), GW 1017) Gentle Wind.
Folk songs for the whole family.

Dile Adios A Tus Temores. abr. ed. Marcos Witt. Read by Marcos Witt. Prologue by Joel Osteen. 5 cds. (Running Time: 18000 sec.). (SPA.). 2007. audio compact disk 24.95 (978-1-933499-55-0(9)) Fonolibro Inc.

Dile Adiós a Tus Temores: Cómo Vencer los Miedos y Vivir Completamente Feliz. abr. ed. Marcos Witt. Read by Marcos Witt. 2007. 17.95 (978-0-7435-6093-1(0)) Pub: S&S Audio. Dist(s): S and S Inc

Dilemma. Jenny Pitman. Read by Lesley Manville. 2 cass. (Running Time: 3 hrs.). (ENG., 2003. (978-1-4050-3373-2(8)) Macmillan UK GBR.

Dilemmas of Leadership: Decision Making & Ethics in the Community College. George B. Vaughan et al. Frwd. by Clark Kerr. (Higher & Adult Education Ser.). 1992. bk. 35.95 (978-1-55542-468-8(6), Jossey-Bass) Wiley US.

Diligence. AIO Team Staff. Created by Focus on the Family Staff. (Running Time: 1 hr. 10 mins. 0 sec.). (Adventures in Odyssey Life Lessons Ser.). (ENG.). (J). 2005. audio compact disk 5.99 (978-1-58997-181-3(7)) Pub: Focus Family. Dist(s): Tyndale Hse

Diligence - Do It to A Finish, Vol. 4. Richard Gorham & Orison Swett Marden. Narrated by Richard Gorham. (ENG.). 2006. audio compact disk 14.95 (978-0-9791934-3-9(5)) LshipTools.

Dillinger Days. collector's ed. John Toland. Read by Michael Prichard. 10 cass. (Running Time: 15 hrs.). 2000. 80.00 (978-0-7366-5582-8(4)) Books on Tape.
The Depression was good to crooks. For thirteen violent months in the 1930s, John Dillinger & his gang swept through the Midwest. From an amateur whose robberies often verged on the comic, Dillinger quickly became an accomplished criminal. He eluded lawmen a half-dozen states, outwitted the FBI & earned for himself the dubious honor of being named Public Enemy Number One. How he captured the American imagination is related in this inside account of a desperate & determined war between the law & the lawless, a struggle that did not end until Dillinger's bloody death outside a Chicago movie house.

Dillon Dillon. unabr. ed. Kathleen Banks. Narrated by Scott Shina. 3 cass. (Running Time: 3 hrs. 30 mins.). 2002. 28.00 (978-1-4025-4136-0(8)) Recorded Bks.
Why would two perfectly smart parents name their child Dillon Dillon? For years, Dillon wonders this as he gets teased by classmates and puts up with curious looks from strangers he meets. But when Dillon finally asks his mom and dad about his name, the answer he gets changes everything Dillon has ever known about himself and how he fits into the world.

DiMaggio: The Last American Knight. unabr. ed. Joseph Durso. Narrated by Richard M. Davidson. 7 cass. (Running Time: 10 hrs. 45 mins.). 2000. 60.00 (978-0-7887-0469-7(9), 94662E7) Recorded Bks.
His name conjures images of world championships & marilyn Monroe. Gives you a personal glimpse at a legend.

***Dimanche & Other Stories.** unabr. ed. Irène Némirovsky. Read by Cassandra Campbell. (Running Time: 10 hrs.). 2010. 29.95 (978-1-4417-4871-3(7)); audio compact disk 29.95 (978-1-4417-4870-6(9)) Blckstn Audio.

Dime. unabr. ed. G. Guardian. (SPA.). 2002. 9.99 (978-0-8297-2202-4(5)) Pub: Vida Pubs. Dist(s): Zondervan

Dime Store Magic. unabr. ed. Kelley Armstrong. Read by Laural Merlington. 9 CDs. (Running Time: 11 hrs. 30 mins. 0 sec.). (Women of the Otherworld Ser.: Bk. 3). (ENG.). 2008. audio compact disk 34.99 (978-1-4001-0742-1(3)) Pub: Tantor Media. Dist(s): IngramPubServ

Dime Store Magic. unabr. ed. Kelley Armstrong. Read by Laural Merlington. Narrated by Laural Merlington. (Running Time: 11 hrs. 30 mins. 0 sec.). (Women of the Otherworld Ser.: Bk. 3). (ENG.). 2008. audio compact disk 69.99 (978-1-4001-3742-8(X)); audio compact disk 24.99 (978-1-4001-5742-6(0)) Pub: Tantor Media. Dist(s): IngramPubServ

Dimelo Tu. Fabián A. Samaniego. (C). bk. 120.95 (978-0-8384-6544-8(7)) Heinle.

Dimelo Tu. 4th ed. Fabián A. Samaniego. (C). bk. 155.95 (978-0-8384-7332-0(6)); bk. 128.95 (978-0-8384-6557-8(9)); bk. 178.95 (978-0-8384-6572-1(2)); bk. 137.95 (978-0-8384-7065-7(3)); bk. 92.95 (978-0-8384-7760-1(7)); bk. 119.95 (978-0-8384-7856-1(5)); bk. 128.95 (978-0-8384-8054-0(3)); bk. 142.95 (978-0-8384-8153-0(1)); bk. 168.95 (978-0-8384-8155-4(8)) Heinle.

Dimelo Tu! A Complete Course. 4th ed. Fabián A. Samaniego. 2001. bk. 91.95 (978-0-03-029191-3(7)) Heinle.

Dimension of Dreams. Jeffrey Lord. Read by Lloyd James. 2 vols. No. 11. 2004. 18.00 (978-1-58807-366-2(1)); (978-1-58807-784-4(5)) Am Pubng Inc.

Dimension of Horror: The Demented Doctor. 1 CD. 1999. (4049-2) Audioscope.
Scary vignettes include: "Open Heart Surgery," "Plastic Surgery," "Invisible Man in Therapy," "New Donor Program," "Wolfman Visit," "Headache Cure," "Vampire," "Hair Transplant," "Eye Surgery," "Transylvania Hope," "Emergency Surgery" & "The Monster is Sick." Plus sound effects & scary music between the vignettes. Includes 3-D graphics.

Dimension X. collector's ed. Ray Bradbury et al. 6 cass. (Running Time: 9 hrs.). Dramatization. 1998. bk. 34.98 (4103) Radio Spirits.
Science fiction series from 1950. 18 adventures in time and space told in future tense.

Dimension X, Set. 2 cass. (Running Time: 2 hrs.). vinyl bd. 10.95 (978-1-57816-047-1(2), DX2401) Audio File.
Includes: "With Folded Hands" (4-15-50) The story of Humanoids, robots that are always at your service. "No Contact" (4-29-50) In the future year of 1982, space expeditions to another planet discover "galactic reefs". "Knock" (5-6-60) The last man on Earth finds himself in a "zoo" run by aliens. "To the Future" (5-27-50) A couple from the year 2155 have returned to the year 1950 & find themselves in Mexico at Fiesta time.

Dimension X: Competition & Universe. 1 cass. (Running Time: 1 hr.). 2001. 6.98 (1973) Radio Spirits.

Dimension X: Dr. Grimshaw's Sanitarium & And the Moon Be Still As Bright. 1 cass. (Running Time: 1 hr.). 2001. 6.98 (1542) Radio Spirits.

Dimension X: Marionettes, Inc. see Science Fiction No. 3

Dimension X: Mars Is Heaven see Science Fiction No. 1

Dimension X: Nightmare & Child's Play. 1 cass. (Running Time: 1 hr.). 2001. 6.98 (2033) Radio Spirits.

Dimension X: The Potters of Firsk & First Contact. 1 cass. (Running Time: 1 hr.). 2001. 6.98 (2007) Radio Spirits.

Dimensions of Consciousness. unabr. ed. Rollo May. 4 cass. (Running Time: 4 hrs. 9 min.). 1966. 36.00 Set. (04004) Big Sur Tapes.
Describing creativity & phenomenology as bridges between the natural world & our personal experience, & myth as the language of the unconscious.

Dimensions of Grief: Adjusting to the Death of a Spouse. Stephen R. Shuchter. (Social & Behavioral Science Ser.). 1986. bk. 47.00 (978-1-55542-003-1(6), Jossey-Bass) Wiley US.

Dimensions of Human Sexuality. Jerry Greenberg & Clint Bruess. (C). 1999. audio compact disk 99.00 (978-0-7637-1254-9(X), 1254-X) Jones Bartlett.

Dimensions of Love. Osho Oshos. Read by Osho Oshos. 1 cass. (Running Time: 90 min.). 10.95 (DCM-0002) Oshos.
Answers Questions such as "How can I feel the love inside of me? How can I really meet & love myself?", "What is Love?" & "Why does it feel like dying when you are in love?".

Dimensions of Scientific Thought. unabr. ed. John T. Sanders. Read by Edwin Newman. (Running Time: 9000 sec.). (Audio Classics: Science & Discovery Ser.). 2006. audio compact disk 25.95 (978-0-7861-6486-8(7)) Pub: Blckstn Audio. Dist(s): NetLibrary CO

Dimensions of Scientific Thought. unabr. ed. John T. Sanders. Read by Edwin Newman. Ed. by Jack Sommer & Mike Hassell. 2 cass. (Running Time: 2 hrs. 45 min.). Dramatization. (Science & Discovery Ser.). (YA). (gr. 11 up). 1993. 17.95 set. (978-1-56823-005-4(2), 10415) Knowledge Prod.
We think of science as a way of discovering certainty in an unpredictable world; experiments are designed to objectively measure cause & effect. Yet science often produces more new questions than answers, & all scientific theories can change with new & better observations. Scientific philosophers say that "objective" observations actually depend heavily on the observer's intuition & point of view. This tape explores the power & limitations of this special type of knowledge called science.

Dimiter. unabr. ed. William Peter Blatty. 6 CDs. (Running Time: 8 hrs. 0 mins. 0 sec.). (ENG.). 2010. audio compact disk 29.99 (978-1-4272-0907-8(3)) Pub: Macmill Audio. Dist(s): Macmillan

Dinah Shore Show: Groucho Marx & Fibber McGee & Molly. Perf. by Groucho Marx et al. Hosted by Dinah Shore. 1 cass. (Running Time: 1 hr.). 2001. 6.98 (2395) Radio Spirits.

Dinah Was. Oliver Goldstick. Contrib. by Yvette Freeman. 2 CDs. (Running Time: 6240 sec.). (L. A. Theatre Works Audio Theatre Collections). 2003. audio compact disk 25.95 (978-1-58081-271-9(6), CDTPT177) Pub: L A Theatre. Dist(s): NetLibrary CO

Dindon, Set. Georges Feydeau. Perf. by Michel Duchaussoy & Michel Aumont. 2 cass. 1991. 26.95 (1050-RF) Olivia & Hill.
A farcical, ingenious, fast-moving comedy written by a master of the late 19th century.

Diné Bizaad: Audio Set Lessons 1-10, 11-20, 21-30. Irvy Goossen. Narrated by Peter Thomas. 6 CDs. (Running Time: 5 hrs.). (NAV.). (C). 2004. audio compact disk 60.00 (978-1-893354-03-6(2)) Pub: Salina Bkshelf. Dist(s): Natl Bk Netwk
The audio lessons to Diné Bizaad: Speak, Read, Write, Navajo emphasize the skills for a communicative approach to learning Navajo. Each of the audio lessons follows along with a chapter in the book. Vocabulary and grammar are introduced and practiced within this context. Diné Bizaad: Speak, Read, Write Navajo and the accompanying audio CDs were created with students in mind to give them the opportunity to use and enjoy the Navajo language.

Dine Bizaad: Speak, Read, Write Navajo. abr. ed. Irvy W. Goossen. Read by Peter Thomas. 2 cass. (Running Time: 2 hrs. 40 min.). 1998. 24.00 Set. (978-0-9644189-8-1(3)); 24.00 Set. (978-0-9644189-7-4(5)) Salina Bkshelf.
To accompany the textbook of the same title.

Dine Bizaad: Speak, Read, Write Navajo, Lessons 1-10. abr. ed. Irvy W. Goossen. Perf. by Peter Thomas. 1 cass. (Running Time: 1 hr. 20 min.). (C). 1996. 12.00 (978-0-9644189-6-7(7)) Salina Bkshelf.

Dine Bizaad Binahoo'aah: Rediscovering the Navajo Language Workbook. Voice by Evangeline Parsons Yazzie & Berlyn Yazzie.Tr. of Rediscovering the Navajo Language. (NAV & ENG.). 2008. audio compact disk (978-1-893354-76-0(8)) Salina Bkshelf.

Diner de Londres. l.t. ed. Jean Piat. (French Ser.). 1995. bk. 30.99 (978-2-84011-104-7(7)) Pub: UlverLrgPrint GBR. Dist(s): Ulverscroft US

Diner de Tetes et La Femme Acephale. Jacques Prevert. Read by Francois Perrier & Sarah Boreo. 1 cass. (FRE.). 1991. 21.95 (1388-LQP) Olivia & Hill.

Dinero Que Hay en Ti! Descybre Tu Personalidad Financiera y Vive Como un Millonario. Julie Stav. Narrated by Vivian Ruiz. Told to Gabriel Sandler. 5 cds. (Running Time: 25200 sec.). (SPA.). 2007. audio compact disk 24.95 (978-1-933499-52-9(4)) Fonolibro Inc.

Ding Bat the Wayward Cat: Moon-Star Records. Sandi Johnson. Narrated by Van Buchanan. 1 cass., 1 CD. (J). (ps-6). 1998. 4.99 (978-1-929063-19-2(9), 119); audio compact disk 9.99 CD. (978-1-929063-20-8(2), 120) Moons & Stars.
This cat is backwards in every way a cat should act. In the end he sails away on a helium balloon as many tom cats often do.

Ding Dong: Caneuon Ding Dong Songs. Acen. 2005. 6.95 (978-88-88046-70-9(4)) Scuola Istruzione ITA.

Dingoes at Dinnertime. unabr. ed. Mary Pope Osborne. Read by Mary Pope Osborne. (Running Time: 38 mins.). (Magic Tree House Ser.: No. 20). (J). (gr. k-3). 2004. pap. bk. 17.00 (978-0-8072-0929-5(5), S FTR 252 SP, Listening Lib) Random Audio Pubg.

Dining & the Opera in Manhattan: Recipes form Manhattan Restaurants, Opera Arias. Sharon O'Connor. Frwd. by Beverly Sills. (Sharon O'Connor's Menus & Music Ser.). 1994. bk. 24.95 (978-1-883914-04-2(3)) Menus & Music.

Dining at Great American Lodges Vol. 18: Recipes from Legendary Lodges; National Parks Lore & Wilderness Landscape Art; Music by the Big Sky Ensemble. Sharon O'Connor. (Sharon O'Connor's Menus & Music Ser.: 18). 2003. pap. bk. 27.95 (978-1-883914-35-6(3)) Menus & Music.
Generous cookbook with music CD. Full-flavored recipes for home cooks from chefs at great American lodges. Luscious food photography. Naitonal Parks descriptions, landscape photography, and a travel guide to lodge retreats. Music by the Big Sky Ensemble sets the mood for lodge cooking and dining.

***Dining with Al-Qaeda: Three Decades Exploring the Many Worlds of the Middle East.** unabr. ed. Hugh Pope. Narrated by Paul Boehmer. (Running Time: 16 hrs. 30 mins. 0 sec.). (ENG.). 2010. audio compact disk 79.99 (978-1-4001-4651-2(8)) Pub: Tantor Media. Dist(s): IngramPubServ

***Dining with Al-qaeda: Three Decades Exploring the Many Worlds of the Middle East.** unabr. ed. Hugh Pope. Narrated by Paul Boehmer. (Running Time: 16 hrs. 0 mins.). 2010. 20.99 (978-1-4001-8651-8(X)); 29.99 (978-1-4001-6651-0(9)); audio compact disk 39.99 (978-1-4001-1651-5(1)) Pub: Tantor Media. Dist(s): IngramPubServ

***Dining with Class to Impress the Brass: Dining Etiquette Tactics & Strategies.** Kathy Pagana. (ENG.). 2010. audio compact disk 15.95 (978-1-933631-98-1(8)) Acanthus Pubg.

Dinner at Mr. Jefferson's: Three Men, Five Great Wines, & the Evening That Changed America. unabr. ed. Charles A. Cerami. Read by William Dufris. (Running Time: 28800 sec.). 2008. 59.95 (978-1-4332-3392-0(4)); audio compact disk & audio compact disk 29.95 (978-1-4332-3396-8(7)); audio compact disk & audio compact disk 80.00 (978-1-4332-3393-7(2)) Blckstn Audio.

Dinner at the Homesick Restaurant. unabr. ed. Anne Tyler. Read by Jill Masters. 9 cass. (Running Time: 13 hrs. 30 min.). 1986. 72.00 (978-0-7366-1072-8(3), 1999) Books on Tape.
Story about two brothers & a sister deserted by their father, raised by their angry mother, moving through the calamities & exaltations of their difficult youth into separate strategies for survival, & finally into a shared humanity.

Dinner at the Panda Palace Book & Tape. abr. ed. Stephanie Calmenson. Read by Russell Horton. Illus. by Nadine Bernard Westcott. Contrib. by Russell Horton. (Running Time: 15 min.). (Tell Me a Story Bks.). (J). (ps-3). 1996. 8.99 (978-0-694-70054-7(1)) HarperCollins Pubs.

Dinner Guest: Me see Poetry & Reflections

Dinner of Herbs, Vol. 1. unabr. ed. Catherine Cookson. Read by Susan Jameson. 10 cass. (Running Time: 10 hrs.). 1995. 84.95 Set. (978-0-7451-4376-7(8), CAB 1059) AudioGO.
In 1807, Roddy Greenbank is brought by his father to the remote village of Langley. But within hours, his father has met a violent death, leaving the boy in shock. Adopted by old Kate Makepace, Roddy finds his closest companions in Hal Roystain & Mary Ellen Lee. But their lives are to be shaped by a legacy of hatred, as they battle against the cruel hand of fate.

Dinner of Herbs, Vol. 2. unabr. ed. Catherine Cookson. Read by Susan Jameson. 10 cass. (Running Time: 10 hrs.). 1997. 84.95 (978-0-7451-4377-4(6), CAB 1060) AudioGO.

Dinner on the Diner. Prod. by Randy Armstrong. 2 CDs. (Running Time: 3 hrs.). 2000. pap. bk. 24.95 (978-1-55961-618-8(0)) Relaxtn Co.

Dinner Party see Ship That Died of Shame

Dinner Party. unabr. ed. Howard Fast. Read by Multivoice Production Staff. (Running Time: 6 hrs.). 2008. 39.25 (978-1-4233-7214-1(X), 9781423372141, BADLE); 39.25 (978-1-4233-7212-7(3), 9781423372127, Brlnc Audio MP3 Lib); 24.95 (978-1-4233-7211-0(5), 9781423372110, Brilliance MP3); 24.95 (978-1-4233-7213-4(1), 9781423372134, BAD) Brilliance Audio.

Dinner with a Perfect Stranger: An Invitation Worth Considering. unabr. ed. David Gregory. Read by Jeff Woodman. 2 CDs. (Running Time: 7200 sec.). (ENG.). 2005. audio compact disk 12.95 (978-0-7393-2284-0(2), Random AudioBks) Pub: Random Audio Pubg. Dist(s): Random

Dinner with Friends. Donald Margulies. 2 CDs. (Running Time: 1 hr. 40 mins.). 2004. audio compact disk 25.95 (978-1-58081-266-5(X), CDTPT182) Pub: L A Theatre. Dist(s): NetLibrary CO
Examines the lives of two couples and the repercussions of divorce on their friendships.

Dinner with Persephone, abr. ed. Patricia Storace. Interview with Patricia Storace. Read by Jill Eikenberry. 2 cass. (Running Time: 2 hrs. 15 min.). 1997. 17.95 (978-1-57453-099-5(2)) Audio Lit.
With blithe humor & bright style, Storace conjures up anarchic cities & idyllic towns & harbors where the Roman, Byzantine & Ottoman empires continue to maintain a presence.

Dinnerladies. Victoria Wood. 2004. audio compact disk 29.95 (978-0-563-52403-8(0)) BBC Worldwide.

Dinners for Two: Recipes from Romantic Country Inns, Music by the San Francisco String Quartet. Sharon O'Connor. (Sharon O'Connor's Menus & Music Ser.). 1991. bk. 24.95 (978-1-883914-07-3(8)) Menus & Music.

Dino: A Christmas Celebration. Perf. by Dino. 1 cass. 1999. (978-0-7601-1884-9(1)); audio compact disk (978-0-7601-1885-6(X)) Brentwood Music.

Dino: Music for All Time. Perf. by Dino Kartsonakis & David T. Clydesdale. 1997. 10.98; audio compact disk 15.98 CD. Brentwood Music.
Collection of timeless songs which cross generational lines, will transport you to places where only truly classic songs can go. Instrumentals.

Dino Collector's Series. Contrib. by Dino. 1 CD. 1998. audio compact disk (978-0-7601-2372-0(1)) Brentwood Music.

Dino Collector's Series. Perf. by DinoRock Performers. 1 cass. 1999. (978-0-7601-2371-3(3)) Brentwood Music.

Dino Dig: Activity Fun Pack. Sally A. Bonkrude. Ed. by Steve Bonkrude & Karla Lange. 1 cass. Dramatization. (J). (ps). 1988. bk. 12.95 (978-0-924829-04-8(4)); 5.95 (978-0-924829-12-3(5)) Musical Imag.
Teacher ideas, reproducible activity pages for the children, songs and a cassette tape covering various prehistoric creatures.

Dino Soarin' Read by Cindy the Songlady. 1 cass. (Running Time: 27 min.). (J). (gr. k-3). 1990. 9.98 Incl. lyric bklet. (978-0-9628207-0-0(9), KFP01) Kid-Fun Prods.
Sing-along songs of self-esteem, including the popular song, "Reading Is In" which encourages literacy in young listeners!.

Dinorock: Dreamosaurus. 1 cass. (J). (ps-2). 1998. audio compact disk 15.98 CD. Rounder Kids Mus Dist.
Learn about dinosaurs through Dinorock musical performers & through the adventures of a young boy named Nelson, who is obsessed with dinosaurs. This will provide hours of enjoyment to all ages.

Dino's Day in London. Stephen Rabley. 1 cass. (Running Time: 1 hr. 30 mins.). 2002. (978-0-582-05859-0(7), PutnaJuv) Penguin Grp USA.

Dinosaur. (Running Time: 60 mins.). 2002. audio compact disk 15.99 (978-1-904972-52-5(7)) Global Jmy GBR GBR.

Dinosaur Bob Mini Book & Tape. William Joyce. Read by Mariel Hemingway. (Running Time: 25 min.). (J). 12.95 (HarperChildAud) HarperCollins Pubs.

Dinosaur Bones. unabr. ed. Bob Barner. Illus. by Bob Barner. Narrated by Jerry Dixon. 1 CD. (Running Time: 10 mins.). (J). (ps-2). 2006. bk. 29.95 (978-0-439-90580-0(X)); bk. 24.95 (978-0-439-90574-9(5)) Weston Woods.
With Lively rhyming text and collage illustrations, the author of Dem Bones reminds us that dinosaur bones used to belong to living, breathing creatures. Full of fun dinosaur facts, this production will make dino-fans of kids and grown-ups alike.

Dinosaur Days. (J). 1990. 9.95 (978-1-887028-22-6(6)) Slim Goodbody.

Dinosaur Days. unabr. ed. Jill Laurimore. Narrated by Julia Franklin & Judith Boyd. 8 cass. (Running Time: 10 hrs. 45 mins.). 2001. 74.00 (978-1-84197-242-8(8), H1216L8) Recorded Bks.
Fliss & Ivor live in the ancient, collapsing Little Wattling Hall, which is proving to be a strain on their financial resources. Their only salvation appears to be an inherited collection of commemorative drinking vessels dating from the early 17th century. But when an American billionaire sends his ambitious lawyer to "sniff the collection out," the consequences are hilarious.

Dinosaur Dream. Dennis Nolen. 1 cass. (J). (ps-3). 1994. 10.95 (978-1-56876-005-6(1)) Soundlines Ent.

Dinosaur Dreams. Tom Szentgyorgyi. Perf. by Judy Blue et al. 1 cass. (Running Time: 88 min.). 1998. 19.95 (978-1-58081-121-7(3), CTA53) L A Theatre.
Bob meets, falls in love with & plans a wedding with Paula - then she disappears. This dark comedy explores how we cope with change & loss.

***Dinosaur Hunter: A Novel.** unabr. ed. Homer Hickam. (Running Time: 9 hrs. 0 mins.). 2010. 15.99 (978-1-4001-8991-5(8)); 24.99 (978-1-4001-6991-7(7)); audio compact disk 34.99 (978-1-4001-1991-2(X)) Pub: Tantor Media. Dist(s): IngramPubServ

***Dinosaur Hunter (Library Edition) A Novel.** unabr. ed. Homer Hickam. (Running Time: 9 hrs. 0 mins.). 2010. 34.99 (978-1-4001-9991-4(3)); audio compact disk 83.99 (978-1-4001-4991-9(6)) Pub: Tantor Media. Dist(s): IngramPubServ

Dinosaur in a Haystack, Pt. 1, Set. unabr. ed. Stephen Jay. Read by Larry McKeever. 8 cass. (Running Time: 12 hrs.). 1999. 64.00 Recorded Bks.
Frankenstein, velvet worms & the theory of punctuated equilibrium.

Dinosaur in a Haystack, Pt. 2, Set. unabr. ed. Stephen Jay. Read by Larry McKeever. 8 cass. (Running Time: 12 hrs.). 1999. 64.00 Recorded Bks.

Dinosaur in a Haystack: Reflections in Natural History. abr. ed. Stephen Jay Gould. Read by Meredith MacRae & Efrem Zimbalist, Jr. 4 cass. (Running Time: 6 hrs.). 1999. 24.95 (978-1-57453-342-2(8)) Audio Lit.
Covers everything from fossils to the phenomena of life on earth today. From fads to fungus, baseball to beeswax, Stephen Jay Gould always circles back to the great themes of time, change, & history. Amused & awestruck, he drifts from trenchant to poignant, making history & science relevant for all.

Dinosaur King Blister. Upper Deck. 2008. 3.99 (978-1-59945-540-2(4)) Pub: Upper Dck Co. Dist(s): Diamond Book Dists

Dinosaur King Starter. Upper Deck. 2008. 9.99 (978-1-59945-666-9(4)) Pub: Upper Dck Co. Dist(s): Diamond Book Dists

Dinosaur Rap. Melissa Caudle et al. Illus. by Anthony Guerra & Bart Harlan. 1 cass. (Rock 'n Learn Ser.). (J). bk. 7.98 Blisterpack. (RNL 959) NewSound.

Dinosaur Rap. unabr. ed. Rock 'N Learn, Inc. Staff. Illus. by Bart Harlan & Anthony Guerra. 1 cass. (Running Time: 42 min.). (Rock 'n Learn Ser.). (J). (gr. 1 up). 1996. pap. bk. 12.99 (978-1-878489-59-3(3), RL959) Rock N Learn.
Cool rap songs teach about fossils, land masses, & neat facts about more than 40 dinosaurs. Audiocassette & full-color illustrated book.

Dinosaur Read Along: With 3-D Dinosound with Book. (J). (ps-3). 2000. pap. bk. 6.98 (978-0-7634-0609-7(0)) W Disney Records.

Dinosaur Rock. Dino Rock. (Running Time: 44 min.). (J). (gr. 4-9). 1998. 9.98 (978-1-57940-015-6(9)); audio compact disk 14.98 (978-1-57940-014-9(0)) Rounder Records.
Fossil findin' fun! Start with two children on vacation at the beach with their parents. Add an eccentric, yodeling paleontologist who is as excited about dinosaurs as the children are. Stir gently with a magic spell that brings dinosaurs (who can sing & dance) to life & you have the makings of a mighty good story. Put that story on an album with catchy tunes & accurate science & you have an award-winning, fun-filled product.

***Dinosaur Rock.** Perf. by Shari Tallon & Jerry Tallon. 1 CD. (Running Time: 58 mins.). (J). (gr. 1-3). 2009. audio compact disk (978-0-9739996-7-9(5)) Narroway ProCN CAN.

Dinosaur Rock. Perf. by Michele Valeri & Michael Stein. 1 cass. (J). (ps-5). 9.98 (218) MFLP CA.
Imagine the giant reptiles coming to life & singing rockabilly, western swing & folk tunes while they tell you about life 100 million years ago.

Dinosaur Show & Tell. Steck-Vaughn Staff. 1 cass. (Running Time: 45 min.). 1996. (978-0-8172-6468-0(X)) SteckVau.

Dinosaur Smarts by Dancing Beetle. Perf. by Eugene Ely. 1 cass. (Running Time: 81 min.). (J). 1995. 10.00 Erthviibz.
Dinosaurs, nature sounds & ecology come together when Ms. Gecko & the spunky musical humans read & sing with Dancing Beetle.

Dinosaur Song Factory. (J). (ps-3). 2000. audio compact disk 12.98 (978-0-7634-0610-3(4)); audio compact disk 12.98 (978-0-7634-0678-3(3)) W Disney Records.

Dinosaur Songs & Other Museum Music. 1 cass. (J). 1997. 10.95 (978-0-9657488-2-7(0)) Kalamazoo River.
Performance set to music.

Dinosaur Soundtrack. 1 CD. (Running Time: 90 mins.). (J). (ps-3). 2000. audio compact disk 17.98 (978-0-7634-0611-0(2)) W Disney Records.

Dinosaur Time Book & Tape. abr. ed. Peggy Parish. Illus. by Arnold Lobel. 1 cass. (I Can Read Bks.). (J). (ps-2). 1990. 8.99 (978-1-55994-262-1(2)) HarperCollins Pubs.

Dinosaur Tracks & Murder. unabr. ed. John Dellinger. Read by Jerry Sciarrio. 4 cass. (Running Time: 4 hrs. 30 min.). 2001. 26.95 (978-1-58116-091-8(7)) Books in Motion.
A murdered body found under the Hogback dinosaur footprints leads private investigator Martin Mayfield on a case of international espionage where he battles foreign agents and the New York mob.

Dinosaur Who Lived in My Backyard. B. G. Hennessy. (J). (ps-3). 2001. pap. bk. 15.95 (VX-87C) Kimbo Educ.
Take a look at what backyard activities might be like if dinosaurs were still here. Includes a read along book.

Dinosaur Who Lived in My Backyard. B. G. Hennessy. Illus. by Susan Davis. 14 vols. (Running Time: 5 mins.). 1991. pap. bk. 35.95 (978-1-59519-027-7(9)); 9.95 (978-1-59112-030-8(6)); audio compact disk 12.95 (978-1-59519-025-3(2)) Live Oak Media.

Dinosaur Who Lived in My Backyard. B. G. Hennessy. Illus. by Susan Davis. 11 vols. (Running Time: 5 mins.). (J). 1991. pap. bk. 18.95 (978-1-59519-026-0(0)) Pub: Live Oak Media. Dist(s): AudioGO

Dinosaur Who Lived in My Backyard. unabr. ed. B. G. Hennessy. Read by Larry Robinson. Illus. by Susan Davis. 11 vols. (Running Time: 5 mins.). (J). (gr. k-3). 1991. pap. bk. 16.95 (978-0-87499-198-7(6)) AudioGO.
Realizing that dinosaurs once may have roamed in what is now a backyard, a child ruminates on what backyard activities might be like today if the dinosaurs had stayed on.

Dinosaur Who Lived in My Backyard. unabr. ed. B. G. Hennessy. 1 cass. (Running Time: 5 min.). (J). (gr. k-3). 1991. 9.95 Live Oak Media.

Dinosaur Who Lived in My Backyard. unabr. ed. B. G. Hennessy. Read by Larry Robinson. Illus. by Susan Davis. 14 vols. (Running Time: 5 mins.). (J). (gr. k-3). 1991. pap. bk. 33.95 Reading Chest. (978-0-87499-200-7(1)) Live Oak Media.

Dinosaurs. 1 cass. Dramatization. (J). pap. bk. 6.95 (978-0-86545-082-0(X)) Spizzirri.
Full of interesting facts about these astonishing prehistorics.

Dinosaurs. Compiled by Benchmark Education Staff. 2005. audio compact disk 10.00 (978-1-4108-5491-9(4)) Benchmark Educ.

Dinosaurs. California Academy of Sciences Staff & Kay Productions Staff. 1 cass. (Running Time: 25 min.). (Science in Action Learning Ser.). (J). (gr. 4-7). 1988. bk. 11.45 Kay Productions.

Dinosaurs. Ed. by Linda Spizzirri. Illus. by Arnie Kohn. 1 cass. Dramatization. (J). (gr. 1-8). pap. bk. 4.98 incl. educational coloring bk. (978-0-86545-019-6(6)) Spizzirri.

Dinosaurs. unabr. ed. Gail Gibbons. 1 cass. (Running Time: 11 mins.). (Follow the Reader Ser.). (J). (ps-2). 1988. pap. bk. 17.00 incl. bk. & guide. (978-0-8072-0159-6(6), FTR 132 SP, Listening Lib) Random Audio Pubg.
Captures the imagination of young dinosaur lovers with an informative text & bright & lively colorful illustrations.

Dinosaurs Vol. 121: Get Kids Excited About Dinosaurs! unabr. ed. Kim Mitzo Thompson & Karen Mitzo Hilderbrand. 1 CD. (Running Time: 36 min.). (Get Kids Excited about Ser.). (J). (ps-4). 1999. audio compact disk 12.99 (978-1-57583-201-2(1)) Twin Sisters.
Through 12 positive and factual songs, children will learn about fossils and explore the habits of many dinosaurs.

Dinosaurs Activity Book Set. 2004. audio compact disk 13.99 (978-1-57583-357-6(3)) Twin Sisters.

Dinosaurs Are Different Book & Tape. abr. ed. Aliki. Illus. by Aliki. 1 cass. (Let's-Read-And-Find-Out-Science Ser.). (J). (gr. k-4). 1990. 8.99 (978-1-55994-244-7(4), TBC 2444) HarperCollins Pubs.

Dinosaurs Before Dark. unabr. ed. Mary Pope Osborne. Read by Mary Pope Osborne. 1 cass. (Running Time: 41 mins.). (Magic Tree House Ser.: No. 1). (J). (gr. k-5). 2004. pap. bk. 17.00 (978-0-8072-0330-9(0), FTR208SP, Listening Lib) Random Audio Pubg.

Dinosaurs Dancing. (J). 1990. 10.95 Creat Teach Pr.

***Dinosaurs Giant Floor Puzzle.** Created by Twin Sisters. (Giant Floor Puzzles Ser.). (ENG.). (J). 2008. audio compact disk (978-1-59922-346-9(5)) Twin Sisters.

Dinosaurs Never Say Please. Bill Harley. (J). 2000. audio compact disk 15.00 (978-1-878126-37-5(7)) Round Riv Prodns.
Stories included are: Dinosaurs Never Say Please; I'm Busy; Bojabi; & Master of All Masters.

Dinosaurs Never Say Please. unabr. ed. Bill Harley. Read by Bill Harley. 1 cass. (Running Time: 47 min.). (J). (gr. k-3). 1987. 10.00 (978-1-878126-25-2(3), RRR103C) Round Riv Prodns.

Dinosaurs U. S. A. Travel Through Sound & Time As the Mystery of These Spectacular Creatures Is Brought to Life. unabr. ed. Roadrunner Audio Staff. 1 cass. (Running Time: 1 hr. 05 min.). (Audio Science Tour Ser.). 1988. 13.95 (978-0-944857-05-2(1), 31001) Matthew Media.
Designed for adults & their children, explaining the mystery of dinosaurs arrival & extinction on earth. Tells where dinosaur remaind are to be found in U. S. A.

***Dinosaurs Write-with-Me Alphabet.** Ed. by Tracee Williams. Des. by Meredith Campbell Britton. (Write-with-Me Ser.). (ENG., (J). 2011. bds. (978-1-59069-922-5(X)) Studio Mouse.

Dinosounds. Ron Schmidtling. (J). 2002. per. 24.95 (978-0-9717154-0-0(8)) Dinosounds Inc.

Dinotopia. James Gurney. Prod. by Tom Lopez. 1 CD. audio compact disk 22.50 (978-1-881137-63-4(5), ZBSF026) ZBS Found.

Dinotopia, Set. James Gurney. Prod. by Tom Lopez. 2 cass. 17.00 (ZBSF025) LuvTwoLisn.

Dinotopia: The World Beneath. unabr. ed. James Gurney. Adapted by Thomas M. Lopez. 2 cass. (Running Time: 2 hr. 30 min.). 1996. 12.95 (978-1-881137-42-9(2), ZBSF017); audio compact disk 22.50 (978-1-881137-43-6(0), ZBSF018) ZBS Found.
Continuing adventures of Arthur & Will Dennison on the mystical island of Dinotopia.

Dio lo Hara Otra Vez. Contrib. by Rut Mixter. Prod. by Rigo Sevilla & Alex Orozco. Contrib. by Jonas Gonzalez Sr. 2005. audio compact disk 14.98 (978-5-559-01290-2(4)) Integrity Music.

Diocesan Priestly Spirituality, Set. George Aschenbrenner. 4 cass. (Running Time: 6 hrs.). (Spirituality of Diocesan Priesthood Ser.). 1998. 35.95 INCL. SCRIPT. (TAH404) Alba Hse Comns.
Clarifies some of the defining elements of spirituality by studying the religious experiences of Christian spiritual history.

Dionne Warwick: Fighting AIDS in the Minority Community. Read by Dionne Warwick. 1 cass. (Running Time: 60 min.). (National Press Club Ser.). 10.95 (NP-88-02-10, HarperThor) HarpC GBR.

Dionysus. Read by Caroline Stevens. 1 cass. (Running Time: 90 min.). (Facing the Gods Ser.: No. 8). 1987. 10.95 (978-0-7822-0304-2(3), 292) C G Jung IL.

Dionysus: Ecstatic God, Archetype of the Conflicted Man. Read by Jean Shinoda Bolen. 2 cass. (Running Time: 2 hrs.). 1989. 16.95 Set. (978-0-7822-0023-2(0), 360) C G Jung IL.

Dios Al Mundo Amó. Zondervan Publishing Staff. 2003. audio compact disk 14.99 (978-0-8297-4332-6(4)) Zondervan.

Dios Al Mundo Amó. unabr. ed. Zondervan Publishing Staff. 2003. 9.99 (978-0-8297-4334-0(0)) Pub: Vida Pubs. Dist(s): Zondervan

Dios de Mi Sustento. unabr. ed. Goldberg. (SPA.). 2000. 7.99 (978-0-8297-3134-7(2)) Pub: Vida Pubs. Dist(s): Zondervan

Dios de Mi Sustento. unabr. ed. Goldberg. 2000. audio compact disk 11.99 (978-0-8297-3132-3(6)) Zondervan.

Dios de Pactos. unabr. ed. Marcos Witt. 2003. 9.99 (978-0-8297-4344-9(8)) Pub: Vida Pubs. Dist(s): Zondervan

Dios Esta en Control, Set. Kenneth Copeland. Tr. by Kenneth Copeland Publications Staff from ENG. 4 cass. (SPA.). 1985. 20.00 (978-0-88114-427-7(4)) K Copeland Pubns.
Biblical study on trusting God.

Dios Esta en Control, Vol. 1. Kenneth Copeland. Tr. by Kenneth Copeland Publications Staff from ENG. 1 cass. (SPA.). 1985. 5.00 (978-0-88114-428-4(2)) K Copeland Pubns.

Dios Esta en Control, Vol. 2. Kenneth Copeland. Tr. by Kenneth Copeland Publications Staff from ENG. 1 cass. (SPA.). 1985. 5.00 (978-0-88114-429-1(0)) K Copeland Pubns.

Dios Esta en Control, Vol. 3. Kenneth Copeland. Tr. by Kenneth Copeland Publications Staff from ENG. 1 cass. (SPA.). 1985. 5.00 (978-0-88114-430-7(4)) K Copeland Pubns.

Dios Esta en Control, Vol. 4. Kenneth Copeland. Tr. by Kenneth Copeland Publications Staff from ENG. 1 cass. (SPA.). 1985. 5.00 (978-0-88114-431-4(2)) K Copeland Pubns.

Dios Habla Hoy. 1987. bk. 10.15 (978-1-58516-118-8(7)) Am Bible.

Dios lo Hara see God Will Make a Way

Dios Para Cordelia. unabr. ed. Malu Huacuja del Toro. Read by Monica Steur. 4 cass. (Running Time: 6 hrs.). (SPA.). 2004. 29.95 (978-1-4025-7669-0(2)) Recorded Bks.
Based upon the sexual abuse story of Latino TV stars controlled and raped by their managers cruelly promoted by their mothers as soon as they reach puberty (the most famous example Mexican singer Gloria Trevi), A God for Cordelia is also a satirical view of Latino women's anti mentality and the effect their religious-patriarchal beliefs.

Dioses Tienen Sed. abr. ed. Anatole France. 3 CDs. (SPA.). 2002. audio compact disk 17.00 (978-958-8161-17-4(7)) YoYoMusic.

Dip: A Little Book That Teaches You When to Quit (and When to Stick) unabr. ed. Seth Godin. Read by Seth Godin. (YA). 2007. 34.99 (978-1-60252-870-3(5)) Find a World.

***DipLCM Electric Guitar Performance Diploma Handbook.** Compiled by Merv Young & Tony Skinner. (Registry of Guitar Tutors Ser.). 2009. pap. bk. 17.50 (978-1-905908-21-9(0)) Mel Bay.

Diplomacy, Pt. 1. unabr. ed. Henry A. Kissinger. Read by Jonathan Reese. 14 cass. (Running Time: 21 hrs.). 1995. 112.00 (978-0-7366-3195-2(X), 3860 A) Books on Tape.
Kissinger shows how America has always based its foreign policy on a fantasy world. Who would know better than he? (Winner, "L.A. Times Book Prize").

Diplomacy, Pt. 2. unabr. ed. Henry A. Kissinger. Read by Jonathan Reese. 14 cass. (Running Time: 21 hrs.). 1995. 112.00 (3860 B) Books on Tape.

Diplomatic Immunity. unabr. ed. Lois McMaster Bujold. Read by Grover Gardner. (Running Time: 39600 sec.). (Vorkosigan Ser.). 2008. 72.95 (978-1-4332-1313-7(3)); audio compact disk 29.95 (978-1-4332-1315-1(X)); audio compact disk & audio compact disk 90.00 (978-1-4332-1314-4(1)) Blckstn Audio.

Direct Action to Save Eagles & to Stop Toxic Pollution. Hosted by Nancy Pearlman. 1 cass. (Running Time: 28 min.). 10.00 (518) Educ Comm CA.

Direct & Indirect Method. Swami Amar Jyoti. 1 cass. 1979. 9.95 (R-26) Truth Consciousness.
How to remain still between the two points of relativity. Delusion of perception. Methods of curing the basic fallacy.

Direct Examination of an Economic Expert Witness. 1 cass. (Running Time: 1 hr.). 1983. 15.00 PA Bar Inst.

Direct Knowledge. Swami Amar Jyoti. 1 cass. 1979. 9.95 (R-22) Truth Consciousness.
Knowing the secret of creation. Why knowledge remains limited. First realizing That, knowing which we know everything. Steps in silencing the mind.

Direct Mail Marketing Secrets: The ultimate crash-course in marketing by Mail. Robert Imbriale. (ENG.). 2008. audio compact disk 19.95 (978-0-9777500-3-0(5)) Ultimate Wealth.

Direct Mail... the Answerable Medium. Michael J. Kuzma & Susan Kryl. 1985. 21.00 (H-509) Bank Mktg Assn.

Direct Perception & Transformation. abr. ed. Jiddu Krishnamurti. 1 CD. (Running Time: 1 hr.). (Living Life Without Conflict Ser.: Vol. 1). 2008. audio compact disk 16.95 (978-1-888004-58-8(4)) Pub: K Publications GBR. Dist(s): SCB Distributors
We are going together to consider what is happening, not only in the outward world, but also what is happening within the world in which we live, the inside world, the world within our skin, the world of our thoughts, feelings, affections, likes and dislikes, hates and violence, we are going to go into all that. And also we are going to talk about meditation, love, and death.

Direct Selling 101: Achieve Financial Success Through Network Marketing. unabr. ed. Neil Phillips & Dana Phillips. Read by Neil Phillips & Dana Phillips. 6 CDs. (Running Time: 8 hrs.). (ENG.). 2005. audio compact disk 29.98 (978-1-59659-027-4(0)) Pub: Gildan Media. Dist(s): HachBkGrp

Directed by God. Elbert Willis. 1 cass. (Divine Guidance Guidelines Ser.). 4.00 Fill the Gap.

Directing. Ed. by Mike Goodridge. (Screencraft Ser.). (ENG., 2002. 50.95 (978-0-240-80498-9(8), FocalSci) Sci Tech Bks.

Directions for Change: Excellence & Optimism. Jennifer James. Read by Jennifer James. 1 cass. (Running Time: 1 hr. 14 min.). 1986. 9.95 (978-0-915423-09-5(X)) Jennifer J.
The way you see your world determines your successes & failures. Check out your perceptions & begin to understand the processes of personal change.

Directive see Twentieth-Century Poetry in English, No. 6, Recordings of Poets Reading Their Own Poetry

***Directive 51.** unabr. ed. John Barnes. Read by Susan Ericksen. (Running Time: 22 hrs.). 2010. 29.99 (978-1-4418-5816-0(4), 9781441858160, Brilliance MP3); 44.97 (978-1-4418-5817-7(2), 9781441858177, Brinc Audio MP3 Lib); 29.99 (978-1-4418-5818-4(0), 9781441858184, BAD); 44.97 (978-1-4418-5819-1(9), 9781441858191, BADLE); audio compact disk 99.97 (978-1-4418-5815-3(6), 9781441858153, BriAudCD Unabrid); audio compact disk 34.99 (978-1-4418-5814-6(8), 9781441858146, Bril Audio CD Unabri) Brilliance Audio.

Director As Producer: Getting Started. MRTW Staff. Prod. by Brian Price. 1 cass. 12.95 (978-1-57677-028-3(1), TAP004) Lodestone Catalog.

Directors' & Officers' Liability Insurance. 4 cass. (Running Time: 5 hrs. 30 min.). 1991. 125.00 (T7-9334) PLI.
This May 1991 program reviews the significant issues that arise in D & O litigation & offers practical solutions to them.

Directors' & Officers' Liability Update. 1987. bk. 75.00 incl. book.; 50.00 cass. only.; 25.00 book only. PA Bar Inst.

Directors in Charge: Skills for Supervision. Dora C. Fowler. 4 cass. (Running Time: 6 hrs.). 1994. pap. bk. 49.00 Set, incl. 43p. bk. (978-1-57323-005-6(7)) Natl Inst Child Mgmt.
Child care management training.

Directory of Alternative Investment Programs: 2000 Edition. Ed. by Steven P. Galante & Keith W. Moore. 2000. audio compact disk 495.00 (978-1-893648-07-4(9)) Dow JonesCo.

Directory of Hospital Personnel, 2002: CD-ROM & Directory Combo. 2002. bk. 2995.00 (978-1-930956-82-7(7)) Grey Hse Pub.

Dirk Gently: the Long Dark Tea-Time of the Soul: A BBC Radio Full-Cast Dramatization. Douglas Adams. (Running Time: 3 hrs. 0 mins. 0 sec.). (ENG.). 2009. audio compact disk 29.95 (978-1-60283-779-9(1)) Pub: AudioGO. Dist(s): Perseus Dist

***Dirk Gently's Holistic Detective Agency.** Douglas Adams. Narrated by Full Cast Production Staff. (Running Time: 3 hrs. 0 mins. 0 sec.). (ENG., 2010. audio compact disk 29.95 (978-1-4056-7743-1(0)) Pub: AudioGO. Dist(s): Perseus Dist

Dirk Gently's Holistic Detective Agency. Douglas Adams. 2004. 9.95 (978-0-7435-4652-2(0)) Pub: S&S Audio. Dist(s): S and S Inc

Dirk Gently's Holistic Detective Agency. unabr. ed. Douglas Adams. Read by Douglas Adams. 5 CDs. (Running Time: 6 hrs.). 2001. audio compact disk 34.95 (N Millennium Audio) New Millenn Enter.

Dirk Gently's Holistic Detective Agency. unabr. ed. Douglas Adams. Read by Douglas Adams. 4 cass. (Running Time: 6 hrs.). 2004. 25.00 (978-1-59007-059-8(3)) Pub: New Millenn Enter. Dist(s): PerseuPGW
The hero is Dirk Gently, a hero who will probably never make his way into the great tradition of hard-boiled, sophisticated detectives. Missing cats & messy divorces are his specialty, but his goal for now is to clear a college friend of suspicion of murder. On the way, he discovers a ghost, a time traveler - & the devastating secret of humankind!.

Dirk Gently's Holistic Detective Agency. unabr. abr. ed. Douglas Adams. Read by Douglas Adams. 6 CDs. (Running Time: 6 hrs.). 2004. 39.95 (978-1-59007-063-5(1)) Pub: New Millenn Enter. Dist(s): PerseuPGW

***Dirt.** abr. ed. Stuart Woods. Read by Tony Roberts. (ENG.). 2005. (978-0-06-084185-0(0), Harper Audio); (978-0-06-084187-4(7), Harper Audio) HarperCollins Pubs.

Dirt. unabr. ed. Stuart Woods. Read by Barrett Whitener. 6 cass. (Running Time: 9 hrs.). (Stone Barrington Ser.: No. 2). 1996. 48.00 (978-0-913369-26-5(8), 4177) Books on Tape.
For Amanda Dart, gossip columnist, the tables have turned. When someone starts faxing details of her affair with a well-known businessman to national opinion-makers, Amanda hires Stone Barrington, lawyer & P.I., to find the faxer.

Dirt. unabr. ed. Stuart Woods. Narrated by Frank Muller. 6 cass. (Running Time: 8 hrs.). (Stone Barrington Ser.: No. 2). 51.00 (978-0-7887-0630-1(6), 94805E7) Recorded Bks.
Welcome to a world where a celebrity's carefully-crafted image, decades in the making, can be destroyed by a single snap of a shutter. Features New York detective Stone Barrington. Available to libraries only.

Dirt Bikes. David Armentrout & Patricia Armentrout. (Motorcycle Mania (CD-ROM) Ser.). (J). 2008. audio compact disk 24.95 (978-1-60472-767-8(5)) Rourke FL.

Dirt Made My Lunch. Perf. by Banana Slug String Band Staff. 1 cass. (J). (gr. k-7). 1989. 9.98 (978-1-877737-29-9(1), 2171) MFLP CA.
It's really very easy to understand how all life is interconnected when the joyful Slugs add humor, upbeat folk, rap & rock music to themes of solar energy, cycles of growth, eagles, rivers & love shared among friends.

Dirt Music. Tim Winton. Read by Suzi Dougherty. (Running Time: 11 hrs. 45 mins.). 2009. 89.99 (978-1-74214-293-7(1), 9781742142937) Pub: Bolinda Pubng AUS. Dist(s): Bolinda Pub Inc

Dirt Music. unabr. ed. Read by Suzi Dougherty. Ed. by Tim Winton. 10 CDs. (Running Time: 11 hrs. 45 mins.). 2004. audio compact disk 98.95 (978-1-74030-854-0(9)) Pub: Bolinda Pubng AUS. Dist(s): Bolinda Pub Inc

Dirt Music. unabr. ed. Ed. by Tim Winton. 8 cass. (Running Time: 11 hrs. 45 mins.). 2004. 64.00 (978-1-74030-776-5(3)) Pub: Bolinda Pubng AUS. Dist(s): Bolinda Pub Inc

Dirt Music. unabr. ed. Tim Winton. Read by Suzi Dougherty. (Running Time: 42300 sec.). 2005. audio compact disk 43.95 (978-1-74093-678-1(7)) Pub: Bolinda Pubng AUS. Dist(s): Bolinda Pub Inc

Dirt/el Suelo: The Scoop on Soil/Tierra y Arena. abr. ed. Natalie M. Rosinsky. Tr. by Sol Robledo. Illus. by Sheree Boyd. (Amazing Science Ser.). (SPA.). (gr. k). 2008. audio compact disk 14.60 (978-1-4048-4471-1(6)) CapstoneDig.

***Dirty Blonde.** abr. ed. Lisa Scottoline. Read by Kate Burton. (ENG.). 2006. (978-0-06-114696-1(X), Harper Audio); (978-0-06-114693-0(5), Harper Audio) HarperCollins Pubs.

Dirty Blonde. abr. ed. Lisa Scottoline. Read by Kate Burton. (Running Time: 21600 sec.). 2008. audio compact disk 14.95 (978-0-06-157123-7(7), Harper Audio) HarperCollins Pubs.

Dirty Blonde. unabr. ed. Lisa Scottoline. Read by Barbara Rosenblat. 9 CDs. (Running Time: 37800 sec.). 2006. audio compact disk 39.95 (978-0-06-089817-5(8)) HarperCollins Pubs.

***Dirty Blonde.** unabr. ed. Lisa Scottoline. Read by Barbara Rosenblat. (ENG.). 2006. (978-0-06-113492-0(9), Harper Audio); (978-0-06-113493-7(7), Harper Audio) HarperCollins Pubs.

Dirty Blonde. unabr. ed. Lisa Scottoline. Read by Barbara Rosenblat. 9 CDs. (Running Time: 10 hrs.). 2006. audio compact disk 99.75 (978-1-4193-9011-1(2), C3710); 79.75 (978-1-4193-9009-8(0), 98356) Recorded Bks.
At 39, Cate has just landed her dream job as a Federal Judge. But when high-profile producer Art Simone is murdered, Cate becomes a prime suspect. Now Cate must protect herself and her loved ones from being caught in the legal system she thought she knew so well.

Dirty Distant War, Pt. 1. unabr. ed. E. M. Nathanson. Read by Wolfram Kandinsky. 10 cass. (Running Time: 15 hrs.). 1990. 80.00 (978-0-7366-1681-2(0), 2529-A) Books on Tape.
Major John Reisman knows the danger that lies behind enemy lines. He found it with the Dirty Dozen. Now Reisman is flying over the Hump into a different theater of the war, where lines of conflict are fuzzy at best. His OSS mission is vague: to find out what strings are being pulled in the knots of China, Burma & French Indonesia, & to start yanking on some that might give an advantage in the war against Japan. But Reisman finds enemies pretending to be friends, friends acting like enemies - a web of crossed purposes, deceit & betrayal.

Dirty Distant War, Pt. 2. E. M. Nathanson. Read by Wolfram Kandinsky. 7 cass. (Running Time: 10 hrs. 30 min.). 1990. 72.00 (2529-B) Books on Tape.

Dirty Dozen, Pt. 2. E. M. Nathanson. Read by Wolfram Kandinsky. 1990. 72.00 (2530-B) Books on Tape.

Dirty Dozen, Pt. 2. unabr. ed. E. M. Nathanson. Read by Wolfram Kandinsky. 9 cass. (Running Time: 13 hrs. 30 min.). 1990. 72.00 (978-0-7366-1683-6(7), 2530-B) Books on Tape.
Project Amnesty is a plan to drop 12 American soldiers-prisoners behind German lines in France just before D- Day. Their trainer-warden, Captain John Reisman resents the assignment & no wonder: it seems doomed to failure & very likely to be terminal personally.

Dirty Girls Make Bad Friends. abr. ed. A. J. Jacobs. Read by A. J. Jacobs. Ed. by Ben Karlin. (Running Time: 15 mins.). (ENG.). 2008. 1.98 (978-1-60024-347-9(9)) Pub: Hachet Audio. Dist(s): HachBkGrp

Dirty Girls on Top. unabr. ed. Alisa Valdes-Rodriguez. Narrated by Cynthia Holloway. (Running Time: 15 hrs. 0 mins. 0 sec.). (ENG.). 2008. audio compact disk 39.99 (978-1-4001-0624-0(9)); audio compact disk 79.99 (978-1-4001-3624-7(5)); audio compact disk 29.99 (978-1-4001-5624-5(6)) Pub: Tantor Media. Dist(s): IngramPubServ

Dirty Girls Social Club see Club Social de las Chicas Temerarias

Dirty Job. Christopher Moore. Narrated by Fisher Stevens. (Running Time: 42600 sec.). 2006. audio compact disk 29.95 (978-0-7927-3975-3(2), CMP 919) AudioGO.

Dirty Job. Christopher Moore. Read by Fisher Stevens. 6 cass. (Running Time: 42600 sec.). (Sound Library). 2006. 54.95 (978-0-7927-3934-0(5),

CSL 919); audio compact disk 74.95 (978-0-7927-3935-7(3), SLD 919) AudioGO.

Dirty Job. unabr. ed. Christopher Moore. Read by Fisher Stevens. 10 CDs. (Running Time: 43200 sec.). 2006. audio compact disk 39.95 (978-0-06-087259-5(4)) HarperCollins Pubs.

***Dirty Job.** unabr. ed. Christopher Moore. Read by Fisher Stevens. (ENG.). 2006. (978-0-06-087851-1(7), Harper Audio); (978-0-06-087852-8(5), Harper Audio) HarperCollins Pubs.

Dirty Laundry. Tori Carrington. Read by Anna Fields. (Running Time: 27000 sec.). 2006. 54.95 (978-0-7861-4598-0(6)); audio compact disk 63.00 (978-0-7861-6990-0(7)) Blckstn Audio.

Dirty Laundry. unabr. ed. Tori Carrington. Read by Anna Fields. (Running Time: 27000 sec.). 2006. audio compact disk 29.95 (978-0-7861-7507-9(9)) Blckstn Audio.

Dirty Laundry. unabr. ed. Paul Thomas. Read by David Tredinnick. 6 cass. (Running Time: 9 hrs.). 2001. 48.00 (978-1-74030-358-3(X)) Pub: Bolinda Pubng AUS. Dist(s): Bolinda Pub Inc

Dirty Little Secret: Uncovering the Truth Behind Porn. unabr. ed. Craig Gross. (Running Time: 4 hrs. 30 mins. 0 sec.). (ENG.). 2006. 12.99 (978-0-310-27774-3(4)) Zondervan.

Dirty Martini. J. A. Konrath. Read by Susie Breck & Dick Hill. (Playaway Adult Fiction Ser.). (ENG.). 2009. 65.00 (978-1-60775-516-6(5)) Find a World.

Dirty Martini. unabr. ed. Read by Susie Breck & Dick Hill. (Running Time: 28800 sec.). (Jacqueline "Jack" Daniels Mystery Ser.). 2007. 69.25 (978-1-4233-1243-7(0), 9781423312437, BrilAudUnabridg); audio compact disk 24.95 (978-1-4233-1246-8(5), 9781423312468, Brilliance MP3); audio compact disk 29.95 (978-1-4233-1244-4(9), 9781423312444, Bril Audio CD Unabri); audio compact disk 87.25 (978-1-4233-1245-1(7), 9781423312451, BriAudCD Unabrid); audio compact disk 39.25 (978-1-4233-1247-5(3), 9781423312475, Brlnc Audio MP3 Lib) Brilliance Audio.

Dirty Martini. unabr. ed. J. A. Konrath. Read by Susie Breck & Dick Hill. (Running Time: 8 hrs.). (Jacqueline "Jack" Daniels Mystery Ser.). 2007. 39.25 (978-1-4233-1249-9(X), 9781423312499, BADLE); 24.95 (978-1-4233-1248-2(1), 9781423312482, BAD) Brilliance Audio.

Dirty Money: A Sully Gomez Mystery. Mel Cebulash. (J). 1993. 10.95 (978-1-56420-003-7(5)) New Readers.

***Dirty Nasty Truth.** abr. ed. J. Barrett Hawkins. Des. by Rick Ford. (J). 2010. 14.95 (978-0-9791718-4-0(9)) DarkPlanet.

Dirty Sally. unabr. ed. Michael Simon. Read by Scott Brick. 6 cass. (Running Time: 9 hrs.). 2004. 54.00 (978-1-4159-0405-3(7)) Books on Tape.
When a young prostitute is found murdered, police detective Dan Reles must find the killer - even if the bloody path leads to Austin's elite.

***Dirty Secrets Club.** Meg Gardiner. Read by Susan Ericksen. (Playaway Adult Fiction Ser.). (ENG.). 2009. 69.99 (978-1-4418-2371-7(9)) Find a World.

Dirty Secrets Club. abr. ed. Meg Gardiner. Read by Susan Ericksen. (Running Time: 6 hrs.). (Jo Beckett Ser.). 2009. audio compact disk 14.99 (978-1-4233-6159-6(8), 9781423361596, BCD Value Price) Brilliance Audio.

Dirty Secrets Club. unabr. ed. Meg Gardiner. Read by Susan Ericksen. (Running Time: 12 hrs.). (Jo Beckett Ser.). 2008. 39.25 (978-1-4233-6157-2(1), 9781423361572, BADLE); 24.95 (978-1-4233-6156-5(3), 9781423361565, BAD); audio compact disk 36.95 (978-1-4233-6152-7(0), 9781423361527, Bril Audio CD Unabri); audio compact disk 97.25 (978-1-4233-6153-4(9), 9781423361534, BriAudCD Unabrid) Brilliance Audio.

Dirty Secrets Club. unabr. ed. Meg Gardiner. Read by Susan Ericksen. Directed By Francesca Amari. Contrib. by Kevon Klemple. (Running Time: 12 hrs.). (Jo Beckett Ser.). 2008. audio compact disk 39.25 (978-1-4233-6155-8(5), 9781423361558, Brlnc Audio MP3 Lib); audio compact disk 24.95 (978-1-4233-6154-1(7), 9781423361541, Brilliance MP3) Brilliance Audio.

***Dirty Sexy Politics WMA.** Meghan McCain. (ENG.). 2010. 21.99 (978-1-4013-9520-9(1)) Pub: Hyperion. Dist(s): HarperCollins Pubs

Dirty Sink, A Bug, & Squirrels: None: God Speaks, Abridged AudioBook. (ENG.). 2008. 12.50 (978-0-9788413-2-4(8)) Powell.

Dirty White Boys. abr. ed. Stephen Hunter. Read by Eric G. Dove. (Running Time: 6 hrs.). 2010. audio compact disk 14.99 (978-1-4418-3939-8(9), 9781441839398) Brilliance Audio.

***Dirty White Boys.** abr. ed. Stephen Hunter. (Running Time: 5 hrs.). 2011. audio compact disk 14.99 (978-1-4418-3940-4(2), 9781441839404, BCD Value Price) Brilliance Audio.

Dirty White Boys. abr. ed. Stephen Hunter. (ENG.). 2006. 14.98 (978-1-59483-774-6(0)) Pub: Hachet Audio. Dist(s): HachBkGrp

Dirty White Boys. unabr. ed. Stephen Hunter. Read by Eric G. Dove. (Running Time: 15 hrs.). 2010. 24.99 (978-1-4418-3935-0(6), 9781441839350, Brilliance MP3); audio compact disk 29.99 (978-1-4418-3933-6(X), 9781441839336) Brilliance Audio.

***Dirty White Boys.** unabr. ed. Stephen Hunter. Read by Eric G. Dove. (Running Time: 15 hrs.). 2010. 39.97 (978-1-4418-3936-7(4), 9781441839367, Brlnc Audio MP3 Lib); 39.97 (978-1-4418-3938-1(0), 9781441839381, BADLE); 24.99 (978-1-4418-3937-4(2), 9781441839374, BAD); audio compact disk 89.97 (978-1-4418-3934-3(8), 9781441839343, BriAudCD Unabrid) Brilliance Audio.

Dirty Work. Larry Brown. Read by Larry Brown. 1 cass. (Running Time: 30 min.). 8.95 (AMF-217) Am Audio Prose.
The author reads from his first novel "Dirty Work" & talks about homage to Vietnam veterans.

Dirty Work. unabr. ed. Larry Brown. Narrated by Ed Sala & Peter Francis James. 4 cass. (Running Time: 5 hrs. 15 mins.). 2000. 35.00 (978-0-7887-0422-2(2), 94614E7) Recorded Bks.
One of the most powerful anti-war novels in American literature. Walter James has no face. Braiden Chaney has no arms or legs. They lost them 22 years ago, in Vietnam. Now, in the course of one long night in a V.A. hospital, these two soldiers - one black, the other white - reveal how they came to be where they are & what they can only hope to become.

Dirty Work. unabr. ed. Stuart Woods. Read by Robert Lawrence & Barrett Whitener. 7 CDs. (Running Time: 7 hrs.). (Stone Barrington Ser.: Bk. 9). 2003. audio compact disk 29.95 (978-1-59086-734-1(3), 1590867343) Brilliance Audio.

Dirty Work. unabr. ed. Stuart Woods. Read by Robert Lawrence. 5 cass. (Running Time: 7 hrs.). (Stone Barrington Ser.: Bk. 9). 2003. 29.95 (978-1-59086-732-7(7), 1590867327, BAU); 69.25 (978-1-59086-733-4(5), 1590867335, CD) Brilliance Audio.
Back in New York City after the London adventures of The Short Forever, cop-turned-lawyer Stone Barrington is approached by a colleague at the firm of Woodman & Weld who needs help with a celebrity divorce case. Heiress Elena Marks needs proof of her layabout husband's infidelity before she can begin divorce proceedings. When the undercover work Stone sets up turns dirty - and catastrophic - leaving the errant husband dead and the mystery woman gone without a trace, Stone must clear his own good name and find a killer hiding among the glitterati of New York's high society. Carpenter - the beautiful British intelligence agent first encountered in The Short Forever - arrives in New York to begin an investigation of her own; Stone suspects that her case is strangely connected to the dead husband. And he and Dino, his former NYPD partner, are set to face the most bizarre and challenging assignment of their very colorful careers.

Dirty Work. unabr. ed. Stuart Woods. Read by Robert Lawrence. 7 CDs, Library ed. (Running Time: 7 hrs.). (Stone Barrington Ser.: No. 9). 2003. audio compact disk 82.25 (978-1-59086-735-8(1), 1590867351, CD Unabrid Lib Ed) Brilliance Audio.

Dirty Work. unabr. ed. Stuart Woods. Read by Robert Lawrence. (Running Time: 7 hrs.). (Stone Barrington Ser.: No. 9). 2004. 39.25 (978-1-59335-442-8(8), 1593354428, Brlnc Audio MP3 Lib) Brilliance Audio.

Dirty Work. unabr. ed. Stuart Woods. Read by Robert Lawrence. (Running Time: 7 hrs.). (Stone Barrington Ser.: No. 9). 2004. 39.25 (978-1-59710-210-0(5), 1597102105, BADLE); 24.95 (978-1-59710-211-7(3), 1597102113, BAD) Brilliance Audio.

Dirty Work. unabr. ed. Stuart Woods. Read by Robert Lawrence. (Running Time: 7 hrs.). (Stone Barrington Ser.: No. 9). 2004. 24.95 (978-1-59335-078-9(3), 1593350783) Soulmate Audio Bks.

Dirty Work & Joe. unabr. ed. Larry Brown. Read by Larry Brown. Illus. by Kay Bonnetti. 2 cass. (Authors Reading Ser.). 1995. 13.95 set. (978-1-55644-411-1(7), 15021) Am Audio Prose.
Distinguished Southern author reads unabridged excerpts from two of his novels.

Dis Papa, l'amour C'est Quoi? 1 CD. (Running Time: 1 hr.).Tr. of Tell Me Daddy, What is Love?. 2001. audio compact disk 14.95 (978-2-89558-004-1(9)) Pub: Coffragants CAN. Dist(s): Penton Overseas

Disagree Without Destroying Set: Healthy Conflict Resolution for Couples. David Grudermeyer & Rebecca Grudermeyer. 2 cass. 18.95 INCL. HANDOUTS. (T-36) Willingness Wrks.

Disagreement. unabr. ed. Nick Taylor. (Running Time: 11 hrs. 0 mins. 0 sec.). (ENG.). 2008. audio compact disk 69.99 (978-1-4001-3710-7(1)) Pub: Tantor Media. Dist(s): IngramPubServ

Disagreement. unabr. ed. Nick Taylor. Read by William Dufris. (Running Time: 11 hrs. 0 mins. 0 sec.). (ENG.). 2008. audio compact disk 34.99 (978-1-4001-0710-0(5)); audio compact disk 24.99 (978-1-4001-5710-5(2)) Pub: Tantor Media. Dist(s): IngramPubServ

Disappear Here. Contrib. by LA Symphony et al. 2005. audio compact disk 13.98 (978-5-558-96603-9(3)) Gotee Records.

Disappearance. J. F. Freedman. Read by Patrick Cullen. 12 cass. (Running Time: 17 hrs. 30 mins.). 2000. 83.95 (978-0-7861-1571-6(8), 2400) Blckstn Audio.
On a soft summer night, she vanishes with her friends sleeping nearby. With her parents' wealth & power guarding her, someone walks into the bedroom of her Montecito home & takes fourteen-year-old Emma Lancaster away.

***Disappearance.** unabr. ed. J. F. Freedman. Read by Patrick Cullen. (Running Time: 17 hrs. 30 mins.). 2010. 44.95 (978-1-4417-4146-2(1)); audio compact disk 123.00 (978-1-4417-4143-1(7)) Blckstn Audio.

Disappearance. unabr. ed. Efrem Sigel. Read by Anthony Heald. (Running Time: 10 hrs. 50 mins.). (ENG.). 2009. 29.95 (978-1-4332-9257-6(2)); 59.95 (978-1-4332-9253-8(X)); audio compact disk 90.00 (978-1-4332-9254-5(8)) Blckstn Audio.

Disappearance. unabr. ed. Collin Wilcox. Read by Larry McKeever. 8 cass. (Running Time: 8 hrs.). (Frank Hastings Ser.). 1996. 48.00 (978-0-7366-3346-8(4), 3996) Books on Tape.
Now that he's made Lieutenant, Frank Hastings assigns routine cases to his subordinates. He saves for himself the puzzlers, like the disappearance of a prominent woman. She is Carol Connelly, wife & mother, rich & elegant, from a family that leans on the mayor for action. Solving the case is politically expedient, but Hastings is stumped. Mrs. Connelly doesn't fit the victim profile. Those close to her say she's cool, aggressive...a predator. Hastings is under pressure to find her - dead or alive.

Disappearance of Childhood. unabr. ed. Neil Postman. Read by Jeff Riggenbach. 5 cass. (Running Time: 7 hrs. 30 min.). 1997. 39.95 (1896) Blckstn Audio.
From the vogue for nubile models to the explosion in the juvenile crime rate, this modern classic of social history & media traces the precipitous decline of childhood in America today & the corresponding threat to the notion of adulthood.

Disappearance of Childhood. unabr. ed. Neil Postman. Read by Jeff Riggenbach. 5 cass. (Running Time: 7 hrs.). 2001. 39.95 (978-0-7861-1131-2(3), 1896) Blckstn Audio.

Disappearance of the Universe Set: Straight Talk about Illusions, Past Lives, Religion, Sex, Politics, & the Miracles of Forgiveness. abr. ed. Gary Renard. Read by Gary Renard. 6 CDs. 2005. audio compact disk 23.95 (978-1-4019-0678-8(8)) Hay House.

Disappearances. unabr. collector's ed. Howard Frank Mosher. Read by Ron Shoop. 9 cass. (Running Time: 9 hrs.). 1986. 54.00 (978-0-7366-1050-6(2), 1978) Books on Tape.
Bill's dad, desperate to preserve his cattle herd through a bitter winter, resorts to smuggling whiskey-a traditional family occupation. He takes his son on a voyage into the vast reaches of the Canadian wilderness & into the demonic & spellbinding past. What they find is the genuine stuff of legends.

Disappearances of Madalena Grimaldi. unabr. ed. Jennifer Rowe. Read by Tracey Callander. 8 cass. (Running Time: 12 hrs.). 1999. (978-1-86442-366-2(8), 590373) Bolinda Pubng AUS.
Claudia Valentine P.I. returns gutsy & glamorous as ever. It is the start of a long, hot summer & Madalena Grimaldi has disappeared. Claudia is hired to find the missing schoolgirl but she's already working on a case, the death of Guy Valentine, her father. As Claudia searches the streets, looking for the ghost of her derelict father & for the man who can lead her to Madalena, she finds herself sinking into a world where, for many, rock bottom is only the beginning.

***Disappeared.** unabr. ed. M. R. Hall. Narrated by Sian Thomas. 11 CDs. (Running Time: 12 hrs. 16 mins.). 2009. audio compact disk 110.95 (978-0-7927-6860-9(4), Chivers Sound Lib) AudioGO.

Disappearing Act. Sid Fleischman. 2 cassette. (Running Time: 2 hours). (J). 2003. 20.00 (978-1-932076-43-1(3)) Full Cast Audio.
Fast, funny, and suspenseful - the brand new novel from Newbery Medalist Sid Fleischman. An unseen man they call the Toad is stalking twelve-year-old Kevin and his older sister, Holly. They flee town in Holly's beat-up old car, driving west until they reach the Pacific Ocean. They change their names and attempt to hide in plain sight as street performers in Venice, California. But have they really eluded the Toad?.

Disappearing Act. unabr. ed. Sid Fleischman. Read by Full Cast Production Staff. (J). 2007. 34.99 (978-1-60252-608-2(7)) Find a World.

Disappearing Acts. Terry McMillan. (Running Time: 30 min.). 8.95 (AMF-225) Am Audio Prose.
Talks about fiction of the Afro-American middle-class.

Disappearing Acts. unabr. ed. Read by Marjorie Johnson & Marc Damon Johnson. Arranged by Terry McMillan. 12 CDs. (Running Time: 18 Hrs.). 2000. audio compact disk 110.95 (978-0-7927-9966-5(6), SLD 017, Chivers Sound Lib) AudioGO.
Zora Banks's musical career was about to take off when she met gorgeous Franklin Swift in a Brooklyn brownstone & there could be no walking away.

Disappearing Acts. unabr. ed. Terry McMillan. Read by Marjorie Johnson. 10 vols. (Running Time: 15 hrs.). 2000. bk. 84.95 (978-0-7927-2272-4(8), CSL 161, Chivers Sound Lib) AudioGO.
Franklin Swift was a sometimes-employed construction worker, not quite divorced daddy of two. Women confused his program, so he was leaving them alone. Zora Banks was a teacher, singer, song-writer. Her musical career was just about to take off, and she was taking a break from heartbreak. Then they met in a Brooklyn brownstone, and there could be no walking away.

***Disappearing Spoon: And Other True Tales of Madness, Love, & the History of the World from the Periodic Table of the Elements.** unabr. ed. Sam Kean. Narrated by Sean Runnette. (Running Time: 12 hrs. 0 mins.). 2010. 34.99 (978-1-4001-9952-5(2)); 17.99 (978-1-4001-8952-6(7)); 24.99 (978-1-4001-6952-6(6)); audio compact disk 83.99 (978-1-4001-4952-0(5)); audio compact disk 34.99 (978-1-4001-1952-3(9)) Pub: Tantor Media. Dist(s): IngramPubServ

Disappearing TV Star. unabr. ed. Emily Rodda. Read by Rebecca Macauley. 3 CDs. (Running Time: 3 hrs. 15 mins.). (Raven Hill Mysteries Ser.: No. 3). (J). (gr. 7-9). 2006. audio compact disk 54.95 (978-1-74093-758-0(9)) Pub: Bolinda Pubng AUS. Dist(s): Bolinda Pub Inc

Disappointment: Parent of Despair. unabr. ed. Lois F. Timmins. 1 cass. (Running Time: 55 min.). 1989. 12.95 (978-0-931814-17-4(0)) Comn Studies.
Discusses the place of disappointment in the gamut of human feelings, how it arises, & how to modify unrealistic expectations in order to avoid despair.

***Disappointment with God: Three Questions No One Asks Aloud.** Philip Yancey. (Running Time: 7 hrs. 32 mins. 0 sec.). (ENG.). 2008. 14.99 (978-0-310-30439-5(3)) Zondervan.

Disarming Principalities Through Love. Francis Frangipane. 1 cass. (Running Time: 90 mins.). (Strategies for our Cities Ser.: Vol. 3). 2000. 5.00 (FF06-003) Morning NC.
This series provides practical, biblical solutions that have been tested & have born fruit for those with a vision for their cities.

Disarming the Past: Command Your Future. As told by Andy Andrews. 2007. audio compact disk 149.99 (978-0-9776246-9-0(2)) Lightning Crown Pub.

Disarming the Power of Fear. Elena Bussolino & Anna Florentis. 2000. 7.99 (978-0-9720314-2-4(1)) Bagatto.

Disarming the Power of Guilt. Elena Bussolino & Anna Florentis. 2000. 7.99 (978-0-9720314-4-8(8)) Bagatto.

Disaster. abr. ed. L. Ron Hubbard. 2 cass. (Running Time: 3 hrs.). (Mission Earth Ser.: Vol. 8). 2002. 15.95 (978-1-59212-064-2(4)) Gala Pr LLC.
The New York Mafia is under aerial assault. The United States is about to declare war. The world's oil supply is rumored to be radioactive. And a mountain of ice is plunging from outer space directly toward Earth!.

Disaster, Deception & Defeat Vol. 1: Tales of Early Southwest Michigan. unabr. ed. Robert C. Myers. Read by Robert C. Myers. 1 cass. (Running Time: 1 hr.). 1997. 10.75 (978-0-9660808-0-3(7)) Berrien Cnty.
Short passages dealing with factual historical sketches of southwest Michigan.

Disaster in Oceania Read Along. Prod. by Laraim Associates. (Barclay Family Adventure Ser.). (YA). 2005. audio compact disk (978-1-56254-989-3(8)) Saddleback Edu.

***Disaster Planning.** PUEI. 2008. audio compact disk 199.00 (978-1-935041-21-4(5), CareerTrack) P Univ E Inc.

***Disaster Preparedness: A Memoir.** unabr. ed. Heather Havrilesky. (Running Time: 8 hrs. 30 mins.). 2010. 29.95 (978-1-4417-6955-8(2)); 54.95 (978-1-4417-6952-7(8)); audio compact disk 29.95 (978-1-4417-6954-1(4)) Blckstn Audio.

***Disaster Preparedness (Library Edition) A Memoir.** unabr. ed. Heather Havrilesky. (Running Time: 8 hrs 30 mins.). 2010. audio compact disk 76.00 (978-1-4417-6953-4(6)) Blckstn Audio.

disastrous Party. unabr. ed. Stephen Axelsen. Read by Stanley McGeagh. (Running Time: 2 hrs. 25 mins.). (Piccolo & Annabelle Ser.). (J). 2007. audio compact disk 43.95 (978-1-74093-832-7(1)) Pub: Bolinda Pubng AUS. Dist(s): Bolinda Pub Inc

***Disastrous Voyage of the Santa Margarita.** Richard Woodman. 2010. 76.95 (978-1-4079-0980-6(0)); audio compact disk 89.95 (978-1-4079-0981-3(9)) Pub: Soundings Ltd GBR. Dist(s): Ulverscroft US

Discernement: Acting Wisely. Sue Anne Steffey Morrow. (Living the Good Life Together Ser.). 2007. 125.00 (978-0-687-64324-0(4)) Abingdon.

Discerning Presence in the Midst of the People, Set. Scripts. George Aschenbrenner. 2 cass. (Running Time: 2 hrs. 53 min.). (Spirituality of Diocesan Priesthood Ser.). 1998. 19.95 (TAH405) Alba Hse Comns.
Focuses on the deepest internal nature of priestly animation - the art of discernment. This faith & ability to discern reveals the core of priestly identity rooted in the human self.

Discerning the Battle. 2000. 14.00 (978-0-9702183-4-6(6)) Aslans Pl.

Discerning the Language of the Spirit. Rick Joyner. 1 cass. (Running Time: 90 mins.). (Hearing God Ser.: Vol. 4). 2000. 5.00 (RJ10-004) Morning NC.
"Principles of Spiritual Warfare" & "Putting on the Full Armor of God." These tapes highlight practical truths that lead to certain victory in spirtual warfare.

Discerning the Times. Bobby Hilton. 4 cass. 2001. 22.00 (978-1-930766-26-6(2)) Pub: Bishop Bobby. Dist(s): STL Dist NA

Discerning Your Prayer Style. Carole Riley. 1 cass. (Running Time: 1 hr.). 2001. 9.95 (A6311) St Anthony Mess Pr.
Apprehend, understand, affirm and apply the best style of prayer that leads us to an interior knowledge of God and of ourselves and to inner peace.

Discernment. Vincent M. Walsh. 1 cass. 1986. 4.00 Key of David.
Personal stories & examples told to promote a full understanding of the basic powers of the Renewal.

Disciple. Contrib. by Disciple. Prod. by Travis Wyrick. 2005. audio compact disk 17.98 (978-5-559-01488-3(5)) Pt of Grace Ent.

Disciple I Adult Tape 1 Pal. bk. 35.00 (978-0-687-71827-6(9)) Abingdon.

Disciple I Adult Tape 2 Pal. bk. 35.00 (978-0-687-71828-3(7)) Abingdon.

Disciple I Adult Tape 3 Pal. bk. 35.00 (978-0-687-71829-0(5)) Abingdon.

Disciple I Revised English Version. bk. 35.00 (978-0-687-78341-0(0)); bk. 35.00 (978-0-687-78342-7(9)); bk. 35.00 (978-0-687-78343-4(7)); bk. 35.00 (978-0-687-78344-1(5)) Abingdon.

Disciple Making: A 10-Step Guide for Churches. Alvin J. Vander Griend. pap. bk. 20.00 (978-1-56212-115-0(4), 216625) FaithAliveChr.

Disciplemaking: Self-Study Course in Understanding & Applying Jesus' Command to "Make Disciples" Ed. by Robert E. Coleman et al. 1994. pap. bk. 41.95 (978-1-879089-12-9(2)) Evangelism & Missions.

Disciples of the Cross. Francis Frangipane. 1 cass. (Running Time: 90 mins.). (Disciples of the Cross Ser.: Vol. 2). 2000. 5.00 (FF01-002) Morning NC.
In this four-part series, Francis releases important information needed to clearly understand the principles of taking up the cross & following Christ.

Disciples of the Cross Series. Francis Frangipane. 4 cass. (Running Time: 6 hrs.). 2000. 20.00 (FF01-000) Morning NC.

Disciples' Prayer. 12 cass. 35.95 (2060, HarperThor) HarpC GBR.

Discipleship. 5 CDs. 2005. audio compact disk (978-0-9767967-6-3(7)) Family Discipleship.

Discipleship. David T. Demola. 7 cass. 28.00 (S-1049) Faith Fellow Min.

Discipleship. unabr. ed. Vivekananda. Read by John Batiste. 1 cass. (Running Time: 45 min.). 1988. 7.95 (978-1-882915-06-4(2)) Vedanta Ctr Atlanta.
Requirements of a spiritual disciple. Relationship of teacher to disciple.

Discipleship: Turning the World Upside Down. Edwina Gateley. 2 cass. (Running Time: 2 hrs.). 2001. 18.95 (A5940) St Anthony Mess Pr.
Includes 4 talks on making space for God, and learning to make room for God and his presence.

Discipleship & the Enneagram. William F. Maestri. 4 cass. (Running Time: 3 hrs. 20 min.). 1992. 26.95 set. (TAH266) Alba Hse Comns.
These insights on the Enneagram will deepen your self-understanding, sharpen your appreciation of your own humanity, & challenge you to be less judgmental & more loving.

Discipleship Evangelism. Created by Andrew Wommack & Don Krow. 2004. audio compact disk 20.00 (978-1-59548-101-6(X)) A Wommack.

Discipleship Evangelism 48 Lesson Set. Based on a work by Andrew Wommack & Don Krow. 2004. spiral bd. 109.40 (978-1-59548-035-4(8)) A Wommack.

Discipleship Journal's Anthology on CD-ROM Libronix Version. ed. Discipleship Journal. (ENG.). 2007. audio compact disk 29.99 (978-1-60006-109-7(5)) NavPress.

Discipleship Journal's Anthology on CD-ROM WORDsearch 7 Version. ed. Discipleship Journal. (ENG.). 2007. audio compact disk 29.99 (978-1-60006-108-0(7)) NavPress.

Disciplina I. Grover Bravo.Tr. of Discipline I. (SPA.). 2009. audio compact disk 15.00 (978-1-935405-50-4(0)) Hombre Nuevo.

Disciplina II. Grover Bravo.Tr. of Discipline II. (SPA.). 2009. audio compact disk 15.00 (978-1-935405-51-1(9)) Hombre Nuevo.

Disciplina Positiva. Jane Nelsen.Tr. of Positive Discipline. (SPA.). 2008. audio compact disk 39.95 (978-0-9816250-8-9(8)) EmpoweringUT.

Discipline: The Glad Surrender. unabr. ed. Elisabeth Elliot. Read by Elisabeth Elliot. 4 cass. (Running Time: 3 hrs. 10 min.). 1989. 18.95 (978-0-8474-2014-8(0)) Back to Bible.
A series that teaches how to discipline one's mind, body, time & feelings & find joy & fulfillment.

Discipline & Delight. Read by Osel Tendzin. 1 cass. 1977. 12.50 (A059) Vajradhatu.
One talk. "Dissatisfaction is the nature of human existence. The reason is clinging to pleasure, avoiding pain, & ignoring what is not understood to be either".

Discipline for Life! Madelyn Swift. 8 cass. (Running Time: 10 hrs.). (One Step at a Time Programs Ser.). bk. 129.95 Set, staff training. (5015); bk. 129.95 Set, parent education. (5018) Natl Inst Child Mgmt.
Innovative ideas & strategies for dealing with children & parents. Includes: "Pt. 1: Gaining Cooperation Without Losing Your Mind," "Pt. 2: Discipline for Life: Don't Start What You Can't Finish," "Pt. 3: Dealing with Angry People: How to be Heard Without Shouting!," & "Pt. 4: Building Self-Esteem: Create the Best Place to Be!".

Discipline I see Disciplina I

Discipline II see Disciplina II

Discipline in the Family: Heb. 13:3-7, 725. Ed Young. 1989. 4.95 (978-0-7417-1725-2(5), 725) Win Walk.

Discipline Is Not a Dirty Word. Edward R. Ritvo & Jean Ritvo. 1988. SMI Intl.

Discipline Is Not a Dirty Word. Edward R. Ritvo & Jean K. Ritvo. 1 cass. (Running Time: 39 min.). 11.00 (978-0-89811-237-5(0), 9438) Meyer Res Grp.
Drs. Edward & Jean Ritvo explain the benefits of proper discipline to the child as well as the parents.

Discipline of Children. unabr. ed. Elisabeth Elliot. Read by Elisabeth Elliot. 3 cass. (Running Time: 2 hrs. 20 min.). 1989. 14.95 (978-0-8474-2015-5(9)) Back to Bible.
Helpful advice on creating a peaceful home & making a happy child through love & discipline.

***Discipline of Grace: God's Role & Our Role in the Pursuit of Holiness.** unabr. ed. Jerry Bridges. Narrated by John Haag. (ENG.). 2010. 14.98 (978-1-59644-891-9(1)); audio compact disk 24.98 (978-1-59644-890-2(3)) christianaud.

Discipline of Market Leaders: Choose Your Customers, Narrow Your Focus, Dominate Your Market. unabr. ed. Michael Treacy & Fred Wiersema. 4 cass. 1995. 21.95 (978-1-55935-164-5(0)) Soundelux.

Discipline of Renewal: The Examination of Conscience. George Maloney. 1 cass. (Running Time: 50 min.). 1995. 8.95 (TAH347) Alba Hse Comns.
Fr. Maloney gives us a step-by-step technology that will enable us to cleanse ourselves of false ego & get in touch with the motivations behind our feelings & actions. Then we will be able to achieve the freedom to find God & to recognize Christ in our lives & in all of creation.

Discipline of Truth Thinking. Elbert Willis. 1 cass. (Truth Thinking Ser.). 4.00 Fill the Gap.

Discipline Required. Elbert Willis. 1 cass. (Controlling Your Mind Guidelines Ser.). 4.00 Fill the Gap.

Discipline Solutions & the Student Brain-Presenter Guides (CD) Eric Jensen. 2002. 64.95 (978-1-890460-19-8(2)) Pub: Corwin Pr. Dist(s): SAGE

Discipline That Lasts a Lifetime: The Best Gift You Can Give Your Kids. abr. ed. Raymond N. Guarendi. 2009. 39.95 (978-0-86716-911-9(7)) St Anthony Mess Pr.

Discipline the Positive Way - A Multimedia Approach to Bringing out the Best in Your Kids. Warren Umansky et al. Read by Warren Umansky. 1 cass. (Running Time: 45 min.). 1998. 39.95 (978-0-9664396-8-7(6)) PPP Enterp.
Includes: game, stickers, charts, activities, rewards, awards, poster & incentives for good behavior.

Discipline Through Childhood. Contrib. by Heidi M. Feldman et al. 1 cass. (American Academy of Pediatrics UPDATE: Vol. 18, No. 1). 1998. 20.00 Am Acad Pediat.

Discipline with a Purpose. unabr. ed. Ray Levy & Joe Cates. 1 cass. (Running Time: 1 hr. 30 mins.). 2002. bk. 12.95 (978-0-9701173-0-4(2)) Cates Levy.

Discipline with Dignity, Set. Richard Curwin & Allen Mendler. Read by Richard Curwin & Allen Mendler. 6 cass. (Running Time: 4 hr. 40 min.). (J). (gr. k-12). 1996. 75.00 Incl. handbk. (978-1-886397-07-1(4)) Bureau of Educ.
Live audio seminar.

Discipline with Love. Stephanie Marston. Read by Stephanie Marston. 1 cass. (Running Time: 45 min.). (Magic of Encouragement Audio Ser.). 1991. 10.95 (978-1-56170-016-5(9), 245) Hay House.
Counselor Stephanie Marston shows you how to avoid power struggles & gives you the twelve keys to effective discipline.

Discipline Yourself for Godliness: Learning the Word Filled Walk. John S. Barnett. (ENG.). 2007. 19.99 (978-1-933561-27-1(0)) BFM Books.

Disciplined Investor: Essential Strategies for Success. adpt. ed. Andrew Horowitz. Narrated by Andrew Horowitz. Footn. by Matty Powers. (ENG.). 2008. (978-0-9787083-9-9(3)) HFactor Pubng.

Disciplined Life: An Overview of Daniel. Ed Young. 1995. 4.95 (978-0-7417-2065-8(5), 1065) Win Walk.

Disciplined Life: Daniel 6:1-6. Ed Young. 1995. 4.95 (978-0-7417-2073-3(6), 1073) Win Walk.

Disciplined Trading: How to Trade Your Way to Financial Freedom. Instructed by Van Tharp. (Trade Secrets Audio Ser.). 2000. 19.95 (978-1-883272-72-2(6)) Marketplace Bks.

Disciplined Trading: How to Trade Your Way to Financial Freedom. Van Tharp. 1. (Running Time: 60). 2005. audio compact disk 19.95 (978-1-59280-236-4(2)) Marketplace Bks.
Synopsis:Van Tharp, one of the original Market Wizards, tells you how you can examine your own beliefs about trading and use them to your advantage. This audio will reveal characteristics about yourself that may already be keeping you from winning trades.

Disciplines of a Godly Man. unabr. ed. R. Kent Huges. 10 CDs. (Running Time: 11 hrs. 0 mins. 0 sec.). (ENG., 2006. audio compact disk 28.98 (978-1-59644-276-4(X), Hovel Audio) christianaud.

***Disciplines of a Godly Man.** unabr. ed. R. Kent Hughes. Narrated by Wayne Shepherd. (ENG.). 2006. 16.98 (978-1-59644-277-1(8), Hovel Audio) christianaud.

***Disciplines of a Godly Woman.** unabr. ed. Barbara Hughes. Narrated by Tamara Adams. (ENG.). 2008. 16.98 (978-1-59644-588-8(2), christianSeed) christianaud.

Disciplines of a Godly Woman. unabr. ed. Barbara Hughes. Read by Tamara Kaye Adams. (Running Time: 5 hrs. 45 mins. 0 sec.). (ENG.). 2008. audio compact disk 28.98 (978-1-59644-587-1(4)) christianaud.

***Disciplines That Make Disciples.** Featuring Arun Andrews. 2009. audio compact disk 6.00 (978-1-61256-006-9(7)) Ravi Zach.

Disciplines to Refresh Our Spirits; Is God Love? Ann Ree Colton & Jonathan Murro. 1 cass. 7.95 A R Colton Fnd.

***Discipling: God's Plan to Train & Transform His People.** Gordon Ferguson. 2009. 10.00 (978-0-9842006-6-5(5)) Illumination MA.

Discipling: Gods' Plan to Train & Transform His People. unabr. ed. Gordon Ferguson. 4 cass. (Running Time: 4 hrs.). 1997. 21.99 Set. (978-1-57782-034-5(7)) Discipleshp.
The author covers all facets of discipling: one-on-one, group & family. Shares refreshingly personal accounts of discipling at work. The principles presented w will change us, our friends & the world.

Disclosing Materials at the Nanoscale. Ed. by P. Vincenzini & G. Marletta. (Advances in Science & Technology Ser.: Vol. 51). audio compact disk 113.00 (978-3-908158-07-3(9)) Trans T Pub CHE.

Disco for Kids. 1 cass. (J). 10.95 incl. manual. (KIM 7035C); lp 11.95 (KIM 7035) Kimbo Educ.
A sequenced approach to disco that presents easy rhythms to great disco sounds. Provides full physical involvement in limited space. Dance to Heel Twist Hustle, Knock Knee Bump, Slow Stomp & more.

Disco for Kids. Georgiana Stewart. 1 cass. (Running Time: 35 min.).Tr. of Disco Para Ninos. (SPA & ENG.). (J). (ps-3). 2001. pap. bk. 10.95 (KMS 7035C); pap. bk. 11.95 (KMS 7035) Kimbo Educ.
Disco music, simple movements for limited spaces. Move to great disco sounds. Side A - English translation. Side B - Spanish narration. Manual in English with narration script in Spanish.

Disco Lummi Stick Activities/Actividades Con Disco para los Palos Lummi. Georgiana Stewart. 1 cass. (Running Time: 35 min.). (SPA & ENG.). (J). (ps-3). 2001. pap. bk. 10.95 (KMS 2035C); pap. bk. 11.95 (KMS 2035) Kimbo Educ.
Popular rhythm stick activities. Side A - English translation. Side B - Spanish narration. Manual in English with narration script in Spanish.

Disco Para Ninos see Disco for Kids

Disco Rhythm Stick Activities. 1 cass. (Running Time: 1 hr.). (J). 2001. pap. bk. 10.95 (KIM 2035C); pap. bk. & pupil's gde. ed. 11.95 (KIM 2035) Kimbo Educ.
Popular rhythm stick activities for middle grades. The Hokey Pokey Disco, Copacabana, Mr. Bojangles & more. Includes manual.

Discomfort Zone: A Personal History. Jonathan Franzen. Read by Jonathan Franzen. (Playaway Adult Nonfiction Ser.). 2008. 39.99 (978-1-60640-508-6(X)) Find a World.

***Disconnect: The Truth about Cell Phone Radiation, What the Industry Has Done to Hide It, & How to Protect Your Family.** unabr. ed. Devra Davis. (Running Time: 8 hrs. 30 mins. 0 sec.). (ENG.). 2010. 19.99 (978-1-4001-6897-2(X)); 15.99 (978-1-4001-8897-0(0)); audio compact disk 29.99 (978-1-4001-1897-7(2)) Pub: Tantor Media. Dist(s): IngramPubServ

***Disconnect (Library Edition) The Truth about Cell Phone Radiation, What the Industry Has Done to Hide It, & How to Protect Your Family.** unabr. ed. Devra Davis. (Running Time: 8 hrs. 30 mins. 0 sec.). (ENG.). 2010. audio compact disk 71.99 (978-1-4001-4897-4(9)) Pub: Tantor Media. Dist(s): IngramPubServ

Discontented Mason see Chinese Fairy Tales

Discordia. Prod. by Union Signal Staff. 1 CD. audio compact disk 15.95 (UNIO002); 12.95 (UNIO001) Lodestone Catalog.
Two episodes, includes "Dead Man's Hole.".

Discordia: The Eleventh Dimension. unabr. ed. Dena K. Salmon. Read by Nick Podehl. 1 MP3-CD. (Running Time: 7 hrs.). 2009. 39.97 (978-1-4233-9357-3(0), 9781423393573, Brinc Audio MP3 Lib); 24.99 (978-1-4233-9356-6(2), 9781423393566, Brilliance MP3); 24.99 (978-1-4233-9358-0(9), 9781423393580, BAD); 39.97 (978-1-4233-9359-7(7), 9781423393597, BADLE); audio compact disk 26.99 (978-1-4233-9354-2(6), 9781423393542, Bril Audio CD Unabri); audio compact disk 82.97 (978-1-4233-9355-9(4), 9781423393559, BriAudCD Unabrid) Brilliance Audio.

***Discord's Apple.** unabr. ed. Carrie Vaughn. (Running Time: 9 hrs.). 2010. 24.99 (978-1-4418-7604-1(9), 9781441876041, BAD); 39.97 (978-1-4418-7605-8(7), 9781441876058, BADLE) Brilliance Audio.

***Discord's Apple.** unabr. ed. Carrie Vaughn. Read by Luke Daniels Dawe & Angela Dawe. 1 MP3-CD. (Running Time: 9 hrs.). 2010. 24.99 (978-1-4418-7602-7(2), 9781441876027, Brilliance MP3) Brilliance Audio.

***Discord's Apple.** unabr. ed. Carrie Vaughn. Read by Luke Daniels & Angela Dawe. 1 MP3-CD. (Running Time: 9 hrs.). 2010. 39.97 (978-1-4418-7603-4(0), 978144187603[illegible]nc Audio MP3 Lib) Brilliance Audio.

***Discord's Apple.** unabr. ed. Carrie Vaughn. Read by Luke Daniels. 8 CDs. (Running Time: 9 hrs.). 2010. audio compact disk 34.99 (978-1-4418-7600-3(6), 9781441876003, Bril Audio CD Unabri) Brilliance Audio.

***Discord's Apple.** unabr. ed. Carrie Vaughn. Read by Luke Daniels Dawe & Angela Dawe. 8 CDs. (Running Time: 9 hrs.). 2010. audio compact disk 89.97 (978-1-4418-7601-0(4), 9781441876010, BriAudCD Unabrid) Brilliance Audio.

Discouraged: Cor. 1:1-9. Ed Young. 1982. 4.95 (978-0-7417-1241-7(5), 241) Win Walk.

Discourager of Hesitancy & Mr. Tolman. (N-21) Jimcin Record.

Discours de la Methode, Set. Rene Descartes. Read by Maurice Petit. 2 cass.Tr. of Discourse on the Method. (FRE.). 1996. 28.95 (1820-LQP) Olivia & Hill.

Discours de Reception a L'academie. Read by Jean Cocteau & Edith Piaf. 1 cass. (FRE.). 1992. 21.95 (1541-LQP) Olivia & Hill.
Cocteau's acceptance speech at the Academie Francaise, together with Edith Piaf reading "Le Bel indifferent".

Discourse on Method, Set. unabr. ed. Rene Descartes. Read by Robert L. Halvorson. 2 cass. (Running Time: 180 min.). 14.95 (5) Halvorson Assocs.

Discourse on the Method see Discours de la Methode

Discourses on Art, Set. unabr. ed. Joshua Reynolds. Read by Robert L. Halvorson. 7 cass. (Running Time: 630 min.). 49.95 (65) Halvorson Assocs.

Discover a Cattle Town: Forth Worth. Compiled by Benchmark Education Staff. 2006. audio compact disk 10.00 (978-1-4108-6622-6(X)) Benchmark Educ.

Discover A Gold Rush Community: San Francisco. Compiled by Benchmark Education Staff. 2006. audio compact disk 10.00 (978-1-4108-6623-3(8)) Benchmark Educ.

Discover A Whaling Community: Nantucket. Compiled by Benchmark Education Staff. 2006. audio compact disk 10.00 (978-1-4108-6621-9(1)) Benchmark Educ.

Discover Adaptation. Compiled by Benchmark Education Staff. 2005. audio compact disk 10.00 (978-1-4108-5517-6(1)) Benchmark Educ.

Discover Ancient China. Compiled by Benchmark Education Staff. 2005. audio compact disk 10.00 (978-1-4108-5557-2(0)) Benchmark Educ.

Discover Ancient Greece. Compiled by Benchmark Education Staff. 2005. audio compact disk 10.00 (978-1-4108-5558-9(9)) Benchmark Educ.

Discover Ancient Rome. Compiled by Benchmark Education Staff. 2005. audio compact disk 10.00 (978-1-4108-5559-6(7)) Benchmark Educ.

Discover Animals. Compiled by Benchmark Education Staff. 2006. audio compact disk 10.00 (978-1-4108-6676-9(9)) Benchmark Educ.

Discover Area Audio CD: Set B. Benchmark Education Co. (Math Explorers Ser.). (J). (gr. 3-8). 2009. audio compact disk 10.00 (978-1-935441-69-4(8)) Benchmark Educ.

Discover Bio. 2nd ed. (C). Date not set. stu. ed. (978-0-393-10460-8(5)) Norton.

Discover Brazil. Compiled by Benchmark Education Staff. 2006. audio compact disk 10.00 (978-1-4108-6652-3(1)) Benchmark Educ.

Discover Canada. Compiled by Benchmark Education Staff. 2006. audio compact disk 10.00 (978-1-4108-6653-0(X)) Benchmark Educ.

Discover Cape Town. Compiled by Benchmark Education Staff. 2006. audio compact disk 10.00 (978-1-4108-6617-2(3)) Benchmark Educ.

Discover Chemistry. 2nd rev. ed. Jeffrey R. Appling & David Frank. (Chemistry Ser.). 1998. audio compact disk 44.40 (978-0-534-36134-1(X)) Brooks-Cole.

Discover Comets. Compiled by Benchmark Education Staff. 2006. audio compact disk 10.00 (978-1-4108-6700-1(5)) Benchmark Educ.

Discover Communities. Compiled by Benchmark Education Staff. 2005. audio compact disk 10.00 (978-1-4108-5536-7(8)) Benchmark Educ.

Discover Congruent & Similar Polygons. Based on a book by Margaret McNamara. (J). 2008. audio compact disk 10.00 (978-1-4108-8081-9(8)) Benchmark Educ.

Discover Congruent & Similar Polygons E-Book: Set A. Benchmark Education Staff. Ed. by Margaret McNamara. (Math Explorers Ser.). (J). 2008. audio compact disk 15.00 (978-1-60437-163-5(3)) Benchmark Educ.

Discover Coral Reefs. Compiled by Benchmark Education Staff. 2005. audio compact disk 10.00 (978-1-4108-5526-8(0)) Benchmark Educ.

Discover Decimals & Fractions Audio CD: Set B. Benchmark Education Co. (Math Explorers Ser.). (J). (gr. 3-8). 2009. audio compact disk 10.00 (978-1-935441-57-1(4)) Benchmark Educ.

Discover Decimals & Place Value Audio CD: Set B. Benchmark Education Co. (Math Explorers Ser.). (J). (gr. 3-8). 2009. audio compact disk 10.00 (978-1-935441-53-3(1)) Benchmark Educ.

Discover Deserts. Compiled by Benchmark Education Staff. 2005. audio compact disk 10.00 (978-1-4108-5524-4(4)) Benchmark Educ.

Discover Dinosaurs. Compiled by Benchmark Education Staff. 2005. audio compact disk 10.00 (978-1-4108-5515-2(5)) Benchmark Educ.

Discover Disease. Compiled by Benchmark Education Staff. 2005. audio compact disk 10.00 (978-1-4108-5532-9(5)) Benchmark Educ.

Discover Division. Based on a book by Tara Funk. (J). 2008. audio compact disk 10.00 (978-1-4108-8065-9(6)) Benchmark Educ.

Discover Division E-Book: Set A. Benchmark Education Staff. Ed. by Tara Funk. (Math Explorers Ser.). (J). 2008. audio compact disk 15.00 (978-1-60437-147-5(1)) Benchmark Educ.

Discover Earth. Compiled by Benchmark Education Staff. 2006. audio compact disk 10.00 (978-1-4108-6671-4(8)) Benchmark Educ.

Discover Earthquakes. Compiled by Benchmark Education Staff. 2005. audio compact disk 10.00 (978-1-4108-5527-5(9)) Benchmark Educ.

Discover English Explorers. Compiled by Benchmark Education Staff. 2005. audio compact disk 10.00 (978-1-4108-5550-3(3)) Benchmark Educ.

Discover Equivalent Fractions. Based on a book by Brett Kelly. (J). 2008. audio compact disk 10.00 (978-1-4108-8073-4(7)) Benchmark Educ.

Discover Equivalent Fractions E-Book: Set A. Benchmark Education Staff. Ed. by Brett Kelly. (Math Explorers Ser.). (J). 2008. audio compact disk 15.00 (978-1-60437-155-0(2)) Benchmark Educ.

Discover Erosion. Compiled by Benchmark Education Staff. 2005. audio compact disk 10.00 (978-1-4108-5528-2(7)) Benchmark Educ.

Discover Estimation Audio CD: Set B. Benchmark Education Co. (Math Explorers Ser.). (J). (gr. 3-8). 2009. audio compact disk 10.00 (978-1-935441-61-8(2)) Benchmark Educ.

Discover Forensic Chemistry. Compiled by Benchmark Education Staff. 2006. audio compact disk 10.00 (978-1-4108-6695-0(5)) Benchmark Educ.

Discover Forests. Compiled by Benchmark Education Staff. 2005. audio compact disk 10.00 (978-1-4108-5533-6(3)) Benchmark Educ.

Discover Fossils. Compiled by Benchmark Education Staff. 2005. audio compact disk 10.00 (978-1-4108-5516-9(3)) Benchmark Educ.

Discover Fractions. Based on a book by Barbara Andrews. (J). 2008. audio compact disk 10.00 (978-1-4108-8069-7(9)) Benchmark Educ.

Discover Fractions E-Book: Set A. Benchmark Education Staff. Ed. by Barbara Andrews. (Math Explorers Ser.). (J). 2008. audio compact disk 15.00 (978-1-60437-151-2(X)) Benchmark Educ.

Discover French Explorers. Compiled by Benchmark Education Staff. 2005. audio compact disk 10.00 (978-1-4108-5549-7(X)) Benchmark Educ.

Discover Gases. Compiled by Benchmark Education Staff. 2005. audio compact disk 10.00 (978-1-4108-5514-5(7)) Benchmark Educ.

Discover George Washington. Compiled by Benchmark Education Staff. 2005. audio compact disk 10.00 (978-1-4108-5553-4(8)) Benchmark Educ.

Discover Glaciers. Compiled by Benchmark Education Staff. 2005. audio compact disk 10.00 (978-1-4108-5529-9(5)) Benchmark Educ.

Discover Heredity. Compiled by Benchmark Education Staff. 2005. audio compact disk 10.00 (978-1-4108-5531-2(7)) Benchmark Educ.

Discover Indonesia: Music of Indonesia. 1 CD. (Running Time: 70 mins.). (YA). 2000. audio compact disk 15.00 (40484) Smithsonian Folkways.
Selections from the widely acclaimed 20 CD Series.

Discover Jamestown. Compiled by Benchmark Education Staff. 2005. audio compact disk 10.00 (978-1-4108-5537-4(6)) Benchmark Educ.

Discover Kitchen Chemistry. Compiled by Benchmark Education Staff. 2006. audio compact disk 10.00 (978-1-4108-6693-6(9)) Benchmark Educ.

Discover Light. Compiled by Benchmark Education Staff. 2006. audio compact disk 10.00 (978-1-4108-6683-7(1)) Benchmark Educ.

Discover Liquids. Compiled by Benchmark Education Staff. 2005. audio compact disk 10.00 (978-1-4108-5513-8(9)) Benchmark Educ.

Discover Local & State GOVT. Compiled by Benchmark Education Staff. 2005. audio compact disk 10.00 (978-1-4108-5540-4(6)) Benchmark Educ.

Discover Mars & Venus. Compiled by Benchmark Education Staff. 2006. audio compact disk 10.00 (978-1-4108-6699-8(8)) Benchmark Educ.

Discover Medical Chemistry. Compiled by Benchmark Education Staff. 2006. audio compact disk 10.00 (978-1-4108-6694-3(7)) Benchmark Educ.

Discover Mesa Verde. Compiled by Benchmark Education Staff. 2005. audio compact disk 10.00 (978-1-4108-5538-1(4)) Benchmark Educ.

Discover Mexico. Compiled by Benchmark Education Staff. 2006. audio compact disk 10.00 (978-1-4108-6651-6(3)) Benchmark Educ.

Discover Mexico City. Compiled by Benchmark Education Staff. 2006. audio compact disk 10.00 (978-1-4108-6615-8(7)) Benchmark Educ.

Discover Minerals. Compiled by Benchmark Education Staff. 2006. audio compact disk 10.00 (978-1-4108-6687-5(4)) Benchmark Educ.

Discover Motion. Compiled by Benchmark Education Staff. 2005. audio compact disk 10.00 (978-1-4108-5521-3(X)) Benchmark Educ.

Discover Multiplication E-Book: Set A. Benchmark Education Staff. Ed. by Carrie Smith. (Math Explorers Ser.). (J). 2008. audio compact disk 15.00 (978-1-60437-143-7(9)) Benchmark Educ.

Discover Multiplication of Multidigit Numbers Audio CD: Set B. Benchmark Education Co. (Math Explorers Ser.). (J). (gr. 3-8). 2009. audio compact disk 10.00 (978-1-935441-65-5(5)) Benchmark Educ.

Discover Music of the Baroque Era. unabr. ed. Clive Unger-Hamilton. (Running Time: 5 hrs.). 2009. audio compact disk 28.98 (978-962-634-959-5(X), Naxos AudioBooks) Naxos.

Discover Music of the Romantic Era. unabr. ed. David McCleery. Read by Jeremy Siepmann. 4 CDs. (Running Time: 5 hrs.). 2009. audio compact disk 28.98 (978-962-634-952-6(2), Naxos AudioBooks) Naxos.

Discover Ocean Pollution. Compiled by Benchmark Education Staff. 2005. audio compact disk 10.00 (978-1-4108-5535-0(X)) Benchmark Educ.

Discover Oil Spills. Compiled by Benchmark Education Staff. 2005. audio compact disk 10.00 (978-1-4108-5534-3(1)) Benchmark Educ.

Discover People. Compiled by Benchmark Education Staff. 2006. audio compact disk 10.00 (978-1-4108-6677-6(7)) Benchmark Educ.

Discover Perimeter Audio CD: Set B. Benchmark Education Co. (Math Explorers Ser.). (J). (gr. 3-8). 2009. audio compact disk 10.00 (978-1-935441-73-1(6)) Benchmark Educ.

Discover Plants. Compiled by Benchmark Education Staff. 2006. audio compact disk 10.00 (978-1-4108-6675-2(0)) Benchmark Educ.

Discover Polygons. Based on a book by Kira Freed. (J). 2008. audio compact disk 10.00 (978-1-4108-8077-2(X)) Benchmark Educ.

Discover Polygons E-Book: Set A. Benchmark Education Staff. Ed. by Kira Freed. (Math Explorers Ser.). (J). 2008. audio compact disk 15.00 (978-1-60437-159-8(5)) Benchmark Educ.

Discover Rock Types. Compiled by Benchmark Education Staff. 2006. audio compact disk 10.00 (978-1-4108-6689-9(0)) Benchmark Educ.

DISCOVER ROMANIAN 10v CD. Rodica Botoman. 2004. audio compact disk 52.95 (978-0-8142-0979-0(3)) Pub: Ohio St U Pr. Dist(s): Chicago Distribution Ctr

Discover Science During the Renaissance. Compiled by Benchmark Education Staff. 2006. audio compact disk 10.00 (978-1-4108-6659-2(9)) Benchmark Educ.

Discover Seoul. Compiled by Benchmark Education Staff. 2006. audio compact disk 10.00 (978-1-4108-6616-5(5)) Benchmark Educ.

Discover Sir Isaac Newton. Compiled by Benchmark Education Staff. 2005. audio compact disk 10.00 (978-1-4108-5522-0(8)) Benchmark Educ.

Discover Solids. Compiled by Benchmark Education Staff. 2005. audio compact disk 10.00 (978-1-4108-5512-1(0)) Benchmark Educ.

Discover Sound. Compiled by Benchmark Education Staff. 2006. audio compact disk 10.00 (978-1-4108-6681-3(5)) Benchmark Educ.

Discover Spanish Explorers. Compiled by Benchmark Education Staff. 2005. audio compact disk 10.00 (978-1-4108-5548-0(1)) Benchmark Educ.

Discover Stars. Compiled by Benchmark Education Staff. 2006. audio compact disk 10.00 (978-1-4108-6701-8(3)) Benchmark Educ.

Discover Storms. Compiled by Benchmark Education Staff. 2005. audio compact disk 10.00 (978-1-4108-5519-0(8)) Benchmark Educ.

Discover Symbols of the United States. Compiled by Benchmark Education Staff. 2005. audio compact disk 10.00 (978-1-4108-5539-8(2)) Benchmark Educ.

Discover the Aztec. Compiled by Benchmark Education Staff. 2005. audio compact disk 10.00 (978-1-4108-5542-8(2)) Benchmark Educ.

Discover the Battle of Gettysburg. Compiled by Benchmark Education Staff. 2006. audio compact disk 10.00 (978-1-4108-6640-0(8)) Benchmark Educ.

Discover the Bill of Rights. Compiled by Benchmark Education Staff. 2006. audio compact disk 10.00 (978-1-4108-6647-9(5)) Benchmark Educ.

Discover the Boston Tea Party. Compiled by Benchmark Education Staff. 2005. audio compact disk 10.00 (978-1-4108-5552-7(X)) Benchmark Educ.

Discover the Circulatory System. Compiled by Benchmark Education Staff. 2006. audio compact disk 10.00 (978-1-4108-6705-6(6)) Benchmark Educ.

Discover the Classics, Vol. 1. 2 CDs. (Running Time: 2 hrs. 30 min.). 2003. pap. bk. (Naxos AudioBooks) Naxos.

Discover the Classics, Vol. 2. 2 CDs. (Running Time: 2 hrs. 30 min.). 2003. pap. bk. (Naxos AudioBooks) Naxos.

Discover the Concerto. 2 CDs. (Running Time: 2 hrs. 30 min.). 2003. pap. bk. (Naxos AudioBooks) Naxos.

Discover the Constitution. Compiled by Benchmark Education Staff. 2006. audio compact disk 10.00 (978-1-4108-6646-2(7)) Benchmark Educ.

Discover the Empire of Egypt. Compiled by Benchmark Education Staff. 2005. audio compact disk 10.00 (978-1-4108-5554-1(6)) Benchmark Educ.

Discover the Empires of Mesopotamia. Compiled by Benchmark Education Staff. 2005. audio compact disk 10.00 (978-1-4108-5556-5(2)) Benchmark Educ.

***Discover the Gift.** unabr. ed. Shajen Joy Aziz & Demian Lichtenstein. (Running Time: 6 hrs.). (ENG.). 2011. audio compact disk 32.00 (978-0-307-93231-0(1), Random AudioBks) Pub: Random Audio Pubg. Dist(s): Random

Discover the Inca. Compiled by Benchmark Education Staff. 2005. audio compact disk 10.00 (978-1-4108-5543-5(0)) Benchmark Educ.

Discover the Iroquois. Compiled by Benchmark Education Staff. 2006. audio compact disk 10.00 (978-1-4108-6635-6(1)) Benchmark Educ.

Discover the Keys to Staying Full of God: Cd Album. Created by Awmi. 2008. audio compact disk 25.00 (978-1-59548-112-2(5)) A Wommack.

Discover the Kingdom of Kush. Compiled by Benchmark Education Staff. 2005. audio compact disk 10.00 (978-1-4108-5555-8(4)) Benchmark Educ.

Discover the Lakota. Compiled by Benchmark Education Staff. 2006. audio compact disk 10.00 (978-1-4108-6634-9(3)) Benchmark Educ.

Discover the Laws of Motion. Compiled by Benchmark Education Staff. 2005. audio compact disk 10.00 (978-1-4108-5523-7(6)) Benchmark Educ.

Discover the Life Cycle of Bees. Compiled by Benchmark Education Staff. 2006. audio compact disk 10.00 (978-1-4108-6663-9(7)) Benchmark Educ.

Discover the Life Cycle of Oak Trees. Compiled by Benchmark Education Staff. 2006. audio compact disk 10.00 (978-1-4108-6664-6(5)) Benchmark Educ.

Discover the Life Cycle of Pine Trees. Compiled by Benchmark Education Staff. 2006. audio compact disk 10.00 (978-1-4108-6665-3(3)) Benchmark Educ.

Discover the Maya. Compiled by Benchmark Education Staff. 2005. audio compact disk 10.00 (978-1-4108-5544-2(9)) Benchmark Educ.

Discover the Midwest Region. Compiled by Benchmark Education Staff. 2005. audio compact disk 10.00 (978-1-4108-5546-6(5)) Benchmark Educ.

Discover the Moon. Compiled by Benchmark Education Staff. 2006. audio compact disk 10.00 (978-1-4108-6670-7(X)) Benchmark Educ.

Discover the Navajo. Compiled by Benchmark Education Staff. 2006. audio compact disk 10.00 (978-1-4108-6633-2(5)) Benchmark Educ.

Discover the Nervous & Digestive Systems. Compiled by Benchmark Education Staff. 2006. audio compact disk 10.00 (978-1-4108-6707-0(2)) Benchmark Educ.

Discover the North & the South. Compiled by Benchmark Education Staff. 2006. audio compact disk 10.00 (978-1-4108-6639-4(4)) Benchmark Educ.

Discover the Northeast Region. Compiled by Benchmark Education Staff. 2005. audio compact disk 10.00 (978-1-4108-5547-3(3)) Benchmark Educ.

Discover the Pacific Northwest Region. Compiled by Benchmark Education Staff. 2005. audio compact disk 10.00 (978-1-4108-5545-9(7)) Benchmark Educ.

Discover the Power of Genesis, Set. unabr. ed. Lawrence Boadt. 3 cass. (Running Time: 4 hrs. 44 min.). 1999. 29.95 (TAH422) Alba Hse Comns.
Thorough study of this revered book, drawing a clear focus on its history, symbolism, & foresight of God's plan. Such a return to the font of revelation will make one more effective in the role of teacher & trainer.

Discover the Power of Imagination & the Art of Interntional Creation: Have a dream. Create a dream. Believe in your dream. Make a dream come true. You are the dreamer & the dream maker of your Life. Melissa Zollo. 2003. audio compact disk 149.00 (978-0-9741449-1-7(6)) Present Mem.

Discover the Renaissance in England. Compiled by Benchmark Education Staff. 2006. audio compact disk 10.00 (978-1-4108-6658-5(0)) Benchmark Educ.

Discover the Renaissance in Italy. Compiled by Benchmark Education Staff. 2006. audio compact disk 10.00 (978-1-4108-6657-8(2)) Benchmark Educ.

Discover the Respiratory System. Compiled by Benchmark Education Staff. 2006. audio compact disk 10.00 (978-1-4108-6706-3(4)) Benchmark Educ.

Discover the Rock Cycle. Compiled by Benchmark Education Staff. 2006. audio compact disk 10.00 (978-1-4108-6688-2(2)) Benchmark Educ.

Discover the Sound Barrier. Compiled by Benchmark Education Staff. 2006. audio compact disk 10.00 (978-1-4108-6682-0(3)) Benchmark Educ.

Discover the Southeast Region. Compiled by Benchmark Education Staff. 2006. audio compact disk 10.00 (978-1-4108-6627-1(0)) Benchmark Educ.

Discover the Southwest Region. Compiled by Benchmark Education Staff. 2006. audio compact disk 10.00 (978-1-4108-6628-8(9)) Benchmark Educ.

Discover the Sun. Compiled by Benchmark Education Staff. 2006. audio compact disk 10.00 (978-1-4108-6669-1(6)) Benchmark Educ.

Discover the Symphony. 2 CDs. (Running Time: 2 hrs. 30 min.). 2003. pap. bk. (Naxos AudioBooks) Naxos.

Discover the Thirteen Colonies. Compiled by Benchmark Education Staff. 2005. audio compact disk 10.00 (978-1-4108-5551-0(1)) Benchmark Educ.

Discover the Underground Railroad. Compiled by Benchmark Education Staff. 2006. audio compact disk 10.00 (978-1-4108-6641-7(6)) Benchmark Educ.

Discover the United States GOVT. Compiled by Benchmark Education Staff. 2005. audio compact disk 10.00 (978-1-4108-5541-1(4)) Benchmark Educ.

***Discover the Wealth Within You.** abr. ed. Ric Edelman. Read by Ric Edelman. (ENG.). 2005. (978-0-06-089266-1(8), Harper Audio); (978-0-06-089265-4(X), Harper Audio) HarperCollins Pubs.

Discover the West Region. Compiled by Benchmark Education Staff. 2006. audio compact disk 10.00 (978-1-4108-6629-5(7)) Benchmark Educ.

Discover Tropical Rain Forests. Compiled by Benchmark Education Staff. 2005. audio compact disk 10.00 (978-1-4108-5525-1(2)) Benchmark Educ.

Discover Water. Compiled by Benchmark Education Staff. 2005. audio compact disk 10.00 (978-1-4108-5520-6(1)) Benchmark Educ.

Discover Weather. Compiled by Benchmark Education Staff. 2005. audio compact disk 10.00 (978-1-4108-5518-3(X)) Benchmark Educ.

Discover Writing the Constitution. Compiled by Benchmark Education Staff. 2006. audio compact disk 10.00 (978-1-4108-6645-5(9)) Benchmark Educ.

Discover Your Angels. Nancy A. Clark. Read by Nancy A. Clark. 1 cass. (Running Time: 60 min.). (Journeys of Rememberance Audio Ser.). 9.95 (LA200) Lghtwrks Aud & Vid.
"Contacting Your Angel" (side A) carries you on a heavenly journey deep into outer space until you arrive at a Crystal Palace located in the Celestial Realms. Out of the many thousands gathered there, you will meet your own special angel - & perhaps one of the Archangels who guide you on your path - from whom you can gain specific guidance before your return. "The Rainbow Bridge to Your Angel" (side B) is a magical journey on a spectrum of light to a special land. As your angel appears to you, you are guided to learn techniques for self loving, understanding personal emotions & creating greater peace, for yourself & for the planet as well.

Discover Your Angels: Contacting Your Angel; The Rainbow Journey. Nancy A. Clark. Read by Nancy A. Clark. 1 cass. (Running Time: 1 hr.). (Journeys of Remembrance Ser.). 1996. 9.95 (978-0-9648307-7-6(9)) Violet Fire Pubns.
Side A: "Contacting Your Angel" is a heavenly journey to the crystal palace to meet your special angel. Side B: "The Rainbow Journey" your guardian angel guides you in self love, understanding emotions, & greater peace.

Discover Your Genius. 2002. audio compact disk 14.95 (978-0-9728185-0-6(2)) InGenius Inc.

Discover Your Genius. Speeches. Greg Joseph. 1 cass. (Running Time: 60 mins.). 2002. 14.95 (978-0-9723168-0-4(9)) InGenius Inc.

***Discover Your Genius.** abr. ed. Michael J. Gelb. Read by Michael J. Gelb. (ENG.). 2005. (978-0-06-085316-7(6), Harper Audio); (978-0-06-085315-0(8), Harper Audio) HarperCollins Pubs.

Discover Your Genius: How to Think Like History's Ten Most Revolutionary Minds. Michael J. Gelb. Narrated by Richard M. Davidson. 9 cass. (Running Time: 12 hrs. 30 mins.). 84.00 (978-1-4025-2161-4(8)) Recorded Bks.

Discover Your Genius: How to Think Like History's Ten Most Revolutionary Minds. abr. ed. Michael J. Gelb. Read by Michael J. Gelb. 5 CDs. (Running Time: 6 hrs.). 2002. 29.95 (978-0-06-001187-1(4)) HarperCollins Pubs.

Discover Your Hidden Secrets. 2004. audio compact disk 15.00 (978-0-9755843-4-7(0)) Dream Theater.

Discover Your Inner Economist: Use Incentives to Fall in Love, Survive Your Next Meeting, & Motivate Your Dentist. Tyler Cowen. Read by David Drummond. (Playaway Adult Nonfiction Ser.). (ENG.). 2009. 59.99 (978-1-60640-977-0(8)) Find a World.

Discover Your Inner Economist: Use Incentives to Fall in Love, Survive Your Next Meeting, & Motivate Your Dentist. unabr. ed. Tyler Cowen. Read by David Drummond. (Running Time: 7 hrs. 30 mins. 0 sec.). (ENG.). 2007. audio compact disk 29.99 (978-1-4001-0537-3(4)); audio compact disk 19.99 (978-1-4001-5537-8(1)); audio compact disk 59.99 (978-1-4001-3537-0(0)) Pub: Tantor Media. Dist(s): IngramPubServ

Discover Your Inner Wisdom: Using Intuition, Logic, & Common Sense to Make Your Best Choices. abr. unabr. ed. Char Margolis. Read by Renée Raudman. Frwd. by John Edward. (Running Time: 7 hrs. 0 mins. 0 sec.). (ENG.). 2008. audio compact disk 19.99 (978-1-4001-5650-4(5)) Pub: Tantor Media. Dist(s): IngramPubServ

Discover Your Inner Wisdom: Using Intuition, Logic, & Common Sense to Make Your Best Choices. abr. unabr. ed. Char Margolis & Victoria St. George. Read by Renée Raudman. Frwd. by John Edward. (Running Time: 7 hrs. 0 mins. 0 sec.). 2008. audio compact disk 49.99 (978-1-4001-3650-6(4)); audio compact disk 24.99 (978-1-4001-0650-9(8)) Pub: Tantor Media. Dist(s): IngramPubServ

Discover Your Learning Genius: Enhance Your Concentration, Memory, & Test-Taking Skills. abr. ed. Judith E. Pearson & Oscar Rodriguez. (ENG.). 2009. audio compact disk 24.95 (978-1-60702-544-3(2)) Crown Hse Pub GBR.

Discover Your Life Purpose. Mary Lee LaBay. 2006. audio compact disk 9.95 (978-1-934705-08-7(X)) Awareness Engin.

Discover Your Perfect Soul Mate. rev. ed. Judith L. Powell. 1 cass. 1994. pap. bk. 12.95 (978-1-56087-078-4(8)) Top Mtn Pub.
Side A contains a 20-minute seminar on finding your perfect mate. You will learn the six steps for programming for a perfect mate, while getting yourself "together" at the same time. You will learn to evaluate your needs & desires; & you will describe specifically what traits & characteristics are important to you in a mate. Side B guides you to a relaxed level of mind where you can visualize you & your perfect mate together. Includes complete handbook & Alphamatic card in book-size box.

Discover Your Sales Strengths: How the World's Greatest Salespeople Develop Winning Careers. abr. ed. Benson Smith & Tony Rutigliano. (ENG.). 2005. 14.98 (978-1-59483-275-8(7)) Pub: Hachet Audio. Dist(s): HachBkGrp

Discover Your Sales Strengths: How the World's Greatest Salespeople Develop Winning Careers. abr. ed. Benson Smith & Tony Rutigliano. (Running Time: 3 hrs.). (ENG.). 2009. 39.98 (978-1-60024-953-2(1)) Pub: Hachet Audio. Dist(s): HachBkGrp

Discover Your Skeleton. Compiled by Benchmark Education Staff. 2005. audio compact disk 10.00 (978-1-4108-5530-5(9)) Benchmark Educ.

Discover Your Special Angel, Vol. 1. Diana Donald. Read by Diana Donald. 1 cass. (Running Time: 1 hr.). (J). 1997. Incls. coloring bk. & crayons. About Face CA.

Discover Your Spirit Animal. Ted Andrews. 1 cass. 1996. 10.00 (978-1-888767-05-6(7)) Life Magic Ent.
Music & music with guided meditation to discover your spirit animal & totem. Exercise drawn from the best selling book "Animal-Speak".

Discoverers Pt. I: A History of Man's Search to Know His World & Himself. unabr. ed. Daniel J. Boorstin. Read by Michael Prichard. 11 cass. (Running Time: 16 hrs. 30 min.). 1984. 88.00 (978-0-7366-1011-7(1), 1944-A) Books on Tape.
The Discoverers is a sweeping, original history of man's greatest adventure: His search to discover the world around him.

Discoverers Pt. II: A History of Man's Search to Know His World & Himself. Daniel J. Boorstin. Read by Michael Prichard. 7 cass. (Running Time: 10 hrs. 30 min.). 1984. 56.00 (1944-B) Books on Tape.

Discoverers Pt. III: A History of Man's Search to Know His World & Himself. Daniel J. Boorstin. Read by Michael Prichard. 8 cass. (Running Time: 12 hrs.). 1984. 64.00 (1944-C) Books on Tape.

Discoverers Set: A History of Man's Search to Know His World & Himself. abr. ed. Scripts. Daniel J. Boorstin. Read by Christopher Cazenove. 4 cass. (Running Time: 6 hrs.). 2004. 24.95 (978-1-59007-358-2(4)) Pub: New Millenn Enter. Dist(s): PerseuPGW

Discoverers Set: A History of Man's Search to Know His World & Himself. abr. ed. Daniel J. Boorstin. Read by Christopher Cazenove. 4 cass. (Running Time: 6 hrs.). 1994. 24.95 (978-1-879371-63-7(4)) Pub Mills.
A vivid & sweeping history of man's greatest adventure: his search to discover the world around him. Boorstin's flair for the vivid anecdote, for fresh points of view, & for the dramatic relationship of ideas has made him the most readable of our eminent historians.

Discoveries. (Dovetales Ser.). pap. bk. 6.95 (978-0-944391-45-7(1)); 4.95 (978-0-944391-25-9(7)) DonWise Prodns.

Discoveries of Colin Wilson. Colin Wilson. 2 cass. 18.00 set. (A0369-88) Sound Photosyn.
A good, white knuckled composite of how a person can stay so productive, creative, & interesting so long.

Discoveries Unknown from Native Plants. Hosted by Nancy Pearlman. 1 cass. (Running Time: 29 min.). 10.00 (241) Educ Comm CA.

Discovering American Culture. Cheryl L. Delk. (Alliance: the Michigan State University Textbook Series of Theme-Based Content Instruction for ESL/EFL). (C). 1997. 15.00 (978-0-472-00258-0(9), 00258) U of Mich Pr.

Discovering American Culture, 2nd Edition. Cheryl L. Delk. (ENG.). 2008. audio compact disk 20.00 (978-0-472-00339-6(9)) U of Mich Pr.

Discovering & Responding to the Alcoholic & Addict. G. Grimm et al. 1986. 10.80 (0701) Assn Prof Chaplains.

Discovering & Using Your Spiritual Gifts. Kenneth C. Kinghorn. 2 cass. 1987. 11.95 (978-0-917851-09-4(9)) Bristol Hse.

Discovering Christ at Christmas: Luke 2:11-12. Ed Young. 1994. 4.95 (978-0-7417-2042-9(6), 1042) Win Walk.

Discovering French Blanc, Euro Edition. (FRE.). (YA). (-12). 2003. audio compact disk (978-0-618-06344-4(7)) Holt McDoug.

Discovering French Blanc, Euro Edition. (FRE.). (YA). (gr. 9-12). 2003. (978-0-618-06341-3(2)) Holt McDoug.

Discovering French, Nouveau! Take-Home Tutor, Rouge 3. Created by McDougal Littell. (Discovering French Ser.). 2006. audio compact disk 29.32 (978-0-618-51589-9(5)) Holt McDoug.

Discovering French, Nouveau! Blanc, Level 2. (FRE.). 2003. audio compact disk (978-0-618-34538-0(8)) Holt McDoug.

Discovering French, Nouveau! Rouge, Level 3. (FRE.). 2003. audio compact disk (978-0-618-34539-7(6)) Holt McDoug.

Discovering French Rouge, Euro Edition. (FRE.). (YA). (-12). 2003. (978-0-618-06342-0(0)); audio compact disk (978-0-618-06345-1(5)) Holt McDoug.

Discovering French: Take-Home Tutor. Created by McDougal Littell. (Discovering French Ser.). 2006. audio compact disk 29.32 (978-0-618-51588-2(7)) Holt McDoug.

Discovering French: Take-Home Tutor: Bleu 1. Created by McDougal Littell. 2006. audio compact disk 29.32 (978-0-618-51587-5(9)) Holt McDoug.

Discovering God's Will. Elbert Willis. 1 cass. (Divine Guidance Guidelines Ser.). 4.00 Fill the Gap.

Discovering God's Will: James 4:11-17, 628. Ed Young. 1987. 4.95 (978-0-7417-1628-6(3), 627) Win Walk.

Discovering Inner Wealth. unabr. ed. Perf. by Eknath Easwaran. 1 cass. (Running Time: 1 hr.). 1985. 7.95 (978-1-58638-526-2(7)) Nilgiri Pr.

Discovering Jewish Music. Marsha Bryan Edelman. 2003. bk. 40.00 (978-0-8276-0727-9(X)) JPS Phila.

Discovering Life Purpose. Douglas W. Phillips. 1 cass. (Running Time: 1 hr.). 2000. 7.00 (978-1-929241-12-5(7)) Pub: Vsn Forum. Dist(s): STL Dist NA

Discovering Life Purpose. Douglas W. Phillips. 1 CD. (Running Time: 1 hr.). 2000. audio compact disk 10.00 (978-1-929241-75-0(5)) Pub: Vsn Forum. Dist(s): STL Dist NA

Most men and women spend decades wondering why God made them. This tape addresses three distinct levels of life purpose, all defined by Scripture, and shows how bibilical leadership is a function of the ability to focus on such priorities.

Discovering Literature: Professional Development Library. 2nd ed. 3 cass. (Literature & the Language Arts Ser.). (J). (gr. 6 up). wbk. ed. 198.99 (978-0-8219-2700-7(0)) EMC-Paradigm.

Discovering Meaning. abr. ed. Tammie Fowles. Read by Tammie Fowles. Read by Kevin Fowles. 1 cass. 1998. 9.95 (978-0-9666900-2-6(8)) SagePlace.

Explores such universal issues as suffering, happiness, living the good life, & finding purpose & meaning on our own unique journey.

Discovering Odyssey: 9 Stories on Family Values, Being Content & More. Focus on the Family Staff & AIO Team Staff. (Running Time: 5 hrs.). (Adventures in Odyssey Ser.). (ENG.). (J). (gr. 1-7). 2007. audio compact disk 14.97 (978-1-58997-470-8(0), Tyndale Ent) Tyndale Hse.

*__Discovering Pig Magic.__ Julie Crabtree. Read by Tavia Gilbert. (Playaway Children Ser.). (ENG.). (J). 2010. 54.99 (978-1-4417-0206-7(7)) Find a World.

Discovering Pig Magic. unabr. ed. Julie Crabtree. (Running Time: 5 hrs. 0 mins.). (ENG.). 2009. 29.95 (978-1-4417-0203-6(2)); 34.95 (978-1-4417-0199-2(0)); audio compact disk 55.00 (978-1-4417-0200-5(8)) Blckstn Audio.

Discovering Rhythm & Rhyme in Poetry. unabr. ed. Poems. Louis Untermeyer. Perf. by Julie Harris & David Wayne. 1 cass. (Running Time: 90 min.). (J). 1984. 8.98 (978-0-694-50664-4(8), CDL5 1156) HarperCollins Pubs.

Discovering the Dance of the Soul. unabr. ed. Gary Arnold. 1 cass. (Running Time: 1 hr.). 1997. pap. bk. 12.95 (978-1-57867-244-8(9)) Windhorse Corp.

In this voyage of discovery, Arnold shares how to reconnect with our soul's deepest yearnings.

Discovering the Inner Kingdom, Prayer of the Heart. Contrib. by Kallistos T. Ware. 2 cass. (Running Time: 60 mins.). 11.95 (978-1-891295-06-5(3), OakPubns) St Vladimirs.

Discovering the Joy Within Us. unabr. ed. Swami Amar Jyoti. 1 cass. (Running Time: 90 mins.). (Satsangs of Swami Amar Jyoti Ser.). 2000. 9.95 (978-0-933572-48-5(4), R-119) Truth Consciousness.

Why is "going outside" easier than "going within?" All gratification really comes from within. Understand the source of misery.

Discovering the Power of Genesis, Set. Lawrence Boadt. 3 cass. (Running Time: 4 hrs. 44 min.). 1999. 29.95 (TAH422) Alba Hse Comns.

Leads us through a thorough study of this revered book, enabling us to draw a clear focus on its history, symbolism & foresight of God's plan.

Discovering the Present. Chiara Lubich. Read by Katie Krokey. (Running Time: 1620 sec.). 2006. audio compact disk 13.95 (978-1-56548-253-1(0)) NewCity.

Discovering the Unknown Self. unabr. ed. Nathaniel Branden. 1 cass. (Running Time: 1 hr. 31 min.). 12.95 (550) J Norton Pubs.

Branden presents a comprehensive analysis of the problem of the "disowned self" or self-alienation, where an individual is out of contact with his own needs & emotions.

Discovering True Self. Jane E. Latimer. Read by Jane E. Latimer. 4 cass. (Running Time: 80 min.). (Filling the Void Ser.). 1990. 9.95 (978-1-882109-31-9(7)) CoreWay Media.

Until we learn to be our true selves in the world, we feel unfulfilled. Recovery involves letting go of the false parts of the self so that the true essence of who we are might express itself in the world. Includes guided healing meditations.

Discovering What You Truly Want. Galexis. 2 cass. (Running Time: 3 hrs.). 1995. 17.95 Set. (978-1-56089-029-4(0)) Visionary FL.

Learn to restore your will, desire, motivation, & focus to embrace your true self & destiny. Includes meditation on Side 4.

Discovering Your Destiny. Creflo A. Dollar. 2 cass. (Running Time: 3 hrs.). 2000. 10.00 (978-1-931172-80-6(3), TS260, Kidz Faith) Pub: Creflo Dollar. Dist(s): STL Dist NA

Discovering Your Human Potential see Unleash Your Potential: The Quest Life Trilogy

Discovering Your Life Purpose. Aretta Swanson. 1 cass. (Running Time: 20 mins.). 1999. 12.00 (978-1-930380-03-5(8)) Performance IL.

Discovering Your Life's Purpose. Marcia Perkins-Reed. Read by Marcia Perkins-Reed. 1 cass. (Running Time: 1 hr.). 1991. 10.95 (978-1-56170-017-2(7), 247) Hay House.

Marcia Perkins-Reed guides you in discovering & fulfilling your life's purpose. She closes with an empowering meditation which clarifies that purpose.

Discovering Your Life's Work. Tara Singh. 2 cass. (Running Time: 2 hrs. 52 min.). (Call to Wisdom Ser.). 1987. 17.95 (978-1-55531-137-7(7), #A107) Life Action Pr.

Explores how man can discover his true function & life-given potential as a human being.

Discovering your Need. Francis Frangipane. 1 cass. (Running Time: 90 mins.). (Seeing the Multitudes Ser.: Vol. 1). 2000. 5.00 (FF07-001) Morning NC.

From the beatitudes, Francis draws applications for ministry to those who need Jesus.

Discovering Your Real Identity. Creflo A. Dollar. 20.00 (978-1-59089-203-9(8)) Pub: Creflo Dollar. Dist(s): STL Dist NA

Discovering Your Special Place: A Soothing Guided Journey to Inner Peace. unabr. ed. Charlotte Reznick. Read by Charlotte Reznick. 1 cass. (Running Time: 23 min.). 1993. 12.95 (978-0-9659691-0-9(X)) Imagery For Kids.

Relaxing guided journey to your own special place of inner peace.

Discovers Papa Noel: Jenny Giraffe & the Streetcar Party. Narrated by Cecilia Casrill Dartez. 1 cass. (Running Time: 24 hrs. NaN mins.). (Jenny Giraffe Ser.). (ENG.). (J). 1997. 9.95 (978-1-56554-263-1(0)) Pelican.

Discovery. Irving Younger. Read by Irving Younger. 3 cass. (Running Time: 3 hrs.). 1985. pap. bk. 70.00 Set. (978-0-943380-43-8(X)) PEG MN.

Methods of conducting discovery.

Discovery. Perf. by Irving Younger. Created by Irving Younger. 3 CDs. (Running Time: 4 hours). 2004. pap. bk. 199.00 (978-1-932831-04-7(5)) PEG MN.

Discovery: Developing Views of the Earth. unabr. collector's ed. John Parker. Read by Dan Lazar. 6 cass. (Running Time: 6 hrs.). 1982. 36.00 (978-0-7366-0414-7(6), 1386) Books on Tape.

The adventures of mariners, merchants, scholars, mapmakers, & other travelers. Charts the contributions each has made to the geography of our lands & seas.

Discovery: Pathways to Better Speech for Children with down Syndrome. (Running Time: 4860 sec.). 2005. 29.99 (978-0-9748071-4-0(1)) Blueberry Shoes.

Discovery Set: A Young Person's Guide to Growing up Today. gif. ed. Isabelle Sennery. Prod. by Odyssey Mind Institute Staff. 4 cass. (J). (gr. 2-9). 2000. pap. bk. 39.95 (978-0-9577945-2-8(5)) Pub: Odyssey Mind Inst AUS. Dist(s): Dana Kerr

Discovery & Process in the Forms of Initiation. unabr. ed. Joseph Henderson. 1 cass. (Running Time: 1 hr. 15 min.). 1973. 11.00 (06604) Big Sur Tapes.

Discovery & Settlement of California. Kenneth Bruce. 1 cass. (Running Time: 58 min.). Dramatization. (Excursions in History Ser.). 12.50 Alpha Tape.

Discovery Cove. (K. I. D. S. Church Ser.: Vol. 4).Tr. of La cueva del descubrimiento. (J). (gr. 1-6). 1998. ring bd. 119.99 (978-1-57405-038-7(9)) CharismaLife Pub.

Discovery of Ancient Civilizations. Instructed by Brian M. Fagan. 12 CDs. (Running Time: 12 hrs.). 2002. bk. 69.95 (978-1-56585-518-2(3), 377) Teaching Co.

Discovery of Ancient Civilizations, Pt. I-II. Instructed by Brian M. Fagan. 12 cass. (Running Time: 12 hrs.). 2002. bk. 54.95 (978-1-56585-517-5(5), 377) Teaching Co.

Discovery of Antarctica. Perf. by Mickey Rooney. 1 cass. 7.95 (DD8855) Natl Recrd Co.

Discovery of Egolessness. Read by Chogyam Trungpa. 5 cass. 1976. 43.50 (A010) Vajradhatu.

Talks include: The experience of ego in America, The Skandhas, Cool Boredom, Undoing the Skandhas, Why Meditation?.

Discovery of Extraterrestials Visting Earth. unabr. ed. Courtney Brown. Read by Connor O'Brien. 7 cass. (Running Time: 10 hrs. 30 min.). 1997. 56.00 Set. (4252) Books on Tape.

Is a dying martian race hiding somewhere on Earth? And who are the Greys, a highly-advanced humanoid people who have nearly destroyed their environment & now seek to enhance their evolution.

Discovery of Penicillin. unabr. ed. Peter Brian Medawar et al. 1 cass. 1990. 12.95 (ECN170) J Norton Pubs.

Discovery of the Americas. unabr. ed. Betsy Maestro & Giulio Maestro. 1 cass. (Running Time: 18 min.). (J). (gr. 1-6). 1993. pap. bk. 17.90 (978-0-8045-6674-2(7), 6674) Spoken Arts.

A look at the movements and migrations to the New World over thousands of years.

Discovery of the Columbia River. Kenneth Bruce. 1 cass. (Running Time: 1 hr.). Dramatization. (Excursions in History Ser.). 12.50 Alpha Tape.

Exciting tape of the exploration of the American west.

Discovery of the Pulsar. unabr. ed. Anthony Hewish & Jocelyn Bell-Burnell. 1 cass. 1990. 12.95 (ECN174-A) J Norton Pubs.

*__Discovery of Witches.__ Deborah Harkness. Contrib. by Jennifer Ikeda. (Running Time: 24 hrs.). (ENG.). 2011. audio compact disk 49.95 (978-0-14-242911-2(2), PengAudBks) Penguin Grp USA.

Discovery Techniques. Read by Irving Younger. 2 cass. (Running Time: 3 hrs.). 60.00 (109) Natl Prac Inst.

Improve your case preparation, insure expeditious settlement & successful litigation.

Discovery Techniques. Irving Younger. 1979. 60.00 (978-1-55917-116-8(2)) Natl Prac Inst.

Discovery to Recovery: Science, Spirituality & 12-Step Facilitated Recovery. Cardwell C. Nuckols. Perf. by Cardwell C. Nuckols. Ed. by Charles Hodge. Executive Producer Dennis S. Miller. Dennis S. Miller. Prod. by Charles Hodge. (ENG.). 2009. audio compact disk 45.00 (978-1-55982-019-6(5)) Grt Lks Training.

Discovery, 1986. Interview with Jack Schwarz & Barbara Schuler. 15.00 (501) Aletheia Psycho.

Discrepant Events - The Science Motivator. unabr. ed. Tik L. Liem. Perf. by Tik L. Liem. 1 cass. (Running Time: 1 hr.). cass. & video 49.00 (978-1-878106-02-5(3)) Sci Inquiry.

Presentation to in-service science teachers, dealing with the rationale of the approach & demonstrating a different set of discrepant events. Observe how the use of discrepant events will bring the students to the teachable moment.

Discretion. Elizabeth Nunez. Narrated by Peter Francis James. 7 cass. (Running Time: 10 hrs. 30 mins.). 64.00 (978-1-4025-1590-3(1)) Recorded Bks.

Discrimination. (701) Yoga Res Foun.

Discussion: Fr. Jack Gallagher, Fr. Dudley Day, Dr. William Coulson & Margaret Hotze. 1 cass. 4.00 (96A3) IRL Chicago.

Discussion about Capitalism, Anarchism, Government & Politics. unabr. ed. Nathaniel Branden. 2 cass. (Running Time: 1 hr. 25 min.). 19.95 (814-815) J Norton Pubs.

A discussion of the psychological motives for entering politics, & the belief in anarcho-capitalism vs. constitutional limited government.

Discussion about Objectivism. unabr. ed. Nathaniel Branden. 4 cass. (Running Time: 2 hrs. 55 min.). 34.00 (820-823) J Norton Pubs.

Deals with the history of objectivism & the relationship among Branden, Ayn Rand & the Biocentric Institute. It traces the history of Branden & his interest in psychology & objectivism & his growth in those fields. It explores the definition of love & the possibility of loving without liking.

Discussion of Modern Greek Poetry. unabr. ed. Read by Kimon Friar. 1 cass. 12.95 (C23163) J Norton Pubs.

Kimon Friar discusses & reads selections from the work of one of the greatest & most celebrated of modern Greek poets, Konstantinos Kavaphes.

Discussion of Polarity in Astrology. unabr. ed. Dane Rudhyar. 1 cass. (Running Time: 1 hr. 25 min.). 1971. 11.00 (10102) Big Sur Tapes.

Deals with the natal chart as an entity divided into sets of polar opposites. In evaluating a chart, he does not regard a configuration as good or bad in itself but looks to its relationship to the chart as a whole.

Discussion of the Federal Vision-mp3. Read by Douglas Wilson & Michael Horton. 2004. 8.00 (978-1-59128-407-9(4)) Canon Pr ID.

Discussion of the Federal Vision-tape. Read by Douglas Wilson & Michael Horton. 2004. 10.00 (978-1-59128-409-3(0)) Canon Pr ID.

Discussion on American Education see Educational Thought of the Founding Fathers

Discussion on American Education, Pt. 2. 1 cass. Incl. Discussion on American Education: Banquet Addresses-Introductory Remarks. Read by David Lowenthal. (142); Discussion on American Education: Education & the Public Man. Read by William Bulger. (142); Discussion on American Education: The State of American Education. Read by John Agresto. (142); 3.00 (142) ISI Books.

Discussion on American Education: Banquet Addresses-Introductory Remarks see Discussion on American Education

Discussion on American Education: Education & the Public Man see Discussion on American Education

Discussion on American Education: The State of American Education see Discussion on American Education

Discussion on Colleges & Universities, Pt. 1. (146) ISI Books.

Discussion on Colleges & Universities, Pt. 2. 1 cass. 3.00 (147) ISI Books.

Discussion on Elementary & Secondary Schools see Elementary & Secondary Schools

Discussion on Holy Father's Message to Bishops, Pts. 1-4. Interview with Robert Faricy et al. 4 cass. (Running Time: 60 min.). 1987. 10.00 (978-1-55794-100-8(9), T51) Eternal Wrd TV.

Discussion on Holy Father's Message to Bishops: Church as Community, Belonging to the Church, Communion of Churches. Interview with Robert Faricy et al. 1 cass. (Running Time: 60 min.). 1987. 10.00 (978-1-55794-096-4(7), T47) Eternal Wrd TV.

Discussion on Holy Father's Message to Bishops: Dissert, Conflict, Church Teaching. Interview with Robert Faricy et al. 1 cass. 1987. 10.00 (978-1-55794-097-1(5), T48) Eternal Wrd TV.

Discussion on Holy Father's Message to Bishops: Pope's Answers, U . S. Problems, Catholic Laity. Interview with Robert Faricy et al. 1 cass. (Running Time: 60 min.). 1987. 10.00 (978-1-55794-098-8(3), T49) Eternal Wrd TV.

Discussion on Holy Father's Message to Bishops: Vocations, Sex Education. Interview with Robert Faricy et al. 1 cass. 1987. 10.00 (978-1-55794-099-5(1), T50) Eternal Wrd TV.

Discussion on Purpose of Education see Transmitting the Western Heritage Through Education

Discussion on Purpose of Education, Pt. 2. 1 cass. Incl. Reflections on a Nation at Risk. Annette Y. Kirk. Read by Russell Kirk. (144); Pt. 1. Elementary & Secondary Schools. Read by Linda Chavez & Donald W. McNemar. (144); 3.00 (144) ISI Books.

Discussion Panel. James Dougherty et al. 1986. 3.00 (153) ISI Books.

Discussion with Men. unabr. ed. Nathaniel Branden. 2 cass. (Running Time: 1 hr. 24 min.). 19.95 (534-35) J Norton Pubs.

Among the topics discussed with men are: the importance of self-esteem in man-woman relationships, monogamy, the relation of the ability to express anger to the capacity to enjoy sex, women's liberation, trial marriages, masturbation, difficulties children create in marriages, & others.

Discussion with Women. unabr. ed. Nathaniel Branden. 4 cass. (Running Time: 2 hrs. 37 min.). 39.90 (536-39) J Norton Pubs.

Among the topics discussed with women are: marital fidelity, bisexuality, masculine-feminine role-playing, ideal marriage age, the importance of privacy in marriage, male impotence, female orgasm, infatuation, the significance of sexual fantasy, emotional repression in marriage & others.

Discussions A-Z Advanced: A Resource Book of Speaking Activities. Adrian Wallwork. (Running Time: 7140 sec.). (Cambridge Copy Collection). (ENG.). 1997. 24.00 (978-0-521-55978-2(2)) Cambridge U Pr.

Discussions A-Z Advanced Audio CD: A Resource Book of Speaking Activities. Adrian Wallwork. (Running Time: 1 hr. 19 mins.). (Cambridge Copy Collection). (ENG.). 2009. audio compact disk 43.00 (978-0-521-13285-5(1)) Cambridge U Pr.

Discussions A-Z Intermediate: A Resource Book of Speaking Activities. abr. ed. Adrian Wallwork. (Running Time: 4680 sec.). 1997. 24.00 (978-0-521-55980-5(4)) Cambridge U Pr.

Discussions A-Z Intermediate Audio CD: A Resource Book of Speaking Activities. Adrian Wallwork. (Running Time: 1 hr. 17 mins.). (Cambridge Copy Collection). (ENG.). 2009. audio compact disk 43.00 (978-0-521-16809-0(0)) Cambridge U Pr.

Discussions with Men on Man-Woman Relationships (audio CD Set) Nathaniel Branden. (ENG.). 2007. audio compact disk 19.95 (978-1-57970-465-0(4), Audio-For) J Norton Pubs.

Discussions with Women on Man-Woman Relationships (audio CD Set) Nathaniel Branden. (ENG.). 2007. audio compact disk 39.00 (978-1-57970-466-7(2), Audio-For) J Norton Pubs.

Disease of Alcoholism. David L. Ohlms. Read by David L. Ohlms. Ed. by JoAnn Moore. 1 cass. (Running Time: 1 hr.). 1994. 10.95 (978-1-56168-000-9(1), A9401) GWC Inc.

Completely updated with cutting-edge information on the neurochemical-genetic aspects of the disease along with signs, symptoms &

diagnostic techniques. This is key to removing the stigma from alcoholism & overcoming denial.

Disease of the World-Process. Swami Jyotirmayananda. 1 cass. (Running Time: 45 min.). 1990. 10.00 Yoga Res Foun.

Disease Profiles. Henry W. Wright. (ENG.). 2008. audio compact disk 17.95 (978-1-934680-51-3(6)) Be in Hlth.

Disease to Please: Curing the People-Pleasing Syndrome. Harriet B. Braiker. Read by Harriet B. Braiker. 2 cass. (Running Time: 3 hrs.). 2004. 24.00 (978-1-932378-20-7(0)) Pub: A Media Intl. Dist(s): Natl Bk Netwk

Disease to Please: Curing the People-Pleasing Syndrome. unabr. ed. Harriet B. Braiker. Read by Harriet B. Braiker. 3 CDs. (Running Time: 3 hrs.). 2004. audio compact disk 28.00 (978-1-932378-21-4(9)) Pub: A Media Intl. Dist(s): Natl Bk Netwk

It is the first book to treat people pleasing as a serious psychological syndrome.

Diseases of Intestinal Absorption: Evaluation & Treatment. Read by Jerry S. Trier. 1 cass. (Running Time: 90 min.). 1986. 12.00 (C8656) Amer Coll Phys.

Diseases of the Liver, Biliary Tract & Pancreas. (Postgraduate Programs Ser.: C85-PG3). 85.00 (8513) Am Coll Surgeons.

Reviews current approaches to the diagnosis & management of those diseases of the pancreas, liver & biliary tree. 12 hours CME category 1 credit.

Diseases of the Liver, Biliary Tract & Pancreas. (Postgraduate Programs Ser.: C84-PG3). 1984. 85.00 (84833C84-PG3) Am Coll Surgeons.

Reviews current therapy of benign & malignant diseases of the liver, biliary tract & pancreas & presents new concepts in pathophysiology & treatment. 12 hours CME category 1 credit.

Diseases of the Liver, Biliary Tract & Pancreas. Moderated by Arthur J. Donovan. (Postgraduate Courses Ser.: C86-PG3). 1986. 115.00 (8613) Am Coll Surgeons.

Reviews current practice on the diagnosis & treatment of diseases of the liver, biliary tract, & pancreas. 12 hours CME credit.

***Diseña con figuras planas Audio CD.** April Barth. Adapted by Benchmark Education Co., LLC. (Content Connections Ser.). (SPA.). (J). 2010. audio compact disk 10.00 (978-1-61672-191-6(X)) Benchmark Educ.

Disengage. Perf. by Circle of Dust. 1 CD. audio compact disk 15.98 Platinum Chrst Dist.

Disengage. Perf. by Circle of Dust. 1 cd. 1998. audio compact disk 15.98 Platinum Chrst Dist.

DisFunctional Attitude movies & television Series. (ENG.). (YA). 2010. DVD 10.95 (978-0-9841748-7-4(7), Fad Prod) Vizzie CA.

Disgrace. J. M. Coetzee. Contrib. by Michael Cumpsty. (Running Time: 7 hrs.). (ENG.). (gr. 12 up). 2008. audio compact disk 34.95 (978-0-14-314345-1(X), PengAudBks) Penguin Grp USA.

Disguise for Death. Susan Kelly. (Soundings (CDs) Ser.). 2006. audio compact disk 84.95 (978-1-84559-453-4(3)) Pub: ISIS Lrg Prnt GBR. Dist(s): Ulverscroft US

Disguise for Death. unabr. ed. Susan Kelly. Read by Gordon Griffin. 8 cass. (Soundings Ser.). 2006. 69.95 (978-1-84559-397-1(9)) Pub: ISIS Lrg Prnt GBR. Dist(s): Ulverscroft US

Dishonest Culture. unabr. ed. Gary Hull. 1 cass. (Running Time: 1 hrs. 30 min.). 1997. 12.95 (978-1-56114-517-1(3), CH51C) Second Renaissance.

How movements such as ebonics, environmentalism & alternative medicine undermine the legitimate fields with which they align themselves.

Dishonest Murderer. unabr. ed. Frances Lockridge & Richard Lockridge. Read by John Michalski. 8 vols. (Running Time: 12 hrs.). (Mr. & Mrs. North Mystery Ser.). 2000. bk. 69.95 (978-0-7927-2208-3(6), CSL 097, Chivers Sound Lib) AudioGO.

It's New Year's Eve and Senator Bruce Kirkhill fails to appear at the home of his fiancee's father, Vice-Admiral Jonathan Satterbee. He is found later in a run-down neighborhood, murdered! Jerry and Pam North are brought into it because the Admiral is writing his memoirs for Jerry's Publishing House. What follows is a mystery packed with unexpected twists with the Norths in the middle of it all.

Dishpan Fantasy. unabr. ed. Thomas M. Lopez & Marcia D. Lopez. Read by Ida Faiella et al. 1 cass. (Running Time: 75 min.). 1991. 10.00 (978-1-881137-31-3(7)); audio compact disk 15.00 CD. (978-1-881137-32-0(5)) ZBS Found.

A funny story about a bored housewife who's whisked away to a paradise filled with trees, flowers & singing breezes.

Disinherited see Jack Conroy: Reading and Interview

***Disintegration: The Splintering of Black America.** unabr. ed. Eugene Robinson. Narrated by Alan Bomar Jones. (Running Time: 8 hrs. 0 mins.). 2010. 15.99 (978-1-4526-7011-9(0)); 29.99 (978-1-4526-2011-4(3)); 19.99 (978-1-4526-5011-1(X)); audio compact disk 71.99 (978-1-4526-3011-3(9)); audio compact disk 29.99 (978-1-4526-0011-6(2)) Pub: Tantor Media. Dist(s): IngramPubServ

Disintegration of the Family Pt. 1: Romans 1:16-32. Ed Young. 1987. 4.95 (978-0-7417-1609-5(7), 609) Win Walk.

Disintegration of the Family Pt. II: Matthew 12:46-50. Ed Young. 1987. 4.95 (978-0-7417-1610-1(0), 610) Win Walk.

Dismantled. Jennifer McMahon. Read by Elisabeth Rodgers. (ENG.). 2009. 59.99 (978-1-61574-920-1(9)) Find a World.

***Dismantled.** unabr. ed. Jennifer McMahon. Read by Elisabeth Rodgers. (ENG.). 2009. (978-0-06-194007-1(0), Harper Audio); (978-0-06-196023-9(3), Harper Audio) HarperCollins Pubs.

***Dismantling America: And Other Controversial Essays.** unabr. ed. Thomas Sowell. (Running Time: 11 hrs.). 2010. 29.95 (978-1-4417-6663-2(4)); 65.95 (978-1-4417-6660-1(X)); audio compact disk 100.00 (978-1-4417-6661-8(8)); audio compact disk 29.95 (978-1-4417-6662-5(6)) Blckstn Audio.

***Dismantling the Empire: America's Last Best Hope.** unabr. ed. Chalmers Johnson. (Running Time: 8 hrs. 0 mins.). 2010. 29.95 (978-1-4417-6111-8(X)); 54.95 (978-1-4417-6107-1(1)); audio compact disk 29.95 (978-1-4417-6110-1(1)); audio compact disk 76.00 (978-1-4417-6108-8(X)) Blckstn Audio.

Dismissed Law Student Essays. Short Stories. 1 CD. (Running Time: 65 mins.). 2003. audio compact disk (978-0-9758533-1-3(7)) Makinrent.

Essays from the creator of the first online resource for academically dismissed law students. The essays chronicle her adventures during: the law application process, first year of law school and the aftermath of academic dismissal.

Dismissed with Prejudice. unabr. ed. J. A. Jance. Read by Gene Engene. 6 cass. (Running Time: 8 hrs.). Dramatization. (J. P. Beaumont Mystery Ser.). 1993. 39.95 (978-1-55686-474-2(4), 752465) Books in Motion.

Computers, poetry & Samurai lore were Tadeo Kurobashi's passions. So it stood to reason the ancient art of hara-kiri would be his suicide method of choice. But Detective Beaumont wasn't certain that the dead software magnate had any choice in the matter.

Dismissed with Prejudice. unabr. collector's ed. J. A. Jance. Read by Connor O'Brien. 7 cass. (Running Time: 10 hrs. 30 min.). (J. P. Beaumont Mystery Ser.). 1997. 56.00 (978-0-7366-3823-4(7), 4491) Books on Tape.

Todeo Kurobashi, a highly successful entrepreneur & executive, had three passions in life: computers, poetry & Samurai lore. So it stands to reason that the ancient art of hara-kiri would be his method of choice for suicide. But J.P. Beaumont isn't certain that the dead software magnate had any say in his own demise. Despite the bloody Samurai sword Kurobashi clutches in his lifeless hand, something just doesn't compute: someone made an error in the time-honored death ritual. It all points away from arcane ceremony & toward cold-blooded homicide, of a most traditional sort.

Disney after Dark. unabr. ed. Ridley Pearson. Read by Gary Littman. (Running Time: 6 hrs.). (Kingdom Keepers Ser.: No. 3). 2005. 39.25 (978-1-4233-0694-8(5), 9781423306948, BADLE); 24.95 (978-1-4233-0693-1(7), 9781423306931, BAD) Brilliance Audio.

Disney at Dawn. unabr. ed. Ridley Pearson. Read by Christopher Lane. 1 MP3-CD. (Running Time: 7 hrs.). (Kingdom Keepers Ser.: No. 2). 2008. 24.95 (978-1-4233-4692-0(0), 9781423346920, Brilliance MP3); 24.95 (978-1-4233-4694-4(7), 9781423346944, BAD); 39.25 (978-1-4233-4695-1(5), 9781423346951, BADLE); 39.25 (978-1-4233-4693-7(9), 9781423346937, Brinc Audio MP3 Lib); audio compact disk 60.97 (978-1-4233-4691-3(2), 9781423346913, BriAudCD Unabrid); audio compact disk 29.95 (978-1-4233-4690-6(4), 9781423346906, Bril Audio CD Unabri) Brilliance Audio.

Disney Babies Personalized Lullabies. unabr. ed. Walt Disney Records Staff. Read by Mary Camire & Lynn McInnis. 1 cass. (Running Time: 30 min.). (J). 1992. 8.95 (978-0-9649745-0-0(9)) Cake & Candle.

Features the first name of a child, both narrated & sung. Four of the six songs feature personalizations.

Disney by Candlelight. 1 cass. (Classic Collections). (J). (978-0-7634-0418-5(7)); Norelco. (978-0-7634-0417-8(9)); audio compact disk (978-0-7634-0419-2(5)); audio compact disk (978-0-7634-0420-8(9)) W Disney Records.

Disney Cars: Read-along. Created by ToyBox Innovations. (Disney's Read Along Ser.). (ENG., (J). (ps-3). 2006. audio compact disk & audio compact disk (978-0-7634-2169-4(3)) W Disney Records.

Disney Classic Songs: High Voice. Created by Hal Leonard Corporation Staff. 2007. pap. bk. 19.95 (978-1-4234-1276-2(1), 1423412761) H Leonard.

Disney Fairies Collection Vol. 3: Rani in the Mermaid Lagoon & Fira & the Full Moon. unabr. ed. Lisa Papademetriou. Read by Quincy Tyler Bernstine & Debra Wiseman. 2 CDs. (Running Time: 2 hrs. 22 mins.). (Disney Fairies Ser.). (J). (gr. 1-3). 2007. audio compact disk 20.40 (978-0-7393-3802-5(1), Listening Lib) Pub: Random Audio Pubg. Dist(s): NetLibrary CO

Disney Fairies Collection Vol. 4: A Masterpiece for Bess & Prilla & the Butterfly. unabr. ed. Lara Bergen & Kitty Richards. Read by Ashley Albert & Quincy Tyler Bernstine. 2 CDs. (Running Time: 2 hrs. 19 mins.). (Disney Fairies Ser.). (J). (gr. 1-3). 2007. audio compact disk 24.00 (978-0-7393-5084-3(6), Listening Lib) Pub: Random Audio Pubg. Dist(s): Random

Disney in Shadow. unabr. ed. Ridley Pearson. Read by MacLeod Andrews. (Running Time: 12 hrs.). (Kingdom Keepers Ser.: No. 3). 2010. 24.99 (978-1-4418-1274-2(1), 9781441812742, Brilliance MP3); 24.99 (978-1-4418-1276-6(8), 9781441812766, BAD); 39.97 (978-1-4418-1275-9(X), 9781441812759, Brinc Audio MP3 Lib); 39.97 (978-1-4418-1277-3(6), 9781441812773, BADLE); audio compact disk 29.99 (978-1-4418-1272-8(5), 9781441812728, Bril Audio CD Unabri); audio compact disk 82.97 (978-1-4418-1273-5(3), 9781441812735, BriAudCD Unabrid) Brilliance Audio.

Disney Karaoke, Vol. 1. 1 CD. (Running Time: 90 mins.). (J). (ps-3). 2000. audio compact disk 12.98 (978-0-7634-0623-3(6)); audio compact disk 12.98 (978-0-7634-0651-6(1)) W Disney Records.

Disney Karaoke, Vol. 2. 1 CD. (Running Time: 90 mins.). (J). (ps-3). 2000. audio compact disk 12.98 (978-0-7634-0652-3(X)); audio compact disk 12.98 (978-0-7634-0655-4(4)) W Disney Records.

Disney Pixar Gift Pack. Created by Toybox Innovations. (ENG., (J). (ps-1). 2001. audio compact disk (978-0-7634-1209-8(0)) W Disney Records.

Disney Pixar 2 Gift Pack. Created by Toybox Innovations. (ENG., (J). (ps-1). 2001. audio compact disk (978-0-7634-1205-0(8)) W Disney Records.

Disney Princess Gift Pack. Created by Toybox Innovations. (ENG., (J). (ps-1). 2001. audio compact disk (978-0-7634-1196-1(5)) W Disney Records.

Disney Songs the Satchmo Way. unabr. ed. 1 cass. (Classic Collections). (J). 13.99 (978-0-7634-0130-6(7)); 13.99 Norelco. (978-0-7634-0129-0(3)); audio compact disk 22.99 CD. (978-0-7634-0131-3(5)); audio compact disk 22.99 (978-0-7634-0132-0(3)) W Disney Records.

Disney War. James B. Stewart. Read by Patrick G. Lawlor. 22 CDs. (Running Time: 26 hrs.). 2005. audio compact disk 140.00 (978-0-7861-7845-2(0)) Blckstn Audio.

Disney War. unabr. ed. James B. Stewart. Read by Patrick G. Lawlor. 18 cass. (Running Time: 26 hrs.). 2005. 75.95 (978-0-7861-3505-9(0)); audio compact disk 79.95 (978-0-7861-7846-9(9)) Blckstn Audio.

Disney War. unabr. ed. James B. Stewart. Read by Patrick G. Lawlor. 2 CDs. (Running Time: 26 hrs.). 2005. audio compact disk 44.95 (978-0-7861-8060-8(9)) Blckstn Audio.

Disney War, Vol. 1. James B. Stewart. Read by Patrick G. Lawlor. (Running Time: 15 hrs.). 2005. reel tape 79.95 (978-0-7861-3506-6(9)) Blckstn Audio.

Disney's Greatest Pop Hits. Prod. by Walt Disney Records Staff. 1 CD. 1998. audio compact disk 22.50 (978-0-7634-0461-1(6)) W Disney Records.

Disney's Greatest Pop Hits. Prod. by Walt Disney Records Staff. 1 cass. (J). 1998. 12.98 (978-0-7634-0460-4(8)) W Disney Records.

Disney's the Original Story of Winnie the Pooh with Book. Contrib. by A. A. Milne & Long John Baldry. 1 cass. (Read-Along Ser.). (J). (ps-3). 1998. bk. 7.99 (978-0-7634-0894-7(8)) W Disney Records.

Disney's Theme Park Sing-Along. 1 cass. (Disney Ser.). (J). 9.58 Blisterpack, incl. 22p. song bk. (DISN 60953) NewSound.

Experience the magic, the music & the fun of Disney Theme Park. Includes: "It's a Small World," "Zip-a-Dee-Doo Dah," "The Bear Band Serenade," & more.

DisneyWar. James B. Stewart. Narrated by Patrick G. Lawlor. (Running Time: 25 hrs. 45 mins.). 2005. 63.95 (978-1-59912-471-1(8)) Iofy Corp.

DisneyWar, Vol. 2. James B. Stewart. Read by Patrick G. Lawlor. (Running Time: 11 hrs.). 2005. reel tape 65.95 (978-0-7861-3513-4(1)) Blckstn Audio.

Disobedience. Naomi Alderman. Read by Roe Kendall. (Running Time: 32400 sec.). 2007. 59.95 (978-1-4332-0128-8(3)); audio compact disk 72.00 (978-1-4332-0129-5(1)); audio compact disk 29.95 (978-1-4332-0130-1(5)) Blckstn Audio.

***Disobedient Girl.** Ru Freeman. Read by Anne Flosnik. (Playaway Adult Fiction Ser.). 2010. 69.99 (978-1-61637-504-1(3)) Find a World.

Disobedient Girl. unabr. ed. Ru Freeman. Narrated by Anne Flosnik. (Running Time: 16 hrs. 0 mins. 0 sec.). (ENG.). 2009. 29.99 (978-1-4001-6368-7(4)); audio compact disk 79.99 (978-1-4001-4368-9(3)); audio compact disk 39.99 (978-1-4001-1368-2(7)) Pub: Tantor Media. Dist(s): IngramPubServ

Disorder Peculiar to the Country: A Novel. unabr. ed. Ken Kalfus. Read by James Boles. (YA). 2008. 54.99 (978-1-60514-771-0(2)) Find a World.

Disorders of Sexual Maturation. Contrib. by Leo Plouffe, Jr. et al. 1 cass. (American College of Obstetrics & Gynecologists UPDATE: Vol. 21, No. 4). 1998. 20.00 Am Coll Obstetric.

Dispassion. 1 cass. (Running Time: 1 hr.). 12.99 (701) Yoga Res Foun.

Dispatches. unabr. ed. Michael Herr. (Running Time: 8 hrs. 0 mins.). (ENG.). 2009. 29.95 (978-1-4332-6816-8(7)) Blckstn Audio.

Dispatches. unabr. ed. Michael Herr. Narrated by Ray Porter. 7 CDs. (Running Time: 8 hrs. 30 mins.). 2009. audio compact disk 19.95 (978-1-4332-6815-1(9)) Blckstn Audio.

Dispatches. unabr. ed. Michael Herr. Read by Ray Porter. 7 cass. (Running Time: 8 hrs. 30 mins.). 2009. 54.95 (978-1-4332-6812-0(4)); audio compact disk 70.00 (978-1-4332-6813-7(2)) Blckstn Audio.

Dispatches. unabr. collector's ed. Michael Herr. Read by Christopher Hurt. 6 cass. (Running Time: 9 hrs.). 1985. 48.00 (978-0-7366-0998-2(9), 1932) Books on Tape.

This is Michael Herr's personal journal chronicling his journey through the nightmare of Vietnam where he was a war correspondent for Esquire magazine.

***Dispatches from the Edge.** unabr. ed. Anderson Cooper. Read by Anderson Cooper. (ENG.). 2006. (978-0-06-121434-9(5), Harper Audio); (978-0-06-121433-2(7), Harper Audio) HarperCollins Pubs.

Dispatches from the Edge: A Memoir of War, Disasters, & Survival. abr. unabr. ed. Anderson Cooper. Read by Anderson Cooper. (Running Time: 21600 sec.). 2006. audio compact disk 29.95 (978-0-06-113780-8(4), Harper Audio) HarperCollins Pubs.

Displaced Persons: Growing up American after the Holocaust. Joseph Berger. Narrated by George Guidall. 9 cass. (Running Time: 13 hrs.). 84.00 (978-1-4025-0988-9(X)) Recorded Bks.

Display: The Missing Link, Track Two. 2 cass. 1990. 17.00 set. Recorded Res.

Display Technologies: Track Two. 2 cass. 1990. 17.00 set. Recorded Res.

Topics covered include new technology.

Dispositional Factors in Human Relationships. Instructed by Manly P. Hall. 8.95 (978-0-89314-041-0(4), C840819) Philos Res.

Dispositor Pattern. Lee Yelenics. 1 cass. 8.95 (727) Am Fed Astrologers.

An AFA Convention workshop tape.

***Dispossessed: A Novel.** unabr. ed. Ursula K. Le Guin. Read by Don Leslie. (ENG.). 2010. (978-0-06-206204-8(2), Harper Audio); (978-0-06-202544-9(9), Harper Audio) HarperCollins Pubs.

Disqualified: 1 Cor. 10:1-13. Ed Young. 1986. 4.96 (978-0-7417-1502-9(3), 502) Win Walk.

Disraeli. unabr. collector's ed. André Maurois. Read by Bill Kelsey. 6 cass. (Running Time: 9 hrs.). 1986. 48.00 (978-0-7366-0656-1(4),) Books on Tape.

The grandson of a Jewish emigre from Italy, the son of a bookish scholar who gave up all links with the Synagogue & had his children baptized as Protestants, Disraeli had more flamboyance & more appeal to the imagination than any other British statesman before Churchill.

Disreputable History of Frankie Landau-Banks. E. Lockhart. Read by Tanya Eby Sirois. (Playaway Children Ser.). (YA). (gr. 7-12). 2008. 64.99 (978-1-60640-890-2(9)) Find a World.

Disreputable History of Frankie Landau-Banks. unabr. ed. E. Lockhart. Read by Tanya Eby Sirois. (Running Time: 6 hrs.). 2008. 39.25 (978-1-4233-6683-6(2), 9781423366836, Brinc Audio MP3 Lib); 39.25 (978-1-4233-6685-0(9), 9781423366850, BADLE); 24.95 (978-1-4233-6684-3(0), 9781423366843, BAD); 24.95 (978-1-4233-6682-9(4), 9781423366829, Brilliance MP3) Brilliance Audio.

Disreputable History of Frankie Landau-Banks. unabr. ed. E. Lockhart. Read by Tanya Eby Sirois. 6 CDs. (Running Time: 6 hrs.). (YA). (gr. 7 up). 2008. audio compact disk 29.95 (978-1-4233-6680-5(8), 9781423366805, Bril Audio CD Unabri); audio compact disk 60.97 (978-1-4233-6681-2(6), 9781423366812, BriAudCD Unabrid) Brilliance Audio.

Disrobed: The New Battle Plan to Break the Left's Stranglehold on the Courts. unabr. ed. Mark W. Smith. Read by Jeff Riggenbach. (Running Time: 36000 sec.). 2006. 59.95 (978-0-7861-4766-3(0)); audio compact disk 29.95 (978-0-7861-7306-8(8)); audio compact disk 72.00 (978-0-7861-6334-2(8)) Blckstn Audio.

Disrobed: The New Battle Plan to Break the Left's Stranglehold on the Courts. unabr. ed. Mark W. Smith. Read by Jeff Riggenbach. (Running Time: 36000 sec.). 2006. 24.95 (978-0-7861-4736-6(9)); audio compact disk 25.95 (978-0-7861-6535-3(9)) Blckstn Audio.

Dissatisfaction, Communicating. unabr. ed. Nathaniel Branden. 1 cass. (Running Time: 1 hr. 1 min.). 12.95 (613) J Norton Pubs.

Includes: complaining; defensiveness; the harmful effects of repressing grievances.

Dissection of the Fetal Pig. (C). 2001. audio compact disk (978-0-929941-35-6(7)) Wood River Assocs.

Dissolution. abr. unabr. ed. C. J. Sansom. 10 CDs. (Running Time: 9 hrs. 30 mins.). (ENG.). 2003. audio compact disk 34.95 (978-1-56511-755-6(7), 1565117557) Pub: HighBridge. Dist(s): Workman Pub

Dissolve Into Love: Communing with Presence. Alex Lukeman. Dramatization. 1996. 10.95 (AL1002) Tigers Nest Aud.

Educational aid for deep relaxation & stress reduction. Presents a guided meditation with music leading to an experience of comfort & nurturing.

Dissolving Anger: Easy. Eldon Taylor. Read by Eldon Taylor. Ed. by Leslie Brice. 1 cass. (Running Time: 1 hr.). 1992. 16.95 (978-1-56705-229-9(0)) Gateways Inst.

Self improvement.

Dissolving Anger: Harmonies. Eldon Taylor. Read by Eldon Taylor. Ed. by Leslie Brice. 1 cass. (Running Time: 1 hr.). 1992. 16.95 (978-1-56705-230-5(4)) Gateways Inst.

Dissolving Anger: Ocean. Eldon Taylor. Read by Eldon Taylor. Ed. by Leslie Brice. 1 cass. (Running Time: 1 hr.). 1992. 16.95 (978-1-56705-231-2(2)) Gateways Inst.

Dissolving Barriers: Discover Your Subconscious Blocks to Love, Health & a Powerful Self-Image. Louise L. Hay. Read by Louise L. Hay. 1 cass. (Running Time: 58 min.). (Conversations on Living Lecture Ser.). 1989. 10.00 (978-0-937611-51-7(4), 218) Hay House.

Discusses & helps you to discover your subconscious blocks to love, health, & self-image.

Dissolving Barriers: Discover Your Subconscious Blocks to Love, Health & a Powerful Self-Image. Louise L. Hay. 1 CD. 2005. audio compact disk 10.95 (978-1-4019-0433-3(5)) Hay House.

Dissolving Barriers to Success. unabr. ed. Linda L. Fudold. 1 cass. (Running Time: 1 hr.). 1997. Rental 14.95 (FUD2) Genesis II.
Experience greater success, self-confidence & self-esteem through this guided process. Fudold communicates hypnotically with your unconscious mind to dissolve the hidden barriers in your life.

Dissolving Boundaries: Solving Global Problems. Bill Moyers. 1 cass. (Running Time: 89 min.). (Bill Moyers World of Ideas Anthology Collection: Vol. 3). 1990. 10.95 (978-1-56176-147-0(8)) Mystic Fire.
Exploring the new global reality of an interdependent planet.

Dissolving the Universe. Gyattrul Rinpoche. 2 cass. 18.00 set. (A0108-86) Sound Photosyn.
Exploring a spiritual technique in Tibetan with translation.

Distance Education in China: A Strategic Reference 2007. Compiled by Icon Group International, Inc. Staff. 2007. ring bd. 195.00 (978-0-497-35878-5(6)) Icon Grp.

Distance Education in Mexico: A Strategic Reference 2006. Compiled by Icon Group International, Inc. Staff. 2007. ring bd. 195.00 (978-0-497-82353-5(5)) Icon Grp.

Distant Battle of Drake's Drum see Poetry of Geoffrey

Distant Beacon. Janette Oke & T. Davis Bunn. Narrated by Suzanne Toren. 5 cass. (Running Time: 7 hrs.). (Song of Acadia Ser.: Vol. 4). 46.00 (978-1-4025-3701-1(8)) Recorded Bks.

Distant Beacon. unabr. ed. Janette Oke & T. Davis Bunn. Read by Marguerite Gavin. (Running Time: 25200 sec.). (Song of Acadia Ser.: Vol. 4). 2007. 44.95 (978-1-4332-0595-8(5)); audio compact disk 55.00 (978-1-4332-0596-5(3)); audio compact disk 29.95 (978-1-4332-0597-2(1)) Blckstn Audio.

***Distant Dawn.** unabr. ed. Zondervan. (Running Time: 7 hrs. 8 mins. 23 sec.). (Westward Dreams Ser.). (ENG.). 2010. 18.99 (978-0-310-87486-7(6)) Zondervan.

Distant Episode. (SAC 43-6) Spoken Arts.

Distant Healing: A Complete Guide. Jack Angelo. 2008. audio compact disk 69.95 (978-1-59179-570-4(2)) Sounds True.

Distant Homeland. Kay Stephens & Julia Franklin. 2009. 54.95 (978-1-84652-477-6(6)); audio compact disk 71.95 (978-1-84652-478-3(4)) Pub: Magna Story GBR. Dist(s): Ulverscroft US

Distant Horizons. Rowena Summers & Tanya Myers. 2009. 61.95 (978-1-84652-540-7(3)); audio compact disk 79.95 (978-1-84652-541-4(1)) Pub: Magna Story GBR. Dist(s): Ulverscroft US

***Distant Hours.** unabr. ed. Kate Morton. Read by Caroline Lee. 2010. audio compact disk 123.95 (978-1-74214-848-9(4), 9781742148489) Pub: Bolinda Pubng AUS. Dist(s): Bolinda Pub Inc

Distant Mirror. 2005. audio compact disk 160.00 (978-0-7861-7526-0(5)) Blckstn Audio.

Distant Mirror. unabr. ed. Barbara W. Tuchman. Read by Larry McKeever. 8 cass. (Running Time: 12 hrs.). 1986. 64.00 (978-0-7366-0784-1(6), 3400) Books on Tape.
Barbara Tuchman dispels the myths of 14th century life and shows us the era in its rhythms, and in the grain and texture of domestic life, what childhood was like, what marriage meant, how money, taxes and war dominated the lives of serf, noble and clergy.

Distant Mirror: Part 1. 2005. 89.95 (978-0-7861-4362-7(2)) Blckstn Audio.

Distant Mirror: Part 2. 2005. 72.95 (978-0-7861-4446-4(7)) Blckstn Audio.

Distant Mirror: The Calamitous 14th Century. unabr. ed. Barbara W. Tuchman. Read by Nadia May. 2005. 44.95 (978-0-7861-7814-8(0)) Blckstn Audio.

Distant Mirror Bk. 1: The Calamitous 14th Century. unabr. ed. Barbara W. Tuchman. Narrated by Aviva Skell. 11 cass. (Running Time: 15 hrs. 30 mins.). 1984. 90.00 (978-1-55690-146-1(1), 84012E7) Recorded Bks.
The first of two books detailing the calamitous 14th Century through the life of Enguerrand de Coucy, a knight.

Distant Mirror Bk. 2: The Calamitous 14th Century. unabr. ed. Barbara W. Tuchman. Narrated by Aviva Skell. 8 cass. (Running Time: 12 hrs.). 1984. 62.00 (978-1-55690-145-4(3), 84023E7) Recorded Bks.
The conclusion of a detailed 2-part account of life in 14th Century Europe.

Distant Mirror Pt. 1: The Calamitous 14th Century. unabr. ed. Barbara W. Tuchman. Read by Larry McKeever. 12 cass. (Running Time: 18 hrs.). 1986. 96.00 (978-0-7366-0783-4(8), 1737-A) Books on Tape.
Tuchman dispels the myths & shows us the 14th century in rhythms & in the grain & texture of domestic life what childhood was like, what marriage meant, how money, taxes & war dominated the lives of serf, noble & clergy.

Distant Mirror Pt. 2: The Calamitous 14th Century. Barbara W. Tuchman. Read by Larry McKeever. 8 cass. (Running Time: 12 hrs.). 1986. 64.00 (1737-B) Books on Tape.
Tuchman dispels the myths & shows us the 14th century in rhythms, & in the grain & texture of domestic life-what childhood was like, what marriage meant, how money, taxes & war dominated the lives of serf, noble & clergy.

Distant Prayer: A Miracles of the 49th Combat Mission. Joseph Banks & Jerry Borrowman. 5 cass. 2004. 19.95 (978-1-57734-906-8(7)); audio compact disk 21.95 (978-1-57734-907-5(5)) Covenant Comms.

Distant Relations. Carlos Fuentes. Read by Carlos Fuentes. 1 cass. (Running Time: 30 min.). 8.95 (AMF-6) Am Audio Prose.
Fuentes talks about how the New World corrupts the Old in his novel & reads from "Distant Relations".

***Distant Shores.** abr. ed. Kristin Hannah. Read by Bernadette Quigley. (Running Time: 6 hrs.). 2010. audio compact disk 9.99 (978-1-4418-6268-6(4), 9781441862686, BCD Value Price) Brilliance Audio.

Distant Shores. unabr. ed. Kristin Hannah. Read by Bernadette Quigley. 7 cass. (Running Time: 10 hrs.). 2002. 32.95 (978-1-58788-943-1(9), 1587889439, BAU); 82.25 (978-1-58788-942-4(0), 1587889420, Unabridge Lib Edns) Brilliance Audio.
Elizabeth and Jackson Shore married young, raised two daughters, and weathered the storms of youth as they built a future together. But after the children leave home, they quietly drift apart. When Jack accepts a wonderful new job offer, Elizabeth puts her needs aside to follow him across the country. Until the sudden death of her father changes everything. Grieving and alone, she retreats to an isolated beach house where she packs away the last remnants of her parents' lives. There, the pieces of a past she never knew unfold to reveal a tender story of lasting devotion, the kind of steadfast commitment that Elizabeth admits is missing from her own marriage. Faced with her own disillusionment, she makes a terrifying decision, risking everything she has for a second chance at happiness.

Distant Shores. unabr. ed. Kristin Hannah. Read by Bernadette Quigley. (Running Time: 10 hrs.). 2004. 39.25 (978-1-59335-571-5(8), 1593355718, Brlnc Audio MP3 Lib) Brilliance Audio.

Distant Shores. unabr. ed. Kristin Hannah. Read by Bernadette Quigley. (Running Time: 10 hrs.). 2004. 39.25 (978-1-59710-213-1(X), 159710213X, BADLE); 24.95 (978-1-59710-212-4(1), 1597102121, BAD) Brilliance Audio.

***Distant Shores.** unabr. ed. Kristin Hannah. Read by Bernadette Quigley. (Running Time: 10 hrs.). 2010. audio compact disk 29.99 (978-1-4418-4016-5(8), 9781441840165); audio compact disk 89.97 (978-1-4418-4017-2(6), 9781441840172, BriAudCD Unabrid) Brilliance Audio.

Distant Shores. unabr. ed. Kristin Hannah. Read by Bernadette Quigley. (Running Time: 10 hrs.). 2004. 24.95 (978-1-59335-099-4(6), 1593350996) Soulmate Audio Bks.

Distant Shores: Music & Photographs from Lake Superior & Lake Michigan. Richard Olsenius. 1990. 9.95 (978-0-9609064-6-8(0)) Bluestem Prod.

***Distant Thunders.** unabr. ed. Taylor Anderson. Narrated by William Dufris. (Running Time: 17 hrs. 0 mins. 0 sec.). (Destroyermen Ser.). (ENG.). 2010. audio compact disk 79.99 (978-1-4001-4502-7(3)) Pub: Tantor Media. Dist(s): IngramPubServ

Distant Valor. unabr. ed. C. X. Moreau. Read by Robert Lawrence. (Running Time: 12 hrs.). 2008. 24.95 (978-1-4233-5419-2(2), 9781423354192, Brilliance MP3); 24.95 (978-1-4233-5421-5(4), 9781423354215, BAD); 39.25 (978-1-4233-5420-8(6), 9781423354208, Brlnc Audio MP3 Lib); 39.25 (978-1-4233-5422-2(2), 9781423354222, BADLE) Brilliance Audio.

Distant Voices: A Short Story Collection. unabr. ed. Barbara Erskine. Read by Rowena Cooper. 14 cass. (Running Time: 14 hrs.). 1998. 110.95 Set, Dolby Sound. (978-0-7540-0170-6(9), CAB 1593) AudioGO.
In this collection of short stories, Barbara Erskine has created a vivid range of worlds & emotions from love, romance, loneliness, betrayal & grief. A biographer investigating a tragic death hears voices from the past; a young boy finds haven in a wasteland; & a young woman finds help from an unexpected source.

Distemper. unabr. ed. Beth Saulnier. Read by Vida Vasaitis. 6 vols. (Running Time: 9 hrs.). 2000. bk. 54.95 (978-0-7927-2417-9(8), CSL 306, Chivers Sound Lib) AudioGO.
After a career-making murder case that proved personal bad news, sharp-witted journalist Alex Bernier swears she's going to report stories, not make them. Then a serial killer declares hunting season in her eccentric upstate New York university town.

Distinguished Guest. unabr. ed. Sue Miller. Read by Frances Cassidy. 7 cass. (Running Time: 10 hrs. 30 mins.). 1995. 56.00 (978-0-7366-3078-8(3), 3759) Books on Tape.
A well-known author in her waning years forces her son to study his past, so he can deal with her inevitable future. Poetic & moving.

Distinguished Guest. unabr. ed. Sue Miller. Narrated by Barbara Caruso. 8 cass. (Running Time: 10 hrs. 30 mins.). 70.00 (978-0-7887-0274-7(2), 94485E7) Recorded Bks.
A profoundly moving story of loss, forgiveness & coming to terms with the death of a parents. Available to libraries only.

Distinguished Guest. unabr. ed. Sue Miller. Narrated by Barbara Caruso. 8 cass. (Running Time: 10 hrs. 30 mins.). 2002. 39.95 (978-0-7887-6919-1(7), RC685) Recorded Bks.
In The Distinguished Guest, Miller has created her most brilliant novel to date-a profoundly moving story of loss, forgiveness, and coming to terms with the death of a parent.

Distinguishing God's Truth from Error. Dan Corner. 1 cass. 3.00 (27) Evang Outreach.

Distortions. unabr. collector's ed. Ann Beattie. Read by Nancy Dannevik. 6 cass. (Running Time: 9 hrs.). 1979. 48.00 (978-0-7366-0200-6(3), 1200) Books on Tape.
A collection of 19 short stories, the characters of which lead lives distorted by dreams, devoid of passion, imagination & vitality.

Distress: The Paralyzing Emotion. Lois F. Timmins. 1 cass. (Running Time: 55 min.). 1986. 12.95 (978-0-931814-09-9(X)) Comn Studies.
If a person can face distress, it will challenge them to overcome their difficulties, & will give a new sense of capability & wholeness. Distress is a cohesive force in human relationships, leading people to feel kinship with others & to express sympathy, empathy, compassion, & many aspects of the close feelings people have toward others. Understanding distress gives insight into needs.

Distributed Energy: Towards a 21st Century Infrastructure. Consumer Energy Council of America Staff. 1 CD. (Running Time: 1 hr. 30 mins.). 2001. audio compact disk 40.00 (978-0-9713963-1-9(0)) Consumer Energy Coun.

Distributed Processing & Local Area Networks. 2 cass. 1990. 16.00 set. Recorded Res.

Distribution & Dealer Termination. Philip F. Zeidman & Harvey M. Applebaum. (Running Time: 11 hrs.). 1992. pap. bk. 295.00 incl. course book. NY Law Pub.

Distribution & Marketing: Antitrust Counseling & Litigation. unabr. ed. Contrib. by Michael D. Blechman & Peter D. Standish. 8 cass. (Running Time: 10 hrs.). 1990. 50.00 course handbk. (T7-9260) PLI.
This recording of PLI's January 1990 program focuses on: vertical non-price restraints, federal & state franchise & dealership laws, dealer termination & treble damage suits, plaintiff's & defendant's perspectives, Robinson-Patman issues, exclusive dealing & tie-ins & government agency perspectives.

Disturber of the Peace: The Life & Times of H. L. Mencken. unabr. collector's ed. William Manchester. Read by John MacDonald. 9 cass. (Running Time: 13 hrs. 30 mins.). 1984. 72.00 (978-0-7366-0713-1(7), 1676) Books on Tape.
William Manchester delivers a portrait of this exceptional individual based on his friendship with him.

Disturber of the Peace: The Life of H. L. Mencken. unabr. ed. William Raymond Manchester. Read by Anthony Heald. (Running Time: 52200 sec.). 2008. audio compact disk & audio compact disk 29.95 (978-1-4332-2569-7(7)) Blckstn Audio.

Disturber of the Peace: The Life of H. L. Mencken. 2nd unabr. ed. William Raymond Manchester. Read by Anthony Heald. (Running Time: 52200 sec.). 2008. 85.95 (978-1-4332-2565-9(4)); audio compact disk & audio compact disk 110.00 (978-1-4332-2566-6(2)) Blckstn Audio.

Disunion! The Coming of the American Civil War, 1789-1859. Elizabeth R. Varon. (Littlefield History of the Civil War Era Ser.). (ENG., 2008. 15.00 (978-0-8078-8722-6(6)); audio compact disk 15.00 (978-0-8078-8724-0(2)) U of NC Pr.

Disuniting of America: Reflections on a Multicultural Society. unabr. ed. Arthur M. Schlesinger, Jr. Read by Jeff Riggenbach. 3 cass. (Running Time: 4 hrs.). 1995. 23.95 (978-0-7861-0885-5(1), 1550) Blckstn Audio.
The promise of America has always been a fresh start on equal footing, & the classic image of the republic is that of the melting pot, where differences of race, wealth, religion, & nationality are submerged in the pursuit & exercise of democracy. But today the idea of the melting pot is under attack, & a new orthodoxy describes America, past & present, as a nation of self-interested groups. The idea of assimilation into the mainstream is giving ground to the celebration of ethnicity.

Disuniting of America: Reflections on a Multicultural Society. unabr. ed. Arthur M. Schlesinger Jr. Read by Jeff Riggenbach. (Running Time: 3 hrs. 30 mins.). 2010. 19.95 (978-1-4417-1766-5(8)); audio compact disk 30.00 (978-1-4417-1763-4(3)) Blckstn Audio.

Ditchdigger's Daughters. unabr. ed. Yvonne S. Thornton & Jo Coudert. Read by Fran L. Washington. (Running Time: 9 hrs.). 2008. 39.25 (978-1-4233-5390-4(0), 9781423353904, BADLE); 39.25 (978-1-4233-5388-1(9), 9781423353881, Brlnc Audio MP3 Lib); 24.95 (978-1-4233-5387-4(0), 9781423353874, Brilliance MP3); 24.95 (978-1-4233-5389-8(7), 9781423353898, BAD) Brilliance Audio.

***Ditchrider's Daughter.** Terry Rich Hartley. Read by Marguerite Gavin. (Running Time: 61). (ENG.). 2010. 2.99 (978-1-61114-019-4(6)); 2.99 (978-0-9825278-9-4(6)) Mind Wings Aud.

Diurnal Charts - What's Going On? John H. Goode. 1 cass. 8.95 (132) Am Fed Astrologers.
Research to determine value of daily charts.

"Divali Awakening to Divine Light" unabr. ed. Swami Amar Jyoti. 1 cass. (Running Time: 1 hr. 30 mins.). (Satsangs of Swami Amar Jyoti Ser.). 1999. 9.95 (978-0-933572-50-8(6), K-167) Truth Consciousness.
Divali celebrates the victory of Light & Truth over untruth & darkness. The power of forgiveness. Bringing Sri Rama's Realm on Earth.

Divas of Gospel. 1 cass. 4.98 (978-1-57908-451-6(6)); audio compact disk 5.98 (978-1-57908-450-9(8)) Platinm Enter.

Dive in the Sun. unabr. ed. Douglas Reeman. Read by David Rintoul. 8 cass. (Running Time: 12 hrs.). 2000. 59.95 (978-0-7451-4028-5(9), CAB 725) Pub: Chivers Audio Bks GBR. Dist(s): AudioGO
With the allies poised for the invasion of Italy, the Germans have one strong-hold: the only dock in the Adriatic large enough to take a major warship. It must be destroyed before the Germans can tow it to a safe harbor. Only one team can do the job and still stand a chance of surviving: the crew of HM Midget Submarine XE 51.

Divergence. unabr. ed. Charles Sheffield. Read by Geoffrey Howard. 7 cass. (Running Time: 10 hrs.). (Heritage Universe Ser.: Bk. 2). 2001. 49.95 (978-0-7861-1981-3(0), 2751); audio compact disk 64.00 (978-0-7861-9743-9(9), 2751) Blckstn Audio.
For millennia, humankind & the other intelligent races have studied the bizarre & unfathomable constructs of the legendary beings known as the Builders. But for all that study, they are still no closer to figuring out who - or what - the Builders have been, or where they have gone. Then, on the world called Quake, in the midst of the violent planetary upheaval that is Summertide, a small group of humans & aliens witness the culmination of all those years of watching & waiting: the planet Quake opens up & something comes out & it looks as if, at long last, the discovery of the Builders themselves is at hand.

Diversification of Activities as a Secret of Mental Health. Instructed by Manly P. Hall. 8.95 (978-0-89314-042-7(2), C821107) Philos Res.

Diversities in the Emerging Church. unabr. ed. Samuel Sandmel. 1 cass. (Running Time: 30 min.). 12.95 (31005) J Norton Pubs.
Points out the differences between the Greek & Jewish world & differences within the Greek world itself.

Diversity & Unity. Richard Rohr. Read by Richard Rohr. 1 cass. (Running Time: 1 hrs.). 1996. pap. bk. (AA2986) Credence Commun.
Meditates on the central need for community & some of the cultural attitudes that block the building of healthy community.

Diverticular Disease of the Colon. 2 cass. (General Sessions Ser.: C85-GS5). 15.00 (8540) Am Coll Surgeons.

Diverticulitis. 2 cass. (Colon & Rectal Surgery Ser.: C84-CR3). 1984. 15.00 (8430) Am Coll Surgeons.

divertirse en la playa Audio CD: Emergent Set A. Benchmark Education Staff. Ed. by Carrie Smith. (Early Explorers Ser.). (J). 2008. audio compact disk 10.00 (978-1-60437-235-9(4)) Benchmark Educ.

Divide. Nicholas Evans. 10 cds. 2005. audio compact disk 90.00 (978-1-4159-2327-6(2)) Books on Tape.

Divide. Nicholas Evans. 2005. 44.99 (978-1-59895-021-2(5)) Find a World.

Divide. unabr. ed. Nicholas Evans. 8 cass. 2005. 99.00 (978-1-4159-2326-9(4)) Books on Tape.

***Divide to Conquer.** Carl Sommer. (Quest for Success Ser.). (ENG.). (YA). 2009. bk. 19.95 (978-1-57537-326-3(2)); pap. bk. 11.95 (978-1-57537-375-1(0)) Advance Pub.

***Divide to Conquer / Divide y Vencerás.** ed. Carl Sommer. (Quest for Success Bilingual Ser.). (ENG & SPA.). (YA). 2009. bk. 21.95 (978-1-57537-425-3(0)) Advance Pub.

***Divided Allegiance.** unabr. ed. Elizabeth Moon. Read by Jennifer Van Dyck. (Running Time: 18 hrs.). (Deed of Paksenarrion Ser.). 2010. 44.97 (978-1-4418-5125-3(9), 9781441851253, Brlnc Audio MP3 Lib); 29.99 (978-1-4418-5124-6(0), 9781441851246, Brilliance MP3); 44.97 (978-1-4418-5126-0(7), 9781441851260, BADLE); audio compact disk 92.97 (978-1-4418-5123-9(2), 9781441851239, BriAudCD Unabrid); audio compact disk 29.99 (978-1-4418-5122-2(4), 9781441851222, Bril Audio CD Unabri) Brilliance Audio.

Divided Heart. unabr. ed. Jean Davidson. 3 cass. 1998. 45.95 Set. (978-1-85903-074-5(2)) Pub: Magna Story GBR. Dist(s): Ulverscroft US

***Divided Heart, Divided Home.** Featuring Ravi Zacharias. 2003. audio compact disk 9.00 (978-1-61256-018-2(0)) Ravi Zach.

Divided House see Tales from a Troubled Land

Divided in Death. abr. ed. J. D. Robb, pseud. (Running Time: 7 hrs.). (In Death Ser.). 2009. audio compact disk 9.99 (978-1-4418-2660-2(2), 9781441826602) Brilliance Audio.

Divided in Death. unabr. ed. J. D. Robb, pseud. Read by Susan Ericksen. (Running Time: 12 hrs.). (In Death Ser.). 2004. audio compact disk 102.25 (978-1-59355-400-2(1), 1593554001, BriAudCD Unabrid); 34.95 (978-1-59355-190-2(8), 1593551908, BAU); audio compact disk 38.95 (978-1-59355-395-1(1), 1593553951, Bril Audio CD Unabri) Brilliance Audio.
Reva Ewing, a former member of the Secret Service, a security specialist for Roarke Enterprises, is a prime suspect in a double homicide. She had every reason to want to kill her husband, the renowned artist Blair Bissel. Not only was he having an affair, he was having it with her best friend. But Lieutenant Eve Dallas, who's on the case, believes Reva is innocent. Eve's instincts tell her that the murder scene looks too perfectly staged, the apparent answers too obvious. And when she digs for more, she discovers that at nearly the exact time a kitchen knife was jammed into the victim's ribs, the passcode to his art studio was changed - and all of the data on his computer deliberately corrupted. To Roarke, it's the computer attack that poses the real threat. Signs show that this is the nightmare his company has secretly been preparing for. He and Reva have been under a code-red government contract to develop a program that would shield against a new breed of hackers, the Doomsday Group. These techno-terrorists with brilliant minds and plenty of financial backing hack into systems, steal data, and corrupt computer units on a large scale and kill anyone who gets too close. Eve and Roarke must infiltrate an extraordinarily secretive government agency to expose the corruption at its core, before the virus spreads from one office to a corporation to the entire country.

Divided in Death. unabr. ed. J. D. Robb, pseud. Read by Susan Ericksen. (Running Time: 12 hrs.). (In Death Ser.). 2004. 39.25 (978-1-59335-547-0(5), 1593355475, Brlnc Audio MP3 Lib); 24.95 (978-1-59335-270-7(0), 1593352700, Brilliance MP3) Brilliance Audio.

Divided in Death. unabr. ed. J. D. Robb, pseud. Read by Susan Ericksen. (Running Time: 12 hrs.). (In Death Ser.). 2004. 39.25 (978-1-59710-214-8(8), 1597102148, BADLE); 24.95 (978-1-59710-215-5(6), 1597102156, BAD) Brilliance Audio.

Divided Lives: The Devastating Impact of Divorce. 1 cass. (Running Time: 1 hr.). 2003. 13.95 (978-1-932631-35-7(6)); audio compact disk 13.95 (978-1-932631-36-4(4)) Ascensn Pr.

Divided Love. unabr. ed. Cynthia Harrod-Eagles. Read by Tanya Myers. 4 cass. (Running Time: 5 hrs. 5 min.). (Storysound Ser.). (J). 1999. 44.95 (978-1-85903-276-3(1)) Pub: Mgna Lrg Print GBR. Dist(s): Ulverscroft US

Divided Mind: The Epidemic of Mindbody Disorders. abr. ed. John E. Sarno. Read by Paul Hecht. (YA). 2008. 59.99 (978-1-60514-021-6(X)) Find a World.

Divided Mind: The Epidemic of Mindbody Disorders. unabr. abr. rev. ed. John E. Sarno. Read by Paul Hecht & James Boles. (Running Time: 5 hrs. 30 mins.). (ENG.). 2007. audio compact disk 29.98 (978-1-59659-090-8(4), GildAudio) Pub: Gildan Media. Dist(s): HachBkGrp

Divided Soul: The Life of Marvin Gaye. unabr. ed. David Ritz. Read by Dion Graham. (Running Time: 7 hrs. NaN mins.). 2009. 29.95 (978-1-4332-0277-3(8)); audio compact disk 44.95 (978-1-4332-0275-9(1)); audio compact disk 60.00 (978-1-4332-0276-6(X)) Blckstn Audio.

Dividing Property on Dissolution of Marriage. Read by M. Dee Samuels et al. 1990. 65.00 Incl. 228p. tape materials. (FA-53265) Cont Ed Bar-CA.

Divina Commedia, Set. Poems. Dante Alighieri. 18 cass. (Running Time: 18 hrs.). (ITA.). 2000. 99.50 (978-1-58085-474-0(5)) Interlingua VA.
Includes: "Inferno," "Purgatorio" & "Paradiso.".

Divina Commedia Set: Inferno. Poems. Dante Alighieri. 6 cass. (Running Time: 6 hrs.). (ITA.). 2000. 39.50 (978-1-58085-471-9(0)) Interlingua VA.

Divina Commedia Set: Paradiso. Poems. Dante Alighieri. 6 cass. (Running Time: 6 hrs.). (ITA.). 2000. 39.50 (978-1-58085-473-3(7)) Interlingua VA.

Divina Commedia Set: Purgatorio. Poems. Dante Alighieri. 6 cass. (Running Time: 6 hrs.). (ITA.). 2000. 39.50 (978-1-58085-472-6(9)) Interlingua VA.

Divination: Beyond Tea Leaves: A Live Workshop with Marion Weinstein. (Dealing with the Future Ser.). (ENG.). 2007. audio compact disk 14.99 (978-1-890733-09-4(1)) Earth Magic.

Divination: Beyond Tea Leaves: A Live Workshop with Marion Weinstein. Marion Weinstein. 1 cass. (Running Time: 1 hrs.). (Dealing with the Future Ser.: Vol. 4). 2000. 10.00 (978-1-890733-04-9(0)) Earth Magic.
Combining the ancient tradition of personal oracles with modern psychological tools: an original & powerful approach to personal growth.

Divination & Dowsing Genius: Imagery to Awaken Your True Psychic Abilities & Soul's Wisdom. Iris K. Barratt. 1 cass. 19.95 (978-1-893087-04-0(2)) Awaken Vis.

Divine. abr. ed. Karen Kingsbury. Read by Sharon Williams. 3. (Running Time: 10800 sec.). 2007. audio compact disk 14.99 (978-1-4233-1699-2(1), 9781423316992, BCD Value Price) Brilliance Audio.

***Divine.** abr. ed. Karen Kingsbury. Read by Sharon Williams. (Running Time: 3 hrs.). 2010. audio compact disk 9.99 (978-1-4418-5691-3(9), 9781441856913, BCD Value Price) Brilliance Audio.

Divine. unabr. ed. Karen Kingsbury. Read by Sharon Williams. (Running Time: 9 hrs.). 2006. 39.25 (978-1-4233-1697-8(5), 9781423316978, BADLE); 24.95 (978-1-4233-1696-1(7), 9781423316961, BAD); 74.25 (978-1-4233-1691-6(6), 9781423316916, BrilAudUnabridg); audio compact disk 92.25 (978-1-4233-1693-0(2), 9781423316930, BriAudCD Unabrid); audio compact disk 39.25 (978-1-4233-1695-4(9), 9781423316954, Brlnc Audio MP3 Lib); audio compact disk 24.95 (978-1-4233-1694-7(0), 9781423316947, Brilliance MP3); audio compact disk 29.95 (978-1-4233-1692-3(4), 9781423316923, Bril Audio CD Unabri) Brilliance Audio.
A contemporary story of Mary Magdalene.

Divine Ambassador: John 16:7. Ed Young. 1991. 4.95 (978-0-7417-1870-9(7), 870) Win Walk.

Divine Assembly. Neville Goddard. 1 cass. (Running Time: 62 min.). 1967. 8.00 (77) J & L Pubns.
Neville taught Imagination Creates Reality. He was a powerfully influential teacher of God as Consciousness.

Divine Bliss: Sacred Songs of Devotion from the Heart of India. unabr. ed. Shri Anandi Ma. Read by Shri Anandi Ma. 1 CD. (Running Time: 1 hr. 4 min.). 1996. audio compact disk 16.98 (978-1-56455-415-4(5), MM00300D) Sounds True.
A female master of Indian devotional singing lifts listeners up on waves of song to taste the peace of the divine. indian chant at its highest level, accompanied by dholak drums, tala bells, tamboura & harmonium.

Divine Blood. unabr. ed. Martinez Hewlett. Read by Lloyd James. 7 cass. (Running Time: 10 hrs. 30 min.). 1999. 49.95 (2356) Blckstn Audio.
The discovery of a bloodstained burial shroud, entombed in the crumbling walls of an historic French monastery. Two men - Father Laurent Carriere & scientist Josh Francis - are plunged into the center of a worldwide religious & political power struggle.

Divine Blood. unabr. ed. Martinez Hewlett. Read by Lloyd James. 7 cass. (Running Time: 10 hrs.). 2004. 49.95 (978-0-7861-1506-8(8), 2356) Blckstn Audio.

Divine Body. Neville Goddard. 1 cass. (Running Time: 62 min.). 1970. 8.00 (82) J & L Pubns.
Neville taught Imagination Creates Reality. He was a powerfully influential teacher of God as Consciousness.

Divine Bovine. Perf. by Bill Lepp. 2005. audio compact disk (978-1-891852-46-6(9)) Quarrier Pr.

Divine Center. Stephen R. Covey. 4 cass. 1998. 24.95 Set. (978-1-57008-529-1(3), Bkcraft Inc) Deseret Bk.

Divine Child. abr. ed. Robert Bly. Read by Marion Woodman. 2 cass. (Running Time: 3 hrs.). 1995. 17.95 (978-0-944993-45-3(1)) Audio Lit.
Bly & Woodman explore the pure spiritual potential within the human being, which they call the Divine Child.

Divine Comedy. Dante Alighieri. Narrated by Grover Gardner. (ENG.). 2008. audio compact disk 32.95 (978-1-60646-032-0(3)) Audio Bk Con.

Divine Comedy. unabr. ed. Poems. Dante Alighieri. Read by Nadia May. 10 cass. (Running Time: 14 hrs. 30 mins.). 1991. 69.95 (978-0-7861-0256-3(X), 1224) Blckstn Audio.
This unique poetic translation is the first that incorporates into the text the biblical, theological & historical allusions of the greatest poem in Christendom. Now it can be read or heard without a glossary or encumbering notes as the liquid lines take you through the horrors of the Inferno, the mysteries of the Purgatorio & the glories of the Paradiso.

Divine Comedy. unabr. ed. Dante Alighieri. Read by Nadia May. 11 CDs. (Running Time: 14 hrs. 30 mins.). 2000. audio compact disk 88.00 (978-0-7861-8991-5(6), 1224) Blckstn Audio.

Divine Comedy. unabr. ed. Dante Alighieri. Read by Ralph Cosham. Tr. by Carlyle Okey-Wicksteed. 11 CDs. (Running Time: 48600 sec.). (Dante Alighieri's Divine Comedy Ser.). 2007. audio compact disk 19.95 (978-1-4332-0023-6(6)); audio compact disk 29.95 (978-1-4332-0636-8(6)); audio compact disk 99.00 (978-1-4332-0635-1(8)) Blckstn Audio.

Divine Comedy. unabr. ed. Dante Alighieri. Read by Heathcote Williams & John Shrapnel. 13 CDs. (Running Time: 12 hrs.). bk. 81.98 (978-962-634-315-9(X), NAX31512) Naxos.

***Divine Comedy.** unabr. ed. Dante Alighieri. Compiled by Charles Eliot Norton. Narrated by Pam Ward. (ENG.). 2009. 16.98 (978-1-59644-679-3(X), Hovel Audio) christianaud.

Divine Comedy. unabr. ed. Dante Alighieri. Read by Ralph Cosham. (YA). 2008. 84.99 (978-1-60514-718-5(4)) Find a World.

Divine Comedy. unabr. ed. Dante Alighieri. Tr. by John Ciardi. (Running Time: 13 hrs. 0 mins. 0 sec.). (ENG.). (YA). 2009. lp 19.98 (978-1-59644-678-6(1), christaudio) christianaud.

Divine Comedy, Set. unabr. ed. Dante Alighieri. Read by Grover Gardner. Tr. by Herbert Kenney. 8 cass. (Running Time: 11 hrs. 30 min.). 1992. 26.95 (978-1-55685-263-3(0)) Audio Bk Con.
This unique poetic translation is the first that incorporates into the text the Biblical, theological, & historical allusions of the greatest poem in Christendom. Now it can be read or heard without a glossary or encumbering notes as the liquid lines take you through the horrors of the Inferno, the mysteries of the Purgatorio, & the glories of the Paradiso.

Divine Comedy: Inferno/Purgatorio/Paradiso. unabr. ed. Dante Alighieri. Read by Ralph Cosham. Tr. by Carlyle et al. (Running Time: 48600 sec.). 2007. 79.95 (978-1-4332-0634-4(X)) Blckstn Audio.

Divine Comedy: The Inferno, the Purgatori, & the Paradiso. unabr. ed. Dante Alighieri. Tr. by John Ciardi. (Running Time: 13 hrs. 0 mins. 0 sec.). (ENG.). 2009. audio compact disk 28.98 (978-1-59644-677-9(3), christaudio) christianaud.

***Divine Comedy: Inferno.** unabr. ed. Dante Alighieri. Narrated by James Langton. (Running Time: 4 hrs. 0 mins. 0 sec.). (ENG.). 2010. 22.99 (978-1-4001-6602-2(0)); audio compact disk 32.99 (978-1-4001-1602-7(3)); audio compact disk 65.99 (978-1-4001-4602-4(X)) Pub: Tantor Media. Dist(s): IngramPubServ

***Divine Comedy: Inferno.** unabr. ed. Dante Alighieri. Narrated by James Langton. (Running Time: 10 hrs. 0 mins.). 2010. 16.99 (978-1-4001-8602-0(1)) Tantor Media.

Divine Comedy Trilogy: Inferno, Purgatory, Paradise, Vols. 1-3. unabr. ed. Dante Alighieri. Read by Heathcote Williams. Tr. by Benedict Flynn. 10 CDs. (Running Time: 13 hrs.). 2001. bk. 58.98 (978-962-634-224-4(2), NAX22412, Naxos AudioBooks) Naxos.

Divine Comedy Trilogy: The Inferno - Purgatory - Paradise. Dante Alighieri. Read by Heathcote Williams. Tr. by Benedict Flynn. 10 cass. (Running Time: 13 hrs.). 2001. 52.98 (978-962-634-724-9(4), NAX22414, Naxos AudioBooks) Naxos.

***Divine Commodity: Discovering a Faith Beyond Consumer Christianity.** Skye Jethani. (Running Time: 7 hrs. 59 mins. 0 sec.). (ENG.). 2009. 18.99 (978-0-310-30230-8(7)) Zondervan.

Divine Compassion. Swami Amar Jyoti. 1 cass. 1978. 9.95 (E-14) Truth Consciousness.
How Master helps us outgrow our fictitious happiness & unhappiness. The meaning of salvation.

Divine Compassion of the Guru. unabr. ed. Swami Amar Jyoti. 1 cass. 1995. 9.95 (E-34) Truth Consciousness.
The highest meaning of compassion. Guru, dispeller of darkness, takes birth to awaken the disciples. True education on this earth.

***Divine Conspiracy.** abr. ed. Dallas Willard. Read by Dallas Willard. (ENG.). 2005. (978-0-06-089454-2(7), Harper Audio); (978-0-06-088692-9(7), Harper Audio) HarperCollins Pubs.

Divine Conspiracy: Rediscovering Our Hidden Life in God. unabr. ed. Dallas Willard. Read by Thomas Penny. (Running Time: 68400 sec.). 2007. audio compact disk 39.95 (978-0-06-133697-3(1), Harper Audio) HarperCollins Pubs.

***Divine Conspiracy: Rediscovering Our Hidden Life in God.** unabr. ed. Dallas Willard. Read by Thomas Penny. (ENG.). 2007. (978-0-06-134163-2(0), Harper Audio); (978-0-06-134164-9(9), Harper Audio) HarperCollins Pubs.

***Divine Conspiracy: Rediscovering Our Hidden Life in God.** unabr. ed. Dallas Willard. Narrated by Thomas Penny. (ENG.). 2007. 19.98 (978-1-59644-450-8(9), Hovel Audio) christianaud.

Divine Conspiracy: Rediscovering Our Hidden Life in God. unabr. ed. Dallas Willard. Narrated by Thomas Penny. (Running Time: 18 hrs. 0 mins. 0 sec.). (ENG.). 2007. lp 24.98 (978-1-59644-449-2(5)) christianaud.

Divine Conspiracy: Rediscovering Our Hidden Life in God. unabr. ed. Dallas Willard. Read by Thomas Anthony Penny. (Running Time: 18 hrs. 0 mins. 0 sec.). (ENG.). 2007. audio compact disk 39.98 (978-1-59644-448-5(7)) christianaud.

Divine Direction. Speeches. Creflo A. Dollar. 4 cass. (Running Time: 5 hrs.). 2003. 25.00 (978-1-59089-757-7(9)); audio compact disk 34.00 (978-1-59089-758-4(7)) Creflo Dollar.

Divine Discipline: Hebrews 12:4-11. Ed Young. 1992. 4.95 (978-0-7417-1936-2(3), 936) Win Walk.

Divine Distraction: Four Ecstatic Talks on the Supreme Means of Real-God Realization. abr. ed. Ruchira Avatar Adi Da Samraj staff. 1 cass. (Guru Devotion Ser.). 1996. 11.95 (978-0-918801-70-8(2), AT-DD) Dawn Horse Pr.
Discourse on the guru devotee relationship.

Divine Drama: Following Jesus, the Son of God, from Genesis to Revelation. 2001. audio compact disk 9.95 (978-1-931047-16-6(2)) Fellow Perform Arts.

Divine Enabling. Elbert Willis. 1 cass. (Victory of Surrender Ser.: Vol. 2). 4.00 Fill the Gap.

Divine Gender: Female Images & Experiences of God. Julia Jewett. Read by Julia Jewett. 2 cass. (Running Time: 2 hrs.). 1991. 16.95 set. (978-0-7822-0358-5(2), 454) C G Jung IL.

Divine Gender: Male Images & Experiences of God. Robert Moore. Read by Robert Moore. 2 cass. (Running Time: 2 hrs.). 1991. 16.95 set. (978-0-7822-0357-8(4), 453) C G Jung IL.

Divine Guidance Guidelines Series, Set. Elbert Willis. 4 cass. 13.00 Fill the Gap.

Divine Gypsy. 1984. 8.50 (2204) Self Realization.
Instrumental arrangements of Paramahansa Yogananda's Cosmic Chants. Selections include: "Divine Gypsy," "I Will Be Thine Always," "Divine Mother's Song to the Devotee," "Thousands of Suns," "They Have Heard Thy Name," "I Am the Sky" & "O God Beautiful.".

Divine Gypsy: Instrumental Arrangements of Selections from Paramahansa Yogananda's Cosmic Chants. Paramhansa Yogananda. (Running Time: 41 mins.). audio compact disk 14.00 (978-0-87612-500-7(3)) Self Realization.

Divine Healing Sermons Volume 1. Tsea. 2006. audio compact disk (978-0-9789883-5-7(3)) TSEA.

Divine Health. Featuring Bill Winston. 3 CDs. 2006. audio compact disk 24.00 (978-1-59544-174-4(3)) Pub: B Winston Min. Dist(s): Anchor Distributors

Divine Health. Bill Winston & Veronica Winston. 3 cass. (Running Time: 4hr.06min.). 2002. 15.00 (978-1-931289-56-6(5)) B Winston Min.

Divine Image. Neville Goddard. 1 cass. (Running Time: 62 min.). 1964. 8.00 (14) J & L Pubns.
Neville taught Imagination Creates Reality. He was a powerfully influential teacher of God as Consciousness.

Divine in Our Image. Sivananda Radha. 1 cass. (Running Time: 1 hr.). 1990. 7.95 (978-0-931454-52-3(2)) Timeless Bks.
How to use an image in meditation.

Divine Incarnation. Swami Jyotirmayananda. 1 cass. (Running Time: 45 min.). 1990. 10.00 Yoga Res Foun.

Divine Incarnations. Speeches. 1. (Running Time: 50). 2003. 9.95 (978-0-87481-357-9(3)) Vedanta Pr.
A LECTURE ON THE CONCEPT THAT THE INFINITE GOD TAKES FORM AT DIFFERENT TIMES TO LEAD HUMANITY BACK TO THEIR REAL NATURE OF DIVINITY.

Divine Inspiration. Billy Graham. 1 cass. (Running Time: 60 mins.). 2000. bk. 19.99 (978-1-930800-09-0(6), Prop Voice); bk. 24.98 (978-1-930800-08-3(8), Prop Voice) Iliad TN.

Divine Inspiration: A Homer Kelly Mystery. unabr. collector's ed. Jane Langton. Read by Frances Cassidy. 7 cass. (Running Time: 10 hrs. 30 min.). 1994. 56.00 (978-0-7366-2722-1(7), 3452) Books on Tape.
Master organist at a Boston church teams with Homer Kelly to solve mysteries of a fire & an unexplained baby.

Divine Is Not the Cause. abr. ed. Adi Da Samraj. (Running Time: 4225 sec.). (Adidam Revelation Discourses Ser.). 2006. audio compact disk 16.95 (978-1-57097-189-1(7)) Dawn Horse Pr.

Divine Justice. abr. ed. David Baldacci. Read by Ron McLarty. (Running Time: 6 hrs.). (Camel Club Ser.). (ENG.). 2008. 14.98 (978-1-60024-425-4(4)) Pub: Hachet Audio. Dist(s): HachBkGrp

Divine Justice. abr. ed. David Baldacci. Read by Ron McLarty. 5 CDs. (Running Time: 6 hrs.). (ENG.). 2009. audio compact disk 14.98 (978-1-60024-820-7(9)) Pub: Hachet Audio. Dist(s): HachBkGrp

Divine Justice. unabr. ed. David Baldacci. Read by Ron McLarty. (Running Time: 11 hrs. 30 mins.). (Camel Club Ser.). (ENG.). 2008. 29.98 (978-1-60024-427-8(0)); audio compact disk 44.98 (978-1-60024-428-5(9)) Pub: Hachet Audio. Dist(s): HachBkGrp

Divine Justice. unabr. ed. David Baldacci. Read by Ron McLarty. 10 CDs. 2008. audio compact disk 110.00 (978-1-4159-6038-7(0), BksonTape) Pub: Random Audio Pubg. Dist(s): Random
Known by his alias, "Oliver Stone," John Carr is the most wanted man in America. With two pulls of the trigger, the men who destroyed Stone's life and kept him in the shadows were finally silenced. But his freedom comes at a steep price: The assassinations he carried out prompt the highest levels of the U. S. government to unleash a massive manhunt. Yet behind the scenes, master spy Macklin Hayes is playing a very personal game of cat and mouse. He, more than anyone else, wants Stone dead. With their friend and unofficial leader in hiding, the members of the Camel Club risk everything to save him. Now, as the hunters close in, Stone's flight from the demons of his past will take him from the power corridors of Washington, D.C., to the small, isolated coal-mining town of Divine, Virginia - and into a world every bit as bloody and lethal as the one he left behind.

***Divine Life of Animals: One Man's Quest to Discover Whether the Souls of Animals Live On.** unabr. ed. Ptolemy Tompkins. (Running Time: 7 hrs.). 2010. 24.99 (978-1-4418-8829-7(2), 9781441888297, Brilliance MP3); 24.99 (978-1-4418-8831-0(4), 9781441888310, BAD); 39.97 (978-1-4418-8830-3(6), 9781441888303, Brinc Audio MP3 Lib); 39.97 (978-1-4418-8832-7(2), 9781441888327, BADLE); audio compact disk 24.99 (978-1-4418-8827-3(6), 9781441888273, Bril Audio CD Unabri); audio compact disk 59.97 (978-1-4418-8828-0(4), 9781441888280, BriAudCD Unabrid) Brilliance Audio.

Divine Light Invocation. Sivananda Radha. 1 cass. 1974. 7.95 (978-0-931454-53-0(0)) Timeless Bks.
Full instruction is given on how to do the Divine Light Invocation which is a powerful spiritual practice for renewing energy & improving visualization & concentration.

Divine Light Invocation: A Healing Meditation. As told by Sivananda Radha & Swami Radhananda. Instructed by Swami Radhananda. 1 CD. (Running Time: 38.25 minutes). 2003. audio compact disk 15.95 (978-1-932018-01-1(8)) Pub: Timeless Bks. Dist(s): Baker Taylor
Provides an in-depth study of a powerful spiritual practice for healing and growth. Presents guided visualizations and mantras for deeper inner exploration.

Divine Liturgy of the Orthodox Church. Ed. by Choirs of St Vladimir's Seminary. 1982. audio compact disk 18.00 (978-0-88141-329-8(1)) St Vladimirs.

Divine Love. Speeches. As told by Swami Prabhavananda. 1. (Running Time: 50). 2003. 9.95 (978-0-87481-358-6(1)) Vedanta Pr.
LECTURES EXPLAINS THE CONCEPT OF DIVINE LOVE AND ITS POWER IN OUR LIVES. BASED ON THE TEACHINGS OF VEDANTA (HINDUISM).

Divine Love. Eldon Taylor. 1 cass. (Running Time: 62 min.). (Inner Talk Ser.). 16.95 incl. script. (978-1-55978-013-1(4), 5413C) Progress Aware Res.
Soundtrack with underlying subliminal affirmations.

Divine Love: Babbling Brook. Eldon Taylor. 1 cass. 16.95 (978-1-55978-757-4(0), 5413F) Progress Aware Res.

Divine Love & Divine Romance. Christopher Love. Read by Christopher Love. 1 cass. (Running Time: 30 min.). 1997. 10.95 (978-1-891820-22-9(2)) World Sangha Pubg.
Self-hypnosis meditation for healing, self-improvement & realizing our full & powerful potential as spiritual beings.

Divine Madness. Alan Watts. 1 cass. (Running Time: 1 hr. 23 min.). 1968. 11.00 (02501) Big Sur Tapes.
Proposes that despite the fact we know little about insanity, we go on putting thousands of people into mental institutions, & destroying them in the process, not because they are mentally ill, but because the rest of us simply do not know how to cope with differences in consciousness.

Divine Matrix: Bridging Time, Space, Miracles, & Belief. Gregg Braden. 2008. audio compact disk 23.95 (978-1-4019-2063-0(2)) Hay House.

Divine Misdemeanors. unabr. ed. Laurell K. Hamilton. Read by Laural Merlington. (Meredith Gentry Ser.: No. 8). (ENG.). 2009. audio compact disk

45.00 (978-0-7393-7048-3(0), Random AudioBks) Pub: Random Audio Pubg. Dist(s): Random

Divine Mother & Shakti. Swami Amar Jyoti. 1 cass. 1981. 9.95 (K-42) Truth Consciousness.
How Divine Mother appears to us. Her benevolence behind all actions. Coming in tune with the dance of Shakti, reaching the source.

Divine Mother Meditation CD. Diane Zimberoff. 2003. audio compact disk 15.00 (978-0-9622728-3-7(3)) Wellness Pr.

Divine Name: Sounds of the God Code. Gregg Braden & Jonathan Goldman. 1 CD. 2004. audio compact disk 15.00 (978-1-4019-0612-2(5), 6125) Hay House.

Divine Order for the Christian Family. Creflo A. Dollar. 50.00 (978-1-59089-000-4(0)) Pub: Creflo Dollar. Dist(s): STL Dist NA

Divine Order of Biblical Prosperity. unabr. ed. Creflo A. Dollar. 10 cass. (Running Time: 15 hrs.). 2001. 50.00 (978-1-931172-95-0(1), Kidz Faith) Pub: Creflo Dollar. Dist(s): STL Dist NA

Divine Parenting: Balancing Justice & Mercy. N. Lee Smith. 1 cass. 7.98 (978-1-55503-783-3(6), 06004997) Covenant Comms.
Guidance for parents.

Divine Plan. Elbert Willis. 1 cass. (Victory of Surrender Ser.: Vol. 1). 4.00 Fill the Gap.

Divine Play of Sri Krishna. unabr. ed. Swami Amar Jyoti. 2 cass. (Running Time: 3 hrs.). (Satsangs of Swami Amar Jyoti Ser.). 1980. 12.95 (978-0-933572-40-9(9), K-166) Truth Consciousness.
The Divine Play of Perfection in every aspect of life. Shri Krishna, His life story & great mission.

Divine Plumbline. unabr. ed. Bruce Thompson. Read by Bruce Thompson. 15 cass. (Running Time: 40 min. per cass.). 1983. bk. 10.00 (978-0-935779-00-4(0)) Crown Min.
Features a series on the breakdown & proper rebuilding of man's personality from a Biblical perspective.

Divine Promises, Set. Bobby Hilton. 4 cass. (Running Time: 6 hrs.). 1999. 18.00 (978-1-930766-05-1(X)) Bishop Bobby.
Religious ministry program.

Divine Relationships. 2004. 14.99 (978-1-58602-156-6(7)); audio compact disk 29.99 (978-1-58602-157-3(5)) E L Long.

Divine Revelation of Hell see Revelacion Divina del Infierno

Divine Revelation of Hell. abr. ed. Mary K. Baxter. 1 cass. (Running Time: 57 mins.). 1998. 7.99 (978-0-88368-342-2(3), 773423) Pub: Whitaker Hse. Dist(s): Anchor Distributors

Divine Revelation of Hell. unabr. ed. Mary K. Baxter. 2 cass. (Running Time: 2 hrs. 11 mins.). 1998. 15.99 (978-0-88368-343-9(1), 773431) Pub: Whitaker Hse. Dist(s): Anchor Distributors

Divine Romance. 1 cass. (Yoga & Christianity Ser.). 9.95 (ST-52) Crystal Clarity.
Include: Talking in tongues as a way to draw God's inspiration; how to work with energy rather than details; the practically of faith; God's "tests" as an essential part of the divine romance; inner communion & the unfolding of the heart's love.

Divine Romance. unabr. ed. Perf. by Eknath Easwaran. 1 cass. (Running Time: 1 hr.). 1990. 7.95 (978-1-58638-527-9(5)) Nilgiri Pr.

***Divine Romance: A Study in Brokeness.** unabr. ed. Gene Edwards. (ENG.). 2011. 9.98 (978-1-61045-107-9(4), Hovel Audio); audio compact disk 15.98 (978-1-61045-106-2(6), Hovel Audio) christianaud.

Divine Ryans. abr. ed. Wayne Johnston & Wayne Johnston. Narrated by David Ross. 3 cass. (Running Time: 4 hrs.). (Between the Covers Collection). (ENG.). 2005. 19.95 (978-0-86492-237-3(X)) Pub: BTC Audiobks CAN. Dist(s): U Toronto Pr

Divine Sarah. unabr. collector's ed. Arthur Gold & Robert Fizdale. Read by Penelope Dellaporta. 11 cass. (Running Time: 16 hrs. 30 min.). 1992. 88.00 (978-0-7366-2216-5(0), 3009) Books on Tape.
Sarah Bernhardt was the first international superstar - a supreme artist of the theater. In this acclaimed biography we see the iron-willed, tempestuous woman who really lived beneath the legend.

Divine Secrets of the Ya-Ya Sisterhood. abr. ed. Rebecca Wells. Read by Rebecca Wells. 2 cass. (Running Time: 3 hrs.). (Ya-Ya Ser.: Bk. 2). 1998. 18.95 (978-0-694-52008-4(X), 396078) HarperCollins Pubs.

***Divine Secrets of the Ya-Ya Sisterhood.** abr. ed. Rebecca Wells. Read by Rebecca Wells. (ENG.). 2009. (978-0-06-196153-3(1), Harper Audio); (978-0-06-196151-9(5), Harper Audio) HarperCollins Pubs.

Divine Secrets of the Ya-Ya Sisterhood. unabr. ed. Rebecca Wells. Read by Judith Ivey. 10 cass. (Running Time: 15 hrs.). (Ya-Ya Ser.: Bk. 2). 2002. 80.00 (978-0-7366-8656-3(8)) Books on Tape.
A 40-year-old actress must repair her relationship with her mother by reading a half-century's-worth of letters and clippings in the Ya-Ya Sisterhood's packet of "Divine Secrets." The Ya-Yas are the wild circle of girls who swirl around narrator Siddalee's mama, Vivi, whose voice is "part Scarlett, part Katherine Hepburn, part Tallulah." As Siddalee reads about these devoted pals, she relives her memories of her irrepressible and irresistible mother, and is rewarded with glimpses of true love and loyalty against the hilarious and poignant backdrop of life in the rural South. A moving exploration of the mother-daughter bond, and of the power of forgiveness to heal our inevitable imperfections - and the secrets are really fun to learn.

Divine Secrets of the Ya-Ya Sisterhood. unabr. ed. Rebecca Wells. Read by Judith Ivey. 10 cass. (Running Time: 15 hrs.). (Ya-Ya Ser.: Bk. 2). 2002. audio compact disk 104.00 (978-0-7366-8658-7(4)) Books on Tape.
Louisiana-born author Rebecca Wells reads her spirited novel about a 40-year-old actress who must repair her relationship with her mother by reading a half-century's-worth of letters and clippings in the Ya-Ya Sisterhood's packet of "Divine Secrets." The Ya-Yas are the wild circle of girls who swirl around narrator Siddalee's mama, Vivi, whose voice is "part Scarlett, part Katherine Hepburn, part Tallulah." As Siddalee reads about these devoted pals, she relives her memories of her irrepressible and irresistible mother, and is rewarded with glimpses of true love and loyalty against the hilarious and poignant backdrop of life in the rural South. A moving exploration of the mother-daughter bond, and of the power of forgiveness to heal our inevitable imperfections.

***Divine Secrets of the Ya-Ya Sisterhood.** unabr. ed. Rebecca Wells. Read by Judith Ivey. (ENG.). 2009. (978-0-06-196154-0(X), Harper Audio); (978-0-06-196152-6(3), Harper Audio) HarperCollins Pubs.

Divine Secrets of the Ya-Ya Sisterhood. unabr. abr. ed. Rebecca Wells. Read by Rebecca Wells. 3 CDs. (Running Time: 3 hrs. 30 mins.). (Ya-Ya Ser.: Bk. 2). 1999. 22.00 (978-0-694-52168-5(X)) HarperCollins Pubs.

Divine Secrets of the Ya-Ya Sisterhood, Set. abr. ed. Rebecca Wells. Read by Rebecca Wells. 2 cass. (Ya-Ya Ser.: Bk. 2). 1999. 18.00 (FS9-43203) Highsmith.

Divine Self Meditation. Mark Earlix. (J). 2000. 12.95 (978-0-9678058-1-8(3)) Art of Healing.

Divine Shakti. unabr. ed. Swami Amar Jyoti. 1 cass. (C). 1996. 9.95 (K-156) Truth Consciousness.
Shakti, the Divine Mother, primal energy of all creation, lifts us to the grace of transformation.

Divine Singing. Chaitanya Kabir. 2007. audio compact disk 69.95 (978-1-59179-505-6(2)) Sounds True.

Divine Sopranos. 1 cass., 1 CD. 7.98 (TA 30407); audio compact disk 12.78 CD Jewel box. (TA 80407) NewSound.

Divine Soul Mind Body Healing & Transmission System: The Divine Way to Heal You, Humanity, Mother Earth, & All Universes. abr. ed. Zhi Gang Sha. Read by Zhi Gang Sha. (Running Time: 7 hrs. 0 mins. 0 sec.). (ENG.). 2009. audio compact disk 29.99 (978-1-4423-0373-7(5)) Pub: S&S Audio. Dist(s): S and S Inc

Divine Soul Songs: Sacred Practical Treasures to Heal, Rejuvenate, & Transform You, Humanity, Mother Earth, & All Universes. abr. ed. Zhi Gang Sha. Read by Zhi Gang Sha. (Running Time: 7 hrs. 0 mins. 0 sec.). (ENG.). 2009. audio compact disk 29.99 (978-0-7435-8302-2(7)) Pub: S&S Audio. Dist(s): S and S Inc

***Divine Transformation.** unabr. ed. Zhi Gang Sha. Read by Zhi Gang Sha. (Running Time: 9 hrs. 30 mins. 0 sec.). (ENG.). 2010. 27.99 (978-1-4423-4057-2(6)) Pub: S&S Audio. Dist(s): S and S Inc

Divine Trinity: Pre-Adamite World. Finis J. Dake, Sr. (J). (gr. k up). 5.95 (978-1-55829-031-0(1)) Dake Publishing.
Bible study.

Divine Virtues. Swami Amar Jyoti. 1 cass. 1980. 9.95 (K-28) Truth Consciousness.
Virtues that take us nearer to God. Seeing what we are now; growing from there. The liability of overindulgence.

Divine Visitation. Derek Prince. 1 cass. (Running Time: 60 min.). 5.95 (I-4257) Derek Prince.

Divine Watchmaker. Chuck Missler & Mark Eastman. 2 cass. (Running Time: 2.5 hours). (Creator Ser.). 1996. vinyl bd. 14.95 Set, incl. study notes. (978-1-880532-35-5(2)) Koinonia Hse.
What do molecular biology, the information sciences, and the design of advanced machines tell us about our origins?Why is "Evolution" the biggest hoax of the century?Review the Neo-Darwinian concepts and how modern discoveries have rendered them obsolete.Modern ScienceModern Microbiology has revealed that even the simplest organisms are complex machines beyond our imagining.

***Divine Watchmaker.** Chuck Missler & Mark Eastman. (ENG.). 2009. audio compact disk 19.95 (978-1-57821-443-3(2)) Koinonia Hse.

Divine Wisdom Pt. I: 1 Cor. 1:18-25. Ed Young. 1985. 4.95 (978-0-7417-1482-4(5), 482) Win Walk.

Divine Wisdom Pt. II: 1 Cor. 1:18-25. Ed Young. 1985. 4.95 (978-0-7417-1483-1(3), 483) Win Walk.

Divine Wisdom of the Bhagavad Gita. Swami Amar Jyoti. 1 cass. 1982. 9.95 (R-46) Truth Consciousness.
The essence of wisdom, given by Sri Krishna, dispelling our self-imposed delusions, driving all the clouds from our minds.

Divine Yoga Flow Practice: With Ateeka. 1999. audio compact disk 14.95 (978-1-893792-41-8(2)) Terra Entmnt.

Divinely Superfluous Beauty see Poetry of Robinson Jeffers

Diviner, & Other Stories. unabr. ed. Short Stories. Brian Friel. Narrated by Donal Donnelly. 5 cass. (Running Time: 6 hrs. 15 mins.). 1994. 44.00 (978-1-55690-987-0(X), 94126E7) Recorded Bks.
A distillation of the best from Friel's previous two short story collections & focuses on the lives of villagers from rural County Donegal in Northwestern Ireland.

Diviner's Son. unabr. ed. Gary Crew. 5 cass. (Running Time: 6 hrs. 15 mins.). 2002. 40.00 (978-1-74030-640-9(6)) Pub: Bolinda Pubng AUS. Dist(s): Bolinda Pub Inc

Diviner's Son. unabr. ed. Gary Crew. Read by Michael Veitch. 6 CDs. (Running Time: 6 hrs. 15 mins.). 2003. audio compact disk 77.95 (978-1-74093-087-1(8)) Pub: Bolinda Pubng AUS. Dist(s): Bolinda Pub Inc

***Diviner's Tale: A Novel.** unabr. ed. Bradford Morrow. (Running Time: 11 hrs.). 2011. 29.95 (978-1-4417-7179-7(4)); 65.95 (978-1-4417-7176-6(X)); audio compact disk 32.95 (978-1-4417-7178-0(6)); audio compact disk 100.00 (978-1-4417-7177-3(8)) Blckstn Audio.

Diving In. unabr. ed. Kate Cann. Read by Amanda Hulme. 5 CDs. (Running Time: 19800 sec.). (GER, ITA & SPA.). (YA). (gr. 9-16). 2006. audio compact disk 63.95 (978-1-74030-907-3(3)) Pub: Bolinda Pubng AUS. Dist(s): Bolinda Pub Inc

Diving Medicine Review. unabr. ed. Kenneth Kizer et al. Ed. by Chris Wachholz. 1 cass. (Running Time: 1 hr. 2 min.). (Hazardous Diving Ser.). (YA). (gr. 8-12). 1987. 8.95 (978-0-939865-04-8(1)) Meunincks Media.
Pre-dive check list & diving information on dysbarism, nitrogen narcosis, drowning, altitude diving, decompression sickness, diving & flying, dive travel & women & diving.

Divining Women. unabr. ed. Kaye Gibbons. 2004. 15.95 (978-0-7435-3937-1(0)) Pub: S&S Audio. Dist(s): S and S Inc

***Divinity of Doubt: The God Question.** Vincent Bugliosi. 2011. audio compact disk 44.99 (978-1-61120-018-8(0)) Dreamscap OH.

Divinium Mysterium. Perf. by Liturgical Organist Consortium. 1 cass. 1998. 11.00 (2920); audio compact disk 16.00 CD. (978-0-937690-52-9(X), 2922) Wrld Lib Pubns.
Christmas music for organ, brass & choir.

Divisadero. unabr. ed. Michael Ondaatje. 7 cass. (Running Time: 10 hrs. 30 mins.). 2007. 90.00 (978-1-4159-4047-1(9)); audio compact disk 90.00 (978-1-4159-3882-9(2)) Books on Tape.

Divisadero. unabr. ed. Michael Ondaatje. Read by Hope Davis. 7 CDs. (Running Time: 8 hrs.). (ENG.). 2007. audio compact disk 39.95 (978-0-7393-4349-4(1), Random AudioBks) Pub: Random Audio Pubg. Dist(s): Random

Division. 1 cass. (Running Time: 1 hr.). (J). (gr. 2-10). 2001. pap. bk. 9.98 (TS 404C) Kimbo Educ.
Dinosaurs add interest as students learn division facts. Side 1 teaches division while Side 2 drills division as it relates to multiplication. Includes book.

Division. Mary Blakely. 1 cass. (978-1-882995-07-3(4)) Azuray Learn.
Multi-sensory education, workbook incl. - Early elementary & up.

Division. J. Krishnamurti. 1 cass. (Running Time: 75 min.). (Krishnamurti & Professor David Bohm - 1980 Ser.: No. 7). 8.50 (ABD807) Krishnamurti.
Krishnamurti & Prof. Bohm offer penetrating, in-depth dialogues which shed light on the fundamental issues of existence.

Division. Kim Mitzo Thompson & Karen Mitzo Hilderbrand. Arranged by Hal Wright. (J). 2000. pap. bk. 13.99 (978-1-57583-334-7(4), TWIN 445CD); audio compact disk 12.99 (978-1-57583-320-0(4), Twin 145CD) Twin Sisters.

Division at the Games. Based on a book by Brett Kelly. (J). 2008. audio compact disk 10.00 (978-1-4108-8068-0(0)) Benchmark Educ.

Division at the Games E-Book: Set A. Benchmark Education Staff. Ed. by Brett Kelly. (Math Explorers Ser.). (J). 2008. audio compact disk 15.00 (978-1-60437-150-5(1)) Benchmark Educ.

Division at the Movies. Based on a book by Brett Kelly. (J). 2008. audio compact disk 10.00 (978-1-4108-8066-6(4)) Benchmark Educ.

Division at the Movies E-Book: Set A. Benchmark Education Staff. Ed. by Brett Kelly. (Math Explorers Ser.). (J). 2008. audio compact disk 15.00 (978-1-60437-148-2(X)) Benchmark Educ.

Division at the Picnic. Based on a book by Tara Funk. (J). 2008. audio compact disk 10.00 (978-1-4108-8067-3(2)) Benchmark Educ.

Division at the Picnic E-Book: Set A. Benchmark Education Staff. Ed. by Tara Funk. (Math Explorers Ser.). (J). 2008. audio compact disk 15.00 (978-1-60437-149-9(8)) Benchmark Educ.

Division in the Ranks: Acts 15:1-35. Ed Young. 1998. 4.95 (978-0-7417-2182-2(1), A1182) Win Walk.

Division of the Spoils. unabr. collector's ed. Paul Scott. Read by Richard Brown. 11 cass. (Running Time: 16 hrs. 30 min.). (Raj Quartet: No. 4). 1992. 88.00 (978-0-7366-2140-3(7), 2939A); 72.00 (978-0-7366-2141-0(5), 2939B) Books on Tape.
Through the eyes of Guy Perron, sergeant in an army intelligence unit, that we view this historic time. Perron's life is bound up with Ronald Merrick, an older man, wounded, enigmatic, a colonel of the police, a person apart. How they work out their conflicts is at one level symbolic of the relationship between English & Indian.

Division Rap. Brad Caudle. 1 CD. (Running Time: 1 hr.). (J). 2001. pap. bk. 13.95; pap. bk. 11.95 (RL 908C) Kimbo Educ.
A number one choice with parents, teachers & students. Learning becomes easy & fun while singing a favorite rap or rock song. The ultimate division tape includes division concepts, story problems, remainders, introduction to long division & exciting rap drills. Includes activity book.

Division Rap. unabr. ed. Brad Caudle & Richard Caudle. Perf. by D. J. Doc Roc and the Get Smart Crew Staff. 1 cass. (Running Time: 57 min.). (Rock n' Learn Ser.). (J). (gr. 3 up). 1992. pap. bk. 12.99 (978-1-878489-08-1(9), RL908) Rock N Learn.
"Top 40" type rap songs with educational lyrics teach division concepts & facts (divisors up to 9). Includes activity book with reproducible worksheets.

Division Rock. unabr. ed. Brad Caudle & Richard Caudle. Perf. by T. J. Rockinstein et al. 1 cass. (Running Time: 30 min.). (Rock 'N Learn Ser.). (J). (gr. 3 up). 1994. pap. bk. 12.99 (978-1-878489-41-8(0), RL941) Rock N Learn.
"Top 40" type songs with educational lyrics teach divisors up to 9. Includes activity book with reproducible worksheets.

Division Songs. 1 cass. (Running Time: 1 hr.). 2001. pap. bk. 9.95 (8) Audio Memory.
Teaches facts from 2 divided by 2 to 144 divided by 12. Songs are sung in sets but facts are sung out of order for additional challenge.

Division Songs. 1 CD. (Running Time: 1 hr.). 2001. pap. bk., tchr. ed., wbk. ed. 12.95 (8CD) Audio Memory.

Division Songs. 2004. bk. 12.95 (978-1-883028-16-9(7)) Audio Memory.

Division Unplugged. Emad Girgis et al. Composed by Mark Shannon & Larry Crowe. Illus. by Glen Wyand. 1 cass. (Running Time: 58 mins. 48 secs.). (Math Unplugged Ser.). (J). (gr. 4-5). 1998. pap. bk. 14.95 (978-1-895523-47-8(8), JMP114K) Jordan Music.
Catchy melodies, drill and student involvement make division facts with divisors to 9 very memorable. A bonus complement of self-quizzing music tracks allows students to quiz themselves.

Division Unplugged. abr. ed. Emad Girgis. Composed by Mark Shannon. Engineer Mark Shannon. Prod. by Sara Jordan. 1 CD. (Running Time: 30 min.). (Songs that Teach Math Ser.). (ENG.). (J). (gr. 4-7). 1998. audio compact disk 13.95 (978-1-895523-77-5(X), JMP 114CD) Pub: S Jordan Publ. Dist(s): CrabtreePubCo

Division Wordbook & Music CD. Twin Sisters Productions Staff. 2006. pap. bk. & wbk. ed. 112.99 (978-1-57583-895-3(8)) Twin Sisters.

Division Wrap-up Rap: Audio CD. Rick Blair. 1 cass. (ENG.). (J). (gr. 4-6). 1985. audio compact disk 9.99 (978-0-943343-24-2(0)) Lrn Wrap-Ups.
Learning aid.

Divisional Harmonics. H. M. Ishikawa. 1 cass. 8.95 (170) Am Fed Astrologers.
Newly developed technique with reference to Addey's Harmonics.

Divisional Harmonics, Pt. 1. H. M. Ishikawa. 1 cass. 8.95 (420) Am Fed Astrologers.
Detailed & precise delineation.

Divisional Harmonics, Pt. 2. H. M. Ishikawa. 1 cass. 8.95 (421) Am Fed Astrologers.

Divorce. Robert S. Sigman. Read by Robert S. Sigman. 1 cass. (Running Time: 55 min.). (Law for the Layman Ser.). 1990. 16.95 (978-1-878135-00-1(7)) Legovac.
What you need to know before you see a lawyer.

Divorce: The Exception, Not the Rule. Creflo A. Dollar & Taffi L. Dollar. 2 cass. (Running Time: 3 hrs.). 2001. 10.00 (978-1-931172-24-0(2), TS297, Kidz Faith) Pub: Creflo Dollar. Dist(s): STL Dist NA

Divorce: The Facts, the Myths, the Deception & What God Says. Creflo A. Dollar. 3 cass. (Running Time: 4 hrs. 30 mins.). 2001. 15.00 (978-1-931172-93-6(5), TS178, Kidz Faith) Pub: Creflo Dollar. Dist(s): STL Dist NA

Divorce - No. Barrie Konicov. 1 cass. 11.98 (978-0-87082-317-6(5), 028) Potentials.
If you do not want a divorce, yet have no choice, this program can quiet your fear, loosen the tension & pressure, making it possible for you to live & love again.

Divorce - The Role of the Pediatrician. Contrib. by Michael Jellinek et al. 1 cass. (American Academy of Pediatrics UPDATE: Vol. 16, No. 6). 1998. 20.00 Am Acad Pediat.

Divorce - Yes. Barrie Konicov. 1 cass. 11.98 (978-0-87082-318-3(3), 029) Potentials.
If you seek a divorce, this program can free you mentally, physically & emotionally from the other person.

Divorce & Bankruptcy. 1 cass. bk. 55.00 (AC-637) PA Bar Inst.

Divorce Code: Amendments of February 12, 1988. 1988. bk. 110.00; 60.00 PA Bar Inst.

Divorce, Confidence & Relaxation. Michael S. Prokop. (Running Time: 42 min.). (J). 9.95 incl. Guide for Kids. (978-0-933879-31-7(8)) Alegra Hse Pubs.

Divorce Court Secrets: Expert answers to women's most pressing divorce law Questions. Interview. Cathi Adams & Jeannie Etter. 2 CDs. 2006. audio compact disk 34.95 (978-0-9770448-1-8(5)) CSL Te Inc.

Divorce, Custody & Support, Side A; Adoption & Name Change, Side B. Frank L. Natter. 1 cass. (Running Time: 90 min.). (Type Law Tapes Ser.: No. 4). 1989. 10.00 (978-1-878287-59-5(1), ATA-4) Type & Temperament.
Implications & insights to understanding one's own personal legal & financial planning on the given subject.

Divorce Express. unabr. ed. Paula Danziger. 1 read-along cass. (Running Time: 1 hr. 21 min.). (Young Adult Cliffhangers Ser.). (YA). (gr. 5-6). 1986. 15.98 incl. bk. & guide. (978-0-8072-1840-2(5), JRH122SP, Listening Lib) Random Audio Pubg.
Since her parents' divorce, Phoebe Brooks has been shuttled back & forth between the home she shares with her father during the week, & her mother's apartment. Then she meets Rosie, who also rides the bus called "The Divorce Express," & she realizes she is not as alone as she thinks.

Divorce, Grieving Through. unabr. ed. Larry Losoncy. 12.95 (1900) J Norton Pubs.
Describes emotional stages people experience after the divorce becomes final & gives positive suggestions for overcoming the painful effects of divorce.

Divorce Party. unabr. ed. Laura Dave. Read by Susan Ericksen. (Running Time: 7 hrs.). 2008. 39.25 (978-1-4233-5239-6(4), 9781423352396, BADLE); 24.95 (978-1-4233-5238-9(6), 9781423352389, BAD); audio compact disk 39.25 (978-1-4233-5237-2(8), 9781423352372, Brinc Audio MP3 Lib); audio compact disk 82.25 (978-1-4233-5235-8(1), 9781423352358, BriAudCD Unabrid); audio compact disk 29.95 (978-1-4233-5234-1(3), 9781423352341, Bril Audio CD Unabri); audio compact disk 24.95 (978-1-4233-5236-5(X), 9781423352365, Brilliance MP3) Brilliance Audio.

Divorce PREP. Interview. Created by DP Publishing Staff. 5 MiniDiscs. (Running Time: 4 hrs. 45 mins.). Dramatization. 2004. 179.00 (978-0-9742048-4-0(6)); 179.00 (978-0-9742048-3-3(8)); audio compact disk 179.00 (978-0-9742048-1-9(1)) DP Pubng.

Divorce 4-Copy Prepack. unabr. ed. Diane Johnson. Narrated by Suzanne Toren. 10 CDs. (Running Time: 11 hrs.). 2001. audio compact disk 97.00 (978-0-7887-7166-8(3), C1419) Recorded Bks.
A witty & insightful look at clashing cultures, was a finalist for the National Book Award. Isabel Walker has flown to Paris to offer moral support for Roxy, her pregnant stepsister. Roxy's husband, Charles-Henri, favorite son of a powerful French family, is having a love affair. Divorce seems imminent. When her entire family arrives to help with legal issues, Isabel feels intense pressure to keep everything from falling apart. And in the background, the unstable husband of Charles-Henri's lover lurks menacingly. A resident of both America & France, Diane Johnson infuses this shrewd comedy of manners with keen observations about cultural differences.

Divorce 4-Copy Prepack. unabr. ed. Diane Johnson. Narrated by Suzanne Toren. 8 cass. (Running Time: 11 hrs.). 2000. 74.00 (978-0-7887-4865-3(3), 96372E7) Recorded Bks.
An insightful comedy of manners. Isabel Walker flies to Paris to support her pregnant stepsister, who plans to divorce her French husband but when the rest of Isabel's family gets involved, French & American cultures collide & the tension escalates toward a gripping conclusion.

Divorced Dad's Rules for Raising Relatively Stable Kids: The Audiobook on Parenting. Patrick Talley. (ENG.). 2009. audio compact disk 24.95 (978-1-934965-24-5(3)) Dreamervision Pub.

Divorced from the Mob. Andrea Giovino & Gary Brozek. Read by Barbara Rosenblat. (Running Time: 9 hrs. 30 mins.). 2004. 30.95 (978-1-59912-472-8(6)) Iofy Corp.

Divorced from the Mob: My Journey from Organized Crime to Independent Woman. Andrea Giovino. Read by Barbara Rosenblat. 7 cass. (Running Time: 10 hrs.). 2004. 49.95 (978-0-7861-2720-7(1), 3253) Blckstn Audio.

Divorced from the Mob: My Journey from Organized Crime to Independent Woman. unabr. ed. Andrea Giovino. Read by Barbara Rosenblat. 8 CDs. (Running Time: 10 hrs.). 2004. audio compact disk 24.95 (978-0-7861-8572-6(4), 3253); audio compact disk 64.00 (978-0-7861-8680-8(1), 3253) Blckstn Audio.
From mob wife with blood on her hands to straight-arrow breadwinner for her four kids?a tale of transformation and empowerment from a woman whose life in organized crime makes Carmella Soprano look like June Cleaver.

Divorced from the Mob: My Journey from Organized Crime to Independent Women. unabr. ed. Andrea Giovino & Gary Brozek. Read by Barbara Rosenblat. 8 CDs. (Running Time: 11 hrs. 30 mins.). 2004. audio compact disk 29.95 (978-0-7861-8726-3(3)) Blckstn Audio.

Divorced from the Mob: My Journey from Organized Crime to Independent Women. unabr. ed. Andrea Giovino & Gary Brozek. Read by Barbara Rosenblat. 7 pieces. (Running Time: 11 hrs. 30 mins.). 2004. reel tape 29.95 (978-0-7861-2648-4(5)) Blckstn Audio.

Divorcing the Elderly. 1995. bk. 99.00 (ACS-954) PA Bar Inst.
Marital discord poses a myriad of unique issues for the elderly. The greater your understanding of those issues & the special needs of the older client, the more effective you will be in representing their interests.

Diwali Satsang. Swami Amar Jyoti. 1 cass. 1985. 9.95 (K-78) Truth Consciousness.
On the glories of the Ramayana & the greatness of its characters. Sri Rama, the utmost pinnacle of goodness & nobility.

Dixie & Other Love Songs. unabr. ed. Christopher L. Woods. Read by Mark Luce & Rick Moock. Ed. by Julie Elaine Fleming. 2 cass. (Running Time: 2 hrs.). Dramatization. (Civil War Era Songs Ser.: Vol. 2). 1994. 19.95 set. (978-1-884649-02-8(5)) Nouveau Glass.
Cassette (A) has 15 popular songs of the Civil War Era sung by the 97th Regimental String Band wihtout interruption. Cassette (B) has the history of each of the songs popular in both the North & South with anecdotes, parodies & sidelights on their creation, plus an overview of Civil War Era music.

Dixie Chicks: The Unauthorized Biography of the Dixie Chicks. Sally Wilford. (Maximum Ser.). (ENG., 2001. audio compact disk 14.95 (978-1-84240-136-1(X)) Pub: Chrome Dreams GBR. Dist(s): IPG Chicago

Dixie Chicks Collectors Box. Sally Wilford & Spencer Leigh. 2 CDs. (ENG., 2003. audio compact disk 30.00 (978-1-84240-207-8(2)) Pub: Chrome Dreams GBR. Dist(s): IPG Chicago

Dixie City Jam. James Lee Burke. 1 cass. (Dave Robicheaux Ser.). 1998. 9.98 (978-0-671-58252-4(6), Audioworks) S&S Audio.
Mystery & detective with police procedure.

Dixie City Jam. abr. ed. James Lee Burke. (Dave Robicheaux Ser.). 2006. 9.95 (978-0-7435-6144-0(9)) Pub: S&S Audio. Dist(s): S and S Inc

Dixie City Jam. unabr. ed. James Lee Burke. Narrated by Mark Hammer. 10 cass. (Running Time: 14 hrs. 30 mins.). (Dave Robicheaux Ser.). 1994. 85.00 (978-0-7887-0060-6(X), 94316E7) Recorded Bks.
A search for a German sub sunk in World War II in the Gulf of Mexico stirs up old hatreds, setting Louisiana detective Dave Robicheaux & his old partner Clete Purcel on a dangerous path.

Dixie City Jam. unabr. ed. James Lee Burke. Read by Mark Hammer. 10 cass. (Running Time: 14 hrs. 30 min.). (Dave Robicheaux Ser.). 1994. Rental 17.50 Set. (94316) Recorded Bks.

Dixieland: The Birth of Jazz. Judith Pasternak et al. 1 cass. (CD Ser.). 1995. pap. bk. 16.98 (978-1-56799-236-6(6), Friedman-Fairfax) M Friedman Pub Grp Inc.

Dixieme Prophetie. James Redfield. (FRE.). pap. bk. 18.95 (978-2-89558-025-6(1)) Pub: Coffragants CAN. Dist(s): Penton Overseas

Dixon Cornbelt League & Other Baseball Stories. unabr. ed. Short Stories. W. P. Kinsella. Narrated by Frank Muller. 3 cass. (Running Time: 4 hrs.). 1999. 26.00 (978-0-7887-0346-1(3), 94538E7) Recorded Bks.
A collection of nine magical stories that amount to nine innings of sheer baseball pleasure.

***DIY Marketing: Grow Your Business Without Spending a Bundle.** Jack Romig. (ENG.). 2010. audio compact disk 39.95 (978-0-9766414-3-8(7)) Tanacacia Pr.

Dizmas. Contrib. by Dizmas. Prod. by Steve Wilson & Rob Hawkins. 2008. audio compact disk 7.99 (978-5-557-43699-1(5)) FF Rcds.

DJ Techniques. Tom Frederikse & Sloly D. 2005. pap. bk. 19.95 (978-1-84492-027-3(5)) Pub: Sanctuary Pubng GBR. Dist(s): H Leonard

***Djibouti.** unabr. ed. Elmore Leonard. (Running Time: 11 hrs.). 2010. 29.95 (978-1-4417-6416-4(X)); 65.95 (978-1-4417-6413-3(5)); audio compact disk 100.00 (978-1-4417-6414-0(3)) Blckstn Audio.

***Djibouti.** unabr. ed. Elmore Leonard. Read by Peter Francis James. 2010. (978-0-06-200603-5(7), Harper Audio); (978-0-06-206803-3(2)) HarperCollins Pubs.

***Djibouti.** unabr. ed. Elmore Leonard. Read by Peter Francis James. 2010. audio compact disk 34.99 (978-0-06-200850-3(1), Harper Audio) HarperCollins Pubs.

Djinn in the Nightingale's Eye: Five Fairy Stories. unabr. ed. Short Stories. A. S. Byatt. Narrated by Virginia Leishman. 5 cass. (Running Time: 6 hrs. 30 mins.). 1997. 44.00 (978-0-7887-1317-0(5), 95175E7) Recorded Bks.
Constructed as a fairy tale within a tale of discovery, it is as beautiful & finely crafted as an oriental ivory puzzle.

DNA Molecule see May Swenson

DNA of Relationships. unabr. ed. Gary Smalley et al. 6 CDs. (Running Time: 7 hrs. 15 mins.). (ENG.). 2004. audio compact disk 22.99 (978-0-8423-5990-0(7)) Tyndale Hse.

DNA of Relationships: Seminar. As told by Gary Smalley. 3 cass. (Running Time: 4 hrs.). 2004. 59.00 (978-1-930784-39-0(2)) Smalley Relat.

DNA Purification. Govinda. Read by Karen Petrella. Ed. by Dietmar R. Rittner. 1 cass. (Running Time: 1 hr. 04 min.). (ViViD-Process Ser.). 1993. 14.95 (978-1-884027-04-8(0)) Magic Sunrise.
Contact the level of your cell consciousness to release trauma from this & former lifetimes. Relies upon newest research in the field of psycho-neuro-immunology.

D'Novo. unabr. ed. D'Novo & José Medero. (SPA.). 2003. 9.99 (978-0-8297-3144-6(X)) Pub: Vida Pubs. Dist(s): Zondervan

Do-Along Songbook. Phil Baron. Ed. by Ken Forse. Illus. by David High et al. (J). (ps). 1986. bk. (978-0-318-60970-6(3)) Alchemy Comms.

Do Americans Over-Use Drugs? unabr. ed. Nathan S. Kline. 1 cass. (Running Time: 26 min.). 12.95 (759) J Norton Pubs.
Kline's surprising answer is "no." In fact, he argues, the anti-drug movement has resulted in a problem of undermedication for many people who could benefit from drugs.

Do & Dont Delgtn. Gary Fellows. 2004. 5.95 (978-0-7435-4653-9(9)) Pub: S&S Audio. Dist(s): S and S Inc

Do Androids Dream of Electric Sheep? see Blade Runner

Do Androids Dream of Electric Sheep? abr. ed. Philip K. Dick. 2006. 14.98 (978-1-59483-775-3(9)) Pub: Hachet Audio. Dist(s): HachBkGrp

Do Animals Have Rights? Contrib. by Edwin Locke & Stephen Sapontzis. 2 cass. (Running Time: 2 hrs.). 19.95 Set. (IL05D) Second Renaissance.
Debate on an issue affecting ever-increasing aspects of our lives. Includes Q&A.

Do Butlers Burgle Banks? unabr. ed. P. G. Wodehouse. Read by Frederick Davidson. 4 cass. (Running Time: 5 hrs. 30 mins.). 1997. 32.95 (978-0-7861-1213-5(1), 1995) Blckstn Audio.
"Unless some kindly burglar takes it into his head to burgle the bank before the examiners arrive, I'm for it," said Mike Bond of Bond's Bank gloomily. Whatever their motives, neither party had reckoned on Horace's susceptibility to steak & kidney pie & to a female person's charms or on the resourcefulness of Mike's betrothed or on the formidable powers of Potter of the Yard.

Do Butlers Burgle Banks?, Set. unabr. ed. P. G. Wodehouse. Read by Frederick Davidson. 4 cass. 1999. 32.95 (FS9-34471) Highsmith.

Do Everything They Tell You Not to Do If You Want to Succeed: Success Is Yours If You Want It. unabr. ed. Sanjay Burman. Read by Sanjay Burman. (Running Time: 2 hrs.). (ENG.). 2008. 19.98 (978-1-59659-313-8(X), GildAudio) Pub: Gildan Media. Dist(s): HachBkGrp

Do Gentlemen Really Prefer Blondes? Bodies, Brains, & Behavior - -the Science Behind Sex, Love & Attraction. unabr. ed. Jena Pincott. Narrated by Laural Merlington. (Running Time: 8 hrs. 30 mins. 0 sec.). (ENG.). 2008. audio compact disk 69.99 (978-1-4001-3825-8(6)); audio compact disk 24.99 (978-1-4001-5825-6(7)) Pub: Tantor Media. Dist(s): IngramPubServ

Do Gentlemen Really Prefer Blondes? Bodies, Brains, & Behavior - -the Science Behind Sex, Love & Attraction. unabr. ed. Jena Pincott. Read by Laural Merlington. (Running Time: 8 hrs. 30 mins. 0 sec.). (ENG.). 2008. audio compact disk 34.99 (978-1-4001-0825-1(X)) Pub: Tantor Media. Dist(s): IngramPubServ

Do Gifted Children Need Special Help? James T. Webb. 2005. 29.95 (978-0-910707-44-2(8)) Great Potential Pr.

Do Goldfish Really Play the Violin? unabr. ed. David Henry Wilson. Read by Andy Crane. 2 cass. (Running Time: 2 hrs.). (Jeremy James Ser.: No. 5). 2001. 18.95 (CCA3328, Chivers Child Audio) AudioGO.

Do Good to Others. 1 cass. (Running Time: 1 hr.). 12.99 (158) Yoga Res Foun.

Do-Gooders: How Liberals Hurt Those They Claim to Help (and the Rest of Us) unabr. ed. Mona Charen. Read by Sandra Burr. (Running Time: 9 hrs.). 2004. 39.25 (978-1-59710-216-2(4), 1597102164, BADLE); 24.95 (978-1-59710-217-9(2), 1597102172, BAD); 24.95 (978-1-59335-774-0(5), 1593357745, Brilliance MP3); 39.25 (978-1-59335-908-9(X), 159335908X, Brinc Audio MP3 Lib); 74.25 (978-1-59355-957-1(7), 1593559577, BrilAudUnabridg); 29.95 (978-1-59355-956-4(9), 1593559569); audio compact disk 29.95 (978-1-59355-958-8(5), 1593559585); audio compact disk 87.25 (978-1-59355-959-5(3), 1593559593, BriAudCD Unabrid) Brilliance Audio.
Please enter a Synopsis.

Do Hard Things: A Teenage Rebellion Against Low Expectations. abr. ed. Alex Harris & Brett Harris. Read by Alex Harris & Brett Harris. (ENG.). 2008. audio compact disk 19.95 (978-0-7393-5906-8(1), Random AudioBks) Pub: Random Audio Pubg. Dist(s): Random

Do I Have to Give up Me to Be Loved by My Kids? Jordan Paul & Margaret Paul. 4 cass. 1987. 20.00 (978-0-912389-03-5(6)) Evolving Pubns.
How to improve parent-child relationships using the intent to learn as described in the book "Do I Have to Give Up Me to Be Loved by My Kids?".

Do I Have What You Need? 11 Cor.8:10-15. Ed Young. 1990. 4.95 (978-0-7417-1792-4(1), 792) Win Walk.

Do I Need to Be Afraid of God? 2007 CCEF Annual Conference. Featuring Bill Smith. (ENG.). 2007. audio compact disk 11.99 (978-1-934885-18-5(5)) New Growth Pr.

Do I Stand Alone? Going to the Mat Against Political Pawns & Media Jackals. Jesse Ventura. Read by Jesse Ventura. 2004. 10.95 (978-0-7435-1976-2(0)) Pub: S&S Audio. Dist(s): S and S Inc

Do It! Let's Get off Our Buts. unabr. ed. Peter McWilliams. Read by Peter McWilliams. 8 cass. (Running Time: 12 hrs.). (Life 101 Ser.). 1995. 24.95 set. (978-0-931580-15-4(3)) Mary Bks.

Do It Motivation. Eldon Taylor. 2 cass. 29.95 Set. (978-1-55978-744-4(9), 4409) Progress Aware Res.

Do It Now! Eldon Taylor. 2 cass. (Running Time: 62 min. per cass.). (Omniphonics Ser.). 29.95 incl. script Set. (978-1-55978-817-5(8), 4018) Progress Aware Res.
3-D soundtrack with underlying subliminal affirmations, night & day versions.

Do It Now! Stop Procrastination with Mind Power, Vol. 34, set. Jonathan Parker. Read by Jonathan Parker. 2 CDs. (Running Time: 2 hrs.). (Success Ser.: Vol. 3). 1999. audio compact disk (978-1-58400-033-4(3)) QuantumQuests Intl.
Disc 1 contains several guided visualizations. Disc 2 contains audible & subliminal positive affirmations with music.

Do it! or Diet: Moderation Not Deprivation, Set. Michelle Present. 2 CDs. (Running Time: 140 min.). 1999. audio compact disk 25.00 (978-0-9659120-4-4(3)) Michelle Present.
A system you can really live with: Controlling weight in the ideal world.

Do-It-Yourself Dust Storm: Acts 6:1-7. Ed Young. 1997. 4.95 (978-0-7417-2157-0(0), A1157) Win Walk.

Do-It-Yourself Japanese Thru Comic. Kazuhiko Nagatomo & Miho T. Steinberg. (JPN & ENG., 20.00 (978-4-7700-1930-1(0)) Pub: Kodansha Intl JPN. Dist(s): Kodansha

Do It Yourself Kids Circus. Georgiana Liccione Stewart. 1 cass. (Running Time: 1 hr.). (J). 2001. pap. bk. 10.95 (KIM 7032C) Kimbo Educ.
Exciting circus activities that children act out as they stage their circus. A wide variety of fine & gross motor skills combine with the child's imagination. Includes manual.

Do It Yourself Kids Circus. Georgiana Liccione Stewart. 1 CD. (Running Time: 1 hr.). (J). (ps-3). 2001. pap. bk. 14.95 (KIM 7032CD) Kimbo Educ.
Exciting circus activities that children act our as they stage their circus. A wide variety of fine & gross motor skills combine with the child's imagination. Includes manual.

Do-It-Yourself Sermon: John 3:16. Ed Young. 1990. 4.95 (978-0-7417-1773-3(5), 773) Win Walk.

Do-It-Yourself Space Clearing Kit: Audiobook 2 CD Set. Excerpts. Narrated by Christan Hummel. 2 CDs. (Running Time: 1 hour 35 mins.). (ENG.). 2004. audio compact disk 19.95 (978-0-9754793-1-5(8)) One Source.
Christan narrates this 2 CD set which accompanies the book, Do It Yourself Space Clearing Kit. Filled with stories, and exercises not in the book, this 2 CD set is a great companion to the book. Not sold separately.

Do No Harm. Andrew Gregg Hurwitz. Read by Jonathan Marosz. 2002. audio compact disk 112.00 (978-0-7366-8794-2(7)) Books on Tape.

Do No Harm. unabr. ed. Gregg Hurwitz. 11 cass. (Running Time: 16 hrs. 30 mins.). 2002. 96.00 (978-0-7366-8752-2(1)) Books on Tape.
When a nurse is brought into the ER at UCLA Medical Center, blinded and with her once lovely face ravaged from an attack by an unknown assailant, ER Chief Dr. David Spier is horrified. Someone is stalking the hospital staff. But things turn monstrous when the assailant is brought into the ER as a patient. The police want him dead; the staff refuses to treat him. But Dr. Spier heals him, and, by so doing, inadvertently abets him in carrying out even more horrible acts. Dr. Spier is now a pariah in the eyes of the city, and the madman's next target. He must plumb the depths of the madman's twisted psyche, and discover the hospital's terrible secret at its base.

Do Not Fear to Hope. Rory Cooney. 1 cass. 9.95 (5273) OR Catholic.
Musically addressing the American Catholic experience, "Do Not Fear to Hope" is an enlivening collection of music for liturgy & prayer. Features Mass parts, songs, & psalms used most often in the lectionary.

Do Not Go Gentle into That Good Night see Child's Christmas in Wales

Do Not Go Gentle into That Good Night see Dylan Thomas Reading His Poetry

Do Not Go Gently: A Starletta Duvall Mystery. unabr. ed. Judith Smith-Levin. Narrated by Marc Damon Johnson. 7 cass. (Running Time: 10 hrs.). 1996. 64.00 (978-0-7887-9039-3(0), F0039L8) Recorded Bks.
Starletta Duvall is an exceptional police lieutenant: tough & professional. But when a serial killer begins targeting successful young black women, the twisted nature of the murders begins to haunt Starletta.

Do Not Remove the Ancient Foundations. Don Nori. 1 cass. 12.00 (978-1-56043-893-9(2)) Destiny Image Pubs.

Do or Die: Sundown Riders. unabr. ed. Ralph Compton Novel. 4 CDs. (Running Time: 4 hrs. 45 mins.). (ENG.). 2003. audio compact disk 22.95 (978-1-56511-807-2(3), 1565118073) Pub: HighBridge. Dist(s): Workman Pub

Do-over. Erik Sellin. (ENG.). 2009. audio compact disk (978-0-9764805-5-6(7)) C CD Bks.

Do-over! How Women Are Reinventing Their Lives. Ann Daly. Read by Ann Daly. (ENG.). 2010. 16.95 (978-0-9797295-2-2(1)) Wollemi Pine Pr.

***Do penguins have Knees?** unabr. ed. David Feldman. Read by David Feldman. (ENG.). 2006. (978-0-06-088319-5(7), Harper Audio); (978-0-06-088320-1(0), Harper Audio) HarperCollins Pubs.

Do Plants Grow under Water? Early Explorers Early Set B Audio CD. Christina Riska. Adapted by Benchmark Education Staff. (J). 2007. audio compact disk 10.00 (978-1-4108-8213-4(6)) Benchmark Educ.

Do-Re-Mi Deux. Barbara J. Lynaugh. 2004. pap. bk. 19.95 (978-0-9755227-0-7(1)) Bravo Drm.

Do Right: A Better Relationship with God: Heb. 13: 9-16. Ed Young. 1992. 4.95 (978-0-7417-1943-0(6), 943) Win Walk.

Do Right: A Better Relationship with Yourself: Heb. 13:5-8. Ed Young. 1992. 4.95 (978-0-7417-1942-3(8), 942) Win Walk.

Do Right Man. Omar R. Tyree. Narrated by Godfrey Simmons. 10 cass. (Running Time: 14 hrs.). 96.00 (978-0-7887-5328-2(2)) Recorded Bks.

Do Right: Your Relationship with Others: Heb. 13:1-4. Ed Young. 1992. 4.95 (978-0-7417-1941-6(X), 941) Win Walk.

***Do Something: Make Your Life Count.** unabr. ed. Miles McPherson. (ENG.). 2009. 12.98 (978-1-59644-826-1(1)); audio compact disk 21.98 (978-1-59644-825-4(3)) christianaud.

Do the Hard Things First: And Other Bloomberg Rules for Business & Politics. abr. ed. Michael Bloomberg. (Running Time: 6 hrs. 0 mins. 0 sec.). (ENG.). 2010. audio compact disk 29.99 (978-0-7435-7996-4(8)) Pub: S&S Audio. Dist(s): S and S Inc

Do the Right Thing: Inside the Movement That's Bringing Common Sense Back to America. unabr. ed. Mike Huckabee. Read by Mike Huckabee. (Running Time: 6 hrs.). (ENG.). (gr. 12 up). 2008. audio compact disk 29.95 (978-0-14-314387-1(5), PengAudBks) Penguin Grp USA.

Do Tôti (book & Tape) Lily Cérat. (CRP.). (J). 2006. 19.00 (978-1-58432-307-5(8)) Educa Vision.

Do unto Otters: A Book about Manners. Laurie Keller. 1 CD. (Running Time: 12 mins.). (J). (ps-3). 2008. bk. 29.95 (978-0-545-09455-9(0)) Weston Woods.

When the Otters move in next door to Mr. Rabbit, he does not know how to act with them. This is the story that highlights how to be a good neighbor and friend - just simply follow the Golden Rule!.

Do We Bring Our Troubles With Us When We Come Into this World. Instructed by Manly P. Hall. 8.95 (978-0-89314-043-4(0), C840603) Philos Res.

Do We Choose Our Lives Before We Are Born? Manly P. Hall. 1 cass. 8.95 (978-0-89314-044-1(9), C870531) Philos Res.

Do We Need More Help Managing Our Dying. 1 cass. (Care Cassettes Ser.: Vol. 21, No. 3). 1994. 10.80 Assn Prof Chaplains.

Do What I Say: Ms. Behavior's Guide to Gay & Lesbian Etiquette. unabr. collector's ed. Meryl Cohn. Read by Frances Cassidy. 5 cass. (Running Time: 7 hrs. 30 min.). 1997. 40.00 (978-0-7366-3657-5(9), 4329) Books on Tape.

learn the do's & dont's of gay & lesbian etiquette with this sometimes serious, often-times hilarious guide.

Do What You Do. 2001. 6.00 (978-1-58602-050-7(1)) E L Long.

Do What You Love, the Money Will Follow. Marsha Sinetar. 2 cass. (Running Time: 1 hr.). 1989. 16.95 Set. (978-0-8091-7858-2(3), 7858-3) Paulist Pr.

The author offers the stories of many men and woman, herself included, who have "revised" their careers and in the process have developed healthy self actualizing personalities. She challenges all of us to make conscious choices that will enable us to express ourselves distinctively through our work. She gives concrete suggestions for building inner confidence and self-esteem.

Do What You Love, the Money Will Follow. Marsha Sinetar. 2009. audio compact disk 16.95 (978-0-8091-8302-9(1)) Paulist Pr.

Do Whatever He Tells You: Contemporary Mariology - A Mini Course. Fred Jelly. 2 cass. (Running Time: 2 hrs. 57 min.). 1991. 18.95 set. (TAH235) Alba Hse Comns.

Perfect for personal, pastoral & theological updating, meditation & parish discussion groups.

Do You! 12 Laws to Access the Power in You to Achieve Happiness & Success. abr. ed. Russell Simmons & Chris Morrow. Read by Black Ice. (Running Time: 6 hrs.). (ENG.). (gr. 8 up). 2007. audio compact disk 29.95 (978-0-14-314213-3(5), PengAudBks) Penguin Grp USA.

Do You Believe in Jesus? Neville Goddard. 1 cass. (Running Time: 62 min.). 1963. 8.00 (98) J & L Pubns.

Neville taught Imagination Creates Reality. He was a powerfully influential teacher of God as Consciousness.

Do You Belong to This Family? Jeanette Oswald. 1 cass. 8.95 (267) Am Fed Astrologers.

Signs are picked up within families; how it influences.

Do You Do It or Does It Do You? How to Let the Universe Meditate You. Alan Watts. 4 CDs. (Running Time: 16200 sec.). 2005. audio compact disk 29.95 (978-1-59179-357-1(2), W964D) Sounds True.

Do You Fear God? Derek Prince. 1 cass. 1991. 5.95 (I-4302) Derek Prince.

The fear of the Lord is the key to the wisdom, knowledge & riches of God. Learn how you can obtain it.

Do You Have a Drinking Problem? 1990. 10.00 (978-1-878400-09-3(6)) Dolphin Pub.

Do You Have a Pit Bull Attitude? unabr. ed. Doug Giles. (YA). 2001. bk. 14.95 (978-0-9667501-2-6(8)) Clash Ministries.

Do You Have the Guts to Be Beautiful? Mitra Ray & Jennifer Daniels. (Running Time: 120 minutes). (ENG.). 2009. audio compact disk 24.99 (978-0-9714342-2-6(0)) Shining Star WA.

Do You Have What It Takes to Be an Entrepreneur? Fun & Guts. unabr. ed. Center for Entrepreneurial Management Staff. 1 cass. (Running Time: 1 hr. 6 min.). 12.95 (1361) J Norton Pubs.

Producers are characterized as strong individualists who strike out on their own, know highs & lows, overextend themselves for worthwhile causes & fail more than they succeed.

Do You Hear What I Hear? Contrib. by Todd Agnew. (Soundtraks Ser.). 2007. audio compact disk 8.99 (978-5-557-56220-1(6)) Christian Wrld.

Do You Hear What I Hear? Jay Welch Chorale. 1 cass. 2.37 (1000624); audio compact disk 12.98 (2800640) Covenant Comms.

Fifteen carols accompanied by the Utah Symphony.

Do You Know God? Read by Ted Gibbons. 1 cass. (Personal Enrichment Ser.). 6.95 (978-0-929985-29-9(X)) Jackman Pubng.

Do we really know God & understand what he wants of us.

Do You Know How to Shut Up?, Vol. 1. 2nd ed. (ENG.). 2008. audio compact disk 14.95 (978-0-9801857-1-3(8)) Mac Daddy.

Do You Know What I Have Done to You? John 13:12-17, 717. Ed Young. 1989. 4.95 (978-0-7417-1717-7(4), 716) Win Walk.

Do You Know Who You Are? Kelley Varner. 1 cass. 1992. 7.00 (978-0-938612-86-5(7)) Destiny Image Pubs.

Do You Know Your Spiritual Gift? Ben Young July 17-18, 1999. Ben Young. 1999. 4.95 (978-0-7417-6142-2(4), B0142) Win Walk.

Do You Love Me? - ShowTrax. Arranged by Mark Brymer. 1 CD. (Running Time: 5 mins.). 2000. audio compact disk 19.95 (08201115) H Leonard.

This 1962 pop hit by the Contours has become one of the favorite party tunes of all time. This easy-to-sing Discovery Series arrangement will be a hit with your younger groups!.

Do You Not Care? Mother Angelica. 1 cass. (Running Time: 60 min.). (Mother Angelica Live Ser.). 10.00 (978-1-55794-053-7(3), T4) Eternal Wrd TV.

Do You Promise Not to Tell? unabr. ed. Mary Jane Clark. Read by Beth Fowler. 6 CDs. (Running Time: 9 hrs.). 2000. audio compact disk 64.95 (978-0-7927-9959-7(3), SLD 010, Chivers Sound Lib) AudioGO.

TV producer Farrell Slater's job at KEY News hangs in the balance when she fails to convince her boss to broadcast the story of the auctioning of hte legendary Faberge Moon Egg. While trying to figure out what she will do with her future, she learns that the multi-million dollar treasure isn't all what it appears to be. Farell seizes the opportunity to expose the story & save her career. The mighty world of television news collides with the art world's secrecy, intrigue & high stakes wheeling & dealing.

Do You Promise Not to Tell?, Set. unabr. ed. Mary Jane Clark. Read by Beth Fowler. 4 vols. (KEY News Ser.: Bk. 2). 1999. bk. 39.95 (978-0-7927-2306-6(6), CSL 195, Chivers Sound Lib) AudioGO.

Do You Really Love God? John 14:15. Ed Young. 1993. 4.95 (978-0-7417-1954-6(1), 954) Win Walk.

Do You Really Want to Be Healed: John 5:1-15, 711. Ed Young. 1989. 4.95 (978-0-7417-1711-5(5), 711) Win Walk.

Do You Really Want to See God, Set. 3 cass. (Running Time: 3 hrs. 50 min.). 1993. 24.95 (978-7-900784-12-4(8), AA2669) Credence Commun.

McKenna tells a story, elicits some reactions from the audience, highlights the theology implicit in the story, & then, after the audience is sensitized by the story, she reads the passage from scripture.

Do You Remember Series: 5600 series. 1 cass. (Running Time: 1 hr.). 5.99 Great Am Audio.

Years available: 1938, 1939, 1940, 1941, 1945, 1950, 1953, 1954, 1955, 1956-1959, 1960-1970.

Do You Remember Springfield? see Poetry of Benet

Do You Remember 1938? abr. ed. Nina Mattikow. 1 cass. (Running Time: 30 min.). (Do You Remember Ser.). 1986. 5.99 (978-1-55569-024-3(6), 5621) Great Am Audio.

FDR is in office, "Alexander's Ragtime Band" is on the jukeboxes, the minimum wage finally hit 25! Hitler was on the march in Europe, Joe Louis fought Max Schmelling & Orson Welles aired the most famous radio show in history, & more. Remember?.

Do You Remember 1939? abr. ed. Nina Mattikow. 1 cass. (Running Time: 30 min.). (Do You Remember Ser.). 1986. 5.99 (978-1-55569-025-0(4), 5622) Great Am Audio.

Remember? "Jeepers Creepers" was the hit tune, "Gone with the Wind" was the big movie & Frank Sinatra joined the Harry James Band. The New York World's Fair opened, Baseball bid a sad farewell to Lou Gehrig & more.

Do You Remember 1940? abr. ed. Nina Mattikow. 1 cass. (Running Time: 30 min.). (Do You Remember Ser.). 1986. 5.99 (978-1-55569-026-7(2), 5623) Great Am Audio.

It was the last peace-time year & Swing was King. Churchill stirred the world with his words & Edward R. Murrow broadcast from London. Ralph Edwards, Walt Disney & Roosevelt Raceway were in the news. Everyone was jitter bugging, Amos n' Andy were on radio & more.

Do You Remember 1941? abr. ed. Nina Mattikow. 1 cass. (Running Time: 30 min.). (Do You Remember Ser.). 1986. 5.99 (978-1-55569-027-4(0), 5624) Great Am Audio.

FDR took office, juke-boxes were playing "Chattanooga Choo-Choo" & "Citizen Kane" was playing the movies theatres. The LP record was invented & teenagers had their first true Pop Idol. On Dec. 7th a "Day of Infamy", The Japanese attacked Pearl Harbor & the world exploded into global war & more. Remember?.

Do You Remember 1945? abr. ed. Nina Mattikow. 1 cass. (Running Time: 30 min.). (Do You Remember Ser.). 1986. 5.99 (978-1-55569-031-1(9), 5628) Great Am Audio.

Do you remember it was the year of victory as our triumphant armies returned home. It began with the Battle of the Bulge, saw the Atomic Bomb drop on Hiroshima & ended with Harry Truman presiding over V-E & V-J Days. The jukeboxes were playing "It's Been a Long, Long Time", Mildred Pierce was playing the movie theatres & more.

Do You Remember 1950? abr. ed. Nina Mattikow. 1 cass. (Running Time: 30 min.). (Do You Remember Ser.). 1986. 5.99 (978-1-55569-036-6(X), 5633) Great Am Audio.

Harry S. Truman was in office, The Weavers were singing "Goodnight Irene" & moviegoers were watching "Sunset Boulevard". The Korean War began, Alger Hiss was convicted of perjury & the minimum wage was raised to $75. A major credit card made its debut, Senator Joseph P. McCarthy was making headlines, & so too were Charlie Chaplin & Zero Mostel & more. Remember?.

Do You Remember 1953? abr. ed. Nina Mattikow. 1 cass. (Running Time: 30 min.). (Do You Remember Ser.). 1986. 5.99 (978-1-55569-039-7(4), 5636) Great Am Audio.

Dwight D. Eisenhower was inaugurated as the 34th President & the Korean War ended. Patti Page was singing "How Much is that Doggie in the Window" & moviegoers were lining up to see "From Here to Eternity". A new magazine featured a nude photo of Marilyn Monroe & Ethel & Julius Rosenberg were executed & more. Do you remember?.

Do You Remember 1954? abr. ed. Nina Mattikow. 1 cass. (Running Time: 30 min.). (Do You Remember Ser.). 1986. 5.99 (978-1-55569-040-3(8), 5637) Great Am Audio.

Remember Bill Haley & The Comets had everyone rocking to "Shake, Rattle & Roll" & moviegoers were lining up to see "On the Waterfront?" The first car with a fuel-injection system debuted & TV dinners were introduced. A Korean evangelist founded a Church in the U.S. & Howard Hughes wrote a personal check for 23,489,478 to buy the 5th largest movie studio & more.

Do You Remember 1955? abr. ed. Nina Mattikow. 1 cass. (Running Time: 30 min.). (Do You Remember Ser.). 1986. 5.99 (978-1-55569-041-0(6), 5638) Great Am Audio.

Bill Haley & the Comets "Rock Around The Clock" was on the jukeboxes & "Rebel without a Cause" was playing the movie houses. The very first McDonalds opened its doors, the minimum wage was raises to $1.00 & the "Adult" westerns arrived on TV. Anaheim, California had a major opening of a new playground for all ages & more.

Do You Remember 1956? abr. ed. Nina Mattikow. 1 cass. (Running Time: 30 min.). (Do You Remember Ser.). 1986. 5.99 (978-1-55569-042-7(4), 5639) Great Am Audio.

Elvis Presley had burst on the music scene & movie lovers were lining up to see "Around the World in 80 Days". Everyone was reading "Confidential" magazine & though we liked Ike, we loved Lucy, & a "Perfect Game" was pitched in the world series & more. Remember?.

Do You Remember 1957? abr. ed. Nina Mattikow. 1 cass. (Running Time: 30 min.). (Do You Remember Ser.). 1986. 5.99 (978-1-55569-043-4(2), 5640) Great Am Audio.

President Dwight D. Eisenhower returned to the White House along with his controversial V.P. Richard M. Nixon. The jukeboxes were rocking to Elvis Presley's "All Shook Up" & "The Bridge Over The River Kwai" was playing the movie screens. It was the year of frisbees, & the space age began & more. Do You Remember?.

Do You Remember 1958? abr. ed. Nina Mattikow. 1 cass. (Running Time: 30 min.). (Do You Remember Ser.). 1986. 5.99 (978-1-55569-044-1(0), 5641) Great Am Audio.

President Eisenhower was in the White House & the hula hoop was the great fad. The U.S. launched Explorer I, & moviegoers were lining up too see "Room At the Top". "Yakatee Yak" by the Coasters was topping the Pop charts & TV was in the midst of a major scandal. Elvis went into the army & the median U.S. income reached 5,087 & more.

Do You Remember 1959? abr. ed. Nina Mattikow. 1 cass. (Running Time: 30 min.). (Do You Remember Ser.). 1986. 5.99 (978-1-55569-045-8(9), 5642) Great Am Audio.

Remember the jukebox set falling in love to the tune of "Put Your Head on my Shoulder", By Paul Anka, & moviegoers were lining up to see "Some Like It Hot". The 49th & 50th States were admitted to the Union. Ike was in the White House & Nixon & the Soviet Premier engaged in their "Kitchen Debate" & more.

Do You Remember 1960? abr. ed. Nina Mattikow. 1 cass. (Running Time: 30 min.). (Do You Remember Ser.). 1986. 5.99 (978-1-55569-046-5(7), 5643) Great Am Audio.

The country had elected its youngest president in history. In a small bar called the Peppermint Lounge, Chubby Checker launched the "Twist" & "Psycho" was packing the movie theatres. Baseball bid farewell to Ted Williams, Wilt Chamberlain was burning up the basketball courts & Nikita Khrushchev was banging his shoe on the table at the U.N. & more. Remember?.

Do You Remember 1961? abr. ed. Nina Mattikow. 1 cass. (Running Time: 30 min.). (Do You Remember Ser.). 1986. 5.99 (978-1-55569-047-2(5), 5644) Great Am Audio.

John F. Kennedy & his wife Jacqueline were in the White House. The chairman of the FCC declared television a "vast wasteland" as Ben Casey arrived on TV. Dion & The Belmonts were topping the charts with "Run Around Sue" & "Breakfast at Tiffany's" was playing the movie theatres & more.

Do You Remember 1962? abr. ed. Nina Mattikow. 1 cass. (Running Time: 30 min.). (Do You Remember Ser.). 1986. 5.99 (978-1-55569-048-9(3), 5645) Great Am Audio.

The jukeboxes were swept by the sound of California as the Beach Boys sang "Surfin" Safari". Moviegoers were lining up to see "Lawrence of Arabia" & 68% of prime time TV was being broadcast in color. The year began with the flight of the Mercury capsule Friendship & the N.Y. Mets played their first season & more. Remember?.

Do You Remember 1963? abr. ed. Nina Mattikow. 1 cass. (Running Time: 30 min.). (Do You Remember Ser.). 1986. 5.99 (978-1-55569-049-6(1), 5646) Great Am Audio.

On Nov. 22nd a shocked nation learned their President had been assassinated in Dallas. There were the first murmurings of Women's Rights. "The Beverly Hillbillies" was the #1 show on TV, 250,000 people gathered on the Lincoln Memorial Mall to hear Martin Luther King Jr. & the minimum wage was $1.15 & more. Do you remember?.

Do You Remember 1964? abr. ed. Nina Mattikow. 1 cass. (Running Time: 30 min.). (Do You Remember Ser.). 1986. 5.99 (978-1-55569-050-2(5), 5647) Great Am Audio.

Lyndon Baines Johnson was in the White House; America was swept by "Beatlemania" & moviegoers were lining up to see "Dr. Strangelove"; Detroit introduced the Mustang; Cassius Clay K.O.'d Sonny Liston & it was a campaign year with a conservative democratic challenger from Arizona & more.

Do You Remember 1965? abr. ed. Nina Mattikow. 1 cass. (Running Time: 30 min.). (Do You Remember Ser.). 1986. 5.99 (978-1-55569-051-9(3), 5648) Great Am Audio.

Remember? President Johnson was returned to office by the largest popular vote in U.S. history. The #1 Pop Tune was "Help"! as "Beatlemania" swept the country & movie'goers were lining up to see "Darling". Soft-Top convertibles were "IT", an oversized Campbell Soup can become fashionable art, & "Get Smart" became a major hit on television & more.

Do You Remember 1966? abr. ed. Nina Mattikow. 1 cass. (Running Time: 30 min.). (Do You Remember Ser.). 1986. 5.99 (978-1-55569-052-6(1), 5649) Great Am Audio.

Simon & Garfunkel had the #1 Pop song with "The Sounds of Silence" & movie'goers were lining up to see "Who's Afraid of Virginia Wolf?" American teenagers were sporting mini-skirts & granny glasses as the spaceship Enterprise sailed on the TV screens. "Folk Rock" was the new sound, & Bob Dylan was the ultimate hipster & more.

Do You Remember 1967? abr. ed. Nina Mattikow. 1 cass. (Running Time: 30 min.). (Do You Remember Ser.). 1986. 5.99 (978-1-55569-053-3(X), 5650) Great Am Audio.

The year began with President Johnson asking for more money for the war in Vietnam. The Rolling Stones "Ruby Tuesday" was the big hit & movie-goers were lining up to see Dustin Hoffman in "The Graduate". Lapel buttons were the new form of expression & a revolutionary new diet book called for drinking 8 glasses of water a day & more.

Do You Remember 1968? abr. ed. Nina Mattikow. 1 cass. (Running Time: 30 min.). (Do You Remember Ser.). 1986. 5.99 (978-1-55569-054-0(8), 5651) Great Am Audio.

Simon & Garfunkel were topping the charts with "Mrs. Robinson", "2001: A Space Odyssey" was packing the movie theatres & men were sporting sideburns & "Nehru Jackets. It was a violent year that witnessed the assassinations of Dr. Martin Luther King Jr. & Robert Kennedy. Richard M. Nixon won the presidential election, "Laugh-In" became the new hit on TV & more. Do you remember?.

Do You Remember 1969? abr. ed. Nina Mattikow. 1 cass. (Running Time: 30 min.). (Do You Remember Ser.). 1986. 5.99 (978-1-55569-055-7(6), 5652) Great Am Audio.

Do you remember it was the Rock concert of the decade at Woodstock, man's first walk on the moon & the inauguration of Richard M. Nixon as the 37th President of the U.S. The 5th Dimension had a monster hit with "Let the Sunshine In", "Easy Rider" was playing the movie theatres & more.

Do You Remember 1970? abr. ed. Nina Mattikow. 1 cass. (Running Time: 30 min.). (Do You Remember Ser.). 1986. 5.99 (978-1-55569-056-4(4), 5653) Great Am Audio.

*Music fans wept at the break-up of the Beatles, & there was a bloody confrontation on a Midwestern college campus. Teenagers rocked to the Jackson Five's "I Want You Back" & movie-goers were lining up to see "M*A*S*H." President Nixon found himself in the center of controversy over Cambodia & more.*

Do You Renounce? Megan McKenna. 4 cass. (Running Time: 5 hrs.). 1992. 29.95 set. (AA2592) Credence Commun.

Real renouncing has the quality of decision, a yes or no: it creates clarity & purpose of life.

Do You Speak Astrology? Doe Koppana. 1 cass. 8.95 (551) Am Fed Astrologers.

Teaching basics using visual aids.

Do You Want God's Best? Jawanza Kunjufu. 1 cass. (Running Time: 60 mins.). 1999. 5.95 (AT24) African Am Imag.

Do You Want to Be Happy? Psalm 1. Ed Young. 1989. 4.95 (978-0-7417-1746-7(8), 746) Win Walk.

Do You Want to Know a Secret? unabr. ed. Mary Jane Clark. Read by Beth Fowler. 6 vols. (Running Time: 9 hrs.). (KEY News Ser.: Bk. 1). 2000. bk. 54.95 (978-0-7927-2285-4(X), CSL 174, Chivers Sound Lib) AudioGO.
Eliza Blake is a newswoman on the rise. She's well liked and respected by her colleagues at Key News. When Bill Kendall, a senior anchorman, dies unexpectedly, Eliza is offered her biggest opportunity ever. Everything seems right, and yet wrong. As Eliza starts to suspect that Kendall's death has ramifications beyond the set of Key News, she begins to unravel a plot of murder, greed and jealously that involves players as high up as the White House.

Do You Wonder? unabr. ed. Read by Peter Himmelman. Perf. by Peter Himmelman. 1 cass. (Running Time: 30 min.). Dramatization. (J). 1986. 8.95 (978-1-58452-002-3(7), 4300); 8.95 Spanish version. (978-1-58452-011-5(6), 5300) Spinoza Co.

Do Your Relationships Work? Jan Snodgrass. 1 cass. 8.95 (578) Am Fed Astrologers.
Elements & modes key to understanding.

Dobro Workshop. Contrib. by Phil Leadbetter. (Running Time: 52 mins.). 2005. 24.95 (978-5-558-08943-1(1)) Mel Bay.

Doc & Dawg. Doc Watson & David Grisman. 2002. bk. 29.95 (978-0-7866-6619-5(6), 97167BCD) Mel Bay.

Doc Holliday. abr. ed. Matt Braun. Read by Jim Gough. 2002. 25.00 (978-1-59183-000-9(1)) Pub: Otis Audio. Dist(s): Lndmrk Audiobks

Doc Holliday & the Earp Brothers. Dave Southworth. 2 cass. (Running Time: 60 min.). (Library of Concise Audio Histories). 13.95 Set. (978-1-890778-10-1(9)) Wld Horse Pub.

Doc in the Box. abr. ed. Elaine Viets. Read by Elaine Viets. 4 cass. (Running Time: 360 min.). (Francesca Vierling Mystery Ser.: No. 4). 2000. 25.00 (978-1-58807-051-7(4)) Am Pubng Inc.
A killer has found a cure for bad doctors - a permanent cure. Medical men are being gunned down in their offices at high noon. there's a healthy list of suspects. It seems almost everyone wants these docs dead.

Doc-Talk Medi-Facts Set: Medical Information. unabr. ed. Joel Zaretsky. Read by Joel Zaretsky. 5 cass. (Running Time: 1 hr.). 1997. 10.00 (978-1-891325-03-8(5)) Our Pal.
Medical information on a variety of human ailments & onditions. .

Doc Watson & Clarence Ashley: The Original Folkways Recordings 1960-1962. Dix Bruce. 2002. per. 43.95 (978-0-7866-6616-4(1), 97056BCD) Mel Bay.

Doc Watson Family. Perf. by Doc Watson. Anno. by Jeff Place. Contrib. by Ralph Rinzler & Mike Seeger. 1 cass. 1990. (0-9307-400120-9307-40012-2-6); audio compact disk (0-9307-40012-2-6) Smithsonian Folkways.
Features 26 Watson Family standards, 11 previously unreleased.

Docile. l.t. ed. Didier Decoin. (French Ser.). 1995. bk. 30.99 (978-2-84011-106-1(3)) Pub: UlverLrgPrint GBR. Dist(s): Ulverscroft US

Docteur Tendresse. Patch Adams. 1 cass. (Running Time: 90 mins.). (French Audiobooks Ser.). (FRE., 2000. pap. bk. 14.95 (978-2-89517-080-8(0)) Pub: Coffragants CAN. Dist(s): Penton Overseas

Docteur Tendresse. Patch Adams. 1 CD. (Running Time: 90 mins.). (French Audiobooks Ser.). 2000. audio compact disk 16.95 (978-2-89517-073-0(8)) Pub: Coffragants CAN. Dist(s): Penton Overseas

Doctor at Large. Richard Gordon. Read by Robin Nedwell. (A-120) Audio Bk.

Doctor Called Caroline. unabr. ed. Elizabeth Harrison. Read by Margaret Holt. 4 cass. (Running Time: 6 hrs.). 2001. 44.95 (26766) Pub: Soundings Ltd GBR. Dist(s): Ulverscroft US
Caroline of the Central London Hospital had planned to become a family doctor at her home in Stonebridge - so what was she doing falling in love with Daniel, registrar to the professor, with his career firmly based in London?.

***Doctor Chopra Says.** abr. ed. Sanjiv Chopra et al. Frwd. by Mehmet C. Oz. (ENG.). 2010. audio compact disk 29.99 (978-1-4272-1033-3(0)) Pub: Macmill Audio. Dist(s): Macmillan

Doctor Copernicus: A Novel. unabr. ed. John Banville. Read by Grover Gardner. 7 cass. (Running Time: 1 hr. 30 min. per cass.). 1987. 56.00 Set. (2129) Books on Tape.
Historical novel telling the story of Copernicus & the affects of his revelations concerning the place of the earth in the universe.

Doctor Copernicus: A Novel. unabr. collector's ed. John Banville. Read by Grover Gardner. 7 cass. (Running Time: 10 hrs. 30 mins.). 1987. 56.00 (978-0-7366-1211-1(4), 2129) Books on Tape.
Genius shaped the life of this lonely, compulsive man - fictional biography.

Doctor de Soto. (J). 2004. bk. 24.95 (978-0-89719-770-0(4)) Weston Woods.

Doctor de Soto. William Steig. (Running Time: 13 mins.). (SPA., (J). (gr. k-3). 1998. 9.95 (978-0-87499-460-5(8)) Live Oak Media.

Doctor de Soto. William Steig. Read by David Cromett. Tr. by Maria Puncel. 14 vols. (Running Time: 13 mins.). (SPA., 1998. pap. bk. & tchr. ed. 37.95 Reading Chest. (978-0-87499-459-9(4)) Live Oak Media.
Dr. De Soto, "un dentista raton," & his wife operate a clinic for all animals except those dangerous to mice. So what do they do when a wailing fox begs for their help?.

Doctor de Soto. William Steig. Illus. by William Steig. 14 vols. (Running Time: 13 mins.). 1998. pap. bk. 39.95 (978-1-59519-161-8(5)); audio compact disk 12.95 (978-1-59519-159-5(3)) Live Oak Media.

Doctor de Soto. William Steig. Illus. by William Steig. 11 vols. (Running Time: 13 mins.). (SPA.). (J). 1998. pap. bk. 18.95 (978-1-59519-160-1(7)) Pub: Live Oak Media. Dist(s): AudioGO

Doctor de Soto. William Steig. 1 cass. (Blue-Ribbon Listen-and-Read Ser.). (J). (ps-2). 1984. 4.95 (978-0-590-37661-7(6)); Scholastic Inc.
The story of Doctor DeSoto, mouse dentist, who must devise a way to treat his patient, a hungry fox, without being devoured.

Doctor de Soto. William Steig. 1 cass., 5 bks. (Running Time: 30 min.). (J). pap. bk. 32.75; bk. 24.95; pap. bk. 15.95 Weston Woods.
Since he is a mouse, dentist De Soto refuses to treat "dangerous" animals. One day, however, a fox shows up writhing in abscessed pain. How can the kind-hearted De Soto & his wife turn him away? But how can they make sure the fox does not exercise his new tooth on them?.

Doctor de Soto. William Steig. 1 cass. (Running Time: 30 min.). (J). (gr. k-4). bk. 24.95 Weston Woods.

Doctor de Soto. William Steig. 1 cass. (Running Time: 30 min.). (J). (gr. k-4). 2000. pap. bk. 12.95 Weston Woods.
A hungry fox with a toothache begs a mouse dentist to relieve his pain in this modern day fable.

Doctor de Soto. William Steig. 1 cass. (J). (gr. k-5). 2004. pap. bk. 14.95 (978-0-89719-771-7(2), PRA284); 8.95 (978-0-89719-921-6(9), RAC284) Weston Woods.
He copes with the toothaches of animals large & small. Since he's a mouse, he refuses to treat "dangerous animals, but one day a fox shows up & begs for relief from the tooth that's killing him.

Doctor de Soto. unabr. ed. William Steig. Read by David Cromett. Tr. by Maria Puncel from ENG. 11 vols. (Running Time: 13 mins.). (SPA., (J). (gr. k-3). 1998. pap. bk. 16.95 (978-0-87499-458-2(6)) Pub: Live Oak Media. Dist(s): AudioGO
Dr. De Soto, "un dentista raton," & his wife operate a clinic for all animals except those dangerous to mice. So what do they do when a wailing fox begs for their help?.

Doctor de Soto Goes to Africa Book & Tape. unabr. abr. ed. William Steig & Steig. Read by Bebe Neuwirth. Illus. by William Steig. Music by Jeremy Steig. 1 cass. (Running Time: 20 min.). (Tell Me a Story Bks.). (J). (ps up). 1995. 8.95 (978-0-694-70003-5(7)) HarperCollins Pubs.

Doctor Desoto. 2004. 8.95 (978-1-56008-385-6(9)); cass. & flmstrp 30.00 (978-0-89719-521-8(3)); audio compact disk 12.95 (978-0-7882-0249-0(9)) Weston Woods.

Doctor Desoto. (J). 2004. pap. bk. 18.95 (978-0-7882-0950-5(7)); pap. bk. 32.75 (978-1-55592-219-1(8)); pap. bk. 32.75 (978-1-55592-220-7(1)); pap. bk. 14.95 (978-1-55592-937-4(0)) Weston Woods.

***Doctor! Doctor!** Hugh Alport. 2010. 54.95 (978-1-4079-0853-3(7)); audio compact disk 64.95 (978-1-4079-0854-0(5)) Pub: Soundings Ltd GBR. Dist(s): Ulverscroft US

Doctor Faustus see Evil, Exploration Of

Doctor Gypsee Gunn's de-Motivational Seminar. (Running Time: 1 hr.). (Stage Ser.). 2004. audio compact disk 14.99 (978-1-894003-08-7(X)) Pub: Scenario Prods CAN. Dist(s): PerseuPGW

Doctor, His Wife, & the Clock. abr. ed. Anna Katharine Green. 2 cass. (Running Time: 180 min.). 1991. 21.95 (978-1-55656-018-7(4)) Dercum Audio.

Doctor Illuminatus: The Alchemist's Son. unabr. ed. Martin Booth. Read by Steven Crossley. 4 cass. (Running Time: 5 hrs. 15 mins.). (J). 2005. 37.75 (978-1-4193-2935-7(9), 97968) Recorded Bks.
Popular English author Martin Booth writes books for young people and adults, and was shortlisted for the Booker Prize. Pip and Tim are siblings who have moved to an old country manor in England with their parents. When they hear a strange knocking sound coming from inside the walls, they are startled to discover a boy emerge named Sebastian. The son of an alchemist, Sebastian has been asleep behind those walls for the last 600 years! And he has a vital message for Pip and Tim - they are in grave danger. Soon, the children find themselves on a quest to defeat a villain who uses the powers of alchemy for evil.

Doctor in Rags. Louise Vernon. Narrated by Fern Ebersole. (ENG.). (J). 2008. audio compact disk 15.95 (978-0-9801244-4-6(1)) IG Publish.

Doctor Is In! unabr. ed. Megan McDonald. 2 cass. (Running Time: 1 hr. 45 mins.). (J). 2005. 19.75 (978-1-4193-2941-8(3)) Recorded Bks.

Doctor, Lawyer. unabr. ed. Collin Wilcox. Read by Larry McKeever. 8 cass. (Running Time: 8 hrs.). (Frank Hastings Ser.). 1997. 48.00 (978-0-7366-3530-1(0), 4168) Books on Tape.
Lt. Frank Hastings finds a killer's extortion notes on the victims, each note successively asking for more money.

Doctor Licks: Guitar Personality. 1997. bk. 16.95 (978-0-7692-0499-4(6), 00698946, Warner Bro) Alfred Pub.

Doctor Mary Courage. Alex Stuart. Read by Margaret Holt. 4 cass. (Running Time: 6 hrs.). 1999. 44.95 (61934) Pub: Soundings Ltd GBR. Dist(s): Ulverscroft US

Doctor Nagler's Brainwashing Weight Reduction Seminar. 2002. audio compact disk 299.95 (978-0-9715023-4-5(X)) Diet Result.

Doctor Nagler's Brainwashing Weight Reduction Seminar. deluxe ed. 2002. 299.95 (978-0-9715023-3-8(1)) Diet Result.

Doctor Nagler's Crash Diet Tapes - Motivating Implosion, Deluxe Box Set. 2001. 29.95 (978-0-9715023-2-1(3)) Diet Result.

Doctor Nagler's Hypnosis for Weight Loss. 2001. audio compact disk 29.95 (978-0-9715023-9-0(0)) Diet Result.

Doctor Nagler's Hypnosis for Weight Loss. 2002. audio compact disk 29.95 (978-0-9715023-6-9(6)) Diet Result.

Doctor Nagler's Hypnosis for Weight Loss. deluxe ed. 2001. 29.95 (978-0-9715023-7-6(4)) Diet Result.

Doctor Nagler's Hypnosis to Stop Smoking. 2002. audio compact disk 29.95 (978-0-9715023-5-2(8)) Diet Result.

Doctor Nagler's Hypnosis to Stop Smoking. deluxe ed. 2002. 29.95 (978-0-9715023-8-3(2)) Diet Result.

Doctor on Horseback. Alex Stuart. Read by Margaret Holt. 4 cass. (Running Time: 6 hrs.). 1999. 44.95 (65751) Pub: Soundings Ltd GBR. Dist(s): Ulverscroft US

Doctor on Horseback. Alex Stuart. 4 cass. (Sound Ser.). 2004. 44.95 (978-1-85496-575-2(1)) Pub: UlverLrgPrint GBR. Dist(s): Ulverscroft US

Doctor Prescribed Death. Perf. by Bela Lugosi. 1 cass. (Running Time: 60 min.). 1943. 7.95 (MM-5760) Natl Recrd Co.
In the story "The Doctor Prescribed Death", a psychologist sets out to prove his unique theory: that an individual intending to commit suicide can be persuaded to commit murder instead . In the story "The Black Cat", a man is driven to madness & murder by the evils of drink & is foiled by a black cat.

***Doctor Proctor's Fart Powder.** Jø Nesbo. Read by William Dufris. (ENG.). (J). 2010. audio compact disk 38.00 (978-1-936223-17-6(1)) Full Cast Audio.

Doctor Rose. Elvi Rhodes. Read by Anne Dover. 7 cass. (Running Time: 9 hrs.). 1999. 61.95 (6657X) Pub: Soundings Ltd GBR. Dist(s): Ulverscroft US

Doctor Thorne. Anthony Trollope. Read by Simon Vance. (Running Time: 73800 sec.). 2007. 105.95 (978-1-4332-0085-4(6)); audio compact disk 120.00 (978-1-4332-0086-1(4)); audio compact disk 44.95 (978-1-4332-0087-8(2)) Blckstn Audio.

Doctor Thorne. Anthony Trollope. 15 cass. (Running Time: 21 hrs.). 1988. 87.95 C to C Cassettes.

Doctor Thorne, Pt. 1. unabr. collector's ed. Anthony Trollope. Read by David Case. 8 cass. (Running Time: 12 hrs.). (Barsetshire Chronicles: Vol. 3). 1993. 64.00 (978-0-7366-2467-1(8), 3231-A) Books on Tape.
Couple intent on marriage confronts sniffish English middle class.

Doctor Thorne, Pt. 2. collector's ed. Anthony Trollope. Read by David Case. 8 cass. (Running Time: 12 hrs.). 1993. 64.00 (978-0-7366-2468-8(6), 3231-B) Books on Tape.

Doctor Thorne, Set. unabr. ed. Anthony Trollope. Read by Flo Gibson. 15 cass. (Running Time: 21 hrs. 30 min.). 1992. 43.95 (978-1-55685-241-1(X)) Audio Bk Con.
This charming novel, one of Trollope's most popular, is full of love & laughter. Will Frank Gresham, heir to an impoverished estate, marry penniless Mary Thorne, despite the protests of all his family? Should Dr. Thorne disclose a secret that may make a difference?.

Doctor Tiene Catarro, EDL Level 12. (Fonolibros Ser.: Vol. 30). (SPA.). 2003. 11.50 (978-0-7652-1019-7(3)) Modern Curr.

Doctor Who: The Dalek Conquests. Contrib. by Nicholas Briggs. 3 CDs. (Running Time: 2 hrs. 35 mins.). 2006. audio compact disk 39.95 (978-0-7927-4340-8(7), BBCD 167) AudioGO.

Doctor Who: The Ice Warriors. Contrib. by Patrick Troughton. 2 CDs. (Running Time: 2 hrs. 30 mins.). 2006. audio compact disk 29.95 (978-0-7927-4332-3(6), BBCD 159) AudioGO.

Doctor Who: The Invasion. Contrib. by Patrick Troughton & Frazer Hines. 3 CDs. (Running Time: 3 hrs. 50 mins.). 2006. audio compact disk 39.95 (978-0-7927-3985-2(X), BBCD 136) AudioGO.

***Doctor Who: The Last Voyage: An Exclusive Audio Adventure Read by David Tennant.** Dan Abnett. Narrated by David Tennant. (Running Time: 2 hrs. 30 mins. 0 sec.). (Doctor Who Ser.). (ENG.). 2010. audio compact disk 24.95 (978-1-4084-0940-4(2)) Pub: AudioGO. Dist(s): Perseus Dist

Doctor Who & the Brain of Morbius: A Doctor Who Radio Adventure. Terrance Dicks. (Running Time: 3 hrs. 55 mins. 0 sec.). (Doctor Who Ser.). (ENG.). 2009. audio compact disk 34.95 (978-1-60283-764-5(3)) Pub: AudioGO. Dist(s): Perseus Dist

Doctor Who & the Creature from the Pit: A Doctor Who Radio Adventure. David Fisher. (Running Time: 4 hrs. 0 mins. 0 sec.). (Doctor Who Ser.). (ENG.). 2009. audio compact disk 34.95 (978-1-60283-765-2(1)) Pub: AudioGO. Dist(s): Perseus Dist

***Doctor Who & the Dalek Invasion of Earth.** Terrance Dicks. Narrated by William Russell & Nicholas Briggs. (Running Time: 4 hrs. 0 mins. 0 sec.). (Doctor Who Ser.). (ENG.). 2010. audio compact disk 34.95 (978-1-4084-0992-3(5)) Pub: AudioGO. Dist(s): Perseus Dist

Doctor who & the Daleks. David Whitaker. Contrib. by William Russell. 4 CDs. (Running Time: 5 hrs. 10 mins.). 2005. audio compact disk 49.95 (978-0-7927-3595-3(1), BBCD 110) AudioGO.

Doctor Who & the Dinosaur Invasion: A Doctor Who Radio Adventure. Malcolm Hulke. (Running Time: 4 hrs. 5 mins. 0 sec.). (Doctor Who Ser.). (ENG.). 2009. audio compact disk 34.95 (978-1-60283-766-9(X)) Pub: AudioGO. Dist(s): Perseus Dist

***Doctor Who & the Ice Warriors: A Classic Doctor Who Novel.** Brian Hayles. Narrated by Frazer Hines. (Running Time: 4 hrs. 0 mins. 0 sec.). (Doctor Who Ser.). (ENG.). 2010. audio compact disk 34.95 (978-1-4084-2670-8(6)) Pub: AudioGO. Dist(s): Perseus Dist

Doctor who & the Pescatons. Victor Pemberton. Contrib. by Tom Baker et al. 2 CDs. (Running Time: 1 hr. 30 mins.). 2005. audio compact disk 29.95 (978-0-7927-3593-9(5), BBCD 108) AudioGO.

***Doctor Who & the Terror of the Autons: A Classic Doctor Who Novel.** Terrance Dicks. (Running Time: 4 hrs. 0 mins. 0 sec.). (Doctor Who Ser.). (ENG.). 2010. audio compact disk 34.95 (978-1-4084-6675-9(9)) Pub: AudioGO. Dist(s): Perseus Dist

***Doctor Who: Dead Air: An Exclusive Audio Adventure Read by David Tennant.** James Goss. Narrated by David Tennant. (Running Time: 1 hr. 10 mins. 0 sec.). (Doctor Who Ser.). (ENG.). 2010. audio compact disk 24.95 (978-1-4084-2680-7(3)) Pub: AudioGO. Dist(s): Perseus Dist

***Doctor Who: Demon Quest: Demon of Paris: A Multi-Voice Audio Original Starring Tom Baker #2.** Paul Magrs. Narrated by Tom Baker & Full Cast. (Running Time: 1 hr. 0 mins. 0 sec.). (Doctor Who Ser.). (ENG.). 2010. audio compact disk 24.95 (978-1-4084-6668-1(6)) Pub: AudioGO. Dist(s): Perseus Dist

***Doctor Who: Demon Quest: Sepulchre: A Multi-Voice Audio Original Starring Tom Baker #5.** Paul Magrs. Narrated by Tom Baker. (Running Time: 1 hr. 0 mins. 0 sec.). (Doctor Who Ser.). (ENG.). 2011. audio compact disk 24.95 (978-1-4084-6671-1(6)) Pub: AudioGO. Dist(s): Perseus Dist

***Doctor Who: Demon Quest: Shards of Ice: A Multi-Voice Audio Original Starring Tom Baker #3.** Paul Magrs. Narrated by Tom Baker & Full Cast. (Running Time: 1 hr. 0 sec.). (Doctor Who Ser.). (ENG.). 2011. audio compact disk 24.95 (978-1-4084-6669-8(4)) Pub: AudioGO. Dist(s): Perseus Dist

***Doctor Who: Demon Quest: Starfall: A Multi-Voice Audio Original Starring Tom Baker #4.** Paul Magrs. Narrated by Tom Baker. (Running Time: 1 hr. 0 mins. 0 sec.). (Doctor Who Ser.). (ENG.). 2011. audio compact disk 24.95 (978-1-4084-6670-4(8)) Pub: AudioGO. Dist(s): Perseus Dist

Doctor Who: Hornets' Nest: the Stuff of Nightmares: A Multi-Voice Audio Original Starring Tom Baker #1. Paul Magrs. Narrated by Tom Baker. (Running Time: 1 hr. 0 mins. 0 sec.). (Doctor Who Ser.). (ENG.). 2010. audio compact disk 24.95 (978-1-60283-866-6(6)) Pub: AudioGO. Dist(s): Perseus Dist

Doctor Who: Pest Control: An Exclusive Audio Adventure. Peter Anghelides. (Running Time: 2 hrs. 0 mins. 0 sec.). (Doctor Who Ser.). (ENG.). 2009. audio compact disk 24.95 (978-1-60283-761-4(9)) Pub: AudioGO. Dist(s): Perseus Dist

***Doctor Who: the Awakening: An Unabridged Classic Doctor Who Novel.** Eric Pringle. (Running Time: 4 hrs. 0 mins. 0 sec.). (Doctor Who Ser.). (ENG.). 2010. audio compact disk 34.95 (978-1-4084-2672-2(2)) Pub: AudioGO. Dist(s): Perseus Dist

Doctor Who: the Day of the Troll: An Exclusive Audio Adventure. unabr. ed. Simon Messingham. Narrated by David Tennant. (Running Time: 1 hr. 30 mins. 0 sec.). (Doctor Who Ser.). (ENG.). 2010. audio compact disk 24.95 (978-1-60283-820-8(8)) Pub: AudioGO. Dist(s): Perseus Dist

***Doctor Who: the Essential Companion: An Audio Guide.** Narrated by Matt Smith & Karen Gillan. (Running Time: 2 hrs. 0 mins. 0 sec.). (Doctor Who Ser.). (ENG.). 2011. audio compact disk 24.95 (978-1-4084-6772-5(0)) Pub: AudioGO. Dist(s): Perseus Dist

Doctor Who: the Nemonite Invasion: An Exclusive Audio Adventure. David Roden. (Running Time: 2 hrs. 0 mins. 0 sec.). (Doctor Who Ser.). (ENG.). 2009. audio compact disk 24.95 (978-1-60283-762-1(7)) Pub: AudioGO. Dist(s): Perseus Dist

Doctor Who: the Rising Night: An Exclusive Audio Adventure. Scott Handcock. (Running Time: 2 hrs. 0 mins. 0 sec.). (Doctor Who Ser.). (ENG.). 2009. audio compact disk 24.95 (978-1-60283-763-8(5)) Pub: AudioGO. Dist(s): Perseus Dist

Doctor Yourself: Natural Healing That Works. unabr. ed. Andrew Saul. Read by Patrick Cullen. (Running Time: 36000 sec.). 2006. audio compact disk 29.95 (978-0-7861-7406-5(4)) Blckstn Audio.

Doctor Yourself: Natural Healing That Works. unabr. ed. Andrew W. Saul. (Running Time: 36000 sec.). 2006. audio compact disk 72.00 (978-0-7861-6743-2(2)) Blckstn Audio.

Doctor Yourself: Natural Healing That Works. unabr. ed. Andrew W. Saul. Read by Patrick Cullen. (Running Time: 36000 sec.). 2006. 59.95 (978-0-7861-4664-2(8)) Blckstn Audio.

Doctor Zhivago. unabr. ed. Boris Pasternak. Read by Philip Madoc. 18 CDs. 2000. audio compact disk 127.95 (978-0-7540-5363-7(6), CCD 054) Pub: Chivers Audio Bks GBR. Dist(s): AudioGO
Evokes the experience of Russia during the first half of the 20th century. It is a vast panorama of a country in the throes of a radical revolution. Seen through the eyes of Yri Zhivago, physician & poet, he must come to terms with the new world & his new embittered self.

Doctored Evidence. Donna Leon. Read by David Colacci. 7 vols. (Commissario Guido Brunetti Mystery Ser.: Bk. 13). 2004. 59.95 (978-0-7927-3210-5(3), CSL 652, Chivers Sound Lib); audio compact disk

79.95 (978-0-7927-3211-2(1), SLD 652, Chivers Sound Lib); audio compact disk 29.95 (978-0-7927-3212-9(X), CMP 652, Chivers Sound Lib) AudioGO.

Doctored Evidence. unabr. ed. Donna Leon. Read by David Colacci. 6 cass. (Running Time: 7 hrs. 46 mins.). (Commissario Guido Brunetti Mystery Ser.: Bk. 13). 2004. 29.95 (978-1-57270-416-9(0)) Pub: Audio Partners. Dist(s): PerseuPGW
Donna Leon's riveting new novel, Doctored Evidence, follows Commissario Guido Brunetti down the winding streets of contemporary Venice as he throws open the doors of a case his superiors would rather leave closed. When a miserly spinster is found brutally murdered in her Venice apartment, police immediately suspect her Romanian housekeeper. They are certain their job is done after the immigrant dies while fleeing arrest, but weeks later; a neighbor comes forward to defend the innocence of the accused. The only investigator who believes the alibi is Brunetti, who will have to go behind the backs of his superiors to vindicate the Romanian and find her employer's actual killer. As always, the indispensable hacking skills of the ever-loyal Signorina Elettra are the perfect complement to Brunetti's meticulous detective work. She discovers mysterious deposits in the old woman's bank account, but who made them? As Brunetti investigates, his wife, at home, reads him teachings on the Seven Deadly Sins. In a modern world of intrigue and nebulous morality, how do they relate to the murder at hand? Doctored Evidence is charged with suspense and evokes a contemporary Venice with Donna Leon's masterful flair.

***Doctored Evidence: Unabridged Value-Priced Edition.** Donna Leon. Narrated by David Colacci. (Running Time: 7 hrs. 46 mins. 0 sec.). (Commissario Guido Brunetti Mystery Ser.). (ENG.). 2010. audio compact disk 14.95 (978-1-60283-994-6(8)) Pub: AudioGO. Dist(s): Perseus Dist

Doctors: The History of Scientific Medicine Revealed Through Biography. Instructed by Sherwin B. Nuland. 6 cass. (Running Time: 6 hrs.). bk. 29.95 (978-1-59803-027-3(2), 8128) Teaching Co.

Doctors: The History of Scientific Medicine Revealed Through Biography. Instructed by Sherwin B. Nuland. 6 CDs. (Running Time: 6 hrs.). 2005. bk. 39.95 (978-1-59803-029-7(9), 8128) Teaching Co.

Doctors & Scientists Oppose Malathion Spraying to Control the Medfly in Urban Areas. Hosted by Nancy Pearlman. 1 cass. (Running Time: 30 min.). 10.00 (1502) Educ Comm CA.

Doctor's Daughter. Hilma Wolitzer. 7 cass. (Running Time: 33300 sec.). 2006. 59.95 (978-0-7927-3912-8(4), CSL 908); audio compact disk 79.95 (978-0-7927-3913-5(2), SLD 908) AudioGO.

Doctor's Daughter: A Novel. Hilma Wolitzer. Read by Anna Fields. 2006. audio compact disk 29.95 (978-0-7927-3968-5(X), CMP 908) AudioGO.

Doctor's Dilemma. unabr. ed. George Bernard Shaw. Perf. by Jane Carr et al. 2 CDs. (Running Time: 1 hr. 46 mins.). Dramatization. 2001. audio compact disk 25.95 (978-1-58081-183-5(3), CDTPT123) Pub: L A Theatre. Dist(s): NetLibrary CO

Doctor's Dilemma, unabr. ed. George Bernard Shaw. Perf. by Martin Jarvis et al. 2 cass. (Running Time: 1 hr. 46 mins.). Dramatization. 2001. 23.95 (978-1-58081-129-3(9), TPT123) L A Theatre.
Satire of the medical profession. A well-respected physician is forced to choose whether to save a bumbling friend or a ne'er-do-well husband.

Doctor's Romance, Set. unabr. ed. Sonia Deane. Read by Tanya Myers. 4 cass. (Running Time: 5 hrs. 15 mins.). 1999. 57.95 (978-1-85903-272-5(9)) Pub: Magna Story GBR. Dist(s): Ulverscroft US
"This cloying romantic nonsense" is Dr. Matthew Thornton's cynical view of love. His new partner, Dr. Lorna Marsden, sympathizes with his feelings. Dealing with so many problems caused by marriage in their work together, it's no wonder they both steer clear of emotional involvement. But given their characters & circumstances, is it any surprise when they find themselves entering into the very situation they deplore?.

Doctors' Story. unabr. ed. Thomas Gallagher. Read by John MacDonald. 8 cass. (Running Time: 12 hrs.). 1987. 64.00 (978-0-7366-1183-1(5), 2103) Books on Tape.
A vivid & comprehensive popular history & covers not only medical education & medical practice, but social, cultural, political & economic life in New York City.

Doctrinal Evidences That Mormons Are Christians. unabr. ed. Duane S. Crowther. Read by Duane S. Crowther. 1 cass. (Running Time: 90 min.). 1984. 13.98 (978-0-88290-399-6(3), 1813) Horizon Utah.
Features a rebuttal to anti-Mormon critics. Seventy-two doctrinal themes concerning Latter-day belief in Jesus Christ are listed. Included is a summary of the role of Jesus Christ in Mormon belief.

***Doctrine: What Christians Should Believe.** unabr. ed. Mark Driscoll & Gerry Breshears. Narrated by Sean Runnette. (ENG.). 2010. 16.98 (978-1-59644-788-2(5), Hovel Audio); audio compact disk 28.98 (978-1-59644-787-5(7), Hovel Audio) christianaud.

Doctrine & Covenants. Narrated by Rex Cambell. 12 CDs. 2004. bk. 24.95 (978-1-59156-347-1(X)) Covenant Comms.

Doctrine & Covenants: Pearl of Great Price. unabr. ed. Read by Lael Woodbury. 16 cass. (Running Time: 16 hrs.). (Scriptures on Cassette Ser.). 1990. 20.95 Set. (978-1-887938-02-0(8)) Snd Concepts.
LDS standard work on cassette.

Doctrine & Covenants & Pearl of Great Price, Set. Narrated by Rex Campbell. 10 cass. 2004. 18.95 (978-1-55503-207-4(9), 050025); audio compact disk 39.95 (978-1-57734-000-3(0), 0200492) Covenant Comms.

Doctrine & Covenants & Pearl of Great Price Set: Dramatized History of the Church. 34 CDs. audio compact disk 99.95 (978-1-57734-020-1(5), 0200514) Covenant Comms.

Doctrine & Spiritual Experience; Conflict or Harmony. Eido Roshi. 1 cass. 1982. 10.00 Vajradhatu.
A panel discussion at the 1982 Conference on Christian & Buddhist Meditation.

Doctrine of New Creation. unabr. ed. Bede Griffiths. 1 cass. (Running Time: 90 min.). 1982. 11.00 (03302) Big Sur Tapes.

Doctrine of Wisdom: Sacred Choral Music of William Mathias. Gloriae Dei Cantores. 1 CD. 1998. audio compact disk 16.95 (978-1-55725-210-4(6), GDCD026) Paraclete MA.

Doctrines of Demons. Jack Deere. 1 cass. (Running Time: 90 mins.). (Demonic Inroads Ser.: Vol. 3). 2000. 5.00 (JD02-003) Morning NC.
First laying a foundation of insight into Satan's overall strategy, Jack then builds upon it with practical knowledge of the Christian's authority over demonic forces.

Doctrines of Hermes Trimegistus. Instructed by Manly P. Hall. 5 cass. 8.50 ea. o.p. Pt. 1: Orientation of the Hermetic Philosophy. (800112-A) Philos Res.

Doctrines of Hermes Trimegistus. Instructed by Manly P. Hall. 5 cass. (Running Time: 150 min.). 1999. 40.00 Set. incl. albun. (978-0-89314-045-8(7), S800112) Philos Res.

Doctrines of Neoplatonism. Instructed by Manly P. Hall. 5 cass. 8.50 ea. o.p. PT 1: Proclus on the Theology of Plato. (800114-A) Philos Res.

Doctrines of Neoplatonism. Instructed by Manly P. Hall. 5 cass. (Running Time: 150 min.). 1999. 40.00 Set. incl. album. (978-0-89314-046-5(5), S800114) Philos Res.

Document Indexing of Image-Based Optical Systems: Designing & Developing a Multimedia Database Engine. 1 cass. 1990. 8.50 Recorded Res.

Documents from & on Economic Thought. Ed. by Warren J. Samuels. 2006. 155.95 (978-0-7623-1355-6(2)) Pub: E G Pubng GBR. Dist(s): TurpinDistUSA

Documents in the Case. unabr. ed. Dorothy L. Sayers. Read by Nigel Anthony. 8 cass. (Running Time: 12 hrs.). 2000. 59.95 (978-0-7451-6746-6(2), CAB 1362) Pub: Chivers Audio Bks GBR. Dist(s): AudioGO
Harrison was an expert on deadly fungi. But how was it that he had eaten such a large quantity of it? Was it an accident, suicide or murder? The documents in the case were a collection of love notes and letters, yet they held a clue to the brilliant murderer who baffled the best minds in London.

Documents in the Case. unabr. ed. Dorothy L. Sayers & Robert Eustace. Read by Nadia May. 5 cass. (Running Time: 7 hrs. 30 min.). 1998. 39.95 (1906) Blckstn Audio.
The grotesquely grinning corpse in the Devonshire shack was of a man who had died horribly - with a dish of muscarine mushrooms at his side. Why would an expert on fungi feast on a large quantity of this particularly poisonous species? A clue to the brilliant murderer, was hidden in a series of letters & documents that no one seemed to care about, except the dead man's son.

Documents of Vatican II-Selections. Read by Al Covaia et al. Ed. by John J. Delaney. 14 cass. 1987. 63.75 (104) Ignatius Pr.
Covers the Dogmatic Constitution on the Church. Dogmatic Constitution of divine revelation, Constitution on the Sacred Liturgy, Pastoral Constitution on the Church in the modern World, and the Decree on the Apostolate of the Laity.

***Documents on British Policy Overseas: Volume 1: the Year of Europe: America, Europe & the Energy Crisis, 1972-74.** Hamilton. 2006. bk. (978-0-415-39148-1(2)) Routledge.

Doddlett Adventures. collector's ed. Short Stories. Andrew Heller. 1. (Running Time: 40 mins). Dramatization. (J). 1996. 7.99 (978-0-9722038-0-7(X)) Mr Do It All Inc.

Dodge City. unabr. ed. Hank Mitchum. Read by Charlie O'Dowd. 4 vols. No. 1. 2003. (978-1-58807-585-7(0)) Am Pubng Inc.

Dodge City. unabr. ed. Hank Mitchum. Read by Charlie O'Dowd. 4 cass. (Running Time: 6 hrs.). (Stagecoach Ser.: No. 1). 2003. 25.00 (978-1-58807-184-2(7)) Am Pubng Inc.
The massive Concord stage thundered across the empty lawless miles of the Great Plains bound for the wickedest town in the West Dodge City. It was a wide-open cattle town always itching for a fight, and a big one was about to start. For Burl Channing was on this stage, a Federal marshal hell-bent on a mission of personal vengeance to bring a vicious murderer to justice. The man he seeks is Frank Killian, a cunning gambler with a killer's finely honed edge. Frightened of one man and betrayed by the other, Emily Barker, a beautiful young widow, is suddenly caught up in their struggle a battle that will soon explode in front of the legendary Long Branch Saloon in one of Dodge City's deadliest gunfights.

Dodge City Trail. abr. ed. Ralph Compton. Read by Jim Gough. 4 cass. (Running Time: 6 hrs.). (Trail Drive Ser.: Bk. 8). 1999. Rental 24.95 (978-1-890990-07-7(8)) Otis Audio.
Returning home after the Civil War, Texas rancher Dan Ember & his neighbors find that their only chance of survival is a dangerous cattle drive north across the Llano, an area overrun with killers, gunslingers & Quanah Parker's Comanches.

Dodger & Me. unabr. ed. Jordan Sonnenblick. Read by William Dufris. 1 MP3-CD. (Running Time: 3 hrs.). 2009. 39.97 (978-1-4233-8245-4(5), 9781423382454, Brlnc Audio MP3 Lib); 39.97 (978-1-4233-8247-8(1), 9781423382478, BADLE); 24.99 (978-1-4233-8246-1(3), 9781423382461, BAD); 24.99 (978-1-4233-8244-7(7), 9781423382447, Brilliance MP3); audio compact disk 19.99 (978-1-4233-8242-3(0), 9781423382423, Bril Audio CD Unabri) Brilliance Audio.

Dodger & Me. unabr. ed. Jordan Sonnenblick. Read by William Dufris. 3 CDs. (Running Time: 3 hrs.). (J). (gr. 3-6). 2009. audio compact disk 44.97 (978-1-4233-8243-0(9), 9781423382430, BriAudCD Unabrid) Brilliance Audio.

Dodging Red Cloud. unabr. ed. Richard S. Wheeler. Narrated by George Guidall. 5 cass. (Running Time: 7 hrs. 30 mins.). 1991. 44.00 (978-1-55690-147-8(X), 91229E7) Recorded Bks.
A group of travelers makes a perilous trek through Indian country. Wiley Smart is as sly & cunning as his fake name. Hannah Larrimer is 12, orphaned & has a chip on his shoulder the size of a two-by-four. These three unlikely bunkmates are thrown together in a hilarious journey through Indian territory, under the vigilant eye of the most feared Indian of all, Red Cloud.

D'Odile et Balivon. Kidzup Productions Staff. 1 CD. (Running Time: 1 hr. 30 mins.). (Kidzup Foreign Language Ser.). (FRE.). (J). 1999. audio compact disk 12.99 (978-1-894281-34-8(9)) Pub: Kidzup CAN. Dist(s): Penton Overseas
This brother and sister team are here with songs and stories. Features traditional & original music from jazz, rock & rap, to classical. Excellent for kids in a French immersion program or as a tutor for a second language.

Dodo la Planete Do (Dream Songs Night Songs) unabr. ed. Roland Stringer. 1 CD. (Running Time: 50 mins.). 2006. audio compact disk 12.98 (978-2-923163-07-9(9)) Pub: MontagnSecrete CAN. Dist(s): Natl Bk Netwk

Dodsworth. Sinclair Lewis. Read by Grover Gardner. (Playaway Adult Fiction Ser.). 2008. 64.99 (978-1-60640-757-8(0)) Find a World.

Dodsworth. unabr. ed. Sinclair Lewis. Read by Grover Gardner. (Running Time: 48600 sec.). 2008. 29.95 (978-1-4332-0812-6(1)); 54.95 (978-1-4332-0815-7(6)); audio compact disk 29.95 (978-1-4332-0813-3(X)); audio compact disk 29.95 (978-1-4332-0814-0(8)); audio compact disk & audio compact disk 63.00 (978-1-4332-0816-4(4)) Blckstn Audio.

Doer of Good see Piece of String

Does America Need a Foreign Policy? Toward a Diplomacy for the 21st Century. unabr. ed. Henry A. Kissinger. Read by Grover Gardner. 8 vols. (Running Time: 12 hrs.). 2001. bk. 69.95 (978-0-7927-2484-1(4), CSL 373, Chivers Sound Lib) AudioGO.
Covers the wide range of problems facing the United States at the beginning of a new millenium and a new presidency, with particular attention to such hot spots as Vladimir Putin's Russia, the new China, the globalized economy, and the demand for humanitarian intervention. He challenges Americans to understand that our foreign policy must be built upon America's permanent national interests, defining what these are, or should be, in the year 2001 and for the foreseeable future.

Does Anybody Hear Her? Contrib. by Casting Crowns. (Mastertrax Ser.). 2005. audio compact disk 9.98 (978-5-558-78698-9(1)) Pt of Grace Ent.

Does Anybody Hear Her? Contrib. by Casting Crowns. (Praise Hymn Soundtracks Ser.). 2005. audio compact disk 8.98 (978-5-558-78707-8(4)) Pt of Grace Ent.

Does Anybody Hear Her. Contrib. by Casting Crowns. (Sound Performance Soundtracks Ser.). 2005. audio compact disk 5.98 (978-5-558-63123-4(6)) Pt of Grace Ent.

Does Anybody Listen, Does Anybody Care? They Will For You! unabr. ed. Jacob Weisberg. Read by Jacob Weisberg. Read by Virginia Schecter. 1 cass. (Running Time: 1 hr. 03 min.). 1985. 14.95 (03-666) Creative CA.
Discusses the skills necessary to get others to listen, to get others to understand & to help others FEEL GOOD when they're involved in a conversation.

Does God Abandon the Heathen? C. S. Lovett. 1 cass. 4.95 (7037) Prsnl Christianity.

Does God Ever Stop Forgiving? Matt. 18:21-35. 1993. 4.95 (978-0-7417-1953-9(3), 953) Win Walk.

Does God Have a Plan for Women? As told by Scarlett Bishop. 3 cass. (Running Time: 1 hr. 30 min.). 2002. 15.00 (978-0-9628301-9-8(4)) M Bishop Minis.

Does God Have a Plan for Women. Speeches. As told by Scarlett Bishop. 3 cass. (Running Time: 90). 2002. 15.00 (978-1-931996-08-2(3)) M Bishop Minis.

Does God Hear Prayer. Read by Thomas Merton. 1 cass. (Running Time: 60 min.). (Thomas Merton Ser.). 8.95 (AA2071) Credence Commun.

Does God Hear the Prayer of a Texan? Col. 1:9-14. Ed Young. 1982. 4.95 (978-0-7417-1249-3(0), 249) Win Walk.

Does God Save from Enemies: Proceedings of 45th Annual Convention National Association of Evangelicals Buffalo, New York. Read by John K. Stoner & Dave Breese. 1 cass. (Running Time: 60 min.). 1987. 4.00 (327) Nat Assn Evan.

Does Jesus Know Us? Do We Know Him? unabr. ed. Hans Urs Von Balthasar. 2 cass. Orig. Title: Kennt Uns Jesus-Kennen wir Inn?. 9.95 set. (952) Ignatius Pr.
Knowing Jesus as a person allows us to truly enter into our Christian faith. Balthasar sets forth the scriptural evidence for our ability to know the Lord & His knowledge of us.

Does Jung Hold Up? How Does the Soul Survive? Christina Middlebrook. Read by Christina Middlebrook. 1 cass. (Running Time: 1 hrs. 20 min.). 1997. 10.95 (978-0-7822-0533-6(X), 601) C G Jung IL.
Focuses on how one can integrate events that ego alien, & provides discussion of how such an illness & experience fits Jung's theoretical framework. Also discusses the process of how healing occurs, the mind-body connection & the cancer war metaphor.

Does Life Enjoy You? (BI05) Master Mind.

Does my head look big in This? Randa Abdel-Fattah. Read by Rebecca Macauley. (Running Time: 9 hrs. 5 mins.). (YA). 2009. 79.99 (978-1-74214-296-8(6), 9781742142968) Pub: Bolinda Pubng AUS. Dist(s): Bolinda Pub Inc

Does My Head Look Big in This? unabr. ed. Randa Abdel-Fattah. Read by Rebecca Macauley. (Running Time: 9 hrs. 5 mins.). 2007. audio compact disk 87.95 (978-1-74093-907-2(7)) Pub: Bolinda Pubng AUS. Dist(s): Bolinda Pub Inc

Does No One at All Ever Feel This Way in the Least see Robert Frost in Recital

Does the Bible Teach the Trinity? Logos Feburary 1, 1998. Ben Young. 1998. 4.95 (978-0-7417-6071-5(1), B0071) Win Walk.

Does the Free Market Maintain a Just Relationship Between Owners, Workers & the Public? Read by T. Patrick Burke. 1 cass. 3.00 (136) ISI Books.

Does the Noise in My Head Bother You? Aerosmith's Notorious Frontman Tells Us How It Was Absolutely Uncut. unabr. ed. Steven Tyler. (ENG.). 2011. audio compact disk 39.99 (978-0-06-184197-2(8), Harper Audio) HarperCollins Pubs.

Does the Triune God Live?-mp3. Read by Douglas Wilson & Dan Barker. 1997. 12.00 (978-1-59128-296-9(9)) Canon Pr ID.

Does the Triune God Live?-tape. Read by Douglas Wilson & Dan Barker. 3 cass. 1997. 15.00 (978-1-59128-298-3(5)) Canon Pr ID.

Does This Cause You to Stumble? John 6:61, 712. Ed Young. 1989. 4.95 (978-0-7417-1712-2(3), 712) Win Walk.

Does Your Name Fix Your Horoscope? Doris C. Doane. Read by Doris C. Doane. 1 cass. (Running Time: 90 min.). 1994. 8.95 (1111) Am Fed Astrologers.
Names & horoscopes.

Does Your Tongue Need Healing? Derek Prince. 2 cass. 11.90 Set. (085-086) Derek Prince.
Since the tongue is the source of both death & life, it is imperative to know how it may be healed.

Dog. Dorling Kindersley Publishing Staff. (Eyewitness Videos Ser.). (ENG.). (J). 2010. 12.99 (978-0-7566-6299-8(0)) DK Pub Inc.

***Dog Appreciation Lessons: Humor & Wisdom from People Who Love Dogs.** 2009. 12.95 (978-0-9785515-1-3(6)) Marion Venture.

Dog Ate My Scriptures: Excuses, Agency, & Responsibility. John Hilton, III. (YA). 2005. audio compact disk 12.95 (978-1-59038-519-7(5)) Deseret Bk.

***Dog Blood.** unabr. ed. David Moody. (Running Time: 9 hrs. 0 mins.). 2010. 29.95 (978-1-4417-4049-6(X)); 59.95 (978-1-4417-4045-8(7)); audio compact disk 32.95 (978-1-4417-4048-9(1)); audio compact disk 90.00 (978-1-4417-4046-5(5)) Blckstn Audio.

Dog Breath & Other Mind-Boggling Hits for Kids. Dav Pilkey. 1 cass. (Running Time: 40 min.). (J). 1997. 9.95; 15.00 CD. Rounder Kids Mus Dist.
Includes jazz recordings such as "Twelfth Street Rag;" "What a Wonderful World;" "Apples & Bananas".

Dog Called Kitty. Bill Wallace. Read by L. J. Ganser. 2 cass. (Running Time: 3 hrs.). (J). 2000. 18.00 (978-0-7366-9149-9(9)) Books on Tape.
An amazing bond develops between Ricky, a boy who is terrified of dogs & an abandoned puppy.

Dog Called Kitty. unabr. ed. Bill Wallace. Read by L. J. Ganser. 2 vols. (Running Time: 2 hrs. 59 mins.). (J). (gr. 3-7). 1996. pap. bk. 29.00 (978-0-8072-7638-9(3), YA907SP, Listening Lib); 23.00 (978-0-8072-7637-2(5), YA907CX, Listening Lib) Random Audio Pubg.
A mangy, half starved puppy wanders onto Ricky's family farm & changes Ricky's life forever. The compelling story of a young boy who overcomes his most terrifying fear with the help of an unlikely friend.

***Dog Days.** Jeff Kinney. (Diary of a Wimpy Kid Ser.). 2010. audio compact disk 14.99 (978-1-4407-8823-9(5)) Recorded Bks.

Dog Days. Geraldine McCaughrean. Read by Glen McCready. 2 CDs. (J). 2004. audio compact disk 21.95 (978-0-7540-6666-8(5), Chivers Child Audio) AudioGO.

Dog Days. unabr. ed. Jeff Kinney. Narrated by Ramon de Ocampo. 2 cass. (Running Time: 2 hrs.). (Diary of a Wimpy Kid Ser.: No. 1). (J). (gr. 5-8). 2008. audio compact disk 25.75 (978-1-4281-8192-2(X)) Recorded Bks.

Dog Days. unabr. ed. Jeff Kinney. Read by Ramon de Ocampo. 2 CDs. (Running Time: 2 hrs.). (Diary of a Wimpy Kid Ser.: No. 1). (J). (gr. 5-8). 2008. audio compact disk 25.75 (978-1-4281-8197-7(0)) Recorded Bks.

Dog Days. unabr. ed. Jeff Kinney. Narrated by Ramon de Ocampo. (Running Time: 7200 sec.). (Diary of a Wimpy Kid Ser.: No. 1). (J). (gr. 3-7). 2008. audio compact disk 14.99 (978-1-4361-0981-9(7)) Pub: Recorded Bks. Dist(s): NetLibrary CO

Dog Days: Dispatches from Bedlam Farm. Jon Katz. Narrated by Tom Stechschulte. (Running Time: 27000 sec.). 2007. audio compact disk 34.99 (978-1-4281-5690-6(9)) Recorded Bks.

Dog Days: Dispatches from Bedlam Farm. unabr. ed. Jon Katz. Read by Tom Stechschulte. 6 cass. (Running Time: 7 hrs. 30 mins.). 2008. 51.75 (978-1-4281-5691-3(7)); audio compact disk 72.75 (978-1-4281-5693-7(3)) Recorded Bks.

Dog den mystery / the phantom mudder / the mugged Pug. Darrel and Sally Odgers. Read by Alan King. (Running Time: 2 hrs. 40 mins.). (Jack Russell: Dog Detective Ser.). (J). 2009. 39.99 (978-1-74214-420-7(9), 9781742144207) Pub: Bolinda Pubng AUS. Dist(s): Bolinda Pub Inc

Dog Friday. unabr. ed. Hilary McKay. Read by Nigel Lambert. 3 cass. (Running Time: 4 hrs., 30 min.). (J). 1997. 24.95 (CCA3372, Chivers Child Audio) AudioGO.
A young boy keeps an abandoned dog left on the beach from being impounded by the police.

Dog Is No Reason to Stay Together (an Essay from Things I've Learned from Women Who've Dumped Me) abr. ed. Damian Kulash. Read by Damian Kulash. Ed. by Ben Karlin. (Running Time: 15 mins.). (ENG.). 2008. 1.98 (978-1-60024-342-4(8)) Pub: Hachet Audio. Dist(s): HachBkGrp

Dog Island. abr. ed. Mike Stewart. 6 cass. (Running Time: 8 hrs.). 2001. 29.95 (978-0-9668567-8-1(3)) MediaBay Audio.

Dog Island. abr. ed. Mike Stewart. Read by Arte Johnson. 6 cass. (Running Time: 9 hrs.). 2004. 29.95 (978-1-931056-40-3(4), N Millennium Audio) New Millenn Enter.
In Dog Island, relative newcomer Mike Stewart sets the likable crew from his critically acclaimed first novel, Sins of the Brothers, on a deadly chase to discover the mastermind behind a brutal murder witnessed by a teenage runaway. As a favor to his friend Susan Fitzsimmons, Tom McInnes idly inquires into a murder that happened the night before at a beach house on the Florida Panhandle. The sheriff is in cahoots with the killers, we learn, because their payback for Tom's pointed questions involves breaking into his office 400 miles away in Mobile, and invading Susan's home, big guns a-blazing.

Dog It Was That Died & Other Plays. unabr. ed. Tom Stoppard. Read by Dinsdale Landen. 1 cass. 10.95 (ECN 216) J Norton Pubs.
On the surface, an amusing & skillful spoof on the school of spy story writers headed by John le Carre, but this is Stoppard & underneath all the wit & verbal dexterity lies a serious moral dilemma.

Dog Like Jack. DyAnne DiSalvo-Ryan. Illus. by DyAnne DiSalvo-Ryan. 11 vols. (Running Time: 13 mins.). 2001. pap. bk. 25.95 (978-0-87499-759-0(3)); pap. bk. 37.95 (978-0-87499-760-6(7)); 9.95 (978-0-87499-757-6(7)) Live Oak Media.

Dog Like Jack. DyAnne DiSalvo-Ryan. Read by George Mazzoli & Barbara Hall. (J). (gr. 4-7). 2006. bk. 28.95 (978-1-59519-300-1(6)) Live Oak Media.

Dog Man: An Uncommon Life on a Faraway Mountain. unabr. ed. Martha Sherrill. Read by Laural Merlington. (Running Time: 6 hrs. 30 mins. 0 sec.). (ENG.). 2008. audio compact disk 29.99 (978-1-4001-0726-1(1)) Pub: Tantor Media. Dist(s): IngramPubServ

Dog Man: An Uncommon Life on a Faraway Mountain. unabr. ed. Martha Sherrill. Read by Laural Merlington. Narrated by Laural Merlington. (Running Time: 6 hrs. 30 mins. 0 sec.). (ENG.). 2008. audio compact disk 19.99 (978-1-4001-5726-6(9)); audio compact disk 59.99 (978-1-4001-3726-8(8)) Pub: Tantor Media. Dist(s): IngramPubServ

Dog Named Christmas. unabr. ed. Greg Kincaid. (Running Time: 3.5 hrs. NaN mins.). 2008. 24.95 (978-1-4332-4892-4(1)); audio compact disk 19.95 (978-1-4332-4895-5(6)); audio compact disk 33.00 (978-1-4332-4893-1(X)); audio compact disk & audio compact disk 19.95 (978-1-4332-4894-8(8)) Blckstn Audio.

Dog of Flanders. abr. ed. Louise De La Ramee. Read by David McCallum. 1 cass. (Running Time: 90 min.). (J). 1984. 9.95 (978-0-694-50817-4(9), CDL5 1575) HarperCollins Pubs.

Dog of My Nightmares: Audio Book Version. Short Stories. Read by Dave Lieber. Based on a book by Dave Lieber. 1 CD. (Running Time: 52 mins.). 2006. audio compact disk 12.95 (978-0-9708530-4-2(1)) Yankee Cowboy.

Dog of the South. Charles Portis. Narrated by Edward Lewis. (Running Time: 9 hrs.). 2001. 30.95 (978-1-59912-651-7(6)) Iofy Corp.

Dog of the South. unabr. ed. Charles Portis. Read by Edward Lewis. 6 cass. (Running Time: 8 hrs. 30 mins.). 2001. 44.95 (978-0-7861-1995-0(0), 2765); audio compact disk 56.00 (978-0-7861-9687-6(4), 2765) Blckstn Audio.
The story of Ray Midge as he tracks down his wife, Norma who has run off with her first husband by following credit card receipts (his credit card!). Midge starts out in Norma's lover's compact car, which has 74,000 miles on it and a quarter-turn slack in the steering wheel (they took his Ford Torino!). The trail leads from Arkansas, down to Mexico, and into Honduras, where Midge stops to help, and of course gets entangled with, Dr. Reo Symes in his broken down bus, "The Dog of the South".

Dog on His Own. unabr. ed. M. J. Auch. Read by William Dufris. 3 CDs. (Running Time: 3 hrs.). (J). (gr. 3-5). 2009. audio compact disk 34.00 (978-1-934180-87-7(4)) Full Cast Audio.

Dog on It. Spencer Quinn, pseud. Narrated by Jim Frangione. (Running Time: 9 hrs. 45 mins.). (Chet & Bernie Mystery Ser.: Bk. 1). 2009. 56.75 (978-1-4361-9507-2(1)) Recorded Bks.

Dog on It. unabr. ed. Spencer Quinn, pseud. Narrated by Jim Frangione. 8 CDs. (Running Time: 9 hrs. 45 mins.). 2009. audio compact disk 92.75 (978-1-4361-7197-7(0)) Recorded Bks.

Dog on It. unabr. ed. Spencer Quinn, pseud. Narrated by Jim Frangione. 8 cass. (Running Time: 9 hrs. 45 mins.). (Chet & Bernie Mystery Ser.: Bk. 1). 2009. 67.75 (978-1-4361-7196-0(2)) Recorded Bks.

Dog on It. unabr. ed. Spencer Quinn, pseud. Narrated by Jim Frangione. 8 CDs. (Running Time: 9 hrs. 45 mins.). (Chet & Bernie Mystery Ser.: No. 1). 2009. audio compact disk 34.99 (978-1-4361-9838-7(0)) Recorded Bks.

Dog Says How. Kevin Kling. Read by Kevin Kling. (Playaway Adult Nonfiction Ser.). 2008. 39.99 (978-1-60640-627-4(2)) Find a World.

Dog Says How. unabr. ed. Kevin Kling. Read by Kevin Kling. 3 CDs. (Running Time: 4 hrs.). (ENG., 2008. audio compact disk 22.95 (978-1-59887-825-7(5), 1598878255) Pub: HighBridge. Dist(s): Workman Pub

Dog Soldiers. unabr. ed. Robert Stone. Read by Paul Shay. 8 cass. (Running Time: 12 hrs.). 1986. 64.00 (978-0-7366-1040-7(5), 1970) Books on Tape.
A dog soldier is a renegade. John Converse: loving the chaos in Nam, he sets up a major heroin deal. Converse's friend, Hicks takes the drugs to California, where he makes a connection with Marge, Converse's wife.

***Dog Soldiers: Unabridged Value-Priced Edition.** Robert Stone. Narrated by Tom Stechschulte. (Running Time: 11 hrs. 25 mins. 0 sec.). (ENG.). 2010. audio compact disk 14.95 (978-1-60283-987-8(5)) Pub: AudioGO. Dist(s): Perseus Dist

Dog Songs. Prod. by Walt Disney Productions Staff. 1 cass. (J). 1997. 5.98 (978-0-7634-0180-1(3)); audio compact disk 11.98 (978-0-7634-0181-8(1)) W Disney Records.

Dog Stars. 1 cass. (Running Time: 27 min.). 14.95 (23561) MMI Corp.
Story of double stars, how this knowledge helps astronomers, Newton's & Kepler's laws are discussed.

Dog Tails. Albert Payson Terhune et al. Music by David Thorn. Engineer Bobbie Frohman. 4 Cds. (Running Time: 4 Hrs.30 Min.). Dramatization. (J). 2004. audio compact disk (978-0-9793777-4-7(9)) Alcazar AudioWorks.

***dog that dumped on my Doona.** Barry Jonsberg. Read by Stig Wemyss. (Running Time: 3 hrs. 10 mins.). (J). 2010. 54.99 (978-1-74214-609-6(0), 9781742146096) Pub: Bolinda Pubng AUS. Dist(s): Bolinda Pub Inc

***Dog That Dumped on My Doona.** unabr. ed. Barry Jonsberg. Read by Stig Wemyss. (Running Time: 3 hrs. 10 mins.). (J). 2008. audio compact disk 54.95 (978-1-74214-115-2(3), 9781742141152) Pub: Bolinda Pubng AUS. Dist(s): Bolinda Pub Inc

Dog That Pitched a No-Hitter. unabr. ed. Matt Christopher. Narrated by Johnny Heller. 1 cass. (Running Time: 15 mins.). (Mike & Harry Ser.). (gr. 2 up). 1997. 10.00 (978-0-7887-0742-1(6), 94919E7) Recorded Bks.
Join the baseball adventures of Mike & his telepathic Airedale, Harry, as Mike pitches against some of the toughest batters in Little League.

Dog That Stole Home. unabr. ed. Matt Christopher. Narrated by Johnny Heller. 1 cass. (Running Time: 15 mins.). (Mike & Harry Ser.). (gr. 1 up). 1997. 10.00 (978-0-7887-0703-2(5), 94877E7) Recorded Bks.
What could be better than having a dog that loves to play baseball? A dog that can talk with you through ESP! And Harry the Airedale is a baseball genius who always knows how to help Mike score the winning run. Valuable lessons on team work, determination & friendship.

Dog Train: And 16 Other Improbable Songs. Michael Ford. Lyrics by Sandra Boynton. (ENG., (J). (ps-3). 2006. audio compact disk 11.95 (978-0-7611-4447-2(1), 0761144471) Workman Pub.

Dog Whisperer. Paul Owens. 2008. audio compact disk 23.95 (978-1-59316-132-3(8)) Listen & Live.

Dog Who Bit a Policeman. unabr. ed. Stuart M. Kaminsky. Narrated by Mark Hammer. 8 cass. (Running Time: 11 hrs. 45 mins.). (Inspector Porfiry Rostnikov Mystery Ser.: No. 12). 2000. 70.00 (978-0-7887-2483-1(5), 95558E7) Recorded Bks.
Deadly fighting amidst the ranks of the Russian Mafia & a popular craze for bloody illegal dog fights, are vicious crimes that are squeezing the resources of Moscow Police Inspector Rostnikov.

***Dog Who Couldn't Stop Loving: How Dogs Have Captured Our Hearts for Thousands of Years.** unabr. ed. Jeffrey Moussaieff Masson. (ENG.). 2010. (978-0-06-200705-6(X), Harper Audio); (978-0-06-206242-0(5), Harper Audio) HarperCollins Pubs.

Dog Who Had Kittens. 1 cass. (Running Time: 35 min.). (J). (ps-3). 2001. pap. bk. 15.95 (VX-84C) Kimbo Educ.
Baxter, the Basset Hound, assumes the role of foster parent to Eloise's kittens. Includes read along book.

Dog Who Had Kittens. Polly M. Robertus. Illus. by Janet Stevens. 14 vols. (Running Time: 14 mins.). 1992. pap. bk. 39.95 (978-1-59112-835-9(8)); 9.95 (978-1-59112-031-5(4)); audio compact disk 12.95 (978-1-59112-832-8(3)) Live Oak Media.

Dog Who Had Kittens. unabr. ed. Polly M. Robertus. Read by Jerry Terheyden. Illus. by Janet Stevens. 11 vols. (Running Time: 14 mins.). (J). (gr. k-3). 1992. pap. bk. 16.95 (978-0-87499-284-7(2)) AudioGO.
Deprived of his share of attention when Eloise has kittens, Baxter the Basset Hound feels miserable until he meets the kittens & assumes the surprising role of foster parent, during Eloise's many absences.

Dog Who Had Kittens. unabr. ed. Polly M. Robertus. Read by Jerry Terheyden. Illus. by Janet Stevens. 11 vols. (Running Time: 14 mins.). (J). (gr. k-3). 1992. bk. 25.95 (978-0-87499-285-4(0)) Live Oak Media.

Dog Who Had Kittens. unabr. ed. Polly M. Robertus. 1 cass. (Running Time: 14 min.). (J). (gr. k-3). 1993. 9.95 Live Oak Media.
Baxter the bassett hound assumes the role of foster parent - with surprising results - when Eloise the cat occasionally tires of her motherly responsibilities.

Dog Who Had Kittens, Grades K-3. unabr. ed. Polly M. Robertus. Read by Jerry Terheyden. Illus. by Janet Stevens. 14 vols. (Running Time: 14 mins.). (J). 1992. pap. bk. & tchr. ed. 37.95 Reading Chest. (978-0-87499-286-1(9)) Live Oak Media.
Deprived of his share of attention when Eloise has kittens, Baxter the Basset Hound feels miserable until he meets the kittens & assumes the surprising role of foster parent, during Eloise's many absences.

Dog Who Loved Too Much: Tales, Treatments & the Psychology of Dogs, abr. ed. Nicholas H. Dodman. Read by Nicholas H. Dodman. 2 cass. (Running Time: 3 hrs.). 1996. 17.95 (978-1-57453-023-0(2), 330091) Audio Lit.
For dog owners whose pets attack ringing telephones, chase imaginary rabbits, are terrified of thunderstorms, or those who just want a better understanding of their canine companions. In engaging case histories, veterinarian & animal behaviorist Dodman identifies disorders & recommends specific treatments.

Dog Who Loved Too Much: Tales, Treatments & the Psychology of Dogs. unabr. ed. Nicholas H. Dodman. Read by Michael Russotto. 6 cass. (Running Time: 9 hrs.). 1996. 48.00 (978-0-7366-3347-5(2), 3997) Books on Tape.
What do you do with a dog that attacks the telephone, chases imaginary rabbits, fears miniblinds, sucks blankets or gets violent with houseguests? Here Nicholas Dodman, Professor at Tufts University School of Veterinary Medicine, tackles the most baffling of dog disorders & presents his unique approach to correcting them. His treatments include key changes in diet, exercise & environment, as well as "human" medications, for canines - as many a dog lover will agree - are not so different from humans after all. This warm & informative resource is complete with lists of symptoms & possible cures.

Dog Who Rescues Cats: The True Story of Ginny, unabr. ed. Philip Gonzalez & Leonore Fleischer. Narrated by Tom Stechschulte. 3 cass. (Running Time: 4 hrs. 15 mins.). 26.00 (978-0-7887-0461-1(3), 94654E7) Recorded Bks.
When a terrible industrial accident nearly ends Philip Gonzalez's life, he becomes a disabled & bitter man until he adopts Ginny, a badly abused one-year-old pup, at the local animal shelter. Ginny reveals a special talent: an almost magical ability to find & nurture stray cats with disabilities. Available to libraries only.

***Dog Years.** unabr. ed. Mark Doty. Read by Mark Doty. (ENG.). 2007. (978-0-06-126252-4(8), Harper Audio); (978-0-06-126251-7(X), Harper Audio) HarperCollins Pubs.

Dog Years: A Memoir. unabr. ed. Mark Doty. Read by Mark Doty. 5 CDs. (Running Time: 21600 sec.). 2007. audio compact disk 39.95 (978-0-06-123401-9(X)) HarperCollins Pubs.

Dogbert's Top Secret Management Handbook. abr. ed. Scott Adams. Read by Scott Adams. 1 cass. (Running Time: 70 min.). 1996. 12.00 (978-0-694-51772-5(0), CPN 10097) HarperCollins Pubs.

***Dogbert's Top Secret Management Handbook.** abr. ed. Scott Adams. Read by Scott Adams. (ENG.). 2005. (978-0-06-089802-1(X), Harper Audio); (978-0-06-089801-4(1), Harper Audio) HarperCollins Pubs.

Dogboy. unabr. ed. Gillian White. 8 cass. (Running Time: 9 hrs. 10 mins.). (Isis Cassettes Ser.). (J). 2004. 69.95 (978-0-7531-1927-3(7)); audio compact disk 84.95 (978-0-7531-2333-1(9)) Pub: ISIS Lrg Prnt GBR. Dist(s): Ulverscroft US

Doge Palace: (Palazzo Duco) Scripts. Jim Sweeney. Contrib. by Katrina Rosati. Created by Whitehot Productions. 1. (Running Time: 3600 sec.). (Great Discoveries Personal Audio Guides: Venice Ser.). 2005. audio compact disk 19.95 (978-1-59971-125-6(7)) AardGP.

Dogeaters. Jessica Hagedorn. Read by Jessica Hagedorn. (Running Time: 30 min.). 1990. 8.95 (AMF-222) Am Audio Prose.
Talks about the Phillipines, multiculturalism, political satire, the Marcoses and the failure of the People's Revolution.

***Dogged Hearts: Poems.** Ellen Dore Watson. (ENG.). 2010. audio compact disk 12.00 (978-1-932195-90-3(4)) Tupelo Pr Inc.

Dogger. 2004. 8.95 (978-0-7882-0303-9(7)) Weston Woods.

Dogless in Metchosin. unabr. ed. Read by Tom Henry. (Running Time: 90 mins.). (ENG., 14.95 (978-1-55017-145-7(3)) Harbour Pub Co CAN.

Dogmatic Theology: 3rd Edition. William G. T. Shedd. Ed. by Alan W. Gomes. 2005. audio compact disk 59.99 (978-1-59638-024-0(1)) P & R Pubng.

Dogs. unabr. ed. Robert Calder. Read by Dan Lazar. 7 cass. (Running Time: 7 hrs.). 1980. 42.00 (978-0-7366-0260-0(7), 1255) Books on Tape.
Dr. Chaim Mandleburg, a genetic sorcerer, creates a super-class of German Shepherds that will kill on command or on their own if unsupervised. One of the puppies gets loose, & is adopted by a college professor. The puppy attacks the professor's small son, then runs off to form a wild canine pack.

Dogs. unabr. ed. Ed. by Linda Spizzirri. 48 cass. (Running Time: 15 min.). Dramatization. (Educational Coloring Book & Cassette Package Ser.). (J). (gr. k-8). 1989. pap. bk. 6.95 (978-0-86545-161-2(3)) Spizzirri.
Explores the History of Man's Best Friend, including the breeds of Pug, Collie & More.

Dogs: 2 Cassettes (unabridged) unabr. ed. Bill Condon. 2 cass. (Running Time: 2 hrs. 24 mins.). 2002. (978-1-74030-623-2(6)) Bolinda Pubng AUS.

Dogs & Goddesses. unabr. ed. Jennifer Crusie, pseud & Anne Stuart. Read by Diane Rich Lani & Renée Raudman. 11 CDs. (Running Time: 13 hrs.). 2009. audio compact disk 82.97 (978-1-4233-9097-8(0), 9781423390978, BriAudCD Unabrid) Brilliance Audio.

Dogs & Goddesses. unabr. ed. Jennifer Crusie, pseud et al. Read by Renée Raudman. (Running Time: 13 hrs.). 2009. 39.97 (978-1-4233-9101-2(2), 9781423391012, BADLE); 24.99 (978-1-4233-9100-5(4), 9781423391005, BAD); 24.99 (978-1-4233-9098-5(9), 9781423390985, Brilliance MP3); 39.97 (978-1-4233-9099-2(7), 9781423390992, Brinc Audio MP3 Lib); audio compact disk 29.99 (978-1-4233-9096-1(2), 9781423390961, Bril Audio CD Unabri) Brilliance Audio.

Dogs Behaving Badly: An A to Z Guide to Understanding & Curing Behavioral Problems in Dogs. Nicholas H. Dodman. Read by Jonathan Marosz. 7 cass. (Running Time: 10 hrs. 30 min.). 1999. 56.00 (5015) Books on Tape.
Dr. Dodman takes 26 intractable & irritating dog behavioral problems & offers easy-to-follow treatment plans to cure each one.

Dog's Best Friend/A Look at Dogs. Steck-Vaughn Staff. 1997. (978-0-8172-7376-7(X)) SteckVau.

***Dogs Don't Lie.** unabr. ed. Clea Simon. Read by To be Announced. (Running Time: 8 hrs. NaN mins.). (Pru Marlowe Pet Noir Ser.). (ENG.). 2011. 29.95 (978-1-4417-8263-2(X)); 54.95 (978-1-4417-8260-1(5)); audio compact disk 76.00 (978-1-4417-8261-8(3)) Blckstn Audio.

Dog's Life. unabr. ed. Paul Bailey. Narrated by Paul Bailey. 5 cass. (Running Time: 6 hrs). 2004. 49.75 (978-1-84505-049-8(5), Clipper Audio) Recorded Bks.

Dog's Life. unabr. collector's ed. Peter Mayle. Read by David Case. 4 cass. (Running Time: 4 hrs.). 1997. 24.00 (978-0-913369-75-3(6), 4330) Books on Tape.

Dog's Life: The Autobiography of a Stray. unabr. ed. Ann M. Martin. Read by Wendy Dillon. 3 cass. (Running Time: 4 hrs. 30 mins.). (J). (gr. 4-7). 2005. 30.00 (978-0-307-28346-7(1), Listening Lib); audio compact disk 30.00 (978-0-307-28283-5(X), Listening Lib); audio compact disk 32.30 (978-0-307-28347-4(X), Listening Lib) Pub: Random Audio Pubg. Dist(s): NetLibrary CO

Dogs Never Lie about Love: Reflections on the Emotional World of Dogs. collector's ed. Jeffrey Moussaieff Masson. Read by Michael Mitchell. 6 cass. (Running Time: 9 hrs.). 1999. 48.00 (978-0-7366-4625-3(6), 5010) Books on Tape.
Masson draws from myth & literature, from scientific studies & from the stories of dog trainers & lovers around the world but the stars of the book are Masson's own three dogs, whose delightful & mysterious behavior provides the way to explore emotions like gratitude, compassion, loneliness & disappointment to speculating what dogs dream of.

Dogs Never Lie about Love: Reflections on the Emotional World of Dogs. unabr. ed. Jeffrey Moussaieff Masson. Read by Michael Mitchell. 7 CDs. (Running Time: 10 hrs. 30 mins.). 2001. audio compact disk 56.00 Books on Tape.
A deadly tide poisons ocean waters, a ghost ship drifts empty in the calm open sea, a Soviet luxury liner explodes into flames & the U. S. President disappears without a trace. As the fate of the U. S. government hangs in the balance, Dirk Pitt must face down a vicious Asian shipping cartel.

Dogs of Babel. unabr. ed. Carolyn Parkhurst. Read by Erik Singer. (ENG.). 2005. 14.98 (978-1-59483-344-1(3)) Pub: Hachet Audio. Dist(s): HachBkGrp

Dogs of Riga. unabr. ed. Henning Mankell. Read by Dick Hill. (Running Time: 37800 sec.). (Kurt Wallander Ser.). 2006. 32.95 (978-0-7861-4732-8(6)); 65.95 (978-0-7861-4839-4(X)); audio compact disk 34.95 (978-0-7861-6539-1(1)); audio compact disk 44.95 (978-0-7861-7309-9(2)); audio compact disk 81.00 (978-0-7861-6132-4(9)) Blckstn Audio.

Dogs of Riga. unabr. ed. Henning Mankell. Read by Dick Hill. (Kurt Wallander Ser.). (YA). 2008. 64.99 (978-1-60514-773-4(7)) Find a World.

Dogs of the South. unabr. ed. Charles Portis. Read by David Hilder. 6 cass. (Running Time: 8 hrs.). 2001. 44.95; audio compact disk 56.95 Blckstn Audio.

Dogs of War. unabr. ed. Frederick Forsyth. Read by Frederick Davidson. 10 cass. (Running Time: 14 hrs. 30 mins.). 1993. 69.95 (978-0-7861-0430-7(9), 1382) Blckstn Audio.
Sir James Manson schemes a coup d'etat in Zangaro, a small West African dictatorship where a secret source of platinum lies waiting to be exploited. The man selected to plan & carry out the sack of Zangaro is Cat Shannon, late of Nigeria & the Congo. There is a deadly parallel about the ways Sir James & Cat set about their tasks: one using all the shady ploys of international finance; the other planning the final blow with a brilliant precision that does not allow for the tiniest slip of timing or tactics.

Dogs of War. unabr. ed. Frederick Forsyth. Read by David Case. 9 cass. (Running Time: 13 hrs. 30 min.). 1989. 72.00 (978-0-7366-1491-7(5), 2367) Books on Tape.
Sir James Manson, a shadowy titan of London's financial district, plots a coup d'etat for an African enclave where a secret source of platinum lies waiting to be exploited.

***Dog's Purpose.** unabr. ed. W. Bruce Cameron. (Running Time: 10 hrs. 0 mins.). 2010. 16.99 (978-1-4001-8645-7(5)); 34.99 (978-1-4001-9645-6(0)) Tantor Media.

***Dog's Purpose.** unabr. ed. W. Bruce Cameron. Narrated by George K. Wilson. 1 MP3-CD. (Running Time: 9 hrs. 30 mins. 0 sec.). 2010. 24.99 (978-1-4001-6645-9(4)); audio compact disk 34.99 (978-1-4001-1645-4(7)); audio compact disk 69.99 (978-1-4001-4645-1(3)) Pub: Tantor Media. Dist(s): IngramPubServ

Dogs' Tale. unabr. ed. Perf. by Mike Anderson. 1 cass. (Running Time: 40 min.). (J). (gr. 3-12). 1999. 10.00 (978-1-929050-05-5(4)) MW Prods.
A live performance containing humorous stories & songs.

Dogs Who Found Me: What I've Learned from Pets Who Were Left Behind. unabr. ed. Ken Foster. Read by Patrick G. Lawlor. (Running Time: 16200 sec.). 2006. audio compact disk 45.00 (978-0-7861-5995-6(2)); audio compact disk 29.95 (978-0-7861-7115-6(4)) Blckstn Audio.

Dogs Who Found Me: What I've Learned from Pets Who Were Left Behind. unabr. ed. Ken Foster. Read by Patrick G. Lawlor. (Running Time: 5 mins. 30 sec.). (YA). 2006. 34.95 (978-0-7861-4885-1(3)) Blckstn Audio.

Dogs Will Be Dogs: A Simple, Effective Guide to Solving Common Dog Behavior Problems. St Hubert's Animal Welfare Center. (Running Time: 10800 sec.). 2007. audio compact disk 19.95 (978-1-59316-091-3(7)) Listen & Live.

Dogsbody, Inc. unabr. ed. L. L. Thrasher. Read by Ron Varela. 6 cass. (Running Time: 7 hrs. 42 min.). 2001. 39.95 (978-1-58116-076-5(3)) Books in Motion.
Were Dr. Sandhoff and P.I. Zach Smith both the target of a would-be assassin at the citizen's rally? And what about the phone message from the doctor placed just before the shooting?.

Dogsong. Gary Paulsen & Distribution Media Staff. (J). 1986. bk. 21.33 (978-0-676-31628-5(X)) RandomHse Pub.

Dogstar. unabr. ed. Philip Dalkin. Read by Alan King. (Running Time: 16620 sec.). 2008. audio compact disk 57.95 (978-1-921415-21-0(5), 9781921415210) Pub: Bolinda Pubng AUS. Dist(s): Bolinda Pub Inc

Dogwatch: Trouble in Pembrook. Adapted by Jeffrey Adams. (ENG.). (J). 2007. audio compact disk 14.99 (978-0-9742012-1-4(9)) Bud C Prod.

Dogwood. Chris Fabry. 2008. audio compact disk 29.99 (978-1-59859-414-0(1)) Oasis Audio.

Dogwood Tree: A Boyhood see Assorted Prose

Dohas of Saraha. Read by T'ai Situ. 2 cass. 1986. (A159) Vajradhatu.

Doin' Dirty. Howard Swindle. Narrated by Richard Ferrone. 9 CDs. (Running Time: 11 hrs.). audio compact disk 89.00 (978-0-7887-9869-6(3)) Recorded Bks.

Doin' Dirty. unabr. ed. Howard Swindle. Narrated by Richard Ferrone. 8 cass. (Running Time: 11 hrs.). 2001. 71.00 (978-0-7887-5013-7(5), 96518E7) Recorded Bks.
Dallas newspaper reporter Richard Carlisle was murdered by such a bizarre method that the autopsy report immediately catches homicide detective Jeb Quinlin's attention.

Doing. Paul R. Scheele. 1 cass. (Running Time: 40 min.). (Personal Celebration Ser.). 1991. 9.95 (978-0-925480-76-7(2)) Learn Strategies.
Helps you do things you want to do & which help you attain goals.

Doing Business in. SRI International Staff & ICE, Inc. Staff. 16 cass. (Running Time: 45 min. per cass.). 1991. 12.95 ea. Set. Intl Cultrl Entpses.
Business customs, protocol & negotiating tactics in 16 different countries.

Doing Business in Australia. SRI International Staff & ICE, Inc. Staff. 1 cass. (Running Time: 45 min.). 14.95 Incl. Essential Facts Bklt. (978-1-879197-05-3(7)) Intl Cultrl Entpses.
Packaged with a booklet of essential facts about the country, this audio tape is delivered in an upbeat, easy to understand style & contains clear, concise information on: How to get things started; How to get things done; Reaching an agreement; How to facilitate mutual understanding; Women in business; Dress; Initial contact; Negotiating; Connections; & much more.

Doing Business in China: How to Profit in the World's Fastest Growing Market. abr. ed. Ted Plafker. (Running Time: 3 hrs.). (ENG.). 2007. 14.98 (978-1-60024-196-3(4)) Pub: Hachet Audio. Dist(s): HachBkGrp

Doing Business in France. SRI International Staff & ICE, Inc. Staff. 1 cass. (Running Time: 45 min.). 14.95 Incl. Essential Facts Bklt. (978-1-879197-01-5(4)) Intl Cultrl Entpses.

Doing Business in Germany. SRI International Staff & ICE, Inc. Staff. 1 cass. (Running Time: 45 min.). 14.95 Incl. Essential Facts Bklt. (978-1-879197-02-2(2)) Intl Cultrl Entpses.

Doing Business in Great Britain. SRI International Staff & ICE, Inc. Staff. 1 cass. (Running Time: 45 min.). 14.95 Incl. Essential Facts Bklt. (978-1-879197-03-9(0)) Intl Cultrl Entpses.

Doing Business in Indonesia. SRI International Staff & ICE, Inc. Staff. 1 cass. (Running Time: 45 min.). 19.95 Incl. Essential Facts Bklt. (978-1-879197-04-6(9)) Intl Cultrl Entpses.

Doing Business in Japan. SRI International Staff & ICE, Inc. Staff. 1 cass. (Running Time: 45 min.). 19.95 Incl. Essential Facts Bklt. (978-1-879197-00-8(6)) Intl Cultrl Entpses.

Doing Business in Japan. unabr. ed. David K. Luhman. Read by David K. Luhman. 4 cass. (Running Time: 3 hrs. 20 min.). 1996. 25.00 Set. (978-1-889297-04-0(6)) Numen Lumen.
Contents from the four programs: "Entering the Japanese Market", "Prospering in the Japanese Market", "Selling to the Japanese Market" & "Understanding Japan's Financial Institutions".

Doing Business in Japan: Telling It Like It Is. unabr. ed. 3 cass. (Running Time: 2 hrs.). 49.50 Set. (978-0-88432-260-3(2), CCJA02) J Norton Pubs.
Business practices & concerns of daily living in Japan are discussed by foreign-born businessmen & journalists.

Doing Business in Korea. SRI International Staff & ICE, Inc. Staff. 1 cass. (Running Time: 45 min.). 19.95 Incl. Essential Facts Bklt. (978-1-879197-06-0(5)) Intl Cultrl Entpses.
Packaged with a booklet of essential facts about the country, this audio tape is delivered in an upbeat, easy to understand style & contains clear, concise information on: How to get things started; How to get things done; Reaching an agreement; How to facilitate mutual understanding; Women in business; Dress; Initial contact; Negotiating; Connections; & much more.

Doing Business in Malaysia. SRI International Staff & ICE, Inc. Staff. 1 cass. (Running Time: 45 min.). 19.95 Incl. Essential Facts Bklt. (978-1-879197-07-7(3)) Intl Cultrl Entpses.

Doing Business in Mexico. SRI International Staff & ICE, Inc. Staff. 1 cass. (Running Time: 45 min.). 19.95 Incl. Essential Facts Bklt. (978-1-879197-08-4(1)) Intl Cultrl Entpses.

Doing Business in Scandinavia. SRI International Staff & ICE, Inc. Staff. 1 cass. (Running Time: 45 min.). 19.95 Incl. Essential Facts Bklt. (978-1-879197-10-7(3)) Intl Cultrl Entpses.

Doing Business in Singapore. SRI International Staff & ICE, Inc. Staff. 1 cass. (Running Time: 45 min.). 19.95 Incl. Essential Facts Bklt. (978-1-879197-11-4(1)) Intl Cultrl Entpses.

Doing Business in Spain. SRI International Staff & ICE, Inc. Staff. 1 cass. (Running Time: 45 min.). 19.95 Incl. Essential Facts Bklt. (978-1-879197-13-8(8)) Intl Cultrl Entpses.

Doing Business in Thailand. SRI International Staff & ICE, Inc. Staff. 1 cass. (Running Time: 45 min.). 19.95 Incl. Essential Facts Bklt. (978-1-879197-14-5(6)) Intl Cultrl Entpses.

Doing Business in the Philippines. SRI International Staff & ICE, Inc. Staff. 1 cass. (Running Time: 45 min.). 19.95 Incl. Essential Facts Bklt. (978-1-879197-09-1(X)) Intl Cultrl Entpses.

Doing Business in the Soviet Union. SRI International Staff & ICE, Inc. Staff. 1 cass. (Running Time: 45 min.). 19.95 Incl. Essential Facts Bklt. (978-1-879197-12-1(X)) Intl Cultrl Entpses.

Doing Business in the United States. SRI International Staff & ICE, Inc. Staff. 1 cass. (Running Time: 45 min.). 14.95 Incl. Essential Facts Bklt. (978-1-879197-15-2(4)) Intl Cultrl Entpses.

Doing Business in 21st-Century India: How to Profit Today in Tomorrow's Most Exciting Market. abr. ed. Gunjan Bagla. (Running Time: 3 hrs.). (ENG.). 2008. 16.98 (978-1-60024-238-0(3)) Pub: Hachet Audio. Dist(s): HachBkGrp

Doing Business in...Audio Guides Series. ICE, Inc. Staff & SRI International Staff. Read by ICE, Inc. Staff. 16 cass. (Running Time: 45 min. per cass.). 1991. Rental 12.95 ea. Intl Cultrl Entpses.
"Doing Business in...audio guides" is a unique set of 16 audio cassettes for business people & international travelers. Each cassette representing a particular country, packaged with a booklet of essential facts is delivered in an upbeat, easy to understand style.

Doing Business on the Net. Wally Bock. 6 cass. 59.95 Set. (150-C47) Natl Seminars.
This practical, easy-to-understand guide to the Internet will show you not only how to get started but how to send profits through the roof as you: Learn what equipment you need to hook up; Learn the benefits of the Internet providers & which is best for you; Forget the frustration of snail mail by setting up your own e-mail address; Get information you need, when you need it, from some of the most sophisticated databases in the world.

Doing Business with Troubled Companies 1991. 1 cass. (Running Time: 3 hrs. 30 min.). 85.00 three audiocass. (T7-9340) PLI.

Doing, Doing, Doing. Read by Odds Bodkin. Created by Odds Bodkin. Contrib. by Perkins School for the Blind. 1 cass. (Running Time: 26 mins.). (J). 2002. (978-0-9743510-3-2(2)) Perkins Schl Blind.
This tape builds on the book also titled "Doing, Doing, Doing." Perkins Panda does activities around the home (eating, washing, dressing, getting ready for bed, etc.). There are two up-tempo songs, "Doing, Doing, Doing" (about daily activities) and "Maybe I'll Go Out" (about getting ready and going outside). The lullaby "Someone Loves You," introduced in the "Belly Button" tape, again ends the program.This tape is also designed to accompany the Doing, Doing, Doing Activity Guide that provides activities that parents and other caregivers can do with children with visual impairments - especially focusing on the home and daily activities.

Doing It. Melvin Burgess. 7 CDs. (Running Time: 7 hrs.). (J). (gr. 10 up). 2004. audio compact disk 51.00 (978-1-4000-8612-2(4), Listening Lib); 36.00 (978-0-8072-2329-1(8), Listening Lib) Random Audio Pubg.
Dino, Jon, and Ben have each got problems - a girlfriend who won't put out, a girlfriend who won't give up, and a predatory teacher . . . just for starters. Award-winning author Melvin Burgess has written a daringly honest and often hilarious account of contemporary teenage life, and the ups and downs that surround DOING IT.

Doing it Now: How to Cure Procrastination & Achieve Your Goals in Twelve Easy Steps. abr. ed. Edwin Bliss. 2004. 7.95 (978-0-7435-4654-6(7)) Pub: S&S Audio. Dist(s): S and S Inc

Doing Our Homework. Swami Amar Jyoti. 2 cass. 1978. 12.95 (E-10) Truth Consciousness.
Master communicates with us always. Homework starts now, wherever we are.

Doing the Works of Jesus, Vol. 1. Kenneth E. Hagin. 8 cass. 32.00 (39H) Faith Lib Pubns.

Doing the Works of Jesus, Vol. 2. Kenneth E. Hagin. 6 cass. 24.00 (40H) Faith Lib Pubns.

Doing Time: The Politics of Imprisonment. Ward Churchill. 1 CD. (Running Time: 1 hr. 8 mins.). (AK Press Audio Ser.). (ENG.). 2002. audio compact disk 14.98 (978-1-902593-47-0(2)) Pub: AK Pr GBR. Dist(s): Consort Bk Sales

Doing Time with the Blues. Bruce E. Arnold. (Time Development Studies). (C). 1999. pap. bk. 20.00 (978-1-890944-17-9(3)) Muse Eek.

Doing Time with the Blues, Vol. 2. Bruce E. Arnold. (Time Development Studies). (C). 1999. pap. bk. 20.00 (978-1-890944-18-6(1)) Muse Eek.

Doing What Is Right in the Sight of God. Kenneth E. Hagin. (Spiritual Life & Scriptual Healing Ser.). 24.00 Faith Lib Pubns.

Dojang Etiquette. James S. Benko. Read by James S. Benko. 1986. 12.95 (TC-14) ITA Inst.
If you have a Dojang (school) you must have this presentation. Master Benko clearly outlines the correct etiquette to be used in all Taekwon-Do Dojangs.

Dolan Debt. unabr. ed. E. R. Slade. Read by Gene Engene. 4 cass. (Running Time: 5 hrs. 42 min.). 1994. 26.95 (978-1-55686-498-8(1)) Books in Motion.
Coe Dolan was an honest cow hand. He didn't like the way his gambler brother Peter made his living, but when Bert Tower shot Pete down like a dog, Coe went on the vengeance trail.

Dolan's Cadillac: And Other Stories. unabr. ed. Stephen King. Stephen King. Read by Tim Curry et al. 5 CDs. (Running Time: 5 hrs. 0 mins. 0 sec.). (ENG.). 2009. audio compact disk 14.99 (978-0-7435-9820-0(2)) Pub: S&S Audio. Dist(s): S and S Inc

Dolces Canciones de Cuna Para los Ninos Queridos. Perf. by David S. Jack & Coral Tuett. Music by David S. Jack. Contrib. by Susan J. Cooper. 1 cass. (Running Time: 30 min.).Tr. of Don't Wake up the Baby. (SPA.). (J). (ps). 1987. 9.98 (978-0-942181-01-2(8), TD 2002) Ta-Dum Prodns.
Spanish version of the original Don't Wake Up the Baby which consists of 11 original lullabies. Stresses positive family values & self-esteem & features both male & female vocalists.

Doll. unabr. ed. Ed McBain, pseud. Read by Jonathan Marosz. 5 cass. (Running Time: 5 hrs.). (87th Precinct Ser.: Bk. 20). 1996. 30.00 (978-0-7366-3512-7(2), 4151) Books on Tape.
Here are the dolls that the 87th Precinct cops have to play with: a model, dead, blood soaking her long blonde hair; her child, Anna, witness to her mother's murder; Anna's plastic doll, which might point to the killer; & a showgirl who mixes love & pain in sen[illegible]oses.

Doll Hair: Styling Tips & Tricks for Your [illegible]. Created by American Girl. (American Girl Library). (J). (gr. 3-7). 200[illegible] bk. 19.95 (978-1-59369-208-7(0), Amer Girl) Amer Girl Pub.

Doll of Salt. Swami Amar Jyoti. 1 cass. 1976. 9.95 (R-69) Truth Consciousness.
"Go within & don't come out." No turning the back to the battlefield. The highest science is discovery of the Self. Finding our Oneness.

Doll People. Ann M. Martin & Laura Godwin. Read by Lynn Redgrave. 3 vols. (Running Time: 3 hrs. 50 mins.). (J). (gr. 3-7). 2004. pap. bk. 37.00 (978-1-4000-9021-1(0), Listening Lib) Random Audio Pubg.

Dollar Daze: The Bottom Dollar Girls in Love. abr. unabr. ed. Karin Gillespie. Read by Carrington MacDuffie. 7 cass. (Running Time: 30600 sec.). (Bottom Dollar Girls Ser.: Bk. 3). 2006. 19.95 (978-0-7861-4538-6(2)); audio compact disk 19.95 (978-0-7861-7140-8(5)) Blckstn Audio.

Dollar Daze: The Bottom Dollar Girls in Love. unabr. ed. Karin Gillespie. Read by Carrington MacDuffie. (Running Time: 30600 sec.). (Bottom Dollar Girls Ser.: Bk. 3). 2006. 59.95 (978-0-7861-4706-9(7)); audio compact disk 29.95 (978-0-7861-7603-8(2)); audio compact disk 72.00 (978-0-7861-6587-2(1)) Blckstn Audio.

Dollar Short: The Bottom Dollar Girls Go Hollywood. Karin Gillespie. Read by Carrington MacDuffie. (Running Time: 30600 sec.). (Bottom Dollar Girls Ser.: Bk. 2). 2006. 54.95 (978-0-7861-4568-3(4)); audio compact disk 63.00 (978-0-7861-7046-3(8)) Blckstn Audio.

Dollar Short: The Bottom Dollar Girls Go Hollywood. abr. unabr. ed. Karin Gillespie. Read by Carrington MacDuffie. 7 cass. (Running Time: 30600 sec.). (Bottom Dollar Girls Ser.: Bk. 2). 2006. 19.95 (978-0-7861-4540-9(4)) Blckstn Audio.

Dollar Short: The Bottom Dollar Girls Go Hollywood. abr. unabr. ed. Karin Gillespie. Read by Carrington MacDuffie. 8 CDs. (Running Time: 600 hrs. NaN mins.). (Bottom Dollar Girls Ser.: Bk. 2). 2006. audio compact disk 19.95 (978-0-7861-7138-5(3)) Blckstn Audio.

Dollar Short: The Bottom Dollar Girls Go Hollywood, Vol. 2. abr. unabr. ed. Karin Gillespie. Read by Carrington MacDuffie. (Running Time: 30600 sec.). (Bottom Dollar Girls Ser.: Bk. 2). 2006. audio compact disk 29.95 (978-0-7861-7602-1(4)) Blckstn Audio.

Dollars & Cents: Early Explorers Early Set B Audio CD. Jamie A. Schroeder. Adapted by Benchmark Education Staff. (J). 2007. audio compact disk 10.00 (978-1-4108-8235-6(7)) Benchmark Educ.

Dollhouse Murders. 9.95 (978-0-87499-595-4(7)); 9.95 (978-0-87499-596-1(5)); 9.95 (978-0-87499-597-8(3)) Live Oak Media.

Dollhouse Murders. Betty Ren Wright. Read by Carol Jordan Stewart. (J). 2008. 34.99 (978-1-60640-637-3(X)) Find a World.

Dollhouse Murders. Betty Ren Wright. Read by Carol Jordan Stewart. (Running Time: 14100 sec.). (Live Oak Mysteries Ser.). (J). 2006. audio compact disk 28.95 (978-1-59519-834-1(2)) Live Oak Media.

Dollhouse Murders. Betty Ren Wright. (Live Oak Mysteries Ser.). (J). 2006. audio compact disk 33.95 (978-1-59519-835-8(0)) Live Oak Media.

Dollhouse Murders, unabr. ed. Betty Ren Wright. Read by Carol Jordan Stewart. 3 cass. (Running Time: 3 hrs.). (J). (gr. 1-8). 1999. 23.95 (OAK 001, Chivers Child Audio) AudioGO.
Amy's Aunt Claire is perfectly suited to the emotionally controlled woman who has hidden the pain of her parents' murders for more than thirty years. Discovering an old-fashioned dollhouse in a dusty attic, Amy is unaware that the dollhouse holds a deadly, forgotten secret about a past murder & the dolls decide that Amy must learn the truth.

Dollhouse Murders. unabr. ed. Betty Ren Wright. Read by Carol Jordan Stewart. 3 vols. (Running Time: 3 hrs. 55 mins.). (J). (gr. 4-6). 1999. bk. 39.95 (978-0-87499-521-3(3)); pap. bk. 30.95 (978-0-87499-520-6(5)) Live Oak Media.
Twelve-year-old Amy knows some connection between Aunt Claire's old dollhouse in the attic & a deadly secret from years ago.

Dollhouse Murders. unabr. ed. Betty Ren Wright. Read by Carol Jordan Stewart. 3 cass. (Running Time: 3 hrs. 55 mins.). (J). (gr. 4-7). 1999. 23.95 (978-0-87499-523-7(X), OAK001) Pub: Live Oak Media. Dist(s): AudioGO

Dollhouse Murders, Grades 4-6. unabr. ed. Betty Ren Wright. Read by Carol Jordan Stewart. 14 vols. (Running Time: 3 hrs. 55 mins.). (J). 1999. pap. bk. & tchr. ed. 41.95 Reading Chest. (978-0-87499-522-0(1)) Live Oak Media.
Twelve-year-old Amy knows some connection between Aunt Claire's old dollhouse in the attic & a deadly secret from years ago.

Dolls. 1 cass. Dramatization. (J). pap. bk. 6.98 (978-0-86545-095-0(1)); Spizzirri.
Filled with facts about dolls from the eighteenth-century American Handcraved Wooden Doll to the Molded Celluloid Kewpie Dolls.

Dolls' Christmas. Tasha Tudor. Read by Davina Porter. 1 cass. (Running Time: 15 mins.). (YA). 1999. stu. ed. 147.80 (978-0-7887-3866-1(6), 47031) Recorded Bks.
Nicey Melinda & Sethany Ann are two very old, but well loved dolls. They are busy planning their yearly Christmas dinner party, with a little help from the two little girls they live with.

Dolls' Christmas. unabr. ed. Tasha Tudor. Narrated by Davina Porter. 1 cass. (Running Time: 15 mins.). (ps up). 2000. 10.00 (978-0-7887-3817-3(8), 96061E7) Recorded Bks.

Dolls' Christmas. unabr. ed. Tasha Tudor. Read by Davina Porter. 1 cass. (Running Time: 15 mins.). (YA). (ps). 2000. pap. bk. 29.95 (978-0-7887-3795-4(3), 41039X4) Recorded Bks.

Doll's Ghost see Classic Ghost Stories, Vol. 2, A Collection

Doll's Ghost see Great Ghost Stories, Volume II

Doll's House see Theatre Highlights

Doll's House. unabr. ed. Henrik Ibsen. Narrated by Flo Gibson. (Running Time: 3 hrs.). 2004. audio compact disk 19.95 (978-1-55685-775-1(6)) Audio Bk Con.

An Asterisk (*) at the beginning of an entry indicates that the title is appearing for the first time.

Doll's House, Set. unabr. ed. Henrik Ibsen. Read by Flo Gibson. 3 cass. (Running Time: 3 hrs. 30 min.). 1993. 16.95 (978-1-55685-276-3(2)) Audio Bk Con.
Nora, Helmer's pampered & petted wife, forges a signature to obtain money for her ailing husband. The results of this act lead to her growth & to her resentment of being treated like a doll in her home.

Dolomite Solution. abr. ed. Trevor Scott. Read by Bruce Watson. 4 vols. No. 3. 2003. (978-1-58807-553-6(2)); 25.00 (978-1-58807-093-7(X)) Am Pubng Inc.
Murder, suspense, and intrigue propel this third Jake Adams mystery thriller from the Dolomite mountains of northern Italy to the winding back streets of Innsbruck, Austria, and across the Atlantic to Boston. Not only have two scientists discovered the DNA link to heart disease, but they have also configured a synthetic version of it. They're up for the Nobel Prize and set to make millions after teaming up with an Austrian biotechnology company. But there are factions who make a good living off the number one killer in America and other companies that would like the solution for themselves. When someone kills one scientist and tries for the second in an attempt to steal The Dolomite Solution, only one man can fight off cunning greed to bring about justice...Jake Adams!.

Dolomite Solution. unabr. ed. Trevor Scott. Read by Stefan Rudnicki. (Running Time: 28800 sec.). 2007. 65.95 (978-1-4332-0580-4(7)); audio compact disk 81.00 (978-1-4332-0581-1(5)); audio compact disk 29.95 (978-1-4332-0582-8(3)) Blckstn Audio.

Dolores: Seven Stories about Her. Bruce Brooks. Narrated by Suzanne Toren. 2 cass. (Running Time: 2 hrs. 45 mins.). (gr. 5 up). 22.00 (978-1-4025-3782-0(4)) Recorded Bks.

Dolores Claiborne. Stephen King. Read by Frances Sternhagen. (Playaway Adult Fiction Ser.). (ENG.). 2009. 60.00 (978-1-60775-561-6(0)) Find a World.

Dolores Claiborne. unabr. ed. Stephen King. Read by Frances Sternhagen. 8 CDs. (Running Time: 9 hrs. 30 mins.). (ENG., 2008. audio compact disk 36.95 (978-1-59887-753-3(4), 1598877534) Pub: HighBridge. Dist(s): Workman Pub

Dolorous Passion of Jesus Christ. unabr. ed. Anne Catherine Emmerich. Read by Nadia May. 7 pieces. (Running Time: 9 hrs. 30 mins.). 2004. reel tape 35.95 (978-0-7861-2760-3(0)); audio compact disk 39.95 (978-0-7861-2761-0(9)) Blckstn Audio.

Dolorous Passion of Our Lord Jesus Christ. Anne Catherine Emmerich. Narrated by Nadia May. (Running Time: 10 hrs.). (C). 2004. 30.95 (978-1-59912-652-4(4)) Iofy Corp.

Dolorous Passion of Our Lord Jesus Christ. Anne Catherine Emmerich. Read by Roger Basick. 1 MP3-CD. (Running Time: 11.5 Hours). 2004. audio compact disk 18.00 (978-0-89555-976-0(5), 2001, TAN Bks) Saint Ben Pr.
Narration of the Last Supper, Passion, Death & Resurrection of Jesus Christ as seen in visions by the Catholic mystic Anne Catherine Emmerich (1784-1824).

Dolorous Passion of Our Lord Jesus Christ. unabr. ed. Anne Catherine Emmerich. Read by Nadia May. (Running Time: 10 hrs.). 2004. audio compact disk 24.95 (978-0-7861-8613-6(5), 3240) Blckstn Audio.

Dolorous Passion of Our Lord Jesus Christ. unabr. ed. Anne Catherine Emmerich. Narrated by Roger Basick. 9 cass. Library ed. (Running Time: 12 hrs.). 2004. 79.75 (978-1-4025-9277-5(9), K1100); audio compact disk 109.75 (978-1-4025-9279-9(5), CK090) Recorded Bks.

Dolorous Passion of Our Lord Jesus Christ. unabr. ed. Anne Catherine Emmerich. Narrated by Roger Basick. 10 CDs. (Running Time: 11 hrs. 30 mins.). 2004. audio compact disk 29.99 (978-1-4025-9193-8(4), 01682) Recorded Bks.
Academy AwardTM-winning filmmaker Mel Gibson's The Passion of the Christ is one of the most controversial and successful motion pictures of all time. Gibson drew inspiration for his film from this striking book, which literally fell off his shelf and into his hands while he reached for another title. During her remarkable life, the Venerable Anne Catherine Emmerich, an Augustinian nun, received a magnificent gift from God-vivid and arresting visions of the enormous suffering of Jesus Christ. Emmerich's incredibly intense visions form an unforgettable picture of the last days of Jesus' life. Collectively, they are a powerful testament to Christ's heroic sacrifice and God's immeasurable love for all His children. The Dolorous Passion of Our Lord Jesus Christ is an extraordinarily moving book. It is impossible to read it and not be deeply touched.

Dolorous Passion Passion of Our Lord Jesus Christ. Anne Catherine Emmerich & Nadia May. 7 cass. (Running Time: 10 hrs.). 2002. 49.95 (978-0-7861-2634-7(5), 3240) Blckstn Audio.

***Dolphin.** unabr. ed. Robert A. Morris. (ENG.). 2008. (978-0-06-169412-7(6)); (978-0-06-172142-7(5)) HarperCollins Pubs.

Dolphin Behavior with Humans. unabr. ed. John Lilly. 1 cass. (Running Time: 90 min.). 1976. 11.00 (03903) Big Sur Tapes.

Dolphin Consciousness: An Ascension Meditation. Sai Maa Lakshmi Devi. 2003. audio compact disk 16.00 (978-1-933488-06-6(9)) HIU Pr.

Dolphin Dreams. Perf. by Spirit Sounds. 1 cass. (Running Time: 1 hr.). 10.00 (MT035) White Dove NM.
This is a sonic birthing environment designed for pregnant women, birthing women, infants & meditators. This unique & powerful tape features the sounds of dolphins, human heart beats, the ocean, a choir, rolling Oms, & quartz crystal. It is an extended play cassette, 30 minutes per side.

Dolphin Experience. unabr. ed. John Lilly. 1 cass. (Running Time: 59 min.). 1969. 11.00 (03902) Big Sur Tapes.
A discussion of the intensive training with six dolphins, a review of the known attributes of dolphins & a comparison of dolphins to people. Included are recordings of dolphins communicating with each other & with humans.

Dolphin in the Deep. Lucy Daniels. Read by Katinka Wolf. 3 cass. (Running Time: 2 hrs. 37 min.). (J). 2001. 15.95 (978-0-7540-5212-8(5)) AudioGO.
A trip to the states is a dream come true for animal lover Mandy Hope & she's been spending a lot of time at the Dolphinarium, playing with the dolphins Bob & Bing but Bob dies & the lonely Bing pines for him.

Dolphin Music, Level 5. Antoinette Moses. Contrib. by Philip Prowse. (Running Time: 3 hrs. 4 mins.). (Cambridge English Readers Ser.). (ENG.). 1999. 15.00 (978-0-521-66492-9(6)) Cambridge U Pr.

Dolphin Named Bob. Twig C. George. Read by Greg Longenhagen. 1 cass. (Running Time: 1 hr. 15 mins.). (YA). 1999. pap. bk. 22.50 (978-0-7887-2997-3(7), 46844) Recorded Bks.
This warm & humorous story of a scrawny dolphin calf's struggle to survive will give you a new appreciation for these amazing creatures. Full of dolphin antics & the joys of working with marine animals, Bob's story is based on real dolphins who live at the National Aquarium.

Dolphin Named Bob. unabr. ed. Twig C. George. Narrated by Greg Longenhagen. 1 cass. (Running Time: 1 hr. 15 mins.). (gr. k up). 1999. 10.00 (978-0-7887-2967-6(5), 95655E7) Recorded Bks.

Dolphin Named Bob, Class set. Twig C. George. Read by Greg Longenhagen. 1 cass. (Running Time: 1 hr. 15 mins.). (YA). 1999. 73.30 (978-0-7887-3027-6(4), 46844) Recorded Bks.

Dolphin Song. unabr. ed. Lauren St. John. Read by Adjoa Andoh. 5 CDs. (Running Time: 6 hrs. 15 mins.). (YA). (gr. 6-9). 2008. audio compact disk 38.00 (978-0-7393-6331-7(X), Listening Lib) Pub: Random Audio Pubg. Dist(s): Random
Just as Martine is settling into life on the wildlife game reserve, she is whisked away on a school trip. She must leave her white giraffe, Jemmy, for two weeks! Her class is going on an ocean voyage to witness the Sardine Run, a spectacular natural phenomenon, off the coast of South Africa. What begins as an exciting adventure quickly turns perilous when a storm blows up and Martine and her classmates are thrown overboard into shark-infested waters. They are saved by a pod of dolphins, only to end up marooned on a deserted island. The castaways, at odds with one another, must figure out not only how to survive, but how to help the dolphins when a terrible danger threatens them. In a gripping tale of courage, friend-ship, and survival, Martine must use her healing gift and her wilderness training to save both humans and animals alike.

Dolphin Song. unabr. ed. Lauren St John. Read by Adjoa Andoh. (Running Time: 23100 sec.). (ENG.). (J). (gr. 4-7). 2008. audio compact disk 35.00 (978-0-7393-6329-4(8), Listening Lib) Pub: Random Audio Pubg. Dist(s): Random

Dolphin Song: A Children's Meditation Tape. 1 cass. (J). (ps-6). 12.95 Aquarius Prods.
Relaxation, games & guided imagery - with specially composed music - teaches children relaxation & concentration techniques. For example, an imaginative game with Frankie the Flute teaches young listeners about their own body rhythms.

Dolphin the Perfect Gamefish. unabr. ed. Jim Sharpe. Read by Jim Sharpe. 1 cass. 1997. 29.95 (978-1-889895-05-5(9)) FIPH.
Dolphins life cycle, spawning, migrations, distribution & fishing seasons, fishing techniques used to catch dolphin.

Dolphins. unabr. ed. Peter M. Spizzirri. Read by Charles Fuller. Ed. by Linda Spizzirri. 1 cass. (Running Time: 15 min.). Dramatization. (Educational Coloring Book & Cassette Ser.). (J). (gr. 1-8). pap. bk. 6.95 (978-0-86545-108-7(7)) Spizzirri.
Filled with the familiar dolphins that play & perform, plus, many lesser known dolphins for your learning pleasure.

Dolphins at Daybreak. unabr. ed. Mary Pope Osborne. 1 cass. (Running Time: 39 mins.). (Magic Tree House Ser.: No. 9). (J). (gr. k-3). 2004. pap. bk. 17.00 (978-0-8072-0534-1(6), Listening Lib) Random Audio Pubg.

Dolphin's First Day: The Story of a Bottlenose Dolphin. Kathleen Weidner Zoehfeld. 1 cass. (Running Time: 35 min.). (J). (ps-2). 2001. bk. 19.95 (SP 4015C) Kimbo Educ.
A newborn dolphin explores his ocean world in the company & protection of his mother. Includes book.

Dolphin's First Day: The Story of a Bottlenose Dolphin. unabr. ed. Kathleen Weidner Zoehfeld. Read by Peter Thomas, Jr. Illus. by Steven James Petruccio. Narrated by Peter Thomas, Jr. 1 cass. (Running Time: 9 min.). Dramatization. (Smithsonian Oceanic Collection). (J). (ps-2). 1994. 5.00 (978-1-56899-033-0(2), BC4001) Soundprints.
Cassette is a dramatized readalong of the storybook, with authentic sound effects added. It consists of two sides - one with & one without page turning signals.

Dolphins of Pern. unabr. ed. Anne McCaffrey. Read by Mel Foster. (Running Time: 11 hrs.). (Dragonriders of Pern Ser.). 2008. 39.25 (978-1-4233-5745-2(0), 9781423357452, Brinc Audio MP3 Lib); 39.25 (978-1-4233-5747-6(7), 9781423357476, BADLE); 24.95 (978-1-4233-5744-5(2), 9781423357445, Brilliance MP3); 24.95 (978-1-4233-5746-9(9), 9781423357469, BAD); audio compact disk 97.25 (978-1-4233-5743-8(4), 9781423357438, BriAudCD Unabrid); audio compact disk 29.99 (978-1-4233-5742-1(6), 9781423357421, Bril Audio CD Unabri) Brilliance Audio.

Dolphins of Pern. unabr. ed. Scripts. Anne McCaffrey. Perf. by Mark Rolston. 6 cass. (Running Time: 9 hrs.). (Pern Ser.). 2003. 29.95 (978-1-59007-353-7(3), N Millennium Audio) Pub: New Millenn Enter. Dist(s): PerseuPGW

Dolphins of Pern, Set. unabr. ed. Anne McCaffrey. Read by Mark Rolston. 6 cass. (Running Time: 9 hrs.). (Pern Ser.). 1994. 29.95 (978-1-879371-81-1(2)) Pub Mills.
An exciting new adventure in the best-selling "Dragonriders of Pern" saga. A decade after the events of All the Weyrs of Pern, two boys, one a dragonrider, reestablish contact with the sapient dolphins & the legendary "shipfish" of Pern.

Dolphins the Homecoming. (Running Time: 60 mins.). 2002. audio compact disk 15.99 (978-1-904972-23-5(3)) Global Jmy GBR GBR.

Dom S Mezoninom. Anton Chekhov. 1 cass. (Running Time: 60 min.). (RUS.). 1996. bk. 19.50 (978-1-58085-567-9(9)) Interlingua VA.
Includes Russian text. The combination of written text & clarity & pace of diction will open the door for intermediate & advanced students to genuine comprehension & the use of literary texts for advancement in rapid understanding of written & oral language materials. The audio text plus written text concept makes foreign languages accessible to a much wider range of students than books alone.

Domain. James Herbert. (Isis (CDs) Ser.). (J). 2006. audio compact disk 99.95 (978-0-7531-2460-4(2)) Pub: ISIS Lrg Prnt GBR. Dist(s): Ulverscroft US

Domain. James Herbert. Read by Steven Pacey. 3 CDs. (Running Time: 3 hrs. 0 mins. 0 sec.). (ENG.). 2008. audio compact disk 27.95 (978-0-230-70428-2(X)) Pub: Macmillan UK GBR. Dist(s): IPG Chicago

Domain. unabr. ed. James Herbert. Read by Gareth Armstrong. 10 cass. (Running Time: 13 hrs. 35 mins.). (Isis Cassettes Ser.). (J). 2006. 84.95 (978-0-7531-3442-9(X)) Pub: ISIS Lrg Prnt GBR. Dist(s): Ulverscroft US

Dombaa Fole: Medicine Music of Mali. Yaya Diallo. 1 cass. (Running Time: 1 hr.). 9.95 (978-1-55961-504-4(4), Ellipsis Arts) Relaxtn Co.

Dombaa Fole: Medicine Music of Mali. Yaya Diallo. 1 CD. (Running Time: 1 hr.). 1998. audio compact disk 14.95 (978-1-55961-501-3(X), Ellipsis Arts) Relaxtn Co.

***Dombey & Son.** abr. ed. Charles Dickens. Read by David Timson. 9 CDs. (Running Time: 11 hrs.). 2009. audio compact disk 54.98 (978-962-634-990-8(5), Naxos AudioBooks) Naxos.

Dombey & Son. unabr. ed. Charles Dickens. Read by Frederick Davidson. (Running Time: 133200 sec.). 2007. audio compact disk 59.95 (978-0-7861-6150-8(7)) Blckstn Audio.

Dombey & Son, Pt. 1. unabr. ed. Charles Dickens. Read by Frederick Davidson. 14 cass. (Running Time: 39 hrs. 30 mins.). 1996. 89.95 (978-0-7861-1003-2(1), 1780A,B) Blckstn Audio.
In this carefully crafted novel, Dickens reveals the complexity of London society in the enterprising 1840s as he takes the listener into the business firm & home of one of its most representative patriarchs, Paul Dombey. A sensitive family drama unfolds between this stem father, his two children & aloof wife in which time & fateful events bring a slow, inexorable pressure to bear upon the hearts of all. In "Paul Dombey" we witness the force of social & personal arrogance ("For Dombey is as proud, Ma'am, as Lucifer") wrestling with his own stubborn, but not unredeemable, heart.

Dombey & Son, Pt. II. Charles Dickens. 12 cass. (Running Time: 16 hrs. 30 mins.). 2000. 77.95 Audio Bk Con.
Laugh with Diogenes the dog, weep with Dombey's unloved daughter Florence, blush with the bashful Mr. Toots, & squirm under the malicious grin of Carker the manager. These, along with the dour Dombey & the bombastic Major Bagstock, are among the myriad characters in this Dickensian masterpiece.

Dombey & Son, Pt. 2. abr. ed. Charles Dickens. 13 cass. (Running Time: 39 hrs. 30 mins.). 1996. 85.95 (978-0-7861-1023-0(6), 1780A,B) Blckstn Audio.
Reveals the complexity of London society in the enterprising 1840's as the listener enters into the business firm & home of one of its most representative patriarchs, Paul Dombey. A sensitive family drama unfolds between this stem father, his two children & aloof wife.

Dombey & Son, Pts. 1 & 2. unabr. ed. 27 cass. (Running Time: 40 hrs. 30 min.). 1996. 155.90 (1780A/B) Blckstn Audio.
Reveals the complexity of London's emerging capitalist society in the 1840s when social relationships were feudal.

Dombey & Son: Part 1. unabr. ed. Charles Dickens & Frederick Davidson. (Running Time: 70200 sec.). 2007. audio compact disk 120.00 (978-0-7861-6123-2(X)) Blckstn Audio.

Dombey & Son (Part 1), Vol. 11. Charles Dickens. Read by Flo Gibson. 12 cass. (Running Time: 18 hrs.). 1990. 39.95 (978-1-55685-173-5(1)) Audio Bk Con.
Laugh with the dog Diogenes, weep with the unloved daughter Florence, blush with the bashful Mr. Toots & squirm under the malicious grin of Carker. These, along with the dour Dembey & bombastic Major Bagstock, are among the myriad characters in this Dickensian masterpiece.

Dombey & Son: Part 2. unabr. ed. Charles Dickens & Frederick Davidson. (Running Time: 63000 sec.). 2007. audio compact disk 120.00 (978-0-7861-6124-9(8)) Blckstn Audio.

Dombey & Son (Part 2), Vol. 2. unabr. ed. Charles Dickens. Narrated by Flo Gibson. (Running Time: 16 hrs. 23 mins.). 1990. 39.95 (978-1-55685-806-2(X)) Audio Bk Con.

Dombey & Son (Parts 1 And 2) unabr. ed. Charles Dickens. Narrated by Flo Gibson. (Running Time: 33 hrs. 32 mins.). 1990. 64.95 (978-1-55685-807-9(8)) Audio Bk Con.

Dombey & Sons. abr. ed. Charles Dickens. Perf. by Paul Scofield. 4 cass. (Running Time: 6 hrs.). 2004. 25.00 (978-1-59007-044-4(5)) Pub: New Millenn Enter. Dist(s): PerseuPGW
The novel tells the story about the rich & powerful Paul Dombey, the head of the House of Dombey. He wants a son & when a daughter (Florence) is born he despises her & rejects her. His wife dies giving birth to his second child, a son (Paul) who is weak & frail & dies as a child. Dombey remarries but his second wife does not love him, refuses him a child and runs off with the manager of the firm. With the manager gone, Paul cannot run the businessand it fails. He ends his days in the care of his neglected daughter Florence.

Dombey & Sons. abr. ed. Charles Dickens. Read by Paul Scofield. 5 CDs. (Running Time: 6 hrs.). 2004. audio compact disk 34.95 (978-1-59007-582-1(X)) Pub: New Millenn Enter. Dist(s): PerseuPGW

Dome. Created by Steck-Vaughn Staff. (Running Time: 3228 sec.). (Power up Extension Ser.). 2003. (978-0-7398-8434-8(4)) SteckVau.

Domestic Affairs. unabr. ed. Eileen Goudge. Read by Susan Ericksen. (Running Time: 67020 sec.). (ENG.). 2008. audio compact disk 34.95 (978-1-60283-408-8(3)) Pub: AudioGO. Dist(s): Perseus Dist

Domestic & Matrimonial Torts. 1998. bk. 99.00 (ACS-2004) PA Bar Inst.
Family law practitioners have traditionally looked only to the Divorce Code & related statutes when confronting the myriad issues arising from the break-up of a marriage. Often overlooked are causes of action arising in tort, which may constitute an untapped source of damages. Lawyers can ill afford to practice family law without a thorough understanding of these important claims & how they may be beneficial to clients.

Domestic Manners of the Americans, Set. unabr. ed. Frances M. Trollope. Read by Flo Gibson. 8 cass. (Running Time: 11 hrs. 30 min.). 1993. 26.95 (978-1-55685-289-3(4)) Audio Bk Con.
A grain of salt, a raised eyebrow & a sense of humor are required for this often derogatory description of the wild, wooly mid-western & eastern United States in the early 1830's as Anthony Trollope's mother reacts from a lofty, haughty plateau.

Domestic Relations Law in Philadelphia County. 1988. bk. 140.00 incl. book.; 65.00 cass. only.; 75.00 book only. PA Bar Inst.

Domestic Violence: Program from the Award Winning Public Radio Series. Interview. Hosted by Peter Kramer. 1 CD. (Running Time: 1 hr). (Infinite Mind Ser.). 2003. audio compact disk 21.95 (978-1-932479-03-4(1), LCM 261) Lichtenstein Creat.
This week on The Infinite Mind: Domestic Violence. Every year, over one million women are battered by someone they know. It's a crime, and for too many Americans, it's also a fact of daily life. Guests include domestic violence survivor Judith whom we agreed would be identified only by her first name; filmmaker Frederick Wiseman, whose most recent documentary films "Domestic Violence" and "Domestic Violence II" will have their premiere broadcasts on PBS in March; Dr. Judith Herman, professor of clinical psychiatry at Harvard University Medical School; Ms. Clare Dalton, professor of law at Northeastern University and executive director of the Domestic Violence Institute at Northeastern University School of Law; singer-songwriter Suzanne Vega, whose song "Luka" put domestic violence on the top ten charts; John, who says he is a former batterer and who asked to be identified only by his first name; and Dr. Edward Gondolf, professor of sociology at Indiana University of Pennsylvania and research director of the Mid-Atlantic Addiction Training Institute. Dr. Peter Kramer is the program's guest host, filling in for Dr. Fred Goodwin, who is traveling.

Domestic Violence 2000: An Integrated Skills Program for Men - Relaxation Exercises. David B. Wexler. (ENG.). 2000. 6.00 (978-0-393-70329-0(0)) Norton.

***Domesticated Jesus.** unabr. ed. Harry L. Kraus, Jr. Narrated by Chris Fabry. (Running Time: 6 hrs. 0 mins. 0 sec.). (ENG.). 2011. audio compact disk 22.99 (978-1-59859-871-1(6)) Oasis Audio.

Dominance: Racism, Sexism & Militarism. Rosemary Haughton. 2 cass. (Running Time: 2 hrs. 12 min.). 1991. 18.95 set. (TAH246) Alba Hse Comns.
The talks on the subjects in the title will put these issues in context which can then be applied to your own particular intentions.

Dominar Los Miedos. unabr. ed. Nader Lucia. Read by Luicia Nader. (SPA.). 2007. audio compact disk 13.00 (978-958-8318-14-1(9)) Pub: Yoyo Music COL. Dist(s): YoYoMusic

Dominate the Law of Sin & Death. Kenneth Copeland. 4 cass. 1986. 20.00 Set incl. study guide. (978-0-88114-746-9(X)) K Copeland Pubns.
Biblical principles for victory over sin.

Dominic. William Steig. Read by Peter Thomas. 2 cass. (Running Time: 2 hrs. 40 mins.). (J). 2000. 18.00 (978-0-7366-9133-8(2)) Books on Tape.
Introduces Dominic, an outgoing mutt who travels the road to "where-eve" & meets all kins of characters.

Dominic. William Steig. 2 cass. (J). 13.58 (BYA 945) NewSound.
Dominic, an outgoing mutt sets off on the road to nowhere in particular. On his way to where-ever, Dominic has all kinds of adventures & meets all kinds of characters: a witch-alligator full of advice, the wretched Doomsday Gang, an invalid pig who leaves Dominic his fortune, & other characters.

Dominic. abr. ed. William Steig. Read by Pat Carroll. 1 cass. (Running Time: 90 min.). (J). 1984. 8.98 (978-0-89845-281-5(3), CP 1738) HarperCollins Pubs.
The first 6 chapters, including the complete stories of Dr. DeSoto & Caleb & Kate & an abridgement of "Dominic".

Dominic. unabr. ed. William Steig. Read by Peter Thomas. 2 cass. (Running Time: 3 hrs.). (J). (gr. 1-8). 1999. 23.00 (LL 0110, Chivers Child Audio) AudioGO.

Dominic. unabr. ed. William Steig. Read by Peter Thomas. 2 cass. (YA). 1999. 16.98 (FS9-34540) Highsmith.

Dominic. unabr. ed. William Steig. Read by Peter Thomas. 2 cass. (Running Time: 2 hrs. 45 mins.). (J). (gr. 2-7). 1998. 23.00 (978-0-8072-7893-2(9), YA945CX, Listening Lib) Random Audio Pubg.
Dominic the dog, bored with his uneventful life sets off to find adventure. He encounters an alligator, Matilda Fox, a widowed goose, Manfred Lion, & a mouse. Everyone Dominic meets along the way has a woeful tale to tell. He also meets his true love Evelyn.

Dominic. unabr. ed. William Steig. Read by Peter Thomas. 2 cass. (Running Time: 2 hrs. 45 mins.). (J). (gr. 3-6). 1998. pap. bk. 28.00 (978-0-8072-7894-9(7), YA945SP, Listening Lib) Random Audio Pubg.

Dominic. unabr. ed. William Steig. Read by Peter Thomas. (ENG.). (J). 2009. audio compact disk 25.00 (978-0-7393-8080-2(X), Listening Lib) Pub: Random Audio Pubg. Dist(s): Random

Dominion. abr. ed. Randy C. Alcorn. Narrated by Frank Muller. (Ollie Chandler Ser.). (ENG.). 2006. 16.09 (978-1-60814-174-6(8)); audio compact disk 22.99 (978-1-59859-146-0(0)) Oasis Audio.

Dominion & Authority to Rule & Reign. David T. Demola. 3 cass. 12.00 (HS-138); 4.00 (5-162) Faith Fellow Min.

Dominion & Services. Stephen Mansfield. 1 cass. (Running Time: 90 mins.). (Studies in Church History Ser.: Vol. 8). 2000. 5.00 (SM02-008) Morning NC.
An in-depth look at different philosophies that have influenced church history, this series provides excellent keys for understanding how to effectively confront the important issues of our times.

Domino: Traditional Children's Songs, Proverbs & Culture from the American Virgin Islands. Karen Ellis. Read by Karen Ellis. Read by St. Croix U. S. V. I. Children. 1 cass. (Running Time: 40 min.). (J). (gr. k-6). 1990. 10.00 (978-0-9625560-0-5(9)) Guavaberry Bks.
Authentic Live Sound Field Recording of childrens - circle games chants & songs, clap pattern chants & songs, jump rope chants & songs collected in 1979 from St. Croix U.S. Virgin Islands. This is the only compilation of west Indian childrens music from the U. S. V. I.

Domino: Traditional Children's Songs, Proverbs & Culture from the American Virgin Islands. Karen S. Ellis. Read by Karen Ellis & St. Croix U. S. V. I. Children. Illus. by Alaria Arpino. 1 cass. (Running Time: 40 min.). (J). (gr. 1-6). 1990. pap. bk. 14.50 (978-0-9625560-3-6(3)) Guavaberry Bks.

Domino Set: Traditional Children's Songs, Proverbs & Culture from the American Virgin Islands. Karen S. Ellis. Read by Karen Ellis & St. Croix U. S. V. I. Children. Illus. by Alaria Arpino. 1 cass. (Running Time: 40 min.). (J). (gr. 1-6). 1990. pap. bk. 21.50 (978-0-9625560-7-4(6)) Guavaberry Bks.

Domino Principle. unabr. ed. Adam Kennedy. Narrated by Frank Muller. 3 cass. (Running Time: 4 hrs. 30 mins.). 1982. 26.00 (978-1-55690-148-5(8), 82030E7) Recorded Bks.
A professional killer is sprung from jail. By the time he discovers the price of his freedom, it is too late to go back.

Domino Vendetta: Sequel to the Domino Principle. unabr. ed. Adam Kennedy. Narrated by Frank Muller. 4 cass. (Running Time: 5 hrs.). 1985. 35.00 (978-1-55690-149-2(6), 85130E7) Recorded Bks.
In this sequel to "The Domino Principle," Roy Tucker takes his revenge on the men who entrapped him in an assassination plot.

Dominoes. Joseph Conrad & Lesley Thompson. (Dominoes Ser.). 2006. 14.25 (978-0-19-424419-0(9)) OUP.

Dominoes. Susan Kingsley & Charles Dickens. Ed. by Susan Kingsley Thomas. (Dominoes Ser.). 2006. 6.50 (978-0-19-424366-7(4)) OUP.

Dominoes. William Shakespeare & Bill Bowler. (Dominoes Ser.). 2005. 12.95 (978-0-19-424372-8(9)) OUP.

Don & Audrey Wood's the Big, Hungry Bear, Quick As a Cricket, 24 Robbers. Illus. by Audrey Wood & Don Wood. 1 cass. (Running Time: 015 min.). (J). (ps-3). 1998. 4.99 (978-0-85953-379-9(4)) Childs Play GBR.

Don Flows Home to the Sea, Pt. A. unabr. collector's ed. Mikhail Sholokhov. Read by Wolfram Kandinsky. 11 cass. (Running Time: 16 hrs. 30 min.). 1980. 88.00 (978-0-7366-0186-3(4), 1186-A) Books on Tape.
Begins with the period immediately after the Russian Revolution & continues through the end of the Civil War. It follows the fortunes of a group of Cossacks & their women - torn between the intense individualism of their Cossack background & the Socialism of the new society.

Don Flows Home to the Sea, Pt. B. collector's ed. Mikhail Sholokhov. Read by Wolfram Kandinsky. 11 cass. (Running Time: 16 hrs 30 min.). 1980. 88.00 (978-0-7366-0187-0(2), 1186-B) Books on Tape.

Don Francisco: Story of St. Francis Xavier. Mary Purcell. 8 cass. 32.95 (741) Ignatius Pr.
The life of this great missionary of the Gospel.

***Don Helms - Your Cheatin Heart - Steel Guitar Song Book.** Don Helms. Compiled by Dewitt Scott. 2010. pap. bk. 19.99 (978-0-7866-8215-7(9)) Mel Bay.

Don Juan. abr. ed. Poems. George Gordon Byron. Read by Alan Howard. Contrib. by Martin Remes. 6 cass. 29.95 set. (SCN 111; SCNSCN 111) J Norton Pubs.
Part I includes "The Dedication & Cantos I to VI" & Part II includes "Cartos VII to XVI." Byron died while in Greece & left Cantos XVII & the whole poem unfinished.

Don Juan. unabr. ed. George Gordon Byron. Read by Frederick Davidson. 10 cass. (Running Time: 16 hrs.). 1996. 69.95 (978-0-7861-0992-0(0), 1769) Blckstn Audio.
Don Juan is a handsome, charming young man, who delights in succumbing to the beautiful women he meets along his journeys which take him from Spain to Greece, Constantinople, Russia, & England. Sprinkled with digressions in which Byron gives his views on wealth, power, society, chastity, poets, & England, "Don Juan" is a poetical novel of satirical fervor & wit. It is Byron's most sustained masterpiece, its structure varied & loose, its language exuberant & lyrical.

Don Juan. unabr. ed. George Gordon Byron. Read by Frederick Davidson. (Running Time: 54000 sec.). 2007. audio compact disk 29.95 (978-0-7861-6064-8(0)); audio compact disk 99.00 (978-0-7861-6063-1(2)) Blckstn Audio.

Don Juan, Set. unabr. ed. George Gordon Byron. Read by Robert L. Halvorson. 2 cass. (Running Time: 180 min.). Incl. Prometheus. George Gordon Byron. Read by Robert L. Halvorson. (42); Rime of the Ancient Mariner. Samuel Taylor Coleridge. Read by Robert L. Halvorson. (42); 14.95 (42) Halvorson Assocs.

Don Juan: And Other Plays, Set. Perf. by Francis Huster & Jacques Toja. Tr. by Jane Molière. 2 cass. (FRE.). 1991. 26.95 (1091-RF) Olivia & Hill.
Moliere concentrates on a certain type of courtier of Louis XIV, the promiscuous & hypocritical nobleman, characterized by Don Juan, who is quick to pursue love affairs despite his wife's devoted love.

Don Juan: Canto I see Poetry of Byron

Don Juan: The Sorcerer. ed. Carlos Castaneda. Interview with Theodore Roszak. 1 CD. (Running Time: 38 mins.). 2005. audio compact disk 9.95 (978-1-57970-350-9(X), C25021D, Audio-For) J Norton Pubs.
Theodore Roszak interviews Carlos Castenda, author of "Teachings of Don Juan." Castaneda's book deals with the author's experiences as an apprentice to a Yaqui Indian sorcerer. Castaneda discusses his experience with hallucinogenic substances which he used under the guidance of his teacher, Don Juan. (Reissue on CD of recording previously available as open-reel tape and as audio cassette.).

Don Juan: The Sorcerer. unabr. ed. Carlos Castañeda. 1 cass. (Running Time: 38 min.). 12.95 (25021) J Norton Pubs.
Theodore Roszak interviews Carlos Castaneda. The author describes his experiences as an apprentice to a Yaqui Indian sorcerer, & with hallucinogenic substances which he used under the guidance of his teacher, Don Juan.

Don Juan Con. Sara Williams. 2007. 9.99 (978-1-59507-091-3(5), ArchBks) ArcheBks Pub.

Don Juan (selections) see Treasury of George Gordon, Lord Byron

Don Juan Tenorio. Zorrilla. audio compact disk 12.95 (978-0-8219-3751-8(0)) EMC-Paradigm.

Don Juan Tenorio. abr. ed. Jose M. Zorilla. Perf. by Francisca Ferrandiz et al. 2 cass. (Running Time: 3 hrs.). Dramatization. (SPA.). 1984. 19.95 (978-0-694-50367-4(3), SWC 2002) HarperCollins Pubs.
Full cast.

Don Leary: Perfect Tennis Strokes. Read by Don Leary. 1 cass. 9.95 (978-0-89811-116-3(1), 7167) Lets Talk Assocs.
Don Leary talks about the people & events which influenced his career, & his own approach to his speciality.

Don Ohlmeyer: Executive Producer, NBC Sports see Scene Behind the Screen: The Business Realities of the TV Industry

Don Quichotte de la Mancha, Set. Miguel de Cervantes Saavedra. Read by Charles Gonzales. 4 cass.Tr. of Don Quijote de la Mancha. (FRE.). 1992. 39.95 (1532-TH) Olivia & Hill.
The first part of the adventures of the immortal characters of Don Quixote & his faithful Sancho Panza.

***Don Quijote.** Miguel de Cervantes Saavedra. 2010. audio compact disk 19.95 (978-1-933499-91-8(5)) Fonolibro Inc.

Don Quijote de la Mancha see Don Quichotte de la Mancha

Don Quijote De la Mancha. Cervantes. audio compact disk 12.95 (978-0-8219-3747-1(2)) EMC-Paradigm.

Don Quijote de la Mancha. Scripts. Composed by Miguel de Cervantes Saavedra. 6 CDs. (Running Time: 6 Hrs). Dramatization. (SPA.). 2005. audio compact disk 24.95 (978-1-933499-00-0(1)) Fonolibro Inc.
FonoLibro in the 400 year anniversary of Don Quixote brings you a masterpiece in audiobook in Spanish. Dramatized with a full cast of actors, music and sound effects brings to life the most famous book of the Spanish literature.

Don Quijote de la Mancha. Composed by Miguel de Cervantes Saavedra. 1 cass. (Running Time: 90 mins.). (SPA.). 2001. 16.95 (SSP225) J Norton Pubs.
For the advanced listener. Includes notes.

Don Quijote de la Mancha. Ed. by William T. Tardy. Composed by Miguel de Cervantes Saavedra. 1 cass. 2001. 15.00 (978-0-8442-7071-5(7)) Glencoe.
Features an adaptation of the first 12 episodes of Don Quijote.

Don Quijote del la Mancha: Intermediate Level. (Leer y Aprender Ser.). (SPA.). pap. bk. 15.95 (978-88-7754-512-1(7), CID5127) Pub: Cideb ITA. Dist(s): Continental Bk

Don Quixote. Miguel de Cervantes Saavedra. Illus. by Miguel de Cervantes Saavedra. Read by Edward De Souza. (Running Time: 3 hrs. 15 mins.). 1999. 24.95 (978-1-60083-727-2(1)) Iofy Corp.

Don Quixote. Miguel de Cervantes Saavedra. Illus. by Miguel de Cervantes Saavedra. (Running Time: 14 hrs. 30 mins.). 2004. 42.95 (978-1-60083-317-5(9), Audiofy Corp) Iofy Corp.

Don Quixote. Miguel de Cervantes Saavedra. Illus. by Miguel de Cervantes Saavedra. Read by Edward De Souza. 3 cass. (Running Time: 3 hrs. 15 mins.). (Classic Fiction Ser.). 1996. 17.98 (978-962-634-522-1(5), NA302214, Naxos AudioBooks) Naxos.
Comic study of delusion & its consequences. Don Quixote, the old gentleman of La Mancha, takes to the road in search of adventure & remains undaunted in the face of repeated danger.

Don Quixote. Miguel de Cervantes Saavedra. Illus. by Miguel de Cervantes Saavedra. Narrated by George Guidall. 35 CDs. (Running Time: 40 hrs. 30 mins.). 2004. audio compact disk 79.99 (978-1-4025-6342-3(6), 01262) Recorded Bks.

Don Quixote. Miguel de Cervantes Saavedra. Illus. by Miguel de Cervantes Saavedra. Read by David Case. (ENG.). 2006. audio compact disk 139.99 (978-1-4001-3217-1(7)) Pub: Tantor Media. Dist(s): IngramPubServ

Don Quixote. abr. ed. Miguel de Cervantes Saavedra. Illus. by Miguel de Cervantes Saavedra. Read by Michael York. 3 vols. (Classics Collection). 1989. audio compact disk 11.99 (978-1-57815-523-1(1), Media Bks Audio) Media Bks NJ.

Don Quixote. abr. ed. Miguel de Cervantes Saavedra. Illus. by Miguel de Cervantes Saavedra. Read by Michael York. 2 cass. (Running Time: 3 hrs.). 2000. 7.95 (978-1-57815-116-5(3), 1078, Media Bks Audio) Media Bks NJ.
Don Quixotes love for the beautiful Dulcinea is confused by his imagination.

Don Quixote. abr. ed. Miguel de Cervantes Saavedra. Illus. by Miguel de Cervantes Saavedra. Read by Edward De Souza. 3 CDs. (Running Time: 3 hrs. 15 mins.). 1995. audio compact disk 22.98 (978-962-634-022-6(3), NA302212, Naxos AudioBooks) Naxos.
Comic study of delusion & its consequences. Don Quixote, the old gentleman of La Mancha, takes to the road in search of adventure & remains undaunted in the face of repeated danger.

Don Quixote. abr. ed. Miguel de Cervantes Saavedra. Illus. by Miguel de Cervantes Saavedra. Read by Christopher Cazenove. 4 cass. (Running Time: 6 hrs.). 2004. 25.00 (978-1-931056-76-2(5), N Millennium Audio) New Millenn Enter.
Don Quixote, a common man from La Mancha, has convinced himself that he is a knight. His escapades astride his aging horse Rosinante are anything but uneventful. With his portly peasant squire, Sancho Panza, who recognizes his master's madness but is nonetheless captivated by promises of kingdoms & riches, Don Quixote mistakes windmills for giants & flocks of sheep for armies. They pursue their chivalrous quest until, in a hilarious conclusion, Don Quixote is returned home.

***Don Quixote.** abr. ed. Miguel de Cervantes Saavedra. Compiled by James Baldwin. Narrated by Johnny Heller. (ENG.). 2010. 12.98 (978-1-59644-963-3(2), MissionAud); audio compact disk 18.98 (978-1-59644-962-6(4), MissionAud) christianaud.

Don Quixote. unabr. ed. Miguel de Cervantes Saavedra. Illus. by Miguel de Cervantes Saavedra. Read by David Case. (YA). 2007. 99.99 (978-1-60252-526-9(9)) Find a World.

Don Quixote. unabr. ed. Miguel de Cervantes Saavedra. Illus. by Miguel de Cervantes Saavedra. Read by David Case. (Running Time: 39 hrs. 30 mins. 0 sec.). (ENG.). 2008. audio compact disk 64.99 (978-1-4001-0901-2(9)) Pub: Tantor Media. Dist(s): IngramPubServ

Don Quixote, Pt. 1. Miguel de Cervantes Saavedra. Illus. by Miguel de Cervantes Saavedra. Narrated by Robert Whitfield. (Running Time: 19 hrs.). 1997. 85.95 (978-1-59912-473-5(4)) Iofy Corp.

Don Quixote, Pt. 1. unabr. collector's ed. Miguel de Cervantes Saavedra. Illus. by Miguel de Cervantes Saavedra. Read by David Case. 13 cass. (Running Time: 19 hrs. 30 min.). 1990. 104.00 (978-0-7366-1658-4(6), 2509A) Books on Tape.
The world's first novel & by far the best-known book in Spanish literature - was originally intended by Cervantes as a skit on traditional popular ballads, yet he also parodied the romances of chivalry. By happy coincidence he produced one of the most entertaining adventure stories of all time & his faithful squire, Sancho Panza, two of the greatest characters in fiction. The first part of Don Quixote was published in 1604.

Don Quixote, Pt. I, set. unabr. ed. Miguel de Cervantes Saavedra. Illus. by Miguel de Cervantes Saavedra. Read by Robert L. Halvorson. 12 cass. (Running Time: 18 hrs.). 84.95 (73) Halvorson Assocs.

Don Quixote, Pt. 2. Miguel de Cervantes Saavedra. Illus. by Miguel de Cervantes Saavedra. Narrated by Robert Whitfield. (Running Time: 19 hrs. NaN mins.). 1997. 80.95 (978-1-59912-474-2(2)) Iofy Corp.

Don Quixote, Pt. 2. unabr. collector's ed. Miguel de Cervantes Saavedra. Illus. by Miguel de Cervantes Saavedra. Read by David Case. 14 cass. (Running Time: 21 hrs.). 1990. 112.00 (978-0-7366-1659-1(4), 2509B) Books on Tape.
The world's first novel & by far the best-known book in Spanish literature - was originally intended by Cervantes as a skit on traditional popular ballads, yet he also parodied the romances of chivalry. By happy coincidence he produced one of the most entertaining adventure stories of all time & his faithful squire, Sancho Panza, two of the greatest characters in fiction. The first part of Don Quixote was published in 1604.

Don Quixote: Four Hundred Years on the Road. Read by Greg Kelly. Contrib. by Barbara Nichol. Prod. by Barbara Nichol. Hosted by Paul Kennedy. Music by Claire Lawrence. Contrib. by David Field. (Running Time: 1 hr.). 2005. audio compact disk 15.95 (978-0-660-19136-2(9)) Pub: Canadian Broadcasting CAN. Dist(s): Georgetown Term

Don Quixote: Part 1 & Part 2. Miguel de Cervantes Saavedra. Read by David Case. (Running Time: 142200 sec.). (Unabridged Classics in Audio Ser.). (ENG.). 2006. audio compact disk 49.99 (978-1-4001-5217-9(8)); audio compact disk 74.99 (978-1-4001-0217-4(0)) Pub: Tantor Media. Dist(s): IngramPubServ

Don Quixote de la Mancha, Pt. 1. unabr. ed. Miguel de Cervantes Saavedra. Read by Robert Whitfield. 27 cass. (Running Time: 19 hrs. 30 min.). (J). (gr. 9-12). 1997. 175.95 (978-0-7861-1242-5(5), 2150A) Blckstn Audio.
"Don Quixote" was originally intended by Cervantes as a skit on traditional popular ballads, yet he also parodied the romances of chivalry.

Don Quixote de la Mancha, Pt. 2. unabr. ed. Miguel de Cervantes Saavedra. Read by Robert Whitfield. 14 cass. (Running Time: 21 hrs.). 1997. 89.95 (978-0-7861-1250-0(6), 2150B) Blckstn Audio.

Don Quixote de la Mancha: Classic Collection. unabr. ed. Miguel de Cervantes Saavedra. Read by Simon Vance. 29 CDs. (Running Time: 39 hrs. 5 mins.). 2008. audio compact disk 59.95 (978-1-4332-1496-7(2)) Blckstn Audio.

Don Quixote de la Mancha Pt. 1. Miguel de Cervantes Saavedra. Read by Robert Whitfield. 14 CDs. (Running Time: 18 hrs.). 2005. audio compact disk 120.00 (978-0-7861-8179-7(6)) Blckstn Audio.

Don Quixote, with EBook. unabr. ed. Miguel de Cervantes Saavedra. Narrated by David Case. (Running Time: 39 hrs. 30 mins. 0 sec.). (ENG.). 2008. audio compact disk 44.99 (978-1-4001-5901-7(6)) Pub: Tantor Media. Dist(s): IngramPubServ

Don Quixote, with eBook. unabr. ed. Miguel de Cervantes Saavedra. Narrated by David Case. (Running Time: 39 hrs. 30 mins. 0 sec.). (ENG.). 2008. audio compact disk 129.99 (978-1-4001-3901-9(5)) Pub: Tantor Media. Dist(s): IngramPubServ

Don Sutton. 1 cass. (Reading with winners: Ser. 1). 1984. 32.95 (978-0-89811-123-1(4), 8802C); Lets Talk Assocs.

Don Sutton: Pitching. Read by Don Sutton. 1 cass. 9.95 (978-0-89811-066-1(1), 7117) Lets Talk Assocs.
Don Sutton talks about the people & events which influenced his career, & his own approach to his speciality.

Dona Luna. Retold by Marianne Mitchell. (SPA.). 2001. 5.95 (978-1-56801-378-7(7), SW4019) Sund Newbrdge.

Donald Barthelme. Read by Donald Barthelme. 1 cass. (Running Time: 30 min.). 1978. 12.95 (L008) TFR.
Barthelme talks about the strange reversals in his work - people as furniture & building as people.

Donald Hall. unabr. ed. Donald Hall. Read by Donald Hall. 1 cass. (Running Time: 29 min.). Incl. Happy Man. 1987. (19); 1987. 10.00 (19) New Letters.
Hall reads & talks about his work & his writing process.

Donald Hall: Prose & Poetry. Donald Hall. Read by Donald Hall. (Running Time: 10800 sec.). 2007. audio compact disk 29.95 (978-0-9761932-4-1(8)) Audio Bkshelf.

Donald Hall: Prose & Poetry. unabr. ed. Poems. Donald Hall. Read by Donald Hall. 2 cass. (Running Time: 3 hrs.). 1997. bk. 23.95 (978-1-883332-26-6(5)) Audio Bkshelf.
Audio describes Hall's life in the country & raising a family. This poetry is immensely accessible.

Donald Justice, Pts. 1 & 11. Donald Justice. Read by Donald Justice. 2 cass. (Running Time: 29 min.). 1985. 10.00 ea. One-sided cass.; 18.00 Two-sided cass. New Letters.
Pulitzer-prize-winning poet Donald Justice reads & talks about his work.

Donald Miller Guitar Ensemble Series. Perf. by Donald Miller. 2 CDs. (Running Time: 3 hrs.). 2003. audio compact disk 19.95 Mel Bay.

Donald Peck - Intermediate Flute Solos Volume 2. Donald Peck. 2007. pap. bk. 24.98 (978-1-59615-300-4(8), 1596153008) Pub: Music Minus. Dist(s): H Leonard

Donald Revell. unabr. ed. Donald Revell. Read by Donald Revell. Interview with Rebekah Presson. 1 cass. (Running Time: 29 min.). 1990. 10.00 (110290) New Letters.
Revell reads from his third book of poems, "New Dark Ages".

Donald Trump- Building a Fortune in Business. (ENG.). 2008. DVD, cd-rom, audio compact disk 59.95 (978-1-60245-116-2(8)) GDL Multimedia.

Donald Trump- Career Success. (ENG.). 2008. DVD, cd-rom, audio compact disk 59.95 (978-1-60245-115-5(X)) GDL Multimedia.

Donald Trump- Real Estate Investing: Master Secrets to Getting Rich. (ENG.). 2008. DVD, cd-rom, audio compact disk 59.95 (978-1-60245-114-8(1)) GDL Multimedia.

Donde Viven?, EDL Level 8. (Fonolibros Ser.: Vol. 14). (SPA.). 2003. 11.50 (978-0-7652-1001-2(0)) Modern Curr.

Donde Viven Los Monstruos. Tr. of Where the Wild Things Are. (SPA.). 2004. 8.95 (978-0-7882-0279-7(0)) Weston Woods.

Done Deal, unabr. ed. Les Standiford. Narrated by Ron McLarty. 7 cass. (Running Time: 9 hrs. 45 mins.). 1998. 60.00 (978-0-7887-1887-8(8), 95309E7) Recorded Bks.
Johnny Deal is salvaging what is left of his family's contracting business. He's about to find himself standing in the way of investors who will do anything to get the property they want.

Donkey-Ride to Disaster. unabr. ed. Kaye Umansky & Kaye Umansky. Read by Nigel Lambert. 2 CDs. (Running Time: 5820 sec.). (J). (gr. 4-7). 2002. audio compact disk 21.95 (978-0-7540-6548-7(0), CHCD 048) AudioGO.

Donkey Skin see Sleeping Beauty & Other Stories

***Donkey Skin.** Illus. by Laura Barella. (Flip-up Fairy Tales Ser.). (ENG.). (J). 2011. audio compact disk 7.99 (978-1-84643-410-5(6)) Childs Play GBR.

Donkey's Dream. unabr. ed. Barbara Helen Berger. 1 cass. (Running Time: 6 min.). (J). (ps-3). 1993. pap. bk. 16.90 (978-0-8045-6661-2(5), 6661) Spoken Arts.
This poetic retelling of the Christmas story from the point of view of the patient donkey is a perfect introduction to the Christmas story for small children.

Donkeys' Tales/the Donkey's Easter Tale. Adele Colvin. Narrated by Suzanne Mann. (Running Time: 34 mins.). (Donkeys' Tales Ser.). (ENG.). (J). 2009. audio compact disk 19.95 (978-1-58980-724-2(3)) Pelican.

Donne by Dancing Beetle. Perf. by Eugene Ely. 1 cass. (Running Time: 77 min.). (J). 1991. 10.00 Erthviibz.
John Donne, nature sounds & parody come together when Ms. Hummingbird & the spunky musical humans read & sing with Dancing Beetle.

Donner Party: First Wagons West & the California Dream. Mark McLaughlin. Read by Mark McLaughlin. 1 cass. (Running Time: 60 min.). 1997. bk. 9.95 (978-0-9657202-3-6(3)) Mic Mac Pub.
Side 1: Covers the early overland emigrants who opened the California Trail. Side 2: Focuses on success of the Donner family's purpose - "Get the Children to California!" Includes poems & letters.

Donner Pass: I-80 from the Foothills over the Sierra. unabr. ed. Joy Wake. Narrated by Elaine West. 1 cass. (Running Time: 1 hr. 10 min.). (TripTape Ser.). 1993. 11.95 (978-1-883605-00-1(8)) Pub: Echo Peak Prods. Dist(s): Bookpeople
Tells motorists about the area as they drive on Interstate 80 from Auburn over Donner Pass to Truckee, California. Features interviews with historians, locals & naturalists along with professional narration & acoustic guitar & piano.

***Donovan's Brain.** Curt Siodmak. 2009. (978-1-60136-575-0(6)) Audio Holding.

Donovan's Brain. Perf. by Orson Welles. 1 cass. (Running Time: 60 min.). (Old Time Radio Classic Singles Ser.). 4.95 (978-1-57816-095-2(2), DB135) Audio File.
A scientist tries to keep a ruthless man alive. Two-part Suspense broadcast (5/18/44 & 5/25/44).

Donovan's Brain. Perf. by Orson Welles. 1 cass. (Running Time: 60 min.). 1944. 7.95 (SF-8030) Natl Recrd Co.
Donovan, a brilliant but ruthless millionaire, is critically injured in an airplane crash. He is brought to the home of a very famous scientist, Dr. Patrick Cory, but the only thing Dr. Cory is able to do is keep alive the brain tissue of this sinister millionaire. Then the brain overcomes Dr. Cory, & causes him to do its bidding.

Donovan's Brain. Perf. by Orson Welles. 1 cass. (Running Time: 60 min.). Dramatization. (Suspense Ser.). 1944. 6.00 Once Upon Rad.
Radio broadcasts - fantasy & science fiction.

Donovan's Station. Robin Mcgrath. Read by Janis Spence. (Running Time: 24120 sec.). 2003. audio compact disk 29.95 (978-0-9734223-2-0(7)) Rattling Bks CAN.

Dons. unabr. ed. Archimede Fusillo. Read by Dino Marnika. 4 CDs. (Running Time: 4 hrs.). 2003. audio compact disk 57.95 (978-1-74093-125-0(4)) Pub: Bolinda Pubng AUS. Dist(s): Bolinda Pub Inc

Dons: 3 Cassettes (unabridged) unabr. ed. Archimede Fusillo. Read by Dino Marnika. 3 cass. (Running Time: 4 hrs.). 2004. 28.00 (978-1-74030-792-5(5)) Pub: Bolinda Pubng AUS. Dist(s): Bolinda Pub Inc

Don't Abort Your Dreams. Speeches. Joel Osteen. 1 Cass. (Running Time: 30 Mins.). 2002. 6.00 (978-1-59349-162-8(X), JA0162) J Osteen.

Don't Ask. unabr. collector's ed. Donald E. Westlake. Read by Michael Kramer. 8 cass. (Running Time: 12 hrs.). (Dortmunder Ser.). 1997. 64.00 (978-0-7366-3491-5(6), 4131) Books on Tape.
Dortmunder has a promising job offer-to heist a bone.

***Don't Bargain with the Devil.** unabr. ed. Sabrina Jeffries. (Running Time: 11 hrs.). (School for Heiresses Ser.). 2011. 19.99 (978-1-4418-4730-0(8), 9781441847300, BAD); 39.97 (978-1-4418-4731-7(6), 9781441847317, BADLE) Brilliance Audio.

***Don't Bargain with the Devil.** unabr. ed. Sabrina Jeffries. Read by Justine Eyre. (Running Time: 11 hrs.). (School for Heiresses Ser.). 2011. 19.99 (978-1-4418-4728-7(6), 9781441847287, BriAudCD Unabrid); 39.97 (978-1-4418-4729-4(4), 9781441847294, Brinc Audio MP3 Lib); audio compact disk 19.99 (978-1-4418-4726-3(X), 9781441847263, Bril Audio CD Unabri); audio compact disk 79.97 (978-1-4418-4727-0(8), 9781441847270, BriAudCD Unabrid) Brilliance Audio.

Don't Be a Hostage to Fear. unabr. ed. Myrtle Smith. Prod. by David Keyston. 1 cass. (Running Time: 58 min.). (Myrtle Smyth Audiotapes Ser.). 1998. , CD. (978-1-893107-17-5(5), M17, Cross & Crown) Healing Unltd.

Don't Be a Leaf. Jean Shepherd. 4 CD. 2006. audio compact disk 16.95 (978-0-9770819-6-7(6)) Choice Vent.

Don't Be Afraid: Solo Track. Larry Shackley. Perf. by Christine Wyrtzen. 1 cass. (50-Day Spiritual Adventure Ser.). 1993. 9.99 (978-1-879050-29-7(3)) Chapel of Air.
Accompaniment track for solo singer.

Dont Be Afraid Brigade. Kathie Hill. 1993. 11.98 (978-0-7673-1312-4(7)) LifeWay Christian.

Don't Be Afraid Brigade. Kathie Hill. 1993. 75.00 (978-0-7673-1253-0(8)) LifeWay Christian.

Don't Be Conformed to This World. Speeches. Joel Osteen. 1 Cass. (Running Time: 30 Mins.). 2001. Rental 6.00 (978-1-59349-091-1(7), JA0091) J Osteen.

Don't be Taken Advantage of - Tips to Healthcare Consumer Savings: Your Health Is in Your Own Hands. Illus. by Angela Brown & Marti Ann Schwartz. 1 cass. (Running Time: 30 mins.). (Words of Wellness - Your Show for Simple Solutions Ser.: 321). 2000. 12.95 (978-1-930995-14-7(8), LLP321) Life Long Pubg.
Don't fall into the tangled web of doctors, rising healthcare costs, insurance premiums & misdiagnosed prescriptions. Learn to take control of your own healthcare.

Don't Believe Your Lying Eyes. Blair S. Walker. Narrated by Marc Johnson. 5 cass. (Running Time: 7 hrs.). 46.00 (978-1-4025-3241-2(5)) Recorded Bks.

Don't bitch just get Rich. unabr. ed. Toney Fitzgerald. Read by Richard Aspel. (Running Time: 8 hrs.). 2007. audio compact disk 87.95 (978-1-74093-945-4(X), 9781740939454) Pub: Bolinda Pubng AUS. Dist(s): Bolinda Pub Inc

Don't bitch just get Rich. unabr. ed. Toney Fitzgerald. Read by Richard Aspel. (Running Time: 8 hrs.). 2009. 43.95 (978-1-74214-126-8(9), 9781742141268) Pub: Bolinda Pubng AUS. Dist(s): Bolinda Pub Inc

Don't Bite the Hook: Finding Freedom from Anger, Resentment, & Other Destructive Emotions. unabr. ed. Pema Chödrön. Read by Pema Chödrön. (YA). 2008. 34.99 (978-1-60514-593-8(9)) Find a World.

Don't Bite the Hook: Finding Freedom from Anger, Resentment, & Other Destructive Emotions. unabr. ed. Pema Chödrön. 3 CDs. (Running Time: 10800 sec.). 2007. audio compact disk 24.95 (978-1-59030-434-1(9)) Pub: Shambhala Pubns. Dist(s): Random

Don't Blame Others: Timothy Chicken Learns to Lead. unabr. ed. Trenna Daniells. Read by Trenna Daniells. 1 cass. Dramatization. (J). (gr. k-6). 1982. 9.95 (978-0-918519-11-5(X)) Trenna Prods.
In a sunny barnyard setting filled with farm animals Timothy chicken finds out the hard way blaming others doesn't work. He also learns the elements of leadership through various lessons such as the power of positive thinking, looking inside for your answers, & creating your own reality.

Don't Blame Others - Timothy Chicken Learns to Lead. Trenna Daniells. (ENG.). (J). 2009. (978-0-918519-18-4(7)) Trenna Prods.

***Don't Blink.** unabr. ed. James Patterson & Howard Roughan. Read by David Patrick Kelly. (Running Time: 7 hrs.). (ENG.). 2010. 24.98 (978-1-60788-235-0(3)); audio compact disk 34.98 (978-1-60788-234-3(5)) Pub: Hachet Audio. Dist(s): HachBkGrp

Don't Bother to Knock. abr. ed. Peter Chambers. Read by John Keyworth. 4 cass. (Running Time: 6 hrs.). (Sound Ser.). 2004. 44.95 (978-1-85496-037-5(7), 60377) Pub: UlverLrgPrint GBR. Dist(s): Ulverscroft US

Don't Close Your Eyes. Besty Brannon Green. 3 cass. 2004. 14.95 (978-1-59156-189-7(2)) Covenant Comms.

Don't Come on Your Cat (an Essay from Things I've Learned from Women Who've Dumped Me) abr. ed. Neal Pollack. Read by Neal Pollack. Ed. by Ben Karlin. (Running Time: 15 mins.). (ENG.). 2008. 1.98 (978-1-60024-334-9(7)) Pub: Hachet Audio. Dist(s): HachBkGrp

Don't Count Your Chicks. 2004. 8.95 (978-1-56008-887-5(7)); cass. & flmstrp 30.00 (978-1-56008-661-1(0)) Weston Woods.

Don't Cry Alone, Set. unabr. ed. Josephine Cox. Read by Maggie Ollerenshaw. 14 cass. 1999. 110.95 (978-0-7540-0281-9(0), CAB1704) AudioGO.

Don't Cut off Your Nose to Spite Your Life. Karen Johns. 1 cass. (Running Time: 1 hr. 30 min.). 8.95 (541) Am Fed Astrologers.

***Don't Cut the Lawn.** Anonymous. 2009. (978-1-60136-582-8(9)) Audio Holding.

Don't Die a Caterpillar: The Power of Transformation. Pastor Lance T. Johnson. 2007. audio compact disk 24.99 (978-1-60247-705-6(1)) Tate Pubng.

Don't Die Broke: How to Turn Your Retirement Savings into Lasting Income. Margaret A. Malaspina. Read by Susan O'Malley. 6 CDs. (Running Time: 7 hrs.). 2000. audio compact disk 48.00 (978-0-7861-9909-9(1), 2520) Blckstn Audio.
Perfect for young professionals seeking to establish a retirement nest egg. Presented in a clever building-block concept designed to guide the expert & novice toward positive net worth growth year after year.

Don't Die Broke: How to Turn Your Retirement Savings into Lasting Income. unabr. ed. Margaret A. Malaspina. Read by Susan O'Malley. 5 cass. (Running Time: 7 hrs.). 2003. 39.95 (978-0-7861-1714-7(1), 2520) Blckstn Audio.
There are dozens of resources for saving & investing in retirement. This one is different. It's about the one-shot decisions you can, should & must make when the time comes to take charge of the money you've worked so hard to save. It explains each option, sorts out its pros & cons & offers sound guidance customized to your own situations. This is the guide that marries vital advice with practical, user-friendly information in an area of retirement planning that few Americans understand.

Don't Die, My Love. Lurlene McDaniel. Read by Alyssa Bresnahan. 4 cass. (Running Time: 5 hrs. 30 mins.). (YA). 2000. pap. bk. 50.24 (978-0-7887-4165-4(9), 41101); 107.70 (978-0-7887-4166-1(7), 47094) Recorded Bks.
High school seniors Julie & Luke have been inseparable since they were 14. Now Luke has been diagnosed with a deadly cancer & their world is crashing down. Addresses the fears of young people faced with life-altering situations.

Don't Die, My Love. unabr. ed. Lurlene McDaniel. Narrated by Alyssa Bresnahan. 4 pieces. (Running Time: 5 hrs. 30 mins.). (gr. 7 up). 2000. 37.00 (978-0-7887-4012-1(1), 96041E7) Recorded Bks.

Don't Diet, Live It: A Conversation with the Authors. abr. ed. Andrea LoBue & Marsea Marcus. Read by Andrea LoBue & Marsea Marcus. 1 cass. (Running Time: 90 min.). 1997. 10.00 (978-0-9655733-2-0(X)) InnerSolutions.
Discussing chapters & personal stories that are based on the book.

Don't Discover Me. Sarah Weeks. (J). (ps-3). Date not set. bk. 15.99 (978-0-06-028139-7(1)) HarperCollins Pubs.

Don't Drink & Drive. abr. ed. Roger W. Breternitz. 1 cass. (Running Time: 45 min.). 1985. pap. bk. 9.95 (978-1-893417-11-3(5)) Vector Studios.
Hypnosis: Side A is introduction & things associated with drinking & driving. Side B hypnosis implants mental suggestions that reform subconscious belief system to control drinking impulses.

Don't Drink the Eye Drops, Dream Rider. unabr. ed. Jon D'Arc. Read by Jon D'Arc. 4 CDs. (Running Time: 4 hrs. 30 mins.). 2001. pap. bk. 40.00 (978-0-915090-67-9(8)) Firefall.
A classic in the medicine of vision. Aaron Rhyder leads a failed life in the shadows, until a sudden strange fogging in his sight, leads him to Dr. Alisa Gray, who lovingly injects visions into his eye with a platinum needle.

Don't Eat Ice Cream with Your Dirty Feet: Strange & Weird Poems for Kids. unabr. ed. Marian L. Clish. Illus. by Lori Clish Robinson. (J). (gr. k-5). 2000. bk. 18.95 (978-1-928632-42-9(4)) Writers Mrktpl.

Don't Eat Ice Cream with Your Dirty Feet: Strange & Weird Poems for Kids. unabr. l.t. ed. Marian L. Clish. Illus. by Lori Clish Robinson. (J). (gr. k-5). 2000. pap. bk. 14.95 (978-1-928632-40-5(8)); pap. bk. 10.95 (978-1-928632-39-9(4)) Writers Mrktpl.

Don't eat the marshmallow... Yet! see No te comas el Marshmallow... Todavia!

Don't Eat the Mystery Meat! unabr. ed. Tom B. Stone. Narrated by Jeff Woodman. 3 cass. (Running Time: 2 hrs. 45 mins.). (Graveyard School Ser.: No. 1). (gr. 3-7). 27.00 (978-0-7887-0596-0(2), 94880E7) Recorded Bks.
An adventure of spooky danger & grisly humor centers around a school so weird that its students are dying to go to class. Available to libraries only.

Don't Enter a Karaoke Contest near Smith College: You Will Lose to Lesbians (An Essay from Things I've Learned from Women Who've Dumped Me) abr. ed. Jason Nash. Read by Jason Nash. Ed. by Ben Karlin. (Running Time: 15 mins.). (ENG.). 2008. 1.98 (978-1-60024-350-9(9)) Pub: Hachet Audio. Dist(s): HachBkGrp

Don't Fall Six Feet Under: Or You Will Miss Your Dreams. Narrated by Francis Whalen. 1. (Running Time: 60 mins). 2004. (978-1-932551-33-4(6)) High King Pub.
Audio Coach teaching how to change your poverty mind set and make your dreams a reality.

Don't Fence Me In: An American Teenager in the Holocaust. Barry Spanjaard. B&B Pub CA.
A first person account of the only American-born boy in three concentration camps.

Don't Fence Me In: An American Teenager in the Holocaust. 12th ed. Barry Spanjaard. Ed. by Bunnie J. Spanjaard. Illus. by Craig Bassuk. pap. bk. 9.95 (978-0-9607008-0-6(3)) B&B Pub CA.

Don't Fidget a Feather! unabr. ed. Erica Silverman. Narrated by John McDonough. 1 cass. (Running Time: 15 mins.). (ps up). 1998. 10.00 (978-0-7887-2061-1(9), 95414E7) Recorded Bks.
Duck & Gander hold a freeze-in-place contest to discover who is the "champion of champions." But when they stand stock still, along comes a host of troublesome visitors. Youngsters discover that winning isn't everything.

Don't Forget How Big God Is! unabr. ed. Keith A. Butler, II. 1 cass. (Running Time: 1 hr. 30 mins.). 2001. 5.00 (A83) Word Faith Pubng.

Don't Forget the Bacon! Pat Hutchins. 1 cass. (Running Time: 35 min.). (J). (ps-3). 2001. pap. bk. 15.95 (VX-83C) Kimbo Educ.
As he sets out for the store, the boy confuses the shopping list. What does he bring home?.

Don't Forget the Bacon! Pat Hutchins. Illus. by Pat Hutchins. 14 vols. (Running Time: 5 mins.). 1992. pap. bk. 35.95 (978-1-59112-710-9(6)); 9.95 (978-1-59112-032-2(2)); audio compact disk 12.95 (978-1-59112-708-6(4)) Live Oak Media.

Don't Forget the Bacon! unabr. ed. Pat Hutchins. Illus. by Pat Hutchins. Read by Larry Robinson. 11 vols. (Running Time: 5 mins.). (Live Oak Readalong Ser.). (J). (gr. k-3). 1992. pap. bk. 16.95 (978-0-87499-252-6(4)) AudioGO.
On a trip to the store, a young boy tries to remember the four items his mother wants only to get hopelessly confused by the things he sees on his trip. He finally gets it all sorted out...almost, that is.

Don't Forget the Bacon! unabr. ed. Pat Hutchins. Illus. by Pat Hutchins. Read by Larry Robinson. 14 vols. (Running Time: 5 mins.). (J). 1992. pap. bk. & tchr. ed. 33.95 Reading Chest. (978-0-87499-254-0(0)) Live Oak Media.

Don't Forget the Bacon! unabr. ed. Pat Hutchins. Illus. by Pat Hutchins. Read by Larry Robinson. 1 cass. (Running Time: 5 mins.). (J). (gr. k-3). 1992. bk. 24.95 (978-0-87499-253-3(2)) Live Oak Media.

Don't Forget the Bacon! unabr. ed. Pat Hutchins. 1 cass. (Running Time: 5 min.). (J). (gr. k-3). 1992. 9.95 Live Oak Media.

Don't Forget the Star. George D. Durrant. 1 cass. 1984. 7.95 (978-1-57008-008-1(9), Bkcraft Inc) Deseret Bk.

Don't Forget to Remember Me. Contrib. by Carrie Underwood. (Praise Hymn Soundtracks Ser.). 2006. audio compact disk 8.98 (978-5-558-20115-4(0)) Pt of Grace Ent.

Don't Get Mad... Get Even & How to Thrive on Rejection, unabr. collector's ed. Alan Abel. Read by Grover Gardner. 6 cass. (Running Time: 6 hrs.). 1988. 36.00 (978-0-7366-1414-6(1), 2301) Books on Tape.
Lances 100 familiar aggravations such as: billed for a debt already paid, stood up on a date, or baggage lost by an airline. Now that we've gotten even, we can turn to dealing with rejection. How to Thrive on Rejection presents perfected techniques for surviving rejection.

Don't Get Me Started. abr. ed. Kate Clinton. Read by Kate Clinton. 2 cass. (Running Time: 3 hrs.). 1998. 16.95 Set. (978-1-57511-050-9(4)) Pub Mills.
Humorous looks at politics, modern living, family issues & much more, by humorist & stand-up comic, Kate Clinton.

***Don't Get Scrooged.** abr. ed. Richard Carlson. Read by Richard Carlson. 2006. (978-0-06-135547-9(X), Harper Audio); (978-0-06-135569-1(0), Harper Audio) HarperCollins Pubs.

***Don't Get Scrooged: How to Survive & Thrive in a World Ful.** abr. ed. Richard Carlson. Read by Richard Carlson. 2006. (978-0-06-123054-7(5), Harper Audio); (978-0-06-123053-0(7), Harper Audio) HarperCollins Pubs.

Don't Get Too Comfortable: The Indignities of Coach Class, the Torments of Low Thread Count, the Never-Ending Quest for Artisanal Olive Oil, & Other First World Problems. unabr. ed. David Rakoff. Read by David Rakoff. 4 CDs. (Running Time: 16200 sec.). (ENG.). 2005. audio compact disk 16.95 (978-0-7393-2335-9(0), Random AudioBks) Pub: Random Audio Pubg. Dist(s): Random

Don't Get Trapped in the Past. Speeches. Joel Osteen. 1 Cass. (Running Time: 30 Mins.). 2002. 6.00 (978-1-59349-145-1(X), JA0145) J Osteen.

Don't Give in - God Wants You to Win! unabr. ed. Thelma Wells. Narrated by Thelma Wells. (Running Time: 5 hrs. 54 mins. 16 sec.). (ENG.). 2009. 16.09 (978-1-60814-523-2(9)) Oasis Audio.

Don't Give In - God Wants You to Win! Preparing for Victory in the Battle of Life. unabr. ed. Thelma Wells. Narrated by Thelma Wells. (Running Time: 5 hrs. 54 mins. 16 sec.). (ENG.). 2009. audio compact disk 22.99 (978-1-59859-506-2(7)) Oasis Audio.

Don't Give Me That Old Time Religion: Luke 5:27-39. Ed Young. 1993. 4.95 (978-0-7417-1951-5(7), 951) Win Walk.

Don't Go near Mrs. Tallie, unabr. ed. Peg Kehret. Narrated by Carine Montbertrand. 2 cass. (Running Time: 2 hrs. 45 mins.). (Frightmares Ser.:

No. 3). (gr. 5 up). 1997. 19.00 (978-0-7887-0681-3(0), 94853E7) Recorded Bks.
Sixth-graders Kayo & Rosie use their wits to protect an elderly neighbor.

Don't Judge a Girl by Her Cover. unabr. ed. Ally Carter. Read by Renée Raudman. (Running Time: 7 hrs.). (Gallagher Girls Ser.: No. 3). 2009. 24.99 (978-1-4233-9685-7(5), 9781423396857, Brilliance MP3); 24.99 (978-1-4233-9687-1(1), 9781423396871, BAD); 39.97 (978-1-4233-9686-4(3), 9781423396864, Brinc Audio MP3 Lib); 39.97 (978-1-4233-9688-8(X), 9781423396888, BADLE); audio compact disk 24.99 (978-1-4233-9683-3(9), 9781423396833, Bril Audio CD Unabri) Brilliance Audio.

Don't Judge a Girl by Her Cover. unabr. ed. Ally Carter. Read by Renée Raudman. 6 CDs. (Running Time: 7 hrs. 24 mins.). (Gallagher Girls Ser.: No. 3). (YA). (gr. 7-10). 2009. audio compact disk 69.97 (978-1-4233-9684-0(7), 9781423396840, BriAudCD Unabrid) Brilliance Audio.

Don't Just Go to Church... Do Something! Mark Crow. 3 cass. (Running Time: 3 hrs.). 2001. (978-1-931537-18-6(6)) Vision Comm Creat.

Don't Just Stand There. . ! David P. Schloss. Read by David P. Schloss. 1 CD. (Running Time: 43 mins.). (ENG.). 2007. audio compact disk 10.95 (978-0-9629230-5-0(2)) D P Schloss.

Don't Just Stand There... ! unabr. ed. David P. Schloss. Read by David P. Schloss. 1 cass. (Running Time: 45 min.). (ENG.). 1997. 9.95 (978-0-9629230-1-2(X)) D P Schloss.
Shows people how to play & win the game of life through the development of a positive winning attitude.This 45 minute motivational audio cassette shares with the listener numerous ways to make their life more successful through the building of a positive winning attitude!Business motivation is more important today that ever before! This is a great tape to motivate your sales force, employees and/or associates!A few of the topics are: How you can win the game of life! How to handle rejections! How to break through self-imposed restrictions! The power of goal setting and the proper way to do it! The secrets of getting what you want in life! How to become a dreamer again! How to quit worrying and start living!Endorsed by: John Milton Fogg, Editor-in-Chief, Upline and author of The Greatest Networker in the World.

***Don't Just Stand There, Pray Something!** Arranged by Polishing the Pulpit. (C). 2010. audio compact disk 25.00 (978-1-60644-123-7(X)) Heart Heart.

Don't Just Talk - "Communicate" unabr. ed. Dorothy Campbell. Read by Dorothy Campbell. 1 cass. (Running Time: 1 hr. 30 mins.). (Self-Power Tape Ser.). 1998. (978-0-9658996-2-8(4)) Positive Pr MA.
Seminar on basic communications skills on both a personal & professional level to produce positive results.

Don't Just Try... Train. Speeches. M. J. Kelly. 1 cass. (Running Time: 1 hr. 20 mins.). 2000. 8.00 (978-1-929266-06-7(5)) Beacon OH.
An audio program in which Matthew Kelly emphasizes the importance of spiritual discipline and training. "Focus," he says, "not on finding the right person but on being the right person.".

Don't Just Try... Train: How Spiritual Discipline Can Transform Your Life. 2003. audio compact disk 6.95 (978-1-932631-71-5(2)) Ascensn Pr.

Don't Kiss Them Good-bye. unabr. ed. Allison DuBois. 2005. 17.95 (978-0-7435-5147-2(8)) Pub: S&S Audio. Dist(s): S and S Inc

Don't Know Much about American History. Kenneth C. Davis. Intro. by Kenneth C. Davis. Read by Oliver Wyman. 4 vols. (Running Time: 7 hrs. 15 mins.). (Don't Know Much about Ser.). (J). (gr. 4-7). 2004. pap. bk. 40.00 (978-0-8072-2092-4(2), Listening Lib) Random Audio Pubg.

Don't Know Much about Anything: Everything You Need to Know but Never Learned about People, Places, Events, & More! abr. ed. Kenneth C. Davis. Intro. by Kenneth C. Davis. Read by Jeff Woodman et al. (Running Time: 16200 sec.). (Don't Know Much about Ser.). (ENG.). 2007. audio compact disk 23.95 (978-0-7393-4283-1(5), Random AudioBks) Pub: Random Audio Pubg. Dist(s): Random

Don't Know Much about Geography. Kenneth C. Davis. Read by Dick Estell. 1999. audio compact disk 80.00 (978-0-7366-5184-4(5)) Books on Tape.

Don't Know Much about Geography: Everything You Need to Know about the World but Never Learned. abr. ed. Kenneth C. Davis. Read by Kenneth C. Davis. 3 CDs. (Running Time: 3 hrs.). (ENG.). 1998. audio compact disk 24.95 (978-0-553-45604-2(0),) Pub: Random Audio Pubg. Dist(s): Random
Was there an Atlantis?What's the smallest country in the world?What's the difference between a jungle and a rain forest? Kenneth C. Davis, author of Don't Know Much About® History, Don't Know Much About® the Civil War and Don't Know Much About® the Bible, turns his inimitable wit and wide-ranging knowledge to the subject of geography, and proves once and for all that there is a lot more to it than labeling countries on a map. From often amusing perceptions people have had through the ages about the world and the universe to the changing map of today, Davis shows how geography is really a great crossroads of many fields: biology, meteorology, astronomy, history, economics, and even politics. In this lively, entertaining, and endlessly fascinating presentation, you'll hear about the personalities that helped shape the world and learn the answers to questions that have vexed most of us since grade school. Along the way, Davis offers an affectionate ode to the earth: a celebration of the earth, a searching investigation of the destruction of our habitat, and a practical guide to saving our home planet. For anyone who has felt geographically ignorant ever since gas stations stopped handing out free maps, Don't Know Much About® Geography is enormously informative entertainment.

Don't Know Much about Geography: Everything You Need to Know about the World but Never Learned. unabr. ed. Kenneth C. Davis. Read by Dick Estell. 8 cass. (Running Time: 12 hrs.). 1999. 64.00 (4983); 64.00 (978-0-7366-4576-8(4), 4983) Books on Tape.
Tackles geography with wit, curiosity and knowledge. In doing so, he proves once and for all that there is a lot more to the subject than labeling countries on a map. Davis explains earthquakes, rain forests, Atlantis and whether there are canaries on the Canary Islands. For anyone who has felt geographically ignorant ever since gas stations stopped handing out free maps.

Don't Know Much about Geography: Everything You Need to Know about the World but Never Learned. unabr. ed. Kenneth C. Davis. Read by Dick Estell. 10 CDs. (Running Time: 11 hrs. 48 mins.). 2001. audio compact disk 80.00 Books on Tape.
There is a lot more to the subject than labeling countries on a map. Davis explains earthquakes, rain forests, Atlantis & whether there are canaries on the Canary Islands. From often amusing perceptions people have had through the ages about the world & the universe to the changing map of today, Davis shows how geography is really a great crossroads of many fields; biology, meteorology, astronomy, history, economics & even politics.

Don't Know Much about History. unabr. rev. ed. Kenneth C. Davis. Read by Jeff Woodman. Told to Jonathan Davis. 14 CDs. (Running Time: 86400 sec.). (ENG.). 2005. audio compact disk 49.95 (978-0-7393-1771-6(7)) Pub: Random Audio Pubg. Dist(s): Random

Don't Know Much about History: Everything You Need to Know about American History but Never Learned. Kenneth C. Davis. Read by Dick Estell. 1999. audio compact disk 112.00 (978-0-7366-5175-2(6)) Books on Tape.

Don't Know Much about History: Everything You Need to Know about American History but Never Learned. rev. abr. ed. Kenneth C. Davis. Read by Jeff Woodman et al. 3 CDs. (Running Time: 3 hrs. 30 mins.). (Don't Know Much about Ser.). (ENG., 2003. audio compact disk 24.95 (978-0-7393-0396-2(1)) Pub: Random Audio Pubg. Dist(s): Random

Don't Know Much about History: Everything You Need to Know about American History but Never Learned. unabr. ed. Kenneth C. Davis. 14 cass. (Running Time: 21 hrs.). 2003. 80.00 (978-0-7366-9249-6(5)) Books on Tape.

Don't Know Much about History: Everything You Need to Know about American History but Never Learned. unabr. ed. Kenneth C. Davis. 14 CDs. (Running Time: 18 hrs.). 1999. audio compact disk 126.00 Books on Tape.
From the first settlements of the continent through Vietnam, Watergate & Reagan, Kenneth Davis takes listeners on a rollicking ride through 600 years of Americana. With wit, candor & fascinating facts, "Don't Know Much about History" explodes long-held misconceptions - revealing the human side of history that textbooks neglect.

Don't Know Much about History: Everything You Need to Know about American History but Never Learned. unabr. ed. Kenneth C. Davis. Read by Dick Estell. 12 cass. (Running Time: 18 hrs.). 2000. 96.00 (978-0-7366-4525-6(X), 4941) Books on Tape.
From Columbus' voyage to the clinton administration, Davis carries the reader on a rollicking ride through 600 year of Americana. With wit, candor & fascinating facts, the author explodes long-held myths & misconceptions, revealing the very human side of history that the textbooks neglect.

***Don't Know Much about History 20th Anniversary Edition: Updated & Revised.** abr. ed. Kenneth C. Davis. (ENG.). 2011. audio compact disk 25.00 (978-0-307-71491-6(8), Random AudioBks) Pub: Random Audio Pubg. Dist(s): Random

***Don't Know Much about History 20th Anniversary Edition: Updated & Revised.** unabr. ed. Kenneth C. Davis. (ENG.). 2011. audio compact disk 50.00 (978-0-307-71493-0(4), Random AudioBks) Pub: Random Audio Pubg. Dist(s): Random

Don't Know Much about Mythology. unabr. ed. Kenneth C. Davis. Read by John Lee. 14 CDs. (Running Time: 73200 sec.). (ENG.). 2005. audio compact disk 49.95 (978-0-7393-1747-1(4)) Pub: Random Audio Pubg. Dist(s): Random

Don't Know Much about Planet Earth. unabr. ed. Kenneth C. Davis. Read by Oliver Wyman. 2 vols. (Running Time: 3 hrs. 26 mins.). (Don't Know Much about Ser.). (J). (gr. 4-7). 2004. pap. bk. 29.00 (978-0-8072-0660-7(1), Listening Lib); 23.00 (978-0-8072-0578-5(8), Listening Lib) Random Audio Pubg.
Learn about the longest river, coldest desert, tallest waterfall, most powerful volcanic eruption - and much more with fascinating anecdotes about the world's most unusual places.

Don't Know Much about Space. unabr. ed. Kenneth C. Davis. Read by Oliver Wyman. 2 vols. (Running Time: 3 hrs. 28 mins.). (Don't Know Much about Ser.). (J). (gr. 4-7). 2004. pap. bk. 29.00 (978-0-8072-0661-4(X), Listening Lib); 23.00 (978-0-8072-0575-4(3), Listening Lib) Random Audio Pubg.
Discover who first charted the stars, why people believed that Earth was the center of the universe and how astronauts may lead us to become pioneers on other planets.

Don't Know Much about the Civil War. Kenneth C. Davis. Read by Dick Estell. 1999. audio compact disk 112.00 (978-0-7366-6219-2(7)) Books on Tape.

***Don't Know Much about the Civil War.** abr. ed. Kenneth C. Davis. Read by Dick Estell. (ENG.). 2011. audio compact disk 14.99 (978-0-307-93290-7(7), Random AudioBks) Pub: Random Audio Pubg. Dist(s): Random

Don't Know Much about the Civil War: Everything You Need to Know about America's Greatest Conflict but Never Learned. abr. ed. Kenneth C. Davis. 4 cass. (Running Time: 6 hrs.). 2000. 30.00 (978-0-8072-8813-9(6), Listening Lib) Random Audio Pubg.
This fresh look at America's greatest conflict will dispel all those misconceptions you acquired by watching "Gone With the Wind". Davis has a genius for bringing history to life, sorting out the players, the politics and the key events.

Don't Know Much about the Civil War: Everything You Need to Know about America's Greatest Conflict but Never Learned. unabr. ed. Kenneth C. Davis. Read by Dick Estell. 12 cass. (Running Time: 18 hrs.). 1999. 96.00 (5017); 96.00 (978-0-7366-4508-9(X), 5017) Books on Tape.

Don't Know Much about the Civil War: Everything You Need to Know about America's Greatest Conflict but Never Learned. unabr. ed. Kenneth C. Davis. Read by Dick Estell. 14 CDs. (Running Time: 21 hrs.). 2001. audio compact disk 112.00 Books on Tape.
Brings history to life, sorts out the players, the politics & the key events - Harpers Ferry, Shiloh, Gettysburg, Emancipation, Reconstruction. Brings to life the people - from Dred Scott to Abraham Lincoln.

Don't Know Much about the Civil War: Everything You Need to Know about America's Greatest Conflict but Never Learned. unabr. ed. Kenneth C. Davis. Read by Dick Estell. 12 cass. (Running Time: 18 hrs.). 1999. 96.00 Books on Tape.

Don't Know Much about the Universe. Kenneth C. Davis. Read by Oliver Wyman. 2001. 56.00 (978-0-7366-7642-7(2)) Books on Tape.

Don't Leave It to Beaver: Prov. 22:6. Ed Young. 1994. 4.95 (978-0-7417-2019-1(1), 1019) Win Walk.

Don't Leave Jesus off Your Christmas List. Contrib. by Johnathan Crumpton & J. Daniel Smith. Prod. by Ed Kee. (ENG.). 2008. audio compact disk 24.99 (978-5-557-38255-7(0), Brentwood-Benson Music) Brentwood Music.

Don't Leave Too Much Room for the Holy Spirit (an Essay from Things I've Learned from Women Who've Dumped Me) abr. ed. Tom McCarthy. Read by Tom McCarthy. Ed. by Ben Karlin. (Running Time: 15 mins.). (ENG.). 2008. 1.98 (978-1-60024-339-4(8)) Pub: Hachet Audio. Dist(s): HachBkGrp

Don't Let Life Lick the Red off Your Candy: Is Your Life Happening Or Are You Making It Happen? (Running Time: 240 mins.). (Don't Let Life Lick The Red Off Your Candy). 2001. 39.95 (978-0-9716019-0-1(9), Div Career Pot); audio compact disk 49.95 (978-0-9716019-1-8(7), Div Career Pot) C P M Enter Inc.

Don't Let Me Go: What My Daughter Taught Me about the Journey Every Parent Must Make. David W. Pierce. (ENG.). 2009. audio compact disk 26.99 (978-1-934384-34-3(8)) Pub: Treasure Pub. Dist(s): STL Dist NA

Don't Let the Enemy Steal Your Joy. Short Stories. Joel Osteen. 1 Cass. (Running Time: 30 Mins.). 2002. 6.00 (978-1-59349-148-2(4), JA0148) J Osteen.

Don't Let the Pigeon Drive the Bus! Narrated by Mo Willems & Jon Scieszka. Music by Peter List. 1 CD. (Running Time: 5 mins.). (J). (ps-1). 2009. bk. 29.95 (978-0-545-13453-8(6)); audio compact disk 12.95 (978-0-545-13443-9(9)) Weston Woods.

Don't Let's Go to the Dogs Tonight: An African Childhood. unabr. ed. Alexandra Fuller. Narrated by Lisette Lecat. 7 cass. (Running Time: 10 hrs. 15 mins.). 2002. 68.00 (978-1-4025-1869-0(2)) Recorded Bks.

Don't Let's Go to the Dogs Tonight: An African Childhood. unabr. ed. Alexandra Fuller. Narrated by Lisette Lecat. 7 cass. (Running Time: 10 hrs. 15 min.). 2004. 37.95 (978-1-4025-1870-6(6)) Recorded Bks.

Don't Let's Go to the Dogs Tonight: An African Childhood. unabr. ed. Alexandra Fuller. Narrated by Lisette Lecat. 9 CDs. (Running Time: 10 hrs. 15 mins.). 2004. audio compact disk 24.99 (978-1-4025-9040-5(7), 01662) Recorded Bks.
Critics around the world hail Don't Let's Go to the Dogs Tonight, an unflinching memoir of a child growing up during the 1970s Rhodesian Civil War. Author Alexandra Fuller shares the remarkable story of a family clinging to a harsh landscape and the dying tenets of colonialism. At the tender age of two, white Alexandra-the daughter of hardworking, yet strikingly unconventional English-bred immigrants-arrives in predominantly black Africa. Shaped by the uncompromising surroundings, she learns to move through life with a hardy resilience. As Rhodesia slowly becomes Zimbabwe, Alexandra survives harrowing family tragedies, including the deaths of siblings, and outbursts of bloody revolution.

Don't Limit God: Cd Album. 2009. audio compact disk 30.00 (978-1-59548-132-0(X)) A Wommack.

Don't Look Back. Karin Fossum. Read by David Rantoul. 6 cass. (Inspector Sejer Mystery Ser.). 54.95 (978-0-7927-3350-8(9), CSL 706); audio compact disk 79.95 (978-0-7927-3351-5(7), SLD 706) AudioGO.

Don't Look Back. Swami Jyotirmayananda. 1 cass. (Running Time: 45 min.). 1990. 10.00 Yoga Res Foun.

Don't Look Back. Amanda Quick, pseud. 8 cass. (Running Time: 12 hrs.). 2002. 64.00 (978-0-7366-8675-4(4)) Books on Tape.
Two lovers Lavinia Lake & Tobias March team up to solve the murder of a beautiful wife whose ancient and mysterious cameo has gone missing.

Don't Look Back. unabr. ed. Amanda Quick, pseud. 10 CDs. (Running Time: 12 hrs.). 2002. audio compact disk 80.00 (978-0-7366-8679-2(7)) Books on Tape.
An intrigue mystery involving an ancient cameo bracelet, known as the Blue Medusa, said to possess terrifying powers. Lavinia Lake and Tobias March join forces again, romantically and intellectually, to solve the murder of the beautiful wife of an old family friend. When she plans to leave her husband, the lovely Celeste Hudson is tragically cut down. The only evidence in the crime is a gentleman's cravat wound around her neck - small compensation for the strange and priceless bracelet that may have been snatched from her wrist as she drew her last breath. Now Lake and March must find both the killer and the missing relic.

Don't Look Back Travel: Albuquerque to Flagstaff. Philip B. Ebersole. Read by Gil Hodges & Eldoo Miller. 2 cass. 1996. bk. (978-0-9656551-0-1(5)) Dont Look Back.
New Mexico & Arizona & some of the sights along the route.

Don't Look Behind You, unabr. ed. Lois Duncan. Narrated by Alyssa Bresnahan. 5 pieces. (Running Time: 6 hrs. 15 mins.). (gr. 10 up). 1998. 44.00 (978-0-7887-2075-8(9), 95428E7) Recorded Bks.
When 11th grader April learns that her father has been working undercover for the FBI, she is shocked. But when she is told that she & her family must take on new identities & move to a new home under the Federal Witness Security Program, she feels everything familiar slipping away.

Don't Look Down. abr. ed. Jennifer Crusie, pseud & Bob Mayer. Read by Patrick G. Lawlor & Renée Raudman. (Running Time: 6 hrs.). 2007. audio compact disk 14.99 (978-1-59600-811-3(3), 9781596008113, BCD Value Price) Brilliance Audio.
Please enter a Synopsis.

Don't Look Down. unabr. ed. Jennifer Crusie, pseud & Bob Mayer. Read by Patrick G. Lawlor & Renée Raudman. (Running Time: 11 hrs.). 2006. 39.25 (978-1-59710-111-0(7), 9781597101110, BADLE); 24.95 (978-1-59710-110-3(9), 9781597101103, BAD); 87.25 (978-1-59355-371-5(4), 9781593553715, BrilAudUnabridg) Brilliance Audio.

Don't Look Down. unabr. ed. Jennifer Crusie, pseud & Bob Mayer. Read by Renée Raudman & Patrick G. Lawlor. 10 CDs. (Running Time: 39600 sec.). 2006. audio compact disk 36.95 (978-1-59355-373-9(0), 9781593553739) Brilliance Audio.

Don't Look Down. unabr. ed. Jennifer Crusie, pseud & Bob Mayer. Read by Patrick G. Lawlor & Renée Raudman. (Running Time: 39600 sec.). 2006. audio compact disk 102.25 (978-1-59355-374-6(9), 9781593553746, BriAudCD Unabrid); audio compact disk 39.25 (978-1-59335-852-5(0), 9781593358525, Brinc Audio MP3 Lib) Brilliance Audio.

Don't Look Down. unabr. ed. Jennifer Crusie, pseud & Bob Mayer. Read by Renée Raudman & Patrick G. Lawlor. (Running Time: 39600 sec.). 2006. audio compact disk 24.95 (978-1-59335-718-4(4), 9781593357184, Brilliance MP3) Brilliance Audio.

Don't Look Now & the Birds & Other Stories. unabr. ed. Short Stories. Daphne Du Maurier. Narrated by Barbara Rosenblat & Margo Sinclair. 7 cass. (Running Time: 10 hrs. 30 mins.). 1989. 60.00 (978-1-55690-150-8(X), 89510E7) Recorded Bks.
Collection includes: "Don't Look Now," "The Birds," "The Apple Tree," "The Blue Lenses," "Not after Midnight" & "The Alibi.".

Don't Look Now or Ever. Anne Schraff. Narrated by Larry A. McKeever. (Standing Tall 1 Mystery Ser.). (J). 2000. audio compact disk 14.95 (978-1-58659-266-0(1)) Artesian.

Don't Look Now or Ever. unabr. ed. Anne Schraff. Narrated by Larry A. McKeever. 1 cass. (Running Time: 40 min.). (Standing Tall Mysteries Ser.). (J). 2000. 10.95 (978-1-58659-094-9(4), 54134) Artesian.

Don't Look Twice. unabr. ed. Andrew Gross. (Running Time: 12 hrs. 0 mins.). (ENG.). 2009. 29.95 (978-1-4332-7904-1(5)); 72.95 (978-1-4332-7902-7(9)); audio compact disk 90.00 (978-1-4332-7903-4(7)) Blckstn Audio.

Don't Look Twice. unabr. ed. Andrew Gross. Read by Christian Hoff. 2009. audio compact disk 34.99 (978-0-06-171265-4(5), Harper Audio) HarperCollins Pubs.

***Don't Look Twice.** unabr. ed. Andrew Gross. Read by Christian Hoff. (ENG.). 2009. (978-0-06-180527-1(0), Harper Audio); (978-0-06-180528-8(9), Harper Audio) HarperCollins Pubs.

Don't Make a Black Woman Take off Her Earrings: Madea's Uninhibited Commentaries on Love & Life. unabr. ed. Tyler Perry. 4 CDs. (Running Time: 5 hrs.). (ENG.). (gr. 8). 2007. audio compact disk 19.95 (978-0-14-305872-4(X), PengAudBks) Penguin Grp USA.

Dont Miss the Bus! Steering Your Child to Success in School. Mary Ann Smialek. 2005. audio compact disk 29.95 (978-1-57886-212-2(4)) Pub: Row & LittleEduc. Dist(s): Rowman

Don't Miss Your Life! An Uncommon Guide to Living with Freedom, Laughter, & Grace. unabr. ed. Charlene Ann Baumbich. Narrated by Charlene Ann Baumbich. (Running Time: 7 hrs. 50 mins. 6 sec.). (ENG.).

2009. 19.59 (978-1-60814-525-6(5)); audio compact disk 27.99 (978-1-59859-585-7(7)) Oasis Audio.

Don't Monkey with Murder. unabr. ed. E. X. Ferrars. Read by Raymond Sawyer. 6 cass. (Running Time: 9 hrs.). 2001. 54.95 (978-0-7531-0916-8(6), 000702) Pub: ISIS Audio GBR. Dist(s): Ulverscroft US

Don't Monkey with Murder. unabr. ed. E. X. Ferrars. Read by Raymond Sawyer. 7 CDs. (Running Time: 18 hrs. 30 mins.). 2001. audio compact disk 69.95 (978-0-7531-0962-5(X), 10962x) Pub: ISIS Audio GBR. Dist(s): Ulverscroft US

Don't Mourn - Organize! Songs of Labor Songwriter Joe Hill. Perf. by Billy Bragg et al. Anno. by Lori E. Taylor. 1 cass. (Running Time: 54 min.). 1993. (0-9307-400260-9307-40026-2-9); audio compact disk (0-9307-40026-2-9) Smithsonian Folkways.

Tribute to the Industrial Workers of the World songwriter & activist Joe Hill.

Don't Panic. Steck-Vaughn Staff. (J). 2003. (978-0-7398-8414-0(X)) SteckVau.

Don't Panic; Cancer, the Lord & Me. Agnes Hamm. 1 cass. 1985. 7.95 (TAH153) Alba Hse Comns.

Account of one Christian's struggle with six bouts of cancer that put her faith & endurance to the test.

Don't Panic Self-Help Kit: The Homework Guide to Conquering Your Fears. R. Reid Wilson. Read by R. Reid Wilson. 4 cass. (Running Time: 4 hrs.). 1997. bk. 45.95 Set, incl. skill cards & recording forms. (978-0-9630683-2-3(6)) Pathway Systs.

Self-help guide on panic attacks.

Don't Point That Thing at Me. Kyril Bonfiglioli. Read by Simon Prebble. (Running Time: 23400 sec.). 2005. 44.95 (978-0-7861-3786-2(X)); audio compact disk 55.00 (978-0-7861-7545-1(1)) Blckstn Audio.

Don't Point That Thing at Me. unabr. ed. Kyril Bonfiglioli. (Running Time: 23400 sec.). (Charlie Mortdecai Mysteries Ser.). 2005. audio compact disk 29.95 (978-0-7861-7822-3(1)) Blckstn Audio.

Don't Point That Thing at Me. unabr. ed. Kyril Bonfiglioli. Read by Simon Prebble. 5 cass. (Running Time: 6 hrs. 30 mins.). (YA). 2006. 24.95 (978-0-7861-4420-4(3)); audio compact disk 25.95 (978-0-7861-7391-4(2)) Blckstn Audio.

Don't Pull on Superman's Cape: Acts 22:1-23:11. Ed Young. 2000. 4.95 (978-0-7417-2249-2(6), 1249) Win Walk.

Don't Push the River. Richard Rohr. 1 cass. (Running Time: 45 min.). 8.95 (AA2851) Credence Commun.

Nothing inside us is as bad as our avoidance of it. When you understand forgiveness, you understand everything. But we need to forgive ourselves as well as others. Only in Faith can we do that. Rohr explains why.

Don't Quit! Stan Crippen. 1 cass. 9.95 (978-1-57734-287-8(9), 06005802) Covenant Comms.

Using failure as a stepping stone to success.

Don't Say I Didn't Warn You: Kids, Carbs, & the Coming Hormonal Apocalypse. unabr. ed. Anita Renfroe. Read by Anita Renfroe. 2009. audio compact disk 29.99 (978-1-4013-9416-5(7), Hyperion Audio) Pub: Hyperion. Dist(s): HarperCollins Pubs

Don't Send a Resume: And Other Contrarian Rules to Help Land a Great Job. abr. rev. ed. Jeffrey J. Fox. Read by Jeffrey J. Fox. 3 CDs. (Running Time: 3 hrs. 0 mins. 0 sec.). (ENG.). 2001. audio compact disk 26.00 (978-1-55927-672-6(X)) Pub: Macmill Audio. Dist(s): Macmillan

Don't Shoot the Dog! The New Art of Teaching & Training. Karen Pryor. Read by Karen Pryor. 2006. audio compact disk 39.95 (978-1-890948-22-1(5)) Sunshine MA.

***Don't Sing at the Table: Life Lessons from My Grandmothers.** unabr. ed. Adriana Trigiani. (ENG.). 2010. (978-0-06-206771-5(0), Harper Audio) HarperCollins Pubs.

Don't Stop Now!, Level 1. Philip Prowse. Contrib. by Philip Prowse. (Running Time: 50 mins.). (Cambridge English Readers Ser.). (ENG., 2005. 9.45 (978-0-521-60565-6(2)) Cambridge U Pr.

Don't Stop the Carnival. unabr. collector's ed. Herman Wouk. Read by Michael Prichard. 10 cass. (Running Time: 15 hrs.). 1981. 80.00 (978-0-7366-0404-8(9), 1380) Books on Tape.

Norman Paperman, a successful & well-known Broadway publicity agent, has long dreamed of escaping his high-pressured Manhattan life. In a fit of bravado, he chucks it all & buys an old hotel on tiny, primitive, lush Amerigo Island.

Don't Sweat Guide to Your Finances. Don't Sweat Press Editors. 3 CDs. (Running Time: 4 Hrs.). 2004. audio compact disk 23.95 (978-1-59316-032-6(1)) Listen & Live.

Finances are often confusing and frustrating. This easy-to follow guidebook will help readers plan, save, and spend. The key is budgeting without obsessing over every bill and expense.

Don't Sweat Guide to Your Job Search. Don't Sweat Press Editors. 3 CDs. (Running Time: 4 Hrs). 2004. audio compact disk 23.95 (978-1-59316-031-9(3)) Listen & Live.

Don't Sweat It! Richard Carlson's Low Stress Strategies for Success. Richard Carlson. 2 cass. 1998. 16.95 (978-1-55977-935-7(7)) CareerTrack Pubns.

Don't Sweat the Small Stuff see Ne Vous Noyez Pas dans une Verre D'Eau

Don't Sweat the Small Stuff see Ne Vous Noyez Pas dans un Verre d'Eau

Don't Sweat the Small Stuff... And It's All Small Stuff - Simple Ways to Keep the Little Things from Taking over Your Life. abr. ed. Richard Carlson. Read by Richard Carlson. 2006. 10.95 (978-0-7435-6217-1(8)) Pub: S&S Audio. Dist(s): S and S Inc

Don't Sweat the Small Stuff... And It's All Small Stuff - Simple Ways to Keep the Little Things from Taking over Your Life. unabr. ed. Richard Carlson. Read by Richard Carlson. 5 CDs. (Running Time: 50 hrs. 0 mins. 0 sec.). 2005. audio compact disk 29.95 (978-0-7435-4065-0(4)) Pub: S&S Audio. Dist(s): S and S Inc

THE #1 NEW YORK TIMES BESTSELLER UNABRIDGED AND ON CD Don't Sweat the Small Stuff...and It's All Small Stuff tells you how to keep from letting the little things in life drive you crazy. Richard Carlson reveals ways to calm down in the midst of your incredibly hurried, stress-filled life. Learn how to put things into perspective by making small daily changes, including advice like "Choose your battles wisely"; "Remind yourself that when you die, your 'in' box won't be empty"; and "Make peace with imperfection". With Don't Sweat the Small Stuff...you'll also learn how to: • Live in the present moment • Let others have the glory at times • Lower your tolerance to stress • Trust your intuitions • Live each day as it might be your last With gentle, supportive suggestions, Dr. Carlson reveals ways to make your actions more peaceful and caring, while making your life more calm and stress-free.

Don't Sweat the Small Stuff... And It's All Small Stuff - Simple Ways to Keep the Little Things from Taking over Your Life. unabr. ed. Richard Carlson. Read by Richard Carlson. 2006. 17.95 (978-0-7435-6129-7(5)) Pub: S&S Audio. Dist(s): S and S Inc

Don't Sweat the Small Stuff... And It's All Small Stuff - Simple Ways to Keep the Little Things from Taking over Your Life. unabr. ed. Richard Carlson. Read by Richard Carlson. 2 CDs. (Running Time: 13 hrs. 0 mins. 0 sec.). 1999. audio compact disk 18.00 (978-0-671-31567-2(6), Sound Ideas) Pub: S&S Audio. Dist(s): S and S Inc

Reveals how to calm down in the midst of today's hurried & stressful world.

Don't Sweat the Small Stuff about Money: Spiritual & practical ways to create abundance & more fun in your Life. abr. ed. Richard Carlson. Read by Richard Carlson. 2006. 10.95 (978-0-7435-6216-4(X)) Pub: S&S Audio. Dist(s): S and S Inc

Don't Sweat the Small Stuff Collection. abr. ed. Richard Carlson. Read by Richard Carlson. 3 cass. (Running Time: 4 hrs. 30 mins.). 1998. 45.00 (978-0-671-71680-6(8), Audioworks) S&S Audio.

Includes: "Don't Sweat the Small Stuff... & It's All Small Stuff," "Don't Worry, Make Money" & "Don't Sweat the Small Stuff with Your Family.".

Don't Sweat the Small Stuff for Men: Simple Ways to Minimize Stress in a Competitive World. abr. ed. Richard Carlson. 2 cass. (Running Time: 3 hrs.). 2001. 17.98 (978-1-58621-184-4(6)) Hachet Audio.

Don't Sweat the Small Stuff for Women: Simple & Practical Ways to Do What Matters Most & Find Time for You. abr. ed. Richard Carlson. 2 cass. (Running Time: 3 hrs.). 2001. 17.98 (978-1-58621-185-1(4)) Hachet Audio.

Don't Take My Grief Away: What to Do When You Lose a Loved One. Doug Manning. Read by Doug Manning. 1 cass. (Running Time: 60 min.). 9.95 HarperCollins Pubs.

Don't Take My Grief Away: What to Do When You Lose a Loved One. abr. ed. Doug Manning. 2 cass. (Running Time: 3 hrs.). 1998. bk. 17.95 (978-1-57453-186-2(7)) Audio Lit.

Don't Take My Grief Away addresses the painful, often disorienting aftermath of the death of a loved one. It covers such areas as the choice of a minister, family dynamics during the time of bereavement, & personalizing the funeral service. Thoughtful advice for understanding & accepting one's feelings as the beginning of rebuilding one's life is also provided.

Don't Take My Grief Away from Me, Vol. 1. Doug Manning. 2 cass,. (Running Time: 1 hr. 28 min.). 1986. 13.95 (978-1-892785-15-2(3)) In-Sight Bks Inc.

Author utilizes his best-selling book by the same title to help individuals walk through the bereavement journey.

Don't Take Our Word for It! Godfrey Harris. Read by Tom Clarke-Hill. 2 cass. (Running Time: 2 hrs.). 1998. Set. Americas Group.

Don't Take Our Word for It! Everything You Need to Know about Making Word of Mouth Advertising Work for You. Godfrey Harris. Read by Tom Clarke-Hill. 2 cass. (Running Time: 2 hrs.). 2000. 17.95 (978-0-935047-26-4(3)) Pub: Americas Group. Dist(s): Penton Overseas

The encyclopedia of word of mouth advertising: how it works, hundreds of ready-to-go ideas for every type of business & basic techniques to use in designing your own word of mouth advertising program.

***Don't Take the Bait: Responding Right to the Trap of Offense.** Jim Hammond. 2010. audio compact disk 18.00 (978-1-57399-461-3(8)) Mac Hammond.

Don't Take Your Elephant to School. unabr. ed. Steve Turner. 1 CD. (Running Time: 37 mins.). (J). (gr. k-4). 2007. audio compact disk 9.95 (978-1-4056-5725-9(1), Chivers Child Audio) AudioGO.

Don't Tell a Soul. David Rosenfelt. 2008. audio compact disk 29.95 (978-1-59316-138-5(7)) Listen & Live.

Don't Tell Me to Suffer Patiently! Richard Rohr. Read by Richard Rohr. 1 cass. (Running Time: 70 min.). 1992. 9.95 (978-7-900781-87-1(0), AA2530) Credence Commun.

Sometimes spiritual depth comes with wrestling with mystery instead of patient suffering.

Don't tell mum I work on the Rigs. Paul Carter. Read by Paul Carter. (Running Time: 4 hrs. 20 mins.). 2009. 59.99 (978-1-74214-200-5(1), 9781742142005) Pub: Bolinda Pubng AUS. Dist(s): Bolinda Pub Inc

***Don't tell mum I work on the Rigs.** unabr. ed. Paul Carter. Read by Paul Carter. (Running Time: 4 hrs. 20 mins.). 2010. 43.95 (978-1-74214-664-5(3), 9781742146645) Pub: Bolinda Pubng AUS. Dist(s): Bolinda Pub Inc

Don't Tell Mum I Work on the Rigs: She Thinks I'm a Piano Player in a Whorehouse. unabr. ed. Paul Carter. Read by Paul Carter. (Running Time: 15600 sec.). 2008. audio compact disk 57.95 (978-1-921334-60-3(6), 9781921334603) Pub: Bolinda Pubng AUS. Dist(s): Bolinda Pub Inc

Don't Tell Mummy, unabr. ed. Tom B. Stone. Narrated by Jeff Woodman. 2 cass. (Running Time: 2 hrs. 30 mins.). (Graveyard School Ser.: No. 16). (gr. 3-7). 2001. 19.00 (978-0-7887-0713-1(2), 94889E7) Recorded Bks.

An adventure of spooky danger & grisly humor centers around a school so weird that its students are dying to go to class.

Don't Think of an Elephant! Know Your Values & Frame the Debate: The Essential Guide for Progressives. George Lakoff. Narrated by George Wilson. 2005. audio compact disk 14.99 (978-1-4193-3978-3(8)) Recorded Bks.

***Don't Throw Away Tomorrow.** unabr. ed. Robert H. Schuller. Read by Tim Jerome. (ENG.). 2005. (978-0-06-083510-1(9), Harper Audio); (978-0-06-083509-5(5), Harper Audio) HarperCollins Pubs.

Don't Touch That Dial. unabr. ed. Steven Thomas Oney. Composed by Mark Birmingham. Photos by David Ellsworth. 1 CD. (Running Time: 1 hr.). (YA). (gr. 3-12). 2003. audio compact disk 12.50 (978-0-9745668-4-9(5)) Cape Cod Radio.

A young boy is locked in a safe and Captain Underhill must crack the combination in time.

***Don't Vote: It Just Encourages the Bastards.** unabr. ed. P. J. O'Rourke. Read by Christopher Lane. (Running Time: 8 hrs.). 2010. 24.99 (978-1-4418-8555-5(2), 9781441885555, Brilliance MP3); 39.97 (978-1-4418-8556-2(0), 9781441885562, Brlnc Audio MP3 Lib); audio compact disk 24.99 (978-1-4418-8553-1(6), 9781441885531, Bril Audio CD Unabri); audio compact disk 59.97 (978-1-4418-8554-8(4), 9781441885548, BriAudCD Unabrid) Brilliance Audio.

***Don't Vote: It Just Encourages the Bastards.** unabr. ed. P. J. O'Rourke. (Running Time: 8 hrs.). 2010. 24.99 (978-1-4418-8557-9(9), 9781441885579, BAD); 39.97 (978-1-4418-8558-6(7), 9781441885586, BADLE) Brilliance Audio.

Don't Wait. Contrib. by Adie. Prod. by Adam Watts et al. 2006. audio compact disk 16.99 (978-5-558-21033-0(8)) BEC Recordings.

Don't Wake up the Baby see Dolces Canciones de Cuna Para los Ninos Queridos

Don't Walk in the Long Grass. unabr. ed. Tenniel Evans. Narrated by Tenniel Evans. 5 cass. (Running Time: 7 hrs.). 2000. 46.00 (978-1-84197-057-8(3), H1049E7) Recorded Bks.

To a boy from a mud & wattle house in the Kenyan wilderness, a British winter was an alarming change. At 10, Tenniel replaced running barefoot through snake-infested grass with a British education. Instead of the exotic, tropical forests & plants were an imposing rectory & an intimidating school. Tenniel had thought of Britain as home, but soon he missed Africa, his family & the old, carefree life. He didn't return for 20 years. In Britain, the climate wasn't the only major shock. Four inquisitive cousins, boring butterflies, wearing shoes & frequent washes in freezing water were, if strange, at least intriguingly different.

Don't Waste Your Life. unabr. ed. John Piper. Read by Lloyd James. (Running Time: 23400 sec.). 2007. audio compact disk & audio compact disk 45.00 (978-1-4332-1285-7(4)) Blckstn Audio.

Don't Waste Your Life. unabr. ed. John Piper. 6 CDs. (Running Time: 6 hrs. 15 mins. 0 sec.). (ENG.). 2006. lp 19.98 (978-1-59644-372-3(3), Hovel Audio) christianaud.

John Piper writes, "I will tell you what a tragedy is. I will show you how to waste your life. Consider this story from the February 1998 Reader's Digest: A couple "took early retirement from their jobs in the Northeast five years ago, when he was 59 and she was 51. Now they live in Punta Gorda, Florida, where they cruise on their 30-foot trawler, play softball and collect shells. . . ." Picture them before Christ at the great day of judgment: "Look, Lord. See my shells." That is a tragedy."God created us to live with a single passion: to joyfully display his supreme excellence in all the spheres of life. The wasted life is the life without this passion. God calls us to pray and think and dream and plan and work not to be made much of, but to make much of him in every part of our lives."? This book is a passionate call for this generation to make their lives count for eternity. John Piper acknowledges that the risks for those who seek to accomplish something in life - risks in relationships for the sake of righteousness and authenticity, risks with money for the cause of the Gospel, and risks in witnessing to the truth and beauty of Christ. Readers will find their passion for the cross of Christ enlarged as a result of reading this book.

***Don't Waste Your Life.** unabr. ed. John Piper. Narrated by Lloyd James. (ENG.). 2006. 14.98 (978-1-59644-373-0(1), Hovel Audio) christianaud.

Don't Waste Your Life. unabr. ed. John Piper. Narrated by Lloyd James. 1 MP3CD. (Running Time: 6 hrs. 15 mins. 0 sec.). (ENG.). 2006. 24.98 (978-1-59644-374-7(X), Hovel Audio) christianaud.

Don't Worry! Cast Your Cares on God. Gloria Copeland. 1 cass. 1992. 5.00 (978-0-88114-907-4(1)) K Copeland Pubns.

Living victoriously over worry.

Don't You Dare Read This, Mrs. Dunphrey. unabr. ed. Margaret Peterson Haddix. Narrated by Christina Moore. 2 cass. (Running Time: 3 hrs.). (J). (gr. 2). 1997. bk. 39.75 (978-0-7887-1251-7(9), 40497) Recorded Bks.

When 16-year old Tish's life is turned upside down, she finds that her dreaded journal assignment becomes her lifeline. An important message for young victims of abuse: "sometimes you need to ask for help".

Don't You Dare Read This, Mrs. Dunphrey. unabr. ed. Margaret Peterson Haddix. Narrated by Christina Moore. 2 cass. (Running Time: 3 hrs.). (YA). (gr. 2). 1997. Rental 8.50 Recorded Bks.

Don't You Dare Read This, Mrs. Dunphrey, unabr. ed. Margaret Peterson Haddix. Narrated by Alyssa Bresnahan. 2 pieces. (Running Time: 3 hrs.). (gr. 7 up). 1997. 19.00 (978-0-7887-1100-8(8), 95093E&) Recorded Bks.

Don't You Forget about Me: A Novel. unabr. ed. Jancee Dunn. (Running Time: 7.5 hrs. 0 mins.). 2008. 29.95 (978-1-4332-1571-1(3)); 26.95 (978-1-4332-1569-8(1)); 54.95 (978-1-4332-1567-4(5)); audio compact disk 26.95 (978-1-4332-1570-4(5)); audio compact disk 60.00 (978-1-4332-1568-1(3)) Blckstn Audio.

Don't You Know There's a War On. unabr. ed. 3 cass. (Running Time: 3 hrs. 33 mins.). 2003. 28.00 (978-1-4025-3231-3(8)) Recorded Bks.

Don't You Wanna Go? Composed by Gerald Crabb. Contrib. by Russell Mauldin. 2007. audio compact disk 24.98 (978-5-557-49188-4(0), Word Music) Word Enter.

Donut Forget Bible Story Lessons: 52 Learn & Sing Lessons. (J). (ps-3). pap. bk. 99.99 (978-0-7847-0999-3(8), 42059) Standard Pub.

Donut Man: the Donut All Stars/at the Zoo. Created by Integrity Music. (J). (ps-3). 2004. 9.99 (978-5-559-50020-1(8)) Integrity Music.

Dooby Dooby Moo. Doreen Cronin. Illus. by Betsy Lewin. Narrated by Randy Travis. 1 cass. (Running Time: 12 mins.). (J). (ps-3). 2007. bk. 24.95 (978-0-545-04283-3(6)) Weston Woods.

When Duck finds out about a talent show at the county fair, he and the animals on the farm start rehearsing. While Farmer Brown tries to figure out what the animals are up to, Duck is determined they will enter the contest and win!.

Dooby Dooby Moo. Doreen Cronin. Illus. by Betsy Lewin. Narrated by Randy Travis. 1 CD. (Running Time: 12 mins.). (J). (ps-3). 2007. bk. 29.95 (978-0-545-04281-9(X)) Weston Woods.

Dooley Fagan. Barbara O'Donnell. 2001. audio compact disk 15.00 (978-0-89914-513-6(2)) Third Party Pub.

***Doolin Waves.** Gerry Shannon. (ENG.). 1992. 11.95 (978-0-8023-7073-0(X)) Pub: Clo Iar-Chonnachta IRL. Dist(s): Dufour

Doom Brigade. abr. ed. Margaret Weis & Don Perrin. Read by Denis De Boisblanc. 2 cass. (DragonLance: Vol. 1). 1998. 17.95 Set. (978-1-55935-218-5(3)) Soundelux.

Spin-off from the dramatic conclusion to "Dragons of Summer Flame".

Doom Stone, unabr. ed. Paul Zindel. Narrated by Simon Prebble. 3 pieces. (Running Time: 3 hrs. 45 mins.). (gr. 6 up). 1998. 27.00 (978-0-7887-1921-9(1), 95342E7) Recorded Bks.

Stonehenge harbors a murderous beast that has killed several people & attacked fifteen-year-old Jackson's anthropologist aunt. He must solve the riddle of the stone before the monster strikes again.

Doom Stone, Set unabr. ed. Paul Zindel. Read by Simon Prebble. 3 cass. (Running Time: 3 hr. 45 mn.). (YA). (gr. 7). 1998. 40.20 HMWK SET . (978-0-7887-1949-3(1), 40656); 97.30 CLASS SET . (978-0-7887-2749-8(4), 46167) Recorded Bks.

Doomed Megalopolis: Soundtrack. 1 CD. 2003. audio compact disk 14.98 (978-1-57813-381-9(5), CDM/001, ADV Music) A D Vision.

Doomed Oasis, unabr. ed. Hammond Innes. Narrated by Jack Foreman. 8 cass. (Running Time: 11 hrs.). 1981. 70.00 (978-1-55690-151-5(8), 81040E7) Recorded Bks.

David Whitaker sets out to track his mysterious father across the Arabian deserts.

Doomed Oasis. unabr. collector's ed. Hammond Innes. Read by Jack Hrkach. 8 cass. (Running Time: 12 hrs.). 1984. 64.00 (978-0-7366-0855-8(9), 1806) Books on Tape.

Charles Whitaker is a Welshman who forsakes his native country for the deserts of Araby. Adapting quickly to this hostile terrain, he soon becomes more Bedouin.

Doomed Planet. abr. ed. L. Ron Hubbard. 2 cass. (Running Time: 3 hrs.). (Mission Earth Ser.: Vol. 10). 2002. 15.95 (978-1-59212-066-6(0)) Gala Pr LLC.

Doomsayer, Vol.. I. unabr. ed. Jerry Ahern. Read by Charlie O'Dowd. 2 vols. 2003. (978-1-58807-815-5(9)) Am Pubng Inc.

Doomsayer, Vol.. II. Jerry Ahern. Read by Charlie O'Dowd. 2 vols. No. 4. 2004. (978-1-58807-816-2(7)) Am Pubng Inc.

Doomsayer, Vol.. II. unabr. ed. Jerry Ahern. Read by Charlie O'Dowd. 2 cass. (Running Time: 3 hrs.). (Survivalist Ser.: No. 4). 2004. 18.00 (978-1-58807-307-5(6)) Am Pubng Inc.

Doomsday Book, unabr. ed. Connie Willis. Narrated by Jenny Sterlin. 18 cass. (Running Time: 26 hrs. 30 mins.). 2000. 149.00 (978-0-7887-4415-0(1), 96115E7) Recorded Bks.
The author takes listeners on a trip through time to discover the things that make us more human. Deftly juggling stories from the 14th & 21st centuries, she weaves action into insightful examination of the things that connect human beings to each other.

Doomsday Horizon. Michael D. Cooper. Read by Carol Eason. 2 cass. (Running Time: 3 hrs.). (Starman Ser.: No. 9). 2004. 18.00 (978-1-58807-482-9(X)) Am Pubng Inc.

Doomsday Key. unabr. ed. James Rollins. Read by Peter Jay Fernandez. 11 CDs. (Running Time: 13 hrs. 30 mins.). (Sigma Force Ser.: Bk. 6). 2009. audio compact disk 39.99 (978-0-06-177452-2(9), Harper Audio) HarperCollins Pubs.

***Doomsday Key.** unabr. ed. James Rollins. Narrated by Peter Jay Fernandez. 1 Playaway. (Running Time: 14 hrs. 30 mins.). 2009. 64.75 (978-1-4407-2719-1(8)); 92.75 (978-1-4407-2716-0(3)); audio compact disk 123.75 (978-1-4407-2717-7(1)) Recorded Bks.

***Doomsday Key.** unabr. ed. James Rollins. Read by Peter Jay Fernandez. 2009. (978-0-06-190223-9(3), Harper Audio); (978-0-06-190221-5(7), Harper Audio) HarperCollins Pubs.

***Doomsday Key.** unabr. collector's ed. James Rollins. Narrated by Peter Jay Fernandez. 11 CDs. (Running Time: 14 hrs. 30 mins.). 2009. audio compact disk 56.95 (978-1-4407-2718-4(X)) Recorded Bks.

***Doomsday Key Unabridged Low Price Cd: A Novel.** unabr. ed. James Rollins. 2010. 19.99 (978-0-06-201091-9(3), Harper Audio) HarperCollins Pubs.

Doomsday Kiss. unabr. collector's ed. Robert Davis. Read by Michael Prichard. 11 cass. (Running Time: 16 hrs. 30 min.). 1999. 88.00 (978-0-7366-4549-2(7), 4957) Books on Tape.
Dr. Alex Seacourt finds himself involved in a plot that threatens the world with a new deadly form of an AIDS virus.

Doomsday Rider. unabr. ed. Ralph Compton & Joseph A. West. (Running Time: 5 hrs.). (ENG.). 2004. audio compact disk 22.95 (978-1-56511-850-8(2), 1565118502) Pub: HighBridge. Dist(s): Workman Pub

Doomsday Warrior 1. Ryder Stacy. 2007. audio compact disk 19.99 (978-1-59950-326-4(3)) GraphicAudio.

Doomsday Warrior 10: American Nightmare. Based on a novel by Ryder Stacy. 2008. audio compact disk 19.99 (978-1-59950-419-3(7)) GraphicAudio.

Doomsday Warrior 11: America's Eden. Based on a novel by Ryder Stacy. 2008. audio compact disk 19.99 (978-1-59950-436-0(7)) GraphicAudio.

Doomsday Warrior 12: Death, American Style. Based on a novel by Ryder Stacy. 2008. audio compact disk 19.99 (978-1-59950-474-2(X)) GraphicAudio.

Doomsday Warrior 13: American Paradise. Based on a novel by Ryder Stacy. (ENG.). 2008. audio compact disk 19.99 (978-1-59950-487-2(1)) GraphicAudio.

Doomsday Warrior 14: American Death Orbit. Based on a book by Ryder Stacy. (ENG.). 2008. audio compact disk 19.99 (978-1-59950-489-6(8)) GraphicAudio.

Doomsday Warrior 15: American Overthrow. Based on a book by Ryder Stacy. (ENG.). 2008. audio compact disk 19.99 (978-1-59950-490-2(1)) GraphicAudio.

Doomsday Warrior 16: American Ultimatum. Ryder Stacy. 2008. audio compact disk 19.99 (978-1-59950-496-4(0)) GraphicAudio.

Doomsday Warrior 17: America's Sword. Ryder Stacy. 2008. audio compact disk 19.99 (978-1-59950-512-1(6)) GraphicAudio.

Doomsday Warrior 18: American Dream Machine. Ryder Stacy. 2009. audio compact disk 19.99 (978-1-59950-520-6(7)) GraphicAudio.

Doomsday Warrior 19: America's Final Defense. Ryder Stacy. 2009. audio compact disk 19.99 (978-1-59950-529-9(0)) GraphicAudio.

Doomsday Warrior 2: Red America. Ryder Stacey. (Running Time: 18000 sec.). (Movie in Your Mind Ser.). 2008. audio compact disk 19.99 (978-1-59950-342-4(5)) GraphicAudio.

Doomsday Warrior 3: The Last American. 2007. audio compact disk 19.99 (978-1-59950-351-6(4)) GraphicAudio.

Doomsday Warrior 3: The Last American. Ryder Stacy. 2007. audio compact disk 19.99 (978-1-59950-298-4(4)) GraphicAudio.

Doomsday Warrior 4: Bloody America. 2007. audio compact disk 19.99 (978-1-59950-360-8(3)) GraphicAudio.

Doomsday Warrior 4: Bloody America. Ryder Stacy. 2007. audio compact disk 19.99 (978-1-59950-299-1(2)) GraphicAudio.

Doomsday Warrior 5: America's Last Declaration. Based on a novel by Ryder Stacy. 2007. audio compact disk 19.99 (978-1-59950-379-0(4)) GraphicAudio.

Doomsday Warrior 6: American Rebellion. Based on a novel by Ryder Stacy. 2007. audio compact disk 19.99 (978-1-59950-386-8(7)) GraphicAudio.

Doomsday Warrior 7: American Defiance. Based on a novel by Ryder Stacy. 2007. audio compact disk 19.99 (978-1-59950-396-7(4)) GraphicAudio.

Doomsday Warrior 8: American Glory. Based on a novel by Ryder Stacy. 2008. audio compact disk 19.99 (978-1-59950-404-9(9)) GraphicAudio.

Doomsday Warrior 9: America's Zero Hour. Based on a novel by Ryder Stacy. 2008. audio compact disk 19.99 (978-1-59950-411-7(1)) GraphicAudio.

Doomwyte. Brian Jacques. (Redwall Ser.). 2008. audio compact disk 39.99 (978-1-4361-6031-5(6)) Recorded Bks.

DoOon Mode. unabr. ed. Piers Anthony. Read by Natalie Ross. (Running Time: 14 hrs.). (Mode Ser.). 2009. 39.97 (978-1-4233-7697-2(8), 9781423376972, Brlnc Audio MP3 Lib) Brilliance Audio.

DoOon Mode. unabr. ed. Piers Anthony. Read by Natalie Ross-Turski. (Running Time: 14 hrs.). (Mode Ser.). 2009. 39.97 (978-1-4233-7699-6(4), 9781423376996, BADLE) Brilliance Audio.

DoOon Mode. unabr. ed. Piers Anthony. Read by Natalie Ross. (Running Time: 14 hrs.). (Mode Ser.). 2009. 24.99 (978-1-4233-7696-5(X), 9781423376965, Brilliance MP3); 24.99 (978-1-4233-7698-9(6), 9781423376989, BAD); audio compact disk 97.97 (978-1-4233-7695-8(1), 9781423376958, BriAudCD Unabrid); audio compact disk 29.99 (978-1-4233-7694-1(3), 9781423376941, Bril Audio CD Unabri) Brilliance Audio.

Door. unabr. ed. Mary Roberts Rinehart. Read by Flo Gibson. 6 cass. (Running Time: 9 hrs.). 1997. 24.95 (978-1-55685-468-2(4), 468-4) Audio Bk Con.
An altered will leads to four murders which baffle Miss Bell, her family & the reader. Will Inspector Harrison be able to save an innocent man from being sent to the electric chair?.

***Door: A Resurrection Celebration.** Contrib. by Dennis and Nan Allen. (ENG.). 1995. audio compact disk 90.00 (978-0-00-511564-0(7)) Lillenas.

Door Between. unabr. ed. Ellery Queen. Read by Blain Fairman. 6 cass. (Running Time: 9 hrs.). 2002. 29.95 (978-1-57270-206-6(0), N61206u) Pub: Audio Partners. Dist(s): PerseuPGW
Writer Karen Leith died in a small, secluded room in her odd Greenwich Village house. Initially the evidence seems to point to the guilt of Karen's friend and future stepdaughter, as Eva is the one with blood on her hands. But Ellery Queen suspects that the accused cannot possibly be guilty. As he penetrates deeper, he becomes certain that Karen was murdered in as clever and horrifying a manner as he has ever encountered. But how? and by whom? Ultimately he proves that logic, intellect, and a bit of intuition can uncover the puzzling truth when all obvious evidence points elsewhere.

Door County Tapestry: A Personality of the County & Its People. Richard Martens et al. Read by Steve Van Beckum. 1 cass. (Running Time: 1 hr. 12 min.). 1994. 9.95 (978-0-9643858-0-1(5)) Trails & Tales.
Recorded quotes from interviews mixed with narration, music & natural sounds.

Door in the Wall. Marguerite De Angeli. Read by Roger Rees. 2 cass. (Running Time: 2 hrs. 13 mins.). (J). 2000. 18.00 (978-0-7366-9026-3(3)) Books on Tape.
For Robin, becoming a knight is his destiny. But when a crippling illness strikes, the world he knows crumbles as even his servants abandon him. Brother Luke rescues Robin & teaches him about patience & strength. When the castle is threatened, Robin who cannot mount or ride a horse, discovers that there is more than one way to serve the king.

Door in the Wall. unabr. ed. Marguerite De Angeli. Read by Roger Rees. 2 vols. (Running Time: 2 hrs. 39 mins.). (J). (gr. 4-7). 2004. pap. bk. 29.00 (978-0-8072-8691-3(5), YA237SP, Listening Lib); 23.00 (978-0-8072-8690-6(7), YA237CX, Listening Lib) Random Audio Pubg.

Door in the Wall & Other Stories. unabr. collector's ed. H. G. Wells. Read by Justin Hecht. 5 cass. (Running Time: 5 hrs.). 1983. 30.00 (978-0-7366-0498-7(1), 1472) Books on Tape.
Other titles are: "The Star," "A Dream of Armageddon," "The Cone," "A Moonlight Fable," "The Diamond Maker," "The Lord of the Dynamos" & Wells' durably celebrated story of true freedom & the human spirit "The Country of the Blind".

Door into Summer. 2006. 44.95 (978-0-7861-3678-0(2)); audio compact disk 55.00 (978-0-7861-7692-2(X)) Blckstn Audio.

Door into Summer. unabr. ed. Robert A. Heinlein. Read by Patrick G. Lawlor. 2006. 29.95 (978-0-7861-7954-1(6)) Blckstn Audio.

Door of No Return. unabr. ed. Sarah Mussi. Read by Dominic Hoffman. 9 CDs. (Running Time: 10 hrs. 48 mins.). (YA). (gr. 5-8). 2008. audio compact disk 55.00 (978-0-7393-6735-3(8), Listening Lib) Pub: Random Audio Pubg. Dist(s): Random

Door Only You Can Open. Derek Prince. 1 cass. 5.95 (119) Derek Prince.
To open or close this door will determine life's destiny.

Door Through Space. Marion Zimmer Bradley. 2007. audio compact disk 27.95 (978-0-8095-7195-6(1)) Diamond Book Dists.

***Door Through Space.** Marion Zimmer Bradley. (Running Time: 5 mins.). 2009. 19.95 (978-1-897331-18-7(5), AudioRealms) Dorch Pub Co.

***Door Through Space.** Marion Zimmer Bradley & Marion Zimmer Bradley. (Running Time: 5 mins.). 2009. audio compact disk 27.95 (978-1-897304-41-9(2), AudioRealms) Dorch Pub Co.

Door to December. unabr. ed. Richard Paige, pseud & Dean Koontz. Read by George Guidall. (Running Time: 13 hrs.). (ENG.). (gr. 8). 2007. audio compact disk 39.95 (978-0-14-314229-4(1), PengAudBks) Penguin Grp USA.

Door to Time. unabr. ed. Pierdomenico Baccalario. Read by Michael Page. (Running Time: 4 hrs.). (Ulysses Moore Ser.: Bk. 1). 2006. 39.25 (978-1-4233-1323-6(2), 9781423313236, BADLE); 24.95 (978-1-4233-1322-9(4), 9781423313229, BAD) Brilliance Audio.

Door to Time. unabr. ed. Pierdomenico Baccalario. Read by Michael Page. 4 cass. (Running Time: 14400 sec.). (Ulysses Moore Ser.: Bk. 1). (J). (gr. 4-7). 2006. 62.25 (978-1-4233-1317-5(8), 9781423313175, BriAudUnabridg); 24.95 (978-1-4233-1316-8(X), 9781423313168, BAU) Brilliance Audio.
In a house on the coast of England, there is a door. It hides unimaginable mysteries, unavoidable danger, and unbelievable surprises. When eleven-year-old twins Jason and Julia move into the old mansion with their family, the door is a secret - locked and hidden behind an old wardrobe. But Jason, Julia, and their friend Rick are about to discover what lies behind it.

Door to Time. unabr. ed. Pierdomenico Baccalario & Iacopo Bruno. (Running Time: 14400 sec.). (Ulysses Moore Ser.: Bk. 1). (J). (gr. 4-7). 2006. audio compact disk 39.25 (978-1-4233-1321-2(6), 9781423313212, Brlnc Audio MP3 Lib); audio compact disk 69.25 (978-1-4233-1319-9(4), 9781423313199, BriAudCD Unabrid); audio compact disk 24.95 (978-1-4233-1320-5(8), 9781423313205, Brilliance MP3); audio compact disk 24.95 (978-1-4233-1318-2(6), 9781423313182, Bril Audio CD Unabri) Brilliance Audio.

***Door Within.** unabr. ed. Wayne Thomas Batson. Narrated by Wayne Thomas Batson. (Running Time: 9 hrs. 49 mins. 31 sec.). (Door Within Trilogy). (ENG.). 2010. 19.59 (978-1-60814-772-4(X)); audio compact disk 27.99 (978-1-59859-809-4(0)) Oasis Audio.

Doorbell Rang see Llaman a la Puerta

Doorbell Rang. Pat Hutchins. Illus. by Pat Hutchins. 11 vols. (Running Time: 5 mins.). (J). (ps-4). 2005. pap. bk. 16.95 (978-0-87499-774-3(7)) AudioGO.
Every time the doorbell rings, another friend arrives to enjoy the cookies Ma has made in this cumulative story.

Doorbell Rang. Pat Hutchins. Illus. by Pat Hutchins. 9.95 (978-1-59112-149-7(3)); 4.50 (978-1-59112-303-3(8)) Live Oak Media.

Doorbell Rang. Pat Hutchins. Illus. by Pat Hutchins. 11 vols. (Running Time: 5 mins.). 2001. pap. bk. 33.95 (978-0-87499-776-7(3)); pap. bk. 33.95 (978-0-87499-803-0(4)); pap. bk. 35.95 (978-1-59112-714-7(9)); audio compact disk 12.95 (978-1-59112-711-6(4)) Live Oak Media.

Doorbell Rang. Pat Hutchins. Illus. by Pat Hutchins. 11 vols. (Running Time: 5 mins.). (J). (ps-3). 2001. bk. 25.95 (978-0-87499-775-0(5)) Live Oak Media.

Doorbell Rang. Pat Hutchins. Tr. by Aida E. Marcuse. 1 cass. (Running Time: 5 mins.). (J). (ps-2). 2001. 9.95 (978-0-87499-773-6(9)) Live Oak Media.

Doorbell Rang. Pat Hutchins. Illus. by Pat Hutchins. 11 vols. (Running Time: 5 mins.). (J). 2005. pap. bk. 18.95 (978-1-59112-712-3(2)) Pub: Live Oak Media. Dist(s): AudioGO

Doorbell Rang. Pat Hutchins. (Metro Reading Ser.). (J). (gr. k). 2000. 8.46 (978-1-58120-990-7(8)) Metro Teaching.

***Doorbell Rang.** unabr. ed. Pat Hutchins. Read by Isabel Keating. (ENG.). 2008. (978-0-06-167368-9(4)); (978-0-06-168783-9(9)) HarperCollins Pubs.

Doorbell Rang. unabr. collector's ed. Rex Stout. Read by Michael Prichard. 4 cass. (Running Time: 6 hrs.). (Nero Wolfe Ser.). 1999. 32.00 (978-0-7366-4462-4(8), 4907) Books on Tape.
A society widow enlists Nero Wolfe & his sidekick, Archie, to help get the Feds off her back.

Doors see Carl Sandburg's Poems for Children

Doors see Gathering of Great Poetry for Children

Doors of Perception: And Heaven & Hell. unabr. ed. Aldous Huxley. Read by Rudolph Schirmer. 2 cass. (Running Time: 2 hrs. 20 mins.). 2004. 17.95 (978-1-57270-065-9(3), E21065u) Pub: Audio Partners. Dist(s): PerseuPGW
This exploratory essay about Huxley's experience with mescaline sparked a generation of drug experimentation & it continues to challenge beliefs about the drugs condoned & forbidden in our society.

***Doors of Perception: The Classic Exploration of Altered Consciousness & Spirituality.** Aldous Huxley. Narrated by Rudolph Schirmer. (Running Time: 2 hrs. 16 mins. 0 sec.). (ENG.). 2011. audio compact disk 19.95 (978-1-60998-191-4(X)) Pub: AudioGO. Dist(s): Perseus Dist

***Doors Open.** unabr. ed. Ian Rankin. Narrated by James McPherson. 8 CDs. (Running Time: 10 hrs.). 2010. 89.99 (978-1-60788-334-0(1)) Hachet Audio.

Doors Open. unabr. ed. Ian Rankin. Read by James MacPherson. (Running Time: 9 hrs. 30 mins.). (ENG.). 2010. 24.98 (978-1-60024-933-4(7)) Pub: Little. Dist(s): HachBkGrp

Doorway to Freedom. Swami Amar Jyoti. 1 cass. 1991. 9.95 (P-59) Truth Consciousness.
Witnessing, the heroic effort to awaken from our alluring dreams. Awakening the upward trend. Mastery of our nature & conditions.

Doorway to the soul how to have a profound spiritual Experience: How to Have a Profound Spiritual Experience. Ron Scolastico. 2004. 9.95 (978-0-7435-4655-3(5)) Pub: S&S Audio. Dist(s): S and S Inc

Doorways to Deception: If the Devil Can't Deceive You, He Can't Defeat You! Mac Hammond. 9 cass. (Running Time: 1 hr.). 1998. 54.00 Set. (978-1-57399-070-7(1)) Mac Hammond.

Dopamine Connection: Program from the Award Winning Public Radio Series. Interview. Hosted by Fred Goodwin. 1 CD. (Running Time: 1 Hour). 2004. audio compact disk 21.95 (978-1-932479-39-3(2), LCM 306) Lichtenstein Creat.
Sex, gambling, drug use, extreme sports. Behind ALL these thrills lurks a brain chemical called dopamine. In this episode of the national, weekly public radio series, The Infinite Mind, we explore the connection between the complex inner working of the brain and our moods, behaviors, and, even, personalities. We look at the science that answers questions like: What is free will? What is the chemistry of love, and does knowing it change how we understand the idea of love? Why does cocaine feel so good? And why do some people like roller coasters and others hate them? Plus, we report on a fascinating study that shows a link between the dopamine medications given for Parkinson's disease and compulsive gambling.Guests include Dr. Daniel Weinberger, chief of the Clinical Brain Disorders Branch of the National Institute of Mental Health; Dr. Hans Breiter, assistant professor of psychiatry at Harvard Medical School and an expert in brain imaging; Dr. Helen Fisher, author of Why We Love: The Nature and Chemistry of Romantic Love; and Mark Decena, the director and co-writer of Dopamine, the movie.

***Dope Sick.** unabr. ed. Walter Dean Myers. Narrated by J. D. Jackson. 1 Playaway. (Running Time: 3 hrs. 30 mins.). (YA). (gr. 9 up). 2009. 54.75 (978-1-4407-2909-6(3)); 30.75 (978-1-4361-6135-0(5)); audio compact disk 30.75 (978-1-4361-6140-4(1)) Recorded Bks.

***Dope Sick.** unabr. collector's ed. Walter Dean Myers. Narrated by J. D. Jackson. 3 CDs. (Running Time: 3 hrs. 30 mins.). (YA). (gr. 9 up). 2009. audio compact disk 28.95 (978-1-4361-6144-2(4)) Recorded Bks.

Doppelganger. unabr. ed. Michael Parker. Read by Alan King. (Running Time: 8 hrs. 25 mins.). (YA). 2007. audio compact disk 83.95 (978-1-74093-938-6(7), 9781740939386) Pub: Bolinda Pubng AUS. Dist(s): Bolinda Pub Inc

Dorado see Classic American Poetry

Dore Schary see Movie Makers Speak: Producers

Dorinda Clark Cole: Recorded Live in Detroit, MI at Bailey Cathedral. Perf. by Dorinda Clark Cole. 2002. audio compact disk Provident Mus Dist.

Doris Grumbach. Interview. Interview with Doris Grumbach & Kay Bonetti. 1 cass. (Running Time: 1 hr. 24 min.). 13.95 (978-1-55644-104-2(5), 4072) Am Audio Prose.
A discussion with well known critic-reviewer-novelist covers problems peculiar to writing contemporary novels from a historical or factual "germ," & her recurring themes, including her biases regarding family life & parent-child relationships.

Doris in Search of Martenarten. unabr. ed. Geoffrey McSkimming. Read by Geoffrey McSkimming. 3 cass. (Running Time: 4 hrs. 8 mins.). (Cairo Jim Ser.). (YA). 2004. 28.00 (978-1-74030-875-5(1)) Pub: Bolinda Pubng AUS. Dist(s): Bolinda Pub Inc

Doris Lessing. unabr. ed. Carole Klein. Read by Anna Fields. 8 cass. (Running Time: 11 hrs. 30 mins.). 2001. 56.95 (978-0-7861-2055-0(X), 2815) Blckstn Audio.
Based on numerous interviews and sources, a timely portrait of a fascinating woman.

Doris Lessing. unabr. ed. Doris Lessing. 1 cass. (Author Speaks Ser.). 1991. 14.95 J Norton Pubs.
Archival recordings of 20th-century authors.

Doris Lessing: A Biography. unabr. ed. Carole Klein & Anna Fields. (Running Time: 10 hrs. NaN mins.). 2008. 29.95 (978-1-4332-5481-9(6)); audio compact disk 90.00 (978-1-4332-5480-2(8)) Blckstn Audio.

Doris Lessing Reads Her Short Stories. unabr. ed. Doris Lessing. Read by Doris Lessing. 1 cass. (Running Time: 32 min.). 1969. 12.95 (23182) J Norton Pubs.
Lessing reads & analyzes one short story & excerpts from other works.

***Dork Diaries: Tales from a Not-So-Fabulous Life.** unabr. ed. Rachel Renée Russell. Read by Lana Quintal. (Running Time: 3 hrs. 0 mins. 0 sec.). (Dork Diaries). (ENG.). (J). 2010. audio compact disk 14.99 (978-1-4423-3896-8(2)) Pub: S&S Audio. Dist(s): S and S Inc

Dork of Cork. unabr. ed. Chet Raymo. Narrated by Donal Donnelly. 9 cass. (Running Time: 12 hrs. 30 mins.). 1995. 78.00 (978-0-7887-0234-1(3), 94458E7) Recorded Bks.
Frank Bois is 43 years old & 43 inches tall, but his yearnings are as wide & deep as the night sky he contemplates from his rooftop in Cork, Ireland.

Dormir-Decider. unabr. ed. Robert A. Monroe. Read by Roland Simon. 1 cass. (Running Time: 30 min.). (Human Plus Ser.). (FRE.). 1993. 14.95 (978-1-56102-104-8(0)) Inter Indus.
Benefit from intuition of your total self.

Dormir Mejor. unabr. ed. Nader Lucia. Read by Luicia Nader. (SPA.). 2007. audio compact disk 13.00 (978-958-8318-12-7(2)) Pub: Yoyo Music COL. Dist(s): YoYoMusic

***Dorothea Benton Frank CD Collection: Shem Creek, Pawleys Island.** abr. ed. Dorothea Benton Frank. (Running Time: 12 hrs.). 2010. audio compact disk 19.99 (978-1-4418-5098-0(8), 9781441850980, BACD) Brilliance Audio.

Dorothy Day: A Radical Devotion. unabr. ed. Robert Coles. Read by C. M. Herbert. 5 cass. (Running Time: 7 hrs.). 1997. 39.95 (978-0-7861-1331-6(6), 2225) Blckstn Audio.
An intellectual & psychological portrait that confronts candidly the central puzzles of her life. Based on many years of conversation & correspondence, as well as tape-recorded interviews.

Dorothy Kirsten in New Orleans. Contrib. by Cornell MacNeil et al. 1 cass. 1998. 16.99 (VAIA1154) VAI Audio.
Features extended scenes from La Traviata.

Dorothy L. Sayers: A Careless Rage for Life. unabr. ed. David Coomes. Read by Nadia May. 5 cass. (Running Time: 7 hrs.). 1993. 39.95 (978-0-7861-0457-4(0), 1409) Blckstn Audio.
Known to millions as the creator of Lord Peter Wimsey & the bestselling author of a dozen detective novels, Dorothy Leigh Sayers was in reality a complex woman - moved, she said, by "a careless rage for life." It is this complex Sayers, brilliant student, controversial apologist, witty, bawdy, intolerant of fools - the woman "terrified of emotion" - who is revealed in this new biography which draws extensively on the thousands of letters Sayers wrote, many of them made public for the first time.

Dorothy Parker. abr. ed. Dorothy Parker. Read by Mary M. Lewis. 2 cass. 12.95 (870) Audio Bk.

Dorothy Parker. unabr. ed. Short Stories. Dorothy Parker. Read by Mary M. Lewis. 10 cass. 59.50 (141) Audio Bk.

Dorothy Parker: What Fresh Hell Is This? unabr. ed. Marion Meade. Read by Grace Conlin. 12 cass. (Running Time: 18 hrs.). 1995. 83.95 (978-0-7861-0870-1(3), 1668) Blckstn Audio.
She was known for her outrageous one-liners, her ruthless theatre criticism, her clever verses & bittersweet stories, but there was another side to Dorothy Parker - a private life set on a course of destruction. She suffered through two divorces, a string of painful affairs, a lifelong problem with alcohol, & several suicide attempts. In this lively, absorbing biography, Marion Meade illuminates both the dark side of Parker & her days of wicked wittiness at the Algonquin Round Table with the likes of Robert Benchley, George Kaufman, & Harold Ross, & in Hollywood with S. J. Perelman, William Faulkner, & Lillian Hellman. At the dazzling center of it all, Meade gives us the flamboyant, self-destructive, & brilliant Dorothy Parker.

***Dorothy Parker Audio Collection.** abr. ed. Dorothy Parker. Read by Christine Baranski. (ENG.). 2005. (978-0-06-084628-2(3), Harper Audio); (978-0-06-084627-5(5), Harper Audio) HarperCollins Pubs.

Dorothy Parker Audio Collection. unabr. abr. ed. Dorothy Parker. Read by Christine Baranski. 1 cass. (Running Time: 1 hr. 30 mins.). 2004. audio compact disk 29.95 (978-0-06-059789-4(5)) HarperCollins Pubs.

Dorothy Parker Stories. unabr. ed. Short Stories. Dorothy Parker. Perf. by Shirley Booth. 1 cass. (Running Time: 39 mins.). 12.00 (H158) Blckstn Audio.
Filled with the insight into people & their interactions that have made her stories so popular, this program offers some of the finest examples of her craft.

Dorothy Thompson: Star Reporter. unabr. ed. Read by Heywood Hale Broun. 1 cass. (Running Time: 56 min.). (Broun Radio Ser.). 12.95 (40030) J Norton Pubs.
With Marion Sanders ("Dorothy Thompson: A Legend in her Time").

Dorp (Lost) Moon-Star Records. Sandi Johnson. Narrated by Lynette Louise. 1 cass., 1 CD. (J). (ps-6). 1996. 8.99 (978-1-929063-31-4(8), 129); audio compact disk 12.99 CD. (978-1-929063-32-1(6), 130) Moons & Stars.
A baby dragon, lost in Scotland in the early 1800's, tries to escape the clutches of Scarface McGuire (dragon slayer) to find his way back to Loch Lomond. Includes songs.

Dorp the Scottish Dragon Bk. 1: Moon-star Records. Sandi Johnson. Narrated by Sybrina Durant. 1 cass., 1 CD. (J). (ps-6). 1986. 9.99 (978-1-929063-42-0(3), 140); audio compact disk 12.99 CD. (978-1-929063-43-7(1), 141) Moons & Stars.
Story of a dragon & many escapes from a dragon slayer bound for glory. All the dragon wants is to be back in Loch Lomond. Includes songs.

Dorp the Scottish Dragon Bk. 2: Moon-Star Records. Sandi Johnson. Narrated by Sybrina Durant. 1 cass., 1 CD. (J). (ps-6). 1987. 4.99 (978-1-929063-28-4(8), 127); audio compact disk 9.99 CD. (978-1-929063-29-1(6), 128) Moons & Stars.
A dragon falls in love. It's springtime in early 1900's in Scotland. Includes songs.

Dorp the Scottish Dragon Bk. 3: Moon-Star Records. Sandi Johnson. Narrated by Sybrina Durant. 1 cass., 1 CD. (J). (ps-6). 1987. 6.99 (978-1-929063-36-9(9), 134); audio compact disk 9.99 CD. (978-1-929063-37-6(7), 135) Moons & Stars.
The dragon goes to Hollywood to be a movie star, where he marries & hatches a baby dragon in 1920's America. Includes songs.

Dorp the Scottish Dragon Bk. 3: Whacky. Sandi Johnson. Perf. by Kenny Britian. 1 cass. (J). 2000. 6.99 (978-1-929063-60-4(1), 159) Moons & Stars.
Story & songs including "Whacky Chicken" & "Earthquake in the 1920s.".

Dorp the Scottish Dragon Bk. 3: Whacky. Sandi Johnson. Perf. by Trina Fillipini. 1 CD. (J). 2000. audio compact disk 12.99 (978-1-929063-61-1(X), 160) Moons & Stars.

Dorp the Scottish Dragon Bk. 4: Moon-Star Records. Sandi Johnson. Narrated by Sybrina Durant. 1 cass., 1 CD. (J). (ps-6). 1987. 8.99 (978-1-929063-40-6(7), 138); audio compact disk 12.99 CD. (978-1-929063-41-3(5), 139) Moons & Stars.
Dorp, his dragonette, & his son live in New York in the 1950's. Another dragon is born on Christmas Eve. Includes songs.

Dorp the Scottish Dragon Bk. 5: Moon-Star Records. Sandi Johnson. Narrated by Sybrina Durant. 1 cass., 1 CD. (J). (ps-6). 1987. 8.99 (978-1-929063-38-3(5), 136); audio compact disk 8.99 CD. (978-1-929063-39-0(3), 137) Moons & Stars.
The family of dragons go on a vacation in Florida, where they are blown out of the sea by a hurricane. Lost in the Bermuda Triangle in the 1970's. Includes songs.

Dorp the Scottish Dragon Bk. 5: Triangle. Sandi Johnson. Perf. by Jon Praker. 1 cass. (J). (ps-6). 2000. 6.99 (978-1-929063-63-5(6), 162) Moons & Stars.
Story & spooky songs including "Witches' Voodoo," "Seminole Warrior," Sun-n-Fun songs" & "Roar.".

Dorp the Scottish Dragon BK. 6: Moon-Star Records. Sandi Johnson. Narrated by Sybrina Durant. 1 cass., 1 CD. (J). (ps-6). 1987. 8.99 (978-1-929063-34-5(2), 132); audio compact disk 12.99 CD. (978-1-929063-35-2(0), 133) Moons & Stars.
The dragon family settles in on a dragon ranch in Texas. The twin dragons are born in the western adventure that takes place in the 1980's.

Dorp the Scottish Dragon Bk. 7: Conquest City. Sandi Johnson. Narrated by Sybrina Durant. 1 cass., 1 CD. (J). (ps-6). 1999. 9.99 (978-1-929063-48-2(2), 143); audio compact disk 12.99 CD. (978-1-929063-45-1(8), 144) Moons & Stars.
Sci Fi adventure of the dragon family takes place in space station Conquest City. They have a secret weapon to the existence of life in the solar system... ZEMO.

Dorrie & the Blue Witch. unabr. ed. Patricia Coombs. 1 read-along cass. (Running Time: 19 min.). (Follow the Reader Ser.). (J). (gr. 1-2). 1983. (Listening Lib) Random Audio Pubg.
Dorrie is up against the mean Blue Witch & needs every trick in the book to outwit her. Shrinking powder, perfume, & ingenuity earn Dorrie the prized gold cauldron for witch catching.

Dorrie & the Blue Witch. unabr. ed. Patricia Coombs. Read by Suzanne Toren. 1 cass. (Running Time: 19 mins.). (Follow the Reader Ser.). (J). (gr. 1-2). 1983. pap. bk. 17.00 (978-0-8072-0042-1(5), FTR 76 SP, Listening Lib) Random Audio Pubg.

Dorrie & the Goblin. unabr. ed. Patricia Coombs. (Running Time: 28 min.). (J). (gr. 1-2). 1987. bk. 15.98 incl. bk. & guide. (978-0-8072-0064-3(6), FTR87SP, Listening Lib) Random Audio Pubg.
Dorrie works some of her own magic when she promises to goblin-sit for a troublesome little creature just hours before Witchville's spectacular Halloween tea party.

Dorrie & the Halloween Plot. unabr. ed. Patricia Coombs. 1 read-along cass. (Running Time: 32 min.). (Follow the Reader Ser.). (J). (gr. 1-2). 1987. bk. 15.98 incl. guide & Bk. (978-0-8072-0062-9(X), FTR86SP, Listening Lib) Random Audio Pubg.
Dorrie & her cat Gink find themselves in a fix when she discovers the Demon's plot to steal the Great Sorceress' Book of Shadows.

Dorrie & the Haunted House. unabr. ed. Patricia Coombs. 1 read-along cass. (Running Time: 24 min.). (Follow the Reader Ser.). (J). (gr. 1-2). 1982. (Listening Lib) Random Audio Pubg.
When the magic blue ruby is stolen, all the witches & wizards in town rush to Dorrie's house for a secret meeting. But little witch Dorrie & her cat are accidentally locked out & wind up face to face with the robbers in a haunted house.

Dorrie & the Haunted House. unabr. ed. Patricia Coombs. Read by Alexandra Cortese. 1 cass. (Running Time: 24 mins.). (Follow the Reader Ser.). (J). (gr. 1-2). 1982. pap. bk. 17.00 (978-0-8072-0020-9(4), FTR 65 SP, Listening Lib) Random Audio Pubg.

***Do's & Don'ts of Records Retention & Destruction.** PUEI. 2008. audio compact disk 199.00 (978-1-935041-37-5(1), CareerTrack) P Univ E Inc.

Do's & Dont's Witnessing to Cults. Walter Ralston Martin. 1 cass. 1997. 6.99 (978-7-5116-0032-5(8), Regal Bks) Gospel Lght.
Cults, demonism & the occult.

Dos Leyendas. Becquer. audio compact disk 12.95 (978-0-8219-3810-2(X)) EMC-Paradigm.

Dos Mundos: A Communicative Approach. unabr. ed. Tracy D. Terrell. 1 cass. (Running Time: 1 hr. 30 mins.). 1999. 38.35 (978-0-07-913183-6(2), Mc-H Human Soc) McGrw-H Hghr Educ.

Dos Mundos: En Breve. Tracy D. Terrell et al. 1 cass. (Running Time: 90 min.). 1998. 44.37 (978-0-07-913223-9(5), Mc-H Human Soc) Pub: McGrw-H Hghr Educ. Dist(s): McGraw

Dos Mundos: En Breve. 4th ed. Tracy D. Terrell et al. (ENG.). (C). 2009. stu. ed. 62.81 (978-0-07-730479-9(9), 0077304799, Mc-H Human Soc) Pub: McGrw-H Hghr Educ. Dist(s): McGraw

Dos Mundos: en Breve Audio Program: Comunicaion y Comunidad. Created by McGraw-Hill Higher Education Staff. 2005. audio compact disk 465.80 (978-0-07-321340-8(3)) McGraw.

DOS Tape. unabr. ed. John Stewart & Alicia Andersen. Read by John Stewart. 1 cass. (Running Time: 1 hr. 14 min.). 1993. 18.95 incl. reference card. (978-1-886173-00-2(1)) Audio Computer.
Handy audio tape guide for new users of IBM/compatible computers by syndicated computer talk show host John Stewart. Covers most important commands used by the Disk Operating System (DOS). Complete with quick reference card.

***Dosadi Experiment.** unabr. ed. Frank Herbert. Narrated by Scott Brick. (Running Time: 11 hrs. 0 mins. 0 sec.). 2010. 24.99 (978-1-4001-6485-1(0)); 17.99 (978-1-4001-8485-9(1)); audio compact disk 34.99 (978-1-4001-1485-6(3)) Pub: Tantor Media. Dist(s): IngramPubServ

***Dosadi Experiment (Library Edition)** unabr. ed. Frank Herbert. Narrated by Scott Brick. (Running Time: 11 hrs. 0 mins.). 2010. 34.99 (978-1-4001-9485-8(7)); audio compact disk 83.99 (978-1-4001-4485-3(X)) Pub: Tantor Media. Dist(s): IngramPubServ

Dosage & Calculations Made Easy, Vol. 5. Patrics A. Hoefler. 2003. spiral bd. (978-1-56533-331-4(4)) MEDS Pubng.

Dostoevsky in 90 Minutes. unabr. ed. Paul Strathern. Read by Robert Whitfield. 2 cass. (Running Time: 1 hr. 30 mins.). 2005. 16.95 (978-0-7861-3432-8(1)) Blckstn Audio.

Dostoevsky in 90 Minutes. unabr. ed. Paul Strathern. Read by Robert Whitfield. 2 CDs. (Running Time: 7200 sec.). 2005. audio compact disk 16.95 (978-0-7861-7982-4(1)) Blckstn Audio.

Dostoevsky in 90 Minutes. unabr. ed. Paul Strathern. Read by Robert Whitfield. (Running Time: 2 hrs. NaN mins.). 2009. audio compact disk 22.95 (978-0-7861-3036-8(9)); audio compact disk 24.00 (978-0-7861-7940-4(6)) Blckstn Audio.

Dostoyevsky: Realism Transfigured. unabr. ed. Ernest J. Simmons. (Running Time: 49 min.). (Classics of Russian Literature Ser.). 1968. 12.95 (23136) J Norton Pubs.
Dostoevsky as an innovator in search of higher "realism" resulting in dramatic portrayals of psychological reality to be found not in the mundane facts of daily existence, but in the tragic absurdity of life.

Dostoyevsky on Stage: The Brothers Karamazov & The Idiot. 3 cass. (Running Time: 4 hrs.). Dramatization. 19.95 Set. (12158FA) Filmic Archives.

Dostoyevsky on Stage: The Brothers Karamazov & the Idiot. unabr. ed. Fyodor Dostoyevsky. Contrib. by David Fishelson. 3 cass. (Running Time: 4 hr.). Dramatization. 1997. 19.95 Set. (978-0-8072-3565-2(2), CB 141 CXR, Listening Lib) Random Audio Pubg.
Prince Myshkin returns to the jaded social whirl of 1860's St. Petersburg after fifteen years of treatment for epilepsy in a Swiss institution.

Dot. 2004. bk. 24.95 (978-0-7882-0331-2(2)); 8.95 (978-0-7882-0333-6(9)); audio compact disk 12.95 (978-0-7882-0334-3(7)) Weston Woods.

Dot & the Kangaroo, Set. unabr. ed. Ethel Pedley. Read by Cindy Killavey. 3 cass. (Running Time: 3 hrs. 30 min.). (J). (gr. 2-4). 1994. in vinyl album. (C-246) Jimcin Record.
Story of a little girl lost in the Australian bush who is befriended by a kindly kangaroo. The kangaroo gives her some berries of understanding & she has many adventures with the animals & the dangers in the outback before the kangaroo helps her find her "lost way".

Dot & the Smugglers. 1 cass. (Running Time: 75 min.). (J). 1989. 29.95 FHE.

Dot. Bomb. abr. ed. J. David Kuo. (ENG.). 2005. 14.98 (978-1-59483-398-4(2)) Pub: Hachet Audio. Dist(s): HachBkGrp

Dot the Fire Dog. 2004. 8.95 (978-1-55592-617-5(7)); audio compact disk 12.95 (978-1-55592-619-9(3)) Weston Woods.

Dot the Fire Dog. (J). 2004. bk. 24.95 (978-1-55592-621-2(5)) Weston Woods.

Dot the I & The Double Expertise: Two One Act Plays. unabr. ed. Gabriel Marcel. Intro. by Katharine Rose Hanley. 1 cass. (Running Time: 1 hr. 10 mins.). Dramatization. 2001. audio compact disk 15.00 (978-0-9715192-0-6(X)) Marcel Srud.

Dottie Walters' The Selling Power of a Woman. Dottie Walters. Read by Dottie Walters. 6 cass. (Running Time: 6 hrs.). 1982. 89.95 (978-0-934344-28-9(0)) Royal Pub.
Specific information for women on becoming sales people. Getting started, capturing a selling job, finding & tracking sales leads, overcoming sales resistance, selling the interview, selling the prospect, keeping people sold.

Dottore: The Double Life of a Mafia Doctor. unabr. ed. Ron Felber. Read by Jim Knobeloch. 7 CDs. (Running Time: 26400 sec.). 2005. audio compact disk 83.95 (978-1-74093-659-0(0)) Pub: Bolinda Pubng AUS. Dist(s): Bolinda Pub Inc

Double. unabr. ed. Marcia Muller & Bill Pronzini. Read by Bernadette Dunne. 8 cass. (Running Time: 12 hrs.). (Nameless Detective Mystery Ser.). 1997. 64.00 (978-0-7366-3710-7(9), 4394) Books on Tape.
Death strikes a PI convention & McCone recruits the Nameless Detective to investigate kinky sex & multiple murder.

Double Agents. unabr. ed. W. E. B. Griffin. Read by Paul Hecht. 10 CDs. (Running Time: 11 hrs. 45 mins.). 2007. audio compact disk 123.75 (978-1-4281-6377-5(8)) Recorded Bks.

Double Agents. unabr. ed. W. E. B. Griffin & William E. Butterworth, IV. Read by W. E. B. Griffin & Paul Hecht. (Running Time: 12 hrs.). (ENG.). (gr. 8). 2007. audio compact disk 32.95 (978-0-14-314204-1(6), PengAudBks) Penguin Grp USA.

Double Agents. unabr. ed. W. E. B. Griffin & William E. Butterworth, IV. Read by Paul Hecht. 10 cass. (Running Time: 11 hrs. 45 mins.). 2007. 82.75 (978-1-4281-6375-1(1)) Recorded Bks.

Double Assassinat dans La. Edgar Allan Poe. pap. bk. 21.95 (978-88-7754-839-9(8)) Pub: Cideb ITA. Dist(s): Distribks Inc

Double-Barreled Detective Story see Classic Detective Stories, Vol. II, A Collection

Double-Barreled Detective Story. Mark Twain. Read by Thomas Becker. (Running Time: 2 hrs. 15 mins.). 2002. 16.95 (978-1-59912-059-1(3), Audiofy Corp) Iofy Corp.

Double-Barreled Detective Story. Mark Twain. Narrated by Ralph Cosham. (Running Time: 8100 sec.). (Unabridged Classics in MP3 Ser.). (ENG.). 2008. audio compact disk 24.00 (978-1-58472-646-3(6), In Aud) Sound Room.

Double-Barreled Detective Story. unabr. ed. Short Stories. Mark Twain. Read by Tom Beyer. 2 cass. (Running Time: 2 hrs. 30 min.). Dramatization. 1991. 16.95 (978-1-55686-385-1(3), 385) Books in Motion.
A single mother uses her grown son to track down & wreak vengeance on the husband who humiliated & abandoned her.

Double-Barreled Detective Story. unabr. ed. Mark Twain. 1 cass. (Running Time: 87 min.). Dramatization. 1977. 7.95 (D-10) Jimcin Record.
A biting, yet hilarious parady of the detective story, in general, & Sherlock Holmes in particular.

Double-Barreled Detective Story. unabr. ed. Mark Twain. 2 CDs. (Running Time: 2 hrs.). 2002. audio compact disk 25.00 (978-1-58472-097-3(2), Commuters Library) Sound Room.

Double-Barreled Detective Story. unabr. ed. Mark Twain. Read by Thomas Becker. 2 cass. (Running Time: 2 hrs. 34 min.). 1994. lib. bdg. 18.95 set incl. vinyl case with notes, author's picture & biography. (978-1-883049-30-0(X)) Sound Room.
An old west parody of the English detective story.

Double-Barreled Detective Story. unabr. ed. Mark Twain. Read by Thomas Becker. Illus. by Lucius Hitchcock. 2 cass. (Running Time: 2 hrs. 14 mins.). (Mark Twain Ser.). 1994. bk. 16.95 (978-1-883049-11-9(3), 390208, Commuters Library) Sound Room.
A first-rate, hilarious, little-known detective story that takes place in the Old West. On the scene is Sherlock Holmes matching wits with Archy Stillman while Ham Sandwich & Wells Fargo look on.

Double-Barreled Detective Story. unabr. ed. Mark Twain. Read by Thomas Becker. 2 cds. (Running Time: 2 hrs 13 mins). (YA). 2002. audio compact disk 18.95 (978-1-58472-241-0(X), 010, In Aud) Pub: Sound Room. Dist(s): Baker Taylor
A parody of Sherlock Holmes set in the Old West.

Double Bass & Other Stories see Contrabajo y Otros Cuentos Humoristicos

Double Bass & Other Stories. Anton Chejov. Read by Carlos J. Vega. (Running Time: 3 hrs.). 2001. 16.95 (978-1-60083-181-2(8), Audiofy Corp) Iofy Corp.

Double Bass Mystery: Level 2. Jeremy Harmer. Contrib. by Philip Prowse. (Running Time: 1 hr. 19 mins.). (Cambridge English Readers Ser.). (ENG.). 1999. 9.45 (978-0-521-65612-2(5)) Cambridge U Pr.

Double Bind: A Novel. abr. ed. Chris Bohjalian. Read by Chris Bohjalian. (Running Time: 23400 sec.). (ENG.). 2008. audio compact disk 14.99 (978-0-7393-6575-5(4), Random AudioBks) Pub: Random Audio Pubg. Dist(s): Random

Double Bind: A Novel. unabr. ed. Chris Bohjalian. Read by Susan Denaker. 9 CDs. (Running Time: 11 hrs.). 2007. audio compact disk 110.00 (978-1-4159-3579-8(3)) Books on Tape.

Double-Bind: Escaping the Contradictory Demands of Manhood. Rodney L. Cooper. 2 cass. (Running Time: 60 min. per cass.). 1996. 14.99 (978-0-310-20489-3(5)) Zondervan.

Double-blind. abr. ed. Loren Coleman. 2 cass. (Running Time: 3 hrs.). (Battletech). 2003. 9.95 (978-1-931953-33-7(3)) Listen & Live.

Double Coffin. unabr. ed. Gwendoline Butler. Read by Nigel Graham. 8 cass. (Running Time: 12 hrs.). (Inspector John Coffin Mystery Ser.). 2000. 69.95 (978-0-7540-0002-0(8), CAB 142559.95) Pub: Chivers Audio Bks GBR. Dist(s): AudioGO
Inspector John Coffin had been content on this sunny October day. But when Richard Lavender, a former prime minister, wants to see him urgently, his contentment is shattered. Lavender confesses that his father was a serial killer, and as a boy he helped bury one of the victims. Wanting to reclaim the past, Lavender asks Coffin to find the body.

***Double Comfort Safari Club.** unabr. ed. Alexander McCall Smith. Read by Lisette Lecat. 8 CDs. (Running Time: 8 hrs. 30 mins.). 2010. audio compact disk 34.99 (978-1-4498-0613-2(9)) Recorded Bks.

Double Cross. James Patterson. (Alex Cross Ser.: No. 13). 2007. audio compact disk 39.99 (978-1-60252-315-9(0)) Find a World.

Double Cross. abr. ed. James Patterson. Read by Peter Jay Fernandez & Michael Stuhlbarg. (Running Time: 6 hrs. 30 mins.). (Alex Cross Ser.: No.

13). (ENG.). 2007. 19.98 (978-1-60024-056-0(9)); audio compact disk 29.98 (978-1-60024-055-3(0)) Pub: Hachet Audio. Dist(s): HachBkGrp

Double Cross. unabr. ed. James Patterson. Read by Peter Jay Fernandez & Michael Stuhlbarg. (Running Time: 8 hrs.). (Alex Cross Ser.: No. 13). (ENG.). 2007. 19.98 (978-1-60024-058-4(5)) Pub: Hachet Audio. Dist(s): HachBkGrp

Double Cross. unabr. ed. James Patterson. Read by Peter Jay Fernandez & Michael Stuhlbarg. (Running Time: 8 hrs.). (Alex Cross Ser.: No. 13). (ENG.). 2009. audio compact disk 19.98 (978-1-60024-849-8(7)) Pub: Hachet Audio. Dist(s): HachBkGrp

Double Cross. unabr. ed. James Patterson. 7 CDs. (Alex Cross Ser.: No. 13). 2007. audio compact disk 70.00 (978-1-4159-4207-9(2), BksonTape) Pub: Random Audio Pubg. Dist(s): Random

Double Cross, Level 3. Philip Prowse. Contrib. by Philip Prowse. (Running Time: 1 hr. 57 mins.). (Cambridge English Readers Ser.). (ENG.). 1999. 15.75 (978-0-521-65616-0(8)) Cambridge U Pr.

Double Cross Blind. Joel N. Ross. 8 cass. (Running Time: 12 hrs.). 2005. 72.00 (978-1-4159-2018-3(4)); audio compact disk 90.00 (978-1-4159-2158-6(X)) Books on Tape.

Double Date. unabr. ed. R. L. Stine. Narrated by Frank Muller. 3 pieces. (Running Time: 3 hrs. 30 mins.). (Fear Street Ser.). (gr. 6 up). 1996. 27.00 (978-0-7887-0207-5(6), 94432E7) Recorded Bks.
Bobby, the good-looking, guitar-playing teenager has taken all the Shadyside High School cheerleaders out on dates & now he's making his way down a list of the most beautiful girls in school. At the top of that list are Bree & Samantha Wade, a pair of gorgeous raven-haired twins. But soon Bobby learns that dating too many girls at once can be deadly.

Double Decker String Band: Chasing Rainbows. 1 cass., 1 CD. 9.98 (C-580); audio compact disk 14.98 CD. (CD-580) Folk-Legacy.
The newest recording of this fine group.

Double Decker String Band: Evolution Girl. 1 cass. 9.98 (C-581) Folk-Legacy.
An earlier recording of our favorite string band.

Double Decker String Band: For an Old Time Call... 1 cass. 9.98 (C-582) Folk-Legacy.
String band music at its very best.

Double Deuce. Robert B. Parker. Contrib. by David Dukes. (Spenser Ser.). 2008. 59.99 (978-1-60640-659-5(0)) Find a World.

Double Deuce. unabr. ed. Robert B. Parker. 4 cass. (Running Time: 6 hrs.). (Spenser Ser.). 2004. 25.00 (978-1-59007-205-9(7)) Pub: New Millenn Enter. Dist(s): PerseuPGW

Double Deuce. unabr. ed. Robert B. Parker. Read by David Dukes. 4 CDs. (Running Time: 6 hrs.). (Spenser Ser.). 2004. audio compact disk 29.95 (978-1-59007-548-7(X)) Pub: New Millenn Enter. Dist(s): PerseuPGW

Double Dutch. unabr. ed. Sharon M. Draper. Narrated by Patricia R. Floyd. 4 pieces. (Running Time: 5 hrs.). (gr. 6 up). 2002. 38.00 (978-1-4025-3127-9(3)) Recorded Bks.
For eighth-grader Delia Douglas, competing in the World Double Dutch Championships with her best friends is a dream that has come true through hours of hard practice. But that dream is now threatened by a terrible secret: Delia can't read. And unless she finds the courage to reach out and get help, she might never jump in another Double Dutch meet again.

***Double Duty Radcliffe Audio Book: 36 Years of Pitching.** Kyle McNary. Prod. by Kyle McNary. (ENG.). (C). 2009. audio compact disk 15.00 (978-0-9642002-3-4(6)) K McNary.

Double Exposure. unabr. ed. Stephen Collins. Read by Susan Ericksen. (Running Time: 9 hrs.). 2008. 24.95 (978-1-4233-5401-7(X), 9781423354017, BAD); 39.25 (978-1-4233-5402-4(8), 9781423354024, BADLE) Brilliance Audio.

Double Exposure. unabr. ed. Stephen Collins. Read by Susan Ericksen. Directed By Laura Grafton. Contrib. by Russell Byers. (Running Time: 28800 sec.). 2008. audio compact disk 24.95 (978-1-4233-5399-7(4), 9781423353997, Brilliance MP3); audio compact disk 39.25 (978-1-4233-5400-0(1), 9781423354000, Brlnc Audio MP3 Lib) Brilliance Audio.

Double Face. Composed by Francis Rimbert. 2005. audio compact disk 14.95 (978-0-9760535-5-2(1), AQM) Pub: Atomic Quill Pr. Dist(s): Pathway Bk Serv

Double Fault. unabr. ed. Lionel Shriver. Read by Renée Raudman. (Running Time: 12 hrs.). 2009. 24.99 (978-1-4233-9703-8(7), 9781423397038, Brilliance MP3); 39.97 (978-1-4233-9704-5(5), 9781423397045, Brlnc Audio MP3 Lib); 24.99 (978-1-4233-9705-2(3), 9781423397052, BAD); 39.97 (978-1-4233-9706-9(1), 9781423397069, BADLE); audio compact disk 97.97 (978-1-4233-9702-1(9), 9781423397021, BriAudCD Unabrid) Brilliance Audio.

Double Fault. unabr. ed. Lionel Shriver & Barrington Sadler. Read by Renée Raudman. 10 CDs. (Running Time: 12 hrs.). 2009. audio compact disk 36.99 (978-1-4233-9701-4(0), 9781423397014, Bril Audio CD Unabri) Brilliance Audio.

Double Fudge. Judy Blume. Read by Judy Blume. 3 vols. (Running Time: 4 hrs. 39 mins.). (Fudge Ser.). (J). (gr. 3-7). 2004. pap. bk. 36.00 (978-0-8072-2036-8(1), Listening Lib) Random Audio Pubg.

Double Fudge. unabr. ed. Judy Blume. 4 CDs. (Running Time: 4 hrs. 39 mins.). (Fudge Ser.). (J). (gr. 3-7). 2004. audio compact disk 35.00 (978-0-8072-1163-2(X), S YA 403 CD, Listening Lib) Random Audio Pubg.

Double Fudge. unabr. ed. Judy Blume. Read by Judy Blume. 3 cass. (Running Time: 4 hrs. 39 mins.). (Fudge Ser.). (J). (gr. 3-7). 2004. 30.00 (978-0-8072-0944-8(9), S YA 403 CX, Listening Lib) Random Audio Pubg.
"Fudge is back and he's discovered money in a big way. He's making his own ""Fudge Bucks,"" dressing as a miser for Halloween and thumbing through catalogs before bed, choosing birthday and Christmas presents years in advance-much to the embarrassment of his family, especially older brother Peter, who's just starting 7th grade. But things begin to change when the Hatchers discover their long-lost relatives, The Howie Hatchers of Honolulu, Hawaii-not exactly your everyday family. With new cousins, Flora and Fauna, and 4 year old Farley Drexel-yes, that's right, another Farley Drexel-the stage is set for a wild and wacky beginning to a new school year.".

Double Fudge. unabr. ed. Judy Blume. Read by Judy Blume. 4 CDs. (Running Time: 4 hrs. 39 mins.). (Fudge Ser.). (ENG.). (J). (gr. 1). 2005. audio compact disk 19.95 (978-0-307-24319-5(2), Listening Lib) Pub: Random Audio Pubg. Dist(s): Random

Double Helix. Nancy Werlin. Narrated by Scott Shina. 7 CDs. (Running Time: 7 hrs. 45 mins.). (YA). 2004. audio compact disk 69.75 (978-1-4193-1830-6(6)) Recorded Bks.

Double Helix. unabr. ed. 6 cass. (Running Time: 8 hrs. 30 min.). 2004. 54.75 (978-1-4025-8377-3(X)) Recorded Bks.

Double Helix: A Personal Account of the Discovery of the Structure of DNA. abr. ed. James D. Watson. 1 cass. 2000. 17.95 (978-1-55935-332-8(5)) Soundelux.
Nobel Prize winner tells the inside story of the discovery of the heredity molecule, DNA.

Double Homicide. unabr. ed. Jonathan Kellerman & Faye Kellerman. Narrated by L. Phillips & J. H. Rubinstein. 9 CDs. (Running Time: 6 hrs.). 2004. audio compact disk 81.00 (978-1-4159-1304-8(8)); 63.00 (978-1-4159-1303-1(X)) Books on Tape.
Novelists Jonathan and Faye Kellerman team up for two novellas featuring different detectives solving crimes in different cities.

Double Homicide. unabr. ed. Jonathan Kellerman & Faye Kellerman. 7 cass. (Running Time: 11 hrs.). 2004. 63.00 (978-1-4159-0449-7(9)); audio compact disk 81.00 (978-1-4159-0450-3(2)) Books on Tape.

Double Homicide. unabr. ed. Jonathan Kellerman & Faye Kellerman. Read by John Rubinstein & Lou Diamond Phillips. (ENG.). 2005. 14.98 (978-1-59483-148-5(3)) Pub: Hachet Audio. Dist(s): HachBkGrp

Double Homicide. unabr. ed. Jonathan Kellerman & Faye Kellerman. Read by John Rubinstein & Lou Diamond Phillips. (Running Time: 6 hrs.). (ENG.). 2009. 49.98 (978-1-60024-646-3(X)) Pub: Hachet Audio. Dist(s): HachBkGrp

Double Identity. Perf. by Double Identity. 1 cass. 5.00 (A0703-90) Sound Photosyn.
Double I.D. makes their debut with this dynamic modern rock demo, with songs "Too Good for Me," & "What I've Been Missing." Expect to be hearing more from these guys!.

Double Image. David Morrell. Read by David Birney. 4 cass. (Running Time: 6 hrs.). 12.99 (978-1-57815-292-6(5), 4438, Media Bks Audio) Media Bks NJ.

Double Image. David Morrell. Read by David Birney. 5 CDs. (Running Time: 6 hrs.). 2002. audio compact disk 14.99 (978-1-57815-549-1(5), 4438CD5, Media Bks Audio) Media Bks NJ.

Double Inconstance, Set. Marivaux. 2 cass. (FRE.). 1991. 26.95 (1077-RF) Olivia & Hill.
A charming 18th-century comedy of light romance & courtship. The Prince, disguised as a nobleman, wants to steal Silvia away from her faithful lover Arlequin.

***Double Indemnity.** unabr. ed. James Cain. Read by James Naughton. (ENG.). 2005. (978-0-06-085454-6(5), Harper Audio); (978-0-06-085453-9(7), Harper Audio) HarperCollins Pubs.

Double Indemnity. unabr. ed. James M. Cain. Read by James Naughton. Contrib. by James Naughton. (Running Time: 012600 sec.). 2005. audio compact disk 29.95 (978-0-06-075668-0(3)) HarperCollins Pubs.

Double Indemnity, Set. abr. ed. James M. Cain. Read by Barry Bostwick. 2 cass. (Running Time: 3 hrs.). 1996. 17.00 (978-0-89845-777-3(7), 390675) HarperCollins Pubs.
Cain's hard-boiled crime classic about two lovers who plan to commit the perfect murder & cash in on an insurance policy that pays double indemnity. A masterpiece of crime fiction which will pilot the listener through a devious & riveting plot of murderous intrigue & erotic compulsion.

Double Indemnity & the Enchanted Isle. James M. Cain. Read by David Hilder. 8 cass. (Running Time: 12 hrs.). 1995. 64.00 (978-0-7366-2937-9(8), 3633) Books on Tape.
In Double Indemnity, a consuming, empty love destroys everything it touches. In the Enchanted Isle, a desperate teen runaway becomes involved in a deadly bank robbery. Where will she turn?.

Double Jeopardy. William Bernhardt. Read by Jonathan Marosz. 7 hrs. (Running Time: 10 hrs. 30 min.). 1999. 56.00 (5057); 56.00 (978-0-7366-4675-8(2)) Books on Tape.

Double Jeopardy. Michael Underwood. Read by Judith Franklyn. 5 cass. (Running Time: 7 hrs. 30 min.). 2001. 49.95 (64968) Pub: Soundings Ltd GBR. Dist(s): Ulverscroft US

Double Jeopardy. abr. ed. Catherine Coulter. Read by Dick Hill & Sandra Burr. (Running Time: 12 hrs.). (FBI Thriller Ser.: Nos. 3-4). 2008. audio compact disk 29.95 (978-1-4233-6686-7(7), 9781423366867, BACD) Brilliance Audio.

Double Jeopardy. unabr. ed. Colin Forbes. Read by Stephen Thorne. 7 cass. (Isis Ser.). (J). 2004. 61.95 (978-1-85089-606-7(2), 9102X) Pub: ISIS Lrg Prnt GBR. Dist(s): Ulverscroft US

Double Jeopardy. unabr. ed. Michael Underwood. 5 cass. (Sound Ser.). 2004. 49.95 (978-1-85496-496-0(8)) Pub: UlverLrgPrint GBR. Dist(s): Ulverscroft US

Double Jeopardy: Program from the Award Winning Public Radio Series. Interview. Hosted by Fred Goodwin. 1 CD. (Running Time: 1 Hour). 2001. audio compact disk 21.95 (978-1-932479-38-6(4), LCM 158) Lichtenstein Creat.
Mental illness and addiction: for 10 million Americans these debilitating disorders, hard enough to cope with on their own, are a deadly team. Sharing their first hand experiences with dual diagnoses are Robert, a client at New York's innovative Institution for Community Living, and writer Emily Carter. Former deputy drug czar Dr. Herbert Kleber and Jean Henry, clinical director of Journey House, in Louisville, Kentucky discuss challenges in diagnosis and treatment. Dr. Alvin F. Poussaint recalls the loss of his schizophrenic older brother to drug related suicide, and the mental health crisis among African-Americans. And Dr. H. Westley Clark, Director of the Center for Substance Abuse Treatment, at the Office of Substance Abuse and Mental Health Services, outlines SAMSHA's strategies to further the mental health field's effectiveness in this field, and answers calls from concerned family members of those living with the double jeopardy of addiction and psychiatric illness.

Double Life of Pocahontas. Jean Fritz. 2004. bk. 24.95 (978-1-56008-189-0(9)); 8.95 (978-1-56008-888-2(5)) Weston Woods.

Double Life of Pocahontas. unabr. ed. Jean Fritz. Read by Melissa Hughes. 2 CDs. (Running Time: 8100 sec.). (J). (gr. 4-7). 2007. audio compact disk 34.95 (978-0-9761932-8-9(0)) Audio Bkshelf.

Double Meprise, Set. Prosper Merimee. Read by Marine Mouton. 2 cass. (FRE.). 1995. 26.95 (1761-KFP) Olivia & Hill.
Julie de Chaverny has been married for six years when a former admirer returns from Constantinople.

Double Minds. unabr. ed. Terri Blackstock. (Running Time: 9 hrs. 30 mins. 0 sec.). (ENG.). 2009. audio compact disk 24.99 (978-0-310-28812-1(6)) Zondervan.

***Double Minds.** unabr. ed. Terri Blackstock. (Running Time: 9 hrs. 31 mins. 0 sec.). (ENG.). 2009. 14.99 (978-0-310-28813-8(4)) Zondervan.

Double or Die. unabr. ed. Charlie Higson. Read by Nathaniel Parker. 7 CDs. (Running Time: 8 hrs. 33 mins.). (Young Bond Ser.: Bk. 3). (YA). (gr. 6-9). 2008. audio compact disk 55.00 (978-0-7393-6193-1(7), Listening Lib) Random Audio Pubg.

Double or Die. unabr. ed. Charlie Higson. Read by Nathaniel Parker. (Running Time: 30780 sec.). (Young Bond Ser.). (ENG.). (J). (gr. 5). 2008. audio compact disk 37.00 (978-0-7393-5055-3(2), Listening Lib) Pub: Random Audio Pubg. Dist(s): Random

Double or Nothing. M. D. Baer. Narrated by Michael Greene. Told to Leif Garrett. (Running Time: 9000 sec.). 2007. 24.95 (978-1-4332-0088-5(0)) Blckstn Audio.

Double or Nothing. M. D. Baer. Read by Leif Garrett. (Running Time: 9000 sec.). 2007. audio compact disk 19.95 (978-1-4332-0090-8(2)) Blckstn Audio.

Double or Nothing. M. D. Baer. Read by Michael Greene. Told to Leif Garrett. (Running Time: 9000 sec.). 2007. audio compact disk 27.00 (978-1-4332-0089-2(9)) Blckstn Audio.

Double or Nothing. M. D. Baer. Perf. by Leif Garrett et al. Prod. by Leif Garrett. 2 cass. (Running Time: 3 hrs.). 2001. 16.95 Lodestone Catalog.
This tale of intrigue & mystery unfolds with delightful comedy-noir overtones. A gifted pianist, a beautiful violinist, a multi-million dollar land deal & EPA violations are entangled with the death of a wealthy developer.

Double or Nothing. unabr. ed. Prod. by M. D. Baer & Leif Garrett. 2 cass. (Running Time: 2 hrs. 45 min.). 1998. 16.95 Set. (978-0-9667581-0-8(2)) Audio Movies.
Greed over a San Diego County land-development deal results in murders, toxic-waste dumping, revenge, a forced marriage, & concealed identity.

Double or Nothing: How Two Friends Risked It All to Buy One of Las Vegas' Legendary Casinos. Tom Breitling. Read by Patrick G. Lawlor. Told to Cal Fussman. (Playaway Adult Nonfiction Ser.). (ENG.). 2009. 59.99 (978-1-60812-794-8(X)) Find a World.

Double or Nothing: How Two Friends Risked It All to Buy One of Las Vegas' Legendary Casinos. unabr. ed. Tom Breitling. Read by Patrick G. Lawlor. (Running Time: 7 hrs. 30 mins. 0 sec.). (ENG.). 2008. audio compact disk 29.99 (978-1-4001-0611-0(7)); audio compact disk 19.99 (978-1-4001-5611-5(4)); audio compact disk 59.99 (978-1-4001-3611-7(3)) Pub: Tantor Media. Dist(s): IngramPubServ

Double Pedal Gold: A Comprehensive Series of Exercises for Developing Double-Pedal Technique. Joe Morton. 2007. pap. bk. 24.95 (978-1-4234-2597-7(9), 1423425979) Pub: Hudson Music. Dist(s): H Leonard

Double Play. unabr. ed. Robert B. Parker. Read by Robert Forster. (YA). 2008. 54.99 (978-1-60514-774-1(5)) Find a World.

Double Play. unabr. ed. Robert B. Parker. Read by Robert Forster. 4 cass. (Running Time: 6 hrs.). 2004. 24.95 (978-1-59007-426-8(2)); audio compact disk 34.95 (978-1-59007-427-5(0)) Pub: New Millenn Enter. Dist(s): PerseuPGW

Double Search: Matthew 2:1-11, 571. Ed Young. 1986. 4.95 (978-0-7417-1571-5(6), 571) Win Walk.

***Double Shot.** abr. ed. Diane Mott Davidson. Read by Patricia Kalember. (ENG.). 2004. (978-0-06-081421-2(7), Harper Audio); (978-0-06-079863-5(7), Harper Audio) HarperCollins Pubs.

Double Shot. abr. ed. Diane Mott Davidson. Read by Patricia Kalembar. (Running Time: 21600 sec.). (Goldy Schulz Culinary Mysteries Ser.: No. 12). 2006. audio compact disk 14.95 (978-0-06-112654-3(3)) HarperCollins Pubs.

***Double Shot.** unabr. ed. Diane Mott Davidson. Read by Barbara Rosenblat. (ENG.). 2004. (978-0-06-081422-9(5), Harper Audio); (978-0-06-079862-8(9), Harper Audio) HarperCollins Pubs.

Double Shot. unabr. ed. Diane Mott Davidson. Prod. by Barbara Rosenblat. 9 CDs. (Running Time: 10 hrs.). (Goldy Schulz Culinary Mysteries Ser.: No. 12). 2004. audio compact disk 39.95 (978-0-06-073876-1(6)) HarperCollins Pubs.

Double Shot. unabr. ed. Diane Mott Davidson. Narrated by Barbara Rosenblat. 7 cass. (Running Time: 10 hrs. 15 mins.). (Goldy Schulz Culinary Mysteries Ser.: No. 12). 2004. audio compact disk 99.75 (978-1-4193-0550-4(6)) Recorded Bks.

Double Shot. unabr. ed. Diane Mott Davidson. Narrated by Barbara Rosenblat. 7 cass. (Running Time: 10 hrs. 15 mins.). (Goldy Schulz Culinary Mysteries Ser.: No. 12). 2004. 69.75 (978-1-4193-0548-1(4), 97856MC) Recorded Bks.

Double Star. unabr. ed. Robert A. Heinlein. Read by Lloyd James. 5 cass. (Running Time: 7 hrs. 30 mins.). 2000. 39.95 (978-0-7861-1745-1(1), 2549); audio compact disk 48.00 (978-0-7861-9902-0(4), z2549) Blckstn Audio.

Double Star. unabr. ed. Robert A. Heinlein. Read by Lloyd James. 5 cass. (Running Time: 7 hrs.). 2000. 27.95 Penton Overseas.

Double Star. unabr. ed. Robert A. Heinlein. Read by Lloyd James. (Running Time: 7 hrs.). 2000. 24.95 (978-0-7861-9503-9(7)) Blckstn Audio.

Double Take. Catherine Coulter. Read by Sandra Burr & Phil Gigante. (FBI Thriller Ser.: No. 11). 2009. 69.99 (978-1-60775-690-3(0)) Find a World.

Double Take. abr. ed. Catherine Coulter. Read by Sandra Burr & Phil Gigante. (Running Time: 6 hrs.). (FBI Thriller Ser.: No. 11). 2008. audio compact disk 14.99 (978-1-4233-0653-5(8), 9781423306535, BCD Value Price) Brilliance Audio.

***Double Take.** unabr. ed. Kevin Michael Connolly. Read by Kevin Michael Connolly. (ENG.). 2009. (978-0-06-198156-2(7), Harper Audio); (978-0-06-198157-9(5), Harper Audio) HarperCollins Pubs.

Double Take. unabr. ed. Catherine Coulter. (Running Time: 39600 sec.). (FBI Thriller Ser.: No. 11). 2007. audio compact disk 24.95 (978-1-59335-753-5(2), 9781593357535, Brilliance MP3) Brilliance Audio.
Please enter a Synopsis.

Double Take. unabr. ed. Catherine Coulter. Narrated by Sandra Burr & Phil Gigante. (Running Time: 39600 sec.). (FBI Thriller Ser.: No. 11). 2007. 82.25 (978-1-59355-723-2(X), 9781593557232, BrilAudUnabridg) Brilliance Audio.

Double Take. unabr. ed. Catherine Coulter. Read by Sandra Burr & Phil Gigante. (Running Time: 11 hrs.). (FBI Thriller Ser.: No. 11). 2007. 39.25 (978-1-59710-848-5(0), 9781597108485, BADLE); 24.95 (978-1-59710-849-2(9), 9781597108492, BAD); audio compact disk 36.95 (978-1-59355-725-6(6), 9781593557256, Bril Audio CD Unabri); audio compact disk 97.25 (978-1-59355-726-3(4), 9781593557263, BriAudCD Unabrid); audio compact disk 39.25 (978-1-59335-887-7(3), 9781593358877, Brlnc Audio MP3 Lib) Brilliance Audio.

Double Tap. Stephen Leather. 15 CDs. (Isis (CDs) Ser.). 2006. audio compact disk 104.95 (978-0-7531-2577-9(3)) Pub: ISIS Lrg Prnt GBR. Dist(s): Ulverscroft US

Double Tap. Stephen Leather. Read by Martyn Read. 13 cass. (Running Time: 17 hrs. 25 mins.). (Isis Cassettes Ser.). 2006. 99.95 (978-0-7531-3592-1(2)) Pub: ISIS Lrg Prnt GBR. Dist(s): Ulverscroft US

Double Tap. abr. ed. Steve Martini. Read by Joe Mantegna. (Paul Madriani Ser.: No. 8). 2005. 15.95 (978-0-7435-5164-9(8)) Pub: S&S Audio. Dist(s): S and S Inc

Double Trouble: L-Book. RJ Nolan. Sheri. (ENG.). 2008. 13.95 (978-1-934889-20-6(2)) Lbook Pub.

Double Victory: A Mulitcultural History of America in World War II. unabr. ed. Ronald T. Takaki. Read by Edward Lewis. 7 CDs. (Running Time: 8 hrs. 30 mins.). 2001. audio compact disk 56.00 (978-0-7861-9708-8(0), 2801) Blckstn Audio.
In Double Victory, there emerges a broad spectrum of American voices to illustrate the various struggles and victories fought during wartime: a

Japanese-American at an internment camp; a Native American code breaker using the Navajo language for the first time; a Mexican-American woman, "Rosarita, the riveter," who was able to work a job during wartime other than as a housecleaner or a maid.

Double Victory: Multicultural History of America in World War II. unabr. ed. Ronald T. Takaki. Read by Edward Lewis. 6 cass. (Running Time: 8 hrs. 30 mins.). 2001. 44.95 (978-0-7861-2041-3(X), 2801) Blckstn Audio.
Through a broad spectrum of American multicultural voices, demonstrates that World War II helped to transform American society and advance the cause of multiculturalism throughout the country.

Double Vision. Pat Barker & Johanna Ward. 6 cass. (Running Time: 8 hrs. 30 mins.). 2002. 44.95 (978-0-7861-2600-2(0), 3196) Blckstn Audio.

Double Vision. abr. ed. Mary Higgins Clark. 2004. 7.95 (978-0-7435-4510-5(9)) Pub: S&S Audio. Dist(s): S and S Inc

Double Vision. unabr. ed. Pat Barker. Read by Johanna Ward. (Running Time: 8 hrs. 30 mins.). 2004. 24.95 (978-0-7861-8769-0(7), 3196) Blckstn Audio.

Double Vision. unabr. ed. Pat Barker. Read by Johanna Ward. 7 CDs. (Running Time: 8 hrs. 30 mins.). 2006. audio compact disk 56.00 (978-0-7861-8938-0(X), 3196) Blckstn Audio.

Double Whammy. unabr. ed. Carl Hiaasen. Narrated by George Wilson. 10 cass. (Running Time: 13 hrs. 30 mins.). 2003. 94.00 (978-1-4025-3778-3(6)) Recorded Bks.
Robert Clinch loved his boat more that anything else in the world more than his wife his kids his girlfiend Even more than the largemouth bass he was pursuing. Thus begins a twisted tale of murder in the world of big-stakes bass fishing tournaments. Filled with exwives, evangelists, and an armed pit-bull.

Double Win. unabr. ed. Denis Waitley. Read by Denis Waitley. 1 cass. (Running Time: 90 mins.). 1987. 9.95 (978-0-07-067829-3(4)) HarperCollins Pubs.
With anecdotes & careful analysis the author shows how "winning by intimidation" is not really winning at all - how "winning by cooperation" everybody wins.

Double Your Catch! How to catch twice as many Striped Bass on the Fly. (ENG.). 2009. audio compact disk 19.00 (978-0-9788060-2-6(6)) Demopoulos.

Double Your Energy. 2004. audio compact disk 15.98 (978-1-55848-710-9(7)) EffectiveMN.

Double Your Energy Auto-Matically. Robert E. Griswold & Deirdre Griswold. Read by Robert E. Griswold & Deirdre Griswold. 1 cass. (Running Time: 60 min.). (While-U-Drive Ser.). 1997. 11.98 (978-1-55848-904-2(5)) EffectiveMN.
Come alive with positive energy & vitality.

Double Your Income Doing What You Love: Raymond Aaron's Guide to Power Mentoring. unabr. ed. Raymond Aaron. Read by Jim Bond. 1 MP3-CD. (Running Time: 6 hrs.). 2008. 39.25 (978-1-4233-5983-8(6), 9781423359838, Brlnc Audio MP3 Lib); 69.25 (978-1-4233-5979-1(8), 9781423359791, BrilAudUnabridg); audio compact disk 74.25 (978-1-4233-5981-4(X), 9781423359814, BriAudCD Unabrid) Brilliance Audio.

Double Your Income Doing What You Love: Raymond Aaron's Guide to Power Mentoring. unabr. ed. Raymond Aaron. Read by Jim Bond. Told to Sue Lacher. 1 MP3-CD. (Running Time: 6 hrs.). 2008. 24.95 (978-1-4233-5982-1(8), 9781423359821, Brilliance MP3); audio compact disk 26.95 (978-1-4233-5980-7(1), 9781423359807) Brilliance Audio.

Double Your Income Doing What You Love: Raymond Aaron's Guide to Power Mentoring. unabr. ed. Raymond Aaron & Sue Lacher. (Running Time: 6 hrs.). 2008. 39.25 (978-1-4233-5985-2(2), 9781423359852, BADLE); 24.95 (978-1-4233-5984-5(4), 9781423359845, BAD) Brilliance Audio.

Double Your Memory Without a Pencil. Paul Stanyard. 1 cass. 12.50 Alpha Tape.

Double Your Reading Speed in Ten Minutes. Paul R. Scheele. 1 cass. (Running Time: 10 min.). 1999. 19.95 (978-0-925480-94-1(0)) Pub: Learn Strategies. Dist(s): Bookworld

Double Your Revenue: Certify Your Woman-Owned Business. 2007. audio compact disk 35.00 (978-0-9729528-2-8(9)) Cantando.

Double Your Sales Potential. Eldon Taylor. Read by Eldon Taylor. Ed. by Leslie Brice. 8 cass. (Running Time: 8 hrs.). 1992. 89.95 set. (978-1-56705-367-8(X)) Gateways Inst.
Self improvement.

Doublet Affair, unabr. ed. Fiona Buckley. Read by Nadia May. 7 cass. (Running Time: 10 hrs.). 2000. 49.95 (978-0-7861-1725-3(7), 2530) Blckstn Audio.
Young Ursula knows it can be treacherous easing herself into the petty foibles at court, but now, having once saved the Virgin Queen from political disaster, she faces an even greater challenge. Some of Ursula's old acquaintances may be plotting to overthrow Elizabeth in favor of Mary, Queen of Scots & the re-establishment of the Catholic faith. Ardent, some would say fanatical, believers will stop at nothing.

Doublet Affair: An Ursula Blanchard Mystery at Queen Elizabeth I's Court. unabr. ed. Fiona Buckley. Read by Nadia May. (Running Time: 10 hrs. 0 mins.). 2010. 29.95 (978-1-4417-1304-9(2)); audio compact disk 90.00 (978-1-4417-1301-8(8)) Blckstn Audio.

Doublevision. unabr. ed. Tallie Thompson. Read by Stephanie Brush. 8 cass. (Running Time: 9 hrs. 30 min.). 2001. 49.95 (978-1-55686-734-7(4)) Books in Motion.
Does the paranormal play a role in the work of a serial killer, even from his jail cell? When an eyewitness appears who claims to have seen the killer. Police Detective Cynthia "Randy" Randquist is in a race against time to find out if a murderer can be in two places at once.

Doubly Dead. unabr. ed. E. X. Ferrars. Read by Hugh Walters. 6 CDs. (Running Time: 6 hrs.). (Isis Ser.). (J). 2001. audio compact disk 64.95 (978-0-7531-0978-6(6), 109786) Pub: ISIS Lrg Prnt GBR. Dist(s): Ulverscroft US
Margot Dalziel, the well-known journalist, was due in London on Friday, returning from a conference abroad; on Saturday she was expected at her rural cottage. By Sunday it had become apparent that something had gone amiss & for some reason, she had vanished.

Doubly Dead. unabr. ed. E. X. Ferrars. Read by Hugh Walters. 6 cass. (Running Time: 9 hrs.). (Isis Ser.). (J). 2004. 54.95 (978-0-7531-0406-4(7), 981012) Pub: ISIS Lrg Prnt GBR. Dist(s): Ulverscroft US
Margot Dalziel, the well-known journalist, was due in London on Friday, returning from a conference abroad; on Saturday she was expected at her rural cottage. But what really happened on Saturday? By Sunday it had become apparent that something had gone amiss &, for some reason, she had vanished. Margot's country neighbors are soon swept into the web of mystery & suspicion.

Doubt: The Thief of God's Greater Blessing Series. Kenneth E. Hagin. 2 cass. 1996. 8.00 Set. (74H) Faith Lib Pubns.

Doubt: The Thief of God's Greater Blessings. Kenneth E. Hagin. 1 cass. 1996. 8.00 (978-0-00-510402-6(5)) Faith Lib Pubns.

Doubt: A History: The Great Doubters & Their Legacy of Innovation from Socrates & Jesus to Thomas Jefferson & Emily Dickinson. unabr. ed. Jennifer Michael Hecht. Read by Martha Harmon Pardee. (Running Time: 20 hrs. 0 mins.). (ENG.). 2009. 44.95 (978-1-4332-9273-6(4)); 99.95 (978-1-4332-9269-9(6)); audio compact disk 123.00 (978-1-4332-9270-5(X)) Blckstn Audio.

Doubting Thomas. unabr. ed. Morris Gleitzman. Read by Morris Gleitzman. (Running Time: 3 hrs. 30 mins.). (J). 2007. audio compact disk 54.95 (978-1-74093-860-0(7)) Pub: Bolinda Pubng AUS. Dist(s): Bolinda Pub Inc

Doug Oldham: He Saw Me. Perf. by Doug Oldham. 1 cass., 1 CD. 1999. 10.98 (978-0-7601-1904-4(X)); audio compact disk 15.98 CD. (978-0-7601-1905-1(8)) Provident Mus Dist.
Collection of hymns & classic songs from one of Southern Gospel's best-known & beloved vocalists.

***Dougaya Daroga Dadomu.** Vasily Bykau. Read by Vasily Bykau. (BEL.). 2010. (978-0-929849-33-1(7)) RFE-RL Inc.

Doughnuts. 2004. pap. bk. 32.75 (978-1-55592-221-4(X)); pap. bk. 32.75 (978-1-55592-222-1(8)); pap. bk. 14.95 (978-1-55592-671-7(1)) Weston Woods.

Doughnuts. Robert McCloskey. 1 cass., 5 bks. (Running Time: 30 min.). (J). pap. bk. 32.75 Weston Woods.

Doughnuts. Robert McCloskey. 1 cass. (Running Time: 30 min.). (J). (gr. k-6). 2000. pap. bk. 12.95 Weston Woods.
A doughnut machine goes berserk & Homer is up to his ears in doughnuts & fun.

Doughnuts, the; Case of the Cosmic Comic. 2004. bk. 24.95 (978-1-56008-173-9(2)); pap. bk. 14.95 (978-1-56008-174-6(0)); 8.95 (978-1-56008-859-2(1)) Weston Woods.

***Douglas Adams at the BBC: A Celebration of the Author's Life & Work.** Douglas Adams. Compiled by British Broadcasting Corporation Staff. Narrated by Simon Jones. 3 CDs. (Running Time: 4 hrs. 0 mins. 0 sec.). (ENG.). 2010. audio compact disk 29.95 (978-0-563-49404-1(2)) Pub: AudioGO. Dist(s): Perseus Dist

Douglas Casey: Why The Great Depression of The 1980's Will Be A Good Thing. (Running Time: 60 min.). (Cal State Univ., Long Beach). 1982. 9.00 (F134) Freeland Pr.
Holding on to real goods, among other suggestions, is a good way to ride-out this inflationary period, according to the author. He also explains the causes & effects of inflation.

Douglas Wood Reads "Old Turtle" & Kaile Schilling Tells the Story of "Family & Owl" Hosted by Nancy Pearlman. 1 cass. (Running Time: 29 min.). 10.00 (1042) Educ Comm CA.

Dougy. unabr. ed. James Moloney. Read by Peter Hardy. 4 cass. (Running Time: 5 hrs. 15 mins.). (YA). 2000. 32.00 (978-1-74030-106-0(4), 500325) Pub: Bolinda Pubng AUS. Dist(s): Bolinda Pub Inc

Dougy. unabr. ed. James Moloney. Read by Peter Hardy. 5 CDs. (Running Time: 5 hrs. 15 mins.). (YA). 2001. audio compact disk 63.95 (978-1-74030-602-7(3)) Pub: Bolinda Pubng AUS. Dist(s): Bolinda Pub Inc

Dougy, Gracey & Angela (bind-up) unabr. ed. James Moloney. Read by Peter Hardy & Kate Hosking. (Running Time: 18 hrs. 55 mins.). (YA). 2008. 43.95 (978-1-74214-024-7(6), 9781742140247) Pub: Bolinda Pubng AUS. Dist(s): Bolinda Pub Inc

***Dov Baron's Resonating Riches: The Quantum Science of Attracting Wealth.** Dov Baron. (ENG.). 2009. audio compact disk 99.95 (978-0-9810313-2-3(3)) In-Phase Pub CAN.

Dove in the Eagle's Nest, Set. unabr. ed. Charlotte M. Yonge. Read by Flo Gibson. 7 cass. (Running Time: 10 hrs. 30 min.). 1989. 25.95 (978-1-55685-158-2(8)) Audio Bk Con.
The lovely Christine is forced to move to a desolate, craggy castle with a family of robber barons. Her influence over these mountain 'eagles' & their descendants weaves a strange tale.

Dover Beach see Treasury of Matthew Arnold

Doves or Serpents: The Dharma in the Self-Genesis Age; Dream Wisdom. Ann Ree Colton & Jonathan Murro. 1 cass. 7.95 A R Colton Fnd.

Dow Thirty-Six Thousand: The New Strategy for Profiting from the Coming Rise in the Stock Market. abr. ed. James K. Glassman & Kevin Hassett. 2 cass. (Running Time: 3 hrs.). 1999. 17.95 Set. (978-1-55935-326-7(0)) Soundelux.
A radically new theory that the Dow Jones Industrial Average could ultimately reach an estimated value of 36,000.

***Down a Dark Hall.** unabr. ed. Lois Duncan. (Running Time: 7 hrs. 30 mins.). (ENG.). (YA). 2011. 17.98 (978-1-60941-799-4(2)) Pub: Hachet Audio. Dist(s): HachBkGrp

Down a Dark Hall. unabr. ed. Lois Duncan. 1 read-along cass. (Running Time: 83 min.). (Young Adult Cliffhangers Ser.). (YA). (gr. 7 up). 1985. 15.98 incl. bk. & guide. (978-0-8072-1832-7(4), JRH116SP, Listening Lib) Random Audio Pubg.
Left at an exclusive boarding school by her honeymooning mother & new father, Kit finds she is one of the only four students who unknowingly share one terrifying quality.

Down an English Lane. Margaret Thornton & Maggie Mash. 2007. 94.95 (978-1-84652-112-6(2)); audio compact disk 104.95 (978-1-84652-111-9(4)) Pub: Magna Story GBR. Dist(s): Ulverscroft US

Down & Dirty Guide to Adult ADD. Michael Gordon & F. Daniel McClure. 1 cass. 1996. (978-1-887306-00-3(5)) GSI Pubns.

Down & Dirty Pictures: Miramax, Sundance, & the Rise of Independent Film. unabr. ed. Peter Biskind. Read by Phil Gigante. (Running Time: 24 hrs.). 2008. 44.25 (978-1-4233-7118-2(6), 9781423371182, BADLE); 44.25 (978-1-4233-7116-8(X), 9781423371168, Brlnc Audio MP3 Lib); 29.95 (978-1-4233-7117-5(8), 9781423371175, BAD) Brilliance Audio.

Down & Dirty Pictures: Miramax, Sundance, & the Rise of Independent Film. unabr. ed. Peter Biskind. Read by Phil Gigante & Philippe Gigantes. (Running Time: 24 hrs.). 2008. 29.95 (978-1-4233-7115-1(1), 9781423371151, Brilliance MP3) Brilliance Audio.

Down & Dirty Pictures: Miramax, Sundance, & the Rise of Independent Film. unabr. ed. Peter Biskind. Read by Phil Gigante. (Running Time: 24 hrs.). 2008. audio compact disk 127.25 (978-1-4233-7114-4(3), 9781423371144, BriAudCD Unabrid); audio compact disk 49.99 (978-1-4233-7113-7(5), 9781423371137, Bril Audio CD Unabri) Brilliance Audio.

Down & Out in Paris & London. unabr. ed. George Orwell. Read by Frederick Davidson. 5 cass. (Running Time: 7 hrs.). 1993. 39.95 (978-0-7861-0302-7(7), 1266) Blckstn Audio.
The "I" of this novel sets down the experiences of a man who finds himself in Paris, in the early 1930s, without a penny. He manages to keep alive & to record, with sensitivity & graphic power, the strange incidents & characters that his poverty brings him in contact with. The latter half of the book takes the English narrator to his home city, London, where the world of poverty is different in externals only.

Down & Out in Paris & London. unabr. ed. George Orwell. Read by Frederick Davidson. (Running Time: 23400 sec.). 2007. audio compact disk 19.95 (978-0-7861-6147-8(7)) Blckstn Audio.

Down & Out in Paris & London. unabr. ed. George Orwell. Read by Frederick Davidson. (Running Time: 23400 sec.). 2007. audio compact disk 29.95 (978-0-7861-5902-4(2)); audio compact disk 45.00 (978-0-7861-6952-8(4)) Blckstn Audio.

Down & Out in Paris & London, unabr. ed. George Orwell. Narrated by Patrick Tull. 5 cass. (Running Time: 6 hrs. 30 mins.). 1986. 44.00 (978-1-55690-152-2(6), 86480E7) Recorded Bks.
A semi-autobiographical account of Orwell's life as a penniless author in the 1930s.

Down & Out in Paris & London. unabr. collector's ed. George Orwell. Read by Richard Green. 7 cass. (Running Time: 7 hrs.). 1978. 42.00 (978-0-7366-0098-9(1), 1106) Books on Tape.
Orwell, a Socialist, believed the lower classes are the wellspring of the world's reform, so he went to live among them in England & on the Continent. Down & Out in Paris & London recounts Orwell's experiences. He describes a world vastly different from the one we know today in a style that is neither sentimental nor polemic.

Down at the End of Lonely Street: The Life & Death of Elvis Presley. unabr. collector's ed. Peter Brown & Pat Broeske. Read by Connor O'Brien. 11 cass. (Running Time: 16 hrs. 30 min.). 1998. 88.00 (978-0-7366-4129-6(7), 4632) Books on Tape.
This rare look at Elvis explores the private man, from his upbringing through his romances & marriage.

Down but Not Out - Help for Those Who Fail: Genesis 12:10-20. Ed Young. 1994. 4.95 (978-0-7417-2026-9(4), 1026) Win Walk.

Down Buttermilk Lane. unabr. ed. Barbara Mitchell. 1 cass. (Running Time: 7 min.). (J). (gr. k-4). 1994. bk. 25.95 (978-0-8045-6823-4(5), 6823) Spoken Arts.

Down by the Creek Bank. Contrib. by David Huntsinger & Dottie Rambo. 1988. 90.00 (978-0-00-658897-9(2), 75609225) Pub: Brentwood Music. Dist(s): H Leonard

Down by the Station: God Made Me to Do What's Right. Perf. by Karyn F. Henley. 1 CD. (Running Time: Approx. 30 minutes). (J). 2004. audio compact disk 8.99 (978-0-9743197-4-2(0), PLCD4) Child Sens Comm.
Down By the Station is part of Karyn Henley's PLAYSONGS(r) Series, music and movement for little ones (ages 2 to 5).

Down Came the Rain: My Journey Through Postpartum Depression. abr. ed. Brooke Shields. Read by Brooke Shields. 4 cass. (Running Time: 6 hrs.). 2005. 26.98 (978-1-4013-8226-1(6)); audio compact disk 31.98 (978-1-4013-8227-8(4), Hyperion Audio) Pub: Hyperion. Dist(s): HarperCollins Pubs

Down Cemetery Road. Mick Herron. 11 CDs. (Running Time: 13 hrs. 34 mins.). (Isis (CDs) Ser.). (J). 2004. audio compact disk 99.95 (978-0-7531-2355-3(X)) Pub: ISIS Lrg Prnt GBR. Dist(s): Ulverscroft US

Down Cemetery Road. unabr. ed. Mick Herron. Read by Anna Bentinck. 10 cass. (Running Time: 12 hrs. 2 mins.). (Isis Cassettes Ser.). (J). 2004. 84.95 (978-0-7531-1978-5(1)) Pub: ISIS Lrg Prnt GBR. Dist(s): Ulverscroft US

Down Country Roads. Short Stories. Contrib. by Roger Welsch & Ken Root. 1 cass. (Running Time: 63 min.). 2003. 14.95 (978-0-911978-08-7(9)) High Plns Pubs Inc.
Syndicated columinist Ken Root takes you on a journey down country roads. Down Country Roads is a look into the past, present and future of country living. Root relies on nostaliga, humor, entertainment, and education to enlighten the listener.

Down for the Count. Stuart M. Kaminsky. Read by Tom Parker. (Running Time: 5 hrs. 30 mins.). (Toby Peters Mystery Ser.: No. 10). 2003. 24.95 (978-1-59912-475-9(0)) Iofy Corp.

Down for the Count. abr. ed. Mark Shaw. Read by Bill Evans. 2 cass. (Running Time: 3 hrs.). Dramatization. bk. 16.95 set. (978-1-56703-013-6(0)) High-Top Sports.

Down for the Count. unabr. ed. Stuart M. Kaminsky. Read by Tom Parker. 4 cass. (Running Time: 5 hrs. 30 mins.). (Toby Peters Mystery Ser.: No. 10). 2003. 32.95 (978-0-7861-2461-9(X), 3096); audio compact disk 40.00 (978-0-7861-9186-4(4), 3096) Blckstn Audio.
Private eye Toby Peters follows boxing as much as the next guy, but he never expected to encounter heavyweight champion Joe Louis this way: covered with blood and standing on a deserted beach next to the corpse of Peters?s ex-wife?s husband. The champ is innocent, but he has something to hide, and Toby agrees to protect the Brown Bomber from the police and the press.

Down from the Hill. unabr. ed. Alan Sillitoe. Read by Richard Earthy. 5 cass. (Running Time: 6 hrs. 30 min.). 1995. 49.95 (978-1-85089-743-9(3), 90104) Pub: ISIS Audio GBR. Dist(s): Ulverscroft US
It's a story about stories. Paul knows that he constructs reality out of lies...Like Ulysses & Huck Finn, Paul is a storyteller who deals with the people he meets on the road by making up identities for himself & for them...Comically & richly faithful to its great tradition.

Down from Troy: A Doctor Comes of Age. unabr. ed. Richard Selzer. Narrated by Sam Gray. 6 cass. (Running Time: 9 hrs.). 1995. Rental 13.50 Set. (94494) Recorded Bks.
In this delightful memoir of a surgeon's formative years, the land lovingly evoked is not the windswept Ilios of Homer but a quiet city huddled beside the banks of the Hudson River, where even the dogs pause to admire the autumn foliage. Selzer has woven into the fabric of remembrance his reflections upon the doctor-patient relationship, the architecture of hospitals, his harrowing immersion in a malpractice suit & the death of an AIDS patient.

Down from Troy: A Doctor Comes of Age, unabr. ed. Richard Selzer. Narrated by Sam Gray. 6 cass. (Running Time: 9 hrs.). 1995. 51.00 (978-0-7887-0301-0(3), 94494E7) Recorded Bks.

Down Here. unabr. ed. Andrew Vachss. Read by Phil Gigante. (Running Time: 10 hrs.). (Burke Ser.). 2011. audio compact disk 29.99 (978-1-4418-2422-6(7), 9781441824226, Bril Audio CD Unabri) Brilliance Audio.

***Down Here.** unabr. ed. Andrew Vachss. Read by Phil Gigante. (Running Time: 10 hrs.). (Burke Ser.). 2011. 24.99 (978-1-4418-2426-4(X), 9781441824264, BAD); 39.97 (978-1-4418-2427-1(8), 9781441824271, BADLE); 24.99 (978-1-4418-2424-0(3), 9781441824240, Brilliance MP3); 39.97 (978-1-4418-2425-7(1), 9781441824257, Brlnc Audio MP3 Lib); audio compact disk 79.97 (978-1-4418-2423-3(5), 9781441824233, BriAudCD Unabrid) Brilliance Audio.

Down Home Dairyland Recordings. James P. Leary. Contrib. by Richard March. (ENG.). 2004. audio compact disk 60.00 (978-0-924119-17-0(9)) Pub: U of Wis Pr. Dist(s): Chicago Distribution Ctr

Down Home Dairyland Recordings. James P. Leary & Richard March. 2004. reel tape 40.00 (978-0-924119-16-3(0)) Pub: Max Kade. Dist(s): U of Wis Pr

Down in the Backpack. Read by Bill Harley. 1 CD. (Running Time: 1 hr. 30 min.). (J). 2001. audio compact disk 15.00 (978-1-878126-43-6(1)); 10.00 (978-1-878126-44-3(X)) Round Riv Prodns.
Eleven new songs showcasing his trademark humor and musicality and featuring favorites like "Down in the Backpack," "Mom and the Radio" and "Milky Way".

Down in the Valley. Perf. by Linda Williams & Robin Williams. (J). 1999. audio compact disk 14.95 (978-0-939065-99-8(1)) Gentle Wind.

Down in the Valley. Robin Williams & Linda Williams. 1 cass. (Running Time: 34 min.). (J). (gr. k up). 1982. 9.95 (978-0-939065-11-0(8), GW 1011) Gentle Wind.
Features songs including Beetle with the Boogie Woogie Beat, C-H-I-C-K-E-N, Nebraska Corn, Frere jacques, Flop Eared Mule & Others.

Down in the Zero. unabr. ed. Andrew Vachss. Read by Phil Gigante. (Running Time: 10 hrs.). (Burke Ser.). 2010. audio compact disk 29.99 (978-1-4418-2121-8(X), 9781441821218, Bril Audio CD Unabri) Brilliance Audio.

***Down in the Zero.** unabr. ed. Andrew Vachss. Read by Phil Gigante. (Running Time: 10 hrs.). (Burke Ser.). 2010. 39.97 (978-1-4418-2124-9(4), 9781441821249, Brlnc Audio MP3 Lib); 24.99 (978-1-4418-2123-2(6), 9781441821232, Brilliance MP3); 24.99 (978-1-4418-2125-6(2), 9781441821256, BAD); 39.97 (978-1-4418-2126-3(0), 9781441821263, BADLE); audio compact disk 79.97 (978-1-4418-2122-5(8), 9781441821225, BriAudCD Unabrid) Brilliance Audio.

Down Memory Lane. Mormon Tabernacle Choir. 1 cass. 4.98 (1500562); audio compact disk 8.98 (1500570) Covenant Comms.
Includes "Singing in the Rain" & "Happy Days Are Here Again".

Down Our Street. unabr. ed. Joan Jonker. Read by Maggie Ollerenshaw. 12 cass. (Running Time: 18 hrs.). 2000. 96.95 (978-0-7540-0540-7(2), CAB 1963) Pub: Chivers Audio Bks GBR. Dist(s): AudioGO
With the Second World War finally over, best friends Molly Bennett & Nellie McDonough are bursting with happiness. Their beloved sons are coming home at last & their eldest children are planning to marry each other.

Down Range: To Iraq & Back. Bridget C. Cantrell & Chuck Dean. Read by Bram Floria. (ENG.). 2009. 39.99 (978-1-61587-755-3(X)) Find a World.

Down River. unabr. ed. John Hart. Read by Scott Sowers. 10 CDs. (Running Time: 12 hrs. 0 mins. 0 sec.). (ENG.). 2007. audio compact disk 39.95 (978-1-4272-0193-5(5)) Pub: Macmill Audio. Dist(s): Macmillan

***Down Sand Mountain.** unabr. ed. Steve Watkins. (Running Time: 11 hrs.). 2011. 39.97 (978-1-4558-0376-7(6), 9781455803767, Candlewick Bril); 19.99 (978-1-4558-0375-0(8), 9781455803750, Candlewick Bril); 19.99 (978-1-4558-0372-9(3), 9781455803729, Candlewick Bril); 39.97 (978-1-4558-0373-6(1), 9781455803736, Candlewick Bril); audio compact disk 24.99 (978-1-4558-0370-5(7), 9781455803705, Candlewick Bril); audio compact disk 54.97 (978-1-4558-0371-2(5), 9781455803712, Candlewick Bril) Brilliance Audio.

Down Syndrome - A Bibliography & Dictionary for Physicians, Patients, & Genome Researchers. Compiled by Icon Group International, Inc. Staff. 2007. ring bd. 28.95 (978-0-497-11369-8(4)) Icon Grp.

Down the Colorado with Major Powell: A Great Storm in Utah see Down the Colorado with Major Powell: Selected Writings of John Muir

Down the Colorado with Major Powell: A Perilous Night on Shasta's Summit see Down the Colorado with Major Powell: Selected Writings of John Muir

Down the Colorado with Major Powell: An Ascent of Mt. Ranier see Down the Colorado with Major Powell: Selected Writings of John Muir

Down the Colorado with Major Powell: Bathing in Salt Lake see Down the Colorado with Major Powell: Selected Writings of John Muir

Down the Colorado with Major Powell: Nevada's Dead Towns see Down the Colorado with Major Powell: Selected Writings of John Muir

Down the Colorado with Major Powell: Puget Sound see Down the Colorado with Major Powell: Selected Writings of John Muir

Down the Colorado with Major Powell: Selected Writings of John Muir. unabr. collector's ed. James R. Ullman & John Muir. Read by Scott Forbes. 8 cass. (Running Time: 8 hrs.). Incl. Down the Colorado with Major Powell: A Great Storm in Utah. 1960. (1051); Down the Colorado with Major Powell: A Perilous Night on Shasta's Summit. 1960. (1051); Down the Colorado with Major Powell: An Ascent of Mt. Ranier. 1960. (1051); Down the Colorado with Major Powell: Bathing in Salt Lake. 1960. (1051); Down the Colorado with Major Powell: Nevada's Dead Towns. 1960. (1051); Down the Colorado with Major Powell: Puget Sound. 1960. (1051); Down the Colorado with Major Powell: Summer Days at Mt. Shasta. 1960. (1051); Down the Colorado with Major Powell: The Forests of Oregon & Their Inhabitants. 1960. (1051); Down the Colorado with Major Powell: The Grand Canyon of the Colorado. 1960. (1051); Down the Colorado with Major Powell: The People & Towns of Puget Sound. 1960. (1051); Down the Colorado with Major Powell: The Rivers of Oregon. 1960. (1051); Down the Colorado with Major Powell: Selected Writings of John Muir. John Muir. 1960. (1051); 1977. 48.00 (978-0-7366-0040-8(X), 1051) Books on Tape.
"Down the Colorado" is the narrative of the first party to explore the Grand Canyon 100 years ago. John Wesley Powell, leader of the expedition, was a one-armed hero of the Civil War. He was also a professional geologist & pioneer - & a fabulous observer.

Down the Colorado with Major Powell: Summer Days at Mt. Shasta see Down the Colorado with Major Powell: Selected Writings of John Muir

Down the Colorado with Major Powell: The Forests of Oregon & Their Inhabitants see Down the Colorado with Major Powell: Selected Writings of John Muir

Down the Colorado with Major Powell: The Grand Canyon of the Colorado see Down the Colorado with Major Powell: Selected Writings of John Muir

Down the Colorado with Major Powell: The People & Towns of Puget Sound see Down the Colorado with Major Powell: Selected Writings of John Muir

Down the Colorado with Major Powell: The Rivers of Oregon see Down the Colorado with Major Powell: Selected Writings of John Muir

Down the Do Re Mi. Red Grammer & Kathy Grammer. 1 cass. (J). (ps-6). 1991. 10.00 (978-1-886146-03-7(9)); audio compact disk 15.00 CD. (978-1-886146-07-5(1)) Red Note Recs.

***Down the Rabbit Hole.** unabr. ed. Peter Abrahams. Read by Mandy Siegfried. (ENG.). 2005. (978-0-06-084300-7(4), Harper Audio); (978-0-06-084299-4(7), Harper Audio) HarperCollins Pubs.

Down the Rabbit Hole. unabr. ed. Peter Abrahams. Read by Mandy Siegfried. 8 CDs. (Running Time: 7 hrs.). (Echo Falls Mystery Ser.: No. 1). (J). 2005. audio compact disk 27.95 (978-0-06-078664-9(7), HarperChildAud) HarperCollins Pubs.

Down the Rabbit Hole. unabr. ed. Peter Abrahams. Narrated by Mandy Siegfried. 6 cass. (Running Time: 8 hrs.). (Echo Falls Mystery Ser.: No. 1). (YA). 2005. 37.75 (978-1-4193-5747-3(6)) Recorded Bks.
In this riveting tale from Edgar nominee Peter Abrahams, 13-year old Ingrid Levin-Hill has landed a part in a local production of Alice in Wonderland. But when a woman associated with the drama group is murdered, and Ingrid is tied to the crime, the teenager embarks on a dizzying investigation that soon makes her feel a lot like the fabled fictional Alice.

Down the River. unabr. collector's ed. Edward Abbey. Read by Paul Shay. 6 cass. (Running Time: 9 hrs.). 1988. 48.00 (978-0-7366-1441-2(9), 2324) Books on Tape.
This book, which takes us up & down rivers & across mountains & deserts, is the perfect antidote to despair.

Down the Yukon. unabr. ed. Will Hobbs. Read by Boyd Gaines. (ENG.). (J). (gr. 5). 2009. audio compact disk 30.00 (978-0-7393-8229-5(2), Listening Lib) Pub: Random Audio Pubg. Dist(s): Random

Down the Yukon. unabr. ed. William Hobbs. Read by Boyd Gaines. 3 vols. (Running Time: 4 hrs. 56 mins.). (Middle Grade Cassette Librariestm Ser.). (J). (gr. 5-9). 2004. pap. bk. 36.00 (978-0-8072-0786-4(1), S YA 310 SP, Listening Lib); 30.00 (978-0-8072-0513-6(3), S YA 310 CX, Listening Lib) Random Audio Pubg.
"As Dawson City goes up in flames, Jason Hawthorn itches to join the new rush for gold in Nome-nearly 2,000 miles away. When a race to Nome is announced with a $20,000 prize, Jason and the girl he loves, Jamie Dunavant, set out to attempt the journey together in their canoe. The Great Race across Alaska will be a grueling test of their courage and skills as they face the hazards of the Yukon River, two very dangerous men, and the terrors of the open sea.".

Down They Rolled. (Language of Mathematics Ser.). 1989. 7.92 (978-0-8123-6403-3(1)) Holt McDoug.

Down to a Soundless Sea: Stories. unabr. ed. Thomas Steinbeck. Read by David Colacci. 6 cass. Library ed. (Running Time: 8 hrs.). 2002. 74.25 (978-1-59086-433-3(6), 1590864336, Unabridge Lib Edns) Brilliance Audio.
Here is a fiction debut that is cause for celebration. Growing up in a family that valued the art of storytelling and the power of oral history, Thomas Steinbeck now follows in his father's footsteps with a brilliant story collection. Down to a Soundless Sea resonates with the rich history and culture of California, recalling vivid details of life in Monterey County from the turn of the century through the 1930s. Steinbeck accomplishes an amazing feat: His stories have the feel of classic literature, but his haunting voice, forceful narrative drive, and dazzling imagery are unmistakably his own. In seven stories, Steinbeck traces the fates and dreams of an eccentric cast of characters, from sailors and ranchers to doctors and immigrants - as each struggles to carve out a living in the often inhospitable environment of rocky cliffs, crashing surf, and rough patches of land along the California coast.

Down to a Soundless Sea: Stories. unabr. ed. Thomas Steinbeck. Read by David Colacci. (Running Time: 8 hrs.). 2004. 39.25 (978-1-59710-218-6(0), 1597102180, BADLE); 24.95 (978-1-59710-219-3(9), 1597102199, BAD) Brilliance Audio.

***Down to a Soundless Sea: Stories.** unabr. ed. Thomas Steinbeck. Read by Jeff Harding. (Running Time: 9 hrs.). 2010. 24.99 (978-1-4418-5359-2(6), 9781441853592, Brilliance MP3); 24.99 (978-1-4418-5361-5(8), 9781441853615, BAD); 39.97 (978-1-4418-5360-8(X), 9781441853608, Brlnc Audio MP3 Lib); 39.97 (978-1-4418-5362-2(6), 9781441853622, BADLE); audio compact disk 29.99 (978-1-4418-5357-8(X), 9781441853578, Bril Audio CD Unabri); audio compact disk 79.97 (978-1-4418-5358-5(8), 9781441853585, BriAudCD Unabrid) Brilliance Audio.

Down to a Soundless Sea: Stories. unabr. ed. Thomas Steinbeck. Read by David Colacci. (Running Time: 8 hrs.). 2004. 24.95 (978-1-59335-045-1(7), 1593350457) Soulmate Audio Bks.

Down to Earth. unabr. ed. Faith Addis. Narrated by Briony Sykes. 6 cass. (Running Time: 8 hrs.). 2000. 56.00 (978-1-84197-113-1(8), H1109E7) Recorded Bks.
The Addises seem determined to try every form of country living possible, putting into practice the most creative & bizarre plans imaginable.

Down to Earth Faith: Genesis 11:31. Ed Young. 1994. 4.95 (978-0-7417-2024-5(8), 1024) Win Walk.

Down-to-Earth Guide to Global Warming. unabr. ed. Laurie David & Cambria Gordon. Narrated by Polly Lee. 2 cass. (Running Time: 2 hrs. 30 mins.). (J). (gr. 4-6). 2008. 25.75 (978-1-4281-9127-3(5)); audio compact disk 25.75 (978-1-4281-9132-7(1)) Recorded Bks.

Down to the Dirt. Thomas J. Hynes. Read by Sherry White & Jonny Harris. (Running Time: 23400 sec.). 2006. audio compact disk 29.95 (978-0-9737586-2-7(7)) Rattling Bks CAN.

Down Will Come Baby. unabr. ed. Gloria Murphy. Read by Julie Finneran. (Running Time: 7 hrs.). 2008. 39.25 (978-1-4233-5900-5(3), 9781423359005, Brlnc Audio MP3 Lib); 24.95 (978-1-4233-5899-2(6), 9781423358992, Brilliance MP3); 39.25 (978-1-4233-5902-9(X), 9781423359029, BADLE); 24.95 (978-1-4233-5901-2(1), 9781423359012, BAD) Brilliance Audio.

Down with High Blood Pressure. 1 cassette. 1985. 12.95 (978-1-55841-003-9(1)); audio compact disk 16.95 (978-1-55841-103-6(8)) Emmett E Miller.
Powerful, drug-free methods use the energy of your mind to help return your blood pressure to normal. Four experiences to reduce tension and pressure, discover the triggers for blood pressure elevation, inactivate those triggers, and enjoy your new level of health.

Down with Perfectionism. Jack Marshall. 1 cass. 7.98 (978-1-55503-416-0(0), 06004644) Covenant Comms.
Help for women who are trying to be perfect now.

Down 42nd Street: Sex, Money, Culture, & Politics at the Crossroads of the World. abr. ed. Marc Eliot. (ENG.). 2005. 14.98 (978-1-59483-392-2(3)) Pub: Hachet Audio. Dist(s): HachBkGrp

Downeast Stand-up. Perf. by Tim Sample. 8.95 (978-0-9607546-9-4(5), 15) Bert and I Inc.
Lively comic tales recorded before a sellout crowd at the Lakewood Theater in Skowhegan, Maine.

Downhill Lie: A Hacker's Return to a Ruinous Sport. unabr. ed. Read by Carl Hiaasen. 5 CDs. (Running Time: 5 hrs. 45 mins.). 2008. audio compact disk 40.00 (978-1-4159-4579-7(9)) Random.

Downhill Lie: A Hacker's Return to a Ruinous Sport. unabr. ed. Carl Hiaasen. Read by Carl Hiaasen. 5 CDs. (Running Time: 6 hrs.). (ENG.). 2008. audio compact disk 29.95 (978-0-7393-5831-3(6), Random AudioBks) Pub: Random Audio Pubg. Dist(s): Random

Downing of TWA Flight 800. abr. ed. James D. Sanders. Read by James D. Sanders. 1 cass. (Running Time: 1 hr. 30 min.). 1997. 9.95 (978-1-882071-95-1(6)) B-B Audio.
On July 17, 1996, minutes after take off, TWA Flight 800 was blown out of the sky, killing all 230 people on board. A naval operation went terribly wrong off the coast of Long Island, releasing an anti-missile missile in the flight path of the doomed TWA.

Downing of TWA Flight 800. unabr. ed. James D. Sanders. Read by James D. Sanders. 2 cass. (Running Time: 3 hrs.). 1997. 17.95 (978-1-882071-99-9(9)) B-B Audio.

Downing Street Years, Pt. 1. unabr. ed. Margaret Thatcher. Read by Donada Peters. 14 cass. (Running Time: 1 hrs. 30 min. per cass.). 1993. 112.00 Set. (3958-A); Rental 14.95 Set. (3958-A) Books on Tape.
Not since Winston Churchill, has a British head of state had such influential a role in U. S. politics & world events as Margaret Thatcher. This gutsy memoir reveals her thoroughness, her tenacity, & her passion for change. It reads like a thriller.

Downing Street Years, Pt. 2. unabr. ed. Margaret Thatcher. Read by Donada Peters. 13 cass. (Running Time: 1 hrs. 30 min. per cass.). 1993. 104.00 Set. (3958-B); Rental 5.00 Set. (3958-B) Books on Tape.

Downriver. unabr. ed. William Hobbs. Narrated by Christina Moore. 4 pieces. (Running Time: 6 hrs.). (gr. 7 up). 1997. 35.00 (978-0-7887-1101-5(6), 95094E7) Recorded Bks.
When 15-year-old Jessie & her six companions "borrow" some gear & attempt to raft the Colorado River through the Grand Canyon, all of them are shocked to find that the whitewater might be the least of their problems.

Downstream. Ed. by Robert A. Monroe. 1 cass. (Running Time: 30 min.). (Meta Music Ser.). 1985. 12.95 (978-1-56102-207-6(1)) Inter Indus.
Carefully blended Hemi-Sync patterns designed to open up areas of your consciousness that contain your possibilities of future activities.

***Downtime: Teaching Teens to Pray.** Mark Yaconelli. (Running Time: 5 hrs. 40 mins. 0 sec.). (ENG.). 2008. 19.99 (978-0-310-30234-6(X)) Zondervan.

***Downtown.** abr. ed. Anne Rivers Siddons. Read by Kate Burton. (ENG.). 2005. (978-0-06-087925-9(4), Harper Audio); (978-0-06-087924-2(6), Harper Audio) HarperCollins Pubs.

Downtown. unabr. ed. Ed McBain, pseud. Read by Michael Prichard. 8 cass. (Running Time: 8 hrs.). (87th Precinct Ser.). 1992. 48.00 (978-0-7366-2142-7(3), 2940) Books on Tape.
Within 24 hours an innocent businessman is swindled, robbed, framed for murder & hunted by an assassin. A sensational change for McBain.

Downtown. unabr. ed. Ed McBain, pseud. Read by David Regal. (Running Time: 8 hrs.). 2009. 39.97 (978-1-4233-8587-5(X), 9781423385875, Brlnc Audio MP3 Lib); 24.99 (978-1-4233-8586-8(1), 9781423385868, Brilliance MP3); 39.97 (978-1-4233-8589-9(6), 9781423385899, BADLE); 24.99 (978-1-4233-8588-2(8), 9781423385882, BAD) Brilliance Audio.

Downtown. unabr. ed. Ed McBain, pseud. Narrated by Richard Ferrone. 8 cass. (Running Time: 10 hrs. 45 mins.). 1991. 70.00 (978-1-55690-153-9(4), 91405E7) Recorded Bks.
A visitor from out of town finds himself a murder suspect in New York City.

Downtown. unabr. ed. Anne Rivers Siddons. Narrated by Barbara Caruso. 12 cass. (Running Time: 17 hrs. 15 mins.). 1994. 97.00 (978-0-7887-0062-0(6), 94318E7) Recorded Bks.
It is a time of great change, both personally & for the United States as well, when a young woman comes to Atlanta in the early 1960's to join the staff of a magazine.

Downtown: My Manhattan. abr. ed. Pete Hamill. (ENG.). 2005. 14.98 (978-1-59483-135-5(1)) Pub: Hachet Audio. Dist(s): HachBkGrp

Downtown: My Manhattan. abr. ed. Pete Hamill. (Running Time: 6 hrs.). (ENG.). 2009. 49.98 (978-1-60024-918-1(3)) Pub: Hachet Audio. Dist(s): HachBkGrp

Downtown: My Manhattan. unabr. ed. Pete Hamill. 6 cass. (Running Time: 10 hrs.). 2004. 72.00 (978-1-4159-0825-9(7)) Books on Tape.

Downtown: My Manhattan. unabr. ed. Pete Hamill. Read by Don Leslie. 7 CDs. (Running Time: 10 hrs.). 2004. audio compact disk 90.00 (978-1-4159-0826-6(5)) Books on Tape.
During his 40 years as a newspaperman, Pete Hamill has been getting to know Manhattan's neighborhoods and inhabitants intimately, witnessing their triumphs as well as tragedies. From the remnants of the British colony, the mansions of the robber barons, to the winding, bohemian streets of Greenwich village and the weathered cobblestones of South Street Seaport, Hamill looks at the history to reveal the city's past, present, and future. More than just a reportage, this is an elegy by a native son who has lived through some of New York's most historic moments.

Downtown Owl. unabr. ed. Chuck Klosterman. Read by Chuck Klosterman. Read by Phillip Baker Hall et al. (Running Time: 9 hrs. 0 mins. 0 sec.). (ENG.). 2008. audio compact disk 39.95 (978-0-7435-7372-6(2)) Pub: S&S Audio. Dist(s): S and S Inc

Downward Path to Wisdom. unabr. ed. Katherine Anne Porter. 1 cass. (Running Time: 90 min.). 1984. 12.95 (978-0-694-50003-1(8), SWC 1006) HarperCollins Pubs.

Dozen a Day for Guitar - Book 1: Technical Exercises for the Guitar to Be Done Each Day Before Practicing. Dale Turner. 2007. pap. bk. 12.99 (978-1-4234-5126-6(0), 1423451260) Pub: Willis Music Co. Dist(s): H Leonard

Dozen Great Ideas. 1 cass. 11.95 (978-1-57025-006-4(5)) Whole Person.
These pointers from seasoned trainers will spark your imagination & sharpen your skills.

Dr. Albert Bartlett Examines the Mythology of Population Growth & the Economy. Hosted by Nancy Pearlman. 1 cass. (Running Time: 29 min.). 10.00 (1216) Educ Comm CA.

Dr. Andrew Weil's Guide to Optimum Health. unabr. ed. Read by Andrew Weil. 8 CDs. (Running Time: 8 hrs.). 2002. audio compact disk 69.95 (978-1-56455-978-4(5), AW00615D) Sounds True.
On this complete 8-hour curriculum, Dr. Weil personally helps you take charge of your total well-being with proven, natural solutions for boosting your body's self-healing function, building energy, and overcoming everyday health challenges.

Dr. Atkins' Age-Defying Diet Revolution: Nature's answer to Drugs. Robert C. Atkins. Read by Jeffrey DeMunn. 2004. 10.95 (978-0-7435-1878-9(0)) Pub: S&S Audio. Dist(s): S and S Inc

Dr. Atkins' New Diet Revolution. abr. ed. Robert C. Atkins. Read by Eric Conger. 2 cass. (Running Time: 3 hrs.). 1998. 18.00 Set. (978-0-694-52001-5(2)) HarperCollins Pubs.
Shows how to reach the ideal weight & how to stay there. The focus is on the overall theory of weight loss & wellness, demonstrating how weight loss can help reduce a variety of health problems, including chronic fatigue syndrome, diabetes & high blood pressure.

***Dr. Atkins' New Diet Revolution.** abr. ed. Robert C. Atkins. Read by Eric Conger. (ENG.). 2004. (978-0-06-078332-7(X), Harper Audio); (978-0-06-082480-8(8), Harper Audio) HarperCollins Pubs.

Dr. Atkins' New Diet Revolution. unabr. ed. Robert C. Atkins. Read by Eric Conger. (Running Time: 10800 sec.). 2008. audio compact disk 14.95 (978-0-06-146771-4(5), Harper Audio) HarperCollins Pubs.

Dr. Benjamin E. Mays at Morehouse. Rex A. Barnett. (Running Time: 40 min.). (YA). 1990. 16.99 (978-0-924198-04-5(4)) Hist Video.
Dr. Benjamin E. Mays' academic genius is analyzed.

Dr. Bill Harrison: Baseball, Vision Dynamics. Read by Bill Harrison. 1 cass. 9.95 (978-0-89811-081-4(5), 7132) Lets Talk Assocs.

Dr. Birute Galdikas' Twenty-Five Years with Wild & Rehabilitated Orangutans in Indonesia; Whooping Crane Update. Hosted by Nancy Pearlman. 1 cass. (Running Time: 28 min.). 10.00 (1419) Educ Comm CA.

Dr. Blair's Chinese Mandarin in No Time: The Revolutionary New Language Instruction Method That's Proven to Work! unabr. ed. Robert Blair. 3 CDs. (Running Time: 3 hrs.). (ENG.). 2005. audio compact disk 17.98 (978-1-59659-012-0(2), GildAudio) Pub: Gildan Media. Dist(s): HachBkGrp

Dr. Blair's Express Lane: Chinese. unabr. ed. Robert Blair. (ENG.). 2006. 4.99 (978-1-59659-061-8(0), GildAudio) Pub: Gildan Media. Dist(s): HachBkGrp

Dr. Blair's Express Lane: French. unabr. ed. Robert Blair. (ENG.). 2006. 4.99 (978-1-59659-059-5(9), GildAudio) Pub: Gildan Media. Dist(s): HachBkGrp

Dr. Blair's Express Lane: German. unabr. ed. Robert Blair. (ENG.). 2006. 4.99 (978-1-59659-064-9(5)) HachBkGrp.

Dr. Blair's Express Lane: Ingles. unabr. ed. Robert Blair. (ENG.). 2006. 4.99 (978-1-59659-063-2(7), GildAudio) Pub: Gildan Media. Dist(s): HachBkGrp

Dr. Blair's Express Lane: Italian. unabr. ed. Robert Blair. (ENG.). 2006. 4.99 (978-1-59659-058-8(0), GildAudio) Pub: Gildan Media. Dist(s): HachBkGrp

Dr. Blair's Express Lane: Japanese. unabr. ed. Robert Blair. (ENG.). 2006. 4.99 (978-1-59659-062-5(9), GildAudio) Pub: Gildan Media. Dist(s): HachBkGrp

Dr. Blair's Express Lane: Spanish. unabr. ed. Robert Blair. (ENG.). 2006. 4.99 (978-1-59659-060-1(2), GildAudio) Pub: Gildan Media. Dist(s): HachBkGrp

Dr. Blair's French in No Time. Robert Blair. Read by Robert Blair. (Running Time: 3 hrs. 15 mins.). (C). 2005. 33.95 (978-1-59912-153-6(0)) Iofy Corp.

Dr. Blair's French in No Time: The Revolutionary New Language Instruction Method That's Proven to Work! unabr. ed. Robert Blair. 3 CDs. (Running Time: 3 hrs.). (ENG.). 2005. audio compact disk 17.98 (978-1-59659-004-5(1), GildAudio) Pub: Gildan Media. Dist(s): HachBkGrp

Dr. Blair's German in No Time: The Revolutionary New Language Instruction Method That's Proven to Work. unabr. ed. Robert Blair. 3 CDs. (Running Time: 3 hrs.). (ENG.). 2005. audio compact disk 17.98 (978-1-59659-032-8(7), GildAudio) Pub: Gildan Media. Dist(s): HachBkGrp

Dr. Blair's Ingles in No Time. Robert Blair. Read by Robert Blair. (Running Time: 3 hrs.). 2005. 33.95 (978-1-59912-164-2(6)) Iofy Corp.

Dr. Blair's Ingles in No Time: Language Learning Comes to Life. unabr. ed. Robert Blair. 3 CDs. (Running Time: 3 hrs.). (ENG.). 2005. audio compact disk 17.98 (978-1-59659-019-9(X), GildAudio) Pub: Gildan Media. Dist(s): HachBkGrp

Dr. Blair's Italian in No Time. Robert Blair. Read by Robert Blair. (Running Time: 3 hrs. 30 mins.). (C). 2005. 33.95 (978-1-59912-163-5(8)) Iofy Corp.

Dr. Blair's Italian in No Time: Language Learning Comes to Life. unabr. ed. Robert Blair. 3 CDs. (Running Time: 3 hrs.). (ENG.). 2005. audio compact disk 17.98 (978-1-59659-018-2(1), GildAudio) Pub: Gildan Media. Dist(s): HachBkGrp

Dr. Blair's Japanese in No Time. Robert Blair. Read by Robert Blair. (Running Time: 3 hrs.). (C). 2005. 33.95 (978-1-59912-159-8(X)) Iofy Corp.

Dr. Blair's Japanese in No Time: The Revolutionary New Language Instruction Method That's Proven to Work! unabr. ed. Robert Blair. 3 CDs. (Running Time: 3 hrs.). (ENG.). 2005. audio compact disk 17.98 (978-1-59659-013-7(0), GildAudio) Pub: Gildan Media. Dist(s): HachBkGrp

Dr. Blair's Mandarin Chinese in No Time. Robert Blair. Read by Robert Blair. (Running Time: 2 hrs.). (C). 2005. 33.95 (978-1-59912-158-1(1)) Iofy Corp.

Dr. Blair's Spanish in No Time. Robert Blair. Read by Robert Blair. (Running Time: 3 hrs. 30 mins.). (C). 2005. 33.95 (978-1-59912-154-3(9)) Iofy Corp.

Dr. Blair's Spanish in No Time: The Revolutionary New Language Instruction Method That's Proven to Work! unabr. ed. Robert Blair. 3 CDs. (Running Time: 3 hrs.). (ENG.). 2005. audio compact disk 17.98 (978-1-59659-005-2(X), GildAudio) Pub: Gildan Media. Dist(s): HachBkGrp

Dr. Bloodmoney: Or How We Got along after the Bomb. unabr. ed. Philip K. Dick. Read by Tom Weiner. (Running Time: 30600 sec.). 2008. 59.95 (978-1-4332-4549-7(3)) Blckstn Audio.

Dr. Bloodmoney: Or, How We Got along after the Bomb. unabr. ed. Philip K. Dick. Read by Tom Weiner. (Running Time: 30600 sec.). 2008. audio compact disk 29.95 (978-1-4332-4551-0(5)); audio compact disk & audio compact disk 70.00 (978-1-4332-4550-3(7)) Blckstn Audio.

Dr. Bob Costanza - Ecological Economics; Controlled Burns; The Hug-a-Tree Program. Hosted by Nancy Pearlman. 1 cass. (Running Time: 28 min.). 10.00 (1303) Educ Comm CA.

Dr. Bob Rotella. abr. gif. ed. Bob Rotella. Read by Bob Rotella. 6 CDs. (Running Time: 53 hrs. 0 mins. 0 sec.). (ENG.). 2005. audio compact disk 39.95 (978-0-7435-4477-1(3)) Pub: S&S Audio. Dist(s): S and S Inc

Dr. Christian. Contrib. by Jean Hersholt. (Running Time: 10800 sec.). 2004. 9.98 (978-1-57019-576-1(5)); audio compact disk 9.98 (978-1-57019-577-8(3)) Radio Spirits.

***Dr. Christian.** RadioArchives.com. (Running Time: 360). (ENG.). 2004. audio compact disk 17.98 (978-1-61081-020-3(1)) Radio Arch.

Dr. Christian: Cupid's Boomerang & Old Battle Ax. Perf. by Jean Hersholt. 1 cass. (Running Time: 1 hr.). 2001. 6.98 (1562) Radio Spirits.

Dr. Colbert's Family Guide to Health, Vol. 2, Pack. abr. unabr. ed. Don Colbert. (Family Guide to Health Ser.). (ENG.). 2007. audio compact disk 19.99 (978-1-59859-269-6(6)) Oasis Audio.

Dr. Colbert's I Can Do This Diet: New Medical Breakthroughs That Use the Power of Your Brain & Body Chemistry to Help You Lose Weight & Keep It off for Life. unabr. ed. Don Colbert. Narrated by Kyle Colbert. (Running Time: 9 hrs. 22 mins. 6 sec.). (ENG.). 2010. 19.59 (978-1-60814-624-6(3)); audio compact disk 27.99 (978-1-59859-678-6(0)) Oasis Audio.

Dr. David Pimentel Advocates Lower Population Totals; David Simcox Urges Reduced Immigration Totals; Reports on Land Stewardship, Texas Wild Rice Protection During Canoe Race & Bear-Human Interactions. Hosted by Nancy Pearlman. 1 cass. (Running Time: 29 min.). 10.00 (1423) Educ Comm CA.

Dr. Davy's Dinosaur Sing-Along. 1 cass. (Running Time: 35 mins.). (J). 2000. 6.98 (978-0-7396-0215-7(2)); audio compact disk 9.98 (978-0-7396-0214-0(4)) Peter Pan.

Dr. Death. Jonathan Kellerman. Read by John Rubinstein. (Alex Delaware Ser.: No. 14). 2000. 64.00 (978-0-7366-5918-5(8)) Books on Tape.

Dr. Death. unabr. ed. Jonathan Kellerman. Read by John Rubinstein. 8 cass. (Running Time: 12 hrs.). (Alex Delaware Ser.: No. 14). 2000. 35.95 (Random AudioBks) Random Audio Pubg.
Milo Sturgis & Dr. Alex Delaware investigate the ironic murder of a doctor responsible for scores of assisted suicides.

Dr. Dimension. 4 cass. (Running Time: 6 hrs.). 2001. 34.95 (HHIR002) Lodestone Catalog.

Dr. Don Colbert's Family Guide to Health Pack: Colds, Weight Loss, Depression & High Cholesterol. unabr. ed. Don Colbert. Read by Steve Hiller. (Family Guide to Health Ser.). (ENG.). 2007. audio compact disk 19.99 (978-1-59859-202-3(5)) Oasis Audio.

Dr Dre: The Unauthorized Biography of Dr Dre. Ben Graham. (Maximum Ser.). (ENG.). 2001. audio compact disk 14.95 (978-1-84240-130-9(0)) Pub: Chrome Dreams GBR. Dist(s): IPG Chicago
Presents the complete story of the man who used hip-hop as his ticket out of the ghetto, from his earliest days right through to his present chart-topping work with Eminem and his Chronic 2001 which further cemented his reputation as an artist of major global proportions.

Dr. Estelle Ramey: How to Help Men Live Longer. Estelle Ramey. 1 cass. (Running Time: 70 min.). 11.95 (K0340B090, HarperThor) HarpC GBR.

Dr. Farran's 30-Day MBA, Set. unabr. ed. Howard Farran. 30 cass. (Running Time: 1 hr. 10 mins. per cass.). 1999. 495.00 (978-1-929023-01-1(4)); audio compact disk 495.00 (978-1-929023-02-8(2)) Farran Ent.
Lecturer, author & practicing dentist, Dr. Farran, presents successful strategies to transform any practice into an economic power house!.

Dr Fell's Cabinet of Smells. Susan P. Gates. Read by Nigel Lambert. 4 CDs. (J). 2004. audio compact disk 34.95 (978-0-7540-6640-8(1), Chivers Child Audio) AudioGO.

Dr. Finlay: Further Adventures of a Black Bag. A. J. Cronin. 2004. audio compact disk 39.95 (978-0-563-52606-3(8)) AudioGO.

Dr. Finlay Adventures of a Black Bag. unabr. ed. A. J. Cronin. 3 vols. (Running Time: 4 hrs.). 2003. audio compact disk 39.95 (978-0-563-49690-8(8), BBCD 035) BBC Worldwide.
Over the course of six episodes, the early years of Dr. Finlay are explored, as he gets to grips with the locals in the Scottish Highland town of Levenford. But the new doctor is full of surprises; caring, stubborn, idealistic and clever, but he proves to be more than a match for the local residents.

Dr. Fritz Reid of Ducks Unlimited's North American Waterfowl Preservation & Wetlands Restoration Efforts. Hosted by Nancy Pearlman. 1 cass. (Running Time: 28 min.). 10.00 (1408) Educ Comm CA.

Dr. fulford's touch of life the healing power of the natural life Force. Robert Fulford. 2004. 7.95 (978-0-7435-4656-0(3)) Pub: S&S Audio. Dist(s): S and S Inc

Dr. George Freibott: Tesla, Koch, 02 Therapies. George Freibott. 1 cass. (Roy Tuckman Interview Ser.). 9.00 (A0688-90) Sound Photosyn.
Live on KPFA.

Dr. Gurgevich's Amazing Hypnotic Tonic to Remove Phobias. Scripts. Steven Gurgevich. Prod. by Steven Gurgevich. 1 CD. (Running Time: 1 hr 14 min). (ENG.). 2003. audio compact disk 24.95 (978-1-932170-04-7(9), HWH) Tranceformation.

Dr. Gurgevich's Amazing Hypnotic Tonic to Remove Tobacco Addiction. Scripts. Steven Gurgevich. Prod. by Steven Gurgevich. 2 CDs. (Running Time: 2 hrs 20 min). (ENG.). 2002. audio compact disk 49.95 (978-1-932170-01-6(4), HWH) Tranceformation.

Dr. Gypsee Gunn's Demotivational Seminar. Gypsee Gunn. 1 CD. (Running Time: 52 mins.). 2001. audio compact disk 14.99 Lodestone Catalog.
Feeling useless, run-down, fatigued, neglected, un-cared for, broken-down, decrepit, tattered or untidy? Now you can harness your innate failure & fail to succumb to the hum & the drum by listening to the Leader of the Beleaguered Masses.

Dr. Hakkak Sadegh Hedayat. (PER.). 2006. DVD & audio compact disk 32.99 (978-1-933429-10-6(0)) Ket Goo Pub.

Dr. Heidegger's Experiment see Tales of Terror & the Supernatural: A Collection

Dr. Heidegger's Experiment see Sredni Vashtar

Dr. Heidegger's Experiment. 1977. (N-12) Jimcin Record.

Dr. Heidegger's Experiment. Nathaniel Hawthorne. Read by David Rosenblatt. 1 cass. (Running Time: 34 min. per cass.). 1980. 10.00 (LSS1106) Esstee Audios.
The author develops an atmosphere of the mysterious & the macabre with Dr. Heidigger giving youth potions to his aged, disenchanted peers.

Dr. Helen Caldicott at the National Press Club. Narrated by Helen Caldicott. 1 cass. (Running Time: 1 hr.). 10.95 (PP-83-02-25, HarperThor) HarpC GBR.

Dr. Jack Payne on Agricultural Conservation Partnerships for Wetlands & a Look At: Ducks Unlimited's "Care" Program. Hosted by Nancy Pearlman. 1 cass. (Running Time: 29 min.). 10.00 (1402) Educ Comm CA.

Dr. Jane Goodall - Thirty Years with the Wild Chimpanzees. Hosted by Nancy Pearlman. 1 cass. (Running Time: 29 min.). 10.00 (807) Educ Comm CA.

Dr. Jean & Friends. Perf. by Jean R. Feldman. 1 cass. (J). 10.95; audio compact disk 14.95 Child Like.

Dr. Jean Sings Silly Songs. Perf. by Jean R. Feldman. 1 cass. 10.95; audio compact disk 14.95 Child Like.

Dr Jean Variety Pack. Jean Feldman. (J). (ps-3). 2007. pap. bk. 56.87 (978-1-59198-719-2(9)) Creat Teach Pr.

Dr. Jeckyll & Mr. Hyde. Perf. by Atlanta Radio Theatre Company Staff. 1 cass. (Running Time: 1 hr.). 2001. 12.95 (ARTC003) Lodestone Catalog.
A gripping story of a gentle doctor & his chemotherapy gone made.

Dr. Jekyll & Mr. Hyde. Robert Louis Stevenson. Read by David Thorn. 2006. audio compact disk (978-0-9787553-1-7(6)) Alcazar AudioWorks.

Dr. Jekyll & Mr. Hyde. Robert Louis Stevenson. Narrated by Grover Gardner. (ENG.). 2008. audio compact disk 16.95 (978-1-60646-059-7(5)) Audio Bk Con.

Dr. Jekyll & Mr. Hyde. Robert Louis Stevenson. Read by Ian Holm. 1 cass. 12.00 (978-1-878427-41-0(5), XC437) Cimino Pub Grp.
The story is generally familiar due to films & stage adaptations, which, however faithful to the plot, have not been able to convey the agony & conflict that permeates the mind of Dr. Jekyll as well as Robert Louis Stevenson's original words, especially when produced by one of our greatest classical actors, Ian Holm, whose voice & performance adds an extra spine-chilling dimension to the text.

Dr. Jekyll & Mr. Hyde. Robert Louis Stevenson. Read by Ralph Cosham. (Running Time: 2 hrs. 30 mins.). 2002. 16.95 (978-1-59912-060-7(7), Audiofy Corp) Iofy Corp.

Dr. Jekyll & Mr. Hyde. Robert Louis Stevenson. Read by Scott Brick. (Running Time: 3 hrs.). 2003. 23.95 (978-1-60083-644-2(5), Audiofy Corp) Iofy Corp.

Dr. Jekyll & Mr. Hyde. Robert Louis Stevenson. Ed. by Raymond Harris. Illus. by Robert J. Pailthorpe. (Classics Ser.). (YA). (gr. 6-12). 1982. bk. 17.96 (978-0-89061-255-2(2), 452) Jamestown.

Dr. Jekyll & Mr. Hyde. Robert Louis Stevenson. Read by John Sessions. 2 cass. (Running Time: 2 hrs. 30 mins.). (Classic Fiction Ser.). (YA). 1996. 13.98 (978-962-634-590-0(X), NA209014, Naxos AudioBooks) Naxos.
Dr. Jekyll wants to rid his soul of evil and in doing so creates the monstrous alter ego, Mr. Hyde. As time goes on, he slides increasingly into this other side of his personality until it finally takes over, with disastrous consequences.

Dr. Jekyll & Mr. Hyde. Robert Louis Stevenson. Narrated by Ralph Cosham. (Running Time: 9000 sec.). (Unabridged Classics in MP3 Ser.). (ENG.). (YA). 2008. audio compact disk 24.00 (978-1-58472-642-5(3), In Aud) Sound Room.

Dr. Jekyll & Mr. Hyde. Robert Louis Stevenson. 10.95 (SAC 1089) Spoken Arts.

Dr. Jekyll & Mr. Hyde. Robert Louis Stevenson. Read by Scott Brick. (ENG.). 2003. audio compact disk 52.00 (978-1-4001-3076-4(X)) Pub: Tantor Media. Dist(s): IngramPubServ

Dr Jekyll & Mr. Hyde. Robert Louis Stevenson. 2007. audio compact disk 25.95 (978-0-8095-7188-8(9)) Diamond Book Dists.

Dr. Jekyll & Mr. Hyde. Robert Louis Stevenson & Alan Venable. (Classic Literature Ser.). 2005. pap. bk. 69.00 (978-1-4105-0117-2(5)); audio compact disk 18.95 (978-1-4105-0118-9(3)) D Johnston Inc.

Dr. Jekyll & Mr. Hyde. abr. ed. Robert Louis Stevenson. 1 cass. (Running Time: 50 min.). Dramatization. (Classics Illustrated Bks.). (J). 5.95; Audio Bk.
Full cast.

Dr. Jekyll & Mr. Hyde. abr. ed. Robert Louis Stevenson. Narrated by Gene Lockhart. 2 cass. (Running Time: 2 hrs. 49 min.). 12.95 (978-0-89926-144-7(2), 832) Audio Bk.

Dr. Jekyll & Mr. Hyde. abr. ed. Robert Louis Stevenson. Read by Roger Rees. 2 cass. (Running Time: 3 hrs.). 2004. 18.00 (978-1-931056-77-9(3), N Millennium Audio) New Millenn Enter.
When the philanthropic, genial Dr. Jekyll becomes intensely interested in the problems of good & evil & their effects on the nature of man, his deliberations soon drive him into his laboratory. There, he pursues an answer to a question that has become his obsession: can the two opposing forces be separated? His experiments produce an astonishing drug that draws out the evil side of his own nature: the evil Mr. Hyde.

Dr. Jekyll & Mr. Hyde. adpt. ed. Robert Louis Stevenson. (Bring the Classics to Life: Level 4 Ser.). (gr. 4-16). 2008. audio compact disk 12.95 (978-1-55576-570-5(X)) EDCON Pubng.

Dr. Jekyll & Mr. Hyde, collector's ed. Robert Louis Stevenson & Henry James. Read by Angela Cheyne. 7 cass. (Running Time: 7 hrs.). 1977. 42.00 (978-0-7366-0058-3(2), 1070) Books on Tape.
The story of a wealthy physician who, with the help of chemical formulations, as a young man begins to live a double life.

Dr. Jekyll & Mr. Hyde. unabr. ed. Robert Louis Stevenson. Featuring William Brown et al. 1 cass. (Running Time: 90 min.). Dramatization. 2002. 12.95 (978-0-929483-19-1(7)) Centauri Express Co.
Suppose you could travel the streets in a perfect disguise; commit any crime, indulge any vice, do whatever you wanted, to anyone you wanted, unburdened by guilt or remorse; and no one would ever know it was you. What would you do? Would you ever stop? Would you still be yourself? Or can a creature without compassion, without self-restraint, without morals, still be called human at all.

Dr. Jekyll & Mr. Hyde. unabr. ed. Robert Louis Stevenson. 2 cass. (Running Time: 3 hrs.). (Horror Library). 1997. pap. bk. 16.95 (978-1-55656-222-8(5)) Pub: Dercum Audio. Dist(s): APG
One of the most horrific depictions of the human potential for evil ever written. In Stevenson's famous supernatural story of good versus evil, meet the well-intentioned, wealthy physician Dr. Jekyll. As he drinks the potion that is the culmination of his research, he unleashes the dark side of his nature, turning into the hideous Mr. Hyde.

Dr. Jekyll & Mr. Hyde. unabr. ed. Robert Louis Stevenson. Read by Patrick Horgan. 2 cass. (Running Time: 2 hrs. 21 min.). (Cassette Bookshelf Ser.). 1987. 15.98 (978-0-8072-3448-8(6), CB116CX, Listening Lib) Random Audio Pubg.
Stevenson's tale of a good doctor who, with the best of intentions, experiments with human nature...& the results are monstrous.

Dr. Jekyll & Mr. Hyde. unabr. ed. Robert Louis Stevenson. Read by Alexander Spencer. 6 Cass. (Running Time: 8.75 Hrs.). 19.95 (978-1-4025-1150-9(7)) Recorded Bks.

Dr. Jekyll & Mr. Hyde, unabr. ed. Robert Louis Stevenson. Narrated by Alexander Spencer. 2 cass. (Running Time: 2 hrs.). 1999. 18.00 (978-1-55690-155-3(0), 80050E7) Recorded Bks.
Saintly Dr. Henry Jekyll is the epitome of dedication, while the frightening Mr. Edward Hyde commits murder. What strange secret binds these two men in the fog of London?.

Dr. Jekyll & Mr. Hyde. unabr. ed. Robert Louis Stevenson. 2 CDs. (Running Time: 2 hrs. 30 mins.). 2002. audio compact disk 25.00 (978-1-58472-101-7(4), Commuters Library) Sound Room.

Dr. Jekyll & Mr. Hyde. unabr. ed. Robert Louis Stevenson. Read by Ralph Cosham. 2 cds. (Running Time: 2 hrs 26 mins). (YA). 2002. pap. bk. (978-1-58472-245-8(2), In Aud) Sound Room.
Intrigue and the split nature of man.

Dr. Jekyll & Mr. Hyde. unabr. ed. Robert Louis Stevenson. Read by Ralph Cosham. 2 cass. (Running Time: 3 hrs.). 1996. bk. 16.95 (978-1-883049-69-0(5), 394107, Commuters Library) Sound Room.
The classic thriller that tells of a man of science who has found a way to live in the two worlds of his nature. Although not as famous, the second story, "Markheim," is a tour-de-force. Markheim murders with the intent to rob on Christmas day & is approached by a strange visitor who offers to show him where the money is hidden.

Dr. Jekyll & Mr. Hyde. unabr. ed. Robert Louis Stevenson. Read by Ralph Cosham. 2 CDs. (Running Time: 2 hrs. 30 mins.). 2000. audio compact disk 18.95 (Commuters Library) Sound Room.

Dr. Jekyll & Mr. Hyde. unabr. ed. Robert Louis Stevenson. Read by Ralph Cosham. 2 cds. (Running Time: 2 hrs 26 mins). (YA). 2002. audio compact disk 18.95 (978-1-58472-243-4(6), 014, In Aud) Pub: Sound Room. Dist(s): Baker Taylor
The classic thriller of the split nature of man.

Dr. Jekyll & Mr. Hyde. unabr. ed. Robert Louis Stevenson. Narrated by Scott Brick. 1 MP3 CD. (Running Time: 3 hrs. 9 mins.). (ENG.). 2003. audio compact disk 20.00 (978-1-4001-5076-2(0)) Pub: Tantor Media. Dist(s): IngramPubServ

Dr. Jekyll & Mr. Hyde. unabr. ed. Robert Louis Stevenson. Narrated by Scott Brick. (Running Time: 3 hrs. 0 mins. 0 sec.). (ENG.). 2008. 17.99 (978-1-4001-5859-1(1)); audio compact disk 17.99 (978-1-4001-0859-6(4)) Pub: Tantor Media. Dist(s): IngramPubServ

Dr. Jekyll & Mr. Hyde. unabr. ed. Robert Louis Stevenson. Read by Tim Behrens. 2 cass. (Running Time: 2 hrs. 30 min.). 1991. 16.95 (978-1-55686-217-5(2), 217) Books in Motion.
Dr. Jekyll, a London physician of good reputation, discovers a drug that changes him from a kindly sane man to a hideous person of cruel & criminal instincts. He must find an antidote before Mr. Hyde takes over.

Dr. Jekyll & Mr. Hyde, Set. Robert Louis Stevenson. 2 cass. 1992. 26.95 (1627-LV) Olivia & Hill.
The strange case of Dr. Jekyll who discovers a drug which enables him to create another personality with all his evil instincts.

Dr. Jekyll & Mr. Hyde, Set. abr. ed. Robert Louis Stevenson. Perf. by St. Charles Players. 2 cass. Dramatization. 1999. 16.95 (FS9-50879) Highsmith.

Dr. Jekyll & Mr. Hyde, Set. abr. ed. Robert Louis Stevenson. Perf. by St. Charles Players. 2 cass. (Running Time: 95 min.). (Mystery Theatre Ser.). 1999. 16.95 (978-1-56994-514-8(4), 32904, Monterey SoundWorks) Monterey Media Inc.
A Classic story of good & evil, where a gentle doctors' experiment transforms him into a hideous monster by night.

Dr. Jekyll & Mr. Hyde, Set. unabr. ed. Robert Louis Stevenson. Read by Grover Gardner. 2 cass. (Running Time: 2 hrs. 30 min.). 1994. 14.95 (978-1-55685-344-9(0)) Audio Bk Con.
Henry Jekyll, convinced of the duality of human nature, attempts an experiment to separate the good & evil aspects of his own character. The shocking results lead to calamity & horror.

***Dr. Jekyll & Mr. Hyde: Bring the Classics to Life.** adpt. ed. Robert Louis Stevenson. (Bring the Classics to Life Ser.). 2008. pap. bk. 21.95 (978-1-55576-611-5(0)) EDCON Pubng.

Dr. Jekyll & Mr. Hyde & Other Tales of the Macabre. unabr. ed. Robert Louis Stevenson. 6 cass. (Running Time: 9 hrs.). Dramatization. 1980. 42.00 (C-36) Jimcin Record.
Includes Stevenson's famous story of a wealthy physician who, through the use of drugs, unleashes the dark, evil side of his nature.

Dr. Jekyll & Mr. Hyde & Travels with a Donkey. abr. ed. Robert Louis Stevenson. 4 cass. (Running Time: 6 hrs. 40 min.). 1995. 26.95 (978-1-885546-04-3(1)) Big Ben Audio.

Dr. Jekyll & Mr Hyde Read Along. (Saddleback's Illustrated Classics Ser.). (J). 2006. (978-1-56254-895-7(6)) Saddleback Edu.

Dr. John Hospers: An Evaluation of The Reagan Administration. (Running Time: 60 min.). (Cal State Univ., Long Beach). 1982. 9.00 (F136) Freeland Pr.
The author begins by citing some positive benefits of the administration on "our" domestic policy in the first term.

Dr. John R. Christopher's Herbal Lectures: Formally New Herb Lectures. John R. Christopher. Read by John R. Christopher. 12 cass. (Running Time: 11 hrs. 32 min.). (ENG.). 1978. 69.95 set. (978-1-879436-02-2(7), 99102) Christopher Pubns.
Lecture tapes covering various systems & organs of the body, & natural healing methods with herbs & diet.

Dr. Laura Audio Collection. unabr. ed. Laura Schlessinger. Read by Laura Schlessinger. 5 cass. (Running Time: 7 hrs.). 1997. 39.95 HarperCollins Pubs.

Dr. Laura Berman: Date with Confidence. Narrated by Laura Berman. 2006. audio compact disk 23.95 (978-1-59987-558-3(6)) Braun Media.

Dr. Laura Berman: Good Sex, Good Relationship. Narrated by Laura Berman. 2006. audio compact disk 23.95 (978-1-59987-547-7(0)) Braun Media.

Dr. Laura Berman: Safe Guard Your Relationship. Narrated by Laura Berman. 2006. audio compact disk 23.95 (978-1-59987-559-0(4)) Braun Media.

Dr. Laura Berman: Spice up Your Relationship. Narrated by Laura Berman. 2006. audio compact disk 23.95 (978-1-59987-557-6(8)) Braun Media.

Dr. Laura Berman: Talk to Teens about Dating & Sex. Narrated by Laura Berman. 2006. audio compact disk 23.95 (978-1-59987-560-6(8)) Braun Media.

Dr. Laura Collection. Laura Schlessinger. 1997. 39.95 (978-0-694-51894-4(8)) HarperCollins Pubs.

Dr. Laura's "Ten Commandments" Leonard Peikoff. 1998. 12.95 (LPXXC85) Second Renaissance.

Dr. Lazlo Szijj on Urban Habitat & "Wildlife Refuges Under Siege" Hosted by Nancy Pearlman. 1 cass. (Running Time: 29 min.). 10.00 (1006) Educ Comm CA.

Dr. Linus Pauling, Vol. 2. 1 cass. (Running Time: 1 hr. 10 min.). (From the Source Ser.). 1987. 9.95 (978-0-944831-13-7(3)) Health Life.

Dr. Looney's Remedy. Perf. by Parachute Express Staff. 1 cass., 1 CD. (J). 7.98 (TLR 1017); audio compact disk 11.18 CD Jewel box. (TLR 1017) NewSound.
Includes: "Working Together," "Me & My Dog," "A Little Night Light" & more.

Dr. Maniac vs. Robby Schwartz. R. L. Stine. (Goosebumps HorrorLand Ser.: No. 5). (J). (gr. 4-7). 2008. audio compact disk 9.95 (978-0-545-11154-6(4)); audio compact disk 29.95 (978-0-545-11329-8(6)) Scholastic Inc.

***Dr. Margaret's Sea Chest.** unabr. ed. Waheed Rabbani. Narrated by Elizabeth Terry. (ENG.). 2010. audio compact disk 41.95 (978-1-60031-072-0(9)) Spoken Books.

Dr. Mary Courage, Set. unabr. ed. Alex Stuart. Read by Margaret Holt. 4 cass. (Sound Ser.). 1987. 44.95 (978-1-85496-193-8(4), US0111) Pub: UlverLrgPrint GBR. Dist(s): Ulverscroft US

Dr. Mays the Legend. Rex A. Barnett. (Running Time: 40 min.). (YA). 16.99 (978-0-924198-06-9(0)) Hist Video.
Academic genius & contributions of Dr. Benjamin E. Mays is reviewed.

Dr. Nathaniel & E. Devers Branden: Honoring The Self: A Participatory Workshop. 2 cass. (Running Time: 2 hrs.). (Cal State Univ., Long Beach). 1982. 18.00 (F142A & B) Freeland Pr.
Can be used to perform home therapy & for problem-solving.

Dr. Nightingale Seeks Greener Pastures. unabr. ed. Lydia Adamson. Read by Laura Hicks. 4 vols. (Running Time: 6 hrs.). 2001. bk. 39.95 (978-0-7927-2489-6(5), CSL 378, Chivers Sound Lib) AudioGO.
Dr. Deirdre "Didi" Nightingale is finding the dwindling dairy industry hard on her practice & her pocketbook. Thinking that racehorses might be the winning ticket to more business, she heads to a vet conference in Atlantic City to find out. But when Didi finds a famous horse doctor mysteriously murdered & his widow offers her a hefty sum to edit his unfinished book, she's pulled into a conspiracy where the stakes are high & life seems to be cheap.

Dr. Nightingale Traps the Missing Lynx. unabr. ed. Lydia Adamson. Read by Laura Hicks. 4 vols. (Running Time: 6 hrs.). (Deirdre Quinn Nightingale Mystery Ser.). 2000. bk. 39.95 (978-0-7927-2386-8(4), CSL 275, Chivers Sound Lib) AudioGO.
Dr. Deidre "Didi" Nightingale leapt at the chance to earn a fat fee by appearing at a plush local fund raiser. Six mixed-breed bobcat kittens were to be auctioned off & all Didi had to do was give the cats a clean bill of health. But when the party's host walks in covered with bloody scratches & promptly drops dead, Didi is mystified. She recognizes the symptoms of rattlesnake venom when she sees them. The poison that killed Buster Purchase didn't come from any feline.

Dr. No. unabr. ed. Ian Fleming. Read by David Rintoul. 6 cass. (Running Time: 6 hrs.). 1993. 54.95 (978-0-7451-5929-4(X), CAB 130) AudioGO.

Dr. No. unabr. ed. Ian Fleming. Read by Robert Whitfield. 5 cass. (Running Time: 7 hrs.). 2001. 39.95 (978-0-7861-1957-8(8), 2728); audio compact disk 56.00 (978-0-7861-9765-1(X), 2728) Blckstn Audio.
M called this case a soft option. Bond can't quite agree. The tropical island is luxurious, the seductive Honey Rider is beautiful and willing, but they are both part of the empire of Dr. No . . . The doctor is a worthy adversary, with a mind as hard and cold as his solid steel hands. Dr. No's obsession is power. His only gifts are strictly pain-shaped.

Dr. No. unabr. ed. Ian Fleming. Read by Simon Vance. (Running Time: 7 hrs. 0 mins.). 2009. audio compact disk 19.95 (978-1-4332-5857-2(9)) Blckstn Audio.

Dr. No. unabr. ed. Ian Fleming. Read by David Rintoul. 6 cass. (Running Time: 9 hrs.). (James Bond Ser.: Bk. 6). 2000. 49.95 (CAB 130) Pub: Chivers Audio Bks GBR. Dist(s): AudioGO
M hasn't forgiven James Bond for the negligence on his last assignment that nearly cost 007 his life. So he decides to send him on a vacation. Bond angrily accepts his orders and flies off the Jamaica. But on the horizon a cloud forms, it is no bigger than a man's hand, the articulated steel hand of Dr. No!.

Dr. Perricone's 7 Secrets to Beauty, Health & Longevity: The Miracle of Cellular Rejuvenation. abr. unabr. ed. Nicholas Perricone. Read by Jeff Woodman. (Running Time: 6 hrs. 0 mins. 0 sec.). (ENG.). 2006. audio compact disk 24.95 (978-1-4272-0074-7(2)) Pub: Macmill Audio. Dist(s): Macmillan

***Dr. Peter Marshall's Sermons Complete Set.** Executive Producer Peter Marshall Ministries. 1999. audio compact disk 189.95 (978-0-9771811-4-8(6)) Pet Mars Mini.

Dr. Quantum Presents: A User's Guide to the Universe. unabr. ed. Fred Alan Wolf. 6 CDs. (Running Time: 7 hrs. 30 min.). 2005. audio compact disk 69.95 (978-1-59179-348-9(3), AF00949D) Sounds True.
At the heart of quantum reality lies an astonishing (and scientifically proven) truth: that the very act of observing events in your life can alter their outcome. Therefore, suggests Dr. Wolf, we can define the fabric of reality at a fundamental level with the choices we make, the things we choose to see or not see, and most importantly, our intentions in each moment.

Dr. Quantum Presents Do-It-Yourself Time Travel. Fred Alan Wolf. (Running Time: 26100 sec.). 2008. audio compact disk 69.95 (978-1-59179-946-7(5)) Sounds True.

Dr. Quantum Presents: Meet the Real Creator - You! Fred Alan Wolf. 4 CDs. (Running Time: 16200 sec.). 2005. audio compact disk 29.95 (978-1-59179-380-9(7), W976D) Sounds True.

Dr. Reginald Cherry's Pathway to Healing Seminar. Reginald B. Cherry. 1 cass. 1997. 29.99 (978-0-88419-512-2(0), CreatHse) Strang Comms Co.

Dr. Robert A Cook's Teaching Series. 12 cass. 27.98 (RC25) Chrstn Dup Intl.

Dr. Robert Gale: American Physician at Chernobyl. Robert Gale. 1 cass. (Running Time: 60 min.). 10.95 (K0280B090, HarperThor) HarpC GBR.

Dr. Rose. unabr. ed. Elvi Rhodes. Read by Anne Dover. 7 cass. (Running Time: 10 hrs. 30 min.). (Sound Ser.). 1992. 61.95 (978-1-85496-657-5(X)) Pub: UlverLrgPrint GBR. Dist(s): Ulverscroft US
The only woman doctor working in the Welfare Center of an industrial Yorkshire town in the 1920s, Rose faces several onerous challenges. Fighting sexism & prejudice from the men on staff, & poverty & illiteracy in the patients she is trying to help, Rose is determined to prove she is talented, committed, & the best person for the job.

Dr. Rosenfeld's Guide to Alternative Medicine: What Works, What Doesn't - What's Right for You. unabr. ed. Isadore Rosenfeld. 6 cass. 1998. 26.95 Set. (978-1-55935-283-3(3)) Soundelux.
Discusses such approaches as hypnosis, acupuncture, aromatherapy, homeopathy, oxygen therapy, & much more.

Dr. Sam Johnson, Detector. unabr. ed. Lillian De La Torre. Narrated by Alexander Spencer. 5 cass. (Running Time: 7 hrs. 30 mins.). 1989. 44.00 (978-1-55690-154-6(2), 89691E7) Recorded Bks.
Nine mysteries featuring Dr. Samuel Johnson & James Boswell as investigators.

Dr. Schiff's Weight Loss Plan for Health, Beauty & Happiness. unabr. collector's ed. Martin Schiff. Read by Martin Schiff. 4 cass. (Running Time: 4 hrs.). 1986. 24.00 (978-0-7366-0739-1(0), 1696) Books on Tape.
Weight loss cannot be achieved by dieting alone. This series shows you how to shed fattening thoughts, attitudes & behavior patterns, then develop positive feelings & a new lifestyle that allows you to lose weight-& keep it off.

Dr. Seuss Audio Collection. unabr. ed. Dr. Seuss. 1 cass. (Running Time: 1 hr. 30 mins.). 2003. 7.99 (978-0-06-058458-0(0)) HarperCollins Pubs.

Dr. Seuss Audio Collection. unabr. abr. ed. Dr. Seuss. Illus. by Hans Conried. 1 cass. (Running Time: 37 min.). Incl. And to Think That I Saw It on Mulberry Street. (J). (ps-1). 1987. (CPN 1287); Big Brag. (J). (ps-1). 1987. (CPN 1287); Gertrude McFuzz. (J). (ps-1). 1987. (CPN 1287); Happy Birthday to You! (J). (ps-1). 1987. (CPN 1287); Scrambled Eggs Super! (J). (ps-1). 1987. (CPN 1287); (Stand Alone Ser.). (J). (gr. k-2). 1986. 12.00 (978-0-89845-168-9(X), CPN 1287) HarperCollins Pubs.

Dr. Seuss How the Grinch Stole Christmas! And Horton Hears a Who! Original Television Soundtracks. 1 cass. (Running Time: 1 hr.). (J). 2002. 7.98 (978-0-7379-0098-9(9), 75968); audio compact disk 11.98 (978-0-7379-0095-8(4), 75969) Rhino Enter.
The first-ever release of the original soundtracks to these favorites. Booklet includes an exclusive interview with Chuck Jones and lyrics to selected Grinch songs.

Dr. Sharman Griselle & Russell Ernst Speak Out on Growth in Los Angeles. Hosted by Nancy Pearlman. 1 cass. (Running Time: 28 min.). 10.00 (1315) Educ Comm CA.

Dr. Spock Talks about Your Baby. unabr. ed. Benjamin M. Spock. 1 cass. (Running Time: 60 min.). 1989. 8.98 (978-0-89845-780-3(7)) HarperCollins Pubs.

Dr. Terry L. Booher Classics, Audio. Prod. by Terry Booher. 2006. audio compact disk 15.00 (978-1-933594-65-1(9)) FBC Pubns.

Dr. Thomas Szasz: The Psychiatric Will: Resolving The Dilemma of Involuntary Interventions. Thomas Szasz. (Running Time: 90 min.). (Cal State Univ., Long Beach). 1982. 10.00 (F135) Freeland Pr.
Focuses mainly on the issues of state interference involving our mental health; the blatant use of institutions to censor dissidents. Suggests a form of "living will" to guard against psychiatric abuses.

Dr. Walton's Hypnocd: Anger Management. James E. Walton. 2002. audio compact disk 19.95 (978-0-9711939-1-8(6)) J E Walton.

Dr. Walton's Stopping Smoking. 2008. audio compact disk (978-0-9711939-4-9(0)) J E Walton.

Dr. Walton's Stress Relief & Deep Sleep. 1 CD. 2003. audio compact disk (978-0-9711939-3-2(2)) J E Walton.

Dr. Walton's Ultimate Weight Loss. (ENG.). 2008. audio compact disk (978-0-9711939-5-6(9)) J E Walton.

Dr. Wasserman's Time Chamber: Preventing Armageddon. Lee Geiger. Narrated by Jim McCabe. (ENG.). 2007. audio compact disk 24.95 (978-1-60031-027-0(3)) Spoken Books.

***Dr. Who: The Eighth Collection.** Big Finish Productions. 2009. audio compact disk 37.95 (978-1-84435-429-0(6)) Pub: Big Finish GBR. Dist(s): Natl Bk Netwk

Dr. Wortle's School. unabr. ed. Anthony Trollope. 6 cass. 1996. 54.95 (978-1-86015-429-4(8)) Pub: UlverLrgPrint GBR. Dist(s): Ulverscroft US
Dr. Wortle's School is Trollope's most merciless attack on the false moralizing & hypocrisy of the Victorian age. When Dr. Wortle, in good faith, hires a couple as teacher & matron at his school, scandal about their marriage is subsequently brought to light.

Dr. Wortle's School, Set. unabr. ed. Anthony Trollope. Narrated by Flo Gibson. 6 cass. (Running Time: 1 hr. 30 min. per cass.). 1988. 24.95 (978-1-55685-004-2(2)) Audio Bk Con.
The discovery of irregularity in the marriage of the newly hired assistant master & matron at Dr. Wortle's school & the ensuing scandal test the character of all involved.

Dr. Wright's Cleaning Out Technique: By Thomas Ashley-Farrand (Namadeva) Voice by Thomas Ashley-Farrand. Thomas Ashley-Farrand. Saraswati Publications. (ENG.). 2004. audio compact disk 18.00 (978-0-9825238-5-8(8)) SaraswaPubns.

Dr. York, Miss Winnie & The Typhoid Shot. Read by Donald Davis. 1 cass. (Running Time: 56 mins.). (gr. 3-7). 1996. 12.00 (978-0-87483-506-9(2)) Pub: August Hse. Dist(s): Natl Bk Netwk
Our young hero learns three valuable lessons: avoiding pain just heightens it, a mother's wrath can hurt worse than a shot & growing up sometimes involves choosing the lesser of two evils.

Dr York, Miss Winnie, & the Typhoid Shot. Donald Davis. (Running Time: 56 mins.). 1996. audio compact disk 16.95 (978-0-87483-718-6(9)) Pub: August Hse. Dist(s): Natl Bk Netwk

Dr. Z on Scoring: How to Pick up, Seduce, & Hook up with Hot Women. unabr. ed. Victoria Zdrok. (Running Time: 11 hrs. 0 mins. 0 sec.). (ENG.). 2008. audio compact disk 69.99 (978-1-4001-3647-6(4)); audio compact disk 24.99 (978-1-4001-5647-4(5)) Pub: Tantor Media. Dist(s): IngramPubServ

Dr. Z on Scoring: How to Pick up, Seduce, & Hook up with Hot Women. unabr. ed. Victoria Zdrok. Read by Victoria Zdrok. (Running Time: 11 hrs. 0 mins. 0 sec.). (ENG.). 2008. audio compact disk 34.99 (978-1-4001-0647-9(8)) Pub: Tantor Media. Dist(s): IngramPubServ

Dr. Zhivago, Poems From. unabr. ed. 1 cass. 1994. 14.95 (978-0-88432-484-3(2), SRU110) J Norton Pubs.
Includes booklet.

Drachenreiter see Dragon Rider

Draco Tavern. unabr. ed. Larry Niven. Read by Tom Weiner. (Running Time: 21600 sec.). 2006. 44.95 (978-0-7861-4908-7(6)); audio compact disk 45.00 (978-0-7861-5947-5(2)); audio compact disk 29.95 (978-0-7861-7069-2(7)) Blckstn Audio.

Draconic Astrology. Pamela Crane. 1 cass. 1992. 8.95 (1021) Am Fed Astrologers.

Drac's Castle. Perf. by Daniel Sjerven. Created by Daniel Sjerven. Prod. by Braun Media. (ENG.). 2008. (978-1-59987-653-5(1)) Braun Media.

Dracula. Fearon Staff. (J). 20.95 (978-0-8359-0959-4(X)) Globe Fearon.

***Dracula.** Bram Stoker. 2009. (978-1-60136-488-3(1)) Audio Holding.

Drácula. Bram Stoker. Contrib. by Frederick Jaeger & Phyllis Logan. 2 CDs. (Running Time: 3 hrs. 20 mins.). 2006. audio compact disk 29.95 (978-0-7927-3993-7(0), BBCD 144) AudioGO.

Drácula. Bram Stoker. Read by Robert Whitfield. 12 CDs. (Running Time: 16 hrs.). 2004. audio compact disk 99.00 (978-0-7861-8148-3(6), 2247) Blckstn Audio.

***Drácula.** Bram Stoker. Tr. by Susan Schuler. Illus. by Alfonso Ruiz. Retold by Michael Burgan. (Classic Fiction Ser.). (SPA.). 2010. audio compact disk 14.60 (978-1-4342-2574-0(7)) CapstoneDig.

Drácula. Bram Stoker. Read by Greg Wise & Saskia Reeves. 16 CDs. (Running Time: 24 hrs.). 2002. audio compact disk 119.95 (978-0-7540-5547-1(7), CCD 238) Pub: Chivers Audio Bks GBR. Dist(s): AudioGO

Drácula. Bram Stoker. Prod. by Spoken Arts Staff. 1 cass. (Running Time: 53 min.). 9.95 (FO-090, HarperThor) HarpC GBR.

Drácula. Bram Stoker. Narrated by Robert Whitfield. (Running Time: 16 hrs.). 1998. 44.95 (978-1-59912-476-6(9)) Iofy Corp.

Drácula. Bram Stoker. Read by Guillermo Piedrahita. (Running Time: 3 hrs.). 2002. 16.95 (978-1-60083-220-8(2), Audiofy Corp) Iofy Corp.

Drácula. Bram Stoker. (Running Time: 4 hrs.). 2005. 24.95 (978-1-60083-728-9(X)) Iofy Corp.

Drácula. Bram Stoker. Perf. by Orson Welles et al. 1 cass. (Running Time: 60 min.). 1938. 7.95 (DF-9060) Natl Recrd Co.
Welles appears as Dr. Stewart & Count Dracula in this faithful adaptation from Bram Stoker's famous novel. Originally broadcast on Mercury Theater on the Air.

Drácula. Bram Stoker. Perf. by Heathcote Williams et al. 3 cass. (Running Time: 4 hrs.). Dramatization. 1997. 17.98 (978-962-634-615-0(9), NA311514, Naxos AudioBooks) Naxos.
Authentic music is combined with a new ballet score & various sound effects to create a gripping dramatization of this classic tale.

Drácula. Bram Stoker. Narrated by Alexander Spencer & Susan Adams. 15 CDs. (Running Time: 18 hrs.). audio compact disk 154.00 (978-1-4025-2301-4(7)) Recorded Bks.

Drácula. Bram Stoker. Read by Susan Adams & Alexander Spencer. 10 Cass. (Running Time: 18 Hrs.). 19.95 (978-1-4025-1661-0(4)) Recorded Bks.

Dracula. Perf. by Orson Welles. 1 cass. 10.00 (MC1018) Esstee Audios.
Radio drama.

Dracula. Perf. by Orson Welles et al. 1 CD. (Running Time: 1 hr.). (Halloween at Radio Spirits Ser.). 2001. audio compact disk 4.98 (978-1-57019-428-3(9), OTR7031) Pub: Radio Spirits. Dist(s): AudioGO

Dracula, abr. ed. Bram Stoker. Perf. by St. Charles Players. 2 cass. (Running Time: 127 Min.). (Mystery Theatre Ser.). 1999. 16.95 (978-1-56994-512-4(8), 313104, Monterey SoundWorks) Monterey Media Inc.
Victorian London by night. Stylish gentlemen & ladies await their carriages. But lurking in the shadows is one of the creatures of the night, one who brings chilling fear to those he encounters, a man who cannot die yet must prey upon the blood of others to prolong his doomed existence...the vampire Dracula.

Drácula. abr. ed. Bram Stoker. Read by Stan Winiarski. 3 cass. (Running Time: 4 hrs.). 1995. 19.95 (978-1-882071-36-4(0)) B-B Audio.
The original story is more terrifying than any movie. Count Dracula has extraordinary needs, along with mysterious powers that allow him to satisfy them. No one really knows the extent of those powers-or those needs-until it is too late. There is nothi.

Drácula. abr. ed. Bram Stoker. Perf. by David McCallum & Carole Shelley. 1 cass. (Running Time: 90 min.). 1984. 8.98 (978-0-89845-215-0(5), CP 1468) HarperCollins Pubs.

Drácula. abr. ed. Bram Stoker. Read by Walter Zimmerman. 1 cass. (Running Time: 87 min.). Dramatization. 1980. 7.95 (N-58) Jimcin Record.
Chilling scenes from the Count's castle.

Drácula. abr. ed. Bram Stoker. Perf. by Heathcote Williams et al. 3 CDs. (Running Time: 4 hrs.). Dramatization. 1997. audio compact disk 22.98 (978-962-634-115-5(7), NA311512, Naxos AudioBooks) Naxos.
Authentic music is combined with a new ballet score & various sound effects to create a gripping dramatization of this classic tale.

Drácula. abr. ed. Bram Stoker. Read by Edward Woodward. 2 cass. (Running Time: 3 hrs.). (Ultimate Classics Ser.). 2004. 18.00 (978-1-931056-84-7(6), N Millennium Audio) New Millenn Enter.
I stood before a great door in silence. Of bell or knocker there was no sign. I felt fears and doubts crowding upon me. Was this a customary incident in the life of a solicitor sent out to explain the purchase of a London estate to a foreigner? Jonathan Harker's rather ordinary past has not prepared him to grapple with the depths of evil he will encounter behind that great door. His straightforward mission must become a valiant campaign to thwart his evil host, Count Dracula. The story that unfolds exposes Harker and his friends to unspeakable horrors, Transylvanian vampires transported to England to seek new, unwary victims, the dead transformed into "the devil's undead", roaming the night with evil intent.

Drácula. abr. ed. Bram Stoker. Contrib. by Andrew Allan. Adapted by George Salverson. 1 CD. (Running Time: 1 hr.). (Stage Ser.). 2004. audio compact disk 14.99 (978-1-894003-24-7(1)) Pub: Scenario Prods CAN. Dist(s): PerseuPGW

Drácula. abr. ed. Bram Stoker. 1 cass. (Running Time: 53 min.). Dramatization. 10.95 (978-0-8045-1087-5(3), SAC 1087) Spoken Arts.
The original story as penned by Stoker, dramatized by Barbara McCaughey, Chris Curran, Robert Somerset, & Ivan de Barca.

Drácula. abr. ed. Bram Stoker. Read by Guillermo Piedrahita. 3 CDs. (SPA.). 2002. audio compact disk 17.00 (978-958-9494-95-0(1)) YoYoMusic.

Drácula. abr. ed. Bram Stoker & Richard Grant. (Running Time: 3 hrs.). (ENG.). (gr. 12 up). 2005. audio compact disk 14.95 (978-0-14-305810-6(X), PengAudBks) Penguin Grp USA.

***Dracula.** unabr. ed. Bram Stoker. Narrated by Greg Wise & Saskia Reeves. 16 CDs. (Running Time: 18 hrs. 0 mins. 0 sec.). (Cover to Cover Ser.). (ENG.). 2010. audio compact disk 29.95 (978-1-60283-880-2(1)) Pub: AudioGO. Dist(s): Perseus Dist

Drácula. unabr. ed. Bram Stoker. Perf. by Big Radio Players Staff. 8 cass. (Running Time: 8 hrs.). Dramatization. 1996. 39.95 (978-1-888928-00-6(X)) BIG RADIO.

Drácula. unabr. ed. Bram Stoker. Read by Robert Whitfield. 11 cass. (Running Time: 16 hrs.). (gr. 9-12). 1998. 76.95 (978-0-7861-1322-4(7), 2247) Blckstn Audio.
The Dracula mythology has inspired a vast subculture, but the story has never been better told than by Stoker. He succeeds entirely in his aim to terrify. His myth is powerful because it allows evil to remain mysterious. Van Helsing's high-thinking & scientific skill cannot resist the dreadful potency of the undead. Only the old magic - a crucifix, garlic, a wooden stake - can provide effective weapons.

Drácula. unabr. ed. Bram Stoker. Read by Robert Whitfield. 11 cass. (Running Time: 52200 sec.). 2005. 29.95 (978-0-7861-3463-2(1), E2247); audio compact disk 29.95 (978-0-7861-8040-0(4), ZE2247); audio compact disk 29.95 (978-0-7861-8164-3(8), ZM2247) Blckstn Audio.

Drácula. unabr. ed. Bram Stoker. 10 cass. (Running Time: 15 hrs.). 2002. 29.95 (978-1-59086-287-2(2), 1590862872, BAU) Brilliance Audio.
Perhaps the most famous vampire story of all time, and the most popular, Dracula is recreated in its entirety in this unabridged audio program. The story of Dracula has been retold and recreated many times in film and on the stage in the last hundred years. Yet, it is essentially a Victorian saga, an awesome tale of a thrillingly bloodthirsty vampire whose nocturnal atrocities embody the dark underside of an outwardly moralistic age. Dracula represents all the hidden and repressed power of male and female sexuality, of animal lust, and passion unleashed. Above all, Dracula is a quintessential story of suspense and horror, boasting one of the most terrifying creatures in literature: centuries-old Count Dracula. Near the beginning of this tale, Jonathan Harker knows little of what is in store when he receives the following letter: "My friend - Welcome to the Carpathians. I am anxiously expecting you. Sleep well tonight. At three tomorrow the diligence will start for Bukovina; a place on it is kept for you. At the Borgo Pass my carriage will await you and bring you to me. Your friend, Dracula.".

Drácula. unabr. ed. Bram Stoker. Read by Multivoice Production Staff. (Running Time: 15 hrs.). 2004. 39.25 (978-1-59335-560-9(2), 1593355602, Brinc Audio MP3 Lib) Brilliance Audio.

Drácula. unabr. ed. Bram Stoker. (Running Time: 15 hrs.). 2004. 24.95 (978-1-59710-220-9(2), 1597102202, BAD) Brilliance Audio.

Drácula. unabr. ed. Bram Stoker. Read by Multivoice Production Staff. (Running Time: 15 hrs.). 2004. 39.25 (978-1-59710-221-6(0), 1597102210, BADLE) Brilliance Audio.

Drácula. unabr. ed. Bram Stoker. Narrated by Tom Casaletto. (Running Time: 54000 sec.). (Classic Collection (Brilliance Audio) Ser.). 2005. audio compact disk 112.25 (978-1-59737-126-1(2), 9781597371261, BriAudCD Unabrid); audio compact disk 44.95 (978-1-59737-125-4(4), 9781597371254, Bril Audio CD Unabri) Brilliance Audio.

Drácula. unabr. ed. Bram Stoker. Read by Greg Wise & Saskia Reeves. 14 cass. (Running Time: 21 hrs.). 2002. 110.95 (978-0-7540-0891-0(6), CAB 2313) Pub: Chivers Audio Bks GBR. Dist(s): AudioGO

Drácula. unabr. ed. Bram Stoker. Read by Robert Whitfield. (YA). 2008. 84.99 (978-1-60514-719-2(2)) Find a World.

Drácula. unabr. ed. Bram Stoker. Read by Walter Zimmerman et al. 10 cass. (Running Time: 16 hrs.). 1980. 56.00 incl. albums. (C-29) Jimcin Record.
The most famous vampire story of all. The count lures an Englishman to his castle & is soon stalking London himself.

Drácula. unabr. ed. Bram Stoker. 8 cass. (Running Time: 12 hrs.). 2001. 39.95 (978-1-57511-094-3(6)) Pub Mills.
Written mostly in the form of diaries & journals, the story dramatically tracks the cruel count from translylvania to England.

Drácula. unabr. ed. Bram Stoker. Narrated by Alexander Spencer & Susan Adams. 12 cass. (Running Time: 18 hrs.). 1980. 97.00 (978-1-55690-156-0(9), 80090E7) Recorded Bks.
Vampire classic set in Transylvanian count's eerie, lonely castle.

Drácula. unabr. ed. Bram Stoker. Read by Multivoice Production Staff. (Running Time: 15 hrs.). 2004. 24.95 (978-1-59335-044-4(9), 1593350449) Soulmate Audio Bks.

Drácula. unabr. ed. Bram Stoker. Read by Eric Martin. 1 cd. (Running Time: 9 hrs 7 mins). 2002. audio compact disk 18.95 (978-1-58472-385-1(8), In Aud) Pub: Sound Room. Dist(s): Baker Taylor
MP3 format.

Drácula. unabr. ed. Bram Stoker. Narrated by John Lee. (Running Time: 15 hrs. 0 mins. 0 sec.). (Tantor Unabridged Classics Ser.). (ENG.). 2008. 27.99 (978-1-4001-5965-9(2)); audio compact disk 35.99 (978-1-4001-0965-4(5)); audio compact disk 72.99 (978-1-4001-3965-1(1)) Pub: Tantor Media. Dist(s): IngramPubServ

Drácula. unabr. collector's ed. Bram Stoker. Read by Charles Garst. 10 cass. (Running Time: 15 hrs.). 1983. 80.00 (978-0-7366-0419-2(7), 1391) Books on Tape.

Drácula, Bk. 1, Episodes 1-16. Bram Stoker. Prod. by Larry Knapp & Lynn Shuck. 8 cass. (Running Time: 8 hrs.). 1996. 49.95 (978-1-57677-059-7(1), BIGR001) Lodestone Catalog.
A full & complete adaptation of Bram Stoker's classic gothic horror novel.

Drácula, Bk. 2, Episodes 9-16. Bram Stoker. Prod. by Larry Knapp & Lynn Shuck. 4 cass. (Running Time: 4 hrs.). 1996. 24.95 (978-1-57677-060-3(5)) Lodestone Catalog.

Drácula, Pt. 1, set. Bram Stoker. 4 cass. (FRE.). 1995. 36.95 (1700-LV) Olivia & Hill.
The classic myth of vampires is read by a cast of actors.

Drácula, Pt. 2, set. Bram Stoker. 4 cass. (FRE.). 1995. 36.95 (1701-LV) Olivia & Hill.
The classic myth of vampires is read by a cast of actors.

Drácula, Pt. 3, set. Bram Stoker. 3 cass. (FRE.). 1995. 34.95 (1702-LV) Olivia & Hill.

Drácula, Pts. 1-3, set. Bram Stoker. 11 cass. (FRE.). 1995. 98.95 (1700/2-LV) Olivia & Hill.

Dracula, Set. Bram Stoker. Read by Flo Gibson. 12 cass. (Running Time: 16 hrs.). 1995. 39.95 (978-1-55685-359-3(9)) Audio Bk Con.
The terrifying tale of Count Dracula & other vampires & werewolves who lust for blood & control of their victims.

Drácula, Set. abr. ed. Bram Stoker. Perf. by St. Charles Players. 2 cass. Dramatization. 1999. 16.95 (FS9-50877) Highsmith.

Dracula: An A+ Audio Study Guide. unabr. ed. F. Abraham & Bram Stoker. (Running Time: 30 mins.). (ENG.). 2006. 5.98 (978-1-59483-707-4(4)) Pub: Hachet Audio. Dist(s): HachBkGrp

***Dracula: Classic BBC Radio Horror.** Bram Stoker. Narrated by Full Cast. (Running Time: 3 hrs. 0 mins. 0 sec.). (ENG.). 2010. audio compact disk 29.95 (978-1-4084-6700-8(3)) Pub: AudioGO. Dist(s): Perseus Dist

Dracula: The Un-Dead. Dacre Stoker & Ian Holt. 2009. audio compact disk 44.99 (978-1-4407-6287-1(2)) Recorded Bks.

Dracula & Frankenstein: Horror Double Bill. Mary Wollstonecraft Shelley & Bram Stoker. Read by David Rintoul & Anthony Valentine. 2008. audio compact disk 33.59 (978-1-906147-29-7(9)) CSA Telltapes GBR.

Dracula Murders. Philip Daniels. Read by John Whitman. 4 cass. (Running Time: 6 hrs.). 1999. 44.95 (6433X) Pub: Soundings Ltd GBR. Dist(s): Ulverscroft US

Dracula Murders. Philip Daniels. 4 cass. (Sound Ser.). 2004. 44.95 (978-1-85496-433-5(X)) Pub: UlverLrgPrint GBR. Dist(s): Ulverscroft US

***Dracula, My Love: The Secret Journals of Mina Harker.** unabr. ed. Syrie James. (Running Time: 16 hrs. 0 mins.). 2010. 20.99 (978-1-4001-8672-3(2)); 29.99 (978-1-4001-6672-5(1)) Pub: Tantor Media. Dist(s): IngramPubServ

***Dracula, My Love: The Secret Journals of Mina Harker.** unabr. ed. Syrie James. Narrated by Justine Eyre. 12 CDs. (Running Time: 14 hrs. 30 mins. 0 sec.). 2010. audio compact disk 39.99 (978-1-4001-1672-0(4)); audio compact disk 95.99 (978-1-4001-4672-7(0)) Pub: Tantor Media. Dist(s): IngramPubServ

Dracula Read Along. (Saddleback's Illustrated Classics Ser.). (YA). 2006. (978-1-56254-897-1(2)) Saddleback Edu.

Dracula's Guest see Tales of Terror & the Supernatural: A Collection

***Dracula's Guest.** Bram Stoker. 2009. (978-1-60136-489-0(X)) Audio Holding.

Dracula's Guest. Bram Stoker. Narrated by Victor Garber. (Running Time: 1 hr.). 2006. 12.95 (978-1-60083-026-6(9)) Iofy Corp.

Dracula's Guest. unabr. ed. Bram Stoker. Read by Walter Zimmerman. 1 cass. (Running Time: 86 min.). Dramatization. 1980. 7.95 (N-37) Jimcin Record.
Tales of horror & suspense by the author.

Drafting: Syllabus. David A. Madsen. (J). 1974. bk. 104.35 (978-0-89420-140-0(9)) Natl Book.

Drafting & Negotiating Commercial Leases. unabr. ed. Contrib. by Morton P. Fisher, Jr. & Richard R. Goldberg. 4 cass. (Running Time: 5 hrs. 30 min.). 1989. 50.00 course handbk. (T7-9247) PLI.
In this recording of PLI's November 1989 lectures, the faculty discusses such areas as: rental terms, including basic rental, percentage rental, rental escalations & pass-throughs such as common area maintenance, real estate taxes, insurance & utilities & use clauses operating covenants; exclusives & radius restrictions; assignment, subletting clauses, convenience cancellation clauses; special issues in office building leases; tenant work letters & tenant improvements; insurance; casualty & restoration clauses; subordination & non-disturbance agreements & mortgagee rights. Selected clauses of an office lease are negotiated by faculty members playing the roles of lessor's & lessee's counsel.

Drafting & Negotiating Commercial Loan Documents. 1990. 125.00 (AC-564) PA Bar Inst.

Drafting & Negotiating Contracts of Sale for Residential & Commercial Real Estate. unabr. ed. Contrib. by Ira Berman. 4 cass. (Running Time: 5 hrs.). 1989. 85.00 (T7-9251) PLI.
This recording of PLI's November 1989 program is designed to provide a hands-on approach to drafting & negotiating contracts of sales. Commencing with the client interview, the discussion takes you through structuring the transaction, drafting & negotiating the contract; clearing title objections; preparing for & the closing itself; & what to do after closing. Differences between commercial & residential contracts are highlighted.

Drafting Documents for Condominiums, PUDs, & Golf Course Communities. 11 cass. (Running Time: 16 hrs. 50 min.). 1997. 315.00 Set, incl. course materials. (MB50) Am Law Inst.
Provides the opportunity to acquire & refine skills needed to draft documents. Also covers unique matters relating to resorts, interval ownership, & other innovative form of community structure & administration. Emphasis on substantive document provision & coverage of the why, when, & how of drafting. Basic knowledge of real estate law & at least limited experience with community association law & practice are presumed.

Drafting Effective Federal Legislation & Amendments in a Nutshell. Ed. by TheCapitol.Net. 2006. 107.00 (978-1-58733-032-2(6)) TheCapitol.

Drafting Escrow Agreements. Read by Fred Blume. 1 cass. 1988. 20.00 (AL-52) PA Bar Inst.

Drafting Findings of Fact & Conclusions of Law. 1 cass. 1990. 15.00 (AL-89) PA Bar Inst.

Drafting Individual Employment Contracts. 1989. 55.00 (AC-506) PA Bar Inst.

Drafting Patent License Agreements. 5th ed. Brian G. Brunsvold & Dennis P. O'Reilley. 2004. bk. 175.00 (978-1-57018-424-6(0), 1424) BNA Books.

Drafting the Estate Plan. David Handler et al. 2005. audio compact disk 279.00 (978-0-8080-8939-1(0)) Toolkit Media.

Drafting Wills & Related Estate Planning Documents. Read by Linn K. Coombs et al. (Running Time: 6 hrs.). 1990. 97.00 Incl. 250p. tape materials. (ES-53255) Cont Ed Bar-CA.

Drafting Wills & Trusts in Plain English. Edward S. Schlesinger. 1 cass. (Running Time: 90 min.). 1985. 17.40 (M643) Am Law Inst.
This tape talks about estate planning documents clearly & concisely so they can be understood by clients, beneficiaries, fiduciaries, & others. It explains how lawyers can improve their drafting skills through the use of checkl ists, proper document organization, & a clear, concise writing style so their documents can accurately reflect a client's wishes & be readily understood.

Drag Racing. Nicki Clausen-Grace. (Rourke Discovery Library (CD-ROM) Ser.). (J). 2008. audio compact disk 24.95 (978-1-60472-773-9(X)) Rourke FL.

Dragnet. 1 cass. (Running Time: 1 hr.). Incl. Dragnet: Gangland Murder. (MM5920); Dragnet: Obscene Literature. (MM5920); 7.95 (MM5920) Natl Recrd Co.

Dragnet. 1 CD. (Running Time: 1 hr.). (Old-Time Radio Blockbusters Ser.). 2002. audio compact disk 4.98 (978-1-57019-392-7(4), OTR7703) Pub: Radio Spirits. Dist(s): AudioGO
"Big Red," Pts. 1 and 2.

Dragnet. Contrib. by Jack Webb. (Running Time: 10800 sec.). 2004. 9.98 (978-1-57019-634-8(6)); audio compact disk 9.98 (978-1-57019-633-1(8)) Radio Spirits.

Dragnet, Set. Perf. by Jack Webb. 2 cass. (Running Time: 2 hrs.). vinyl bd. 10.95 (978-1-57816-046-4(4), DN2401) Audio File.
Includes: "Master Jewel Thief" (8-18-49); "The Big Picture" (12-7-50); "The Big Speech" (4-19-51); "The Big Almost No Show" (1-31-52).

Dragnet, Vol. 2. collector's ed. Perf. by Jack Webb & Barton Yarborough. 6 cass. (Running Time: 9 hrs.). 1999. bk. 34.98 (4185) Radio Spirits.
18 police dramas.

Dragnet, Vol. 3. collector's ed. Perf. by Jack Webb & Barton Yarborough. 6 cass. (Running Time: 9 hrs.). 2001. bk. 34.98 (4426) Radio Spirits.
Sergeant Joe Friday of the L.A.P.D. and Sergeant Ben Romano in 18 police dramas.

Dragnet: Big Seventeen & Big Hit & Run Killer. Perf. by Jack Webb. 1 cass. (Running Time: 1 hr.). 2001. 6.98 (2613) Radio Spirits.

Dragnet: Big Watch & The Big Badge. Perf. by Jack Webb. 1 cass. (Running Time: 1 hr.). 2001. 6.98 (2514) Radio Spirits.

Dragnet: Big Winchester & Big In-Laws. Perf. by Jack Webb. 1 cass. (Running Time: 1 hr.). 2001. 6.98 (2597) Radio Spirits.

Dragnet: City Hall Bombing. 6 cass. (Running Time: 6 hrs.). 1999. 19.98 (AB199) Radio Spirits.

Dragnet: Claude Jimmerson, Child Killer & Big Girl. Perf. by Jack Webb. 1 cass. (Running Time: 1 hr.). 2001. 6.98 (2494) Radio Spirits.

Dragnet: Gangland Murder see Dragnet

Dragnet: Garbage Chuted & Big Boys. Perf. by Jack Webb. 1 cass. (Running Time: 1 hr.). 2001. 6.98 (2574) Radio Spirits.

Dragnet: Obscene Literature see Dragnet

Dragnet: The Big Blast & The Big Mailman. Perf. by Jack Webb. 1 cass. (Running Time: 1 hr.). 2001. 6.98 (2176) Radio Spirits.

Dragnet: The Big Bunco & The Big Elevator. Perf. by Jack Webb. 1 cass. (Running Time: 1 hr.). 2001. 6.98 (1901) Radio Spirits.

Dragnet: The Big Donation & The Big Roll. Perf. by Jack Webb. 1 cass. (Running Time: 1 hr.). 2001. 6.98 (2194) Radio Spirits.

Dragnet: The Big Drive & The Big Paper. Perf. by Jack Webb. 1 cass. (Running Time: 1 hr.). 2001. 6.98 (2435) Radio Spirits.

Dragnet: The Big Fraud & the Big Rain. Perf. by Jack Webb. 1 cass. (Running Time: 1 hr.). 2001. 6.98 (2235) Radio Spirits.

Dragnet: The Big Kill & The Big Thank You. Perf. by Jack Webb. 1 cass. (Running Time: 1 hr.). 2001. 6.98 (2396) Radio Spirits.

Dragnet: The Big Mail & The Big Shakedown. Perf. by Jack Webb. 1 cass. (Running Time: 1 hr.). 2001. 6.98 (2076) Radio Spirits.

Dragnet: The Big Meet & The Big Church. Perf. by Jack Webb. 1 cass. (Running Time: 1 hr.). 2001. 6.98 (2534) Radio Spirits.

Dragnet: The Big Safe & The Big Gamble. Perf. by Jack Webb. 1 cass. (Running Time: 1 hr.). 2001. 6.98 (1927) Radio Spirits.

Dragnet: The Big Saint & The Big Speech. Perf. by Jack Webb. 1 cass. (Running Time: 1 hr.). 2001. 6.98 (1867) Radio Spirits.

Dragnet: The Big Smart Guy & The Big Chance. Perf. by Jack Webb. 1 cass. (Running Time: 1 hr.). 2001. 6.98 (2008) Radio Spirits.

Dragnet: The Big 4th & The Big Whiff. Perf. by Jack Webb. 1 cass. (Running Time: 1 hr.). 2001. 6.98 (2276) Radio Spirits.

Dragnet: The Roseland Roof Murder & The Big Picture. Perf. by Jack Webb. 1 cass. (Running Time: 1 hr.). 2001. 6.98 (2133) Radio Spirits.

Dragnet: The Werewolf & Homicide. Perf. by Jack Webb. 1 cass. (Running Time: 1 hr.). 2001. 6.98 (2474) Radio Spirits.

Dragnet Pt. 1 & 2: Big Red. 1 CD. (Running Time: 1 hr.). (Old-Time Radio Blockbusters Ser.). 2001. audio compact disk 4.98 (7703) Radio Spirits.

Dragnet Pt. 1 & 2: The Big Gangster. Perf. by Jack Webb. 1 cass. (Running Time: 1 hr.). 2001. 6.98 (2254) Radio Spirits.

Dragnet Pt. 1 & Pt. 2: Big Man. Perf. by Jack Webb. 1 cass. (Running Time: 1 hr.). 2001. 6.98 (2455) Radio Spirits.

Dragnet & Gunsmoke. unabr. ed. Perf. by Jack Webb & William Conrad. 1 cass. (Running Time: 60 min.). Dramatization. 7.95 Norelco box. (MW-4433) Natl Recrd Co.
Dragnet: Dum de dum dum! "Saturday, September 5th. It was a mild day in Los Angeles..." Tune in to the documented drama of an actual crime. Travel step-by-step on the side of the law as Friday investigates a hit & run accident. Fatima cigarette commercials. Gunsmoke: U.S. Marshall Dillon, of Dodge City...The story of the violence that moved west with young America, & the man who moved with it. Matt discovers there is a reward out to anyone that will kill him. With all the regulars...Chester, Doc & Kitty. L&M Filter cigarette commercials.

Dragnet on Radio. Perf. by Jack Webb. 20 cass. (Running Time: 30 hrs.). 2001. 59.98 (4477); audio compact disk 69.98 (4478) Radio Spirits.
Dum-de-dum-dum. That's the famous theme that starts each episode of the most popular police series in history, based on actual crime cases from the Los Angeles Police Department.

***Dragnet, Volume 1.** RadioArchives.com. (Running Time: 600). (ENG.). 2007. audio compact disk 29.98 (978-1-61081-102-6(X)) Radio Arch.

***Dragnet, Volume 2.** RadioArchives.com. (Running Time: 600). (ENG.). 2008. audio compact disk 29.98 (978-1-61081-136-1(4)) Radio Arch.

***Dragnet, Volume 3.** RadioArchives.com. (Running Time: 600). (ENG.). 2008. audio compact disk 29.98 (978-1-61081-147-7(X)) Radio Arch.

***Dragnet, Volume 4.** RadioArchives.com. (Running Time: 360). (ENG.). 2010. audio compact disk 17.98 (978-1-61081-180-4(1)) Radio Arch.

Dragon see Dragon

Dragon. unabr. ed. Clive Cussler. Read by Michael Prichard. 11 cass. (Running Time: 16 hrs. 30 min.). (Dirk Pitt Ser.).Tr. of Dragon. 1990. 88.00 (978-0-7366-1791-8(4), 2628) Books on Tape.
August 1945: A lone B-29 takes off from Alaska for the long flight to Japan, bearing the third atomic bomb as back-up to the Hiroshima & Nagasaki bombs. Shot down just short of its target, the plane crashes into the sea, taking its secret to the bottom. In the aftermath of the war, its very existence is denied, then forgotten. October 1993: A new Japanese empire has emerged, one relying upon financial power rather than military prowess. An uneasy America, increasingly under siege from the economic might of its "ally," remains unaware of the lengths to which some Japanese may be willing to go to ensure Japan's dominance. Unaware, that is, until a huge Japanese auto carrier is destroyed - by a nuclear explosion.

Dragon, Set. abr. ed. Clive Cussler. Read by John Rubinstein. 2 cass. (Running Time: 3 hrs.). (Dirk Pitt Ser.).Tr. of Dragon. 1999. (978-0-671-57763-6(8), 390679, Audioworks) S&S Audio.
From the ocean depths to the Arctic Circle, daredevil explorer & master adventurer Dirk Pitt is the U.S.'s secret weapon in the war on terrorism.

Dragon: Chinese Feng Shui Music. Jian-ming Wang. Perf. by Shanghai Chinese Traditional Orchestra. Conducted by Xia Fei-yun. 1 CD. (Running Time: 1 hr.). audio compact disk (978-1-57606-048-3(9)) Wind Recs.
This music is composed based on the combination of the theories of the five elements & the five tones of traditional Chinese music. Dragon is beneficial for people whose homes are built on or near a swampy lowland, or whose front doors face west or northwest. The detailed liner notes explain feng shui, I Ching & the five elements, as well as additional indications for listening to Dragon music.

***Dragon Age: the Calling.** unabr. ed. David Gaider. Narrated by Stephen Hoye. (Running Time: 14 hrs. 30 mins.). (Dragon Age Ser.). 2010. 19.99 (978-1-4001-8620-4(X)); 29.99 (978-1-4001-6620-6(9)); audio compact disk 39.99 (978-1-4001-1620-1(1)) Pub: Tantor Media. Dist(s): IngramPubServ

***Dragon Age: the Stolen Throne.** unabr. ed. David Gaider. Narrated by Stephen Hoye. (Running Time: 12 hrs. 30 mins.). (Dragon Age Ser.). 2010. 34.99 (978-1-4001-9621-0(3)); 18.99 (978-1-4001-8621-1(8)) Tantor Media.

***Dragon Age: the Stolen Throne.** unabr. ed. David Gaider. Narrated by Stephen Hoye. (Running Time: 13 hrs. 0 mins. 0 sec.). (Dragon Age Ser.). (ENG.). 2010. 24.99 (978-1-4001-6621-3(7)); audio compact disk 34.99 (978-1-4001-1621-8(X)) Pub: Tantor Media. Dist(s): IngramPubServ

Dragon & the Raven. unabr. ed. G A Henty. Narrated by John Bolen. (Running Time: 7 hrs. 30 mins. 0 sec.). (ENG.). (J). (gr. 4-7). 2008. 19.99 (978-1-4001-5870-6(2)); audio compact disk 55.99 (978-1-4001-3870-8(1)) Pub: Tantor Media. Dist(s): IngramPubServ

Dragon & the Raven. unabr. ed. G A Henty. Narrated by John Bolen. (Running Time: 7 hrs. 30 mins. 0 sec.). (ENG.). (J). (gr. 4-7). 2008. audio compact disk 27.99 (978-1-4001-0870-1(5)) Pub: Tantor Media. Dist(s): IngramPubServ

Dragon & the Raven: Or the Days of King Alfred. G. A. Henty. Read by John Bolen. (Running Time: 7 hrs. 24 mins.). 2002. 27.95 (978-1-60083-609-1(7), Audiofy Corp) Iofy Corp.

Dragon & the Raven: Or the Days of King Alfred. unabr. ed. G. A. Henty. Narrated by John Bolen. 1 CD (MP3). (Running Time: 7 hrs 19 mins.). (ENG.). 2002. audio compact disk 20.00 (978-1-4001-5038-0(8)) Pub: Tantor Media. Dist(s): IngramPubServ

Dragon & the Raven: Or the Days of King Alfred. unabr. ed. G. A. Henty. Narrated by John Bolen. 7 CDs. (Running Time: 7 hrs. 19 mins.). (ENG.). 2002. audio compact disk 39.00 (978-1-4001-0038-5(0)) Pub: Tantor Media. Dist(s): IngramPubServ

Dragon & the Unicorn. Lynne Cherry. 1 cass. (Running Time: 15 min.). (J). (gr. 1-5). 2001. pap. bk. 17.95 (6838) Spoken Arts.
This lavish original fairy tale is a stirring environmental story.

Dragon Apparent: Travels in Cambodia, Laos & Vietnam. unabr. collector's ed. Norman Lewis. Read by Richard Brown. 8 cass. (Running Time: 12 hrs.). 1990. 64.00 (978-0-7366-1685-0(3), 2531) Books on Tape.
A Dragon Apparent, a best seller when published, describes Norman Lewis's journeys in the Far East at a time when the countries he visited were passing out of the reach of the ordinary traveler, & which will never again be seen as they were then. In his preface to the 1982 edition, Lewis wrote, "Henry Kissinger had said that the dominoes were falling, so now it was the turn of Cambodia & Laos. The holocaust visited on them consumed not only the present, but the past; it obliterated their cultures & values even more than physical things. From the ashes that remained no phoenix would ever rise. Not enough survived even to recreate the memory of what the world had lost".

Dragon Avenger. unabr. ed. E. E. Knight. Narrated by Wanda McCaddon & David Drummond. (Running Time: 13 hrs. 30 mins. 0 sec.). (Age of Fire Ser.). (ENG.). 2009. 24.99 (978-1-4001-6201-7(7)); audio compact disk 37.99 (978-1-4001-1201-2(X)); audio compact disk 75.99 (978-1-4001-4201-9(6)) Pub: Tantor Media. Dist(s): IngramPubServ

Dragon Bones. Lisa See. Read by Liza Ross. 11 CDs. (Running Time: 45900 sec.). (Red Princess Ser.: Bk. 3). 2005. audio compact disk 99.95 (978-0-7531-2431-4(9)) Pub: ISIS Lrg Prnt GBR. Dist(s): Ulverscroft US

Dragon Bones. unabr. ed. Lisa See. Read by Liza Ross. 10 cass. (Running Time: 12 hrs. 42 mins.). (Red Princess Ser.: Bk. 3). (J). 2004. 84.95 (978-0-7531-1875-7(0)) Pub: ISIS Lrg Prnt GBR. Dist(s): Ulverscroft US

***Dragon Bones: Hurog Duology.** Patricia Briggs. As told by Joe Manganiello. (Running Time: 610). (ENG.). (C). 2010. audio compact disk 39.99 (978-0-9827792-1-7(6), Buzzy Audio) Buzzy Multimed.

Dragon Champion. unabr. ed. E. E. Knight. Narrated by Wanda McCaddon & David Drummond. (Running Time: 13 hrs. 30 mins. 0 sec.). (Age of Fire Ser.). (ENG.). 2009. audio compact disk 79.99 (978-1-4001-4200-2(8)); audio compact disk 29.99 (978-1-4001-6200-0(9)); audio compact disk 39.99 (978-1-4001-1200-5(1)) Pub: Tantor Media. Dist(s): IngramPubServ

Dragon Factor. John S. Fischer. 1 cass. 8.95 (660) Am Fed Astrologers.
An AFA Convention workshop tape.

***Dragon Fate.** unabr. ed. E. E. Knight. (Running Time: 10 hrs. 0 mins.). (Age of Fire Ser.). 2011. 16.99 (978-1-4001-8578-8(5)); audio compact disk 34.99 (978-1-4001-1578-5(7)); audio compact disk 83.99 (978-1-4001-4578-2(3)) Pub: Tantor Media. Dist(s): IngramPubServ

***Dragon Fate.** unabr. ed. E. E. Knight. (Running Time: 10 hrs. 0 mins. 0 sec.). (Age of Fire Ser.). (ENG.). 2011. 24.99 (978-1-4001-6578-0(4)) Pub: Tantor Media. Dist(s): IngramPubServ

***Dragon Fate (Library Edition)** unabr. ed. E. E. Knight. (Running Time: 10 hrs. 0 mins.). (Age of Fire Ser.). 2011. 34.99 (978-1-4001-9578-7(0)) Tantor Media.

Dragon Harper. Anne McCaffrey & Todd McCaffrey. Read by Susan Ericksen. (Dragonriders of Pern Ser.). 2008. 69.99 (978-1-60640-785-1(6)) Find a World.

Dragon Harper. abr. ed. Anne McCaffrey & Todd McCaffrey. Read by Susan Ericksen. (Running Time: 6 hrs.). (Dragonriders of Pern Ser.). 2008. audio compact disk 14.99 (978-1-4233-1473-8(5), 9781423314738, BCD Value Price) Brilliance Audio.

Dragon Harper. unabr. ed. Anne McCaffrey. Read by Susan Ericksen. 1 MP3-CD. (Running Time: 36000 sec.). (Dragonriders of Pern Ser.). 2007. audio compact disk 24.95 (978-1-4233-1468-4(9), 9781423314684, Brilliance MP3) Brilliance Audio.

Dragon Harper. unabr. ed. Anne McCaffrey & Todd McCaffrey. (Running Time: 10 hrs.). (Dragonriders of Pern Ser.). 2007. 39.25 (978-1-4233-1471-4(9), 9781423314714, BADLE); 24.95 (978-1-4233-1470-7(0), 9781423314707, BAD) Brilliance Audio.

Dragon Harper. unabr. ed. Anne McCaffrey & Todd McCaffrey. Read by Susan Ericksen. 9 cass. (Running Time: 36000 sec.). (Dragonriders of Pern Ser.). 2007. 92.25 (978-1-4233-1465-3(4), 9781423314653, BrilAudUnabridg); audio compact disk 36.95 (978-1-4233-1466-0(2), 9781423314660, Bril Audio CD Unabri); audio compact disk 39.25 (978-1-4233-1469-1(7), 9781423314691, Brlnc Audio MP3 Lib); audio compact disk 97.25 (978-1-4233-1467-7(0), 9781423314677, BriAudCD Unabrid) Brilliance Audio.

***Dragon Haven.** unabr. ed. Robin Hobb. (Running Time: 21 hrs. 0 mins.). (Rain Wild Chronicles: Vol. 2). 2010. 24.99 (978-1-4001-8334-0(0)); 49.99 (978-1-4001-9334-9(6)); audio compact disk 49.99 (978-1-4001-1334-7(2)) Pub: Tantor Media. Dist(s): IngramPubServ

***Dragon Haven.** unabr. ed. Robin Hobb. Narrated by Anne Flosnik. (Running Time: 20 hrs. 0 mins. 0 sec.). (Rain Wild Chronicles: Vol. 2). (ENG.). 2010. 34.99 (978-1-4001-6334-2(X)); audio compact disk 99.99 (978-1-4001-4334-4(9)) Pub: Tantor Media. Dist(s): IngramPubServ

***Dragon Heir.** unabr. ed. Cinda Williams Chima. Narrated by Robert Ramirez. 1 Playaway. (Running Time: 15 hrs. 15 mins.). (Heir Chronicles: No. 3). (YA). (gr. 7 up). 2009. 64.75 (978-1-4407-0385-0(X)); 102.75 (978-1-4361-8764-0(8)); audio compact disk 108.75 (978-1-4361-8768-8(0)) Recorded Bks.

***Dragon Heir.** unabr. collector's ed. Cinda Williams Chima. Narrated by Robert Ramirez. 13 CDs. (Running Time: 15 hrs. 15 mins.). (Heir Chronicles: No. 3). (YA). (gr. 7 up). 2009. audio compact disk 59.95 (978-1-4361-8772-5(9)) Recorded Bks.

Dragon Hunter. Charles Gallenkamp. Read by Scott Brick. 2001. audio compact disk 96.00 (978-0-7366-7618-2(X)) Books on Tape.

Dragon Hunter. unabr. collector's ed. Charles Gallenkamp. Read by Scott Brick. 10 cass. (Running Time: 15 hrs.). 2001. 80.00; audio compact disk 96.00 Books on Tape.
The life story of Roy Chapman Andrews, one of the twentieth century's most acclaimed explorers.

Dragon Hunter: Roy Chapman Andrews & the Central Asiatic Expeditions. unabr. ed. Charles Gallenkamp. 10 cass. (Running Time: 15 hrs.). 2001. 80.00 (978-0-7366-7179-8(X)) Books on Tape.
Andrews became world famous after leading five central Asiatic expeditions between 1922 and 1930 for the American Museum of Natural History. Perhaps the model for Indiana Jones, he explored the uncharted Gobi Desert of Outer and Inner Mongolia in a successful search for extinct mammals. Andrews not only found dinosaur eggs and the first Velociraptor, he also publicized and popularized his finds to an eager audience.

***Dragon in the Desert.** Michael Dahl. Illus. by Tou Vue. (Dragonblood Ser.). (ENG.). 2010. audio compact disk 14.60 (978-1-4342-2568-9(2)) CapstoneDig.

Dragon in the Family. Jackie French Koller. Narrated by Jeff Woodman. (Running Time: 30 mins.). (gr. 3 up). 10.00 (978-0-7887-9448-3(5)) Recorded Bks.

Dragon in the Sea. unabr. ed. Frank Herbert. Narrated by Scott Brick. (Running Time: 7 hrs. 30 mins. 0 sec.). (ENG.). 2008. audio compact disk 59.99 (978-1-4001-3567-7(2)) Pub: Tantor Media. Dist(s): IngramPubServ

Dragon in the Sea. unabr. ed. Frank Herbert. Read by Scott Brick. (Running Time: 7 hrs. 30 mins. 0 sec.). (ENG.). 2008. audio compact disk 19.99 (978-1-4001-5567-5(3)) Pub: Tantor Media. Dist(s): IngramPubServ

Dragon in the Sea. unabr. ed. Frank Herbert. Narrated by Scott Brick. 6 CDs. (Running Time: 7 hrs. 30 mins. 0 sec.). (ENG.). 2008. audio compact disk 29.99 (978-1-4001-0567-0(6)) Pub: Tantor Media. Dist(s): IngramPubServ

Dragon in the Sea. unabr. ed. Frank Herbert. Read by Scott Brick. (YA). 2008. 54.99 (978-1-60514-861-8(X)) Find a World.

Dragon in the Sock Drawer. unabr. ed. Kate Klimo. Read by Walter M. Mayes. (Running Time: 3 hrs.). (Dragon Keepers Ser.). 2009. 19.99 (978-1-4418-0220-0(7), 9781441802200, Brilliance MP3); 39.97 (978-1-4418-0221-7(5), 9781441802217, Brlnc Audio MP3 Lib); 19.99 (978-1-4418-0222-4(3), 9781441802224, BAD) Brilliance Audio.

Dragon in the Sock Drawer. unabr. ed. Kate Klimo. Read by Walter Mayes. (Running Time: 3 hrs.). (Dragon Keepers Ser.). 2009. 39.97 (978-1-4418-0223-1(1), 9781441802231, BADLE); audio compact disk 19.99 (978-1-4418-0218-7(5), 9781441802187, Bril Audio CD Unabri) Brilliance Audio.

Dragon in the Sock Drawer. unabr. ed. Kate Klimo. Read by Walter M. Mayes. 3 CDs. (Running Time: 3 hrs.). (Dragon Keepers Ser.). (J). (gr. 3-6). 2009. audio compact disk 39.97 (978-1-4418-0219-4(3), 9781441802194, BriAudCD Unabrid) Brilliance Audio.

Dragon Inside. Created by Steck-Vaughn Staff. (Running Time: 4688 sec.). (Power up Extension Ser.). 2003. (978-0-7398-8426-3(3)) SteckVau.

Dragon Keeper. unabr. ed. Robin Hobb. Narrated by Anne Flosnik. (Running Time: 21 hrs. 0 mins. 0 sec.). (Rain Wild Chronicles: Vol. 1). 2010. 34.99 (978-1-4001-6333-5(1)); 24.99 (978-1-4001-8333-3(2)); 49.99 (978-1-4001-9333-2(8)); audio compact disk 49.99 (978-1-4001-1333-0(4)); audio compact disk 99.99 (978-1-4001-4333-7(0)) Pub: Tantor Media. Dist(s): IngramPubServ

Dragon Keeper. unabr. ed. Carole Wilkinson. Narrated by Nancy Wu. 7 cass. (Running Time: 10 hrs.). 2005. 65.75 (978-1-4193-6679-6(3)) Recorded Bks.
Carole Wilkinson has created a fascinating work of historical fantasy. In ancient China, a young slave girl who doesn¿t even know her own name courageously helps a dragon escape. The Han Emperor orders her capture and an evil dragon slayer is hot on her trail. As she journeys with the dragon, the girl discovers the magic within herself, outsmarts her vile pursuers, and becomes the Dragon Keeper.

***Dragon King.** unabr. ed. R. A. Salvatore. Narrated by David Drummond. (Running Time: 13 hrs. 30 mins.). (Crimson Shadow Ser.). 2010. 18.99 (978-1-4001-8358-6(8)); 24.99 (978-1-4001-6358-8(7)); audio compact disk 75.99 (978-1-4001-4358-0(6)); audio compact disk 37.99 (978-1-4001-1358-3(X)) Pub: Tantor Media. Dist(s): IngramPubServ

***Dragon Kiss.** unabr. ed. E. D. Baker. Narrated by Katherine Kellgren. 1 Playaway. (Running Time: 6 hrs. 30 minis.). (J). (gr. 4-6). 2009. 59.75 (978-1-4407-5776-1(3)) Recorded Bks.

***Dragon Kiss.** unabr. ed. E. D. Baker. Narrated by Katherine Kellgren. 6 cass. (Running Time: 6 hrs. 30 mins.). (Frog Princess Ser.: Bk .7). (J). (gr. 4-6). 2009. 51.75 (978-1-4407-5767-9(4)) Recorded Bks.

***Dragon Kiss.** unabr. ed. E. D. Baker. Narrated by Katherine Kellgren. 6 CDs. (Running Time: 6 hrs. 30 mins.). (Frog Princess Ser.: Bk. 7). (J). (gr. 4-6). 2009. audio compact disk 66.75 (978-1-4407-5771-6(2)) Recorded Bks.

***Dragon Kiss.** unabr. collector's ed. E. D. Baker. Narrated by Katherine Kellgren. 6 CDs. (Running Time: 6 hrs. 30 mins.). (Frog Princess Ser.: Bk. 7). (J). (gr. 4-6). 2009. audio compact disk 41.95 (978-1-4407-5772-3(0)) Recorded Bks.

Dragon Lady: The Life & Legends of the Last Empress of China, Pt. II. unabr. ed. Sterling Seagrave. Read by Alexander Adams. 8 cass. (Running Time: 12 hrs.). 1993. 64.00 (3111B) Books on Tape.
The historical record is set straight about China's Empress Tzu Hsi (1835-1908), once falsely accused of reigning over an empire of murder, poison & intrigue.

Dragon Lady Pt. I: The Life & Legend of the Last Empress of China. unabr. ed. Sterling Seagrave. Read by Alexander Adams. 8 cass. (Running Time: 12 hrs.). 1993. 64.00 (978-0-7366-2331-5(0), 3111A) Books on Tape.

Dragon-Lover's Treasury. 2000. (978-1-57042-900-2(6)) Hachet Audio.

Dragon-Lover's Treasury of the Fantastic. abr. ed. Anne McCaffrey et al. Ed. by Margaret Weis. 2 cass. 2001. 7.95 (978-1-57815-199-8(6), Media Bks Audio) Media Bks NJ.

Dragon-Lover's Treasury of the Fantastic. unabr. ed. Margaret Weis. Read by John F. Cygan. 3 CDs. (Running Time: 3 hrs.). 2000. audio compact disk 11.99 (978-1-57815-516-3(9), 1138 CD3, Media Bks Audio) Media Bks NJ.
The dragon is one of the most enduring creatures in the fantasy world. This collection of stories by some of the best fantasy writers of our time. There is high drama, exotic adventures of peril & daring & even a light touch of humor.

Dragon of the Red Dawn. unabr. ed. Mary Pope Osborne. Read by Mary Pope Osborne. (Running Time: 4620 sec.). (Magic Tree House Ser.: No. 37). (ENG.). (J). (gr. 1-4). 2007. audio compact disk 14.95 (978-0-7393-3870-4(6), Listening Lib) Pub: Random Audio Pubg. Dist(s): Random

Dragon of the Red Dawn: Monday with a Mad Genius - Dark Day in the Deep Sea - Eve of the Emperor Penguin. unabr. ed. Mary Pope Osborne. Read by Mary Pope Osborne. (Magic Tree House Ser.: Nos. 37-40). (ENG.). (J). (gr. 1). 2009. audio compact disk 30.00 (978-0-7393-7259-3(9), Listening Lib) Pub: Random Audio Pubg. Dist(s): Random

Dragon Outcast. unabr. ed. E. E. Knight. Narrated by Todd McLaren & David Drummond. (Running Time: 11 hrs. 0 mins. 0 sec.). (Age of Fire Ser.). (ENG.). 2009. audio compact disk 69.99 (978-1-4001-4202-6(4)); audio compact disk 34.99 (978-1-4001-1202-9(8)) Pub: Tantor Media. Dist(s): IngramPubServ

Dragon Outcast. unabr. ed. E. E. Knight. Narrated by Todd McLaren & David Drummond. (Running Time: 11 hrs. 0 mins. 0 sec.). (Age of Fire Ser.). (ENG.). 2009. audio compact disk 24.99 (978-1-4001-6202-4(5)) Pub: Tantor Media. Dist(s): IngramPubServ

Dragon Place. Gioia Timpanelli. 2 cass. 9.00 (A0309-83) Sound Photosyn.

Dragon Reborn. abr. ed. Robert Jordan. Read by Mark Rolston. 2 cass. (Running Time: 3 hrs.). (Wheel of Time Ser.: Bk. 3). 1992. 15.95 Set. (978-1-879371-29-3(4), 40120) Pub Mills.
Rand al'Thor must face the Dark One & Perrin faces the loss of his own humanity.

Dragon Reborn. unabr. rev. ed. Robert Jordan. Read by Kate Reading & Michael Kramer. Ed. by Harriet Mcdougal. 22 CDs. (Running Time: 27 hrs. 0 mins. 0 sec.). (Wheel of Time Ser.: Bk. 3). (ENG.). 2004. audio compact disk 79.99 (978-1-59397-531-9(7)) Pub: Macmill Audio. Dist(s): Macmillan

Dragon Reborn, Pt. 1. unabr. ed. Robert Jordan. Read by Kate Reading & Michael Kramer. 9 cass. (Running Time: 13 hrs. 30 min.). (Wheel of Time Ser.: Bk. 3). 1997. 72.00 (978-0-7366-3601-8(3), 4256-A) Books on Tape.
When the Dark One's forces attack Rand's encampment, Rand loses his nerve, escaping under the cover of battle. After a journey of soul-searching & self-discovery.

Dragon Reborn, Pt. 2. unabr. ed. Robert Jordan. Read by Kate Reading & Michael Kramer. 9 cass. (Running Time: 13 hrs. 30 min.). (Wheel of Time Ser.: Bk. 3). 1997. 72.00 (978-0-7366-3602-5(1), 4256-B) Books on Tape.

Dragon Rider. Cornelia Funke. 7 cass. Orig. Title: Drachenreiter. (J). 2004. 50.00 (978-1-4000-9091-4(1), Listening Lib); audio compact disk 59.50 (978-1-4000-9494-3(1), Listening Lib) Pub: Random Audio Pubg. Dist(s): NetLibrary CO

Dragon Rider. unabr. ed. Cornelia Funke. Read by Brendan Fraser. (Running Time: 11 hrs. 35 mins.). Orig. Title: Drachenreiter. (ENG.). (J). (gr. 5). 2005. audio compact disk 40.00 (978-1-4000-9868-2(8), Listening Lib) Pub: Random Audio Pubg. Dist(s): Random

***Dragon Rule.** unabr. ed. E. E. Knight. Narrated by David Drummond. (Running Time: 8 hrs. 0 mins. 0 sec.). (Age of Fire Ser.). (ENG.). 2010. 24.99 (978-1-4001-6577-3(6)); 15.99 (978-1-4001-8577-1(7)); 34.99 (978-1-4001-9577-0(2)); audio compact disk 34.99 (978-1-4001-1577-8(9)) Pub: Tantor Media. Dist(s): IngramPubServ

***Dragon Rule.** unabr. ed. E. E. Knight. Narrated by David Drummond. (Running Time: 8 hrs. 0 mins. 0 sec.). (Age of Fire Ser.). (ENG.). 2010. audio compact disk 69.99 (978-1-4001-4577-5(5)) Pub: Tantor Media. Dist(s): IngramPubServ

Dragon Sea: A True Tale of Treasure, Archeology, & Greed off the Coast of Vietnam. unabr. ed. Frank Pope. Read by Johnny Heller. (Running Time: 11 hrs. 0 mins. 0 sec.). (ENG.). 2007. audio compact disk 24.99 (978-1-4001-5356-5(5)); audio compact disk 69.99 (978-1-4001-3356-7(4)) Pub: Tantor Media. Dist(s): IngramPubServ

Dragon Sea: A True Tale of Treasure, Archeology, & Greed off the Coast of Vietnam. unabr. ed. Frank Pope & Johnny Heller. (Running Time: 11 hrs. 0 mins. 0 sec.). (ENG.). 2007. audio compact disk 34.99 (978-1-4001-0356-0(8)) Pub: Tantor Media. Dist(s): IngramPubServ

***Dragon Seed.** unabr. ed. Pearl S. Buck. Narrated by Adam Verner. (Running Time: 14 hrs. 5 mins. 55 sec.). (ENG.). 2010. 27.99 (978-1-60814-759-5(2), SpringWater); audio compact disk 39.99 (978-1-59859-776-9(0), SpringWater) Oasis Audio.

Dragon Seekers. Christopher McGowan. Read by Stuart Langston. 7 cass. (Running Time: 8 hrs.). 2004. 44.95 (978-0-7861-2638-5(8), 3244) Blckstn Audio.

Dragon Seekers. Christopher McGowan. Read by Stuart Langston. 7 CDs. (Running Time: 8 hrs.). 2004. audio compact disk 56.00 (978-0-7861-8735-5(2), 3244) Blckstn Audio.

Dragon Singer. unabr. ed. James Comey. Contrib. by Christopher McGovern. 1 cass. (Running Time: 1 hrs. 6 min.). (Stages Audio Bks.: Vol. 2). (J). (ps-5). 1996. 10.00 (978-0-9652093-1-1(8)) Stages Imag.
A musical adventure in learning & fun, about cooperation & the determination to act on convictions.

Dragon Strike. unabr. ed. E. E. Knight. Narrated by Todd McLaren & David Drummond. (Running Time: 12 hrs. 30 mins. 0 sec.). (Age of Fire Ser.).

(ENG.). 2009. 24.99 (978-1-4001-6203-1(3)) Pub: Tantor Media. Dist(s): IngramPubServ

Dragon Strike. unabr. ed. E. E. Knight. Narrated by Todd McLaren & David Drummond. (Running Time: 12 hrs. 30 mins. 0 sec.). (Age of Fire Ser.). (ENG.). 2009. audio compact disk 75.99 (978-1-4001-4203-3(2)); audio compact disk 37.99 (978-1-4001-1203-6(6)) Pub: Tantor Media. Dist(s): IngramPubServ

***Dragon Strike.** unabr. ed. E. E. Knight. Narrated by David Drummond. (Running Time: 12 hrs. 30 mins.). (Age of Fire Ser.). 2009. 18.99 (978-1-4001-8203-9(4)); 37.99 (978-1-4001-9203-8(X)) Tantor Media.

Dragon Tales. 1 cass. (Running Time: 1 hr.). (J). 2002. 9.98; audio compact disk 13.98 Rhino Enter.

Dragon Tales. unabr. ed. Kenneth Grahame & Edith Nesbit. (Running Time: 2 hrs. 30 mins.). 2009. audio compact disk 17.98 (978-962-634-949-6(2), Naxos AudioBooks) Naxos.

Dragon Tunes. 1 cass. (Running Time: 45 min.). (J). (ps). 2001. 9.98 (978-0-7379-0175-7(6)) Rhino Enter.
Songs from the musical segments shown on the PBS series.

Dragon Tunes. 1 CD. (Running Time: 45 min.). (J). (ps-2). 2001. audio compact disk 13.98 (978-0-7379-0176-4(4)) Rhino Enter.
Companion to the video series. Most of the 20 tunes have a bouncy rock beat and involve some kind of movement activities for listeners to perform.

Dragon Wakes: China & the West, 1793-1911. unabr. ed. Christopher Hibbert. Narrated by Ed Blake. 11 cass. (Running Time: 15 hrs. 15 mins.). 1995. 91.00 (978-0-7887-0315-7(3), 94507E7) Recorded Bks.
Hear the fascinating daily lives of the self-sufficient people and the ruthless, dynastic politics of this world power.

Dragon with One Ruby Eye. unabr. ed. Paul W. Moomaw. Read by Kevin Foley. 8 cass. (Running Time: 11 hrs. 30 min.). 2001. 49.95 (978-1-55686-755-2(7)) Books in Motion.
CIA operative Adam Pray is assigned to recover stolen plutonium when he uncovers a plot which could destroy a nuclear power plant, and with it, half of Europe.

Dragon Wytch. Yasmine Galenorn. Read by Cassandra Campbell. (Playaway Adult Fiction Ser.). (ENG.). 2009. 64.99 (978-1-60847-890-3(4)) Find a World.

Dragon Wytch. unabr. ed. Yasmine Galenorn. Narrated by Cassandra Campbell. (Running Time: 11 hrs. 0 mins. 0 sec.). (Sisters of the Moon Ser.). (ENG.). 2009. audio compact disk 34.99 (978-1-4001-0999-9(X)); audio compact disk 69.99 (978-1-4001-3999-6(6)); audio compact disk 24.99 (978-1-4001-5999-4(7)) Pub: Tantor Media. Dist(s): IngramPubServ

Dragondrums. Anne McCaffrey. Read by Allison Green. 5 cass. (Running Time: 7 hrs.). (Harper Hall Trilogy: Vol. 3). 1993. 44.20 Set. (978-1-56544-041-8(2), 550012); Rental 7.80 30 day rental Set. (550012) Literate Ear.
Again the deadly Thread threatens the Kingdom of Pern. But now, the oldtimers who defeated the deadly force in years gone by are breeding rebellion. The Master Harper must send young Piemur, a drum apprentice. Can Piemur meet the task of rescuing his beloved Pern, & still return to the safety & home of his little fire lizard?

Dragondrums. unabr. ed. Anne McCaffrey. Narrated by Sally Darling. 6 cass. (Running Time: 9 hrs.). (Harper Hall Trilogy: Vol. 3). (gr. 7). 1992. 53.00 (978-1-55690-618-3(8), 92311E7) Recorded Bks.
Piemur, the drummer's apprentice, comes of age on a journey to Pern's uncharted Southern Continent.

DragonFire. unabr. ed. Donita K. Paul. Read by Ellen Grafton. (Running Time: 11 hrs.). (DragonKeeper Chronicles Ser.). 2009. 39.97 (978-1-4233-9274-3(4), 9781423392743, Brlnc Audio MP3 Lib); 19.99 (978-1-4233-9273-6(6), 9781423392736, Brilliance MP3); 39.97 (978-1-4233-9276-7(0), 9781423392767, BADLE); 19.99 (978-1-4233-9275-0(2), 9781423392750, BAD); audio compact disk 19.99 (978-1-4233-9271-2(X), 9781423392712, Bril Audio CD Unabri); audio compact disk 59.97 (978-1-4233-9272-9(8), 9781423392729, BriAudCD Unabrid) Brilliance Audio.

Dragonflight. abr. ed. Anne McCaffrey. Read by Adrienne Barbeau. 4 cass. (Running Time: 6 hrs.). (Dragonriders of Pern Ser.). 2002. 25.00 (978-1-57453-532-7(3)) Audio Lit.
Lessa emerges from hiding after ten long Turns, ready to reclaim her birthright, impress the Dragon Queen, and eventually become Weyrwoman of Benden. As the deadly Threads begin to turn again, the bold dragonriders take to the air, belching flames that destroy the strands before they touch the ground.

Dragonflight. unabr. ed. Anne McCaffrey. Read by Dick Hill. 6 cass. (Running Time: 9 hrs.). (Dragonriders of Pern Ser.: Vol. 1). 2002. 29.95 (978-1-59086-288-9(0), 1590862880, BAU) Brilliance Audio.
On the beautiful planet Pern, colonized for centuries, Land Holders and Craftsmen have traditionally tithed food and supplies to the dragonweyrs to which they are bound. In times past, the mighty telepathic dragons and their riders were the only protection from the dreaded, life-threatening Thread. But it has been over 400 years since the last Threadfall, and some people have come to doubt that the menace will every strike again. But F'lar, rider of Pern's greatest bronze dragon, has no such illusions. The Red Star is near; Thread will fall soon.

Dragonflight. unabr. ed. Anne McCaffrey. Read by Dick Hill. (Running Time: 9 hrs.). (Dragonriders of Pern Ser.). 2005. 39.25 (978-1-59737-950-2(6), 9781597379502, BADLE); 24.95 (978-1-59737-949-6(2), 9781597379496, BAD); audio compact disk 34.95 (978-1-59737-951-9(4), 9781597379519, Bril Audio CD Unabri) Brilliance Audio.

Dragonflight. unabr. ed. Anne McCaffrey. Read by Dick Hill. (Running Time: 32400 sec.). (Dragonriders of Pern Ser.: Vol. 1). 2005. audio compact disk 92.25 (978-1-59737-952-6(2), 9781597379526, BriAudCD Unabrid) Brilliance Audio.

Dragonflight. unabr. ed. Anne McCaffrey. Read by Dick Hill. (Running Time: 32400 sec.). (Dragonriders of Pern Ser.: Vol. 1). 2005. audio compact disk 24.95 (978-1-59737-947-2(6), 9781597379472, Brilliance MP3); audio compact disk 39.25 (978-1-59737-948-9(4), 9781597379489, Brlnc Audio MP3 Lib) Brilliance Audio.

Dragonfly in Amber see Dragonfly in Amber

Dragonfly in Amber. Diana Gabaldon. Read by Davina Porter. (Running Time: 141300 sec.). (Outlander Ser.: Bk. 2).Tr. of Dragonfly in Amber. 2006. audio compact disk 59.99 (978-1-4193-8102-7(4)) Recorded Bks.

Dragonfly in Amber. unabr. ed. Diana Gabaldon. Read by Davina Porter. 27 cass. (Running Time: 39 hrs. 15 mins.). (Outlander Ser.: Bk. 2).Tr. of Dragonfly in Amber. 1998. 186.00 (978-0-7887-2170-0(4), 95466E7) Recorded Bks.
Sweep back into the 18th-century as Claire, determined to share the secret of time travel with her daughter, returns to Scotland 20 years later.

Dragonfly in Amber, Set. Diana Gabaldon. Read by Davina Porter. 27 cass. (Running Time: 39 hrs. 15 min.). (Outlander Ser.: Bk. 2).Tr. of Dragonfly in Amber. 1998. 87.00 (978-0-7887-2472-5(X), 95587) Recorded Bks.
Determined to share the secret of her time travel with her daughter, Claire returns to Scotland 20 years later to relive her stay in the intrigue-ridden court of Charles Stuart.

Dragonfly Pool. unabr. ed. Eva Ibbotson. Narrated by Patricia Conolly. (Running Time: 10 hrs.). (YA). (gr. 5-8). 2008. 56.75 (978-1-4361-9887-5(9)); 67.75 (978-1-4361-5203-7(8)); audio compact disk 97.75 (978-1-4361-5208-2(9)) Recorded Bks.

Dragonfly Pool. unabr. collector's ed. Eva Ibbotson. Narrated by Patricia Conolly. 9 CDs. (Running Time: 10 hrs.). (YA). (gr. 5-8). 2008. audio compact disk 42.95 (978-1-4361-5212-9(7)) Recorded Bks.

Dragonfly's Tale. unabr. ed. Kristina Rodanas. 1 cass. (Running Time: 14 min.). (J). (gr. k-4). 1994. pap. bk. 17.90 (978-0-8045-6813-5(8), 6813) Spoken Arts.
1992 Southwest Book Award.

Dragongirl. abr. ed. Todd McCaffrey. (Running Time: 6 hrs.). 2011. audio compact disk 14.99 (978-1-4233-7342-1(1), 9781423373421, BCD Value Price) Brilliance Audio.

Dragongirl. unabr. ed. Todd McCaffrey. Read by Emily Durante. (Running Time: 16 hrs.). 2010. 24.99 (978-1-4233-7337-7(5), 9781423373377, Brilliance MP3); 24.99 (978-1-4233-7339-1(1), 9781423373391, BAD); 39.97 (978-1-4233-7338-4(3), 9781423373384, Brlnc Audio MP3 Lib); 39.97 (978-1-4233-7340-7(5), 9781423373407, BADLE); audio compact disk 38.99 (978-1-4233-7335-3(9), 9781423373353, Bril Audio CD Unabri); audio compact disk 92.97 (978-1-4233-7336-0(7), 9781423373360, BriAudCD Unabrid) Brilliance Audio.

Dragonheart. Todd McCaffrey. Read by Emily Durante. (Playaway Adult Fiction Ser.). (ENG.). 2009. 79.99 (978-1-60812-685-9(4)) Find a World.

Dragonheart. unabr. ed. Todd McCaffrey. Read by Emily Durante. (Running Time: 20 hrs.). 2008. 29.99 (978-1-4233-7330-8(8), 9781423373308, BAD); 29.99 (978-1-4233-7328-5(6), 9781423373285, Brilliance MP3); 44.97 (978-1-4233-7329-2(4), 9781423373292, Brlnc Audio MP3 Lib); 44.97 (978-1-4233-7331-5(6), 9781423373315, BADLE); audio compact disk 112.25 (978-1-4233-7327-8(8), 9781423373278, BriAudCD Unabrid); audio compact disk 39.99 (978-1-4233-7326-1(X), 9781423373261, Bril Audio CD Unabri) Brilliance Audio.

DragonKnight. unabr. ed. Donita K. Paul. Read by Ellen Grafton. (Running Time: 13 hrs.). (DragonKeeper Chronicles Ser.). 2009. 39.97 (978-1-4233-9268-2(X), 9781423392682, Brlnc Audio MP3 Lib); 19.99 (978-1-4233-9267-5(1), 9781423392675, Brilliance MP3); 39.97 (978-1-4233-9270-5(1), 9781423392705, BADLE); 19.99 (978-1-4233-9269-9(8), 9781423392699, BAD); audio compact disk 19.99 (978-1-4233-9265-1(5), 9781423392651, Bril Audio CD Unabri); audio compact disk 59.97 (978-1-4233-9266-8(3), 9781423392668, BriAudCD Unabrid) Brilliance Audio.

DragonLight. unabr. ed. Donita K. Paul. Read by Ellen Grafton. (Running Time: 11 hrs.). (DragonKeeper Chronicles Ser.). 2009. 39.97 (978-1-4233-9280-4(9), 9781423392804, Brlnc Audio MP3 Lib); 19.99 (978-1-4233-9279-8(5), 9781423392798, Brilliance MP3); 39.97 (978-1-4233-9282-8(5), 9781423392828, BADLE); 19.99 (978-1-4233-9281-1(7), 9781423392811, BAD); audio compact disk 19.99 (978-1-4233-9277-4(9), 9781423392774, Bril Audio CD Unabri); audio compact disk 59.97 (978-1-4233-9278-1(7), 9781423392781, BriAudCD Unabrid) Brilliance Audio.

Dragonling. unabr. ed. Jackie French Koller. Narrated by Jeff Woodman. (Running Time: 1 hr.). audio compact disk 12.75 (978-1-4025-2302-1(5)) Recorded Bks.

Dragonling. unabr. ed. Jackie French Koller. Narrated by Jeff Woodman. 1 cass. (Running Time: 1 hr.). (J). (gr. 2 up). 2002. 12.75 (978-0-7887-9447-6(7)) Recorded Bks.
Darek is envious when quest wearing dragon claws for a necklace. His brother has killed a Great Blue, the largest and most feared of all dragons. Only Darek knows that the slain beast has a newborn dragonling. Darek decides to return the dragonling to its home, a terrifying valley filled with deadly beasts.

Dragonmede. unabr. ed. Rona Randall. Read by Susanna Dawson. 9 cass. (Running Time: 12 hrs.). 1998. 90.95 Set. (978-1-85903-227-5(3)) Pub: Magna Story GBR. Dist(s): Ulverscroft US
Luella Rochdale, gay, immoral & generous-hearted, runs a gambling house in Victorian London. Luella's sole ambition - a successful marriage for her daughter, Eustacia - is achieved when Eustacia becomes the wife of Julian Kershaw, heir to Dragonmede. But the marriage is passionate, stormy & disillusioning. Eustacia discovers that life in country society is no more respectable than in London. Worse, at Dragonmede it is accompanied by sinister legend & fear, plus the shock of learning how her marriage was manipulated, & why.

Dragonplague. unabr. ed. Terence Strong. Read by John Cormack. 12 cass. (Running Time: 14 hrs. 31 mins.). (Isis Cassettes Ser.). (J). 2004. 94.95 (978-0-7531-1903-7(X)); audio compact disk 99.95 (978-0-7531-2252-5(9)) Pub: ISIS Lrg Prnt GBR. Dist(s): Ulverscroft US

Dragonquest. unabr. ed. Anne McCaffrey. Read by Dick Hill. (Running Time: 12 hrs.). (Dragonriders of Pern Ser.). 2005. 39.25 (978-1-59600-987-5(X), 9781596009875, BADLE); 24.95 (978-1-59600-986-8(1), 9781596009868, BAD) Brilliance Audio.

Dragonquest. unabr. ed. Anne McCaffrey. Read by Dick Hill. (Running Time: 43200 sec.). (Dragonriders of Pern Ser.: Vol. 2). 2005. audio compact disk 39.25 (978-1-59600-985-1(3), 9781596009851, Brlnc Audio MP3 Lib); audio compact disk 24.95 (978-1-59600-984-4(5), 9781596009844, Brilliance MP3); audio compact disk 102.25 (978-1-59600-983-7(7), 9781596009837, BriAudCD Unabrid); audio compact disk 37.95 (978-1-59600-982-0(9), 9781596009820, Bril Audio CD Unabri) Brilliance Audio.
Another Turn, and the deadly silver Threads began falling again. So the bold dragonriders took to the air once more and their magnificent flying dragons swirled and swooped, belching flames that destroyed the shimmering strands before they reach the ground. But F'lar knew he had to find a better way to protect his beloved Pern, and he had to find it before the rebellious Oldtimers could breed anymore dissent... before his brother F'nor would be foolhardy enough to launch another suicide mission... and before those dratted fire-lizards could stir up any more trouble!.

DragonQuest. unabr. ed. Donita K. Paul. Read by Ellen Grafton. (Running Time: 12 hrs.). (DragonKeeper Chronicles Ser.). 2009. 39.97 (978-1-4233-9262-0(0), 9781423392620, Brlnc Audio MP3 Lib); 19.99 (978-1-4233-9261-3(2), 9781423392613, Brilliance MP3); 39.97 (978-1-4233-9264-4(7), 9781423392644, BADLE); 19.99 (978-1-4233-9263-7(9), 9781423392637, BAD); audio compact disk 19.99 (978-1-4233-9259-0(0), 9781423392590, Bril Audio CD Unabri); audio compact disk 59.97 (978-1-4233-9260-6(4), 9781423392606, BriAudCD Unabrid) Brilliance Audio.

Dragons. Patricia C. Wrede. 4 cass. (Running Time: 6 hrs.). (YA). 2001. (Listening Lib) Random Audio Pubg.

Dragons & Kings. Jackie French Koller. Narrated by Jeff Woodman. 2 CDs. (Running Time: 1 hr. 30 mins.). audio compact disk 22.00 (978-1-4025-1959-8(1)) Recorded Bks.

Dragons & Kings. unabr. ed. Jackie French Koller. Narrated by Jeff Woodman. 1 cass. (Running Time: 1 hr. 30 mins.). (gr. 3 up). 2002. 10.00 (978-0-7887-9451-3(5)) Recorded Bks.
Darek and his dragon have escaped from Krad, a neighboring kingdom, after being held captive. But on their return home they find their village under the control of Zarnak, a wicked tyrant.

***Dragon's Apprentice.** unabr. ed. James A. Owen. Read by James Langton. (Running Time: 10 hrs. 0 mins. 0 sec.). (Chronicles of the Imaginarium Geographica Ser.). (ENG.). (YA). 2010. audio compact disk 39.99 (978-1-4423-3413-7(4)) Pub: S&S Audio. Dist(s): S and S Inc

Dragons Are Singing Tonight. unabr. ed. Jack Prelutsky. Read by Jack Prelutsky. (Running Time: 37 min.). (Follow the Reader Ser.). (J). (gr. k-3). 1994. 9.95 (978-0-8072-0222-7(3), FTR 168 CXR, Listening Lib) Random Audio Pubg.
Dragons, dragons, everywhere! These poems honoring the fire-breathing medieval wonders are fun for dragon-lovers everywhere - a book filled with humor, magic & originality.

Dragons Are Singing Tonight. unabr. ed. Jack Prelutsky. Read by Jack Prelutsky. 1 cass. (Running Time: 51 mins.). (Follow the Reader Ser.). (J). (ps-3). 1994. 11.00 Library ed. (978-0-8072-0220-3(7), FTR168CX, Listening Lib) Random Audio Pubg.

Dragon's Ascension. Ed Greenwood. Read by Simon Vance. (Running Time: 11 hrs.). 2003. 34.95 (978-1-59912-373-8(8)) Iofy Corp.

Dragon's Ascension. unabr. ed. Ed Greenwood. Read by Simon Vance. 9 CDs. (Running Time: 12 hrs.). 2004. audio compact disk 72.00 (978-0-7861-8889-5(8)); audio compact disk 24.95 (978-0-7861-8724-9(7)); 56.95 (978-0-7861-2624-8(8)) Blckstn Audio.
Aglirta, known as the Kingless Land, has fallen into lawlessness. Now, a powerful warlord has come to take control through force, while the diabolic minions of the Serpent move into position for a climactic battle that will scar the valiant Band of Four forever.

Dragons at the Party. unabr. ed. Jon Cleary. Read by Gordon Griffin. 9 cass. (Running Time: 13 hrs. 30 mins.). 1999. 79.95 (68386) Pub: Soundings Ltd GBR. Dist(s): Ulverscroft US

Dragons at the Party. unabr. ed. Jon Cleary. Read by Gordon Griffin. 9 cass. (Sound Ser.). 2004. 76.95 (978-1-85496-838-6(8)) Pub: UlverLrgPrint GBR. Dist(s): Ulverscroft US

Dragon's Breath. unabr. ed. E. D. Baker. Narrated by Katherine Kellgren. 7 CDs. (Running Time: 7 hrs. 15 mins.). (YA). (gr. 5-8). 2005. audio compact disk 69.75 (978-1-4193-5577-6(5), C3408); 54.75 (978-1-4193-3561-7(8), 98012) Recorded Bks.
This sequel to Book Sense 76 Children¿s Pick The Frog Princess is "as magically adventurous as fantasy can get," according to VOYA. Princess Emma, a witch in training, is having some trouble controlling her skills. She even puts herself in the dungeon by mistake. When her kingdom is threatened, she will need the aid of her magical aunt to protect everyone.

Dragon's Breath: Read-Along/Homework Pack. unabr. ed. E. D. Baker. Narrated by Katherine Kellgren. 6 cass. (Running Time: 7 hrs. 15 mins.). (YA). (gr. 5-8). 2005. bk. 92.70 (978-1-4193-3563-1(4), 42041) Recorded Bks.

Dragon's Bride. Jo Beverley. Narrated by Simon Prebble. 8 cass. (Running Time: 11 hrs.). 72.00 (978-1-4025-3916-9(9)) Recorded Bks.

***Dragon's Dagger.** unabr. ed. R. A. Salvatore. Narrated by Paul Boehmer. (Running Time: 11 hrs. 0 mins. 0 sec.). (Spearwielder's Tale Ser.). (ENG.). 2010. 24.99 (978-1-4001-6636-7(5)); 16.99 (978-1-4001-8636-5(6)); audio compact disk 69.99 (978-1-4001-4636-9(4)); audio compact disk 34.99 (978-1-4001-1636-2(8)) Pub: Tantor Media. Dist(s): IngramPubServ

Dragon's Doom: A Band of Four Novel. unabr. ed. Ed Greenwood. Read by Simon Vance. (Running Time: 16 hrs.). (Band of Four Ser.). 2004. 24.95 (978-0-7861-8604-4(6)); 76.95 (978-0-7861-2711-5(2)); audio compact disk 104.00 (978-0-7861-8643-3(7)) Blckstn Audio.

Dragon's Eye. unabr. ed. Kaza Kingsley. Read by Simon Jones. (Running Time: 10 hrs. 0 mins. 0 sec.). (Erec Rex Ser.). (ENG.). (J). 2009. audio compact disk 39.99 (978-0-7435-8139-4(3)) Pub: S&S Audio. Dist(s): S and S Inc

Dragon's Fire. abr. ed. Anne McCaffrey. Read by Dick Hill. (Running Time: 21600 sec.). (Dragonriders of Pern Ser.). 2007. audio compact disk 14.99 (978-1-4233-1463-9(8), 9781423314639, BCD Value Price) Brilliance Audio.

Dragon's Fire. unabr. ed. Anne McCaffrey & Todd McCaffrey. Read by Dick Hill. (Running Time: 12 hrs.). (Dragonriders of Pern Ser.). 2006. 39.25 (978-1-4233-1461-5(1), 9781423314615, BADLE); 24.95 (978-1-4233-1460-8(3), 9781423314608, BAD); 87.25 (978-1-4233-1455-4(7), 9781423314554, BrilAudUnabridg); audio compact disk 102.25 (978-1-4233-1457-8(3), 9781423314578, BriAudCD Unabrid); audio compact disk 39.25 (978-1-4233-1459-2(X), 9781423314592, Brlnc Audio MP3 Lib); audio compact disk 38.95 (978-1-4233-1456-1(5), 9781423314561, Bril Audio CD Unabri); audio compact disk 24.95 (978-1-4233-1458-5(1), 9781423314585, Brilliance MP3) Brilliance Audio.
Please enter a Synopsis.

Dragon's Gate. Laurence Yep. Narrated by George Guidall. 7 CDs. (Running Time: 7 hrs. 15 mins.). (Golden Mountain Chronicles). (gr. 7 up). audio compact disk 69.00 (978-1-4025-2303-8(3)) Recorded Bks.

Dragon's Gate. unabr. ed. Laurence Yep. Narrated by George Guidall. 5 pieces. (Running Time: 7 hrs. 15 mins.). (Golden Mountain Chronicles). (gr. 7 up). 1994. 44.00 (978-0-7887-0132-0(0), 94357E7) Recorded Bks.
A young Chinese boy follows his father & uncle to the United States, where he joins their work crew building the Transcontinental Railroad through the Rocky Mountains. An excellent introduction to 19th-century American history & Chinese-American cultural heritage.

Dragon's Keep. unabr. ed. Janet Lee Carey. Narrated by Bianca Amato. 8 CDs. (Running Time: 9 hrs. 15 mins.). (YA). (gr. 6-10). 2008. audio compact disk 87.75 (978-1-4281-8317-9(5)); 61.75 (978-1-4281-8312-4(4)) Recorded Bks.
A winner of the Mark Twain Award, Janet Lee Carey pens a richly imagined tale of princesses and dragons. On Wilde Island, Rosalind and her mother live their lives in exile, awaiting the time they can reclaim their rightful place on the throne. And there is reason to hope - a 600-year-old prophesy has decreed that they will do just that. But little do they know, their destinies hinge on Rosalind's amazing, shameful secret. Beneath her gold gloves, the fourth finger of her left hand is in truth a dragon's claw.

Dragon's Kin. unabr. ed. Anne McCaffrey & Todd McCaffrey. Read by Dick Hill. 6 cass. (Running Time: 8 hrs.). (Dragonriders of Pern Ser.). 2003. 29.95 (978-1-59355-180-3(0), 1593551800, BAU); 74.25 (978-1-59355-181-0(9), 1593551819, BrilAudUnabridg); audio compact disk 31.95 (978-1-59355-480-4(X), 159355480X, Bril Audio CD Unabri); audio compact disk 87.25 (978-1-59355-481-1(8), 1593554818, BriAudCD Unabrid) Brilliance Audio.

Beginning with the classic Dragonriders of Pern, Anne McCaffrey has created a complex, endlessly fascinating world uniting humans and great telepathic dragons. Millions of devoted readers have soared on the glittering wings of Anne's imagination, following book by book the evolution of one of science fiction's most beloved and honored series. Now, for the first time, Anne has invited another writer to join her in the skies of Pern, a writer with an intimate knowledge of Pern and its history: her son, Todd. Young Kindan has no expectations other than joining his father in the mines of Camp Natalon, a coal mining settlement struggling to turn a profit far from the great Holds where the presence of dragons and their riders means safety and civilization. Mining is fraught with danger. Fortunately, the camp has a watch-wher, a creature distantly related to dragons and uniquely suited to specialized work in the dark, cold mineshafts. Kindan's father is the watch-wher's handler, and his son sometimes helps him out. But even that important job promises no opportunity outside the mine. Then disaster strikes. In one terrible instant, Kindan loses his family and the camp loses its watch-wher. Fathers are replaced by sons in the mine - except for Kindan, who is taken in by the camp's new Harper. Grieving, Kindan finds a measure of solace in a burgeoning musical talent . . . and in a new friendship with Nuella, a mysterious girl no one seems to know exists. It is Nuella who assists Kindan when he is selected to hatch and train a new watch-wher, a job that forces him to give up his dream of becoming a Harper; and it is Nuella who helps him give new meaning to his life. Meanwhile, sparked by the tragedy, long-simmering tensions are dividing the camp. Far below the surface, a group of resentful miners hides a deadly secret. As warring factions threaten to explode, Nuella and Kindan begin to discover unknown talents in the misunderstood watch-wher-talents that could very well save an entire Hold. During their time teaching the watch-wher, the two learn some things themselves: that even a seemingly impossible dream is never completely out of reach . . . and that light can be found even in the deepest darkness.

Dragon's Kin. unabr. ed. Anne McCaffrey & Todd McCaffrey. Read by Dick Hill. (Running Time: 8 hrs.). (Dragonriders of Pern Ser.). 2004. 39.25 (978-1-59335-640-8(4), 1593356404, Brinc Audio MP3 Lib) Brilliance Audio.

Dragon's Kin. unabr. ed. Anne McCaffrey & Todd McCaffrey. Read by Dick Hill. (Running Time: 8 hrs.). (Dragonriders of Pern Ser.). 2004. 39.25 (978-1-59710-222-3(9), 1597102229, BADLE); 24.95 (978-1-59710-223-0(7), 1597102237, BAD) Brilliance Audio.

Dragon's Kin. unabr. ed. Anne McCaffrey & Todd McCaffrey. Read by Dick Hill. (Running Time: 8 hrs.). (Pern Ser.). 2004. 24.95 (978-1-59335-255-4(7), 1593352557) Soulmate Audio Bks.

Dragon's Night. unabr. ed. Anne McCaffrey & Todd McCaffrey. (Running Time: 15 hrs.). (Dragonriders of Pern Ser.). 2010. audio compact disk 99.97 (978-1-4233-4698-2(X), 9781423346982, BriAudCD Unabrid) Brilliance Audio.

Dragons of a Fallen Sun. abr. ed. Margaret Weis & Tracy Hickman. 4 cass. (Running Time: 6 hrs.). (DragonLance: Vol. 1). 2000. 24.95 (978-1-55935-345-8(7)) Soundelux.

Dragons of Blueland. Ruth Stiles Gannett. Illus. by Ruth Chrisman Gannett. (Tales of My Father's Dragon Ser.: Bk. 3). (J). (gr. 3-6). pap. bk. 4.99 (978-0-8072-1287-5(3), Listening Lib) Random Audio Pubg.

Dragons of Blueland. unabr. ed. Ruth Stiles Gannett. Read by Robert Sevra. 1 cass. (Running Time: 51 mins.). (Tales of My Father's Dragon Ser.: Bk. 3). (J). (gr. 2-5). 1997. pap. bk. 17.00 (978-0-8072-0238-8(X), FTR 177 SP, Listening Lib) Random Audio Pubg.

Dragons of Summer Flame. abr. ed. Margaret Weis & Tracy Hickman. Read by Wanda McCaddon. 4 cass. (DragonLance Chronicles: Vol. 4). 1998. 21.95 Set. (978-1-55935-206-2(X)) Soundelux.

Palin Majere seeks to enter the Abyss in search of his lost uncle. The Dark Queen has found new champions. Devoted followers, loyal to the death, The Knights of Takhisis, follow the Vision to victory.

Dragons of the Dwarven Depths. abr. ed. Margaret Weis & Tracy Hickman. Read by Sandra Burr. (Running Time: 21600 sec.). (DragonLance: Vol. 1). 2007. audio compact disk 14.99 (978-1-4233-1617-6(7), 9781423316176, BCD Value Price) Brilliance Audio.

Dragons of the Dwarven Depths. unabr. ed. Margaret Weis & Tracy Hickman. Read by Sandra Burr. (Running Time: 15 hrs.). (DragonLance: Vol. 1). 2006. 39.25 (978-1-4233-1615-2(0), 9781423316152, BADLE); 24.95 (978-1-4233-1614-5(2), 9781423316145, BAD); 97.25 (978-1-4233-1609-1(6), 9781423316091, BriAudUnabridg); audio compact disk 117.25 (978-1-4233-1611-4(8), 9781423316114, BriAudCD Unabrid); audio compact disk 39.25 (978-1-4233-1613-8(4), 9781423316138, Brinc Audio MP3 Lib); audio compact disk 24.95 (978-1-4233-1612-1(6), 9781423316121, Brilliance MP3); audio compact disk 39.95 (978-1-4233-1610-7(X), 9781423316107, Bril Audio CD Unabri) Brilliance Audio.

Please enter a Synopsis.

Dragons of the Highlord Skies. abr. ed. Margaret Weis & Tracy Hickman. Read by Sandra Burr. (Running Time: 6 hrs.). (DragonLance: Vol. 2). 2008. audio compact disk 14.99 (978-1-4233-1627-5(4), 9781423316275, BCD Value Price) Brilliance Audio.

Dragons of the Highlord Skies. unabr. ed. Margaret Weis & Tracy Hickman. Read by Sandra Burr. (Running Time: 16 hrs.). (DragonLance: Vol. 2). 2007. 39.25 (978-1-4233-1625-1(8), 9781423316251, BADLE); 24.95 (978-1-4233-1624-4(X), 9781423316244, BAD); 97.25 (978-1-4233-1619-0(3), 9781423316190, BriAudUnabridg); audio compact disk 39.95 (978-1-4233-1620-6(7), 9781423316206, Bril Audio CD Unabri); audio compact disk 24.95 (978-1-4233-1622-0(3), 9781423316220, Brilliance MP3); audio compact disk 39.25 (978-1-4233-1623-7(1), 9781423316237, Brinc Audio MP3 Lib); audio compact disk 117.25 (978-1-4233-1621-3(5), 9781423316213, BriAudCD Unabrid) Brilliance Audio.

Dragons of the Hourglass Mage. abr. ed. Margaret Weis & Tracy Hickman. (Running Time: 6 hrs.). 2008. audio compact disk 26.95 (978-1-4233-1636-7(3), 9781423316367, BACD) Brilliance Audio.

Dragons of the Hourglass Mage. abr. ed. Margaret Weis & Tracy Hickman. (Running Time: 6 hrs.). 2009. audio compact disk 14.99 (978-1-4233-1637-4(1), 9781423316374, BCD Value Price) Brilliance Audio.

Dragons of the Hourglass Mage. unabr. ed. Margaret Weis & Tracy Hickman. (Running Time: 15 hrs.). 2008. 112.25 (978-1-4233-1629-9(0), 9781423316299, BriAudUnabridg) Brilliance Audio.

Dragons of the Hourglass Mage. unabr. ed. Margaret Weis & Tracy Hickman. Read by Sandra Burr. (Running Time: 11 hrs.). (Lost Chornicles Ser.). 2009. 39.97 (978-1-4233-1635-0(5), 9781423316350, BADLE); 39.97 (978-1-4233-1633-6(9), 9781423316336, Brinc Audio MP3 Lib); 24.99 (978-1-4233-1634-3(7), 9781423316343, BAD); audio compact disk 99.97 (978-1-4233-1631-2(2), 9781423316312, BriAudCD Unabrid) Brilliance Audio.

Dragons of the Hourglass Mage. unabr. ed. Margaret Weis & Tracy Hickman. Read by Sandra Burr. (Running Time: 12 hrs.). (Lost Chronicles: Vol. 3). 2009. 24.99 (978-1-4233-1632-9(0), 9781423316329, Brilliance MP3); audio compact disk 39.99 (978-1-4233-1630-5(4), 9781423316305, Bril Audio CD Unabri) Brilliance Audio.

Dragon's School. unabr. ed. Anne McCaffrey & Todd McCaffrey. (Running Time: 15 hrs.). (Dragonriders of Pern Ser.). 2011. audio compact disk 99.97 (978-1-4233-4707-1(2), 9781423347071, BriAudCD Unabrid); audio compact disk 38.99 (978-1-4233-4706-4(4), 9781423347064, Bril Audio CD Unabri) Brilliance Audio.

Dragon's Teeth see Tanglewood Tales

Dragon's Teeth: A Problem in Deduction. unabr. ed. Ellery Queen. Read by Blain Fairman. 6 cass. (Running Time: 8 hrs. 14 min.). 2001. 29.95 (978-1-57270-197-7(8), N61197u) Pub: Audio Partners. Dist(s): PerseuPGW

Eccentric multimillionaire Cadmus Cole hires Ellery Queen to investigate a case but won't say what it is. When Cole dies mysteriously at sea, Queen & his partner, Beau Rummell, must navigate a thicket of complications that includes a $50 million legacy, two beautiful, avaricious women vying for it & even a phony Ellery Queen.

Dragons' Truth. Teel McClanahan, 3rd. Read by Teel McClanahan, 3rd. (ENG.). (YA). 2008. 12.99 (978-1-934516-75-1(9)); audio compact disk 24.99 (978-1-934516-76-8(7)) Modern Evil.

Dragonsblood. unabr. ed. Todd McCaffrey. Read by Dick Hill. (Running Time: 15 hrs.). (Dragonriders of Pern Ser.). 2005. 39.25 (978-1-59710-225-4(3), 9781597102254, BADLE); 24.95 (978-1-59710-224-7(5), 9781597102247, BAD); 24.95 (978-1-59335-802-0(4), 9781593358020, Brilliance MP3); 97.25 (978-1-59600-115-2(1), 9781596001152, BriAudUnabridg); 36.95 (978-1-59600-114-5(3), 9781596001145); audio compact disk 38.95 (978-1-59600-116-9(X), 9781596001169); audio compact disk 112.25 (978-1-59600-117-6(8), 9781596001176, BriAudCD Unabrid) Brilliance Audio.

Something terrible is happening to the dragons of Pern - and the only person who can save them has been dead for over four hundred Turns. The dragonriders of the Third Pass have only the lyrics of a disquieting song and strange hints of marvelous rooms hidden in Benden Weyr to aid them. And the lyrics point to one thing - that to save the dragons of Pern, one young woman must sacrifice everything, including those she loves.

Dragonsblood. unabr. ed. Todd McCaffrey. Read by Dick Hill. 1 CD. (Running Time: 15 hrs.). (Pern Ser.). 2005. 39.25 (978-1-59335-936-2(5), 9781593359362) Soulmate Audio Bks.

In Dragon's Kin, bestselling author Anne McCaffrey did the unthinkable: for the first time ever, she invited another writer to join her in the skies of her most famous fictional creation. That writer was her son, Todd McCaffrey. Together, they penned a triumphant new chapter in the annals of the extraordinarily popular Dragonriders of Pern. Now, for the first time, Todd McCaffrey flies alone. And Dragonsblood is proof that the future of Pern is in good hands. After all, dragons are in his blood... Never in the dramatic history of Pern has there been a more dire emergency than that which faces the young dragonrider Lorana. A mysterious fatal illness is striking dragons. The epidemic is spreading like wildfire . . . and the next deadly cycle of Threadfall is only days away. Somehow, Lorana must find a cure before the dragons - including her own beloved Arith - succumb to the sickness, leaving Pern undefended. The lyrics of an all-but-forgotten song seem to point toward an answer, an answer from nearly five hundred years in the past, when Kitti Ping and her daughter Wind Blossom bred the first dragons from their smaller cousins, the fire-lizards. No doubt the first Pern colonists possessed the advanced technology to find the cure Lorana seeks, but over the centuries, that knowledge has been lost. Or has it? For in the distant past, an aged Wind Blossom worries that the germs that affect the fire-lizards may one day turn against larger prey - and unleash a plague that will destroy the dragons, Pern's only defenders against Thread. But as her people struggle to survive, Wind Blossom has neither the time nor the resources to expend on a future that may never arrive - until suddenly she uncovers evidence that her worst fears will come true. Now two brave women, separated by hundreds of years but joined by bonds transcending time, will become unknowing allies in a desperate race against sickness and Threadfall, with nothing less than the survival of all life on Pern at stake. "The torch has been passed and burns more brightly than ever in this latest chapter of the venerable Pern saga, the first of what one hopes will be many solo efforts by the son of series creator Anne McCaffrey." - Publishers Weekly (starred review).

Dragonsdale. unabr. ed. Salamanda Drake. Read by Jill Shilling. 5 cds. (Running Time: 5 hrs. 50 mins.). 2007. audio compact disk 45.00 (978-0-7393-5098-0(6), Random AudioBks) Pub: Random Audio Pubg. Dist(s): Random

Dragonsdale: Where Dragons & Dreams Take Flight! unabr. ed. Salamanda Drake. Read by Jill Shilling. (Running Time: 21000 sec.). (ENG.). (J). (gr. 4-7). 2007. audio compact disk 35.00 (978-0-7393-4886-4(8), Listening Lib) Pub: Random Audio Pubg. Dist(s): Random

Dragonsdawn. Anne McCaffrey. Read by Allison Green. 9 cass. (Running Time: 14 hrs.). (Pern Ser.). 1993. 63.40 Set. (978-1-56544-009-8(9), 550014); Rental 10.40 30 day rental Set. (550014) Literate Ear.

The planet Pern. Untouched by industrial development or intergalactic war, Pern seemed ideal to the travellers from earth. Then horror: Threads began to destroy all that lived. Fire is discovered to destroy Thread, but they need a colony-wide defense against an attack that lasts for fifty years. Small dragon-like lizards are discovered breathing fire on Thread, destroying it.

Dragonsdawn. unabr. ed. Anne McCaffrey. Read by Dick Hill. (Running Time: 15 hrs.). (Dragonriders of Pern Ser.). 2005. 39.25 (978-1-59600-993-6(4), 9781596009936, BADLE); 24.95 (978-1-59600-992-9(6), 9781596009929, BAD); audio compact disk 39.25 (978-1-59600-991-2(8), 9781596009912, Brinc Audio MP3 Lib); audio compact disk 24.95 (978-1-59600-990-5(X), 9781596009905, Brilliance MP3); audio compact disk 117.25 (978-1-59600-989-9(6), 9781596009899, BriAudCD Unabrid); audio compact disk 44.95 (978-1-59600-988-2(8), 9781596009882, Bril Audio CD Unabri) Brilliance Audio.

The beautiful planet Pern seemed a paradise to its new colonists - until unimaginable terror turned it into hell. Suddenly deadly spores were falling like silver threads from the sky, devouring everything - and everyone - in their path. It began to look as if the colony, cut off from Earth and lacking the resources to combat the menace, was doomed. Then some of the colonists noticed that the small, dragonlike lizards that inhabited their new world were joining the fight against Thread, breathing fire on it and teleporting to safety. If only, they thought, the dragonets were big enough for a human to ride and intelligent enough to work as a team with a rider... And so they set their most talented geneticist to work to create the creatures Pern so desperately needed - Dragons!.

Dragonsdawn & Renegades of Pern. abr. ed. Anne McCaffrey. Read by Adrienne Barbeau. 4 cass. (Running Time: 6 hrs.). (Pern Ser.). 2002. 25.00 (978-1-57453-533-4(1)) Audio Lit.

The beautiful planet Pern seems a paradise to its new colonists - until deadly spores fall like silver threads from the sky, devouring everything in their path. In renegades of Pern, having lot their hold, Aramina's family fears both outlaws and the dreaded Threadfall.

Dragonseye. unabr. ed. Anne McCaffrey. Read by Dick Hill. 10 cass. (Running Time: 14 hrs.). (Dragonriders of Pern Ser.). 1997. 89.25 (978-1-56100-808-7(7), 1561008087, Unabridge Lib Edns) Brilliance Audio.

Thread: deadly silver strands that fall from the sky like rain, devouring every organic thing in their path - animals, plants, and people alike. Who could believe that such a horrible thing could exist? After all, it's been two hundred years since Thread supposedly fell on Pern. No one alive remembers that first onslaught. There's no sign of it anywhere in the world. Only the dragons, originally created to be a weapon against Thread, are still around to remind people that once before their population was decimated, their hopes and dreams and livelihoods almost destroyed forever. For two centuries the dragonriders have been practicing and training, passing down from generation to generation the Threadfighting techniques learned on the fly by their besieged ancestors. And most of the Lord Holders are prepared to protect their people, to provide sanctuary, to assemble groundcrews to search out and destroy any Thread that might be missed by the dragons soaring overhead. All but one. Even now the ominous signs are appearing: the violent winter storms and volcanic eruptions that are said to herald the approach of the Red Star and its lethal spawn. Impossibly, one stubborn Lord Holder, Chalkin of Bitra, refuses to believe - and that disbelief could spell disaster for all of Pern. So while the dragonriders desperately train to face an enemy they've never fought before, they and the other Lord Holders must find a way to deal with Chalkin and protect Bitra.

Dragonseye. unabr. ed. Anne McCaffrey. Read by Dick Hill. 10 cass. (Running Time: 14 hrs.). (Dragonriders of Pern Ser.). 2003. 29.95 (978-1-59086-581-1(2), 1590865812, BAU) Brilliance Audio.

Dragonseye. unabr. ed. Anne McCaffrey. Read by Dick Hill. (Running Time: 14 hrs.). (Dragonriders of Pern Ser.). 2004. 39.25 (978-1-59335-439-8(8), 1593354398, Brinc Audio MP3 Lib) Brilliance Audio.

Dragonseye. unabr. ed. Anne McCaffrey. Read by Dick Hill. (Running Time: 14 hrs.). (Dragonriders of Pern Ser.). 2004. 39.25 (978-1-59710-226-1(1), 1597102261, BADLE); 24.95 (978-1-59710-227-8(X), 159710227X, BAD) Brilliance Audio.

Dragonseye. unabr. ed. Anne McCaffrey. Read by Dick Hill. (Running Time: 14 hrs.). (Dragonriders of Pern Ser.). 2007. audio compact disk 102.25 (978-1-4233-3382-1(9), 9781423333821, BriAudCD Unabrid); audio compact disk 38.95 (978-1-4233-3381-4(0), 9781423333814, Bril Audio CD Unabri) Brilliance Audio.

Dragonseye. unabr. ed. Anne McCaffrey. Read by Dick Hill. (Running Time: 14 hrs.). (Pern Ser.). 2004. 24.95 (978-1-59335-077-2(5), 1593350775) Soulmate Audio Bks.

Dragonsinger. unabr. ed. Anne McCaffrey. Narrated by Sally Darling. 6 CDs. (Running Time: 10 hrs.). (Harper Hall Trilogy: Vol. 2). (gr. 7 up). 1977. audio compact disk 89.00 (978-1-4025-1491-3(3), C1616) Recorded Bks.

Young listeners who have heard Dragonsong always ask what happens to Menolly after she and the fire lizards meet the masterharper of Harper Hall. The second volume answers this question with a captivating tale of how Menolly and her fire lizards find happiness at Harper Hall.

Dragonsinger, unabr. ed. Anne McCaffrey. Narrated by Sally Darling. 7 cass. (Running Time: 10 hrs.). (Harper Hall Trilogy: Vol. 2). (gr. 7 up). 1992. 62.00 (978-1-55690-617-6(X), 92310) Recorded Bks.

How Menolly & her fire lizards find happiness at Harper Hall.

Dragonslayers. Bruce Coville. Read by Bruce Coville. 2 cass. (J). 12.78 Set, blisterpack. (BYA 958) NewSound.

Grizelda decides to get revenge on King Mildred, but she doesn't go halfway. She makes the fiercest dragon the kingdom has ever seen. Now someone's got to kill the thing, but the knights are too frightened, which leaves the job to an old squire, a young page boy, & the most willful princess who ever strapped on a sword.

Dragonslayers. unabr. ed. Bruce Coville. Read by Bruce Coville. Perf. by WTW Repertory Company. 2 vols. (Running Time: 2 hrs. 40 mins.). (Words Take Wingtm Ser.). (J). (gr. 3-6). 2004. pap. bk. 29.00 (978-0-8072-7988-5(9), S YA 958 SP, Listening Lib) Random Audio Pubg.

"To get revenge on King Mildred, Grizelda creates the fiercest dragon the kingdom has ever seen. He is such a terror that he must be killed, but none of the knights have the courage to do it. Only an old squire, a page boy, and a very willful princess are up for the battle.".

Dragonslayers, Set. unabr. ed. Bruce Coville. 2 cass. (J). (gr. 1-8). 1999. 16.98 (LL 0120, Chivers Child Audio) AudioGO.

Dragonslayers, Set. unabr. ed. Bruce Coville. 2 cass. (YA). 1999. 16.98 (FS9-34633) Highsmith.

***Dragonslayer's Return.** unabr. ed. R. A. Salvatore. Narrated by Paul Boehmer. (Running Time: 10 hrs. 30 mins.). (Spearwielder's Tale Ser.). 2010. 16.99 (978-1-4001-8637-2(4)); 24.99 (978-1-4001-6637-4(3)) Pub: Tantor Media. Dist(s): IngramPubServ

***Dragonslayer's Return.** unabr. ed. R. A. Salvatore. Narrated by Paul Boehmer. (Running Time: 11 hrs. 0 mins. 0 sec.). (Spearwielder's Tale Ser.). (ENG.). 2010. audio compact disk 69.99 (978-1-4001-4637-6(2)); audio compact disk 34.99 (978-1-4001-1637-9(6)) Pub: Tantor Media. Dist(s): IngramPubServ

Dragonsong. Anne McCaffrey. Read by Allison Green. 4 cass. (Running Time: 6 hrs.). (Harper Hall Trilogy: Vol. 1). 1993. 41.00 Set. (978-1-56544-029-6(3), 550010); Rental 7.30 30 day rental Set. (550010) Literate Ear.

Menolly's world is in grave danger from Threadfall, the killing ropes of death falling from a nearby star. What miraculous discovery will help her save the world of Pern?.

Dragonsong. Anne McCaffrey. Narrated by Sally Darling. 7 CDs. (Running Time: 7 hrs. 15 mins.). (Harper Hall Trilogy: Vol. 1). audio compact disk 69.00 (978-0-7887-9515-2(5)) Recorded Bks.

Dragonsong, unabr. ed. Anne McCaffrey. Narrated by Sally Darling. 5 cass. (Running Time: 7 hrs. 15 mins.). (Harper Hall Trilogy: Vol. 1). 1992. 46.00 (978-1-55690-588-9(2), 92125E7) Recorded Bks.

Menolly befriends a pack of fire-lizards.

DragonSpell. unabr. ed. Donita K. Paul. Read by Ellen Grafton. (Running Time: 11 hrs.). (DragonKeeper Chronicles Ser.). 2009. 19.99 (978-1-4233-9255-2(8), 9781423392552, Brilliance MP3); 39.97 (978-1-4233-9256-9(6), 9781423392569, Brinc Audio MP3 Lib); 39.97 (978-1-4233-9258-3(2), 9781423392583, BADLE); 19.99 (978-1-4233-9257-6(4), 9781423392576, BAD); audio compact disk 19.99 (978-1-4233-9253-8(1), 9781423392538, Bril Audio CD Unabri); audio compact disk 59.97 (978-1-4233-9254-5(X), 9781423392545, BriAudCD Unabrid) Brilliance Audio.

Dragonwings 1903. unabr. ed. Laurence Yep. Read by B. D. Wong. (J). 2007. 39.99 (978-1-60252-829-1(2)) Find a World.

Dragonwings 1903. unabr. ed. Laurence Yep. Read by B. D. Wong. (Running Time: 25200 sec.). (Golden Mountain Chronicles). (J). (gr. 4-7). 2007. audio compact disk 29.95 (978-0-06-149336-2(8), HarperChildAud) HarperCollins Pubs.

Dragonwyck, Set. unabr. ed. Anya Seton. Read by Bonnie Hurren. 10 cass. 1999. 84.95 (978-0-7540-0402-8(3), CAB 1825) AudioGO.
It is May of 1844. 18 year-old Miranda Wells receives a letter from Nicholas Van Ryn, a distant cousin, inviting, her for a visit. Happily accepting the invitation, she travels to Dragonwyck, his manor of Gothic magnificence & eerie manifestations. What evil could possibly befall Miranda in a rich gentleman's house on the Hudson River?.

Drake. unabr. collector's ed. Ernle Bradford. Read by Bill Kelsey. 7 cass. (Running Time: 10 hrs. 30 mins.). 1992. 56.00 (978-0-7366-2101-4(6), 2906) Books on Tape.
Drake was the first Englishman to circle the globe, also a great commander against the Armada. Fascinating biography.

Drama City. abr. ed. George P. Pelecanos. Read by Chad Coleman. (ENG.). 2005. 14.98 (978-1-59483-129-4(7)) Pub: Hachet Audio. Dist(s): HachBkGrp

Drama City. abr. ed. George P. Pelecanos. Read by Chad Coleman. (Running Time: 6 hrs.). (ENG.). 2009. 49.98 (978-1-60788-028-8(8)) Pub: Hachet Audio. Dist(s): HachBkGrp

Drama City. unabr. ed. George P. Pelecanos. Narrated by J. D. Jackson. 7 CDs. (Running Time: 8 hrs. 30 mins.). 2005. audio compact disk 69.75 (978-1-4193-3349-1(6)); 59.75 (978-1-4193-3347-7(X)) Recorded Bks.
As kids, Lorenzo and Nigel dealt drugs together on the streets of Washington, DC. Lorenzo did eight years in prison and now tries to stay straight, serving out his parole working with the Humane Society, rescuing abused dogs and ticketing their owners. Nigel moved up in the drug hierarchy and has an operation of his own, though respecting Lorenzo's decisions. Lorenzo's parole officer, Rachel, has her issues, too: addictions to sex and alcohol. Pelecanos steps away from his Derek Strange series (except for a brief cameo at the end) to tell their stories.

Drama in Nigeria. unabr. ed. Narrated by Gerald Moore. 1 cass. 12.95 (ECN 113) J Norton Pubs.
Looks at current trends in Nigerian drama exemplified by the works of Femi Osofisan & Kole Omotoso. Also includes a discussion with Robert Speaight, David Jones & Michael Billington on the way productions of Shakespeare have changed over the years & the ideas that have influenced these changes.

Drama of Pretense. Swami Amar Jyoti. 1 cass. 1989. 9.95 (M-77) Truth Consciousness.
Pretense, the game of ego, is always guided by self interest. A relaxed attitude for growth.

Dramarama. E. Lockhart. Read by Kate Reinders. (Playaway Children Ser.). (J). 2008. 59.99 (978-1-60640-786-8(4)) Find a World.

Dramarama. unabr. ed. E. Lockhart. Read by Kate Reinders. (Running Time: 6 hrs.). 2008. 39.25 (978-1-4233-6729-1(4), 9781423367291, BADLE); 39.25 (978-1-4233-6727-7(8), 9781423367277, Brinc Audio MP3 Lib); 24.95 (978-1-4233-6728-4(6), 9781423367284, BAD); 24.95 (978-1-4233-6726-0(X), 9781423367260, Brilliance MP3); audio compact disk 82.25 (978-1-4233-6725-3(1), 9781423367253, BriAudCD Unabrid); audio compact disk 29.99 (978-1-4233-6724-6(3), 9781423367246, Bril Audio CD Unabri) Brilliance Audio.

Dramatic Life of Anton Chekhov, Vol. 58. Narrated by Elliot Engel. 1 CD. (Running Time: 66 mins). 2002. audio compact disk 15.00 (978-1-890123-53-6(6)) Media Cnslts.
Examination of life of this giant of Russian literature who revolutionized not one but two different types of 20th-century literature.

Dramatic Readings from Scripture: With Musical Backgrounds. Mark Friedman & Janet Vogt. Read by Mark Friedman & Janet Vogt. 1 cass. 1995. 14.95 (10086) OR Catholic.
16 passages from scripture, both Old & New Testament, truly come to life through the excellent dramatic interpretation and tasteful musical background.

Dramatic Weight Loss (Hypnosis) Dynamic Weight Loss, Vol. 7. Jayne Helle. 1 cass. (Running Time: 28 min.). 1997. 15.00 (978-1-891826-06-1(9)) Introspect.
With this self-hypnosis program the pounds melt away as you develop a life style of good eating habits & exercise. Two sides to this tape.

***Dramatist.** Ken Bruen. 2010. 38.95 (978-1-4450-0164-7(0)); audio compact disk 51.95 (978-1-4450-0165-4(9)) Pub: Isis Pubng Ltd GBR. Dist(s): Ulverscroft US

Dramatist. unabr. ed. Ken Bruen. 1 MP3-CD. (Running Time: 4 hrs. 30 mins.). (Jack Taylor Ser.: Bk. 4). 2006. 29.95 (978-0-7927-3967-8(1), Chivers Sound Lib) AudioGO.

Dramatist. unabr. ed. Ken Bruen. Narrated by Michael Deehy. 4 CDs. (Running Time: 17280 sec.). (Jack Taylor Ser.: Bk. 4). 2006. audio compact disk 49.95 (978-0-7927-3911-1(6), Chivers Sound Lib); 29.95 (978-0-7927-3910-4(8), Chivers Sound Lib) AudioGO.
In The Dramatist Bruen manages to weave together an intriguing and wholly coherent story line with the kind of in-depth character study that is so much a part of what makes this series so blasted good. This novel is still largely character-driven, to be sure, but in it Bruen uses plot in service of character and not merely as a necessary but regrettable evil. All the pieces fit together here and all of Jack's chickens come home to roost. It's in this novel, in other words, that all of the fragmented, jagged and jarring aspects of Jack Taylor's life and personality - so painstakingly depicted in those three earlier books - coalesce and redound to Jack like some kind of high-voltage karmic thunderbolt. This is crime fiction written on the scale of Sophoclean tragedy.

Dramatist Norman Corwin. Read by Norman Corwin. (AF1725) J Norton Pubs.

Dramatized Audio Bible. unabr. ed. Zondervan Publishing Staff. (Running Time: 76 hrs. 0 mins. 0 sec.). (ENG.). 2004. 49.99 (978-0-310-92264-3(X)) Zondervan.

Dramatized Bible-KJV. Dramatization. 2006. audio compact disk 99.95 (978-1-56563-974-4(X)) Hendrickson MA.

Dramatized Bible-KJV. Narrated by Stephen Johnston. 2006. audio compact disk 74.97 (978-1-59856-068-8(9)) Hendrickson MA.

Dramatized Bible Stories. 1 cass. 1993. 9.98; 9.98; 11.98 Chrstn Dup Intl.

Dramatized Bible Stories. 3 cass. (Running Time: 4 hrs. 30 min.). (SPA.). 2000. 24.99 (978-7-902031-28-8(3)) Chrstn Dup Intl.

Dramatized Bible Stories. Contrib. by Christian Duplications International Staff. 1 cass. Dramatization. 1993. 9.98 (978-7-902031-90-5(9)) Chrstn Dup Intl.
Religion.

Dramatized Bible Stories. Contrib. by Christian Duplications International Staff. 1 cass. Dramatization. (J). (ps-3). 1993. 9.98 (978-7-902031-76-9(3)); 9.98 (978-7-902031-83-7(6)) Chrstn Dup Intl.

Dramatized Bible Stories. Contrib. by Christian Duplications International Staff. 12 cass. (J). (ps up). 1994. 19.98 Set. (978-7-902032-04-9(2)) Chrstn Dup Intl.

Dramatized Bible Stories, Vol. 1, Tapes 1-4. (Historias de la Biblia Ser.). (SPA.). 2000. 9.99 (978-7-902032-11-7(5)) Chrstn Dup Intl.

Dramatized Bible Stories, Vol. 2, Tapes 5-8. 4 cass. (Historias de la Biblia Ser.). (SPA.). (J). (ps-3). 2000. 9.99 (978-7-902032-32-2(8)) Chrstn Dup Intl.

Dramatized Bible Stories, Vol. 3, Tapes 9-12. 4 cass. (Historias de la Biblia Ser.). (SPA.). (J). (ps-3). 2000. 9.99 (978-7-902032-88-9(3)) Chrstn Dup Intl.

Dramatized Bible Stories Set. 3 cass. (Running Time: 4 hrs. 30 mins.). (J). (ps-3). 2000. 24.99 (978-7-902031-97-4(6)) Chrstn Dup Intl.

Dramatized History of John Taylor. Petrea Kelly. 2004. 5.98 (978-1-57734-931-0(8)); audio compact disk 5.98 (978-1-57734-932-7(6)) Covenant Comms.

Dramatized History of the Church. 31 cass. 69.95 set. (978-1-55503-513-6(2), 0400386) Covenant Comms.

Dramatized History of the Church, Set. 18 cass. 49.95 (978-1-57734-043-0(4), 0400475); audio compact disk 69.95 (978-1-57734-001-0(9), 0400459) Covenant Comms.

Dramatized Life of Christ, Set. 4 cass. 10.77 (978-1-57734-325-7(5), 0400521); audio compact disk 12.57 (978-1-57734-292-2(5), 0400513) Covenant Comms.

Dramatized Life of Christ: Journey to Bethany. 8 cass. 29.95 set. (978-1-55503-296-8(6), 040037) Covenant Comms.
Great for older children & adults.

Dramatized New Testament-KJV. Narrated by Stephen Johnston. Dramatization. 2006. audio compact disk & audio compact disk 24.97 (978-1-59856-069-5(7)) Hendrickson MA.

Draping. Milady Publishing Company Staff. 1 cass. (Standard Ser.: Chapter 5). 1995. 6.95 (978-1-56253-277-2(4), Milady) Pub: Delmar. Dist(s): CENGAGE Learn

Drastic Dragon of Draco, Texas. deluxe unabr. ed. Elizabeth Ann Scarborough. 6 cass. (Running Time: 7 hrs. 30 min.). 2002. lib. bdg. 35.00 (978-0-932079-14-5(8), 79148) TimeFare AudioBks.

Drastic Park: A Gil Beckman Mystery. W. E. Davis. Narrated by L. J. Ganser. 5 cass. (Running Time: 6 hrs. 30 mins.). 45.00 (978-1-4025-1782-2(3)) Recorded Bks.

Drat! You Copycat!; Doggone It! unabr. ed. Nancy Krulik. Read by Anne Bobby. 2 CDs. (Running Time: 1 hr. 52 mins.). (Katie Kazoo, Switcheroo Ser.: Nos. 7-8). (J). (gr. 2-4). 2006. audio compact disk 24.00 (978-0-7393-3622-9(3), Listening Lib) Pub: Random Audio Pubg. Dist(s): Random
Katie is an ordinary third-grader - except for one very extraordinary problem! She accidentally wished on a shooting star to be anyone but herself. But what Katie soon learns is that wishes really do come true - and in the strangest ways... Drat! You Copycat! Becky, the new girl in class 3A, is a great big copycat! She copies everything Suzanne does. Suzanne can't stand Becky! Then the magic wind turns Katie into Becky. Will Suzanne change her mind about the new girl? Will Katie turn back into herself without causing too much trouble? Doggone It! When Katie's teacher, Mrs. Derkman, moves in next door, Katie can't believe her bad luck! Mrs. Derkman hates dogs, and she wants the dogs on their street to be kept on leashes at all times! When the magic wind blows and turns Katie into her own dog, Pepper, will Katie convince her teacher that dogs are not all bad?.

Draught of Death. unabr. ed. Ray Harrison. Read by Terry Wale. 5 cass. (Running Time: 7 hrs. 30 mins.). 2000. 49.95 (978-1-86042-614-8(X), 2614X) Pub: Soundings Ltd GBR. Dist(s): Ulverscroft US

Draw Me Close. 2002. audio compact disk (Brentwood Records) Brentwood Music.

Draw Me Up. 2004. audio compact disk 16.99 (978-7-5124-0246-1(5)) Destiny Image Pubs.

Draw Me Up. Perf. by Morningstar. 1 cass. (Running Time: 90 mins.). 1999. 10.99; audio compact disk 15.99 Destiny Image Pubs.

Draw Near. Perf. by Among Thorns Staff. 2002. audio compact disk Provident Mus Dist.

Draw Near. Stanton Lanier. (Running Time: 50 mins.). 2004. audio compact disk 15.00 (978-0-9746289-3-6(X)) S Lanier.

Draw Near. 5800th ed. Music by Steven Janco. 2001. audio compact disk 16.00 (978-1-58459-037-8(8)) Wrld Lib Pubns.

Draw Near. 5801st ed. Music by Steven Janco. 2001. 11.00 (978-1-58459-038-5(6)) Wrld Lib Pubns.

Draw near unto Me. Steven A. Cramer. 3 cass. 2004. 8.98 (978-1-57734-878-8(8)) Covenant Comms.

Draw Near unto Me. Scott Simmons. 1 cass. 1997. 9.95 (978-1-57008-319-8(3), Bkcraft Inc) Deseret Bk.

Draw the Line: About Social Issues. Perf. by Peter Alsop. 1 cass. 11.00 Moose Schl Records.

Drawing Basics with Thomas Kin. 2004. audio compact disk 51.95 (978-0-7403-0707-2(X)) Alpha OmeGa Pub.

Drawing Closer to God: Custody of the Eyes. Jeffrey T. Robideau. Read by Jeffrey T. Robideau. 3 cass. (Running Time: 2 hr. 30 mins.). 1999. 10.00 (978-0-9704588-0-3(0)) Get Holy.
The purpose of custody of the eyes in ones moral life & how to develop it in one's spiritual life.

Drawing in the Dust. unabr. ed. Zoe Klein. Narrated by Justine Eyre. (Running Time: 14 hrs. 0 mins. 0 sec.). (ENG.). 2009. 24.99 (978-1-4001-6344-1(7)); audio compact disk 75.99 (978-1-4001-4344-3(6)); audio compact disk 37.99 (978-1-4001-1344-6(X)) Pub: Tantor Media. Dist(s): IngramPubServ

Drawing Lessons. unabr. ed. Tracy Mack. Read by Marguerite Gavin. (Running Time: 9000 sec.). (YA). (gr. 8-12). 2006. 22.95 (978-0-7861-4904-9(3)); audio compact disk 24.00 (978-0-7861-5976-5(6)); audio compact disk 29.95 (978-0-7861-7073-9(5)) Blckstn Audio.

Drawing near CD Series. 2007. audio compact disk 44.99 (978-1-933185-19-4(8)) Messengr Intl.

Drawing near CD Series. 2004. audio compact disk 32.00 (978-1-59834-043-3(3)) Walk Thru the Bible.

Drawing on the Powers of Heaven. Grant Von Harrison. 1 cass. (Personal Enrichment Ser.). 6.95 (978-0-929985-39-8(7)) Jackman Pubng.
Living so we can obtain the blessings of Heaven.

Drawing with Shapes. (J). 2005. audio compact disk (978-1-933796-03-1(0)) PC Treasures.

Drawn in Blood. unabr. ed. Andrea Kane. Read by Joyce Bean. (Running Time: 13 hrs.). 2009. 24.99 (978-1-4418-0190-6(1), 9781441801906, Brilliance MP3); 39.97 (978-1-4418-0191-3(X), 9781441801913, Brinc Audio MP3 Lib); 24.99 (978-1-4418-0192-0(8), 9781441801920, BAD); 39.97 (978-1-4418-0193-7(6), 9781441801937, BADLE); audio compact disk 38.99 (978-1-4418-0188-3(X), 9781441801883, Bril Audio CD Unabri); audio compact disk 87.97 (978-1-4418-0189-0(8), 9781441801890, BriAudCD Unabrid) Brilliance Audio.

Drawn to the Lord: Six Stories of Vocation. unabr. ed. Carlo Maria Martini. Read by Maureen O'Leary. 2 cass. (J). 9.95 set. (518) Ignatius Pr.
Young people in Milan asked their Cardinal to "teach them how to pray", resulting in this collection of six stories focusing on the meaning of prayer in the lives of special saints, followed by scripture texts & homilies.

Drawn with the Sword: Reflections on the American Civil War. unabr. collector's ed. James M. McPherson. Read by Dick Estell. 6 cass. (Running Time: 9 hrs.). 1997. 48.00 (978-0-913369-76-0(4), 4331) Books on Tape.
Brings to life Ulysses S. Grant, Robert E. Lee, & Abraham Lincoln himself - & shows them in all their complexities.

Dread Lad see Twentieth-Century Poetry in English, No. 24, Recordings of Poets Reading Their Own Poetry

Dread Mountain. unabr. ed. Emily Rodda. Read by Ron Haddrick. 2 cass. (Running Time: 3 hrs.). (Deltora Quest Ser.: Bk. 5). 2002. (978-1-74086-026-0(8)) Bolinda Pubng AUS.
Dread Mountain finds the three heroes Lief, Barda and Jasmine on a perilous quest to find the seven lost gems of the magic belt of Deltora. Four gems have now been found. To find the fifth stone the heroes must venture almost to the border of Shadowlands and plunge into the darkness and terror of the realm of the monstrous toad Gellick.

Dread Murder. unabr. ed. Gwendoline Butler. 5 CDs. 2007. audio compact disk 59.95 (978-1-84559-524-1(6)) Pub: Soundings Ltd GBR. Dist(s): Ulverscroft US

Dread Murder. unabr. ed. Gwendoline Butler. Read by Michael Tudor Barnes. 5 cass. 2007. 49.95 (978-1-84559-421-3(5)) Pub: Soundings Ltd GBR. Dist(s): Ulverscroft US

Dreaded Lurgie. unabr. ed. Jamie Rix. Read by Nigel Planer. 4 cass. (Running Time: 4 hrs.). (J). 1997. 32.95 (CCA 3374, Chivers Child Audio) AudioGO.

Dreadful Acts. Philip Ardagh. Read by Martin Rayner. 2 cass. (Running Time: 2 hrs. 30 mins.). (Eddie Dickens Trilogy: Bk. 2). (J). (gr. 4 up). 2004. 23.00 (978-0-8072-1890-7(1), Listening Lib) Pub: Random Audio Pubg. Dist(s): Random

Dreadful Acts. unabr. ed. Philip Ardagh. Read by Martin Rayner. 3 CDs. (Running Time: 2 hrs. 30 mins.). (Eddie Dickens Trilogy: Bk. 2). (J). (gr. 4 up). 2004. audio compact disk 30.00 (978-0-8072-2004-7(3), Listening Lib) Pub: Random Audio Pubg. Dist(s): Random

Dreadful Lemon Sky. John D. MacDonald. Read by Darren McGavin. 2 cass. (Running Time: 180 min.). (Travis McGee Ser.: Vol. 16). 2001. 9.99 (978-0-375-41672-9(2), Random AudioBks) Random Audio Pubg.

Dreadful Lemon Sky. unabr. collector's ed. John D. MacDonald. Read by Michael Prichard. 7 cass. (Running Time: 7 hrs.). (Travis McGee Ser.: Vol. 16). 1977. 42.00 (978-0-7366-0047-7(7), 1059) Books on Tape.
Travis McGee, a man of universal interest & independent means, lives on an old houseboat he won in a poker game. One evening, a distraught young woman appears on McGee's houseboat with an extraordinary sum of money that she wishes McGee to hold in safekeeping. She dictates what should be done with the funds should she not return within a month. When the woman does not reappear, McGee is drawn into an intrigue replete with murder, drugs, fear, & passion.

Dreadnought Britain, Germany & the Coming of the Great War, Pt. 1. unabr. ed. Robert K. Massie. Read by Grover Gardner. 11 cass. (Running Time: 16 hrs. 30 min.). 1992. 88.00 (978-0-7366-2217-2(9), 3010-A) Books on Tape.
Dramatic recreation of the diplomatic minuets & military brinkmanship that preceded WW II, making inevitable the catastrophes of this century.

Dreadnought Britain, Germany & the Coming of the Great War, Pt. 2. unabr. ed. Robert K. Massie. Read by Grover Gardner. 10 cass. (Running Time: 15 hrs.). 1992. 80.00 (3010-B) Books on Tape.

Dreadnought Britain, Germany & the Coming of the Great War, Pt. 3. unabr. ed. Robert K. Massie. Read by Grover Gardner. 10 cass. (Running Time: 15 hrs.). 1992. 80.00 (3010-C) Books on Tape.

***Dream.** Gilbert Morris. (Running Time: 10 hrs. 27 mins. 0 sec.). (Singing River Ser.). (ENG.). 2009. 14.99 (978-0-310-30524-8(1)) Zondervan.

***Dream.** Carl Sommer. (Quest for Success Ser.). (ENG.). (YA). 2009. bk. 19.95 (978-1-57537-327-0(0)); pap. bk. 11.95 (978-1-57537-376-8(9)) Advance Pub.

Dream, No. 1. Swami Jyotirmayananda. 1 cass. (Running Time: 45 min.). 1990. 10.00 Yoga Res Foun.

Dream, No. 2. Swami Jyotirmayananda. 1 cass. (Running Time: 45 min.). 1990. 10.00 Yoga Res Foun.

Dream: Have You Caught Gods Vision? Its Not What You Think. unabr. ed. Kenny Luck. Read by Kenny Luck. (Running Time: 24000 sec.). (God's Man Ser.). (ENG.). 2008. audio compact disk 26.99 (978-1-934384-12-1(7)) Pub: Treasure Pub. Dist(s): STL Dist NA

Dream: Structure, Nature & Dynamics. Read by John Van Eenwyk. 2 cass. (Running Time: 4 hrs.). 1986. 21.95 Set. (978-0-7822-0312-7(4), 208) C G Jung IL.

***Dream / Sueña.** ed. Carl Sommer. (Quest for Success Bilingual Ser.). (ENG & SPA.). (YA). 2009. bk. 21.95 (978-1-57537-426-0(9)) Advance Pub.

Dream a Little Dream. Joe Wolff & Burt Wolff. Illus. by Bill Oates. 1 cass. (J). (gr. 2-12). 1992. 10.98 (978-1-878573-62-9(4)); audio compact disk 12.98 (978-1-878573-63-6(2)) Transitions Music.
A collection of beautiful new songs enhanced by recorded womb sounds, to aid in relaxtion & induce sleep.

Dream a Little Dream. collector's ed. Susan Elizabeth Phillips. Read by Anna Fields. 10 CDs. (Running Time: 15 hrs.). (Chicago Stars Bks.: No. 4). 2000. audio compact disk 80.00 (978-0-7366-5153-0(5)) Books on Tape.
Rachel Stone, whose late husband embezzled five million dollars from the ministry, is desperate. An outcast in a hostile town, she is flat broke with a five-year-old son to raise & in need of a job. When fate & a dead car engine leave her at Gabriel Bonner's drive-in theater, Rachel gets a job & a second chance at love.

Dream a Little Dream. unabr. collector's ed. Susan Elizabeth Phillips. Read by Anna Fields. 8 cass. (Running Time: 12 hrs.). (Chicago Stars Bks.: No. 4). 1999. 64.00 (978-0-7366-4280-4(3), 4778) Books on Tape.

Dream a World: A Child's Journey to Self-Discovery Dreamer's Activity Kit. Bunny Hull. Composed by Bunny Hull. Illus. by Synthia Saint James. 1 CD. (Running Time: 50 minutes). (KCC Ser.). (J). 2004. audio compact disk 15.95 (978-0-9721478-4-2(5), BH107) BrassHeart.
A mystical, musical adventure from Grammy(r) Award-winning songwriter Bunny Hull and acclaimed illustrator Synthia Saint James. A full 16-track album of classic original songs and 24 pages of interactive creative arts and story combine to convey the importance of having a dream and how to achieve that dream!.

Dream & Deep Sleep. Swami Jyotirmayananda. 1 cass. (Running Time: 45 min.). 1990. 10.00 Yoga Res Foun.

Dream & Drink of Freedom. Johnny Dolphin. 12.95 Synerg CA.

Dream & the Dreamer. Swami Amar Jyoti. 1 cass. 1976. 9.95 (R-5) Truth Consciousness.
The secret of creation. How the dream starts. The highest climax of Vedanta. On pain, suffering, angels & Enlightened Ones.

Dream & the Nightmare: The Sixties' Legacy to the Underclass. unabr. ed. Myron Magnet. Read by Jeff Riggenbach. 5 cass. (Running Time: 7 hrs.). 1994. 39.95 (978-0-7861-0737-7(5), 1494) Blckstn Audio.
Shows how the influences of the Sixties decade have become accepted wisdom, adversely affecting the fabric of all American life but most egregiously harming the people who were presumably being helped. Magnet explores how key '60s ideas have pervaded our thinking about crime, the homeless, the mentally ill, welfare, & education & provides a startling illustration about the directions roads take when they are paved with good intentions. He also shows how today's political correctness is only an intensification of such thought.

Dream Angus: The Celtic God of Dreams. unabr. ed. Alexander McCall Smith. Read by Michael Page. (Running Time: 3 hrs.). (Myths Ser.). 2006. 39.25 (978-1-4233-2105-7(7), 9781423321057, BADLE); 24.95 (978-1-4233-2104-0(9), 9781423321040, BAD); audio compact disk 19.95 (978-1-4233-2100-2(6), 9781423321002, Bril Audio CD Unabri) Brilliance Audio.
Angus is one of the earliest Celtic deities and one of the most beloved. Son of the Dagda, the chief of the Celtic gods, and Boann, a water spirit, Angus is the god of love, youth, and beauty. He is a trickster and a romantic, a combination of Eros and Apollo. He is much loved by women, a breaker of hearts. He will reveal to you in a dream your true love, if asked, and if in the mood. Around his head there are four birds fluttering - each of which is a kiss. In Alexander McCall Smith's retelling, five different young men named Angus find themselves living the myths of Angus, from his search for the girl he loves to his discovery that the man who raised him is not his father.

Dream Angus: The Celtic God of Dreams. unabr. ed. Read by Michael Page. (Running Time: 10800 sec.). (Myths Ser.). 2006. 44.25 (978-1-4233-2099-9(9), 9781423320999, BrilAudUnabridg); audio compact disk 62.25 (978-1-4233-2101-9(4), 9781423321019, BriAudCD Unabrid); audio compact disk 39.25 (978-1-4233-2103-3(0), 9781423321033, Brinc Audio MP3 Lib); audio compact disk 24.95 (978-1-4233-2102-6(2), 9781423321026, Brilliance MP3) Brilliance Audio.

Dream Answers Meditation. Laura Kern. Read by Laura Kern. 1 cass. (Running Time: 1 hr.). 1995. 10.00 (978-1-887541-02-2(0)) L Kern.
Spoken audio cassette with background music for relaxation & meditation. Subject: finding answers to your life challenges through your nighttime dreams.

Dream Around the World/Silly Aunt Tilly. Created by Steck-Vaughn Staff. (Running Time: 483 sec.). (Primary Take-Me-Home Books Level A Ser.). 1998. 9.80 (978-0-8172-8664-4(0)) SteckVau.

Dream Awake. unabr. ed. Owen Dodson. Read by James Earl Jones & Josephine Premice. Dramatization. 10.95 (978-0-8045-1095-0(4), SAC 7175) Spoken Arts.
Major events in Black American history in song, verse & dramatization.

***Dream Bearer.** abr. ed. Walter Dean Myers. Read by Peter Francis James. (ENG.). 2005. (978-0-06-083917-8(1)); (978-0-06-083915-4(5)) HarperCollins Pubs.

Dream Bearer. unabr. ed. 3 cass. (Running Time: 3 hrs. 45 min.). 2003. 28.00 (978-1-4025-5582-4(2)) Recorded Bks.

Dream Bearer. unabr. ed. Walter Dean Myers. Read by Peter Francis James. (J). 2008. 54.99 (978-1-60514-571-6(8)) Find a World.

Dream Bearer. unabr. ed. Walter Dean Myers. Narrated by Peter Francis James. 2003. 24.95 (978-1-4025-5583-1(0)) Recorded Bks.
Twelve-year-old David can?t understand why his older brother is acting like someone with a bad secret and why his father is filled with rage and manic energy. Then David meets a man who claims to be a 300-year-old bearer of dreams. If he looks deeply enough to understand Ty?s and Rueben?s dreams, David wonders, can he keep his family from flying apart?.

Dream Bold in God. 2000. audio compact disk 15.00 (978-1-58302-149-1(3)) One Way St.
All of the songs are based on the theme of dreaming big along with God of everything you can be.

Dream Boogie see Poetry of Langston Hughes

Dream Book. Helen Barolini. Read by Jennifer Lagier et al. 1 cass. (Running Time: 30 min.). 13.95 (978-1-55644-357-2(9), 10041) Am Audio Prose.
Readings from an anthology of writings by Italian-American women.

***Dream Breakers.** Elizabeth Gill. Read by Colleen Predergast. 2010. 54.95 (978-1-84652-623-7(X)); audio compact disk 71.95 (978-1-84652-624-4(8)) Pub: Magna Story GBR. Dist(s): Ulverscroft US

Dream Castle. G. Saul Snatsky. (ENG.). 2007. audio compact disk (978-0-9761674-7-1(6)) Sauls Audio.

Dream Catcher. Perf. by Jack Grunsky. 1 cass. (J). (gr. 4 up). 1995. 10.98 (978-0-945267-17-1(7), YM033-CN); audio compact disk 13.98 (978-0-945267-18-8(5), YM033-CD) Youngheart Mus.
Songs include: "Carnival Parade"; "The Way We Get Together"; "Down in the Valley"; "Dream Catcher"; "Lets Play"; "My Tree"; "Mbira - The Walker's Friend"; "Alligator Stomp"; "Storyteller"; "Lazy Island Melody"; "Chili Chili, Hot Hot Hot" & more.

Dream Catcher. Perf. by Kevin Locke. 1 cass. (Running Time: 44 min.). 1992. 9.98 (978-1-877737-04-6(6), MLP2696) MFLP CA.
Flute songs & chants of the Northern Plains Indians.

Dream Catcher. abr. ed. Terry Johnston. (ENG.). 2006. 14.98 (978-1-59483-776-0(7)) Pub: Hachet Audio. Dist(s): HachBkGrp

Dream Catcher. abr. ed. Terry C. Johnston. Read by John R. Jones. 2 cass. (Running Time: 3 hrs.). 1994. 17.00 Set. (978-1-57042-080-1(7), 4-520807) Hachet Audio.
A decade has passed since Confederate soldier Jonah Hook returned to find his wife & children gone - kidnapped by a man of unspeakable brutality. The trail is cold, but driven by his eternal love for his wife & his undying hatred of the man who stole her away, Jonah Hook will ride one last time with his firstborn son Jeremiah & his friend Tow Sleep. However, Jonah alone must face the demon he has chased so long in a final showdown of blood & fury that will finally bring peace to his restless soul... in his life or death.

Dream Catcher. unabr. ed. Maria Barrett. Read by Liz Holliss. 10 cass. (Running Time: 12 hrs.). (Isis Ser.). (J). 2002. 84.95 (978-0-7531-1533-6(6)) Pub: ISIS Lrg Prnt GBR. Dist(s): Ulverscroft US
Firm friends from the school run to Wynchcombe Primary, Sarah, Roz and Janie each have a dream. Sarah dreams of finding a way through the constant struggle to bring up her partially deaf son, Rory, alone; Roz dreams of keeping her farm afloat; Janie, a GP's wife, dreams of escaping the ever-growing emptiness in her life that she cannot explain. Then Janie's brother Marcus, a top city analyst, suggests that they set up an investment group - pooling their money and playing the stock market together - and introduces them to his stockbroker friend, Alex. With a mixture of luck, instinct and research, the group begin to make some serious money: the sort of money that makes dreams come true. But good dreams can easily turn bad. When the gains are high, so are the risks.

Dream Change: Shamanic Journeying Techniques from the Amazon & Andes. John Perkins. (Running Time: 3600 sec.). 2003. 10.95 (978-0-89281-394-0(6), Heal Arts VT) Inner Tradit.

Dream Chants: East & West. 2000. audio compact disk (978-0-9746047-1-8(2)) Sacred Sound.

Dream Children. Gail Godwin. Read by Gail Godwin. 1 cass. 1986. 13.95 (978-1-55644-159-2(2), 6071) Am Audio Prose.
Author reads her own short story.

Dream Control. 1 cass. 10.00 (978-1-58506-042-9(9), 82) New Life Inst OR.
Remember & control your dreams. Expand your awareness & self-understanding.

Dream Control. Bruce Goldberg. (ENG.). 2005. audio compact disk 17.00 (978-1-57968-080-0(1)) Pub: B Goldberg. Dist(s): Baker Taylor

Dream Control. Bruce Goldberg. Read by Bruce Goldberg. 1 cass. (Running Time: 25 min.). (ENG.). 2007. 13.00 (978-1-885577-81-8(8)) Pub: B Goldberg. Dist(s): Baker Taylor
Obtain information from dreams through self-hypnosis.

Dream Control Techniques Through Hypnosis. Created by Victoria Wizell. Voice by Victoria Wizell. 2 CDs. 2004. audio compact disk 59.00 (978-0-9679176-9-6(7)) Hyptalk.
We spend 1/3 of our life sleeping and a good part of that time dreaming ... Learn how to use your dream state to benefit you through four powerful sessions.

Dream Country. abr. ed. Luanne Rice. Read by Laural Merlington. (Running Time: 21600 sec.). 2006. audio compact disk 16.99 (978-1-4233-0989-5(8), 9781423309895) Brilliance Audio.
No one understands all the complexities of love, resentments, heartaches, and healing better than New York Times bestseller Luanne Rice, whose Follow the Stars Home was praised by People magazine as a story of "heartbreak and redemption." In Dream Country, she once again draws us into a splintered family's search for hope. Daisy had gone to the Wyoming wilderness in search of inspiration for her jewelry making. She found rancher James Tucker, a man with the wilderness inside him. Their life together was close to paradise - until their three-year-old son Jake disappeared and was never found. Her marriage in tatters, Daisy returned home to Connecticut, taking with her from Wyoming two things: her daughter, Jake's twin, and her livelihood, the jewelry she etches with symbols of Indian legend. Wyoming had taken everything else. Thirteen years later, Wyoming wants more. Sage, now sixteen, has run away, and Daisy fears that Sage's thirst to see the land and father of her dreams is driving her westward on freight trains and farm roads. Terrified, her mother flies out to where James Tucker rides the range with a heart turned to stone, still scouring the canyons for Jake. Wary of each other, Daisy and James wait and pray for the safe arrival of their one remaining child. And they'll need all the strength and wisdom they can find, to learn that you cannot close the door on the past. In fact, sometimes, if you're willing to step through it, that door to the past can lead you home.

Dream Country. unabr. ed. Luanne Rice. Read by Laural Merlington. 8 cass. (Running Time: 12 hrs.). 2001. 35.95 (978-1-58788-007-0(5), 1587880075, BAU); 87.25 (978-1-58788-008-7(3), 1587880083) Brilliance Audio.

Dream Country. unabr. ed. Luanne Rice. Read by Laural Merlington. (Running Time: 12 hrs.). 2005. 39.25 (978-1-59600-670-6(6), 9781596006706, BADLE); 24.95 (978-1-59600-669-0(2), 9781596006690, BAD); audio compact disk 24.95 (978-1-59600-667-6(6), 9781596006676, Brilliance MP3); audio compact disk 39.25 (978-1-59600-668-3(4), 9781596006683, Brinc Audio MP3 Lib) Brilliance Audio.

Dream Country. unabr. ed. Luanne Rice. Read by Laural Merlington. (Running Time: 13 hrs.). 2010. audio compact disk 89.97 (978-1-4418-3588-8(1), 9781441835888, BriAudCD Unabrid); audio compact disk 29.99 (978-1-4418-3587-1(3), 9781441835871, Bril Audio CD Unabri) Brilliance Audio.

Dream Cruise. unabr. collector's ed. Brainard Chapman. Read by Bob Erickson. 8 cass. (Running Time: 8 hrs.). 1985. 48.00 (978-0-7366-0550-2(9), 1524) Books on Tape.
The Chapmans sailed their ketch-rigged Fisher 37 from Norway to Florida on their first transatlantic passage in 1977-78. It begins in Norway & carries them to Sweden, Denmark, Germany, England, then to Madeira, the Canary Islands, the West Indies, the Bahamas & Florida.

Dream Dance Meditation. 1 cass. (Tara Sutphen Meditation Tapes Ser.). 11.98 (978-0-87554-482-3(7), TS203) Valley Sun.

Dream Days. Kenneth Grahame. Read by Anais 9000. 2008. 27.95 (978-1-60112-198-1(9)) Babblebooks.

Dream Days, Set. unabr. ed. Kenneth Grahame. Read by Flo Gibson. 3 cass. (Running Time: 4 hrs. 30 min.). (YA). (gr. 6-9). 1989. 16.95 (978-1-55685-134-6(0)) Audio Bk Con.
"The Reluctant Dragon", "The Magic Ring" & "The Saga of the Seats" are part of this collection.

Dream Discoveries: God in Us. unabr. ed. Jonathan Murro & Ann Ree Colton. 1 cass. 7.95 (978-0-917189-10-4(8)) A R Colton Fnd.

Dream Divination. Robert Michael Place. Perf. by Robert Michael Place. Ed. by Leisa/Anne ReFalo. Prod. by Leisa/Anne ReFalo. (ENG., 2009. 50.00 (978-1-935194-05-7(4), Hermes Pubns) Tarot Connect.

Dream Drumming see Poetry & Voice of Muriel Rukeyser

Dream Endures. unabr. ed. Kevin Starr. 10 cass. (Running Time: 15 hrs.). 2001. 80.00 (978-0-7366-6723-4(7)); 80.00 (978-0-7366-6724-1(5)) Books on Tape.
In the 1930s, what we now call "the good life" first took root, emerged and flowered in California. Film, fiction, leisure and architecture fed the legend. In a sense, American culture and society emulated California then and for years to come. He shows us the rich urban colors of San Francisco and the pastels of communities like Carmel.

Dream Fish & Road Trips: Fly-Fishing Tales from Alaska, Montana, & Beyond. E. Donnall Thomas & E. Donnall Thomas, Jr. Narrated by Christopher Lane. (Running Time: 16200 sec.). 2006. audio compact disk 28.00 (978-1-932378-90-0(1)) Pub: A Media Intl. Dist(s): Natl Bk Netwk

Dream for the World: Luke 5:4-10. Ed Young. 1988. 4.95 (978-0-7417-1676-7(3), 676) Win Walk.

Dream Gates. Perf. by Robert Moss. 6 cass. (Running Time: 9 hrs.). 1999. 59.95 Set. (83-0018) Explorations.
Can dreams be a portal to another reality, where the past, present & future fuse into a secret frontier of unlimited possibilities? Moss shows how to use dream work practices & one's own skills to explore this infinite realm. Enhance dream recall. Embark on conscious dreams. Return to a dream to resolve it & clarify its messages.

Dream Gates. Robert Moss. 2006. audio compact disk 69.95 (978-1-59179-489-9(7)) Sounds True.

Dream Gates. Robert Moss. 2007. audio compact disk 69.95 (978-1-59179-326-7(2)) Sounds True.

Dream Giver: Following Your God-Given Destiny. Bruce Wilkinson. Contrib. by David Kopp & Heather Kopp. (ENG.). 2003. audio compact disk 18.99 (978-1-59052-203-5(6), Mltnmah) Pub: Doubday Relig. Dist(s): Random
Bruce Wilkinson shows how to identify and overcome the obstacles that keep millions from living the life God created them for.

***Dream House.** E. Jean Beres. Read by Aaron Tucker & Gale Van Cott. (Running Time: 71). (ENG.). 2009. 2.99 (978-1-61114-006-4(4)) Mind Wings Aud.

Dream House. E. Jean Beres. Read by Aaron Tucker & Gale Van Cott. (ENG.). 2009. audio compact disk 5.49 (978-0-9821192-5-9(9)) Mind Wings Aud.

Dream House. unabr. ed. Rochelle Krich. Read by Deanna Hurst. (Running Time: 10 hrs.). (Molly Blume Ser.). 2004. 39.25 (978-1-59710-229-2(6), 1597102296, BADLE); 24.95 (978-1-59710-228-5(8), 1597102288, BAD) Brilliance Audio.

Dream House. unabr. ed. Rochelle Majer Krich. Read by Deanna Hurst. 6 cass. (Running Time: 10 hrs.). (Molly Blume Ser.: No. 2). 2003. 32.95 (978-1-59086-453-1(0), 1590864530, BAU); 82.25 (978-1-59086-454-8(9), 1590864549, Unabridge Lib Edns) Brilliance Audio.
Friday, October 31. 9:37 p.m., 100 block of South Martel. A vandal threw a pumpkin through the front window of a house and several eggs at the front door. The police report read like just another Halloween prank - a nasty, petty act. But the attack is one in a recent spate of increasingly violent vandalisms targeting residents who have paid millions of dollars for their dream homes in the ritziest enclaves of Los Angeles. Residents are already seething, hotly divided about the growing number of Historical Architectural Restoration and Preservation (HARP) boards that prevent homeowners from remodeling their expensive real estate, forcing them to preserve the traditional integrity of neighborhoods where Hollywood legends once lived. So impassioned are pro- and anti-HARP forces that Crime Sheet columnist Molly Blume suspects that members from both sides of the debate may be perpetrating the vandalism that claims new victims almost daily. But the arson that destroys a house on Fuller Street doesn't fit the pattern. This beautiful property belongs to Margaret Reston and her husband, Hank; and the sick old man who dies when it burns is Margaret's father. Margaret herself has disappeared. She was last seen working in her garden five months ago - and although traces of her blood were found in her car, the police have no idea what has happened to the missing woman. This intrigue all makes good copy for hard-hitting newshound Molly. Almost in love again with the high-school sweetheart who dumped her and is now a rabbi, Molly can't stop thinking about Margaret and Hank Reston and the old man whose life was tragically, though accidentally, cut short. But was it an accident? What has happened to Margaret Reston? Where does malice end and evil begin?.

Dream House. unabr. ed. Rochelle Majer Krich. Read by Deanna Hurst. (Running Time: 10 hrs.). (Molly Blume Ser.: No. 2). 2004. 39.25 (978-1-59335-508-1(4), 1593355084, Brinc Audio MP3 Lib) Brilliance Audio.

Dream House. unabr. ed. Rochelle Majer Krich. Read by Deanna Hurst. (Running Time: 10 hrs.). (Molly Blume Ser.: No. 2). 2004. 24.95 (978-1-59335-240-0(9), 1593352409) Soulmate Audio Bks.

Dream Imagery Constellated by the Analytic Process. Read by Donald Kalsched. 1 cass. (Running Time: 90 min.). 1987. 10.95 (978-0-7822-0105-5(9), 256) C G Jung IL.

Dream in a Dream: On the Nature of Consciousness. Josip Pasic & Murray Stein. Read by Josip Pasic & Murray Stein. 2 cass. (Running Time: 2 hrs.). 1992. 16.95 set. (978-0-7822-0405-6(8), 500) C G Jung IL.
Drawing on psychological case material, Jungian analyst Josip Pasic explores the broader implications of the network of psychological identities well known as human Consciousness & its consequences in our personal, social, & spiritual endeavors. Followed by a response from author & analyst Murray Stein.

Dream Interpretation. Michael P. Marshall. Read by Michael P. Marshall. Ed. by Jonathan C. Renaud. Music by Ted Crook. 1 cass. (Running Time: 52 min.). 1995. 9.00 (978-0-912403-17-5(9)) Prod Renaud.
A new approach to what our dreams mean & how they affect our lives & self-understanding.

Dream Interpretation. Jackie Woods. 2003. audio compact disk 14.95 (978-0-9659665-5-9(0)) Adawehi Pr.

Dream Interpretation & Amplification. Read by Thomas P. Lavin. 2 cass. (Running Time: 4 hrs.). 1986. 21.95 Set. (978-0-7822-0135-2(0), 211) C G Jung IL.

Dream Is a Wish Your Heart Makes: My Story. abr. ed. Annette Funicello. (ENG.). 2006. 14.98 (978-1-59483-763-0(5)) Pub: Hachet Audio. Dist(s): HachBkGrp

Dream Is a Wish Your Heart Makes...Annette Funicello. abr. ed. Annette Funicello & Patricia Romanowski. 2 cass. (Running Time: 3 hrs.). 1994. 17.00 Set. (978-1-57042-056-6(4), 4-520564) Hachet Audio.
For the first time ever, America's sweetheart Annette Funicello tells her life story, from the Mickey Mouse Club to her recent battle with Multiple Sclerosis.

Dream Lover. unabr. ed. Lawrence Sanders. Read by William Dufris. 6 vols. (Running Time: 9 hrs.). 2000. bk. 54.95 (978-0-7927-2284-7(1), CSL 173, Chivers Sound Lib) AudioGO.
For studio executive Eli Hebron, there was no escape. Not from the bewitching dream web of Hollywood in 1927, on the eve of sound. Not from the irresistible lure of power that sparked the garish circus of studio politics. Not from the seductive Gladys Divine, the hopeful young starlet whose beauty threatened to lead Eli, still stunned from his movie-star wife's suicide, to ultimate disaster.

Dream Lovers: The Magnificent Shattered Lives of Bobby Darin & Sandra Dee. abr. ed. Dodd Darin. (ENG.). 2006. 14.98 (978-1-59483-777-7(5)) Pub: Hachet Audio. Dist(s): HachBkGrp

***Dream Machine: The Untold History of the Notorious V-22 Osprey.** unabr. ed. Richard Whittle. (Running Time: 17 hrs. 0 mins.). 2010. 21.99 (978-1-4001-8416-3(9)) Tantor Media.

***Dream Machine: The Untold History of the Notorious V-22 Osprey.** unabr. ed. Richard Whittle. Narrated by Kevin Foley. (Running Time: 18 hrs. 30 mins. 0 sec.). (ENG.). 2010. 29.99 (978-1-4001-6416-5(8)); audio compact disk 39.99 (978-1-4001-1416-0(0)); audio compact disk 79.99 (978-1-4001-4416-7(7)) Pub: Tantor Media. Dist(s): IngramPubServ

Dream Man. unabr. ed. Linda Howard. Read by Phil Gigante. 1 MP3-CD. (Running Time: 11 hrs.). 2009. 39.97 (978-1-4233-6317-0(5), 9781423363170, Brinc Audio MP3 Lib); 24.99 (978-1-4233-6316-3(7), 9781423363163, Brilliance MP3); 24.99 (978-1-4233-6318-7(3), 9781423363187, BAD); audio compact disk 92.97 (978-1-4233-6315-6(9), 9781423363156, BriAudCD Unabrid); audio compact disk 29.99 (978-1-4233-6314-9(0), 9781423363149, Bril Audio CD Unabri) Brilliance Audio.

Dream Man. unabr. ed. Linda Howard. Read by Phil Gigante. (Running Time: 11 hrs.). 2009. 39.97 (978-1-4418-5026-3(0), 9781441850263, BADLE) Brilliance Audio.

Dream Man: Songs for the Very Young. Betsy Jacobs. 1 cass. (J). (ps-2). 1992. (978-0-9641011-0-4(6)) J H Prods.

Dream Manager: Archive Results Beyond Your Dreams by Helping Your Employees Fulfill Theirs. rev. unabr. ed. Matthew Kelly. Read by David Slavin. Frwd. by Patrick Lencioni. (Running Time: 12600 sec.). 2007. 22.95 (978-1-4013-8844-7(2), Hyperion Audio) Pub: Hyperion. Dist(s): HarperCollins Pubs

Dream Master: Arabian Nights. Theresa Breslin. Read by Clifford Norgate. (Running Time: 15480 sec.). (J). (gr. 4-7). 2001. audio compact disk 34.95 (978-0-7540-6694-1(0)) AudioGo GBR.

Dream Mysteries: A Guide to Exploring Your Dreams. Alex Lukeman. 1 cass. 1996. 9.95 (AL1001) Llewellyn Pubns.
Practical system that enables you to understand your dreams & the symbolism your dreams contain.

Dream Mysteries: An Audio Guide to Exploring Your Dreams. Alex Lukeman. Interview with Pali Montoya-Bowman. 1989. 9.95 (978-1-878309-00-6(5), AL1001) Tigers Nest Aud.
Educational aid which assists the listener in understanding & remembering dreams.

***Dream of Darkness.** Reginald Hill. 2010. 54.95 (978-1-4450-0121-0(7)); audio compact disk 71.95 (978-1-4450-0122-7(5)) Pub: Isis Pubng Ltd GBR. Dist(s): Ulverscroft US

Dream of Past Lives. 1 cass. (Tara Sutphen Sleep Programming Tapes Ser.). 11.98 (978-0-87554-553-0(X), 2102) Valley Sun.

***Dream of Perpetual Motion: A Novel.** unabr. ed. Dexter Palmer. Narrated by William Dufris. 2 MP3-CDs. (Running Time: 14 hrs. 0 mins. 0 sec.). 2010. 24.99 (978-1-4001-6496-7(6)); 34.99 (978-1-4001-9496-4(2)); 17.99 (978-1-4001-8496-5(7)); audio compact disk 34.99 (978-1-4001-1496-2(9)); audio compact disk 69.99 (978-1-4001-4496-9(5)) Pub: Tantor Media. Dist(s): IngramPubServ

Dream of Reason: A History of Philosophy from the Greeks to the Renaissance. unabr. ed. Anthony Gottlieb. Read by Nadia May. 15 CDs. (Running Time: 19 hrs.). 2003. audio compact disk 120.00 (978-0-7861-9326-4(3), 3056); 85.95 (978-0-7861-2379-7(6), 3056) Blckstn Audio.
A stunning successor to Bertrand Russell's 1945 classic. In this landmark new study of Western thought. The author looks afresh at the writings of the great thinkers, questions much of conventional wisdom, and explains his findings with unbridled brilliance and clarity. From the pre-Socratic philosophers through the celebrated days of Socrates, Plato, and Aristotle, up to Renaissance visionaries like Erasmus and Bacon, philosophy emerges here as a phenomenon unconfined by any one discipline.

Dream of Scipio. unabr. ed. Iain Pears. 16 CDs. (Isis (CDs) Ser.). (J). 2003. audio compact disk 109.95 (978-0-7531-1718-7(5)) Pub: ISIS Lrg Prnt GBR. Dist(s): Ulverscroft US

Dream of Scipio. unabr. ed. Iain Pears. 14 cass. (Isis Ser.). (J). 2003. 99.95 (978-0-7531-1594-7(8)) Pub: ISIS Lrg Prnt GBR. Dist(s): Ulverscroft US

Dream of the Earth, abr. ed. Thomas Berry. Read by Thomas Berry. 2 cass. (Running Time: 3 hrs.). 1995. 15.95 (978-0-944993-60-6(5)) Audio Lit.
A visionary statement of our threatened planet's needs from its human inhabitants.

Dream of the Rood see Beowulf & Other Poetry

Dream on the Water. unabr. ed. Read by Peter Himmelman. Perf. by Peter Himmelman. 1 cass. (Running Time: 28 min.). Dramatization. (J). 1985. 8.95 (978-1-58452-003-0(5), 4315); 8.95 Spanish version. (978-1-58452-012-2(4), 5315) Spinoza Co.

Dream Play. Paul R. Scheele. 1 cass. (Running Time: 40 min.). (Paraliminal Tapes Ser.). 1992. 24.95 (978-0-925480-20-0(7)) Learn Strategies.
Helps you program your dreams for success in almost any endeavor.

Dream Power. Bruce Goldberg. (ENG.). 2005. audio compact disk 17.00 (978-1-57968-095-4(X)) Pub: B Goldberg. Dist(s): Baker Taylor

Dream Power. Bruce Goldberg. Read by Bruce Goldberg. 1 cass. (Running Time: 25 min.). (ENG.). 2007. 13.00 (978-1-885577-60-3(5)) Pub: B Goldberg. Dist(s): Baker Taylor
Through self-hypnosis use the nightly REM cycle to solve problems & empower oneself.

Dream Power. Stuart Wilde. Read by Stuart Wilde. 2 cass. (Self-Help Tape Ser.). 1992. 21.95 Set. (978-0-930603-54-0(0)) White Dove NM.
We spend a third of our lives asleep, much of it dreaming. As a first step to better understanding your life & the relationships you are involved in, Stuart explains how to interpret & harness the power of your dreams.

Dream Power - Improve Your Luck. Robert E. Griswold. Read by Robert E. Griswold. 1 cass. (Super Strength Ser.). 1996. 10.95 (978-1-55848-322-4(5)) EffectiveMN.
Side One: You can program yourself to have positive, creative dreams. Side Two: Easy techniques & positive programming that has helped thousands of people unblock their natural flow of good luck & become more successful.

Dream Rider: Don't Drink the Eye Drops. unabr. ed. Jon D'Arc. Read by Elihu Blotnick. 4 CDs. (Running Time: 4 hrs. 35 min.). (Pseudonymous Ser. - TM). 2002. audio compact disk 21.00 (978-0-915090-86-0(4)) Firefall.
A procedural romance: son of a famous photographer, Aaron Rhyder leads a failed life in the shadows, until a sudden fogging of his sight sends him to Dr. Alisa Grey, who lovingly injects visions into his eye with a platinum needle.

Dream River. Maria Illo & William Brizendine. 1 cass. (C). 1994. per. 9.95 (978-0-9613159-2-4(X)) Emerald Forest.
Original songs with varied acoustic accompaniment.

Dream River. Perf. by Maria Illo & William Brizendine. 1 cass. (Running Time: 60 min.). 1994. 8.95 (978-0-9613159-4-8(6)) Emerald Forest.
Original songs with acoustic accompaniment.

Dream Sellers. unabr. ed. Ruth Hamilton. Read by Marlene Sidaway. 12 cass. (Running Time: 12 hrs.). 1999. 96.95 Set. (978-0-7540-0272-7(1), CAB1695) AudioGO.
The Shawcross family was a strange & unhappy one. But as the new generation begins to grow up, the truth behind the old family scandals begins to emerge.

Dream Solutions: Find your Answers in your Dreams. Dick Sutphen. 1 cass. (Running Time: 1 hr.). (RX17 Ser.). 1986. 14.98 (978-0-87554-297-3(2), RX106) Valley Sun.
You have the power & ability to find your answers in your dreams. Before going to sleep, you focus on what you desire to resolve. When seeking answers, you ask to receive them in dreams. You receive positive solutions in vivid dreams. You remember your dreams upon awakening. You can dream the solution to any problem.

Dream Songs & Healing Sounds in the Rainforests of Malaysia. Anno. by Marina Roseman. 1 cass. 1995. (0-9307-404170-9307-40417-2-7); audio compact disk (0-9307-40417-2-7) Smithsonian Folkways.
The Temiar people of central Malaysia's rainforest have developed a musical landscape that evolves from their dreams - dreamsongs - which celebrate all important occasions in Temiar society.

Dream Stalker. unabr. ed. Margaret Coel. Read by Stephanie Brush. 6 cass. (Running Time: 7 hrs. 30 min.). (Wind River Ser.). 1999. 39.95 (978-1-55686-873-3(1)) Books in Motion.
Father John discovers a frozen body on the Arapaho Reservation, a corpse that later disappears.

Dream Team. abr. ed. Chuck Daly & Alex Sachare. Read by Donald V. Allen. 2 cass. (Running Time: 3 hrs.). Dramatization. bk. 15.95 set. (978-1-56703-025-9(4)) High-Top Sports.

Dream Team: The University of Michigan 1989 NCAA Basketball National Championship Run. unabr. ed. Read by Frank Beckman & Larry Henry. 1 cass. (Running Time: 60 min.). 1994. 9.95 (978-1-885408-04-4(8)) Listen & Live.
It was a Cinderella tournament run for the 1989 Michigan Basketball team. Join WJR's Frank Beckman as he narrates the heart-stopping story of Coach Steve Fisher & the Wolverine's improbable last-second victory over Seton Hall.

Dream the Impossible. Emmett Smith. 1 cass. 3.95 (978-1-57734-401-8(4), 34441425); 5.98 (978-1-55503-240-1(0), 0600229) Covenant Comms.
Inspiring stories of handicapped people who have overcome & excelled.

Dream Theory & Demonstration. Frederick Perls. 1 cass. (Running Time: 60 min.). 1968. 11.00 (04402) Big Sur Tapes.

Dream Therapy CD Album. Bruce Goldberg. (ENG.). 2005. audio compact disk 75.00 (978-1-57968-053-4(4)) Pub: B Goldberg. Dist(s): Baker Taylor

Dream Therapy Program Album, Set. Bruce Goldberg. Read by Bruce Goldberg. 6 cass. (Running Time: 3 hrs.). (ENG.). 2005. 65.00 (978-1-885577-91-7(5)) Pub: B Goldberg. Dist(s): Baker Taylor
Self-hypnosis program training to use dreams to improve creativity, lucid dream and take charge of life.

Dream Time. Perf. by Paul Fitzgerald & Mark Flanagan. Created by Matthew Manning. Prod. by Stuart Wilde. 1 cass. 10.95 (CN608) White Dove NM.
Hypnotic voices, gentle, distant rhythms, & haunting pipes lead you to Alchringa - the sacred dreamtime of the Aborigines. Paul Fitzgerald & Mark Flanagan have worked together for 10 years to develop new experimental techniques combined with natural & organic sounds.

Dream Time Fairy Tale Classics: Jack & the Beanstalk, the Frog Prince, Puss 'N Boots. unabr. ed. Short Stories. Perf. by Julie Just. Prod. by Bob E. Flick & Adam Mayefsky. 1 cass. (Running Time: 1 hr.). Dramatization. (Dream Time Fairy Tales Ser.: Vol. 1). (J). (gr. k-6). 2000. 9.99 (978-1-884214-07-3(X)) Ziggurat Prods.
Includes"Jack & the Beanstalk," "The Frog Prince," "Puss N Boots.".

Dream Time Fairy Tale Classics Vol. 1: Jack & the Beanstalk, The Frog Prince, Puss 'N Boots. Short Stories. Perf. by Julie Just. Engineer Bob E. Flick. Music by Bob E. Flick. Des. by Adam Mayefsky. 1 CD. (Running Time: 47 mins.). Dramatization. (Dream Time Fairy Tales Ser.: Vol. 1). (J). 2000. audio compact disk 15.00 (978-1-884214-13-4(4)) Ziggurat Prods.
Classic Fairy Tales for children (and adults!) to enjoy. Includes "Jack and the Beanstalk", "The Frog Prince", and "Puss 'N Boots".

Dream Time Fairy Tale Classics Vol. 2: Hansel & Gretel, Rumpelstiltskin, Rapunzel. Short Stories. Perf. by Julie Just. Engineer Bob E. Flick. Music by Bob E. Flick. Des. by Adam Mayefsky. 1 CD. (Running Time: 30 mins.). Dramatization. (Dream Time Fairy Tales Ser.: Vol. 2). (J). 2000. audio compact disk 15.00 (978-1-884214-12-7(6)) Ziggurat Prods.
Classic Fairy Tales for children and adults to enjoy. Includes "Hansel & Gretel", "Rapunzel", and "Rumpelstiltskin.".

Dream Time Fairy Tale Classics Vol. 2: Hansel & Gretel, Rumpelstiltskin, Rapunzel. unabr. ed. Short Stories. Perf. by Julie Just. Engineer Bob E. Flick. Music by Bob E. Flick. Des. by Adam Mayefsky. 1 cass. (Running Time: 1 hr.). Dramatization. (Dream Time Fairy Tales Ser.: Vol. 2). (J). (gr. k-6). 2000. 9.99 (978-1-884214-11-0(8)) Ziggurat Prods.
Includes: "Hansel and Gretel," "Rapunzel," & "Rumpelstiltskin.".

Dream Time Fairy Tales Vol. 3: Little Red Riding Hood, Goldilocks & the Three Bears, the Adventures of Tom Thumb, the Three Little Pigs. Short Stories. Perf. by Janellen Steininger & Reg Green. Engineer Bob E. Flick. Music by Bob E. Flick. Adapted by Adam Mayefsky. Des. by Adam Mayefsky. 1 CD. (Running Time: 42 mins.). Dramatization. (Dream Time Fairy Tales Ser.: Vol. 3). (J). (gr. k-9). 2001. audio compact disk 15.00 (978-1-884214-22-6(3)) Ziggurat Prods.
Classic Fairy Tales for children and adults alike to enjoy! Includes:Little Red Riding Hood:A little girl with red cloak and hood,Ventures deep into the wood.To Grandmother's house she is to go,But waiting inside....oh no, oh no!!Goldilocks & The Three Bears:A mischievous girl with golden hair,Disturbs the home of three big bears.When they return to what's been done,Watch out, Goldilocks....you better run!The Adventures of Tom Thumb:A boy named Thumb who is very small,Has great adventures and is loved by all.The King, his court, and the Fairy too,Are amazed by Tom, and so will you!The Three Little Pigs:The big bad wolf has come to town,To blow the three pigs' houses down.Which house still stands when all is done,The straw, the wood, the brick...or none?!.

Dream Time Fairy Tales Vol. 4: Aladdin & the Magic Lamp, the Emperor's New Clothes, Ali Baba & the 40 Thieves. Short Stories. Perf. by Janellen Steininger et al. Engineer Bob E. Flick. Music by Bob E. Flick. Des. by Adam Mayefsky. 1 CD. (Running Time: 40 mins.). Dramatization. (Dream Time Fairy Tales Ser.: Vol. 4). (J). (gr. k-9). 2001. audio compact disk 15.00 (978-1-884214-23-3(1)) Ziggurat Prods.
Classic Fairy Tales for children & adults alike to enjoy! Includes...Aladdin and the Magic Lamp:A boy took a lamp from an evil man,And discovered great power now in his hand.All was well when the genie was near,Until the lamp and the princess disappeared!The Emperor's New Clothes:The Emperor was rich, and vain to boot,He ordered clothes that cost a loot.But when he flaunted his brand new gown,He was laughed at by the entire town!Ali Baba & the 40 Thieves:"Open Sesame" were the magic words,Ali Baba one day overheard.A cave of treasure lay in the sand,But 40 thieves were very close at hand!.

Dream to Call My Own. abr. ed. Tracie Peterson. Narrated by Aimee Lilly. (Running Time: 6 hrs. 40 mins. 24 sec.). (Brides of Gallatin County Ser.: No. 3). (ENG.). 2009. audio compact disk 27.99 (978-1-59859-560-4(1)) Oasis Audio.

Dream to Call My Own. abr. ed. Tracie Peterson. Narrated by Aimee Lilly. (Running Time: 6 hrs. 40 mins. 24 sec.). (Brides of Gallatin County Ser.). (ENG.). 2009. 19.59 (978-1-60814-478-5(X)) Oasis Audio.

Dream to Share. unabr. ed. June Francis. Contrib. by Margaret Sircom. 9 cass. (Story Sound Ser.). 2006. 76.95 (978-1-85903-971-7(5)) Pub: Mgna Lrg Print GBR. Dist(s): Ulverscroft US

Dream to Share. unabr. ed. June Francis & Margaret Sircom. Contrib. by Margaret Sircom. 11 CDs. (Story Sound CD Ser.). 2006. audio compact disk 99.95 (978-1-84652-036-5(3)) Pub: Mgna Lrg Print GBR. Dist(s): Ulverscroft US

Dream Train: A Novel of the Orient Express. unabr. ed. Charlotte Vale Allen. Read by Liza Ross. 10 cass. (Running Time: 15 hrs.). (Isis Ser.). (J). 1999. 84.95 (978-0-7531-0525-2(X), 990211) Pub: ISIS Lrg Prnt GBR. Dist(s): Ulverscroft US
It's a plum assignment for photojournalist Joanna James: a ride on the Orient-Express with a stop in Venice for five days at the exclusive Cipriani Hotel - all expenses paid. A stop in London renews her friendship with two very different lovers who both want a commitment she is not ready to give. But then she boards the luxurious train & enters its romantic world, where strangers become friends, where confidences are shared, where hearts are broken, & where love is lost...& found.

Dream Trilogy CD Collection: Daring to Dream; Holding the Dream; Finding the Dream. abr. ed. Nora Roberts. Read by Sandra Burr. (Running Time: 9 hrs.). (Dream Trilogy). 2009. audio compact disk 34.99 (978-1-4233-7902-7(0), 9781423379027, BACD) Brilliance Audio.

Dream Variations see Poetry of Langston Hughes

Dream Waking. Galek Rinpoche. 1 cass. 1992. 9.00 (OC296-66) Sound Horizons AV.

***Dream Wave Meditation.** Kelly Howell. (ENG.). 2010. audio compact disk 14.95 (978-1-60568-064-4(8)) Brain Sync.

Dream When You're Feeling Blue: A Novel. unabr. ed. Elizabeth Berg. Read by Elizabeth Berg. 11 CDs. (Running Time: 13 hrs. 30 mins.). 2007. audio compact disk 110.00 (978-1-4159-3857-7(1)); 110.00 (978-1-4159-3845-4(8)) Books on Tape.
As the novel opens, Kitty and Louise Heaney say good-bye to their boyfriends Julian and Michael, who are going to fight overseas. On the domestic front, meat is rationed, children participate in metal drives, and Tommy Dorsey and Glenn Miller play music that offers hope and lifts spirits. For Kitty, a confident, headstrong young woman, the departure of her boyfriend and the lessons she learns about love, resilience, and war will bring a surprise and uncover a secret, and will lead her to a radical action on behalf of those she loves that will change the Heaney family forever. The lifelong consequences of the choices the sisters make are at the heart of this superb novel about the power of love and the enduring strength of family.

Dream When You're Feeling Blue: A Novel. unabr. ed. Elizabeth Berg. Read by Elizabeth Berg. (Running Time: 36000 sec.). (ENG.). 2007. audio compact disk 34.95 (978-0-7393-2546-9(9), Random AudioBks) Pub: Random Audio Pubg. Dist(s): Random

Dream Within a Dream see Purloined Letter & Other Works

Dream Woman. unabr. ed. Wilkie Collins. Read by Walter Covell. 1 cass. (Running Time: 90 min.). Dramatization. 1981. 7.95 (S-6) Jimcin Record.
Strange happenings & eerie creatures.

Dream Woman & Mad Monkton. Wilkie Collins. 1 cass. (Running Time: 1 hr.). (Radiobook Ser.). 1987. 4.98 (978-0-929541-29-7(4)) Radiola Co.
Two complete stories.

Dream Work. Jeremy Taylor. 4 cass. (Running Time: 4 hrs. 52 min.). 1994. 33.95 Set. (TAH313) Alba Hse Comns.
This cassette program will help you explore the possible meaning & significance of your dreams & the dreams of others. Excellent for anyone interested in growing through a better knowledge of their dreams.

Dream Yoga: The Practice of Lucid Dreaming as a Path to Enlightenment. Speeches. Tenzin Wangyal. 2 CDs. (Running Time: 2 hours 4 minutes). 2007. audio compact disk 19.95 (978-0-9753771-3-0(2)) Ligmincha Ins.

Dreamcatcher. unabr. ed. Stephen King. Read by Jeffrey DeMunn. 16 vols. (Running Time: 24 hrs.). 2001. bk. 124.95 (978-0-7927-2457-5(7), CSL 346, Chivers Sound Lib) AudioGO.
Once upon a time, in the haunted city of Derry, four boys stood together & did a brave thing. Twenty-five years later, the boys are now men with separate lives & troubles. Each hunting season the foursome reunite in the woods of Maine. This year, a stranger stumbles into their camp & before long, these men will be plunged into a horrifying struggle.

Dreamcatcher. unabr. ed. Stephen King. Read by Jeffrey DeMunn. 3 CDs. (Running Time: 9 hrs.). 2002. audio compact disk 69.95 (978-0-7927-2762-0(2), CMP 346, Chivers Sound Lib) AudioGO.
Each hunting season, four friends reunite in the woods of Maine. This year, a stranger stumbles into their camp, mumbling something about lights in the sky. Before long, these men will be plunged into a horrifying struggle with a creature from another world. Their only chance of survival is locked in their shared past, and in the Dreamcatcher.

Dreamcatcher. unabr. movie tie-in ed. Stephen King. Read by Jeffrey DeMunn. 2006. 23.95 (978-0-7435-6331-4(X), Audioworks) Pub: S&S Audio. Dist(s): S and S Inc

Dreamdark: Silksinger. Laini Taylor. Read by Cassandra Campbell. (Playaway Top Children's Picks Ser.). (ENG.). (J). 2009. 59.99 (978-1-4418-1017-5(X)) Find a World.

Dreamer. Neville Goddard. 1 cass. (Running Time: 62 min.). 1965. 8.00 (57) J & L Pubns.
Neville taught Imagination Creates Reality. He was a powerfully influential teacher of God as Consciousness.

***Dreamer.** Pam Muñoz Ryan. Illus. by Peter Sís. (ENG.). 2010. audio compact disk 39.99 (978-0-545-22339-3(3)) Scholastic Inc.

Dreamer. abr. ed. Brian Evans. Read by Brian Evans. Prod. by Greg Knowles. 2 cass. (Running Time: 3 hrs.). 1995. 14.95 Set. (978-1-882320-02-8(6)) Helion Audio.
The autobiography of a young actor who found Hollywood to be rough & unforgiving of his naivete' & adolescent mistakes. When Brian Evans was just three years old, he knew he wanted to be a star. Leaving Haverhill, Mass. to make it big, he embarked on an incredible journey - one that would take him from featured roles in films & TV to prison. Brian's story is one of a young man's struggle to succeed in show business, while battling his own personal demons. In his own words, Brian tells of his youthful recklessness, & his attempts to turn his life around. Features two original songs.

Dreamer: A Novel about Martin Luther King, Jr. Charles Johnson. 2004. 15.95 (978-0-7435-4657-7(1)) Pub: S&S Audio. Dist(s): S and S Inc

Dreamer Has a Nightmare. Dave Blevins. 1 cass. (Running Time: 1 hr.). (J). 2000. pap. bk. 8.99 David C Cook.
A sleepy rhinoceros named Dreamer has a nightmare about a flood. Dreamer can't go back to sleep & sleeping is his favoite thing to do! After he shares his dream with others, they too begin to have this dream about a flood.Finally, Ponder helps them understand that they actually lived this event. Included: read-along book.

Dreamers of the Day. abr. ed. Mary Doria Russell. Read by Ann Marie Lee. (Running Time: 23400 sec.). (ENG.). 2008. audio compact disk 29.95 (978-0-7393-5839-9(1), Random AudioBks) Pub: Random Audio Pubg. Dist(s): Random

Dreamfever. Karen Marie Moning. Read by Natalie Ross & Phil Gigante. (Playaway Adult Fiction Ser.). (ENG.). 2009. 69.99 (978-1-4418-2937-5(7)) Find a World.

Dreamfever. unabr. ed. Karen Marie Moning. (Running Time: 9 hrs.). (Fever Ser.: No. 4). 2009. 39.97 (978-1-4233-4212-0(7), 9781423342120, BADLE) Brilliance Audio.

Dreamfever. unabr. ed. Karen Marie Moning. Read by Phil Gigante & Natalie Ross. (Running Time: 9 hrs.). (Fever Ser.: No. 4). 2009. 24.99 (978-1-4233-4209-0(7), 9781423342090, Brilliance MP3); 39.97 (978-1-4233-4210-6(0), 9781423342106, Brinc Audio MP3 Lib) Brilliance Audio.

Dreamfever. unabr. ed. Karen Marie Moning. Read by Natalie Ross & Phil Gigante. (Running Time: 9 hrs.). (Fever Ser.: No. 4). 2009. 24.99 (978-1-4233-4211-3(9), 9781423342113, BAD); audio compact disk 34.99 (978-1-4233-4207-6(0), 9781423342076, Bril Audio CD Unabri); audio compact disk 92.97 (978-1-4233-4208-3(9), 9781423342083, BriAudCD Unabrid) Brilliance Audio.

DreamGiver. Bruce Wilkinson. (Study Ser.). 2004. audio compact disk 19.99 (978-1-932131-24-6(8)) Pub: Glob Vision. Dist(s): STL Dist NA

Dreamgivers: The Wells Fargo Trail. unabr. ed. Jim Walker. Narrated by Jack Garrett. 5 cass. (Running Time: 6 hrs. 45 mins.). 2001. 45.00 (978-0-7887-5150-9(6), K0037E7) Recorded Bks.
Still having bad memories of the Appomattox battle, Zachary Cobb heads west to start over & start a new career as an undercover Wells Fargo agent.

Dreamhunter. Elizabeth Knox. Read by Edwina Wren. (Running Time: 11 hrs. 10 mins.). (Dreamhunter Duet Ser.: No. 1). (YA). 2009. 84.99 (978-1-74214-253-1(2), 9781742142531) Pub: Bolinda Pubng AUS. Dist(s): Bolinda Pub Inc

Dreamhunter. unabr. ed. Elizabeth Knox. Read by Edwina Wren. (Running Time: 11 hrs. 10 mins.). (Dreamhunter Duet Ser.: No. 1). 2007. audio compact disk 93.95 (978-1-74093-828-0(3)) Pub: Bolinda Pubng AUS. Dist(s): Bolinda Pub Inc

Dreaming Child see Winter's Tales

Dreaming Detective. H. R. F. Keating. Read by Sheila Mitchell. 6 cass. 54.95 (978-0-7927-3393-5(2), CSL 724); audio compact disk 74.95 (978-0-7927-3394-2(0), SLD 724); audio compact disk 29.95 (978-0-7927-3411-6(4), CMP 724) AudioGO.

***Dreaming in English: A Novel.** unabr. ed. Laura Fitzgerald. (Running Time: 11 hrs.). 2011. 24.99 (978-1-4418-3961-9(5), 9781441839619, BAD); 39.97 (978-1-4418-3962-6(3), 9781441839626, BADLE); 39.97 (978-1-4418-3960-2(7), 9781441839602, Brinc Audio MP3 Lib); 24.99 (978-1-4418-3959-6(3), 9781441839596, Brilliance MP3); audio compact disk 79.97 (978-1-4418-3958-9(5), 9781441839589, BriAudCD Unabrid); audio compact disk 29.99 (978-1-4418-3957-2(7), 9781441839572, Bril Audio CD Unabri) Brilliance Audio.

Dreaming of a Stranger. unabr. ed. Sheila O'Flanagan. Narrated by Caroline Lennon. 14 cass. (Running Time: 19 hrs. 30 mins.). 2004. 99.75 (978-1-84505-160-0(2), H1723MC, Clipper Audio) Recorded Bks.

Dreaming of the Bones. Deborah Crombie. Narrated by Jenny Sterlin. 12 CDs. (Running Time: 14 hrs. 30 mins.). (Duncan Kincaid/Gemma James Novel Ser.). 2001. audio compact disk 116.00 (978-0-7887-5203-2(0), C1360E7) Recorded Bks.
After 12 years, Scotland Yard Superintendent Duncan Kincaid receives a phone call from his ex-wife Victoria asking for his help. She's working on a biography of the late poet Lydia Brooke & has uncovered information that has her convinced Lydia's death was not a suicide. When a second death occurs that is clearly murder, Duncan & his partner find themselves searching for clues to a 30-year-old mystery to find the killer.

Dreaming of the Bones. unabr. ed. Deborah Crombie. Narrated by Jenny Sterlin. 10 cass. (Running Time: 14 hrs. 30 mins.). (Duncan Kincaid/Gemma James Novel Ser.). 2000. 85.00 (978-0-7887-4085-5(7), 95946E7) Recorded Bks.

***Dreaming of You.** unabr. ed. Lisa Kleypas. Read by Rosalyn Landor. (Running Time: 11 hrs.). 2011. 24.99 (978-1-4418-5209-0(3), 9781441852090, Brilliance MP3); 39.97 (978-1-4418-5210-6(7), 9781441852106, Brinc Audio MP3 Lib); audio compact disk 29.99 (978-1-4418-5207-6(7), 9781441852076); audio compact disk 79.97 (978-1-4418-5208-3(5), 9781441852083, BriAudCD Unabrid) Brilliance Audio.

Dreaming Pictures: Paul Klee. P. Klee. (Adventures in Art Ser.). 1998. audio compact disk 25.00 (978-3-7913-1943-8(4)) Prestel Pub NY.

Dreaming the Dream. Kenneth Wapnick. 4 CDs. 2006. audio compact disk 23.00 (978-1-59142-251-8(5), CD69) Foun Miracles.

Dreaming the Dream. Kenneth Wapnick. 1 CD. (Running Time: 3 hrs 53 mins 38 secs,). 2006. 19.00 (978-1-59142-263-1(9), 3m69) Foun Miracles.

Dreaming up the Tunes. Contrib. by Johnny Og Connolly. (ENG.). 1998. 13.95 (978-0-8023-7133-1(7)); audio compact disk 20.95 (978-0-8023-8133-0(2)) Pub: Clo Iar-Chonnachta IRL. Dist(s): Dufour

Dreaming Void. unabr. ed. Peter F. Hamilton. Narrated by John Lee. 2 MP3-CDs. (Running Time: 22 hrs. 30 mins. 0 sec.). (Void Ser.: Pt. 1). (ENG.). 2008. 39.99 (978-1-4001-5727-3(7)) Pub: Tantor Media. Dist(s): IngramPubServ

Dreaming Void. unabr. ed. Peter F. Hamilton. Read by John Lee. 18 CDs. (Running Time: 22 hrs. 30 mins. 0 sec.). (Void Ser.: Pt. 1). (ENG.). 2008. audio compact disk 109.99 (978-1-4001-3727-5(6)); audio compact disk 54.99 (978-1-4001-0727-8(X)) Pub: Tantor Media. Dist(s): IngramPubServ

Dreaming with Don Miguel Ruiz. Don Miguel Ruiz. 1 CD. (Running Time: 1 hr.). 2001. audio compact disk (978-1-878424-40-2(8)) Amber-Allen Pub.
Meditations to aid you in transforming the dream of your life.

Dreaming with God. Bill Johnson. (Running Time: 5 hours, 31 minutes). 2007. 24.99 (978-1-4245-0702-3(2)) Tre Med Inc.

Dreaming with God: Secrets to Redesigning Your World Through God's Creative Flow. Bill Johnson. Frwd. by James W. Goll. (Running Time: 19920 sec.). 2007. audio compact disk 39.99 (978-0-7684-2600-7(6)) Destiny Image Pubs.

Dreamland. Sarah Dessen. (Running Time: 9 hrs.). (ENG.). (YA). (gr. 7 up). 2009. audio compact disk 29.95 (978-0-14-314469-4(3), PengAudBks) Penguin Grp USA.

Dreamland. abr. ed. Kevin Baker. Read by John Rubinstein. 4 cass. 1999. 18.00 (FS9-43375) Highsmith.

***Dreamland.** abr. ed. Kevin Baker. Read by John Rubinstein. (ENG.). 2006. (978-0-06-088676-9(5), Harper Audio); (978-0-06-088675-2(7), Harper Audio) HarperCollins Pubs.

Dreamland. abr. ed. Dale Brown & Jim DeFelice. Read by J. K. Simmons. 4 cass. (Running Time: 6 hrs.). (Dale Brown's Dreamland Ser.). 2001. 25.95 (978-0-694-52471-6(9)) HarperCollins Pubs.

***Dreamland.** collector's unabr. ed. Sarah Dessen. Narrated by Liz Morton. 7 CDs. (Running Time: 8 hrs. 30 mins.). (YA). (gr. 7 up). 2009. audio compact disk 41.95 (978-1-4407-2563-0(2)) Recorded Bks.

***Dreamland.** unabr. ed. Sarah Dessen. Narrated by Liz Morton. 1 Playaway. (Running Time: 8 hrs. 30 mins.). (YA). (gr. 7 up). 2009. 56.75 (978-1-4407-2101-4(7)); 51.75 (978-1-4407-2092-5(4)); audio compact disk 66.75 (978-1-4407-2096-3(7)) Recorded Bks.

Dreamland: World Lullabies & Soothing Songs. Putumayo. (Running Time: 37 min). 2004. audio compact disk 15.95 (978-1-58759-071-9(9)) Putumayo Wrld.

DreamLearning. Michael DeLuca & Mark Richardson. Read by Michael DeLuca & Mark Richardson. Read by Sara Harrell Banks. Ed. by Richard Ridington. 4 cass. (Running Time: 4 hrs. 45 min.). 1996. pap. bk. & wbk. ed. 12.95 DREAM JOURNAL. (978-1-888864-02-1(8), DLJ-1) InnrQuest.
8 sessions dealing with how to remember, interpret, direct & receive guidance & healing through your dreams. Set price includes instructional dream journal/workbook.

DreamLearning. Michael DeLuca & Mark Richardson. Read by Michael DeLuca & Mark Richardson. Read by Sara Harrell Banks. Ed. by Richard Ridington. 4 cass. (Running Time: 4 hrs. 45 min.). 1996. pap. bk. 89.95 (978-1-888864-00-7(1), DL) InnrQuest.
Eight sessions dealing with how to remember, interpret, direct & receive guidance & healing through your dreams. Set price includes instructional dream journal/workbook.

DreamLearning: Dream Interpretation. Michael DeLuca & Mark Richardson. Read by Michael DeLuca & Mark Richardson. Read by Sara Harrell Banks. Ed. by Richard Ridington. 1 cass. (Running Time: 50 min.). 1996. 12.00 (978-1-888864-03-8(6)) InnrQuest.
How to remember, record, & interpret your dreams using the DreamLearning Dream Journal.

Dreamosaurus. DinoRock Performers. (J). 1998. 9.98 Rounder Kids Mus Dist.
Learn about dinosaurs through music & dialogue. This is based on the adventures of ayoung boy named Nelson, who is obsessed with dinosaurs. It is sure to provide enjoyment for a variety of listeners.

Dreamosaurus. Perf. by DinoRock Performers. 1 CD. (Running Time: 51 mins.). (J). 1998. audio compact disk 15.98 (978-1-57940-017-0(5)) Rounder Records.

Dreamosaurus. Perf. by DinoRock Performers. Lyrics by Mike Stein et al. 1 CD. (J). (ps-2). 1998. audio compact disk 9.98 (978-1-57940-016-3(7)) Rounder Records.
Learn about dinosaurs through Dinorock musical performers & through the adventures of a young boy named Nelson, who is obsessed with dinosaurs. This will provide hours of enjoyment to all ages.

Dreamquake. Elizabeth Knox. Read by Edwina Wren. (Running Time: 13 hrs.). (Dreamhunter Duet Ser.: No. 2). (YA). 2009. 94.99 (978-1-74214-254-8(0), 9781742142548) Pub: Bolinda Pubng AUS. Dist(s): Bolinda Pub Inc

Dreamquake. unabr. ed. Elizabeth Knox. Read by Edwina Wren. (Running Time: 46800 sec.). (Dreamhunter Duet Ser.: No. 2). (YA). (gr. 7). 2008. audio compact disk 103.95 (978-1-921334-20-7(7), 9781921334207) Pub: Bolinda Pubng AUS. Dist(s): Bolinda Pub Inc

Dreams. John Bradshaw. (Running Time: 18000 sec.). 2008. audio compact disk 120.00 (978-1-57388-366-5(2)) J B Media.

Dreams. Sigmund Freud. Read by Jonathan Reese. (Running Time: 23400 sec.). (Unabridged Classics in Audio Ser.). (ENG.). 2005. audio compact disk 59.99 (978-1-4001-3166-2(9)) Pub: Tantor Media. Dist(s): IngramPubServ

Dreams. unabr. ed. Sigmund Freud. Read by Jonathan Reese. 6 cass. (Running Time: 6 hrs.). 1997. 36.00 (4132) Books on Tape.
According to Freud, our unconscious impulses are not random, but packed with meaning, taking on color, form & even a storyline. All dreams are actually wish fulfillments & interpreting them can bridge the gap to the conscious, resulting in more meaningful living.

Dreams. unabr. ed. Sigmund Freud. Read by Jonathan Reese. (Running Time: 6 hrs. 30 mins. 0 sec.). (Tantor Unabridged Classics Ser.). (ENG.). 2009. audio compact disk 27.99 (978-1-4001-0911-1(6)); audio compact disk 55.99 (978-1-4001-3911-8(2)); audio compact disk 19.99 (978-1-4001-5911-6(3)) Pub: Tantor Media. Dist(s): IngramPubServ

Dreams: Gifts from the Unconscious. Read by June Singer. 1 cass. (Running Time: 90 min.). 1975. 10.95 (978-0-7822-0257-1(8), 012) C G Jung IL.

Dreams: Program from the Award Winning Public Radio Series the Infinite Mind. Interview. Hosted by Fred Goodwin. 1 CD. (Running Time: 1 hr.). (Infinite Mind Ser.: 99). 2000. 21.95 (978-1-888064-94-0(3), LCM 99) Lichtenstein Creat.
All of us dream: four or five times each night, 100,000 times over the course of a lifetime, about four solid years of dreaming. In this program, host Dr. Fred Goodwin explores the mystery and the science of dreams, with guests Rita Dwyer, Dr. Alan Siegel, lucid dream expert Dr. Stephen LaBerge, author Spalding Gray and musical guest Carrie Newcomer. With commentary by John Hockenberry.

Dreams & Active Imagination. Read by Lois Khan. 2 cass. (Running Time: 1 hr. 45 min.). 1991. 16.95 (978-0-7822-0125-3(3), 444) C G Jung IL.

Dreams & Dreaming. unabr. ed. Christopher Evans. 1 cass. (Running Time: 30 min.). 12.95 (33030) J Norton Pubs.

Dreams & ESP. Read by Stanley Krippner. 1 cass. (Running Time: 90 min.). 1976. 10.95 (978-0-7822-0133-8(4), 014) C G Jung IL.

Dreams & How to Interpret Them. Stephen Hawley Martin. 2008. 2.95 (978-1-892538-28-4(8)) Pub: Oaklea Pr. Dist(s): Midpt Trade

Dreams & Illusions: Tales of the Pacific Rim. Perf. by Brenda Wong Aoki. 1 cass. (Running Time: 45 min.). (Family Ser.). (J). (gr. k-7). 1990. 9.98 (8019); audio compact disk 14.98 (8019) Rounder Records.
This is the debut album from performance artist Brenda Wong Aoki (featured in the movie "Living in Tokyo"), who brings alive tales from Japan, China, Korea, Cambodia & California.

Dreams & Meditations. Ole Nydahl. 2 cass. 18.00 set. (A0695-90) Sound Photosyn.
The subtle distinctions from a Tibetan Buddhist viewpoint & how to use them.

Dreams & Messages from God. Maureen Schuler. 3 cass. (Running Time: 2 hrs. 58 min.). 1993. 26.95 Set. (TAH290) Alba Hse Comns.
An excellent program for anyone desiring to come to a deeper understanding of self. For the adventurous journeyer inquisitive of the meaning of their own dreams & the revealing aspects of their own emotions. For those who desire harmony & balance in order to find the God who calls them to wholeness.

Dreams & Shadows: The Future of the Middle East. Robin Wright. Read by Laural Merlington. (Playaway Adult Nonfiction Ser.). 2008. 69.99 (978-1-60640-149-1(1)) Find a World.

Dreams & Shadows: The Future of the Middle East. unabr. ed. Robin Wright. (Running Time: 18 hrs. 0 mins. 0 sec.). (ENG.). 2008. audio compact disk 39.99 (978-1-4001-0597-7(8)) Pub: Tantor Media. Dist(s): IngramPubServ

Dreams & Shadows: The Future of the Middle East. unabr. ed. Robin Wright. Read by Laural Merlington. (Running Time: 18 hrs. 0 mins. 0 sec.). (ENG.). 2008. audio compact disk 29.99 (978-1-4001-5597-2(5)); audio compact disk 79.99 (978-1-4001-3597-4(4)) Pub: Tantor Media. Dist(s): IngramPubServ

Dreams & Visions. 2003. (978-1-59024-121-9(5)); audio compact disk (978-1-59024-122-6(3)) B Hinn Min.

Dreams & Visions. 2002. (978-1-59024-042-7(1)); audio compact disk (978-1-59024-043-4(X)) B Hinn Min.

Dreams & Visions. Lester Sumrall. 5 cass. (Running Time: 7 hrs. 30 mins.). 1999. 20.00 (978-1-58568-036-8(2)) Sumrall Pubng.

Dreams & Visions: An Advent Retreat. Megan McKenna. Read by Megan McKenna. 6 cass. (Running Time: 7 hrs.). 1996. pap. bk. (AA2991) Credence Commun.
Offers a bracing challenge to live up to the prophetical message in Isaiah & Matthew.

Dreams are Letters from the Soul Audio Set: Discover the Connections Between Your Dreams & Your Spiritual Life. Connie Kaplan. 9 CDs. 2006. audio compact disk 32.95 (978-0-9786239-6-8(7)) Generosity Inc.

Dreams Come True: Gen. 41:41-57. Ed Young. 1988. 0.95 (978-0-7417-1682-8(8), 682) Win Walk.

Dreams Do Come True. Edwards-Ticehur. 2002. audio compact disk 12.95 (978-0-646-19145-4(4)) Joshua Bks AUS.

Dreams from My Father: A Story of Race & Inheritance. Barack Obama. Read by Barack Obama. 2008. audio compact disk (978-1-84767-328-2(7)) CanongateBooks GBR.

Dreams from My Father: A Story of Race & Inheritance. abr. ed. Barack Obama. Read by Barack Obama. (YA). 2007. 49.99 (978-0-7393-7471-9(0)) Find a World.

Dreams from My Father: A Story of Race & Inheritance. abr. ed. Barack Obama. Read by Barack Obama. 5 CDs. (Running Time: 7 hrs. 30 mins.). 2005. audio compact disk 25.95 (978-0-7393-2100-3(5)) Pub: Random Audio Pubg. Dist(s): Random

Dreams... God Speaks in the Night. Jack Deere. 1 cass. (Running Time: 90 mins.). (Hearing God's Voice Ser.: Vol. 3). 2000. 5.00 (JD04-003) Morning NC.
These messages are an outstanding collection that lay a solid & practical foundation for discerning God's voice.

Dreams in Time. 1 cass. (Running Time: 50 min.). 1998. (978-1-892450-26-5(7), 125) Promo Music.
Relaxation music.

Dreams into Action Vol. 1, Set: The Two Day Seminar. unabr. ed. Milton Katselas. 4 cass. (Running Time: 6 hr.). 1997. 25.00 (978-0-9676705-2-2(7)) Katselas.

Dreams of a Final Theory. unabr. ed. Steven Weinberger. Read by Jonathan Tindle. 1 CD. (Running Time: 9 hrs. 30 min.). 2001. audio compact disk 19.95 (zm2558) Blckstn Audio.
The Nobel Prize-winning physicist & author of "The First Three Minutes," describes the grand quest for a unifying theory of nature, one that can explain forces as different as the cohesion inside the atom & the gravitational tug between the sun & the earth.

Dreams of a Final Theory: The Scientist's Search for the Ultimate Laws of Nature. unabr. ed. Steven M. Weinberg. Read by Jonathan Tindle. 8 CDs. (Running Time: 10 hrs.). 2000. audio compact disk 64.00 (978-0-7861-9898-6(2), 2558) Blckstn Audio.
The Novel Prize-winning physicist & author of "The First Three Minutes," describes the grand quest for a unifying theory of nature, one that can explain forces as different as the cohesion inside the atom & the gravitational tug between the sun & the earth.

Dreams of a Final Theory: The Scientist's Search for the Ultimate Laws of Nature. unabr. ed. Steven Weinberger. Read by Jonathan Tindle. 7 cass. (Running Time: 10 hrs.). 2000. 49.95 (978-0-7861-1754-3(0), 2558) Blckstn Audio.

Dreams of Bali. Thomas M. Lopez. 2 CDs. (Running Time: 2 hrs.). 2001. audio compact disk 24.95 (ZBSF020) Lodestone Catalog.
Mojo Sam encounters some amazing physical & psychic twists & turns in New Mexico. You can follow Mojo the VooDoo man into his discovery of Native American spirituality.

Dreams of Bali. unabr. ed. Thomas M. Lopez. Read by Robert Lorick et al. 2 CDs. (Running Time: 2 hr.). Dramatization. (Travels with Jack Ser.). (J). (gr. 4 up). 1992. audio compact disk 24.95 (978-1-881137-90-0(2), ZBSF020) ZBS Found.
A two-hour adventure story with Jack Flanders in Bali. Environmental sounds & music digitally recorded at various locations in Bali. Ruth Maleczech is also a reader.

Dreams of Bali, Set. unabr. ed. Thomas M. Lopez. Read by Robert Lorick et al. 2 cass. (Running Time: 2 hr.). Dramatization. (Travels with Jack Ser.). (J). (gr. 4 up). 1992. 15.95 (978-1-881137-02-3(3), ZBSF019) ZBS Found.

Dreams of Bali: A Travels with Jack Adventure. Thomas M. Lopez. 2 cass. (Running Time: 2 hrs. 5 min.). 1996. 16.95 (978-1-57677-064-1(8)) Lodestone Catalog.
Travel with Jack to Bali to visit his old friend Tiffany, & hang on as the trip spins out of control when Jack is confronted with jealous rivalries, black magic, dreams, & spectral visits from a Balinese holy man. A marvelous blend of profound native wisdom & the mesmerizing music of Bali, digitally recorded on location, it will transport your mind directly into another culture, into a place where mystery, metaphysics, & humor freely mingle.

***Dreams of Home.** Migdalia Cruz. Contrib. by Lisa Marie Ackel et al. (Running Time: 2820 sec.). (L. A. Theatre Works Audio Theatre Collections). (ENG.). 2010. audio compact disk (978-1-58081-709-7(2)) L A Theatre.

Dreams of India. Thomas M. Lopez. 2 cass. (Running Time: 2 hrs.). 2001. 15.95 (ZBSF033); audio compact disk 25.00 (ZBSF034) Lodestone Catalog.
When an Indian woman hands Jack Flanders his own business card, claiming that he gave it to her aunt forty years ago, there is no doube in Jack's mind that another quest is about to unfold. He's off to New Delhi, Bombay & Bangalore! In an abandoned palace, he discovers a presence that speaks to him with his own voice.

Dreams of India. unabr. ed. Thomas M. Lopez. Read by Robert Lorick et al. 2 cass. (Running Time: 2 hrs.). Dramatization. (Travels with Jack Ser.). (J). (gr. 4 up). 1992. 15.00 Set. (978-1-881137-01-6(5)); audio compact disk 22.50 (978-1-881137-89-4(9)) ZBS Found.
From the radio series, "Travels with Jack," an adventure story with Jack Flanders in India. Environmental sounds & music digitally recorded at various locations throughout the subcontinent.

***Dreams of Joy: A Novel.** unabr. ed. Lisa See. (ENG.). 2011. audio compact disk 40.00 (978-0-7393-5935-8(5), Random AudioBks) Pub: Random Audio Pubg. Dist(s): Random

Dreams of My Russian Summers. Andreï Makine. Read by Geoffrey Howard. 6 cass. (Running Time: 9 hrs.). 1998. 48.00 (978-0-7366-4437-2(7), 4690) Books on Tape.
Coming of age story of a boy growing up amid the harsh realities of Soviet life in the 1960s & 1970s, softened only by summer visits with his grandmother. Through her subtly woven tales of war & revolution he learns of a Russia he has never known.

Dreams of My Russian Summers. abr. ed. Andreï Makine. Read by Alfred White. 2 cass. 1998. 17.95 Set. (978-1-55935-301-4(5)) Soundelux.
Chronicles a young Russian boy's summers spent with his beloved French grandmother & the stories she shares of an earlier time.

Dreams of My Russian Summers, unabr. collector's ed. Andreï Makine. Read by Geoffrey Howard. 6 cass. (Running Time: 9 hrs.). 1998. 48.00 (978-0-7366-4192-0(0), 896053) Books on Tape.
Coming of age story of a boy growing up amid the harsh realities of Soviet life in the 1960s & 1970s, softened only by summer visits with his grandmother. Through her subtly woven tales of war & revolution he learns of a Russia he has never known.

Dreams of Past Existence: The Archetypal Child in Wordsworth, Teaching & Ourselves. Read by Daniel Lindley, Jr. 1 cass. (Running Time: 90 min.). 1989. 10.95 (978-0-7822-0146-8(6), 363) C G Jung IL.

Dreams of Rio. Thomas M. Lopez. 5 cass. (Running Time: 6 hrs.). 2001. 29.95 (ZBSF013); audio compact disk 35.00 (ZBSF014) Lodestone Catalog.
Hypnotic voodoo beats, lush jungle noises, tropical rains, an alluring female anthropologist, as Jack Flanders travels through the mysterious wilds of Brazillian rainforests in search of the Lost City.

Dreams of Rio. unabr. ed. Meatball Fulton. Read by Robert Lorick et al. 5 cass., 5 CDs. (Running Time: 6 hrs.). Dramatization. (J). (gr. 4 up). 1987. 29.95 set. (978-1-881137-12-2(0)) ZBS Found.
Dreams of Rio is an engaging romp through the forests & samba clubs of Brazil. Music by Tim Clark is featured along with the luscious ambient sounds recorded by Fulton & Clark on location in Brazil.

Dreams of Rio, Set. Meatball Fulton. Read by Robert Lorick et al. Music by Tim Clark. 5 cass. (Running Time: 6 hr.). (Jack Flanders Ser.). 29.95 (ZBSF013) ZBS Ind.

Dreams of Rio, Set. unabr. ed. Meatball Fulton. Read by Robert Lorick et al. 6 CDs. (Running Time: 6 hr.). Dramatization. (J). (gr. 4 up). 1987. audio compact disk 35.00 (978-1-881137-47-4(3), ZBSF014) ZBS Found.

Dreams of Sleep & Rich in Love. Josephine Humphreys. Read by Josephine Humphreys. 1 cass. (Running Time: 81 min.). 1988. 13.95 (978-1-55644-295-7(5), 8061) Am Audio Prose.
A warm, precise & often sly reading of the first chapters of these two wonderful novels.

Dreams of Sumatra. unabr. ed. Thomas M. Lopez. Read by Robert Lorick et al. 2 cass. (Running Time: 2 hrs.). Dramatization. (Travels with Jack Ser.). (J). (gr. 4 up). 1993. 15.00 set. (978-1-881137-03-0(1)); audio compact disk 22.50 (978-1-881137-91-7(0)) ZBS Found.
From the radio series, "Travels with Jack". A two-hour adventure story with Jack Flanders in Sumatra. Environment sounds & music digitally recorded at various locations in Sumatra.

Dreams of the Amazon. unabr. ed. Thomas M. Lopez. Read by Robert Lorick et al. 2 cass. (Running Time: 2 hrs.). Dramatization. (Travels with Jack Ser.). 1992. 15.00 Set. (978-1-881137-00-9(7)); audio compact disk 22.50 (978-1-881137-88-7(0)) ZBS Found.
From the radio series, "Travels with Jack" a two-hour adventure story with Jack Flanders in India. Environmental sounds & music digitally recorded at various locations throughout the subcontinent.

Dreams of the Animals see Poetry & Voice of Margaret Atwood

Dreams that No One Can Steal. Elaine A. Scott. 2008. audio compact disk 34.99 (978-1-60604-090-4(1)) Tate Pubng.

Dreams Underfoot. unabr. ed. Charles de Lint. (Running Time: 14 hrs. 0 mins.). 2009. 29.95 (978-1-4332-6013-1(1)); audio compact disk 79.95 (978-1-4332-6009-4(3)); audio compact disk 99.00 (978-1-4332-6010-0(7)) Blckstn Audio.

Dreamscape. Windham Hill Staff. 1 cass. 1998. 15.00 (978-1-56170-558-0(6)) Hay House.

Dreamscapes-Music. 2007. audio compact disk 16.95 (978-1-56136-429-9(0)) Master Your Mind.

Dreamsnake. unabr. ed. Vonda N. McIntyre. Read by Anna Fields. 7 cass. (Running Time: 10 hrs. 30 mins.). 2000. 49.95 (978-0-7861-1809-0(1), 2608) Blckstn Audio.
The healer Snake is summoned & she travels the blasted landscape to save a sick child. With her she carries two serpents from whose venom she distills her medicine & a third, even more precious, the alien dreamsnake, whose bite can ease the fear & pain of death. But when her dreamsnake is killed by the primitive ignorance of those she has come to help, her powers as a healer are all but lost.

Dreamsnake. unabr. ed. Vonda N. McIntyre & Anna Fields. (Running Time: 10 hrs. NaN mins.). 2008. 29.95 (978-1-4332-5488-8(3)); audio compact disk 80.00 (978-1-4332-5487-1(5)) Blckstn Audio.

Dreamsongs. Perf. by Laurie Burke. Contrib. by Tony Carito. 1 cass., 1 CD. (J). 1998. 9.98; audio compact disk 15.98 CD. Music Design Inc.
A new family music collection of soothing original melodies & storybook imagery. Each lullaby has a positive, life-affirming message along with simple, regular rhythms akin to nursery rhymes & sweet melodies.

DreamTending. Stephen Aizenstat. 2007. audio compact disk 69.95 (978-1-59179-500-1(1)) Sounds True.

Dreamtime Journey: The Path of Direct Experience: A Shamanic Inner Journey. Jeremiah R. Abrams. Music by SoulFood. 2005. bk. 39.95 (978-0-9761015-9-8(9)) Zur Inst.

Dreamwalker: The Path of Sacred Power. abr. ed. Mary S. Rain. Read by Nancy Fish. 2 cass. (Running Time: 3 hrs.). 1997. 17.95 (978-1-57453-167-1(0)) Audio Lit.
Dreamwalkers travel the path of knowledge & go where the spirit of truth leads them. Brian Many Heart teaches Mary Summer Rain the magic & power of the Dreamwalker.

Dreamwork. Zoilita Grant. (ENG.). 2009. audio compact disk 16.95 (978-1-890575-40-3(2)) Zoilita Grant.

Dresden 1945: The Devil's Tinderbox. unabr. collector's ed. Alexander McKee. Read by Derek Morton. 9 cass. (Running Time: 13 hrs. 30 min.). 1988. 72.00 (978-0-7366-1349-1(8), 2250) Books on Tape.
Discusses what it was like to be in the flaming streets & smoke filled cellars of Dresden & in the cockpits & gun turrets of the warplanes overhead.

Dress Her in Indigo. unabr. collector's ed. John D. MacDonald. Read by Michael Prichard. 7 cass. (Running Time: 10 hrs. 30 min.). (Travis McGee Ser.: Vol. 11). 1980. 56.00 (978-0-7366-0243-3(7), 1239) Books on Tape.
Travis McGee is again the star in this adventure. This modern-day Sam Spade, accompanied by his friend Meyer, travels to the Mexican village of Oaxaca. There they meet all kinds - the gay, the depraved, the violent - in trying to determine the cause of a client's violent & tragic death.

Dress Lodger. Sheri Holman. Narrated by Nadia May. (Running Time: 13 hrs.). 2000. 41.95 (978-1-59912-653-1(2)) Iofy Corp.

Dress Lodger. unabr. ed. Sheri Holman. Read by Nadia May. 9 cass. (Running Time: 13 hrs.). 2000. 62.95 (978-0-7861-1819-9(9), 2618); audio compact disk 88.00 (978-0-7861-9852-8(4), 2618) Blckstn Audio.
Fifteen-year-old Gustine is a "dress lodger," a young prostitute who rents a beautiful blue dress from her landlord to attract a higher class of clientele. Gustine works to support her fragile only child, born with a remarkable anatomical defect. Surgeon Henry Chiver has come to Sunderland to escape his past & start a new life. During the worst epidemic since the bubonic plague, Gustine secures bodies for the doctor's school, until Henry's greed & his growing obsession with her child challenge her loyalty to him. With cholera bearing down on the city, Gustine must turn to her mortal enemy in her battle for the life & afterlife of her child.

Dress Rehearsal (Hypnosis), Vol. 32. Jayne Helle. 1 cass. (Running Time: 28 min.). 1996. 15.00 (978-1-891826-31-3(X)) Introspect.
A mental practice before an upcoming event. Used for any situation you are worried about, or want the most positive exercise for.

Dress Your Family in Corduroy & Denim. David Sedaris. 2005. 34.99 (978-1-59895-026-7(6)) Find a World.

Dress Your Family in Corduroy & Denim. unabr. ed. David Sedaris. Read by David Sedaris. (YA). 2005. 44.99 (978-1-59895-139-4(4)) Find a World.

Dress Your Family in Corduroy & Denim. unabr. ed. David Sedaris. (ENG.). 2005. 14.98 (978-1-59483-158-4(0)) Pub: Hachet Audio. Dist(s): HachBkGrp

Dress Your Family in Corduroy & Denim. unabr. ed. David Sedaris. (Running Time: 6 hrs. 30 mins.). (ENG.). 2009. 49.98 (978-1-60024-616-6(8)) Pub: Hachet Audio. Dist(s): HachBkGrp

***Dress Your Family in Corduroy & Denim.** unabr. ed. David Sedaris. Read by Author. (Running Time: 6 hrs. 30 mins.). (ENG.). 2011. audio compact disk 54.99 (978-1-61113-823-8(X)) Pub: Hachet Audio. Dist(s): HachBkGrp

Dress Your Family in Corduroy & Denim. unabr. rev. ed. David Sedaris. Read by David Sedaris. 5 cass. (Running Time: 6 hrs. 30 mins.). (ENG.). 2004. 26.98 (978-1-58621-501-9(9)); audio compact disk 31.98 (978-1-58621-502-6(7)) Pub: Hachet Audio. Dist(s): HachBkGrp

Dressage Formula: CD Audio. Erik Herbermann. (Running Time: 7 hrs. 0 mins. 0 sec.). (ENG.). 2008. audio compact disk 24.95 (978-0-9723875-1-4(X)) Pub: Traf Sq Bks. Dist(s): IPG Chicago

Dressed for Death, unabr. collector's ed. Donna Leon. Read by Anna Fields. 6 cass. (Running Time: 9 hrs.). (Commissario Guido Brunetti Mystery Ser.: Bk. 3). 1999. 48.00 (978-0-7366-4317-7(6), 4785) Books on Tape.
Respectable Venetians hardly notice the murder of a transvestite prostitute until the body is identified as the staid director of the Banca di Verona. Only Guido Brunetti suspects foul play.

Dressed to Steal. unabr. ed. Carolyn Keene. Read by Rebecca Rogers. (Running Time: 12600 sec.). (Nancy Drew: Girl Detective Ser.). (J). (gr. 3-7). 2007. audio compact disk 29.95 (978-1-4332-0039-7(2)) Blckstn Audio.

Dressed to Steal. unabr. ed. Carolyn Keene. Read by Rebecca Rogers. (Running Time: 12600 sec.). (Nancy Drew: Girl Detective Ser.). (J). (gr. 4-7). 2007. 24.95 (978-1-4332-0035-9(X)); audio compact disk 27.00 (978-1-4332-0036-6(8)) Blckstn Audio.

Dressed to Steal. unabr. ed. Carolyn Keene. Read by Rebecca Rogers. 3 CDs. (Running Time: 12600 sec.). (Nancy Drew: Girl Detective Ser.). (J). (gr. 3-7). 2007. audio compact disk 19.95 (978-1-4332-0038-0(4)) Blckstn Audio.

Dressed up Sammy, Cassette. Short Stories. 1 cassette tape. (Running Time: 13 mins.). (J). 2006. 4.95 (978-1-57874-275-2(7)) Kaeden Corp.

Dressed up Sammy, CD. Short Stories. Kathleen Urmston & Karen Evans. Narrated by Rick Sellers & Wesley McCraw. 1 CD. (Running Time: 16 mins). (J). 2005. audio compact disk 7.95 (978-1-57874-099-4(1)) Kaeden Corp.

Dressing Do's: How to Dress Without the Stress. Text by Twin Sisters Productions Staff. 1 CD. (Running Time: 30 mins). (J). 2004. audio compact disk 12.99 (978-1-57583-730-7(7)) Twin Sisters.
Great new songs for parent and child to enjoy together each morning. Kids will have fun while learning color and pattern matching; to dress for the weather; what clothes go on first and last; the sequence of zip, button, buckle and tie! Enhanced CD includes activities, coloring pages, and a parent guide that can be printed from any home computer.

Dressing up for the Carnival, unabr. ed. Carol Shields. 4 cass. (Running Time: 6 hrs.). 2000. 25.00 (978-1-57453-352-1(5)) Audio Lit.
This playful yet tender collection distills her elegance, wisdom & insouciant humor into 22 compact & delicious stories. Through them all runs a preoccupation with identity. In the title story a procession of characters try on new selves.

***Dressler's Sum & Substance Audio on Criminal Law.** 5th rev. ed. Joshua Dressler. (Sum & Substance Ser.). 2010. audio compact disk 74.00 (978-0-314-26690-3(9), West Lglwrks) West.

***Dressler's Sum & Substance Audio on Criminal Law.** 5th rev. ed. West. (Sum & Substance Ser.). 2010. audio compact disk 74.00 (978-0-314-26691-0(7), West Lglwrks) West.

Dressmaker. unabr. ed. Beryl Bainbridge. Read by Jacqueline King. 5 cass. (Running Time: 5 hrs. 10 mins.). (Sound Ser.). 2002. 49.95 (978-1-86042-610-0(7)) Pub: UlverLrgPrint GBR. Dist(s): Ulverscroft US
If Liverpool, 1944, was grim for Rita and her two aunts, Nellie and Margo, Rita knew that life in America was gay and rich, she's seen it all in the films. So when her G.I. came to call, she was sure that love and escape had come at last. But Nellie, who slaved for them all and kept the town in clothes, knew different: the boy would have to go. And in the end, it wasn't really her fault.

Dressmaker. unabr. ed. Beryl Bainbridge. Read by Jacqueline King. 5 CDs. (Running Time: 18600 sec.). (Sound Ser.). 2003. audio compact disk 59.95 (978-1-84283-169-4(0)) Pub: UlverLrgPrint GBR. Dist(s): Ulverscroft US

***Dressmaker of Khair Khana: Five Sisters, One Remarkable Family, & the Woman Who Risked Everything to Keep Them Safe.** unabr. ed. Gayle Tzemach Lemmon. (ENG.). 2011. (978-0-06-202745-0(X), Harper Audio) HarperCollins Pubs.

Drew Pearson: Wide Receiver. Read by Drew Pearson. 1 cass. 9.95 (978-0-89811-082-1(3), 7133) Lets Talk Assocs.
Drew Pearson talks about the people & events which influenced his career, & his approach to his speciality.

Drew Smith's "Play by Ear" Autoharp Workshop. 2 cass. 22.95 Set, incl. illustrated guide. (C-572) Folk-Legacy.

Dreyfus Case. 1 cass. (Running Time: 39 min.). 10.00 (HE801) Esstee Audios.
Details abound regarding French politics, army intrigue, religious factionalism, Dreyfus' personality, conflict with Germany, the two court trials, Dreyfus' reinstatement, & some reference to debates among Dreyfusards & revisionist historians.

DRG Desk Reference: The Ultimate Resource for Improving MS-DRG Assignment Practices. Created by Ingenix. 2008. audio compact disk 199.95 (978-1-60151-150-8(7)) Ingenix Inc.

DRG Expert: A Comprehensive Guidebook to the DRG Classification System. Created by Ingenix. 2008. audio compact disk 119.95 (978-1-60151-146-1(9)) Ingenix Inc.

Drift. John Ridley. Narrated by J. D. Jackson. 8 cass. (Running Time: 10 hrs. 30 mins.). 64.00 (978-1-4025-3676-2(3)) Recorded Bks.

***Drift.** Penni Russon. Read by Melissa Eccleston. (Running Time: 8 hrs. 35 mins.). (YA). 2009. 59.99 (978-1-74214-355-2(5), 9781742143552) Pub: Bolinda Pubng AUS. Dist(s): Bolinda Pub Inc

Drift. unabr. ed. Penni Russon. Read by Melissa Eccleston. (Running Time: 30900 sec.). 2008. audio compact disk 83.95 (978-1-921334-99-3(1), 9781921334993) Pub: Bolinda Pubng AUS. Dist(s): Bolinda Pub Inc

Drift Fence. unabr. collector's ed. Zane Grey. Read by Dan Lazar. 7 cass. (Running Time: 7 hrs.). 1929. 42.00 (978-0-7366-0325-6(5), 1311) Books on Tape.
When the first drift fence was built across a free cattle range, bitter feelings burst forth among the ranchers. Jim Traft, the tenderfoot in charge of building the fence, found himself in deep trouble. It took all his wits to stay alive, let alone complete the fence.

Drift House: The First Voyage. unabr. ed. Dale Peck. Narrated by Richard Poe. 10 CDs. (Running Time: 11 hrs. 45 mins.). 2005. audio compact disk 116.75 (978-1-4193-6653-6(X), C3488); 71.75 (978-1-4193-6639-0(4), 98236) Recorded Bks.
New York-based author and teacher Dale Peck was inspired to write this amazing story after the events of September 11, 2001. The three Oakenfeld children - Susan, Charles and Murray - are perplexed. Their parents aren't letting them turn on the television. Something strange is going on in the city, that's for sure. And now Mom and Dad are sending them off to Canada to stay with their Uncle Farley - who they've never even met!.

Drifter: Men of the Saddle. unabr. ed. Lori Copeland. 6 cass. (Running Time: 9 hrs.). 2005. 59.75 (978-1-4193-4835-8(3)) Recorded Bks.

Drifters. unabr. ed. James A. Michener. Read by Larry McKeever. 13 cass. (Running Time: 19 hrs. 30 min.). 1994. 104.00 (3492A); 96.00 (978-0-7366-2772-6(3), 3492B) Books on Tape.
Six disenchanted young runaways live in a dark, private world created out of dreams, drugs & dedication to pleasure.

Drifting Cowboy, unabr. collector's ed. Short Stories. Will James. Read by Connor O'Brien. 4 cass. (Running Time: 6 hrs.). (Tumbleweed Ser.). 1999. 32.00 (978-0-7366-4400-6(8), 4861) Books on Tape.
Seven stories revolving around the adventures of a lanky cowboy named Bill, whose drifting takes him throughout the West, from Montana to Arizona, as he lives the hard life of a working cowboy.

Drifting off to Sleep. unabr. ed. Mitch Meyerson. 1 cass. (Running Time: 50 min.). (Unassigned Ser.). (ENG.). 2001. reel tape 11.95 (978-1-57224-225-8(6)) New Harbinger.
This soothing tape provides those who have difficulty falling asleep with guided imagery, relaxing music, and gentle natural sounds that will ease them into a good night's rest.

Driftless. unabr. ed. David Rhodes. (Running Time: 15 hrs. 30 mins.). 2010. 29.95 (978-1-4417-2165-5(7)); 85.95 (978-1-4417-2161-7(4)); audio compact disk 118.00 (978-1-4417-2162-4(2)) Blckstn Audio.

***Driftwood Cottage: A Chesapeake Shores Novel.** abr. ed. Sherryl Woods. (Running Time: 6 hrs.). (Chesapeake Shores Ser.). 2011. 9.99 (978-1-4558-0488-7(6), 9781455804887, BAD); audio compact disk 14.99 (978-1-61106-994-5(7), 9781611069945, BACD) Brilliance Audio.

***Driftwood Cottage: A Chesapeake Shores Novel.** unabr. ed. Sherryl Woods. (Running Time: 11 hrs.). (Chesapeake Shores Ser.). 2011. 39.97 (978-1-61106-993-8(9), 9781611069938, BADLE); 24.99 (978-1-61106-990-7(4), 9781611069907, Brilliance MP3); 39.97 (978-1-61106-991-4(2), 9781611069914, Brlnc Audio MP3 Lib); 24.99 (978-1-61106-992-1(0), 9781611069921, BAD); audio compact disk 29.99 (978-1-61106-988-4(2), 9781611069884, Bril Audio CD Unabri); audio compact disk 79.97 (978-1-61106-989-1(0), 9781611069891, BriAudCD Unabrid) Brilliance Audio.

***Driftwood Summer.** unabr. ed. Patti Callahan Henry. (Running Time: 10 hrs.). 2010. 24.99 (978-1-4418-6190-0(4), 9781441861900, BAD); 39.97 (978-1-4418-6191-7(2), 9781441861917, BADLE) Brilliance Audio.

***Driftwood Summer.** unabr. ed. Patti Callahan Henry. Read by Julia Whelan. (Running Time: 10 hrs.). 2010. 24.99 (978-1-4418-6188-7(2), 9781441861887, Brilliance MP3); 39.97 (978-1-4418-6189-4(0), 9781441861894, Brlnc Audio MP3 Lib); audio compact disk 29.99 (978-1-4418-6186-3(6), 9781441861863, Bril Audio CD Unabri); audio compact disk 79.97 (978-1-4418-6187-0(4), 9781441861870, BriAudCD Unabrid) Brilliance Audio.

Drill Here, Drill Now, Pay Less: A Handbook for Slashing Gas Prices & Solving Our Energy Crisis. unabr. ed. Newt Gingrich. Narrated by Newt Gingrich. Narrated by Callista Gingrich. (Running Time: 3 hrs. 53 mins. 31 sec.). (ENG.). 2008. 12.59 (978-1-60814-175-3(6), SpringWater) Oasis Audio.

Drill Here Drill Now Pay Less: Slashing Gas Prices & Solving Our Energy Crisis. unabr. ed. Newt Gingrich. Narrated by Newt Gingrich. Narrated by Callista Gingrich. (Running Time: 3 hrs. 53 mins. 31 sec.). (ENG.). 2008. instr.'s hndbk. ed. 17.99 (978-1-59859-524-6(5)) Oasis Audio.

Drillmaster of Valley Forge: The Baron de Steuben & the Making of the American Army. unabr. ed. Paul Douglas Lockhart. (Running Time: 12 hrs. 0 mins. 0 sec.). (ENG.). 2008. audio compact disk 69.99 (978-1-4001-3968-2(6)) Pub: Tantor Media. Dist(s): IngramPubServ

Drillmaster of Valley Forge: The Baron de Steuben & the Making of the American Army. unabr. ed. Paul Douglas Lockhart. Read by Norman Dietz. (Running Time: 12 hrs. 0 mins. 0 sec.). (ENG.). 2008. audio compact disk 34.99 (978-1-4001-0968-5(X)); audio compact disk 24.99 (978-1-4001-5968-0(7)) Pub: Tantor Media. Dist(s): IngramPubServ

Drink in the Passage see Tales from a Troubled Land

Drink, Play, F@#K: One Man's Search for Anything Across Ireland, Las Vegas, & Thailand. unabr. ed. Andrew Gottlieb. Read by Dick Hill. (Running Time: 6 hrs.). 2009. 19.99 (978-1-4233-8300-0(1), 9781423383000, BAD); 39.97 (978-1-4233-8301-7(X), 9781423383017, BADLE); 19.99 (978-1-4233-8298-0(6), 9781423382980, Brilliance MP3); 39.97 (978-1-4233-8299-7(4), 9781423382997, Brlnc Audio MP3 Lib); audio compact disk 74.97 (978-1-4233-8297-3(8), 9781423382973, BriAudCD Unabrid); audio compact disk 19.99 (978-1-4233-8296-6(X), 9781423382966, Bril Audio CD Unabri) Brilliance Audio.

Drink with the Devil. Jack Higgins. Read by Patrick Macnee. (Sean Dillon Ser.). 2008. 59.99 (978-1-60640-660-1(4)) Find a World.

Drink with the Devil. unabr. ed. Jack Higgins. Perf. by Patrick Macnee. 6 cass. (Running Time: 9 hrs.). (Sean Dillon Ser.). 2001. 32.00 (978-1-59040-065-4(8), Phoenix Audio) Pub: Amer Intl Pub. Dist(s): PerseuPGW
The hijacked barge Irish Rose is at the disposal of terrorists who are planning an Irish civil war.

***Drink with the Devil.** unabr. ed. Jack Higgins. Read by Michael Page. (Running Time: 7 hrs.). (Sean Dillon Ser.). 2010. 24.99 (978-1-4418-4348-7(5), 9781441843487, BAD); 39.97 (978-1-4418-4347-0(7), 9781441843470, Brlnc Audio MP3 Lib); 39.97 (978-1-4418-4349-4(3), 9781441843494, BADLE); 24.99 (978-1-4418-4346-3(9), 9781441843463, Brilliance MP3); audio compact disk 87.97 (978-1-4418-4345-6(0), 9781441843456, BriAudCD Unabrid);

audio compact disk 29.99 (978-1-4418-4344-9(2), 9781441843449, Bril Audio CD Unabri) Brilliance Audio.

Drink with the Devil. unabr. ed. Jack Higgins. Perf. by Patrick Macnee. 6 cass. (Running Time: 9 hrs.). (Sean Dillon Ser.). 2004. 32.95 (978-1-59007-189-2(1)) Pub: New Millenn Enter. Dist(s): PerseuPGW
Sean Dillon, master of disguise and steady Higgins hero (Angel of Death, etc.), returns for another go against political mayhem in the author's latest action-fest. A 1985 hijacking of gold bullion, masterminded by Irish Protestant terrorist Michael Ryan, ends with the ship that's carrying the booty sinking off Ireland. Ryan and his niece Kathleen flee to America while their presumed henchman, seemingly a sailor but actually a disguised Dillon, then an IRA enforcer, ostensibly returns to sea. Ten years later, Ryan is sprung from an American medical prison by a Mafia lawyer intent on retrieving the bullion. Soon the gold is the object of desire of the mob, a retired IRA chief of staff and British Intelligence, for whom Dillon now works.

Drink with the Devil, Set. unabr. ed. Jack Higgins. Read by Patrick Macnee. 6 cass. (Sean Dillon Ser.). 1999. 29.95 (FS9-34529) Highsmith.

Drinking Coffee Elsewhere. unabr. ed. Z. Z. Packer. Read by Shirley Jordan. (YA). 2006. 44.99 (978-1-59895-569-9(1)) Find a World.

Drinking Deeply from the Chalice Well. Jean S. Bolen. 4 cass. (Running Time: 6 hrs.). 1990. 31.95 Set. (978-0-7822-0025-6(7), 428) C G Jung IL.
Pure spring water flows from the Chalice Well at Glastonbury where the Grail was purportedly once hidden. Taking this image as a symbol for our own spiritual wellsprings, San Francisco analyst & author Bolen shares myths, stories, & guided meditations which provide the opportunity for listeners to venture inward & reconnect with their personal sacred places.

Drinking from a Cup Made Cinchy see Assorted Prose

***Drinking Gourd.** unabr. ed. F. N. Monjo. Read by Rick Adamson. Illus. by Fred Brenner. (ENG.). 2008. (978-0-06-166921-7(0)); (978-0-06-166922-4(9)) HarperCollins Pubs.

Drinking Gourd: A Story of the Underground Railroad. unabr. abr. ed. F. N. Monjo. Illus. by Fred Brenner. 1 cass. (I Can Read Bks.). (J). (gr. k-3). 1991. 8.99 (978-1-55994-355-0(6), TBC 3556) HarperCollins Pubs.

Drinking Song. (23297-A) J Norton Pubs.

Drinking with the Moon: A Guide to Classical Chinese Poetry. Jeannette L. Faurot. (CHI & ENG.). 1998. bk. 9.95 (978-0-8351-2640-3(4), DRMOT) China Bks.

Drioball na Faineoige. Contrib. by Johnny Connolly. (ENG.). 1998. 13.95 (978-0-8023-7127-0(2)); audio compact disk 21.95 (978-0-8023-8127-9(8)) Pub: Clo Iar-Chonnachta IRL. Dist(s): Dufour

***Drip, Drop.** unabr. ed. Sarah Weeks. (ENG.). 2008. (978-0-06-172958-4(2)); (978-0-06-169415-8(0)) HarperCollins Pubs.

Drive. unabr. ed. James Sallis. Read by Paul Michael Garcia. (Running Time: 12600 sec.). 2007. 24.95 (978-1-4332-0865-2(2)); audio compact disk 19.95 (978-1-4332-0867-6(9)); audio compact disk 27.00 (978-1-4332-0866-9(0)) Blckstn Audio.

Drive: The Surprising Truth about What Motivates Us. unabr. ed. Daniel H. Pink. Contrib. by Daniel H. Pink. 5 CDs. (Running Time: 6 hrs.). (ENG.). (gr. 12 up). 2010. audio compact disk 29.95 (978-0-14-314508-0(8), PengAudBks) Penguin Grp USA.

***Drive: The Surprising Truth about What Motivates Us.** unabr. ed. Daniel H. Pink. Read by Daniel H. Pink. 5 CDs. (Running Time: 6 hrs.). 2010. audio compact disk 50.00 (978-0-307-70216-6(2), BksonTape) Pub: Random Audio Pubg. Dist(s): Random

Drive Away Back Pain. Robert L. Swezey. Read by Robert L. Swezey. 2 cass. (Running Time: 1 hr. 05 min.). 1994. 16.95 Set. (978-1-881206-02-6(5)) Cequal Pubng.
A whole new concept - back relief as you drive! Dr. Swezey's self-care audio program shows you how to reduce muscle tension & tight ligaments that are a major factor in back & neck pain. It takes you step by step through conditioning & safeguarding your back while you drive.

Drive Business Performance: Enabling a Culture of Intelligent Execution. unabr. abr. ed. Bruno Aziza & Joey Fitts. Read by Jim Bond. (Running Time: 7 hrs.). 2008. 39.25 (978-1-4233-6034-6(6), 9781423360346, BADLE); 24.95 (978-1-4233-6033-9(8), 9781423360339, BAD); audio compact disk 39.25 (978-1-4233-6032-2(X), 9781423360322, Brinc Audio MP3 Lib); audio compact disk 82.25 (978-1-4233-6030-8(3), 9781423360308, BriAudCD Unabrid); audio compact disk 24.95 (978-1-4233-6031-5(1), 9781423360315, Brilliance MP3); audio compact disk 29.95 (978-1-4233-6029-2(X), 9781423360292, Bril Audio CD Unabri) Brilliance Audio.

Drive-By. unabr. ed. Lynne Ewing. Narrated by Robert Ramirez. 4 cass. (Running Time: 1 hr. 30 mins.). (gr. 3 up). 2002. 12.00 (978-1-4025-0739-7(9)) Recorded Bks.
Jimmy is dead - a victim of gang violence in Los Angeles. Gunned down in front of his family, he was accused of skimming drug-money from Ice Breaker Joe and Lamar. Jimmy's younger brother Tito knows Jimmy hated gangs - how could he have been involved with these criminals? Now the gangbangers are looking for Tito. He needs to find their missing money soon, or his family may be hurt. Dodging taggers, hustlers and dealers along the way, Tito comes up with a plan that may save his family and put the gangbangers away forever.

***Drive by Church History.** Prod. by Burning Bush Communications. Instructed by Todd Friel. (ENG.). 2010. audio compact disk (978-0-9824991-3-9(2)) Burn Bush Comm.

Drive-by Comedy: Qyick Wit from David Brenner, George Carlin, Margaret Cho, Al Franken, Amy Sedaris, Paul Dinello & Stephen Colbert. unabr. ed. David Brenner et al. 1 CD. (Running Time: 1 hr.). (ENG.). 2003. audio compact disk 9.99 (978-1-56511-818-8(9), 1565118189) Pub: HighBridge. Dist(s): Workman Pub

Drive by Theology. Prod. by Burning Bush Communications. Instructed by Todd Friel & R. W. Glenn. (ENG.). 2009. audio compact disk (978-0-9786075-9-3(7)) Burn Bush Comm.

Drive Factor: Getting Your Life in Gear for the 7 Areas That Matter Most. Rick Sarkisian. 2 CDs. (Running Time: 2 hours). 2004. audio compact disk 19.95 (978-0-9743962-2-4(2)) LifeWork Pr.
Audio book version of The Drive Factor by Rick Sarkisian, Ph.D., as read by the author.

Drive-In French for Kids. (J). 2000. 9.95 (978-0-658-01080-4(8), 010808) M-H Contemporary.

Drive-In French for Kids: Songs & Games for On-the-Go Children. NTC Publishing Group Staff. 1. (Running Time: 45 min.). (Drive-In Ser.). (FRE & ENG., (ps-2). 2000. pap. bk. 9.95 (978-0-658-00868-9(4), 008684) McGraw.

Drive-In Spanish for Kids. (J). 2000. audio compact disk 9.95 (978-0-658-01079-8(4), 010794) M-H Contemporary.

Drive Me Crazy. Eric Jerome Dickey. Read by Richard Allen. (Playaway Adult Fiction Ser.). 2008. 69.99 (978-1-60640-801-8(1)) Find a World.

Drive Me Crazy. unabr. ed. Eric Jerome Dickey. Read by Richard Allen. 7 cass. (Running Time: 10 hrs.). 2004. 32.95 (978-1-59355-833-8(3), 1593558333, BAU); audio compact disk 97.25 (978-1-59355-837-6(6), 1593558376, BACDLib Ed); 24.95 (978-1-59335-760-3(5), 1593357605, Brilliance MP3); 39.25 (978-1-59335-894-5(6), 1593358946, Brinc Audio MP3 Lib); 82.25 (978-1-59355-834-5(1), 1593558341, BAudLibEd); audio compact disk 36.95 (978-1-59355-836-9(8), 1593558368, Bril Audio CD Unabri) Brilliance Audio.
"Driver" is an ex-con trying to make his life right but who shares an expensive secret and a past affair with his boss's wife - a woman who is nothing but trouble. Dickey's rich characters make listeners feel as if they are present in the hustle-filled pool hall, the bedroom, and the Lincoln Town Car that "Driver" chauffeurs his wealthy and notorious clients around in. Dickey's millions of fans will be happy to see the reappearance of a femme fatale from Thieves' Paradise, who adds spice and surprises every time she turns up.

Drive Me Crazy. unabr. ed. Eric Jerome Dickey. Read by Richard Allen. (Running Time: 10 hrs.). 2004. 39.25 (978-1-59710-231-5(8), 1597102318, BADLE); 24.95 (978-1-59710-230-8(X), 159710230X, BAD) Brilliance Audio.

Drive Safely. 1 cass. (Running Time: 60 min.). 10.95 (053) Psych Res Inst.
Reinforcement of safe driving principles with a release of tension, frustration & stress.

Drive Time, Vol. 7. Perf. by Focus on the Family Staff. 6 cass. (Running Time: 6 hrs.). (Adventures in Odyssey Ser.). (YA). (gr. 2-6). 2004. 24.99 (978-1-56179-976-3(9)); audio compact disk 24.99 (978-1-56179-977-0(7)) Pub: Focus Family. Dist(s): Tommy Nelson
Bringing favorite stories together in new ways & characters learn valuable lessons while on vacation or traveling in the car. Each volume containing 6 hrs. (12 episodes) of radio drama, packed with powerful lessons for kids.

Drive Time: German - Learn German While You Drive. unabr. l.t. ed. Living Language Staff. (All-Audio Courses Ser.). (GER & ENG.). 2006. audio compact disk 21.95 (978-1-4000-2162-8(6), LivingLang) Pub: Random Info Grp. Dist(s): Random

Drive-Time De-Stress Hypnosis. Scripts. Marjorie Baker Price. 2 cassettes. (Running Time: 60 minutes). 1992. 16.95 (978-0-9713013-2-0(8)) Centering Pubns.
Leave stress behind, clear and center yourself with this powerful, relaxing 2 tape audio set; "Drive-Time: Clearing and Centering Yourself" and "Drive-Time: Leaving Your Work Behind". Put in the tape at the end of your work day and arrive home relaxed and recharged.

Drive-Time Message for Men: Daily Devotions for Your Commute. Jeff Atwood & Smith Management. Read by Matt Moran. Prod. by Jeff Atwood. Contrib. by Ron Smith. Prod. by Steven V. Taylor. (ENG.). 2006. audio compact disk 7.99 (978-1-60006-071-7(4)) NavPress.

Drive-Time Message for Men Vol. 2: Daily Devotions for Your Commute. Jeff Atwood & Smith Management. Read by Matt Moran. (ENG.). 2007. audio compact disk 7.99 (978-1-60006-142-4(7)) NavPress.

Drive-Time Message for Women No. 1: Daily Devotions for Your Commute. Eugene H. Peterson & Smith Management. 2006. audio compact disk 7.99 (978-1-60006-072-4(2)) NavPress.

Drive-Time Message for Women No. 2: Daily Devotions for Your Commute. Jeff Atwood & Smith Management. Read by Faith Murphy. 2007. audio compact disk 7.99 (978-1-60006-143-1(5)) NavPress.

***Driven.** Larry Miller. 2010. audio compact disk 49.99 (978-1-60641-787-4(8)) Deseret Bk.

Driven Patriot Pt. 2: The Life & Times of James Forrestal. unabr. collector's ed. Townsend Hoopes & Douglas Brinkley. Read by Jonathan Reese. 9 cass. (Running Time: 13 hrs. 30 min.). 1993. 72.00 (978-0-7366-2520-3(8), 3275A); 64.00 (978-0-7366-2521-0(6), 3275-B) Books on Tape.
The life & tragic death of James Forrestal, our first Secretary of Defense. A classic about the Truman era.

Driven to Death. abr. ed. Engle & Barnes. (Running Time: 2 hrs.). (Strange Matter Ser.). 2006. 9.95 (978-1-4233-0884-3(0), 9781423308843, BAD) Brilliance Audio.

Driven to Death. abr. ed. Engle & Julian Barnes. Read by Multivoice Production Staff. (Running Time: 2 hrs.). (Strange Matter Ser.). 2006. 25.25 (978-1-4233-0885-0(9), 9781423308850, BADLE) Brilliance Audio.

Driven to Death. abr. ed. Marty M. Engle & Johnny Ray Barnes, Jr. (Running Time: 7200 sec.). (Strange Matter Ser.). (J). (gr. 4-7). 2006. audio compact disk 25.25 (978-1-4233-0883-6(2), 9781423308836, BACDLib Ed); audio compact disk 9.95 (978-1-4233-0882-9(4), 9781423308829, BACD) Brilliance Audio.
Darren Donaldson is staring out his bedroom window at 2 o'clock in the morning, panicked, looking down the street for any sign of his brother. His older brother, David, snuck out of the house at midnight, taking the car as usual, making Darren promise he wouldn't tell. He's been gone for three hours, the longest he's even been gone. Something must have happened. Something dreadful. Wait! There's David now! The car is coming down the street. He's killed the engine, coasting toward the driveway. He's scrambling out of the car, pushing it from behind. He looks frantic, terrified! What's going on? He's signaling for help, looking over his shoulder as if... Headlights snap on at the end of street as an engine roars to life. David is screaming! Something is chasing him... and it isn't stopping.

Driven to Distraction: Recognizing & Coping with Attention Deficit Disorder from Childhood Through Adulthood. Edward M. Hallowell & John J. Ratey. Narrated by John McDonough. 10 cass. (Running Time: 13 hrs. 45 mins.). 92.00 (978-1-4025-0986-5(3)) Recorded Bks.

Driven to Distraction: Recognizing & Coping with Attention Deficit Disorder from Childhood Through Adulthood. abr. ed. Edward M. Hallowell & John J. Ratey. 1 cass. (Running Time: 2 hrs.). 1999. 16.00 (61218) Courage-to-Change.
A guide to recognizing & coping with Attention Deficit Disorder from childhood through adulthood.

Driven to Distraction: Recognizing & Coping with Attention Deficit Disorder from Childhood Through Adulthood. unabr. abr. ed. Edward M. Hallowell & John J. Ratey. Read by Edward M. Hallowell. 2 CDs. (Running Time: 20 hrs. 0 mins. 0 sec.). (ENG.). 2003. audio compact disk 19.95 (978-0-7435-2900-6(6), Sound Ideas) Pub: S&S Audio. Dist(s): S and S Inc
THE NATIONAL AUDIO BESTSELLER Procrastination. Disorganization. Distractibility. Millions of adults have long considered these the hallmarks of a lack of self-discipline. But for many, these and other problems in school, at work and in social relationships are actually symptoms of an inborn neurological problem: ADD, or Attention Deficit Disorder. Through vivid stories of the experiences of their patients - both adults and children - Dr. Edward R. Hallowell and Dr. John J. Ratey show the varied forms ADD takes - from the hyperactive search for high stimulation to the floating inattention of daydreaming - and the transforming impact of precise diagnosis and treatment. Driven to Distraction is a must listen for everyone intrigued by the workings of the human mind.

Driven to Perfection: From Road Rage to Road Sage. Solo. Ed. by Judith Slater. Photos by Judith Slater. 2000. bk. 15.95 (978-1-893359-00-0(X)) Winward Ways.

Driven to Perfection: Graduation from Hell. Jack Mothershed & Jean Bolin. 2 CDs. (Running Time: 2 hrs.). 2000. audio compact disk 15.95 (978-1-893359-30-7(1)) Winward Ways.

Driven to Perfection: Messages from the Mountains. Jack Mothershed & Connard Hogan. 2 CDs. (Running Time: 2 hrs.). 2000. audio compact disk 15.95 (978-1-893359-20-8(4)) Winward Ways.

Driven to Perfection: Mourning, Meaning, Moving On. Judith Slater & Jack Mothershed. 2 CDs. (Running Time: 2 hrs.). 2000. audio compact disk 15.95 (978-1-893359-05-5(0)) Winward Ways.

Driven to Perfection: Paragliders, Paracletes, Paradoxes. 2 CDs. (Running Time: 2 hrs.). 2000. audio compact disk 15.95 (978-1-893359-25-3(5)) Winward Ways.

Driven to Puff-X-shun: From Sucks to Success. Jack Mothershed. 2 CDs. (Running Time: 2 hrs.). 2000. audio compact disk 15.95 (978-1-893359-15-4(8)) Winward Ways.

Driven to Purr-fection: Lessons in Feline Finesse. Judith Slater. 2 CDs. (Running Time: 2 hrs.). 2000. audio compact disk 15.95 (978-1-893359-10-9(7)) Winward Ways.

***Driven West: Andrew Jackson's Trail of Tears to the Civil War.** unabr. ed. A. J. Langguth. (Running Time: 14 hrs. 0 mins.). 2010. 39.99 (978-1-4001-9849-8(6)); 29.99 (978-1-4001-6849-1(X)); 19.99 (978-1-4001-8849-9(0)); audio compact disk 39.99 (978-1-4001-1849-6(2)); audio compact disk 95.99 (978-1-4001-4849-3(9)) Pub: Tantor Media. Dist(s): IngramPubServ

Driver. Perf. by Ferron. 1 cass. (Running Time: 62 min.). 1994. 9.98 Norelco. (978-1-56628-050-1(8), EB 2272/WB 4EB D2272/WB 42564-2); 15.98 (978-1-56628-051-8(6), EB D2272/WB 42564-2) MFLP CA.
Original folk music.

Driver #8. abr. ed. Dale Earnhardt & Jade Gurss. Read by David Thomas. (ENG.). 2005. 14.98 (978-1-59483-379-3(6)) Pub: Hachet Audio. Dist(s): HachBkGrp

Driver's Ed. Caroline B. Cooney. Narrated by George Guidall. 5 CDs. (Running Time: 5 hrs. 45 mins.). (gr. 9 up). 2000. audio compact disk 48.00 (978-0-7887-4965-0(X), C1310E7) Recorded Bks.
When 15-year-old Remy Marland goes along with a driver's ed class prank of stealing road signs, it looks to be harmless fun. However, when fun turns to vandalism, events spiral out of control to a deadly conclusion. Available to libraries only.

Driver's Ed. unabr. ed. Caroline B. Cooney. Narrated by George Guidall. 4 pieces. (Running Time: 5 hrs. 45 mins.). (gr. 9 up). 35.00 (978-0-7887-0542-7(3), 94737E7) Recorded Bks.

Driving Force. unabr. ed. Dick Francis. Read by David Case. 8 cass. (Running Time: 12 hrs.). 1994. 64.00 (978-0-7366-2613-2(1), 3355) Books on Tape.
Freddie Croft, a young ex-jockey, owns a profitable fleet of horse vans. A man with few illusions about racing's dark side, Freddie is a stickler for security. So imagine his anger when a driver not only breaks the rules (never pick up a hitchhiker), but the hitchhiker dies in the van.

Driving Force. unabr. ed. Dick Francis. Narrated by Simon Prebble. 7 cass. (Running Time: 10 hrs. 30 mins.). 1993. 60.00 (978-1-55690-788-3(5), 93107E7) Recorded Bks.
Former jockey Freddie Croft, a race horse transporter, comes to realize his vans are smuggling an unusual cargo: a horse virus, whose discovery has led to the murder of one of his employees.

Driving Growth Through Leadership. 2005. audio compact disk (978-0-9755044-1-3(X)) Leadership Strtgies.

Driving Home: Six Visits with Dr. Martin Marty on Health, Faith & Ethics. Martin E. Marty. 3 cass. (Running Time: 6 hrs.). 2000. 39.95 (978-0-945482-03-1(5)) Park Ridge Ctr.
Six topics related to health, faith & ethics.

Driving in the Dark. unabr. ed. Deborah Moggach. Read by Richard Earthy. 6 cass. (Running Time: 8 hrs.). 1994. 54.95 (978-1-85695-813-4(2), 941011) Pub: ISIS Audio GBR. Dist(s): Ulverscroft US
Desmond never did have much luck with women - except for getting them through their driving tests. Now a bus driver, he is at the most crucial crossroads of his life, for his wife had thrown him out. He sees as a way out of his despair - to steer the bus on a spectacularly reckless quest for the son he has never seen.

***Driving Like Crazy: Thirty Years of Vehicular Hell-Bending Celebrating America the Way It's Supposed to Be - with & Oil Well in Every Backyard, a Cadillac Escalade in Every Carport, & the Chairman of the Federal Reserve Mowing Our Lawn.** P. J. O'Rourke. Read by Christopher Lane. (Playaway Adult Nonfiction Ser.). (ENG.). 2009. 54.99 (978-1-4418-2969-6(5)) Find a World.

Driving Like Crazy: Thirty Years of Vehicular Hell-Bending, Celebrating America the Way It's Supposed to Be - with an Oil Well in Every Backyard, a Cadillac Escalade in Every Carport, & the Chairman of the Federal Reserve Mowing Our Lawn. unabr. ed. P. J. O'Rourke. Read by Christopher A. Lane. 1 MP3-CD. (Running Time: 8 hrs.). 2009. 14.99 (978-1-4233-9673-4(1), 9781423396734, Brilliance MP3) Brilliance Audio.

Driving Like Crazy: Thirty Years of Vehicular Hell-Bending, Celebrating America the Way It's Supposed to Be - with an Oil Well in Every Backyard, a Cadillac Escalade in Every Carport, & the Chairman of the Federal Reserve Mowing Our Lawn. unabr. ed. P. J. O'Rourke. Read by Christopher Lane. 1 MP3-CD. (Running Time: 8 hrs.). 2009. 39.97 (978-1-4233-9674-1(X), 9781423396741, Brinc Audio MP3 Lib); 39.97 (978-1-4233-9676-5(6), 9781423396765, BADLE); 14.99 (978-1-4233-9675-8(8), 9781423396758, BAD) Brilliance Audio.

Driving Like Crazy: Thirty Years of Vehicular Hell-Bending, Celebrating America the Way It's Supposed to Be - with an Oil Well in Every Backyard, a Cadillac Escalade in Every Carport, & the Chairman of the Federal Reserve Mowing Our Lawn. unabr. ed. P. J. O'Rourke. Read by Christopher A. Lane. 7 CDs. (Running Time: 8 hrs.). 2009. audio compact disk 24.99 (978-1-4233-9671-0(5), 9781423396710, Bril Audio CD Unabri) Brilliance Audio.

Driving Like Crazy: Thirty Years of Vehicular Hell-Bending, Celebrating America the Way It's Supposed to Be - with an Oil Well in Every Backyard, a Cadillac Escalade in Every Carport, & the Chairman of the Federal Reserve Mowing Our Lawn. unabr. ed. P. J. O'Rourke. Read by Christopher Lane. 7 CDs. (Running Time: 8 hrs.). 2009. audio compact disk 74.97 (978-1-4233-9672-7(3), 9781423396727, BriAudCD Unabrid) Brilliance Audio.

***Driving Like Crazy: Thirty Years of Vehicular Hell-bending Celebrating America the Way It¿s Supposed to Be¿with an Oil Well in Every Backyard, a Cadillac Escalade in Every Carport, & the Chairman of the Federal Reserve Mowing Our Lawn.** unabr. ed. P. J. O'Rourke. Read by Christopher Lane. (Running Time: 8 hrs.). 2010. audio compact disk 14.99 (978-1-4418-8559-3(5), 9781441885593, BCD Value Price) Brilliance Audio.

Driving on the Wrong Side of the Road: Humorous Views on Love, Lust, & Lawn Care. Estill Diana. (ENG.). 2007. audio compact disk 16.95 (978-0-9799708-0-1(6)) Totally Sk.

Driving over Lemons: An Optimist in Andalucia. unabr. ed. Chris Stewart. Read by Chris Stewart. 6 cass. (Running Time: 9 hrs.). 2000. 54.95 (978-0-7540-0542-1(9), CAB 1965) Pub: Chivers Audio Bks GBR. Dist(s): AudioGO
Being retired as the drummer of Genesis, the author launched a career as a sheep-shearer & travel writer. He has no regrets about this. Had he become a big-time rock star he might never have moved with his wife Ana to a remote mountain farm in Andalucia.

Driving over Lemons: An Optimist in Andalucia. unabr. ed. Chris Stewart. Read by Chris Stewart. 6 CDs. (Running Time: 9 hrs.). 2000. audio compact disk 64.95 (978-0-7540-5393-4(8), CCD 084) Pub: Chivers Audio Bks GBR. Dist(s): AudioGO
At age seventeen, he was retired as the drummer of Genesis & launched a career as a sheep-shearer & travel writer. Had he become a big-time rock star he might never have moved with his wife Ana to a remote mountain farm in Andalucia.

Driving Tips from Grampa. Gerry Stewart. 2007. audio compact disk 19.99 (978-1-60247-679-0(9)) Tate Pubng.

Driving under the Influence. 1998. bk. 99.00 (ACS-2197) PA Bar Inst.
Whether you deal with DUI cases every day or only occasionally, you cannot afford to be out-of-step with the current state of law. The "how tos" of handling a DUI case have been the target of several significant legislative & case law changes in the past year, making your job as prosecutor or defender that much more complex. Don't miss this opportunity to catch up on developments in the areas of blood alcohol levels, roadblocks, revere extrapolation & other issues.

Driving under the Influence & Other Traffic Cases: Current Law & Practice. 1987. bk. 90.00; 45.00 PA Bar Inst.

Driving Without Anxiety Through CHAANGE. Ann Seagrave & Faison Covington. Read by Ann Seagrave & Faison Covington. (Anxiety Treatment Ser.). 15.50 CHAANGE.
Presents an understanding of the problem, a segment about dialogue related to driving fears, a relaxation segment, & a practice session which is designed to desensitize the participant to the feared situation.

Droichead (The Bridge) unabr. ed. 1 cass., 1 mag. (Running Time: 1 hr.). (IRI.). 1989. pap. bk. 19.95 (AFIR63-Winter, AFIR64-Summer, AFIR65-Spring) J Norton Pubs.
Presents a recording in three Irish dialects (Ulster, Connaught, Munster) of bilingual magazine covering history, music, art, literature, book reviews, food articles, cultural events.

Drole a Equipe. 15.00 (Natl Textbk Co) M-H Contemporary.
Features short dialogues designed for intermediate students.

Drole De Mission. Christiane Szeps-Fralin. 59.95 (978-0-8219-3628-3(X)) EMC-Paradigm.

Drole de Mission. unabr. ed. Christiane Szeps-Fralin. 3 cass. (Running Time: 3 hrs.). (Mystery Thrillers in French Ser.). (FRE.). pap. bk. 49.95 (SFR116) J Norton Pubs.
Short-episode thriller, intermediate level, in a radio-play format, especially created to develop listening comprehension skills. Accompanying book provides a transcript of the recording, exercises & French vocabulary.

Droles de Poemes pour Enfants Sages. Poems. Guillaume Apollinaire et al. Read by Companie Rene Bourdet. 1 cass. (FRE.). 1995. 21.95 (1718-LQP) Olivia & Hill.
Selection of poems including: Queneau - "Un Enfant a dit"; Desnos - "La Sauterelle"; Apollinaire - Le Dromadaire; Vian - "Un Poisson d'avril.".

Drood. abr. ed. Dan Simmons. Read by Simon Prebble. (Running Time: 10 hrs. 30 mins.). (ENG.). 2009. 19.98 (978-1-60024-464-3(5)) Pub: Hachet Audio. Dist(s): HachBkGrp

Drood. abr. ed. Dan Simmons. Read by Simon Prebble. (Running Time: 10 hrs. 30 mins.). (ENG.). 2010. audio compact disk 19.98 (978-1-60024-834-4(9)) Pub: Hachet Audio. Dist(s): HachBkGrp

Drop City. T. C. Boyle. Narrated by Richard Poe. 13 cass. (Running Time: 19 hrs. 15 mins.). 2003. 118.00 (978-1-4025-2024-2(7)) Recorded Bks.

Drop City. T. C. Boyle. 11 cass. (Running Time: 19 hrs. 15 mins.). 2004. 39.99 (978-1-4025-3631-1(3), 02604) Recorded Bks.

Drop Dead Beautiful. abr. ed. Jackie Collins. Read by Jackie Collins. Read by Sydney Tamila Poitier et al. (Running Time: 5 hrs. 0 mins. 0 sec.). Bk. 6. (ENG.). 2007. audio compact disk 24.95 (978-1-4272-0049-5(1)) Pub: Macmill Audio. Dist(s): Macmillan

Drop Dead Beautiful. unabr. ed. Jackie Collins. 2 MP3 CDs. (Running Time: 18 hrs.). (Lucky Santangelo Ser.: Bk. 6). 2007. 69.95 (978-0-7927-4762-8(3)); 89.95 (978-0-7927-4785-7(2)); audio compact disk 115.95 (978-0-7927-4683-6(X)) AudioGO.

Drop Dead Beautiful. unabr. ed. Jackie Collins. Read by Jonathan Davis. (Running Time: 15 hrs. 0 mins. 0 sec.). Bk. 6. (ENG.). 2007. audio compact disk 49.95 (978-1-4272-0051-8(3)) Pub: Macmill Audio. Dist(s): Macmillan

Drop Dead Gorgeous. abr. ed. Linda Howard. Read by Joyce Bean. (Running Time: 14400 sec.). 2007. audio compact disk 14.99 (978-1-4233-0584-2(1), 9781423305842, BCD Value Price) Brilliance Audio.

Drop Dead Gorgeous. unabr. ed. Linda Howard. Read by Joyce Bean. (Running Time: 9 hrs.). 2006. 39.25 (978-1-4233-0582-8(5), 9781423305828, BADLE); 24.95 (978-1-4233-0581-1(7), 9781423305811, BAD); 74.25 (978-1-4233-0576-7(0), 9781423305767, BrilAudUnabridg); audio compact disk 39.25 (978-1-4233-0580-4(9), 9781423305804, Brinc Audio MP3 Lib); audio compact disk 92.25 (978-1-4233-0578-1(7), 9781423305781, BriAudCD Unabrid); audio compact disk 36.95 (978-1-4233-0577-4(9), 9781423305774, Bril Audio CD Unabri); audio compact disk 24.95 (978-1-4233-0579-8(5), 9781423305798, Brilliance MP3) Brilliance Audio.

Drop Edge of Yonder. unabr. ed. Donis Casey. Read by Pamela Ward. (Running Time: 28800 sec.). (Alafair Tucker Mysteries Ser.). 2007. audio compact disk 55.00 (978-1-4332-1136-2(X)) Blckstn Audio.

Drop Edge of Yonder. unabr. ed. Donis Casey & Pamela Ward. (Running Time: 28800 sec.). (Alafair Tucker Mysteries Ser.). 2007. 44.95 (978-1-4332-1135-5(1)); audio compact disk 29.95 (978-1-4332-1137-9(8)) Blckstn Audio.

Drop Shot. unabr. ed. Harlan Coben. Read by Jonathan Marosz. 6 cass. (Running Time: 9 hrs.). (Myron Bolitar Ser.: No. 2). 1999. 48.00 (978-0-7366-4789-2(9), 5136) Books on Tape.
Tennis has been good to sports agent Myron Bolitar. He represents two of the hottest young stars in the game. But when his female player is murdered in broad daylight at the U.S. Open and his male player becomes the prime suspect, Myron's got a whole new match to win. His investigation leads to an old murder, the mob, a crooked senator, and someone who's determined to shut down his search for good.

Drop Shot. unabr. ed. Harlan Coben. Read by Jonathan Marosz. 6 cass. (Running Time: 9 hrs.). (Myron Bolitar Ser.: No. 2). 2001. 29.95 (978-0-7366-6794-4(6)) Books on Tape.
Sports agent Myron Bolitar uncovers a connection between a murdered tennis player, another star player, a senator & the Mafia.

Drop Shot. unabr. ed. Harlan Coben. Read by Jonathan Marosz. (Running Time: 28800 sec.). (Myron Bolitar Ser.: No. 2). (ENG.). 2006. audio compact disk 19.99 (978-0-7393-4096-7(4), Random AudioBks) Pub: Random Audio Pubg. Dist(s): Random

Dropped a Bombshell. unabr. ed. Lilian Jackson Braun & Lilian Jackson Braun. Read by George Guidall. (Running Time: 4 hrs.). (ENG.). (gr. 8). 2006. audio compact disk 14.95 (978-0-14-305930-1(0), PengAudBks) Penguin Grp USA.

Dropping Your Guard see Baje la Guardia

Dropping Your Guard. 2005. 42.00 (978-1-57972-554-9(6)); audio compact disk 42.00 (978-1-57972-551-8(1)) Insight Living.

Dropping Your Guard. Charles R. Swindoll. 1 cass. 1984. 10.99 (978-2-01-018173-3(5)) Nelson.
With material from the opening chapters of his book, Chuck Swindoll challenges us to drop the masks & break the bonds of fear which keep us from relating to others.

Drops of Emptiness. Thich Nhat Hanh & Chan Khong. 1 CD. (Running Time: 42 min.). 2003. audio compact disk 17.00 Parallax Pr.
Includes poetry, Vietnamese folk-songs, Buddhist hymns, and chants performed in English, French, and Vietnamese.

Drops of Emptiness: Songs, Chants & Poetry from Plum Village, France. unabr. ed. Contrib. by Chan Khong & Thich Nhat Hanh. Told to Monks and Nuns of Plum Village. 1 CD. (Running Time: 2520 sec.). 1997. audio compact disk 16.98 (978-1-56455-562-5(3), MM00003D) Sounds True.
Vietnamese Zen songs, chants, hymns, & poetry from Plum Village monastery in southwestern France.

Drops of Nectar. Shiva Rea. 2003. audio compact disk 24.95 (978-1-59179-052-5(2)) Sounds True.

Drowned Hopes. unabr. collector's ed. Donald E. Westlake. Read by Michael Kramer. 11 cass. (Running Time: 16 hrs. 30 min.). (Dortmunder Ser.). 1997. 88.00 (978-0-7366-3677-3(3), 4357) Books on Tape.
John Dortmunder strikes it unlucky again when he gets a visit from an old cellmate, Tom Jimson.

Drowned Maiden's Hair. unabr. ed. Laura Amy Schlitz. Read by Alma Cuervo. 8 cass. (Running Time: 9 hrs.). (J). (gr. 4-8). 2007. 56.75 (978-1-4281-6301-0(8)); audio compact disk 87.75 (978-1-4281-6306-5(9)) Recorded Bks.

Drowned Rat. unabr. ed. E. X. Ferrars. Read by Frances Jeater. 5 CDs. (Running Time: 6 hrs.). (Isis Ser.). (J). 2000. audio compact disk 59.95 (978-0-7531-0798-0(8), 107988) Pub: ISIS Lrg Prnt GBR. Dist(s): Ulverscroft US
Someone is out to kill Douglas Cable, recently returned from Australia to inherit beautiful Havershaw House. By displacing his cousin's wife & daughter from their home & introducing strangers to the village, he is stirring up trouble. Catherine Gifford, daughter of the local doctor, acts as the unwilling catalyst for crisis. Her involvement with the visiting Australians can lead only to danger.

Drowned Rat. unabr. ed. Elizabeth Ferrars. Read by Frances Jeater. 5 cass. (Running Time: 6 hrs.). 2000. 49.95 (978-0-7531-0535-1(7), 991008) Pub: ISIS Audio GBR. Dist(s): Ulverscroft US
Someone is out to kill Douglas Cable. Recently returned from Australia to inherit beautiful Havershaw House. By displacing his cousin's wife & daughter from their home & introducing strangers to the village, he is stirring up trouble. Catherine Gifford, daughter of the local doctor, acts as the unwilling catalyst for crisis. Her involvement with the visiting Australians can lead only to danger.

Drowned Wednesday. unabr. collector's ed. Garth Nix. Read by Allan Corduner. 5 cass. (Running Time: 8 hrs. 41 mins.). (Keys to the Kingdom Ser.: No. 3). (J). (gr. 4-7). 2005. 40.00 (978-0-8072-1732-0(8), BksonTape) Random Audio Pubg.
With his unlimited imagination and thrilling storytelling, Garth Nix has created a character and a world that become even more compelling with each audiobook. As Arthur gets closer to the heart of his quest, the suspense and mystery grow more and more intense . . . This is the third audiobook in the thrilling, triumphantly imaginative Keys to the Kingdom series by Garth Nix, the bestselling author of Sabriel, Lirael, and Abhorsen.

Drowning People. abr. ed. Richard Mason. (Running Time: 4 hrs.). (ENG.). 2006. 14.98 (978-1-59483-700-5(7)) Pub: Hachet Audio. Dist(s): HachBkGrp

Drowning Pool. unabr. ed. Ross MacDonald, pseud. Read by Tom Parker. 5 cass. (Running Time: 7 hrs.). 2002. 39.95 (978-0-7861-2297-4(8), 2986); audio compact disk 48.00 (978-0-7861-9475-9(8), 2986) Blckstn Audio.
When a millionaire matriarch is found floating face down in the family pool, the prime suspects are her good-for-nothing son and his seductive teenage daughter.

Drowning Ruth. unabr. ed. Christina Schwarz. Read by Joanne McQuinn. 8 cass. (Running Time: 11 hrs. 30 mins.). 2001. (978-0-7531-1160-4(8)) ISIS Audio GBR.
A frozen lake, a winter's night, and a tragedy that will haunt a child's life. Apparently worn out by caring for wounded soldiers, Amanda retreats from her nursing job at the close of the First World War to her family's farm on a lake in Wisconsin, hoping that life with her beloved sister Mattie and her niece, three-year-old Ruth, will restore her.

Drowning Sorrows. unabr. ed. Douglas Post. Perf. by Keli Garrett et al. 1 cass. (Running Time: 1 hr. 23 min.). 1996. 19.95 (978-1-58081-083-8(7)) L A Theatre.
A woman stumbles into a remote bar on the Caribbean island of St. John & faints. It isn't the tropical drinks that befell Emily Miles, but the sight of the bartender, Duncan Grant. In the restless Duncan, Emily is sure she recognizes the young man she has been searching for ever since he left her at the altar, twenty years ago.

Drowning Tree. Carol Goodman. Read by Christine Marshall. 12 vols. 2004. bk. 49.95 (978-0-7927-3291-4(X), SLD 682, Chivers Sound Lib) AudioGO.

Drowning World. unabr. ed. Ed. by Alan Dean Foster. 6 cass. (Running Time: 10 hrs.). 2002. 32.00 (978-1-59040-550-5(1)) Audio Lit.

Drowning World. unabr. ed. Alan Dean Foster. 6 cass. (Running Time: 9 hrs.). 2003. 32.00 (978-1-57453-550-1(1), Fantastic Audio) Audio Lit.

Drug Abuse. 1 cass. (Running Time: 60 min.). 10.95 (046) Psych Res Inst.
Designed to eliminate the tendencies toward substance abuses.

Drug & Alcohol Testing in the Schools & Public Sector. 5 cass. (Running Time: 5 hrs.). 1987. 89.95 (5330029) Amer Bar Assn.
Covers case law, implications for human rights, employer & employee issues.

Drug Free & Happy to Be. 1 cass. (Running Time: 20 min.). (YA). (gr. 10-12). 1991. 15.95 Prosperity & Profits.
Poet's workshop.

Drug Free & Happy to Be. Read by Poet's Workshop Staff. 1 cass. (Running Time: 20 min.). (J). (gr. 10-12). 1991. 15.95 (37SOR306T) Sell Out Recordings.
A poem on possibilities if a person is Drug Free & Happy to Be.

Drug-Proofing Your Children. David Freudberg. Perf. by Berry Brazelton et al. 1 cass. (Running Time: 45 min.). 1994. 11.95 (978-0-9640914-3-6(7)) Human Media.
Thoughtful guide to parents & sensible suggestions from experts in parenting & substance abuse prevention.

Drug Testing in the Workplace. 1987. bk. 100.00 incl. book.; 50.00 cass. only.; 50.00 book only. PA Bar Inst.

Drugs & Alcohol. unabr. ed. Rod L. Evans. Read by Robert Guillaume. Ed. by John Lachs & Mike Hassell. 2 cass. (Running Time: 3 hrs.). Dramatization. (Morality in Our Age Ser.). 1995. 17.95 Set. (978-1-56823-028-3(1), 10507) Knowledge Prod.
Drugs & alcohol involve personal habits that have significant social consequences. Some have said that we are a society of drinkers & pill takers; much of this consumption is legal. Should the use of intoxicants, stimulants & drug medications be governed by personal choice or regulation? Alcohol, tobacco, & coffee all are consumed legally in the U.S. - yet all these have been banned at some point in world history (to no avail). Which drugs should be legal, & which should be illegal? Is law or persuasion a better method of reform?.

Drugs & Alcohol: Knowledge Products Production. unabr. ed. Rod L. Evans. Read by Robert Guillaume. (Running Time: 4 mins.). (J). 2006. audio compact disk 25.95 (978-0-7861-6532-2(4)) Pub: Blckstn Audio. Dist(s): NetLibrary CO

Drugs & Society. 5th ed. Glen Hanson & Peter Venturelli. (C). 1998. audio compact disk 99.00 (978-0-7637-0730-9(9), 0730-9) Jones Bartlett.

Drugs & Society. 6th ed. Glen Hanson & Peter Venturelli. (C). 2000. audio compact disk 99.00 (978-0-7637-1509-0(3), 1509-3) Jones Bartlett.

Druid Circle see Sound of Modern Drama: The Crucible

Druid Circle. (J). (SAC 7145) Spoken Arts.

Drum: A Mini-Musical based on a Tale of Generosity for Unison & 2-Part Voices. Composed by Sally K. Albrecht et al. (ENG.). 2009. audio compact disk 54.95 (978-0-7390-5840-4(1)) Alfred Pub.

Drum! How to Play the Rhythms of Africa & Latin America. unabr. ed. Intro. by Geoff Johns. 1 CD. (Running Time: 1 hr. 6 mins.). 1997. audio compact disk 16.98 (978-1-56455-456-7(2), MM00323D) Sounds True.
The only step-by-step audiotape teaching how to play the most popular rhythms & percussion structures of Ghana, Cuba, Guinea, Haiti, & Brazil.

*__Drum Basics.__ Oliver Kolsch. (ENG., 2008. pap. bk. 12.95 (978-3-8024-0674-4(5)) Voggenreiter Pubs DEU.

Drum Circle: A Guide to World Percussion. Chalo Eduardo & Frank Kumor. (ENG.). 2001. audio compact disk 10.00 (978-0-7390-2319-8(5)) Alfred Pub.

Drum Circle Sing-A-Long. Composed by Norman Jones. (J). 2004. audio compact disk 14.95 (978-0-9763522-1-1(4)) R C Network.

Drum Circle Spirit: Facilitating Human Potential Through Rhythm. Arthur E. Hull. 1 CD. (Running Time: 1 hr.). (Performance in World Music Ser.: No. 10). 1998. pap. bk. 29.95 (978-0-941677-84-4(2)) White Cliffs Media.

Drum Damba. David Locke. Contrib. by Abubakari Lunna. 1 cass.; 1 CD. 1989. audio compact disk 15.95 CD. (978-0-941677-50-9(8)) White Cliffs Media.

Drum Duets Vol 1. John Wackerman. (ENG.). 2007. audio compact disk 14.95 (978-0-7390-5056-9(7)) Alfred Pub.

Drum Grooves Presents: Groovin' to the Music. Dana J. Oliver. 1 CD. 1999. audio compact disk Drum Grooves.
Includes 50 songs with accompanying scores to challenge the beginning through intermediate drummer. Learn to play a broad variety of musical styles. Emphasis is on playing with music.

Drum Meditations, Vols. 1 & 2. unabr. ed. Paul D. Kurth & Joan E. Kurth. Read by Joan E. Kurth. 3 cass. (Running Time: 3 hrs. 20 min.). 1991. 49.95 Set, incl. instruction bklt. (978-1-880375-00-6(1), 375001) Tuffin Media.
Exercise, Stress Reduction, Creative Imaging, & Shamanic Experiences Through Drum Rhythms.

*__Drum Sessions.__ bk. 14.95 (978-0-8497-2900-3(9)) Kjos.

Drum Set Dailies - Rudimental Book. Frank Briggs. 2000. pap. bk. 5.95 (978-0-7866-5248-8(9), 98581BCD) Mel Bay.

Drum Stories, No. 1. Bill Matthews. 2005. audio compact disk 16.50 (978-0-9765971-0-0(1)) Fremont Drum.
Companion CD #1 for Drum Stories: 50 solos & phrases.

Drum Stories, No. 2. Bill Matthews. 2005. audio compact disk 16.50 (978-0-9765971-1-7(X)) Fremont Drum.
Companion CD #2 for "Drum Stories: 50 solos & phrases.

Drum Talk: Hand Drum Dialogues 1-17. Created by Bill Matthews. 1998. audio compact disk 15.00 (978-0-9718861-6-2(4)) Fremont Drum.

Drum Talk No. 2: Hand Drum Dialogues 18-33. 1998. audio compact disk 15.00 (978-0-9718861-7-9(2)) Fremont Drum.

Drum Taps see Twentieth-Century Poetry in English, No. 16, Walt Whitman Speaks for Himself

*__Drum-Taps & Memoranda During the War.__ Walt Whitman. (Running Time: 5 hrs. 0 mins. 0 sec.). (ENG.). 2011. audio compact disk 19.95 (978-1-60998-163-1(4)) Pub: AudioGO. Dist(s): Perseus Dist

Drumlin Woodchuck see Robert Frost in Recital

Drumlin Woodchuck see Twentieth-Century Poetry in English, No. 6, Recordings of Poets Reading Their Own Poetry

Drummer Hoff see Tambor Diego

Drummer Hoff. 2004. bk. 24.95 (978-1-56008-191-3(0)); 8.95 (978-1-56008-889-9(3)); 8.95 (978-0-7882-0090-8(9)); cass. & flmstrp 30.00 (978-1-56008-662-8(9)); audio compact disk 12.95 (978-1-55592-907-7(9)) Weston Woods.

Drummer Hoff. (J). 2004. pap. bk. 18.95 (978-1-55592-405-8(0)); pap. bk. 38.75 (978-1-55592-406-5(9)); pap. bk. 32.75 (978-1-55592-223-8(6)); pap. bk. 14.95 (978-1-56008-192-0(9)) Weston Woods.

Drummer Hoff. Ed Emberley. Illus. by Ed Emberley. 1 cass., 5 bks. (Running Time: 30 min.). (J). pap. bk. 32.75 Weston Woods.

Drummer Hoff. Ed Emberley. Illus. by Ed Emberley. 1 cass. (Running Time: 30 min.). (J). bk. 24.95; pap. bk. 12.95 Weston Woods.
Told in lively folk verse, several soldiers each bring a different part for a remarkable machine called a cannon but only one of them gets to fire it off.

Drummer Hoff Error. (J). 2004. pap. bk. 18.95 (978-1-55592-409-6(3)); pap. bk. 38.75 (978-1-55592-410-2(7)) Weston Woods.

Drummers Collective 25th Anniversary Celebration & Bass Day 2002. Created by Hal Leonard Corporation Staff. 2003. audio compact disk 12.95 (978-0-634-06637-5(4), 0634066374) Pub: Hudson Music. Dist(s): H Leonard

Drummer's Path: African & Diaspora Percussive Music. Sule G. Wilson. 1 cass. (Running Time: 1 hr.). 1992. 9.95 (978-0-89281-362-9(8)) Inner Tradit.
Rhythms from diverse cultures of Puerto Rico, Brazil, Africa & India, & traditional African-American dance featuring hand & body percussion.

Drummer's Path: African & Diaspora Percussive Music. Sule G. Wilson. 1 CD. (Running Time: 1 hr.). 1992. audio compact disk 15.95 (978-0-89281-502-9(7), Heal Arts VT) Inner Tradit.
Wilson is joined by an all-star cast of international musicians on this eclectic recording of traditional rhythms.

Drumming up Character Teacher's Guide, CD & DVD: A Hip-Hop Music Approach to Character Education. Lindsay Marie Rust & Stephen Bennett Campbell. Des. by Lindsay Marie Rust. Lyrics by Stephen Bennett Campbell. Prod. by Dancing Drum. Dancing Drum. 2008. pap. bk. 49.95 (978-0-9816724-0-3(X)) Dancing.

Drums: Rhythm of the Heartbeat. 1 cass. (Running Time: 30 min.). 9.95 (C0610B090, HarperThor) HarpC GBR.

Drums Across the Tundra. Bernie Krause. 1 cass. (Running Time: 60 min.). (Music & Word Ser.). 1994. 9.95 (2309, NrthWrd Bks) TandN Child.
Chuna McIntyre learned these intriguing Yup'ik Eskimo songs & stories from his 91-year-old grandmother. Songs resonate with strong beats suitable for dancing, & his storytelling is pure poetry.

Drums from Day One. Jim Payne. 2002. bk. 19.95 (978-0-7866-4851-1(1), 98356BCD) Mel Bay.

Drums from Day One. Jim Payne. 2003. pap. bk. 29.95 (978-0-7866-6862-5(8), 98356SET) Mel Bay.

Drums, Girls, & Dangerous Pie. Jordan Sonnenblick. Read by Joel Johnstone. (ENG.). (YA). (gr. 7-12). 2006. audio compact disk 29.95 (978-0-439-89550-7(2)) Scholastic Inc.

***Drums, Girls, & Dangerous Pie.** unabr. ed. Jordan Sonnenblick. (Running Time: 5 hrs.). 2011. 19.99 (978-1-61106-164-2(4), 9781611061642, BAD); 39.97 (978-1-61106-165-9(2), 9781611061659, BADLE); 19.99 (978-1-61106-162-8(8), 9781611061628, Brilliance MP3); 39.97 (978-1-61106-163-5(6), 9781611061635, Brlnc Audio MP3 Lib); audio compact disk 49.97 (978-1-61106-161-1(X), 9781611061611, BriAudCD Unabrid); audio compact disk 19.99 (978-1-61106-160-4(1), 9781611061604, Bril Audio CD Unabri) Brilliance Audio.

Drums, Girls, & Dangerous Pie. unabr. ed. Jordan Sonnenblick. Read by Joel Johnstone. (J). 2007. 49.99 (978-1-60252-830-7(6)) Find a World.

Drums of Autumn. unabr. ed. Diana Gabaldon. Narrated by Davina Porter. 33 cass. (Running Time: 45 hrs. 45 mins.). (Outlander Ser.: Bk. 4). 1999. 198.00 (978-0-7887-3473-1(3), 95755E7) Recorded Bks.
Claire has twice used an ancient stone circle to travel back to the 18th century. The first time she found love with a Scottish warrior but had to return to the present to save their unborn child. The second time she went back to find her lost love but had to leave their daughter behind. Now Brianna, from her 1960's vantage point, has found her parents' obituary & will risk everything to change history.

Drums of Change: The Story of Running Fawn. unabr. ed. Janette Oke. Narrated by Barbara Caruso. 5 cass. (Running Time: 7 hrs. 30 mins.). 1997. 44.00 (978-0-7887-0846-6(5), 94992E7) Recorded Bks.
Running Fawn dreams of someday sharing a tepee fire with handsome Silver Fox in the lush forests of the Northwest. But in the late 1800s, pale-faced men come with their strange ideas. When Silver Fox embraces their beliefs, she suddenly finds herself alone, clinging to the traditions of her people.

Drums of Defiance: Maroon Music from Jamaica. Contrib. by Kenneth Bilby. 1 cass. or CD. 1992. (0-9307-404120-9307-40412-2-2); audio compact disk (0-9307-40412-2-2) Smithsonian Folkways.
Reveals a long history of struggle. During the 17th & 18th centuries, some of the Africans brought to Jamaica as slaves escaped to the mountains. There they settled, & over time became known as "Maroons".

Drums of Morning: Growing up in the Thirties. unabr. ed. Vernon Scannell. Read by Martyn Read. 8 cass. (Running Time: 10 hrs.). 2000. 54.95 (978-0-7531-0767-6(8), 000112) Pub: ISIS Audio GBR. Dist(s): Ulverscroft US
Vernon Scannell recalls his childhood & early manhood, culminating in his joining the Army in 1940. He explores the relationship between himself, his siblings & his sadistic & probably psychotic father, set against the vivid backdrop of Britain between the wars. What emerges is a frank, sometimes comical, but always powerful portrait of a boy with few material advantages finding his own salvation through literature, music, boxing & the grace of love.

Drums of Passion. unabr. ed. Babatunde Olatunji & Elizabeth Gips. 1 cass. (Running Time: 90 min.). 1998. 11.00 (32005) Big Sur Tapes.

Drumset Essentials. Peter Erskine. (ENG.). 2002. audio compact disk 10.00 (978-0-7390-2685-4(2)) Alfred Pub.

Drumset Essentials. Peter Erskine. (ENG.). 2002. audio compact disk 10.00 (978-0-7390-2904-6(5)) Alfred Pub.

Drumset for the 21st Century: Intermediate Level. Rob Silverman & Mike Silverman. 1997. spiral bd. 19.95 (978-0-7866-1872-9(8), 95790BCD) Mel Bay.

Drumset Rudiments/Rudiments on the Drum Set: Grundlegende Technik Spielend Lernen!/Learn the Basic Techniques in a Fun Way! Andreas Berg. 2003. pap. bk. 22.95 (978-3-89922-009-4(9)) AMA Verlag DEU.

Drunk with Love. unabr. collector's ed. Ellen Gilchrist. Read by Ruth Stokesberry. 8 cass. (Running Time: 8 hrs.). 1987. 48.00 (978-0-7366-1216-6(5), 2135) Books on Tape.
Short Stories, including "Nineteen Forty-One", "The Expansion of the Universe", "Adoration" & more.

Drunk with Power. Perf. by Margaret Cho. 2000. audio compact disk 16.98 (978-1-929243-12-9(X)) Uproar Ent.

Drunkard's Funeral see Poetry of Vachel Lindsay

Drunkard's Walk: How Randomness Rules Our Lives. unabr. ed. Leonard Mlodinow. Read by Sean Pratt. (Running Time: 9 hrs.). (ENG.). 2008. 24.98 (978-1-59659-253-7(2), GildAudio) Pub: Gildan Media. Dist(s): HachBkGrp

Drunkard's Walk: How Randomness Rules Our Lives. unabr. ed. Leonard Mlodinow. Read by Sean Pratt. (Running Time: 9 hrs.). (ENG.). 2009. audio compact disk 39.98 (978-1-59659-279-7(6)) Pub: Gildan Media. Dist(s): HachBkGrp

Drunken Chrysanthemum: The Teacher & the Preacher. Read by David Miller. 1 cass. (Running Time: 90 min.). 1984. 10.95 (978-0-7822-0167-3(9), ND7905) C G Jung IL.

Dry: A Memoir. unabr. rev. ed. Augusten Burroughs. Read by Augusten Burroughs. 7 CDs. (Running Time: 8 hrs. 30 mins. 0 sec.). (ENG., 2003. audio compact disk 29.95 (978-1-55927-901-7(X)) Pub: Macmill Audio. Dist(s): Macmillan

Dry as a Desert. Compiled by Benchmark Education Staff. 2005. audio compact disk 10.00 (978-1-4108-5471-1(X)) Benchmark Educ.

Dry Bones That Dream see Final Account

Dry Cleaning - Small Businesses Cleaning Up & Recycling. Hosted by Nancy Pearlman. 1 cass. (Running Time: 29 min.). 10.00 (1103) Educ Comm CA.

Dry Drunk Revisited & Shame: A Spiritual Block to Serenity. 1 cass. (Recovery Is Forever Ser.). 1981. 8.95 (1535G) Hazelden.

Dry Ice. Stephen White. Read by Dick Hill. (Dr. Alan Gregory Ser.). 2008. 74.99 (978-1-60640-911-4(5)) Find a World.

Dry Ice. abr. ed. Stephen White. Read by Dick Hill. (Running Time: 21600 sec.). (Dr. Alan Gregory Ser.). 2008. audio compact disk 14.99 (978-1-4233-2886-5(8), 9781423328865, BCD Value Price) Brilliance Audio.

Dry Ice. unabr. ed. Stephen White. Read by Dick Hill. 1 MP3-CD. (Running Time: 12 hrs.). (Dr. Alan Gregory Ser.). 2007. 39.25 (978-1-4233-2882-7(5), 9781423328827, Brlnc Audio MP3 Lib); 24.95 (978-1-4233-2881-0(7), 9781423328810, Brilliance MP3); 49.97 (978-1-4233-2884-1(1), 9781423328841, BADLE); 24.95 (978-1-4233-2883-4(3), 9781423328834, BAD); 87.25 (978-1-4233-2878-0(7), 9781423328780, BriAudUnabridg); audio compact disk 102.25 (978-1-4233-2880-3(9), 9781423328803, BriAudCD Unabrid); audio compact disk 38.95 (978-1-4233-2879-7(5), 9781423328797, Bril Audio CD Unabri) Brilliance Audio.

Dry, Quiet War. Tony Daniel. Narrated by Jared Doreck. (Great Science Fiction Stories Ser.). 2006. audio compact disk 10.99 (978-1-884612-53-4(9)) AudioText.

Drylands. unabr. ed. Thea Astley. Read by Beverly Dunn. 4 cass. (Running Time: 7 hrs. 20 mins.). 2004. 32.00 (978-1-74030-157-2(9), 500741) Pub: Bolinda Pubng AUS. Dist(s): Lndmrk Audiobks

Drylands. unabr. ed. Thea Astley. Read by Beverley Dunn. (Running Time: 7 hrs. 20 mins.). 2009. audio compact disk 77.95 (978-1-74214-118-3(8), 9781742141183) Pub: Bolinda Pubng AUS. Dist(s): Bolinda Pub Inc

DSI - Date Scene Investigation: The Diagnostic Manual of Dating Disorders. unabr. ed. Ian Kerner. Read by Ian Kerner. (Running Time: 25200 sec.). 2006. audio compact disk 29.95 (978-0-06-112080-0(4)) HarperCollins Pubs.

***DSI - Date Scene Investigation.** unabr. ed. Ian Kerner. Read by Ian Kerner. (ENG.). 2006. (978-0-06-117147-5(6), Harper Audio); (978-0-06-117150-5(6), Harper Audio) HarperCollins Pubs.

DSM-IV: Diagnosis & Treatment Planning: Exam. Linda H. Seligman. 8 cass. 1996. 70.00 exam. (74228) Am Coun Assn.
The ability to make accurate diagnoses is an essential skill for counselors. This dynamic home-study unit is designed to extend your mastery of diagnostic principles & facilitate your use of the DSM-IV in developing effective treatment plans & documenting progress.

DSM-IV: Diagnosis & Treatment Planning: Tapes & Exam. Linda H. Seligman. 8 cass. 1996. 94.00 Set. (74227) Am Coun Assn.

DSM-IV Training Program Complete, Set. Richard Reid. 1995. audio compact disk 620.00 (978-0-87630-772-4(1)) Pub: Brunner-Routledge. Dist(s): Taylor and Fran

Du Cote de Chez Swann, Combray, Pt. 1, Set. Marcel Proust. Read by Andre Dussollier. 4 cass. (FRE.). 1995. 39.95 (1600-TH) Olivia & Hill.
"Longtemps, je me suis couche de bonne heure." With this famous sentence noted actor Andre Dussollier launches into the haunting reading of Proust.

Du Cote de Chez Swann, Combray, Pt. 2, Set. Marcel Proust. Read by Andre Dussollier. 4 cass. (FRE.). 1995. 39.95 (1601-TH) Olivia & Hill.
"Longtemps, je me suis couche de bonne heure." With this famous sentence noted actor Andre Dussollier launches into the haunting reading of Proust.

Du Cote de Chez Swann, Combray, Pts. 1-2, Set. Marcel Proust. Read by Andre Dussollier. 4 cass. (FRE.). 1995. 69.95 (1600/01) Olivia & Hill.

Du Laser a la Fermeture Eclair. Pierre-Gilles de Gennes. 1 cass. (Running Time: 60 mins.). (College de France Lectures). (FRE.). 1996. 21.95 (1854-LQP) Olivia & Hill.

Du Tac Au Tac: Managing Conversations in French. 2nd ed. Bragger. 1 cass. (Running Time: 90 mins.). 2002. stu. ed. 19.00 (978-0-8384-2122-2(9)) Heinle.

Dual Enigma. abr. ed. Michael Underwood. Read by Judith Franklyn. 4 cass. (Running Time: 6 hrs.). (Sound Ser.). 1992. 44.95 (978-1-85496-576-9(X)) Pub: UlverLrgPrint GBR. Dist(s): Ulverscroft US

Dual Programming & Problem Solving: C++ Data Structures. Nell Dale et al. (C). 1999. audio compact disk 101.00 (978-0-7637-0981-5(6), 0981-6) Jones Bartlett.

Duality as Metaphor in A Course in Miracles. Kenneth Wapnick. 10 CDs. 2005. audio compact disk 60.00 (978-1-59142-184-9(5), CD39) Foun Miracles.

***Duality as Metaphor in A Course in Miracles.** Kenneth Wapnick. 2010. 54.00 (978-1-59142-480-2(1)) Foun Miracles.

Duane-Radial Ray Syndrome - A Bibliography & Dictionary for Physicians, Patients, & Genome Researchers. Compiled by Icon Group International, Inc. Staff. 2007. ring bd. 28.95 (978-0-497-11370-4(8)) Icon Grp.

Duane Shinn's Crash Course in Basic Music. Duane Shinn. 1 cass. (Running Time: 60 min.). 19.95 incl. 48 flash cards incl. 48 flash cards. (MU-1) Duane Shinn.
A concentrated course in note reading, rhythm, etc., for beginners or for those who want to brush up on the fundamentals of music.

Duane's Depressed. unabr. ed. Larry McMurtry. Read by Joe Barrett. 8 cass. (Running Time: 12 hrs.). (Last Picture Show Trilogy: No. 3). 2001. 40.00 (978-1-59040-044-9(5), Phoenix Audio) Pub: Amer Intl Pub. Dist(s): PerseuPGW
McMurtry brings the Thalia saga to an end. Utterly unsentimental, often hilarious, sometimes tragic and shocking... and in the end full of hope.

Duane's Depressed. unabr. ed. Larry McMurtry. Read by Joe Barrett. 8 cass. (Last Picture Show Trilogy: No. 3). 1999. 36.00 (FS9-50952) Highsmith.

Dubious Legacy. unabr. ed. Mary Wesley. Read by Anna Massey. 8 cass. (Running Time: 12 hrs.). 2000. 59.95 (978-0-7451-4109-1(9), CAB 792) Pub: Chivers Audio Bks GBR. Dist(s): AudioGO
James and Matthew arrive for the weekend at the Tillotson's country house with anticipation, for they plan to propose to their girlfriends. However, the lives of all those gathered are about to take some astonishing turns.

Dublin Mystery see Classic Detective Stories, Vol. I, A Collection

Dublin Mystery. 1981. (N-79) Jimcin Record.

Dublin 4. unabr. ed. Maeve Binchy. Read by Kate Binchy. 4 cass. (Running Time: 6 hrs.). 2000. 34.95 (CAB 308) Pub: Chivers Audio Bks GBR. Dist(s): AudioGO
A vintage collection of four short stories set in the heart of Dublin's fashionable Southside. A society hostess entertains her husband's mistress to dinner; a country girl savors the delights of city life; a student faces the dilemma of unmarried pregnancy; and an alcoholic photographer tries to relaunch his shattered career.

Dubliners. James Joyce. 2 cass. (Running Time: 3 hrs.). 1998. 16.85 Set. (978-1-901768-12-1(0)) Pub: CSA Telltapes GBR. Dist(s): Ulverscroft US

Dubliners. James Joyce. 1 cass. 1996. pap. bk. 5.95 Boxed set. (29121-9) Dover.

Dubliners. James Joyce. Read by Ralph Cosham. (Running Time: 6 hrs. 15 mins.). 2003. 24.95 (978-1-59912-061-4(5), Audiofy Corp) Iofy Corp.

Dubliners. James Joyce. Read by Jim Norton. (Running Time: 7 hrs.). 2005. 38.95 (978-1-60083-729-6(8)) Iofy Corp.

Dubliners. James Joyce. Read by Jim Norton. 3 cass. (Running Time: 3 hrs. 30 mins.). (Works of James Joyce). 1999. 17.98 (978-962-634-673-0(6), NA317314, Naxos AudioBooks) Naxos.
This volume contains the first ten short stories from Dubliners: The Sisters, An Encounter, Araby, Eveline, After the Race, Two Gallante,The Boarding House, A Little Cloud, Counterparts and Clay.

Dubliners. James Joyce. Narrated by Ralph Cosham. (Running Time: 22500 sec.). (Unabridged Classics in MP3 Ser.). (ENG.). 2008. audio compact disk 24.00 (978-1-58472-517-6(5), In Aud) Sound Room.

Dubliners. unabr. ed. Short Stories. James Joyce. Read by Frederick Davidson. 6 cass. (Running Time: 9 hrs.). 1992. 44.95 (978-0-7861-0359-1(0), 1316) Blckstn Audio.
Each of these fifteen stories is permeated with what Joyce called "epiphanies," deep universal truths which become visible through events & circumstances which seem outwardly insignificant. He combines this with some sharp humor & some sensitive poignancy & the effect is powerful & masterful. It is little wonder why "Dubliners" is often hailed as one of the greatest short story collections in the English language.

Dubliners. unabr. ed. James Joyce. Read by Frederick Davidson. (Running Time: 27000 sec.). 2007. audio compact disk 29.95 (978-0-7861-6119-5(1)) Blckstn Audio.

Dubliners. unabr. ed. James Joyce. Read by Frederick Davidson. (Running Time: 27000 sec.). 2007. audio compact disk 55.00 (978-0-7861-6118-8(3)) Blckstn Audio.

Dubliners. unabr. ed. James Joyce. Narrated by T. P. McKenna. (Running Time: 7 hrs. 0 mins. 0 sec.). (ENG.). 2009. audio compact disk 31.95 (978-1-934997-47-5(1)) Pub: CSAWord. Dist(s): PerseuPGW

Dubliners. unabr. ed. James Joyce. Read by Ralph Cosham. (YA). 2007. 59.99 (978-1-59895-851-5(8)) Find a World.

Dubliners. unabr. ed. James Joyce. Read by Frank McCourt et al. 7 cds. (Running Time: 8 hrs). 2005. audio compact disk 39.95 (978-0-06-078956-5(5)) HarperCollins Pubs.

Dubliners. unabr. ed. James Joyce. Read by Jim Killavey. 5 cass. (Running Time: 7 hrs. 20 min.). (YA). (gr. 10-12). 1991. 29.00 set. (C-210) Jimcin Record.
Fifteen short stories by Ireland's premier novelist including "The Dead" & "Ivy Day in the Committee Room.".

Dubliners. unabr. ed. James Joyce. Read by Jim Norton. 6 CDs. bk. 41.98 (978-962-634-313-5(3), NAX31312) Naxos.

Dubliners. unabr. ed. James Joyce. Read by Jim Norton. 3 CDs. (Running Time: 3 hrs. 15 mins.). (Works of James Joyce). 1999. audio compact disk 22.98 (978-962-634-173-5(4), NA3173[illegible], Naxos AudioBooks) Naxos.
This volume contains the first ten short stories from Dubliners: The Sisters, An Encounter, Araby, Eveline, After the Race, Two Gallante,The Boarding House, A Little Cloud, Counterparts and Clay.

Dubliners, unabr. ed. Short Stories. James Joyce. Narrated by Donal Donnelly. 7 cass. (Running Time: 9 hrs. 15 mins.). 1999. 60.00 (978-1-55690-157-7(2), 91223E7) Recorded Bks.
A collection of short stories that offers a unified vision across the Joycean literary landscape, where a claustrophobic & "paralyzed" Dublin spirals outward to a wide ranging, boundless universe.

Dubliners. unabr. ed. Short Stories. James Joyce. Read by Ralph Cosham. 6 cds. (Running Time: 6 hrs 15 mins.). 2002. audio compact disk 33.95 (978-1-58472-246-5(0), 019, In Aud) Pub: Sound Room. Dist(s): Baker Taylor
Fifteen stories by James Joyce. The Sisters, An Encounter, Araby, Eveline, After the Race, Two Gallants, The Boarding House, A Little Cloud, Counter Parts, Clay, A Painful Case, Ivy Day in the Committee Room, A Mother, Grace, The Dead.

Dubliners. unabr. ed. James Joyce. Read by Ralph Cosham. 1 cd. (Running Time: 6 hrs 15 mins). 2002. audio compact disk 18.95 (978-1-58472-386-8(6), In Aud) Pub: Sound Room. Dist(s): Baker Taylor
MP3 format.

***Dubliners.** unabr. ed. James Joyce. Read by Malachy Mccourt et al. (ENG.). 2003. (978-0-06-073560-9(0), Caedmon) HarperCollins Pubs.

***Dubliners.** unabr. ed. James Joyce. Read by Malachy Mccourt. (ENG.). 2003. (978-0-06-079946-5(3), Caedmon) HarperCollins Pubs.

Dubliners. unabr. abr. ed. James Joyce. Read by Gerard McSorley. 3 CDs. (Running Time: 3 hrs.). (ENG.). 2004. audio compact disk 22.95 (978-1-56511-940-6(1), 1565119401) Pub: Penguin-HghBrdg. Dist(s): Workman Pub

Dubliners. unabr. collector's ed. James Joyce. Read by David Case. 8 cass. (Running Time: 8 hrs.). 1993. 48.00 (978-0-7366-2333-9(7), 3112) Books on Tape.
These 15 stories, Joyce's first published prose, are "a series of chapters in the moral history of his community".

Dubliners, No. 2. James Joyce. 2 cass. (Running Time: 3 hrs.). 1998. 16.85 Set. (978-1-901768-13-8(9)) Pub: CSA Telltapes GBR. Dist(s): Ulverscroft US

Dubliners, Pt. II. James Joyce. Read by Jim Norton. 3 cass. (Running Time: 3 hrs. 45 mins.). (Works of James Joyce). 1999. 17.98 (978-962-634-683-9(3), NA318314, Naxos AudioBooks) Naxos.
This volume continues the masterly unabridged reading of short stories & contains the last 6 stories from the Dubliners collection: Clay, A Painful Case, Ivy Day in the Committee Room, A Mother, Grace and perhaps the most well-known of all, The Dead.

Dubliners, Pt. II. unabr. ed. James Joyce. Read by Jim Norton. 3 CDs. (Running Time: 3 hrs. 45 mins.). (Works of James Joyce). 1999. audio compact disk 22.98 (978-962-634-183-4(1), NA318312, Naxos AudioBooks) Naxos.
This volume continues the masterly unabridged reading of short stories and contains the last 6 stories from The Dubliners collection: Clay, A Painful Case, Ivy Day in the Committee Room, A Mother, Grace and perhaps the most well-known of all, The Dead.

Dubliners: Selected Short Stories, Set. unabr. ed. Short Stories. James Joyce. Read by Flo Gibson. 4 cass. (Running Time: 5 hrs. 30 min.). 1993. 19.95 (978-1-55685-299-2(1)) Audio Bk Con.
This enchanting collection of Irish tales includes: "Eveline," "After the Race," "Two Gallants," "The Boarding House," "Counterparts," "Clay," "A Painful Case," "Ivy in the Committee Room," "A Mother," "Grace," & "The Dead".

Dubliners - Selected Short Stories. James Joyce. Narrated by Flo Gibson. (ENG.). 2009. audio compact disk 24.95 (978-1-60646-096-2(X)) Audio Bk Con.

Dubrovsky. Alexander Pushkin. 4 cass. (Running Time: 4 hrs.). (RUS.). bk. 49.50 set. Interlingua VA.
Historical novel relates the career of a nobleman who turns to brigandage after he is ruined & turned out of his estate in a lawsuit. Panoramic view of social life & the relationship of masters & serfs. Includes Russian text with English vocabulary & notes.

Duce: The Life of Benito Mussolini. collector's ed. Christopher Hibbert. Read by David Case. 11 cass. (Running Time: 16 hrs. 30 min.). 2000. 88.00 (978-0-7366-5436-4(4)) Books on Tape.
The first full length biography of Mussolini following World War II. A straightforward account of a complicated, contradictory man from Mussolini's childhood to his imprisonment in Switzerland, from his experience as a soldier to his founding of the Fascist party & his rise to

power, from his control over the Italian people to his arrest & escape from Gran Sasso & finally, to his grim end at the hands of a mob.

Duchess. Jude Deveraux. 2004. 9.95 (978-0-7435-4660-7(1)) Pub: S&S Audio. Dist(s): S and S Inc

Duchess. unabr. ed. Amanda Foreman. Narrated by Wanda McCaddon. (Running Time: 16 hrs. 0 mins. 0 sec.). (ENG.). 2009. audio compact disk 79.99 (978-1-4001-4161-6(3)); audio compact disk 29.99 (978-1-4001-6161-4(4)); audio compact disk 39.99 (978-1-4001-1161-9(7)) Pub: Tantor Media. Dist(s): IngramPubServ

Duchess & the Dragon. unabr. ed. Jamie Carie. Narrated by Peter Sandon. (ENG.). 2008. 18.19 (978-1-60814-176-0(4)); audio compact disk 25.99 (978-1-59859-374-7(9)) Oasis Audio.

Duchess of Duke Street. unabr. ed. Mollie Hardwick. Read by Valerie Singleton. 8 cass. 47.60 (A-120) Audio Bk.

Duchess of Duke Street, Vol. 1. unabr. ed. Mollie Hardwick. Read by Carole Boyd. 6 cass. (Sound Ser.). 2004. 54.95 (978-1-85496-537-0(9)) Pub: UlverLrgPrint GBR. Dist(s): Ulverscroft US

Duchess of Duke Street, Vol. 1 Mollie Hardwick. Read by Carole Boyd. 6 cass. (Running Time: 9 hrs.). 1999. 54.95 (65379) Pub: Soundings Ltd GBR. Dist(s): Ulverscroft US

Duchess of Duke Street, Vol. 2. Mollie Hardwick. Read by Anne Dover. 5 cass. (Running Time: 7 hrs. 30 mins.). 2001. 49.95 (65573) Pub: Soundings Ltd GBR. Dist(s): Ulverscroft US

Duchess of Malfi. John Webster. Perf. by Peggy Ashcroft & Paul Scofield. Prod. by Donald McWhinnie. 3 cass. (Running Time: 2 hrs. 30 min.). Dramatization. 1973. 21.95 (978-1-57970-098-0(5), SCN122) J Norton Pubs.
John Webster was intrigued by the cruelty, decadence and violence of the Italian courts of his age. he collaborated with other dramatists, including Dekker, in a number of comedies, but it is for his two great tragedies, "The Duchess of Malfi" and "The White Divel," that he is best remembered. Based on Italian novelle, both plays have plots of extreme horror and bloodiness. However, in a sound reproduction the ludicrous and sometimes repellent visual aspects of "The Duchess" are circumvented, and the listener is free to concentrate on Webster's superb poetry.

Duchess of Malfi. unabr. ed. John Webster. Perf. by Paul Scofield & Peggy Ashcroft. Prod. by Donald McWhinnie. 3 cass. 19.95 (SCN 122) J Norton Pubs.
Tragedy that portrays the decadence cruelty & violence of the Italian court through a plot of horror & bloodiness.

Duchess of Wilshire's Diamonds see Classic Detective Stories, Vol. II, A Collection

Duchess of Wrexe, Set. unabr. ed. Hugh Walpole. Read by Flo Gibson. 10 cass. (Running Time: 15 hrs.). 1994. 29.95 (978-1-55685-327-2(0)) Audio Bk Con.
The indomitable grandeur of the irascible, intimidating Duchess all but controls the lives of her family & London society. Only Rachel, her grandaughter, can escape perhaps through love.

Duchesse de Langeais, Set. Excerpts. Honoré de Balzac. Read by Fanny Ardant. 2 cass. (FRE.). 1991. 38.95 (1008-EF) Olivia & Hill.
Excerpts from this French classic tale of love & passion. After many years of searching, the Marquis de Montriveau finally tracks down the woman he loves. Once a fashionable Parisian hostess, she is now in a Carmelite convent from which the Marquis plans to kidnap her.

Duck for President see Pato para Presidente

Duck for President. 2004. bk. 24.95 (978-0-7882-0539-2(0)); 8.95 (978-0-7882-0544-6(7)); audio compact disk 12.95 (978-0-7882-0545-3(5)) Weston Woods.

***Duck Song.** (ENG., (J). 2010. bk. 18.95 (978-0-9843955-9-0(8)) Flinders.

Duck That Stayed Behind. Becky Hill. (J). 2007. audio compact disk 9.99 (978-1-60462-094-8(3)) Tate Pubng.

Ducklings Grow Up: Early Explorers Emergent Set B Audio CD. Cameron Swain. Adapted by Benchmark Education Staff. (J). 2007. audio compact disk 10.00 (978-1-4108-8208-0(X)) Benchmark Educ.

Ducks & Diamonds Mystery: Abbie Girl Spy Mystery. Darren J. Butler. Narrated by Daisy Eagan. Voice by Lindsay Lohan et al. 1 CD. (Running Time: 90 mins.). (J). 2000. audio compact disk 24.95 (978-0-9700752-7-7(8)) Onstage Pubng.

Duc's Homecoming: On the Ho Chi Minh Trail. Duc Nguyen. 1 cass. (Running Time: 30 min.). 9.95 (HO-060, HarperThor) HarpC GBR.

***Dude Abides: The Gospel According to the Coen Brothers.** unabr. ed. Cathleen Falsani. (Running Time: 6 hrs. 40 mins. 0 sec.). (ENG.). 2009. 14.99 (978-0-310-77345-0(8)) Zondervan.

Dude Ranger, Set. unabr. ed. Zane Grey. Read by William Dufris. 5 cass. (Sagebrush Western Ser.). (J). 1999. 49.95 (978-1-57490-224-2(5)) Pub: ISIS Lrg Prnt GBR. Dist(s): Ulverscroft US

Dude, Where's My Country? Michael Moore. 6 cassettes. (Running Time: 9 hrs). 2004. 56.00 (978-0-7366-9642-5(3)); audio compact disk 72.00 (978-0-7366-9643-2(1)) Books on Tape.

Dude, Where's My Country? unabr. ed. Michael Moore. Read by D. David Morin. (ENG.). 2005. 14.98 (978-1-59483-299-4(4)) Pub: Hachet Audio. Dist(s): HachBkGrp

Dude, Where's My Country? unabr. ed. Michael Moore. Read by D. David Morin. (Running Time: 9 hrs.). (ENG.). 2009. 64.98 (978-1-60024-984-6(1)) Pub: Hachet Audio. Dist(s): HachBkGrp

Dude, Where's My Walker?, The Infinite Mind Vol. 234. Interview. Hosted by Peter Kramer. 1. (Running Time: 59 mins). 2006. 21.95 (978-1-933644-27-1(3)) Lichtenstein Creat.
This week on The Infinite Mind, "Dude, Where's My Walker?": the science of memory loss for the baby boom generation. The Baby Boomers are hitting their 50's & 60's... and the 50's and 60's are hitting back. No aspect of aging scares the boomers more than memory loss. In this program, we look at what they're doing about it. We visit a memory workshop to find out if two days of coaching can really improve the brain's recall. Dr. Gary Small takes less time than that - in just 15 minutes, he teaches our host, Dr. Peter Kramer, an on-air trick for remembering unrelated words, and also explains how memory works (and why it sometimes doesn't). Dr. Antonio Convit tells us that when it comes to memory, you are what you eat. The ladies of "Menopause: The Musical" sing about their own memory woes. And Drs. Gary Lynch and Roger Stoll, of Cortex Pharmaceuticals, say that someday a revolutionary "smart pill" could make all these worries a thing of the past. With commentary from John Hockenberry.

Due, No. 4. Gruppo META Staff. (ENG.). 1996. 33.99 (978-0-521-57805-9(1)) Cambridge U Pr.

Due, Pack. Gruppo META Staff. 4 cass. (Running Time: 6 hrs.). (ENG.). 1996. 74.00 (978-0-521-57806-6(X)) Cambridge U Pr.

Due Diligence in Business Transactions, Vol. 629. rev. ed. Gary M. Lawrence. 1994. audio compact disk 249.00 (978-1-58852-066-1(8)) IncisiveMed.

Due preparations for the Plague. Janette Turner Hospital. Read by Sean Mangan. (Running Time: 12 hrs. 30 mins.). 2009. 89.99 (978-1-74214-244-9(3), 9781742142449) Pub: Bolinda Pubng AUS. Dist(s): Bolinda Pub Inc

Due Preparations for the Plague. unabr. ed. Janette Turner Hospital. 9 cass. (Running Time: 12 hrs. 30 mins.). 2004. 72.00 (978-1-74093-203-5(X)) Pub: Bolinda Pubng AUS. Dist(s): Bolinda Pub Inc

Due Preparations for the Plague. unabr. ed. Janette Turner Hospital. Read by Sean Mangan. 10 CDs. (Running Time: 12 hrs. 30 mins.). 2004. audio compact disk 98.95 (978-1-74093-377-3(X)) Pub: Bolinda Pubng AUS. Dist(s): Bolinda Pub Inc

Due Season: Seven Ways to Get from the Bottom to the Top. Creflo A. Dollar. 4 cass. (Running Time: 6 hrs.). 2001. 20.00 (978-1-931172-92-9(7), TS76, Kidz Faith) Pub: Creflo Dollar. Dist(s): STL Dist NA

Duel see Contes de Maupassant

Duel see Selected European Short Stories

Duel. unabr. ed. John Lukacs. Read by Grover Gardner. 7 cass. (Running Time: 10 hrs. 30 min.). 1992. 56.00 (978-0-7366-2143-4(1), 2941) Books on Tape.
Hitler vs. Churchill. A frightening view of just how close England came to losing the war.

Duel: 10 May -31 July, 1940: The Eighty-Day Struggle Between Churchill & Hitler. unabr. ed. John Lukacs. Narrated by John McDonough. 9 cass. (Running Time: 13 hrs.). 1999. 78.00 (978-0-7887-0358-4(7), 94550E7) Recorded Bks.
This is the story of the 80-day struggle between Adolph Hitler & Winston Churchill. One was poised on the edge of victory; the other was threatened by invasion & defeat, with the freedom of the world hanging in the balance. A history of exceptional scholarship & power. The Duel reveals the truth about how close England-& all democratic nations-came to losing the war. It is a classic account of a moment in the history of World War II & the 20th century.

Duel: 10 May-31 July 1940: The Eighty-Day Struggle Between Churchill & Hitler. unabr. ed. John Lukacs. Narrated by John McDonough. 11 CDs. (Running Time: 13 hrs.). 2000. audio compact disk 99.00 (978-0-7887-3402-1(4), C1008) Recorded Bks.
Story of the 80-day struggle between Adolph Hitler & Winston Churchill. One was poised on the edge of victory; the other was threatened by invasion & defeat, with the freedom of the world hanging in the balance.

Duel & The Womanhater. Perf. by Ann Southern. 1 cass. (Running Time: 60 min.). Dramatization. (Adventures of Maisie Ser.). 6.00 Once Upon Rad.
Radio broadcasts - humor.

Duel of Eagles: The Mexican & U. S. Fight for the Alamo. unabr. ed. Jeff Long. Narrated by George Wilson. 12 cass. (Running Time: 18 hrs. 15 mins.). 1991. 97.00 (978-1-55690-158-4(5), 91309E7) Recorded Bks.
A history of the Texas Revolution & the Battle of the Alamo.

Duel of the Fates. 1999. 19.95 (978-0-7692-8933-5(9), Warner Bro) Alfred Pub.

Dueling Princes. unabr. ed. Tyne O'Connell. Read by Nicky Talacko. 6 CDs. (Running Time: 7 hrs. 25 mins.). (Calypso Chronicles: Bk. 3). (J). (gr. 4-7). 2007. audio compact disk 77.95 (978-1-74093-987-4(5), 9781740939874) Pub: Bolinda Pubng AUS. Dist(s): Bolinda Pub Inc

Duende: The Spirit of Flamenco. Silhouette Staff. 3 cass. 1994. 29.95 (978-1-55961-273-9(8)) Relaxtn Co.

Duende; The Spirit of Flamenco. 3 CDs. 1994. audio compact disk 44.95 (978-1-55961-272-2(X)) Relaxtn Co.

Duerme. unabr. ed. Carmen Boullosa. Narrated by Carmen Boullosa. 3 cass. (Running Time: 4 hrs.). (SPA.). 2003. 28.00 (978-1-4025-1598-9(7)) Recorded Bks.
Set in the Baroque era, a woman recounts her relationships. Set against a backdrop of the Spanish invasion and mexican Indian culture.

Duérmete, Mi Niño! Arranged by Hal Wright. Executive Producer Kim Mitzo Thompson. Prod. by Twin Sisters Productions Staff. Executive Producer Karen Mitzo Hilderbrand. 1 CD. (Running Time: 60). (SPA.). (J). 2005. audio compact disk 6.99 (978-1-57583-831-1(1)) Twin Sisters.
Duermete, Mi Ni?o!De el regalo de una buena noche de sue?o con esta nueva coleccion de canciones de cuna y de ni?os. Primero, las doce canciones tradicionales y originales son cantadas suave y tiernamente para ti y el bebe. Despues, cada cancion es repetida como una pista instrumental con la cual se pueda cantar. Alivie el bebe durante paseos de coche, en la hora de siesta, comida, o la hora de acostarse. SHIPPING APRIL '05! Incluye 60 minutos de musica cantada e instrumental, y 44 paginas de partituraSleep, my little one! Give the gift of a good night's sleep with this new collection of lullabies and children?s songs. First, the twelve traditional and original songs are gently, tenderly sung for you and baby. Next each song is repeated as a sing along instrumental. Comfort baby during car rides, nap time, meal time, and bedtime.Includes 60 minutes of vocal and instrumental music and 44 pages of sheet music.

Duet. unabr. ed. Kimberley Freeman. Read by Caroline Lee. (Running Time: 72000 sec.). 2008. audio compact disk 123.95 (978-1-921334-56-6(8), 9781921334566) Pub: Bolinda Pubng AUS. Dist(s): Bolinda Pub Inc

Duets. Perf. by Mike Marshall. 1 cass.; 1 CD. 1998. 10.98 (978-1-56628-125-6(3), 71674); audio compact disk 15.98 CD. (978-1-56628-124-9(5), 71674D) MFLP CA.

Duets. unabr. ed. Told to Garrison Keillor. (Running Time: 3600 sec.). (ENG.). 2006. audio compact disk 16.95 (978-1-59887-066-4(1), 1598870661) Pub: HighBridge. Dist(s): Workman Pub

***Duff.** unabr. ed. Kody Keplinger. Read by Ellen Grafton. (Running Time: 8 hrs.). 2010. 22.99 (978-1-4418-5822-1(9), 9781441858221, Brilliance MP3); 22.99 (978-1-4418-5824-5(5), 9781441858245, BAD); 39.97 (978-1-4418-5823-8(7), 9781441858238, Brinc Audio MP3 Lib); 39.97 (978-1-4418-5825-2(3), 9781441858252, BADLE); audio compact disk 22.99 (978-1-4418-5820-7(2), 9781441858207, Bril Audio CD Unabri); audio compact disk 69.97 (978-1-4418-5821-4(0), 9781441858214, BriAudCD Unabrid) Brilliance Audio.

Duffy & the Devil. unabr. ed. Harve Zemach & Margot Zemach. Narrated by Virginia Leishman. 1 cass. (Running Time: 30 mins.). (gr. 1 up). 2001. 10.00 (978-0-7887-0638-7(1), 94817E7) Recorded Bks.
New twists & turns & a hilarious ending give new vitality to this Cornish version of "Rumpelstiltskin".

Duffy's Tavern. Perf. by Ed Gardner. 2008. audio compact disk 35.95 (978-1-57019-861-8(6)) Radio Spirits.

Duffy's Tavern. Created by Radio Spirits. (Running Time: 10800 sec.). 2004. 9.98 (978-1-57019-709-3(1)); audio compact disk 9.98 (978-1-57019-708-6(3)) Radio Spirits.

Duffy's Tavern, Vol. 1. collector's ed. Perf. by Ed Gardner et al. 6 cass. (Running Time: 9 hrs.). 1998. bk. 34.98 (4011) Radio Spirits.
Never a dull moment at the hilarious tavern on New York's 3rd Avenue, "Where the Elite Meet to Eat," with Archie the Manager. The basis for the hit TV show, Cheers. 18 episodes.

Duffy's Tavern, Vol. 2. collector's ed. Perf. by Ed Gardner et al. 6 cass. (Running Time: 9 hrs.). 2001. bk. 34.98 (4199) Radio Spirits.

Duffy's Tavern: Archie Wants to Patent Electricity & No More IOU's at Tavern. Perf. by Ed 'Archie' Gardner. 1 cass. (Running Time: 1 hr.). 2001. 6.98 (1643) Radio Spirits.

Duffy's Tavern: Archie's Philosophy & Archie's Yearbook. Perf. by Ed 'Archie' Gardner. 1 cass. (Running Time: 1 hr.). 2001. 6.98 (2515) Radio Spirits.

Duffy's Tavern: Chester Morris & Duffy Takes Up Reading. Perf. by Ed 'Archie' Gardner & Chester Morris. 1 cass. (Running Time: 1hr.). 2001. 6.98 (1644) Radio Spirits.

Duffy's Tavern: Col. Stoopnagle & Bert Gordon. Perf. by Ed 'Archie' Gardner et al. 1 cass. (Running Time: 1 hr.). 2001. 6.98 (1641) Radio Spirits.

Duffy's Tavern: Duffy's For Sale & Floor Show. Perf. by Ed 'Archie' Gardner. 1 cass. (Running Time: 1 hr.). 2001. 6.98 (1928) Radio Spirits.

Duffy's Tavern: Ed Wynn & Father's Day. Perf. by Ed 'Archie' Gardner & Ed Wynn. 1 cass. (Running Time: 1 hr.). 2001. 6.98 (2009) Radio Spirits.

Duffy's Tavern: Jean Sablon & Jimmy Durante & Ann Sothern. Perf. by Ed 'Archie' Gardner et al. 1 cass. (Running Time: 1 hr.). 2001. 6.98 (1974) Radio Spirits.

Duffy's Tavern: Minerva Pious & Bob Crosby. Perf. by Ed 'Archie' Gardner et al. 1 cass. (Running Time: 1 hr.). 2001. 6.98 (1642) Radio Spirits.

Duffy's Tavern & This Is Your F. B. I. "A Christmas Visitor" & "The Return of St. Nick" unabr. ed. Perf. by Ed Gardner & Jeff Chandler. 1 cass. (Running Time: 60 min.). Dramatization. 7.95 Norelco box. (CM-5570) Natl Recrd Co.
Duffy's Tavern: Archie is in a bad mood because Duffy didn't come through with a Christmas gift. To make matters worse, everyone's going to a party but Archie. Then a visitor drops in, & he & Archie take a walk around town. A sentimental show in the best tradition of radio. Sponsored by Bristol Meyers. This Is Your F.B.I.: Eddie, a ten-year-old youngster asks the F.B.I. to investigate the disappearance of a favorite settlement-house worker, Pops Norton, who plays Santa for the children every year. A vacationing F.B.I. agent discovers that the old man has been accused of being a forger, but this being the Christmas season, well, it just has to have a happy ending. Sponsored by Equitable Life Assurance Society & broadcast December 24, 1948.

Dug down Deep: Unearthing What I Believe & Why It Matters. unabr. ed. Joshua Harris. Read by Joshua Harris. (ENG.). 2010. audio compact disk 25.00 (978-0-307-71401-5(2), Random AudioBks) Pub: Random Audio Pubg. Dist(s): Random

Duggan's Trad. Contrib. by Family Duggan. (ENG.). 1993. 13.95 (978-0-8023-7090-7(X)); audio compact disk 21.95 (978-0-8023-8090-6(5)) Pub: Clo Iar-Chonnachta IRL. Dist(s): Dufour

***Duggars: 20 & Counting! Raising One of America's Largest Families - How they Do It.** unabr. ed. Jim Bob Duggar & Michelle Duggar. Narrated by Michelle Duggar. (Running Time: 5 hrs. 0 mins. 0 sec.). (ENG.). 2010. 16.09 (978-1-60814-788-5(6)); audio compact disk 22.99 (978-1-59859-879-7(1)) Oasis Audio.

Duino Elegies & the Sonnets to Orpheus. unabr. ed. Poems. Rainer Maria Rilke. Read by Stephen Mitchell. Tr. by Stephen Mitchell. 2 cass. (Running Time: 3 hrs.). 1997. 17.95 (978-1-57453-158-9(1)) Audio Lit.
Rilke addresses the problems of death, God & "destructive time" & attempts to overcome & transform these problems into an indestructible inner world.

Duke: The Life & Image of John Wayne. unabr. ed. Ronald L. Davis. Read by Adams Morgan. 11 cass. (Running Time: 16 hrs.). 1999. 76.95 (978-0-7861-1529-7(7), 2379) Blckstn Audio.
Focuses on Wayne's human side, portraying a personality defined by frailty & insecurity as well as by courage & strength.

Duke Diet. unabr. ed. Howard J. Eisenson & Martin Binks. (Running Time: 9 hrs. 30 mins. 0 sec.). (ENG.). 2007. audio compact disk 29.99 (978-1-4001-0420-8(3)) Pub: Tantor Media. Dist(s): IngramPubServ

Duke Diet: The World-Renowned Program for Healthy & Lasting Weight Loss. unabr. ed. Howard J. Eisenson & Martin Binks. Read by Dick Hill. (Running Time: 9 hrs. 30 mins. 0 sec.). (ENG.). 2007. audio compact disk 19.99 (978-1-4001-5420-3(0)); audio compact disk 59.99 (978-1-4001-3420-5(X)) Pub: Tantor Media. Dist(s): IngramPubServ

Duke Ellington. 2004. audio compact disk 12.95 (978-1-55592-908-4(7)) Weston Woods.

Duke Ellington. (J). 2004. pap. bk. 32.75 (978-1-55592-212-2(0)); pap. bk. 14.95 (978-1-55592-090-6(X)) Weston Woods.

Duke Ellington. Andrea Davis Pinkney. Narrated by Forest Whitaker. 1 CD. (Running Time: 15 mins.). (J). (gr. 1-5). 2004. bk. 29.95 (978-1-55592-408-9(5)); bk. 24.95 (978-1-55592-057-9(8)) Weston Woods.

Duke Ellington: The Piano Prince & His Orchestra. Andrea Davis Pinkney. Perf. by Forest Whitaker. Music by Duke Ellington & Joel Goodman. Illus. by Brian Pinkney. 1 cass. (Running Time: 18 mins.). (J). (gr. k-4). 2004. bk. 8.95 (978-1-55592-995-4(8), QHRA393) Weston Woods.
A swirl of words & music introduces Duke Ellington. A combination of the early years of the 20th century, a history of the Jazz age & a biography of Ellington as it whirls through the glittering era of the Harlem Renaissance.

Duke of Deception. unabr. ed. Geoffrey Wolff. Read by Jonathan Marosz. 7 cass. (Running Time: 10 hrs. 30 min.). 1994. 56.00 (978-0-7366-2614-9(X), 3356) Books on Tape.
Take "The Duke" first. Geoffrey's father was right out of Dickens. He was like the Wizard of Oz, all smoke & curtains, but not funny. He drank, stole, scammed - but also was warm & loving. He was tragic.

***Duke's Children.** Anthony Trollope. Read by Anais 9000. 2009. 33.95 (978-1-60112-273-5(X)) Babblebooks.

Duke's Children. unabr. collector's ed. Anthony Trollope. Read by David Case. 15 cass. (Running Time: 22 hrs. 30 min.). 1994. 120.00 (978-0-7366-2865-5(7), 3571) Books on Tape.
When his wife dies, the Duke of Omnium looks after his children. They see to his continuing education in ways he never dreamed!.

Duke's Children, Set. unabr. ed. Anthony Trollope. Read by Flo Gibson. 15 cass. (Running Time: 21 hrs.). 1993. 43.95 (978-1-55685-295-4(9)) Audio Bk Con.
The Duke of Omnium, ever the perfect gentleman, is sorely tested by his children's college escapades & the matrimonial choices of his son, Lord Silverbridge, & his daughter, Lady Mary. Love & laughter triumph.

Duke's Shorts. unabr. ed. Perf. by Dan Elliott et al. 2 cass. (Running Time: 3 hrs.). Dramatization. 1993. 14.95 set. (978-0-9630499-1-9(7)) B J Fitz.
A variety of short stories from this very diverse, talented author. The stories range from humor to intense drama, & from romance to science fiction, all with the same powerful ability to capture the reader's interest without exception.

Dulce Amore: Sugar Series. Short Stories. 1 CD. (Running Time: 73:05). Dramatization. 2004. audio compact disk 15.95 (978-0-9759671-2-6(6)) Sounds Pubng Inc.
SoundsErotic original short, erotic audio stories are sensual stories for lovers. Our original short stories are written by award winning authors and read by professional voices.

Dulce Domum: From the Wind in the Willows. Kenneth Grahame. 2007. 5.99 (978-1-60339-163-4(0)) Listenr Digest.

Dulce Domum: From the Wind in the Wilows. Kenneth Grahame. 2007. audio compact disk 5.99 (978-1-60339-164-1(9)) Listenr Digest.

Dulce Ridentem see Poetry of Benet

Dulcie's Taste of Magic/Silvermist & the Ladybug Curse. unabr. ed. Gail Herman. Read by Ashley Albert & Kathleen McInerney. (Running Time: 8760 sec.). (Disney Fairies Ser.). (ENG.). (J). (gr. 2). 2008. audio compact disk 14.95 (978-0-7393-6503-8(7), Listening Lib) Pub: Random Audio Pubg. Dist(s): Random

Dulcimer Chords. Contrib. by Joe Carr. (Running Time: 30 mins.). 2005. 9.95 (978-5-558-08944-8(X)) Mel Bay.

Dulcimer Fiddle Tunes. Lois Hornbostel. 1998. pap. bk. 19.95 (978-0-7866-4501-5(6), 93713BCD) Mel Bay.

Duma Key. unabr. ed. Stephen King. Read by John Slattery. 18 CDs. (Running Time: 23 hrs. 0 mins. 0 sec.). (ENG.). 2008. audio compact disk 49.95 (978-0-7435-6974-3(1)) Pub: S&S Audio. Dist(s): S and S Inc

Dumb Bunny. unabr. ed. Barbara Park. Read by Lana Quintal. (Running Time: 4680 sec.). (Junie B. Jones Ser.: No. 27). (ENG.). (J). (gr. 1-4). 2007. audio compact disk 14.95 (978-0-7393-3869-8(2), Listening Lib) Pub: Random Audio Pubg. Dist(s): Random

Dumb-ettes. Perf. by Rich Little. 2000. audio compact disk 16.98 (978-1-929243-31-0(6)) Uproar Ent.

Dumb Witness: A BBC Full-Cast Radio Drama. unabr. ed. Agatha Christie. Narrated by Full Cast. (Running Time: 2 hrs. 0 mins. 0 sec.). (ENG.). 2010. audio compact disk 24.95 (978-1-60283-808-6(9)) Pub: AudioGO. Dist(s): Perseus Dist

Dumb Witness: A Hercule Poirot Mystery. unabr. ed. Agatha Christie. Read by Hugh Fraser. 2006. 29.95 (978-1-57270-513-5(2)) Pub: Audio Partners. Dist(s): PerseuPGW

Dumb Witness: A Hercule Poirot Mystery. unabr. ed. Agatha Christie. Narrated by Hugh Fraser. (Mystery Masters Ser.). (ENG.). 2006. audio compact disk 29.95 (978-1-57270-512-8(4)) Pub: AudioGO. Dist(s): Perseus Dist
In this intricate mystery first published in 1937, Poirot receives a letter - two months after it was written - from rich spinster Emily Arundell about a possible attempt on her life. Suspicious, Poirot heads for her hometown of Market Basing to find her already dead. A now cold trail of clues leads Poirot through a colorful cast of characters and one of Christie's typically cozy villages as he attempts to solve a murder that confounds even his superior skills. Reader Hugh Fraser masterfully evokes Christie's distinctive world.

Dumbo. 1 cass. (J). 3.98 Clamshell. (978-1-55886-107-7(6), BB/PT 434) Smarty Pants.

Dumbo. 1 cass. (Read-Along Ser.). (J). bk. 7.99 W Disney Records.

Dumbo Soundtrack. Prod. by Walt Disney Productions Staff. 1 CD. (J). 1997. audio compact disk 19.95 (978-0-7634-0333-1(4)) W Disney Records.
Music - Popular.

Dumbo Soundtrack. Prod. by Walt Disney Productions Staff. 1 cass. (J). (ps-3). 1997. 12.98 (978-0-7634-0332-4(6)) W Disney Records.

***Dummy.** 2010. audio compact disk (978-1-59171-180-3(0)) Falcon Picture.

Dumping Billy. unabr. ed. Olivia Goldsmith. Read by Bernadette Quigley. (Running Time: 11 hrs.). 2004. 34.95 (978-1-59355-809-3(0), 1593558090, BAU); 87.25 (978-1-59355-810-9(4), 1593558104, BrilAudUnabridg) Brilliance Audio.
There's something magical about Billy Nolan. It's not just that the Brooklyn bar owner is wickedly handsome; it is also that any woman he dates and dumps - and he dumps them all - immediately goes on to marry the next man she meets. But Kate Jameson is immune to his charms. She left Brooklyn for upward-mobility in Manhattan at the first chance she got, and she's not about to fall for some cad from the old neighborhood. But when her best friend Bina's engagement is broken off, Kate hatches a plan: all she has to do is get Billy to date and dump Bina. Then they'll wait for Bina's wayward fiance to return for the magic to happen. But the one thing Kate hasn't counted on is how Billy feels about the whole plot - and how she begins to feel about Billy. She may have changed her style, but her roots are showing.

Dumping Billy. unabr. ed. Olivia Goldsmith. Read by Bernadette Quigley. (Running Time: 11 hrs.). 2004. 24.95 (978-1-59335-309-4(X), 159335309X, Brilliance MP3); 39.25 (978-1-59335-468-8(1), 1593354681, Brinc Audio MP3 Lib) Brilliance Audio.

Dumping Billy. unabr. ed. Olivia Goldsmith. Read by Bernadette Quigley. (Running Time: 11 hrs.). 2004. 39.25 (978-1-59710-232-2(6), 1597102326, BADLE); 24.95 (978-1-59710-233-9(4), 1597102334, BAD) Brilliance Audio.

Dumping Debt. Featuring Dave Ramsey. 2002. audio compact disk (978-0-9720044-7-3(5)) Lampo Inc.

Dumping Princes. unabr. ed. Tyne O'Connell. Read by Nicky Talacko. (Running Time: 6 hrs. 40 mins.). (Calypso Chronicles). (YA). (gr. 7-12). 2008. audio compact disk 77.95 (978-1-921415-00-5(2), 9781921415005) Pub: Bolinda Pubng AUS. Dist(s): Bolinda Pub Inc

Dunbar Out Loud. Perf. by Bobby Norfolk. 1 CD. (Running Time: 54 mins.). 2004. audio compact disk 14.95 (978-0-87483-721-6(9)) Pub: August Hse. Dist(s): Natl Bk Netwk

Dunbar Out Loud. unabr. ed. Paul Laurence Dunbar. Read by Bobby Norfolk. (J). 2007. 34.99 (978-1-59895-852-2(6)) Find a World.

Dunc & Amos Hit the Big Top; Dunc's Dump. unabr. ed. Gary Paulsen. Read by Bill Fantini. 2 cass. (Culpepper Adventures Ser.: Nos. 9-10). (gr. 3-5). lib. bdg. 16.95 set. (978-1-55656-191-7(1), DAB 079) Pub: Dercum Audio. Dist(s): APG

Dunc & Amos Hit the Big Top; Dunc's Dump. unabr. ed. Gary Paulsen. Read by Bill Fantini. 2 cass. (Running Time: 3 hrs.). (Culpepper Adventures Ser.: Nos. 9-10). (gr. 3-5). 1993. pap. bk. 9.95 (978-1-55656-190-0(3)) Pub: Dercum Audio. Dist(s): APG
The two "best friends for life" crack a burglary ring & investigate illegal dumping at the town dump.

Dunc & the Flaming Ghost; Amos Gets Famous. unabr. ed. Gary Paulsen. Read by Bill Fantini. 2 cass. (Culpepper Adventures Ser.: Nos. 7-8). (gr. 3-5). lib. bdg. 16.95 set. (978-1-55656-189-4(X), DAB 078) Pub: Dercum Audio. Dist(s): APG

Dunc & the Flaming Ghost; Amos Gets Famous. unabr. ed. Gary Paulsen. Read by Bill Fantini. 2 cass. (Running Time: 3 hrs.). (Culpepper Adventures Ser.: Nos. 7-8). (gr. 3-5). 1993. pap. bk. 9.95 (978-1-55656-188-7(1), 396028) Pub: Dercum Audio. Dist(s): APG
The two best friends check out the haunted house & take a turn at the circus.

Dunc & the Scam Artist; Dunc & Amos & the Red Tattoos. unabr. ed. Gary Paulsen. Read by Bill Fantini. 2 cass. (Culpepper Adventures Ser.: Nos. 11-12). (gr. 3-5). lib. bdg. 16.95 set. (978-1-55656-193-1(8), DAB 080) Pub: Dercum Audio. Dist(s): APG

Dunc & the Scam Artist; Dunc & Amos & the Red Tattoos. unabr. ed. Gary Paulsen. Read by Bill Fantini. 2 cass. (Running Time: 3 hrs.). (Culpepper Adventures Ser.: Nos. 11-12). (gr. 3-5). 1993. pap. bk. 9.95 (978-1-55656-192-4(X)) Pub: Dercum Audio. Dist(s): APG
Dune & Amos are on the trail of con artists. Then they head for camp for fresh air & a change of pace.

Duncan's Greatest Hits. Perf. by Rob Evans. (J). (ps-3). 1997. cass. & video 11.95 (978-84-7200-035-3(4)) Integrity Music.

Dunce Cap Kelly. unabr. ed. Dave Kinnoin & Jimmy Hammer. 1 cass., 1 CD. (Running Time: 48 min.). (J). (gr. 1-6). 1993. 9.98 (978-1-881304-02-9(7), SW103-4); audio compact disk 12.98 CD. (978-1-881304-12-8(4), SW103-2) Song Wizard Recs.
Fun & inspiring original songs, sung by Dave Kinnoin.

Dunc's Halloween; Dunc Breaks the Record. unabr. ed. Gary Paulsen. Read by Bill Fantini. 2 pieces. (Running Time: 3 hrs.). (Culpepper Adventures Ser.: Nos. 5-6). (gr. 3-5). 1993. 9.95 (978-1-55656-186-3(5)) Pub: Dercum Audio. Dist(s): APG
The two best friends "celebrate" Halloween & try hang-gliding. Along the way they learn about werewolves & wilderness survival.

Dune. Frank Herbert. Read by Scott Brick. 2002. 36.00 (978-0-7366-8959-5(1)); audio compact disk 160.00 (978-0-7366-9240-3(1)) Books on Tape.

Dune. unabr. ed. Frank Herbert. Read by George Guidall. 13 Cass. (Running Time: 23.25 Hrs). 44.95 (978-1-4025-2360-1(2)); audio compact disk 59.95 (978-1-4025-2380-9(7)) Recorded Bks.

Dune. unabr. ed. Frank Herbert. Narrated by George Guidall. 16 cass. (Running Time: 23 hrs. 30 mins.). 1993. 128.00 (978-1-55690-933-7(0), 93429E7) Recorded Bks.
On the planet Arrakis, a new leader emerges to overthrow the evil House of Harkonnen, liberate the Fremen from the deserts & bring to fulfillment the prophecy of the Bene Gesserit.

Dune. unabr. ed. Frank Herbert & Frank Herbert. Read by Orlagh Cassidy et al. 18 CDs. (Running Time: 22 hrs. 0 mins. 0 sec.). (ENG.). 2007. audio compact disk 59.95 (978-1-4272-0143-0(9)) Pub: Macmill Audio. Dist(s): Macmillan

Dune. unabr. collector's ed. Frank Herbert. Read by Connor O'Brien. 13 cass. (Running Time: 19 hrs. 30 min.). 1997. 104.00 (978-0-7366-3763-3(X), 4437) Books on Tape.
This first book is set on the desert planet Arrakis, a world drawn as vividly & terrifyingly as any in literature. Dune begins the story of the man known as Maud'dib, a hero who will guide his great family in their ambition to bring about humankind's most ancient & unattainable dream to found the perfect society.

Dune: House Atreides. Brian Herbert & Kevin J. Anderson. Read by Michael Prichard. 2000. 144.00 (978-0-7366-9258-8(4)) Books on Tape.

Dune: House Atreides. unabr. ed. Brian Herbert & Kevin J. Anderson. Narrated by Scott Brick. 3 MP3-CDs. (Running Time: 26 hrs. 30 mins. 0 sec.). (Prelude to Dune Ser.). (ENG.). 2009. 39.99 (978-1-4001-6361-8(7)); audio compact disk 109.99 (978-1-4001-4361-0(6)); audio compact disk 54.99 (978-1-4001-1361-3(X)) Pub: Tantor Media. Dist(s): IngramPubServ

Dune: House Corrino. Brian Herbert & Kevin J. Anderson. Read by Michael Prichard. 2001. 128.00 (978-0-7366-9260-1(6)) Books on Tape.

***Dune: House Corrino.** unabr. ed. Brian Herbert & Kevin J. Anderson. Narrated by Scott Brick. (Running Time: 24 hrs. 0 mins.). (Prelude to Dune Ser.). 2009. 54.99 (978-1-4001-9363-9(X)) Tantor Media.

Dune: House Corrino. unabr. ed. Brian Herbert & Kevin J. Anderson. Narrated by Scott Brick. (Running Time: 24 hrs. 0 mins. 0 sec.). (Prelude to Dune Ser.). (ENG.). 2010. audio compact disk 54.99 (978-1-4001-1363-7(6)) Pub: Tantor Media. Dist(s): IngramPubServ

***Dune: House Harkonnen.** unabr. ed. Brian Herbert & Kevin J. Anderson. Narrated by Scott Brick. (Running Time: 26 hrs. 30 mins.). (Prelude to Dune Ser.). 2009. 28.99 (978-1-4001-8362-3(6)) Tantor Media.

Dune: House Harkonnen. unabr. ed. Brian Herbert & Kevin J. Anderson. Narrated by Scott Brick. (Running Time: 26 hrs. 30 mins. 0 sec.). (Prelude to Dune Ser.). (ENG.). 2009. 39.99 (978-1-4001-6362-5(5)); audio compact disk 109.99 (978-1-4001-4362-7(4)) Pub: Tantor Media. Dist(s): IngramPubServ

Dune: The Banquet see Dune Trilogy

Dune Pt. 1: House Atreides. unabr. ed. Brian Herbert & Kevin J. Anderson. Read by Michael Prichard. 10 cass. (Running Time: 90 mins. per cass.). (Dune Chronicles: 4). 2000. 60.00 (5153-A) Books on Tape.
Chronicles the early life of Leto Atreides, prince of a minor house in the galactic Imperium. Leto comes to confront the realities of power when House Vernius is betrayed in an imperial plot involving a quest for an artificial substitute to melange, a substance vital in interstellar trade that is found only on the planet Dune.

Dune Pt. 2: House Atreides. unabr. ed. Brian Herbert & Kevin J. Anderson. Read by Michael Prichard. 8 cass. (Running Time: 90 mins. per cass.). (Dune Chronicles: 4). 2000. 48.00 (5153-B) Books on Tape.
Chronicles the early life of Leto Atreides, prince of a minor house in galactic Imperium. Leto comes to confront the realities of power when House Vernius is betrayed in an imperial plot involving a quest for an artificial substitute to melange, a substance vital in interstellar trade that is found only on the planet Dune.

Dune Pt. 2: House Harkonnen. Brian Herbert & Kevin J. Anderson. Read by Michael Prichard. 2000. 144.00 (978-0-7366-9259-5(2)) Books on Tape.

Dune Pt. 2: House Harkonnen. unabr. ed. Brian Herbert & Kevin J. Anderson. Read by Michael Prichard. 10 cass. (Running Time: 15 hrs.). 2000. 80.00 (978-0-7366-5654-2(5), 5453-A); 64.00 (978-0-7366-5948-2(X), 5453-B) Books on Tape.
Second in the prequeil trilogy, a huge number of characters in a complex story continue the journey to Dune.

***Dune Audio Collection.** abr. ed. Frank Herbert. Read by Frank Herbert. (ENG.). 2007. (978-0-06-084586-5(4), Harper Audio); (978-0-06-084587-2(2), Harper Audio) HarperCollins Pubs.

Dune Messiah. rev. unabr. ed. Frank Herbert & Frank Herbert. Read by Euan Morton et al. 7 CDs. (Running Time: 9 hrs. 0 mins. 0 sec.). (ENG.). 2007. audio compact disk 34.95 (978-1-4272-0236-9(2)) Pub: Macmill Audio. Dist(s): Macmillan

Dune Messiah. unabr. collector's ed. Frank Herbert. Read by Connor O'Brien. 6 cass. (Running Time: 9 hrs.). (Dune Chronicles: Bk. 2). 1998. 48.00 (978-0-7366-4018-3(5), 4516) Books on Tape.
Second installment explores new developments on the desert planet Arrakis, with its intricate social order & its strange threatening environment. Picks up the story of the man known as Maud'dib, heir to a power unimaginable, bringing to fruition an ambition of unparalleled scale, the centuries old scheme to create a superbeing who reigns not in the heavens but among men. But the question is, do all paths of glory lead to the grave.

Dune Road. unabr. ed. Jane Green. Contrib. by Cassandra Campbell. 9 CDs. (Running Time: 11 hrs.). (ENG.). (gr. 12 up). 2009. audio compact disk 39.95 (978-0-14-314464-9(2), PengAudBks) Penguin Grp USA.

Dune: the Butlerian Jihad. Brian Herbert & Kevin J. Anderson. Read by Scott Brick. (Dune Ser.). 2003. 24.95 (978-1-59397-042-0(0)) Pub: Macmill Audio. Dist(s): Macmillan

Dune Trilogy. unabr. ed. 4 cass. HarperCollins Pubs.

Dune Trilogy. unabr. ed. Sbc116 Cae. 4 cass. (Running Time: 6 hrs.). Incl. Battles of Dune. (SBC 116); Dune: The Banquet. (SBC 116); Sandworms of Dune. (SBC 116); Truths of Dune. (SBC 116); 1985. 29.95 (978-0-89845-018-7(7), SBC 116) HarperCollins Pubs.

Dunedin. unabr. ed. Shena Mackay. Read by Nicolette McKenzie. 10 cass. (Running Time: 10 hrs.). 2000. 84.95 (978-0-7531-0816-1(X), 000514) Pub: ISIS Audio GBR. Dist(s): Ulverscroft US
The author's perceptive black comedy takes us between New Zealand in 1909 where Jack McKenzie arrives from Glasgow to become a pastor in the New World & present-day London where his descendants are leading very different existences.

Dung (Texas Block Party) Ed Young. 1992. 4.95 (978-0-7417-1935-5(5), 935) Win Walk.

Dungeon of Doom. John R. Erickson. Read by John R. Erickson. 2 cassettes. (Running Time: approx 3 hours). (Hank the Cowdog Ser.: No. 44). (J). 2004. 17.99 (978-1-59188-344-9(X)); audio compact disk 19.99 (978-1-59188-644-0(9)) Maverick Bks.

Dunk. unabr. ed. David Lubar. Read by Full Cast Production Staff. (YA). 2007. 44.99 (978-1-60252-499-6(8)) Find a World.

Dunnet Landing Sketches. unabr. ed. Sarah Orne Jewett. Read by Shaela Connor. 3 cass. (Running Time: 3 hrs. 6 min.). Dramatization. 1993. 21.95 (978-1-55686-457-5(4), 457) Books in Motion.
Sequel to The Country of the Pointed Firs. Once again the author draws her audience deep into the lives of the inhabitants of Dunnet Landing, a small village situated on the northern coast of turn-of-the-century Maine.

Duns Scotus & Medieval Christianity. unabr. ed. Ralph McInerny. Read by Lynn Redgrave. (Running Time: 10800 sec.). (World of Philosophy Ser.). 2006. audio compact disk 25.95 (978-0-7861-6387-8(9)) Pub: Blckstn Audio. Dist(s): NetLibrary CO

Dunwich Horror. abr. ed. H. P. Lovecraft. Read by David McCallum. 2 cass. (Running Time: 1 hr. 54 min.). 1987. 15.95 (978-0-89845-656-1(8), A 2102) HarperCollins Pubs.
In the first story one learns of the spooky town & of the life & times of the dark & goatish & not entirely human, William Waitley. The second story concerns a renovated ancestral home, inside of which many horrors have passed.

Dupes of Communism. unabr. ed. Louis Budenz. 1 cass. (Running Time: 43 min.). 12.95 (141) J Norton Pubs.

Duplicate Death. unabr. ed. Georgette Heyer. Read by Clifford Morgate. 8 cass. (Running Time: 10 hrs.). 1992. 69.95 (978-0-7451-6009-2(3), CAB 643) AudioGO.
The game was Duplicate Bridge - & it led to a double murder.

Duplicate Keys. unabr. ed. Jane Smiley. Narrated by Ruth Ann Phimister. 7 cassettes. (Running Time: 11.5 hrs). 29.95 (978-1-4025-2540-7(0)) Recorded Bks.

Duplicate Keys. unabr. ed. Jane Smiley. Narrated by Ruth Ann Phimister. 8 cass. (Running Time: 11 hrs. 30 mins.). 1998. 70.00 (978-0-7887-2177-9(1), 95473E7) Recorded Bks.
When Alice unlocks the door to a friend's New York apartment & finds two corpses in the living room, she must sort through a tangle of relationships & motives to find out why they were killed.

Duplicate Keys. unabr. ed. Jane Smiley. Narrated by Ruth Ann Phimister. 10 CDs. (Running Time: 11 hrs. 30 mins.). 2000. audio compact disk 90.00 (978-0-7887-3961-3(1), C1116E7) Recorded Bks.

***Duplicate This! Showing Your Friends How to Live Like Jesus.** unabr. ed. Andy Braner. (Running Time: 5 hrs. 41 mins. 0 sec.). (Invert Ser.). (ENG.). 2009. 12.99 (978-0-310-77217-0(6)) Zondervan.

Duplication Nation CD. Randy Gage. 12 CD's. 2004. audio compact disk 147.00 (978-0-9762299-0-2(0)) Prime Concepts Grp.

Duplication Nation Leadership Kit. Randy Gage. (ENG.). 2002. audio compact disk 477.00 (978-0-9744363-9-5(9)) Prime Concepts Grp.

Duplicity of Hargraves see O. Henry Favorites

Duplicity of Hargraves & Others. unabr. ed. H. G. Wells et al. Read by Gene Engene & Jack Sondericker. 4 cass. (Running Time: 4 hrs.). Dramatization. 1990. 26.95 (978-1-55686-091-1(9), 091) Books in Motion.
Series of short stories: The Duplicity of Hargraves, The Man Who Could Work Miracles, A Deal in Wheat, What Was It, Mateo Falcone, A Lodging for the Night, Behind the Shade.

Durable Goods. unabr. ed. Elizabeth Berg. Read by Jen Taylor. 6 CDs. (Running Time: 9 hrs.). 2001. audio compact disk 64.95 (978-0-7927-9902-3(X), SLD 053, Chivers Sound Lib); bk. 39.95 (978-0-7927-2460-5(7), CSL 349, Chivers Sound Lib) AudioGO.
In the heat of summer, on a small army base in rural Texas, Katie waits inpatiently for her life to change. Still feeling the pain of the recent death of her mother, her spirit remains miraculously strong. She is filled with longings.

Durango. Hank Mitchum. Read by Charlie O'Dowd. 4 vols. No. 17. 2004. 25.00 (978-1-58807-200-9(2)); (978-1-58807-960-2(0)) Am Pubng Inc.

Durango. Scripts. Hank Mitchum. 5 CDs. (Running Time: 6 hrs.). (Stagecoach Ser.: No. 17). 2005. 14.99 (978-1-58807-483-6(8)) Am Pubng Inc.
Stage driver pushes his rig north through a freak early autumn blizzard. The stage is held up and the horses stolen. The driver and passengers are left to survive or not until help can arrive.

Duraznos: Level 4, Vol. 7. 2003. 11.50 (978-0-7652-0994-8(2)) Modern Curr.

Dusk see Piece of String

Dusk of Dawn: An Essay Toward an Autobiography of a Race Concept see Black Pioneers in American History, Vol. 2, 19th - 20th Centuries

***Dust.** 2010. audio compact disk (978-1-59171-236-7(X)) Falcon Picture.

Dust. Charles R. Pellegrino. 2004. 11.95 (978-0-7435-4663-8(6)) Pub: S&S Audio. Dist(s): S and S Inc

Dust. unabr. ed. Martha Grimes. Read by John Lee. 8 CDs. (Running Time: 10 hrs.). (ENG.). (gr. 12 up). 2007. audio compact disk 39.95 (978-0-14-305903-5(3), PengAudBks) Penguin Grp USA.

***Dust.** unabr. ed. Joan Frances Turner. (Running Time: 10 hrs.). (ENG.). 2010. audio compact disk 39.95 (978-0-14-242853-5(1), PengAudBks) Penguin Grp USA.

***Dust & Shadow: An Account of the Ripper Killings by Dr. John H. Watson.** unabr. ed. Lyndsay Faye. Read by Simon Vance. (Running Time: 9 hrs. 30 mins.). 2010. 29.95 (978-1-4417-6813-1(0)); 59.95 (978-1-4417-6810-0(6)); audio compact disk 90.00 (978-1-4417-6811-7(4)) Blckstn Audio.

Dust Disappears. Carilda O. Labra. Ed. by Stanley H. Barkan. Tr. by Daniela Gioseffi & Enildo A García. Frwd. by Gregory Rabassa. Illus. by Plumido De Cobo. (Review Latin-American Writers Chapbook Ser.: No. 1). (ENG & SPA.). 1991. 10.00 (978-0-89304-154-0(8)) Cross-Cultrl NY.

Dust in the Lion's Paw. unabr. ed. Freya Stark. Read by Rosemary Davis. 12 cass. (Running Time: 18 hrs.). (Isis Ser.). (J). 1989. 94.95

(978-1-85089-701-9(8), 89081) Pub: ISIS Lrg Prnt GBR. Dist(s): Ulverscroft US

Dust in the Lion's Paw. unabr. collector's ed. Freya Stark. Read by Donada Peters. 9 cass. (Running Time: 13 hrs. 30 mins.). 1990. 72.00 (978-0-7366-1686-7(1), 2532) Books on Tape.
Dust in the Lion's Paw forms the fourth & perhaps most recent part of Freya Stark's autobiography. It covers WW II, recalling the vicissitudes of 1939 & the tide of war. When war broke out, Stark was in the Middle East, working for the British Foreign Office. She specialized in education & propaganda directed toward the native populations. This background forms the perspective from which she tells her tale of the war & of Britain's role in it.

Dust of Death see Asimov's Mysteries

Dust on the Sea. Douglas Reeman. 2 cass. (Running Time: 3 hrs.). 1999. 16.95 (978-1-85686-731-3(5), Audiobks) Pub: Random GBR. Dist(s): Trafalgar

Dust on the Sea. unabr. ed. Edward L. Beach, Jr. Read by Wolfram Kandinsky. 12 cass. (Running Time: 18 hrs.). 1989. 96.00 (978-0-7366-1522-8(9), 2393) Books on Tape.
The time: the grim middle years of WWII. The ship: the U.S.S Eel, most lethal weapon in America's submarine arsenal on a perilous mission into Japan's tightly guarded inner sea. The crew: hand-picked professionals to the last - led by a captain tormented by his own secret doubts. The cargo: a deadly payload of electromagnetic torpedoes.

Dust on the Sea. unabr. ed. Douglas Reeman. 10 cass. (Running Time: 37680 sec.). (Thrush Green Chronicles Ser.). 2000. 84.95 (978-0-7540-0442-4(2), CAB 1865) Pub: Chivers Audio Bks GBR. Dist(s): AudioGO
It is 1943. Captain Mike Blackwood, Royal Marine Commando, is ready to head down the ramp of a landing craft & launch an assault on a Sicilian beach. Here, Mike Blackwood must find within himself the qualities of leadership which will inspire those marines who are once again the first to land & among the first to die.

Dust Particles in Sunlight: Poems of Rumi. Poems. Jalal Al-Din Rumi. Read by Coleman Bark. 1 cass. (Running Time: 60 min.). (Handbook of Poetry Audio Book Ser.: Vol. 3). 1997. 12.00 (978-0-930872-60-1(6)) Omega Pubns NY.

Dust to Dust. abr. ed. Heather Graham. Read by Tanya Eby and Luke Daniels. (Running Time: 5 hrs.). (Prophecy Ser.). 2010. audio compact disk 9.99 (978-1-4418-2602-2(5), 9781441826022, BCD Value Price) Brilliance Audio.

Dust to Dust. abr. ed. Tami Hoag. Read by Jon Tenney. 2004. 15.95 (978-0-7435-4664-5(4)) Pub: S&S Audio. Dist(s): S and S Inc

Dust to Dust. unabr. ed. Heather Graham. (Running Time: 11 hrs.). (Prophecy Ser.). 2009. 39.97 (978-1-4233-9749-6(5), 9781423397496, BADLE) Brilliance Audio.

Dust to Dust. unabr. ed. Heather Graham. Read by Luke Daniels & Tanya Eby. (Running Time: 11 hrs.). (Prophecy Ser.). 2009. 39.97 (978-1-4233-9747-2(9), 9781423397472, Brinc Audio MP3 Lib) Brilliance Audio.

Dust to Dust. unabr. ed. Heather Graham. Read by Tanya Eby and Luke Daniels. (Running Time: 11 hrs.). (Prophecy Ser.). 2009. 24.99 (978-1-4233-9746-5(0), 9781423397465, Brilliance MP3) Brilliance Audio.

Dust to Dust. unabr. ed. Heather Graham. Read by Luke Daniels & Tanya Eby. (Running Time: 11 hrs.). (Prophecy Ser.). 2009. 24.99 (978-1-4233-9748-9(7), 9781423397489, BAD); audio compact disk 97.97 (978-1-4233-9745-8(2), 9781423397458, BriAudCD Unabrid) Brilliance Audio.

Dust to Dust. unabr. ed. Tami Hoag. Read by Nick Sullivan. 10 vols. (Running Time: 15 hrs.). 2001. bk. 84.95 (978-0-7927-2410-0(0), CSL 299, Chivers Sound Lib) AudioGO.
Together with his partner, Nikki Liska, detective Sam Kovac begin to dig at the too-neat edges of a Minneapolis Internal Affairs cop whose death was either suicide or a kinky act turned tragic.

Dust to Dust. unabr. ed. Tami Hoag. Read by Nick Sullivan. 12 CDs. (Running Time: 18 hrs.). 2001. audio compact disk 110.95 (978-0-7927-9935-1(6), SLD 086, Chivers Sound Lib) AudioGO.
Sorry. The single word is written on the mirror. In front of it hung the body of Andy Fallon, a Minneapolis Internal Affairs cop. Was it suicide? Or a kinky act turned tragic accident? As Nikki Liska and Sam Kovac begin to investigate they find their lives on the line because a killer wants the truth left dead and buried. Ashes to ashes.

Dust to Dust. unabr. ed. Tami Hoag. Read by Jeff Harding. 10 cass. (Running Time: 14 hrs.). 2001. (978-0-7531-1181-9(0)) ISIS Audio GBR.
The death on internal affairs investigator Andy Fallon is a potential political bomb for the Minneapolis Police Department. Fallon was gay, and he was investigating a possible police connection in the brutal murder of another gay officer. But Andy?s death looks like suicide or an embarrassing accident: death by auto-erotic misadventure and the pressure is on from the top brass to close the case. But Andy Fallon?s ex-lover doesn?t believe that Andy died by his own hand and presses lead detective Sam Kovac to find another answer. Kovac begins to investigate Andy?s cases and the deeper he digs, the more suspicious he becomes. It looks like Andy hit on something that got him killed and he might not be the final victim. Someone wants the truth left dead and buried. Ashes to ashes, dust to dust.

Dusty & Lefty: The Lives of the Cowboys. abr. unabr. ed. Tim Russell. Told to Garrison Keillor. 1 CD. (Running Time: 4500 sec.). (ENG.). 2006. audio compact disk 14.95 (978-1-59887-043-5(2), 1598870432) Pub: HighBridge. Dist(s): Workman Pub

Dusty Answer. unabr. ed. Rosamond Lehmann. Read by Jenny Agutter. 10 cass. (Running Time: 15 hrs.). 2001. 84.95 (978-0-7540-0569-8(0), CAB1992) AudioGO.

Dusty Death. J. M. Gregson & Jonathan Keeble. 2009. 54.95 (978-1-84652-514-8(4)); audio compact disk 71.95 (978-1-84652-515-5(2)) Pub: Magna Story GBR. Dist(s): Ulverscroft US

Dusty Letters, Set. unabr. ed. Elisabeth McNeill. Read by Julia Sands. 7 cass. (Running Time: 9 hrs. 15 min.). 1999. 76.95 (978-1-85903-300-5(8)) Pub: Magna Story GBR. Dist(s): Ulverscroft US
Sir Henry Gwillim, his wife Elizabeth & her frivolous sister, Polly, sailed from Portsmouth on a freezing February day in 1801 to a new life in the East, Sir Henry had been appointed to an influential judiciary post in the East India Company. Seven years in India change everything. Sir Henry becomes embroiled in bribery & corruption, Elizabeth finds new interests studying botany & Indian customs while Polly is constantly let down by a succession of admirers. Faced with an uncertain future, all three look for ways to escape..but only one succeeds.

Dutch. 2 cass. (Running Time: 80 min.). (Language - Thirty Library). bk. 16.95 set in vinyl album. Moonbeam Pubns.
Using the proven method based on the famous U.S. Military accelerated language learning program, Language/30 courses stress conversationally useful words & phrases.

Dutch. Ed. by Berlitz Publishing. (In 60 MINUTES Ser.). 2008. audio compact disk 9.95 (978-981-268-397-7(6)) Pub: APA Pubns Serv SGP. Dist(s): Langenscheidt

Dutch. Berlitz Publishing Staff. 1 CD. (Running Time: 1 hr. 14 mins.). (Berlitz Travel Pack CD Ser.). (DUT & ENG., 2004. audio compact disk 21.95 (978-981-246-590-0(1), 465901) Pub: Berlitz Pubng. Dist(s): Langenscheidt

Dutch. unabr. ed. Ed. by Charles Berlitz. 2 cass. (Running Time: 1 hr. 30 mins.). (Language/30 Brief Course Ser.). pap. bk. 21.95 (AF1034) J Norton Pubs.
Quick, highly condensed introduction to the words & phrases you'll need to communicate effectively in the country you're visiting. Cassettes & phrase guide book are in a vinyl album.

Dutch: A Memoir of Ronald Reagan. unabr. ed. Edmund Morris. Read by Edmund Morris. 6 cass. (Running Time: 9 hrs.). 1999. 48.00 (978-0-7366-4800-4(3), 5150) Books on Tape.
This, the only biography ever authorized by a sitting president, is as revolutionary in method as it is formidable in scholarship. Morris, the Pulitzer Prize-winning biographer of Theodore Roosevelt, finds the President to be a man of extraordinary power and mystery. During thirteen years of archival research and interviews with Reagan and his family, friends admirers and enemies, Morris studied the young "Dutch" the middle-aged "Ronnie," and the septuagenarian Chief Executive with a closeness and dispassion unmatched by any other presidential biographer.

Dutch: Language/30. rev. ed. Educational Services Corporation Staff. Intro. by Charles Berlitz. 2 cass. (DUT.). 1994. pap. bk. 21.95 (978-0-910542-63-0(5)) Educ Svcs DC.
Dutch self-teaching language course.

Dutch: Learn to Speak & Understand Dutch. unabr. ed. Pimsleur Staff. (Running Time: 5 hrs. 0 mins. 0 sec.). (Basic Ser.). (ENG.). 2007. audio compact disk 24.95 (978-0-671-04778-8(7), Pimsleur) Pub: S&S Audio. Dist(s): S and S Inc

Dutch: Learn to Speak & Understand Dutch with Pimsleur Language Programs. unabr. ed. Pimsleur Staff. (Running Time: 8 hrs. 0 mins. 0 sec.). (Conversational Ser.). (ENG.). 2007. audio compact disk 49.95 (978-0-7435-5252-3(0), Pimsleur) Pub: S&S Audio. Dist(s): S and S Inc

Dutch: Learn to Speak & Understand Dutch with Pimsleur Language Programs. unabr. ed. Created by Pimsleur Staff. (Running Time: 16 hrs. 0 mins. 0 sec.). (Comprehensive Ser.). (ENG.). 2007. audio compact disk 345.00 (978-0-671-04779-5(5), Pimsleur) Pub: S&S Audio. Dist(s): S and S Inc

Dutch: Short Course. Paul Pimsleur. 5 cass. (Pimsleur Language Learning Ser.). 1993. pap. bk. 149.95 (0671-57913-4) SyberVision.

Dutch for Speakers of English, Compact. unabr. ed. 5 cass. (Running Time: 5 hrs.). (Pimsleur Tapes Ser.). (DUT.). 1993. 129.00 set. (19300, Pimsleur) S&S Audio.
A ten-lesson-unit program based upon the Pimsleur Spoken Language Programmed Instructional Method, providing basic beginning language training to the ACTFL Novice Level.

Dutch Phrase Book Pack. rev. ed. Collins Publishers Staff. (ENG & DUT.). 2003. pap. bk. 13.99 (978-0-00-765081-1(7)) Pub: HarpC GBR. Dist(s): Trafalgar

Dutch Twins & the Japanese Twins, Set. unabr. ed. Lucy Fitch Perkins. Read by Flo Gibson. 3 cass. (Running Time: 3 hrs. 30 min.). (J). (gr. 1-3). 1989. 16.95 (978-1-55685-147-6(2)) Audio Bk Con.
Features a visit to foreign lands at the turn of the century to learn their customs, surrounding & playthings through the eye of little twins.

Dutchman's Flat; His Brother's Debt; Big Medicine; The Turkey Feather Riders. abr. ed. Louis L'Amour. 3 vols. (Great Mysteries - Louis L'Amour Ser.). 2001. audio compact disk 11.99 (978-1-57815-529-3(0), Media Bks Audio) Media Bks NJ.

Dutchman's Flat; Man Riding West. abr. ed. Louis L'Amour. 2 cass. (Running Time: 3 hrs.). (Louis L'Amour Collector Ser.:). 2000. 7.95 (978-1-57815-100-4(7), 1071, Media Bks Audio) Media Bks NJ.
The adventures of the brave men & women who settled the American frontier.

Duty: A Father, His Son, & the Man Who Won the War. abr. ed. Bob Greene. 2 cass. (Running Time: 3 hrs.). 2000. 18.00 (978-1-55935-336-6(8)) Soundelux.
The true story of Paul Tibbets & the dropping of the world's first atomic bomb. It is also a salute to the heroes of that generation.

Duty, Honor, Country (audio CD) Douglas MacArthur. (ENG.). 2007. audio compact disk 12.95 (978-1-57970-476-6(X), Audio-For) J Norton Pubs.

***Duty to the Dead.** unabr. ed. Charles Todd. Narrated by Rosalyn Landor. 1 Playaway. (Running Time: 10 hrs.). (Bess Crawford Mystery Ser.: No. 1). 2009. 79.95 (978-0-7927-6840-1(X)); 49.95 (978-0-7927-6764-0(0)); audio compact disk 79.95 (978-0-7927-6687-2(3)) AudioGO.

DVD- Pediatric Emergencies I DVD. 9th ed. AAOS Staff. 2005. 153.95 (978-0-7637-2990-5(6)) Jones Bartlett.

DVD- the EMS Call DVD. 9th ed. AAOS Staff. 2005. 153.95 (978-0-7637-2982-0(5)) Jones Bartlett.

DVD- Trauma MGMT & Spinal Immobilization DVD. 9th ed. AAOS Staff. 2005. 92.95 (978-0-7637-2989-9(2)) Jones Bartlett.

DVD-Airway Management DVD. 9th ed. AAOS Staff. 2005. 92.95 (978-0-7637-2985-1(X)) Jones Bartlett.

DVD Guide to the Citizenship Test & Interview. Narrated by Roger Steffenf. Contrib. by Oscar Castagna. Prod. by Oscar Castagna. (Running Time: 33 mins.). 2005. reel tape, video, DVD 35.00 (978-0-9707073-7-6(1)) O Castagna.

DVD-Patient Assessment DVD. 9th ed. AAOS Staff. 2005. 92.95 (978-0-7637-2986-8(8)) Jones Bartlett.

DVD-Wilderness First AID DVD. 2nd ed. AAOS Staff. 2005. 86.50 (978-0-7637-2834-2(9)) Jones Bartlett.

Dvorak: An Introduction to Symphony No. 9 "From the New World" Jeremy Siepmann. 2 CDs. (Running Time: 3 hrs.). (Classics Explained Ser.). 2003. pap. bk. (978-1-84379-014-3(9)) NaxMulti GBR.

Dvorak: The Greatest Hits. 1 cass. audio compact disk 10.98 CD. (978-1-57908-164-5(9), 3610) Platinm Enter.

Dvorak: Two String Quartets, Opus 34 & Opus 51. abr. ed. Pro Arte Quartet UW-Madisoin School of Music Staff. 2001. audio compact disk 15.00 (978-1-931569-01-9(0)) Pub: U of Wis Pr. Dist(s): Chicago Distribution Ctr

Dwads. Edward Helin. 1 cass. 8.95 (870) Am Fed Astrologers.

Dwads - Refining Delineation. Mary L. Lewis. 1 cass. 8.95 (210) Am Fed Astrologers.
An AFA Convention workshop tape.

Dwads in Transit. Betty Penner. 1 cass. 8.95 (745) Am Fed Astrologers.

Dwarf see Fantastic Tales of Ray Bradbury

Dwarka. Music by Atul Desai. 1 cass. (Tirth Ser.: Vol. 2). 1996. (D96002) Multi-Cultural Bks.

Dwelling in the Holy of Holies. 2003. (978-1-931713-75-7(8)) Word For Today.

Dwelling in the Holy of Holies, Pack. 2003. audio compact disk (978-1-931713-74-0(X)) Word For Today.

Dwelling in the Secret Place. Gloria Copeland. 2 cass. 1993. 10.00 Set. (978-0-88114-930-2(6)) K Copeland Pubns.
Biblical teaching on knowing God.

Dwelling in the Secret Place. Mark Crow. 3 cass. (Running Time: 4 hrs. 30 mins.). (978-1-931537-33-9(X)) Vision Comm Creat.

Dwelling Place. unabr. ed. Catherine Cookson. Read by Elizabeth Henry. 10 cass. (Running Time: 15 hrs.). (Sound Ser.). 2004. 84.95 (978-1-85496-752-7(5), 67525) Pub: UlverLrgPrint GBR. Dist(s): Ulverscroft US
When her parents both die in 1832, 15-year-old Cissie builds a dwelling for her 9 brothers & sisters on the open Northumbrian fells to escape being taken to the workhouse. This is the story of her heroic fight to rear them under appalling conditions.

Dwelling Place. unabr. collector's ed. Catherine Cookson. Read by Mary Woods. 8 cass. (Running Time: 12 hrs.). 1985. 64.00 (978-0-7366-0943-2(1), 1886) Books on Tape.
Cissie Brodie is a fighter. With mother & father gone, she is left alone with her several brothers & sisters & her whole sense of duty pushed her to find an answer that will save the family from the workhouse. Enter the local Lord who declares he is a true protector, extending his help to the deserving poor. But Cissie senses his motives are less than pure, still she must do something for the brood for which she is provider.

Dwelling Place, Set. Catherine Cookson. Read by Elizabeth Henry. 10 cass. 1999. 84.95 (67525) Pub: Soundings Ltd GBR. Dist(s): ISIS Pub

Dwight D. Eisenhower: Ike. 2005. audio compact disk 15.95 (978-1-885959-27-0(3)) Soundworks Intl.

Dwight Swain: Master Writing Teacher. Dwight V. Swain. 2003. audio compact disk 49.95 (978-1-880717-48-6(4)) Writers AudioShop.

Dybbuk. unabr. ed. S. Ansky. Read by Ed Asner. 2 cass. (Running Time: 3 hrs.). 2001. 18.00 (978-1-59040-178-1(6), Phoenix Audio) Pub: Amer Intl Pub. Dist(s): PerseuPGW

Dybbuk. unabr. ed. S. Ansky. Read by Yuri Rasovsky. Adapted by Yuri Rasovsky. 2 CDs. (Running Time: 1 hr.). 2001. audio compact disk 16.00 (978-0-7861-8845-1(6), 3204) Blckstn Audio.

Dybbuk. unabr. ed. S. Ansky. Read by Yuri Rasovsky. Adapted by Yuri Rasovsky. (Running Time: 1 hr.). 2003. 14.95 (978-0-7861-2613-2(2), 3204) Blckstn Audio.

Dying Breed. Declan Hughes. 2008. 69.95 (978-0-7531-2943-2(4)); audio compact disk 89.95 (978-0-7531-2944-9(2)) Pub: Isis Pubng Ltd GBR. Dist(s): Ulverscroft US

Dying Earth. unabr. ed. Jack Vance. Read by Arthur Morey. (Running Time: 7 hrs.). (Tales of the Dying Earth Ser.). 2010. 24.99 (978-1-4418-1457-9(4), 9781441814579, Brilliance MP3); 24.99 (978-1-4418-1459-3(0), 9781441814593, BAD); 39.97 (978-1-4418-1458-6(2), 9781441814586, Brinc Audio MP3 Lib); 39.97 (978-1-4418-1460-9(4), 9781441814609, BADLE); audio compact disk 29.99 (978-1-4418-1455-5(8), 9781441814555, Bril Audio CD Unabri); audio compact disk 79.97 (978-1-4418-1456-2(6), 9781441814562, BriAudCD Unabrid) Brilliance Audio.

Dying for Chocolate. abr. ed. Diane Mott Davidson. Read by Barbara Rosenblat. 2 cass. (Running Time: 3 hrs.). (Goldy Schulz Culinary Mysteries Ser.: No. 2). 2000. 7.95 (978-1-57815-142-4(2), 1101, Media Bks Audio) Media Bks NJ.
A murderously delicious suspense chock full of mystery & complete with genuine, delicious recipes for everyone to try.

Dying for Chocolate. abr. ed. Diane Mott Davidson. Read by Barbara Rosenblat. 3 CDs. (Running Time: 3 hrs.). (Goldy Schulz Culinary Mysteries Ser.: No. 2). (YA). 2000. audio compact disk 11.99 (978-1-57815-502-6(9), 1101 CD3, Media Bks Audio) Media Bks NJ.
A murderously delicious suspense chock full of mystery & chocolate - complete with genuine, delicious recipes.

Dying for Chocolate. abr. ed. Diane Mott Davidson. Read by Barbara Rosenblat. 2 cass. (Running Time: 3 hrs.). (Goldy Schulz Culinary Mysteries Ser.: No. 2). 1995. 16.95 (978-1-879371-78-1(2), 393464) Pub Mills.
Goldy Bear's personal life has become a recipe for disaster. She's got an abusive ex-husband who's into making tasteless threats, a rash of mounting bills that are taking a huge bite out of her budget & two enticing men at her door. Just as her catering business is starting to take off, a murder sends her life into yet another tailspin.

Dying for Chocolate. unabr. ed. Diane Mott Davidson. Read by Barbara Rosenblat. 9 CDs. (Running Time: 9 hrs. 30 min.). (Goldy Schulz Culinary Mysteries Ser.: No. 2). 2004. audio compact disk 55.00 (978-1-59007-438-1(6)) Pub: New Millenn Enter. Dist(s): PerseuPGW

Dying for Chocolate. unabr. ed. Diane Mott Davidson. Narrated by Barbara Rosenblat. 8 cass. (Running Time: 9 hrs. 30 mins.). (Goldy Schulz Culinary Mysteries Ser.: No. 2). 1996. 60.00 (978-0-7887-0576-2(8), 94754E7) Recorded Bks.
Trouble mars caterer Goldy Bear's success at the Aspen Meadows Country Club when her boyfriend perishes in a suspicious accident.

Dying for Chocolate. unabr. abr. ed. Diane Mott Davidson. Read by Barbara Rosenblat. 8 cass. (Running Time: 9 hrs. 30 mins.). (Goldy Schulz Culinary Mysteries Ser.: No. 2). 2004. 34.95 (978-1-59007-348-3(7)) Pub: New Millenn Enter. Dist(s): PerseuPGW

***Dying for Mercy.** unabr. ed. Mary Jane Clark. Read by Isabel Keating. (ENG.). 2009. (978-0-06-190250-5(0), Harper Audio); (978-0-06-190251-2(9), Harper Audio) HarperCollins Pubs.

Dying for Mercy. unabr. ed. Mary Jane Clark. Read by Isabel Keating. 2009. audio compact disk 39.99 (978-0-06-176818-7(9), Harper Audio) HarperCollins Pubs.

Dying for Millions. unabr. ed. Judith Cutler. 5 cass. (Isis Ser.). (J). 2002. 49.95 (978-0-7531-1371-4(6)) Pub: ISIS Lrg Prnt GBR. Dist(s): Ulverscroft US

Dying for Power. Judith Cutler. 8 CDs. (Running Time: 8 hrs. 57 mins.). (Isis (CDs) Ser.). (J). 2004. audio compact disk 79.95 (978-0-7531-2360-7(6)) Pub: ISIS Lrg Prnt GBR. Dist(s): Ulverscroft US

Dying for Power. unabr. ed. Judith Cutler. Read by Diana Bishop. 7 cass. (Running Time: 8.5 hrs.). (Isis Ser.). (J). 2002. 61.95 (978-0-7531-1450-6(X)) Pub: ISIS Lrg Prnt GBR. Dist(s): Ulverscroft US
For Sophie Rivers, tackling newly imposed profit margins and a disruptive fundamentalist movement means that teaching comes low on the agenda. And when a young teacher dies, victim of a series of arson attacks at William Murdock College of Further Education, another teacher is attacked, and a women's safe hostel is razed to the ground, Sophie has more than school politics on her mind. Could these events be connected to the group of muggers she witnessed in action, or the fundamentalist students? Meanwhile Sophie's love life is no less complex as three men vie for her attention. But when the murderer targets Sophie, she's on her own.

Dying for Revenge. Eric Jerome Dickey. Read by Dion Graham & Susan Ericksen. (Playaway Adult Fiction Ser.). 2009. 84.99 (978-1-60812-674-3(9)) Find a World.

Dying for Revenge. unabr. ed. Eric Jerome Dickey. 1 MP3-CD. (Running Time: 16 hrs.). (Gideon Ser.). 2008. 24.95 (978-1-4233-6708-6(1),

9781423367086, Brilliance MP3); audio compact disk 34.99 (978-1-4233-6706-2(5), 9781423367062, Bril Audio CD Unabri) Brilliance Audio.

Dying for Revenge. unabr. ed. Eric Jerome Dickey. Narrated by Dion Graham & Susan Ericksen. (Running Time: 16 hrs.). (Gideon Ser.). 2008. 24.95 (978-1-4233-6710-9(3), 9781423367109, BAD) Brilliance Audio.

Dying for Revenge. unabr. ed. Eric Jerome Dickey. Read by Susan Ericksen & Dion Graham. (Running Time: 16 hrs.). (Gideon Ser.). 2008. 39.25 (978-1-4233-6711-6(1), 9781423367116, BADLE) Brilliance Audio.

Dying for Revenge. unabr. ed. Eric Jerome Dickey. Read by Dion Graham & Dion Susan Ericksen. 1 MP3-CD. (Running Time: 16 hrs.). (Gideon Ser.). 2008. 39.25 (978-1-4233-6709-3(X), 9781423367093, Brlnc Audio MP3 Lib) Brilliance Audio.

Dying for Revenge. unabr. ed. Eric Jerome Dickey. Read by Dion Graham & Susan Ericksen. 13 CDs. (Running Time: 16 hrs.). (Gideon Ser.). 2008. audio compact disk 117.25 (978-1-4233-6707-9(3), 9781423367079, BriAudCD Unabrid) Brilliance Audio.

Dying Ground. Nichelle D. Tramble. Narrated by J. D. Jackson. 6 cass. (Running Time: 8 hrs. 45 mins.). 62.00 (978-1-4025-3272-6(5)) Recorded Bks.

***Dying in the Wool.** Frances Brody & Sandra Hunt. 2010. 84.95 (978-1-84652-863-7(1)); audio compact disk 89.95 (978-1-84652-864-4(X)) Pub: Magna Story GBR. Dist(s): Ulverscroft US

Dying Inside. abr. ed. Robert A. Silverberg. 1 cass. 1984. 12.95 (978-0-694-50327-8(4), SWC 1612) HarperCollins Pubs.

Dying into the River of Existence: A Weekend Inquiry with Adyashanti. Featuring Adyashanti. (ENG.). 2008. audio compact disk 65.00 (978-1-933986-51-7(4)) Open Gate Pub.

Dying Light. Stuart MacBride & Stuart Macbride. Read by Kenny Blyth. 10 cass. (Running Time: 12 hrs. 50 mins.). (Isis Cassettes Ser.). 2006. 84.95 (978-0-7531-3602-7(3)) Pub: ISIS Lrg Prnt GBR. Dist(s): Ulverscroft US

Dying Light. Stuart MacBride & Stuart Macbride. 12 CDs. (Isis (CDs) Ser.). 2006. audio compact disk 99.95 (978-0-7531-2601-1(X)) Pub: ISIS Lrg Prnt GBR. Dist(s): Ulverscroft US

Dying Light in Corduba. unabr. ed. Lindsey Davis. Narrated by Donal Donnelly. 12 cass. (Running Time: 16 hrs. 30 mins.). (Marcus Didius Falco Ser.). 1996. 97.00 (978-0-7887-3108-2(4), 95819E7) Recorded Bks.
Falco must travel to a distant province to investigate corruption in the olive oil trade with his very pregnant aristocratic girlfriend in tow.

Dying Night see Asimov's Mysteries

Dying Night see Best of Isaac Asimov

Dying Thunder. abr. ed. Terry C. Johnston. Read by Dick Wilkinson. 2002. (978-1-59183-005-4(2)) Otis Audio.

***Dying to Cross.** unabr. ed. Jorge Ramos. Read by Jonathan Davis. (ENG.). 2005. (978-0-06-084285-7(7), Harper Audio); (978-0-06-084284-0(9), Harper Audio) HarperCollins Pubs.

Dying to Cross: The Worst Immigrant Tragedy in American History. unabr. ed. Jorge Ramos. Read by Jonathan Davis. 2005. audio compact disk 29.95 (978-0-06-079232-9(9)) HarperCollins Pubs.

Dying to Eat: Women & Eating Disorders. 1 cass. (Running Time: 30 min.). 9.95 (HO-87-06-02, HarperThor) HarpC GBR.

Dying to Please. abr. ed. Linda Howard. Read by Susan Ericksen. 5 CDs Library ed. (Running Time: 6 hrs.). 2002. audio compact disk 69.25 (978-1-59086-164-6(7), 1590861647, CD Lib Edit) Brilliance Audio.

Dying to Please. abr. ed. Linda Howard. Read by Susan Ericksen. (Running Time: 6 hrs.). 2005. audio compact disk 16.99 (978-1-59355-705-8(1), 9781593557058, BCD Value Price) Brilliance Audio.
Loyal. Beautiful. Professional. Impeccably organized. Potentially lethal. Sarah Stevens is a woman with many distinct qualities. First and foremost a butler par excellence, skilled at running large households smoothly and efficiently, she is also a trained bodyguard and expert marksman - indispensable to her elderly employer, a courtly gentleman whom Sarah has come to respect and love. Then one night she thwarts a burglary in progress, a courageous act that awards Sarah her requisite "fifteen minutes of fame" with the local press. But the exposure is enough to catch the attention of a tortured soul who, unbeknownst to Sarah, will stop at nothing to have her for himself. Sarah's perfectly ordered life is shattered when tragedy strikes: her beloved employer is brutally murdered. The detective investigating the case assures Sarah that she is not a suspect. Until lightning strikes twice. There's a second killing - and this time, despite a lack of evidence connecting her to the crime, Sarah cannot escape the shadow of guilt. The only option left for Sarah is to carry on with her life. But she doesn't realize that a deranged stalker is luring her into an elaborate trap...one in which she, once ensnared, might never escape. For Sarah soon finds herself at the mercy of a man who will tend to her every whim, smother her with affection, and crush her in his all-consuming embrace.

Dying to Please. unabr. ed. Linda Howard. Read by Susan Ericksen. 7 cass. (Running Time: 10 hrs.). 2002. 32.95 (978-1-59086-160-8(4), 1590861604, BAU); 78.25 (978-1-59086-161-5(2), 1590861612, Unabridge Lib Edns) Brilliance Audio.

Dying to Please. unabr. ed. Linda Howard. Read by Susan Ericksen. (Running Time: 10 hrs.). 2004. 39.25 (978-1-59335-443-5(6), 1593354436, Brlnc Audio MP3 Lib) Brilliance Audio.

Dying to Please. unabr. ed. Linda Howard. Read by Susan Ericksen. (Running Time: 10 hrs.). 2004. 39.25 (978-1-59710-235-3(0), 1597102350, BADLE); 24.95 (978-1-59710-234-6(2), 1597102342, BAD) Brilliance Audio.

Dying to Please. unabr. ed. Linda Howard. Read by Susan Ericksen. (Running Time: 10 hrs.). 2010. audio compact disk 29.99 (978-1-4418-2693-0(9), 9781441826930, Bril Audio CD Unabri); audio compact disk 89.97 (978-1-4418-2694-7(7), 9781441826947, BriAudCD Unabrid) Brilliance Audio.

Dying to Please. unabr. ed. Linda Howard. Read by Susan Ericksen. (Running Time: 10 hrs.). 2004. 24.95 (978-1-59335-079-6(1), 1593350791) Soulmate Audio Bks.

***Dying to Please-ABR.** Linda Howard & Romantic-Suspense. 2010. audio compact disk 9.99 (978-1-4418-5648-7(X)) Brilliance Audio.

Dying to Retire. Jessica Fletcher & Donald Bain. Read by Cynthia Darlow. 7 vols. (Murder, She Wrote Ser.). 2004. pap. bk. 59.95 (978-0-7927-3198-6(0), CSL 648, Chivers Sound Lib); pap. bk. 79.95 (978-0-7927-3199-3(9), SLD 648, Chivers Sound Lib) AudioGO.

Dying to Tell. unabr. ed. Robert Goddard. Narrated by Gerard Doyle. 8 cass. (Running Time: 11 hrs. 15 mins.). 2002. 72.00 (978-1-4025-1804-1(8)) Recorded Bks.

Dying Trade. David Donachie. 2009. 89.95 (978-1-4079-0564-8(3)); audio compact disk 99.95 (978-1-4079-0565-5(1)) Pub: Soundings Ltd GBR. Dist(s): Ulverscroft US

Dying Was the Best Thing That Ever Happened to Me: Stories of Healing & Wisdom along Life's Journey. Frwd. by John Harricharan. (ENG.). 2007. audio compact disk (978-0-9772185-2-3(X)) Sunshine Ridge.

Dying Well in the Nursing Home. 1 cass. (Care Cassettes Ser.: Vol. 22, No. 8). 1995. 10.80 Assn Prof Chaplains.

Dylan. unabr. ed. Read by Cassandra Morris. Created by Lisi Harrison. (Running Time: 3 hrs. 30 mins.). (Clique Summer Collection: No. 2). (ENG.). 2009. 9.98 (978-1-60024-697-5(4)) Pub: Hachet Audio. Dist(s): HachBkGrp

Dylan Thomas. Dylan Thomas. 4 cass. Incl. Child's Christmas in Wales. Dylan Thomas. (SBC 102); Death Shall Have No Dominion. (SBC 102); Over Sir John's Hill. (SBC 102); Quite Early One Morning. (SBC 102); 29.95 incl. program bklet. (SBC 102) HarperCollins Pubs.

Dylan Thomas: A New Life. Andrew Lycett. Narrated by Simon Vance. (Running Time: 18 hrs.). 2004. 48.95 (978-1-59912-478-0(5)) Iofy Corp.

Dylan Thomas: A New Life. Andrew Lycett. Read by Simon Vance. 13 cass. (Running Time: 18 hrs.). 2005. 95.95 (978-0-7861-2919-5(0), 3401); audio compact disk 120.00 (978-0-7861-8225-1(3), 3401) Blckstn Audio.

Dylan Thomas: An Appreciation. unabr. ed. Poems. Dylan Thomas. Read by Dylan Thomas. Read by Sian Phillips & Sion Probert. Comment by Paul Ferris. 1 cass. 12.95 (ECN 060) J Norton Pubs.
A performance of Dylan Thomas reading his own poems forms part of this feature & other extracts from his works.

Dylan Thomas: The Caedmon Collection. unabr. ed. Dylan Thomas. Read by Dylan Thomas. 10 CDs. (Running Time: 14 hrs.). 2002. audio compact disk 49.95 (978-0-694-52659-8(2)) HarperCollins Pubs.
On February 22, 1952, Dylan Thomas made his first recording for Caedmon Records, A Child's Christmas in Wales and Five Poems. It was the first of many albums Thomas was to record for Caedmon. This recording launched not only Caedmon, but the spoken-word industry as well.Here, at long last, in celebration of 50 years of spoken-word publishing, Caedmon presents Dylan Thomas: The Caedmon Collection.This collection includes Thomas' poetry: "Fern Hill" and "Do Not Go Gentle Into That Good Night," his prose: Adventures in the Skin Trade and Quite Early One Morning, and his final work - Under Milk Wood, a play. The recording of Under Milk Wood included here is the only one in existence with Dylan Thomas in the cast. It owes its remarkable existence to the serendipitous placement of a microphone at center stage minutes before the curtain was raised.

Dylan Thomas: The Caedmon Collection. unabr. ed. Dylan Thomas. Read by Dylan Thomas. 2004. audio compact disk 29.95 (978-0-06-079083-7(0)) HarperCollins Pubs.

Dylan Thomas Reading. unabr. ed. Dylan Thomas. Read by Dylan Thomas. 1 cass. Incl. Child Lovers. W. H. Davies. (SWC 1294); Child on the Cliffs. Edward Thomas. (SWC 1294); Collier. Vernon Watkins. (SWC 1294); Comus. John Milton. (SWC 1294); John Kensella's Lament for Mrs. Mary Moore. W. B. Yeats. (SWC 1294); Leaden Echo & the Golden Echo. Gerard Manley Hopkins. (SWC 1294); Paradise Lost. John Milton. (SWC 1294); Sacco Writes to His Son. Alun Lewis. (SWC 1294); Ship of Death. D. H. Lawrence. (SWC 1294); Pts. 1 & 2. Strange Meeting. Wilfred Owen. (SWC 1294); 1970. 14.00 (978-0-694-50199-1(9), SWC 1294) HarperCollins Pubs.

Dylan Thomas Reading, Vol. 4. unabr. ed. Dylan Thomas. Read by Dylan Thomas. 1 cass. Incl. As I Walked Out One Evening: Songs, Ballads, Lullabies, Limericks & Other Light Verse. W. H. Auden. (SWC 1061); Bards. Walter de la Mare. (SWC 1061); Broken Appointment. Thomas Hardy. (SWC 1061); Chard Witlow: Mr. T. S. Elliot's Sunday Evening Broadcast Postscript. Henry Reid. (SWC 1061); In Death Divided. Thomas Hardy. (SWC 1061); Master & Bos'n Song. W. H. Auden. (SWC 1061); Naming of Parts. Henry Reid. (SWC 1061); Owl. Edward Thomas. (SWC 1061); To Lizbie Brown. Thomas Hardy. (SWC 1061); Visit to America. Dylan Thomas. (SWC 1061); 1972. 14.00 (978-0-694-50049-9(6), SWC 1061) HarperCollins Pubs.

Dylan Thomas Reading, Vol. 5. unabr. ed. Dylan Thomas. Read by Dylan Thomas. 1 cass. Incl. Holiday Memory. (SWC 1132); Reminiscences of Childhood. (SWC 1132); Visit to Grandpa's. (SWC 1132); 1988. 14.00 (978-0-694-50933-1(7), SWC 1132) HarperCollins Pubs.

Dylan Thomas Reading: And Death Shall Have No Dominion & Other Poems. unabr. ed. Dylan Thomas. Read by Dylan Thomas. 1 cass. Incl. And Death Shall Have No Dominion. (CDL5 1018); If I Were Tickled by the Rub of Love. (CDL5 1018); Lament. (CDL5 1018); Poem on His Birthday. (CDL5 1018); Refusal to Mourn the Death, by Fire, of a Child in London. (CDL5 1018); Should Lanterns Shine. (CDL5 1018); There Was a Savior. (CDL5 1018); Winter's Tale. (CDL5 1018); (J). 1984. 11.95 (978-1-55994-106-8(5), CDL5 1018) HarperCollins Pubs.

Dylan Thomas Reading from King Lear & The Duchess of Malfi. abr. ed. William Shakespeare & John Webster. Read by Dylan Thomas. 1 cass. 1984. 12.95 (978-0-694-50116-8(6), SWC 1158) HarperCollins Pubs.

Dylan Thomas Reading His Poetry. unabr. ed. Poems. Dylan Thomas. Read by Dylan Thomas. 2 cass. Incl. After the Funeral. (SWC 2014); Alterwise by Owl Light. (SWC 2014); And Death Shall Have No Dominion. (SWC 2014); Ballad of the Long-Legged Bait. (SWC 2014); Ceremony after a Fire Raid. (SWC 2014); Dawn Raid. (SWC 2014); Do Not Go Gentle into That Good Night. (SWC 2014); Fern Hill. Dylan Thomas. (SWC 2014); Hand That Signed the Paper. (SWC 2014); Hunchback in the Park. (SWC 2014); If I Were Tickled By the Rub of Love. (SWC 2014); If My Head Hurt a Hair's Foot. (SWC 2014); In Country Sleep. (SWC 2014); In My Craft of Sullen Art. (SWC 2014); Lament. (SWC 2014); Light Breaks Where No Sun Shines. (SWC 2014); Love in the Asylum. (SWC 2014); On the Marriage of a Virgin. (SWC 2014); Over Sir John's Hill. (SWC 2014); Poem in October. (SWC 2014); Poem on His Birthday. (SWC 2014); Refusal to Mourn the Death, by Fire, of a Child in London. (SWC 2014); Should Lanterns Shine. (SWC 2014); There Was a Savior. (SWC 2014); This Side of the Truth. (SWC 2014); Tombstone Told When She Died. (SWC 2014); Winter's Tale. (SWC 2014); 1984. 19.95 (978-0-694-50765-8(2), SWC 2014) HarperCollins Pubs.

Dylan Thomas Reading On the Marriage of a Virgin, Over Sir John's Hill, In Country Sleep & Others, Vol. 3. unabr. ed. Dylan Thomas. Read by Dylan Thomas. 1 cass. Incl. After the Funeral. (SWC 1043); Few Words of a Kind. (SWC 1043); Hunchback in the Park. (SWC 1043); In Country Sleep. (SWC 1043); Light Breaks Where No Sun Shines. (SWC 1043); On the Marriage of a Virgin. (SWC 1043); 1972. 14.00 (978-0-694-50034-5(8), SWC 1043) HarperCollins Pubs.

Dylan Thomas Reads. unabr. ed. Poems. Dylan Thomas. Read by Dylan Thomas. 2 cass. (Running Time: 1 hr. 52 mins.). 19.00 (H167) Blckstn Audio.
Selections include "And Death Shall Have No Dominion," "A Winter's Tale," "On Reading Poetry Aloud" & others.

Dylan Thomas Reads. unabr. ed. Read by Dylan Thomas. 2 cass. (Running Time: 1 hr. 32 min.). 1992. 19.00 (978-1-55994-564-6(8), DCN 2286) HarperCollins Pubs.

Dylan Thomas Reads the Poetry of W. B. Yeats & Others. unabr. ed. W. B. Yeats. Read by Dylan Thomas. 1 cass. Incl. At the Keyhole. Walter de la Mare. (SWC 1353); Circus Animals. W. B. Yeats. (SWC 1353); Dialogue of Self & Soul. W. B. Yeats. (SWC 1353); For Ann Gregory. W. B. Yeats. (SWC 1353); Leda & the Swan. W. B. Yeats. (SWC 1353); Libertine. Louis MacNeice. (SWC 1353); Long-Legged Fly. W. B. Yeats. (SWC 1353); News of the World. George Barker. (SWC 1353); Novelette. Louis MacNeice. (SWC 1353); September 1, 1939. W. H. Auden. (SWC 1353); Solomon & the Witch. W. B. Yeats. (SWC 1353); Speech of Oedipus at Colonus. W. B. Yeats. (SWC 1353); Three Bushes. W. B. Yeats. (SWC 1353); Three Things. W. B. Yeats. (SWC 1353); Whales, Weep Not. D. H. Lawrence. (SWC 1353); Woman's History. W. H. Davies. (SWC 1353); 1972. 12.95 (978-0-694-50225-7(1), SWC 1353) HarperCollins Pubs.

Dynamic Astronomy. Robert T. Dixon. 1971. (978-0-13-221218-2(8)) P-Hall.

Dynamic Communications in Industry. unabr. ed. Charles C. Gibbons. 1 cass. (Running Time: 22 min.). 12.95 (13007) J Norton Pubs.
The nature, importance & variety of communications in business & industrial organizations.

Dynamic Decision-Making. 1 cass. 10.00 (978-1-58506-033-7(X), 65) New Life Inst OR.
Learn how to make decisions quickly & well.

Dynamic Development Series CD Volume 1: Achieve Your True Potential with the Dynamic Development Series. Randy Gage. (ENG.). 2003. audio compact disk 147.00 (978-0-9744363-5-7(6)) Prime Concepts Grp.

Dynamic Development Series CD Volume 2: Journey to Enlightenment... Achieve Your True Potential. Randy Gage. 2003. audio compact disk 147.00 (978-0-9744363-6-4(4)) Prime Concepts Grp.

Dynamic Family. Gary V. Whetstone. Instructed by Faye Whetstone. 9 cass. (Running Time: 13 hrs. 30 mins.). (Practical Ministry Ser.: Vol. PM102). 1996. 180.00 (978-1-58866-024-4(9), BM 102 A00) Gary Whet Pub.
In over 80% of all prayer requests, the greatest cause of abuse, alcoholism, depression & general dysfunction is summed up in one misunderstood word, "family".

Dynamic Health & Radiant Vitality. Gil Boyne. Read by Gil Boyne. 1 cass. (Running Time: 45 min.). (Hypnosis Motivation Cassettes Ser.). 1977. 9.95 (109) Westwood Pub Co.
Discusses how to subconsciously develop the mental imagery, feeling tone, & mental expectancy for the radiant, vibrant expression of perfect health & wellness.

Dynamic Human Anatomy: Electronic Supplement to Grant's Atlas of Anatomy, Eleventh Edition. Arthur F. Dalley & Douglas J. Gould. (ENG.). 2003. audio compact disk 4.00 (978-0-7817-5012-7(1)) Lppncott W W.

Dynamic Intuition: Creating a Joyous & Successful Life. abr. ed. Laura Day. 2004. 11.95 (978-0-7435-4076-6(X)) Pub: S&S Audio. Dist(s): S and S Inc

Dynamic-Kundalini. 1 cass. (Running Time: 2 hrs.). (Meditations from Osho Ser.). 10.95 (TRR-0001) Oshos.
Designed as morning & evening meditations, Dynamic & Kundalini enhance your awareness, creativity & vitality, create a sense of joyful well-being & promote the flowering of your consciousness.

Dynamic Laws of Prosperity Lectures [MP3 CD - AUDIO]. Catherine Ponder. 2006. bds. 19.99 (978-956-291-195-5(0)) Edit Benei CHL.

Dynamic Laws of Prosperity [MP3 AUDIO] (Audio CD) Catherine Ponder. 2006. bds. 19.99 (978-956-291-155-9(1)) Edit Benei CHL.

Dynamic Leadership - 60 Minutes with John C. Maxwell: Summary of 360 Degree Leader; Talent Is Never Enough; Winning with People. unabr. ed. John Maxwell. Read by John Maxwell. (YA). 2008. 34.99 (978-1-60514-529-7(7)) Find a World.

Dynamic Learning. Evelyn Wood. 6 cass. (Running Time: 6 hrs.). 1992. 195.00 set. (273A) Nightingale-Conant.

Dynamic of Shadow & Its Impact on the Body. Judith Shaw. Read by Judith Shaw. 2 cass. (Running Time: 2 hrs. 30 min.). 1991. 18.95 set. (978-0-7822-0382-0(5), 470) C G Jung IL.
Shadow is always linked with the unknown, darkness, & danger. For people with eating disturbances, body is in the shadow-feared, despised, & dominated. The dynamic process of the shadow as "suffering & a passion" will be explored using the symptoms of anorexia, bulimia, & obesity as potential bringers of light. In this workshop, the one-sidedness behind these symptoms & the subsequent reaction in the psyche are illustrated using Shakespeare's Taming of the Shrew.

Dynamic Personality. unabr. ed. Judith L. Powell. Read by Judith L. Powell. 1 cass. (Running Time: 40 min.). (Powell Life Improvement Programs Ser.). 1987. pap. bk. 12.95 (978-0-914295-34-1(9)) Top Mtn Pub.
Side A presents a mental training exercise designed to shape a personality & Side B presents subliminal suggestions hidden in ocean-type sound.

Dynamic Trial Practice. Ronald Carlson & Edward Imwinkelreid. 1 cass. 1993. 39.95 bk. (3327) Natl Prac Inst.

Dynamic Trial Practice. Ronald Carlson & Edward A. Imwinkelried. 1993. 125.00 Natl Prac Inst.

Dynamic Vocabulary! Peter Funk & Mary Funk. 2 cass. (Running Time: 2 hrs.). (Learn in Your Car Ser.: Vol. 1). (ENG.). 1991. 15.95 (978-1-56015-204-0(4)) Penton Overseas.
Vocabulary enhancement program.

Dynamic Vocabulary! Peter Funk & Mary Funk. 2 cass. (Running Time: 2 hrs.). (Learn in Your Car Ser.: Vol. 2). (ENG.). 1993. 15.95 (978-1-56015-210-1(9)) Penton Overseas.

Dynamic Vocabulary!, Set. Peter Funk & Mary Funk. 4 cass. (Running Time: 4 hrs.). (Learn in Your Car - Discovery Ser.). (ENG.). 1993. 29.95 (978-1-56015-211-8(7)) Penton Overseas.

Dynamic Worship for Guitar. Strand Michael. 2004. bk. 29.95 (978-1-57921-543-9(2)) WinePress Pub.

***Dynamics.** L. Ron Hubbard. 2010. audio compact disk 15.00 (978-1-4031-6793-4(1)); audio compact disk 15.00 (978-1-4031-6785-9(0)); audio compact disk 15.00 (978-1-4031-6789-7(3)); audio compact disk 15.00 (978-1-4031-6786-6(9)); audio compact disk 15.00 (978-1-4031-6796-5(6)); audio compact disk 15.00 (978-1-4031-6784-2(2)); audio compact disk 15.00 (978-1-4031-6782-8(6)); audio compact disk 15.00 (978-1-4031-6788-0(5)); audio compact disk 15.00 (978-1-4031-6794-1(X)); audio compact disk 15.00 (978-1-4031-6792-7(3)); audio compact disk 15.00 (978-1-4031-6783-5(4)); audio compact disk 15.00 (978-1-4031-6787-3(7)); audio compact disk 15.00 (978-1-4031-6791-0(5)); audio compact disk 15.00 (978-1-4031-6781-1(8)); audio compact disk 15.00 (978-1-4031-6780-4(X)); audio compact disk 15.00 (978-1-4031-6798-9(2)); audio compact disk 15.00 (978-1-4031-6797-2(4)); audio compact disk 15.00 (978-1-4031-6795-8(8)); audio compact disk 15.00 (978-1-4031-6790-3(7)) Bridge Pubns Inc.

Dynamics for Personal Success Vol. 4: Empowerment; The Challenge; The Leaders Edge. Frederick G. Elias. Read by Peter Bie. Interview with Gary Fruen. 6 cass. 59.95 Set. (978-1-881241-01-0(7)) ODC Pub.
Goal setting, overcoming barriers to growth, leadership development, & empowering messages.

Dynamics of Confession: Dynamic Movement Toward Realized Absolution. George Bowman. 1986. 10.80 (0203) Assn Prof Chaplains.

Dynamics of Crisis Intervention: The Suicidal Person. Kenneth Reed et al. 1986. 10.80 (0207) Assn Prof Chaplains.

Dynamics of Effective Listening. Tony Alessandra. 6 cass. 1994. 59.95 (10640AX) Nightingale-Conant.
Sales trainers, business leaders & marriage counselors all agree: Listening is the key personal development skill. Effective listening can help you make better, more informed decisions...alert you to profitable opportunities...&

prevent misunderstandings between you & your spouse, children & co-workers. In this new program, Tony Alessandra shows you how to double your communication power by mastering the art of "active" listening. Discover how to block out speaker-related barriers like accents & "paraphrase" key points discussed. You'll even learn to detect subtle nuances in speech, where a person's vocal intonation reveals one of 30 different emotional states.

Dynamics of Legislation: Leadership & Policy Change in the Congressional Process. Charles R. Wise. (Public Administration Ser.). 1991. bk. 47.00 (978-1-55542-335-3(3), Jossey-Bass) Wiley US.

Dynamics of Self-Discovery. Gil Boyne. Read by Gil Boyne. 1 cass. (Running Time: 45 min.). (Hypnosis Motivation Cassettes Ser.). 1977. 9.95 (108) Westwood Pub Co.
Explores overcoming your identity crisis & creates a powerful belief in your own abilities. Discover your real self & your true capacity.

Dynamics of Spiritual Direction Ministry. Carole Riley. 4 cass. (Running Time: 5 hrs. 30 min.). 1995. 34.95 Set. (TAH355) Alba Hse Comns.
A model of group spiritual direction is presented which will be helpful to hospice care workers, clergy, chaplains, RCIA participants, retreat centers, seminaries & groups preparing for one-to-one direction, as well as for people in locations where fewer persons are skilled in the ministry of self direction.

Dynamics of Stigma & Its Treatment. David Belgum. 1986. 10.80 (0401) Assn Prof Chaplains.

Dynamics of Stock Market Forecasting. Lloyd Cope. 1 cass. 8.95 (061) Am Fed Astrologers.
Forecasting national trends and company prospects.

Dynamics of the Spiritual Life: Stories, Insights, Reflections. John Shea. 6 cass. 1996. 29.95 set, vinyl binder. (978-0-87946-137-9(3), 326) ACTA Pubns.
Master storyteller & theologian John Shea describes various strategies for developing one's spirituality.

Dynamite Customer Service. abr. ed. Linda L. McNeil. Read by Linda L. McNeil. 2 cass. (Running Time: 1 hrs. 30 min.). 1995. pap. bk. 29.95 Set. (978-1-891446-05-4(3)) Open Mind.
Especially for physical therapists. an entertaining overview of what it takes to really connect with your customers so they are not just satisfied, they are delighted. Includes information for improving front office procedures & telephone etiquette.

Dynamite Customer Service. abr. ed. Linda L. McNeil. Read by Linda L. McNeil. 2 cass. (Running Time: 1 hrs. 30 min.). 1996. pap. bk. 29.95 Set. (978-1-891446-07-8(X)) Open Mind.
Especially for small businesses, an entertaining overview of what it takes to really connect with your customers so they are not just satisfied, they are delighted. Includes information for improving front office procedures & telephone etiquette.

DynaMoments, Vol. 1. Warren W. Wiersbe. Read by Warren W. Wiersbe. 3 cass. (Running Time: 4 hrs. 30 min.). 1987. 14.95 (978-0-8474-2455-9(3)) Back to Bible.
Features short daily meditations for use as brief family devotions. Vol. 1 discusses Psalms 1-19; Matt. 1-7; & Philippians.

DynaMoments, Vol. 2. Warren W. Wiersbe. Read by Warren W. Wiersbe. 3 cass. (Running Time: 4 hrs. 30 min.). 1987. 14.95 (978-0-8474-2460-3(X)) Back to Bible.
Features short daily meditations for use as brief family devotions. Vol. 2 discusses Psalms 20-34; Matthew 8-11; & Colossians.

DynaMoments, Vol. 3. Warren W. Wiersbe. Read by Warren W. Wiersbe. 3 cass. (Running Time: 4 hrs. 30 min.). 1987. 14.95 (978-0-8474-2465-8(0)) Back to Bible.
Features short daily meditations for use as brief family devotions. Vol. 3 discusses Psalms 35-45; Matthew 12-15; & I Thessalonians.

DynaMoments, Vol. 4. Warren W. Wiersbe. Read by Warren W. Wiersbe. 3 cass. (Running Time: 4 hrs. 30 min.). 1987. 14.95 (978-0-8474-2470-2(7)) Back to Bible.
Features short daily meditations for use as brief family devotions. Vol. 4 discusses Psalms 46-56; Matthew 16-20; & James.

DynaMoments, Vol. 5. Warren W. Wiersbe. Read by Warren W. Wiersbe. 3 cass. (Running Time: 4 hrs. 30 min.). 1987. 14.95 (978-0-8474-2475-7(8)) Back to Bible.
Features short daily meditations for use as brief family devotions. Vol. 5 discusses Psalms 57-76; Matthew 21-26; & Titus-Philemon.

DynaMoments, Vol. 6. Warren W. Wiersbe. Read by Warren W. Wiersbe. 3 cass. (Running Time: 4 hrs. 30 min.). 1987. 14.95 (978-0-8474-2480-1(4)) Back to Bible.
Features short daily meditations for use as brief family devotions. Vol. 6 discusses Psalms 77-89; Matthew 27-28 & Ephesians 1: 1-4:16.

DynaMoments, Vol. 7. Warren W. Wiersbe. Read by Warren W. Wiersbe. 3 cass. (Running Time: 4 hrs. 30 min.). 1988. 14.95 (978-0-8474-2485-6(5)) Back to Bible.
Features short daily meditations for use as brief family devotions. Vol. 7 discusses Psalms 90-104: John 1-4 & Ephesians.

DynaMoments, Vol. 8. Warren W. Wiersbe. Read by Warren W. Wiersbe. 3 cass. (Running Time: 4 hrs. 30 min.). 1988. 14.95 (978-0-8474-2490-0(1)) Back to Bible.
Features short daily meditations for use as brief family devotions. Vol. 8 discusses Psalms 105-118; John 5-9 & Galatians.

DynaMoments, Vol. 9. Warren W. Wiersbe. Read by Warren W. Wiersbe. 3 cass. (Running Time: 4 hrs. 30 min.). 1988. 14.95 (978-0-8474-2495-5(2)) Back to Bible.
Features short daily meditations for use as brief family devotions. Vol. 9 discusses Psalms 119-128; John 10-12 & I Peter.

DynaMoments, Vol. 10. Warren W. Wiersbe. Read by Warren W. Wiersbe. 3 cass. (Running Time: 4 hrs. 30 min.). 1988. 14.95 (978-0-8474-2500-6(2)) Back to Bible.
Features short daily meditations for use as brief family devotions. Vol. 10 discusses Psalms 129-150; John 13-16 & Romans 1-6.

DynaMoments, Vol. 11. Warren W. Wiersbe. Read by Warren W. Wiersbe. 3 cass. (Running Time: 4 hrs. 30 min.). 1989. 14.95 (978-0-8474-2505-1(3)) Back to Bible.
Features short daily meditations for use as brief family devotions. Vol. 11 discusses Proverbs 1-10; John 17-19 & Romans 7-11.

DynaMoments, Vol. 12. Warren W. Wiersbe. Read by Warren W. Wiersbe. 3 cass. (Running Time: 4 hrs. 30 min.). 1989. 14.95 (978-0-8474-2510-5(X)) Back to Bible.
Features short daily meditations for use as brief family devotions. Vol. 12 discusses Proverbs 11-15; John 20, 21 & Romans 12-16.

Dynasties: Fortunes & Misfortunes of the World's Great Family Businesses. David S. Landes. Read by Alan Sklar. (Playaway Adult Nonfiction Ser.). (ENG.). 2009. 65.00 (978-1-60775-640-8(4)) Find a World.

Dynasties: Fortunes & Misfortunes of the World's Great Family Businesses. unabr. ed. David S. Landes. Narrated by Alan Sklar. (Running Time: 13 hrs. 30 mins. 0 sec.). (ENG.). 2006. audio compact disk 69.99 (978-1-4001-3279-9(7)) Pub: Tantor Media. Dist(s): IngramPubServ

Dynasties: Fortunes & Misfortunes of the World's Great Family Businesses. unabr. ed. David S. Landes. Read by Alan Sklar. (Running Time: 13 hrs. 30 mins. 0 sec.). (ENG.). 2006. audio compact disk 34.99 (978-1-4001-0279-2(0)); audio compact disk 24.99 (978-1-4001-5279-7(8)) Pub: Tantor Media. Dist(s): IngramPubServ

Dyslexia: How to Make the Most of a Learning Disability. Illus. by Angela Brown. Voice by Cary Westbrook. Prod. by Les Lingle. 1 cass. (Running Time: 30 mins.). (Words of Wellness Ser.: Vol. 305). 2000. 12.95 (978-1-930995-04-8(0), LLP305) Life Long Pubg.
Do you have trouble learning new words, spelling them, use analogies to talk & explain things...do you have a creative streak or a surplus of great ideas?.

Dyslexia: Program from the Award Winning Public Radio Series. Interview. Hosted by Fred Goodwin. 1CD. (Running Time: 1 hr). (Infinite Mind Ser.: Vol. 206). 2002. audio compact disk 21.95 (978-1-888064-89-6(7), LCM 223) Lichtenstein Creat.
As many as 1 in 7 American children are affected to some degree by dyslexia, which disables language skills but often bestows special abilities in the visual and spatial realm. This program explores what dyslexia is, and what it is not, with guests including author and producer Stephen J. Cannell, Thomas Viall of the International Dyslexia Association, Yale researcher Dr. Sally Shaywitz, Toronto entrepreneur Jay Mandarino, author Thomas G. West, virtual reality pioneer Daniel Sandin, children's author Jeanne Betancourt and her daughter, filmmaker Nicole Betancourt.

Dyslexia, My Life: One Man's Story of Life with a Learning Disability. 3rd ed. Scripts. Girard J. Sagmiller. 2 cass. (Running Time: 160 mins). 2002. 11.95 (978-0-9643087-4-9(6), 1002) DML.

Dysphagia Assessment & Treatment Planning: A Team Approach. 2nd rev. ed. Ed. by Rebecca Leonard & Katherine Kendall. 2007. bk. 149.95 (978-1-59756-153-2(3)) Plural Pub Inc.

Dysthymia: Program from the Award Winning Public Radio Series. Interview. Hosted by Fred Goodwin. 1 CD. (Running Time: 1 Hour). 2001. audio compact disk 21.99 (978-1-932479-40-9(6), LCM 182) Lichtenstein Creat.
Do you know someone who never seems to experience joy? Whether it be a new pair of shoes, a new job, or even a raise - they never look happy and their personality always seems "blah." It's something that used to be thought to be a personality disorder, but the mental health community now recognizes these symptoms to be a mood disorder. It's a chronic low-level depression called "dysthymia." And if left untreated, or misdiagnosed, which is what often happens, it can last for a lifetime. Guests include; web designer Kristy Mclean, who has dysthymia; research psychiatrist Dr. John Markowitz of Payne-Whitney Clinic in New York; composer and author Mary Rodgers on her depression and that of her father, composer Richard Rodgers; author and psychiatrist Dr. Peter Kramer and comedian Lisa Kaplan, who makes depression part of her act.

Dzogchen Dream & Sleep Practices. unabr. ed. Geshe T. Wangyal. 1 cass. 1993. 9.00 (OC322-69) Sound Horizons AV.

E

E- ACLS Cdrom CD. Natl Safety Council. (C). 2004. audio compact disk 99.95 (978-0-7637-3229-5(X)) Jones Bartlett.

E. A. R. T. H. Songs & Stories. Short Stories. Created by Hawk Hurst. 1. (Running Time: 65 minutes). 1997. 10.00 (978-0-9710716-0-5(8)) Silv Watr Ret.
Native American influenced stories include: The Cherokee Legend of the First Flute; Rainforest Rainstick; and Earth Drum.Native American influenced stories include:Fifteen traditional and original each accompanied by Native American-style flutes, drums, and rattles.Great for kids and families, as well as music and social studes teachers. Lyrics included.

E. A. Robinson. Robert Pack. 1 cass. (Running Time: 55 min.). 1962. 12.95 (23199) J Norton Pubs.
Pack believes Edwin Arlington Robinson is a very underrated poet whose work resembles Frost's, & who has been totally eclipsed by him. He examines Robinson's major theme of isolation, & reads specific examples of his work.

E 'Ai I Kekahi, E Kapi I Kekahi. Lilinoe Andrews. Illus. by Leimomi Respicio. (HAW.). (J). (gr. 1-3). 1997. pap. bk. 8.95 (978-1-890270-03-2(2)) Aha Punana Leo.

E. B. White & the Essay: A Light & Enlightening Lecture, Featuring Elliot Engel. 2001. bk. 15.00 (978-1-890123-43-7(9)) Media Cnslts.

E-Commerce as a Business Strategy an Overview. unabr. ed. Jack Shaw. Perf. by Jack Shaw. 1 cass. (Running Time: 57 mins). 2000. 17.95 (978-0-9664890-4-0(7)) Elctrnic Commerce.
Learn how the different E-Commerce technologies work in not technical terms; how businesses are using Electronic Commerce to redesign their business processes & how successful organizations plan for & manage the transition to E-Business.

E-Commerce for Banks, Credit Unions & Insurance Companies: An Overview. unabr. ed. Jack Shaw. Perf. by Jack Shaw. 1 cass. (Running Time: 57 mins.). 2000. 17.95 (978-0-9664890-6-4(3)) Elctrnic Commerce.
For you if you want to hear, in non-technical terms, how E-Commerce technologies work & how leaders in your industry are using them for strategic advantage.

E-Commerce for Manufacturers an Overview. unabr. ed. Jack Shaw. Perf. by Jack Shaw. 1 cass. (Running Time: 57 mins.). 2000. 17.95 (978-0-9664890-5-7(5)) Elctrnic Commerce.
Learn about the technologies. You'll hear examples of how manufacturers are increasing inventory to hundreds or even thousands of times per year, redesigning products in real time with customers hundreds of miles away & managing most of their orders without any human intervention in the process.

E-Commerce in Czech Republic: A Strategic Reference 2007. Compiled by Icon Group International, Inc. Staff. 2007. ring bd. 195.00 (978-0-497-35905-8(7)) Icon Grp.

E. E. Cummings Reads: A Poetry Collection. unabr. abr. ed. E. E. Cummings. Read by E. E. Cummings. 3 cass. (Running Time: 3 hrs. 30 min.). 2001. 22.00 (978-0-694-52431-0(X)) HarperCollins Pubs.

E. Ethelbert Miller. unabr. ed. Ed. by Jim McKinley. Prod. by Rebekah Presson. 1 cass. (Running Time: 29 min.). (New Letters on the Air Ser.). 1994. 10.00 (032894) New Letters.
Miller, a professor at Howard University & a frequent commentator on NPR news, reads from his newly-published volume, "First Light: New & Selected Poems." He also talks about editing the anthology, "In Search of Color Everywhere: A Collection of African-American Poetry" & about his efforts to start creative writing programs at traditionally Black universities.

E. G. Seidensticker. Read by E. G. Seidensticker. 1981. (L014) TFR.

E Ho'opili Mai. William H. Wilson et al. 1 cass. (HAW., (J). (gr. k-2). 1999. pap. bk. 6.95 (978-1-58191-077-3(0)) Aha Punana Leo.

E Is for Elisa. unabr. ed. Johanna Hurwitz. Narrated by Barbara Caruso. 1 cass. (Running Time: 1 hr. 30 mins.). (ps up). 1998. 10.00 (978-0-7887-1955-4(6), 95350 E7) Recorded Bks.
Four-year-old Elisa is already in school & is learning to read, but can she ever catch up with her big brother who teases her? She decides to prove herself by taking him up on a dare.

E Is for Elisa. unabr. ed. Johanna Hurwitz. Read by Barbara Caruso. 1 cass. (Running Time: 1 hr. 30 min.). (J). (gr. 3). 1998. 22.24 HMWK SET . (978-0-7887-1963-9(7), 40662); 70.70 CLASS SET . (978-0-7887-3292-8(7), 46177) Recorded Bks.
Four-year-old Elisa hates it when her big brother teases her & calls her a crybaby. She decides to prove herself by taking him up on a dare.

E Is for Evidence. unabr. collector's ed. Sue Grafton. Read by Mary Peiffer. 7 cass. (Running Time: 7 hrs.). (Kinsey Millhone Mystery Ser.). 1994. 56.00 (978-0-7366-2615-6(8), 3357) Books on Tape.
Someone salts Kinsey Millhone's bank account with an extra $5000 & suddenly she has a new client: herself! The evidence leads to the wealthy Woody family, ex-husband #2 & possibly murder.

E Kanikapila Play-along Series. (HAW.). (YA). 2007. audio compact disk 22.95 (978-0-9791692-0-5(8)) Nohili Heizer.

E Ku'u Tutu, Aloha Nui 'la: A Legacy to our Grandchildren. Music by Partners In Development Foundation. (HAW.). (J). 2009. audio compact disk 14.95 (978-1-933835-11-2(7)) Part Dev.

E. L. Doctorow. Interview with E. L. Doctorow. 1 cass. (Running Time: 25 min.). 1977. 11.95 (L017) TFR.
Doctorow talks about Ragtime & other books & discusses the literary device of weaving fact & fiction.

E. L. Doctorow: Interview. (Running Time: 45 min.). 13.95 (978-1-55644-349-7(8), 10012) Am Audio Prose.
Doctorow provides an informative overview of his work in this interview including specific discussion of several of his books - "Welcome to Hard Times," "Ragtime," "World's Fair," "Lives of the Poet," & "Billy Bathgate.".

E. L. Doctorow Reading: The Writer in the Family & The Leather Man. E. L. Doctorow. Read by E. L. Doctorow. 1 cass. (Running Time: 47 min.). 13.95 (978-1-55644-348-0(X), 10011) Am Audio Prose.
The author reads "The Writer in the Family & "The Leather Man" from "Lives of the Poets - A Novella & Six Stories.".

E. L. Mayo. unabr. ed. Read by E. L. Mayo & David Ray. Ed. by Cynthia Sosland. 1 cass. (Running Time: 29 min.). 1985. 10.00 New Letters.
Readings from "The Collected Poems of E. L. Mayo" published by New Letters in 1980.

E-Learning Educational Services in Italy: A Strategic Reference 2006. Compiled by Icon Group International, Inc. Staff. 2007. ring bd. 195.00 (978-0-497-36036-8(5)) Icon Grp.

E. M. Bounds: Man of Prayer. unabr. ed. Lyle W. Dorsett. Narrated by Jonathan Marosz. 2 CDs. (Running Time: 2 hrs. 30 mins. 0 sec.). (ENG.). 2005. audio compact disk 15.98 (978-1-59644-097-5(X), Hovel Audio) christianaud.
The name of E.M. Bounds is familiar to anyone who has an interest in prayer. In a world awash in books that jam the isles of bookstores everywhere, few will even begin to survive the lifetime of the authors, but that is not true of E.M. Bounds. After a century, many of his books are still in print. Their long life is a testimony to the timeliness of the prayer lessons he learned from his own deep Christian spirituality. In view of the popularity of E.M. Bounds writings, it seems incredible that so little of him has been published. To remedy that amazing state of affairs, Lyle W. Dorsett has read every scrap of paper related to Bounds, and the family has made available to him for the first time a private collection of the Bounds correspondence. From that, Dorsett wrote this account of Mr. Boundsâ€(tm) life.

***E. M. Bounds: Man of Prayer.** unabr. ed. Lyle W. Dorsett. Narrated by Jonathan Marosz. (ENG.). 2005. 9.98 (978-1-59644-095-1(3), Hovel Audio) christianaud.

E. M. Forster. unabr. ed. Stephen Spender. 1 cass. (Running Time: 1 hr.). 1953. 12.95 (23014) J Norton Pubs.
Forster rejects the inhuman existence of a world conditioned by the cruelly powerful methods of business & politics. He also rejects the simplification of spiritual salvationism, whether in religion or in art, & reinforces personal relations as the center of his vision.

E-mail Marketing Mastery: If You Thought E-mail Was Dead Think Again. Speeches. 2 cds. (Running Time: 2hrs). 2006. audio compact disk 29.95 (978-0-9777500-0-9(0)) Ultimate Wealth.

E-Mail Murders. unabr. ed. Paul Zindel. Narrated by Jeff Woodman. 2 pieces. (Running Time: 2 hrs. 45 mins.). (P. C. Hawke Mysteries Ser.). (gr. 8 up). 2002. 19.00 (978-1-4025-1808-9(0)) Recorded Bks.
A trip to the French Riviera should be a nice vacation for high-school super-sleuth P.C. Hawke and his best friend Mackenzie. But when a woman is murdered at their hotel, P.C. and Mac can't just sit around and wait for the cops to solve the crime.

E-Motion Vol. 1: Mind & Body Fitness. Laura D. Sachs. Read by Laura D. Sachs. Music by Steven Halpern. 1 cass. (Running Time: 36 min.). 1998. 14.95 (978-0-9676421-1-6(6)) E Motion.
A wake-up (Side A) is a 7 gentle stretches & a guided focus for theday, standing mediation. Relaxation (Side B) is a lying down guided progressive relaxation sharing similar focus.

E-Motion Mind - Body Fitness. Read by Laura D. Sachs. Created by Laura D. Sachs. (Running Time: 16:31). 2003. audio compact disk 14.95 (978-0-9676421-2-3(4)) E Motion.

***E-Myth Accountant: Why Most Accounting Practices Don¿t Work & What to Do about It.** unabr. ed. Michael E. Gerber. Read by Michael E. Gerber. (Running Time: 7 hrs.). 2011. 29.95 (978-1-4417-1087-1(6)); 44.95 (978-1-4417-1083-3(3)); audio compact disk 69.00 (978-1-4417-1084-0(1)); audio compact disk 24.95 (978-1-4417-1086-4(8)) Blckstn Audio.

***E-Myth Attorney: Why Most Legal Practices Don¿t Work & What to Do about It.** unabr. ed. Michael E. Gerber et al. (Running Time: 7 hrs. 0 mins.). 2010. 44.95 (978-1-4417-1215-8(1)); audio compact disk 69.00 (978-1-4417-1216-5(X)) Blckstn Audio.

***E-Myth Attorney: Why Most Legal Practices Don't Work & What to Do about It.** unabr. ed. Michael Gerber et al. (Running Time: 7 hrs. 0 mins.). 2010. 29.95 (978-1-4417-1219-6(4)); audio compact disk 29.95 (978-1-4417-1218-9(6)) Blckstn Audio.

***E-Myth Enterprise.** unabr. ed. Michael E. Gerber. Read by John H. Mayer. (ENG.). 2009. (978-0-06-190225-3(X), Harper Audio); (978-0-06-190226-0(8), Harper Audio) HarperCollins Pubs.

E-Myth Enterprise: How to Turn a Great Idea into a Thriving Business. abr. unabr. ed. Michael E. Gerber. Read by John H. Mayer & John H. Mayer. 2009. audio compact disk 22.99 (978-0-06-178009-7(X), Harper Audio) HarperCollins Pubs.

***E-Myth Mastery.** abr. ed. Michael E. Gerber. Read by Michael E. Gerber. (ENG.). 2005. (978-0-06-083923-9(6), Harper Audio); (978-0-06-083926-0(0), Harper Audio) HarperCollins Pubs.

E Myth Mastery: The Seven Essential Disciplines for Building a World Class Company. abr. ed. Michael E. Gerber. Read by Michael E. Gerber. 2005. audio compact disk 29.95 (978-0-06-075924-7(0)) HarperCollins Pubs.

***E-Myth Revisited: Why Most Small Businesses Don't Work And.** unabr. ed. Michael E. Gerber. Read by Michael E. Gerber. (ENG.). 2005. (978-0-06-083922-2(8), Harper Audio); (978-0-06-083924-6(4), Harper Audio) HarperCollins Pubs.

E-Myth Revisited: Why Most Small Businesses Don't Work & What to Do about It. abr. ed. Michael E. Gerber. 4 CDs. (Running Time: 6 hrs.). 2003. audio compact disk 22.00 (978-0-06-057490-1(9)) HarperCollins Pubs.
In this first compact disc edition of the totally revised one million copy underground bestseller The E-Myth, Michael Gerber dispels the myths surrounding starting your own business and shows how commonplace assumptions can get in the way of running a business. He walks you through the steps in the life of a business - from entrepreneurial infancy, through adolescent growing pains, to the mature entrepreneurial perspective, the guiding light of all businesses that succeed - and shows how to apply the lessons of franchising to any business, whether or not it is a franchise. Finally, Gerber draws the vital, often overlooked distinction between working on your business and working in your business. After you have listened to The E-Myth Revisited, you will truly be able to grow your business in a predictable and productive way.

E-Myth Revisited: Why Most Small Businesses Don't Work & What to Do about It. unabr. ed. Michael E. Gerber. Read by Michael E. Gerber. 2004. audio compact disk 34.95 (978-0-06-075559-1(8)) HarperCollins Pubs.

E-Myth Revisited & E-Myth Mastery. 2005. 39.99 (978-1-59895-031-1(2)) Find a World.

E-Myth Revisited, the & E-Myth Mastery: Why Most Small Businesses Don't Work & What to Do about it & the Seven Essential Disciplines for Building a World Class Company. unabr. ed. Michael E. Gerber. Read by Michael E. Gerber. (YA). 2005. 44.99 (978-1-59895-140-0(8)) Find a World.

E Pluribus Unum, unabr. ed. Forrest McDonald. Read by Phillip J. Sawtelle. 7 cass. (Running Time: 10 hrs.). 1989. 49.95 (978-0-7861-0015-6(X), 1015) Blckstn Audio.
A thoroughly researched reconstruction of the pivotal fourteen years in which our nation was formed.

E. T. Extra-Terrestrial. 1 CD. (Running Time: 1 hr. 30 mins.). (J). 2002. audio compact disk (978-0-7634-1853-3(6)) W Disney Records.

***E. T. Scenario.** Chuck Missler. (ENG.). 2009. audio compact disk 19.95 (978-1-57821-452-5(1)) Koinonia Hse.

E. T. Scenario. Chuck Missler. 2 cass. (Running Time: 2.5 hours). (Briefing Packages by Chuck Missler). 1993. vinyl bd. 14.95 Incls. notes . (978-1-880532-96-6(4)) Koinonia Hse.
" Have we actually received a message of extra-terrestrial origin? " Can we really review history before it happens?" Has science finally discovered the supernatural?Explore the discovery of a message system of extra-terrestrial origin that we know as the Bible; 66 books penned by 40 authors over several thousands of years, from outside our time domain.The Originator of this message system has demonstrated His mastery of time and space by writing out history for us in advance. We call this prophecy!.

E-Views Version 6. 0. 4th ed. audio compact disk (978-0-324-78397-1(3)) South-West.

E-2, Vol. 7. Pace International Research, Inc. Staff. (E-2 Video Ser.). 1984. 8.00 (978-0-89209-265-9(3)) Pace Grp Intl.

E-2, Vol. 8. Pace International Research, Inc. Staff. (E-2 Video Ser.). 1984. 8.00 (978-0-89209-266-6(1)) Pace Grp Intl.

E-2, Vol. 15. Pace International Research, Inc. Staff. (E-2 Video Ser.). 1984. 8.00 (978-0-89209-267-3(X)) Pace Grp Intl.

E-2, Vol. 19. Pace International Research, Inc. Staff. (E-2 Video Ser.). 1984. 8.00 (978-0-89209-268-0(8)) Pace Grp Intl.

Eaarth: Making a Life on a Tough New Planet. unabr. ed. Bill McKibben. Read by Adam Grupper. Narrated by Oliver Wyman. (Running Time: 9 hrs. 0 mins. 0 sec.). (ENG.). 2010. audio compact disk 34.99 (978-1-4272-0949-8(9)) Pub: Macmill Audio. Dist(s): Macmillan

Each & All see Poetry of Ralph Waldo Emerson

Each & All see Ralph Waldo Emerson: Poems and Essays

Each Art & Science Has a Moral Structure of Its Own. Manly P. Hall. 1 cass. 8.95 (978-0-89314-047-2(3), C891105) Philos Res.

Each Day a Journey: Inspirational Speech. Anna Dunwell. 1 cass. (Running Time: 2 hrs.). 1997. 12.95 (978-1-891657-14-6(3), AC6042) Lift Every Voice.
Renowed diversity consultant presented this speech to Boston College graduate school of education students planning to teach in urban areas with students from diverse cultural backgrounds. Covers topics of racism comfort with self & others, educational challenges & self imposed limitations.

Each Day a New Beginning: Daily Meditations for Women. abr. ed. Read by Kitt Weagant. 2 cass. (Running Time: 3 hrs.). (Hazelden Meditations Book). 1998. 17.95 (978-1-57453-285-2(5)) Audio Lit.
Daily meditations drawing on the common experiences, shared struggles & unique strengths of women.

Each Day Is Your Creation, Vol. 2. Susan Lipshutz. 1 cass. (Running Time: 52 min.). 1996. S Lipshutz.
Daily meditations to awaken & harmonize body, mind & spirit.

Each Day You Face. Perf. by Amanda Greene. 2003. audio compact disk Provident Mus Dist.

Each Little Bird That Sings. unabr. ed. Deborah Wiles. Read by Kim Mai Guest. 3 cass. (Running Time: 4 hrs. 30 mins.). (J). (gr. 4-7). 2005. 35.00 (978-0-307-28373-3(9), Listening Lib); audio compact disk 38.25 (978-0-307-28374-0(7), Listening Lib) Pub: Random Audio Pubg. Dist(s): NetLibrary CO

Each One of Us Matters to God. abr. ed. A. W. Tozer. 1 cass. (Running Time: 40 min.). (C). 4.97 (978-1-55748-379-9(5)) Barbour Pub.

Each Peach Pear Plum. Janet Ahlberg. 2004. pap. bk. 14.95 (978-1-56008-194-4(5)); 8.95 (978-0-89719-917-9(0)); cass. & flmstrp 30.00 (978-0-89719-517-1(5)) Weston Woods.

Each Peach Pear Plum. Janet Ahlberg. (J). 2004. bk. 24.95 (978-1-56008-193-7(7)) Weston Woods.

EACLS(TM) Instructor's ToolKit CD-ROM. 2nd rev. ed. ACEP. (C). 2007. audio compact disk 220.50 (978-0-7637-5154-8(5)) Jones Bartlett.

Eagle & the Raven. abr. ed. James A. Michener. Read by Michael Rider. 2 cass. (Running Time: 3 hrs.). 1996. 7.95 Set. (978-1-57815-039-7(6), 1024) Media Bks NJ.

Eagle & the Raven, Pt. 1. unabr. collector's ed. Pauline Gedge. Read by Donada Peters. 9 cass. (Running Time: 13 hrs. 30 min.). 1986. 72.00 (978-0-7366-0876-3(1), 1825A) Books on Tape.
This spans three generations of Celts. First comes Caradoc, a king's son, who sets out to unite the people of the Raven & lead them against Rome. Eurgain, his gentle wife, alone for months at a time, seeks solace with Caradoc's best friend. Gladys, Caradoc's warrior sister, falls in love with the Roman general who is her prisoner. Aricia, the vain & soft queen of the northern country, aligns her tribe with Rome. Finally, Boudicca, a strong-willed woman, carries to its conclusion the cause that is Caradoc's legacy.

Eagle & the Raven, Pt. 2. collector's ed. Pauline Gedge. Read by Donada Peters. 7 cass. (Running Time: 10 hrs. 30 mins.). 1986. 56.00 (978-0-7366-0877-0(X), 1825-B) Books on Tape.

Eagle & the Raven, Pt. 3. collector's ed. Pauline Gedge. Read by Donada Peters. 9 cass. (Running Time: 13 hrs. 30 mins.). 1986. 72.00 (978-0-7366-0878-7(8), 1825-C) Books on Tape.

Eagle & the Rose: A Remarkable True Story. abr. ed. Rosemary Altea. Read by Rosemary Altea. 2 cass. 2001. 7.95 (978-1-57815-200-1(3), Media Bks Audio) Media Bks NJ.

Eagle Bird: Mapping a New West. abr. ed. Charles F. Wilkinson. 2 cass. (Running Time: 2 hrs.). 1993. 16.95 (978-0-939643-47-9(2), NrthWrd Bks) TandN Child.

Eagle Can Fly Again (audio) David R. Whalen. 2008. audio compact disk 27.99 (978-1-60696-111-7(X)) Tate Pubng.

Eagle Catcher. unabr. ed. Margaret Coel. Read by Stephanie Brush. 6 cass. (Running Time: 6 hr. 54 min.). (Wind River Ser.). 1998. 39.95 (978-1-55686-822-1(7)) Books in Motion.
A search for the murderer of a tribal chief who uncovered land deals & oil.

Eagle Catcher, Set. unabr. ed. Margaret Coel. Read by Stephanie Brush. 6 cass. (Wind River Ser.). 1999. 36.95 Books in Motion.
Father John & Vicki investigate the murder of the Arapaho Tribal Chairman.

Eagle Christian. Nathaniel Holcomb. 7 cass. (Running Time: 10 hrs. 30 mins.). 1998. (978-1-930918-29-0(1)) Its All About Him.

Eagle Christians. 2001. (978-1-59024-025-0(1)); audio compact disk (978-1-59024-026-7(X)) B Hinn Min.

Eagle Has Flown. Jack Higgins. Read by David McCallum. (Liam Devlin Ser.: Bk. 4). 2004. 10.95 (978-0-7435-4721-5(7)) Pub: S&S Audio. Dist(s): S and S Inc

***Eagle Has Flown.** unabr. ed. Jack Higgins. Read by Michael Page. (Running Time: 8 hrs.). (Liam Devlin Ser.: Bk. 4). 2010. 39.97 (978-1-4418-4381-4(7), 9781441843814, Brlnc Audio MP3 Lib); 24.99 (978-1-4418-4380-7(9), 9781441843807, Brilliance MP3); 24.99 (978-1-4418-4383-8(3), 9781441843838, BAD); 39.97 (978-1-4418-4385-2(X), 9781441843852, BADLE); audio compact disk 87.97 (978-1-4418-4378-4(7), 9781441843784, BriAudCD Unabrid); audio compact disk 29.99 (978-1-4418-4377-7(9), 9781441843777, Bril Audio CD Unabri) Brilliance Audio.

Eagle Has Landed. Jack Higgins. Contrib. by Christopher Cazenove. (Liam Devlin Ser.: Bk. 1). 2008. 64.99 (978-1-60640-661-8(2)) Find a World.

***Eagle Has Landed.** unabr. ed. Jack Higgins. Read by Michael Page. (Running Time: 14 hrs.). (Liam Devlin Ser.: Bk. 1). 2010. 24.99 (978-1-4418-4362-3(0), 9781441843623, Brilliance MP3); 24.99 (978-1-4418-4364-7(7), 9781441843647, BAD); 39.97 (978-1-4418-4363-0(9), 9781441843630, Brlnc Audio MP3 Lib); 39.97 (978-1-4418-4365-4(5), 9781441843654, BADLE); audio compact disk 29.99 (978-1-4418-4360-9(4), 9781441843609, Bril Audio CD Unabri); audio compact disk 87.97 (978-1-4418-4361-6(2), 9781441843616, BriAudCD Unabrid) Brilliance Audio.

Eagle Has Landed. unabr. ed. Jack Higgins. Perf. by Christopher Cazenove. 9 cass. (Running Time: 12 hrs.). (Liam Devlin Ser.: Bk. 1). 2004. 39.95 (978-1-59007-190-8(5)) Pub: New Millenn Enter. Dist(s): PerseuPGW
The story of a daring Nazi commando raid into a small English village in 1943 has some surprising consequences. The prelude to the actual landing is staged in German and English scenes, perfectly suited to radio-style dramatization. Nazi generals with thick accents, an undercover IRA assassin using a lilting brogue and a German agent in the guise of the perfect English country woman offer excellent roles for the talented cast.

Eagle Heist. Raymond Austin. Narrated by Raymond Todd. (Running Time: 8 hrs. 30 mins.). 2000. 27.95 (978-1-59912-654-8(0)) Iofy Corp.

Eagle Heist. unabr. ed. Raymond Austin. Read by Raymond Todd. 6 cass. (Running Time: 8 hrs. 30 mins.). 2002. 44.95 (978-0-7861-2245-5(5), 2968); audio compact disk 56.00 (978-0-7861-9490-2(1), 2968) Blckstn Audio.
An ex-cop turned P.I., Sloan investigates the mysterious theft of an armored truck full of diamonds and the death of an Eagle Security guard. Set in Washington, DC, the case takes the cunning Beauford to Morocco and finally to Spain where he makes the shocking discovery of the mastermind behind the Eagle heist.

Eagle in the Sky. Wilbur Smith. Read by Michael Jayston. 2 cass. (Running Time: 3 hrs.). (ENG., 2001. 16.99 (978-0-333-78266-8(6)) Pub: Macmillan UK GBR. Dist(s): Trafalgar

Eagle in the Sky. unabr. ed. Wilbur Smith. Read by Nigel Davenport. 8 cass. (Running Time: 12 hrs.). (Ballantyne Novel Ser.). 2000. 59.95 (978-0-7451-6291-1(6), CAB 209) Pub: Chivers Audio Bks GBR. Dist(s): AudioGO
Young David Morgan, a gifted heir to a South African fortune, rebels against the boardroom future mapped out for him by his family. And after meeting Debra, a young Israeli writer, David fights to preserve their love from the destruction of war, and replant it in the peaceful South African wilds.

Eagle in the Sky. unabr. ed. Wilbur Smith. Read by Nigel Davenport. 10 CDs. (Ballantyne Novel Ser.). 2000. audio compact disk 79.95 (978-0-7540-5368-2(7), CCD 059) Pub: Chivers Audio Bks GBR. Dist(s): AudioGO
David Morgan, heir to a South African fortune, rebels against the future mapped out for him by his family. After meeting Debra, a young Israeli writer, David fights to preserve their love from the destruction of war & replant it in the peaceful South African wilds.

Eagle in the Sky. unabr. collector's ed. Wilbur Smith. Read by Richard Brown. 9 cass. (Running Time: 13 hrs. 30 mins.). (Ballantyne Novels Ser.). 1989. 72.00 (978-0-7366-1588-4(1), 2451) Books on Tape.
Young men hate giving up their freedom, & David Morgan is more forceful than most. Heir to a South African fortune, privileged & indulged, he senses the trap posed by his inheritance. No boardroom or pinstripes for him! Besides, he wants to fly. So with a fine disregard for patrimony he trades it all for a career in aviation. Then he meets a beautiful young Israeli, Debra. She threatens his freedom in an even more fundamental way. David's flight to preserve his independence & his passionate attachment to Debra, carried out against a background of war & destruction, provides the tension in this fine story of two young people in a turbulent time.

***Eagle Named Freedom: My True Story of a Remarkable Friendship.** unabr. ed. Jeff Guidry. (Running Time: 10 hrs. 0 mins.). 2010. 16.99 (978-1-4001-8623-5(4)) Tantor Media.

***Eagle Named Freedom: My True Story of a Remarkable Friendship.** unabr. ed. Jeff Guidry. Narrated by John Pruden. (Running Time: 5 hrs. 30 mins. 0 sec.). (ENG.). 2010. 19.99 (978-1-4001-6623-7(3)); audio compact disk 49.99 (978-1-4001-4623-9(2)); audio compact disk 24.99 (978-1-4001-1623-2(6)) Pub: Tantor Media. Dist(s): IngramPubServ

Eagle of the Ninth. abr. ed. Rosemary Sutcliff. Read by Charlie Simpson. (J). 2007. 34.99 (978-1-60252-528-3(5)) Find a World.

Eagle of the Ninth. abr. ed. Rosemary Sutcliff. Read by Charlie Simpson. (Running Time: 16339 sec.). (Classic Literature with Classical Music Ser.). (YA). (gr. 7-12). 2006. audio compact disk 28.98 (978-962-634-423-1(7), Naxos AudioBooks) Naxos.

Eagle on a Frozen Limb (Stewardship) Deuteronomy 6:1-11, 713. Ed Young. 1989. 4.95 (978-0-7417-1713-9(1), 713) Win Walk.

Eagle Pass. abr. ed. Matthew S. Hart. Read by Charlton Griffin. Abr. by Odin Westgaard. 2 vols. No. 8. 2004. 18.00 (978-1-58807-250-4(9)); (978-1-58807-745-5(4)) Am Pubng Inc.

Eagle Strike. unabr. ed. Anthony Horowitz. Narrated by Simon Prebble. 6 CDs. (Running Time: 6 hrs. 45 mins.). (Alex Rider Ser.: Bk. 4). (J). 2005. audio compact disk 58.75 (978-1-4193-3848-9(X), C3277); 52.75 (978-1-4193-3585-3(5), 98016) Recorded Bks.
Alex Rider, the hero of award-winning author Anthony Horowitz's best-selling adventure series, has been called a teenaged James Bond. In Eagle Strike the 14-year-old secret agent has his hands full with former pop idol Sir Damian Cray, who claims to want to save the world. Only Alex knows the truth - it's the world that needs saving from Cray.

Eagle That Is Forgotten see Poetry of Vachel Lindsay

Eagle Trap, Set. unabr. ed. Geoffrey Archer. Read by Christian Rodska. 12 cass. (Running Time: 12 hrs.). 1999. 96.95 (978-0-7540-0262-8(4), CAB1685) AudioGO.
One night British Sea Harriers reduced his Beirut headquarters to rubble & his evil drug empire to ruins. But Abdul Habib still had enough money & hate for an elaborate plan which would destroy Gibraltar & the British aircraft carrier which had committed the fatal strike.

Eaglerly Waiting: Romans 8:16-25. Ed Young. 1984. 4.95 (978-0-7417-1379-7(9), 379) Win Walk.

Eagle's Claw: A Musical Adventure in Learning & Fun. unabr. ed. James Comey. Composed by Christopher McGovern. 3 cass,. (Running Time: 1 hr.). (Audio Adventures Ser.: Vol. 3). (J). (ps-5). 1998. 10.00 Set. (978-0-9652093-2-8(6)) Stages Imag.

Eagle's Cry. David Nevin. Read by Geoffrey Howard. (Running Time: 20 hrs. 30 mins.). 2000. 48.95 (978-1-59912-479-7(3)) Iofy Corp.

Eagle's Cry. unabr. ed. David Nevin. Read by Geoffrey Howard. 14 cass. (Running Time: 20 hrs. 30 mins.). 2001. 89.95 (978-0-7861-2625-5(6), 3233); audio compact disk 128.00 (978-0-7861-8744-7(1), 3233) Blckstn Audio.

Eagle's Daughter. Judith Tarr & Anna Fields. 9 cass. (Running Time: 13 hrs.). 2002. 62.95 (978-0-7861-1137-4(2), 1904) Blckstn Audio.

Eagle's Daughter. unabr. ed. Judith Tarr. Read by Anna Fields. 9 cass. (Running Time: 13 hrs. 30 min.). 1998. 62.95 (1904) Blckstn Audio.
Story of the tenth-century Byzantine princess, Theophano, wife of Otto II, the Holy Roman Emperor. When her husband was killed in battle, Theophano became Regent for her infant son, Otto III, & ruled the Holy Roman Empire for a decade. The climax is one of the great Dark Ages wars of succession, when her son became a pawn in the hands of the Frankish king.

Eagle's Daughter. unabr. ed. Judith Tarr. (Running Time: 46800 sec.). 2007. audio compact disk 29.95 (978-0-7861-5964-2(2)) Blckstn Audio.

Eagle's Daughter: War & Romance in the Holy Roman Empire. unabr. ed. Judith Tarr. (Running Time: 46800 sec.). 2007. audio compact disk 90.00 (978-0-7861-5963-5(4)) Blckstn Audio.

Eagles over Crooked Creek. Max Bonham. (Running Time: 0 hr. 12 mins.). 1999. 10.95 (978-1-60083-502-5(3)) Iofy Corp.

***Eagles over Crooked Creek.** Max Brand. 2009. (978-1-60136-434-0(2)) Audio Holding.

Eagles 1: Eyes of Eagles. 2006. audio compact disk 19.99 (978-1-59950-175-8(9)) GraphicAudio.

Eagles 10: Revenge of Eagles. William W. Johnstone. Directed By Bob Supan. Contrib. by Mort Shelby et al. (Running Time: 18000 sec.). (Eagles Ser.: No. 10). 2007. audio compact disk 19.99 (978-1-59950-353-0(0)) GraphicAudio.

Eagles 11: Pride of Eagles. William W. Johnstone. Directed By Bob Supan. Contrib. by Mort Shelby et al. (Running Time: 21600 sec.). (Eagles Ser.: No. 11). 2007. audio compact disk 19.99 (978-1-59950-361-5(1)) GraphicAudio.

Eagles 12: Crusade of Eagles. (Running Time: 18000 sec.). (Eagles Ser.). 2007. audio compact disk 19.99 (978-1-59950-376-9(X)) GraphicAudio.

Eagles 13: Thunder of Eagles. Based on a novel by William W. Johnstone. (Eagles Ser.: No. 13). 2008. audio compact disk 19.99 (978-1-59950-475-9(8)) GraphicAudio.

Eagles 14: Bloodshed of Eagles. Based on a novel by William W. Johnstone. (Eagles Ser.: No. 14). 2009. audio compact disk 19.99 (978-1-59950-617-3(3)) GraphicAudio.

***Eagles 15: Slaughter of Eagles.** William W. Johnstone. 2010. audio compact disk 19.99 (978-1-59950-717-0(X)) GraphicAudio.

Eagles 2: Dreams of Eagles. 2006. audio compact disk 19.99 (978-1-59950-186-4(4)) GraphicAudio.

Eagles 4: Scream of Eagles. William W. Johnstone. Directed By Bob Supan. Contrib. by David Coyne et al. (Running Time: 21600 sec.). (Eagles Ser.: No. 4). 2007. audio compact disk 19.99 (978-1-59950-204-5(6)) GraphicAudio.

Eagles 5: Rage of Eagles. William W. Johnstone. Directed By Bob Supan. Contrib. by Mort Shelby et al. (Running Time: 21600 sec.). (Eagles Ser.: No. 5). 2007. audio compact disk 19.99 (978-1-59950-215-1(1)) GraphicAudio.

Eagles 6: Song of Eagles. William W. Johnstone. Directed By Bob Supan. Contrib. by Mort Shelby et al. (Running Time: 18000 sec.). (Eagles Ser.: No. 6). 2007. audio compact disk 19.99 (978-1-59950-226-7(7)) GraphicAudio.

Eagles 7: Cry of Eagles. William W. Johnstone. Directed By Bob Supan. Contrib. by Mort Shelby et al. (Running Time: 21600 sec.). (Eagles Ser.: No. 7). 2007. audio compact disk 19.99 (978-1-59950-316-5(6)) GraphicAudio.

Eagles 8: Blood of Eagles. William W. Johnstone. Directed By Bob Supan. Contrib. by Mort Shelby et al. (Running Time: 25200 sec.). (Eagles Ser.: No. 8). 2007. audio compact disk 19.99 (978-1-59950-325-7(5)) GraphicAudio.

Eagles 9: Destiny of Eagles. William W. Johnstone. Directed By Bob Supan. Contrib. by Mort Shelby et al. (Running Time: 21600 sec.). (Eagles Ser.: No. 9). 2007. audio compact disk 19.99 (978-1-59950-343-1(3)) GraphicAudio.

Ear Candy. (Running Time: 74 mins.). 2001. 7.95 (978-1-886238-19-0(7)); audio compact disk 11.95 (978-1-886238-20-6(0)) Passion Press.

Ear, the Eye, & the Arm. Nancy Farmer. (J). audio compact disk 89.75 (978-1-4025-4914-4(8)) Recorded Bks.

Ear, the Eye, & the Arm. unabr. ed. Nancy Farmer. Narrated by George Guidall. 7 pieces. (Running Time: 10 hrs.). (J). (gr. 4 up). 1997. 60.75 (978-0-7887-0431-4(1), 94623E7) Recorded Bks.
African tribal folklore meets futuristic technology in this tale of mutant superheroes searching for three kidnapped children in 2194 Zimbabwe.

Ear to the Ground: Malvina Reynolds. Perf. by Malvina Reynolds. 1 CD. (Running Time: 1 hr. 2 mins.). 2000. audio compact disk 15.00 (40124) Smithsonian Folkways.
Malvina Reynolds is a well-known songwriter & activist for social justice & the environment.

Ear Training: Middle C to C, Vol. 1. Barry Wehrli. (ENG.). (J). 2003. audio compact disk 14.95 (978-0-9673826-6-1(1)) Wehrli Pubns.

Ear Training Two Note Beginning Vol. 5: With Audio CD. l.t. ed. Bruce E. Arnold. (ENG.). 1998. spiral bd. 23.99 (978-1-890944-35-3(1)) Muse Eek.

Ear Training Two Note Beginning Volume 2 Vol. 2: With Audio CD. l.t. ed. Bruce E. Arnold. (ENG.). 1998. spiral bd. 23.99 (978-1-890944-32-2(7)) Muse Eek.

Ear Training Two Note Beginning Volume 3 Vol. 3: With Audio CD. l.t. ed. Bruce E. Arnold. (ENG.). 1998. spiral bd. 23.99 (978-1-890944-33-9(5)) Muse Eek.

Ear Training Two Note Beginning Volume 4 Vol. 4: With Audio CD. l.t. ed. Bruce E. Arnold. (ENG.). 1998. spiral bd. 23.99 (978-1-890944-34-6(3)) Muse Eek.

Ear Training Two Note Beginning Volume 6 Vol. 6: With Audio CD. l.t. ed. Bruce E. Arnold. (ENG.). 1998. spiral bd. 23.99 (978-1-890944-36-0(X)) Muse Eek.

Earl Nightingale on Success. Earl Nightingale. 6 cass. 59.95 Set. Nightingale-Conant.
A comprehensive cross section of Earl's incredible 40-year career, this "encyclopedia of success" features six carefully selected works on self-mastery. Includes: The Boss, The Strangest Secret, Direct Line, 20 Minutes That Can Change Your Life, As a Man Thinketh & Think & Grow Rich.

Earl Nightingale Video Classics. Earl Nightingale. 1 cass. 1993. 174.95 incl. 5 videos. (G5900T) Nightingale-Conant.

Earl of Louisiana. unabr. ed. A. J. Liebling. Read by Walter Zimmerman. 6 cass. (Running Time: 9 hrs.). 1988. 48.00 (978-0-7366-1415-3(X), 2302) Books on Tape.
Earl Long lived all his life under the shadow of his more brilliant & famous brother. It had been that way when they were boys-Huey led, Earl followed. But Earl lived 25 years longer than his brother, & thus did some things that Huey could not do.

Earl the Squirrel. Don Freeman. Illus. by Don Freeman. Read by J. J. Myers. 1 cass. (Running Time: 11 mins.). (J). (ps-2). 2008. pap. bk. 16.95 (978-1-4301-0411-7(2)); pap. bk. 18.95 (978-1-4301-0414-8(7)) Live Oak Media.

Early African Literature: Its Political Source & Commitment. unabr. ed. Claude Wauthier. 1 cass. (Running Time: 20 min.). 1968. 12.95 (23144) J Norton Pubs.
Traces the development of early African writing from its first expressions of indigenous thought & culture to the post-independence period of passionate patriotism following World War II.

Early American: Early Short Stories by Well-Known & Lesser-Known American Authors. unabr. ed. Ed. by Gary Gabriel. 6 cass. (Running Time: 6 hrs.). (Audio Drama 101 Ser.: Vol. 2). 1998. 14.95 (978-1-892077-01-1(9)) Lend-A-Hand Soc.

Early American Christmas for Guitar. John Mock. 1996. pap. bk. 20.95 (978-0-7866-2668-7(2), 96518CDP) Mel Bay.

Early American Roots. 2002. audio compact disk 15.98 (978-0-7866-3216-9(X), 97212CD) Mel Bay.

Early Austrian Economics. unabr. ed. Israel M. Kirzner. Ed. by Mike Hassell. Narrated by Louis Rukeyser. 2 cass. (Running Time: 80 min. per cass.). Dramatization. (Great Economic Thinkers Ser.). 1988. 17.95 (978-0-938935-33-9(X), 10203) Knowledge Prod.
Carl Menger, Eugene von Bohm-Bawerk & other pioneers in Vienna believed capitalism is governed by consumer demand. These economists said that value can never be objectively determined - it is always dependent on the subjective preferences of consumers.

Early Austrian Economics: Knowledge Products. Izrael Kirzner. Read by Louis Rukeyser. (Running Time: 9000 sec.). (Great Economic Thinkers Ser.). 2006. audio compact disk 25.95 (978-0-7861-6930-6(3)) Pub: Blckstn Audio. Dist(s): NetLibrary CO

Early Autumn. unabr. collector's ed. Robert B. Parker. Read by Michael Prichard. 5 cass. (Running Time: 5 hrs.). (Spenser Ser.). 1989. 40.00 (978-0-7366-1589-1(X), 2452) Books on Tape.
A bitter divorce is only the beginning. First the father hires thugs to kidnap his son. Then the mother hires Spenser to get the boy back. But as soon as Spenser senses the lay of the land, he decides to do some kidnapping of his own. With a contract out on his life, he heads for the Maine woods, determined to give a puny 15-year-old a crash course in survival & to beat his dangerous opponents at their own brutal game.

Early Ayn Rand: A Selection from Her Unpublished Fiction (Revised Edition) unabr. ed. Ayn Rand. Read by Bernadette Dunne. (Running Time: 19 hrs. 30 mins.). 2010. 99.95 (978-1-4332-2637-3(5)); audio compact disk 123.00 (978-1-4332-2638-0(3)) Blckstn Audio.

Early Ayn Rand: A Selection from Her Unpublished Fiction (Revised Edition) unabr. rev. ed. Ayn Rand. Read by Bernadette Dunne. (Running Time: 19 hrs. 5 mins.). (ENG.). 2011. 44.95 (978-1-4332-2641-0(3)) Blckstn Audio.

***Early Ayn Rand, Revised Edition: A Selection from Her Unpublished Fiction.** unabr. ed. Ayn Rand. Read by Bernadette Dunne. (Running Time: 19 hrs. 5 mins.). (ENG.). 2011. audio compact disk 34.95 (978-1-4332-2640-3(5)) Blckstn Audio.

Early Bird's Alarm Clock/Amazing Bird. Steck-Vaughn Staff. (J). 1999. (978-0-7398-2439-9(2)) SteckVau.

Early Childhood Books Collection. K. Hague et al. Illus. by Pat Hutchins & M. Hague. 77 vols. (Running Time: 41 mins.). 2000. pap. bk. 106.95 (978-0-87499-820-7(4)) Live Oak Media.

Early Childhood Classic. Perf. by Hap Palmer. 1 cass. (Running Time: 1 hr.). (J). 2001. 9.95 (HP 111); audio compact disk 14.95 (HP 111 CD) Hap-Pal Music.
Here is a joyful collection of all time favorite activity songs for young children. In these unique renditions Hap Palmer preserves the charm & simplicity of the traditional songs while adding new, original lyrics & melodies to extend & enrich familiar classics.

Early Childhood Music Curriculum, Tape 1. Karen Rupprecht & Val Smalkin. Read by Kinde-Singers. Perf. by Val & Pam. 1 cass. (Running Time: 52 min.). (J). (ps-2). 1995. 10.00 (978-1-887882-01-9(4)) Small Kin Music.
A children's audio tape of 15 songs designed for parents & teachers of 3 to 8 year olds. Side A - vocals & accompaniment. Side B - accompaniment only.

Early Childhood Songs. Ella Jenkins. 1 CD. (Running Time: 1 hr.). (J). 2001. audio compact disk 15.00 (FC 45015CD) Kimbo Educ.

Early Christian Writings & the King James Bible. Speeches. David W. Bercot. 2 CDs. (Running Time: 2 hrs. 20 mins.). 2002. audio compact disk 14.95 (978-0-924722-14-1(2)) Scroll Pub.
A discussion of what the writings of the pre-Nicene church (A.D. 100-325) reveal about the text types used by the early Christians for both the Old and New Testaments. Does the King James Bible more closely follow the texts used by the early Christians - or do modern translations?.

Early Christianity Pts. I-II: The Experience of the Divine. Instructed by Luke Timothy Johnson. 12 CDs. (Running Time: 12 hrs.). 2002. bk. 69.95 (978-1-56585-364-5(4), 647) Teaching Co.

Early Christianity Pts. I-II, Vol. 1: The Experience of the Divine. Instructed by Luke Timothy Johnson. 12 cass. (Running Time: 12 hrs.). bk. 54.95 (978-1-56585-177-1(3), 647) Teaching Co.

Early Christianity Vol. 2: The Experience of the Divine. Instructed by Luke Timothy Johnson. 6 cass. (Running Time: 6 hrs.). 2002. 129.95 (978-1-56585-178-8(1)) Teaching Co.

Early Church: The the Book of Acts. unabr. rev. ed. 2002. audio compact disk 14.99 (978-0-310-94486-7(4)) Zondervan.

Early Church Audio Download. Zondervan Publishing Staff. (Running Time: 3 hrs. 0 mins. 0 sec.). (NIV Audio Bible Ser.). (ENG.). 2006. 8.99 (978-0-310-27229-8(7)) Zondervan.

Early Church Biographies-CD. 2003. 35.00 (978-1-59128-386-7(8)) Canon Pr ID.

Early Churchills. unabr. ed. A. L. Rowse. Read by David Case. 11 cass. (Running Time: 16 hrs. 30 min.). 1996. 70.40 (978-0-7366-3603-2(X), 4257) Books on Tape.
The death of Ambassador Pamela Harriman, Winston Churchill's daughter-in-law, has renewed interest in one of England's most remarkable families.

Early Days - Mescaline Opens Huxley's Doors of Perception. Humphrey Osmond. 1 cass. 9.00 (A0096-83) Sound Photosyn.
At the 1983 Psychedelic Conference.

Early, Early Childhood Songs. Perf. by Ella Jenkins. 1 cass. (Running Time: 32 min.). (J). (ps). 1990. (0-9307-450150-9307-45015-2-8); audio compact disk (0-9307-45015-2-8) Smithsonian Folkways.
Eight favorites performed with nursery school children. Features melodies performed on folk instruments followed by playful group exercises for melody recognition. Includes "Mary Had a Little Lamb," "Farmer in the Dell" & "Skip to My Lou".

Early Explorers Audio CD Theme Set: Set of 6 Set A. Adapted by Benchmark Education Staff. (English Explorers Ser.). (J). (gr. 3-6). 2007. audio compact disk 60.00 (978-1-4108-9843-2(1)) Benchmark Educ.

Early Explorers Early Take Home Book CD-ROM. Compiled by Benchmark Education Company Staff. (Early Explorers Set C Ser.). (J). (gr. 1). 2008. audio compact disk (978-1-60437-652-4(X)) Benchmark Educ.

Early Explorers Early/Fluent Take Home Book CD-ROM. Compiled by Benchmark Education Company Staff. (Early Explorers Set C Ser.). (J). (gr. 2). 2008. audio compact disk (978-1-60437-653-1(8)) Benchmark Educ.

Early Explorers Emergent Take Home Book CD-ROM. Compiled by Benchmark Education Company Staff. (Early Explorers Set C Ser.). (J). (gr. k-1). 2008. audio compact disk (978-1-60437-651-7(1)) Benchmark Educ.

Early Explorers Take Home Book CD: Set A Early. Benchmark Education Staff. (J). 2006. audio compact disk 10.00 (978-1-4108-7248-7(3)) Benchmark Educ.

Early Explorers Take Home Book CD: Set A Emergent. Benchmark Education Staff. (J). 2006. audio compact disk 10.00 (978-1-4108-7247-0(5)) Benchmark Educ.

Early Explorers Take Home Book CD: Set A Fluent. Benchmark Education Staff. (J). 2006. audio compact disk 10.00 (978-1-4108-7249-4(1)) Benchmark Educ.

Early Explorers Take Home Book CD: Set B Bluent. Compiled by Benchmark Education Staff. (J). 2006. audio compact disk 10.00 (978-1-4108-7791-8(4)) Benchmark Educ.

Early Explorers Take Home Book CD: Set B Early. Compiled by Benchmark Education Staff. (J). 2006. audio compact disk 10.00 (978-1-4108-7790-1(6)) Benchmark Educ.

Early Explorers Take Home Book CD: Set B Emergent. Compiled by Benchmark Education Staff. (J). 2006. audio compact disk 10.00 (978-1-4108-7789-5(2)) Benchmark Educ.

Early Fluency Stage 3. Steck-Vaughn Staff. 1997. (978-0-8172-7379-8(4)) SteckVau.

Early French Libertarian Thought. unabr. ed. Leonard Liggio. 1 cass. (Running Time: 1 hr. 21 min.). 12.95 (383) J Norton Pubs.

Early Horror Works. Short Stories. H. P. Lovecraft. 1 CD. (Running Time: 74 mins). 2005. audio compact disk 11.99 (978-0-9764805-2-5(2)) C CD Bks.
Five chilling, unabridged stories from one of America's greatest horror writers. Listen to the story of a curious tourist's confrontation with The Beast in the Cave. In Dagon, a naval prisoner escapes his captors... but to what? The Statement of Randolph Carter recounts the horrifying experience of two researchers. A group of thieves get more than they bargain for when they choose The Terrible Old Man as their next victim. A meta-physics student is eerily intrigued by The Music of Erich Zann. "The five stories practically come to life as the words flow from the peakers. (Narrator) Sellin does a marvelous job of making each sentence breathe through his emotion and pitch." - Robert Denson, Sunpiper Press Book Review.

Early JZ & HT Tunes Trombone, Bass, Tuba & Bass Instruments - Backup Trax. Dix Bruce. 1995. pap. bk. 17.95 (978-0-7866-1428-8(5), 95644BCD) Mel Bay.

Early Learning. Robert M. Miller. Prod. by Rick Lamb. 1 cass. (Running Time: 1 hr. 30 min.). 1998. 14.95 (978-0-9679487-2-0(X)) Horse Show.
Dr. Miller offers an in-depth discussion of the theory and technique behind Imprint Training, a swift and effective way to permanently shape a young horse's lifetime behavior. Abridged from the best-selling book.

Early Literacy Preparing Young Children for Success in Reading. Nikisha Jackson. (ENG.). 2009. spiral bd. 39.95 (978-0-9796689-1-3(3)) REASAQ.

Early Middle Ages, Vol. I-II. Instructed by Philip Daileader. 12 cass. (Running Time: 12 hrs.). 2004. bk. 54.95 (978-1-56585-912-8(X), 8267); bk. 69.95 (978-1-56585-914-2(6), 8267) Teaching Co.

Early Moon see Carl Sandburg's Poems for Children

Early Morning in the Rain Forest. 1 cass. (Running Time: 61 min.). 1994. audio compact disk 15.95 CD. (2620, Creativ Pub) Quayside.
Restful listening experience. Gentle music from Ken Davis' Crystal Piano accompanying the unique sounds of Australia's Daintree Rain Forest.

Early Morning in the Rain Forest. 1 cass. (Running Time: 61 min.). 1994. 9.95 (2619, NrthWrd Bks) TandN Child.

Early Music Favorites for Acoustic Guitar: Intermediate Level. Richard L. Matteson, Jr. 1998. pap. bk. 19.95 (978-0-7866-2085-2(4), 95779BCD) Mel Bay.

Early Narratives of the Northwest: 1634-1699. unabr. collector's ed. Read by Grover Gardner. Ed. by Louise P. Kellogg. 9 cass. (Running Time: 13 hrs. 30 min.). 1983. 72.00 (978-0-7366-0457-4(X), 1429) Books on Tape.
A collection of stories by 17th century adventurers who discovered the Great Lakes, the plains of Illinois & the astonishing Mississippi River.

Early One Morning. Rob Ryan. Read by Steven Pacey. 10 vols. (Running Time: 15 hrs.). 2003. 84.95 (978-0-7540-8373-3(X)) Pub: Chivers Audio Bks GBR. Dist(s): AudioGO

Early-Onset Glaucoma - A Bibliography & Dictionary for Physicians, Patients, & Genome Researchers. Compiled by Icon Group International, Inc. Staff. 2007. ring bd. 28.95 (978-0-497-11204-2(3)) Icon Grp.

Early Psychedelic History. unabr. ed. Humphrey Osmond. 1 cass. (Running Time: 57 min.). 1976. 1.01 (07301) Big Sur Tapes.

Early Quakerism Reconsidered. John M. Moore. 5 cass. Incl. Early Quakerism Reconsidered: From Movement to Sect: Social Development in Early Quakerism. 1974.; Early Quakerism Reconsidered: Quakers & Social Radicals: How Radical Were the Early Friends? 1974.; Early Quakerism Reconsidered: Sources of Quakerism: Mystics & Puritans. 1974.; Early Quakerism Reconsidered: The Early Quakers & Politics. 1974.; Early Quakerism Reconsidered: Was George Fox the Founder of Quakerism? 1974.; 1974. 17.50 Set.; 4.50 ea. Pendle Hill.

Early Quakerism Reconsidered: From Movement to Sect: Social Development in Early Quakerism see Early Quakerism Reconsidered

Early Quakerism Reconsidered: Quakers & Social Radicals: How Radical Were the Early Friends? see Early Quakerism Reconsidered

Early Quakerism Reconsidered: Sources of Quakerism: Mystics & Puritans see Early Quakerism Reconsidered

Early Quakerism Reconsidered: The Early Quakers & Politics see Early Quakerism Reconsidered

Early Quakerism Reconsidered: Was George Fox the Founder of Quakerism? see Early Quakerism Reconsidered

Early Railroad Maps: Get Ready to Ride the Railroads with this Amazing Set! Compiled by Scott Reid. Created by A2ZCDS Staff. 5cds. 2004. audio compact disk 29.95 (978-1-932731-72-9(5)) A2ZCDS.

Early Reader Collection, Level A. Steck-Vaughn Staff. 2004. audio compact disk 19.95 (978-0-7398-8211-5(2)) SteckVau.

Early Reader Collection, Level B. Steck-Vaughn Staff. 2004. audio compact disk 32.95 (978-0-7398-8212-2(0)) SteckVau.

Early Reader Program Collection, Level C. Steck-Vaughn Staff. 2004. audio compact disk 64.95 (978-0-7398-8280-1(5)) SteckVau.

***Early Reader's Collection (Playaway)** (Playaway Ser.). (ENG.). audio compact disk 87.60 (978-1-4342-3005-8(8)) CapstoneDig.

Early Recognition of AIDS-Related Problems. Dan William. (AIDS: The National Conference for Practitioners). 1986. 9.00 (978-0-932491-50-3(2)) Res Appl Inc.

Early Recordings, 1965-1973. British Library Sound Archive Staff. (British Library - British Library Sound Archive Ser.). 2009. audio compact disk 15.00 (978-0-7123-0594-5(7)) Pub: Britis Library GBR. Dist(s): Chicago Distribution Ctr

Early Retirement Syndrome: Luke 12:13-34. Ed Young. 1993. 4.95 (978-0-7417-1957-7(6), 957) Win Walk.

Early River Civilizations Audio CD Theme Set: Set of 6 Set A. Adapted by Benchmark Education Staff. (English Explorers Ser.). (J). (gr. 3-6). 2007. audio compact disk 60.00 (978-1-4108-9846-3(6)) Benchmark Educ.

Early Roots of Robert Johnson. Woody Mann. (Stefan Grossman's Guitar Workshop Ser.). 1999. pap. bk. 24.95 (978-0-7866-4999-0(2)) Mel Bay.

Early Short Stories by Willa Cather. unabr. ed. Willa Cather. Narrated by Flo Gibson. (Running Time: 2 hrs. 45 mins.). 2004. audio compact disk 16.95 (978-1-55685-776-8(4)) Audio Bk Con.

Early Short Stories by Willa Cather, Set. unabr. ed. Willa Cather. Read by Flo Gibson. 2 cass. (Running Time: 3 hrs.). (gr. 8 up). 1991. 14.95 (978-1-55685-197-1(9)) Audio Bk Con.
"A Singer's Romance", "The Sentimentality of William Tavener", "The Count of Crow's Nest", "A Resurrection", "The Prodigies" & "Nanette: an Aside" are told with extraordinary human insight.

Early Spanish Adventures Home Connection Kit. Created by Music. (ENG.). 2009. audio compact disk 19.95 (978-1-935572-09-1(1)) MMnM Bks.

Early Spanish Adventures Supplemental Curriculum Kit. 2nd rev. ed. Created by Music Movement and Magination. (ENG.). 2009. spiral bd. 179.95 (978-1-935572-03-9(2)) MMnM Bks.

Early Stages. unabr. ed. John Gielgud. Read by John Gielgud. 7 cass. (Running Time: 8 hrs. 40 min.). (Isis Ser.). (J). 2004. 61.95 (978-1-85089-818-4(9), 89121) Pub: ISIS Lrg Prnt GBR. Dist(s): Ulverscroft US

***Early to Death, Early to Rise.** unabr. ed. Kim Harrison. Read by Mandy Siegfried. (ENG.). 2010. (978-0-06-198398-6(5)); (978-0-06-199750-1(1)) HarperCollins Pubs.

Early U&H Tunes for Clarinet, Tenor Sax & B Flat Instruments - Backup Trax. Dix Bruce. 1995. pap. bk. 17.95 (978-0-7866-1427-1(7), 95643BCD) Mel Bay.

Early Warning System: Matt. 26:75. Ed Young. 1988. Rental 4.95 (978-0-7417-1694-1(1), 694) Win Walk.

Early Winter. Marion Dane Bauer. Read by Jeff Woodman. 2 cass. (Running Time: 2 hrs. 45 mins.). (YA). 2000. pap. bk. 42.00 (978-0-7887-4328-3(7), 41123); 178.30 (978-0-7887-4429-7(1), 47120) Recorded Bks.
When 11-year-old Tim visits his grandparents, Grandma whispers about Alzheimer's disease & Granddad no longer seems sure of himself. Tim decides to prove his grandfather is still the man he always was. He will take him on a secret fishing trip.

Early Winter. unabr. ed. Marion Dane Bauer. Narrated by Jeff Woodman. 2 pieces. (Running Time: 2 hrs. 45 mins.). (gr. 5 up). 2000. 20.00 (978-0-7887-4245-3(0), 96213E7) Recorded Bks.

Early Years 1958-1962. Perf. by New Lost City Ramblers. Anno. by Jon Pankake. Contrib. by Moses Asch et al. 1 cass. 1991. (0-9307-400360-9307-40036-2-6); audio compact disk (0-9307-40036-2-6) Smithsonian Folkways.

Earmarks: Capitol Learning Audio Course. William LaForge. Prod. by TheCapitol.Net. (ENG.). 2008. 47.00 (978-1-58733-018-6(0)) TheCapitol.

***Earn What You're Worth: How to Maximize Your Income at Any Time in Any Market.** unabr. ed. Brian Tracy. Read by Author. (Running Time: 6 hrs.). (ENG.). 2011. 27.00 (978-1-59659-638-2(4), GildAudio); audio compact disk 29.98 (978-1-59659-637-5(6), GildAudio) Pub: Gildan Media. Dist(s): HachBkGrp

***Ears Cd Set.** Phoenix Learning Resources Staff. (ENG.). 2009. audio compact disk 108.00 (978-0-7915-1458-0(7)) Phoenix Lrn.

Ears of the City. unabr. ed. Ron Ellis. Read by Geoffrey Annis. 6 cass. (Running Time: 8 hrs.). (Story Sound Ser.). (J). 2006. 54.95 (978-1-85903-871-0(9)) Pub: Mgna Lrg Print GBR. Dist(s): Ulverscroft US

Earth. Compiled by Benchmark Education Staff. 2006. audio compact disk 10.00 (978-1-4108-6668-4(8)) Benchmark Educ.

Earth. Composed by Vanraj Bhatia. 1 cass. (Elements Ser.: Vol. 1). 1995. (M95007); audio compact disk (CD M95007) Multi-Cultural Bks.
At the Dawn of Creation, Earthquake, Rainforest, Earth & Water, Earth & Heaven.

Earth: It's Importance in the Chart. Bernice P. Grebner. 1 cass. (Running Time: 90 min.). 8.95 (665) Am Fed Astrologers.

Earth: The Late Summer Season. Ann Bailey. Read by Ann Bailey. Read by Jon Bailey. 1 cass. (Running Time: 60 min.). (Wellness Through the Seasons Ser.). 1994. 12.00 incl. script. (978-1-889643-05-2(X)) SourcePoint.
Music, sounds & spoken words illustrate the connection between the late summer season & health within the body, mind & spirit.

Earth: The Sequel: The Race to Reinvent Energy & Stop Global Warming. unabr. ed. Fred Krupp & Miriam Horn. Narrated by Dick Hill. (Running Time: 9 hrs. 30 mins. 0 sec.). (ENG.). 2001. audio compact disk 34.99 (978-1-4001-0708-7(3)) Pub: Tantor Media. Dist(s): IngramPubServ

Earth: The Sequel: The Race to Reinvent Energy & Stop Global Warming. unabr. ed. Fred Krupp & Miriam Horn. Narrated by Dick Hill. (Running Time: 9 hrs. 30 mins. 0 sec.). (ENG.). 2008. audio compact disk 69.99 (978-1-4001-3708-4(X)) Pub: Tantor Media. Dist(s): IngramPubServ

Earth: The Sequel: The Race to Reinvent Energy & Stop Global Warming. unabr. ed. Fred Krupp & Miriam Horn. Read by Dick Hill. (Running Time: 9 hrs. 30 mins. 0 sec.). (ENG.). 2008. audio compact disk 24.99 (978-1-4001-5708-2(0)) Pub: Tantor Media. Dist(s): IngramPubServ

Earth Abides. unabr. ed. George R. Stewart. Read by Jonathan Davis. (Running Time: 16 hrs.). 2009. audio compact disk 99.97 (978-1-4418-0615-4(6), 9781441806154, BriAudCD Unabrid) Brilliance Audio.

Earth Abides-UAB. George R. Stewart. 2009. audio compact disk 39.99 (978-1-4418-0614-7(8)) Brilliance Audio.

Earth, Air, Fire & Custard. Tom Holt. Read by Raymond Sawyer. 14 cass. (Running Time: 19 hrs. 45 mins.). (Isis Cassettes Ser.). (J). 2005. 99.95 (978-0-7531-2196-2(4)) Pub: ISIS Lrg Prnt GBR. Dist(s): Ulverscroft US

Earth, Air, Fire & Custard. unabr. ed. Tom Holt. Read by Raymond Sawyer. 16 CDs. (Running Time: 19 hrs. 14 mins.). (Isis (CDs) Ser.). (J). 2005. audio compact disk 109.95 (978-0-7531-2439-0(4)) Pub: ISIS Lrg Prnt GBR. Dist(s): Ulverscroft US

Earth & Me. 1 cass. (Running Time: 52 min.). (J). (gr. k-12). 1997. 9.98 Shadow Box.
As featured at the Shadow Box Theatre, a musical description of the birth of the earth, animals, & humans, as joyfully witnessed by a child. The child later laments the destruction of the planet by human carelessness, vowing to help the earth renew itself. Complete soundtrack.

Earth & Me. Sandra Robbins. Arranged by Jeff Olmsted. (J). 2004. bk. 23.95 (978-1-882601-49-3(1)); pap. bk. 16.95 (978-1-882601-52-3(1)); audio compact disk 11.95 (978-1-882601-45-5(9)) See-Mores Wrkshop.

Earth & Me: A Child Learns about Our World. unabr. ed. Sandra Robbins. (See-More's Stories Ser.). (J). 1997. audio compact disk 9.95 (978-1-882601-44-8(0)) See-Mores Wrkshop.

Earth & Me (Hard Cover Book & Tape Set) Sandra Robbins. Arranged by Jeff Olmsted. (J). 2004. mass mkt. 21.95 (978-1-882601-50-9(5)) See-Mores Wrkshop.

Earth & Me (Soft Cover Book & CD Set) Told to Sandra Robbins. Arranged by Jeff Olmsted. (J). 2004. pap. bk. 18.95 (978-1-882601-51-6(3)) See-Mores Wrkshop.

Earth & Sky. Douglas Post. Perf. by Ed Begley, Jr. et al. 1 cass. (Running Time: 1 hr. 22 min.). 1998. 19.95 (978-1-58081-046-3(2), TPT30) L A Theatre.
Head in the clouds, Sara McKeon lives in the rarified world of library work & poetry readings. She seems completely unsuited to investigating the sudden brutal murder of her lover. A haunting mystery, infused with humor, poetry & an urban gift.

Earth & Soil. unabr. ed. Alan Gemmell. 1 cass. 1990. 12.95 (TSE009) J Norton Pubs.
Vital role of soil in the food chain.

Earth as an Integrated Organism - A Look At: Peter Russell's "The Global Brain" Hosted by Nancy Pearlman. 1 cass. (Running Time: 29 min.). 10.00 (1030) Educ Comm CA.

Earth as Ruler of Libra. Beverly J. Farrell. 1 cass. 8.95 (112) Am Fed Astrologers.
Closer look at Libra and Earth as possible ruler.

Earth Blood 1. James Axler. 2009. audio compact disk 19.99 (978-1-59950-563-3(0)) GraphicAudio.

***Earth Book.** unabr. ed. Todd Parr. (Running Time: 4 mins.). (ENG.). (J). 2010. 0.98 (978-1-60788-887-1(4)) Pub: Hachet Audio. Dist(s): HachBkGrp

Earth Cell. unabr. ed. Charles Brass. Read by Jack Labbe. 4 cass. (Running Time: 4 hrs. 24 min.). 1994. 26.95 (978-1-55686-524-4(4)) Books in Motion.
Miles the Immortal attempts to stop a cat-like race of beings known as the Quirill from using Earth as a source for slaves to aid in their war with the Dnarr, their mortal enemies.

Earth Centered Astrology. Janet Brundage. 1 cass. 8.95 (495) Am Fed Astrologers.
Life on earth is based on polarity & balance.

Earth Changes. unabr. ed. Robert A. Monroe. Read by Robert A. Monroe. (Running Time: 45 min.). (Explorer Ser.). 1983. 12.95 (978-1-56113-008-5(7), 9) Monroe Institute.
Four Explorers discuss earth changes.

Earth Changes: Your Wake-Up Call. abr. ed. Lee Carroll. Read by Lee Carroll. 1 cass. (Running Time: 1 hr. 18 min.). (Kryon Tapes Ser.). 1995. 10.00 (978-0-9636304-6-9(6)) Kryon Writings.
Live recording of channelled event.

Earth Child: Songs & Stories about Living Lightly on Planet Earth. unabr. ed. Kathryn Sheehan. Read by Lesley Smith. 2 cass. (Running Time: 1 hr. 25 min.). (J). (ps-5). 1994. 16.95 set. (978-1-57178-004-1(1)) Coun Oak Bks.
Includes 14 songs & 10 interactive stories to entertain & educate children, while fostering an awareness of nature. The songs contain new words set to familiar tunes of childhood so that children can quickly learn to sing-along.

Earth Dance. Perf. by Nick Ashron. Created by Matthew Manning. Prod. by Stuart Wilde. 1 cass. 10.95 (CN602) White Dove NM.
A moving musical interpretation of the cycles of nature. Earthly acoustic waves of sound are punctuated by softly plucked strings in tumbling patterns. Nick Ashron first gained recognition with Britain's first New Age rock group Pegasus.

Earth Day. Linda Lowery. Illus. by Mary Bergherr. (J). (gr. 2-4). 1993. bk. 22.95 (978-0-87499-303-5(2)) Live Oak Media.

Earth Day. unabr. ed. Linda Lowery. 1 cass. (Running Time: 15 min.). (J). (gr. 3-6). 1993. 9.95 Live Oak Media.
A history & examination of the importance of this now international holiday.

Earth Day. unabr. ed. Linda Lowery. Read by Randye Kaye. Illus. by Mary Bergherr. 1 cass. (Running Time: 15 mins.). (J). (gr. 1-6). 1993. pap. bk. 15.95 (978-0-87499-302-8(4)) Live Oak Media.
First celebrated in the United States in 1970, Earth Day called attention to the importance of respecting our environment. Now Earth Day is an annual event celebrated every April 22nd. This book explains the history & the importance of the holiday.

Earth Day - Then & Now. Hosted by Nancy Pearlman. 1 cass. (Running Time: 30 min.). 10.00 (717) Educ Comm CA.

Earth Day, Grades 1-6. unabr. ed. Linda Lowery. Read by Randye Kaye. Illus. by Mary Bergherr. 14 vols. (Running Time: 15 mins.). (J). 1993. pap. bk. & tchr. ed. 33.95 Reading Chest. (978-0-87499-304-2(0)) Live Oak Media.

Earth Fathers: A Transformative Archetype in Contemporary Society. Read by Arthur Colman. 1 cass. (Running Time: 90 min.). 1987. 10.95 (978-0-7822-0036-2(2), 244) C G Jung IL.

Earth Fire, Jerry Ahern. Read by Charlie O'Dowd. 2 cass. (Running Time: 3 hrs.). 2003. 18.00 (978-1-58807-317-4(3)) Am Pubng Inc.

Earth Fire, Vol. I. Jerry Ahern. Read by Charlie O'Dowd. 2 vols. 2004. 18.00 (978-1-58807-316-7(5)) Am Pubng Inc.

Earth Fire, Vol. I. Jerry Ahern. Read by Charlie O'Dowd. 2 vols. No. 9. 2004. (978-1-58807-931-2(7)) Am Pubng Inc.

Earth Fire, Vol. II. Jerry Ahern. Read by Charlie O'Dowd. 2 vols. No. 9. 2004. (978-1-58807-932-9(5)) Am Pubng Inc.

Earth First! Activists Speak Out about Habitat Conservation Plans & Hunt Sabotage & Sagewing Performs Songs about Trees & Canyons. Hosted by Nancy Pearlman. 1 cass. (Running Time: 28 min.). 10.00 (1203) Educ Comm CA.

Earth Healing. 3 cass. (Running Time: 4 hrs. 30 mins.). 2000. 24.95 (978-1-55961-617-1(2)); audio compact disk 29.95 (978-1-55961-616-4(4)) Relaxtn Co.

Earth in Ascensions. unabr. ed. Nancy A. Clark. Read by Nancy A. Clark. 2 cass. (Running Time: 1 hr.). 1975. 16.00 set. Violet Fire Pubns.
Four chapters from book of same name.

Earth in the Balance: Ecology & the Human Spirit. abr. ed. Ed. by Al Gore. 2 cass. (Running Time: 3 hrs.). 2000. 17.95 (978-1-57453-382-8(7)) Audio Lit.

Earth in the Balance: Ecology & the Human Spirit. abr. ed. Al Gore. Read by Al Gore. (YA). 2008. 34.99 (978-1-60514-775-8(3)) Find a World.

Earth in the Balance: Ecology & the Human Spirit. unabr. ed. Read by Ed Begley, Jr. Ed. by Al Gore. 9 cass. (Running Time: 10 hrs. 30 min.). 1999. 49.95 (978-1-57453-313-2(4)) Audio Lit.
Vice President Gore argues that the engines of human civilization have brought on imminent catastrophe, & that only a worldwide mobilization can save the earth for future generations. His analysis of environmental crises along political, scientific, & economic lines leads to a plan for action.

Earth Is Heaven: A Meditational Journey. Read by Kathy Scharlau. 1 cass. (Running Time: 68 min.). 1997. 9.95 (978-1-890339-01-2(6)); audio compact disk 13.95 CD. (978-1-890339-00-5(8)) Orchid Lane.
A self-guided meditation with a blend of background music.

Earth Is the Lord's. Dianne Bergant. 6 cass. (Running Time: 9 hrs. 30 min.). 1992. 38.95 set. (TAH258) Alba Hse Comns.
At last! We have clear precise instruction from Scripture about OUR obligation for OUR earth. What is our responsibility for the earth? How is this determined? Whose rules are we going to play by? This is a compelling program everyone should hear.

Earth is the Lord's. unabr. ed. Perf. by Eknath Easwaran. 1 cass. (Running Time: 1 hr.). 1985. 7.95 (978-1-58638-528-6(3)) Nilgiri Pr.

Earth Is the Lord's & the Fullness Thereof. Instructed by Manly P. Hall. 8.95 (978-0-89314-048-9(1), C861123) Philos Res.

Earth Island Journal, Headwaters Forest Coalition & Safer!-CBE Representatives Explore Issues of Tree-Free Paper, Pacific Ancient Forests & Multi-Ethnicity in the Environmental Movement; Protecting Blue Elbow Swamp on the Texas-Louisiana Border. Hosted by Nancy Pearlman. 1 cass. (Running Time: 28 min.). 10.00 (1407) Educ Comm CA.

Earth Kinship. unabr. ed. Catherine Bateson. 1 cass. 9.00 (OC65) Sound Horizons AV.

Earth Magic: Sacred Rituals for Connecting to Nature's Power. Starhawk. 4 CDs. (Running Time: 17100 sec.). 2006. audio compact disk 29.95 (978-1-59179-415-8(3), W1000D) Sounds True.

Earth Mama. Joyce J. Rouse. 1 cass. (Running Time: 26 min.). (J). (gr. 1-12). 1994. 9.95 (978-1-887712-00-2(3)) Rouse Hse Prodns.
Positive, encouraging environmental songs for families & kids of all ages. 9 songs.

Earth Mother Lullabies from Around the World. unabr. ed. 2 cass. (J). 19.95 (S11053) J Norton Pubs.
Lullabies are from diverse ethnic traditions: Japanese, Russian, Swedish, Icelandic, Slovakian, Yiddish, Iroquois Indian, Afro-American & Spanish, among others. The program which received the American Literary Association's Notable Children's Recording Award, includes what is believed to be the oldest musically notated song ever translated.

Earth Mother Lullabies from Around the World, Vol. 1. Pamala Ballingham & Timothy Ballingham. Perf. by Pamala Ballingham. 1 cass. (J). (ps up). 1987. 9.95 (978-0-922104-00-0(X), EMP 01B) Earth Mother Prodns.
Features ten folk lullabies accompanied by mandolin, harp, flute & guitar (norelco box).

Earth Mother Lullabies from Around the World, Vol. 2. Pamala Ballingham & Timothy Ballingham. Perf. by Pamala Ballingham. 1 cass. (Running Time: 49 min.). (J). (ps up). 1989. 9.95 Bookpack pkg. (978-0-922104-03-1(4), EMP 02B); 9.95 norelco box, 08/1987. (978-0-922104-02-4(6), EMP 02B2) Earth Mother Prodns.
Lullabies from Sweden, South Africa, Slovakia, the British Isles, the United States, & ancient Near East have been arranged for soprano harmonies, harp, guitar, & flute.

Earth Mother Lullabies from Around the World, Vol. 3. Pamala Ballingham & Timothy Ballingham. Perf. by Pamala Ballingham. 1 cass. (Running Time: 50 min.). (J). (ps up). 1990. 9.95 Norelco box. (978-0-922104-07-9(7), EMP 04B); 9.95 Bookpack pkg. (978-0-922104-08-6(5), EMP 04B4) Earth Mother Prodns.
Ten traditional lullabies from England, Poland, Spain, Norway, Germany, Nigeria, & the United States. Vocals accompanied by guitar, piano, harmonica, soothing sound effects. Stress reducer, sleep inducer for all ages.

Earth Mother Lullabies Series, Vol. 1. Timothy Ballingham & Pamala Ballingham. Perf. by Pamala Ballingham. 1 cass. (Running Time: 49 min.). (J). (ps up). 1989. 9.95 Bookpack pkg. (978-0-922104-01-7(8), EMP 01B1) Earth Mother Prodns.

Earth Moving Equipment in Argentina: A Strategic Reference 2007. Compiled by Icon Group International, Inc. Staff. 2007. ring bd. 195.00 (978-0-497-35797-9(6)) Icon Grp.

Earth, My Butt & Other Big Round Things. Carolyn Mackler. Narrated by Johanna Parker. 5 CDs. (Running Time: 6 hrs.). (YA). 2003. audio compact disk 48.75 (978-1-4193-1817-7(9)) Recorded Bks.

Earth, My Butt & Other Big Round Things. unabr. ed. Carolyn Mackler. 5 cassettes. (Running Time: 6 hrs). (J). 2004. 45.75 (978-1-4193-0306-7(6)) Recorded Bks.

Earth Mysteries (Lecture) unabr. ed. Paul Devereux. 2 cass. 18.00 (OC42L) Sound Horizons AV.

Earth Mysteries (Workshop) unabr. ed. Paul Devereux. 4 cass. 36.00 (OC42W) Sound Horizons AV.

Earth Rhythms. 1 cass. (Running Time: 42 min.). (Elements of Nature Ser.). 1994. audio compact disk 15.95 CD. (2814, Creativ Pub) Quayside.
A tour of Mother Earth & her voices. Bruce Kurnow's compositions.

Earth Rhythms. 1 cass. (Running Time: 42 min.). (Elements of Nature Ser.). 1994. 9.95 (2812, NrthWrd Bks) TandN Child.

Earth Rhythms, Vol. 4. Created by Vicki Corona. (Running Time: 30 min). (Celebrate the Cultures Ser.: 4). 1999. audio compact disk 16.95 (978-1-58513-125-9(3)) Dance Fantasy.
Polynesian Music CD to accompany our books and/or videos setting out the choreographies. Includes the songs: SunshineSiva Lapalapa, NaWaka, Pineapple Beach, Pa'u Mango, 'Olu'olu Congrats, Coconutz, Tabu, Lautilifoa, Magic Islands, Tokere Lagoon, Aloha Gram, Christmas in Tahiti, and Silent Night Island Style Sing-a-Long.

Earth-Ruler of Libra. Beverly J. Farrell. 1 cass. 8.95 (403) Am Fed Astrologers.
New 'cookbook' for Earth in signs & houses.

Earth Science: Audio Summary. 6th ed. Holt, Rinehart and Winston Staff. Date not set. audio compact disk 115.93 (978-0-03-036359-7(4)) Holt McDoug.

Earth Science Experiments on File. Diagram Group. (gr. 6-12). 2004. audio compact disk 149.95 (978-0-8160-5000-0(7)) Facts On File.

Earth Science Mapping for Planning, Development & Conservation. Ed. by G. J. McCall & B. R. Marker. (C). 1989. 289.00 (978-0-86010-989-1(5)) Graham & Trotman GBR.

Earth Science on File#153;, New Edition, CD-ROM. Diagram Staff. (gr. 6-12). 2004. audio compact disk 149.95 (978-0-8160-5812-9(1)) Facts On File.

Earth-Shaking Facts about Earthquakes with Max Axiom, Super Scientist. Katherine Krohn. Illus. by Tod Smith & Al Milgram. Contrib. by Dennis Spears & Colleen Buckman. (Graphic Science Ser.). (ENG.). (gr. 3-4). 2008. audio compact disk 6.95 (978-1-4296-3190-7(2)) CapstoneDig.

Earth Shall Weep: A History of Native America. James Wilson. Narrated by Nelson Runger. 15 cass. (Running Time: 22 hrs.). 125.00 (978-1-4025-1879-9(X)) Recorded Bks.

Earth Songs. Doug Wood. 2005. audio compact disk 14.95 (978-0-9719971-3-4(6)) Pub: Wind In The Pines. Dist(s): Adventure Pubns

Earth Speaks. Perf. by Michel Sherman. 1 cass. (Running Time: 1 hr.). 1996. 10.95; audio compact disk 15.95 CD. AnimaMundi.
Multi-layered, transcendent music of lute & guitar, composed in collaboration with animal helpers & the spirits of Nature, to relax, focus, tune in, & deepen your connection with your fellow species. Recover the true spirit of ecological awareness, & attune yourself to the language, message, & heart of the earth. Interwoven with sounds of nature, the music invites entrancement until the Earth herself & all her creatures speak to you.

Earth Stories. Jay O'Callahan. Perf. by Jay O'Callahan. 1 cass. (Running Time: 49 min.). Dramatization. (J). (gr. k up). 1984. 10.00 (978-1-877954-05-4(5)); audio compact disk 15.00 (978-1-877954-28-3(4)) Pub: Artana Prodns. Dist(s): Yellow Moon
The wonder of the Earth. Meet two very special friends - a worm and a caterpillar - in HERMAN AND MARGUERITE Plus THE BOY WHO LOVED FROGS and more.

Earth the Creative Planet: The Ellipsis Arts Sampler. Ellipsis Arts Staff. 1 CD. (Running Time: 1 hr.). 1999. audio compact disk 7.95 (978-1-55961-506-8(0)) Relaxtn Co.

Earth Tracks. Christine E. Campbell. 1 CD. (Running Time: 45 mins.). (Tracks Along the Way Ser.: Vol. 2). 2001. audio compact disk 16.00 (978-1-890066-26-0(5)) Spectrm Pubs.

Earth Will Shake: The Historical Illuminatus Chronicles, Volume I. Robert Anton Wilson. (Running Time: 12 hrs.). 2006. 29.95 (978-0-9796694-0-8(5)) Deepleaf Prod.

Earth with One Spirit. Narrated by Mike Pinder. Music by Mike Pinder. 1 cass. (J). 9.98; audio compact disk 15.98 CD. One Step Recs.

Earth with One Spirit: Stories from Around the World for the Child Within Us All. Mike Pinder. 1 cass. (J). 1996. (978-1-888057-02-7(5)) One Step Recs.
Mike Pinder, singer-songwriter of the Moody Blues narrates seven uplifting & imaginative stories for children over a musical atmosphere created by Mike.

Earthblood 2: Deep Trek. James Axler. 2009. audio compact disk 19.99 (978-1-59950-581-7(9)) GraphicAudio.

Earthblood 3: Aurora Quest. Based on a novel by James Axler. 2009. audio compact disk 19.99 (978-1-59950-615-9(7)) GraphicAudio.

Earthborn Vol. 5: Homecoming. unabr. ed. Orson Scott Card. (Running Time: 14 hrs. 0 mins.). 2009. 29.95 (978-1-4332-1905-4(0)); audio compact disk 79.95 (978-1-4332-1901-6(8)); audio compact disk 110.00 (978-1-4332-1902-3(6)) Blckstn Audio.

Earthbound. Sabine Helling. (Alliance: the Michigan State University Textbook Series of Theme-Based Content Instruction for ESL/EFL). (C). 1997. 15.00 (978-0-472-00272-6(4)) U of Mich Pr.

***Earthbound.** unabr. ed. Richard Matheson. Read by Bronson Pinchot. (Running Time: 7 hrs. 30 mins.). 2010. 29.95 (978-1-4417-5689-3(2)); audio compact disk 24.95 (978-1-4417-5688-6(4)) Blckstn Audio.

***Earthbound.** unabr. ed. Richard Matheson. Read by Bronson Pinchot. (Running Time: 7 hrs. 30 mins.). 2010. 54.95 (978-1-4417-5685-5(X)); audio compact disk 69.00 (978-1-4417-5686-2(8)) Blckstn Audio.

Earthfall Vol. 4: Homecoming. unabr. ed. Orson Scott Card & Stefan Rudnicki. (Running Time: 12 hrs. NaN mins.). 2008. 29.95 (978-1-4332-1897-2(6)); 72.95 (978-1-4332-1893-4(3)); audio compact disk 90.00 (978-1-4332-1894-1(1)) Blckstn Audio.

Earthlight. unabr. collector's ed. Arthur C. Clarke. Read by Dan Lazar. 6 cass. (Running Time: 6 hrs.). 1979. 48.00 (978-0-7366-0239-6(9), 1235) Books on Tape.
There are permanent populations established on the Moon, Venus & Mars. The outer space inhabitants have formed a new political entity (the Federation), & between the Federation & Earth a growing rivalry has developed.

Earthlodge. Perf. by Keith Bear. Contrib. by Lisa Dowhaniuk. 1 cass. (Running Time: 49 mins.). 2000. 9.98 (978-0-9650872-6-1(3), MM0153C); audio compact disk 14.98 (978-0-9650872-5-4(5), MM0153D) Scoria.
Bear, a Mandan Hibatsa storyteller & flute player shares stories & songs of his people as they were first played & heard in a Mandan Earthlodge built on the plains of the Dakotas.

Earthly Delights: Music for the Garden. Windham Hill Staff. 1 cass. 1998. 15.00 (978-1-56170-557-3(8)) Hay House.

Earthly Joys. unabr. ed. Philippa Gregory. Narrated by Steven Crossley. 14 cass. (Running Time: 20 hrs. 15 mins.). 1999. 116.00 (978-1-84197-021-9(2), H1021E7) Recorded Bks.
The engrossing story of John Tradescant, the greatest gardening pioneer of his day. Though a man of humble origins, John Tradescant rises to the court of King Charles I, as we follow his travels throughout the known world in search of new plants. Set against the backdrop of England as civil war looms, this is a book rich in historical detail.

Earthly Joys, Set. unabr. ed. Philippa Gregory. Narrated by Steven Crossley. 14 cass. 1999. 116.00 (Clipper Audio) Recorded Bks.

Earthly Possessions. unabr. ed. Anne Tyler. Read by Jeanne Hopson. 8 cass. (Running Time: 8 hrs.). 1987. 48.00 (978-0-7366-1070-4(7), 1997) Books on Tape.
Charlotte has been meaning to run away from home: from the ceaseless looking-after & the immense faith it takes just to keep everything going.

Earthly Purpose. Dick Sutphen. Read by Dick Sutphen. 2 stereo cass. (Running Time: 3 hrs.). (New Age Nonfiction Ser.). 1991. 14.95 set. (978-0-87554-469-4(X), N112) Valley Sun.
From Dick Sutphen's bestselling book about group reincarnation & his personal search for his ties to Teotihuacan. 250 past-life regressions form the basis for this story about a metaphysical society of 1400 years ago. With 3-D sound effects.

Earthmother Lullabies I. Perf. by Pamala Ballingham. 1 cass. (J). 9.98 (220) MFLP CA.
Pamela Ballingham sings lullabies from all over the world, includes: Ho Ho Watanay (Iroquois), Lulla Lulla Lullaby (Jewish), Sleep My Darling Baby Sleep (Icelandic), The Mockingbird Song (Appalachian), Arorro, Mi Nino (Latin American) & more.

Earthquake! Compiled by Benchmark Education Staff. 2005. audio compact disk 10.00 (978-1-4108-5470-4(1)) Benchmark Educ.

Earthquake! Godwin Chu. (Natural Disasters Ser.). 2001. audio compact disk 18.95 (978-1-4105-0166-0(3)) D Johnston Inc.

Earthquake! Godwin Chu. Ed. by Jerry Stemach. Illus. by Jeff Ham. Narrated by Denise Jordan Walker. 2001. audio compact disk 200.00 (978-1-58702-533-4(7)) D Johnston Inc.

Earthquake!, Level 1. 2 cass. (Running Time: 1 hr. 30 mins.). (SmartReader Ser.). (J). 1999. pap. bk. & tchr. ed. 19.95 (978-0-7887-0766-7(3), 79351T3) Recorded Bks.
Rosie is on her way home from work when an earthquake strikes her home. How will her family survive the damage caused by the tremors?.

Earthquake!, Level 2. 2 cass. (Running Time: 1 hr. 30 mins.). (SmartReader Ser.). (J). 1999. pap. bk. & tchr. ed. 19.95 (978-0-7887-0114-6(2), 79302T3) Recorded Bks.

Earthquake!, Vol. 1. Godwin Chu. Ed. by Jerry Stemach et al. Illus. by Jeff Ham & Susan Baptist. Narrated by Denise Jordan Walker. Contrib. by Ted S. Hasselbring. (Start-to-Finish Books). (J). (gr. 2-3). 2001. 35.00 (978-1-58702-534-1(5)) D Johnston Inc.

Earthquake!, Vol. 1. Godwin Chu. Ed. by Jerry Stemach et al. Illus. by Jeff Ham & Susan Baptist. Narrated by Denise Jordan Walker. Contrib. by Ted S. Hasselbring. (Start-to-Finish Books). (J). (gr. 2-3). 2002. 100.00 (978-1-58702-954-7(5)) D Johnston Inc.

Earthquake!, Vol. 1. unabr. ed. Godwin Chu. Ed. by Jerry Stemach et al. Illus. by Jeff Ham & Susan Baptist. Narrated by Denise Jordan Walker. Contrib. by Ted S. Hasselbring. 1 cass. (Running Time: 1 hr.). (Start-to-Finish Books). (J). (gr. 2-3). 2001. (978-1-58702-379-8(2), F39K2) D Johnston Inc.
Your students are bound to enjoy learning about earthquakes from this action-packed, fact-filled book. The history of earthquakes is brought to like in exciting tales of people surviving famous earthquakes. The science of earthquakes come to lie in clear, compelling descriptions. Finally, your students will learn what to do in case of an earthquake. This book tells about many aspects of earthquake science and history, including the seismograph, the Richter scale and the Ring of Fire.

Earthquake Experts. (Greetings Ser.: Vol. 2). (gr. 3-5). 10.00 (978-0-7635-2061-8(6)) Rigby Educ.

Earthquake in the Early Morning. unabr. ed. Mary Pope Osborne. Read by Mary Pope Osborne. (Running Time: 40 mins.). (Magic Tree House Ser.: No. 24). (J). (gr. k-3). 2004. pap. bk. 17.00 (978-0-8072-0933-2(3), S FTR 256 SP, Listening Lib) Random Audio Pubg.

Earthquake Prediction. Ann E. Parker. 1 cass. (Running Time: 90 min.). 1990. 8.95 (759) Am Fed Astrologers.

Earthquakes. Anne Schraff. Narrated by Larry A. McKeever. (Natural Disaster Ser.). (J). 2004. 10.95 (978-1-58659-117-5(7)); audio compact disk 14.95 (978-1-58659-351-3(X)) Artesian.

Earthquakes & Volcanoes. H. M. Ishikawa. 1 cass. 8.95 (422) Am Fed Astrologers.
An AFA Convention workshop tape.

Earthquakes & Your Water, Gas & Electricity. Hosted by Nancy Pearlman. 1 cass. (Running Time: 29 min.). 10.00 (608) Educ Comm CA.

Earthquakes, Weather & Divisional Harmonics. H. M. Ishikawa. 1 cass. 8.95 (171) Am Fed Astrologers.

Earth's Activists Alive & Well in the 80's. Hosted by Nancy Pearlman. 1 cass. (Running Time: 29 min.). 10.00 (239) Educ Comm CA.

Earth's Atmosphere: Syllabus. Robin Sladd. (J). 1978. 41.25 (978-0-89420-141-7(7), 235000) Natl Book.

Earth's Birthday Sing-Along. unabr. ed. Dave Kinnoin. Read by Dave Kinnoin. 1 cass., 1 CD. (Running Time: 34 min.). (J). (gr. k-6). 1998. 9.98 (978-1-881304-05-0(1), SW105-4); audio compact disk 12.98 CD. (978-1-881304-07-4(8), SW105-2) Song Wizard Recs.
Fun & inspiring original songs for kids sung by Dave Kinnoin.

Earth¿s Changing Climate. Instructed by Richard Wolfson. 6 cass. (Running Time: 6 hrs.). 2007. 89.95 (978-1-59803-293-2(3)); audio compact disk 39.95 (978-1-59803-294-9(1)) Teaching Co.

Earth's Changing Environment. Compiled by Encyclopaedia Britannica, Inc. 2006. audio compact disk 29.95 (978-1-59339-305-2(9)) Pub: Ency Brit Inc. Dist(s): NetLibrary CO

***Earth's Changing Surface: CD add-on Set.** Perf. by Millmark Education Staff. (ConceptLinks Ser.). 2009. audio compact disk 50.00 (978-1-61618-349-3(7)) Millmark Educ.

***Earth's Changing Surface Audio CD.** Perf. by Millmark Education Staff. (ConceptLinks Ser.). 2007. audio compact disk 28.00 (978-1-4334-0075-9(8)) Millmark Educ.

***Earth's Changing Surface SB1 Audio CD Weathering & Erosion.** Perf. by Millmark Education Staff. (Content Literacy Libraries Ser.). 2008. audio compact disk (978-1-4334-0408-5(7)) Millmark Educ.

***Earth's Changing Surface SB2 Audio CD the Rock Cycle.** Perf. by Millmark Education Staff. (Content Literacy Libraries Ser.). 2008. audio compact disk (978-1-4334-0409-2(5)) Millmark Educ.

***Earth's Changing Surface SB3 Audio CD Rocks & Minerals.** Perf. by Millmark Education Staff. (Content Literacy Libraries Ser.). 2008. audio compact disk (978-1-4334-0410-8(9)) Millmark Educ.

***Earth's Changing Surface SB4 Audio CD Fossils & History.** Perf. by Millmark Education Staff. (Content Literacy Libraries Ser.). 2008. audio compact disk (978-1-4334-0411-5(7)) Millmark Educ.

Earth's Hidden Treasures - Salvage Archaeology. Hosted by Nancy Pearlman. 1 cass. (Running Time: 29 min.). 10.00 (211) Educ Comm CA.

Earth's Water Cycle Audio CD. Adapted by Benchmark Education Company Staff. Based on a work by Kira Freed. (Early Explorers Set C Ser.). (J). (gr. 2). 2008. audio compact disk 10.00 (978-1-60437-551-0(5)) Benchmark Educ.

Earthsong. Miriam Winter. 1995. 11.95 (978-0-8245-3002-0(0), Crossroad Classic) Pub: Crossroad NY. Dist(s): IPG Chicago

Earthsongs. Perf. by Doug Wood. 1 cass. 1994. audio compact disk 15.95 CD. (2713, Creativ Pub) Quayside.
21-song compilation of his best work - a masterpiece of nature-conscious music for the entire family.

Earthsongs. Perf. by Doug Wood. 1 cass. 1994. 9.95 (2712, NrthWrd Bks) TandN Child.

Earthstone: A Musical Adventure Story. Odds Bodkin. Read by Odds Bodkin. 2 cass. (Running Time: 2 hrs.). Dramatization. (Odds Bodkin Musical Story Collection). (ps up). 2003. bk. 18.95 (978-1-882412-07-5(9)) Pub: Rivertree. Dist(s): Penton Overseas
Fully-produced parable of ecological balance, with Odds Bodkin & cast & nine original songs.

Earthworks. John Widdowson. 3 pieces. (J). 2000. audio compact disk 214.00 (978-0-7195-7566-2(4), HodderMurray) Pub: Hodder Edu GBR. Dist(s): Trans-Atl Phila

Earthy Tunes. Mary Miche. 1 cass. (J). (ps-6). 1987. 11.50 (978-1-883505-03-5(8)) Song Trek Music.
Selection of 17 educational songs about plants & animals for children.

Eartraining. 4 cass. (Running Time: 90 min. per cass.). (YA). (gr. 9 up). 135.00 ea. Brown & Benchmark.
Four-90 minute cassettes with ear training exercises. These tapes accompany Benward: Ear Training: A technique for listening & Basic Sightsinging & Ear Training.

Eas-Broadway. 2001. bk. 21.95 (978-1-85909-801-1(0), Warner Bro) Alfred Pub.

Easier Childbirth. (Running Time: 45 min.). (Relationship Ser.). 9.98 (978-1-55909-104-6(5), 86) Randolph Tapes.
Enjoying & experiencing the miracle & joy of birth.

***Easier Than You Think.** unabr. ed. Richard Carlson. Read by Richard Carlson. (ENG.). 2005. (978-0-06-084575-9(6), Harper Audio); (978-0-06-084573-5(2), Harper Audio) HarperCollins Pubs.

Easier Than You Think: Small Changes that Add up to a World of Difference in Life. unabr. ed. Richard Carlson. Read by Richard Carlson. 2005. audio compact disk 22.95 (978-0-06-079430-9(5)) HarperCollins Pubs.

Easier to Kill. Valerie Wilson Wesley. Read by Rebecca Nicholas. 5 cass. (Running Time: 7 hrs. 30 min.). 1999. 40.00 (978-0-7366-4415-0(6), 4876) Books on Tape.
Radio talk show host Mandy Magic seems to have it all. But she is stalked by a past that won't let her go. A threatening note & repeated acts of vandalism call into question the recent, apparently robbery-related death of her stylist. Fearing for her own safety, Magic calls Newark P.I. Tamara Hayle for help. But as Tamara soon discovers, Magic is a woman of secrets & half-truths with more shady characters in her life than she cares to admit. And the more truth Tamara seeks, the more of Magic's lies she uncovers, until she faces a killer hellbent on taking a cruel revenge & destroying everyone that stands in the way.

Easier Visualization. (Running Time: 45 min.). (Success Ser.). 9.98 (978-1-55909-129-9(0), 105) Randolph Tapes.
Lets you visualize what you want to happen in your life.

Easiest Classic Guitar Solo. Kent Murdick. 1997. audio compact disk 14.95 (978-0-7866-2097-5(8)) Mel Bay.

Easiest Pan Flute. Costel Puscoiu. 1996. pap. bk. 14.95 (978-0-7866-1627-5(X), 95681BCD) Mel Bay.

***Easiest Way to Grow.** Katz Mabel. (ENG & SPA., (J). 2010. pap. bk. 19.95 (978-0-9825910-6-2(3)) Your Business.

Easiest Way to Understanding Ho'oponopono: The Clearest Answers to Your Most Frequently Asked Questions - Volume I, Vol. 1. Mabel Katz. (ENG.). 2009. 10.00 (978-0-9748820-4-8(6)) Your Business.

Easiest Way to Understanding Ho'oponopono: The Clearest Answers to Your Most Frequently Asked Questions-Volume I, Vol. 1. Mabel Katz. (ENG & SPA.). 2009. 9.95 (978-0-9748820-2-4(X)) Your Business.

Easing into Sleep. 1 cassette. 1981. 12.95 (978-1-55841-020-6(1)) Emmett E Miller.
Often called "the cure for insomnia" most users never hear the end of this tape. Two experiences to help you learn to put your day to rest, choose your dreams and mentally project a perfect tomorrow.

Easing into Sleep. 1 CD. 1981. audio compact disk 16.95 (978-1-55841-113-5(5)) Emmett E Miller.
Two experiences to help you learn to put your day to rest, choose your dreams and mentally project a perfect tomorrow.

Easing into Sleep. Emmett E. Miller. Read by Emmett E. Miller. 1 cass. (Running Time: 1 hr.). 1996. 10.00 (978-1-56170-365-4(6), 390) Hay House.
Guided meditations & deep breathing to relax your body & your mind.

Easing P.M.S. Read by Mary Richards. (Subliminal Impact Ser.). 12.95 (638) Master Your Mind.

East. unabr. ed. Edith Pattou. 7 cass. (Running Time: 10 hrs. 49 mins.). (J). (gr. 4-7). 2005. 50.00 (978-0-307-24666-0(3), Listening Lib) Random Audio Pubg.
A young woman journeys to a distant castle on the back of a great white bear who is the victim of a cruel enchantment.

East African Bird Sounds. Finch. 2002. audio compact disk (978-0-85661-142-1(5), Acad Press) Sci Tech Bks.

East & West. Chris Patten. Read by Chris Patten. 2 cass. (Running Time: 3 hrs.). (ENG., 1998. 16.85 Set. (978-0-333-74859-6(X)) Pub: Macmillan UK GBR. Dist(s): Macmillan NJ
From the last Governor of Hong Kong, a controversial analysis of the Asian phenomenon & the future of economic & political liberty in China & East Asia in the next century. Examines the implications of China's economic reforms, & sets out the key political agendas for the futures, not only for the East, but also for the West.

East & West: Two Borders of the River. Michael J. Dudick. 1 cass. (Inspiring Presentations from the National Rosary Congress Ser.). 2.50 (978-1-56036-101-5(8)) AMI Pr.

East Bay Grease: A Novel. unabr. ed. Eric M. Williamson. Narrated by Johnny Heller. 6 cass. (Running Time: 7 hrs. 45 mins.). 2000. 57.00 (978-0-7887-4312-2(0), 96131E7) Recorded Bks.
Coming-of-age story written through the eyes of blue-collar hardship. Highlights the turbulent experiences of T-Bird Murphy in 60s & 70s Oakland.

East by West. Ed. by Robert A. Monroe. 1 cass. (Running Time: 30 min.). (Meta Music Ser.). 1985. 12.95 (978-1-56102-208-3(X)) Inter Indus.
The way of the Orient as first perceived by the Occidental mind, followed by a small integration of the two cultures. The relaxed listener begins to understand & enjoy the musical imagery of another culture.

East Coast Workshop. John C. Lilly. 6 cass. (Running Time: 6 hrs.). (John Lilly Tape Ser.). 1973. 64.95 set. Dolphin Tapes.
Includes Matter, Energy & the Black Hole; Superspace, Space & States; The Use of Indeterminancy; I Have Thunk, I Cannot Am; Inner & Outer Realities & Handbooks, People & So Forth.

East End Girl. Sally Worboyes. 2007. audio compact disk 79.95 (978-1-84559-591-3(2)) Pub: ISIS Audio GBR. Dist(s): Ulverscroft US

East End Girl: Growing up the Hard Way. Sally Worboyes. Read by Annie Aldington. 7 cass. 2007. 61.95 (978-1-84559-552-4(1)) Pub: ISIS Audio GBR. Dist(s): Ulverscroft US

East Indiaman. unabr. ed. Richard Woodman. Read by Terry Wale. 10 cass. (Running Time: 12 hrs.). (William Kite Trilogy: Bk. 3). (J). 2003. 84.95 (978-1-84283-512-8(2)); audio compact disk 89.95 (978-1-84283-521-0(1)) Pub: ISIS Lrg Prnt GBR. Dist(s): Ulverscroft US

East Is West. unabr. collector's ed. Freya Stark. Read by Donada Peters. 6 cass. (Running Time: 9 hrs.). 1991. 48.00 (978-0-7366-1881-6(3), 2710) Books on Tape.
Once described as "a traveler of genius" Dame Freya Stark's vivid accounts of journeys in Persia, Arabia & the Near East opened up new vistas for a wide readership. Long before it was fashionable to be a solo traveler, much less a woman alone, she roamed the world. East is West is the story of her war-time experiences in Egypt, Palestine & Syria. Stark tells her story with the freedom & independence of an intrepid traveler & with the authority of an official of the British Diplomatic Corps.

East Java I - Songs before Dawn: Gandrung Banyuwangi. Perf. by Gadrung Temu. Anno. by Philip Yampolsky. 1 cass. (Running Time: 65 min.). (Music of Indonesia Ser.: Vol. 1). 1991. (0-9307-400550-9307-40055-2-1); audio compact disk (0-9307-40055-2-1) Smithsonian Folkways.
An unmarried female singer performs a beautiful suite of songs backed by a small ensemble of musicians who play violins, drums & metal percussion.

East Lynne, Pt. 2. Geoffrey Wood. 8 cass. (Running Time: 12 hrs.). 2000. 53.95 Audio Bk Con.
Perhaps the greatest soap opera ever told! The lovely Lady Isabel Vane, her compassionate, noble husband Archibald Carlyle, the evil Francis Levinson & the irascible Cornelia are just a few who people this remarkable novel of love, adultery, mystery & murder. This was a blockbuster of the late 1800's.

East Lynne (Part 1), Vol. 11. unabr. ed. Geoffrey Wood. Read by Flo Gibson. 8 cass. (Running Time: 12 hrs.). 1989. 26.95 (978-1-55685-136-0(7)) Audio Bk Con.
The lovely Lady Isabel Vane, her compassionate noble husband, Archibald Carlyle, the evil Francis Levison & the irascible Miss Cornelia are just a few in this story of love, adultery, mystery & murder.

East Lynne (Part 2), Vol. 2. unabr. ed. Ellen Wood. Narrated by Flo Gibson. (Running Time: 11 hrs. 44 mins.). 1989. 26.95 (978-1-55685-808-6(6)) Audio Bk Con.

East Lynne (Parts 1 And 2) unabr. ed. Ellen Wood. Narrated by Flo Gibson. (Running Time: 23 hrs. 42 mins.). 1989. 46.95 (978-1-55685-809-3(4)) Audio Bk Con.

East Meet West Meditation Audio. Robert Speigel. 2009. 13.00 (978-0-937977-20-0(9)) Speigel&Assoc.

East of A. Russell Atwood. Read by Adams Morgan. 5 cass. (Running Time: 7 hrs. 30 min.). 2000. 27.95 (978-0-7861-1777-2(X)) Pub: Blckstn Audio. Dist(s): Penton Overseas

East of A. unabr. ed. Russell Atwood. Read by Adams Morgan. 5 cass. (Running Time: 7 hrs.). 2000. 39.95 (978-0-7861-1711-6(7), 2527) Blckstn Audio.
Payton returns to the Lower East Side after a short absence to find himself an outsider. When he takes a wrong turn on a side street, he stumbles into trouble in the form of three bull-necked heavies & a tough sixteen-year-old runaway named Gloria Manlow. After a savage beating, he is robbed of his Rolex watch & left bleeding on the sidewalk. For Payton, trying to retrieve his three-thousand-dollar wristwatch has its perils. So does tracking Gloria, whose trail zigzags from a stray dog to a psycho boyfriend to an ice-hearted killer.

East of A. unabr. ed. Russell Atwood. Read by Adams Morgan. 6 CDs. (Running Time: 7 hrs.). 2000. audio compact disk 48.00 (978-0-7861-9911-2(3), 2527) Blckstn Audio.

East of A. unabr. ed. Russell Atwood. Read by Adams Morgan. 5 cass. (Running Time: 7 hrs.). 2000. 27.95 Penton Overseas.

East of Algiers. unabr. ed. Francis Durbridge & Douglas Rutherford. Read by Michael Tudor Barnes. 6 CDs. (Running Time: 6 hrs. 17 mins.). (Isis (CDs) Ser.). (J). 2006. audio compact disk 64.95 (978-0-7531-2506-9(4)) Pub: ISIS Lrg Prnt GBR. Dist(s): Ulverscroft US

East of Algiers: A Paul Temple Mystery. unabr. ed. Francis Durbridge & Douglas Rutherford. Read by Michael Tudor Barnes. 5 cass. (Running Time: 6 hrs.). (Isis Cassettes Ser.). (J). 2006. 49.95 (978-0-7531-3441-2(1)) Pub: ISIS Lrg Prnt GBR. Dist(s): Ulverscroft US

***East of Chosin: Entrapment & Breakout in Korea 1950.** unabr. ed. Roy E. Appleman. Narrated by Sean Runnette. (Running Time: 14 hrs. 0 mins.). 2010. 19.99 (978-1-4001-8934-2(9)); 29.99 (978-1-4001-6934-4(8)); audio compact disk 39.99 (978-1-4001-1934-9(0)) Pub: Tantor Media. Dist(s): IngramPubServ

***East of Chosin (Library Edition) Entrapment & Breakout in Korea 1950.** unabr. ed. Roy E. Appleman. Narrated by Sean Runnette. (Running Time: 14 hrs. 0 mins. 0 sec.). 2010. audio compact disk 95.99 (978-1-4001-4934-6(7)) Pub: Tantor Media. Dist(s): IngramPubServ

East of Desolation. abr. ed. Jack Higgins. (Running Time: 6 hrs.). 2011. audio compact disk 9.99 (978-1-4418-1785-3(9), 9781441817853, BCD Value Price) Brilliance Audio.

East of Desolation. unabr. ed. Jack Higgins. Read by Michael Page. (Running Time: 6 hrs.). 2010. audio compact disk 29.99 (978-1-4418-1778-5(6), 9781441817785, Bril Audio CD Unabri) Brilliance Audio.

***East of Desolation.** unabr. ed. Jack Higgins. Read by Michael Page. (Running Time: 5 hrs.). 2010. 24.99 (978-1-4418-1780-8(8), 9781441817808, Brilliance MP3); 39.97 (978-1-4418-1781-5(6), 9781441817815, Brinc Audio MP3 Lib); 24.99 (978-1-4418-1782-2(4), 9781441817822, BAD); 39.97 (978-1-4418-1783-9(2), 9781441817839, BADLE); audio compact disk 92.97 (978-1-4418-1779-2(4), 9781441817792, BriAudCD Unabrid) Brilliance Audio.

East of Desolation. unabr. ed. Jack Higgins. Read by Stephen Rea. 6 cass. (Running Time: 9 hrs.). 2000. 49.95 (978-0-7451-6014-6(X), CAB 267) Pub: Chivers Audio Bks GBR. Dist(s): AudioGO

East of Desolation. unabr. collector's ed. Jack Higgins. Read by Ian Whitcomb. 6 cass. (Running Time: 6 hrs.). 1982. 36.00 (978-0-7366-0482-6(0), 1457) Books on Tape.
The life of a private eye is threatened when he investigates the mystery surrounding a fatal planecrash and a batch of priceless emeralds.

East of Eden. unabr. ed. John Steinbeck. Narrated by Richard Poe. 18 cass. (Running Time: 25 hrs.). 69.95 (978-0-7887-8912-0(0)) Recorded Bks.
Written in his later years, Steinbeck's novel follows the intertwined affairs of two families in southern California. As the saga unfolds, it also becomes a retelling of two powerful stories from Genesis: the fall of Adam and Eve, and the rivalry of Cain and Abel. Available to libraries only.

East of Eden. unabr. ed. John Steinbeck. Narrated by Richard Poe. 18 cass. (Running Time: 25 hrs.). 146.00 (978-0-7887-4883-7(1)) Recorded Bks.
Available to libraries only.

East of the Mountains. David Guterson. 2 cass. (Running Time: 3 hrs.). 1999. 16.85 Set. (978-0-00-105559-9(3)) Ulvrscrft Audio.
Involves prose & narrative genius. Unravel the mysteries & reveal the potential powers of the human spirit even as it ebbs, in a moving & action-filled drama set against an unforgettable landscape.

East of the Mountains. abr. ed. David Guterson. Read by Edward Hermann. 4 cass. 1999. 25.00 (FS9-43399) Highsmith.

East Point: Hidden Side of the Personality. Jan Popelka. 1 cass. (Running Time: 90 min.). 1984. 8.95 (281) Am Fed Astrologers.

East to the Dawn: The Life of Amelia Earhart. unabr. ed. Susan Butler. Read by Anna Fields. 13 cass. (Running Time: 19 hrs.). 1998. 85.95 (978-0-7861-1325-5(1), 2221) Blckstn Audio.
Experience Amelia Earhart not just as a pilot, but also as an educator, a social worker, a lecturer, a businesswoman, & a tireless promoter of women's rights.

East to the Dawn: The Life of Amelia Earhart. unabr. ed. Susan Butler. Read by Anna Fields. (Running Time: 19 hrs. 0 mins.). (ENG.). 2009. 44.95 (978-1-4417-0690-4(9)); audio compact disk 123.00 (978-1-4417-0687-4(9)); audio compact disk & audio compact disk 39.95 (978-1-4417-0689-8(5)) Blckstn Audio.

East to West. Contrib. by Casting Crowns. (Mastertrax Ser.). 2007. audio compact disk 9.98 (978-5-557-60390-4(5)) Beach St.

East to West. Contrib. by Casting Crowns. (Sound Performance Soundtracks Ser.). 2007. audio compact disk 5.98 (978-5-557-60314-0(X)) Pt of Grace Ent.

East to West: A Journey Round the World. unabr. collector's ed. Arnold J. Toynbee. Read by David Case. 7 cass. (Running Time: 10 hrs. 30 mins.). 1989. 56.00 (978-0-7366-1590-7(3), 2453) Books on Tape.
In February 1956 Arnold Toynbee, just retired after more than 30 years at the Royal Institute of International Affairs in London, set out on a 17-month journey around the world. He wanted to visit Asia & Latin America. We travel with him to Ecuador, Peru, New Zealand, Australia, Vietnam, Manila, Hong Kong, Japan, India & the Middle East. The journey is very worthwhile. Toynbee was a great historian, known best for his 12-volume A Study of History, completed in 1961. What made him famous was his comfortable style. Thus to travel with him through the world of his day, is to see that world in a fresh & vivid way.

East 43rd Street, Level 5. Alan R. Battersby. Contrib. by Philip Prowse. (Running Time: 2 hrs. 40 mins.). (Cambridge English Readers Ser.). (ENG., 2001. 15.75 (978-0-521-78364-4(X)) Cambridge U Pr.

Easter. Monks of Solesmes Staff. 1 CD. 1985. audio compact disk 16.95 (978-1-55725-102-2(9), 930-066) Paraclete MA.

Easter: A Treasured Anthology: Tenor. Contrib. by J. Daniel Smith et al. 2007. audio compact disk 7.50 (978-5-557-56211-9(7), Brentwood-Benson Music) Brentwood Music.

Easter: Alto. Contrib. by J. Daniel Smith et al. 2007. audio compact disk 7.50 (978-5-557-56212-6(5), Brentwood-Benson Music) Brentwood Music.

Easter: Bass. Contrib. by J. Daniel Smith et al. 2007. audio compact disk 7.50 (978-5-557-56210-2(9), Brentwood-Benson Music) Brentwood Music.

Easter: Jesus His Power Unleashed. abr. ed. Narrated by Kailey Bell & Todd Busteed. (Running Time: 7200 sec.). (Kidz Rock Ser.). (ENG.). (J). 2008. audio compact disk 8.99 (978-1-59859-325-9(0)) Oasis Audio.

Easter: Soprano. Contrib. by J. Daniel Smith et al. 2007. audio compact disk 7.50 (978-5-557-56213-3(3), Brentwood-Benson Music) Brentwood Music.

Easter He Lives: 1 Cor. 15:51-57. Ed Young. (J). 1980. 4.95 (978-0-7417-1111-3(7), A0111) Win Walk.

Easter Anthem. Randy Smith. 1997. 6.00 (978-0-7673-3569-0(4)) LifeWay Christian.

Easter Audio Bible Pack AWBC. Zondervan Publishing Staff. 2004. audio compact disk 349.96 (978-0-310-63929-9(8)) Zondervan.

Easter Bunny. unabr. ed. Winifred Wolfe. 1 cass. (Running Time: 4 min.). (J). (ps-3). 1991. bk. 19.90 (978-0-8045-6663-6(1), 6663) Spoken Arts.

Easter Collection: Velveteen Rabbit; Peter Cottontail; Clifford's Happy Easter. unabr. ed. Margery Williams et al. Read by Oliver Wyman. (J). 2008. 34.99 (978-1-60514-703-1(6)) Find a World.

Easter Egg Farm. Mary Jane Auch. Illus. by Mary Jane Auch. Read by Larry Robinson. 11 vols. (Running Time: 10 mins.). (Egg Ser.). (J). (gr. k-3). 1995. pap. bk. 16.95 (978-0-87499-343-1(1)) AudioGO.
Pauline the Hen seems unable to lay eggs until she fully concentrates on the task. Her efforts result not only in eggs, but in unusual eggs that bear the image of whatever she happened to be looking at while concentrating. While this proves to be a windfall for her Easter egg-selling owner, a bigger surprise lies in store when some of the eggs start to hatch.

Easter Egg Farm. Mary Jane Auch. 1 cass. (Running Time: 35 min.). (J). (ps-3). 2001. pap. bk. 15.95 (VX-48C) Kimbo Educ.
Pauline, the Hen, lays eggs that bear the image of whatever she was looking at while concentrating. Includes read along book.

Easter Egg Farm. Mary Jane Auch. Illus. by Mary Jane Auch. 11 vols. (Running Time: 10 mins.). 1995. bk. 28.95 (978-1-59519-031-4(7)); pap. bk. 39.95 (978-1-59519-030-7(9)); 9.95 (978-1-59112-034-6(9)); audio compact disk 12.95 (978-1-59519-028-4(7)) Live Oak Media.

Easter Egg Farm. Mary Jane Auch. Illus. by Mary Jane Auch. 11 vols. (Running Time: 10 mins.). (J). 1995. pap. bk. 18.95 (978-1-59519-029-1(5)) Pub: Live Oak Media. Dist(s): AudioGO

Easter Egg Farm. Mary Jane Auch. Illus. by Mary Jane Auch. Read by Larry Robinson. 14 vols. (Running Time: 10 mins.). (Egg Ser.). (J). 1995. pap. bk. & tchr. ed. 37.95 Reading Chest. (978-0-87499-345-5(8)) Live Oak Media.
Pauline the Hen seems unable to lay eggs until she fully concentrates on the task. Her efforts result not only in eggs, but in unusual eggs that bear the image of whatever she happened to be looking at while concentrating. While this proves to be a windfall for her Easter egg-selling owner, a bigger surprise lies in store when some of the eggs start to hatch.

Easter Egg Farm. Mary Jane Auch. Illus. by Mary Jane Auch. Read by Larry Robinson. 11 vols. (Running Time: 10 mins.). (Egg Ser.). (J). (gr. k-3). 1995. bk. 25.95 (978-0-87499-344-8(X)) Live Oak Media.

Easter Message 2007. Charles R. Swindoll. (ENG.). 2007. audio compact disk 12.00 (978-1-57972-766-6(2)) Insight Living.

***Easter Messages 2010.** Charles R. Swindoll. 2010. audio compact disk 12.00 (978-1-57972-883-0(9)) Insight Living.

Easter Miracle. Contrib. by Mike Gay & Sue Gay. 1996. audio compact disk 35.00 (978-0-00-513563-1(X), 75608633) Pub: Brentwood Music. Dist(s): H Leonard

Easter Miracle. Contrib. by Mike Gay & Sue Gay. 1996. 30.00 (978-0-00-513562-4(1), 75608635) Pub: Brentwood Music. Dist(s): H Leonard

Easter Miracle: Through the Eyes of the Children. Prod. by Mike Gay & Sue Gay. 1 cass., 1 CD. (J). 1998. 3.99 (978-0-7601-2214-3(8)); audio compact disk 5.99 CD. (978-0-7601-2215-0(6)) Provident Mus Dist.
The message of the real miracle of Easter.

Easter Praise Parade. Contrib. by Allen Dennis & Nan & Nancy Gordon. (ENG.). (J). 1998. audio compact disk 90.00 (978-5-551-92060-1(7)) Lillenas.

Easter Praise Parade: A Resurrection Celebration for Kids. Nan Allen et al. 1 cass. (Running Time: 35 min.). (J). 2001. 80.00 (MU-9247C); audio compact disk 80.00 (MU-9247T) Lillenas.
Everybody loves a parade! Through a variety of musical styles, accompanied by an imaginative script. An Easter musical that represents in a straightforward manner great truth-truths that our kids & congregations can understand & experience for themselves. Everyone involved will appreciate the great new songs & the fresh treatment of timeless hymns. Accompaniment cassette with side 1, stereo trax & side 2, split-channel.

Easter Procession: Encounters with the Risen Christ a Devotion in Paschaltide (from Byzantine Sources) Schola Cantorum of St. Peter the Apostle Staff. Directed By J. Michael Thompson. Composed by James E. Clemens. (Running Time: 1 hr.). 2005. audio compact disk 16.95 (978-0-8146-7957-9(9)) Liturgical Pr.

Easter Reflections. 2005. 29.95 (978-1-59649-732-0(7)); audio compact disk 24.95 (978-1-59649-731-3(9)) Whspmg Pine.

Easter Story see Passion & Glory

Easter Story. unabr. ed. Zondervan Publishing Staff. 2003. audio compact disk 71.64 (978-0-310-92801-0(X)); audio compact disk 1.99 (978-0-310-92888-1(5)) Zondervan.

Easter Story: What Really Happened? Chuck Missler. 2 CD's. (Running Time: 120 min. aprox.). 2007. audio compact disk 19.95 (978-1-57821-371-9(1)) Koinonia Hse.

Easter Story Rhymes. unabr. ed. Alfreda C. Doyle. Read by Alfreda C. Doyle. 1 cass. (Running Time: 35 min.). (Alfreda's Radio Ser.: Vol. 8). (J). (gr. 5-9). 1998. bk. 16.95 (978-1-56820-312-6(8)) Story Time.
Stories that educate, entertain, inform & rhyme.

Easter 2009 Message: Suddenly One Morning. Charles R. Swindoll. 2009. audio compact disk 7.99 (978-1-57972-849-6(9)) Insight Living.

Easter 2010 Messages see Semana Santa 2010

Eastern & Western Science. unabr. ed. Elmer Green & Swami Rama. 1 cass. (Running Time: 90 min.). 1970. 11.00 (06402) Big Sur Tapes.
Green presents data on his psycho-physiological research in which Swami Rama, a Hindu religious teacher, demonstrated his ability to control various involuntary processes of his body & nervous system. The Swami then translates Eastern Chakra & psychic nerve control into useful exercises.

Eastern Approaches, Pt. 1. unabr. collector's ed. Fitzroy Maclean. Read by Richard Brown. 8 cass. (Running Time: 12 hrs.). 1990. 64.00 (978-0-7366-1854-0(6), 2687A) Books on Tape.
In 1943 Brigadier Fitzroy Maclean parachuted into Yugoslavia as Churchill's personal representative to Tito - then a guerrilla leader known variously as a man, a woman & a committee. This classic true adventure story of WW II ranges from Yugoslavia to Russia, China & the sands of the Sahara. It is the story of an adventurer, soldier & diplomat who left his mark on the 20th century.

Eastern Approaches, Pt. 2. unabr. collector's ed. Fitzroy Maclean. Read by Richard Brown. 8 cass. (Running Time: 12 hrs.). 1990. 64.00 (978-0-7366-1855-7(4), 2687-B) Books on Tape.

Eastern Arabic. unabr. ed. Frank A. Rice & Majed F. Sa'id. 8 cass. (Running Time: 7 hrs.). (ARA.). (YA). (gr. 10-12). 1985. pap. bk. 225.00 (978-0-88432-201-6(7), AFA450) J Norton Pubs.
Learn the same way that you learned English, by listening & repeating. Native speakers ensure that you hear the correct pronunciation, while the cassette player becomes your own private "tireless tutor," repeating the same phrase time after time until you have mastered it. The text uses a transcription, rather than the Arabic alphabet, to represent the sounds & forms of the modern spoken language & includes an Arabic-English glossary.

Eastern Arabic: Learn to Speak & Understand Arabic with Pimsleur Language Programs. 2nd ed. Pimsleur Staff. (Running Time: 400 hrs. 0 mins. NaN sec.). (Quick & Simple Ser.). (ARA & ENG.). 2003. audio compact disk 19.95 (978-0-7435-2942-6(1), Pimsleur) Pub: S&S Audio. Dist(s): S and S Inc

Eastern Arabic No. 1: Learn to Speak & Understand Arabic with Pimsleur Language Programs. 2nd ed. Pimsleur Staff & Pimsleur. 16 CDs. (Running Time: 160 hrs. 0 mins. 0 sec.). (Comprehensive Ser.). (ARA & ENG.). 2003. audio compact disk 345.00 (978-0-7435-2944-0(8), Pimsleur) Pub: S&S Audio. Dist(s): S and S Inc

Eastern Armenian. unabr. ed. 6 cass. (ARM.). bk. 115.00 Set. (AFAR10) J Norton Pubs.

Eastern Armenian: Learn to Speak & Understand Armenian with Pimsleur Language Programs. Pimsleur Staff & Pimsleur. (Running Time: 500 hrs. 0 mins. NaN sec.). (Compact Ser.). (ENG.). 2004. audio compact disk 115.00 (978-0-7435-3687-5(8), Pimsleur) Pub: S&S Audio. Dist(s): S and S Inc

Eastern Caribbean in Focus: A Guide to the People, Politics & Culture. James Ferguson. (In Focus Guides). (ENG., 1997. audio compact disk 12.95 (978-1-56656-263-8(5)) Interlink Pub.

Eastern Europe under Gorbachev. 1 cass. (Running Time: 61 min.). 10.95 (K0880B09, HarperThor) HarpC GBR.

Eastern Myth & Mythology. Joseph Campbell. 1991. 10.95 (978-1-55927-141-7(8)) Macmill Audio.

Eastern Opus. Created by Matthew Manning. Prod. by Stuart Wilde. 1 cass. 10.95 (CN616) White Dove NM.
Spirited music begins against a backdrop of crying gulls & the buzz of bamboo jungles of the Orient. Simple repeated themes with eastern drums, gongs, strings & pipes create a sense of mystery & the exotic unknown.

Eastern Path to Lifelong Achievement. George Leonard. 6 cass. (Running Time: 6 hrs.). 1995. 59.95 Set incl. pamphlet. (12130AM) Nightingale-Conant.
This transformational program provides powerful insights for finding true happiness & success by focusing on the journey itself - not the end results. George Leonard draws on a unique blend of marital arts, Eastern wisdom & Western research to help you release your limitless potential.

Eastern Religion & Western Therapy. Alan Watts. 2 cass. (Running Time: 2 hrs.). 1971. 18.00 set. (02502) Big Sur Tapes.

Eastern River System; New York's Hackensack Meadowlands; & California's Santa Cruz Island. Hosted by Nancy Pearlman. 1 cass. (Running Time: 30 min.). 10.00 (420) Educ Comm CA.

***Eastern Stars: How Baseball Changed the Dominican Town of San Pedro de Macoris.** unabr. ed. Mark Kurlansky. (Running Time: 9 hrs. 0 mins.). 2010. 15.99 (978-1-4001-8431-6(2)); 34.99 (978-1-4001-9431-5(8)) Tantor Media.

***Eastern Stars: How Baseball Changed the Dominican Town of San Pedro de Macoris.** unabr. ed. Mark Kurlansky. Narrated by Ed Sala. 1 MP3-CD. (Running Time: 9 hrs. 0 mins. 0 sec.). 2010. 24.99 (978-1-4001-6431-8(1)); audio compact disk 34.99 (978-1-4001-1431-3(4)); audio compact disk 69.99 (978-1-4001-4431-0(0)) Pub: Tantor Media. Dist(s): IngramPubServ

Eastertide. Monks of Solesmes Staff. 1 CD. 1985. audio compact disk 16.95 (978-1-55725-108-4(8), 930-071) Paraclete MA.

Eastward. unabr. collector's ed. Roger F. Duncan. Read by Jonathan Reese. 6 cass. (Running Time: 6 hrs.). 1979. 36.00 (978-0-7366-0169-6(4), 1171) Books on Tape.
Roger Duncan & his wife set out to explore the Maine coast in Eastward, their sloop. Their story is a handbook for skippers sailing their ships in East Coast waters.

Easy Aces, Set. unabr. ed. Perf. by Goodman Ace & Jane Ace. 3 cass. (Running Time: 3 hrs.). Dramatization. 15.95 (978-1-57816-145-4(2), EA103) Audio File.
Old time radio broadcast comedy series.

***Easy & Effective Debt Collection Strategies.** PUEI. 2009. audio compact disk 199.00 (978-1-935041-53-5(3), CareerTrack) P Univ E Inc.

Easy A's Vol. 22: Get Good Grades. Jonathan Parker. 2 cass. (Running Time: 1 hr. 45 min.). (J). 1992. 17.00 Set. (978-1-58400-021-1(X)) QuantumQuests Intl.

***Easy as A-B-C.** unabr. ed. Laura Lippman. Read by Linda Emond & Francois Battiste. (ENG.). 2008. (978-0-06-176298-7(9), Harper Audio); (978-0-06-176297-0(0), Harper Audio) HarperCollins Pubs.

***Easy Baroque Pieces for Classical Guitar.** Ed. by Jerry Willard. Created by Hal Leonard Corp. (ENG.). 2010. pap. bk. 17.99 (978-0-8256-3743-8(0), 0825637430) Pub: Music Sales. Dist(s): H Leonard

Easy Beats & Breaks. Frank Biggs. 1998. pap. bk. 17.95 (978-0-7866-3271-8(2), 97060BCD) Mel Bay.

Easy Blues Rhythms for Guitar. Ed Lozano. 2004. audio compact disk 16.95 (978-0-8256-1901-4(7), AM971432) Pub: Music Sales. Dist(s): H Leonard

Easy Blues Songbook. Ed Lozano. 2004. audio compact disk 17.95 (978-0-8256-1573-3(9)) Pub: Music Sales. Dist(s): H Leonard

Easy Chairs, Hard Words AudioBook: Conversations on the Liberty of God. Douglas Wilson. Read by Gene Helsel & Josiah Helsel. 3 CDs. (ENG.). 1997. audio compact disk 20.00 (978-1-59128-537-3(2)) Canon Pr ID.

Easy Chairs, Hard Words-mp3: Conversations of the Liberty of God. Read by Gene Helsel & Josiah Helsel. 4 cass. 1997. 20.00 (978-1-59128-535-9(6)) Canon Pr ID.

Easy Chairs, Hard Words-tape: Conversations of the Liberty of God. Read by Gene Helsel & Josiah Helsel. 3 cass. 1997. 20.00 (978-1-59128-538-0(0)) Canon Pr ID.

Easy Chart Insight. Thomas Seers. Read by Thomas Seers. 1 cass. (Running Time: 90 min.). 1994. 8.95 (1109) Am Fed Astrologers.
Reading the horoscope.

Easy Childbirth Through Hypnosis. Scripts. Created by Zoilita Grant. 1 CD. 2001. audio compact disk 15.95 (978-1-890575-23-6(2)) Zoilita Grant.

Easy Christmas Favorites. Larry Clark. Contrib. by David Feldstein. 2004. audio compact disk 12.95 (978-0-8258-2170-7(3)); audio compact disk 12.95 (978-0-8258-3595-7(X)); audio compact disk 12.95 (978-0-8258-3596-4(8)); audio compact disk 12.95 (978-0-8258-3597-1(6)); audio compact disk 12.95 (978-0-8258-3598-8(4)) Fischer Inc NY.

Easy Christmas Favorites. Larry Clark. Arranged by Larry Clark. Contrib. by David Feldstein. 2004. audio compact disk 14.95 (978-0-8258-4695-3(1)) Fischer Inc NY.

Easy Christmas Melodies Piano: With Duet Accompaniments. Cynthia Pace. 2007. pap. bk. 12.95 (978-1-4234-2603-5(7), 1423426037) H Leonard.

Easy Classic Tunes for Clarinet. Stephen Duro. 2004. audio compact disk 12.95 (978-0-8256-1777-5(4), M961895) Pub: Music Sales. Dist(s): H Leonard

Easy Classical Guitar. (iSong Ser.). 1999. audio compact disk 24.95 (978-0-634-01151-1(0), 00451031) Pub: iSong. Dist(s): H Leonard

Easy Classical Piano. 1999. audio compact disk 24.95 (978-0-634-01483-3(8)) Pub: iSong. Dist(s): H Leonard

Easy Classical Piano, Vol. 2. 1999. audio compact disk 24.95 (978-0-634-01484-0(6), 00451036) Pub: iSong. Dist(s): H Leonard

Easy Company Soldier: The Endless Combat of a Sergeant from World War II's Band of Brothers. unabr. ed. Don Malarkey & Bob Welch. Read by Scott Grimes. 6 CDs. (Running Time: 8 hrs. 0 mins. 0 sec.). (ENG.). 2008. audio compact disk 29.95 (978-1-4272-0450-9(0)) Pub: Macmill Audio. Dist(s): Macmillan

Easy Concert Pieces for Violin & Orchestra. Created by Hal Leonard Corporation Staff. 2006. pap. bk. 24.98 (978-1-59615-151-2(X), 159615151X) Pub: Music Minus. Dist(s): H Leonard

Easy Death. Da Avabhasa. 1 cass. 1992. 11.95 (978-0-918801-56-2(7)) Dawn Horse Pr.

Easy Decision see Gathering of Great Poetry for Children

Easy Does It. Perf. by Hap Palmer. 1 cass., 1 CD. (J). 11.95 (EA 581C); lp 11.95 (EA 581); audio compact disk 14.95 CD. (EA581CD) Kimbo Educ.
Birds in the Circle - The Bean Bag - Move Around the Color - Circle Your Way & more.

***Easy E-Newsletters.** PUEI. 2008. audio compact disk 199.00 (978-1-935041-02-3(9), CareerTrack) P Univ E Inc.

Easy English for Busy People Vol. 1: English to Polish. Helen Costello. Read by Pawel Bawalec & Jenny Bryce. 2 CDs. (Running Time: 1 hr. 23 mins. 0 sec.). (ENG.). 2008. audio compact disk 21.95 (978-0-230-71164-8(2)) Pub: Macmillan UK GBR. Dist(s): IPG Chicago

Easy English for Busy People Vol. 1: English to Russian. Helen Costello. Read by Max Bollinger & Julie Maisey. 2 CDs. (Running Time: 1 hr. 21 mins. 32 sec.). (ENG.). 2008. audio compact disk 16.95 (978-0-230-71170-9(7)) Pub: Macmillan UK GBR. Dist(s): IPG Chicago

Easy English for Busy People Vol. 2: English to Polish. Helen Costello. Read by Pawel Bawalec & Jenny Bryce. 2 CDs. (Running Time: 1 hr. 8 mins. 26 sec.). (ENG.). 2008. audio compact disk 21.95 (978-0-230-71167-9(7)) Pub: Macmillan UK GBR. Dist(s): IPG Chicago

Easy English for Busy People Vol. 2: English to Russian. Helen Costello. Read by Max Bollinger & Julie Maisey. 2 CDs. (Running Time: 1 hr. 5 mins. 0 sec.). (ENG.). 2008. audio compact disk 21.95 (978-0-230-71173-0(1)) Pub: Macmillan UK GBR. Dist(s): IPG Chicago

Easy English Vocabulary. unabr. ed. Living Language Staff. (ESL Ser.). 2009. audio compact disk & audio compact disk 9.99 (978-1-4000-0660-1(0), LivingLang) Pub: Random Info Grp. Dist(s): Random

Easy Enhanced Learning. 1 cass. 12.95 (978-1-884305-65-8(2)) Changeworks.
This tape will help you learn faster & retain more of what you learn.

Easy Fingerstyle Guitar Solos. Dick Weissman. 1998. pap. bk. 9.95 (978-0-7866-2695-3(X), 96549BCD) Mel Bay.

Easy Flamenco Solos. Mel Agen. 1998. audio compact disk 12.95 (978-0-7866-2830-8(8)) Mel Bay.

Easy flute Solos: Beginning students, vol. i (digitally remastered version - 2 CD Set) Katarzyna Bury. 2 vols. 2002. pap. bk. 34.98 (978-1-59615-292-2(3), 586-009) Pub: Music Minus. Dist(s): Bookworld

Easy Go - Learn or Improve Bridge. Scripts. Keith Hanson. 1 cass. (Running Time: 55 min.). 2000. (978-1-890095-21-5(4), 19205-4); audio compact disk (978-1-890095-20-8(6), 19205-2) Nesak Intl.

Easy Go French. Scripts. 1 cass. (FRE.). 1999. (978-1-890095-13-0(3), 19200-4); audio compact disk (978-1-890095-17-8(6), 19200-2) Nesak Intl.
The most popular words & phrases - two way booklet enclosed.

Easy Go German. Scripts. 1 cass. (GER.). 1999. (978-1-890095-14-7(1), 19202-4); audio compact disk (978-1-890095-18-5(4), 19202-2) Nesak Intl.

Easy Go Italian. Scripts. 1 cass. (ITA.). 1999. (978-1-890095-15-4(X), 19203-4); audio compact disk (978-1-890095-19-2(2), 19203-2) Nesak Intl.

Easy Go Spanish. Scripts. 1 cass. (SPA.). 1999. (978-1-890095-12-3(5), 19201-4); audio compact disk (978-1-890095-16-1(8), 19201-2) Nesak Intl.

Easy in Your Harness: Ericksonian & NLP Tools for Working with the Enneagram. Thomas R. Condon. 12 cass. (Running Time: 12 hrs.). 84.95 set. (978-1-884305-87-0(3)) Changeworks.
Tapes to help you: Better understand yourself & others; Combine NLP & Ericksonian tools with the Enneagram; Study & learn at leisure.

Easy in Your Harness: NLP & the Enneagram. Thomas R. Condon. 6 cass. (Running Time: 16 hrs.). 1993. 84.95 set. (AA2607) Credence Commun.
We can never be free of our enneagram proclivities - our harness, if you will - but we can adjust our compulsions so we can be comfortable & productive.

Easy jazz duets for two tenor saxophones & rhythm Section. Zoot Sims. 1994. pap. bk. 34.98 (978-1-59615-608-1(2), 586-059) Pub: Music Minus. Dist(s): Bookworld

Easy jazz duets for two trumpets & rhythm Section. Burt Collins. 2002. pap. bk. 34.98 (978-1-59615-419-3(5), 586-016) Pub: Music Minus. Dist(s): Bookworld

Easy Jazz Guitar Solos: Beginning-Intermediate Level. Alan De Mause. (Value Line Ser.). 1998. pap. bk. 9.95 (978-0-7866-1840-8(X), 95700BCD) Mel Bay.

***Easy Lessons Learned the Hard Way.** (ENG.). 2009. 15.00 (978-0-9843553-2-7(4)) Saranese Cult.

Easy Meat. unabr. ed. John Harvey. Narrated by Ron Keith. 9 cass. (Running Time: 12 hrs. 30 mins.). (Charlie Resnick Mystery Ser.: Vol. 8). 1997. 78.00 (978-0-7887-0818-3(X), 94968E7) Recorded Bks.
When Nottingham detective Charlie Resnik investigates a teen suicide, it appears to be just another case of fear winning out over reason in juvenile hall.

Easy Meditation CD Set, Set. Based on a book by Robert Morgen. 4 CD's. (Running Time: 5 Hours). 2006. audio compact disk 174.95 (978-0-9773801-6-9(5)) MysticWolf.
Simple, easy and effective guided meditations to help you connect your Mind, Body and Spirit, from the author of ?Kundalini Awakening for Personal Mastery? (ISBN: 0-9773801-0-6), "Basic Meditation for Druids" (ISBN: 0-9773801-9-X) and "Easy Meditation for Martial Artists" (ISBN: 0-9773801-3-0)The exercises on these CD's allow anyone to quickly and easily learn to connect to the energy that surrounds and permeates us. Guided meditations allow the user to relax and simply follow along, while at the same time learning the simple skills that allow them to meditate anywhere and at any time.Topics covered include;"Easy Introduction to Meditation" (ISBN 0-9773801-2-2) (66:20) $19.95 DescriptionRobert Morgen's "Easy Introduction to Meditation" provides the novice through high intermediate meditator with directions, exercises and guided meditations to help one learn to clear and control the mind, develop a great degree of higher self awareness and take more control over one's life. The CD includes:1. Introduction and Concepts of Meditation 5:062. Meditation Positions 5:443. Breathing for Meditation 5:454. Full Body Awareness 4:145. Intention and Awareness 5:456. Grounding 5:137. Progressive Relaxation 9:018. The Brain Scrub 3:569. The Secret Smile 21:31"Advanced Meditation Exercises" (74:40) $19.95 DescriptionRobert Morgen's ?Advanced Meditation Exercises" provides exercises and guided meditations for the high intermediate to expert meditator. Using this CD will allow one to develop stronger abilities in concentration, visualization, moving, feeling and seeing energy and much more. The CD includes:1. Introduction to the Advanced Exercises 1:172. Feeling and Seeing Energy 10:063. Drawing Energy 9:354. Skin Breathing 5:555. The Microcosmic Orbit 10:506. Damo?s Cave 37:12?Timed Meditations? (76:27) $14.95DescriptionRobert Morgen's ?Timed Meditations " is designed to allow one to make time for meditation in and easily controlled manner. With timed music tracks that range from 5 minutes to 25 minutes, this CD allows one to take a few minutes and meditate any time, without worrying about how much time is available. With this simple CD it?s easy to grab a quick 5, 10 or 15 minutes to meditate during lunch breaks or other time sensitive periods. 1. Introduction to Meditation 5:062. 5 Minute Meditation3. 10 Minute Meditation 4. 15 Minute Meditation5. 20 Minute Meditation 6. 25 Minute Meditation"Opening the Chakras" $29.95 DescriptionRobert Morgen's ?Opening the Chakras " introduce intermediate meditators to their chakra system. With brief, simple explanations Morgen guides listeners through the process of working with and opening the chakras. The powerful guided meditations on this CD have been the highlight of Morgen?s Seminars and classes. The CD includes:1. Intro to the Chakras 1:302. Drawing Energy into the Chakras 10:583. Hugging the Tree 10:584. Opening the Chakras 14:305. Becoming the Universe 36:00Anyone who is truly serious about meditation and kundalini awakening will want this valuable tool.

Easy Memory Improvement for Busy People. Bob Griswold. Read by Deirdre M. Griswold. 1 Cass. (Running Time: 1 Hr.). 2000. 11.98 (978-1-55848-212-8(1)) EffectiveMN.

Easy Money. Jenny Siler. Read by Betty Bobbitt. (Running Time: 8 hrs.). 2009. 79.99 (978-1-74214-284-5(2), 9781742142845) Pub: Bolinda Pubng AUS. Dist(s): Bolinda Pub Inc

Easy Money. abr. ed. Jenny Siler. Read by Alyssa Bresnahan. 4 cass. (Running Time: 6 hrs.). 2001. 25.00 (978-1-59040-121-7(2), Phoenix Audio) Pub: Amer Intl Pub. Dist(s): PerseuPGW

Easy Money. unabr. ed. Jenny Siler. Read by Betty Bobbitt. 6 cass. (Running Time: 8 hrs.). 2005. 48.00 (978-1-74093-616-3(7)); audio compact disk 87.95 (978-1-74093-617-0(5)) Pub: Bolinda Pubng AUS. Dist(s): Bolinda Pub Inc

Easy Money. unabr. ed. Jenny Siler. Read by Betty Bobbitt. 8 x CDs. (Running Time: 28800 sec.). 2006. audio compact disk 49.95 (978-1-74094-839-5(4)) Bolinda Pubng AUS.

Easy Piano Christmas: 25 Christmas Favorites for Piano Solo with Play-along CD. Arranged by Lauren Keiser. 2004. audio compact disk 14.95 (978-0-8258-4915-2(2)) Fischer Inc NY.

Easy Piano Classics: 30 Famous Piano Pieces from Bach to Gretchaninoff. Ed. by Marianne Magolt. Created by Hal Leonard Corporation Staff. 2008. pap. bk. 14.95 (978-3-7957-5488-4(7), 3795754887) Pub: Schott Music Corp. Dist(s): H Leonard

Easy Prey. John Sandford, pseud. Narrated by Richard Ferrone. 11 CDs. (Running Time: 12 hrs. 45 mins.). (Prey Ser.). 2001. audio compact disk 111.00 (978-0-7887-5164-6(6), C1326E7) Recorded Bks.
Two young women have been found dead at a party. One was Alie'e Mason, a model on the fast track to stardom. While Chief Davenport hunts the killer, another murderer begins targeting anyone who was close to Alie'e. As he tries to protect Alie'e's girlfriend, he finds himself drawn personally into the investigation.

Easy Prey. unabr. ed. John Sandford, pseud. Narrated by Richard Ferrone. 9 cass. (Running Time: 12 hrs. 45 mins.). (Prey Ser.). 2000. 83.00 (978-0-7887-4359-7(7), 96311E7) Recorded Bks.

Easy Problem Solving. Read by Mary Richards. (Subliminal Impact Ser.). 12.95 Master Your Mind.
Explains how to solve problems with ease.

Easy Pronunciation: English as a Second Language. unabr. ed. Living Language Staff. Read by Living Language Staff. (YA). 2007. 49.99 (978-1-59895-813-3(5)) Find a World.

Easy Reading Selections in English, Set. Robert James Dixson. 6 cass. (SPA.). 86.85 (978-0-13-222910-4(2), PH7647) Longman.

Easy Rock Bass. Dieter Petereit. 1999. pap. bk. 19.95 (978-0-7866-5263-1(2)) Voggenreiter Pubs DEU.

Easy Russian for English Speakers: Results Focused Audio Training; Learn to Meet, Greet, Do Business in Russian; Make Friends, Dates & Discover Mysterious Russian Soul. Max Bollinger. Perf. by Max Bollinger. (ENG & RUS.). 2008. DVD & cd-rom 24.00 (978-0-9561165-0-5(7)) Max Bollinger GBR.

Easy Silence. Angela Huth. Read by Angela Huth. 10 CDs. (Running Time: 11 hrs. 44 mins.). (Isis (CDs) Ser.). (J). 2004. audio compact disk 89.95 (978-0-7531-2319-5(3)) Pub: ISIS Lrg Prnt GBR. Dist(s): Ulverscroft US

Easy Silence. unabr. ed. Angela Huth. Read by Angela Huth. 10 cass. (Running Time: 15 hrs.). 2001. 84.95 (978-0-7531-0757-7(0), 000512) Pub: ISIS Audio GBR. Dist(s): Ulverscroft US

Easy Sin. Jon Cleary. Read by Christian Rodska. (Chivers Audio Bks.). 2003. 69.95 (978-0-7540-8394-8(2)) Pub: Chivers Audio Bks GBR. Dist(s): AudioGO

Easy Sleep. Michael Rosenbaum & Cindy Rosenbaum. Perf. by Michael Rosenbaum. (Running Time: 25 min.). (J). (ps-5). 9.95 Happy Kids Prods.
Guided relaxation songs, poetry & music that gently relaxes a child to sleep, & help with nightmares.

Easy Songs for Beginning Singers - Baritone/Bass. Compiled by Joan Boytim. 1 CD. (Running Time: 90 mins.). 2000. pap. bk. 16.95 (00740121) H Leonard.
Ideal for middle school students & beginning voice students of all ages. Piano accompaniments, recorded by a top vocal coach that are perfect for practice. Songs appropriately chosen for each voice-type include: "Beautiful Dreamer"; "Funiculi, Funicula"; "Go Down Moses"; "The Minstrel Boy"; "Out of My Soul's Great Sadness"; "Simple Gifts"; "Sometimes I Feel Like a Motherless Child"; "Where Did You Get That Hat?".

Easy Songs for Beginning Singers - Mezzo Soprano. Compiled by Joan Boytim. 1 CD. (Running Time: 90 mins.). (YA). 2000. pap. bk. 16.95 (00740119) H Leonard.

Easy Songs for Beginning Singers - Soprano. Compiled by Joan Boytim. 1 CD. (Running Time: 90 mins.). (YA). (gr. 7 up). 2000. pap. bk. 16.95 (00740118) H Leonard.

Easy Songs for Beginning Singers - Tenor. Compiled by Joan Boytim. 1 CD. (Running Time: 90 mins.). (YA). 2000. pap. bk. 16.95 (00740120) H Leonard.

Easy Spanish Stories: The Dog House & Other Stories see Cuentos Faciles, Vol. 2, La Casilla del Perro y Otros Cuentos

Easy Spanish Stories: The Rope & Other Stories see Cuentos Faciles, Vol. 4, La Cuerda y Otros Cuentos

Easy Spanish Stories: The Stolen Ass & Other Stories see Cuentos Faciles, Vol. 3, El Asno Robado y Otros Cuentos

Easy Spanish Stories: Time is Money & 15 Other Stories see Cuentos Faciles, Vol. 1, El Tiempo es Oro y 15 Cuentos Mas

Easy Speedy French. abr. ed. Created by Language Dynamics. 2 CDs. (Running Time: 7200 sec.). 2003. audio compact disk 19.00 (978-1-893564-87-9(8)) Macmill Audio.

Easy Speedy French: Complete Tapescript & Listening Guide. Mark Frobose. 2 cass. (Running Time: 2 hrs.). (FRE.). 1993. stu. ed. 19.99 (978-1-893564-11-4(8)) Macmill Audio.

Easy Speedy German. Mark Frobose. 2 CDs. (Running Time: 2 hrs). 2003. audio compact disk 19.00 (978-1-893564-88-6(6)) Macmill Audio.

Easy Speedy German 1. Mark Frobose. 2 cass. (Running Time: 2 hrs.). (GER.). 1999. 19.99 (978-1-893564-13-8(4)) Macmill Audio.

Easy Speedy Italian. Mark Frobose. 2 CDs. (Running Time: 2 hrs.). 2003. audio compact disk 19.00 (978-1-893564-90-9(8)) Macmill Audio.

Easy Speedy Italian. Mark Frobose. 2 cass. 2004. 19.99 (978-1-893564-43-5(6)) Macmill Audio.

Easy Speedy Italian 1. Mark Frobose. 2 cass. (Running Time: 2 hrs.). 1999. 19.99 (978-1-893564-12-1(6)) Macmill Audio.

Easy Speedy Portuguese. Mark Frobose. 2 CDs. (Running Time: 2 hrs.). 2003. audio compact disk 19.00 (978-1-893564-95-4(9)) Macmill Audio.

Easy Speedy Spanish. Mark Frobose. 2 CDs. (Running Time: 2 hrs.). 2003. audio compact disk 19.00 (978-1-893564-84-8(3)) Macmill Audio.

Easy Speedy Spanish: Complete Listening Guide & Tapescript. Mark Frobose. 2 cass. (Running Time: 2 hrs.). 1993. stu. ed. 19.99 (978-1-893564-10-7(X)) Macmill Audio.

Easy Stories Plus: Readings & Activities for Language Skills - Low Beginning. 2001. 17.00 (978-1-56420-254-3(2)); audio compact disk 17.00 (978-1-56420-251-2(8)) New Readers.

Easy Stress Relief for Busy People. Bob Griswold. Read by Deirdre M. Griswold. 2000. 11.98 (978-1-55848-215-9(6)) EffectiveMN.

Easy Stress Solutions for You. Ruth Hoskins. 1 cass. (Running Time: 40 mins.). 2000. 10.99 (978-0-9677629-0-6(1)) Pub: Gefen Pub Hse ISR. Dist(s): Gefen Bks

Easy System to Control Your Debts. unabr. ed. Vernon K. Jacobs. 1 cass. (Running Time: 32 min.). 12.95 (965) J Norton Pubs.
If you're in over your head, here's a simple 12-point program for getting out of debt.

Easy tenor saxophone Solos: Student edition, vol. II, Vol. 2. Harriet Wingreen. 1994. pap. bk. & stu. ed. 34.98 (978-1-59615-607-4(4), 586-025) Pub: Music Minus. Dist(s): Bookworld

Easy Times: A Beginning Multiplication Tutorial. 1 CD. (Running Time: 1 hr.). (J). (gr. 2-5). 2008. audio compact disk 12.00 (978-0-9794672-1-9(7)) AudioBookMan.

Easy to Learn Construction Spanish. 1 CD. (Running Time: 60 mins.). 2002. audio compact disk 14.95 (978-0-9724199-0-1(X)) Ablemos Inc.
Learn all the sounds needed to be able to read anything in Spanish. Practice along with the audio CD and the refrence list of Construction terms and phrases such as rooms of the house, materials, tools, etc.Increase productivity with your workers!!!Learn about Hispanic culture traits and beliefs.

Easy Travel to Other Planets. Ted Mooney. Read by Ted Mooney. 1 cass. (Running Time: 30 min.). 8.95 (AMF-7) Am Audio Prose.
Mooney reads from "Easy to Travel to Other Planets" & talks about New Wave fiction & processing information in a future-shock world.

Easy Visualization. Betty L. Randolph. Read by Betty L. Randolph. Read by Leonard Baron. Ed. by Success Education Institute International Staff. 1 cass. (Running Time: 60 min.). 1990. bk. 9.98 (978-1-55909-276-0(9), 105B) Randolph Tapes.
Sixty thousand messages left-right brain; Male-female voice tracks. Messages subliminally parallel music. Orchestrated, specially arranged Baroque classical music with 60 beats for accelerated learning. Exclusively recorded for Success Education Institute by a world class symphony orchestra. All messages heard audibly for 3-5 minutes before covered by music.

Easy Way to Correct Chinese Pronunciation. Liu Liying. 3 pieces. (CHI & ENG.). 2002. reel tape 17.95 (978-7-88703-144-0(3), EAWACT) China Bks.

Easy Way to Kurdish. unabr. ed. Soraya Mofty. Read by Soraya Mofty. Read by Cyrus Salam. 2 cass. (Running Time: 1 hr. 30 mins.). (KUR.). (gr. 9-12). 1997. pap. bk. 55.00 (978-0-88432-940-4(2), AFKU10) J Norton Pubs.
Mini-course features basic vocabulary for travel & day-to-day living.

Easy Way to Kurdish CDs & Text. Soraya Mofty. Voice by Soraya Mofty. Voice by Cyrus Salam. 2 CDs. (Running Time: 1 hr. 30 mins.). (KUR.). 2005. audio compact disk 55.00 (978-1-57970-264-9(3), AFKU10D, Audio-For) J Norton Pubs.
This mini-course in the Surani dialect of Kurdish features basic vocabulary for travel and day-to-day living.

Easy Way to Latvian. unabr. ed. Liga K. Streips. 12 cass. (Running Time: 12 hrs.). (Self-Instructional Language Courses). (LAV & ENG.). 1980. pap. bk. 245.00 (978-0-88432-442-3(7), AFLV10) J Norton Pubs.
Spoken Latvian for English-speaking learners. Organized around 24 lessons that teach the basic phrases needed for beginning communication. Text uses Roman script & contains transcripts of all dialogs, grammatical notes, additional vocabulary & self-test exercises.

Easy Way to Lithuanian. 6 cass. (Running Time: 9 hrs.). pap. bk. 165.00 J Norton Pubs.
Features phrases & sentences that can be memorized easily & used in everyday conversation.

Easy Way to Lithuanian. unabr. ed. Lithuanian Educational Council of the USA Staff. 6 cass. (Running Time: 9 hrs.). (Self-Instructional Language Courses). (LIT.). (J). 1992. pap. bk. 185.00 (978-0-88432-458-4(3), AFLT10) J Norton Pubs.
Features phrases & sentences that can be memorized easily & used in everyday conversation. In addition to dialogs, vocabulary & grammar, each lesson contains self-test exercises.

***Easy Way to Lithuanian Cds & Book.** Lithuanian Educational Council. (ENG & LIT.). 2005. pap. bk. 185.00 (978-1-57970-315-8(1), Audio-For) J Norton Pubs.

Easy Wedding Planner: With Free Planning Software. Alex A. Lluch & Elizabeth H. Lluch. 2000. pap. bk. 17.95 (978-1-887169-15-8(6)) Pub: Wedding Solns. Dist(s): Natl Bk Netwk

Easy Weight Loss. Read by Mary Richards. 1 cass. (Running Time: 48 min.). (Energy Break Ser.). 2007. audio compact disk 19.95 (978-1-56136-153-3(4)) Master Your Mind.

Easy Yoga Workbook: The Perfect Introduction to Yoga. Tara Fraser. 2003. pap. bk. (978-0-00-766235-7(1), HarperThor) HarpC GBR.

EasyFlow Meditation: Guided Relaxation for Nourishing Sleep & Instant Stress Relief. Monique Danielle. 2007. audio compact disk 19.98 (978-0-9797033-0-0(1)) Easy Flow.

EasyLearn French. Arlene Jullie. Read by Arlene Jullie. 6 cass. (Running Time: 2 hrs.). (FRE.). 1990. 89.95 Set. Learn Strategies.
Accelerated learning program for introductory French.

EasyLearn German. Helga Boege. Read by Helga Boege. 6 cass. (Running Time: 2 hrs.). (GER.). 1990. 89.95 Set. Learn Strategies.
Accelerated learning program for introductory German.

EasyLearn Spanish. Arlene Jullie. Read by Arlene Jullie. 6 cass. (Running Time: 2 hrs.). (SPA.). 1990. 89.95 Set. Learn Strategies.
Accelerated learning program for introductory Spanish.

Eat A Bowl of Cherries. Prod. by Norman Jones & The Rhythm Child Network. (ENG.). (J). 2009. audio compact disk 14.95 (978-0-9763522-0-4(6)) R C Network.

Eat & Be Lean. 2nd rev. ed. Chriscilla M. Thornock & Dana Thornock. 1994. pap. bk. 49.95 (978-0-9629060-2-2(6)) Thornock Intl.

Eat & Lose Weight see Je Mange Donc je Maigris

Eat Cake. unabr. ed. Jeanne Ray. Read by Jeanne Ray. (Running Time: 7 hrs.). 2004. 39.25 (978-1-59335-357-5(X), 159335357X, Brlnc Audio MP3 Lib) Brilliance Audio.
Ruth loves to bake cakes. When she is alone, she dreams up variations on recipes. When she meditates, she imagines herself in the warm, comforting center of a gigantic bundt cake. If there is a crisis, she bakes a cake; if there is a reason to celebrate, she bakes a cake. Ruth sees it as an outward manifestation of an inner need to nurture her family - which is a good thing, because all of a sudden that family is rapidly expanding. First, her mother

moves in after robbers kick in her front door in broad daylight. Then Ruth's father, a lounge singer, who she's seen only occasionally throughout her life, shatters both wrists and, having nowhere else to go, moves in, too. Her mother and father just happen to hate each other with a deep and poisonous emotion reserved only for life-long enemies. Oh, yes indeed! Add to this mix two teenagers, a gainfully employed husband who is suddenly without a job, and a physical therapist with the instincts of a Cheryl Richardson and you've got a delightful and amusing concoction that comes with its own delicious icing.

Eat Cake. unabr. ed. Jeanne Ray. Read by Jeanne Ray. (Running Time: 7 hrs.). 2004. 39.25 (978-1-59710-237-7(7), 1597102377, BADLE); 24.95 (978-1-59710-236-0(9), 1597102369, BAD) Brilliance Audio.

Eat Cake. unabr. ed. Jeanne Ray. Read by Jeanne Ray. (Running Time: 7 hrs.). 2004. 24.95 (978-1-59335-029-1(5), 1593350295) Soulmate Audio Bks.

Eat Cake: A Novel. unabr. ed. Jeanne Ray. Read by Jeanne Ray. 4 cass. (Running Time: 7 hrs.). 2003. 69.25 (978-1-59086-085-4(3), 1590860853); audio compact disk 29.95 (978-1-59086-827-0(7), 1590868277, BriAudCD Unabrid); audio compact disk 82.25 (978-1-59086-828-7(5), 1590868285, CD Unabrid Lib Ed) Brilliance Audio.

Eat Cake: A Novel. unabr. ed. Read by Jeanne Ray. Narrated by Jeanne Ray. 5 cass. (Running Time: 7 hrs.). 2003. 27.95 (978-1-59086-084-7(5), 1590860845, BAU) Brilliance Audio.

Eat, Drink, & Be Healthy: The Harvard Medical School Guide to Healthy Eating. abr. ed. Walter C. Willett. Narrated by Christopher Lane. Told to Patrick J. Skerrett. (Running Time: 10800 sec.). 2001. audio compact disk 22.95 (978-1-933310-09-1(X)) STI Certified.

***Eat, Drink, & Be Merry: America's Doctor Tells You Why the Healt.** abr. ed. Dean Edell. (ENG.). 2004. (978-0-06-075233-0(5), Harper Audio) HarperCollins Pubs.

***Eat, Drink, & Be Merry: America's Doctor Tells You Why the Healt.** abr. ed. Dean Edell. (ENG.). 2004. (978-0-06-081338-3(5), Harper Audio) HarperCollins Pubs.

Eat for Health. 1 cass. (Health Ser.). 12.98 (113) Randolph Tapes.
A motivator for lowering cholesterol! Dynamic program! Instills good eating healthy habits & patterns for fitness for life.

***Eat for Health Audio - Book 1.** Joel Fuhrman. (ENG.). 2010. audio compact disk 24.95 (978-0-9825541-1-1(7)) NutritExcell.

Eat No Eat. abr. ed. Robert A. Monroe. Read by Robert A. Monroe. (Running Time: 30 min.). (Human Plus Ser.). 1989. 14.95 (978-1-56102-008-9(7)) Inter Indus.
Control your appetite.

Eat, Play, & Be Healthy: The Harvard Medical School Guide to Healthy Eating for Kids. abr. ed. W. Allan Walker. Narrated by Lawrence Bullock. Told to Courtney Humphries. Frwd. by Walter C. Willett. (Running Time: 10800 sec.). 2006. audio compact disk 22.95 (978-1-933310-04-6(9)) A Media Intl.

Eat, Pray, Love: One Woman's Search for Everything Across Italy, India & Indonesia. unabr. ed. Elizabeth Gilbert. Read by Elizabeth Gilbert. 8 cass. (Running Time: 12 hrs.). 2006. 72.00 (978-1-4159-2669-7(7)); audio compact disk 99.00 (978-1-4159-2670-3(0)) Books on Tape.

Eat, Pray, Love: One Woman's Search for Everything Across Italy, India & Indonesia. unabr. ed. Elizabeth Gilbert. Read by Elizabeth Gilbert. 11 CDs. (Running Time: 13 hrs.). (ENG.). (gr. 12 up). 2006. audio compact disk 39.95 (978-0-14-305852-6(5), PengAudBks) Penguin Grp USA.

***Eat Right for Your Type.** abr. ed. Peter D'adamo. Read by Polly Adams. (ENG.). 2008. (978-0-06-157301-9(9)); (978-0-06-157302-6(7)) HarperCollins Pubs.

Eat Right for Your Type: The Individualized Diet Solution to Staying Healthy, Living Longer & Achieving Your Ideal Weight. unabr. abr. ed. Peter D'Adamo. Read by Polly Adams. Told to Catherine Whitney. (Running Time: 10800 sec.). 2008. audio compact disk 14.95 (978-0-06-144184-4(8), Harper Audio) HarperCollins Pubs.

Eat Smart, Think Smart, Set. abr. ed. Robert Haas. Read by Robert Haas. 2 cass. (Running Time: 3 hrs.). 1994. 16.95 (978-1-879371-67-5(7)) Pub Mills.
"Smart nutrients" can actually improve mental capacity. Robert Haas, a bestselling author of nutritional books, offers the first comprehensive blueprint for building a safe & effective dietary program for increasing & improving your mental facilities.

Eat That Frog! 21 Great Ways to Stop Procrastinating & Get More Done in Less Time. unabr. ed. Brian Tracy. Read by Brian Tracy. (Running Time: 9600 sec.). (ENG.). 2006. audio compact disk 24.95 (978-1-57270-720-7(8)) Pub: AudioGO. Dist(s): Perseus Dist

Eat the Cookie... Buy the Shoes: Giving Yourself Permission to Lighten Up. unabr. ed. Joyce Meyer. Read by Sandra McCollom. (Running Time: 6 hrs.). (ENG.). 2010. 16.98 (978-1-60788-186-5(1)); audio compact disk 24.98 (978-1-60788-185-8(3)) Pub: Hachet Audio. Dist(s): HachBkGrp

Eat the Dark. unabr. ed. Joe Schreiber. Read by Renée Raudman. (Running Time: 6 hrs. 30 mins. 0 sec.). (ENG.). 2007. audio compact disk 29.99 (978-1-4001-0482-6(3)); audio compact disk 59.99 (978-1-4001-3482-3(X)); audio compact disk 19.99 (978-1-4001-5482-1(0)) Pub: Tantor Media. Dist(s): IngramPubServ

***Eat This Book: A Conversation in the Art of Spiritual Reading.** unabr. ed. Eugene H. Peterson. Narrated by Grover Gardner. (ENG.). 2006. 14.98 (978-1-59644-243-6(3), Hovel Audio) christianaud.

Eat This Book: The Art of Spiritual Reading. unabr. ed. Eugene H. Peterson. 5 CDs. (Running Time: 6 hrs. 0 mins. 0 sec.). (ENG.). 2006. audio compact disk 24.98 (978-1-59644-242-9(5), Hovel Audio) christianaud.
Is it enough that we read the Bible, or does it also matter how we read the Bible? Translator of The Message, pastor, and theologian Eugene Peterson is convinced that how we read the Bible is just as important as that we read the Bible. Eat This Book rejects disinterested Bible study and instead offers a stirring call to live what the Bible says.

Eat this Book: The Holy Community at Table with Holy Scripture. Instructed by Eugene H. Peterson. 2001. audio compact disk 28.50 (978-1-57383-600-5(1), Regent Audio) Regent College CAN.

Eat This Book Set: The Holy Community at Table with Holy Scripture. Instructed by Eugene Patterson. 4 cass. 1999. 24.95 (978-1-57383-500-8(5), RGT1, Regent Audio) Regent College CAN.
The translator of the popular Bible paraphrase "The Message" lectures on the authority of Holy Scripture & its place in the life of a Christian.

Eat to Win. Robert Haas. Intro. by A. E. Whyte. (Listen & Learn USA! Ser.). 1984. 8.95 (978-0-88684-030-3(9)) Listen USA.
Explains how to know your own body chemistry & benefit from the newest nutritional discoveries, as well as how to stay young by eating right.

Eat to Win for Permanent Fat Loss: The Revolutionary Fat-Burning Diet for Peak Mental & Physical Health. abr. ed. Robert Haas. 2 cass. (Running Time: 3 hrs.). 2000. 18.00 (978-1-55935-337-3(6)) Soundelux.
Offers a remarkably flexible, healthy food plan.

Eat with Your Head: How to Develop & Maintain Weight Loss Motivation. Interview. Glenn Livingston. 6. (Running Time: 5 hours). 2003. 97.00 (978-0-9727192-2-3(9)) Psy Tech.
Approximately 5 hours of a recorded teleseminar in which Dr. Glenn Livingston demonstrates his innovative techniques for developing and maintaining weight loss motivation.

Eat Your Way Through the Second House. Susan Aiu. 1 cass. 8.95 (019) Am Fed Astrologers.
An AFA Convention workshop tape.

Eaten Alive: Parasitic Killers Your Doctors Won't Tell You About. Perf. by Clive Buchanan. 2 cass. (Running Time: 1 hr. 55 min.). (Wellness Audio Ser.). 1999. 16.95 Set. (978-1-56889-013-5(3), AW5162); 33.90 Set, incl. public performance rights for schools & libraries. Lghtwrks Aud & Vid.
Buchanan's invaluable information includes: how your children's problems could be caused by parasitic invaders like hookworms & pinworms; how to reduce your risk of cancer; how to eradicate the causes of mysterious intestinal disorders; & how to lose weight, gain energy & improve your disposition.

Eaters of the Dead. unabr. ed. Michael Crichton. Narrated by George Guidall. 4 cass. (Running Time: 5 hrs. 45 mins.). 1999. 40.00 (978-0-7887-3459-5(8), 95882E7) Recorded Bks.
What if the mythical exploits of Beowulf were inspired by actual events & documented by an eyewitness? Crichton offers an imaginative fictional answer to this question. At once a thrilling travel narrative & provocative retelling of the oldest of English epics, lets you enjoy ancient Norse culture as never before.

Eaters of the Dead. unabr. ed. Michael Crichton. Narrated by George Guidall. 5 CDs. (Running Time: 5 hrs. 45 mins.). 2000. audio compact disk 46.00 (978-0-7887-3977-4(8), C1096E7) Recorded Bks.

Eating: Guided Imagery for Making Peace with Food. Read by Nancy L. Tubesing & Sandy S. Christian. Music by Steven Halpern. 1 cass. (Running Time: 56 min.). 1996. 11.95 (978-1-57025-108-5(8)) Whole Person.
Relax & imagine your way to healthy, joy-filled eating! These four meditations are designed to help you make peace with food. Use daily or occasionally to tune in to your body & its hungers, to soothe eating anxieties & to reaffirm your ability to make healthy choices.

***Eating Animals.** unabr. ed. Jonathan Safran Foer. Narrated by Jonathan Todd Ross. 1 Playaway. (Running Time: 10 hrs. 15 mins.). 2009. 59.75 (978-1-4407-3636-0(7)); 72.75 (978-1-4407-3633-9(2)); audio compact disk 102.75 (978-1-4407-3634-6(0)) Recorded Bks.

***Eating Animals.** unabr. collector's ed. Jonathan Safran Foer. Narrated by Jonathan Todd Ross. 9 CDs. (Running Time: 10 hrs. 15 mins.). 2009. audio compact disk 51.95 (978-1-4407-3635-3(9)) Recorded Bks.

Eating Disorders. Frank Minirth & Paul Meier. Read by Frank Minirth & Paul Meier. 1 cass. (Running Time: 59 min.). (Minirth & Meier Home Counseling Audio Library). 1994. 9.95 (978-1-56707-033-0(7)) Dallas Christ Recs.
Causes, symptoms, & treatments from a clinical & spiritual perspective.

Eating Disorders: Anorexia to Obesity. Read by Kathleen L. Wishner. 1 cass. (Running Time: 9 min.). 1985. 12.00 (C8531) Amer Coll Phys.

Eating, Drinking, Overthinking: The Toxic Triangle of Food, Alcohol, & Depression - And How Women Can Break Free. abr. ed. Susan Nolen-Hoeksema. Read by Eliza Foss. 3 CDs. (Running Time: 3 hrs. 0 mins. 0 sec.). (ENG.). 2005. audio compact disk 19.95 (978-1-59397-869-3(3)) Pub: Macmill Audio. Dist(s): Macmillan

Eating, Drinking, Overthinking: The Toxic Triangle of Food, Alcohol, & Depression - and How Women Can Break Free. abr. ed. Susan Nolen-Hoeksema. 2005. 11.95 (978-1-59397-870-9(7)) Pub: Macmill Audio. Dist(s): Macmillan

Eating on the Run: Healthy Habits for Hectic Lifestyles. Evelyn Tribole. 2 cass. (Running Time: 3 hrs.). 1998. 15.95 (978-1-55977-750-6(8)) CareerTrack Pubns.

Eating Problems: To Improve Food-Related Behavior. unabr. ed. Robert B. Speigel. Read by Robert B. Speigel. 2 cass. (Running Time: 1 hr.). (Audio Suggestion Bedtime Stories Tape Ser.). (J). 1993. 16.95 set incl. coloring poster. (978-0-937977-05-7(5)) Speigel&Assoc.
Psychotherapist Robert B. Speigel tells a story from his own childhood & leads children through a series of relaxation & positive visualization exercises designed to help them gain confidence to overcome bad habits & negative thinking. A helpful "Parent Information" cassette is included that provides positive daytime techniques & facts about each problem compiled from current research.

Eating Right. (For Your Information Ser.). 1993. 16.00 (978-1-56420-022-8(1)) New Readers.

Eating the Loser Tape Series, Vol . 1, Set. abr. ed. 6 cass. (Running Time: 3 hr. 23 min.). 1999. pap. bk. 195.00 (978-0-9672837-1-5(X)) Speculative Holdings.
Created to help the student of trading uncover his personal trade art form. This is always unique to the student & cannot be taught.

Eating Well for Optimum Health: The Essential Guide to Food, Diet & Nutrition. unabr. ed. Andrew Weil. Read by Alexander Marshall. 6 cass. (Running Time: 9 hrs.). 2000. 44.95 (978-0-7366-4919-3(0), 5227) Books on Tape.
Dr. Weil provides us with a program for improving our well-being by making smart choices about how and what we eat. He explains the safest and most effective ways to lose weight; how diet can affect energy and sleep; how foods can exacerbate or minimize specific physical problems; how much fat to include in our diet; what nutrients are in which foods, and much more. He makes clear that an optimal diet will both supply the body's needs and mortify the body's defenses and healing mechanisms.

EatRight Analysis Version 12. 0. Ed. by Esha Research Staff. (C). 2006. audio compact disk 39.95 (978-0-7637-4685-8(1)) Jones Bartlett.

Eats, Shoots & Leaves: The Zero Tolerance Approach to Punctuation. unabr. ed. Lynne Truss. (Running Time: 1 hr.). (ENG.). (gr. 12 up). 2004. audio compact disk 14.95 (978-0-14-280082-9(1), PengAudBks) Penguin Grp USA.

Eavan Boland. unabr. ed. Eavan Boland. Read by Rebekah Presson. Ed. by James McKinley. 1 cass. (Running Time: 29 min.). (New Letters on the Air Ser.). 1994. 10.00 (112894); 18.00 2-sided cass. New Letters.
Boland is interviewed by Rebekah Presson & reads from her new book, In a Time of Violence.

EB Standard Edition 2004. Compiled by Encyclopaedia Britannica, Inc. 2004. audio compact disk (978-1-59339-087-7(4)) Ency Brit Inc.

Ebb Tide. Richard Woodman. (Nathaniel Drinkwater Ser.: Bk. 14). (J). 2005. 69.95 (978-1-84559-049-9(X)); audio compact disk 79.95 (978-1-84559-073-4(2)) Pub: ISIS Lrg Prnt GBR. Dist(s): Ulverscroft US

Ebba Eban Reads the Psalms & Ecclesiastes. 1 cass. (Running Time: 90 mins.). (HEB & ENG.). 16.95 J Norton Pubs.

Ebdon's England. unabr. ed. John Ebdon. Read by John Westbrook. 5 cass. (Running Time: 5 hrs. 45 min.). (Isis Ser.). (J). 2004. 49.95 (978-1-85089-608-1(9), 89095) Pub: ISIS Lrg Prnt GBR. Dist(s): Ulverscroft US

Ebdon's Odyssey. unabr. ed. John Ebdon. Read by Peter Barker. 6 cass. (Running Time: 6 hrs. 45 min.). 2001. 54.95 (978-1-85695-445-7(5), 92082) Pub: ISIS Audio GBR. Dist(s): Ulverscroft US
Following two cruises around the Hellenic lands, John Ebdon turned his attention to tourist-free Greece. He set off on a single-handed expedition, staying in two villages on the islands of Andros & Kos. He fell irretrievably in love with the country, with the island people & with their way of life.

Ebeneezer Sneezer. Perf. by Fred Penner. 1 cass. (J). (ps-5). 1983. 10.98 (978-0-945267-56-0(8), YM086-CN); audio compact disk 13.98 (978-0-945267-57-7(6), YM086-CD) Youngheart Mus.
Songs include: "Car, Car" (Riding in My Car); "Polly Wolly Doodle"; "The Old Sow"; "The Old Chisholm Trail"; "My Grandfather's Clock"; "This Old Man"; "Ebeneezer Sneezer"; "Holiday"; "I've Got No Strings"; "The Fox" & more.

Ebenezer, Jr. Musical for Young Voices. Paul M. Miller. Contrib. by Tom Fettke. 1 cass. (Running Time: 1 hr.). 1985. 12.99 (978-0-685-68495-5(4), TA-9064C) Lillenas.
This adaptation of Dicken's A Christmas Carol combines contemporary & biblical elements to communicate the true meaning of Christmas. Script, concept & music allows for a salvation emphasis ideal for either children or junior high choir ages 8 to 14. Features unison/optional 2-part arrangements of attractive songs such as "It's a Great Day"; "Reach Out for the Gift"; "Joy to the World"; "Christmas Isn't Christmas"; "Sharing is the Best Part"; "Come to My Heart, Lord Jesus"; "O Holy Night" & more.

Ebenezer, Jr. Musical for Young Voices. Lyrics by Paul M. Miller. Arranged by Tom Fettke. 1 cass. (Running Time: 40 min.). (J). 1985. 80.00 (MU-9064C) Lillenas.

Ebon Storms. Music by Scott Spear & Edward Haser. 7 CDs. (Running Time: 8 hrs.). 2001. audio compact disk 55.00 (LSUM004) Lodestone Catalog.
Truth & deceit, balance & chaos, sacrifice & betrayal all play a part in this high fantasy adventure.

Ebony Swan. unabr. ed. Phyllis A. Whitney. Read by Anna Fields. 7 cass. (Running Time: 10 hrs.). 1997. 49.95 (978-0-7861-1237-1(9), 1984) Blckstn Audio.
Susan Prentice has come home to Virginia's eastern shores. Twenty-five years ago, her mother fell to her death down the steps of the family's home. Susan has little memory of the accident, or of her maternal grandmother, Alex Montoro. But Susan's arrival has alarmed people who fear what may lie dormant in Susan's memory. They believe that the fall was no accident. Susan must pry open the locked doors of the past, where burning passions, dark secrets & hidden danger must be challenged to set the present free.

Ebony Swan. unabr. ed. Phyllis A. Whitney. Read by Anna Fields. (Running Time: 9 hrs. 0 mins.). 2010. 29.95 (978-1-4417-0755-0(7)); audio compact disk 90.00 (978-1-4417-0752-9(2)) Blckstn Audio.

Ebony Warrior. unabr. ed. Fred R. Hoffman. Read by Ron Varela. 4 cass. (Running Time: 4 hrs. 30 min.). 2001. 26.95 (978-1-55686-938-9(X)) Books in Motion.
Warrior Kanga turns the tide in battle a... Arab slavers, and gains the respect of his people. But Kanga's natu... uses great trouble when he kidnaps the lovely Toma from the Kandu tribe.

Ebook Lectures: Adobe Photoshop Technique Training. rev. ed. Stephanie Torta. 2009. 49.95 (978-0-7637-8194-1(0)) Jones Bartlett.

EBS Adult. cass. & reel tape 12.40 (978-0-7673-4916-1(4)) LifeWay Christian.

EBS Adult. 2003. cass. & reel tape 12.75 (978-0-633-07747-1(X)) LifeWay Christian.

EBS Adult. 2004. 13.30 (978-0-633-08119-5(1)) LifeWay Christian.

EBS Adult. 2004. cass. & reel tape 13.30 (978-0-633-08372-4(0)) LifeWay Christian.

EBS Adult. 2004. cass. & reel tape 13.30 (978-0-633-08621-3(5)) LifeWay Christian.

EBS Adult. 2004. cass. & reel tape 13.30 (978-0-633-17429-3(7)) LifeWay Christian.

EBS Adult. 2005. cass. & reel tape 13.30 (978-0-633-17624-2(9)) LifeWay Christian.

EBS Adult. 2005. cass. & reel tape 13.30 (978-0-633-17822-2(5)) LifeWay Christian.

Ecce Puer see James Joyce Reads James Joyce

Ecce Romani, Level I. (LAT.). 2000. 36.97 (978-0-673-57597-5(7)) Addson-Wesley Educ.

Ecce Romani, Level II. (LAT.). 2000. 36.97 (978-0-201-37492-6(7)) AddisonWesley.

Ecce Romani: Audio Program on CDs. 4 CDs. audio compact disk 37.97 (978-0-13-116374-4(4)); audio compact disk 37.97 (978-0-13-116384-3(1)) PH School.

Ecclesiastes: A Profound & Futile Joy: A Profound & Futile Joy-mp3. Read by Douglas Wilson. 12. 1997. 32.00 (978-1-59128-446-8(5)) Canon Pr ID.

Ecclesiastes: A Profound & Futile Joy: A Profound & Futile Joy-tape. Read by Douglas Wilson. 12 cass. 1997. 40.00 (978-1-59128-448-2(1)) Canon Pr ID.

Ecclesiastes & the Song of Solomon. unabr. ed. Poems. Read by George Vafiadis. 1 cd. (Running Time: 56 mins). 2002. audio compact disk 16.95 (978-1-58472-248-9(7), 033, In Aud) Pub: Sound Room. Dist(s): Baker Taylor
King James Version.

Ecclesiastes & the Song of Solomon: King James Version. unabr. ed. Narrated by Adrian Cronauer. 1 cass. (Running Time: 1 hr.). 10.00 (978-1-55690-159-1(3), 87550E7) Recorded Bks.
Available to libraries only.

Ecclesiastes Commentary: Through the Bible with Chuck Missler. Chuck Missler. 1 MP3 CD-ROM. (Running Time: 8 hours). (Chuck Missler Commentaries). 2002. cd-rom 29.95 (978-1-57821-204-0(9)) Koinonia Hse.
From the human point of view, life ("under the sun") does appear futile; and it is easy for us to get pessimistic. Ecclesiastes goes beyond the other wisdom literature to emphasize the fact that human life and human goals, as ends in themselves apart from God, are meaningless. What a relief to turn and hear Jesus Christ say, "I am come that they might have life, and that they might have it more abundantly."

Ecclesiastical Physiology: 1 Cor. 12:12-31. Ed Young. 1986. 4.95 (978-0-7417-1509-8(0), 509) Win Walk.

Ecclesiazusae see Assembly of Women: Ecclesiazusae

Ecclesiogenic Neurosis: The Dark Side of Organized Religion. Read by Thomas P. Lavin. 1 cass. (Running Time: 90 min.). 1987. 10.95 (978-0-7822-0136-9(9), 260) C G Jung IL.

Eccoci! Beginning Italian. Paola Blelloch & Rosetta D'Angela. (ENG.). (C). 1997. 44.95 (978-0-471-16823-2(8), JWiley) Wiley US.

ECG Made Easy. 2nd ed. Atul Luthra. 2004. audio compact disk 6.00 (978-81-8061-342-5(9)) Jaypee Brothers IND.

Echo. Minette Walters. Narrated by Simon Prebble. 10 CDs. (Running Time: 11 hrs. 30 mins.). 2000. audio compact disk 97.00 (978-0-7887-4750-2(9), C1238E7) Recorded Bks.
When a journalist investigates the unusual death of a homeless man, he embarks on a perilous journey through unsolved crimes of the past & the shadowy world of London's down & out. Best-selling, award-winning novelist Minette captivates mystery aficionados with this finely-wrought web of secrets & betrayals.

***Echo.** unabr. ed. Jack McDevitt. (Running Time: 11 hrs. 0 mins.). 2010. 17.99 (978-1-4001-8473-6(8)); 24.99 (978-1-4001-6473-8(7)); audio compact disk 34.99 (978-1-4001-1473-3(X)) Pub: Tantor Media. Dist(s): IngramPubServ

Echo, unabr. ed. Minette Walters. Narrated by Simon Prebble. 8 cass. (Running Time: 11 hrs. 30 mins.). 1997. 67.00 (978-0-7887-4044-2(X), 96153E7) Recorded Bks.

Echo Burning. Lee Child. Read by Dick Hill. (Jack Reacher Ser.). 2008. 99.99 (978-1-60640-914-5(X)) Find a World.

Echo Burning. Lee Child. 12 CDs. (Jack Reacher Ser.). (J). 2002. audio compact disk 99.95 (978-1-84283-234-9(4)) Pub: ISIS Lrg Prnt GBR. Dist(s): Ulverscroft US

Echo Burning. abr. ed. Lee Child. Read by Dick Hill. 5. (Running Time: 21600 sec.). (Jack Reacher Ser.). 2007. audio compact disk 14.99 (978-1-4233-1952-8(4), 9781423319528, BCD Value Price) Brilliance Audio.

Echo Burning. unabr. ed. Lee Child. Read by Dick Hill. (Running Time: 13 hrs.). (Jack Reacher Ser.). 2004. 39.25 (978-1-59335-559-3(9), 1593355599, Brlnc Audio MP3 Lib) Brilliance Audio.

Echo Burning. unabr. ed. Lee Child. Read by Dick Hill. (Running Time: 13 hrs.). (Jack Reacher Ser.). 2004. 39.25 (978-1-59710-239-1(3), 1597102393, BADLE); 24.95 (978-1-59710-238-4(5), 1597102385, BAD) Brilliance Audio.

Echo Burning. unabr. ed. Lee Child. Read by Dick Hill. (Running Time: 13 hrs.). (Jack Reacher Ser.). 2007. audio compact disk 107.25 (978-1-4233-3386-9(1), 9781423333869, BriAudCD Unabrid); audio compact disk 38.95 (978-1-4233-3385-2(3), 9781423333852, Bril Audio CD Unabri) Brilliance Audio.

Echo Burning. unabr. ed. Lee Child. Read by Dick Hill. (Running Time: 13 hrs.). (Jack Reacher Ser.). 2004. 24.95 (978-1-59335-043-7(0), 1593350430) Soulmate Audio Bks.
Jack Reacher, hailed as "a wonderfully epic hero" by People, confronts Texan hatred and hidden crimes in this superb new thriller. Ex-military cop Jack Reacher returns in this latest in the award-winning series critics call "spectacular" (The Seattle Times), "relentless" (Denver Post), and "perfect" (The New York Times Book Review). Reacher is hitching through the heat of West Texas and getting desperate for a ride. The last thing he's worried about is exactly who picks him up. She's called Carmen. She's a good-looking young woman, she has a beautiful little girl . . .and she has married into the wrong family. They're called the Greers. They're a bitter and miserly clan, and they've made her life a living hell. Worse, her monster of a husband is soon due out of prison. So she needs protection, and she needs it now. Lawyers can't help. Cops can't be trusted. So Reacher goes home with her to the lonely ranch where nothing is as it seems, and where evil swirls around them like dust in a storm. Within days, Carmen's husband is dead - and simmering secrets send Echo, Texas, up in flames.

***Echo in the Bone.** unabr. ed. Diana Gabaldon. Narrated by Davina Porter. 1 Playaway. (Running Time: 46 hrs.). 2009. 69.75 (978-1-4407-2896-9(8)); 113.75 (978-1-4407-2893-8(3)); audio compact disk 123.75 (978-1-4407-2894-5(1)); audio compact disk 79.99 (978-1-4407-4552-2(8)) Recorded Bks.

Echo in the Chimney: And, the Magic in the Mirror. Read by Hilary McKay & Sophie Aldred. 2 CDs. 2006. audio compact disk 21.95 (978-0-7540-6733-7(5), Chivers Child Audio) AudioGO.

Echo in the Darkness, Set. abr. ed. Francine Rivers. Read by Wayne Shepherd. 2 cass. (Running Time: 1 hr. 30 mins. per cass.). (Mark of the Lion Ser.: Vol. 2). 1995. 17.99 (978-1-886463-17-2(4)) Oasis Audio.
Through the courageous faith of the Christian slave girl Hadassah & the troubled lives of her Roman masters, continues this moving tale of first-century Rome.

***Echo (Library Edition)** unabr. ed. Jack McDevitt. (Running Time: 11 hrs. 0 mins.). 2010. 34.99 (978-1-4001-9473-5(3)); audio compact disk 83.99 (978-1-4001-4473-0(6)) Pub: Tantor Media. Dist(s): IngramPubServ

Echo Made Easy. Atul Luthra. 2005. audio compact disk 15.00 (978-81-8061-436-1(0)) Jaypee Brothers IND.

Echo Maker. unabr. ed. Richard Powers. Narrated by Bernadette Dunne. 15 CDs. (Running Time: 72360 sec.). 2006. audio compact disk 117.95 (978-0-7927-4483-2(7), SLD 1013); audio compact disk 74.95 (978-0-7927-4570-9(1), CMP 1013) AudioGO.

Echo of an Angry God. unabr. ed. Beverley Harper. 9 cass. (Running Time: 13 hrs. 10 mins.). 2004. 72.00 (978-1-74030-567-9(1)) Pub: Bolinda Pubng AUS. Dist(s): Lndmrk Audiobks

Echo of Greece. unabr. ed. Edith Hamilton. Read by Nadia May. 4 cass. (Running Time: 5 hrs. 30 mins.). 1994. 32.95 (978-0-7861-0746-9(4), 1501) Blckstn Audio.
With the clarity & grace for which she is admired, Edith Hamilton writes of Plato & Aristotle, of Demosthenes & Alexander the Great, of the much-loved playwright Menander, of the Stoics, & finally of Plutarch. She brings these figures vividly to life, not only placing them in relation to their own times but also conveying very poignantly their meaning for our world today.

***Echo of Violence.** unabr. ed. Jordan Dane. Read by Paula Christensen. (ENG.). 2010. (978-0-06-200709-4(2), Harper Audio); (978-0-06-206215-4(8), Harper Audio) HarperCollins Pubs.

Echo Park. abr. ed. Michael Connelly. Read by Len Cariou. (Running Time: 6 hrs.). (Harry Bosch Ser.: No. 12). (ENG.). 2006. 14.98 (978-1-59483-586-5(1)) Pub: Hachet Audio. Dist(s): HachBkGrp

Echo Park. abr. ed. Michael Connelly. Read by Len Cariou. 5 CDs. (Running Time: 6 hrs.). No. 12. (ENG.). 2008. audio compact disk 14.98 (978-1-60024-525-1(0)) Pub: Hachet Audio. Dist(s): HachBkGrp

Echo Park. unabr. ed. Michael Connelly. Read by Len Cariou. 10 cass. (Running Time: 15 hrs.). (Harry Bosch Ser.: No. 12). 2006. 90.00 (978-1-4159-3468-5(1)); audio compact disk 96.00 (978-1-4159-3469-2(X)) Books on Tape.

Echo Park. unabr. ed. Michael Connelly. Read by Len Cariou. (Running Time: 10 hrs. 30 mins.). (Harry Bosch Ser.: No. 12). (ENG.). 2006. 16.98 (978-1-59483-588-9(8)); audio compact disk 39.98 (978-1-59483-589-6(6)) Pub: Hachet Audio. Dist(s): HachBkGrp

Echo Park. unabr. ed. Michael Connelly. Read by Len Cariou. (Running Time: 10 hrs. 30 mins.). (Harry Bosch Ser.: No. 12). (ENG.). 2009. 59.98 (978-1-60788-270-1(1)) Pub: Hachet Audio. Dist(s): HachBkGrp

Echo Platoon. Richard Marcinko & John Weisman. Read by Richard Marcinko. (Rogue Warrior Ser.). 2004. 10.95 (978-0-7435-1940-3(X)) Pub: S&S Audio. Dist(s): S and S Inc

Echoes. Danielle Steel. Read by Simon Prebble. 7 cass. 2005. 63.00 (978-1-4159-1331-4(5)) Books on Tape.

Echoes. Danielle Steel & Simon Prebble. 9 cds. 2005. audio compact disk 81.00 (978-1-4159-1332-1(3)) Books on Tape.

Echoes, Set. Maeve Binchy. Read by Kate Binchy. 14 cass. 110.95 (CAB 1030) Pub: Chivers Audio Bks GBR. Dist(s): AudioGO

Echoes: Sometimes Death Is Not the End. novel ed. William E. Darke. 9 CDs. (Running Time: 10 hrs. 30 mins.). Dramatization. 2006. pap. bk. 14.95 (978-0-9777974-0-0(6), 20616) Darke Arch Aud.

***Echoes of Betrayal.** Una-Mary Parker. 2010. 69.95 (978-1-4450-0072-5(5)); audio compact disk 84.95 (978-1-4450-0073-2(3)) Pub: Isis Pubng Ltd GBR. Dist(s): Ulverscroft US

Echoes of Glacier. 1 cass. (Running Time: 60 min.). 1994. audio compact disk 15.95 CD. (2632, Creativ Pub) Quayside.
Original music by Chuck Lange. Contemporary, easy music complements the dozens of pure, natural sounds from this park.

Echoes of Glacier. 1 cass. (Running Time: 60 min.). 1994. 9.95 (2631, NrthWrd Bks) TandN Child.

Echoes of Heaven. Florian Monheim. 2006. pap. bk. 49.95 (978-3-937406-11-4(5)) Pub: edel CLASS DEU. Dist(s): Natl Bk Netwk

Echoes of Heaven: The Fine Art of Cathedrals & Their Hymns. Florian Monheim. 2007. bk. 14.95 (978-3-937406-52-7(2)) Pub: edel CLASS DEU. Dist(s): Natl Bk Netwk

Echoes of His Presence: Stories of the Messiah from the People of His Day, That the World May Know Him. unabr. ed. Raynard Vander Laan. 2 cass. 1998. 17.99 (978-0-310-67887-8(0)) Zondervan.

Echoes of Light. unabr. ed. Perf. by Ghaze Husrev Bey Choir. 1 cass. (Running Time: 50 min.). 1994. 6.95 (978-1-889720-16-6(X)) Amirah Pubng.
Chants & dramatizations in Arabic, Serbo-Croation & English with Islamic Themes.

Echoes of My Heart. unabr. ed. Barbara Francis. Read by Jean DeBarbieris. 8 cass. (Running Time: 10 hrs. 30 min.). Dramatization. 1993. 49.95 (978-1-55686-484-1(1), 484) Books in Motion.
Sequel to Voice of My Heart. A single act of fate threatens to destroy any hopes of an heir to the Hinton Dynasty & by 1948 an aging Sara encounters the same dilemma faced by old Jonas half a century earlier - who will take over the reins of the Hinton Industrial Empire.

Echoes of Olympia. 1 cass. (Running Time: 60 min.). 1994. audio compact disk 15.95 CD. (2633, Creativ Pub) Quayside.
Original music. Sounds of the ocean, animals, rivers, & birds highlight this light, contemporary music.

Echoes of Olympia. 1 cass. (Running Time: 60 min.). 1994. 9.95 (2663, NrthWrd Bks) TandN Child.

Echoes of Silence: A Mystery Featuring DI Tom Richmonds. Marjorie Eccles. Read by Christopher Kay. 8 cass. (Sound Ser.). 2002. 69.95 (978-1-84283-035-2(X)) Pub: UlverLrgPrint GBR. Dist(s): Ulverscroft US

Echoes of St. Hildegard. Perf. by The Lady Chapel Singers. Directed By Lisa Thomas. 1. 2003. audio compact disk 17.00 (978-0-89869-425-3(6)) Church Pub Inc.

Echoes of the Andes. (Running Time: 60 mins.). 2002. audio compact disk 15.99 (978-1-904972-22-8(5)) Global Jrny GBR GBR.

Echoes of the Eternal: Bliss. Swami Chetanananda. 1 cass. (Running Time: 59 min.). (Echoes of the Eternal Ser.). 1984. 8.95 (978-0-916356-67-5(1)) Vedanta Soc St Louis.
45 Sanskrit chants, hymns & prayers with English translation.

Echoes of the Eternal: Harmony. Swami Chetanananda. 1 cass. (Running Time: 57 min.). (Echoes of the Eternal Ser.). 1984. 8.95 (978-0-916356-68-2(X)) Vedanta Soc St Louis.
22 Sanskrit chants, hymns, & prayers with English translation.

Echoes of the Eternal: Peace. Swami Chetanananda. 1 cass. (Running Time: 58 min.). (Echoes of the Eternal Ser.). 1984. 8.95 (978-0-916356-66-8(3)) Vedanta Soc St Louis.
41 Sanskrit chants, hymns & prayers with English translation.

Echoes of the Eternal Series. unabr. ed. Music by Swami Chetanananda. 3 cass. (Running Time: 2 hrs. 54 min.). 1984. 22.00 Set. (978-0-916356-74-3(4)) Vedanta Soc St Louis.
108 Sanskrit chants, hymns, & prayers from the Vedas, Upanishads, Epics, Puranas, & other sources with English translation. The three cassettes in this series are also listed separately with these subtitles: Peace; Bliss; Harmony.

Echoes of the Forest: Music of the Central African Pygmies. Louis Sarno & Jean-Pierre Hallet. 1 CD. (Running Time: 1 hr.). pap. bk. 19.95 (978-1-55961-276-0(2), Ellipsis Arts) Relaxtn Co.
This collection, which calls attention to a people currently engaged in a battle against extinction, preserves forever the rarely heard & surprisingly accessible rhythms of the songs of the Ba-Benjelle Pygmies.

Echoes of the Forests. Musical Expeditions Staff. 1 cass. (Running Time: 1 hr.). 1995. pap. bk. 16.95 (978-1-55961-277-7(0), Ellipsis Arts) Relaxtn Co.
This collection, which calls attention to a people currently engaged in a battle against extinction, preserves forever the rarely heard and surprisingly accessible rhythms of the songs of the Ba-Benjelle Pygmies.

***Echoes of the Fourth Magic.** unabr. ed. R. A. Salvatore. Narrated by Lloyd James. (Running Time: 11 hrs. 30 mins. 0 sec.). (Chronicles of Ynis Aielle Ser.). (ENG.). 2010. 24.99 (978-1-4001-6638-1(1)); 17.99 (978-1-4001-8638-9(2)); audio compact disk 69.99 (978-1-4001-4638-3(0)); audio compact disk 34.99 (978-1-4001-1638-6(4)) Pub: Tantor Media. Dist(s): IngramPubServ

Echoes of the Mekong. unabr. ed. Peter A. Huchthausen. Read by Marguerite Gavin. (Running Time: 23400 sec.). 2007. audio compact disk 29.95 (978-0-7861-0308-9(6)) Blckstn Audio.

Echoes of the Mekong. unabr. ed. Peter A. Huchthausen & Nguyen T. Lung. Read by Lloyd James & Marguerite Gavin. 5 cass. (Running Time: 7 hrs.). 1998. 39.95 (978-0-7861-1432-0(0), 2318) Blckstn Audio.
In alternating chapters, Huchthausen & Lung recall the experience of war on the vast Mekong River & Lung recalls the terrifying years that followed. Here is a fresh light on the American involvement in Vietnam as it follows two people caught in the war from youth to maturity.

Echoes of the Mekong. unabr. ed. Peter A. Huchthausen & Nguyen Thi Lung. Read by Marguerite Gavin & Lloyd James. Frwd. by Sylvana Foa. (Running Time: 23400 sec.). 2007. audio compact disk 45.00 (978-0-7861-0284-6(5)) Blckstn Audio.

Echoes of the Past. unabr. ed. Jessica Blair. Read by Trudy Harris. 11 cass. (Running Time: 14 hrs. 35 mins.). (Story Sound Ser.). (J). 2005. 89.95 (978-1-85903-763-8(1)) Pub: Mgna Lrg Print GBR. Dist(s): Ulverscroft US

Echoes of Tiger Stadium. Joe Falls. 1999. 12.95 (978-0-9673996-1-4(0)) PrimeauProd.

Echoes of Yellowstone. 1 cass. (Running Time: 60 min.). 1994. audio compact disk 15.95 CD. (2404, Creativ Pub) Quayside.
Bald eagle, red-tailed hawk, & Canada goose as a medley of music & nature lifts one's spirit. Elk & bison, paint pots, bubbling geysers, & melting snow.

Echoes of Yellowstone. 1 cass. (Running Time: 60 min.). 1994. 9.95 (2402, NrthWrd Bks) TandN Child.

Echoing. Contrib. by Colm O'Foghlu. (ENG.). 1997. 14.95 (978-0-8023-7120-1(5)); audio compact disk 21.95 (978-0-8023-8120-0(0)) Pub: Clo Iar-Chonnachta IRL. Dist(s): Dufour

Echoing Green: The Untold Story of Bobby Thomson, Ralph Branca, & the Shot Heard Round the World. abr. ed. Joshua Prager. Read by Joshua Prager. 2006. 17.95 (978-0-7435-6431-1(6)) Pub: S&S Audio. Dist(s): S and S Inc

Eckhart Tolle Audio Collection. Eckhart Tolle. Read by Eckhart Tolle. (Playaway Adult Nonfiction Ser.). (ENG.). 2009. 69.99 (978-1-60812-782-5(6)) Find a World.

Eckhart Tolle Audio Collection. unabr. ed. Eckhart Tolle. 7 CDs. (Running Time: 10 hrs. 30 mins.). 2002. audio compact disk 59.95 (978-1-59179-003-7(4), AW00637D) Sounds True.
The author continues to reach listeners from all walks of life with his simple and profound message: that only in the present moment can we free ourselves to seek our highest potential as human beings.

Eckhart Tolle's Findhorn Retreat: Stillness Amidst the World. unabr. ed. Eckhart Tolle. 4 CDs. (Running Time: 3 hrs. 30 mins. 0 sec.). (ENG.). 2005. audio compact disk 24.95 (978-1-57731-508-7(1)) Pub: New Wrld Lib. Dist(s): PerseuPGW
Best-selling author and spiritual guide Eckhart Tolle led a remarkable two-day retreat at Findhorn, Scotland, a community on the leading edge of personal and global transformation. His weekend talks, captured on audio, create a deeply moving experience for listeners. Speaking on the subject of stillness, which he describes as a doorway into the Now and to true personal enlightenment, Tolle shows listeners how to find stillness in the present moment and enter a deeper dimension of peace and fulfillment.

Eclipse. (ENG.). 2007. (978-1-60339-043-9(X)); cd-rom & audio compact disk (978-1-60339-044-6(8)) Listenr Digest.

Eclipse. abr. ed. Richard North Patterson. Read by Peter Francis James. (Running Time: 7 hrs. 0 mins. 0 sec.). (ENG.). 2009. audio compact disk 29.95 (978-1-4272-0611-4(2)) Pub: Macmill Audio. Dist(s): Macmillan

Eclipse. unabr. ed. Stephenie Meyer. Read by Ilyana Kadushin. (Running Time: 58980 sec.). (Twilight Saga: No. 3). (ENG.). (J). (gr. 7-12). 2007. audio compact disk 57.00 (978-0-7393-5616-6(X), Listening Lib) Pub: Random Audio Pubg. Dist(s): Random

Eclipse. unabr. ed. Stephenie Meyer. Read by Ilyana Kadushin. 13 CDs. (Twilight Saga: No. 3). (YA). (gr. 7-12). 2007. audio compact disk 80.00 (978-0-7393-6099-6(X), Listening Lib) Pub: Random Audio Pubg. Dist(s): Random

Eclipse. unabr. ed. Richard North Patterson. Read by Peter Francis James. 2 MP3-CDs. (Running Time: 14 hrs.). 2009. 59.95 (978-0-7927-6166-2(9), Chivers Sound Lib); 74.95 (978-0-7927-6167-9(7), Chivers Sound Lib); audio compact disk 99.95 (978-0-7927-6000-9(X), Chivers Sound Lib) AudioGO.

Eclipse. unabr. ed. Richard North Patterson. Read by Peter Francis James. 11 CDs. (Running Time: 13 hrs. 30 mins. 0 sec.). (ENG.). 2009. audio compact disk 39.95 (978-1-4272-0609-1(0)) Pub: Macmill Audio. Dist(s): Macmillan

Eclipse. unabr. collector's ed. Alan Moorehead. Read by Bill Kelsey. 8 cass. (Running Time: 12 hrs.). 1990. 64.00 (978-0-7366-1715-4(9), 2556) Books on Tape.
Eclipse was the code name given by the Allies to their last operation of the war in Europe - the occupation of Germany. Alan Moorehead's original intention was to chronicle the collapse of German Europe sociologically & politically, psychologically & even emotionally. He was after atmosphere more than fact, especially since Eclipse was written too soon after the fact for responsible history. In the final tally, Eclipse is a commentary. Starting with the collapse in Italy, Moorehead advances through France, the Rhine, finally into the heart of Germany where the last Nazis were finally extirpated.

Eclipse Bay. Jayne Ann Krentz. Read by Mary Peiffer. (Eclipse Bay Ser.: Vol. 1). 2001. audio compact disk 64.00 (978-0-7366-7507-9(8)) Books on Tape.

Eclipse Bay. abr. ed. Jayne Ann Krentz. Read by Joyce Bean. (Running Time: 6 hrs.). (Eclipse Bay Ser.: Vol. 1). 2007. 39.25 (978-1-4233-3590-0(2), 9781423335900, BADLE); 24.95 (978-1-4233-3589-4(9), 9781423335894, BAD) Brilliance Audio.

Eclipse Bay. abr. ed. Jayne Ann Krentz. Read by Joyce Bean. (Running Time: 6 hrs.). (Eclipse Bay Ser.: Vol. 1). 2007. 39.25 (978-1-4233-3588-7(0), 9781423335887, Brlnc Audio MP3 Lib); 24.95 (978-1-4233-3587-0(2), 9781423335870, Brilliance MP3) Brilliance Audio.

Eclipse Bay. abr. ed. Jayne Ann Krentz. Read by Joyce Bean. (Running Time: 6 hrs.). (Eclipse Bay Ser.: Vol. 1). 2008. audio compact disk 14.99 (978-1-4233-6231-9(4), 9781423362319, BCD Value Price) Brilliance Audio.

Eclipse Bay. unabr. ed. Jayne Ann Krentz. Read by Mary Peiffer. 7 cass. (Running Time: 10 hrs. 30 mins.). (Eclipse Bay Ser.: Vol. 1). 2001. 56.00 (978-0-7366-6039-6(9)) Books on Tape.
A rich girl & the town's bad boy jointly inherit an old house & must now determine who is trying to kill them.

Eclipse Bay. unabr. ed. Jayne Ann Krentz. Read by Joyce Bean. (Running Time: 10 hrs.). (Eclipse Bay Ser.: Vol. 1). 2009. 39.97 (978-1-4233-8672-8(8), 9781423386728, Brlnc Audio MP3 Lib); 24.99 (978-1-4233-8671-1(X), 9781423386711, Brilliance MP3); 39.97 (978-1-4233-8674-2(4), 9781423386742, BADLE); 24.99 (978-1-4233-8673-5(6), 9781423386735, BAD); audio compact disk 87.97 (978-1-4233-8670-4(1), 9781423386704, BriAudCD Unabrid); audio compact disk 29.99 (978-1-4233-8669-8(8), 9781423386698) Brilliance Audio.

Eclipse Bay: Eclipse Bay, Dawn in Eclipse Bay, Summer in Eclipse Bay. abr. ed. Jayne Ann Krentz. Read by Joyce Bean. (Running Time: 18 hrs.). (Eclipse Bay Ser.: Vols. 1-3). 2008. audio compact disk 34.95 (978-1-4233-6213-5(6), 9781423362135, BACD) Brilliance Audio.

Eclipse of Fatherhood: Society's Assault on Manhood. 1 cass. (Running Time: 1 hr.). 2003. 13.95 (978-1-932631-49-4(6)); 13.95 (978-1-932631-50-0(X)) Ascensn Pr.

Eclipse of the Supernatural in Religious Life. Brian Mullady. 1 cass. (National Meeting of the Institute, 1995 Ser.). 4.00 (95N3) IRL Chicago.

Eclipses. Eugene Moore. 1 cass. (Running Time: 90 min.). 1984. 8.95 (241) Am Fed Astrologers.

Eclipses. Sandra L. Serio. 1 cass. 1992. 8.95 (1088) Am Fed Astrologers.

Eclipses & Occultations. Rose Lineman. 1 cass. 8.95 (441) Am Fed Astrologers.

Eco-Busters - Environmental Law Enforcement. Hosted by Nancy Pearlman. 1 cass. (Running Time: 29 min.). 10.00 (316) Educ Comm CA.

Eco-Ethics & Sustainability - Dr. Donald Conray, Ms. Faith Sand, & Rev. Al Cohen. Hosted by Nancy Pearlman. 1 cass. (Running Time: 29 min.). 10.00 (1007) Educ Comm CA.

Eco-Hysteria: A Scientist Examines the Global Warming Hypothesis. Jay L. Wile. (ENG.). 2008. audio compact disk 8.00 (978-1-932012-93-4(1)) Apologia Educ.

Ecohysteria. 2006. audio compact disk 7.20 (978-1-932012-70-5(2)) Apologia Educ.

Ecological Intelligence: How Knowing the Hidden Impacts of What We Buy Can Change Everything. abr. ed. Daniel Goleman. Read by Daniel Goleman. (Running Time: 5 hrs. 0 mins. 0 sec.). (ENG.). 2009. audio compact disk 24.95 (978-1-4272-0738-8(0)) Pub: Macmill Audio. Dist(s): Macmillan

Ecological Intelligence: How Knowing the Hidden Impacts of What We Buy Can Change Everything. unabr. ed. Daniel Goleman. Read by Daniel Goleman. (Running Time: 8 hrs. 30 mins. 0 sec.). (ENG.). 2009. audio compact disk 39.95 (978-1-4272-0685-5(6)) Pub: Macmill Audio. Dist(s): Macmillan

Ecological Picolo see Picolo-Ecolo

Ecological Ranching & Race Relations. Hosted by Nancy Pearlman. 1 cass. (Running Time: 28 min.). 10.00 (525) Educ Comm CA.

Ecological Vision. unabr. ed. Fritjof Capra. 1 cass. (Running Time: 1 hr.). 1984. 11.00 (03002) Big Sur Tapes.

Ecology & Health. University of Iowa, CEEDE Staff. 1 cass. (Neighbors & Friends Ser.). (SPA.). (YA). (gr. 7-12). 1988. 8.95 (978-0-7836-1161-7(7), 8103); 8.95 (978-0-7836-1160-0(9), 8102); 8.95 (978-0-7836-1159-4(5), 8101); 8.95 (978-0-7836-1158-7(7), 8100); 8.95 (978-0-7836-1156-3(0), 8098) Triumph Learn.
Stories told in English about everyday problems & situations.

Ecology & the Environment: A Look at Ecosystems of the World. Amy L. Tickle. (Alliance: the Michigan State University Textbook Series of Theme-Based Content Instruction for ESL/EFL). (C). 1996. pap. bk. 15.00 (978-0-472-00256-6(2), 00256) U of Mich Pr.

Ecology Awareness. Eldon Taylor. 1 cass. (Running Time: 62 min.). (Inner Talk Ser.). 16.95 incl. script. (978-1-55978-618-8(3), 53868F) Progress Aware Res.
Soundtrack - Brook with underlying subliminal affirmations.

Ecology Center of Southern California. Hosted by Nancy Pearlman. 1 cass. (Running Time: 29 min.). 10.00 (404) Educ Comm CA.

Ecology Smarts by Dancing Beetle. Perf. by Eugene Ely. 1 cass. (J). 1995. 10.00 Erthviibz.
Ecology, science, myth & nature sounds come together when Ms. Seahorse & the spunky musical humans read & sing with Dancing Beetle.

Economic & Financial Crimes see Delitos Economicos y Financieros en la Empresa Publica y Privada

Economic & Financial Crimes. Danilo Lugo. Read by Danilo Lugo. (Running Time: 1 hr.). (C). 2003. 14.95 (978-1-60083-306-9(3), Audiofy Corp) Iofy Corp.

***Economic & Political Concepts.** unabr. ed. Various Authors. (Running Time: 1 hr. 30 mins.). (GetAbstract Ser.). 2009. 78.00 (978-1-4417-3370-2(1)); audio compact disk 80.00 (978-1-4417-3367-2(1)) Blckstn Audio.

Economic Consequences of Price Inflation. John Chamberlain et al. 1 cass. (Running Time: 1 hr. 25 min.). 12.95 (285) J Norton Pubs.

Economic Consequences of the Peace. John Maynard Keynes. Read by Anais 9000. 2008. 27.95 (978-1-60112-206-3(3)) Babblebooks.

Economic Corollaries of the Axiom. John Robbins. 1 cass. (Introduction to Economics Ser.: No. 4). 5.00 Trinity Found.

Economic Crisis. Milton Friedman. Interview with William F. Buckley, Jr. 1 CD. (Running Time: 54 MINS.). 2005. audio compact disk 12.95 (978-1-57970-223-6(6), C32083D) J Norton Pubs.

Economic Crisis?, What Will Be the Next. unabr. ed. Murray Newton Rothbard. 1 cass. (Running Time: 52 min.). 12.95 (360) J Norton Pubs.

Economic Determinism & the Conspiracy Theory of History Revisited. unabr. ed. Murray Newton Rothbard. 2 cass. (Running Time: 1 hr. 54 min.). 19.95 (211) J Norton Pubs.
Discusses the history of economic determinism & the various conspiracy theories & examines the relationship between economics & history.

Economic Development Finance Programs. Read by Norman L. Oakes. 1 cass. 1990. 20.00 (AL-93) PA Bar Inst.

Economic Facts & Fallacies. unabr. ed. Thomas Sowell. Read by Jeff Riggenbach. (Running Time: 36000 sec.). 2008. 59.95 (978-1-4332-4534-3(5)); audio compact disk 29.95 (978-1-4332-4536-7(1)); audio compact disk & audio compact disk 80.00 (978-1-4332-4535-0(3)) Blckstn Audio.

Economic Growth: How to Foster it - How to Destroy it. M. Northrup Buechner. 1 cass. (Running Time: 1 hr. 30 min.). 1997. 13.95 (978-1-56114-388-7(X), DB45C) Second Renaissance.
A clarifying analysis of the policies that destroy economic growth in America.

Economic Liberties & the Constitution. Bernard Siegan. 1 cass. (Running Time: 60 min.). 1987. 9.95 (978-0-945999-07-2(0)) Independent Inst.
The Constitution's Defense of Property Rights & Economic Liberties Has Been Undetermined by Erroneous Decisions Based on Political Interests Instead of Justice & Legal Precedent.

Economic Man - An Obituary. Richard M. Salsman. 2 cass. (Running Time: 3 hrs.). 1995. 24.95 Set. (978-1-56114-366-5(9), DS10D) Second Renaissance.
The connection between particular philosophic conceptions of man's nature & economics.

Economic Naturalist's Field Guide: Common Sense Principles for Troubled Times. unabr. ed. Robert H. Frank. (Running Time: 8 hrs. 30 mins. 0 sec.). (ENG.). 2009. 19.99 (978-1-4001-6186-7(X)); audio compact disk 29.99 (978-1-4001-1186-2(2)); audio compact disk 59.99 (978-1-4001-4186-9(9)) Pub: Tantor Media. Dist(s): IngramPubServ

Economic Revolution, Nature of Government. unabr. ed. Robert LeFevre. 1 cass. (Running Time: 1 hr. 52 min.). 12.95 (1009) J Norton Pubs.
A third revolution in the offing; force & fraud in government.

Economic Sanctions Reconsidered. 3rd ed. Gary Clyde Hufbauer et al. 2009. pap. bk. 39.95 (978-0-88132-431-0(0)) Peterson Inst.

Economic Strength of the Republic of China. unabr. ed. K. T. Li. 1 cass. (Running Time: 45 min.). 12.95 (417) J Norton Pubs.

Economic Thought of the Roman State-Church. John Robbins. 1 cass. (Conference on Christianity & Roman Catholicism Ser.: No. 8). 5.00 Trinity Found.

Economics. Instructed by Timothy Taylor. 2 cass. (Running Time: 13 hrs.). 2000. 129.95 Teaching Co.

Economics. 3rd ed. Instructed by Timothy Taylor. 18 cass. (Running Time: 18 hrs.). 2005. 199.95 (978-1-59803-124-9(4)); audio compact disk 99.95 (978-1-59803-126-3(0)) Teaching Co.

Economics, Course No. 523. Timothy Taylor. 2 pts., 20 lectures. 84.91 Set. Teaching Co.
Do free markets cause pollution & poverty? How can we fix the trade imbalance with Japan...should we? Does the minimum wage cause unemployment? Is Alan Greenspan more powerful than Bill Clinton & Newt Gingrich? Why is there always so much disagreement among economists? Professor Taylor is the perfect person to explain these & other questions on economics. He starts by describing how economists think making it clear why economists have a different perspective. He goes through 20 lectures explaining micro- & macroeconomics in a way that makes the fundamentals of these complicated topics clear for everyone.

Economics, Pts. I-II. Instructed by Timothy Taylor. 10 pieces. (Running Time: 15 hrs.). (C). 1994. bk. 54.95 (978-1-56585-150-4(1), 523) Teaching Co.

Economics, Pts. I-III. Instructed by Timothy Taylor. 20 CDs. (Running Time: 15 hrs.). (C). 1994. bk. 99.95 (978-1-56585-358-4(X), 523) Teaching Co.

Economics, Vol. 33. Tracy Herrick. 1 cass. (Running Time: 60 min.). (Money Talk Ser.). 1986. 7.95 B & H Comm.
Explains in clear, easy-to-understand terms, how wealth is created & destroyed. The six key principles that underlie every financial & business decision. How to unravel the mysteries of economics.

Economics: Government Budget, Deficit & Trade Policy. Instructed by Timothy Taylor. 2 cass., 4 lectures. (Running Time: 3 hrs.). (SuperStar Teachers Ser.). 19.95 Set. (978-1-56585-145-0(5)) Teaching Co.
The goal of this course is to make you economically literate - to make you absorb, understand & accept or reject the arguments of economists & others who use economic arguments. The four lectures specifically focus on...The Federal Budget, The Deficit, Fiscal Policy, The Federal Reserve, Monetary Policy, The Unemployment-Inflation Tradeoff & Trade Policy.

Economics: HM ClassPrep CD with Test Generator. 4th ed. (gr. 6-12). 2004. audio compact disk (978-0-618-23011-2(4), 3-52020) CENGAGE Learn.

Economics: Norton Media Library. 3rd ed. Joseph E. Stiglitz & Carl E. Walsh. (YA). 2002. audio compact disk (978-0-393-10455-4(9)) Norton.

Economics & Politics of Race. unabr. ed. Thomas Sowell. Read by Robert Morris. 7 cass. (Running Time: 10 hrs.). 1989. 49.95 (978-0-7861-0072-9(9), 1067) Blckstn Audio.
Using an international framework to analyze a group of differences, Sowell has pioneered a new approach for pursuing his important studies. His goal is to utilize historical experience & empirical data to determine how much of each of the racial groups' economic fate has been determined by the surrounding society & how much by internal patterns that follow the same group around the world.

Economics & Politics of the Carter Administration. unabr. ed. Murray Newton Rothbard. 1 cass. (Running Time: 46 mins.). 12.95 (970) J Norton Pubs.

Economics & Rational Self-Interest. Richard M. Salsman. 4 cass. (Running Time: 5 hrs. 30 min.). 1996. 49.95 Set. (978-1-56114-433-4(9), DS12D) Second Renaissance.
Economics & the proper understanding of man, knowledge & value.

Economics & the Public Purpose. unabr. ed. John Kenneth Galbraith. 12.95 (40108) J Norton Pubs.
The problems of our modern consumer economy & the need to realign a system directed to the public interest.

Economics & the Public Purpose (audio CD) ed. Interview. John Kenneth Galbraith. Interview with Heywood Hale Broun. 1 CD. (Running Time: 55 min.). (Heywood Hale Broun Ser.). 2007. audio compact disk 12.95 (978-1-57970-456-8(5), C40108D, Audio-For) J Norton Pubs.

Economics & the Theory of Value, The Nature Of. unabr. ed. Percy L. Greaves, Jr. 1 cass. (Running Time: 1 hr. 29 min.). 12.95 (153) J Norton Pubs.
Focuses on the economics of Austrian economist Ludwig von Mises. It presents his basis for studying economics, compares the Misesian subjective theory of value with the Marxian labor theory of value, & cites laws of human action which govern economic exchange.

Economics in One Lesson. Henry Hazlitt. 5 cass. (Running Time: 90 min.). 2001. 39.95 Set. (DH41W) Second Renaissance.

Economics in One Lesson. unabr. ed. Henry Hazlitt. Read by Jeff Riggenbach. 5 cass. (Running Time: 7 hrs.). 1996. 39.95 (978-0-7861-0953-1(X), 1730) Blckstn Audio.
Explains basic truths about economics & the economic fallacies responsible for unemployment, inflation, high taxes & recession. Writes about key classical liberal thinkers like John Locke, Adam Smith, Thomas Jefferson, John Stuart Mill, Alexis de Tocqueville & Herbert Spencer.

Economics in One Lesson. unabr. ed. Henry Hazlitt. Read by Jeff Riggenbach. 6 CDs. (Running Time: 7 hrs.). 2000. audio compact disk 48.00 (978-0-7861-9917-4(2), 1730) Blckstn Audio.

Economics in One Lesson. unabr. ed. Henry Hazlitt. 1 cass. (Running Time: 1 hr. 1 min.). 12.95 (106) J Norton Pubs.
The art of economics, Hazlitt contends consists in looking not merely at the immediate but at the longer run effects of any action or policy; in tracing the consequences of that policy not merely for one group but for all groups. On the other side of the tape Prof. Rogge refutes the charge that a free society would be controlled by private monopolies.

Economics in One Lesson. unabr. ed. Eilen G. Purdy. Ed. by Mike Hassell. Narrated by Louis Rukeyser. 2 cass. (Running Time: 75 min. per cass.). Dramatization. (YA). (gr. 10 up). 1988. 17.95 (978-0-938935-45-2(3), 10230) Knowledge Prod.
Economics in One Lesson has been called "the shortest & surest way to understand basic economics." And now, for the first time, Henry Hazlitt's masterpiece is available on audio cassette, complete with the background story of the author, his book, & how it came to be a modern classic. Henry Hazlitt's Economics in One Lesson was first published in 1946. This was just ten years after John Maynard Keynes' General Theory of Employment, Interest & Money had revolutionized economic thinking. But Hazlitt saw many fallacies in the conventional wisdom of his day, including fallacies in Keynes' thinking & other fallacies that had persisted for centuries.

Economics in One Lesson: The Shortest & Surest Way to Understand Basic Economics. unabr. ed. Henry Hazlitt. Read by Jeff Riggenbach. (Running Time: 7 hrs. 0 mins.). 2009. audio compact disk 19.95 (978-1-4332-7246-2(6)) Blckstn Audio.

Economics of a Free Society. unabr. ed. Nathaniel Branden. 1 cass. (Running Time: 59 min.). 12.95 (574) J Norton Pubs.
Basic principles of exchange - Division of labor - The mechanism of a free market - Politics & wealth - "The pyramid of ability".

Economics of Crisis. unabr. collector's ed. Eliot Janeway. Read by James Cunningham. 8 cass. (Running Time: 12 hrs.). 1978. 64.00 (978-0-7366-0107-8(4), 1115) Books on Tape.
Discusses policy for management of our economy in World War II. Recalling not only that we were shifting almost overnight from a peace to war footing, & also that we had just completed 8 years of grinding depression, managerial tasks necessarily were controversial.

Economics of Fantasy: Rape in Twentieth-Century Literature. Sharon Stockton. 2006. audio compact disk 9.95 (978-0-8142-9094-1(9)) Pub: Ohio St U Pr. Dist(s): Chicago Distribution Ctr

Economist on Wall Street: Notes on the Sanctity of Gold, the Value of Money, the Security of Investments, & Other Delusions. unabr. ed. Peter L. Bernstein. Read by Sean Pratt. (Running Time: 8 hrs. 30 mins.). (ENG.). 2008. 29.98 (978-1-59659-317-6(2), GildAudio) Pub: Gildan Media. Dist(s): HachBkGrp

Economy & Taxation, Set. unabr. ed. David Ricardo. Read by Robert L. Halvorson. 2 cass. (Running Time: 180 min.). 14.95 (83) Halvorson Assocs.

Economy of Love. P Ferrini. audio compact disk 16.95 (978-1-879159-56-3(2)) Heartways Pr.

Econopower: How a New Generation of Economists Is Transforming the World. unabr. ed. Mark Skousen. Read by Jeff Riggenbach. (Running Time: 30600 sec.). 2008. 54.95 (978-1-4332-2853-7(X)); audio compact disk & audio compact disk 29.95 (978-1-4332-2857-5(2)); audio compact disk & audio compact disk 60.00 (978-1-4332-2854-4(8)) Blckstn Audio.

Ecosystems. Steck-Vaughn Staff. 2002. (978-0-7398-6219-3(7)) SteckVau.

***Ecosystems: CD add-on Set.** Perf. by Millmark Education Staff. (ConceptLinks Ser.). 2009. audio compact disk 50.00 (978-1-61618-342-4(X)) Millmark Educ.

***Ecosystems Audio CD.** Perf. by Millmark Education Staff. (ConceptLinks Ser.). 2007. audio compact disk 28.00 (978-1-4334-0005-6(7)) Millmark Educ.

***Ecosystems SB1 Audio CD Populations & Communities.** Perf. by Millmark Education Staff. (Content Literacy Libraries Ser.). 2008. audio compact disk (978-1-4334-0388-0(9)) Millmark Educ.

***Ecosystems SB2 Audio CD Food Chains & Food Webs.** Perf. by Millmark Education Staff. (Content Literacy Libraries Ser.). 2008. audio compact disk (978-1-4334-0389-7(7)) Millmark Educ.

***Ecosystems SB3 Audio CD Energy Flow & Use.** Perf. by Millmark Education Staff. (Content Literacy Libraries Ser.). 2008. audio compact disk (978-1-4334-0390-3(0)) Millmark Educ.

***Ecosystems SB4 Audio CD Changing & Conserving.** Perf. by Millmark Education Staff. (Content Literacy Libraries Ser.). 2008. audio compact disk (978-1-4334-0391-0(9)) Millmark Educ.

Ecotourism in Suriname & Barbados with Anna Harlowe, Lynn Cason & Peter Rothholtz. Hosted by Nancy Pearlman. 1 cass. (Running Time: 29 min.). 10.00 (1204) Educ Comm CA.

Ecouter pour s'exprimer: Listening, Conversation & Composition in a Cultural Context - Student Tapes. Patrick Blanche. 1996. bk. (978-0-07-005861-3(X)) McGraw.

Ecoutez Bien Messieurs. Sacha Guitry. 1 cass. (FRE.). 1995. 21.95 (1721-LQP) Olivia & Hill.
Sacha Guitry calls this short play a "divertissement." A discarded mistress leaves her actor companion a note saying that she plans to kill him while he is on stage. When she interrupts the performance the audience is confused as to whether what they are seeing is real or part of the play. Brilliantly interpreted by Guitry & a small cast.

Ecstasies. James Broughton. 1 cass. 1986. 9.95 SPD-Small Pr Dist.

Ecstasy: Music for Tantra. Kelly Howell. 2000. audio compact disk 14.95 (978-1-881451-65-5(8)) Brain Sync.

Ecstasy: Supercharge Love & Sexuality. unabr. ed. Kelly Howell. 1 cass. (Running Time: 60 min.). 1993. 11.95 (978-1-881451-12-9(7)) Brain Sync.
Experience a euphoric rush of "releasing" & exaltation as endorphins flood into your system. This rapturous state of delight removes deeply entrenched inhibitions & fears & transports listeners to a realm of sensual inspiration.

Ecstasy & Education. unabr. ed. George Leonard. 1 cass. (Running Time: 90 min.). 1970. 11.00 Big Sur Tapes.

Ecstasy Business. unabr. collector's ed. Richard Condon. Read by Richard Green. 6 cass. (Running Time: 9 hrs.). 1988. 48.00 (978-0-7366-1283-8(1), 2192) Books on Tape.
Satirical novel of Hollywood, from the author of "Prizzi's Honor" & "The Manchurian Candidate".

Ecstasy Is a New Frequency Set: Teachings of The Light Institute. abr. ed. Chris Griscom. Read by Chris Griscom. 4 cass. (Running Time: 4 hrs. 33 min.). 1998. bk. 32.00 (978-0-9623696-6-7(7)) Light Inst Pr.
Multi-incarnational exploration; clearing imprints from the body & exploring themes such as depression, fear, drug abuse & disease.

Ecstasy of Not Being Anybody. abr. ed. Scott Morrison. 1 cass. (Running Time: 1 hr.). 1998. 7.50 (978-1-882496-14-3(0)) Twnty Frst Cntry Ren.
Letting go of the pretense & the burden of imagining there is something incomplete or lacking, that there is something wrong with you, & compensating by the endless process of trying to be somebody.

Ecstasy of Victory: Joshua 6:1-20. Ed Young. 1985. 4.95 (978-0-7417-1449-7(3), A0449) Win Walk.

***Ecstasy Unveiled.** unabr. ed. Larissa Ione. (Running Time: 13 hrs.). (Demonica Ser.). (ENG.). 2011. 24.98 (978-1-60941-478-8(0)) Pub: Hachet Audio. Dist(s): HachBkGrp

Ecstatic Moment. unabr. ed. Paul Ferrini. Read by Paul Ferrini. 1 cass. (Running Time: 90 min.). (Christ Mind Talks & Workshops Ser.). 1997. audio compact disk 10.00 (978-1-879159-27-3(9)) Heartways Pr.
A workshop given at Agape International Center of Truth in May 1997.

Ecstatic Sex: Breathing Exercises for Heightened Pleasure & Deeper Intimacy. Gay Hendricks. 1 CD. (Running Time: 1 hr. 15 mins.). 2004. audio compact disk 15.95 (978-1-59179-139-3(1), W774D) Sounds True.

ECT-Electro-Convulsive Therapy: Program from the Award Winning Public Radio Series. Interview. Hosted by Peter Kramer. 1 CD. (Running Time: 1 Hour). 2005. audio compact disk 21.95 (978-1-932479-41-6(4), LCM 373) Lichtenstein Creat.
Electroshock therapy: It's a charged topic. Is it something out of Frankenstein, or a modern medical miracle? Research shows today's electroconvulsive therapy is the quickest, most effective way to treat major depression. But there are risks; for one, nearly everyone experiences memory loss. We'll investigate the very real pros and cons of electroconvulsive therapy. With Oscar-nominated actress Marsha Mason reading the work of Sylvia Plath.

Ecume des Jours. Boris Vian. Read by A. Faraoun & C. Deis. 4 cass. (FRE.). 1991. 34.95 (1396-VSL) Olivia & Hill.
A love story between Colin & Chloe, two characters who live in a world of fantasy where everyday life becomes magical through the distortion of feelings, situations & things.

Ecumenical Church of the Third Millennium. Perf. by John Vennari. 1 cass. (Running Time: 90 mins.). 7.00 (20206) Cath Treas.
This lecture demonstrates that we are now only in the early stages of the post-Vatican II revolution. There are more radical, ecumenical changes to come that Catholics must be made aware of - including the "permission" for a single Church to be owned & used by Catholics & non-Catholics. Answers some of the false tenets of ecumenism. Learn what is in store in the future.

Ecumenical Journey. Edward C. Casey. 3 cass. (Running Time: 4 hrs. 11 min.). 1994. 27.95 Set. (RAH322) Alba Hse Comns.
A remarkable discussion starter as well as primer on developing ecumenical spirit & conduct by one of the church's leading authorities on the subject. Must hearing for all priests & those interested in ecumenism.

Ecumenism: The One Mediator, the Saints & Mary - A Lutheran-Roman Catholic Dialogue. Fred Jelly & John Reuman. 2 cass. (Running Time: 2 hrs.). 1993. 14.95 Set. (TAH297) Alba Hse Comns.
This insightful dialogue presents Catholic & Lutheran positions on Christ the One Mediator & Mary & the Saints. It places in relief the Salient Lutheran & Roman Catholic convergences & differences in belief & practice.

Ed Fox. Ed. by Dian Hanson. (ENG., 2008. 39.99 (978-3-8228-4507-3(8)) Pub: Taschen DEU. Dist(s): IngramPubServ

Ed Meese: Irresponsible Conduct of the Independent Counsel. 1 cass. (Running Time: 1 hr.). 10.95 (NP-88-07-25, HarperThor) HarpC GBR.

Ed Miller: Border Background. 1 cass. 9.98 (C-115) Folk-Legacy.
Songs of the Scots folksong revival by a fine Scottish singer.

Ed Miller: Home & Away. 1 cass. 9.98 (C-517) Folk-Legacy.
Songs of Scotland by a fine Scottish singer who now lives in Texas.

Ed Miller: Life at the Cactus Cafe. 1 cass., 1 CD. 9.98 (C-5172); audio compact disk 14.98 CD. (CD-5172) Folk-Legacy.
"Scottish Songs, None Too Serious," by an excellent singer.

Ed Miller: Scottish Voice. 1 cass., 1 CD. 9.98 (C-546); audio compact disk 14.98 CD. (CD-546) Folk-Legacy.
Scottish songs, old & new, by a man who sings from the heart.

Ed Ochester. unabr. ed. Read by Ed Ochester. 1 cass. (Running Time: 29 min.). 1985. 10.00 New Letters.
Pennsylvania poet Ed Ochester here reads from Weehawken Ferry.

Ed Roberts: Wheelchair Genius. Steven E. Brown. (J). (gr. 4-7). 2006. audio compact disk 20.00 (978-1-931145-27-5(X)) Institute Disabilty.

Ed Trickett: Gently Down the Stream of Time. 1 cass. 9.98 (C-64) Folk-Legacy.
Thoughtful & moving "cycle of life" program.

Ed Trickett: People Like You. 1 cass. 9.98 (C-92) Folk-Legacy.
Nicely varied program of excellent material, with Barton & Para.

Ed Trickett: The Telling Takes Me Home. 1 cass. 9.98 (C-46) Folk-Legacy.
A fine program of old & new songs.

Ed Young & Craig Reynolds. Ed Young. 1995. 4.95 (978-0-7417-2043-6(4), 1043) Win Walk.

Edden Hammons Collection Vol. 2: The Legendary West Virginia Fiddler from 1947 Field Recordings. Instructed by John Cuthbert. Prod. by Danny Williams. 2 vols. (West Virginia University Press Sound Archives Ser.: Vol. 2). 2001. audio compact disk 24.95 (978-0-937058-54-1(8)) Pub: West Va U Pr. Dist(s): Chicago Distribution Ctr

Eddie Cantor, Set. 2 cass. (Running Time: 2 hrs.). vinyl bd. 10.95 (978-1-57816-048-8(0), EC2401) Audio File.
The show business legend with wonderful guest stars. Commercials for Bristol Myers, Pabst Blue Ribbon Beer. "March 7, 1945" Harry Von Zell entered his child in a baby picture contest, but submitted Cantor's baby photo instead of his son's & they land in jail for mail fraud! "March 14, 1945" Cantor, Von Zell & the baby are in jail as Eddie's lawyer, the Russian, tries all kinds of legal maneuvers. "January 30, 1947" It's Eddie Cantor's 55th birthday & to celebrate the occasion he wants to start a new radio network. On hand to extend birthday greetings & to help with the new venture are guests Jack Benny, Peter Lind Hayes & Ralph Edwards. "March 6, 1946" Eddie's special guest is Al Jolson as the two great entertainers exchange stories on how they met to prove who is the older.

Eddie Cantor Radio Show. 2 episodes on 1 cas. (Running Time: 60 min. per cass.). 1998. 7.98 Boxed set. (4337); audio compact disk 15.98 CD Boxed set. (4338) Radio Spirits.
Never-before released shows include: "Cantor Loves Lucy" & "All Star Show".

Eddie Cantor Radio Show; Chase & Sanborn Radio Show. collector's ed. Prod. by Brian Gari. 4 CDs. (Running Time: 4 hrs.). 2001. bk. 29.99 (4419) Radio Spirits.
Digitally remastered shows form 1931 through 1933. Features rare live versions of Eddie's movie songs as well as songs he introduced but never recorded.

Eddie Cantor Radio Show 1942-1943. 3 cass. 1994. 23.95 (978-1-887958-05-9(3)) B Gari.
Old time radio.

Eddie Fantastic, Set. abr. ed. Chris Heimerdinger. 2 cass. 11.98 (978-1-55503-412-2(8), 0700843) Covenant Comms.

Eddie Kantar Teaches Modern Bridge Defence: Interactive CD-ROM Edition. Eddie Kantar. 1999. audio compact disk 34.95 (978-1-894154-09-3(6)) Master Pt Pr CAN.

Eddie Munster aka Butch Patrick. Helen Darras. Read by Butch Patrick. 2007. 29.95 (978-1-933918-27-3(6)) Bloomimg Twig Bks.

Eddie Munster aka Butch Patrick: The Hollywood-a Should-a Could-a Years. Helen Darras. Read by Butch Patrick. 2007. 29.95 (978-1-933918-28-0(4)) Bloomimg Twig Bks.

***Eddie Palmieri - Hot Salsa ... Caliente!** Eddie Palmieri. (ENG.). 2010. pap. bk. 16.99 (978-1-4234-9767-7(8), 1423497678) H Leonard.

Eddie Rickenbacker: Boy Pilot & Racer. Kathryn Cleven Sisson. Read by Patrick G. Lawlor. (Running Time: 7200 sec.). (Young Patriots Ser.). (J). (gr. 4-7). 2007. 22.95 (978-1-4332-0153-0(4)); audio compact disk 24.00 (978-1-4332-0154-7(2)) Blckstn Audio.

Eddie Rickenbacker: Boy Pilot & Racer. unabr. ed. Kathryn Cleven Sisson. Read by Patrick G. Lawlor. (Young Patriots Ser.). (J). 2007. 34.99 (978-1-60252-636-5(2)) Find a World.

Eddie Signwriter: A Novel. unabr. ed. Adam Schwartzman. (Running Time: 10 hrs. 30 mins.). 2010. 29.95 (978-1-4417-2676-6(4)); 65.95 (978-1-4417-2672-8(1)); audio compact disk 34.95 (978-1-4417-2675-9(6)); audio compact disk 100.00 (978-1-4417-2673-5(X)) Blckstn Audio.

Eddy L. Harris. unabr. ed. Eddy L. Harris. 1 cass. (Running Time: 29 min.). (New Letters on the Air Ser.). 1992. 10.00 (050892) New Letters.
In his latest book, "Native Stranger: A Black American's Journey into the Heart of Africa," Harris tells of his year-long trek around the African continent.

Eddys. Ed. by Robert A. Monroe. 1 cass. (Running Time: 30 min.). (Meta Music Ser.). 1985. 12.95 (978-1-56102-209-0(8)) Inter Indus.
A cue to the transitory, the spiral energy formed by the experience of thoughts or events, which still echo uniquely within the private reality of the listener.

Edelweiss, Level 1. (Yamaha Clavinova Connection Ser.). 2004. disk 1.04 (978-0-634-09581-8(1)) H Leonard.

Eden Burning. unabr. ed. Elizabeth Lowell. Read by James Daniels. 6 cass. (Running Time: 9 hrs.). 2002. 29.95 (978-1-58788-261-6(2), 1587882612, BAU); 69.25 (978-1-58788-262-3(0), 1587882620, Unabridge Lib Edns) Brilliance Audio.
Paradise calls to Chase Wilcox. A man of science fascinated by the rebirth of life in the wake of cataclysmic natural upheaval, he is drawn to the lush beauty of the island of Hawaii and the secrets it holds - while escaping the destruction of his own personal world. The island is home to many unexpected wonders, which is why Nicole Ballard could never leave. A research assistant, an artist, a dancer - a tall and stunning redhead who goes by the stage name Pele, goddess of fire - she, too, hides a secret pain, releasing her pent-up sensuality to the accompaniment of native drums before a mesmerized audience. Joined on a scientific project that carries them both into the moist, verdant heart of a tropical wonderland, Nicole and Chase will be forced to confront their own lingering inner darkness, while resisting a newly inflamed need to touch, to give...to care. In the shadow of Mount Kilauea, all restraints will be broken, as emotions flow hot and free as rivers of molten rock. And desire will erupt, as unpredictable and dangerous as the living volcano, transforming the very landscape of their lives.

Eden Burning. unabr. ed. Elizabeth Lowell. Read by James Daniels. (Running Time: 9 hrs.). 2004. 39.25 (978-1-59335-358-2(8), 1593353588, Brlnc Audio MP3 Lib) Brilliance Audio.

Eden Burning. unabr. ed. Elizabeth Lowell. Read by James Daniels. (Running Time: 9 hrs.). 2004. 39.25 (978-1-59710-241-4(5), 1597102415, BADLE); 24.95 (978-1-59710-240-7(7), 1597102407, BAD) Brilliance Audio.

Eden Burning. unabr. ed. Elizabeth Lowell. Read by James Daniels. (Running Time: 9 hrs.). 2010. audio compact disk 29.99 (978-1-4418-3572-7(5), 9781441835727, Bril Audio CD Unabri); audio compact disk 89.97 (978-1-4418-3573-4(3), 9781441835734, BriAudCD Unabrid) Brilliance Audio.

Eden Burning. unabr. ed. Elizabeth Lowell. Read by James Daniels. (Running Time: 9 hrs.). 2004. 24.95 (978-1-59335-030-7(9), 1593350309) Soulmate Audio Bks.

Eden Burning. unabr. collector's ed. Belva Plain. Read by Jeanne Hopson. 10 cass. (Running Time: 15 hrs.). 1985. 80.00 (978-0-7366-1058-2(8), 1985) Books on Tape.
This is the story of two men & one woman. Eden is St. Felice, a lush Caribbean island with extremes of privilege & want. Patrick, the fiery black prime minister, seeks a better life for his people. Francis, scion of a prominent New York family, feels the tug of that other island. & Tee-15 years old when we meet her, wise beyond her years-charged with a passion for life.

Eden Close. collector's unabr. ed. Anita Shreve. Read by Mary Peiffer. 6 cass. (Running Time: 9 hrs.). 2000. 48.00 (978-0-7366-4777-9(5), 5122) Books on Tape.
After many years away, Andrew returns to his hometown to attend his mother's funeral. Unwittingly, he is drawn into the tragic legacy of his childhood friend, the beautiful Eden Close. He recalls the night he was awakened by gunshots & screams from the next farm: Mr. Close was killed & Eden blinded. Now, seventeen years later, Andrew begins to uncover the grisly story. As the truth about Eden's past comes to light, so too does Andrew's strange & blinding attachment to the girl herself.

Eden Close. unabr. ed. Anita Shreve. Read by Mary Peiffer. 6 cass. (Running Time: 9 hrs.). 2001. 24.00 (978-0-7366-4960-5(3)) Books on Tape.
Andrew unravels the layers of thwarted love between a husband, wife & tormented girl in the hometown he left seventeen years ago.

***Eden Diet: You Can Eat Treats, Enjoy Your Food, & Lose Weight.** Rita M. Hancock. (Running Time: 6 hrs. 47 mins. 44 sec.). (ENG.). 2010. 14.99 (978-0-310-58977-8(0)) Zondervan.

***Edexcel Spanish, Set.** Mike Thacker et al. 2008. cd-rom 250.00 (978-0-340-96888-8(5)) Pub: Hodder Edu GBR. Dist(s): Trans-Atl Phila

Edgar Allan Poe. abr. ed. Edgar Allan Poe. Read by Basil Rathbone & Vincent Price. 5 CDs. (Running Time: 360 min.). 2000. audio compact disk 29.95 (978-0-694-52419-8(0)) HarperCollins Pubs.

Edgar Allan Poe. unabr. ed. John Ostrom. 1 cass. (Running Time: 40 min.). 1953. 12.95 (23040) J Norton Pubs.
A re-examination of the legend of Poe & alcohol based on evidence from Poe's correspondence. Issue is taken with the oversimplified portrayal of Poe as a drunkard.

Edgar Allan Poe. unabr. ed. Edgar Allan Poe. Illus. by Edgar Allan Poe. 4 cass. 1999. HarperCollins Pubs.

Edgar Allan Poe. unabr. abr. ed. Edgar Allan Poe. Read by Vincent Price & Basil Rathbone. 4 cass. (Running Time: 6 hrs.). 2000. 25.95 (978-0-694-52403-7(4)) HarperCollins Pubs.

Edgar Allan Poe, 4 cass. unabr. ed. Edgar Allan Poe. Illus. by Edgar Allan Poe. 4 cass. Incl. Fall of the House of Usher. (SBC 106); Gold Bug. (SBC 106); Pit & the Pendulum. Edgar Allan Poe. (SBC 106); Raven. (SBC 106); 1999. 29.95 (978-0-89845-037-8(3), SBC 106) HarperCollins Pubs.

Edgar Allan Poe: James Stewart Reads Edgar Allan Poe. unabr. ed. Edgar Allan Poe. Read by Jimmy Stewart. 1 cass. 12.95 (ECN 057) J Norton Pubs.
Features "The Tell-Tale Heart" & "The Black Cat".

Edgar Allan Poe: Short Stories & Poems. unabr. ed. Edgar Allan Poe. Read by Edward Blake. 2 cass. (Running Time: 1 hr. 41 min.). (Cassette Bookshelf Ser.). 1985. 15.95 Set. (CB 104 CXR, Listening Lib) Random Audio Pubg.
A collection of the masterworks of Poe's bone-chilling, spine-tingling thrillers.

Edgar Allan Poe A Love Story: The Nightmares of Edgar Allan Poe. unabr. ed. Xavier Joseph Carbajal. Perf. by Sherry Jodway & Joe H. Maylea. 3 cass. (Running Time: 3 hrs.). Dramatization. (Works of Edgar Allan Poe). 2000. 24.95 (978-0-9654507-3-7(2), 2222) New Future Pub.
Hilarious, spine-tingling account of Poe's last days & his love for a ghost named Lenore. Also features "The Tell Tale Heart," "The Premature Burial," "Hop-Frog" & twenty rare, never performed works by the Master of horror.

Edgar Allan Poe Set: Short Stories & Poems. unabr. ed. Edgar Allan Poe. Read by Edward Blake. 2 cass. (Running Time: 1 hr. 41 min.). Incl. Bells. 1985. (CB 104CX); Black Cat. 1985. (CB 104CX); Case of M. Valdemar. 1985. (CB 104CX); Cask of Amontillado. 1985. (CB 104CX); Masque of the Red Death. 1985. (CB 104CX); Raven. 1985. (CB 104CX); Tell-Tale Heart. 1985. (CB 104CX); Ulalume. 1985. (CB 104CX); (Cassette Bookshelf Ser.). 1985. 15.98 Library ed. (978-0-8072-3412-9(5), CB 104CX, Listening Lib) Random Audio Pubg.
A collection of the masterworks of Poe's bone-chilling, spine-tingling thrillers. Includes "The Tell-Tale Heart," "The Cask of Amontillado," "The Masque of the Red Death," "Facts in the Case of M. Valdemar," "The Black Cat," "The raven," "Annabel Lee," "Ulalume," & "The Bells."

Edgar Allan Poe Vol. 1: The Tell-Tale Heart, the Pit & the Pendulum, the Sleeper. Short Stories. Edgar Allan Poe. Read by Eddie Albert. Engineer Bob E. Flick. Music by Bob E. Flick. Des. by Adam Mayefsky. 1 CD. (Running Time: 1 hr. 14 mins.). Dramatization. (Edgar Allan Poe Ser.: Vol. 1). 1997. audio compact disk 15.00 (978-1-884214-19-6(3)) Ziggurat Prods.
Classic tales from the eerie, haunted, and wildlytormented world of the Master of Horror thatwill leave you afraid of the dark forever!"The Tell-Tale Heart": After hiding his murder victim underneath the floor boards, aman is tormented by the incessant beating of a "tell-tale" heart."The Pit and the Pendulum": Bear witness to the executioner's dungeon torture as a sharp pendulum swings closer...and closer...and closer!"The Sleeper": A chilling poem recited.

Edgar Allan Poe Vol. 1: The Tell-Tale Heart, the Pit & the Pendulum, the Sleeper. unabr. ed. Short Stories. Edgar Allan Poe. Read by Eddie Albert. Contrib. by Bob E. Flick. Prod. by Bob E. Flick. Des. by Adam Mayefsky. 1 cass. (Running Time: 1 hr. 20 min.). Dramatization. (Gold Ser.: Vol. 1). 1997. 9.99 (978-1-884214-03-5(7)) Ziggurat Prods.

Edgar Allan Poe Vol. 2: The Masque of the Red Death, the Cask of Amontillado, Silence. Short Stories. Edgar Allan Poe. Perf. by Jim Gallant. Engineer Bob E. Flick. Music by Bob E. Flick. Des. by Adam Mayefsky. 1 CD. (Running Time: 51 mins.). Dramatization. (Edgar Allan Poe Ser.: Vol. 2). 2003. audio compact disk 15.00 (978-1-884214-27-1(4)) Ziggurat Prods.
Classic tales from the Master of Horror himself! Includes..."The Masque of the Red Death":With the Red Death plague ravaging society outside, a corrupt prince and a thousand of his privileged subjects indulge in a bizarre masquerade party on the inside?seemingly safe from harm. The party is soon interrupted, however, by a shadowy, masked figure intent on teaching the crowd the meaning of true horror!"The Cask of Amontillado":One man's insults prompt another to plot revenge of the most premeditated sort, making skillful use of a cask of Amontillado wine!"Silence":In this tormented fable, a demon expresses thepain and desolation of a land ruled by silence.

Edgar Allan Poe - Collected Stories & Poems. unabr. ed. Edgar Allan Poe. Read by Ralph Cosham. (YA). 2006. 39.99 (978-1-59895-189-9(0)) Find a World.

***Edgar Allan Poe Audio Collection.** abr. ed. Edgar Allan Poe. Read by Vincent Price & Basil Rathbone. (ENG.). 2003. (978-0-06-079952-6(8), Harper Audio); (978-0-06-074270-6(4), Harper Audio) HarperCollins Pubs.

Edgar Allan Poe Audiobook Collection 1: The Pit & the Pendulum/the Black Cat. Edgar Allan Poe. Perf. by Christopher Aruffo. (ENG.). (YA). 2007. audio compact disk 9.95 (978-0-9761435-5-0(0)) Acoustic Learn.

Edgar Allan Poe Audiobook Collection 1-3: The Black Cat & Other Stories. Short Stories. Edgar Allan Poe. Read by Christopher Aruffo. 3 CDs. (Running Time: 3 hrs. 17 mins.). (YA). 2007. audio compact disk 19.99 (978-0-9800581-0-9(4)) Acoustic Learn.

Edgar Allan Poe Audiobook Collection 2: William Wilson/the Masque of the Red Death. Edgar Allan Poe. Perf. by Christopher Aruffo. (ENG.). (YA). 2007. audio compact disk 9.95 (978-0-9761435-6-7(9)) Acoustic Learn.

Edgar Allan Poe Audiobook Collection 3: The Fall of the House of Usher/the Imp of the Perverse. Edgar Allan Poe. Perf. by Christopher Aruffo. (ENG.). (YA). 2007. audio compact disk 9.95 (978-0-9761435-7-4(7)) Acoustic Learn.

Edgar Allan Poe Audiobook Collection 4: Poe on Poetry. Short Stories. Edgar Allan Poe. Read by Christopher Aruffo. 5 CDs. (Running Time: 5 hrs. 13 mins.). (YA). 2007. audio compact disk 24.95 (978-0-9761435-8-1(5)) Acoustic Learn.

Edgar Allan Poe Audiobook Collection 5: Eureka. Short Stories. Edgar Allan Poe. Read by Christopher Aruffo. 5 CDs. (Running Time: 6 hrs. 6 mins.). (YA). 2007. audio compact disk 29.99 (978-0-9761435-9-8(3)) Acoustic Learn.

Edgar Allan Poe Audiobook Collection 6: Message Found in a Bottle/the Oblong Box. Edgar Allan Poe. Read by Christopher Aruffo. (ENG.). (YA). 2008. audio compact disk 9.95 (978-0-9800581-1-6(2)) Acoustic Learn.

Edgar Allan Poe Audiobook Collection 7: The Cask of Amontillado/the Premature Burial. Narrated by Christopher Aruffo. (Running Time: 66). (ENG.). (C). 2009. audio compact disk 9.95 (978-0-9800581-2-3(0)) Acoustic Learn.

Edgar Allan Poe Audiobook Collection 8: Ligeia/Eleonora. Edgar Allan Poe. Narrated by Christopher Aruffo. (Running Time: 76). (ENG.). (C). 2009. audio compact disk 9.95 (978-0-9800581-3-0(9)) Acoustic Learn.

Edgar Allan Poe Audiobook Collection 9: The Pioneers. Edgar Allan Poe. Narrated by Christopher Aruffo. (ENG.). (C). 2009. audio compact disk 29.99 (978-0-9800581-5-4(5)) Acoustic Learn.

Edgar Allan Poe Collected Stories & Poems. Edgar Allan Poe. Narrated by Ralph Cosham. (Running Time: 23460 sec.). (Unabridged Classics in MP3 Ser.). (ENG.). 2008. audio compact disk 14.95 (978-1-58472-612-8(1), In Aud); audio compact disk 24.00 (978-1-58472-613-5(X), In Aud) Sound Room.

Edgar Allan Poe Collection. Richard Ganci. Edgar Allan Poe. (Famous Short Stories Ser.). 1999. audio compact disk 18.95 (978-1-4105-0134-9(5)) D Johnston Inc.

Edgar Allan Poe Collection. Edgar Allan Poe. Ed. by Jerry Stemach et al. Retold by Richard Ganci. Illus. by Ed Smaron. Contrib. by Ted S. Hasselbring. (J). (gr. 2-3). 2000. 35.00 (978-1-58702-438-2(1)) D Johnston Inc.

Edgar Allan Poe Collection. Edgar Allan Poe. Ed. by Jerry Stemach et al. Retold by Richard Ganci. Illus. by Jeff Ham. Contrib. by Ed Smaron & Ted S. Hasselbring. (Start-to-Finish Books: Vol. 3). 2002. 100.00 (978-1-58702-961-5(8)) D Johnston Inc.

Edgar Allan Poe Collection. abr. ed. Edgar Allan Poe. Ed. by Jerry Stemach et al. Retold by Richard Ganci. Illus. by Jeff Ham. Contrib. by Ed Smaron & Ted S. Hasselbring. (J). (gr. 2-3). 1999. (978-1-893376-46-5(X), F07K2) D Johnston Inc.
On an island off South Carolina, the narrator meets Legrand and his servant Jupiter. Once rich, now poor, Legend develops "grand" ideas of newfound riches when he is "bitten" by a gold bug he finds near a treasure map. The man leads the trio to a skull in a tree below which they unearth the treasure of Captain Kidd.

Edgar Allan Poe Collection 6-8: The Cask of Amontillado & Other Stories. Edgar Allan Poe. Narrated by Christopher Aruffo. (Running Time: 211). (ENG.). (C). 2009. audio compact disk 19.99 (978-0-9800581-4-7(7)) Acoustic Learn.

Edgar Allan Poe Short Stories. Edgar Allan Poe. Read by Edward Blake. 2 cass. 15.95 set. (8147Q) Filmic Archives.
Includes: "The Tell Tale Heart"; "The Cask of Amontillado"; "The Masque of Red Death"; "The Raven"; "Annabel Lee"; "Facts in the Case of M. Valdemar"; "Ulalume"; "The Black Cat"; "The Bells".

Edgar Allan Poe Stories. abr. ed. Poems. Edgar Allan Poe. Perf. by Basil Rathbone. 2 cass. (Running Time: 2 hrs 05 min.). (J). (gr. 9-12). 1998. 18.00 (978-1-55994-091-7(3), CPN 2104) HarperCollins Pubs.

Edgar Allan Poe's Stories & Tales, Vol. II. abr. ed. Short Stories. Edgar Allan Poe. Perf. by St. Charles Players. 2 cass. (Running Time: 1 hrs. 40 mins.). (YA). (gr. 7). 2000. 16.95 (978-1-56994-525-4(X), 313254) Monterey Media Inc.
A cat, seemingly innocent, black as night, chasing the demon within man's worst nature. Four stories & tales. Classic intrigue, suspense, deduction mystery & murder.

Edgar Allan Poe's Stories & Tales I, abr. ed. Short Stories. Edgar Allan Poe. Perf. by St. Charles Players. 2 cass. Dramatization. 1999. 16.95 (FS9-42728) Highsmith.

Edgar Allan Poe's Stories & Tales I, abr. ed. Perf. by St. Charles Players. 2 cass. (Running Time: 2 hrs). (YA). (gr. 6 up). 1998. 16.95

(978-1-56994-500-1(4), 313234, Monterey SoundWorks) Monterey Media Inc.
Whether searching for the buried treasure of Captain Kidd in " "The Gold Bug", seeking revenge in "The cask of Amontillado", entering a web of murder & betrayal from within "The Tell-Tale Heart", or caught in a place of chilling madness in "The Fall of the House of Usher", the words of the master storyteller will thrill & envelop the listener.

Edgar Allan Poe's Tales of Terror. 1 CD. (Running Time: 1 hr. 30 mins.). (Sound Curriculum Ser.). (YA). (gr. 5-12). 2002. audio compact disk 61.00 (978-0-7833-0027-6(1)) T S Klise Co.

Edgar Allen Poe Set: Classic Stories & Poems. unabr. ed. Poems. Edgar Allan Poe. Read by Ralph Cosham. 6 cass. (Running Time: 6 hrs. 30 min.). (Great Authors Ser.). 1997. 34.95 Set, incl. literary notes, author's picture, author's biography, & collector's box. (978-1-883049-73-7(3), Commuters Library) Sound Room.
Eighteen of Poe's best known works ranging from horror to the sublime.

Edgar & Ellen: The Tourist Trap. unabr. ed. Charles Ogden. Read by Ariadne Meyers. (J). 2007. 34.99 (978-1-60252-749-2(0)) Find a World.

***Edgar Bergen & Charlie Mccarthy: Ladies Men.** Perf. by Edgar Bergen & Bette Davis. 2009. audio compact disk 39.98 (978-1-57019-915-8(9)) Radio Spirits.

Edgar Bergen & Charlie McCarthy Show. Read by Edgar Bergen. 3 cass. (Running Time: 3 hrs.). (3-Hour Collectors' Editions Ser.). 2002. 9.98 (978-1-57019-578-5(1), 27824) Radio Spirits.

Edgar Bergen & Charlie McCarthy Show. Perf. by Bette Davis. 1 CD. (Running Time: 1 hr.). (Old-Time Radio Blockbusters Ser.). 2002. audio compact disk 4.98 (978-1-57019-391-0(6), OTR7702) Pub: Radio Spirits. Dist(s): AudioGO

Edgar Bergen & Charlie McCarthy Show. Radio Spirits Staff. Read by Edgar Bergen. 3 CDs. (Running Time: 3 hrs.). (3-Hour Collectors' Editions Ser.). 2005. audio compact disk 9.98 (978-1-57019-579-2(X), 27822) Radio Spirits.

Edgar Bergen & Charlie McCarthy Show. collector's ed. Perf. by Edgar Bergen et al. 1 DVD. (Running Time: 3 hrs.). (TV from Yesteryear Ser.). 2001. bk. 9.98 (7803) Radio Spirits.
Contains three classic television shows and three complete old time radio shows.

Edgar Bergen & Charlie McCarthy Show: Bette Davis. Perf. by Edgar Bergen et al. 1 CD. (Running Time: 1 hr.). (Old-Time Radio Blockbusters Ser.). 2001. audio compact disk 4.98 (7702) Radio Spirits.

Edgar Cayce & the Planets. Emma B. Donath. 1 cass. 8.95 (518) Am Fed Astrologers.

Edgar Cayce on the Akashic Records. Kevin J. Todeschi. (Running Time: 22920 sec.). 2008. audio compact disk 79.95 (978-0-87604-577-0(8)) ARE Pr.

Edgar Cayce on the Millennium: The Famed Prophet Visualizes a Bright New World. unabr. ed. Jess Stearn. Read by Alyssa Bresnahan. 4 cass. (Running Time: 6 hrs.). 2000. 24.95 (978-1-57453-312-5(6)) Audio Lit.

Edgar Cayce on the Millennium Set: The Famed Prophet Visualizes a Bright New World. unabr. ed. Jess Stearn. Read by Alyssa Bresnahan. 4 cass. (Running Time: 6 hrs.). 1999. 24.95 Audio Lit.
More than six decades ago, psychic Edgar Cayce looked forward to the millennium, with hope, not fear. Having predicted many disastrous phenomena, Cayce also believed that humans have the capacity to harness spiritual powers & alter the fate of the world.

Edgar Cayce Whole Health Weight-Loss Plan, Set. Anne E. Hunt. 3 cass. (Running Time: 2 hr. 20 min.). 1991. pap. bk. 29.95 (978-0-87604-263-2(9), 354) ARE Pr.
This remarkable diet plan, based on the Edgar Cayce readings, can reshape the entire you - body, mind & spirit. This unique plan includes the book Weight No More, plus three audiocassettes that contain revealing self-study exercises to help you design a personal strategy to a new self-image.

Edgar Huntly. Charles Brockden Brown. Read by Anais 9000. 2008. 27.95 (978-1-60112-152-3(0)) Babblebooks.

Edgar Scherick see Movie Makers Speak: Producers

Edge. Rick Barrera & Tony Alessandra. Read by Rick Barrera & Tony Alessandra. 6 cass. (Running Time: 5 hrs.). 1993. 79.95 set incl. action guide. (2023) Dartnell Corp.
Get a vital edge over the competition by developing this non-manipulative, "human" approach to selling.

Edge. abr. ed. 2 cass. (Running Time: 4.00). 1999. 29.95 Set. (799PAB) Nightingale-Conant.
More than 750 of the world's most successful competitors tell you how to get "the edge." Dozens of motivating mini-essays & stories describe the lives of these achievers.

Edge. abr. ed. Catherine Coulter. Read by Dick Hill & Sandra Burr. (Running Time: 21600 sec.). (FBI Thriller Ser.: No. 4). 2007. audio compact disk 14.99 (978-1-4233-1364-9(X), 9781423313649, BCD Value Price) Brilliance Audio.

***Edge.** abr. ed. Jeffery Deaver. (Running Time: 6 hrs. 30 mins. 0 sec.). (ENG.). 2010. audio compact disk 29.99 (978-1-4423-3535-6(1)) Pub: S&S Audio. Dist(s): S and S Inc

Edge. unabr. ed. Catherine Coulter. Read by Robert Lawrence. 7 cass. (Running Time: 10 hrs.). (FBI Thriller Ser.: No. 4). 1999. 39.95 (978-1-56740-430-2(8), 1567404308, BAU); 73.25 (978-1-56740-653-5(X), 156740653X, Unabridge Lib Edns) Brilliance Audio.
Baffled by a seemingly supernatural connection to his critically injured sister, an FBI special agent heads to the Oregon coast in search of a more plausible explanation for his sudden ESP, only to discover more puzzling mysteries. FBI agent Ford MacDougal - "Mac" - is recovering from a terrorist car bombing when his sister appears to purposely drive her Porsche off an Oregon cliff. Curiously, Mac felt as if he were in the car with her as she sailed toward the sea, even though he was really in a hospital bed on the other side of the country. By the time Mac arrives in Portland, his sister - Dr. Jilly Bartlett, a medical researcher - has come out of the coma she's been in for four days. But after a few scant hours with her brother, Jilly vanishes without a trace. In searching for her, Mac gets a different story from everyone he encounters. When the local sheriff enlists Mac's aid in a puzzling murder of an elderly resident, Mac little suspects that the case connects to his sister's disappearance. FBI agents Lacey Sherlock and Dillon Savich (last seen in The Target) join Mac to ride shotgun, only to find their search leading from a small town on the Oregon coast to the rain forests of Costa Rica. Together, they must escape relentless pursuers as well as the hostile jungle itself before discovering the true nature of the evil at The Edge.

Edge. unabr. ed. Catherine Coulter. Read by Robert Lawrence. (Running Time: 10 hrs.). (FBI Thriller Ser.: No. 4). 2006. 39.25 (978-1-4233-1362-5(3), 9781423313625, BADLE); 24.95 (978-1-4233-1361-8(5), 9781423313618, BAD); 39.25 (978-1-4233-1360-1(7), 9781423313601, Brlnc Audio MP3 Lib); audio compact disk 24.95 (978-1-4233-1359-5(3), 9781423313595, Brilliance MP3); audio compact disk 36.95 (978-1-4233-1357-1(7), 9781423313571, Bril Audio CD Unabri) Brilliance Audio.

***Edge.** unabr. ed. Jeffery Deaver. Read by Skipp Sudduth. (Running Time: 14 hrs. 30 mins. 0 sec.). (ENG.). 2010. audio compact disk 39.99 (978-1-4423-3537-0(8)) Pub: S&S Audio. Dist(s): S and S Inc

Edge. unabr. ed. Dick Francis. Narrated by Simon Prebble. 8 cass. (Running Time: 11 hrs. 30 mins.). 2000. 71.00 (978-0-7887-3998-9(0), H1077E7) Recorded Bks.
As the journey begins, the passengers look forward to enjoying their adventure & solving the mystery. But meanwhile, a ruthless leader of the racing underworld is hatching his own plans for the Mystery Race. Tor Kelsey, an undercover security agent on the luxurious train, is about to encounter the most perilous challenge of his career.

Edge. unabr. ed. Alan Gibbons. Read by Jerome Pride. 5 CDs. (Running Time: 20100 sec.). (YA). (gr. 7-13). 2002. audio compact disk 63.95 (978-1-74093-322-3(2)) Pub: Bolinda Pubng AUS. Dist(s): Bolinda Pub Inc

Edge, Set. unabr. ed. Catherine Coulter. 8 cass. (FBI Thriller Ser.: No. 4). 1999. 39.95 (FS9-51009) Highsmith.

Edge in Creativity, No. 6. Carl Faber. 1 cass. (Running Time: 90 min.). (Edges Ser.). 1982. 9.50 (978-0-918026-38-5(5)) Perseus Pr.

Edge in Love: Cruelty & Devouring Mo. Carl Faber. 1 cass. (Running Time: 90 min.). (Edges Ser.). 1982. 9.50 (978-0-918026-31-6(8), SR 42-809) Perseus Pr.

Edge in Madness: The Dangerous Opening of the Mind. Carl Faber. 1 cass. (Running Time: 90 min.). (Edges Ser.). 1982. 9.50 (978-0-918026-32-3(6), SR 42-809) Perseus Pr.

Edge in Madness: The Experience of Unbearable Pain. Carl Faber. 1 cass. (Running Time: 90 min.). (Edges Ser.). 1982. 9.50 (978-0-918026-33-0(4), SR 42-809) Perseus Pr.

Edge of Adventure Group Experience Disc Three: Taking the First Steps in Christian Formation. Speeches. Keith Miller & Bruce Larson. Perf. by Keith Miller & Bruce Larson. 2005. bk. 14.95 (978-0-9766211-5-7(0)) Formation Pr.
Keith Miller and Bruce Larson have input in a study course designed for small groups, Sessions 11, 12, 13.

Edge of Adventure Group Experince-Disc One: Taking the First Steps in Christian Formation. 2nd ed. Speeches. Keith Miller & Bruce Larson. Perf. by Keith Miller & Bruce Larson. 2005. bk. Rental 14.95 (978-0-9766211-3-3(4)) Formation Pr.
Keith Miller and Bruce Larson have input in the study course designed for small groups, sessions 1, 2, 3, 4, 5, 6.

Edge of Adventure Grtoup Experience Disc Two: Taking the First Steps in Christian Formation. Speeches. Keith Miller & Bruce Larson. Perf. by Keith Miller & Bruce Larson. 2005. bk. 14.95 (978-0-9766211-4-0(2)) Formation Pr.
Keith Miller and Bruce Larson have input in the study course designed for small groups, sessions 7, 8, 9, 10.

***Edge of Apocalypse.** Tim LaHaye & Craig Parshall. (Running Time: 11 hrs. 5 mins. 6 sec.). (End Ser.). (ENG.). 2010. 24.99 (978-0-310-32630-4(3)) Zondervan.

***Edge of Apocalypse.** unabr. ed. Tim LaHaye & Craig Parshall. (Running Time: 11 hrs. 5 mins. 6 sec.). (End Ser.). (ENG.). 2010. audio compact disk 29.99 (978-0-310-32629-8(X)) Zondervan.

Edge of Battle. Dale Brown. Narrated by Michael McShane. 10 cass. (Running Time: 52200 sec.). (Sound Library). 2006. 84.95 (978-0-7927-4223-4(0), CSL 953); audio compact disk & audio compact disk 49.95 (978-0-7927-4224-1(9), CMP 953) AudioGO.

Edge of Battle. unabr. ed. Dale Brown. Narrated by Michael McShane. 14 CDs. (Running Time: 52200 sec.). (Sound Library). 2006. audio compact disk 112.95 (978-0-7927-4047-6(5), SLD 953) AudioGO.

Edge of Battle. unabr. ed. Dale Brown. Read by Michael Mcshane. 12 CDs. (Running Time: 52200 sec.). 2006. audio compact disk 44.95 (978-0-06-075645-1(4), Harper Audio) HarperCollins Pubs.

***Edge of Battle.** unabr. ed. Dale Brown. Read by Michael Mcshane. (ENG.). 2006. (978-0-06-113038-0(9), Harper Audio); (978-0-06-113037-3(0), Harper Audio) HarperCollins Pubs.

Edge of Danger. Jack Higgins. Narrated by Gerard Doyle. 6 CDs. (Running Time: 6 hrs. 30 mins.). (Sean Dillon Ser.). 2004. audio compact disk 62.00 (978-1-4025-2910-8(4)) Recorded Bks.
The Rashids are a powerful Arab family who pride themselves on financial success and an international reputation. So when they are sidestepped in critical oil-drilling negotiations, they swear an oath of vengeance against the one they hold responsible. Now it¿s up to operative Sean Dillion and a Washington colleague to keep the Rashids from their target - the President of the United States.

Edge of Danger. unabr. ed. Jack Higgins. Narrated by Gerard Doyle. 5 cass. (Running Time: 6 hrs. 30 mins.). (Sean Dillon Ser.). 2001. 48.00 (978-0-7887-5259-9(6)) Recorded Bks.
When a powerful Arab family is sidestepped in oil-drilling negotiations, they swear an oath of destruction against the one they hold responsible - the President of the United States.

Edge of Darkness. unabr. ed. Tim LaHaye & Bob Phillips. Read by Paul Michael. (Running Time: 34200 sec.). (Babylon Rising Ser.: Bk. 4). (ENG.). 2006. audio compact disk 44.95 (978-0-7393-3199-6(X), Random AudioBks) Pub: Random Audio Pubg. Dist(s): Random

Edge of Disaster. unabr. ed. Stephen Flynn. Read by Dick Hill. (Running Time: 7 hrs. 30 mins. 0 sec.). (ENG.). 2007. audio compact disk 19.99 (978-1-4001-5412-8(X)); audio compact disk 59.99 (978-1-4001-3412-0(9)) Pub: Tantor Media. Dist(s): IngramPubServ

Edge of Disaster: Rebuilding a Resilient Nation. unabr. ed. Stephen Flynn. Read by Dick Hill. (Running Time: 7 hrs. 30 mins. 0 sec.). (ENG.). 2007. audio compact disk 29.99 (978-1-4001-0412-3(2)) Pub: Tantor Media. Dist(s): IngramPubServ

Edge of Eternity. abr. ed. Randy C. Alcorn. (Running Time: 21600 sec.). (ENG.). 2008. audio compact disk 24.99 (978-1-934384-11-4(9)) Pub: Treasure Pub. Dist(s): STL Dist NA

Edge of Evil. J. A. Jance. Read by Susanna Burney. (Ali Reynolds Ser.: No. 1). 2006. audio compact disk 29.95 (978-0-7927-3956-2(6), CMP 888) AudioGO.

Edge of Evil. J. A. Jance. Read by Susanna Burney. 7 CDs. (Running Time: 29340 sec.). (Ali Reynolds Ser.: No. 1). 2006. audio compact disk 74.95 (978-0-7927-3881-7(0), SLD 888) AudioGO.

Edge of Evil. abr. unabr. ed. J. A. Jance. Read by Kristen Kairos. (Ali Reynolds Ser.: No. 1). 2008. audio compact disk 19.95 (978-0-06-168436-4(8), Harper Audio) HarperCollins Pubs.

Edge of Evil. unabr. ed. J. A. Jance. Read by Kris Faulkner. 1 MP3-CD. (Running Time: 7 hrs.). (Ali Reynolds Ser.: No. 1). 2006. 24.95 (978-1-59607-561-0(9)); 39.95 (978-1-59607-559-7(7)); audio compact disk 43.95 (978-1-59607-560-3(0)) Books in Motion.
Successful, high-profile TV journalist Alison Reynolds' career came to an abrupt stop when top executives decided they needed a "younger face." As if that wasn't enough, it seems her husband wants a "younger face" as well. With a dead career and a divorce pending, Ali feels she has no reason to stay in Los Angeles and heads back home to Sedona, Arizona when she hears of the mysterious death of a childhood friend. But now it appears that the dark and ominous circumstances surrounding her friend's death are encircling her as well...and a killer is closing in for the kill.

***Edge of Evil.** unabr. ed. J. A. Jance. Read by Kristen Kairos. (ENG.). 2008. (978-0-06-170236-5(6)); (978-0-06-170238-9(2)) HarperCollins Pubs.

Edge of Evolution: The Search for the Limits of Darwinism. Michael J. Behe. Read by Patrick G. Lawlor. (Playaway Adult Nonfiction Ser.). 2008. 64.99 (978-1-60640-996-1(4)) Find a World.

Edge of Evolution: The Search for the Limits of Darwinism. unabr. ed. Michael J. Behe. Read by Patrick G. Lawlor. (Running Time: 11 hrs. 0 mins. 0 sec.). (ENG.). 2007. audio compact disk 34.99 (978-1-4001-0500-7(5)); audio compact disk 24.99 (978-1-4001-5500-2(2)); audio compact disk 69.99 (978-1-4001-3500-4(1)) Pub: Tantor Media. Dist(s): IngramPubServ

Edge of God, No. 11. Carl Faber. 1 cass. (Running Time: 90 min.). 1983. 9.50 (978-0-918026-34-7(2), SR 52-605) Perseus Pr.

Edge of Honor. Gilbert Morris. Narrated by Ed Sala. 9 cass. (Running Time: 12 hrs. 30 mins.). 78.00 (978-0-7887-5182-0(4)) Recorded Bks.

Edge of Honor. unabr. ed. P. T. Deutermann. Read by Multivoice Production Staff. (Running Time: 22 hrs.). 2009. 29.99 (978-1-4233-8610-0(8), 9781423386100, Brilliance MP3); 29.99 (978-1-4233-8612-4(4), 9781423386124, BAD); 44.97 (978-1-4233-8613-1(2), 9781423386131, BADLE) Brilliance Audio.

***Edge of Honor.** unabr. ed. P. T. Deutermann. Read by multivoice. (Running Time: 22 hrs.). 2009. 44.97 (978-1-4233-8611-7(6), 9781423386117, Brlnc Audio MP3 Lib) Brilliance Audio.

Edge of Honor, Set. unabr. ed. P. T. Deutermann. 14 cass. 1999. 130.55 (FS9-43254) Highsmith.

Edge of Justice. Clinton McKinzie. 2002. 25.00 (978-0-553-71343-5(4), Random AudioBks) Random Audio Pubg.

Edge of Justice. unabr. ed. Clinton McKinzie. 8 cass. (Running Time: 12 hrs.). 2002. 64.00 (978-0-7366-8660-0(6)); audio compact disk 80.00 (978-0-7366-8663-1(0)) Books on Tape.
A routine investigation into a young woman's accidental climbing death in Wyoming turns into a murder chase.

Edge of Love No. 8: Cruelty & Devouring II. Carl Faber. 1 cass. (Running Time: 90 min.). 1983. 9.50 (978-0-918026-35-4(0), SR 52-605) Perseus Pr.

Edge of Magic: The Transformation of Music. unabr. ed. Mickey Hart. 2 cass. 20.00 (OC155) Sound Horizons AV.
Describes the search for magical music.

Edge of Night. Carol Warburton. 3 cass. 2004. 14.95 (978-1-57734-987-7(3)) Covenant Comms.

Edge of Redemption No. 9: The Soul in Mortal Crisis. Carl Faber. 1 cass. (Running Time: 90 min.). 1983. 9.50 (978-0-918026-36-1(9), SR 52-605) Perseus Pr.

Edge of Regret. Janet Woods. 2009. 61.95 (978-1-4079-0447-4(7)); audio compact disk 71.95 (978-1-4079-0448-1(5)) Pub: Soundings Ltd GBR. Dist(s): Ulverscroft US

***Edge of the Plate: Making Humble Food into Something Wonderful.** Judith Henderson. (ENG.). 2010. audio compact disk 0.00 (978-1-4507-2941-3(X)) Indep Pub IL.

Edge of the Rain. unabr. ed. Beverly Harper. Read by Jerome Pride. 9 cass. (Running Time: 13 hrs.). 2000. (978-1-876584-94-8(7), 591211) Bolinda Pubng AUS.
The blood scent was fresh. Hunger ached in her belly, the lioness slid forward as close as she dared. The little boy, seconds away from death, was two, maybe three years old. He was lost in the vast Kalahari desert.

Edge of the River. Bob Hartman & Michael McGuire. 1 cass. (J). (ps-3). 1994. bk. 11.99 (3-1213) David C Cook.
Children's Bible story.

Edge of the Stage, No. 10. Carl Faber. 1 cass. (Running Time: 90 min.). 1983. 9.50 (978-0-918026-37-8(7), SR 52-605) Perseus Pr.

Edge of the World. unabr. ed. Kevin J. Anderson. Read by Scott Brick. (Running Time: 20 hrs.). (Terra Incognita Ser.). (ENG.). 2009. 29.98 (978-1-60024-908-2(6)) Pub: Hachet Audio. Dist(s): HachBkGrp

Edge of the World. unabr. ed. Charles Neider. Read by Walter Zimmerman. 15 cass. (Running Time: 22 hrs. 30 mins.). 1988. 120.00 (978-0-7366-1284-5(X), 2193 A&B) Books on Tape.
Presents a varied portrait of Antarctica.

Edge of the World, Pt. 1. unabr. ed. Charles Neider. Read by Walter Zimmerman. 7 cass. (Running Time: 10 hrs. 30 mins.). 1988. 56.00 (2193-A) Books on Tape.

Edge of the World, Pt. 2. unabr. ed. Charles Neider. Read by Walter Zimmerman. 8 cass. (Running Time: 12 hrs.). 1988. 64.00 (2193-B) Books on Tape.

Edge of Time: Wormholes, Time Machines & Parallel Universes. Ed. by Marco A. V. Bitetto. 1 cass. 1999. (978-1-58578-116-4(9)) Inst of Cybernetics.

Edge of War. unabr. ed. Peter Biskind. (Running Time: 16 hrs.). 2008. 112.25 (978-1-4233-7015-4(5), 9781423370152, BrilAudUnabridg); audio compact disk 44.95 (978-1-4233-7016-1(3), 9781423370169, Bril Audio CD Unabri) Brilliance Audio.

Edge of War. unabr. ed. Peter Biskind. Read by Dick Hill. (Running Time: 24 hrs.). 2008. 44.25 (978-1-4233-7111-3(9), 9781423371113, BADLE); 29.95 (978-1-4233-7110-6(0), 9781423371106, BAD); 44.25 (978-1-4233-7109-0(7), 9781423371090, Brlnc Audio MP3 Lib); 29.95 (978-1-4233-7108-3(9), 9781423371083, Brilliance MP3); audio compact disk 49.99 (978-1-4233-7106-9(2), 9781423371069, Bril Audio CD Unabri); audio compact disk 117.25 (978-1-4233-7107-6(0), 9781423371076, BriAudCD Unabrid) Brilliance Audio.

Edge of War. unabr. ed. Peter Biskind et al. Read by Luke Daniels. (Running Time: 12 hrs.). (Red Dragon Ser.). 2010. 99.97 (978-1-4233-7019-2(8), 9781423370192, Brlnc Audio MP3 Lib) Brilliance Audio.

Edge on the Sword. unabr. ed. Rebecca Tingle. Narrated by Emily Gray. 6 pieces. (Running Time: 7 hrs. 45 mins.). (gr. 9 up). 2002. 54.00 (978-1-4025-1457-9(3)) Recorded Bks.
The daughter of King Alfred, 15-year-old Aethelflaed is faced with changing surroundings as her people will soon be at war with the Danish Hordes from northern England. At her father's command, Aethelflaed is sent away to Mercia in southern England to the home of her father's allies. There, she learns to fight with the help of her tough new bodyguard Red. In time, she gains the title of Lady of the Mercians and becomes one of the most important women in Old English military history.

***Edges.** unabr. ed. Léna Roy. (ENG.). (J). 2010. audio compact disk 30.00 (978-0-307-74687-0(9), Listening Lib) Pub: Random Audio Pubg. Dist(s): Random

Edges O Israel O Palestine. Leora Skolkin-Smith. Narrated by Tovah Feldshuh. Directed By Charles Potter. Prod. by Marjorie Van Halteren. Music by Raed El-Khazen. Engineer David Shinn. (ENG.). 2008. audio compact disk 24.95 (978-0-9802409-0-(5)) Midsummer NY.

Edible France: A Traveller's Guide. Glynn Christian. (ENG., 1997. audio compact disk 15.00 (978-1-56656-221-8(X)) Interlink Pub.

Edible History of Humanity. unabr. ed. Tom Standage. (Running Time: 10 hrs. 30 mins. 0 sec.). (ENG.). 2009. audio compact disk 59.99 (978-1-4001-4308-5(X)) Pub: Tantor Media. Dist(s): IngramPubServ

Edible History of Humanity. unabr. ed. Tom Standage. Narrated by George K. Wilson. (Running Time: 10 hrs. 30 mins. 0 sec.). (ENG.). 2009. audio compact disk 19.99 (978-1-4001-6308-3(0)) Pub: Tantor Media. Dist(s): IngramPubServ

Edible History of Humanity. unabr. ed. Tom Standage. Read by George K. Wilson. 9 CDs. (Running Time: 10 hrs. 30 mins. 0 sec.). (ENG.). 2009. audio compact disk 29.99 (978-1-4001-1308-8(3)) Pub: Tantor Media. Dist(s): IngramPubServ

Ediciones para el estudiante en Casetes: Student & Teacher Support Resources. 7 cass. (McGraw-Hill Ciencias Ser.). (ENG & SPA.). (gr. 3 up). 2000. (978-0-02-277919-1(1)) Macmillan McGraw-Hill Schl Div.

Ediciones para el estudiante en Casetes: Student & Teacher Support Resources. 14 cass. (McGraw-Hill Ciencias Ser.). (ENG & SPA.). (gr. 4 up). 2000. (978-0-02-277921-4(3)) Macmillan McGraw-Hill Schl Div.

Ediciones para el estudiante en Casetes: Student & Teacher Support Resources. 21 cass. (McGraw-Hill Ciencias Ser.). (ENG & SPA.). (gr. 5 up). 2000. (978-0-02-277922-1(1)) Macmillan McGraw-Hill Schl Div.

Ediciones para el Estudiante en Casetes: Student & Teacher Support Resources. 6 cass. (McGraw-Hill Ciencias Ser.). (ENG & SPA.). (gr. 2 up). 2000. (978-0-02-277918-4(3)) Macmillan McGraw-Hill Schl Div.

Edinburgh Excursion. Lucilla Andrews. Read by Tracey Shaw. 4 cass. (Running Time: 6 hrs.). (Sound Ser.). 1986. 44.95 (978-1-85496-008-5(3), 60083) Pub: UlverLrgPrint GBR. Dist(s): Ulverscroft US

Edison. unabr. ed. Paul Israel. Read by Raymond Todd. 16 cass. (Running Time: 23 hrs. 30 mins.). 2000. 99.95 (978-0-7861-1794-9(X), 2593) Blckstn Audio.
History about the most prolific inventor, he received an astounding 1,093 U.S. patents, comes to life as never before. Only biography to cover the whole of Edison's career in invention, including his early, foundational work in telegraphy.

Edison. unabr. ed. Paul Israel. Read by Raymond Todd. (Running Time: 22 hrs. 50 mins.). 2008. 44.95 (978-1-4332-4577-0(9)); cass. & audio compact disk 130.00 (978-1-4332-4576-3(0)) Blckstn Audio.

Edison: Inventing the Century. unabr. collector's ed. Neil Baldwin. Read by Michael Russotto. 14 cass. (Running Time: 21 hrs.). 1996. 112.00 (978-0-7366-3317-8(0), 3969) Books on Tape.
He introduced talking dolls, but the fragile phonograph inside their bodies fell apart, rendering them mute. During WWI, he promised an automated battlefield to minimize casualties, but he never delivered. This hardly sounds like Thomas Alva Edison, the "Wizard of Menlo Park." But it was, late in his life, when he had lost focus.

Edited from Re-Empowering. Carl Whitaker. 1 cass. 9.00 (A0437-88) Sound Photosyn.
Some great bits from the master of family counseling.

Edith Sitwell Reads Her Poems. unabr. ed. Edith Sitwell. Read by Edith Sitwell. 1 cass. (Running Time: 49 min.). 1971. 12.95 (23084) J Norton Pubs.

Edith Stein. Teresa De Spiritu Sancto. 9 cass. 36.95 (314) Ignatius Pr.
Recollections of the life of this Carmelite philosopher and Saint.

Edith Stein: Scholar, Feminist, Saint. unabr. ed. Freda M. Oben. Read by Maureen O'Leary. 2 cass. 9.95 set. (767) Ignatius Pr.
This celebrated 20th century saint started her career as an intellectual, in company with the most brilliant minds of the century - then WWI & her estrangement from Judaism brought a conversion to Catholicism & finally, the vows of the Carmelite Order.

Edith Wharton. abr. ed. Hermione Lee. Read by Kate Reading. 7 CDs. (Running Time: 30600 sec.). (ENG.). 2007. audio compact disk 34.95 (978-0-7393-5409-4(4), Random AudioBks) Pub: Random Audio Pubg. Dist(s): Random

Edith Wharton. unabr. ed. Read by Heywood Hale Broun & R. W. B. Lewis. 1 cass. (Running Time: 56 min.). (Broun Radio Ser.). 12.95 (40207) J Norton Pubs.
Wharton talks with Professor R. W. B. Lewis, her biographer.

Edith Wharton: A Celebration of the Short Story. abr. ed. Edith Wharton. Read by Kathleen Chalfant et al. 2 CDs. (Running Time: 7200 sec.). (Selected Shorts Ser.: 21). (ENG.). 2007. audio compact disk 19.95 (978-0-9719218-7-0(3)) Pub: Symphony Space. Dist(s): IPG Chicago
Selected Shorts is an award-winning series of classic and contemporary short fiction read by acclaimed actors, recorded live at Peter Norton Symphony Space in New York City, and aired on public radio stations nationwide. Selected Shorts has toured to the Mount, the home of the great American writer Edith Wharton, for the last several summers, presenting readings of short stories by Edith Wharton and other writers. This 2-CD set features four of Wharton's short stories, all read by acclaimed actresses. Fans of Wharton and of the Selected Shorts Series are sure to love this new release.

***Edith Wharton on Audio Vol. 1: The Last Asset, Autre Temps, Expiation.** (ENG.). 2010. lib. bdg. 25.00 (978-0-9818091-5-1(4)) BMA Studios.

Edith Wharton: Stories. Edith Wharton. Read by Ralph Cosham. (Playaway Adult Fiction Ser.). 2008. 39.99 (978-1-60640-822-3(4)) Find a World.

Edith Wharton, Stories. unabr. ed. Short Stories. Edith Wharton. Read by Ralph Cosham. 2 cds. (Running Time: 2 hrs 18 mins). 2002. audio compact disk 18.95 (978-1-58472-250-2(9), 012, In Aud) Pub: Sound Room. Dist(s): Baker Taylor
Four stories by Edith Wharton. The Moving Finger, The Debt, The Daunt Diana, and The Eyes.

Edith Wharton: Stories: Stories. Edith Wharton. Read by Ralph Cosham. (Running Time: 2 hrs. 30 mins.). 2002. 18.95 (978-1-59912-062-1(3), Audiofy Corp) Iofy Corp.

Edith Wharton: Stories: The Eyes; the Daunt Diana; the Moving Finger; the Debt. Edith Wharton. Narrated by Ralph Cosham. (Running Time: 9000 sec.). (Unabridged Classics in MP3 Ser.). (ENG.). (YA). 2008. audio compact disk 24.00 (978-1-58472-643-2(1), In Aud) Sound Room.

Editha see Great American Short Stories, Vol. III, A Collection

Editha. William Dean Howells. Read by Donna Barkman. 1 cass. (Running Time: 72 min.). 1986. 7.95 (S-62) Jimcin Record.
Stories of psychological insight.

Edith's Book: The True Story of How One Young Girl Survived the War. unabr. ed. Edith Velmans. Read by Miriam Margolyes. 8 cass. (Running Time: 29400 sec.). (Mitchell Grant Adventures Ser.). 2000. 69.95 (978-0-7540-0345-8(0), CAB 1768) Pub: Chivers Audio Bks GBR. Dist(s): AudioGO
Edith Van Hessen began her first diary at the age of thirteen in 1938. A carefree Dutch teenager, even the German invasion of Holland in 1940 did not immediately threaten Edith's happy-go-lucky existence. But her family was Jewish & by 1942 it became clear that they were all in danger. Early one morning, Edith was sent into hiding with a family in a small town in the south of Holland.

Edith's Story: Love & Survival During World War II. unabr. ed. Edith Velmans. Intro. by Edith Velmans. Read by Miriam Margolyes. 6 cass. (Running Time: 8 hrs. 10 mins.). 2000. 29.95 (978-1-57270-177-9(3), E61177u, Audio Editions) Pub: Audio Partners. Dist(s): PerseuPGW
A moving & deeply engaging first-person account of courage & survival. Teenager Edith van Hessen was a Dutch high school student in 1939 & she was Jewish. When Hitler's army invaded Holland, Edith lived with a courageous Protestant family in another town, taking a new identity, hidden in the open. This is her unforgettable true story based on her teen-age diaries, wartime letters & later reflections as an adult survivor.

Editing & Postproduction. Declan McGrath. (Screencraft Ser.). (ENG., 2001. 58.95 (978-0-240-80468-2(6), FocalSci) Sci Tech Bks.

Edmund Burke: A Genius Reconsidered. unabr. ed. Russell Kirk. Read by Frederick Davidson. 5 cass. (Running Time: 7 hrs.). 1994. 39.95 (978-0-7861-0472-7(4), 1424) Blckstn Audio.
This volume makes vivid the four great struggles in the life of Burke: his work for conciliation with the American colonies; his involvement in cutting down the domestic power of George III; his prosecution of Warren Hastings, the Governor-General of India; & his resistance to Jacobinism, the French Revolution's "armed doctrine." In each of these great phases of his public life, Burke fought with passionate eloquence & relentless logic for justice & for the proper balance of order & freedom.

Edmund Campion. unabr. collector's ed. Evelyn Waugh. Read by David Case. 6 cass. (Running Time: 6 hrs.). 1991. 36.00 (978-0-7366-1945-5(3), 2766) Books on Tape.
Edmund Campion, a brilliant scholar & orator, a deacon in the Church of England, a true subject of Queen Elizabeth I, was torn by conscience: though professing Protestantism, his heart was Catholic. At last he declared himself & went to Rome for training as a Jesuit.

Edmund Campion: Hero of God's Underground. Harold C. Gardiner. 4 cass. 18.95 (722) Ignatius Pr.
Life of the Jesuit martyr's dangerous work in persecuted England.

Edmund Rubbra - The Sacred Muse. Gloriae Dei Cantores. 1 CD. 1997. audio compact disk 16.95 (978-1-55725-194-7(0), GDCD024) Paraclete MA.

Edmund White: Interview with Edmund White & Kay Bonetti. unabr. ed. 1 cass. 1989. 13.95 (978-1-55644-341-1(2), 9072) Am Audio Prose.

Edmund Wilson: Letters on Literature & Politics, 1912-1972. unabr. ed. Read by Heywood Hale Broun et al. 1 cass. (Running Time: 56 min). (Broun Radio Ser.). 12.95 (40305) J Norton Pubs.
A conversation with Elena Wilson, Edmund's wife & editor, & Phillip Hamburger, staff writer of the New York Times.

Edna O'Brien. unabr. ed. Read by Edna O'Brien & Rebekah Presson. Ed. by James McKinley. 1 cass. (Running Time: 29 min.). (New Letters on the Air Ser.). 1994. 10.00 (090594); 18.00 2-sided cass. New Letters.
O'Brian is interviewed by Rebekah Presson & reads from House of Splendid Isolation.

Edna Ritchie of Viper, KY. 1 cass. 9.98 (C-3) Folk-Legacy.
Traditional ballads sung by a member of the famous Ritchie family.

***EDRA41: Policy & the Environment: Proceedings of the 41st Annual Conference of the Environmental Design Research Association Washington DC June 2-6, 2010 (Digital Version)** Compiled by Environmental Design Research Association Staff. 2010. cd-rom 75.00 (978-0-9827851-0-2(0)) EDRA.

Educación para el Amor. P. Juan Rivas. (SPA.). 2009. audio compact disk 18.95 (978-1-935405-48-1(9)) Hombre Nuevo.

Educar para Triunfar. P. Juan Rivas. (SPA.). 2006. audio compact disk 18.95 (978-1-935405-66-5(7)) Hombre Nuevo.

Educate & Train Your Recreated Human Spirit. Kenneth E. Hagin. 5 cass. (Developing the Human Spirit Ser.). 20.00 (#826) Faith Lib Pubns.
The moment you were born again was just the beginning of your development in spiritual things."Developing the Human Spirit Series" show you how to.

Educated Child: A Parents Guide from Preschool Through Eighth Grade. William J. Bennett. 2004. 15.95 (978-0-7435-4666-9(0)) Pub: S&S Audio. Dist(s): S and S Inc

Educated Eye: Seven-Part Program on Connoisseurship & Collection. Created by Kendall Taylor. 1 cass. 1995. (0-9307-90003-4-7) Smithsonian Folkways.
Trains general listeners, collectors, dealers, museum docents & art lovers to refine their aesthetic awareness & make subtle distinctions about quality, advising what & how to collect & when to enter the collectibles market.

Educated Heart: Provencal Love Poetry of the 12th Century. Robert Bly. 1 cass. 10.95 (978-1-879323-05-6(2)) Sound Horizons AV.

Educating a Whole Person in Freedom. 1 cass. (Running Time: 50 min.). (JPN.). 1997. 25.00 (978-1-888947-81-6(0)) Sudbury Valley.

Educating Esme Set: Diary of a Teacher's First Year. abr. ed. Esmé Raji Codell. Read by Esmé Raji Codell. 2 cass. 1999. 18.95 (FS9-51019) Highsmith.

Educating Gifted Children. unabr. ed. Sylvia Rimm. Read by Sylvia Rimm. 2 cass. (Running Time: 1 hr. 57 min.). 1989. 20.00 (978-0-937891-04-9(5), SR104) Apple Pub Wisc.
Two-sided tapes of the questions most asked of Dr. Sylvia Rimm by parents & teachers on Educating Gifted Children.

Educating the Proper Woman Reader: Victorian Family Literary Magazines & the Cultural Health of the Nation. Jennifer Phegley. 2004. audio compact disk 9.95 (978-0-8142-9055-2(8)) Pub: Ohio St U Pr. Dist(s): Chicago Distribution Ctr

Education. Ellen G. White. Narrated by Eric Martin. 8 CDs. 2004. audio compact disk 39.95 (978-1-883012-24-3(4)); audio compact disk 39.95 (978-1-883012-25-0(2)) Remnant Pubns.

***Education.** unabr. ed. Lynn Barber. Read by Carolyn Seymour. (Running Time: 6 hrs. 30 mins.). 2010. 29.95 (978-1-4417-5211-6(0)); 44.95 (978-1-4417-5207-9(2)); audio compact disk 24.95 (978-1-4417-5210-9(2)); audio compact disk 69.00 (978-1-4417-5208-6(0)) Blckstn Audio.

Education: Practical Approaches for the Future. Read by Frank Fortkamp & Allan E. Harrison. (Running Time: 60 min.). 1981. 9.00 (F119) Freeland Pr.
Restructuring the public school system is the main theme of this discussion, which offers alternatives of special interest to the free-market advocate. Panel discussion.

Education & Children. Read by Sylvia Goodman et al. 2 cass. (Running Time: 59 min.). (Wilhelm Reich: His Life & Work Ser.). 1974. 18.00 set. (1934) Big Sur Tapes.
In this seminar, Sylvia Goodman begins by emphasizing the importance of a good birth experience to a happy life. She gives several guidelines to follow in delivering & raising a healthy infant. Eva Reich then follows with a discussion of social reforms necessary to bring out the full potential of every child. In Tape 2, Peter Marin criticizes some of the previously expressed ideas, & gives suggestions as to how education could be improved. Keleman then attacks the "myth of the Garden of Eden", which implies that civilization destroys an otherwise perfect relationship between mother & child. A question & answer period follows.

Education & Politics see Ralph Waldo Emerson: Poems and Essays

Education & Return of Hymankaplan. Leo Rosten. Read by Leo Rosten. 10.95 (978-0-8045-0950-3(6), SAC 43-4) Spoken Arts.

Education & the Control of Human Behavior. unabr. ed. Carl Ransom Rogers & B. F. Skinner. 6 cass. (Running Time: 4 hrs.). 49.50 (29244) J Norton Pubs.

Education & the Founding Fathers. unabr. ed. David Barton. Read by David Barton. 1 cass. 1992. 4.95 (978-0-925279-20-0(X)) Wallbuilders.
A look at the Bible-based educational system which produced America's great heroes & what they said & did (in their writings, laws, & court decisions) to ensure that America would always continue to have that same Christian system of education.

Education As Liberation According to John. Carolyn Osiek. Read by Carolyn Osiek. 1 cass. (Running Time: 60 min.). 7.95 (TAH182) Alba Hse Comns.

Education by Remote Control. (23291-A) J Norton Pubs.

Education for an Enlightened Society. Vajracarya. 1978. 10.00 (A080) Vajradhatu.
A seminar by the scholar & mediatation master trained in the philosophical & meditative traditions of Buddhism in Tibet.

Education for Living. unabr. ed. Perf. by Eknath Easwaran. 1 cass. (Running Time: 1 hr.). 1991. 7.95 (978-1-58638-529-3(1)) Nilgiri Pr.

Education in America. Stephen Mansfield. 1 cass. (Running Time: 90 mins.). (Studies in Church History Ser.: Vol. 7). 2000. 5.00 (SM02-007) Morning NC.
An in-depth look at different philosophies that have influenced church history, this series provides excellent keys for understanding how to effectively confront the important issues of our times.

Education Law. 2007th rev. ed. Michael Kaufman. (Law School Legends Ser.). 2008. 52.00 (978-0-314-18097-1(4), gilbert) West.

Education Must Prepare for the World of Tomorrow. Instructed by Manly P. Hall. 8.95 (978-0-89314-101-1(1), C830605) Philos Res.

Education of a British-Protected Child. unabr. ed. Chinua Achebe. Narrated by Michael Page. 1 MP3-CD. (Running Time: 5 hrs. 0 mins. 0 sec.). 2009. 19.99 (978-1-4001-6377-9(3)); audio compact disk 29.99 (978-1-4001-1377-4(6)); audio compact disk 59.99 (978-1-4001-4377-1(2)) Pub: Tantor Media. Dist(s): IngramPubServ

***Education of a British-Protected Child: Essays.** unabr. ed. Chinua Achebe. Narrated by Michael Page. (Running Time: 5 hrs. 0 mins.). 2009. 13.99 (978-1-4001-8377-7(4)); 29.99 (978-1-4001-9377-6(X)) Tantor Media.

Education of a Coach. abr. ed. David Halberstam. Read by Eric Conger. (Running Time: 10800 sec.). 2006. audio compact disk 14.98 (978-1-4013-8495-1(1)) Pub: Hyperion. Dist(s): HarperCollins Pubs

Education of a Coach. unabr. ed. David Halberstam. Narrated by Tom Stechschulte. 7 cass. (Running Time: 9 hrs. 50 mins.). 2006. 69.75 (978-1-4193-7581-1(4)) Recorded Bks.

Education of a Tyrant. unabr. ed. Gilbert Highet. Read by Gilbert Highet. 1 cass. (Running Time: 30 min.). 9.95 (23308-AB) J Norton Pubs.
The Emperor Nero started his reign as a brilliant & much loved prince, with a weakness to his character. Seneca & Petronius wrote books through which he could sublimate his own conflicts & grow but it did not succeed.

Education of an Accidental CEO: Lessons Learned from the Trailer Park to the Corner Office. abr. ed. David Novak & John Boswell. Read by Howard Ross. (Running Time: 25200 sec.). (ENG.). 2007. audio compact disk 31.95 (978-0-7393-5476-6(0), Random AudioBks) Pub: Random Audio Pubg. Dist(s): Random

Education of Children. unabr. ed. Alfred Adler. Read by Robin Lawson. 5 cass. (Running Time: 7 hrs.). 1991. 39.95 (978-0-7861-0273-0(X), 1239) Blckstn Audio.
Presents some of Adler's most powerful insights on numerous aspects relating to the education of children, including the development of personality; the relationship between the inferiority complex & striving for superiority; preventing the inferiority complex; obstacles to social development; the child's position in the family; the child at school; adolescence & sex education; & educating the parent.

Education of Henry Adams. unabr. ed. Henry Adams. Narrated by David Colacci. (Running Time: 70320 sec.). (ENG.). 2007. audio compact disk 49.95 (978-1-60283-266-4(8)) Pub: AudioGO. Dist(s): Perseus Dist

Education of Henry Adams. unabr. ed. Henry Adams. Read by Wolfram Kandinsky. 16 cass. (Running Time: 23 hrs. 30 mins.). 1994. 99.95 (978-0-7861-0461-1(9), 1413) Blckstn Audio.
The great-grandson of John Adams & grandson of John Quincy Adams, Henry Adams asserts that his conventional education was defective. Considering his best Boston & Quincy background, Harvard, German post-graduate training, & his position as secretary to his father, Charles Francis Adams, this is a rather puzzling claim; especially when one considers that he wrote what many consider to be one of the three greatest autobiographies ever - "The Autobiography of Benjamin Franklin" & Rousseau's "Confessions" being the other two.

Education of Henry Adams. unabr. ed. Henry Adams. Read by Wolfram Kandinsky. (Running Time: 22 hrs. 0 mins.). 2008. 44.95 (978-1-4332-4998-3(7)); audio compact disk 130.00 (978-1-4332-4997-6(9)) Blckstn Audio.

Education of Henry Adams. unabr. collector's ed. Henry Adams. Read by Jonathon Reese. 13 cass. (Running Time: 19 hrs. 30 mins.). 1999. 104.00 (978-0-7366-4377-1(X), 4841) Books on Tape.
Author & historian, Henry Adams, was also the son of Charles Francis Adams & the grandson of an American President.

Education of Joe. 1979. 4.95 (978-0-7417-1003-1(X)) Win Walk.

Education of Julius Caesar, Pt. 1. unabr. collector's ed. Arthur D. Kahn. Read by Walter Zimmerman. 10 cass. (Running Time: 15 hrs.). 1990. 80.00 (978-0-7366-1733-8(7), 2573-A) Books on Tape.
The author spent ten years preparing this comprehensive biography of Julius Caesar. Kahn traces Caesar's education from birth to death. The result is a rich exploration of the man & his times, for "Caesar deserves to be studied not only for the knowledge of history but for himself.

Education of Julius Caesar, Pt. 2. unabr. collector's ed. Arthur D. Kahn. Read by Walter Zimmerman. 10 cass. (Running Time: 15 hrs.). 1990. 80.00 (978-0-7366-1734-5(5), 2573-B) Books on Tape.

Education of Little Tree, abr. ed. Forrest Carter. Read by Peter Coyote. 2 cass. (Running Time: 3 hrs.). 1999. reel tape 16.95 (978-0-944993-51-4(6)) Audio Lit.
The tale of the education of a young boy by his Cherokee grandparents. A unique blend of American simplicity & spiritual profundity.

Education of Little Tree, unabr. ed. Forrest Carter. Narrated by Jeff Woodman. 5 pieces. (Running Time: 7 hrs. 15 mins.). (gr. 5 up). 1998. 46.00 (978-0-7887-2225-7(5), 95524E7) Recorded Bks.
A remembrance of a young boy's years with his Cherokee grandparents. Listeners of all ages will value Granpa's timeless teachings of "The Way," honoring the mysteries of the subtle balance of all living things.

Education of Little Tree, Class Set. unabr. ed. Forrest Carter. Read by Jeff Woodman. 5 cass., 10 bks. (Running Time: 7 hrs. 15 min.). (YA). 1998. bk. 196.30 (978-0-7887-2547-0(5), 46717) Recorded Bks.
A remembrance of a young boy's years with his Cherokee grandparents.

Education of Little Tree, Homework Set. unabr. ed. Forrest Carter. Read by Jeff Woodman. 5 cass. (Running Time: 7 hrs. 15 min.). (YA). 1998. bk. 67.20 (978-0-7887-2242-4(5), 40726) Recorded Bks.

Education of Mary: A Little Miss of Color, 1832. unabr. ed. Ann Rinaldi. 5 cass. (Running Time: 7 hrs.). (YA). (gr. 7 up). 2003. 50.00 (978-1-4025-2478-3(1)) Recorded Bks.
Though 13-year-old Mary is happy to keep quiet about the secret instruction she receives at Miss Prudence Crandall?s private school for the daughters of the richest families in New England, Mary?s sister Sarah glories in the fuss she creates when she is openly admitted. When Miss Prudence replaces the school?s white students with little misses of color, all sides of the anti-slavery movement want to use the school to further their own agendas?with Mary and Sarah caught in the middle!.

***Education of the Heart.** abr. ed. Thomas Moore. Read by Thomas Moore. (ENG.). 2005. (978-0-06-089375-0(3), Harper Audio); (978-0-06-089376-7(1), Harper Audio) HarperCollins Pubs.

Education of the Heart. unabr. ed. Perf. by Eknath Easwaran. 1 cass. (Running Time: 1 hr.). 1992. 7.95 (978-1-58638-530-9(5)) Nilgiri Pr.

Education of the Soul. Guy Finley. (ENG.). 2004. 79.95 (978-1-929320-38-7(8)) Life of Learn.

Education of the Soul. Guy Finley. 9 cass. (Running Time: 12 hours). 2004. 79.00 (978-1-929320-31-8(0)); audio compact disk 95.00 (978-1-929320-32-5(9)) Life of Learn.
A comprehensive program that distills the fundamental concepts that form the core of the invisible spiritual curriculum. In this complete course in self-realization, best-selling author Guy Finley integrates key principles from eastern and western traditions and shines new Light on their hidden meaning. This life-changing material reveals essential secrets of Love, Will, Relationships, the Present Moment, Rebirth, and much more.

Éducation Sentimentale, Pt. 1, set. Gustave Flaubert. Read by Maurice Antoni. 4 cass. (FRE.). 1995. 39.95 (1650-TH) Olivia & Hill.
Frederic Moreau, student in Paris around 1840, worried, unhappy, unambitious, fed only by vague literary, artistic & mundane aspirations. His deep love for Mme. Arnoux seems to be the only light in his life.

Éducation Sentimentale, Pt. 2, set. Gustave Flaubert. Read by Maurice Antoni. 4 cass. (FRE.). 1995. 39.95 (1651-TH) Olivia & Hill.

Éducation Sentimentale, Pt. 3, set. Gustave Flaubert. Read by Maurice Antoni. 4 cass. (FRE.). 1996. 39.95 (1796-TH) Olivia & Hill.
Frederick Moreau, student in Paris around 1840, worried, unhappy, unambitious, fed only by vague literary, artistic & mundane aspirations. His deep love for Mme. Arnoux seems to be the only light in his life.

Éducation Sentimentale, Pts. 1-2, set. Gustave Flaubert. Read by Maurice Antoni. 8 cass. (FRE.). 1995. 69.95 (1650/51) Olivia & Hill.
Frederic Moreau, student in Paris around 1840, worried, unhappy, unambitious, fed only by vague literary, artistic & mundane aspirations. His deep love for Mme. Arnoux seems to be the only light in his life.

Education Without Compromise: From Chaos to Coherence in Higher Education. William D. Schaefer. (Higher Education Ser.). 1990. bk. 30.95 (978-1-55542-197-7(0), Jossey-Bass) Wiley US.

Education Without Enlightenment Can Be Dangerous. Manly P. Hall. 1 cass. 8.95 (978-0-89314-102-8(X), C891008) Philos Res.

Educational Establishment vs. Civilization. John Robbins. 1 cass. (Christianity & Education Ser.: No. 1). 5.00 Trinity Found.

Educational Interventions for NLD: Getting the Most Out of School Experiences. Sue Thompson. 1 cass. (Running Time: 1 hr. 15 min.). 1998. bk. 20.00 (978-1-58111-056-2(1)) Contemporary Medical.
Describes how to help students in school, evaluate students with NLD, curriculum modifications & teaching strategies.

Educational Interventions for the Child with Nonverbal Learning Disorder. Sue Thompson & Judith Paton. 1 cass. (Running Time: 84 min.). 1997. bk. 15.00 (978-1-58111-010-4(3)) Contemporary Medical.
Auditory effects of NLD; ways to compensate, accommodate, modify & strategize within various environments, intervention within educational arena.

Educational Interventions for the Child with Nonverbal Learning Disorders. Contrib. by Sue Thompson & Judith Paton. 1 cass. (Running Time: 1 hrs. 30 min.). 20.00 (19-004A) J W Wood.
Auditory effects of this dysfunction, ways to compensate, accomodate, modify & strategize within various environments, interventions within the educational arena & recommendations to transition into other activities.

Educational Leader Fluency Cards Audio. Benchmark Education Staff. 2004. audio compact disk 10.00 (978-1-4108-3595-6(2)) Benchmark Educ.

Educational Leader Poetry Audio. Benchmark Education Staff. 2004. audio compact disk 10.00 (978-1-4108-3596-3(0)) Benchmark Educ.

Educational Psychology: Windows on Classrooms. 7th ed. Paul Eggen & Don Kauchak. 2006. pap. bk. 115.33 (978-0-13-234094-6(1)) P-H.

Educational Thought of the Founding Fathers. Read by Ralph Lerner. 1 cass. Incl. Historical Development of American Education. Read by Richard H. Powers. (141); Pt. 1. Discussion on American Education. (141); 3.00 (141) ISI Books.

Edutainment: How to Teach Language with Fun & Games. 2nd ed. Ian Hewitt. 2 cass. 1999. pap. bk. 34.95 (978-0-9586492-0-9(0)) Language Direct JPN.

Edward de Bono's Smart Thinking. Edward De Bono. 1 cass. 1993. 10.95 Macmill Audio.

Edward, Edward see Poetry of Robert Burns & Border Ballads

Edward Field. unabr. ed. Ed. by Jim McKinley. Prod. by Rebekah Presson. 1 cass. (Running Time: 29 min.). (New Letters on the Air Ser.). 1994. 10.00 (041894) New Letters.
Although he lives in New York, Field says he's very popular on the West Coast & has been credited as the father of the Long Beach poetry scene. Field won the Lamont Poetry prize in 1963 & now his selected poems, titled "Counting Myself Lucky" have been published. Field is a master of the narrative poem & takes as his subjects movie stars, gay life, being Jewish & Buddhism.

Edward Hirsch. unabr. ed. Edward Hirsch. 1 cass. (Running Time: 29 min.). 1985. 10.00 (030891) New Letters.

Edward Hopper Pt. A: An Intimate Biography. unabr. collector's ed. Gail Levin. Read by Anna Fields. 10 cass. (Running Time: 15 hrs.). 1997. 80.00 (978-0-7366-3561-5(0), 4207A) Books on Tape.
In the art of Edward Hopper, unhappy men & women play out mysterious dramas in stark spaces. It makes us wonder what kind of life engendered this art.

Edward Hopper Pt. B: An Intimate Biography. unabr. collector's ed. Gail Levin. Read by Anna Fields. 8 cass. (Running Time: 12 hrs.). 1997. 64.00 (978-0-7366-3562-2(9), 4207B) Books on Tape.

Edward Kennedy. Cerebellum Academic Team Staff. Prod. by Ronald Miller. (Running Time: 30 mins.). (Just the Facts Ser.). 2010. 24.95 (978-1-59163-103-3(3)) Cerebellum.

Edward Mills & George Benton: A Tale see Man That Corrupted Hadleyburg & Other Stories

Edward Mills & George Benton: A Tale see Favorite Stories by Mark Twain

Edward Morin. unabr. ed. Read by Edward Morin. 1 cass. (Running Time: 29 min.). 10.00 New Letters.
One of a weekly half-hour radio program with authors talking & presenting their own works. Edward Morin here reads from "Hot Songs for Motown".

Edward R. Murrow. 1 cass. (Running Time: 1 hr.). 10.95 (F0360B090, HarperThor) HarpC GBR.

Edward R. Murrow. unabr. ed. Bob Edwards. (Running Time: 4 hrs. 31 mins. 12 sec.). (ENG.). 2004. audio compact disk 24.99 (978-1-4001-0136-8(0)) Pub: Tantor Media. Dist(s): IngramPubServ

Edward R. Murrow: And the Birth of Broadcast Journalism. unabr. ed. Bob Edwards. Read by Bob Edwards. (Running Time: 4 hrs. 31 mins. 12 sec.). (ENG.). 2004. audio compact disk 49.99 (978-1-4001-3136-5(7)) Pub: Tantor Media. Dist(s): IngramPubServ

Edward R Murrow & the Birth of Broadcast Journalism. unabr. ed. Bob Edwards. (Running Time: 4 hrs. 31 mins. 12 sec.). (ENG.). 2004. audio compact disk 19.99 (978-1-4001-5136-3(8)) Pub: Tantor Media. Dist(s): IngramPubServ

Edward S. Schlesinger, Esq., on Estate Planning. Contrib. by Edward S. Schlesinger. 10 cass. (Running Time: 15 hrs.). 1998. 149.00 Set; includes album & practice aids. (M212) Am Law Inst.
Lectures offer a wealth of practical information& planning tips in a conversational & convenient format for busy lawyers. Schlesinger has practiced, taught, & written in the estate planning field for more than 35 years.

Edward Wilkins: Starre Augen. unabr. ed. 1 cass. (Running Time: 1 hr.). (GER.). 18.95 (CGE355) J Norton Pubs.

Edward's Eyes. unabr. ed. Patricia MacLachlan. Narrated by Milo Ventmiglia. 2 CDs. (Running Time: 1 hr. 30 mins.). (J). (gr. 4-6). 2008. audio compact disk 25.75 (978-1-4281-8227-1(6)); 25.75 (978-1-4281-8222-6(5)) Recorded Bks.
A widely admired author of children's books, Patricia MacLachlan won the Newbery Medal for Sarah, Plain and Tall. Edward's Eyes is a tale of brothers and the magic of summer days filled with reading and pick-up games of baseball. But summer can't last forever, and an unforeseen tragedy throws a curveball into the lives of Edward's family - and afterwards nothing will ever be the same.

Edward's Eyes. unabr. ed. Patricia MacLachlan. Read by Milo Ventimiglia. 2 CDs. (Running Time: 1 hr. 30 mins. 0 sec.). (ENG.). (J). (gr. 3-7). 2007. audio compact disk 17.99 (978-0-7435-6911-8(3)) Pub: S&S Audio. Dist(s): S and S Inc

Edwin Drood, The Mystery Of. unabr. ed. Gilbert Highet. Read by Gilbert Highet. 1 cass. (Running Time: 30 min.). 9.95 (23295-A) J Norton Pubs.

Edwin of the Iron Shoes. unabr. ed. Marcia Muller. Read by Bernadette Dunne. 6 cass. (Running Time: 6 hrs.). (Sharon McCone Mystery Ser.: No. 1). 1996. 48.00 (978-0-7366-3408-3(8), 4054) Books on Tape.
Sharon McCone, a tough-minded investigator for a legal services cooperative, noses her way through the tainted underbelly of a San Francisco street occupied by an eclectic assortment of dealers in antiques, pseudo art & junk. She's after a killer who slashed a diminutive victim, antique dealer Joan Albritton, with the victim's own bone-handled knife.

***EEO Regulatory Compliance & Reporting.** PUEI. 2009. audio compact disk 199.00 (978-1-935041-62-7(2), CareerTrack) P Univ E Inc.

***Eerie Silence: Renewing Our Search for Alien Intelligence.** unabr. ed. Paul Davies. Narrated by George K. Wilson. (Running Time: 10 hrs. 0 mins.). 2010. 34.99 (978-1-4001-9551-0(9)); 16.99 (978-1-4001-8551-1(3)); 24.99 (978-1-4001-6551-3(2)); audio compact disk 69.99 (978-1-4001-4551-5(1)); audio compact disk 34.99 (978-1-4001-1551-8(5)) Pub: Tantor Media. Dist(s): IngramPubServ

Effacer. unabr. ed. Robert A. Monroe. Read by Roland Simon. 1 cass. (Running Time: 30 min.). (Human Plus Ser.). (FRE.). 1993. 14.95 (978-1-56102-071-3(0)) Inter Indus.
Release restrictive & destructive patterns.

Effect of the New Tax Law on Church & Clergy: Proceedings of the 45th Annual Convention National Association of Evangelical Buffalo, New York. Read by Phil Temple. 1 cass. (Running Time: 60 min.). 1987. 4.00 (339) Nat Assn Evan.

Effect of Various Diseases on Thyroid Function Tests. Read by Robert D. Utiger. 1 cass. (Running Time: 90 min.). 1986. 12.00 (C8648) Amer Coll Phys.

Effective Academic Advising Strategies: NACADA Webinar No. 30. Moderated by Jayne Drake. (ENG.). 2010. audio compact disk 140.00 (978-1-935140-72-6(8)) Nat Acad Adv.

Effective Business Presentations. Jim Savage & Bryan Flanagan. 3 cass. 1987. 89.95 (978-1-56207-211-7(0)) Zig Ziglar Corp.
This program is a dynamic self-study designed to teach you all the vital skills of group presentations.

Effective Communication. Betty L. Randolph. Read by Betty L. Randolph. Read by Leonard Baron. Ed. by Success Education Institute International Staff. 1 cass. (Educational Ser.). 1989. bk. 14.98 Ocean Format. (978-1-55909-254-8(8), 420P); bk. Music Format. (420PM) Randolph Tapes.
Features 60,000 messages with the left-right brain.

Effective Communication: Easy. Eldon Taylor. Read by Eldon Taylor. Ed. by Leslie Brice. 1 cass. (Running Time: 1 hr.). 1992. 16.95 (978-1-56705-143-8(X)) Gateways Inst.
Self improvement.

Effective Communication: Ocean. Eldon Taylor. Read by Eldon Taylor. Ed. by Leslie Brice. 1 cass. (Running Time: 1 hr.). 1992. 16.95 (978-1-56705-144-5(8)) Gateways Inst.

Effective Communication: Stream. Eldon Taylor. Read by Eldon Taylor. Ed. by Leslie Brice. 1 cass. (Running Time: 1 hr.). 1992. 16.95 (978-1-56705-145-2(6)) Gateways Inst.

Effective Communication: The Master's Keys to Becoming a Master Communicator. Mac Hammond. 5 cass. (Running Time: 1 hr.). 1997. 30.00 Set. (978-1-57399-061-5(2)) Mac Hammond.
How to be more effective through communication.

Effective Communication: The Master's Keys to Becoming a Master Communicator. Mac Hammond. (ENG.). 2007. audio compact disk 25.00 (978-1-57399-333-3(6)) Mac Hammond.

Effective Communication - Critical Skills You Need to Succeed, in Less Than One Hour: Stuff for Busy People. Interview. Created by Sylvia Henderson. Interview with Alicia Dixon. 1. (Running Time: 40 mins). (Stuff for Busy People Ser.). 2003. audio compact disk 15.00 (978-1-932197-24-2(9), V-Twin Pr) Springbrd Training.
Effective Communication: Critical Skills You Need to Succeed, in Less Than One HourCDROM (Computer). Computer-based CD. Takes less than one hour to complete.Included on the CD:Audio program (via computer). Accompanying handout (for note taking) - print one copy per participant. An article on the related topic. Bonus! An article you can use in your own newsletter. A continuing education resource from Springboard Training. Sylvia Henderson, CEO of Springboard Training, tells you how you can be a more-effective communicator as a result of her 20+ years as a corporate trainer, manager and communicator. The interview format makes the message more interesting and relevant for you than a "straight lecture".In this program you will learn about the benefits of and specific ways to communicate more effectively in your personal and professional lives.Program objectives include:Identify verbal and non-verbal factors for communicating effectively. Recognize how to communicate in a variety of contexts and situations. Receive resources that facilitate your continued study of interpersonal and written communication skills. This is a good small-group educational tool.

Effective Communication Between Parents & Children. C. Eugene Walker. 2 cass. 21.95 Self-Control Sys.
Provides information for parents who want to assure that they & their teenagers will survive the difficult teenage years.

Effective Communication Skills for Couples. Pat Heim. 1 cass. (Running Time: 50 min.). 1995. 12.95 (978-1-891531-04-0(2)) Heim Gp.
Covers common communication problems couples encounter & what we can do to communicate more.

Effective Coping with Anger. R. Donnenwirth & H. B. Marksberry. 1986. 10.80 (0602A) Assn Prof Chaplains.

Effective Deposition: Techniques & Strategies That Work. David Malone & Peter Hoffman. 5 cass. (Running Time: 6 hrs. 36 min.). (Practical Guide Ser.). 1996. 73.95 Set. (2310S) Natl Inst Trial Ad.
A thorough guide that explores every aspect of depositions.

Effective Deposition Practice. Henry Hecht. 1 cass. 1994. 135.00 (4931) Natl Prac Inst.

Effective Direct & Cross-Examination. Read by Ken M. Kawaichi et al. (Running Time: 4 hrs. 45 min.). 1989. 95.00 Incl. 93p. tape materials. (CP-53122) Cont Ed Bar-CA.
Covers witness selection & preparation; sequence of presenting evidence; direct examination; cross-examination; experts; recurring issues & pitfalls.

Effective Evaluation: Improving the Usefulness of Evaluation Results Through Responsive & Naturalistic Approaches. Egon G. Guba & Yvonna S. Lincoln. (Social & Behavioral Science Ser.). 1992. pap. bk. 27.00 (978-1-55542-442-8(2), Jossey-Bass) Wiley US.

Effective Executive. unabr. ed. Peter F. Drucker. Read by Michael Prichard. 6 cass. (Running Time: 6 hrs.). 1981. 36.00 (978-0-7366-0352-2(2), 1338) Books on Tape.
Guide on how to escape common management traps. Analyzing what makes for effectiveness, Drucker asserts it is an acquired self-discipline that enables the executive not only to avoid what is unproductive, but to perceive & accomplish what really needs doing.

Effective Jury Selection: Mastering the Power of the Process. Joseph V. Guastaferro. 1993. pap. bk. 185.00 (978-0-943380-95-7(2)) PEG MN.

Effective Jury Selection: Mastering the Power of the Process. unabr. ed. Joseph V. Guastaferro. Read by Joseph V. Guastaferro. Ed. by P. E. G. Staff. 6 cass. (Running Time: 6 hrs.). 1993. pap. bk. 179.00 set. (978-0-943380-80-3(4)) PEG MN.
This program can help you to achieve a greater measure of success in the courtroom. Evaluating & understanding the individuals deciding your case is crucial to your success as an advocate.

Effective Jury Voir Dire. Read by Michael Virga et al. (Running Time: 2 hrs. 30 min.). 1991. 89.00 Incl. 155p. tape materials. (CP-55200) Cont Ed Bar-CA.

Effective Leadership. Gary V. Whetstone. (Practics Ser.). 1996. 170.00 (978-1-58866-069-5(9)) Gary Whet Pub.

Effective Leadership. Bill Winston. 3 cass. (C). 1995. 15.00 (978-1-931289-63-4(8)) Pub: B Winston Min. Dist(s): Anchor Distributors

Effective Legal Negotiation & Settlement. Charles Craver. 1 cass. 1994. 135.00 (4004) Natl Prac Inst.

Effective Life Management. Gary V. Whetstone. Adapted by Faye Whetstone. (Practics Ser.: Vol. PR101). 1997. 170.00 (978-1-58866-049-7(4)) Gary Whet Pub.

Effective Listening. Kevin J. Murphy. 2004. 7.95 (978-0-7435-4667-6(9)) Pub: S&S Audio. Dist(s): S and S Inc

Effective Listening Skills. Ron Meiss. 4 cass. 79.95 set. (C10105) CareerTrack Pubns.
Reduce mistakes, sharpen your concentration & "hear" more. These skills will help you understand people's true needs; minimize misunderstandings; get better results in sales & negotiations; enjoy honest feedback from friends, family & coworkers.

Effective Listening Skills & How to Listen Powerfully. Ron Meiss. 4 cass. 64.95 set. (V10105) CareerTrack Pubns.
The skills presented in these programs will help you & your team avoid mistakes, minimize wasted time & repair strained relationships.

Effective Management of Chemical Analysis Laboratories. unabr. ed. Read by John H. Taylor, Jr. & Mary M. Routson. 4 cass. (Running Time: 4 hrs. 48 min.). 455.00 Set, incl. 120p. manual. (94) Am Chemical.

Effective Marketing for Small Business. Speeches. Featuring Melvin J. Gravely, 2nd. 2 cass. (Running Time: 75 min.). 1998. 24.95 (978-0-9656194-2-4(7)) Impact Grp.

Effective Meditations for Creative Visualizing. Deirdre M. Griswold & Robert E. Griswold. Read by Deirdre M. Griswold. 1 cass. (Effective Meditations Ser.). 1996. 11.98 (978-1-55848-405-4(1)) EffectiveMN.
Relaxing way to learn & experience the power of visualization....& get the results you choose.

Effective Meditations for Health & Healing. Robert E. Griswold & Deirdre M. Griswold. Read by Deirdre M. Griswold. 1 cass. (Contemporary Meditation Ser.). 1995. 11.98 (978-1-55848-402-3(7)) EffectiveMN.
Relaxing program offers easy techniques for focusing your mind towards better health & well-being.

Effective Meditations for Inner Peace & Happiness. Robert E. Griswold & Deirdre M. Griswold. Read by Deirdre M. Griswold. 1 cass. (Contemporary Meditation Ser.). 1995. 11.98 (978-1-55848-403-0(5)) EffectiveMN.
Great techniques for calming the mind & enabling you to reach & maintain inner peace & joy.

Effective Meditations for Overcoming Self-Doubt. Deirdre M. Griswold & Robert E. Griswold. Read by Deirdre M. Griswold. 1 cass. (Effective Meditations Ser.). 1996. 11.98 (978-1-55848-406-1(X)) EffectiveMN.
Negative feelings quickly melt away as you experience these relaxing, confidence building meditations.

Effective Meditations for Positive Living. Deirdre M. Griswold & Robert E. Griswold. Read by Deirdre M. Griswold. 1 cass. (Effective Meditations Ser.). 1996. 11.98 (978-1-55848-404-7(3)) EffectiveMN.
It's been said that the mind can make a heaven of hell & a hell of heaven. This helps to make your life more like a heaven.

Effective Meditations for Stress Relief. Robert E. Griswold & Deirdre M. Griswold. Read by Deirdre M. Griswold. 1 cass. (Contemporary Meditation Ser.). 1995. 11.98 (978-1-55848-401-6(9)) EffectiveMN.
Helps relax, free from excessive stress & in immediate control of physical & mental well-being.

Effective Meditations for Weight Control. Robert E. Griswold. Read by Deirdre M. Griswold. 1 cass. (Contemporary Meditation Ser.). 1995. 11.95 (978-1-55848-400-9(0)) EffectiveMN.
The key to permanent weight control is in your mind. Easy, natural method will do what diets could never accomplish.

Effective Negotiating. Jeremy Comfort. Told to York Associates Staff. (Oxford Business English Skills Ser.). 1999. 24.50 (978-0-19-457277-4(3)) OUP.

Effective Networking Freeway Guide. David Nour. Contrib. by David Nour. (Freeway Guides: Practical Audio for People on the Go Ser.). (ENG.). 2009. 34.99 (978-1-60812-505-0(X)) Find a World.

Effective Opening Statements & Closing Arguments. Read by Kevin Dunne et al. (Running Time: 3 hrs.). 1992. 89.00 Incl. 131p. tape materials. (CP-55255) Cont Ed Bar-CA.
Using videotaped demonstrations by leading California trial lawyers, experienced litigators explain the key elements of planning & presenting your opening statement & closing argument. They help you avoid common mistakes & learn when to respond to your opponent's statement or argument.

Effective Oral Presentations. unabr. ed. Read by W. F. Oettle. 3 cass. (Running Time: 3 hrs.). 350.00 Set, incl. 50p. manual. (B3) Am Chemical.

Effective Parenting in a Defective World CD Series. 2004. audio compact disk 22.00 (978-1-59834-011-2(5)) Walk Thru the Bible.

Effective Parenting Tips That Build Self-Esteem. James Battle. 1985. 9.50 (978-0-87562-091-6(4)) Spec Child.
Stresses the importance of parents & parent-figures as role models in putting children in the right frame of mind to learn by fostering a can-do attitude based on good self-regard. Includes many examples of specific things parents (& teachers) can say to children. Help improve their academic performance.

Effective Praise: A Study of a Christian's Life from Praise to His Presence. Gary V. Whetstone. 4 cass. (Running Time: 6 hrs.). (Empowerment Ser.). 1995. pap. bk. 35.00 (978-1-58866-179-1(2), VE007A) Gary Whet Pub.
Throughout the Old & New Testaments, praise played a significant role in the battles of life. Praise is biblically declared to release God's awesome authority.

Effective Prayer. Elbert Willis. 1 cass. (Outcome of Abiding in Jesus Ser.). 4.00 Fill the Gap.

Effective Prayer Series. Kenneth W. Hagin, Jr. 3 cass. 12.00 Set. (24J) Faith Lib Pubns.

***Effective Presentation Skills: Speaking in Public with Confidence.** Avril Carson. 1995. 98.70 (978-1-85811-105-6(6)) Pub: EMIS GBR. Dist(s): Intl Spec Bk

Effective Presentations. Jeremy Comfort. (Oxford Business English Skills Ser.). 1996. 24.50 (978-0-19-457066-4(5)) OUP.

Effective Project Management. Bill Hendricks. 8 cass. 10.95 wkbk. (901-C47) Natl Seminars.
Discover how to use "people resources" wisely so projects are completed on schedule & within budget every time.

Effective Salesmanship. 1 cass. (Running Time: 60 min.). 10.95 (012) Psych Res Inst.
Increase sales potential through a relaxed, courteous, & informative sales performance.

Effective Salesperson: Ten Quick Steps to Profitable Selling. Income Opportunities Editors. 1 cass. (Running Time: 60 min.). (Business Opportunities Ser.: Vol. 45). 1987. 7.95 (978-0-939963-13-3(2)) B & H Comm.
Describes why sales are lost, how to close a sale, creative selling technique, selling in hard times, beat the competition.

Effective Self-Hypnosis: Pathways to the Unconscious: With Steps to Self Hypnosis. C. Alexander Simpkins & Annellen M. Simpkins. 1 cass. 2000. bk. 44.95 (978-0-9679113-1-1(1)) Radiant Dolphin Pr.

Effective Short Selling. Instructed by Michael Smith. (Trade Secrets Audio Ser.). 2000. 19.95 (978-1-883272-75-3(0)) Marketplace Bks.

Effective Short Selling: Profiting in Bull & Bear Markets. Instructed by Michael Smith. 2005. audio compact disk 19.95 (978-1-59280-237-1(0)) Marketplace Bks.

Effective Social Action by Community Groups. Alvin Zander. (Management-Social & Behavioral Science Ser.). 1990. bk. 36.95 (978-1-55542-223-3(3), Jossey-Bass) Wiley US.

Effective Socializing. Jeremy Comfort. Told to York Associates Staff. (Oxford Business English Skills Ser.). 1997. 24.50 (978-0-19-457098-5(3)) OUP.

Effective Speaking. Barrie Konicov. 1 cass. 11.98 (978-0-87082-428-9(7), 030) Potentials.
This program is a guide for those who experience the incredible fear of speaking before a group.

Effective Speaking. Barrie Konicov. 1 CD. 2003. audio compact disk 16.98 (978-0-87082-971-0(8)) Potentials.
If you experience debilitating fear when you must speak before a group, this program was designed for you. You will find the self-hypnosis on track 1 and the subliminal on track 2. The easy-listening music of the subliminal, together with the self-hypnosis, is the original format which most people love and with which they are most familiar.

Effective Speaking. Betty L. Randolph. 1 cass. (Running Time: 45 min.). (Educational Ser.). 1989. 9.98 (978-1-55909-204-3(1), 76S) Randolph Tapes.
Learn to communicate ideas clearly & enjoy giving presentations. Subliminal messages are heard 3-5 minutes before becoming ocean sounds or music.

Effective Speaking: Without Fear. Robert E. Griswold. Read by Robert E. Griswold. 1 cass. 1992. 10.95 (978-1-55848-012-4(9)) EffectiveMN.
Speaking to one thousand people will be as easy & enjoyable as speaking to one person when you apply the communication skills presented in this program.

Effective Speaking & Writing. 1 cass. (Running Time: 60 min.). 10.95 (035) Psych Res Inst.
Unleash natural abilities to transfer information through the written & spoken word concisely & confidently.

Effective Speaking for Managers. unabr. ed. Robert L. Montgomery. 4 cass. 49.95 incl. guidebk. (S01810) J Norton Pubs.
Learn how to coordinate the elements of any speech; become more effective in one-on-one communication; conduct a meeting, control methods & problem-solving applications.

Effective Speaking for Managers. unabr. ed. Robert L. Montgomery. Read by Robert L. Montgomery. 4 cass. (Running Time: 60 min. per cass.). 1982. 49.95 incl. guide bk. (978-1-55678-026-4(5), 1587, Lrn Inc) Oasis Audio.
Analyze, capture & hold your audience, coordinate the elements of any speech for any purpose, conduct a meeting, discussion or conference using new control methods & problem solving applications.

Effective Speaking (Individual or Groups) Norman J. Caldwell. Read by Norman J. Caldwell. Ed. by Achieve Now Institute Staff. 1 cass. (Running Time: 20 min.). (Self-Directed Improvement Ser.). 1988. 9.97 (978-1-56273-061-1(4)) My Mothers Pub.
Express yourself & show confidence.

Effective Studying. Betty L. Randolph. Read by Betty L. Randolph. Read by Leonard Baron. Ed. by Success Education Institute International. 1 cass. (Running Time: 60 min.). (Educational Ser.). 1989. bk. 9.98 90 min. extended length stereo music. (58X); 9.98 (978-1-55909-194-7(0), 58S) Randolph Tapes.
"High-performance" learning with "brain-friendly" strategies. Subliminal messages are heard 3-5 minutes before becoming ocean sounds or music.

Effective Studying & Test Taking. Read by Robert E. Griswold. 1 cass. 1992. 10.95 (978-1-55848-013-1(7)) EffectiveMN.
Parents say this program has brought amazing results for their children. They now have a more positive attitude toward learning, & they are enjoying school & getting better grades.

Effective Teaching Methods: Research-Based Practice. 6th ed. Gary D. Borich. 2006. pap. bk. 88.00 (978-0-13-238859-7(6)) P-H.

Effective Team Building, Set. 6 cass. (Running Time: 6 hrs.). Incl. Effective Team Building: Definition of a Team. (80090); Effective Team Building: Developing an Open Atmosphere. (80090); Effective Team Building: Developing One-to-One Relationships. (80090); Effective Team Building: Developing the Team's Creative Potential. (80090); Effective Team Building: Improving Communication. (80090); Effective Team Building: Motivation & Change within a Team. (80090); Effective Team Building: Principles of Followership. (80090); Effective Team Building: Putting Together an Effective Team. (80090); Effective Team Building: The Communication Process. (80090); Effective Team Building: Using Leadership Skills. (80090); Establishing & Maintaining the Team. (80090); Understanding People. (80090); 165.00 (978-0-7612-0536-4(5), 80090) AMACOM.
Helps you to: align personal & corporate goals; find & build on employee strengths; reduce conflicts & politicking; increase morale & lower absenteeism by helping everyone recognize his or her importance to the team.

Effective Team Building: Definition of a Team see Effective Team Building

Effective Team Building: Developing an Open Atmosphere see Effective Team Building

Effective Team Building: Developing One-to-One Relationships see Effective Team Building

Effective Team Building: Developing the Team's Creative Potential see Effective Team Building

Effective Team Building: Improving Communication see Effective Team Building

Effective Team Building: Motivation & Change within a Team see Effective Team Building

Effective Team Building: Principles of Followership see Effective Team Building

Effective Team Building: Putting Together an Effective Team see Effective Team Building

Effective Team Building: The Communication Process see Effective Team Building

Effective Team Building: Using Leadership Skills see Effective Team Building

Effective Teamwork. Contrib. by Michael D. Magnin. 1 cass. (Running Time: 39 mins.). pap. bk. 99.95 (1027AV) J Wilson & Assocs.

Effective Technical Management. unabr. ed. Read by Augustus C. Walker. 5 cass. (Running Time: 5 hrs. 6 min.). 435.00 Set, incl. 165p. manual. (B4) Am Chemical.

Effective Techniques for Dealing with Difficult Customers. PUEI. 2007. audio compact disk 199.00 (978-1-934147-21-4(4), CareerTrack); audio compact disk 199.00 (978-1-934147-03-0(6), CareerTrack) P Univ E Inc.

***Effective Telephone Techniques.** Tony Hackett. 1995. 84.60 (978-1-85811-106-3(4)) Pub: EMIS GBR. Dist(s): Intl Spec Bk

Effective Telephoning. Jeremy Comfort. Told to York Associates Staff. (Oxford Business English Skills Ser.). 1996. 24.50 (978-0-19-457095-4(9)) OUP.

Effective Time Management. Norman J. Caldwell. Read by Norman J. Caldwell. Ed. by Achieve Now Institute Staff. 1 cass. (Running Time: 20 min.). (Success Now Ser.). 1988. 9.97 (978-1-56273-068-0(1)) My Mothers Pub.
Controlling your time & directing your future.

Effective Time Management for CPAs. Frank Sanitate. Read by Frank Sanitate. 6 cass. (Running Time: 10 hrs.). 1990. 135.00 set. (0941) Toolkit Media.

Effective Time Management in the Professional Firm, Set. Tony Hackett. 2 cass. 1999. 105.73 (978-1-85811-204-6(4)) Pub: EMIS GBR. Dist(s): Intl Spec Bk
In these days of fixed price work & close attention to costs by clients, fee-earners & support staff alike must use their time effectively. The first & most vital step is to take control of their time by thoroughly reviewing the way they work. Effective time management practices need to be put in place, including strategies for managing priorities, scheduling resources, delegating effectively & dealing with interruptions. Provides a cost effective solution, without bringing in an external trainer or sending everyone to courses.

Effective Transfer Tax Valuation Discount Planning. 2 cass. (Running Time: 1 hr. 54 min.). (Business Valuation Discount Planning & Tax Dispute Techniques Ser.). 1995. 125.00 Set, incl. study materials. (M231) Am Law Inst.
This fundamental program explains the principles of valuation to aid lawyers in developing effective valuation planning strategies & techniques. It provides an overview of the transfer tax "fair market value" tradition for estate, gift, & GST purposes & examines the willing buyer-willing seller principles. Also discusses Revenue Rulings 59-60 & 93-12 (& their judicial interpretation) in the context of the fair market value tradition. Also explores choice of entity issues, special valuation rules (including the gift tax & transfer tax provisions of Chapter 14, IRC Sections 2701-2704), & asset selection & funding issues.

Effective Use of Paralegals in the Law Office. Read by Stanley A. Smith et al. 1 cass. 1989. 20.00 (AL-68) PA Bar Inst.

Effective Use of Real Evidence at Trial. 1986. bk. 65.00; 35.00 PA Bar Inst.

Effective Way of Learning, Reading, Writing, & Speaking Chinese Level 1: Practical Chinese. Wendy Lin. 2000. 5.00 (978-0-9715058-3-4(7)); 5.00 (978-0-9715058-5-8(3)) Creative Wrld Ent.

Effective Way of Learning, Reading, Writing, & Speaking Chinese Level 2: Practical Chinese. Wendy Lin. 2000. 5.00 (978-0-9715058-6-5(1)); 5.00 (978-0-9715058-4-1(5)) Creative Wrld Ent.

Effective Weight Loss. Mary Lee LaBay. 2006. audio compact disk 12.95 (978-1-934705-13-1(6)) Awareness Engin.

Effective Writing for Business, College, & Life. unabr. ed. William Stanek. Read by Ron Knowles. (YA). 2008. 39.99 (978-1-60514-572-3(6)) Find a World.

Effective Writing for Business, College, & Life. unabr. ed. William Stanek. Narrated by Ron Knowles. (Running Time: 2 hrs. 44 mins.). (ENG.). 2006. 16.95 (978-1-57545-320-0(7), RP Audio Pubng) Pub: Reagent Press. Dist(s): OverDrive Inc

Effectively Teaching the Faith. Steve Kellmeyer. 2005. 11.95 (978-0-9767368-8-2(8)) Bridegroom.

Effectively Using Persuasion in Your Oral Presentations: Capitol Learning Audio Course. James B. Lees. Prod. by TheCapitol.Net. (ENG.). 2007. 47.00 (978-1-58733-065-0(2)) TheCapitol.

Effectively Using Your Psychic Healing Power. 1 CD. (Running Time: 30 minutes). 1999. 14.95 (978-0-9779472-4-9(6)) Health Wealth Inc.
Combine the power of your subconscious mind with your psychic (intuitive/spiritual) abilities! Learn how to tune up in vibration, quickly and easily, to experience well-being on all levels. A great tool to maintain your mind and emotions in peace and calm. You will be guided to enter into a positive trance state and use simple and effective techniques to clear away any stress or foreign energy you may have collected during your day.

Effectiveness of Chaplaincy. 1 cass. (Care Cassettes Ser.: Vol. 13, No. 1). 1986. 10.80 Assn Prof Chaplains.

Effects of Absent Father. Donna Henson. Read by Donna Henson. 1 cass. (Running Time: 90 min.). 1994. 8.95 (1139) Am Fed Astrologers.

Effects of Divorce. 1 cass. (Running Time: 90 min.). (Mother Angelica Live Ser.). 10.00 (978-1-55794-055-1(X), T6) Eternal Wrd TV.

Effects of Emotion on Physiology. Ingrid Naiman. 4 cass. (Running Time: 5 hrs.). 30.00 (978-1-882834-96-9(8)) Seventh Ray.
How feelings affect the functioning of the body.

Effects of Exercise on the Female. 2 cass. (Gynecology & Obstetrics Ser.). 15.00 (8563 (C85-GO5)) Am Coll Surgeons.

Effects of Federal Aid to Education. unabr. ed. Roger A. Freeman. 1 cass. (Running Time: 43 min.). 12.95 (136) J Norton Pubs.
Freeman discusses the trends in modern education & the effects of federal aid, the public's loss of confidence in school & university administrators, & campus unrest.

Effects of Maternal Depression on Children. Contrib. by Douglas M. Teti et al. 1 cass. (American Academy of Pediatrics UPDATE: Vol. 17, No. 1). 1998. 20.00 Am Acad Pediat.

Effects of Praise. Andrew Wommack. 3 cass. (Running Time: 4 hrs. 20 min.). 14.00 Set. (978-0-9623936-9-3(X), 1004) A Wommack.
Satan is trying to cut us off from one of our greatest sources of power. This three-tape series will help you fight back. Praise is God's antidote & prevention for depression.

Effects of Praise: New Updated Compact Disk. 3 CDs. 2004. audio compact disk 21.00 (978-1-59548-011-8(0)) A Wommack.

Effects of Stimulants & Narcotic Drugs on the Human Psyche. Instructed by Manly P. Hall. 8.95 (978-0-89314-103-5(8), S800133) Philos Res.

Effectual Fervent Prayer. 4 cass. 2000. 18.00 (978-1-930766-21-1(1)) Bishop Bobby.

Effectual Grace; His Name is Wonderful. Ann Ree Colton & Jonathan Murro. 1 cass. 7.95 A R Colton Fnd.

Effi Briest. Theodor Fontane. audio compact disk 12.95 (978-0-8219-3797-6(9)) EMC-Paradigm.

Efficient Thinking. unabr. ed. Nathaniel Branden. 1 cass. (Running Time: 1 hr. 28 min.). (Basic Principles of Objectivism Ser.). 12.95 (566) J Norton Pubs.
The nature of clear thinking; psuedo-thinking; the nature of definitions; common thinking errors. Guest lecture by Barbara Branden.

Efficient Thinking, Principles Of. unabr. ed. Barbara Branden. 10 cass. (Running Time: 15 hrs.). 79.50 (978-0-88432-215-3(7), S01528) J Norton Pubs.
Deals with thinking in both its theoretical & practical aspects.

Effort & Freedom. Read by Osel Tendzin. 3 cass. 1984. 34.00 (A096) Vajradhatu.
How to practice meditation without struggle.

Effort & Grace. Speeches. As told by Swami PRABHVANANDA. 1. (Running Time: 50 MINS.). 2003. 9.95 (978-0-87481-351-7(4)) Vedanta Pr.
A LECTURE ON HOW TO PRACTICE SPIRITUALITY, AND THE ROLE OF GRACE IS SPIRITUAL GROWTH.

Effortless Change. Created by AWMI. (ENG.). 2001. 25.00 (978-1-59548-059-0(5)) A Wommack.

Effortless Change. Created by AWMI. (ENG.). 2004. audio compact disk 25.00 (978-1-59548-010-1(2)) A Wommack.

Effortless Prosperity, Set, Bk. 1, Vol. 1. 16 cass. (Running Time: 16 hrs.). 1997. 75.00 (978-1-930455-07-8(0)) E P Inc Pubng Co.
30 lessons on 16 tapes which describes the effortless prosperity lessons in detail.

Effortless Prosperity, Set, Bk. 2, Vol. 2. 16 cass. (Running Time: 15 hrs. 30 min.). 1999. 75.00 (978-1-930455-08-5(9)) E P Inc Pubng Co.
This companion for Effortless Prosperity Book 2 consists of lessons 31-60 on 15 tapes.

Effortless Prosperity: Effortless Health. 1 cass. (Running Time: 1 hr.). 1999. 10.00 (978-1-930455-12-2(7)) E P Inc Pubng Co.
Effortless health by good nutrition and peace of mind.

Effortless Prosperity Set, Vol. 1, Seminars 1, 2, 3, 4: How to Open to Receive. 4 cass. (Running Time: 5 hrs. 30 min.). 1997. 35.00 (978-1-930455-09-2(7)) E P Inc Pubng Co.

Effortless Prosperity Vol. 2: How to Open to Receive. 4 cass. (Running Time: 4 hrs.). 1997. 35.00 (978-1-930455-10-8(0)) E P Inc Pubng Co.

Effortless Relaxation. Steven Halpern. 1 cass. (Soundwave Two Thousand, the Audio Active Subliminal Ser.). 1990. (2014) Inner Peace Mus.
Beautiful new age music with subliminal affirmations.

Effortless Success: How to Get What You Want & Have a Great Time Doing It! Michael Neill. 6 CDs. 2008. audio compact disk 34.95 (978-1-4019-1908-5(1)) Hay House.

Effortless Weight Loss. Barry Tesar. 1 cass. (Running Time: 1 hr.). (Subliminal Inspiration Ser.). 1992. 9.98 (978-1-56470-001-8(1)) Success Cass.
Subliminal program.

Efforts & Emancipation. Swami Amar Jyoti. 1 cass. 1987. 9.95 (M-73) Truth Consciousness.
The Vedic formula; Artha, Kama, Dharma, Moksha. Linking virtue & Liberation. Freedom from death. Study & control of mind & body. The ingredients of wisdom.

Efforts & Surrender. Swami Amar Jyoti. 1 cass. 1978. 9.95 (C-14) Truth Consciousness.
Effacing the line between ego & God. After surrender, efforts are guided & sanctified.

Eflexx Awareness Meditation. unabr. ed. Mike Angulo. (Running Time: 40 mins.). (ENG.). 2007. 9.98 (978-1-59659-155-4(2), GildAudio) Pub: Gildan Media. Dist(s): HachBkGrp

Eflexx Empowerment Meditation. unabr. ed. Mike Angulo. (Running Time: 32 mins.). (ENG.). 2007. 9.98 (978-1-59659-157-8(9), GildAudio) Pub: Gildan Media. Dist(s): HachBkGrp

Eflexx Meditation Bundle: Awareness Meditation, Empowerment Meditation, Sound Meditation. Mike Angulo. Read by Mike Angulo. (Playaway Adult Nonfiction Ser.). (ENG.). 2009. 69.99 (978-1-60775-719-1(2)) Find a World.

Eflexx Sound Meditation. unabr. ed. Mike Angulo. (Running Time: 48 mins.). (ENG.). 2007. 9.98 (978-1-59659-156-1(0), GildAudio) Pub: Gildan Media. Dist(s): HachBkGrp

Egalitarianism & Inflation. Ayn Rand. Read by Ayn Rand. 1 cass. (Running Time: 80 min.). 12.95 (978-1-56114-076-3(7), AR16C) Second Renaissance.
What is the source of the phenomenon of inflation? Seeking a more fundamental explanation than that provided by politics or economics, Ayn Rand says the answer is: the pre-conceptual epistemology of primitives. She presents a stunning analysis of the cognitive processes underlying the evolution of economic production, including the recognition of the nature of time & saving.

Egalitarianism & Inflation. Comment by Ayn Rand. 1 cass. (Running Time: 80 min.). (Ford Hall Forum Ser.). 1974. 12.95 (AR16C) Second Renaissance.
How the preconceptual epistemology of primitives is the fundamental source of inflation. Analysis of how production - requiring a grasp of the link between time & savings - evolved. Includes Q&A.

Egermeier's ABC Bible Storybook: Favorite Stories Adapted for Young Children. Elsie Egermeier. Ed. by Karen Rhodes. Illus. by Laura Gibbons Nikiel. Adapted by Arlene S. Hall. (ENG.). (J). (ps-5). 2007. bk. 14.99 (978-1-59317-198-8(6)) Warner Pr.

Egg Money. JoAnne Lower. 1 cass. 1997. (978-1-888940-03-9(4)); audio compact disk (978-1-888940-04-6(2)) J Lower Ent.
Personal stories of growing up on a small Midwestern farm set to the music of hammered dulcimer, banjo, fiddle, mandolin & harmonica.

Egg Series, Set. Mary Jane Auch. Illus. by Mary Jane Auch. Read by Larry Robinson. 2 vols. (Running Time: 24 mins.). (J). (gr. k-3). 2000. pap. bk. 29.95 (978-0-87499-572-5(8)) Live Oak Media.
Includes: "The Easter Egg Farm" & "Eggs Mark the Spot.".

Eggs. unabr. ed. Jerry Spinelli. Read by Cassandra Morris & Suzanne Toren. (Running Time: 4 hrs.). (ENG.). (J). (gr. 3-7). 2007. 9.98 (978-1-59483-971-9(9)) Pub: Hachet Audio. Dist(s): HachBkGrp

Eggs. unabr. ed. Jerry Spinelli. Read by Suzanne Toren & Cassandra Morris. 4 cass. (Running Time: 4 hrs. 50 mins.). (J). (gr. 4-7). 2007. 30.75 (978-1-4281-4820-8(5)); audio compact disk 46.75 (978-1-4281-4825-3(6)) Recorded Bks.

Eggs, Beans & Crumpets. unabr. ed. P. G. Wodehouse. Read by Jonathan Cecil. 6 cass. (Running Time: 9 hrs.). 2001. 54.95 (978-0-7540-0658-9(1), CAB 2080) Pub: Chivers Audio Bks GBR. Dist(s): AudioGO
Funny short stories feature a cast of outrageous characters, all plotting to save themselves from wedlock, poverty or ignominy with various degrees of success.

Eggs, Eggs, Eggs. (Sails Literacy Ser.). (gr. 1 up). 10.00 (978-0-7578-2659-7(8)) Rigby Educ.

Eggs Mark the Spot. Mary Jane Auch. Illus. by Mary Jane Auch. Read by Larry Robinson. 14 vols. (Running Time: 14 mins.). (Egg Ser.). 1997. pap. bk. & tchr. ed. 37.95 Reading Chest. (978-0-87499-389-9(X)) Live Oak Media.
Pauline is a hen that can lay an egg that bears the image of whatever she is looking at. How she provides clues to a burglary, makes her a heroine.

Eggs Mark the Spot. unabr. ed. Mary Jane Auch. Illus. by Mary Jane Auch. Read by Larry Robinson. 1 cass. (Running Time: 14 mins.). (Egg Ser.). (J). (gr. k-3). 1997. bk. 24.95 (978-0-87499-388-2(1)); pap. bk. 15.95 (978-0-87499-387-5(3)) Live Oak Media.

Eggs Must Be Broken... (an Essay from Things I've Learned from Women Who've Dumped Me) abr. ed. Tom Shillue. Read by Tom Shillue. Ed. by Ben Karlin. (Running Time: 15 mins.). (ENG.). 2008. 1.98 (978-1-60024-335-6(5)) Pub: Hachet Audio. Dist(s): HachBkGrp

Eglantine. Catherine Jinks. Read by Melissa Chambers. (Running Time: 3 hrs. 20 mins.). (Allie's Ghost Hunters Ser.: Bk. 1). (J). 2009. 54.99 (978-1-74214-408-5(X), 9781742144085) Pub: Bolinda Pubng AUS. Dist(s): Bolinda Pub Inc

Eglantine. unabr. ed. Catherine Jinks. Read by Melissa Chambers. 3 CDs. (Running Time: 3 hrs. 20 mins.). (Allie's Ghost Hunters Ser.: Bk. 1). (J). (gr. 4-7). 2007. audio compact disk 54.95 (978-1-74093-997-3(2), 9781740939973) Pub: Bolinda Pubng AUS. Dist(s): Bolinda Pub Inc

Ego. unabr. ed. Aldous Huxley. 1 cass. (Running Time: 1 hr. 3 min.). (Human Situation Ser.). 1959. 11.00 (01115) Big Sur Tapes.

Ego, A Quaint Absurdity. Kenneth Wapnick. 2008. 12.00 (978-1-59142-354-6(6)); audio compact disk 15.00 (978-1-59142-353-9(8)) Foun Miracles.

Ego & Desire, Cosmos Connections. Ann Ree Colton & Jonathan Murro. 1 cass. 7.95 A R Colton Fnd.

Ego & Forgiveness see Ego und die Vergebung

Ego & Forgiveness. Kenneth Wapnick. 2 cass. (Running Time: 3 hrs.). 1985. 10.00 (978-0-933291-55-3(8), T-5) Foun Miracles.
Overview of the principles of A Course in Miracles.

Ego & Forgiveness. Kenneth Wapnick. 3 CDs. 2005. audio compact disk 17.00 (978-1-59142-189-4(6), CD5) Foun Miracles.

***Ego & Forgiveness.** Kenneth Wapnick. 2010. 13.00 (978-1-59142-478-9(X)) Foun Miracles.

Ego & Its Projections. Read by Chogyam Trungpa. 5 cass. 1976. 45.00 (A025) Vajradhatu.
Five talks. "Who are we? What are We? We have to come to some kind of understanding of that".

Ego & Its Relations with the Unconscious. Read by Robert Moore. 2 cass. (Running Time: 2 hrs.). 1991. 16.95 Set. (978-0-7822-0207-6(1), 439) C G Jung IL.

Ego & Self Abandonment. Swami Amar Jyoti. 1 cass. 1989. 9.95 (R-93) Truth Consciousness.
Ego, the crucial & most missed point; a nondualistic approach.

Ego & Soul. Richard Rohr. 1 cass. (Running Time: 60 min.). 8.95 (AA2849) Credence Commun.
The psychological laws we learn to fit into a competitive world work wonderfully there. But as we approach God, the rules change. What worked so well in the world of achievement is subverted as we learn a new way of being, seeing & relating. Rohr explains these new movements of the soul. Profoundly refreshing.

Ego & the Unbound Self. Swami Amar Jyoti. 1 cass. 1977. 9.95 (N-18) Truth Consciousness.
Topics include: what is ego? Returning to the True Self; the need for a Master; spirituality in the USA; spirituality & science; faith, suffering & grace; finding God in our world; intelligence & enlightenment.

Ego As Hero. Read by John Van Eenwyk. 1 cass. (Running Time: 2 hrs.). 1984. 12.95 (978-0-7822-0311-0(6), 157) C G Jung IL.

Ego Scriptor Cantilenae: The Music of Ezra Pound. Ezra Pound. 2004. audio compact disk 21.99 (978-84-390-1005-0(2)) Pub: Cupsa Edit ESP. Dist(s): SPD-Small Pr Dist

Ego, Self, & Essence. John C. Lilly. 6 cass. (Running Time: 6 hrs.). 1971. 56.00 set. (03910) Big Sur Tapes.
Includes Introduction to Satori States; Relationship of States; Through the Screen of Words; Programming the Work; Samples of the Work & A Clean 48 & the Narrow Slot.

Ego-States & Hidden Observers & the Women in Black & the Lady in White. unabr. ed. John G. Watkins & Helen H. Watkins. (Sound Seminars Ser.). 34.50 (978-0-88432-065-4(0)) J Norton Pubs.

Ego Strikes Back: The Return of the Repressed. Kenneth Wapnick. 2008. 20.00 (978-1-59142-344-7(9)); audio compact disk 25.00 (978-1-59142-343-0(0)) Foun Miracles.

Ego und die Vergebung. 1 cass. (Running Time: 1 hr.).Tr. of Ego & Forgiveness. 2001. (978-3-923662-50-0(5)) Foun Miracles.

Ego...Cause & Effect/Love Relationships. Marianne Williamson. Read by Marianne Williamson. 1 cass. (Running Time: 90 mins.). (Lectures on a Course in Miracles). 1999. 10.00 (978-1-56170-187-2(4), M715) Hay House.

Egoism, The Ethics Of. unabr. ed. Robert LeFevre & George H. Smith. 1 cass. (Running Time: 1 hr. 23 min.). 12.95 (337) J Norton Pubs.

Egoist, Set. unabr. ed. George Meredith. Read by Flo Gibson. 13 cass. (Running Time: 19 hrs.). 1992. 41.95 (978-1-55685-248-0(7)) Audio Bk Con.
To be jilted twice (or thrice?) is a ghastly nightmare for Sir Willoughby Patterne, the handsome, wealthy egoist, who is deeply concerned about his image & stature in the county.

Egoist: A Comedy in Narrative see Cambridge Treasury of English Prose: Dickens to Butler

Ægypt. John Crowley. Read by John Crowley. (Running Time: 61200 sec.). 2007. 89.95 (978-1-4332-0110-3(0)); audio compact disk 120.00 (978-1-4332-0111-0(9)); audio compact disk 44.95 (978-1-4332-0112-7(7)) Blckstn Audio.

Egypt. (Running Time: 60 mins.). 2002. audio compact disk 15.99 (978-1-904972-57-0(8)) Global Jrny GBR GBR.

Egypt. Contrib. by Time-Life Audiobooks Staff. (Lost Civilizations Ser.). 1999. (978-1-57042-726-8(7)) Hachet Audio.

Egypt Game. Zilpha Keatley Snyder. Narrated by Alyssa Bresnahan. 5 CDs. (Running Time: 5 hrs. 15 mins.). (gr. 5 up). 1967. audio compact disk 48.00 (978-1-4025-1483-8(2), C1608) Recorded Bks.
This lively, funny tale of six children who create a game centered on ancient Egyptian lore showcases all the reasons why critics hail Zilpha Keatley Snyder as one of America's most talented children's author.

Egypt Game, unabr. ed. Zilpha Keatley Snyder. Narrated by Alyssa Bresnahan. 4 pieces. (Running Time: 5 hrs. 15 mins.). (gr. 5 up). 1994. 35.00 (978-0-7887-0077-4(4), 94310E7) Recorded Bks.
A group of children find themselves involved in a mystery while playing an elaborate game in the empty lot behind an old curiosity shop.

Egyptian Arabic. unabr. ed. Pimsleur Staff. 4 CDs. (Running Time: 400 hrs. 0 mins. NaN sec.). (Pimsleur Language Program Ser.). (ENG.). 2001. audio compact disk 19.95 (978-0-7435-0816-2(5), Pimsleur) Pub: S&S Audio. Dist(s): S and S Inc

Egyptian Arabic: Learn to Speak & Understand Egyptian Arabic with Pimsleur Language Programs. unabr. ed. Pimsleur. Created by Pimsleur. 8 CDs. (Running Time: 80 hrs. 0 mins. 0 sec.). (Instant Conversation Ser.). (ARA, EGY & ENG.). 2006. audio compact disk 49.95 (978-0-7435-5115-1(X), Pimsleur) Pub: S&S Audio. Dist(s): S and S Inc

Egyptian Arabic: Learn to Speak & Understand Egyptian Arabic with Pimsleur Language Programs. unabr. ed. Pimsleur Staff. 16 CDs. (Running Time: 160 hrs. 0 mins. 0 sec.). (Comprehensive Ser.). (ENG.). 2001. audio compact disk 345.00 (978-0-7435-0659-5(6), Pimsleur) Pub: S&S Audio. Dist(s): S and S Inc

Egyptian Arabic: Learn to Speak & Understand Egyptian Arabic with Pimsleur Language Programs. unabr. ed. Pimsleur Staff. 5 CDs. (Running Time: 50 hrs. 0 mins. 0 sec.). (Basic Ser.). (ARA, EGY & ENG.). 2005. audio compact disk 24.95 (978-0-7435-5078-9(1), Pimsleur) Pub: S&S Audio. Dist(s): S and S Inc

Egyptian Myths & Magic. Katie Green. Perf. by Tony Vacca. 2 CDs. (Running Time: 98 min.). 2002. audio compact disk 25.00 (978-0-9722032-0-3(6)) Oak Stars.

Egyptian Shamanism As a Way of Knowledge. Nicki Scully. 2 cass. 18.00 set. (A0452-89) Sound Photosyn.

Egyptian Tarot. unabr. ed. Angeles Arrien. 2 cass. (Running Time: 2 hrs.). 1982. 18.00 Set. (00201) Big Sur Tapes.
Referring to the Thoth tarot deck, Arrien explains how the tarot symbols provide a visual map of specific tools for aiding growth & transformation.

Egyptian Treasures: Mummies & Myths. unabr. ed. Short Stories. As told by Jim Weiss. 1 cass. (Running Time: 1 hr.). Dramatization. (J). (gr. 2 up). 1999. 10.95 (978-1-882513-22-2(3), 1124-22) Greathall Prods.
Come face to face with a mummy! Meet ancient Egyptian gods, pyramid builders, an expert thief and a modern detective in true stories. Includes "The Great Myths of Egypt," "Osiris and Set," "The Secret Name of Ra-Amun," "A Rival for the Throne," "The Courage of Isis," The Pyramid Builders" and "The Mummy's Tomb".

Egyptian Treasures: Mummies & Myths. unabr. ed. Short Stories. As told by Jim Weiss. 1 CD. (Running Time: 1 hr.). Dramatization. (J). (gr. 2 up). 2001. audio compact disk 14.95 (978-1-882513-47-5(9), 1124-022) Greathall Prods.

Egyptological Bibliography 1822-1997. 1 CD. (Running Time: 1 hr. 30 mins.). 2001. audio compact disk 99.00 (978-90-6258-961-6(8)) Pub: Netherlands Inst NLD. Dist(s): Eisenbrauns

Egyptologie. Jean Yoyotte. 1 cass. (Running Time: 60 mins.). (College de France Lectures). (FRE.). 1996. 21.95 (1850-LQP) Olivia & Hill.

Egyptologist: A Novel. Arthur Phillips. 12 CDs. (Running Time: 15 hrs.). 2004. audio compact disk 34.99 (978-1-4025-8956-0(5), 02502) Recorded Bks.

Egypt's Eternal Light: 2009 Calendar. 2008. 16.95 (978-977-416-147-6(5)) Pub: Am Univ Cairo Pr EGY. Dist(s): Intl Pubs Mktg

Eh Canada. Pierre Berton. 2 CDs. (Running Time: 3 hrs.). 2005. audio compact disk 15.95 (978-0-660-18321-3(8)) Pub: Canadian Broadcasting CAN. Dist(s): Georgetown Term

Ehlers-Danlos Syndrome - A Bibliography & Dictionary for Physicians, Patients, & Genome Researchers. Compiled by Icon Group International, Inc. Staff. 2007. ring bd. 28.95 (978-0-497-11205-9(1)) Icon Grp.

EHypnotapes: Tension Relief. James E. Walton. 2001. audio compact disk 24.95 (978-0-9711939-0-1(8)) J E Walton.

Eifelheim. unabr. ed. Michael Flynn. Read by Anthony Heald. (Running Time: 63000 sec.). 2007. 59.95 (978-1-4332-0610-8(2)); audio compact disk 72.00 (978-1-4332-0611-5(0)); audio compact disk 29.95 (978-1-4332-0612-2(9)) Blckstn Audio.

Eiger Dreams: Ventures among Men & Mountains. unabr. ed. Jon Krakauer. Read by Philip Franklin. 6 cass. (Running Time: 9 hrs.). 1998. 48.00 (978-0-7366-4126-5(2), 4630) Books on Tape.
The author of "Into Thin Air" examines mountaineering & the drive to climb above the clouds & look death in the eye.

Eiger Dreams: Ventures among Men & Mountains. unabr. ed. Jon Krakauer. Read by Philip Franklin. 6 cass. (Running Time: 9 hrs.). Set. North Star.
Krakaver explores mountaineering from the unique perspective of one who has himself battled peaks like k2, Denali, Everest & the Eiger - always with a keen eye; an open heart & a hunger for the ultimate experience.

Eiger Sanction. unabr. ed. Trevanian. Read by Joe Barrett. (Running Time: 11 hrs. 0 mins.). 2009. 29.95 (978-1-4332-5942-5(7)); audio compact disk 65.95 (978-1-4332-5938-8(9)); audio compact disk 90.00 (978-1-4332-5939-5(7)) Blckstn Audio.

Eight Black Horses. Ed McBain, pseud. Read by Jonathan Marosz. (87th Precinct Ser.: Bk. 38). 1999. 56.00 (978-0-7366-4873-8(9)); 56.00 (5097) Books on Tape.
Acts of revenge against the cops on the trial of a psychopathic killer.

Eight Brocades Taoist Yoga Guided Practice CD. Created by Valley Spirit Arts. (ENG.). 2007. audio compact disk 19.95 (978-1-889633-24-4(0)) Valley SpiritA.

Eight Cousins. Louisa May Alcott. Narrated by Flo Gibson. (ENG.). (J). 2008. audio compact disk 27.95 (978-1-60646-013-9(7)) Audio Bk Con.

Eight Cousins, unabr. ed. Louisa May Alcott. Read by Flo Gibson. 5 cass. (Running Time: 6 hrs. 30 min.). 1997. 20.95 (978-1-55685-436-1(6)) Audio Bk Con.
Orphaned at thirteen, Rose goes to live with her uncle Alec. Here she meets her seven spirited boy cousins with whom she has home-spun fun & many exciting adventures.

Eight Cousins. unabr. ed. Louisa May Alcott. Narrated by Barbara Caruso. 6 pieces. (Running Time: 8 hrs.). (gr. 7 up). 2002. 54.00 (978-1-4025-1987-1(7)) Recorded Bks.
Recently orphaned, young Rose Campbell is sent to the "Aunt Hill," where Uncle Alex, her six aunts and seven boy cousins live in noisy confusion. It is nothing like the quiet girls' boarding school that has been Rose's home for the past year. Surrounded by a bewildering array of pets, relatives, and unfamiliar foods, the fragile girl wonders if she will ever get used to this new life. Fortunately, Uncle Alex is her guardian. He keeps the aunts from coddling her too much, and makes sure that she has plenty of time to play outside with her cousins. Day by day, learning how to care for each of these people, Rose begins to bloom.

Eight Days of Hanukkah. George David Weiss. 1 cass. (J). 1991. 8.95 (978-1-879756-00-7(5)) Holiday Time.

Eight Days to Live. abr. ed. Iris Johansen. Read by Jennifer Van Dyck. 5 CDs. (Running Time: 6 hrs.). (Eve Duncan Ser.). 2010. audio compact disk 24.99 (978-1-4233-2948-0(1), 9781423329480, BACD) Brilliance Audio.

Eight Days to Live. abr. ed. Iris Johansen. (Running Time: 6 hrs.). (Eve Duncan Ser.). 2010. audio compact disk 14.99 (978-1-4233-2949-7(X), 9781423329497, BCD Value Price) Brilliance Audio.

***Eight Days to Live.** abr. ed. Iris Johansen. Read by Jennifer Van Dyck. (Running Time: 6 hrs.). (Eve Duncan Ser.). 2010. 14.99 (978-1-4418-8321-6(5), 9781441883216, BAD) Brilliance Audio.

Eight Days to Live. unabr. ed. Iris Johansen. Read by Jennifer Van Dyck. 1 MP3-CD. (Running Time: 12 hrs.). (Eve Duncan Ser.). 2010. 24.99 (978-1-4233-2944-2(9), 9781423329442, Brilliance MP3); 24.99 (978-1-4233-2946-6(5), 9781423329466, BAD); 39.97 (978-1-4233-2945-9(7), 9781423329459, Brinc Audio MP3 Lib); 39.97 (978-1-4233-2947-3(3), 9781423329473, BADLE); audio compact disk 36.99 (978-1-4233-2942-8(2), 9781423329428, Bril Audio CD Unabri) Brilliance Audio.

***Eight Days to Live.** unabr. ed. Iris Johansen. Read by Jennifer Van Dyck. 11 CDs. (Running Time: 12 hrs.). (Eve Duncan Ser.). 2010. audio compact disk 97.97 (978-1-4233-2943-5(0), 9781423329435, BriAudCD Unabrid) Brilliance Audio.

Eight Deadly Supervisory Traps. Joseph Procaccini. 1986. 9.75 (978-0-932491-40-4(5)) Res Appl Inc.
Supervisors can "walk on water" if they know where the stones are. Avoid being "all wet" as a manager by identifying common pitfalls: Super-rational Perspective, Resource Myopia, Persian King Syndrome, Action Addiction... & much more.

Eight Faces of Faith: Connecting Catechesis & Learning. Gretchen Hailer. 2 cass. (Running Time: 2 hrs.). 2001. 16.95 (A6810) St Anthony Mess Pr.
Discusses ways of learning: linguistic, mathematical, musical, bodily, spatial, interpersonal, intrapersonal and naturalist.

Eight Feet in the Andes. unabr. ed. Dervla Murphy. Read by Kate Binchy. 12 cass. (Running Time: 12 hrs. 50 min.). (Isis Ser.). (J). 2004. 94.95 (978-1-85089-782-8(4), 89011) Pub: ISIS Lrg Prnt GBR. Dist(s): Ulverscroft US

Eight-Fold Cycle of Transformation. Maria K. Simms. 1 cass. 1992. 8.95 (1089) Am Fed Astrologers.

***Eight for Eternity.** unabr. ed. Mary Reed. (Running Time: 10 hrs. 0 mins.). (John the Lord Chamberlain Mystery Ser.). 2010. 29.95 (978-1-4417-2652-0(7)); 59.95 (978-1-4417-2648-3(9)); audio compact disk 90.00 (978-1-4417-2649-0(7)) Blckstn Audio.

Eight-Great. abr. ed. Robert A. Monroe. Read by Robert A. Monroe. (Running Time: 30 min.). (Human Plus Ser.). 1989. 14.95 (978-1-56102-009-6(5)) Inter Indus.
Redirect mental & physical states to express your best.

Eight Great False Responsibilities of Life. Guy Finley. (ENG.). 2006. 7.49 (978-1-929320-55-4(8)) Life of Learn.

Eight Great Plays: As Literature & As Philosphy. Leonard Peikoff. 18 cass. (Running Time: 18 hrs.). 1994. 195.00 Set. (978-1-56114-212-5(3), LP39D) Second Renaissance.
Designed to enhance the ability to understand, judge & savor the values offered by great drama. Plays discussed: "Antigone"; "Othello"; "Le Cid"; "Don Carlos"; "An Enemy of the People"; "Saint Joan"; "Monna Vanna"; "Cyrano de Bergerac".

Eight Hour Supervisor. Gib Whiteman. 8 cass. 39.95 incl. study guide. (3044) SyberVision.
Just a few of the contents: leadership & motivation, effective supervisory listening, managing supervisory stress, managing supervisory time, effective communication for supervisors & managers, management skills for supervisors & managers.

Eight Laws of Leadership. Elmer L. Towns. 3 cass. 99.95 Set, incl. planning & promotional materials, gifts & personality inventories, textbk. (421) Chrch Grwth VA.

Eight Little Piggies. unabr. collector's ed. Stephen Jay Gould. Read by Larry McKeever. 13 cass. (Running Time: 19 hrs. 30 min.). 1993. 104.00 (978-0-7366-2469-5(4), 3232) Books on Tape.
Collection of 31 essays drawn from Gould's columns in Natural History magazine.

Eight Men Out. unabr. ed. Eliot Asinof. Read by Harold N. Cropp. 8 cass. (Running Time: 11 hrs. 30 mins.). 1996. 56.95 (978-0-7861-0995-1(5), 1772) Blckstn Audio.
"The Most Gigantic Sporting Swindle in the History of America!" These headlines proclaiming the 1919 fix of the World Series startled millions of readers & focused the attention of the entire country on one of the most incredible episodes ever to be enacted in the public eye. After painstaking research, Eliot Asinof has reconstructed the entire scene-by-scene story of this fantastic scandal in which eight Chicago White Sox players arranged with the nation's leading gamblers to throw the series to Cincinnati.

Eight Men Out. unabr. ed. Eliot Asinof. Read by Paul Shay. 9 cass. (Running Time: 13 hrs. 30 min.). 1991. 72.00 (978-0-7366-1882-3(1), 2711) Books on Tape.
"Say it ain't so, Joe, say it ain't so." But to the horror of their teammates & all of America, eight members of the champion Chicago White Sox gave in to greed & threw the 1919 World Series. Eliot Asinof vividly describes the tense meetings, the hitches in the plot, the actual plays in which the series was thrown, the grand jury indictment & the famous 1921 trial. Here, too, is a graphic picture of the American underworld that managed the fix, the shocked newspapermen who uncovered the story & the war-exhausted nation that turned to the Series for relief, only to be rocked by the scandal.

Eight Million Ways to Die. unabr. ed. Lawrence Block. Read by Lawrence Block. 8 vols. (Running Time: 12 hrs.). (Matthew Scudder Mystery Ser.: No. 5). 2000. bk. 69.95 (978-0-7927-2224-3(8), CSL 113, Chivers Sound Lib) AudioGO.
Kim was a young hooker who wanted out, seeking Matthew Scudder's protection. She didn't deserve to live the way she did, or die the way she did: slashed to ribbons in the seedy waterfront district. Now Scudder wants to find her killer. But her investigation into Kim's shady past reveals lethal secrets even dirtier than her clients. And there's more than young flesh for sale, because now Scudder's life is on the market.

Eight Million Ways to Die. unabr. ed. Lawrence Block. 10 CDs. (Running Time: 15 hrs.). (Matthew Scudder Mystery Ser.: No. 5). 2000. audio compact disk 94.95 (978-0-7927-9976-4(3), SLD 027, Chivers Sound Lib) AudioGO.

Eight New Rules of Real Estate. John Tuccillo. 1 cass. (Running Time: 118 min.). 2000. 17.30 (978-0-7931-4081-7(1)) Kaplan Pubng.

Eight Nights of Hanukah. 1 cass. (Running Time: 5 min.). 1983. 8.00 (978-0-932360-38-0(6)) Archae Edns.
Two audio interpretations of traditional sacred texts.

Eight-Phase Cycle of the Moon. Claire Abbate. 1 cass. (Running Time: 60 min.). 1992. 8.95 (1001) Am Fed Astrologers.

Eight-Phase Moon Cycle. Claire Abbate. 1 cass. 1992. 8.95 (1002) Am Fed Astrologers.

Eight Principles of Reformation. unabr. ed. David Barton. Read by David Barton. 1 cass. (Running Time: 60 min.). 1992. 4.95 (978-0-925279-21-7(8)) Wallbuilders.
Provides eight Biblical guidelines for restoring Christian principles to society & public affairs in America. A national revival, although badly needed, cannot be sustained if not accompanied by a national reformation.

Eight Selves Within Us. Robert A. Wilson. 2 cass. 1980. 18.98 (TP52) Union Label.
Robert Anton Wilson gives an introduction to his theories of the eight circuits of the evolving human nervous system, & examines the impact of society & education upon the being, with specific attention to the first two circuits. Given at the Cosmicon Convention in San Francisco, 1980.

Eight-Sided Heart. unabr. ed. Poems. Louise Bogan. Read by Louise Bogan. 1 cass. (Running Time: 58 min.). 1968. 12.95 (23654) J Norton Pubs.
One of this century's poets.

Eight Stages of Man. John E. Bradshaw. (Running Time: 14400 sec.). 2008. audio compact disk 100.00 (978-1-57388-144-9(9)) J B Media.

Eight Steps to Better Business Writing, Set. abr. ed. Michelle Fairfield Poley. Read by Michelle Fairfield Poley. 2 cass. (Running Time: 3 hrs.). 1996. bk. 21.95 (978-1-878542-73-1(7),) SkillPath Pubns.

Eight Steps to Happiness: The Buddhist Way of Loving Kindness. Geshe Kelsang Gyatso. 8 CDs. (Running Time: 9 hrs. 0 mins. 0 sec.). (ENG., 2003. audio compact disk 34.95 (978-0-948006-83-8(8)) Pub: Tharpa Pubns GBR. Dist(s): IPG Chicago

Eight Transneptunian Planets: The Uranian System. Arlene Kramer. 1 cass. 8.95 (206) Am Fed Astrologers.
An AFA Convention workshop tape.

Eight Universals That Sustain Health. Angeles Arrien. 1 cass. (Running Time: 1 hr.). 1990. 11.00 (00203) Big Sur Tapes.

Eight Verses for Training the Mind. Dalai Lama XIV. 4 CDs. (Running Time: 4 hrs.). 2006. audio compact disk 29.95 (978-1-55939-240-2(1)) Pub: Snow Lion Pubns. Dist(s): Natl Bk Netwk

Eight Verses for Training the Mind, Set. unabr. ed. Dalai Lama XIV. 4 cass. (Running Time: 4 hrs. 30 min.). 1999. 24.95 (978-1-55939-134-4(0)) Pub: Snow Lion Pubns. Dist(s): Natl Bk Netwk

Eight Week Cholesterol Cure. Robert E. Kowalski. Read by Richard Gebhart. 8 cass. 1989. 29.95 (2091); 49.95 (2089) SyberVision.
Describes what cholesterol is, the different types, its biological function, affect on the body & relationship to disease. Also provides seven steps to reducing cholesterol. Includes video & study guide.

Eight Weeks to Optimum Health: A Proven Program for Taking Full Advantage of Your Body's Natural Healing Power. abr. rev. exp. ed. Andrew Weil. Read by Andrew Weil. (Running Time: 10800 sec.). (ENG.). 2006. audio compact disk 19.95 (978-0-7393-4055-4(7), Random AudioBks) Pub: Random Audio Pubg. Dist(s): Random

***Eight White Nights.** unabr. ed. Andre Aciman. Narrated by Paul Boehmer. (Running Time: 17 hrs. 0 mins. 0 sec.). (ENG.). 2010. audio compact disk 79.99 (978-1-4001-4573-7(2)) Pub: Tantor Media. Dist(s): IngramPubServ

***Eight White Nights: A Novel.** unabr. ed. Andre Aciman. Narrated by Paul Boehmer. (Running Time: 17 hrs. 0 mins.). 2010. 21.99 (978-1-4001-8573-3(4)); 39.99 (978-1-4001-9573-2(X)); 29.99 (978-1-4001-6573-5(3)); audio compact disk 39.99 (978-1-4001-1573-0(6)) Pub: Tantor Media. Dist(s): IngramPubServ

***Eighteen Acres.** unabr. ed. Nicolle Wallace. 2010. (978-0-06-202352-0(7), Harper Audio) HarperCollins Pubs.

Eighteen Millimeter Blues. unabr. ed. Gerald A. Browne. Read by Michael McConnohie. 9 cass. (Running Time: 13 hr. 37 mins.). 1993. 72.00 (978-0-7366-2907-2(6), 3604); Rental 17.50 Set. (3604) Books on Tape.
Off the coast of Burma, two Japanese women pearl divers come up with the precious, incredible "blues" & are killed for their pains. But the spirit of one diver, Setsu, refuses to rest until revenged. Setsu's spirit chooses Julia Elkins - beautiful, impetuous & sexually inspired by gem dealer Grady Bowman - as her vehicle for vengeance. Julia accompanies Grady on a gem-buying trip to Rangoon, little suspecting the intrigues & perils that lie ahead.

Eighteenth & Early Nineteenth Century. 1 cass. (Golden Treasury of Poetry & Prose Ser.). 1991. 16.95 (1059-SA) Olivia & Hill.

***Eighteenth Century Flute Pieces with Orchestra.** Katarzyna Bury. 2010. pap. bk. 34.98 (978-1-59615-812-2(3), 1596158123) Pub: Music Minus. Dist(s): H Leonard

Eighth Annual Criminal Law Symposium. 1991. 45.00 (AC-641) PA Bar Inst.

Eighth Annversary Special: Program from the Award Winning Public Radio Series. Hosted by Fred Goodwin & Peter Kramer. 1 CD. (Running Time: 1 Hour). 2005. audio compact disk 21.95 (978-1-932479-42-3(2), LCM 369) Lichtenstein Creat.
The Infinite Mind Eighth Anniversary Special (beginning April 6, 2005): Hosted jointly by Dr. Fred Goodwin, our host since the program's premiere in 1998, and by our new host Dr. Peter Kramer, this retrospective features some of the best moments from The Infinite Mind's first seven years, including the Firesign Theatre on what's funny and why; top sleep researchers on how much sleep we really need; a Baptist school teacher describes her bout with hypersexuality; and fame through the ages with Howard Bloom (Alexander the Great traveled with his own publicist). Also, batting champ Wade Boggs on the mindset it takes to hit a fastball; former hostage Terry Anderson on forgiveness; Oliver Sacks on Tourette's syndrome; managed care and suicide; Frederick Wiseman talks about his documentary on "Domestic Violence"; Suzanne Vega talks and sings about autism, and Alex, the world-famous talking parrot, speaks out on animal intelligence.

Eighth Day. unabr. ed. John Case. Read by Dick Hill. 9 cass. (Running Time: 12 hrs.). 2002. 34.95 (978-1-59086-229-2(5), 1590862295, BAU); 92.25 (978-1-59086-230-8(9), 1590862309, CD Unabrid Lib Ed) Brilliance Audio.
For Danny Cray, a struggling artist and part-time private investigator, the offer is too good to be true. A wealthy, enigmatic lawyer, Jude Belzer, would like to retain Danny for a little damage control. His client, an elusive billionaire, is the target of a vicious campaign by the Italian press that threatens to destroy his reputation. Belzer wants Danny to find out who is responsible - and he will pay handsomely. Danny's only lead is the meager estate of a recently deceased professor of religious studies, a man so deeply terrified that he buried himself alive in the basement of an isolated farmhouse. Belzer swears that if Danny can get the late professor's files, the conspiracy against his own reclusive client will unravel. It's the perfect assignment, in a way, and Danny can sure use the money. But the more he probes, the more apparent it becomes that nothing is what it seems. There is something he isn't being told. Something that's not quite right. Something dark, fast, and sinister that's coming at him from behind. From the powerful world of Washington D.C., to the ancient grandeur of Rome, from the mysteries of Istanbul to the high-stakes drama of Silicon Valley, The Eighth Day is a briskly paced, globe-trotting thriller of electrifying suspense. Packed with unexpected reversals and astonishing twists of plot, this is John Case's most gripping novel to date.

Eighth Day. unabr. ed. John Case. Read by Dick Hill. (Running Time: 12 hrs.). 2004. 39.25 (978-1-59335-558-6(0), 1593355580, Brlnc Audio MP3 Lib) Brilliance Audio.

Eighth Day. unabr. ed. John Case. Read by Dick Hill. (Running Time: 12 hrs.). 2004. 39.25 (978-1-59710-243-8(1), 1597102431, BADLE); 24.95 (978-1-59710-242-1(3), 1597102423, BAD) Brilliance Audio.

Eighth Day. unabr. ed. John Case. Read by Dick Hill. (Running Time: 12 hrs.). 2004. 24.95 (978-1-59335-042-0(2), 1593350422) Soulmate Audio Bks.

Eighth Dwarf, unabr. ed. Ross Thomas. Narrated by Frank Muller. 6 cass. (Running Time: 8 hrs.). 1984. 51.00 (978-1-55690-160-7(7), 84120E7) Recorded Bks.
If Jackson had just left Ploscaru to drown in the Beverly Hills pool, he would never have gotten himself locked up in a basement in bombed-out Berlin with a naked asssassin. But then, he would never have met the dwarf either.

***Eighth Grade Bites.** unabr. ed. Heather Brewer. Read by Kevin Pariseau. (Running Time: 5 hrs.). (Chronicles of Vladimir Tod: Bk. 1). 2010. 19.99 (978-1-4418-6843-5(7), 9781441868435, Brilliance MP3); 39.97 (978-1-4418-6844-2(5), 9781441868442, Brlnc Audio MP3 Lib); 39.97 (978-1-4418-6846-6(1), 9781441868466, BADLE); audio compact disk 54.97 (978-1-4418-6842-8(9), 9781441868428, BriAudCD Unabrid) Brilliance Audio.

***Eighth Grade Bites.** unabr. ed. Heather Brewer. Read by Kevin Pariseau. (Running Time: 5 hrs.). (Chronicles of Vladimir Tod: Bk. 1). (YA). 2010. audio compact disk 19.99 (978-1-4418-6841-1(0), 9781441868411, Bril Audio CD Unabri) Brilliance Audio.

Eighth International in Situ & on-Site Bioremediation Symposium: June 6-9, 2005; Baltimore, Maryland. Ed. by Bruce C. Alleman & Mark E. Kelley. 2006. audio compact disk 295.00 (978-1-57477-152-7(3)) Battelle.

Eighth Shepherd. unabr. ed. Bodie Thoene & Brock Thoene. Narrated by Sean Barrett. (Running Time: 9 hrs. 30 mins. 0 sec.). (A. D. Chronicles Ser.). (ENG.). 2009. 20.99 (978-1-60814-473-0(9)); audio compact disk 29.99 (978-1-59859-555-0(5)) Oasis Audio.

Eighty Acres: Elegy for a Family Farm. unabr. collector's ed. Ronald Jager. Read by Rob McQuay. 7 cass. (Running Time: 10 hrs. 30 mins.). 1999. 56.00 (978-0-7366-4875-2(5), 5099) Books on Tape.
The authors brings to life his childhood on an eight-acre Dutch family farm in western Michigan.

Eighty Million Eyes. unabr. ed. Ed McBain, pseud. Read by Jonathan Marosz. 5 cass. (Running Time: 5 hrs.). (87th Precinct Ser.: Bk. 21). 1997. 40.00 (978-0-7366-3565-3(3), 4209) Books on Tape.
When someone kills a popular comedian live on nationwide TV, it's no joke to the boys of the 87th Precinct. Although fans loved the funny man, everyone from his gag writer to his wardrobe lady wanted him dead.

Eighty-One Famous Poems: An Audio Companion to The Norton Anthology of Poetry. Poems. Read by Alexander Scourby et al. 2 cass. (Running Time: 2 hrs. 20 min.). 19.95 set. (8006Q) Filmic Archives.
Includes 39 major British & American poets from Shakespeare, Milton, Blake & Wordsworth, to Keats, the Brownings, Whitman, Dickinson, & Yeats.

Eigse Dhiarmuidin. (ENG.). 2002. 13.95 (978-0-8023-7151-5(5)); audio compact disk 23.95 (978-0-8023-8151-4(0)) Pub: Clo Iar-Chonnachta IRL. Dist(s): Dufour

Eine und die Andere: Textbuch mit Handreichungen. H. Mueller. (GER.). (C). 1994. 29.00 (978-3-12-675421-7(X)) Pub: Klett Ernst Verlag DEU. Dist(s): Intl Bk Import

Einfachste Weg Ho'oponopono zu Verstehen: Die verstandlichsten Antworten auf die am meisten gestellten Frangen-Volumen I, Vol. 1. Mabel Katz. (GER.). 2009. 9.95 (978-0-9818210-1-6(4)) Your Business.

Einfuhrung in Die Evangelische Theologie see Evangelical Theology: An Introduction

Einniu. Contrib. by Einniu. (ENG.). 1993. 13.95 (978-0-8023-7086-0(1)); audio compact disk 21.95 (978-0-8023-8086-9(7)) Pub: Clo Iar-Chonnachta IRL. Dist(s): Dufour

Einstein: His Life & Universe. abr. ed. Walter Isaacson. 2007. 17.95 (978-0-7435-6097-9(3)) Pub: S&S Audio. Dist(s): S and S Inc

Einstein: His Life & Universe. abr. ed. Walter Isaacson. Read by Edward Herrmann. (Running Time: 7 hrs. 0 mins. 0 sec.). (ENG.). 2007. audio compact disk 29.95 (978-0-7435-6096-2(5)) Pub: S&S Audio. Dist(s): S and S Inc

Einstein: His Life & Universe. unabr. ed. Walter Isaacson. 2007. 29.95 (978-0-7435-6139-6(2)) Pub: S&S Audio. Dist(s): S and S Inc

Einstein: His Life & Universe. unabr. ed. Walter Isaacson. Read by Edward Herrmann. 18 CDs. (Running Time: 22 hrs. 0 mins. 0 sec.). (ENG.). 2007. audio compact disk 49.95 (978-0-7435-6138-9(4)) Pub: S&S Audio. Dist(s): S and S Inc

Einstein & the Buddha. unabr. ed. Fritjof Capra. 1 cass. 1990. 12.95 (ECN182) J Norton Pubs.
Parallels between the world views of scientists & mystics.

Einstein & the Buddha CD. Interview. Fritjof Capra. Interview with Jocelyn Ryder-Smith. 1 CD. (Running Time: 40 mins.). (Basic Principles of Objectiveness Ser.). 2006. audio compact disk 12.95 (978-1-57970-419-3(0), ECN182D, Audio-For) J Norton Pubs.
Modern physicists and Eastern mystics seem strange bedfellows, but Dr. Fritjof Capra, who lecturer and researcher in particle physics at the Lawrence Berkeley Laboratories in California, has detected what he believes are very powerful parallels between their world views. In this interview, he discusses some of the ideas he originally put forward in his bestselling book, "The Tao of Physics." He claims there are two basic themes which run through both modern science and mystical traditions: the fundamental unity and interdependence of all phenomena, and the intrinsically dynamic nature of reality. He goes on to suggest that experts in the fields of medicine, economics, and politics may have something to learn from the physicist and the mystic.

Einstein Factor. abr. ed. Win Wenger & Richard Poe. Read by Win Wenger. (Running Time: 80 hrs. 0 mins. 0 sec.). (ENG.). 2002. audio compact disk 39.95 (978-0-7435-2523-7(X), Nightgale) Pub: S&S Audio. Dist(s): S and S Inc

Einstein Lived Here. unabr. collector's ed. Abraham Pais. Read by Jonathan Reese. 9 cass. (Running Time: 13 hrs. 30 min.). 1997. 72.00 (978-0-7366-4008-4(8), 4506) Books on Tape.
The author discusses Einstein's developed opinions on issues from physics to civil liberties.

Einstein's Dreams. unabr. ed. Alan P. Lightman. Read by Alexander Adams. 3 cass. (Running Time: 3 hrs.). 1994. 24.95 (978-0-7366-2673-6(5), 3410) Books on Tape.
Enchanting vision of what time has been or might be, as imagined by Albert Einstein.

Einstein's Relativity & the Quantum Revolution: Modern Physics for Non-Scientists, Course No. 153. Instructed by Richard Wolfson. 2 cass. (Running Time: 12 hrs.). 1996. 129.95 Set. Teaching Co.
Introduces & explains modern physics to non-scientists. The path of our progress from Copernicus to Newton to Einstein to Planck & Heisenberg & Schroedinger is compressed into an exciting 12 hours during which we are able to walk alongside these giants with Professor Wolfson as our guide.

Einstein's Relativity & the Quantum Revolution Pts. I-II: Modern Physics for Non-Scientists. 2nd rev. ed. Instructed by Richard Wolfson. 12 CDs. (Running Time: 12 hrs.). 2000. bk. 69.95 (978-1-56585-280-8(X), 153) Teaching Co.

Einstein's Relativity & the Quantum Revolution Pts. I-II, Vol. 1: Modern Physics for Non-Scientists. Instructed by Richard Wolfson. 12 cass. (Running Time: 12 hrs.). 54.95 (978-1-56585-006-4(8), 153) Teaching Co.

Einstein's Relativity & the Quantum Revolution Vol. 2: Modern Physics for Non-Scientists. Instructed by Richard Wolfson. 6 cass. (Running Time: 6 hrs.). 2000. 129.95 (978-1-56585-007-1(6)) Teaching Co.

Einstein's Relativity & the Quantum Revolution Vol. 2: Modern Physics for Non-Scientists. 2nd rev. ed. Instructed by Richard Wolfson. 6 CDs. (Running Time: 6 hrs.). 2000. audio compact disk 179.95 (978-1-56585-281-5(8)) Teaching Co.

Einstein's Revolution. unabr. ed. John T. Sanders. Read by Edwin Newman. (Running Time: 10800 sec.). (Audio Classics: Science & Discovery Ser.). 2006. audio compact disk 25.95 (978-0-7861-6431-8(X)) Pub: Blckstn Audio. Dist(s): NetLibrary CO

Einstein's Revolution. unabr. ed. John T. Sanders. Read by Edwin Newman. Ed. by Jack Sommer & Mike Hassell. 2 cass. (Running Time: 2 hrs. 45 min.). Dramatization. (Science & Discovery Ser.). (YA). (gr. 11 up). 1993. 17.95 Set. (978-1-56823-001-6(X), 10411) Knowledge Prod.
Isaac Newton's world had operated in a fixed, rigid, "absolute" framework of space & time. Yet discoveries about electromagnetism in the late 19th century created new & troubling inconsistencies. In 1905, Einstein's name became synonymous with "genius" when his Special Theory of Relativity challenged old concepts in physics. Hertz, Lorentz, Mach, Poincare, & others illuminate the ideas that so captivated Albert Einstein & shook our conventional ideas about space & time.

Einstein's Wife. unabr. ed. Andrea Gabor. Read by Kate Reading. 9 cass. (Running Time: 13 hrs. 30 min.). 1996. 72.00 (978-0-7366-3318-5(9), 3970) Books on Tape.
Does marriage to a brilliant man, committed to his work, preclude a wife's aspirations? What if the wife is equally brilliant? How does she balance her marriage & children with her own goals?.

Eirerobics Soundtrack: Music for Eirerobics Irish Dance Exercise Program. Composed by Diane Laverty. 2006. audio compact disk 17.95i (978-0-9785251-0-1(8)) Eirerobics.

Eisenhower. unabr. ed. Geoffrey Perret. Narrated by Nelson Runger. 21 cass. (Running Time: 30 hrs.). 2000. 164.00 (978-0-7887-4950-6(1), 96465E7) Recorded Bks.
Drawing from fresh sources, this is the first complete biography of Dwight D. Eisenhower in two decades. It is the story of the individualistic West Point cadet, the Supreme Commander of Allied forces in World War II & the much loved thirty-fourth president of the United States.

Eisenhower. unabr. ed. John Wukovitz. Read by Brian Emerson. (Running Time: 25200 sec.). (Great Generals Ser.). 2006. audio compact disk 63.00 (978-0-7861-6396-0(8)) Blckstn Audio.

Eisenhower. unabr. ed. John Wukovitz. Read by Brian Emerson. Frwd. by Wesley K. Clark. 6 cass. (Running Time: 25200 sec.). (Great Generals Ser.). 2006. 25.95 (978-0-7861-4617-8(6)); 54.95 (978-0-7861-4836-3(5)); audio compact disk 25.95 (978-0-7861-6849-1(8)); audio compact disk 29.95 (978-0-7861-7458-4(7)) Blckstn Audio.

Eisenhower, Pt. 1. unabr. ed. Geoffrey Perret. Read by Jeff Riggenbach. 10 cass. (Running Time: 14 hrs. 30 mins.). 1999. 69.95 (978-0-7861-1631-7(5), 2459-A,B) Blckstn Audio.
Eisenhower seems on the surface to have had an impenetrable demeanor, but here he is brought to life: the story about his supposed affair with Kay Summersby; his remarkable sojourn in the Philippines with MacArthur; his rise to commander of all the Allied Forces in Europe - something for which he alone was uniquely equipped - & finally his political life & presidency, a story never fully understood until now.

Eisenhower, Pt. 2. unabr. ed. Geoffrey Perret. Read by Jeff Riggenbach. 8 cass. (Running Time: 14 hrs. 30 mins.). 1999. 56.95 (978-0-7861-1696-6(X), 2459-A,B) Blckstn Audio.
Like Robert E. Lee, Eisenhower seems on the surface to have had an impenetrable demeanor, but here he is brought to life; the story about his supposed affair with Kay Summersby; his remarkable sojourn in the Philippines with MacArthur; his rise to commander of all the Allied Forces in Europe - something for which he alone was uniquely equipped & his political life.

Eisenhower: A Closer Look. unabr. ed. Read by Peter Lyon. 1 cass. (Running Time: 56 min.). 1985. 12.95 (40076) J Norton Pubs.
Lyon discusses with Heywood Hale Broun the merits of the late president as soldier, statesman, & politician. Lyon's scholarly approach unearths new insights into the military hero & enigmatic public man.

Eisenhower Vol. 1: Soldier, General of the Army, President-Elect, 1890-1952. unabr. collector's ed. Stephen E. Ambrose. Read by Jay Robertson. 15 cass. (Running Time: 22 hrs. 30 mins.). 1991. 120.00 (978-0-7366-1977-6(1), 2795) Books on Tape.
Dwight Eisenhower was not exactly born into poverty, but the family's circumstances were at least austere. He was one of seven children; his father, a railway worker. But the family was strong & unified, the youngsters energetic & ambitious, the corrosion of self-pity entirely absent from their thought. Ike made it to West Point, where he excelled in sports. He was a natural leader. But it was at Leavenworth years later, as a student at the war college, that his intellectual talent showed itself. He graduated first in his class. The author draws on a wealth of previously unpublished information to give us this beautifully realized portrait of Eisenhower.

Eisenhower Vol. 1: The President. unabr. collector's ed. Stephen E. Ambrose. Read by John MacDonald. 11 cass. (Running Time: 16 hrs. 30 mins.). 1993. 88.00 (978-0-7366-2426-8(0), 3191-A) Books on Tape.
The people & events of the 1950s become clear in this second volume of Ambrose's biography.

Eisenhower Vol. 2: The President. unabr. collector's ed. Stephen E. Ambrose. Read by John MacDonald. 10 cass. (Running Time: 15 hrs.). 1993. 80.00 (978-0-7366-2427-5(9), 3191-B) Books on Tape.

Eisenhower at War, 1943-1945, Pt. 1. unabr. ed. Read by John MacDonald. Ed. by Dwight D. Eisenhower. 9 cass. (Running Time: 13 hrs. 30 mins.). Incl. Pt. 2. Eisenhower at War, 1943-1945. 10 cass. (Running Time: 15 hrs.). Read by John MacDonald. Ed. by Dwight D. Eisenhower. 1987. 80.00 (2158-B); Pt. 3. Eisenhower at War, 1943-1945. 8 cass. (Running Time: 12 hrs.). Read by John MacDonald. Ed. by Dwight D. Eisenhower. 1987. 64.00 (2158-C); 1987. 72.00 (978-0-7366-1241-8(6), 2158-A) Books on Tape.
"Eisenhower at War" reshapes our thinking about WWII in Europe & its legacy - the divided continent with which the world had precariously lived. This book also revises established portraits of the wartime leaders: Roosevelt, Churchill, Marshall, Montgomery & Eisenhower himself, of whom his grandson draws a far more complex & subtle portrait than seen before.

Eisenhower Deception, Set. unabr. ed. Clive Egleton. Read by Frank Muller. 5 cass. (Running Time: 6 hrs. 30 mins.). 1984. 42.00 (978-1-55690-161-4(5), 84180) Recorded Bks.
Set in 1956, an English plot to invade the Suez Canal turns up some embarrassing skeletons in a President's closet.

Eisenhower Era. (Presidency Ser.). 10.00 Esstee Audios.
A look at Ike & how he reflected America.

Either/or Investor: How to Succeed in Global Investing, One Decision at a Time. unabr. ed. Clark Winter. Narrated by Stephen Hoye. (Running Time: 7 hrs. 0 mins. 0 sec.). (ENG.). 2008. audio compact disk 59.99 (978-1-4001-3811-1(6)); audio compact disk 19.99 (978-1-4001-5811-9(7)) Pub: Tantor Media. Dist(s): IngramPubServ

Either/or Investor: How to Succeed in Global Investing, One Decision at a Time. unabr. ed. Clark Winter. Narrated by Stephen Hoye. (Running Time: 7 hrs. 0 mins. 0 sec.). (ENG.). 2008. audio compact disk 29.99 (978-1-4001-0811-4(X)) Pub: Tantor Media. Dist(s): IngramPubServ

Ej, Lasko, Lasko - O, Love, Love. unabr. ed. Perf. by Anita Smisek & Steven Zdenek Eckels. 1 cass. 1994. 10.00 (978-1-57193-082-8(5), AP-005/CS); audio compact disk 15.00 CD. (978-1-57193-086-6(8), AP-006/CD) Alliance Pubns.
Folksongs from Bohemia, Moravia, & Slovakia sung in their native dialects by Anita Smisek & accompanied by Steven Zdenek Eckels original classical guitar stylings.

EKG Prep: On Audio. unabr. ed. Instructed by Jill S. Flateland. 3 cass. (Running Time: 7 hrs.). 1990. 79.00 cass. & soft-bound bk. (HT49) Ctr Hlth Educ.
Learn how to interpret advanced EKGs & get a good review of the basics. It's so simple with this specially designed course. There are case studies galore! You'll discover: everything from ischemia, injury, & infarct to axis deviation, all in one handy program; how to detect combination infarcts; how the location of an MI determines the complications you need to anticipate.

El McMeen Acoustic Guitar/Playing Favorites. El McMeen. 1997. pap. bk. 23.95 (978-0-7866-2944-2(4), 95973CDP) Mel Bay.

El Nino: Stormy Weather for People & Wildlife. unabr. ed. Caroline Arnold. Narrated by Nelson Runger. 1 cass. (Running Time: 1 hr.). (gr. 4 up). 10.00 (978-0-7887-2626-2(9), 95630E7) Recorded Bks.
Chances are you have probably experienced the disruptive effects of El Nino. The notorious "boy child" has spawned wacky weather & natural disasters around the globe. In easy-to-understand language, explains how this powerful weather pattern is formed & what its far reaching effects are. Available to libraries only.

El Salvador. Donna Pena. 1995. 10.95 (336); audio compact disk 15.95 (336) GIA Pubns.

Elaborations on the Mind. Wisdom Master Maticintin. 1. (Running Time: 78:08). 2002. audio compact disk 16.00 (978-0-932927-18-7(1)) Dharmavidya.
Buddhist Teachings.

Elaine Elias. 1 cass. (Running Time: 1 hr.). (Marian McPartland's Piano Jazz Ser.). 13.95 (MM-88-05-07, HarperThor) HarpC GBR.

Elantris, Vol. 1. unabr. ed. Brandon Sanderson. Read by James Konicek. 6 CDs. (Running Time: 7 hrs.). 2009. audio compact disk 19.99 (978-1-59950-555-8(X)) GraphicAudio.

Elantris, Vol. 2. Brandon Sanderson. 2009. audio compact disk 19.99 (978-1-59950-562-6(2)) GraphicAudio.

Elantris, Vol. 3. Brandon Sanderson. 2009. audio compact disk 19.99 (978-1-59950-570-1(3)) GraphicAudio.

***ELAP Plus Assessment Links: Individual CD.** Continental Press Staff. 2008. stu. ed. 49.95 (978-0-8454-5786-3(1)); stu. ed. 49.95 (978-0-8454-5785-6(3)); stu. ed. 49.95 (978-0-8454-5784-9(5)); stu. ed. 49.95 (978-0-8454-5781-8(0)); stu. ed. 49.95 (978-0-8454-5783-2(7)); stu. ed. 49.95 (978-0-8454-5782-5(9)) Continental Pr.

Elder Care: Helping Our Aging Folks. Ina Jaffe. Read by Ina Jaffe. 1 cass. (Running Time: 37 min.). 9.95 (IO-140, HarperThor) HarpC GBR.

Elder Harold's Revolver. unabr. ed. Boyd Richardson. Read by Nathan Smith Jones. 4 cass. (Running Time: 5 hrs. 12 mins.). (YA). 2005. 19.95 (978-1-932280-67-8(7), 80677) Granite UT.

Elder Law Leadership Seminar: Top Partners on Best Practices & Winning Legal Strategies for Achieving Client Success. Ed. by ReedLogic Staff. 2006. pap. bk. 249.95 (978-1-59701-084-9(7)) Aspatore Bks.

Elder Olson. unabr. ed. Read by Elder Olson. 1 cass. (Running Time: 29 min.). 1985. 10.00 New Letters.
Distinguished critic & poet, Elder Olson here reads from Olson's Penny Arcade & his Collected Poems.

Eldercare. T. J. Terry. 10 cass. (C). 1996. 120.00 Set. (978-1-887258-19-7(1)); 29.95 ea. T J Terry.
Age related biological changes & those diseases most likely to be encountered by student nurses when caring for hospitalized elders.

Eldercare in Food & Exercise. (Caregiving to the Elderly Ser.). 1989. 9.95 (978-1-877843-03-7(2)) Elder Care Solutions.
The importance of diet & good nutrition. Kitchen safety. Food preperation & serving ideas. Exercise.

Eldercare Nursing Series. T. J. Terry. 14 cass. or CD. 1998. 99.95 Set.; audio compact disk 59.95 CD. (978-1-887258-27-2(2)) T J Terry.
Each individual subject includes the age-related biological changes of one body system & the most common diseases of that body system requiring hospitalization; also covers all age-related biological changes without relative disease entities & polypharmacology in elders comprehensively.

Elderly Suicide: Who Would Miss Me? 1 cass. (Running Time: 30 min.). 9.95 Natl Public Radio.

Elders Speak, No. 1. Frances Cree & Mary Louise Defender Wilson. 1 cass. 10.00 (978-1-885357-94-6(X)) Rational Isl.
Shared experiences of older people & their allies, & about older people using re-evaluation counseling.

Elders Speak, No. 4. 3 cass. 10.00 ea. (978-1-885357-95-3(8)) Rational Isl.

Eldest. Christopher Paolini. (Inheritance Cycle Ser.: Bk. 2). (YA). 2005. 54.99 (978-1-59895-037-3(1)) Find a World.

Eldest. Christopher Paolini. 5. (Inheritance Cycle Ser.: Bk. 2). 2007. audio compact disk 24.95 (978-1-933499-48-2(6)) Fonolibro Inc.

Eldest. unabr. ed. Christopher Paolini. Read by Gerald Doyle. (J). 2005. 64.99 (978-0-7393-7473-3(7)) Find a World.

Eldest. unabr. ed. Christopher Paolini. Read by Gerard Doyle. 20 CDs. (Running Time: 84420 sec.). (Inheritance Cycle Ser.: Bk. 2). (ENG.). (J). (gr. 5-12). 2005. audio compact disk 55.00 (978-0-307-28072-5(1), Listening Lib) Pub: Random Audio Pubg. Dist(s): Random

Eldest. unabr. collector's ed. Christopher Paolini. Read by Gerard Doyle. 20 CDs. (Inheritance Cycle Ser.: Bk. 2). (YA). (gr. 7 up). 2005. audio compact disk 72.25 (978-0-307-28288-0(0), Listening Lib); 65.00 (978-1-4000-9863-7(7), Listening Lib) Pub: Random Audio Pubg. Dist(s): Random
Darkness falls... despair abounds... evil reigns... Eragon and his dragon, Saphira, have just saved the rebel state from destruction by the mighty forces of King Galbatorix, cruel ruler of the Empire. Now Eragon must travel to Ellesmera, land of the elves, for further training in the skills of the Dragon Rider: magic and swordsmanship. Soon he is on the journey of a lifetime, his eyes open to awe-inspring new places and people, his days filled with fresh adventure. But chaos and betrayal plague him at every turn, and nothing is what it seems. Before long, Eragon doesn't know whom he can trust. Meanwhile, his cousin Roran must fight a new battle - one that might put Eragon in even graver danger. Will the king's dark hand strangle all resistance? Eragon may not escape with even his life.

Eldorado see Raven & Other Works

Eldredge Collection: Waking the Dead - Wild at Heart - Captivating. unabr. ed. John Eldredge & Stasi Eldredge. (Running Time: 97200 sec.). (ENG.). 2005. audio compact disk 59.99 (978-1-59859-099-9(5)) Oasis Audio.

Eleanor. Barbara Cooney. Read by Christina Moore. 1 cass. (Running Time: 15 mins.). (YA). 2000. pap. bk. 25.24 (978-0-7887-4330-6(9), 41125) Recorded Bks.
Eleanor Roosevelt's mother called her Granny because she looked so funny & old-fashioned. Young Eleanor was very shy, awkward & lonely. Poignant story of a sad little girl who grew up with a compassion & strength that eventually made her one of America's most beloved First Ladies.

Eleanor. unabr. ed. Barbara Cooney. Read by Christina Moore. 1 cass. (Running Time: 15 mins.). (YA). 2000. 11.00 (978-0-7887-4431-0(3), 47122) Recorded Bks.

Eleanor. unabr. ed. Barbara Cooney. Narrated by Christina Moore. 1 cass. (Running Time: 15 mins.). (gr. 1 up). 2000. 11.00 (978-0-7887-4229-3(9), 96178E7) Recorded Bks.

Eleanor: Her Secret Journey. unabr. ed. Rhoda Lerman. Read by Jean Stapleton. 2 cass. (Running Time: 1 hr. 20 mins.). 2001. 20.95 (978-1-58081-202-3(3), WTA11) L A Theatre.
Account of a fascinating woman, involved in a complicated marriage with one of history's most influential men & his family, at a tumultuous time in world history.

Eleanor & Hattie & the Wild Waves. unabr. ed. Barbara Cooney. Read by Barbara Cooney. Music by Paul Sullivan. 1 CD. (Running Time: 46 min.). 1997. audio compact disk 15.95 (978-1-883332-67-9(2)) Audio Bkshelf.
Based on the tragic childhood of famous First Lady & world ambassador Eleanor Roosevelt.

Eleanor & Hattie & the Wild Waves. unabr. ed. Barbara Cooney. Read by Barbara Cooney. Music by Paul Sullivan. 1 cass. (Running Time: 46 min.). (YA). 1997. reel tape 13.95 (978-1-883332-31-0(1)) Audio Bkshelf.

Eleanor of Aquitaine: By the Wrath of God, Queen of England. Alison Weir. Narrated by Jill Tanner. 6 cass. (Running Time: 8 hrs. 30 mins.). 107.00 (978-1-4025-3394-5(2)) Recorded Bks.

Eleanor Roosevelt: A Life of Discovery, unabr. ed. Russell Freedman. Narrated by Barbara Caruso. 3 pieces. (Running Time: 3 hrs. 45 mins.). (gr. 8 up). 1998. 27.00 (978-0-7887-1816-8(9), 95284E7) Recorded Bks.
Almost anything scares shy, young Eleanor. But as a young woman, she makes a lasting discovery that later enables her to redefine the role of America's first lady - being shy doesn't matter when she's helping others.

Eleanor Roosevelt: A Personal & Public Life. unabr. ed. J. William T. Youngs. Read by Donada Peters. 7 cass. (Running Time: 10 hrs. 30 mins.). 1986. 56.00 (978-0-7366-0759-9(5), 1716) Books on Tape.

Eleanor Roosevelt: First Lady of the World. Ryan Jacobson. Illus. by Barbara Schulz & Gordon Purcell. (Graphic Biographies Ser.). (ENG.). (gr. 3-4). 2007. audio compact disk 6.95 (978-1-4296-1468-9(4)) CapstoneDig.

Eleanor Roosevelt Homework Set: A Life of Discovery. unabr. ed. Russell Freedman. Read by Barbara Caruso. 3 cass. (Running Time: 3 hrs. 45 min.). (YA). 1997. bk. 46.20 (978-0-7887-1849-6(5), 40629) Recorded Bks.

Eleanor Roosevelt Homework Set: A Life of Discovery, Class Set. unabr. ed. Russell Freedman. Read by Barbara Caruso. 3 cass., 10 bks. (Running Time: 3 hrs. 45 min.). (YA). (gr. 8). 1997. bk. 157.30 (978-0-7887-2575-3(0), 46180) Recorded Bks.
Almost anything scares shy, young Eleanor. But as a young woman, she makes a lasting discovery that later enables her to redefine the role of America's first lady.

Eleanor Roosevelt Pt. 2: 1884-1933. unabr. collector's ed. Blanche Wiesen Cook. Read by Kate Reading. 8 cass. (Running Time: 12 hrs.). 1994. 64.00 (978-0-7366-2617-0(4), 5023-A) Books on Tape.
Eleanor Roosevelt emerges as a woman dedicated to social injustice, but still sustaining enduring relationships.

Eleanor Roosevelt Vol. 1, Pt. 1: 1884-1933, unabr. collector's ed. Blanche Wiesen Cook. Read by Kate Reading. 8 cass. (Running Time: 12 hrs.). 1994. 64.00 (978-0-7366-2616-3(6), 3358A/B) Books on Tape.
Eleanor Roosevelt is arguably the most important woman in American political history. She polarized people during her life, & as this biography proves, continues to do so to this day. Cook rescues Roosevelt from her role as long-suffering matron. In her place stands a woman fully realized - evolving, self-directed. Her life celebrated social justice combined with enduring emotional relationships.

Eleanor Roosevelt Vol. 2, Pt. 1: 1884-1933. collector's ed. Blanche Wiesen Cook. Read by Kate Reading. 10 cass. (Running Time: 15 hrs.). 1999. 80.00 (978-0-7366-4642-0(6)) Books on Tape.
Eleanor Roosevelt emerges as a woman dedicated to social injustice, but still sustaining enduring relationships.

Eleanor Roosevelt Vol. 2, Pt. 2: 1884-1933. collector's ed. Blanche Wiesen Cook. Read by Kate Reading. 10 cass. (Running Time: 15 hrs.). 1999. 80.00 (978-0-7366-4721-2(X)) Books on Tape.

Eleanor Roosevelt (INK Audiocassette) First Lady of the World. (Graphic Library Biographies I Ser.). (ENG.). 2006. audio compact disk 5.95 (978-0-7368-7450-2(X)) CapstoneDig.

Eleanor Roosevelt Remembered. 1 cass. (Running Time: 30 min.). 10.95 (F0190B090, HarperThor) HarpC GBR.

Eleanor Smeal: The Feminization of Power. Eleanor Smeal. Read by Eleanor Smeal. 1 cass. (Running Time: 1 hr.). 10.95 (K0370B090, HarperThor) HarpC GBR.

Eleanor's Love of Money. VCI Invest.

Election Chart. Carolyn Dodson. 1 cass. 8.95 (091) Am Fed Astrologers.
Emphasis on business, moves, travel, personal activity.

Election Intrigue. unabr. ed. Sandy Laurence. 1 cass. (Running Time: 20 min.). (J). (gr. 4-8). 1983. bk. 16.99 (978-0-934898-53-9(7)); pap. bk. 9.95 (978-0-934898-21-8(9)) Jan Prods.
While doing volunteer work for a local candidate, a teenager uncovers a devious plot by the supporters of the other candidate.

Election 1984 - With the Uranium Dial. Maria K. Simms. 1 cass. 8.95 (184) Am Fed Astrologers.
An AFA Convention workshop tape.

Electional Astrology. V. Austin-Chatham. 1 cass. 8.95 (379) Am Fed Astrologers.

Electional Chart. Carolyn Dodson. 1 cass. 8.95 (517) Am Fed Astrologers.
Select best timing for events.

Electional Horary. Mary L. Lewis. 1 cass. 8.95 (211) Am Fed Astrologers.
Best time to marry, buy, travel, mail income tax, etc.

Elective Surgery. John H. Goode. 1 cass. (Running Time: 90 min.). 1990. 8.95 (861) Am Fed Astrologers.

Electn Classroom Manager to AC. David Maxwell & Eiki Satake. 2005. audio compact disk (978-1-4018-1568-4(5)) Delmar.

Electoral Reform & Minority Representation: Local Experiments with Alternative Elections. Shaun Bowler et al. 2003. audio compact disk 9.95 (978-0-8142-9000-2(0)) Pub: Ohio St U Pr. Dist(s): Chicago Distribution Ctr

Electric & Other Non-Polluting Alternatives to Gasoline-Powered Vehicles. Hosted by Nancy Pearlman. 1 cass. (Running Time: 29 min.). 10.00 (1008) Educ Comm CA.

***Electric Barracuda.** unabr. ed. Tim Dorsey. (ENG.). 2011. (978-0-06-206372-4(3), Harper Audio); (978-0-06-202724-5(7), Harper Audio) HarperCollins Pubs.

Electric Bass: A Dictionary of Grooves & Techniques. John Patitucci. (SPA & ITA.). audio compact disk 26.95 (978-88-7207-555-5(6), ML1425) Nuova Carisch ITA.

***Electric Bass Basics.** Martin Engelien. (ENG., 2008. pap. bk. 12.95 (978-3-8024-0676-8(1)) Voggenreiter Pubs DEU.

Electric Bass for the Young Beginner. Dino Monoxelos. (ENG.). 2010. pap. bk. 14.99 (978-0-7866-7689-7(2)) Mel Bay.

Electric Bass Method, Vol. 1. Roger Filiberto. 1963. pap. bk. 20.95 (978-0-7866-1725-8(X), 93234CDP) Mel Bay.

Electric Bass Method, Vol. 2. Roger Filiberto. 1965. pap. bk. 14.95 (978-0-7866-0911-6(7), 93235P); pap. bk. 20.95 (978-0-7866-1726-5(8), 93235CDP) Mel Bay.

Electric Bass Method: 1 And 2, Vols. 1 & 2. 1995. audio compact disk 15.98 (978-0-7866-1701-2(2), 932345CD) Mel Bay.

Electric Blues. Erikka Haa. (CD Ser.). 2001. bk. 16.98 (978-1-56799-299-1(4), Friedman-Fairfax) M Friedman Pub Grp Inc.

Electric Blues Guitar Method. William Bay. 1997. pap. bk. 17.95 (978-0-7866-2958-9(4)) Mel Bay.

Electric Brain: Program from the Award Winning Public Radio Series. Interview. Hosted by Fred Goodwin. 1 CD. (Running Time: 1 hr.). 2001. audio compact disk 21.95 (978-1-932479-43-0(0), LCM 163) Lichtenstein Creat.
The Electric Brain probes the brain's natural electricity and how scientists are learning to bypass faulty wiring to help deaf people to hear, blind people to see, and depressed people to feel joy again.

***Electric Church.** unabr. ed. Jeff Somers. Narrated by Todd McLaren. (Running Time: 11 hrs. 0 mins.). (Avery Cates Ser.). 2010. 17.99 (978-1-4001-8674-7(9)); 34.99 (978-1-4001-9674-6(4)); 24.99 (978-1-4001-6674-9(8)); audio compact disk 34.99 (978-1-4001-1674-4(0)); audio compact disk 69.99 (978-1-4001-4674-1(7)) Pub: Tantor Media. Dist(s): IngramPubServ

Electric City. Perf. by Jack Poley. 1 cass. 1993. 10.00 (JP/42444); audio compact disk 15.00 CD. (JP/42444) Talisman IN.
Guitar & synthesizers. A fusion of jazz, space, Latin, classical, & rhythm & blues.

Electric Guitar. Peter Gelling. (Progressive Ser.). 2004. pap. bk. 24.95 (978-1-86469-161-0(1), 256-055) Kolala Music SGP.

***Electric Guitar Basics.** Georg Wolf. (ENG., 2007. pap. bk. 12.95 (978-3-8024-0607-2(9)) Voggenreiter Pubs DEU.

Electric Kool-Aid Acid Test. unabr. collector's ed. Tom Wolfe. Read by Michael Prichard. 9 cass. (Running Time: 13 hrs. 30 min.). 1992. 72.00 (978-0-7366-2102-1(4), 2907) Books on Tape.
Author of "One Flew over the Cuckoo's Nest," dropped-out in the 1960's. Tom Wolfe tells the dead-end story.

***Electric Literature Aloud! Ten Great Short Stories - Unabridged.** Colson Whitehead et al. (ENG.). 2010. 21.95 (978-0-9824980-5-7(5)) Electric Lit.

***Electric Literature No. 2.** Lydia Davis & Colson Whitehead. (Running Time: 3.10). (ENG.). 2010. 14.95 (978-0-9824980-2-6(0)) Electric Lit.

***Electric Literature No. 3.** Aimee Bender et al. (ENG.). 2010. 14.95 (978-0-9824980-4-0(7)) Electric Lit.

Electric Power Equipment in India: A Strategic Reference 2006. Compiled by Icon Group International, Inc. Staff. 2007. ring bd. 195.00 (978-0-497-36010-8(1)) Icon Grp.

Electric Power Production & Services in Ecuador: A Strategic Reference 2006. Compiled by Icon Group International, Inc. Staff. 2007. ring bd. 195.00 (978-0-497-35919-5(7)) Icon Grp.

Electric Power Production & Services in Vietnam: A Strategic Reference 2006. Compiled by Icon Group International, Inc. Staff. 2007. ring bd. 195.00 (978-0-497-82472-3(8)) Icon Grp.

Electric Services in Indonesia: A Strategic Reference 2007. Compiled by Icon Group International, Inc. Staff. 2007. ring bd. 195.00 (978-0-497-36028-3(4)) Icon Grp.

Electric Universe: The Shocking True Story of Electricity. unabr. ed. David Bodanis. Read by Del Roy. 4 cass. (Running Time: 7 hrs.). 2005. 72.00 (978-0-7366-9834-4(5)) Books on Tape.
From the author of the bestselling E=MC2, comes a mesmerizing journey of discovery illuminating the wondrous yet unseen force that permeates our world and the scientists who've probed its secrets. Before 1790, when Alessandro Volta began the scientific investigation that spurred an explosion of knowledge and invention, electricity was perceived as little more than a property of certain substances that sparked when rubbed. Now we know that this formerly thought an inconsequential force is responsible for everything from the structure of the atom to the functioning of our brains. Bodanis, a superb storyteller, tells a story filled with romance, divine inspiration, fraud, and scientific breakthroughs revealing how we learned to harness its powers. The great scientists such as Michael Faraday and Samuel Morse come to life, complete with all their brilliance and idiosyncrasy.

Electric Universe: The Shocking True Story of Electricity. unabr. collector's ed. David Bodanis. Read by Del Roy. 5 CDs. (Running Time: 7 hrs.). 2005. audio compact disk 38.25 (978-1-4159-1626-1(8)) Pub: Books on Tape. Dist(s): NetLibrary CO

Electrical Engineering Dictionary: CRCnetBASE 2000. Ed. by Phillip A. Laplante. 1999. audio compact disk 199.95 (978-0-8493-2170-2(0), 2170) Pub: CRC Pr. Dist(s): Taylor and Fran

Electrical Power Distribution (EPD) Equipment in Brazil: A Strategic Reference 2006. Compiled by Icon Group International, Inc. Staff. 2007. ring bd. 195.00 (978-0-497-35836-5(0)) Icon Grp.

Electrical Systems, Heating & Air Conditioning. rev. ed. Bob Leigh et al. Ed. by Roger L. Fenneman & Harris E. Dark. Illus. by Ralph J. Butterworth. (Automobile Mechanics Refresher Course Ser.: Bk. 3). 1981. pap. bk. 13.90 (978-0-88098-070-8(2), H M Gousha) Prntice Hall Bks.

Electricity. Gilda Berger. (Smart Science Ser.). (gr. k-1). 2000. 12.00 (978-1-58273-504-7(2)) Sund Newbrdge.

Electricity & Magnetism. unabr. ed. Eric Laithwaite. 1 cass. 1990. 12.95 (ECN024) J Norton Pubs.

Electricity Deregulation: Is There Life for Restructuring after California? 1 cass. (Running Time: 60 min.). 2001. 5.00 (978-1-56986-212-4(5)) Federal Bar.
This forum sponsored by the Environment, Energy, and Natural Resources Section features panelists that discuss why implementation of electricity deregulation in New England has been successful, what key building blocks are necessary to implement deregulation elsewhere in light of Californiaís deregulation experience, the federal governmentís role in California, and the outlook for restructuring in the future.

***Electricity Is Everywhere CD.** Nadia Higgins. Illus. by Andres Martinez Ricci. (Science Rocks! Set 2 CD Ser.). 2010. cd-rom 27.07 (978-1-60270-963-8(7)) ABDO Pub Co.

***Electricity Is Everywhere Site CD.** Nadia Higgins. Illus. by Andres Martinez Ricci. (Science Rocks! Set 2 Site CD Ser.). 2010. cd-rom 57.07 (978-1-60270-977-5(7)) ABDO Pub Co.

Electro-Auriculotherapy: Explanation of Auriculotherapy for the Lay Person. unabr. ed. Julian Padowicz & David L. Camhi. Read by Julian Padowicz. 1 cass. (Running Time: 15 min.). 1999. 7.95 (978-1-881288-23-7(4), BFI AudioBooks) BusnFilm Intl.

Electroanalytical Chemistry. Instructed by Fred Anson. 6 cass. (Running Time: 5 hrs. 6 min.). 185.00 incl. 145pp. manual. (29) Am Chemical.
Discusses areas in electroanalytical chemistry, including Faraday's Law, voltammetry, controlled potential electrolysis, coulometric titrations & polarography.

Electrocardiographic Interpretation: A Self-Study Approach to Clinical Electrocardiography. Emanuel Stein. 10 cass. 1991. 130.00 Set. Lppncott W W.
This package offers a self-study course on practical concepts of ECG interpretation, using the vector analysis approach. It covers the normal ECG, hypertrophy, repolarization alterations, myocardial infarction, conduction disturbances & arrhythmias.

Electrocardiographic Interpretation: A Self-Study Approach to Clinical Electrocardiography. Emanuel Stein. 10 cass. 1991. bk. 155.00 incl. cardiac vector analysis model. (978-0-8121-1380-8(2)); bk. & stu. ed. 39.95 cardiac vector analysis model only. (978-0-8121-1378-5(0)) Lppncott W W.

Electron Mass. Saint Silicon. 1 cass. 9.00 (A0308-88) Sound Photosyn.
If you are a computer abuser you'll love what St. Silicon has to say at the Reality Hackers Forum.

Electronic & Biometric Security Equipment & Services in Saudi Arabia: A Strategic Reference 2006. Compiled by Icon Group International, Inc. Staff. 2007. ring bd. 195.00 (978-0-497-82406-8(X)) Icon Grp.

Electronic & Biometric Security Equipment & Services in Switzerland: A Strategic Reference 2007. Compiled by Icon Group International, Inc. Staff. 2007. ring bd. 195.00 (978-0-497-82425-9(6)) Icon Grp.

Electronic Arc Welding Explained Basic Procedures. Richard Hunter. (Series No. 904A). 1977. bk. 379.00 (978-0-8064-0374-8(8), DelLearn) Delmar.

Electronic Business (EB) Services for Small & Medium Enterprises (SMEs) in Taiwan: A Strategic Reference 2006. Compiled by Icon Group International, Inc. Staff. 2007. ring bd. 195.00 (978-0-497-82429-7(9)) Icon Grp.

Electronic Cassette for Children. unabr. ed. Esther Nelson & Bruce Haack. Read by Esther Nelson & Bruce Haack. 1 cass. (Running Time: 40 min.). Dramatization. (Dance Sing & Listen Ser.). (J). (gr. 1-8). 1987. 9.95 (978-0-945110-07-1(3)) Granny Pr.
From traditional melodies of long ago to the space sounds of tomorrow, from all-out action tunes to soothing lullabies, these songs & stories are set against a background of electronic sound.

Electronic Chemicals in Taiwan: A Strategic Reference 2007. Compiled by Icon Group International, Inc. Staff. 2007. ring bd. 195.00 (978-0-497-82430-3(2)) Icon Grp.

Electronic Cinema: Track Three. 2 cass. 1990. 17.00 set. Recorded Res.

Electronic Components & Semiconductors in Japan: A Strategic Reference 2006. Compiled by Icon Group International, Inc. Staff. 2007. ring bd. 195.00 (978-0-497-82325-2(X)) Icon Grp.

Electronic Dairy Herd Management. 2001. audio compact disk 25.00 (978-1-59215-066-3(7)) Babcock Inst.

Electronic Devices Lab Source. (C). 2004. audio compact disk 53.95 (978-1-4180-0534-4(7)) Pub: Delmar. Dist(s): CENGAGE Learn

Electronic Ignition Explained. Richard Hunter. 1978. bk. 139.00 (978-0-8064-0118-8(4), DelLearn) Delmar.

Electronic Keyboard: Method for Young Beginners: Supplementary Songbook A. Gary Turner. Illus. by Ann Lee. 2008. pap. bk. 17.95 (978-1-86469-275-4(8)) Kolala Music SGP.

***Electronic Record Keeping for HR Professionals.** Created by Park University Enterprises. 2010. 199.95 (978-1-60959-008-6(2)) P Univ E Inc.

Electronic Security Equipment & Services in Argentina: A Strategic Reference 2007. Compiled by Icon Group International, Inc. Staff. 2007. ring bd. 195.00 (978-0-497-35798-6(4)) Icon Grp.

Electronic Security Equipment & Services in Ecuador: A Strategic Reference 2006. Compiled by Icon Group International, Inc. Staff. 2007. ring bd. 195.00 (978-0-497-35920-1(0)) Icon Grp.

Electronic Security in Chile: A Strategic Reference 2006. Compiled by Icon Group International, Inc. Staff. 2007. ring bd. 195.00 (978-0-497-35856-3(5)) Icon Grp.

Electronic Technical Dairy Guides. (FRE & SPA.). 1999. audio compact disk 50.00 (978-1-59215-054-0(3)) Babcock Inst.

Electronics. Eric H. Glendinning & John McEwan. 1993. 17.50 (978-0-19-457386-3(9)) OUP.

Electronics Components in France: A Strategic Reference 2006. Compiled by Icon Group International, Inc. Staff. 2007. ring bd. 195.00 (978-0-497-35948-5(0)) Icon Grp.

Electronics into the Future: Network Version. 3rd ed. Intellipro, Inc. Staff & Paula Collins. (C). 1999. audio compact disk 1045.00 (978-0-7668-0657-3(X)) Pub: Delmar. Dist(s): CENGAGE Learn

Electronics Testing Equipment in China: A Strategic Reference 2007. Compiled by Icon Group International, Inc. Staff. 2007. ring bd. 195.00 (978-0-497-35879-2(4)) Icon Grp.

Electronics Trainer Circuit Board. Carlo Sapijaszko. (C). 2004. audio compact disk 265.95 (978-1-4018-3979-6(7)) Pub: Delmar. Dist(s): CENGAGE Learn

Elefantito Del Circo. Tr. of Circus Baby, the. (SPA.). 2004. 8.95 (978-0-7882-0260-5(X)) Weston Woods.

Elegance: A Novel. unabr. abr. ed. Kathleen Tessaro. Illus. by Elizabeth McGovern. 5 cass. (Running Time: 7 hrs. 30 min.). 2003. 25.95 (978-0-06-055418-7(5)) HarperCollins Pubs.

Elegance of the Hedgehog. unabr. ed. Muriel Barbery. Read by Cassandra Morris & Barbara Rosenblat. 8 CDs. (Running Time: 9 hrs. 30 mins.).Tr. of L'élégance du Hérisson. (ENG.). 2009. audio compact disk 29.95 (978-1-59887-925-4(1), 1598879251) Pub: HighBridge. Dist(s): Workman Pub

Elegant Aging: How to Grow Deeper, Stronger, Wiser. William G. DeFoore. (ENG.). 2007. audio compact disk 29.99 (978-0-9814740-2-1(0)) Halcyon Life.

Elegiac Cityscape: Propertius & the Meaning of Roman Monuments. Tara S. Welch. 2005. audio compact disk 9.95 (978-0-8142-9087-3(6)) Pub: Ohio St U Pr. Dist(s): Chicago Distribution Ctr

Elegy see Twentieth-Century Poetry in English, No. 27, Recordings of Poets Reading Their Own Poetry

***Elegy.** (ENG.). 2010. audio compact disk (978-1-59171-251-0(3)) Falcon Picture.

Elegy for a Dead Soldier see Twentieth-Century Poetry in English, No. 7, Recordings of Poets Reading Their Own Poetry

***Elegy for April.** unabr. ed. Benjamin Black. Read by Timothy Dalton. 7 CDs. (Running Time: 9 hrs.). 2010. audio compact disk 74.95 (978-0-7927-7127-2(3)) AudioGO.

Elegy for April. unabr. ed. Benjamin Black. Read by Timothy Dalton. 8 CDs. (Running Time: 9 hrs. 30 mins. 0 sec.). 2010. audio compact disk 39.99 (978-1-4272-0945-0(6)) Pub: Macmill Audio. Dist(s): Macmillan

Elegy for G. B. Shaw see Twentieth-Century Poetry in English, No. 27, Recordings of Poets Reading Their Own Poetry

Elegy for Iris, unabr. ed. John Bayley. Read by David Case. 5 cass. (Running Time: 7 hrs. 30 min.). 1999. 40.00 (978-0-7366-4471-6(7), 4914) Books on Tape.
The author was married to Iris Murdock, the eminent novelist & philosopher, for more than 40 years. When Murdoch was stricken with Alzheimer's disease, the author assumed sole care of her. With great compassion he re-creates their life together & poignantly describes the mask that descended over Iris' being with the progression of her disease.

Elegy for Iris. unabr. collector's ed. John Bayley. Read by David Case. 5 cass. (Running Time: 7 hrs. 30 min.). 1999. 29.95 (978-0-7366-4472-3(5)) Books on Tape.
When Murdoch was stricken with Alzheimer's disease, Bayley assumed sole care of her. With great compassion he re-creates their life together & poignantly describes the mask that descended over Iris's being with the progression of her disease.

Elegy for Janis Joplin see Poetry & Voice of Marilyn Hacker

Elegy for Mr. Goodbeare see Osbert Sitwell Reading His Poetry

Elegy I: Jealosie see Love Poems of John Donne

Elegy in a Country Churchyard. (23289-A) J Norton Pubs.

Elegy on the Death of a Mad Dog see Treasury of Oliver Goldsmith, Thomas Gray & William Collins

Elegy VII: Natures Lay Ideot see Love Poems of John Donne

Elegy VIII: The Comparison see Love Poems of John Donne

Elegy Written in a Country Churchyard see Treasury of Oliver Goldsmith, Thomas Gray & William Collins

Elektra. Perf. by Inge Borkh et al. Contrib. by Knud Andersson. Composed by Johann Strauss. 2 CDs. 1966. audio compact disk 33.95 STEREO. (VAIA 1170-2) VAI Audio.
Live from the New Orleans Opera. Bonus tracks: Borkh in excerpts from Verdi's "Macbeth.".

Element: How Finding Your Passion Changes Everything. unabr. ed. Ken Robinson. Read by Ken Robinson. Told to Lou Aronica. (Running Time: 8 hrs. 30 mins. 0 sec.). (ENG.). 2009. audio compact disk 24.99 (978-1-4001-6060-0(X)) Pub: Tantor Media. Dist(s): IngramPubServ

Element: How Finding Your Passion Changes Everything. unabr. ed. Ken Robinson & Lou Aronica. (Running Time: 8 hrs. 30 mins. 0 sec.). (ENG.). 2009. audio compact disk 69.99 (978-1-4001-4060-2(9)); audio compact disk 34.99 (978-1-4001-1060-5(2)) Pub: Tantor Media. Dist(s): IngramPubServ

Element of Playfulness. J. Krishnamurti. 1 cass. (Running Time: 85 min.). 8.50 (ARE84) Krishnamurti.
British television producer Ronald Eyre asks Krishnamurti about playfulness & the significance of life. This conversation recorded on October 18, 1984, explores time, freedom from fear, life, death & ending.

Elementally 8. 8 CD's. 2003. audio compact disk (978-1-932616-00-2(4)) Feng Shui Para.
The ELEMENTALLY 8 empowerment audio book is the perfect tool for anyone who wants to improve their communication skills and their understanding of what makes their friends, family and co-workers "tick". In classical Feng Shui, the five Chinese elements express themselves 8 different ways as...FIRE, MOTHER EARTH, SOFT METAL, HARD METAL, WATER, MOUNTAIN EARTH, HARD WOOD and SOFT WOOD.In this audio collection, you will discover the human characteristics and qualities of these elements and how to use these qualities to enhance your relationships with others. You'll learn specific power directions to help you negotiate a sale, communicate with your friends and family, increase your wealth, and improve your health, and you'll discover which locations, colors, and people support you and which ones deplete you.

Elementals: Stories of Fire & Ice. unabr. ed. Short Stories. A. S. Byatt. Narrated by Virginia Leishman. 3 cass. (Running Time: 4 hrs. 45 mins.). 1999. 30.00 (978-1-84197-052-3(2), H1035E7) Recorded Bks.
A collection of imaginative stories probing the motivations of a most unlikely but intriguing set of people.

Elementals: Stories of Fire & Ice. unabr. ed. Short Stories. A. S. Byatt. Narrated by Virginia Leishman. 4 CDs. (Running Time: 4 hrs. 45 mins.). 1999. audio compact disk 34.00 (978-1-84197-094-3(8), C1124E7) Recorded Bks.

Elementary: 1, 200-Word Vocabulary. Sue Arengo. 2003. 14.75 (978-0-19-422078-1(8)) OUP.

Elementary Algebra. 2nd ed. Created by Pearson/Addison Wesley. (Math XL Ser.). 2006. audio compact disk 26.67 (978-0-321-37537-7(8)) AddisonWesley.

Elementary Algebra Chpater Test Prep Video. Michael Sullivan, III & Katherine R. Struve. 2006. audio compact disk 17.40 (978-0-13-134608-6(3)) Pearson Educ CAN CAN.

Elementary Algebra for College Students. 6th ed. Allen R. Angel. (CD Lecture Ser.). 2003. audio compact disk 42.20 (978-0-13-140032-0(0)) Pearson Educ CAN CAN.

Elementary Algebra for College Students: Early Graphing. 2nd ed. Allen R. Angel. (Mathpro 5 Ser.). 2003. audio compact disk 36.80 (978-0-13-141111-1(X)) Pearson Educ CAN CAN.

Elementary & Intermediate Algebra: Chapter Test Prep. Michael Sullivan et al. 2006. audio compact disk 10.40 (978-0-13-227112-7(5)) Pearson Educ CAN CAN.

Elementary & Intermediate Algebra for College Students. 2nd ed. Allen R. Angel. (CD Lecture Ser.). 2003. audio compact disk 44.00 (978-0-13-141120-3(9)) Pearson Educ CAN CAN.

Elementary & Secondary Schools see Discussion on Purpose of Education

Elementary & Secondary Schools, Pt. 2. Read by Donald W. McNemar et al. 1 cass. Incl. Discussion on Elementary & Secondary Schools. (145); Pt. 1. Elementary & Secondary Schools: Colleges & Universities. Read by David Lowenthal. (145); 3.00 (145) ISI Books.

Elementary & Secondary Schools: Colleges & Universities see Elementary & Secondary Schools

Elementary Anecdotes in American English. Leslie A. Hill. (Anecdotes in American English Ser.). (C). 1980. 17.50 (978-0-19-502828-7(7)) OUP.

Elementary Bulgarian 1. Charles Gribble & Lyubomira P. Gribble. 4 cass. 1984. 20.00 (978-0-87415-015-5(9), 12B) Foreign Lang.

Elementary Bulgarian 2. Charles Gribble & Lyubomira P. Gribble. 3 cass. 1984. 15.00 (978-0-87415-018-6(3), 13B) Foreign Lang.

Elementary Chinese Readers, Vol. 1. 29.95 (978-0-8351-0820-1(1)) China Bks.

Elementary Czech 1. Charles E. Townsend & Elaine McKee. 7 cass. 1984. 35.00 (978-0-87415-027-8(2), 16B) Foreign Lang.

Elementary Czech 2. Charles E. Townsend & Elaine McKee. 7 cass. 1984. 35.00 (978-0-87415-030-8(2), 17B) Foreign Lang.

Elementary Edition, Vol. 1. Cathy Ellis & Tammy Cherry. Perf. by Rick Krive. 1 cass. (Complete Guide for the Guitar Ser.). (J). (gr. 3-6). 1998. 23.95 (978-1-879542-66-2(8), EFM7001TP) Ellis Family Mus.
Follow up to "The Adventures of Gilly, the Guitar." Follow along on the guitar or bass-guitar with the instrumentals split mix. The 19 ensemble performance pieces include some vocals.

Elementary Greek Koine for Beginners: Year One. Christine Gatchell. 2005. audio compact disk 12.95 (978-0-9742391-9-4(4)) Pub: Open Texture. Dist(s): Natl Bk Netwk

Elementary Greek: Koine for Beginners: Year Three Audio Companion. Christine Gatchell. Read by Ian Bogost. 2007. audio compact disk 12.95 (978-1-933900-06-3(7)) Pub: Open Texture. Dist(s): Natl Bk Netwk

Elementary Greek Koine for Beginners: Year Two: Audio Companion. Christine Gatchell. 2006. audio compact disk 12.95 (978-1-933900-02-5(4)) Pub: Open Texture. Dist(s): Natl Bk Netwk

Elementary Modern Standard Arabic, Vol. 1. Peter F. Abboud et al. 15 cass. 1983. 116.09 Set. U MI Lang Res.

Elementary Modern Standard Arabic, Vol. 2. Peter F. Abboud et al. 6 cass. 1983. 61.58 Set. U MI Lang Res.

Elementary Modern Standard Arabic, Vols. 1 & 2. Peter F. Abboud et al. 21 cass. 1983. 138.14 Set. U MI Lang Res.

Elementary Ojibwa. 3 cass. 40.49 Set. U MI Lang Res.

Elementary Polish 1. Jerzy R. Krzyzanowski et al. 4 cass. 1986. 20.00 (978-0-87415-097-1(3), 41B) Foreign Lang.

Elementary Polish 2. Jerzy R. Krzyzanowski et al. 6 cass. (Running Time: 8 hrs.). (OSU Foreign Language Publications). (POL.). 1986. 30.00 (978-0-87415-100-8(7), 42B) Foreign Lang.
Polish language tapes.

Elementary Reader in English, Set. Lolita Dixson. (C). 1987. 105.00 (978-0-13-259466-0(8)) Longman.

Elementary School Classroom in a Slum see Twentieth-Century Poetry in English, No. 9, Recordings of Poets Reading Their Own Poetry

Elementary Serbo-Croatian 1. Biljana Sljivic-Simsic & Krinka Vidakovic. 6 cass. 1986. 30.00 (978-0-87415-064-3(7), 28B) Foreign Lang.

Elementary Serbo-Croatian 2. Biljana Sljivic-Simsic & Krinka Vidakovic. 6 cass. 1986. 30.00 (978-0-87415-067-4(1), 29B) Foreign Lang.

Elementary Slovak 1. Louise B. Hammer. 6 cass. (Running Time: 1 hr.). 1995. 30.00 (978-0-87415-263-0(1), 112B) Foreign Lang.
Audio cassettes to accompany Elementary Slovak I student manual.

Elementary Slovak 2. Louise B. Hammer. 8 cass. (Running Time: 12 hrs.). (Foreign Language Publications). 1996. 40.00 (978-0-87415-285-2(2), 122B) Foreign Lang.
Exercises to supplement student manual.

Elementary Statistics. 9th ed. Mario F. Triola. 2004. audio compact disk 14.97 (978-0-321-12210-0(0)) P-H.

Elementary Statistics: PowerPoint. 9th rev. ed. Triola. audio compact disk 14.97 (978-0-321-12215-5(1)) P-H.

Elementary Swahili Newspaper Reader. 1985. 24.00 (978-0-931745-15-7(2)) Dunwoody Pr.

Elementary Swahili Newspaper Reader, Set. Agnes Musyoki & John D. Murphy. 3 cass. (Running Time: 1 hr. 30 min. per cass.). (SWA.). 1985. 24.00 (3074) Dunwoody Pr.
Twenty readings provide the student with a broad selection of articles together with the necessary lexical & grammatical aids. The subject matter covers a variety of fields, including discussions of political, economic, military & human interest topics.

Elementary Task Listening. Jacqueline St. Clair Stokes. (Running Time: 33 mins.). (ENG.). 1984. 25.20 (978-0-521-25594-3(5)) Cambridge U Pr.

***Elementary Task Listening Audio CD.** Jacqueline St. Clair Stokes. (Running Time: 32 mins.). (ENG.). 2010. audio compact disk 23.00 (978-0-521-15604-2(1)) Cambridge U Pr.

Elementary Ukranian 1. Assya Humesky & Val Bolen. 1 cass. 1984. 5.00 (978-0-87415-051-3(5), 24B) Foreign Lang.

Elementary Ukranian 2. Assya Humesky & Val Bolen. 1 cass. 1984. 5.00 (978-0-87415-055-1(8), 25B) Foreign Lang.

Elementos Esencales del Ministerio. Charles R. Swindoll.Tr. of Ministry Essentials. (SPA.). 2007. audio compact disk 27.00 (978-1-57972-802-1(2)) Insight Living.

Elements: Constitutional Type & Temperament. Ingrid Naiman. 4 cass. (Running Time: 6 hrs.). 40.00 (978-1-882834-98-3(4)) Seventh Ray.
Detailed description of the air, fire, earth, & water types. Psychological & physiological.

Elements & Crosses. K. Hamaker-Zondag. 1 cass. 8.95 (670) Am Fed Astrologers.
An AFA Convention workshop tape.

Elements of Effort: Reflections on the Art & Science of Running. unabr. ed. John Jerome. Narrated by L. J. Ganser. 3 cass. (Running Time: 4 hrs. 15 mins.). 1999. 26.00 (978-0-7887-3056-6(8), 95750E7) Recorded Bks.
Celebrate the simplicity & freedom of running with this engaging collection of essays. For years the author & athlete, recorded the wisdom he gained during his daily runs. His wry reflections take you on a joyous journey through the most elemental aspects of the sport.

***Elements of Investing.** unabr. ed. Burton G. Malkiel & Charles D. Ellis. Read by Erik Synnestvedt. (Running Time: 2 hrs. 30 mins.). (ENG.). 2009. 19.98 (978-1-59659-501-9(9), GildAudio) Pub: Gildan Media. Dist(s): HachBkGrp

Elements of Investing. unabr. ed. Burton G. Malkiel & Charles D. Ellis. Read by Sean Pratt & Erik Synnestvedt. (Running Time: 2 hrs. 30 mins.). (ENG.). 2009. audio compact disk 24.98 (978-1-59659-458-6(6)) Pub: Gildan Media. Dist(s): HachBkGrp

Elements of Jazz: From Cakewalks to Fusion. Instructed by Bill Messenger. 4 cass. (Running Time: 6 hrs.). 29.95 (978-1-56585-209-9(5)) Teaching Co.

Elements of Jazz: From Cakewalks to Fusion. Instructed by Bill Messenger. 8 CDs. (Running Time: 6 hrs.). audio compact disk 39.95 (978-1-59803-148-5(1)) Teaching Co.

Elements of Jazz: From Cakewalks to Fusion, Course 728. Perf. by Ursula Ricks & Ashton Fletcher. Instructed by Bill Messenger. 6 cass. (Running Time: 6 hrs.). 2000. 19.95 Teaching Co.
Eight lectures for a look at this uniquely American art form.

Elements of Language: Macintosh Version. Holt, Rinehart and Winston Staff. 1997. cd-rom & audio compact disk 50.40 (978-0-03-095485-6(1)) Holt McDoug.

Elements of Language: Select Readings Sampler. Holt, Rinehart and Winston Staff. (YA). (gr. 7-12). 1993. 11.13 (978-0-03-043027-5(5)) Holt McDoug.

Elements of Literature. Holt, Rinehart and Winston Staff. 1997. 291.80 (978-0-03-095564-8(5)) Holt McDoug.
A complete range of transparencies that enliven your presentation of selections and enhance lessons, including: Graphic Organizers that help students to organize information visually.

Elements of Literature. Holt, Rinehart and Winston Staff. 20 cass. 1997. 169.73 (978-0-03-052008-2(8)) Holt McDoug.
Recordings of captivating poems, short stories, and essays written by inspiring classic and contemporary authors Dramatic readings by professional actors and actresses.

Elements of LIterature: Audoi CD Library. 5th ed. Holt, Rinehart and Winston Staff. 2004. audio compact disk 347.80 (978-0-03-073817-3(2)) Holt McDoug.

Elements of Literature: Comprehensive Audio Program. Holt, Rinehart and Winston Staff. 1997. 169.73 (978-0-03-052014-3(2)); 169.73 (978-0-03-052017-4(7)) Holt McDoug.

Elements of Literature: Comprehensive Audio Program. Holt, Rinehart and Winston Staff. 1998. 169.73 (978-0-03-052018-1(5)) Holt McDoug.

Elements of Literature: Daily Language Activities. 5th ed. Holt, Rinehart and Winston Staff. 2003. audio compact disk 282.60 (978-0-03-073871-5(7)); audio compact disk 282.60 (978-0-03-073872-2(5)); audio compact disk 282.60 (978-0-03-073873-9(3)) Holt McDoug.

Elements of Literature: Holt Adapted Reader. 3rd ed. Holt, Rinehart and Winston Staff. (J). 2003. 100.20 (978-0-03-073403-8(7)) Holt McDoug.

Elements of Literature: Holt Adapted Reader. 3rd ed. Holt, Rinehart and Winston Staff. (gr. 1). 2003. 100.20 (978-0-03-073404-5(5)) Holt McDoug.

Elements of Literature: Holt Adapted Reader. 3rd ed. Holt, Rinehart and Winston Staff. (gr. 2). 2003. 100.20 (978-0-03-073406-9(1)) Holt McDoug.

Elements of Literature: Holt Adapted Reader. 3rd ed. Holt, Rinehart and Winston Staff. (gr. 3). 2003. 100.20 (978-0-03-073407-6(X)) Holt McDoug.

Elements of Literature: Holt Adapted Reader. 3rd ed. Holt, Rinehart and Winston Staff. (gr. 4). 2003. 100.20 (978-0-03-073408-3(8)) Holt McDoug.

Elements of Literature: Holt Adapted Reader. 3rd ed. Holt, Rinehart and Winston Staff. (gr. 5). 2003. 100.20 (978-0-03-073409-0(6)) Holt McDoug.

Elements of Literature: Holt Adapted Reader. 3rd ed. Holt, Rinehart and Winston Staff. (gr. 6). 2003. 100.20 (978-0-03-073411-3(8)) Holt McDoug.

Elements of Literature: Holt Reader's Audio CD Library. 3rd ed. Holt, Rinehart and Winston Staff. 2002. audio compact disk 168.26 (978-0-03-068472-2(2)); audio compact disk 168.26 (978-0-03-068473-9(0)); audio compact disk 168.26 (978-0-03-068474-6(9)); audio compact disk 168.26 (978-0-03-068476-0(5)); audio compact disk 168.26 (978-0-03-068477-7(3)); audio compact disk 168.26 (978-0-03-068478-4(1)); audio compact disk 168.26 (978-0-03-068479-1(X)) Holt McDoug.

Elements of Literature: Library. 5th ed. Holt, Rinehart and Winston Staff. 2003. audio compact disk 376.13 (978-0-03-073818-0(0)); audio compact disk 376.13 (978-0-03-073819-7(9)); audio compact disk 376.13 (978-0-03-073821-0(0)); audio compact disk 376.13 (978-0-03-073822-7(9)) Holt McDoug.

Elements of Literature: Library. 5th ed. Holt, Rinehart and Winston Staff. 2003. audio compact disk 347.80 (978-0-03-073814-2(8)) Holt McDoug.

Elements of Literature: Library. 5th ed. Holt, Rinehart and Winston Staff. 2004. audio compact disk 347.80 (978-0-03-073816-6(4)) Holt McDoug.

Elements of Literature: One-Stop Lesson Planner: Missouri Edition. Holt, Rinehart and Winston Staff. (J). (gr. 1). 2002. tchr. ed. 286.65 (978-0-03-073632-2(3)) Holt McDoug.

Elements of Literature: Selections & Summaries. 5th ed. Holt, Rinehart and Winston Staff. (SPA.). 2003. audio compact disk 220.66 (978-0-03-073984-2(5)); audio compact disk 220.66 (978-0-03-073986-6(1)); audio compact disk 220.66 (978-0-03-073987-3(X)); audio compact disk 220.66 (978-0-03-073992-7(6)) Holt McDoug.

Elements of Literature: Selections & Summaries. 5th ed. Holt, Rinehart and Winston Staff. (SPA.). 2003. cd-rom 216.33 (978-0-03-073963-7(2)); audio compact disk 216.33 (978-0-03-073967-5(5)); audio compact disk 216.33 (978-0-03-073968-2(3)) Holt McDoug.

Elements of Literature: Unit Introduction. Holt, Rinehart and Winston Staff. 1993. 54.80 (978-0-03-094648-6(4)) Holt McDoug.
A program that uses inspiring selections as models for teaching literary elements, the writing process, and language skills.

Elements of Literature: Unit Introduction. Holt, Rinehart and Winston Staff. 1993. 57.53 (978-0-03-094644-8(1)) Holt McDoug.

Elements of Literature: Unit Introduction Cassettes. Holt, Rinehart and Winston Staff. 1993. 57.53 (978-0-03-094647-9(6)) Holt McDoug.

Elements of Literature Course 1: The Voice of Meaningful Literature. Holt, Rinehart and Winston Staff. (J). (gr. 5-6). 1997. 291.80 (978-0-03-095561-7(0)) Holt McDoug.
Provides a bold yet thoughtful mix of familiar classics and outstanding contemporary voices from diverse backgrounds that will put the light back in any student?s eyes. Captivating poems, short stories, and essays are grouped together by universal themes so that students can enter into a meaningful dialogue with the world of ideas.

Elements of Literature Course 2: The Voice of Meaningful Literature. Holt, Rinehart and Winston Staff. (YA). (gr. 6-7). 1997. 291.80 (978-0-03-095562-4(9)) Holt McDoug.

Elements of Literature Course 3: The Voice of Meaningful Literature. Holt, Rinehart and Winston Staff. (YA). (gr. 7-8). 2000. 291.80 (978-0-03-095563-1(7)) Holt McDoug.

Elements of Literature Course 4: The Voice of Meaningful Literature. Holt, Rinehart and Winston Staff. (YA). (gr. 9-10). 1997. 291.80 (978-0-03-095565-5(3)) Holt McDoug.

Elements of Literature Course 5: The Voice of Meaningful Literature. Holt, Rinehart and Winston Staff. (YA). (gr. 11-12). 1997. 291.80 (978-0-03-095566-2(1)) Holt McDoug.
A mix of familiar classics and outstanding contemporary voices from diverse backgrounds that will put the light back in any student's eyes. • Captivating poems, short stories, and essays are grouped together by universal themes so that students can enter into a meaningful dialogue with the world of ideas.

Elements of Literature Course 6: The Voice of Meaningful Literature. Holt, Rinehart and Winston Staff. (YA). (gr. 11-12). 1997. 291.80 (978-0-03-095567-9(X)) Holt McDoug.

Elements of Literature, Grade 10: Selections Library. 3rd ed. Holt, Rinehart and Winston Staff. (SPA.). 2002. audio compact disk 147.00 (978-0-03-067717-5(3)) Holt McDoug.

Elements of Literature, Grade 11: Selections Library. 3rd ed. Holt, Rinehart and Winston Staff. (SPA.). 2002. audio compact disk 147.00 (978-0-03-067718-2(1)) Holt McDoug.

Elements of Literature, Grade 12: Selections Library. 3rd ed. Holt, Rinehart and Winston Staff. (SPA.). 2002. audio compact disk 147.00 (978-0-03-067719-9(X)) Holt McDoug.

Elements of Literature, Grade 6: Selections Library. 3rd ed. Holt, Rinehart and Winston Staff. (SPA.). 2002. audio compact disk 147.00 (978-0-03-067712-0(2)) Holt McDoug.

Elements of Literature, Grade 7: Selections Library. 3rd ed. Holt, Rinehart and Winston Staff. (SPA.). 2002. audio compact disk 147.00 (978-0-03-067713-7(0)) Holt McDoug.

Elements of Literature, Grade 8: Selections Library. 3rd ed. Holt, Rinehart and Winston Staff. (SPA.). 2002. audio compact disk 147.00 (978-0-03-067714-4(9)) Holt McDoug.

Elements of Literature, Grade 9: Selections Library. 3rd ed. Holt, Rinehart and Winston Staff. (SPA.). 2002. audio compact disk 147.00 (978-0-03-067716-8(5)) Holt McDoug.

Elements of Literature 2: Audio CD Library: Summaries in Spanish. 3rd ed. Holt, Rinehart and Winston Staff. 2002. audio compact disk 49.13 (978-0-03-067983-4(4)); audio compact disk 49.13 (978-0-03-067988-9(5)); audio compact disk 49.13 (978-0-03-067989-6(3)); audio compact disk 49.13 (978-0-03-067991-9(5)); audio compact disk 49.13 (978-0-03-067984-1(2)); audio compact disk 49.13 (978-0-03-067986-5(9)) Holt McDoug.
Provides a thoughtfully selected, diverse mix of familiar classics and contemporary voices. Collections of poems, short stories, and non-fiction encourage students to enter into a meaningful dialogue with the ideas and themes of literature.

Elements of Literature 2: Library: Summaries in Spanish. 3rd ed. Holt, Rinehart and Winston Staff. 2002. audio compact disk 49.13 (978-0-03-067987-2(7)) Holt McDoug.

Elements of Medical Term. 1994. 112.50 (978-0-8273-6551-3(9)) Delmar.

Elements of Music. abr. ed. Joseph N. Straus. 2003. audio compact disk 19.60 (978-0-13-184091-1(6)) Pearson Educ CAN CAN.

Elements of New Testament Greek: For the Elements of New Testament Greek. 3rd rev. ed. Jeremy Duff. As told by Jonathan T. Pennington. (ENG & GEC.). 2005. audio compact disk 29.99 (978-0-521-61473-3(2)) Cambridge U Pr.

Elements of Poetry. 2 CDs. (Running Time: 3 hrs.). (YA). (gr. 5-12). 2002. audio compact disk 71.00 (978-0-7833-0022-1(0)) T S Klise Co.
This audio kit explains the basic terms used in poetry including simile, metaphor, rhyme, rhythm, alliteration, and more. Students work through a series of Response Sheets, finding examples of what they've learned in poems like The Highwayman, October, The Raven, The Wreck of the Hesperus.

Elements of Pronunciation: Intensive Practice for Intermediate & More Advanced Students. Colin Mortimer. 4 cass. (ENG., 1985. 59.00 (978-0-521-26334-4(4)) Cambridge U Pr.

Elements of Style. unabr. ed. Wendy Wasserstein. Read by Kathe Mazur. 8 cass. (Running Time: 10 hrs.). 2006. 72.00 (978-1-4159-2990-2(4), BksonTape); audio compact disk 90.00 (978-1-4159-2991-9(2), BksonTape) Pub: Random Audio Pubg. Dist(s): Random

Elements of the Sky. 1 cass. (Running Time: 33 min.). 14.95 (13429) MMI Corp.
Planetary rotation, creation of Universe, stellar explosions & more discussed by Hayden Planetarium astronomers.

Elements of True Prayer. John MacArthur, Jr. 4 cass. (John MacArthur's Bible Studies). 16.25 (HarperThor) HarpC GBR.

Elemyntal. 1 CD. 2000. audio compact disk 13.99 (978-0-7601-3444-3(8)) Pub: Brentwood Music. Dist(s): Provident Mus Dist
Songs include: "Elemyntal," "Slow It Down," "Leave Her Alone," "Good n' Plenty" & more.

Elena Castedo: Paradise. unabr. ed. Elena Castedo. Read by Elena Castedo. Interview with Rebekah Presson. 1 cass. (Running Time: 29 min.). 1991. 10.00 (061491) New Letters.
Recently, Paradise won the Book of the Year Award in Castedo's native Chile where it has topped best-seller lists for months. Castedo translated the book.

Elena's Song. Peggy Stoks. Narrated by Christina Moore. 7 cass. (Running Time: 9 hrs. 15 mins.). (Abounding Love Ser.: Vol. 3). 62.00 (978-0-7887-9023-2(4)) Recorded Bks.

Eleni. unabr. ed. Nicholas Gage. Read by [illegible]ael Prichard. 15 cass. (Running Time: 22 hrs. 30 min.). 1991. 120.00 (97[illegible]-7366-1978-3(X), 2796) Books on Tape.
With Glasnost & Gorby all the rage, it's easy to forget how real the Communist threat was. Yet following WW II, millions of people were brutalized by it, nowhere more viciously than in Greece, where the Soviets subsidized a Civil War that nearly succeeded. Among its victims was Eleni Gatzoyiannis, suspect beause her husband was in America, & finally executed for her lack of cooperation. Nicki, still a child, made it to New York. He vowed that when he grew up he would find her killer & settle the score. Thirty years later he did.

Elephant & the Dragon: The Rise of India & China, & What It Means for All of Us. unabr. ed. Robyn Meredith. Read by Laural Merlington. (Running Time: 9 hrs. 0 mins. 0 sec.). (ENG.). 2007. audio compact disk 59.99 (978-1-4001-3485-4(4)); audio compact disk 19.99 (978-1-4001-5485-2(5)) Pub: Tantor Media. Dist(s): IngramPubServ

Elephant & the Dragon: The Rise of India & China, & What It Means for All of Us. unabr. ed. Robyn Meredith. Read by Laural Merlington. (YA). 2008. 54.99 (978-1-60514-183-1(6)) Find a World.

Elephant & the Dragon: The Rise of India & China, & What It Means for All of Us. unabr. ed. Read by Laural Merlington. (Running Time: 9 hrs. 0 mins. 0 sec.). (ENG.). 2007. audio compact disk 29.99 (978-1-4001-0485-7(8)) Pub: Tantor Media. Dist(s): IngramPubServ

Elephant Games: And Other Playful Poems to Perform. unabr. ed. Brod Bagert. Read by Brod Bagert. 1 cass. (Running Time: 30 min.). (ENG.). (J). (gr. k-6). 1997. reel tape 9.00 (978-1-887746-04-5(8)) Juliahouse Pubs.

Elephant in Aisle Four: And Other Whimsical Animal Songs. Perf. by Lisa Atkinson. 1 cass. (Running Time: 40 mins.). (J). (ps-3). 2000. 9.95 (978-1-58467-006-3(1)); audio compact disk 14.95 (978-1-58467-007-0(X)) Gentle Wind.
Animal songs that convey a underlying message of unity & peace.

Elephant Is Stuck! Jill Eggleton. (Sails Literacy Ser.). (gr. k up). 10.00 (978-0-7578-4039-5(6)) Rigby Educ.

Elephant Man. abr. ed. Frederick Treves. Narrated by Daniel Chodos. 2 cass. (Running Time: 2 hrs. 4 min.). 12.95 (978-0-89926-152-2(3), 840) Audio Bk.
John Merrick was a circus freak when Frederick Treves, a distinguished Medical College Lecturer discovered him. Nicknamed the Elephant Man, Merrick's story was the inspiration for the award-winning stage play & feature film.

Elephant Shooter see Tales from a Troubled Land

Elephant Song. unabr. ed. Wilbur Smith. Read by Richard Brown. 15 cass. (Running Time: 22 hrs. 30 min.). (Ballantyne Novels Ser.). 1993. 120.00 (978-0-7366-2470-1(8), 3233) Books on Tape.
When a friend is murdered by African ivory poachers, renowned ecologist seeks justice.

***Elephant to Hollywood: The Autobiography.** abr. ed. Michael Caine. (Running Time: 6 hrs. 0 mins. 0 sec.). 2010. audio compact disk 29.99 (978-1-4272-1178-1(7)) Pub: Macmill Audio. Dist(s): Macmillan

Elephant Vanishes. Haruki Murakami. Read by Teresa Gallagher et al. (Running Time: 13 hrs.). 2006. 54.95 (978-1-60083-916-0(9)) Iofy Corp.

Elephant Vanishes. unabr. ed. Haruki Murakami. Read by Theresa Gallagher et al. (YA). 2007. 69.99 (978-1-59895-853-9(4)) Find a World.

Elephant Vanishes. unabr. ed. Haruki Murakami. Read by John Chancer et al. 8 CDs. (Running Time: 37919 sec.). 2006. audio compact disk 54.98 (978-962-634-406-4(7), NA840612, Naxos AudioBooks) Naxos.

Elephants. Sydnie M. Kleinhenz. Contrib. by Colleen Buckman. (African Animals Ser.). (ENG.). (gr. k-1). 2008. audio compact disk 14.65 (978-1-4296-3196-9(1)) CapstoneDig.

Elephants Can Remember. Agatha Christie. Read by John Moffatt. 6 CDs. (Running Time: 9 hrs.). 2001. audio compact disk 64.95 (978-0-7540-5425-2(X), CCD 116) Pub: Chivers Audio Bks GBR. Dist(s): AudioGO

Hercule Poirot stood on the cliff top. Here, many years earlier, there had been a tragic accident. Poirot delves back into the past and discovers that "old sins leave long shadows".

Elephants Can Remember. unabr. ed. Agatha Christie. Read by John Moffatt. 5 cass. (Running Time: 6 hrs. 30 mins.). 2003. 27.95 (978-1-57270-341-4(5), 691157) Pub: Audio Partners. Dist(s): PerseuPGW

Elephants Can Remember. unabr. ed. Agatha Christie. Narrated by John Moffatt. 6 CDs. (Running Time: 6 hrs. 30 mins.). (Mystery Masters Ser.). (ENG.). 2003. audio compact disk 29.95 (978-1-57270-342-1(3), 750812) Pub: AudioGO. Dist(s): Perseus Dist

Elephants Can Remember. unabr. ed. Agatha Christie. Read by John Moffatt. 6 cass. (Running Time: 9 hrs). 1999. 49.95 (978-0-7540-0334-2(5), CAB1757) Pub: Chivers Audio Bks GBR. Dist(s): AudioGO

Hercule Poirot stood on the cliff-top. Here, many years earlier, there had been a tragic accident. This was followed by the grisly discovery of two more bodies: a husband & wife shot dead. But who had killed them? Was it a suicide pact, crime of passion, or murder? Poirot delves back into the past & discovers that old sins leave long shadows.

Elephants Can Remember: A BBC Full-Cast Radio Drama. unabr. ed. Agatha Christie. Narrated by John Moffatt & Full Cast. (Running Time: 2 hrs. 0 mins. 0 sec.). (ENG.). 2010. audio compact disk 24.95 (978-1-60283-809-3(7)) Pub: AudioGO. Dist(s): Perseus Dist

Elephant's Child see Favorite Children's Stories: A Collection

Elephant's Child see Just So Stories, Set, For Little Children

Elephant's Child see Favorite Just So Stories

***Elephant's Child.** Anonymous. 2009. (978-1-60136-595-8(0)) Audio Holding.

Elephant's Child. Rudyard Kipling. (J). bk. 14.00 Windham Hill.

Elephant's Child. unabr. ed. Rudyard Kipling. (Running Time: 18 min.). (World of Just So Stories Ser.: No. 2). (J). bk. 15.00 (SAC 6504A) Spoken Arts.

Kipling's famous story in book-cassette format with illustrations.

Elephant's Child & the Cat that Walked by Himself. (J). 2005. audio compact disk (978-1-933796-43-7(X)) PC Treasures.

Eleven. Lauren Myracle. Narrated by Jen Taylor. (Running Time: 4 hrs. 57 mins.). (J). (gr. 4-7). 2009. 49.99 (978-1-60775-990-4(X)) Find a World.

Eleven. unabr. ed. Patricia Reilly Giff. Read by Staci Snell. 3 CDs. (Running Time: 3 hrs. 20 mins.). (J). (gr. 5-7). 2008. audio compact disk 45.00 (978-0-7393-6282-2(8), Listening Lib) Pub: Random Audio Pubg. Dist(s): Random

Eleven. unabr. ed. Patricia Reilly Giff. Read by Staci Snell. (Running Time: 12000 sec.). (ENG.). (J). (gr. 3-8). 2008. audio compact disk 25.00 (978-0-7393-6280-8(1), Listening Lib) Pub: Random Audio Pubg. Dist(s): Random

Eleven. unabr. ed. Lauren Myracle. Narrated by Jen Taylor. 4 CDs. (Running Time: 4 hrs. 57 mins.). (ENG.). (J). (gr. 4-7). 2009. audio compact disk 49.95 (978-0-545-11524-7(8)) Scholastic Inc.

Eleven on Top. abr. ed. Janet Evanovich. Read by Lorelei King. 3 CDs. (Running Time: 3 hrs. 0 mins. 0 sec.). (Stephanie Plum Ser.: No. 11). (ENG.). 2005. audio compact disk 19.95 (978-1-59397-697-2(6)) Pub: Macmill Audio. Dist(s): Macmillan

Eleven on Top. unabr. ed. Janet Evanovich. Read by Lorelei King. (Stephanie Plum Ser.: No. 11). 2005. 29.95 (978-0-7927-3647-9(8), CMP 805); audio compact disk 74.95 (978-0-7927-3646-2(X), SLD 805) AudioGO.

Eleven on Top. unabr. ed. Janet Evanovich. Read by Lorelei King. 7 CDs. (Running Time: 8 hrs. 30 mins. 0 sec.). (Stephanie Plum Ser.: No. 11). (ENG.). 2005. audio compact disk 34.95 (978-1-55927-787-7(4)) Pub: Macmill Audio. Dist(s): Macmillan

Eleven Turtle Tales: Adventure Tales from Around the World. Short Stories. Read by Pleasant DeSpain. 1 cass. (Running Time: 1 hr. 10 mins.). (gr. 4-7). 1996. bk. 12.00 (978-0-87483-425-3(2)) Pub: August Hse. Dist(s): Natl Bk Netwk

Turtle, the slow but steady, is wise beyond her years in these world folktales.

Eleventh Commandment. unabr. ed. Jeffrey Archer. Narrated by Paul Hecht. 9 CDs. (Running Time: 10 hrs. 45 mins.). 1999. audio compact disk 83.00 (978-0-7887-3440-3(7), C1046E7) Recorded Bks.

Follows a skilled assassin on his whirlwind journey from the inner circles of the CIA to the front lines of international espionage.

Eleventh Commandment. unabr. ed. Jeffrey Archer. Read by Paul Hecht. 8 cass. (Running Time: 10 hrs. 45 mins.). 1998. 75.00 (978-0-7887-1968-4(8), 95355E7) Recorded Bks.

***Eleventh Grade Burns.** unabr. ed. Heather Brewer. (Running Time: 8 hrs.). (Chronicles of Vladimir Tod: Bk. 4). (YA). 2010. 19.99 (978-1-4418-6863-3(1), 9781441868633, BAD) Brilliance Audio.

***Eleventh Grade Burns.** unabr. ed. Heather Brewer. (Running Time: 8 hrs.). (Chronicles of Vladimir Tod: bk. 4). (YA). 2010. 39.97 (978-1-4418-6864-0(X), 9781441868640, BADLE) Brilliance Audio.

***Eleventh Grade Burns.** unabr. ed. Heather Brewer. Read by Kevin Pariseau. (Running Time: 9 hrs.). (Chronicles of Vladimir Tod: Bk. 4). (YA). 2010. 19.99 (978-1-4418-6861-9(5), 9781441868619, Brilliance MP3); 39.97 (978-1-4418-6862-6(3), 9781441868626, Brlnc Audio MP3 Lib); audio compact disk 19.99 (978-1-4418-6859-6(3), 9781441868596, Bril Audio CD Unabri); audio compact disk 54.97 (978-1-4418-6860-2(7), 9781441868602, BriAudCD Unabrid) Brilliance Audio.

Eleventh Hour. Perf. by Jars of Clay. 2002. audio compact disk 17.98 Essential Recs.

Eleventh Hour. abr. ed. Catherine Coulter. Read by Sandra Burr. (Running Time: 21600 sec.). (FBI Thriller Ser.: No. 7). 2006. audio compact disk 16.99 (978-1-4233-1936-8(2), 9781423319368, BCD Value Price) Brilliance Audio.

When FBI agent Dane Carver's twin brother, Father Michael Joseph, is brutally murdered in his San Francisco church, husband-and-wife agents Lacey Sherlock and Dillon Savich take a personal interest in the investigation. Then Nicola "Nick" Jones, a homeless woman and the only witness to the shooting, is scared out of her mind because she is trying to hide from her own monsters - who are drawing closer and closer. The chase goes from San Francisco to the Premiere Studios in Los Angeles and its new television hit, a show all about murder.

Eleventh Hour. unabr. ed. Catherine Coulter. Read by Sandra Burr. 7 cass. (Running Time: 10 hrs.). (FBI Thriller Ser.: No. 7). 2002. 32.95 (978-1-58788-840-3(8), 1587888408, BAU); 82.25 (978-1-58788-841-0(6), 1587888416, Unabridge Lib Edns); audio compact disk 97.25 (978-1-58788-844-1(0), 1587888440, CD Unabrid Lib Ed) Brilliance Audio.

Eleventh Hour. unabr. ed. Catherine Coulter. Read by Sandra Burr. (Running Time: 10 hrs.). (FBI Thriller Ser.: No. 7). 2004. 39.25 (978-1-59335-619-4(6), 1593356196, Brlnc Audio MP3 Lib) Brilliance Audio.

Eleventh Hour. unabr. ed. Catherine Coulter. Read by Sandra Burr. (Running Time: 10 hrs.). (FBI Thriller Ser.: No. 7). 2004. 39.25 (978-1-59710-244-5(X), 159710244X, BADLE); 24.95 (978-1-59710-245-2(8), 1597102458, BAD) Brilliance Audio.

***Eleventh Hour.** unabr. ed. Catherine Coulter. Read by Sandra Burr. (Running Time: 10 hrs.). (FBI Thriller Ser.). 2010. audio compact disk 19.99 (978-1-4418-7840-3(8), 9781441878403, Bril Audio CD Unabri) Brilliance Audio.

Eleventh Hour. unabr. ed. Catherine Coulter. Read by Sandra Burr. (Running Time: 10 hrs.). (FBI Thriller Ser.: No. 7). 2004. 24.95 (978-1-59335-207-3(7), 1593352077) Soulmate Audio Bks.

Eleventh Hour-ABR. Catherine Coulter & #7 Fbi Thriller. 2010. audio compact disk 9.99 (978-1-4418-4179-7(2)) Brilliance Audio.

Eleventh Man. Ivan Doig. 2008. audio compact disk 39.99 (978-1-4361-4961-7(4)) Recorded Bks.

Eleventh Month, Eleventh Day, Eleventh Hour: Armistice Day, 1918 World War. unabr. ed. Joseph Persico. Read by Jonathan Marosz. 12 cass. (Running Time: 18 hrs.). 2004. 104.00 (978-1-4159-0362-9(X)); audio compact disk 128.00 (978-1-4159-0781-8(1)) Books on Tape.

Ttraces the last day of World War I, weaving together the experiences of the famous, such as President Wilson, General Pershing, and Douglas MacArthur and the unsung and unremembered. With peace talks underway, the beaten Germans proposed an interim cease-fire to spare lives, but the French Allied commander, General Ferdinand Foch, refused. Hostilities would not cease, Foch insisted, before the appointed hour of the Armistice.

Eleventh Plague. unabr. ed. John S. Marr & John Baldwin. Read by Adams Morgan. 10 cass. (Running Time: 14 hrs. 30 mins.). 2000. 69.95 (978-0-7861-1683-6(8), 2504) Blckstn Audio.

Two children die of a disease thought to be nonexistent in the United States. Within hours, thoroughbreds at the legendary Churchill Downs are dying of a virus that cannot be identified, even by the most expert veterinarians. Called in to help shed light on these gruesome enigmas, noted virologist Jack Bryne discovers that the two events are not only connected, they are deliberate acts of bioterrorism.

***Eleventh Victim.** abr. ed. Nancy Grace. Read by Kate Mcintyre. 2010. audio compact disk 14.99 (978-1-4013-9522-3(8)) Pub: Hyperion. Dist(s): HarperCollins Pubs

Elfquest. 8 cass. (Running Time: 11 hrs.). 2001. 59.95 (LIST001) Lodestone Catalog.

Elfquest: Journey to Sorrow's End. Wendy Pini & Richard Pini. 8 cass. (Running Time: 11 hrs. 25 mins.). (Elfquest Ser.). (J). 2000. 50.00 (978-0-7366-9102-4(2)) Books on Tape.

Unravels the tale of the gallant band of elves called Wolfriders, who search for place not contaminated by humans.

Elfquest: Journey to Sorrow's End. unabr. ed. Richard Pini & Wendy Pini. 2 cass. (Running Time: 3 hr.). (Elfquest Ser.: Vol. 7 & 8). (J). 1997. 15.95 Set; trade pkg. (978-0-8072-7837-6(8), BTYA930CXR, Listening Lib) Random Audio Pubg.

Elfquest: Journey to Sorrow's End. unabr. ed. Richard Pini & Wendy Pini. 2 cass. (Running Time: 3 hr.). (Elfquest Ser.: Vols. 5 & 6). (J). 1997. 15.95 Trade pkg. (978-0-8072-7817-8(3), BTYA924CXR, Listening Lib) Random Audio Pubg.

The desert village of Sorrow's End lies in the path of thundering destruction from the burning sands & the only answer to its salvation may lie in the Wolfriders' deep forest past.

Elfquest: Journey to Sorrow's End. unabr. ed. Wendy Pini. Read by Richard Pini. 8 cass. (Running Time: 11 hrs., 24 mins.). (Elfquest Ser.). (J). (gr. 7-12). 1998. 53.00 (978-0-8072-7865-9(3), LL0105, Listening Lib) Random Audio Pubg.

Elfquest began as a comic about elves, but has grown into a series of full-length novels, created by the authors. Unravels the tale of the gallant band of elves called Wolfriders, who search for a place not contaminated by humans.

Elfquest: Journey to Sorrow's End. unabr. ed. Wendy Pini & Richard Pini. 2 cass. (Running Time: 3 hrs.). Dramatization. (Elfquest Ser.: Vols. 3 & 4). (J). (gr. 3). 1996. 15.95 Set, retail box. (978-0-8072-7640-2(5), YA916CXR, Listening Lib) Random Audio Pubg.

Elfquest Vols. 5 & 6: Journey to Sorrow's End. Wendy Pini & Richard Pini. 2 cass. (Elfquest Ser.: Vols. 5 & 6). 12.78 Set, blisterpack. (BYA 924) NewSound.

Elfquest - Complete Set. unabr. ed. Wendy Pini & Richard Pini. 8 cass. (Running Time: 8 hrs.). (Elfquest Ser.). 1997. 64.98 Set. AudioGO.

Elgar - Violoncello Concerto in E Minor, Op. 85: 2-CD Set. Composed by Edward Elgar. 2006. pap. bk. 34.98 (978-1-59615-411-7(X), 159615411X) Pub: Music Minus. Dist(s): H Leonard

Eli. Bill Myers. 4 cass. (Running Time: 6 hrs.). 2000. 24.99 Zondervan.

Eli. abr. ed. Bill Myers & Zondervan Publishing Staff. (Running Time: 6 hrs. 0 mins. 0 sec.). (ENG.). 2003. 10.99 (978-0-310-26029-5(9)) Zondervan.

Eli. unabr. ed. Bill Myers. Narrated by Ed Sala. 8 cass. (Running Time: 12 hrs.). 2000. 68.00 (978-0-7887-4961-2(7), K0016) Recorded Bks.

The author imagines a fascinating scenario that reaches to the heart of a basic question of Christian faith. When TV newsman Conrad Davis crashes his car, he should be dead. Instead, he awakens in a world exactly like ours except for one detail, Jesus Christ did not come 2000 years ago, but today. For Conrad, it's a chance to answer a question many have considered over the last two millennia. How would I react if I lived in the time of Jesus.

Eli. unabr. ed. Bill Myers. 2000. 24.99 (978-0-310-23622-1(3)) Zondervan.

***Eli Manning CD.** Sarah Tieck. (Big Buddy Biographies CD Ser.). 2010. cd-rom 27.07 (978-1-61613-073-2(3)) ABDO Pub Co.

***Eli Manning Site CD.** Sarah Tieck. (Big Buddy Biographies Site CD Ser.). 2010. cd-rom 57.07 (978-1-61613-253-8(1)) ABDO Pub Co.

***Eli the Good.** unabr. ed. Silas House. (Running Time: 7 hrs.). 2011. 19.99 (978-1-4558-0117-6(8), 9781455801176, Candlewick Bril); 39.97 (978-1-4558-0118-3(6), 9781455801183, Candlewick Bril); 19.99 (978-1-4558-0114-5(3), 9781455801145, Candlewick Bril); 39.97 (978-1-4558-0115-2(1), 9781455801152, Candlewick Bril); audio compact disk 22.99 (978-1-4558-0112-1(7), 9781455801121, Candlewick Bril); audio compact disk 54.97 (978-1-4558-0113-8(5), 9781455801138, Candlewick Bril) Brilliance Audio.

Eli Wallach see Movie Makers Speak: Actors

Eli Whitney & the Cotton Gin. Jessica Gunderson et al. Illus. by Gerry Acerno. (Inventions & Discovery Ser.). (ENG.). (gr. 3-4). 2007. audio compact disk 6.95 (978-1-4296-1114-5(6)) CapstoneDig.

Eli Whitney & the Cotton Gin (INK Audiocassette) (Inventions & Discovery Ser.). (ENG.). 2007. audio compact disk 5.95 (978-0-7368-7987-3(0)) CapstoneDig.

Elias. (Heroes de la Fe Ser.). 2000. (978-1-57697-780-4(3)) Untd Bible Amrcas Svce.

Elias Boudinott Cherokee & His America. Read by Willena Robinson. Ed. by Willena Robinson. 2005. 24.00 (978-1-882182-15-2(4)) Cherokee Lang & Cult.

Elidor. Alan Garner. Read by Garard Green. 3 cass. (J). 19.18 Set, blisterpack. (BYA 921) NewSound.

Elidor. unabr. ed. Alan Garner. Read by Garard Green. 3 cass. (Running Time: 4 hrs. 13 mins.). (YA). (gr. 7-12). 1997. 24.00 (978-0-8072-7790-4(8), YA921CX, Listening Lib) Random Audio Pubg.

Presents four youths who must save the bleak world of Elidor by guarding four treasures that hold the key to its liberation.

Elidor. unabr. ed. Alan Garner. Read by Garard Green. 3 cass. (Running Time: 4 hr. 13 mins.). (J). 1997. pap. bk. 29.00 (978-0-8072-7791-1(6), YA921SP, Listening Lib) Random Audio Pubg.

Elidor, Set. Alan Garner. Read by Garard Green. 3 cass. (J). 19.18 Blisterpack. (BYA 921) NewSound.

Elie Wiesel: A Holocaust Survivor Cries Out for Peace. Sarah Houghton. (High Five Reading - Green Ser.). (ENG.). (gr. 3-4). 2007. audio compact disk 5.95 (978-1-4296-1441-2(2)) CapstoneDig.

Elie Wiesel: On Remembering. Read by Elie Wiesel. 1 cass. (Running Time: 1 hr.). 10.95 (K0150B090, HarperThor) HarpC GBR.

Elie Wiesel [Audible. com Overdrive. com]: A Holocaust Survivor Cries Out for Peace. Sarah Houghton. (High Five Reading - Green Ser.). 2009. audio compact disk 7.93 (978-1-4296-4946-9(1)) CapstoneDig.

Elie Wiesel Reading from His Works. abr. ed. Elie Wiesel. Read by Elie Wiesel. 1 cass. (Running Time: 39 min.). 10.95 (978-0-8045-1005-9(9), SAC 1005) Spoken Arts.

The Nobel Prize winner & holocaust survivor reads excerpts from his works, "The Gates of the Forest," "The Song of the Dead," "The Accident" & "The Town Beyond the Wall".

Elijah: A Man of Heroism & Humility. 2001. 25.95 (978-1-57972-353-8(5)) Insight Living.

Elijah: A Man of Heroism & Humility CD. Charles R. Swindoll. (ENG.). 2007. audio compact disk 38.00 (978-1-57972-789-5(1)) Insight Living.

Elijah of Buxton. unabr. ed. Christopher Paul Curtis. Read by Mirron Willis. (J). 2008. 54.99 (978-0-7393-7095-7(2)) Find a World.

Elijah of Buxton. unabr. ed. Christopher Paul Curtis. Read by Mirron Willis. 8 CDs. (Running Time: 8 hrs. 58 mins.). (J). (gr. 4-7). 2007. audio compact disk 55.00 (978-0-7393-6415-4(4), Listening Lib) Pub: Random Audio Pubg. Dist(s): Random

When you first walk into a room in a house, or into a stable, they have a way of telling you they know you're there. It ain't nothing particular noticeable, but the air inside of 'em changes like it's saying, "I'm watching you." But I'd got into this stable so quiet and sneakish that nothing knowed I'd cracked open the door, held my breath, and took a step inside. Then I heard a humming sound so near that my blanged legs and breathing frozed up all over again. Whatever it was that was making that sound was so close that even my eyeballs locked where they were at. Then I started sliding my eyes off to the left. Someone had leaned some dark bundles or sacks up 'gainst the left hand side of the stable. There were five of 'em. The noise commenced again, sounding like someone fishing 'round trying to figure which song they were 'bout to hum. It was one of the bundles! It had four live, moving arms! I couldn't believe I'd come all they way to the United States of America to see my first haint!.

Elijah of Buxton. unabr. ed. Christopher Paul Curtis. Read by Mirron Willis. (Running Time: 32280 sec.). (ENG.). (J). (gr. 5-7). 2008. audio compact disk 50.00 (978-0-7393-6719-3(6), Listening Lib) Pub: Random Audio Pubg. Dist(s): Random

Eliminate Eating Disorders. Bruce Goldberg. (ENG.). 2005. audio compact disk 17.00 (978-1-57968-076-3(3)) Pub: B Goldberg. Dist(s): Baker Taylor

Eliminate Eating Disorders. Bruce Goldberg. Read by Bruce Goldberg. 1 cass. (Running Time: 25 min.). (ENG.). 2007. Rental 13.00 (978-1-885577-43-6(5)) B Goldberg.

Remove bulimic and anorexic behavior, and maintain ideal weight through self-hypnosis.

Eliminate Eating Disorders. Dick Sutphen. 1 cass. (Running Time: 1 hr.). (RX17 Ser.). 14.98 (978-0-87554-398-7(7), RX162) Valley Sun.

Eliminate Fear & Worry. Dick Sutphen. 1 cass. (Running Time: 1 hr.). (RX17 Ser.). 14.98 (978-0-87554-394-9(4), RX158) Valley Sun.

Eliminate Guilt & Worry. Bruce Goldberg. (ENG.). 2005. audio compact disk 17.00 (978-1-57968-093-0(3)) Pub: B Goldberg. Dist(s): Baker Taylor

Eliminate Guilt & Worry. Bruce Goldberg. Read by Bruce Goldberg. 1 cass. (Running Time: 25 min.). (ENG.). 2007. 13.00 (978-1-885577-58-0(3)) Pub: B Goldberg. Dist(s): Baker Taylor

Through self-hypnosis remove these two useless emotions.

***Eliminate the Confusion of FMLA.** Created by CareerTrack. 2010. audio compact disk 199.95 (978-1-60959-020-8(1)) P Univ E Inc.

Eliminate the Confusion of FMLA. PUEI. audio compact disk 199.00 (978-1-934147-77-1(X), CareerTrack) P Univ E Inc.

Eliminate the Confusion of FMLA. PUEI. 2006. audio compact disk 199.00 (978-1-934147-07-8(9), CareerTrack) P Univ E Inc.

Eliminate the Confusion of FMLA. PUEI. 2007. audio compact disk 199.00 (978-1-934147-51-1(6), CareerTrack) P Univ E Inc.

Eliminate TMJ & Teeth Grinding. Scott Sulak. 1998. 15.00 (978-1-932659-10-8(2)) Change For Gd.

Eliminating Destructive Negative Emotions - Loving Myself & Others. unabr. ed. Lilburn S. Barksdale. Read by Mark Denis. 1 cass. (Running Time: 41 min.). 1977. 9.95 (978-0-918588-30-2(8), 124) NCADD.

This cassette tells how to overcome negative emotions such as resentment, anger, hate & bitterness. It then gives an exercise to help you feel more kind & loving toward yourself & others.

Eliminating the Break. unabr. ed. Jeannie Deva. 1 cass. (Running Time: 1 hr.). (Deva Method Advanced Vocal Exercises Ser.: Vol. 1). 1996. 12.00 (978-1-882224-15-9(9)) Jeannie Deva.

Vocal exercise tape to complement "The Contemporary Vocalist Improvement Course".

Elimine las Emociones Negativas Destructivas: Amese a Usted Mismo y a los Demas. unabr. ed. Lilburn S. Barksdale. Read by Juan Francisco Estrada & Betty Teague. Tr. by George Teague. 1 cass. (Running Time: 38 min.). (SPA.). 1994. 9.95 (978-0-918588-44-9(8), 124S) NCADD.

This cassette tells how to overcome negative emotions such as resentment, anger, hate & bitterness. It then gives an exercise to help you feel more kind & loving toward yourself & others.

Elisabeth & Mouse. 1 cass. (Running Time: 1 hr. 30 mins.). (SmartReader Ser.). (J). 1999. pap. bk. & tchr. ed. 19.95 (978-0-7887-1151-0(2), 79415T3) Recorded Bks.

When her brother Harry returns from the New World with tales of adventure, 17-year-old Elisabeth is determined to see America for herself. Can she & her faithful companion, Mouse, stow away on a boat & survive the perilous voyage?.

Elisha: Giver of Life. Larry Randolph. 1 cass. (Running Time: 90 mins.). (Church in Transition Ser.: Vol. 3). 2000. 5.00 (LR01-003) Morning NC.
Larry prepares us for the needed changes we must accept in order to receive our bridegroom.

Elite Minds-Elite Minds & Who Are the Elected Ones/Soul at Death: Volume 9, Vol. 9. Speeches. As told by Bhagat Singh Thind. (Running Time: 60 mins.). (ENG., 2003. 6.50 (978-1-932630-33-6(3)) Pub: Dr Bhagat Sin. Dist(s): Baker Taylor

Elixir. abr. ed. Davis Bunn. Read by David Colacci. 3 CDs. (Running Time: 3 hrs.). 2004. audio compact disk 62.25 (978-1-59355-843-7(0), 1593558430); 17.95 (978-1-59355-841-3(4), 1593558414); audio compact disk 19.95 (978-1-59355-842-0(2), 1593558422) Brilliance Audio.
When Revell Pharmaceuticals, the multi-billion dollar giant owned by the Revells, approaches Taylor Knox and his company with the possibility of a merger, the future has never looked better. Not only will the merger benefit Taylor and his company - the promise of a personal share of the proceeds makes the move even more worthwhile. But in order to obtain this personal share, Taylor must find the missing pharmaceutical heiress, Kirra Revell - once the love of his life - who seems to have disappeared without a trace. According to her sister, Kirra has been kidnapped. But as Taylor travels the globe in pursuit of the missing woman, he realizes that Kirra simply doesn't want to be found. As the search continues, Taylor's life is threatened at every turn. Who is behind these deadly attacks? When Taylor finally locates Kirra and discovers the secret of her research with indigenous plants, he realizes what a threat she is to her family's pharmaceutical empire. And now, he too is a threat. How far are these corporate killers willing to go to protect their empire?

Elixir. unabr. ed. Davis Bunn. Read by David Colacci. 5 cass. (Running Time: 7 hrs.). 2004. 27.95 (978-1-59355-839-0(2), 1593558392); 69.25 (978-1-59355-840-6(6), 1593558406) Brilliance Audio.

Elixir. unabr. ed. Davis Bunn. Read by David Colacci. (Running Time: 6 hrs.). 2004. 24.95 (978-1-59335-285-1(9), 1593352859, Brilliance MP3); 39.25 (978-1-59335-544-9(0), 1593355440, Brlnc Audio MP3 Lib) Brilliance Audio.

Elixir. unabr. ed. Davis Bunn. Read by David Colacci. (Running Time: 6 hrs.). 2004. 39.25 (978-1-59710-247-6(4), 1597102474, BADLE); 24.95 (978-1-59710-246-9(6), 1597102466, BAD) Brilliance Audio.

***Elixir.** unabr. ed. T. Davis Bunn. Read by David Colacci. (Running Time: 7 hrs.). 2010. audio compact disk 29.99 (978-1-4418-4029-5(X), 9781441840295); audio compact disk 89.97 (978-1-4418-4030-1(3), 9781441840301, BriAudCD Unabrid) Brilliance Audio.

***Elixir.** unabr. ed. Hilary Duff. Read by Julia Whelan. (Running Time: 7 hrs. NaN mins.). (ENG.). 2010. 29.95 (978-1-4417-7413-2(0)); 44.95 (978-1-4417-7410-1(6)) Blckstn Audio.

***Elixir.** unabr. ed. Hilary Duff. Read by Julia Whelan. (Running Time: 10 hrs. 5 mins.). (YA). 2010. audio compact disk 19.95 (978-1-4417-7412-5(2)) Blckstn Audio.

***Elixir (Library Edition)** unabr. ed. Hilary Duff. Read by Julia Whelan. (Running Time: 7 hrs. NaN mins.). (ENG.). 2010. audio compact disk 69.00 (978-1-4417-7411-8(4)) Blckstn Audio.

Eliza Stanhope. Joanna Trollope. Read by Lindsay Duncan. 2 cass. (Running Time: 3 hrs.). (ENG., 1995. 18.00 (978-1-85998-162-7(3), HoddrStoughton) Pub: Hodder General GBR. Dist(s): IPG Chicago

Elizabeth. abr. ed. J. Randy Taraborrelli. Read by Lynne Maclean. (Running Time: 6 hrs.). (ENG.). 2006. 14.98 (978-1-59483-527-8(6)) Pub: Hachet Audio. Dist(s): HachBkGrp

Elizabeth. abr. ed. J. Randy Taraborrelli. Read by Lynne Maclean. (Running Time: 6 hrs.). (ENG.). 2009. 19.98 (978-1-60788-140-7(3)) Pub: Hachet Audio. Dist(s): HachBkGrp

Elizabeth. unabr. ed. Evelyn Anthony. Read by Sarah Sherborne. 10 cass. (Running Time: 15 hrs.). 2001. 84.95 (978-0-7540-0264-2(0), CAB 1687) Pub: Chivers Audio Bks GBR. Dist(s): AudioGO
In 1558, the time of the accession of Elizabeth I, England was impoverished and torn by religious strife. 30 years later, that same country was the equal of the European powers who had hoped to destroy it.

Elizabeth. unabr. ed. Sarah Bradford. Read by Donada Peters. 9 cass. (Running Time: 13 hrs. 30 mins.). 1997. 72.00 (4296-A); 64.00 (4296-B) Books on Tape.
Examines the woman who has reigned over Britain for the past forty years.

Elizabeth: A Biography of Britain's Queen. unabr. ed. Sarah Bradford. Read by Donada Peters. 17 cass. (Running Time: 25 hrs. 30 min.). 1997. 136.00 (978-0-7366-3633-9(1), 4296A/B) Books on Tape.

Elizabeth & Essex. unabr. ed. Lytton Strachey. Narrated by Flo Gibson. 5 cass. (Running Time: 7 hrs. 30 mins.). 2003. 20.95 (978-1-55685-726-3(8)) Audio Bk Con.
The Queen and the Earl's tempestuous love affair commingled with the Irish campaign and the Spanish Armada is full of dramatic developments.

Elizabeth & Essex. unabr. collector's ed. Lytton Strachey. Read by Jill Masters. 6 cass. (Running Time: 9 hrs.). 1985. 48.00 (978-0-7366-0863-3(X), 1814) Books on Tape.
This is an analysis of the relationship between the Earl of Essex & Queen Elizabeth. He was 21, spoiled & ambitious, but shrewd with an eye toward the main chance. He thought he could use the Queen to get power for himself. She was in her mid-50's, imperious & demanding.

Elizabeth & Her German Garden. unabr. ed. Elizabeth von Arnim. Narrated by Flo Gibson. 3 cass. (Running Time: 20 hrs. 57 mins.). (YA). 2001. 59.95 (978-1-55685-673-0(3)) Audio Bk Con.
Charming, witty & often lyrical, we enjoy Elizabeth's leisure & love of flowers, while she copes with her husband's overbearing nature (named "The Man of Wrath) & her pesty houseguests.

Elizabeth & Her German Garden. unabr. ed. Elizabeth von Arnim. Read by Nadia May. 3 cass. (Running Time: 4 hrs.). 2001. 23.95 (978-0-7861-1974-5(8), 2744) Blckstn Audio.
"May 7th - There were days last winter when I danced for sheer joy out in my frostbound garden in spite of my years & children. Through Elizabeth's eyes we watch the seasons, from May's "osis of bird-cherries & greenery" to the time when "snow carpets her Pomeranian wilderness." Each season brings with it new events as friends & neighbors come & go.

Elizabeth & Her German Garden. unabr. ed. Elizabeth Von Arnim. Read by Nadia May. (Running Time: 14400 sec.). 2008. audio compact disk 19.95 (978-1-4332-4528-2(0)); audio compact disk & audio compact disk 33.00 (978-1-4332-4527-5(2)) Blckstn Audio.

Elizabeth & Her German Garden, Vol. 1. unabr. ed. Elizabeth von Arnim. Narrated by Flo Gibson. (J). 2001. 16.95 (978-1-55685-739-3(X)) Audio Bk Con.

Elizabeth & Mary: Cousins, Rivals, Queens. abr. ed. Jane Dunn. Read by Isla Blair. 7 cass. (Running Time: 30 hrs.). (ENG.). 2004. audio compact disk 29.95 (978-0-7393-0982-7(X)) Pub: Random Audio Pubg. Dist(s): Random
The first dual biography of two of the world’s most remarkable women—Elizabeth I of England and Mary Queen of Scots—by one of Britain’s “best biographers” (The Sunday Times). In a rich and riveting narrative, Jane Dunn reveals the extraordinary rivalry between the regal cousins. It is the story of two queens ruling on one island, each with a claim to the throne of England, each embodying dramatically opposing qualities of character, ideals of womanliness (and views of sexuality) and divinely ordained kingship. As regnant queens in an overwhelmingly masculine world, they were deplored for their femaleness, compared unfavorably with each other and courted by the same men. By placing their dynamic and ever-changing relationship at the center of the book, Dunn illuminates their differences. Elizabeth, inheriting a weak, divided country coveted by all the Catholic monarchs of Europe, is revolutionary in her insistence on ruling alone and inspired in her use of celibacy as a political tool—yet also possessed of a deeply feeling nature. Mary is not the romantic victim of history but a courageous adventurer with a reckless heart and a magnetic influence over men and women alike. Vengeful against her enemies and the more ruthless of the two queens, she is untroubled by plotting Elizabeth’s murder. Elizabeth, however, is driven to anguish at finally having to sanction Mary’s death for treason. Working almost exclusively from contemporary letters and writings, Dunn explores their symbiotic, though never face-to-face, relationship and the power struggle that raged between them. A story of sex, power and politics, of a rivalry unparalleled in the pages of English history, of two charismatic women—told in a masterful double biography. From the Hardcover edition.

Elizabeth & Mary: Cousins, Rivals, Queens. unabr. ed. Jane Dunn. 14 cass. (Running Time: 21 hrs.). 2004. 96.00 (978-0-7366-9730-9(6)) Books on Tape.

Elizabeth Barrett Browning & Christina Rossetti. abr. ed. Christina Rossetti & Elizabeth Barrett Browning. Narrated by Rachel Bavidge & Georgina Sutton. 1 CD. (Running Time: 1 hr. 15 mins.). (Great Poets Ser.). 2009. audio compact disk 14.98 (978-962-634-920-5(4), Naxos AudioBooks) Naxos.

Elizabeth Berg: Say When - The Art of Mending - The Year of Pleasures. unabr. ed. Elizabeth Berg. Read by David Colacci et al. (Running Time: 21 hrs.). 2006. audio compact disk 36.95 (978-1-4233-1681-7(9), 9781423316817, Bril Audio CD Unabri) Brilliance Audio.

Elizabeth Bishop. 1 cass. 1997. 10.95 (978-1-57523-165-5(4)) Unapix Enter.

Elizabeth Browning: Selected Poems. unabr. ed. Poems. Elizabeth Barrett Browning. Read by Nadia May. 5 cass. (Running Time: 7 hrs.). 1995. 39.95 (978-0-7861-0863-3(0), 1661) Blckstn Audio.

Elizabeth Cady Stanton: Women's Rights Pioneer. Connie Colwell Miller. Illus. by Cynthia Martin. (Graphic Biographies Ser.). (ENG.). (gr. 3-4). 2007. audio compact disk 6.95 (978-1-4296-1467-2(6)) CapstoneDig.

Elizabeth Cady Stanton (INK Audiocassette) Women's Rights Pioneer. (Graphic Library Biographies I Ser.). (ENG.). 2006. audio compact disk 5.95 (978-0-7368-7455-7(0)) CapstoneDig.

Elizabeth George. Elizabeth George. Read by Derek Jacobi. 6 cass. 1998. (978-1-84032-136-4(9), HoddrStoughton) Hodder General GBR.
Includes "Payment in Blood," "Well-Schooled in Murder," & "A Suitable Vengeance.

Elizabeth I. 2005. (978-1-4025-2165-2(0)) Recorded Bks.

***Elizabeth I.** Margaret George. (Running Time: 25 hrs.). (ENG.). 2011. audio compact disk 49.95 (978-0-14-242913-6(9), PengAudBks) Penguin Grp USA.

Elizabeth I: Red Rose of the House of Tudor, England 1544. unabr. ed. Kathryn Lasky. Read by Josephine Bailey. (J). 2008. 44.99 (978-1-60514-573-0(4)) Find a World.

Elizabeth I: Red Rose of the House of Tudor, England 1544. unabr. ed. Kathryn Lasky. Narrated by Josephine Bailey. 4 CDs. (Running Time: 4 hrs. 16 mins. 12 sec.). (Royal Diaries). (ENG.). (J). 2005. audio compact disk 49.99 (978-1-4001-3135-8(9)) Pub: Tantor Media. Dist(s): IngramPubServ
Welcome to the bizarre court of Henry VIII, where even a princess fears losing her head like her mother. Elizabeth hides her tenacious personality from everyone, especially her father. Your 21st-century kid will enjoy Elizabeth's "treasonous thoughts" and glimpse the daily life of a young woman who ascended the throne at 25 and went on to rule her country for 45 years.

Elizabeth I: Red Rose of the House of Tudor, England 1544. unabr. ed. Kathryn Lasky. Narrated by Josephine Bailey. 1 MP3 CD. (Running Time: 4 hrs. 16 mins. 12 sec.). (Royal Diaries). (ENG.). (J). (gr. 2-6). 2005. 19.99 (978-1-4001-5135-6(X)); audio compact disk 24.99 (978-1-4001-0135-1(2)) Pub: Tantor Media. Dist(s): IngramPubServ

Elizabeth I, CEO: Strategic Lessons from the Leader Who Built an Empire. unabr. ed. Alan Axelrod. Narrated by Nelson Runger. 6 cass. (Running Time: 8 hrs.). 2001. 59.00 (978-0-7887-5010-6(0), 96515E7) Recorded Bks.
A guide for today's business manager & leaders that will show that Elizabeth's lessons are as relevant today as they were four centuries ago.

Elizabeth I, CEO: Strategic Lessons from the Leader Who Built an Empire. unabr. ed. Alan Axelrod. Read by Nelson Runger. 5 cass. (Running Time: 8 hrs.). 2004. 24.95 (978-0-7887-5089-2(5), 00034) Recorded Bks.
When Elizabeth ascended the throne in 1558, England was the laughing stock of Europe. Economic, political, and religious calamities were numerous, and Elizabeth endured constant criticism. But by the end of her 45-year reign, England was one of the world's mightiest nations. Axelrod uses the legendary Queen's life as a model for modern leadership, and a powerful example of how one person can make an extraordinary difference. Elizabeth I CEO is an indispensable guide for today's business managers and leaders.

***Elizabeth Lowell: Untamed, Forbidden, Enchanted.** abr. ed. Elizabeth Lowell & 3-In-1 Cd Coll. (Running Time: 19 hrs.). 2010. audio compact disk 29.99 (978-1-4418-5041-6(4), 9781441850416) Brilliance Audio.

Elizabeth Lowell CD Collection 1: Desert Rain; Lover in the Rough; Beautiful Dreamer. abr. ed. Elizabeth Lowell. Read by Laural Merlington. (Running Time: 12 hrs.). 2009. audio compact disk 34.99 (978-1-4233-7735-1(4), 9781423377351, BACD) Brilliance Audio.

Elizabeth Lowell CD Collection 2: To the Ends of the Earth; This Time Love; Forget Me Not. abr. ed. Elizabeth Lowell. Read by Laural Merlington. (Running Time: 12 hrs.). 2009. audio compact disk 34.99 (978-1-4233-9727-4(4), 9781423397274, BACD) Brilliance Audio.

Elizabeth Lowell CD Collection 3: Tell Me No Lies; A Woman Without Lies; Autumn Lover. abr. ed. Elizabeth Lowell. Read by Laural Merlington. (Running Time: 17 hrs.). 2009. audio compact disk 34.99 (978-1-4418-0151-7(0), 9781441801517, BACD) Brilliance Audio.

Elizabeth Rex. abr. ed. Timothy Findley. 2 CDs. (Running Time: 3 hrs.). (gr. 9-12). 2005. audio compact disk 15.95 (978-0-660-18535-4(0)) Canadian Broadcasting CAN.

Elizabeth Tallent. unabr. ed. Elizabeth Tallent. Read by Elizabeth Tallent. 1 cass. (Running Time: 29 min.). 1989. 10.00 (111289) New Letters.
Tallent reads from the title story of her collection, "Time with Children" & talks with New Letters Magazine Editor, James McKinley about developing her prose style & voice.

Elizabethan Love Poems. unabr. ed. Christopher Marlowe et al. Read by Maxine Audley & Robert Speaight. 1 cass. (Running Time: 50 min.). 10.95 (978-0-8045-0896-4(8), SAC 8005) Spoken Arts.

Elizabethans & America. unabr. ed. A. L. Rowse. Read by Jill Masters. 7 cass. (Running Time: 10 hrs. 30 min.). 1980. 56.00 (978-0-7366-0589-2(4), 1556) Books on Tape.
England staged a renaissance under the Virgin Queen. Everything flowered, particularly the institutions of government. Elizabeth mid-wifed the notion that individuals had inherent worth, that citizens were free, & that the right to govern flowed from them. Once out, the genie never went back into the bottle.

Elizabeti's Doll. 2004. bk. 24.95 (978-1-55592-053-1(5)); audio compact disk 12.95 (978-1-55592-909-1(5)) Weston Woods.

Elizabeti's Doll. (J). 2004. pap. bk. 14.95 (978-1-55592-716-5(5)) Weston Woods.

Elizabeti's Doll. Stephanie Stuve-Bodeen. Illus. by Christy Hale. Narrated by Lynn Whitfield. Music by Crystal Taliefero. 1 cass. (Running Time: 30 min.). (J). (ps-1). bk. 24.95 Weston Woods.

Elizabeti's Doll. Stephanie Stuve-Bodeen. Tr. by Esther Sarfatti. Illus. by Christy Hale. (J). (gr. k-1). 2004. 8.95 (978-0-7882-0099-1(2), WW6521) Weston Woods.

Elk-Dog Heritage. unabr. ed. Don Coldsmith. Read by Rusty Nelson. 8 cass. (Running Time: 5 hrs. 48 min.). (Spanish Bit Saga Ser.). 2001. 49.95 (978-1-58116-153-3(0)); audio compact disk 32.50 (978-1-58116-154-0(9)) Books in Motion.
Chief Heads Off has introduced horses - the "elk dogs" to his people, with very positive results. Now able to fend off their traditional enemy, the "Head Splitters," the chief must now convince various tribal factions that this new war-like mentality could lead to doom.

Elkan: The Adventure of a Lifetime. John Eytchison & Kathy Eytchison. (Running Time: 13140 sec.). 2008. audio compact disk 24.99 (978-1-60247-622-6(5)) Tate Pubng.

Ella Enchanted. Gail Carson Levine. Read by Eden Riegel. 4 cass. (Running Time: 6 hrs.). (J). 2000. 30.00 (978-0-7366-9041-6(7)) Books on Tape.
Spunky heroine Ella might be mistaken for Cinderella with a stubborn streak in this fresh & romantic fantasy. Conveys the many shades of Ella's frustration & sharp wit.

Ella Enchanted. Gail Carson Levine. Read by Eden Riegel. 5 CDs. (Running Time: 5 hrs. 42 mins.). (J). (gr. 4-7). 2004. audio compact disk 38.25 (978-0-8072-2018-4(3), Listening Lib) Pub: Random Audio Pubg. Dist(s): NetLibrary CO

Ella Enchanted. movie tie-in unabr. ed. Gail Carson Levine. Read by Eden Riegel. 5 CDs. (Running Time: 5 hrs. 42 mins.). (ENG.). (J). (gr. 3). 2004. audio compact disk 28.00 (978-1-4000-9059-4(8), Listening Lib) Pub: Random Audio Pubg. Dist(s): Random

Ella Enchanted. unabr. ed. Gail Carson Levine. (YA). 2002. 17.99 (978-0-8072-0879-3(5), Listening Lib) Random Audio Pubg.
Against a bold tapestry of princes, ogres, giants, wicked stepsisters, and fairy godmothers, Ella's spirited account of her quest to break the curse is a funny, poignant, and enchanting tale about an unforgettable heroine who is determined to be herself.

Ella Enchanted. unabr. ed. Gail Carson Levine. Read by Eden Riegel. 4 vols. (Running Time: 5 hrs. 42 mins.). (J). (gr. 4-7). 2004. pap. bk. 38.00 (978-0-8072-8694-4(X), YA238SP, Listening Lib); 32.00 (978-0-8072-8693-7(1), YA238CX, Listening Lib) Random Audio Pubg.

Ella Fitzgerald: The Tale of a Vocal Virtuosa. 2004. 8.95 (978-1-55592-832-2(3)); audio compact disk 12.95 (978-1-55592-888-9(9)) Weston Woods.

Ella in Bloom. Shelby Hearon. Narrated by Alyssa Bresnahan. 7 CDs. (Running Time: 8 hrs. 30 mins.). audio compact disk 69.00 (978-1-4025-2096-9(4)) Recorded Bks.

Ella in Bloom. Shelby Hearon. Narrated by Alyssa Bresnahan. 6 cass. (Running Time: 8 hrs. 30 mins.). 2000. 57.00 (978-1-4025-0664-2(3), 96716) Recorded Bks.
Terrell asks her younger sister Ella to conceal her adulterous affair, then dies in a plane crash just hours later. As the lie takes on a life of its own, love blossoms between Ella and Rufus, Terell's grieving spouse.

Ella Jenkins: Songs, Rhythms & Chants for the Dance. Perf. by Ella Jenkins. 1 cass. (Running Time: 68 mins.). 2000. 10.00 (SFWMC 45004); audio compact disk 10.00 (SFWCD 45004) Smithsonian Folkways.

Ella Jenkins Holiday Times. 1 cass. (Running Time: 60 min.). (J). (ps up). 1996. 14.00 CD. Smithsonian Folkways.
Traditional songs alternate with Ella Jenkins' original compositions.

Ella the Elegant Elephant. Carmela D'Amico & Steve D'Amica. 1 CD. (Running Time: 10 mins.). (J). (gr. k-3). 2005. bk. 29.95 (978-0-8045-4128-2(0), SACD4128) Spoken Arts.
The littlest elephant in Little Village is also just a little bit shy. She¿s moved to a new neighborhood, and has to start at a brand-new school. Good thing she has her grandma¿s lucky hat to take along. But Belinda Blue the bully doesn¿t like Ella. And she doesn¿t like the hat. And that means trouble with a capital "B". Hang onto your hats, readers.... this adventure is just beginning.

Ella the Elegant Elephant. Carmela D'Amico & Steven D'Amico. 1 cass. (Running Time: 10 mins.). (J). (gr. k-3). 2005. bk. 27.95 (978-0-8045-6933-0(9), SAC6933) Spoken Arts.

Elle s'appelait Sarah. unabr. ed. Tatiana de Rosnay. Read by Odile Cohen. (YA). 2007. 79.99 (978-2-35569-001-3(4)) Find a World.

Ellen & the Barber: Three Love Stories of the Thirties. Frank O'Rourke. Read by Mary Woods. 4 cass. (Running Time: 5 hrs. 30 mins.). 1999. 32.95 (978-0-7861-1660-7(9), 2488) Blckstn Audio.
Evokes a small midwest town during the Great Depression & World War II & introduces three strong & surprising young women & the men in their lives: Ellen, who has no good reason to deny her natural instincts; Miriam, torn between the promise of a loving future & the demands of family & home & Vera, whose intelligence & restless hunger for life plunges her into disaster.

Ellen Bryant Voigt. unabr. ed. Ellen B. Voigt. Read by Ellen B. Voigt. 1 cass. (Running Time: 29 min.). 1988. 10.00 New Letters.
Voigt reads poetry from The Lotus Flowers & is interviewed.

Ellen Foster. Kaye Gibbons. 2004. 10.95 (978-0-7435-4669-0(5)) Pub: S&S Audio. Dist(s): S and S Inc

Ellen Foster. unabr. ed. Kaye Gibbons. Narrated by Ruth Ann Phimister. 3 cass. (Running Time: 4 hrs.). 1998. 32.00 (978-0-7887-2019-2(8), 95396E7) Recorded Bks.
Growing up in a small southern town, 11-year-old Ellen has already learned the world's most difficult lesson: life is unfair.

Ellen Foster. unabr. ed. Kaye Gibbons. Narrated by Ruth Ann Phimister. 4 CDs. (Running Time: 4 hrs.). 2000. audio compact disk 36.00 (978-0-7887-3965-1(4), C1120E7) Recorded Bks.

Ellen Gilchrist. Interview. Interview with Ellen Gilchrist & Kay Bonetti. 1 cass. 1986. 13.95 (978-1-55644-158-5(4), 6062) Am Audio Prose.
In this interview Gilchrist discusses her characters as having lives of their own which she merely transcribes. She also talks about her late blooming development as a writer.

Ellen Gilchrist: Collected Stories. unabr. ed. Ellen Gilchrist. Read by Mary Peiffer. 13 cass. (Running Time: 19 hrs. 30 mins.). 104.00 (978-0-7366-6028-0(3)) Books on Tape.
With uncanny insights into human character & the part played in it by love, Ellen Gilchrist occupies a unique place in American fiction. Assembled by the author herself, these stories provide a much-needed retrospective on an important voice.

Ellen Gilchrist: I Cannot Get You Close Enough. unabr. ed. Ellen Gilchrist. Read by Ellen Gilchrist. Interview with James McKinley. Prod. by Rebekah Presson. 1 cass. (Running Time: 29 min.). 1991. 10.00 (052491) New Letters.
One of the most popular southern women writers, Ellen Gilchrist is loved by National Public Radio listeners for her readings of journal entries. Here, she reads from her new book of three novellas.

***Ellen Tebbits.** unabr. ed. Beverly Cleary. Read by Andrea Martin. (ENG.). 2005. (978-0-06-085455-3(3)); (978-0-06-085456-0(1)) HarperCollins Pubs.

Ellen Tebbits. unabr. ed. Beverly Cleary. Read by Andrea Martin. Contrib. by Andrea Martin. (Running Time: 007200 sec.). (J). (ps-7). 2005. audio compact disk 17.95 (978-0-06-078595-6(0), HarperChildAud) HarperCollins Pubs.

Ellen Tebbits. unabr. ed. Beverly Cleary. 1 read-along cass. (Running Time: 46 min.). (Soundways to Reading Ser.). (J). (gr. 2-4). 1982. 15.98 (978-0-8072-1090-1(0), SWR 26 SP, Listening Lib); (Listening Lib) Random Audio Pubg.
Ellen & Augustine are very best friends, until Ellen slaps Augustine in the middle of a quarrel. How can she ever begin to apoligize?.

Ellery Queen. 1 cass. (Running Time: 60 min.). (Old Time Radio Classic Singles Ser.). 4.95 (978-1-57816-097-6(9), EQ107) Audio File.
Two exciting mysteries solved by the super-sleuth. "The Singing Rat," 1/7/43 & "The Scarecrow & the Snowman," 1/20/44. Bromo Seltzer c ommercials.

Ellery Queen. 1 cass. (Running Time: 60 min.). Incl. Scarecrow & the Snowman. 1943. (M-7920); Singing Rat. 1943. (M-7920); 1943. 7.95 (M-7920) Natl Recrd Co.
In "The Singing Rat", Ellery Queen, his father (Inspector Queen), & his adventurous secretary Nikki are involved in this story of a stool pigeon, a gangster named Moose, & a crooked bankruptcy scheme. In "The Scarecrow & the Snowman", a scarecrow is found stabbed & bleeding, but it turns out to be a mysterious man. He recovers, disappears & re-appears six months later as a snowman.

Ellery Queen. unabr. ed. Ellery Queen. 1 cass. (Running Time: 53 min.). Incl. Mischief Maker. (J). (#751); Nick the Knife. (J). (#751); (J). 12.95 (#751) J Norton Pubs.
In the first episode, Ellery Queen tries to find out why the residents of a rooming house are receiving mysterious & frightening letters. In the second episode, Ellery is after the murderer of several young women.

Ellery Queen Armchair Detective & F. B. I. in Peace & War: The Case of the Three Frogs & Help Wanted. unabr. ed. 1 cass. (Running Time: 60 min.). Dramatization. 7.95 Norelco box. (MM-9973) Natl Recrd Co.
Ellery Queen: Listen carefully & see if you can solve this case before Detective Ellery Queen does. It is not any easy case to solve, but if you concentrate you may discover that you are an excellent "Armchair Detective!" F.B.I. in Pease & War: The Federal Bureau of Investigation is called in to investigate a series of robberies of very valuable items from fashionable homes. The familiar theme music & the L-A-V-A...Lava Soap commercial...will surely be like hearing from an old friend once again.

Ellery Queen's Mystery Magazine: Murder in Hollywood & Murder with a Twist. unabr. ed. Haskell Barken & Robert Bloch. Read by Morgan Fairchild & Roddy McDowall. 5 vols. (Great Mystery Ser.). 2001. audio compact disk 14.99 (978-1-57815-537-8(1), Media Bks Audio) Media Bks NJ.

Elles Sont Folles. 1 cass. (Running Time: 60 mins.). Dramatization. (Maitres du Mystere Ser.). (FRE.). 1996. 11.95 (1837-MA) Olivia & Hill.
Popular radio thriller, interpreted by France's best actors.

Ellington Was Not a Street. Ntozake Shange. Illus. by Kadir Nelson. Narrated by Phylicia Rashad. 1 CD. (Running Time: 8 mins.). (J). 2005. bk. 29.95 (978-0-439-77582-3(5), WHCD672); bk. 24.95 (978-0-439-77576-2(0), WHRA672) Weston Woods.
In this reflective poetic tribute, the author remembers growing up when many of the great figures in African-American history gathered in her family home to talk and share ideas and even sing. Narrated by Phylicia Rashad with the music of Duke Ellington. Video includes documentary segment, More About a few of the Men Who Changed the World. Audio CD includes bonus track of the poem ready by the author, Ntozake Shange.

***Elliot Allagash: A Novel.** unabr. ed. Simon Rich. Read by Paul Michael Garcia. (Running Time: 8 hrs. NaN mins.). (ENG.). 2011. 29.95 (978-1-4417-7406-4(8)); 54.95 (978-1-4417-7403-3(3)); audio compact disk 24.95 (978-1-4417-7405-7(X)); audio compact disk 76.00 (978-1-4417-7404-0(1)) Blckstn Audio.

Ellis Marsalis. Read by Ellis Marsalis. 1 cass. (Running Time: 60 min.). (Marian McPartland's Piano Jazz Ser.). 13.95 (MM-87-05-28, HarperThor) HarpC GBR.

Ellis-van Creveld Syndrome - A Bibliography & Dictionary for Physicians, Patients, & Genome Researchers. Compiled by Icon Group International, Inc. Staff. 2007. ring bd. 28.95 (978-0-497-11373-5(2)) Icon Grp.

Ellison the Elephant. Eric Drachman. Illus. by James Muscarello. Giovanna Imbesi & Bryon Holley. 2004. bk. 18.95 (978-0-9703809-1-3(7)) Pub: Kidwick Bks. Dist(s): Natl Bk Netwk

Elmer & the Dragon. Ruth Stiles Gannett. Illus. by Ruth Chrisman Gannett. (Tales of My Father's Dragon Ser.: Bk. 2). (J). (gr. 3-6). pap. bk. 4.99 (978-0-8072-1288-2(1), Listening Lib) Random Audio Pubg.

Elmer & the Dragon. unabr. ed. Ruth Stiles Gannett. Read by Robert Sevra. 1 cass. (Running Time: 46 mins.). (Tales of My Father's Dragon Ser.: Bk. 2). (J). (gr. 2-5). 1997. pap. bk. 17.00 (978-0-8072-0244-9(4), FTR178SP, Listening Lib) Random Audio Pubg.
Elmer & the flying baby dragon help the king of the canaries find treasure.

Elmer Gantry. unabr. ed. Sinclair Lewis. Read by Flo Gibson. 11 cass. (Running Time: 16 hrs. 5 mins.). (YA). (gr. 10 up). 2002. vinyl bd. 71.95 (978-1-55685-666-2(0)) Audio Bk Con.
A study of hypocrisy that scandalized readers when first published. A philandering preacher has difficulty practicing what he preaches. Despite his convincing orations from the pulpit, his love affairs increase & yet he rises in the ranks of his church.

Elmer Gantry. unabr. ed. Sinclair Lewis. Read by Anthony Heald. (Running Time: 57600 sec.). 2008. 85.95 (978-1-4332-2213-9(2)); audio compact disk & audio compact disk 110.00 (978-1-4332-2214-6(0)); audio compact disk & audio compact disk 29.95 (978-1-4332-2217-7(5)) Blckstn Audio.

Elmer Gantry. unabr. ed. Sinclair Lewis. Read by Anthony Heald. (Running Time: 16 hrs.). 2009. audio compact disk 34.95 (978-1-4332-2216-0(7)) Blckstn Audio.

Elmer Green on Biofeedback: The Rationale for Psychophysiologic Self-Regulation. Elmer Green. Read by Elmer Green. Ed. by Stephen Lerner. 1 cass. (Running Time: 54 min.). 1987. 10.00 (978-1-56948-001-4(X)) Menninger Clinic.
Elmer Green presents his model of why the body responds to self-regulation techniques. The application of biofeedback to psychosomatic conditions is explored.

Elmer Kelton Tells the Truth: Five Talks on the Old West, Cowboys & Writing the Western Novel. Elmer Kelton. Read by Elmer Kelton. 4 CDs. 2003. spiral bd. 49.95 (978-1-880717-50-9(6), 829-038) Writers AudioShop.

Elmer Kelton Tells the Truth: His Best Talks on the Old West, Cowboys & Writing. Elmer Kelton. Hosted by Mike Blakely. Music by Mike Blakely. 2 cass. (Running Time: 3 hrs.). (ENG.). 2000. 17.95 (978-1-880717-41-7(7), 32) Writers AudioShop.
The best of this famous author's speeches: finely-crafted, humorous talks that encompass fact, fiction & folklore. Known for his award-winning western fiction such as "The Good Old Boys," "The Wolf & the Buffalo" & "The Time It Never Rained.".

Elmer the Great. Perf. by Joe E. Brown et al. 1 cass. (Running Time: 1 hr.). 1999. 6.98 (4167) Radio Spirits.

Elmo & the Baby Animals. 1 cass. (Sesame Street Ser.). (J). 1995. bk. 6.98 (Sony Wonder) Sony Music Ent.
It's time for exploration on the farm & learning what sounds the baby animals make for Elmo & friends.

Elmo & the Orchestra. Perf. by Boston Pops Orchestra. Conducted by Keith Lockhart. 1 CD. (Running Time: 45). (J). 2001. audio compact disk 13.98 (Sony Wonder) Sony Music Ent.
Features Elmo, Baby Bear, Big Bird, Telly Monster & more of your "Sesame Street" friends.

Elmo Saves Christmas. (Sesame Street Ser.). (J). (gr. 3 up). 1997. 6.98 (Sony Wonder) Sony Music Ent.

Elmo Saves Christmas: Holiday Favorites. 1 cass. (Running Time: 1 hr.). (J). 2000. 9.98 (Sony Wonder); audio compact disk 13.98 (Sony Wonder) Sony Music Ent.

Elmo Says BOO! 1 cass., 1 CD. (Running Time: 30 min.). (J). 1997. 13.98 Inc. coupon bks., mini-catalog, & poster. (Sony Wonder); audio compact disk 9.98 CD. Sony Music Ent.

Elmopalooza. Perf. by Elmo. 1 cass.; 1 CD. 1998. 9.98 (978-1-57330-617-1(7), 39373); audio compact disk 15.98 CD. (978-1-57330-616-4(9), 39373D) MFLP CA.

Elmopalooza! Perf. by Rosie O'Donnell et al. 1 cass., 1 CD. (J). 7.98 (SME 63432); audio compact disk 11.18 CD Jewel box. (SME 63432) NewSound.
Included: "Mambo I, I, I," "I Want a Monster to Be My Friend," "Zig Zag Dan" & more songs with other celebrity singers.

Elmopalooza! Perf. by Rosie O'Donnell et al. 1 cass., 1 CD. (J). 1998. 9.98 (Sony Wonder); audio compact disk 13.98 CD. Sony Music Ent.
A rock 'n' roll extravaganza celebrating 30 years of songs & laughs on Sesame Street.

Elmore Leonard's Western Roundup: The Bounty Hunters; Forty Lashes Less One; Gunsights. abr. ed. Elmore Leonard. Read by Peter Renaday. (Playaway Adult Fiction Ser.). 2008. 54.99 (978-1-60640-509-3(8)) Find a World.

Elmore Leonard's Western Roundup: The Bounty Hunters; Forty Lashes Less One; Gunsights. abr. ed. Elmore Leonard. Read by Peter Renaday. 2008. audio compact disk 18.95 (978-1-59887-590-4(6), 1598875906) Pub: HighBridge. Dist(s): Workman Pub

Elmo's Favorite Sing-Alongs. 1 cass. (Sesame Street Ser.). (J). 1995. bk. 9.98 (Sony Wonder); audio compact disk 13.98 CD. Sony Music Ent.
Includes a lyric book for the little red monster's favorite tunes. Sing along to hits such as "Elmo's Song," "The Hokey Pokey," "To Sing a Simple Song" & "Sing Along".

Elmo's Lowdown Hoedown. 1 cass., 1 CD. (J). 1998. 9.98 (Sony Wonder); audio compact disk 13.98 CD. Sony Music Ent.
Inclues 12 new down home favorites with Sesame Street characters Oscar the Grouch, Big Bird, Elmo & Polly Parton.

Elmo's Music to Move By. 1 cass. (Running Time: 11 min.). (Golden's Sesame Street Ser.). (J). 1994. bk. 6.99 (14429, Gold Bks) RH Chldrns.
How can you have a fun picnic when it's raining? Elmo finds out when Big Bird & Herry Monster come over to his house. Together, they have lots of fun playing pretend while they listen to some beautiful music.

Elocution Exercises. Read by Chogyam Trungpa. 1 cass. 1983. 14.50 incl. booklet. (A113) Vajradhatu.

Elohim: Experience Worship from the Heart of Israel. 1 CD. (Running Time: 60 mins.). 2000. audio compact disk (978-0-7601-2531-1(7)) Brentwood Music.
Songs include: "Sing to God," "Arise O Lord," "As the Deer Pants," "My God, My God," "Tree of Life" & more.

Eloisa to Abelard. (39) Halvorson Assocs.

Eloise. Catherine Jinks. Read by Melissa Chambers. (Running Time: 4 hrs. 10 mins.). (Allie's Ghost Hunters Ser.: Bk. 3). (J). 2009. 59.99 (978-1-74214-410-8(1), 9781742144108) Pub: Bolinda Pubng AUS. Dist(s): Bolinda Pub Inc

Eloise. Kay Thompson. (Eloise Ser.). (J). (ps). 2001. bk. 22.00 (978-0-689-84311-2(9), SSChildren) SandS Childrens.

Eloise. unabr. ed. Catherine Jinks. Read by Melissa Chambers. (Running Time: 14940 sec.). (Allie's Ghost Hunters Ser.: Bk. 3). (J). 2008. audio compact disk 57.95 (978-1-921415-37-1(1), 9781921415371) Pub: Bolinda Pubng AUS. Dist(s): Bolinda Pub Inc

Eloquent Silence. unabr. ed. Sandra Brown. Read by Joyce Bean. (Running Time: 6 hrs.). 2005. 39.25 (978-1-59710-248-3(2), 9781597102483, BADLE); 24.95 (978-1-59710-249-0(0), 9781597102490, BAD); audio compact disk 82.25 (978-1-59355-907-6(0), 9781593559076, BriAudCD Unabrid); 24.95 (978-1-59335-766-5(4), 9781593357665, Brilliance MP3); 39.25 (978-1-59335-900-3(4), 9781593359003, Brinc Audio MP3 Lib); 29.95 (978-1-59355-904-5(6), 9781593559045, BAU); 69.25 (978-1-59355-905-2(4), 9781593559052, BrilAudUnabridg) Brilliance Audio.
Lauri is a dedicated young teacher for the deaf. Her past conceals a wound still unhealed, her present is a facade, and she uses her career to hide her loneliness. Drake, daytime TV's most popular star, has two heartaches - the daughter he believes will never have a normal life and the dead wife he can't forget. Jennifer is the beautiful hearing-impaired child who may become a pawn between the man and the woman she needs the most. Now, in the heart of a New Mexico arts community, the three may become a family...but only if each one dares to find a voice and lets his or her fears and needs speak for themselves.

Eloquent Silence. unabr. ed. Sandra Brown. Read by Joyce Bean. (Running Time: 28800 sec.). 2007. audio compact disk 14.99 (978-1-4233-3352-4(7), 9781423333524, BCD Value Price) Brilliance Audio.

Elric of Melnibone. Michael Moorcock. 2007. audio compact disk 19.95 (978-0-8095-6273-2(1)) Pub: Wildside. Dist(s): Diamond Book Dists

***Elric of Melnibone.** Michael Moorcock. (Running Time: 6 mins.). 2009. 19.95 (978-1-897331-08-8(8), AudioRealms) Dorch Pub Co.

Elric of Melnibone. unabr. ed. Michael Moorcock & Michael Moorcock. Read by Jeffrey West. 5 CDs. (Running Time: 6 hrs.). (Elric Ser.: Vol. 1). 2006. audio compact disk 24.95 (978-0-8095-6274-9(X)) Pub: Wildside. Dist(s): Diamond Book Dists

Elric of Menibone. unabr. ed. Michael Moorcock. 6 CDs. (Running Time: 6 mins.). 2003. audio compact disk 29.95 (978-0-9731596-0-8(X), AudioRealms) Dorch Pub Co.
Elric, Emperor of Melnibone, cursed with a keen and cynical intelligence, schooled in the art of sorcery.

Elric Volume 3: Weird of the White Wolf: Weird of the White Wolf. Michael Moorcock. 2007. audio compact disk 29.95 (978-0-8095-7196-3(X)) Diamond Book Dists

Elric Volume 4: the Vanishing Tower: The Vanishing Tower. Michael Moorcock. 2007. audio compact disk 29.95 (978-0-8095-7173-4(0)) Diamond Book Dists.

Elsa Lanchester Herself. Interview. Elsa Lanchester. 1 CD. (Running Time: 59 min.). 2005. audio compact disk 12.95 (978-1-57970-277-9(5), C23085D, Audio-For) J Norton Pubs.
Elsa Lanchester, widow of Charles Laughton, unburdens herself of her very literate and multi-faceted opinions on Laughton, Sitwell, T.S. Eliot, and others. (Pacifica, KPFK, 59 min., recorded 1967.).

Elsa Lanchester Reminisces. unabr. ed. Elsa Lanchester. 1 cass. (Running Time: 59 min.). 1967. 12.95 (23085) J Norton Pubs.
Elsa Lanchester, widow of Charles Laughton, unburdens herself of her very literate & multifaceted opinions on Laughton, Sitwell, T. S. Eliot & others.

Elsewhere. collector's unabr. ed. Gabrielle Zevin. Read by Cassandra Morris. 6 CDs. (Running Time: 6 hrs.). (YA). (gr. 7-10). 2005. audio compact disk 42.50 (978-0-307-28370-2(4), Listening Lib) Pub: Random Audio Pubg. Dist(s): NetLibrary CO
Welcome to Elsewhere. It is usually warm with a breeze, the sun and the stars shine brightly, and the beaches are marvelous. It's quiet and peaceful here. And you can't get sick or any older. Curious to see new paintings by Picasso? Swing by one of Elsewhere's museums. Need to talk to someone about your problems? Stop by Marilyn Monroe's psychiatric practice. Elsewhere. It's where fifteen-year-old Liz Hall ends up, after she has died. It is a place so like Earth, yet completely different from it. Here Liz will age backward from the day of her death until she becomes a baby again and returns to Earth. But Liz wants to turn sixteen, not fourteen (again). She wants to get her driver's license. She wants to graduate from high school and go to college. She wants to fall in love. And now that she's dead, Liz is being forced to live a life she doesn't want with a grandmother she has only just met. And it is not going well. How can Liz let go of the only life she has ever known and embrace a new one? Is it possible that a life lived in reverse is no different from a life lived forward?.

Elsewhere. collector's unabr. ed. Gabrielle Zevin. Read by Cassandra Morris. 4 cass. (Running Time: 6 hrs.). (YA). (gr. 7-10). 2005. 35.00 (978-0-307-28369-6(0), Listening Lib) Pub: Random Audio Pubg. Dist(s): Random

Elsewhere, U. S. A. How We Got from the Company Man, Family Dinners, & the Affluent Society to the Home Office, BlackBerry Moms, & Economic Anxiety. unabr. ed. Dalton Conley. Read by Christopher Lane. (Running Time: 7 hrs.). 2009. 39.97 (978-1-4233-7767-2(2), 9781423377672, BADLE); 39.97 (978-1-4233-7765-8(6), 9781423377658, Brinc Audio MP3 Lib); 24.99 (978-1-4233-7764-1(8), 9781423377641, Brilliance MP3); 24.99 (978-1-4233-7766-5(4), 9781423377665, BAD); audio compact disk 82.97 (978-1-4233-7763-4(X), 9781423377634, BriAudCD Unabrid); audio compact disk 29.99 (978-1-4233-7762-7(1), 9781423377627, Bril Audio CD Unabri) Brilliance Audio.

Elsie Dinsmore. Martha Finley. Narrated by Anna Fields. (Running Time: 8 hrs. 30 mins.). (J). 2000. 27.95 (978-1-59912-480-3(7)) Iofy Corp.

Elsie Dinsmore. unabr. ed. Martha Finley. Read by Anna Fields. (Running Time: 7 hrs. 30 mins.). (Elsie Dinsmore Ser.). 2001. 29.95 (978-0-7861-8222-0(9), 2785) Blckstn Audio.

Elsie Dinsmore. unabr. ed. Martha Finley. Read by Susan O'Malley. 6 cass. (Running Time: 8 hrs. 30 mins.). 2001. 44.95 (978-0-7861-2017-8(7), 2785) Blckstn Audio.
Elsie Dinsmore is an endearing eight-year-old girl with several bewildering problems. She has never known her mother, who died when Elsie was a baby & she longs for a close, loving relationship with her father. He, however, has sent her off to be raised at Roselands, his brother's Southern plantation.

Elsie Dinsmore. unabr. ed. Martha Finley. Read by Anna Fields. 6 CDs. (Running Time: 7 hrs. 30 mins.). (Elsie Dinsmore Ser.). 2004. audio compact disk 55.00 (978-0-7861-8127-8(3), 2785) Blckstn Audio.

Elsie Dinsmore, Bk. I. Martha Finley. Read by Bill Potter. 6 cass. (Running Time: 8 hrs. 30 mins.). 2001. 25.00 (978-0-9665233-7-9(7)) Pub: Vsn Forum. Dist(s): STL Dist NA

Elsie Dinsmore, Bk. II. Martha Finley. Read by Bill Potter. 6 cass. (Running Time: 8 hrs.). 2001. 25.00 (978-1-929241-42-2(9)) Pub: Vsn Forum. Dist(s): STL Dist NA

Elsie Dinsmore, Bk. III. Martha Finley. Read by Bill Potter. 6 cass. (Running Time: 8 hrs.). 2001. 25.00 (978-1-929241-43-9(7)) Pub: Vsn Forum. Dist(s): STL Dist NA

Elsie in New York & the Purple Dress. O. Henry. Read by Susan McCarthy et al. (Running Time: 1800 sec.). (J). (gr. 4-7). 2006. 15.95 (978-0-7861-4523-2(4)); audio compact disk 17.00 (978-0-7861-7181-1(2)) Blckstn Audio.

Elsie in New York & the Purple Dress. unabr. ed. O. Henry. Read by Susan McCarthy et al. (Running Time: 1800 sec.). (J). (gr. 4-7). 2006. audio compact disk 19.95 (978-0-7861-7615-1(6)) Blckstn Audio.

Elsie Piddock Skips in Her Sleep. Eleanor Farjeon. Read by Ellin Greene. 1 cass. (Running Time: 60 min.). (J). (gr. k-6). 1986. 9.95 (978-0-939065-21-9(5), GW 1025) Gentle Wind.
Includes: "Elsie Piddock Skips in Her Sleep", "Nella's Dancing Shoes's", "The Sea-Baby", "A Dragon Fly", "The Tide In The River", "The Quarrel", "The Night Will Never Stay".

Elsie Piddock Skips in Her Sleep. Eleanor Farjeon. Read by Ellin Greene. (J). 1999. audio compact disk 14.95 (978-0-939065-74-5(6)) Gentle Wind.

Elsie's Children. unabr. ed. Martha Finley. Read by Marguerite Gavin. 5 cass. (Running Time: 7 hrs.). (Elsie Dinsmore Ser.: Vol. 6). 2006. 39.95 (978-0-7861-2408-4(3), 3078); audio compact disk 48.00 (978-0-7861-8389-0(6), 3078) Blckstn Audio.

Elsie's Girlhood. Martha Finley. Narrated by Marguerite Gavin. (Running Time: 10 hrs.). (J). 2001. 30.95 (978-1-59912-481-0(5)) Iofy Corp.

Elsie's Girlhood. unabr. ed. Martha Finley. Narrated by Marguerite Gavin. 7 cass. (Running Time: 10 hrs.). 2001. 49.95 (978-0-7861-2147-2(5), 2898) Blckstn Audio.
As Elsie Dinsmore grows up and becomes a young woman, her family undergoes major changes. Her father, Horace Dinsmore, falls in love and marries sweet Rose Allison, whom Elsie has loved since childhood. Soon two new members, Horace Jr. and Rosebud, join the happy family. Elsie spends a summer with her eccentric aunt Wealthy, where she experiences the joy of first love and the deep pain of betrayal. In an attempt to cure her broken heart, Elsie's family takes her on a tour of Europe. Upon her return, where and when she least expects it, Elsie discovers the delightful wonder of a true and enduring love.

Elsie's Girlhood. unabr. ed. Martha Finley. Read by Marguerite Gavin. 8 CDs. (Running Time: 10 hrs.). (Elsie Dinsmore Ser.: Vol. 3). 2000. audio compact disk 72.00 (978-0-7861-8125-4(7), 2898) Blckstn Audio.

Elsie's Holidays at Roselands. Martha Finley. Read by Marguerite Gavin. (Running Time: 10 hrs.). (J). 2002. 30.95 (978-1-59912-482-7(3)) Iofy Corp.

Elsie's Holidays at Roselands. unabr. ed. Martha Finley. Read by Marguerite Gavin. 7 cass. (Running Time: 10 hrs.). 2001. 49.95 (978-0-7861-2126-7(2), 2886); audio compact disk 64.00 (978-0-7861-9630-2(0), 2886) Blckstn Audio.
Eight-year-old Elsie Dinsmore is enjoying a blissful Christmas holiday season with her family and friends when a crisis arises that threatens life as she knows it. She believes that obeying a request her father has made would violate her conscience, and she must refuse him. He, in turn, believes Elsie is being willful and disobedient, and he fails to see her refusal as a matter of her deep, abiding faith in God.

Elsie's Motherhood. unabr. ed. Martha Finley. Read by Marguerite Gavin. 6 cass. (Running Time: 8 hrs. 30 mins.). (Original Elsie's Classics Ser.: Bk. 5). 2002. 44.95 (978-0-7861-2249-3(8), 2972) Blckstn Audio.
In a frightening incident, Elsie's husband, Edward Travilla, narrowly survives an accidental shooting when friends tease son Edward, Jr., into firing a loaded pistol. The shot grazes Edward's head, and he survives with only minor damage. Soon life in the Travilla household returns to its calm routine. In the meantime, Elsie welcomes a cousin from Scotland who brings a very special talent with him as well as news of her mother's ancestral family.

Elsie's Motherhood. unabr. ed. Martha Finley. Read by Marguerite Gavin. 7 CDs. (Running Time: 8 hrs. 30 mins.). (Elsie Dinsmore Ser.: Vol. 5). 2003. audio compact disk 56.00 (978-0-7861-9493-3(6), 2972) Blckstn Audio.

Elsie's Womanhood. unabr. ed. Martha Finley. Read by Marguerite Gavin. 7 cass. (Running Time: 10 hrs.). 2002. 49.95 (978-0-7861-2168-7(8), 2918) Blckstn Audio.
It is time for celebration as Elsie prepares to marry her beloved Edward. Following their wedding, the happy couple honeymoons at Viamede, childhood home of Elsie's mother in the bayou region of Louisiana. Here Elsie's faith matures, and she learns to share her belief with others in a meaningful way.

***Elsie's Womanhood.** unabr. ed. Martha Finley. Read by Marguerite Gavin. (Running Time: 9 hrs.). 2010. 29.95 (978-1-4417-2629-2(2)); audio compact disk 76.00 (978-0-7861-6794-4(7)) Blckstn Audio.

Elusion: 2-Disc Special Edition. Directed By Tex Thayer. (ENG.). 2008. DVD & audio compact disk 11.99 (978-0-9800765-0-9(1)) April Third.

Elusive Bride. unabr. ed. Stephanie Laurens. Read by Simon Prebble. (Running Time: 13 hrs. 30 mins.). 2010. 29.95 (978-1-4417-2582-0(2)); 79.95 (978-1-4417-2578-3(4)); audio compact disk 109.00 (978-1-4417-2579-0(2)) Blckstn Audio.

***Elusive Bride.** unabr. ed. Stephanie Laurens. Read by Simon Prebble. (ENG.). 2010. (978-0-06-197867-8(1), Harper Audio); (978-0-06-198541-6(4), Harper Audio) HarperCollins Pubs.

Elusive Childhood: Impossible Representations in Modern Fiction. Susan Honeyman. 2005. audio compact disk 9.95 (978-0-8142-9082-8(5)) Pub: Ohio St U Pr. Dist(s): Chicago Distribution Ctr

***Elusive Isabel.** Jacques Futrelle. Read by Anais 9000. 2009. 27.95 (978-1-60112-233-9(0)) Babblebooks.

Elusive Love. unabr. collector's ed. Catherine Lanigan. Read by Anna Fields. 8 cass. (Running Time: 12 hrs.). 1997. 64.00 (978-0-7366-3764-0(8), 4438) Books on Tape.
Susannah Parker & Michael West are waiting for the perfect love to find them. Susannah thought she'd found it in Greg Walton but was wrong.

Elusive Mrs. Pollifax. Dorothy Gilman. Narrated by Barbara Rosenblat. 4 cass. (Running Time: 6.5 hrs.). 19.95 (978-1-4025-6283-9(7)) Recorded Bks.

Elusive Mrs. Pollifax. unabr. ed. Dorothy Gilman. Narrated by Barbara Rosenblat. 5 cass. (Running Time: 6 hrs. 30 mins.). (Mrs. Pollifax Mystery Ser.: Vol. 3). 1990. 44.00 (978-1-55690-162-1(3), 90005E7) Recorded Bks.
Mrs. Pollifax - America's first "senior" spy - is dispatched to Bulgaria with a precious cargo in her hat.

Elusive Pimpernel. unabr. ed. Emmuska Orczy. Read by Johanna Ward. 7 cass. (Running Time: 10 hrs.). 1998. 49.95 (978-0-7861-1279-1(4), 2169) Blckstn Audio.
In this sequel to "The Scarlet Pimpernel," Sir Percy Blakeney's arch-enemy travels to England in pursuit of the impudent enemy of the French Republic. Monsieur Chauvelin devises a dastardly plot to annihilate, once & for all, both Sir Percy & his beautiful wife Marguerite. Lured to France, where the entire town of Boulogne is held hostage on their behalf, they seem to be hopelessly trapped. Will the Scarlet Pimpernel prevail.

Elusive Pimpernel. unabr. ed. Emmuska Orczy. Read by Johanna Ward. (Running Time: 32400 sec.). 2007. audio compact disk 72.00 (978-0-7861-5804-1(2)); audio compact disk 29.95 (978-0-7861-5805-8(0)) Blckstn Audio.

***Elvenbane.** unabr. ed. Mercedes Lackey & Andre Norton. Read by Aasne Vigesaa. (Running Time: 19 hrs.). (Half Blood Chronicles Ser.). 2010. audio compact disk 29.99 (978-1-4418-1425-8(6), 9781441814258, Bril Audio CD Unabri) Brilliance Audio.

***Elvenbane.** unabr. ed. Andre Norton & Mercedes Lackey. Read by Aasne Vigesaa. (Running Time: 19 hrs.). (Half Blood Chronicles Ser.). 2010. 24.99 (978-1-4418-1429-6(9), 9781441814296, BAD); 39.97 (978-1-4418-1430-2(2), 9781441814302, BADLE); 24.99 (978-1-4418-1427-2(2), 9781441814272, Brilliance MP3) Brilliance Audio.

***Elvenbane.** unabr. ed. Andre Norton & Mercedes Lackey. Read by Aasne Vigesaa. (Running Time: 19 hrs.). (Half Blood Chronicles Ser.). 2011. audio compact disk 89.97 (978-1-4418-1426-5(4), 9781441814265, BriAudCD Unabrid) Brilliance Audio.

***Elvenbane.** unabr. ed. Andre Norton et al. (Running Time: 19 hrs.). (Half Blood Chronicles Ser.). 2010. 39.97 (978-1-4418-1428-9(0), 9781441814289, Brlnc Audio MP3 Lib) Brilliance Audio.

***Elvenblood.** unabr. ed. Andre Norton and Mercedes Lackey. (Running Time: 14 hrs.). (Half Blood Chronicles Ser.). 2010. 24.99 (978-1-4418-1435-7(3), 9781441814357, BAD); 39.97 (978-1-4418-1436-4(1), 9781441814364, BADLE) Brilliance Audio.

***Elvenblood.** unabr. ed. Andre Norton and Mercedes Lackey. Read by Aasne Vigesaa. (Running Time: 13 hrs.). (Half Blood Chronicles Ser.). 2011. 39.97 (978-1-4418-1434-0(5), 9781441814340, Brlnc Audio MP3 Lib); 24.99 (978-1-4418-1433-3(7), 9781441814333, Brilliance MP3); audio compact disk 92.97 (978-1-4418-1432-6(9), 9781441814326, BriAudCD Unabrid); audio compact disk 29.99 (978-1-4418-1431-9(0), 9781441814319, Bril Audio CD Unabri) Brilliance Audio.

Elves & the Shoemaker. 2004. bk. 24.95 (978-0-7882-0546-0(3)); bk. 24.95 (978-1-56008-195-1(3)); pap. bk. 32.75 (978-1-55592-196-5(5)); pap. bk. 14.95 (978-1-56008-196-8(1)); 8.95 (978-0-89719-955-1(3)); 8.95 (978-0-7882-0548-4(X)); 8.95 (978-1-56008-449-5(9)); cass. & flmstrp 30.00 (978-0-89719-567-6(1)); audio compact disk 12.95 (978-0-7882-0549-1(8)) Weston Woods.

***Elves & the Shoemaker.** Anonymous. 2009. (978-1-60136-578-1(0)); (978-1-60136-591-0(8)) Audio Holding.

Elves & the Shoemaker. Arlene Capriola & Rigmor Swenson. Ed. by Cherisse Mastry. Illus. by Kathy Burns. 1 cass. (Once Upon a Time Ser.). (J). (gr. k-2). 1998. 6.95 (978-1-57022-161-3(8), ECS1618) ECS Lrn Systs.

Elves & the Shoemaker. Arlene Capriola & Rigmor Swenson. Ed. by Cherisse Mastry. Illus. by Kathy Burns. 1 cass. (Once upon a Time Ser.). (J). (gr. k-2). 1998. pap. bk. & wbk. ed. 12.95 (978-1-57022-172-9(3)) ECS Lrn Systs.

Elves & the Shoemaker. Retold by Paul Galdone. 1 cass. (Running Time: 5 min.). (J). (ps-3). pap. bk. 12.95 Weston Woods.
The shoemaker & his wife reward two little elves who have helped them become rich & prosperous.

Elves & the Shoemaker. Retold by Paul Galdone. 1 cass. (Running Time: 30 min.). (J). bk. 24.95; pap. bk. 12.95 Weston Woods.

Elves & the Shoemaker. Freya Littledale. Illus. by Brinton Turkle. 1 cass. (Blue-Ribbon Listen-and-Read Ser.). (J). (ps-2). 1984. Scholastic Inc.

Elves & the Shoemaker. Freya Littledale & Brinton Turkle. Illus. by Brinton Turkle. 1 cass. (Blue-Ribbon Listen-and-Read Ser.). (J). (ps-2). 1984. 4.95 (978-0-590-37662-4(4)) Scholastic Inc.

Elves in the Shelves see Necklace of Raindrops & Other Stories

Elves of Cintra. abr. ed. Terry Brooks. Read by Phil Gigante. (Running Time: 6 hrs.). (Genesis of Shannara Ser.: Bk. 2). 2008. audio compact disk 14.99 (978-1-4233-2272-6(X), 9781423322726, BCD Value Price) Brilliance Audio.

Elves of Cintra. unabr. ed. Terry Brooks. Read by Phil Gigante. 1 MP3-CD. (Running Time: 14 hrs.). (Genesis of Shannara Ser.: Bk. 2). 2007. 39.25 (978-1-4233-2268-9(1), 9781423322689, Brlnc Audio MP3 Lib); 39.25 (978-1-4233-2270-2(3), 9781423322702, BADLE); 24.95 (978-1-4233-2269-6(X), 9781423322696, BAD); 92.25 (978-1-4233-2264-1(9), 9781423322641, BrilAudUnabridg); audio compact disk 38.95 (978-1-4233-2265-8(7), 9781423322658, Bril Audio CD Unabri); audio compact disk 24.95 (978-1-4233-2267-2(3), 9781423322672, Brilliance MP3); audio compact disk 112.25 (978-1-4233-2266-5(5), 9781423322665, BriAudCD Unabrid) Brilliance Audio.

Elvis: Love Him Tender. Parton and Associates. 3 cass. (Running Time: 3 hrs. 40 min.). Dramatization. 62.50 Alpha Tape.
Explores Presley's career & life.

Elvis in the Morning. unabr. ed. William F. Buckley, Jr. Narrated by Lloyd James. 7 cass. (Running Time: 11 hrs. 30 mins.). 2001. 49.95 (978-0-7861-2113-7(0), 2874); audio compact disk 72.00 (978-0-7861-9640-1(8), 2874) Blckstn Audio.
Orson is a young boy whose mother works at the U.S. Army base in Germany in the 1950s. There, he becomes a fan of a G.I. stationed at the base, one Elvis Presley, whose music is played over and over on the radio. When Orson is caught stealing recordings of Elvis's tunes from the PX, the attendant publicity catches the star's attention, and he comes to visit his young fan. Thus begins a lifelong friendship. As Elvis's career rockets ever higher and his behavior becomes ever more erratic, the two share many adventures.The sixties explode, and Elvis becomes the icon of the nation, while Orson, a college demonstrator, drifts away from regular life while looking for something of substance in which to believe. Each man is an emblem of his times, as social conventions crumble, barriers fall, and the cultural landscape changes forever. A panorama of change and dissent, of the ability of friends to stay true despite distance and time, portrays a nation in change and the effects of celebrity on innocence.

Elvis Is Dead & I Don't Feel So Good Myself. unabr. collector's ed. Lewis Grizzard. Read by Lawrence M. Vanella. 8 cass. (Running Time: 8 hrs.). 1985. 48.00 (978-0-7366-0424-6(3), 1396) Books on Tape.
This is Grizzard's account of coping with a changing world. The 50's were simple times to grow up in & the 60's exploded with assassinations, terrorism, & free love. We may not feel so good ourselves, but his commentary & humor help make us feel better.

Elvis Music & Interview. 1 CD. (Running Time: 45mins). (Maximum Ser.). 2005. audio compact disk (978-1-84240-318-1(4)) Chrome Dreams GBR.
Although he was without doubt the world?s most electrifying performer throughout his life, it was the years from 1954 -1958 that Elvis changed the face of popular music forever. This CD contains rare interviews with Elvis, recorded during those early years of his career, interspersed with music from the 1954 Sun Sessions ? surely the most pivotal recording sessions everWith huge interest in The King ongoing, year after year, and fans constantly hungry for new collector?s items, Elvis: Music And Interview is certain to delight both the old school enthusiasts and the new generations, growing up to his music in 2005.

Elvis Presley. Pamela Clarke Keogh. Narrated by Anna Fields. (Running Time: 8 hrs. NaN mins.). 2005. 37.95 (978-1-59912-483-4(1)) Iofy Corp.

Elvis Presley. unabr. ed. Bobbie Ann Mason. 2 cass. (Running Time: 2 hrs. 30 mins.). (J). 2000. 18.00 (978-0-7366-9070-6(0)) Books on Tape.

***Elvis Presley: Pro Vocal Men's Edition Volume 23.** Elvis Presley. (ENG.). 2010. pap. bk. 14.99 (978-0-634-09974-8(4), 0634099744) H Leonard.

Elvis Presley: The Man, the Life, the Legend. Pamela Clark Keogh. Read by Anna Fields. (Running Time: 28800 sec.). 2005. audio compact disk 63.00 (978-0-7861-7840-7(X)) Blckstn Audio.

Elvis Presley: The Man, the Life, the Legend. Pamela Clarke Keogh. Read by Anna Fields. (Running Time: 8 mins. 30 sec.). 2005. 54.95 (978-0-7861-3511-0(5)) Blckstn Audio.

Elvis Presley: The Man, the Life, the Legend. unabr. ed. Clarke Clarke Keogh. Read by Anna Fields. 13 vols. (Running Time: 28800 sec.). 2005. audio compact disk 29.95 (978-0-7861-8055-4(2), ZM3486) Blckstn Audio.

Elvis Presley: The Man, the Life, the Legend. unabr. ed. Pamela Clark Keogh. Read by Anna Fields. 6 cass. (Running Time: 28800 sec.). 2005. 29.95 (978-0-7861-3549-3(2), E3486); audio compact disk 29.95 (978-0-7861-7738-7(1), ZE3486) Blckstn Audio.

Elvis Presley Pt. 1: Last Train to Memphis. unabr. ed. Peter Guralnick. Read by Christopher Lane. 8 cass. (Running Time: 12 hrs.). 1994. 64.00 (3702-A) Books on Tape.
They were the years of his self-invention & unshakable self-confidence, during which it seemed everything Elvis Presley tried succeeded wildly. Until he was 24 - when he was drafted & his mother died - it was all blue skies. Guralnick focuses on this formative period of Presley's life. He unveils the man behind the legend - a walking contradiction: a trustful, shy mama's boy given to loud clothes; a chaste romantic, but a frequent swinger; an all-night partyer but rarely smoking or drinking; & a lonely soul despite throngs of fans.

Elvis Presley Pt. 2: Last Train to Memphis. unabr. ed. Peter Guralnick. Read by Christopher Lane. 8 cass. (Running Time: 12 hrs.). 1994. 64.00 (3702-B) Books on Tape.

Elvis Presley Set: Love Songs. 2 cass. (Running Time: 1 hr. 30 min.). 1999. 14.99 (YXAZ96); audio compact disk 16.99 (YYA0B9) Time-Life.

Elvis Presley - The Missing Years, Set. collector's ed. Perf. by Elvis Presley & Blue Moon Boys. 2002. bk. 29.95 (WHE1030DVD) MVD Ent.

Elvis Takes a Back Seat. unabr. ed. Leanna Ellis. Narrated by Pam Turlow. (ENG.). 2008. 18.19 (978-1-60814-177-7(2)); audio compact disk 25.99 (978-1-59859-339-6(0)) Oasis Audio.

Elvis the Rooster & the Magic Words. unabr. ed. Denys Cazet. 1 cass. (Running Time: 16 mins.). (Readalongs for Beginning Readers Ser.). (J). 2006. pap. bk. 16.95 (978-1-59519-690-3(0)) Live Oak Media.

Elvis...In His Own Words, Set. Elvis Presley. 2 CDs. 2002. audio compact disk 12.99 (978-0-9726530-0-8(7)) Passport Intl Prod.

Elvis's Man Friday. unabr. ed. Gene Smith. Narrated by Tom Stechschulte. 5 cass. (Running Time: 7 hrs. 15 mins.). 2000. 44.00 (978-0-7887-0641-7(1), 94755E7) Recorded Bks.

Elyon. unabr. ed. Ted Dekker & Kaci Hill. Narrated by Tim Gregory. (Books of History Chronicles: Bk. 6). (ENG.). 2009. 16.09 (978-1-60814-565-2(4)); audio compact disk 22.99 (978-1-59859-531-4(8)) Oasis Audio.

Elyon Vol. 1: The Most High God. Creflo A. Dollar & Taffi L. Dollar. 4 cass. (Running Time: 6 hrs.). 2000. 20.00 (978-1-931172-36-3(6), TS 258, Kidz Faith) Pub: Creflo Dollar. Dist(s): STL Dist NA

Elyon Vol. 2: The Significance of the Tithe. Creflo A. Dollar. 4 cass. (Running Time: 6 hrs.). 2000. 20.00 (978-1-931172-38-7(2), TS264, Kidz Faith) Pub: Creflo Dollar. Dist(s): STL Dist NA

Elyon Vol. 3: The Highest Authority of All. Creflo A. Dollar & Taffi L. Dollar. 4 cass. (Running Time: 6 hrs.). 2000. 20.00 (978-1-931172-66-0(8), TS265, Kidz Faith) Pub: Creflo Dollar. Dist(s): STL Dist NA

Elyon Vol. 4: The Most High God. Creflo A. Dollar. 4 cass. (Running Time: 6 hrs.). 2000. 20.00 (978-1-931172-68-4(4), TS266, Kidz Faith) Pub: Creflo Dollar. Dist(s): STL Dist NA

***Elysiana.** unabr. ed. Chris Knopf. (Running Time: 7 hrs.). 2010. 29.95 (978-1-4417-6460-7(7)); 44.95 (978-1-4417-6457-7(7)) Blckstn Audio.

***Elysiana.** unabr. ed. Chris Knopf. Read by Jim Meskimen. (Running Time: 7 hrs.). 2010. audio compact disk 69.00 (978-1-4417-6458-4(5)) Blckstn Audio.

***Elysium.** Catherine Jinks. Read by Melissa Chambers. (Running Time: 3 hrs. 35 mins.). (Allie's Ghost Hunters Ser.). (J). 2009. 54.99 (978-1-74214-549-5(3), 9781742145495) Pub: Bolinda Pubng AUS. Dist(s): Bolinda Pub Inc

Elysium. unabr. ed. Catherine Jinks. Read by Melissa Chambers. 3 CDs. (Running Time: 3 hrs. 35 mins.). (Allie's Ghost Hunters Ser.: Bk. 4). (J). (gr. 4-7). 2009. audio compact disk 54.95 (978-1-74214-142-8(0), 9781742141428) Pub: Bolinda Pubng AUS. Dist(s): Bolinda Pub Inc

Elysium: Abode of the Angels. Erik Berglund & John Mazzei. 1 cass. 9.95 (LA201); audio compact disk 15.95 (LA201D) Lghtwrks Aud & Vid.
Elysium, the heaven realm of ancient Greece, is the point of outpouring of angelic energies through music. Woven throughout this CD are angelic voices singing the language of angels - music unfettered by the separation caused by words. Featured in "Opening to Angels" this album combines Erik's harp & voice & the synthesizer of John Mazzei.

Email & Voicemail Tools. unabr. ed. Michael Podolinsky. 2 cass. (Running Time: 3 hrs.). (Smart Audio Ser.). 2004. 19.99 (978-1-58926-341-3(3)); audio compact disk 19.99 (978-1-58926-342-0(1)) Oasis Audio.
Today's business professionals rely on the conveniences of e-mail and voicemail. Instead of having your message deleted learn the secrets of getting the response you want.

Emancipation from Economic Slavery. unabr. ed. E. C. Harwood. 1 cass. (Running Time: 40 min.). 12.95 (1108) J Norton Pubs.
Harwood examines the historic means of enslaving people & the four prolonged inflation stages. He concludes that freedom & gold are inseparable.

Emayghee Chah Tjr2x: A Universal Second Language. Elmer J. Hankes. Illus. by James McBurney. 1 cass. (C). 1992. pap. bk. 15.00 (978-0-925837-10-3(5)) Hankes Found.

Embarrassment of Riches: An Interpretation of Dutch Culture in the Golden Age. unabr. ed. Simon Schama. Read by Nadia May. 16 cass. (Running Time: 86400 sec.). 1991. 99.95 (978-0-7861-0936-4(X), 1203) Blckstn Audio.
The brilliantly detailed interpretation of the seventeenth century Dutch Republic. Rebellion against Spanish rule led, in only a few generations, to the creation of a powerful world empire, its culture admired throughout the West. Making themselves up as they went along the Dutch drew creativity, according to Schama, from the moral ambiguity of materialism.

Embarrassment of Riches Pt. 1: An Interpretation of Dutch Culture in the Golden Age. unabr. ed. Simon Schama. 1991. audio compact disk 63.00 (978-0-7861-0230-3(6)) Blckstn Audio.

Embarrassments. Henry James. Narrated by Flo Gibson. (ENG.). 2007. 20.95 (978-1-55685-923-6(6)) Audio Bk Con.

Embassy Row: A Mycroft Holmes Novel. Quinn Fawcett. Narrated by Simon Prebble. 10 CDs. (Running Time: 12 hrs.). audio compact disk 97.00 (978-1-4025-0000-8(9)) Recorded Bks.

Embassy Row: A Mycroft Holmes Novel. unabr. ed. Quinn Fawcett. Narrated by Simon Prebble. 9 cass. (Running Time: 12 hrs.). 2000. 82.00 (978-0-7887-4934-6(X), H1133E7) Recorded Bks.
Attending secret high level negotiations with the Japanese ambassador, Mycroft hopes to secure English access to Japanese waters. On the night the agreement is to be signed, a British diplomat who was opposed to the treaty, is found dead with a Japanese dagger in his back.

Embassy Series: Essentials of U. S. Governance for Foreign Diplomats & Embassy Staff: Part I: the U. S. Government in a Nutshell; Part II: the Dynamics of the Legislative Process; Part III: The Federal Regulatory Process. Todd Tatelman et al. Prod. by TheCapitol.Net. (ENG.). 2008. 127.00 (978-1-58733-089-6(X)) TheCapitol.

Embedded Development with GNU: Cross-Development for Windows & Linux. William Gatliff et al. 2003. audio compact disk (978-1-57820-126-6(8)) C M P Books.

Embers. 2005. 29.95 (978-1-59649-024-6(1)); audio compact disk 24.95 (978-1-59649-023-9(3)) Whsprng Pine.

Embers. abr. ed. Sándor Márai. Read by Paul Scofield. 4 cass. 2002. (978-0-14-180400-2(9)) Pnguin Bks Ltd GBR.
As darkness settles on a forgotten castle at the foot of the Carpathian mountains, two men sit down to a final meal together. They have not seen

one another in forty-one years. At their last meeting, in the company of a beautiful woman, an unspoken act of betrayal left all three lives shattered - and each of them alone. Tonight, as wine stirs the blood, it is time to talk of old passions and that last, fateful meeting.

Embers of the Dead. unabr. ed. Roy Lewis. Read by Jack Paulin. 6 cass. (Story Sound Ser.). (J). 2006. 54.95 (978-1-85903-896-3(4)) Pub: Mgna Lrg Print GBR. Dist(s): Ulverscroft US

Embers of the Dead. unabr. ed. Roy Lewis & Jack Paulin. Read by Jack Paulin. 7 CDs. (Running Time: 8 hrs.). (Story Sound CD Ser.). (J). 2006. audio compact disk 71.95 (978-1-85903-946-5(4)) Pub: Mgna Lrg Print GBR. Dist(s): Ulverscroft US

Embezzler. unabr. ed. Louis Auchincloss. Read by Dan Lazar. 7 cass. (Running Time: 10 hrs. 30 mins.). 1979. 56.00 (978-0-7366-0165-8(1), 1167) Books on Tape.
Guy Prime, convicted of misappropriating bonds during the Depression, gives his apologia, followed by the narratives of his closest friend, Rex Geer & Prime's wife, Angelica, who marries Geer after Prime's self-exile.

Embodiment of All the Siddhas. Read by Chogyam Trungpa. 4 cass. 1975. 40.50 (A103) Vajradhatu.
Four talks. A seminar given on the "Sadhana of Mahamudra".

Embodiment Practices from the Trance of Scarcity. Victoria Castle. (ENG.). 2006. 10.00 (978-0-9771331-1-6(7)) Sagacious Pr.

Embouchure: Poems on Jazz & Other Musics. Poems. Akua L. Hope. 1 cass. 1995. 12.95 (978-0-9647876-1-2(X)) ArtFarm Pr.

Embrace. Perf. by Mac Powell & Age of Faith Staff. 1 cass. Brentwood Music.
Guitar driven pop rock with uncompromising lyrics. Includes The Love of Jesus, with guest vocals by Mac Powell of Third Day.

Embrace the Grim Reaper. unabr. ed. Judy Clemens. (Running Time: 7.5 hrs. 0 mins.). (ENG.). 2009. 29.95 (978-1-4332-6557-0(5)); 54.95 (978-1-4332-6553-2(2)); audio compact disk 60.00 (978-1-4332-6554-9(0)) Blckstn Audio.

Embrace the Night. unabr. ed. Karen Chance. Narrated by Cynthia Holloway. 12 CDs. (Running Time: 16 hrs. 0 mins. 0 sec.). (Cassandra Palmer Ser.). (ENG.). 2008. audio compact disk 79.99 (978-1-4001-3819-7(1)) Pub: Tantor Media. Dist(s): IngramPubServ

Embrace the Night. unabr. ed. Karen Chance. Read by Cynthia Holloway. 12 CDs. (Running Time: 16 hrs. 0 mins. 0 sec.). (Cassandra Palmer Ser.). (ENG.). 2008. audio compact disk 39.99 (978-1-4001-0819-0(5)); audio compact disk 29.99 (978-1-4001-5819-5(2)) Pub: Tantor Media. Dist(s): IngramPubServ

Embrace the Serpent. unabr. ed. Quayle & Northcott. Read by J. Charles. (Running Time: 10 hrs.). 2008. 24.95 (978-1-4233-5969-2(0), 9781423359692, BAD); 24.95 (978-1-4233-5967-8(4), 9781423359678, Brilliance MP3); 39.25 (978-1-4233-5970-8(4), 9781423359708, BADLE); 39.25 (978-1-4233-5968-5(2), 9781423359685, Brlnc Audio MP3 Lib) Brilliance Audio.

Embrace the Struggle: Living Life on Life's Terms. unabr. ed. Zig Ziglar & Julie Ziglar Norman. Read by Zig Ziglar. (Running Time: 7 hrs. 0 mins. 0 sec.). (ENG.). 2009. audio compact disk 29.99 (978-0-7435-9748-7(6)) Pub: S&S Audio. Dist(s): S and S Inc

Embrace the Wind. Perf. by Pat Ferreri et al. Composed by L. A. Wendt. 1 cass. (Running Time: 45 min.). (Quiet Times Ser.). 1989. 9.98 (978-1-878328-03-8(4)) Realmusic.
A graceful sloop embraces the ever elusive wind. Its stretched rigging resonates with the warmth of classical guitar. Guitar & clarinets with environmental sounds recorded on Lake Michigan.

Embrace Tiger - Return to Mountain: Spiritual Conflict Management. Gary Simmons. 2 cass. (Running Time: 3 hrs.). 1999. 13.95 (978-0-87159-827-1(2)) Unity Schl Christ.

Embrace Tiger, Return to Mountan: Spiritual Conflict Management. Gary Simmons. 2009. audio compact disk 15.95 (978-0-9824797-2-8(7)) Q Effect.

***Embraced by Darkness.** unabr. ed. Keri Arthur. Narrated by Angela Dawe. (Running Time: 11 hrs. 0 mins.). (Riley Jenson Guardian Ser.). 2010. 17.99 (978-1-4526-7005-8(6)); 24.99 (978-1-4526-5005-0(5)); 34.99 (978-1-4526-0005-5(8)) Tantor Media.

***Embraced by Darkness (Library Edition)** unabr. ed. Keri Arthur. Narrated by Angela Dawe. (Running Time: 11 hrs. 0 mins.). (Riley Jenson Guardian Ser.). 2010. 34.99 (978-1-4526-2005-3(9)); 83.99 (978-1-4526-3005-2(4)) Tantor Media.

Embraced by the Light. Betty J. Eadie. 2004. 12.95 (978-0-7435-4684-3(9)) Pub: S&S Audio. Dist(s): S and S Inc

Embraced by the Light: The Musical Journey. Stan Zenk. Composed by Bryce Neubert. 1 cass. 1993. 9.95 (978-1-882723-07-2(4)); audio compact disk 14.95 (978-1-882723-08-9(2)) Onjinjinkta.

***Embraced by the Spirit: The Untold Blessings of Intimacy with God.** Charles R. Swindoll. (ENG.). 2011. 18.99 (978-0-310-42773-5(8)) Zondervan.

Embracing Change: Using the Treasures Within You. unabr. ed. Louise L. Hay. 2010. audio compact disk 16.95 (978-1-4019-2577-2(4)) Hay House.

Embracing Change/Feeling Forgiven. Marianne Williamson. Read by Marianne Williamson. 1 cass. (Running Time: 90 mins.). (Lectures on a Course in Miracles). 1999. 10.00 (978-1-56170-188-9(2), M716) Hay House.

Embracing Chaos Set: How to Shake Things up & Make Things Happen. Tom Peters. 6 cass. 59.95 (10450AX) Nightingale-Conant.
The global business environment is revolutionizing the way products are entering the market. If you want to profit from new opportunities being born out of the chaos, you have to move at a frantic pace. Here are specific strategies & cutting-edge techniques used successfully by today's most innovative companies. Tom Peters even shows you how to take the initiative for change & spot today's golden opportunities.

Embracing Defeat. unabr. ed. John W. Dower. Read by Edward Lewis. (Running Time: 21 hrs. 50 mins.). 2008. 44.95 (978-1-4332-4568-8(X)) Blckstn Audio.

Embracing Defeat: Japan in the Wake of World War II. unabr. ed. John W. Dower. Read by Edward Lewis. 16 cass. (Running Time: 23 hrs. 30 mins.). 2003. 99.95 (978-0-7861-1684-3(6), 2505) Blckstn Audio.
Embracing Defeat lies in its vivid portrayal of the countless ways in which the Japanese met the challenge of starting over from top-level manipulations concerning the fate of Emperor Hirohito to the hopes, fears, & activities of ordinary men & women in every walk of life.

Embracing Defeat: Japan in the Wake of World War II. unabr. ed. John W. Dower. Read by Edward Lewis. (Running Time: 77400 sec.). 2008. audio compact disk & audio compact disk 125.00 (978-1-4332-4567-1(1)) Blckstn Audio.

Embracing Freedom Within Depression. Carole Riley. 3 cass. (Running Time: 3 hrs. 8 min.). 1997. 28.95 Set. (TAH375) St Pauls Alba.
Sr. Carole balances the series of discussions with musical sections & poetry. Perfect as a learning & meditation tool for those who suffer depression & those who love them.

Embracing Stress. Music by Steve Greene. (ENG.). 1994. audio compact disk 19.95 (978-0-9789606-2-9(9)) Heartwork Inst.

Embracing the Sovereing Scripture: Knowing God' Will Series, Sept. Ben Young. 2000. 4.95 (978-0-7417-6197-2(1), B0197) Win Walk.

Embracing the Spirit, Pt. 3. abr. ed. Tammie Fowles. Read by Tammie Fowles. Read by Kevin Fowles. 1 cass. 1998. 11.95 (978-0-9666900-3-3(6)) SagePlace.
Addresses the meaning, magic, & mystery that confronts those who seek to awaken & reclaim their spirituality.

Embracing the Spirit of Abundance. Bobby Hilton. 6 cass. 2001. 30.00 (978-1-930766-23-5(8)) Pub: Bishop Bobby. Dist(s): STL Dist NA

Embracing Your Inner Mediocrity: Making Peace with Reality. (ENG.). 2009. audio compact disk 22.95 (978-0-9821290-1-2(7)) Sterling TN.

Embroidered Truths. unabr. ed. Monica Ferris. Read by Melissa Hughes. 5 cass. (Needlecraft Mystery Ser.). 2005. 49.95 (978-0-7927-3662-2(1), CSL 811); audio compact disk 64.95 (978-0-7927-3663-9(X), SLD 811) AudioGO.

E=mc2: A Biography of the World's Most Famous Equation. David Bodanis. Read by Dan Cashman. 2001. audio compact disk 48.00 (978-0-7366-7079-1(3)) Books on Tape.

E=mc2: A Biography of the World's Most Famous Equation. unabr. ed. David Bodanis. Read by Dan Cashman. 6 CDs. (Running Time: 9 hrs.). 2001. audio compact disk 48.00 Books on Tape.
A lucid, interesting and concise explanation of Einstein's famous equation that rescues the masses from ignorance.

E=mc2: A Biography of the World's Most Famous Equation. unabr. ed. David Bodanis. 5 cass. (Running Time: 7hrs. 30 mins.). 2001. 40.00 (978-0-7366-6211-6(1)) Books on Tape.
A lucid, interesting, and concise explanation of Einstein's famous equation that rescues the masses from ignorance.

EMD Short Report. 1 cass. 2000. 15.95 Prof Pride.
Record 20 EMD short reports. Very useful learning medical jargon.

***Emerald.** unabr. ed. Dennis Lehane. (ENG.). 2007. (978-0-06-136931-5(4), Harper Audio) HarperCollins Pubs.

***Emerald Atlas.** unabr. ed. John Stephens. (Running Time: 11 hrs.). (Books of Beginning Ser.). (ENG.). (J). 2011. audio compact disk 48.00 (978-0-307-87976-9(3), Listening Lib) Pub: Random Audio Pubg. Dist(s): Random

Emerald Beauty-Music. 2007. audio compact disk 19.95 (978-1-56136-402-2(9)) Master Your Mind.

Emerald Cave Collections Box 1: 6 Volume Set including EC1 - EC6, Prod. by Thomas W. Gustin. 6 CDs. (Running Time: 7 hrs, 56 mins, 27 secs). 2004. audio compact disk 48.00 (978-0-9761848-0-5(X), ECC) Gustech.
Emerald Cave "Nature" Recordings SeriesCollection Box 1 consists of 6 different audio format CDs featuring "ONLY" the sounds of nature; no music, no mixing, no loops, no enhancements. See EC1-EC6 descriptions for further details.

Emerald City of Oz. unabr. ed. L. Frank Baum. Read by Tim Hunter et al. 4 cass. (Running Time: 5 hrs. 30 min.). Dramatization. (Oz Ser.). (YA). (gr. 5-8). 1995. 24.95 Set. (978-1-886354-06-7(5)) Piglet Pr.
The Piglet Press audio version of this Baum classic provides a cast of over 80 characters. These include, Dorothy (our heroine), Ozma (the Girl Princess ruler of Oz), & the familiar Wizard of Oz, Tin Woodman, Scarecrow, & Cowardly Lion. Baum delights in engaging word play with his uniquely eponymous characters of Oz, including the Flutterbudgets, Rigmaroles, Fuddles, Cuttenclips, & the inhabitants of Utensia, Bunnybury, & Bunbury. The "bad guys" are wantonly absent of socially redeeming value, & get their ultimate come-upance without resorting to violence. As the storyline shifts back & forth from the scheming of the Nome King & his allies, & the delightful discoveries Dorothy & her friends make as they explore new regions of Oz, the listener's imagination will be in full play.

Emerald Eyes. unabr. ed. Richard Bamberg & Joy Bamberg. Read by Laurie Klein. 6 cass. (Running Time: 6 hrs. 42 min.). 1995. 39.95 (978-1-55686-586-2(4)) Books in Motion.
Charlene Rodgers is frantically pursued through the Peruvian jungle by bandits who are attempting to gain possession of an original artifact belonging to an ancient Mayan culture.

Emerald Flame. unabr. ed. Virginia Coffman. Read by Harriet Grey. 7 cass. (Storysound Ser.). (J). 2000. 61.95 (978-1-85903-385-2(7)) Pub: Mgna Lrg Print GBR. Dist(s): Ulverscroft US

Emerald Green. 1 cass. (Running Time: 60 min.). (Interludes Music Ser.). 1989. 9.95 (978-1-55569-279-7(6), MOD-3900) Great Am Audio.

Emerald Peacock. unabr. ed. Katharine Gordon. Read by Patricia Gallimore. 8 cass. (Running Time: 11 hrs.). 2000. 69.95 (978-1-86042-273-7(X), 2273X) Pub: Soundings Ltd GBR. Dist(s): Ulverscroft US
A great & dangerous love between a beautiful Irish girl & an Indian prince.

***Emerald Windows.** Zondervan. (Running Time: 8 hrs. 38 mins. 39 sec.). (ENG.). 2010. 9.99 (978-0-310-86916-0(1)) Zondervan.

Emeralds & Espionage, Set. Lynn Gardner. 2 cass. 11.98 (978-1-55503-799-4(2), 07001053) Covenant Comms.
A romantic thriller.

Emerged & Emerging New Uniform Commercial Code. 12 cass. (Running Time: 16 hrs.). 1998. 395.00 Set; incl. study guide 1052p. (MD30) Am Law Inst.
Advanced course designed for practitioners needing to keep current with the substantive changes in the UCC, as well as for others concerned with the manner in which commercial law meets business needs & adjusts to technological change.

Emergency. Tana Reiff. 1 cass. (That's Life Ser.: Bk. 1). 1994. 10.95 (978-0-7854-1095-9(3)) Am Guidance.

***Emergency.** abr. ed. Neil Strauss. Read by Neil Strauss. (ENG.). 2009. (978-0-06-190098-3(2), Harper Audio); (978-0-06-186397-4(1), Harper Audio) HarperCollins Pubs.

Emergency: Injury. abr. ed. Robert A. Monroe. Read by Robert A. Monroe. (Running Time: 30 min.). (Human Plus Ser.). 1989. 14.95 (978-1-56102-010-2(9)) Inter Indus.
Increase body's natural healing & balancing abilities.

Emergency: This Book Will Save Your Life. abr. ed. Neil Strauss. Read by Neil Strauss. 7 CDs. (Running Time: 8 hrs.). 2010. audio compact disk 34.99 (978-0-06-199531-6(2), Harper Audio) HarperCollins Pubs.

Emergency: Toxic. abr. ed. Robert A. Monroe. Read by Robert A. Monroe. (Running Time: 30 min.). (Human Plus Ser.). 1989. 14.95 (978-1-56102-011-9(7)) Inter Indus.
Assist in protecting & discharging foreign & harmful substances.

Emergency Care & Transportation of the Sick & Injured. 9th rev. ed. American Academy of Orthopaedic Surgeons Staff. (C). 2005. stu. ed. 50.95 (978-0-7637-2970-7(1)) Jones Bartlett.

Emergency Consumer Remedies for Torts & Breach of Contract. Read by Gary E. Klein & Susan L. DeJamatt. 1 cass. 1990. 20.00 (AL-81) PA Bar Inst.

Emergency Medicine. 2nd ed. Ed. by Judith E. Tintinalli et al. 2000. 195.00 (978-0-07-135711-1(4)) Pub: McGraw-Hill Prof. Dist(s): McGraw

Emergency Medicine Review, Vol. A226. unabr. ed. 36 cass. 1995. 795.00 set. (978-1-57664-364-8(6)) CME Info Svcs.
Continuing medical education home-study. Complete package contains audiotapes, syllabus, self-assessment examination to earn CME Category 1 credit.

Emergency Series. abr. ed. Robert A. Monroe. Read by Robert A. Monroe. 6 cass. (Running Time: 30 min.). 1989. 69.00 Set. (978-1-56102-712-5(X)) Inter Indus.
Contains: Pre Op, Intra Op, Recovery, Recuperation, Energy Walk & Surf tapes.

Emergent Stage 2. Steck-Vaughn Staff. 1996. (978-0-8172-6597-7(X)) SteckVau.

Emergent Voices: CBC Canadian Literary Award Stories, 1979-1999. abr. ed. Ed. by Robert Weaver. 3 cass. (Running Time: 4 hrs. 30 mins.). (Between the Covers Collection). (ENG.). 2005. 19.95 (978-0-86492-276-2(0)) Pub: BTC Audiobks CAN. Dist(s): U Toronto Pr

Emerging & Reemerging Infections. Contrib. by Mary A. Jackson et al. 1 cass. (American Academy of Pediatrics UPDATE: Vol. 19, No. 1). 1998. 20.00 Am Acad Pediat.

Emerging Framework of World Power. Noam Chomsky. (AK Press Audio Ser.). 2003. audio compact disk 14.98 (978-1-902593-75-3(8)) Pub: AK Pr GBR. Dist(s): Consort Bk Sales

Emerging from Pain: A Healing Visualization. Heraty Eugenie. (ENG.). 2007. 16.98 (978-1-934332-05-4(4), Heal Voice) Inter Med Pub.

Emerging from Shadows-tape: The Shroud of Turin. Read by Nathan D. Wilson. 2005. 10.00 (978-1-59128-436-9(8)) Canon Pr ID.

Emerging Theories of Sellers' & Brokers' Liability in Residential Real Estate Transactions. Read by William J. Maffucci. 1 cass. 1989. 20.00 (AL-58) PA Bar Inst.

Emerging Viruses & Vaccinations. Leonard G. Horowitz. 2 cass. (Running Time: 3 hrs.). 1997. cass. & video 19.95 (978-0-923550-17-2(8)) Tetrahedron Pub.
Contaminated vaccines are spreading new immune-system-related disorders.

Emerging Voices: Short Stories by Turn-of-the-Century Women Writers. Short Stories. Ed. by Gary Gabriel. (Running Time: 60 min.). (Audio-Drama 101 Ser.: Vol. 5). 14.95 Lend-A-Hand Soc.

Emerging Voices: Verbatim Dramatizations of 101 Familiar & Unfamiliar Short Stories. unabr. ed. 6 cass. (Running Time: 6 hrs.). (AudioDrama 101 Ser.: Vol. 7). 2001. 14.95 (978-1-892077-07-3(8)) Lend-A-Hand Soc.
Emerging voices: Stories by Twentieth Century Women Writers.

Emersion in the Sand: Amplification to revitalize & Deepen Your Experience of Sandplay. Interview. Dee Preston-Dillon. Voice by Dee Preston-Dillon. Executive Producer Center for Culture and Sandplay Staff. Engineer Nick Johnson. Illus. by Ellen LaCapria. Des. by Eric Kriemelmeyer. Music by Karl Kriemelmeyer. 1 CD. (Running Time: 1 hour). 2004. audio compact disk (978-0-9764157-0-1(4)) C C Sandplay.
How do therapists interpret a client's sand scene? Dr. Preston-Dillon discusses the therapeutic skill of amplification to help clinicians understand the complex symbolic meanings in their client's sand scenes. She introduces four archetypes to support sandplay practice, inviting the listener to explore these images with guided exercises through sand work, drawing, and journaling. This CD is part of the "Efficacy in Sandplay" series for professionals using Sand Therapy. www.cultureplay.com.

Emerson. Tara Singh. 2 cass. (Running Time: 2 hrs.). (Minds That Have Touched the Earth Ser.). 1993. 19.95 set. (978-1-55531-266-4(7), 1A422) Life Action Pr.
An illuminating profile of Ralph Waldo Emerson's contribution to generations striving to live ethical lives.

Emerson by Dancing Beetle. Perf. by Eugene Ely. 1 cass. (Running Time: 73 min.). (J). 1991. 10.00 Erthviibz.
Ralph Waldo Emerson, parody & nature sounds come together when Ms. Firefly & the spunky musical humans read & sing with Dancing Beetle.

Emerson, Thoreau, & the Transcendentalist Movement. Instructed by Ashton Nichols. 12 CDs. (Running Time: 12 hrs.). 2006. 69.95 (978-1-59803-242-0(9)); 129.95 (978-1-59803-241-3(0)) Teaching Co.

Emery-Dreifuss Muscular Dystrophy - A Bibliography & Dictionary for Physicians, Patients, & Genome Researchers. Compiled by Icon Group International, Inc. Staff. 2007. ring bd. 28.95 (978-0-497-11206-6(X)) Icon Grp.

Emil & Karl. Yankev Glatshteyn. Read by Humphrey Bower. (Running Time: 4 hrs. 35 mins.). (YA). 2009. 59.99 (978-1-74214-316-3(4), 9781742143163) Pub: Bolinda Pubng AUS. Dist(s): Bolinda Pub Inc

Emil & Karl. unabr. ed. Read by Humphrey Bower. Ed. by Yankev Glatshteyn. Tr. by Jeffrey Shandler. (Running Time: 16500 sec.). (YA). (gr. 7). 2008. audio compact disk 57.95 (978-1-921334-61-0(4), 9781921334610) Pub: Bolinda Pubng AUS. Dist(s): Bolinda Pub Inc

Emile see Treasury of French Prose

Emily. unabr. ed. Valerie Wood. Read by Kim Hicks. 12 cass. (Running Time: 18 hrs.). 2002. 96.95 (978-0-7540-0807-1(X), CAB 2229) AudioGO.

***Emily & Einstein.** unabr. ed. Linda Francis Lee. (Running Time: 9 hrs. 30 mins.). 2011. 34.99 (978-1-4526-0035-2(X)); 16.99 (978-1-4526-7035-5(8)); 24.99 (978-1-4526-5035-7(7)) Tantor Media.

***Emily & Einstein (Library Edition)** unabr. ed. Linda Francis Lee. (Running Time: 9 hrs. 30 mins.). 2011. 34.99 (978-1-4526-2035-0(0)); 83.99 (978-1-4526-3035-9(6)) Tantor Media.

Emily Dickinson. 1 cass. 1997. 10.95 (978-1-57523-164-8(6)) Unapix Enter.

Emily Dickinson. unabr. ed. Poems. Emily Dickinson. Read by Mary Woods. 4 cass. (Running Time: 5 hrs. 30 mins.). 1993. 32.95 (978-0-7861-0397-3(3), 1349) Blckstn Audio.
The subjects of these poems are as wide-ranging as their author's life was constrained: beginning always with particulars of personal experience, her poems encompass life & death, love & longing, joyfulness & sorrow. With spare, precise language, she conveyed a penetrating vision of the natural world & an actue understanding of the most profound human truths.

Emily Dickinson: A Light & Enlightening Lecture, Featuring Elliot Engel. 2000. bk. 15.00 (978-1-890123-33-8(1)) Media Cnslts.

Emily Dickinson: A Self-Portrait. Emily Dickinson. Read by Julie Harris. 2 cass. (Running Time: 90 min.). 24.95 set. (8120Q) Filmic Archives.
This is a fine portrait of the gifted poet composed of selections from her letters & poems. They are lovingly interpreted by Julie Harris, & this recording went on to inspire the William Luce play "The Belle of Amherst," for which Ms. Harris won the Tony Award for her portrayal of Dickinson. Poems include "This is my letter to the world"; "Some Keep the Sabbath going to church"; "I cautious scanned my little life"; "To make a prairie it takes a clover & one bee", & many others.

Emily Dickinson: My Letter to the World. 1 CD. (Running Time: 71 mins.). 2002. audio compact disk 15.00 (978-0-9665212-9-0(3), EssayAudiocom) EssayAudio.

Emily Dickinson: 75 Poems. unabr. ed. Poems. Emily Dickinson. Narrated by Alexandra O'Karma. 2 cass. (Running Time: 2 hrs. 15 mins.). 1990. 18.00 (978-1-55690-163-8(1), 90010E7) Recorded Bks.
A selection from the long-hidden works of the belle of Amherst.

Emily Dickinson Is Dead. unabr. collector's ed. Jane Langton. Read by Ruth Stokesberry. 6 cass. (Running Time: 9 hrs.). 1987. 48.00 (978-0-7366-1077-3(4), 2004) Books on Tape.
A murder occurs at a memorial symposium for Emily Dickinson.

Emily Dickinson Recalled in Song. unabr. ed. Hosted by Joseph Jones. 1 cass. (Running Time: 30 min.). 12.95 (23854) J Norton Pubs.
A literary scholar meets the ghost of the poet & they discuss & demonstrate through song how her poetry may have been influenced in its rhythm & rhyme schemes by church music written by Lowell Mason & other well-known composers of the 19th century.

***Emily Hudson.** unabr. ed. Melissa Jones. Narrated by Lorna Raver. (Running Time: 11 hrs. 0 mins. 0 sec.). (ENG.). 2010. audio compact disk 83.99 (978-1-4001-4926-1(6)) Pub: Tantor Media. Dist(s): IngramPubServ

***Emily Hudson: A Novel.** unabr. ed. Melissa Jones. Narrated by Lorna Raver. (Running Time: 11 hrs. 0 mins. 0 sec.). (ENG.). 2010. 24.99 (978-1-4001-6926-9(7)); 17.99 (978-1-4001-8926-7(8)); audio compact disk 34.99 (978-1-4001-1926-4(X)) Pub: Tantor Media. Dist(s): IngramPubServ

Emily of New Moon. unabr. ed. L. M. Montgomery. Read by Susan O'Malley. 9 cass. (Running Time: 13 hrs.). (gr. 4-7). 1999. 62.95 (978-0-7861-1488-7(6), 2339) Blckstn Audio.
Emily discovers loneliness when she is left an orphan, & her mother's snobbish relatives takes her to live with them at New Moon Farm.

Emily of New Moon. unabr. ed. L. M. Montgomery. Read by Susan O'Malley. (Running Time: 12 hrs. 0 mins.). (ENG.). 2009. 29.95 (978-1-4417-0308-8(X)); audio compact disk 105.00 (978-1-4417-0305-7(5)) Blckstn Audio.

Emily of New Moon, Set. unabr. ed. L. M. Montgomery. Read by Flo Gibson. 7 cass. (Running Time: 10 hrs. 20 min.). (YA). (gr. 8 up). 1989. bk. 47.95 Audio Bk Con.
In this story of Emily Starr, orphaned as a little girl, learn her adventures & thoughts in her letters to her dead father & see her growth as a would-be author.

Emily of New Moon, Set. unabr. ed. L. M. Montgomery. Read by Susan O'Malley. 9 cass. (J). 1999. 62.95 (FS9-43391) Highsmith.

Emily of New Moon, Set unabr. ed. L. M. Montgomery. Read by Flo Gibson. 7 cass. (Running Time: 10 hrs. 30 min.). (J). (gr. 5-6). 1999. pap. bk. 25.95 (978-1-55685-579-5(6)) Audio Bk Con.
In this charming & moving story of Emily Starr, orphaned as a little girl, we learn her adventures & thoughts in her letters to her dead father & we see her growth as a would-be author.

Emily Post: Daughter of the Gilded Age, Mistress of American Manners. unabr. ed. Laura Claridge. (Running Time: 18 hrs. NaN mins.). 2008. audio compact disk 44.95 (978-1-4332-4919-8(7)); audio compact disk & audio compact disk 39.95 (978-1-4332-4918-1(9)) Blckstn Audio.

Emily Post: Daughter of the Guilded Age, Mistress of American Manners. unabr. ed. Laura Claridge. (Running Time: 18 hrs NaN mins.). 2008. 95.95 (978-1-4332-4916-7(2)); audio compact disk 120.00 (978-1-4332-4917-4(0)) Blckstn Audio.

***Emily Post's the Guide to Good Manners for Kids.** abr. ed. Cindy Post Senning. (ENG.). 2006. (978-0-06-135551-6(8)) HarperCollins Pubs.

***Emily the Strange: Stranger & Stranger.** unabr. ed. Rob Reger. Read by Angela Goethals. Illus. by Jessica Gruner. (ENG.). 2010. (978-0-06-196751-1(3)); (978-0-06-193828-3(9)) HarperCollins Pubs.

***Emily the Strange: the Lost Days.** unabr. ed. Rob Reger. Read by Angela Goethals. (ENG.). 2009. (978-0-06-190194-2(6)); (978-0-06-182465-4(8)) HarperCollins Pubs.

***Emily Windsnap & the Castle in the Mist.** unabr. ed. Liz Kessler. Read by Finty Williams. 4 CDs. (Running Time: 4 hrs. 18 mins.). (Emily Windsnap Ser.: Bk. 3). (YA). (gr. 8 up). 2009. audio compact disk 87.97 (978-0-307-70617-1(6), Listening Lib) Pub: Random Audio Pubg. Dist(s): Random

Emily Windsnap & the Castle in the Mist. unabr. ed. Liz Kessler. (Emily Windsnap Ser.: Bk. 3). (ENG.). (J). (gr. 3). 2009. audio compact disk 28.00 (978-0-307-70627-0(3), Listening Lib) Pub: Random Audio Pubg. Dist(s): Random

Emily Windsnap & the Monster from the Deep. unabr. ed. Liz Kessler. Read by Finty Williams. 4 CDs. (Running Time: 4 hrs. 13 mins.). (Emily Windsnap Ser.: Bk. 2). (J). 2006. audio compact disk 38.00 (978-0-7393-3558-1(8), Listening Lib); 30.00 (978-0-7393-3567-3(7), Listening Lib) Pub: Random Audio Pubg. Dist(s): Random
All I wanted was to impress my best friend, Shona, and the other mermaids who live in the sea around Allpoints Island. But what did I do instead? I woke up the kraken, a terrifying octopus-like monster the size of an apartment building. Now he's coming after everything and everyone I love. And who can stop him? You guessed it. Me. Well, me and Shona, and another person too - someone I'd hoped never, ever to see again.

Emily Windsnap & the Monster from the Deep. unabr. ed. Liz Kessler. Read by Finty Williams. (Running Time: 15180 sec.). (Emily Windsnap Ser.: Bk. 2). (ENG.). (J). (gr. 3). 2009. audio compact disk 28.00 (978-0-307-28234-7(1), Listening Lib) Pub: Random Audio Pubg. Dist(s): Random

***Emily Windsnap & the Siren's Secret.** unabr. ed. Liz Kessler. (ENG.). (J). 2011. audio compact disk 28.00 (978-0-307-91702-7(9), Listening Lib) Pub: Random Audio Pubg. Dist(s): Random

Emily's First 100 Days of School. Rosemary Wells. Narrated by Diana Canova. 1 CD. (Running Time: 36 mins.). (J). (ps-4). 2006. bk. 29.95 (978-0-439-84900-5(4), WHCD654); pap. bk. 14.95 (978-0-439-84902-9(0), WPRA654); pap. bk. 18.95 (978-0-439-84903-6(9), WPCD654); bk. 24.95 (978-0-439-84898-5(9), WHRA654) Weston Woods.
With so much to do on her first day of school, Emily feels like it will take forever to reach 100, when her teacher announces they will have a party after 100 days. As the days and weeks go by, Emily and her new classmates learn new ideas, expand their world, and grow closer together one day at a time.

***Emily's First 100 Days of School.** Weston Woods Staff. (J). audio compact disk 12.95 (978-0-439-84893-0(8)) Weston Woods.

Emily's Fortune. unabr. ed. Phyllis Reynolds Naylor. Read by Lee Adams. (ENG.). (J). 2010. 20.00 (978-0-307-73801-1(9), Listening Lib) Pub: Random Audio Pubg. Dist(s): Random

***Emily's Runaway Imagination.** unabr. ed. Beverly Cleary. Read by Christina Moore. (ENG.). 2009. (978-0-06-180530-1(0)); (978-0-06-174464-8(6)) HarperCollins Pubs.

Emily's Runaway Imagination. unabr. ed. Beverly Cleary. 1 cass. (Running Time: 49 min.). (Soundways to Reading Ser.). (J). (gr. 2-4). 1986. 15.98 incl. bk. & guide. (978-0-8072-1140-3(0), SWR48SP, Listening Lib) Random Audio Pubg.
Emily Bartlett's life has been one incredible scheme after another usually ending in fiasco - until she gets it into her head that the little town of Pitchfork needs a library.

Emily's Runaway Imagination, unabr. ed. Beverly Cleary. Narrated by Christina Moore. 4 pieces. (Running Time: 4 hrs. 45 mins.). (gr. 4 up). 1992. 35.00 (978-1-55690-609-1(9), 92302E7) Recorded Bks.
Eight year old Emily lives in a village way out in Oregon, but no town is too small for her to find mischief in. Her mother blames it on her runaway imagination. Set in the early years of this century, it is the story of an adventurous girl who decides her town needs a library & she's the one to make it happen.

Eminem: The Unauthorized Biography of Eminem. Scott Gigney. (Maximum Ser.). (ENG., 2001. audio compact disk 14.95 (978-1-84240-094-4(0)) Pub: Chrome Dreams GBR. Dist(s): IPG Chicago

Eminem X-Posed. Eminem & Chrome Dreams Staff. (ENG., 2002. audio compact disk 14.95 (978-1-84240-133-0(5)) Pub: Chrome Dreams GBR. Dist(s): IPG Chicago

Eminence. unabr. ed. William X. Kienzle. Read by Edward Holland. 8 cass. (Running Time: 8 hrs.). (Father Koesler Mystery Ser.: No. 11). 2001. 64.00 (978-0-7366-8379-1(8)) Books on Tape.
From the spare quarters of a makeshift monastery in downtown Detroit, four religious Brothers and a priest are doing the impossible - working miracles of the sight-to-the-blind, health-to-the-sick variety. People are flocking to this "monastery of St. Stephen" to be cured. But there are rumors of rather more nefarious practices taking place at St. Stephen's: embezzlement, torture, and murder. Father Koesler once again is called on to investigate this rumor of monks and priests making miracles. Father Koesler is experienced, but even he has never faced such a pure polarity.

Eminence. unabr. ed. Morris West. Narrated by Graeme Malcolm. 8 cass. (Running Time: 10 hrs. 45 mins.). 1999. 71.00 (978-1-84197-007-3(7), H1007E7) Recorded Bks.
In the closing years of this Pontiff's reign a story is told of the next Papal election & of certain characters who may well have a part to play in it. Most important of these is the eminence of the title, Luca, Cardinal Rosini, a man who suffered torture & degradation as a young priest in Argentina, who lived in exile in Rome & was promoted to high office in the Vatican. By his own admission he is a flawed man, but he is still a man of power & a possible candidate for election. There is, however, much more to this novel than Vatican politics. Love & passion, tenderness & intrigue, heavy suspense & high drama, all are here.

Eminence, Set. unabr. ed. Morris West. Narrated by Graeme Malcolm. 8 cass. 1999. 71.00 (H1007K4, Clipper Audio) Recorded Bks.

Eminent Dogs, Dangerous Men, unabr. ed. Donald McCaig. Narrated by Nelson Runger. 6 cass. (Running Time: 8 hrs.). 1991. 51.00 (978-1-55690-164-5(X), 91301E7) Recorded Bks.
An American travels to Scotland in search of a hard to find sheepdog. How he finds his "wee bonny Gael" is a story of determination & faith.

Eminent Domain & Land Valuation Litigation, Set. 18 cass. (Running Time: 23 hrs. 30 min.). 1999. stu. ed. 395.00 (MD40) Am Law Inst.
Advanced course covers both the substantive & practice issues & includes presentations by appraisers as well as practicing attorneys.

Eminent Elizabethans. unabr. ed. A. L. Rowse. Read by Bill Kelsey. 8 cass. (Running Time: 12 hrs.). 1983. 64.00 (978-0-7366-1348-4(X), 2249) Books on Tape.
Presents a quintet of Elizabethans, notable in their day & characteristic of their time.

Eminent Historian. unabr. ed. Gilbert Highet. Read by Gilbert Highet. 1 cass. (Running Time: 30 min.). 9.95 (23297-A) J Norton Pubs.

***Eminent Lives: the Presidents Collection.** unabr. ed. James Atlas. Read by Sam Tsoutsouvas. (ENG.). 2006. (978-0-06-117341-7(X), Harper Audio); (978-0-06-117340-0(1), Harper Audio) HarperCollins Pubs.

Eminent Victorian Soldiers. unabr. ed. Byron Farwell. Read by Bill Kelsey. 7 cass. (Running Time: 10 hrs. 30 min.). 1993. 56.00 (978-0-7366-2570-8(4), 3319) Books on Tape.
Eight of Queen Victoria's generals virtually created the British empire.

Eminent Victorians. unabr. ed. Lytton Strachey. Read by Nadia May. 7 cass. (Running Time: 10 hrs.). 1992. 49.95 (978-0-7861-0387-4(6), 1339) Blckstn Audio.
One of the most famous biographical studies ever published. "Eminent Victorians" is a collection of four biographical essays, on Cardinal Manning, a churchman "of smiling asceticism" & ruthless personal ambition; Florence Nightingale, the founder of modern nursing, a woman of indomitable will; of General "Chinese" Gordon the martyr of Khartoum; & Thomas Arnold, headmaster at Rugby, whose zeal for Christian morality changed the whole atmosphere of education in England. According to Strachey, all in some measure demonstrated some of the outstanding traits of the Victorian period but also shared an excess of moral righteousness that in some way impaired their sense of humanity.

Eminent Victorians. unabr. ed. Lytton Strachey. Narrated by Samuel Gillies. 9 cass. (Running Time: 12 hrs. 15 mins.). 2000. 79.00 (978-1-84197-051-6(4), H1061E7) Recorded Bks.
"The History of the Victorian Age will never be written: we know too much about it", says Strachey in his preface. Instead, he provides an insight into Victorian Society through four of its key characters. Using each figure as a focus, Strachey shows the church's vacuous, manipulative hypocrisy, a nurse's paranoia & paradoxical lack of feeling, the inadequate, bigoted education system & the imperialistic, kudos-seeking nature of Victorian war.

Eminent Victorians. unabr. collector's ed. Lytton Strachey. Read by Jill Masters. 9 cass. (Running Time: 13 hrs. 30 mins.). 1985. 72.00 (978-0-7366-0864-0(8), 1815) Books on Tape.
Irreverent essays on Cardinal Manning, Florence Nightingale, Dr. Arnold & General Gordon found an eager audience in the post-W.W. I generation. Strachey debunks the myths surrounding these Victorian personalities. His estimates now require considerable revision, but retain authority.

Eminent Victorians, Set. unabr. ed. Lytton Strachey. 7 cass. (Running Time: 10 hrs.). 1993. 25.95 (978-1-55685-285-5(1)) Audio Bk Con.
Vivid, ironic & sometimes scathing studies of four legendary figures: Dr. Arnold, Florence Nightingale, Cardinal Manning, & General Gordon.

Emissary of Light: My Adventure with the Secret Peacemakers. abr. ed. James F. Twyman. (ENG.). 2006. 14.98 (978-1-59483-840-8(2)) Pub: Hachet Audio. Dist(s): HachBkGrp

Emissary of Light: My Adventures with the Secret Peacemakers. abr. ed. James F. Twyman. Read by James F. Twyman. 2 cass. (Running Time: 3 hrs.). 1997. 17.00 (978-1-57042-330-7(X)) Hachet Audio.
For thousands of years, the mystical community known as the Emissaries of Light has worked in secret, invoking the greatest spiritual power to bring peace to areas of devastating bloodshed. Jimmy Twyman is the first outsider to have the privilege of learning with them. In the mountains of Bosnia & Croatia, he observes their amazing meditations & the foundations of their ancient work.

Emissary: star trek, deep space Nine. J. M. Dillard. 2004. 10.95 (978-0-7435-4622-5(9)) Pub: S&S Audio. Dist(s): S and S Inc

Emlyn's Moon. Jenny Nimmo & Jenny Nimmo. Read by John Keating. (Running Time: 15600 sec.). (Snow Spider Trilogy: Bk. 2). (ENG.). (J). (gr. 4-7). 2007. audio compact disk 49.95 (978-0-439-02316-0(5)) Scholastic Inc.

Emlyn's Moon. Jenny Nimmo & Jenny Nimmo. Read by John Keating. Narrated by John Keating. (Running Time: 15600 sec.). (Snow Spider Trilogy: Bk. 2). (ENG.). (J). (gr. 4-7). 2007. audio compact disk 24.95 (978-0-439-92496-2(0)) Scholastic Inc.

Emlyn's Moon. unabr. ed. Jenny Nimmo. Read by John Keating. (J). 2007. 44.99 (978-1-60252-681-5(8)) Find a World.

Emma see Cambridge Treasury of English Prose: Austen to Bronte

Emma. Jane Austen. Contrib. by Angharad Rees. 4 CDs. (Running Time: 4 hrs. 15 mins.). 2006. audio compact disk 49.95 (978-0-7927-4341-5(5), BBCD 168) AudioGO.

Emma. Jane Austen. Read by Nadia May. 11 cass. (Running Time: 16 hrs.). 2000. 76.95 (978-0-7861-1842-7(3), 2641) Blckstn Audio.
Humorous portrayal of a heroine whose injudicious interferences in the life of a young parlour-boarder in a neighboring village ofted lead to substantial mortification.

Emma. Jane Austen. Read by Donada Peters. 2002. audio compact disk 120.00 (978-0-7366-8766-9(1)) Books on Tape.

Emma. Jane Austen. Read by Jane Lapotaire. 12 cass. (Running Time: 16 hrs. 5 min.). 69.95 (CC/014) C to C Cassettes.
The self deluding but not unkindly Emma Woodhouse imagines that she dominates those around her in the small town of Highbury, but her inept match making creates problems not only for others but for herself as well.

Emma. Jane Austen. Narrated by Jill Masters. (Running Time: 18 hrs.). 1983. 25.95 (978-1-59912-806-1(3)) Iofy Corp.

Emma. Jane Austen. Read by Juliet Stevenson. (Running Time: 3 hrs. 45 mins.). 2000. 24.95 (978-1-60083-730-2(1)) Iofy Corp.

Emma. Jane Austen. Read by Juliet Stevenson. 3 cass. (Running Time: 3 hrs. 45 mins.). (Works of Jane Austen). 1996. 17.98 (978-962-634-595-5(0), NA309514, Naxos AudioBooks) Naxos.

Emma. Jane Austen. Read by Juliet Stevenson. (Running Time: 60006 sec.). 2006. audio compact disk 81.98 (978-962-634-394-4(X), Naxos AudioBooks) Naxos.

Emma. abr. ed. Jane Austen. Narrated by Angharad Rees. (Running Time: 18900 sec.). (BBC Radio Classics Ser.). (ENG.). 2007. audio compact disk 29.95 (978-1-60283-281-7(1)) Pub: AudioGO. Dist(s): Perseus Dist

Emma. abr. ed. Jane Austen. 4 cass. (Running Time: 6 hrs. 40 min.). 1996. 26.95 Set. (978-1-885546-10-4(6)) Big Ben Audio.
Austen's spirited young heroine encounters comic trials & tribulations in her search for true love, against the sharply observed backdrop of Jane Austen's small town England.

Emma. abr. ed. Jane Austen. Read by Anna Massey. 4 cass. 22.95 (SCN 015) J Norton Pubs.
Emma displays both her gift of gentle irony & her knowledge of the psychology of both sexes.

Emma. abr. ed. Jane Austen. Read by Juliet Stevenson. 3 CDs. (Running Time: 3 hrs. 45 mins.). (Works of Jane Austen). (J). (gr. 9-12). 1996. audio compact disk 22.98 (978-962-634-095-0(9), NA309512) Naxos.

Emma. abr. ed. Jane Austen. Read by Samantha Eggar. 4 cass. (Running Time: 6 hrs.). 2004. 25.00 (978-1-59007-114-4(X)) Pub: New Millenn Enter. Dist(s): PerseuPGW
Charming, willful Emma Woodehouse amuses herself by planning other people's lives. When her interfering backfires, she learns a bitter lesson: well-intentioned busybodies are as resented as those motivated by ill will, and everyone should learn to respect the individuality of others.

Emma. unabr. ed. Jane Austen. Read by Prunella Scales. 10 cass. (Running Time: 14 hrs. 30 mins.). (gr. 9-12). 2004. 39.95 (978-1-57270-071-0(8), F91071u) Pub: Audio Partners. Dist(s): PerseuPGW
When Emma sets about matchmaking among her friends, she discovers her own inadequacies in the art. Austen captures perfectly the laughter & gossip as the ladies wrestle with love & marriage.

Emma. unabr. ed. Jane Austen. Read by Prunella Scales. (Running Time: 52200 sec.). (Cover to Cover Classics Ser.). (ENG.). 2006. audio compact disk 37.95 (978-1-57270-532-6(9)) Pub: AudioGO. Dist(s): Perseus Dist

Emma. unabr. ed. Jane Austen. Read by Nadia May. (Running Time: 55800 sec.). 2008. audio compact disk & audio compact disk 99.00 (978-0-7861-6266-6(X)) Blckstn Audio.

Emma. unabr. ed. Jane Austen. Read by Nadia May. (Running Time: 14 hrs. 15 mins.). 2010. audio compact disk 29.95 (978-0-7861-6267-3(8)) Blckstn Audio.

***Emma.** unabr. ed. Jane Austen. Read by Nadia May. (Running Time: 14 hrs. 15 mins.). 2010. audio compact disk 32.95 (978-1-4417-5536-0(5)) Blckstn Audio.

Emma. unabr. ed. Jane Austen. 11 cass. (Running Time: 11 hrs.). 2002. 104.00 (978-0-7366-8765-2(3)) Books on Tape.
"Emma Woodhouse, handsome, clever and rich, with a comfortable house and happy disposition, seemed to unite some of the best blessings of existence; and had lived nearly twenty-one years in the world with very little to distress or vex her. Emma fancies herself a superb judge of human character and becomes entrenched in the amorous affairs of her friends. In doing so, she remains oblivious to her own romantic possibilities, and the resulting comical misunderstandings are highly entertaining.

Emma. unabr. ed. Jane Austen. Read by Michael Page. 12 cass. (Running Time: 15 hrs.). 2002. 34.95 (978-1-59086-290-2(2), 1590862902, BAU) Brilliance Audio.
The funny and heartwarming story of a young lady whose zeal, snobbishness and self-satisfaction lead to several errors in judgment. Emma takes Harriet Smith, a parlour boarder and unknown, under her wing and schemes for advancement through a good marriage. The attempts at finding Harriet a suitor occupy all of Emma's time. However, in the midst of the search she settles on a most unlikely union with her own constant critic: Mr. Knightly. Jane Austen's works have claimed a renewed popularity and audience with the release of motion pictures Sense and Sensibility, Emma, and Clueless based upon Austen's classic novels. Emma was originally published in 1816.

Emma. unabr. ed. Jane Austen. Read by Michael Page. (Running Time: 15 hrs.). 2004. 39.25 (978-1-59335-556-2(4), 1593355564, Brlnc Audio MP3 Lib) Brilliance Audio.

Emma. unabr. ed. Jane Austen. Read by Michael Page. (Running Time: 15 hrs.). 2004. 39.25 (978-1-59710-251-3(2), 1597102512, BADLE); 24.95 (978-1-59710-250-6(4), 1597102504, BAD) Brilliance Audio.

Emma. unabr. ed. Jane Austen. Read by Michael Page. (Running Time: 54000 sec.). (Classic Collection (Brilliance Audio) Ser.). 2005. audio compact disk

112.25 (978-1-59737-128-5(9), 9781597371285, BriAudCD Unabrid); audio compact disk 44.95 (978-1-59737-127-8(0), 9781597371278, Bril Audio CD Unabri) Brilliance Audio.

Emma. unabr. ed. Jane Austen. Read by Juliet Stevenson. (YA). 2006. 94.99 (978-1-59895-629-0(9)) Find a World.

Emma. unabr. ed. Jane Austen. Read by Jill Masters. 13 cass. (Running Time: 19 hrs. 30 min.). 1984. 69.00 (C-124) Jimcin Record.
A comedy of manners which satirizes the self-deceptions of vanity. A mellower book than "Pride & Prejudice", it equals it in its rich humor & vivid portraiture of character.

Emma. unabr. ed. Jane Austen. Narrated by Victoria Morgan. 12 cass. (Running Time: 15 hrs. 30 mins.). 1987. 97.00 (978-1-55690-165-2(8), 87350E7) Recorded Bks.
Emma Woodhouse is thrown into despair when her long-time companion marries. Now she needs a new subject for her attentions.

Emma. unabr. ed. Jane Austen. Read by Michael Page. (Running Time: 15 hrs.). 2004. 24.95 (978-1-59335-041-3(4), 1593350414) Soulmate Audio Bks.
The funny and heartwarming story of a young lady whose zeal, snobbishness and self-satisfaction lead to several errors in judgment. Emma takes Harriet Smith, a parlour boarder and unknown, under her wing and schemes for advancement through a good marriage. The attempts at finding Harriet a suitor occupy all of Emma's time. However, in the midst of the search she settles on a most unlikely union with her own constant critic: Mr. Knightly. Jane Austen's works have claimed a renewed popularity and audience with the release of motion pictures Sense and Sensibility, Emma, and Clueless based upon Austen's classic novels. Emma was originally published in 1816.

Emma. unabr. ed. Jane Austen. Read by Wanda McCaddon. Narrated by Wanda McCaddon. (Running Time: 15 hrs. 0 mins. 0 sec.). (Tantor Unabridged Classics Ser.). (ENG.). 2008. 27.99 (978-1-4001-5687-0(4)); audio compact disk 35.99 (978-1-4001-0687-5(7)); audio compact disk 72.99 (978-1-4001-3687-2(3)) Pub: Tantor Media. Dist(s): IngramPubServ

***Emma.** unabr. ed. Jane Austen. Narrated by Jenny Agutter. (Running Time: 14 hrs. 50 mins. 0 sec.). (ENG.). 2010. audio compact disk 39.95 (978-1-4084-2716-3(8)) Pub: AudioGO. Dist(s): Perseus Dist

Emma. unabr. collector's ed. Jane Austen. Read by Jill Masters. 13 cass. (Running Time: 19 hrs. 30 mins.). 1983. 104.00 (978-0-7366-3894-4(6), 134507) Books on Tape.
This comedy of manners satirizes the self-deceptions of vanity. It presents a picture of mixed family & social life. Emma is recognizable as a vamp, a pretty & capricious young woman who defines the limits of reality by banging against them. Enter the small world of the provincial country village, described in anything but a provincial manner.

Emma, Set. unabr. ed. Jane Austen. Narrated by Flo Gibson. 10 cass. (Running Time: 15 hrs.). 1986. 29.95 (978-1-55685-005-9(0)) Audio Bk Con.
A fascinating portrait of a headstrong young woman who is convinced that she can order the society around her & manage the lives & loves of her friends. Each failure helps her character to develop into a lady of compassion. With the inexhaustable Miss Bates, who speaks in medleys, & other villagers this is a perfect satiric picture of English village life in the 19th century.

Emma, Set. unabr. ed. Jane Austen. Read by Jill Masters. 13 cass. 1999. 85.95 (FS9-51114) Highsmith.

Emma: Level 2: 700 Headwords. Jane Austen & Barbara MacKay. Contrib. by Bill Bowler & Sue Parminter. (Dominoes Ser.). 2002. 14.25 (978-0-19-424359-9(1)) OUP.

Emma & Joseph Set: Their Divine Mission. Gracia Jones. 5 cass. 2004. 19.95 (978-1-57734-530-5(4), 07002181) Covenant Comms.

***Emma-Jean Lazarus Fell in Love.** unabr. ed. Lauren Tarshis. Read by Mamie Gummer. 3 CDs. (Running Time: 4 hrs. 44 mins.). (YA). (gr. 5-8). 2009. audio compact disk 30.00 (978-0-7393-8133-5(4), Listening Lib) Pub: Random Audio Pubg. Dist(s): Random

Emma-Jean Lazarus Fell in Love. unabr. ed. Lauren Tarshis. (ENG.). (J). (gr. 3). 2009. audio compact disk 25.00 (978-0-7393-8131-1(8), Listening Lib) Pub: Random Audio Pubg. Dist(s): Random

Emma-Jean Lazarus Fell Out of a Tree. unabr. ed. Lauren Tarshis. Read by Mamie Gummer. 3 CDs. (Running Time: 3 hrs. 4 mins.). (J). (gr. 4-7). 2007. audio compact disk 24.00 (978-0-7393-5122-2(2), Random AudioBks) Pub: Random Audio Pubg. Dist(s): Random

Emma-Jean Lazarus Fell Out of a Tree. unabr. ed. Lauren Tarshis. Read by Mamie Gummer. (Running Time: 11040 sec.). (ENG.). (J). (gr. 3-7). 2007. audio compact disk 27.00 (978-0-7393-4796-6(9), Listening Lib) Pub: Random Audio Pubg. Dist(s): Random

Emmanuel. Contrib. by Amy Grant. (Ultimate Tracks (Word Tracks) Ser.). 2006. audio compact disk 8.98 (978-5-558-14986-9(8), Word Music) Word Enter.

Emmanuel. Contrib. by Darlene Zschech. (Praise Hymn Soundtracks Ser.). 2002. audio compact disk 8.98 (978-5-550-12893-0(4)) Pt of Grace Ent.

Emmanuel Christmas: Matthew 1:23, 641. Ed Young. 1987. 4.95 (978-0-7417-1641-5(0), 641) Win Walk.

Emmanuel Fried. unabr. ed. Read by Emmanuel Fried. 1 cass. (Running Time: 29 min.). 1985. 10.00 New Letters.
Emmanuel Fried reads from his play, "The Dodo Bird" & also poems & other stories from the Buffalo Labor Writers' Workshop.

Emmanuel, God with Us. Contrib. by Amy Grant. (Mastertrax Ser.). 2007. audio compact disk 9.98 (978-5-557-58526-2(5)) Pt of Grace Ent.

Emma's Child. Kristine Thatcher. Perf. by David Darlow et al. 1 cass. (Running Time: 60 min.). 1998. 22.95 (978-1-58081-120-0(5), CTA54) L A Theatre.
Explores the idea of commitment - in a marriage - as a parent. The story of a childless couple struggling to decide whether to continue the adoption process when the baby they had hoped for is born severely disabled.

Emma's Christmas Rose. unabr. ed. Elizabeth Daish. Read by Julia Sands. 5 cass. (Running Time: 6 hrs. 35 min.). 63.95 (978-1-85903-185-8(4)) Pub: Magna Story GBR. Dist(s): Ulverscroft US
In her haven on the Isle of Wight, Emma's Aunt Emily cultivates a unique Christmas Rose, guaranteed to bloom at a time of bleak scarcity in gardens - a sign of hope and future promise.

Emma's Nightmare: The Voyage of the Titanic. 1 cass. (Running Time: 1 hr. 30 mins.). (SmartReader Ser.). (J). 1999. pap. bk. & tchr. ed. 19.95 (978-0-7887-0555-7(5), 79336T3) Recorded Bks.
When the "unsinkable" ship hits an iceberg, young Emma & her family struggle to survive the disaster.

Emma's Peace. unabr. ed. Elizabeth Daish. 6 cass. (Storysound Ser.). (J). 1998. 54.95 (978-1-85903-139-1(0)) Pub: Mgna Lrg Print GBR. Dist(s): Ulverscroft US

Emma's Pet. David M. McPhail. Illus. by David M. McPhail. Read by Rick Adamson. 11 vols. (Running Time: 4 mins.). (J). (gr. k-3). 1988. pap. bk. 16.95 (978-0-87499-106-2(4)) AudioGO.
Emma seeks out the cuddliest, most lovable pet she can find. None fills the bill, however, until she runs into the biggest, cuddliest pet of all, her very own father!.

Emma's Pet. David M. McPhail. Illus. by David M. McPhail. (Running Time: 4 mins.). (J). (gr. k-2). 1988. 9.95 (978-1-59112-036-0(5)) Live Oak Media.

Emma's Pet. David M. McPhail. Illus. by David M. McPhail. 14 vols. (Running Time: 4 mins.). 1988. pap. bk. 35.95 (978-1-59519-252-3(2)); audio compact disk 12.95 (978-1-59519-250-9(6)) Live Oak Media.

Emma's Pet. David M. McPhail. Illus. by David M. McPhail. 11 vols. (Running Time: 4 mins.). (J). 1988. pap. bk. 18.95 (978-1-59519-251-6(4)) Pub: Live Oak Media. Dist(s): AudioGO

Emma's Pet, Grades K-3. David M. McPhail. Illus. by David M. McPhail. Read by Rick Adamson. 14 vols. (Running Time: 4 mins.). 1988. pap. bk. & tchr. ed. 33.95 Reading Chest. (978-0-87499-108-6(0)) Live Oak Media.

Emma's Secret. unabr. abr. rev. ed. Barbara Taylor Bradford. Read by Kate Burton. 5 CDs. (Running Time: 6 hrs. 0 mins. 0 sec.). No. 4. (ENG.). 2004. audio compact disk 29.95 (978-1-55927-796-9(3)) Pub: Macmill Audio. Dist(s): Macmillan

Emma's War: A True Story. unabr. ed. Deborah Scroggins. (Running Time: 52200 sec.). 2007. audio compact disk & audio compact disk 99.00 (978-1-4332-1294-9(3)) Blckstn Audio.

Emma's War: A True Story. unabr. ed. Deborah Scroggins. Read by Kate Reading. (Running Time: 52200 sec.). 2007. 85.95 (978-1-4332-1293-2(5)); audio compact disk 29.95 (978-1-4332-1295-6(1)) Blckstn Audio.

Emmet Fox's Golden Keys to Successful Living. Emmet Fox. 1 cass. (Running Time: 60 min.). (Sermon on the Mount Ser.). 9.95 HarperCollins Pubs.

***Emmy & the Incredible Shrinking Rat.** unabr. ed. Lynn Jonell. 6 CDs. (Running Time: 7 hrs.). (J). (gr. 3-6). 2009. audio compact disk 45.00 (978-1-934180-68-6(8)) Full Cast Audio.

Emotional Alchemy. unabr. ed. Tara Bennett-Goleman. Read by Anna Fields. 10 cass. (Running Time: 15 hrs.). 2001. 80.00 (978-0-7366-8487-3(5)) Books on Tape.
A psychotherapist shows how difficult emotions can be made to disappear through the Buddhist practice of "mindfulness".

Emotional Alchemy: How the Mind Can Heal the Heart. abr. rev. ed. Tara Bennett-Goleman. Read by Tara Bennett-Goleman. Frwd. by Dalai Lama XIV. 3 CDs. (Running Time: 3 hrs. 0 mins. 0 sec.). (ENG.). 2001. audio compact disk 26.00 (978-1-55927-690-0(8)) Pub: Macmill Audio. Dist(s): Macmillan

Emotional Awareness: Overcoming the Obstacles to Emotional Balance & Compassion. unabr. ed. Dalai Lama XIV & Paul Ekman. Read by Richard Gere. 7 CDs. (Running Time: 10 hrs.). 2008. audio compact disk 59.95 (978-0-7927-5643-9(6)) AudioGO.
Take this transformative journey in the understanding of emotions! The Dalai Lama and renowned psychologist Paul Ekman share their thinking about science and spirituality, the bonds between East and West, and the nature and quality of our emotional lives. In this unparalleled series of conversations, these two leading thinkers prod and push toward answers to the central questions of emotional experience. What are the sources of hate and compassion? Should a person extend her compassion to a torturer? What does science reveal about the benefits of Buddhist meditation? As they come to grips with these issues, they invite us to join them in an unfiltered view of two great traditions and two great minds.

Emotional Awareness: Overcoming the Obstacles to Psychological Balance & Compassion. abr. unabr. ed. Dalai Lama XIV & Paul Ekman. Read by Richard Gere. 6 CDs. (Running Time: 10 hrs. 0 mins. 0 sec.). 2008. audio compact disk 39.95 (978-1-4272-0522-3(1)) Pub: Macmill Audio. Dist(s): Macmillan

Emotional Body & the Beginnings of Social Consciousness. Manly P. Hall. 1 cass. 8.95 (978-0-89314-104-2(6), C890507) Philos Res.

***Emotional Calendar: Understanding Seasonal Influences & Milestones to Become Happier, More Fulfilled, & in Control of Your Life.** unabr. ed. John R. Sharp & John Butman. (Running Time: 8 hrs. 30 mins.). 2011. 15.99 (978-1-4526-7050-8(1)); 19.99 (978-1-4526-5050-0(0)); audio compact disk 29.99 (978-1-4526-0050-5(3)) Pub: Tantor Media. Dist(s): IngramPubServ

***Emotional Calendar (Library Edition) Understanding Seasonal Influences & Milestones to Become Happier, More Fulfilled, & in Control of Your Life.** unabr. ed. John R. Sharp & John Butman. (Running Time: 8 hrs. 30 mins.). 2011. 29.99 (978-1-4526-2050-3(4)); audio compact disk 71.99 (978-1-4526-3050-2(X)) Pub: Tantor Media. Dist(s): IngramPubServ

Emotional Confidence: Know How Your Feelings Work So You Can Tame Your Temperment. Gael Lindenfield. 1 cass. 1998. (978-0-7225-9911-2(0), HarperThor) HarpC GBR.

Emotional Control for Busy People. Bob Griswold. Read by Deirdre M. Griswold. 2000. 11.98 (978-1-55848-214-2(8)) EffectiveMN.

Emotional First Aid Kit for Mothers. Linda Eyre. 2 cass. 1998. 14.95 Set. (978-1-57008-433-1(5), Bkcraft Inc) Deseret Bk.

Emotional Fitness - Basic Assertive Training, Set. Arynne Simon. 4 cass. 1995. bk. 59.95 (978-1-882389-12-4(3)) Wilarvi Communs.
Learn to develop a new set of 'emotional muscles.'.

Emotional Freedom: Liberate Yourself from Negative Emotions & Transform Your Life. abr. ed. Judith Orloff. Read by Judith Orloff. (ENG.). 2009. audio compact disk 19.95 (978-0-7393-5794-1(8), Random AudioBks) Pub: Random Audio Pubg. Dist(s): Random

Emotional Freedom Practices: How to Transform Difficult Emotions into Positive Energy. Judith Orloff. (Running Time: 2:00:00). 2009. audio compact disk 19.95 (978-1-59179-763-0(2)) Sounds True.

Emotional Healing. Jean Munzer. 2 cass. (Running Time: 2 hrs. 30 min.). 1994. 19.95 set. (978-1-57124-014-9(4)) Creat Seminars.
Healing from within.

Emotional Impact of Adoption. Hosted by Mardie Caldwell. (ENG.). 2008. audio compact disk 12.95 (978-1-935176-04-6(8)) Pub: Am Carrage Hse Pubng. Dist(s): STL Dist NA

***Emotional Intelligence: The Keys to Working Effectively with Others.** Puei. (ENG.). 2010. audio compact disk 199.95 (978-1-60959-000-0(7)) P Univ E Inc.

Emotional Intelligence: Why It Can Matter More Than IQ. abr. rev. ed. Daniel Goleman. Read by Daniel Goleman. 3 CDs. (Running Time: 3 hrs. 0 mins. 0 sec.). (ENG.). 2001. audio compact disk 26.00 (978-1-55927-642-9(8)) Pub: Macmill Audio. Dist(s): Macmillan

Emotional Intelligence: Why It Can Matter More Than IQ. unabr. ed. Daniel Goleman. Read by Barrett Whitener. 9 cass. (Running Time: 13 hrs. 30 min.). 1996. 72.00 (978-0-913369-17-3(9), 4055) Books on Tape.
How should we define intelligence? For years, we've looked to the I.Q. test. That's too narrow, says Daniel Goleman, a Harvard Ph.D. & former senior editor of "Psychology Today." He proposes a new standard, based on years of research: Emotional Intelligence.

Emotional Intelligence: Why It Can Matter More Than IQ. 10th anniv. unabr. ed. Daniel Goleman. Read by Daniel Goleman. Read by Barrett Whitener. Contrib. by Jon Kabat-Zinn. 11 CDs. (Running Time: 13 hrs. 30 mins. 0 sec.). (ENG.). 2005. audio compact disk 44.95 (978-1-59397-780-1(8)) Pub: Macmill Audio. Dist(s): Macmillan

Emotional Intelligence Set: Traits of Emotionally Mature Relationships. David Grudermeyer & Rebecca Grudermeyer. 2 cass. 18.95 INCL. HANDOUTS. (T-49) Willingness Wrks.

Emotional Intelligence Quick Book: Everything You Need to Know to Put Your EQ to Work. unabr. ed. Travis Bradberry & Jean Greaves. Read by Thom Pinto. Frwd. by Patrick Lencioni. (Running Time: 3 hrs. 0 mins. 0 sec.). (ENG.). 2007. audio compact disk 19.95 (978-1-4272-0094-5(7)) Pub: Macmill Audio. Dist(s): Macmillan

***Emotional Intelligence 2. 0.** unabr. ed. Jean Greaves. Read by Travis Bradberry & Tom Parks. (Running Time: 4 hrs.). 2010. 39.97 (978-1-4418-4228-2(4), 9781441842282, BADLE) Brilliance Audio.

***Emotional Intelligence 2. 0.** unabr. ed. Jean Greaves. Read by Travis Bradberry & Tom Parks. (Running Time: 4 hrs.). 2010. 19.99 (978-1-4418-4227-5(6), 9781441842275, BAD) Brilliance Audio.

***Emotional Intelligence 2.0.** unabr. ed. Jean Greaves. Read by Travis Bradberry & Tom Parks. 1 MP3-CD. (Running Time: 4 hrs.). 2010. 39.97 (978-1-4418-4226-8(8), 9781441842268, Brinc Audio MP3 Lib); 19.99 (978-1-4418-4225-1(X), 9781441842251, Brilliance MP3); audio compact disk 59.97 (978-1-4418-4224-4(1), 9781441842244, BriAudCD Unabrid); audio compact disk 19.99 (978-1-4418-4223-7(3), 9781441842237, Bril Audio CD Unabri) Brilliance Audio.

Emotional Literacy Hour: Teaching for Achievement in Bristol Schools. rev. ed. Ed. by Barbara Maines et al. 2000. 35.95 (978-1-873942-87-1(7)) Pub: P Chapman GBR. Dist(s): SAGE

Emotional Mastery: With Optimal Thinking. unabr. ed. Rosalene Glickman. (Running Time: 45 mins.). (ENG.). 2009. 6.95 (978-1-59659-480-7(2), GildAudio) Pub: Gildan Media. Dist(s): HachBkGrp

Emotional Patterns in Pediatrics. Paul Derrickson. 1986. 10.80 (0312) Assn Prof Chaplains.

Emotional Repression. unabr. ed. Nathaniel Branden. 1 cass. (Running Time: 1 hr. 5 min.). 12.95 (611) J Norton Pubs.
The nature & causes of repression; the symptoms of repression in a romantic relationship.

Emotional Security. Doris C. Doane. 1 cass. 8.95 (087) Am Fed Astrologers.

Emotional Self-Control. unabr. ed. Judith L. Powell. Read by Judith L. Powell. 1 cass. (Running Time: 40 min.). (Successful Living Ser.). 1987. pap. bk. 12.95 (978-0-914295-28-0(4), 28-4) Top Mtn Pub.
Side A presents exercises designed to provide self-control by controlling negative mood swings & avoiding unjustified anger. Side B presents subliminal emotions suggestions hidden in New Age Music.

Emotional Stress. Manly P. Hall. 1 cass. 8.95 (978-0-89314-471-5(1), C900805) Philos Res.

***Emotionally Healthy Church: A Strategy for Discipleship That Actually Changes Lives.** Peter Scazzero. Told to Warren Bird. (Running Time: 7 hrs. 43 mins. 0 sec.). (ENG.). 2008. 17.99 (978-0-310-30440-1(7)) Zondervan.

Emotionally Weird. unabr. ed. Kate Atkinson. Read by Kara Wilson. 10 cass. (Running Time: 15 hrs.). 2000. 84.95 (978-0-7540-0546-9(1), CAB 1969) Pub: Chivers Audio Bks GBR. Dist(s): AudioGO
On an island off the west coast of Scotland, Effie & her mother Nora take refuge in the large house of their ancestors & tell each other stories.

Emotionally Weird. unabr. ed. Kate Atkinson. Read by Kara Wilson. 10 CDs. (Running Time: 15 hrs.). 2001. audio compact disk 94.95 (978-0-7540-5395-8(4), CCD086) Pub: Chivers Audio Bks GBR. Dist(s): AudioGO

Emotions. Timmothy B. McCann. Narrated by Kevin R. Free. 6 cass. (Running Time: 8 hrs.). 56.00 (978-0-7887-9966-2(5)) Recorded Bks.

Emotions. unabr. ed. Timmothy B. McCann. Narrated by Kevin R. Free. 7 CDs. (Running Time: 8 hrs.). 2004. audio compact disk 69.00 (978-1-4025-2471-4(4)) Recorded Bks.
Emotions follows Joi Weston as she faces the crisis of her life. Should she continue to stay in a marriage gone stale, or taste the passion that a vibrant, sensual writer stirs in her?.

Emotions: Messengers from Inner Space. Created by Louise LeBrun. (Women & Power Ser.: Vol. 5). 1999. 10.95 (978-0-9685566-4-1(7)) Par3tners Renewal CAN.

Emotions: Program from the Award Winning Public Radio Series. Interview. Hosted by Fred Goodwim. 1 CD. (Running Time: 1 hr.). 2000. audio compact disk 21.95 (978-1-932479-44-7(9), LCM 114) Lichtenstein Creat.
Emotions are an integral part of being human. But what makes us happy, sad, or angry? What can science tell us about what happens in the brain when we experience emotion? In this program, we talk about the science of emotions. Guests include: Dr. Antonio Damasio, head of the Department of Neurology at the University of Iowa, and the author of The Feeling of What Happens: Body, Emotion, and the Making of Consciousness published by Harcourt Brace; Candace Pert, research professor in the department of physiology at Georgetown University Medical School, and the author of Molecules of Emotion, published by Simon & Schuster; Jack Katz, professor of sociology at UCLA, and the author of How Emotions Work, published by the University of Chicago Press; and Dempsey Rice, a producer for The Infinite Mind and producer/director of the HBO documentary film Daughter of Suicide. Plus, actors from the Classic Stage Company's recent production of Naked.

Emotions As Signals. Michael P. Marshall. Read by Michael P. Marshall. Ed. by Jonathan C. Renaud. Music by Ted Crook. 1 cass. (Running Time: 52 min.). 1995. 9.00 (978-0-912403-08-3(X)) Prod Renaud.
Emotions are more than they appear. They are keys to our deepest understanding of selves & others.

Emotions As Tools of Cognition. unabr. ed. Barbara Branden. 1 cass. (Running Time: 1 hr. 41 min.). (Principles of Efficient Thinking Ser.). 12.95 (706) J Norton Pubs.
The manner in which wishes & fears can distort the thinking process; emotional-perceptual thinking, its nature, causes, mechanism & consequences.

Empathizing. abr. ed. Robert A. Monroe. Read by Robert A. Monroe. (Running Time: 30 min.). (Human Plus Ser.). 1989. 14.95 (978-1-56102-012-6(5)) Inter Indus.
Perceive & respond to emotional, mental & physical states of others.

Empathy Gap: Building Bridges to the Good Life & the Good Society. unabr. ed. J. D. Trout. Read by J. D. Trout. (Running Time: 9 hrs.). 2009. 39.97 (978-1-4233-7681-1(1), 9781423376811, BADLE); 39.97 (978-1-4233-7679-8(X), 9781423376798, Brinc Audio MP3 Lib); 24.99 (978-1-4233-7680-4(3), 9781423376804, BAD); 24.99 (978-1-4233-7678-1(1), 9781423376781, Brilliance MP3); audio compact disk 82.97 (978-1-4233-7677-4(3), 9781423376774, BriAudCD Unabrid); audio compact disk 29.99 (978-1-4233-7676-7(5), 9781423376767, Bril Audio CD Unabri) Brilliance Audio.

Empathy in Priestly Ministry. Patrick Collins. 3 cass. (Running Time: 4 hrs. 7 min.). 1999. 29.95 (TAH416) Alba Hse Comns.
Looks at the nature, degrees, effects & typical blocks to empathy while indicating how to become more empathetic.

Emperor, unabr. ed. Short Stories. Frederick Forsyth. Narrated by Frank Muller. 3 cass. (Running Time: 4 hrs. 30 mins.). 1984. 26.00 (978-1-55690-166-9(6), 84062E7) Recorded Bks.
A bank manager finds there is more to life in an exhausting struggle with a giant fish.

Emperor & the Nightingale. 1 cass. (J). 1989. bk. 14.00 Windham Hill.

Emperor Julian's Oration on the Mother of the Gods. Manly P. Hall. 1 cass. 8.95 Philos Res.

Emperor Mage. unabr. ed. Tamora Pierce. Narrated by Tamora Pierce. 8 CDs. (Running Time: 7 hrs. 45 mins.). (Immortals Ser.: No. 3). (J). (gr. 7). 2008. audio compact disk 55.00 (978-1-934180-20-4(3)) Full Cast Audio.

Emperor Norton's Ghost, unabr. ed. Dianne Day. Read by Anna Fields. 7 cass. (Running Time: 10 hrs. 30 min.). (Fremont Jones Mystery Ser.). 1999. 56.00 (978-0-7366-4505-8(5), 4920) Books on Tape.
Two years after the Great Earthquake that destroyed San Francisco, Fremont Jones & Michael Archer are back in the City by the Bay, committed to being "partners in life & work." Their life is shared as equals & their work is the private investigations agency they have opened together. It's Fremont's friendship with a flighty, troubled young woman that gets her involved in her first murder investigation. When two well-known mediums are murdered, Fremont finds herself in the thick of the investigation & dangerously embroiled in her friend's illicit affair.

***Emperor of All Maladies: A Biography of Cancer.** unabr. ed. Siddhartha Mukherjee. (Running Time: 20 hrs. 0 mins.). 2010. 23.99 (978-1-4001-8917-5(9)); 34.99 (978-1-4001-6917-7(8)); audio compact disk 119.99 (978-1-4001-4917-9(7)) Pub: Tantor Media. Dist(s): IngramPubServ

***Emperor of All Maladies: A Biography of Cancer.** unabr. ed. Siddhartha Mukherjee. Narrated by Stephen Hoye. (Running Time: 20 hrs. 0 mins. 0 sec.). (ENG.). 2010. audio compact disk 49.99 (978-1-4001-1917-2(0)) Pub: Tantor Media. Dist(s): IngramPubServ

***Emperor of All Maladies (Library Edition) A Biography of Cancer.** unabr. ed. Siddhartha Mukherjee. (Running Time: 20 hrs. 0 mins.). 2010. 49.99 (978-1-4001-9917-4(4)) Tantor Media.

***Emperor of Nihon-Ja.** John Flanagan. Contrib. by John Keating. (Ranger's Apprentice Ser.: Bk. 10). (ENG.). 2011. audio compact disk 39.95 (978-0-14-242896-2(5), PengAudBks) Penguin Grp USA.

Emperor of Ocean Park. abr. ed. Stephen L. Carter. Read by Peter Francis James. (Running Time: 6 hrs.). (ENG.). 2007. audio compact disk 19.99 (978-0-7393-4374-6(2), Random AudioBks) Pub: Random Audio Pubg. Dist(s): Random

Emperor of Ocean Park. unabr. ed. Stephen L. Carter. 20 CDs. (Running Time: 30 hrs.). 2002. audio compact disk 160.00 (978-0-7366-8646-4(0)) Books on Tape.
The sudden death of a black former Supreme Court nominee leads to a murder investigation set in the upper-crust East Coast legal community.

Emperor of Ocean Park, Pt. 1. unabr. ed. Stephen L. Carter. 10 cass. (Running Time: 15 hrs.). 2002. 80.00 (978-0-7366-8645-7(2)) Books on Tape.
Donald Wolfe, a young lawyer, arrives in New York City. Idealistic and ambitious, he marries Lillian out of infatuation and little else. Their marriage is shaky, but they have a child, Tina, and for her, Donald would give up everything. When his flawed marriage begins to fail, he must consider a step that would force him into flight and a life of hiding. Tina develops into an exceptional young woman, who at university falls in love with the lawyer Gilbert. Together, they go to New York, where she learns the truth about her family's past - a truth that must change her regard for the father who has protected and cherished her.

Emperor of Ocean Park, Pt. 2. unabr. ed. Stephen L. Carter. 2002. 80.00 (978-0-7366-8740-9(8)) Books on Tape.
The sudden death of a black former Supreme Court nominee leads to a murder investigation set in the upper-crust East Coast legal community.

Emperors & Idiots: The Hundred-Year Rivalry Between the Yankees & Red Sox. unabr. ed. Mike Vaccaro. Read by Scott Brick. 7 CDs. (Running Time: 13 hrs. 30 mins.). 2005. audio compact disk 63.00 (978-1-4159-1680-3(2)); 54.00 (978-1-4159-1596-7(2)) Books on Tape.
Vaccaro weaves together the various strands of the Red Sox-Yankees rivalry from 1903 through the seven games of the American League Championship Series in 2004 in masterful fashion. Some strands are repeated and nuanced to emphasize their interrelationships in this drama of day-in/day-out, in-season and off-season competition and individual and team mutual hatred society.

Emperor's Children. Claire Messud. Read by Suzanne Toren. (Running Time: 67500 sec.). 2006. audio compact disk 39.99 (978-1-4193-9803-2(2)) Recorded Bks.

Emperor's Clothes. Reuven Doron. 1 cass. (Running Time: 90 mins.). (Back to the Garden Ser.: Vol. 1). 2000. 5.00 (RD05-001) Morning NC.
The message presented in this series will woo you back to the intimacy & innocence of the Garden.

Emperor's Last Island. unabr. ed. Julia Blackburn. Read by Nadia May. 6 cass. (Running Time: 8 hrs. 30 mins.). 1995. 44.95 Set. (978-0-7861-0711-7(1), 1588) Blckstn Audio.
In October 1814 Napoleon Bonaparte arrived on St. Helena & began the melancholy & surreal exile that would last until his death six years later. The story of a deposed emperor holding court amid the shabbiness & paranoia of an island prison would be fascinating enough. But Julia Blackburn interweaves it with a history of St. Helena itself & with an intensely personal account of her own voyage in search of Napoleon's ghost.

Emperor's New Clothes see Favorite Children's Stories: A Collection

Emperor's New Clothes see Storytime Favorites

Emperor's New Clothes see Favorite Tales by Hans Christian Andersen

Emperor's New Clothes. 1 cass. (J). 12.95 (SASH001) S&S Audio.

Emperor's New Clothes. 2004. bk. 24.95 (978-0-89719-772-4(0)); 8.95 (978-0-7882-0076-2(3)); cass. & flmstrp 30.00 (978-0-89719-573-7(6)) Weston Woods.

Emperor's New Clothes. Scripts. Hans Christian Andersen. 1 cass. or 1 CD. (Running Time: 20 mins.). (J). (gr. 2-6). 2000. pap. bk. & tchr. ed. 29.95 Bad Wolf Pr.
The Emperor thinks he needs a new outfit & the Crooks have just the thing in mind! But will the Emperor catch on to their scheme before he embarrasses himself at the big Harvest Day Parade? Sheet music available.

Emperor's New Clothes. unabr. ed. Read by Julie Harris. Based on a story by Hans Christian Andersen. 1 read-along cass. (Running Time: 15 min.). (World of Words Ser.). (J). (gr. k-3). bk. 15.00 (SAC 6500J) Spoken Arts.
Jullie Harris reads the famous tale of the bamboozling tailors-page turn bell tones.

Emperor's New Clothes: An All-Star Retelling of the Classic Fairy Tale. Hans Christian Andersen. Perf. by Liam Neeson et al. Prod. by Steven Spielberg. 1 cass. (Running Time: 1 hr.). 2001. 12.95 Lodestone Catalog.
Kids will love it & adults will find an extra level of brilliant satire.

Emperor's New Clothes: Listening. Dave Perry & Jean Perry. (ENG.). 2002. audio compact disk 12.95 (978-0-7390-2258-0(X)) Alfred Pub.

Emperor's New Clothes: SoundTrax. Dave Perry & Jean Perry. (ENG.). 2002. audio compact disk 59.95 (978-0-7390-2257-3(1)) Alfred Pub.

***Emperor's New Clothes: The Graphic Novel.** Hans Christian Andersen. Illus. by Jeffrey Stewart Timmins. Retold by Stephanie True Peters. (Graphic Spin Ser.). (ENG.). 2010. audio compact disk 14.60 (978-1-4342-2579-5(8)) CapstoneDig.

Emperor's New Clothes & Other Tales. unabr. ed. Hans Christian Andersen. Read by Michael Redgrave. Tr. by R. P. Keigwin. 1 cass. (Running Time: 56 min.). Incl. Emperor's Nightingale. Based on a story by Hans Christian Andersen. (J). (ps-3). 1989. (CPN 1073); Steadfast Tin Soldier. Based on a story by Hans Christian Andersen. (J). (ps-3). 1989. (CPN 1073); Tinder-Box. Based on a story by Hans Christian Andersen. (J). (ps-3). 1989. (CPN 1073); (J). (ps-3). 1989. 9.95 (978-0-89845-863-3(3), CPN 1073) HarperCollins Pubs.

Emperor's New Clothes & The Princess & the Pea. Hans Christian Andersen. (J). 1988. bk. 20.00 (978-0-394-07801-4(2)) SRA McGraw.

Emperor's New Clothes & The Twelve Dancing Princesses. unabr. ed. Perf. by Elaine Stritch et al. Based on a story by Hans Christian Andersen. 2 cass. (Running Time: 1 hr. 30 min.). (J). 2001. 14.95 (978-1-885608-00-0(4)) Airplay.
Two fully produced radio plays based on the original children's classics.

Emperor's New Clothes Collection. Narrated by Margot Kidder. (Running Time: 1 hr.). 2006. 14.95 (978-1-60083-004-4(8)) Iofy Corp.

Emperor's New Groove. unabr. ed. 1 cass. (Running Time: 1 hr. 30 mins.). (J). 2000. pap. bk. 9.98 (978-0-7634-0710-0(0)) W Disney Records.

Emperor's New Mind: Concerning Computers, Minds & the Laws of Physics. abr. ed. Rosen Penrose. Read by Michael Jackson. 4 cass. (Running Time: 6 hrs.). 2004. 25.00 (978-1-931056-78-6(1), N Millennium Audio) New Millenn Enter.
Physicist Roger Penrose's 1989 treastise attacks the foundations of strong artificial intelligence & is crucial listening for anyone interested in the history of thinking about AI & consciousness. Part survey of modern physics, part explorations of the philosophy of mind, this audio is not for the casually interested. Though it's not overly technical, it's pace is quick. This overview of relativity & quantum theory, written by a master, is priceless & uncontroversial.

Emperor's Nightingale see Emperor's New Clothes & Other Tales

Emperors of Rome. Instructed by Garrett G. Fagan. 79.95 (978-1-59803-312-0(3)) Teaching Co.

Emperors of Rome. Instructed by Garrett G. Fagan. 2007. audio compact disk 99.95 (978-1-59803-313-7(1)) Teaching Co.

Emperors of the Ice: A True Story of Disaster & Survival in the Antarctic, 1910-13. unabr. ed. Richard Farr. Read by Michael Page. 1 MP3-CD. (Running Time: 5 hrs.). 2009. 39.97 (978-1-4233-8239-3(0), 9781423382393, Brlnc Audio MP3 Lib); 24.99 (978-1-4233-8238-6(2), 9781423382386, Brilliance MP3); 39.97 (978-1-4233-8241-6(2), 9781423382416, BADLE); 24.99 (978-1-4233-8240-9(4), 9781423382409, BAD); audio compact disk 24.99 (978-1-4233-8236-2(6), 9781423382362, Bril Audio CD Unabri); audio compact disk 48.97 (978-1-4233-8237-9(4), 9781423382379, BriAudCD Unabrid) Brilliance Audio.

Emperor's Pearl. unabr. ed. Robert H. Van Gulik. Narrated by Frank Muller. 3 cass. (Running Time: 4 hrs. 45 mins.). (Judge Dee Mysteries Ser.). 1986. 26.00 (978-1-55690-167-6(4), 86870E7) Recorded Bks.
A member of the dragonboat crew is murdered on festival night. As Judge Dee attempts to solve the crime, he is thrown back into time & the century-old theft of the legendary Emperor's Pearl.

Emperor's Teacup: And More Tales from near & Far. abr. ed. Dembar Greene. Illus. by April Hartmann. (Rigby Literacy Ser.). 2001. audio compact disk 10.40 (978-0-7578-2046-5(8), Rigby PEA) Pearson EdAUS AUS.

***Emperor's Tomb.** abr. ed. Steve Berry. Read by Scott Brick. (ENG.). 2010. audio compact disk 32.00 (978-0-7393-2920-7(0), Random AudioBks) Pub: Random Audio Pubg. Dist(s): Random

***Emperor's Tomb.** unabr. ed. Steve Berry. Read by Scott Brick. (ENG.). 2010. audio compact disk 50.00 (978-0-7393-2922-1(7), Random AudioBks) Pub: Random Audio Pubg. Dist(s): Random

Empieza a Tocar: Armonica. (SPA.). 2004. pap. bk. 12.95 (978-0-8256-2951-8(9), AM978197, Schirmer Trade Bks) Pub: Music Sales. Dist(s): H Leonard

Empieza a Tocar: Bajo. (SPA.). 2004. pap. bk. 12.95 (978-0-8256-2898-6(9), AM978208, Schirmer Trade Bks) Pub: Music Sales. Dist(s): H Leonard

Empieza a Tocar: Bateria. (SPA.). 2004. pap. bk. 12.95 (978-0-8256-2899-3(7), AM978219, Schirmer Trade Bks) Pub: Music Sales. Dist(s): H Leonard

Empieza a Tocar: Guitarra. (SPA.). 2004. pap. bk. 12.95 (978-0-8256-2896-2(2), AM978692, Schirmer Trade Bks) Pub: Music Sales. Dist(s): H Leonard

Empieza a Tocar: Saxofon Alto. (SPA.). 2004. pap. bk. 12.95 (978-0-8256-2950-1(0), AM978230, Schirmer Trade Bks) Pub: Music Sales. Dist(s): H Leonard

Empieza a Tocar: Teclado. (SPA.). 2004. pap. bk. 12.95 (978-0-8256-2897-9(0), AM978241, Schirmer Trade Bks) Pub: Music Sales. Dist(s): H Leonard

Empire. unabr. ed. Donaldl L. Barlett & James B. Steele. Read by Christopher Hurt. (Running Time: 30 hrs. 30 mins.). 1998. audio compact disk 160.00 (978-0-7861-7726-4(8)) Blckstn Audio.

Empire. unabr. ed. Orson Scott Card. Narrated by Stefan Rudnicki. 8 CDs. (Running Time: 10 hrs.). (Empire Ser.: No. 1). 2006. audio compact disk 79.95 (978-0-7927-4377-4(6), SLD 1001) AudioGO.

Empire. unabr. ed. Orson Scott Card. Read by Orson Scott Card. Read by Stefan Rudnicki. 1 MP3-CD. (Running Time: 40680 sec.). (Empire Ser.: No. 1). 2006. audio compact disk 49.95 (978-0-7927-4576-1(0), CMP 1001) AudioGO.

Empire. unabr. ed. Orson Scott Card. Read by Stefan Rudnicki. 9 CDs. (Running Time: 11 hrs. 0 mins. 0 sec.). No. 1. (ENG.). 2006. audio compact disk 39.95 (978-1-59397-980-5(0)) Pub: Macmill Audio. Dist(s): Macmillan

Empire. unabr. ed. Gore Vidal. Read by Grover Gardner. 14 cass. (Running Time: 21 hrs.). (American Chronicles Ser.: Vol. 3). 1993. 112.00 (978-0-7366-2471-8(6), 3234) Books on Tape.
Turn-of-the-century American newspaperwoman struggles to control her destiny.

Empire: The Life, Legend, & Madness of Howard Hughes. abr. ed. Donald L. Barlett & James B. Steele. Read by Christopher Hurt. 1 MP3. (Running Time: 32400 sec.). 2005. audio compact disk 29.95 (978-0-7861-8061-5(7)) Blckstn Audio.

Empire: The Life, Legend, & Madness of Howard Hughes. abr. ed. James B. Steele & Donald L. Barlett. Read by Christopher Hurt. 7 cass. (Running Time: 32400 sec.). 2005. 29.95 (978-0-7861-3504-2(2)); audio compact disk 29.95 (978-0-7861-7847-6(7)) Blckstn Audio.

Empire: The Life, Legend & Madness of Howard Hughes. unabr. ed. Donald L. Barlett & James B. Steele. Read by Christopher Hurt. 2 MP3. (Running Time: 102600 sec.). 2005. audio compact disk 44.95 (978-0-7861-8106-3(0), ZM1384) Blckstn Audio.

***Empire: The Novel of Imperial Rome.** unabr. ed. Steven Saylor. Read by James Langton. (Running Time: 24 hrs. 0 mins. 0 sec.). (Novels of Ancient Rome Ser.). (ENG.). 2010. audio compact disk 69.99 (978-1-4272-1091-3(8)) Pub: Macmill Audio. Dist(s): Macmillan

Empire: The Rise & Demise of the British World Order & the Lessons for Global Power. Niall Ferguson. Read by Sean Barrett. 14 vols. 2004. pap. bk. 110.95 (978-0-7927-3203-7(0), CSL 650, Chivers Sound Lib); pap. bk. 115.95 (978-0-7927-3204-4(9), SLD 650, Chivers Sound Lib) AudioGO.

Empire Part II: The Life, Legend & Madness of Howard Hughes. unabr. ed. Donald L. Barlett & James B. Steele. 11 cass. (Running Time: 30 hrs. 30 mins.). 1994. 76.95 (978-0-7861-0736-0(7), 1384A, B) Blckstn Audio.
Howard Hughes had always been different. Raised by overprotective parents, pathologically fearful of germs, in awe of his father, unable to make friends, he grew into a man ruled by madness. Orphaned & a millionaire at eighteen, Hughes repudiated his relatives, seized control of the Hughes Tool Company & went on to become a movie producer, accomplished pilot, owner of TWA, a key defense contractor, Hollywood's most pursued bachelor & partner of the U.S. government. This is an epic biography of an epic figure.

Empire Pt. I: The Life, Legend & Madness of Howard Hughes. unabr. ed. Donald L. Barlett & James B. Steele. Read by Christopher Hurt. 10 cass. (Running Time: 30 hrs. 30 mins.). 1994. 69.95 (978-0-7861-0432-1(5), 1384A, B) Blckstn Audio.

Empire Brass on Broadway. Perf. by Empire Brass Quintet. 1 cass., 1 CD. 7.98 (TA 30303); audio compact disk 12.78 CD Jewel box. (TA 80303) NewSound.

Empire Builders. unabr. ed. Ben Bova. Read by Stefan Rudnicki. (Running Time: 14 hrs. 0 mins.). 2010. 29.95 (978-1-4332-2953-4(6)); 79.95 (978-1-4332-2949-7(8)); audio compact disk 118.00 (978-1-4332-2950-3(1)) Blckstn Audio.

Empire Falls. Richard Russo. Narrated by Ron McLarty. 18 CDs. (Running Time: 21 hrs.). audio compact disk 166.00 (978-1-4025-3487-4(6)) Recorded Bks.

***Empire Falls.** abr. ed. Richard Russo. Read by Ron Mclarty. (ENG.). 2005. (978-0-06-085019-7(1), Harper Audio); (978-0-06-085018-0(3), Harper Audio) HarperCollins Pubs.

Empire Falls. unabr. ed. Richard Russo. Narrated by Ron McLarty. 15 cass. (Running Time: 21 hrs.). 2001. 122.00 (978-0-7887-8928-1(7)) Recorded Bks.
Once a prosperous mill town, Empire Falls has been on a steady decline since its factories closed. Miles Roby dreams of escape, but life has conspired to keep him in the small, dying town. The diner Miles runs, like the majority of the town, is owned by Mrs. Whiting, a vindictive widow. After years of tolerating her controlling ways, Miles looks into the past to find out why she has such an interest in his life. As he faces an impending divorce, a failing business, and the resurrection of long buried secrets, he discovers the joy of raising his teenage daughter offsets it all.

Empire Falls. unabr. ed. Richard Russo. Read by Ron McLarty. 10 cass. (Running Time: 14 hrs.). 2001. 42.95 (978-0-694-52559-1(6), Harper Audio) HarperCollins Pubs.

Empire of Blue Water: Captain Morgan's Great Pirate Army, the Epic Battle for the Americas, & the Catastrophe That Ended the Outlaws' Bloody Reign. abr. ed. Stephan Talty. Read by John H. Mayer. (Running Time: 23400 sec.). (ENG.). 2007. audio compact disk 29.95 (978-0-7393-4165-0(0), Random AudioBks) Pub: Random Audio Pubg. Dist(s): Random

Empire of Bones: A Novel of Sam Houston & the Texas Revolution. unabr. ed. Jeff Long. Narrated by George Guidall. 7 cass. (Running Time: 10 hrs.). 1993. 60.00 (978-1-55690-909-2(8), 93405E7) Recorded Bks.
Fictional account of the Battle of San Jacinto, April 21, 1836, in which Sam Houston & his Texans defeated Santa Anna & the Mexican Army.

Empire of Egypt. Compiled by Benchmark Education Staff. 2005. audio compact disk 10.00 (978-1-4108-5476-6(0)) Benchmark Educ.

Empire of Lies. abr. ed. Andrew Klavan. (Running Time: 6 hrs.). 2008. audio compact disk 14.99 (978-1-4233-1296-3(1), 9781423312963, BCD Value Price) Brilliance Audio.

Empire of Lies. unabr. ed. Andrew Klavan. Read by Andrew Klavan. 1 MP3-CD. (Running Time: 11 hrs.). (Weiss & Bishop Ser.). 2008. 24.95 (978-1-4233-1291-8(0), 9781423312918, Brilliance MP3); 39.25 (978-1-4233-1292-5(9), 9781423312925, Brlnc Audio MP3 Lib); 39.25 (978-1-4233-1294-9(5), 9781423312949, BADLE); 24.95 (978-1-4233-1293-2(7), 9781423312932, BAD); audio compact disk 34.95 (978-1-4233-1289-5(9), 9781423312895, Bril Audio CD Unabri); audio compact disk 92.25 (978-1-4233-1290-1(2), 9781423312901, BriAudCD Unabrid) Brilliance Audio.

Empire of Sun. Peggy Ballard. 2004. 8.95 (978-0-7435-4685-0(7)) Pub: S&S Audio. Dist(s): S and S Inc

Empire of the Air: The Men Who Made Radio. Tom Lewis. Perf. by Steve Allen. Adapted by David Ossman. 1 cass. (Running Time: 90 min.). 1996. 12.95 (978-1-57677-050-4(8), OWME005) Lodestone Catalog.
This brilliant adaptation tells the story of the visionaries who turned a hobbyists' toy into Radio, a whole broadcasting industry & launched the modern communications age. The story traces the lives of Lee DeForest, a poor clergyman's flamboyant son; Edwin Howard Armstrong, a reclusive genius; & David Sarnoff, the immigrant who rose from delivery boy to head of RCA.

Empire of the Air - Audio Documentary. Adapted by David Ossman. Directed By David Ossman. 2 CDs. (Running Time: 90 mins.). Dramatization. 2004. audio compact disk 19.95 (978-1-59938-044-5(7)) Lode Cat.

Empire of the Czar. Marquis Decustine. 17 cass. (Running Time: 25.5 hrs.). 2001. 64.00 (978-0-7366-6721-0(0)); 72.00 (978-0-7366-6722-7(9)) Books on Tape.

Empire of the East. Fred Saberhagen. Read by Raymond Todd. (Running Time: 66600 sec.). 2005. cass., cass., DVD 95.95 (978-0-7861-3497-7(6));

DVD & audio compact disk 44.95 (978-0-7861-8066-0(8)); DVD, audio compact disk, audio compact disk 120.00 (978-0-7861-7883-4(3)) Blckstn Audio.

Empire of the East. Fred Saberhagen. Narrated by Raymond Todd. (Running Time: 18 hrs. 30 mins.). 2005. 48.95 (978-1-59912-484-1(X)) Iofy Corp.

Empire of the Song: Victorian Songs & Music. Olivia Bailey. 2004. audio compact disk 14.99 (978-1-84067-468-2(7)) Pub: Caxton Editions GBR. Dist(s): Bk Sales Inc

***Empire of the Summer Moon: Quanah Parker & the Rise & Fall of the Comanches, the Most Powerful Indian Tribe in American History.** unabr. ed. S. C. Gwynne. Narrated by David Drummond. (Running Time: 15 hrs. 0 mins.). 2010. 39.99 (978-1-4001-9655-5(8)); 29.99 (978-1-4001-6655-8(1)); 20.99 (978-1-4001-8655-6(2)); audio compact disk 79.99 (978-1-4001-4655-0(0)); audio compact disk 39.99 (978-1-4001-1655-3(4)) Pub: Tantor Media. Dist(s): IngramPubServ

Empire of the Sun. unabr. ed. J. G. Ballard. Read by David Case. 8 cass. (Running Time: 12 hrs.). 1996. 64.00 (978-0-7366-3319-2(7), 3971) Books on Tape.
For a child, living in a foreign country - with its strange customs & a mysterious language - is tough enough. But now add to this the horror of losing your parents in a war zone & spending three years in a prison camp.

Empire of the Sun. unabr. ed. J. G. Ballard. Read by Peter Egan. 8 cass. (Running Time: 12 hrs.). 2001. 59.95 (978-0-7451-5767-2(X), CAB 152) Pub: Chivers Audio Bks GBR. Dist(s): AudioGO
Japan invaded China in 1937 and for Jim, 11 years old, British and born and raised in Shanghai, this was the real war. Then came the Japanese attack on Pearl Harbor, followed by the sinking of British and American ships anchored in the Yangtze harbor. Separated from his parents, Jim is taken to the camps. For the next four years this will be his home. The horrors of war are seen through the eyes of Jim, to whom they become a normal way of life.

Empire of Their Own: How the Jews Invented Hollywood. unabr. collector's ed. Neal Gabler. Read by Richard Brown. 14 cass. (Running Time: 21 hrs.). 1991. 112.00 (978-0-7366-2003-1(6), 2820) Books on Tape.
Adolph Zukor, Louis B. Mayer, the brothers Warner, Carl Laemmle, Harry Cohn - these men created not only Hollywood but also what might be called the great American myth. (It's alive & well today). What these empire builders had in common was their origins...East European & Russian Jewish. But borscht & bagels didn't sell. What did was cowboys & Indians, the frontier, virile men & chaste women, red-blooded two-fisted opportunity, patriotism & America. This was the myth, in which the creators had a dangerous psychological stake. In perfecting it, they largely lost themselves.

Empire Rising: A Novel. unabr. ed. Thomas Kelly. Read by Michael Deehy. 2 pieces. 2005. 49.95 (978-0-7927-3468-0(8), CMP 744); 69.95 (978-0-7927-3445-1(9), CSL 744); audio compact disk 112.95 (978-0-7927-3446-8(7), SLD 744) AudioGO.

***Empire State NYSESLAT: Audio CD.** Continental Press Staff. 2008. stu. ed. 9.50 (978-0-8454-5652-1(0)); stu. ed. 9.50 (978-0-8454-5656-9(3)); stu. ed. 9.50 (978-0-8454-5655-2(5)); stu. ed. 9.50 (978-0-8454-5657-6(1)); stu. ed. 9.50 (978-0-8454-5651-4(2)); stu. ed. 9.50 (978-0-8454-6037-5(4)); stu. ed. 9.50 (978-0-8454-5658-3(X)); stu. ed. 9.50 (978-0-8454-5654-5(7)); stu. ed. 9.50 (978-0-8454-5653-8(9)) Continental Pr.

***Empire State NYSESLAT: Classroom Package.** Continental Press Staff. 2008. pap. bk. & stu. ed. 499.95 (978-0-8454-5665-1(2)); pap. bk. & stu. ed. 499.95 (978-0-8454-5664-4(4)); pap. bk. & stu. ed. 499.95 (978-0-8454-6039-9(0)); pap. bk. & stu. ed. 499.95 (978-0-8454-5662-0(8)); pap. bk. & stu. ed. 499.95 (978-0-8454-5663-7(6)); pap. bk. & stu. ed. 499.95 (978-0-8454-5661-3(X)); pap. bk. & stu. ed. 499.95 (978-0-8454-5666-8(0)); pap. bk. & stu. ed. 499.95 (978-0-8454-5660-6(1)) Continental Pr.

***Empire State NYSESLAT: Package.** Continental Press Staff. 2008. pap. bk. 499.95 (978-0-8454-5659-0(8)) Continental Pr.

Empire Strikes Back. 1 cass. (Play Pack Star Wars Ser.). (J). bk. 14.99 (978-0-7634-0198-6(6)) W Disney Records.

Empire Strikes Back. Ed. by Disney Staff. Characters created by George Lucas. 1 cass. (Read Along Star Wars Ser.). (J). bk. 7.99 (978-0-7634-0194-8(3)) W Disney Records.

Empire Strikes Back: The Original Radio Drama. unabr. abr. ed. George Lucas. Perf. by Anthony Daniels et al. Created by National Public Radio Staff. 5 CDs. (Running Time: 5 hrs.). Dramatization. (ENG.). 1993. audio compact disk 59.95 (978-1-56511-007-6(2), 1565110072) Pub: HighBridge. Dist(s): Workman Pub

***Empire Strikes Out: How Baseball Sold U. S. Foreign Policy & Promoted the American Way Abroad.** unabr. ed. Robert Elias. (Running Time: 15 hrs.). 2010. 29.95 (978-1-4417-6155-2(1)); 85.95 (978-1-4417-6152-1(7)); audio compact disk 118.00 (978-1-4417-6153-8(5)); audio compact disk 32.95 (978-1-4417-6154-5(3)) Blckstn Audio.

Empire: the Life, Legend, & Madness of Howard Hughes: Part 1. Donald L. Barlett & James B. Steele. Read by Christopher Hurt. 24 CDs. (Running Time: 50400 sec.). 1994. audio compact disk 160.00 (978-0-7861-7928-2(7)) Blckstn Audio.

Empires of Mesopotamia. Compiled by Benchmark Education Staff. 2005. audio compact disk 10.00 (978-1-4108-5490-2(6)) Benchmark Educ.

Empires of Sand. unabr. ed. David Ball. Narrated by George Guidall. 21 cass. (Running Time: 28 hrs. 15 mins.). 2000. 159.00 (978-0-7887-4873-8(4), 96233E7) Recorded Bks.
After four trips to the Sahara & extensive historical research, he crafted this sweeping adventure novel spanning two continents & 15 years. Set against a backdrop of the crumbling French Empire's attempts to colonize the Sahara Desert & following the lives of two cousins who are raised as brothers but destined to become enemies.

Empires of the Mind. Denis Waitley. Read by Denis Waitley. 6 cass. (Running Time: 6 hrs.). 1995. 59.95 Set. (12190AM) Nightingale-Conant.
Access today's global power source of instant information & convert it into knowledge for achieving your goals. Discover how to multiply your power by sharing it & to "benchmark" your talents against the talents of industry leaders. Learn lessons for self-leadership that will enable you to control your time, actions & habits so that success becomes second nature.

Empires of the Mind. abr. ed. Dennis Waitley. 2 cass. 1996. 13.95 set. (53685) Books on Tape.
Waitley says that, to succeed, individuals must reinvent themselves as their companies restructure job descriptions.

Empires of the Sea: The Siege of Malta, the Battle of Lepanto, & the Contest for the Center of the World. Roger Crowley. Read by John Lee. (ENG.). 2009. 64.99 (978-1-60775-772-6(9)) Find a World.

Empires of the Sea: The Siege of Malta, the Battle of Lepanto, & the Contest for the Center of the World. unabr. ed. Roger Crowley. Narrated by John Lee. (Running Time: 11 hrs. 0 mins. 0 sec.). (ENG.). 2008. audio compact disk 24.99 (978-1-4001-5722-8(6)) Pub: Tantor Media. Dist(s): IngramPubServ

Empires of the Sea: The Siege of Malta, the Battle of Lepanto, & the Contest for the Center of the World. unabr. ed. Roger Crowley. Read by John Lee. (Running Time: 11 hrs. 0 mins. 0 sec.). (ENG.). 2008. audio compact disk 34.99 (978-1-4001-0722-3(9)) Pub: Tantor Media. Dist(s): IngramPubServ

Empires of the Sea: The Siege of Malta, the Battle of Lepanto, & the Contest for the Center of the World. unabr. ed. Roger Crowley. Read by John Lee. Narrated by John Lee. (Running Time: 11 hrs. 0 mins. 0 sec.). (ENG.). 2008. audio compact disk 69.99 (978-1-4001-3722-0(5)) Pub: Tantor Media. Dist(s): IngramPubServ

Empirical Evidence of Easter: 1 Cor. 15:3-8. Ed Young. 1993. 4.95 (978-0-7417-1965-2(7), 965) Win Walk.

Empirically Based Assessment. Thomas M. Achenbach & Stephanie H. McConaughy. 2 cass. (Running Time: 1 hr. 30 mins.). 1999. 41.00 (9-23318) Riverside Pub Co.
A package of: Development & Applications of Empirically Based Assessment and School-Centered Applications of Empirically Based Assessment.

Empiricism. Gordon Clark. 1 cass. (Lectures on Apologetics: No. 5). 5.00 Trinity Found.

Employee Benefit & Retirement Planning: A Basic Guide. Nathan M. Bisk & Richard Feldheim. 6 cass. 1995. bk. 199.00 set. (CPE5040) Bisk Educ.
Provides you with the tools & techniques you need to put together a cost-effective benefit & compensation package. We cover employee benefit agreements for both small & large companies.

Employee Benefits - 1989 & Beyond. 1989. 55.00 (AC-479) PA Bar Inst.

Employee Benefits Litigation. 10 cass. (Running Time: 15 hrs.). 1998. 315.00 Incl. course materials. (MC44) Am Law Inst.
Examines the principal claims, defenses, pleading, discovery, motions, pre-trial, & settlement approaches. Also considered are pension & retirement plans, health & medical plans, & other employee benefit plans.

Employee Benefits Reports Series Subscription, 1989-90. 4 cass. 55.00 set. (T6-9065) PLI.

Employee Benefits Reports 1990-91 Series Subscription. 4 cass. 55.00 (T6-9063) PLI.

Employee Enrollment Presentation. Robert A. Robinson. Read by H. Paul Springer & Jonathan Robinson. Ed. by John Campbell. 1 cass. (Running Time: 20 min.). (ECA Benefit Communications Ser.). 1990. pap. bk. 10.95 (978-1-884780-09-7(1)) Phoenix Pubng.
Instructional audio cassette of insurance sales presentation for selling payroll deduction insurance products to employees.

Employee Guide to Mergers & Acquisitions - Playaway. Price Pritchett. Voice by Eric Conger. 2007. (978-0-944002-37-7(4)) Pritchett.

Employee Guide to Mergers & Acquisitions Audible. Price Pritchett. Narrated by Eric Conger. (ENG.). 2007. 9.95 (978-0-944002-43-8(9)) Pritchett.

Employee-Management Relations, The Psychology Of. Roger M. Bellows. 1 cass. (Running Time: 20 min.). 12.95 (13027) J Norton Pubs.
This is a discussion of psychological management versus autocratic management in relation to employee motivation & employee dynamics.

Employee Motivation: The Role of the Supervisor. unabr. ed. Roger M. Bellows. 12.95 (13028) J Norton Pubs.
Emphasizes how to manage the interpersonal relationships in the working milieu.

Employee of the Month. Perf. by Austin Lounge Lizards Staff. 1 cass., 1 CD. 7.98 (SUH 3874); audio compact disk 12.78 CD. (SUH 3874) NewSound.

Employee Policies & Manuals. Ed. by Socrates Media Editors. 2005. audio compact disk 29.95 (978-1-59546-095-0(0)) Pub: Socrates Med LLC. Dist(s): Midpt Trade

Employee Relations Law in the Health Care Industry. 1987. bk. 120.00; 45.00 PA Bar Inst.

Employee Retirement & Welfare Plans of Tax-Exempt & Governmental Employers. 11 cass. (Running Time: 16 hrs. 30 min.). 1998. 395.00 Set; incl. study guide 827p. (MD18) Am Law Inst.
Examines recent developments affecting qualified plans, nonqualified plans, & welfare plans. Designed for attorneys, accountants, actuaries, consultants, & administrators responsible for understanding Code, ERISA, & other federal rules.

Employee Retirement & Welfare Plans of Tax-Exempt & Governmental Employers: Featuring Practical Solutions to Problems under the Internal Revenue Code, ERISA, & Other Federal Laws. 1 cass. (Running Time: 17 hrs. 30 min.). 1999. 395.00 Incl. study guide. (AE04) Am Law Inst.

Employee Stock Ownership Plans - Practical Applications. Rebecca J. Miller. 3 cass. (Running Time: 8 hrs.). 1995. 119.00 set, incl. wkbk. (751216EZ) Am Inst CPA.
In this course, you find out all the advantages (& disadvantages) of ESOPs: when to recommend them to clients; how they benefit the employer, business owners, & employees. A typical case study shows how to transfer the ownership of a healthy, closely held corporation using an ESOP. This is a common situation when a key stockholder-executive wants to retire & an ESOP is uniquely able to meet the needs of all concerned.

Employee Welfare Benefit Plans 1989. unabr. ed. Contrib. by Cynthia M. Combe. 4 cass. (Running Time: 5 hrs. 30 min.). 1989. 50.00 course handbk. (T7-9221) PLI.
This recording of PLI's March 1989 satellite program provides a thorough overview of the basic concepts underlying Code Section 89 as well as a detailed analysis of how to conduct the Section 89 nondiscrimination testing process. Major topics discussed include: Section 89: qualification rules, anti-discrimination rules & regulations, retiree benefits, Medicare secondary & funding issues, cafeteria plans, FASB exposure draft on new requirements for accounting retiree benefits other than pensions & welfare benefit plans in mergers & acquisitions.

Employees vs. Independent Contractors: Problems & Resolutions. Sidney Kess & Barbara Weltman. 1 cass. (Running Time: 1 hr.). 1993. 60.00 (0972) Toolkit Media.
Provides practitioners with an understanding of various issues relating to independent contractor problems & enables them to spot issues of concern to the IRS. Provides four hours of CPE credit.

Employer Compliance with the Americans with Disabilities Act. 4 cass. (Running Time: 5 hrs. 30 min.). 60.00 Set incl. four audiocass. plus 480-page course handbook. (T6-9171); 95.00 video incl. course handbook. (V8-2354) PLI.

Employer-Employee Relationship. Elbert Willis. 1 cass. (Relationship Ser.). 4.00 Fill the Gap.

Employer Responsibilities under the New "Right to Know" Act. Terry R. Bossert. 1 cass. (Running Time: 1 hr.). 1987. 20.00 PA Bar Inst.

Employer Strategies. Contrib. by Charles R. Church. (Running Time: 4 hrs.). 1984. 70.00 incl. program handbook. NJ Inst CLE.
This seminar helps attorneys provide management clients with truly professional legal service.

Employment & Labor Relations Law for the Corporate Counsel & the General Practitioner. 13 cass. (Running Time: 18 hrs.). 1999. 345.00 Set; incl. study guide. (MD64) Am Law Inst.
Gives lawyers on the firing line an introduction to the myriad laws & governmental regulations that affect the employment relationship. Also brings more experienced practitioners up to the minute on current developments in this rapidly changing field.

Employment at Will. Read by Debra K. Wallett. 1 cass. 1991. 20.00 (AL-110) PA Bar Inst.

Employment Discrimination & Civil Rights Actions in Federal & State Courts. 11 cass. (Running Time: 16 hrs.). 1998. 315.00 Incl. course materials. (MC59) Am Law Inst.
Features an overview of recent U.S. Supreme Court opinions & high-profile cases in the employment discrimination field, a discussion of new directions, both federal and state, for affirmative action & reverse discrimination, a comparative review of sexual harassment & age discrimination litigation, examination of the Americans With Disabilities Act, analysis of emerging controversies involving the Family & Medical Leave Act & other statues.

Employment Law. Ed. by Socrates Media Editors. 2005. audio compact disk 29.95 (978-1-59546-105-6(1)) Pub: Socrates Med LLC. Dist(s): Midpt Trade

Employment Law Litigation. Moderated by Jay W. Waks. 8 cass. (Running Time: 12 hrs.). 1992. pap. bk. 295.00 incl. course book. NY Law Pub.
Covers the impact of recent case law & statutory developments; building a defensible termination record; settlements; depositions; preparing witnesses; trial strategy; jury selection; evidentiary issues; cross-examination; jury instructions; damages & ADR.

Employment Law Practice: Recent Developments (1992) Read by Ralph H. Baxter, Jr. et al. (Running Time: 2 hrs. 30 min.). 1992. 89.00 (BU-55244) Cont Ed Bar-CA.
If you represent employers, employees, corporate policy makers, or labor unions, you need to follow the constant changes in employment law. Experienced employer & employee counsel analyze recent civil rights, disability rights, & sexual harassment developments; workplace safety & health issues; reductions in force (notice, older worker's benefit protection laws); drugs & alcohol policies; privacy; wrongful termination; & attorneys' fees.

Empower: Enabling Methods of Planning & Organizing Within Everyone's Reach. Robert S. Gold et al. (C). 1997. audio compact disk 74.95 (978-0-7637-0410-0(5), 0763704105) Jones Bartlett.

***Empower the Children Now.** Prod. by Victoria Hazlett. Composed by Victoria Hazlett. (ENG.). 2009. (978-0-9768148-7-0(0)) Golden Star.

Empower Your Sales: Dynamic Psychological Breakthrough to Accelerate Your Sales. 3rd rev. ed. Michele Blood. Ed. by Michele Blood. Illus. by Musivation International Staff. 2 cass. (Running Time: 2 hrs.). 2001. 19.95 (978-1-890679-12-5(7)) Micheles.

Empower Your Self Affirmations & Meditation. Suzanne E. Harrill. 1 cass. 1998. (978-1-883648-07-7(6)) Innerworks Pub.

***Empowered: Unleash Your Employees, Energize Your Customers, & Transform Your Business.** unabr. ed. Josh Bernoff & Ted Schadler. Read by Josh Bernoff. (Running Time: 6 hrs. 30 mins.). (ENG.). 2010. 26.98 (978-1-59659-668-9(6), GildAudio) Pub: Gildan Media. Dist(s): HachBkGrp

Empowered by Empathy. Narrated by Rose Rosetree. Prod. by Marilyn Cooley. 6 CDs. 2006. 49.00 (978-0-9752538-1-6(6)) Womens Intuition.
Empaths can directly experience what it?s like to be other people;;1 in 20 Americans has at least one gift for doing this. Unskilled, empaths pick up pain belonging to those people, and therefore suffer from such problems as emotional instability, apparent co-dependence, low self-esteem, or hypochondria. But this book, Empowered by Empathy, explains how to improve the quality of life by becoming a skilled empath. Rose Rosetree offers how-to techniques that she has used with students on three continents to turn empathy ON. At will. Bigger than ever before. Interspersed with these techniques, Rosetree describes elusive spiritual travels that are sometimes humorous, sometimes moving, and consistently fascinating.

Empowered for Victorious Christian Living. 2001. (978-1-59024-032-8(4)) B Hinn Min.

Empowered to Serve. John MacArthur, Jr. 5 cass. 16.95 (20147, HarperThor) HarpC GBR.

Empowering Boards for Leadership, 120 Minutes: Redefining Excellence in Governance. John Carver & J. Carver. Read by John Carver. 2 cass. (Running Time: 2 hrs.). (J-B Carver Board Governance Ser.). (ENG.). 1992. 47.00 (978-1-55542-447-3(3), Jossey-Bass) Wiley US.

Empowering Children to Cope. Dlugokinski. 1997. audio compact disk 17.95 (978-1-56032-630-4(1)) Taylor and Fran.

Empowering Employees: Enhance Productivity & Motivate Your Employees. Contrib. by L. Kristi Long. 1 cass. (Running Time: 30 mins.). pap. bk. 99.95 (1032AV); pap. bk. 99.95 (1032AV) J Wilson & Assocs.

Empowering Lay Volunteers. bk. 2.00 (978-0-687-76228-6(6)) Abingdon.

Empowering Older Adults: Practical Strategies for Counselors. Elinor B. Waters & Jane Goodman. (Social & Behavioral Science Ser.). 1990. bk. 47.00 (978-1-55542-286-8(1), Jossey-Bass) Wiley US.

Empowering Successful Leaders. As told by Frank Damazio. 6 cass. 2002. 59.99 (978-1-886849-95-2(1)) CityChristian.

Empowering Teenagers: A lecture by Dr. Jane Nelsen. Jane Nelsen. Ed. by Kenneth Ainge, Jr. (ENG.). 2006. audio compact disk 14.95 (978-0-9816250-1-0(0)) EmpoweringUT.

Empowering Women Gift Collection. abr. ed. Caroline Myss et al. 4 CDs. 2008. audio compact disk 23.95 (978-1-4019-1901-6(4)) Hay House.

Empowering Your Preaching. As told by Frank Damazio. 5 cass. 2002. 25.00 (978-1-886849-92-1(7)) CityChristian.
Revitalize your preaching ministry through this seminar! It is filled with inspirational and practical tips to enlarge your preaching abilities. Your sprit will be empowered and you will receive a fresh new hunger to preach the Word with power and clarity. 12 Samples of Frank Damazio's actual preaching notes included!.

Empowering Your Team. Pat Heim. 1 cass. (Running Time: 50 min.). 1995. 12.95 (978-1-891531-02-6(6)) Heim Gp.
Helps to anticipate & deal with barriers your team encounters, & the importance of conflict in group development.

Empowerment. Read by Chogyam Trungpa. 1 cass. 1976. 12.50 (A106) Vajradhatu.
Three talks, the process of transmission of the teaching from master to disciple is discussed.

Empowerment. abr. ed. David Gershon & Gail Straub. Read by David Gershon & Gail Straub. 2 cass. (Running Time: 3 hrs.). 1995. 15.95 set. (978-0-944993-71-2(0)) Audio Lit.
The authors, creators of the massive global initiative, the First Earth Run, have addressed the issue of personal empowerment not just theoretically, but practically.

Empowerment. abr. ed. Phil Murray. Read by Phil Murray. 10 cass. (Running Time: 1 hr. 12 mins.). 1999. 16.99 (978-1-84032-162-3(8), HoddrStoughton) Pub: Hodder General GBR. Dist(s): Trafalgar
Basing his advice on the teachings of ancient wisdom, shows how we can directly apply them to modern-day life, & empower ourselves as never before.

Empowerment Meditations from When Life Becomes Overwhelming Set: Empowerment Meditations. unabr. ed. Brian Sheen. 3 cass. (YA). 22.95 (978-1-928787-01-3(0), 001) Quan Pubg.
Meditation techniques that incorporate power metaphors & visualizations to expand awareness of highest consciousness of oneself to promote a positive transformation.

Empowerment Through My Subconscious System: Audio Material. Erika Niemann. Perf. by Erika Niemann. Engineer Steve Dronzek. (ENG.). 2007. (978-1-931267-02-1(2)) Close Connects.

Empowered Leader. Created by Barry Neil Kaufman. 2 CDs. (Running Time: 49 mins., 55 mins.). 2005. audio compact disk 35.00 (978-1-887254-18-2(8)) Epic Century.
Leaders are not just born! Leadership is a skill that can be developed, improved and expanded. The way we perform and the nature of our leadership skills affect every area of our lives.Leadership skills presented from an Option Process perspective are the very same skills that empower us in everyday experiences. This series is an essential resource or gift for educators, business people, administrators, helping professionals, therapists and group leaders or supervisors in any field. Barry Neil Kaufman defines the skills of leadership as achievable attributes, detailing methods that would maximize anyone' s performance in any interpersonal or group experience.

Empreinte de l'Ange see Mark of the Angel

Empreinte de L'Ange see Mark of the Angel

Empresa. (SPA.). 2002. bk. 8.90 (978-84-494-2381-9(3), 1402); bk. 8.90 (978-84-494-2379-6(1), 1402) Oceano Grupo ESP.

Empress. unabr. ed. Karen Miller. Narrated by Josephine Bailey. (Running Time: 20 hrs. 0 mins. 0 sec.). (Godspeaker Ser.). (ENG.). 2009. 34.99 (978-1-4001-6316-8(1)); audio compact disk 49.99 (978-1-4001-1316-3(4)); audio compact disk 99.99 (978-1-4001-4316-0(0)) Pub: Tantor Media. Dist(s): IngramPubServ

Empress Orchid. Anchee Min. Narrated by Alexandra O'Karma. 11 cass. (Running Time: 18 hrs.). 2004. 34.99 (978-1-4025-7202-9(6), 03954) Recorded Bks.

Emptied Soul: The Psychopath in Everyone's Life. Adolph Guggenbuhl-Craig & James Hillman. Read by James Hillman & Adolph Gugenbuhl-Craig. 1 cass. (Running Time: 70 min.). 1995. pap. bk. 10.95 (978-1-879816-16-9(4)) Spring Audio.
Why do psychopaths fascinate us? James Hillman & Adolph Guggenbuhl-Craig ask themselves why our society is simultaneously horrified & obsessed with psychopaths; coming up with some unique & disturbing answers.

Emptiness & Compassion. Read by Osel Tendzin. 3 cass. 1987. 34.00 (A098) Vajradhatu.
Emptiness is not cold & vacant, but contains warmth & self-existing compassion.

Empty & Beautiful. Contrib. by Matt Maher. Prod. by Jeff Thomas. 2008. audio compact disk 11.99 (978-5-557-46347-8(X)) Essential Recs.

Empty Chair. Jeffery Deaver. Read by Joe Mantegna. (Lincoln Rhyme Ser.: No. 3). 2004. 15.95 (978-0-7435-1961-8(2)) Pub: S&S Audio. Dist(s): S and S Inc

Empty Chair. unabr. ed. Jeffery Deaver. Read by Richard Perry Turner. 12 vols. (Running Time: 18 Hrs.). (Lincoln Rhyme Ser.: No. 3). 2000. bk. 96.95 (978-0-7927-2371-4(6), CSL 260, Chivers Sound Lib) AudioGO.
A quadriplegic since a beam crushed his spinal cord years ago, Rhyme is desperate to improve his condition & goes to the University of North Carolina Medical Center for high-risk experimental surgery.

Empty Chair. unabr. ed. Jeffery Deaver. Read by Richard Perry Turner. 14 CDs. (Running Time: 21 Hrs.). (Lincoln Rhyme Ser.: No. 3). 2000. audio compact disk 115.95 (978-0-7927-9951-1(8), SLD 002, Chivers Sound Lib) AudioGO.
In a twenty-four hour period, the sleepy town of Tanner's Corner has seen a local teen murdered & two women abducted.

Empty Copper Sea. unabr. collector's ed. John D. MacDonald. Read by Michael Prichard. 8 cass. (Running Time: 8 hrs.). (Travis McGee Ser.: Vol. 17). 1979. 48.00 (978-0-7366-0331-7(X), 1318) Books on Tape.
When Hub Lawless falls overboard off the Florida coast, it's called a drowning. But no one quite believes it. Not Travis McGee, whose old friend Van Harder, skipper of Hub's boat, is blamed for the mishap.

Empty Hours. unabr. ed. Ed McBain, pseud. Read by Jonathan Marosz. 6 cass. (Running Time: 6 hrs.). (87th Precinct Ser.: Bk. 15). 1996. 36.00 (978-0-7366-3409-0(6), 4056) Books on Tape.
Three murders. Few clues. No connections. The boys at the 87th Precinct have their hands full.

Empty House see Return of Sherlock Holmes

Empty House. unabr. ed. Rosamunde Pilcher. Read by Lindsay Duncan. 4 cass. (Running Time: 4 hrs.). 1996. 39.95 (978-0-7451-4233-3(8), CAB 916) AudioGO.
Virginia Keile's secret dream was to have a second chance at loving the Cornish farmer she had met, & foolishly lost, back when she was a debutante. Marriage to a man chosen by her mother that ended in her husband's accidental death, taught her a lot about life.

Empty House. unabr. ed. Rosamunde Pilcher. Read by Donada Peters. 5 cass. (Running Time: 5 hrs.). 1992. 40.00 (978-0-7366-2144-1(X), 2942) Books on Tape.
Released from a miserable marriage, Virginia Keile returns to Cornwall seeking the love she lost years ago. Warm & touching.

Empty House & Other Ghost Stories. Algernon Blackwood. (Running Time: 7 mins.). 2009. audio compact disk 31.95 (978-1-897304-68-6(4)) Dorch Pub Co.

***Empty House & Other Ghost Stories.** Algernon Blackwood. (Running Time: 7 mins.). 2009. 19.95 (978-1-897331-19-4(3), AudioRealms) Dorch Pub Co.

Empty Pinata. Alma Flor Ada. Illus. by Vivi Escrivá. (Stories for the Year 'Round Ser.). (J). (gr. k-3). 4.95 (978-1-58105-320-3(7)) Santillana.

Empty Pot. unabr. ed. Demi. 1 cass. (Running Time: 7 min.). (J). (ps-2). 1993. pap. bk. 17.90 (978-0-8045-6751-0(4), 6751) Spoken Arts.
Ping's talent as a gardener is put to the test when the Chinese Emperor announces an unusual test to choose an heir.

Empty Quiver: Genesis 21:1-8. Ed Young. 1994. 4.95 (978-0-7417-2037-5(X), 1037) Win Walk.

Empty Saddles. L. Ron Hubbard. Read by Geoffrey Lewis. 1 cass. 1995. 8.99 (978-0-88404-940-1(X)) Bridge Pubns Inc.
Teeming with action, "Empty Saddles" is the story of Cavalry Officer Major Lee Stuart - sole survivor of a raid led by the renegade, "El Falcon." Publicly branded a traitor by his C.O., Stuart sets out on a single-handed search for "El Falcon" - little knowing that the brutal leader plans to wipe out all U.S. forces in Texas.

Empty Saddles. abr. ed. L. Ron Hubbard. Read by Geoffrey Lewis. 1 cass. (Running Time: 1 hr.). 1993. 9.95 (978-0-88404-829-9(2)) Bridge Pubns Inc.

Empty Saddles. abr. ed. L. Ron Hubbard. Read by Geoffrey Lewis. 1 cass. (Running Time: 1 hr.). 1994. 9.95 (978-1-59212-010-9(5)) Gala Pr LLC.
Cavalry Officer Major Lee Stuart, stationed at remote Fort Torando, barely escapes with his life when his entire troop is massacred during a desert sortie by a hostile horde, headed by the mysterious renegade "El Falcon.".

Empty Saddles. abr. ed. L. Ron Hubbard. (Running Time: 3600 sec.). (Western Audiobooks Ser.). 2006. audio compact disk 9.95 (978-1-59212-225-7(6)) Gala Pr LLC.

Emptying the Ocean with a Bowl. Swami Amar Jyoti. 1 dolby cass. 1983. 9.95 (J-45) Truth Consciousness.
Cleaning the mind, from moment to moment, humming the Lord's Name. How to deal with the patterns of existence. Spiritual education. The difference between becoming & Being.

EMS Scenarios: Case Studies for Prehospital Providers. American Academy of Orthopaedic Surgeons (AAOS). 2008. audio compact disk 104.95 (978-0-7637-5555-3(9)) Jones Bartlett.

EMT - Basic Student Review Manual. 3rd ed. AAOS Staff. (C). 1999. stu. ed. 40.95 (978-0-7637-1043-9(1), 1043-1) Jones Bartlett.

EMT-Basic Practical Skills Review DVD. 9th rev. ed. American Academy of Orthopaedic Surgeons Staff. 2005. 69.95 (978-0-7637-2980-6(9)) Jones Bartlett.

EMTB: Tool Kit with Power Point. 7th ed. AAOS Staff. (C). 1999. audio compact disk 281.95 (978-0-7637-0929-7(8), 0929-8) Jones Bartlett.

En: Affinity. Music by John Falconer & Elizabeth Falconer. 1 CD. (Running Time: 60:24). 2005. audio compact disk 15.00 (978-0-9770499-8-1(1)) Koto World.
EN means "Affinity" and this husband-wife duo have an affinity for Japanese music based on years of study in Japan. Award-winning artist Elizabeth Falconer (koto) and John Falconer (shakuhachi bamboo flute) perform original compositons and well-known pieces from Japan, as well as their own arrangements of American spirituals, a romantic classical work, and a lilting Cuban melody. Reaching beyond the style of "meditation music," this is an utterly refreshing take on the versatile sounds of these traditional Japanese instruments. A warm, inspired performance to refresh for the mind and spirit. The CD includes:Enigma, Whispering Trees, Silver River, Spring Sea, Danza Lucumi, Sukiyaki Song, Amazing Grace/Swing Low, Lost Lake Reflections, Scharborough Fair, Je Crois Encore Entendre, Nightingale's Return. Performed by the duo EN.

En Activo: Practical Business Spanish. Esther Santamaria Iglesias & Helen Jones. (SPA & ENG.). 2008. audio compact disk 44.95 (978-0-415-40886-8(5), 0415408865) Pub: Routledge. Dist(s): Taylor and Fran

En Attendant Godot, Set. Samuel Beckett. Read by G. Bejean et al. 2 cass.Tr. of Waiting for Godot. (FRE.). 1992. 26.95 (1524-VSL) Olivia & Hill.
The famous play about two hoboes, Estragon & Vladimir, who await the arrival of Godot. They have never seen him, nor do they know why they are waiting for him. A classic from the theater of the absurd.

En Bonne Forme. (FRE.). 2003. (978-0-618-01246-6(X)) CENGAGE Learn.

En Bonne Forme. 4th ed. Simone R. Dietiker. (C). 1990. 2.66 (978-0-669-12019-6(7)) HM Harcourt.

En Bretagne. pap. bk. 27.95 (978-88-7754-756-9(1)) Pub: Cideb ITA. Dist(s): Distribks Inc

En Busca de Bravo, EDL Level 12. (Fonolibros Ser.: Vol. 27). (SPA.). 2003. 11.50 (978-0-7652-1016-6(9)) Modern Curr.

En busca de la iglesia de Cristo. P. Juan Rivas. (SPA.). (YA). 2006. audio compact disk 18.95 (978-1-935405-73-3(X)) Hombre Nuevo.

En busca de paz: Descubra el plan de Dios para darle felicidad y esperanza. Margarita Trevino. Ed. by Elizabeth Rivera. (SPA.). 1999. reel tape 9.99 (978-1-56309-332-6(4)) Womans Mission Union.

En Busca De Unicornios: Level 6, Vol. 2. 2003. 11.50 (978-0-7652-0988-7(8)) Modern Curr.

En Busca Tiempo Perdido. unabr. ed. Proust Marcel. Read by Daniel Quintero. (SPA.). 2007. 39.99 (978-958-8318-22-6(X)) Pub: Yoyo Music COL. Dist(s): YoYoMusic

En Camino. 3rd ed. Holt, Rinehart and Winston Staff. 2002. audio compact disk 195.73 (978-0-03-065969-0(8)) Holt McDoug.

En Contacto: Gramatica. 7th ed. Gill. bk. 77.95 (978-0-8384-8823-2(4)) Heinle.

En Contacto: Gramatica. 7th ed. Gill. (C). bk. 65.95 (978-0-8384-7109-8(9)); bk. 73.95 (978-0-8384-7578-2(7)); bk. 106.95 (978-0-8384-7596-6(5)); bk. 102.95 (978-0-8384-7794-6(1)); bk. 113.95 (978-0-8384-8029-8(2)); bk. 100.00 (978-0-8384-6394-9(0)); bk. 119.95 (978-0-8384-8454-8(9)) Heinle.

En Diestra Dios Padre. unabr. ed. Abuelo Historias Del. (SPA.). 2007. audio compact disk 13.00 (978-958-8318-02-8(5)) Pub: Yoyo Music COL. Dist(s): YoYoMusic

***En el mar Audio CD.** Cynthia Swain. Adapted by Benchmark Education Company, LLC. (My First Reader's Theater Ser.). (SPA.). (J). 2009. audio compact disk 10.00 (978-1-935470-75-5(2)) Benchmark Educ.

En el Tranvia. Created by Rigby Staff. 1994. 10.40 (978-0-435-05937-8(8), Rigby PEA) Pearson EdAUS AUS.

En Espanol!, Level 1A. (SPA.). 2003. stu. ed. (978-0-618-01792-8(5)) Holt McDoug.

En Espanol!, Level 2. (SPA.). 2003. (978-0-395-95345-7(6)); audio compact disk (978-0-618-34552-6(3)); audio compact disk (978-0-395-95348-8(0)) Holt McDoug.

En Espanol!, Level 3. (SPA.). 2003. (978-0-395-95346-4(4)); audio compact disk (978-0-618-34562-5(0)); audio compact disk (978-0-395-95349-5(9)) Holt McDoug.

En Espanol!, Level 4. (SPA.). 2003. audio compact disk (978-0-618-35372-9(0)); audio compact disk (978-0-618-35378-1(X)) Holt McDoug.

***En la escuela Audio CD.** Francisco Blane. Adapted by Benchmark Education Company, LLC. (My First Reader's Theater Ser.). (SPA.). (J). 2009. audio compact disk 10.00 (978-1-935470-62-5(0)) Benchmark Educ.

En la Playa. (Cuenta y Canta una Historia Ser.). 18.95 (978-88-536-0222-0(8)) EMC-Paradigm.

En Las Alas Del Amor. Julissa Arce. 1 CD. (Running Time: 1 hr. 30 min.). 2002. audio compact disk 14.99 (978-0-8297-3802-5(9)) Zondervan.

En Manos de la Cocinera & Other Short Stories. Short Stories. Miguel de Unamuno. Read by Leopoldo Perdomo. 1 cass. (Running Time: 1 hr.).Tr. of In the Cook's Hands. (SPA.). 2000. 19.50 INCL. TRANSCRIPT. (978-1-58085-263-0(7)) Interlingua VA.

En medio del Silencio. Jez. (SPA.). 2006. audio compact disk 14.99 (978-0-8297-5053-9(3)) Zondervan.

En Mi Mente Estas. unabr. ed. Hector David Aguilar. (SPA.). 2001. 7.99 (978-0-8297-3214-6(4)) Pub: Vida Pubs. Dist(s): Zondervan

En Mi Mente Estas. unabr. ed. Hector David Aguilar. 1 CD. 2001. audio compact disk 11.99 (978-0-8297-3212-2(8)) Zondervan.

***En Mode Book/CD Set: 22 Easy Character Pieces for Guitar.** Stanley Yates. 2010. pap. bk. 14.99 (978-0-7866-8243-0(4)) Mel Bay.

En Parejas Emergent: Stage 2. Steck-Vaughn Staff. (SPA.). 1999. (978-0-7398-0774-3(9)) SteckVau.

En Provence. pap. bk. 27.95 (978-88-7754-335-6(3)) Pub: Cideb ITA. Dist(s): Distribks Inc

En Provence. (Running Time: 60 mins.). 2002. audio compact disk 15.99 (978-1-904972-58-7(6)) Global Jmy GBR GBR.

En Tu Presencia. unabr. ed. Jocelyn Arias. 2001. audio compact disk 14.99 (978-0-8297-3602-1(6)); 9.99 (978-0-8297-3604-5(2)) Zondervan.
Praise and Worship.

En una Palabra, Sevilla, Espana: A CD-ROM for Exploring Culture in Spanish. Emmanuel Paris-Bouvret & Ana Maria Pérez-Gironés. 1. 2006. audio compact disk 29.95 (978-1-58901-136-6(8)) GeorgetownUPr.

En Voyage see Treasury of French Prose

Enabling Lay People in Ministry. Ann Engh et al. 1986. 10.80 (0708) Assn Prof Chaplains.

Encephalitis: Program from the Award Winning Public Radio Series. Interview. Hosted by Fred Goodwin. 1 CD. (Running Time: 1 hr). (Infinite Mind Ser.). 1999. audio compact disk 21.95 (978-1-932479-16-4(3), LCM 83) Lichtenstein Creat.
This special report of The Infinite Mind focuses on the mosquito-borne virus that?s sickened dozens of New Yorkers with symptoms ranging from headache and fever to encephalitis and death. In this hour, we hear from residents of affected neighborhoods, from the scientific detectives on the front lines, from a physician who specializes in infectious diseases, and from experts on the chemicals used to kill infected mosquitoes. We also look at the likelihood of the disease spreading to other parts of the U.S.

Enchanted. abr. ed. Elizabeth Lowell. Read by Anne Flosnik. (Running Time: 7 hrs.). (Medieval Ser.). 2009. audio compact disk 14.99 (978-1-4233-3242-8(3), 9781423332428, BCD Value Price) Brilliance Audio.

Enchanted. abr. ed. Elizabeth Lowell. Read by Deborah McLiam. 1 cass. (Running Time: 90 min.). 1995. 5.99 (978-1-57096-024-6(0), RAZ 924) Romance Alive Audio.
Beautiful heiress Ariane has been betrayed & brutalized, & is forced into an arranged marriage with ruggedly handsome Simon the Loyal. The mystical forces of the time in which they live combine to conjure peace for their people & a bewitching love for them.

Enchanted. unabr. ed. Elizabeth Lowell. (Running Time: 12 hrs.). (Medieval Ser.). 2008. 39.25 (978-1-4233-3238-1(5), 9781423332381, Brlnc Audio MP3 Lib); audio compact disk 107.25 (978-1-4233-3236-7(9), 9781423332367, BriAudCD Unabrid) Brilliance Audio.

Enchanted. unabr. ed. Elizabeth Lowell. Read by Anne Flosnik. (Running Time: 12 hrs.). (Medieval Ser.). 2008. 24.95 (978-1-4233-3237-4(7), 9781423332374, Brilliance MP3); 39.25 (978-1-4233-3240-4(7), 9781423332404, BADLE); 24.95 (978-1-4233-3239-8(3), 9781423332398, BAD); audio compact disk 29.99 (978-1-4233-3235-0(0), 9781423332350, Bril Audio CD Unabri) Brilliance Audio.

Enchanted: The Best of Robert Gass. Robert Gass. (Running Time: 53 min.). 1999. audio compact disk (978-1-891319-19-8(1)) Spring Hill CO.

Enchanted: The Best of Robert Gass & On Wings of Song. Perf. by Robert Gass. 1 cass. (Running Time: 53 min.). 1999. (978-1-879560-22-2(4)) Spring Hill CO.

***Enchanted Apple Tree.** Anonymous. 2009. (978-1-60136-588-0(8)) Audio Holding.

Enchanted April. Elizabeth von Arnim. Read by Anais 9000. 2009. 27.95 (978-1-60112-224-7(1)) Babblebooks.

Enchanted April. Elizabeth von Arnim. Read by Amy von Lecteur. 2009. 27.95 (978-1-60112-995-6(5)) Babblebooks.

Enchanted April. Elizabeth Von Arnim. Narrated by Flo Gibson. 2008. audio compact disk 37.95 (978-1-55685-904-5(X)) Audio Bk Con.

Enchanted April. abr. unabr. ed. Elizabeth Von Arnim. Read by Nadia May. 6 cass. (Running Time: 30600 sec.). (Classic Collection (Brilliance Audio) Ser.). 2006. 19.95 (978-0-7861-4460-0(2)); audio compact disk 24.95 (978-0-7861-9473-5(1), 1428); audio compact disk 19.95 (978-0-7861-7292-4(4)) Blckstn Audio.

Enchanted April, unabr. ed. Elizabeth von Arnim. Read by Johanna Ward. 6 cass. (Running Time: 8 hrs. 30 mins.). 1994. 44.95 (978-0-7861-0476-5(7), 1428) Blckstn Audio.
Four very diverse women, all seeking revitalization & escape from the dreary February rains of 1920s London, rent the small medieval castle of San Salvatore, nestled high about the bay of Portofino, Italy.

Enchanted April. unabr. ed. Elizabeth von Arnim. Read by Nadia May. 7 CDs. (Running Time: 8 hrs. 30 mins.). 2000. audio compact disk 56.00 (978-0-7861-9927-3(X), 1428) Blckstn Audio.

Enchanted April, Set. unabr. ed. Elizabeth von Arnim. Read by Flo Gibson. 5 cass. (Running Time: 7 hrs. 30 min.). 1998. 20.95 (978-1-55685-519-1(2)) Audio Bk Con.
Four English ladies, strangers to each other, rent a villa for a month near Portofino. Their lives & loves change as they fall under the spell of this enchanting place.

Enchanted April, Set. unabr. ed. Elizabeth von Arnim. Read by Nadia May. 6 cass. 1999. 44.95 (FS9-23905) Highsmith.

Enchanted Castle. E. Nesbit. Narrated by Virginia Leishman. 7 CDs. (Running Time: 7 hrs. 45 mins.). (gr. 3 up). audio compact disk 69.00 (978-1-4025-1964-2(8)) Recorded Bks.

Enchanted Castle. abr. ed. Edith Nesbit. Read by Joanna Page. (Running Time: 9409 sec.). (J). (gr. 4-7). 2008. audio compact disk 17.98 (978-962-634-858-1(5), Naxos AudioBooks) Naxos.

Enchanted Castle. unabr. ed. E. Nesbit. Narrated by Flo Gibson. 6 cass. (Running Time: 7 hrs. 30 min.). (J). 1986. 24.95 (978-1-55685-051-6(4)) Audio Bk Con.
Young Gerald, Cathy & Jimmy find an enchanted castle & awaken a princess from a hundred-year sleep only to have her made invisible by a magic ring. Her rescue is often funny & sometimes frightening.

Enchanted Castle, unabr. ed. E. Nesbit. Read by Johanna Ward. 6 cass. (Running Time: 8 hrs. 30 mins.). 1994. 44.95 (978-0-7861-0492-5(9), 1443) Blckstn Audio.
Jimmy, Gerald, & Cathy discover an enchanted garden & wake a beautiful princess from a hundred-year-sleep - only to have her immediately made invisible by a magic ring. The quest to rescue her from her own magic proves difficult, humorous, & at times very frightening.

Enchanted Castle. unabr. ed. E. Nesbit. Read by Shaela Connor. 6 cass. (Running Time: 6 hrs. 36 min.). Dramatization. 1992. 39.95 (978-1-55686-443-8(4), 443) Books in Motion.
Four children, their lovely French governess, & a love-sick English lord find adventure, friendship & ultimately love in a truly enchanted garden where anything can & does happen.

Enchanted Castle. unabr. ed. E. Nesbit. Narrated by Virginia Leishman. 6 pieces. (Running Time: 7 hrs. 45 mins.). (gr. 3 up). 2001. 52.00 (978-0-7887-5252-0(9), 96540E7) Recorded Bks.
Jerry, Jimmy & Kathleen can't go home for their school holiday because their cousin is sick with the measles there. Instead, they stay at Kathleen's school. One morning, as they set out to find adventure, they find an enchanted place. Soon, the four friends are surrounded by strange, wonderful things - & magic too!.

Enchanted Christmas. Prod. by Walt Disney Productions Staff. 1 cass. (J). 1997. 6.98 (978-0-7634-0344-7(X)) W Disney Records.
Music - Popular.

Enchanted Evening: Volume III of the Autobiography of M. M. Kaye. M. M. Kaye. 10 cass. (Running Time: 15 hrs.). 2001. 80.00 (978-0-7366-6386-1(X)) Books on Tape.

Enchanted Evening: Volume III of the Autobiography of M. M. Kaye. unabr. ed. M. M. Kaye. Read by Kate Reading. 2001. 60.00 Books on Tape.
The third volume of M.M. Kaye's memoirs takes Kaye from early womanhood to a budding career & marriage.

Enchanted Fish. unabr. ed. 1 cass. (Running Time: 20 min.). Dramatization. (Magic Looking Glass Ser.). (J). (gr. 2-6). 1989. 9.95 (978-0-7810-0046-8(7), NIM-CW-130-4-C) NIMCO.
A Spanish folk tale.

Enchanted Forest: Classic Fairytales from Many Lands. Short Stories. Donald O'Donovan. 1. (Running Time: 60min). (J). 2005. audio compact disk 12.00 (978-1-892226-21-1(9)) New Centry Pr.
The Enchanted Forest, Classic Fairytales from Many Lands. Volumes One of a 6 Volume series. Narrated by Dana Johnson and Donald O'Donovan. Music, sound effects and character voices. 60 minutes.Enrich your children's lives with the mystery and wonder of these timeless tales performed by two accomplished voice actors.

Enchanted Forest Vol. 2: Classic Fairytales from Many Lands. Short Stories. Donald O'Donovan. 2. (Running Time: 60). (J). 2005. audio compact disk 12.00 (978-1-892226-20-4(0)) New Centry Pr.
The Enchanted Forest, Classic Fairytales from Many Lands. Volumes Two of a 6 Volume series. Narrated by Dana Johnson and Donald O'Donovan. Music, sound effects and character voices. 60 minutes.Enrich your children's lives with the mystery and wonder of these timeless tales performed by two accomplished voice actors.

Enchanted Forest Vol. 3: Classic Fairytales from Many Lands. Short Stories. Donald O'Donovan. (Running Time: 60). 2005. audio compact disk 12.00 (978-1-892226-19-8(7)) New Centry Pr.
The Enchanted Forest, Classic Fairytales from Many Lands. Volumes Three of a 6 Volume series. Narrated by Dana Johnson and Donald O'Donovan. Music, sound effects and character voices. 60 minutes.Enrich your children's lives with the mystery and wonder of these timeless tales performed by two accomplished voice actors.Volume ThreeThe Farmer, His Son and Their DonkeySnow White and Rose RedThe Three Little PigsThe Frog PrinceThe Little Red HenThe Stupid BoyRapunzel.

Enchanted Land. abr. ed. Jude Deveraux. Read by Victoria Pryne. 1 cass. (Running Time: 90 min.). 1995. 5.99 (978-1-57096-022-2(4), RAZ 922) Romance Alive Audio.
From the bluegrass splendor of her Kentucky home to the rugged beauty of sun drenched New Mexico, Morgan Wakefield must endure hardship & cruelty before finding lasting love with the man who defies a continent's dangers to possess her.

Enchanted Meditations for Kids. Christiane Kerr. (J). 2005. audio compact disk 17.95 (978-1-901923-89-6(4), 247-044) Pub: Divinit Pubing GBR. Dist(s): Bookworld

Enchanted Mule. unabr. ed. 1 cass. (Running Time: 20 min.). Dramatization. (Magic Looking Glass Ser.). (J). (gr. 2-6). 1989. 9.95 (978-0-7810-0048-2(3), NIM-CW-130-6-C) NIMCO.
A Spanish folk tale.

Enchanted Night. abr. ed. Steven Millhauser. Read by Stefan Rudnicki. 2 cass. (Running Time: 3 hrs.). 2001. 18.00 (978-1-59040-148-4(4), Phoenix Audio) Pub: Amer Intl Pub. Dist(s): PerseuPGW

Enchanted Night. unabr. ed. Steven Millhauser. Narrated by Linda Stephens. 2 cass. (Running Time: 3 hrs.). 1999. 23.00 (978-0-7887-4042-8(3), 96152E7) Recorded Bks.
Creates a magical spell of the moon in this beguiling short work. One hot summer night, as the full moon rises over a small Connecticut town, people are pulled outside by its radiant force.

Enchanted Tales. unabr. ed. Read by Julie Harris et al. 4 cass. (Running Time: 1 hr. 31 min.). (J). 1996. 24.95 Set. (978-1-888453-04-1(4), BMP Audio) BMP Music.
Enter the magical & whimsical world of classic fairy tales as read by our most beloved actors. Includes: "The Nightingale" by Hans Christian Andersen; "The Elfin Grove" & "The Bremen Town Musicians" by the Brothers Grimm; "The Hunting of the Snark" by Lewis Carroll.

Enchanted Vagabonds. unabr. collector's ed. Dana Lamb. Read by Larry McKeever. 12 cass. (Running Time: 18 hrs.). 1984. 96.00 (978-0-7366-0623-3(8), 1585) Books on Tape.
In the 1930's Dana Lamb & his wife build a sailing canoe & set out on a summer voyage along the pacific coast. This junket almost end in disaster but for their intelligence, & a "can do" sense of the possible.

Enchanted Wood. Ruth Sanderson. 1 cass. (J). (ps-3). 1998. 10.95 (978-1-56876-012-4(4)) Soundlines Ent.

*__Enchanter.__ unabr. ed. Vladimir Nabokov. Read by Christopher Lane. (Running Time: 3 hrs.). 2010. 39.97 (978-1-4418-7259-3(0), 9781441872593, BADLE); 19.99 (978-1-4418-7258-6(2), 9781441872586, BAD); 19.99 (978-1-4418-7256-2(6), 9781441872562, Brilliance MP3); 39.97 (978-1-4418-7257-9(4), 9781441872579, Brinc Audio MP3 Lib); audio compact disk 19.99 (978-1-4418-7254-8(X), 9781441872548, Bril Audio CD Unabri); audio compact disk 59.97 (978-1-4418-7255-5(8), 9781441872555, BriAudCD Unabrid) Brilliance Audio.

Enchanting Song of the Magical Bird: A Story from Nelson Mandela's Favorite African Folktales. Read by Jurnee Smollett. Compiled by Nelson Mandela. (Running Time: 6 mins.). (ENG.). 2009. 1.99 (978-1-60024-856-6(X)) Pub: Hachet Audio. Dist(s): HachBkGrp

Enchantment. abr. ed. Orson Scott Card. 4 cass. (Running Time: 6 hrs.). 2002. 25.00 (978-1-57453-510-5(2)) Audio Lit.
The moment Ivan stumbled upon a clearing in the dense Carpathian forest, his life was forever changed Atop a pedestal encircled by fallen leaves, the beautiful princess Katerina lay still as death. Beyond a malevolent presence stirred, sending the ten-year-old scrambling for the safety of his Cousin Marek's farm. Now, years later, Ivan is an American graduate student, engaged to be married. yet he cannot forget that day long ago. Compelled to return to his native land, Ivan finds the clearing just as he left it, but this time he does not run. This time he awakens the beauty with a kiss & steps into a world that banished a thousand years ago.

Enchantment. abr. ed. Christina Skye. 2 cass. (Running Time: 3 hrs.). 1998. 16.95 Ohio U Special Pubns.

Enchantment. abr. ed. Christina Skye. Perf. by Rena Sofer & Wally Kurth. 2 cass. (Running Time: 3 hrs.). (My Romance Ser.: Vol. 2). 1999. 16.95 Set. (978-0-9661644-1-1(5)) Renaiss Prodns.
Romances narrated by daytime television stars.

*__Enchantment.__ unabr. ed. Orson Scott Card. Read by Stefan Rudnicki. (Running Time: 14 hrs. 30 mins.). 2010. 29.95 (978-1-4417-3949-0(1)); 85.95 (978-1-4417-3945-2(9)); audio compact disk 118.00 (978-1-4417-3946-9(7)) Blckstn Audio.

Enchantment. unabr. ed. Monica Dickens. Read by Jane Asher. 5 cass. (Running Time: 5 hrs. 30 min.). (Isis Ser.). 1993. 49.95 set. (978-1-85089-770-5(0), 90082) Eye Ear.
During the day Tim sells fabric by the meter; at night he writes letters. What begins as harmless escapism, however, gradually takes over his life, until he is in danger of losing his grip on reality & sliding fulltime into fantasy.

Enchantment. unabr. ed. Monica Dickens. Read by Jane Asher. 5 cass. (Running Time: 7 hrs. 30 mins.). 2001. 69.95 (90082) Pub: ISIS Audio GBR. Dist(s): Ulverscroft US

Enchantment, Set. abr. ed. Orson Scott Card. Read by Alyssa Bresnahan. 4 cass. 1999. 25.00 (FA9-50916) Highsmith.

*__Enchantment Emporium.__ unabr. ed. Tanya Huff. Read by Teri Clark Linden. (Running Time: 14 hrs.). 2010. 24.99 (978-1-4418-7979-0(X), 9781441879790, BAD); 39.97 (978-1-4418-7980-6(3), 9781441879806, BADLE) Brilliance Audio.

*__Enchantment Emporium.__ unabr. ed. Tanya Huff. Read by Teri Clark Linden. (Running Time: 14 hrs.). 2010. 24.99 (978-1-4418-7983-7(8), 9781441879837, Brilliance MP3); 39.97 (978-1-4418-7984-4(6), 9781441879844, Brinc Audio MP3 Lib); audio compact disk 29.99 (978-1-4418-7981-3(1), 9781441879813, Bril Audio CD Unabri); audio compact disk 82.97 (978-1-4418-7982-0(X), 9781441879820, BriAudCD Unabrid) Brilliance Audio.

Enchantment of Lily Dahl. unabr. ed. Siri Hustvedt. Read by Siri Hustvedt. 4 cass. (Running Time: 6 hrs.). 1996. 21.95 (978-1-885608-16-1(0)) Airplay.
Lily Dahl, fully embraces the tough-beautiful-brave qualities of an irresistible old style heroine.

Enchantress from the Stars. unabr. ed. Sylvia Engdahl. Read by Jennifer Ikeda. 9 CDs. (Running Time: 10 hrs.). (YA). (gr. 6-9). 2006. audio compact disk 94.75 (978-1-4193-9921-3(7)); 65.75 (978-1-4193-9916-9(0)) Recorded Bks.
Three alien races meet on the small green world of Andrecia. The Imperial Exploration Corps wants to claim the planet for their own, but the Anthropological Service stands in their way. And when young Elana makes contact with native Georyn, a love story exploring the very depths of human emotion unfolds.

Enchantress of Florence. unabr. ed. Salman Rushdie. Read by Firdous Bamji. (Running Time: 13 hrs. 30 mins.). 2008. 61.75 (978-1-4361-3254-1(1)) Recorded Bks.

Enchantress of Florence. unabr. ed. Salman Rushdie. Read by Firdous Bamji. 12 cass. (Running Time: 13 hrs. 30 mins.). 2008. 92.75 (978-1-4025-7655-3(2)); audio compact disk 123.75 (978-1-4361-1937-5(5)); audio compact disk 39.99 (978-1-4361-4870-2(7)) Recorded Bks.
Salman Rushdie is one of the world¿s most revered literary masters, with a Booker Prize and two Whitbread Awards among his accolades. His unique brand of magic realism is particularly effective in The Enchantress of Florence, the story of a European traveler and the extraordinary tale he shares with 16th-century Mughal emperor Akbar the Great. The traveler claims to be the son of a Mughal princess forgotten by time. If his tale is true, what happened to the princess?.

Encíclica Dios es Amor. Papa Benedicto Xvi. Comment by P. Antonio Rivero. (SPA.). 2008. audio compact disk 11.95 (978-1-935405-74-0(8)) Hombre Nuevo.

Enciclopedia Compacta Britannica. Compiled by Encyclopaedia Britannica, Inc. 2008. audio compact disk 19.95 Ency Brit Inc.

Enciende tu Vida. Grover Bravo.Tr. of Light up your Life. (SPA.). 2009. audio compact disk 15.00 (978-1-935405-57-3(8)) Hombre Nuevo.

Enciende Una Luz. Marcos Witt. (SPA.). 2003. 9.99 (978-0-8297-4354-8(5)) Pub: Vida Pubs. Dist(s): Zondervan

Encina see Poesia y Drama de Garcia Lorca

Encontrando a Dios en Lugares Conocidos. Charles R. Swindoll.Tr. of Meeting God in Familiar Places. 2009. audio compact disk 27.00 (978-1-57972-848-9(0)) Insight Living.

Encopresis. Contrib. by Leonard A. Rappaport et al. 1 cass. (American Academy of Pediatrics UPDATE: Vol. 17, No. 6). 1998. 20.00 Am Acad Pediat.

Encore, Level 2. Jane Magratn & Kim Newman. 1 CD. (Running Time: 1 hr. 30 mins.). (Encore! Ser.). (ENG.). 1992. audio compact disk 10.95 (978-0-7390-1453-0(6), 4049) Alfred Pub.

Encore, Level 3. Jane Magrath & Kim Newman. 1 CD. (Running Time: 1 hr. 30 mins.). (Encore! Ser.). (ENG.). 1992. audio compact disk 10.95 (978-0-7390-1507-0(9), 4050) Alfred Pub.

Encore: A Guide to Enjoying Music. Jack Boyd. 1 cass. 1991. 37.95 CD. (978-1-55934-101-1(7), 1101) Mayfield Pub.

Encore: A Guide to Enjoying Music. Jack Boyd. Read by Jack Boyd. 1 cass. 1991. 22.95 (978-1-55934-062-5(2), 1062) Mayfield Pub.

Encore: Inding Work That Matters in the Second Half of Life. unabr. ed. Marc Freedman. Read by Sean Pratt. (Running Time: 5 hrs.). (ENG.). 2008. 24.98 (978-1-59659-228-5(1), GildAudio) Pub: Gildan Media. Dist(s): HachBkGrp

Encore at the Blue Note. Perf. by Oscar Peterson. 1 cass., 1 CD. 7.98 (TA 33356); audio compact disk 12.78 CD Jewel box. (TA 83356) NewSound.

Encore Effect: How to Achieve Remarkable Performance in Anything You Do. unabr. ed. Mark Sanborn. Read by Mark Sanborn. 3 CDs. (Running Time: 3 hrs.). 2008. audio compact disk 40.00 (978-1-4159-5722-6(3), BksonTape) Pub: Random Audio Pubg. Dist(s): Random

Encore on Something's Happening! Dave Emory. 1 cass. (Roy Tuckman Interview Ser.). 9.00 (A0709-90) Sound Photosyn.

Encore on Something's Happening! Oscar Janiger. 1 cass. (Roy Tuckman Interview Ser.). 9.00 (A0483-88) Sound Photosyn.
Another appearance from the man who turned on Hollywood.

Encore Provence: New Adventures in the South of France. Peter Mayle. Read by David Case. 4 cass. (Running Time: 6 hrs.). 2000. 26.95 (N110) Blckstn Audio.
Account of the author's homecoming which includes visits that reveal surprising secrets.

Encore Provence: New Adventures in the South of France. Peter Mayle. Read by David Case. 1999. audio compact disk 48.00 (978-0-7366-5170-7(5)) Books on Tape.

Encore Provence: New Adventures in the South of France. abr. ed. Peter Mayle. Read by David Chase. 3 cass. (Running Time: 4 hrs.). 1999. 24.00 (978-0-679-46083-1(7), Random AudioBks) Random Audio Pubg.
A mix of Gallic characters, adventure, & culinary treats.

Encore Provence: New Adventures in the South of France. unabr. ed. Peter Mayle. Read by David Case. 6 CDs. (Running Time: 7 hrs. 12 mins.). 2001. audio compact disk 48.00 Books on Tape.
Mayle recounts his return to France in a collection of essays that celebrates the unique lifestyle & habits of the Provence natives.

Encore Provence: New Adventures in the South of France. unabr. ed. Peter Mayle. Read by David Case. 5 cass. (Running Time: 7 hrs. 30 mins.). 1999. 40.00 (978-0-7366-4484-6(9), 4924) Books on Tape.

Encore 1. Kim O'Reilly. 1 CD. (Running Time: 90 mins.). (Encore! Ser.). (ENG.). 1992. audio compact disk 10.95 (978-0-7390-0708-2(4), 4048) Alfred Pub.

Encores for Solo Singers: Medium High Voice. Ed. by Jay Althouse. (For Solo Singers Ser.). (ENG.). 2003. audio compact disk 12.95 (978-0-7390-3237-4(2)) Alfred Pub.

Encores for Solo Singers: Medium Low Voice. Ed. by Jay Althouse. (For Solo Singers Ser.). (ENG.). 2003. audio compact disk 12.95 (978-0-7390-3240-4(2)) Alfred Pub.

Encounter see Twentieth-Century Poetry in English, No. 24, Recordings of Poets Reading Their Own Poetry

*__Encounter.__ (ENG.). 2010. audio compact disk (978-1-59171-276-3(9)) Falcon Picture.

Encounter in the Cage Country see James Dickey Reads His Poetry & Prose

Encounter in the Spirit: The Jesus Prayer. George Maloney. 1 cass. (Running Time: 1 hr.). 1995. 8.95 (TAH348) Alba Hse Comns.
Fr. Maloney explores the Jesus prayer in depth, focusing on its roots in the young church & through the developing spirituality of the early Christian community. It concludes with a brief guided meditation, this audio cassette program is wonderful material for developing the spirit in our lives.

Encounter the Goddess. Bruce Goldberg. (ENG.). 2005. audio compact disk 17.00 (978-1-57968-063-3(1)) Pub: B Goldberg. Dist(s): Baker Taylor

Encounter the Goddess. Bruce Goldberg. Read by Bruce Goldberg. 1 cass. (Running Time: 25 min.). (ENG.). 2006. 13.00 (978-1-885577-94-8(X)) Pub: B Goldberg. Dist(s): Baker Taylor
Through self-hypnosis meets one's own personal goddess. Training in the art of psychic empowerment.

Encounter with an Interviewer see Best of Mark Twain

Encounter with Tiber, Pt. 1. unabr. ed. Buzz Aldrin, Jr. & John Barnes. Read by Jonathan Reese. 9 cass. (Running Time: 13 hrs. 30 min.). 1997. 72.00 (978-0-7366-3635-3(8), 4297-A) Books on Tape.
Buzz Aldrin, Apollo 11 astronaut, & John Barnes, sci-fi author, make a perfect team. One has explored other worlds in space; the other one has created them in books.

Encounter with Tiber, Pt. 2. Buzz Aldrin, Jr. & J. Barnes. Read by Jonathan Reese. 8 cass. (Running Time: 12 hrs.). 1997. 64.00 (4297-B) Books on Tape.

Encountering Christ in the Gospels. Scott Hahn. 6 cass. 1995. 29.95 Set. (5268-C) Ignatius Pr.
Scott Hahn shows you how to come into contact with the living Christ through a careful reading of the four Gospels. In this series, you will learn how each Gospel stresses different aspects of Christ's life & message - & why these varying accounts actually deepen our grasp of the mystery of God's love in Christ in a complementary way. You will learn how to distinguish the different Christological themes & emphasis in each of the four Gospels & to see the distinctive contribution of each evangelist.

*__Encountering Heaven & the Afterlife: True Stories from People Who Have Glimpsed the World Beyond.__ unabr. ed. James L. Garlow & Keith Wall. Narrated by James L. Garlow. (Running Time: 8 hrs. 6 mins. 43 sec.). (ENG.). 2010. 19.59 (978-1-60814-716-8(9)); audio compact disk 27.99 (978-1-59859-761-5(2)) Oasis Audio.

Encountering the Risen Jesus. Vincent M. Walsh. 3 cass. (Running Time: 30 min.). 10.00 Key of David.

Encountering the Wisdom Jesus: Quickening the Kingdom of Heaven Within. Cynthia Bourgeault. 6 CDs. (Running Time: 24300 sec.). 2005. audio compact disk 69.95 (978-1-59179-293-2(2), F918D) Sounds True.

Encounters Erotica. 1 CD. (Running Time: 90 min.). 2001. audio compact disk 16.95 Passion Press.

Encounters in Modern Hebrew: Level 1. Edna A. Coffin. (ENG., 1993. 34.50 (978-0-472-00251-1(1), 00251) U of Mich Pr.

Encounters in Modern Hebrew: Level 2. Edna A. Coffin. (ENG., 1994. 21.95 (978-0-472-00252-8(X), 00252) U of Mich Pr.

Encounters with Animals. unabr. ed. Gerald Durrell. Read by Nigel Davenport. 4 cass. (Running Time: 6 hrs.). 2000. 34.95 (978-0-7540-0085-3(0), CAB 1508) Pub: Chivers Audio Bks GBR. Dist(s): AudioGO
Based on the broadcasts made by Gerald Durrell for the BBC, this is a vividly entertaining account of the animals he discovered and observed in places like Argentina, Africa and Guiana. A cornucopia of creatures are featured: dancing birds of paradise, mosaic-like lizards, snakes of all sizes, and many more. Their characters, conflicts and peculiar courtship rituals are revealed here.

Encounters with Animals. unabr. ed. Gerald Durrell & Nigel Davenport. Read by Nigel Davenport. 4 CDs. (Running Time: 6 hrs.). 2002. audio compact disk 49.95 (978-0-7540-5514-3(0), CCD 205) Pub: Chivers Pr GBR. Dist(s): AudioGO

*__Encounters with Pan & Elemental Kingdom.__ R. Ogilvie Crombie. (Running Time: 1 hr. 55 mins. 0 sec.). (ENG.). 2010. audio compact disk 19.95 (978-1-84409-199-7(6)) Pub: Findhorn Pr GBR. Dist(s): IPG Chicago

Encounters with the Archdruid. unabr. ed. John McPhee. Read by Dan Lazar. 7 cass. (Running Time: 7 hrs.). 1986. 42.00 (978-0-7366-1068-1(5), 1995) Books on Tape.
David Brower is a man with a mission to save the unspoiled regions of the world. A militant conservationist, he takes on anyone who threatens his vision of our wilderness heritage. John McPhee arranged for Brower, the Archdruid of the story, to meet on contested turf with three of Brower's chief opponents.

Encourage a Passion for God. Speeches. Frank Hamrick. 1 cass. (Running Time: 90 mins.). 2001. (978-1-929784-78-3(3)); audio compact disk (978-1-929784-79-0(1)) Psitive Action.
Message for School teachers.

Encouragement. unabr. ed. Poems. Sri Chinmoy Centre Staff. Read by Sri Chinmoy Centre Staff. 1 cass. 1998. 9.95 (978-0-9664613-6-7(3)) Jharna Kala.

Encouragement for Single Parents. Joyce Meyer. 2 cass. (Running Time: 2 hrs.). 2001. 12.00 (TJM-152) Harrison Hse.
Single parents, are you ready to exchange your "mess" for a miracle? Well, now is the time for you to meet the God of unreasonable exchange. He wants you to exchange all of your weaknesses for His strength... all of your hurts, wounds, and disappointments for His mercy, hope and healing... your bitterness, resentment and unforgiveness for His unconditional love, peace and forgiveness. He'll take your ashes and give you His beauty. He really can turn all of your messes into miracles.

Encouraging Creative Response to Illness. William Trotter & Martha Trotter. 1986. 10.80 (090) Assn Prof Chaplains.

Encouraging Spiritual Communication. Rick Joyner. 1 cass. (Running Time: 90 mins.). (Hearing God Ser.: Vol. 3). 2000. 5.00 (RJ10-003) Morning NC.
"Principles of Spiritual Warfare" & "Putting on the Full Armor of God." These tapes highlight practical truths that lead to certain victory in spirtual warfare.

***Encouraging the Heart: A Leader's Guide to Rewarding & Recognizing Others.** unabr. ed. James M. Kouzes & Barry Z. Posner. Read by Erik Synnestvedt. (Running Time: 5 hrs. 30 mins.). (ENG.). 2010. 27.98 (978-1-59659-585-9(X), GildAudio) Pub: Gildan Media. Dist(s): HachBkGrp

Encouraging Words for Discouraging Days. Charles R. Swindoll. 2009. audio compact disk 24.00 (978-1-57972-824-3(3)) Insight Living.

Encuentro Inesperado! Barbara Velasquez. 55.95 (978-0-8219-3635-1(2)) EMC-Paradigm.

Encuentros. 4th ed. Spinelli. (C). bk. 118.95 (978-0-8384-6554-7(4)); bk. 110.95 (978-0-8384-8191-2(4)) Heinle.

Encuentros: An Introduction to Spanish Language & Culture. 4th ed. Emily Spinelli & Marta Rosso-O'Laughlin. (SPA.). 2001. lab manual ed. (978-0-03-028666-7(2)) Harcourt Coll Pubs.

Encuentros: An Introduction to Spanish Language & Culture, Instructor Resource Manual. 4th ed. Emily Spinelli & Marta Rosso-O'Laughlin. (SPA.). 2001. bk. (978-0-03-029282-8(4)) Harcourt Coll Pubs.

Encuentros de un Caracol Aventurero see Poesia y Drama de Garcia Lorca

Encuentros Maravillosos: Gramatica a Traves de la Literatura: Audio Program. Kanter. 2 CDs. (SPA.). audio compact disk 39.97 (978-0-13-116366-9(3)) PH School.

Encyclopaedia Britannica. Compiled by Encyclopaedia Britannica, Inc. 2003. audio compact disk (978-1-59339-067-9(X)); audio compact disk (978-1-59339-062-4(9)) Ency Brit Inc.

Encyclopaedia Britannica. Compiled by Encyclopaedia Britannica, Inc. 2004. audio compact disk (978-1-59339-069-3(6)) Ency Brit Inc.

Encyclopaedia Britannica. Compiled by Encyclopaedia Britannica, Inc. 2004. audio compact disk (978-1-59339-076-1(9)) Ency Brit Inc.

Encyclopaedia Britannica AB Games. Compiled by Encyclopaedia Britannica, Inc. 2006. audio compact disk (978-1-59339-303-8(2)) Ency Brit Inc.

Encyclopaedia Britannica Almanac 2004. Compiled by Encyclopaedia Britannica, Inc. 2004. audio compact disk (978-1-59339-128-7(5)) Ency Brit Inc.

Encyclopaedia Britannica Almanac 2005. Compiled by Encyclopaedia Britannica, Inc. 2005. audio compact disk (978-1-59339-438-7(1)) Ency Brit Inc.

Encyclopaedia Britannica Almanac 2008. Compiled by Encyclopaedia Britannica, Inc. 2008. audio compact disk 11.95 Ency Brit Inc.

Encyclopaedia Britannica Atlas Visual de la Cinema. Compiled by Encyclopaedia Britannica, Inc. 2007. audio compact disk (978-1-59339-564-3(7)) Ency Brit Inc.

Encyclopaedia Britannica Children's Encyclopedia. Compiled by Encyclopaedia Britannica, Inc. 2008. audio compact disk (978-1-59339-418-9(7)) Ency Brit Inc.

Encyclopaedia Britannica Deluxe Edition 2004 CD: A World of Knowledge at Your Fingertips. deluxe ed. Compiled by Encyclopaedia Britannica, Inc. 3 CDs. 2003. audio compact disk 34.95 (978-1-59339-068-6(8), 041704 80 ONR) Ency Brit Inc.

Encyclopaedia Britannica Dinosaurs. Compiled by Encyclopaedia Britannica, Inc. 2004. audio compact disk (978-1-59339-123-2(4)) Ency Brit Inc.

Encyclopaedia Britannica Education Series: GCSE Biology, Chemistry, Physics. Compiled by Encyclopaedia Britannica, Inc. (gr. 14-16). 2007. audio compact disk (978-1-59339-561-2(2)) Ency Brit Inc.

Encyclopaedia Britannica Education Series: GCSE French, History, English. Compiled by Encyclopaedia Britannica, Inc. (gr. 14-16). 2007. audio compact disk (978-1-59339-559-9(0)) Ency Brit Inc.

Encyclopaedia Britannica Education Series: GCSE Maths, German, Geography. Compiled by Encyclopaedia Britannica, Inc. (gr. 14-16). 2007. audio compact disk (978-1-59339-560-5(4)) Ency Brit Inc.

Encyclopaedia Britannica Education Series: GCSE Spanish, Electronics, Music. Compiled by Encyclopaedia Britannica, Inc. (gr. 14-16). 2007. audio compact disk (978-1-59339-562-9(0)) Ency Brit Inc.

Encyclopaedia Britannica Education Series: Key Stage 1 English PC CD-ROM. Compiled by Encyclopaedia Britannica, Inc. (gr. 4-7). 2007. audio compact disk (978-1-59339-544-5(2)) Ency Brit Inc.

Encyclopaedia Britannica Education Series: Key Stage 1 English PC CD-ROM. Compiled by Encyclopaedia Britannica, Inc. (gr. 7-11). 2007. audio compact disk (978-1-59339-547-6(7)) Ency Brit Inc.

Encyclopaedia Britannica Education Series: Key Stage 1 Information Technology PC CD-ROM. Compiled by Encyclopaedia Britannica, Inc. (gr. 4-7). 2007. audio compact disk (978-1-59339-545-2(0)) Ency Brit Inc.

Encyclopaedia Britannica Education Series: Key Stage 1 Maths PC CD-ROM. Compiled by Encyclopaedia Britannica, Inc. (gr. 4-7). 2007. audio compact disk (978-1-59339-546-9(9)) Ency Brit Inc.

Encyclopaedia Britannica Education Series: Key Stage 2 English PC CD-ROM. Compiled by Encyclopaedia Britannica, Inc. (gr. 11-14). 2007. audio compact disk (978-1-59339-550-6(7)) Ency Brit Inc.

Encyclopaedia Britannica Education Series: Key Stage 2 Maths PC CD-ROM. Compiled by Encyclopaedia Britannica, Inc. (gr. 7-11). 2007. audio compact disk (978-1-59339-548-3(5)) Ency Brit Inc.

Encyclopaedia Britannica Education Series: Key Stage 2 Sciences PC CD-ROM. Compiled by Encyclopaedia Britannica, Inc. (gr. 7-11). 2007. audio compact disk (978-1-59339-549-0(3)) Ency Brit Inc.

Encyclopaedia Britannica Education Series: Key Stage 3 Maths PC CD-ROM. Compiled by Encyclopaedia Britannica, Inc. (gr. 11-14). 2007. audio compact disk (978-1-59339-551-3(5)) Ency Brit Inc.

Encyclopaedia Britannica Educational Series: GCSE Biology PC CD-ROM. Compiled by Encyclopaedia Britannica, Inc. 2006. audio compact disk (978-1-59339-326-7(1)) Ency Brit Inc.

Encyclopaedia Britannica Educational Series: GCSE Electronics PC CD-ROM. Compiled by Encyclopaedia Britannica, Inc. 2006. audio compact disk (978-1-59339-328-1(8)) Ency Brit Inc.

Encyclopaedia Britannica Educational Series: GCSE Music PC CD-ROM. Compiled by Encyclopaedia Britannica, Inc. 2006. audio compact disk (978-1-59339-327-4(X)) Ency Brit Inc.

Encyclopaedia Britannica English-Hindi Dictionary. Compiled by Encyclopaedia Britannica, Inc. 2009. audio compact disk Ency Brit Inc.

Encyclopaedia Britannica Familiy Encyclopedia Suite. Compiled by Encyclopaedia Britannica, Inc. 2007. audio compact disk (978-1-59339-415-8(2)) Ency Brit Inc.

Encyclopaedia Britannica Geometry. Compiled by Encyclopaedia Britannica, Inc. 2006. audio compact disk (978-1-59339-304-5(0)) Ency Brit Inc.

Encyclopaedia Britannica Hispanic Heritage. Compiled by Encyclopaedia Britannica, Inc. 2006. audio compact disk 19.95 (978-1-59339-302-1(4)) Ency Brit Inc.

Encyclopaedia Britannica Homework Essentials Plus. Compiled by Encyclopaedia Britannica, Inc. 2007. audio compact disk 19.95 (978-1-59339-543-8(4)) Ency Brit Inc.

Encyclopaedia Britannica Homework Essentials 2004. Compiled by Encyclopaedia Britannica, Inc. 2004. audio compact disk (978-1-59339-071-6(8)) Ency Brit Inc.

Encyclopaedia Britannica Homework Essentials 2004 CD- Mini Box. Compiled by Encyclopaedia Britannica, Inc. 2004. audio compact disk (978-1-59339-094-5(7)) Ency Brit Inc.

Encyclopaedia Britannica Let the Games Begin. Compiled by Encyclopaedia Britannica, Inc. 2004. audio compact disk (978-1-59339-129-4(3)) Ency Brit Inc.

Encyclopaedia Britannica Let the Games Begin 2008. Compiled by Encyclopaedia Britannica, Inc. 2008. audio compact disk 14.95 (978-1-59339-614-5(7)) Ency Brit Inc.

Encyclopaedia Britannica My Body. Compiled by Encyclopaedia Britannica, Inc. 2004. audio compact disk (978-1-59339-126-3(9)) Ency Brit Inc.

Encyclopaedia Britannica Nature. Compiled by Encyclopaedia Britannica, Inc. 2004. audio compact disk (978-1-59339-124-9(2)) Ency Brit Inc.

Encyclopaedia Britannica Presents: Hollywood & the World of Movies. Compiled by Encyclopaedia Britannica, Inc. 2004. audio compact disk 19.95 (978-1-59339-119-5(6)) Ency Brit Inc.

Encyclopaedia Britannica Presents: Let the Games Begin. Compiled by Encyclopaedia Britannica, Inc. 2004. audio compact disk (978-1-59339-118-8(8)) Ency Brit Inc.

Encyclopaedia Britannica Profiles Series D-Day: the Turning Point of WWII ordered by Traci Mysliwiec 10-24-05: The Invasions That Changed History Forever. Compiled by Encyclopaedia Britannica, Inc. 2006. audio compact disk 19.95 (978-1-59339-284-0(2)) Ency Brit Inc.

Encyclopaedia Britannica Ready Reference 2004. Compiled by Encyclopaedia Britannica, Inc. 2004. audio compact disk 49.99 (978-1-59339-099-0(8)) Ency Brit Inc.

Encyclopaedia Britannica Standard. Compiled by Encyclopaedia Britannica, Inc. 2008. audio compact disk 19.95 (978-1-59339-628-2(7)) Ency Brit Inc.

Encyclopaedia Britannica Student Library. Compiled by Encyclopaedia Britannica, Inc. (gr. 1-9). 2008. audio compact disk 19.95 (978-1-59339-430-1(6)) Ency Brit Inc.

Encyclopaedia Britannica Student Library2006. Compiled by Encyclopaedia Britannica, Inc. 2006. audio compact disk (978-1-59339-262-8(1)) Ency Brit Inc.

Encyclopaedia Britannica Touch the Sky. Compiled by Encyclopaedia Britannica, Inc. 2004. audio compact disk (978-1-59339-125-6(0)) Ency Brit Inc.

Encyclopaedia Britannica Ultimate Reference Suite 2004: A Complete Reference Library for All Ages. Compiled by Encyclopaedia Britannica, Inc. 6 pieces. 2003. audio compact disk 49.95 (978-1-59339-064-8(5), 041804 80 ONR) Ency Brit Inc.

Encyclopaedia Britannica Weather. Compiled by Encyclopaedia Britannica, Inc. 2008. audio compact disk Ency Brit Inc.

Encyclopaedia Britannica World Religions. Compiled by Encyclopaedia Britannica, Inc. 2004. audio compact disk (978-1-59339-127-0(7)) Ency Brit Inc.

Encyclopaedia Britannica World Religions. Compiled by Encyclopaedia Britannica, Inc. 2008. audio compact disk 14.95 Ency Brit Inc.

Encyclopaedia Britannica 2003 Almanac. Compiled by Encyclopaedia Britannica, Inc. 2004. audio compact disk 10.95 (978-1-59339-078-5(5)) Ency Brit Inc.

Encyclopaedia Britannica 2004 Homework Essentials Plus 2004. Compiled by Encyclopaedia Britannica, Inc. 2004. audio compact disk 19.95 (978-1-59339-077-8(7)) Ency Brit Inc.

Encyclopaedia Britannica 2004 Ultimate Reference Suite. Compiled by Encyclopaedia Britannica, Inc. 2003. audio compact disk (978-1-59339-063-1(7)) Ency Brit Inc.

Encyclopaedia Britannica 2004 Ultimate Reference Suite. Compiled by Encyclopaedia Britannica, Inc. 2004. audio compact disk 69.95 (978-1-59339-074-7(2)) Ency Brit Inc.

Encyclopaedia Britannica 2006 Deluxe. Compiled by Encyclopaedia Britannica, Inc. 2006. audio compact disk (978-1-59339-450-9(0)) Ency Brit Inc.

Encyclopaedia Britannica 2006 Standard. Compiled by Encyclopaedia Britannica, Inc. 2006. audio compact disk (978-1-59339-256-7(7)) Ency Brit Inc.

Encyclopaedia Britannica 2006 Universal Reference Suite. Compiled by Encyclopaedia Britannica, Inc. 2006. audio compact disk (978-1-59339-254-3(0)) Ency Brit Inc.

Encyclopaedia Britannica 2008 Children's Learning Suite. Compiled by Encyclopaedia Britannica, Inc. (gr. 1-9). 2008. audio compact disk 24.95 (978-1-59339-421-9(7)) Ency Brit Inc.

Encyclopaedia Britannica 2008 Concise Encyclopedia. Compiled by Encyclopaedia Britannica, Inc. 2008. audio compact disk 19.95 (978-1-59339-422-6(5)) Ency Brit Inc.

Encyclopaedia Britannica 2008 Desktop Encyclopedia. Compiled by Encyclopaedia Britannica, Inc. 2008. audio compact disk 29.95 (978-1-59339-423-3(3)) Ency Brit Inc.

Encyclopaedia Britannica 2008 Ready Reference. Compiled by Encyclopaedia Britannica, Inc. 2008. audio compact disk 9.95 Ency Brit Inc.

Encyclopaedia Britannica 2009 Concise. Compiled by Encyclopaedia Britannica, Inc. 2008. audio compact disk 19.95 Ency Brit Inc.

Encyclopaedia Britannica 2009 Deluxe. Compiled by Encyclopaedia Britannica, Inc. 2008. audio compact disk 27.99 Ency Brit Inc.

Encyclopaedia Britannica 2009 Desktop Encyclopedia. Compiled by Encyclopaedia Britannica, Inc. 2008. audio compact disk 29.95 Ency Brit Inc.

Encyclopaedia Britannica 2009 Family Encyclopedia. Compiled by Encyclopaedia Britannica, Inc. audio compact disk Ency Brit Inc.

Encyclopaedia Britannica 2009 Homework Essentials Plus. Compiled by Encyclopaedia Britannica, Inc. audio compact disk Ency Brit Inc.

Encyclopaedia Britannica 2009 Student Library. Compiled by Encyclopaedia Britannica, Inc. audio compact disk 19.95 Ency Brit Inc.

Encyclopaedia Britannnica Homework Essentials Plus. Compiled by Encyclopaedia Britannica, Inc. 2008. audio compact disk Ency Brit Inc.

Encyclopedia Britannica English Arabic Dictionary. Compiled by Encyclopaedia Britannica, Inc. (gr. 1). audio compact disk (978-1-59339-383-0(0)) Ency Brit Inc.

Encyclopedia Brown & the Case of the Missing Clues. Donald J. Sobol. (J). 1979. 44.43 (978-0-394-64547-6(2)) SRA McGraw.

Encyclopedia Brown & the Case of the Secret Pitch. Donald J. Sobol. Read by Jason Harris. (Running Time: 1 hr.). (Encyclopedia Brown Ser.: No. 2). (J). (gr. 3-7). 2004. pap. bk. 17.00 (978-0-8072-1985-0(1), Listening Lib); 23.00 (978-0-8072-1875-4(8), Listening Lib) Random Audio Pubg.

Encyclopedia Brown, Boy Detective. Donald J. Sobol. Read by Jason Harris. (Running Time: 1 hr.). (Encyclopedia Brown Ser.: No. 1). (J). (gr. 3-7). 2004. pap. bk. 17.00 (978-0-8072-1984-3(3), Listening Lib) Random Audio Pubg.

Encyclopedia Brown Cracks the Case. unabr. ed. Donald J. Sobol. Narrated by Greg Steinbruner. 2 cass. (Running Time: 1 hrs. 30 mins.). (J). (gr. 3-5). 2008. 25.75 (978-1-4281-8791-7(X)); audio compact disk 25.75 (978-1-4281-8796-2(0)) Recorded Bks.

Encyclopedia Brown Finds the Clues. unabr. ed. Donald J. Sobol. Narrated by Greg Steinbruner. 2 CDs. (Running Time: 1 hr. 30 mins.). (J). (gr. 1-5). 2007. audio compact disk 25.95 (978-1-4281-7221-0(1)); 20.95 (978-1-4281-7217-3(3)) Recorded Bks.
When the Mystery Writers of America bestowed a Special Edgar Award on Donald J. Sobol's Encyclopedia Brown series, its reputation as a classic of children's literature was assured. This fun read finds 10-year-old Leroy Brown (known to the people of his town as Encyclopedia Brown) honing his impressive detective skills.

***Encyclopedia Brown Keeps the Peace.** unabr. ed. Donald J. Sobol. Narrated by Greg Steinbruner. 1 Playaway. (Running Time: 1 hr. 15 mins.). (J). (gr. 3-5). 2009. 54.75 (978-1-4407-0326-3(4)); 25.75 (978-1-4361-8745-9(1)); audio compact disk 25.75 (978-1-4361-8749-7(4)) Recorded Bks.

Encyclopedia Brown Saves the Day. unabr. ed. Donald J. Sobol. Narrated by Greg Steinbruner. (Running Time: 1 hrs. 30 mins.). (J). (gr. 3-5). 2008. 51.75 (978-1-4361-9886-8(0)); 25.75 (978-1-4361-5192-4(9)); audio compact disk 25.75 (978-1-4361-5197-9(X)) Recorded Bks.

Encyclopedia Brown Saves the Day. unabr. collector's ed. Donald J. Sobol. Narrated by Greg Steinbruner. 2 CDs. (Running Time: 1 hrs. 30 mins.). (J). (gr. 3-5). 2008. audio compact disk 19.95 (978-1-4361-5201-3(1)) Recorded Bks.

***Encyclopedia Brown Solves Them All.** unabr. ed. Donald J. Sobol. Narrated by Greg Steinbruner. 1 cass. (Running Time: 1 hrs. 15 mins.). (J). (gr. 3-5). 2009. 25.75 (978-1-4407-2154-0(8)); audio compact disk 25.75 (978-1-4407-2158-8(0)) Recorded Bks.

***Encyclopedia Brown Solves Them All.** unabr. collector's ed. Donald J. Sobol. Narrated by Greg Steinbruner. 1 CD. (Running Time: 1 hr. 15 mins.). (J). (gr. 3-5). 2009. audio compact disk 22.95 (978-1-4407-2559-3(4)) Recorded Bks.

Encyclopedia Brown Tracks Them Down. unabr. ed. Donald J. Sobol. Narrated by Greg Steinbruner. 2 CDs. (Running Time: 1 hrs. 15 mins.). (J). (gr. 3-6). 2008. audio compact disk 25.75 (978-1-4361-1463-9(2)); 25.75 (978-1-4361-1458-5(6)) Recorded Bks.
Edgar Award-winning author Donald J. Sobol's Encyclopedia Brown mysteries star a humble 10-year-old genius. Here Encyclopedia employs all of his detective skills to investigate 10 more brain-twisting cases with his friend Sally. Thieves and crooks of all ages better beware if they roll into Idaville thinking the town is easy pickings. Encyclopedia hasn't met a case yet that he couldn't crack - or a criminal he couldn't help put behind bars.

Encyclopedia of Guitar Picture Chords in Color. 2004. pap. bk. 29.95 (978-0-8256-1931-1(9), AM973819, Amsco Music) Pub: Music Sales. Dist(s): H Leonard

Encyclopedia of Picture Chords for All Keyboardists. Leonard Vogler. 1996. pap. bk. 29.95 (978-0-8256-1503-0(8), AM931403, Schirmer Trade Bks) Pub: Music Sales. Dist(s): H Leonard

Encyclopedia of Solar Inventions. Compiled by Wayne A. Biszick. Concept by Wayne A. Biszick. 2007. cd-rom 39.[illegible] (978-0-615-20436-9(8)) Global Power.

Encyclopedia of the Russian Market, Vo[illegible] 1. 6th rev. ed. BIA. (J). 2006. audio compact disk 289.00 (978-1-4187-5191-3(X)) Bus Info Agency.

Encyclopedia of the Russian Market, Volume 1. 6th rev. ed. BIA. (J). 2006. audio compact disk 289.00 (978-1-4187-5190-6(1)) Bus Info Agency.

Encyclopedia of the Russian Market, Volume 2. 6th rev. ed. BIA. (J). 2006. audio compact disk 289.00 (978-1-4187-5193-7(6)) Bus Info Agency.

Encyclopedia of the Russian Market, Volume 2. 6th rev. ed. BIA. (J). 2006. audio compact disk 289.00 (978-1-4187-5192-0(8)) Bus Info Agency.

Encyclopedia of the Russian Market, Volume 3. 6th rev. ed. BIA. (J). 2006. audio compact disk 289.00 (978-1-4187-5195-1(2)) Bus Info Agency.

Encyclopedia of the Russian Market, Volume 3. 6th rev. ed. BIA. (J). 2006. audio compact disk 289.00 (978-1-4187-5194-4(4)) Bus Info Agency.

Encyclopedie Racontee, Vol. 2. Christiane Duchesne & Carmen Marois. 1 CD. (Running Time: 1 hrs. 30 mins.). (Children's French Ser.). (FRE.). (J). (gr. k-12). 2000. 16.95 (978-2-89517-031-0(2)) Pub: Coffragants CAN. Dist(s): Penton Overseas
Cyrus will brighten the days of curious children, tired parents & desperate baby sitters. He will charm grandparents & teachers too!.

Encylopaedia Britannica Student Encyclopaedia 2004. Compiled by Encyclopaedia Britannica, Inc. 2004. audio compact disk (978-1-59339-098-3(X)) Ency Brit Inc.

Encylopaedia Britannica the Universe. Compiled by Encyclopaedia Britannica, Inc. 2008. audio compact disk 14.95 Ency Brit Inc.

End. Arthur J. Cockfield. 7 CDs. (Running Time: 7 hrs. 9 mins.). 2002. audio compact disk 23.99 (978-0-9725163-0-3(1)) SSI Pubng.
An apocalyptic environmental catastrophy bringing us closer to the final days of earth?s existance. Splashed with present scientific information weaved through biblical prophesies, this story has been liken to H. G. Well?s ?War Of The Worlds? by Jack Osbourn, President of AudioPulp.com.

End. Yisrayl Hawkins. 10 cass. (Running Time: 10 hrs. 58 min.). 1998. Set. (978-1-890967-23-9(8)) Hse of Yahweh.
This book is a desperate warning to all mankind. It describes in detail the curses that are coming upon them because they fail to heed the every word of Yahweh.

End. abr. ed. Lemony Snicket, pseud. Read by Tim Curry & Tim Curry. (Running Time: 21600 sec.). (Series of Unfortunate Events Ser.: Bk. 13). (J). (gr. 5-9). 2006. 20.00 (978-0-06-057950-0(1), HarperChildAud) HarperCollins Pubs.

End. unabr. ed. Lemony Snicket, pseud. Read by Tim Curry. 5 cass. (Running Time: 6 hrs.). (Series of Unfortunate Events Ser.: Bk. 13). (J). (gr. 4-7). 2006.

39.75 (978-1-4281-2138-6(2)); audio compact disk 49.75 (978-1-4281-2143-0(9)) Recorded Bks.

End. unabr. abr. ed. Lemony Snicket, pseud. Read by Tim Curry & Tim Curry. 5 CDs. (Running Time: 21600 sec.). (Series of Unfortunate Events Ser.: Bk. 13). (J). (gr. 5-9). 2006. audio compact disk 25.95 (978-0-06-057952-4(8), HarperChildAud) HarperCollins Pubs.

End: The Book of Revelation. Scott Hahn. 11 cass. 1995. 49.95 Set. (5265-C) Ignatius Pr.
Scott discovers the unifying principles of the book of Revelation - history, liturgy, & covenant - to present the "big picture" of this multi-dimensional & oft-mysterious book.

End & the Beginning: Pope John Paul II - The Struggle for Freedom, the Last Years, the Legacy. unabr. ed. George Weigel. Read by Stefan Rudnicki. (ENG.). 2010. audio compact disk 45.00 (978-0-307-71549-4(3), Random AudioBks) Pub: Random Audio Pubg. Dist(s): Random

End Clenching & Grinding Your Teeth with Guided Meditation. abr. ed. Paisha Rochlin. Read by Paisha Rochlin. Perf. by Mimi Dye. 1 cass. (Running Time: 36 min.). (C). 1997. (978-0-9675925-1-0(8)) Program for Well.
Guided meditation with viola background to help listener relax, use the power of imagination & suggestion to end the habit of clenching & grinding teeth & stress in general. Stress reduction & dental health guided meditation.

End Depression. 1 cass. 10.00 (978-1-58506-017-7(8), 44) New Life Inst OR.
Use this program to throw off depression & enjoy life again.

End Fear of Failure. 1 cass. 10.00 (978-1-58506-039-9(9), 71) New Life Inst OR.
Use this program to help end your fear of failure. Become confident & brave.

End Games. Michael Dibdin. (Aurelio Zen Mystery Ser.). 2008. 76.95 (978-0-7531-3032-2(7)); audio compact disk 89.95 (978-0-7531-3033-9(5)) Pub: ISIS Audio GBR. Dist(s): Ulverscroft US

End Gossip. Eldon Taylor. 1 cass. (Running Time: 62 min.). (Inner Talk Ser.). 16.95 incl. script. (978-1-55978-614-0(0), 53874F) Progress Aware Res.
Soundtrack - Brook with underlying subliminal affirmations.

End in Tears. unabr. ed. Ruth Rendell. Read by John Lee. 8 cass. (Running Time: 11 hrs.). (Inspector Wexford Mystery Ser.: Bk. 20). 2006. 72.00 (978-1-4159-3077-9(5)); audio compact disk 76.50 (978-1-4159-3078-6(3)) Pub: Books on Tape. Dist(s): NetLibrary CO

End Is Coming, Vol. I. Jerry Ahern. Read by Charlie O'Dowd. 2 vols. No. 8. 2004. 18.00 (978-1-58807-314-3(9)) Am Pubng Inc.

End Is Coming, Vol.. I. Jerry Ahern. Read by Charlie O'Dowd. 2 vols. No. 8. 2004. (978-1-58807-873-5(6)) Am Pubng Inc.

End Is Coming, Vol. II. Jerry Ahern. Read by Charlie O'Dowd. 2 vols. No. 8. 2004. 18.00 (978-1-58807-315-0(7)) Am Pubng Inc.

End Is Coming, Vol.. II. Jerry Ahern. Read by Charlie O'Dowd. 2 vols. No. 8. 2004. (978-1-58807-874-2(4)) Am Pubng Inc.

***End Is Now.** Rob Stennett. (Running Time: 9 hrs. 41 mins. 0 sec.). (ENG.). 2009. 14.99 (978-0-310-77321-4(0)) Zondervan.

End Is the Beginning. Katherine De Jersey & Dale Richardson. 1 cass. 8.95 (512) Am Fed Astrologers.
Prenatal influences affect relationships.

End Maternal Depression. Eldon Taylor. 1 cass. (Running Time: 62 min.). (Inner Talk Ser.). 16.95 incl. script. (978-1-55978-621-8(3), 53865F) Progress Aware Res.
Soundtrack - Brook with underlying subliminal affirmations.

End Mental Blocks & Soar Freely. 2005. audio compact disk 11.95 (978-0-911203-95-0(8)) New Life.

End of a Drought. 2002. 6.00 (978-1-58602-111-5(7)); audio compact disk 9.99 (978-1-58602-113-9(3)) E L Long.

End of All Conceptions. Swami Amar Jyoti. 1 cass. 1982. 9.95 (M-28) Truth Consciousness.
How unbounded Consciousness is limited by our conceptions in a never-ending play.

End of America: A Letter of Warning to a Young Patriot. unabr. ed. Naomi Wolf. Read by Karen White. (Running Time: 6 hrs. 30 mins. 0 sec.). (ENG.). 2008. audio compact disk 24.99 (978-1-4001-0646-2(X)) Pub: Tantor Media. Dist(s): IngramPubServ

End of America: A Letter of Warning to a Young Patriot: A Citizen's Call to Action. unabr. ed. Naomi Wolf. Read by Karen White. (Running Time: 6 hrs. 30 mins. 0 sec.). (ENG.). 2008. audio compact disk 49.99 (978-1-4001-3646-9(6)); audio compact disk 19.99 (978-1-4001-5646-7(7)) Pub: Tantor Media. Dist(s): IngramPubServ

End of America: Letter of Warning to a Young Patriot. unabr. ed. Naomi Wolf. Read by Karen White. (YA). 2008. 44.99 (978-1-60514-862-5(8)) Find a World.

End of Christendom. unabr. ed. Malcolm Muggeridge. Read by Frederick Davidson. 2 cass. (Running Time: 2 hrs. 30 mins.). 1988. 17.95 (978-0-7861-0028-6(1), 1027) Blckstn Audio.
Muggeridge contends that Christendom is of this world & like every other human creation, subject to decay & ruin.

End of Days: Predictions & Prophecies about the End of the World. abr. ed. Sylvia Browne. Read by Jeanie Hackett. (ENG., 2008. audio compact disk 26.95 (978-1-59887-609-3(0), 1598876090) Pub: HighBridge. Dist(s): Workman Pub

***End of Everything: A Novel.** unabr. ed. Megan Abbott. Read by To be announced. (Running Time: 7 hrs. NaN mins.). (ENG.). 2011. 29.95 (978-1-4417-8172-7(2)) Blckstn Audio.

***End of Everything: A Novel.** unabr. ed. Megan Abbott. Read by To be Announced. (Running Time: 7 hrs. NaN mins.). (ENG.). 2011. 44.95 (978-1-4417-8169-7(2)) Blckstn Audio.

***End of Everything: A Novel.** unabr. ed. Megan Abbott. Read by To be announced. (Running Time: 7 hrs. NaN mins.). 2011. audio compact disk 24.95 (978-1-4417-8171-0(4)) Blckstn Audio.

***End of Everything: A Novel.** unabr. ed. Megan Abbott. Read by To be Announced. (Running Time: 7 hrs. NaN mins.). (ENG.). 2011. audio compact disk 69.00 (978-1-4417-8170-3(6)) Blckstn Audio.

End of Food. unabr. ed. Paul Roberts. Narrated by William Dufris. (Running Time: 15 hrs. 0 mins. 0 sec.). (ENG.). 2008. audio compact disk 39.99 (978-1-4001-0599-1(4)) Pub: Tantor Media. Dist(s): IngramPubServ

End of Food. unabr. ed. Paul Roberts. Read by Lloyd James. Narrated by William Dufris. (Running Time: 15 hrs. 0 mins. 0 sec.). (ENG.). 2008. 29.99 (978-1-4001-5599-6(1)); audio compact disk 79.99 (978-1-4001-3599-8(0)) Pub: Tantor Media. Dist(s): IngramPubServ

End of Iraq: How American Incompetence Created a War Without End. Peter W. Galbraith. Read by Alan Sklar. (Playaway Adult Nonfiction Ser.). (ENG.). 2009. 64.99 (978-1-60812-544-9(0)) Find a World.

End of Iraq: How American Incompetence Created a War Without End. unabr. ed. Peter W. Galbraith. Read by Alan Sklar. Narrated by Alan Sklar. (Running Time: 9 hrs. 30 mins. 0 sec.). (ENG.). 2008. audio compact disk 34.99 (978-1-4001-0777-3(6)); audio compact disk 24.99 (978-1-4001-5777-8(3)); audio compact disk 69.99 (978-1-4001-3777-0(2)) Pub: Tantor Media. Dist(s): IngramPubServ

End of Life Care Issues Hospice & Palliative Care. Daniel Farb et al. 2006. audio compact disk 49.95 (978-1-59491-286-3(6)) Pub: UnivofHealth. Dist(s): AtlasBooks

End of Life Care Issues Physiologic Change. Daniel Farb et al. 2006. audio compact disk 49.95 (978-1-59491-285-6(8)) Pub: UnivofHealth. Dist(s): AtlasBooks

End of Nature, unabr. ed. Bill McKibben. Narrated by Nelson Runger. 6 cass. (Running Time: 8 hrs. 30 mins.). 1990. 51.00 (978-1-55690-168-3(2), 90096E7) Recorded Bks.
Technology has brought an end to "natural" events. McKibben not only tells us what we can do now to benefit future generations, but he also provides a persuasive explanation as to how we got ourselves in our current environmental pickle to begin with.

***End of Overeating: Taking Control of the Insatiable American Appetite.** unabr. ed. David A. Kessler. Narrated by Blair Hardman. 6 CDs. (Running Time: 7 hrs.). 2009. audio compact disk 72.75 (978-1-4407-5120-2(X)) Recorded Bks.

End of Overeating: Taking Control of the Insatiable American Appetite. unabr. ed. David A. Kessler. Read by Blair Hardman. 7 hrs. (Running Time: 7 hrs. 0 mins. 0 sec.). (ENG.). 2009. audio compact disk 29.99 (978-0-7435-9679-4(X)) Pub: S&S Audio. Dist(s): S and S Inc

***End of Overeating: Taking Control of the Insatiable American Appetite.** unabr. collector's ed. David A. Kessler. Narrated by Blair Hardman. 6 CDs. (Running Time: 7 hrs. 30 mins.). 2009. audio compact disk 41.95 (978-1-4407-5121-9(8)) Recorded Bks.

End of Poverty: Economic Possibilites for Our Time. unabr. ed. Jeffrey D. Sachs. Read by Malcolm Hillgartner. Frwd. by Bono. (Running Time: 50400 sec.). 2008. audio compact disk & audio compact disk 99.00 (978-1-4332-3353-1(3)) Blckstn Audio.

End of Poverty: Economic Possibilities for Our Time. unabr. ed. Jeffrey D. Sachs. Read by Malcolm Hillgartner. Frwd. by Bono. (Running Time: 50400 sec.). 2008. 79.95 (978-1-4332-3352-4(5)); audio compact disk & audio compact disk 29.95 (978-1-4332-3356-2(8)) Blckstn Audio.

End of Poverty: Economic Possibilities for Our Time. unabr. ed. Jeffrey D. Sachs. Read by Malcolm Hilgartner. (Running Time: 14 hrs.). (ENG.). (gr. 12 up). 2008. audio compact disk 49.95 (978-0-14-314304-8(2), PengAudBks) Penguin Grp USA.

***End of Reason: A Response to the New Atheists.** Zondervan. (Running Time: 2 hrs. 35 mins. 50 sec.). (ENG.). 2010. 14.99 (978-0-310-86998-6(6)) Zondervan.

End of Reincarnation: Breaking the Cycle of Birth & Death. Gary Renard. (Running Time: 9000 sec.). 2006. audio compact disk 19.95 (978-1-59179-462-2(5)) Sounds True.

End of Silence. Contrib. by Red & Jason McArthur. Prod. by Rob Graves. 2007. audio compact disk 15.98 (978-5-557-52689-0(7)) Essential Recs.

End of State: Necessary Evils. Neesa Hart. 2005. audio compact disk 30.99 (978-1-4143-0041-2(7)) Tyndale Hse.

End of Suffering - Nov 2001: The Work of Byron Katie. Byron Katie. 2001. audio compact disk 15.00 (978-1-890246-13-6(1)) B Katie Int Inc.

End of Summer see Twentieth-Century Poetry in English, No. 29, Recordings of Poets Reading Their Own Poetry

End of Summer. unabr. ed. Rosamunde Pilcher. Read by Stella Gonet. 4 cass. (Running Time: 4 hrs.). 1997. 39.95 (978-0-7451-6595-0(8), CAB 1211) AudioGO.
Sitting on a California beach at summer's end, Jane Marsh recalled her childhood at the Elvie estate in Scotland. She remembered the heather-covered hills, the lonely loch, her grandmother, & Sinclair. She had dreamed of marrying Sinclair & settling at Elvie forever. Now an urgent visit from her grandmother's lawyer has become a catalyst for her return to Scotland. Awaiting her is the chilling realization that she might be ready to wed the wrong man.

End of Summer. unabr. ed. Rosamunde Pilcher. Read by Donada Peters. 5 cass. (Running Time: 5 hrs.). 1991. 40.00 (978-0-7366-2004-8(4), 2821) Books on Tape.
Jane Marsh thinks back to her childhood - to a remote corner of Scotland & an estate called Elvie. She can see the heather hills & the lonesome loch, but most of all she pictures her grandmother - & Sinclair. Once she dreamed of marrying Sinclair & living at Elvie forever...once, no longer. But now an urgent visit from her grandmother's attorney prompts her return to Scotland - where waiting for her are memories - & Sinclair. Dare she make the return permanent?.

End of the Affair. unabr. ed. Graham Greene. Read by Michael Kitchen. 6 cass. (Running Time: 9 hrs.). 2000. 49.95 (CAB 1748) Pub: Chivers Audio Bks GBR. Dist(s): AudioGO
Novelist Maurice Bendrix's love affair with his friend's wife, Sarah, had begun in London during the Blitz. But one day, without warning, Sarah had broken off the relationship. Two years later, driven by obsessive jealousy & grief, Bendrix hires a private detective to follow Sarah & find out why she ended their affair.

End of the Affair, Set. unabr. ed. Graham Greene. Read by Michael Kitchen. 6 cass. 1999. 54.95 (978-0-7540-0325-0(6), CAB1748) AudioGO.

End of the Battle. unabr. collector's ed. Evelyn Waugh. Read by David Case. 6 cass. (Running Time: 9 hrs.). (World War II Trilogy). 1992. 48.00 (978-0-7366-2250-9(0), 3039) Books on Tape.
Final volume in trilogy. Guy Crouchback gets one last assignment in Yugoslavia with Tito's forces.

***End of the Beginning.** unabr. ed. Harry Turtledove. Narrated by John Allen Nelson. (Running Time: 19 hrs. 30 mins.). (Days of Infamy Ser.). 2010. 23.99 (978-1-4001-8393-7(6)); 34.99 (978-1-4001-6393-9(5)); audio compact disk 49.99 (978-1-4001-1393-4(8)); audio compact disk 99.99 (978-1-4001-4393-1(4)) Pub: Tantor Media. Dist(s): IngramPubServ

***End of the Free Market: Who Wins the War Between States & Corporations?** unabr. ed. Ian Bremmer. Read by Willis Sparks. (Running Time: 7 hrs.). (ENG.). 2010. 29.98 (978-1-59659-605-4(8), GildAudio) Pub: Gildan Media. Dist(s): HachBkGrp

End of the Harvest. 2004. DVD & audio compact disk 9.99 (978-0-01-223326-9(9)) D Christiano Films.

End of the Line. abr. ed. Matthew S. Hart. Read by Charlton Griffin. Abr. by Odin Westgaard. 2 vols. No. 7. 2004. 18.00 (978-1-58807-249-8(5)); (978-1-58807-744-8(6)) Am Pubng Inc.

End of the Matter. unabr. ed. Alan Dean Foster. (Running Time: 8 hrs.). (Pip & Flinx Ser.: No. 3). 2010. 39.97 (978-1-4233-9562-1(X), 9781423395621, BADLE) Brilliance Audio.

End of the Matter. unabr. ed. Alan Dean Foster. Read by Stefan Rudnicki. (Running Time: 8 hrs.). (Pip & Flinx Ser.: No. 3). 2010. 39.97 (978-1-4233-9561-4(1), 9781423395614, Brlnc Audio MP3 Lib); 24.99 (978-1-4233-9560-7(3), 9781423395607, Brilliance MP3) Brilliance Audio.

End of the Matter. unabr. ed. Alan Dean Foster. Read by Christian Rummel & Stefan Rudnicki. (Running Time: 8 hrs.). (Pip & Flinx Ser.: No. 3). 2010. audio compact disk 29.99 (978-1-4233-9558-4(1), 9781423395584, Bril Audio CD Unabri); audio compact disk 87.97 (978-1-4233-9559-1(X), 9781423395591, BriAudCD Unabrid) Brilliance Audio.

End of the Rainbow. unabr. ed. V. C. Andrews. Read by Liza Ross. 8 cass. (Running Time: 37500 sec.). (Hudson Ser.). 2002. 69.95 (978-0-7531-1123-9(3)); audio compact disk 84.95 (978-0-7531-1339-4(2)) Pub: ISIS Lrg Prnt GBR. Dist(s): Ulverscroft US
Rain's precious daughter, Summer, is about to turn sixteen. Her future lies wide open before her and she carries her mother's wise advice to her heart: life is hardship, but above all, life is hope. A devastating tragedy will force Summer to stare into the cold eyes of adulthood long before she is ready. She will learn very quickly about hardship - but what of hope? Is she as strong as her courageous mother? Or will she crumble?.

End of the Tether. Joseph Conrad. Read by Anais 9000. 2008. 27.95 (978-1-60112-143-1(1)) Babblebooks.

End of the Tether. Joseph Conrad. 1986. (1527) Books on Tape.

End of the Twentieth Century & The End of a Modern Age. unabr. ed. John Lukacs. Read by Bill Kelsey. 8 cass. (Running Time: 12 hrs.). 1997. 64.00 (978-0-7366-3604-9(8), 4258) Books on Tape.
For the West, the period between the end of World War II & the collapse of the Soviet Union was marked by relative peace, high standards of living & high economic productivity.

End of the U. S. Dollar Monopoly: Toward Free Market Monetary System. Friedrich A. Hayek. 1 cass. (Running Time: 40 min.). 10.95 (1104) J Norton Pubs.

End of the Whole Mess: And Other Stories. unabr. ed. Stephen King. Read by Stephen King. Read by Matthew Broderick et al. (Running Time: 5 hrs. 0 mins. 0 sec.). (ENG.). 2009. audio compact disk 14.99 (978-0-7435-9823-1(7)) Pub: S&S Audio. Dist(s): S and S Inc

End of the World: August 20, 2000. Ben Young. 2000. 4.95 (978-0-7417-6194-1(7), B0194) Win Walk.

***End of the World Club.** unabr. ed. Jon Voelkel & Pamela Voelkel. Narrated by Scott Brick. 9 CDs. (Jaguar Stones Trilogy: Bk. 2). (J). (gr. 3-6). 2010. audio compact disk 44.00 (978-0-307-71204-2(4), Listening Lib) Pub: Random Audio Pubg. Dist(s): Random

End of Time: Understanding God's Plan for the Future. James A. Scudder. Illus. by Timothy Bowden. (Christian Living Ser.). 2000. pap. bk. 2.50 (978-0-9679145-0-3(7)) Victin Grace Min.

End of Time: Understanding God's Plan for the Future. abr. ed. James A. Scudder. 1 cass. (Running Time: 1 hr.). 2000. 30.00 (978-0-9679145-1-0(5)) Victin Grace Min.
This easy-to-comprehend guide is a great source for the beginner Bible student or new believer.

End of Time, the Start of Time. Megan McKenna. 4 cass. (Running Time: 5 hrs.). 1992. 29.95 set. (AA2591) Credence Commun.
A perfect retreat to reclaim Advent & learn to enjoy & profit from powerful apocalyptic images.

End of War: A Novel of the Race for Berlin. unabr. ed. David L. Robbins. Narrated by George Guidall. 16 CDs. (Running Time: 19 hrs. 30 mins.). 2001. audio compact disk 139.00 (978-0-7887-6182-9(X)) Recorded Bks.
The End of War focuses on the final months of World War II. Using both real & fictional characters, Robbins tells the riveting story of the race for Berlin. In 1945, world leaders Churchill, Roosevelt & Stalin are poised like gods, shaping the course of history as they consider the military value of Berlin. Their momentous decisions will be realized on a very human level in the lives of a Russian soldier, a German cellist & an American photojournalist. The accuracy creates unforgettable visions of the warfare in this superb thriller.

End of War: A Novel of the Race for Berlin. unabr. ed. David L. Robbins. Narrated by George Guidall. 14 cass. (Running Time: 19 hrs. 30 mins.). 2000. 110.00 (978-0-7887-4862-2(9), 96451E7) Recorded Bks.
Using both real & fictional characters, the author tells the riveting story of the race for Berlin during the final months of World War II. Based on interviews with survivors, historical documents, biographies & analysis, this creates unforgettable visions of warfare.

End of War Set: A Novel of the Race for Berlin. abr. ed. David L. Robbins. 2 cass. 2000. 18.00 (978-1-55935-340-3(6)) Soundelux.
In the final months of war in Europe, the Grand Alliance between Stalin, Churchill & Roosevelt teeters under the burdens of death & desolation, politics & personality.

End of World War Two. 1 cass. (Running Time: 60 min.). 1945. 6.00 Once Upon Rad.
Radio broadcasts - headlines - NBC coverage of the surrender of Japan & the celebration that followed.

End of Your World: Uncensored Straight Talk on the Nature of Enlightenment. Adyashanti & Adyashanti. (Running Time: 27000 sec.). 2008. audio compact disk 69.95 (978-1-59179-945-0(7)) Sounds True.

End Procrastination. Dean A. Montalbano. 2 cds. (Running Time: 2.25 hrs). (Hypnotic Sensory Response Audio Ser.). 2004. audio compact disk 39.95 (978-1-932086-15-7(3)) L Lizards Pub Co.

End Procrastination. Eldon Taylor. Read by Eldon Taylor. Interview with XProgress Aware Staff. 1 cass. (Running Time: 62 min.). 16.95 incl. script. (978-1-55978-299-9(4), 020113) Progress Aware Res.
Verbal coaching soundtrack with underlying subliminal affirmations & sound matrix frequencies for brain entrainment.

End Procrastination: Self Hypnosis. Speeches. Dean A. Montalbano. 2 cass. (Running Time: 2 hours). 2003. 39.95 (978-1-932086-10-2(2)) L Lizards Pub Co.
A self Hypnosis audio set designed to help you END procrastination.

End Sexual Guilt. 1 cass. 10.00 (978-1-58506-024-5(0), 54) New Life Inst OR.
Until your realize you have a right to enjoy sex, you can't have a completely happy love life. For sale only to adults.

End Smoking. 2001. audio compact disk 15.95 (978-1-890575-29-8(1)) Zoilita Grant.

End Smoking. Eldon Taylor. Read by Eldon Taylor. Interview with XProgress Aware Staff. Music by Steven Halpern. Interview with XProgress Aware. 1 cass. (Running Time: 62 min.). (EchoTech Ser.). 16.95 incl. script. (978-1-55978-339-2(7), 9903) Progress Aware Res.
Gentle coaching & soundtrack with underlying subliminal affirmations with tones & frequencies to alter brain wave activity.

End the Fed. unabr. ed. Ron Paul. Read by Bob Craig. (Running Time: 7 hrs.). (ENG.). 2009. 18.98 (978-1-60024-867-2(5)); audio compact disk 26.98 (978-1-60024-866-5(7)) Pub: Hachet Audio. Dist(s): HachBkGrp

End the War with Yourself. 2005. audio compact disk 15.00 (978-1-890246-39-6(5)) B Katie Int Inc.

End Time: The Book of Revelation. Richard Rohr. 4 cass. (Running Time: 3 hrs. 43 min.). 1988. 19.00 Vinyl album. (AA2029) Credence Commun.
Takes the central themes & concerns of the Book of Revelation & preaches a weekend retreat.

End-Time Events. Kenneth Copeland & Charles Capps. 3 cass. (Running Time: 4 hrs. 30 min.). 2001. 15.00 (978-1-57562-270-5(X), TKC270X) K Copeland Pubns.

End Time Faith, Pt. 1. Elbert Willis. 1 cass. 4.00 Fill the Gap.

End Time Faith, Pt. 2. Elbert Willis. 1 cass. 4.00 Fill the Gap.

End Time Faith, Pt. 3. Elbert Willis. 1 cass. 4.00 Fill the Gap.

End Time Faith, Pt. 4. Elbert Willis. 1 cass. 4.00 Fill the Gap.

End Time Faith Series, Set. Elbert Willis. 4 cass. 13.00 Set. Fill the Gap.

End-Time Pressures That Shape Us. Derek Prince. 1 cass. (B-7008) Derek Prince.

End-Time Strategies. 2003. 65.00 (978-0-9742635-9-5(1)) TSEA.

End Times. unabr. ed. Chuck Smith. 4 cass. (Running Time: 3 hrs.). 2001. 12.95 (978-0-936728-88-9(4)) Word For Today.
A four part collection on end times prophesies.

End Times: The the Book of Revelation. unabr. rev. ed. 2002. audio compact disk 14.99 (978-0-310-94487-4(2)) Zondervan.

***End Times Audio Download.** Zondervan Publishing Staff. (Running Time: 30 hrs. 0 mins. 0 sec.). (NIV Audio Bible Ser.). (ENG.). 2006. 8.99 (978-0-310-27230-4(0)) Zondervan.

***End to Al-Qaeda: Destroying Bin Laden's Jihad & Restoring America's Honor.** unabr. ed. Malcolm Nance. (Running Time: 12 hrs.). 2010. 24.99 (978-1-4418-4338-8(8), 9781441843388, BAD) Brilliance Audio.

End to Al-Qaeda: Destroying Bin Laden's Jihad & Restoring America's Honor. unabr. ed. Malcolm Nance. Read by Arthur Morey. 1 MP3-CD. (Running Time: 12 hrs.). 2010. 24.99 (978-1-4418-3422-5(2), 9781441834225, Brilliance MP3); 39.97 (978-1-4418-3423-2(0), 9781441834232, Brlnc Audio MP3 Lib); 39.97 (978-1-4418-3424-9(9), 9781441834249, BADLE); audio compact disk 36.99 (978-1-4418-3420-1(6), 9781441834201, Bril Audio CD Unabri); audio compact disk 89.97 (978-1-4418-3421-8(4), 9781441834218, BriAudCD Unabrid) Brilliance Audio.

End-User Computing with Optical Disk - Implementation. 2 cass. 1990. 17.00 set. Recorded Res.

End-User Computing with Optical Disk - Selection. 2 cass. 1990. 17.00 set. Recorded Res.

Endangered Dreams Pt. A: The Great Depression in California. Kevin Starr. Read by Lloyd James. 10 cass. (Running Time: 15 hrs.). 2000. 80.00 (978-0-7366-5976-5(5)) Books on Tape.
Kevin Starr carries his account into the 1930s, when the political extremes that threatened so much of the Depression-ravaged world loomed large across the California landscape. In capturing the powerful forces that swept the state during the 1930s, Starr weaves an insightful analysis into his narrative fabric. Out of a shattered decade of economic and social dislocation, he constructs a coherent whole and a mirror for understanding our own time.

Endangered Dreams Pt. B: The Great Depression in California. unabr. collector's ed. Kevin Starr. Read by Lloyd James. 8 cass. (Running Time: 12 hrs.). 2000. 80.00 (978-0-7366-5977-2(3)) Books on Tape.
Covers one of the most vibrant decades in California's history, the 1920s. Focusing mainly on Los Angeles, Starr reveals how this city arose almost defiantly on a site lacking many of the advantages normally required for urban development. He describes the importance of water & what it took to get the precious liquid to the arid South. He examines the discovery of oil, the boosters & land developers, the evangelists & the countless other colorful figures of the period.

Endangered Reptiles & Amphibians As Presented by Dr. Glenn Stewart. Hosted by Nancy Pearlman. 1 cass. (Running Time: 29 min.). 10.00 (1022) Educ Comm CA.

Endangered Species. 1 cass. Dramatization. (J). pap. bk. 6.95 (978-0-86545-103-2(6)) Spizzirri.
Facts about American wildlife that is faced with extinction, like the wolf, walrus, condor & crocodile.

Endangered Species. Nevada Barr. Narrated by Barbara Rosenblat. 9 CDs. (Running Time: 10 hrs.). (Anna Pigeon Ser.: Vol. 5). audio compact disk 89.00 (978-1-4025-1567-5(7)) Recorded Bks.

Endangered Species. Ed. by Linda Spizzirri. 1 cass. Dramatization. (J). (gr. 1-8). pap. bk. 4.98 incl. educational coloring bk. (978-0-86545-041-7(2)) Spizzirri.

Endangered Species. abr. ed. Nevada Barr. Read by Cindy Williams. 2 cass. (Running Time: 3 hrs.). (Anna Pigeon Ser.: No. 5). 2001. 18.00 (978-1-59040-129-3(8), Phoenix Audio) Pub: Amer Intl Pub. Dist(s): PerseuPGW

Endangered Species. abr. ed. Rex Burns. Read by Charlton Griffin. Abr. by Edward McClure. 2 vols. 2003. (978-1-58807-672-4(5)) Am Pubng Inc.

Endangered Species. unabr. ed. Nevada Barr. Narrated by Barbara Rosenblat. 7 cass. (Running Time: 10 hrs.). (Anna Pigeon Ser.: No. 5). 2001. 66.00 (978-0-7887-5407-4(6)) Recorded Bks.
In the midst of a dangerously dry season, national park ranger Anna Pigeon has been posted to Cumberland Island off the Georgia coast for a monotonous, 21-day fire watch. But her boredom is short-lived, for this remote island spawns eccentricity and secrets, greed, suspicion - and murder.

Endangered Species: Legal Requirements & Policy Guidance. Ed. by Danny C. Reinke & Lucinda Low Swartz. 2001. bk. 45.00 (978-1-57477-108-4(6)) Battelle.

Endangered Species & Friends. Karen Scott. 1 cass. (J). (ps-4). bk. 19.95 (978-1-889667-63-8(3), 616629) Second Ark.
ABC book on endangered species interactive glossary, pull-out map.

Endearing Lessons of Kiddush Hashem from the Life of Rav Shimon Schwab, ZT"L. Myer J. Schwab. 1 cass. (Running Time: 90 mins.). 1999. 6.00 (R60FU) Torah Umesorah.

Ender Collection. Orson Scott Card. (Ender Ser.). (978-1-59397-499-2(X)) Macmill Audio.

Ender in Exile. unabr. ed. Orson Scott Card. 1 MP3-CD. (Running Time: 15 hrs. 30 mins.). 2008. 69.95 (978-0-7927-5824-2(2), Chivers Sound Lib); 69.95 (978-0-7927-5932-4(X), Chivers Sound Lib); audio compact disk 112.95 (978-0-7927-5663-7(0), Chivers Sound Lib) AudioGO.

Ender in Exile. unabr. ed. Orson Scott Card. Narrated by Stefan Rudnicki & Harlan Ellison. 13 CDs. (Running Time: 14 hrs. 0 mins. 0 sec.). (Ender Ser.). (ENG.). 2008. audio compact disk 49.95 (978-1-4272-0512-4(4)) Pub: Macmill Audio. Dist(s): Macmillan

Ender's Game. Orson Scott Card. 7 cass. (Running Time: 8 hrs.). (Ender Ser.: Bk. 1). 1993. 55.00 Set. (978-1-56544-043-2(9), 550001); Rental 9.75 30 day rental Set. (550001) Literate Ear.
Earth's government prepares for a third attack by aliens who have almost succeeded in destroying the planet. Child geniuses are raised in military training grounds & intensively prepared for the confrontation. Ender Wiggins stands out among them. Ender is six years old & has no real idea of what he is being trained for. It seems like a game.

Ender's Game. unabr. ed. Orson Scott Card. Read by Stephen Rudnicki et al. (Ender Ser.: Bk. 1). 29.95 (978-0-7927-3360-7(6)); 59.95 (978-0-7927-3358-4(4)); audio compact disk 89.95 (978-0-7927-3359-1(2)) AudioGO.

Ender's Game. unabr. ed. Orson Scott Card. Narrated by Harlan Ellison & Stefan Rudnicki. 9 CDs. (Running Time: 10 hrs. 30 mins. 0 sec.). (Ender Quartet Ser.). (ENG.). (J). (gr. 7 up). 2008. audio compact disk 39.95 (978-1-4272-0526-1(4)) Pub: Macmill Audio. Dist(s): Macmillan

Ender's Game. unabr. rev. ed. Orson Scott Card. Read by Stefan Rudnicki & Harlan Ellison. 9 CDs. (Running Time: 10 hrs. 30 mins. 0 sec.). (Ender Ser.: Bk. 1). (ENG.). 2004. audio compact disk 39.95 (978-1-59397-474-9(4)) Pub: Macmill Audio. Dist(s): Macmillan

Ender's Shadow. unabr. ed. Orson Scott Card. Read by Scott Brick & Gabrielle De Cuir. 13 CDs. (Running Time: 15 hrs. 30 mins. 0 sec.). (Shadow Ser.). (ENG.). 2005. audio compact disk 49.95 (978-1-59397-664-4(X)) Pub: Macmill Audio. Dist(s): Macmillan

Ending Addictions. Scripts. Marjorie Baker Price. Perf. by Marjorie Baker Price. 2 cassettes. (Running Time: 60 minutes). 1990. 16.95 (978-0-9713013-6-8(0)) Centering Pubns.
This two-tape set "Freedom From Drugs and Alcohol" and "Ending An Addictive Relationship" will powerfully provide an inner directed ability to recover from addictions. Each tape offers tremendously healing self-hypnosis exercises to return you to an internal center of control and safety. Here you can , from a restored awareness, clarity and personal power, recover your own unique spirituality and a newly- freed life, which can now offer real possibilites for health, love and success.

Ending Anorexic Patterns. Eldon Taylor. 1 cass. (Running Time: 62 min.). (Inner Talk Ser.). 16.95 (53799C) Progress Aware Res.
Soundtrack - Musical Themes with underlying subliminal affirmations.

Ending Anorexic Patterns: Babbling Brook. Eldon Taylor. 1 cass. 16.95 (978-1-55978-518-1(7), 53799F) Progress Aware Res.

Ending Anorexic Patterns: Music Theme. Eldon Taylor. 1 cass. 16.95 (978-1-55978-186-2(6), 53799C) Progress Aware Res.

Ending Attack Thought/Evolving Wings. Marianne Williamson. Read by Marianne Williamson. 1 cass. (Running Time: 90 mins.). (Lectures on a Course in Miracles). 1999. 10.00 (978-1-56170-292-3(7), M804) Hay House.

Ending Bad Dreams. Eldon Taylor. 1 cass. (Running Time: 62 min.). (Inner Talk Ser.). 16.95 incl. script. (978-1-55978-615-7(9), 53866F) Progress Aware Res.
Soundtrack - Brook with underlying subliminal affirmations.

***Ending in Marriage.** Debbie Macomber. 2011. audio compact disk 9.99 (978-1-4418-5344-8(8)) Brilliance Audio.

***Ending in Marriage.** unabr. ed. Debbie Macomber. Read by Dan John Miller. (Running Time: 5 hrs.). 2010. 14.99 (978-1-4418-5342-4(1), 9781441853424, Brilliance MP3); 14.99 (978-1-4418-5343-1(X), 9781441853431, BAD); audio compact disk 14.99 (978-1-4418-5341-7(3), 9781441853417, Bril Audio CD Unabri) Brilliance Audio.

Ending Jet Lag: Eight Simple Rules. Douglas Westfall. 2008. 10.00 (978-1-891030-68-0(X), PAP) Paragon Agency.

Ending Our Resistance to Love. Kenneth Wapnick. 2008. 10.00 (978-1-59142-364-5(3)) Foun Miracles.

Ending Self Destructive Patterns. Eldon Taylor. 1 cass. (Running Time: 62 min.). (Inner Talk Ser.). 16.95 incl. script. (978-1-55978-435-1(0), 53802F) Progress Aware Res.
Brook Soundtrack with underlying subliminal affirmations.

Ending Self Destructive Patterns. Eldon Taylor. Read by Eldon Taylor. Interview with XProgress Aware Staff. Music by Steven Halpern. Interview with XProgress Aware. 1 cass. (Running Time: 62 min.). (EchoTech Ser.). 16.95 incl. script. (978-1-55978-349-1(4), 9909) Progress Aware Res.
Gentle coaching & soundtrack with underlying subliminal affirmations with tones & frequencies to alter brain wave activity.

Ending Self Destructive Patterns. Eldon Taylor. 1 CD. (Running Time: 52 min.). (Whole Brain Innertalk Ser.). 1998. audio compact disk (978-1-55978-857-1(7)) Progress Aware Res.

Ending Self Destructive Patterns. Eldon Taylor. 1 CD. (Running Time: 52 min.). (Whole Brain Innertalk Ser.). 1999. audio compact disk (978-1-55978-915-8(8)) Progress Aware Res.

Ending Self Destructive Patterns: Pastoral Theme. Eldon Taylor. 1 cass. 16.95 (978-1-55978-434-4(2), 53802M) Progress Aware Res.

Ending Self-Sabotage: Easy. Eldon Taylor. Read by Eldon Taylor. Ed. by Leslie Brice. 1 cass. (Running Time: 1 hr.). 1992. 16.95 (978-1-56705-186-5(3)) Gateways Inst.
Self improvement.

Ending Self-Sabotage: Ocean. Eldon Taylor. Read by Eldon Taylor. Ed. by Leslie Brice. 1 cass. (Running Time: 1 hr.). 1992. 16.95 (978-1-56705-187-2(1)) Gateways Inst.

Ending Self-Sabotage: Stream. Eldon Taylor. Read by Eldon Taylor. Ed. by Leslie Brice. 1 cass. (Running Time: 1 hr.). 1992. 16.95 (978-1-56705-188-9(X)) Gateways Inst.

Ending the Betrayal of Self. unabr. ed. Paul Ferrini. Read by Paul Ferrini. 2 cass. (Running Time: 3 hrs.). (Christ Mind Talks & Workshops Ser.). 1997. audio compact disk 16.95 Set. (978-1-879159-28-0(7)) Heartways Pr.
A workshop given at the Learning Annex in April 1997.

Ending the Cycle of Generational Curses. Creflo A. Dollar. 5 cass. (Running Time: 7 hrs. 30 mins.). 2001. 25.00 (978-1-931172-96-7(X), TS204, Kidz Faith) Pub: Creflo Dollar. Dist(s): STL Dist NA

Ending the War on Drugs. Dirk Chase Eldredge. Read by Jeff Riggenbach. 5 cass. (Running Time: 7 hrs.). 2005. 54.95 (978-0-7861-2937-9(9), 3412); audio compact disk 63.00 (978-0-7861-8185-8(0), 3412) Blckstn Audio.

Ending Up, unabr. collector's ed. Kingsley Amis. Read by David Case. 5 cass. (Running Time: 5 hrs.). 1988. 30.00 (978-0-7366-1312-5(9), 2218) Books on Tape.
A comic, semi-tragic novel detailing the lives of four eccentric geriatrics in a retirement cottage.

Ending Well, Starting Strong: Your Personal Pastorate Start-up Workshop. Roy M. Oswald. 1995. pap. bk. 89.95 (978-1-56699-143-8(9), AL157) Alban Inst.

Endings Man. Frederic Lindsay. Read by Joe Dunlop. 6 cass. 2007. 54.95 (978-1-84559-548-7(3)) Pub: Soundings Ltd GBR. Dist(s): Ulverscroft US

***Endless Forest.** unabr. ed. Sara Donati. Narrated by Kate Reading. 18 CDs. (Running Time: 22 hrs.). 2010. audio compact disk 100.00 (978-1-4159-6615-0(X)) Random.

Endless Forms Most Beautiful: The New Science of Evo Devo & the Making of the Animal Kingdom. unabr. ed. Sean B. Carroll. Read by Arthur Morey. 7 CDs. (Running Time: 9 hrs.). 2009. audio compact disk 92.97 (978-1-4233-7811-2(3), 9781423378112, BriAudCD Unabrid) Brilliance Audio.

Endless Forms Most Beautiful: The New Science of Evo Devo & the Making of the Animal Kingdom. unabr. abr. ed. Sean B. Carroll. Read by Arthur Morey. (Running Time: 8 hrs.). 2009. 39.97 (978-1-4233-7815-0(6), 9781423378150, BADLE); 39.97 (978-1-4233-7813-6(X), 9781423378136, Brlnc Audio MP3 Lib); 24.99 (978-1-4233-7812-9(1), 9781423378129, Brilliance MP3); 24.99 (978-1-4233-7814-3(8), 9781423378143, BAD); audio compact disk 29.99 (978-1-4233-7810-5(5), 9781423378105, Bril Audio CD Unabri) Brilliance Audio.

Endless Game. abr. ed. Bryn Forbes. Read by Bryn Forbes. 1 cass. 1993. 12.00 (978-1-878427-29-8(6), XC407) Cimino Pub Grp.

Endless Knot. Stephen R. Lawhead. Narrated by Robert Whitfield. (Running Time: 12 hrs. 30 mins.). 2001. 34.95 (978-1-59912-655-5(9)) Iofy Corp.

Endless Knot. unabr. ed. Stephen R. Lawhead. Read by Robert Whitfield. 9 cass. (Running Time: 13 hrs. 30 mins.). 2002. 62.95 (978-0-7861-2374-2(5)); audio compact disk 88.00 (978-0-7861-9379-0(4)) Blckstn Audio.

Endless Knot. unabr. ed. Stephen R. Lawhead. Read by Robert Whitfield. 1 MP3. (Running Time: 16 hrs. 30 min.). (Song of Albion Ser.). 2002. audio compact disk 24.95 (978-0-7861-9110-9(4)) Blckstn Audio.

***Endless Knot: The Song of Albion Trilogy, Book 3.** unabr. ed. Stephen R. Lawhead. Read by Robert Whitfield. (Song of Albion Ser.). 2010. audio compact disk 29.95 (978-1-4417-5137-9(8)) Blckstn Audio.

Endless Love. unabr. ed. Scott Spencer. Narrated by Scott Shina. 11 cass. (Running Time: 16 hrs.). 2001. 99.00 (978-0-7887-4995-7(1), 95678E7) Recorded Bks.
Memories of a deeply damaged man & his obsession with a beautiful unstable young woman & her unconventional family.

Endless Mercy. Perf. by Vinny Flynn and Still Waters. 1 cass., 1 CD. (Running Time: 40 min.). 1999. 12.00 (978-1-884479-05-2(7)); audio compact disk 16.00 CD. (978-1-884479-06-9(5)) Spirit Song.
Meditative religious songs.

***Endless Night.** Agatha Christie. Narrated by Hugh Fraser. (Running Time: 7 hrs. 0 mins. 0 sec.). (ENG.). 2011. audio compact disk 29.95 (978-1-60283-939-7(5)) Pub: AudioGO. Dist(s): Perseus Dist

***Endless Night.** Agatha Christie & Lizzie Watts. Narrated by Jonathan Forbes. (Running Time: 2 hrs. 0 mins. 0 sec.). (ENG.). 2010. audio compact disk 24.95 (978-1-4084-0080-7(4)) Pub: AudioGO. Dist(s): Perseus Dist

Endless Steppe: Growing up in Siberia, unabr. ed. Esther Hautzig. Narrated by Alyssa Bresnahan. 6 pieces. (Running Time: 7 hrs. 45 mins.). (gr. 7 up). 1997. 51.00 (978-0-7887-0413-0(3), 94605E7) Recorded Bks.
Explore the history of World War II & celebrate the triumph of the human spirit with this poignant autobiography. In 1941, Russian soldiers invaded 10-year-old Esther Hautzig's peaceful home in Poland. Arrested & deported to a remote Siberian village, her family struggles against all odds to survive the war.

Endless Tunnel. unabr. ed. Howard H. Hilton. Read by Gene Engene. 6 cass. (Running Time: 7 hrs. 30 min.). 1996. 36.95 Set. (978-1-55686-712-5(3)) Books in Motion.
Boston's Callahan Tunnel becomes the scene of a fiery holocaust where twenty-three holiday travelers become trapped when an oversized trailer overturns & blocks the tunnel.

Endoscopic Sinus Surgery. Nikhil J. Bhatt. 1997. audio compact disk 235.95 (978-1-56593-898-4(4), Singular) Delmar.

Endoscopic Urology: Transurethral, Transureteral & Percutaneous. Moderated by Martin I. Resnick. 2 cass. (Urologic Surgery Ser.: UR-2). 1986. 19.00 (8669) Am Coll Surgeons.

Endowed from On High Set: Understanding the Symbols of the Endowment, unabr. ed. John D. Charles. Read by Mark Van Wagoner. 2 cass. (Running Time: 2 hrs.). 1998. 16.98 (978-0-88290-646-1(1), 1870) Horizon Utah.
The scriptural basis for each aspect of the temple endowment is examined.

Endurance. (702) Yoga Res Foun.

Endurance. Derek Prince. 1 cass. (I-4053); 5.95 (080) Derek Prince.
God has a specific process by which this essential ingredient for a successful Christian character may be produced.

Endurance. abr. ed. Caroline Alexander. Read by Michael Tezla & Martin Ruben. 5 CDs. (Running Time: 6 hrs.). 2000. audio compact disk 29.95 HighBridge.
A riveting account of explorer Ernest Shackleton's expedition of the South Atlantic & twenty month survival on ice flows.

Endurance. unabr. ed. Caroline Alexander. Read by Stuart Langton. 2001. audio compact disk 40.00 Books on Tape.
An unflinching account of Shackleton's 1914 expedition - one of history's greatest epics of survival.

***Endurance.** unabr. ed. Jack Kilborn. 1 CD MP3. (Running Time: 7 hrs.). 2010. 39.97 (978-1-4233-8317-8(6), 9781423383178, Brlnc Audio MP3 Lib); 24.99 (978-1-4233-8316-1(8), 9781423383161, Brilliance MP3); 39.97 (978-1-4233-8319-2(2), 9781423383192, BADLE) Brilliance Audio.

Endurance. unabr. ed. Jack Kilborn. (Running Time: 9 hrs.). 2011. audio compact disk 24.99 (978-1-4233-8314-7(1), 9781423383147, Bril Audio CD Unabri) Brilliance Audio.

***Endurance.** unabr. ed. Jack Kilborn. (Running Time: 9 hrs.). 2011. 24.99 (978-1-4233-8318-5(4), 9781423383185, BAD) Brilliance Audio.

***Endurance.** unabr. ed. Jack Kilborn. Read by Christopher Lane. 6 CDs. (Running Time: 9 hrs.). 2011. audio compact disk 69.97 (978-1-4233-8315-4(X), 9781423383154, BriAudCD Unabrid) Brilliance Audio.

Endurance. unabr. ed. Alfred Lansing. Read by Richard Brown. (Running Time: 39600 sec.). 2007. 25.95 (978-0-7861-4716-8(4)); audio compact disk 27.95 (978-0-7861-6580-3(4)); audio compact disk 29.95 (978-0-7861-7323-5(8)) Blckstn Audio.

Endurance. unabr. ed. Alfred Lansing. Read by Simon Prebble. (Running Time: 10 hrs. 30 mins.). 2007. audio compact disk 19.95 (978-1-4332-0818-8(0)) Blckstn Audio.

Endurance: Shackleton's Incredible Voyage. abr. ed. Alfred Lansing. Read by Patrick Malahide. 4 cass. (Running Time: 6 hrs.). 2000. 24.95 (978-1-57270-133-5(1), E41133) Pub: Audio Partners. Dist(s): PerseuPGW
In August 1914, Ernest Shackleton & his crew set sail from England for Antarica, where he hoped to be the first man to cross the uncharted continent on foot. Five months later - just a day short of its destination - the Endurance became locked in an island of ice. For ten months it drifted until it was finally crushed. Shackleton & his crew made an 850-mile journey in a 20-foot craft to survive for over a year on the ice-bound Antarctic seas.

Endurance: Shackleton's Incredible Voyage. abr. ed. Alfred Lansing. Read by Tim Pigott-Smith. 5 CDs. (Running Time: 6 hrs.). 2002. audio compact disk 29.95 (978-1-57270-290-5(7)) Pub: Audio Partners. Dist(s): PerseuPGW
A phenomenal adventure/survival story. Polar explorer Ernest Shackleton enabled all 27 men on his crew to survive for over a year on the ice-bound Antarctic seas. This gripping account of the journey is based on contemporaneous diaries that were kept by the survivors.

Endurance: Shackleton's Incredible Voyage. unabr. ed. Alfred Lansing. Read by Richard Brown. 8 cass. (Running Time: 11 hrs. 30 mins.). 1991. 56.95 (978-0-7861-0180-1(6), 1160) Blckstn Audio.
This fabulous account of Sir Ernest Shackleton's epic adventure recreates one of the most astonishing feats of exploration & human courage ever recorded. In August, 1914, the "Endurace" set sail for the South Atlantic. In October, 1915, still half a continent away from its intended base, the ship was trapped, then crushed in the ice. For five months Shackleton & his men, drifting on ice packs, were castaways in one of the most savage regions of the world.

Endurance: Shackleton's Incredible Voyage. unabr. ed. Alfred Lansing. Read by Grover Gardner. 7 cass. (Running Time: 10 hrs. 30 mins.). 1988. 56.00 (978-0-7366-1350-7(1), 2251) Books on Tape.
Ernest Shackleton made his first expedition to the Antarctic with Scott in 1901. Fifteen years later he returned, but this time in command of his own party. First, ice crushed his ship. Shackleton led his men 180 miles across the ice to Elephant Island. From there he & a few others sailed 800 miles on the wildest of seas, crossed South Georgia Island to a whaling station, & returned to Elephant Island to rescue the survivors.

Endurance: Shackleton's Incredible Voyage. unabr. ed. Alfred Lansing. Read by Simon Prebble. (Running Time: 37800 sec.). 2007. 65.95 (978-1-4332-0628-3(5)); audio compact disk 81.00 (978-1-4332-0629-0(3)); audio compact disk 29.95 (978-1-4332-0630-6(7)) Blckstn Audio.

Endurance: Shackleton's Incredible Voyage. unabr. ed. Alfred Lansing. Read by Simon Prebble. (Running Time: 37800 sec.). 2007. 19.95 (978-1-4332-0817-1(2)) Blckstn Audio.

Endurance: Shackleton's Legendary Antarctic Expedition. Caroline Alexander. Read by Stuart Langton. 1999. audio compact disk 40.00 (978-0-7366-6294-9(4)) Books on Tape.

Endurance: Shackleton's Legendary Antarctic Expedition. abr. ed. Caroline Alexander. Read by Michael Tezla & Martin Ruben. 5 CDs. (Running Time: 6 hrs.). (ENG.). 2000. audio compact disk 29.95 (978-1-56511-418-0(3), 1565114183) Pub: HighBridge. Dist(s): Workman Pub

Endurance: Shackleton's Legendary Antarctic Expedition, unabr. ed. Caroline Alexander. Read by Stuart Langton. 4 cass. (Running Time: 6 hrs.). 1999. 32.00 (978-0-7366-4485-3(7), 4916) Books on Tape.
An unflinching account of Shackleton's 1914 expedition - one of history's greatest epics of survival.

Endurance: Shipwreck & Survival on a Sea of Ice. Matt White. (High Five Reading - Purple Ser.). (ENG.). (gr. 4 up). 2001. audio compact disk 5.95 (978-0-7368-9505-7(1)) CapstoneDig.

Endurance: Shipwreck & Survival on a Sea of Ice. Matt White. (High Five Reading - Purple Ser.). (ENG.). (gr. 4-5). 2007. audio compact disk 5.95 (978-1-4296-1425-2(0)) CapstoneDig.

Endurance Training: Hebrews 12:1-3. Ed Young. 1992. 4.95 (978-0-7417-1934-8(7), 934) Win Walk.

Enduring Adversity, Matters of the Heart Vol. 4: Keys to Staying Steady in Tough Times. Mac Hammond. 2 cass. 2004. 10.00 (978-1-57399-139-1(2)); audio compact disk 10.00 (978-1-57399-141-4(4)) Mac Hammond.
Mac Hammond explains how you can cultivate a thankful heart and a merry heart - two key heart conditions that unlock the doors to winning any fight of faith.

Enduring Grace. Carol L. Flinders. 2 cass. (Running Time: 3 hrs.). 1995. 18.95 Set. (AA2844) Credence Commun.
The lives & teachings of six great women saints. St. Catherine of Siena, Julian of Norwich, Clare of Assisi, Mechtild of Magdeburg, Teresa of Avila & St. Catherine of Genoa. Their letters, their lives, their times & above all, their life of faith & prayer - fully Catholic, fully feminine, fully orthodox. And so nourishing.

Enduring Love. Ian McEwan. Read by Steven Crossley. 6 Cass. (Running Time: 9 Hrs.). 29.95 (978-1-4025-3931-2(2)) Recorded Bks.

Enduring Love. movie tie-in ed. Ian McEwan. Read by Richard E. Grant. 2 cass. (Running Time: 3 hrs.). 1999. 16.85 Set. (978-0-00-105565-0(8)) Ulvrscrft Audio.
Totally compelling, utterly & terrifyingly convincing, is the story of how an ordinary man can be driven to the brink of murder & madness by another's delusions.

Enduring Love. unabr. ed. Ian McEwan. Narrated by Steven Crossley. 6 cass. (Running Time: 9 hrs.). 1998. 51.00 (978-0-7887-2176-2(3), 95472E7) Recorded Bks.
One idyllic British afternoon, when Joe Rose rushes to aid an elderly man & his grandson, he encounters a zealous stranger who will cast a shadow over Joe's life far beyond the limits of that fateful day.

Enduring Love, Set. Michele Ashman Bell. 2 cass. 12.95 (978-1-57734-334-9(4), 07001932) Covenant Comms.

Enduring Love, Set. abr. ed. Ian McEwan. Read by Maxwell Caulfield. 4 cass. (Running Time: 6 hrs.). 1997. 24.95 (978-1-57511-040-0(7)) Pub Mills.
A freak accident brings a mysterious stranger into the life of a young couple, with distrubing consequences.

Enduring Passions. David Wiltshire. 2009. 61.95 (978-1-4079-0320-0(9)); audio compact disk 79.95 (978-1-4079-0321-7(7)) Pub: Soundings Ltd GBR. Dist(s): Ulverscroft US

Endymion. unabr. ed. Dan Simmons. Read by Victor Bevine. (Running Time: 23 hrs.). (Hyperion Cantos Ser.). 2009. 29.99 (978-1-4233-8164-8(5), 9781423381648, Brilliance MP3); 44.97 (978-1-4233-8165-5(3), 9781423381655, Brlnc Audio MP3 Lib); 44.97 (978-1-4233-8166-2(1), 9781423381662, BADLE); audio compact disk 99.97 (978-1-4233-8163-1(7), 9781423381631, BriAudCD Unabrid); audio compact disk 49.99 (978-1-4233-8162-4(9), 9781423381624, Bril Audio CD Unabri) Brilliance Audio.

Endymion: Hymn to Pan see Poetry of Keats

Endymion Spring. unabr. ed. Matthew Skelton. Read by Richard Easton. 6 cass. (YA). 2006. 45.00 (978-0-7393-3807-0(2), Listening Lib); audio compact disk 60.00 (978-0-7393-3775-2(0), Listening Lib) Pub: Random Audio Pubg. Dist(s): Random

Enemies. unabr. ed. Keith Douglass. Read by David Hilder. 6 cass. (Running Time: 9 hrs.). (Carrier Ser.: No. 15). 2001. 48.00 Books on Tape.
"Tombstone" Magruder and Carrier Battle Group Fourteen are sent to maintain the peace between Greece and Macedonia.

Enemies: A Love Story. unabr. ed. Isaac Bashevis Singer. Read by Wolfram Kandinsky. 8 cass. (Running Time: 8 hrs.). 1986. 48.00 (978-0-7366-0389-8(1), 1366) Books on Tape.
Herman Broder, whose family was wiped out in the Nazi Holocaust in Poland, escaped death by hiding in a village hayloft for two years. When we meet him he is living in an apartment in the Coney Island section of Brooklyn with his cloistered wife, Yadwiga, a Polish peasant girl who helped him escape. He is also deeply involved with Masha Toshiner. He finds out his first wife, Tamara, has survived & is in America. The three women discover the truth & each proposes her own solution.

***Enemies: How America's Foes Steal Our Vital Secrets-and How We Let It Happen.** unabr. ed. Bill Gertz. Read by James Adams. (Running Time: 10 hrs. 0 mins.). 2010. 29.95 (978-1-4417-2269-0(6)); 59.95 (978-1-4417-2265-2(3)); audio compact disk 90.00 (978-1-4417-2266-9(1)) Blckstn Audio.

Enemies of Eros. unabr. ed. Maggie Gallagher. Read by Mary Woods. 5 cass. (Running Time: 7 hrs.). 1992. 39.95 (978-0-7861-0286-0(1), 1251) Blckstn Audio.
The sexual revolution is killing family, marriage & sex, contends Maggie Gallagher. By giving motherhood a low social status, argues Gallagher, our culture dismisses the work that family-centered mothers perform. In the process, she attacks sacred cows with humor & style & demonstrates how the feminist movement (among other forces) has failed women & children first, with men not far behind.

Enemies of "Extremism" Ayn Rand. 1 cass. (Running Time: 28 min.). 1962. 12.95 (978-1-56114-116-6(X), AR36C) Second Renaissance.

Enemies of the People: My Family's Journey to America. unabr. ed. Kati Marton. Narrated by Laural Merlington. 1 MP3-CD. (Running Time: 9 hrs. 0 mins. 0 sec.). (ENG.). 2009. 24.99 (978-1-4001-6335-9(8)); audio compact disk 69.99 (978-1-4001-4335-1(7)); audio compact disk 34.99 (978-1-4001-1335-4(0)) Pub: Tantor Media. Dist(s): IngramPubServ

***Enemies of the People: My Family's Journey to America.** unabr. ed. Kati Marton. Narrated by Laural Merlington. (Running Time: 9 hrs. 0 mins.). 2009. 34.99 (978-1-4001-9335-6(4)); 15.99 (978-1-4001-8335-7(9)) Tantor Media.

Enemies We Face. Derek Prince. 4 cass. 1989. 19.95 set. (I-EF1) Derek Prince.
This four-part series exposes Satan's kingdom - its origin, organization, & operation - & the requirements for a victorious church.

Enemies Within the Home: Ephesians 4:31. Ed Young. (J). 1981. 4.95 (978-0-7417-1160-1(5), A0160) Win Walk.

Enemy. abr. ed. Lee Child. Read by Dick Hill. (Running Time: 6 hrs.). (Jack Reacher Ser.). 2007. audio compact disk 14.99 (978-1-4233-1961-0(3), 9781423319610, BCD Value Price) Brilliance Audio.

Enemy. abr. ed. Lee Child. Read by Dick Hill. (Running Time: 6 hrs.). (Jack Reacher Ser.). 2009. audio compact disk 9.99 (978-1-4418-2643-5(2), 9781441826435, BCD Value Price) Brilliance Audio.

Enemy. unabr. ed. Lee Child. Read by Dick Hill. 8 cass. (Running Time: 14 hrs.). (Jack Reacher Ser.). 2004. 97.25 (978-1-59086-410-4(7), 1590864107, BrilAudUnabridg); 34.95 (978-1-59086-409-8(3), 1590864093, BAU); audio compact disk 39.95 (978-1-59355-394-4(3), 1593553943, Bril Audio CD Unabri); audio compact disk 112.25 (978-1-59355-399-9(4), 1593553994, BriAudCD Unabrid) Brilliance Audio.
Jack Reacher. Hero. Loner. Soldier. Soldier's son. An elite military cop, he was one of the army's brightest stars. But in every cop's life there is a turning point. One case. One messy, tangled case that can shatter a career. Turn a lawman into a renegade. And make him question words like honor, valor, and duty. For Jack Reacher, this is that case... New Year's Day, 1990. The Berlin Wall is coming down. The world is changing. And in a North Carolina "hot-sheets" motel, a two-star general is found dead. His briefcase is missing. Nobody knows what was in it. Within minutes Jack Reacher has his orders: Control the situation. But this situation can't be controlled. Within hours the general's wife is murdered hundreds of miles away. Then the dominoes really start to fall... Two Special Forces soldiers - the toughest of the tough - are taken down, one at a time. Top military commanders are moved from place to place in a bizarre game of chess. And somewhere inside the vast worldwide fortress that is the U.S. Army, Jack Reacher - an ordinarily untouchable investigator for the 110th Special Unit - is being set up as a fall guy with the worst enemies a man can have. But Reacher won't quit. He's fighting a new kind of war. And he's taking a young female lieutenant with him on a deadly hunt that leads them from the ragged edges of a rural army post to the winding streets of Paris to a confrontation with an enemy he didn't know he had. With his French-born mother dying - and divulging to her son one last, stunning secret - Reacher is forced to question everything he once believed...about his family, his career, his loyalties - and himself. Because this soldier's son is on his way into the darkness, where he finds a tangled drama of desperate desires and violent death - and a conspiracy more chilling, ingenious, and treacherous than anyone could have guessed.

Enemy. unabr. ed. Lee Child. Read by Dick Hill. (Running Time: 14 hrs.). (Jack Reacher Ser.). 2004. 24.95 (978-1-59335-315-5(4), 1593353154, Brilliance MP3); audio compact disk 39.25 (978-1-59335-474-9(6), 1593354746, Brlnc Audio MP3 Lib) Brilliance Audio.

Enemy. unabr. ed. Lee Child. Read by Dick Hill. (Running Time: 14 hrs.). (Jack Reacher Ser.). 2004. 39.25 (978-1-59710-253-7(9), 1597102539, BADLE); 24.95 (978-1-59710-252-0(0), 1597102520, BAD) Brilliance Audio.

Enemy at Green Knowe. L. M. Boston. Read by Simon Vance. (Running Time: 18000 sec.). (Green Knowe Chronicles). (J). (ps-7). 2006. audio compact disk 27.95 (978-1-59316-064-7(X)) Listen & Live.

Enemy at Green Knowe. unabr. ed. L. M. Boston. Read by Simon Vance. (J). 2007. 34.99 (978-1-59895-922-2(0)) Find a World.

Enemy at Home: The Cultural Left & Its Responsibility For 9/11. unabr. ed. Dinesh D'Souza. Read by Michael Kramer. (Running Time: 11 hrs. 0 mins. 0 sec.). (ENG.). 2007. audio compact disk 24.99 (978-1-4001-5366-4(2)); audio compact disk 79.99 (978-1-4001-3366-6(1)) Pub: Tantor Media. Dist(s): IngramPubServ

Enemy at Home: The Cultural Left & Its Responsibility For 9/11. unabr. ed. Read by Michael Kramer. (Running Time: 11 hrs. 0 mins. 0 sec.). (ENG.). 2007. audio compact disk 39.99 (978-1-4001-0366-9(5)) Pub: Tantor Media. Dist(s): IngramPubServ

Enemy Called Average. John Mason. 2 cass. 1995. 12.99 Set. (978-0-88419-365-4(9), 6040) Nelson.

Enemy in Sight. unabr. ed. Alexander Kent, pseud. Read by Michael Jayston. 10 vols. (Running Time: 14 hrs.). (Richard Bolitho Ser.: Bk. 10). 2003. 84.95 (978-0-7540-0995-5(5), CAB 2417, Chivers Sound Lib) AudioGO.

***Enemy of God.** abr. ed. Bernard Cornwell. Read by Tim Pigott-Smith. (ENG.). 2010. (978-0-06-200946-3(X), Harper Audio); (978-0-06-201472-6(2), Harper Audio) HarperCollins Pubs.

Enemy of God. unabr. ed. Robert Daley. 8 cass. (Running Time: 44040 sec.). 2005. 69.95 (978-0-7927-3680-6(X), CSL 819); audio compact disk 94.95 (978-0-7927-3681-3(8), SLD 819) AudioGO.

Enemy of God. unabr. ed. Robert Daley. 2005. 29.95 (978-0-7927-3682-0(6), CMP 819) AudioGO.

Enemy of God. unabr. collector's ed. Bernard Cornwell. Read by David Case. 12 cass. (Running Time: 18 hrs.). (Warlord Chronicles: Vol. 2). 1997. 96.00 (978-0-7366-4073-2(8), 4582) Books on Tape.
In this sequel to "The Winter King," King Arthur has subdued civil war, but unrest continues.

Enemy of the People. unabr. ed. Read by Flo Gibson. Ed. by Henrik Ibsen. 3 cass. (Running Time: 3 hrs.). 2000. 24.95 Audio Bk Con.

Enemy of the People. unabr. ed. Ed. by Henrik Ibsen. Narrated by Flo Gibson. 3 cass. (Running Time: 3 hrs. 30 mins.). (gr. 10 up). 2000. 16.95 (978-1-55685-640-2(7)) Audio Bk Con.
Dr. Stockman is ridiculed & persecuted by the politicians & townspeople for telling the truth about the towns contaminated public baths.

Enemy of the State. unabr. ed. Kenneth W. Kalcheim. 1 cass. (Running Time: 31 min.). 12.95 (404) J Norton Pubs.

Enemy Spy. Wendelin Van Draanen. Read by Daniel Young. (Shredderman Ser.: Bk. 4). (J). 2008. 34.99 (978-1-60640-649-6(3)) Find a World.

Enemy Spy. Wendelin Van Draanen. Read by Daniel Young. Illus. by Brian Biggs. (Running Time: 7800 sec.). (Shredderman Ser.: Bk. 4). (J). (gr. 3-6). 2007. audio compact disk 22.95 (978-1-4301-0114-7(8)) Live Oak Media.

Enemy Spy. Wendelin Van Draanen. Read by Daniel Young. Illus. by Brian Biggs. (Running Time: 7800 sec.). (Shredderman Ser.: Bk. 4). (J). 2007. 18.95 (978-1-4301-0112-3(1)) Live Oak Media.

Enemy Within. abr. ed. Larry Bond. Read by David Purdham. 4 cass. (Running Time: 4 hrs. 30 mins.). (493929) S&S Audio.

Enemy Within. abr. ed. L. Ron Hubbard. 2 cass. (Running Time: 3 hrs.). (Mission Earth Ser.: Vol. 3). 2002. 15.95 (978-1-59212-059-8(8)) Gala Pr LLC.
Heller has been sent to eliminate pollution on Earth to make it habitable for the coming invaders, but Voltarian killer/spy Soltan Gris (our evil narrator) is bent on sabotaging his mission. Will Heller discover the giant heroin operation in Turkey that Gris is hooked into? Does the exotic belly dancer, Utanc, lure Gris away from his vengeful plans?.

Enemy Within. abr. ed. Robert K. Tanenbaum. 2004. 15.95 (978-0-7435-4686-7(5)) Pub: S&S Audio. Dist(s): S and S Inc

Enemy Within. abr. ed. Phillip Thompson. 2 cass. (Running Time: 3 hrs.). 2004. 18.00 (978-1-58807-338-9(6)) Am Pubng Inc.
After a successful career as a Marine Corps officer, Wade Stuart, an ATF special agent, finds himself working undercover in his home territory, the Mississippi Delta, infiltrating a militia unit with lofty goals. When Stuart uncovers a plot to assassinate the governor of Mississippi and take over the state as part of a people's revolution, Washington plans to send in the 2nd Marine Division to attack the militia. Stuart sees a bloodbath coming, begs for more time to quash the plan, but the president sees this as a good opportunity to set an example. Isolated and unsure of the decision out of Washington, Stuart must race to shut down the militia before the military arrives. Enemy Within rushes forward at breakneck speed, and only one man can stop these domestic terrorists...Wade Stuart!.

Enemy Within. unabr. ed. Larry Bond & Patrick Larkin. Read by Michael Russotto. 13 cass. (Running Time: 19 hrs. 30 min.). 1996. 104.00 (978-0-7366-3388-8(X), 4038) Books on Tape.
With riots & fires on the one hand & a failing communications system on the other, the Feds target our fringe groups as the cause. They focus on disaffected loonies & that's just what Gen. Amir Taleh, Iran's new leader, wants them to do. It leaves his agents free to get on with their work.

Enemy Within. unabr. ed. Robert K. Tanenbaum. Read by Nick Sullivan. 12 vols. (Running Time: 18 hrs.). 2001. bk. 96.95 (978-0-7927-2515-2(8), CSL 404, Chivers Sound Lib); audio compact disk 115.95 (978-0-7927-9938-2(0), SLD 089, Chivers Sound Lib) AudioGO.
When a black man is shot multiple times in the back on the streets of New York by an NYPD golden boy, chaos erupts throughout the city. And in an election year, a year of secret handshakes and politically motivated favors, no one feels the pressure more than the men and women who vow to protect and serve. For Butch Karp, chief assistant district attorney for New York County, bullet holes aren't the only holes in this volatile case, nor in a second shocking puzzle.

Enemy Women. unabr. ed. Paulette Jiles. 12 CDs. (Running Time: 15 hrs.). 2002. audio compact disk 96.00 (978-0-7366-8733-1(5)) Books on Tape.
A Missouri girl is imprisoned for her Confederate sympathies, and her jailer falls in love with her.

Enemy Women. unabr. ed. Paulette Jiles. Read by Karen White. 10 cass. (Running Time: 15 hrs.). 2002. 80.00 (978-0-7366-8616-7(9)) Books on Tape.
Adair Randolph Colley is the eighteen-year-old daughter of a mild-mannered justice of the peace during the Civil War. One day in November 1864 the Union militia sweeps through the quiet Ozarks backwoods, burns the Colleys' home, steal their possessions, and arrest Squire Colley. When Adair and her sisters set out to find their father in hope of securing his release, Adair herself is denounced as a Confederate spy and sent to prison in St. Louis. There, she meets her Union interrogator, Major William Neumann, and the two fall in love. Before he is sent back to the front, Neumann helps Adair plan an escape and, not long after he leaves, she makes her break. Weakened and alone, Adair must now travel through dangerous territory as she journeys home - not knowing who or what she will find there.

Energetic Core Exercise Series. Scripts. Created by Karen D. Custer. 3 CDs. (Running Time: 2 hrs. 46 mins.). 2005. audio compact disk 30.00 (978-0-9777330-0-2(9)) Light Riders.
16 Guided Imagery exercises designed to enhance clarity, deepen listener's sense of well-being and strengthen the body/mind/spirit connection. These exercises help the listener become more aware of the inner, essential Self.

Energi. unabr. ed. Paul Williams. Read by Paul Williams. 1 cass. (Running Time: 90 min.). 1996. 11.95 (978-1-57453-060-5(7)) Audio Lit.

Energies of Enactment. Read by Eleanor Irwin. 1 cass. (Running Time: 90 min.). 1976. 10.95 (978-0-7822-0096-6(6), 020) C G Jung IL.
Part of the "Energy" conference set.

Energize. Windham Hill Staff. 1 cass. 1998. 15.00 (978-1-56170-556-6(X)) Hay House.

***Energize Your Heart: In 4 Dimensions.** Puran Bair & Susanna Bair. Read by Asatar Bair & Jeanie Underwood. (ENG.). 2007. 13.95 (978-0-9795269-4-7(9)) Lvng Hrt Med.

Energized by Grace: Christ's Church: Men & Women Energized by Grace to do the Impossible. 2007. 19.99 (978-1-933561-26-4(2)) BFM Books.

Energized Hypnosis: Basic Techniques Complete Package, Vol.1 complete. Christopher S. Hyatt. Ed. by Nick Tharcher. Nick Tharcher. (ENG.). 2008. pap. bk. 93.99 (978-1-935150-94-7(4)) Orig Falcon.

Energized Hypnosis: The Complete 4 Volume Package. Christopher S. Hyatt. (ENG.). 2008. pap. bk. 199.99 (978-1-935150-15-2(4)) Orig Falcon.

Energized Hypnosis: The Innate Power Response, Vol. 2. Christopher S. Hyatt & Calvin Iwema. (ENG.). 2008. DVD & audio compact disk 49.99 (978-1-935150-17-6(0)) Orig Falcon.

Energized Hypnosis Audios. Christopher S. Hyatt & Calvin Iwema. Ed. by Nick Tharcher. (ENG.). 2008. audio compact disk 31.00 (978-1-935150-01-5(4)) Orig Falcon.

***Energized Life Audio CD.** Susan Diane Matz. Read by Susan Diane Matz. (ENG.). 2010. 15.95 (978-0-9841054-2-7(5)) Abriev Ent.

Energizers to Go. S. Higby. 2003. 14.95 (978-1-890460-22-8(2)) Pub: Corwin Pr. Dist(s): SAGE

Energizing: Heart Rhythm Meditation. Contrib. by Susanna Bair & Puran Bair. 2007. audio compact disk 24.95 (978-0-9795269-0-9(6)) Lvng Hrt Med.

Energy. 1 cass. (Running Time: 60 min.). 10.95 (034) Psych Res Inst.
Techniques to promote a high energy performance level..

Energy! 1 cass. 10.00 (978-1-58506-010-8(0), 16) New Life Inst OR.
Don't let fatigue slow you down & take the fun from your life.

Energy. Sundance/Newbridge, LLC Staff. (Early Science Ser.). (gr. k-3). 2007. audio compact disk 12.00 (978-1-4007-6553-9(6)); audio compact disk 12.00 (978-1-4007-6551-5(X)); audio compact disk 12.00 (978-1-4007-6552-2(8)) Sund Newbrdge.

Energy. Eldon Taylor. 1 cass. (Running Time: 62 min.). (Neurophonics Ser.). 16.95 (978-1-55978-651-5(5), 1002) Progress Aware Res.
Sound patterns for Altered States of Consciousness with underlying subliminal affirmations & frequency response signals. Use with headphones only.

Energy. Stuart Wilde. 1 cass. (Running Time: 1 hr.). 11.95 (978-0-930603-07-6(9)) White Dove NM.
A subliminal tape. Relaxing musical background. Your conscious mind hears only the music while your subconscious mind, accepts the powerful affirmations.

***Energy: CD add-on Set.** Perf. by Millmark Education Staff. (ConceptLinks Ser.). 2009. audio compact disk 50.00 (978-1-61618-356-1(X)) Millmark Educ.

Energy Anatomy. Read by Caroline Myss. 6 cass. (Running Time: 9 hrs.). 1999. 59.95 Set, incl. study guide 8p. (83-0019) Explorations.
Learn to view health through a spiritual-biological lens to gain a clear picture of how the body heals.

Energy Anatomy. unabr. ed. Caroline Myss. 9 CDs. (Running Time: 9 hrs.). 2001. audio compact disk 69.95 (978-1-56455-880-0(0), AW00533D) Sounds True.

Energy & Childhood. Read by Edith Sullwold. 1 cass. (Running Time: 90 min.). 1976. 10.95 (978-0-7822-0307-3(8), 017) C G Jung IL.
Part of the "Energy" conference set.

Energy & Climate: Science for Citizens in the Age of Global Warming. Instructed by Richard Wolfson. 5 cass. (Running Time: 7 hrs. 30 mins.). 1996. 39.95 (978-1-56585-008-8(4)) Teaching Co.

Energy & Imagination: The Myth of an Energy Crisis. Read by Sam Keen. 1 cass. (Running Time: 90 min.). 1976. 10.95 (978-0-7822-0112-3(1), 016) C G Jung IL.

Energy & Lighting - Design & Management. 1 cass. (America's Supermarket Showcase '96 Ser.). 1996. 11.00 (NGA96-050) Sound Images.

Energy & Me: Relaxation. Roxanne E. Daleo. 1 cass. (J). 1999. 12.95 Hlth Jrnys.

Energy & Me: Relaxation. unabr. ed. Roxanne E. Daleo. Read by Roxanne E. Daleo. 1 cass. (Running Time: 29 min.). (MindWorks for Children Ser.: Vol. 4). 1988. 12.95 (978-1-889447-14-8(5)) Mindwrks Chldrn.
Designed to give children the tools they need to relax body & mind. Regular use of these tapes will help children develop self-confidence & a healthy mental attitude, improve concentration & problem-solving abilities, & stimulate creativity.

Energy & Power Generation Equipment & Services in Russia: A Strategic Reference 2007. Compiled by Icon Group International, Inc. Staff. 2007. ring bd. 195.00 (978-0-497-82400-6(0)) Icon Grp.

Energy & Power (the Ultimate Healer Subliminal Series, 3 Of 6) Feel more energetic & Powerful! Kyrah Malan. 1 CD. (Running Time: 27 mins). 2006. audio compact disk 39.95 (978-0-9787324-3-1(X), SPS3) K Malan.
The ultimate in subliminal affirmations. Music, messages and binaural beats are specifically designed to work together to help you move through your day with ease and joy. Let yourself remain unaffected by negative people or situations. Create and KEEP your power.What you hear is beautiful music that has been proven in university studies or harmonize and organize your energy field, putting you in a calm, receptive state quickly and easily.What your subconscious hears are specially designed affirmations and suggestions, designed to rewrite subconscious beliefs and change behavior faster and more effectively than any subliminal program available today.The Foundation set is designed to be used in order, each CD building on the effects of the previous CDs, and includes Love Your Life, Release & Relax, Energy & Power, Manifest & Magnetize, Live Your Life, and Spirit & Soul. Can be used independently. Unlike typical subliminal programs which recommend you listen to them for at least 30 days, Ultimate healer CDs help create positive results in only 17 days; some people report results in as little as 2 or 3 days!You can play them during everyday activities, while driving, reading, or at work, or listen to them with headphones. You have freedom and flexibility with The Ultimate Healer Subliminal Series.

Energy & the Physical Body. unabr. ed. Robert A. Monroe. Read by Robert A. Monroe. (Running Time: 45 min.). (Explorer Ser.). 1983. 12.95 (978-1-56113-014-6(1), 15) Monroe Institute.
Relation of energy & the physical body.

***Energy Audio CD.** Perf. by Millmark Education Staff. (ConceptLinks Ser.). 2008. audio compact disk 28.00 (978-1-4334-0190-9(8)) Millmark Educ.

Energy Bar Tool. unabr. ed. Robert A. Monroe. Read by Robert A. Monroe. (Running Time: 45 min.). (Gateway Experience - Threshold Ser.). 1983. 14.95 (978-1-56113-260-7(8)) Monroe Institute.
Find your own energy bar tool to direct your non-physical energies.

Energy Bus: 10 Rules to Fuel Your Life, Work, & Team with Positive Energy. unabr. ed. Jon Gordon. Read by Jon Gordon. (Running Time: 3 hrs.). (ENG.). 2008. 19.98 (978-1-59659-314-5(8), GildAudio) Pub: Gildan Media. Dist(s): HachBkGrp

Energy Cleansing Process & Object Meditation. 1 cass. (Running Time: 1 hr.). 2004. 8.95 (978-0-9617713-5-5(6), WT-102) Perelandra Ltd.
Energy Cleansing Process and the Object Meditation.

Energy Clearing. unabr. ed. Cyndi Dale. (Running Time: 2:36:50). 2009. audio compact disk 19.95 (978-1-59179-697-8(0)) Sounds True.

Energy Conference. 7 cass. (Running Time: 9 hrs.). 1976. 59.95 Set. (978-0-7822-0001-0(X), ENERGY) C G Jung IL.

Energy Crisis. unabr. ed. James Buckley et al. 1 cass. (Running Time: 50 min.). 12.95 (222) J Norton Pubs.
Two senators discuss the causes & solutions to our present energy crisis. The discussion is made livelier by the comments of moderator Friedman, who chastises both speakers on some points.

Energy Crisis & Related Investment Opportunities. unabr. ed. C. Vern Myers. 1 cass. (Running Time: 56 min.). 12.95 (367) J Norton Pubs.

***Energy Efficient Homes for Dummies.** abr. ed. Rik Degunther. (ENG.). 2008. (978-0-06-176490-5(6), Harper Audio); (978-0-06-176491-2(4), Harper Audio) HarperCollins Pubs.

Energy Food. unabr. ed. Robert A. Monroe. Read by Robert A. Monroe. (Running Time: 45 min.). (Gateway Experience - Freedom Ser.). 1983. 14.95 (978-1-56113-266-9(7)) Monroe Institute.
Perceive, absorb & store non-physical energy.

Energy from A Tree. Read by Mary Richards. (Stress Reduction Ser.). 9.95 (100) Master Your Mind.

Energy from a Tree. Read by Mary Richards. 1 cass. (Running Time: 60 min.). (Energy Break Ser.). 2007. audio compact disk 19.95 (978-1-56136-158-8(5)) Master Your Mind.

Energy Generation Equipment & Transmission Services in Greece: A Strategic Reference 2007. Compiled by Icon Group International, Inc. Staff. 2007. ring bd. 195.00 (978-0-497-35992-8(8)) Icon Grp.

Energy Generation Equipment & Transmission Services in Italy: A Strategic Reference 2006. Compiled by Icon Group International, Inc. Staff. 2007. ring bd. 195.00 (978-0-497-36037-5(3)) Icon Grp.

***Energy Healing.** Ann Marie Chiasson, MD. (Running Time: 6:00:00). 2011. DVD & audio compact disk 99.00 (978-1-59179-771-5(3)) Sounds True.

Energy Healing: An Intimate Conversational Journey into Healing Wisdom. unabr. ed. Rahul Patel. 8 cass. (Running Time: 12 hrs.). 2000. 69.95 (978-1-55525-014-0(9), 21300A) Nightingale-Conant.
Heal your body, mind, and soul with a unique fusion of scientific methods and timeless techniques.

Energy Healing & the Sixth Sense. Edward Strachar. 6 CDs. (Running Time: 6 hrs.). 2003. 129.00 (978-0-9723168-7-3(6)) InGenius Inc.

Energy Investments. unabr. ed. Larry Abraham. 1 cass. (Running Time: 1 hr. 21 min.). 11.95 (412) J Norton Pubs.

Energy-Key to Personal Magnetism & Energy. Kriyananda, pseud. (Running Time: 2 hrs.). 14.95 (ST-16) Crystal Clarity.

Energy Management Reference Libraray. Wayne C. Turner. 2006. audio compact disk 450.00 (978-1-4200-4466-9(4)) Pub: Fairmont Pr. Dist(s): Taylor and Fran

Energy Matters: How to Tap the Power Within. Robert A. Rausch. 2002. per. 19.95 (978-0-9717752-4-4(9)) Exec Energy.

Energy Medicine. Perf. by Larry Dossey et al. 6 cass. (Running Time: 7 hrs.). 1999. 59.95 Set. (83-0053) Explorations.
Is the human body merely a complex biological machine, or is our health sustained by "subtle energies" that can be guided for healing? Features some of the most prominent healers of our time & other experts in thought-provoking presentations & discussions.

Energy Meditation. Read by Mary Richards. 12.95 (206) Master Your Mind.
Presents two exercises for opening one's energy centers.

Energy Meditation. Eldon Taylor. 1 cass. (Running Time: 62 min.). (Inner Talk Ser.). 16.95 incl. script. (978-1-55978-000-1(2), 5400C) Progress Aware Res.
Soundtrack - Musical Themes with underlying subliminal affirmations.

Energy Meditation: Babbling Brook. Eldon Taylor. 1 cass. 16.95 (978-1-55978-756-7(2), 5400F) Progress Aware Res.

Energy Moves for Self Healing Audio: Meditation Audio. Energy Moves Staff. 2009. 9.95 (978-1-4276-4129-8(3)) AardGP.

Energy of Beginning. Read by Leland Roloff. 1 cass. (Running Time: 1 hr.). 1976. 9.95 (978-0-7822-0231-1(4), 022) C G Jung IL.

Energy, Power & Spirit see Unleash Your Potential: The Quest Life Trilogy

Energy Production & Services in Belgium: A Strategic Reference 2006. Compiled by Icon Group International, Inc. Staff. 2007. ring bd. 195.00 (978-0-497-35825-9(5)) Icon Grp.

Energy Production & Services in Finland: A Strategic Reference 2006. Compiled by Icon Group International, Inc. Staff. 2007. ring bd. 195.00 (978-0-497-35936-2(7)) Icon Grp.

Energy Production & Services in France: A Strategic Reference 2007. Compiled by Icon Group International, Inc. Staff. 2007. ring bd. 195.00 (978-0-497-35949-2(9)) Icon Grp.

Energy Resources for the Future: Syllabus. Walter Youngquist. (J). 1977. bk. 196.75 (978-0-89420-144-8(1), 231000) Natl Book.

***Energy SB1 Audio CD Kinetic Energy & Potential Energy.** Perf. by Millmark Education Staff. (Content Literacy Libraries Ser.). 2008. audio compact disk (978-1-4334-0432-0(X)) Millmark Educ.

***Energy SB2 Audio CD Many Different Forms.** Perf. by Millmark Education Staff. (Content Literacy Libraries Ser.). 2008. audio compact disk (978-1-4334-0433-7(8)) Millmark Educ.

***Energy SB3 Audio CD Changing Forms.** Perf. by Millmark Education Staff. (Content Literacy Libraries Ser.). 2008. audio compact disk (978-1-4334-0434-4(6)) Millmark Educ.

***Energy SB4 Audio CD Sources of Energy.** Perf. by Millmark Education Staff. (Content Literacy Libraries Ser.). 2008. audio compact disk (978-1-4334-0435-1(4)) Millmark Educ.

Energy Secrets for Women on the Run. unabr. ed. Kaye Olson. Read by Kaye Olson. Read by Leanor Reizen & Bruce Joseph. 2 cass. (Running Time: 1 hr. 42 min.). 1997. 14.95 Set. (978-0-9660264-0-5(3)) Working Well.
Topics include Stress, Preventing Burnout, Deep Breathing, Managing Time, Self-talk, Eat for Energy, Exercise, Sleep, Humor & Laughter & Self-nurturing Exercises.

Energy Walk. abr. ed. Robert A. Monroe. Read by Robert A. Monroe. (Mind Food Ser.). 1983. 14.95 (978-1-56102-406-3(6)) Inter Indus.
An Interior journey to greater personal strength.

Energy Walk, Tape 5. abr. ed. Robert A. Monroe. Read by Robert A. Monroe. 6 cass. (Emergency Ser.). 1983. 69.00 Set. (978-1-56102-704-0(9)); Inter Indus.
Provides special techniques for pain reduction.

Energy/la Energia: Heat, Light, & Fuel/Calor, Luz y Combustible. abr. ed. Darlene Stille. Tr. by Sol Robledo. Illus. by Sheree Boyd. (Amazing Science Ser.). (SPA.). (gr. k). 2008. audio compact disk 14.60 (978-1-4048-4476-6(7)) CapstoneDig.

Enfance. Jacques Prevert. Read by Jacques Prevert. Perf. by Juliette Greco et al. 1 cass. (FRE.). 1995. 16.95 (1665-RF) Olivia & Hill.
Prevert grew up in Neuilly between a religious school & city streets, a period important to his life & work.

Enfant & His City. 1 cass. 10.00 Esstee Audios.
The creation of Washington, DC.

Enfant de la Montagne Noire. l.t. ed. Lauent Cabrol. (French Ser.). 2001. bk. 30.99 (978-2-84011-432-1(1)) Pub: UlverLrgPrint GBR. Dist(s): Ulverscroft US

Enfant de Xena, Set. Dan Dastier. Read by Yves Belluardo. 3 cass. (FRE.). 1995. 29.95 (1793-CO) Olivia & Hill.
What is happening? - The atomic shelters have been taken over. Paris is suffering through a heat wave & it is raining in the Sahara.

Enfant et la Riviere, Set. Henri Bosco. Read by Henri Gougaud. 2 cass. (FRE.). 1992. bk. 35.95 (1GA068) Olivia & Hill.
Pascalet, a little boy who lives in Provence, is fascinated by the neighboring river he has never seen. And one day when his parents are away... a delightful story.

Enfants D'Izieu. Rolande Causse. Perf. by Bulle Ogier. 1 cass. (FRE.). 1995. 16.95 (1435-DI) Olivia & Hill.
The true story of a group of Jewish children between the ages of 4 & 17 hiding in southern France during World War II.

Enfoque. Stephen R. Covey. 2008. audio compact disk 24.95 (978-1-933499-71-0(0)) Fonolibro Inc.

Enforcing Family Law Orders. Read by Patricia Berkowitz et al. (Running Time: 2 hrs. 45 min.). 1991. 89.00 Incl. 217p. tape materials. (FA-55218) Cont Ed Bar-CA.

Enforcing Rules Audio CD. Adapted by Benchmark Education Company Staff. Based on a work by Vickey Herold. (Early Explorers Set C Ser.). (J). (gr. 2). 2008. audio compact disk 10.00 (978-1-60437-553-4(1)) Benchmark Educ.

Enfrente a Sus Gigantes. abr. ed. Max Lucado. (Running Time: 13200 sec.).Tr. of Facing Your Giants. (SPA.). 2007. audio compact disk 22.99 (978-0-89922-622-4(1)) Pub: Grupo Nelson. Dist(s): Nelson

Engagements: Husband & Wife 1. 1. (ENG.). 2007. audio compact disk 24.99 (978-0-9801995-0-5(6)) Live Fully En.

Engagements: Husband & Wife 2. 1. (ENG.). 2007. audio compact disk 24.99 (978-0-9801995-1-2(4)) Live Fully En.

Engagements: Parent & Child 1. 1. (ENG.). 2007. audio compact disk 24.99 (978-0-9801995-2-9(2)) Live Fully En.

Engaging Spirituality During HIV-AIDS Progression. 1 cass. (Care Cassettes Ser.: Vol. 21, No. 7). 1994. 10.80 Assn Prof Chaplains.

***Engaging the Enemy.** Elizabeth Moon. 2010. audio compact disk 19.99 (978-1-59950-672-2(6)) GraphicAudio.

Engaging the Enemy. unabr. ed. Elizabeth Moon. Narrated by Cynthia Holloway. (Running Time: 16 hrs. 0 mins. 0 sec.). (Vatta's War Ser.). (ENG.). 2008. audio compact disk 37.99 (978-1-4001-0829-9(2)); audio compact disk 75.99 (978-1-4001-3829-6(9)); audio compact disk 24.99 (978-1-4001-5829-4(X)) Pub: Tantor Media. Dist(s): IngramPubServ

***Engaging the Enemy (Part 2 Of 2) Vatta's War.** Elizabeth Moon. 2010. audio compact disk 19.99 (978-1-59950-680-7(7)) GraphicAudio.

Engaging the Organization in Change, Pt. 2. unabr. ed. Dick Axelrod. 1 cass. (Running Time: 1 hrs. 15 min.). (Transforming Local Government Ser.: Vol. 20). 1999. 10.00 (978-1-882403-76-9(2), IG9921) Alliance Innov.

Engaging Torah: Contemporary Insights. 28 cass. (Running Time: 25 min. per cass.). (C). 1999. Set. (571799) URJ Pr.
Explores each parashah in great depth & chronicles Judaism's episodes in a way that is both accessible & challenging to the listener. Now, for the first time many of the world's greatest scholars & community leaders provide their insight & knowledge into the study of the Torah.

Engineered for Murder. unabr. ed. Aileen Schumacher. Read by Stephanie Brush. 8 cass. (Running Time: 9 hrs. 30 min.). (Tory Travers Mystery Ser.: Bk. 1). 2001. 49.95 (978-1-55686-969-3(X)) Books in Motion.
Engineer Tory Travers is assigned inspection duty for a university's new football stadium. Finding not only structural problems, but also the murder of the quality control technician, Travers turns to Police Detective David Alvarez for protection and to review the blueprints of the crime.

Engineer's Thumb see Adventures of Sherlock Holmes

Engines, Lubricating & Coding Systems. rev. ed. Bob Leigh et al. Ed. by Roger L. Fennema & Leslie A. Wiseman. Illus. by Ralph J. Butterworth. (Automobile Mechanics Refresher Course Ser.: Bk. 2). 1981. pap. bk. 13.90 (978-0-88098-069-2(9), H M Gousha) Prntice Hall Bks.

England Tape 1: London to Glastonbury. 1 cass. (Running Time: 90 min.). (Guided Auto Tape Tour). 12.95 (GB1); Comp Comms Inc.

England Tape 2: Glastonbury to Stratford. 1 cass. (Running Time: 90 min.). (Guided Auto Tape Tour). 12.95 (GB2); Comp Comms Inc.

England Tape 3: Stratford to London. 1 cass. (Running Time: 90 min.). (Guided Auto Tape Tour). 12.95 (GB3); Comp Comms Inc.

England before World War Two. 10.00 (HE820) Esstee Audios.
How did England respond to Hitler's challenge?.

England Explores the Americas. Compiled by Benchmark Education Staff. 2005. audio compact disk 10.00 (978-1-4108-5488-9(4)) Benchmark Educ.

England, First & Last. unabr. collector's ed. Anthony Bailey. Read by Grover Gardner. 7 cass. (Running Time: 7 hrs.). 1987. 42.00 (978-0-7366-1235-7(1), 2153) Books on Tape.
Autobiographical account of a young boy brought up in the United States during World War II, who returns to England at the age of 11. Sequel to "America, Lost & Found".

England, My England. unabr. collector's ed. D. H. Lawrence. Read by Richard Brown. 8 cass. (Running Time: 8 hrs.). 1988. 48.00 (978-0-7366-1264-7(5), 2176) Books on Tape.
Collection of short stories, including "Fanny & Annie" & "The Horse Dealer's Daughter".

England of Elizabeth, Pt. 1. unabr. ed. A. L. Rowse. Read by Jill Masters. 10 cass. (Running Time: 15 hrs.). 1984. 80.00 (978-0-7366-0587-8(8), 1555-A) Books on Tape.
Under Elizabeth, England experienced its own Renaissance in art, literature & commerce. By the time she died, the nation was established along lines that brought it to prominence in world affairs & kept it there for two centuries.

England of Elizabeth, Pt. 2. unabr. ed. A. L. Rowse. Read by Jill Masters. 10 cass. (Running Time: 15 hrs.). 1984. 80.00 (1555-B) Books on Tape.

England Their England. A. G. Macdonell. 2 cass. 2002. (978-1-901768-05-3(8)) CSA Telltapes GBR.
The English as seen by the 'outsider' in the person of a young Scotsman in 1920's England - a richly comic, classic satire on society, politics, nationalism. Includes uncut the famously hilarious cricket match.

England's Mistress: The Infamous Life of Emma Hamilton. unabr. ed. Kate Williams. Narrated by Josephine Bailey. (Running Time: 15 hrs. 0 mins. 0 sec.). (ENG.). 2006. audio compact disk 39.99 (978-1-4001-0302-7(9)); audio compact disk 79.99 (978-1-4001-3302-4(5)); audio compact disk 29.99 (978-1-4001-5302-2(6)) Pub: Tantor Media. Dist(s): IngramPubServ

Englisch Ohne Muhe Heute. 1 CD. (Running Time: 1 hr. 30 min.).Tr. of English with Ease. (ENG & GER.). 2000. pap. bk. 95.00 (978-2-7005-1051-5(8)) Pub: Assimil FRA. Dist(s): Distribks Inc

Englisch Ohne Muhe Heute. Assimil Staff. 1 cass. (Running Time: 1 hr. 30 min.).Tr. of English with Ease. (ENG & GER.). 1999. pap. bk. 75.00 (978-2-7005-1001-0(1)) Pub: Assimil FRA. Dist(s): Distribks Inc

Englische in der Praxis. Assimil Staff. 1 cass. (Running Time: 1 hr. 30 min.).Tr. of Using English. 1999. pap. bk. 75.00 (978-2-7005-1017-1(8)); pap. bk. 95.00 (978-2-7005-1076-8(3)) Pub: Assimil FRA. Dist(s): Distribks Inc

English see Kingpins of the Pimps: The william perry Story

English see Death As an Ally, Vol. 2, Meeting at Holocaust Museum

English. unabr. ed. 1 cass. (Survival Vietnamese English Ser.). (ENG & VIE.). 1975. pap. bk. 24.50 (978-0-88432-419-5(2), AFE552) J Norton Pubs.
Features a course on basic Vietnamese vocabulary used in everyday life for English speakers.

***English.** unabr. ed. Wang Gang. Read by Michael Sun Lee. Tr. by Martin Merz & Jane Weizhen Pan from CHI. 8 CDs. (Running Time: 10 hrs.). 2009. audio compact disk 80.00 (978-1-4159-6183-4(2), BksonTape) Pub: Random Audio Pubg. Dist(s): Random

English, Set. Ilona Davydova. 11 cass. (Running Time: 12 hr.). 1990. pap. bk. 179.00 (978-0-9675296-0-8(3)) Express Method.

English: English for Speakers of Korean. Pimsleur Staff. 16 CDs. (Running Time: 16 hrs.). 2002. audio compact disk 345.00 (978-0-7435-0616-8(2), Pimsleur) S&S Audio.

English: Syllabus. Norman H. Crowhurst. (J). 1974. bk. 135.90 (978-0-89420-145-5(X), 171000) Natl Book.

English - Quick & Easy & Getting There Book 1 CD Bk. 1: English Language Teaching. 2005. audio compact disk (978-0-7428-1508-7(0)) CCLS Pubg Hse.

Getting There for native speakers of panish BeginnersThis four-book series is geared to the needs of teachers working with Spanish-speaking students in grades 5?8 in public and private schools.English teaching in schools in Spanish-speaking countries and communities requires carefully researched, customized materials that take into account the special needs of young native speakers of Spanish and the teaching constraints in schools.Getting There capitalizes on the energy and curiosity of young learners and fits the realities of larger classes and limited time often found in schoolsSimple, organized, sustainableGetting There is a simple, easy-to-teach, structurally graded seriesEach of the 10 lessons per book opens with humorous, lighthearted texts followed by oral practice of the new vocabulary and grammarNeatly organized, the oral and written texts are followed by grammar study with explanations in SpanishAbundant practice of the new structures and vocabulary through written exercisesReading passages consolidate the new input of each lessonEach book of Getting There has 10 lessons, 4 refresher sections and a vocabulary list to assure sustainable learningteacher?s resourcesTest/Picture Kit: includes suggestions for working with flashcards, suggestions for testing, correction key and answer key for all exercisesPicture CardsCD with lesson texts, additional words, oral activities, reading texts and songs (Books 1 and 2)Video (optional)student?s materialStudent?s Books 1?4CD and video (optional).

English - Quick & Easy & Getting There Book 2 CD Bk. 2: English Language Teaching. 2005. audio compact disk (978-0-7428-1509-4(9)) CCLS Pubg Hse.

English - Quick & Easy & Getting There Book 3 CD, Vol. 3. 2005. audio compact disk (978-0-7428-1510-0(2)) CCLS Pubg Hse.

English - Quick & Easy & Getting There Book 4 CD Bk. 4: English Language Teaching. 2005. audio compact disk (978-0-7428-1511-7(0)) CCLS Pubg Hse.

English - Spanish. Agustina Tocalli-Beller. (Running Time: 26 mins.). (Songs that Teach Spanish Ser.). (SPA.). (J). 2002. audio compact disk 13.95 (978-1-894262-64-4(6)) Pub: S Jordan Publ. Dist(s): CrabtreePubCo

English - Spanish, Vol. 2. Agustina Tocalli-Beller. (Running Time: 1 hr. 8 mi). (Songs that Teach Spanish Ser.). (SPA.). (J). 2002. audio compact disk 13.95 (978-1-894262-69-9(7)) Pub: S Jordan Publ. Dist(s): CrabtreePubCo

English Accent: Sounds of American Speech: English for Tagalog Speakers. unabr. ed. Harold Stearns. 4 cass. (Running Time: 1 hr. 30 min. per cass.). 1990. 89.50 set, incl. 144p. bk. & 42 visual aid cards. (SEN210) J Norton Pubs.

English Accent Arabic. unabr. ed. Harold Stearns. 4 cass. (Running Time: 6 hrs.). (Accent English Ser.). (ARA & ENG.). 1991. bk. 89.50 set, incl. visual aids cards. (SEN125) J Norton Pubs.

English as a second language instructional program.

English, Accent in Greek, Set. unabr. ed. 4 cass. (Running Time: 90 min.). 1994. bk. 89.50 (SEN245) J Norton Pubs.

Includes 144-page book, 42 visual-aid cards, & mirror.

English Accent Series: Learning the Sounds of American English. unabr. ed. 4 cass. bk. 89.50 incl. 144-pg bk, 42 visual aid cards & mirror. (SEN170) J Norton Pubs.

English Air. unabr. ed. D. E. Stevenson. Read by Peter Joyce. 7 cass. 1997. 62.95 Set. (978-1-86015-424-9(7)) T T Beeler.

Wynne & Franz fall in love. Unfortunately, it is 1938 & he is half German. An accurate portrait of wartime England.

English as a Second Language: Pronunciation Pairs. unabr. ed. 4 cass. bk. 89.50 Set, incl. 152p. student's bk. & 127p. tchr's. manual. (SEN400) J Norton Pubs.

English as a Second Language: Sing, Dance, Laugh, & Eat Cheeseburgers. unabr. ed. 1 cass. (Running Time: 1 hr.). (J). bk. 19.95 (SEN285) J Norton Pubs.

Traditional songs for young learners.

English As a Second Language No. 2: American History for ESL Learners. unabr. ed. Kenneth Bruce. 6 cass. (Running Time: 9 hrs.). 1996. pap. bk. 69.50 (978-0-88432-937-4(2), S19215) J Norton Pubs.

Helps persons adjusting to life in the U.S.A. improve their understanding of spoken American English while learning facts about U.S. history.

English As a Second Language - Chinese (Mandarin) Comprehensive, Set. unabr. ed. Pimsleur Staff. 16 cass. (CHI.). 1997. 295.00 (978-0-671-57914-2(2), Pimsleur) S&S Audio.

English As a Second Language - Japanese Comprehensive, Set. unabr. ed. Pimsleur Staff. 16 cass. 1997. 295.00 (978-0-671-57916-6(9), Pimsleur) S&S Audio.

English As a Second Language - Spanish Comprehensive, Set. abr. ed. Pimsleur Staff. 16 cass. (SPA.). 1997. 295.00 (978-0-671-57918-0(5), Pimsleur) S&S Audio.

English As a Second Language, El Ingles Practico. unabr. ed. 2 cass. (Running Time: 1 hr. 30 min.). 26.95 (1043); J Norton Pubs.

Developed for Spanish-speaking persons who wish to begin their study of English or to improve upon their knowledge, the material of this course has been carefully selected for relevance to everyday conversational situations.

English As She Is Spoke. Donald Monat & June Dixon. Perf. by Donald Monat & June Dixon. 1 cass. (Running Time: 1 hr. 30 min.). 1998. 10.95 (978-1-57511-031-8(8)) Pub Mills.

A funny examination of the various incarnations of the language we call "English" & all of its diverse usage in different regions, countries and/or cultures.

English ASAP, Level 1, set. Steck-Vaughn Staff. 1997. 22.90 (978-0-8172-7961-5(X)) SteckVau.

English ASAP, Level 2, set. Steck-Vaughn Staff. 1997. 22.90 (978-0-8172-7962-2(8)) SteckVau.

English ASAP, Level 4. Steck-Vaughn Staff. 2 cass. (Running Time: 3 hrs.). (J). 1999. (978-0-7398-0195-6(3)) SteckVau.

English ASAP Literacy. Steck-Vaughn Staff. Cass. 1. 1997. 11.40 (978-0-8172-7963-9(6)); 11.40 (978-0-8172-7964-6(4)) SteckVau.

English ASAP Literacy, Set. Steck-Vaughn Staff. 1997. 22.90 (978-0-8172-7960-8(1)) SteckVau.

English ASAPLevel 3. Steck-Vaughn Staff. 2 cass. (Running Time: 2 hrs.). (J). 1999. (978-0-7398-0189-5(9)) SteckVau.

English Assassin. unabr. ed. Daniel Silva. Read by John Lee. 7 cass. (Running Time: 10 hrs. 30 mins.). (Gabriel Allon Ser.: No. 2). 2002. 56.00 (978-0-7366-8547-4(2)); audio compact disk 61.20 (978-0-7366-8558-0(8)) Pub: Books on Tape. Dist(s): NetLibrary CO

Israeli art restorer and secret agent Gabriel Allon has a problem. A prominent Swiss banker has called him to Switzerland to restore his Raphael. The problem is that Allon finds the banker dead in front of his Raphael, and he's the prime suspect. After some diplomatic intervention, Allon is freed. However, the banker's daughter, tells him that her father's cache of French Impressionist paintings, acquired during the World War, has been stolen by the murderers. Once Allon knows about the banker's wartime misdeeds, he attracts the attention of a secret Swiss organization dedicated to suppressing knowledge of all such crimes, and he is pursued by a killer known only as "the Englishman.

English-Cantonese. unabr. ed. 4 cass. (Survival English Ser.). 1989. bk. 49.50 (E556) J Norton Pubs.

Features a course on basic English vocabulary used in everyday life in the United States.

English Carols for Piano Solo. Gail Smith. 1993. pap. bk. 22.95 (978-0-7866-1185-0(5), 95040CDP) Mel Bay.

English-Chinese (Cantonese) Phrasebook with Useful Word List see English for Cantonese Speakers CDs & Text

English Creek. Ivan Doig. Read by Ivan Doig. 2 cass. (Running Time: 3 hrs.). 16.95 (978-0-939643-31-8(6)) Audio Pr.

English Creek. unabr. collector's ed. Ivan Doig. Read by Paul Shay. 10 cass. (Running Time: 15 hrs.). 1987. 80.00 (978-0-7366-1202-9(5), 2120) Books on Tape.

Coming-of-age novel set in Montana during the 1930s, where a 14-year old boy in at odds with his family.

English Creek, Set. Ivan Doig. Read by Ivan Doig. 2 cass. (Running Time: 3 hrs.). 1994. 16.95 (3538, NrthWrd Bks) TandN Child.

Doig's stories capture the essence of Montana ranch country in the years between the Depression & World War II.

English Explorers Audio CD's. Compiled by Benchmark Education Staff. 2006. audio compact disk 775.00 (978-1-4108-6983-8(0)) Benchmark Educ.

English Extra. Grace Tanaka & Kay A. Ferrell. 2002. audio compact disk 66.15 (978-0-13-870411-7(2)) Longman.

English Fairy Tales, Pt. 1. unabr. ed. 1 cass. (Running Time: 50 min.). Dramatization. Incl. English Fairy Tales: History of Tom Thumb. (J). (SAC 920); English Fairy Tales: Jack & the Beanstalk. (J). (SAC 920); English Fairy Tales: King O' the Cats. (J). (SAC 920); English Fairy Tales: Mr. Vinegar. (J). (SAC 920); English Fairy Tales: Teeny-Tiny. (J). (SAC 920); English Fairy Tales: The Old Woman & Her Pig. (J). (SAC 920); English Fairy Tales: The Three Wishes. (J). (SAC 920); (J). 10.95 (978-0-8045-0920-6(4), SAC 920) Spoken Arts.

English Fairy Tales, Pt. 2. unabr. ed. Read by Christopher Casson et al. 1 cass. (Running Time: 46 min.). Dramatization. Incl. English Fairy Tales: Childe Rowland. (J). (SAC 925); English Fairy Tales: Master of All Masters. (J). (SAC 925); English Fairy Tales: Scrapefoot. (J). (SAC 925); English Fairy Tales: The Ass, the Table & the Stick. (J). (SAC 925); English Fairy Tales: The Laidly Worm of Spindleston Heugh. (J). (SAC 925); English Fairy Tales: The Little Bull Calf. (J). (SAC 925); English Fairy Tales: The Three Sillies. (J). (SAC 925); (J). 10.95 (978-0-8045-0925-1(5), SAC 925) Spoken Arts.

English Fairy Tales: Childe Rowland see English Fairy Tales

English Fairy Tales: History of Tom Thumb see English Fairy Tales

English Fairy Tales: Jack & the Beanstalk see English Fairy Tales

English Fairy Tales: King O' the Cats see English Fairy Tales

English Fairy Tales: Master of All Masters see English Fairy Tales

English Fairy Tales: Mr. Vinegar see English Fairy Tales

English Fairy Tales: Scrapefoot see English Fairy Tales

English Fairy Tales: Teeny-Tiny see English Fairy Tales

English Fairy Tales: The Ass, the Table & the Stick see English Fairy Tales

English Fairy Tales: The Laidly Worm of Spindleston Heugh see English Fairy Tales

English Fairy Tales: The Little Bull Calf see English Fairy Tales

English Fairy Tales: The Old Woman & Her Pig see English Fairy Tales

English Fairy Tales: The Three Sillies see English Fairy Tales

English Fairy Tales: The Three Wishes see English Fairy Tales

English Fast & Easy, for Spanish Speakers Vol. 1: Basico, Set. unabr. ed. 8 cass. pap. bk. 165.00 (AFE375) J Norton Pubs.

English, Fast & Easy for Spanish Speakers Vol. II: Intermedio, Set. unabr. ed. 16 cass. pap. bk. 215.00 (AFE380) J Norton Pubs.

English, Fast & Easy for Spanish Speakers Vol. III: Avanzado, Set. unabr. ed. 16 cass. pap. bk. 215.00 (AFE385) J Norton Pubs.

English Fiddle. Chris Bartram. (ENG.). 2009. lib. bdg. 22.99 (978-0-7866-8027-6(X)) Mel Bay.

English Firsthand 1: Gold Edition. Marc Helgesen et al. 2002. (978-962-00-1537-3(1)) Longman.

English Firsthand 2: Gold Edition, Level 2. Marc Helgesen et al. 2002. (978-962-00-1538-0(X)) Longman.

English Folk Tunes for Accordion: 88 Traditional Pieces Book/CD Pack. David Oliver. 2008. pap. bk. 26.95 (978-1-84761-017-1(X), 184761017X) Pub: Schott Music Corp. Dist(s): H Leonard

English for All Book 1 Audio for All CD: Elt. 2002. audio compact disk (978-1-929310-56-2(0)) ALL Pubng House.

English for All Book 2 Audio for All CD: Elt. 2002. audio compact disk (978-1-929310-57-9(9)) ALL Pubng House.

English for All Book 3 Audio for All CD: Elt. 2002. audio compact disk (978-1-929310-58-6(7)) ALL Pubng House.

English for All Book 4 Audio for All CD: Elt. 2002. audio compact disk (978-1-929310-59-3(5)) ALL Pubng House.

English for All Book 5 Audio for All CD: Elt. 2002. audio compact disk (978-1-929310-60-9(9)) ALL Pubng House.

English for All Book 5 Listening Comprehension Test CD: Elt - english language Teaching. 2006. audio compact disk (978-1-59943-018-8(5)) ALL Pubng House.

English for All Book 6 Audio for All CD: Elt. 2004. audio compact disk (978-1-929310-61-6(7)) ALL Pubng House.

English for All Book 6 Listening comprehension Test CD: Elt - english language Teaching. 2006. audio compact disk (978-1-59943-026-3(6)) ALL Pubng House.

English for All Book 6 Student's Book (with CD) Elt. 2004. pap. bk. (978-1-929310-80-7(3)) ALL Pubng House.

English for Arabic, Q&S: Learn to Speak & Understand English for Arabic with Pimsleur Language Programs. Pimsleur Staff & Pimsleur. 4 CDs. (Running Time: 400 hrs. 0 mins. NaN sec.). (Quick & Simple, English As a Second Lang Ser.). (ARA.). 2001. audio compact disk 19.95 (978-0-7435-0497-3(6), Pimsleur) Pub: S&S Audio. Dist(s): S and S Inc

English for Arabic Speakers: Learn to Speak & Understand English As a Second Language with Pimsleur Language Programs. unabr. ed. Pimsleur Staff. 16 CDs. (Running Time: 160 hrs. 0 mins. 0 sec.). (Comprehensive, English As a Second Langu Ser.). (ARA.). 2001. audio compact disk 345.00 (978-0-7435-1005-9(4), Pimsleur) Pub: S&S Audio. Dist(s): S and S Inc

English for Beginners Level 1 & 2: English for Portuguese Native Speakers - Beginners, Intermediate & Advance Level. (POR & ENG.). 2003. audio compact disk (978-0-9720962-4-9(8)) BES.

English for Bengali Speakers, unabr. ed. British Broadcasting Corporation Staff. 3 cass. (Running Time: 3 hrs.). (English: Tiger's Eye Ser.). (BEN.). 1993. pap. bk. 59.50 (978-0-88432-778-3(7), SEN330) J Norton Pubs.

For learners of English from South & South-east Asia, requires a basic working knowledge of English. Includes 200-page bilingual text.

English for Burmese. Gordon F. Schmader. 10 dual track cass. (Spoken English As a Foreign Language Ser.). (BUR & ENG.). 1980. 90.00 (978-0-87950-600-1(8)) Spoken Lang Serv.

English for Burmese. Gordon F. Schmader. 10 dual track cass. (Spoken English As a Foreign Language Ser.). (BUR & ENG.). 1980. pap. bk. 110.00 (978-0-87950-601-8(6)) Spoken Lang Serv.

English for Business see Wirtschaftsenglisch

English for Business Communication, Set. 2nd rev. ed. Simon Sweeney. (Running Time: hrs. mins.). (ENG.). 2003. 42.00 (978-0-521-75451-4(8)) Cambridge U Pr.

English for Business Communication, Set. 2nd rev. ed. Simon Sweeney. (Running Time: hrs. mins.). (ENG., 2003. audio compact disk 42.00 (978-0-521-75452-1(6)) Cambridge U Pr.

English for Business (Double) see Inglés para Negocios (Double)

English for Business Studies Audio CD Set, Set. 2nd rev. ed. Ian MacKenzie. (Running Time: 1 hr. 43 mins.). (ENG.). 2002. audio compact disk 44.00 (978-0-521-75288-6(4)) Cambridge U Pr.

***English for Business Studies Audio CDs (2) A Course for Business Studies & Economics Students.** 3rd rev. ed. Ian Mackenzie. (Running Time: 1 hr. 38 mins.). (ENG.). 2010. audio compact disk 42.00 (978-0-521-74343-3(5)) Cambridge U Pr.

English for Business Studies103 Vol. 1: A Course for Business Studies & Economics Students. 2nd rev. ed. Ian MacKenzie. (Running Time: 1 hr. 43 mins.). (ENG.). 2002. 44.00 (978-0-521-75287-9(6)) Cambridge U Pr.

English for Business Success: Introductory Course, Set. 2nd rev. ed. Lin Lougheed. (Longman Preparation Series for the Toeic Test Ser.). 1996. 57.75 (978-0-201-87790-8(2)) Longman.

English for Business Success Set: Advanced Course. 2nd rev. ed. Lin Lougheed. (Longman Preparation Series for the Toeic Test Ser.). 1996. 57.75 (978-0-201-87792-2(9)) Longman.

English for Business Success Set: More Practice Tests. 2nd rev. ed. Lin Lougheed. (Longman Preparation Series for the Toeic Test Ser.). 1996. 39.90 (978-0-201-87794-6(5)) Longman.

English for Cantonese. Center for Applied Linguistics Staff. 4 cass. (Running Time: 4 hrs.). 2001. pap. bk. 49.50 (E556) Ctr Appl Ling.

Introduces basic English vocabulary necessary for day-to-day life in the United States.

English for Cantonese Speakers CDs & Text. 4 CDs. (Running Time: 4 hrs.). (Survival English Ser.). Orig. Title: English-Chinese (Cantonese) Phrasebook with Useful Word List. 2005. audio compact disk 75.00 (978-1-57970-175-8(2), AFE605) J Norton Pubs.

English for Chinese (Cantonese) Speakers: Learn to Speak & Understand English As a Second Language. Pimsleur Staff. (Running Time: 160 hrs. 0 mins. 0 sec.). (Pimsleur Language Program Ser.). (ENG.). 2001. audio compact disk 345.00 (978-0-7435-0043-2(1), Pimsleur) Pub: S&S Audio. Dist(s): S and S Inc

English for Chinese (Cantonese) Speakers: Learn to Speak & Understand English As a Second Language with Pimsleur Language Programs. Pimsleur Staff. 4 cass. (Running Time: 400 hrs. 0 mins. NaN sec.). (Pimsleur Language Program Ser.). (ENG.). 2001. audio compact disk 19.95 (978-0-7435-0024-1(5), Pimsleur) Pub: S&S Audio. Dist(s): S and S Inc

English for Chinese (Mandarin) Speakers: Learn to Speak & Understand English as a Second Language with Pimsleur Language Programs. 3rd ed. Pimsleur Staff. 16 CDs. (Running Time: 160 hrs. 0 mins. 0 sec.). (Comprehensive, English As a Second Langu Ser.). (ENG.). 2001. audio compact disk 345.00 (978-0-7435-0877-3(7), Pimsleur) Pub: S&S Audio. Dist(s): S and S Inc

English for Chinese (Mandarin) Speakers: Learn to Speak & Understand English As a Second Language with Pimsleur Language Programs. 3rd unabr. ed. Pimsleur Staff & Pimsleur. 4 cass. (Running Time: 400 hrs. 0 mins. NaN sec.). (Quick & Simple, English As a Second Lang Ser.). (ENG.). 2001. audio compact disk 19.95 (978-0-7435-0875-9(0), Pimsleur) Pub: S&S Audio. Dist(s): S and S Inc

English for Chinese People. unabr. ed. Conversa-Phone Institute Staff. 3 cass. (Running Time: 2 hrs. 40 min.). (English for Foreigners Ser.). (ENG & CHI.). 1990. 23.98 Set. (978-1-56752-072-9(3), COC-6011) Conversa-phone.

2 manuals containing 65 lessons in English conversation with grammar notes.

English for Chinese Speakers. 2 cass. (Running Time: 2 hrs.). 2001. 26.95 (SEN600, LivingLang) Random Info Grp.

Brief course teaches the rudiments of language quickly & easily.

English for Cleaning & Maintenance see Ingles para Limpieza y Mantenimiento

English for Construction Jewel Case see Ingles para Restaurante Jewel Case

English for Construction Jewel Case see Ingles para Construccion Jewel Case

English for Czech People. unabr. ed. Conversa-Phone Institute Staff. 3 cass. (Running Time: 2 hrs. 40 min.). (English for Foreigners Ser.). (ENG & CZE.). 1990. 23.98 Set. (978-1-56752-076-7(6), COC-6018) Conversa-phone.

2 manuals containing 65 lessons in English conversation with grammar notes.

English for Educators Jewel Case see Ingles para Educadores Jewel Case

English for Everyday Activities: Low Beginning. 2001. stu. ed. 17.00 (978-1-56420-287-1(9)); stu. ed. 17.00 (978-1-56420-288-8(7)) New Readers.

English for Everyone see Ingles Para Todos

English for French: Learn to Speak & Understand English for French. Pimsleur Staff. 4 CDs. (Running Time: 400 hrs. 0 mins. NaN sec.). (Basic, English As a Second Language Ser.). (ITA & FRE.). 2002. audio compact disk 19.95 (978-0-671-77631-2(2), Pimsleur) Pub: S&S Audio. Dist(s): S and S Inc

English for French People. unabr. ed. Conversa-Phone Institute Staff. 3 cass. (Running Time: 2 hrs. 40 min.). (English for Foreigners Ser.). (ENG & FRE.). 1990. 23.98 Set. (978-1-56752-067-5(7), COC-6002) Conversa-phone.

English for French, Q & S: Learn to Speak & Understand English for French. unabr. ed. Pimsleur Staff. 16 CDs. (Running Time: 160 hrs. 0 mins. 0 sec.). (Comprehensive, English As a Second Langu Ser.). (FRE.). 2002. audio compact disk 345.00 (978-0-7435-2527-5(2), Pimsleur) Pub: S&S Audio. Dist(s): S and S Inc

English for French Speakers see Nouvel Anglais sans Peine

English for French Speakers. 2 cass. (Running Time: 2 hrs.). 2001. pap. bk. 29.95 (SEN605, LivingLang) Random Info Grp.
Brief course with dictionary/phrase book teaches the rudiments of language quickly & easily.

English for French Speakers. unabr. ed. 4 cass. bk. 64.50 Set. (SEN310); 24.50 250p. bk. (BEN310) J Norton Pubs.

English for German People. unabr. ed. Conversa-Phone Institute Staff. 3 cass. (Running Time: 2 hrs. 40 min.). (English for Foreigners Ser.). (ENG & GER.). 1990. 23.98 Set. (978-1-56752-068-2(5), COC-6003) Conversa-phone.
2 manuals containing 65 lessons in English conversation with grammar notes.

English for German Speakers. 2 cass. (Running Time: 2 hrs.). 2001. pap. bk. 29.95 (SEN610, LivingLang) Random Info Grp.
Brief course with dictionary/phrase book teaches the rudiments of language quickly & easily.

English for German Speakers: Learn to Speak & Understand English as a Second Language with Pimsleur Language Programs. Pimsleur Staff & Pimsleur. 16 CDs. (Running Time: 160 hrs. 0 mins. 0 sec.). (Pimsleur Language Program Ser.). (GER.). 2001. audio compact disk 345.00 (978-0-7435-0502-4(6), Pimsleur) Pub: S&S Audio. Dist(s): S and S Inc

English for German Speakers: Learn to Speak & Understand English As a Second Language with Pimsleur Language Programs. unabr. ed. Pimsleur Staff & Pimsleur. 4 CDs. (Running Time: 400 hrs. 0 mins. NaN sec.). (Pimsleur Language Program Ser.). (GER.). 2001. audio compact disk 19.95 (978-0-7435-0501-7(8), Pimsleur) Pub: S&S Audio. Dist(s): S and S Inc

English for Global Business. Emily Lites & Kathy Thorpe. (ENG., 2001. 30.00 (978-0-472-00287-0(2), 00287); audio compact disk 35.00 (978-0-472-00307-5(0), 00307) U of Mich Pr.
English for Global Business is a business English textbook for non-native speakers who are learning English in order to conduct business, communicate with international professionals, advance in a career, prepare for the TOEIC exam, or pursue an MBA or other university professional degree in English. This textbook emphasizes the oral communication skills that are most needed for international business. This focus on the language of business and social interactions enables the businessperson to understand international associates clearly and to speak naturally and with confidence. The book also familiarizes learners with American English usage and with aspects of U.S. business protocol and etiquette. English for Global Business is for intermediate-level students and contains chapters on: Getting acquainted Describing your work Telephoning Traveling internationally Entertaining a business associate Discussing issues Exercises for listening, vocabulary, language mastery, and communication encourage increased knowledge and fluency. Sections on professional protocols introduce learners to cross-cultural issues and the etiquette appropriate for common business interactions in the United States.

English for Greek People. unabr. ed. Conversa-Phone Institute Staff. 3 cass. (Running Time: 2 hrs. 40 min.). (English for Foreigners Ser.). (ENG & GRE.). 1990. 23.98 Set. (978-1-56752-077-4(4), COC-6020) Conversa-phone.
2 manuals containing 65 lessons in English conversation with grammar notes.

English for Greeks. F. W. Householder, Jr. 7 dual track cass. (Spoken English As a Foreign Language Ser.). (ENG & GRE.). 1980. 90.00 (978-0-87950-604-9(0)) Spoken Lang Serv.

English for Greeks. F. W. Householder, Jr. 7 dual track cass. (Spoken English As a Foreign Language Ser.). (ENG & GRE.). 1980. bk. 110.00 incl. bk. (978-0-87950-605-6(9)) Spoken Lang Serv.

English for Haitian: Learn to Speak & Understand English As a Second Language with Pimsleur Language Programs. unabr. ed. Pimsleur Staff. 16 cass. (Running Time: 160 hrs. 0 mins. 0 sec.). (Comprehensive, English As a Second Langu Ser.). (ENG.). 2002. 295.00 (978-0-7435-2342-4(3), Pimsleur) Pub: S&S Audio. Dist(s): S and S Inc

English for Haitian Speakers: Learn to Speak & Understand English as a Second Language with Pimsleur Language Programs. Pimsleur Staff. 4 cass. (Running Time: 400 hrs. 0 mins. NaN sec.). (Quick & Simple, English As A Second Lang Ser.). (ITA & ENG.). 2004. 19.95 (978-0-7435-2340-0(7), Pimsleur) Pub: S&S Audio. Dist(s): S and S Inc

English for Haitian Speakers: Learn to Speak & Understand English as a Second Language with Pimsleur Language Programs. Pimsleur Staff. 4 CDs. (Running Time: 400 hrs. 0 mins. NaN sec.). (Quick & Simple, English As A Second Lang Ser.). (ITA & ENG.). 2005. audio compact disk 19.95 (978-0-7435-2341-7(5), Pimsleur) Pub: S&S Audio. Dist(s): S and S Inc

English for Haitian Speakers: Learn to Speak & Understand English as a Second Language with Pimsleur Language Programs. unabr. ed. Pimsleur Staff & Pimsleur. 16 CDs. (Running Time: 160 hrs. 0 mins. 0 sec.). (Comprehensive, English As a Second Langu Ser.). (ENG.). 2002. audio compact disk 345.00 (978-0-7435-2343-1(1), Pimsleur) Pub: S&S Audio. Dist(s): S and S Inc

English for Hindi Speakers, unabr. ed. British Broadcasting Corporation Staff. 3 cass. (Running Time: 3 hrs.). (English: Tiger's Eye Ser.). (HIN.). 1993. pap. bk. 59.50 (978-0-88432-779-0(5), SEN340) J Norton Pubs.
For learners of English from South & South-east Asia, requires a basic working knowledge of English. Includes 200-page bilingual text.

English for Hindi Speakers: Learn to Speak & Understand English for Hindi. abr. ed. Pimsleur Staff. (Running Time: 400 hrs. 0 mins. NaN sec.). (Pimsleur Language Program Ser.). (HIN.). 2001. audio compact disk 19.95 (978-0-671-79082-0(X), Pimsleur) Pub: S&S Audio. Dist(s): S and S Inc

English for Hmong. Center for Applied Linguistics Staff. 4 cass. (Running Time: 4 hrs.). 2001. pap. bk. 49.50 (E554) Ctr Appl Ling.
Introduces basic English vocabulary necessary for day-to-day life in the United States.

English for Hospitality Jewel Case see Ingles para Hospitalidad Jewel Case

English for Housekeeping Jewel Case see Ingles para el Trabajo Domestico Jewel Case

English for Hungarian People. unabr. ed. Conversa-Phone Institute Staff. 3 cass. (Running Time: 2 hrs. 40 min.). (English for Foreigners Ser.). (ENG & HUN.). 1990. 23.98 Set. (978-1-56752-071-2(5), COC-6010) Conversa-phone.
2 manuals containing 65 lessons in English conversation with grammar notes.

English for Indonesians. G. E. Williams. 9 dual track cass. (Spoken English As a Foreign Language Ser.). (ENG & IND.). 1980. 90.00 (978-0-87950-606-3(7)) Spoken Lang Serv.

English for Indonesians. G. E. Williams. 9 dual track cass. (Spoken English As a Foreign Language Ser.). (ENG & IND.). 1980. bk. 110.00 incl. bk. (978-0-87950-607-0(5)) Spoken Lang Serv.

English for Information Technology. Eric H. Glendinning & John McEwan. 2002. audio compact disk 21.95 (978-0-19-457378-8(8)) OUP.

English for International Communication. Jack C. Richards et al. 1 cass. (Running Time: hrs. mins.). (Changes Ser.). 1995. stu. ed. 24.15 (978-0-521-44939-7(1)); 40.00 (978-0-521-44942-7(1)) Cambridge U Pr.

English for International Communication. Jack C. Richards et al. 1 cass. (Running Time: hrs. mins.). (Changes Ser.). 1995. stu. ed. 23.00 (978-0-521-44940-3(5)); 42.00 (978-0-521-44943-4(X)) Cambridge U Pr.

English for Iranians. Created by Spoken Language Services Inc. 7 dual track cass. (Spoken English As a Foreign Language Ser.). (ENG & PER.). 1981. 90.00 (978-0-87950-618-6(0)) Spoken Lang Serv.

English for Iranians. Herbert H. Paper & Mohammad A. Jazayery. 7 dual track cass. (Spoken English As a Foreign Language Ser.). (ENG & PER.). 1980. pap. bk. 110.00 incl. bk. (978-0-87950-619-3(9)) Spoken Lang Serv.

English for Italian People. unabr. ed. Conversa-Phone Institute Staff. 3 cass. (Running Time: 2 hrs. 40 min.). (English for Foreigners Ser.). (ENG & ITA.). 1990. 23.98 Set. (978-1-56752-069-9(3), COC-6004) Conversa-phone.

English for Italian Speakers. 2 cass. (Running Time: 2 hrs.). 2001. pap. bk. 29.95 (SEN615, LivingLang) Random Info Grp.
Brief course with dictionary/phrase book teaches the rudiments of language quickly & easily.

English for Italian Speakers. unabr. ed. Pimsleur Staff. 16 CDs. (Running Time: 160 hrs. 0 mins. 0 sec.). (Comprehensive, English As a Second Langu Ser.). (ITA.). 2002. audio compact disk 345.00 (978-0-7435-2529-9(9), Pimsleur) Pub: S&S Audio. Dist(s): S and S Inc

English for Italian Speakers: Learn to Speak & Understand English as a Second Language with Pimsleur Language Programs. Pimsleur Staff. 4 CDs. (Running Time: 400 hrs. 0 mins. NaN sec.). (Pimsleur Language Program Ser.). (ITA.). 2001. audio compact disk 19.95 (978-0-671-77640-4(1), Pimsleur) Pub: S&S Audio. Dist(s): S and S Inc

English for Italian Speakers II: Learn to Speak & Understand English as a Second Language with Pimsleur Language Programs. Pimsleur Staff. 16 cass. (Running Time: 160 hrs. 0 mins. 0 sec.). (Pimsleur Language Program Ser.). (ITA.). 2000. 295.00 (978-0-671-04711-5(6), Pimsleur) Pub: S&S Audio. Dist(s): S and S Inc

English for Japanese People. unabr. ed. Conversa-Phone Institute Staff. 3 cass. (Running Time: 2 hrs. 40 min.). (English for Foreigners Ser.). 1990. 23.98 Set. (978-1-56752-073-6(1), COC-6012) Conversa-phone.
2 manuals containing 65 lessons in English conversation with grammar notes.

English for Job Interviews Jewel Case see Ingles para Entrevistas de Trabajo Jewel Case

English for Jugo-Slavs. Charles E. Bidwell & Sheldon Wise. 9 dual track cass. (Spoken English As a Second Language Ser.).Tr. of Kurs Govornog Engleskog Jezika. (CRO, ENG & SER.). 1980. pap. bk. 110.00 incl. bk. (978-0-87950-609-4(1)); 90.00 (978-0-87950-608-7(3)) Spoken Lang Serv.

English for Khmer. Center for Applied Linguistics Staff. 3 cass. (Running Time: 3 hrs.). 2001. pap. bk. 39.50 (E553) Ctr Appl Ling.
Introduces basic English vocabulary necessary for day-to-day life in the United States.

English for Kids: And the Whole Family. unabr. ed. Pamela Rand. Perf. by Harmony Grisman. 1 cass. (Running Time: 45 min.). (J). (ps-6). 1997. pap. bk. 14.95 Incl. activity wkbk., parental guide. (978-1-878245-03-8(1)) OptimaLearning.
Original songs & lively conversations by native speakers. Based on renown OptimaLearning method. Course is highly motivational for children & whole family.

English for Korean People. unabr. ed. Conversa-Phone Institute Staff. 3 cass. (Running Time: 2 hrs. 40 min.). (English for Foreigners Ser.). (ENG & KOR.). 1990. 23.98 Set. (978-1-56752-075-0(8), COC-6015) Conversa-phone.
2 manuals containing 65 lessons in English conversation with grammar notes.

English for Korean Speakers: Learn to Speak & Understand English As a Second Language with Pimsleur Language Programs. Luis Ricardo Alonso & Pimsleur Staff. 5 CDs. (Running Time: 400 hrs. 0 mins. NaN sec.). (Pimsleur Language Program Ser.). (KOR.). 2001. audio compact disk 19.95 (978-0-671-77619-0(3), Pimsleur) Pub: S&S Audio. Dist(s): S and S Inc

English for Korean Speakers No. 1: Learn to Speak & Understand English as a Second Language with Pimsleur Language Programs. Pimsleur Staff & Pimsleur. (Running Time: 160 hrs. 0 mins. 0 sec.). (Pimsleur Language Program Ser.). (KOR.). 2001. audio compact disk 345.00 (978-0-7435-0040-1(7), Pimsleur) Pub: S&S Audio. Dist(s): S and S Inc

English for Koreans. Fred Lukoff. 9 dual track cass. (Spoken English As a Foreign Language Ser.). (ENG & KOR.). 1980. bk. & stu. ed. 110.00 incl. bk. (978-0-87950-611-7(3)) Spoken Lang Serv.

English for Koreans. Fred Lukoff. 9 dual track cass. (Spoken English As a Foreign Language Ser.). (ENG & KOR.). 1980. bk. 90.00 (978-0-87950-610-0(5)) Spoken Lang Serv.

English for Landscaping Jewel Case see Ingles para Jardineria Jewel Case

English for Lao. Center for Applied Linguistics Staff. 3 cass. (Running Time: 3 hrs.). 2001. pap. bk. 39.50 (E557) Ctr Appl Ling.
Introduces basic English vocabulary necessary for day-to-day life in the United States.

English for Lao Speakers. 6 CDs. (Running Time: 4 hrs. 30 min.). (Survival English Ser.). 2005. audio compact disk 65.00 (978-1-57970-179-6(5), AFE606) J Norton Pubs.

English for Manufacturing (Double) see Inglés para Industrias Manufactureras (Double)

English for Manufacturing (Single) see Inglés para Industrias Manufactureras

English for Marathi Speakers, unabr. ed. British Broadcasting Corporation Staff. 3 cass. (Running Time: 3 hrs.). (English: Tiger's Eye Ser.). (MAR.). 1993. pap. bk. 59.50 (978-0-88432-780-6(9), SEN350) J Norton Pubs.
For learners of English from South & South-east Asia, requires a basic working knowledge of English. Includes 200-page bilingual text.

English for Native Chinese Speakers. 2 CDs. (Living Language Ser.). 2005. audio compact disk 39.95 (978-1-57970-174-1(4), SEN600D) J Norton Pubs.

English for Native Chinese Speakers: Living Language Courses. unabr. ed. 2 cass. pap. bk. 29.95 (SEN600) J Norton Pubs.
An extremely effective way for the non-English-speaking individual to learn the rudiments of the language quickly & easily.

English for Native French Speakers: Living Language Courses. unabr. ed. 2 cass. 29.95 (SEN605) J Norton Pubs.

English for Native German Speakers: Living Language Courses. unabr. ed. 2 cass. 29.95 (SEN610) J Norton Pubs.
An extremely effective way for the non English-speaking individual to learn the rudiments of the language quickly & easily.

English for Native Italian Speakers: Living Language Courses. unabr. ed. 2 cass. pap. bk. 29.95 (SEN615) J Norton Pubs.
An extremely effective way for the non-English-speaking individual to learn the rudiments of the language quickly & easily.

English for Native Spanish Speakers: Living Language Courses. unabr. ed. 2 cass. pap. bk. 29.95 (AFE620) J Norton Pubs.

English for Persian Speakers. unabr. ed. Created by Pimsleur Staff. (Running Time: 16 hrs. 0 mins. 0 sec.). (Comprehensive Ser.). (PER & ENG.). 2006. audio compact disk 345.00 (978-0-7435-5384-1(5), Pimsleur) Pub: S&S Audio. Dist(s): S and S Inc

English for Pofessionals in General Book 4 Student's Audio CD: English Language Teaching. Waldyr Lima. 2008. audio compact disk (978-0-7428-0047-2(4)) CCLS Pubg Hse.

English for Polish People. unabr. ed. Conversa-Phone Institute Staff. 3 cass. (Running Time: 2 hrs. 40 min.). (English for Foreigners Ser.). (ENG & POL.). 1990. 23.98 Set. (978-1-56752-070-5(7), COC-6009) Conversa-phone.
2 manuals containing 65 lessons in English conversation with grammar notes.

English for Portuguese (Brazilian) Speakers: Learn to Speak & Understand English As a Second Language with Pimsleur Language Programs. Pimsleur Staff. 4 cass. (Running Time: 160 hrs. 0 mins. 0 sec.). (Pimsleur Language Program Ser.). (POR & ENG.). 2001. 295.00 (978-0-671-04783-2(3), Pimsleur); audio compact disk 19.95 (978-0-7435-0610-6(3), Pimsleur) Pub: S&S Audio. Dist(s): S and S Inc

English for Portuguese (Brazilian) Speakers: Learn to Speak & Understand English As a Second Language with Pimsleur Language Programs. Pimsleur Staff & Pimsleur. 16 CDs. (Running Time: 160 hrs. 0 mins. 0 sec.). (Comprehensive, English As a Second Langu Ser.). (ENG.). 2001. audio compact disk 345.00 (978-0-7435-0611-3(1), Pimsleur) Pub: S&S Audio. Dist(s): S and S Inc

English for Portuguese Speakers, Set. unabr. ed. Conversa-Phone Institute Staff. 3 cass. 1994. 29.95 (978-1-56752-080-4(4)) Conversa-phone.
Full study language course for Portuguese speakers to learn English. Includes 96 page manual & 1 pocket dictionary (Collins Gem Ingles Portuguese).

English for Professionals in General Book 1 Listening Comprehension Test CD-A: English Language Teaching. 2004. audio compact disk (978-0-7428-1064-8(X)) CCLS Pubg Hse.

English for Professionals in General Book 1 Student's Audio CD: English Language Teaching. Waldyr Lima. 2008. audio compact disk (978-0-7428-0043-4(1)) CCLS Pubg Hse.

English for Professionals in General Book 2 Listening Comprehension Test CD-A: English Language Teaching. 2004. audio compact disk (978-0-7428-1309-0(6)) CCLS Pubg Hse.

English for Professionals in General Book 2 Student's Audio CD: English Language Teaching. Waldyr Lima. 2008. audio compact disk (978-0-7428-0044-1(X)) CCLS Pubg Hse.

English for Professionals in General Book 3 Listening Comprehension Test CD-A: English Language Teaching. 2004. audio compact disk (978-0-7428-1310-6(X)) CCLS Pubg Hse.

English for Professionals in General Book 3 Student's Audio CD: English Language Teaching. Waldyr Lima. 2008. audio compact disk (978-0-7428-0046-5(6)) CCLS Pubg Hse.

English for Professionals in General Book 4 Listening Comprehension Test CD-A: English Language Teaching. 2004. audio compact disk (978-0-7428-1263-5(4)) CCLS Pubg Hse.

English for Russian. Center for Applied Linguistics Staff. 2 cass. (Running Time: 2 hrs.). 2001. pap. bk. 34.50 (E565) Ctr Appl Ling.
Introduces basic English vocabulary necessary for day-to-day life in the United States.

English for Russian People. unabr. ed. Conversa-Phone Institute Staff. 3 cass. (Running Time: 2 hrs. 40 min.). (English for Foreigners Ser.). (ENG & RUS.). 1990. 23.98 Set. (978-1-56752-074-3(X), COC-6014) Conversa-phone.
2 manuals containing 65 lessons in English conversation with grammar notes.

English for Russian Speakers: Learn to Speak & Understand English as a Second Language with Pimsleur Language Programs. Pimsleur Staff. 16 CDs. (Running Time: 160 hrs. 0 mins. 0 sec.). (Pimsleur Language Program Ser.). (RUS.). 2001. audio compact disk 345.00 (978-0-671-77655-8(X), Pimsleur) Pub: S&S Audio. Dist(s): S and S Inc

English for Russian Speakers: Learn to Speak & Understand English for Russian with Pimsleur Language Programs. Pimsleur Staff. 4 CDs. (Running Time: 400 hrs. 0 mins. NaN sec.). (Pimsleur Language Program Ser.). (RUS.). 2000. audio compact disk 19.95 (978-0-7435-1773-7(3), Pimsleur) Pub: S&S Audio. Dist(s): S and S Inc

English for Russian Speakers: Multilingual Books Language Course. 2 CDs. (Multilingual Books Intensive Language Courses). (RUS.). (C). 1991. spiral bd. 59.00 (978-1-58214-160-2(6)) Language Assocs.

English for Russian Speakers CDs & Text. 4 CDs. (Running Time: 4 hrs.). (Survival English Ser.). 2005. audio compact disk 55.00 (978-1-57970-180-2(9), AFE607) J Norton Pubs.

English for Sales & Cashiers see Ingles para Vendedores y Cajeros Amaray Case

English for Sales People & Cashiers see Ingles para Vendedores y Cajeros

English for Science & Engineering-Audio. Ivor Williams. 2007. audio compact disk (978-1-4130-2086-1(0)) South-West.

English for Spanish. Center for Applied Linguistics Staff. 4 cass. (Running Time: 4 hrs.). 2001. pap. bk. 49.50 (E555) Ctr Appl Ling.
Introduces basic English vocabulary necessary for day-to-day life in the United States.

English for Spanish III: Learn to Speak & Understand English As a Second Language with Pimsleur Language Programs. Pimsleur Staff. 16 CDs. (Running Time: 160 hrs. 0 mins. 0 sec.). (Comprehensive, English As a Second Langu Ser.). (SPA.). 2001. audio compact disk 345.00 (978-0-7435-0532-1(8), Pimsleur) Pub: S&S Audio. Dist(s): S and S Inc

English for Spanish Speakers. 2 cass. (Running Time: 2 hrs.). 2001. pap. bk. 29.95 (AFE620, LivingLang) Random Info Grp.
Brief course with dictionary/phrase book teaches the rudiments of language quickly & easily.

English for Spanish Speakers. 2 cass. (Running Time: 90 min. per cass.). (Basic Courses Ser.). 1993. bk. 20.00 set incl. 2 bks. (LivingLang) Random Info Grp.

English for Spanish Speakers: Learn to Speak & Understand English as a Second Language. 2nd ed. Pimsleur Staff. 4 cass. (Running Time: 400 hrs. 0 mins. NaN sec.). (Pimsleur Language Program Ser.). (SPA & ITA.). 2000. 19.95 (978-0-7435-1023-3(2), Pimsleur) Pub: S&S Audio. Dist(s): S and S Inc

English for Spanish Speakers: Learn to Speak & Understand English as a Second Language with Pimsleur Language Programs. 2nd ed. Pimsleur Staff. 4 CDs. (Running Time: 400 hrs. 0 mins. NaN sec.). (Pimsleur Language Program Ser.). (SPA.). 2000. audio compact disk 19.95 (978-0-7435-1774-4(1), Pimsleur) Pub: S&S Audio. Dist(s): S and S Inc

English for Spanish Speakers: Learn to Speak & Understand English as a Second Language with Pimsleur Language Programs. 2nd ed. Pimsleur Staff. 16 CDs. (Running Time: 160 hrs. 0 mins. 0 sec.). (Pimsleur Language Program Ser.). (SPA.). 2001. audio compact disk 345.00 (978-0-671-78476-8(5), Pimsleur) Pub: S&S Audio. Dist(s): S and S Inc

English for Spanish Speakers: Learn to Speak & Understand English as a Second Language with Pimsleur Language Programs. 2nd ed. Pimsleur Staff. 8 cass. (Running Time: 800 hrs. 0 mins. NaN sec.). (Conversational Ser.). (SPA.). 2002. 49.95 (978-0-7435-2909-9(X), Pimsleur) Pub: S&S Audio. Dist(s): S and S Inc

English for Spanish Speakers I: Learn to Speak & Understand English as a Second Language with Pimsleur Language Programs. 2nd ed. Pimsleur Staff. 16 cass. (Running Time: 160 hrs. 0 mins. 0 sec.). (Pimsleur Language Program Ser.). (SPA.). 1999. 295.00 (978-0-671-58117-6(1), Pimsleur) Pub: S&S Audio. Dist(s): S and S Inc

English for Spanish Speakers II: Learn to Speak & Understand English As a Second Language with Pimsleur Language Programs. Pimsleur Staff. (Running Time: 160 hrs. 0 mins. 0 sec.). (Comprehensive, English As a Second Langu Ser.). (SPA.). 2001. audio compact disk 345.00 (978-0-671-77625-1(8), Pimsleur) Pub: S&S Audio. Dist(s): S and S Inc

English for Speakers of Mandarin Chinese. Isabella Y. Yen. 9 dual track cass. (Spoken English As a Foreign Language Ser.). (CHI & ENG.). 1981. bk. 90.00 (978-0-87950-602-5(4)); pap. bk. 110.00 incl. bk. (978-0-87950-603-2(2)) Spoken Lang Serv.

English for Speakers of Spanish. Frederick Browning Agard et al. 5 dual track cass. (Spoken English As a Foreign Language Ser.). 1975. bk. 70.00 (978-0-87950-311-6(4)); bk. 90.00 incl. bk. (978-0-87950-312-3(2)) Spoken Lang Serv.

English for Speakers of Thai. William J. Gedney. 9 dual track cass. (Spoken English As a Foreign Language Ser.). 1981. 90.00 (978-0-87950-612-4(1)) Spoken Lang Serv.

English for Speakers of Thai. William J. Gedney. 9 dual track cass. (Spoken English As a Foreign Language Ser.). (ENG & THA.). 1980. pap. bk. 110.00 incl. bk. (978-0-87950-613-1(X)) Spoken Lang Serv.

English for Speakers of Vietnamese. William W. Gage. 9 dual track cass. (Spoken English As a Foreign Language Ser.). 1981. bk. 110.00 incl. bk. (978-0-87950-617-9(2)); 90.00 (978-0-87950-616-2(4)) Spoken Lang Serv.

English for Tamil Speakers, British Broadcasting Corporation Staff. 3 cass. (Running Time: 3 hrs.). (English: Tiger's Eye Ser.). (TAM.). 1993. pap. bk. 59.50 (978-0-88432-781-3(7), SEN360) J Norton Pubs.
For learners of English from South & South-east Asia, requires a basic working knowledge of English. Includes 200-page bilingual text.

English for Teluga Speakers, British Broadcasting Corporation Staff. 3 cass. (Running Time: 3 hrs.). (English: Tiger's Eye Ser.). (TEL.). 1993. pap. bk. 59.50 (978-0-88432-782-0(5), SEN370) J Norton Pubs.

English for the Financial Sector Audio CD. Ian MacKenzie. (Running Time: 1 hr. 10 mins.). (ENG.). 2008. audio compact disk 25.00 (978-0-521-54728-4(8)) Cambridge U Pr.

English for the Medical Office Jewel Case see Ingles para la Oficina Medica Jewel Case

English for the Real World. unabr. ed. Living Language Staff. Read by Living Language Staff. (YA). 2007. 49.99 (978-1-59895-816-4(X)) Find a World.

English for the Spanish Speaker Bk. 1: For Ages 10 - Adult. 1 cass. (Running Time: 1 hr. 30 mins.). 10.95 Fisher Hill.
Includes vocabulary, conversation, and story pages for each lesson.

English for the Spanish Speaker Book 1. Kathleen S. Fisher & Kathrane Wilcoxon.Tr. of Inglés para el Hispanohablante Libro 1. (ENG & SPA.). 2009. audio compact disk 12.95 (978-1-878253-55-2(7)) Fisher Hill.

English for the Spanish Speaker Book 1, Vol. 1. (ENG & SPA.). (gr. 7 up). 2001. 10.95 (978-1-878253-21-7(2)) Fisher Hill.

English for the Spanish Speaker Book 2. Kathleen S. Fisher & Kathrane Wilcoxon.Tr. of Inglés para el Hispanohablante Libro 2. (ENG & SPA.). 2009. audio compact disk 12.95 (978-1-878253-56-9(5)) Fisher Hill.

English for the Spanish Speaker Book 2, Vol. 2. (ENG & SPA.). 2004. 10.95 (978-1-878253-32-3(8)) Fisher Hill.

English for the Spanish Speaker Book 3. Kathleen S. Fisher & Kathrane Wilcoxon.Tr. of Inglés para el Hispanohablante Libro 3. (ENG & SPA.). 2009. audio compact disk 12.95 (978-1-878253-57-6(3)) Fisher Hill.

English for the Spanish Speaker Book 3, Vol. 3. (ENG & SPA.). 2004. 10.95 (978-1-878253-33-0(6)) Fisher Hill.

English for the Spanish Speaker Book 4. Kathleen S. Fisher.Tr. of Inglés para el Hispanohablante Libro 4. (ENG & SPA.). 2009. audio compact disk 12.95 (978-1-878253-58-3(1)) Fisher Hill.

English for the Spanish Speaker Book 4, Vol. 4. (ENG & SPA.). 2004. 10.95 (978-1-878253-34-7(4)) Fisher Hill.

English for the Teacher: A Language Development Course. Mary Spratt. 1 cass. (Running Time: 5340 sec.). (Cambridge Teacher Training & Development Ser.). (ENG., 1994. 26.00 (978-0-521-42677-0(4)) Cambridge U Pr.

***English for the Teacher Audio CDs (2) A Language Development Course.** Mary Spratt. (Running Time: 1 hr. 28 mins.). (Cambridge Teacher Training & Development Ser.). (ENG.). 2005. audio compact disk 24.00 (978-0-521-15497-0(9)) Cambridge U Pr.

English for the Vestibular Book 1 CD: English Language Teaching. 2006. audio compact disk (978-0-7428-1596-4(X)) CCLS Pubg Hse.

English for the Vestibular Book 2 CD: English Language Teaching. 2006. audio compact disk (978-0-7428-1597-1(8)) CCLS Pubg Hse.

English for the Vestibular Book 3 CD: English Language Teaching. 2006. audio compact disk (978-0-7428-1598-8(6)) CCLS Pubg Hse.

English for the Work Place see Ingles Para los Trabajadores

***English for the World of Work.** Created by AGS Publishing. (Teacher's Resource Library). (ENG.). 2006. audio compact disk (978-0-7854-3082-7(2)) Am Guidance.

English for Turks. Robert B. Lees. 9 dual track cass. (Running Time: 9 hrs.). (Spoken English As a Foreign Language Ser.).Tr. of Konusulan Ingilizce. (ENG & TUR.). 1980. pap. bk. 110.00 (978-0-87950-615-5(6)); 90.00 (978-0-87950-614-8(8)) Spoken Lang Serv.

English for Vietnamese. Center for Applied Linguistics Staff. 3 cass. (Running Time: 3 hrs.). 2001. 39.50 (E551) Ctr Appl Ling.
Introduces basic English vocabulary necessary for day-to-day life in the United States.

English for Vietnamese Speakers: Learn to Speak & Understand English As a Second Language with Pimsleur Language Programs. abr. ed. Pimsleur Staff & Pimsleur. (Running Time: 400 hrs. 0 mins. NaN sec.). (Quick & Simple, English As a Second Lang Ser.). (ITA & VIE.). 2003. audio compact disk 19.95 (978-0-7435-2345-5(8), Pimsleur) Pub: S&S Audio. Dist(s): S and S Inc

English for Vietnamese Speakers: Learn to Speak & Understand English as a Second Language with Pimsleur Language Programs. unabr. ed. Pimsleur Staff. 16 CDs. (Running Time: 160 hrs. 0 mins. 0 sec.). (Comprehensive, English As a Second Langu Ser.). (VIE.). 2002. audio compact disk 345.00 (978-0-7435-2347-9(4), Pimsleur) Pub: S&S Audio. Dist(s): S and S Inc
Programs provide a method of self-practice with an expert teacher and native speakers in lessons specially designed to work with the way the mind naturally acquires language information.

English for Vietnamese Speakers CDs & Text. 5 CDs. (Running Time: 5 hrs.). (Survival English Ser.). Orig. Title: English-Vietnamese Phrasebook with Useful Word List. 2005. audio compact disk 65.00 (978-1-57970-181-9(7), AFE601) J Norton Pubs.

English Governess. unabr. ed. Anna Leon Owens. Read by Nadia May. 9 cass. (Running Time: 13 hrs.). 2001. 56.95 (978-0-7861-2051-2(7), 2811); audio compact disk 72.00 (978-0-7861-9702-6(1), 2811) Blckstn Audio.
Vividly recounts the experiences of one Anna Harriette Leonowens as governess for the sixty-plus children of King Mongkut of Siam, and translator and scribe for the King himself. Bright, young and energetic, Leonowens was well-suited to her role and her writings convey a heartfelt interest in the lives, legends and languages of Siam's rich and poor.

English-Hmong. unabr. ed. 4 cass. (Survival English Ser.). 1981. pap. bk. 49.50 (978-0-88432-415-7(X), AFE554) J Norton Pubs.
Features a course on basic English vocabulary used in everyday life in the United States.

English-Hmong Phrasebook with Useful Word List see Survival English for Hmong Speakers CDs & Text

English Humorists, Set. abr. ed. William Makepeace Thackeray. Read by Robert L. Halvorson. 4 cass. (Running Time: 360 min.). 28.95 (60) Halvorson Assocs.

English II. Pimsleur Staff. 16 cass. (Running Time: 16.5 hrs.). (Pimsleur Language Program Ser.). 2000. 295.00 (978-0-671-04710-8(8), Pimsleur) S&S Audio.

English II. unabr. ed. 16 cass. 2001. 295.00 (978-0-7435-0035-7(0), Pimsleur) S&S Audio.
The Pimsleur programs provide a method of self-practice with an expert teacher and native speakers in lessons specially designed to work with the way the mind naturally acquires language information.

English II for Italian Speakers: Learn to Speak & Understand English As a Second Language with Pimsleur Language Programs. unabr. ed. Pimsleur Staff. 16 CDs. (Running Time: 160 hrs. 0 mins. 0 sec.). (Comprehensive, English As a Second Langu Ser.). (ITA.). 1999. audio compact disk 345.00 (978-0-7435-0042-5(3), Pimsleur) Pub: S&S Audio. Dist(s): S and S Inc

English in Action. Barbara H. Foley & Elizabeth Neblett. 2 cass. (Running Time: 3 hrs.). 2002. pap. bk. 23.95 (978-0-8384-5190-8(X)); audio compact disk 23.95 (978-0-8384-0534-5(9)) Heinle.

English in Action. Elizabeth Neblett & Barbara H. Foley. 1 cass. (Running Time: 1 hr.). 2002. bk. 26.95 (978-0-8384-0728-8(5)) Heinle.

English in Action, Bk. 1. Barbara H. Foley & Elizabeth Neblett. 1 CD. (Running Time: 1 hr.). 2002. pap. bk. 26.95 (978-0-8384-0722-6(6)) Heinle.

English in Action, Bk. 2. Elizabeth Neblett & Barbara H. Foley. 1 CD. (Running Time: 1 hr.). 2002. pap. bk. 26.95 (978-0-8384-0723-3(4)) Heinle.

English in Action, Bk. 3. Barbara H. Foley & Elizabeth Neblett. 1 CD. (Running Time: 1 hr.). 2003. bk. 26.95 (978-0-8384-0724-0(2)) Heinle.

English in Action, Bk. 3. Elizabeth Neblett & Barbara H. Foley. 1 cass. (Running Time: 1 hr.). 2003. bk. 26.95 (978-0-8384-0731-8(5)) Heinle.

English in Action, Bk. 4. Barbara H. Foley & Elizabeth Neblett. 1 CD. (Running Time: 1 hr.). 2003. pap. bk. 26.95 (978-0-8384-0725-7(0)) Heinle.

English in Action, Bk. 4. Elizabeth Neblett & Barbara H. Foley. 1 cass. (Running Time: 1 hr.). 2003. bk. 26.95 (978-0-8384-0732-5(3)) Heinle.

English in Action Book 1. Elizabeth Neblett & Barbara H. Foley. 1 cass. (Running Time: 1 hr.). 2002. pap. bk. 26.95 (978-0-8384-0726-4(9)) Heinle.

English in Medicine. 3rd rev. ed. Eric H. Glendinning & Beverly A. S. Holmstrom. (Running Time: 1 hr. 15 mins.). (ENG.). 2004. 25.00 (978-0-521-60667-7(5)) Cambridge U Pr.

English in Medicine. 3rd rev. ed. Eric H. Glendinning & Beverly A. S. Holmstrom. (Running Time: 1 hr. 15 mins.). (ENG., 2004. audio compact disk 25.00 (978-0-521-60668-4(3)) Cambridge U Pr.

English in Mind. Alessandr Del Lungo et al. (English in Mind Ser.). 2004. (978-88-8433-350-6(4)) Cambridge U Pr.

English in Mind, Bk. 1. Herbert Puchta & Jeff Stranks. (English in Mind Ser.). 2004. (978-0-521-61218-0(7)) Cambridge U Pr.

English in Mind, Bk. 2. Herbert Puchta & Jeffrey Stranks. (Running Time: 2 hrs. 30 mins.). (ENG.). 2004. 42.00 (978-0-521-75062-2(8)) Cambridge U Pr.

English in Mind, Bk. 3. Herbert Puchta et al. (Running Time: 2 hrs. 30 mins.). (ENG.). 2005. 40.00 (978-0-521-75068-4(7)) Cambridge U Pr.

English in Mind, Vol. 1. Herbert Puchta & Jeffrey Stranks. (Running Time: 2 hrs. 30 mins.). (ENG.). 2004. 42.00 (978-0-521-75053-0(9)) Cambridge U Pr.

English in Mind: Class Audio CDs 1A And 1B. abr. ed. Herbert Puchta & Jeff Stranks. (English in Mind Ser.). 2007. audio compact disk 40.00 (978-0-521-70697-1(1)) Cambridge U Pr.

English in Mind: Class Audio CDs 4. Herbert Puchta et al. (Running Time: 2 hrs. 30 mins.). (ENG., 2007. audio compact disk 40.00 (978-0-521-68274-9(6)) Cambridge U Pr.

English in Mind: Starter A & Starter B. Herbert Puchta & Jeff Stranks. (Running Time: 7713 sec.). (English in Mind Ser.). 2007. audio compact disk 40.00 (978-0-521-70686-5(6)) Cambridge U Pr.

English in Mind: American Voices: Starter A & Starter B. Herbert Puchta & Jeff Stranks. (Running Time: 1 hr. 59 mins.). (ENG.). 2007. audio compact disk 40.00 (978-0-521-70696-4(3)) Cambridge U Pr.

English in Mind: American Voices: 1A And 1B. Herbert Puchta & Jeff Stranks. (Running Time: 9120 sec.). (English in Mind Ser.). 2007. audio compact disk 40.00 (978-0-521-70698-8(X)) Cambridge U Pr.

English in Mind Class Audio CDs Starter. Herbert Puchta & Jeff Stranks. (Running Time: 2 hrs. 30 mins.). (ENG.). 2004. audio compact disk 42.00 (978-0-521-54503-7(X)) Cambridge U Pr.

English in Mind Combos 2A & 2B, American Voices Class Audio CDs. Herbert Puchta & Jeff Stranks. (English in Mind Ser.). 2007. audio compact disk 40.00 (978-0-521-70700-8(5)) Cambridge U Pr.

English in Mind Combos 2A & 2B Class Audio CDs. Herbert Puchta et al. (English in Mind Ser.). 2007. audio compact disk 40.00 (978-0-521-70699-5(8)) Cambridge U Pr.

English in Mind Combos 3A & 3B, American Voices Class Audio CDs. Herbert Puchta & Jeff Stranks. (English in Mind Ser.). 2007. audio compact disk 40.00 (978-0-521-70702-2(1)) Cambridge U Pr.

English in Mind Combos 3A & 3B Class Audio CDs. Herbert Puchta et al. (English in Mind Ser.). 2007. audio compact disk 40.00 (978-0-521-70701-5(3)) Cambridge U Pr.

***English in Mind for Spanish Speakers Level 1 Teacher's Resource Book with Audio CDs (3)** Brian Hart. Told to Mario Rinvolucri et al. (ENG.). 2010. spiral bd. 43.00 (978-84-8323-681-9(8)) Cambridge U Pr.

English in Mind Level 1 Audio CDs (3) 2nd rev. ed. Herbert Puchta & Jeff Stranks. (Running Time: 3 hrs. 50 mins.). (ENG.). 2010. audio compact disk 51.00 (978-0-521-18868-5(7)) Cambridge U Pr.

English in Mind Level 2 Audio CDs (3) 2nd rev. ed. Herbert Puchta & Jeff Stranks. (Running Time: 3 hrs. 50 mins.). (ENG.). 2010. audio compact disk 51.00 (978-0-521-18336-9(7)) Cambridge U Pr.

***English in Mind Level 3 Audio CDs (3)** 2nd rev. ed. Herbert Puchta & Jeff Stranks. Told to Richard Carter & Peter Lewis-Jones. (Running Time: 2 hrs. 30 mins.). (ENG.). 2010. audio compact disk 40.00 (978-0-521-18337-6(5)) Cambridge U Pr.

English in Mind Level 4 Class Audio CDs Italian Edition: Volume 0, Part 0. Herbert Puchta & Jeff Stranks. 2007. audio compact disk 41.00 (978-0-521-69926-6(6)) Cambridge U Pr.

English in Mind, Level 5. Herbert Puchta et al. (Running Time: 3 hrs. 54 mins.). (ENG.). 2008. audio compact disk 43.05 (978-0-521-70901-9(6)) Cambridge U Pr.

English in Mind Starter. Herbert Puchta & Jeffrey Stranks. (Running Time: 2 hrs. 30 mins.). (ENG.). 2004. 42.00 (978-0-521-75044-8(X)) Cambridge U Pr.

English in Mind Starter Class Audio CDs American Voices Edition. Herbert Puchta & Jeffrey Stranks. (Running Time: 2 hrs. 30 mins.). (English in Mind Ser.). 2006. audio compact disk 11.00 (978-0-521-67644-1(4)) Cambridge U Pr.

English in Mind Starter Class Cassettes American Voices Edition. Herbert Puchta & Jeffrey Stranks. (Running Time: 2 hrs. 30 mins.). (English in Mind Ser.). 2007. 11.00 (978-0-521-67643-4(6)) Cambridge U Pr.

***English in Mind Starter Level Audio CDs (3)** 2nd rev. ed. Herbert Puchta & Jeff Stranks. (Running Time: 3 hrs. 24 mins.). (ENG.). 2010. audio compact disk 40.00 (978-0-521-12749-3(1)) Cambridge U Pr.

English in Mind 1. Herbert Puchta & Jeff Stranks. (Running Time: 2 hrs. 30 mins.). (ENG.). 2004. audio compact disk 42.00 (978-0-521-54504-4(8)) Cambridge U Pr.

English in Mind 1 Audio CDs Egyptian Version. Herbert Puchta & Jeff Stranks. (English in Mind Ser.). 2004. audio compact disk (978-0-521-61219-7(5)) Cambridge U Pr.

English in Mind 1 Class Audio CDs American Voices Edition. Herbert Puchta & Jeffrey Stranks. (Running Time: 2 hrs. 30 mins.). 2006. audio compact disk 11.00 (978-0-521-67646-5(0)) Cambridge U Pr.

English in Mind 1 Class Audio CDs Italia. Herbert (Pad Puchta. (English in Mind Ser.). 2004. audio compact disk (978-88-8433-351-3(2)) Cambridge U Pr.

English in Mind 1 Class Cassettes American English Edition. Herbert Puchta & Jeff Stranks. (Running Time: 2 hrs. 30 mins.). (English in Mind Ser.). 2007. 11.00 (978-0-521-67645-8(2)) Cambridge U Pr.

English in Mind 2. Herbert Puchta & Jeff Stranks. 2 CDs. (Running Time: 2 hrs. 30 mins.). (ENG.). 2004. audio compact disk 42.00 (978-0-521-54505-1(6)) Cambridge U Pr.

English in Mind 2 Class Audio CDs American Voices Edition. Herbert Puchta & Jeffrey Stranks. (Running Time: 2 hrs. 27 mins.). 2006. audio compact disk 11.00 (978-0-521-67648-9(7)) Cambridge U Pr.

English in Mind 2 Class Cassettes American Voices Edition. Herbert Puchta & Jeff Stranks. (Running Time: 2 hrs. 30 mins.). (English in Mind Ser.). 2007. 11.00 (978-0-521-67647-2(9)) Cambridge U Pr.

English in Mind 2 Class Cassettes Italia. Herbert (Pad Puchta & Jeff Stranks. (English in Mind Ser.). 2004. (978-88-8433-356-8(3)) Cambridge U Pr.

English in Mind 3: Class Audio CDs. Herbert Puchta et al. (Running Time: 2 hrs. 30 mins.). (ENG.). 2005. audio compact disk 42.00 (978-0-521-54506-8(4)) Cambridge U Pr.

English in Mind 3 Class Audio Cassettes Egyptian Edition: Volume 0, Part 0. Herbert Puchta et al. 2006. 56.00 (978-0-521-69437-7(X)) Cambridge U Pr.

English in Mind 3 Class Audio CDs American Voices Edition. Herbert Puchta & Jeff Stranks. (Running Time: 2 hrs. 24 mins.). 2006. audio compact disk 11.00 (978-0-521-67650-2(9)) Cambridge U Pr.

English in Mind 3 Class Cassettes American Voices Edition. Herbert Puchta et al. (Running Time: 2 hrs. 30 mins.). (English in Mind Ser.). 2007. 11.00 (978-0-521-67649-6(5)) Cambridge U Pr.

English in Mind 4 Class Audio Cassettes (2) Herbert Puchta et al. (Running Time: 2 hrs. 30 mins.). (ENG.). 2007. 42.00 (978-0-521-68273-2(8)) Cambridge U Pr.

English in Tune. 1 cass. (Running Time: 25 min.). (ITA.). (J). Incl. guide with lyrics, music, language learning activities. (978-88-8148-162-0(6)) Midwest European Pubns.
Songs, games & activities which exploit the structures & functions of everyday English.

English Job Interview Techniques: The Gold Standard of Job Interviewing. DGS Consulting LLC. Transcribed by Hongki Kim & Hongki Kim. (KOR & ENG.). 2007. audio compact disk 24.99 (978-0-9797897-9-3(6)) DGS Con.

English KnowHow, Level 1. Angela Blackwell & Therese Naber. 2003. audio compact disk 39.95 (978-0-19-453693-6(9)) OUP.

English KnowHow, Level 2. Angela Blackwell & Therese Naber. Ed. by Margaret Brooks. 2004. 39.95 (978-0-19-453682-0(3)) OUP.

English KnowHow, No. 2. Angela Blackwell & Therese Naber. 2005. audio compact disk 39.95 (978-0-19-453692-9(0)) OUP.

English KnowHow, No. 3. Angela Blackwell & Therese Naber. 2 cds. 2005. audio compact disk 39.95 (978-0-19-453694-3(7)) OUP.

English KnowHow, No. 3. Angela Blackwell & Therese Naber. Ed. by Margaret Brooks. 2005. 39.95 (978-0-19-453688-2(2)) OUP.

English Knowhow: English Knowhow Opener Reserved. Therese Naber & Angela Blackwell. Ed. by Margaret Brooks. 2005. cd-rom, audio compact disk, audio compact disk 21.95 (978-0-19-453672-1(6)) OUP.

English Knowhow: English Knowhow 1: English Knowhow 1 Reserved. Therese Naber & Angela Blackwell. Ed. by Margaret Brooks. 2005. audio compact disk 21.95 (978-0-19-453678-3(5)) OUP.

English Knowhow Opener. Angela Blackwell & Therese Naber. 2003. audio compact disk 39.95 (978-0-19-453691-2(2)) OUP.

English KnowHow 2. Angela Blackwell & Therese Naber. 2005. stu. ed. 20.50 (978-0-19-453852-7(4)) OUP.

English KnowHow 3: Student Book with CD. Angela Blackwell & Therese Naber. 2005. audio compact disk 20.50 (978-0-19-453853-4(2)) OUP.

English Language. unabr. ed. Read by Heywood Hale Broun et al. 1 cass. (Running Time: 56 min.). (Broun Radio Ser.). 12.95 (40221) J Norton Pubs.
With William & Mary Morris ("Harper's Dictionary of Contemporary Usage") & Theodore Bemstein ("The Reverse Dictionary").

English Literature. Benjamin W. Griffith. (Running Time: 18000 sec.). (Barron's EZ-101 Study Keys Ser.). 2005. audio compact disk 36.00 (978-0-7861-7598-7(2)) Blckstn Audio.

English Literature. unabr. ed. Benjamin W. Griffith. 4 cass. (Running Time: 18000 sec.). (Barron's EZ-101 Study Keys Ser.). 2005. 24.95 (978-0-7861-3662-9(6), E3529) Blckstn Audio.

English Literature. unabr. ed. Benjamin W. Griffith. Read by Stuart Langston. 4 CDs. (Running Time: 18000 sec.). (Barron's EZ-101 Study Keys Ser.). 2005. audio compact disk 25.95 (978-0-7861-7735-6(7), ZE3529); audio compact disk 29.95 (978-0-7861-7960-2(0), ZM3529) Blckstn Audio.

English Literature (Barron's EZ-101 Study Keys) 2005. 34.95 (978-0-7861-3770-1(3)) Blckstn Audio.

English Major. unabr. ed. Jim Harrison. (Running Time: 7.5 hrs. NaN mins.). (ENG.). 2008. 29.95 (978-1-4332-4666-1(X)); 54.95 (978-1-4332-4663-0(5)); audio compact disk 29.95 (978-1-4332-4665-4(1)) Blckstn Audio.

English Major. unabr. ed. Jim Harrison. Read by Mark Bramhall. 6 CDs. (Running Time: 7 hrs. 30 mins.). 2008. audio compact disk 60.00 (978-1-4332-4664-7(3)) Blckstn Audio.

English Novel. Instructed by Timothy Spurgin. 12 cass. (Running Time: 12 hrs.). 54.95 (978-1-59803-215-4(1)) Teaching Co.

English Novel. Instructed by Timothy Spurgin. 12 CDs. (Running Time: 12 hrs.). 2006. audio compact disk 69.95 (978-1-59803-216-1(X)) Teaching Co.

English Novel Today: From Dickens to Snow. unabr. ed. Angus Wilson. 1 cass. (Running Time: 27 min.). 1960. 12.95 (23255) J Norton Pubs.
The post WW II British novel is examined in the light of recent history. Wilson believes that the most significant change in this area since the war has been a move toward a greater concern with social & political problems.

English Panorama Set: A Course for Advanced Learners. Felicity O'Dell. 2 cass. (Running Time: hrs. mins.). (ENG.). 1998. 44.10 (978-0-521-47692-8(5)) Cambridge U Pr.

English Passengers. Matthew Kneale. Narrated by Matthew Kneale. 17 CDs. (Running Time: 20 hrs. 30 mins.). audio compact disk 168.00 (978-1-4025-1541-5(3)) Recorded Bks.

English Passengers. unabr. ed. Matthew Kneale. Narrated by Matthew Kneale. 15 cass. (Running Time: 20 hrs. 30 mins.). 2001. 126.00 (978-1-84197-258-9(4)) Recorded Bks.
It is 1857, and Reverend Geoffrey Wilson sets out on his mission to prove scientifically the literal historical truth of the Bible by locating the Garden of Eden. However, the Reverent has placed Eden in Van Diemen's Land or Tasmania, a British prison colony.

English Patient. abr. ed. Michael Ondaatje. Read by Ralph Fiennes. (Running Time: 14400 sec.). (ENG.). 2007. audio compact disk 22.95 (978-0-7393-4394-4(7), Random AudioBks) Pub: Random Audio Pubg. Dist(s): Random

English Phrase-a-Day for Hispanic Children. unabr. ed. Judith White. Illus. by Carol Macbain. 2 cass. (Umbrella Parade Ser.). (J). (gr. k-6). 1993. pap. bk. 24.95 set incl. activity-coloring bk. (978-0-88432-498-0(2), SEN850) J Norton Pubs.
This audio-cassete-coloring book program makes learning English fun. Children learn a variety of everyday expressions by listening & coloring. The illustrations, vocabulary, & activities are organized by season of the year. All the voices on the tapes are native speakers & the music & sound effects are original.

English Pronunciation: Learning the Sounds of American English. unabr. ed. British Broadcasting Corporation Staff. 3 cass. (YA). pap. bk. 49.50 (978-0-88432-674-8(8), S32560) J Norton Pubs.
This course, originally developed for presentation on BBC radio by J.D. O'Connor, serves as a model for pronunciation of English words for ESL students.

English Pronunciation Exercises for Japanese Students. Harriet Gordon Grate. (C). (gr. 12 up). 1987. bk. 150.00 (978-0-685-42245-8(3), 58138) Prentice ESL.

English Pronunciation Exercises for Japanese Students, Set. Harriet Gordon Grate. 2001. 326.65 (978-0-13-281361-7(0)) Longman.

English Pronunciation for International Students, Set. Paulette Dale & Lillian Poms. 2001. bk. 43.85 (978-0-13-279910-2(3)) Longman.

English Pronunciation for Japanese Speakers, Set. Paulette Dale & Lillian Poms. 2001. 43.85 (978-0-13-034380-2(3)) Longman.

English Pronunciation for Spanish Speakers: Consonants, Set. Paulette Dale & Lillian Poms. 2 cass. (Running Time: 3 hrs.). 1986. bk. 55.25 (978-0-13-281338-9(6)) Longman.

English Pronunciation for Spanish Speakers: Vowels, Set. Paulette Dale & Lillian Poms. 2001. 43.85 (978-0-13-281353-2(X)) Longman.

English Pronunciation Illustrated. John Trim. 2 cass. (Running Time: 2 hrs. 3 mins.). (ENG.). 1984. 44.10 (978-0-521-26350-4(6)) Cambridge U Pr.

***English Pronunciation Illustrated Audio CDs (2)** John Trim. (Running Time: 2 hrs. 1 min.). (ENG.). 2010. audio compact disk 41.00 (978-0-521-16878-6(3)) Cambridge U Pr.

English Pronunciation in Use, Set. Mark Hancock. 1 cass. (Running Time: 90 mins.). (ENG., 2003. 56.00 (978-0-521-00660-6(0)); audio compact disk 56.00 (978-0-521-00659-0(7)) Cambridge U Pr.

English Pronunciation in Use Advanced 5 Audio CDs. Martin Hewings. (Running Time: 5 hrs. 8 mins.). (ENG., 2007. audio compact disk 53.00 (978-0-521-61958-5(0)) Cambridge U Pr.

English Pronunciation in Use Elementary 5 Audio CD Set. Jonathan Marks. (Running Time: 6 hrs. 10 mins.). (ENG., 2007. audio compact disk 55.65 (978-0-521-67264-1(3)) Cambridge U Pr.

English Prose & Poetry of the Victorian Age. abr. ed. Alfred Lord Tennyson et al. Read by Peter Speaight et al. 6 cass. (Running Time: 4 hrs. 24 min.). Incl. English Prose & Poetry of the Victorian Age: Dickens Duets. Charles Dickens. Read by Frank Pettingell. 1986. (PCC 15); English Prose & Poetry of the Victorian Age: Sonnets from the Portuguese. Elizabeth Barrett Browning. Read by Penelope Lee. 1986. (PCC 15); English Prose & Poetry of the Victorian Age: Treasury of Lewis Carroll. Lewis Carroll, pseud. Read by Christopher Casson. 1986. (PCC 15); English Prose & Poetry of the Victorian Age: Treasury of Robert Browning. Robert Browning. Read by Robert Speaight. 1986. (PCC 15); English Prose & Poetry of the Victorian Age. Alfred Lord Tennyson. Read by Robert Speaight. 1986. (PCC 15); English Prose & Poetry of the Victorian Age. Matthew Arnold. Read by Robert Speaight. 1986. (PCC 15); 1986. 55.00 (978-0-8045-0015-9(0), PCC 15) Spoken Arts.

English Prose & Poetry of the Victorian Age: Dickens Duets see English Prose & Poetry of the Victorian Age

English Prose & Poetry of the Victorian Age: Sonnets from the Portuguese see English Prose & Poetry of the Victorian Age

English Prose & Poetry of the Victorian Age: Treasury of Lewis Carroll see English Prose & Poetry of the Victorian Age

English Prose & Poetry of the Victorian Age: Treasury of Robert Browning see English Prose & Poetry of the Victorian Age

English Quick & Easy: EFL for Native Speakers of Spanish, Levels 1-2. (English Quick & Easy). (J). (gr. 5-9). 2000. 8.99 (978-1-928882-94-7(3)) CCLS Pubg Hse.

English Quick & Easy: ESL for Native Speakers of Spanish, Levels 3-4. (Getting There / English Quick & Easy). (J). 2000. 8.99 (978-1-928882-93-0(5)) CCLS Pubg Hse.

***English Quick & Easy Book 1 - CD De Áudio.** (SPA.). 2005. audio compact disk (978-0-7428-1498-1(X)) CCLS Pubg Hse.

***English Quick & Easy Book 2 - CD De Áudio.** (SPA.). 2005. audio compact disk (978-0-7428-1499-8(8)) CCLS Pubg Hse.

***English Quick & Easy Book 3 - CD De Áudio.** (SPA.). 2005. audio compact disk (978-0-7428-1500-1(5)) CCLS Pubg Hse.

***English Quick & Easy Book 4 - CD De Áudio.** (SPA.). 2005. audio compact disk (978-0-7428-1529-2(3)) CCLS Pubg Hse.

English Rebel Songs, 1381-1984. Chumbawamba. (Running Time: 0 hr. 42 mins. 0 sec.). (PM Audio Ser.). (ENG.). 2008. audio compact disk 14.98 (978-1-60486-000-9(6)) Pub: Pm Pre. Dist(s): IPG Chicago

English Romantic Poetry, Vol. 2. Instructed by Willard Spiegelman. 6 cass. (Running Time: 6 hrs.). 2002. 129.95 (978-1-56585-042-2(4)) Teaching Co.

English Say Hello. Louis Aarons. 4 cass. (Running Time: 5 hrs.). (WordMate Ser.). (YA). 2000. pap. bk. & wbk. ed. 49.95 (978-1-887447-04-1(0)) WordMate.
Basic English for native speakers of Spanish include pronunciation guide, word lists, dialogs for communication, useful expressions, proverbs, & idioms.

English Set. unabr. ed. University of Iowa, CEEDE Staff. 2 cass. (Constitution Ser.). 1988. 15.95 Set. (978-0-7836-1106-8(4), 9998) Triumph Learn.
English readings about the American Constitution.

English Society in the Eighteenth Century. unabr. ed. Roy Porter. Read by Wanda McCaddon. (Running Time: 16 hrs. 0 mins.). (ENG.). 2009. 29.95 (978-1-4332-1921-4(2)); 89.95 (978-1-4332-1917-7(4)); audio compact disk 118.00 (978-1-4332-1918-4(2)) Blckstn Audio.

English Spanish, 3. Sara Jordan & Diana Isaza-Shelton. (Songs that Teach Spanish Ser.). (SPA.). (J). 2005. audio compact disk 13.95 (978-1-55386-034-1(9)) Pub: S Jordan Publ. Dist(s): CrabtreePubCo

English, Spoken 'Round the World: In a Manner of Speaking. unabr. ed. 1 cass. 12.95 (32660); J Norton Pubs.
The program demonstrates through readings the accents & dialects of English.

English Teacher. unabr. ed. Lily King. Read by Christina Moore. 6 cass. (Running Time: 8 hrs.). 2006. 59.75 (978-1-4193-6965-0(2), 98259) Recorded Bks.
In The English Teacher, King pens an emotionally devastating tale of a mother and son - and the turns of fate that threaten their carefully constructed existence. English teacher and single mother Vida Avery has insulated herself and her 15-year-old son from almost all outside influence. But her sudden marriage to Tom Belou - and the subsequent integration into Tom¿s family - radically alters the course of all of their lives.

English Teaching Set. unabr. ed. University of Iowa, CEEDE Staff. 5 cass. (Tales of Marvel & Wonder Ser.). 1988. 99.00 Set, incl. tchr's. guide, activity masters, ESL grammar activity masters & the ESL grammar activity masters tchr's. guide. (978-0-7836-1089-4(0), 9989) Triumph Learn.
Twenty-three Indochinese fables.

English the Berlitz Way: Level 1. Berlitz Editors. 2 cass. (Running Time: 120 min.). (Basic Ser.). (J). 1999. bk. 29.95 (978-2-8315-7363-2(7)) Berlitz Intl Inc.

English the Berlitz Way: Level 2. Berlitz Editors. 2 cass. (Running Time: 120 min.). (Basic Ser.). (J). 1999. bk. 29.95 (978-2-8315-7364-9(5)) Berlitz Intl Inc.

English the Berlitz Way: Level 3. Berlitz Editors. 2 cass. (Running Time: 120 min.). (Basic Ser.). (J). 1999. bk. 29.95 (978-2-8315-7365-6(3)) Berlitz Intl Inc.

English the Berlitz Way 1 for Japanese Speakers. 2000. bk. 29.95 (978-2-8315-7311-3(4)) Berlitz Intl Inc.

English Time, Level 4. Susan Rivers & Setsuko Toyama. 2008. 39.95 (978-0-19-436422-5(4)); audio compact disk 39.95 (978-0-19-436423-2(2)) OUP.

English Time, Level 5. Susan Rivers & Setsuko Toyama. 2008. 39.95 (978-0-19-436430-0(5)); audio compact disk 39.95 (978-0-19-436431-7(3)) OUP.

English Time, Level 6. Susan Rivers & Setsuko Toyama. 2008. 39.95 (978-0-19-436438-6(0)) OUP.

English Time 1, No. 1. Susan Rivers. 2008. 39.95 (978-0-19-436309-9(0)); audio compact disk 39.95 (978-0-19-436310-5(4)) OUP.

English Time 2. Susan Rivers. 2008. 39.95 (978-0-19-436406-5(2)) OUP.

English Time 2, Vol. 2. Susan Rivers. 2008. audio compact disk 39.95 (978-0-19-436407-2(0)) OUP.

English Time 3. Susan Rivers & Setsuko Toyama. 2008. 39.95 (978-0-19-436414-0(3)); audio compact disk 39.95 (978-0-19-436415-7(1)) OUP.

***English Unlimited Elementary Class Audio CDs (3)** Alex Tilbury et al. (Running Time: 2 hrs. 55 mins.). (ENG.). 2010. audio compact disk 56.00 (978-0-521-69775-0(1)) Cambridge U Pr.

***English Unlimited for Spanish Speakers Elementary Class Audio CDs (3)** Theresa Clementson et al. (Running Time: 3 hrs.). (ENG.). 2010. audio compact disk 64.00 (978-84-8323-912-4(4)) Cambridge U Pr.

***English Unlimited for Spanish Speakers Pre-intermediate Class Audio CDs (3)** David Rea et al. (Running Time: 2 hrs. 58 mins.). (ENG.). 2010. audio compact disk 64.00 (978-84-8323-978-0(7)) Cambridge U Pr.

***English Unlimited for Spanish Speakers Starter Class Audio CDs (2)** Adrian Doff. (Running Time: 1 hr. 48 mins.). (ENG.). 2010. audio compact disk 64.00 (978-84-8323-871-4(3)) Cambridge U Pr.

***English Unlimited Pre-intermediate Class Audio CDs (3)** Alex Tilbury et al. (Running Time: 2 hrs. 58 mins.). (ENG.). 2010. audio compact disk 56.00 (978-0-521-69779-8(4)) Cambridge U Pr.

***English Unlimited Starter Class Audio CDs (2)** Adrian Doff. (Running Time: 1 hr. 47 mins.). (ENG.). 2010. audio compact disk 43.00 (978-0-521-72636-8(0)) Cambridge U Pr.

***English Unlimited Upper Intermediate Class Audio CDs (3)** Alex Tilbury & Leslie Anne Hendra. Told to David Rea & Theresa Clementson. (Running Time: 3 hrs. 1 min.). (ENG.). 2011. audio compact disk 40.00 (978-0-521-73992-4(6)) Cambridge U Pr.

English-Vietnamese Phrasebook with Useful Word List see English for Vietnamese Speakers CDs & Text

English Village Christmas Carols: Traditional Christmas Carolling from the Southern Pennines. Perf. by Carollers from Castleton Staff & Foolow Carollers, The. Compiled by Ian Russell. 1 CD. (Running Time: 71 min.). 1999. audio compact disk 49.99 Smithsonian Folkways.

English with a Smile. Barbara Zaffran & David Krulik. (English with a Smile Ser.: Bk. 2). 1993. bk. 60.00 (978-0-685-62873-7(6), Natl Textbk Co) M-H Contemporary.

English with a Smile, Bk. 1. National Textbook Company Staff. 3 cass. 45.00 (Natl Textbk Co) M-H Contemporary.
With a variety of exercises that help enhance speaking, listening, reading & writing skills, this lively volume builds & reinforces total language development in English.

English with a Smile, Bk. 2. National Textbook Company Staff. 3 cass. 1999. 45.00 (978-0-8325-0302-3(9), Natl Textbk Co) M-H Contemporary.

English with Ease see Englisch Ohne Muhe Heute

English with Ease see Nuovo Inglese Senza Sforzo

English with Ease see Nuevo Ingles sin Esfuerzo

English with Ease see Jezyk Anglielski

English with Ease see Englisch Ohne Muhe Heute

English with Ease see O Novo Ingles Sem Custo

English with Ease for Polish Speakers. 4 cass. (POL & ENG.). 1997. pap. bk. 75.00 Set. Distribks Inc.

English, Yes! Level 1: Basic: Learning English Through Literature. rev. ed. Created by Jamestown Publishers. 2003. audio compact disk 43.96 (978-0-07-860856-8(2), 9780078608568) Pub: Jamestown. Dist(s): McGraw

English, Yes! Level 4: Intermediate A, rev. ed. Burton Goodman. 2003. audio compact disk 43.96 (978-0-07-861509-2(7), 9780078615092) Pub: Jamestown. Dist(s): McGraw
Level 4 Something Funny based on a story by Elizabeth Van Steenwyk Three Hundred Pesos based on a story by Manuela Williams Crosno Younde Goes to Town based on an African Folktale retold by Harold Courlander and George Herzog Dr. Heidegger's Experiment based on a story by Nathaniel Hawthorne Six Rows of Flowers based on a story by Toshio Mori Space Star based on a story by Lael J. Littke The Contest based on a story by William Hoffman Irregular Verbs Present and Past Tenses Score Chart.

English, Yes! Level 6: Advanced: Learning English Through Literature, rev. ed. Burton Goodman. 2003. audio compact disk 43.96 (978-0-07-861511-5(9), 9780078615115) Pub: Jamestown. Dist(s): McGraw
Level 6 Unit 1: Talking in the New Land based on a story by Edite Cunhã Unit 2: Keesh based on a story by Jack London Unit 3: The Force of Luck based on a story by Rudolfo A. Anaya and José Griego y Maestas Unit 4: Sixteen based on a story by Maureen Daly Bread and Music (poem) by Conrad Aiken Alone (poem) by Maya Angelou Unit 5: The Stolen Letter based on a story by Edgar Allan Poe Unit 6: The Sanctuary based on a story by Jesse Stuart Lineage (poem) by Margaret Walker The Courage That My Mother Had (poem) by Edna St. Vincent Millay Unit 7: The Lady or the Tiger? based on a story by Frank Stockton The Road Not Taken (poem) by Robert Frost Unit 8: The Surveyor by Alma Flor Ada IrregularVerbs Present and Past Tenses Score Chart.

English 365, Set. Bob Dignen et al. 2 cass. (Running Time: 1 hr. 46 mins.). (ENG.). 2004. 45.15 (978-0-521-75370-8(8)) Cambridge U Pr.

English 365, Set. 2nd ed. Bob Dignen et al. 2 cds. (Running Time: 1 hr. 46 mins.). (ENG.). 2004. audio compact disk 45.15 (978-0-521-75371-5(6)) Cambridge U Pr.

English 365: For Work & Life. Bob Dignen et al. (Running Time: 1 hr. 46 mins.). (ENG.). 2004. 45.15 (978-0-521-75365-4(1)); audio compact disk 45.15 (978-0-521-75366-1(X)) Cambridge U Pr.

Englisher. Beverly Lewis. 8. (Running Time: 9 hrs. 50 mns.). (Annie's People Ser.: No. 2). 2006. 61.75 (978-1-4281-0650-5(2)) Recorded Bks.

Englisher. unabr. ed. Beverly Lewis. 8 cass. (Running Time: 9 hrs. 30 mins.). (Annie's People Ser.: No. 2). 2006. 59.75 (978-1-4193-0650-1(2)) Recorded Bks.

Englishman see De Maupassant Short Stories

English365, Level 3. Steve Flinders et al. 2 cass. (Running Time: 2 hrs. 30 mins.). (ENG.). 2005. 45.15 (978-0-521-54920-2(5)) Cambridge U Pr.

English365: Professional English for Work & Life, 2 cds. Steve Flinders et al. 2 CDs. (Running Time: 2 hrs. 30 mins.). (ENG.). 2005. audio compact disk 45.15 (978-0-521-54919-6(1)) Cambridge U Pr.

***Englits - All Quiet on the Western Front (Audio) Detailed Summaries of Great Literature.** 2010. 2.99 (978-1-60299-252-8(5), Interlingua) InterLinguacom.

***EngLits - All's Well That Ends Well (Audio) Detailed Summaries of Great Literature: All's Well That Ends Well (Audio)** 2010. 2.99 (978-1-60299-240-5(1), Interlingua) InterLinguacom.

***EngLits - Animal Farm (Audio) Detailed Summaries of Great Literature.** 2010. 2.99 (978-1-60299-250-4(9), Interlingua) InterLinguacom.

***EngLits - Anna Karenina (Audio) Detail Summaries of Great Literature.** 2010. 2.99 (978-1-60299-234-4(7), Interlingua) InterLinguacom.

***EngLits - Brave New World (Audio) Detailed Summaries of Great Literature.** 2010. 2.99 (978-1-60299-210-8(X), Interlingua) InterLinguacom.

***EngLits - Candide (Audio) Detail Summaries of Great Literature.** 2010. 2.99 (978-1-60299-226-9(6), Interlingua) InterLinguacom.

EngLits - Hamlet (mp3) 2007. 2.99 (978-1-60299-040-1(9)) InterLinguacom.

***EngLits - Robinson Crusoe (Audio) Detail Summaries of Great Literature.** 2010. 2.99 (978-1-60299-235-1(5), Interlingua) InterLinguacom.

EngLits - Romeo & Juliet (mp3) (ENG.). 2007. 2.99 (978-1-60299-041-8(7)) InterLinguacom.

***EngLits - Tess of the D'Urbervilles (Audio) Detailed Summaries of Great Literature: Tess of the D'Urbervilles (Audio)** 2010. 2.99 (978-1-60299-238-2(X), Interlingua) InterLinguacom.

***EngLits - the Age of Innocence (Audio) Detail Summaries of Great Literature.** 2010. 2.99 (978-1-60299-236-8(3), Interlingua) InterLinguacom.

***EngLits - the Great Gatsby (Audio) Detailed Summaries of Classic Literature: the Great Gatsby (Audio)** 2010. 2.99 (978-1-60299-228-3(2), Interlingua) InterLinguacom.

***EngLits - the Sun Also Rises (Audio) Detail Summaries of Great Literature.** 2010. 2.99 (978-1-60299-232-0(0), Interlingua) InterLinguacom.

***EngLits - Uncle Tom's Cabin (Audio) Detailed Summaries of Great Literature: Uncle Tom's Cabin by Harriet Beecher Stowe (Audio)** 2010. 2.99 (978-1-60299-239-9(8), Interlingua) InterLinguacom.

***EngLits - White Fang (Audio) Detail Summaries of Great Literature.** 2010. 2.99 (978-1-60299-237-5(1), Interlingua) InterLinguacom.

***EngLits -Tthe Stranger (Audio) Detail Summaries of Great Literature.** 2010. 2.99 (978-1-60299-230-6(4), Interlingua) InterLinguacom.

EngLits-A Christmas Carol (mp3) (ENG.). 2007. (978-1-60299-060-9(3)) InterLinguacom.

EngLits-A Tale of Two Cities (mp3) (ENG.). 2007. (978-1-60299-062-3(X)) InterLinguacom.

EngLits-As you like It (mp3) (ENG.). 2007. (978-1-60299-052-4(2)) InterLinguacom.

EngLits-BillyBudd, Sailor (mp3) (ENG.). 2007. 2.99 (978-1-60299-083-8(2)) InterLinguacom.

EngLits-Crime & Punishment (mp3) (ENG.). 2007. 2.99 (978-1-60299-089-0(1)) InterLinguacom.

EngLits-Daisy Miller (mp3) (ENG.). 2007. 2.99 (978-1-60299-085-2(9)) InterLinguacom.

EngLits-David Copperfield (mp3) (ENG.). 2007. (978-1-60299-061-6(1)) InterLinguacom.

EngLits-Don Quixote (mp3) (ENG.). 2007. 2.99 (978-1-60299-066-1(2)) InterLinguacom.

EngLits-Dr. Jekyll & Mr. Hyde (mp3) (ENG.). 2007. 2.99 (978-1-60299-071-5(9)) InterLinguacom.

EngLits-Dubliners (mp3) (ENG.). 2007. 2.99 (978-1-60299-076-0(X)) InterLinguacom.

EngLits-Emma (mp3) (ENG.). 2007. (978-1-60299-057-9(3)) InterLinguacom.

EngLits-Ethan Frome (mp3) (ENG.). 2007. 2.99 (978-1-60299-087-6(5)) InterLinguacom.

EngLits-Frankenstein (mp3) (ENG.). 2007. 2.99 (978-1-60299-068-5(9)) InterLinguacom.

EngLits-Great Expectations (mp3) (ENG.). 2007. (978-1-60299-063-0(8)) InterLinguacom.

EngLits-Gulliver's Travels (mp3) (ENG.). 2007. 2.99 (978-1-60299-067-8(0)) InterLinguacom.

EngLits-HenryIV, part II(mp3) (ENG.). 2007. (978-1-60299-044-9(1)) InterLinguacom.

EngLits-HenryIV, Part 1 (mp3) (ENG.). 2007. (978-1-60299-043-2(3)) InterLinguacom.

EngLits-HenryV (mp3) (ENG.). 2007. (978-1-60299-045-6(X)) InterLinguacom.

EngLits-Jane Eyre (mp3) (ENG.). 2007. 2.99 (978-1-60299-072-2(7)) InterLinguacom.

EngLits-Julius Ceasar (mp3) (ENG.). 2007. (978-1-60299-046-3(8)) InterLinguacom.

EngLits-King Lear (mp3) (ENG.). 2007. (978-1-60299-047-0(6)) InterLinguacom.

EngLits-Macbeth (mp3) (ENG.). 2007. (978-1-60299-048-7(4)) InterLinguacom.

EngLits-Madame Bovary (mp3) (ENG.). 2007. 2.99 (978-1-60299-069-2(7)) InterLinguacom.

EngLits-Middlemarch (mp3) (ENG.). 2007. 2.99 (978-1-60299-074-6(3)) InterLinguacom.

EngLits-Moby Dick (mp3) (ENG.). 2007. 2.99 (978-1-60299-082-1(4)) InterLinguacom.

EngLits-Much Ado about Nothing (mp3) (ENG.). 2007. (978-1-60299-049-4(2)) InterLinguacom.

EngLits-Notes from Underground (mp3) (ENG.). 2007. 2.99 (978-1-60299-088-3(3)) InterLinguacom.

EngLits-Oliver Twist (mp3) (ENG.). 2007. (978-1-60299-059-3(X)) InterLinguacom.

EngLits-Othello(mp3) (ENG.). 2007. (978-1-60299-050-0(6)) InterLinguacom.

EngLits-Persuasion (mp3) (ENG.). 2007. (978-1-60299-058-6(1)) InterLinguacom.

EngLits-Pride & Prejudice (mp3) (ENG.). 2007. (978-1-60299-056-2(5)) InterLinguacom.

EngLits-Sense & Sensibility (mp3) (ENG.). 2007. (978-1-60299-055-5(7)) InterLinguacom.

EngLits-Silas Marner (mp3) (ENG.). 2007. 2.99 (978-1-60299-075-3(1)) InterLinguacom.

EngLits-the Adventures of Huckleberry Finn (mp3) (ENG.). 2007. 2.99 (978-1-60299-079-1(4)) InterLinguacom.

EngLits-the Adventures of Tom Sawyer (mp3) (ENG.). 2007. 2.99 (978-1-60299-080-7(8)) InterLinguacom.

EngLits-the Awakening (mp3) (ENG.). 2007. 2.99 (978-1-60299-086-9(7)) InterLinguacom.

EngLits-the Death of Ivan Ilyich (mp3) (ENG.). 2007. 2.99 (978-1-60299-090-6(5)) InterLinguacom.

EngLits-the Merchant of Venice. (ENG.). 2007. (978-1-60299-051-7(4)) InterLinguacom.

EngLits-the Odyssey (mp3) (ENG.). 2007. (978-1-60299-064-7(6)) InterLinguacom.

EngLits-the Oedipus Plays (mp3) (ENG.). 2007. 2.99 (978-1-60299-065-4(4)) InterLinguacom.

EngLits-the Red Badge of Courage (mp3) (ENG.). 2007. 2.99 (978-1-60299-081-4(6)) InterLinguacom.

EngLits-the Scarlet Letter (mp3) (ENG.). 2007. 2.99 (978-1-60299-077-7(8)) InterLinguacom.

EngLits-the Tempest (mp3) 2007. (978-1-60299-054-8(9)) InterLinguacom.

EngLits-the Turn of the Screw (mp3) (ENG.). 2007. 2.99 (978-1-60299-084-5(0)) InterLinguacom.

EngLits-Treasure Island (mp3) (ENG.). 2007. 2.99 (978-1-60299-070-8(0)) InterLinguacom.

EngLits-Twelfth Night (mp3) (ENG.). 2007. (978-1-60299-053-1(0)) InterLinguacom.

EngLits-Wuthering Heights (mp3) (ENG.). 2007. 2.99 (978-1-60299-073-9(5)) InterLinguacom.

Enhance Creativity. Zoilita Grant. 2001. audio compact disk 15.95 (978-1-890575-35-9(6)) Zoilita Grant.

Enhance Creativity: Increase Creativity with Hypnosis. Trevor H. Scott. 2003. audio compact disk 19.95 (978-0-9763138-9-2(8)) Beverly Hills CA.

Enhance Sensory Perception. 1 cass. (Running Time: 60 min.). 10.95 (013) Psych Res Inst.
Designed to develop awareness of all the senses plus psychic potential.

Enhance Your Spiritual Growth by Applying Scriptual Truths. Kenneth E. Hagin. (Developing the Human Spirit Ser.). 20.00 Faith Lib Pubns.

Enhanced Academic Performance. Michael P. Kelly. 1 cass. 1992. 14.95 (978-1-883700-17-1(5)) ThoughtForms.
Self help.

Enhancing & Expanding Access to Online Catalogs & In-House Datafiles. 2 cass. 1990. 16.00 set. Recorded Res.

Enhancing Astro-Intuition. Terrie Brill. 1 cass. 1992. 8.95 (1012) Am Fed Astrologers.

Enhancing Creativity. Steven Halpern. 1 cass. (Soundwave Two Thousand, the Audio Active Subliminal Ser.). 1990. (2015) Inner Peace Mus.
Beautiful, relaxing new age music with subliminal affirmations.

Enhancing Creativity, Vol. 116. 1998. 24.95 (978-1-58557-023-2(0)) Dynamic Growth.

Enhancing Faculty Careers: Strategies for Development & Renewal. Jack H. Schuster et al. (Higher & Adult Education Ser.). 1990. bk. 43.45 (978-1-55542-210-3(1), Jossey-Bass) Wiley US.

Enhancing Health & Well-Being. Read by Steven Halpern. 1 cass. (Running Time: 60 min.). (Soundwave Two Thousand Subliminal Ser.). 1993. 9.98 (SRXB 2025) Inner Peace Mus.
Beautiful music with subliminal affirmations.

Enhancing Instruction in Your Foreign Language Classroom: Increasing Effective Communication Through Interactive Learner-Centered Activities, Set. Barbara Snyder. 6 cass. (Running Time: 4 hr.). (J). (gr. 6-12). 1998. 75.00 Incl. handbk. (978-1-886397-21-7(X)) Bureau of Educ.

Enhancing Intimacy. Steven Halpern. Read by Steven Halpern. 1 cass. (Running Time: 1 hr.). (Soundwave Two Thousand Subliminal Ser.). 1994. pap. bk. 9.98 (SRX-2068) Inner Peace Mus.
Relaxing music plus positive affirmations, recorded subliminally.

Enhancing Intimacy. Roger Mellot. 2 cass. (Running Time: 3 hrs.). 1995. 15.95 (978-1-55977-049-1(X)) CareerTrack Pubns.

Enhancing Massage. Steven Halpern. 1 cass. (Soundwave Two Thousand, the Audio Active Subliminal Ser.). 1990. (2010) Inner Peace Mus.
Beautiful, relaxing music with subliminal affirmations.

Enhancing Math Learning Set: Strategies That Strengthen Student Motivation, Involvement & Success, Lola May. Read by Lola May. 6 cass. (Running Time: 4 hr. 8 min.). (J). (gr. 3-8). 1996. 75.00 Incl. handbk. (978-1-886397-08-8(2)) Bureau of Educ.
Live audio seminar.

Enhancing Recovery, Set. unabr. ed. Interview. Shirley G. McCann. Interview with James L. Shearer & Cindy M. Sullivan. 2 cass. (Running Time: 17 mins. per cass.). 1999. 17.95 (978-0-9675380-0-6(9), 51795) Luna Prom.
Tape 1 is pre-surgery. Tape 2 is post surgical self-healing.

Enhancing Self-Esteem. Read by Steven Halpern. 1 cass. (Running Time: 60 min.). (Soundwave Two Thousand Subliminal Ser.). 1992. 9.98 (SRX 2024) Inner Peace Mus.
Relaxing music plus subliminal affirmations.

Enhancing Sensual Pleasure. Read by Steven Halpern. 1 cass. (Running Time: 60 min.). (Soundwave Two Thousand Subliminal Ser.). 1993. 9.98 (SRXB 2069) Inner Peace Mus.
Beautiful music plus subliminal affirmations for consenting adults.

Enhancing Success. Steven Halpern. 1 cass. (Soundwave Two Thousand, the Audio Active Subliminal Ser.). 1990. (2017) Inner Peace Mus.
Beautiful music with subliminal affirmations.

Enhancing the Literacy Development of Your Preschoolers & Kindergarteners. Read by Cecile Mielenn. 6 cass. (Running Time: 4 hrs. 26 min.). 2003. 89.00 (978-1-886397-53-8(8)) Bureau of Educ.

Enhancing Your Effectiveness As an Elementary School Principal, Set. John Blaydes. 6 cass. (Running Time: 4 hr. 32 min.). 1999. 75.00 Incl. live workshop & hdbk. (978-1-886397-25-5(2)) Bureau of Educ.

ENIAC: The Triumphs & Tragedies of the World's First Computer. unabr. ed. Scott McCartney. Read by Adams Morgan. 5 cass. (Running Time: 7 hrs.). 1999. 39.95 (978-0-7861-1633-1(1), 2461) Blckstn Audio.
For all his genius, John von Neumann was not, as he is generally credited, the true father of the modern computer. That honor belongs to the two men - John Mauchly & Presper Eckert - who built the world's first programmable computer, the lengendary ENIAC (Electronic Numerical Integrator & Computer). Based on original interviews with surviving participants.

Enid Blyton. unabr. ed. George Greenfield. Read by Tracey Lloyd. 2 cass. (Running Time: 2 hrs. 20 min.). (Isis Ser.). (J). 2003. 24.95 (978-0-7531-0720-1(1)) Pub: ISIS Lrg Prnt GBR. Dist(s): Ulverscroft US
Describes Enid Blyton's background and career, her inspirations and her style. It also deals with the multi-million dollar business that the Enid Blyton industry has become since her death.

Enigme en Perigord. Parodi & Vallacco. audio compact disk 12.95 (978-0-8219-3777-8(4)) EMC-Paradigm.

Enj. 8th ed. David Hamilton. (C). 2002. audio compact disk 48.00 (978-0-393-94087-9(X)) Norton.

Enjoy Peace of Mind. Eldon Taylor. Read by Eldon Taylor. Ed. by Leslie Brice. 6 cass. (Running Time: 6 hrs.). 1992. 69.95 set. (978-1-56705-368-5(8)) Gateways Inst.
Self improvement.

Enjoy Successful Parenting: Practical Strategies for Parents of Children 2-12. Roger W. MacIntire. 4 cass. 1997. 24.95 Set. (978-0-9640558-8-9(0)) Summit Crossrds.

Enjoy the Impact You Have on Your Kids: Put An End to Passive Parenting. Illus. by Angela Brown & Barbara Lynn Taylor. Prod. by Les Lingle. 1 cass. (Running Time: 30 mins.). (Words of Wellness - Your Show for Simple Solutions Ser.: Vol. 319). 2000. 12.95 (978-1-930995-11-6(3), LLP319) Life Long Pubg.
Say good-bye to dysfunctional families, you can start today being a good role model for your children - regardless of their age.

Enjoy the Journey!, Set. Lucile Johnson. 2 cass. 1997. 11.98 Set. (978-1-57734-018-8(3), 07001428) Covenant Comms.
Ideas for women from one of the most beloved LDS speakers.

Enjoy the Zoo. unabr. ed. 1 cass. (Romper Room Sing & Read-Alongs Ser.). (J). 1986. 5.95 incl. bk. & sheet music. (978-0-89845-312-6(7), RRC 3127) HarperCollins Pubs.

Enjoy Your Job! Michael E. Bernard. 4 cass. 49.95 Set. (C052) Inst Rational-Emotive.
Provides methods for learning to take control over the stress-producing aspects of the job while at the same time handling your work - & your life - with increased motivation, energy, & enthusiasm.

Enjoy Your Job!, Set. Michael E. Bernard. 4 cass. 35.95 (C052) A Ellis Institute.
This informative & lively set for teachers provides methods for learning to take control over the stress-producing aspects of the job while at the same time tackling your work & your life with increased energy & enthusiasm.

Enjoy Your Life: Cultivate Relaxed, Mindful & Harmonious Living. Mark Bancroft. Read by Mark Bancroft. 1 cass., bklet. (Running Time: 1 hr.). (General Self-Development/Improvement Ser.). 1999. 12.95 (978-1-58522-029-8(9), 915, EnSpire Aud) EnSpire Pr.
Two complete sessions plus printed instruction manual/guidebook. With healing music soundtrack.

Enjoy Your Life: Cultivate Relaxed, Mindful, & Harmonious Living. Mark Bancroft. Read by Mark Bancroft. 1 CD, bklet. (Running Time: 1 hr.). (General Self-Development/Improvement Ser.). 2006. audio compact disk 20.00 (978-1-58522-069-4(8)) EnSpire Pr.
Two complete sessions plus printed instructionmanual/guidebook. With healing music soundtrack.

Enjoying Exercise: Ocean. Eldon Taylor. Read by Eldon Taylor. Ed. by Leslie Brice. 1 cass. (Running Time: 1 hr.). 1992. 15.95 (978-1-56705-110-0(3)) Gateways Inst.
Self improvement.

Enjoying Exercise: Rhythm. Eldon Taylor. Read by Eldon Taylor. Ed. by Leslie Brice. 1 cass. (Running Time: 1 hr.). 1992. 16.95 (978-1-56705-111-7(1)) Gateways Inst.

Enjoying Exercise: Stream. Eldon Taylor. Read by Eldon Taylor. Ed. by Leslie Brice. 1 cass. (Running Time: 1 hr.). 1992. 16.95 (978-1-56705-112-4(X)) Gateways Inst.

Enjoying Opera. Sarah Caldwell. 1 cass. (Running Time: 1hr. 16 mins.). 2001. 12.95 Smithson Assocs.

Enjoying Poetry. David Steindl-Rast. 4 cass. (Running Time: 4 hrs. 30 min.). 1992. 38.95 set. Dolphin Tapes.

Enjoying the Ride. Win Straube. 2006. (978-0-9777031-1-1(8)) Straube Ctrs.

***Enjoying True Peace.** unabr. ed. Stephanie Perry Moore. Narrated by Robin Miles. (Running Time: 4 hrs. 30 mins. 0 sec.). (Yasmin Peace Ser.). (ENG.). 2010. audio compact disk 18.98 (978-1-61045-081-2(7), christaudio) christianaud.

Enjoying Your Career As a Health Professional. unabr. ed. Bernard Virshup. Read by William Huss & Randy Thomas. 1 cass. (Running Time: 82 min.). 1994. pap. bk. 17.95 (978-0-9641270-0-5(8)) Praxis Pubs.
Gives useful strategies for coping with the pressures of a health professional's life & career. It deals with, among other things, stress, self-worth, feelings, criticism, & difficult people.

Enjoyment of Scripture. unabr. ed. Samuel Sandmel. 1 cass. (Running Time: 1 hr. 4 min.). 1970. 12.95 (23123) J Norton Pubs.
A lecture on the great literary aspects of the Hebrew Bible, & the way in which they are great. It is an exposition of the literary mandates of biblical narrators & poets.

Enlaces. 2nd ed. Eileen W. Glisan & Judith L. Shrum. bk. & wbk. ed. 92.95 (978-0-8384-0542-0(8)); bk., wbk. ed., lab manual ed. 79.20 (978-0-8384-0336-5(0)) Heinle.

Enlarge the Borders of Your Heart: Yielding to the Holy Spirit in Your Everyday Life. Lynne Hammond. 2 cass. (Running Time: 2 hrs.). 2005. 5.00 (978-1-57399-188-9(0)); audio compact disk 10.00 (978-1-57399-189-6(9)) Mac Hammond.
Being led by the Spirit is bottom-line Christianity for this time and this hour. In this two-message series by Lynne Hammond, you'll learn how you can enlarge your daily experience with God. If you are ready to stop waiting for God to move in your life and start acting, then get this series and begin to enlarge the border of your heart!.

Enlarge Your Vision, Pt. 1. Speeches. Joel Osteen. 1 Cass. (Running Time: 30 Mins.). (J). 2000. 6.00 (978-1-59349-043-0(7), JA0043) J Osteen.

Enlarge Your Vision, Pt. 2. Speeches. Joel Osteen. 1 Cass. (Running Time: 30 Mins.). (J). 2000. 6.00 (978-1-59349-044-7(5), JA0044) J Osteen.

Enlarger of Faith. Elbert Willis. 1 cass. (Humility of Heaven Ser.). 4.00 Fill the Gap.

Enlarger of the Soul. Elbert Willis. 1 cass. (Gentleness & Goodness Ser.). 4.00 Fill the Gap.

Enlightened Companion: A Companion to Beyond Skepticism. Stephen H. Martin. 1 cass. (Running Time: 90 min.). 1995. 11.95 (978-0-9646601-5-1(6)) Oaklea Pr.
Metaphysical insights, meditations to aid in spiritual growth - self-actualization.

Enlightened Heart: An Anthology of Sacred Poetry. abr. ed. Poems. Read by Stephen Mitchell et al. Ed. by Stephen Mitchell. 2 cass. (Running Time: 3 hrs.). 1995. 16.95 (978-0-944993-34-7(6)) Audio Lit.
This treasury of sacred poetry contains selections from the world's most profound cultural & religious traditions.

Enlightened Jesus: & the Kingdom of Heaven on Earth. Steve S. Sadleir. (ENG.). 2008. audio compact disk 37.00 (978-1-883544-13-3(0)) Self Awareness.

Enlightened Mind: An Anthology of Sacred Prose. unabr. ed. Poems. Read by Jacob Needleman et al. Ed. by Stephen Mitchell. 2 cass. (Running Time: 3 hrs.). 2001. 16.95 (978-0-944993-48-4(6)) Audio Lit.

Enlightened Sex. David Deida. 6 CDs. 2004. audio compact disk 69.95 (978-1-59179-083-9(2), AF00839D) Sounds True.

Enlightening Postmodernism. Alan Mckenzie. (ENG.). (C). 2004. 24.95 (978-1-55753-325-8(3)) Pub: Purdue U Pr. Dist(s): AtlasBooks

Enlightening the Listener: Contemporary North Indian Classical Vocal Music Performance. Prabha Atre. 2000. bk. 34.00 (978-81-215-0940-4(8)) Pub: M Manoharial IND. Dist(s): Coronet Bks

Enlightenment. Swami Amar Jyoti. 2 cass. 1988. 12.95 (M-75) Truth Consciousness.
The highest subject & the lightest, Thou art That. Following the right way. The real value of the living Master.

Enlightenment Invention of the Modern Self, Parts I-II. Instructed by Leo Damrosch. 12 CDs. (Running Time: 12 hrs.). 2003. bk. 69.95 (978-1-56585-660-8(0), 4117) Teaching Co.

Enlightenment Invention of the Modern Self, Pts. I-II. Instructed by Leo Damrosch. 12 cass. (Running Time: 12 hrs.). 2003. bk. 54.95 (978-1-56585-658-5(9), 4117) Teaching Co.

Enlightenment Is Unconditional Intimacy with This Moment. Scott Morrison. 1 cass. 7.50 (978-1-882496-20-4(5)) Twnty Frst Cntry Ren.
Enlightenment, spiritual awakening & liberation does not take time, but rather absolute willingness, openness, & honesty.

Enlightenment of the Buddha. Vajracarya. Read by Chogyam Trungpa. 3 cass. 1975. 27.00 (A017) Vajradhatu.
Talks include: Life of the Buddha, Wakefulness, The Enlightened Ones.

Enlightenment Series. unabr. ed. George Walsh. Read by George Walsh. 1 cass. (Running Time: 1 hr.). 1996. 14.95 (978-1-57724-003-7(0), Prncpal Srce Audio) Objectivist Ctr.
The author analyzes the central doctrines of Enlightenment culture, their spread among the educated classes, & weaknesses that led to the disintegration of the movement.

Enlightenment Series 10 CD Set: Talks & Guided Meditations. Steven S. Sadleir. (ENG.). 2006. audio compact disk 195.00 (978-1-883544-16-4(5)) Pub: Self Awareness. Dist(s): New Leaf Dist

Enlightenment Unfolding: A 3-CD Album. Featuring Adyashanti. (ENG.). 2007. audio compact disk 29.00 (978-1-933986-19-7(0)) Open Gate Pub.

Enlisting Client Participation. Jan Spiller. 1 cass. 8.95 (587) Am Fed Astrologers.
Dynamic approach uses mutual involvement.

Enlisting Client Participation in Astrology Readings. Jan Spiller. 1 cass. 8.95 (327) Am Fed Astrologers.

Enlivening the Chakras. unabr. ed. Stan Kendz. Read by Stan Kendz. 1 cass. (Running Time: 60 min.). 1994. 10.00 (978-1-57582-003-3(X)) HAPPE Progs.
Learn what the Chakras are, how they work with your body, & how they help us release blocks & enhance our lives.

Enlivening the 7 Chakras. Stan Kendz. 1 cass. (Running Time: 090 min.). 1999. 17.95 (978-1-893527-46-1(8)) Namaste Pr NY.

Enna Burning. unabr. ed. Shannon Hale. Read by Cynthia Bishop. (Books of Bayern Ser.: Bk. 2). (J). 2007. 54.99 (978-1-60252-895-6(0)) Find a World.

Enneagram: A Gentle Introduction, Robert Olson. Read by Robert Olson. 2 cass. (Running Time: 2 hrs.). 39.95 (AA8365) Credence Commun.
Therapist-professor Olson relates the enneagram information to clinical insights into personal growth.

Enneagram: Building Health Family Relationships. unabr. ed. William F. Maestri. 4 cass. (Running Time: 4 hrs. 33 min.). 1992. 33.95 set. (TAH285) Alba Hse Comns.
Hardly anybody disputes the central importance of the family for human living, & that is why today's dysfunctional family marred by divorce, violence, generational conflict & many other ills, must cause all of us deep concern. We need to begin family relationships, & that is where the Enneagram can prove exceptional assistance-though this at first sight may not appear to be the case.

Enneagram: Naming Our Illusions. Richard Rohr. 6 cass. (Running Time: 5 hrs.). 49.95 Set. (AA2226) Credence Commun.
Provacative, lively, & spiritually penetrating introduction to the ancient Sufi tradition.

Enneagram: Naming Our Illusions. Richard Rohr. 6 cass. (Running Time: 6 hrs.). 2001. 49.95 (A8090) St Anthony Mess Pr.
The enneagram says only 9 types of personalities exist. Each type suffers from one major illusion about the way the world is. Once you know your enneagram style, you begin to free yourself from your illusion.

Enneagram Set: A Gentle Introduction. Robert Olson. Read by Robert Olson. 2 cass. (Running Time: 2 hrs.). 17.95 (978-7-900787-56-9(9), AA2704) Credence Commun.
Therapist-professor Olson relates the enneagram information to clinical insights into personal growth.

Enneagram & DSM - III. unabr. ed. Claudio Naranjo. 1 cass. (Running Time: 42 min.). 1994. 11.00 (34203) Big Sur Tapes.
Examines the profound usefulness of the enneggram in shedding light on the character types described in the "Diagnostic & Statistical Manual of Mental Disorders".

Enneagram & Placement of Attention. unabr. ed. Helen Palmer. 1 cass. (Running Time: 1 hr. 3 min.). 1991. 11.00 (08602) Big Sur Tapes.
Discusses the inner placement of attention of the Enneagramm, the preoccupation of mind & heart.

Enneagram as a Tool for Students of the Fourth Way. unabr. ed. Gloria Cuevas-Barnett. 1 cass. (Running Time: 90 min.). 1994. 10.00 (CR013) Big Sur Tapes.
Gurdjieff used the enneagram with his students as a tool for self-observation & self-verification. Cuevas-Barnett, a long-time teacher of Gurdjieff's Fourth Way practice, discusses how she uses the enneagram to facilitate the work.

Enneagram Basics. Patrick O'Leary. Read by Patrick O'Leary. 8 cass. (Running Time: 7 hrs. 30 min.). 1992. 59.95 Set. (978-7-900781-59-8(5), AA2523) Credence Commun.
O'Leary introduces the Enneagram.

Enneagram II: Tool of Conversion. Richard Rohr. Read by Richard Rohr. 9 cass. (Running Time: 9 hrs. 17 min.). 1991. 64.95 Set. (978-7-900782-84-7(2), AA2442) Credence Commun.
A workshop about the Enneagram with Rohr, & 100 Enneagram teachers & advanced students.

Enneagram II: Tool of Conversion. Richard Rohr. 9 cass. (Running Time: 9 hrs.). 2001. 64.95 (A8110) St Anthony Mess Pr.
Panel Q&A discussion on this personality typing system.

Enneagram of Patriarchal Society. unabr. ed. Claudio Naranjo. 2 cass. (Running Time: 1hr. 51 min.). 1995. 18.00 Set. (34202) Big Sur Tapes.
Naranjo, who introduced the enneagram to North America in 1971, gives a brilliant, personable address that examines the anatomy of American society according to the map provided by the enneagram.

Enneagram Strategy to Access Higher States of Awareness. unabr. ed. Helen Palmer. 1 cass. (Running Time: 1 hr.). 1989. 11.00 (HP006) Big Sur Tapes.
Places the Enneagram in the context of the two major lines of meditation practice: that which emphasizes emptying the mind & that which emphasizes concentration as a way of accomplishing the same spiritual ends.

Enneagram Tools for Change: Eights. Thomas R. Condon. 1 cass. 12.95 (978-1-884305-58-0(X)) Changeworks.
The Enneagram is an ancient, powerful overview of human psychological types. The system describes distinct personality styles, their inner motivations & talents.

Enneagram Tools for Change: Fives. Thomas R. Condon. 1 cass. 12.95 (978-1-884305-55-9(5)) Changeworks.

Enneagram Tools for Change: Fours. Thomas R. Condon. 1 cass. 12.95 (978-1-884305-54-2(7)) Changeworks.

Enneagram Tools for Change: Introduction. Thomas R. Condon. 2 cass. 16.95 set. (978-1-884305-50-4(4)) Changeworks.

Enneagram Tools for Change: Nines. Thomas R. Condon. 1 cass. 12.95 (978-1-884305-59-7(8)) Changeworks.

Enneagram Tools for Change: Ones. Thomas R. Condon. 2 cass. 16.95 set. (978-1-884305-51-1(2)) Changeworks.

Enneagram Tools for Change: Sevens. Thomas R. Condon. 1 cass. 12.95 (978-1-884305-57-3(1)) Changeworks.

Enneagram Tools for Change: Sixes. Thomas R. Condon. 1 cass. 12.95 (978-1-884305-56-6(3)) Changeworks.

Enneagram Tools for Change: Threes. Thomas R. Condon. 1 cass. 12.95 (978-1-884305-53-5(9)) Changeworks.

Enneagram Tools for Change: Twos. Thomas R. Condon. 1 cass. 12.95 (978-1-884305-52-8(0)) Changeworks.

Enneagram Tools for Change: Waking from Trances. Thomas R. Condon. 1 cass. 12.95 (978-1-884305-60-3(1)) Changeworks.

Enneagrams. unabr. ed. Helen Palmer. 2 cass. 1987. 18.00 set. (A0276-88) Sound Photosyn.
Using the Gurgieffian system of personality categorization.

Enneagrams Workshop. unabr. ed. Eli J. Bear & Jerry Perkins. 5 cass. 1987. 45.00 set. (978-1-56964-571-0(X), A0011-87) Sound Photosyn.
Interest in Enneagrams is building! Gurgief might be amused by this workshop. Elsewhere, Eli teaches Neurolinguistics Programming & Jerry is a Rolfer.

Enoch's Ghost. unabr. ed. Bryan Davis. Narrated by Peter Sandon. (Running Time: 12 hrs. 43 mins. 29 sec.). (Oracles of Fire Ser.). (ENG.). 2008. 10.49 (978-1-60814-178-4(0)) Oasis Audio.

Enoch's Ghost. unabr. ed. Bryan Davis. Narrated by Peter Sandon. (Running Time: 12 hrs. 43 mins. 29 sec.). (Oracles of Fire Ser.). (ENG.). 2009. audio compact disk 39.99 (978-1-59859-529-1(6)) Oasis Audio.

Enorme Escarajabo Negro. Created by Rigby Staff. 1993. 10.40 (978-0-435-05933-0(5), Rigby PEA) Pearson EdAUS AUS.

Enormous Crocodile see Roald Dahl

Enormous Crocodile & the Magic Finger. Roald Dahl. Read by Roald Dahl. (Running Time: 40 min.). (J). 11.95 (HarperChildAud) HarperCollins Pubs.

Enormous Egg. unabr. ed. Oliver Butterworth. Read by Joshua Swanson. (Running Time: 3 hrs. 30 mins.). (ENG.). 2009. 9.98 (978-1-60024-674-6(5)); audio compact disk 15.98 (978-1-60024-673-9(7)) Pub: Hachet Audio. Dist(s): HachBkGrp

Enormous Egg. unabr. ed. Oliver Butterworth. 1 read-along cass. (Running Time: 45 min.). (Soundways to Reading Ser.). (J). (gr. 3-5). 1981. 15.98 (978-0-8072-1082-6(X), SWR 21 SP, Listening Lib); 24.00 (978-0-8072-8775-0(X), YA264CX, Listening Lib) Random Audio Pubg.
One morning Nate checks on his hen & finds the biggest egg he's ever seen. And no one - not scientists nor senators - expects the twentieth century Triceratops that hatches.

Enormous Egg. unabr. ed. Oliver Butterworth. 3 cass. (J). 2000. pap. bk. 29.00 (978-0-8072-8776-7(8), YA264SP, Listening Lib); 22.00 (978-0-8072-6173-6(4), Listening Lib) Random Audio Pubg.
When Nate Twitchell discovers that one of his family's hens has laid the biggest egg he has ever seen, he is determined to see it hatch. And when it does, neither he nor his parents, the townspeople, the scientists or the politicians from Washington are prepared for what comes out!.

***Enormous Radio.** abr. ed. John Cheever. Read by Meryl Streep et al. (ENG.). 2009. (978-0-06-125288-4(3), Caedmon) HarperCollins Pubs.

***Enormous Radio.** unabr. ed. John Cheever. Read by Meryl Streep et al. (ENG.). 2009. (978-0-06-196860-0(9), Caedmon) HarperCollins Pubs.

Enormous Red Dragon. Dan Corner. 1 cass. 3.00 (28) Evang Outreach.

Enormous Turnip: Three Billy-Goats. Sue Arengo. (Classic Tales Ser.). 1999. 14.75 (978-0-19-422031-6(1)) OUP.

Enormous Watermelon. (gr. k-1). 10.00 (978-0-7635-5073-8(6)) Rigby Educ.

Enormous Watermelon Audio CD. Benchmark Education Company. Based on a work by Brenda Parkes. (Shared Reading Classics Ser.). (J). (gr. k-2). 2009. audio compact disk 10.00 (978-1-60634-764-5(0)) Benchmark Educ.

Enough. Contrib. by Barlow Girl. (Sound Performance Soundtracks Ser.). 2006. audio compact disk 5.98 (978-5-558-35306-8(6)) Pt of Grace Ent.

Enough. abr. rev. ed. Bill McKibben. (ENG.). 2003. 25.95 (978-1-55927-913-0(3)) Pub: Macmill Audio. Dist(s): Macmillan

Enough: True Measures of Money, Business, & Life. unabr. ed. John C. Bogle. Read by John C. Bogle. Read by Alan Sklar. (ENG.). 2008. audio compact disk 26.95 (978-1-59887-854-7(9), 1598878549) Pub: HighBridge. Dist(s): Workman Pub

Enough Already! Clearing Mental Clutter to Become the Best You. abr. ed. Peter Walsh. Read by Peter Walsh. 5 CDs. (Running Time: 6 hrs. 0 mins. 0 sec.). (ENG.). 2009. audio compact disk 29.99 (978-0-7435-8077-9(X)) Pub: S&S Audio. Dist(s): S and S Inc

Enough Rope: Collected Stories. unabr. ed. Lawrence Block. Read by Alan Sklar. 4 CDs. (Running Time: 18 hrs.). 2002. audio compact disk 89.95 (978-0-7927-2768-2(1), CMP 505, Chivers Sound Lib) AudioGO.

Enough Rope Vol. 1: Collected Stories. unabr. ed. Lawrence Block. Read by Alan Sklar. 18 vols. (Running Time: 18 hrs.). 2002. bk. 127.95 (978-0-7927-2719-4(3), CSL 505, Chivers Sound Lib) AudioGO.
In this collection that includes nearly a dozen new works, the acclaimed Lawrence Block offers mesmerizing tales of mystery and murder featuring Scudder, Keller, and Bernie, as well as a whole new cast of compelling and memorable characters. Arranged by character in the order in which they were written.

Enough to Make a Cat Laugh. unabr. ed. Deric Longden. Read by Deric Longden. 5 CDs. (Running Time: 5 hrs. 15 min.). 2000. audio compact disk 59.95 (978-0-7531-0695-2(7), 106957) Pub: ISIS Audio GBR. Dist(s): Ulverscroft US

Enough to Make a Cat Laugh. unabr. ed. Deric Longden. Read by Deric Longden. 6 cass. (Running Time: 7 hr. 30 min.). (Isis Ser.). (J). 1997. 54.95 (978-0-7531-0172-8(6), 970303) Pub: ISIS Lrg Prnt GBR. Dist(s): Ulverscroft US
Throughout the 1990's Deric Longden has been living with his wife, author Aileen Armitage & an array of cats. Ever since Thermal entered his life, Deric has seen his world increasingly taken over by cats. He has little time left over for his professional life as a writer.

Enquiry. (713) Yoga Res Foun.

Enquiry. Dick Francis. Contrib. by William Nighy & Philip Voss. 2 CDs. (Running Time: 1 hr. 35 mins.). 2006. audio compact disk 29.95 (978-0-7927-3980-7(9), BBCD 131) AudioGO.

Enquiry. Swami Jyotirmayananda. 1 cass. (Running Time: 1 hr.). 1990. 12.99 Yoga Res Foun.

Enquiry. unabr. ed. Dick Francis. Read by Geoffrey Howard. 4 cass. (Running Time: 5 hrs. 30 mins.). 1996. 32.95 Set. (978-0-7861-0959-3(9), 1736) Blckstn Audio.
Jockey Kelly Hughes & trainer Dexter Cranfield had been barred from racing - a devastating event for them both. The charge at the secret enquiry? Throwing a race for personal profit. It was a vicious frame-up & worse, they had nowhere to turn to clear their names.

Enquiry. unabr. ed. Dick Francis. Read by Geoffrey Howard. 5 CDs. (Running Time: 5 hrs. 30 mins.). 2000. audio compact disk 40.00 (978-0-7861-9933-4(4), 1736) Blckstn Audio.

Enquiry. unabr. ed. Dick Francis. Read by Tony Britton. 6 cass. (Running Time: 9 hrs.). 1993. 49.95 (978-0-7451-5949-2(4), CAB 051) Pub: Chivers Audio Bks GBR. Dist(s): AudioGO
To a jockey, losing his license is the equivalent of being disbarred. When steeplechase rider, Kelly Hughes, lost his license, he was bewildered, for he was not guilty of the charges. But as Kelly investigates, he learns that he was framed. And the closer he comes to a solution, the fiercer the retaliation grows. But Kelly was left with nothing much to lose, the only serious mistake his enemy had made.

Enquiry. unabr. ed. Dick Francis. Narrated by Simon Prebble. 5 cass. (Running Time: 6 hrs. 45 mins.). 1990. 44.00 (978-1-55690-169-0(0), 90088E7) Recorded Bks.
Kelly Hughes & his trainer have been charged with throwing a race for profit, an offense that will get them barred from a racing for the rest of their lives. Disbarment is a personal tragedy when racing is your life; it is a bloody outrage when you know you've been framed.

Enquiry of "Who Am I?" (195) Yoga Res Foun.

Enquiry of "Who Am I?", No. 2. Swami Jyotirmayananda. 1 cass. (Running Time: 1 hr.). 1990. 12.99 Yoga Res Foun.

Enrico Caruso. David Timson. 4 CDs. audio compact disk 35.99 (978-1-84379-064-8(5), 8.558131-34) NaxMulti GBR.

Enrique Lagardere. Paul Feval. 2008. audio compact disk 16.95 (978-1-933499-69-7(9)) Fonolibro Inc.

***Enrique Lagardere - el Jorobado: Digital Version.** Paul Feval. Prod. by FonoLibro Inc. (SPA.). 2010. 11.95 (978-1-61154-011-6(9)) Fonolibro Inc.

Enriquecer Goce Sexual. unabr. ed. Nader Lucia. Read by Lulcia Nader. (SPA.). 2007. audio compact disk 13.00 (978-958-8318-13-4(0)) Pub: Yoyo Music COL. Dist(s): YoYoMusic

Ensemble. Ed. by Christian Marclay. (ENG., 2008. audio compact disk 20.00 (978-0-88454-112-7(6)) Pub: U of Pa Contemp Art. Dist(s): Dist Art Pubs

Ensemble. 6th ed. Comeau. (FRE.). 1999. pap. bk. 48.95 (978-0-470-00302-2(2), JWiley) Wiley US.

Ensemble. 7th ed. Raymond F. Comeau & Normand J. Lamoureux. (FRE.). (C). 2005. lab manual ed. 30.95 (978-0-471-77754-0(4), JWiley) Wiley US.

Ensemble: Easy & Intermediate Pieces for Orff Ensemble Grades 4 - 8. Brent M. Holl. Bergen White. (ENG.). (J). 2002. pap. bk. 19.95 (978-0-9795470-6-5(7)) Beatin Path.

Ensemble Grammaire: Tapescript. 6th ed. Raymond F. Comeau. 1998. pap. bk. 42.95 (978-0-470-00294-0(8), JWiley) Wiley US.

Ensemble Litterature. 6th ed. Raymond F. Comeau. 2001. pap. bk. & stu. ed. 33.95 (978-0-470-00286-5(7), JWiley) Wiley US.

Ensembles, Large & Small. (YA). 1994. 17.00 (978-0-89898-807-9(1), BMR05098, Warner Bro) Alfred Pub.

Ensuite: Cours Intermediaire de Francais. 3rd ed. Thompson. 1 cass. (Running Time: 90 min.). (FRE.). (C). 1998. stu. ed. 68.75 (978-0-07-913146-1(8), Mc-H Human Soc) Pub: McGrw-H Hghr Educ. Dist(s): McGraw

Ensuring Advisor Success: NACADA Webinar Series 14. Featuring Pat Folsom & Jennifer Joslin. (ENG.). 2008. audio compact disk 140.00 (978-1-935140-56-6(6)) Nat Acad Adv.

Entendiendo a Sus Angeles y Conociendo a Sus Guias. unabr. ed. John Edward. 2 cass. (Running Time: 2 hrs.).Tr. of Understanding Your Angels & Meeting Your Guides. (SPA & ENG.). 2000. reel tape 18.95 (978-1-56170-766-9(X)) Hay House.
Learn how to use tools such as meditation and visualization to contact your angels and guides.

***Enter a Murderer.** abr. ed. Ngaio Marsh. Read by Anton Lesser. (Running Time: 4 hrs. 0 mins. 0 sec.). (ENG.). 2010. audio compact disk 19.95 (978-1-4055-0798-1(5)) Pub: Little BrownUK GBR. Dist(s): IPG Chicago

Enter a Murderer. unabr. ed. Ngaio Marsh. Read by James Saxon. 6 cass. (Running Time: 8 hrs.). 2000. 29.95 (978-1-57270-163-2(3), N61163u) Pub: Audio Partners. Dist(s): PerseuPGW
The brilliant Inspector Roderick Alleyn must discover who put the real bullet in a prop gun when a quarrel in a star's dressing room echoes the script of a new play.

Enter a Murderer. unabr. ed. Ngaio Marsh. Read by James Saxon. 6 cass. (Running Time: 9 hrs.). (Inspector Alleyn Mystery Ser.). 2000. 49.95 (978-0-7451-6574-5(5), CAB 1190) Pub: Chivers Audio Bks GBR. Dist(s): AudioGO
The crime was committed on stage at the Unicorn Theater, when an unloaded gun fired a real bullet. The victim was Arthur Surbanadler, an actor clawing his way to stardom through blackmail. The stage was set for one of Chief Inspector Alleyn's most baffling cases.

Enter His Courts. Rick Joyner. 1 cass. (Running Time: 90 mins.). (Foundation Ser.: Vol. 7). 2000. 5.00 (RJ05-007) Morning NC.

Enter the Asian Food Market. 6th rev. ed. BIA. (J). 2006. audio compact disk 289.00 (978-1-4187-4832-6(3)) Bus Info Agency.

Enter the Asian Food Market. 6th rev. ed. BIA. (J). 2006. audio compact disk 249.00 (978-1-4187-4831-9(5)) Bus Info Agency.

Enter the Metallurgical & Fabricated Metal Companies of Russia & the Former Soviet Republics. 6th rev. ed. BIA. (J). 2006. audio compact disk 289.00 (978-1-4187-5031-2(X)) Bus Info Agency.

Enter the Metallurgical & Fabricated Metal Companies of Russia & the Former Soviet Republics. 6th rev. ed. BIA. (J). 2006. audio compact disk 249.00 (978-1-4187-5030-5(1)) Bus Info Agency.

Enter the Russian Communications Market: Key Providers. 6th rev. ed. BIA. (J). 2006. audio compact disk 289.00 (978-1-4187-5039-8(5)) Bus Info Agency.

Enter the Russian Communications Market: Key Providers. 6th rev. ed. BIA. (J). 2006. audio compact disk 249.00 (978-1-4187-5038-1(7)) Bus Info Agency.

Enter the Russian Transportation Market. 6th rev. ed. BIA. (J). 2006. audio compact disk 289.00 (978-1-4187-5177-7(4)) Bus Info Agency.

Enter the Russian Transportation Market. 6th rev. ed. BIA. (J). 2006. audio compact disk 249.00 (978-1-4187-5176-0(6)) Bus Info Agency.

Enter the Saint. unabr. ed. Leslie Charteris. Read by David Case. 6 cass. (Running Time: 6 hrs.). (Saint Ser.). 1991. 36.00 (978-0-7366-1883-0(X), 2712) Books on Tape.
The Man Who Was Clever & The Lawless Lady stand out in the history of crime as the first parties of interest to that "ruthless association of reckless young men, brilliantly led, who worked on the side of the law & who were yet outside the law." Before long the mere mention of The Saint was enough to disturb the sleep of the most dull-witted crook, to say nothing of Chief Inspector Claud Eustace Teal, New Scotland Yard - but these are the halcyon days. So share adventure with Simon Templar, The Saint, & his co-horts Roger Conway, Patricia Holm & Dick Tremayne.

Enter the Western Europe Manufacturing Market: Measuring, Analyzing, & Controlling Instruments. 6th rev. ed. BIA. (J). 2006. audio compact disk 289.00 (978-1-4187-4686-5(X)) Bus Info Agency.

Enter the Western Europe Manufacturing Market: Measuring, Analyzing, & Controlling Instruments. 6th rev. ed. BIA. (J). 2006. audio compact disk 249.00 (978-1-4187-4685-8(1)) Bus Info Agency.

Enter This Temple. Contrib. by Leeland. (Mastertrax Ser.). 2008. audio compact disk 9.98 (978-5-557-47323-1(8)) Essential Recs.

Enter Three Witches: A Story of Macbeth. unabr. ed. Caroline B. Cooney. Narrated by Charlotte Parry. 7 cass. (Running Time: 7 hrs. 30 mins.). (YA). (gr. 8 up). 2007. 56.75 (978-1-4281-6331-7(X)); audio compact disk 77.75 (978-1-4281-6336-2(0)) Recorded Bks.

Enter Through the Narrow Gate. 1 cass. (J). 1999. 3.00 Evang Outreach.

Enter Through the Narrow Gate. Dan Corner. 1 cass. 3.00 (116) Evang Outreach.

Enter-View. Read by Sheikh Al-Wahshi. 1 cass. (Running Time: 1 hr.). 9.98 (TP063) Union Label.
Pacifica Radio interview with Sheikh Al-Wahshi demonstrates that words cannot express the Sheikh's unique message. Side 2: Reading from the book Spontaneous Surrender.

Entering God's Rest. 4 cass. 15.95 (20148, HarperThor) HarpC GBR.

Entering His Courts. Rick Joyner. 1 cass. (Running Time: 90 mins.). (Foundation Ser.: Vol. 7). 2000. 5.00 (RJ05-007) Morning NC.
As an overview of God's plan for His church, this series contains essential truths for everyone who wants to see the church become all that she is called to be.

Entering into Rest. David T. Demola. 1 cass. 4.00 (S-1070) Faith Fellow Min.

***Entering into the Moment.** Created by Laura Davis. Prod. by Laura Davis. (ENG.). 2009. audio compact disk 15.00 (978-0-9843234-3-2(0)) Imm Suc Enter.

Entering the Castle: Exploring Your Mystical Experience of God. Caroline Myss. 8 CDs. 2007. audio compact disk 39.95 (978-1-4019-1722-7(4)) Hay House.

Entering the Cave. Marina Bokelman. Read by Marina Bokelman. 1 cass. (Running Time: 1 hr.). (Seasonal Medicine Wheel Ser.). 1991. 9.95 (978-1-886139-04-6(0), SMW-4) Sacred Paw.
Attunement with seasonal energy, Winter healing issues, transformational process work.

Entering the Domain of Spirit. Featuring Adyashanti. (ENG.). 2009. audio compact disk 29.00 (978-1-933986-63-0(8)) Open Gate Pub.

Entering the Fifth Dimension. unabr. ed. Gary Arnold. 1 cass. (Running Time: 1 hr.). 1997. pap. bk. 12.95 (978-1-57867-356-8(9)) Windhorse Corp.
The fifth dimension, sought by Einstein & Newton & cryptically referenced by ancient cabalistic texts is that state of consciousness superseding space in time.

Entering the Fourth Dimension. Swami Amar Jyoti. 1 cass. 1978. 9.95 (O-14) Truth Consciousness.
Horizontal & vertical consciousness. Evolving from third to fourth dimension. Real superman on earth. On collectivity, ecology & universal consciousness.

Entering the Gates of Jewish Spirituality. unabr. ed. Zalman Schachter-Shalomi. Read by Zalman Schachter-Shalomi. 6 cass. (Running Time: 8hrs. 11min.). 1994. 56.00 Set. (31001) Big Sur Tapes.
Introduces the "tools we need as adults to express our soul's concern".

Entering the Japanese Market. unabr. ed. David K. Luhman. Read by David K. Luhman. 1 cass. (Running Time: 45 min.). (Doing Busines in Japan Ser.: Vol. 1). 1993. 10.00 (978-1-889297-00-2(3)) Numen Lumen.
Marketing overview, barriers, the high yen, keiretsu issues, entry vehicle, licensing, yugen kaisha, kabushiki kaisha, earning repatriation, merger & acquisition.

Entering the Millenium or Flying. Robert Thurman. 18.95 (978-1-56176-942-1(8)) Mystic Fire.

Entering the Now. unabr. ed. Eckhart Tolle. Read by Eckhart Tolle. 2 CDs. (Running Time: 2 hrs. 15 mins.). 2003. audio compact disk 24.95 (978-1-59179-098-3(0), W732D) Sounds True.
Shares practices and insights to take listeners into "the timeless dimension"a luminous place found only in this very moment that transcends the struggles and anxiety of our busy lives.

Entering the Realm of the Spirit. 2002. (978-1-59024-049-6(9)) B Hinn Min.

Entering the Vajra World. Read by Chogyam Trungpa. 4 cass. 1978. 38.50 (A022) Vajradhatu.
With some personal understanding of wakefulness (which is known as buddha nature) we are inspired to journey; despite the obstacles of resentment, anger, laziness, & doubt, we are able to enter the brilliance of the vajra world.

Entering Tree of Life. Ted Andrews. 1 cass. (Running Time: 1 hr. 50 min.). 1997. bk. 10.00 (978-1-888767-06-3(5)) Life Magic Ent.
Meditation & music to assist in exploring the ancient mystical Cabala & the Tree of Life. Based on best selling books "Simplified Magic," & "More Simplified Magic".

Entering Truth Thinking. Elbert Willis. 1 cass. (Truth Thinking Ser.). 4.00 Fill the Gap.

Enterprise Success System. Harry C. Green. 8 CDs. 2003. audio compact disk 195.00 (978-1-893847-00-2(4)) Mr Entrep.
The Enterprise Success System? contains audio CDs in which Harry Green will personally mentor you through the tools, strategies and resources that comprise the system. As you listen to the CDs at home, in your car or while working out, Harry will guide you through this indispensable system that is sure to save you time and money and put you on the fast track to turning your vision into action.The Enterprise Success System? contains manuals, business plan templates, PowerPoint presentations and specimen legal documents that have been used successfully to help entrepreneurs start, fund and grow their businesses at all stages. It includes the exclusive Capital Made Easy Program and tools used by Harry Green himself for years to successfully raise capital and grow his businesses from startup to private placements and public offerings.The presentation and document CDs contain sample presentations and specimen documents that you can easily adapt to meet your needs. These documents and presentations will literally save you tens of thousands of dollars. You will learn how you can use these documents to help reduce your attorney?s preparation time and substantially slash your legal bills.

Enterprise the First Adventure. Vonda N. McIntyre. (Star Trek Ser.). 2004. 7.95 (978-0-7435-4276-0(2)) Pub: S&S Audio. Dist(s): S and S Inc

Enterprise, the First Adventure. Vonda McIntyre. Read by Leonard Nimoy & George Takei. (Running Time: 2 hrs.). 1992. 19.95 (978-1-60083-430-1(2), Audiofy Corp) Iofy Corp.

***Enterprise 2. 0: New Collaborative Tools for Your Organization's Toughest Challenges.** unabr. ed. Andrew McAfee. Read by Erik Synnestvedt. (Running Time: 6 hrs.). (ENG.). 2010. 27.98 (978-1-59659-545-3(0), GildAudio) Pub: Gildan Media. Dist(s): HachBkGrp

Entertainer & the Dybbuk. Sid Fleischman. Narrated by Banna Rubinow. 2 CDs. (Running Time: 1 hr. 45 mins.). (J). (gr. 5 up). 2009. audio compact disk 29.00 (978-1-934180-38-9(6)) Full Cast Audio.

Entertaining Angels: Hebrews 13:2. Ed Young. (J). 1981. 4.95 (978-0-7417-1185-4(0), A0185) Win Walk.

***Entertaining Easy Classics - Volume 1.** Steve Rawlins. (ENG.). 2010. pap. bk. 12.99 (978-1-4234-9759-2(7), 1423497597) H Leonard.

***Entertaining Easy Classics - Volume 2.** Steve Rawlins. (ENG.). 2010. pap. bk. 12.99 (978-1-4234-9760-8(0), 1423497600) H Leonard.

Entertainment: Movies Basic Terms. Douglas Moore. Illus. by Sydney M. Baker. (All about Language Ser.). (J). (gr. 7 up). 1986. pap. bk. 22.00 (978-0-939990-48-1(2)) Intl Linguistics.

Entertainment, Arts, & Sports Law. 12 cass. (Running Time: 17 hrs.). 1999. 345.00 Set; incl. study guide 605p. (MD58) Am Law Inst.
Provides information regarding intellectual property, tax planning, labor, employment, & workplace laws.

Entertainment Capital Made Easy: How to Find the Right Investors for Your FILM or TV Show. Speeches. Mervin L. Evans. 5 Audio CD. (Running Time: 300 M). 2002. (978-0-914391-18-0(6)) Comm People Pr.

Entertainment Capital Made EZ - Mervin Evans: Getting Your Entertainment Deal Funded Made Easy. Mervin L. Evans. 1 Audio CD. (Running Time: 1 Hours). 2004. 79.99 (978-0-914391-14-2(3)) Comm People Pr.

Entheogens: The Spiritual Psychedelics. Andrew Weil et al. 6 cass. (Running Time: 7 hrs.). (Psychedelic Conference II Ser.). 1983. 56.00 set. Big Sur Tapes.
Sponsored by Associated Students Program Board, UCSB, Santa Barbara. Includes Psychoactive Drugs Thru Human History; Entheogens in Eleusinian Mysteries, Entheogens in Vedic Culture; The Early Years-Mescaline & Huxley; Hallucinogens: Return to the Logos, Drugs of Perception; LSD: My Problem Child; Psychospiritual Transformation, Chemical Ecstasy, Religious Freedom.

Entheogens & Psychospiritual Transformation. Ralph Metzner. 1 cass. 7.00 (A0087-83) Sound Photosyn.
From the Psychedelic Conference '83. Walter Clark contributes.

Entheogens in Vedic Culture. Jonathan Ott. 1 cass. 9.00 (A0097-83) Sound Photosyn.
Psychedelic Convention '83.

Enthusast: Power of the Enneagram Individual Type Audio Recording. Scripts. Based on a work by Enneagram Institute Staff. 1 CD. (Running Time: 60 mins.). 2004. audio compact disk 10.00 (978-0-9755222-6-4(4)) Enneagr.
Type Seven Individual Type Audio Recording (ITAR) in CD format from the audio tapeset The Power of the Enneagram. Includes a 25 minute introduction to the system as a whole, as well as a 35 minute exposition on Type Seven. An excellent way for therapists or business consultants to introduce the Enneagram to clients, or to work with the Enneagram in ongoing situations.

Enthusiasm. 1 cass. 10.00 (978-1-58506-038-2(0), 70) New Life Inst OR.
Release the bubbling enthusiasm locked within you.

Enthusiasm. 1 cass. (Running Time: 45 min.). (Educational Ser.). 9.98 (978-1-55909-040-7(5), 42); 9.98 90 min. extended length stereo music. (42X) Randolph Tapes.
Learn to be enthusiastic, motivated & excited. Subliminal message are heard 3-5 minutes before becoming ocean sounds or music.

Enthusiasm. Betty L. Randolph. 1 stereo cass. (Running Time: 45 min.). (Self-Hypnosis Ser.). 9.98 (978-1-55909-153-4(3), 813) Randolph Tapes.
An aid to discovering enthusiasm & excitement. Music background & spoken word.

Enthusiasm. unabr. ed. Polly Shulman. Read by Jennifer Ikeda. 6 CDs. (Running Time: 6 hrs. 45 mins.). (YA). (gr. 9 up). 2006. audio compact disk 64.75 (978-1-4281-2213-0(3)); 49.75 (978-1-4281-2208-6(7)) Recorded Bks.
Julie is a quiet bookworm. Her best friend Ashleigh, on the other hand, is an "Enthusiast." As long as they have known each other, Ash has been obsessed with one thing or another. Now it is Jane Austen's Pride and Prejudice, which just happens to be Julie's favorite book. Before Julie knows what hit her, she and Ash are decked-out in 19th-century garb, smelling like mothballs, and crashing the local all-boys prep school formal dance. Their mission is to find their personal Misters Darcy. But when they set their sights on the same young gentleman, their journey into the world of proper English courtship looks like it might cause a broken heart or two.

Enthusiasm Sells. 1974. audio compact disk (978-0-89811-278-8(8)) Meyer Res Grp.

Enthusiastic & Motivated. Eldon Taylor. 1 cass. (Running Time: 62 min.). (Inner Talk Ser.). 16.95 (978-1-55978-101-5(7), 5315A) Progress Aware Res.
Soundtrack - Tropical Lagoon with underlying subliminal affirmations.

Enthusiastic & Motivated: Babbling Brook. Eldon Taylor. 1 cass. 16.95 (978-1-55978-464-1(4), 5315F) Progress Aware Res.

Enthusiastic & Motivated: Music Theme. Eldon Taylor. 1 cass. 16.95 (978-1-55978-103-9(3), 5315C) Progress Aware Res.

***Entice.** unabr. ed. Carrie Jones. Read by Julia Whelan. (Running Time: 8 hrs.). 2010. 24.99 (978-1-4418-6107-8(6), 9781441861078, BAD); 39.97 (978-1-4418-6108-5(4), 9781441861085, BADLE); 24.99 (978-1-4418-6105-4(X), 9781441861054, Brilliance MP3); 39.97 (978-1-4418-6106-1(8), 9781441861061, Brlnc Audio MP3 Lib); audio compact disk 29.99 (978-1-4418-6103-0(3), 9781441861030, Bril Audio CD Unabri); audio compact disk 87.97 (978-1-4418-6104-7(1), 9781441861047, BriAudCD Unabrid) Brilliance Audio.

Enticements. unabr. ed. Una-Mary Parker. Read by Anita Wright. 10 cass. (Running Time: 15 hrs.). 2001. 84.95 (978-0-7531-0846-8(1), 000503) Pub: ISIS Audio GBR. Dist(s): Ulverscroft US

Entities, Energy, & Information Sources. unabr. ed. Robert A. Monroe. Read by Robert A. Monroe. (Running Time: 45 min.). (Explorer Ser.). 1986. 12.95 (978-1-56113-030-6(3), 31) Monroe Institute.
Explores the nature of channels & their information.

EntLits-the House of the Seven Gables (mp3) (ENG.). 2007. 2.99 (978-1-60299-078-4(6)) InterLinguacom.

Entombed. abr. ed. Linda Fairstein. Read by Blair Brown & Blair Brown. (Running Time: 6 hrs. 0 mins. 0 sec.). (Alexandra Cooper Mysteries Ser.). 2009. audio compact disk 14.99 (978-0-7435-6959-0(8)) Pub: S&S Audio. Dist(s): S and S Inc

Entombed. unabr. ed. Linda Fairstein. Narrated by Barbara Rosenblat. 10 CDs. (Running Time: 11 hrs.). (Alexandra Cooper Mysteries Ser.). 2005. audio compact disk 109.75 (978-1-4193-1582-4(X), C3010); 79.75 (978-1-4193-1580-0(3), 97911) Recorded Bks.
Linda Fairstein's thrilling novels featuring sex crimes prosecutor Alexandra Cooper consistently crack the New York Times best-seller list. A former prosecutor herself, Fairstein delivers tales that are chillingly authentic. When a former residence of Edgar Allan Poe is demolished, a human skeleton is found behind the walls. Soon, Cooper is digging into Poe's tormented life, hoping to discover a clue that will break open the case.

Entomologist. 1 cass. (Science Ser.). (J). bk. Incl. 24p. bk. (TWIN 422) NewSound.
Gain an understanding of the importance of insects.

Entrance into God's Kingdom. Derek Prince. 1 cass. (B-2001) Derek Prince.

Entranced. unabr. ed. Nora Roberts. Read by MacLeod Andrews. (Running Time: 7 hrs.). (Donovan Legacy Ser.). 2010. audio compact disk 24.99 (978-1-4418-3808-7(2), 9781441838087, Bril Audio CD Unabri) Brilliance Audio.

***Entranced.** unabr. ed. Nora Roberts. Read by MacLeod Andrews. (Running Time: 7 hrs.). (Donovan Legacy Ser.). 2010. 24.99 (978-1-4418-3810-0(4), 9781441838100, Brilliance MP3); 39.97 (978-1-4418-3811-7(2), 9781441838117, Brlnc Audio MP3 Lib); 39.97 (978-1-4418-3812-4(0), 9781441838124, BADLE); audio compact disk 79.97 (978-1-4418-3809-4(0), 9781441838094, BriAudCD Unabrid) Brilliance Audio.

Entrapment. unabr. ed. Jerry Ahern. Read by Alan Zimmerman. 4 vols. No. 5. 2002. (978-1-58807-517-8(6)) Am Pubng Inc.

Entrapment. unabr. ed. Jerry Ahern. Read by Alan Zimmerman. 3 vols. (Running Time: 4 hrs. 30 mins.). (Defender Ser.: No. 5). 2002. 22.00 (978-1-58807-025-8(5)) Am Pubng Inc.
David Holden and his Patriots have hit the subversive FLNA hard by knocking out their headquarters on an exclusive resort island. But, the FLNAs leader is devising a horrifying plan to assassinate Americas President and capture Holden. Now, with the enemy a heartbeat away from his evil victory in North America, Holden is lured toward a fatal trap.

Entrapment. unabr. ed. Jerry Ahern. Read by Alan Zimmerman. 4 vols. No. 5. 2003. audio compact disk 28.00 (978-1-58807-267-2(3)); audio compact disk (978-1-58807-698-4(9)) Am Pubng Inc.

Entrapment Syndromes. 2 cass. (Orthopaedic Surgery Ser.: C85-OR2). 1985. 15.00 (8571) Am Coll Surgeons.

Entre Amigos, Level 1. M. L. Lagartos et al. 1 cass. (Running Time: 1 hr. 30 mins.). (SPA & ENG., (J). (gr. 4). (978-84-7143-625-2(6)) Sociedad General ESP.

Entre Amigos, Level 2. M. L. Lagartos et al. 1 cass. (Running Time: 1 hr. 30 mins.). (SPA.). (J). (gr. 4). (978-0-00-069811-7(3)) Sociedad General ESP.

Entre Amigos, Level 3. M. L. Lagartos et al. 1 cass. (Running Time: 1 hr. 30 mins.). (SPA & ENG., (J). (gr. 4). (978-84-7861-046-4(4)) Coloquio Edit ESP.

Entre las Sabanas: Una Coleccion de Historias Eroticas. abr. ed. Penthouse Magazine Staff. Narrated by Mayra De Libero et al. 6 CDs. (Running Time: 25200 sec.). (SPA.). 2008. audio compact disk 24.95 (978-1-933499-65-9(6)) Pub: Fonolibro Inc. Dist(s): Downtown Bk

Entre Mar y Coordillera. Roberto Orellana. 2003. 2.00 (978-0-8297-3905-3(X)); audio compact disk 3.60 (978-0-8297-3903-9(3)) Zondervan.

Entre Mundos: An Integrated Approach for the Native Speaker. 2nd ed. Alonso-Lyrintzis & Zaslow. (SPA.). audio compact disk 10.97 (978-0-13-183430-9(4)) PH School.

Entre Nous, Vol. 1. 1 cass. (FRE.). 1995. bk. 18.95 (1496-AF) Olivia & Hill.
Introductory & intermediate programs recorded in Paris. You hear French spoken as the French speak it - idiomatically with colloquialisms & even slang. Dialogues take you from the train station to the hotel to the theater to the restaurant & so on. Includes cultural notes for the beginner.

Entre Nous, Vol. 2. 1 cass. (FRE.). 1995. bk. 18.95 (1497-AF) Olivia & Hill.

Entre Nous I CD & Booklet. Colette Crosnier. 1 CD. (Running Time: 1 hr.). (FRE.). 2005. audio compact disk 21.95 (978-1-57970-121-5(3), FR0622D) J Norton Pubs.

Entre Nous II CD & Booklet. Colette Crosnier. 1 CD. (Running Time: 1 hr.). (FRE.). 2005. audio compact disk Rental 21.95 (978-1-57970-122-2(1), FR0623D) J Norton Pubs.

Entrepreneur Starter Kit. Lyn Christian. Read by Lyn Christian. (Running Time: 6 hrs. 15 mins.). (C). 2005. 36.95 (978-1-59912-166-6(2)) Iofy Corp.

Entrepreneurial Conversation: The Powerful Way to Create Mutually Beneficial, Long-Term Business Relationships. Narrated by Michael Corbett & Edward Rogoff. (ENG.). 2008. 10.46 (978-0-9791522-4-5(0)) Rowhouse Pub.

***Entrepreneurial Management & Leadership.** Jay Christensen-Szalanski & Lon D. Moeller. (ENG.). 2010. audio compact disk 59.95 (978-0-7575-7711-6(3)) Kendall-Hunt.

Entrepreneurial Thinking Set: The Way to Wealth & Opportunity. Mike Vance. 6 cass. 59.95 (15040AX) Nightingale-Conant.
Mike Vance has worked with many of America's most successful entrepreneurs - including Walt Disney, Buckminster Fuller & Steven Jobs. In this program, he shares their secrets with you & demonstrates how to apply entrepreneurial thinking to your workplace. He explains the skills, actions & attitudes entrepreneurs use to define success. He also illustrates the specific steps you must take to think more like an entrepreneur. Discover how to spot trends, find the opportunities hidden in new technologies, unlock your creative genius & maintain a healthy attitude toward change.

Entrepreneurs & Intrapreneurs: The Business of Innovation. Speeches. Joan Koerber-Walker. 1 CD. (Running Time: 55 mins). 2005. audio compact disk 19.95 (978-0-9747056-7-5(5), AUD BOI 2005) CorePurpose.
*In this Audio session - recorded live at Arizona State University, noted entrepreneur and speaker Joan Koerber-Walker explores the mindsets of Entreprenuers and Intraprenuers and the Business of Innovation. Ms. Koerber-Walker has spent her career taking businesses in new directions. As a corporate executive, she launched new processes and programs around the world for a rapidly growing Fortune 500 company before setting out to launch her own company, CorePurpose, Inc., in 2002. CorePurpose, Inc. is a consulting and services aggregator specializing in building solutions that enable its clients to focus more of their resources and energy on what they are passionate about and invest in a way that makes financial sense. She shares secrets for success in the Business of Innovation: * Refining your Focus * Finding the "-preneur" inside of you * Creating a culture of innovation * Connecting the dots An author, speaker and life long intrapreneur/entrepreneur, Joan Koerber-Walker is passionate about finding innovative ways to help companies grow. CorePurpose, the company she founded in 2002, was recognized in 2003 by the Arizona Technology Council as one of the most innovative new companies in Arizona.In 2004, Ms. Koerber-Walker was named one of the top women entrepreneurs in the country as a national finalist for the Stevie considered the "Oscar" for Women Entrepreneurs. In addition to her activities as CEO of CorePurpose, she serves on advisory boards at Arizona State University, Texas A&M, Parenting Arizona and on the Board of Directors of the Arizona Technology Council and the National Speakers Association - Arizona chapter.She was awarded a BA in Economics from the University of Delaware, and an MBA from the W. P. Carey School of Business.*

Entrepreneur's Guide to Venture Capital: Finding the Money You Need. unabr. ed. Center for Entrepreneurial Leadership, Inc. Staff. Hosted by Jeffry A. Timmons. 3 cass. (Running Time: 2 hrs. 32 min.). 1997. 29.95 Set. (978-1-891616-06-8(4)) Kauffman Ctr.
Mysteries of venture capital funding are revealed through interviews with the men & women who seek to raise it & also, from those who decide where to invest it.

Entrepreneur's Starter Kit: Expert Insights into Small Business Success. unabr. ed. Lyn Christian. 8 CDs. (Running Time: 6 hrs.). (ENG.). 2005. audio compact disk 19.98 (978-1-59659-021-2(1), GildAudio) Pub: Gildan Media. Dist(s): HachBkGrp

Entretien, Set. Blaise Cendrars. 2 CDs. (FRE.). 1995. audio compact disk 44.95 (1790-RF) Olivia & Hill.
Radio interview of Cendrars, inveterate traveler & poet. In his poems travel becomes a mystical experience.

Entretien, Set. Jean Giono. Interview with Jean Carriere. 2 CDs. (Running Time: 90 mins.). (FRE.). 1995. audio compact disk 44.95 (1649-LQP) Olivia & Hill.
A fascinating interview in which Giono reveals his talent as a storyteller.

Entretiens, Set. Andre Breton. 2 cass. 1992. 26.95 (1526-RF) Olivia & Hill.
The poet, founder & theorist of the Surrealist movement speaks of the beginning of the movement, its political commitment as of 1927 & its subsequent break with Communism.

Entretiens, Set. Louis De Vilmorin. 2 CDs. (FRE.). 1995. bk. 44.95 (1791-RF) Olivia & Hill.
Radio interview of this famous "femme de lettres" & friend of Malraux.

Entretiens, Set. Jules Roy. Interview with Thierry Pfister. 2 cass. (FRE.). 1995. 26.95 (1661-RF) Olivia & Hill.
Roy speaks of the important themes that have marked his life: his Algerian childhood & the war, his literary life in Paris, his search for God & his love of women.

Entretiens, Set. Jean Vilar & Agnes Varda. 2 cass. (FRE.). 1991. 26.95 (1298-RF) Olivia & Hill.
Fascinating for anyone interested in 20th-century French theater.

Entretiens Text. Siskin. (C). 1994. bk. 50.00 (978-0-15-502054-2(4)) Harcourt.

Entrevistas: Listening Comprehension (Component) Robert Davis. 1 cass. (Running Time: 1 hr.). (C). 2000. 13.43 (978-0-07-230841-9(9), Mc-H Human Soc) Pub: McGrw-H Hghr Educ. Dist(s): McGraw

Entropy Effect. Vanda N. McIntyre. 3 CDs. (Running Time: 3 hrs.). (Star Trek Ser.: 27). 2005. 25.00 (978-1-58807-890-2(6)) Am Pubng Inc.
The Enterprise is summoned to transport a dangerous criminal from Starbase prison to a rehabilitation center: brilliant physicist Dr. Georges Mordeaux, accused of promising to send people back in time - then killing them instead. But there's more at stake than just a few lives. For Mordeaux's experiments have somehow throw the entire universe into a deadly time warp. All of existence is closing in on itself - and only Spock can stop The Entropy Effect!.

Entropy Effect. Vonda N. McIntyre. (Star Trek Ser.). 2004. 7.95 (978-0-7435-4536-5(2)) Pub: S&S Audio. Dist(s): S and S Inc

***Entwined.** unabr. ed. Heather Dixon. (ENG.). (J). 2011. audio compact disk 44.00 (978-0-307-91583-2(2), Listening Lib) Pub: Random Audio Pubg. Dist(s): Random

Enusth Multimedia. Prod. by ENUSTH Staff. 2002. cd-rom & audio compact disk (978-0-9763986-2-2(1)) Enusth.

Enusth Screensaver. Prod. by ENUSTH Staff. 2002. cd-rom & audio compact disk (978-0-9763986-3-9(X)) Enusth.

Envelope Addressing: Your Guide to Ideas & Possibilities. 1 cass. (Running Time: 23 min.). 32.95 (CFSS/CS26) Ctr Self Suff.

Envious Casca. unabr. ed. Georgette Heyer. Read by Clifford Norgate. 10 cass. (Running Time: 15 hrs.). (Inspector Hemingway Mysteries Ser.). 2000. 69.95 (978-0-7451-4212-8(5), CAB 895) Pub: Chivers Audio Bks GBR. Dist(s): AudioGO
The large, rambling home seemed the perfect setting for the Christmas gathering. Unfortunately, the host hated both the festivity and his guests. And when a corpse is added to the scene, the season of goodwill becomes the setting for murder.

Environment - External & Internal. unabr. ed. Perf. by Eknath Easwaran. 1 cass. (Running Time: 1 hr.). 1985. 7.95 (978-1-58638-531-6(3)) Nilgiri Pr.

Environment & I CD see Die Umwelt und ich CD

Environment, the Audio CD Theme Set: Set of 6 Set A. Adapted by Benchmark Education Staff. (English Explorers Ser.). (J). (gr. 3-6). 2007. audio compact disk 60.00 (978-1-4108-9838-8(5)) Benchmark Educ.

Environmental & Toxic Tort Claims: Insurance Coverage in 1989 & Beyond. unabr. ed. Contrib. by Richard D. Williams. 4 cass. (Running Time: 5 hrs.). 1989. 50.00 course handbk. (T7-9211) PLI.
This recording of PLI's May 1989 program explores the rapidly developing legal issues which arise when corporations seek insurance coverage for environmental & toxic tort liability claims. Topics covered include: the terms, conditions & exclusions of general liability & property insurance policies, tactical, strategic & ethical aspects of insurance coverage litigation from both insurer & insured perspectives, environmental regulation & toxic tort case law, technical & expert testimony issues & techniques for evidence development in an environmental insurance coverage case, disputes among primary insurers, excess insurers & reinsurers in allocation & resolution of multi-party & multi-year insurance claims.

Environmental & Toxic Tort Matters - Advanced Civil Litigation: Thursday-Saturday, March 28-30, 1996 - Red Lion's La Posada Resort, Scottsdale (Phoenix), Set. ALI-ABA Committee on Continuing Professional Education. 10 cass. (Running Time: 15 hrs.). 1996. 197.50 Incl. course materials. (MA88) Am Law Inst.
This advanced course of study is designed to provide experienced practitioners with an update on important current developments while covering in depth a number of advanced environmental & toxic tort topics: organizing multi-party litigation, procedures for multi-district litigation & litigation pursuant to the Manual for Complex Litigation, disclosure rules & alternative procedural tracks under the Federal Rules of Civil Procedure, expert & scientific evidence issues, contribution claims, alternative dispute resolution, settlements & consent decrees, Superfund reauthorization, & more.

Environmental Artists: Pass It Along. Hosted by Nancy Pearlman. 1 cass. (Running Time: 28 min.). 10.00 (330) Educ Comm CA.

Environmental Claims: Liability Issues in a Post-Transaction Scenario. Read by Jose Allen et al. (Running Time: 3 hrs.). 1991. 89.00 Incl. 438p. tape materials. (BU-55226) Cont Ed Bar-CA.
Experts explain claims, procedures, & litigation techniques for the business lawyer facing environmental litigation. Covers damages (statutory & common law); clean-up cost recovery; insurance coverage & defense; bankruptcy; & enforcement (civil & criminal).

Environmental Concerns of Fiduciaries. 1 cass. (Running Time: 50 min.). 1993. 95.00 Incl. study guide. (Y505) Am Law Inst.
Examines the potential environmental libilities of executives & trustees & suggests ways to minimize risks.

Environmental Consequences of Nuclear War. Hosted by Nancy Pearlman. 1 cass. (Running Time: 28 min.). 10.00 (206) Educ Comm CA.

Environmental Engineers' Handbook. Bela G. Liptak & David H. F. Liu. 1999. audio compact disk 199.95 (978-0-8493-2157-3(3), 2157) Pub: CRC Pr. Dist(s): Taylor and Fran

Environmental Filmmaking - Uranium Mining. Hosted by Nancy Pearlman. 1 cass. (Running Time: 30 min.). 10.00 (305) Educ Comm CA.

Environmental Hearing Board. 1 cass. (Running Time: 1 hr.). (Advocacy Before Administrative Agencies Ser.). 1984. 20.00 PA Bar Inst.

Environmental Issues in Bankruptcy. 1 cass. 1990. bk. 45.00 (AC-578) PA Bar Inst.

Environmental Issues on File. Diagram Group. (YA). (gr. 6-12). 2004. audio compact disk 149.95 (978-0-8160-5120-5(8)) Facts On File.

Environmental Law. 13 cass. (Running Time: 18 hrs. 30 min.). 1999. 345.00 Set; incl. study guide 614p. (MD47) Am Law Inst.
Recorded at the longest standing & largest annual conference of environmental law practitioners, surveys the continually expanding practice field of environmental law.

Environmental Law. William H. Rodgers. 4 cass. (Running Time: 5 hrs.). (Outstanding Professor Ser.). 1997. pap. bk. 49.95 Set. (978-1-57793-028-0(2)) Sum & Substance.
Lecture given by a prominent American law school professor.

Environmental Law. 3rd rev. ed. Rodgers. (Audio Tape Ser.). 2000. bk. 63.00 (978-0-314-24345-4(3), West Lglwrks) West.

Environmental Law: Groundwater Protection & Industrial Contamination. 1984. bk. 55.00; 30.00 PA Bar Inst.

Environmental Law Series. 9 cass. (Running Time: 10 hrs. 50 min.). 1995. 289.00 set, incl. study materials. (M239) Am Law Inst.
Leading practitioners & EPA counsel lead viewers through the law & practice of Superfund, RCRA, the Clean Water Act, & the Clean Air Act with real-world insight & useful advice.

Environmental Law Update: Municipal Waste-Hazardous Waste-Storage Tanks-Citizen Suits-Wetlands-Liability Insurance. 1988. bk. 125.00; 70.00; 55.00 book only. PA Bar Inst.

Environmental Law Update: PA Safe Drinking Water Act-Pretreatment-EPA NPDES-Air Pollution-Hazardous & Solid Waste 1984 Amendments. 1986. bk. 80.00; 55.00 PA Bar Inst.

Environmental Law Update: The Hot Issues in 1988. 1 cass. 1988. 25.00 (AC-448) PA Bar Inst.

Environmental Liability. Michael Ramos. 3 cass. (Running Time: 8 hrs.). 1995. bk. 119.00 set. (740914EZ) Am Inst CPA.
This course will enable both outside & staff accountants of business enterprises to recognize environmental problems, measure & account for clean-up costs, & apply relevant accounting & audit guidance. A major new section covers the tax treatment of remediation steps.

Environmental Liability in Business Transactions. 1986. bk. 80.00; 55.00 PA Bar Inst.

Environmental Litigation. 19 cass. (Running Time: 29 hrs. 30 min.). 1995. 230.00 Set; incl. study guide. (M206) Am Law Inst.
Advanced course designed to assist private & governmental litigators in meeting the special problems & demands of environmental litigation. Integrates recent developments & new information with practical litigation issues including discovery, examination of expert witnesses, & settlement negotiation.

Environmental Management Systems: Strategies for Improving Environmental Performance. 1997. bk. 99.00 (ACS-1230) PA Bar Inst.
Learn how environmental management systems can be used to identify & address potential environmental liabilitites as well as opportunities for cost effective pollution prevention. Experienced environmental lawyers analyze the legal issues associated with environmental managemanent systems & new regulatory agency initiatives.

Environmental Overkill, unabr. ed. Dixy L. Ray & Lou Guzzo. Read by Jeff Riggenbach. 6 cass. (Running Time: 8 hrs. 30 mins.). 1994. 44.95 (978-0-7861-0830-5(4), 1551) Blckstn Audio.
This book tells you what actually happened at the Earth Summit, provides you with a close look at the environmentalism of Vice President Al Gore & it will help you make your own informed decisions on air pollution, global warming, endangered species, wetlands, overpopulation & other contentious environmental issues.

Environmental Overkill: Whatever Happened to Common Sense? unabr. ed. Dixy Lee Ray. Read by Jeff Riggenbach. Told to Lou Guzzo. (Running Time: 27000 sec.). 2007. audio compact disk 29.95 (978-0-7861-6111-9(6)); audio compact disk 55.00 (978-0-7861-6110-2(8)) Blckstn Audio.

Environmental Planning. unabr. ed. William D. Ruckelshaus. 1 cass. (Running Time: 49 min.). 12.95 (453) J Norton Pubs.

Environmental Private Rights of Action. 1998. bk. 99.00 (ACS-2129) PA Bar Inst.
What's new & what's hot in environmental private rights of action? Here's an opportunity to find out about this very active area of environmental practice designed to protect the public at large. Not only does this update the latest developments in citizens suits, including remedies, damages & attorneys fees, but it explores the hot topic of environmental justice.

Environmental Private Rights of Action in Pennsylvania. 1991. 95.00 (AC-609) PA Bar Inst.

Environmental Science. Michael McKinney & Robert Schoch. (C). 1998. audio compact disk 126.95 (978-0-7637-0701-9(5), 0701-5) Jones Bartlett.

Environmental Science: Guided Reading Program. 4th ed. Holt, Rinehart and Winston Staff. 2003. audio compact disk 235.66 (978-0-03-068064-9(6)) Holt McDoug.

Environmental Science: Instructor's Toolkit. 6th ed. Daniel D. Chiras. (C). 2001. tchr. ed. 99.00 (978-0-7637-1775-9(4), 1775-4) Jones Bartlett.

Environmental Services in China: A Strategic Reference 2006. Compiled by Icon Group International, Inc. Staff. 2007. ring bd. 195.00 (978-0-497-35880-8(8)) Icon Grp.

Environmental Songs for Kids. Coco Kallis & Mark Greenberg. 1 cass. (Running Time: 37 min.). (J). 1999. 8.50; 14.00 Smithsonian Folkways.
Notes include lyrics & resource list.

Environmental Sounds. Bruce Goldberg. (ENG.). 2005. 13.00 (978-1-57968-119-7(0)); audio compact disk 17.00 (978-1-57968-106-7(9)) Pub: B Goldberg. Dist(s): Baker Taylor

Environmental Technologies in Uruguay: A Strategic Reference 2006. Compiled by Icon Group International, Inc. Staff. 2007. ring bd. 195.00 (978-0-497-82463-1(9)) Icon Grp.

Environmentally Friendly Building Products in Philippines: A Strategic Reference 2007. Compiled by Icon Group International, Inc. Staff. 2007. ring bd. 195.00 (978-0-497-82388-7(8)) Icon Grp.

Environmentally Sustainable Buildings in Singapore: A Strategic Reference 2007. Compiled by Icon Group International, Inc. Staff. 2007. ring bd. 195.00 (978-0-497-82412-9(4)) Icon Grp.

Envy. Sandra Brown. Narrated by Victor Slezak. 13 CDs. (Running Time: 15 hrs.). audio compact disk 124.00 (978-1-4025-2902-3(3)) Recorded Bks.

Envy. Sandra Brown. Narrated by Victor Slezak. 11 cass. (Running Time: 15 hrs.). 2001. 94.00 (978-1-4025-0742-7(9), 96910) Recorded Bks.
Intrigued by a provocative partial manuscript she has received from a mysterious unknown sender, New York book editor Maris Matherly-Reed ventures to an obscure island off the Georgia coast to find this incredible new author. On the island, maria learns more about him, and her husband, than she ever wanted to.

Envy. Judy Corbett. 2007. 44.95 (978-0-7531-3798-7(4)); audio compact disk 59.95 (978-0-7531-2779-7(2)) Pub: ISIS Audio GBR. Dist(s): Ulverscroft US

Envy. abr. ed. Sandra Brown. (Running Time: 60 hrs. 0 mins. 0 sec.). 2004. audio compact disk 14.95 (978-0-7435-3757-5(2), S&S Encore) Pub: S&S Audio. Dist(s): S and S Inc
SANDRA BROWN'S BLOCKBUSTER BESTSELLER AT A NEW LOW PRICE! ENVY Read by Victor Slezak Book editor Maris Matherly-Reed receives a tantalizing partial manuscript submitted by a writer identified only as P.M.E. Curiosity compels her to track down the author, Parker Evans, and work with him to complete the tale. But as the story unfolds, Maris becomes convinced it is more than just fiction. When someone close to her dies, the presence of evil looms even closeri??.

***Envy: A Luxe Novel.** unabr. ed. Anna Godbersen. Read by Nina Siemaszko. (ENG.). 2009. (978-0-06-170960-9(3)); (978-0-06-172483-1(1)) HarperCollins Pubs.

Envy, or Yiddish in America & The Pagan Rabbi. unabr. ed. Cynthia Ozick et al. Read by Ron Rifkin & Mitchell Greenberg. 3 cass. (Running Time: 4 hrs.). 2000. 29.95 (978-1-893079-06-9(6), JCCAUDIOBOOKS) Jewish Contempry Classics.
The Pagan Rabbi - Isaac Kornfield, a learned rabbi, hanged himself in a park. His friend pays a condolence call upon the bereaved wife & is shocked to find her cold, unforgiving, as she tells of her husband's great struggle, between the nymph of his passions & the book-laden old Jew of his soul. Envy, or Yiddish in America - Ostrover the Story Teller is the only Yiddish writer in America whose wok is regularly translated & published. Edelshtein seethes with jealousy, if he had a translator, he'd be famous too! Imprisoned in Yiddish, Edelshtein plots & yearns & staggers through the snows of Manhattan, looking for a translator to save him from his fate.

Encyclopaedia Britannica Planet Earth. Compiled by Encyclopaedia Britannica, Inc. 2008. audio compact disk Ency Brit Inc.

Encyclopaedia Britannica the Human Body. Compiled by Encyclopaedia Britannica, Inc. 2008. audio compact disk Ency Brit Inc.

Eon: Dragoneye Reborn. Alison Goodman. Read by Nancy Wu. (Playaway Young Adult Ser.). (ENG.). (J). (gr. 4-7). 2009. 70.00 (978-1-60775-527-2(0)) Find a World.

Eon: Dragoneye Reborn. unabr. ed. Alison Goodman. Read by Nancy Y. Wu. (Running Time: 15 hrs.). 2008. 39.97 (978-1-4233-7960-7(8), 9781423379607, BADLE); 39.97 (978-1-4233-7958-4(6), 9781423379584, Brlnc Audio MP3 Lib); 24.99 (978-1-4233-7959-1(4), 9781423379591, BAD); 24.99 (978-1-4233-7957-7(8), 9781423379577, Brilliance MP3); audio compact disk 97.97 (978-1-4233-7956-0(X), 9781423379560, BriAudCD Unabrid) Brilliance Audio.

Eon: Dragoneye Reborn. unabr. ed. Alison Goodman. Read by Nancy Wu. (Running Time: 15 hrs.). 2008. audio compact disk 36.99 (978-1-4233-7955-3(1), 9781423379553, Bril Audio CD Unabri) Brilliance Audio.

Eona. unabr. ed. Alison Goodman. (Running Time: 15 hrs.). 2010. 24.99 (978-1-4233-7963-8(2), 9781423379638) Brilliance Audio.

Eona. unabr. ed. Alison Goodman. (Running Time: 15 hrs.). 2011. audio compact disk 39.99 (978-1-4233-7961-4(6), 9781423379614) Brilliance Audio.

Eona: The Last Dragoneye. unabr. ed. Alison Goodman. (Running Time: 15 hrs.). 2010. 39.97 (978-1-4233-7964-5(0), 9781423379645, Brlnc Audio MP3 Lib); 39.97 (978-1-4233-7966-9(7), 9781423379669, BADLE); 24.99 (978-1-4233-7965-2(9), 9781423379652, BAD); audio compact disk 99.97 (978-1-4233-7962-1(4), 9781423379621, BriAudCD Unabrid) Brilliance Audio.

EPA Section 608 Certification Exam. ESCO Institute Staff. 1. 2003. 12.95 (978-1-930044-19-7(4), 608CASS) ESCO PR.
Contains all the information necessary to pass the Section 608 Universal Certification Exam.

Epaminondas, Br'er Rabbit's Lafin Place, the Little Red Hen, Penny's Travels, Puss in Boots, Mother Hulda. EDCON Publishing Group Staff. (ENG.). 2008. audio compact disk 12.95 (978-0-8481-0420-7(X)) EDCON Pubng.

Epele: Evaluacion del Dominio del Espanol como Lenguaje Extranjero, Cuadernillo 1. George Luder. (SPA.). 1997. pap. bk. 15.00 (978-1-884083-36-5(6)) Maval Pub.

Epele: Evaluacion del Dominio del Espanol como Lenguaje Extranjero, Cuadernillo 2. George Luder. 1997. pap. bk. 15.00 (978-1-884083-37-2(4)) Maval Pub.

Epele: Evaluacion del Dominio del Espanol como Lenguaje Extranjero, Cuadernillo 3. George Luder. 1997. pap. bk. 15.00 (978-1-884083-38-9(2)) Maval Pub.

Ephesians: The Unity of the Spirit. unabr. ed. Warren W. Wiersbe. Read by Warren W. Wiersbe. 10 cass. (Running Time: 12 hrs. 20 min.). 1989. 39.95 (978-0-8474-2348-4(4)) Back to Bible.
A challenge & encouragement to find out how to be equipped for Christian living.

Ephesians Commentary: Verse by Verse Through the Bible with Chuck Missler. Chuck Missler. 1 MP3 CD-ROM. (Running Time: 8 hrs.). (Chuck Missler Commentaries). 2001. cd-rom [illegible] (978-1-57821-138-8(7)) Koinonia Hse.
Have you ever wished you could win a [illegible]? Or inherit a great fortune? We have already won an inheritance that is beyond our comprehension! An inheritance that transcends any quantitative measurement. In fact, it was set aside for us before the world began! Ephesians is regarded by many as the loftiest pinnacle of the New Testament, and yet is also a practical manual for personal combat.

Ephesians I & II. (LifeLight Bible Studies: Course 18). 13.95 Set. (20-2542) Concordia.

Ephraim's Seed, Set. abr. ed. Pam Blackwell. Read by Pam Blackwell. 8 cass. (Running Time: 3 hrs.). (Millennial Ser.). 1999. 34.95 B F Pubng.
Science Fiction story portrays Latter-Day Saints living at the end of the Earth's existence.

Epic: Stories of Survival from the World's Highest Peaks. 2009. audio compact disk 24.95 (978-1-59316-454-6(8)) Listen & Live.

Epic: Stories of Survival from the World's Highest Peaks. unabr. ed. Read by Rick Adamson et al. Ed. by Clint Willis. Contrib. by Greg Child et al. 4 cass. (Running Time: 6 hrs.). 2000. pap. bk. 38.95 (LC026) Listen & Live.
The climb that went wrong: fighting blinding snowstorms & horrific avalanches; days spent tentbound running low on food, water & oxygen; surviving broken bones & shattered spirits. A collection of accounts of legend-making expeditions.

Epic: Stories of Survival from the World's Highest Peaks. unabr. ed. Short Stories. Alfred Lansing et al. Read by Eric Conger et al. 4 cass. (Running Time: 6 hrs.). (Adrenaline Ser.). 1999. 24.95 (978-1-885408-33-4(1), LL026) Listen & Live.

Epic: The Story God Is Telling & the Role That Is Yours to Play. unabr. ed. John Eldredge. (Running Time: 2 hrs. 20 mins.). 2004. audio compact disk 14.99 (978-0-7852-0910-2(7)) Nelson.
We don't usually identify with the author of a great story. Instead we bond with the hero and heroine-the ones that the story is about . We share in their

An Asterisk (*) at the beginning of an entry indicates that the title is appearing for the first time.

heartaches and triumphs. We cheer their accomplishments and mourn their losses. When we think about our own story, we may see God as the author-an omniscient and omnipotent cosmic mastermind-but fail to recognize Him as the central character. In Epic , a retelling of the gospel in four acts, John Eldredge invites us to revisit the drama of life, viewing God not only as the author but also as the lead actor, exploring His motives and His heart. This unabridged CD read by the author examines the power of story, the universal longing for a "plot" that makes sense deep inside us, our desire for a meaningful role to play, our love of books and movies, and how all of this points us to the gospel itself. It's a story better than any fairy tale! Our human hearts are made for great drama, and the gospel, with its tragedy and grandeur, truly is epic. Hardcover print editions available, including one in Spanish.

Epic Adventures: Stories from the Survivors. 10 cass. (Running Time: 15 hrs.). 2001. 39.95 (978-1-56015-917-9(0)) Penton Overseas.
From the world's highest peaks to its oceans deep, "Epic Adventures" invites you to share in the intense experiences of those who challenge the edge and survive.

Epic in Literature. Narrated by Ralph Bates. 1 cass. (Running Time: 56 mins.). (Sound Seminars Lectures on the Classics). 14.95 (C23110) J Norton Pubs.
A discussion of the excitement & trend created by Homer, his attributes as an artist & writer along with cultural life influence.

Epic Inspirational Movie Theme. 1 cass. (Running Time: 90 mins.). 2000. audio compact disk 16.95 (978-1-56015-735-9(6)) Penton Overseas.
Featuring themes from "The Prince of Egypt," "Ben Hur," "Spartacus" & "The Bible.".

Epic Inspirational Movie Themes & Other Spiritual Music. 1 cass. (Running Time: 90 mins.). 2000. audio compact disk 9.95 (978-1-56015-736-6(4)) Penton Overseas.

Epic Live. Short Stories. John Eldredge. 1 Cd. (Running Time: 50 mins.). 2004. audio compact disk 13.00 (978-1-933207-00-1(0)) Ransomed Heart.
This live conference audio is based on the book Epic by John Eldredge and invites readers to live from the stories their hearts have been longing for. Eldredge says that life, for most of us, feels like a movie we've arrived to forty minutes late. We find ourselves in the middle of a story that is sometimes wonderful, sometimes awful, usually a confusing mixture of both, and we haven't a clue how to make sense of it all. We need to know the rest of the story. We were born into the midst of a great story - a Larger Story. And we have a crucial role to play.

Epic of a Crime. (23311-A) J Norton Pubs.

Epic of Inanna: Queen of Heaven & Earth. Diane Wolkstein & Samuel Noah-Krammer. Music by Geoffrey Gordon. (Running Time: 20 min.). 1987. (978-1-879846-01-2(2)) Cloudstone NY.
4000 year old epic of Sumerian Goddess brought to life by this interweaving of performance, interview, & Sumerian art & landscape.

Epic of the Eternal People, Vol. 1. Shmuel Irons. 16 cass. (Running Time: 22 hrs.). (From the Exile of the Ten Tribes to the Reign of Herod Ser.). 1993. 120.00 Set, incl. source bk. (978-1-889648-05-7(1)) Jwish Her Fdtn.
Using original sources, Rabbi Irons traces Jewish history from the exile of the ten lost tribes to the end of the reign of Herod.

Epic of the Eternal People, Vol. 2. unabr. ed. Shmuel Irons. 16 cass. (Running Time: 22 hrs.). (From Yavneh to Betar Ser.). 1995. 120.00 Set, incl. source bk. (978-1-889648-06-4(X)) Jwish Her Fdtn.
Using original sources, Rabbi Irons traces Jewish history from the years prior to the destruction of the second temple to the years prior to the Bar Kochba revolt.

Epic of the Eternal People, Vol. 3. Shmuel Irons. 12 cass. (Running Time: 18 hrs.). (Creation of the Mishna Ser.). 1996. 90.00 Set, incl. source bk. (978-1-889648-07-1(8)) Jwish Her Fdtn.
Using original sources, Rabbi Irons traces Jewish history from the fall of Betar to the creation of the Mishna.

Epic Poems of the Renaissance Vol. 5: Multilingual Books Literature, Ed. by Maurizio Falyhara & Christina Giocometti. 1 CD. (Audio Anthology of Italian Literature Ser.: 5). (ITA.). 1999. spiral bd. 29.95 (978-1-58214-111-4(8)) Language Assocs.

Epic Poems of the Renaissance Vol. 5: Multilingual Books Literature, Ed. by Maurizio Falyhera & Cristina Giocometti. 1 cass. (Running Time: 90). (Audio Anthology of Italian Literature Ser.: 5). (ITA.). 1999. spiral bd. 19.95 (978-1-58214-108-4(8)) Language Assocs.

Epicenter: Why the Current Rumblings in the Middle East Will Change Your Future. unabr. ed. Joel C. Rosenberg. Narrated by Joel C. Rosenberg. (Running Time: 10 hrs. 42 mins. 53 sec.). (ENG.). 2006. audio compact disk 24.99 (978-1-59859-178-1(9)) Oasis Audio.

Epicenter 2. 0: Why the Current Rumblings in the Middle East Will Change Your Future. unabr. ed. Joel C. Rosenberg. Read by Joel C. Rosenberg. (Running Time: 32400 sec.). 2006. audio compact disk 63.00 (978-0-7861-5986-4(3)) Blckstn Audio.

Epicenter 2. 0: Why the Current Rumblings in the Middle East Will Change Your Future. unabr. ed. Joel C. Rosenberg. Narrated by Joel C. Rosenberg. (ENG.). 2006. 17.49 (978-1-60814-179-1(9)) Oasis Audio.

Epictetus: The Art of Living. abr. ed. Read by Richard Nelson Bolles. Tr. by Sharon Lebell from GRE. Interview with Jacob Needleman. 1 cass. (Running Time: 1 hr. 30 min.). 1997. 11.95 (978-1-57453-088-9(7)) Audio Lit.
The timeless words of ancient philosopher Epictetus can help modern people effectively meet the challenges of daily life.

Epicurus & Socrates. unabr. ed. Comment by Gilbert Highet. 1 cass. 9.95 (C23306) J Norton Pubs.
Discusses the work of Greek philosopher Epicurus in the field of nuclear physics; on the second side, Highet reviews the trial of Socrates at which he was condemned to death.

Epiglottis & Upper Airway Obstruction - Diabetic Ketocidosis. Steven Selbst & Robert Luten. (Pediatric Emergencies: The National Conference for Practioners Ser.). 1986. 9.00 (978-0-932491-72-5(3)) Res Appl Inc.

Epilepsy: Program from the Award Winning Public Radio Series. Interview. Hosted by Fred Goodwin. Comment by John Hockenberry. 1 CD. (Running Time: 1 hr). (Infinite Mind Ser.). 1999. audio compact disk 21.95 (978-1-932479-15-7(5), LCM 81) Lichtenstein Creat.
One out of every hundred people in the U.S. has epilepsy. Seizures have been attributed to everything from divinity to demonic possession. In this hour, we'll hear about the latest in epilepsy treatment and research. Plus, a look at cultural perceptions of epilepsy, and commentary by John Hockenberry.

Epilogue: A Memoir. unabr. ed. Anne Roiphe. (Running Time: 5 hrs. NaN mins.). 2008. 29.95 (978-1-4332-4639-5(2)); 34.95 (978-1-4332-4636-4(8)); audio compact disk 50.00 (978-1-4332-4637-1(6)); audio compact disk & audio compact disk 19.95 (978-1-4332-4638-8(4)) Blckstn Audio.

Epilogue A see Robert Lowell: A Reading

Epiphany. Contrib. by Manafest. 2005. audio compact disk 13.98 (978-5-558-92020-8(3)) BEC Recordings.

Epiphany. unabr. ed. David Hewson. Narrated by Peter Marinker. 14 CDs. (Running Time: 16 hrs. 45 mins.). 2009. audio compact disk 123.75 (978-1-4361-9227-9(7), Clipper Audio) Recorded Bks.

Epiphany. unabr. collector's ed. David Hewson. Narrated by Peter Marinker. 14 CDs. (Running Time: 16 hrs. 45 mins.). 2009. audio compact disk 59.95 (978-1-4361-9228-6(5), Clipper Audio) Recorded Bks.

Episode of War see Great American Short Stories

Episode of War see Fourteen American Masterpieces

Episodes. John James Audubon. 2 cass. (Running Time: 2 hrs. 30 min.). 1994. 17.95 Set. (978-1-879557-19-2(3)) Audio Scholar.
A collection of vignettes Audubon wrote throughout his lifetime. It is a view of life in the wilderness as told by an artist with a pioneering vision of nature. Colorful like his paintings, "Episodes" is Audubon's self-portrait in words.

Episodes: My Life as I See It. unabr. ed. Blaze Ginsberg. Read by MacLeod Andrews. (Running Time: 8 hrs.). 2009. 39.97 (978-1-4418-0173-9(1), 9781441801739, Brlnc Audio MP3 Lib); 24.99 (978-1-4418-0174-6(X), 9781441801746, BAD); 39.97 (978-1-4418-0175-3(8), 9781441801753, BADLE) Brilliance Audio.

Episodes: My Life as I See It. unabr. ed. Blaze Ginsberg. Read by MacLeod Andrews. 1 MP3-CD. (Running Time: 8 hrs.). (J). (gr. 4-7). 2009. 24.99 (978-1-4418-0172-2(3), 9781441801722, Brilliance MP3); audio compact disk 29.99 (978-1-4418-0170-8(7), 9781441801708, Bril Audio CD Unabri); audio compact disk 69.97 (978-1-4418-0171-5(5), 9781441801715, BriAudCD Unabrid) Brilliance Audio.

Episodes from Dream of Red Chamber. 1 cass. 8.95 incl. script. (978-0-88710-151-9(8)) Yale Far Eastern Pubns.

Epistemology Workshop: Excerpt Tape. abr. ed. Ayn Rand. 1 cass. (Running Time: 30 min.). 1969. 12.95 (978-1-56114-313-9(8), AR50X) Second Renaissance.
Three excerpts from her epistemology workshops for professionals in philosophy, physics & mathematics.

Epistle of Barnabas: One of the important writings of the Apostolic Fathers. Narrated by Gerard VanHalsema. (ENG.). 2007. audio compact disk Rental 15.00 (978-1-931848-10-7(6)) Christ Class Ethereal.

Epistle to Be Left in the Earth see Caedmon Treasury of Modern Poets Reading Their Own Poetry

Epistle to Be Left in the Earth see Twentieth-Century Poetry in English: Recordings of Poets Reading Their Own Poetry

Epistles of John. Gary V. Whetstone. Instructed by June Austin. (New Testament Ser.: Vol. NT 204). (C). 1997. 80.00 (978-1-928774-83-9(0)) Gary Whet Pub.

Epitaph for a Spy, unabr. ed. Eric Ambler. Narrated by Alexander Spencer. 5 cass. (Running Time: 7 hrs.). 1982. 49.75 (978-1-55690-170-6(4), RD685) Recorded Bks.
Joseph Vadassy looked forward to a quiet vacation beside the Mediterranean. Instead, he is branded a spy & suddenly he was on everybody's list.

Epitaph for a Spy. unabr. collector's ed. Eric Ambler. Read by Richard Brown. 8 cass. (Running Time: 8 hrs.). 1987. 48.00 (978-0-7366-1203-6(3), 2121) Books on Tape.
Spy thriller featuring a retiring teacher who inadvertently becomes involved in espionage.

Epitaph That Ends All Epitaphs: Matthew 28:5-6. Ed Young. 1985. 4.95 (978-0-7417-1446-6(9), 446) Win Walk.

Epitaphs. Bill Pronzini. Read by Nick Sullivan. 5 cass. (Nameless Detective Mystery Ser.). 2004. 49.95 (978-0-7927-3275-4(8), CSL 676, Chivers Sound Lib); audio compact disk 64.95 (978-0-7927-3276-1(6), SLD 676, Chivers Sound Lib) AudioGO.

Epithalamion see Twentieth-Century Poetry in English, No. 28, Recordings of Poets Reading Their Own Poetry

Epopee de la France Libre, Set. 7 cass. (FRE.). 1991. 59.95 (1219-RF) Olivia & Hill.
A fascinating ten-hour document broadcast on France-Culture. The history of "Free France" told by those who were its main participants. Details of daily life are mixed with acts of heroism & the major events of the times.

Epossumondas. Coleen Salley. Narrated by Cynthia Darlow. (Running Time: 15 mins.). (J). 2002. 10.75 (978-1-4193-1614-2(1)) Recorded Bks.

Epossumondas Saves the Day. unabr. ed. Coleen Salley. Read by Cynthia Darlow. 2 CDs. (Running Time: 30 mins.). (J). (gr. k-3). 2007. audio compact disk 15.75 (978-1-4281-4908-3(2)); 15.75 (978-1-4281-4903-8(1)) Recorded Bks.
Coleen Salley's wonderful Epossumondas books are audio treats for young listeners. Mama is preparing a birthday cake for her sweet patootie, when she realizes she's out of baking soda. So she sends two friends to the store to help out, but neither returns because they get swallowed by a huge snapping turtle.Mama then ventures out herself, only to meet the same fate. Now it's up to Epossumondas to save the day and rescue everyone.

Epoxy Resins: Chemistry & Technology. unabr. ed. Read by Ronald S. Bauer. 3 cass. (Running Time: 3 hrs.). 435.00 Set, incl. 140p. manual. (B1) Am Chemical.

Epreuve, Le Gâteau, La Serre, L'Enfant, Set. Short Stories. Guy de Maupassant. Read by B. Dautun & M. Barbulee. 2 cass. (Bonnes Nouvelles, Grands Commédiens Ser.). (FRE.). 1991. 26.95 (1254-RF) Olivia & Hill.
Four short stories.

Equal Music. unabr. ed. Vikram Seth. Narrated by Steven Crossley. 12 cass. (Running Time: 16 hrs. 30 mins.). 2000. 102.00 (978-0-7887-4493-8(3), H1080E7) Recorded Bks.
Violinist Michael Holme & the Maggiore Quartet are tackling a piece by Beethoven. For Michael, the music resurrects memories of his days as a student in Vienna, where he developed an intense love for Julia McNicholl, a mesmerizing beauty & gifted pianist. After years apart, they share a chance encounter & Julia agrees to accompany the quartet on tour. As they sweep through various concert halls, they are forced to examine their relationship & confront the inevitable consequences of their love.

Equal Parts/Charts & Maps. Steck-Vaughn Staff. 2002. (978-0-7398-5994-0(3)) SteckVau.

Equal Rites. Terry Pratchett. 2 cass. (Running Time: 3 hrs.). (Discworld Ser.). (ENG.). 1993. 16.99 (978-0-552-14016-4(3)) Pub: Transworld GBR. Dist(s): IPG Chicago

Equal Rites. unabr. ed. Terry Pratchett. Read by Celia Imrie. 6 cass. (Running Time: 7 hrs. 45 min.). (Discworld Ser.). (J). 1998. 54.95 (978-1-85695-828-8(0), 951001) Pub: ISIS Lrg Prnt GBR. Dist(s): Ulverscroft US

Equal Rites. unabr. ed. Terry Pratchett. Read by Celia Imrie. 7 CDs. (Running Time: 28200 sec.). (Discworld Ser.). 2003. audio compact disk 71.95 (978-0-7531-0737-9(6)) Pub: ISIS Lrg Prnt GBR. Dist(s): Ulverscroft US

Equal Vision. Swami Jyotirmayananda. 1 cass. (Running Time: 45 min.). 1990. 10.00 Yoga Res Foun.

Equality: The Challenge of Our Time. unabr. ed. Rudolf Dreikurs. 1 cass. (Running Time: 53 min.). 12.95 (29138) J Norton Pubs.
Discussion of evolution of the concept of human equality & the implications involved for child-training & education.

Equality or Heresy. Joan Chittister. 3 cass. (Running Time: 4 hrs.). 1995. Set. (AA2777) Credence Commun.
These talks were given by, given to & given about powerful spiritual women. Three women - Eve, Mary Magdalene & the Samaritan woman have clear, powerful, electrifying messages for the church today.

***Equation for Manifestation Audio Technology.** Dov Baron. (ENG.). 2009. spiral bd. 299.00 (978-0-9810313-3-0(1)) In-Phase Pub CAN.

***Equation for Manifestation Home Study Course.** Dov Baron. (ENG.). 2009. pap. bk. 249.00 (978-0-9810313-7-8(4)) In-Phase Pub CAN.

Equilibrium. John Ralston Saul. 1 CD. (Running Time: 1 hr. 30 mins.). 2005. audio compact disk 12.95 (978-0-660-18797-6(3)) Pub: Canadian Broadcasting CAN. Dist(s): Georgetown Term

Equipment Leasing 1989. unabr. ed. Contrib. by William E. Flowers & Ian Shrank. 8 cass. (Running Time: 12 hrs.). 1989. 50.00 course handbk. (T7-9241) PLI.
In this October 1989 recording of a PLI program, the experienced faculty considers: impact of changes in the Tax Act & regulations, judicial decisions relating to lease provisions, third-party liability & the Uniform Commercial Code, effect of the Bankruptcy Code on enforcement of lessor's remedies & lessee's rights, current status of FASB statements & interpretations on accounting treatment of leases, issues relating to assignments of leases & financing by lessors, peripheral documentation in connection with leasing transactions, leveraged leasing issues, ethical aspects of due diligence & conflict of interest concerns.

Equipped for Deliverance: Breaking Demonic Assignments over a Person,Place or Church. Susan Gaddis. 13. 2003. 50.00i (978-1-932505-07-8(5)) Et Fnd Cu.

***Equipping Church: Serving Together to Transform Lives.** Sue Mallory. (Running Time: 8 hrs. 8 mins. 0 sec.). (ENG.). 2008. 21.99 (978-0-310-30442-5(3)) Zondervan.

Equipping the Saints for the Work of the Ministry. Jim Babansia. 4 cass. (Running Time: 96 mins. per cass.). 1998. 20.00 (978-0-9676380-1-0(1)) Step By Step Min.
Teaching based on scripture.

Equitable Distribution. rev. ed. 1996. bk. 99.00 (ACS-1131) PA Bar Inst.
Who gets the house? Do I get to keep my pension? These are among the first questions your divorce client will ask you. You need to know the latest cases to give your clients accurate answers & effective advice. This offers help, an update on the state of equitable distribution law in Pennsylvania. The knowledgeable faculty will emphasize the latest Pennsylvania appellate cases essential to your practice.

Equitable Distribution of Pensions: Avoiding the Pitfalls of Deferred Distribution. 1990. 65.00 (AC-568) PA Bar Inst.

Equitable Distribution Update. 1991. 49.00 (AC-657) PA Bar Inst.

Equivocal Death. unabr. ed. Amy Gutman. Read by Amy McWhirter. (Running Time: 11 hrs.). 2005. 39.25 (978-1-59600-703-1(6), 9781596007031, BADLE); 24.95 (978-1-59600-702-4(8), 9781596007024, BAD); audio compact disk 24.95 (978-1-59600-700-0(1), 9781596007000, Brilliance MP3); audio compact disk 39.25 (978-1-59600-701-7(X), 9781596007017, Brlnc Audio MP3 Lib) Brilliance Audio.
Just out of Harvard Law School, Kate Paine is on the fast track at Samson & Mills, the nation's richest, most powerful law firm. Assigned to assist the charismatic managing partner in a high-profile sexual harassment case, Kate can hardly believe her luck. But with the brutal murder of Madeline Waters, a beautiful female partner, Kate's carefully constructed world begins to collapse. A mysterious warning from the dead woman just hours before her death leaves Kate terrified and confused - could she be the killer's next target? Finding herself in a race against time to unlock the secrets of Madeline's violent death, Kate delves far beneath Samson & Mills' smooth veneer discovering a shocking legacy of abuse and betrayal - a legacy that may hold the key to solving the murder, as well as, to Kate's own survival.

Equivocal Death: A Novel. unabr. ed. Amy Gutman. Read by Amy McWhirter. 7 cass. (Running Time: 11 hrs.). 2001. 73.25 (978-1-58788-128-2(4), 1587881284); 32.95 (978-1-58788-127-5(6), 1587881276, BAU) Brilliance Audio.

Er-Lang & the Suns: A Tale from China. Retold by Tony Guo & Euphine Cheung. 1 cass. (Running Time: 30 mins.). (Folktales Ser.). (J). (ps-4). 1999. 7.95 (978-1-57255-181-7(X)) Mondo Pubng.
Where did nighttime come from? The people of China suffer from the burning heat of the seven suns until Er-Lang uses his courage, strength & wisdom to save his people.

Er-Lang & the Suns: A Tale from China. Tony Guo & Euphine Cheung. Illus. by Karl Edwards. (J). 1995. 7.95 (978-1-879531-13-0(5)) Mondo Pubng.

Era of Good Feelings. Kenneth Bruce. 1 cass. (Running Time: 1 hr.). Dramatization. (Excursions in History Ser.). 12.50 Alpha Tape.

Era of the Crusades, Parts I-III. Instructed by Kenneth Harl. 18 cass. (Running Time: 18 hrs.). bk. 79.95 (978-1-56585-830-5(1), 390) Teaching Co.

Era of the Crusades, Pts. I-III. Instructed by Kenneth Harl. 18 CDs. (Running Time: 18 hrs.). 2003. bk. 99.95 (978-1-56585-832-9(8), 390) Teaching Co.

Era of the Mountain Men. Kenneth Bruce. 1 cass. (Running Time: 1 hr. 10 min.). Dramatization. (Excursions in History Ser.). 12.50 Alpha Tape.
Exploring the west.

Eragon. Christopher Paolini. Read by Gerard Doyle. 14 CDs. (Running Time: 16 hrs. 23 mins.). (Inheritance Cycle Ser.: Bk. 1). (YA). (gr. 7 up). 2004. audio compact disk 72.25 (978-1-4000-8624-5(8), Listening Lib) Pub: Random Audio Pubg. Dist(s): NetLibrary CO

Eragon. abr. ed. Christopher Paolini. Narrated by Karl Hofmann. (Playaway Children Ser.). (SPA.). (J). (gr. k). 2009. 59.99 (978-1-60812-504-3(1)) Find a World.

Eragon. unabr. ed. Christopher Paolini. Read by Gerald Doyle. (YA). 2006. 54.99 (978-0-7393-7475-7(3)) Find a World.

Eragon. unabr. ed. Christopher Paolini. Perf. by Gerard Doyle. 14 CDs. (Running Time: 16 hrs. 23 mins.). (Inheritance Cycle Ser.: Bk. 1). (ENG.). (YA). 2004. audio compact disk 39.95 (978-1-4000-9068-6(7), Listening Lib) Pub: Random Audio Pubg. Dist(s): Random
Fifteen-year-old Eragon believes that he is merely a poor farm boy—until his destiny as a Dragon Rider is revealed. Gifted with only an ancient sword, a loyal dragon, and sage advice from an old storyteller, Eragon is soon swept into a dangerous tapestry of magic, glory, and power. Now his choices could save—or destroy—the Empire. This deluxe edition of Eragon includes an excerpt from Eldest, the next volume in the Inheritance trilogy; an exclusive foldout map of Alagaësia; never-before-seen art by the author depicting Zar’roc, Eragon’s sword; and an expanded pronunciation guide to the Ancient and Dwarf languages. “An authentic work of great talent.”—The New York Times Book Review

“Christopher Paolini make[s] literary magic with his precocious debut.”—People H “Unusual, powerful, fresh, and fluid.”—Booklist, Starred “An auspicious beginning to both career and series.”—Publishers Weekly A New York Times Bestseller A USA Today Bestseller A Wall Street Journal Bestseller A Book Sense Bestseller From the Hardcover edition.

Eragon. unabr. ed. Christopher Paolini. 10 cass. (Running Time: 16 hrs. 23 mins.). (Inheritance Cycle Ser.: Bk. 1). (YA). (gr. 7 up). 2004. 55.00 (978-0-8072-1963-8(0), Listening Lib) Random Audio Pubg.
Fifteen-year-old Eragon believes that he is merely a poor farm boy until his destiny as a Dragon Rider is revealed. Gifted with only an ancient sword, a loyal dragon, and sage advice from an old storyteller, Eragon is soon swept into a dangerous tapestry of magic, glory, and power. Now his choices could save or destroy the Empire.

Eragon. unabr. abr. ed. Christopher Paolini. 7 CDs. (Running Time: 28800 sec.). (Inheritance Cycle Ser.: Bk. 1). (SPA.). (YA). (gr. 7-12). 2006. audio compact disk 29.95 (978-1-933499-28-4(1)) Fonolibro Inc.

Eragon/Eldest/Brisingr. unabr. ed. Christopher Paolini. Read by Gerard Doyle. (ENG.). (J). 2008. audio compact disk, audio compact disk, audio compact disk 154.95 (978-0-7393-5234-2(2), Listening Lib) Pub: Random Audio Pubg. Dist(s): Random

Eranos Yi Ching: The Use, History & Psychology of the Classic Chinese Oracle. unabr. ed. Rudolf Ritsema & Stephen Karcher. 2 cass. (Running Time: 3 hrs.). 1992. pap. bk. 19.95 (978-1-879816-07-7(5)) Pub: Spring Audio. Dist(s): Daimon Verlag
In these recorded talks, Ritsema and Karcher of the Eranos Foundation have woven together a series of essays which explain the psychology, history and practical use of the Yi Ching in a clear and coherent manner.

Erectile Function. Scripts. Steven Gurgevich. Prod. by Steven Gurgevich. 1 CD. (Running Time: 45 min). (ENG.). 2002. audio compact disk 19.95 (978-1-932170-09-2(X), HWH) Tranceformation.

Eres Todopoderoso. unabr. ed. Danilo Montero. (SPA.). 2003. 9.99 (978-0-8297-4364-7(2)) Pub: Vida Pubs. Dist(s): Zondervan

Ereth's Birthday. unabr. ed. Avi. Narrated by John McDonough. 3 pieces. (Running Time: 4 hrs. 30 mins.). (gr. 3 up). 2002. 28.00 (978-1-4025-2203-1(7)) Recorded Bks.
Belching beavers, this is the worst birthday ever for Ereth, the prickly old porcupine! Even his best friend, Poppy the deer mouse, seems to have forgotten about him. If Ereth wants a present, it looks like he'll just have to get it for himself. But when his quest for salt leads him instead to foster parenthood of a litter of boisterous fox kits, a bad birthday becomes the least of Ereth's worries.

Ereth's Birthday. unabr. ed. Avi. Narrated by John McDonough. 3 cass. (Running Time: 4 hrs. 30 mins.). (J). 2003. 28.00 (978-1-4025-2210-9(X)) Recorded Bks.

Erewhon. Samuel Butler. 1996. pap. bk. 79.95 (978-1-86015-006-7(3)) Ulverscroft US.

Erewhon. unabr. ed. Samuel Butler. 6 cass. 1996. 54.95 (978-1-86015-432-4(8)) Pub: UlverLrgPrint GBR. Dist(s): Ulverscroft US
Not only is Erewhon an adventure but also Butler's satirical inversion of English customs & philosophy in the 19th century. the explorer, Higgs, discovers a well organized & civilized country, apparently idyllic. However, the body politic has two ruling obsessions, disease is considered a crime & machinery is seen as a threat to the supremacy of man.

Eric. Terry Pratchett. Read by Tony Robinson. (Running Time: 3 hrs.). (Discworld Ser.). (ENG., 2006. audio compact disk 24.95 (978-0-552-15334-8(6)) Pub: Transworld GBR. Dist(s): IPG Chicago

Eric. unabr. ed. Terry Pratchett. Read by Stephen Briggs. 4 CDs. (Running Time: 3 hrs. 36 mins.). (Discworld Ser.). (J). 2002. audio compact disk 51.95 (978-0-7531-1266-3(3)) Pub: ISIS Lrg Prnt GBR. Dist(s): Ulverscroft US
Eric is fourteen, lives on the famed and magical Discworld and is the first ever demonology hacker. Fortunately, he doesn't succeed in raising any devils, but he does raise Rincewind (the most incompetent wizard in the universe) and the Luggage (the world's most dangerous travel accessory). The idea is that Rincewind will grant him his three rather adolescent wishes. Getting marooned at the dawn of Time, changing the future and meeting history's most embarrassing god is only the start.

Eric Bogosian. Eric Bogosian. Interview with Kay Bonetti. 1-2 cass. (Author Interview Ser.). 1995. 13.95 (978-1-55644-443-2(5)) Am Audio Prose.

Eric Bogosian: An American Audio Prose Library Reading & Interview. Eric Bogosian. Read by Eric Bogosian. 2 cass. (Running Time: 2 hrs. 30 min.). 1997. 25.00 (978-1-55644-419-7(2)) Am Audio Prose.
Fascinating glimpse into the life & work of a unique American artist.

Eric Bogosian Reading & Interview. Eric Bogosian. Read by Eric Bogosian. Interview with Kay Bonetti-Callison. 2 cass. (Running Time: 2 hrs.). 1996. 25.00 Set. (978-1-55644-444-9(3)) Am Audio Prose.

Eric Bogosian Reads & Performs from "Solos" & "Notes from Underground" Eric Bogosian. Read by Eric Bogosian. Interview with Kay Bonetti-Callison. 1 cass. (Running Time: 60 min.). 1996. 13.95 (978-1-55644-442-5(7)) Am Audio Prose.

Eric Brighteyes. H. Rider Haggard. Read by Shelly Frasier. (Running Time: 10 hrs. 45 mins.). 2001. 29.95 (978-1-60083-600-8(3), Audiofy Corp) Iofy Corp.

Eric Brighteyes. H. Rider Haggard. Read by Shelly Frasier. (ENG.). 2005. audio compact disk 90.00 (978-1-4001-3028-3(X)) Pub: Tantor Media. Dist(s): IngramPubServ

Eric Brighteyes. unabr. ed. H. Rider Haggard. Narrated by Shelly Frasier. 9 CDs. (Running Time: 10 hrs. 48 mins.). (ENG.). 2001. audio compact disk 45.00 (978-1-4001-0028-6(3)); audio compact disk 23.00 (978-1-4001-5028-1(0)) Pub: Tantor Media. Dist(s): IngramPubServ
This deftly crafted Viking tale depicts the terror, tragedy and vanity of life. The ill fated lovers, Eric and "Gudruda the Fair", fall victim to the jealous Swanhild's sorcery. Eric and his 'thrall' must overcome treachery, bloodthirsty foes, the open sea and blizzards as he battles to win his beloved Gudruda. Will the star-crossed lovers triumph over the fate of the Norns and the spite of Swanhild?.

Eric Brighteyes. unabr. ed. H. Rider Haggard. Narrated by Shelly Frasier. (Running Time: 11 hrs. 0 mins. 0 sec.). (ENG.). 2009. audio compact disk 22.99 (978-1-4001-6102-7(9)); audio compact disk 32.99 (978-1-4001-1102-2(1)); audio compact disk 65.99 (978-1-4001-4102-9(8)) Pub: Tantor Media. Dist(s): IngramPubServ

Eric Champion: Natural. Perf. by Eric Champion. 1 cass., 1 Cd. 1998. 10.98 (978-0-7601-1491-9(9)); audio compact disk 15.98 Cd. (978-0-7601-1492-6(7)) Provident Mus Dist.
A unique blend of '80's influenced modern rock.

Eric Martin Bible-Nab: Catholic. Narrated by Eric Martin. 2006. audio compact disk 99.99 (978-1-930034-17-4(2)) Casscomm.

Eric Martin KJV Bible + DVD. Narrated by Eric Martin. 2006. audio compact disk 79.99 (978-1-930034-13-6(X)) Casscomm.

Eric Martin New Testament-Nab. Narrated by Eric Martin. 2006. audio compact disk 34.99 (978-1-930034-20-4(2)) Casscomm.

Eric Martin NKJV Bible. Narrated by Eric Martin. (ENG.). 2003. 79.99 (978-1-930034-21-1(0)) Casscomm.

Eric Vaughn's Complete Guide to Managing Everything, Everyone & Every Task System & Tool Kit, Set. Eric Vaughn. 6 cass. 2001. ring bd. 149.00 (978-0-9701079-0-9(0)) Jet Pubng.

Erica Jong. Interview with Erica Jong. 1 cass. (Running Time: 45 min.). 12.95 (L039) TFR.
Jong discusses in separate interviews, "Fear of Flying" & "Fanny". She remembers that, as the baby in her family, she had to be funny or outrageous in order to get attention.

Erica Jong, Set, Vol. I & II. unabr. ed. Ed. by Jim McKinley. Prod. by Rebekah Presson. 2 cass. (Running Time: 29 min.). (New Letters on the Air Ser.). 1994. 18.00 (052193, 090393) New Letters.
Jong is best known for her six novels & especially for the provocative "Fear of Flying." But she is also an acclaimed poet with seven volumes of poetry to her credit. Here she reads from "Becoming Light: Poems New & Selected" & talks about the need for poetry, the perils of being a feminist who likes men & her interest in witchcraft.

Erich Ist Verschwunden. Bottcher & Lang. audio compact disk 12.95 (978-0-8219-3795-2(2)) EMC-Paradigm.

Erich Segal. Interview with Erich Segal. 1 cass. (Running Time: 22 min.). 1971. 11.95 (L066) TFR.
Segal talks about "Love Story" & why he thinks it will last a lot longer than the harsh words from the critics.

Erie Canal. 2004. bk. 24.95 (978-0-7882-0562-0(5)); pap. bk. 14.95 (978-1-56008-197-5(X)); 8.95 (978-1-56008-890-5(7)); cass. & flmstrp 30.00 (978-1-56008-663-5(7)) Weston Woods.

Erie Canal, the; Star-Spangled Banner, the; Clementine; She'll Be Comin' 'Round the Mountain. 2004. (978-0-89719-838-7(7)); cass. & flmstrp (978-0-89719-746-5(1)) Weston Woods.

Erik Erikson - Psychological Stages. Robert Stone. 1985. 10.00 (978-0-938137-10-8(7)) Listen & Learn.
Stages of Psychosocial Development: Basic Trust vs. Basic Mistrust, Autonomy vs. Shame & Doubt, Initiative vs. Guilt, Industry vs. Inferiority, Identity vs. Role Confusion, Intimacy vs. Isolation, Generativity vs. Stagnation, Ego Integrity vs. Despair.

Erika: Poems of the Holocaust. William Heyen. 1991. 12.95 (978-1-877770-23-4(X)) Time Being Bks.

Erika Hofer Discusses Psychological Practices in Vienna. unabr. ed. 1 cass. (Running Time: 1 hr.). (GER.). 14.95 (29098) J Norton Pubs.

ERISA Fiduciary Responsibility Issues Update: Qualified Pension & 401(k) Plans, ESOPs, & Health Plans. 3 cass. (Running Time: 3 hrs. 30 min.). 1999. 165.00 Set; incl. study guide 286p. (D286) Am Law Inst.
Explores the most timely & important fiduciary issues that regularly arise in the design & administration of various types of employee benefit plans. The discussion is intended for attorneys & plan consultants; plan service providers & administrators; employers & plan sponsors; trustees, investment advisors, & other fiduciaries; & insurers, mutual funds, brokers, & other investment personnel.

Ernest & Celestine. (J). 2004. pap. bk. 14.95 (978-1-56008-039-8(6)); 8.95 (978-0-89719-922-3(7)) Weston Woods.

Ernest & Celestine's Picnic. 2004. bk. 24.95 (978-1-56008-198-2(8)); 8.95 (978-1-56008-891-2(5)); cass. & flmstrp 30.00 (978-0-89719-522-5(1)); cass. & flmstrp 30.00 (978-1-56008-664-2(5)) Weston Woods.

Ernest & Celestine's Picnic. (J). 2004. pap. bk. 14.95 (978-1-56008-199-9(6)) Weston Woods.

Ernest Gaines Interview with Kay Bonetti. Interview. Interview with Ernest J. Gaines & Kay Bonetti. 1 cass. 1986. 13.95 (978-1-55644-156-1(8)) Am Audio Prose.
Gaines discusses "The Autobiography of Miss Jane Pittman".

Ernest Hemingway: A Life Story. unabr. ed. Carlos Baker. Read by Christopher Hurt. (Running Time: 29 hrs. 5 mins.). 2008. 44.95 (978-1-4332-5810-7(2)); audio compact disk 160.00 (978-1-4332-5807-7(2)) Blckstn Audio.

Ernest Hemingway: A Writer's Life. unabr. ed. Catherine Reef. Narrated by Jill Shellabarger. (Running Time: 4 hrs. 0 mins. 44 sec.). (ENG.). 2009. 16.09 (978-1-60814-579-9(4), SpringWater); audio compact disk 22.99 (978-1-59859-538-3(5), SpringWater) Oasis Audio.

Ernest Hemingway Pt. 1: A Life Story, unabr. ed. Carlos Baker. Read by Christopher Hurt. 11 cass. (Running Time: 36 hrs.). 1992. 76.95 (978-0-7861-0384-3(1), 1337A, B) Blckstn Audio.
Now hailed as a classic, Carlos Baker's bestselling "Ernest Hemingway: A Life Story" brings into sharp focus one of the titans of twentieth-century American literature, a writer whose life itself was the stuff of legend. Baker draws not only on Hemingway's diaries, letters, & unpublished writings, but unlike more recent biographers, on the personal testimony of the artists & writer, sportsmen & soldiers - indeed, virtually all the men & women who played a part in Hemingway's career.

Ernest Hemingway Pt. 2: A Life Story, unabr. ed. Carlos Baker. Read by Christopher Hurt. 10 cass. (Running Time: 36 hrs.). 1992. 69.95 (978-0-7861-0385-0(X), 1337A, B) Blckstn Audio.

Ernest Hemingway Reads. unabr. ed. Ernest Hemingway. Read by Ernest Hemingway. 1 cass. (Running Time: 45 mins.). 11.95 (H101) Blckstn Audio.
This collection contains, in addition to the Nobel Prize acceptance speech, five recordings made from 1948 to 1961. One is a second poem to his wife, Mary, another a selection from a work in progress.

Ernest Hemingway Reads. unabr. ed. Ernest Hemingway. Read by Ernest Hemingway. 1 cass. (Running Time: 45 min.). 1992. 12.00 (978-1-55994-573-8(7), DCN 1185, Caedmon) HarperCollins Pubs.

Ernest Hemingway Reads. unabr. abr. ed. Ernest Hemingway. Read by Ernest Hemingway. 1 cass. (Running Time: 45 min.). Incl. Ernest Hemingway Reads: In Harry's Bar in Venice. (CDL5 1185); Ernest Hemingway Reads: Nobel Prize Acceptance Speech. (CDL5 1185); Ernest Hemingway Reads: Saturday Night at the Whorehouse in Billings, Montana. (CDL5 1185); Ernest Hemingway Reads: Second Poem to Mary. (CDL5 1185); Ernest Hemingway Reads: The Fifth Column. (CDL5 1185); Ernest Hemingway Reads: Work in Progress. (CDL5 1185); (gr. 9-12). 1998. 12.00 (978-0-89845-958-6(3), CDL5 1185) HarperCollins Pubs.

Ernest Hemingway Reads: In Harry's Bar in Venice see Ernest Hemingway Reads

Ernest Hemingway Reads: Nobel Prize Acceptance Speech see Ernest Hemingway Reads

Ernest Hemingway Reads: Saturday Night at the Whorehouse in Billings, Montana see Ernest Hemingway Reads

Ernest Hemingway Reads: Second Poem to Mary see Ernest Hemingway Reads

Ernest Hemingway Reads: The Fifth Column see Ernest Hemingway Reads

Ernest Hemingway Reads: Work in Progress see Ernest Hemingway Reads

Ernest Hemingway Short Stories, Set. unabr. ed. Ernest Hemingway. Read by Alexander Scourby. 2 cass. (Running Time: 1 hr. 25 min.). (Cassette Bookshelf Ser.). 1984. 15.95 (978-0-8072-3497-6(4), CB 100 CXR, Listening Lib) Random Audio Pubg.
Features two of Hemingway's best loved, flowing chronicles of human nature, "The Short Happy Life of Francis Macomber" & "The Snows of Kilimanjaro.".

Ernest J. Gaines. unabr. ed. Ernest J. Gaines. Read by Ernest J. Gaines. 1 cass. (Running Time: 29 min.). 1989. 10.00 (121089) New Letters.
Reads from a collection of short stories, "Bloodline," & discusses the obsessions of southern writers (place, race, & the past).

Ernest Lehman see Movie Makers Speak: Writers

Ernestine & Amanda, unabr. ed. Sandra Belton. Narrated by Kim Staunton. 3 pieces. (Running Time: 3 hrs. 45 mins.). (gr. 3 up). 1998. 27.00 (978-0-7887-2068-0(6), 95421E7) Recorded Bks.
A vital glimpse into the realities of life for young African-American girls growing up in the late 50s.

Ernie Gets Lost. 1 cass. (J). bk. 5.58 Blisterpack. (SME 63434) NewSound.
What happens when Ernie gets separated from Maria at the department store. Voices help children learn what to do if they get lost.

Ernie Haase & Signature Sound. Contrib. by Ernie Haase & Signature Sound. Prod. by Lari Goss. 2005. audio compact disk 13.98 (978-5-558-77749-9(4)) Gaither Music Co.

Ernie Harwell's Diamond Gems. abr. ed. Ernie Harwell. 2 cass. (Running Time: 3 hrs.). 1991. 14.95 (978-1-879094-03-1(7)) Momentum Bks.
Baseball seems to differ from other sports in the quality & quantity of the anecdotes it generates. Here Harwell, longtime broadcaster for the Detroit Tigers, presents some of his favorites.

Eros Affair, Set. unabr. ed. Philip McCutchan. 6 cass. (Storysound Ser.). (J). 1998. 54.95 (978-1-872672-00-7(0)) Pub: Mgna Lrg Print GBR. Dist(s): Ulverscroft US

Eros, Love & Lies. unabr. ed. R. D. Laing. Read by R. D. Laing. 1 cass. (Running Time: 55 min.). (C). 1995. bk. 10.95 (978-1-56176-912-4(6), MYS-76912) Mystic Fire.
Psychiatrist R. D. Laing explores the dynamics of human relationships & the vital necessity of bringing honesty to our lives. He speaks of the incompatible contradictions that enmesh us in a web of lies, a system of double-binds programmed to self-destruct. Laing was devastated to find that the behavior he considered "mad" was found not so much in his "insane" patients, but with the so-called "normal" families he studied.

Erotic & the Holy. Marc Gafni. 6 CDs. (Running Time: 7 hrs. 30 mins.). 2006. audio compact disk 69.95 (978-1-59179-289-5(4), AF00914D) Sounds True.

Erotic Edge Set: Erotica for Couples, Ed. by Lonnie Barbach. 2 CDs. (Running Time: 3 hrs.). 2001. audio compact disk 24.95 (978-1-886238-34-3(0)) Passion Press.

Erotic Edge Set: Erotica for Couples, abr. ed. Read by Carol J. Stewart & Gino Scandur. Ed. by Lonnie Barbach. 2 cass. (Running Time: 3 hrs.). 1995. 16.95 (978-1-886238-07-7(3)) Passion Press.
Nationally known sex therapist Lonnie Barbach's first work of arousing fiction for & by both men & women. The collection is a graphically intense exploration of seduction, romance & erotic fantasy with no limits on each couples shared pleasure.

Erotic Poems of the Earl of Rochester. unabr. ed. Read by Ian Magilton. 1 cass. (Running Time: 1 hrs.). 1994. pap. bk. 12.95 (978-1-879816-11-4(3)) Pub: Spring Pubns. Dist(s): Natl Bk Netwk
The Earl of Rochester was King Charles' drinking pal & poet - raw, loud, yet elegant as only the rakes of the Restoration could be.

Erotic Psychology. unabr. ed. Sam Keen. 1 cass. (Running Time: 57 min.). 1980. 11.00 (05702) Big Sur Tapes.
With great humor & insight, Keen speaks of human growth from the tantric sexual viewpoint. He also discusses sexual bonding in terms of the chakra system.

Erotic Reader, Set. 2 cass. (Running Time: 3 hrs.). 1995. 16.95 (978-1-886238-00-8(6), 8006) Passion Press.
Selected excerpts from banned Victorian erotica featuring the 'best parts' of many classics including The Diary of Mata Hari, Memoirs of a Young Don Juan & Confessions of an English Maid.

Erotic Tales see Cuentos Eroticos

Erotic Tales. Read by Laura García. (Running Time: 3 hrs.). (C). 2001. 16.95 (978-1-60083-176-8(1), Audiofy Corp) Iofy Corp.

Erotica. unabr. ed. D. H. Lawrence et al. Read by J. P. Linton & Michelle Gay. 1 cass. (Running Time: 1 hr. 30 min.). (Love Story Classics Ser.). 1995. 13.95 (978-0-9637488-4-3(X)) Love Story Class.
The third volume of an unabridged anthology on the theme of love, containing a collection of written sensuality by famous authors.

Eroticization of Logos in Modern Times, Set. Diane Martin. Read by Diane Martin. 2 cass. (Running Time: 2 hrs.). 1994. 16.95 (978-0-7822-0446-9(5), 524) C G Jung IL.

Erotikos Logos see George Seferis

Error of Judgement. unabr. ed. Dexter Dias. Read by William Gaminara. 8 cass. (Running Time: 12 hrs.). 2000. 59.95 (CAB 1367) Pub: Chivers Audio Bks GBR. Dist(s): AudioGO
On Christmas Eve, a disturbed man walks into a brothel with a claw hammer and confesses a murder. He knows he has buried a corpse and he knows the location, but he can't identify the victim or himself. At the Old Bailey, disillusioned barrister Nick Downes is briefed to defend the unknown man accused of murder, and the prosecuting counsel is Sally Fielding, Nick's partner. But when the corpse's skull is reconstructed, the dead man's face reappears, a face identical to that of Nick's client.

Ersatz Elevator. unabr. ed. Lemony Snicket, pseud. 4 cass. (Running Time: 4 hrs. 30 mins.). (Series of Unfortunate Events Ser.: Bk. 6). (YA). (gr. 5 up). 2003. 35.00 (978-1-4025-3738-7(7)) Recorded Bks.

Ersatz Elevator. unabr. abr. ed. Lemony Snicket, pseud. Read by Lemony Snicket, pseud. Read by Tim Curry. 3 cass. (Running Time: 4 hrs.). (Series of Unfortunate Events Ser.: Bk. 6). (J). (gr. 3-8). 2002. 20.00 (978-0-694-52593-5(6)) HarperCollins Pubs.

Ersatz Elevator. unabr. abr. ed. Lemony Snicket, pseud. Read by Tim Curry. 3 CDs. (Running Time: 5 hrs.). (Series of Unfortunate Events Ser.: Bk. 6). (J). (gr. 3-8). 2003. audio compact disk 25.95 (978-0-06-056621-0(3)) HarperCollins Pubs.

Erskine Caldwell. Interview. Interview with Erskine Caldwell & Kay Bonetti. 1 cass. (Running Time: 1 hr.). 13.95 (978-1-55644-069-4(3), 3042) Am Audio Prose.
Wide-ranging discussion about the life, craft, & social vision of one of America's most controversial, influential, ground breaking, & fiercely independent writers.

Erskine Caldwell. unabr. ed. Erskine Caldwell. 1 cass. (Author Speaks Ser.). 1991. 14.95 J Norton Pubs.
Archival recordings of 20th-century authors.

Erskine Caldwell. unabr. ed. Erskine Caldwell. Read by Erskine Caldwell. 1 cass. (Running Time: 50 min.). Incl. It Happened Like This. (SAC 43-3); People vs. Abe Latham, Colored. (SAC 43-3); Small Day. (SAC 43-3); 10.95 (978-0-8045-0721-9(X), SAC 43-3) Spoken Arts.
Author reads four of his short stories.

***Es la hora Audio CD.** Francisco Blane. Adapted by Benchmark Education Company, LLC. (My First Reader's Theater Ser.). (SPA.). (J). 2009. audio compact disk 10.00 (978-1-935470-69-4(8)) Benchmark Educ.

Esa Mosca!, EDL Level 3. (SPA.). 2003. 11.50 (978-0-7652-1002-9(9)) Modern Curr.

Esau. Philip Kerr. 2004. 13.95 (978-0-7435-4687-4(3)) Pub: S&S Audio. Dist(s): S and S Inc

Esau. unabr. collector's ed. Philip Kerr. Read by Geoffrey Howard. 9 cass. (Running Time: 3 hrs. 30 min.). 1998. 72.00 (978-0-7366-4121-0(1), 4625) Books on Tape.
Mountaineer Jack Furness finds proof that the Abominable Snowman may exist, but nuclear war & secret agents threaten to derail his quest.

Escapade. unabr. ed. Walter Satterthwait. Narrated by Jeff Woodman & Emily Gray. 9 cass. (Running Time: 13 hrs.). 2001. 82.00 (978-0-7887-9892-4(8)) Recorded Bks.
Hired to guard Harry Houdini from rival magicians death threats, Phil Beaumont finds his hands full at a stately country home where Sir Arthur Conan Doyle is among the guests. When the host is murdered, Phil must sort through the clues without upsetting his boss.

Escape. (Running Time: 0 hr. 30 mins.). 2005. 16.95 (978-1-59912-925-9(6)) Iofy Corp.

Escape. 1 cass. (Running Time: 60 min.). Incl. Orient Express. 1949. (M-7930); Shipment of Mute Fate. 1949. (M-7930); 1949. 7.95 (M-7930) Natl Recrd Co.

Escape. Perf. by William Conrad & Hans Conreid. 1 cass. (Running Time: 60 min.). (Old Time Radio Classic Singles Ser.). 4.95 (978-1-57816-098-3(7), ES108) Audio File.
Includes: 1) "Orient Express" (2/19/49). 2) "Shipment of Mute Fate" famous story about a deadly snake loose in the hold of a cargoship (3/28/48).

Escape. Perf. by William Conrad & Hans Conried. 1 cass. (Running Time: 60 min.). Incl. Orient Express. 1949. (M-7930); Shipment of Mute Fate. 1949. (M-7930); 1949. 7.95 (M-7930) Natl Recrd Co.
Orient Express is an action packed story with the complete mystique of the famous train itself. In "Shipment of Mute Fate", a ship voyage starts from Venezuela carrying a cargo of death, a 12 foot deadly Bushmaster snake. The crew & passengers live in a state of terror when the snake escapes & cannot be found.

Escape. Gordon Korman. (Island Ser.). (ENG.). (J). (gr. 4-7). 2008. audio compact disk 29.95 (978-0-545-03325-1(X)) Scholastic Inc.

Escape. Created by Radio Spirits. (Running Time: 10800 sec.). 2004. 9.98 (978-1-57019-636-2(2)); audio compact disk 9.98 (978-1-57019-635-5(4)) Radio Spirits.

Escape. Contrib. by Rush of Fools. (Mastertrax Ser.). 2008. audio compact disk 9.98 (978-5-557-36654-0(7)) Pt of Grace Ent.

Escape. abr. ed. Carolyn Jessop. Read by Alison Fraser. (Running Time: 18000 sec.). (ENG.). 2007. audio compact disk 27.95 (978-0-7393-5457-5(4), Random AudioBks) Pub: Random Audio Pubg. Dist(s): Random

Escape. unabr. ed. Jerry Ahern. Read by Alan Zimmerman. 3 vols. (Running Time: 4 hrs. 30 mins.). (Defender Ser.: No. 6). 2000. 22.00 (978-1-58807-026-5(3)) Am Pubng Inc.
David Holden was supposed to be a dead man. The subversive FLNA had taken him captive, and their master torturer tried to make him talk. But, it would take more than chains to keep Holden jailed and more than pain to make him tell. Now that hes free and on the run with a beautiful woman, he's ready to kill anyone who tries to stop him. This time the FLNA is going to pay for their terrorist cruelty in cold blood.

Escape. unabr. ed. Jerry Ahern. Read by Alan Zimmerman. 4 vols. No. 6. 2003. (978-1-58807-521-5(4)); audio compact disk 28.00 (978-1-58807-268-9(1)); audio compact disk (978-1-58807-699-1(7)) Am Pubng Inc.

Escape. unabr. ed. James Clavell. Read by John Lee. 11 cass. (Running Time: 16 hrs. 30 mins.). 88.00 (978-0-7366-6025-9(9)) Books on Tape.

***Escape.** unabr. ed. Barbara Delinsky. (ENG.). 2011. audio compact disk 40.00 (978-0-307-73513-3(3), Random AudioBks) Pub: Random Audio Pubg. Dist(s): Random

Escape. unabr. ed. Robert K. Tanenbaum. Narrated by Charles Leggett. 18 CDs. (Running Time: 22 hrs. 30 mins.). (ENG.). 2008. audio compact disk 39.95 (978-1-60283-393-7(1)) Pub: AudioGO. Dist(s): Perseus Dist

Escape, Set. 2 cass. (Running Time: 2 hrs.). (Old Time Radio Classic Singles Ser.). vinyl bd. 10.95 (978-1-57816-049-5(9), ES2401) Audio File.
Includes: "Three Skeleton Key" (11/15/49) This is the chilling story about the rats against the occupants of a lighthouse. "Pressure" (3/22/53) This is the story of the USS Swordfish, a submarine out of Pearl Harbor, on its fourth war patrol. "The Birds" (7/10/54) This is the famous story that Alfred Hitchcock made into a film classic. "Red Wine" (8/11/49) The bad guy's connoisseur taste does him in!.

Escape, Vol. 1. collector's ed. Perf. by Raymond Lawrence et al. 6 cass. (Running Time: 9 hrs.). Dramatization. 1999. bk. 34.98 (4150) Radio Spirits.
18 classic episodes of radio's greatest series of high adventure.

Escape, Vol. 2. 1 cass. (Running Time: 60 min.). (Old Time Radio Classic Singles Ser.). 4.95 (978-1-57816-099-0(5), ES222) Audio File.
Includes: 1) "Wild Oranges" Trapped in a dark Plantation house with a homicidal maniac. (12/17/47). 2) "The Follower" - A dead man, a missing wife & a trip to Mexico. (2/18/51).

Escape, Vol. 2. collector's ed. Perf. by Vic Perrin et al. Narrated by William Conrad. 6 cass. (Running Time: 9 hrs.). Dramatization. 1999. bk. 34.98 (4186) Radio Spirits.
18 classic episodes of radio's greatest series of high adventure with Conrad as the "Voice of Escape".

Escape, Vol. 3. collector's ed. 6 cass. (Running Time: 9 hrs.). Dramatization. 2000. bk. 34.98 (4546) Radio Spirits.
18 classic tales.

Escape: A Passenger to Bali & Conqueror's Isle. Read by John Dehner & Harry Bartell. 1 cass. (Running Time: 1 hr.). 2001. 6.98 (2475) Radio Spirits.

Escape: Barcelina & the Fisherman & Bloodwaters. 1 cass. (Running Time: 1 hr.). 2001. 6.98 (1957) Radio Spirits.

Escape: Casting the Runes & Occurrence at Owl Creek Bridge. Perf. by John McIntire. 1 cass. (Running Time: 1 hr.). 2001. 6.98 (2255) Radio Spirits.

Escape: Clear for Action & The Far Away Island. Perf. by William Conrad & Ted De Corsia. 1 cass. (Running Time: 1 hr.). 2001. 6.98 (2415) Radio Spirits.

Escape: Confession & Action. Perf. by William Conrad & Joseph Kearns. 1 cass. (Running Time: 1 hr.). 2001. 6.98 (2277) Radio Spirits.

Escape: Confidential Agent & When the Man Comes, Follow Him. 1 cass. (Running Time: 1 hr.). 2001. 6.98 (2034) Radio Spirits.

Escape: Conquest & A Bullet for Mr. Smith. Perf. by William Conrad. 1 cass. (Running Time: 1 hr.). 2001. 6.98 (2057) Radio Spirits.

Escape: Dead of Night & Pollack & the Porrah Man. 1 cass. (Running Time: 1 hr.). 2001. 6.98 (2236) Radio Spirits.

Escape: El Guitarrero & The Derelict. 1 cass. (Running Time: 1 hr.). 2001. 6.98 (2135) Radio Spirits.

Escape: Into Health & Wellbeing. unabr. ed. Twin Sisters. Read by Twin Sisters. (YA). 2008. 44.99 (978-1-59922-318-6(X)) Find a World.

***Escape: Journey into Fear.** Perf. by William Conrad et al. 2010. audio compact disk 39.98 (978-1-57019-937-0(X)) Radio Spirits.

Escape: Leinengen vs. the Ants. (CD-4736) Natl Recrd Co.

Escape: Misfortune's Isle & A Shipment of Mute Fate. 1 cass. (Running Time: 1 hr.). 2001. 6.98 (2575) Radio Spirits.

Escape: Operation Feur de Lys & Diamond as Big as the Ritz. 1 cass. (Running Time: 1 hr.). 2001. 6.98 (2011) Radio Spirits.

Escape: The Bird of Paradise & Violent Night. Perf. by John Dehner & William Conrad. 1 cass. (Running Time: 1 hr.). 2001. 6.98 (2495) Radio Spirits.

Escape: The Boiling Sea & Ted de Corsia. 1 cass. (Running Time: 1 hr.). 2001. 6.98 (2195) Radio Spirits.

Escape: The Cave & Up Periscope. 1 cass. (Running Time: 1 hr.). 2001. 6.98 (1646) Radio Spirits.

Escape: The Dark Wall & Two & Two Make Four. Perf. by John Dehner & Shep Menken. 1 cass. (Running Time: 1 hr.). 2001. 6.98 (2598) Radio Spirits.

Escape: The King of Owanatu & Heart of Kali. Perf. by Tony Barrett et al. 1 cass. (Running Time: 1 hr.). 2001. 6.98 (2614) Radio Spirits.

Escape: The Lost Special & The Orient Express. 1 cass. (Running Time: 1 hr.). 2001. 6.98 (1975) Radio Spirits.

Escape: The Scarlet Plague with Vic Perrin & Affair at Mandrake. Perf. by Vic Perrin. 1 cass. (Running Time: 1 hr.). 2001. 6.98 (2535) Radio Spirits.

Escape: The Second Shot with John Dehner & The Return with Lawrence Dobkin. Perf. by John Dehner & William Conrad. 1 cass. (Running Time: 1 hr.). 2001. 6.98 (2516) Radio Spirits.

Escape! The Story of the Great Houdini. unabr. ed. Sid Fleischman. Read by Sid Fleischman. Read by Taylor Mali. 3 CDs. (Running Time: 12600 sec.). (J). (gr. 4-8). 2007. audio compact disk 39.95 (978-0-9761932-5-8(6)) Audio Bkshelf.

Escape! The Story of the Great Houdini. unabr. ed. Sid Fleischman. Read by Sid Fleischman. Read by Taylor Mali. (J). 2008. 59.99 (978-1-60514-720-8(6)) Find a World.

Escape: The Thirteenth Truck & The Man from Tomorrow. 1 cass. (Running Time: 1 hr.). 2001. 6.98 (2177) Radio Spirits.

Escape: The 4th Man & John Jack Todd. 1 cass. (Running Time: 1 hr.). 2001. 6.98 (2325) Radio Spirits.

Escape: Three Skeleton Key. Perf. by Vincent Price & Beau Geste. 1 cass. (Running Time: 1 hr.). 2001. 6.98 (1645) Radio Spirits.

Escape Artist. David Wagoner. Read by David Wagoner. 1 cass. (Running Time: 50 min.). 13.95 (978-1-55644-027-4(8), 1151) Am Audio Prose.
Jailbreak scene in this picaresque novel recently adapted as a motion picture by Francis Ford Coppola.

***Escape Artist.** unabr. ed. Read by To be Announced. Ed. by Ifkovic. (Running Time: 8 hrs. NaN mins.). (Edna Ferber Mysteries Ser.). (ENG.). 2011. 29.95 (978-1-4417-8256-4(7)); 54.95 (978-1-4417-8253-3(2)); audio compact disk 76.00 (978-1-4417-8254-0(0)) Blckstn Audio.

***Escape Clause.** 2010. audio compact disk (978-1-59171-167-4(3)) Falcon Picture.

Escape from Alcatraz. J. Campbell Bruce. Read by Patrick Cullen. (Running Time: 30600 sec.). 2006. 54.95 (978-0-7861-4515-7(3)); audio compact disk 63.00 (978-0-7861-7189-7(8)) Blckstn Audio.

Escape from Alcatraz. unabr. abr. ed. J. Campbell Bruce. Read by Patrick Cullen. (Running Time: 30600 sec.). 2006. audio compact disk 29.95 (978-0-7861-7623-6(7)) Blckstn Audio.

Escape from Andersonville: A Novel of the Civil War. abr. ed. Gene Hackman & Daniel Lenihan. Read by Christopher Lane. (Running Time: 6 hrs.). 2009. audio compact disk 14.99 (978-1-4233-5085-9(5), 9781423350859, BCD Value Price) Brilliance Audio.

Escape from Andersonville: A Novel of the Civil War. unabr. ed. Gene Hackman & Daniel Lenihan. Read by Christopher Lane. 1 MP3-CD. (Running Time: 10 hrs.). 2008. 24.95 (978-1-4233-5080-4(4), 9781423350804, Brilliance MP3); 24.95 (978-1-4233-5082-8(0), 9781423350828, BAD); 39.25 (978-1-4233-5081-1(2), 9781423350811, Brinc Audio MP3 Lib); 39.25 (978-1-4233-5083-5(9), 9781423350835, BADLE); audio compact disk 38.95 (978-1-4233-5078-1(2), 9781423350781, Bril Audio CD Unabri); audio compact disk 102.25 (978-1-4233-5079-8(0), 9781423350798, BriAudCD Unabrid) Brilliance Audio.

Escape from Castle Cant. unabr. ed. K. P. Bath. Read by Kerin McCue. 8 CDs. (Running Time: 9 hrs.). (YA). (gr. 6-9). 2006. 59.75 (978-1-4281-2168-3(4)) Recorded Bks.

Escape from Castle Cant. unabr. ed. K. P. Bath. Read by Kerin McCue. 8 cass. (Running Time: 9 hrs.). (YA). (gr. 6-9). 2007. audio compact disk 87.75 (978-1-4281-2173-7(0)) Recorded Bks.

Escape from Christiandome. Robert E. Burnell. 1 cass. 1991. 5.00 (978-951-24-0007-2(3)) Mrngstar Pubns.

Escape from Cubicle Nation: From Corporate Prisoner to Thriving Entrepreneur. unabr. ed. Pamela Slim. Read by Sandra Burr. 1 MP3-CD. (Running Time: 12 hrs.). 2009. 24.99 (978-1-4233-9328-3(7), 9781423393283, Brilliance MP3); 39.97 (978-1-4233-9329-0(5), 9781423393290, Brinc Audio MP3 Lib); 24.99 (978-1-4233-9330-6(9), 9781423393306, BAD); 39.97 (978-1-4233-9331-3(7), 9781423393313, BADLE); audio compact disk 29.99 (978-1-4233-9326-9(0), 9781423393269); audio compact disk 92.97 (978-1-4233-9327-6(9), 9781423393276, BriAudCD Unabrid) Brilliance Audio.

***Escape from Cubicle Nation: From Corporate Prisoner to Thriving Entrepreneur.** unabr. ed. Pamela Slim. Read by Sandra Burr. (Running Time: 12 hrs.). 2010. audio compact disk 14.99 (978-1-61106-444-5(9), 9781611064445, BCD Value Price) Brilliance Audio.

Escape from Depression. 2 CDs. 2004. audio compact disk 25.50 (978-1-55841-134-0(8)) Emmett E Miller.
This program weaves vital information based on clinical experience and the latest neuropsychiatric research with powerful self-healing tools like cognitive-behavioral self-therapy, meditation, deep relaxation, self-imagery, self-hypnosis, autogenic training and prayer. It offers a new perspective on the mechanism of depression as a state of being cut off from your spirit or heart, a kind of learned helplessness, based on a belief in loss and a failure to grieve properly. Because it is learned, depression can be unlearned.

Escape from Egypt. unabr. ed. Sonia Levitin. Read by Grace Conlin. 6 cass. (Running Time: 8 hrs. 30 mins.). 1995. 44.95 (978-0-7861-0762-9(6), 1611) Blckstn Audio.
Jesse, a Hebrew slave, & Jennat, a half-Egyptian, half-Syrian girl, live in vastly different worlds. Jesse's life is filled with cruelty inflicted upon him by Egyptian task-masters. His mother believes that God will someday rescue His people & guide them to their own land. Jesse's father believes only in survival & will stop at nothing to gain favors from the rich & powerful. Jennat, too, serves an Egyptian - her wealthy mistress, Memnet - but she is content to share in the glitter of Egyptian life & idol worship. When Jesse & Jennat work together in Memnet's household, their worlds collide, & they are attracted to each other, despite their differences.

Escape from Fire Mountain. unabr. ed. Gary Paulsen. Narrated by Jeff Woodman. 1 cass. (Running Time: 1 hr.). (Gary Paulsen's World of Adventure Ser.: Bk. 3). (gr. 4 up). 1997. 10.00 (978-0-7887-0797-1(3), 94947E7) Recorded Bks.
When 13-year-old Nikki Roberts hears a call for help on her CB radio, the young hunting guide rushes into a Wabash Mountain forest fire to find two lost children. But there are other dangers waiting for Nikki on the mountain.

Escape from Hell. unabr. ed. Larry Niven & Jerry Pournelle. Read by Tom Weiner. (Running Time: 9.5 hrs. 0 mins.). (ENG.). 2009. 29.95 (978-1-4332-5899-2(4)); 59.95 (978-1-4332-5895-4(1)); audio compact disk 80.00 (978-1-4332-5896-1(X)) Blckstn Audio.

Escape from Home. unabr. ed. Avi. Narrated by Simon Prebble. 7 pieces. (Running Time: 10 hrs. 30 mins.). (Beyond the Western Sea Ser.: Bk. 1). (gr. 6 up). 1997. 60.00 (978-0-7887-1159-6(8), 95119E7) Recorded Bks.
A vivid picture of life in the 19th century Ireland & England. When their father sends money from the United States, 12-year old Patrick O'Connell & his sister journey to Liverpool to board an American-bound ship. But along the way, Patrick meets some strangers who are more than eager to help him care for his new fortune.

Escape from HorrorLand. R. L. Stine. (Goosebumps HorrorLand Ser.: No. 11). (ENG.). (J). (gr. 4-7). 2009. audio compact disk 29.95 (978-0-545-02389-4(0)); audio compact disk 9.95 (978-0-545-13854-3(X)) Scholastic Inc.

Escape from Love: Dissociating A Course in Miracles. Kenneth Wapnick. 2 CDs. 2004. audio compact disk 13.00 (978-1-59142-137-5(3), CD95) Foun Miracles.
This talk was originally part of a three-day Academy class on "The Face of Innocence," held in 2004. The focus of these excerpts was our need to dissociate A Course in Miracles, splitting off its teachings from our daily practice by unconsciously erecting a wall of denial that keeps us from seeing what we are doing. Discussion focused on the paradox of sincere students committing themselves to Jesus and his Course, at the same time not making the attitudinal changes he advocates; most specifically holding on to lives of judgment and specialness. Looking at this dissociation with the love of Jesus beside us undoes it, enabling the wall of fear and judgment to dissolve as we learn to forgive ourselves for being afraid.

***Escape from Love: Dissociating A Course in Miracles.** Kenneth Wapnick. 2010. 10.00 (978-1-59142-479-6(8)) Foun Miracles.

Escape from Mediocrity: Advice on Living the above Average Life. Clay Campbell. 1 CD. (Running Time: 1 hr.). 2005. audio compact disk 12.95 (978-1-932226-48-5(6)) Wizard Acdmy.
Escape From Mediocrity: Advice On Living The Above Average Life will help business owners, management and employees to bring UP the level of productivity and put an end to mediocrity in their personal life and career.YOU?LL learn how to have a "don't kid yourself day?. Raise the bar and find BALANCE in six areas: Family, Finances, Friends, Career, Spiritual, and Physical/Health.Clay is one of many partners that make up the Wizard of Ads? organization, with offices around the world.Clay helps people to grow in personal development to achieve their goals and dreams as individuals and as a company.As a successful business owner himself, his marketing, promotional strategies, and creative writing skills have helped several businesses, besides his own, to achieve their goals and increase their profits.Clay is available for speaking for noon lunches, after dinner, Chamber of Commerce, Rotary, Men?s groups, church groups, and small business advertising seminars. He is witty, funny, down to earth, and will add excitement to any event.

Escape from Singapore. unabr. collector's ed. Ian Skidmore. Read by Richard Green. 6 cass. (Running Time: 6 hrs.). 1981. 36.00 (978-0-7366-0304-1(2), 1292) Books on Tape.
The narrative of a minor but heroic detail of World War II. A small band of British soldiers refuses to obey an order to surrender to the Japanese at Singapore. One step ahead of the enemy, they take a frail sailing canoe across the Bay of Bengal to Ceylon. The journey takes 36 days & nearly ends in disaster.

Escape from Sonora. unabr. ed. Will Bryant. Read by Gene Engene. 2001. 64.95 (978-1-55686-793-4(X)) Books in Motion.
1916 Mexico is the setting when four drifters on the run from the law are captured by outcasts of Pancho Villa's army. The group's ingenious escape plan just might work.

Escape from the Carnivale. unabr. ed. Dave Barry & Ridley Pearson. 2 cass. (Running Time: 7200 sec.). (Never Land Ser.). (J). (gr. 4-7). 2006. 25.25 (978-1-4233-0949-9(9), 9781423309499, BrilAudUnabridg); audio compact disk 9.95 (978-1-4233-0950-5(2), 9781423309505, Bril Audio CD Unabri) Brilliance Audio.
Life on Mollusk Island has settled into a regular rhythm after all the excitement surrounding the arrival of Peter, Molly, and the pirates. But one day when Little Scallop and a few of her mermaid friends venture beyond the boundaries set by their parents, big trouble awaits them. Then the young mermaid Surf is grabbed by Crookshank's men and taken aboard his ship, the Carnivale. To her shock, Surf finds that he plans to make her part of his circus at sea - just another sideshow attraction. With quick thinking and her indomitable spirit, Little Scallop, Teacher, James, and Surf's twin Aqua devise a plan and rescue Surf in the nick of time. Designed for readers 7 to 10, Escape from the Carnivale takes us on a memorable journey filled with adventure, danger, and offers up a very satisfying conclusion.

Escape from the Carnivale. unabr. ed. Dave Barry & Ridley Pearson. Read by Jim Dale. 2 CDs. (Running Time: 7200 sec.). (Never Land Ser.). (J). (gr. 4-7). 2006. audio compact disk 25.25 (978-1-4233-0951-2(0), 9781423309512, BriAudCD Unabrid); audio compact disk 25.25 (978-1-4233-0953-6(7), 9781423309536, Brinc Audio MP3 Lib); audio compact disk 9.95 (978-1-4233-0952-9(9), 9781423309529, Brilliance MP3) Brilliance Audio.

Escape from the Carnivale. unabr. ed. Dave Barry & Ridley Pearson. Read by Jim Dale. (Running Time: 2 hrs.). (Never Land Ser.). 2006. 25.25 (978-1-4233-0955-0(3), 9781423309550, BADLE); 9.95 (978-1-4233-0954-3(5), 9781423309543, BAD) Brilliance Audio.

Escape from the Earth. Created by Saddleback Educational Publishing. 1 cass. (Running Time: 3907 sec.). (PageTurner Science Fiction Ser.). (J).

2002. audio compact disk 10.95 (978-1-56254-486-7(1), SP 4861) Saddleback Edu.
Word-for-word read-along of Escape From Earth.

Escape from the Tyranny of Our Own Thoughts. Instructed by Manly P. Hall. 8.95 (978-0-89314-106-6(2), C830911) Philos Res.

Escape from Vulture's Roost. Lavaille Lavette. Narrated by Tammi Reiss. 1 cass. (Running Time: 840 sec.). (Adventures of Roopster Roux Ser.). (ENG.). (J). (ps-3). 1998. 5.95 (978-1-56554-404-8(8)) Pelican.

Escape High Adventure. Perf. by William Conrad et al. 2008. audio compact disk 39.98 (978-1-57019-875-5(6)) Radio Spirits.

Escape, Illusion & Reality: Luke 16:25. Ed Young. 1980. 4.95 (978-0-7417-1129-8(X)) Win Walk.

Escape, No. 2. 1 cass. (Running Time: 60 min.). Incl. Follower. (MM-5145); Homicidal Maniac. (MM-5145); 7.95 (MM-5145) Natl Recrd Co.
In "The Homicidal Maniac" somewhere in the pitch black room is a homicidal maniac with a knife groping for his victim, trying to prevent escape. In "The Follower", Mark Litton discovers a dead man in his apartment & his wife missing.

Escape of Arsene Lupin see Extraordinary Adventures of Arsene Lupin

Escape of the Aliens. unabr. ed. Loren Robinson. Read by Gene Engene. 6 cass. (Running Time: 7 hrs.). Dramatization. 1990. 39.95 (978-1-55686-325-7(X), 325) Books in Motion.
Three peaceful aliens are stranded on earth. However they are pursued by both the U. S. & Russia. The U. S. military believes the downed craft to be of Russian design, & the Russians believe the craft to be an advanced U. S. fighter jet & both groups rush to find the missing pilots.

Escape of the Slinkys. unabr. ed. Nancy Tucker. 1 CD. (Running Time: 38 mins.). (J). (gr. 2-7). 2005. audio compact disk 14.95 (978-1-58467-026-1(6)) Gentle Wind.
Clever lyrics abound with goofy puns, zany word plays, and tongue twisters sure to delight the upper elementary ages. With inventive tunes and fabulous guitar work, Nancy shares her hilariously upside down perspective with sensitivity to values such as personal integrity and ecological awareness.

Escape Route. Peter F. Hamilton. Narrated by Jared Doreck. (Great Science Fiction Stories Ser.). 2007. audio compact disk 17.99 (978-1-884612-56-5(3)) AudioText.

Escape the Second Death. Jack Van Impe. 1 cass. 7.00 J Van Impe.
Sermons proving that holy living & love are proofs of salvation.

Escape to God. Jim Hohnberger. Ed. by Tim Canuteson & Julie Canuteson. 6 CDs. (Running Time: 9 hrs.). (ENG.). 2002. 39.95 (978-1-883012-00-7(7)) Remnant Pubns.
The principle of soul-surrender will inspire and challenge you to the very core of your being.

Escape to Sun City. unabr. ed. Cecile Bauer. Read by Rusty Nelson. 8 cass. (Running Time: 10 hrs. 6 min.). 2001. 49.95 (978-1-58116-081-9(X)) Books in Motion.
When a community bank buys the work contract of seven elderly school bus drivers and eliminates their pensions, the "Old Fogies Motorcycle Gang" decides to get even and embarks on the most hilarious holdup in bank history.

***Escape to Witch Mountain.** unabr. ed. Alexander Key. Read by Marc Thompson. (Running Time: 4 hrs.). 2010. 19.99 (978-1-4418-5877-1(6), 9781441858771, Brilliance MP3); 39.97 (978-1-4418-5878-8(4), 9781441858788, Brlnc Audio MP3 Lib); 39.97 (978-1-4418-5879-5(2), 9781441858795, BADLE); audio compact disk 19.99 (978-1-4418-5875-7(X), 9781441858757, Bril Audio CD Unabri); audio compact disk 59.97 (978-1-4418-5876-4(8), 9781441858764, BriAudCD Unabrid) Brilliance Audio.

Escape Tyranny: Volume 2, Vol. 2. Bhagat Singh Thind. Clark Walker. (Running Time: 60). (ENG.). 2003. audio compact disk 12.00 (978-1-932630-03-9(1)) Pub: Dr Bhagat Sin. Dist(s): Baker Taylor

Escape Tyranny: Volume 2, Vol. 2. Speeches. As told by Bhagat Singh Thind. (Running Time: 60 mins). (ENG., 2003. 6.50 (978-1-932630-26-8(0)) Pub: Dr Bhagat Sin. Dist(s): Baker Taylor

Escape with H. G. Wells. Created by Radio Spirits. (Running Time: 10800 sec.). 2004. audio compact disk 9.98 (978-1-57019-772-7(5)) Radio Spirits.

Escape 101: The Four Secrets to Taking a Career Break Without Losing Your Money or Your Mind. unabr. ed. Dan Clements & Tara Gignac. Read by Erik Synnestvedt. (Running Time: 5 hrs.). (ENG.). 2008. 24.98 (978-1-59659-258-2(3), GildAudio) Pub: Gildan Media. Dist(s): HachBkGrp

Escaping the Delta: Robert Johnson & the Invention of the Blues. Elijah Wald. 1 CD. 2005. pap. bk. 14.99 (978-0-06-052427-2(8), AmistadHarper) HarperCollins Pubs.

Escaping the Family Trap. unabr. ed. Jack Boland. Read by Jack Boland. 2 cass. (Running Time: 2 hrs.). 19.95 set. (978-0-88152-061-3(6), BA31) Master Mind.

Escaping the Giant Wave. unabr. ed. Kehret Peg. Narrated by Bregy Terry. 3 CDs. (Running Time: 2 hrs. 45 mins.). (YA). (gr. 5-8). 2009. audio compact disk 39.95 (978-0-9814890-5-6(2)) Audio Bkshelf.

Escaping the Prision of the Intellect see Como Escapar de la Prision del Intelecto

Escaping the Prison of the Intellect: A Journey from Here to Here. unabr. ed. Deepak Chopra. 1 CD. (Running Time: 172800 sec.). (Chopra, Deepak Ser.). (ENG.). 2006. audio compact disk 12.95 (978-1-878424-56-3(4)) Amber-Allen Pub.
This recording shows why Deepak Chopra is considered one of the great pioneers in the field of mind-body medicine. Here he offers compelling answers to the eternal questions of identity, origin, and meaning. Chopra's thesis is that people rely on their senses to define their experience of reality - limiting their experience of the material world and making them prisoners, out of touch with realities that lie beyond the material. He explains that there is no difference between observer and observed; it is all one shared experience. Realizing this truth, says Chopra, frees people from their sensory-created prison to experience a more nurturing and fulfilling life. The author's calm, uplifting voice gives these ideas heft and power, and his inclusion of relaxed guitar interludes let listeners pause to contemplate more deeply. Chopra expands the discussion by citing T. S. Eliot, Nietzsche, Rumi, Tagore, and Patanjali, as well as scientific experiments and spiritual texts.

***Escaping the Trap: The US Army X Corps in Northeast Korea 1950.** unabr. ed. Roy E. Appleman. Narrated by Kevin Foley. (Running Time: 16 hrs. 30 mins. 0 sec.). 2010. 29.99 (978-1-4001-6935-1(6)); 21.99 (978-1-4001-8935-9(7)); audio compact disk 39.99 (978-1-4001-1935-6(9)) Pub: Tantor Media. Dist(s): IngramPubServ

***Escaping the Trap (Library Edition) The US Army X Corps in Northeast Korea 1950.** unabr. ed. Roy E. Appleman. Narrated by Kevin Foley. (Running Time: 16 hrs. 30 mins.). 2010. 39.99 (978-1-4001-9935-8(2)); audio compact disk 95.99 (978-1-4001-4935-3(5)) Pub: Tantor Media. Dist(s): IngramPubServ

***Escenarios Cotidianos en Nuestra Comunidad Cd.** rev. ed. Kennedy-Messer. (ENG.). 2010. audio compact disk 54.58 (978-0-7575-5529-9(2)) Kendall-Hunt.

Eschatology. Neville Goddard. 1 cass. (Running Time: 62 min.). 1969. 8.00 (3) J & L Pubns.
Neville taught Imagination Creates Reality. He was a powerfully influential teacher of God as Consciousness.

Escher Twist: A Homer Kelly Mystery. unabr. ed. Jane Langton. Read by Michael Prichard. 5 cass. (Running Time: 7 hrs. 30 mins.). 2002. 40.00 (978-0-7366-8553-5(7)) Books on Tape.
Homer Kelly is back - a distinguished Thoreau scholar, and also an ex-detective for Middlesex County. This time, he must probe into the mysteries city of Cambridge, Massachusetts. His friend Leonard is fascinated by the drawings of M.C. Escher, mathematical drawings as complex as multifarious Cambridge. Leonard attends an Escher exhibition in Cambridge, and is enthralled by the drawings of a mysterious female Escher fan in a green coat who will not give Leonard anything but her first name: Frieda. Leonard wants to find her again, and engages Homer to do so. But Homer finds that the case takes on an Escher-like complexity of its own, with past murders and present secrets interlocking.

Esclava Isaura. Scripts. Based on a novel by Bernardo Guimaraes. Adapted by Ligia Lesama. 3 CDs. (Running Time: 2 hrs 40 Min). Dramatization. (SPA.). 2003. audio compact disk 16.95 (978-0-9728598-1-3(0)) Fonolibro Inc.
Isaura the Slave, Audio book dramatized in Spanish based on the famous story wrote during the abolitionist campaign of 1875 by the Brazilian Bernardo Guimaraes. It is the story of a beautiful and educated white slave, Isaura (Performed by Mayra Alejandra Rodriguez), daughter of a mestiza that passed through terrible times because she didnot give herself to the sordid desires of the owner of thehouse, Mr. Almeida. Isaura was brought up and educated by his wife, a kind woman that in addition to desire the freedom of the beautiful slave, taught her to read, to write and to play the piano. Isaura?s freedom dreams were truncated by Leoncio (Mr. Almeida?s son), who, after his marriage, assumed the management of the house. Leoncio became obsessed with the slave, and hurt by her denial made her life miserable. Isaura escaped with the help of her father to another city, where she assumed the name of Elvira and met Alvaro (Performed by Raul Amundaray), a handsome young noble man, who fell in love with Elvira. The story takes intensity when Isaura?s identity is revealed and found by Leoncio. (3 CDs - 2 Horas 40 Minutos).

Escritos y Proclamas. unabr. ed. Simon Bolivar. Read by Pedro Montoya. 3 CDs.Tr. of Writngs & Speeches. (SPA.). 2001. audio compact disk 17.00 (978-958-9494-19-6(6)) YoYoMusic.

Escuela de Sanidad Por Gloria Copeland. Gloria Copeland. Tr. by Kenneth Copeland Publications Staff from ENG. 6 cass. (SPA.). 1987. 30.00 Set. (978-0-88114-643-1(9)) K Copeland Pubns.
Indepth study of biblical healing.

***Escuela para Padres: Como Desarrollar la Autoestima en los Adolescentes.** Germain Duclos et al. (SPA.). 2010. audio compact disk 15.99 (978-607-457-045-8(0)) Lectorum MEX.

ESEA Implementation Guide. Julie A. Miller & Lois Berkowitz. Contrib. by American Association of School Administrators Staff. 2002. pap. bk. 299.00 (978-0-8108-4566-4(0)) Pub: Scarecrow. Dist(s): Rowman

Esencia de la Aromaterapia. Dona Carolina da Silva. Narrated by Monica Steuer. 3 cass. (Running Time: 4 hrs. 30 mins.). 28.00 (978-0-7887-9972-3(X)) Recorded Bks.

Esha Eatright Analysis 2003 Update, Version 2.0. Esha. (C). 2002. audio compact disk 44.95 (978-0-7637-2535-8(8), 0763725358) Jones Bartlett.

***Esio Trot & the Minpins.** abr. ed. Roald Dahl. Read by Joanna Lumley. (ENG.). 2005. (978-0-06-088647-9(1)); (978-0-06-088648-6(X)) HarperCollins Pubs.

Eskimo Stories: Tales of Magic. E. Kiethan. Perf. by Diane Wolkstein. (Running Time: 35 min.). (J). (gr. 1-12). 10.00 (978-1-879846-02-9(0)) Cloudstone NY.
Includes: A Brother & a Sister, A Tale of Two Old Women, & The Man Who Became a Caribou. Shamanic folklore of Eskimo tribal groups.

Eskimos. unabr. ed. Ed. by Linda Spizzirri. 48 cass. (Running Time: 15 min.). Dramatization. (Educational Coloring Book & Cassette Package Ser.). (J). (gr. k-8). 1989. pap. bk. 6.95 (978-0-86545-153-7(2)) Spizzirri.
Presents information on dwellers of the cold artic region.

Eskimos: Far & Forgotten. 1 cass. (Running Time: 30 min.). 8.00 (B0100B090, HarperThor) HarpC GBR.

ESL for Japanese Speakers, Set. 1997th ed. Paul Pimsleur. 16 cass. (Pimsleur Language Learning Ser.). 1997. pap. bk. & stu. ed. 345.00 (0671-57916-9) SyberVision.

ESL for Mandarin Speakers, Set. Paul Pimsleur. 16 cass. (Pimsleur Language Learning Ser.). 1996. pap. bk. & stu. ed. 345.00 (0671-57914-2) SyberVision.

ESL for Spanish Speakers, Set. Paul Pimsleur. 16 cass. (Pimsleur Language Learning Ser.). 1991. pap. bk. & stu. ed. 345.00 (0671-57918-5) SyberVision.

ESL Ingles en Tres Meses, Vol. 2. unabr. ed. 16 cass. (Running Time: 16 hrs.). 215.00 (E320); J Norton Pubs.

ESL Ingles en Tres Meses, Vol. 3. unabr. ed. 16 cass. (Running Time: 16 hrs.). 215.00 (E340); J Norton Pubs.

ESL Ingles para Emergencias. unabr. ed. 1 cass. 19.95 (E360); J Norton Pubs.
A brief, practical course in Spanish & English for the Spanish-speaker living in an American city.

ESL Japanese Lessons 31 to 90 Prepack 2. Pimsleur Staff. 2006. 400.00 (978-0-7435-5282-0(2), Pimsleur) Pub: S&S Audio. Dist(s): S and S Inc

ESL Level B. M. Walker. 3 cass. per set. (Running Time: 11 hrs. 31 mins.). (Addison Wesley ESL Ser.). (J). (gr. 1-6). 1991. 67.84 EA. SET. (978-0-201-19394-7(9)) Longman.
Fingerplays, songs, poems, stories & comprehension exercises that go with the AW ESL program.

ESL, One Potato. unabr. ed. British Broadcasting Corporation Staff. 1 cass. (J). 1992. pap. bk. 19.95 (978-0-88432-763-9(9), 504070) J Norton Pubs.
ESL program for children including 34-page book.

ESL Teaching Techniques, Practical. unabr. ed. 4 cass. 39.50 (S07012) J Norton Pubs.
Presents background information & recommended techniques for teaching seven fundamental ESL skills. Most of the suggested techniques are readily adapted to ESL education from the primary grades through adult education classes & to vocationally oriented programs in which ESL education is included.

Esophagus, Benign & Malignant Disease. 3 cass. (Thoracic Surgery Ser.: C85-TH3). 1985. 22.50 (8587) Am Coll Surgeons.

Esoteric Alchemy: Transmutation of Attitudes. Instructed by Manly P. Hall. 8.95 (978-0-89314-107-3(0), C840708) Philos Res.

Esoteric Anthropology. Manly P. Hall. 5 cass. (Running Time: 150 min.). 1999. 40.00 Set. (978-0-89314-108-0(9)) Philos Res.
Includes: "The Beginning of Human Life;" "The Rise of Mankind in Nature;" "The Origin of Race & Languages;" "Ensouling of Humanity;" & "The Future of the Human Race".

Esoteric Astrology. Gayle Garrison. 1 cass. 1992. 8.95 (1033) Am Fed Astrologers.

Esoteric Astrology. Paul Grell. 1 cass. 8.95 (669) Am Fed Astrologers.

Esoteric History of Western Spirituality. Interview. Tim Wallace-Murphy & Marilyn Hopkins. Created by Tim Wallace-Murphy & Marilyn Hopkins. Created by Laura Lee. Interview with Laura Lee. Prod. by Paul Robear. Contrib. by Scott Sanders. 2 cass. (Running Time: 2 hrs.). 2001. 19.95 (978-1-889071-20-6(X), 6315) Radio Bookstore.
British researchers Tim Wallace-Murphy and Marilyn Hopkins join host Laura Lee for a lively discussion examining the spiritual quest in Western culture. What perennial wisdom comes through all spiritual traditions? What are the roots of Christianity? What earlier religions contributed to its development? How did the Esoteric Teachings survive centuries of suppression? What can we learn from examining this long and often hidden history? What impact might this examination have on our own personal quest today?Tape 1Tim Wallace-Murphy and Marilyn Hopkins recount the common threads of all spiritual teachings, and a newly connected chronology of the West?s spiritual history, tracing the contributions of Megalithic cultures, fertility cults celebrating the death/rebirth cycle of Nature, and Egyptian cosmology. They continue with Judaic history and custom, new insights on the life of Jesus, and Rome?s restructuring of Early Christianity. Tape 2Here we examine the influence of the hidden streams of spirituality on Western culture: The cathedral building spurred by ancient construction secrets. The use of what we regard today as light, color and sound therapy for physiological transformation to support higher states of consciousness. The clues that specific temples were designed as a sequential Pilgrimage Initiation in Europe and in Egypt. The influence of the Order of Knights Templar on business and banking that led to opportunities for trade, travel, reading and the flowering of the Renaissance. The push and pull through the ages of freedom and oppression. The opportunities today for spiritual advancement.

***Esoteric Path to a New Life.** (ENG.). 2010. 19.95 (978-1-934162-49-1(3)) New Life.

Esoteric Path to a New Life (Tape Album) 2000. 19.95 (978-0-911203-53-0(2)) New Life.

Esoteric Philosophy of H. P. Blavatsky. Instructed by Manly P. Hall. 5 cass. 8.50 ea. o.p. Pt. 1: Source of the Secret Doctrine. (800162-A) Philos Res.

Esoteric Realm: Elusive Aspect of the Self. Kenneth James. 1 cass. (Running Time: 1 hr. 35 min.). (Language & Life of Symbols Ser.). 1995. 10.95 (978-0-7822-0494-0(5), 570) C G Jung IL.

Espagnol des Affaires. 1 cass. (Running Time: 1 hr., 30 min.). (FRE & SPA.). 2000. bk. 75.00 (978-2-7005-1369-1(X)) Pub: Assimil FRA. Dist(s): Distribks Inc

Espana a Tu Alcance: Spanish Skills for Intermediate Students. Michael Truman & Concha Perez Valle. 2004. 20.95 (978-0-415-16374-3(9)) Pub: Routledge. Dist(s): Taylor and Fran

Espana Viva. Derek Utley. (Running Time: 3 hrs. 0 mins. 0 sec.). (ENG.). 2003. (978-0-563-47268-1(5)) BBC WrldWd GBR.

Español a lo Vivo. 7th ed. Ernest J. Wilkins & Jerry W. Larson. (SPA & ENG.). (C). 1990. 506.95 (978-0-471-51878-5(6), JWiley) Wiley US.

***Español Activo Libro 1 - CD De Áudio.** (SPA.). 2005. audio compact disk (978-0-7428-1704-3(0)) CCLS Pubg Hse.

***Español Activo Libro 2 - CD De Áudio.** (SPA.). 2005. audio compact disk (978-0-7428-1705-0(9)) CCLS Pubg Hse.

***Español Activo Libro 3 - CD De Áudio.** 2005. audio compact disk (978-0-7428-1712-8(1)) CCLS Pubg Hse.

***Español Activo Libro 4 - CD De Áudio.** (SPA.). 2005. audio compact disk (978-0-7428-1713-5(X)) CCLS Pubg Hse.

Español Activo Libros 1 y 2 CD: Spanish Language Teaching. (SPA.). 2005. audio compact disk (978-0-7428-1512-4(9)) CCLS Pubg Hse.

Español Activo Libros 3 y 4 CD: Spanish Language Teaching. (SPA.). 2005. audio compact disk (978-0-7428-1513-1(7)) CCLS Pubg Hse.

Espanol Alegre. 3rd ed. Lonnie D. Zovi. (SPA.). (J). 1992. pap. bk. 15.95 (978-0-935301-74-8(7)) Vibrante Pr.

Espanol Analitico Hecho Mas Facil see Analytical Spanish Made Easier

Español Completo Libro 1 CD: Spanish Language Teaching. (SPA.). 2005. audio compact disk (978-0-7428-1534-6(X)) CCLS Pubg Hse.

Español Completo Libro 2 CD: Spanish Language Teaching. (SPA.). 2005. audio compact disk (978-0-7428-1535-3(8)) CCLS Pubg Hse.

Español Completo Libro 3 CD: Spanish Language Teaching. (SPA.). 2005. audio compact disk (978-0-7428-1536-0(6)) CCLS Pubg Hse.

Espanol de los Negocios. J. S. Artes et al. 1 cass. (Running Time: 1 hr.). (SPA.). 2001. 27.95 Pub: Sociedad General ESP. Dist(s): Continental Bk
This business course was designed for the adolescent & adult student that is geared to reinforce the communicative skills & terminology needed in the business world.

Español del Río de la Plata Audio CD: Spanish Language Teaching. Waldyr Lima. (SPA.). 2007. audio compact disk (978-0-7428-1675-6(3)) CCLS Pubg Hse.

Español del Río de la Plata Libro del Alumno (con CD de Audio) Spanish Language Teaching. Waldyr Lima. (SPA., 2007. pap. bk. & stu. ed. (978-0-7428-1708-1(3)) CCLS Pubg Hse.

Espanol en Directo: Dialogos. Equipo de Expertos 2100 Staff. 1 cass. (Running Time: 1 hr. 30 mins.). (SPA.). (978-84-7143-636-8(1)) Sociedad General ESP.

Espanol en Directo: Dialogos. Aquilino Sanchez Perez. 2 vols. (Running Time: 3 hrs.). (SPA.). (978-84-7143-635-1(3)) Sociedad General ESP.

Espanol en Directo: Ejercicios Estructurales. Aquilino Sanchez. 3 vols. (Running Time: 4 hrs. 30 mins.). (SPA.). (978-84-7143-637-5(X)) Sociedad General ESP.

Espanol Escrito, Curso para Hispanohablantes Bilingues: Dictation Cassette. 5th ed. Guadalupe Valdés & Richard V. Teschner. (SPA.). 6.97 (978-0-13-049500-6(X)) PH School.

***Español Internacional - Libro 4 - Más Práctica Oral CD ROM.** (ENG.). 2008. audio compact disk (978-0-7428-0039-7(3)) CCLS Pubg Hse.

***Español Internacional Libro 3 CALL CD ROM: Spanish Language Teaching.** Waldyr Lima. (SPA.). 2008. audio compact disk (978-0-7428-0027-4(X)) CCLS Pubg Hse.

***Español Internacional Libro 5 Prueba de Comprensión Auditiva Audio CD: Spanish Language Teaching.** Waldyr Lima. (SPA.). 2009. audio compact disk (978-0-7428-1742-5(3)) CCLS Pubg Hse.

Español Internacional Libros 1 y 2 Prueba de Comprensión Auditiva Audio CD: Spanish Language Teaching. Waldyr Lima. (SPA.). 2007. audio compact disk (978-0-7428-1679-4(6)) CCLS Pubg Hse.

Español Internacional Libros 3 y 4 Prueba de Comprensión Auditiva Audio CD: Spanish language Teaching. Waldyr Lima. (SPA.). 2009. audio compact disk (978-0-7428-0108-0(X)) CCLS Pubg Hse.

Espanol para el Bilingue. Marie E. Barkes. 5 cass. (Running Time: 1 hr.). 2001. 99.95 (978-0-8442-7202-3(7)) Glencoe.
Designed for native Spanish speakers who want to develop universal Spanish skills.

Espanol para Principiantes. abr. ed. Sara Jordan. Composed by Sara Jordan. 1 CD. (Running Time: 30 min.). (Songs that Teach Spanish Ser.). (SPA.). (J). (gr. 4-7). 1993. audio compact disk 13.95 (978-1-894262-11-8(5), JMP S05CD) Pub: S Jordan Publ. Dist(s): CrabtreePubCo

Espanol para Principiantes: Canciones y Juegos. Sara Jordan. Prod. by Sara Jordan. Tr. by Ramiro Puerto. Illus. by Hector Obando. Engineer Mark Shannon. 1 cass. (Running Time: 44 min. 50 secs.). (SPA.). (J). 1993. 14.95 (978-1-895523-35-5(4), JMP S05K) Jordan Music.
Great for beginners. Learn the alphabet, farm animals, counting, family members, parts of the body, days of the week, colors, fruit, opposites and shapes in Spanish. Packaged with an activity/lyrics book.

Español para Todos Libro 1 Audio para Todos CD: Spanish Language Teaching. 2005. audio compact disk (978-1-929310-92-0(7)) ALL Pubng House.

Español para Todos Libro 2 Audio para Todos CD: Spanish Language Teaching. 2005. audio compact disk (978-1-929310-93-7(5)) ALL Pubng House.

Español para Todos Libro 3 Audio para Todos CD: Spanish Language Teaching. 2005. audio compact disk (978-1-929310-94-4(3)) ALL Pubng House.

Español para Todos Libro 4 Audio para Todos CD: Spanish Language Teaching. 2005. audio compact disk (978-1-929310-95-1(1)) ALL Pubng House.

Español para Todos Libro 5 Audio para Todos CD: Spanish Language Teaching. 2005. audio compact disk (978-1-929310-96-8(X)) ALL Pubng House.

Español para Todos Libro 6 Audio para Todos CD: Spanish Language Teaching. 2005. audio compact disk (978-1-929310-97-5(8)) ALL Pubng House.

Espanol Sin Fronteras: Level 1. J. Sánchez Lobato et al. 2 cass. (Running Time: 3 hrs.). (SPA, ENG & JPN., 2001. 44.95 (978-84-7143-608-5(6), SGS6086E) Pub: Sociedad General ESP. Dist(s): Continental Bk
A fast and effective progression will allow students to master spoken and written Spanish upon completion of the three levels. Each lesson contains situations and short dialogues, grammar, exercises, vocabulary and culture.

Espanol Sin Fronteras: Level 3. J. Sánchez Lobato et al. 1 cass. (Running Time: 1 hr. 30 min.). (SPA, ENG & JPN.). 2001. 26.95 (978-84-7143-771-6(6), SGS7716E) Pub: Sociedad General ESP. Dist(s): Continental Bk

Espanol Sin Fronteras: Level 3. J. Sánchez Lobato et al. 1 cass. (Running Time: 1 hr. 30 min.). (SPA, ENG & JPN., 2001. wbk. ed. 26.95 (978-84-7143-786-0(4), SGS7864) Pub: Sociedad General ESP. Dist(s): Continental Bk

Espanol 2000: Nivel Elemental (Alumno) Nieves Garcia Hernandez & Jesús Sánchez Lobato. 1 cass. (Running Time: 1 hr. 30 mins.). (SPA & ENG.). 2000. (978-84-7143-619-1(1)) Sociedad General ESP.

Espanol 2000: Nivel Elemental (Ejercicios) Nieves Garcia Hernandez & Jesús Sánchez Lobato. 2 vols. (Running Time: 3 hrs.). (SPA & ENG.). 2000. (978-84-7143-620-7(5)) Sociedad General ESP.

Espanol 2000: Nivel Medio (Alumno) Nieves Garcia Hernandez & Jesús Sánchez Lobato. 2 vols. (Running Time: 3 hrs.). (SPA & ENG., 2000. (978-84-7143-621-4(3)) Sociedad General ESP.

Espanol 2000: Nivel Medio (Ejercicios) Nieves Garcia Hernandez & Jesús Sánchez Lobato. 2 vols. (Running Time: 3 hrs.). (SPA & ENG.). 2000. (978-84-7143-622-1(1)) Sociedad General ESP.

Espanola Inglesa. Cervantes. audio compact disk 12.95 (978-0-8219-3749-5(9)) EMC-Paradigm.

Espanola Inglesa. Miguel de Cervantes Saavedra. (SPA.). pap. bk. 20.95 (978-88-7754-898-6(3)) Pub: Cideb ITA. Dist(s): Distribks Inc

Especially for Children: Classic Moments from the Bill Gaither Trio. Perf. by Bill Gaither Trio, The. 1 CD. 1999. audio compact disk (978-0-7601-3163-3(5)) Brentwood Music.
Original performances includes: "I Am a Promise," "Jesus Loves Me," & "This Little Light of Mine.".

Especially for Helping Professionals: Understanding Parents' Feelings & Emotional Stresses. John F. Taylor. 1 cass. (Running Time: 49 min.). (Answers to ADD Ser.). 1993. 9.95 (978-1-883963-10-1(9)) ADD Plus.
Lecture tape.

Especially for Missionaries, Vol. 1. Ed Pinegar. 1 cass. 4.98 (978-1-55503-345-3(8), 06004326) Covenant Comms.
The Book of Mormon as a key to conversion.

Especially for Missionaries, Vol. 2. Ed Pinegar. 1 cass. 4.98 (978-1-55503-346-0(6), 06004334) Covenant Comms.
Communication with God, companions & investigators.

Especially for Missionaries, Vol. 3. Ed Pinegar. 1 cass. 4.98 (978-1-55503-347-7(4), 06004342) Covenant Comms.
Teaching by the Spirit with the power of God.

Especially for Missionaries, Vol. 4. Ed Pinegar. 1 cass. 4.98 (978-1-55503-348-4(2), 06004350) Covenant Comms.
Your capacity & potential as a missionary.

Especially for Missionaries, Vol. 5. Ed Pinegar. 1 cass. 4.98 (978-1-55503-349-1(0), 06004369) Covenant Comms.
A gospel overview. Talks on 12 basic doctrines.

Especially for Missionaries, Vol. 6. Ed Pinegar. 1 cass. 2004. 4.98 (978-1-55503-375-0(X), 06004377) Covenant Comms.
The power of faith & unconditional love.

Especially for Missionaries, Vols. 1 & 2. Ed Pinegar. 1 CD. audio compact disk 10.98 (978-1-55503-963-9(4), 2500698) Covenant Comms.
Two of the best talks given to missionaries.

Especially for Mothers. 6 cass. 15.98 Set. (978-1-55503-802-1(6), 344554) Covenant Comms.
A collection of great talks by Covenant's finest.

Especially for Parents. 6 cass. 15.95 Set. (978-1-55503-672-0(4), 3444414) Covenant Comms.
Talks for successful parenting.

Especially for Teachers: Motivating the ADD-ADHD Student. John F. Taylor. 1 cass. (Running Time: 34 min.). (Answers to ADD Ser.). 1993. 9.95 (978-1-883963-11-8(7)) ADD Plus.
Lecture tape.

Especially for Teachers: Understanding the ADD-ADHD Student. John F. Taylor. 1 cass. (Running Time: 44 min.). (Answers to ADD Ser.). 1993. 9.95 (978-1-883963-03-3(6)) ADD Plus.

Especially for Teens: Shortcuts to School Success. John F. Taylor. 1 cass. (Running Time: 68 min.). (Answers to ADD Ser.). 1993. 9.95 (978-1-883963-01-9(X)) ADD Plus.

Especially for Young Children. Eldon Taylor. 1 CD. (Running Time: 52 min.). (Whole Brain Innertalk Ser.). 1998. audio compact disk (978-1-55978-872-4(0)) Progress Aware Res.

Especially for Young Children. Eldon Taylor. 1 CD. (Running Time: 52 min.). (Whole Brain Innertalk Ser.). 1999. audio compact disk (978-1-55978-945-5(X)) Progress Aware Res.

Esperanto. Perf. by Shadowfax. 1 cass. (Running Time: 46 min.). 1992. 9.98 (978-1-877737-25-1(9), EB2518/WB4-42523) MFLP CA.
A unique blend of jazz, new age contemporary & world music. Mixing rhythms & sounds of many different cultures.

Esperanto: Jen Nia Mondo, Pt. B, Lessons 13-25. J. C. Wells. 1 cass., bklet. (Running Time: 34 mins.). (ESP & ENG.). (YA). (gr. 10-12). 2001. pap. bk. 24.95 (AFES30) J Norton Pubs.

Esperanto Part A Course: Jen Nia Mondo, Vol. 1012. J. C. Wells. (ESP.). 1992. pap. bk. 29.00 (978-0-88432-997-8(6), AFES10) J Norton Pubs.
Consists of 25 lessons made up of dialogs, vocabulary, grammar & exercises. Esperanto is an easy language to learn. Each one of its 28 alphabet letters has only one sound; grammar is streamlined because there are only 16 basic rules without exceptions or irregularities & every word is pronounced as it is spelled.

Esperanto sans Peine. 1 cass. (Running Time: 1 hr., 30 min.). (ESP & FRE.). 2000. bk. 75.00 (978-2-7005-1341-7(X)) Pub: Assimil FRA. Dist(s): Distribks Inc

Esperanza: A Gift of Spanish Song. Glori Dei Cantores. 2005. audio compact disk 16.95 (978-1-55725-367-5(6), GDCD037) Paraclete MA.

Esperanza en Tiempos de Afflicion. 2003. audio compact disk 48.00 (978-1-57972-549-5(X)) Insight Living.

***esperanza que necesitas, audio CD: En el Padre Nuestro.** Zondervan. (SPA.). 2010. audio compact disk 19.99 (978-0-8297-5267-0(6)) Pub: Vida Pubs. Dist(s): Zondervan

***esperanza que necesitas, audio Download: From the Lord's Prayer.** unabr. ed. Zondervan. (ENG.). 2010. 18.99 (978-0-8297-5268-7(4)) Pub: Vida Pubs. Dist(s): Zondervan

Esperanza Rising. Pam Muñoz Ryan. Read by Trini Alvarado. 4 CDs. (Running Time: 4 hrs. 42 mins.). (J). (gr. 4-7). 2004. audio compact disk 35.00 (978-0-8072-1769-6(7), Listening Lib) Random Audio Pubg.

Esperanza Rising. unabr. ed. Pam Muñoz Ryan. Read by Trini Alvarado. 3 vols. (Running Time: 4 hrs. 42 mins.). (Middle Grade Cassette Librariestm Ser.). (J). (gr. 4-7). 2004. pap. bk. 36.00 (978-0-8072-1726-9(3), S YA 281 SP, Listening Lib); 30.00 (978-0-8072-8862-7(4), Listening Lib) Random Audio Pubg.
When Esperanza & Mama are forced to flee to the bountiful region of Aguascalientes, Mexico, to a Mexican farm labor camp in California, they must adjust to a life without fancy dresses & servants they were accustomed to on Rancho de las Rosas. Now they must confront the challenges of hard work, acceptance by their own people & economic difficulties brought on by the Great Depression. When Mama falls ill & a strike for better working conditions threatens to uproot their new life, Esperanza must relinquish her hold on the past learn to embrace a future ripe with the riches of family & community.

Esperanza Rising. unabr. ed. Pam Muñoz Ryan. Read by Trini Alvarado. (Running Time: 4 hrs. 42 mins.). (ENG.). (J). (gr. 3-7). 2007. audio compact disk 25.00 (978-0-7393-3896-4(X), Listening Lib) Pub: Random Audio Pubg. Dist(s): Random

Espiritu de Martirio: Sin Miedo Amor. David Witt & Mujahid El Masih. Narrated by Bill Witt. 2008. audio compact disk 14.99 (978-1-930034-60-0(1)) Casscomm.

Espiritu Santo y Fuego. unabr. ed. Marco Barriento. (SPA.). 1999. 7.99 (978-0-8297-2501-8(6)) Pub: Vida Pubs. Dist(s): Zondervan

Espoir Pour L'Afrique see Hope for Africa: High Hope for Africa

Espoir Pour L'Afrique see Hope for Africa (French): High Hope for Africa

Espresso Tales. Narrated by Alexander McCall Smith. (Running Time: 54000 sec.). (44 Scotland Street Ser.: Bk. 2). 2006. 29.99 (978-1-4193-9615-1(3)) Recorded Bks.

Espresso Tales. unabr. ed. Alexander McCall Smith. Read by Robert Ian MacKenzie. 12 cass. (Running Time: 15 hrs.). (44 Scotland Street Ser.: Bk. 2). 2006. 89.75 (978-1-4281-0285-9(X)); audio compact disk 119.75 (978-1-4281-0287-3(6)) Recorded Bks.

Espresso Tales. unabr. ed. Alexander McCall Smith. 12 CDs. (Running Time: 54000 sec.). (44 Scotland Street Ser.: Bk. 2). 2006. audio compact disk 34.99 (978-1-4193-9614-4(5), C3779) Recorded Bks.
New York Times best-selling author Alexander McCall Smith, creator of the beloved No. 1 Ladies' Detective Agency novels, crafts the second irresistible installment in his Scotland Street series. Espresso Tales follows the charming and immensely popular 44 Scotland Street, as all the favorite residents of that Edinburgh address return.

Esprit '90. Ed. by Information Industries and Innovation, Directorate-G. 1990. audio compact disk 309.00 (978-0-7923-1039-6(X)) Spri.

Essay of Dramatic Poesy see Cambridge Treasy Burton

Essay Writing Super Seminar, 2nd ed. Ira Shafiroff. 4 cass. (Running Time: 6 hrs.). (Audio Tape Ser.). 1998. pap. bk. & wbk. ed. 50.00 (978-1-57793-035-8(5), 28417) Pub: Sum & Substance. Dist(s): West Pub

Essays. (20) Halvorson Assocs.

Essays. abr. ed. Francis Bacon. Read by Robert L. Halvorson. 4 cass. (Running Time: 360 min.). 28.95 (58) Halvorson Assocs.

Essays. unabr. ed. Wallace Shawn. Read by Wallace Shawn. 4 CDs. (Running Time: 5 hrs.). 2009. audio compact disk 36.00 (978-1-60846-004-5(5)) Pub: Haymarket Bks. Dist(s): Consort Bk Sales

Essays: Second Series (1844), Set. unabr. ed. Ralph Waldo Emerson. Read by Robert L. Halvorson. 5 cass. 35.95 (8) Halvorson Assocs.

Essays Set: First Series (1841), unabr. ed. Ralph Waldo Emerson. Read by Robert L. Halvorson. 7 cass. (Running Time: 10 hr. 30 min.). 49.95 (7) Halvorson Assocs.

Essays & Criticisms, Set. abr. ed. Robert Louis Stevenson. Read by Robert L. Halvorson. 2 cass. (Running Time: 180 min.). 14.95 (81) Halvorson Assocs.

Essays for the Ear: Youth's the Tune, Age the Song. (Running Time: 30 min.). 1989. 11.95 ea. (C070AB090, HarperThor); 47.00 Set. (C070BB090, HarperThor) HarpC GBR.

Essays in Criticism see Cambridge Treasury of English Prose: Dickens to Butler

Essays, of Counsel Civil & Moral see Cambridge Treasy Malory

Essays on Education, Set. unabr. ed. Herbert Spencer. Read by Robert L. Halvorson. 4 cass. (Running Time: 360 min.). 28.95 (38) Halvorson Assocs.

Essays on Education & Self-Reliance. unabr. ed. Ralph Waldo Emerson. Perf. by Archibald Macleish. 1 cass. 1972. 12.95 (978-0-694-50228-8(6), SWC 1358) HarperCollins Pubs.

Essays or Counsels Civil & Moral. unabr. ed. Francis Bacon. Read by Bernard Mayes. 4 cass. (Running Time: 6 hrs.). 1999. 32.95 (1208) Blckstn Audio.
Bacon's education was grounded in the classical texts of ancient Greece & Rome, but his writings bring clarity & color to the dry scholasticism of medieval learning. Among his lofty subjects are truth, death, nobility, travel, marriage, health, riches, beauty, negotiating, ambition & gardens.

Essays Out Loud: On Having Adventures & a Necessary End. Nancy Mairs. (ENG.). 2009. audio compact disk 14.00 (978-1-888553-17-8(0)) Pub: Kore Pr. Dist(s): Chicago Distribution Ctr

Esselen Indians. unabr. ed. Loretta Wyer et al. 1 cass. 1997. 11.00 (32008) Big Sur Tapes.
Wyer is the current Chairwoman of the Esselen Indian Tribe of Big Sur, California, a tribe considered officially extinct since the 1800s. With the help of anthropoligist Levinthal, the Esselen Indians are coming out of secrecy & seeking their rightful status as an intact tribe.

Essence. Perf. by Don Campbell. 1 cass. (Running Time: 57 min.). 1998. (978-1-891319-10-5(8)); audio compact disk (978-1-891319-09-9(4)) Spring Hill CO.

Essence, Octave & Consciousness. Guy Spiro. 1 cass. 8.95 (260) Am Fed Astrologers.
Basic hands-on esoteric Astrology.

Essence of Being in Balance: Creating Habits to Match Your Desires. Wayne W. Dyer. 6 CDs. 2006. audio compact disk 39.95 (978-1-4019-1069-3(6)) Hay House.

Essence of Compassion. unabr. ed. Osho Oshos. Read by Osho Oshos. 1 cass. (Running Time: 1 hr. 20 min.). 1993. 10.95 (DQL-062088B) Oshos.
Osho speaks about the essential qualities of compassion & the challenge this presents the modern seeker.

***Essence of Happiness: A Guidebook for Living.** unabr. ed. Dalai Lama XIV & Howard C. Cutler. (Running Time: 1 hr. 0 mins. 0 sec.). (ENG.). 2010. audio compact disk 14.99 (978-1-4423-4080-0(0)) Pub: S&S Audio. Dist(s): S and S Inc

Essence of Intuition. unabr. ed. Charles Faulkner. 2 cass. (Running Time: 2 hrs. 20 mins.). 1998. 29.95 N L P Comp.
Learn to actually listen to your intuition, use emotions to encourage rather than block intuition & know how to sort out false intuitions from real ones.

Essence of Nature Series. unabr. ed. Gail Taylor. Read by Gail Taylor. Ed. by James B. Kirgan. 15 cass. (Running Time: 22 hrs. 30 min.). (J). (gr. 9). 1989. 149.99 set, stereo. (978-1-878362-00-1(3)) Emerald Ent.
This is a series of fifteen children's stories about Thumper, the adventure dog. Thumper leaves the pack of Samoyed sled dogs in Alaska to begin his adventures. These tapes include the actual sounds from designated areas in the United States & Canada.

Essence of Stonehenge Pt. 1: Part I: the Significant Principles. unabr. ed. Dianthus. 1 cass. (Running Time: 1 hr. 13 min.). (ENG.). 1996. 11.00 (978-1-890372-04-0(8)) Dianthus.
Addresses why Stonehenge, a prehistoric monument, was built; what it represents, & what it teaches.

Essence of Stonehenge Pt. II: Part 2: the Future of Mankind. Dianthus. 1 cass. (Running Time: 1 hr. 17 min.). (ENG.). 1996. 11.00 (978-1-890372-05-7(6)) Dianthus.
Presents mankind's future in four analogies. Also discusses the benefits of future sight.

Essence of Success: The Earl Nightingale Library. Earl Nightingale. Read by Earl Nightingale. 20 cass. (Running Time: 20 hrs.). 159.95 (978-1-55525-041-6(6), 861A) Nightingale-Conant.
Each volume is a program for mastering one key aspect of successful living. Includes: Attitude & Excellence; Courage & Self-Esteem; Creativity; Opportunity & Goal-Setting; Personal Growth; Interpersonal Communication & Relationships; The Mind; Writing & Public Speaking; Success; Happiness.

Essence of Tai Chi Chi Kung. Jwing-Ming Yang. Read by Leslie Takao. 2 cass. (Running Time: 2 hrs.). 1996. bk. 15.95 (978-1-886969-40-7(X), A003) Pub: YMAA Pubn. Dist(s): Natl Bk Netwk
General Chinese Qigong theory & how it applies to the practice of Tai Chi Chuan.

Essence of the Bhagavad Gita: Explained by Paramhansa Yogananda, as Remembered by His Disciple, Swami Kriyananda. Swami Kriyananda. 2007. audio compact disk 59.95 (978-1-56589-221-7(6)) Pub: Crystal Clarity. Dist(s): Natl Bk Netwk

Essence of the Nyingma Teachings. Read by Dudjom Rinpoche. 2 cass. 1976. 22.50 (A174) Vajradhatu.

***Essence of Thought.** unabr. ed. Douglas Hofstadter & Emmanuel Sander. (ENG.). 2011. audio compact disk 36.95 (978-1-61573-092-6(3), 1615730923) Pub: HighBridge. Dist(s): Workman Pub

Essence of Yoga. 2 cass. (Running Time: 2 hrs.). (Essence of Yoga Ser.). 14.95 (ST-25) Crystal Clarity.
What yogis mean by "living impersonally"; understanding the true nature of joy; why outward pleasures don't bring happiness; turning weaknesses into strengths; specific meditations to neutralize likes & dislikes; how yoga leads you inward to the essence of "you-ness".

Essence of Yoga Series. 14 cass. 82.00 incl. vinyl storage album. (LS-6) Crystal Clarity.
Explains: The Essence of Yoga; Ashtanga Yoga; The Paths of Yoga; The Art & Science of Meditation; Awakening Kundalini; Guru-Disciple; Yoga Postures as an Aid to Spiritual Growth.

Essential Abraham Lincoln. unabr. ed. Abraham Lincoln. (Running Time: 4 hrs.). 2009. audio compact disk 22.98 (978-962-634-943-4(3), Naxos AudioBooks) Naxos.

Essential Abraham Lincoln: Speeches, Letters, Biography. Hagon Garrick & Peter Whitfield. Read by Garrick Hagon & Peter Marinker. (Playaway Young Adult Ser.). (ENG.). 2009. 59.99 (978-1-60775-749-8(4)) Find a World.

Essential Agatha Christies Best Short Sleuths Crack Twenty-Two Famous Cases. unabr. ed. Agatha Christie. 12 CDs. (ENG.). 2009. audio compact disk 49.95 (978-1-60283-663-1(9)) Pub: AudioGO. Dist(s): Perseus Dist

Essential Am, Pt. 5. David Shi. (C). Date not set. audio compact disk (978-0-393-10392-2(7)) Norton.

Essential America, Pt. 1. George Tindall. (C). Date not set. audio compact disk (978-0-393-10388-5(9)) Norton.

Essential America, Pt. 2. George Tindall. (C). Date not set. audio compact disk (978-0-393-10389-2(7)) Norton.

Essential America, Pt. 3. David Shi. (C). Date not set. audio compact disk (978-0-393-10390-8(0)) Norton.

Essential America, Pt. 4. David Shi. (C). Date not set. audio compact disk 0.00 (978-0-393-10391-5(9)) Norton.

Essential America, Vol. 2, Pts. 5-7. David Shi. (C). Date not set. audio compact disk (978-0-393-10396-0(X)) Norton.

Essential Kabbalah. abr. ed. Daniel Chanan Matt. Read by Edward Asner. 2 cass. (Running Time: 3 hrs.). 1996. 17.95 (978-1-57453-034-6(8), 330103) Audio Lit.
Here is the Kabbalah in all its beauty, presented with poetic nuances, exotic imagery & bold innovation. The translator provides insightful accounts of the primary aspects of Jewish mysticism, including the radical transcendence of God, the ten divine attributes & the feminine aspect of God.

Essential Kamasutra. Wendy Doniger. 2003. audio compact disk 24.95 (978-1-59179-065-5(4)) Sounds True.

Essential Keats. Read by Philip Levine. 1 cass. (Essential Poets Ser.). 9.95 Filmic Archives.

Essential Keyboard Repertoire, Vol. 2. Perf. by Kim O'Reilly. Ed. by Lynn Freeman Olson. 1 CD. (Running Time: 1 hr. 30 mins.). (Essential Keyboard Repertoire Ser.). (ENG.). 1993. audio compact disk 10.95 (978-0-7390-0620-7(7), 4092) Alfred Pub.

Essential Keyboard Repertoire, Vol. 3. Perf. by Kim O'Reilly. (Essential Keyboard Repertoire Ser.). (ENG.). 1995. audio compact disk 10.95 (978-0-7390-0549-1(9), 14025) Alfred Pub.

Essential Keyboard Repertoire, Vol. 4. Perf. by Kim O'Reilly. 1 CD. (Essential Keyboard Repertoire Ser.). (ENG.). 1996. audio compact disk 15.95 (978-0-7390-0888-1(9), 14027) Alfred Pub.

Essential Keyboard Repertoire, Vol 1: 100 Early Intermediate Selections in Their Original Form - Baroque to Modern. Kim O'Reilly. Contrib. by Kim O'Reilly. Ed. by Lynn Freeman Olson. (Essential Keyboard Repertoire Ser.). (ENG.). 1993. audio compact disk 10.95 (978-0-88284-858-7(5)) Alfred Pub.

Essential Kidz 2: DVD Resource. Contrib. by Luke Gambill. Prod. by Luke Gambill. (ENG.). (J). 2008. 39.99 (978-5-557-48403-9(5), Brentwood-Benson Music) Brentwood Music.

Essential King James Bible: Classic Stories from the Bible. Read by Martin Jarvis & Rosalind Ayres. (CSA Word Classics (Playaway) Ser.). (ENG.). (J). (gr. 3-7). 2009. 65.00 (978-1-60775-555-5(6)) Find a World.

Essential King James Bible: Complete Stories from the Old & New Testaments. Read by Martin Jarvis & Rosalind Ayres. 2006. audio compact disk 24.95 (978-1-57270-556-2(6)) Pub: Audio Partners. Dist(s): PerseuPGW

Essential King James Bible: Complete Stories from the Old & New Testaments. Read by Martin Jarvis & Rosalind Ayres. 2007. audio compact disk 19.99 (978-1-906147-01-3(9)) CSA Telltapes GBR.

Essential King James Bible: Complete Stories from the Old & New Testaments. unabr. ed. Read by Martin Jarvis & Rosalind Ayres. 4 cass. (Running Time: 6 hrs.). 2002. 24.95 (978-1-57270-245-5(1)) Pub: Audio Partners. Dist(s): PerseuPGW
Carefully chosen selection of the best-known, most important stories of the King James Bible.

***Essential Kipling.** Rudyard Kipling. Read by Rupert Degas et al. (Playaway Adult Fiction Ser.). (ENG.). 2009. 59.99 (978-1-61545-905-6(7)) Find a World.

Essential Kipling. unabr. ed. Rudyard Kipling. Read by Martin Jarvis & Richard Pasco. Narrated by Rupert Degas & Liza Goddard. 4 CDs. (Running Time: 5 hrs. 0 mins. 0 sec.). (ENG.). 2009. audio compact disk 26.95 (978-1-934997-30-7(7)) Pub: CSAWord. Dist(s): PerseuPGW

Essential Kyrgyz Manufacturers. 6th rev. ed. BIA. (J). 2006. audio compact disk 249.00 (978-1-4187-4862-3(5)) Bus Info Agency.

Essential Kyrgyz Manufacturers. 6th rev. ed. BIA. (J). 2006. audio compact disk 219.00 (978-1-4187-4861-6(7)) Bus Info Agency.

Essential Latin: Companion Cassettes to the Essential Latin Textbook. 2nd ed. G. D. A. Sharpley. (YA). (gr. 13 up). 2000. 39.95 (978-0-415-22270-9(2)) Pub: Routledge. Dist(s): Taylor and Fran

Essential Leather Manufacturers of Western Europe. 6th rev. ed. BIA. (J). 2006. audio compact disk 289.00 (978-1-4187-4668-1(1)) Bus Info Agency.

Essential Leather Manufacturers of Western Europe. 6th rev. ed. BIA. (J). 2006. audio compact disk 249.00 (978-1-4187-4667-4(3)) Bus Info Agency.

Essential Letters from America: The 1940s And 1950s. Read by Alistair Cooke. (Running Time: 2 hrs. 30 mins. 0 sec.). (ENG.). 2009. audio compact disk 24.95 (978-1-60283-769-0(4)) Pub: AudioGO. Dist(s): Perseus Dist

Essential Letters from America: The 1960s. unabr. ed. Alistair Cooke. Read by Alistair Cooke. Narrated by Matt Frei. (Running Time: 2 hrs. 30 mins. 0 sec.). (ENG.). 2010. audio compact disk 24.95 (978-1-60283-805-5(4)) Pub: AudioGO. Dist(s): Perseus Dist

***Essential Letters from America: The 1970s.** John Betjeman. Read by Alistair Cooke. (Running Time: 5 hrs. 0 mins. 0 sec.). (ENG.). 2010. audio compact disk 34.95 (978-1-4084-0076-0(6)) Pub: AudioGO. Dist(s): Perseus Dist

Essential Lewis & Clark: Selections. unabr. ed. Landon Y. Jones. Read by Tom Wopat & Peter Friedman. 5 CDs. (Running Time: 6 hrs.). 2003. audio compact disk 29.95 (978-0-06-055936-6(5)) HarperCollins Pubs.

***Essential Lewis & Clark Selections.** abr. ed. Landon Y. Jones. Read by Tom Wopat & Peter Friedman. (ENG.). 2004. (978-0-06-081371-0(7), Harper Audio) HarperCollins Pubs.

***Essential Lewis & Clark Selections.** unabr. ed. Landon Y. Jones. Read by Tom Wopat & Peter Friedman. (ENG.). 2004. (978-0-06-075494-5(X), Harper Audio) HarperCollins Pubs.

Essential Lumber & Wood Manufacturers of Western Europe. 6th rev. ed. BIA. (J). 2006. audio compact disk 289.00 (978-1-4187-4650-6(9)) Bus Info Agency.

Essential Lumber & Wood Manufacturers of Western Europe. 6th rev. ed. BIA. (J). 2006. audio compact disk 249.00 (978-1-4187-4649-0(5)) Bus Info Agency.

Essential Manufacturers of Belarus. 6th rev. ed. BIA. (J). 2006. audio compact disk 289.00 (978-1-4187-4607-0(X)) Bus Info Agency.

Essential Manufacturers of Belarus. 6th rev. ed. BIA. (J). 2006. audio compact disk 249.00 (978-1-4187-4606-3(1)) Bus Info Agency.

Essential Manufacturers of Denmark. 6th rev. ed. BIA. (J). 2006. audio compact disk 289.00 (978-1-4187-4736-7(X)) Bus Info Agency.

Essential Manufacturers of Denmark. 6th rev. ed. BIA. (J). 2006. audio compact disk 249.00 (978-1-4187-4735-0(1)) Bus Info Agency.

Essential Manufacturers of Serbia & Montenegro. 6th rev. ed. BIA. (J). 2006. audio compact disk 289.00 (978-1-4187-5252-1(5)) Bus Info Agency.

Essential Manufacturers of Serbia & Montenegro. 6th rev. ed. BIA. (J). 2006. audio compact disk 249.00 (978-1-4187-5251-4(7)) Bus Info Agency.

Essential Manufacturers of the Czech Republic. 6th rev. ed. BIA. (J). 2006. audio compact disk 259.00 (978-1-4187-4622-3(3)) Bus Info Agency.

Essential Manufacturers of the Czech Republic. 6th rev. ed. BIA. (J). 2006. audio compact disk 259.00 (978-1-4187-4621-6(5)) Bus Info Agency.

Essential Manufacturers of the Netherlands. 6th rev. ed. BIA. (J). 2006. audio compact disk 289.00 (978-1-4187-4813-5(7)) Bus Info Agency.

Essential Manufacturers of the Netherlands. 6th rev. ed. BIA. (J). 2006. audio compact disk 249.00 (978-1-4187-4812-8(9)) Bus Info Agency.

Essential Metallurgical Companies of Western Europe. 6th rev. ed. BIA. (J). 2006. audio compact disk 289.00 (978-1-4187-4674-2(6)) Bus Info Agency.

Essential Metallurgical Companies of Western Europe. 6th rev. ed. BIA. (J). 2006. audio compact disk 249.00 (978-1-4187-4673-5(8)) Bus Info Agency.

Essential Mining Companies of Western Europe. 6th rev. ed. BIA. (J). 2006. audio compact disk 289.00 (978-1-4187-4688-9(6)) Bus Info Agency.

Essential Mining Companies of Western Europe. 6th rev. ed. BIA. (J). 2006. audio compact disk 249.00 (978-1-4187-4687-2(8)) Bus Info Agency.

Essential Musicianship for Band - Masterwork Studies: Alto Clarinet. Paula Crider & Jack Saunders. 2007. pap. bk. 14.95 (978-0-634-08860-5(2), 0634088602) H Leonard.

Essential Musicianship for Band - Masterwork Studies: Alto Saxophone. Paula Crider & Jack Saunders. 2007. pap. bk. 14.95 (978-0-634-08862-9(9), 0634088629) H Leonard.

Essential Musicianship for Band - Masterwork Studies: Baritone B. C. Paula Crider & Jack Saunders. 2007. pap. bk. 14.95 (978-0-634-08868-1(8), 0634088688) H Leonard.

Essential Musicianship for Band - Masterwork Studies: Baritone Saxophone. Paula Crider & Jack Saunders. 2007. pap. bk. 14.95 (978-0-634-08864-3(5), 0634088645) H Leonard.

Essential Musicianship for Band - Masterwork Studies: Baritone T. C. Paula Crider & Jack Saunders. 2007. pap. bk. 14.95 (978-0-634-08869-8(6), 0634088696) H Leonard.

Essential Musicianship for Band - Masterwork Studies: Bass Clarinet. Paula Crider & Jack Saunders. 2007. pap. bk. 14.95 (978-0-634-08861-2(0), 0634088610) H Leonard.

Essential Musicianship for Band - Masterwork Studies: Bassoon. Paula Crider & Jack Saunders. 2007. pap. bk. 14.95 (978-0-634-08858-2(0), 0634088580) H Leonard.

Essential Musicianship for Band - Masterwork Studies: Clarinet. Paula Crider & Jack Saunders. 2007. pap. bk. 14.95 (978-0-634-08859-9(9), 0634088599) H Leonard.

Essential Musicianship for Band - Masterwork Studies: Conductor Score. Paula Crider & Jack Saunders. 2007. pap. bk. 49.95 (978-0-634-08855-1(6), 0634088556) H Leonard.

Essential Musicianship for Band - Masterwork Studies: F Horn. Paula Crider & Jack Saunders. 2007. pap. bk. 14.95 (978-0-634-08866-7(1), 0634088661) H Leonard.

Essential Musicianship for Band - Masterwork Studies: Flute. Paula Crider & Jack Saunders. 2007. pap. bk. 14.95 (978-0-634-08856-8(4), 0634088564) H Leonard.

Essential Musicianship for Band - Masterwork Studies: Oboe. Paula Crider & Jack Saunders. 2007. pap. bk. 14.95 (978-0-634-08857-5(2), 0634088572) H Leonard.

Essential Musicianship for Band - Masterwork Studies: Percussion/Mallet Percussion. Paula Crider & Jack Saunders. 2007. pap. bk. 14.95 (978-0-634-08872-8(6), 0634088726) H Leonard.

Essential Musicianship for Band - Masterwork Studies: String Bass. Paula Crider & Jack Saunders. 2007. pap. bk. 14.95 (978-0-634-08871-1(8), 0634088718) H Leonard.

Essential Musicianship for Band - Masterwork Studies: Tenor Saxophone. Paula Crider & Jack Saunders. 2007. pap. bk. 14.95 (978-0-634-08863-6(7), 0634088637) H Leonard.

Essential Musicianship for Band - Masterwork Studies: Trombone. Paula Crider & Jack Saunders. 2007. pap. bk. 14.95 (978-0-634-08867-4(X), 063408867X) H Leonard.

Essential Musicianship for Band - Masterwork Studies: Trumpet. Paula Crider & Jack Saunders. 2007. pap. bk. 14.95 (978-0-634-08865-0(3), 0634088653) H Leonard.

Essential Musicianship for Band - Masterwork Studies: Tuba. Paula Crider & Jack Saunders. 2007. pap. bk. 14.95 (978-0-634-08870-4(X), 063408870X) H Leonard.

Essential Mystics: The Soul's Journey into Truth. abr. ed. Andrew Harvey. Read by Andrew Harvey. 2 cass. (Running Time: 3 hrs.). 1996. 17.95 (978-1-57453-026-1(7), 330095) Audio Lit.

Essential Nature of Creation. Swami Amar Jyoti. 1 cass. 1991. 9.95 (O-33) Truth Consciousness.
Creation is endless, eternal. Essence & image, objective & subjective, are all simultaneously One. All paths are overlapping.

Essential Norwegian Manufacturers. 6th rev. ed. BIA. (J). 2006. audio compact disk 289.00 (978-1-4187-4959-0(1)) Bus Info Agency.

Essential Norwegian Manufacturers. 6th rev. ed. BIA. (J). 2006. audio compact disk 249.00 (978-1-4187-4958-3(3)) Bus Info Agency.

Essential Odetta. 1 cass. (Running Time: 60 min.). (Vanguard Folk Ser.). (J). 10.98 (2245); audio compact disk 16.98 (D2245) MFLP CA.

Essential Parker: Big Blonde - Mrs. Post Enlarges on Etiquette - Horsie. unabr. ed. Dorothy Parker. Read by Christine Baranski & Cynthia Nixon. 1 CD. (Running Time: 3600 sec.). 2006. audio compact disk 12.95 (978-0-06-115352-5(4)) HarperCollins Pubs.

Essential Patti Smith: Poetry. Patti Smith. Read by Smith Patti. 2006. audio compact disk 12.95 (978-0-06-117067-6(4)) HarperCollins Pubs.

Essential Pete Seeger. Perf. by Pete Seeger. 1 cass. (Running Time: 60 min.). (Vanguard Folk Ser.). (J). 10.98 (2246); audio compact disk 16.98 (D2246) MFLP CA.

Essential Polish Manufacturers. 6th rev. ed. BIA. (J). 2006. audio compact disk 289.00 (978-1-4187-4630-8(4)) Bus Info Agency.

Essential Polish Manufacturers. 6th rev. ed. BIA. (J). 2006. audio compact disk 249.00 (978-1-4187-4629-2(0)) Bus Info Agency.

Essential Portuguese Manufacturers. 6th rev. ed. BIA. (J). 2006. audio compact disk 289.00 (978-1-4187-4947-7(8)) Bus Info Agency.

Essential Portuguese Manufacturers. 6th rev. ed. BIA. (J). 2006. audio compact disk 249.00 (978-1-4187-4946-0(X)) Bus Info Agency.

Essential Portuguese Phrase Book. 10 cass. 150.00 (Natl Textbk Co) M-H Contemporary.
Stresses functional communication for mastery of Brazilian Portuguese.

Essential Portuguese Phrase Book. 2 cass. (Running Time: 80 min.). (Language - Thirty Library). bk. 16.95 set in vinyl album. Moonbeam Pubns.
Using the proven method based on the famous U.S. Military accelerated language learning program, Language/30 courses stress conversationally useful words & phrases.

Essential Portuguese Phrase Book. 1 cass. (Running Time: 90 min.). (TravelTalk Ser.). 1993. 15.00 incl. script incl. 288-page phrasebook-dictionary. (LivingLang) Random Info Grp.

Essential Printing & Publishing Companies of Western Europe. 6th rev. ed. BIA. (J). 2006. audio compact disk 289.00 (978-1-4187-4659-9(2)) Bus Info Agency.

Essential Printing & Publishing Companies of Western Europe. 6th rev. ed. BIA. (J). 2006. audio compact disk 249.00 (978-1-4187-4658-2(4)) Bus Info Agency.

Essential Psychopharmacology. Paschal Preston. 1998. 70.00 (978-0-8002-4430-9(3)) Taylor and Fran.

Essential Pulp & Paper Manufacturers of Western Europe. 6th rev. ed. BIA. (J). 2006. audio compact disk 289.00 (978-1-4187-4656-8(8)) Bus Info Agency.

Essential Pulp & Paper Manufacturers of Western Europe. 6th rev. ed. BIA. (J). 2006. audio compact disk 249.00 (978-1-4187-4655-1(X)) Bus Info Agency.

Essential Question. Dudley Hall. 1 cass. (Running Time: 90 mins.). (Keys to the Kingdom Ser.: Vol. 1). 2000. 5.00 (DH01-001) Morning NC.
These messages outline three essentials for successful Christian living.

Essential Reading. Frank Biggs. 1999. pap. bk. 14.95 (978-0-7866-3273-2(9), 97062BCD) Mel Bay.

Essential Reiki: A Complete Guide to an Ancient Healing Art. unabr. ed. Diane Stein. 1 CD. (Running Time: 1 hr.). 2001. audio compact disk 14.95 (978-1-58091-100-9(5), CrossingPr) Ten Speed Pr.
Reiki is the ancient system of "laying on of hands" derived from Tibetan Buddhism. The author discusses the three degrees of Reiki and her experiences as a master teacher.

Essential Repertoire for the Concert Choir: Artist Level. Glenda Casey & Bobbie Douglass. 1999. audio compact disk 79.95 (978-0-7935-9708-6(0)) H Leonard.

Essential Repertoire for the Concert Choir: Artist Level. Glenda Casey & Bobbie Douglass. (Essential Elements for Choir Ser.). 1999. audio compact disk 59.95 (978-0-7935-9709-3(9)); audio compact disk 59.95 (978-0-7935-9710-9(2)) H Leonard.

Essential Repertoire for the Concert Choir: Mixed Voices, Level 3. Glenda Casey & Bobbie Douglass. (Essential Elements for Choir Ser.). 1999. audio compact disk 29.95 (978-0-7935-9687-4(4)) H Leonard.

Essential Repertoire for the Concert Choir: Tenor Bass Voices, Level 3. Glenda Casey & Bobbie Douglass. (Essential Elements for Choir Ser.). 1999. audio compact disk 29.95 (978-0-7935-9696-6(3)); audio compact disk 59.95 (978-0-7935-9707-9(2)) H Leonard.

Essential Repertoire for the Concert Choir: Treble Voices, Level 3. Glenda Casey & Bobbie Douglass. (Essential Elements for Choir Ser.). 1999. audio compact disk 29.95 (978-0-7935-9695-9(5)); audio compact disk 59.95 (978-0-7935-9706-2(4)) H Leonard.

Essential Repertoire for the Concert Choir Level 3: Mixed Voices, Glenda Casey & Bobbie Douglass. (Essential Elements for Choir Ser.). 1999. audio compact disk 79.95 (978-0-7935-9688-1(2)) H Leonard.

Essential Repertoire for the Concert Choir Level 4: Mixed Voices - Artist Level, Glenda Casey & Bobbie Douglass. (Essential Elements for Choir Ser.). 1999. audio compact disk 29.95 (978-0-7935-9697-3(1)) H Leonard.

Essential Repertoire for the Concert Choir Level 4: Tenor Bass Voices - Artist Level, Glenda Casey & Bobbie Douglass. (Essential Elements for Choir Ser.). 1999. audio compact disk 29.95 (978-0-7935-9699-7(8)) H Leonard.

Essential Repertoire for the Concert Choir Level 4: Treble Voices - Artist Level, Glenda Casey & Bobbie Douglass. (Essential Elements for Choir Ser.). 1999. audio compact disk 29.95 (978-0-7935-9698-0(X)) H Leonard.

Essential Repertoire for the Developing Choir: Mixed Voices, Level 2. Janice Killian & Michael O'Hern. (Essential Elements for Choir Ser.). 1999. audio compact disk 29.95 (978-0-7935-9692-8(0)); audio compact disk 79.95 (978-0-7935-9703-1(X)) H Leonard.

Essential Repertoire for the Developing Choir: Tenor Bass Voices, Level 2. Janice Killian & Michael O'Hern. (Essential Elements for Choir Ser.). 1999. audio compact disk 29.95 (978-0-7935-9694-2(7)) H Leonard.

Essential Repertoire for the Developing Choir: Treble, Level 2. Janice Killian & Michael O'Hern. (Essential Elements for Choir Ser.). 1999. audio compact disk 29.95 (978-0-7935-9693-5(9)); audio compact disk 59.95 (978-0-7935-9704-8(8)) H Leonard.

Essential Repertoire for the Developing Choir Level 2: Tenor Bass Voices, Janice Killian & Michael O'Hern. (Essential Elements for Choir Ser.). 1999. audio compact disk 59.95 (978-0-7935-9705-5(6)) H Leonard.

Essential Repertoire for the Tenor Bass Level 1: Choir Part Learning, 1998. audio compact disk 0.01 (978-0-7935-9733-8(1)) H Leonard.

Essential Repertoire for the Young Choir, Level 1. (Essential Elements for Choir Ser.). 1998. audio compact disk 0.01 (978-0-7935-9732-1(3)) H Leonard.

Essential Repertoire for the Young Choir: Learning Part. 1998. audio compact disk 0.01 (978-0-7935-9731-4(5)) H Leonard.

Essential Repertoire for the Young Choir: Mixed Voices, Level 1. Janice Killian & Michael O'Hern. (Essential Elements for Choir Ser.). 1998. audio compact disk 29.95 (978-0-7935-9689-8(0)); audio compact disk 79.95 (978-0-7935-9700-0(5)) H Leonard.

Essential Repertoire for the Young Choir: Part-Learning, Level 2. (Essential Elements for Choir Ser.). 1999. audio compact disk 0.01 (978-0-7935-9739-0(0)) H Leonard.

Essential Repertoire for the Young Choir: Performed/Accompaniment, Level 2. (Essential Elements for Choir Ser.). 1999. audio compact disk 0.01 (978-0-7935-9740-6(4)) H Leonard.

Essential Repertoire for the Young Choir: Performed/Accompaniment, Level 2. (Essential Elements for Choir Ser.). 1999. audio compact disk 0.01 (978-0-7935-9742-0(0)) H Leonard.

Essential Repertoire for the Young Choir: Performed/Accompaniment, Level 3. (Essential Elements for Choir Ser.). 1999. audio compact disk 0.01 (978-0-7935-9774-1(9)) H Leonard.

Essential Repertoire for the Young Choir: Performed/Accompaniment, Level 3. (Essential Elements for Choir Ser.). 1999. audio compact disk 0.01 (978-0-7935-9776-5(5)) H Leonard.

Essential Repertoire for the Young Choir: Repertoire Artist Mixed, Part-Learning, Level 4. (Essential Elements for Choir Ser.). 1999. audio compact disk 0.01 (978-0-7935-9781-9(1)) H Leonard.

Essential Repertoire for the Young Choir: Repertoire Artist Mixed, Performed/Accompaniment, Level 4. (Essential Elements for Choir Ser.). 1999. audio compact disk 0.01 (978-0-7935-9780-2(3)) H Leonard.

Essential Repertoire for the Young Choir: Repertoire Artist, Tenor Bass, Part-Learning, Level 4. (Essential Elements for Choir Ser.). 1999. audio compact disk 0.01 (978-0-7935-9785-7(4)) H Leonard.

Essential Repertoire for the Young Choir: Repertoire Artist, Tenor Bass, Performed/Accompaniment, Level 4. (Essential Elements for Choir Ser.). 1999. audio compact disk 0.01 (978-0-7935-9784-0(6)) H Leonard.

Essential Repertoire for the Young Choir: Repertoire Artist Treble, Part-Learning, Level 4. (Essential Elements for Choir Ser.). 1999. audio compact disk 0.01 (978-0-7935-9783-3(8)) H Leonard.

Essential Repertoire for the Young Choir: Repertoire Artist Treble, Performed/Accompaniment, Level 4. (Essential Elements for Choir Ser.). 1999. audio compact disk 0.01 (978-0-7935-9782-6(X)) H Leonard.

Essential Repertoire for the Young Choir: Repertoire for Young Tenor Bass, Level 1. (Essential Elements for Choir Ser.). 1998. audio compact disk 0.01 (978-0-7935-9737-6(4)) H Leonard.

Essential Repertoire for the Young Choir: Repertoire for Young Treble, Level 1. (Essential Elements for Choir Ser.). 1998. audio compact disk 0.01 (978-0-7935-9734-5(X)) H Leonard.

Essential Repertoire for the Young Choir: Repertoire for Young TreblePart-Learning, Pt. 2. (Essential Elements for Choir Ser.). 1998. audio compact disk 0.01 (978-0-7935-9735-2(8)) H Leonard.

Essential Repertoire for the Young Choir: Tenor/ Bass Performed/Accompaniment, Level 3. (Essential Elements for Choir Ser.). 1999. audio compact disk 0.01 (978-0-7935-9778-9(1)) H Leonard.

Essential Repertoire for the Young Choir: Tenor Bass Voices, Level 1. Janice Killian & Michael O'Hern. (Essential Elements for Choir Ser.). 1998. audio compact disk 29.95 (978-0-7935-9691-1(2)); audio compact disk 59.95 (978-0-7935-9702-4(1)) H Leonard.

Essential Repertoire for the Young Choir: Tenor/Bass Part-Learning, Level 3. (Essential Elements for Choir Ser.). 1999. audio compact disk 0.01 (978-0-7935-9779-6(X)) H Leonard.

Essential Repertoire for the Young Choir: Treble Voices, Level 1. Janice Killian & Michael O'Hern. (Essential Elements for Choir Ser.). 1998. audio compact disk 29.95 (978-0-7935-9690-4(4)); audio compact disk 39.95 (978-0-7935-9701-7(3)) H Leonard.

Essential Repertoire for the Young Choir Level 2: Part-Learning, 1999. audio compact disk 0.01 (978-0-7935-9741-3(2)) H Leonard.

Essential Repertoire for the Young Choir Level 2: Part-Learning, (Essential Elements for Choir Ser.). 1999. audio compact disk 0.01 (978-0-7935-9743-7(9)) H Leonard.

Essential Repertoire for the Young Choir Level 2: Performed/Accompaniment, (Essential Elements for Choir Ser.). 1999. audio compact disk 0.01 (978-0-7935-9738-3(2)) H Leonard.

Essential Repertoire for the Young Choir Level 3: Part-Learning, (Essential Elements for Choir Ser.). 1999. audio compact disk 0.01 (978-0-7935-9775-8(7)) H Leonard.

Essential Repertoire for the Young Choir Level 3: Part-Learning, (Essential Elements for Choir Ser.). 1999. audio compact disk 0.01 (978-0-7935-9777-2(3)) H Leonard.

Essential Romanian Manufacturers. 6th rev. ed. BIA. (J). 2006. audio compact disk 289.00 (978-1-4187-5248-4(7)) Bus Info Agency.

Essential Romanian Manufacturers. 6th rev. ed. BIA. (J). 2006. audio compact disk 249.00 (978-1-4187-5247-7(9)) Bus Info Agency.

Essential Rubber & Plastic Manufacturers of Western Europe. 6th rev. ed. BIA. (J). 2006. audio compact disk 289.00 (978-1-4187-4665-0(7)) Bus Info Agency.

Essential Rubber & Plastic Manufacturers of Western Europe. 6th rev. ed. BIA. (J). 2006. audio compact disk 249.00 (978-1-4187-4664-3(9)) Bus Info Agency.

Essential Russian Manufacturers. 6th rev. ed. BIA. (J). 2006. audio compact disk 289.00 (978-1-4187-5250-7(9)) Bus Info Agency.

Essential Russian Manufacturers. 6th rev. ed. BIA. (J). 2006. audio compact disk 249.00 (978-1-4187-5249-1(5)) Bus Info Agency.

Essential Sales Professional's Companion, Set. abr. ed. Herb Cohen et al. Read by Herb Cohen et al. 4 cass. (Running Time: 4 hrs.). 1995. 39.00 (978-0-694-51566-0(3), BGS 006, Harper Audio) HarperCollins Pubs.

Essential Sanskrit - Prayers & Invocations. (SAN.). 2005. audio compact disk (978-0-9746047-2-5(0)) Sacred Sound.

Essential Sanskrit for Yoga Posture Pronunciation. Speeches. 2 CDs. (Running Time: 2 hours 7 minutes). 2003. audio compact disk 24.99 (978-0-9746047-0-1(4)) Sacred Sound.

Essential Self & the Machine. E. J. Gold. 1 cass. (Running Time: 1 hr. 30 min.). 9.98 (TP114) Union Label.
The nature & behavior of the machine, the chronic & the essential self are explored in this talk.

Essential Shakespeare. abr. ed. William Shakespeare. Contrib. by Simon Callow et al. (Running Time: 8100 sec.). (ENG.). 2005. audio compact disk 18.95 (978-1-59887-008-4(4), 1598870084) Pub: HighBridge. Dist(s): Workman Pub

Essential Shakespeare Live: The Royal Shakespeare Company in Performance. abr. ed. British Library Staff & Vrej Nersessian. Perf. by Peggy Ashcroft et al. Contrib. by Royal Shakespeare Company Staff. 2 CDs. (Running Time: 8160 sec.). (ENG., 2010. audio compact disk 25.00 (978-0-7123-0524-2(6)) Pub: Britis Library GBR. Dist(s): Chicago Distribution Ctr

***Essential Shakespeare Live Encore.** The British Library. (ENG.). 2010. audio compact disk 25.00 (978-0-7123-5100-3(0)) Pub: Britis Library GBR. Dist(s): Chicago Distribution Ctr

Essential Singaporean Manufacturers. 6th rev. ed. BIA. (J). 2006. audio compact disk 99.00 (978-1-4187-4864-7(1)) Bus Info Agency.

Essential Singaporean Manufacturers. 6th rev. ed. BIA. (J). 2006. audio compact disk 219.00 (978-1-4187-4863-0(3)) Bus Info Agency.

Essential Slovenian Manufacturers. 6th rev. ed. BIA. (J). 2006. audio compact disk 249.00 (978-1-4187-4632-2(0)) Bus Info Agency.

Essential Slovenian Manufacturers. 6th rev. ed. BIA. (J). 2006. audio compact disk 219.00 (978-1-4187-4631-5(2)) Bus Info Agency.

Essential Slowakisch Manufacturers. 6th rev. ed. BIA. (J). 2006. audio compact disk 259.00 (978-1-4187-4618-6(5)) Bus Info Agency.

Essential Slowakisch Manufacturers. 6th rev. ed. BIA. (J). 2006. audio compact disk 259.00 (978-1-4187-4617-9(7)) Bus Info Agency.

Essential South Korean Manufacturers. 6th rev. ed. BIA. (J). 2006. audio compact disk 289.00 (978-1-4187-4860-9(9)) Bus Info Agency.

Essential South Korean Manufacturers. 6th rev. ed. BIA. (J). 2006. audio compact disk 249.00 (978-1-4187-4859-3(5)) Bus Info Agency.

Essential Spanish for Healthcare. 2 cass. (At Work Ser.). 1997. bk. 35.00 (LivingLang) Random Info Grp.

Essential Spanish Manufacturers. 6th rev. ed. BIA. (J). 2006. audio compact disk 289.00 (978-1-4187-4929-3(X)) Bus Info Agency.

Essential Spanish Manufacturers. 6th rev. ed. BIA. (J). 2006. audio compact disk 249.00 (978-1-4187-4928-6(1)) Bus Info Agency.

Essential Stone, Clay, Glass & Concrete Manufacturers of the Eastern Europe. 6th rev. ed. BIA. (J). 2006. audio compact disk 289.00 (978-1-4187-5305-4(X)) Bus Info Agency.

Essential Stone, Clay, Glass & Concrete Manufacturers of the Eastern Europe. 6th rev. ed. BIA. (J). 2006. audio compact disk 249.00 (978-1-4187-5304-7(1)) Bus Info Agency.

Essential Stone, Clay, Glass, & Concrete Manufacturers of Western Europe. 6th rev. ed. BIA. (J). 2006. audio compact disk 289.00 (978-1-4187-4671-1(1)) Bus Info Agency.

Essential Stone, Clay, Glass & Concrete Manufacturers of Western Europe. 6th rev. ed. BIA. (J). 2006. audio compact disk 249.00 (978-1-4187-4670-4(3)) Bus Info Agency.

Essential Sunday Gospel Brunch. 1 CD. audio compact disk 18.98 (978-1-57908-492-9(3), 1465) Platinm Enter.

Essential Sunday Gospel Brunch, Set. unabr. ed. 1 cass. 12.98 (978-1-57908-493-6(1), 1465) Platinm Enter.

Essential Swedish Manufacturers. 6th rev. ed. BIA. (J). 2006. audio compact disk 289.00 (978-1-4187-4917-0(6)) Bus Info Agency.

Essential Swedish Manufacturers. 6th rev. ed. BIA. (J). 2006. audio compact disk 249.00 (978-1-4187-4916-3(8)) Bus Info Agency.

Essential Swiss Manufacturers. 6th rev. ed. BIA. (J). 2006. audio compact disk 289.00 (978-1-4187-4902-6(8)) Bus Info Agency.

Essential Swiss Manufacturers. 6th rev. ed. BIA. (J). 2006. audio compact disk 249.00 (978-1-4187-4901-9(X)) Bus Info Agency.

Essential Taylor II, Vol. 1. Read by Gardner C. Taylor. 1 cass. (Running Time: 2 hrs. 20 mins.). 2001. 18.00; audio compact disk 20.00 Judson.

Essential Taylor II, Vol. 2. Read by Gardner C. Taylor. 1 cass. (Running Time: 2 hrs. 20 mins.). 2001. 18.00; audio compact disk 20.00 Judson.

Essential Technique Bk. 3: Play along Trax, Band Method. Paul Lavender. 1999. audio compact disk 12.95 (978-0-634-03233-2(X)) H Leonard.

Essential Technique Play-Along Trax, Disc 1. Paul Lavender. 1999. audio compact disk 14.95 (978-0-634-09087-5(9)) H Leonard.

Essential Technique, 2000. 2002. spiral bd. 14.95 (978-0-634-04423-6(0)) H Leonard.

Essential Telephoning in English. Barbara Garside & Tony Garside. (Running Time: 1 hr. 12 mins.). (ENG.). 2002. stu. ed. 25.00 (978-0-521-78390-3(9)) Cambridge U Pr.

Essential Telephoning in English: Student's Book. Barbara Garside & Tony Garside. (Running Time: 4560 sec.). (ENG.). 2002. stu. ed. 25.00 (978-0-521-78391-0(7)) Cambridge U Pr.

Essential Tennessee Williams. abr. ed. Tennessee Williams. Read by Tennessee Williams. (Running Time: 3600 sec.). (Caedmon Essentials Ser.). 2007. audio compact disk 12.95 (978-0-06-123267-1(X)) HarperCollins Pubs.

Essential Textile Manufacturers of Western Europe. 6th rev. ed. BIA. (J). 2006. audio compact disk 289.00 (978-1-4187-4644-5(4)) Bus Info Agency.

Essential Textile Manufacturers of Western Europe. 6th rev. ed. BIA. (J). 2006. audio compact disk 249.00 (978-1-4187-4643-8(6)) Bus Info Agency.

Essential Tin Whistle Toolbox, Set. Told to Grey Larsen. 2004. per. 29.95 (978-0-7866-6891-5(1), 99129BCD) Mel Bay.

Essential Tolkien: The Hobbit & the Fellowship of the Ring. abr. ed. J. R. R. Tolkien. Read by J. R. R. Tolkien. (Running Time: 3600 sec.). 2007. audio compact disk 12.95 (978-0-06-137649-8(3), Caedmon) HarperCollins Pubs.

Essential Transportation Companies of Western Europe. 6th rev. ed. BIA. (J). 2006. audio compact disk 289.00 (978-1-4187-4694-0(0)) Bus Info Agency.

Essential Transportation Companies of Western Europe. 6th rev. ed. BIA. (J). 2006. audio compact disk 249.00 (978-1-4187-4693-3(2)) Bus Info Agency.

Essential Transportation Equipment Manufacturers of Western Europe. 6th rev. ed. BIA. (J). 2006. audio compact disk 289.00 (978-1-4187-4684-1(3)) Bus Info Agency.

Essential Transportation Equipment Manufacturers of Western Europe. 6th rev. ed. BIA. (J). 2006. audio compact disk 249.00 (978-1-4187-4683-4(5)) Bus Info Agency.

Essential Turkish Manufacturers. 6th rev. ed. BIA. (J). 2006. audio compact disk 289.00 (978-1-4187-5256-9(8)) Bus Info Agency.

Essential Turkish Manufacturers. 6th rev. ed. BIA. (J). 2006. audio compact disk 249.00 (978-1-4187-5255-2(X)) Bus Info Agency.

Essential Twain. abr. ed. Mark Twain. Read by Ed Begley, Jr. (Running Time: 3600 sec.). (Caedmon Essentials Ser.). 2007. audio compact disk 12.95 (978-0-06-123218-3(1)) HarperCollins Pubs.

Essential Ukrainian & Moldavian Manufacturers. 6th rev. ed. BIA. (J). 2006. audio compact disk 289.00 (978-1-4187-4628-5(2)) Bus Info Agency.

Essential Ukrainian & Moldavian Manufacturers. 6th rev. ed. BIA. (J). 2006. audio compact disk 249.00 (978-1-4187-4627-8(4)) Bus Info Agency.

Essential Uzbek Manufacturers. 6th rev. ed. BIA. (J). 2006. audio compact disk 249.00 (978-1-4187-4868-5(4)) Bus Info Agency.

Essential Uzbek Manufacturers. 6th rev. ed. BIA. (J). 2006. audio compact disk 219.00 (978-1-4187-4867-8(6)) Bus Info Agency.

Essential Verbs & Other Grammatical Structures. 3 cass. (Running Time: 4 hrs.). 2000. 50.00 Aviation Lang Sch.

Essential Verbs! French: No Sentence Is Complete without that One Key Word: the VERBS! see Acting with an Accent

Essential Verbs! French: No Sentence Is Complete without that One Key Word: the VERBS! Penton Overseas, Inc. Staff. 2 cass. (Running Time: 80 min.). (Language - Thirty Library). bk. 16.95 set in vinyl album. Moonbeam Pubns.
Using the proven method based on the famous U.S. Military accelerated language learning program, Language/30 courses stress conversationally useful words & phrases.

Essential Verbs! French: No Sentence Is Complete without that One Key Word: the VERBS! Penton Overseas, Inc. Staff. 1 cass. (Running Time: 1 hr.). (Listen & Learn a Language Ser.). (FRE.). (J). bk. (TWIN 410) NewSound.

Essential Verbs! French: No Sentence Is Complete without that One Key Word: the VERBS! Penton Overseas, Inc. Staff. (Vocabulearn-CE Ser.). 1996. audio compact disk 39.95 (978-1-56015-891-2(3)); audio compact disk 39.95 (978-1-56015-841-7(7)) Penton Overseas.

Essential Verbs! French: No Sentence Is Complete without that One Key Word: the VERBS! Penton Overseas, Inc. Staff. 1 cass. (Running Time: 30 min.). (Vocabulearn Beginners Series 1). (FRE & ENG.). (J). 1999. 10.95 Incl. listening guide. Penton Overseas.

Essential Verbs! German: No Sentence Is Complete Without That One Key Word: the VERBS! see Acting with an Accent

Essential Verbs! German: No Sentence Is Complete Without That One Key Word: the VERBS! Penton Overseas, Inc. Staff. 2 cass. (Running Time: 80 min.). (Language - Thirty Library). bk. 16.95 set in vinyl album. Moonbeam Pubns.

Essential Verbs! German: No Sentence Is Complete Without That One Key Word: the VERBS! Penton Overseas, Inc. Staff. 1 cass. (Running Time: 1 hr.). (Listen & Learn a Language Ser.). (GER.). (J). bk. (TWIN 411) NewSound.

Essential Vonnegut. unabr. ed. Kurt Vonnegut & Walter James Miller. Read by Kurt Vonnegut. 1 CD. (Running Time: 3600 sec.). (Caedmon Essentials Ser.). 2006. audio compact disk 12.95 (978-0-06-115351-8(6)) HarperCollins Pubs.

***Essential Vonnegut Interviews.** unabr. ed. Kurt Vonnegut. Read by Kurt Vonnegut. (ENG.). 2006. (978-0-06-133625-6(4), Harper Audio); (978-0-06-133624-9(6), Harper Audio) HarperCollins Pubs.

Essential Walt Whitman. unabr. abr. ed. Walt Whitman. Read by Ed Begley. (Running Time: 3600 sec.). (Caedmon Essentials Ser.). 2008. audio compact disk 12.95 (978-0-06-156641-7(1), Caedmon) HarperCollins Pubs.

***Essential Welty: Powerhouse & Petrified Man.** unabr. ed. Eudora Welty. Read by Eudora Welty. (ENG.). 2006. (978-0-06-113547-7(X), Harper Audio); (978-0-06-113548-4(8), Harper Audio) HarperCollins Pubs.

Essential Welty: Why I Live at the P. O. - A Memory - Powerhouse & Petrified Man. unabr. ed. Eudora Welty. Read by Eudora Welty. (Running Time: 3600 sec.). 2006. audio compact disk 12.95 (978-0-06-112419-8(2)) HarperCollins Pubs.

Essential Western European Manufacturers. 6th rev. ed. BIA. (J). 2006. audio compact disk 289.00 (978-1-4187-4638-4(X)) Bus Info Agency.

Essential Western European Manufacturers. 6th rev. ed. BIA. (J). 2006. audio compact disk 249.00 (978-1-4187-4637-7(1)) Bus Info Agency.

Essential Word on the Street. abr. ed. Rob Lacey. (Running Time: 1 hr. 12 mins. 0 sec.). (ENG.). 2005. 7.99 (978-0-310-26070-7(1)) Zondervan.

Essential Worship Keyboard & CD: Instruction for the Worship Musician. Sandy Hoffman & Marc Hoffman. (ENG., 2007. spiral bd. (978-1-932096-43-9(4)) Emerald WA.

Essential Yolanda Adams. Contrib. by Yolanda Adams. 2006. audio compact disk 24.98 (978-5-558-86485-4(0), Verity) Brentwood Music.

Essentials for an Astrologer. J. Mukherjee. 1 cass. 1992. 8.95 (1072) Am Fed Astrologers.

Essentials for Heatlh & Wellness. 2nd ed. Gordon Edlin et al. (C). 1999. audio compact disk 99.00 (978-0-7637-1255-6(8), 1255-8) Jones Bartlett.

Essentials for Nursing Assistants: A Humanistic Approach to Caregiving. 2nd ed. Pamela J. Carter. 2009. pap. bk. 61.95 (978-1-60547-619-3(6)) Lppncott W W.

Essentials for Self-Realization. Swami Jyotirmayananda. 1 cass. (Running Time: 45 min.). 1990. 10.00 Yoga Res Foun.

Essentials of American Government: Continuity & Change. 7th ed. Larry J. Sabato. 2006. audio compact disk 53.40 (978-0-321-37148-5(8)) Longman.

Essentials of Credibility, Composure & Confidence, Set. abr. ed. Lani Arredondo. Perf. by Lani Arredondo. 2 cass. (Running Time: 3 hrs.). 1996. bk. 21.95 (978-1-878542-67-0(2),) SkillPath Pubns.
Practical tips to make a more professional, creditable impression.

Essentials of Human Communication: TestGen EQ. 5th rev. ed. Devito. audio compact disk 49.97 (978-0-205-41871-8(6)) Longman Higher Ed.

Essentials of Musculoskeletal Care. 3rd ed. Letha Y. Griffin. 2005. bk. 140.00 (978-0-89203-352-2(5)) Amer Acad Ortho Surg.

Essentials of Music Theory: Ear Training. Andrew Surmani & Karen Farnum Surmani. (Essentials of Music Theory Ser.). (ENG.). 1998. audio compact disk 18.95 (978-0-7390-2013-5(7)) Alfred Pub.

Essentials of Music Theory, Bk 1-2: Ear Training. Andrew Surmani et al. (Essentials of Music Theory Ser.). (ENG.). 1998. audio compact disk 10.95 (978-0-7390-2727-1(1)) Alfred Pub.

Essentials of Organic Chemistry: Comprehensive Treatment by a Master Teacher. Instructed by Maitland Jones. 8 cass. (Running Time: 8 hrs. 6 min.). 240.00 incl. 315pp. manual. (56) Am Chemical.
A condensed course on the basic principles of organic chemistry.

Essentials of Recovery & Recovery. 1 cass. (Overcoming Roadblocks in Recovery Ser.). 1984. 8.95 (1528G) Hazelden.

Essentials of the Islamic Faith. M. Fethullah Gulen & Lee Crooks. (ENG.). 2007. audio compact disk 19.95 (978-1-59784-042-2(4)) Pub: Tughra. Dist(s): Natl Bk Netwk

Essentials of Using & Understanding Mathematics Digital Video Tour. Created by Addison Wesley. 2002. audio compact disk 37.80 (978-0-321-11621-5(6)) AddisonWesley.

Essie. unabr. ed. Flora Pearce. Read by Diana Bishop. 8 cass. (Running Time: 9 hrs. 32 min.). 2001. 69.95 (978-1-85089-672-2(0), 20991) Pub: ISIS Audio GBR. Dist(s): Ulverscroft US
It is 1913 when thirteen-year-old Essie leaves her impoverished family for a job as a kitchen maid. But her traumatic childhood has left deep scars, & it is many years before Essie can finally come to terms with her own past & accept with open arms the love she is offered.

Esssential Byron. Read by Paul Muldoon. 1 cass. (Essential Poets Ser.). 9.95 (8623Q) Filmic Archives.

Est-ce dans ce monde là que nous voulons Vivre? unabr. ed. Eva Joly. Read by Helen Ginier-Gillet. (YA). 2007. 79.99 (978-2-35569-069-3(3)) Find a World.

Esta Es Mi Tierra (This Is My Land) 1 cass. (Running Time: 1 hr. 30 mins.). (SPA & ENG.). (J). (ps-3). 12.00 (978-1-57417-022-1(8), AC7606); audio compact disk 16.00 (978-1-57417-011-5(2), AC0539) Arcoiris Recs.

Establish Contact with Aliens. Bruce Goldberg. (ENG.). 2005. audio compact disk 17.00 (978-1-57968-060-2(7)) Pub: B Goldberg. Dist(s): Baker Taylor

Establish Contact with Aliens. Bruce Goldberg. Read by Bruce Goldberg. 1 cass. (Running Time: 25 min.). (ENG.). 2006. 13.00 (978-1-885577-68-9(0)) Pub: B Goldberg. Dist(s): Baker Taylor
Through self-hypnosis invite communication with extraterrestrial beings in a safe & mutually growth oriented environment.

Establish Healing Foundation. Elbert Willis. 1 cass. (Learning Divine Healing Ser.). 4.00; 4.00 Fill the Gap.

Establishing an Effective Nutrition Education - Counseling Program: Skills for the RD. Katherine R. Curry & Susan P. Himburg. Read by James Ryan et al. 2 cass. (Running Time: 2 hrs.). (Study Kit Ser.). 1988. bk. 56.00 Set, in plastic binder. (978-0-88091-042-2(9), 1311-SK11) Am Dietetic Assn.
An interactive program on planning nutrition education & counseling programs & effective counseling techniques for both group & one-on-one situations.

Establishing & Maintaining the Team see Effective Team Building

Establishing Benchmark Tests & Selection Criteria: Procurement Evaluation for Jukebox Selection. 1 cass. 1990. 8.50 Recorded Res.

Establishing Inner Safety: Freeing Your Life. unabr. ed. Galexis. 2 cass. (Running Time: 3 hrs.). (Fortress Ser.: Vol. 1). 1996. 19.95 Set. (978-1-56089-047-8(9), G125) Visionary FL.
Practical living of spiritual principles workshop. Identifying the Fortress & issues surrounding safety & security. Then, leave your self-made prison into love & safety. Meditation included.

Establishing Priorities: Neh. 9:38; 10:39. Told to Ed Young. 1990. 4.95 (978-0-7417-1819-8(7), 819) Win Walk.

Establishing Your Heart on God's Word. Kenneth Copeland. 8 cass. 1988. 40.00 Set. (978-0-88114-913-5(6)) K Copeland Pubns.
Biblical teaching on spiritual maturity.

Establishing Your Heritage. Mark Crow. 4 cass. (Running Time: 4 hrs.). 2001. (978-1-931537-06-3(2)) Vision Comm Creat.

Establishing Your Professional Image. Dora C. Fowler. 1 cass. (Running Time: 60 min.). 9.95 (4005) Natl Inst Child Mgmt.
Looks at the specific verbal & non-verbal skills that can be acquired to come across with more confidence & personal power.

Establishment. unabr. ed. Howard Fast. Read by Sandra Burr. (Running Time: 12 hrs.). 2008. 39.25 (978-1-4233-7220-2(4), 9781423372202, Brlnc Audio MP3 Lib); 39.25 (978-1-4233-7222-6(0), 9781423372226, BADLE); 24.95 (978-1-4233-7221-9(2), 9781423372219, BAD); 24.95 (978-1-4233-7219-6(0), 9781423372196, Brilliance MP3) Brilliance Audio.

Establishment's War Against Laetrile. unabr. ed. Michael Culbert. 1 cass. 12.95 (942) J Norton Pubs.

Estate. unabr. ed. Isaac Bashevis Singer. Read by Noah Waterman. 8 cass. (Running Time: 11 hrs. 30 mins.). 1995. 56.95 (978-0-7861-0808-4(8), 1631) Blckstn Audio.
This is the sequel to & the conclusion of "The Manor." The human condition, in a particular time & place - man's estate - is the theme of this major novel. As one character says, "It's not child's play to be born, to marry, to bring forth generations, to grow old, to die.".

Estate & Financial Planning for the Aging or Incapacitated Client. unabr. ed. Contrib. by David P. Callahan & Peter J. Strauss. 6 cass. (Running Time: 8 hrs. 30 min.). 1990. 50.00 course handbk. (T7-9262) PLI.
Designed to guide attorneys & related professionals through the maze of legal & financial problems that affect the aging or incapacitated client of moderate or substantial means, this recording of the February 1990 program discusses such issues as: Property Management Alternatives (Judicial & Non-Judicial); Medicaid; Medicare; Death with Dignity; Private Care Management; Health Insurance & Planning for the Disabled Adult Child, as well as Special Ethical Issues.

Estate & Financial Planning for the Elderly. 1990. 40.00 (AC-550) PA Bar Inst.

Estate & Financial Planning for the Elderly. 1999. bk. 99.00 (ACS-2183) PA Bar Inst.
This overview of the newest practice specialty prepares you to answer your clients' questions about government benefits & the financial planning they require.

Estate & Gift Tax. 2nd rev. ed. John K. McNulty. 6 cass. (Running Time: 9 hrs. 20 mins.). (Outstanding Professor Audio Tape Ser.). 1997. 63.00 (978-1-57793-022-8(3), 28428, West Lglwrks) West.
Lecture given by a prominent American law school professor on the subjects of Civil Procedure, Contracts, Criminal, Real Property, Torts, and Exam Skill: Essay Writing.

Estate Planner Library. Ed. by Socrates Media Editors. 2005. audio compact disk 49.95 (978-1-59546-112-4(4)) Pub: Socrates Med LLC. Dist(s): Midpt Trade

Estate Planning: A Basic Guide. Nathan M. Bisk & Scott Barnett. 6 cass. 1995. bk. 199.00 set. (CPE5020) Bisk Educ.
Learn the 10 most common estate planning mistakes & how to avoid them plus how the federal estate tax laws work, how to select an executor, trustee & attorney. Coverage on buysell agreements charitable contributions, deferred compensation, profit-sharing & pension plans are also included & much more.

Estate Planning after the Tax Reform Act of 1986. Robert A. Stein & John R. Price. 1987. 115.00 (978-1-55917-156-4(1)) Natl Prac Inst.

Estate Planning & Administration: Recent Developments (1992) Read by James Allen et al. (Running Time: 3 hrs.). 1992. 89.00 Incl. 165p. tape materials. (ES-55235) Cont Ed Bar-CA.
Analyzes significant changes in state & federal statutory & case law affecting trusts, estates, conservatorships, & estate, gift, & income tax. Covers creditors' claims, predeath transfers, pension & insurance proceeds, elder law, & more. Explains new IRS procedures, forms, & regulations, & highlights important letter rulings.

Estate Planning for Children with Disabilities. 1 cass. 1989. bk. 45.00 (AC-528) PA Bar Inst.

Estate Planning for Closely Held Business Interests. Jerry A. Kasner. 2 cass. 99.00 set, incl. wkbk. (754126KQ) Am Inst CPA.
This course will give you the knowledge of the income tax rules relating to partnerships, C corporations, & S corporations that will enhance estate planning opportunities & may open new sources of business to you as part of the estate planning team.

Estate Planning for Distributions from Qualified Plans & IRAs. 2 cass. (Running Time: 3 hrs.). 1999. 165.00 Set; incl. study guide 194p. (D284) Am Law Inst.

Estate Planning for Subsequent Marriages. 1997. bk. 99.00 (ACS-1259) PA Bar Inst.
Unique estate planning issues arise for clients in multiple marriages regardless of whether the subsequent marriage follows a divorce or the death of a spouse.

Estate Planning for the Family Business Owner. 12 cass. (Running Time: 16 hrs. 30 min.). 1998. 395.00 Set; incl. study guide 1035p. (MC81) Am Law Inst.
Advanced course provides a comprehensive overview, with special attention to changes wrought by TRA '97. Covers the life cycle of the closely held business from choice of entity to estate administration, with primary attention to tax & estate planning issues & the due attention to non-tax issues.

Estate Planning for the Family Business Owner. 1 cass. (Running Time: 18 hrs.). 1999. 395.00 Set; incl. study guide. (AE08) Am Law Inst.

Estate Planning for the Family Business Owner: Thursday - Saturday, March 12-14, 1998, San Francisco (Fairmont Hotel) 12 cass. 1998. 395.00 Incl. course materials. (MC81) Am Law Inst.
Provides an overview of estate planning techniques for the family business owner, with special attention to changes wrought by the Taxpayer Relief Act of 1997.

Estate Planning for the Owner of a Family Business. 1998. bk. 99.00 (ACS-2137); bk. 99.00 (ACS-2137) PA Bar Inst.
If you represent the owners of small, family-owned businesses, then this is the book for you. It offers new, creative tax, & estate planning techniques that enhance the growth of your clients' businesses & save them money.

Estate Planning in Depth. 28 cass. (Running Time: 40 hrs.). 1999. 495.00 Set; incl. study guide 1578p. (AD85) Am Law Inst.
Advanced course includes recent wealth transfer tax developments.

Estate Planning in the Nineties. Read by Robert A. Stein & Clint Schroeder. bk. 125.00 (NO. 0324) Natl Prac Inst.

Estate Planning, Private Rights & Public Benefits for the Elderly. 1987. bk. 80.00; 45.00 PA Bar Inst.

Estate Planning under the Taxpayer Relief Act of 1997. Contrib. by Edward S. Schlesinger. 1 cass. (Running Time: 1 hrs. 20 min.). 1997. 27.40 (M168) Am Law Inst.
Surveys the newly enacted provisions affecting estates & gifts with helpful tips, cautions, & commentary.

Estate Tax Preparation Course. Sidney Kess & Barbara Weltman. 3 cass. (Running Time: 3 hrs.). 1994. 95.00 set. (0960) Toolkit Media.

Estates & Trusts: Dispute Resolution & Litigation. Read by Dominic Campisi et al. (Running Time: 5 hrs.). 1991. 115.00 Incl. Ethics: 1 hr., & 263p. tape materials. (ES-55207) Cont Ed Bar-CA.
Experts explain tactics to avoid disputes in the planning stage & to resolve or litigate conflicts during administration. Covers conflicts of interest & other ethical problems; disputes among beneficiaries & fiduciaries that can be resolved or mitigated through drafting; & probate & trust issues that can only be resolved before the courts.

Esteem. Eldon Taylor. 1 cass. (Running Time: 62 min.). (Neurophonics Ser.). 16.95 (978-1-55978-656-0(6), 1007) Progress Aware Res.
Sound patterns for Altered States of Consciousness with underlying subliminal affirmations & frequency response signals. Use with headphones only.

Esteem, Awareness, Support, Empowerment (E. A. S. E.), Phase 1. Frank Dane. 1998. pap. bk. & wbk. ed. 29.95 (978-0-9672749-0-4(7)) POUVANT.

Esteem, Awareness, Support, Empowerment (E. A. S. E.), Phase 2. Frank Dane. 1999. bk. & wbk. ed. 29.95 (978-0-9672749-1-1(5)) POUVANT.

Ester, una Mujer de Fortaleza y Dignidad. 2004. audio compact disk 34.00 (978-1-57972-671-3(2)) Insight Living.

Esther: A Biblical Interpretation. Concept by Ermance Rejebian. (ENG.). 2007. 5.00 (978-1-60339-133-7(9)); audio compact disk 5.00 (978-1-60339-134-4(7)) Listenr Digest.

Esther: A Novel. Henry Adams. (Literary Classics Ser.). (ENG.). 1997. 14.98 (978-1-57392-132-9(7)) Prometheus Bks.

Esther: A Woman of Strength & Dignity. 2003. audio compact disk 42.00 (978-1-57972-542-6(2)) Insight Living.

Esther: A Woman of Strength & Dignity. 2005. 42.00 (978-1-57972-672-0(0)); audio compact disk 42.00 (978-1-57972-610-2(0)) Insight Living.

Esther: God's Woman at God's Time. Nancy Leigh DeMoss. (ENG.). 2006. audio compact disk 31.99 (978-0-940110-74-8(1)) Life Action Publishing.

Esther: It's Tough Being a Woman. Beth Moore. 2008. pap. bk. 277.75 (978-1-4158-5289-7(8)) LifeWay Christian.

Esther - Nehemiah. abr. ed. Laura Williams. 1 cass. (Running Time: 1 hr.). Dramatization. (Best Loved Bible Stories Ser.). (J). (ps-3). 1995. 9.99 (978-0-8423-6075-3(1)) Tyndale Hse.
Fully dramatized Bible stories for kids with original music & songs. Two stories & a 48-page activity booklet.

Esther: Portrait of a Queen Pt. 1: The Queen God is Seeking. Derek Prince. 1 cass. (I-5041) Derek Prince.

Esther: Portrait of a Queen Pt. 2: The Queen Meets the Challenge. Derek Prince. 1 cass. (I-5042) Derek Prince.

Esther's Story. unabr. ed. Diane Wolkstein. Narrated by Linda Stephens. 1 cass. (Running Time: 45 mins.). (gr. 3 up). 1997. 10.00 (978-0-7887-0701-8(9), 94875E7) Recorded Bks.
This first-person retelling of the legend of Esther brings a chapter of Jewish history to life. The young Jewish woman chosen as queen by the king of Persia must summon all her courage to prevent the massacre of her people.

Esthetician's Guide to Business Management. Gambino. 1 cass. (SalonOvations Ser.). 1995. 10.95 (978-1-56253-303-8(7), Milady) Pub: Delmar. Dist(s): CENGAGE Learn

***Estima totales y diferencias Audio CD.** April Barth. Adapted by Benchmark Education Co., LLC. (Content Connections Ser.). (SPA.). (J). 2010. audio compact disk 10.00 (978-1-61672-192-3(8)) Benchmark Educ.

Estimation at the Factory Audio CD: Set B. Benchmark Education Co. (Math Explorers Ser.). (J). (gr. 3-8). 2009. audio compact disk 10.00 (978-1-935441-60-1(4)) Benchmark Educ.

Estimation in Space Audio CD: Set B. Benchmark Education Co. (Math Explorers Ser.). (J). (gr. 3-8). 2009. audio compact disk 10.00 (978-1-935441-59-5(0)) Benchmark Educ.

Estimation in the Ancient World Audio CD: Set B. Benchmark Education Co. (Math Explorers Ser.). (J). (gr. 3-8). 2009. audio compact disk 10.00 (978-1-935441-58-8(2)) Benchmark Educ.

Es...Todo. 2001. audio compact disk 129.00 (CZW11510) Am Guidance.

Estonian Basic Course CDs & Text. 32 CDs. (Running Time: 30 hrs.). (EST.). 2005. audio compact disk 295.00 (978-1-57970-237-3(6), AFET10D) J Norton Pubs.

Estrategias de Producto - una Estrategia del Nuevo Milenio. unabr. ed. Juan A. Gutierrez.Tr. of Product Strategies - A Strategy for the New Millenium. (SPA.). audio compact disk 13.00 (978-958-43-0223-6(X)) YoYoMusic.

***Estrategias de resta Audio CD.** April Barth. Adapted by Benchmark Education Co., LLC. (Content Connections Ser.). (SPA.). (J). 2010. audio compact disk 10.00 (978-1-61672-193-0(6)) Benchmark Educ.

***Estrategias de suma Audio CD.** April Barth. Adapted by Benchmark Education Co., LLC. (Content Connections Ser.). (SPA.). (J). 2010. audio compact disk 10.00 (978-1-61672-194-7(4)) Benchmark Educ.

Estrategias para Triunfar. Miguel Angel Cornejo. 1 cass. (Running Time: 1 hr. 30 mins.).Tr. of Strategies for Success. (SPA.). 2001. Astran.

Estrategias para Triunfar. Miguel Angel Cornejo. 2 cass. (Running Time: 2 hrs.).Tr. of Strategies for Success. (SPA.). 2002. (978-968-6210-14-9(8)) Taller del Exito.
Leaders are made, not born. When facing difficulties they get stronger and reach beyond the limits of what is possible.

Estrogen Replacement Therapy: Good or Bad? 2 cass. (Gynecology & Obstetrics Ser.: C84-GO1). 1984. 15.00 (8432) Am Coll Surgeons.

Estuche de Salud. 3 cass. (Running Time: 1 hr. 36 min.). (SPA.). 1996. pap. bk. 29.95 Set. (978-1-56491-062-2(8)) Imagine Pubs.
Mental drills to help the person feel better about the illness.

Estuche Del Amor. Carlos González. Ed. by Dina Gonzalez. 4 cass. (Running Time: 1 hr. 28 min.). (SPA.). 1991. 39.00 Set. (978-1-56491-055-4(5)) Imagine Pubs.
Gives the person the clue to not be ignored as an individual & to communicate more easily with anyone.

Estuche del Amor. 3rd ed. Carlos Gonzalez. 4 CDs. (Running Time: 2 hrs., 15 mins.). (SPA.). 2004. audio compact disk 49.00 (978-1-56491-123-0(3)) Imagine Pubs.

Estudiemos juntos la Biblia. P. Juan Rivas. (SPA.). (YA). 2000. audio compact disk 18.95 (978-1-935405-77-1(2)) Hombre Nuevo.

Estudios Sociales Scott Foresman: Technology. (Scott Foresman Social Study Ser.). (SPA.). (gr. 1 up). 2003. audio compact disk (978-0-328-05739-9(8), Scott Frsmn) Addson-Wesley Educ.

Estudios Sociales Scott Foresman: Technology. (Scott Foresman Social Study Ser.). (SPA.). (gr. 2 up). 2003. audio compact disk (978-0-328-05740-5(1), Scott Frsmn) Addson-Wesley Educ.

Estudios Sociales Scott Foresman: Technology. (Scott Foresman Social Study Ser.). (SPA.). (gr. 3 up). 2003. audio compact disk (978-0-328-05741-2(X), Scott Frsmn) Addson-Wesley Educ.

Estudios Sociales Scott Foresman: Technology. (Scott Foresman Social Study Ser.). (SPA.). (gr. 4 up). 2003. audio compact disk (978-0-328-05785-6(1), Scott Frsmn) Addson-Wesley Educ.
Easy-to-follow recordings of all lessons in the Pupil Edition enable all students to access contents. Dramatic readings of Estas ahi (You Are There) features and biographies help to make social studies content meaningful.

Estudios Sociales Scott Foresman: Technology. (Scott Foresman Social Study Ser.). (SPA.). (gr. 5 up). 2003. audio compact disk (978-0-328-05743-6(6), Scott Frsmn) Addson-Wesley Educ.

Estuve en el Fin del Mundo. Eduardo Robles. (SPA.). 2009. 60.00 (978-1-60775-583-8(1)) Find a World.

***ESV Bible: New Testament.** unabr. ed. Crossway Books Staff. Narrated by Marquis Laughlin. (ENG.). 2003. 19.99 (978-1-60814-663-5(4)) Oasis Audio.

ESV Hear the Word Audio Bible. 2008. audio compact disk 99.99 (978-1-4335-0294-1(1)) CrosswayIL.

Et les Cigales Qui Chantent. Mary Alice Fontenot. Narrated by Julie F. Landry. 1 cass. (Running Time: 30 min.). (Clovis Ecrivesse AudioCassette Ser.).Tr. of Et Petit Papillon. (FRE.). (J). (gr. 4-7). 1997. 9.95 (978-1-56554-104-7(9)) Pelican.

Et Petit Papillon see Et les Cigales Qui Chantent

Etait une Fois. Francois Savigny. 1 cass. 2001. 15.00 (978-0-8442-1335-4(7), Natl Textbk Co) M-H Contemporary.
Presents three popular fairy tales.

etc Program, Level 1: Life Skills Audiotape/CD. Elaine Kirn. 1988. audio compact disk 12.00 (978-1-891077-59-3(7)) Authors Editors.

etc Program, Level 2: Listening/Speaking, 2 Audiotapes/CDs. 1988. audio compact disk 24.00 (978-1-891077-62-3(7)) Authors Editors.

etc Program, Level 3: Listening/Speaking, 5 Audiotapes/CDs. Elaine Kirn. 1988. audio compact disk 60.00 (978-1-891077-65-4(1)) Authors Editors.

etc Program, Level 4: Listening/Speaking, 1 Audiotape/CD. Elaine Kirn. 1989. audio compact disk 12.00 (978-1-891077-68-5(6)) Authors Editors.

etc Program, Level 5: Listening/Speaking, 2 Audiotapes/CDs. Elaine Kirn. 1989. audio compact disk 24.00 (978-1-891077-71-5(6)) Authors Editors.

etc Program, Level 6: Listening/Speaking, 2 Audiotapes/CDs. Elaine Kirn. 1989. audio compact disk 24.00 (978-1-891077-74-6(0)) Authors Editors.

Ete see Albert Camus: Reading from His Novel and Essays

Ete Indien. Short Stories. Truman Capote. Read by Jean-Claude Rey. 1 cass. (FRE.). 1995. 18.95 (1731-DI) Olivia & Hill.
The brutal separation of a child & grandfather gives a nostalgic atmosphere to this magnificent short story which takes the form of a dream in the mind of the narrator.

Ete 39, Set. Henri Amouroux. 2 cass. (Francais sous l'occupation Ser.). (FRE.). 1991. 26.95 (1220-RF) Olivia & Hill.
The last Sunday of peace; the French people in 1939.

Eternal Body-Imagination. Neville Goddard. 1 cass. (Running Time: 62 min.). 1965. 8.00 (102) J & L Pubns.
Neville taught Imagination Creates Reality. He was a powerfully influential teacher of God as Consciousness.

Eternal City. Domenica De Rosa. (Isis (CDs) Ser.). 2007. audio compact disk 64.95 (978-0-7531-2688-2(5)) Pub: ISIS Lrg Prnt GBR. Dist(s): Ulverscroft US

Eternal City. unabr. ed. Domenica De Rosa. Read by Aileen Gonsalves. 6 cass. (Running Time: 7 hrs.). (Isis Cassettes Ser.). (J). 2006. 54.95 (978-0-7531-3538-9(8)) Pub: ISIS Lrg Prnt GBR. Dist(s): Ulverscroft US

Eternal Flame: Acts 7:1-60. Ed Young. 1997. Rental 4.95 (978-0-7417-2159-4(7), A1159) Win Walk.

Eternal Flames. (Running Time: 60 mins.). 2002. audio compact disk 15.99 (978-1-904972-28-0(4)) Global Jrny GBR GBR.

Eternal Forest. (Running Time: 60 mins.). 2002. audio compact disk 15.99 (978-1-904972-42-6(X)) Global Jrny GBR GBR.

Eternal Funk. Perf. by Unity Klan. 1 cass. 1997. audio compact disk 15.99 (D8858) Diamante Music Grp.
Their original style appeals to a variety of categories, which provides an opportunity for their Christ-centered lyrics to bring the name of Jesus back to the hip-hop scene.

Eternal Husband. Fyodor Dostoyevsky. Read by Jim Killavey. 6 cass. (Running Time: 6 hrs. 30 min.). 1989. 36.00 incl. album. (C-139) Jimcin Record.
Story of revenge & passion.

Eternal Husband. unabr. collector's ed. Fyodor Dostoyevsky. Read by Jim Killavey. 6 cass. (Running Time: 6 hrs.). 1985. 36.00 (978-0-7366-3906-4(3), 9139) Books on Tape.
A psychological study of a betrayed husband who seeks revenge on his wife's seducer. The author, with psychological & philosophical insight, plumbs the depths & complexities of the human soul.

***Eternal Kiss: 13 Vampire Tales of Blood & Desire.** unabr. ed. Trish Telep. (Running Time: 11 hrs.). 2010. 39.97 (978-1-4418-7222-7(1), 9781441872227, BADLE) Brilliance Audio.

***Eternal Kiss: 13 Vampire Tales of Blood & Desire.** unabr. ed. Trish Telep Editors. (Running Time: 12 hrs.). 2010. 24.99 (978-1-4418-7220-3(5), 9781441872203, Brilliance MP3); 39.97 (978-1-4418-7221-0(3), 9781441872210, Brlnc Audio MP3 Lib); audio compact disk 79.97 (978-1-4418-7219-7(1), 9781441872197, BriAudCD Unabrid) Brilliance Audio.

***Eternal Kiss: 13 Vampire Tales of Blood & Desire.** unabr. ed. Trish Telep Editors. (Running Time: 12 hrs.). (YA). 2010. audio compact disk 29.99 (978-1-4418-7218-0(3), 9781441872180, Bril Audio CD Unabri) Brilliance Audio.

***Eternal Kiss of Darkness.** unabr. ed. Jeaniene Frost. Read by Tavia Gilbert. (Running Time: 12 hrs. 30 mins.). (Night Huntress World Ser.). 2010. 29.95 (978-1-4417-7336-4(3)); 72.95 (978-1-4417-7333-3(9)); audio compact disk 32.95 (978-1-4417-7335-7(5)); audio compact disk 105.00 (978-1-4417-7334-0(7)) Blckstn Audio.

Eternal Law of Faith. unabr. ed. Swami Amar Jyoti. 1 cass. (Satsangs of Swami Amar Jyoti Ser.). 1996. 9.95 (D-18) Truth Consciousness.
The uncompromising attitude of faith, the only way to our Sweet Home. Faith, the greatest healer, bestows strength, erases ego.

***Eternal Life: A New Vision.** unabr. ed. John Shelby Spong. Read by John Morgan. (ENG.). 2009. (978-0-06-196155-7(8), Harper Audio); (978-0-06-184559-8(0), Harper Audio) HarperCollins Pubs.

Eternal Light. Glori Dei Cantores. 2005. audio compact disk 12.99 (978-1-55725-435-1(4), GDCD111) Paraclete MA.
For nearly thirty years, Gloriae Dei Cantores has traveled extensively, performing in the world's finest concert halls-from London to Moscow, Belgium to Venice, and all over the United States-stirring the hearts of thousands of listeners, delighting classical music fans, and astounding critics with its versatility and interpretive sensitivity. Now, in Eternal Light, Gloriae Dei Cantores presents a "collector's edition" of some of its most

beloved meditative choral works. This must-have volume is ideal for playing at home, on a commute, at the office, or any place that would be enhanced by the lush choral melodies of Palestrina, Rachmaninoff, Brahms, Argento, and others.

Eternal Love. 2 CDs. (Running Time: 3 hrs.). 1998. audio compact disk 16.98 (978-1-57908-438-7(9)) Platinm Enter.

Eternal Mercenary. abr. ed. Barry Sadler. Read by Bruce Watson. 2 vols. (Casca Ser.: No. 1). 2002. (978-1-58807-503-1(6)) Am Pubng Inc.

Eternal Mercenary. abr. ed. Barry Sadler. Read by Bruce Watson. 2 vols. (Running Time: 3 hrs.). (Casca Ser.: No. 1). 2002. 18.00 (978-1-58807-101-9(4)) Am Pubng Inc.
From the moment Casca ran his spear through the torso of Jesus, the self-proclaimed Son of God, he began an endless lifelong journey filled with war, death, love, and heartache. At every turn of his sword, at every miraculously healed wound on his body, at every escape from death, the words of Jesus echo madly through his mind, Soldier, you are content with what you are. Then that you shall remain until we meet again. After the crucifixion of Jesus, Cascas first love and homethe Roman tenth legionis cruelly seized from him when he defies authority and responds to untimely opposition with murder, landing him a life sentence of slavery. However, what he deems the end of his life is only the beginning. Spanning a journey of one-hundred and fifty years, his battles take him from the great empire of Rome to Greece, Khmer, Vietnam, and finally to Israel. Defying the torture of never ending sameness, a man who cannot die, does not age, and lives by the sword, can only become known as THE ETERNAL MERCENARY.

Eternal Mercenary. abr. ed. Barry Sadler. Read by Bruce Watson. 3 vols. (Casca Ser.: No. 1). 2003. audio compact disk (978-1-58807-706-6(3)) Am Pubng Inc.

Eternal Mercenary. abr. ed. Barry Sadler. Read by Bruce Watson. 3 vols. (Running Time: 3 hrs.). (Casca Ser.: No. 1). 2003. audio compact disk 25.00 (978-1-58807-275-7(4)) Am Pubng Inc.

Eternal Om: To Purify & Balance the Chakras. unabr. ed. Yogi Hari. 2003. audio compact disk 14.95 (978-1-57777-039-8(0), 407-009) Pub: Nada Prodns. Dist(s): Bookworld

***Eternal Ones.** Kirsten Miller. (ENG.). (YA). 2010. audio compact disk 29.95 (978-0-14-314576-9(2), PengAudBks) Penguin Grp USA.

Eternal Pleasure. Nina Bangs. 2008. audio compact disk 43.95 (978-1-897304-63-1(3)) Pub: AudioRealms CN CAN. Dist(s): Natl Bk Netwk

Eternal Praise. Perf. by London Philharmonic Orchestra, The. 2000. 4.99 (978-1-930800-03-8(7), Prop Voice); audio compact disk 5.99 (978-1-930800-02-1(9), Prop Voice) Iliad TN.

***Eternal Prison.** unabr. ed. Jeff Somers. Narrated by Todd McLaren. (Running Time: 12 hrs. 0 mins. 0 sec.). (Avery Cates Ser.). (ENG.). 2010. 24.99 (978-1-4001-6676-3(4)); 34.99 (978-1-4001-9676-0(0)); 17.99 (978-1-4001-8676-1(5)); audio compact disk 69.99 (978-1-4001-4676-5(3)); audio compact disk 34.99 (978-1-4001-1676-8(7)) Pub: Tantor Media. Dist(s): IngramPubServ

Eternal Religion. Swami Amar Jyoti. 1 cass. 1977. 9.95 (R-57) Truth Consciousness.
On Vedanta; where all systems end & realization begins. Nondualism, One without a second. Transcendence without condemnation.

Eternal Return. Roger Woolger. 2008. audio compact disk 69.95 (978-1-59179-514-8(1)) Sounds True.

Eternal Security. Chuck Missler. (ENG.). 2008. audio compact disk 19.95 (978-1-57821-416-7(5)) Koinonia Hse.

Eternal Security: Once Save; Always Saved. Lloyd A. Olson. 2007. audio compact disk 40.99 (978-1-60247-943-2(7)) Tate Pubng.

Eternal Summer. Curt Sampson. Read by Dennis Mckee. (Running Time: 9 hrs.). 2000. 30.95 (978-1-59912-656-2(7)) Iofy Corp.

Eternal Summer: Palmer, Nicklaus & Hogan in 1960, Golf's Golden Year. unabr. ed. Curt Sampson. Narrated by Dennis McKee. 6 cass. (Running Time: 8 hrs. 30 mins.). 2001. 44.95 (978-0-7861-2122-9(X), 2882); audio compact disk 56.00 (978-0-7861-9634-0(3), 2882) Blckstn Audio.
1960 was the year that golf and its vivid personalities exploded onto the consciousness of the nation as television chronicled the colorful and exciting careers of Arnie Palmer, Ben Hogan and newcomer, Jack Nicklaus, "what golf used to be".

Eternal Unchanging Word. Derek Prince. 1 cass. (I-4061) Derek Prince.

Eternally Successful Organization. Philip B. Crosby. 1 cass. (Running Time: 86 min.). 1988. 9.95 (978-0-07-014534-4(2)) McGraw.
Crosby offers practical strategies based on his lifetime study of management & his own personal quest for the best way to run his successful international firm. Crosby creates a fictional model company complete with a realistic cast of characters to show you how companies, like individuals, choose between healthy or destructive behavior.

Eternity see Poetry of Hart Crane

Eternity: Discipler Altar Worker Training Seminar. Tim Nashif & Marc Estes. 2 cass. (Running Time: 3 hrs.). 2000. pap. bk. (978-1-886849-69-3(2)) CityChristian.

Eternity CD. (CHI.). 2009. audio compact disk 15.00 (978-0-9721862-8-5(X)) Lamb Music & Min.

Eternity Code. Eoin Colfer. Read by Nathaniel Parker. 4 cass. (Running Time: 6 hrs. 54 mins.). (Artemis Fowl Ser.: Bk. 3). (J). (gr. 6 up). 2004. 32.00 (978-1-4000-8595-8(0), Listening Lib); audio compact disk 45.00 (978-1-4000-8597-2(7), Listening Lib) Random Audio Pubg.

Eternity Code. unabr. ed. Eoin Colfer. Read by Nathaniel Parker. 6 CDs. (Running Time: 6 hrs. 53 mins.). (Artemis Fowl Ser.: Bk. 3). (YA). (gr. 7). 2004. audio compact disk 30.00 (978-1-4000-8596-5(9), Listening Lib) Pub: Random Audio Pubg. Dist(s): Random

Eternity in Death. J. D. Robb, pseud. Read by Susan Ericksen. (In Death Ser.). 2009. 44.99 (978-1-60775-857-0(1)) Find a World.

Eternity in Death. unabr. ed. J. D. Robb, pseud. (Running Time: 3 hrs.). (In Death Ser.). 2007. 39.25 (978-1-4233-5175-7(4), 9781423351757, BADLE); 24.95 (978-1-4233-5174-0(6), 9781423351740, BAD) Brilliance Audio.

Eternity in Death. unabr. ed. J. D. Robb, pseud. Read by Susan Ericksen. (Running Time: 10800 sec.). (In Death Ser.). 2007. audio compact disk 39.25 (978-1-4233-5173-3(8), 9781423351733, Brinc Audio MP3 Lib); audio compact disk 19.95 (978-1-4233-5170-2(3), 9781423351702, Bril Audio CD Unabri); audio compact disk 24.95 (978-1-4233-5172-6(X), 9781423351726, Brilliance MP3) Brilliance Audio.

Eternity in Death. unabr. ed. R. D. Robb. Read by Susan Ericksen. (Running Time: 10800 sec.). (In Death Ser.). 2007. audio compact disk 62.25 (978-1-4233-5171-9(1), 9781423351719, BriAudCD Unabrid) Brilliance Audio.

Eternity in Man's Mind. Neville Goddard. 1 cass. (Running Time: 62 min.). 1964. 8.00 (22) J & L Pubns.
Neville taught Imagination Creates Reality. He was a powerfully influential teacher of God as Consciousness.

Eternity Is Now. Contrib. by Telecast. Prod. by Zach Hodges & Josh White. 2005. audio compact disk 13.98 (978-5-558-86599-8(7)) BEC Recordings.

Eternity Ring. Patricia Wentworth. 8 CDs. (Isis (CDs) Ser.). 2006. audio compact disk 79.95 (978-0-7531-2605-9(2)) Pub: ISIS Lrg Prnt GBR. Dist(s): Ulverscroft US

Eternity Ring. Patricia Wentworth. Read by Diana Bishop. 7 cass. (Running Time: 31200 sec.). (Isis Cassettes Ser.). 2006. 61.95 (978-0-7531-3580-8(9)) Pub: ISIS Lrg Prnt GBR. Dist(s): Ulverscroft US

***Eternity Soup: Inside the Quest to End Aging.** unabr. ed. Greg Critser. Narrated by Erik Synnestvedt. (Running Time: 6 hrs. 30 mins.). 2010. 14.99 (978-1-4001-8561-0(0)); 19.99 (978-1-4001-6561-2(X)); audio compact disk 59.99 (978-1-4001-4561-4(9)); audio compact disk 29.99 (978-1-4001-1561-7(2)) Pub: Tantor Media. Dist(s): IngramPubServ

***Eternity's Edge.** Bryan Davis. (Running Time: 10 hrs. 10 mins. 0 sec.). (Echoes from the Edge Ser.). (ENG.). (YA). 2009. 12.99 (978-0-310-29426-9(6)) Zondervan.

***Ethan Allen: The Green Mountain Boys & Vermont's Path to Statehood.** unabr. ed. Emily Raabe. Read by Benjamin Becker. (Running Time: 2 hrs.). 2011. audio compact disk 29.97 (978-1-4558-0478-8(9), 9781455804788, BriAudCD Unabrid); audio compact disk 24.99 (978-1-4558-0477-1(0), 9781455804771, Bril Audio CD Unabri) Brilliance Audio.

Ethan Frome. Edith Wharton. 2 cass. 19.95 set. (8111Q) Filmic Archives.
In a typical New England village, Ethan Frome barely makes a living out of his stony farm & exists at odds with his wife Zeena, a whining hypochondriac. When Mattie, Zeena's cousin, comes to live with them, love develops between her & Ethan. They try to end their hapless romance by steering a bobsled into a tree, but both end up cripples, tied to a long life of despair with Zeena. Zeena, however, is transformed into a devoted nurse, while Mattie becomes the nagging invalid.

Ethan Frome. Edith Wharton. Read by William Hope. (Running Time: 2 hrs. 30 mins.). 1999. 22.95 (978-1-60083-732-6(8)) Iofy Corp.

Ethan Frome. Edith Wharton. Read by Scott Brick. (Running Time: 3 hrs. 48 mins.). 2002. 25.95 (978-1-60083-632-9(1), Audiofy Corp) Iofy Corp.

Ethan Frome. Edith Wharton. Narrated by Jim Killavey. (Running Time: 3 hrs. 30 mins.). (C). 2006. 20.95 (978-1-59912-807-8(1)) Iofy Corp.

Ethan Frome. Edith Wharton. Narrated by Irene Worth. (Running Time: 3 hrs.). 2006. 14.95 (978-1-59912-981-5(7)) Iofy Corp.

Ethan Frome. Edith Wharton. Narrated by Scott Brick. (ENG.). 2005. audio compact disk 58.00 (978-1-4001-3063-4(8)) Pub: Tantor Media. Dist(s): IngramPubServ

Ethan Frome. unabr. ed. Edith Wharton. Read by C. M. Herbert. 3 cass. (Running Time: 4 hrs.). 1997. 23.95 t. (978-0-7861-1179-4(8), 1938) Blckstn Audio.
A portrait of the simple inhabitants of a nineteenth-century New England village.

Ethan Frome. unabr. ed. Edith Wharton. Read by C. M. Hebert. (Running Time: 10800 sec.). 2007. audio compact disk 19.95 (978-0-7861-6068-6(3)); audio compact disk 27.00 (978-0-7861-6067-9(5)) Blckstn Audio.

Ethan Frome. unabr. ed. Edith Wharton. Read by Marilyn Langbehn. 3 cass. (Running Time: 3 hrs. 30 min.). Dramatization. 1992. 21.95 (978-1-55686-391-2(8), 391) Books in Motion.
Considered one of the author's finest stories, Ethan Frome is the tragic drama of three ordinary people involved in a love triangle in rural New England of 1900.

Ethan Frome. unabr. ed. Edith Wharton. Read by Wanda McCaddon. 4 cass. (Running Time: 6 hrs.). 2001. 24.95 (978-0-7366-6767-8(9)) Books on Tape.
The story of a man torn between two women in rural New England.

Ethan Frome. unabr. ed. Edith Wharton. Read by Scott Brick. (YA). 2007. 44.99 (978-1-59895-796-9(1)) Find a World.

Ethan Frome. unabr. ed. Edith Wharton. Read by William Roberts. 3 cass. (Running Time: 3 hrs. 45 min.). (Isis Ser.). (J). 1994. 34.95 (978-1-85695-727-4(6), 940110) Pub: ISIS Lrg Prnt GBR. Dist(s): Ulverscroft US

Ethan Frome. unabr. ed. Edith Wharton. Read by Jim Killavey. 4 cass. (Running Time: 4 hrs. 7 min.). (YA). (gr. 10-12). 1991. 24.00 set. (C-214) Jimcin Record.
Considered the finest of Wharton's many novels & short stories.

Ethan Frome. unabr. ed. Edith Wharton. Read by Richard Thomas. 4 cass. (Running Time: 6 hrs.). 2004. 25.00 (978-1-931056-79-3(X), N Millennium Audio) New Millenn Enter.
This is a wonderful tale set near the turn of century and the bleak winter landscape of New England. A story of a poor farmer - lonely & downtrodden, his wife Zeena & her cousin, the enchanting Mattie Silver. Ethan Fromme is certainly a man who is at odds with social mores & his personal desires.

Ethan Frome, unabr. ed. Edith Wharton. Narrated by George Guidall. 3 cass. (Running Time: 4 hrs. 30 mins.). 1993. 26.00 (978-1-55690-813-2(X), 93123E7) Recorded Bks.
A tragedy of young love denied, set against the bleak winter landscape of a New England hardscabble farm at the turn of the century.

Ethan Frome. unabr. ed. Edith Wharton. Narrated by Scott Brick. 1 MP3 CD. (Running Time: 3 hrs. 49 mins.). (ENG.). 2002. audio compact disk 20.00 (978-1-4001-5063-2(9)) Pub: Tantor Media. Dist(s): IngramPubServ
Ethan Frome, a poor, downtrodden New England farmer is trapped in a loveless marriage to his invalid wife, Zeena. His ambition and intelligence are oppressed by Zeena's cold, conniving character. When Zeena's young cousin Mattie arrives to help care for her, Ethan is immediately taken by Mattie's warm, vivacious personality. They fall desperately in love as he realizes how much is missing from his life and marriage. Tragically, their love is doomed by Zeena's ever-lurking presence and by the social conventions of the day. Ethan remains torn between his sense of obligation and his urge to satisfy his heart's desire up to the suspenseful and unanticipated conclusion. Perhaps reflective of Wharton's own loveless marriage, this sophisticated, star-crossed love story vividly depicts her abhorrence of society's relentless standards of loyalty. Ethan Frome is one of Wharton's most popular and best-known works.This audiobook is on one CD, encoded in MP3 format and will only play on computers and CD players that have the ability to play this unique format.

Ethan Frome. unabr. ed. Edith Wharton. Narrated by Scott Brick. (Running Time: 4 hrs. 0 mins. 0 sec.). (ENG.). 2008. 19.99 (978-1-4001-5852-2(4)); audio compact disk 19.99 (978-1-4001-0852-7(7)); audio compact disk 39.99 (978-1-4001-3852-4(3)) Pub: Tantor Media. Dist(s): IngramPubServ

Ethan Frome. unabr. collector's ed. Edith Wharton. Read by Wanda McCaddon. 4 cass. (Running Time: 4 hrs.). 1982. 24.00 (978-0-7366-0405-5(7), 1381) Books on Tape.
A portrayal of lonely lives in half-deserted New England villages before the coming of the motor & the telephone: Ethan Frome, his wife, & his wife's cousin Mattoe, whom Ethan loves.

Ethan Frome, Set. unabr. ed. Edith Wharton. Narrated by John MacDonald. 3 cass. (Running Time: 4 hr.). (gr. 10-12). 1987. 16.95 (978-1-55685-074-5(3)) Audio Bk Con.
Love & deep tragedy in a small New England town.

Ethan of Athos. unabr. ed. Lois McMaster Bujold. Read by Grover Gardner. (Running Time: 8.5 hrs. NaN mins.). (Vorkosigan Ser.). 2009. 29.95 (978-1-4332-5093-4(4)); audio compact disk 70.00 (978-1-4332-5091-0(8)); audio compact disk 54.95 (978-1-4332-5090-3(X)) Blckstn Audio.

Ethan of Athos. unabr. ed. Lois McMaster Bujold. 1 CD (MP3). (Running Time: 7 hrs.). (Vorkosigan Ser.). 1999. audio compact disk 19.95 (978-1-885585-18-9(7)) Readers Chair.
Obstetrician Ethan Urquhart is one of the busiest men on Athos, even though the planet is forbidden to women. That is, until a mysterious genetic crisis threatens Athos with extinction.

Ethan of Athos, unabr. ed. Lois McMaster Bujold. Read by Michael Hanson & Carol Cowan. 6 cass. (Running Time: 7 hrs.). (Vorkosigan Ser.). (YA). 1999. 36.00 (978-1-885585-05-9(5)) Readers Chair.
The ovarian cultures on Athos are dying & Dr. Ethan Urquhart must go off planet to buy more. Along the way, he encounters twisted interplanetary political machinations, Cetagandan covert operatives & perhaps most disturbing, Elli Quinn, a Dendarii mercenary & woman.

Ethel Barrett Tells Favorite Old Testament Stories. Perf. by Ethel Barrett. 1 cass. (Running Time: 90 mins.). 1983. 7.99 (978-7-5116-0002-8(6)) Gospel Lght.
Bible stories from the Old Testament.

Ethel Barrett Tells Favorite Old Testament Stories. 1999th ed. Perf. by Ethel Barrett. 1 cass. (J). 1999. 7.99 Gospel Lght.
Includes the stories of Creation, Abraham & Lot, Joseph & His Brothers & more.

Ethel Barrett Tells Missionary Adventure Stories, Vol. 1. Short Stories. Perf. by Ethel Barrett. 1 cass. (Running Time: 90 mins.). (J). 1999. 7.99 Gospel Lght.
Stories about prayers, pilots, nurses & missionaries to delight young imaginations.

Ethel Barrett Tells Missionary Adventure Stories, Vol. 2. 1999th ed. Short Stories. Perf. by Ethel Barrett. 1 cass. (J). 1999. 7.99 Gospel Lght.

Ethel Barrett Tells Modern-Day Parables, Vol. 1. Ethel Barrett. 2 cass. (J). 7.99 (978-7-5116-0006-6(9), A127583, Gospel Light) Gospel Lght.
Eight parables that communicate Christian values through the antics of animal characters.

Ethel Barrett Tells Modern-Day Parables, Vol. 2. Ethel Barrett. 2 cass. (J). 7.99 (978-7-5116-0007-3(7)) Gospel Lght.

Ethel Kvalheim, Rosemaler. Jocelyn Riley. 1 cass. (Running Time: 18 min.). (YA). 1992. 8.00 (978-1-877933-25-7(2)) Her Own Words.
Documentary.

Etherealizing see Robert Frost Reads

Etheridge Knight. abr. ed. Read by Etheridge Knight. 1 cass. (Running Time: 29 min.). Incl. Poems from Prison; 1987. 10.00 New Letters.
Poetess gives a public reading in Chicago.

Etheridge Knight II. unabr. ed. Etheridge Knight. Read by Etheridge Knight. 1 cass. (Running Time: 29 min.). 1989. 10.00 New Letters.
Knight reads his poetry & is interviewed.

Ethical Assassin. abr. ed. David Liss. Read by William Dufris. 5. (Running Time: 21600 sec.). 2007. audio compact disk 14.99 (978-1-4233-0936-9(7), 9781423309369, BCD Value Price) Brilliance Audio.

Ethical Assassin. unabr. ed. David Liss. Read by William Dufris. (Running Time: 13 hrs.). 2006. 39.25 (978-1-4233-0934-5(0), 9781423309345, BADLE); 24.95 (978-1-4233-0933-8(2), 9781423309338, BAD); 92.25 (978-1-4233-0928-4(6), 9781423309284, BrilAudUnabridg); audio compact disk 107.25 (978-1-4233-0930-7(8), 9781423309307, BriAudCD Unabrid); audio compact disk 39.25 (978-1-4233-0932-1(4), 9781423309321, Brinc Audio MP3 Lib); audio compact disk 38.95 (978-1-4233-0929-1(4), 9781423309291, Bril Audio CD Unabri); audio compact disk 24.95 (978-1-4233-0931-4(6), 9781423309314, Brilliance MP3) Brilliance Audio.
No one is more surprised than Lem Altick when it turns out he's actually good at peddling encyclopedias door to door. He hates the predatory world of sales, but he needs the money to pay for college. Then things go horribly wrong. In a sweltering trailer in rural Florida, a couple Lem has spent hours pitching to is shot dead before his eyes, and the unassuming young man is suddenly pulled into the dark world of conspiracy and murder. Not just murder: assassination - or so claims the killer, the mysterious and strangely charismatic Melford Kean, who has struck without remorse and with remarkable good cheer. But the self-styled ethical assassin hadn't planned on a witness, and so he makes Lem a deal: Stay quiet and there will be no problems. Go to the police and take the fall. Before Lem can decide, he is drawn against his will into the realm of the assassin, a post-Marxist intellectual with whom he forms an unlikely (and perhaps unwise) friendship. The ethical assassin could be a charming sociopath, eco-activist, or vigilante for social justice. Lem isn't sure what is motivating Melford, but Lem realizes that to save himself, he must unravel the mystery of why the assassinations have occurred. To do so, he descends deeper into a bizarre world he never knew existed, where a group of desperate schemers are involved in a plot that could keep Lem from leaving town alive.

Ethical Considerations for Criminal Law Practitioners Under the New Rules. 1 cass. (Running Time: 1 hr. 30 min.). 1988. 25.00 PA Bar Inst.

Ethical Decision Making in Pastoral Care. 1 cass. (Care Cassettes Ser.: Vol. 16, No. 1). 1989. 10.80 Assn Prof Chaplains.

Ethical Dilemmas for the Surgeon: Panel Discussion Sponsored by the Committee on Young Surgeons. Moderated by Donald T. Trunkey. 2 cass. (Spring Sessions Ser.: SP-4). 1986. 19.00 (8675) Am Coll Surgeons.

Ethical Issues in Life & Death. 1 cass. (Care Cassettes Ser.: Vol. 22, No. 1). 1995. 10.80 Assn Prof Chaplains.

Ethical Issues in Medical Research & Practice. C. Grimm et al. 1986. 10.80 (0801) Assn Prof Chaplains.

Ethical Issues in Ministry to Persons with AIDS. 1 cass. (Care Cassettes Ser.: Vol. 14, No. 1). 1987. 10.80 Assn Prof Chaplains.

Ethical Issues in Your Practice. 1987. bk. 40.00; 30.00 PA Bar Inst.

Ethical-Legal Considerations. Harold Ginzburg. (AIDS: The National Conference for Practitioners). 1986. 9.00 (978-0-932491-60-2(X)) Res Appl Inc.

Ethical Responsibility of Being an Astrologer. Rosetta Connors. 1 cass. 8.95 (060) Am Fed Astrologers.
An AFA Convention workshop tape.

Ethical Spirituality: How to Not Worry. Sharon Sarles. (ENG.). 1997. pap. bk. 29.95 (978-0-9657770-0-1(6)) Organztnl Strategies.

Ethics. Aristotle. Narrated by Jim Killavey. (Running Time: 10 hrs.). 1990. 29.95 (978-1-59912-808-5(X)) Iofy Corp.

Ethics. unabr. ed. Aristotle. Read by Jim Killavey. 8 cass. (Running Time: 12 hrs.). 1990. 56.95 (978-0-7861-0611-0(5), 2101) Blckstn Audio.
Aristotle set out to discover the good life for mankind: the life of happiness. What he deduces is that happiness derives from the activity of the soul in accordance with virtue. Virtue is manifest in the deliberate choice of actions as part of a well-planned life, a life whose plan takes a middle course between excess & deficiency.

Ethics. unabr. ed. Aristotle. Read by Jim Killavey. 8 cass. (Running Time: 10 hrs. 30 min.). (YA). (gr. 9). 1991. 56.00 set. (C-211) Jimcin Record.
Treatise on justice & morality.

Ethics. unabr. collector's ed. Aristotle. Read by Jim Killavey. 8 cass. (Running Time: 12 hrs.). 1992. 64.00 (978-0-7366-3959-0(4), 9210) Books on Tape.
Born in 384 B.C., Aristotle pushed open new doors of thought, always a risky enterprise. He gained access to Alexander, then a young man, later to become "the Great." Aristotle's ideas were liberal & they had consequences. Generations of Christians, Muslims & Jews have benefited from them, transmitted as they were by a man who under another tutor might have been known as merely "the Conqueror".

Ethics, Pt. 1, set. abr. ed. Benedictus de Spinoza. Read by Robert L. Halvorson. 2 cass. (Running Time: 180 min.). 14.95 (80) Halvorson Assocs.

Ethics, Set. abr. ed. Aristotle. Read by Robert L. Halvorson. 8 cass. (Running Time: 720 min.). 56.95 (51) Halvorson Assocs.

Ethics: Program from the Award Winning Public Radio Series. Interview. Hosted by Fred Goodwin. Comment by John Hockenberry. 1 CD. (Running Time: 1 hr.). (Infinite Mind Ser.). 2002. audio compact disk 21.95 (978-1-888064-63-6(3), LCM 235) Lichtenstein Creat.
the second program in our three-part series Mental Health in Troubled Times: One Year After.In the days and weeks following the terrorist attacks of last year, Americans around the country joined together in grief, righteous anger, and patriotism. But over the past 12 months, we have witnessed one scandal after another - Arthur Anderson, Enron, the Catholic Church, Martha Stewart, WorldCom - capturing public attention and eroding public trust. This week we look at what it means to behave ethically and where some church and corporate leaders have gone wrong.Correspondent Phillip Martin reports on an "ethical fitness" seminar at the Institute for Global Ethics, where Americans from around the country gather to talk about ethics. Dr. Goodwin's guests include Kim Clark, Dean of the Harvard Business School; Steven Pinker, professor of psychology in the department of brain and cognitive sciences at the Massachusetts Institute of Technology; Father Robert Drinan, Professor of Ethics and Law, Georgetown University Law Center, Jed Emerson, a fellow at the Hewlett Foundation and a leading proponent of social responsibility in business; Mary Flood, a reporter for the Houston Chronicle who broke much of the Enron story; and singer-songwriters Suzzy and Maggie Roche perform their song "Anyway." Commentary by John Hockenberry.

Ethics & Counseling in an Elder Law Practice: Value Added Concepts. 1 cass. (Running Time: 2 hrs.). 1999. 25.00 Set; incl. outline. (ACX992) Am Law Inst.
Live recording from the Elder Law Update teleseminar series.

Ethics & Morality in Architecture. unabr. ed. Read by Frank Lloyd Wright. 1 cass. (Running Time: 34 min.). 12.95 J Norton Pubs.

Ethics & Professionalism for the Pennsylvania Lawyer. American Law Institute-American Bar Association, Committee on Continuing Professional Education Staff. 1 cass. (Running Time: 90 mins.). Am Law Inst.
Five different case studies explore the ethical issues of practice through dramatized practice scenarios, stimulating discussions, expert instruction.

Ethics & Trends in Human Genetics. 1 cass. (Care Cassettes Ser.: Vol. 10, No. 9). 1983. 10.80 Assn Prof Chaplains.

Ethics in Action. Gerald Corey et al. 2002. audio compact disk 35.95 (978-0-534-59895-2(1)) Wadsworth Pub.

Ethics in Astrology. ACT Staff. 1 cass. 8.95 (477) Am Fed Astrologers.
How do we confront issues raised?.

Ethics in Counseling. 1 cass. (Professional Issues Ser.). 1981. 8.95 (1467G) Hazelden.

Ethics in Counseling. Barbara Herlihy & Gerald Corey. 6 cass. pap. bk. 109.00 (74230); 79.00 incl. script. (74231); 55.00 exam. (74232) Am Coun Assn.
Ethical behavior guidelines & techniques for ethical decision making.

Ethics in Education. Ayn Rand. Read by Ayn Rand. 1 cass. (Running Time: 50 min.). 1966. 12.95 (978-1-56114-065-7(1), AR02C) Second Renaissance.
The role of Romantic art in the early development of a moral "sense of life".

Ethics of Aristotle. Joseph Koterski. 6 cass. (Running Time: 6 hrs.). 2001. 29.95 (978-1-56585-092-7(0), 408) Teaching Co.

Ethics of Aristotle. Instructed by Joseph Koterski. 6 CDs. (Running Time: 6 hrs.). 2001. bk. 39.95 (978-1-56585-341-6(5), 408) Teaching Co.

Ethics of Competition. John Robbins. 1 cass. (Introduction to Economics Ser.: No. 10). 5.00 Trinity Found.

Ethics of Excellence Audible. Price Pritchett. (ENG.). 2007. 9.95 (978-0-944002-39-1(0)) Pritchett.

Ethics of Libertarianism. unabr. ed. Walter Block. 1 cass. (Running Time: 41 min.). 12.95 (172) J Norton Pubs.
This lecture is an introductory overview of libertarian ideas. Defining libertarianism as "the philosophical view that it is immoral to commit aggression against nonaggressors".

Ethics of the Enlightened World. Read by Chogyam Trungpa. 3 cass. 1980. 31.50 (A024) Vajradhatu.
Five talks. To relate clearly with the environment as simple, decent, & ordinary human beings is extraordinarily powerful.

Ethics of the Enlightened World. Vajracarya. Read by Chogyam Trungpa. 3 cass. 1980. 31.50 Vajradhatu.
Explains that relating clearly with the environment as simple, decent, & ordinary human beings is extraordinarily powerful, & that clarity is our natural state of being.

Ethics of Unity. Swami Amar Jyoti. 1 cass. 1991. 9.95 (K-141) Truth Consciousness.
On "turning the other cheek". Ethics & morality depend upon the consciousness of unity; lacking this, they will never work.

Ethics to Excellence: The Key to Productivity. Layne A. Longfellow. Read by Layne A. Longfellow. 1 cass. (Running Time: 90 min.). 1986. 12.00 Lect Theatre.
Lecture asserting that leaders in the private & public sectors must bring together a nation's divergent motivations to achieve excellence.

Ethiopia. unabr. ed. Wendy McElroy. Read by Peter Hackes. Prod. by Pat Childs. (Running Time: 10800 sec.). (World's Political Hot Spots Ser.). 2006. audio compact disk 25.95 (978-0-7861-6448-6(4)) Pub: Blckstn Audio. Dist(s): NetLibrary CO

Ethiopia. unabr. ed. Wendy McElroy. Read by Peter Hackes. Ed. by Mike Hassell. 2 cass. (Running Time: 3 hrs.). Dramatization. (World's Political Hot Spots Ser.). (YA). (gr. 11 up). 1992. 17.95 (978-0-938935-97-1(6), 10362) Knowledge Prod.
This rich culture of Africa, known in the Bible as Abyssinia, claims descent from King Solomon & the Queen of Sheba. Under a Marxist regime, however, these ancient people are dying from famine & genocide.

Ethnic America, unabr. ed. Thomas Sowell. Read by James Bundy. 9 cass. (Running Time: 13 hrs.). 1989. 62.95 (978-0-7861-0048-4(6), 1046) Blckstn Audio.
A useful & concise record tracing the history of nine ethnic groups - the Irish, the Germans, the Japanese, the Blacks, the Puerto Ricans & the Mexicans. Provides us with perspective-building facts & explains each ethnic group's varied experiences in adapting to American society.

Ethnic America. unabr. ed. Thomas Sowell. Read by James Bundy. (Running Time: 45000 sec.). 2006. audio compact disk 90.00 (978-0-7861-6639-8(8)); audio compact disk 29.95 (978-0-7861-7356-3(4)) Blckstn Audio.

***Ethnic Blends: Mixing Diversity into Your Local Church.** unabr. ed. J. Mark DeYmaz & Harry Li. (Running Time: 6 hrs. 57 mins. 14 sec.). (Leadership Network Innovation Ser.). (ENG.). 2010. 18.99 (978-0-310-32124-8(7)) Zondervan.

Ethnic Dances of Black People Around the World. 2 cass. (Running Time: 2 hrs.). 2001. pap. bk. 18.95 (KIM 9040C) Kimbo Educ.
Eight ethnic dances are introduced by talk-thru, walk-thru instructions. Includes Calypso (Trinidad), Shango (African Voodoo Ritual), Samba (Brazil), Ibo (Haiti), & more. Includes manual.

Ethnobotany. unabr. ed. Terence McKenna. 5 cass. 1984. 45.00 set. (978-1-56964-037-1(8), A0174-84) Sound Photosyn.
A complete course with a guest talk by Dennis McKenna.

Ethnobotany & Shamanism. Terence McKenna. 1 cass. 54.00 (A0228-87) Sound Photosyn.
Another excellent full course presented as a 'round the world exploration. No wasted time, it's all information.

Ethnobotany of Shamanism. Terence McKenna. 2 cass. 18.00 set. (A0395-88) Sound Photosyn.
An integral opening to the workshop.

Ethnobotany of Shamanism Workshop. Terence McKenna. 6 cass. 54.00 set. (A0396-88) Sound Photosyn.
A further non-repetitive, complete course in fascinating facts from afar.

Ethylmalonic Encephalopathy - A Bibliography & Dictionary for Physicians, Patients, & Genome Researchers. Compiled by Icon Group International, Inc. Staff. 2007. ring bd. 28.95 (978-0-497-11207-3(8)) Icon Grp.

Etica, la Unica Regla para Tomar Decisiones. unabr. ed. John C. Maxwell. (SPA.). 2005. audio compact disk 16.99 (978-987-557-063-4(X)) Pub: Vida Pubs. Dist(s): Zondervan

Etiquette Powerpoint. Melanie Nelson. (YA). 2007. audio compact disk 49.95 (978-1-57175-582-7(9), 7172) Learning ZoneXpress.

Etiquette Scholar's Dining Etiquette, Vol. 1. unabr. ed. Michael T. Lininger, 1st. Compiled by Yellowstone Publishing LLC, 1st. Kari L. Lininger, 1st & Richard W. Mitchell, 1st. (ENG.). 2010. stu. ed. & training bk. ed. 14.95 (978-0-9801951-1-8(X)) Yellowstone Pub.

Etrange Disparition. Blanche & Guilmault. audio compact disk 12.95 (978-0-8219-3783-9(9)) EMC-Paradigm.

Etranger see Albert Camus: Reading from His Novel and Essays

Etranger, Set. Albert Camus. Read by Michael Lonsdale. 3 cass. (FRE.). 1991. 29.95 (1016-AV) Olivia & Hill.
In this modern classic, Camus describes Meursault, a stranger in a society whose values he rejects. Lonsdale's voice reflects the detachment of Meursault, even when faced by his own execution.

Etta: A Novel. unabr. ed. Gerald Kolpan. (Running Time: 10 hrs. 5 mins.). 2009. 29.95 (978-1-4332-5933-3(8)); audio compact disk 29.95 (978-1-4332-5932-6(X)); audio compact disk 90.00 (978-1-4332-5930-2(3)); audio compact disk 65.95 (978-1-4332-5929-6(X)) Blckstn Audio.

Etudes for the Twenty-First Century Clarinet. Phillip Rehfeldt. 2 cass. (Editions for Clarinet Ser.). 1992. 50.00 Set. (978-0-933251-12-0(2)) Mill Creek Pubns.
Includes thirty-three musical scores.

Etudiant Etranger, Set. Philippe Labro. Read by Philippe Labro. 6 cass. (FRE.). 1991. 49.95 (1068-KFP) Olivia & Hill.
In a small, prestigious university in Virginia a young French student discovers campus life during the quiet 50s. Autobiographical.

Eucharist: The Role of the Priest in the Sacrifice of the Mass. Avery Dulles. 1 cass. (Running Time: 1 hr. 13 min.). 1995. 8.95 (TAH334) Alba Hse Comns.
Fr. Dulles praises Vatican II's middle course between clericalism & laicism. It balances the role of the community & the priest in a most profound & authentic manner.

Eucharist - Gift of Love. William Marra. 1 cass. (Inspiring Presentations from the National Rosary Congress Ser.). 2.50 (978-1-56036-087-2(9)) AMI Pr.

Eucharist - "In Memory of Me" Eugene LaVerdiere. 4 cass. (Running Time: 3 hrs. 24 min.). 1994. 34.95 Set. (TAH304) Alba Hse Comns.
The Eucharist is a story of mission & ministry, the assembly of the church, the breaking of the bread "in memory of me," & the last supper, which is the first of many more suppers done in memory of me.

Eucharist of Jesus. Robert Fabing. 9.95 (5362, North Am Liturgy) OR Catholic.
Presents a program for instruction & understanding the action of the Sunday Eucharist.

Eucharistic Devotion & the Spiritual Life. Frederick L. Miller. 1 cass. (National Meeting of the Institute, 1990 Ser.). 4.00 (90N7) IRL Chicago.

Eudora Welty Reading from Her Works. unabr. ed. Eudora Welty. Read by Eudora Welty. 1 cass. Incl. Memory. (V 1010); Why I Live at the P. O. (V 1010); Worn Path. (V 1010); 11.95 (978-1-55994-093-1(X), V 1010) HarperCollins Pubs.

Eudora Welty Reads. abr. ed. Eudora Welty. Read by Eudora Welty. 1 cass. (Authors Reading Authors Ser.). 1986. 9.95 (978-0-89845-555-7(3), A 1010) HarperCollins Pubs.

Eudora Welty Reads. abr. ed. Eudora Welty & Eudora Welty. Read by Eudora Welty. 2 cass. (Running Time: 3 hrs.). 1998. 18.00 (978-0-694-52014-5(4)) HarperCollins Pubs.

Eudora Welty Reads. unabr. ed. Short Stories. Eudora Welty. Read by Eudora Welty. 2 cass. (Running Time: 1 hr. 38 mins.). 18.00 (H130) Blckstn Audio.
Relates, in her sweetly vibrant Mississippi drawl, five of her finest stories: "Why I Live at the P.O.," "A Memory," "A Worn Path," "Powerhouse" & "Petrified Man.".

Eudora Welty Reads. unabr. ed. Eudora Welty. Read by Eudora Welty. 2 cass. (Running Time: 38 min.). 1996. 19.00 (978-1-55994-568-4(0), DCN 2289) HarperCollins Pubs.
Includes "Why I Live at the P. O.", "Powerhouse", "Petrified Man" & other stories.

Eudora Welty Reads Her Stories Powerhouse & Petrified Man. abr. ed. Eudora Welty. 1 cass. 1984. 12.95 (978-0-694-50331-5(2), SWC 1626) HarperCollins Pubs.

Eugen Gomringer. unabr. ed. Eugen Gomringer. Read by Eugen Gomringer. Interview with Rebekah Presson. 1 cass. (Running Time: 29 min.). 1990. 10.00 (092890) New Letters.
Swiss poet & father of "Concrete" poetry, Gomringer talks about his fascination with minimalism that began during World War II & became very popular in Europe during the 50's.

Eugene Onegin: A Novel in Verse. abr. ed. Perf. by Jerome Hines. Tr. by Alexander Pushkin. Intro. by Alexander Pushkin. 1 cass. 1978. 12.95 (978-0-694-50289-9(8), SWC 1532) HarperCollins Pubs.

Eugene-Portland. Dan Heller. 1 cass. 1994. 9.95 (978-1-885433-00-8(X)) Takilma East.

Eugene Returns!, Vol. 44. Focus on the Family & AIO Team Staff. Prod. by Dave Arnold & Marshal Younger. 4 cass. (Running Time: 5 hrs.). (Adventures in Odyssey Ser.). (ENG.). (J). (gr. 3-7). 2005. audio compact disk 24.99 (978-1-58997-300-8(3)) Pub: Focus Family. Dist(s): Tyndale Hse

Eugene Rhodes: Talkin' about My Time. 1 cass. 9.98 (C-12) Folk-Legacy.
Blues from a northern penitentiary inmate.

Eugenia Grandet. abr. ed. Honoré de Balzac. 3 CDs.Tr. of Eugenie Grandet. (SPA.). 2002. audio compact disk 17.00 (978-958-8161-49-5(5)) YoYoMusic.

Eugenics Wars, Vol. I. Greg Cox. 3 CDs. (Running Time: 3 hrs.). (Star Trek Ser.: No. 22). 2005. 25.00 (978-1-58807-885-8(X)) Am Pubng Inc.
Now, as an ancient and forbidden technology tempts mankind once more, Captain James T. Kirk of the Starship Enterprise(tm) must probe deep into the secrets of the past, to discover the true origins of the dreaded Eugenics Wars - and of perhaps the greatest foe he has ever faced.

Eugenics Wars, Vol. II. Greg Cox. 3 CDs. (Running Time: 3 hrs.). (Star Trek Ser.: No.23). 2005. 25.00 (978-1-58807-886-5(8)) Am Pubng Inc.
Volume Two proves to be every bit as exciting, entertaining, and humorous as the first volume of this saga. The second portion of this engrossing story takes the reader from the beginnings of Khan's consolidation of his power, through the events that lead to his flight from Earth. From beginning to end, this novel is eminently satisfying.

Eugenics Wars Vol. 1: The Rise & Fall of Khan Noonien Singh. Greg Cox. (Star Trek Ser.). 2004. 10.95 (978-0-7435-1866-6(7)) Pub: S&S Audio. Dist(s): S and S Inc

Eugenie Grandet see Eugenia Grandet

Eugénie Grandet. Honoré de Balzac. Read by Laura García. (Running Time: 3 hrs.). 2002. 16.95 (978-1-60083-258-1(X), Audiofy Corp) Iofy Corp.

Eugénie Grandet. unabr. ed. Read by Honoré de Balzac. 5 cass. 1998. 47.95 Set. (978-1-86015-440-9(9)) T T Beeler.
A young woman in rural France finds that she can no longer stifle her emotions after meeting her gallant cousin.

Eugénie Grandet, Set. Honoré de Balzac. Read by J. Castalo. 3 cass. (FRE.). 1991. 31.95 (1009-OH) Olivia & Hill.
One of the most famous works of the "Comedie Humaine." It is a study of provincial life, of the miser M. Grandet & his daughter, Eugenie, enamored of her spendthrift cousin Charles.

Eugenio Montale's Dora Markus from "Imitations" see Twentieth-Century Poetry in English, No. 32-33, Recordings of Poets Reading Their Own Poetry

Euided Writing, Interactive Writing & Independent Writing: the Keys to Writing: Success. abr. ed. Intro. by Vaime Bailey. 6 cass. (Running Time: 3 hrs. 40 mins.). (gr. 3-6). 2004. 89.00 (978-1-886397-59-0(7)) Bureau of Educ.

Eulalia! A Tale from Redwall. Brian Jacques. Narrated by Brian Jacques. (Running Time: 45000 sec.). (Redwall Ser.). (J). (gr. 4-7). 2007. audio compact disk 34.99 (978-1-4281-7705-5(1)) Recorded Bks.

Eulalia! A Tale from Redwall. unabr. ed. Brian Jacques. 11 CDs. (Running Time: 12 hrs. 30 mins.). (Redwall Ser.: Bk. 19). (YA). (gr. 5-8). 2007. audio compact disk 108.75 (978-1-4281-7708-6(6)); 88.75 (978-1-4281-7706-2(X)) Recorded Bks.
From the mind of Brian Jacques - the New York Times best-selling author of the Redwall series - comes another exhilarating adventure in this beloved saga. At the legendary fortress of Salamandastron, aging Lord Asheye has a prophecy. A new, young badger lord must take his place, but Lord Asheye does not know who the young warrior is. Meanwhile, unaware of his destiny, the future lord is captured by infamous fox Vizka Longtooth, who intends to lay siege to Redwall Abbey.

Eulalie & the Hopping Head. David Small. Read by Martin Jarvis & Rosalind Ayres. 11 vols. (Running Time: 14 mins.). (J). (ps-2). 2003. pap. bk. 18.95 (978-1-59112-509-9(X)) Pub: Live Oak Media. Dist(s): AudioGO

Eulalie & the Hopping Head. David Small. 11 vols. (Running Time: 14 mins.). (J). 2003. bk. 25.95 (978-1-59112-217-3(1)) Live Oak Media.

Eulalie & the Hopping Head. David Small. Read by Martin Jarvis & Rosalind Ayres. 11 vols. (Running Time: 14 mins.). (J). 2003. bk. 28.95 (978-1-59112-510-5(3)) Live Oak Media.

Eulalie & the Hopping Head. David Small. Illus. by David Small. 14 vols. (Running Time: 14 mins.). 2003. pap. bk. 35.95 (978-1-59112-520-4(0)) Live Oak Media.

Eulalie & the Hopping Head. David Small. Illus. by David Small. 14 vols. (Running Time: 14 mins.). (J). 2003. pap. bk. 33.95 (978-1-59112-218-0(X)); 9.95 (978-1-59112-215-9(5)); audio compact disk 12.95 (978-1-59112-508-2(1)) Live Oak Media.

Eulalie & the Hopping Head. David Small. Read by Martin Jarvis & Rosalind Ayres. 11 vols. (Running Time: 14 mins.). (J). 2005. pap. bk. 16.95 (978-1-59112-216-6(3)) Pub: Live Oak Media. Dist(s): AudioGO

Eule. Jacob W. Grimm & Wilhelm K. Grimm. 1 cass. (Running Time: 60 min.). (Bruder Grimm Kinder & Hausmarchen Ser.). (GER.). 1996. pap. bk. 19.50 (978-1-58085-215-9(7), GR-10) Interlingua VA.
Includes German transcription. Includes title story, Das Waldhaus, Der Mond, Der Grabhugel, Meister Pfriem. The combination of written text & clarity & pace of diction will open the door for intermediate & advanced students to genuine comprehension & the use of literary texts for advancement in rapid understanding of written & oral language materials. The audio text plus written text concept makes foreign languages accessible to a much wider range of students than books alone.

Eulenburg Audio & Score Presentation Case: Eulenburg Audio Scores Complete Box Set - - 50 Scores. 2008. audio compact disk 599.00 (978-3-7957-6498-2(X), 379576498X) Pub: Schott Musik DEU. Dist(s): H Leonard

Eunoia. Christian Bök. 2003. audio compact disk 16.95 (978-1-55245-124-3(0)) Pub: Coach Hse Bks CAN. Dist(s): Chicago Distribution Ctr
Five stories of which uses only one vowel!.

Euology for the Young Victims of the 16th Street Baptist Church Bombing: An Unabridged Selection from A Call to Conscience - the Landmark Speeches of Dr. Martin Luther King, Jr. unabr. ed. Read by Fred Shuttleworth & Martin Luther King, Jr. (Running Time: 30 mins.). (ENG.). 2006. 1.98 (978-1-59483-486-8(5)) Pub: Hachet Audio. Dist(s): HachBkGrp

Euphoria. Roderick Borrie. Music by Hugh Fraser. 2000. audio compact disk (978-1-893238-11-4(3)) Doc Borrie.

Euphues & His England see Cambridge Treasy Malory

Eupsychian Ethic. Abraham H. Maslow. 6 cass. (Running Time: 5 hrs. 42 min.). 1969. 56.00 set. (01404) Big Sur Tapes.

Eureka! Brian Tell. 1999. pap. bk. 14.95 (978-0-9676065-0-7(0)) Busy Flower Pubng.

Eureka. abr. ed. William Diehl. Read by Cotter Smith. 4 cass. (Running Time: 6 hrs.). 2002. 25.95 (978-0-06-009938-1(0)) HarperCollins Pubs.

Eureka: A Prose Poem. Edgar Allan Poe. (Literary Classics Ser.). (ENG.). 1997. 14.98 (978-1-57392-134-3(3)) Prometheus Bks.

Eureka! Discovering American English & Culture Through Proverbs, Fables, Myths, & Legends. Planaria J. Price. (ENG., 1999. 30.00 (978-0-472-00285-6(6)) U of Mich Pr.

Eureka Seven OST II. Prod. by Bandai Entertainment. (YA). 2007. 19.98 (978-1-59409-713-3(5)) Bandai Ent.

Euripides' Hekabe. unabr. ed. Read by Stephen G. Daitz. Ed. by Stephen G. Daitz. 2 cass. (Running Time: 2 hrs.). (Living Voice of Greek & Latin Ser.). (GRE.). (YA). (gr. 10-12). pap. bk. 39.95 (978-0-88432-084-5(7), S23650) J Norton Pubs.

Eurodollar Market: The Coming Deflationary Storm. unabr. ed. John Exter. 1 cass. (Running Time: 36 min.). 12.95 (1101) J Norton Pubs.

Eurodollar Market-Epicenter of World-Wide Deflation. unabr. ed. John Exter. 1 cass. (Running Time: 54 min.). 12.95 (368) J Norton Pubs.

Europa Conspiracy. unabr. ed. Tim LaHaye & Bob Phillips. 6 cass. (Running Time: 9 hrs.). (Babylon Rising Ser.: Bk. 3). 2005. 54.00 (978-1-4159-2437-2(6)); audio compact disk 72.00 (978-1-4159-2438-9(4)) Books on Tape.

Europa (Earth's Cry Heaven's Smile) Ed. by Aaron Stang. Arranged by Bill Purse. (Warner Bros. Publications 21st Century Guitar Ensemble Ser.). (ENG.). 2002. audio compact disk 19.95 (978-0-7579-9786-0(4), Warner Bro) Alfred Pub.

Europa Rising: Rebuilding the Empire. Chuck Missler. 2 CD's. (Running Time: 2 hrs.). (Briefing Packages by Chuck Missler). 2003. audio compact disk 19.95 (978-1-57821-215-6(4)) Koinonia Hse.
Who Conquered The Romans?Just as Daniel had predicted, the Babylonian Empire was ultimately conquered by the Persians; the Persians were, in turn, conquered by the Greeks; and, the Greeks were conquered by the Romans. But who conquered the Romans?The Roman Empire ultimately disintegrated into pieces, and each segment seems to have had its "day in the sun." The ensuing struggles for power, and the influx of external tribes into the cohesion that once was Rome, continued over almost two millennia. In our series reviewing the rise of the "New Europe," we'll take a brief glimpse at the caldron that has been stewing with tensions and ambitions for many centuries.

Europe & the Wars of Religion (1500-1700), Part I-II. Instructed by Govind Sreenivasan. 12 cass. (Running Time: 12 hrs.). 2003. bk. 54.95 (978-1-56585-664-6(3), 8247) Teaching Co.

Europe & the Wars of Religion (1500-1700), Parts I-II. Instructed by Govind Sreenivasan. 12 CDs. (Running Time: 12 hrs.). 2003. bk. 69.95 (978-1-56585-666-0(X), 8247) Teaching Co.

Europe & Western Civilization in the Modern Age, Pts. I-IV. Instructed by Thomas Childers. 24 cass. (Running Time: 24 hrs.). 99.95 (978-1-56585-238-9(9), 820) Teaching Co.

Europe & Western Civilization in the Modern Age, Vol. 2. Instructed by Thomas Childers. 6 cass. (Running Time: 6 hrs.). 1998. 249.95 (978-1-56585-239-6(7)) Teaching Co.

Europe & Western Civilization in the Modern Age, Vol. 3. Instructed by Thomas Childers. 6 cass. (Running Time: 6 hrs.). 1998. 249.95 (978-1-56585-240-2(0)) Teaching Co.

Europe & Western Civilization in the Modern Age, Vol. 4. Instructed by Thomas Childers. 6 cass. (Running Time: 6 hrs.). 1998. 249.95 (978-1-56585-241-9(9)) Teaching Co.

Europe & Western Europe in the Modern Age, Pts. I-IV. Instructed by Thomas Childers. 24 CDs. (Running Time: 24 hrs.). 1998. bk. 129.95 (978-1-56585-389-8(X), 820) Teaching Co.

Europe Central. unabr. ed. William T. Vollmann. (Running Time: 115200 sec.). 2008. audio compact disk 44.95 (978-1-4332-1321-2(4)) Blckstn Audio.

Europe Central. unabr. ed. William T. Vollmann. Read by Ralph Cosham. (Running Time: 115200 sec.). 2008. audio compact disk & audio compact disk 160.00 (978-1-4332-1320-5(6)) Blckstn Audio.

Europe Central: Part 1, Part A. unabr. ed. William T. Vollmann. (Running Time: 59400 sec.). 2008. 89.95 (978-1-4332-1319-9(2)) Blckstn Audio.

Europe Central: Part 2, Part B. unabr. ed. William T. Vollmann. Read by Ralph Cosham. (Running Time: 55800 sec.). 2008. 85.95 (978-1-4332-1361-8(3)) Blckstn Audio.

European Agreement Concerning the International Carriage of Dangerous Goods by Road (ADR) Applicable as from 1 January 2009 (CD-ROM) United Nations. (ENG & FRE.). 2009. audio compact disk 155.00 (978-92-1-039723-0(1)) Untd Nat Pubns.

European & Japanese Reports on Manufacturing & Coordination: Track One. 2 cass. 1990. 17.00 set. Recorded Res.

European Christmas. Rick Steves. (Rick Steves Ser.). (ENG.). 2006. audio compact disk 12.95 (978-1-59880-041-8(8)) Pub: Westview. Dist(s): PerseuPGW

European Economic Community: Products Liability Rules & Environmental Policy. 9 cass. (Running Time: 12 hrs.). bk. 75.00 incl. 468-page course handbook. (T6-9144) PLI.

European History & European Lives Pts. I-III: 1715-1914. Instructed by Jonathan Steinberg. 18 cass. (Running Time: 18 hrs.). bk. 79.95 (978-1-56585-755-1(0), 8270) Teaching Co.

European History & European Lives Pts. I-III: 1715-1914. Instructed by Jonathan Steinberg. 18 CDs. (Running Time: 18 hrs.). 2003. bk. 99.95 (978-1-56585-756-8(9), 8270) Teaching Co.

European Limnofauna: A Pictorial Key to the Families. H. Visser & H. Veldhuijsen. Ed. by ETI Staff. 2000. audio compact disk 379.00 (978-3-540-14708-4(X)) Spri.

European Musical Heritage, C. 800 - C. 1750. Sarah Fuller. (C). 1988. 95.31 (978-0-07-555102-7(0), Mc-H Human Soc) Pub: McGrw-H Hghr Educ. Dist(s): McGraw

European Mysticism. unabr. ed. Perf. by Eknath Easwaran. 1 cass. (Running Time: 1 hr.). 1987. 7.95 (978-1-58638-532-3(1)) Nilgiri Pr.

European Security Journal. Special Markets Staff. (978-0-9999999-6-7(6), Rout) Tay Francis Ltd GBR.

European Thought & Culture in the 19th Century, Pts. I-II. Instructed by Lloyd Kramer. 12 CDs. (Running Time: 12 hrs.). 2001. bk. 69.95 (978-1-56585-348-5(2), 4423); 54.95 (978-1-56585-103-0(X), 4423) Teaching Co.

European Thought & Culture in the 19th Century, Vol. 2. Instructed by Lloyd Kramer. 6 cass. (Running Time: 6 hrs.). 2001. 129.95 (978-1-56585-104-7(8)) Teaching Co.

European Thought & Culture in the 20th Century, Pts. I-II. Instructed by Lloyd Kramer. 12 CDs. (Running Time: 12 hrs.). 2002. bk. 69.95 (978-1-56585-349-2(0), 4427) Teaching Co.

European Thought & Culture in the 20th Century, Vol. 2. Instructed by Lloyd Kramer. 6 cass. (Running Time: 6 hrs.). 2002. 129.95 (978-1-56585-106-1(4)) Teaching Co.

European Thought & Culure in the 20th Century: Parts I-II. Instructed by Lloyd Kramer. 12 cass. (Running Time: 12 hrs.). 2002. bk. 54.95 (978-1-56585-105-4(6), 4427) Teaching Co.

***Europeans.** Henry James. Narrated by Eleanor Bron. (Running Time: 6 hrs. 0 mins. 0 sec.). (Cover to Cover Ser.). (ENG.). 2011. audio compact disk 29.95 (978-1-60283-943-4(3)) Pub: AudioGO. Dist(s): Perseus Dist

Europeans. unabr. ed. Henry James. Read by Susan O'Malley. 4 cass. (Running Time: 390 min.). 1997. 26.95 Set. (978-1-885546-14-2(9)) Big Ben Audio.
Eugenia, an expatriated American & morganatic wife of a German prince, has her marriage repudiated in favor of a state marriage. She goes to America in hopes of making a wealthy marriage. Set in the beautiful countryside around Boston in the mid-nineteenth century & focuses on the effects of Old World experience on New World innocence.

Europeans. unabr. ed. Henry James. Read by Lloyd James. 6. (Running Time: 25200 sec.). 2007. audio compact disk 55.00 (978-0-7861-5800-3(X)); audio compact disk 29.95 (978-0-7861-5801-0(8)) Blckstn Audio.

Europeans. unabr. ed. Henry James. Read by Diane Burroughs. 5 cass. (Running Time: 6 hrs.). Dramatization. 1982. 32.00 incl. album. (C-86) Jimcin Record.
The old world vs. the new world is the theme in this novel of manners.

Europeans. unabr. ed. Henry James. Read by Lloyd James. (Running Time: 7 hrs.). 2001. 39.95 (978-0-7861-1909-7(8)) Blckstn Audio.

Europeans, unabr. collector's ed. Henry James. Read by Diane Burroughs. 7 cass. (Running Time: 7 hrs.). 1982. 42.00 (978-0-7366-3875-3(X), 9086) Books on Tape.
Concerns an expatriate American, Eugenia & her artist brother, Felix Young. Eugenia is the morganatic wife of a German prince, but she is to be repudiated in favor of a state marriage; thus she leaves for Boston to make an appropriate match of her own.

Europeans, Set. Henry James. Narrated by Flo Gibson. 4 cass. (Running Time: 1 hr. 30 min. per cass.). 1987. 19.95 (978-1-55685-080-6(8)) Audio Bk Con.
The old world of experience, personified by Felix & his sister, Baroness Munster, meets the innocent new world as they visit their American cousins in New England.

Europe's Last Summer. unabr. ed. David Fromkin. Read by Sklar Alan. 9 CDs. (Running Time: 11 hrs. 30 mins.). 2004. audio compact disk 72.00 (978-0-7861-8679-2(8), 3279); 56.95 (978-0-7861-2718-4(X), 3279) Blckstn Audio.
The early summer of 1914 was the most glorious Europeans could remember. But, behind the scenes, the most destructive war the world had yet known was moving inexorably into being, a war that would continue to resonate into the twenty-first century. The question of how it began has long vexed historians. Most have cited the assassination of Archduke Ferdinand; some concluded that it was nobody?s fault. But David Fromkin, whose account is based on the latest scholarship, provides a different answer. He shows that hostilities were started deliberately.

Euroskop: Kassetten. Paul Webster & Joerg Jahn. 4 cass. (Cambridge Express German Ser.). (GER., 1998. 133.00 (978-0-521-48429-9(4)) Cambridge U Pr.

Eustace. Catherine Jinks. Read by Melissa Chambers. (Running Time: 3 hrs. 45 mins.). (Allie's Ghost Hunters Ser.: Bk. 2). (J). 2009. 54.99 (978-1-74214-409-2(8), 9781742144092) Pub: Bolinda Pubng AUS. Dist(s): Bolinda Pub Inc

Eustace. unabr. ed. Catherine Jinks. Read by Melissa Chambers. (Running Time: 13500 sec.). (Allie's Ghost Hunters Ser.: Bk. 2). (J). (gr. 4-7). 2008. audio compact disk 54.95 (978-1-74093-990-4(5), 9781740939904) Pub: Bolinda Pubng AUS. Dist(s): Bolinda Pub Inc

Eustace Diamonds. Anthony Trollope. 2007. 19.95 (978-1-60112-032-8(X)) Babblebooks.

Eustace Diamonds, Pt. 1. unabr. collector's ed. Anthony Trollope. Read by David Case. 9 cass. (Running Time: 13 hrs. 30 min.). 1993. 72.00 (978-0-7366-2638-5(7), 3377-A) Books on Tape.
Young & widowed, Lizzie Eustace makes bold to keep a family necklace given to her by her late husband. The in-laws consolidate against her.

Eustace Diamonds, Pt. 2. Anthony Trollope. 9 cass. (Running Time: 11 hrs. 30 min.). 1999. 59.95 Audio Bk Con.
Young, beautiful, wealthy, & widowed Lady Lizzie Eustace plots and lies to keep a fabulous necklace & to gain the love & protection of her imagined "corsair." Her in-laws' solicitor fights for the return of the diamonds to their reighful heirs. Their theft causes further complications.

Eustace Diamonds, Pt. 2. collector's unabr. ed. Anthony Trollope. Read by David Case. 9 cass. (Running Time: 13 hrs. 30 min.). 1994. 72.00 (978-0-7366-2639-2(5), 3377-B) Books on Tape.
Young & widowed, Lizzie Eustace makes bold to keep a family necklace given to her by her late husband. The in-laws consolidate against her.

Eustace Diamonds (Part 1), Vol. 11. unabr. ed. Anthony Trollope. Read by Flo Gibson. 8 cass. (Running Time: 12 hrs). 1994. 26.95 (978-1-55685-313-5(0)) Audio Bk Con.
Young, beautiful, wealthy & widowed Lady Lizzie Eustace plots & lies to keep a fabulous necklace & to gain the love & protection of her imagined "corsair". Her in-laws' solicitor fights for the return of the diamonds to the rightful heirs. Their theft causes further complications.

Eustace Diamonds (Part 2), Vol. 2. unabr. ed. Anthony Trollope. Narrated by Flo Gibson. (Running Time: 12 hrs. 17 mins.). 1994. 28.95 (978-1-55685-810-9(8)) Audio Bk Con.

Eustace Diamonds (Parts 1 And 2) unabr. ed. Anthony Trollope. Narrated by Flo Gibson. (Running Time: 24 hrs. 11 mins.). 1994. 49.95 (978-1-55685-811-6(6)) Audio Bk Con.

Euthanasia: The Distinction Between Killing & Letting Die. Donnie Self. 1986. 10.80 (0302B) Assn Prof Chaplains.

Eva, unabr. ed. Peter Dickinson. Narrated by Jill Tanner. 6 pieces. (Running Time: 8 hrs.). (gr. 8 up). 1992. 51.00 (978-1-55690-602-2(1), 92207E7) Recorded Bks.
Thirteen year-old Eva wakes up after an accident to an astounding surprise. Her memories & personality have been implanted into the body of a chimp!.

Eva Peron, unabr. ed. Nicholas Fraser & Marysa Navarro. Read by Nadia May. 7 cass. (Running Time: 10 hrs. 30 mins.). 1995. 49.95 (1801) Blckstn Audio.
Story of the rise of Eva Duarte, from poverty to actress, to mistress of Colonel Peron, & finally in 1945, the president's wife. In postwar Argentina she wielded a power - spiritual & practical - with few parallels outside of hereditary monarchy. Idolized by millions, she was hated & feared by many - she was Evita, the legend.

Eva Peron. unabr. ed. Nicholas Fraser & Marysa Navarro. Read by Nadia May. 7 cass. (Running Time: 10 hrs.). 2000. 49.95 (978-0-7861-1026-1(0), 1801) Blckstn Audio.

Eva Peron: A Biography. unabr. collector's ed. Alicia Dujovne Ortiz. Read by Mary Peiffer. 10 cass. (Running Time: 15 hrs.). 1997. 80.00 (978-0-913369-36-4(5), 4210) Books on Tape.
No twentieth-century figure enjoys a more romantic reputation than Eva Peron, the wife of Argentina's dictator, Juan Peron in the 1950s.

Evaluacion de los Recursos de Productos Forestales no Madereros Vol. 13: Experiencia y Principios Biometricos. 2001. cd-rom 18.00 (978-92-5-304614-0(7)) Pub: FAO ITA. Dist(s): Bernan Associates

Evaluating Abdominal Pain. Contrib. by Keith Ashcraft et al. 1 cass. (American Academy of Pediatrics UPDATE: Vol. 19, No. 7). 1998. 20.00 Am Acad Pediat.

Evaluating Intoxication Evidence in Civil & Criminal Cases. Contrib. by Edward F. Fitzgerald & David N. Hume. (Running Time: 5 hrs. 30 min.). 1985. 110.00 incl. program handbook. NJ Inst CLE.
Assists in cases involving alcohol consumption, including its absorption & elimination; pre-trial motions regarding chemical test evidence; examination & cross examination of expert witnesses on chemical test evidence.

Evaluating Software for Optical Disk Jukeboxes. 1 cass. 1990. 8.50 Recorded Res.

Evaluation & Emergency Treatment of Head Injuries: Symposium. Moderated by Howard M. Eisenberg. 3 cass. (Neurological Surgery Ser.: NS-1). 1986. 28.50 (8647) Am Coll Surgeons.

Evaluation des Ressources en Produits Forestiers non Ligneux Vol. 13: Experience et Principes de Biometrie. (ITA.). 2001. cd-rom 18.00 (978-92-5-204614-1(3)) Pub: FAO ITA. Dist(s): Bernan Associates

Evaluation of the Patient with Carcinoma of the Abdominal Colon. 2 cass. (Colon & Rectal Surgery Ser.: C85-CR2). 15.00 (8556) Am Coll Surgeons.

Evan Brain: Adventures of a Delusional Kid Superhero. 2007. audio compact disk 11.95 (978-0-9794716-1-2(3)) BDA Pubng.

Evan S. Connell. unabr. ed. Evan S. Connell. Read by Evan S. Connell. Read by Jim Birdsall. Interview with Rebekah Presson. 1 cass. (Running Time: 29 min.). 1991. 10.00 (051791) New Letters.
Author of "Mrs. Bridge" & "Mr. Bridge" is featured in a rare interview. Program features a reading from his latest work, "The Alchymist's Journal".

Evangelical Discovers the Faith. 2004. audio compact disk 27.95 (978-1-888992-51-9(4)) Catholic Answers.

Evangelical Feast Days-mp3. Read by Douglas Wilson. 12. 2003. 32.00 (978-1-59128-452-9(X)) Canon Pr ID.

Evangelical Feast Days-tape. Read by Douglas Wilson. 12 cass. 2003. 40.00 (978-1-59128-454-3(6)) Canon Pr ID.

Evangelical Foreign Missions Association (EFMA) Annual Meeting: National Association of Evangelicals, 47th Annual Convention, Columbus, Ohio, March 7-9, 1989. Wade T. Coggins. 1 cass. (Workshops Ser.: No. 18-Wednesd). 1989. 4.25 ea. 1-8 tapes.; 4.00 ea. 9 or more tapes. Nat Assn Evan.

Evangelical Imperatives in Diocesan Priestly Spirituality, Set. Scripts. George Aschenbrenner. 3 cass. (Running Time: 3 hrs. 52 min.). (Spirituality of Diocesan Priesthood Ser.). 1998. 29.95 (TAH407) Alba Hse Comns.
Chastity, poverty, & obedience, recognized as the evangelical imperatives are the response to the universal call to holiness & serious discipleship of Jesus.

Evangelical Is Not Enough. Thomas Howard. Read by Christopher Codol. 6 cass. 1984. pap. bk. 11.95 (978-0-89870-221-7(6), 121) Ignatius Pr.
A deeply moving narrative that unfolds the conversion to Catholicism of two Protestant Evangelical Christians.

Evangelical Response to Human Need: Proceedings of the 45th Annual Convention National Association of Evangelicals Buffalo, New York. Read by Dennis Ripley. 1 cass. (Running Time: 60 min.). 1987. 4.00 (311) Nat Assn Evan.

Evangelical Theology: American Lectures 1962. Karl Barth. Read by Karl Barth. 2007. audio compact disk 75.00 (978-1-55635-318-5(9), Wipf and Stock) Wipf Stock.

Evangelical Theology: An Introduction. unabr. ed. Karl Barth. Narrated by Jonathan Marosz. 6 CDs. (Running Time: 7 hrs. 45 mins. 0 sec.).Tr. of Einfuhrung in Die Evangelische Theologie. (ENG.). 2005. audio compact disk 24.98 (978-1-59644-328-0(6), Hovel Audio) christianaud.

***Evangelical Theology: An Introduction.** unabr. ed. Karl Barth. Narrated by Jonathan Marosz. (ENG.). 2005. 14.98 (978-1-59644-329-7(4), Hovel Audio) christianaud.

Evangelical Theology, American Lectures 1962. Speeches. Karl Barth & Markus Barth. Voice by Karl Barth. Photos by John Opie. 7 CDs. (Running Time: 5 hrs. 32 mins.). 2007. audio compact disk 75.00 (978-0-9785738-0-5(3)) Concise Logic.
5 lectures by Dr. Karl Barth, and his answers to questions, on 7 audio CDs. Images and text of companion booklet by Markus Barth, and additional images and information from Dr. Karl Barth's 1962 tour of the USA, on 1 data CD. Sturdy Unikeep CD case with cover art encloses the set.

***Evangelicalism: What Is it & Is it worth Keeping?** unabr. ed. D. A. Carson. Narrated by Dave Heath. (Running Time: 3 hrs. 30 mins. 0 sec.). (ENG.). 2011. audio compact disk 18.98 (978-1-59644-172-9(0), Hovel Audio) christianaud.

Evangeline see Treasury of Henry Wadsworth Longfellow

Evangeline Adams. Bonnie Wilson. Read by Bonnie Wilson. 1 cass. (Running Time: 90 min.). 1994. 8.95 (1124) Am Fed Astrologers.
A look at the life of astrologer Evangeline Adams.

Evangeline & Poems, Set Poems. Henry Wadsworth Longfellow & Oliver Wendell Holmes. Read by Flo Gibson. 2 cass. (Running Time: 2 hrs.). 1999. pap. bk. 14.95 (978-1-55685-613-6(X)) Audio Bk Con.
A fine historic narrative poem full of love & hope after early Americans were purged from their homes, with some scenes that bring to mind the tragedy of Kosovo.

Evangelio de Los Andrajosos. unabr. ed. Brennan Manning. Read by Scott Brick. (Running Time: 23400 sec.).Tr. of Ragamuffin Gospel. 2006. audio compact disk 55.00 (978-0-7861-6729-6(7)) Blckstn Audio.

Evangelio de Los Andrajosos. unabr. ed. Brennan Manning. Frwd. by Michael W. Smith. Contrib. by Rich Mullins. 6 CD's. (Running Time: 6 hrs. 42 mins. 0 sec.).Tr. of Ragamuffin Gospel. (ENG.). 2005. audio compact disk 24.98 (978-1-59644-133-0(X), Hovel Audio) christianaud.
Only when we truly embrace God's grace can we bask in the joy of a gospel that enfolds the neediest of His flock - the "ragamuffins." The Ragamuffin Gospel - now with the author's own reflective epilogue, "Ragamuffin Ten Years Later" beckons us to God's "furious love" that burns brightly and constantly.

Evangelism: Building Bridges. 2007. audio compact disk 17.99 (978-1-934570-03-6(6)) Lanphier Pr.

***Evangelism & the Sovereignty of God.** unabr. ed. J. I. Packer. Narrated by Grover Gardner. (ENG.). 2005. 10.98 (978-1-59644-089-0(9), Hovel Audio) christianaud.

Evangelism & the Sovereignty of God. unabr. ed. J. I. Packer. Narrated by Grover Gardner. 1 MP3CD. (Running Time: 3 hrs. 9 mins. 0 sec.). (ENG.). 2005. lp 19.98 (978-1-59644-090-6(2), Hovel Audio); audio compact disk 18.98 (978-1-59644-091-3(0), Hovel Audio) christianaud.
If God is in control of everything, does that mean the Christian can sit back and not bother to evangelize? Or does active evangelism simply imply that God is not sovereign at all? J.I. Packer shows in this classic study how false both these attitudes are. In a careful review of the biblical evidence, he shows how a right understanding of Goda??s sovereignty is not so much a barrier to evangelism as an incentive and powerful support for it.

Evangelism by Fire CD. Reinhard Bonnke. (ENG.). 2004. audio compact disk 29.99 (978-0-9758789-2-7(1)) E-R-Productions.
Ignite your passion to reach those who do not know Christ. Gain spiritual understanding and discover a new dimension of Spirit-led evangelism. This book is a must for every believer.

Evangelist Come Forth! Narrated by Jim Barbarossa. 12 cass. (Running Time: 1 hr. per cass.). 72.00 (978-0-9676380-7-2(0)) Step By Step Min.

Evangelist Dave Benoit, My Personal Testimony & Two Types of Christians: Careless & Concerned. David Benoit. 1 cass. (YA). (gr. 7 up). 1987. 6.00 (978-0-923105-06-8(9)) Glory Ministries.
Side one contains Dave Benoit's story of his salvation from pills to the pulpit, from reform school to Bible college. Side two contains a message to motivate people to be concerned for a lost & dying world.

Evangelistic Praying. John MacArthur, Jr. 4 cass. (John MacArthur's Bible Studies). 16.25 (HarperThor) HarpC GBR.

Evangelium Vitae: The Gospel of Life. James Kehoe. 11 cass. 44.00 Set. (95G) IRL Chicago.

Evangelium Vitae: The Gospel of Life. William F. Maestri. 2 cass. (Running Time: 2 hrs. 58 min.). 1996. 17.95 Set. (TAH358) Alba Hse Comns.
A thoughtful reflection & application of the gospel of life to current moral issues in the church. Must be viewed within the overall Catholic moral tradition as well as the urgent message of John Paul II. Human life is a sacred gift from God to be respected in all its forms & the church is entrusted with the mission to proclaim & live the gospel life.

Evangelium Vitae: The Gospel of Life. William B. Smith. 1 cass. 4.00 (96C1) IRL Chicago.

Evangelization & Culture. Chaput Bishop. 1 cass. (National Meeting of the Institute, 1992 Ser.). 4.00 (92N2) IRL Chicago.

Evangelization & Vocations. Assumpta Long. 1 cass. (National Meeting of the Institute, 1992 Ser.). 4.00 (92N7) IRL Chicago.

Evangelization of Americas. J. Hitchcock. 1 cass. (National Meeting of the Institute, 1992 Ser.). 4.00 (92N3) IRL Chicago.

Evangelizing in the Midst of the Culture of Death. Jeff Cavins. 2004. audio compact disk 14.95 (978-1-932927-36-8(0)) Ascensn Pr.

Evangelizing the Baptized. Scott Hahn. 3 cass. 1995. 19.95 Set. (137-C) Ignatius Pr.
Titles include: "Dealing with Bible Christians: Why Are They Anti-Catholic?:" Scott will tell you how to show your Protestant friends that the Catholic Church is, in fact, the voice of Christ on earth. "Cradle Catholics - What to Do with the Lukewarm?:" Shows how to re-ignite the fire of Faith in the hearts of lukewarm Catholics. "Fallen Away Catholics: Why Are So Many Leaving?:" Explores the reasons behind the exodus of so many Catholics from the Church, & how to help them.

Evans Business Starter Kit: How to Raise Vc! Mervin L. Evans. 2002. audio compact disk 19.99 (978-0-914391-28-9(3)) Comm People Pr.

Evans Credit Repair Kit: AAA+ Credit in 30 Days. Mervin Evans. 1 CDs. (Running Time: 90 hrs.). 2006. audio compact disk 19.99 (978-0-914391-88-3(7)) Comm People Pr.

Eva's Cousin: A Novel. unabr. ed. Sibylle Knauss. Read by Kim Edwards-Fukei. Tr. by Anthea Bell from GER. 10 vols. (Running Time: 15 hrs.). 2002. bk. 84.95 (978-0-7927-2704-0(5), CSL 490, Chivers Sound Lib); audio compact disk 110.95 (978-0-7927-2729-3(0), SLD 490, Chivers Sound Lib) AudioGO.
In the summer of 1944, twenty-year-old Marlene is thrilled to visit her older cousin, Eva Braun - Adolf Hitler's mistress - at the Fuhrer's Bavarian mountain retreat. But soon a clandestine mission of mercy forces her to question her allegiance to both her cousin and her country - and to face the chilling reality that exists outside her sheltered world.

***Eve.** abr. ed. Iris Johansen. (Running Time: 6 hrs.). (Eve Duncan Ser.). 2011. 9.99 (978-1-4418-8608-8(7), 9781441886088, BAD) Brilliance Audio.

***Eve.** unabr. ed. Iris Johansen. (Running Time: 12 hrs.). (Eve Duncan Ser.). 2011. audio compact disk 36.99 (978-1-4418-8600-2(1), 9781441886002, Bril Audio CD Unabri) Brilliance Audio.

Eve: A Novel of the First Woman. unabr. ed. Elissa Elliott. Read by Sandra Burr & Tanya Eby Sirois. (Running Time: 16 hrs.). 2009. 24.99 (978-1-4233-7850-1(4), 9781423378501, Brilliance MP3) Brilliance Audio.

Eve: A Novel of the First Woman. unabr. ed. Elissa Elliott. Read by Sandra Burr et al. (Running Time: 16 hrs.). 2009. 39.97 (978-1-4233-7851-8(2), 9781423378518, Brinc Audio MP3 Lib); 39.97 (978-1-4233-7853-2(9), 9781423378532, BADLE); 24.99 (978-1-4233-7852-5(0), 9781423378525, BAD); audio compact disk 117.97 (978-1-4233-7849-5(0), 9781423378495, BriAudCD Unabrid); audio compact disk 38.99 (978-1-4233-7848-8(2), 9781423378488, Bril Audio CD Unabri) Brilliance Audio.

Eve of Saint Agnes see Treasury of John Keats

Eve of Saint Venus & Nothing Like the Sun. abr. ed. Anthony Burgess. 1 cass. 1974. 12.95 (978-0-694-50261-5(8), SWC 1442) HarperCollins Pubs.

Eve of St. Agnes see Poetry of Keats

Eve of the Emperor Penguin. unabr. ed. Mary Pope Osborne. Read by Mary Pope Osborne. (Magic Tree House Ser.: No. 40). (ENG.). (J). (gr. 1). 2008. audio compact disk 14.95 (978-0-7393-7290-6(4), Listening Lib) Pub: Random Audio Pubg. Dist(s): Random

***Eve of the Isle.** Carol Rivers. Read by Annie Aldington. 2010. audio compact disk 89.95 (978-1-84652-804-0(6)) Pub: Magna Story GBR. Dist(s): Ulverscroft US

***Eve of the Isle.** Carol Rivers & Annie Aldington. 2010. 84.95 (978-1-84652-803-3(8)) Pub: Magna Story GBR. Dist(s): Ulverscroft US

***Evel Knievel.** unabr. ed. Leigh Montville. (ENG.). 2011. audio compact disk 40.00 (978-0-307-73892-9(2), Random AudioBks) Pub: Random Audio Pubg. Dist(s): Random

Evelina. Fanny Burney. Read by Anais 9000. 2008. 33.95 (978-1-60112-211-7(X)) Babblebooks.

Evelina: Or the History of a Young Lady's Entrance into the World, Set. unabr. ed. Fanny Burney. Read by Flo Gibson. 11 cass. (Running Time: 16 hrs.). (gr. 9 up). 1989. 34.95 (978-1-55685-140-7(5)) Audio Bk Con.
Eighteenth Century England as seen through the cusiosity & the romantic view of a young girl who leaves the quiet countryside to be introduced to the excitement & often strange ways of London & Bristol Society.

Eveline's Visit see Classic Ghost Stories, Vol. 3, A Collection

Evelyn. unabr. ed. Evelyn Doyle. Narrated by Marie McCarthy. 4 cass. (Running Time: 6 hrs.). 2003. (978-1-85903-655-6(4)) Magna Story GBR.
Ireland 1953. Desmond Doyle is married with six children and living in the infamous Fatima Mansions in Dublin. His wife deserts him and Desmond's world falls apart when he is advised to put his children in the care of State industrial schools as a temporary measure while he finds work in England. Upon his return, to his horror he finds that the children have been consigned to care until the age of sixteen. Told through the eyes of Evelyn, Desmond's nine year old daughter, this is the heartrending true story of one man's fight to change the law and reunite his family.

Evelyn Waugh. unabr. ed. Stephen Spender. 1 cass. (Running Time: 59 min.). 12.95 (23017) J Norton Pubs.
The group of Waugh's novels from "Decline & Fall" to "Brideshead Revisited" contrast idealized vision of the past with a gaudy present & an England still dreaming of its past greatness with a England of the 1920's & early 1930's in which people lived their lives as though part of an absurd dream.

Evelyn Wood Dynamic Learning, Set. 6 cass. 195.00 (273AX) Nightingale-Conant.
Go beyond speed reading to improving your total learning skills in this powerful program. It is a total learning system that picks up right where the world-famous Evelyn Wood Reading Dynamics leaves off - & is specifically designed for anyone who wants to maximize their time, advance their career & earn more money. Enhance the learning performance of your mind. Harness your innate brain power with the very latest scientific techniques of advanced learning. Become an "active listener." Supercharge all aspects of your learning & mental processing. Includes 192-page guidebook & permanent storage case.

Evelyn Wood Memory Dynamics. PUEI. 2006. audio compact disk 89.95 (978-1-933328-45-4(2), EvelynWood) P Univ E Inc.

Evelyn Wood Reading Dynamics. 6 cass. 159.95 Set, incl. 152p. study guide. (903-C47) Natl Seminars.
Learn new habits that allow you to gobble up whole paragraphs faster than ever before. Tap into breakthrough techniques learned by thousands, including key aides of three U.S. Presidents, judges, congressmen & corporate CEOs. With more time to use the information you learn, you'll have a powerful, competitive edge!.

Evelyn Wood Reading Dynamics. Evelyn Wood. 6 cass. 195.00 Set, incl. 152p. course guide, Progress Report Chart & Storage Case. (463AD) Nightingale-Conant.
Research shows that we read slowly because that's the way we were taught to read. "Evelyn Wood Reading Dynamics" breaks those old habits & teaches new, more efficient ones. Before you know it, you'll be breezing through material that used to require hours. And while you're increasing your speed, you'll also improve your retention & comprehension.

Evelyn Wood Reading Dynamics. Evelyn Wood. 6 cass. 159.95 Set incl. course guide, progress report & storage case. (463AS) Pryor Resources.
You'll learn how to determine your current reading rate, then increase it immediately. Your reading speed will double - guaranteed! Plus there's an advanced comprehension & retention system that will help you understand more.

Evelyn Wood Reading Dynamics Accelerator. PUEI. 2007. audio compact disk 199.95 (978-1-934147-22-1(2), EvelynWood) P Univ E Inc.

Evelyn Wood Reading Dynamics Guide for Parents & Teachers. PUEI. 2007. audio compact disk 69.95 (978-1-934147-25-2(7), EvelynWood) P Univ E Inc.

Evelyn Wood Reading Dynamics Master Series. PUEI. 2006. audio compact disk 199.95 (978-1-933328-30-0(4), EvelynWood) P Univ E Inc.

Evelyn Wood Vocabulary Dynamics. PUEI. 2006. audio compact disk 89.95 (978-1-933328-44-7(4), EvelynWood) P Univ E Inc.

Evelyn Wood's Speed-Reading & Learning Program: Remember Everything You Read. abr. ed. Stanley D. Frank. Read by Byron Paul. 4 cass. (Running Time: 6 hrs.). 1997. 22.95 Set. (978-1-55935-258-1(2), 258-2BK) Soundelux.

Even. unabr. ed. Andrew Grant. (Running Time: 11 hrs. 0 mins.). 2009. 29.95 (978-1-4332-7960-7(6)); 65.95 (978-1-4332-7956-0(8)); audio compact disk 29.95 (978-1-4332-7959-1(2)); audio compact disk 90.00 (978-1-4332-7957-7(6)) Blckstn Audio.

Even Better Parents. rev. ed. Barbara Maines & George Robinson. 1997. 92.95 (978-1-873942-02-4(8)) Pub: P Chapman GBR. Dist(s): SAGE

Even Buffett Isn't Perfect: What You Can - and Can't - Learn from the World's Greatest Investor. unabr. ed. Vahan Janjigian. Read by Lloyd James & Kent Cassella. Frwd. by Steve Forbes. (Running Time: 6 hrs. 30 mins. 0 sec.). (ENG.). 2008. audio compact disk 29.99 (978-1-4001-0737-7(7)); audio compact disk 59.99 (978-1-4001-3737-4(3)) Pub: Tantor Media. Dist(s): IngramPubServ

Even Buffett Isn't Perfect: What You Can - and Can't - Learn from the World's Greatest Investor. unabr. ed. Vahan Janjigian. Read by Lloyd James. Narrated by Kent Cassella. (Running Time: 6 hrs. 30 mins. 0 sec.). (ENG.). 2008. audio compact disk 19.99 (978-1-4001-5737-2(4)) Pub: Tantor Media. Dist(s): IngramPubServ

Even Cowgirls Get the Blues. unabr. ed. Tom Robbins. Perf. by Michael Nouri. 9 cass. (Running Time: 13 hrs.). 2001. 43.00 (978-1-59040-053-1(4), Phoenix Audio) Pub: Amer Intl Pub. Dist(s): PerseuPGW
Follow Sissy Hankshaw's amazing odyssey from Virginia to chic Manhattan to the Dakota Badlands, where FBI agents, cowgirls and ecstatic whooping cranes explode in a deliciously drawn-out climax.

Even Cowgirls Get the Blues. unabr. ed. Scripts. Tom Robbins. Perf. by Michael Nouri. 9 cass. (Running Time: 13 hrs. 30 mins.). 2004. 36.95 (978-1-59007-362-9(2)) Pub: New Millenn Enter. Dist(s): PerseuPGW

Even Deeper Sleep. Created by Victoria Wizell. Voice by Victoria Wizell. 1 CD. 2001. audio compact disk 39.00 (978-0-9679176-6-5(2)) Hyptalk.
Allow the relaxing effects of hypnosis to put you into a deep trance and into a deep sleep. Improve your sleep nightly by listening to this night time hypnosis program, filled with suggestions that will program your subconscious mind to help you fall asleep faster and easier than ever.

Even Eagles Need a Push. David McNally. 2 cass. (Running Time: 2 hrs.). 1998. 18.95 Set. (978-0-9626921-1-6(5)) Trans-Form Pr.
The tool one needs to envision a life of happiness & successes, & then create that life for oneself through one's gifts & talents. Presents a unique & personal process for self-appreciation that has helped thousands of people cut through negativism, break the shackles of doubt & guilt, & burst forth into the future with a vigor & purpose previously unknown to them.

Even Further up the Organization: The Resourceful Manager's Guide to Corporate Success. Robert Townsend. Read by Robert Townsend. 6 cass. 59.95 Set. (727AD) Nightingale-Conant.
Now, the man who transformed tiny Avis Rent-a-Car into the number-two auto-leasing company in America gives you his winning game plan for corporate success.

Even in Darkness. abr. ed. Read by Jeff Leever. 4 CDs. 2002. audio compact disk 18.95 (978-0-9707616-6-8(X)) Kingplus Multimedia.

Even Money. Dick Francis & Felix Francis. (Running Time: 11 hrs.). (ENG.). (gr. 12 up). 2009. audio compact disk 39.95 (978-0-14-314483-0(9), PengAudBks) Penguin Grp USA.

***Even Money.** unabr. ed. Dick Francis & Felix Francis. Read by Martin Jarvis. 9 CDs. (Running Time: 10 hrs. 30 mins.). 2009. audio compact disk 100.00 (978-1-4159-5994-7(3), BksonTape) Pub: Random Audio Pubg. Dist(s): Random

Even More Legends of the Great Lakes. 2008. audio compact disk 15.00 (978-0-9728212-7-8(9)) Old Country Bks.

Even More Notes from the Universe: Dancing Life's Dance. unabr. ed. Mike Dooley. Read by Mike Dooley. (Running Time: 2 hrs. 0 mins. 0 sec.). (ENG.). 2008. audio compact disk 19.99 (978-0-7435-7485-3(0)) Pub: S&S Audio. Dist(s): S and S Inc

Even More Pretty Good Jokes. unabr. ed. Garrison Keillor. Read by Garrison Keillor. Read by Roy Blount, Jr. & Ensemble Cast Staff. 2 CDs. (Running Time: 2 hrs.). (ENG.). 2009. audio compact disk 24.95 (978-1-59887-875-2(1), 1598878751) Pub: HighBridge. Dist(s): Workman Pub

Even More Short & Shivery: Thirty Spine-Tingling Stories. unabr. ed. Short Stories. Robert D. San Souci. 3 pieces. (Running Time: 4 hrs.). (gr. 5 up). 1997. 27.00 (978-0-7887-1590-7(9), 95202E7) Recorded Bks.
Compiled from macabre legends & international folktales that have thrilled listeners for generations.

Even More Short & Shivery: Thirty Spine-Tingling Stories, Class Set. unabr. ed. Robert D. San Souci. 3 cass., 10 bks. (Running Time: 4 hrs.). (J). 1997. bk. 184.80 (978-0-7887-2613-2(7), 46188) Recorded Bks.
Compiled from macabre legends & international folktales that have thrilled listeners for generations.

Even More Short & Shivery Homework Set: Thirty Spine-Tingling Stories. unabr. ed. Robert D. San Souci. 3 cass. (Running Time: 4 hrs.). (J). (gr. 5). 1997. bk. 48.95 (978-0-7887-1834-2(7), 40614) Recorded Bks.

Even Now. unabr. ed. Karen Kingsbury. Read by Kathy Garver. (Running Time: 13 hrs. 0 mins. 0 sec.). (ENG.). 2005. audio compact disk 29.99 (978-0-310-25404-1(3)) Zondervan.

Even Now. unabr. ed. Karen Kingsbury. (Running Time: 13 hrs. 0 mins. 0 sec.). (ENG.). 2006. 14.99 (978-0-310-26753-9(6)) Zondervan.

Even Roses Bleed. unabr. ed. Michael Bracken. Read by Maynard Villers. 4 cass. (Running Time: 4 hrs. 6 min.). 1995. 26.95 (978-1-55686-603-6(8)) Books in Motion.
Here is an intriguing group of electrifying short stories. Included are five short stories of Nathaniel Rose detective mysteries, two novelettes & one supernatural mystery.

***Even Silence Has an End: My Six Years of Captivity in the Colombian Jungle.** Ingrid Betancourt. (Running Time: 9 hrs.). 2010. audio compact disk 29.95 (978-0-14-242835-1(3), PengAudBks) Penguin Grp USA.

***Even Silence Has an End: My Six Years of Captivity in the Colombian Jungle.** unabr. ed. Ingrid Betancourt. (Running Time: 9 hrs.). 2010. 29.95 (978-1-101-43674-5(3)) Penguin Grp USA.

Even the Demons Believe. Timothy Williams. Narrated by Kerry Williams. 2001. audio compact disk 6.99 (978-1-57921-436-4(3)) WinePress Pub.

***Even the Dog Won't Touch Me.** Tom Bradley. 2009. audio compact disk 10.00 (978-0-9811704-9-7(8)) Pub: Ahadada CAN. Dist(s): SPD-Small Pr Dist

Even the Queen & Other Short Stories. unabr. ed. Connie Willis. 2 cass. (Running Time: 3 hrs.). (J). (gr. 10 up). 1997. 17.95 Wyrmhole.
Award-winning author acclaimed by the Denver Post as one of science fiction's best writers, reads five of her most popular short fiction stories.

Even the Seagulls Cried. unabr. ed. Dorothy R. Kliewer. Read by Juanita Parker. 6 cass. (Running Time: 6 hrs. 24 min.). 2001. 39.95 (978-1-55686-913-6(4)) Books in Motion.
Vacationing to get away from threatening phone calls, Darcy Nichols enlists the support of the Reef Cliff Sheriff when an observer is seen, and a murder takes place on the seashore.

Even the Sun Will Die: An Interview with Eckhart Tolle. unabr. ed. Interview. Eckhart Tolle. 2 CDs. (Running Time: 2 hrs 30 min). (Power of Now Teaching Ser.). 2002. audio compact disk 24.95 (978-1-56455-968-5(8), AW00607D) Sounds True.
When Eckhart Tolle agreed to be interviewed on September 11, 2001, he could not foresee the historic nature of this date or the suffering that would follow. As the day?s events unfolded, in real time, he responded with a calm and clear voice, helping to make sense out of the fear and chaos that will forever define this date.Documents this historic meeting with Eckhart Tolle and the comforting wisdom he revealed that day. We live in a time, he says, when we define ourselves through our enemies; and science and technology are in the service of human madness.

Even the Wicked. unabr. ed. Lawrence Block. Narrated by Mike Hammersmith. 7 cass. (Running Time: 12 hrs.). (Matthew Scudder Mystery Ser.: No. 13). 29.95 (978-1-4025-5841-2(4)) Recorded Bks.

Even the Wicked. unabr. ed. Lawrence Block. Narrated by Mark Hammer. 9 cass. (Running Time: 12 hrs.). (Matthew Scudder Mystery Ser.: No. 13). 1997. 83.00 (978-0-7887-1299-9(3), 95134E7) Recorded Bks.
A demented serial killer is shocking the "Big Apple" with death threats sent to the Daily News. When one of Matt's old friends is named as the next victim, the private eye suddenly finds himself matching wits with the wily murderer.

Even Trolls Have Moms. Joe Scruggs. 1 cass. (Running Time: 40 min.). (J). (ps-2). 1988. 9.95 (978-0-916123-09-3(X), PJS-730) Ed Graphics Pr.
Features 11 activity & listening songs for kindergarten & elementary school age children & their parents & teachers.

Even unto Death see Great American Short Stories, Vol. III, A Collection

Even Yuppies Die. unabr. ed. Marian Babson. Read by Diana Bishop. 6 cass. (Running Time: 9 hrs.). 2002. 54.95 (978-0-7540-0878-1(9), CAB 2300) Pub: Chivers Pr GBR. Dist(s): AudioGO

Evening. abr. ed. Susan Minot. Read by Katherine D. Walker. 2 cass. 1999. 18.00 (FS9-43286) Highsmith.

Evening Angels. Perf. by Kurt Bestor. 1 cass. 9.98; audio compact disk 17.98 Lifedance.
Orchestra, electronic instruments & children's choir. Based on the painting "Evening Angels," has the rich tonal qualities of a film soundtrack, & emotionally uplifting music that inspires. Demo CD or cassette available.

Evening at Esalen. unabr. ed. Robert Bly. 2 cass. (Running Time: 2 hrs. 23 min.). 1982. 18.00 (00307) Big Sur Tapes.

Evening by Evening. Charles H. Spurgeon. (Pure Gold Classics). (ENG.). 2005. pap. bk. 14.99 (978-0-88270-877-5(5)) Bridge-Logos.

Evening Class. unabr. ed. Maeve Binchy. Narrated by Barbara Caruso. 11 cass. (Running Time: 15 hrs. 30 mins.). 2000. 95.00 (978-0-7887-3999-6(9), H1076K8) Recorded Bks.
Hoping to revitalize a dead-end career, Latin teacher Aidan Dunne is forming an evening Italian class. But the prospect of attracting students to his small secondary school on the seamy side of Dublin is daunting, until the

appearance of Signora. This mysterious Irish woman, who happens to speak fluent Italian, has a contagious passion for Italy & for life. When she agrees to teach the class to a motley group of Dubliners, the consequences are life-altering for all of them.

Evening Discussion. 2 cass. 1990. 17.00 set. Recorded Res.
Topics covered include finance for HDTV.

Evening Family Rosary. Mother Angelica. 1 cass. (Running Time: 60 min.). 10.00 (978-1-55794-054-4(1), T5) Eternal Wrd TV.

Evening Forest. Read by Mary Richards. 1 cass. (Running Time: 60 min.). (Energy Break Ser.). 2007. audio compact disk 19.95 (978-1-56136-162-5(3), 104) Master Your Mind.

Evening in Byzantium. unabr. ed. Irwin Shaw. Read by Wolfram Kandinsky. 8 cass. (Running Time: 12 hrs.). 1978. 64.00 Set. (978-0-7366-0152-8(X), 1152) Books on Tape.
The setting is Cannes, the time is the annual film festival & the hero is 48-year-old Jesse Craig, a successful but fading film producer. His story is told in a series of flashbacks which reveal the pressures of his life: his shattered marriage, his two daughters whom he scarcely knows, his mistress & a familiar world disintegrating around him.

Evening in December. Composed by Tom Fettke et al. (ENG.). 2008. audio compact disk 19.95 (978-0-7390-5656-1(5)) Alfred Pub.

Evening in December. Composed by Tom Fettke et al. (ENG.). 2008. audio compact disk 59.95 (978-0-7390-5474-1(0)) Alfred Pub.

Evening in December. Composed by Tom Fettke et al. (ENG.). 2008. audio compact disk 90.00 (978-0-7390-5471-0(6)) Alfred Pub.

Evening in December: CD-ROM. Composed by Tom Fettke et al. (ENG.). 2008. audio compact disk 250.00 (978-0-7390-5473-4(2)) Alfred Pub.

Evening in December: Preview Pack, Choral Score & CD. Composed by Tom Fettke et al. (ENG.). 2008. audio compact disk 12.00 (978-0-7390-5469-7(4)) Alfred Pub.

Evening in December: 10 CDs. Composed by Tom Fettke et al. (ENG.). 2008. audio compact disk 60.00 (978-0-7390-5470-3(8)) Alfred Pub.

Evening in Italy. Donald Walters. 2002. audio compact disk 15.95 (978-1-56589-767-0(6)) Pub: Crystal Clarity. Dist(s): Natl Bk Netwk

Evening News. abr. ed. Marly Swick & JoBeth Williams. 2 cass. 1999. 17.98 (FS9-43369) Highsmith.

Evening News. unabr. ed. Marly Swick. Narrated by Barbara Caruso. 9 cass. (Running Time: 12 hrs. 15 mins.). 1999. 83.00 (978-0-7887-3132-7(7), 95687E7) Recorded Bks.
After years of an unhappy marriage, Giselle Trias has a caring new husband & a young daughter - even her son Teddy gets along with his half-sister. But one sunny day, Teddy plays with a neighbor's gun. Suddenly Giselle is fighting to keep her family together & to forgive the unforgivable.

Evening News: A Novel. abr. ed. Marly Swick. (Running Time: 4 hrs.). (ENG.). 2006. 14.98 (978-1-59483-701-2(5)) Pub: Hachet Audio. Dist(s): HachBkGrp

Evening of Cowboy Entertainment: Wyoming Read & Andy Nelson "Live" Andrew G. Nelson et al. (Running Time: 60 mins). 2003. audio compact disk 15.00 (978-0-9706459-1-3(0)) Pseudo Pubng.

Evening of Poetry. Robert Bly. 2 cass. 18.00 (OC124) Sound Horizons AV.
Robert returns the poetry "reading" to the more ancient event in which memorization and some form of music take part.

Evening of Poetry & Talk about Men, Women & Relationships. Read by Robert Bly. 1 cass. (Running Time: 90 min.). 1988. 10.95 (978-0-7822-0015-7(X), 311) C G Jung IL.
Poet & best-selling author Robert Bly performs love & "not-love" poems of his own & of others.

Evening of Stories. Robert Bly. 2 cass. 18.00 (OC70) Sound Horizons AV.

Evening Plenaries: National Association of Evangelicals, 47th Annual Convention, Columbus, Ohio, March 7-9, 1989 (Thursday), No. 117. Oswald Hoffmann. 1 cass. 1989. 4.25 ea. 1-8 tapes.; 4.00 ea. 9 tapes or more. Nat Assn Evan.

Evening Plenaries: National Association of Evangelicals, 47th Annual Convention, Columbus, Ohio, March 7-9, 1989 (Tuesday), No. 101. Paul A. Cedar. 1 cass. 1989. 4.00 ea. 1-8 tapes.; 4.00 9 tapes or more. Nat Assn Evan.

Evening Plenaries: National Association of Evangelicals, 47th Annual Convention, Columbus, Ohio, March 7-9, 1989 (Wednesday), No. 110. David A. Seamands. 1 cass. 1989. 4.25 ea. 1-8 tapes.; 4.00 ea. 9 tapes or more. Nat Assn Evan.

Evening Plenaries: Proceeding of the 45th Annual Convention National Association of Evangelicals Buffalo, New York. Read by Ravi Zacharias. 1 cass. (Running Time: 60 min.). 1987. 4.00 (348) Nat Assn Evan.

Evening Plenaries: Proceedings of the 45th Annual Convention National Association of Evangelicals Buffalo, New York. Read by Richard Halverson. 1 cass. (Running Time: 60 min.). 1987. 4.00 (304) Nat Assn Evan.

Evening Plenaries: Proceedings of the 45th Annual Convention National Association of Evangelicals Buffalo, New York. Read by Howard Jones. 1 cass. (Running Time: 60 min.). 1987. 4.00 (332) Nat Assn Evan.

Evening Primrose see Fancies & Goodnights

Evening Ragas, Vol. 1. Music by Pandit Jasraj. 1 cass. (From Dawn to Midnight Ser.). 1990. (A90009); audio compact disk (CD A92080) Multi-Cultural Bks.

Evening Ragas, Vol. 2. Music by Rajan Mishra. 1 cass. (From Dawn to Midnight Ser.). 1990. (A90010); audio compact disk (CD A92081) Multi-Cultural Bks.

Evening Ragas, Vol. 3. Music by Padma Talwalkar. 1 cass. (From Dawn to Midnight Ser.). 1990. (A90011); audio compact disk (CD A92082) Multi-Cultural Bks.

Evening Ragas, Vol. 4. Music by Shahid Parvez. 1 cass. (From Dawn to Midnight Ser.). 1990. (A90012); audio compact disk (CD A92083) Multi-Cultural Bks.

Evening Reflections: A Collection of Inspirational Poetry, Prayers, & Bible Verses for Daily Reflection. Narrated by Karen Jean Matsko Hood. 2002. audio compact disk 24.95 (978-1-930948-80-8(8)) Whsprng Pine.

Evening Reflections: A Collection of Inspirational Poetry, Prayers, & Bible Verses for Daily Reflection. Karen Jean Matsko Hood. 2003. 29.95 (978-1-59210-157-3(7)) Whsprng Pine.

Evening Reflections-Music. 2007. audio compact disk 16.95 (978-1-56136-416-9(9)) Master Your Mind.

Evening Star. unabr. ed. Larry McMurtry. Read by Roses Prichard. 15 cass. (Running Time: 22 hrs. 30 min.). 1993. 120.00 (978-0-7366-2472-5(4), 3235) Books on Tape.
Terms of Endearment's Aurora Greenway comes to grips with the passing of time as she faces her 70s.

Evening Star. unabr. ed. Larry McMurtry & Will Patton. 2004. 27.95 (978-0-7435-4688-1(1)) Pub: S&S Audio. Dist(s): S and S Inc

Evening Waterfall see Carl Sandburg's Poems for Children

***Evening with Alice Taylor Cassette Ctpk.** Alice Taylor. (ENG.). 1989. 9.95 (978-0-86322-111-8(4)) Pub: BrandonMt IRL. Dist(s): Dufour

Evening with Angels. Megan McKenna. 2 cass. (Running Time: 2 hrs.). 1995. Set. (AA2925) Credence Commun.
McKenna enchants a Chicago Loyola University crowd with eight stories of winged things, most of them angels.

Evening with Doc Watson & David Holt. Perf. by Doc Watson & David Holt. 1 CD. (Running Time: 90 mins.). 2000. audio compact disk 15.98 High Windy Audio.
A collection of stories & music.

Evening with Dylan Thomas. abr. ed. Dylan Thomas. Read by Dylan Thomas. 1 cass. Incl. As I Walked Out One Evening: Songs, Ballads, Lullabies, Limericks & Other Light Verse. W. H. Auden. (SWC 1157); Glass of Beer. James Stephens. (SWC 1157); If My Head Hurt a Hair's Foot. Dylan Thomas. (SWC 1157); In My Craft or Sullen Art. (SWC 1157); In Tara's Halls. W. B. Yeats. (SWC 1157); Introduction to Thomas Hardy. Dylan Thomas. (SWC 1157); Irreverent Introduction. Dylan Thomas. (SWC 1157); Lapis Lazuli. W. B. Yeats. (SWC 1157); Lent. W. R. Rodgers. (SWC 1157); Master & Bos'n Song. W. H. Auden. (SWC 1157); On Reading Poetry Aloud. Dylan Thomas. (SWC 1157); One Poet Visits Another. W. H. Davies. (SWC 1157); Passing the Graveyard. Andrew Young. (SWC 1157); Poem in October. Dylan Thomas. (SWC 1157); Ruined Maid. Thomas Hardy. (SWC 1157); Song. Alun Lewis. (SWC 1157); This Side of the Truth. Dylan Thomas. (SWC 1157); Three Bushes. W. B. Yeats. (SWC 1157); To Lizbie Brown. Thomas Hardy. (SWC 1157); To My Son Aged Eight. John Betjeman. (SWC 1157); Traveler's Curse after Misdirection. Dylan Thomas. (SWC 1157); 1988. 12.95 (978-0-694-50934-8(5), SWC 1157) HarperCollins Pubs.

Evening with Frederick Douglass. 1 cass. (Running Time: 1 hr.). 10.95 (OP-79-02-01, HarperThor) HarpC GBR.

Evening with R. A. W. Robert A. Wilson. 2 cass. 18.00 set. (A0234-87) Sound Photosyn.
At the cosmic podium at San Jose.

Evening with Robert Frost. unabr. ed. Read by Robert Frost. 1 cass. (Running Time: 55 min.). 12.95 (C23066) J Norton Pubs.

Evening with Three Alumni. 1 cass. (Running Time: 1 hr. 30 min.). 1996. 10.00 (978-1-888947-58-8(6)) Sudbury Valley.
Former students at Sudbury Valley School talk, March 23, 1996.

Evening with W. O. Mitchell. abr. ed. W. O. Mitchell. Narrated by W. O. Mitchell. Intro. by Stuart McLean. 1 cass. (Running Time: 1 hr. 30 mins.). (ENG.). 2001. 14.95 (978-0-86492-328-8(7)) Pub: BTC Audiobks CAN. Dist(s): U Toronto Pr
"W.O. Mitchell's public readings were unforgettably colourful and enjoyable. This spirited recording of five of his favourite stories, which includes ""The Day I Spoke for Mister Lincoln,"" ""How to Fail at Public Speaking,"" and ""Melvin Arbunkle's First Course in Shock Therapy,"" captures him at his most amusing.".

Evening with W. O. Mitchell. abr. ed. W. O. Mitchell. Perf. by W. O. Mitchell. Intro. by Stuart McLean. 2 CDs. (Running Time: 1 hr. 30 mins.). (ENG.). 2001. audio compact disk 16.95 (978-0-86492-329-5(5)) Pub: BTC Audiobks CAN. Dist(s): U Toronto Pr

Evening with W. S. Merwin. W. S. Merwin. Read by W. S. Merwin. 1 cass. 9.00 (A0249-87) Sound Photosyn.
The visionary poet, often in The New Yorker & author of many collections & translations, reciting his exquisite poetry.

Evening's Love: Prologue see Poetry of John Dryden

***Event Planning.** PUEI. 2008. audio compact disk 199.00 (978-1-935041-22-1(3), CareerTrack) P Univ E Inc.

Eventide. Kent Haruf. Read by George Hearn. 2004. audio compact disk 72.00 (978-1-4159-0003-1(5)) Books on Tape.

Events: Fate or Free Will. Joanne Stover. 1 cass. 8.95 (333) Am Fed Astrologers.

Events of Space: Metaphors: A System for Teaching the Learning Skills of Focus, Attention & Completion. Patricia Bracken Oleksy. 2007. audio compact disk (978-1-59971-477-6(9)) AardGP.

Events That Shaped Our Lives. Created by Radio Spirits. (History Channel Presents...Ser.). 2004. 9.98 (978-1-57019-737-6(7)) Radio Spirits.

EVEolution: The Eight Truths of Marketing to Women, Set. abr. ed. Faith Popcorn. Read by Faith Popcorn. 2 cass. (Running Time: 3 hrs.). 2000. 18.00 (978-1-55935-339-7(2)) Soundelux.
Leading trend forecaster predicts the next revolution in American business.

Ever. Gail Carson Levine. Read by Jenna Lamia & Oliver Wyman. (Running Time: 5 hrs. 7 mins.). (Playaway Children Ser.). (J). (gr. 3-7). 2009. 50.00 (978-1-60775-489-3(4)) Find a World.

Ever. Gail Carson Levine. (J). (gr. 4-7). 2009. audio compact disk 25.95 (978-0-545-09320-0(1)) Scholastic Inc.

Ever. unabr. ed. Gail Carson Levine. Read by Jenna Lamia & Oliver Wyman. 4 CDs. (Running Time: 5 hrs. 7 mins.). (J). (gr. 4-7). 2009. audio compact disk 49.95 (978-0-545-09338-5(4)) Scholastic Inc.

Ever After. unabr. ed. Karen Kingsbury. (Running Time: 10 hrs. 0 mins. 0 sec.). (ENG.). 2007. 14.99 (978-0-310-26756-0(0)) Zondervan.

Ever After. unabr. ed. Karen Kingsbury. Read by Kathy Garver. (Running Time: 10 hrs. 0 mins. 0 sec.). (ENG.). 2007. audio compact disk 29.99 (978-0-310-25405-8(1)) Zondervan.

***Ever After.** unabr. ed. Nora Roberts. (Running Time: 3 hrs.). 2010. 19.99 (978-1-4418-6736-0(8), 9781441867360, Brilliance MP3); 19.99 (978-1-4418-6738-4(4), 9781441867384, BAD); 39.97 (978-1-4418-6739-1(2), 9781441867391, BADLE); audio compact disk 19.99 (978-1-4418-6734-6(1), 9781441867346, Bril Audio CD Unabri) Brilliance Audio.

***Ever After.** unabr. ed. Nora Roberts. Read by Justine Eyre. (Running Time: 3 hrs.). 2010. 39.97 (978-1-4418-6737-7(6), 9781441867377, Brlnc Audio MP3 Lib); audio compact disk 62.97 (978-1-4418-6735-3(X), 9781441867353, BriAudCD Unabrid) Brilliance Audio.

Ever Faithful, Ever Sure. Composed by David Hampton. Contrib. by David Shipps & John Milton. 2007. audio compact disk 24.98 (978-5-557-49187-7(2), Word Music) Word Enter.

Ever since Darwin: Reflections in Natural History. unabr. collector's ed. Stephen Jay Gould. Read by Larry McKeever. 6 cass. (Running Time: 9 hrs.). 1989. 48.00 (978-0-7366-1637-9(3), 2492) Books on Tape.
The kernel of Darwin's theory is that those who survive are better adapted to life than those who do not. But the theory is as threatening as it is simple, for it takes us, so to speak, out of the action. We like to think of ourselves as tops on evolution's ladder. In fact, we are only the last surviving branch on a bush. We rarely consider how short a time, geologically speaking, we have been on earth, or how soon we may disappear.

Everafter. unabr. ed. Amy Huntley. Read by Tavia Gilbert. (Running Time: 5 hrs.). 2009. 24.99 (978-1-4418-0186-9(3), 9781441801869, BAD); 39.97 (978-1-4418-0187-6(1), 9781441801876, BADLE) Brilliance Audio.

Everafter. unabr. ed. Amy Huntley. Read by Tavia Gilbert. 5 CDs. (Running Time: 5 hrs.). (J). (gr. 4-7). 2009. audio compact disk 54.97 (978-1-4418-0183-8(9), 9781441801838, BriAudCD Unabrid) Brilliance Audio.

Everafter. unabr. ed. Amy Huntley. Read by Tavia Gilbert. 1 MP3-CD. (Running Time: 5 hrs.). (J). (gr. 4-7). 2009. 24.99 (978-1-4418-0184-5(7), 9781441801845, Brilliance MP3); 39.97 (978-1-4418-0185-2(5), 9781441801852, Brlnc Audio MP3 Lib); audio compact disk 24.99 (978-1-4418-0182-1(0), 9781441801821, Bril Audio CD Unabri) Brilliance Audio.

***Everafter War.** unabr. ed. Michael Buckley. Read by L. J. Ganser. 1 Playaway. (Running Time: 6 hrs. 45 mins.). (Sisters Grimm Ser.: Bk. 7). (YA). (gr. 5-8). 2009. 59.75 (978-1-4407-2141-0(6)); 56.75 (978-1-4407-2132-8(7)); audio compact disk 77.75 (978-1-4407-2136-6(X)) Recorded Bks.

***Everafter War.** unabr. collector's ed. Michael Buckley. Read by L. J. Ganser. 6 CDs. (Running Time: 6 hrs. 45 mins.). (Sisters Grimm Ser.: Bk. 7). (YA). (gr. 5-8). 2009. audio compact disk 44.95 (978-1-4407-2553-1(5)) Recorded Bks.

***Evercrossed.** unabr. ed. Elizabeth Chandler. (Running Time: 7 hrs. 0 mins. 0 sec.). (Kissed by an Angel Ser.). (YA). 2011. audio compact disk 29.99 (978-1-4423-3959-0(4)) Pub: S&S Audio. Dist(s): S and S Inc

***Everest: A Sound History.** Michael R. Breckon. 2009. (978-1-60136-383-1(4)) Audio Holding.

Everglades. unabr. ed. Randy Wayne White. Read by Dick Hill. 7 cass. (Running Time: 10 hrs.). (Doc Ford Ser.: No. 10). 2003. 32.95 (978-1-59086-958-1(3), 1590869583, BAU); 82.25 (978-1-59086-959-8(1), 1590869591, Unabridge Lib Edns) Brilliance Audio.
Doc Ford returns to his stilt house on Dinkin Bay to find an old friend and one-time lover waiting for him. Her real-estate developer husband has disappeared and been pronounced dead, and she's sure there is worse to follow - and she's right. Following the trail, Ford ends up deep in the Everglades, at the gates of a community presided over by a man named Bhagwan Shiva (formerly Jerry Singh). Shiva is big business, but that business has been a little shaky lately, and so he's come up with a scheme to enhance both his cash and his power. Of course, there's the possibility that some people could get hurt and the Everglades itself damaged, but Shiva smells a killing. And if that should turn out to be literally, as well as figuratively, true...well, that's just too damned bad.

Everglades. unabr. ed. Randy Wayne White. Read by Dick Hill. (Running Time: 10 hrs.). (Doc Ford Ser.: No. 10). 2004. 39.25 (978-1-59335-384-1(7), 1593353847, Brlnc Audio MP3 Lib) Brilliance Audio.

Everglades. unabr. ed. Randy Wayne White. Read by Dick Hill. (Running Time: 10 hrs.). (Doc Ford Ser.: No. 10). 2004. 39.25 (978-1-59710-254-4(7), 1597102547, BADLE); 24.95 (978-1-59710-255-1(5), 1597102555, BAD) Brilliance Audio.

Everglades. unabr. ed. Randy Wayne White. Read by Dick Hill. (Running Time: 10 hrs.). (Doc Ford Ser.: No. 10). 2004. 24.95 (978-1-59335-104-5(6), 1593351046) Soulmate Audio Bks.

Evergreen. unabr. ed. Belva Plain. 16 cass. 95.20 Audio Bk.
Epic novel of a woman's rise from poverty to wealth covering several decades of hope & tragedy.

Evergreen, Pt. 1. unabr. collector's ed. Belva Plain. Read by Dick Estell. 8 cass. (Running Time: 12 hrs.). 1987. 64.00 (978-0-7366-1087-2(1), 2012-A) Books on Tape.
The dramatic saga of Anna who comes to America at the turn of the century. We witness her marriage, her children & her deceit.

Evergreen, Pt. 2. collector's ed. Belva Plain. Read by Dick Estell. 8 cass. (Running Time: 12 hrs.). 1987. 64.00 (978-0-7366-1088-9(X), 2012-B) Books on Tape.
The dramatic saga of Anna who comes to America at the turn of the century. We witness her marriage, her children & her deceit.

Evergreen: Mandolin Music for Christmas. Butch Baldassari. 1995. pap. bk. 15.95 (978-0-7866-0629-0(0), 95535P); pap. bk. 20.95 (978-0-7866-0631-3(2), 95535CDP) Mel Bay.

Evergreen: Mandolin Music for Christmas. Butch Baldassari. 2002. bk. 20.95 (978-0-7866-6569-3(6), 95535BCD) Mel Bay.

Evergreen, Everblue. Raffi. 1 cass, 1 CD. (J). 2001. 10.95 (KSR 10060); audio compact disk 16.95 (KSR 10060CD) Kimbo Educ.
Big Beautiful Planet, Clean Rain, Where I Live, What's the Matter With Us, Mama's Kitchen, We Are Not Alone & more.

Evergreen, Everblue. Perf. by Raffi. 1 cass., 1 CD. (J). 7.98 (RDR 8060); audio compact disk 12.78 CD Jewel box. (RDR 8060) NewSound.

Evergreen, Everblue. Perf. by Raffi. 1 cass. (Running Time: 39 mins.). (J). 1999. (978-1-886767-49-2(1)); audio compact disk (978-1-886767-48-5(3)) Rounder Records.
An ecology album - a musical celebration of our power to act together to preserve the earth for all generations.

Evergreen, Everblue: Songs for the Environment. Perf. by Raffi. 1 cass. (J). (ps up). 10.98 (2176); audio compact disk 17.98 (D2176) MFLP CA.
Raffi delights his fans with a recent recording in celebration of the earth & all its miracles. Original, mostly new songs in a fresh upbeat style remind us of the precious natural wonders surrounding us all.

Evergreens: Gentle Tales of Nature. unabr. ed. Odds Bodkin. Read by Odds Bodkin. 1 cass. (Running Time: 40 mins.). Dramatization. (Odds Bodkin Storytelling Library). (J). (ps up). 2003. bk. 9.95 (978-1-882412-22-8(2), EVCS) Pub: Rivertree. Dist(s): Penton Overseas
Folk tales include "The Evergreens," "The Name of the Tree," "The Woman Who Fell from the Sky," "The Lion Makers" & "The Wind & the Sun". Odds narrates & plays the 12 string guitar, kalimba & Celtic harp.

Evergreens: Gentle Tales of Nature. unabr. ed. Odds Bodkin. Read by Odds Bodkin. 1 CD. (Running Time: 40 mins.). Dramatization. (Odds Bodkin Musical Story Collection). (ps up). 2003. bk. 14.95 (978-1-882412-23-5(0), EVCD) Pub: Rivertree. Dist(s): Penton Overseas

Everlasting see Twentieth-Century Poetry in English, No. 28, Recordings of Poets Reading Their Own Poetry

Everlasting. Iris Johansen. Narrated by Angela Brazil. (ENG.). 2009. audio compact disk 19.95 (978-1-60283-627-3(2)) Pub: AudioGO. Dist(s): Perseus Dist

***Everlasting.** abr. ed. Kathleen E. Woodiwiss. Read by Xanthe Elbrick. (ENG.). 2007. (978-0-06-155578-7(9)); (978-0-06-155579-4(7)) HarperCollins Pubs.

Everlasting. abr. ed. Kathleen E. Woodiwiss. Read by Xanthe Elbrick. (Running Time: 21600 sec.). 2007. audio compact disk 29.95 (978-0-06-142960-6(0), Harper Audio) HarperCollins Pubs.

Everlasting Glory: Vermont Soldiers who were Awarded the Congressional Medal of Honor during the Civil War 1861-1865. Phil Rogers. 2007. per. 14.95 (978-0-9728347-4-2(5)) Blue Hill.

Everlasting God. Contrib. by Lincoln Brewster. (Praise Hymn Soundtracks Ser.). 2007. audio compact disk 8.98 (978-5-557-70337-6(3)) Pt of Grace Ent.

Everlasting God. Contrib. by Lincoln Brewster. (Sound Performance Soundtracks Ser.). 2007. audio compact disk 5.98 (978-5-557-71911-7(3)) Pt of Grace Ent.

Everlasting God. Contrib. by Brenton Brown. Prod. by Nathan Nockels & Hanif Williams. Contrib. by Les Moir & Brad O'Donnell. 2006. audio compact disk 16.99 (978-5-558-45804-6(6)) Pt of Grace Ent.

Everlasting God. Contrib. by Chris Tomlin. (Mastertrax Ser.). 2006. audio compact disk 9.98 (978-5-558-02883-6(1)) Pt of Grace Ent.

Everlasting God: 25 Modern Worship Favorites. 2008. audio compact disk 13.99 (978-5-557-48827-3(8)) Pt of Grace Ent.

Everlasting God with O God, Our Help in Ages Past. Contrib. by Michael Lawrence. 2007. audio compact disk 24.99 (978-5-557-54329-3(5)) Allegis.

Everlasting Gospel see Poetry of William Blake

***Everlasting Man.** G k Chesterton. 2009. audio compact disk 39.95 (978-1-58617-422-4(3)) Pub: Ignatius Pr. Dist(s): Midpt Trade

Everlasting Man. unabr. ed. G. K. Chesterton. Read by Thomas Whitworth. 7 cass. (Running Time: 10 hrs.). 1990. 49.95 (978-0-7861-0200-6(4), 1176) Blckstn Audio.
Widely recognized as one of the most powerful & profound theological works ever written. Perhaps G.K. Chesterton was able to see the world through spiritual eyes better than anyone else.

***Everlasting Man.** unabr. ed. G. K. Chesterton. Read by Thomas Whitworth. (Running Time: 10 hrs.). 2010. 29.95 (978-1-4417-0470-2(1)); audio compact disk 90.00 (978-1-4417-0467-2(1)) Blckstn Audio.

Everlasting Melody - ShowTrax. Conducted by Henry Leck. Contrib. by Rollo Dilworth. 1 CD. (Running Time: 5 mins.). (Henry Leck Choral Ser.). 2000. audio compact disk 19.95 (08551345) H Leonard.
Now available for SATB, this gospel-style original will set every toe tapping & fill every heart with harmony. Well-written vocal & piano parts ensure success!.

Everlost. unabr. ed. Neal Shusterman. Read by Nick Podehl. (Running Time: 8 hrs.). (Skinjacker Trilogy: Bk. 1). 2009. 39.97 (978-1-4233-7316-2(2), 9781423373162, Brlnc Audio MP3 Lib); 39.97 (978-1-4233-7318-6(9), 9781423373186, BADLE); 24.99 (978-1-4233-7315-5(4), 9781423373155, Brilliance MP3); 24.99 (978-1-4233-7317-9(0), 9781423373179, BAD); audio compact disk 87.97 (978-1-4233-7313-1(8), 9781423373131, BriAudCD Unabrid); audio compact disk 29.99 (978-1-4233-7314-8(6), 9781423373148, Bril Audio CD Unabri) Brilliance Audio.

Everly Brothers: Ladies Love Outlaws. abr. ed. Consuelo Dodge. Read by Dennis Dean. 4 cass. (Running Time: 3 hrs. 36 min.). 1993. pap. bk. 30.00; 20.00 set. (978-1-879347-11-3(3)) Cin-Dav.
Covers the lives of rock's singing duo legends, the Everly Brothers from birth to the present. It delves into their personal & professional lives, ups & downs, past, present & future. It shows why there will never be another duo quite like the Everly Brothers.

***Evermore.** unabr. ed. Alyson Noël. Read by Katie Schorr. (Immortals Ser.: Bk. 1). (YA). 2009. 14.99 (978-1-4272-0841-5(7)) Pub: Macmill Audio. Dist(s): Macmillan

Evermore. unabr. ed. Alyson Noël. Read by Katie Schorr. (Running Time: 11 hrs. 0 mins. 0 sec.). (Immortals Ser.: Bk. 1). (ENG., (YA). (gr. 7-12). 2009. audio compact disk 29.99 (978-1-4272-0840-8(9)) Pub: Macmill Audio. Dist(s): Macmillan

Everwild. unabr. ed. Neal Shusterman. Read by Nick Podehl. (Running Time: 11 hrs.). (Skinjacker Trilogy: Bk. 2). 2009. 24.99 (978-1-4418-0214-9(2), 9781441802149, Brilliance MP3); 39.97 (978-1-4418-0215-6(0), 9781441802156, Brlnc Audio MP3 Lib); 24.99 (978-1-4418-0216-3(9), 9781441802163, BAD); 39.97 (978-1-4418-0217-0(7), 9781441802170, BADLE); audio compact disk 29.99 (978-1-4418-0212-5(6), 9781441802125, Bril Audio CD Unabri) Brilliance Audio.

Everwild. unabr. ed. Neal Shusterman. Read by Nick Podehl. 10 CDs. (Running Time: 11 hrs.). (Skinjacker Trilogy: Bk. 2). (YA). (gr. 8 up). 2009. audio compact disk 87.97 (978-1-4418-0213-2(4), 9781441802132, BriAudCD Unabrid) Brilliance Audio.

Every Base Covered Pt. II: Philippians 3:13-14. Ed Young. 1985. 4.95 (978-0-7417-1478-7(7), 478) Win Walk.

Every Base Covered (Paul) Pt. I: Philippians 3:13-14. Ed Young. 1985. 4.95 (978-0-7417-1477-0(9), 477) Win Walk.

Every Body Has Parasites: If You're Alive, You're at Risk! Valerie Saxion. 2005. audio compact disk 29.95 (978-1-932458-47-3(6)) Pub: Bronze Bow Pubng. Dist(s): STL Dist NA

Every Breath You Take. abr. ed. Judith McNaught. Read by Laura Dean. (Running Time: 21600 sec.). (ENG.). 2006. audio compact disk 14.99 (978-0-7393-4093-6(X), Random AudioBks) Pub: Random Audio Pubg. Dist(s): Random

Every Child Needs a Praying Mom. abr. ed. Fern Nichols & Zondervan Publishing Staff. (Running Time: 3 hrs. 0 mins. 0 sec.). (ENG.). 2003. 14.99 (978-0-310-26030-1(2)) Zondervan.

Every Child Needs a Praying Mom. abr. unabr. ed. Fern Nichols. 2 CDs. (Running Time: 3 hrs.). 2003. audio compact disk 24.99 (978-0-310-25445-4(0)) Zondervan.
Fern Nichols now shares how she has taught women to pray in a way that changes their lives and the lives of those they love. She teaches the principles and practices that will not only revolutionize the way people think about prayer but the way they do pray, leading them into a deeper intimacy with Jesus, who is always interceding on our behalf.

Every Creeping Thing: True Tales of Faintly Repulsive Wildlife. Richard Conniff. Narrated by Richard M. Davidson. 8 cass. (Running Time: 9 hrs.). 2001. 65.00 (978-0-7887-4674-1(X), 96365E7) Recorded Bks.

Every Day Deserves a Chance: Wake up to the Gift of 24 Hours. unabr. ed. Max Lucado. Read by Wayne Shepherd. (Running Time: 9344 sec.). 2007. audio compact disk 19.99 (978-0-8499-6392-6(3)) Nelson.

Every Day in Tuscany: Seasons of an Italian Life. unabr. ed. Frances Mayes. Read by Frances Mayes. 2010. 35.00 (978-0-307-70296-8(0), Random AudioBks) Pub: Random Audio Pubg. Dist(s): Random

Every Day Is Earth Day! Joyce J. Rouse. 1 cass. (J). (gr. 1-12). 1995. 9.95 (978-1-887712-01-9(1)) Rouse Hse Prodns.
More fun songs encouraging a sustainable lifestyle & teaching about resources & our global environment from "Earth Mama." 10 songs.

Every Day the World see Poetry & Voice of Ted Hughes

Every Day's a Blessing: Jim Koerner, Ex-Prisoner of War. abr. ed. Aaron Elson. Interview with Jim Koerner. 2 cass. (Running Time: 2 hrs.). 1998. 12.50 Set. (978-0-9640611-4-9(7)) Chi Chi Pr.

Every Dead Thing. John Connolly. (Charlie Parker Ser.). 2004. 14.95 (978-0-7435-4689-8(X)) Pub: S&S Audio. Dist(s): S and S Inc

Every Dog Has His Day. John R. Erickson. 2 cass. (Running Time: 2 hrs.). (Hank the Cowdog Ser.: No. 10). (J). (gr. 2-5). 1989. 16.95 (978-0-87719-152-0(2)) Lone Star Bks.

Every Dog Has His Day. unabr. ed. John R. Erickson. 2 cass. (Running Time: 2 hrs.). (Hank the Cowdog Ser.: No. 10). (J). (gr. 2-5). 2001. 24.00 (978-0-7366-6134-8(4)) Books on Tape.
After being wrongly accused of murder, Hank resigns his position as Head of Ranch Security and joins the outlaw coyotes.

Every Dog Has His Day. unabr. ed. John R. Erickson. Read by John R. Erickson. 2 cass. (Running Time: 3 hr.). (Hank the Cowdog Ser.: No. 10). (J). 2001. 16.95 (978-0-7366-6899-6(3)) Books on Tape.
It's roundup time at the ranch, but Hank has been left behind! Hotshot Benny is running the show while Hank is tied to a fence post.

Every Dog Has His Day. unabr. ed. John R. Erickson. Read by John R. Erickson. 2 cass. (Running Time: 3 hrs.). (Hank the Cowdog Ser.: No. 10). (J). 2002. 17.99 (978-1-59188-310-4(5)) Maverick Bks.
It's roundup time at the ranch and Hank is left behind, tied to a post, while a high-bred border collie named Bennie takes his place.

Every Dog Has His Day. unabr. ed. John R. Erickson. Read by John R. Erickson. 3 CDs. (Running Time: Approx 3 hours). (Hank the Cowdog Ser.: No. 10). (J). 2002. audio compact disk 19.99 (978-1-59188-610-5(4)) Maverick Bks.
It?s roundup time, and Hank the Cowdog is ready to strut his stuff. So what?s Benny?a world-class cattle dog with the papers to prove it?doing at the ranch? As Head of Ranch Security, Hank knows it?s his job to find out. But what Hank learns isn?t easy to swallow?Benny has been brought in to take his place in the roundup! Hank refuses to let some pedigreed pooch get the best of him. He?s got to find a way to prove that he?s a dog worth keeping around?before his days on the ranch run out for good.Hear the songs ?Saddle Up Overture in C-Maybe? and ?Daddy Packed His Suitcase ?Cause Momma Was a Mean Old Bag? in this hilarious adventure for the whole family.

Every Dog Has His Day. unabr. ed. John R. Erickson. 2 cass. (Running Time: 3 hrs.). (Hank the Cowdog Ser.: No. 10). (J). (gr. 2-5). 1998. 17.00 (21652) Recorded Bks.

Every Dog Has His Day. unabr. collector's ed. John R. Erickson. 3 CDs. (Running Time: 4 hrs. 30 mins.). (Hank the Cowdog Ser.: No. 10). (J). (gr. 2-5). 2001. audio compact disk 28.00 Books on Tape.
Hank is literally at the end of his rope. It's roundup time at the ranch and Hank is left behind, tied to a post, while a high-bred border collie named Bennie takes his place. How can Hank restore himself as Head of Ranch Security and reclaim his fame and fortune?.

Every Fixed Star. abr. ed. Jane Kirkpatrick. 6 cass. (Running Time: 7 hrs.). 2003. 29.99 (978-1-58926-141-9(0), W68L-0120) Oasis Audio.
Tells the story of Marie, the first mother to cross the Rocky Mountains and remain in the Pacific Northwest.

Every Fixed Star. abr. ed. Jane Kirkpatrick. Read by Barbara Rosenblat. 8 CDs. (Running Time: 7 hrs.). 2003. audio compact disk 34.99 (978-1-58926-142-6(9), W68L-012D) Oasis Audio.

Every Flower Is Beautiful: All Kinds. Steck-Vaughn Staff. 1 cass. (Running Time: 1 hr. 30 min.). (J). 1999. (978-0-7398-2445-0(7)) SteckVau.

Every Good Girl. unabr. ed. Judy Astley. Read by Phyllida Nash. 8 cass. (Running Time: 8 hrs.). 1999. 69.95 (978-0-7540-0248-2(9), CAB1671) AudioGO.
After ending twenty years of marriage to Joe, a serial philanderer, Nina was happy to concentrate on her own hectic life. But some disturbing elements began to appear, & home no longer felt safe.

Every Good Thing. (Paws & Tales Ser.: No. 42). 2002. 3.99 (978-1-57972-502-0(3)); audio compact disk 5.99 (978-1-57972-503-7(1)) Insight Living.

Every Good Woman Deserves a Lover. unabr. ed. Diana Appleyard. Read by Trudy Harris. 6 cass. (Running Time: 9 hrs. 3 mins.). (Isis Cassettes Ser.). (J). 2006. 54.95 (978-0-7531-3414-6(4)) Pub: ISIS Lrg Prnt GBR. Dist(s): Ulverscroft US

Every Knee Shall Bow: The Truth & Tragedy of Ruby Ridge & the Randy Weaver Family. unabr. ed. Jess Walter. Read by Edward Lewis. 10 cass. (Running Time: 15 hrs.). 1996. 80.00 (978-0-7366-3410-6(X), 4057) Books on Tape.
The definitive book on the Ruby Ridge seige.

***Every Last Drop: A Novel.** unabr. ed. Charlie Huston. Read by Scott Brick. (Running Time: 9 hrs.). 2010. 29.95 (978-1-4417-5330-4(3)); 59.95 (978-1-4417-5327-4(3)); audio compact disk 90.00 (978-1-4417-5328-1(1)) Blckstn Audio.

***Every Last One.** unabr. ed. Anna Quindlen. Read by Hope Davis. 8 CDs. (Running Time: 10 hrs.). 2010. audio compact disk 92.75 (978-1-4498-1022-1(5)) Recorded Bks.

***Every Last One.** unabr. ed. Anna Quindlen. Read by Hope Davis. (Running Time: 9 hrs. 30 mins. 0 sec.). 2010. audio compact disk 39.99 (978-1-4423-3400-7(2)) Pub: S&S Audio. Dist(s): S and S Inc

***Every Last One.** unabr. collector's ed. Anna Quindlen. Read by Hope Davis. 8 CDs. (Running Time: 10 hrs.). 2010. audio compact disk 44.95 (978-1-4498-1023-8(3)) Recorded Bks.

Every Little Thing about You. Lori Wick. Narrated by Ed Sala. 8 CDs. (Running Time: 9 hrs. 15 mins.). (Yellow Rose Trilogy: No. 1). audio compact disk 79.00 (978-0-7887-9858-0(8)) Recorded Bks.

Every Little Thing about You. unabr. ed. Lori Wick. Narrated by Ed Sala. 7 cass. (Running Time: 9 hrs. 15 mins.). (Yellow Rose Trilogy: No. 1). 2001. 63.00 (978-0-7887-5310-7(X), K0053E7) Recorded Bks.
Shotgun, Texas is a rough place, but Liberty Drake, a female deputy, has no trouble holding her own, until she meets a handsome ex-Texas Ranger.

Every Little Thing in the World. unabr. ed. Nina de Gramont. Read by Abby Craden. (ENG.). (J). (gr. 9). 2010. 37.00 (978-0-307-71018-5(1), Listening Lib) Pub: Random Audio Pubg. Dist(s): Random

Every Living Thing. unabr. ed. James Herriot. Read by Jonathan Reese. 9 cass. (Running Time: 13 hrs. 30 min.). 1997. 72.00 (4471) Books on Tape.
For the first time in over a decade, the world's favorite veterinarian, James Herriot, returns us to that rural green enclave called Yorkshire for more irresistible tales of animals & people.

Every Living Thing. unabr. ed. James Herriot & James Herriot. Read by Christopher Timothy. 10 CDs. (Running Time: 12 hrs. 0 mins. 0 sec.). (ENG.). (YA). 2005. audio compact disk 39.95 (978-1-59397-777-1(8)) Pub: Macmill Audio. Dist(s): Macmillan

Every Man. Contrib. by Casting Crowns. (Mastertrax Ser.). 2007. audio compact disk 9.98 (978-5-557-60389-8(1)) Beach St.

Every Man a Tiger. abr. ed. Tom Clancy. Read by Murphy Guyer. 4 cass. 1999. 25.00 (FS9-43427) Highsmith.

Every Man a Tiger. unabr. ed. Tom Clancy & Chuck Horner. 15 cass. (Running Time: 22 hrs. 30 min.). 1999. 120.00 (978-0-7366-4577-5(2), 4984) Books on Tape.
Never before has the Gulf air war & its planning been revealed in such rich, provocative detail. The story of how the Air Force, damaged by Vietnam, reinvented itself through vision, determination, & brutally hard work.

Every Man's Battle Audio. abr. ed. Stephen Arterburn & Fred Stoeker. Read by John Fuller. Told to Mike Yorkey. 3 CDs. (Running Time: 3 hrs. 38 mins.). (ENG.). 2003. audio compact disk 16.99 (978-1-57856-714-0(9), WaterB Pr) Pub: Doubday Relig. Dist(s): Random
Shares the stories of dozens who have escaped the trap of sexual immorality and presents a practical, detailed plan for any man who desires sexual purity.

Every Man's Marriage. abr. ed. Stephen Arterburn & Fred Stoeker. Read by John Fuller. Told to Mike Yorkey. 3 CDs. (Running Time: hrs. mins.). (Every Man Ser.). (ENG.). 2003. audio compact disk 16.99 (978-1-57856-715-7(7), WaterB Pr) Pub: Doubday Relig. Dist(s): Random
A terrific resource for establishing mutual respect and sacrifice in your marriage based on Christ's example of His bride, the church.

Every Missionary Can Baptize. Grant Von Harrison. Read by Ted Gibbons. 1 cass. (Missionary Success Ser.). 6.95 (978-0-929985-35-0(4)) Jackman Pubng.
Gives steps to insure success as missionary.

Every Mother Is a Daughter: The Never-Ending Quest for Success, Inner Peace, & a Really Clean Kitchen. unabr. ed. Perri Klass. Told to Sheila Solomon Klass. 8 cass. (Running Time: 11 hrs.). (YA). 2006. 29.95 (978-0-7861-4401-3(7)); audio compact disk 29.95 (978-0-7861-7437-9(4)) Blckstn Audio.

Every Mother Is a Daughter: The Neverending Quest for Success, Inner Peace, & a Really Clean Kitchen. Perri Klass & Sheila Solomon Klass. Read by Anna Fields & Carrington MacDuffie. (Running Time: 39600 sec.). 2006. 65.95 (978-0-7861-4559-1(5)); audio compact disk 81.00 (978-0-7861-7082-1(4)) Blckstn Audio.

Every Move I Make CD & Move It Like This DVD. Willow Creek Association. 2003. DVD & audio compact disk 40.98 (978-0-310-64548-1(4)) Zondervan.

Every Move I Make CD & Move It Like This DVD Combo Pack (ZCS) Zondervan Publishing Staff. 2006. DVD & audio compact disk 40.98 (978-0-310-64844-4(0)) Zondervan.

Every Move Must Have a Purpose: Strategies from Chess for Business & Life. abr. unabr. ed. Bruce Pandolfini. 2 CDs. (Running Time: 2 hrs.). 2003. audio compact disk 19.95 (978-1-59316-016-6(X), 490368) Listen & Live.
Fluid and elegant, yet rigorous and rule-bound, chess is a game that seduces, confounds, and hooks. Now, world-renowned chess master and Fortune 500 business consultant Bruce Pandolfini shows readers how chess principles can be simply and logically applied to any business or life situation.

Every Move You Make. abr. ed. M. William Phelps. (Running Time: 6 hrs.). 2009. audio compact disk 14.99 (978-1-4233-4949-5(0), 9781423349495) Brilliance Audio.

Every Move You Make. unabr. ed. M. William Phelps. Read by J. Charles. (Running Time: 14 hrs.). 2008. 39.25 (978-1-4233-4947-1(4), 9781423349471, BADLE); 24.95 (978-1-4233-4946-4(6), 9781423349464, BAD); 24.95 (978-1-4233-4944-0(X), 9781423349440, Brilliance MP3); 39.25 (978-1-4233-4945-7(8), 9781423349457, Brlnc Audio MP3 Lib); audio compact disk 38.95 (978-1-4233-4942-6(3), 9781423349426, Bril Audio CD Unabri); audio compact disk 102.25 (978-1-4233-4943-3(1), 9781423349433, BriAudCD Unabrid) Brilliance Audio.

Every Nation, Tribe & Tongue. Perf. by Bill Drake. 2002. audio compact disk 15.00 (978-1-884543-72-2(3)) AuthenticMedia.

Every Nobody Is a Somebody & In Search of God. Emmett Smith. 1 cass. 2004. 7.98 (978-1-55503-225-8(7), 06002919) Covenant Comms.
Stories of individual worth & transformation.

***Every Now & Then.** unabr. ed. Karen Kingsbury. (Running Time: 9 hrs. 33 mins. 0 sec.). (9/11 Ser.). (ENG.). 2008. 14.99 (978-0-310-28819-0(3)) Zondervan.

Every Now & Then. unabr. ed. Ralph P. Martin & Karen Kingsbury. (9/11 Ser.). (ENG.). 2008. audio compact disk 24.99 (978-0-310-28818-3(5)) Zondervan.

***Every Other Monday: Twenty Years of Life, Lunch, Faith, & Friendship.** unabr. ed. John Kasich & Daniel Paisner. (Running Time: 8 hrs. 0 mins.). 2010. 15.99 (978-1-4001-8795-9(8)); 29.99 (978-1-4001-9795-8(3)) Tantor Media.

***Every Other Monday: Twenty Years of Life, Lunch, Faith, & Friendship.** unabr. ed. John Kasich & Daniel Paisner. Narrated by John Pruden. (Running Time: 6 hrs. 30 mins. 0 sec.). (ENG.). 2010. 19.99 (978-1-4001-6795-1(7)); audio compact disk 71.99 (978-1-4001-4795-3(6)); audio compact disk 29.99 (978-1-4001-1795-6(X)) Pub: Tantor Media. Dist(s): IngramPubServ

Every Pastor Needs a Pastor. Louis McBurney. 2 cass. 9.25 Self-Control Sys.
Helps pastors to cope with their calling, offers comfort & encouragement to every clergyman courageous enough to admit his need.

Every Second Counts. abr. ed. Lance Armstrong & Sally Jenkins. Read by Oliver Wyman. 3 CDs. (Running Time: 4 hrs.). (ENG.). 2003. audio compact disk 27.50 (978-0-7393-0362-7(7), 53608034) Pub: Random Audio Pubg. Dist(s): Random

Every Second Counts. unabr. ed. Lance Armstrong & Sally Jenkins. 6 cass. (Running Time: 9 hrs.). 2003. 63.00 (978-0-7366-9440-7(4)) Books on Tape.

Every Secret Thing. Lila Shaara. Narrated by Julia Gibson. (Running Time: 68400 sec.). 2006. audio compact disk 39.99 (978-1-4193-9328-0(6)) Recorded Bks.

Every Secret Thing. unabr. ed. Laura Lippman. Read by Laurence Bouvard. 9 cass. (Running Time: 11 hrs. 46 mins.). (Isis Cassettes Ser.). (J). 2004. 76.95 (978-0-7531-1874-0(2)); audio compact disk 89.95 (978-0-7531-2264-8(2)) Pub: ISIS Lrg Prnt GBR. Dist(s): Ulverscroft US

Every Secret Thing. unabr. ed. Ann Tatlock. Narrated by Linda Stephens. 9 cass. (Running Time: 10 hrs.). 2007. 72.75 (978-1-4281-9549-3(1)); audio compact disk 102.75 (978-1-4281-9551-6(3)) Recorded Bks.

Every Single Girl's Guide to Her Future Husband's Last Divorce. Adryenn Ashley. Abr. by Adryenn Ashley. 2007. audio compact disk 7.95 (978-0-9715679-1-7(3), Cloudy Bend Pr) ChickLit Media.

***Every Soul a Star.** unabr. ed. Wendy Mass. Narrated by Jessica Almasy et al. 1 Playaway. (Running Time: 8 hrs. 45 mins.). (YA). (gr. 5-8). 2009. 59.75 (978-1-4407-0979-1(3)); 51.75 (978-1-4407-0970-8(X)); audio compact disk 66.75 (978-1-4407-0974-6(2)) Recorded Bks.

***Every Soul a Star.** unabr. collector's ed. Wendy Mass. Narrated by Jessica Almasy et al. 6 CDs. (Running Time: 8 hrs. 45 mins.). (YA). (gr. 5-8). 2009. audio compact disk 41.95 (978-1-4407-2554-8(3)) Recorded Bks.

Every Spy a Prince. abr. ed. Dan Raviv & Yossi Melman. Read by Dan Raviv. 2 cass. (Running Time: 3 hrs.). 1991. 15.95 set. (978-0-9627187-8-6(5)) Pub Mills.
This book, a New York Times bestseller for 4 months, explores the Israeli intelligence operations, relating its history & some of its most famous & intricate exploits.

Every Spy a Prince. unabr. ed. Dan Raviv & Yossi Melman. Read by Richard Brown. 15 cass. (Running Time: 22 hrs. 30 min.). 1991. 120.00 (978-0-7366-1979-0(8), 2797) Books on Tape.
The Israeli secret service dented its reputation in 1973 when the Mossad failed to foresee the Yom Kippur War. This set off bitter feuds among the country's intelligence agencies: Aman, the intelligence-gathering arm of the military; Shin Bet, the agency in charge of internal security; & the Mossad, responsible for foreign operations. Every Spy a Prince tells the story of Israeli Intelligence. It also gives us a framework for understanding developments in the Mideast & in this context evaluates new weapons systems, conventional as well as chemical, biological & nuclear.

***Every Thought Captive: Battling the Toxic Belief that Separates Us from the Life We Crave.** unabr. ed. Jerusha Clark. (ENG.). 2006. 14.98 (978-1-59644-349-5(9), Hovel Audio) christianaudio.

Every Thought Captive: Battling the Toxic Beliefs That Separate Us from the Life We Crave. unabr. ed. Jerusha Clark. 6 CDs. (Running Time: 7 hrs. 30 mins. 0 sec.). (ENG.). 2006. audio compact disk 24.98 (978-1-59644-348-8(0), Hovel Audio) christianaud.

Every Tone a Testimony: An African American Aural History. Compiled by Robert H. Cataliotti. 2 CDs. (Running Time: 2 hrs. 27 min.). (YA). (gr. 7 up). 2001. pap. bk. 23.00 (978-0-9704942-1-4(1), CD47003) Smithsonian Folkways.
Creates a history of African American life & culture in sound - an aural history. An unparalleled assembly of voices in music, oratory, poetry & prose by historically renowned African American musicians, writers & activists. Includes lyrics, bklet.

***Every Tongue Got to Confess.** unabr. ed. Zora Neale Hurston. Read by Ruby Dee & Ossie Davis. (ENG.). 2005. (978-0-06-084273-4(3), Harper Audio); (978-0-06-084274-1(1), Harper Audio) HarperCollins Pubs.

Every Tongue Got to Confess: Negro Folk-Tales from the Gulf States. Zora Neale Hurston. Narrated by Ruby Dee & Ossie Davis. 6 cass. (Running Time: 7 hrs.). 52.00 (978-1-4025-0238-5(9)) Recorded Bks.

Every Tongue Got to Confess: Negro Folk-Tales from the Gulf States. unabr. ed. Zora Neale Hurston. 5 cass. (Running Time: 7 hrs.). 2002. 32.95 (978-1-4025-0239-2(7)) Recorded Bks.
This collection of folk-tales was compiled in the late 1920s by noted anthropologist and author Zora Neale Hurston. In this work, published over 40 years after her death, she has collected a spectacular sampling of tales, yarns, fables and testimonies from all over the Gulf-states region.

Every Trace. abr. ed. Gregg Main. Read by Fee Waybill. 4 cass. (Running Time: 6 hrs.). 1999. 24.95 (978-1-57511-047-9(4)) Pub Mills.
A woman vanishes when she attempts to avenge the murder of her father. Her husband sets out to find her, & so does the killer.

Every Tree Has a Life Cycle Audio CD. Adapted by Benchmark Education Company Staff. Based on a work by Cynthia Swain. (Early Explorers Set C Ser.). (J). (gr. k-1). 2008. audio compact disk 10.00 (978-1-60437-520-6(5)) Benchmark Educ.

Every Which Way but Dead. unabr. ed. Kim Harrison. Read by Marguerite Gavin. (Hollows Ser.: Bk. 3). (YA). 2008. 84.99 (978-1-60514-634-8(X)) Find a World.

Every Which Way but Dead. unabr. ed. Kim Harrison. Read by Marguerite Gavin. 13 CDs. (Running Time: 16 hrs. 0 mins. 0 sec.). (Hollows Ser.: Bk. 3). (ENG.). 2007. audio compact disk 39.99 (978-1-4001-0473-4(4)); audio compact disk 79.99 (978-1-4001-3473-1(0)); audio compact disk 29.99 (978-1-4001-5473-9(1)) Pub: Tantor Media. Dist(s): IngramPubServ

Every Woman for Herself. Trisha Ashley. Read by Joolz Denby. 6 cass. (Running Time: 8 hrs.). (Story Sound Ser.). (J). 2004. 54.95 (978-1-85903-697-6(X)) Pub: Mgna Lrg Print GBR. Dist(s): Ulverscroft US

Every Woman's Battle: Discovering God's Plan for Sexual & Emotional Fulfillment. Shannon Ethridge. (Running Time: 24000 sec.). (Every Woman's Ser.). (ENG.). 2008. audio compact disk 26.99 (978-1-934384-13-8(5)) Pub: Treasure Pub. Dist(s): STL Dist NA

Every Woman's Marriage: Igniting the Joy & Passion You Both Desire. Shannon and Greg Ethridge. (ENG.). 2008. audio compact disk 26.99 (978-1-934384-14-5(3)) Pub: Treasure Pub. Dist(s): STL Dist NA

Every Young Man's Battle: Strategies for Victory in the Real World of Sexual Temptation. abr. ed. Stephen Arterburn & Fred Stoeker. Read by J. Charles Steve Yankee. (Running Time: 3 hrs.). (Every Man Ser.). 2006. 39.25 (978-1-4233-0396-1(2), 9781423303961, BADLE); 24.95 (978-1-4233-0395-4(4), 9781423303954, BAD) Brilliance Audio.

Every Young Man's Battle: Strategies for Victory in the Real World of Sexual Temptation. abr. ed. Stephen Arterburn & Fred Stoeker. Read by J. Charles Yankee & Steve Yankee. Told to Mike Yorkey. (Running Time: 10800 sec.). (Every Man Ser.). 2006. audio compact disk 39.25 (978-1-4233-0394-7(6), 9781423303947, Brlnc Audio MP3 Lib) Brilliance Audio.
In this world you're surrounded by sexual images that open the door to temptation. They're everywhere - on TV, billboards, magazines, music, the Internet - and so easy to access that it sometimes feels impossible to escape their clutches. Yet God expects His children to be sexually pure. So how can you survive the relentless battle against temptation? Here's powerful ammunition. Stephen Arterburn and Fred Stoeker examine the standard of Ephesians 5:3 - "there must not be even a hint of sexual immorality" - in a positive and sensitive light. And they explain how an authentic, vibrant relationship with Jesus Christ is the key to victory over temptation. Every Young Man's Battle will show you how to train your eyes and your mind, how to clean up your thought life, and how to develop a realistic battle plan for remaining pure in today's sexually soaked culture. As a result, you'll experience hope - real hope - for living a strong, pure life God's way.

Every Young Man's Battle: Strategies for Victory in the Real World of Sexual Temptation. abr. ed. Stephen Arterburn & Fred Stoeker. Read by J. Charles & Steve Yankee. Told to Mike Yorkey. (Running Time: 10800 sec.). (Every Man Ser.). 2006. audio compact disk 24.95 (978-1-4233-0393-0(8), 9781423303930, Brilliance MP3) Brilliance Audio.

Every Young Man's Battle: Strategies for Victory in the Real World of Sexual Temptation. abr. ed. Stephen Arterburn et al. Read by J. Charles & Steve Yankee. 3 CDs. (Running Time: 3 hrs.). (Everyman Ser.). 2003. audio compact disk 24.95 (978-1-59086-691-7(6), 1590866916); audio compact disk 62.25 (978-1-59086-692-4(4), 1590866924) Brilliance Audio.

Everybody Dance! 1 LP. (J). 2001. pap. bk. 11.95 (KIM 9131) Kimbo Educ.
Cool songs & dances starring a super bunch of kids just having fun & performing 10 lively dances. Celebrate an exuberant approach to fitness with high-tech action. Achy Breaky Heart, Hot, Hot, Hot, The Loco Motion, La Bamba, YMCA, Everybody Dance Now & More. The step-by-step demonstration of the more complicated routines makes learning these dances a snap. Includes guide with lyrics & instructions.

Everybody Dance. 1 cass . (J). 1993. pap. bk. 10.95 (KIM9131C); pap. bk. 14.95 (KIM 9131CD) Kimbo Educ.

Everybody Dies. unabr. ed. Lawrence Block. Narrated by Mark Hammer. 8 cass. (Running Time: 11 hrs. 30 mins.). (Matthew Scudder Mystery Ser.: No. 14). 1999. 70.00 (978-0-7887-2484-8(3), 95559E7) Recorded Bks.
When an old hoodlum buddy asks P.I. Matt Scudder to investigate the deaths of his employees, Matt suddenly finds himself in a world where no man's survival can be taken for granted.

Everybody Had a Gun. unabr. ed. Richard S. Prather. Read by Maynard Villers. 6 cass. (Running Time: 7 hrs. 6 min.). (Shell Scott Ser.: Bk. 3). 2001. 39.95 (978-1-55686-898-6(7)) Books in Motion.
When an unpleasant little man enters Shell's office toting a .45 with the P.I. in its sites, a red-headed bombshell distracts the hit man, to foil the plan. But the woman quickly disappears.

Everybody Has Music Inside: Featuring Songs of Greg & Steve. 1994. bk. 35.00 (978-0-7935-3599-6(9)) H Leonard.

Everybody Needs a Little Tenderness. unabr. ed. Read by Peter Himmelman. Perf. by Peter Himmelman. 1 cass. (Running Time: 29 min.). Dramatization. (J). 1985. 8.95 (978-1-58452-004-7(3), 4330); 8.95 Spanish version. (978-1-58452-013-9(2), 5330) Spinoza Co.

Everybody Needs a Rock. unabr. ed. Byrd Baylor. Narrated by Will Rogers. 1 cass. (Running Time: 10 min.). (Byrd Baylor Ser.). (J). (gr. k-6). 1988. 5.95 (978-0-929937-13-7(9)) SW Series.
Describes the intimate feeling a child has for his own just-right rock.

Everybody Needs Somebody. Lucile Johnson. 1 cass. 6.98 (978-1-55503-282-1(6), 06004253) Covenant Comms.
Lucile's best on the amazing impact we have on each other.

Everybody Needs Somebody. Lucile Johnson. 1 cass. 2004. 3.95 (978-1-57734-386-8(7), 34441255) Covenant Comms.

Everybody Once Was a Kid: Gemini-Fun Songs & Activities for Kids. (MusicTivity Ser.). (J). 1993. pap. bk. 9.95 (978-0-7935-2875-2(5)); pap. bk. 12.95 (978-0-7935-2874-5(7)) H Leonard.

Everybody Ought to Know. Heritage Christ. 2004. audio compact disk 16.99 (978-1-880809-37-2(0)) Leg Pubs Intl.

Everybody Sing & Dance! Esther Nelson & Jacques Trapp. 1 cass. (Running Time: 1 hr.). (J). (ps-3). 1989. bk. 10.95 (978-0-945110-09-5(X), D511) Granny Pr.
Designed to introduce children to the joys of song, dance, rhythm, & creative movement. Contains 68 songs to sing & dance to, fingerplays, group dances, rhythm band songs, & songs that encourage young imaginations.

Everybody Smokes in Hell. John Ridley. Narrated by Peter Jay Fernandez. 9 CDs. (Running Time: 9 hrs.). audio compact disk 78.00 (978-1-4025-1551-4(0)) Recorded Bks.

Everybody Smokes in Hell. unabr. ed. John Ridley. Narrated by Peter Jay Fernandez. 6 cass. (Running Time: 9 hrs.). 2001. 52.00 (978-0-7887-5336-7(3), F0035) Recorded Bks.
When Filthy White Guy blows up the microwave of the convenience store where Paris Scott has worked for 30 long nights, Paris decides his life couldn't be more of a mess. But when he gives Filthy White Guy a ride home to a Bel Air mansion, things really start to explode.

Everybody Wins: The Chapman Guide to Solving Conflicts Without Arguing. unabr. ed. Gary Chapman. Narrated by Maurice England. (Marriage Savers Ser.). (ENG.). 2007. 9.79 (978-1-60814-181-4(0)); audio compact disk 13.99 (978-1-59859-191-0(6)) Oasis Audio.

***Everybody's Different.** Cerebellum Academic Team. (Running Time: 16 mins.). (Lesson Booster Ser.). 2010. cd-rom 79.95 (978-1-59443-693-2(2)) Cerebellum.

Everybody's favorite songs - low voice, vol. I. John Wustman. 2005. pap. bk. 34.98 (978-1-59615-498-8(5), 586-061) Pub: Music Minus. Dist(s): Bookworld

Everybody's favorite songs - low voice, vol. II, Vol. 2. John Wustman. 2001. pap. bk. 34.98 (978-1-59615-500-8(0), 586-063) Pub: Music Minus. Dist(s): Bookworld

Everybody's Gettin' Some. 1 cass., 1 CD. 7.98 (TA 33360); audio compact disk 12.78 CD Jewel box. (TA 83360) NewSound.

Everybody's Normal till You Get to Know Them. unabr. ed. John Ortberg. 5 cass. (Running Time: 7 hrs. 30 min.). 2003. 29.99 (978-0-310-25082-1(X)) Zondervan.
This is not a book for normal people to learn how to handle difficult people, there is no such thing. This is a book about how imperfect people can pursue community with other imperfect people. To love and be loved is the fiercest longing of the soul. Community living in vital relationship with others is essential to human life. In his new book John Ortberg explores the biblical vision of community as the place God made for us and the place where God meets us.

Everybody's Normal till You Get to Know Them. unabr. ed. Zondervan Publishing Staff & John Ortberg. (Running Time: 8 hrs. 14 mins. 0 sec.). (ENG.). 2003. 10.99 (978-0-310-26147-6(3)) Zondervan.

Everybody's Special. unabr. ed. Janice Buckner. Perf. by Janice Buckner. 1 cass. (Running Time: 35 min.). (Janice Buckner Educational Entertainment Ser.). (J). (gr. k-6). 1988. pap. bk. 15.99 (978-1-56479-001-9(0), MR102SB) Moonlight Rose.
12 songs teaching concepts of self esteem, appreciation of others, & respect for the world we live in.

Everybody's Special: Self-Esteem. Janice Buckner. 1 cass. (Running Time: 70 min.). (Learn along Song Ser.: Vol. 2). (J). 1992. 9.98 (978-1-56479-102-3(5), MR102-4) Moonlight Rose.
Collection of original songs on self-esteem & the appreciation of others that celebrates life & understanding each person's worth. Includes sing-it-yourself side.

Everybreath. Perf. by James McNally. 1 cass., 1 CD. 8.78 (WH 11292); audio compact disk 13.58 CD Jewel box. (WH 11292) NewSound.

Everyday. HarperCollins Pubs.

Everyday Conversations in Russian. Nicholas Maltzoff. (J). (gr. 7-12). 1984. 20.95 (978-0-8442-4278-1(0)) Glencoe.
Designed for students, tourists, business travelers & anyone who wants to develop an ability to speak Russian.

Everyday Death Sentence. Perf. by CMC'S Staff. 1 cass. 1999. 10.98 (KMGC9506); audio compact disk 16.98 (KMGD9506) Provident Mus Dist.

Everyday English, Bk. 1. 2nd ed. Barbara Zaffran. 1990. 29.38 (978-0-8442-0653-0(9), 9780844206530, ESL/ELT) Pub: McGrw-H Hghr Educ. Dist(s): McGraw

Everyday English, Bk. 3. 2nd ed. Barbara Zaffran. (C). 1990. 24.97 (978-0-8442-0664-6(4), ESL/ELT) Pub: McGrw-H Hghr Educ. Dist(s): McGraw

Everyday English Book 1 Unit 1-3, Bk. 1. 2nd ed. Created by McGraw-Hill Staff. 1990. 29.38 (978-0-8442-0652-3(0), 9780844206523, ESL/ELT) Pub: McGrw-H Hghr Educ. Dist(s): McGraw

Everyday English Conversation. Susan Stempleski. (Talk Time Ser.). 2007. audio compact disk 39.95 (978-0-19-438211-3(7)) OUP.

Everyday English Conversation. Susan Stempleski. (Talk Time Ser.). 2007. audio compact disk 39.95 (978-0-19-438219-9(2)) OUP.

Everyday Enlightenment: The Twelve Gateways to Personal Growth. abr. ed. Dan Millman. (Running Time: 2 hrs. 30 mins.). (ENG.). 2006. 14.98 (978-1-59483-702-9(3)) Pub: Hachet Audio. Dist(s): HachBkGrp

Everyday Enlightment. 1999. (978-1-57042-734-3(8)) Hachet Audio.

Everyday Grace. Marianne Williamson. (ENG.). 2003. audio compact disk 10.95 (978-1-4019-0306-0(1)) Hay House.

Everyday Grace: Having Hope, Finding Forgiveness, & Making Miracles. Marianne Williamson. 48.00 (978-0-7366-8867-3(6)) Books on Tape.

Everyday Grace: Having Hope, Finding Forgiveness, & Making Miracles. Marianne Williamson. 2002. audio compact disk 48.00 (978-0-7366-8868-0(4)) Books on Tape.

Everyday Healing Foods. David Freudberg. Perf. by Jean Carper et al. 1 cass. (Running Time: 1 hr.). 1995. 11.95 (978-0-9640914-0-5(2)) Human Media.
Learn which common fruits, vegetables & spices comprise a "food pharmacy" that can actively help safeguard your health.

Everyday Italian, Vol. 1. Loana Kane. 3 cass. (ITA.). (C). 1994. 29.50 Set. (978-0-930329-54-9(6)) Kabel Pubs.
Italian textbook on tape.

Everyday Italian, Vol. 2. Loana Kane. 3 cass. (C). 1994. 29.50 Set. (978-0-930329-56-3(2)) Kabel Pubs.
Italian textbook on tapes.

Everyday Japanese. Edward A. Schwarz & Reiko Ezawa. 1 cass. (Running Time: 60 min.). 1989. 9.95 (978-0-8442-8499-6(8), Natl Textbk Co) M-H Contemporary.
Acquaints students with a range of Japanese accents by using native male & female speakers.

Everyday Journey from Death into Life. Jose Hobday. Read by Jose Hobday. 8 cass. (Running Time: 7 hrs. 30 min.). 49.95 incl. bibliography in vinyl album. (AA0548) Credence Commun.
Discusses memory, revelation, transformation, harmony, brokeness & fertility as it helps one understand oneself as the body of Christ.

Everyday Kowa Phrases. unabr. ed. 1 cass. (Running Time: 1 hr.). 14.95 (CKW001) J Norton Pubs.
The selection of words & phrases revolve around the themes of everyday living.

Everyday Leadership. unabr. ed. Contrib. by Pat Wagner & Alan Dumas. 1 cass. (Running Time: 55 min.). 1999. 12.95 (978-0-9642678-8-6(8)) Pattern Res.
Eliciting the best from other people.

Everyday Life: American Standard. 1 cass. 1999. 10.98 (KMGC9702); audio compact disk 16.98 (KMGD9702) Provident Mus Dist.

Everyday Life: Disgruntled. 1 CD. 1999. audio compact disk 16.98 (KMGD9603) Provident Mus Dist.

Everyday Man. Perf. by Gary Chapman. 1 cass. 1988. audio compact disk Brentwood Music.
Produced by Gary Chapman, Brown Bannister & Mark Wright, Chapman wrote the majority of these songs, & a highlight is the song, Your Love Stays With Me.

Everyday Mandarin. unabr. ed. Singapore Broadcasting Corporation Staff. 2 cass. pap. bk. 375.00 Set, incl. 3 VHS video cass. (SV0022) J Norton Pubs.

Everyday Meditation. unabr. ed. 1 cass. (Running Time: 40 min.). (Inner Mastery Ser.). 1994. 9.95 Norelco size. (978-1-886198-12-8(8)) Soft Stone Pub.
Teaches meditation techniques that increase your quality and appreciation of life. Effective, unique skills for living each day more fully, with increased energy, awareness and balance. For the beginning or advanced meditator, this is the ideal choice to play in whole or in part every day. Background music composed to facilitate your practice. Endorsed by hospitals, airlines and psychologists. This tape was made in response to requests from those who come to my retreats and enjoy my guided meditations. They wanted something to play when they weren't at retreat that would refocus them and "provide mileage" (as one long-term meditator told me) for their daily meditations. The purpose of these tapes is not only that you feel results after each listen, but that you develop increasingly deeper skills to serve you in all of life's challenges and excursions. Commonly considered negatives such as pain, stress and insomnia are experienced in a new, non-judgmental way that invites insight and is both growth-promoting and freeing. Once perceived enemies turn into welcome teachers. Similarly, positive and everyday events such as watching a bird soar, hitting a ball or conducting business are experienced in a more complete way; a way that enriches your relationship to self and thus the outside world.

Everyday Meditation. unabr. ed. Krs Edstrom. Read by Krs Edstrom. 1 cass. (Running Time: 40 min.). (Inner Mastery Ser.). 1994. 12.95 Bk. box size. (978-1-886198-04-3(7), IMS05) Soft Stone Pub.

Everyday Meditation: A Mini-Retreat to Calm the Mind & Nourish the Soul. K. R. S. Edstrom. 1 CD. (Running Time: 40 mins.). 2009. audio compact disk 16.95 (978-1-886198-19-7(5)) Pub: Soft Stone Pub. Dist(s): Ingram Bk Co

***Everyday Mindfulness: Meditation for Beginners.** unabr. ed. Beryl Bender Birch. (Running Time: 55 mins.). 2010. 9.99 (978-1-61544-020-7(8)) Better Listen.

Everyday Oneness: Selected Talks & Dialogues with Adyashanti. 3 Audio CDs. Featuring Adyashanti. (ENG.). 2008. audio compact disk 29.00 (978-1-933986-49-4(2)) Open Gate Pub.

Everyday Problems & Their Solutions. 1 cass. (Running Time: 30 min.). 1985. (0283) Evang Sisterhood Mary.
Subjects are: Ten tips for a Life of Reconciliation; Give Me! Give Me! Don't Repress-Confess!; A Challenge & An Inspiration.

Everyday Songs: Sing & Learn. Composed by Sally K. Albrecht. (ENG.). 2005. audio compact disk 13.99 (978-0-7390-3790-4(0)) Alfred Pub.

Everyday Survival: Why Smart People Do Stupid Things. unabr. ed. Laurence Gonzales. Narrated by Kevin T. Collins. 8 CDs. (ENG.). 2008. audio compact disk 29.95 (978-1-60283-494-1(6)) Pub: AudioGO. Dist(s): Perseus Dist

Everyday Ukrainian. unabr. ed. Zirka Derlycia. 10 cass. (Running Time: 10 hrs.). (UKR & ENG.). (YA). (gr. 10-12). 1993. pap. bk. 245.00 (978-0-88432-491-1(5), AFUK10) J Norton Pubs.
New self-study course, designed for the beginner. Features practical, everyday Ukranian with emphasis on the spoken language. Vocabulary & grammar are illustrated with dialogs & basic sentences & drilled in a variety of exercises. Text includes an answer key, grammar appendix & glossary.

Everyday Ukrainian CDs & Text. Zirka Derlycia. 10 CDs. (Running Time: 10 hrs.). (UKR.). 2005. audio compact disk 245.00 (978-1-57970-158-1(2), AFUK10D) J Norton Pubs.

Everyday Video Course: Mandarin. unabr. ed. 2 cass. (Running Time: 2 hrs.). bk. 375.00 (SVO022) J Norton Pubs.

Everyday Wisdom. Wayne W. Dyer. 1 CD. 2005. audio compact disk 10.95 (978-1-4019-0428-9(9)) Hay House.

Everyday Wisdom. unabr. ed. Wayne W. Dyer. Read by Wayne W. Dyer. 1 cass. (Running Time: 65 min.). 1994. 10.95 (978-1-56170-086-8(X), 354) Hay House.
The international renowned author of Real Magic & Your Erroneous Zones reads his collection of over 200 insightful quotes & observations. A must for the millions who have enjoyed Dr. Dyer's books.

Everyman. Philip Roth. Narrated by George Guidall. (Running Time: 15300 sec.). 2006. audio compact disk 29.99 (978-1-4193-8723-4(5)) Recorded Bks.

Everyman. unabr. ed. Philip Roth. Read by George Guidall. 3 cass. (Running Time: 4 hrs. 25 mns.). 2006. 30.75 (978-1-4193-8899-6(1)); audio compact disk 51.75 (978-1-4193-8901-6(7)) Recorded Bks.

Everyone. J Parker.

Everyone Communicates, Few Connect. abr. ed. John C. Maxwell. 2010. audio compact disk 24.99 (978-1-4002-0255-3(8)) Nelson.

Everyone Dies. unabr. ed. Michael McGarrity. Read by Patrick G. Lawlor. 6 cass. (Running Time: 8 hrs.). (Kevin Kerney Ser.: Bk. 8). 2003. 29.95 (978-1-59086-779-2(3), 1590867793, BAU); 74.25 (978-1-59086-780-8(7), 1590867807, BrilAudUnabridg) Brilliance Audio.
Santa Fe Police Chief Kevin Kerney and his wife, Lieutenant Colonel Sara Brannon, are on leave and eagerly awaiting the birth of their son when a prominent gay attorney is gunned down outside his office by an unknown assailant. Called to the crime scene and faced with scanty evidence and no apparent motive, Kerney directs his chief of detectives to delve into the victim's personal and professional life, a decision that ultimately leads to a SWAT team screw-up and the death of two innocent people. But the killer has just begun. Kerney's horse, a mustang he'd gentled and trained, is vicously and senselessly destroyed; a dead rabbit is left on his doorstep; and a second victim with ties to the criminal justice system is found in her bed with her throat cut along with the warning: EVERYONE DIES. As a time of joy turns into a nightmare, Kerney and Sara search desperately for a seemingly unstoppable chameleonlike killer who promises to murder them and their unborn son.

Everyone Dies. unabr. ed. Michael McGarrity. Read by Patrick G. Lawlor. (Running Time: 8 hrs.). (Kevin Kerney Ser.: Bk. 8). 2004. 39.25 (978-1-59335-496-1(7), 1593354967, Brinc Audio MP3 Lib) Brilliance Audio.

Everyone Dies. unabr. ed. Michael McGarrity. Read by Patrick G. Lawlor. (Running Time: 8 hrs.). (Kevin Kerney Ser.). 2004. 24.95 (978-1-59710-256-8(3), 1597102563, BAD) Brilliance Audio.

Everyone Dies. unabr. ed. Michael McGarrity. Read by Patrick G. Lawlor. (Running Time: 8 hrs.). (Kevin Kerney Ser.: Bk. 8). 2004. 39.25 (978-1-59710-257-5(1), 1597102571, BADLE) Brilliance Audio.

Everyone Dies. unabr. ed. Michael McGarrity. Read by Patrick G. Lawlor. (Running Time: 8 hrs.). (Kevin Kerney Ser.: Bk. 8). 2004. 24.95 (978-1-59335-233-2(6), 1593352336) Soulmate Audio Bks.

***Everyone Is Beautiful.** unabr. ed. Katherine Center. Read by Kirsten Potter. 6 CDs. (Running Time: 7 hrs. 30 mins.). 2009. audio compact disk 70.00 (978-1-4159-5996-1(X), BksonTape) Pub: Random Audio Pubg. Dist(s): Random

Everyone Knows Gato Pinto. unabr. ed. Joe Hayes. Read by Joe Hayes. 1 cass. (Running Time: 1 hr. 20 min.). (J). (gr. 2-7). 1993. 10.95 (978-0-939729-23-4(7), CPP9237) Pub: Trails West Pub. Dist(s): Continental Bk
Nine Hispanic folktales from New Mexico.

***Everyone Loves You When You're Dead: Journeys into Fame & Madness.** unabr. ed. Neil Strauss. (ENG.). 2011. (978-0-06-200715-5(7), Harper Audio) HarperCollins Pubs.

Everyone Needs a Friend, Friend. George Bloomer. audio compact disk Whitaker Hse.

Everyone Needs a Friend, Friend. George Bloomer. 2003. audio compact disk 14.99 (978-0-88368-968-4(5)) Whitaker Hse.

Everyone Worth Knowing. abr. ed. Lauren Weisberger. Read by Eliza Dushku. 2005. 15.95 (978-0-7435-5249-3(0)) Pub: S&S Audio. Dist(s): S and S Inc

Everyone Worth Knowing. abr. ed. Lauren Weisberger. Read by Eliza Dushku. (Running Time: 50 hrs. 0 mins. 0 sec.). (ENG.). 2008. audio compact disk 14.99 (978-0-7435-7363-4(3)) Pub: S&S Audio. Dist(s): S and S Inc

Everyone's a Coach: You Can Inspire Anyone to Be a Winner. abr. ed. Ken Blanchard & Don Shula. (Running Time: 2 hrs. 40 mins. 0 sec.). (ENG.). 2003. 9.99 (978-0-310-26032-5(9)) Zondervan.

Everything about Playing Blues. Wilbur M. Savidge & Randy L. Vradenburg. 2004. bk. 24.95 (978-1-884848-09-4(5), BS90001) Pub: Praxis Music. Dist(s): Music Sales

Everything Belongs. Richard Rohr. 5 cass. (Running Time: 5 hrs.). 39.95 Set. (AA2847) Credence Commun.
Richard Rohr gave a retreat to 300 people from all over the country. It was a retreat on contemplative prayer to people who had no organized tradition of contemplative discipline, just good Christian hunger for a stronger life of prayer. Richard doesn't give you formulas for prayer, because he is undoing the cultural belief in formulas. Instead - using parables, analogies, contrasts, poems, koans, allusions & metaphors - he creates an experience through simple, spontaneous lectures. When you listen, you will probably not be able to define contemplative prayer, or even easily summarize what you have learned.

Everything but the Truth. unabr. ed. Joe Bright. Read by Ric Benson. 8 cass. (Running Time: 7 hrs. 6 min.). 2001. 49.95 (978-1-58116-139-7(5)) Books in Motion.
A case of stolen gems from the site of a Hollywood party find young actor Sam Simmons in the lead of a humorous plot where Hollywood celebrities, wanna-be's, and the criminal underworld all converge while "taking care of business".

Everything Changes. unabr. ed. Jonathan Tropper. Read by Scott Brick. 11 CDs. (Running Time: 10 hrs.). 2005. audio compact disk 99.00 (978-1-4159-1670-4(5)); 81.00 (978-1-4159-1585-1(7)) Books on Tape.
To all appearances, Zachary King is a man with luck on his side. A steady, well-paying job, a rent-free Manhattan apartment, and Hope, his stunning, blue-blooded fiancée: smart, sexy, and completely out of his league. But as the wedding day looms, Zack finds himself haunted by the memory of his best friend, Rael, killed in a car wreck two years earlier - and by his increasingly complicated feelings for Tamara, the beautiful widow Rael left behind. Then Norm - Zack's freewheeling, Viagra-popping father - resurfaces after a twenty-year absence, looking to make amends. Norm's overbearing, often outrageous efforts to reestablish ties with his sons infuriate Zack, and yet, despite twenty years of bad blood, he finds something compelling in his father's maniacal determination to transform his own life. Inspired by Norm, Zack boldly attempts to make some changes of his own, and the results are instantly calamitous. Soon fists are flying, his love life is a shambles, and his once carefully structured existence is spinning hopelessly out of control.

Everything Comes to Those Who Wait **see Paddington for Christmas**

Everything Drums Book: From Tuning & Timing to Fills & Solos, All You Need to Keep the Beat. Eric Starr. 1 CD. 2003. pap. bk. 19.95 (978-1-58062-886-0(9)) Pub: Adams Media. Dist(s): FplusW Media

Everything for a Dog. unabr. ed. Ann M. Martin. Read by David Pittu. (Running Time: 5 hrs.). 2009. 19.99 (978-1-4233-9239-2(6), 9781423392392, BAD) Brilliance Audio.

Everything for a Dog. unabr. ed. Ann M. Martin. Read by David Pittu. 5 CDs. (Running Time: 5 hrs.). (J). (gr. 4-6). 2009. audio compact disk 59.97 (978-1-4233-9236-1(1), 9781423392361, BriAudCD Unabrid) Brilliance Audio.

Everything for a Dog. unabr. ed. Ann M. Martin. Read by David Pittu. 1 MP3-CD. (Running Time: 5 hrs.). (J). (gr. 4-7). 2009. 39.97 (978-1-4233-9238-5(8), 9781423392385, Brinc Audio MP3 Lib) Brilliance Audio.

Everything for a Dog. unabr. ed. Ann M. Martin. Read by David Pittu. 5 CDs. (Running Time: 5 hrs.). (gr. 4-7). 2009. audio compact disk 19.99 (978-1-4233-9235-4(3), 9781423392354, Bril Audio CD Unabri) Brilliance Audio.

Everything for a Dog. unabr. ed. Read by David Pittu. Ed. by Ann M. Martin. Narrated by Ann M. Martin. (Running Time: 5 hrs.). 2009. 19.99 (978-1-4233-9237-8(X), 9781423392378, Brilliance MP3); 39.97 (978-1-4233-9240-8(X), 9781423392408, BADLE) Brilliance Audio.

Everything Get-a-Job Book. abr. ed. Dawn Rosenberg McKay. Narrated by Michael Coon. (Everything Bks.). (ENG.). 2007. 13.99 (978-1-60814-182-1(9)) Oasis Audio.

Everything Glorious. Contrib. by David Crowder Band. (Mastertrax Ser.). (ENG.). 2008. audio compact disk 9.98 (978-5-557-43320-4(1)) Pt of Grace Ent.

Everything Green Living Book: Transform Your Lifestyle - Easy Ways to Conserve Energy, Protect Your Family's Health, & Help Save. abr. ed. Diane Gow McDilda. Narrated by Rick Plastina. (Everything Bks.). (ENG.). 2008. 13.99 (978-1-60814-183-8(7)) Oasis Audio.

Everything Green Living Book: Transform Your Lifestyle - Easy Ways to Conserve Energy, Protect Your Family's Health, & Help Save the Environment. abr. ed. Diane Gow McDilda. Narrated by Rick Plastina. (Running Time: 5 hrs. 0 mins. 0 sec.). (Everything Bks.). (ENG.). 2008. audio compact disk 19.99 (978-1-59859-315-0(3)) Oasis Audio.

Everything Grows. Perf. by Raffi. 1 cass, 1 CD. (J). 10.95 (KSR 8134C); lp 10.95 (KSR 8134) Kimbo Educ.
Bathtime, Brown Girl in the Ring, Let's Make Some Noise, Ha Ha Thisaway, Teddy Bear Hug, Harv Ga Kita & more.

Everything Grows. Perf. by Raffi. 1 cass, 1 CD. (J). 2001. audio compact disk 16.95 (KSR 8134 CD) Kimbo Educ.

Everything Grows. Perf. by Raffi. 1 cass. (J). (ps-6). 10.98 (222); audio compact disk 17.98 (D222) MFLP CA.
The incredible music of the pied piper of children's music. Songs include: "Bath Time," "Teddy Bear Hug," "Everything Grows," "The Mountain Polka," "Eight Piggies in a Row," & many more.

Everything Grows. Perf. by Raffi. 1 cass., 1 CD. (J). 7.98 (RDR 8058); audio compact disk 12.78 CD Jewel box. (RDR 8058) NewSound.

Everything Grows. Perf. by Raffi. 1 cass. (Running Time: 33 mins.). (J). 1999. (978-1-886767-45-4(9)); (978-1-886767-71-3(8)) Rounder Records.
Singable, danceable, lovable. This collection bubbles with delightful music for every childhood mood. Here is Raffi at his most enchanting.

Everything Grows. Perf. by Raffi. 1 CD. (Running Time: 33 mins.). (J). 1999. audio compact disk (978-1-886767-44-7(0)); audio compact disk (978-1-886767-70-6(X)) Rounder Records.

Everything Guide to Being a Sales Rep: Winning Secrets to a Successful & Profitable Career. abr. ed. Ruth Klein. Narrated by Rick Plastina. (Running Time: 5 hrs. 2 mins. 30 sec.). (Everything (Oasis Audio) Ser.). (ENG.). 2007. audio compact disk 19.99 (978-1-59859-267-2(X)) Oasis Audio.

Everything Guide to C. S. Lewis & Narnia. abr. ed. Jon Kennedy. Narrated by Mark Warner. (Everything Bks.). (ENG.). 2008. 13.99 (978-1-60814-180-7(2), SpringWater) Oasis Audio.

Everything I Needed to Know in Life I Didn't Learn in School... Are We Teaching Real Life Skills? Miriam Gettinger. 1 cass. (Running Time: 90 mins.). 1999. 6.00 (W60FW) Torah Umesorah.

Everything Improve Your Credit Book: Boost Your Score, Lower Your Interest Rates, & Save Money. abr. ed. Justin Pritchard. Narrated by Rick Plastina. (Everything Bks.). (ENG.). 2007. 13.99 (978-1-60814-185-2(3)); audio compact disk 19.99 (978-1-59859-265-8(3)) Oasis Audio.

Everything in Order! Sundance/Newbridge, LLC Staff. (Early Math Ser.). (gr. k-1). 2000. 12.00 (978-1-58273-984-7(6)) Sund Newbrdge.

***Everything Is Broken: A Tale of Catastrophe in Burma.** unabr. ed. Emma Larkin. (Running Time: 8 hrs. 30 mins.). 2010. 15.99 (978-1-4001-8704-1(4)); 29.99 (978-1-4001-9704-0(X)) Tantor Media.

***Everything Is Broken: A Tale of Catastrophe in Burma.** unabr. ed. Emma Larkin. Narrated by Emily Durante. (Running Time: 8 hrs. 30 mins. 0 sec.). (ENG.). 2010. 19.99 (978-1-4001-6704-3(3)); audio compact disk 59.99 (978-1-4001-4704-5(2)); audio compact disk 29.99 (978-1-4001-1704-8(6)) Pub: Tantor Media. Dist(s): IngramPubServ

Everything Is Fine. unabr. ed. Ann Dee Ellis. Read by Carrington MacDuffie. 3 CDs. (Running Time: 3 hrs. 35 mins.). (YA). (gr. 6-9). 2009. audio compact disk 38.00 (978-0-7393-7907-3(0), Listening Lib) Pub: Random Audio Pubg. Dist(s): Random

Everything Is Fine. unabr. ed. Ann Dee Ellis. (J). (gr. 7). 2009. audio compact disk 27.00 (978-0-7393-7906-6(2), Listening Lib) Pub: Random Audio Pubg. Dist(s): Random

Everything Is Going to Be O.K.! Dan Litchford, Jr. 1 cass. 3.95 (978-1-57734-389-9(1), 34441298); 7.98 (978-1-55503-787-1(9), 06005012) Covenant Comms.
Staying happily on the straight & narrow.

Everything Is Illuminated. unabr. ed. Jonathan Safran Foer. Narrated by Jeff Woodman & Scott Shina. 9 cass. (Running Time: 11 hrs. 45 mins.). 2002. 76.00 (978-1-4025-2851-4(5)) Recorded Bks.
Jonathan is a Jewish college student searching Europe for the one person he believes can explain his roots. Alex, a lover of all things American and unsurpassed butcher of the English language, is his lovable Ukrainian guide. On their quixotic quest, the two young men look for Augustine, a woman who might have saved Jonathan's grandfather from the Nazis.

Everything Is Illuminated. unabr. ed. Jonathan Safran Foer. Read by Jeff Woodman Scott Shina. 7 cass. (Running Time: 11 hrs. 45 mins.). 2004. 29.99 (978-1-4025-2499-8(4), 01804) Recorded Bks.

Everything Is Illuminated. unabr. ed. Jonathan Safran Foer. 2004. audio compact disk 29.99 (978-1-4193-2676-9(7)) Recorded Bks.

Everything Is Impersonal. unabr. ed. Andrew Cohen. 2 cass. (Running Time: 1 hr. 36 min.). (Bodhgaya Ser.: Vol. 4). 16.00 Set. (978-1-883929-13-8(X)) Moksha Pr.
A look far beyond the fundamentally limited & personal dimension of existence to discover a radically new & liberating perspective on life that is absolutely impersonal.

Everything Is Wild **see Middle-Aged Man on the Flying Trapeze**

Everything Leadership Book. Eric Yaverbaum & Eric Sherman. Read by Mark Warner. (Playaway Adult Nonfiction Ser.). 2008. 59.99 (978-1-60640-950-3(6)) Find a World.

Everything Leadership Book. abr. ed. Eric Yaverbaum & Erik Sherman. (Everything Bks.). (ENG.). 2008. 13.99 (978-1-60814-186-9(1), SpringWater) Oasis Audio.

Everything Leadership Book. abr. ed. Eric Yaverbaum & Erik Sherman. Read by Mark Warner. (Everything Bks.). (ENG.). 2008. audio compact disk 19.99 (978-1-59859-391-4(9)) Oasis Audio.

Everything Managing People Book. abr. ed. Gary McLain & Deborah S. Romaine. (Everything Bks.). (ENG.). 2007. 13.99 (978-1-60814-187-6(X)) Oasis Audio.

Everything Managing People Book. 2nd abr. ed. Gary McClain & Deborah S. Romaine. Read by Michael Coon. (Running Time: 18000 sec.). (Everything Bks.). (ENG.). 2007. audio compact disk 19.99 (978-1-59859-193-4(2)) Oasis Audio.

Everything Martin Luther King Jr. Book: The Struggle, the Dream, the Legacy. unabr. ed. Jessica McElrath. Narrated by Dwain Contribution by Kyles. (Everything Bks.). (ENG.). 2007. 24.49 (978-1-60814-188-3(8)) Oasis Audio.

Everything Martin Luther King Jr. Book: The Struggle, the Dream, the Legacy. unabr. ed. Jessica McElrath. Narrated by Dwain Contribution by Kyles. Frwd. by Dale P. Andrews. (Running Time: 9 hrs. 0 mins. 0 sec.). (Everything Bks.). (ENG.). 2007. audio compact disk 34.99 (978-1-59859-313-6(7)) Oasis Audio.

Everything Martin Luther King Jr. Book: The Struggle. the Dream. the Legacy. unabr. ed. Jessica McElrath & Dale P. Andrews. Read by Dwain J. Kyles. (YA). 2008. 39.99 (978-1-60514-883-0(0)) Find a World.

Everything Matters! Ron Currie, Jr. Contrib. by Abby Craden et al. (Running Time: 13 hrs.). (ENG.). (gr. 12 up). 2009. audio compact disk 39.95 (978-0-14-314478-6(2), PengAudBks) Penguin Grp USA.

***Everything Matters!** unabr. ed. Ron Currie, Jr. 11 CDs. (Running Time: 13 hrs.). 2009. audio compact disk 80.00 (978-1-4159-6470-5(X), BksonTape) Pub: Random Audio Pubg. Dist(s): Random

***Everything Must Change: Jesus, Global Crises, & a Revolution of Hope.** unabr. ed. Brian McLaren. Narrated by Lloyd James. (ENG.). 2007. 16.98 (978-1-59644-516-1(5), Hovel Audio) christianaud.

Everything Must Change: Jesus, Global Crises, & a Revolution of Hope. unabr. ed. Brian D. McLaren. Read by Lloyd James. (Running Time: 10 hrs. 0 mins. 0 sec.). (ENG.). 2007. audio compact disk 26.98 (978-1-59644-515-4(7), Hovel Audio) christianaud.

***Everything New: Reimagining Heavan & Hell.** unabr. ed. Jeff V. Cook. (ENG.). 2010. 14.99 (978-0-310-32611-3(7)) Zondervan.

Everything on a Waffle. unabr. ed. Polly Horvath. 2 cass. (Running Time: 3 hrs. 15 mins.). (J). (gr. 3-7). 2004. 23.00 (978-0-8072-0715-4(2), Listening Lib) Random Audio Pubg.

Everything on a Waffle. unabr. ed. Polly Horvath. Read by Kathleen McInerney. 3 CDs. (Running Time: 3 hrs. 15 mins.). (Middle Grade Cassette Librariestm Ser.). (J). (gr. 3-7). 2004. audio compact disk 30.00 (978-0-8072-1598-2(8), S YA 363 CD, Listening Lib) Random Audio Pubg.

Everything on a Waffle. unabr. ed. Polly Horvath. Read by Kathleen McInerney. (Running Time: 11700 sec.). (ENG.). (J). (gr. 5-9). 2008. audio compact disk 25.00 (978-0-7393-5965-5(7), Listening Lib) Pub: Random Audio Pubg. Dist(s): Random

Everything Retirement Planning Book. abr. ed. Judith R. Harrington & Stanley Contribution by Steinberg. (Everything Bks.). (ENG.). 2007. 13.99 (978-1-60814-189-0(6)) Oasis Audio.

Everything Retirement Planning Book. abr. ed. Judith R. Harrington & Stanley J. Steinberg. Read by Michael Coon. (Running Time: 18000 sec.). (Everything Bks.). (ENG.). 2007. audio compact disk 19.99 (978-1-59859-194-1(0)) Oasis Audio.

Everything(r) Rock & Blues Guitar Book: From Chords to Scales & Licks to Tricks, All You Need to Play Like the Greats. Marc Schonbrun. 2003. pap. bk. 19.95 (978-1-58062-883-9(4)) Pub: Adams Media. Dist(s): FplusW Media

***Everything She Thought She Wanted.** Elizabeth Buchan. Read by Katherine Kellgren & Ruth Moore. (Playaway Adult Fiction Ser.). (ENG.). 2010. 59.99 (978-1-61637-684-0(8)) Find a World.

***Everything That Rises Must Converge.** unabr. ed. Flannery O'Connor. (Running Time: 9 hrs.). 2010. 29.95 (978-1-4417-5379-3(6)); 59.95 (978-1-4417-5375-5(3)); audio compact disk 29.95 (978-1-4417-5378-6(8)); audio compact disk 90.00 (978-1-4417-5376-2(1)) Blckstn Audio.

Everything That Santa Knows. Contrib. by Johnathan Crumpton & J. Daniel Smith. Prod. by Ed Kee. (ENG.). 2008. audio compact disk 24.99 (978-5-557-38261-8(5), Brentwood-Benson Music) Brentwood Music.

Everything to Gain. unabr. ed. Barbara Taylor Bradford. Read by Kate Reading. 9 cass. (Running Time: 13 hrs. 30 mins.). 1995. 72.00 (978-0-7366-3009-2(0), 3695) Books on Tape.
Mallory Keswick has a dream life: a devoted husband, two beautiful children & a home that's picture perfect. Then disaster strikes. With no choice but to carry on, Mallory begins rebuilding her life. But until she discovers her own strength, she won't find love again.

Everything to Gain. unabr. ed. Barbara Taylor Bradford. Narrated by Barbara Rosenblat. 9 cass. (Running Time: 12 hrs. 45 mins.). 1995. 78.00 (978-0-7887-0197-9(5), 94421E7) Recorded Bks.
The senseless murder of her family sends a young successful woman in a tailspin.

Everything to Know about Nodes. Elizabeth Gauerke. 1 cass. 8.95 (129) Am Fed Astrologers.
An AFA Convention workshop tape.

Everything You Always Wanted to Know about Speakers Bureaus - but Didn't Know to Ask **see How to Be Booked by Speakers Bureaus**

Everything You Always Wanted to Know about the "Miracle Course" unabr. ed. Carol Howe. 4 cass. (Running Time: 6 hrs.). 1995. 31.95 Set. (978-1-889642-16-1(9)) C Howe.
Provides clear direction for moving from theory & intellectual understanding to the experience of a happier, more peaceful life. Includes: An "eye-opening" presentation of the way we create our experience & how to change it. A detailed explanation of how our choices for guilt & fear produce our every problem & how to choose again for a happy life. The meaning of miracles & how we invite them into our lives.

Everything You Ever Wanted to Know about Divorce: Matthew 19:8. Ed Young. (J). 1982. 4.95 (978-0-7417-1224-0(5), 224) Win Walk.

Everything You Need to Know about Nursing Fundamentals: Administration of Meds. Patricia Hoefler. 1993. (978-1-56533-159-4(1)) MEDS Pubng.

Everything You Need to Know about Nursing Fundamentals: Bedmaking, Body Mechanics, Body Positions & Transfer Activities. Patricia Hoefler. 1993. (978-1-56533-155-6(9)) MEDS Pubng.

Everything You Need to Know about Nursing Fundamentals: Care of the Skin, Mouth, Hair, Nails & Bathing. Patricia Hoefler. 1993. (978-1-56533-156-3(7)) MEDS Pubng.

Everything You Need to Know about Nursing Fundamentals: Infection Control. Patricia Hoefler. 1993. (978-1-56533-158-7(3)) MEDS Pubng.

Everything You Need to Know about Nursing Fundamentals: Vital Signs. Patricia Hoefler. 1993. (978-1-56533-157-0(5)) MEDS Pubng.

Everything You Need to Know about the Nclex-pn: Cardiovascular/Respiratory Disorders. Patricia Hoefler. 1988. (978-1-56533-101-3(X)) MEDS Pubng.

Everything You Need to Know about the Nclex-pn: Complications of Obstetrics. Patricia Hoefler. 1988. (978-1-56533-110-5(9)) MEDS Pubng.

Everything You Need to Know about the Nclex-pn: Endocrine & Renal Disorders. Patricia Hoefler. 1991. (978-1-56533-133-4(8)) MEDS Pubng.

Everything You Need to Know about the Nclex-pn: Growth & Development. Patricia Hoefler. 1988. (978-1-56533-106-8(0)) MEDS Pubng.

Everything You Need to Know about the Nclex-pn: Math & Calculations. Patricia Hoefler. 1989. (978-1-56533-107-5(9)) MEDS Pubng.

Everything You Need to Know about the Nclex-pn: Musculoskeletal Disorders. Patricia Hoefler. 1988. (978-1-56533-102-0(8)) MEDS Pubng.

Everything You Need to Know about the Nclex-pn: Normal Pregnancy. Patricia Hoefler. 1988. (978-1-56533-111-2(7)) MEDS Pubng.

Everything You Need to Know about the Nclex-pn: Pharmacology. Patricia Hoefler. 1988. (978-1-56533-104-4(4)) MEDS Pubng.

Everything You Need to Know about the Nclex-pn: Psychiatric Nursing. Patricia Hoefler. 1988. (978-1-56533-112-9(5)) MEDS Pubng.

Everything You Need to Know about the Nclex-pn: Psycho-Social Component. Patricia Hoefler. 1988. (978-1-56533-113-6(3)) MEDS Pubng.

Everything You Need to Know about the Nclex-pn: The Aging Client. Patricia Hoefler. 1991. (978-1-56533-114-3(1)) MEDS Pubng.

Everything You Need to Know about the Nclex-pn Pt. 1: Pediatrics. Patricia Hoefler. 1988. (978-1-56533-108-2(7)) MEDS Pubng.

Everything You Need to Know about the Nclex-pn Pt. 1: Pediatrics, Pt. 2. Patricia Hoefler. 1988. (978-1-56533-109-9(5)) MEDS Pubng.

Everything You Need to Know about the Nclex-pn Vol. 2: Neurological Disorders. Patricia Hoefler. 1988. (978-1-56533-064-1(1)); (978-1-56533-065-8(X)) MEDS Pubng.

Everything You Need to Know about the Nclex-pn Vol. 2: Neurological Disorders. Patricia Hoefler. 1988. (978-1-56533-105-1(2)) MEDS Pubng.

Everything You Need to Know about the NCLEX-PNpn: Test-Taking Strategies for NCLEX-PN. Patricia Hoefler. 1988. audio compact disk (978-1-56533-115-0(X)) MEDS Pubng.

Everything You Need to Know about the Nclex-rn: Blood Disorders. Patricia Hoefler. 1988. (978-1-56533-061-0(7)) MEDS Pubng.

Everything You Need to Know about the Nclex-rn: Cardiovascular Disorders. Patricia Hoefler. 1988. (978-1-56533-056-6(0)) MEDS Pubng.

Everything You Need to Know about the Nclex-rn: Communicable Diseases. Patricia Hoefler. 2002. (978-1-56533-095-5(1)) MEDS Pubng.

Everything You Need to Know about the Nclex-rn: Emergencies. Patricia Hoefler. 1989. (978-1-56533-077-1(3)) MEDS Pubng.

Everything You Need to Know about the Nclex-rn: Endocrine Disorders. Patricia Hoefler. 1988. (978-1-56533-058-0(7)) MEDS Pubng.

Everything You Need to Know about the Nclex-rn: GI, Hepatic & Pancreatic. Patricia Hoefler. 1989. (978-1-56533-060-3(9)) MEDS Pubng.

Everything You Need to Know about the Nclex-rn: GI, Hepatic & Pancreatic, Pt. 1. Patricia Hoefler. 1988. (978-1-56533-103-7(6)) MEDS Pubng.

Everything You Need to Know about the Nclex-rn: How to Study. Patricia Hoefler. 1991. (978-1-56533-052-8(8)) MEDS Pubng.

Everything You Need to Know about the Nclex-rn: Math & Calculations. Patricia Hoefler. 1992. (978-1-56533-074-0(9)) MEDS Pubng.

Everything You Need to Know about the Nclex-rn: Musculoskeletal Disorders. Patricia Hoefler. 1988. (978-1-56533-062-7(5)) MEDS Pubng.

Everything You Need to Know about the Nclex-rn: Normal Pregnancy. Patricia Hoefler. 1988. (978-1-56533-071-9(4)) MEDS Pubng.

Everything You Need to Know about the Nclex-rn: Nutrition. Patricia Hoefler. 1991. (978-1-56533-055-9(2)) MEDS Pubng.

Everything You Need to Know about the Nclex-rn: Pediatric Bacterial Diseases. Patricia Hoefler. 1988. (978-1-56533-076-4(5)) MEDS Pubng.

Everything You Need to Know about the Nclex-rn: Pediatric Chronic Illness. Patricia Hoefler. 1998. (978-1-56533-078-8(1)) MEDS Pubng.

Everything You Need to Know about the Nclex-rn: Pediatric Viral Diseases. Patricia Hoefler. 1988. (978-1-56533-079-5(X)) MEDS Pubng.

Everything You Need to Know about the Nclex-rn: Pharmacology. Patricia Hoefler. 1988. (978-1-56533-075-7(7)) MEDS Pubng.

Everything You Need to Know about the Nclex-rn: Postoperative Positioning. Patricia Hoefler. 1991. (978-1-56533-053-5(6)) MEDS Pubng.

Everything You Need to Know about the Nclex-rn: Psycho-Social Component. Patricia Hoefler. 1987. (978-1-56533-066-5(8)) MEDS Pubng.

Everything You Need to Know about the Nclex-rn: Questions & Answers. Patricia Hoefler. 1991. (978-1-56533-067-2(6)) MEDS Pubng.

Everything You Need to Know about the Nclex-rn: Renal Disorders. Patricia Hoefler. 1988. (978-1-56533-063-4(3)) MEDS Pubng.

Everything You Need to Know about the Nclex-rn: Respiartory Disorders. Patricia Hoefler. 1988. (978-1-56533-059-7(5)) MEDS Pubng.

Everything You Need to Know about the Nclex-rn: The Aging Client. Patricia Hoefler. 1991. (978-1-56533-094-8(3)) MEDS Pubng.

Everything You Need to Know about the Nclex-rn: The Newborn. Patricia Hoefler. 1993. (978-1-56533-072-6(2)) MEDS Pubng.

Everything You Need to Know about the Nclex-rn Pt. 2: Nursing Management. Patricia Hoefler. 2002. (978-1-56533-096-2(X)); (978-1-56533-097-9(8)) MEDS Pubng.

Everything You Need to Know about the Nclex-rn Pt. 3: Nursing Mangement. Patricia Hoefler. 2002. (978-1-56533-098-6(6)) MEDS Pubng.

Everything You Need to Know about the Nclex-rn Vol. 2: Complications of Pregnancy. Patricia Hoefler. 1988. (978-1-56533-070-2(6)) MEDS Pubng.

Everything You Need to Know about the Nclex-rn Vol. 2: Complications of Pregnancy. Patricia Hoefler. 1993. (978-1-56533-073-3(0)) MEDS Pubng.

Everything You Need to Know about the Nclex-rn Vol. 2: Psychiatric Disorders. Patricia Hoefler. 1988. (978-1-56533-068-9(4)); (978-1-56533-069-6(2)) MEDS Pubng.

***Everything you need to know about the World.** Simon Eliot. Read by Stig Wemyss. (Running Time: 2 hrs. 35 mins.). (J). 2009. 34.99 (978-1-74214-373-6(3), 9781742143736) Pub: Bolinda Pubng AUS. Dist(s): Bolinda Pub Inc

Everything You Need to Know about the World. unabr. ed. Simon Eliot. Read by Stig Wemyss. (Running Time: 9300 sec.). (J). (gr. 3-7). 2007. audio compact disk 54.95 (978-1-74093-981-2(6), 9781740939812) Pub: Bolinda Pubng AUS. Dist(s): Bolinda Pub Inc

Everything You Need to Know about Writing Better Test Questions Using the Nursing Process: Part 1. Patricia Hoefler. 1989. (978-1-56533-084-9(6)) MEDS Pubng.

Everything You Need to Know about Writing Better Test Questions Using the Nursing Process: Part 2. Patricia Hoefler. 1989. (978-1-56533-085-6(4)) MEDS Pubng.

Everything You Need to Know about Writing Better Test Questions Using the Nursing Process: Part 3. Patricia Hoefler. 1989. (978-1-56533-086-3(2)) MEDS Pubng.

Everything You Need to Know to Become a Best-Selling Author. Compiled by Scott Jeffrey. 2005. audio compact disk 150.00 (978-0-9776246-8-3(4)) Lightning Crown Pub.

Everything You Pretend to Know & Are Afraid Someone Will Ask. abr. ed. Lynette Padwa. Read by Cynthia Lauren Tewes. (Running Time: 10800 sec.). 2008. audio compact disk 23.95 (978-1-59316-125-5(5)) Listen & Live.

Everything You Should Know about Publishing, Publicity, Promotion & Building a Platform: A Step-by-Step Guide for Authors. Interview. Arielle Ford. 5 CDs. (Running Time: 3 hrs. 33 mins.). 2005. ring bd. 497.00 (978-0-9768204-0-6(4), EYSK-KICKSTART) KickStart.

Everything You Should Know about the Nclex-rn: Pediatric Surgical Conditions. Patricia Hoefler. 1988. (978-1-56533-081-8(1)) MEDS Pubng.

Everything You Wanted to Know about Credit but Were Too Ashamed to Ask: Live Interactive Consumer Credit Instructional Seminar. Renee Crenshaw & Anthony Miles. Executive Producer Anthony Miles. 2006. audio compact disk 9.95 (978-0-9747086-2-1(3)) Pub: Rising Star Found. Dist(s): AtlasBooks

Everything You Wanted to Know about Developing Your Life's Purpose. Speeches. Renee Crenshaw & Anthony Miles. 1. (Running Time: 2hrs). 2004. audio compact disk 9.95 (978-0-9747086-0-7(7)) Rising Star Found.

Everything You've Ever Wanted to Know about Heaven: Luke 23:43. Ed Young. 1999. 4.95 (978-0-7417-2207-2(0), 1207) Win Walk.

Everything's Eventual. Stephen King. 10 cass. (Running Time: 11 hrs. 45 mins.). 93.00 (978-1-4025-2213-0(4)); 64.00 (978-1-4025-2244-4(4)) Recorded Bks.

Everything's Eventual. unabr. ed. Stephen King. Read by Justin Long et al. 6 CDs. (Running Time: 73 hrs. 0 mins. 0 sec.). (ENG.). 2002. audio compact disk 39.95 (978-0-7435-2589-3(2), Audioworks) Pub: S&S Audio. Dist(s): S and S Inc

Everything's Eventual. unabr. ed. Stephen King. 2006. 23.95 (978-0-7435-6332-1(8), Audioworks) Pub: S&S Audio. Dist(s): S and S Inc

Everything's Eventual Pt. 2: 14 Dark Tales. unabr. ed. Stephen King. 2002. 34.95 (RG062) Recorded Bks.

Everything's Growing. Niki Davies. 1 cass. (Running Time: 90 mins.). 2000. bk. 17.95 (978-1-85909-607-9(7), Warner Bro) Alfred Pub.

Everything's Negotiable. Herb Cohen. 1 cass. 1986. 8.95 (978-0-88684-086-0(4)) Listen USA.
Shows how & why everything is negotiable.

Everything's Negotiable. unabr. ed. L. Wayne Gertmanian. Read by L. Wayne Gertmanian. 6 cass. (Running Time: 6 hrs.). 2000. (978-1-931187-16-9(9), NEG) Word Success.

***Everywhere That Mary Went.** abr. ed. Lisa Scottoline. Read by Kate Burton. (ENG.). 2004. (978-0-06-078639-7(6), Harper Audio) HarperCollins Pubs.

Everywhere That Mary Went. abr. ed. Lisa Scottoline. Read by Kate Burton. 2004. audio compact disk 14.95 (978-0-06-072637-9(7)) HarperCollins Pubs.

***Everywhere That Mary Went.** abr. ed. Lisa Scottoline. Read by Kate Burton. (ENG.). 2004. (978-0-06-081807-4(7), Harper Audio); (978-0-06-081808-1(5), Harper Audio) HarperCollins Pubs.

Everywoman's Celebration of Life. Diane Y. Chapman. Read by Diane Y. Chapman. 1 cass. (Running Time: 50 min.). 1996. 10.95 (978-0-9653239-0-1(0)) Pub: Wrds to Yr Adv. Dist(s): Penton Overseas
Self-help, inspirational tape with meditations, life experiences & prayer to help women see their lives in a positive way!.

Eve's Daughter. Michael Taylor. Read by Julia Sands. 11 cass. (Running Time: 14 hrs. 35 min.). (Storysound Ser.). (J). 2001. 89.95 (978-1-85903-450-7(0)) Pub: Mgna Lrg Print GBR. Dist(s): Ulverscroft US

Eve's Ransom. George R. Gissing. Read by Anais 9000. 1 CD. (Running Time: 5.8 hours). 2006. 16.95 (978-1-60112-002-1(8)) Babblebooks.

Eve's Ransom. George R. Gissing. Read by Jill Masters. 6 cass. (Running Time: 9 hrs.). 1989. 29.00 incl. album. (C-96) Jimcin Record.
Victorian love triangle.

Evidence. Instructed by Steven Goode. 5 cass. (Running Time: 7 hrs. 50 min.). (Outstanding Professors Ser.). 1995. 49.95 Set. (978-0-940366-62-6(2)) Sum & Substance.
Lecture given by a prominent American law school professor.

Evidence. Perf. by Cody Moffett. 1 cass., 1 CD. 7.98 (TA 33343); audio compact disk 12.78 CD Jewel box. (TA 83343) NewSound.

Evidence. Charles R. Nesson. (Running Time: 6 hrs.). 125.00 incl. 1 Colorado ethics credit & bk. (7306) Natl Prac Inst.
A well known & much liked Harvard Law School scholar & public television moderator offers this update on the law of evidence. He provides background for the less experienced trial lawyer & the new challenges for the veteran litigator.

Evidence. abr. ed. Jonathan Kellerman. Read by John Rubinstein. (Alex Delaware Ser.: No. 25). (ENG.). 2009. audio compact disk 32.00 (978-0-7393-6897-8(4), Random AudioBks) Pub: Random Audio Pubg. Dist(s): Random

Evidence. unabr. ed. Jonathan Kellerman. Read by John Rubinstein. (Alex Delaware Ser.: No. 25). (ENG.). 2009. audio compact disk 45.00 (978-0-7393-6899-2(0), Random AudioBks) Pub: Random Audio Pubg. Dist(s): Random

Evidence. 4th rev. ed. Steven J. Goode. (Running Time: 31680 sec.). (Sum & Substance Ser.). 2007. 74.00 (978-0-314-18953-0(X), West Lglwrks) West.

Evidence - A Comprehensive Survey. 1990. 45.00 (AC-557) PA Bar Inst.

Evidence Against Her: A Novel. unabr. ed. Robb Forman Dew. Read by Kate Fleming. 8 vols. (Running Time: 12 hrs.). 2001. bk. 69.95 (978-0-7927-2535-0(2), CSL 424, Chivers Sound Lib) AudioGO.

Evidence for the Trial Lawyer. Faust Rossi. 1994. bk. 135.00 (978-1-55917-171-7(5)) Natl Prac Inst.

Evidence for Trial Lawyers. Read by Irving Younger. 125.00 incl. study guide. (NO. 320) Natl Prac Inst.
Learn how to respond instantly in the hectic circumstances of the courtroom.

Evidence for Trial Lawyers. Irving Younger. 1982. 125.00 (978-1-55917-165-6(0)) Natl Prac Inst.

Evidence in State & Federal Courts. (Running Time: 5 hrs.). 1993. 92.00 Incl. 310p. coursebk. (29348) NYS Bar.
Concentrates on explaining what is admissible evidence at trial & how to introduce it. Practical, specific examples are considered & effective courtroom skills are highlighted.

Evidence Law: Artistry & Advocacy in the Courtroom. unabr. ed. Thomas A. Mauet. Read by Thomas A. Mauet. 6 cass. (Running Time: 6 hrs.). pap. bk. 165.00 Set. PEG MN.
Examines evidence from the judges point of view.

Evidence Not Seen: A Woman's Miraculous Faith in the Jungles of World War II. unabr. ed. Darlene Deibler Rose. (Running Time: 8 hrs. NaN mins.). 2009. 29.95 (978-1-4332-4949-5(9)); audio compact disk 54.95 (978-1-4332-4946-4(4)); audio compact disk 70.00 (978-1-4332-4947-1(2)) Blckstn Audio.

***Evidence of Mercy.** Terri Blackstock. (Running Time: 10 hrs. 0 mins. 0 sec.). (Sun Coast Chronicles Ser.). (ENG.). 2008. 14.99 (978-0-310-30529-3(2)) Zondervan.

Evidence of Saving Grace. Dan Comer. 1 cass. 3.00 (29) Evang Outreach.

Evidence to Destroy. unabr. ed. Margaret Yorke. Read by Carolanne Lynn. 4 cass. (Running Time: 6 hrs.). 2001. 44.95 (978-0-7531-0922-9(0), 000814) Pub: ISIS Audio GBR. Dist(s): Ulverscroft US

Evidence, 1988. Charles R. Nesson. 1988. 135.00 (978-1-55917-162-5(6)) Natl Prac Inst.

Evidence, 2d (Law School Legends Audio Series) 2nd rev. ed. Faust F. Rossi. 2002. 45.95 (978-0-15-901013-6(6)) West.

Evidence, 2005 ed. (Law School Legends Audio Series) Faust F. Rossi. (Law School Legends Audio Ser.). 2005. 58.00 (978-0-314-16094-2(9), gilbert); 57.95 (978-0-314-16093-5(0), gilbert) West.

Evidences & Witnesses of the Book of Mormon. 2 cass. 2004. 14.95 (978-1-59156-331-0(3)); audio compact disk 14.95 (978-1-59156-332-7(1)) Covenant Comms.

Evidentiary Privileges. Thomas B. Rutter. 1 cass. (Running Time: 1 hr.). 1983. 20.00 PA Bar Inst.

Evil Acts. unabr. ed. Lesley Grant-Adamson. Read by Jilly Bond. 6 cass. (Running Time: 7 hrs. 15 min.). (Isis Ser.). (J). 1997. 54.95 (978-0-7531-0064-6(9), 960901) Pub: ISIS Lrg Prnt GBR. Dist(s): Ulverscroft US
Grace discovers she has been tricked into buying the home of a serial killer. Her obsession with the previous occupant, leads to delusion. Convinced of the murderer's continuing presence & his efforts to destroy her, she unwittingly teeters towards mental breakdown.

***Evil & the Justice of God.** unabr. ed. N. T. Wright. Narrated by Simon Vance. (ENG.). 2007. 14.98 (978-1-59644-471-3(1), Hovel Audio) christianaud.

Evil & the Justice of God. unabr. ed. N. T. Wright. Read by Simon Vance. (Running Time: 4 hrs. 30 mins. 0 sec.). (ENG.). 2007. audio compact disk 23.98 (978-1-59644-470-6(3)) christianaud.

Evil at Heart. unabr. ed. Chelsea Cain. Read by Carolyn McCormick. (Running Time: 9 hrs. 0 mins. 0 sec.). No. 3. (ENG.). 2009. audio compact disk 39.99 (978-1-4272-0782-1(8)) Pub: Macmill Audio. Dist(s): Macmillan

Evil Elves. Bruce Coville. 1 cassette. (Running Time: 1 hour). (Moongobble & Me Ser.: Bk. 2). (J). 2004. 9.50 (978-1-932076-85-1(9)) Full Cast Audio.
Unabridged, multi-voiced recording. Read by Ryan Sparkes and the Full Cast Family. Moongobble and Edward are off on another Mighty Task, even more dangerous than the first.Urk the toad, Fireball the dragon, and the Rusty Knight are coming along too, of course.This time their adventures will lead them right into the fearsome Forest of Night. They're expecting danger. They're expecting adventure. What they aren't expecting is a discovery that will change Edward's life forever! Filled with laughs and suspense, enhanced by original music, and spiced with Bruce Coville's unique blend of heart and humor, this enchanting production is sure to bring the entire family under its spell. Pop it in and let the magic begin!.

Evil Elves. Bruce Coville. 1 cass. (Running Time: 1 hr). (Moongobble & Me Ser.: Bk. 3). (J). 2005. 9.50 (978-1-932076-88-2(3)) Full Cast Audio.

Evil, Exploration Of. unabr. ed. John Simon. 1 cass. (Running Time: 59 min.). Incl. Changeling. 1970. (23094); Doctor Faustus. 1970. (23094); King Lear. 1970. (23094); 1970. 12.95 (23094) J Norton Pubs.
Discussion of these classic landmarks in English drama, marking the attempt to "come to terms" with evil, the substance of tragedy.

***Evil Eye.** unabr. ed. Jason Goodwin. (Running Time: 11 hrs. 0 mins.). (Yashim the Eunuch Ser.). 2010. 34.99 (978-1-4001-9590-9(X)); 17.99 (978-1-4001-8590-0(4)) Tantor Media.

***Evil Eye.** unabr. ed. Jason Goodwin. (Running Time: 11 hrs. 0 mins. 0 sec.). (Yashim the Eunuch Ser.). (ENG.). 2011. 24.99 (978-1-4001-6590-2(3)); audio compact disk 34.99 (978-1-4001-1590-7(6)); audio compact disk 69.99 (978-1-4001-4590-4(2)) Pub: Tantor Media. Dist(s): IngramPubServ

Evil Forces at the End Time. Derek Prince. 1 cass. (I-7006) Derek Prince.

Evil Genius. Wilkie Collins. Read by John Bolen. (Running Time: 11 hrs. 15 mins.). 2001. 29.95 (978-1-60083-589-6(9), Audiofy Corp) Iofy Corp.

Evil Genius. Wilkie Collins. Read by John Bolen. (ENG.). 2005. audio compact disk 96.00 (978-1-4001-3017-7(4)) Pub: Tantor Media. Dist(s): IngramPubServ

Evil Genius. unabr. ed. Wilkie Collins. Narrated by John Bolen. 1 CD (MP3). (Running Time: 11 hrs. 14 mins.). (ENG.). 2001. audio compact disk 23.00 (978-1-4001-5017-5(5)) Pub: Tantor Media. Dist(s): IngramPubServ

Evil Genius. unabr. ed. Wilkie Collins. Narrated by John Bolen. 10 CDs. (Running Time: 11 hrs. 14 mins.). (ENG.). 2001. audio compact disk 48.00 (978-1-4001-0017-0(8)) Pub: Tantor Media. Dist(s): IngramPubServ

Evil Genius. unabr. ed. Wilkie Collins. Narrated by John Bolen. (Running Time: 11 hrs. 0 mins. 0 sec.). (ENG.). 2009. audio compact disk 22.99 (978-1-4001-6085-3(5)); audio compact disk 32.99 (978-1-4001-1085-8(8)); audio compact disk 65.99 (978-1-4001-4085-5(4)) Pub: Tantor Media. Dist(s): IngramPubServ

Evil Genius. unabr. ed. Catherine Jinks. Read by Justine Eyre. 13 CDs. (Running Time: 16 hrs. 41mins). (YA). (gr. 7-10). 2007. audio compact disk 85.00 (978-0-7393-5082-9(X)) Pub: Random Audio Pubg. Dist(s): Random

Evil Inc. unabr. ed. Glenn Kaplan. Read by Glenn Kaplan. (Running Time: 39600 sec.). 2007. 29.95 (978-1-4332-0317-6(0)); 72.95 (978-1-4332-0315-2(4)); audio compact disk 29.95 (978-1-4332-0318-3(9)); audio compact disk 90.00 (978-1-4332-0316-9(2)); audio compact disk 29.95 (978-1-4332-0319-0(7)) Blckstn Audio.

Evil Intent. unabr. ed. Kate Charles. Read by Annie Aldington. 9 cass. (Running Time: 12 hrs.). (Story Sound Ser.). (J). 2005. 76.95 (978-1-85903-869-7(7)) Pub: Mgna Lrg Print GBR. Dist(s): Ulverscroft US

Evil Intent. unabr. ed. Kate Charles & Annif Aldington. Read by Annif Aldington. 10 CDs. (Running Time: 12 hrs.). (Story Sound CD Ser.). (J).

2005. audio compact disk 89.95 (978-1-85903-910-6(3)) Pub: Mgna Lrg Print GBR. Dist(s): Ulverscroft US

Evil of Procrastination. Swami Jyotirmayananda. Read by Swami Jyotirmayananda. 1 cass. (Running Time: 60 min.). 12.99 (732) Yoga Res Foun.

Evil of Self-Sacrifice. unabr. ed. Nathaniel Branden. 1 cass. (Running Time: 1 hr. 17 min.). (Basic Principles of Objectivism Ser.). 12.95 (572) J Norton Pubs.

The ethics of altruism; altruism as anti-man & anti-life.

Evil Star. unabr. ed. Anthony Horowitz. Read by Simon Prebble. 8 CDs. (Running Time: 9 hrs.). (Power of Five Ser.: Bk. 2). (YA). (gr. 5-9). 2006. audio compact disk 84.74 (978-1-4281-1028-1(3), C3837); 59.75 (978-1-4281-1023-6(2), 98470) Recorded Bks.

When Matt closed Raven's Gate, an ancient portal to the world of evil, he thought the trouble was over. But sinister forces are still hot on Matt's trail and will stop at nothing to destroy him. Somehow five children from across the globe must join forces, as the threat of the Old Ones still looms near. Now Matt and the second of the five, Pedro - who speaks no English - must find the second gate in the lost city of the Incas before the evil star rises.

Evil under the Sun. unabr. ed. Agatha Christie. Read by David Suchet. 6 CDs. (Running Time: 6 hrs. 30 min.). (Hercule Poirot Mystery Ser.). 2002. audio compact disk 39.95 (978-1-57270-248-6(6), Audio Editions) Pub: Audio Partners. Dist(s): PerseuPGW

The body of a beautiful and flirtatious actress is found strangled to death. Everybody is a suspect as voodoo practices, drug-smuggling, and religious mania are noted as part of the relevant evidence. Poirot unravels the crime with all the genius that his reputation has led us to expect. Agatha Christie never wrote a more cleverly woven story than this grim, yet delicious revelation of evil under the sun.

Evil under the Sun. unabr. ed. Agatha Christie. Read by David Suchet. 5 cass. (Running Time: 7 hrs. 30 min.). 2002. 27.95 (978-1-57270-247-9(8), Audio Editions) Pub: Audio Partners. Dist(s): PerseuPGW

Evil under the Sun. unabr. ed. Agatha Christie. Narrated by David Suchet. (Running Time: 23220 sec.). (Hercule Poirot Mystery Ser.). (ENG.). 2005. audio compact disk 29.95 (978-1-57270-477-0(2)) Pub: AudioGO. Dist(s): Perseus Dist

At Devon's Jolly Roger resort, Arlena Stuart Marshall openly cavorts with Patrick Redfern while her husband and Patrick's wife helplessly watch. Later Arlena's lifeless body is found in the sand at a nearby cove. The evidence seems to point to Arlena's husband as the murderer, but Hercule Poirot, who just happens to be on holiday at the tony hotel, doesn't settle for such an easy answer. Everyone is a suspect, and the evidence includes voodoo practices, drug-smuggling, religious mania, bank withdrawals, mysterious love letters, and two murders from the past.

Evil under the Sun. unabr. ed. Agatha Christie. 2 vols. (Running Time: 3 hrs.). Dramatization. 2003. audio compact disk 29.95 (978-0-563-49680-9(0), BBCD 030) BBC Worldwide.

An exclusive hotel on a tiny, picturesque island seems to be the ideal retreat from the stresses of criminal detection for Hercule Poirot. But with the appearance of the beautiful Arlena Stuart, the quiet and peaceful atmosphere becomes charged with an indefinable erotic tension. And when she is found viciously strangled in a secluded cove. there are few, especially among the women, who seem to feel either surprise or regret.

Evil Ways. Ed. by Aaron Stang. Arranged by Rob Goldsmith. (Warner Bros. Publications 21st Century Guitar Ensemble Ser.). (ENG.). 2002. audio compact disk 19.95 (978-0-7579-0046-4(1), Warner Bro) Alfred Pub.

Evils of the New Age Movement. Mother Angelica & Father Michael. 1 cass. (Running Time: 60 min.). (Mother Angelica Live Ser.). 1988. 10.00 (978-1-55794-107-7(6), T58) Eternal Wrd TV.

Criticizes the New Age Movement & offers insights into the signs that are appearing in modern times.

Evita: The Real Life of Eva Peron. collector's ed. N. Fraser & M. Navarro. Read by Kathleen O'Malley. 7 cass. (Running Time: 10 hrs. 30 mins.). 1997. 56.00 (978-0-7366-3838-8(5), 4558) Books on Tape.

Looks beyond the myth of Eva Peron & into the less attractive facts of her life.

Evolution: The Remarkable History of a Scientific Theory. Edward J. Larson. Narrated by John McDonough. 6 cds. (Running Time: 6.25 hrs.). 2005. audio compact disk 69.75 (978-1-4025-9651-3(0)) Recorded Bks.

Evolution & Christian Faith. Joan Roughgarden. 2007. audio compact disk 15.95 (978-1-59726-158-6(0)) Pub: Island Pr. Dist(s): Chicago Distribution Ctr

Evolution & Extinction: Essays. unabr. ed. Stephen Jay Gould. Read by Jeff Riggenbach. 2 cass. (Running Time: 3 hrs.). 1998. 17.95 (978-1-879557-48-2(7)) Pub: Audio Scholar. Dist(s): Penton Overseas

Essays on evolution & extinction, impact theory, punctuated equilibrium & natural selection by today's most popular writer of science.

Evolution & the Future of Humanity: Homo sapiens' galactic Future. George F. Hart. (ENG., 2008. audio compact disk 10.00 (978-0-9818642-0-4(1)) Science Pubs Co.

Evolution & the Origin of Life. unabr. ed. J. Marvin Weller. 1 cass. (Running Time: 22 min.). 12.95 (33003) J Norton Pubs.

The development of evolutionary thought is traced & life is explained as having originated on earth more than three billion years ago as the result of a long process of chemical evolution.

Evolution, Me & Other Freaks of Nature. unabr. ed. Robin Brande. Read by Kaili Vernoff. 5 CDs. (Running Time: 6 hrs. 25 mins.). (YA). (gr. 7 up). 2007. audio compact disk 45.00 (978-0-7393-5134-5(6), Listening Lib) Pub: Random Audio Pubg. Dist(s): Random

Evolution of a Cat Named Monkey Face. unabr. ed. Chief Little Summer & Warm Night Rain. 1 CD. (J). (gr. k-4). 1999. audio compact disk 11.95 CD. (978-1-880440-18-6(0)) Piqua Pr.

Stray cat befriended by a little girl who tames him.

Evolution of a Graphic Concept: The Stonecutter. 2004. 8.95 (978-1-56008-892-9(3)); cass. & flmstrp 30.00 (978-1-56008-665-9(3)) Weston Woods.

Evolution of a Graphic Concept: the Stonecutter; Stonecutter. 2004. cass. & flmstrp 30.00 (978-1-56008-807-3(9)) Weston Woods.

***Evolution of Bruno Littlemore.** unabr. ed. Benjamin Hale. Read by Robert Petkoff. (Running Time: 20 hrs.). (ENG.). 2011. 29.98 (978-1-60788-689-1(8)) Pub: Hachet Audio. Dist(s): HachBkGrp

Evolution of Calpurnia Tate. unabr. ed. Jacqueline Kelly. Read by Natalie Ross. 1 MP3-CD. (Running Time: 9 hrs.). 2009. 24.99 (978-1-4418-0244-6(4), 9781441802446, Brilliance MP3); 39.97 (978-1-4418-0245-3(2), 9781441802453, Brlnc Audio MP3 Lib); 24.99 (978-1-4418-0246-0(0), 9781441802460, BAD); 39.97 (978-1-4418-0247-7(9), 9781441802477, BADLE) Brilliance Audio.

Evolution of Calpurnia Tate. unabr. ed. Jacqueline Kelly. Read by Natalie Ross. 8 CDs. (Running Time: 9 hrs.). (gr. 4-7). 2009. audio compact disk 24.99 (978-1-4418-0242-2(8), 9781441802422, Bril Audio CD Unabri) Brilliance Audio.

Evolution of Calpurnia Tate. unabr. ed. Jacqueline Kelly. Read by Natalie Ross. 8 CDs. (Running Time: 9 hrs.). (YA). (gr. 5-8). 2009. audio compact disk 54.97 (978-1-4418-0243-9(6), 9781441802439, BriAudCD Unabrid) Brilliance Audio.

Evolution of Customer Service: Beyond Customer Service to Customer Satisfaction. Janet S. Rush. Read by Janet S. Rush. 6 cass. 1991. 59.95 set. (978-1-56207-218-6(8)) Zig Ziglar Corp.

Janet will expose you to hundreds of both ancient & modern customer relations tools. These tapes are fast-paced & guaranteed to equip you with skills you can start using immediately.

Evolution of God. unabr. ed. Robert Wright. Narrated by Arthur Morey. 2 MP3-CDs. (Running Time: 19 hrs. 0 mins. 0 sec.). (ENG.). 2009. 34.99 (978-1-4001-6281-9(5)); audio compact disk 49.99 (978-1-4001-1281-4(8)); audio compact disk 99.99 (978-1-4001-4281-1(4)) Pub: Tantor Media. Dist(s): IngramPubServ

Evolution of Health Services Research: Personal Reflections on Applied Social Science. Odin W. Anderson. Frwd. by James R. Greenley. (Jossey-Bass Health Ser.). 1991. bk. 47.00 (978-1-55542-340-7(X), Jossey-Bass) Wiley US.

Evolution of Human Culture. unabr. ed. William I. Thompson. 1 cass. (Running Time: 1 hr. 24 min.). 1998. 11.00 (12401) Big Sur Tapes.

A fascinating talk about cultural evolution as an archetypal process in which three critical transformations - hominization, agriculture, & writing - have been initiated by the feminine.

***Evolution of Jazz Drumming.** Danny Gottlieb. (ENG.). 2011. pap. bk. 29.99 (978-1-61774-273-6(2), 1617742732) Pub: Hudson Music. Dist(s): H Leonard

Evolution of Mind: Program from the Award Winning Public Radio Series. Hosted by Fred Goodwin. Comment by John Hockenberry. Contrib. by Randolph Nesse et al. 1 cass. (Running Time: 1 hr.). (Infinite Mind Ser.). 1998. audio compact disk 21.95 (978-1-888064-48-3(X), LCM 7) Lichtenstein Creat.

Just what is "the mind," & how did it come to be the complex system that it is today? Dr. Pinker, author of "How the Mind Works," & Dr. Nesse, an evolutionary psychiatrist. Also inhuman conditions in psychiatric facilities around the world.

Evolution of Poi Aloha Shirt. 2000. audio compact disk 18.99 (978-0-89610-945-2(3)) Island Heritage.

Evolution of Poi G/C Cd. 2002. audio compact disk 21.00 (978-0-89610-683-3(7)) Island Heritage.

Evolution of Political Knowledge: Theory & Inquiry in American Politics, Vol. 1 & 2. Edward D. Mansfield & Richard Sisson. 2003. audio compact disk 19.95 (978-0-8142-9025-5(6)) Ohio St U Pr.

***Evolution of Self: As applied to CG Jung & Teilhard de Chardin.** Ira Progoff. 2010. audio compact disk 15.00 (978-1-935859-11-6(0)) Dialogue Assoc.

Evolution of the Soul. June Singer. Read by June Singer. 1 cass. (Running Time: 90 min.). 1993. 10.95 (978-0-7822-0425-4(2), 508) C G Jung IL.

The unknown writers of the Gnostic book, The Exegesis of the Soul, might well have titled it "The Evolution of the Soul." They wrote of the feminine soul that incorporated all the charms, beauty, & grace of the Hellenic lady, as well as the dark, shaming aspect of the sinful woman of Judaic lore. Jungian analyst June Singer, author of The Gnostic Book of Hours, explores this tale of violation & redemption.

Evolution Reprints. Ed. by Marco A. V. Bitetto. 1 cass. 2000. (978-1-58578-047-1(2)) Inst of Cybernetics.

Evolution, Secularism & the Attack on the Church. Perf. by John Vennari. 1 cass. (Running Time: 90 mins.). 7.00 (20198) Cath Treas.

Not only demonstrates the falsehood of evolution, but shows that communism, Modernism, Secularism Humanism, the New Age Movement & even the United Nations are all based on the theory of evolution. Also shows how modern Churchmen have compromised with this false theory rather than oppose it.

Evolution to Spiritual Being. Swami Amar Jyoti. 1 cass. 1997. 9.95 (M-102) Truth Consciousness.

Evolution beyond human: the alluring psychic level is not true spiritual Being. Taking responsibility, facing ourselves, getting to higher consciousness.

Evolution to the Fourth Dimension. Swami Amar Jyoti. 1 cass. 1981. 9.95 (C-27) Truth Consciousness.

The process that leads to surrender & the plunge into full illumination. The meaning of evolving. Breaking the walls of ignorance.

***Evolutionary Void.** unabr. ed. Peter F. Hamilton. (Running Time: 25 hrs. 0 mins.). (Void Ser.: Pt. 3). 2010. 27.99 (978-1-4001-8184-1(4)); 54.99 (978-1-4001-9184-0(X)) Tantor Media.

***Evolutionary Void.** unabr. ed. Peter F. Hamilton. (Running Time: 24 hrs. 0 mins. 0 sec.). (Void Ser.: Pt. 3). 2010. 39.99 (978-1-4001-6184-3(3)); audio compact disk 54.99 (978-1-4001-1184-8(6)); audio compact disk 131.99 (978-1-4001-4184-5(2)) Pub: Tantor Media. Dist(s): IngramPubServ

Evolutions. unabr. ed. Karen Traviss et al. (Running Time: 14 hrs. 0 mins. 0 sec.). (ENG.). 2010. audio compact disk 49.99 (978-1-4272-0786-9(0)) Pub: Macmill Audio. Dist(s): Macmillan

Evolution's End. Joseph C. Pearce. 2 cass. 1993. 18.00 set. (OC341-72) Sound Horizons AV.

***Evolving in Monkey Town: How a Girl Who Knew All the Answers Learned to Ask the Questions.** unabr. ed. Rachel Held Evans. (Running Time: 4 hrs. 27 mins. 55 sec.). (ENG.). 2010. 14.99 (978-0-310-77371-9(7)) Zondervan.

Evolving Models of Organizational Behavior. unabr. ed. Keith Davis. 1 cass. (Running Time: 27 min.). 12.95 (13030) J Norton Pubs.

Presents four different approaches to working with people in organizations: autocratic, custodial, supportive & collegial.

Ev'rybody Wants to Be a Cat (from The Aristocats) Arranged by Cristi Cary Miller. 1 CD. 2000. audio compact disk 19.95 H Leonard.

With its bluesy accompaniment, this 2-part setting of the cute song from Walt Disney's "The Aristocrats" will be "purr-fectly" wonderful to perform!.

Ewe Lamb. unabr. ed. Margaret Bacon. Read by Julia Sands. 7 cass. (Storysound Ser.). (J). 2000. 61.95 (978-1-85903-391-3(1)) Pub: Mgna Lrg Print GBR. Dist(s): Ulverscroft US

Ex. unabr. ed. John Lutz. Read by Edward Lewis. 8 cass. (Running Time: 8 hrs.). 1996. 48.00 (978-0-913369-27-2(6), 4178) Books on Tape.

Ex-Files. unabr. ed. Pete Johnson. Narrated by Gillian Walton & Tom Lawrence. 4 CDs. (Running Time: 4 hrs. 30 mins.). (YA). (gr. 9 up). 2007. audio compact disk 34.95 (978-1-4056-5680-1(8)) AudioGO.

Ex Libris: Confession of a Common Reader. unabr. ed. Anne Fadiman. Narrated by Suzanne Toren. 3 cass. (Running Time: 4 hrs. 30 mins.). 1998. 28.00 (978-0-7887-3113-6(0), 95824 E7) Recorded Bks.

Reveals a collection of essays celebrating the joy of reading. From building castles with books as a child, to the trauma of marrying her library with her husbands, the author reveals the intimate details of her lifelong affair with books.

Ex-Mas Feast (A Story from Say You're One of Them) unabr. ed. Uwem Akpan. Read by Dion Graham. (Running Time: 1 hr.). (ENG.). 2008. 3.98 (978-1-60024-301-1(0)) Pub: Hachet Audio. Dist(s): HachBkGrp

Ex-Mrs. Hedgefund. unabr. ed. Jill Kargman. Read by Susan Ericksen. (Running Time: 9 hrs.). 2009. 39.97 (978-1-4233-7709-2(5), 9781423377092, BADLE); 39.97 (978-1-4233-7707-8(9), 9781423377078, Brlnc Audio MP3 Lib); 24.99 (978-1-4233-7706-1(0), 9781423377061, Brilliance MP3); 24.99 (978-1-4233-7708-5(7), 9781423377085, BAD); audio compact disk 87.97 (978-1-4233-7705-4(2), 9781423377054, BriAudCD Unabrid); audio compact disk 29.99 (978-1-4233-7704-7(4), 9781423377047) Brilliance Audio.

Ex-Wives. unabr. ed. Deborah Moggach. Narrated by Diana Bishop. 7 cass. (Running Time: 9 hrs. 45 mins.). 2000. 63.00 (978-1-84197-161-2(8), H1155E7) Recorded Bks.

Russell Buffery's career as an actor has been both eminent & extensive, but his personal life isn't looking rosy, bachelorhood beckons as the latest of his three wives leaves him. Then he meets Celeste, young, beautiful & fascinated by his past.

Exact Replica of a Figment of My Imagination: A Memoir. unabr. ed. Elizabeth McCracken. Read by Elizabeth McCracken. (Running Time: 4 hrs. 30 mins.). (ENG.). 2008. 16.98 (978-1-60024-472-8(6)) Pub: Hachet Audio. Dist(s): HachBkGrp

Exact Revenge. abr. ed. Tim Green. Read by Stephen Lang. (ENG.). 2005. 14.98 (978-1-59483-166-9(1)) Pub: Hachet Audio. Dist(s): HachBkGrp

Exact Revenge. abr. ed. Tim Green. Read by Stephen Lang. (Running Time: 6 hrs.). (ENG.). 2009. 44.98 (978-1-60788-043-1(1)) Pub: Hachet Audio. Dist(s): HachBkGrp

Exactly What Is Your Business? Neh. 7:1-73; 11:1-12. Ed Young. 1990. 4.95 (978-0-7417-1815-0(4), 815) Win Walk.

Exaltation. 1 CD. 1999. audio compact disk 16.98 (978-1-57908-504-9(0), 5347) Platinm Enter.

Exaltation: Songs of Women-Sacred Solos. Perf. by Susan Anthony et al. Prod. by S. T. Kimbrough, Jr. (Classical Praise Ser.). 2005. audio compact disk (978-1-890569-94-5(1), GBGMusik) Gnl Brd Glbl Minis.

Exaltation & the Kingdoms of Glory. Duane S. Crowther. Read by Duane S. Crowther. 1 cass. (Running Time: 90 min.). 1991. 13.98 (978-0-88290-417-7(5), 1820) Horizon Utah.

An inspiring & motivational discourse that explains many facets of eternal life & encourages listeners to strive for perfection. Explains the LDS belief of heaven & man's final rewards.

Exalted: Col. 1:15-20. Ed Young. (J). 1982. 4.95 (978-0-7417-1251-6(2), 251) Win Walk.

Exalted above All: Living Light School of Worship 05. Living Light School of Worship Staff. 2005. audio compact disk 16.98 (978-1-4245-0177-9(6)) Tre Med Inc.

1. Exalted Above All2. You Reign3. I Stand in Wonder4. You Are5. Always6. To Worship You, My King7. Your Ways are Higher8. You're Holy9. Thank You10. God of Love.

Exalted Worship: So great a Salvation. Kirk Cameron & Scott Krippayne. Prod. by Todd Friel. Executive Producer Joel Anderson. Engineer David Shannon. Compiled by Rick Appleton. Joe Potter. (ENG.). 2009. audio compact disk 14.99 (978-0-9824991-1-5(6)) Burn Bush Comm.

Exaltemos Al Rey de Reyes. unabr. ed. Claudio Freidzon. (SPA.). 2002. 9.99 (978-0-8297-3484-3(8)) Pub: Vida Pubs. Dist(s): Zondervan

Exalting Christ the Lamb of God. 2003. audio compact disk 54.00 (978-1-57972-530-3(9)) Insight Living.

Exalting Christ... the Lamb of God. unabr. ed. Charles R. Swindoll. 6 cass. (Running Time: 5 hrs.). 2000. 30.95 (978-1-57972-333-0(0)) Insight Living.

Exam Skills: Essay Writing. Steve Bracci. 2 cass. (Running Time: 2 hrs. 45 min.). (Outstanding Professors Ser.). 1996. 46.00 (978-1-57793-030-3(4), 28418, West Lglwrks) West.

Lecture given by a prominent law school professor.

Exam Skills: Multi-Choice & MBE. unabr. ed. Steven Finz. 1 cass. (Running Time: 1 hr. 30 mins.). (Outstanding Professors Ser.). 1996. 35.00 (978-1-57793-031-0(2), 28419, West Lglwrks) West.

Lecture by a prominent American law school professor.

***Exam Solutions.** 2nd ed. Fleming's Fundamentals of Law. 2010. pap. bk. 85.00 (978-1-932440-67-6(4)) Flmngs Fdmntls Law.

Exam Solutions: Community Property. 1989. audio compact disk 67.95 (978-1-932440-10-2(0)) Flmngs Fdmntls Law.

Exam Solutions: Community Property. 4 CDs. (Running Time: 4 hours). 2000. 67.95 (978-1-932440-11-9(9)) Flmngs Fdmntls Law.

Exam Solutions: Corporations. 3 audio tapes. (Running Time: 5 hours). 1982. 67.95 (978-1-932440-19-5(4)) Flmngs Fdmntls Law.

Audio lecture of Corporations (business Org) covering Formations, Promoter transactions, pre/post incorporation agreements, powers adn management, duty of care/loyality, SEC violations, closed corporations, capitalization, regulation of securities, shares and dividends, redemption/repurchases, fundamental changes in the corporate structure.

Exam Solutions: Criminal Procedure. 3 audio tapes. (Running Time: 4.5 hours). 1982. 67.95 (978-1-932440-22-5(4)) Flmngs Fdmntls Law.

Audio lecture of Criminal Procedure covering 4th, 5th, 6th and 8th amendments, Standing , exclusionary rule, harmless vs reversible error, post convicitions issues and exam approaches.

Exam Solutions: Criminal Procedure. 4 CDs. (Running Time: 4 hours). 1982. audio compact disk 72.95 (978-1-932440-21-8(6)) Flmngs Fdmntls Law.

Audio lecture of Criminal Procedure covering 4t, 5th, 6th and 8th amendments, Standing , exclusionary rule, harmless vs reversible error, post convicitions issues and exam approaches.

Exam Solutions: Evidence. 3 audio tapes. (Running Time: 5 hours). 1982. 67.95 (978-1-932440-24-9(0)) Flmngs Fdmntls Law.

Audio Lecture of Evidence covering, relevancy, character, impeachment, opinion, authentication, best evidence, type of evidence, burdens/presumptions, judicaila notice, jearsay: exclusions, exemptions, exceptions, and privileges.

Exam Solutions: Evidence. 5 CDs. (Running Time: 5 hours). 1982. audio compact disk 72.95 (978-1-932440-23-2(2)) Flmngs Fdmntls Law.

Exam Solutions: Professional Responsibility. 2 audio tapes. (Running Time: 4 hours). 1982. spiral bd. 94.95 (978-1-932440-25-6(9)) Flmngs Fdmntls Law.

Audio lecture of Professioanal Responsibility covering ethical standards promugulated under the ABA model rules of professional conduct ad the model rule of judicial conduct and leading supreme courts cases. With MBE questions for the MPRE.

Exam Solutions: Property. 1989. audio compact disk 72.95 (978-1-993244-02-2(6)) Flmngs Fdmntls Law.

Exam Solutions: Remedies. 3 audio tapes. (Running Time: 5 hours). 1982. 89.95 (978-1-932440-30-0(5)) Flmngs Fdmntls Law.
Lecture of Remedies covering Tort remedies, damages, restitiution, Injuncitns/ contract remedies damages, rescission, restitution, reformation, specific performance.

Exam Solutions: Remedies. 5 CDs. (Running Time: 5 hours). 1982. audio compact disk 84.95 (978-1-932440-29-4(1)) Flmngs Fdmntls Law.
Audio Lecture of Remedies outline covering Tort remedies, damages, restitiution, Injuncitns/ contract remedies damages, rescission, restitution, reformation, specific performance.

Exam Solutions: Trust. 4 CDs. (Running Time: 4 hours). 1982. audio compact disk 72.95 (978-1-932440-33-1(X)) Flmngs Fdmntls Law.
Audio Lecture of trust law covering creation, types of trust, trustee supervisions, beneficiaries rights, modification and termination of right.

Exam Solutions: Trust. 2 audio tapes. (Running Time: 4 hours). 1982. 72.95 (978-1-932440-34-8(8)) Flmngs Fdmntls Law.

Exam Solutions: Wills. 2 audio tapes. (Running Time: 4 hours). 1982. 67.95 (978-1-932440-36-2(4)) Flmngs Fdmntls Law.
Audio lecture on Wills- Californina Emphasis covering Validity, what a will consists of, Revocation, DRR, revival, distributions, intestate succession.

Exam Solutions: Wills. 3 cds. (Running Time: 4 hours). 1982. audio compact disk 72.95 (978-1-932440-35-5(6)) Flmngs Fdmntls Law.

Exam Solutions Vol. 1: Civil Procedure. 3 Cassettes. (Running Time: 4 hours). 1982. 67.95 (978-1-932440-07-2(0)); audio compact disk 72.95 (978-1-932440-08-9(9)) Flmngs Fdmntls Law.
Civil Procedure 1 on CDs. Civil Procedure Hardcopy outline with Civil Procedure 1 exams reviewed. Subject Matter Jurisdiction, Supplemental Jurisdiction, Removal Jurisdiciton, Personal Jurisdiction, In Rem and Quasi in Rem Jurisdiction, Notice: Service of Process, Challenging the Personal Jurisdiction, Venue, Choice of Law, Pleading, Joinder of Claims and Parties.

Exam Solutions Vol. 1: Constitutional Law. 3 Audio Tapes. (Running Time: 4.5 hours). 1982. audio compact disk 72.95 (978-1-932440-12-6(7)) Flmngs Fdmntls Law.
Lecture of the Outline on Community Property.

Exam Solutions Vol. 1: Constitutional Law. 3 Audio Tapes. (Running Time: 4.5 hours). 1982. 67.95 (978-1-932440-13-3(5)) Flmngs Fdmntls Law.
Lecture of Constitutional Law 1 Ouline covering Procedure, Federal Power source, Federal-State Conflicts, Intergovernmental Immunities, Separation of Powers, Due process, Eminent domain, Contract Clause.

Exam Solutions Vol. 1: Contracts. 3 Audio Tapes. (Running Time: 4.5 hours). 1982. 67.95 (978-1-932440-16-4(X)) Flmngs Fdmntls Law.

Exam Solutions Vol. 1: Contracts. 5 cd's. (Running Time: 4 hours). 1982. audio compact disk 72.95 (978-1-932440-15-7(1)) Flmngs Fdmntls Law.
Audio Outline Lecture covering on Contracts 1 covering formation, defenses, third party beneficiaries, breach and rememdies.

Exam Solutions Vol. 1: Property. 2 audio tapes. (Running Time: 4 hours). 1982. 67.95 (978-1-932440-27-0(5)) Flmngs Fdmntls Law.
Audio lecture on Property 1 covering: conncurrent interest, future interest, class gifts, adverse possession, landloard-tenant relations.

Exam Solutions Vol. 1: Torts. 1982. 67.95 (978-1-932440-32-4(1)) Flmngs Fdmntls Law.
Audio Lecture of Torts 1 covering Intentional tort, defenses, Nelfigence-causation emphasis, defenses.

Exam Solutions Vol. 1: Torts. 4 CDs. (Running Time: 4 hours). 1982. audio compact disk 72.95 (978-1-932440-31-7(3)) Flmngs Fdmntls Law.

Exam Solutions Vol. 2: Civil Procedure. 1982. 67.95 (978-1-932440-09-6(7)) Flmngs Fdmntls Law.

Exam Solutions Vol. 2: Constitutional Law. 3 Audio Tapes. (Running Time: 4.5 hours). 1982. 67.95 (978-1-932440-14-0(3)) Flmngs Fdmntls Law.

Exam Solutions Vol. 2: Contracts. 4 CDs. (Running Time: 4 hours). 1982. audio compact disk 72.95 (978-1-932440-17-1(8)) Flmngs Fdmntls Law.
Audio Lecture of Contracts 2 Outline of Contracts 2 covering Assignment/Delegation, third party beneficiaries, conditions, discharge, breach, remedies. Also, the lecture covers exams on this area.

Exam Solutions Vol. 2: Contracts. 3 audio tapes. (Running Time: 4.5 hours). 1982. 67.95 (978-1-932440-18-8(6)) Flmngs Fdmntls Law.
Audio Lecture of contracts 2 covering assignment/delegation, third party beneficiaries, conditions, discharge, breach, remedies.

Exam Solutions Vol. 2: Property. 2 audio tapes. (Running Time: 4 hours). 1982. 67.95 (978-1-932440-28-7(3)) Flmngs Fdmntls Law.
Outline of Property 2 covering sale of land, deed, recording act, easements, profits and licenses, covenants, equitable servitudes, implied peciprocal negative easements, water rights, lateral and subjacent supports, and eminent domain/zoning.

Exam Solutions Vol. 2: Torts. 1989. 67.95 (978-1-932440-39-3(9)) Flmngs Fdmntls Law.

***Examen stratégique décennal de l'Etude Machel: Les enfants et les conflits dans un monde en Mutation.** United Nations Children's Fund Staff & Office of the Special Representative of the Secretary- for Children and Armed Conflict.Tr. of Machel Study 10-Year Strategic Review: Children & Conflict in a Changing World. (FRE., 2009. pap. bk. 35.00 (978-92-806-4364-0(9)) Pub: UNICEF. Dist(s): Untd Nat Pubns

Examination of Psyche from Kaballah. 2 cass. 18.00 (OC82) Sound Horizons AV.

Examine Yourself. 2 cass. 7.95 (22-1, HarperThor) HarpC GBR.

Examining Religions. Standard Publishing Staff. 2006. cd-rom 24.99 (978-0-7847-1877-3(6)) Standard Pub.

Examining the Charismatic - Ecumenical Movement. Dan Corner. 1 cass. 3.00 (30) Evang Outreach.

Examining the Expert Witness. 1986. bk. 75.00 incl. only.; 35.00 cass. only.; 40.00 book only. PA Bar Inst.

Examining the Plaintiff. James McElhaney et al. 1 cass. (Running Time: 59 min.). (Winning at Trial Ser.). 1986. 20.00 (FAWAT03) Natl Inst Trial Ad.

Examkrackers MCAT Audio Osmosis with Jordan & Jon. 12 CDs. (Audio Osmosis). 2001. audio compact disk 199.95 (978-1-893858-23-7(5)) Osote Pubg.

Examples of the Nature of Jesus. unabr. ed. Read by Gayle D. Erwin. 1 cass. (Running Time: 1 hr.). 1992. 4.95 (978-1-56599-518-5(X), C-18) Yahshua Pub.

Exams. Eldon Taylor. 1 cass. (Running Time: 62 min.). (Inner Talk Ser.). 16.95 (978-1-55978-357-6(5), 5370A) Progress Aware Res.
Soundtrack - Tropical Lagoon with underlying subliminal affirmations.

Excalibur see Tales of King Arthur & His Knights

Excalibur see King Arthur

***Excalibur.** abr. ed. Bernard Cornwell. Read by Tim Pigott-Smith. (ENG.). 2010. (978-0-06-201473-3(0), Harper Audio); (978-0-06-200948-7(6), Harper Audio) HarperCollins Pubs.

Excalibur, unabr. collector's ed. Bernard Cornwell. Read by David Case. 12 cass. (Running Time: 18 hrs.). (Warlord Chronicles: Vol. 3). 1998. 96.00 (978-0-7366-4276-7(5), 4774) Books on Tape.
The story of King Arthur's consolidation of power, also of the endless conspiracies that nearly brought him down, weaving the magic & desperation of King Arthur's era into immediately convincing realism.

Excalibur: Book 3: Restoration. abr. ed. Peter David. Read by Joe Morton. 2004. 10.95 (978-0-7435-4676-8(8)) Pub: S&S Audio. Dist(s): S and S Inc

***Excavation.** unabr. ed. James Rollins. Read by John Meagher. (ENG.). 2010. (978-0-06-196157-1(4), Harper Audio); (978-0-06-195859-5(X), Harper Audio) HarperCollins Pubs.

Excavations at Tall Jawa, Jordan: The Iron Age Town. P. M. Michele Daviau. Contrib. by Paul-Eugene Dion et al. (Culture & History of the Ancient near East Ser.: Vol. 11). 2003. bk. 310.00 (978-90-04-13012-8(8)) Pub: Brill Academic NLD. Dist(s): Brill Acad Pub

Exceed Customer Expectations. pap. bk. & tchr.'s training gde. ed. 99.95 J Wilson & Assocs.
Provides "business skills" training to teach & reinforce the basic knowledge required to thrive in any type of work environment.

Exceeding Customer Expectations: What Enterprise, America's #1 Car Rental Company, Can Teach You about Creating Lifetime Customers. abr. ed. Kirk Kazanjian. Read by Alan Sklar. (Running Time: 21600 sec.). (ENG.). 2007. audio compact disk 29.95 (978-0-7393-4203-9(7), Random AudioBks) Pub: Random Audio Pubg. Dist(s): Random

Exceeding Love. Creflo A. Dollar. (ENG.). 2000. 10.00 (978-1-59089-017-2(5)) Pub: Creflo Dollar. Dist(s): STL Dist NA

Excel in Exams: Classic. Eldon Taylor. Read by Eldon Taylor. Ed. by Leslie Brice. 1 cass. (Running Time: 1 hr.). 1992. 16.95 (978-1-56705-149-0(9)) Gateways Inst.
Self improvement.

Excel in Exams: Ocean. Eldon Taylor. Read by Eldon Taylor. Ed. by Leslie Brice. 1 cass. (Running Time: 1 hr.). 1992. 16.95 (978-1-56705-150-6(2)) Gateways Inst.

Excel in Exams: Stream. Eldon Taylor. Read by Eldon Taylor. Ed. by Leslie Brice. 1 cass. (Running Time: 1 hr.). 1992. 16.95 (978-1-56705-151-3(0)) Gateways Inst.

Excel in School, Vol. 4. Jonathan Parker. Read by Jonathan Parker. 1 CD. (Running Time: 1 hr.). (Subliminal Ser.: Vol. 4). 1999. audio compact disk (978-1-58400-045-7(7)) QuantumQuests Intl.
Positive subliminal messages with classical music on compact disc.

Excel-lerated Learning - French. Barrie Konicov. 1 cass. (Support Program for Language Learning Ser.). (YA). 16.98 (978-0-87082-590-3(9), 302); 11.98 (978-0-87082-580-4(1), 302) Potentials.
Self-hypnosis techniques designed to allow you to learn while you sleep.

Excel-lerated Learning - German. Barrie Konicov. 1 cass. (Support Program for Language Learning Ser.). (YA). 16.98 (303); 11.98 (978-0-87082-576-7(3), 303) Potentials.
Self hypnosis techniques designed to allow you to learn while you sleep.

Excel-lerated Learning - Hebrew. Barrie Konicov. 1 cass. (Running Time: 90 min.). (YA). 16.98 (978-0-87082-595-8(X), 308) Potentials.
Self hypnosis techniques designed to allow learning while sleeping.

Excel-lerated Learning - Italian. Barrie Konicov. 2 cass. (Running Time: 90 min.). (Support Programs for Language Learning Ser.). (YA). 16.98 (978-0-87082-593-4(3)); 11.98 (978-0-87082-568-2(2), 305) Potentials.
Self-hypnosis techniques designed to allow learning while you sleep.

Excel-lerated Learning - Japanese. Barrie Konicov. 1 cass. 11.98 (978-0-87082-572-9(0), 307) Potentials.
Self-hypnosis techniques designed to allow you to learn while you sleep.

Excel-lerated Learning - Japanese. Barrie Konicov. 2 cass. (Running Time: 90 min.). (Support Programs for Language Learning Ser.). (YA). 16.98 (978-0-87082-589-7(5)) Potentials.

Excel-lerated Learning - Portuguese. Barrie Konicov. 2 cass. (Running Time: 90 min.). (Support Programs for Language Learning Ser.). (YA). 16.98 (978-0-87082-594-1(1)); 11.98 (978-0-87082-570-5(4), 304) Potentials.

Excel-lerated Learning - Russian. Barrie Konicov. 2 cass. (Running Time: 90 min.). (Support Programs for Language Learning Ser.). (YA). 16.98 (978-0-87082-596-5(8)); 11.98 (978-0-87082-574-3(7), 306) Potentials.

Excel-lerated Learning - Spanish. Barrie Konicov. 2 cass. (Running Time: 90 min.). (Support Programs for Language Learners Ser.). (YA). 16.98 (978-0-87082-591-0(7)); 11.98 (978-0-87082-578-1(X), 301) Potentials.

Excel No. 1. 1 cass. (Running Time: 1 hr. 30 mins.). (SPA.). 2001. Astran.

Excel No. 2. 1 cass. (Running Time: 1 hr. 30 mins.). (SPA.). 2001. Astran.

Excelencia. Marcos Witt. (Serie de Predicaciones Ser.). 2009. audio compact disk 19.99 (978-0-8297-5399-8(0)) Zondervan.

Excelencia del Vendedor Profesional. unabr. ed. Hugo Tapias.Tr. of Excellence of the Professional Salesman. (SPA.). 2001. audio compact disk 13.00 (978-958-43-0145-1(4)) YoYoMusic.

Excelente Es Tu Nombre. unabr. ed. Doris Machin. 1999. 7.99 (978-0-8297-2503-2(2)) Pub: Vida Pubs. Dist(s): Zondervan

Excellence. AIO Team Staff. Created by Focus on the Family Staff. (Running Time: 1 hr. 10 mins. 0 sec.). (Adventures in Odyssey Life Lessons Ser.). (ENG.). (J). 2006. audio compact disk 5.99 (978-1-58997-374-9(7)) Pub: Focus Family. Dist(s): Tyndale Hse

Excellence: Character-The Only Concrete Worth Building On. Gary V. Whetstone. 4 cass. (Running Time: 6 hrs.). (Empowerment Ser.). 1993. pap. bk. 35.00 (978-1-58866-180-7(6), VE003A) Gary Whet Pub.
Do you want to know the secret of success or failure? It lies in a person's character. Identify & develop character traits that will eliminate failure & will lead.

Excellence: Commissioned under Command. Gary V. Whetstone. 4 cass. (Running Time: 6 hrs.). (Empowerment Ser.). 1993. bk. 35.00 (978-1-58866-182-1(2), VE004A) Gary Whet Pub.
Have you ever been sent to the store only to return with both the wrong item & the wrong attitude? This series reveals how to achieve a standard of excellence by doing.

Excellence: Commitment to Completion. Gary V. Whetstone. 4 cass. (Running Time: 6 hrs.). (Empowerment Ser.). 1993. pap. bk. 35.00 (978-1-58866-184-5(9), VE005A) Gary Whet Pub.
Jesus said, " Well done!" we all have a project, only to quit before its completion. Learn the secret of stamina & how to guard yourself from fainting.

Excellence Challenge. Tom Peters. Read by Tom Peters. 6 cass. 69.95 Set. (142A) Nightingale-Conant.

Excellence in Advertising: The Winners. 1 cass. (America's Supermarket Showcase '96 Ser.). 1996. 11.00 (NGA96-034) Sound Images.

Excellence in Merchandising: The Winners. 1 cass. (America's Supermarket Showcase '96 Ser.). 1996. 11.00 (NGA96-017) Sound Images.

Excellence in Ministry: A Study of I Timothy. unabr. ed. Charles R. Swindoll. 10 cass. (Running Time: 8 hrs. 30 mins.). 1998. 48.95 (978-1-57972-269-2(5)) Insight Living.

Excellence in Supervision. Conlow. 2001. pap. bk. 249.00 (978-1-56052-614-8(9)) Crisp Pubns.

Excellence of the Professional Salesman see Excelencia del Vendedor Profesional

Excellence of the Professional Salesman. Hugo Tapias. Read by Fernando Gutierrez, Jr. (Running Time: 1 hr.). 2001. 14.95 (978-1-60083-268-0(7), Audiofy Corp) Iofy Corp.

Excellent English - Level 3 (Low Intermediate) - Audio CDs (2) Jan Forstrom et al. (Excellent English Ser.). (C). 2008. audio compact disk 36.88 (978-0-07-329186-4(2), 0073291862, ESL/ELT) Pub: McGrw-H Hghr Educ. Dist(s): McGraw

Excellent Exam Results with Mind Power, Vol. 38, set. Jonathan Parker. Read by Jonathan Parker. 2 CDs. (Running Time: 2 hrs.). (Success Ser.: Vol. 3). (YA). (gr. 1 up). 1999. audio compact disk (978-1-58400-037-2(6)) QuantumQuests Intl.
Disc 1 contains several guided visualizations. Disc 2 contains audible & subliminal positive affirmations with music.

Excellent Manager. Brian S. Tracy. Read by Brian S. Tracy. 2 cass. (Effective Manager Seminar Ser.: No. 4). 95.00 Set, incl. 1-hr. videotape & 2 wkbks., program notes & study guide. (746VD) Nightingale-Conant.
Traits of top-rated managers.

Excellent Mystery. Ellis Peters, pseud. Narrated by Roe Kendall. (Running Time: 8 hrs. 30 mins.). 2000. 27.95 (978-1-59912-410-0(6)) Iofy Corp.

Excellent Mystery. unabr. ed. Ellis Peters. Read by Vanessa Benjamin. 7 CDs. (Running Time: 8 hrs. 30 mins.). 2001. audio compact disk 56.00 (978-0-7861-9780-4(3), 2711) Blckstn Audio.
In the year of our Lord 1141, August comes in golden as a lion & two monks ride in the Benedictine Abbey bringing with them disturbing news of war.

Excellent Mystery. unabr. ed. Ellis Peters. Read by Roe Kendall. 6 cass. (Running Time: 8 hrs. 30 mins.). (Chronicles of Brother Cadfael Ser.). 2001. 44.95 (978-0-7861-1940-0(3), 2711) Blckstn Audio.

Excellent Mystery. unabr. ed. Ellis Peters, pseud. Read by Stephen Thorne. 6 cass. (Running Time: 7 hrs.). (Chronicles of Brother Cadfael Ser.: Vol. 11). 2000. 29.95 (978-1-57270-140-3(4), N61140u) Pub: Audio Partners. Dist(s): PerseuPGW
From the moment Brother Cadfael meets two monks who are seeking refuge at Saint Peter & Paul, he believes that something deeper than their common vows binds the two brothers. Brother Cadfael faces a test of beliefs, as he must distinguish between the innocent & the guilty.

Excellent Mystery. unabr. ed. Ellis Peters, pseud. Read by Stephen Thorne. 6 cass. (Running Time: 9 hrs.). (Chronicles of Brother Cadfael Ser.: Bk. 11). 2000. 49.95 (978-0-7451-4184-8(6), CAB 867) Pub: Chivers Audio Bks GBR. Dist(s): AudioGO
It's 1141 in England, and King Stephen and Empress Maud are struggling over the throne. Many innocent people are victimized, and property is destroyed. Then a latent tragedy becomes a reality, and Brother Cadfael must distinguish between the innocent and the evil.

Excellent Mystery. unabr. ed. Ellis Peters, pseud. Narrated by Patrick Tull. 6 cass. (Running Time: 8 hrs. 15 mins.). (Chronicles of Brother Cadfael Ser.: Vol. 11). 1994. 51.00 (978-0-7887-0112-2(6), 94353E7) Recorded Bks.
When the nearby Abbey of Hyde Meade is totally destroyed, two of its brothers seek refuge at the Abbey of Saint Peter & Saint Paul & mystery soon follows; Brother Cadfael investigates.

Excellent Posture. Eldon Taylor. 1 cass. (Running Time: 62 min.). (Inner Talk Ser.). 16.95 incl. script. (978-1-55978-170-1(X), 5371C) Progress Aware Res.
Soundtrack - Musical Themes with underlying subliminal affirmations.

Excellent Posture: Ocean. Eldon Taylor. Read by Eldon Taylor. Ed. by Leslie Brice. 1 cass. (Running Time: 1 hr.). 1992. 16.95 (978-1-56705-302-9(5)) Gateways Inst.
Self improvement.

***Excellent Wife: A Biblical Perspective.** unabr. ed. Martha Peace. Narrated by Tamara Adams. (ENG.). 2007. 16.98 (978-1-59644-436-2(3), Hovel Audio) christianaud.

Excellent Wife: A Biblical Perspective. unabr. ed. Martha Peace. Read by Tamara Kaye Adams. (Running Time: 8 hrs. 18 mins. 0 sec.). (ENG.). 2007. audio compact disk 26.98 (978-1-59644-435-5(5)) christianaud.

Excellent 11: Qualities Teachers & Parents Use to Motivate, Inspire, & Educate Children, Vol. 11. abr. ed. Ron Clark. Read by Ron Clark. 2 CDs. (Running Time: 2 hrs. 30 mins.). 2004. audio compact disk 19.98 (978-1-4013-9898-9(7), Hyperion Audio) Pub: Hyperion. Dist(s): HarperCollins Pubs

Excelling at Sports: OZO. Eldon Taylor. Read by Eldon Taylor. Ed. by Leslie Brice. 1 cass. (Running Time: 1 hr.). 1992. 19.95 (978-1-56705-016-5(6)) Gateways Inst.

Except for Me & Thee. unabr. ed. Jessamyn West. Read by Roses Prichard. 7 cass. (Running Time: 10 hrs. 30 min.). 1980. 56.00 (978-0-7366-0240-2(2), 1236) Books on Tape.
A Quaker couple looks back on their marriage.

Exception to the Rulers: Exposing Oily Politicians, War Profiteers, & the Media That Love Them. unabr. ed. Amy Goodman & David Goodman. (ENG.). 2008. audio compact disk 40.00 (978-1-931859-67-7(1)) Pub: Haymarket Bks. Dist(s): Consort Bk Sales

Exceptional Assistant: Achieving Respect As an Indispensable Secretary, Administrative Assistant, or Support Staff Member. 6 cass. 59.95 Set incl. wkbk. (11360AS) Pryor Resources.
Learn success skills the quick, proven way with the practical, hands-on ideas presented here. Become more productive, better organized, more valuable to your boss, & happier in your job.

Exceptional Clearance. unabr. ed. William J. Caunitz. Narrated by George Guidall. 7 cass. (Running Time: 9 hrs. 45 mins.). 2001. 64.00 (978-0-7887-8865-9(5)) Recorded Bks.
When three young women are found murdered in New York, Detective Lieutenant John Vinda is determined to do anything that's necessary to stop the killing - even if it means bending the rules.

Exceptional Customer Service. Fred Pryor. 6 cass. (Running Time: 6 hrs.). 1993. 59.95 set. (10430A) Nightingale-Conant.

Exceptional Customer Service. PUEI. 2006. audio compact disk 89.95 (978-1-933328-40-9(1), Fred Pryor) P Univ E Inc.

Exceptional Customer Service: A Must for Everyone Who Communicates with Customers. 6 cass. 59.95 Set incl. wkbk. (10430AS) Pryor Resources.
Learn to see yourself & your organization as others see you. Keep your cool even when handling complaints. Sharpen your listening skills with 11 creative techniques. Build excellent rapport & utilize easy ways to ensure crystal-clear, positive communications.

Excerpts & Conversations, 1980's. unabr. ed. John Lilly & Toni Lilly. 1 cass. 1986. 10.00 (978-1-56964-615-1(5), A0076-86) Sound Photosyn.
Moments from this cyclonic dyad.

Excerpts from Toning Workshop. Excerpts. Laurel Elizabeth Keyes. Voice by Laurel Elizabeth Keyes. 1 cass. (Running Time: 90 mins.). 1983. 10.00 (978-0-9791360-4-7(0)) Gentle Living.
Laurel Keyes is actually demonstrating Toning techniques in a workshop. This is a good tape to experience her voice and how she uses Toning with other people and how it can make a difference in your life.

Excess Baggage. Judy Astley. Read by Laura Brattan. 8 CDs. (Running Time: 9 hrs.). (Isis (CDs) Ser.). (J). 2005. audio compact disk 79.95 (978-0-7531-2434-5(3)) Pub: ISIS Lrg Prnt GBR. Dist(s): Ulverscroft US

Excess Baggage. unabr. ed. Judy Astley. 6 cass. (Running Time: 9 hrs.). 2001. 54.95 (978-0-7531-0928-1(X), 000910) Pub: ISIS Audio GBR. Dist(s): Ulverscroft US
A Proper Family Holiday was the last thing Lucy was expecting to have. But as a penniless house-painter with an expired lease on her flat and a twelve-year-old daughter, she could hardly turn down her parents' offer to take them on a trip to the Caribbean. In the fabulous heat and beautiful surroundings, family tensions should just melt away. But some problems just refuse to be left at home.

Excessive Force, Set. unabr. ed. Thomas Ian Griffith. Read by Tony Todd. 2 cass. (Running Time: 3 hrs.). 1993. 16.95 (978-1-56876-002-5(7)) Soundlines Ent.
Terry McCain is a streetwise Chicago cop whose short fuse & fast fists put him in conflict with the Mob when three million dollars worth of drug money disappears during a botched drug bust.

Exchange at the Cross. Derek Prince. 1 cass. (Running Time: 60 min.). 5.95 (I-4256) Derek Prince.

Exchange Monthly Newsletter. Ann Seagrave & Faison Covington. (Anxiety Treatment Ser.). 15.00 CHAANGE.
Includes hints in dealing with anxiety-related difficulties.

Exchange Your Inner Critic for Compassion. 2007. audio compact disk 14.00 (978-0-9786744-7-2(2)) HFTBLU.

Exchanged Life. Lee Lefebre. 1 cass. (Running Time: 1 hr. 25 min.). (Exchanged Life Conference Ser.: Vol. 4). 1993. 6.00 (978-1-57838-008-4(1)) CrossLife Express.
Christian living.

Exchanged Life. Read by Lee Lefebre. 1 cass. (Running Time: 1 hr. 25 min.). (GraceLife Conference Ser.: Vol. 4). 1993. 6.00 (978-1-57838-109-8(6)) CrossLife Express.

Exchanged Life: Romans Chapter 5. Richard Hall. Read by Richard Hall. 1 cass. (Running Time: 1 hr.). 1994. 6.00 (978-1-57838-014-5(6)) CrossLife Express.
Commentary on Romans Chapter 5.

Exchanged Life: Romans Chapter 5 Through 8. Richard Hall. Read by Richard Hall. 4 cass. (Running Time: 4 hrs.). 1994. 23.99 Set. (978-1-57838-013-8(8)) CrossLife Express.
Commentary on Romans Chapters 5-8.

Exchanged Life: Romans Chapter 6. Richard Hall. Read by Richard Hall. 1 cass. (Running Time: 1 hr.). 1994. 6.00 (978-1-57838-015-2(4)) CrossLife Express.
Commentary on Romans Chapter 6.

Exchanged Life: Romans Chapter 7. Richard Hall. Read by Richard Hall. 1 cass. (Running Time: 1 hr.). 1994. 6.00 (978-1-57838-016-9(2)) CrossLife Express.
Commentary on Romans Chapter 7.

Exchanged Life: Romans Chapter 8. Richard Hall. Read by Richard Hall. 1 cass. (Running Time: 1 hr.). 1994. 6.00 (978-1-57838-017-6(0)) CrossLife Express.
Commentary on Romans Chapter 8.

Exchanged Life Conference - Album, Vol. 1. Read by Lee Lefebre. 8 cass. 1993. 39.99 Set. (978-1-57838-004-6(9)) CrossLife Express.
Christian living.

***Excited about Energy CD.** Nadia Higgins. Illus. by Andres Martinez Ricci. (Science Rocks! Set 2 CD Ser.). 2010. cd-rom 27.07 (978-1-60270-964-5(5)) ABDO Pub Co.

***Excited about Energy Site CD.** Nadia Higgins. Illus. by Andres Martinez Ricci. (Science Rocks! Set 2 Site CD Ser.). 2010. cd-rom 57.07 (978-1-60270-978-2(5)) ABDO Pub Co.

Exciting Piano! 1 cass. pap. bk. 39.95 (EP-1) Duane Shinn.
Learn the seven secrets of exciting piano playing! Just one secret will make a big difference in your playing, with all of them you're on your way to becoming a truly exciting piano player.

***Exclusive.** abr. ed. Sandra Brown. Read by Tanya Eby. 5 CDs. (Running Time: 6 hrs.). 2010. audio compact disk 14.99 (978-1-4418-1405-0(1), 9781441814050, BACD) Brilliance Audio.

***Exclusive.** abr. ed. Sandra Brown. (Running Time: 6 hrs.). 2011. audio compact disk 9.99 (978-1-4418-1406-7(X), 9781441814067, BCD Value Price) Brilliance Audio.

***Exclusive.** abr. ed. Fern Michaels. Read by Natalie Ross. (Running Time: 4 hrs.). (Godmothers Ser.: Bk. 2). 2010. audio compact disk 14.99 (978-1-4233-4546-6(0), 9781423345466, BACD) Brilliance Audio.

***Exclusive.** unabr. ed. Sandra Brown. Read by Tanya Eby. 1 MP3-CD. (Running Time: 13 hrs.). 2010. 39.97 (978-1-4418-1402-9(7), 9781441814029, Brlnc Audio MP3 Lib); 24.99 (978-1-4418-1401-2(9), 9781441814012, Brilliance MP3); 24.99 (978-1-4418-1403-6(5), 9781441814036, BAD); 39.97 (978-1-4418-1404-3(3), 9781441814043, BADLE); audio compact disk 97.97 (978-1-4418-1400-5(0), 9781441814005, BriAudCD Unabrid); audio compact disk 39.99 (978-1-4418-1399-2(3), 9781441813992, Bril Audio CD Unabri) Brilliance Audio.

***Exclusive.** unabr. ed. Fern Michaels. (Running Time: 8 hrs.). (Godmothers Ser.: Bk. 2). 2010. 24.99 (978-1-4233-4544-2(4), 9781423345442, BAD); 39.97 (978-1-4233-4545-9(2), 9781423345459, BADLE) Brilliance Audio.

***Exclusive.** unabr. ed. Fern Michaels. Read by Natalie Ross. (Running Time: 8 hrs.). (Godmothers Ser.: Bk. 2). 2010. 39.97 (978-1-4233-4543-5(6), 9781423345435, Brlnc Audio MP3 Lib); 24.99 (978-1-4233-4542-8(8), 9781423345428, Brilliance MP3); audio compact disk 97.97 (978-1-4233-4541-1(X), 9781423345411, BriAudCD Unabrid); audio compact disk 29.99 (978-1-4233-4540-4(1), 9781423345404, Bril Audio CD Unabri) Brilliance Audio.

Exclusive, Set. unabr. ed. Sandra Brown. Read by Denise Crosby. 9 cass. 1999. 49.95 (FS9-34535) Highsmith.

Excursion to Tindari. unabr. ed. Andrea Camilleri. Read by Grover Gardner. (Running Time: 10 hrs. 50 mins.). (Inspector Montalbano Mystery Ser.). 2009. 29.95 (978-1-4332-1833-0(X)); 65.95 (978-1-4332-1829-3(1)); audio compact disk 100.00 (978-1-4332-1830-9(5)) Blckstn Audio.

Excursions in World Music. 4th ed. 2003. audio compact disk 41.60 (978-0-13-140307-9(5), P-H) Pearson Educ CAN CAN.

Excusas, Excusas. Created by Rigby Staff. 1993. 10.40 (978-0-435-05949-1(1), Rigby PEA) Pearson EdAUS AUS.

Excuse. unabr. ed. Allan Baillie. (Running Time: 35 mins.). (Aussie Bites Ser.). (YA). 2005. audio compact disk 39.95 (978-1-74030-965-3(0)) Pub: Bolinda Pubng AUS. Dist(s): Bolinda Pub Inc

***Excuse Me, but I Was Next... . How to Handle the Top 100 Manners Dilemmas.** abr. ed. Peggy Post. Read by Susan Bennett. (ENG.). 2006. (978-0-06-123049-3(9), Harper Audio); (978-0-06-123050-9(2), Harper Audio) HarperCollins Pubs.

Excuse Me, but I Was Next... . CD: How to Handle the Top 100 Manners Dilemmas. abr. ed. Peggy Post. Read by Susan Bennett. 2006. audio compact disk 22.95 (978-0-06-114267-3(0)) HarperCollins Pubs.

Excuses Begone! How to Change Lifelong, Self-Defeating Thinking Habits. Wayne W. Dyer. 2009. audio compact disk (978-1-4019-2556-7(1), 1033) Hay Hse GBR.

Excuses Begone! How to Change Lifelong, Self-Defeating Thinking Habits. abr. ed. Wayne W. Dyer & Ram Dass. Read by Wayne W. Dyer. (ENG.). 2009. audio compact disk 45.00 (978-1-4019-2557-4(X), 1035) Hay House.

Excuses Begone! How to Change Lifelong, Self-Defeating Thinking Habits. unabr. ed. Wayne W. Dyer. Read by Wayne W. Dyer. 8 CDs. 2009. audio compact disk 39.95 (978-1-4019-2310-5(0), 879) Hay House.

Excuses, Excuses: Luke 14:6. Ed Young. 1989. 4.95 (978-0-7417-1757-3(3), 757) Win Walk.

Excuses/Self-Justification: Luke 14:1-35. Ed Young. 1996. 4.95 (978-0-7417-2091-7(4), 1091) Win Walk.

Exectioner 309: Flames of Fury. 2006. audio compact disk 19.99 (978-1-59950-335-6(2)) GraphicAudio.

Executing the Basics of Healing: A Game Plan for Walking in Divine Health. Kenneth W. Hagin, Jr. 6 cass. (Running Time: 6 hrs.). 2002. 30.00 (48J) Faith Lib Pubns.

***Execution.** (ENG.). 2010. audio compact disk (978-1-59171-302-9(1)) Falcon Picture.

Execution. Larry Bossidy. 2006. cd-rom 34.99 (978-1-59895-483-8(0)) Find a World.

Execution. unabr. ed. Larry Bossidy & Ram Charan. Read by Larry Bossidy & Ram Charan. (YA). 2006. 44.99 (978-0-7393-7477-1(X)) Find a World.

Execution: The Discipline of Getting Things Done. unabr. ed. Larry Bossidy & Ram Charan. Read by Larry Bossidy et al. Read by John Bedford Lloyd et al. 7 CDs. (Running Time: 8 hrs.). (ENG.). 2002. audio compact disk 34.95 (978-0-7393-0275-0(2), Random AudioBks) Pub: Random Audio Pubg. Dist(s): Random

Execution by Hunger. unabr. collector's ed. Miron Dolot. Read by Larry McKeever. 8 cass. (Running Time: 12 hrs.). 1988. 64.00 (978-0-7366-1451-1(6), 2333) Books on Tape.
In 1929, in an effort to destroy self-sufficient peasant farmers, Stalin ordered the collectivization of all Ukrainian farms. In the ensuing years, a brutal Soviet campaign of confiscations, terror & murder spread through the villages. What food remained was insufficient to support the population. In the resulting famine as many as seven million Ukrainians starved to death.

Execution Dock. unabr. ed. Anne Perry. Read by David Colacci. 1 MP3-CD. (Running Time: 13 hrs.). (William Monk Novel Ser.). 2008. 39.97 (978-1-59335-986-7(1), 9781593359867, Brlnc Audio MP3 Lib); audio compact disk 97.97 (978-1-59600-287-6(5), 9781596002876, BriAudCD Unabrid) Brilliance Audio.
Please enter a Synopsis.

Execution Dock. unabr. ed. Anne Perry. Read by David Colacci. (Running Time: 13 hrs.). (William Monk Ser.). 2009. 39.97 (978-1-59710-913-0(4), 9781597109130, BADLE); 24.99 (978-1-59710-912-3(6), 9781597109123, BAD) Brilliance Audio.

Execution Dock. unabr. ed. Anne Perry. Read by David Colacci. 11 CDs. (Running Time: 13 hrs.). (William Monk Novel Ser.: No. 15). 2009. audio compact disk 39.99 (978-1-59600-286-9(7), 9781596002869, Bril Audio CD Unabri) Brilliance Audio.

Execution Dock. unabr. ed. Anne Perry. Read by David Colacci. 1 MP3-CD. (Running Time: 13 hrs.). (William Monk Novel Ser.: No. 16). 2009. 24.99 (978-1-59335-985-0(3), 9781593359850, Brilliance MP3) Brilliance Audio.

Executioner Box Set 1. Don Pendleton. (Executioner Ser.: Nos. 300-304). 2007. audio compact disk (978-1-59950-432-2(4)) GraphicAudio.

Executioner 300: Warriors Requiem. 2006. audio compact disk 19.99 (978-1-59950-144-4(9)) GraphicAudio.

Executioner 300-309: MP3 CD Long Haul Boxset. Based on a book by Don Pendleton. (ENG.). 2007. 94.99 (978-1-59950-484-1(7)) GraphicAudio.

Executioner 301: Blast Radius. Don Pendleton. (Executioner Ser.: No. 301). 2004. audio compact disk 19.99 (978-1-933059-55-6(9)) GraphicAudio.

Executioner 302: Shadow Search. Don Pendleton. (Executioner Ser.: No. 302). 2004. audio compact disk 19.99 (978-1-933059-63-1(X)) GraphicAudio.

Executioner 303: Sea of Terror. Don Pendleton. (Executioner Ser.: No. 303). 2005. audio compact disk 19.99 (978-1-933059-71-6(0)) GraphicAudio.

Executioner 304: Soviet Specter. Don Pendleton. (Executioner Ser.: No. 304). 2005. audio compact disk 19.99 (978-1-933059-79-2(6)) GraphicAudio.

Executioner 305: Point Position. Don Pendleton. (Executioner Ser.: No. 305). 2005. audio compact disk 19.99 (978-1-933059-87-7(7)) GraphicAudio.

Executioner 306: Mercy Mission. Don Pendleton. (Executioner Ser.: No. 306). 2005. audio compact disk 19.99 (978-1-933059-95-2(8)) GraphicAudio.

Executioner 308: Into the Fire. Don Pendleton. (Executioner Ser.: No. 308). 2006. audio compact disk 19.99 (978-1-59950-029-4(9)); audio compact disk 19.99 (978-1-59950-093-5(0)) GraphicAudio.

Executioner 309: Flames of Fury. Don Pendleton. (Executioner Ser.: No. 309). 2006. audio compact disk 19.99 (978-1-59950-094-2(9)) GraphicAudio.

Executioner 310: Killing Heat. 2006. audio compact disk 19.99 (978-1-59950-128-4(7)) GraphicAudio.

Executioner 311: Night of Knives. 2006. audio compact disk 19.99 (978-1-59950-173-4(2)) GraphicAudio.

Executioner 312: Death Gamble. 2006. audio compact disk 19.99 (978-1-59950-184-0(8)) GraphicAudio.

Executioner 313: Lockdown. Don Pendleton. (Executioner Ser.: No. 313). 2006. audio compact disk 19.99 (978-1-59950-194-9(5)); audio compact disk 19.99 (978-1-59950-199-4(6)) GraphicAudio.

Executioner 314: Lethal Payload. 2007. audio compact disk 19.99 (978-1-59950-202-1(X)) GraphicAudio.

Executioner 315: Agent of Peril. Don Pendleton. (Executioner Ser.: No. 315). 2007. audio compact disk 19.99 (978-1-59950-213-7(5)) GraphicAudio.

Executioner 316: Poison Justice. Don Pendleton. (Executioner Ser.: No. 316). 2007. audio compact disk 19.99 (978-1-59950-224-3(0)) GraphicAudio.

Executioner 317: Hour of Judgement. Don Pendleton. (Executioner Ser.: No. 317). 2007. audio compact disk 19.99 (978-1-59950-145-1(7)) GraphicAudio.

Executioner 317: Hour of Judgment. Don Pendleton. (Executioner Ser.: No. 317). 2007. audio compact disk 19.99 (978-1-59950-317-2(4)) GraphicAudio.

Executioner 318: Code of Resistance. Don Pendleton. (Executioner Ser.: No. 318). 2007. audio compact disk 19.99 (978-1-59950-328-8(X)) GraphicAudio.

Executioner 319: Entry Point. Don Pendleton. (Executioner Ser.: No. 319). 2007. audio compact disk 19.99 (978-1-59950-346-2(8)) GraphicAudio.

Executioner 320: Exit Code. Based on a novel by Don Pendleton. (Executioner Ser.: No. 320). 2007. audio compact disk 19.99 (978-1-59950-373-8(5)) GraphicAudio.

Executioner 321: Suicide Highway. Based on a novel by Don Pendleton. (Executioner Ser.: No. 321). 2008. audio compact disk 19.99 (978-1-59950-392-9(1)) GraphicAudio.

Executioner 322: Time Bomb. Based on a novel by Don Pendleton. (Executioner Ser.: No. 322). 2008. audio compact disk 19.99 (978-1-59950-408-7(1)) GraphicAudio.

Executioner's Song. unabr. ed. Norman Mailer. Read by Jonathan Reese. 12 cass. (Running Time: 18 hrs.). 1998. 96.00 (978-0-7366-4090-9(8), 4598-A); 104.00 (978-0-7366-4091-6(6), 4598-B) Books on Tape.
This classic piece of "New Journalism" follows the last nine months of a convicted murderer's life.

Executive Break (Hypnosis), Vol. 12. Jayne Helle. 1 cass. (Running Time: 10 min.). 1997. 15.00 (978-1-891826-11-5(5)) Introspect.
Gives you a break any time you feel a need to relax during your busy day. Take five minutes & feel refreshed & more confident.

Executive Charisma: Six Steps to Mastering the Art of Leadership. D. A. Benton. 2004. audio compact disk 28.00 (978-1-932378-31-3(6)); 24.00 (978-1-932378-30-6(8)) Pub: A Media Intl. Dist(s): Natl Bk Netwk
Drawing on her years of experiences coaching clients from top companies worldwide, executive development coach D.A. Benton outlines a proven process for acquiring the style, flair, and credibility needed to make it to the top.

Executive Coaching Techniques. Daniel Farb. Created by University of Health Care Staff. (Secrets of a Leadership Coach Ser.). 2004. 49.95 (978-1-932634-00-6(2)) Pub: UnivofHealth. Dist(s): AtlasBooks

Executive Compensation Plans. 1999. bk. 99.00 (ACS-1396) PA Bar Inst.
It is under increasing scrutiny by shareholders, the government & the public. Business must retain & reward key management, & executives seek compensation plans that minimize & taxes while assuring payment in the event of a severance or change in control. These sometimes competing interests assure rapid change & a surplus of difficult issues.

Executive Conference Call Leadership. Byron Van Arsdale. (ENG.). 2005. audio compact disk 399.00 (978-0-9725081-7-9(1)) RossdalePress.

Executive Director's Report: National Association of Evangelicals, 47th Annual Convention, Columbus, Ohio, March 7-9, 1989. Billy A. Melvin. 1 cass. (General Sessions Ser.: No. 111). 1989. 4.25 ea 1-8 tapes.; 4.00 ea. 9 tapes or more. Nat Assn Evan.

Executive Director's Report: Proceedings of the 45th Annual Convention National Association of Evangelicals Buffalo, New York. Read by Billy A. Melvin. 1 cass. (Running Time: 60 min.). 1987. 4.00 (350) Nat Assn Evan.

Executive ESP: Access Your Intuition for Business Success. abr. ed. Gerald Jackson. 1 cass. 1990. 10.95 (978-0-671-68464-8(7), Sound Ideas) S&S Audio.

Executive ESP: Access Your Intuition for Business Success. unabr. ed. Gerald Jackson. Perf. by Gerald Jackson. 6 cass. (Running Time: 5 hrs.). 1989. 59.95 set. (978-0-671-68470-9(1)) S&S Audio.

Executive Intent. unabr. ed. Dale Brown. Read by William Dufris. 2010. audio compact disk 39.99 (978-0-06-162962-4(6), Harper Audio) HarperCollins Pubs.

***Executive Intent.** unabr. ed. Dale Brown. Read by William Dufris. (ENG.). 2010. (978-0-06-199304-6(2), Harper Audio) HarperCollins Pubs.

***Executive Intent: A Novel.** unabr. ed. Dale Brown. Read by William Dufris. (ENG.). 2010. (978-0-06-199303-9(4), Harper Audio) HarperCollins Pubs.

Executive Japanese, Vol. 1. unabr. ed. Hajime Takamizawa. 2 cass. (Running Time: 1 hr. 30 mins.). bk. 85.00 (978-0-88432-400-3(1), AFJ510) J Norton Pubs.
Created specifically for business purposes, this program, which starts at the beginner's level & continues to more advanced levels, can be used by anyone: professionals, students, office workers & others working with the Japanese or living in Japan.

Executive Japanese, Vol. 1-3, Set. Hajime Takamizawa. 2 cass. (Running Time: 2 hrs.). 2001. pap. bk. 225.00 (AFJ500) J Norton Pubs.

Executive Japanese, Vol. 2. unabr. ed. Hajime Takamizawa. 2 cass. (Running Time: 2 hrs.). pap. bk. 85.00 (978-0-88432-401-0(X), AFJ520) J Norton Pubs.

Executive Japanese, Vol. 3. unabr. ed. Hajime Takamizawa. 2 cass. (Running Time: 2 hrs.). bk. 85.00 (978-0-88432-402-7(8), AFJ530) J Norton Pubs.

Executive Memory Guide. abr. ed. Hermine Hilton. 2004. 7.95 (978-0-7435-4690-4(3)) Pub: S&S Audio. Dist(s): S and S Inc

Executive Memory Guide. unabr. ed. Hermine Hilton. Read by Hermine Hilton. 6 cass. (Running Time: 4 hrs. 30 min.). 1988. 59.95 set. (978-0-671-66413-8(1)) S&S Audio.

Executive Orders, Pt. 1. unabr. ed. Tom Clancy. Read by Michael Prichard. 13 cass. (Running Time: 19 hrs. 30 min.). 1996. 104.00 (978-0-7366-3513-4(0), 4152-A) Books on Tape.
"Debt of Honor" ends as Jack Ryan is confirmed as Vice President minutes before a mammoth act of terrorism kills the President, most of his cabinet, all but a few members of Congress, the entire Supreme Court & all of the Joint Chiefs of Staff. Suddenly Ryan is President, which is where "Executive Orders" begins.

Executive Orders, Pt. 2. Tom Clancy. Read by Michael Prichard. 13 cass. (Running Time: 19 hrs. 30 min.). 1996. 104.00 (978-0-7366-3514-1(9), 4152-B) Books on Tape.

Executive Orders, Pt. 3. Tom Clancy. Read by Michael Prichard. 10 cass. (Running Time: 15 hrs.). 1996. 104.00 (978-0-7366-3515-8(7), 4152-C) Books on Tape.

Executive Orders, Set. abr. ed. Tom Clancy. Read by Edward Herrmann. 4 cass. (Running Time: 6 hrs.). (Tom Clancy Ser.). (ENG., 1996. audio compact disk 29.95 (978-0-679-45789-3(5)) Pub: Random Audio Pubg. Dist(s): Random

Executive Orders, Set. abr. ed. Tom Clancy. 4 cass. (Running Time: 6 hrs.). 2000. 25.95 (978-0-375-43696-3(0), Random AudioBks) Random Audio Pubg.

Executive Power. abr. ed. Vince Flynn. Read by Armand Schultz. (Mitch Rapp Ser.: No. 4). 2004. 15.95 (978-0-7435-4691-1(1)) Pub: S&S Audio. Dist(s): S and S Inc

Executive Power. abr. ed. Vince Flynn. Read by Armand Schultz. 5 CDs. (Running Time: 5 hrs. 0 mins. 0 sec.). No. 4. (ENG.). 2006. audio compact disk 14.95 (978-0-7435-5205-9(9), S&S Encore) Pub: S&S Audio. Dist(s): S and S Inc

Executive Power. unabr. ed. Vince Flynn. 9 cass. (Running Time: 13 hrs. 15 min.). (Mitch Rapp Ser.: No. 4). 2003. 83.00 (978-1-4025-5929-7(1)) Recorded Bks.

Executive Power: Use the Greatest Collection of Psychological Strategies to Create an Automatic Advantage in Any Business Situation. unabr. ed. David J. Lieberman. Read by David J. Lieberman. (Running Time: 4 hrs. 30 mins.). (ENG.). 2009. 19.98 (978-1-59659-388-6(1), GildAudio); audio compact disk 19.98 (978-1-59659-272-8(9)) Pub: Gildan Media. Dist(s): HachBkGrp

***Executive Privilege.** unabr. ed. Phillip Margolin. Read by Jonathan Davis. (ENG.). 2008. (978-0-06-163058-3(6)); (978-0-06-163069-9(1)) HarperCollins Pubs.

Executive Privilege. unabr. ed. Phillip Margolin. Read by Jonathan Davis. 10 CDs. (Running Time: 11 hrs.). 2008. audio compact disk 39.95 (978-0-06-155583-1(5), Harper Audio) HarperCollins Pubs.

Executive Report on Strategies in Afghanistan. Compiled by Icon Group International, Inc. Staff. 2007. ring bd. 430.00 (978-0-497-35563-0(9)) Icon Grp.

Executive Report on Strategies in Andorra. Compiled by Icon Group International, Inc. Staff. 2007. ring bd. 430.00 (978-0-497-35564-7(7)) Icon Grp.

Executive Report on Strategies in Anguilla. Compiled by Icon Group International, Inc. Staff. 2007. ring bd. 430.00 (978-0-497-35565-4(5)) Icon Grp.

Executive Report on Strategies in Antigua & Barbuda. Compiled by Icon Group International, Inc. Staff. 2007. ring bd. 430.00 (978-0-497-35566-1(3)) Icon Grp.

Executive Report on Strategies in Aruba. Compiled by Icon Group International, Inc. Staff. 2007. ring bd. 430.00 (978-0-497-35567-8(1)) Icon Grp.

Executive Report on Strategies in Azerbaijan. Compiled by Icon Group International, Inc. Staff. 2007. ring bd. 430.00 (978-0-497-35568-5(X)) Icon Grp.

Executive Report on Strategies in Belarus. Compiled by Icon Group International, Inc. Staff. 2007. ring bd. 430.00 (978-0-497-35569-2(8)) Icon Grp.

Executive Report on Strategies in Bermuda. Compiled by Icon Group International, Inc. Staff. 2007. ring bd. 430.00 (978-0-497-35570-8(1)) Icon Grp.

Executive Report on Strategies in Bhutan. Compiled by Icon Group International, Inc. Staff. 2007. ring bd. 430.00 (978-0-497-35571-5(X)) Icon Grp.

Executive Report on Strategies in Brunei. Compiled by Icon Group International, Inc. Staff. 2007. ring bd. 430.00 (978-0-497-35572-2(8)) Icon Grp.

Executive Report on Strategies in Burundi. Compiled by Icon Group International, Inc. Staff. 2007. ring bd. 430.00 (978-0-497-35573-9(6)) Icon Grp.

Executive Report on Strategies in Christmas Island. Compiled by Icon Group International, Inc. Staff. 2007. ring bd. 430.00 (978-0-497-35574-6(4)) Icon Grp.

Executive Report on Strategies in Cocos (Keeling) Island. Compiled by Icon Group International, Inc. Staff. 2007. ring bd. 430.00 (978-0-497-35575-3(2)) Icon Grp.

Executive Report on Strategies in Comoros. Compiled by Icon Group International, Inc. Staff. 2007. ring bd. 430.00 (978-0-497-35576-0(0)) Icon Grp.

Executive Report on Strategies in Congo (formerly Zaire) Compiled by Icon Group International, Inc. Staff. 2007. ring bd. 430.00 (978-0-497-35577-7(9)) Icon Grp.

Executive Report on Strategies in Cook Islands. Compiled by Icon Group International, Inc. Staff. 2007. ring bd. 430.00 (978-0-497-35578-4(7)) Icon Grp.

Executive Report on Strategies in Cuba. Compiled by Icon Group International, Inc. Staff. 2007. ring bd. 430.00 (978-0-497-35579-1(5)) Icon Grp.

Executive Report on Strategies in Djibouti. Compiled by Icon Group International, Inc. Staff. 2007. ring bd. 430.00 (978-0-497-35580-7(9)) Icon Grp.

Executive Report on Strategies in Dominica. Compiled by Icon Group International, Inc. Staff. 2007. ring bd. 430.00 (978-0-497-35581-4(7)) Icon Grp.

Executive Report on Strategies in Gabon. Compiled by Icon Group International, Inc. Staff. 2007. ring bd. 430.00 (978-0-497-35582-1(5)) Icon Grp.

Executive Report on Strategies in Georgia. Compiled by Icon Group International, Inc. Staff. 2007. ring bd. 430.00 (978-0-497-35583-8(3)) Icon Grp.

Executive Report on Strategies in Gibraltar. Compiled by Icon Group International, Inc. Staff. 2007. ring bd. 430.00 (978-0-497-35584-5(1)) Icon Grp.

Executive Report on Strategies in Greenland. Compiled by Icon Group International, Inc. Staff. 2007. ring bd. 430.00 (978-0-497-35585-2(X)) Icon Grp.

Executive Report on Strategies in Grenada. Compiled by Icon Group International, Inc. Staff. 2007. ring bd. 430.00 (978-0-497-35586-9(8)) Icon Grp.

Executive Report on Strategies in Guinea. Compiled by Icon Group International, Inc. Staff. 2007. ring bd. 430.00 (978-0-497-35587-6(6)) Icon Grp.

Executive Report on Strategies in Guinea-Bissau. Compiled by Icon Group International, Inc. Staff. 2007. ring bd. 430.00 (978-0-497-35588-3(4)) Icon Grp.

Executive Report on Strategies in Guyana. Compiled by Icon Group International, Inc. Staff. 2007. ring bd. 430.00 (978-0-497-35589-0(2)) Icon Grp.

Executive Report on Strategies in Iceland. Compiled by Icon Group International, Inc. Staff. 2007. ring bd. 430.00 (978-0-497-35590-6(6)) Icon Grp.

Executive Report on Strategies in Iran. Compiled by Icon Group International, Inc. Staff. 2007. ring bd. 430.00 (978-0-497-35591-3(4)) Icon Grp.

Executive Report on Strategies in Iraq. Compiled by Icon Group International, Inc. Staff. 2007. ring bd. 430.00 (978-0-497-35592-0(2)) Icon Grp.

Executive Report on Strategies in Kiribati. Compiled by Icon Group International, Inc. Staff. 2007. ring bd. 430.00 (978-0-497-35593-7(0)) Icon Grp.

Executive Report on Strategies in Kyrgyzstan. Compiled by Icon Group International, Inc. Staff. 2007. ring bd. 430.00 (978-0-497-35594-4(9)) Icon Grp.

Executive Report on Strategies in Latvia. Compiled by Icon Group International, Inc. Staff. 2007. ring bd. 430.00 (978-0-497-35595-1(7)) Icon Grp.

Executive Report on Strategies in Lebanon. Compiled by Icon Group International, Inc. Staff. 2007. ring bd. 430.00 (978-0-497-35596-8(5)) Icon Grp.

Executive Report on Strategies in Lesotho. Compiled by Icon Group International, Inc. Staff. 2007. ring bd. 430.00 (978-0-497-35597-5(3)) Icon Grp.

Executive Report on Strategies in Liberia. Compiled by Icon Group International, Inc. Staff. 2007. ring bd. 430.00 (978-0-497-35598-2(1)) Icon Grp.

Executive Report on Strategies in Libya. Compiled by Icon Group International, Inc. Staff. 2007. ring bd. 430.00 (978-0-497-35599-9(X)) Icon Grp.

Executive Report on Strategies in Luxembourg. Compiled by Icon Group International, Inc. Staff. 2007. ring bd. 430.00 (978-0-497-35600-2(7)) Icon Grp.

Executive Report on Strategies in Macau. Compiled by Icon Group International, Inc. Staff. 2007. ring bd. 430.00 (978-0-497-35601-9(5)) Icon Grp.

Executive Report on Strategies in Macedonia. Compiled by Icon Group International, Inc. Staff. 2007. ring bd. 430.00 (978-0-497-35602-6(3)) Icon Grp.

Executive Report on Strategies in Madagascar. Compiled by Icon Group International, Inc. Staff. 2007. ring bd. 430.00 (978-0-497-35603-3(1)) Icon Grp.

Executive Report on Strategies in Malawi. Compiled by Icon Group International, Inc. Staff. 2007. ring bd. 430.00 (978-0-497-35604-0(X)) Icon Grp.

Executive Report on Strategies in Maldives. Compiled by Icon Group International, Inc. Staff. 2007. ring bd. 430.00 (978-0-497-35605-7(8)) Icon Grp.

Executive Report on Strategies in Mali. Compiled by Icon Group International, Inc. Staff. 2007. ring bd. 430.00 (978-0-497-35606-4(6)) Icon Grp.

Executive Report on Strategies in Malta. Compiled by Icon Group International, Inc. Staff. 2007. ring bd. 430.00 (978-0-497-35607-1(4)) Icon Grp.

Executive Report on Strategies in Marshall Islands. Compiled by Icon Group International, Inc. Staff. 2007. ring bd. 430.00 (978-0-497-35608-8(2)) Icon Grp.

Executive Report on Strategies in Mauritania. Compiled by Icon Group International, Inc. Staff. 2007. ring bd. 430.00 (978-0-497-35609-5(0)) Icon Grp.

Executive Report on Strategies in Mauritius. Compiled by Icon Group International, Inc. Staff. 2007. ring bd. 430.00 (978-0-497-35610-1(4)) Icon Grp.

Executive Report on Strategies in Micronesia Federation. Compiled by Icon Group International, Inc. Staff. 2007. ring bd. 430.00 (978-0-497-35611-8(2)) Icon Grp.

Executive Report on Strategies in Moldova. Compiled by Icon Group International, Inc. Staff. 2007. ring bd. 430.00 (978-0-497-35612-5(0)) Icon Grp.

Executive Report on Strategies in Mongolia. Compiled by Icon Group International, Inc. Staff. 2007. ring bd. 430.00 (978-0-497-35613-2(9)) Icon Grp.

Executive Report on Strategies in Montserrat. Compiled by Icon Group International, Inc. Staff. 2007. ring bd. 430.00 (978-0-497-35614-9(7)) Icon Grp.

Executive Report on Strategies in Mozambique. Compiled by Icon Group International, Inc. Staff. 2007. ring bd. 430.00 (978-0-497-35615-6(5)) Icon Grp.

Executive Report on Strategies in Namibia. Compiled by Icon Group International, Inc. Staff. 2007. ring bd. 430.00 (978-0-497-35616-3(3)) Icon Grp.

Executive Report on Strategies in Nauru. Compiled by Icon Group International, Inc. Staff. 2007. ring bd. 430.00 (978-0-497-35617-0(1)) Icon Grp.

Executive Report on Strategies in Nepal. Compiled by Icon Group International, Inc. Staff. 2007. ring bd. 430.00 (978-0-497-35618-7(X)) Icon Grp.

Executive Report on Strategies in New Caledonia. Compiled by Icon Group International, Inc. Staff. 2007. ring bd. 430.00 (978-0-497-35619-4(8)) Icon Grp.

Executive Report on Strategies in Nicaragua. Compiled by Icon Group International, Inc. Staff. 2007. ring bd. 430.00 (978-0-497-35620-0(1)) Icon Grp.

Executive Report on Strategies in Niger. Compiled by Icon Group International, Inc. Staff. 2007. ring bd. 430.00 (978-0-497-35621-7(X)) Icon Grp.

Executive Report on Strategies in Niue. Compiled by Icon Group International, Inc. Staff. 2007. ring bd. 430.00 (978-0-497-35622-4(8)) Icon Grp.

Executive Report on Strategies in Norfolk Island. Compiled by Icon Group International, Inc. Staff. 2007. ring bd. 430.00 (978-0-497-35623-1(6)) Icon Grp.

Executive Report on Strategies in North Korea. Compiled by Icon Group International, Inc. Staff. 2007. ring bd. 430.00 (978-0-497-35624-8(4)) Icon Grp.

Executive Report on Strategies in Oman. Compiled by Icon Group International, Inc. Staff. 2007. ring bd. 430.00 (978-0-497-35625-5(2)) Icon Grp.

Executive Report on Strategies in Palau. Compiled by Icon Group International, Inc. Staff. 2007. ring bd. 430.00 (978-0-497-35626-2(0)) Icon Grp.

Executive Report on Strategies in Papua New Guinea. Compiled by Icon Group International, Inc. Staff. 2007. ring bd. 430.00 (978-0-497-35627-9(9)) Icon Grp.

Executive Report on Strategies in Paraguay. Compiled by Icon Group International, Inc. Staff. 2007. ring bd. 430.00 (978-0-497-35628-6(7)) Icon Grp.

Executive Report on Strategies in Qatar. Compiled by Icon Group International, Inc. Staff. 2007. ring bd. 430.00 (978-0-497-35629-3(5)) Icon Grp.

Executive Report on Strategies in Rwanda. Compiled by Icon Group International, Inc. Staff. 2007. ring bd. 430.00 (978-0-497-35630-9(9)) Icon Grp.

Executive Report on Strategies in Sao Tome E Principe. Compiled by Icon Group International, Inc. Staff. 2007. ring bd. 430.00 (978-0-497-35631-6(7)) Icon Grp.

Executive Report on Strategies in Senegal. Compiled by Icon Group International, Inc. Staff. 2007. ring bd. 430.00 (978-0-497-35632-3(5)) Icon Grp.

Executive Report on Strategies in Serbia & Montenegro. Compiled by Icon Group International, Inc. Staff. 2007. ring bd. 430.00 (978-0-497-35633-0(3)) Icon Grp.

Executive Report on Strategies in Seychelles. Compiled by Icon Group International, Inc. Staff. 2007. ring bd. 430.00 (978-0-497-35634-7(1)) Icon Grp.

Executive Report on Strategies in Sierra Leone. Compiled by Icon Group International, Inc. Staff. 2007. ring bd. 430.00 (978-0-497-35635-4(X)) Icon Grp.

Executive Report on Strategies in Slovenia. Compiled by Icon Group International, Inc. Staff. 2007. ring bd. 430.00 (978-0-497-35636-1(8)) Icon Grp.

Executive Report on Strategies in Solomon Islands. Compiled by Icon Group International, Inc. Staff. 2007. ring bd. 430.00 (978-0-497-35637-8(6)) Icon Grp.

Executive Report on Strategies in Somalia. Compiled by Icon Group International, Inc. Staff. 2007. ring bd. 430.00 (978-0-497-35638-5(4)) Icon Grp.

Executive Report on Strategies in Sri Lanka. Compiled by Icon Group International, Inc. Staff. 2007. ring bd. 430.00 (978-0-497-35639-2(2)) Icon Grp.

Executive Report on Strategies in St. Helena. Compiled by Icon Group International, Inc. Staff. 2007. ring bd. 430.00 (978-0-497-35641-5(4)) Icon Grp.

Executive Report on Strategies in St. Kitts & Nevis. Compiled by Icon Group International, Inc. Staff. 2007. ring bd. 430.00 (978-0-497-35642-2(2)) Icon Grp.

Executive Report on Strategies in St. Lucia. Compiled by Icon Group International, Inc. Staff. 2007. ring bd. 430.00 (978-0-497-35643-9(0)) Icon Grp.

Executive Report on Strategies in St Pierre & Miquelon. Compiled by Icon Group International, Inc. Staff. 2007. ring bd. 430.00 (978-0-497-35640-8(6)) Icon Grp.

Executive Report on Strategies in St. Vincent & the Grenadines. Compiled by Icon Group International, Inc. Staff. 2007. ring bd. 430.00 (978-0-497-35644-6(9)) Icon Grp.

Executive Report on Strategies in Sudan. Compiled by Icon Group International, Inc. Staff. 2007. ring bd. 430.00 (978-0-497-35645-3(7)) Icon Grp.

Executive Report on Strategies in Suriname. Compiled by Icon Group International, Inc. Staff. 2007. ring bd. 430.00 (978-0-497-35646-0(5)) Icon Grp.

Executive Report on Strategies in Swaziland. Compiled by Icon Group International, Inc. Staff. 2007. ring bd. 430.00 (978-0-497-35647-7(3)) Icon Grp.

Executive Report on Strategies in Tajikistan. Compiled by Icon Group International, Inc. Staff. 2007. ring bd. 430.00 (978-0-497-35648-4(1)) Icon Grp.

Executive Report on Strategies in the British Virgin Islands. Compiled by Icon Group International, Inc. Staff. 2007. ring bd. 430.00 (978-0-497-35649-1(X)) Icon Grp.

Executive Report on Strategies in the Cayman Islands. Compiled by Icon Group International, Inc. Staff. 2007. ring bd. 430.00 (978-0-497-35650-7(3)) Icon Grp.

Executive Report on Strategies in the Falkland Islands. Compiled by Icon Group International, Inc. Staff. 2007. ring bd. 430.00 (978-0-497-35651-4(1)) Icon Grp.

Executive Report on Strategies in the Faroe Islands. Compiled by Icon Group International, Inc. Staff. 2007. ring bd. 430.00 (978-0-497-35652-1(X)) Icon Grp.

Executive Report on Strategies in the Gambia. Compiled by Icon Group International, Inc. Staff. 2007. ring bd. 430.00 (978-0-497-35653-8(8)) Icon Grp.

Executive Report on Strategies in the Northern Mariana Island. Compiled by Icon Group International, Inc. Staff. 2007. ring bd. 430.00 (978-0-497-35654-5(6)) Icon Grp.

Executive Report on Strategies in the Pitcairn Islands. Compiled by Icon Group International, Inc. Staff. 2007. ring bd. 430.00 (978-0-497-35655-2(4)) Icon Grp.

Executive Report on Strategies in the United States. Compiled by Icon Group International, Inc. Staff. 2007. ring bd. 430.00 (978-0-497-35656-9(2)) Icon Grp.

Executive Report on Strategies in Togo. Compiled by Icon Group International, Inc. Staff. 2007. ring bd. 430.00 (978-0-497-35657-6(0)) Icon Grp.

Executive Report on Strategies in Tokelau. Compiled by Icon Group International, Inc. Staff. 2007. ring bd. 430.00 (978-0-497-35658-3(9)) Icon Grp.

Executive Report on Strategies in Tonga. Compiled by Icon Group International, Inc. Staff. 2007. ring bd. 430.00 (978-0-497-35659-0(7)) Icon Grp.

Executive Report on Strategies in Tunisia. Compiled by Icon Group International, Inc. Staff. 2007. ring bd. 430.00 (978-0-497-35660-6(0)) Icon Grp.

Executive Report on Strategies in Turkmenistan. Compiled by Icon Group International, Inc. Staff. 2007. ring bd. 430.00 (978-0-497-35661-3(9)) Icon Grp.

Executive Report on Strategies in Turks & Caicos Islands. Compiled by Icon Group International, Inc. Staff. 2007. ring bd. 430.00 (978-0-497-35662-0(7)) Icon Grp.

Executive Report on Strategies in Tuvalu. Compiled by Icon Group International, Inc. Staff. 2007. ring bd. 430.00 (978-0-497-35663-7(5)) Icon Grp.

Executive Report on Strategies in Uganda. Compiled by Icon Group International, Inc. Staff. 2007. ring bd. 430.00 (978-0-497-35664-4(3)) Icon Grp.

Executive Report on Strategies in Vanuatu. Compiled by Icon Group International, Inc. Staff. 2007. ring bd. 430.00 (978-0-497-35665-1(1)) Icon Grp.

Executive Report on Strategies in Wallis & Futuna. Compiled by Icon Group International, Inc. Staff. 2007. ring bd. 430.00 (978-0-497-35666-8(X)) Icon Grp.

Executive Report on Strategies in Western Sahara. Compiled by Icon Group International, Inc. Staff. 2007. ring bd. 430.00 (978-0-497-35667-5(8)) Icon Grp.

Executive Report on Strategies in Yemen. Compiled by Icon Group International, Inc. Staff. 2007. ring bd. 430.00 (978-0-497-35668-2(6)) Icon Grp.

Executive Report on Strategies in Zambia. Compiled by Icon Group International, Inc. Staff. 2007. ring bd. 430.00 (978-0-497-35669-9(4)) Icon Grp.

Executive Report on Strategies in Zimbabwe. Compiled by Icon Group International, Inc. Staff. 2007. ring bd. 430.00 (978-0-497-35670-5(8)) Icon Grp.

Executive Selection. unabr. ed. Robert N. McMurry. 1 cass. (Running Time: 31 min.). 12.95 (13039) J Norton Pubs.
Mr. McMurry is a specialist with his own firm in industrial relations, personnel administration & market research. He discusses in detail how to recruit, screen, select & place qualified incumbents in positions.

Executive Seminar Series. Roy W. Menninger et al. Read by Roy W. Menninger et al. 4 cass. (Running Time: 3 hrs. 4 min.). 1987. 35.00 set. (978-1-56948-006-9(0)) Menninger Clinic.

Executive Speedbriefings: Purchasing CRM Software - the World's Top CRM CEOs on Need to Know Information When Buying Products in Their Industry, Competitive Analysis & More¿. ReedLogic. 1. (Running Time: 2 hrs., 30 mins). 2005. audio compact disk 299.95 (978-1-59701-052-8(9)) Aspatore Bks.
*The goal of this Executive SpeedBriefing is to quickly and efficiently provide you with critical information on purchasing CRM software. Upon completion of viewing the SpeedBriefing, you will have a solid grasp of the big picture concepts you need to understand and be able to speak intelligently with anyone on the topic. The 2.5 hours worth of speeches have been produced on CD-ROM and can be viewed in PowerPoint by any PC-based computer. Each speaker shares their insight for successful strategies and industry expertise in a format similar to a radio address, with graphics displayed in the background - a speech within a presentation. ReedLogic?s proprietary SpeedBriefing process, privately used for years by top C-Level executives (CEO, CFO, CTO, CMO, Partner) from the world?s largest companies, walks you through critical advice provided by industry veterans of current CRM software companies on information they would want to know if purchasing a product from one of their competitors and the industry in general. Each speaker provides an in-depth competitive analysis based on past trends and the prospective future. Topics include:*How to generate growing profits and revenues for your company*The 5 most important things to know about CRM, sales and marketing software*The most useful resources for achieving success in the industry*Due diligence items necessary for choosing the right software provider for your company*The eight pitfalls to avoid when purchasing CRM software*The direct impact of CRM software on your company's bottom line.This CD features speeches and presentations by:1.) Mike Adams, President and CEO: Arial Software2.) Gene Austin, CEO: Convio, Inc. 3.) John Bailye, CEO: Dendrite, Inc. 4.) Arturo Coto, CEO: Inquisite, Inc. 5.) Scott Dorsey, Co-Founder and President: ExactTarget 6.) Keith Eades, Chairman and Senior Managing Partner: SPI 7.) Stephen Gold, President and CEO: Azerity8.) Lauren Goldstein, Director of Account Services and Denise Barnes, COO: Babcock and Jenkins9.) Robert LoCascio, CEO and Chairman: LivePerson10.) Robert Rappaport, President and CEO: Conversive, Inc.*

Executive Speedbriefings: Presenting to an Arbitrator: Winning Strategies to Achieve the Best Decision Possible in Arbitration. Speeches. ReedLogic. 1 CD. (Running Time: 2 hrs., 30 mins). 2005. audio compact disk 99.95 (978-1-59701-053-5(7)) Aspatore Bks.
*The goal of this Executive SpeedBriefing is to quickly and efficiently provide you with critical information on what you need to know when presenting to an arbitrator. Upon completion of viewing the SpeedBriefing, you will have a solid grasp of the big picture concepts you need to understand and be able to speak intelligently with anyone on the topic. The 2.5 hours worth of speeches have been produced on CD-ROM and can be viewed in PowerPoint by any PC-based computer. Each speaker shares their insight for successful strategies and industry expertise in a format similar to a radio address, with graphics displayed in the background - a speech within a presentation. ReedLogic?s proprietary SpeedBriefing process, privately used for years by top C-Level executives (CEO, CFO, CTO, CMO, Partner) from the world?s largest companies, walks you through critical advice provided by attorneys from the top 200 law firms in the country. The speeches walk you through, step-by-step, how an arbitration case proceeds and prepares you for a myriad of situations with no-nonsense advice based on the speakers' wealth of industry experience. Topics include: * Effective methods of proving your case to an arbitrator* The 5 questions your client needs to be prepared to answer* Financial implications of arbitration and saving your client money* The biggest mistakes clients often make and how to prevent them* The 3 most important things to know going into arbitration. The CD features 10-15 Minute speeches and presentations by:1.) Katherine Benesch, Partner; Duane Morris LLP 2.) Robert Berk, Partner; Jones, Skelton & Hochuli, P.L.C. 3.) The Honorable Thomas R. Brett, Of Counsel to Crowe & Dunlevy 4.) Larry W. Bridgesmith, Member; Waller Lansden Dortch & Davis 5.) Scott Cessar, Member in Charge; Eckert Seamans 6.) Richard T. Franch, Partner; Jenner & Block 7.) The Honorable Stewart F. Hancock, Jr., Of Counsel to Hancock Estabrook, LLP 7.) B. Ted Howes, Partner; McDermott Will & Emery 9.) Thomas J. Pryor, Shareholder; Stark & Stark 10.) Adam P. Schiffer, Partner; King & Spalding LLP.*

Executive Success Diet. June Roth & Harvey Roth. 1 cass. 1987. 8.95 (978-0-88684-104-1(6)) Listen USA.
Outlines eight steps to good health & nutrition.

Executive Summary Made Easy. Mervin L. Evans. 2 cass. (Running Time: 2 + 1/2 hr.). 2001. (978-0-914391-52-4(6)) Comm People Pr.

Executive Time Management. Brian S. Tracy. Read by Brian S. Tracy. 2 cass. (Effective Manager Seminar Ser.: No. 10). 95.00 Set, incl. 1-hr. videotape & 2 wkbks., program notes & study guide. (752VD) Nightingale-Conant.
Shows you how to gain two hours a day right now...& more later.

Executive Voice Trainer. unabr. ed. Jeffrey Jacobi. 4 cass. (Running Time: 6 hrs.). 2001. 25.00 (978-1-59040-090-6(9), Phoenix Audio) Pub: Amer Intl Pub. Dist(s): PerseuPGW

Executor. unabr. ed. Jesse Kellerman. Contrib. by Kirby Heyborne. 9 CDs. (Running Time: 11 hrs.). (ENG.). 2010. audio compact disk 39.95 (978-0-14-242773-6(X), PengAudBks) Penguin Grp USA.

Executricks: Or How to Retire While You're Still Working. Stanley Bing. Read by Alan Sklar. (Playaway Adult Nonfiction Ser.). 2008. 39.99 (978-1-60640-690-8(6)) Find a World.

Executricks: Or How to Retire While You're Still Working. unabr. ed. Stanley Bing. Read by Alan Sklar. (Running Time: 4 hrs. 30 mins. 0 sec.). (ENG.). 2008. audio compact disk 24.99 (978-1-4001-0703-2(2)) Pub: Tantor Media. Dist(s): IngramPubServ

Executricks: Or How to Retire While You're Still Working. unabr. ed. Stanley Bing. Read by Alan Sklar. Narrated by Alan Sklar. (Running Time: 4 hrs. 30 mins. 0 sec.). (ENG.). 2008. audio compact disk 19.99 (978-1-4001-5703-7(X)); audio compact disk 49.99 (978-1-4001-3703-9(9)) Pub: Tantor Media. Dist(s): IngramPubServ

Exemplary Novels. Miguel de Cervantes Saavedra. Read by Santiago Munevar. (Running Time: 3 hrs.). 2003. 16.95 (978-1-60083-290-1(3), Audiofy Corp) Iofy Corp.

Exercise & Fitness Motivation: Hypnotherapy. Glenn Harrold. 2007. audio compact disk 17.95 (978-1-901923-72-8(X)) Pub: Divinit Pubing GBR. Dist(s): Bookworld

Exercise & the Mind: Program from the Award Winning Public Radio Series. Hosted by Peter Goodwin. 1 CD. (Running Time: 1 Hour). 2001. audio compact disk 21.95 (978-1-932479-45-4(7), LCM 189) Lichtenstein Creat.
In this hour, we explore Exercise and the Mind. Guests include Olypmic athlete Marla Runyan; Dr. John Ratey, associate clinical professor of psychiatry at Harvard Medical School and author of A User's Guide to the Brain; Dr. James Blumenthal, professor of medical psychology at Duke University Medical Center; Dr. Kristine Yaffe, assistant professor of psychiatry, neurology and epidemiology at the University of California at San Francisco; Dr. Monika Fleshner, assistant professor in the Department of Kinesiology and Applied Physiology and the Center for Neurosciences at the University of Colorado at Boulder. We'll also talk to New York Giants football player Greg Comella about yoga. Our guest host is Dr. Susan Vaughan.

Exercise for Life. Mark L. Hendrickson et al. Frwd. by David Watts. (Health Plus Enrichment Ser.). 1986. pap. bk. 5.95 (978-0-932090-17-1(6)) Health Plus.
Suitable for both young & old alike. Improve strength, endurance, energy & flexibility. Reduce stress & tension. Promote more restful sleep. Increase the efficiency of your heart. Reduce the risk of heart disease. Improve your appearance & self image.

Exercise in Self-Discovery. unabr. ed. Nathaniel Branden. 1 cass. (Running Time: 43 min.). 12.95 (541) J Norton Pubs.
Branden discusses his most well known & innovative therapeutic technique, the "sentence-completion exercise" & explains how an individual may use this technique at home to work on personal problems. Special attention is given to the use of this technique for couples who wish to improve the quality of their communication as well as solve personal problems.

Exercise in Self-Discovery (audio CD) Nathaniel Branden. (ENG.). 2007. audio compact disk 12.95 (978-1-57970-467-4(0), Audio-For) J Norton Pubs.

Exercise Made Easy. Norman J. Caldwell. Read by Norman J. Caldwell. Ed. by Achieve Now Institute Staff. 1 cass. (Running Time: 20 min.). (Better Health Ser.). 1988. 9.97 (978-1-56273-051-2(7)) My Mothers Pub.
Feel the freedom of body movement, enjoy releasing body & mind comfortably picking your exercise release!.

Exercise Motivation. 1998. 24.95 (978-1-58557-002-7(8)) Dynamic Growth.

Exercise Motivation. Bob Griswold. Read by Bob Griswold. 1 CD. (Running Time: 69 mins.). (Love Tapes Ser.). 2005. audio compact disk 15.98 (978-1-55848-151-0(6), Love Tapes) EffectiveMN.
Although we all know the amazing physical and emotional benefits of a consistent exercise program, most of us find it very difficult to get started and/or stay with a program. This program makes it easy! It gets to the root of the problem by helping you reprogram your inner mind to make daily exercise a fun and automatic activity. You'll quickly achieve the health, energy and shape you desire.This CD contains 3 programs. The first is a guided meditation with powerful imagery and techniques for reaching your fitness goals. It also includes two excellent subliminal programs, one with the sound of ocean waves and the other with relaxing original music.

Exercise Motivation. Robert E. Griswold. Read by Robert E. Griswold. 1 cass. 1992. 10.95 (978-1-55848-015-5(3)) EffectiveMN.
Created to make it easy for you to exercise so you can achieve the health, energy & shape your desire.

Exercise Motivation (Subliminal), Vol. 27. Jayne Helle. 1 cass. (Running Time: 28 min.). 1995. 15.00 (978-1-891826-26-9(3)) Introspect.
Let the job of exercise overflow at the subconscious level where the heart & mind work as one.

Exercise with Me: Think Fit While You Workout with Ann Myers. unabr. ed. H. Ann Myers. Read by H. Ann Myers. Music by Paul Conly. 1 cass. (Running Time: 50 min.). 1994. 9.95 (978-1-887011-01-3(3)) Fresh Aer Hlth.
This tape exercises the "mind muscle" while you work your body! It's about making your attitude more positive & exercise more enjoyable. Upbeat music! Use with indoor equipment or outdoors with earphones.

Exercise Your Voice to Health. Sally A. Stefanini. (J). (gr. 3-8). 1994. 21.95 (978-0-937857-49-6(1), 1432) Speech Bin.

Exercises & Action Steps from Breaking Through: Getting Past the Stuck Points in Your Life. Short Stories. Based on a book by Barbara Stanny. 1CD. (Running Time: 70 mins.). 2006. audio compact disk 15.95 (978-1-934126-02-8(0)) Pwful Woman.
This CD is a collection of a dozen exercises which will propel you to affect actual change in your life. Do all 12 exercises and you're sure to gain new insights on your problems and enter the solution zone.

Exercises for Natural Playing Drums. Dave Weckl. audio compact disk 14.95 (978-0-8258-5098-1(3)) Fischer Inc NY.

Exercises in American English Pronunciation: Listening & Pronunciation Drills. Michael F. Sudlow. 1990. 65.00 (978-1-877591-22-8(X)) Excellence Education.

Exercises in English Conversation, Bk. 1, Set. Robert James Dixson. 4 cass. (YA). (gr. 7 up). 1987. 105.00 (978-0-13-294654-4(8), PH6548) Longman.

Exercises in English Conversation, Bk. 2, Set. Robert James Dixson. 4 cass. (YA). (gr. 7 up). 1987. 105.00 (978-0-13-294695-7(5), PH6955) Longman.

Exercises in Flexibility. unabr. ed. Perf. by Eknath Easwaran. 1 cass. (Running Time: 1 hr.). 1991. 7.95 (978-1-58638-533-0(X)) Nilgiri Pr.

Exercises in Spanish. Susanne Vasi & Joseph Tomasino. (C). (gr. 11-12). 1980. 25.00 (978-0-686-70158-3(5), 58639) Prentice ESL.

Exercising Good Relationship Skills- Green Collection: Developing A Child's Relationship Skills. Trenna Daniells. Narrated by Trenna Daniells. (ENG.). (J). 2009. (978-0-918519-69-6(1)) Trenna Prods.

Exercising Good Relationship Skills -the Green Collection: Developing A Child's Relationship Skills. Trenna Daniells. Narrated by Trenna Daniells. (ENG.). (J). 2009. audio compact disk (978-0-918519-65-8(9)) Trenna Prods.

Exercising Spiritual Gifts. Derek Prince. 3 cass. 14.95 Set. (ESGI) Derek Prince.
The Holy Spirit - inbreathed by the resurrected Christ, outpoured by the ascended Christ - manifests Himself in nine supernatural gifts.

Exercising Your Authority. Speeches. Joel Osteen. 1 Cass. (Running Time: 30 Mins.). (J). 2000. 6.00 (978-1-59349-045-4(3), JA0045) J Osteen.

Exercising Your Authority, Pt. 3. Speeches. Joel Osteen. 1 Cass. (Running Time: 30 Mins.). (J). 2000. 6.00 (978-1-59349-047-8(X), JA0047) J Osteen.

Exercising Your Faith, Pt. 4. Speeches. Joel Osteen. 1 Cass. (Running Time: 30 Mins.). (J). 2000. 6.00 (978-1-59349-048-5(8), JA0048) J Osteen.

Exercising Your Soul: Fifteen Minutes a Day to a Spiritual Life. unabr. ed. Gary Jansen. (Running Time: 3 hrs.). (ENG.). 2010. 19.98 (978-1-59659-345-9(8), GildAudio) Pub: Gildan Media. Dist(s): HachBkGrp

Exfoliate. Music by Robert J. Bixby. 1. (Running Time: 45). 2000. audio compact disk 10.00 (978-1-882983-71-1(8)) Pub: March Street Pr. Dist(s): Baker Taylor
Electronic/industrial music with a driving beat.

Exhale (Zen Heart Simplicity) 2005. audio compact disk (978-1-59250-617-0(8)) Gaiam Intl.

Exhausting Our Temperament. Swami Amar Jyoti. 1 cass. 1978. 9.95 (G-5) Truth Consciousness.
Everyone acts; the important part is how we act. Ways to finish our tendencies, barriers to realization of our true nature.

Exhaustion Cure: Up Your Energy from Low to Go in 21 Days. abr. ed. Laura Stack. (Running Time: 4 hrs.). (ENG.). 2008. 10.00 (978-0-7393-5876-4(6)) Pub: Random Audio Pubg. Dist(s): Random

Exhaustion Cure: Up Your Energy from Low to Go in 21 Days. abr. ed. Laura Stack. Read by Laura Stack. (Running Time: 14400 sec.). (ENG.). 2008. audio compact disk 19.95 (978-0-7393-5875-7(8), Random AudioBks) Pub: Random Audio Pubg. Dist(s): Random

Exhaustion Cure: Up Your Energy from Low to Go in 21 Days. unabr. ed. Laura Stack. Read by Bernadette Dunne. 8 CDs. (Running Time: 9 hrs. 15 mins.). 2008. audio compact disk 90.00 (978-1-4159-4813-2(5), BksonTape) Pub: Random Audio Pubg. Dist(s): Random
Feeling fatigued? Wish you could have more get-up-and-go? If you're like millions of Americans, you get home from a long day with barely enough energy to lift the remote control. But with Laura Stack's comprehensive plan, you can regain your vitality in just three weeks. Let The Productivity Pro(r) help you eliminate the "energy bandits" from all aspects of your life - from your diet and your work schedule to your environment and your relationships - so you can start living in a way that will boost your energy. Focusing on simple changes that make a huge difference, The Exhaustion Cure presents manageable ways to: Cut down on "energy bandits" and fill up on "energy boosters." Stop relying on caffeine, cigarettes and other substances to keep you going. Avoid letting negative situations or people control your thoughts and actions. Sneak in time for fitness during the busiest days. Accomplish your goals and find more time to devote to your family.

Exhibition of Radio Art. 1 cass. (Running Time: 60 min.). 10.95 (OP-78-04-27, HarperThor) HarpC GBR.

***ExhibitorEd: Tips, Tools & Action Plans.** Marlys Arnold. (ENG.). 2010. ring bd. 247.00 (978-0-9712905-3-7(9)) Tiff Harb Prod.

Exhortation on Faith. David T. Demola. 1 cass. 4.00 (2-140) Faith Fellow Min.

Exile. Allan Folsom. 2004. audio compact disk 160.00 (978-1-4159-0336-0(0)) Books on Tape.

Exile. Denise Mina. Read by Katy Anderson. 11 CDs. (Running Time: 12 hrs. 49 mins.). (Isis (CDs) Ser.). (J). 2005. audio compact disk 99.95 (978-0-7531-2426-0(2)) Pub: ISIS Lrg Prnt GBR. Dist(s): Ulverscroft US

Exile. abr. ed. Aaron Allston. Read by Marc Thompson. (Running Time: 21600 sec.). (Star Wars Ser.). (ENG.). 2007. audio compact disk 29.95 (978-0-7393-2398-4(9), Random AudioBks) Pub: Random Audio Pubg. Dist(s): Random

Exile. abr. ed. Richard North Patterson. Read by Dennis Boutsikaris. (Running Time: 7 hrs. 0 mins. 0 sec.). (ENG.). 2007. audio compact disk 29.95 (978-1-4272-0059-4(9)) Pub: Macmill Audio. Dist(s): Macmillan

***Exile.** abr. ed. Richard North Patterson. (Running Time: 7 hrs. 0 mins. 0 sec.). (ENG.). 2011. audio compact disk 14.99 (978-1-4272-1191-0(4)) Pub: Macmill Audio. Dist(s): Macmillan

Exile. unabr. ed. Allan Folsom. 2004. 136.00 (978-1-4159-0335-3(2)) Books on Tape.

Exile. unabr. ed. Denise Mina. 9 cass. (Running Time: 12 hrs. 49 mins.). (Isis Cassettes Ser.). (J). 2005. 76.95 (978-0-7531-2013-2(5)) Pub: ISIS Lrg Prnt GBR. Dist(s): Ulverscroft US

Exile. unabr. ed. Richard North Patterson. Read by Dennis Boutsikaris. 17 CDs. (Running Time: 21 hrs. 0 mins. 0 sec.). (ENG.). 2007. audio compact disk 59.95 (978-1-4272-0061-7(0)) Pub: Macmill Audio. Dist(s): Macmillan

Exiled. (StarLiner Boundless Ser.). 2000. audio compact disk 10.99 (978-0-9705222-0-7(7)) Starliner.

Exiles see Poetry & Voice of Marilyn Hacker

Exile's Return see Robert Lowell: A Reading

Exile's Return: Andrei Codrescu in Revolutionary Romania. Andrei Codrescu. Read by Andrei Codrescu. 1 cass. (Running Time: 1 hr.). 10.95 (FO-060, HarperThor) HarpC GBR.

Existence; Astrology: Fact or Fiction. Ann Ree Colton & Jonathan Murro. 1 cass. 7.95 A R Colton Fnd.

Existence, Consciousness & Bliss. Swami Amar Jyoti. 1 cass. 1994. 9.95 (R-109) Truth Consciousness.
Sat-Chit-Ananda-attributes of the Ultimate. The true purpose of the Sadguru. Do not grieve-be awakened.

Existential Psychology. unabr. ed. Viktor E. Frankl. 2 cass. 1987. 18.00 set. (978-1-56964-764-6(X), A0317-87) Sound Photosyn.
The well respected psychologist in a rare statement.

Existential Vacuum: A Challenge to Psychiatry. unabr. ed. Viktor E. Frankl. 1 cass. (Running Time: 1 hr. 24 min.). 1969. 11.00 (09101) Big Sur Tapes.
Describes the feeling of emptiness & loss of faith that plagues us in this age of affluence & success, & suggests how psychiatry can deal with the resulting vacuum in human existence.

Existentialism. Robert Stone. 1 cass. 1983. 10.00 (978-0-938137-00-9(X)) Listen & Learn.
Discusses the major contributions, reviews famous works & philosophical thoughts - Oedipus the King, Macbeth, Hamlet, War & Peace, the Plague, existence precedes essence, life has no inherent meaning, man has freedom of choice, personal myth, awareness, goals of psychotherapy.

Existentialist Writing. Norman Mailer. Read by Norman Mailer. 1 cass. (Running Time: 39 min.). 1963. 12.95 (23046) J Norton Pubs.
Mailer attempts to convey the emotional implications of the existentialist position through excerpts from his work. Mailer reads from a Hassidic story by Buber to illustrate that our society is making a mistaken attempt to deal with the mystical on a logical positivist basis.

Existing Light. unabr. ed. Madeline De Frees. Read by Madeline DeFrees. 1 cass. (Running Time: 45 min.). (Watershed Tapes of Contemporary Poetry). 12.95 (23617) J Norton Pubs.

Exit A. unabr. ed. Anthony Swofford. 2007. 23.95 (978-0-7435-6351-2(4), Audioworks) Pub: S&S Audio. Dist(s): S and S Inc

Exit Ghost. unabr. ed. Philip Roth. Narrated by George Guidall. (Running Time: 27900 sec.). 2007. audio compact disk 34.99 (978-1-4281-6516-8(9)) Recorded Bks.

Exit Lines. unabr. ed. Reginald Hill. Read by Colin Buchanan. 8 cass. (Running Time: 12 hrs.). (Dalziel & Pascoe Ser.). 2000. 69.95 (978-0-7540-0525-4(9), CAB 1948) Pub: Chivers Audio Bks GBR. Dist(s): AudioGO
Three old men die on a stormy November night: one by deliberate violence, one in a road accident & one by unknown cause.

Exit Lines. unabr. ed. Reginald Hill. Read by Colin Buchanan. 8 CDs. (Running Time: 12 hrs.). (Dalziel & Pascoe Ser.). 2000. audio compact disk 79.95 (978-0-7540-5389-7(X), CCD 080) Pub: Chivers Audio Bks GBR. Dist(s): AudioGO
Three old men die on a stormy November night: one by deliberate violence, one in a road accident & the other by an unknown cause. But when the dying words of the accident victim suggest that a drunken Superintendent Dalziel had been behind the wheel, the integrity of the entire Mid-Yorkshire CID is called into question.

Exit Music. abr. ed. Ian Rankin. Read by James MacPherson. (Running Time: 7 hrs. 30 mins.). (ENG.). 2008. 24.98 (978-1-60024-455-1(6)) Pub: Hachet Audio. Dist(s): HachBkGrp

Exit Wounds. J. A. Jance. Read by Debra Monk. (Joanna Brady Mystery Ser.). 1975. 9.99 (978-0-06-074350-5(6)); audio compact disk 9.99 (978-0-06-074349-9(2)) HarperCollins Pubs.

***Exit Wounds.** abr. ed. J. A. Jance. Read by Debra Monk. (ENG.). 2004. (978-0-06-074635-3(1), Harper Audio); (978-0-06-079971-7(4), Harper Audio) HarperCollins Pubs.

Exito Mas Grande del Mundo. Og Mandino. 1 cass. (Running Time: 60 min.).Tr. of Greatest Success in the World. (SPA.). 2003. 12.00 (978-1-931059-06-0(3)) Taller del Exito.

Exito y Abundancia para la Mujer. Irene Martinez.Tr. of Success & Abundance for the Woman of Today. (SPA.). 2009. audio compact disk 12.95 (978-0-9823920-0-3(1)) Mestiza Prods.

Exode, Set. Henri Amouroux. 2 cass. (Francais sous l'occupation Ser.). (FRE.). 26.95 (1222-RF) Olivia & Hill.
A portrait of Petain.

Exodus. Josepha Sherman & Susan Schwartz. Read by Boyd Gaines. (Running Time: 4 hrs.). 2007. 19.95 (978-1-60083-437-0(X), Audiofy Corp) Iofy Corp.

Exodus. abr. ed. Josepha Sherman & Susan Schwartz. Read by Boyd Gaines. 2004. 14.95 (978-0-7435-3990-6(7)) Pub: S&S Audio. Dist(s): S and S Inc

Exodus. unabr. ed. 5 cass. (Running Time: 7 hrs. 30 mins.). (Little Rock Scripture Study Ser.). 2002. 65.00 (978-0-8146-7604-2(9)) Liturgical Pr.
Lent is the perfect time to study the central themes of liberation, wilderness, Passover, covenant and God's dwelling. Israel's journey from bondage to freedom invites you to examine your own faith journey.

Exodus. unabr. ed. Leon Uris. Read by Dan Lazar. 9 cass. (Running Time: 13 hrs. 30 min.). 1979. 72.00 (978-0-7366-0308-9(5), 1297-A); 64.00 (1297-B) Books on Tape.
The time is 1946; the British on Cyprus have set up a more "humane" concentration camp for the Jewish refugees of World War II. Agents of the Mussad Aliyah Bet are determined to set their people free.

Exodus: A Biblical Interpretation. Concept by Ermance Rejebian. (ENG.). 2007. 5.99 (978-1-60339-135-1(5)); audio compact disk 5.99 (978-1-60339-136-8(3)) Listenr Digest.

Exodus: Ambivalence & Wholeness. Read by John Van Eenwyk. 1 cass. (Running Time: 90 min.). (Patterns of Divinity Ser.: No. 8). 1988. 10.95 (978-0-7822-0317-2(5), 308) C G Jung IL.

Exodus, A Jet Tour Through. Dan Corner. 1 cass. 3.00 (101) Evang Outreach.

Exodus Commentary: Verse by verse with Chuck Missler. Chuck Missler. 1 CD Rom. (Running Time: 24 hours aprox). (Chuck Missler Commentaries). 2000. cd-rom 39.95 (978-1-57821-107-4(7)) Koinonia Hse.
The Book of Exodus is the bedrock of God's plan of redemption and is seen as a 'type' of the early church. It is also an adventure of discovery, since the dramatic narrative is laced with numerous hidden messages in the form of microcodes and macrocodes, each anticipating the New Testament climax.

Exodus I. (LifeLight Bible Studies: Course 10). 13.95 (20-2292) Concordia.

***Exodus Quest.** unabr. ed. Will Adams. Narrated by David Colacci. (Running Time: 12 hrs. 0 mins.). (Daniel Knox Ser.). 2010. 17.99 (978-1-4001-8700-3(1)); 34.99 (978-1-4001-9700-2(7)); 24.99 (978-1-4001-6700-5(0)); audio compact disk 34.99 (978-1-4001-1700-0(3)); audio compact disk 69.99 (978-1-4001-4700-7(X)) Pub: Tantor Media. Dist(s): IngramPubServ

Exodus XV. Perf. by Lori Wilke. 1 cass. (Running Time: 5 min.). 1988. 9.98 Sound track. (978-1-891916-20-5(3)) Spirit To Spirit.

Exodus 2. (LifeLight Bible Studies: Course 11). bk. & stu. ed. 13.95 (978-0-570-09281-0(7), 20-2296) Concordia.

Exorcism & Magic: Acts 19:13-20. Ed Young. 2000. 4.95 (978-0-7417-2244-7(5), 1244) Win Walk.

Exorcism & the Christ; Stewardship. Jonathan Murro & Ann Ree Colton. 1 cass. 7.95 A R Colton Fnd.
Discusses the goal of God-Realization.

Exorcist. abr. ed. William Peter Blatty. Read by William Peter Blatty. Prod. by Brad Fregger. 4 cass. (Running Time: 6 hrs. 12 min.). 1995. 24.00 Set. (978-1-886392-03-8(X), Parrot Bks) Walberg Pubng.
The number one modern classic of horror fiction, this audiobook is a riveting narrative that will thrill readers everywhere. A story of the struggle of the ordinary against extraordinary evil.

Exorcist. unabr. ed. William Peter Blatty. Read by William Peter Blatty. 8 cass. (Running Time: 12 hrs.). 2001. 40.00 (978-1-59040-056-2(9), Phoenix Audio) Pub: Amer Intl Pub. Dist(s): PerseuPGW
A terrifying battle with an obscene, unspeakable evil that must end in victory... or madness and death.

Exorcist, Set. unabr. ed. William Peter Blatty. Read by William Peter Blatty. 8 cass. 1999. 36.00 (FS9-51204) Highsmith.

Exotic. unabr. ed. Carter Brown. Narrated by Sean Mangan. 3 cass. (Running Time: 4 hrs.). 2001. 28.00 (978-1-74030-366-8(0)) Pub: Bolinda Pubng AUS. Dist(s): Bolinda Pub Inc

Exotic Dances of Tonga Booklet. Vicki Corona. (Celebrate the Cultures Ser.: II-24-B). 1989. pap. bk. 24.95 (978-1-58513-153-2(9)) Dance Fantasy.

Exotic Dances of Tonga w/Music CD & Dance Demo DVD. Vicki Corona. Vicki Corona. (Celebrate the Cultures Ser.: 2-24C). 1989. pap. bk. 32.95 (978-1-58513-109-0(7)) Dance Fantasy.

Exotica: World Music Divas. 1 cass., 1 CD. 7.18 (RCA 68988); audio compact disk 9.58 CD Jewel box. (RCA 68988) NewSound.

Expand Your Mind Power: Develop an Amazing Memory. Kreskin. 1 cass. (Running Time: 55 min.). 8.95 (T-81) Listen USA.

Expanded Intuition Training Tape Series. Thomas R. Condon. 6 cass. 69.95 set, incl. wkbk. (978-1-884305-77-1(6)) Changeworks.
The tapes & workbook will teach you how to: Identify your own "intuitive style;" Allow intuitions to come through for you; Know which signals to look for & trust; Ask questions & receive guidance; Have intuitions on demand; Get quality information for any purpose.

Expanding Consciousness. Swami Amar Jyoti. 1 cass. (Satsangs of Swami Amar Jyoti Ser.). 1996. 9.95 (M-101) Truth Consciousness.
Breaking out of ignorance, moving from understanding to insight & true intelligence. Reassessing our lives. Qualifications on the spiritual path.

Expanding Consciousness, Vol. 1. Sage. 1996. (978-1-890808-01-3(6)) AhhhMuse.

Expanding Horizons. abr. ed. James A. Long. 5 cass. (Running Time: 7 hrs. 30 min.). 1990. 30.00 (978-0-911500-49-3(9)) Theos U Pr.
Widely used as an introduction to theosophy, it features short essays & roundtable talks with varying age groups. It presents practical insights on those basic questions which go to the root of the human predicament.

Expanding Human Intelligence. 1 cass. (Running Time: 1 hr.). 11.95 (ME-84-08-13, HarperThor) HarpC GBR.

Expanding in Light. Swami Amar Jyoti. 1 cass. Orig. Title: Darkness to Light. 1982. 9.95 (R-43) Truth Consciousness.
Groping in our darkness we don't see earth is already the Kingdom of God. Nitya Lila, dancing in ecstasy in His joyful creation.

Expanding into Cosmic Living. Swami Amar Jyoti. 1 cass. 1995. 9.95 (A-48) Truth Consciousness.
Swadharma - living one's part for the good of all-forms the basis for Rta Dharma (cosmic order).

Expanding Tactics for Listening. 2nd rev. ed. Jack C. Richards. 2003. audio compact disk 54.95 (978-0-19-437542-9(0)) OUP.

Expanding Technique Through Pieces. John Griggs. 1998. pap. bk. 17.95 (978-0-7866-1685-5(7), 95709BCD) Mel Bay.

Expanding Your Comfort Zone: NACADA Webinar Series 05. Featuring Blane Harding. (ENG.). 2007. audio compact disk 140.00 (978-1-935140-47-4(7)) Nat Acad Adv.

Expanding Your Creativity see Creative Problem Solving

Expanding Your Faith. Creflo A. Dollar. 20.00 (978-1-59089-005-9(1)) Pub: Creflo Dollar. Dist(s): STL Dist NA

Expanding Your Faith's Capacity: Creating an Inner Image. Creflo A. Dollar. 2008. audio compact disk 21.00 (978-1-59944-723-0(1)) Creflo Dollar.

Expanding Your Nonprofit Organization Skills: An Audio Survey Course. unabr. ed. Arnold J. Olenick. Read by Donald Wescott et al. 6 cass. (Running Time: 3 hrs. 33 min.). Dramatization. 1995. 39.95 Set. (978-1-880561-01-0(8)) CashFlow Bks.
A self-study course for nonprofit administrators & board members, covering all aspects of establishing, organizing, planning & managing the activities of a nonprofit organization. Includes legal & tax aspects, fund raising, personnel policies, planning, budgeting & accounting, via interviews & enactments.

Expanding Zero. 1 cass. (Running Time: 1 hr.). 14.95 (CBC670) MMI Corp.
Dramatized talk by CBC-TV Science producer covers a journey from the infinitely small to the infinitely big.

Expansion of Elizabethan England. unabr. ed. A. L. Rowse. Read by Jill Masters. 15 cass. (Running Time: 22 hrs. 30 min.). 1985. 120.00 (978-0-7366-0590-8(8), 1557) Books on Tape.
Elizabeth ruled from 1558 to 1603. It is moot whether she inspired the tremendous increase in national energy or whether it would have occurred without her.

Expect a Miracle. 1999. 11.98 (978-0-633-03940-0(3)) LifeWay Christian.

Expect a Miracle: The Miraculous Things That Happen to Ordinary People. abr. ed. Dan Wakefield. Read by Dan Wakefield. 2 cass. (Running Time: 3 hrs.). 1996. 17.95 (978-1-57453-040-7(2), 330094) Audio Lit.

Expect a Miracle: The Miraculous Things That Happen to Ordinary People. unabr. ed. Dan Wakefield. Narrated by Robert Sevra. 8 cass. (Running Time: 10 hrs. 45 mins.). 70.00 (978-0-7887-0463-5(X), 94656E7) Recorded Bks.
Includes miracle stories ranging from the birth of a child to the gift of friendship, along with testaments from celebrities such as singer Judy Collins & best-selling author Michael Crichton. Available to libraries only.

Expect a Miracle: Unwavering Faith through Fetal Surgery. Andrea Merkord. 2007. audio compact disk 34.99 (978-1-60247-388-1(9)) Tate Pubng.

Expect a Miracle Cassette Kit. 1999. 54.95 (978-0-633-03936-3(5)) LifeWay Christian.

Expect a Miracle Cd Kit. 1999. audio compact disk 59.95 (978-0-633-03935-6(7)) LifeWay Christian.

Expect a Miracle Cd Promo Pak. 1999. audio compact disk 12.00 (978-0-633-03933-2(0)) LifeWay Christian.

Expect a Miracle Choral Cd. 1999. audio compact disk 16.98 (978-0-633-03939-4(X)) LifeWay Christian.

Expect a Miracle Stereo/Split Acc Cassette) 1999. 40.00 (978-0-633-03938-7(1)) LifeWay Christian.

Expect a Miracle Stereo/Split Acc Cd. 1999. audio compact disk 50.00 (978-0-633-03937-0(3)) LifeWay Christian.

Expect Miracles: The Missing Secret to Astounding Success. unabr. ed. Joe Vitale, Jr.. Read by Joe Vitale, Jr. (Running Time: 4 hrs.). (ENG.). 2008. 24.98 (978-1-59659-297-1(4), GildAudio) Pub: Gildan Media. Dist(s): HachBkGrp

Expect Miracles: The Missing Secret to Astounding Success. unabr. ed. Joe Vitale. Read by Joe Vitale. (Running Time: 5 hrs.). (ENG.). 2009. audio compact disk 29.98 (978-1-59659-282-7(6), GildAudio) Pub: Gildan Media. Dist(s): HachBkGrp

Expect the Impossible. Contrib. by Stellar Kart & Otto Price. Prod. by Ian Eskelin. 2008. audio compact disk 13.99 (978-5-557-47082-7(4), Word Records) Word Enter.

Expectant Father: Facts, Tips, & Advice for Dads-to-Be. Armin Brott & Jennifer Ash. 9 CDs. (Running Time: 10 hrs.). (New Father Ser.). (ENG.). 2008. audio compact disk 36.95 (978-0-7892-0967-2(5)) Pub: Abbeville Pr. Dist(s): Perseus Dist

Expectation Gap Series: SASs 53-61. Dave Dennis & John E. Ellingsen. 12 cass. (Running Time: 36 hrs.). 269.00 Set, incl. textbks. & 3 quizzers. (CPE2120) Bisk Educ.
The most comprehensive changes in auditing standards to come about in 40 years are analyzed.

Expectations in Marriage: Ways to Deal with Disappointment & Anger in Loving Relationships. William G. DeFoore. (ENG.). 2005. audio compact disk 19.99 (978-0-9785244-5-6(4)) Halcyon Life.

Expected One: A Novel. abr. ed. Kathleen McGowan, pseud. Read by Linda Emond. (Magdalene Line Ser.: Bk. 1). 2006. 17.95 (978-0-7435-6523-3(1), Audioworks) Pub: S&S Audio. Dist(s): S and S Inc

Expected One: A Novel. unabr. ed. Kathleen McGowan, pseud. Read by Linda Stephens. 15 cass. (Running Time: 18 hrs.). (Magdalene Line Ser.: Bk. 1). 2006. 109.75 (978-1-4281-1279-7(0)); audio compact disk 119.75 (978-1-4281-1281-0(2)) Recorded Bks.
Kathleen McGowan has spent more than 20 years researching the life of Mary Magdalene and her descendants, inspiring Kathleen to write this fictionalized account of her own experiences. The writings of Mary Magdalene have been hidden for more than two thousand years, protected by supernatural forces. Only The Expected One can uncover the ancient scrolls, revealing secrets of early Christianity, of the heroes and antiheroes of the Bible, and of Christ himself. It is a secret many have died to protect.

Expected One: A Novel. unabr. ed. Kathleen McGowan, pseud. Read by Linda Emond. (Magdalene Line Ser.: Bk. 1). 2006. 29.95 (978-0-7435-6385-7(9), Audioworks) Pub: S&S Audio. Dist(s): S and S Inc

Expected One: A Novel. unabr. ed. Kathleen McGowan, pseud. Read by Linda Emond. (Running Time: 17 hrs. 30 mins. 0 sec.). (Magdalene Line Ser.: Bk. 1). 2008. audio compact disk 21.99 (978-0-7435-8163-9(6)) Pub: S&S Audio. Dist(s): S and S Inc

Expedition! abr. ed. Dana Fuller Ross, pseud. Read by Sambrook Erikson. 4 vols. (Wagons West: Bk. 2). 2003. (978-1-58807-643-4(1)); audio compact disk 30.00 (978-1-58807-399-0(8)); audio compact disk (978-1-58807-631-1(8)) Am Pubng Inc.

Expedition! abr. ed. Dana Fuller Ross, pseud. Read by Sambrook Erickson. 4 vols. (Running Time: 6 hrs.). (Wagons West: Bk. 2). 2003. 25.00 (978-1-58807-143-9(X)) Am Pubng Inc.
Once there was a wilderness so vast no white man had ever crossed it. Then Lewis and Clark became the pathfinders for a nation, opening up a land of possibilities that called with a siren's song to brave young men and women looking for a dream. In the heart of this majestic land, Clay and his Sioux wife, Shining Moon, lead a perilous expedition up the Yellowstone River. While Clay and his band confront fierce storms and the plots of adversaries, brother Jeff Holt heads back east on a treacherous quest; impetuous young cousin Ned takes to the high seas; and in the east, Melissa Holt struggles against the unscrupulous business man who means to have her.

Expedition. unabr. ed. Loren Robinson. Read by Maynard Villers. 6 cass. (Running Time: 7 hrs. 30 min.). 1995. 39.95 (978-1-55686-635-7(6)) Books in Motion.
In the year 2007, two astronauts & their spaceship, Charger II, disappear on re-entry after a routine mission. In 2009 evidence is discovered that reveals they were thrust back in time.

Expedition of Humphrey Clinker. unabr. ed. Tobias George Smollett. Narrated by Flo Gibson. 11 cass. (Running Time: 16 hrs.). 2003. 34.95 (978-1-55685-716-4(0)) Audio Bk Con.
Considered Smollett's finest book, this collection of letters from members of the Bramble household takes them through England and Scotland with vivid descriptions. Their observations are intriguing and often witty.

***Expeditionary Man: The Adventure a Man Wants, the Leader His Family Needs.** unabr. ed. Rich Wagner. (Running Time: 6 hrs. 51 mins. 0 sec.). (ENG.). 2009. 18.99 (978-0-310-77207-1(9)) Zondervan.

Expendable Spy. Jack D. Hunter. Narrated by Brian Emerson. (Running Time: 8 hrs. 30 mins.). (C). 2000. 27.95 (978-1-59912-657-9(5)) Iofy Corp.

Expendable Spy. unabr. ed. Jack D. Hunter. Read by Brian Emerson. 6 cass. (Running Time: 8 hrs. 30 mins.). 1997. 44.95 (978-0-7861-1160-2(7), 1931) Blckstn Audio.
A hair-raising novel of an audacious American who discovers a secret so big & so appalling that his own intelligence office orders his execution.

Experience high Self-esteem. Branden. 2004. 7.95 (978-0-7435-4692-8(X)) Pub: S&S Audio. Dist(s): S and S Inc

Experience His Presence: The Best from a New Generation of Hosanna! Music. Contrib. by Don Moen. 2007. audio compact disk 12.99 (978-5-557-60929-6(6)) Integrity Music.

Experience in Sound & Drama: A Novel of the Earth's Last Days. adpt. ed. Tim LaHaye & Jerry B. Jenkins. 4 CDs. (Running Time: 4 hrs.). (Left Behind Ser.: Bk. 1). (ENG., 1999. audio compact disk 19.99 (978-0-8423-5146-1(9)) Tyndale Hse.

Experience Joy: Guided Meditation. Concept by Vicky Thurlow. Voice by Vicky Thurlow. (ENG.). 2008. audio compact disk 14.95 (978-0-9817055-0-7(2)) DVT Invest.

Experience of A Course in Miracles. Kenneth Wapnick. 1 CD. (Running Time: 11 hrs. 19 mins. 55 secs.). 2007. 54.00 (978-1-59142-308-9(2), 3m56) Foun Miracles.

Experience of A Course in Miracles: A Commentary on the section, Development of Trust. Kenneth Wapnick. 10 CDs. 2007. audio compact disk 61.00 (978-1-59142-300-3(7), CD56) Foun Miracles.

Experience of Actual Time in the Rorschach Test. unabr. ed. Samuel J. Beck. 1 cass. (Running Time: 26 min.). 1963. (29239) J Norton Pubs.
An explanation & clarification of the concept derived from Rorschach's Experience Balance. Experience Actual is the test's technique for penetrating to a person's emotional resources in their full breadth, depth, & intensities.

Experience of Christ. Benedict J. Groeschel. 1 cass. (Running Time: 1 hr. 24 min.). 1996. 9.95 (TAH367) Alba Hse Comns.
Fr. Groeschel addresses what it means to experience Christ with faith, & how that experience is defined by cultural & other factors. We must be ready to encourage the diversity of experience that welcomes all.

Experience of Enlightenment. Swami Jyotirmayananda. Read by Swami Jyotirmayananda. 1 cass. (Running Time: 60 min.). 12.99 (737) Yoga Res Foun.

Experience of Gnosis: Self-Knowledge [illegible]owledge of God. Stephan Hoeller. 1 cass. 1999. (40027) Big Sur [illegible]
1993 Los Angeles.

Experience of Hospitalization: Its Implications for a Pastoral Ministry. D. Middleton et al. 1986. 10.80 (0405) Assn Prof Chaplains.

Experience of Religious Faith-Moral Component of Religious Response. Benedict J. Groeschel. 2 cass. (Running Time: 1 hr. 56 min.). 1996. 18.95 Set. (TAH368) Alba Hse Comns.
We must reclaim the sense of faith as mystery to dispel the trends towards minimalism, skepticism & rationalism. The priest is challenged today to live

in this way so that his pastoral activity can result in the careful formation of the faithful's consciences.

Experience the Peace. 1 cass. (Running Time: 1 hr.). 9.95 (M1) Nada Prodns. *Guided meditation with Leela Mata to heal yourself.*

Experience the Power of Grace. Cheryl Richardson. 4 CDs. 2006. audio compact disk 29.95 (978-1-4019-1114-0(5)) Hay House.

Experience Yoga Nidra: Guided Deep Relaxation. Swami Janakananda Saraswati. Voice by Swami Janakananda Saraswati. 1 CD. (Running Time: 73 mins). 1996. audio compact disk 20.00 (978-91-630-9488-0(6)) Pub: Bindu Pubs SWE. Dist(s): Grnlf Bk Grp
Two genuine relaxation methods from the Nyasa Tantra, 20 minutes and 45 minutes - and a piece of music. 20 page information booklet. Swami Janakananda guides you into a deep relaxation of body and mind. He also uses the tantric mantras and visual symbols to awaken and harmonize the chakras. With nature sounds and music in the background. Roop Verma, on sitar, is the first musician to record the chakras' ancient music symbols. ?Yoga Nidra is much more than a deep relaxation; it is a total experience that touches and awakens all parts of your being.? Swami Janakananda.

Experience Your Greatness III: Give Yourself Permission to Forgive. Gary Quinn. Ed. by Elizabeth Day. 2004. audio compact disk 17.95 (978-0-9745943-0-9(X)) Pub: DayBue Pubg. Dist(s): Grnlf Bk Grp

Experience Your Greatness IV: Give Yourself Permission to Trust. Gary Quinn. Ed. by Elizabeth Day. 1. 2004. audio compact disk (978-0-9745943-1-6(8)) DayBue Pubg.
Guided Meditation.

Experiences. unabr. collector's ed. Arnold J. Toynbee. Read by David Case. 11 cass. (Running Time: 16 hrs. 30 min.). 1991. 88.00 (978-0-7366-1917-2(8), 2741) Books on Tape.
Published on the author's 80th birthday, Experiences is the sequel to Acquaintances. In the first & third parts of Experiences, the author writes, "I am the subject as well as the narrator. In the second part I am an observer & an appraiser, but not of particular persons, as I am in Acquaintances. This second part of the present book is a survey of, & commentary on human affairs in my lifetime." That lifetime was remarkable - the advances of medical science & the unprecedented rapidity of change in science, technology, education & public affairs. An observer such as Toynbee has had more change to observe than in any previous generation, & because of his outstanding work as a historian, the perspective he brings is unique & incomparably valuable.

Experiences of the McWillamses with Membranous Croup see $30,000 Bequest & Other Stories

Experiencing Balance. 1998. 24.95 (978-1-58557-011-9(7)) Dynamic Growth.

Experiencing Dance: From Student to Dance Artist. Helene Scheff et al. 2005. tchr. ed. (978-0-7360-5454-6(5)) HumanKinUSA.

Experiencing Divine Joy Through Humor. Kriyananda, pseud. 1 cass. (Running Time: 60 min.). 9.95 (SC-9) Crystal Clarity.
Discusses why humor satisfies us; the importance of being able to laugh at yourself; dangers of "put-down" humor; humor as a route to inwardness; & avoiding over-indulgence in humor.

***Experiencing Forgiveness: A Meditation on Ephesians 2:4.** Deborah Kukal. (ENG.). 2008. 14.95 (978-0-9801278-0-5(7)) Hydration.

Experiencing God: How to Live the Full Adventure of Knowing & Doing the Will of God. unabr. ed. Henry T. Blackaby et al. Narrated by Wayne Shepherd. (Running Time: 11 hrs. 3 mins. 19 sec.). (ENG.). 2008. 24.49 (978-1-60814-190-6(X)) Oasis Audio.

Experiencing God: How to Live the Full Adventure of Knowing & Doing the Will of God. unabr. ed. Henry Blackaby et al. Read by Henry Blackaby. Narrated by Wayne Shepherd. (Running Time: 11 hrs. 3 mins. 19 sec.). (ENG.). 2008. audio compact disk 34.99 (978-1-59859-369-3(2)) Oasis Audio.

Experiencing God: How to Live the Full Adventure of Knowing & Doing the Will of God. 15th anniv. ed. Henry T. Blackaby & Claude V. King. 1998. 15.99 (978-0-8054-1150-8(X)) BH Pubng Grp.

Experiencing God: Knowing & Doing the Will of God. Henry Blackaby et al. Read by Wayne Shepherd. (Playaway Adult Nonfiction Ser.). (ENG.). 2009. 60.00 (978-1-60775-596-8(3)) Find a World.

Experiencing God in Daily Life. Robert Fabing. 1 cass. 9.95 (5360) OR Catholic.
Drawing from his experience as a retreat master, Bob Fabing makes the "Examination of Conscience" accessible for everyday use. Excellent for building a daily sense of spirituality, as well as for retreat or spiritual direction!.

Experiencing God the Musical. Gary Rhodes. 2000. audio compact disk 85.00 (978-0-633-00715-7(3)) LifeWay Christian.

Experiencing God's Power. Elbert Willis. 1 cass. (Miracle Land Ser.). 4.00 Fill the Gap.

Experiencing Health & Healing: OZO. Eldon Taylor. Read by Eldon Taylor. Ed. by Leslie Brice. 1 cass. (Running Time: 1 hr.). 1992. 19.95 (978-1-56705-010-3(7)) Gateways Inst.
Self improvement.

Experiencing Inner Peace: OZO. Eldon Taylor. Read by Eldon Taylor. Ed. by Leslie Brice. 1 cass. (Running Time: 1 hr.). 1992. 19.95 (978-1-56705-014-1(X)) Gateways Inst.

Experiencing Marketing at the Marketplace Cd-rom. Ernest R. Cadotte. 2000. audio compact disk 27.95 (978-0-324-10881-1(8)) South-West.

Experiencing Marketing Strategy at the Marketplace Cd-Rom. Ernest R. Cadotte. 2000. audio compact disk 27.95 (978-0-324-10880-4(X)) South-West.

Experiencing Prayer with Jesus. unabr. ed. Henry T. Blackaby & Norman Blackaby. (ENG.). 2005. 13.99 (978-1-60814-191-3(8)) Oasis Audio.

Experiencing Relaxation: Enhancing Your Ability to Relax & Manage Stress by Using Hypnosis. 2005. audio compact disk 19.95 (978-0-9771008-0-4(4)) A M Tamalonis.

Experiencing Spiritual Breakthroughs Audio Album. Instructed by Bruce Wilkinson. 2000. 15.95 (978-1-885447-62-3(0)) Walk Thru the Bible.
Every year, dedicated Christian parents raise kids who bitterly rebel against them and God. And for thousands of moms and dads, it continues to be their single greatest fear. But it doesn't have to be. If you put into practice your God-intended role and purpose as a mom or dad, you can parent with confidence. But it will require real courage on your part. When you understand how God wants you to parent your child, will you be willing to change? If so, the prospects for your family are very promising indeed. Experiencing Spiritual Breakthroughs uses engaging drama, powerful teaching, and eye-catching graphics to help you understand how to fulfill your parent roles the way God intended.

Experiencing the Cross: Your Greatest Opportunity for Victory over Sin. unabr. ed. Henry T. Blackaby. Narrated by Wayne Shepherd. (ENG.). 2005. 19.59 (978-1-60814-192-0(6)) Oasis Audio.

Experiencing the Cross: Your Greatest Opportunity for Victory over Sin. unabr. ed. Henry T. Blackaby. Read by Henry T. Blackaby. Narrated by Wayne Shepherd. (Running Time: 16200 sec.). (ENG.). 2005. audio compact disk 27.99 (978-1-59859-019-7(7)) Oasis Audio.

Experiencing the Fullness of Love. Taffi L. Dollar. 30.00 (978-1-59089-024-0(8)) Pub: Creflo Dollar. Dist(s): STL Dist NA

***Experiencing the Joy.** unabr. ed. Stephanie Perry Moore. Narrated by Robin Miles. (Running Time: 4 hrs. 25 mins. 0 sec.). (Yasmin Peace Ser.). (ENG.). 2010. 12.98 (978-1-61045-013-3(2), christaudio); audio compact disk 18.98 (978-1-61045-079-9(5), christaudio) christianaud.

Experiencing the Resurrection: The Everyday Encounter That Changes Your Life. unabr. ed. Henry Blackaby. Narrated by Wayne Shepherd. (ENG.). 2008. 13.99 (978-1-60814-193-7(4)) Oasis Audio.

Experiencing the Resurrection: The Everyday Encounter That Changes Your Life. unabr. ed. Henry Blackaby & Melvin Blackaby. Read by Chris Fabry. Narrated by Wayne Shepherd. (Running Time: 18000 sec.). (ENG.). 2008. audio compact disk 19.99 (978-1-59859-320-4(X)) Oasis Audio.

Experiencing the Ripple Effect: Everyday, in some way, you're getting better & Better. 2006. audio compact disk 19.95 (978-0-9771008-1-1(2)) A M Tamalonis.

Experiencing the Spirit. unabr. ed. Henry Blackaby. Narrated by Wayne Shepherd. (Running Time: 4 hrs. 2 mins. 0 sec.). (ENG.). 2009. 13.99 (978-1-60814-507-2(7)); audio compact disk 19.99 (978-1-59859-514-7(8)) Oasis Audio.

Experiencing the Word: The Letters of Paul. David Payne. 4 CDs. (Running Time: 4 hrs.). (Holman CSB Audio Ser.). 2004. bk. 14.99 (978-1-58640-017-0(7)) BH Pubng Grp.

Experiencing the Word Bible. Read by David Payne. Michael Stanton. 64 CDs. (ENG., 2005. audio compact disk 99.97 (978-1-55819-947-7(0)) BH Pubng Grp.

Experiencing the Word Through the Gospels. David Payne. 8 CDs. (Holman CSB Audio Ser.). 2004. bk. 19.99 (978-1-58640-016-3(9)) BH Pubng Grp.

***Experiential Storytelling: (Re) Discovering Narrative to Communicate God's Message.** Zondervan. (Running Time: 3 hrs. 3 mins. 0 sec.). (ENG.). 2010. 9.99 (978-0-310-86921-4(8)) Zondervan.

Experiment. John Darnton. Narrated by Barbara Caruso & George Guidall. 16 CDs. (Running Time: 17 hrs. 15 mins.). 2000. audio compact disk 142.00 (978-0-7887-4761-8(4), C1254E7) Recorded Bks.
Sklyer & Jude have never met, yet they're identical, both victims of a horrifying science experiment. As their story of genetic manipulation unfolds, listeners realize with dawning horror that its premise lies disturbingly within the realm of possibility. Includes an exclusive interview with the author.

Experiment. abr. ed. John Darnton. 2002. 12.99 (978-1-57815-261-2(5)) Media Bks NJ.

Experiment, unabr. ed. John Darnton. Narrated by George Guidall. 12 cass. (Running Time: 17 hrs. 15 mins.). 1999. 102.00 (978-0-7887-3763-3(5), 95980E7) Recorded Bks.

Experiment in Treason. Bruce Alexander. Read by John Lee. 2002. 56.00 (978-0-7366-8853-6(6)) Books on Tape.

Experiment with Death. unabr. ed. E. X. Ferrars. Read by Anne Dover. 4 cass. (Running Time: 6 hrs.). (Sound Ser.). 2004. 44.95 (978-1-85496-674-2(X), 6674x) Pub: UlverLrgPrint GBR. Dist(s): Ulverscroft US
When Sam Partlett joined the staff at the Institute of Pomology at King's Weltham, he brought nothing but discord. But it was not Sam who was found dead at the Institute, throat slashed with one of the laboratory razors. In the close-knit scientific community, Inspector Day quietly set to work to probe the secrets of people busy with different experiments - but had someone carried out an experiment with death.

Experimental Aeronautical Sciences. Ed. by Marco A. V. Bitetto. 1 cass. 2000. (978-1-58578-290-1(4)) Inst of Cybernetics.

Experimental Disassociation (Astral Projection) Eldon Taylor. 1 cass. (Running Time: 62 min.). (Neurophonics Ser.). 16.95 (978-1-55978-654-6(X), 1005) Progress Aware Res.
Sound patterns for Altered States of Consciousness with underlying subliminal affirmations & frequency response signals. Use with headphones only.

Experimental Medicine, Set. abr. ed. Claude Bernard. Read by Robert L. Halvorson. 7 cass. 49.95 (29) Halvorson Assocs.

Experimental Prose. Richard Kostelanetz. Read by Richard Kostelanetz. 1 cass. (Running Time: 40 min.). 1976. 8.00 (978-0-932360-93-9(9)) Archae Edns.
Contains several experiments with multi-trackings which are not "straight readings" of his texts but audio realizations produced mostly at radio stations & in electronic music studios. Includes "Milestones in a Life", "Excelsior" & "Declaration of Independence".

Expert. unabr. ed. Lee Gruenfeld. Read by Barrett Whitener. 15 cass. (Running Time: 22 hrs.). 1999. 95.95 (978-0-7861-1479-5(7), 2331) Blckstn Audio.
Combines the worlds of high-stakes law, international intrigue, & cutting-edge technology.

***Expert.** unabr. ed. Lee Gruenfeld. Read by Barrett Whitener. (Running Time: 21 hrs. 0 mins.). 2010. 44.95 (978-1-4417-0344-6(6)); audio compact disk 123.00 (978-1-4417-0341-5(1)) Blckstn Audio.

Expert Tells You How to Get Published. unabr. ed. Hubert Bermont. 1 cass. (Running Time: 49 min.). 12.95 (730) J Norton Pubs.
Bermont discusses how to find the right publishers, working with editors, illustrators, lawyers, agents, contracts & money.

Expert Witness Challenges. unabr. ed. Dan Poynter. Read by Dan Poynter. 1 cass. (Running Time: 1 hr.). 1993. 9.95 (978-0-915516-77-3(2), E-101) Para Pub.
You will learn how expert witness work is changing & how you can adapt to the challenges. Then Poynter will share ten tips & techniques for making your testimony easier & more effective. Includes resources.

Expert Witnesses. Read by Irving Younger. (Running Time: 3 hrs.). 60.00 (108); 195.00 video. (NO. 108) Natl Prac Inst.
Focuses his experience as professor, judge, prosecutor & world famous trial attorney on expert witnesses, covering both law & technique.

Expert Witnesses. Irving Younger. 1978. 60.00 (978-1-55917-168-7(5)) Natl Prac Inst.

Expert Witnesses. Irving Younger. Read by Irving Younger. 3 cass. (Running Time: 3 hrs.). 1985. pap. bk. 70.00 Set. (978-0-943380-40-7(5)) PEG MN.
Enhancing or attacking the credibility of experts.

Expert Witnesses. Speeches. Perf. by Irving Younger. Created by Irving Younger. 2 CDs. (Running Time: 3 hours). 2004. pap. bk. 199.00 (978-1-932831-01-6(0)) PEG MN.

Expert Witnesses: A Handbook for Litigators. 1 cass. 1991. 45.00 incl. script. (AC-646) PA Bar Inst.

Expert Witnesses & Discovery in Family Law Litigation. 1987. bk. 85.00 incl. book.; 55.00 cass. only.; 30.00 book only. PA Bar Inst.

Expert Witnesses, Cross Examination & Impeachment. 1 cass. (Running Time: 52 min.). (Basic Concepts in the Law of Evidence Ser.). 1975. 15.00 (EYX04) Natl Inst Trial Ad.

Expertas en Terremotos: Audiocassette. (Saludos Ser.: Vol. 2). (SPA.). (gr. 3-5). 10.00 (978-0-7635-2067-0(5)) Rigby Educ.

Experts & Hearsay: What Every Trial Lawyer Must Know. Faust Rossi. 1994. 150.00 Natl Prac Inst.

Experts' Guide to 100 Things Everyone Should Know How to Do. unabr. ed. Samantha Ettus. Read by Ensemble Cast. (YA). 2007. 39.99 (978-1-60252-683-9(4)) Find a World.

Experts' Guide to 100 Things Everyone Should Know How to Do. unabr. ed. Samantha Ettus. Created by Samantha Ettus. (Running Time: 6 hrs.). (ENG.). 2005. audio compact disk 24.95 (978-1-56511-993-2(2), 1565119932) Pub: Penguin-HghBrdg. Dist(s): Penguin Grp USA

Explain Pain Audio. David S. Butler & G. Lorimer Moseley. (ENG.). 2009. 70.00 (978-0-9750910-6-7(9)) Noigroup AUS.

Explaining Hitler, Pt. 1. unabr. collector's ed. Ron Rosenbaum. Read by Barrett Whitener. 9 cass. (Running Time: 13 hrs. 30 min.). 1999. 72.00 (978-0-7366-4667-3(1), 5049-A) Books on Tape.
Two-part examination, Rosenbaum analyzes why Hitler "managed to escape explanation" for his rabid anti-Semitism & his role in the Holocaust. Examines various theories & supporting evidence while trying to understand the man whose name is synonymous with the incarnation of evil.

Explaining Hitler, Pt. 2. collector's ed. Ron Rosenbaum. Read by Barrett Whitener. 8 cass. (Running Time: 12 hrs.). 1999. 64.00 (978-0-7366-4724-3(4), 5049-B) Books on Tape.

Explaining Revocable Trusts to Clients. Edward S. Schlesinger. 2 cass. (Running Time: 2 hrs.). 1999. 25.00 (M762) Am Law Inst.
Designed for estate planning lawyers & their clients, this audiotape defines the revocable trust & thoroughly describes its functions & important features.

Explaining Social Deviance. Instructed by Paul Root Wolpe. 6 cass. (Running Time: 6 hrs.). 1995. 39.95 (978-1-56585-189-4(7)) Teaching Co.

Explanation of Love. Elbert Willis. 1 cass. (Faithfulness Through Love Ser.). 4.00 Fill the Gap.

Expletives & coloquialisms all Hispanics should learn to live & work in the United States see Ingles Callejero: Vulgaridades y coloquialismos que todo hispano debe aprender para vivir y trabajar en Estados Unidos

Explode Your Practice: More Clients Than You Can Handle. David Wood. (ENG.). 2005. audio compact disk 197.00 (978-0-9817647-3-3(8)) SolBox.

Exploded. abr. ed. Read by Tom Bodett. 2 cass. (Running Time: 1 hr. 53 min.). 1996. 17.95 (978-1-57453-085-8(2)) Audio Lit.
Looks at births, deaths, marriages, divorces, windfalls & calamities the defining events that leave us shell-shocked for a time.

Exploding the Myth of Self-Defense: A Survival Guide for Every Woman. Judith Fein. Ed. by Jean Gilliam. 1 cass. (Running Time: 1 hr.). 1994. pap. bk. 14.95 (978-0-929523-24-8(5)) Torrance Pub.
Dr. Judith Fein gives you the key to the secrets of self-esteem & personal power. "Fein's book is a gift for women who want control over their lives".

Exploitation & Trade in Walruses, Polar Bears & Koalas. Hosted by Nancy Pearlman. 1 cass. (Running Time: 29 min.). 10.00 (1013) Educ Comm CA.

Exploiting the Devil's Weakness. C. S. Lovett. 1 cass. (Running Time: 60 min.). 6.95 (7033) Prsnl Christianity.
Expands on truths of the "Dealing with the Devil" book.

Exploits of Brigadier General, Set. Arthur Conan Doyle. Narrated by Richard Brown. 6 cass. (Running Time: 8 hrs.). 1988. 24.95 (978-1-55685-129-2(4)) Audio Bk Con.
With his tongue unobtrusively tucked in his cheek, Doyle assists an imaginary French Brigadier to recall his deeds of valor & gallantry while a young officer in Napoleon's army.

***Exploits of Brigadier Gerard.** unabr. ed. Arthur Conan Doyle. Read by Rupert Degas. 6 CDs. (Running Time: 7 hrs. 13 mins.). 2010. audio compact disk 34.98 (978-1-84379-385-4(7), Naxos AudioBooks) Naxos.

Explora el Mundo: Personas, Lugares y Culturas: Student Edition on Audio CD. stu. ed. 207.97 (978-0-13-068410-3(4)) PH School.

Exploramos. Alma Flor Ada. 1 cass. (Running Time: 25 min.). (SPA.). (J). (gr. 3-4). 1987. 3.28 incl. script. (978-0-201-16875-4(8)) AddisonWesley.

Exploration see Twentieth-Century Poetry in English, No. 28, Recordings of Poets Reading Their Own Poetry

Exploration & Discovery. unabr. ed. University of Iowa, CEEDE Staff. 1 cass. (VIE.). 1986. 8.95 (978-0-7836-0606-4(0), 8733); 8.95 (978-0-7836-0605-7(2), 8732); 8.95 (978-0-7836-0604-0(4), 8730) Triumph Learn.
An American history based English fluency development program.

Exploration & Discovery: Cambodian Cassette Tape. unabr. ed. University of Iowa, CEEDE Staff. 1 cass. (CAM.). 1986. 8.95 (978-0-7836-0603-3(6)) Triumph Learn.

Exploration & Discovery: Complete Cambodian Set. unabr. ed. University of Iowa, CEEDE Staff. 1 cass. (CAM.). 1989. 95.00 incl. tchr's. guide, student text, activity masters, CAI disk, ESL grammar activity masters & tchr's. guide for ESL grammar activity masters. (978-0-7836-0749-8(0), 8945) Triumph Learn.

Exploration & Discovery: Complete Hmong Set. unabr. ed. University of Iowa, CEEDE Staff. 1 cass. 1989. 95.00 incl. tchr's. guide, student text, activity masters, CAI disk, ESL grammar activity masters & tchr's. guide for ESL grammar activity masters. (978-0-7836-0750-4(4), 8946) Triumph Learn.

Exploration & Discovery: Complete Lao Set. unabr. ed. University of Iowa, CEEDE Staff. 1 cass. (LAO.). 1989. 95.00 incl. tchr's. guide, student text, activity masters, CAI disk, ESL grammar activity masters & tchr's. guide for ESL grammar activity masters. (978-0-7836-0751-1(2), 8947) Triumph Learn.

Exploration & Discovery: Complete Vietnamese Set. unabr. ed. University of Iowa, CEEDE Staff. 1 cass. (VIE.). 1989. 95.00 incl. tchr's. guide, student text, activity masters, CAI disk, ESL grammar activity masters & tchr's. guide for ESL grammar activity masters. (978-0-7836-0752-8(0), 8948) Triumph Learn.

Exploration Earth & Genesis. Doctor Who. (Running Time: 1 hr. 20 mins.). 2001. audio compact disk 9.99 (978-0-563-47857-7(8)) London Brdge.

***Exploration Fawcett: Journey to the Lost City of Z.** unabr. ed. Co. P. H. Fawcett. (Running Time: 15 hrs. 30 mins.). 2010. 85.95 (978-1-4417-6376-1(7)); audio compact disk 118.00 (978-1-4417-6377-8(5)) Blckstn Audio.

***Exploration Fawcett: Journey to the Lost City of Z.** unabr. ed. Percy Fawcett. (Running Time: 15 hrs. 30 mins.). 2010. 29.95 (978-1-4417-6379-2(1)); audio compact disk 34.95 (978-1-4417-6378-5(3)) Blckstn Audio.

Exploration for Buried Archaeological Sites in the Great Lakes Region: Modeling Archaeological Site Burial in Southern Michigan. G. William Monaghan et al. 2005. bk. 35.95 (978-0-87013-738-9(7)) Mich St U Pr.

Exploration of Higher Potentials of Individuals. unabr. ed. Nathaniel Branden. 1 cass. (Running Time: 1 hr. 1 min.). 12.95 (557) J Norton Pubs.
Covers the importance of overcoming defense mechanisms of childhood which are harmful to the adult; the importance of respect for individuality & development of autonomy & self-responsibility; the effect of insanity in childhood environments upon adults.

Exploration of the Heart. Perf. by Lew Childre. 4 cass. (Running Time: 3 hrs. 30 min.). 1999. 49.95 Set. (83-0070) Explorations.
Eliminate stress, facilitate change & live life to its fullest potential with the power of your heart.

Exploration Sleep. unabr. ed. Robert A. Monroe. Read by Robert A. Monroe. (Running Time: 45 min.). (Gateway Experience - Discovery Ser.). 1981. 14.95 (978-1-56113-254-6(3)) Monroe Institute.
Learn techniques for out of body exploration.

Explorations in Eastern Mysticism: Taoism. Paul Hourihan. 4 cass. (Running Time: 4 hrs.). 2003. (978-1-931816-06-9(9)) Vedantic Shores.

Explorations in Eastern Mysticism: Taoism. Paul Hourihan. 4 cass. (Running Time: 1 hr. per cass.). 2003. (978-1-931816-07-6(7)) Vedantic Shores.
Part II, Lectures 3 & 4 of a four-lecture course focusing on the poetically enigmatic mystic philosophy of Taoism. Many insights from Western mysticism are included as points of correlation and comparison.

Explorations in Eastern Mysticism: Taoism, Pt. I. Paul Hourihan. 4 CDs. (Running Time: 1 hr.). 2003. audio compact disk (978-1-931816-04-5(2)) Vedantic Shores.
Part I of a 2-part, four-lecture course focusing on the poetically enigmatic mystic philosophy of Taoism. Many insights from Western mysticism are included as points of correlations and comparison.

Explorations in Eastern Mysticism Pt. II: Taoism. Paul Hourihan. 4 CDs. (Running Time: approx. 1 hr. per CD). 2003. audio compact disk (978-1-931816-05-2(0)) Vedantic Shores.
Part II, Lectures 3 & 4 of a four-lecture course focusing on the poetically enigmatic mystic philosophy of Taoism. Many insights from Western mysticism are included as points of correlation and comparison.

Explorations in Eating Journal, Calendar, & Audio Program. 2008. ring bd. 49.95 (978-0-9794787-2-7(3)) Horizons DRC.

Explorations 1. Linda Lee et al. 2000. audio compact disk 39.95 (978-0-19-435036-5(3)) OUP.

Explore: Stories of Survival from off the Map. unabr. ed. Redmond O'Hanlon et al. Ed. by Jennifer Schwamm Willis. Narrated by Grover Gardner et al. 4 cass. (Running Time: 6 hrs.). (Adrenaline Ser.). 2000. 24.95 (978-1-885408-55-6(2), LL046) Listen & Live.
Offers first-hand accounts from the world's boldest explorers, men & women encountering storms, starvation, cannibals, predators & disease in their pursuit of mystery & adventure.

Explore a Past Life. Mary Lee LaBay. 2006. audio compact disk 12.95 (978-1-934705-12-4(8)) Awareness Engin.

Explore America Audio Tape of Historical Music. 3rd rev. ed. Pamella C. Beall & Susan H. Nipp. 2002. reel tape 10.95 (978-1-55501-543-5(3)) BallardTighe.

Explore! Microsoft PowerPoint 2000 - Brief. John Zeanchock. 2001. audio compact disk 22.95 (978-0-619-02071-2(7)) Pub: Course Tech. Dist(s): CENGAGE Learn

Explore, Strengthen, Renew: An Introduction to Chemical Dependency. 6 cass. 42.95 Set. (1521G) Hazelden.

Explore, Strengthen, Renew: Professional Issues. 6 cass. 42.95 Set. (1568G) Hazelden.

Explore, Strengthen, Renew: Recovery - The New Life. 6 cass. 42.95 Set. (1597G) Hazelden.

Explore, Strengthen, Renew: Renewing Ourselves. 6 cass. 42.95 Set. (5600G) Hazelden.

Explore the Book CD Series. 2005. audio compact disk 24.95 (978-1-59834-057-0(3)) Walk Thru the Bible.

Explore with Math, Level 4. Ann Edson & Allan A. Schwartz. 8 cass. 89.95 incl. 8 activity bks., & guide. (978-0-89525-033-9(0), AKC 63) Ed Activities.
Products & dividends; mutliplying by one, two & 2-digit numbers; dividing; roman numerals; equivalent fractions; locating points & coordinates; working with mixed numbers; metric measures; averages etc.

Explore Your Past Lives. unabr. ed. Dick Sutphen. Read by Dick Sutphen. 1 cass. (Running Time: 1 hr.). (Spirit Guide Meditations). 1999. 14.98 (978-0-87554-639-1(0), SG112) Valley Sun.
A spirit guide assists in the regression process.

Explorer. unabr. collector's ed. W. Somerset Maugham. Read by Jill Masters. 6 cass. (Running Time: 9 hrs.). 1985. 48.00 (978-0-7366-0790-2(0), 1742) Books on Tape.
Story of the Allertons, Fred & his children, as they deal with the loss of their birthright. Fred squanders the family fortune & dishonors the family name. His children, Lucy & George, try to pick up the pieces when what they assume is theirs is taken from them.

Explorer. 13th ed. Atkinson & Daryl J. Bem. (C). 1999. audio compact disk 36.95 (978-0-15-506841-4(5)) Pub: Harcourt Coll Pubs. Dist(s): CENGAGE Learn

Explorer on Main Street see Richard Eberhart Reading His Poetry

Explorers & Discoverers Vols. 1-4: From Alexander the Great to Sally Ride. Ed. by Peggy Saari & Daniel B. Baker. (J). (gr. 4-8). 1995. bk. 145.00 (978-0-8130-9787-9(8), GML00402-107443, UXL) Gale.

Explorers & Innovators. Compiled by Encyclopaedia Britannica, Inc. 2008. audio compact disk Ency Brit Inc.

Explorers in Dinosaur World. (J). 2005. cass. & cd-rom 25.95 (978-0-9771381-2-8(7)) Geoffrey Williams.

Explorers in Dinosaur World. Geoffrey T. Williams. 1 cass. (J). 1989. 7.00 (PSS) Penguin Grp USA.
Takes children on a journey through a world where prehistoric creatures still roam the earth.

Explorer's Past Life Regressions. unabr. ed. Robert A. Monroe. Read by Robert A. Monroe. (Running Time: 45 min.). (Explorer Ser.). 1983. 12.95 (978-1-56113-001-6(X), 2) Monroe Institute.
The Explorer is taken into several pastlife regressions.

Explorers to 1815 History. Marlin Detweiler & Laurie Detweiler. Perf. by Meshell Watt. 1998. 6.95 (978-1-930710-08-5(9)) Veritas Pr PA.

Exploring a Course in Miracles. Read by Tara Singh. 3 cass. (Running Time: 3 hrs.). 1996. 21.95 (978-1-55531-278-7(0)) Pub: Life Action Pr. Dist(s): APG
Discover how & why "A Course in Miracles" came into being, the most productive way to read & practice it, & the challenge of living its principles.

Exploring Album. unabr. ed. Robert A. Monroe. Read by Robert A. Monroe. 6 cass. (Running Time: 45 min.). (Gateway Experience - Exploring Ser.). 1984. 72.00 (978-1-56113-284-3(5)) Monroe Institute.
Exploring album for 6 cassettes.

Exploring & Developing Your Senses. Trenna Daniells. Read by Trenna Daniells. 1 cass. (Running Time: 30 min.). (One to Grow on Ser.). (J). (gr. k-6). 1982. 9.95 (978-0-918519-10-8(1), SR68522) Trenna Prods.
Unique exploration works with children to focus their minds & expand the awareness of their senses. Several exploratory exercises bring a more acute comprehension of touch, sound, taste, feeling, body movement, meditation, & intuition.

Exploring & Developing Your Senses. Trenna Daniells. Narrated by Trenna Daniells. (ENG.). (J). 2009. (978-0-918519-52-8(7)) Trenna Prods.

Exploring & Mapmaking. unabr. ed. Ian Jackson. Read by Edwin Newman. (Running Time: 10800 sec.). (Audio Classics: Science & Discovery Ser.). 2006. audio compact disk 25.95 (978-0-7861-6437-0(9)) Pub: Blckstn Audio. Dist(s): NetLibrary CO

Exploring & Mapmaking. unabr. ed. Ian Jackson. Read by Edwin Newman. Ed. by Jack Sommer & Mike Hassell. 2 cass. (Running Time: 2 hrs. 45 min.). Dramatization. (Science & Discovery Ser.). (YA). (gr. 11 up). 1993. 17.95 set. (978-0-938935-68-1(2), 10403) Knowledge Prod.
While astronomers charted the heavens, geographers & cartographers mapped the earth's exotic lands & seas. Commerce & navigation exploded as mapmakers & bold explorers built on each other's achievements; in the process, our very concept of the earth changed from a flat surface to a sphere.

Exploring Arabic. Hisham A. Khalek & Joan G. Sheeran. 59.95 (978-0-8219-4136-2(4)); pap. bk. 779.95 (978-0-8219-4142-3(9)) EMC-Paradigm.

Exploring Arabic. Joan G. Sheeran & Hisham A. Khalek. pap. bk. 239.95 (978-0-8219-3886-7(X)); pap. bk. 219.95 (978-0-8219-4148-5(8)); pap. bk. 799.95 (978-0-8219-3887-4(8)) EMC-Paradigm.

Exploring Chinese. Joan G. Sheeran. 59.95 (978-0-8219-4135-5(6)); pap. bk. 239.95 (978-0-8219-3893-5(2)); pap. bk. 219.95 (978-0-8219-4147-8(X)); pap. bk. 799.95 (978-0-8219-3894-2(0)); pap. bk. 779.95 (978-0-8219-4141-6(0)) EMC-Paradigm.

Exploring Chinese Philosophy. unabr. ed. John Blofeld. Narrated by Al Huang. 6 cass. (Running Time: 7 hrs. 16 min.). 1978. 56.00 Set. (02903) Big Sur Tapes.
Describes his great love of China, his writing reflects what he saw during his many years there. He explores Chinese, Buddhist, & related Eastern philosophies, with Al Huang participating in the discussion.

Exploring Creation Biology. 2005. audio compact disk 15.00 (978-1-932012-63-7(X)) Apologia Educ.

Exploring Creation with Biology 2nd edition audio CD. 2nd ed. Jay Wile & Marilyn Durnell. Read by Kathleen Wile. (ENG.). 2005. 15.00 (978-1-932012-65-1(6)) Apologia Educ.

Exploring Creation with Chemistry 2nd edition audio CD. Jay L. Wile. Read by Candice Jones. (C). 2004. 15.00 (978-1-932012-51-4(6)) Apologia Educ.

Exploring Creation with General Science audio CD. Jay L. Wile. Read by Candice Jones. 2004. 15.00 (978-1-932012-50-7(8)) Apologia Educ.

Exploring Creation with General Science 2nd edition audio CD. 2nd ed. Jay L. Wile. Read by Candice Jones. (ENG.). 2008. 15.00 (978-1-932012-92-7(3)) Apologia Educ.

Exploring Creation with Physical Science: Audio CD. Jay L. Wile. Read by Michael A. Wilson. 2003. 15.00 (978-1-932012-41-5(9)) Apologia Educ.

Exploring Creation with Physical Science 2nd edition audio CD. 2nd ed. Jay L. Wile. Read by Kathleen Wile. (ENG.). 2007. 15.00 (978-1-932012-83-5(4)) Apologia Educ.

Exploring Creation with Physics 2nd edition audio CD. 2nd ed. Jay Wile. Read by Kathleen Wile. (ENG.). 2005. 15.00 (978-1-932012-64-4(8)) Apologia Educ.

Exploring Dimensions of Consciousness. Instructed by Manly P. Hall. 5 cass. 8.50 ea. o.p. Pt. 1: Universal & Personal Consciousness. (800164-A) Philos Res.

Exploring Ecosystems with Max Axiom, Super Scientist. Agnieszka Biskup. Illus. by Tod Smith. (Graphic Science Ser.). (ENG.). (gr. 3-4). 2007. audio compact disk 6.95 (978-1-4296-1125-1(1)) CapstoneDig.

Exploring Fatima: A National Fatima Symposium at Marymount University, Arlington, VA. Eamon R. Carroll et al. Read by Eamon R. Carroll et al. 6 cass. (Running Time: 6 hrs.). 1989. 16.95 (978-1-56036-036-0(4), 361915) AMI Pr.
The message of Fatima presented in depth at a National Fatima Symposium - Must Catholics believe in Fatima? Reflections on the Fatima children; Setting the stage for Fatima; The World situation in 1917; Mary as Catechist at Fatima; The Scriptural context of Fatima & Speakers' panel.

Exploring "Focusing" & Bodily Meanings. 1 cass. (Care Cassettes Ser.: Vol. 22, No. 6). 1995. 10.80 Assn Prof Chaplains.

Exploring French. Joan G. Sheeran. 59.95 (978-0-8219-4133-1(X)); bk. 239.95 (978-0-8219-3483-8(X)); bk. 219.95 (978-0-8219-4145-4(3)); bk. 879.95 (978-0-8219-4153-9(4)); bk. 859.95 (978-0-8219-4151-5(8)); pap. bk. 799.95 (978-0-8219-3863-8(0)); pap. bk. 779.95 (978-0-8219-4139-3(9)); audio compact disk 89.95 (978-0-8219-3915-4(7)) EMC-Paradigm.

Exploring Freshwater Habitats. Patti Seifert. Illus. by Peg Doherty. (J). 1995. 7.95 (978-1-879531-31-4(3)) Mondo Pubng.

Exploring German. Joan G. Sheeran. 89.90 (978-0-8219-3921-5(1)); 59.95 (978-0-8219-4132-4(1)) EMC-Paradigm.

Exploring German. 3rd ed. Joan G. Sheeran. bk. 239.95 (978-0-8219-3488-3(0)); bk. 219.95 (978-0-8219-4144-7(5)); bk. 879.95 (978-0-8219-4154-6(2)); bk. 859.95 (978-0-8219-4150-8(X)); pap. bk. 799.95 (978-0-8219-3864-5(9)); pap. bk. 779.95 (978-0-8219-4138-6(0)) EMC-Paradigm.

Exploring Italian. 2nd ed. Joan G. Sheeran. 89.95 (978-0-8219-3919-2(X)); 59.95 (978-0-8219-4134-8(8)); pap. bk. 239.95 (978-0-8219-3493-7(7)); pap. bk. 219.95 (978-0-8219-4146-1(1)); pap. bk. 799.95 (978-0-8219-3865-2(7)); pap. bk. 779.95 (978-0-8219-4140-9(2)) EMC-Paradigm.

Exploring Jasper. unabr. ed. Gail Taylor. Read by Gail Taylor. Ed. by James B. Kirgan. 1 cass. (Running Time: 1 hr. 30 min.). (Essence of Nature Ser.: Vol. 2). (J). 1989. 12.99 stereo. (978-1-878362-02-5(X)) Emerald Ent.
On this tape Thumper, the adventure dog, explores Jasper National Park in Canada. This tape includes the actual sounds of nature in this Canadian National Park.

Exploring Land Habitats. Margaret Phinney. Illus. by Terri Talas. (J). 1995. 7.95 (978-1-879531-40-6(2)) Mondo Pubng.

Exploring Microsoft Office XP. Robert T. Grauer & Mary Ann Barber. 2002. audio compact disk 22.80 (978-0-13-141494-5(1), P-H) Pearson Educ CAN CAN.

Exploring Music & Sound on Your PC! unabr. ed. John Stewart. Read by John Stewart. Ed. by Alicia Andersen. 1 cass. (Running Time: 1 hr. 14 min.). (ACI Tape Ser.). 1998. 18.95 Incl. ref. card. (978-1-886173-07-1(9)) Audio Computer.
Covers all aspects of audio recording & editing with a standard PC. Also introduction to MIDI & MOD music. Covers copyright information, microphones, background music & more.

Exploring Numerical Methods. Peter Linz. (C). 2002. audio compact disk 44.95 (978-0-7637-1529-8(8), 1529-8) Jones Bartlett.

Exploring Our Divine Biology: Learning the Language of Power & Health. Caroline Myss. (Exploring Our Divine Biology). 1996. 55.00 (978-1-893869-55-4(5)) Celbrtng Life.

Exploring Our World: A Musical Adventure Through Science & History. Diana Carter Coates & Brad Schultz. 1 cass/. (J). 1999. 14.99 (978-0-9675874-1-7(7)) Edna.
Original educational children's music.

Exploring Panaceas for Health. Ralph Alan Dale. Read by Ralph Alan Dale. 1 cass. (Running Time: 90 min.). 1976. 9.00 (9) Dialectic Pubng.
Myths & truths for maintaining health.

Exploring Perception: For the Macintosh & Microsoft Windows. Colin Ryan. audio compact disk 77.95 student's ed. (978-0-534-32104-8(6)) Brooks-Cole.

Exploring Perception: For the Macintosh & Microsoft Windows. Colin Ryan. 1996. audio compact disk 991.95 site license with instr's. notes. (978-0-534-32103-1(8)) Brooks-Cole.

Exploring Saltwater Habitats. Sue Smith. Illus. by Cynthia A. Belcher. 1 cass. (Running Time: 30 min.). (J). 1995. 7.95 (978-1-879531-34-5(8)) Mondo Pubng.
A visit to the briny deep uncovers a tremendous variety of habitats brimming with life. Discover Australia's Great Barrier Reef, the deep sea of the Pacific, Antarctica's icy waters, tide pools in Maine, and kelp forests.

Exploring Spanish. Joan G. Sheeran. 59.95 (978-0-8219-4131-7(3)); audio compact disk 89.95 (978-0-8219-3917-8(3)) EMC-Paradigm.

Exploring Spanish. 3rd ed. Joan G. Sheeran. bk. 239.95 (978-0-8219-3478-4(3)); bk. 219.95 (978-0-8219-4143-0(7)); bk. 879.95 (978-0-8219-4152-2(6)); bk. 859.95 (978-0-8219-4149-2(6)); pap. bk. 799.95 (978-0-8219-3862-1(2)); pap. bk. 779.95 (978-0-8219-4137-9(2)) EMC-Paradigm.

***Exploring Spoken English Audio CDs (2)** Ronald Carter & Michael McCarthy. (Running Time: 1 hr. 36 mins.). (ENG.). 2010. audio compact disk 41.00 (978-0-521-12169-9(8)) Cambridge U Pr.

Exploring the Archetypes: For Life's Lesson. Caroline Myss. (Exploring The Archetypes). 1997. 55.00 (978-1-893869-59-2(8)) Celbrtng Life.

Exploring the Chaos of Something Extraordinary. Naomi R. Steinfeld. Read by Neva Duyndam. 1 cass. 1989. 9.95 (978-1-878159-02-1(X)) Duvall Media.
A beautifully written, sensitive account of Naomi Steinfeld's search for meaning after her fears became reality & she was admitted to a psychiatric hospital.

Exploring the Composite Chart. Jeanne Darling. 1 cass. 8.95 (073) Am Fed Astrologers.
Casting, delineating, progressing - personal & business.

Exploring the Dark Side in Dreams. Hal Stone & Sidra Stone. 1 cass. (Running Time: 1 hrs.). 1993. 10.95 (T32) Dragonhawk Pub.
The unconscious has its own special way of calling attention to the "dark" aspects of our psyches - the natural instinctual energies that we have disowned over time. These dreams, drawn from a number of countries, are remarkable for their clarity & intensity. They give a picture of the disowning process itself & of the importance of reclaiming our lost instinctual heritage.

Exploring the Hermetic Tradition. Terence McKenna. 4 cass. 1992. 36.00 set. (OC289-64) Sound Horizons AV.

Exploring the Inner World. unabr. ed. Linda H. Wind. 4 cass. (Running Time: 4 hrs. 10 min.). (Inner Work Tape Ser.: Pt. 1). 1996. 24.95 Set. (978-1-890027-01-8(4)) Heron Pr NY.
Provide an introduction to meditation & connecting with inner guidance.

Exploring the Levels of Creation. abr. ed. Sylvia Browne. Read by Sylvia Browne. 2 CDs. 2006. audio compact disk 18.95 (978-1-4019-0893-5(4)) Hay House.

Exploring the Magic of the Inner World - Blue Collection: Exploring the child's World of Dreams, Senses & Change. Trenna Daniells. Narrated by Trenna Daniells. (J). 2009. audio compact disk (978-0-918519-63-4(2)) Trenna Prods.

Exploring the Meaning of Money. Siegfried E. Finser. 2 cass. 1992. 18.00 set. (OC318-96) Sound Horizons AV.

Exploring the Roots of Religion. Instructed by John R. Hale. 2009. 199.95 (978-1-59803-575-9(4)); audio compact disk 269.95 (978-1-59803-576-6(2)) Teaching Co.

Exploring the Unknown: Dark Curtain & The Bells Toll. Perf. by Veronica Lake & Melvin Douglas. 1 cass. (Running Time: 1 hr.). 2001. 6.98 (1647) Radio Spirits.

***Exploring the World of Music: Cd Set.** 2nd rev. ed. Efc (Hast). (ENG.). 2010. audio compact disk 89.73 (978-0-7575-6328-7(7)) Kendall-Hunt.

Exploring Tomorrow. (SF-8020) Natl Recrd Co.

Exploring Tree Habitats. Patti Seifert. Illus. by Peg Doherty. (J). (gr. 1-5). 1995. 7.95 (978-1-879531-37-6(2)) Mondo Pubng.

Exploring Vibrational Medicine. Richard Gerber. 4 CDs. 2004. audio compact disk 29.95 (978-1-59179-258-1(4), AW00332D) Sounds True.
A pioneering physician shares thought-provoking research into energy-based medicine. Topics include: acupuncture meridians, chakras, prayer, meditation & much more.

Exploring with Marci, Volume 1 - Audio Version: Fun & Adventure in the Wild, Wild West. Short Stories. Marci Mesnard. Read by Marci Mesnard. Ed. by Michael Brenner. Executive Producer Michael Brenner. 3 CD's. (Running Time: 3 hrs. 44 mins.). 2005. audio compact disk 19.95 (978-0-9764461-1-8(1)) Brenner Pr.
Exploring with Marci, Vol. 1, is a collection of colorful travel essays about Marci and her husband Jim's adventures in the Western United States, Alaska, and Hawaii. Join Marci and her husband Jim on their adventures in the Wild, Wild West. Encounter the phantoms of old Piute Springs. Paddle a kayak up a river in Kauai. Hike up an ice-cold river in Zion National Park. Climb the highest mountain in the Continental U.S. Explore the darkness of a lava tube cave.Marci Mesnard and her husband, Jim, live in Southern California, in the midst of the pastel beauty of the Mojave Desert. Together they have experienced unique and exciting adventures for over 25 years.This audio version is read by the author.

Exploring Your Past Lives, Vol. I. unabr. ed. Dean Marshall & Marie Kirkendoll. 3 cass. (Running Time: 3 hrs.). 1986. 29.95 incl. bklet. (978-1-55585-077-7(4)) Quest NW Pub.
Explanation & instruction on how to relax & guide your memory back through time to remember & re-experience past lives.

Explosion. l.t. ed. Karine Naouri. (French Ser.). 2000. bk. 30.99 (978-2-84011-365-2(1)) Pub: UlverLrgPrint GBR. Dist(s): Ulverscroft US

Explosion at Donner Pass. unabr. ed. Gary McCarthy. Read by Gene Engene. 6 cass. (Running Time: 6 hrs.). (Derby Man Ser.: Bk. 6). 1995. 39.95 set. (978-1-55686-565-7(1)) Books in Motion.
Darby Buckingham working with the Central Pacific Railroad, endures vicious fighting, sabotage & murder as track is laid over the notorious Donner Pass.

Explosion Prevention. unabr. ed. Read by Wilfred E. Baker. 3 cass. (Running Time: 3 hrs. 20 min.). 415.00 Set, incl. 122p. manual. (95) Am Chemical.

***Exponential: How to Accomplish the Jesus Mission.** unabr. ed. Dave Ferguson & Jon Ferguson. (Running Time: 7 hrs. 40 mins. 27 sec.). (Exponential Ser.). (ENG.). 2010. 16.99 (978-0-310-58638-8(0)) Zondervan.

Export-Import & Joint-Venture Companies. 6th rev. ed. BIA. (J). 2006. audio compact disk 289.00 (978-1-4187-5182-1(0)) Bus Info Agency.

Export-Import & Joint-Venture Companies. 6th rev. ed. BIA. (J). 2006. audio compact disk 249.00 (978-1-4187-5181-4(2)) Bus Info Agency.

Exporting Using Commercial Letters of Credit. Donald M. Gartrell. 1 cass. (Running Time: 30 min.). 1998. bk. 12.38 (978-1-893461-02-4(5)) Gartrell.
Discusses: how a company should select a bank to serve their international needs, how they should have their L/Cs issued to assure payment, cost saving tips & ways to save time & stress on trade transactions, use of freight forwarders, & transferring & assigning proceeds of a L/C.

Expose on Satan, Set. T. D. Jakes. 4 cass. 1999. 20.00 (978-1-57855-321-1(0)) T D Jakes.

Exposed. abr. ed. Alex Kava. (Running Time: 6 hrs.). (Maggie O'Dell Ser.: Bk. 6). 2007. audio compact disk 87.25 (978-1-59600-904-2(7), 9781596009042, BACDLib Ed) Brilliance Audio.
Please enter a Synopsis.

Exposed. abr. ed. Alex Kava. Read by Tanya Eby. (Running Time: 6 hrs.). (Maggie O'Dell Ser.: Bk. 6). 2009. audio compact disk 14.99 (978-1-59600-905-9(5), 9781596009059, BCD Value Price) Brilliance Audio.

Exposed. unabr. ed. Katherine L. James. Read by Stephanie Brush. 6 cass. (Running Time: 6 hrs. 42 min.). (Cait Dramis Mystery Ser.). 2001. 39.95 (978-1-55686-879-5(0)) Books in Motion.
Cait Dramis' temporary position selling time-shares at an Oregon State Fair booth is interesting. Especially when one of her booth partners turns up dead. Cait investigates with a young cop's help.

Exposed. unabr. ed. Alex Kava. (Running Time: 10 hrs.). (Maggie O'Dell Ser.: Bk. 6). 2007. audio compact disk 39.25 (978-1-59600-907-3(1), 9781596009073, Brinc Audio MP3 Lib) Brilliance Audio.
Please enter a Synopsis.

Exposed. unabr. ed. Alex Kava. (Running Time: 8 hrs.). (Maggie O'Dell Ser.: Bk. 6). 2008. 24.95 (978-1-59600-906-6(3), 9781596009066, Brilliance MP3) Brilliance Audio.

Exposed. unabr. ed. Alex Kava. Read by Tanya Eby Sirois. (Running Time: 8 hrs.). (Maggie O'Dell Ser.: Bk. 6). 2008. 39.25 (978-1-59600-909-7(8), 9781596009097, BADLE); 24.95 (978-1-59600-908-0(X), 9781596009080, BAD); audio compact disk 34.95 (978-1-4233-4445-2(6), 9781423344452, Bril Audio CD Unabri) Brilliance Audio.

Exposed! Helping Junior Highers Understand God's Plan for Sex. abr. ed. Kurt Johnston. (Super-Ser.). 2006. audio compact disk 30.00 (978-5-558-25700-7(8)) Group Pub.

Exposing False Spiritual Leaders. 6 cass. 19.95 (20139, HarperThor) HarpC GBR.

Exposing the Religious Spirit Series. Jack Deere. 2 cass. (Running Time: 3 hrs.). 2000. 10.00 (JD11-000) Morning NC.
"Characteristics of a Religious Spirit" & "Dealing with a Religious Spirit." This series exposes one of the greatest enemies of every move of God.

Exposing the Spirit of Fornication- Spanish. Speeches. Creflo A. Dollar. 1 cass. (Running Time: 1 hr. 20 mins.). 2001. 5.00 (978-1-59089-690-7(4)) Creflo Dollar.

Exposition, Narration, Scene. Brenda Wilbee. 1 cass. (Running Time: 45 min.). (Writing for Publication: Fiction that Sells Ser.: No. 5). 1987. 7.95 (978-0-943777-05-4(4)) byBrenda.
Writing narration, exposition, telescoping narrative, major & minor scenes in fiction.

Expositions of the Heart. LiShawn Scott. Ed. by LiShawn Scott. 2001. audio compact disk (978-0-9646405-2-8(X)) Bawn Pubs.

Expositors Bible Commentary: The Complete Award-Winning 12-Volume Commentary. Frank E. Gaebelein. (Expositor's Bible Commentary Ser.). 2006. audio compact disk 129.99 (978-0-310-27449-0(4)) Zondervan.

Expositor's Bible Commentary for Macintosh(r). unabr. ed. Zondervan Publishing Staff et al. 1999. audio compact disk 199.99 (978-0-310-23012-0(8)) Zondervan.

Expositor's Bible Commentary for Windows. unabr. ed. Ed. by Frank E. Gaebelein. 1998. audio compact disk 199.99 (978-0-310-21987-3(6)) Zondervan.

Exposure. abr. ed. R. J. Pineiro. Perf. by William R. Moses. 2 cass. (Running Time: 3 hrs.). 1997. 17.00 Set. (978-1-56876-064-3(7)) Soundlines Ent.
Harrison Beckett finds himself protecting Pamela Sasser, a computer scientist he was hired to kill, in order to expose a flaw in a computer chip which has already killed thousands.

Exposure. unabr. ed. Evelyn Anthony. Read by Sian Thomas. 10 cass. (Running Time: 10 hrs.). 1994. 84.95 (978-0-7451-4318-7(0), CAB 1001) AudioGO.
Journalist Julia Hamilton is thrilled when she is given the job of heading a new feature called Exposure, aimed at rooting out corruption. Exposure's first target is media tycoon, Harold King, alias Hans Koenig. He has deliberately covered up his dark past in Germany. And when Julia travels there to find the truth, she learns that her boss, Lord Western, is dangerously involved.

***Exposure.** unabr. ed. Mal Peet. (Running Time: 11 hrs.). 2011. 19.99 (978-1-4558-0063-6(5), 9781455800636, Candlewick Bril); 39.97 (978-1-4558-0064-3(3), 9781455800643, Candlewick Bril); 19.99 (978-1-4558-0060-5(0), 9781455800605, Candlewick Bril); 39.97 (978-1-4558-0061-2(9), 9781455800612, Candlewick Bril); audio compact disk 24.99 (978-1-4558-0058-2(9), 9781455800582, Candlewick Bril); audio compact disk 54.97 (978-1-4558-0059-9(7), 9781455800599, Candlewick Bril) Brilliance Audio.

Exposure. unabr. ed. R. J. Pineiro. Read by Brian Emerson. 7 cass. (Running Time: 10 hrs.). 1997. 49.95 (978-0-7861-1042-1(2), 1814) Blckstn Audio.
Riveting thriller of a woman who stands between a powerful billionaire presidential candidate & the millions of Americans whose lives are at stake - unless his secret is exposed.

Expresate, Level 1. 6th ed. Holt, Rinehart and Winston Staff. (SPA.). Date not set. audio compact disk 375.13 (978-0-03-074431-0(8)) Holt McDoug.

Expresate, Level 1. 6th ed. Humbach. (Holt Spanish Ser.). (SPA.). Date not set. audio compact disk 75.13 (978-0-03-039797-4(9)) Holt McDoug.

Expresate, Level 2. 6th ed. Holt, Rinehart and Winston Staff. (SPA.). Date not set. audio compact disk 375.13 (978-0-03-074432-7(6)) Holt McDoug.

Expresate, Level 2. 6th ed. Humbach. (Holt Spanish Ser.). (SPA.). Date not set. audio compact disk 76.80 (978-0-03-039798-1(7)) Holt McDoug.

Expresate, Level 3. 6th ed. Holt, Rinehart and Winston Staff. (SPA.). Date not set. audio compact disk 375.13 (978-0-03-074461-7(X)) Holt McDoug.

Expresate, Level 3. 6th ed. Humbach. (Holt Spanish Ser.). (SPA.). Date not set. audio compact disk 77.46 (978-0-03-039799-8(5)) Holt McDoug.

Expresate: Audio CD Program. 6th ed. Holt, Rinehart and Winston Staff. (SPA.). Date not set. audio compact disk 199.66 (978-0-03-074368-9(0)) Holt McDoug.

Expresate: Audio CD Program, Level 1A. 6th ed. Holt, Rinehart and Winston Staff. (Holt Spanish Ser.). (SPA.). 2004. audio compact disk 199.66 (978-0-03-074367-2(2)) Holt McDoug.
A consistent chapter structure gives students the confidence to succeed.

Express: Ainsi Va la France. Ross Steele. 3 cass. (Running Time: 60 min. per cass.). (FRE.). 29.95 (978-0-8442-1258-6(X), Natl Textbk Co) M-H Contemporary.

Express: The Ernie Davis Story. unabr. ed. Robert C. Gallagher. Narrated by Paul Boehmer. 5 CDs. (Running Time: 5 hrs. 30 mins. 0 sec.). (ENG.). 2008. audio compact disk 24.99 (978-1-4001-0877-0(2)); audio compact disk 49.99 (978-1-4001-3877-7(9)) Pub: Tantor Media. Dist(s): IngramPubServ

Express: The Ernie Davis Story. unabr. ed. Robert C. Gallagher. Read by Paul Boehmer. 1 MP3-CD. (Running Time: 5 hrs. 30 mins. 0 sec.). (ENG.). 2008. 19.99 (978-1-4001-5877-5(X)) Pub: Tantor Media. Dist(s): IngramPubServ

Express Advanced: Aujourd'hui la France. Ross Steele & Jose Pavis. 3 cass. (Running Time: 4 hrs.). (FRE.). (YA). 1994. 46.60 (978-0-8442-1278-4(4), Natl Textbk Co) M-H Contemporary.

Express French: Learn to Speak & Understand French with Pimsleur Language Programs. Pimsleur Staff & Pimsleur. (Running Time: 115 hrs. 0 mins. NaN sec.). (Express Ser.). (ENG.). 2003. audio compact disk 11.95 (978-0-7435-3390-4(9), Pimsleur) Pub: S&S Audio. Dist(s): S and S Inc

Express, Grades 10-12: Aujourd' hui la France. (FRE.). 1993. pap. bk. & tchr. ed. 59.50 (978-0-88432-999-2(2), SFR300) J Norton Pubs.
Increase your reading comprehension while learning about contemporary French culture as portrayed in L'Express, France's popular weekly news magazine. Forty-six informative & interesting articles discuss a broad range of trends in education, the arts, industry & the changing face of French politics. Each article is accompanied by photos, culture & vocabulary notes, comprehension & discussion questions & writing exercises. Includes transcript of interviews.

Express Track to German: A Teach-Yourself Program. Hilke Opitz et al. 4 cass. (Running Time: 6 hrs.). (ENG & GER., 1992. bk. 35.00 (978-0-8120-7858-9(6)) Barron.

Express Track to Italian. 4 cass. (Running Time: 60 min. per cass.). (ITA.). 1990. bk. 35.00 Set. Barron.

Express Yourself in America, Vol. 1. Short Stories. Elaine de Araujo. Created by Elaine de Araujo. Perf. by Wayne A. Ferrara. Narrated by Wayne A. Ferrara. 1 CD. (Running Time: 68 mins.). Dramatization. 2005. per. 39.95 (978-0-9770512-0-5(X)) Ferrara Araujo.
The Express Yourself in America Volume One CD is included and packaged with the Express Yourself in America Volume One book. It includes all narrations, dialogues and activity questions that are in the printed book so the student can practice listening skills.

Expression vs. Equality: The Politics of Campaign Finance Reform. J. Tobin Grant & Thomas J. Rudolph. 2004. audio compact disk 9.95 (978-0-8142-9051-4(5)) Pub: Ohio St U Pr. Dist(s): Chicago Distribution Ctr

Expressions, Level 1. 2 cass. (Running Time: 3 hrs.). 2002. 48.95 (978-0-8384-2243-4(8)) Heinle.
Using a task-based approach, Expressions' integrated four-skills syllabus provides learners with abundant opportunities for communicative and meaningful language practice.

Expressions, Level 1. David Nunan. 2 CDs. (Running Time: 3 hrs.). audio compact disk 50.95 (978-0-8384-2390-5(6)) Heinle.

Expressions, Level 2. Nunan. 48.95 (978-0-8384-2273-1(X)) Heinle.

Expressions, Level 2. David Nunan. 2 CDs. (Running Time: 3 hrs.). audio compact disk 50.95 (978-0-8384-2389-9(2)) Heinle.

Expressions, Level 3. 48.95 (978-0-8384-2287-8(X)) Heinle.

Expressions, Level 3. David Nunan. 3 CDs. (Running Time: 4 hrs.). audio compact disk 50.95 (978-0-8384-2388-2(4)) Heinle.

Expressions: Assessment Program, Levels 1, 2, & 3. David Nunan. 23.95 (978-0-8384-2300-4(0)) Heinle.

Expressions Intro 1-2-3. David Nunan & Linse. 2002. audio compact disk (978-0-8384-0583-3(5)) Heinle.

Expressions Introduction. David Nunan & Beatty. 1 CD. (Running Time: 1 hr.). pap. bk. 21.95 (978-0-8384-6537-0(4)) Heinle.

Expressions Introduction. David Nunan & Beatty. 2002. stu. ed. 18.00 (978-0-8384-2841-2(X)); 13.95 (978-0-8384-2599-2(2)) Heinle.

Expressions Introduction. David Nunan & Beatty. 1 CD. (Running Time: 1 hr.). 2002. tchr. ed. 13.95 (978-0-8384-2598-5(4)) Heinle.

Expressions Introduction 1, 2, 3: Assessment Package. David Nunan & Linse. 1 cass. (Running Time: 1 hr.). 2002. 23.95 (978-0-8384-4464-1(4)) Heinle.

Expressions of Love. Elbert Willis. 1 cass. (Oasis of Love Guidelines Ser.). 4.00 Fill the Gap.

Expressions of Worship. 1999. 11.98 (978-0-7673-9299-0(X)) LifeWay Christian.

Expressions of Worship. Gary Rhodes. 1999. 75.00 (978-0-633-03963-9(2)); audio compact disk 16.98 (978-0-633-03964-6(0)); audio compact disk 85.00 (978-0-633-03962-2(4)) LifeWay Christian.

Expressive Politics. Boatright Robert. 2004. audio compact disk 9.95 (978-0-8142-9050-7(7)) Pub: Ohio St U Pr. Dist(s): Chicago Distribution Ctr

Expressways, Level 2. 2nd ed. Steven J. Molinsky & Bill Bliss. 2 cass. 2002. bk., wbk. ed., act. bk. ed. 40.80 (978-0-13-744210-2(6)) Longman.

Expressways, Level 4. 2nd ed. Steven J. Molinsky & Bill Bliss. 2 cass. 2002. bk., wbk. ed., act. bk. ed. 40.80 (978-0-13-744236-2(X)); 40.80 (978-0-13-386368-0(9)) Longman.

Expressways: Level 4, Level 1. 2nd ed. Steven J. Molinsky & Bill Bliss. 2 cass. 2002. bk., wbk. ed., act. bk. ed. 40.80 (978-0-13-740861-0(7)); 40.80 (978-0-13-385329-2(2)) Longman.

Expressways: Level 4, Level 3. 2nd ed. Steven J. Molinsky & Bill Bliss. 2 cass. 2002. bk. & tchr.'s training gde. ed. 20.90 (978-0-13-385684-2(4)) Longman.

Expressways: Student Course Book, Level 2. 2nd ed. Steven J. Molinsky & Bill Bliss. 2 cass. (C). 1996. bk. & stu. ed. 40.80 (978-0-13-385386-5(1)) Longman.

Extasie see Love Poems of John Donne

Extended Chords: How to Form Them & Use Them. Duane Shinn. 1 cass. 19.95 (HAR-3) Duane Shinn.
Explains how to form 7ths, 9ths, 11ths, & 13ths & then learn to voice them.

Extended (Experiential) Awareness, Purposeful Relaxation, Differential (Multiple) Bodily Feeling States & Communication, Set-EA. Russell E. Mason. Read by Russell E. Mason. 6 cass. (Running Time: 5 hrs. 54 min.). (Train-Ascendance Ser.). 1975. pap. bk. 55.00 Set. (978-0-89533-013-0(X), GT-LE) F I Comm.
For individual use or group discussion. Both broad understanding & specific training for awareness & for daily purposeful applications to solve problems involving negative feelings & to accomplish goals with positive feelings.

Extending Connection to an Area of Your Life. 2001. 20.00 (978-0-9714058-1-3(6)) Vanati.

Extension Learning. ZWL Publishing and Professional Speech Center Staff. 1 CD. spiral bd. 1500.00 (978-1-884643-05-7(1)); 1500.00 Incl. advanced level ZWL's Power Talk Audio Learning System, ppd envelopes, blank audio cass. tapes, student learning guide & personal KWL speech coach. (978-1-884643-06-4(X)) Voicesvoices.
Courses build vocabulary, increase vocal expression, minimize accents & dialects, boost self-confidence. Completion of each level can be rated at 1.8 Continuing Education Units (CEUs).

Extensive Radio Visit. Dennis J. McKenna. 3 cass. (Roy Tuckman Interview Ser.). 27.00 set. (A0482-85) Sound Photosyn.
Clear thinking, straightforward talk from the wildest ethnobotanist in town.

Exterminators: (Justice League of America) unabr. ed. Based on a novel by Christopher Golden. 5 CDs. (Running Time: 5 hrs.). 2008. audio compact disk 19.99 (978-1-59950-444-5(8)) GraphicAudio.

Extinguishers DVD. International Association of Fire Chiefs Staff & National Fire Protection Association. 2005. 315.95 (978-0-7637-3610-1(4)) Jones Bartlett.

Extortioners. unabr. collector's ed. John Creasey. Read by Richard Green. 6 cass. (Running Time: 6 hrs.). 1984. 36.00 (978-0-7366-0344-7(1), 1330) Books on Tape.
Inspector Roger "Handsome" West is embroiled in a hectic race to trap a clutch of ruthless hoodlums who apparently will stop at nothing to achieve their objective. West's search for their motive leads him to the high places of London society & to the world's most illustrious anthropologists.

Extra. unabr. ed. Michael Shea. (Running Time: 10 hrs. 0 mins.). 2010. 29.95 (978-1-4417-2526-4(1)); 59.95 (978-1-4417-2522-6(9)); audio compact disk 90.00 (978-1-4417-2523-3(7)) Blckstn Audio.

Extra Class Audio Theory Course: FCC Amateur Radio License Preparation for Element 4. 4th ed. Gordon West. 7 CDs. (Running Time: 9 hrs). (ENG & AFA.). 2005. audio compact disk 39.95 (978-0-945053-44-6(4)) Master Pub Inc.
Audio Theory Course for FCC Extra Class Amateur Radio Element 4 license exam. Narrated by Gordon West, WB6NOA, this audio course follows the contents and organization of his Extra Class book and is a great study companion to the book.

Extra Credit. unabr. ed. Andrew Clements. Read by Gabra Zackman. 3 CDs. (Running Time: 3 hrs. 30 mins. 0 sec.). (ENG.). (J). 2009. audio compact disk 19.99 (978-0-7435-8204-9(7)) Pub: S&S Audio. Dist(s): S and S Inc

Extra Innings. unabr. ed. Robert Newton Peck. Narrated by Tom Stechschulte. 4 cass. (Running Time: 5 hrs.). (gr. 7 up). 38.00 (978-0-7887-5020-5(8)) Recorded Bks.
In a shocking instant, 16-year-old Tate Stonemason loses his entire family when their private plane crashes. He is the only survivor of the accident, but his leg is crushed and, along with it, his hopes of pitching in the big leagues. Emotionally shattered over his family and angry about his leg, Tate wonders if the healing process will ever begin.

***Extract from Captain Stormfield's Visit to Heaven: Narrated by Richard Henzel.** Text by Mark Twain. (ENG.). 2010. audio compact disk 12.99 (978-0-9826688-5-6(6)) R Henzel.

Extract of Hindu Krishnamurti Paddhati. U. Vaidya. 1 cass. 8.95 (469) Am Fed Astrologers.
Secrets to a successful marriage.

Extracting the Gold from Life's Crisis. Gary V. Whetstone. 4 cass. (Running Time: 6 hrs.). (Freedom Ser.). 1993. pap. bk. 35.00 (978-1-58866-212-5(8), VROO3A) Gary Whet Pub.
Learn how to correctly handle pressure, stress, conflict, & temptation so they work for your benefit! This series will teach you how to draw the wealth out of distresses.

Extracts from Adam's Diary see Man That Corrupted Hadleyburg & Other Stories

Extracts from Adam's Diary & Eve's Diary. unabr. ed. Mark Twain. Read by Walter Zimmerman & Cindy Hardin. 1 cass. (Running Time: 72 min.). 1977. 7.95 (N-1) Jimcin Record.
Humorous & often touching look at the first man & woman.

Extrana Visita. Alma Flor Ada. (Libros Para Contar Ser.). (SPA., (J). (gr. k-3). 4.95 (978-1-58105-259-6(6)) Santillana.

Extranjero. unabr. ed. Albert Camus & Francois Mauriac. Read by Hernando Iván Cano. 3 CDs.Tr. of Outsider. (SPA.). 2002. audio compact disk 17.00 (978-958-8161-48-8(7)) YoYoMusic.

Extraño Caso Del Dr. Jekyll y Mr Hyde. unabr. ed. Roberto Louis Stevenson. 3 CDs.Tr. of Satrange Case of Dr. Jekyll & Mr. Hyde. (SPA.). 2001. audio compact disk 17.00 (978-958-9494-40-0(4)) YoYoMusic.

***Extraordinary.** unabr. ed. Nancy Werlin. Read by Emily Bauer, Jennifer Van Dyck, Kate Reinders, MacLeod Andrews, and Daniel di Tomasso. (Running Time: 9 hrs.). (YA). 2010. 24.99 (978-1-4418-8232-5(4), 9781441882325, BAD); 39.97 (978-1-4418-8233-2(2), 9781441882332, BADLE) Brilliance Audio.

***Extraordinary.** unabr. ed. Nancy Werlin. Read by Emily Bauer et al. 1 MP3-CD. (Running Time: 9 hrs.). (YA). 2010. 39.97 (978-1-4418-8231-8(6), 9781441882318, Brinc Audio MP3 Lib); 24.99 (978-1-4418-8230-1(8), 9781441882301, Brilliance MP3); audio compact disk 72.97 (978-1-4418-8229-5(4), 9781441882295, BriAudCD Unabrid); audio compact disk 29.99 (978-1-4418-8228-8(6), 9781441882288, Bril Audio CD Unabri) Brilliance Audio.

Extraordinary Adventures of Alfred Kropp. unabr. ed. Rick Yancey. Read by Paul Michael. 5 cass. (Running Time: 7 hrs.). (J). (gr. 4-7). 2006. 40.00 (978-0-307-28455-6(7), Listening Lib); audio compact disk 50.00 (978-0-307-28456-3(5), Listening Lib) Pub: Random Audio Pubg. Dist(s): Random

Extraordinary Adventures of Alfred Kropp. unabr. ed. Rick Yancey. Read by Paul Michael. 6 CDs. (Running Time: 25200 sec.). (ENG.). (J). (gr. 5-12). 2006. audio compact disk 34.00 (978-0-307-28449-5(2), Listening Lib) Pub: Random Audio Pubg. Dist(s): Random

Extraordinary Adventures of Arsene Lupin. unabr. ed. Maurice Leblanc. Read by Walter Covell. 4 cass. (Running Time: 6 hrs.). Incl. Arrest of Arsene Lupin. 1984. (C-97); Arsene Lupin in Prison. 1984. (C-97); Black Pearl. 1984. (C-97); Escape of Arsene Lupin. 1984. (C-97); Madame Imbert's Safe. 1984. (C-97); Mysterious Traveller. 1984. (C-97); Queen's Necklace.

1984. (C-97); Seven of Hearts. 1984. (C-97); Sherlock Holmes Arrives Too Late. 1984. (C-97); 1984. 28.00 (C-97) Jimcin Record.
An inventive genius, a master of disguise & an accomplished actor, Lupin operates only in the choice Chateaux & Salons. He scorns sham, & with great disdain, leaves his card in a Baron's residence. The card reads "Arsene Lupin, Gentlemanburglar, will return when the furniture is genuine".

Extraordinary Adventures of Arsene Lupin. unabr. collector's ed. Maurice Leblanc. Read by Walter Covell. 6 cass. (Running Time: 6 hrs.). (Jimcin Recording Ser.). 1983. 36.00 (978-0-7366-3877-7(6), 9097) Books on Tape.
The stories include: "The Arrest of Arsene Lupin," "Arsene Lupin in Person," "The Escape of Arsene Lupin," "The Mysterious Traveller," "The Queen's Necklace," "The Seven of Hearts," "Madame Imbert's Safe," "The Black Pearl" & "Sherlock Holmes Arrives Too Late".

Extraordinary Customer Service: An Attitude, Not a Department. Laurie Murphy & Jack Mackey. 8 cass. 59.95 Set, incl. wkbk. (505-C47) Natl Seminars.
This program is brimming with practical skills to increase the productivity & professionalism of your entire customer service team. Recent consumer studies show that your customers just want to trust you. Are you doing all you can to gain their confidence? Make customer service an attitude, not a department - give extraordinary customer service!.

Extraordinary Leader: Turning Good Managers into Great Leaders. John H. Zenger. 2005. audio compact disk 28.00 (978-1-932378-83-2(9)) A Media Intl.

Extraordinary Leader: Turning Good Managers into Great Leaders. abr. ed. John H. Zenger & Joseph Folkman. Read by Barrett Whitener. (Running Time: 16200 sec.). 2007. audio compact disk 28.00 (978-1-933309-01-9(6)) Pub: A Media Intl. Dist(s): Natl Bk Netwk

***Extraordinary Love.** Contrib. by John Angotti. (ENG.). 2010. audio compact disk 17.00 (978-1-58459-489-5(6)) Wrld Lib Pubns.

***Extraordinary, Ordinary People: A Memoir of Family.** unabr. ed. Condoleezza Rice. Read by Condoleezza Rice. (Running Time: 9 hrs.). 2010. audio compact disk 35.00 (978-0-307-75063-1(9), RandomAudioBks) Pub: Random Audio Pubg. Dist(s): Random

Extraordinary Popular Delusions & the Madness of Crowds, Pt. 1. unabr. collector's ed. Charles MacKay. Read by Bill Kelsey. 10 cass. (Running Time: 15 hrs.). 1993. 80.00 (978-0-7366-2522-7(4), 3276-A) Books on Tape.
A study of crowd psychology & a guide to understanding mass movements. As good today as when written over a century ago.

Extraordinary Popular Delusions & the Madness of Crowds, Pt. 2. collector's ed. Charles MacKay. Read by Bill Kelsey. 9 cass. (Running Time: 13 hrs. 30 min.). 1993. 72.00 (978-0-7366-2523-4(2), 3276-B) Books on Tape.

***Extraordinary Powers.** abr. ed. Joseph Finder. (Running Time: 6 hrs. 0 mins. 0 sec.). (ENG.). 2010. audio compact disk 14.99 (978-1-4272-1173-6(6)) Pub: Macmill Audio. Dist(s): Macmillan

Extraordinary Relationships: A New Way of Thinking about Human Interactions. Roberta Gilbert. (ENG.). 2006. audio compact disk (978-0-9763455-4-1(4)) Leading Systems.

Extras. unabr. ed. Scott Westerfeld. Narrated by Carine Montbertrand. 10 CDs. (Running Time: 11 hrs. 45 mins.). (Uglies Ser.: Bk. 4). (YA). (gr. 5-8). 2007. audio compact disk 108.75 (978-1-4281-7241-8(6)); 88.75 (978-1-4281-7236-4(X)) Recorded Bks.
Critically acclaimed, award-winning author Scott Westerfeld continues his New York Times best-selling Uglies series with Extras. The only thing that matters in the world is fame, and all people are constantly monitored as though they are contestants in a global talent competition. In the blink of an eye, absolutely anyone can suddenly become famous.

Extravagant Grace: Devotions That Celebrate God's Gift of Grace. abr. ed. Patsy Clairmont et al. (Running Time: 12 hrs. 30 mins. 0 sec.). (ENG.). 2003. 14.99 (978-0-310-26033-2(7)) Zondervan.

Extravagant Grace: Devotions That Celebrate God's Gift of Grace. unabr. ed. Barbara Johnson et al. 2000. 17.99 (978-0-310-23126-4(4)) Zondervan.

Extravagant Love. Derek Prince. 1 cass. 5.95 (123) Derek Prince.
God's love is vast, boundless, extravagant! How shall we measure it? How shall we respond?.

Extravagant Worship. abr. unabr. ed. Darlene Zschech. Narrated by Darlene Zschech. (Running Time: 5 hrs. 18 mins. 0 sec.).Tr. of Adoracion sin reservas. (ENG.). 2005. audio compact disk 19.99 (978-1-58926-876-0(8), 6876) Oasis Audio.

***Extravagant Worship.** unabr. ed. Darlene Zschech. Narrated by Darlene Zschech.Tr. of Adoracion sin reservas. (ENG.). 2005. 13.99 (978-1-60814-734-2(7)) Oasis Audio.

Extreme! Contrib. by Steven V. Taylor. 1997. 11.98 (978-0-7601-1497-1(8), 75602104); 85.00 (978-0-7601-1500-8(1), 75606318); 85.00 (978-0-7601-1540-4(0), 75606452); audio compact disk 85.00 (978-0-7601-1499-5(4), 75606319); audio compact disk 16.98 (978-0-7601-1559-6(1), 75601598) Pub: Brentwood Music. Dist(s): H Leonard

Extreme Channel Surfing. Perf. by Mack Jamie. 1 CD. (Running Time: 1 hr.). 2002. audio compact disk 16.95 (978-1-929243-43-3(X)) Uproar Ent.
Fast paced comedy from Mack & Jamie, two of the brightest comic minds arounds.

Extreme Denial. abr. ed. David Morrell. Read by Peter Boyle. 4 cass. (Running Time: 6 hrs.). 2001. 25.00 (978-1-59040-133-0(6), Phoenix Audio) Pub: Amer Intl Pub. Dist(s): PerseuPGW

Extreme Dreams Depend on Teams: Foreword by Doc Rivers & Patrick Lencioni. unabr. ed. Pat Williams & Jim Denney. (Running Time: 8 hrs. 30 mins.). (ENG.). 2009. 27.98 (978-1-59659-464-7(0), GildAudio) Pub: Gildan Media. Dist(s): HachBkGrp

Extreme Dreams Depend on Teams: Foreword by Doc Rivers & Patrick Lencioni. unabr. ed. Pat Williams & Jim Denney. (Running Time: 8 hrs. 30 mins.). (ENG.). 2009. audio compact disk 29.98 (978-1-59659-342-8(3), GildAudio) Pub: Gildan Media. Dist(s): HachBkGrp

Extreme Faction. 2006. 59.95 (978-0-7861-4434-1(3)); audio compact disk 63.00 (978-0-7861-7376-1(9)) Blckstn Audio.

Extreme Faction. abr. ed. Trevor Scott. Read by Bruce Watson. 4 vols. No. 2. 2002. (978-1-58807-552-9(4)) Am Pubng Inc.

Extreme Faction. abr. ed. Trevor Scott. Read by Bruce Watson. 4 vols. (Running Time: 6 hrs.). (Jake Adams International Thriller Ser.: No. 2). 2002. 25.00 (978-1-58807-092-0(1)) Am Pubng Inc.
Guarding two agribusiness honchos at a conference in Odessa, Ukraine, Jake Adams witnesses the strange death of a former Soviet biochemist. The problem is, Jake isn't the only one standing next to the biochemist when he is swiftly and cleverly assassinated. Under presidential orders, Jake is brought back into the CIA to hunt down the killer. From the U.S. to Germany, Kurdish terrorists are attacking world leaders with the same deadly nerve gas that the Soviet biochemist developed just days before his untimely death. With little time to spare and double agents running interference, will Jake discover the faction of political connections and take down the terrorists' dire scheme?.

Extreme Faction. unabr. ed. Trevor Scott. Read by Stefan Rudnicki. 2006. 29.95 (978-0-7861-7751-6(9)) Blckstn Audio.

Extreme Justice. William Bernhardt. Read by Jonathan Marosz. (Ben Kincaid Ser.: No. 7). 2001. 56.00 (978-0-7366-6845-3(4)) Books on Tape.

Extreme Life Collection. Kelly Regan Barnhill et al. (Playaway Children Ser.). (ENG.). (J). 2009. 39.99 (978-1-60847-558-2(1)) Find a World.

Extreme Makeover CD Series. 2007. audio compact disk 19.99 (978-1-933185-21-7(X)) Messengr Intl.

***Extreme Makeover Life Message Series.** Lisa Bevere. 2010. audio compact disk 0.00 (978-1-933185-65-1(1)) Messengr Intl.

Extreme Makeover of Hillary (Rodham) Clinton. unabr. ed. Bay Buchanan. (Running Time: 25200 sec.). 2007. 54.95 (978-1-4332-1337-3(0)) Blckstn Audio.

Extreme Makeover of Hillary (Rodham) Clinton. unabr. ed. Bay Buchanan. Read by Pam Ward. (Running Time: 25200 sec.). 2007. audio compact disk 29.95 (978-1-4332-1339-7(7)); audio compact disk & audio compact disk 55.00 (978-1-4332-1338-0(9)) Blckstn Audio.

Extreme Management. Mark Stevens. 2 cass. (Running Time: 3 hrs.). 2002. 17.98 (978-1-58621-169-1(2)) Hachet Audio.
The Advanced Management Program is an exhaustive 10 week boot-camp (six days a week, 14 hours a day) that prepares the business elite for the highly competitive global marketplace. For the first time, the closely guarded secrets will be available to executives and would-be executives everywhere.

Extreme Management: What They Teach at Harvard Business School's Advanced Management Program. abr. ed. Mark Stevens. Read by Sam Chew et al. (ENG.). 2005. 14.98 (978-1-59483-441-7(5)) Pub: Hachet Audio. Dist(s): HachBkGrp

Extreme Measures. abr. ed. Vince Flynn. Read by Armand Schultz. (Running Time: 6 hrs. 0 mins. 0 sec.). No. 9. (ENG.). 2008. audio compact disk 29.99 (978-0-7435-6873-9(7)) Pub: S&S Audio. Dist(s): S and S Inc

***Extreme Measures.** abr. ed. Vince Flynn. Read by Armand Schultz. (Running Time: 6 hrs. 0 mins. 0 sec.). (ENG.). 2010. audio compact disk 14.99 (978-1-4423-3551-6(3)) Pub: S&S Audio. Dist(s): S and S Inc

Extreme Measures. unabr. ed. Vince Flynn. Read by George Guidall. 11 CDs. (Running Time: 13 hrs. 0 mins. 0 sec.). No. 9. (ENG.). 2008. audio compact disk 49.99 (978-0-7435-7481-5(8)) Pub: S&S Audio. Dist(s): S and S Inc

Extreme Measures. unabr. ed. Michael Palmer. Read by Michael Kramer. 9 cass. (Running Time: 13 hrs. 30 min.). 1997. 72.00 (978-0-7366-3725-1(7), 4406) Books on Tape.
A medical thriller in which a young, dedicated doctor has what it takes to join the secret society of murderous, brutal medical professionals who have plans for him well beyond the normal call of duty.

Extreme Measures. unabr. ed. Michael Palmer. Narrated by George Guidall. 9 cass. (Running Time: 12 hrs. 15 mins.). 78.00 (978-0-7887-0634-9(9), 94810E7) Recorded Bks.
Secrecy, intrigue & doctors blurring edges of medical ethics are the ingredients in Palmer's prescription for riveting medical thrillers. Using his decades of emergency room experiences, he creates a haunting world of life & death. Available to libraries only.

Extreme Toyota: Radical Contradictions That Drive Success at the World's Best Manufacturer. unabr. ed. Emi Osono et al. Read by Sean Pratt. (Running Time: 8 hrs.). (ENG.). 2008. 24.98 (978-1-59659-247-6(8), GildAudio) Pub: Gildan Media. Dist(s): HachBkGrp

Extremely Goofy Movies Dance Party. 1 CD. (Running Time: 90 mins.). (J). (ps-3). 2000. audio compact disk 12.98 (978-0-7634-0645-5(7)); audio compact disk 12.98 (978-0-7634-0646-2(5)) W Disney Records.

Extremely Loud & Incredibly Close. unabr. ed. Jonathan Safran Foer. Read by Jeff Woodman et al. 10 cds. (Running Time: 11 hrs). 2005. audio compact disk 34.99 (978-1-4193-2879-4(4)) Recorded Bks.

Exxon Valdez & American Trader Oil Spills. Hosted by Nancy Pearlman. 1 cass. (Running Time: 30 min.). 10.00 (711) Educ Comm CA.

Eye. D. Hastings-Nield. (Anatomy Project). 1998. audio compact disk 199.95 (978-1-85070-830-8(4), Parthenon Pbng) Pub: CRC Pr. Dist(s): Taylor and Fran

***Eye.** unabr. ed. Vladimir Nabokov. (Running Time: 2 hrs.). 2011. 39.97 (978-1-4418-7302-6(3), 9781441873026, BADLE); 19.99 (978-1-4418-7301-9(5), 9781441873019, BAD); 19.99 (978-1-4418-7299-9(X), 9781441872999, Brilliance MP3); 39.97 (978-1-4418-7300-2(7), 9781441873002, Brlnc Audio MP3 Lib); audio compact disk 19.99 (978-1-4418-7297-5(3), 9781441872975, Bril Audio CD Unabri); audio compact disk 49.97 (978-1-4418-7298-2(1), 9781441872982, BriAudCD Unabrid) Brilliance Audio.

Eye - Ear - Hand Phonics: Completely Individualized Phonics System. 15 cass. Incl. Eye - Ear - Hand Phonics: Consonant Digraphs & Blends. 4 cass. (J). 69.00 set, incl. activity worksheets & guide. (978-0-89525-255-5(4), AMC 13); Eye - Ear - Hand Phonics: Initial Consonants. 5 cass. (J). 79.00 set, incl. 20 lessons, activity worksheets & guide. (978-0-89525-147-3(7), AMC 12); Eye - Ear - Hand Phonics: Long & Short Vowels. 6 cass. (J). 89.00 set, incl. activity worksheets & guide. (978-0-89525-146-6(9), AMC 15); (J). (gr. k-2). 189.00 incl. activity bks. or dittos Set. (CEYEAR) Ed Activities.
Teaches students to learn the various phonic sounds. Listening skills & following directions are emphasized as decoding skills are taught; humorous characters are used to help reinforcement through association. Includes initial consonant sounds; consonant Digraph CH, Blends (SW, SM, SN, SC, SK, ST, SP), Consonant Digraph SH, Blends (PL, BL, CL, SL, PL, FL), Consonant Digraph TH, Blends (FR, GR, CR, TR, BR, DR, PR), Consonant Digraph WH; long & short vowels (story form).

Eye - Ear - Hand Phonics: Consonant Digraphs & Blends see Eye - Ear - Hand Phonics: Completely Individualized Phonics System

Eye - Ear - Hand Phonics: Initial Consonants see Eye - Ear - Hand Phonics: Completely Individualized Phonics System

Eye - Ear - Hand Phonics: Long & Short Vowels see Eye - Ear - Hand Phonics: Completely Individualized Phonics System

Eye & Tooth see Robert Lowell: A Reading

Eye Care Revolution. Robert Abel. Narrated by Jeff Riggenbach. (Running Time: 19 hrs.). 2002. 50.95 (978-1-59912-658-6(3)) Iofy Corp.

Eye Contact, abr. ed. Stephen Collins. Read by Stephen Collins. 2 cass. (Running Time: 3 hrs.). 2000. 7.95 (978-1-57815-143-1(0), 1102, Media Bks Audio) Media Bks NJ.
Enter the world of a New York actress whose best performances are off-screen, in her dangerous relations with men.

Eye Contact. unabr. ed. Stephen Collins. Read by Susan Ericksen. (Running Time: 12 hrs.). 2008. 39.25 (978-1-4233-5354-6(4), 9781423353546, BADLE); 24.95 (978-1-4233-5353-9(6), 9781423353539, BAD) Brilliance Audio.

Eye Contact. unabr. ed. Stephen Collins. Read by Susan Ericksen. Directed By Sandra Burr. Contrib. by Paige Sherwood. (Running Time: 11 hrs.). 2008. audio compact disk 39.25 (978-1-4233-5352-2(8), 9781423353522, Brlnc Audio MP3 Lib); audio compact disk 24.95 (978-1-4233-5351-5(X), 9781423353515, Brilliance MP3) Brilliance Audio.

Eye Contact. unabr. ed. Cammie McGovern. Read by Julia Fletcher. (YA). 2006. 49.99 (978-1-59895-208-7(0)) Find a World.

Eye for an Eye. Janet Lorimer. 1 cass. (Running Time: 4101 sec.). (PageTurner Spy Ser.). (J). 2002. 10.95 (978-1-56254-490-4(X), SP 490X) Saddleback Edu.
Word-for-word read-along of An Eye for An Eye.

Eye for an Eye. Anthony Trollope. Narrated by Flo Gibson. 2007. 20.95 (978-1-55685-887-1(6)) Audio Bk Con.

Eye for an Eye. Anthony Trollope. Narrated by Flo Gibson. (ENG.). 2008. audio compact disk 27.95 (978-1-60646-037-5(4)) Audio Bk Con.

Eye for an Eye. unabr. ed. Erika Holzer. Read by Sandra Burr & Multivoice Production Staff. (Running Time: 10 hrs.). 2009. 39.97 (978-1-4233-8619-3(1), 9781423386193, Brlnc Audio MP3 Lib) Brilliance Audio.

Eye for an Eye. unabr. ed. Erika Holzer. Read by Sandra Burr. (Running Time: 10 hrs.). 2009. 39.97 (978-1-4233-8621-6(3), 9781423386216, BADLE) Brilliance Audio.

Eye for an Eye. unabr. ed. Erika Holzer. Read by Sandra Burr & Multivoice Production Staff. (Running Time: 10 hrs.). 2009. 24.99 (978-1-4233-8618-6(3), 9781423386186, Brilliance MP3) Brilliance Audio.

Eye for an Eye. unabr. ed. Erika Holzer. Read by Sandra Burr. (Running Time: 10 hrs.). 2009. 24.99 (978-1-4233-8620-9(5), 9781423386209, BAD) Brilliance Audio.

***Eye for Glory: The Civil War Chronicles of a Citizen Soldier.** Zondervan. (ENG.). 2011. 16.99 (978-0-310-41263-2(3)) Zondervan.

Eye Hath Not Seen: 1 Cor. 2:6-13. Ed Young. 1985. 4.95 (978-0-7417-1485-5(X), 485) Win Walk.

Eye in the Door. unabr. ed. Pat Barker. Narrated by Steven Crossley. 6 cass. (Running Time: 9 hrs. 15 mins.). 1997. 51.00 (978-0-7887-0819-0(8), 94969E7) Recorded Bks.
Second book in the author's World War I trilogy.

Eye in the Graveyard. Michael Dahl. Illus. by Fernando Molinari. (Library of Doom Ser.). (gr. 1-3). 2008. audio compact disk 14.60 (978-1-4342-0604-6(1)) CapstoneDig.

Eye of Jade. unabr. ed. Diane Wei Liang. Read by Cindy Cheung. (YA). 2008. 59.99 (978-1-60514-940-0(3)) Find a World.

Eye of Love. Margery Sharp. Read by Anne Dover. 6 cass. (Running Time: 7 hrs.). (Soundings Ser.). (J). 2004. 54.95 (978-1-84283-779-5(6)); audio compact disk 64.95 (978-1-84283-863-1(6)) Pub: ISIS Lrg Prnt GBR. Dist(s): Ulverscroft US

Eye of the Beholder. Read by Heather Forest. 1 cass. (Running Time: 80 mins.). (J). (gr. 6 up). 1991. 9.95 (978-0-938756-31-6(1), 007) Yellow Moon.
Collection of classic tales, musically told, about the beauty in us all.

Eye of the Beholder. Excerpts. As told by Heather Forest. Music by Heather Forest. 1 CD. (Running Time: 78 mins). 2005. audio compact disk 14.95 (978-0-938756-72-9(9), 007CD) Yellow Moon.

Eye of the Beholder. Jayne Ann Krentz. Read by Jayne Atkinson. 2004. 14.95 (978-0-7435-4693-5(8)) Pub: S&S Audio. Dist(s): S and S Inc

Eye of the Beholder. abr. ed. David Ellis. Read by Dick Hill. (Running Time: 6 hrs.). 2008. audio compact disk 14.99 (978-1-4233-3641-9(0), 9781423336419, BCD Value Price) Brilliance Audio.

Eye of the Beholder. abr. ed. Jayne Ann Krentz. Read by Jayne Atkinson. 4 cass. 1999. 24.00 (FS9-43415) Highsmith.

Eye of the Beholder. unabr. ed. David Ellis. Read by Dick Hill. (Running Time: 12 hrs.). 2007. 39.25 (978-1-4233-3639-6(9), 9781423336396, BADLE); 24.95 (978-1-4233-3638-9(0), 9781423336389, BAD); 87.25 (978-1-4233-3633-4(X), 9781423336334, BrilAudUnabridg); audio compact disk 24.95 (978-1-4233-3636-5(4), 9781423336365, Brilliance MP3); audio compact disk 34.95 (978-1-4233-3634-1(8), 9781423336341, Bril Audio CD Unabri); audio compact disk 39.25 (978-1-4233-3637-2(2), 9781423336372, Brlnc Audio MP3 Lib); audio compact disk 107.25 (978-1-4233-3635-8(6), 9781423336358, BriAudCD Unabrid) Brilliance Audio.

Eye of the Beholder. unabr. ed. Jayne Ann Krentz. Read by Jen Taylor. 8 vols. (Running Time: 12 hrs.). 2000. bk. 69.95 (978-0-7927-2411-7(9), CSL 300, Chivers Sound Lib) AudioGO.
At a luxurious Arizona resort, a hard-edged businessman & a beautiful art consultant make a tantalizing mind-body connection, while a killer threatens their piece of paradise.

Eye of the Beholder. unabr. ed. Bryan Lysaght. Read by Arthur Addison. 9 cass. (Running Time: 13 hrs. 30 min.). 1996. 72.00 (978-0-7366-3286-7(7), 3941) Books on Tape.
Days before opening the case that would have made her a celebrity, Julie Beck, assistant U.S. attorney, learned that her quarry - Robert Vargo, criminal financier - fled to Cuba with millions in fraudulently gleaned funds, leaving three dead witnesses in his wake. Four years later, Vargo is back in the U.S. & the one man who can lead Beck to him sits behind bars - where Beck put him for tipping off Vargo to his impending arrest.

Eye of the Cricket: A Lew Griffin Mystery. unabr. ed. James Sallis. Read by G. Valmont Thomas. (Running Time: 4 hrs. 0 mins.). (ENG.). 2009. 19.95 (978-1-4332-3033-2(X)); 24.95 (978-1-4332-3029-5(1)); audio compact disk 40.00 (978-1-4332-3030-1(5)) Blckstn Audio.

Eye of the Elephant. unabr. ed. Delia Owens & Mark Owens. Read by Frances Cassidy. 7 cass. (Running Time: 10 hrs. 30 min.). 1994. 56.00 (978-0-7366-2866-2(5), 3572) Books on Tape.
When the Owenses go public about poachers killing a thousand elephants each year, they nearly pay with their lives.

Eye of the Gator. unabr. collector's ed. E. C. Ayres. Read by Barrett Whitener. 6 cass. (Running Time: 9 hrs.). 1997. 48.00 (978-0-7366-3588-2(2), 4242) Books on Tape.
Though habitually laid back, Tony Lowell, photographer/P.I., jumps in the fray when a friend's nephew, Timothy, disappears.

Eye of the Needle. Ken Follett. Narrated by Eric Lincoln. Told to Roslyn Alexander et al. (Playaway Adult Fiction Ser.). (ENG.). 2009. 64.99 (978-1-60775-687-3(0)) Find a World.

Eye of the Needle. Ken Follett. Narrated by Graeme Malcolm. 10 CDs. (Running Time: 11 hrs. 15 mins.). audio compact disk 119.75 (978-0-7887-9875-7(8)) Recorded Bks.

Eye of the Needle. unabr. ed. Ken Follett. Read by Tim Behrens. 8 cass. (Running Time: 11 hrs.). 1985. 49.95 (978-1-55686-225-0(3), 112672) Books in Motion.
His code name was "The Needle." The handsome, intelligent German aristocrat knows the secret that can win the war for Hitler. Lucy, a beautiful Englishwoman, is the only one who can stop him.

Eye of the Needle. unabr. ed. Ken Follett. Read by Richard Green. 7 cass. (Running Time: 10 hrs. 30 min.). 1980. 56.00 (978-0-7366-0428-4(6), 1400) Books on Tape.
The time is early 1944, the place a secluded area on the east coast of England. In order to keep the impending invasion of Normandy a secret, American & British forces have constructed a fake military site here - complete with imitation ships, plywood airplanes, barracks & equipment.

The Germans are meant to discover this operation through aerial photographs. However, a German spy has uncovered this deception & is trying to meet up with a German U-Boat to report the Allied plan to his superiors.

Eye of the Needle. unabr. ed. Ken Follett. Read by Multivoice Production Staff. (Running Time: 9 hrs.). 2004. 29.95 (978-1-59355-650-1(0), 1593556500, BAU) Brilliance Audio.
One enemy spy knows the secret of the Allies' greatest deception, a brilliant aristocrat and ruthless assassin - code name: "The Needle" - who holds the key to the ultimate Nazi victory. Only one person stands in his way: a lonely Englishwoman on an isolated island, who is coming to love the killer who has mysteriously entered her life. Ken Follett's unsurpassed and unforgettable masterwork of suspense, intrigue, and dangerous machinations of the human heart.

Eye of the Needle. unabr. ed. Ken Follett. Read by Multivoice Production Staff. (Running Time: 9 hrs.). 2004. 24.95 (978-1-59335-278-3(6), 1593352786, Brilliance MP3); 39.25 (978-1-59335-539-5(4), 1593355394, Brlnc Audio MP3 Lib) Brilliance Audio.

Eye of the Needle. unabr. ed. Ken Follett. (Running Time: 9 hrs.). 2004. 24.95 (978-1-59710-259-9(8), 1597102598, BAD) Brilliance Audio.

Eye of the Needle. unabr. ed. Ken Follett. Read by Multivoice Production Staff. (Running Time: 9 hrs.). 2004. 39.25 (978-1-59710-258-2(X), 159710258X, BADLE) Brilliance Audio.

Eye of the Needle. unabr. ed. Ken Follett. Read by Multivoice Production Staff. (Running Time: 9 hrs.). 2007. audio compact disk 38.95 (978-1-4233-2861-2(2), 9781423328612, Bril Audio CD Unabri) Brilliance Audio.

Eye of the Needle. unabr. ed. Ken Follett. Read by Roslyn Alexander & Richard Lavin. Narrated by Eric Lincoln. (Running Time: 32400 sec.). 2007. audio compact disk 92.25 (978-1-4233-2862-9(0), 9781423328629, BriAudCD Unabrid) Brilliance Audio.

Eye of the Needle, unabr. ed. Ken Follett. Narrated by Graeme Malcolm. 8 cass. (Running Time: 11 hrs. 15 mins.). 1990. 79.75 (978-1-55690-171-3(2), 90054E7) Recorded Bks.
A German agent in Britain alone knows that Britain's D-Day preparations are a hoax. He must be stopped before he can relay his discovery to Berlin.

Eye of the Oracle. unabr. ed. Bryan Davis. Narrated by Peter Sandon. (Oracles of Fire Ser.). (ENG.). 2008. 10.49 (978-1-60814-194-4(2)) Oasis Audio.

Eye of the Oracle. unabr. ed. Bryan Davis. Narrated by Peter Sandon. (Running Time: 19 hrs. 31 mins. 34 sec.). (Oracles of Fire Ser.). (ENG.). 2009. audio compact disk 49.99 (978-1-59859-528-4(8)) Oasis Audio.

Eye of the Prophet. unabr. ed. Khalil Gibran. Read by Johnny Cash. 1 cass. (Running Time: 1 hr. 30 min.). 1996. 11.95 (978-1-57453-012-4(7)) Audio Lit.
Writing of youth, love, marriage & truth, Gibran skillfully weaves a great spiritual tapestry that transcends cultural divisions.

Eye of the Red Tsar: A Novel of Suspense. unabr. ed. Sam Eastland. Read by Paul Michael. (ENG.). 2010. audio compact disk 35.00 (978-0-307-73596-6(6), Random AudioBks) Pub: Random Audio Pubg. Dist(s): Random

Eye of the Storm. Perf. by Kenny Ainge. Lyrics by Kenny Ainge. Prod. by Kenneth Ainge, Jr. (ENG.). 2008. audio compact disk 14.95 (978-0-9816250-9-6(6)) EmpoweringUT.

Eye of the Storm. Catherine Jones. 2008. 69.95 (978-1-84559-948-5(9)); audio compact disk 79.95 (978-1-84559-949-2(7)) Pub: Soundings Ltd GBR. Dist(s): Ulverscroft US

Eye of the Storm. abr. ed. Jack Higgins. Perf. by Patrick Macnee. 2 cass. (Running Time: 3 hrs.). (Sean Dillon Ser.). 2004. 18.00 (978-1-59007-191-5(3)) Pub: New Millenn Enter. Dist(s): PerseuPGW
Former allies in the IRA, Sean Dillon and Martin Brosnan have chosen different paths. Now Dillon is a terrorist for hire, a master of diguise employed by Saddam Hussein. Brosnan is the one man who knows Dillon's strengths and weaknesses...and brilliant mastery of espionage. Once friends, now enemies, they are playing the deadliest game of their careers. A game that culminates in a frightening - and true - event: Iraq's attempted mortar attack on the British war cabinet at 10 Downing Street in Februrary 1991.

Eye of the Storm. unabr. ed. V. C. Andrews. Read by Liza Ross. 8 cass. (Running Time: 9 hrs. 30 min.). (Hudson Ser.). (J). 2002. 69.95 (978-0-7531-1122-2(5)); audio compact disk 84.95 (978-0-7531-1274-8(4)) Pub: ISIS Lrg Prnt GBR. Dist(s): Ulverscroft US
In the wake of a terrible loss, Rain is left alone to bear the Hudson family secrets, as dark and forbidding as storm clouds on the horizon . . .After the death of her beloved Grandmother Hudson, Rain finds herself caught in a battle for the vast Hudson family wealth. Marked to inherit millions, Rain faced the fury of her unaccepting mother, her manipulative stepfather and her vicious Aunt Victoria. But no amount of money can keep Rain's world from crashing down when tragedy strikes.

Eye of the Storm. unabr. ed. Jack Higgins. Read by Michael Page. (Running Time: 8 hrs.). (Sean Dillon Ser.). 2010. audio compact disk 87.97 (978-1-4418-3886-5(4), 9781441838865, BriAudCD Unabrid); audio compact disk 29.99 (978-1-4418-3885-8(6), 9781441838858) Brilliance Audio.

***Eye of the Storm.** unabr. ed. Jack Higgins. Read by Michael Page. (Running Time: 8 hrs.). (Sean Dillon Ser.). 2010. 24.99 (978-1-4418-3887-2(2), 9781441838872, Brilliance MP3); 39.97 (978-1-4418-3888-9(0), 9781441838889, Brlnc Audio MP3 Lib); 39.97 (978-1-4418-3890-2(2), 9781441838902, BADLE); 24.99 (978-1-4418-3889-6(9), 9781441838896, BAD) Brilliance Audio.

***Eye of the Storm.** unabr. ed. Jack Higgins. (Running Time: 8 hrs.). (Sean Dillon Ser.). 2011. audio compact disk 14.99 (978-1-4418-3892-6(9), 9781441838926, BCD Value Price) Brilliance Audio.

Eye of the Storm. unabr. ed. Jack Higgins. Read by Sean Barrett. 7 CDs. (Running Time: 7 hrs. 30 min.). (Sean Dillon Ser.). 2001. audio compact disk (978-0-7531-0889-5(5)) ISIS Audio GBR.
The IRA, ETA, the PLO, Sean Dillon has worked for them all. His assassin's bullet is highly respected and highly priced. Now, in the middle of the Gulf War, the Iraqis need his services for a vicious terrorist strike; Target Britain. The plan is to shake the world - wipe out key Western Government figures and gain a massive propaganda coup. But on Dillon's tail are British Intelligence. They've found a killer to stalk a killer, a man with personal reasons to enter the storm . .

Eye of the Storm. unabr. ed. Marcia Muller. Read by Bernadette Dunne. 7 cass. (Running Time: 10 hrs. 30 min.). (Sharon McCone Mystery Ser.: No. 7). 1998. 56.00 (978-0-7366-4135-7(1), 4640) Books on Tape.
Once a magnificent home of a tycoon & planter, Appleby Island is a place of history & mystery in the Sacramento delta. Now Patsy McCone, her new lover & a group of investors are turning the old mansion into an elegant B & B. Summoned by her eccentric younger sister, San Francisco's sharon McCone arrives in the teeth of a gale. She's been called in to take a short vacation & investigate mysterious acts of vandalism that are running the project to ruin.

Eye of the Storm. unabr. ed. John Ringo. Read by Mark Vietor. (Running Time: 15 hrs.). (Posleen War Ser.: No. 11). 2009. 24.99 (978-1-4233-9520-1(4), 9781423395201, Brilliance MP3); 39.97 (978-1-4233-9521-8(2), 9781423395218, Brlnc Audio MP3 Lib); 39.97 (978-1-4233-9522-5(0), 9781423395225, BADLE); audio compact disk 29.99 (978-1-4233-9518-8(2), 9781423395188, Bril Audio CD Unabri); audio compact disk 99.97 (978-1-4233-9519-5(0), 9781423395195, BriAudCD Unabrid) Brilliance Audio.

Eye of the Storm Vol. 2: Storm, E Weather, Set. abr. ed. Jones Desmond. Read by Jones Desmond. 2 cass. Dramatization. (YA). (gr. 7-12). 1999. pap. bk. 30.00 (978-0-9669585-3-9(5)) Eye Storm.

Eye of the Storm Vol. 2: Storm, E Weather, Set. 2nd abr. rev. ed. Jones Desmond. Read by Jones Desmond. Tr. by Golden Arts Photos and Graphics Staff. 2 cass. Dramatization. (YA). (gr. 7-12). 1999. bk. 22.00 (978-0-9669585-4-6(3)) Eye Storm.

Eye of the Tiger. (Paws & Tales Ser.: No. 31). 2002. 3.99 (978-1-57972-480-1(9)); audio compact disk 5.99 (978-1-57972-481-8(7)) Insight Living.

Eye of the Tiger. unabr. ed. Wilbur Smith. Read by Nigel Davenport. 8 cass. (Running Time: 12 hrs.). (Ballantyne Novel Ser.). 2000. 59.95 (978-0-7451-6295-9(9), CAB 157) Pub: Chivers Audio Bks GBR. Dist(s): AudioGO
Harry Fletcher, a man with a tainted past, has reformed and is making an honest living as a charter skipper. Suddenly, men from his violent past overturn his good intentions, involving him in the race to recover a fantastic treasure form the ancient wreck.

Eye of the Tiger. unabr. collector's ed. Wilbur Smith. Read by Richard Brown. 9 cass. (Running Time: 13 hrs. 30 min.). (Ballantyne Novels Ser.). 1990. 72.00 (978-0-7366-1821-2(X), 2657) Books on Tape.
"Death by misadventure" is the convenient ruling on two fatalities aboard Wave Dancer, whose skipper, Harry Fletcher, skirts shoals of coral in remote waters of the South Indian Ocean. No stranger to violence, Harry knows this "misadventure" means he's playing with the big boys where the stakes are high. His problem is only that he doesn't know exactly what game is being played. His only certainty is that to fail is to die.

***Eye of the Virgin.** unabr. ed. Frederick Ramsay. (Running Time: 8 hrs. 30 mins.). 2010. 29.95 (978-1-4417-4976-5(4)); 54.95 (978-1-4417-4972-7(1)); audio compact disk 76.00 (978-1-4417-4973-4(X)) Blckstn Audio.

Eye of the Wind. Jane Jackson. Read by Patricia Gallimore. 10 cass. (Sound Ser.). (J). 2003. 84.95 (978-1-84283-356-8(1)) Pub: ISIS Lrg Prnt GBR. Dist(s): Ulverscroft US

Eye of the Wolf. unabr. ed. Margaret Coel. Read by Stephanie Brush. 1 MP3-CD. (Running Time: 9 hrs.). (Wind River Ser.). 2005. 24.95 (978-1-59607-459-0(0)); audio compact disk 51.95 (978-1-59607-458-3(2)); 49.95 (978-1-59607-457-6(4)) Books in Motion.
"This is for the Indian Priest..." The cryptic message on the answering machine was clearly meant for Father O' Malley. The unemotional voice was speaking of revenge against old enemies, and wanted O'Malley to visit the site of the 1874 Bates Battle where Captain Bate's cavalry, lead by Shoshone warriors massacred nearly everyone living on an Arapaho tribal grounds. Now, someone has left three dead Shoshones on the battlefield, positioned to mimic the bodies of those Arapahos killed in the historic slaughter. Frankie Montana, attorney Vicky Holden's latest client, is a frequent guest of the reservation's holding cells, and after a recent heated encounter with the three dead men, is the number one suspect in their deaths. Despite his faults, Vicky doesn't believe he is capable of murder. Instead, she suspects that someone is trying to stir up a war between the Arapaho and Shoshone people, ripping open the still painful wounds of the past...the question is why?.

Eye of the World, abr. ed. Robert Jordan. Read by Mark Rolston. 2 cass. (Running Time: 3 hrs.). (Wheel of Time Ser.: Bk. 1). 2000. 7.95 (978-1-57815-132-5(5), 1091, Media Bks Audio) Media Bks NJ.
Only two kinds of magic exist. one female & the other male. The hero Rand is on an epic quest to unite the diverse people of his planet against the Dark One, who threatens to destroy their world.

Eye of the World. abr. ed. Robert Jordan. Read by Mark Rolston. 2 cass. (Running Time: 3 hrs.). (Wheel of Time Ser.: Bk. 1). 1994. 16.95 Set. (978-1-879371-52-1(9), 40020) Pub Mills.
Rand al'Thor & his friends begin to learn of their destinies.

Eye of the World. unabr. ed. Robert Jordan. (Wheel of Time Ser.: Bk. 1). 2001. audio compact disk 69.95 (978-1-57511-098-1(9)) Pub Mills.

Eye of the World. unabr. rev. ed. Robert Jordan. Read by Michael Kramer & Kate Reading. 25 CDs. (Running Time: 31 hrs. 0 mins. 0 sec.). (Wheel of Time Ser.: Bk. 1). (ENG.). 2004. audio compact disk 59.95 (978-1-59397-432-9(9)) Pub: Macmill Audio. Dist(s): Macmillan

Eye of the World, Pt. 1. unabr. ed. Robert Jordan. Read by Kate Reading & Michael Kramer. 11 cass. (Running Time: 16 hrs. 30 min.). (Wheel of Time Ser.: Bk. 1). 1996. 88.00 (978-0-7366-3533-2(5), 4179-A) Books on Tape.
Three boys, forced to flee from their village, hold the key to defeating ultimate evil.

Eye of the World, Pt. 2. unabr. ed. Robert Jordan. Read by Kate Reading & Michael Kramer. 10 cass. (Running Time: 15 hrs.). (Wheel of Time Ser.: Bk. 1). 1996. 80.00 (978-0-7366-3534-9(3), 4179-B) Books on Tape.

Eye of Vengeance. abr. ed. Jonathon King. Read by Mel Foster. (Running Time: 21600 sec.). 2007. audio compact disk 14.99 (978-1-4233-1349-6(6), 9781423313496, BCD Value Price) Brilliance Audio.

Eye of Vengeance. unabr. ed. Jonathon King. Read by Mel Foster. (Running Time: 9 hrs.). 2006. 39.25 (978-1-59600-380-4(4), 9781596003804, BADLE); 24.95 (978-1-59600-379-8(0), 9781596003798, BAD); 74.25 (978-1-59600-374-3(X), 9781596003743, BriAudUnabridg); audio compact disk 92.25 (978-1-59600-376-7(6), 9781596003767, BriAudCD Unabrid); audio compact disk 34.95 (978-1-59600-375-0(8), 9781596003750); audio compact disk 24.95 (978-1-59600-377-4(4), 9781596003774, Brilliance MP3); audio compact disk 39.25 (978-1-59600-378-1(2), 9781596003781, Brlnc Audio MP3 Lib) Brilliance Audio.
Please enter a Synopsis.

Eye to Eye. unabr. ed. Catherine Jinks. Read by Simon Oats. 5 cass. (Running Time: 4 hrs. 30 mins.). 2002. (978-1-86442-349-5(8), 581264) Bolinda Pubng AUS.
While scavenging in the desert, Jansi stumbles across PIM, a Stelcorp star ship, embedded in the sand. PIM is damaged & needs the boy's help, but Jansi has never encourtered a star ship before, much less one capable of thought & expression. Together they forge an unlikely friendship, until a Stelcorp ship arrives, threatening PIM with destruction. For the boy & the star ship, there will be no future unless they triumph against the galaxy's mightiest force.

Eyes. unabr. ed. Edith Wharton. Read by Ralph Cosham. 2 cass. (Running Time: 2 hrs. 18 min.). 1994. lib. bdg. 18.95 Set, incl. vinyl case with notes, author's picture & biography. (978-1-883049-37-9(7)) Sound Room.
A collection of Wharton's finest stories: "The Debt", "The Daunt Diana", "The Moving Finger", & the classic, "The Eyes".

Eyes, Set. unabr. ed. Short Stories. Edith Wharton. 2 cass. (Running Time: 2 hrs. 30 mins.). (Edith Wharton Ser.). 1994. 16.95 (978-1-883049-16-4(4), 390228) Sound Room.
"The Eyes" is the first story & the most famous of Edith Wharton's ghost stories. "The Moving Finger" is a story of a man's love for his dead wife. "The Daunt Diana" tells the story of an art collector who learns of art's true value & "The Debt" is a story of loyalty.

Eyes & Ears of the Heart. Dan Comer. 1 cass. 3.00 (102) Evang Outreach.

Eyes Have It see Your Own World

Eyes Like Stars. unabr. ed. Lisa Mantchev. Read by Cynthia Bishop. 8 CDs. (Running Time: 10 hrs. 30 mins.). (YA). (gr. 7 up). 2009. audio compact disk 55.00 (978-1-936223-00-8(7)) Full Cast Audio.

Eyes of Darkness. unabr. ed. Dean Koontz. Read by Tanya Eby. (Running Time: 10 hrs.). 2010. 39.97 (978-1-4418-1719-8(0), 9781441817198, Brlnc Audio MP3 Lib); 24.99 (978-1-4418-1718-1(2), 9781441817181, Brilliance MP3); 24.99 (978-1-4418-1720-4(4), 9781441817204, BAD); audio compact disk 38.99 (978-1-4418-1716-7(6), 9781441817167, Bril Audio CD Unabri); audio compact disk 97.97 (978-1-4418-1717-4(4), 9781441817174, BriAudCD Unabrid) Brilliance Audio.

***Eyes of Darkness.** unabr. ed. Dean Koontz. Read by Tanya Eby. (Running Time: 10 hrs.). 2010. 39.97 (978-1-4418-1721-1(2), 9781441817211, BADLE) Brilliance Audio.

Eyes of Eagles. abr. ed. William W. Johnstone. 2 cass. (Running Time: 3 hrs.). (Eagles Ser.: No. 1). 2004. 18.00 (978-1-58807-441-6(2)) Am Pubng Inc.
A new series from one of today's most popular Western writers. Orphaned at the age of seven and adopted by Indians, Jamie MacCallister grew into a man more at ease in the wilderness than in the 'civilized' world. When he headed west and crossed the Arkansas Territory, he finally found himself a home. But the Mexican province of Texas in the late 1820s was a dangerous place, changing as more and more Americans settled there. And there are people from back east who have reason to want MacCallister dead. Eagles: A sweeping saga of the men who were part of history in the making, who pushed back the horizons of an extraordinary new land.

***Eyes of Heisenberg.** unabr. ed. Frank Herbert. Narrated by Scott Brick. (Running Time: 6 hrs. 30 mins. 0 sec.). (ENG.). 2010. 19.99 (978-1-4001-6487-5(7)); 13.99 (978-1-4001-8487-3(8)); audio compact disk 24.99 (978-1-4001-1487-0(X)) Pub: Tantor Media. Dist(s): IngramPubServ

***Eyes of Heisenberg (Library Edition)** unabr. ed. Frank Herbert. Narrated by Scott Brick. (Running Time: 6 hrs. 30 mins. 0 sec.). (ENG.). 2010. audio compact disk 49.99 (978-1-4001-4487-7(6)) Pub: Tantor Media. Dist(s): IngramPubServ

***Eyes of Prey.** abr. ed. John Sandford, pseud. Read by Ken Howard. (ENG.). 2006. (978-0-06-122896-4(6), Harper Audio); (978-0-06-122897-1(4), Harper Audio) HarperCollins Pubs.

Eyes of Prey. unabr. ed. John Sandford, pseud. Narrated by Richard Ferrone. 10 cass. (Running Time: 14 hrs.). (Prey Ser.). 1993. 85.00 (978-1-55690-826-2(1), 93141K8) Recorded Bks.
Lt. Lucas Davenport of the Minneapolis police takes on a macabre case, tracking down a serial killer who maims the eyes of his victims after he has murdered them.

Eyes of Prey. unabr. ed. John Sandford, pseud. Narrated by Richard Ferrone. 12 CDs. (Running Time: 14 hrs.). (Prey Ser.). 2000. audio compact disk 109.00 (978-0-7887-3962-0(X), C1117E7) Recorded Bks.

Eyes of the Amaryllis, unabr. ed. Natalie Babbitt. Narrated by Alyssa Bresnahan. 3 pieces. (Running Time: 3 hrs. 15 mins.). (gr. 5 up). 1993. 27.00 (978-1-55690-871-2(7), 93313E7) Recorded Bks.
Geneva goes to spend the summer with her grandmother on the rugged New England coast & encounters a ghostly mystery.

Eyes of the Cat. unabr. ed. Will C. Knott. Read by Maynard Villers. 4 cass. (Running Time: 4 hrs. 30 min.). (Golden Hawk Ser.: Bk. 7). 1996. 26.95 (978-1-55686-700-2(X)) Books in Motion.
Hawk is concerned when he realizes a white, ex-cavalry officer is training the Blackfoot Indians how to fight with organized military precision.

***Eyes of the Dragon.** unabr. ed. Stephen King. (Running Time: 10 hrs. 0 mins.). 2010. 29.95 (978-1-4417-3889-9(4)); 59.95 (978-1-4417-3885-1(1)); audio compact disk 60.00 (978-1-4417-3886-8(X)) Blckstn Audio.

Eyes of the Dragon. unabr. ed. Stephen King. (Running Time: 11 hrs.). (ENG.). 2010. audio compact disk 39.95 (978-0-14-242788-0(8), PengAudBks) Penguin Grp USA.

Eyes of the Emperor. unabr. ed. Graham Salisbury. Read by Robert Ramirez. 5 CDs. (Running Time: 5 hrs. 15 mins.). (YA). 2006. audio compact disk 49.75 (978-1-4193-8486-8(4), C3664); 39.75 (978-1-4193-8481-3(3), 98327) Recorded Bks.
After the attack on Pearl Harbor, Eddy Okubo, a Japanese American teenager, is more determined than ever to prove his loyalty and worth as an American soldier. Graham Salisbury poignantly pens the historically accurate but fictional account of the special mission given to 26 Japanese American soldiers in the midst of WWII and a young man's struggle between heritage and patriotism.

Eyes of the Overworld. unabr. ed. Jack Vance. Read by Arthur Morey. (Running Time: 8 hrs.). (Tales of the Dying Earth Ser.). 2010. 39.97 (978-1-4418-1464-7(7), 9781441814647, Brlnc Audio MP3 Lib); 24.99 (978-1-4418-1463-0(9), 9781441814630, Brilliance MP3); 24.99 (978-1-4418-1465-4(5), 9781441814654, BAD); audio compact disk 79.97 (978-1-4418-1462-3(0), 9781441814623, BriAudCD Unabrid); audio compact disk 29.99 (978-1-4418-1461-6(2), 9781441814616, Bril Audio CD Unabri) Brilliance Audio.

***Eyes of the Overworld.** unabr. ed. Jack Vance. Read by Arthur Morey. (Running Time: 7 hrs.). (Tales of the Dying Earth Ser.). 2010. 39.97 (978-1-4418-1466-1(3), 9781441814661, BADLE) Brilliance Audio.

Eyes of the Panther & Other Stories. unabr. ed. Ambrose Bierce. Read by Walter Zimmerman & Donna Barkman. 4 cass. (Running Time: 5 hrs. 30 mins.). 1983. 32.95 (978-0-7861-0547-2(X), 2041) Blckstn Audio.
Known for his wit and sardonic humor, Ambrose Bierce wrote with the intensity of Edgar Allan Poe. He is primarily remembered as a controversial journalist for a San Francisco newspaper. Few realize that he wrote numerous short stories best described as potboilers.

Eyes of the Panther & Other Stories. unabr. ed. Ambrose Bierce. Read by Walter Zimmerman & Donna Barkman. 4 cass. (Running Time: 1 hr. per cass.). 24.00 (9121) Books on Tape.
Titles include "The Eyes of the Panther," "A Watcher by the Dead," "The Death of Halpern Frayser," "Moxon's Master," "Mysterious Disappearances," "The Suitable Surroundings," "The Famous Gilson Bequest" & "The Secret of Macarger's Gulch".

Eyes of the Panther & Other Stories. unabr. ed. Ambrose Bierce. Read by Walter Zimmerman & Donna Barkman. 4 cass. (Running Time: 1 hr. 30 min.

per cass.). Incl. Death of Halpern Frayser. 1984. (C-121); Famous Gilson Bequest. 1984. (C-121); Moxon's Master. 1984. (C-121); Mysterious Disappearances. 1984. (C-121); Secret of Macarger's Gulch. 1984. (C-121); Suitable Surroundings. 1984. (C-121); Watcher by the Dead. 1984. (C-121); 1984. 28.00 (C-121); 33.00 incl. album. Jimcin Record.
Stories of the macabre from Edgar Allan Poe's greatest rival.

Eyes of the World. unabr. ed. Harold Bell Wright. Read by Tim Behrens. 12 cass. (Running Time: 14 hrs. 30 min.). Dramatization. 1992. 64.95 (978-1-55686-409-4(4), 409) Books in Motion.
Artist & painter Aaron King, is bequeathed a strange legacy by his mother: he must discover by himself, a precious truth. He fights his way through hypocrisy, deception & self-delusion until, in an enthralling mountain top confrontation, he discovers a part of himself he almost lost.

***Eyes of Willie McGee: A Tragedy of Race, Sex, & Secrets in the Jim Crow South.** unabr. ed. Alex Heard. Read by J. D. Jackson. (ENG.). 2010. (978-0-06-201601-0(6), Harper Audio); (978-0-06-201133-6(2), Harper Audio) HarperCollins Pubs.

Eyes on the Horizon: Serving on the Front Lines of National Security. unabr. ed. Richard B. Myers. Read by Arthur Morey. Told to Malcolm McConnell. (Running Time: 14 hrs. 0 mins. 0 sec.). (ENG.). 2009. audio compact disk 75.99 (978-1-4001-4177-7(X)); audio compact disk 24.99 (978-1-4001-6177-5(0)); audio compact disk 37.99 (978-1-4001-1177-0(3)) Pub: Tantor Media. Dist(s): IngramPubServ

Eyes on the Peacock's Tail. Vayu Naidu. 1 cass. (Running Time: 022 min.). (Under the Banyan Ser.). (YA). (gr. 2 up). 1998. bk. 11.99 (978-81-86838-27-3(9)) APG.
Fairy tales & folklore.

Eyes Still Have It: The Shamus Award-Winning Stories. unabr. ed. Short Stories. Robert J. Randisi. 7 cass. (Running Time: 9 hrs. 30 mins.). 60.00 (978-0-7887-0568-7(7), 94745E7) Recorded Bks.
In this mystery anthology, Robert J. Randisi has compiled the past twelve winners of the Shamus Award for Best Detective Fiction into one spellbinding collection to die for. Mystery buffs will revel in these riveting stories featuring unforgettable characters such as Mickey Spillane's Mike Hammer, Marcia Muller's Sharon McCone, Lawrence Block's Matthew Scudder & Loren D. Estleman's Amos Walker. Available to libraries only.

Eyesight-Vision & Astrology. Ginger Chalford. 1 cass. 8.95 (046) Am Fed Astrologers.
Aspects, patterns, retrogrades, fixed stars show visual problems.

Eyewitness. Stephen Leather. 10 CDs. (Running Time: 11 hrs. 36 mins.). (Isis (CDs) Ser.). (J). 2004. audio compact disk 89.95 (978-0-7531-2354-6(1)) Pub: ISIS Lrg Prnt GBR. Dist(s): Ulverscroft US

Eyewitness. unabr. ed. Stephen Leather. 10 cass. (Running Time: 11 hrs. 36 mins.). (Isis Cassettes Ser.). (J). 2004. 84.95 (978-0-7531-1743-9(6)) Pub: ISIS Lrg Prnt GBR. Dist(s): Ulverscroft US

Eyewitness: 1900-1909. Comment by Joanna Bourke. Contrib. by Tim Pigott-Smith. 3 CDs. (Running Time: 3 hrs. 45 mins.). 2005. audio compact disk 39.95 (978-0-7927-3589-2(7), BBCD 105) AudioGO.

Eyewitness: 1910-1919. Comment by Joanna Bourke. Contrib. by Tim Pigott-Smith. 4 CDs. (Running Time: 5 hrs.). 2005. audio compact disk 49.95 (978-0-7927-3592-2(7), BBCD 107) AudioGO.

Eyewitness: 1920-1929. Comment by Joanna Bourke. Contrib. by Tim Pigott-Smith. 3 CDs. (Running Time: 3 hrs. 45 mins.). 2005. audio compact disk 39.95 (978-0-7927-3594-6(3), BBCD 109) AudioGO.

Eyewitness: 1930-1939. Comment by Joanna Bourke. Contrib. by Tim Pigott-Smith. 4 CDs. (Running Time: 4 hrs. 55 mins.). 2005. audio compact disk 49.95 (978-0-7927-3596-0(X), BBCD 111) AudioGO.

Eyewitness: 1940-1949. Comment by Joanna Bourke. Contrib. by Tim Pigott-Smith. 4 CDs. (Running Time: 5 hrs.). 2005. audio compact disk 49.95 (978-0-7927-3598-4(6), BBCD 113) AudioGO.

Eyewitness: 1980-1989. Comment by Joanna Bourke. Contrib. by Tim Pigott-Smith. 4 CDs. (Running Time: 4 hrs.). 2005. audio compact disk 49.95 (978-0-7927-3730-8(X), BBCD 122) AudioGO.

Eyewitness: 1990-1999. Comment by Joanna Bourke. Contrib. by Tim Pigott-Smith. 4 CDs. (Running Time: 4 hrs.). 2005. audio compact disk 49.95 (978-0-7927-3732-2(6), BBCD 124) AudioGO.

Eyewitness Collection. unabr. ed. 38 CDs. 2006. audio compact disk 450.00 (978-0-7927-4262-3(1), BBCD153) AudioGO.

Eyewitness Dvd Amphibian. Dorling Kindersley Publishing Staff. (Eyewitness Videos Ser.). (ENG.). (J). (gr. k). 2008. 12.99 (978-0-7566-4503-8(4)) DK Pub Inc.

Eyewitness Dvd Arctic. Dorling Kindersley Publishing Staff. (Eyewitness Videos Ser.). (ENG.). (J). (gr. 1-12). 2008. 12.99 (978-0-7566-3889-4(5)) DK Pub Inc.

Eyewitness Dvd Bird. Dorling Kindersley Publishing Staff. (DK Eyewitness Bks.). (ENG.). (J). (gr. 1-12). 2006. 12.99 (978-0-7566-2825-3(3)) DK Pub Inc.

Eyewitness Dvd Butterfly. Dorling Kindersley Publishing Staff. (DK Eyewitness Bks.). (ENG.). (J). (gr. 1). 2006. 12.99 (978-0-7566-2826-0(1)) DK Pub Inc.

Eyewitness Dvd Dinosaur. Dorling Kindersley Publishing Staff. (Eyewitness Videos Ser.). (ENG.). (J). (gr. 1-12). 2008. 12.99 (978-0-7566-3892-4(5)) DK Pub Inc.

***Eyewitness DVD: Elephant: Elephant.** DK Publishing. (Eyewitness Videos Ser.). (ENG.). (J). 2011. 12.99 (978-0-7566-8271-2(1)) DK Pub Inc.

Eyewitness Dvd Fish. Dorling Kindersley Publishing Staff. (DK Eyewitness Bks.). (ENG.). (J). (gr. 1-12). 2006. 12.99 (978-0-7566-2827-7(X)) DK Pub Inc.

***Eyewitness DVD: Flight: Flight.** DK Publishing. (Eyewitness Videos Ser.). (ENG.). (J). 2011. 12.99 (978-0-7566-8272-9(X)) DK Pub Inc.

Eyewitness Dvd Human Machines. Dorling Kindersley Publishing Staff. (Eyewitness Videos Ser.). (ENG.). (J). (gr. k). 2008. 12.99 (978-0-7566-4504-5(2)) DK Pub Inc.

***Eyewitness DVD: Life: Life.** DK Publishing. (Eyewitness Videos Ser.). (ENG.). (J). 2011. 12.99 (978-0-7566-8273-6(8)) DK Pub Inc.

Eyewitness Dvd Mammal. Dorling Kindersley Publishing Staff. (Eyewitness Videos Ser.). (ENG.). (J). (gr. 1-12). 2006. 12.99 (978-0-7566-2829-1(6)) DK Pub Inc.

Eyewitness Dvd Pond & River. Dorling Kindersley Publishing Staff. (DK Eyewitness Bks.). (ENG.). (J). (gr. 1). 2006. 12.99 (978-0-7566-2831-4(8)) DK Pub Inc.

Eyewitness Dvd Reptile. Dorling Kindersley Publishing Staff. (Eyewitness Videos Ser.). (ENG.). (J). (gr. 1-12). 2007. 12.99 (978-0-7566-3891-7(7)) DK Pub Inc.

Eyewitness Dvd Shark. Dorling Kindersley Publishing Staff. (DK Eyewitness Bks.). (ENG.). (J). (gr. 1-12). 2006. 12.99 (978-0-7566-2832-1(6)) DK Pub Inc.

***Eyewitness DVD: Tree: Tree.** DK Publishing. (Eyewitness Videos Ser.). (ENG.). (J). 2011. 12.99 (978-0-7566-8274-3(6)) DK Pub Inc.

Eyewitness to Power: The Essence of Leadership: Nixon to Clinton. abr. ed. David Gergen. Read by David Gergen. 4 cass. (Running Time: 6 hrs.). 2000. 24.95 (978-1-55935-350-2(3)) Soundelux.
White House adviser to Nixon, Ford, Reagan & Clinton, David Gergen assesses the key leadership lessons they offer for coming presidents.

Eyre Affair. Jasper Fforde. Contrib. by Susan Duerden. (Running Time: 12 hrs.). No. 1. (ENG.). 2009. audio compact disk 39.95 (978-0-14-314570-7(3), PengAudBks) Penguin Grp USA.

Eyre Affair. unabr. abr. ed. Jasper Fforde. Read by Elizabeth Sastre. 8 CDs. (Running Time: 10 hrs.). (Thursday Next Ser.: No. 1). 2002. audio compact disk 36.95 (978-1-56511-546-0(5), 1565115465) Pub: HighBridge. Dist(s): Workman Pub

EZ EMS Protocols. William Porter. 2008. audio compact disk 556.95 (978-0-7637-5456-3(0)) Jones Bartlett.

Ezekiel Commentary. Chuck Missler. (ENG.). 2009. audio compact disk 89.95 (978-1-57821-413-6(0)) Koinonia Hse.

Ezekiel Commentary: Verse by-Verse with Chuck Missler. Chuck Missler. 1 MP3 CD-ROM. (Running Time: over 24 hours). (Chuck Missler Commentaries). 2000. cd-rom 44.95 (978-1-57821-113-5(1)) Koinonia Hse.
The book of Ezekiel contains some of the most incredible prophecies in the Bible, including detailed description of a Nuclear War and the cleanup afterward. Ezekiel ministered to a nation experiencing judgment for their sins, and may have some lessons for us today.

Ezekiel Option. abr. ed. Joel C. Rosenberg. Read by Patrick G. Lawlor. (Running Time: 6 hrs.). 2005. audio compact disk 74.25 (978-1-59600-309-5(X), 9781596003095, BACDLib Ed) Brilliance Audio.
The first book in a new series of apocalyptic thrillers leading up to the rapture.

Ezekiel Option. abr. ed. Joel C. Rosenberg. (Running Time: 6 hrs.). 2009. audio compact disk 9.99 (978-1-4418-2650-3(5), 9781441826503) Brilliance Audio.

Ezekiel Option. unabr. ed. Joel C. Rosenberg. Read by Patrick G. Lawlor. (Running Time: 10 hrs.). 2005. 39.25 (978-1-59710-444-9(2), 9781597104449, BADLE); 24.95 (978-1-59710-445-6(0), 9781597104456, BAD); 82.25 (978-1-59600-306-4(5), 9781596003064, BrilAudUnabridg); 32.95 (978-1-59600-305-7(7), 9781596003057, BAU); audio compact disk 39.25 (978-1-59335-998-0(5), 9781593359980, Brinc Audio MP3 Lib); audio compact disk 24.95 (978-1-59335-997-3(7), 9781593359973, Brilliance MP3) Brilliance Audio.

***Ezekiel Option.** unabr. ed. Joel C. Rosenberg. Read by Patrick Lawlor. (Running Time: 12 hrs.). 2010. audio compact disk 89.97 (978-1-4418-4070-7(2), 9781441840707, BriAudCD Unabrid); audio compact disk 29.99 (978-1-4418-4069-1(9), 9781441840691, Bril Audio CD Unabri) Brilliance Audio.

Ezra & Nehemiah Commentary. Chuck Missler. 1 CD. (Running Time: 10 hours). (Chuck Missler Commentaries). 2003. 24.95 (978-1-57821-243-9(X)) Koinonia Hse.
*The books of Ezra and Nehemiah (and Esther) cover about 100 years, closing the Old Testament historical books. The books of Samuel, Kings, and Chronicles closed with the Southern Kingdom (Judah)'s going into captivity. The two post-exile books of Ezra and Nehemiah record the return from Babylon after its fall to the Persians under Cyrus, the rebuilding of the Temple and Jerusalem, and the reestablishment of the national life of Israel.This MP3 CD is self-contained and includes: * Over 10 hours of Verse-by-Verse audio teaching through Ezra and Nehemiah as MP3 files. * Extensive searchable study notes as PDF files. A special message from Chuck Missler.Listings of other MP3 resources. * All software included to play MP3 files. * Adobe Acrobat(r) Reader.This program will read the PDF notes.*

Ezra Pound. 1 cass. 1997. 10.95 (978-1-57523-162-4(X)) Unapix Enter.

Ezra Pound, On. unabr. ed. Theodore Weiss. 1 cass. (Running Time: 1 hr. 7 min.). 1966. 12.95 (23232) J Norton Pubs.
Weiss considers Pound one of the most controversial figures in letters; a man seriously involved with the life & death struggle. He was a prolific letter writer, & influenced every major writer of his time.

Ezra Pound Reads, Set. unabr. ed. Ezra Pound. Read by Ezra Pound. 2 cass. (Running Time: 90 min.). 1993. 19.00 (978-1-55994-845-6(0), DCN 2088) HarperCollins Pubs.
The Cantos were Ezra Pound's most ambitious poetic project. This recording offers the writer's dramatic reading of "Cantos XLV, LI" & the second half of "Canto LXXVI", as well as his performance of poems titled "The Gypsy" & "The Exile's Letter.".

Ezra Pound Reads Selected Cantos & Others. unabr. ed. Poems. Ezra Pound. Read by Ezra Pound. 2 cass. (Running Time: 1 hr. 13 min.). 19.00 (H105) Blckstn Audio.
The importance of a major poet's voice has never been better illustrated. Included: "Hugh Selwyn Mauberley," "Cantico del Sole," "Moeurs Contemporaines," "Canto I," "Canto IV," "The Gypsy," "The Exile's Letter" & more.

Ezra Taft Benson: A Personal Glimpse. Reed A. Benson. 1 cass. 6.98 (978-1-55503-344-6(X)) Covenant Comms.
Personal stories of the prophet.

Ezra Taft Benson: A Personal Glimpse. Reed A. Benson. 1 cass. 2004. 3.95 (978-1-57734-374-5(3), 34441123) Covenant Comms.

Ezra/Nehemiah: Reformation in Nehemiah: Rebuilding the Walls: Rebuilding the Walls-Tape-Vol. 2. Read by Douglas Wilson. 11 cass. 2006. 38.00 (978-1-59128-526-7(7)) Canon Pr ID.

Ezra/Nehemiah: Reformation of Worship-MP3, Vol. 1. Narrated by Douglas Wilson. 2006. (978-1-59128-521-2(6)) Canon Pr ID.

Ezra/Nehemiah: The Message of Ezra: Reformation of Worship, Vol. 1. Read by Douglas Wilson. 11. 2006. 38.00 (978-1-59128-522-9(4)) Canon Pr ID.

Ezra/Nehemiah: The Message of Ezra: Reformation of Worship: Reformation of Worship-mp3-Vol. 2. Read by Douglas Wilson. 11 cass. 2006. 38.00 (978-1-59128-524-3(0)) Canon Pr ID.

E2 Genius Series: E2 Genius. Edwin T. Cornelius & Pace International Research, Inc. Staff. 2 cass. 1991. 12.00 audio cass. I. (978-0-89209-839-2(2)); 12.00 audio cass. II. (978-0-89209-840-8(6)); 12.00 audio cass. 3. (978-0-89209-841-5(4)); 12.00 audio cass. 4. (978-0-89209-842-2(2)); 12.00 audio cass. 5. Pace Grp Intl.

F

F. Chopin. Lene Mayer-Skumanz. Illus. by Winfried Opgenoorth. (J). 2007. bk. 30.99 (978-84-96646-07-0(6)) Loguez Ediciones ESP.

F. Clifton White: Presidential Politics see Buckley's Firing Line

F. Grillparzer: Konig Ottokars Gluck und Ende. unabr. ed. M. Garland. 1 cass. (ENG & GER.). 1986. 11.95 (G7752) J Norton Pubs.
Analyzes the play as Grillparzer's first venture into the genre of historical drama. Discusses aspects of the central figure of the play - King Ottokar - & his inner development.

F Is for Fugitive. abr. ed. Sue Grafton. Read by Judy Kaye. 2 cass. (Running Time: 3 hrs.). (Kinsey Millhone Mystery Ser.). 1989. 17.00 (978-0-394-58173-6(3), Random AudioBks) Random Audio Pubg.
Kinsey Millhone, private investigator and wise-cracking ex-cop tries to prove the innocence of a man already found guilty of murder.

F Is for Fugitive. unabr. collector's ed. Sue Grafton. Read by Mary Peiffer. 8 cass. (Running Time: 8 hrs.). (Kinsey Millhone Mystery Ser.). 1994. 64.00 (978-0-7366-2620-0(4), 3360) Books on Tape.
Baily's girlfriend was found dead on Floral Beach. Unfortunately, already having a bad record & no alibi, he was found guilty of murder. A year later, he escaped & successfully disappeared. He now needs Kinsey to find the real killer.

F. Lee Bailey: Role of the Advocate see Buckley's Firing Line

F. Scott Fitzgerald: Stories. unabr. ed. F. Scott Fitzgerald. Read by Kimberly Schraf. 2 CDs. (Running Time: 1 hr 59 mins). 2002. audio compact disk 18.95 (978-1-58472-211-3(8), 056, In Aud) Pub: Sound Room. Dist(s): Baker Taylor
Bernice Bobs Her Hair and The Jelly-Bean.

F. Scott Fitzgerald: The Great American Dreamer. Tobias Wolff. Narrated by Jack Perkins. 1 cass. 1998. 9.95 (978-0-7670-0736-8(0)) A & E Home.
Literary.

F. Scott Fitzgerald Short Stories. Read by Alexander Scourby. 2 cass. (Running Time: 1 hr. 53 min.). 1995. 15.95 set. (8627Q) Filmic Archives.
Includes "The Bridal Party", "Three Hours Between Planes", "Babylon Revisited", & "The Lost Decade".

F. Scott Fitzgerald Stories. F. Scott Fitzgerald. Narrated by Kimberly Schraf. (Running Time: 7200 sec.). (Unabridged Classics in MP3 Ser.). (YA). 2008. audio compact disk 24.00 (978-1-58472-644-9(X), In Aud) Sound Room.

F. Scott Fitzgerald: Stories: Stories. F. Scott Fitzgerald. Read by Kimberly Schraf. (Running Time: 2 hrs.). 2002. 18.95 (978-1-59912-063-8(1), Audiofy Corp) Iofy Corp.

***F. U. B. A. R.** abr. ed. Sam Seder & Stephen Sherrill. Read by Sam Seder. (ENG.). 2006. (978-0-06-113509-5(7), Harper Audio); (978-0-06-113508-8(9), Harper Audio) HarperCollins Pubs.

F. U. B. A. R. America's Right-Wing Nightmare. unabr. ed. Sam Seder & Stephen Sherrill. Read by Sam Seder. (Running Time: 21600 sec.). 2006. audio compact disk 29.95 (978-0-06-087635-7(2)) HarperCollins Pubs.

F Word. unabr. ed. Louis Anderson & Carl Kurlander. (ENG.). 2005. 14.98 (978-1-59483-361-8(3)) Pub: Hachet Audio. Dist(s): HachBkGrp

Fabian. Joan Wolf & Carla Korb. (J). 2003. 5.95 (978-0-9744465-3-0(X)) Cruzane Mtn Pubng.

Fable of the Vision Drink. unabr. ed. Henry Munn. 1 cass. (Running Time: 1 hr. 28 min.). 1977. 11.00 (01701) Big Sur Tapes.

Fablehaven. Brandon Mull. Contrib. by E. B. Stevens. (Running Time: 34200 sec.). (Fablehaven Ser.: Bk. 1). (J). (gr. 3-7). 2006. audio compact disk 39.95 (978-1-59038-594-4(2)) Deseret Bk.

Fables. Arnold Lobel. (J). 1985. 19.04 (978-0-394-07666-9(4)) SRA McGraw.

***Fables.** unabr. ed. Arnold Lobel. Read by Mark Linn-baker. (ENG.). 2009. (978-0-06-196703-0(3)); (978-0-06-190163-8(6)) HarperCollins Pubs.

Fables, Set. abr. ed. Aesop. Read by Robert L. Halvorson. 4 cass. (Running Time: 360 min.). (J). 28.95 (97) Halvorson Assocs.

Fables, Tome I. Jean De La Fontaine. Retold by Albert Milaire. Illus. by Anne Cote. 1 CD. (Running Time: 1 hr. 30 mins.). (FRE.). (J). (gr. 1-7). 1998. 16.95 (978-2-921997-43-0(6)) Pub: Coffragants CAN. Dist(s): Penton Overseas
Features classic children's fables recorded completely in French by well-known artists.

Fables, Tome 1. Jean De La Fontaine. Retold by Albert Milaire. Illus. by Anne Cote. 1 cass. (Running Time: 90 mins.). (FRE.). (J). (gr. 1-7). 1998. cass. & audio compact disk 12.95 (978-2-921997-44-7(4)) Pub: Coffragants CAN. Dist(s): Penton Overseas

Fables, Tome II. Jean De La Fontaine. Retold by Albert Milaire. Illus. by Anne Cote. 1 cass. (Running Time: 1 hr. 30 mins.). (J). (gr. 1-7). 2000. bk. & pap. bk. 12.95 (978-2-89517-061-7(4)) Pub: Coffragants CAN. Dist(s): Penton Overseas

Fables, Vol. 1. Arnold Lobel. (FRE.). (J). 2002. bk. 18.95 (978-2-89558-027-0(8)) Pub: Al Stanke CAN. Dist(s): Penton Overseas

Fables, Vol. 2. Arnold Lobel. 1 CD. (Coffragants Ser.). (FRE.). (J). 1998. 16.95 Plastic case. (978-2-921997-54-6(1)) Penton Overseas.

fables de la Fontaine. unabr. ed. Jean De La Fontaine. Read by Yves Belluardo & Martine Chide. 2007. 69.99 (978-2-35569-041-9(3)) Find a World.

Fables de la Fontaine, Vol. I. unabr. ed. 1cass. (Running Time: 1 hr.). (FRE.). pap. bk. 16.95 (SFR380) J Norton Pubs.
Beginning level. Includes: "La Cigale et la Fourmi," "Le Loup et le Chien" &"Le Coq et le Renard.".

Fables de La Fontaine, Vol. I. unabr. ed. Jean De La Fontaine. Read by Georges Riquier. 1 cass. (Running Time: 30 min.). Incl. Cigale et la Fourmi. (SAC 895); Coq et le Renard. (SAC 895); Loup et la Chien. (SAC 895); (FRE.). 11.95 incl. text. (978-0-8045-0895-7(X), SAC 895) Spoken Arts.
Fables written by the first lyrical poet of France. Includes fables listed & 16 others.

Fables de la Fontaine, Vol. II. unabr. ed. 1 cass. (Running Time: 1 hr.). (FRE.). pap. bk. 16.95 (SFR385) J Norton Pubs.
Beginning level. Includes: "Le Heron," "Les Deux pigeons," "Le Lievre et la Tortue" & "Le Coche et la Mouche.".

Fables de La Fontaine, Vol. II. unabr. ed. Jean De La Fontaine. (Running Time: 26 min.). (FRE.). 11.95 (978-0-8045-0909-1(3), SAC 909) Spoken Arts.
Le Heron, Les Deux Pigeons, Le Lievre et la Tortue, Le Coche et la Mouche. & eight others.

Fables for Our Time see Thurber Carnival

Fables for Our Time & Further Fables for Our Time. unabr. collector's ed. Short Stories. James Thurber. Read by Wolfram Kandinsky. 4 cass. (Running Time: 4 hrs.). 1983. 24.00 (978-0-7366-0678-3(5), 1637) Books on Tape.
A collection of humorous tales in the style of Aesop, laced through with barbs of memorable satire.

Fables of Aesop. unabr. ed. Read by John Franklyn et al. Based on a story by Aesop. (Running Time: 40 min.). 10.95 (978-0-8045-1013-4(X), 7003) Spoken Arts.
The thirty-seven Aesop fables contained in this recording include: "The Town Mouse & the Country Mouse", "The Fox & the Crow", "The Lion & the Mouse", "The Fox & the Stork", "Adrocles", & others.

Fables of Aesop the Slave. Instructed by Manly P. Hall. Based on a story by Aesop. 8.95 (978-0-89314-111-0(9), C820509) Philos Res.

Fables of God: Spiritual fairy tales for the Sleeping. Gary Arnold. (ENG.). 2009. audio compact disk 24.95 (978-1-57867-004-8(7)) Windhorse Corp.

Fables of India. abr. ed. Perf. by Zia Mohyeddin. 1 cass. Incl. Fables of India: Good-Speed & the Elephant King. (J). (CDL5 1168); Fables of India: The Adder & the Fox. (J). (CDL5 1168); Fables of India: The Blue Jackal. (J). (CDL5 1168); Fables of India: The Brahmin & the Villain. (J). (CDL5 1168); Fables of India: The Camel & His Neighbor. (J). (CDL5 1168); Fables of India: The Long-Eared Cat & the Vulture. (J). (CDL5 1168); Fables of India: The Monkey's Heart. (J). (CDL5 1168); Fables of India: The Restless Pigeon. (J). (CDL5 1168); Fables of India: The Twin Parrots. (J). (CDL5 1168); (J). 1972. 9.95 (978-0-694-50666-8(4), CDL5 1168) HarperCollins Pubs.

Fables of India: Good-Speed & the Elephant King see Fables of India

Fables of India: The Adder & the Fox see Fables of India

Fables of India: The Blue Jackal see Fables of India

Fables of India: The Brahmin & the Villain see Fables of India

Fables of India: The Camel & His Neighbor see Fables of India

Fables of India: The Long-Eared Cat & the Vulture see Fables of India

Fables of India: The Monkey's Heart see Fables of India

Fables of India: The Restless Pigeon see Fables of India

Fables of India: The Twin Parrots see Fables of India

Fables of Leonardo da Vinci. abr. ed. Leonardo da Vinci. Perf. by Alfred Drake. 1 cass. 8.98 (CDL5 1437) HarperCollins Pubs.

Fables, Tales, Stories. Leo Tolstoy. 2 cass. (Running Time: 2 hrs.). (RUS.). 1994. bk. 29.50 set. (978-1-58085-575-4(X)) Interlingua VA.
Includes Russian text, notes & vocabulary in English. The combination of written text & clarity & pace of diction will open the door for intermediate & advanced students to genuine comprehension & the use of literary texts for advancement in rapid understanding of written & oral language materials. The audio text plus written text concept makes foreign languages accessible to a much wider range of students than books alone.

Fables, Tome I. 1 cass. (Running Time: 1 hr. 30 mins.).Tr. of Fables, Vol. I. (FRE.). (J). (gr. 1-7). 2000. pap. bk. 12.95 (978-2-921997-10-2(X)) Pub: Coffragants CAN. Dist(s): Penton Overseas
Features classic children's fables recorded completely in French by well-known artists.

Fables, Tome II. Jeannine De La Fontaine. 1 CD. (Running Time: 1 hr.).Tr. of Fables, Vol. II. (FRE.). (J). (gr. 1-7). 2001. pap. bk. 18.95 (978-2-89558-020-1(0)) Pub: Coffragants CAN. Dist(s): Penton Overseas

Fables, Vol. I see Fables, Tome I

Fables, Vol. II see Fables, Tome II

Fabric of Our Mind. Swami Amar Jyoti. 1 cass. 1979. 9.95 (J-19) Truth Consciousness.
Stilling the mind to go within. Each one's way is through one's own mind.

Fabric of Reality: A Weekend Inquiry with Adyashanti recorded November 18-19 2006. Featuring Adyashanti. 7 CDs. (Running Time: 8 hours). (ENG.). 2006. audio compact disk 65.00 (978-1-933986-13-5(1)) Open Gate Pub.

Fabric of Sin. Phil Rickman. (Merrily Watkins Ser.). 2008. 89.95 (978-0-7531-3022-3(X)); audio compact disk 99.95 (978-0-7531-3023-0(8)) Pub: ISIS Audio GBR. Dist(s): Ulverscroft US

Fabric of Sin. Phil Rickman. Read by Julie Maisey. (Running Time: 5 hrs. 20 mins. 0 sec.). (Merrily Watkins Ser.). (ENG.). 2008. audio compact disk 34.95 (978-1-84724-457-4(2)) Pub: Quercus GBR. Dist(s): IPG Chicago

Fabric of the Cosmos: Space, Time, & the Texture of Reality. abr. ed. Brian Greene. Read by Erik Davies. 5 CDs. (Running Time: 6 hrs.). (ENG.). 2005. audio compact disk 20.00 (978-0-7393-2365-6(2), Random AudioBks) Pub: Random Audio Pubg. Dist(s): Random

Fabric of the Cosmos: Space, Time, & the Texture of Reality. unabr. ed. Brian Greene. 16 cass. (Running Time: 24 hrs.). 2004. 120.00 (978-0-7366-9749-1(7)) Books on Tape.

Fabricant. unabr. ed. Claire Carmichael. Read by Francis Greenslade. 4 cass. (Running Time: 4 hrs.). 2002. (978-1-74030-232-6(X)) Bolinda Pubng AUS.

Fabricated Metal Products in Germany: A Strategic Reference 2007. Compiled by Icon Group International, Inc. Staff. 2007. ring bd. 195.00 (978-0-497-35972-0(3)) Icon Grp.

Fabrication et Utilisation de l'outillage en Matieres Osseuses du Neolithique de Chypre: Khirokitia et Cap Andreas-Kastros. Alexandra Legrand. (Bar S Ser.). (C). 1678. audio compact disk 87.50 (978-1-4073-0116-7(0)) Pub: British Arch Reports GBR. Dist(s): David Brown

Fabrics of Fairy Tales: Stories Spun from Far & Wide. unabr. ed. Retold by Tanya Robyn Batt. Illus. by Rachel Griffin. 2 CDs. (Running Time: 1 hr. 45 mins.). (J). (gr. 4-6). 2001. audio compact disk 19.99 (978-1-84148-407-5(5)) BarefootBksMA.
Stories about fabrics. Shows how storytelling is a magical weaving process.

Fabry Disease - A Bibliography & Dictionary for Physicians, Patients, & Genome Researchers. Compiled by Icon Group International, Inc. Staff. 2007. ring bd. 28.95 (978-0-497-11208-0(6)) Icon Grp.

Fabula de la Sirena y los Borrachos see Pablo Neruda Reading His Poetry

Fabulation or the Re-Education of Undine. abr. ed. Lynn Nottage. 2 CDs. (Running Time: 6780 sec.). (L. A. Theatre Works Audio Theatre Collections). 2005. audio compact disk 25.95 (978-1-58081-304-4(6), LA 070) Pub: L A Theatre. Dist(s): NetLibrary CO

Fabulous Families! Six Steps to Raising (Almost) Perfect Kids. 2003. 13.95 (978-1-932631-57-9(7)) Ascensn Pr.

Fabulous Families! Six Steps to Raising (Almost) Perfect Kids! 2003. audio compact disk 13.95 (978-1-932631-58-6(5)) Ascensn Pr.

Fabulous Family Holomolaiset: A Minnesota Finnish Family's Oral Tradition. Patricia J. Eilola. 1 cass. 1997. 12.95 (978-0-9660402-0-3(1)) Superior Prodn.
A young Finnish-American girl, pioneering in Northern Minnesota, learns important lessons with the help of stories her parents tell about a mythical Sami family, the Holomoiaiset. Emphasis on overcoming challenges through love & humor.

Fabulous Fifties. 4 cass. (Running Time: 4 hrs.). 16.95 Set. (978-1-55569-104-2(8), 6650-01) Great Am Audio.
Fads, headlines, sports, lifestyles, political scene of the 50s.

Fabulous Food. 1 CD. (Running Time: 24 min.). (J). 2005. audio compact disk 14.95 (978-0-9765887-0-2(6)) S Edu Res LLC.

Fabulous Forty Pictures. Art Freifeld. Illus. by Paul Leung. 1988. 10.95 (978-0-916177-22-5(X)) Am Eng Pubns.

Fabulous Fox Twins. Ken McCoy & Ken Mccoy. 2008. audio compact disk 79.95 (978-1-84652-194-2(7)) Pub: Magna Story GBR. Dist(s): Ulverscroft US

Fabulous Fox Twins. Ken McCoy & Ken Mccoy. 2008. 61.95 (978-1-84652-193-5(9)) Pub: Magna Story GBR. Dist(s): Ulverscroft US

Fabulous Funtime Tales. 1 cass. (Barney Ser.). (J). (ps-k). bk. 6.38 Blisterpack. (LY9572) NewSound.
Includes: "The Three Little Pigs," & "Chicken Little" - a delightful collection of stories told by Barney himself.

Fabulous Idiot. abr. ed. Theodore Sturgeon. Perf. by Theodore Sturgeon. 1 cass. 8.98 (CP 1634) HarperCollins Pubs.

Fabulous Inheritance: 1 Peter 1:1-5. Ed Young. 1982. 4.95 (978-0-7417-1263-9(6), 263) Win Walk.

***Fabulous Reinvention of Sunday School: Transformational Techniques for Reaching & Teaching Kids.** unabr. ed. Aaron Reynolds. (Running Time: 6 hrs. 23 mins. 25 sec.). (ENG.). 2009. 14.99 (978-0-310-77200-2(1)) Zondervan.

Fabulous Things. unabr. ed. Kelly Braffet. Read by Edwina Wren. (Running Time: 33300 sec.). 2006. audio compact disk 87.95 (978-1-74093-775-7(9)) Pub: Bolinda Pubng AUS. Dist(s): Bolinda Pub Inc

Face. unabr. ed. Dean Koontz. Read by Dylan Baker. 12 cass. (Running Time: 18 hrs.). 2003. 104.00 (978-0-7366-9144-4(8)) Books on Tape.

Face at the Window. unabr. ed. Sarah Graves. Narrated by Lindsay Ellison. 1 MP3-CD. (Running Time: 9 hrs. 30 mins.). (Home Repair Is Homicide Mystery Ser.). 2009. 49.95 (978-0-7927-6172-3(3), Chivers Sound Lib); audio compact disk 79.95 (978-0-7927-5976-8(1), Chivers Sound Lib) AudioGO.

***Face-Changers.** Thomas Perry. Narrated by Joyce Bean. (Running Time: 15 hrs. 30 mins.). (Jane Whitefield Ser.). 2009. 39.99 (978-1-4001-9022-5(3)) Tantor Media.

Face-Changers. unabr. ed. Thomas Perry. Narrated by Joyce Bean. (Running Time: 15 hrs. 30 mins. 0 sec.). (Jane Whitefield Ser.). (ENG.). 2009. audio compact disk 79.99 (978-1-4001-4022-0(6)) Pub: Tantor Media. Dist(s): IngramPubServ

***Face-Changers.** unabr. ed. Thomas Perry. Narrated by Joyce Bean. (Running Time: 15 hrs. 30 mins.). (Jane Whitefield Ser.). 2009. 20.99 (978-1-4001-8022-6(8)) Tantor Media.

Face-Changers. unabr. abr. ed. Thomas Perry. Narrated by Joyce Bean. (Running Time: 15 hrs. 30 mins. 0 sec.). (Jane Whitefield Ser.). (ENG.). 2009. 29.99 (978-1-4001-6022-8(7)); audio compact disk 39.99 (978-1-4001-1022-3(X)) Pub: Tantor Media. Dist(s): IngramPubServ

Face Down. Arrow Records. 2008. audio compact disk 13.99 (978-1-59944-732-2(0)) Creflo Dollar.

Face I Know see Savagery of Love: Brother Antoninus Reads His Poetry

Face in the Cemetery: A Mamur Zapt Mystery. unabr. ed. Michael Pearce. Read by Nigel Carrington. 6 cass. (Running Time: 9 hrs.). 2002. 54.95 (978-0-7540-0832-3(0)) AudioGO.

Face in the Frost. unabr. ed. John Bellairs. Narrated by George Guidall. 4 cass. (Running Time: 5 hrs. 15 mins.). (gr. 6 up). 1995. 36.00 (978-0-7887-0209-9(2), 94434E7) Recorded Bks.

Face Is Familiar see Suspense

Face of a Stranger. unabr. ed. Anne Perry. Narrated by Davina Porter. 9 cass. (Running Time: 13 hrs. 30 mins.). (William Monk Novel Ser.). 1995. 78.00 (978-0-7887-0321-8(8), 94513E7) Recorded Bks.
A tragic accident leaves Inspector Monk with amnesia just moments after he solves the murder of a popular Crimean war hero.

Face of Battle: A Study of Agincourt, Waterloo & the Somme. John Keegan. Read by Robert Whitfield. (Playaway Adult Nonfiction Ser.). 2008. 69.99 (978-1-60640-775-2(9)) Find a World.

Face of Battle: A Study of Agincourt, Waterloo & the Somme. unabr. ed. John Keegan. Read by Robert Whitfield. 9 cass. (Running Time: 13 hrs.). 2001. 62.95 (978-0-7861-2109-0(2), 2871); audio compact disk 80.00 (978-0-7861-9642-5(4), 2871) Blckstn Audio.
Military history focuses on what a set battle is like for the man in the thick of it, his fears, his wounds and their treatment, the mechanics of being taken prisoner, the nature of leadership at the most junior level, the role of compulsion in getting men to stand their ground, the intrusions of cruelty and compassion, the very din and blood.

Face of Battle: A Study of Agincourt, Waterloo & the Somme. unabr. collector's ed. John Keegan. Read by Victor Rumbellow. 10 cass. (Running Time: 15 hrs.). 1982. 80.00 (978-0-7366-0315-7(8), 1302) Books on Tape.
What is it like to be in battle? John Keegan, a senior instructor at Sandhurst, the British Military Academy speaks for soldiers who were present in the fray. For examples, Keegan selects Agincourt in 1415, Waterloo in 1815 & the Somme in 1916. Agincourt was hand-to-hand combat, a personal encounter. At Waterloo, 400 years later, the battle was still largely personal. The Somme, however, stands as the distillation of wars in the industrial age: long-distance killing of faceless men by others who merely activate the instruments of destruction.

Face of Betrayal. unabr. ed. Lis Wiehl & April Henry. Narrated by Pam Turlow. (Triple Threat Ser.). (ENG.). 2009. 19.59 (978-1-60814-564-5(6)); audio compact disk 27.99 (978-1-59859-613-7(6)) Oasis Audio.

Face of Christ & Master of the Blue Cape. Instructed by Manly P. Hall. 8.95 (978-0-89314-112-7(7), C800103) Philos Res.

Face of Death. abr. ed. Cody McFadyen. Read by Joyce Bean. (Running Time: 6 hrs.). (Smoky Barrett Ser.: No. 2). 2008. audio compact disk 14.99 (978-1-4233-3886-4(3), 9781423338864) Brilliance Audio.

Face of Death. unabr. ed. Cody McFadyen. 12. (Running Time: 15 hrs.). (Smoky Barrett Ser.: No. 2). 2007. audio compact disk 39.95 (978-1-4233-3879-6(0), 9781423338796, Bril Audio CD Unabri) Brilliance Audio.

Face of Death. unabr. ed. Cody McFadyen. Read by Joyce Bean. (Running Time: 15 hrs.). (Smoky Barrett Ser.: No. 2). 2007. 39.25 (978-1-4233-3884-0(7), 9781423338840, BADLE); 24.95 (978-1-4233-3883-3(9), 9781423338833, BAD); 97.25 (978-1-4233-3878-9(2), 9781423338789, BrilAudUnabridg); audio compact disk 117.25 (978-1-4233-3880-2(4), 9781423338802, BriAudCD Unabrid); audio compact disk 39.25 (978-1-4233-3882-6(0), 9781423338826, Brinc Audio MP3 Lib); audio compact disk 24.95 (978-1-4233-3881-9(2), 9781423338819, Brilliance MP3) Brilliance Audio.

Face of Deception. unabr. ed. Iris Johansen. Read by Laurel Lefkow. 10 CDs. (Running Time: 15 hrs.). (Eve Duncan Ser.). 2002. audio compact disk 94.95 (978-0-7927-2752-1(5), SLD 218, Chivers Sound Lib) AudioGO.
Forensic sculptor Eve Duncan has been approached by billionaire magnate John Logan to reconstruct the face of an adult murder victim. but when she begins to uncover the identity of the skull, she is thrust into a frightening web of murder and deceit . .

Face of Deception, Set. unabr. ed. Iris Johansen. Read by Laurel Lefkow. 8 vols. (Running Time: 12 hr.). (Eve Duncan Ser.). 1999. bk. 69.95 (978-0-7927-2329-5(5), CSL 218, Chivers Sound Lib) AudioGO.
Forensic sculptor Eve Duncan has the unique ability to reconstruct the identity of the long dead from their skulls. For Eve whose own daughter was murdered & her body never found, her job is a way of healing. She is approached by a billionaire magnate John Logan to reconstruct the face of an adult murder victim. When she begins to uncover the identity of the skull, she is thrust into a frightening web of murder & deceit.

Face of God. Ed Boluduc. 1 cass., 1 CD. 1999. 11.00 (978-0-937690-97-0(X), 7442); audio compact disk 16.00 CD. (978-0-937690-98-7(8), 7444) Wrld Lib Pubns.

Face of God. unabr. ed. Zondervan Publishing Staff & Bill Myers. (Running Time: 12 hrs. 17 mins. 0 sec.). (ENG.). 2004. 26.99 (978-0-310-26148-3(1)) Zondervan.

Face of God; Encounter at Saint Matthew's. Jonathan Murro. 1 cass. 7.95 A R Colton Fnd.
Discusses the goal of God-Realization.

Face of Jesus, Set. Gregory Elmer. Read by Gregory Elmer. 6 cass. (Running Time: 5 hrs. 30 min.). 1993. 49.95 (978-7-900783-91-2(1), AA2666) Credence Commun.
Father Elmer gently uncovers the images, touches, memories, feelings & metaphors of scripture, art & poetry for a prolonged & powerful meditation on the face of Christ.

Face of Jesus Christ: 11 Cor. 4:1-6. Ed Young. 1990. 4.95 (978-0-7417-1780-1(8), 780) Win Walk.

Face of Love. Contrib. by Sanctus Real. Prod. by Christopher Stevens. 2006. audio compact disk 13.99 (978-5-558-54373-5(6)) Pt of Grace Ent.

Face of the Assassin. unabr. ed. David Lindsey. Read by Dick Hill. (Running Time: 11 hrs.). 2004. 32.95 (978-1-59355-785-0(X), 159355785X, BAU); 87.25 (978-1-59355-786-7(8), 1593557868, BrilAudUnabridg) Brilliance Audio.
The faceless are Paul Bern's business. As a forensic artist in Austin, Texas, Paul painstakingly reconstructs the likenesses of unfortunate souls whose features have been obliterated by crime or accident. As macabre as his vocation may be, it has become a comfortable and lucrative routine - until the day a mysterious woman arrives at his studio. The visitor brings two gifts. The first is a human skull she has smuggled out of Mexico. The second is a staggering secret that brings him eyeball to eyeball with a past he never knew he had. Suddenly, Paul's own government blackmails him into cooperating in a clandestine mission against a Middle Eastern terrorist group that has made the drug jungles of South America its staging ground. By using his own face as bait to lure the enemy, he will become all too intimate with the underworld of violence that he seeks to destroy, while thousands of lives hang in the balance of his intricate and dangerous deception.

Face of the Assassin. unabr. ed. David Lindsey. Read by Dick Hill. (Running Time: 11 hrs.). 2004. 39.25 (978-1-59335-465-7(7), 1593354657, Brinc Audio MP3 Lib); 24.95 (978-1-59335-307-0(3), 1593353073, Brilliance MP3) Brilliance Audio.

Face of the Assassin. unabr. ed. David Lindsey. Read by Dick Hill. (Running Time: 11 hrs.). 2004. 39.25 (978-1-59710-260-5(1), 1597102601, BADLE) Brilliance Audio.

Face of the Assassin. unabr. ed. David Lindsey. Read by Dick Hill. (Running Time: 11 hrs.). 2004. 24.95 (978-1-59710-261-2(X), 159710261X, BAD) Brilliance Audio.

Face of the Next Move of God. Paul Cain. 1 cass. (Running Time: 90 mins.). (next move of God Ser.: Vol. 1). 2000. 5.00 (PC02-001) Morning NC.
"The Face of the Next Move of God" & "Standards of Leadership." The requirements to be part of the next move of God are examined in these powerful messages.

Face of Trespass. unabr. ed. Ruth Rendell. Read by Ric Jerrom. 6 cass. (Running Time: 9 hrs.). 1998. 49.95 (978-0-7540-0090-7(7), CAB1513) Pub: Chivers Audio Bks GBR. Dist(s): AudioGO
Two years ago he had been a promising young novelist. Now he was living in a derelict cottage with only his obsessive thoughts for company. Two years of loving Drusilla: the spoiled, rich, unstable woman with a husband she wanted dead. The affair was over, but the long slide into deception & violence had just begun.

Face on the Milk Carton, unabr. ed. Caroline B. Cooney. Narrated by Alyssa Bresnahan. 4 pieces. (Running Time: 5 hrs. 30 mins.). (gr. 7 up). 1998. 35.00 (978-0-7887-1916-5(5), 95337E7) Recorded Bks.
Alyssa Bresnahan brings to life the character of 15 year-old Janie Johnson, a teenager whose typical angst is compounded when she discovers her picture on a milk carton as a missing child.

Face on the Milk Carton. unabr. ed. Caroline B. Cooney. Narrated by Alyssa Bresnahan. 6 CDs. (Running Time: 5 hrs. 30 mins.). (gr. 7 up). 2000. audio compact disk 45.00 (978-0-7887-3447-2(4), C1053E7) Recorded Bks.
When 15-year-old Janie Johnson sees her own face in the missing children ad on the milk carton, her world begins to blur. Could she have been kidnapped? Her search for the answers begin.

Face on the Milk Carton, Set. unabr. ed. Caroline B. Cooney. Read by Alyssa Bresnahan. 4 casss. . (Running Time: 5 hr. 30 min.). (YA). (gr. 6). 1998. 49.24 (978-0-7887-1944-8(0), 40651); 115.70 (978-0-7887-2463-3(0), 46190) Recorded Bks.
When 15-year-old Janie Johnson sees her own face in the missing children & on the milk carton, her world begins to blur.

Face on the Wall: A Homer Kelly Mystery, unabr. ed. Jane Langton. Read by Lloyd James. 6 cass. (Running Time: 9 hrs.). 1999. 48.00 (978-0-7366-4369-6(9), 4827) Books on Tape.
Homer Kelly's niece Annie Swann has decided to paint a large-scale mural on the wall of her new home recreating scenes from famous children's stories. But again & again, however often she paints it out, a mysterious, eerie face appears on the wall. When Annie finds her tenants' retarded eight-year-old-son dead beneath it, she is sued for all she's worth by his parents & it becomes a case for Uncle Homer.

Face on Your Plate: The Truth about Food. unabr. ed. Jeffrey Moussaieff Masson. Read by Fred Stella. 1 MP3-CD. (Running Time: 6 hrs.). 2009. 39.97 (978-1-4233-8423-6(7), 9781423384236, Brinc Audio MP3 Lib); 24.99 (978-1-4233-8422-9(9), 9781423384229, Brilliance MP3); 39.97 (978-1-4233-8425-0(3), 9781423384250, BADLE); 24.99 (978-1-4233-8424-3(5), 9781423384243, BAD); audio compact disk 87.97 (978-1-4233-8421-2(0), 9781423384212, BriAudCD Unabrid); audio compact disk 29.99 (978-1-4233-8420-5(2), 9781423384205, Bril Audio CD Unabri) Brilliance Audio.

Face the Fire. abr. ed. Nora Roberts. Read by Sandra Burr. 4 CDs. (Running Time: 4 hrs.). (Three Sisters Island Trilogy: Vol. 3). 2004. audio compact disk 14.99 (978-1-59355-323-4(4), 1593553234, BCD Value Price) Brilliance Audio.
Mia Devlin knows what it is like to love with your whole heart - and then watch your love walk away. Years ago, she and Sam Logan shared an incredible bond built on passion, legend, and fate. But then one day he fled Three Sisters Island, leaving her lost in memories of the magic they shared - and determined to live without love. The new owner of the island's only hotel, Sam has returned to Three Sisters with hopes of winning back Mia's affections. He is puzzled when she greets him with icy indifference - for the chemistry between them is still sizzling and true. Angry, hurt and deeply confused, Mia refuses to admit that a passion for Sam still burns in her heart. But she'll need his help - and his powers - to face her greatest, most terrifying challenge. And as the deadline for breaking a centuries-old curse

draws near, they must take the first steps toward destiny - and come together to turn back the dark.

Face the Fire. unabr. ed. Nora Roberts. Read by Sandra Burr. 7 cass. (Running Time: 10 hrs.). (Three Sisters Island Trilogy: Vol. 3). 2002. 74.25 (978-1-58788-228-9(0), 1587882280, Unabridge Lib Edns) Brilliance Audio.

Face the Fire. unabr. ed. Nora Roberts. Read by Sandra Burr. (Running Time: 36000 sec.). (Three Sisters Island Trilogy: Vol. 3). 2004. audio compact disk 39.25 (978-1-59335-491-6(6), 1593354916, Brlnc Audio MP3 Lib) Brilliance Audio.

Face the Fire. unabr. ed. Nora Roberts. Read by Sandra Burr. (Running Time: 10 hrs.). (Three Sisters Island Trilogy: Vol. 3). 2004. 39.25 (978-1-59710-263-6(6), 1597102636, BADLE); 24.95 (978-1-59710-262-9(8), 1597102628, BAD) Brilliance Audio.

Face the Fire. unabr. ed. Nora Roberts. Read by Sandra Burr. (Running Time: 36000 sec.). (Three Sisters Island Trilogy: Vol. 3). 2007. audio compact disk 97.25 (978-1-4233-3416-3(7), 9781423334163, BriAudCD Unabrid); audio compact disk 36.95 (978-1-4233-3415-6(9), 9781423334156, Bril Audio CD Unabri) Brilliance Audio.

Face the Fire. unabr. ed. Nora Roberts. Read by Sandra Burr. (Running Time: 10 hrs.). (Three Sisters Island Trilogy: Vol. 3). 2004. 24.95 (978-1-59335-040-6(6), 1593350406) Soulmate Audio Bks.

Face the Issues Set: Intermediate Listening & Critical Thinking Skills. Carol Numrick. (J). (gr. 7-9). 1990. 38.00 (978-0-8013-0301-2(X), 75951) Longman.

Face the Issues Set: Intermediate Listening & Critical Thinking Skills. 2nd ed. Carol Numrich. Contrib. by National Public Radio Staff. 2 cass. 2002. 36.40 (978-0-201-69518-2(9)) Longman.

Face the Nation: My Favorite Stories from the First 50 Years of the Award-winning News Broadcast. unabr. ed. Bob Schieffer. Narrated by Bob Schieffer. 4 cass. (Running Time: 6 hrs.). 2004. 39.75 (978-1-4193-0742-3(8), 97868MC) Recorded Bks.

Face to Face. unabr. ed. Ellery Queen. Read by Patrick Cullen. 5 cass. (Running Time: 7 hrs.). 1996. 39.95 (978-0-7861-0969-2(6), 1746) Blckstn Audio.
When Gloria Guild, the singing "Glory" of the thirties & millionairess wife of Count Carlos Armando, is murdered, she leaves only one clue - the word "face" written in her dying scrawl. Who or what is "face"? Ellery & his father the Inspector British agent Harry Burke, & Sergeant Velle all get involved. Ellery's search takes him from the Bowery to a way-out wedding before he arrives at a shocking conclusion.

***Face to Face.** unabr. ed. Ellery Queen. Read by Patrick Cullen. (Running Time: 7 hrs.). 2010. 29.95 (978-1-4417-4498-2(3)); audio compact disk 69.00 (978-1-4417-4495-1(9)) Blckstn Audio.

Face to Face Retreat. Lawrence Gillick. Read by Lawrence Gillick. 7 cass. (Running Time: 7 hrs. 30 min.). 1991. 49.95 Set. (978-7-900783-19-6(9), AA2451) Credence Commun.
Father Gillick begins helping us let go of our false faces & let God see our real faces.

***Face to Face with God: The Ultimate Quest to Experience His Presence.** unabr. ed. Bill Johnson. Narrated by Arthur Morey. (ENG.). 2010. 12.98 (978-1-59644-921-3(7)); audio compact disk 21.98 (978-1-59644-920-6(9)) christianaud.

Face to the Sky. (Greetings Ser.: Vol. 3). (gr. 2-3). 10.00 (978-0-7635-5874-1(5)) Rigby Educ.

Face upon the Floor (The Face upon the Barroom Floor) see Favorite American Poems

Facebook Factor: How to harness the power of Facebook, Twitter, & other social networks to build your business Fast! Narrated by Robert Imbriale. 2009. audio compact disk 19.95 (978-0-9777500-7-8(8)) Ultimate Wealth.

Facedown. Contrib. by Matt Redman et al. Prod. by Matt Hemsley & Andy Hutch. (Running Time: 3 hrs. 49 mins.). 2004. 14.98 (978-5-559-52306-4(2)) Pt of Grace Ent.

Faceless Killers. unabr. ed. Henning Mankell. (Running Time: 32400 sec.). (Kurt Wallander Ser.). 2006. 59.95 (978-0-7861-4831-8(4)) Blckstn Audio.

Faceless Killers. unabr. ed. Henning Mankell. Read by Dick Hill. (Running Time: 32400 sec.). (Kurt Wallander Ser.). 2006. 32.95 (978-0-7861-4731-1(8)); audio compact disk 34.95 (978-0-7861-6540-7(5)); audio compact disk 29.95 (978-0-7861-7310-5(6)); audio compact disk 72.00 (978-0-7861-6139-3(6)) Blckstn Audio.

Faceless Strangers. unabr. ed. Nigel McCrery. Read by Paddy Glynn. 6 cass. (Running Time: 8 hrs. 34 mins.). (Isis Ser.). (J). 2002. 54.95 (978-0-7531-1167-3(5)); audio compact disk 79.95 (978-0-7531-1401-8(1)) Pub: ISIS Lrg Prnt GBR. Dist(s): Ulverscroft US
When the beautiful wife of a local MP is found naked and murdered in their home, the entire resources of the Cambridge Constabulary are brought to bear. But when the decomposed body of a homeless drug addict is discovered, it is an entirely different matter. Police resources are stretched and there is no money left to deal with the case. Nevertheless Detective Sergeant Stanley Sharman is determined to solve the murder and he approaches Dr Sam Ryan, now working independently in Cambridge, to help him. Between them they form an uneasy alliance, working together to track down the killer of a girl without a past and without an identity.

Facelift Naturally: The At-Home or Anywhere, Painless, Natural Facelift for Men & Women That Really Works! Julia M. Busch. Photos by Busch, Scherley, Photography, Inc. Staff. 2 cass. (Running Time: 1 hr. 40 min.). 1992. bk. 59.98 set incl. charts, bk. illustrations in lock-tight vinyl binder. (978-0-9632907-6-2(2)) Anti Aging Pr.
Guides you step-by-step to a facelift that rivals cosmetic surgery. Using only your hands, Julia, on cassette, "talks" you through a rejuvenating, relaxing, invigorating Facelift; coaxes stubborn areas with Mini-Lifts; offers Tune-Up-the-Body Points to realign & rebalance energy; dissolves tension with the Back of the Head & Neck Ritual; & gives Hints for a Fabulous Face. Just place your Quick Reference Facial Chart in front of the mirror & turn on the cassettes. Soon you'll press your "lift" buttons anytime, anywhere: at the office, carpooling the kids, at formal occasions - no one will suspect. A must for youth seekers who want to reverse their age or maintain taut wrinkle-free skin.

Faces. abr. ed. Martina Cole. Read by Nicola Duffett. (Running Time: 5 hrs. 52 mins. 0 sec.). (ENG.). 2009. audio compact disk (978-1-4055-0615-1(6)) Little BrownUK GBR.

Faces at Gettysburg. Ernest Yaniger. Tr. by Repertory Theatre Staff. 1 cass. (Running Time: 25 min. per cass.). 1985. 10.00 (RAH911) Esstee Audios.
Relates the war experiences of a housewife, a confederate soldier, a farm boy, a Northern lawyer, an English observer, & a Baltimore nurse. Music & angelic choir background.

Faces in the Crowd-4 CD audio Book. Thomas Henry Kelly. 2004. audio compact disk 35.00 (978-1-56142-198-5(7)) T Kelly Inc.

Faces, Mirrors, Masks: Twentieth-Century Latin American Fiction. 1 cass. (Running Time: 1 hr.). 10.95 (F007AB090, HarperThor); 10.95 (F007BB090, HarperThor); 10.95 (F007CB090, HarperThor); 10.95 (F007DB090, HarperThor); 10.95 (F007EB090, HarperThor); 10.95 (F007FB090, HarperThor) HarpC GBR.

Faces, Mirrors, Masks Programs 1-13: Twentieth-Century Latin American Fiction. Read by Jorge Luis Borges et al. 7 cass. 75.00 Set. (F007SB090, HarperThor) HarpC GBR.

Faces, Mirrors, Masks: Twentieth-Century Latin American Fiction Program 13: The Voice of the Powerless. Read by Elena Poniatowska. 1 cass. (Running Time: 30 min.). 9.95 (F007GB090, HarperThor) HarpC GBR.

Faces of Christmas Past. Short Stories. Bill Holm. Read by Bill Holm. Prod. by Scott Beyers. 1 CD. (Running Time: 65 mins.). 2002. audio compact disk 15.00 (978-0-9665212-6-9(9), 5) EssayAudio.
An exceptional memoir that speaks with wit and grace to the perils of Christmas and self-imposed burdens of ritual duty (like the newsy Christmas Xerox). The unabridged audiobook is read by its author, Bill Holm. Mr. Holm's storytelling lends itself to audio perfectly. Because of this being Holm's first unadbridged audiobook, we've wrapped up and stuffed a few of the wonderful holiday songs that are mentioned in the story, performed and sung by the author, at the end of the reading. The Track List:1. Preface2. Interior Christmas3. The Gavel of Christmas Tradition Bangs on the Table4. Icelandic Christmas Ghost Stories5. Music and Rites of Christmas6. The Winter of 1996-97, a Humdinger7. A Benediction8. In The Bleak Midwinter - Rossetti / Holst9. Christmas Bells - Longfelllow10. Ehemals ("Formerly") from Weihnachtsbaum - Liszt.

Faces of Eve. abr. ed. John L. Lund. 4 cass. (Running Time: 5 hrs. 26 min.). 1996. bk. 24.95 Set. (978-1-891114-32-8(8)) Commun Co.
Includes "Daughter of God", "Wife & Companion", "Mother in Zion", "Sister in the Kingdom".

Faces of Fear. abr. ed. John Saul. Read by Laural Merlington. (Running Time: 5 hrs.). 2009. audio compact disk 14.99 (978-1-4233-0462-3(4), 9781423304623, BCD Value Price) Brilliance Audio.

Faces of Fear. unabr. ed. John Saul. Read by Laural Merlington. 1 MP3-CD. (Running Time: 10 hrs.). 2008. 24.95 (978-1-4233-0457-9(8), 9781423304579, Brilliance MP3); 39.25 (978-1-4233-0460-9(8), 9781423304609, BADLE); 24.95 (978-1-4233-0459-3(4), 9781423304593, BAD); 39.25 (978-1-4233-0458-6(6), 9781423304586, Brlnc Audio MP3 Lib); audio compact disk 36.95 (978-1-4233-0455-5(1), 9781423304555, Bril Audio CD Unabri); audio compact disk 97.25 (978-1-4233-0456-2(X), 9781423304562, BriAudCD Unabrid) Brilliance Audio.

Faces of Fire. Michael Jan Friedman. (Star Trek Ser.). 2004. 10.95 (978-0-7435-4661-4(X)) Pub: S&S Audio. Dist(s): S and S Inc

Faces of Raga. Music by Tarun Bhattachanya. 1 cass. 1997. Multi-Cultural Bks.

Faces of Raga. Music by Budhaditya Mukherjee. 1 cass. 1997. (A-97018) Multi-Cultural Bks.

Faces of Raga. Music by Ajay Pohankar. 1 cass. 1997. (A-97019) Multi-Cultural Bks.

Faces of Rega. Music by Prabhakar Karekar. 1 cass. 1997. (A97017) Multi-Cultural Bks.

Faces of the Enemy: Esalen Symposium. unabr. ed. UBC Staff & Tarrytown Staff. Moderated by Sam Keen. 8 cass. 1983. 77.00 Vinyl Album Set. Big Sur Tapes.
Convened at the Palace of Fine Arts, San Francisco, this conference examines the darkness, the shadow within us, which leads to the destruction of ourselves & others. From personal to planetwide, in the arts, sciences, philosophy, religion, & the governments of the Soviet Union & the United States, the creation & perception of enemies.

Faces of the USA. Elizabeth Laird. (YA). (gr. 7-12). 1987. 24.95 (978-0-582-01896-9(X), 78271) Longman.

Faces Pressed Against the Glass: Black Folks Caught Between the Chaos & the Cosmos. Paul D. Thompson. 6 cass. 1997. Set. (978-1-887111-10-2(7)) Dogon Pub.
Analysis of the state of Black Americans at the close of the 20th century.

Facets. abr. ed. Barbara Delinsky. Read by Joyce Bean. (Running Time: 6 hrs.). 2008. audio compact disk 14.99 (978-1-59600-874-8(1), 9781596008748, BCD Value Price) Brilliance Audio.
Hillary Cox...A successful writer, she could not escape her obsession for one man, and all the pain and passion he offered. John St. George...Not content with his father's fortune in tourmaline mines and a chain of jewelry stores, he wanted his father's young second wife, too. Pam St. George... Her father's death left her at her half-brother's mercy, and John would rule her like a tyrant, and a lover. Cutter Reid... Transformed from a kid with no future to a man with distinction, he was the object of John's undying hatred, and Pam's tempestuous love. When John St. George announces his engagement on national TV, Hillary Cox threatens to bring him down in disgrace - while a three-decade-old family drama of power, duplicity, and money comes to its explosive conclusion.

Facets. unabr. ed. Barbara Delinsky. Read by Joyce Bean. (Running Time: 14 hrs.). 2007. 39.25 (978-1-59710-265-0(2), 9781597102650, BADLE); 24.95 (978-1-59710-264-3(4), 9781597102643, BAD); 97.25 (978-1-58788-829-8(7), 9781587888298, BrilAudUnabridg); audio compact disk 112.25 (978-1-59600-875-5(X), 9781596008755, BriAudCD Unabrid); audio compact disk 38.95 (978-1-59600-872-4(5), 9781596008724, Bril Audio CD Unabri); audio compact disk 39.25 (978-1-59335-813-6(X), 9781593358136, Brlnc Audio MP3 Lib); audio compact disk 24.95 (978-1-59335-679-8(X), 9781593356798, Brilliance MP3) Brilliance Audio.

Facets of Ayn Rand. Mary Ann Sures & Charles Sures. Read by Susan O'Malley. (Running Time: 4 hrs.). 2003. 22.95 (978-1-59912-485-8(8)) Iofy Corp.

Facets of Ayn Rand. Mary Ann Sures et al. 3 cass. (Running Time: 4 hrs.). 2002. 23.95 (978-0-7861-2589-0(6), 3190) Blckstn Audio.

Facets of Ayn Rand. unabr. ed. Mary Ann Sures & Charles Sures. Read by Susan O'Malley. (Running Time: 4 hrs. NaN mins.). (ENG.). 2000. 24.95 (978-0-7861-8805-5(7), 3190) Blckstn Audio.

Facets of Ayn Rand. unabr. ed. Mary Ann Sures & Charles Sures. Read by Susan O'Malley. 4 CDs. (Running Time: 4 hrs.). 2006. audio compact disk 32.00 (978-0-7861-8977-9(0), 3190) Blckstn Audio.

***Facets of Ayn Rand: Memoirs.** unabr. ed. Mary Ann Sures. Read by Susan O'Malley. (Running Time: 4 hrs. NaN mins.). (ENG.). 2011. audio compact disk 19.95 (978-1-4417-0217-3(2)) Blckstn Audio.

Facets of Murder. unabr. ed. Ray Harrison. Read by Terry Wale. 7 cass. (Running Time: 10 hrs. 30 min.). 2001. 61.95 (978-1-86042-694-0(8), 26948) Pub: Soundings Ltd GBR. Dist(s): Ulverscroft US
Murder, theft & abduction are the last things on Constable Morton's mind when he takes his fiancee Catherine to choose an engagement ring. But as they inspect the biggest diamond they have ever seen, disaster strikes.

Face2face Advanced Class Audio CDs (3) Gillie Cunningham & Jan Bell. (ENG.). 2009. audio compact disk 73.50 (978-0-521-71282-8(3)) Cambridge U Pr.

Face2face Elementary. Gillie Cunningham & Chris Redstone. (Running Time: 2 hrs. 50 mins.). (ENG.). 2005. audio compact disk 33.60 (978-0-521-60338-6(2)) Cambridge U Pr.

Face2face Intermediate. Chris Redston & Gillie Cunningham. (Running Time: 3 hrs. 20 mins.). (ENG., 2006. audio compact disk 43.05 (978-0-521-60340-9(4)) Cambridge U Pr.

Face2face Intermediate Class Cassettes. Chris Redston & Gillie Cunningham. (Running Time: 3 hrs. 42 mins.). (ENG.). 2006. 58.80 (978-0-521-60344-7(7)) Cambridge U Pr.

Face2face Pre-Intermediate. Chris Redston & Gillie Cunningham. (Running Time: 2 hrs. 50 mins.). (ENG.). 2005. audio compact disk 33.60 (978-0-521-60339-3(0)) Cambridge U Pr.

Face2face Pre-Intermediate Class Cassettes. Chris Redston & Gillie Cunningham. (Running Time: 2 hrs. 30 mins.). (ENG.). 2005. 33.60 (978-0-521-60343-0(9)) Cambridge U Pr.

Face2face Starter Class Audio CDs. Chris Redston. Told to Gillie Cunningham. (Running Time: 3 hrs. 10 mins.). (ENG.). 2009. audio compact disk 56.00 (978-0-521-71277-4(7)) Cambridge U Pr.

Face2face Upper Intermediate Class. Chris Redston & Gillie Cunningham. (Running Time: 3 hrs. 20 mins.). (ENG., 2007. audio compact disk 56.70 (978-0-521-60341-6(2)) Cambridge U Pr.

Face2face Upper Intermediate Class Cassettes. Chris Redston & Gillie Cunningham. (Running Time: 3 hrs. 20 mins.). (ENG.). 2007. 56.70 (978-0-521-60345-4(5)) Cambridge U Pr.

Facial Make-Up. Milady Publishing Company Staff. 1 cass. (Standard Ser.: Chapter 20). 1995. 14.95 (978-1-56253-292-5(8), Milady) Pub: Delmar. Dist(s): CENGAGE Learn

Facial Reanimation. 2 cass. (Plastic & Maxillofacial Surgery Ser.: C85-PL4). 1985. 15.00 (8583) Am Coll Surgeons.

Facial Skeletal Reconstruction after Traumatic or Surgical Ablation: Interdisciplinary Panel Discussion. Moderated by Paul L. Manson. 2 cass. (Plastic & Maxillofacial Surgery Ser.: PL-4). 1986. 19.00 (8663) Am Coll Surgeons.

Facial Tic. Barrie Konicov. 1 cass. 11.98 (978-0-87082-319-0(1), 031) Potentials.
Demonstrates how your nerves & muscles can repair themselves if you tell them what to do. Your body could respond to a spoken word, telling your nerves to relax.

Facilitating SoulCollage in Groups. Speeches. Seena B. Frost. Voice by Seena B. Frost. (Running Time: 70 min). 2003. 12.95 (978-0-9643158-8-4(2)) Pub: Hanford Mead. Dist(s): Baker Taylor
Side 1 - Frost shares her decade of experience facilitating SoulCollage(r) in groups: how to gather participants, introduce the work, support group members, collect materials needed, and create "sacred space". Always honoring each person's unique process, she poses and answers common questions about SoulCollage and its use in different group formats. Side 2 - Frost answers more questions about SoulCollage(r), talks about the "I Am One Who..." exercise, how to use SoulCollage in advanced and on-going groups, and gives many practical suggestions.

Facilitator Training for Getting Ahead in a Just-Gettin-by-World Audio Workshop. Philip E. DeV ol. (ENG.). 2007. audio compact disk 99.00 (978-1-929229-83-3(6)) aha Process.

Facilitator's Guide to Accompany the Moral Imperative of School Leadership. Michael Fullan. 2004. 16.95 (978-1-4129-1477-2(9)) Pub: Corwin Pr. Dist(s): SAGE

Facilitator's Guide to Cultural Proficiency. 2nd ed. Randall B. Lindsey et al. (C). 2005. 16.95 (978-1-4129-1657-8(7)) Pub: Corwin Pr. Dist(s): SAGE

Facilitator's Guide to Failure Is Not an Option(TM) Six Principles That Guide Student Achievement in High-Performing Schools. Alan M. Blankstein. 2006. 16.95 (978-1-4129-3780-1(9), B09333F) Pub: Corwin Pr. Dist(s): SAGE

Facilitator's Guide to the Student Evaluation Standards. Lori A. Wingate & Arlen R. Gullickson. Contrib. by Joint Committee on Standards for Educational Evaluation Staff. 2003. 16.95 (978-0-7619-3131-7(7), B46624M) Pub: Corwin Pr. Dist(s): SAGE

Facilitator's Guide to Ways to Think about Mathematics. Steven Benson et al. (1-Off Ser.). 2004. 49.95 (978-1-4129-0520-6(6), B3104XM) SAGE.

Facilitator's Guide to What Every Principal Should Know about Leadership. Jeffrey Glanz. 2006. 19.95 (978-1-4129-4136-5(9)) Pub: Corwin Pr. Dist(s): SAGE

Facing Death. Gangaji Foundation Staff. Read by Gangaji Foundation Staff. 1 cass. (Running Time: 1 hr. 19 min.). 2001. 12.00 (978-1-887984-10-2(0)); audio compact disk 14.00 (978-1-887984-11-9(9)) The Gangaji Fnd.
Compilation of segments concerning illness, pain, and death.

Facing Death without Fear: 2007 CCEF Annual Conference. Featuring David Powlison. (ENG.). 2007. audio compact disk 11.99 (978-1-934885-15-4(0)) New Growth Pr.

Facing down Evil: Life on the Edge as an FBI Hostage Negotiator. unabr. ed. Clint Van Zandt. Read by Alan Sklar. Told to Daniel Paisner. (Running Time: 10 hrs. 30 mins. 0 sec.). (ENG.). 2006. audio compact disk 69.99 (978-1-4001-3286-7(X)) Pub: Tantor Media. Dist(s): IngramPubServ

Facing down Evil: Life on the Edge as an FBI Hostage Negotiator. unabr. ed. Clint Van Zandt & Daniel Paisner. Narrated by Alan Sklar. (Running Time: 10 hrs. 30 mins. 0 sec.). (ENG.). 2006. audio compact disk 34.99 (978-1-4001-0286-0(3)); audio compact disk 24.99 (978-1-4001-5286-5(0)) Pub: Tantor Media. Dist(s): IngramPubServ

Facing God's Judgement. Derek Prince. 1 cass. 5.95 (4389) Derek Prince.
Is there hope for America? If Jesus said "Would you ask Me to give you My heart for America?" how would you answer? There is hope for this nation. If we have Jesus' heart for America, lives will be changed.

Facing Illness Series. Created by Laura Boynton King. 6 CD's. 2003. audio compact disk 109.95 (978-0-9748885-5-2(9)) Summit Dynamics.
A 6-volume series of Self-Hypnosis CD's using the proven benefits of self-hypnosis to foster a positive, healthy mind set that greatly speed recovery and ease pain.

Facing Life Problems with God's Hope see Como Enfrentar Problemas con la Ayuda de Dios

Facing Life's Problems with God's Hope. 2003. audio compact disk 54.00 (978-1-57972-570-9(8)) Insight Living.

Facing Life's Problems with God's Hope. 2004. 54.00 (978-1-57972-569-3(4)) Insight Living.

Facing Nature see John Updike

Facing Our Blocks. Swami Amar Jyoti. 1 dolby cass. 1984. 9.95 (J-46) Truth Consciousness.
Being specific about our blocks & taking responsibility. The purpose of life is the same in every birth, till we reach the Goal.

Facing Perilous Times. Derek Prince. 1 cass. 5.95 (4337) Derek Prince.
Self-love & occult power have inundated this generation with a flood of moral corruption. One rock remains unshaken: the authority of Scripture.

Facing Terror. Carrie McDonnall. 2005. audio compact disk 24.99 (978-1-59859-024-1(3)) Oasis Audio.

Facing Terror: The True Story of Carrie & David Mcdonnall's Sacrifice in Iraq. abr. ed. Carrie McDonnall & Kristin Billerbeck. (ENG.). 2005. 17.49 (978-1-60814-195-1(0)) Oasis Audio.

Facing the Facts. Swami Amar Jyoti. 1 cass. 1979. 9.95 (J-21) Truth Consciousness.
Finding relief from pressures. God's blueprint for us.

Facing the Fire. John Lee. 4 cass. 1993. 36.00 set. (OC330-70) Sound Horizons AV.

Facing the Flood/Nature's Power. Steck-Vaughn Staff. (J). 1999. (978-0-7398-0928-0(8)) SteckVau.

Facing the Funnell Clouds & Losing: Acts 5:1-11. Ed Young. 1997. 4.95 (978-0-7417-2155-6(4), A1155) Win Walk.

Facing the Future. Derek Prince. 4 cass. 19.95 Set. (062; 063; 064; 065) Derek Prince.
Do you wonder what the future holds? The Bible's record of proven correctness, extending over many centuries, validates its claim to predict the future with authority & accuracy.

Facing the Future. Read by Basilea Schlink. 1 cass. (Running Time: 30 min.). 1985. (0234) Evang Sisterhood Mary.
Trained in spiritual warfare; the marvellous purposes of god.

Facing the Future: Four Kids Face Earth's Last Days Together. unabr. ed. Jerry B. Jenkins & Tim LaHaye. Narrated by Scott Shina. 3 pieces. (Running Time: 3 hrs. 15 mins.). (Left Behind Ser.: Bk. 4). (gr. 6 up). 2002. 28.00 (978-1-4025-1991-8(5)) Recorded Bks.
Ever since the Rapture, four teenagers have been focusing on Christ's return. When they hear one man's eyewitness account of the nightmares he has seen, they are also driven to discover the identity of the Antichrist.

Facing the Future CD Series. 2003. audio compact disk 14.00 (978-1-59834-030-3(1)) Walk Thru the Bible.

Facing the Illusion of Fear. Featuring Adyashanti. (ENG.). 2009. audio compact disk 35.00 (978-1-933986-55-5(7)) Open Gate Pub.

Facing the Light - The Third Force of Life. Read by Leland Roloff. 4 cass. (Running Time: 4 hrs.). 1991. 28.95 Set. (978-0-7822-0237-3(3), 429S) C G Jung IL.

Facing the Music. unabr. ed. Henri Temianka. Read by Henri Temianka. 7 cass. (Running Time: 10 hrs. 30 min.). 1991. 29.95 Set. (978-0-936939-00-1(1), AB7000) Cambria Records.
Maestro Henri Temianka traces his life story as a virtuoso violinist/conductor & offers an inside view of the real concert world.

Facing the Public-Subliminal. 2007. audio compact disk 19.95 (978-1-56136-047-5(3)) Master Your Mind.

Facing the Shadow in Men & Women. unabr. ed. Robert Bly & Marion Woodman. Read by Robert Bly & Marion Woodman. Ed. by Richard Chelew. 4 cass. (Running Time: 4 hrs. 30 min.). 1993. 29.95 Bookpack, set. (978-1-880155-06-6(0), OTA 302) Oral Trad Arch.
In this lively & funny presentation, Bly & Woodman, using stories, music & discussion, challenge us to face the shadow in all areas of our lives, from politics to parenting. They perform a tale of love between a young woman & the White Bear King Valeman, & recite poems of Bly, Dickinson, Kabir & others, accompanied by musicians Marcus Wise on tabla & David Whetstone on sitar.

***Facing the Sky (8-CD Audio Book) A True Story - A Journey to Find Healing from a Broken Past.** Rainee Grason. (Running Time: 800). (ENG.). 2009. audio compact disk 49.00 (978-0-9814988-1-2(7)) Prec Grace Pub.

Facing the Truth. Swami Amar Jyoti. 1 cass. 1987. 9.95 (A-40) Truth Consciousness.
Putting an end to beating about the bushes. Truth as a way of life. On selfishness. Using God's bounties as He wants. Justifying our human birth. Qualifications for Liberation.

Facing the Wind: A True Story of Tragedy & Reconciliation. unabr. ed. Julie Salamon. Read by Sandra Burr. 7 cass. (Running Time: 10 hrs.). 2001. 32.95 (978-1-58788-160-2(8), 1587881608, BAU); 78.25 (978-1-58788-161-9(6), 1587881616, Unabridge Lib Edns) Brilliance Audio.
Bob Rowe and his wife Mary worked hard to build their American dream. A suburban home, barbecues in the summer, and a fast track corporate job made their life look ideal to outsiders. Yet they faced one of the most difficult challenges for a couple: their son Christopher was born severely handicapped and disabled. As a family, they managed to navigate through the tough times by being hands-on parents. Their efforts were emboldened by a group of extraordinary women - all of whom also had disabled children - who acted as a support system for one another. Yet something slowly began to happen to Rowe . . . His deceased mother's voice started to reverberate in his head instructing him to murder his family; reality disintegrated and a new job was lost when it proved too overwhelming. Finally a short stay in a psychiatric hospital did nothing to quell his sudden volatility . . . In a horribly violent act, he killed his wife and children. Seen through the eyes and thoughts of Rowe's friends and second wife (whom he married on release from the psychiatric hospital where he spent just a few years for the murder of his family), Salamon braids the story of a man's roller coaster life (from ideal family man to murderer to someone struggling for redemption) with the touching and heroic tales of the mothers who were left looking on in shock at the tragedy no one ever could have anticipated.

Facing the Wind: The True Story of Tragedy & Reconciliation. unabr. ed. Julie Salamon. Read by Sandra Burr. (Running Time: 10 hrs.). 2004. 39.25 (978-1-59335-449-7(5), 1593354495, Brinc Audio MP3 Lib) Brilliance Audio.

Facing the Wind: The True Story of Tragedy & Reconciliation. unabr. ed. Julie Salamon. Read by Sandra Burr. (Running Time: 10 hrs.). 2004. 39.25 (978-1-59710-267-4(9), 1597102679, BADLE); 24.95 (978-1-59710-266-7(0), 1597102660, BAD) Brilliance Audio.

Facing the Wind: The True Story of Tragedy & Reconciliation. unabr. ed. Julie Salamon. Read by Sandra Burr. (Running Time: 10 hrs.). 2004. 24.95 (978-1-59335-080-2(5), 1593350805) Soulmate Audio Bks.

Facing Today & the Future Through Self-Hypnosis. John G. Kappas. 1 cass. (Running Time: 60 min.). 1986. 9.95 (978-0-937671-67-2(3), 67-3) Panorama Van Nuys.
Teaches how to self-hypnotize, word suggestions for best effect, when & when not to use self-hypnosis. Also conditioning exercises.

Facing up. Bear Grylls. 2 cass. (Running Time: 3 hrs.). 2001. (978-0-333-78255-2(0)) Macmillan UK GBR.

Facing Up: A Remarkable Journey to the Summit of Mount Everest. unabr. ed. Bear Grylls. Read by Julian Rhind-Tutt. 8 cass. (Running Time: 8 hrs.). 2001. 69.95 (978-0-7540-0624-4(7), CAB2047) Pub: Chivers Audio Bks GBR. Dist(s): AudioGO
For every six mountaineers who make it to the top of Mount Everest, one will die. The author is the youngest British climber to reach the summit & return alive, a feat made all the more remarkable by the fact that only two years earlier he broke his back in a parachuting accident. He endured over seventy days on Everest's southeast face & only avoided death when he fell into a crevasse at 19,000 feet.

Facing Your Challenges Head On. Speeches. Joel Osteen. 1 Cass. (Running Time: 30 Mins.). 2002. 6.00 (978-1-59349-140-6(9)) J Osteen.

Facing Your Giants see Enfrente a Sus Gigantes

Facing Your Giants. unabr. abr. ed. Max Lucado. Read by Wayne Shepherd. (Running Time: 10800 sec.). 2006. audio compact disk 24.99 (978-0-8499-6387-2(7)) Nelson.

Facing Your Middle Years with Hope: 2007 CCEF Annual Conference. Featuring Paul Tripp. (ENG.). 2007. audio compact disk 11.99 (978-1-934885-07-9(X)) New Growth Pr.

Fact & Fiction in the Da Vinci Code. Steve Kellmeyer. 2005. 16.95 (978-0-9767368-7-5(X)) Bridegroom.

Fact & the Idea of the Fact. J. Krishnamurti. 1 cass. (Running Time: 75 min.). (Madras - the Last Talks 1986 Ser.: No. 1). 8.50 (AMT861) Krishnamurti.
Krishnamurti traveled to India in November, 1985, for the last time. These, his final public talks, were given a little over a month before his death. He addresses the fact that despite the amazing technological achievements of modern times, man has remained, psychologically, the barbarian he was when he first appeared on earth. Krishnamurti maintains that each of us is responsible for the brutality & divisiveness of the society in which we live, a society which is only a reflection of ourselves & as such, incapable of being saved from chaos except through a profound change in each human psyche. His lifelong work is the foundation for his insistence that such a change is possible.

Fact Families. Sundance/Newbridge, LLC Staff. (Early Math Ser.). (gr. k-1). 2000. 12.00 (978-1-58273-865-9(3)) Sund Newbrdge.

***Factor de Atraccion.** Joe Vitale. 2010. audio compact disk 24.95 (978-1-933499-97-0(4)) Fonolibro Inc.

Factoring Case Studies. Ernest Zerenner & Jeff Callender. Read by Jeff Callender. 1 cass. (Running Time: 1 hr.). 1996. 6.95 (978-1-889095-03-5(6)) Dash Point Pubng.
Five case studies of clients' use of factoring. Audience: new factors.

Factory Girls: From Village to City in a Changing China. unabr. ed. Leslie T. Chang. Read by Susan Ericksen. 2 MP3-CDs. (Running Time: 15 hrs. 0 mins. 0 sec.). (ENG.). 2009. 24.99 (978-1-4001-6045-7(6)); audio compact disk 37.99 (978-1-4001-1045-2(9)); audio compact disk 75.99 (978-1-4001-4045-9(5)) Pub: Tantor Media. Dist(s): IngramPubServ

***Facts: A Novelist's Autobiography.** unabr. ed. Philip Roth. (Running Time: 7 hrs.). 2010. 24.99 (978-1-4418-0573-7(7), 9781441805737, BAD); 39.97 (978-1-4418-0574-4(5), 9781441805744, BADLE) Brilliance Audio.

***Facts: A Novelist's Autobiography.** unabr. ed. Philip Roth. Read by Mel Foster. (Running Time: 7 hrs.). 2010. 24.99 (978-1-4418-0571-3(0), 9781441805713, Brilliance MP3); 39.97 (978-1-4418-0572-0(9), 9781441805720, Brinc Audio MP3 Lib); audio compact disk 24.99 (978-1-4418-0569-0(9), 9781441805690); audio compact disk 82.97 (978-1-4418-0570-6(2), 9781441805706, BriAudCD Unabrid) Brilliance Audio.

Facts & Fictions of Minna Pratt, unabr. ed. Patricia MacLachlan. Narrated by Christina Moore. 3 pieces. (Running Time: 3 hrs. 30 mins.). (gr. 5 up). 1993. 27.00 (978-1-55690-855-2(5), 93223E7) Recorded Bks.
Minna Pratt struggles with the difficult realities of her life: her eccentric parents, playing Mozart on the cello & her first boyfriend.

Facts Behind the Helsinki Roccamatios. Yann Martel. Read by Jeff Woodman et al. (Playaway Adult Fiction Ser.). 2008. 39.99 (978-1-60640-628-1(0)) Find a World.

Facts Can't Speak for Themselves: Reveal the Stories That Give Facts Their Meaning. Eric Oliver. (ENG.). 2008. audio compact disk 65.00 (978-1-934833-03-2(7)) Trial Guides.

Facts Concerning the Recent Carnival of Crime in Connecticut. Narrated by Richard Henzel. Prod. by Richard Henzel. (ENG.). 2009. audio compact disk 9.99 (978-0-9747237-8-5(9)) R Henzel.

Facts, Fables & Fancies about Our Early Presidents. Frank Morgan. 3 cass. (Running Time: 60 min. per cass.). 1989. 18.95 Set. (978-0-88432-269-6(6), S01600) J Norton Pubs.
Rarely told stories about early U. S. presidents, laden with tales, quotes & historical insights.

Facts in the Case of M. Valdemar see Pit & the Pendulum

Facts in the Case of M. Valdemar see Best of Edgar Allan Poe

Facts in the case of M. Valdemar. 1979. (N-24) Jimcin Record.

Facts in the Case of the Great Beef Contract see Best of Mark Twain

Facts in the Green Beef Contract see $30,000 Bequest & Other Stories

Facts of Faith. Nathaniel Holcomb. 7 cass. (Running Time: 10 hrs. 30 mins.). 1998. (978-1-930918-19-1(4)) Its All About Him.

Facts of Nature Are Not Man Made - Story of Bringing Nephews to America: Volume 11, Vol. 11. Speeches. As told by Bhagat Singh Thind. (Running Time: 60 mins). (ENG., 2003. 6.50 (978-1-932630-35-0(X)); audio compact disk 12.00 (978-1-932630-12-1(0)) Pub: Dr Bhagat Sin. Dist(s): Baker Taylor

Faculty Club. unabr. ed. Danny Tobey. Read by Rich Orlow. (Running Time: 8 hrs. 0 mins. 0 sec.). (ENG.). 2010. audio compact disk 29.99 (978-1-4423-0608-0(4)) Pub: S&S Audio. Dist(s): S and S Inc

FAD Cartoons. (ENG.). (YA). 2010. DVD 10.95 (978-0-9841748-3-6(4), Fad Prod) Vizzie CA.

FAD the Movie. (ENG, APA, ARA, ARM & EGY.). (YA). 2010. DVD 10.95 (978-0-9841748-0-5(X), Fad Prod) Vizzie CA.

FAD 2 the Return of the Angels. (ENG.). (YA). 2010. DVD 10.95 (978-0-9841748-1-2(8), Fad Prod) Vizzie CA.

Fade. Kyle Mills. 8 cass. (Running Time: 12 hrs.). 2005. Rental 72.00 (978-1-4159-2100-5(8)); audio compact disk 90.00 (978-1-4159-2101-2(6)) Books on Tape.

Fade. unabr. ed. Lisa McMann. Read by Ellen Grafton. (Running Time: 5 hrs.). (Wake Trilogy: Bk. 2). 2010. 19.99 (978-1-4418-1987-1(8), 9781441819871, BAD); 39.97 (978-1-4418-1986-4(X), 9781441819864, Brinc Audio MP3 Lib); 39.97 (978-1-4418-1988-8(6), 9781441819888, BADLE); audio compact disk 19.99 (978-1-4418-1983-3(5), 9781441819833, Bril Audio CD Unabri); audio compact disk 44.97 (978-1-4418-1984-0(3), 9781441819840, BriAudCD Unabrid) Brilliance Audio.

Fade. unabr. ed. Lisa McMann. Read by Ellen Grafton. (Running Time: 5 hrs.). (Wake Trilogy: Bk. 22). 2010. 19.99 (978-1-4418-1985-7(1), 9781441819857, Brilliance MP3) Brilliance Audio.

Fade Away. unabr. ed. Harlan Coben. Read by Jonathan Marosz. 6 cass. (Running Time: 9 hrs.). (Myron Bolitar Ser.: No. 3). 2000. 48.00 (978-0-7366-4995-7(6), 5253) Books on Tape.
The home was top-notch New Jersey suburban. The living room was Martha Stewart. The basement was legos, and blood. For sports agent Myron Bolitar, the disappearance of a man he once competed against was bringing back memories, of the sport he and Greg Downing had both played and the woman they both loved. Now, among the stars, the wanna-bes, the gamblers and the groupies, Mayron is unraveling the strange, violent ride of a sports hero gone wrong, and coming face-to-face with a past he can't relive and a present he may not survive.

Fade Away. unabr. ed. Harlan Coben. Read by Jonathan Marosz. 6 cass. (Running Time: 9 hrs.). (Myron Bolitar Ser.: No. 3). 2001. 29.95 (978-0-7366-4951-3(4)) Books on Tape.
Sports Agent Myron Bolitar goes undercover with an NBA team when a star player disappears without a trace.

Fade Away. unabr. ed. Harlan Coben. Read by Jonathan Marosz. 7 CDs. (Running Time: 31500 sec.). (Myron Bolitar Ser.: No. 3). (ENG.). 2007. audio compact disk 19.99 (978-0-7393-4098-1(0), Random AudioBks) Pub: Random Audio Pubg. Dist(s): Random

***Fade Out.** unabr. ed. Rachel Caine. Narrated by Cynthia Holloway. (Running Time: 8 hrs. 30 mins.). (Morganville Vampires Ser.). 2010. 15.99 (978-1-4001-8197-1(6)); 19.99 (978-1-4001-6197-3(5)); audio compact disk 29.99 (978-1-4001-1197-8(8)); audio compact disk 59.99 (978-1-4001-4197-5(4)) Pub: Tantor Media. Dist(s): IngramPubServ

***Fadeaway Girl.** Martha Grimes. (Running Time: 10 hrs.). (ENG.). 2011. audio compact disk 29.95 (978-0-14-242914-3(7), PengAudBks) Penguin Grp USA.

Faded Coat of Blue. Owen Parry. Read by Paul Boehmer. 2000. 56.00 (978-0-7366-5920-8(X)) Books on Tape.

Faded Flower; When the Last Leaf Falls. unabr. ed. Paul McCusker & Myers. 2001. 24.99 (978-0-310-24046-4(8)) Zondervan.

Faded Love. John R. Erickson. 2 cass. (Running Time: 2 hrs.). (Hank the Cowdog Ser.: No. 5). (J). (gr. 2-5). 1989. 16.95 (978-0-87719-137-7(9)) Lone Star Bks.

Faded Love. unabr. ed. John R. Erickson. 2 cass. (Running Time: 3 hrs.). (Hank the Cowdog Ser.: No. 5). (J). (gr. 2-5). 2001. (978-0-7366-6139-3(5)) Books on Tape.
Hank's thoughts turn to romance. He decides that he has been working too hard and needs a vacation. He goes to visit his true love, Miss Beulah the Collie, the pitter in the patter of his heart. On the way, Hank encounters all kinds of challenging situations. Will his intuition and investigative powers be enough?.

Faded Love. unabr. ed. John R. Erickson. Read by John R. Erickson. 2 cass. (Running Time: 3 hrs.). (Hank the Cowdog Ser.: No. 5). (J). (gr. 2-5). 2001. 16.95 (978-0-7366-6894-1(2)) Books on Tape.
Hank goes courting Beulah the Collie, mistakenly believing that the smell of dead skunk is an ancient coyote love potion.

Faded Love. unabr. ed. John R. Erickson. Read by John R. Erickson. Illus. by Gerald L. Holmes. 2 cass. (Hank the Cowdog Ser.: No. 5). (J). (gr. 2-5). 1985. 13.95 (978-0-916941-12-3(4)) Maverick Bks.

Faded Love. unabr. ed. John R. Erickson. Read by John R. Erickson. 2 cassettes. (Running Time: approx. 3 hours). (Hank the Cowdog Ser.: No. 5). (J). 2002. 17.99 (978-1-59188-305-0(9)) Maverick Bks.

Faded Love. unabr. ed. John R. Erickson. Read by John R. Erickson. 3 CDs. (Running Time: Approx. 3 hours). (Hank the Cowdog Ser.: No. 5). (J). 2002. audio compact disk 19.99 (978-1-59188-605-1(8)) Maverick Bks.
Duped by Drover, mocked by Pete the Barncat, and busted yet again by Sally May, the Head of Ranch Security decides it?s time for a break from the grueling daily grind. Heading into the wild outback, Hank goes in search if his true love, the charming Miss Beulah. Finding her was easy, but luring her away from Plato, the annoying bird dog, is not. Hank is sure he can win Beulah?s heart with the help of a powerful aphrodisiac. But other forces are conspiring against him, and getting the girl turns out to be more difficult than Hank imagined?.Hank and the coyote brothers belt out a polka number called, ?Rotten Meat? and believe it or not, Hank sings a tender love song called ?Beulah?s Song.?.

Faded Love. unabr. ed. John R. Erickson. 2 cass. (Hank the Cowdog Ser.: No. 5). (J). (gr. 2-5). 1998. 17.00 (21647) Recorded Bks.

Faded Love. unabr. collector's ed. John R. Erickson. 3 CDs. (Running Time: 4 hrs. 30 mins.). (Hank the Cowdog Ser.: No. 5). (J). (gr. 2-5). 2001. audio compact disk 28.00 Books on Tape.
Hank's thoughts turn to romance. He decides that he has been working too hard and needs a vacation. He goes to visit his true love, Miss Beulah the Collie, the pitter in the patter of his heart. On the way, Hank encounters all kinds of challenging situations. Will his intuition and investigative powers be enough?.

Faded Love & Let Sleeping Dogs Lie. unabr. ed. John R. Erickson. Read by John R. Erickson. 4 cass. (Running Time: 6 hrs.). (Hank the Cowdog Ser.: Nos. 5-6). (J). 2002. 26.99 (978-0-916941-63-5(9)); audio compact disk 31.99 (978-0-916941-83-3(3)) Maverick Bks.
Duped by Drover, mocked by Pete the Barncat, and busted yet again by Sally May, the head of ranch security decides it's time for a break from the grueling daily grind. Heading into the wild outback, Hank goes in search if his true love, the charming Miss Beulah. Finding her was easy, but luring her away from Plato, the annoying bird dog, is not.

Fadeout: A Dave Brandstetter Mystery. unabr. ed. Joseph Hansen. Read by Jim Zeiger. 4 cass. (Running Time: 5 hrs. 15 min.). (Dave Brandstetter Mystery Ser.: No. 1). 1995. 24.95 (978-1-888348-01-9(1), HCB201) Hall Closet.
Dave attempts to discover the missing body of small town personality Fox Olson, thought to have died in a car crash on a stormy night. Instead, he finds much more in the small town & eventually murder.

***Fading Echoes.** unabr. ed. Erin Hunter. Read by Kathleen Mcinerney. (ENG.). 2010. (978-0-06-193826-9(2)); (978-0-06-198811-0(1)) HarperCollins Pubs.

Fado: Portugal. Véronique Mortaigne & Jacques Péron. Tr. by Maria Oliver Marcuello. (SPA., 2003. bk. 49.80 (978-84-494-2410-6(0), 1150) Oceano Grupo ESP.

Fado Portugues: Songs from the Soul of Portugal. Donald Cohen. 2004. audio compact disk 36.95 (978-0-7119-8229-1(5)) Pub: Music Sales. Dist(s): H Leonard

Faefever. Karen Marie Moning. Read by Joyce Bean. (Fever Ser.: No. 3). 2009. 64.99 (978-1-60775-867-9(9)) Find a World.

Faefever. unabr. ed. Karen Marie Moning. Read by Joyce Bean. 1 MP3-CD. (Running Time: 10 hrs.). (Fever Ser.: No. 3). 2008. 39.25 (978-1-4233-4203-8(8), 9781423342038, Brinc Audio MP3 Lib); 39.25 (978-1-4233-4205-2(4), 9781423342052, BADLE); 24.95 (978-1-4233-4204-5(6), 9781423342045, BAD); 24.95 (978-1-4233-4202-1(X), 9781423342021, Brilliance MP3); audio compact disk 92.25 (978-1-4233-4201-4(1), 9781423342014, BriAudCD Unabrid); audio compact disk 34.95 (978-1-4233-4200-7(3), 9781423342007, Bril Audio CD Unabri) Brilliance Audio.

Faerie Lord. unabr. ed. Herbie Brennan. Narrated by James Daniel Wilson. 11 cass. (Running Time: 12 hrs. 15 mins.). (Faerie Wars Ser.: Bk. 4). (YA). (gr. 6-10). 2008. 88.75 (978-1-4361-5418-5(9)); audio compact disk 108.75 (978-1-4361-5423-9(5)) Recorded Bks.

Faerie Queene. Edmund Spenser. Read by John Moffatt. (Running Time: 4 hrs.). 2002. 24.95 (978-1-60083-733-3(6)) Iofy Corp.

Faerie Wars. unabr. ed. Herbie Brennan. 8 cass. (Running Time: 11 hrs. 15 min.). (YA). (gr. 5-8). 2004. 73.00 (978-1-4025-7361-3(8)) Recorded Bks.
The Faerie Wars is an introduction to the complex world of the Faerie Realm, which is inhabited by the Faeries of the Night and the Faeries of the

Light. The two main characters are teenaged boys, Henry Atherton, a likable, forthright, British boy whose family is breaking up as a result of his mother's les-bian affair with his father's secretary, and Prince Pyrgus Malvae, heir to the Purple Emperor, a brave, socially conscious Faerie of the Light.

Fahrenheit 451. Ray Bradbury. Read by Christopher Hurt. (Running Time: 18000 sec.). 2005. 34.95 (978-0-7861-4351-1(7)); 45.00 (978-0-7861-7537-6(0)) Blckstn Audio.

Fahrenheit 451. Ray Bradbury. Read by Michael Prichard. 1988. audio compact disk 82.00 (978-0-7366-7493-5(4)) Books on Tape.

Fahrenheit 451. Ray Bradbury. Read by Christopher Hurt. 2008. 44.99 (978-1-60640-883-4(6)) Find a World.

Fahrenheit 451. Ray Bradbury. Narrated by Paul Hecht. 4 cass. (Running Time: 5 hrs. 45 mins.). 35.00 (978-0-7887-3274-4(9)) Recorded Bks.

Fahrenheit 451. unabr. ed. Ray Bradbury. Read by Scott Brick. 4 cass. (Running Time: 6 hrs.). 2004. 28.00 (978-1-4159-1618-6(7)); audio compact disk 32.00 (978-1-4159-1619-3(5)) Books on Tape.
In Bradbury's classic, frightening vision of the future where trivial information is valued and true knowledge perceived as subversive, firemen don't put out fires but start them- to burn books. Guy Montag is a fireman with a wife who's goading him to work harder so they could afford another television set. When Montag befriends their neighbor Clarisse, whose love for books and knowledge is contrasted to the Montags' mindless existence, Clarisse suddenly disappears. As a result, Guy begins to hide her books. When his wife turns him in, Guy is ordered to hand them over. Refusing, he runs away, joining an outlawed group of intellectuals who store the contents of the books in their heads, waiting for the time the society will want to.

Fahrenheit 451. unabr. ed. Ray Bradbury. Read by William Roberts. 4 cass. (Running Time: 6 hrs.). 2000. 34.95 (SAB 013) Pub: Chivers Audio Bks GBR. Dist(s): AudioGO
Resisting a totalitarian state that burns all the books is a group of rebels who memorize works of literature and philosophy. Then one day, Montag, trained by the State to destroy books, throws down his can of kerosene and begins reading.

Fahrenheit 451. unabr. ed. Ray Bradbury. Read by Thierry Blanc. (YA). 2007. 79.99 (978-2-35569-093-8(6)) Find a World.

Fahrenheit 451. unabr. ed. Ray Bradbury. Read by Ray Bradbury. 5 CDs. (Running Time: 6 hrs.). (gr. 9-12). 2001. audio compact disk 29.95 (978-0-694-52627-7(4)) HarperCollins Pubs.

Fahrenheit 451. unabr. ed. Ray Bradbury. Read by Alexander Spencer. 4 cass. (Running Time: 5 hrs. 30 mins.). 1982. 35.00 (978-1-55690-172-0(0), 82021) Recorded Bks.
A darkly imagined future where books are outlawed & free speech unheard.

***Fahrenheit 451.** unabr. ed. Ray Bradbury. Narrated by Stephen Hoye. (Running Time: 5 hrs. 30 mins.). 2010. 13.99 (978-1-4001-8818-5(0)); 19.99 (978-1-4001-6818-7(X)); audio compact disk 59.99 (978-1-4001-4818-9(9)); audio compact disk 24.99 (978-1-4001-1818-2(2)) Pub: Tantor Media. Dist(s): IngramPubServ

***Fahrenheit 451.** unabr. ed. Ray Bradbury. Read by Ray Bradbury. (ENG.). 2005. (978-0-06-085508-6(8), Harper Audio); (978-0-06-085506-2(1), Harper Audio) HarperCollins Pubs.

Fahrenheit 451. unabr. abr. ed. Ray Bradbury. Read by Ray Bradbury. 4 cass. (Running Time: 6 hrs.). 2001. 25.95 (978-0-694-52626-0(6), RH266) HarperCollins Pubs.

Fahrenheit 451. unabr. anniv. ed. Ray Bradbury. 4 cass. (Running Time: 18000 sec.). 2005. 19.95 (978-0-7861-3762-6(2), E3556) Blckstn Audio.
The system was simple. Everyone understood it. Books were for burning, along with the houses in which they were hidden. Guy Montag was a fireman whose job it was to start fires. And he enjoyed his job. He had been a fireman for ten years, and he had never questioned the pleasure of the midnight runs nor the joy of watching pages consumed by flames... never questioned anything until he met a seventeen-year-old girl who told him of a past when people were not afraid. Then Guy met a professor who told him of a future in which people could think. And Guy Montag suddenly realized what he had to do.

Fahrenheit 451. unabr. anniv. ed. Ray Bradbury. Read by Christopher Hurt. 5 CDs. (Running Time: 18000 sec.). 2005. audio compact disk 19.95 (978-0-7861-7627-4(X), ZE3556); audio compact disk 29.95 (978-0-7861-7868-1(X), ZM3556) Blckstn Audio.

Fahrenheit 451. unabr. collector's ed. Ray Bradbury. Read by Michael Prichard. 5 cass. (Running Time: 5 hrs.). (J). 1988. 40.00 (978-0-7366-1397-2(8), 2286) Books on Tape.
The system was simple. Everyone understood it. Books were for burning...along with the houses in which they were hidden. Guy Montag enjoyed his job. He had been a fireman for 10 years & he had never questioned the pleasure of the midnight runs nor the joy of watching pages consumed by flames, never questioned anything until he met a 17-year-old girl who told him of a past when people were not afraid. Then he met a professor who told him of a future in which people could think & Guy Montag suddenly realized what he had to do.

Failed State: America. Noam Chomsky. 2006. 17.95 (978-1-59397-940-9(1)) Pub: Macmill Audio. Dist(s): Macmillan

Failed States: The Abuse of Power & the Assault on Democracy. unabr. ed. Noam Chomsky. Read by Alan Sklar. 6 CDs. (Running Time: 14 hrs. 0 mins. 0 sec.). (ENG.). 2006. audio compact disk 39.95 (978-1-59397-939-3(8)) Pub: Macmill Audio. Dist(s): Macmillan

Failing America's Faithful: How Today's Churches Are Mixing God with Politics & Losing Their Way. unabr. ed. Kathleen Kennedy Townsend. Read by Renée Raudman. (Running Time: 5 hrs. 30 mins. 0 sec.). (ENG.). 2007. audio compact disk 24.99 (978-1-4001-0410-9(6)); audio compact disk 49.99 (978-1-4001-3410-6(2)); audio compact disk 19.99 (978-1-4001-5410-4(3)) Pub: Tantor Media. Dist(s): IngramPubServ

Failing Forward: Turning Mistakes into Stepping Stones for Success. abr. ed. John C. Maxwell. (Running Time: 10200 sec.). 2007. audio compact disk 24.99 (978-0-7852-8932-6(1)) Nelson.

Failte. Contrib. by Peadar O. Flatharta. (ENG.). 1998. 13.95 (978-0-8023-7134-8(5)); audio compact disk 21.95 (978-0-8023-8134-7(0)) Pub: Clo Iar-Chonnachta IRL. Dist(s): Dufour

Failure. Scripts. Leslie Gries. Narrated by Leslie Gries. Omaha Choirs of St. Paul U.M.C. 4 CDs. (Running Time: 4 hrs. 40 min.). 2006. audio compact disk 18.50 (978-0-9787656-0-6(5)) Jewels Pr.
"Dona Nobis Pacem Now!" presents everything one needs to know about mounting both a large-scale production of classical music and a recording in one novella. Presented here in a fictionalized version is the story of the author's attempt to produce her very real composition "Dona nobis pacem." What ensues are moments of hilarity and heartbreak amid a spoof of all things Nebraskan.

Failure of Recollection, Best Evidence Rule, Perception. 1 cass. (Running Time: 1 hr.). (Basic Concepts in the Law of Evidence Ser.). 1975. 15.00 (EYX03) Natl Inst Trial Ad.

Failure, Restoration, Forgiveness, Set. George Verwer. Read by George Verwer. 2 cass. 1995. 12.95 (978-1-886463-10-3(7)) Oasis Audio.
Takes you on a journey of self-discovery, honest confession & submission to God & dedicated to weak people everywhere.

Failure to Appear. unabr. ed. J. A. Jance. Read by Gene Eugene. 8 cass. (Running Time: 10 hrs. 12 mins.). (J. P. Beaumont Mystery Ser.). 1995. 49.95 (978-1-55686-562-6(7), 892559) Books in Motion.
When Seattle-based detective J.P. Beaumont's missing teenage daughter, Kelly, turns up at the Shakespeare Festival in Ashland, Oregon, she is pregnant, about to be married & living in a communal boarding house. Her talented actress friend, Tania, seems to be the center of intrigue as accidents, mystery, murders, child pornography, theatre & middle-aged romance combine for an intriguing listening experience.

Failure to Appear. unabr. collector's ed. J. A. Jance. Read by Connor O'Brien. 7 cass. (Running Time: 10 hrs. 30 min.). (J. P. Beaumont Mystery Ser.). 1998. 56.00 (978-0-7366-4042-8(8), 4541) Books on Tape.
J.P. Beaumont's teenaged daughter Kelly has run off. Her tracks lead the sober-but-struggling sleuth to the Oregon Shakespeare festival. That's where he finds her all right. But in addition to one very headstrong offspring, something else iswaiting backstage for Beau, a case of murder.

Failure to Project Psychological Visibility. unabr. ed. Nathaniel Branden. 1 cass. (Running Time: 1 hr. 16 min.). 12.95 (610) J Norton Pubs.
Why romance so often vanishes; the importance of thought & effort to sustain a relationship; the importance of leisure.

Faint Cold Fear. abr. ed. Robert Daley. Read by Michael McConnohie. 2 cass. (Running Time: 3 hrs.). 1991. 7.95 Set. (978-1-57815-038-0(8), 1010) Media Bks NJ.

***Faint Cold Fear.** abr. ed. Karin Slaughter. Read by Dana Ivey. (ENG.). 2004. (978-0-06-078295-5(1), Harper Audio) HarperCollins Pubs.

***Faint Cold Fear.** abr. ed. Karin Slaughter. Read by Dana Ivey. (ENG.). 2004. (978-0-06-081443-4(8), Harper Audio) HarperCollins Pubs.

Faint Heart Never Kissed a Pig. unabr. ed. Ann Drysdale. Read by Anne Dover. 5 cass. (Running Time: 7 hrs.). (Isis Audio Reminiscence Ser.). (J). 2001. 49.95 (978-0-7531-0852-9(6), 000513) Pub: ISIS Lrg Prnt GBR. Dist(s): Ulverscroft US
The author, her three children, with Snuff the sheep, Emily the goat, Rosalie the pig, Magnus the pony & many other animals live in a remote farmhouse on the North York Moors. This book is a moving & hilarious account of how Ann established the farm, without previous experience & of how the animals arrived, many of them waifs & strays from across the Dales.

Fainting Goats Tale: Unique Narrative of Tennessee's Nervous Native,the Fainting Goat. Short Stories. Wanda Wood. 1. (Running Time: 49 mins). Dramatization. (YA). 2004. audio compact disk 15.00i (978-1-59971-143-0(5)) AardGP.
Unique narrative of Tennessees nervous native, the fainting goat. Myotonic goats hold a place in history as well as in the hearts of mankind. Follow their journey from the heart of Tennessee, to the Tex/Mex border, to Canada and back again. This cd cronicles the travels and disappearance of Jon Tinsley who is well known for his contribution to the myotonic.

Fair Barbarian. unabr. ed. Frances Hodgson Burnett. Read by Laurie Klein. 4 cass. (Running Time: 4 hrs. 42 min.). Dramatization. 1992. 26.95 (978-1-55686-430-8(2), 430) Books in Motion.
When free spirited Octavea Bassett of Bloody Gulch, Nevada visits her maiden Aunt Belinda in England, the sleepy little town of Slowbridge is shaken to its foundations. It is not considered good taste to know Americans - especially this one.

Fair Country. Jon Robin Baitz. Perf. by Kurt Deutsch et al. 1 cass. (Running Time: 1 hr. 35 min.). 1996. 25.95 (978-1-58081-125-5(6), TPT114) Pub: L A Theatre. Dist(s): NetLibrary CO
A well-meaning American diplomat in South Africa tries to pacify his unstable wife & anti-apartheid son by being reassigned to The Hague. But peace is hard to come by & at an elegant New Year's Eve party, a harrowing betrayal is revealed.

Fair Day's Work. unabr. collector's ed. Nicholas Monsarrat. Read by Richard Green. 7 cass. (Running Time: 7 hrs.). 1979. 42.00 (978-0-7366-0177-1(5), 1179) Books on Tape.
Two novels by the author of "The Cruel Sea", both serious but widely separate in theme. "A Fair Day's Work" pivots on a wildcat strike that cripples the liner Good Hope. At berth in Liverpool, the festive passengers and determined strikers offer memorable contrasts. "The Time Before This" tackles a grimmer subject: extermination by thermonuclear war. Focus is on Grant Shepherd, a visionary loner, who discovers evidence in Canada's vast wilderness that a sophisticated civilization dwelt there before us. He attributes its demise to nuclear holocaust, "because it discovered more than it knew how to use." Will these words be our own epitaph?.

Fair Exchange. Tom Blackburn. (Running Time: 0 hr. 30 mins.). 2000. 10.95 (978-1-60083-535-3(X)) Iofy Corp.

***Fair Exchange.** Tom W. Blackburn. 2009. (978-1-60136-435-7(0)) Audio Holding.

Fair Game. Created by Trina Porte. 2006. audio compact disk 9.00 (978-0-9705352-2-1(8)) Chickaree Pr.

Fair Game: My Life As a Spy, My Betrayal by the White House. abr. ed. Valerie Plame Wilson. 2007. 17.95 (978-0-7435-7123-4(1)) Pub: S&S Audio. Dist(s): S and S

***Fair Game: My Life as a Spy, My Betrayal by the White House.** abr. movie tie-in ed. Valerie Plame Wilson. Read by Valerie Plame Wilson. (Running Time: 7 hrs. 0 mins. 0 sec.). 2010. audio compact disk 14.99 (978-1-4423-4002-2(9)) Pub: S&S Audio. Dist(s): S and S Inc

Fair Girls & Grey Horses. unabr. ed. Diana Pullein-Thompson et al. Read by Margaret Sircom. 8 cass. (Running Time: 10 hrs. 35 min.). 1999. 83.95 (978-1-85903-271-8(0)) Pub: Magna Story GBR. Dist(s): Ulverscroft US
Are your twins normal? Mrs. Pullein-Thompson was asked, "Good God, I hope not" she retorted. The twins were Diana & Christine who, with their elder sister, Josephine, have written over 150 books, selling throughout the world. Now, over 50 years after the publication of their first book, the three sisters have decided to write about their extraordinary childhood with loveable but often unreliable animals & unforgettable humans. Every one who grew up with the Pullein-Thompson sisters' stories will find this account of their lives absorbing.

Fair Housing Litigation. (Running Time: 30 min.). 1988. 15.00 cass. only. PA Bar Inst.

***Fair Maiden.** Joyce Carol Oates. Narrated by Angela Goethals. (Running Time: 5 hrs. 37 mins. 0 sec.). (ENG.). 2011. audio compact disk 29.95 (978-1-60998-166-2(9)) Pub: AudioGO. Dist(s): Perseus Dist

***Fair Maiden.** unabr. ed. Joyce Carol Oates. Narrated by Angela Goethals. 1 Playaway. (Running Time: 5 hrs. 37 mins.). 2010. 64.95 (978-0-7927-6891-3(4), Chivers Sound Lib); 39.95 (978-0-7927-6890-6(6), Chivers Sound Lib); audio compact disk 59.95 (978-0-7927-6407-6(2), Chivers Sound Lib) AudioGO.

Fair Skies over Fizzy Mountain: The Truthsayer Trilogy - Book One, Bk. 1. Anna Winston Falawful. Read by Davina Hunt Porter. (ENG.). (J). 2009. audio compact disk 29.95 (978-0-9825440-0-6(6)) CityKidCreat.

Fair Stood the Wind for France. unabr. ed. H. E. Bates. Read by Nigel Havers. 8 cass. (Running Time: 8 hrs.). 1993. 69.95 (978-0-7451-5779-5(3), CAB 211) AudioGO.

Fair Stood the Wind for France. unabr. ed. H. E. Bates. Read by Geoffrey Howard. 6 cass. (Running Time: 8 hrs. 30 mins.). 1999. 44.95 (978-0-7861-1494-8(0), 2345) Blckstn Audio.
When a bomber is forced to land in occupied France during World War II, the crew are taken in by a family of French peasants. As Francoise cares for the wounded pilot, Franklin, her courage and her faith save him not only from the enemy but from himself.

Fair Stood the Wind for France. unabr. ed. H. E. Bates. Read by Geoffrey Howard. 8 CDs. (Running Time: 8 hrs. 30 mins.). 2000. audio compact disk 64.00 (978-0-7861-9935-8(0), 2345) Blckstn Audio.

Fair Stood the Wind for France. unabr. ed. H. E. Bates. Read by Geoffrey Howard. 1 CD. (Running Time: 9 hrs.). 2001. audio compact disk 19.95 (zm2345) Blckstn Audio.
End of mission. The great bomber had been giving the crew trouble since leaving Italy. Finally over occupied France, it settles like a weary, wounded edge on what seemed to Franklin a hard, smooth field.

Fair Stood the Wind for France. unabr. ed. H. E. Bates. Read by Geoffrey Howard. 6 cass. (Running Time: 8 hrs. 30 mins.). 2005. 29.95 (978-0-7861-3468-7(2), E2345); audio compact disk 29.95 (978-0-7861-8045-5(5), Z2345); audio compact disk 24.95 (978-0-7861-9656-2(4), 2345) Blckstn Audio.

***Fair Tax Book: Saying Goodbye to the Income Tax & The.** abr. ed. Neal Boortz. (ENG.). 2005. (978-0-06-089883-0(6), Harper Audio); (978-0-06-089884-7(4), Harper Audio) HarperCollins Pubs.

Fair Weather. Richard Peck. Read by Estelle Parsons. 3 vols. (Running Time: 3 hrs. 30 mins.). (J). (gr. 5-9). 2004. pap. bk. 36.00 (978-0-8072-2038-2(8), Listening Lib) Random Audio Pubg.

Fair Weather. abr. ed. Richard Peck. Read by Estelle Parsons. 3 cass. (Running Time: 3 hrs. 30 mins.). (J). (gr. 5-9). 2004. 30.00 (978-0-8072-0952-3(X), Listening Lib) Random Audio Pubg.
Amidst the wonders of the 1893 Chicago's World Fair, Rosie discovers herself and the world.

Fairest. unabr. ed. Gail Carson Levine. Read by Sarah Naughton. (YA). 2007. 54.99 (978-1-60252-896-3(9)) Find a World.

Fairfield Triangle. abr. ed. Engle & Barnes. Read by Full Cast Production Staff. Directed By Sandra Bovee. (Running Time: 7200 sec.). (Strange Matter Ser.). (YA). (gr. 8-12). 2007. audio compact disk 25.25 (978-1-4233-0879-9(4), 9781423308799, BACDLib Ed) Brilliance Audio.

Fairfield Triangle. abr. ed. Engle & Julian Barnes. Read by Multivoice Production Staff. (Running Time: 2 hrs.). (Strange Matter Ser.). 2007. 25.25 (978-1-4233-0881-2(6), 9781423308812, BADLE); 9.95 (978-1-4233-0880-5(8), 9781423308805, BAD) Brilliance Audio.

Fairfield Triangle. abr. ed. Engle et al. Directed By Sandra Bovee. (Running Time: 7200 sec.). (Strange Matter Ser.). (YA). (gr. 8-12). 2007. audio compact disk 9.95 (978-1-4233-0878-2(6), 9781423308782, BACD) Brilliance Audio.

Fairies. Read by Julie Harris. 1 read-along cass. (Running Time: 7 min.). Dramatization. bk. 15.00 (SAC 6500H) Spoken Arts.

Fairies. unabr. ed. Narrated by Julie Harris. 1 cass. (Running Time: 15 min.). (World of Words Ser.). (J). (gr. k-3). 2001. pap. bk. 10.00 (978-0-8045-6608-7(9), 6500-H); pap. bk. 22.00 (978-0-8045-6708-4(5), 6500-H/10) Spoken Arts.

Fairies & the Quest for Never Land. unabr. ed. Gail Carson Levine. (ENG.). (J). 2010. audio compact disk 25.00 (978-0-307-71155-7(2), Listening Lib) Pub: Random Audio Pubg. Dist(s): Random

Fairies Collection No. 2: Vidia & the Fairy Crown & Lily's Pesky Plant. unabr. ed. Read by Alissa Hunnicutt & Ashley Albert. 2 CDs. (Running Time: 2 hrs. 27 mins.). (J). 2006. audio compact disk 24.00 (978-0-307-28587-4(1), Listening Lib); 23.00 (978-0-307-28586-7(3), Listening Lib) Pub: Random Audio Pubg. Dist(s): Random
Vidia and the Fairy Crown, by Laura Driscoll and read by Alissa Hunnicutt - When Queen Clarion's fairy crown goes missing, everyone in Pixie Hollow thinks sour-tempered Vidia is to blame. Now it's up to Vidia to clear her name. But time is running out. Vidia has only two days to solve the mystery of the missing fairy crown. If she doesn't, she will be banished from the fairy kingdom - forever. Lily's Pesky Plant by Kirsten Larsen, read by Ashley Albert - Lily has a talent for making things grow. So when she finds a mysterious seed during a walk in the forest, she plants it right away. The ugly seedling that comes up is a surprise, but Lily treasures all plants and has an extra-special feeling about this one. Bust all the other fairies don't like the mysterious plant one bit! Will Lily have to pull up her poor, ugly, stinky, pesky plant?.

Fairies Collection No. 4: A Masterpiece for Bess, Prilla & the Butterfly Lie. unabr. ed. Kitty Richards & Lara Rice Bergen. Read by Ashley Albert & Quincy Tyler Bernstine. (Running Time: 8400 sec.). (Disney Fairies Ser.). (ENG.). (J). (gr. 1-3). 2007. audio compact disk 19.95 (978-0-7393-5057-7(9), Listening Lib) Pub: Random Audio Pubg. Dist(s): Random

Fairies 101: An Introduction to Connecting, Working, & Healing with the Fairies & Other Elementals. abr. ed. Doreen Virtue. Read by Doreen Virtue. 1 CD. 2007. audio compact disk 10.95 (978-1-4019-0762-4(8)) Hay House.

Fairtax - the Truth: Answering the Critics. unabr. ed. Neal Boortz et al. Read by Neal Boortz. Told to Rob Woodall. (Running Time: 21600 sec.). 2008. audio compact disk 19.95 (978-0-06-166247-8(X), Harper Audio) HarperCollins Pubs.

Fairy Collection. Shirley Barber. (J). 2005. bk. (978-1-86503-572-7(6)) Five MileAUS AUS.

Fairy Dreams. Gwyneth Rees. Read by Sophie Ward. (Running Time: 9720 sec.). (J). 2001. audio compact disk 29.95 (978-0-7540-6784-9(X)) AudioGo GBR.

Fairy Dust. Gwyneth Rees. Read by Sophie Ward. 3 CDs. (Running Time: 9180 sec.). (J). 2005. DVD, audio compact disk, audio compact disk 29.95 (978-0-7540-6671-2(1), Chivers Child Audio) AudioGO.

Fairy Dust & the Quest for the Egg. collector's unabr. ed. Gail Carson Levine. Read by Hannah Gordon. 3 cass. (Running Time: 4 hrs. 30 mins.). (Disney Fairies Ser.). (J). (gr. 4-7). 2005. 30.00 (978-0-307-28293-4(7), Listening Lib); audio compact disk 25.50 (978-0-307-28294-1(5), Listening Lib) Pub: Random Audio Pubg. Dist(s): NetLibrary CO

Fairy Dust & the Quest for the Egg. unabr. ed. Gail Carson Levine. Read by Hannah Gordon. 6 CDs. (Running Time: 13200 sec.). (Disney Fairies Ser.). (ENG.). (J). (gr. 3). 2005. audio compact disk 25.00 (978-0-307-28167-8(1), Listening Lib) Pub: Random Audio Pubg. Dist(s): Random
Prilla, the newest fairy to arrive in Neverland, is so odd that Neverland itself isn't certain whether to let her into Fairy Haven. Prilla shakes hands when

she meets other fairies, and she says "Pleased to meet you," instead of "Fly with you." What's more, she calls Tinker Bell Miss Bell. Altogether, she acts more like a Clumsy than a self-respecting Never fairy should. To make matters worse, Prilla doesn't know what her talent is - or if she has a talent at all. Mother Dove, the wisest creature in Neverland, thinks Prilla has a talent, but even she isn't certain. A diabolical hurricane, a selfish fairy, Captain Hook, snobby mermaids, a fierce golden hawk, and the evil dragon Kyto combine in a tantalizing elixir that tests Mother Dove's wisdom, Tink's courage, and Prilla's mettle. Even Clumsy children on the mainland - even listeners, wherever they may be - play a crucial role in deciding Neverland's fate.

Fairy Frog see Black Fairy Tales

Fairy Garden. (Running Time: 60 mins.). 2002. audio compact disk 15.99 (978-1-904972-38-9(1)) Global Jrny GBR GBR.

Fairy Haven & the Quest for the Wand. unabr. ed. Gail Carson Levine. Narrated by Rosalyn Landor. 3 CDs. (Running Time: 3 hrs. 33 mins.). (J). (gr. 2-4). 2007. audio compact disk 30.00 (978-0-7393-6107-8(4)) Pub: Random Audio Pubg. Dist(s): Random

Fairy Haven & the Quest for the Wand. unabr. ed. Gail Carson Levine. Read by Rosalyn Landor. (Running Time: 12780 sec.). (ENG.). (J). (gr. 2-1). 2007. audio compact disk 27.00 (978-0-7393-5652-4(6), Listening Lib) Pub: Random Audio Pubg. Dist(s): Random

Fairy Mountain. Read by Jake Warner. (J). 2007. audio compact disk 12.95 (978-1-933781-12-9(2)) TallTales Aud.

Fairy Nightsongs. Perf. by Gary Stadler & Singh Kaur. 1 cass., 1 CD. 7.98 (SQR 103); audio compact disk 11.98 CD Jewel box. (SQR 103) NewSound.

***Fairy Reader.** unabr. ed. Brothers Grimm. Compiled by James Baldwin. Narrated by Cassandra Campbell. (ENG.). 2010. 10.98 (978-1-59644-965-7(9), MissionAud); audio compact disk 12.98 (978-1-59644-964-0(0), MissionAud) christianaud.

Fairy Rebel. unabr. ed. Lynne Reid Banks. Read by Lynne Reid Banks. 2 cass. (Running Time: 2 hrs. 30 mins.). (J). (gr. 4-6). 1995. 18.00 (978-0-8072-7593-1(X), YA888CX, Listening Lib) Random Audio Pubg.
Jan's dream of having a little baby girl suddenly came true after meeting an extraordinary fairy named Tiki. But Tiki had defied & angered the Fairy Queen by using her power to help a human. Now her human friends are against the chilling powers of a terrifying leader.

Fairy Rebel. unabr. ed. Read by Lynne Reid Banks. Ed. by Lynne Reid Banks. 2 cass. (Running Time: 2 hrs. 30 mins.). (J). (gr. 4-6). 1995. pap. bk. 23.00 (978-0-8072-7594-8(8), YA888SP, Listening Lib) Random Audio Pubg.

Fairy Rebel, Set. unabr. ed. Lynne Reid Banks. Read by Lynne Reid Banks. 2 cass. (YA). 1999. 16.98 (FS9-31420) Highsmith.

Fairy Stories, Vol. 2. Shirley Barber. 1 Cd. (J). audio compact disk (978-1-86503-779-0(6)) Five MileAUS AUS.

Fairy Tale. Read by Lesley Ann Fogle. Prod. by Lesley Ann Fogle. Tr. by Catherine Hutter. Johann Wolfgang von Goethe. 1 cd. (Running Time: 57 min).Tr. of Marchen. (ENG., 2007. (978-0-9796025-0-4(5)) L A Fogle.

Fairy Tale Characters in Songs for Children of All Ages see Personagges de Contes en Chanson pour les Petits et les Grandes

Fairy-Tale Detectives. unabr. ed. Michael Buckley. Read by L. J. Ganser. 6 CDs. (Running Time: 6 hrs. 15 mins.). (Sisters Grimm Ser.: Bk. 1). 2006. audio compact disk 64.75 (978-1-4193-8746-3(4), C3677); 49.75 (978-1-4193-6194-4(5), 98195) Recorded Bks.
The recently orphaned Sisters Grimm find out from their Granny, who they thought was dead, that they're descendents of the legendary Brothers Grimm. Now they must take over the family responsibility of being fairy tale detectives in a town where fairy tales are real. Their first case: a giant is destroying the town and it may have something to do with a boy named Jack and a certain famous beanstalk.

Fairy Tale Mix Ups. (J). 2005. audio compact disk (978-1-933796-00-0(6)) PC Treasures.

Fairy Tale Rap: Jack & the Beanstalk & Other Stories. unabr. ed. Barbara Leeds. Read by Fairy Tale Rappers. 1 cass. (Running Time: 20 min.). (J). (gr. k-8). 1990. 8.95 (978-0-9624932-1-8(X)) Miramonte Pr.
Rhythmic dramatizations of fairy tales: Go, Jack, Go (Jack & the Beanstalk); The Real Princess (The Princess & the Pea); Cider from the Cellar (The Three Sillies); The King's New Clothes (The Emperor's New Clothes).

Fairy Tale Rap, No. 2: The Fisherman & His Wife & Other Stories. unabr. ed. Barbara Leeds. Read by Fairy Tale Rappers. 1 cass. (Running Time: 21 min.). (J). (gr. k-6). 1992. 8.95 (978-0-9624932-5-6(2)) Miramonte Pr.
Rhythmic dramatizations of fairy tales: The Fisherman & His Wife, A Rabbit with an Attitude (The Hare & the Tortoise), The Three Little Pigs, The Little Red Hen, Chicken-Licken, Belling the Cat, The Boy Who Cried Wolf.

Fairy Tale Weddings. unabr. ed. Debbie Macomber. Read by Teri Clark Linden. (Running Time: 10 hrs.). 2009. 39.97 (978-1-4418-0769-4(1), 9781441807694, Brlnc Audio MP3 Lib); 24.99 (978-1-4418-0768-7(3), 9781441807687, Brilliance MP3); 39.97 (978-1-4418-0771-7(3), 9781441807717, BADLE); 24.99 (978-1-4418-0770-0(5), 9781441807700, BAD); audio compact disk 29.99 (978-1-4418-0766-3(7), 9781441807663, Bril Audio CD Unabri); audio compact disk 97.97 (978-1-4418-0767-0(5), 9781441807670, BriAudCD Unabrid) Brilliance Audio.

Fairy Tales. Carolyn Graham. (Jazz Chants Ser.). 1988. 39.95 (978-0-19-434299-5(9)) OUP.

Fairy Tales. Carolyn Graham. (Jazz Chants Ser.). 2003. audio compact disk 39.95 (978-0-19-438606-7(6)) OUP.

Fairy Tales. Ed. by Publications International Staff. (J). 2007. audio compact disk 3.98 (978-1-4127-3795-1(8)) Pubns Intl Ltd.

Fairy Tales. unabr. ed. Prod. by Listening Library Staff. 9 cass. (Running Time: 13 hrs. 13 mins.). 2005. 60.00 (978-0-307-24589-2(6), Listening Lib) Pub: Random Audio Pubg. Dist(s): Random

Fairy Tales. unabr. ed. Prod. by Listening Library Staff. 11 CDs. (Running Time: 13 hrs. 13 mins.). (YA). (gr. 4 up). 2005. audio compact disk 75.00 (978-0-307-24590-8(X), Listening Lib) Pub: Random Audio Pubg. Dist(s): Random

Fairy Tales, Vol. 1. 4 cass. (Four-to-Go Ser.). (J). (ps-2). 11.98 Set. (978-1-55886-045-2(2)) Smarty Pants.
Children's fairy tales.

Fairy Tales, Vol. 1. 4 cass. (Four-to-Go Ser.). (J). (ps-2). 11.98 Set. (978-1-55886-041-4(X)) Smarty Pants.

Fairy Tales, Vol. 2. 4 cass. (Four-to-Go Ser.). (J). (ps-2). 11.98 Set. (978-1-55886-042-1(8)) Smarty Pants.

Fairy Tales by Oscar Wilde. Oscar Wilde. Narrated by Christopher Hurt. (ENG.). (J). 2009. audio compact disk 16.95 (978-1-60646-104-4(4)) Audio Bk Con.

Fairy Tales by Oscar Wilde, Set. unabr. ed. Oscar Wilde. Read by Flo Gibson. 2 cass. (Running Time: 3 hrs.). (J). (gr. 2-4). 1986. 14.95 (978-1-55685-052-3(2)) Audio Bk Con.
Includes such tales as "The Young King," "The Happy Prince," "The Fisherman & His Soul," "The Selfish Giant" & "The Nightingale & the Rose.".

Fairy Tales for Men & Women. Robert Bly. Read by Robert Bly. Ed. by William Booth & Paul Feroe. (Running Time: 1 hr. 20 min.). 1986. 9.00 Ally Pr.
Bly reads two fairytales for men, "The Man Who Loved a Star" & "Jack in the Beanstalk", & two for women, "The Moon Palace" & "King Threshbeard".

Fairy Tales for Men & Women. Robert Bly. 1 cass. 9.00 (A0602-86) Sound Photosyn.
Bly introduces stories about male & female psychic development by talking about the psychological importance of fairy tales. The stories include: "The Man Who Loved a Star," "Jack & the Beanstalk," "King Thrush-Beard," & "The Moon Palace".

Fairy Tales for Men & Women. unabr. ed. Robert Bly. 2 cass. (Running Time: 2 hrs. 52 min.). 1982. 18.00 (00303) Big Sur Tapes.

Fairy Tales from Estonia. Diane Wolkstein. 1 cass. (Running Time: 52 min.). (J). (gr. k-6). pap. bk. 10.00 (978-1-879846-03-6(9)) Cloudstone NY.
The sweet sound of the Estonian kannel leads the listener through these magical, enchanted fairy tales.

Fairy Tales from France. unabr. ed. William Trowbridge Larned. Read by Dorothy Ann Jackson. (J). 2007. 34.99 (978-1-60252-897-0(7)) Find a World.

Fairy Tales, Individuation in Later Life, & the Return of the Inner Child. Read by Allan B. Chinen. 1 cass. (Running Time: 90 min.). 1990. 10.95 (978-0-7822-0034-8(6), 413) C G Jung IL.

Fairy Tales of Ireland. unabr. ed. Perf. by Cyril Cusack. Ed. by Joseph Jacobs. 1 cass. Incl. Fairy Tales of Ireland: Hudden & Dudden & Donald O'Neary. (J). (CDL5 1368); Fairy Tales of Ireland: The Legend of Knockgrafton. (J). (CDL5 1368); Fairy Tales of Ireland: The Leprechaun & the Field of Boliauns. (J). (CDL5 1368); (J). 1972. 9.95 (978-0-694-50884-6(5), CDL5 1368) HarperCollins Pubs.

Fairy Tales of Ireland: Hudden & Dudden & Donald O'Neary see Fairy Tales of Ireland

Fairy Tales of Ireland: The Legend of Knockgrafton see Fairy Tales of Ireland

Fairy Tales of Ireland: The Leprechaun & the Field of Boliauns see Fairy Tales of Ireland

Fairy Tales, Vol. 2. 4 cass. (Four-to-Go Ser.). (J). (ps-2). 11.98 Set. (978-1-55886-046-9(0)) Smarty Pants.
Children's fairy tales.

Fairy Tales World-Wide by Dancing Beetle. Perf. by Eugene Ely. 1 cass. (Running Time: 81 min.). (J). 1992. 10.00 Erthviibz.
Fairy tales, science & nature sounds come together when Ms. Lacewing & the spunky musical humans read & sing with Dancing Beetle.

Fairy Treasure: A Fairy Who Needs a Friend. Gwyneth Rees. 3 CDs. 2006. audio compact disk 29.95 (978-0-7540-6718-4(1), Chivers Child Audio) AudioGO.

Fairytale Analysis from Self Psychology: The Fisherman & His Wife. Read by Lionel Corbett & Cathy Rives. 2 cass. (Running Time: 2 hrs.). 1989. 16.95 Set. (978-0-7822-0046-1(X), 382-4) C G Jung IL.

Fairytale Classics. unabr. ed. 4 cass. (Running Time: 4 hr.). (Crated Gift Cassette Ser.). (J). 1985. 16.95 (978-1-55569-079-3(3), 5750-01) Great Am Audio.
Dramatized productions of "Alice in Wonderland, "Snow White", Beauty & the Beast", "Rapunzel", "Sleeping Beauty" & "Cinderella".

Fairytale Favorites in Story & Song. Read by Jim Weiss. 1 cass. (J). (gr. 1-6). 1999. 9.95; audio compact disk 14.95 CD. (6624-012) Greathall Prods.

Fairytale Favorites in Story & Song. Short Stories. As told by Jim Weiss. 1 cass. (Running Time: 1 hr.). Dramatization. (Storyteller's Version Ser.). (J). (gr. k up). 1993. 10.95 (978-1-882513-12-3(6), 1124-12) Greathall Prods.
A unique telling of the classics of imagination and wonder, including hilarious versions of "Puss in Boots" (includes song: "The Pussycat Rag"), "Stone Soup" (includes song: "Stone Soup"), the romance of "Rapunzel" and the magic of "The Shoemaker and the Elves".

Fairytale Favorites in Story & Song. Read by Jim Weiss. 1 cass., CD. (Running Time: 1 hr.). (J). (GHP12) NewSound.

Fairytale of the Morley Dog CD. M. I. ke Dudek. (YA). 2007. audio compact disk 1.75 (978-0-9740380-2-5(4)) M Dudek.

Fairytales. 1 cass. (Running Time: 48 min.). (Picture Book Parade Ser.). (J). (ps-4). 1986. 8.95 (978-0-89719-929-2(4), WW735C) Weston Woods.
An anthology including "Beauty & the Beast," "The Selfish Giant," "Red Riding Hood," & "The Ugly Duckling".

Faith. Ariel. (702) Yoga Res Foun.

Faith. Kenneth Copeland. 12 cass. 1982. 60.00 Set incl. study guide. (978-0-938458-64-7(7)) K Copeland Pubns.
Biblical faith.

Faith. Creflo A. Dollar. cass. & video 25.00 (978-1-59089-123-0(6)) Pub: Creflo Dollar. Dist(s): STL Dist NA

Faith. Neville Goddard. 1 cass. (Running Time: 62 min.). 1968. 8.00 (41) J & L Pubns.
Neville taught Imagination Creates Reality. He was a powerfully influential teacher of God as Consciousness.

Faith. Rick Joyner. 6 cass. (Running Time: 9 hrs.). (Growing in Faith Ser.: Vol. 1). 2000. 5.00 (RJ14-001) Morning NC.
With fresh & practical messages centering on faith, this tape series will enable you to better understand essential principles of the Christian walk.

Faith. Connell Lewis. (Running Time: 55 min.). 2003. audio compact disk 15.99 (978-0-9729876-0-8(6)) Pub: Corner Music Grp. Dist(s): STL Dist NA

Faith. Derek Prince. 1 cass. (Running Time: 60 min.). 5.95 (B-4180) Derek Prince.

Faith: Believe in Your Power. Kelly Howell. 2000. audio compact disk 14.95 (978-1-881451-71-6(2)) Brain Sync.

Faith: How It Works. Kenneth Copeland. (ENG.). 2007. audio compact disk 20.00 (978-1-57562-950-6(X)) K Copeland Pubns.

Faith: Our Access to God. Gloria Copeland. Perf. by Gloria Copeland. 1 cass. (Ingredients for Success: Faith, Patience & Love Ser.: Tape 1). 1995. cass. & video 5.00 (978-1-57562-017-6(0)) K Copeland Pubns.
Biblical teaching on success.

Faith: Our Heavenly Substance. Kenneth Copeland. 4 cass. 1992. pap. bk. study guide. (978-0-88114-950-0(0)); 20.00 Set. (978-0-88114-916-6(0)) K Copeland Pubns.
Biblical teaching on faith.

Faith: Recovering the Language of Belief. Richard Rohr. 1 cass. (Running Time: 1 hr.). 2001. 8.95 (A6551) St Anthony Mess Pr.
Offers four guidelines in this time of transition to rebuild the Church from the bottom up.

Faith: Songs for the Spirit. Compiled by Dean Diehl & Ed Kee. 1 CD. 2000. audio compact disk 9.99 (978-0-7601-3181-7(3), SO33210) Pub: Brentwood Music. Dist(s): Provident Mus Dist
Includes: "Creed," "Hand of Providence," "I Will Choose Christ," "Where There Is Faith," "I Believe" & more.

Faith: Stories from the Collection More News from Lake Wobegon. Garrison Keillor. (Running Time: 4380 sec.). (ENG., 2008. audio compact disk 13.95 (978-1-59887-606-2(6), 1598876066) Pub: HighBridge. Dist(s): Workman Pub

Faith: The Internal Belief in Eternal Good. Manly P. Hall. 8.95 (978-0-89314-113-4(5), C880320) Philos Res.
Inspirational & mystical beliefs - includes fiction, myths, & poetry.

Faith: The Prescriptions for Life. Creflo A. Dollar. 6 cass. (Running Time: 9 hrs.). 2000. 30.00 (978-1-931172-34-9(X), TS257, Kidz Faith) Pub: Creflo Dollar. Dist(s): STL Dist NA

Faith: The Servant of the Believer. Kenneth Copeland. 4 cass. 1982. bk. 20.00 Set incl. study guide. (978-0-938458-33-3(7)) K Copeland Pubns.
God's purpose for faith.

Faith: What Christians Believe, Why They Believe it, & Why It Matters. unabr. ed. Charles W. Colson. Told to Harold Fickett III. (Running Time: 6 hrs. 30 mins. 0 sec.). (ENG.). 2008. 18.99 (978-0-310-27609-8(8)) Zondervan.

Faith: What Christians Believe, Why They Believe It, & Why It Matters. unabr. ed. Charles Colson et al. Read by Charles Colson. (Running Time: 6 hrs. 30 mins. 0 sec.). (ENG.). 2008. audio compact disk 24.99 (978-0-310-27608-1(X)) Zondervan.

Faith - Not by Sight. Read by Basilea Schlink. 1 cass. (Running Time: 30 min.). 1985. (0229) Evang Sisterhood Mary.
Easter for disbelieving hearts; the creative working of the Holy Spirit in our lives today.

Faith Adventure. Mark Bradford. 1 CD. (Running Time: 1 hr.). Dramatization. (Target Trax Ser.). 1997. pap. bk. 15.00 (978-1-58302-132-3(9), DTT-07) One Way St.
Collection of six religious musical puppetry performance pieces.

***Faith Alone: A Daily Devotional.** Martin Luther. Ed. by James C. Galvin. (Running Time: 13 hrs. 0 mins. 0 sec.). (ENG.). 2009. 14.99 (978-0-310-30443-2(1)) Zondervan.

Faith Alone: Is It Justifiable? 2004. 23.95 (978-1-888992-46-5(8)); audio compact disk 27.95 (978-1-888992-50-2(6)) Catholic Answers.

Faith Amidst Adversity. Larry Chesley. 1 cass. 7.98 (978-1-55503-384-2(9), 06004407) Covenant Comms.
True story of courage & spiritual triumph.

***Faith & Doubt.** John Ortberg. (Running Time: 4 hrs. 47 mins. 0 sec.). (ENG.). 2008. 16.99 (978-0-310-28982-1(3)) Zondervan.

Faith & Doubt. unabr. ed. John Ortberg. (ENG.). 2008. audio compact disk 27.99 (978-0-310-28981-4(5)) Zondervan.

Faith & Force: The Destroyers of the Modern World. Ayn Rand. Read by Ayn Rand. 2 cass. (Running Time: 1 hr. 55 min.). 24.95 Incl. Questions & Answers cass. (55 min.). (978-1-56114-011-4(2), AR07D) Second Renaissance.
Why is the modern world characterized by such widespread anxiety about impending disaster - combined with an evasive refusal to search for the means of averting it? Because, Ayn Rand answers, today's intellectuals dare not acknowledge the fact that such disaster is the consequence of their moral code of altruism. An extensive question & answer period covers such topics as Ayn Rand's recommended books on capitalism; the meaning of the virtue of productiveness for a businessman whose wealth is already assured; why the use of force is not in a rational individual's interests; breaking with society versus breaking with the culture; the psychology of Dominique in The Fountainhead.

Faith & Freedom. Kenneth Copeland. Perf. by Kenneth Copeland. 1 cass. (Take Hold of Your Victory! Ser.: Tape 2). 1995. cass. & video 5.00 (978-1-57562-001-5(4)) K Copeland Pubns.
Biblical teaching on victory.

Faith & Media. Bernard R. Bonnot. 1 cass. (Running Time: 1 hr. 18 min.). 1995. 8.95 (TAH351) Alba Hse Comns.
In our modern world the impact of the media on our lives cannot be denied. Increasingly our value systems are being shaped by what we read & what we view. The media have become an important part of human development, often overtaking family, school & faith communities in terms of influence on the development of our value systems.

Faith & Miracles. Vincent M. Walsh. 1 cass. Incl. Faith & Miracles: Wisdom & Knowledge. 1986.; 1986. 4.00 Key of David.
Personal stories & examples told to promote a full understanding of the basic powers of the Renewal.

Faith & Miracles: Wisdom & Knowledge see Faith & Miracles

Faith & Patience. Kenneth Copeland. 10 CDs. 2006. audio compact disk 30.00 (978-1-57562-839-4(2)) K Copeland Pubns.

Faith & Patience. Kenneth Copeland. 6 cass. 1983. 30.00 Set incl. study guide. (978-0-938458-54-8(X)) K Copeland Pubns.
How Biblical faith & patience work.

Faith & Poetry. Poems. Robert F. Morneau. 1 cass. (Running Time: 54 min.). 1995. 9.95 (TAH343) Alba Hse Comns.
Rev. Morneau's reflective discussion is peppered with citations from the works of several notable writers - Gerard Manley Hopkins, Robert Frost, George Herbert & Thomas Merton to name but a few. A thoroughly delightful audio-cassette program.

Faith & Politics: How the Moral Values Debate Divides America & How to Move Forward Together. unabr. ed. John Danforth. Read by John Danforth. 8 CDs. (Running Time: 36000 sec.). 2006. audio compact disk 29.95 (978-1-59316-089-0(5)) Listen & Live.

Faith & the Magic of Language. 1 cass. 1993. 32.99 Chalice Pr.

Faith & Treason. unabr. ed. Antonia Fraser. Read by Donada Peters. 10 cass. (Running Time: 15 hrs.). 1997. 80.00 Set. (978-0-7366-3658-2(7), 4332) Books on Tape.
Re-creates the 1605 terrorist conspiracy known as the Gunpowder Plot, a plan to blow up the House of Parliament foiled when the English government arrested Guy Fawkes.

***Faith & Values of Sarah Palin: What She Believes & What It Means for America.** unabr. ed. Stephen Mansfield & David A. Holland. Narrated by Stephen Mansfield. (Running Time: 5 hrs. 47 mins. 32 sec.). (ENG.). 2010. 16.09 (978-1-60814-753-3(3)); audio compact disk 22.99 (978-1-59859-786-8(8)) Oasis Audio.

Faith Builders. 4 Cassette Tape. 2004. (978-1-59548-044-6(7)); audio compact disk (978-1-59548-045-3(5)) A Wommack.

Faith Builders from Psalms 91. Lula Brooks. 1989. Youth Alive Prods.
Bible based audible & subliminal affirmations based on Psalms 91.

Faith Classics. Kenneth E. Hagin. 6 cass. 24.00 (16H) Faith Lib Pubns.

Faith Comes by Hearing. 12 cass. (Running Time: 18 hrs.). 2000. 29.95 (978-1-57449-082-4(6)); 29.95 (978-1-57449-174-6(1)) Am Bible.

Faith, Covenant & Community in Exodus & Deuteronomy. Richard Rohr. 10 cass. (Running Time: 9 hrs. 12 min.). 69.95 Set. (AA2300) Credence Commun.
Rohr explains what the text meant when written & how it applies to American culture today.

Faith Doing Justice. Evelyn Mattern & Ronald T. Krietemeyer. 2 cass. (Running Time: 1 hr. 26 min.). 1996. 18.95 Set. (TAH374) St Pauls Alba.
In this series you are invited to explore your call to be a person of faith doing justice, to exhibit the courage to answer the challenge of the gospel.

Faith Factor. Vic Reasoner. 1 cass. 3.00 (VR1) Evang Outreach.

Faith, Focus & Healing. Swami Amar Jyoti. 1 dolby cass. 1986. 9.95 (D-14) Truth Consciousness.
The healing power within everyone; the way to get well. Healing our whole being.

Faith for Guidance. Elbert Willis. 1 cass. (Divine Guidance Guidelines Ser.). 4.00 Fill the Gap.

Faith for Living. Featuring Bill Winston. 2. 2004. 10.00 (978-1-59544-077-8(1)); audio compact disk 16.00 (978-1-59544-078-5(X)) Pub: B Winston Min. Dist(s): Anchor Distributors

Faith for Living: The Ultimate Way of Life. Creflo A. Dollar. (ENG.). 2005. 15.00 (978-1-59944-079-8(2)) Creflo Dollar.

Faith for Living: The Ultimate Way of Life. Creflo A. Dollar. (ENG.). 2006. audio compact disk 21.00 (978-1-59944-080-4(6)) Creflo Dollar.

Faith for the Final Hour. 4 cass. 14.00 Set. (978-1-884137-86-0(5)) J Van Impe.

Faith for Today: The Strong Pillar for Your Life. Kenneth Copeland et al. Perf. by Gloria Copeland & Creflo A. Dollar. . 1997. cass. & video 70.00 Set. (978-1-57562-219-4(X), 02-1600) K Copeland Pubns.
A journey that will open your eyes to the simplicity of faith & how to put it to work in your life today. Includes: "Faith is Our Servant"; "Faith Talks"; "Faith - Is It A Take-It-Or-Leave-It Deal?," Pts 1 & 2; "How to Live by Faith"; "Prerequisite for Manifestations of the Supernatural"; "We Stand by Faith"; "The Source of True Power," A & B; "We Walk by Faith"; & "Dominating the Laws of Death".

Faith Found New. Speeches. Isaiah Showell, Sr. Featuring La-Trease Showell. Illus. by Clayton Nichols. 1 compact disc. (Running Time: 45 minutes). (YA). 2004. per. 15.00 (978-0-9754489-0-8(0)) Divine Intertwine.
the compact disc contains the reading of each poem by the author, followed by a brief sermonette by Elder Isaiah Showell and Elder La-Trease D. Showell.

Faith Fuse. abr. ed. Reinhard Bonnke. (Running Time: Approx: 60 min.). 2001. audio compact disk 7.00 (978-1-933106-02-1(6)) E-R-Productions.
According to Jesus, moving mountains requires mustard seed size faith. Reinhard Bonnke clarifies the real issues that activate a living, working faith to move mountains in your life and lives of others.

Faith Healing: Help from the other Side. Gary Arnold. (ENG.). 2008. audio compact disk 24.95 (978-1-57867-057-4(8)) Pub: Windhorse Corp. Dist(s): New Leaf Dist

Faith, Hope & Cancer. Carol Westfahl. 2008. audio compact disk 19.95 (978-1-59598-075-5(X), RHP) HenschelHAUS.

Faith, Hope, & Healing: Inspiring Lessons Learned from People Living with Cancer. unabr. ed. Bernie Siegel. Read by Bernie Siegel. (Running Time: 7 hrs. 30 mins.). (ENG.). 2009. 29.98 (978-1-59659-416-6(0), GildAudio) Pub: Gildan Media. Dist(s): HachBkGrp

***Faith, Hope, & Ivy June.** unabr. ed. Phyllis Reynolds Naylor. Read by Karen White. 5 CDs. (Running Time: 6 hrs. 22 mins.). (J). (gr. 5-7). 2009. audio compact disk 50.00 (978-0-7393-8053-6(2), Listening Lib) Pub: Random Audio Pubg. Dist(s): Random

Faith, Hope, & Ivy June. unabr. ed. Phyllis Reynolds Naylor. Read by Karen White. (ENG.). (J). (gr. 4). 2009. audio compact disk 34.00 (978-0-7393-8051-2(6), Listening Lib) Pub: Random Audio Pubg. Dist(s): Random

Faith, Hope, & Love: The Three Keys to Living a Holy Life. 1 cass. (Running Time: 1 hr.). 2003. 13.95 (978-1-932631-20-3(8)); audio compact disk 13.95 (978-1-932631-22-7(4)) Ascensn Pr.

Faith, How It Works. Kenneth Copeland. 4 cass. 1982. bk. 20.00 Set incl. study guide. (978-0-938458-26-5(4)) K Copeland Pubns.
Biblical teaching on faith.

Faith in God & Faithfulness in Medicine. 1 cass. (Care Cassettes Ser.: Vol. 15, No. 6). 1988. 10.80 Assn Prof Chaplains.

Faith in God's Love. Kenneth Copeland. 4 cass. 1983. 20.00 Set incl. study guide. (978-0-938458-62-3(0)) K Copeland Pubns.
Faith in God's love.

Faith in Miracles/Remembering the Basics. Marianne Williamson. Read by Marianne Williamson. 1 cass. (Running Time: 90 mins.). (Lectures on a Course in Miracles). 1999. 10.00 (978-1-56170-189-6(0), M717) Hay House.

Faith in Our True Being. Swami Amar Jyoti. 1 cass. 1987. 9.95 (D-15) Truth Consciousness.
Faith can move mountains. It carries us to the Goal, past all the side issues. Where nonsense ends, faith begins. Many ways to leave our cage. Be what you truly are.

***Faith in Real Life: Creating Community in the Park, Coffee Shop, & Living Room.** unabr. ed. Mike Tatlock. (Running Time: 6 hrs. 30 mins. 16 sec.). (ENG.). 2010. 14.99 (978-0-310-77341-2(5)) Zondervan.

Faith in Search of Understanding see Assorted Prose

***Faith in the Land of Make Believe: What God Can Do... Even in Hollywood.** unabr. ed. Lee Stanley. (ENG.). 2011. 19.99 (978-0-310-32546-8(3)) Zondervan.

Faith in the Light. Swami Amar Jyoti. 1 cass. 1981. 9.95 (D-6) Truth Consciousness.
Faith is the instrument to make darkness flee.

Faith in the Night Seasons: Understanding God's Will. 7 audio CDs. (Running Time: 7 hours). (King's High Way Ser.). 2007. audio compact disk 29.95 (978-0-9760994-2-0(X)); audio compact disk & audio compact disk 19.95 (978-0-9760994-6-8(2)) Kings High Way.

Faith in the Night Seasons: Understanding God's Will. Nancy Missler. 8 cass. (Running Time: 7 hours). 2002. 29.95 (978-0-9752534-6-5(8)) Kings High Way.
What are ?night seasons?? How are they different from other trials? Why would a loving heavenly Father put His children through such a difficult time? Does God ?single out? certain people for night seasons or will we all go through such times? Trials can push us closer to God or farther away from Him. What is the ?key? to staying in fellowship? If we find ourselves in a ?night season,? what are some of the things we should do? ----------------------------------?I am so excited over ?Faith in the Night Seasons;? ecstatic over it is more like it! I have never experienced anything, other than the Bible, that has so changed my life.?B.D., New Mexico.

Faith in the Service: True Stories from Latter-day Saint Servicemen & Women. Chad Hawkins. 2008. audio compact disk 16.95 (978-1-59038-948-5(4)) Deseret Bk.

Faith Instinct: How Religion Evolved & Why It Endures. unabr. ed. Nicholas Wade. Narrated by Alan Sklar. (Running Time: 12 hrs. 30 mins. 0 sec.). (ENG.). 2009. 24.99 (978-1-4001-6349-6(8)); audio compact disk 69.99 (978-1-4001-4349-8(7)); audio compact disk 34.99 (978-1-4001-1349-1(0)) Pub: Tantor Media. Dist(s): IngramPubServ

***Faith Instinct: How Religion Evolved & Why It Endures.** unabr. ed. Nicholas Wade. Narrated by Alan Sklar. (Running Time: 12 hrs. 30 mins.). 2009. 18.99 (978-1-4001-8349-4(9)); 34.99 (978-1-4001-9349-3(4)) Tantor Media.

Faith is Scientific. Swami Amar Jyoti. 1 cass. 1982. 9.95 (D-7) Truth Consciousness.
Faith in our own True Self. How faith cures. The perfect science of resigning unto Him. The problem of 'proof'.

Faith Life. Contrib. by Alvin Slaughter et al. 2005. audio compact disk 13.99 (978-5-558-80726-4(1)) Integrity G.

Faith Like a Rock. Kenneth Copeland. 1 cass. 1988. 5.00 (978-0-88114-807-7(5)) K Copeland Pubns.
Foundational study of faith.

Faith of Barack Obama. unabr. ed. Stephen Mansfield. Narrated by Stephen Mansfield. 4 CDs. (Running Time: 3 hrs. 46 mins. 5 sec.). (ENG.). 2008. audio compact disk 22.99 (978-1-59859-496-6(6), SpringWater) Oasis Audio.

Faith of Condoleezza Rice. Leslie Montgomery. Read by Wayne Shepherd. (Running Time: 6 hrs. 28 mins.). 2007. audio compact disk 26.99 (978-1-58134-916-0(5)) CrosswayIL.

Faith of George W. Bush. unabr. ed. Stephen Mansfield. Read by J. Charles. 4 cass. (Running Time: 5 hrs.). 2004. 24.95 (978-1-59355-920-5(8), 1593559208); 62.25 (978-1-59355-921-2(6), 1593559216); audio compact disk 74.25 (978-1-59355-923-6(2), 1593559232) Brilliance Audio.
The first audiobook to explore the religious ideals that drive the policies and politics of Bush as president and that have privately shaped Bush as a man. His life demonstrates the power of faith to create change, to build a family and political career, and to shape the destiny of a nation with his leadership. This audiobook shows us how George W. Bush interjects his faith and belief in God into every detail of his life. From the President's devotional time alone each morning to his frequent incorporation of Scripture into his speeches, Bush relies upon his faith to direct his actions and goals. From the tragedy of September 11th to the present-day conflict in Iraq, President Bush has learned to use his personal faith to help him live his life - both in office and in private. This audiobook will inspire others to do the same.

Faith of George W. Bush. unabr. ed. Stephen Mansfield. Read by J. Charles. (Running Time: 5 hrs.). 2004. 39.25 (978-1-59335-534-0(3), 1593355343, Brlnc Audio MP3 Lib); 24.95 (978-1-59335-301-8(4), 1593353014, Brilliance MP3) Brilliance Audio.

Faith of George W. Bush. unabr. ed. Stephen Mansfield. Read by J. Charles. (Running Time: 5 hrs.). 2004. 39.25 (978-1-59710-269-8(5), 1597102695, BADLE); 24.95 (978-1-59710-268-1(7), 1597102687, BAD) Brilliance Audio.

Faith of George W. Bush. unabr. ed. Stephen Mansfield. Read by J. Charles. (Running Time: 21600 sec.). 2007. audio compact disk 14.99 (978-1-4233-1564-3(2), 9781423315643, BCD Value Price) Brilliance Audio.

Faith of My Fathers. abr. ed. John S. McCain & Mark Salter. Read by John S. McCain. 4 CDs. (Running Time: 18000 sec.). (ENG.). 2008. audio compact disk 19.99 (978-0-7393-2088-4(2)) Pub: Random Audio Pubg. Dist(s): Random
John McCain is one of the most admired leaders in the United States government, but his deeply felt memoir of family and war is not a political one and ends before his election to Congress. With candor and ennobling power, McCain tells a story that, in the words of Newsweek, "makes the other presidential candidates look like pygmies."   John McCain learned about life and honor from his grandfather and father, both four-star admirals in the U.S. Navy. This is a memoir about their lives, their heroism, and the ways that sons are shaped and enriched by their fathers.   John McCain's grandfather was a gaunt, hawk-faced man known as Slew by his fellow officers and, affectionately, as Popeye by the sailors who served under him. McCain Sr. played the horses, drank bourbon and water, and rolled his own cigarettes with one hand. More significant, he was one of the navy's greatest commanders, and led the strongest aircraft carrier force of the Third Fleet in key battles during World War II.   John McCain's father followed a similar path, equally distinguished by heroic service in the navy, as a submarine commander during World War II. McCain Jr. was a slightly built man, but like his father, he earned the respect and affection of his men. He, too, rose to the rank of four-star admiral, making the McCains the first family in American history to achieve that distinction. McCain Jr.'s final assignment was as commander of all U.S. forces in the Pacific during the Vietnam War.   It was in the Vietnam War that John McCain III faced the most difficult challenge of his life. A naval aviator, he was shot down over Hanoi in 1967 and seriously injured. When Vietnamese military officers realized he was the son of a top commander, they offered McCain early release in an effort to embarrass the United States. Acting from a sense of honor taught him by his father and the U.S. Naval Academy, McCain refused the offer. He was tortured, held in solitary confinement, and imprisoned for five and a half years.   60;   Faith of My Fathers is about what McCain learned from his grandfather and father, and how their example enabled him to survive those hard years. It is a story of three imperfect men who faced adversity and emerged with their honor intact. Ultimately, Faith of My Fathers shows us, with great feeling and appreciation, what fathers give to their sons, and what endures. From the Hardcover edition.

Faith of My Fathers. unabr. ed. Lynn Austin. Read by Suzanne Toren. 10 cass. (Running Time: 12 hrs. 50 mns.). (Chronicles of the Kings: Bk. 4). 2006. 79.75 (978-1-4193-9785-1(0)) Recorded Bks.

Faith of Our Fathers. 1 cass., 1 CD. 9.58 (VLT 15020); audio compact disk 13.58 CD Jewel box. (VLT 15020) NewSound.

Faith of Our Fathers, Vol. 1. 1 cass., 1 CD. 14.95 (FOFR-C); audio compact disk 19.95 CD. (FOFR-D) Ignatius Pr.
Twenty traditional Catholic hymns sung by Ireland's finest musicians & singers. Includes: "Tantum Ergo, "Salve Regina," "Holy God We Praise Thy Name," "Soul of My Savior," "Faith of Our Fathers" & fifteen more.

Faith of Our Fathers, Vol. 2. 1 cass., 1 CD. 14.95 (FOFR2-C); audio compact disk 19.95 CD. (FOFR2-D) Ignatius Pr.
Twenty traditional Catholic hymns sung by Ireland's finest musicians & singers. Includes: "O Salutaris Hostia," "Ave Maria," "Panis Angelicus," "Lady of Knock," "Sweet Sacrament Divine" & fifteen more.

Faith of Our Fathers, Vol. 2. 1 cass., 1 CD. 9.58 (VLT 15022); audio compact disk 13.58 CD Jewel box. (VLT 15022) NewSound.

Faith of Our Fathers: A House Divided. N. C. Allen. 8 cass. 2004. 29.95 (978-1-57734-898-6(2)); audio compact disk 29.95 (978-1-57734-899-3(0)) Covenant Comms.

Faith of Our Fathers: To Make Men Free, Vol. 2. N. C. Allen. 8 cass. 2004. 29.95 (978-1-59156-122-4(1)) Covenant Comms.

Faith of Our Fathers Vol. 2: Through the Perilous Fight. N. C. Allen. 11 CDs. 2004. audio compact disk 29.95 (978-1-59156-309-9(7)) Covenant Comms.

Faith of Our Fathers Vol. 2: To Make Men Free. N. C. Allen. 9 CDs. 2004. audio compact disk 29.95 (978-1-59156-123-1(X)) Covenant Comms.

Faith of Our Fathers Vol. 3: Through the Perilous Fight. N. C. Allen. 7 cass. 2004. 29.95 (978-1-59156-336-5(4)) Covenant Comms.

Faith of the American Soldier. unabr. ed. Stephen Mansfield. Read by Phil Gigante. (Running Time: 4 hrs.). 2005. 39.25 (978-1-59600-392-7(8), 9781596003927, BADLE); 24.95 (978-1-59600-391-0(X), 9781596003910, BAD); 39.25 (978-1-59600-390-3(1), 9781596003903, Brlnc Audio MP3 Lib); 24.95 (978-1-59600-389-7(8), 9781596003897, Brilliance MP3); 49.25 (978-1-59600-386-6(3), 9781596003866, BriAudUnabridg); 19.95 (978-1-59600-385-9(5), 9781596003859, BAU); audio compact disk 69.25 (978-1-59600-388-0(X), 9781596003880, BriAudCD Unabrid) Brilliance Audio.
Please enter a Synopsis.

Faith of the American Soldier. unabr. ed. Stephen Mansfield. Read by Phil Gigante. Contrib. by Phil Gigante. 4 CDs. (Running Time: 4 hrs.). 2005. audio compact disk 21.95 (978-1-59600-387-3(1), 9781596003873, Bril Audio CD Unabri) Brilliance Audio.

Faith of the Fallen. unabr. ed. Terry Goodkind. Read by John Kenneth. 20 cass. (Running Time: 27 hrs.). (Sword of Truth Ser.: Bk. 6). 2000. 39.95 (978-1-58788-010-0(5), 1587880105, BAU); 169.25 (978-1-58788-011-7(3), 1587880113, Unabridge Lib Edns) Brilliance Audio.
Terry Goodkind, author of the enormously popular Sword of Truth novels, has forged perhaps his best yet, pitting Richard Rahl and Kahlan Amnell against threats to the freedom of the world. They both must struggle at opposite ends of the world against the relentless, monolithic forces of the Imperial Order. A Sister of the Dark captures Richard and takes him deep into the Old World, to the very heart of the Order, while his beloved Kahlan remains behind. Free because of Richard's sacrifice for her, but unwilling to abandon the cause of the Midlands, Kahlan violates not only prophecy but her last pledge to Richard, and raises an army against the advancing horde of the Imperial Order. Separated and fighting for their lives, Richard and Kahlan will be pushed to the limits of their endurance, and tested in their love for one another. Once again, the master storyteller weaves a riveting spell that will captivate even more fans for this incredible series.

Faith of the Fallen. unabr. ed. Terry Goodkind. Read by John Kenneth. (Running Time: 27 hrs.). (Sword of Truth Ser.: Bk. 6). 2004. 29.95 (978-1-59335-304-9(9), 1593353049, Brilliance MP3); audio compact disk 44.25 (978-1-59335-467-1(3), 1593354673, Brlnc Audio MP3 Lib) Brilliance Audio.

Faith of the Fallen. unabr. ed. Terry Goodkind. Read by John Kenneth. (Running Time: 27 hrs.). (Sword of Truth Ser.). 2004. 44.25 (978-1-59710-270-4(9), 1597102709, BADLE); 29.95 (978-1-59710-271-1(7), 1597102717, BAD) Brilliance Audio.

Faith of the Fallen. unabr. ed. Terry Goodkind. Read by John Kenneth. (Running Time: 27 hrs.). (Sword of Truth Ser.: Bk. 6). 2007. audio compact disk 38.95 (978-1-4233-2169-9(3), 9781423321699, Bril Audio CD Unabri); audio compact disk 112.25 (978-1-4233-2170-5(7), 9781423321705, BriAudCD Unabrid) Brilliance Audio.

Faith Opens Prison Doors. Gloria Copeland. 2 cass. 1990. 10.00 Set. (978-0-88114-929-6(2)) K Copeland Pubns.
Biblical teaching on Galatians 3:23.

Faith or Efforts? Swami Amar Jyoti. 1 cass. 1981. 9.95 (P-42) Truth Consciousness.
Plunging into the unknown vs. efforts & study. Learning to mold ourselves to the needs of the path. Letting go of blocks for love of God.

Faith Precedes the Miracle & Making Changes in Our Lives. Hyrum Smith. 1 cass. 7.98 (978-1-55503-199-2(4), 06003842) Covenant Comms.

Faith, Reason & Catholic Education: Side 2: Questions & Answers: Br. Jas. Curran, Sr. Assumpta Long, Fr. Jude Mead, Sr. Marie Edward. Ronald P. McArthur. 1 cass. (National Meeting of the Institute, 1990 Ser.). 4.00 (90N2) IRL Chicago.

Faith Refresher, 3. Featuring Bill Winston. 4 CDs. 2006. audio compact disk 24.00 (978-1-59544-188-1(3)) Pub: B Winston Min. Dist(s): Anchor Distributors

Faith Refresher, 5. Featuring Bill Winston. 3 cass. 2005. 15.00 (978-1-59544-095-2(X)) Pub: B Winston Min. Dist(s): Anchor Distributors

Faith Refresher, Vol. 1. Bill Winston. 3 cass. (C). 2001. 15.00 (978-1-931289-28-3(X)) Pub: B Winston Min. Dist(s): Anchor Distributors

Faith Refresher, Vol. 3. Bill Winston. 3 cass. (Running Time: 3hr.07min.). (C). 2003. 15.00 (978-1-931289-16-0(6)) B Winston Min.

Faith Refresher Volume 2, Vol. 2. Bill Winston. 3 cass. (Running Time: 3hr.20min.). (C). 2002. 15.00 (978-1-931289-29-0(8)) Pub: B Winston Min. Dist(s): Anchor Distributors

Faith Refresher Volume-4. Bill Winston. 3. 2004. audio compact disk 24.00 (978-1-59544-008-2(9)) Pub: B Winston Min. Dist(s): Anchor Distributors
In this powerful and prophetic series you will learn how to avoid temptation and strife which cancels your faith, the importance of allowing God to be your true source and supply, that you were created with a wealth of potential, and fatih is the master key and currency used to gain true riches.

Faith Refresher Volume-4. Featuring Bill Winston. 3. 2004. 15.00 (978-1-59544-007-5(0)) Pub: B Winston Min. Dist(s): Anchor Distributors

Faith Refresher Volume 4. Featuring Bill Winston. 3. 2002. 15.00 (978-1-59544-057-0(7)) Pub: B Winston Min. Dist(s): Anchor Distributors
In this powerfuland prophetic series you will learn how to avoid temptation and strife which cancels your faith, the importance of allowing God to be your true source and supply,that you were created with a wealth of potential, and faith is the master key and currency used to gain true riches.

Faith School Series, Vol. 1. Elbert Willis. 4 cass. 13.00 Set. Fill the Gap.

Faith School Series, Vol. 2. Elbert Willis. 4 cass. 13.00 Fill the Gap.

Faith Speaks. Gloria Copeland. Perf. by Gloria Copeland. 1 cass. (Ingredients for Success: Faith, Patience & Love Ser.: Tape 3). 1995. cass. & video 5.00 (978-1-57562-019-0(7)) K Copeland Pubns.

Faith Standing: Hebrews 11:32. Ed Young. 1992. 4.95 (978-0-7417-1931-7(2), 931) Win Walk.

Faith Takes Back What the Devil's Stolen Series. Kenneth W. Hagin, Jr. 3 cass. 1992. 12.00 Set. (26J) Faith Lib Pubns.

Faith That Attracts God. Rick Joyner. 1 cass. (Running Time: 90 mins.). (Growing in Faith Ser.: Vol. 6). 2000. 5.00 (RJ14-006) Morning NC.
With fresh & practical messages centering on faith, this tape series will enable you to better understand essential principles of the Christian walk.

Faith That Makes Sense: Micah 6:8. Ed Young. (J). 1981. 4.95 (978-0-7417-1174-8(5), A0174) Win Walk.

Faith That Purifies: Genesis 15:16, Rom.4:3, Galatians 3:6. Ed Young. 1980. 4.95 (978-0-7417-1142-7(7)) Win Walk.

Faith that Works. Kenneth W. Hagin, Jr. 3 cass. 12.00 (22J) Faith Lib Pubns.

Faith, the Life of A Believer Series. Smith Chuck. (ENG.). 2001. audio compact disk 22.99 (978-1-932941-09-8(6)) Word For Today.

Faith the link with God's Power. Reinhard Bonnke. 2009. audio compact disk 7.00 (978-1-933106-75-5(1)) E-R-Productions.

Faith to Change the World. Lester Sumrall. 12 cass. (Running Time: 18 hrs.). 1999. 48.00 (978-1-58568-043-6(5)) Sumrall Pubng.

Faith to Move Mountains. Featuring Bill Winston. 2 cass. 2005. 10.00 (978-1-59544-162-1(X)); audio compact disk 16.00 (978-1-59544-163-8(8)) Pub: B Winston Min. Dist(s): Anchor Distributors

Faith under Fire: Women's Bible Studies in the Books of Peter & Jude. Brodersen Cheryl. (ENG.). 2007. DVD 39.99 (978-1-59751-967-0(7)) Word For Today.

Faith Unfurled: New Testament Survey. Speeches. Douglas Jacoby. 8 CDs. (Running Time: 8 Hours). 2005. audio compact disk 32.00 (978-0-9767583-4-1(2)) Illumination MA.

Faith vs. Fear, Vol. 2. Creflo A. Dollar. 20.00 (978-1-59089-026-4(4)) Pub: Creflo Dollar. Dist(s): STL Dist NA

Faith vs. Fear Opposing Forces. Kenneth Copeland. 2 cass. 1988. 10.00 Set. (978-0-88114-920-3(9)) K Copeland Pubns.
Biblical teaching on overcoming faith.

Faith Walking Power Walk: Hebrews 11:5-6. Ed Young. 1992. 4.95 (978-0-7417-1915-7(0), 915) Win Walk.

Faith Worshipping Power Walk: Hebrews 11:4. Ed Young. 1992. 4.95 (978-0-7417-1914-0(2), 914) Win Walk.

Faith Zone, Set. Bobby Hilton. 4 cass. (Running Time: 6 hrs.). 2002. 22.00 (978-1-930766-02-0(5)) Pub: Bishop Bobby. Dist(s): STL Dist NA

Faithful: Two Diehard Boston Red Sox Fans Chronicle the Historic 2004 Season. unabr. ed. Stewart O'Nan & Stephen King. Read by Ron McLarty & Adam Grupper. 12 cass. (Running Time: 16 hrs.). 2005. 99.75 (978-1-4193-2709-4(7), 97960) Recorded Bks.
New York Times best-selling authors and rabid Boston Red Sox fans, Stewart O'Nan and Stephen King began work on this fans' journal in the spring of 2003, with only a faint hope that their beloved team would end an 86-year drought and win a World Series. Filled with insightful and humorous e-mail correspondences and diary entries, Faithful conjures up the smell of the infield grass, and the sound of cracking bats and roaring crowds.

Faithful: Two Diehard Boston Red Sox Fans Chronicle the Historic 2004 Season. unabr. ed. Stewart O'Nan & Stephen King. Read by Ron McLarty & Adam Grupper. 2004. 23.95 (978-0-7435-4509-9(5)) Pub: S&S Audio. Dist(s): S and S Inc

Faithful: Two Diehard Boston Red Sox Fans Chronicle the Historic 2004 Season. unabr. collector's ed. Stewart O'Nan & Stephen King. Read by Ron McLarty & Adam Grupper. 14 CDs. (Running Time: 16 hrs.). 2005. audio compact disk 59.95 (978-1-4193-2712-4(7), CD202) Recorded Bks.

Faithful Attraction: The Prevention of an Affair: Hebrews 13:4. Ed Young. 1995. 4.95 (978-0-7417-2051-1(5), 1051) Win Walk.

Faithful Follower. Swami Amar Jyoti. 1 cass. 1976. 9.95 (D-12) Truth Consciousness.
Truth cannot be argued nor faith reasoned out. What we meditate upon manifests through us.

Faithful Gardener. Clarissa Pinkola Estes. 2 CDs. (Running Time: 1 hr 30 mins). 2005. audio compact disk 19.95 (978-1-59179-388-5(2)) Sounds True.
What in life is unconquerable; what survives? On The Faithful Gardener, Dr. Clarissa Pinkola Estes mines the rich storytelling tradition of her own family to unearth a series of lyrical stories that illustrate how faith is the one immortal force in our lives. Raised by a family of refugee immigrants who revered stories as healing instruments, Dr. Estes tells these ageless tales first told "... to nourish, repair, and strengthen - whatever is most needed and wanted." Like Matriochka dolls, The Faithful Gardener stories nest inside one another. What begins as a simple tale from the lips of a child, becomes the greater saga of Uncle Zovar, a quiet refugee from the Nazi slave camps, and his refusal to let bitterness darken his devotion to the earth. The final story, told in the form of a vivid old country tale about "that which can never die," holds an unforgettable lesson about sacrifice and spiritual regeneration. The Faithful Gardener captures the spirit of a long-ago time, while deeply expressing our common desire to know that grappling with sudden and unexpected twists of fate and challenging transitions - however painful - is never in vain.

Faithful Heart: Seeking Wisdom & Integrity. Charles R. Swindoll. 2 cass. 1998. 11.95 (978-1-57972-142-8(7)) Insight Living.

Faithful Is Our God. Contrib. by Hezekiah Walker. (Soundtraks Ser.). 2007. audio compact disk 8.99 (978-5-557-56225-6(7)) Christian Wrld.

Faithful One see Chinese Fairy Tales

Faithful to All Things: Buddhism & the Western Poetic Imagination. Speeches. Featuring David Whyte. 1 CD. 1998. audio compact disk 15.00 (978-1-932887-05-1(9)) Pub: Many Rivers Pr. Dist(s): Partners-West

Faithful unto Death. unabr. ed. Caroline Graham. Read by Hugh Ross. 10 cass. (Running Time: 10 hrs.). (Chief Inspector Barnaby Ser.: Bk. 5). 1997. 84.95 Set. (978-0-7540-0015-0(X), CAB 1438) AudioGO.
When Simone Hollingsworth misses bell-ringing practice, her friends in Fawcett Green aren't surprised. Bell-ringing, it seems, is Simone's latest hobby to have fallen by the wayside. Only her neighbors suspect the worst. The discovery of a body draws Inspector Barnaby to the village, & it's soon apparent that unraveling the mystery will stretch Barnaby's powers of persuasion to the limit.

Faithful unto Death. unabr. ed. Caroline Graham. Read by Hugh Ross. 10 cass. (Running Time: 15 hrs.). (Chief Inspector Barnaby Ser.: Bk. 5). 2000. 69.95 (CAB 1438) Pub: Chivers Audio Bks GBR. Dist(s): AudioGO

Faithful unto the End. Elizabeth Roberts. 1 cass. (Running Time: 1 hr.). 2001. 10.00 (978-0-9706641-1-2(7)) E Roberts.

***Faithfully, Judith.** Ernest Haycox. 2009. (978-1-60136-436-4(9)) Audio Holding.

Faithfully, Judith. Ernest Haycox. (Running Time: 0 hr. 42 mins.). 1998. 10.95 (978-1-60083-471-4(X)) Iofy Corp.

Faithfulness in Church Attendance. Creflo A. Dollar. 2008. audio compact disk 14.00 (978-1-59944-734-6(7)) Creflo Dollar.

Faithfulness of God: 11 Tim. 2:10-13; Gen. 18:25. Ed Young. 1990. 4.95 (978-0-7417-1829-7(4), 829) Win Walk.

Faithfulness Series. Creflo A. Dollar. 20.00 (978-1-59089-009-7(4)) Pub: Creflo Dollar. Dist(s): STL Dist NA

Faithfulness Series, Vol. 2. Creflo A. Dollar. 25.00 (978-1-59089-020-2(5)) Pub: Creflo Dollar. Dist(s): STL Dist NA

Faithfulness Series, Vol. 3. Creflo A. Dollar. 20.00 (978-1-59089-022-6(1)) Pub: Creflo Dollar. Dist(s): STL Dist NA

Faithfulness Through Love, Set. Elbert Willis. 4 cass. 13.00 Fill the Gap.

FaithHome. Debra Ball-Kilbourne & MaryJane Pierce Norton. Created by Dan Solomon & Joy Solomon. 1997. bk. 10.00 (978-0-687-06570-7(4)) Abingdon.

Faithkeeper. adpt. ed. Interview with Bill Moyers & Oren Lyons. 1 cass. (Running Time: 58 min.). 1994. 10.95 (978-1-56176-905-6(3)) Mystic Fire.
Lyons discusses ancient Native American prophecies of the ecological disasters we now face, tells the legend of his clan, & speaks of responsibility to future generations.

Faith's Launching Pad. Elbert Willis. 1 cass. (Faith School Ser.: Vol. 2). 4.00 Fill the Gap.

Faith's Possible Dream: Realizing God's Vision for Your Marriage, Your Ministry, & Your Life, 4 of Faith Series. Mac Hammond. 4 cass. (Running Time: 4 hrs). 2005. 10.00 (978-1-57399-233-6(X)) Mac Hammond.
Learn how to identify your God-given dream and to grow the kind of mature faith that makes that dream a reality.

Faith's Possible Dream: Realizing God's Vision for Your Marriage, Your Ministry, & Your Life, 4 of the faith series. Mac Hammond. 4 CDs. 2006. audio compact disk Rental 20.00 (978-1-57399-314-2(X)) Mac Hammond.

Faith's Supportive Graces. Elbert Willis. 1 cass. (Faith School Ser.: Vol. 1). 4.00 Fill the Gap.

Faiths That Lead to Certainties. Manly P. Hall. 1 cass. 8.95 (978-0-89314-114-1(3)) Philos Res.

Fakes & Originals. Umberto Eco. 1 cass. 9.00 (A0179-87) Sound Photosyn.
The very Italian author of "The Name of the Rose" discusses a point of law.

Faking It. Pete Johnson. Read by Paul Chequer. (Running Time: 14580 sec.). (J). 2001. audio compact disk 34.95 (978-0-7540-6686-6(X)) AudioGo GBR.

Faking It. unabr. ed. Jennifer Crusie, pseud. Read by Aasne Vigesaa. 7 cass. (Running Time: 10 hrs.). 2002. 32.95 (978-1-59086-026-7(8), 1590860268, BAU); 82.25 Library ed. (978-1-59086-027-4(6), 1590860276, Unabridge Lib Edns) Brilliance Audio.
Publishers Weekly (starred review) raves "Crusie charms with her brisk, edgy style..." Kirkus (starred review) of Crusie's latest, New York Times bestselling Fast Women states "Move over, Susan Isaacs. Crusie is just as smart and sassy about the things a woman has to do to make love work, and a lot funnier to boot." Reformed art forger Tilda Goodnight reluctantly joins forces with semi-reformed con man Davy Dempsey to steal a dubious painting and several million embezzled dollars from a lethal widow named Clea who has targeted a mild-mannered art collector as her next dearly departed. Complications include her sister, the female impersonator; his best friend, the reformed cat burglar; a recidivist embezzler named Rabbit; a hit man, some lousy sex, and a juke box. Trouble ensues.

Faking It. unabr. ed. Jennifer Crusie, pseud. Read by Aasne Vigesaa. (Running Time: 10 hrs.). 2004. 39.25 (978-1-59335-455-8(X), 159335455X, Brlnc Audio MP3 Lib) Brilliance Audio.

Faking It. unabr. ed. Jennifer Crusie, pseud. Read by Aasne Vigesaa. (Running Time: 10 hrs.). 2004. 39.25 (978-1-59710-273-5(3), 1597102733, BADLE); 24.95 (978-1-59710-272-8(5), 1597102725, BAD) Brilliance Audio.

Faking It. unabr. ed. Jennifer Crusie, pseud. Read by Aasne Vigesaa. (Running Time: 12 hrs.). 2010. audio compact disk 89.97 (978-1-4418-3569-7(5), 9781441835697, BriAudCD Unabrid); audio compact disk 29.99 (978-1-4418-3568-0(7), 9781441835680, Bril Audio CD Unabri) Brilliance Audio.

Faking It. unabr. ed. Jennifer Crusie, pseud. Read by Aasne Vigesaa. (Running Time: 10 hrs.). 2004. 24.95 (978-1-59335-109-0(7), 1593351097) Soulmate Audio Bks.

Fala Factor. Stuart M. Kaminsky. Narrated by Tom Parker. (Running Time: 9 hrs.). (Toby Peters Mystery Ser.: No. 9). (C). 2001. 30.95 (978-1-59912-659-3(1)) Iofy Corp.

Fala Factor. unabr. ed. Stuart M. Kaminsky. Read by Tom Parker. 6 cass. (Running Time: 8 hrs. 30 mins.). (Toby Peters Mystery Ser.: No. 9). 2001. 44.95 (978-0-7861-2045-1(2), 2805); audio compact disk 56.00 (978-0-7861-9705-7(6), 2805) Blckstn Audio.
The year is 1942, and Eleanor Roosevelt is convinced that there is an imposter in the White House masquerading as Fala, FDR's prized Scottie. Positive that a shady veterinarian has absconded with the genuine pooch, Eleanor turns for help to that much-battered and near penniless private eye: Toby Peters.

Falcon. Created by Radio Spirits. Contrib. by Les Damon. (Running Time: 36000 sec.). 2004. 39.98 (978-1-57019-677-5(X)) Radio Spirits.

Falcon, Vol. 1. 6 cass. 24.98 Set. Moonbeam Pubns.

Falcon, Vol. 1. collector's ed. Perf. by Les Damon. Created by Michael J. Arlen. 6 cass. (Running Time: 9 hrs.). 1999. bk. 34.98 (4133) Radio Spirits.
18 broadcasts with Michael Waring, the freelance detective, also known as the Falcon.

Falcon, Vol. 2. 6 cass. 24.98 Set. Moonbeam Pubns.

Falcon, Vol. 2. collector's ed. Perf. by Les Damon. Created by Michael J. Arlen. 6 cass. (Running Time: 9 hrs.). 2000. bk. 34.98 (4548) Radio Spirits.

Falcon: Count Me Out Tonight, Angel. Perf. by Les Damon & Jackson Beck. 2009. audio compact disk 31.95 (978-1-57019-886-1(1)) Radio Spirits.

Falcon: Invisible Thug & Babbling Brook. 1 cass. (Running Time: 1 hr.). 2001. 6.98 (2615) Radio Spirits.

Falcon: The Case of the Curious Cop & Sweet Swindle. Perf. by Les Damon. 1 cass. (Running Time: 1 hr.). 2001. 6.98 (2278) Radio Spirits.

Falcon: The Flaming Club & The Practical Choker. Perf. by Les Damon. 1 cass. (Running Time: 1 hr.). 2001. 6.98 (1739) Radio Spirits.

Falcon: The Running Waters & The Case of the Broken Key. Perf. by Les Damon. 1 cass. (Running Time: 1 hr.). 2001. 6.98 (1544) Radio Spirits.

Falcon: The Worried Wife & The Missing Miss. Perf. by Les Damon. 1 cass. (Running Time: 1 hr.). 2001. 6.98 (1902) Radio Spirits.

Falcon at the Portal, unabr. ed. Elizabeth Peters, pseud. Narrated by Barbara Rosenblat. 11 cass. (Running Time: 15 hrs. 30 mins.). (Amelia Peabody Ser.: No. 11). 1999. 96.00 (978-0-7887-3744-2(9), 95650E7) Recorded Bks.
Join the spunky Amelia and her charming family for a thrilling new archaeological adventure in exotic Edwardian Egypt. Even as they celebrate David's marriage, someone impersonating him is peddling fake antiquities.

Falcon at the Portal. unabr. ed. Elizabeth Peters, pseud. Narrated by Barbara Rosenblat. 13 CDs. (Running Time: 15 hrs. 30 mins.). (Amelia Peabody Ser.: No. 11). 2000. audio compact disk 119.00 (978-0-7887-4206-4(X), C1135E7) Recorded Bks.
Join the spunky Amelia & her charming family for a thrilling new archaeological adventure in exotic Edwardian Egypt. Even as they celebrate David's marriage, someone impersonating him is peddling fake antiquities.

Falcon Flies. Wilbur Smith. Read by Stephen Thorne. 18 CDs. (Running Time: 27 hrs.). 2001. audio compact disk 127.95 (978-0-7540-5432-0(2), CCD 123) Pub: Chivers Audio Bks GBR. Dist(s): AudioGO
The story of one family's conquest of the untamed lands of Africa.

Falcon Flies. Wilbur Smith. 2 cass. (Running Time: 3 hrs.). (ENG., 2001. (978-0-333-78237-8(2)) Macmillan UK GBR.

Falcon Flies. unabr. ed. Wilbur Smith. Read by Stephen Thorne. 16 cass. (Running Time: 24 hrs.). (Ballantyne Novel Ser.). 1999. 99.95 (978-0-7540-0247-5(0), CAB1670) Pub: Chivers Audio Bks GBR. Dist(s): AudioGO
Set in the untamed wilderness of pre-colonial Africa. Saga of exploration & adventure, elephant hunting & slave trading, of fierce & ruthless men & one courageous & determined woman.

Falcon Flies, Pt. 1. unabr. collector's ed. Wilbur Smith. Read by Richard Brown. 8 cass. (Running Time: 12 hrs.). (Ballantyne Novels Ser.). 1988. 64.00 (978-0-7366-1416-0(8), 2303-A) Books on Tape.
The green swells of the South Atlantic, the fever-ridden shores of the Indian Ocean & the vanished Eden that was the African interior are the setting for this adventure story.

Falcon Flies, Pt. 2. collector's ed. Wilbur Smith. Read by Richard Brown. 9 cass. (Running Time: 13 hrs. 30 min.). (Ballantyne Novels Ser.). 1988. 72.00 (978-0-7366-1417-7(6), 2303-B) Books on Tape.

Falcon for the Hawks. unabr. ed. Clive Egleton. Read by Michael Tudor Barnes. 6 cass. (Running Time: 9 hrs.). 2000. 54.95 (978-1-86042-453-3(8), 24538) Pub: Soundings Ltd GBR. Dist(s): Ulverscroft US
In March 1917, a Zeppelin loses its way & drifts helplessly out of control over Hertfordshire. A hair-raising campaign of dogged courage & intrepid airmanship ensues.

***Falcon Seven.** unabr. ed. James Huston. Read by Scott Sowers. (Running Time: 12 hrs. 30 mins. 0 sec.). (ENG.). 2010. audio compact disk 39.99 (978-1-4272-1012-8(8)) Pub: Macmill Audio. Dist(s): Macmillan

Falcondance. unabr. ed. Amelia Atwater-Rhodes. Read by Andy Paris. 4 cass. (Running Time: 6 hrs.). (Kiesha'ra Ser.: Bk. 3). 2005. 37.75 (978-1-4193-3067-4(5), 97992) Recorded Bks.
Acclaimed author Amelia Atwater-Rhodes' previous novels have been chosen as ALA Quick Picks - and Hawksong was a School Library Journal Best Book of the Year and VOYA Best Science Fiction, Fantasy, and Horror Selection. In the stunning novel Falcondance, a falcon named Nicias travels to the land of his heritage to meet someone who will help him to understand his newfound magical powers and unlock the secrets of his destiny.

Falconer. unabr. collector's ed. John Cheever. Read by Walter Zimmerman. 7 cass. (Running Time: 7 hrs.). 1988. 42.00 (978-0-7366-1351-4(X), 2252) Books on Tape.
Falconer is a prison & Farragut is the convicted man. This is the story of what happens to him.

Falconer & the Great Beast. unabr. ed. Ian Morson. Read by Stephen Thorne. 6 cass. (Running Time: 6 hrs. 45 min.). (Isis Ser.). (J). 2003. 54.95 (978-0-7531-1693-7(6)); audio compact disk 64.95 (978-0-7531-2229-7(4)) Pub: ISIS Lrg Prnt GBR. Dist(s): Ulverscroft US
It is 1268. Oxford is forced to host the Tartars, whose legendary fierceness has already wreaked havoc in France and Germany. This time they claim a peaceful mission - they merely wish to gain an audience with the king.A sense of foreboding hovers: whilst the Tartars stage a banquet outside the city walls, the town is unusually quiet. But only the Tartar ambassador himself falls victim to evil. When he is found dead, it looks like murder. How was it possible except by magic?.

Falconfar. unabr. ed. Ed Greenwood. Read by Phil Gigante. (Running Time: 12 hrs.). (Falconfar Saga Ser.). 2010. 24.99 (978-1-4233-5124-5(X), 9781423351245, Brilliance MP3); 24.99 (978-1-4233-5126-9(6), 9781423351269, BAD); 39.97 (978-1-4233-5125-2(8), 9781423351252, Brlnc Audio MP3 Lib); 39.97 (978-1-4233-5127-6(4), 9781423351276, BADLE); audio compact disk 29.99 (978-1-4233-5122-1(3), 9781423351221, Bril Audio CD Unabri); audio compact disk 99.97 (978-1-4233-5123-8(1), 9781423351238, BriAudCD Unabrid) Brilliance Audio.

Falcons of Montabard. Elizabeth Chadwick. Read by Christopher Scott. 14 cass. (Running Time: 18 hrs.). (Soundings Ser.). (J). 2004. 99.95 (978-1-84283-641-5(2)) Pub: ISIS Lrg Prnt GBR. Dist(s): Ulverscroft US

***Falcons of Montabard.** Elizabeth Chadwick. 2010. audio compact disk 104.95 (978-1-4079-1520-3(7)) Pub: Soundings Ltd GBR. Dist(s): Ulverscroft US

Fall. Garrison Keillor. 1 cass., 1 CD. 8.78 Blisterpack. (PHC 2107); audio compact disk 11.18 CD Jewel box. (PHC 55458) NewSound.

Fall. Simon Mawer. Read by Robert Glenister. 2003. 96.95 (978-0-7540-8376-4(4)); audio compact disk 110.95 (978-0-7540-8771-7(9)) Pub: Chivers Audio Bks GBR. Dist(s): AudioGO

Fall. abr. unabr. ed. Garrison Keillor. Contrib. by Garrison Keillor. 1 CD. (Running Time: 1 hr.). (ENG.). 1997. audio compact disk 13.95 (978-1-56511-214-8(8), 1565112148) Pub: HighBridge. Dist(s): Workman Pub

***Fall.** unabr. ed. Guillermo del Toro & Chuck Hogan. Read by Peter Francis James. (Strain Trilogy: Bk. 2). (ENG.). 2010. (978-0-06-198871-4(5), Harper Audio); (978-0-06-204203-3(3), Harper Audio) HarperCollins Pubs.

***Fall.** unabr. ed. David Fulmer. Read by To be Announced. (Running Time: 8.5 hrs. NaN mins.). (ENG.). 2011. 29.95 (978-1-4417-8270-0(2)); 54.95 (978-1-4417-8267-0(2)); audio compact disk 76.00 (978-1-4417-8268-7(0)) Blckstn Audio.

***Fall & Rise of China.** Instructed by Richard Baum. 2010. 249.95 (978-1-59803-639-8(4)); audio compact disk 359.95 (978-1-59803-640-4(8)) Teaching Co.

Fall & Winter. Contrib. by Jon Foreman & Charlie Peacock. 2008. audio compact disk 13.99 (978-5-557-50593-2(8)) Sigma F RUS.

***Fall Asleep, Stay Asleep: Relax into Sleep, Sleep Through the Night, & Awaken Refreshed.** Martin L. Rossman. (Running Time: 2:00:00). 2010. audio compact disk 14.95 (978-1-59179-745-6(4)) Sounds True.

Fall from Grace. Nora Kay. Read by Lesley Mackie. 10 cass. (Sound Ser.). (J). 2002. 84.95 (978-1-84283-213-4(1)) Pub: ISIS Lrg Prnt GBR. Dist(s): Ulverscroft US

Fall in Love, Stay in Love. abr. ed. Willard F. Harley, Jr.. Read by Willard F. Harley, Jr. 2002. 24.99 (978-0-8007-4424-3(1)) Revell.

Fall in the Arms of Jesus. Coldwater Media. (ENG.). 2009. audio compact disk 15.00 (978-0-9822283-1-9(7)) ColdWater Media.

Fall of a Cosmonaut. unabr. ed. Stuart M. Kaminsky. Read by Nick Sullivan. 8 vols. (Running Time: 12 hrs.). (Inspector Porfiry Rostnikov Mystery Ser.: No. 13). 2001. bk. 69.95 (978-0-7927-2369-1(4), CSL 258, Chivers Sound Lib) AudioGO.
Post-Yeltsin Russia is a place where law governs neither nature nor man. A place where a brief, sudden storm can blow an iron bench down a city street.

Fall of a Philanderer. Carola Dunn. Read by Bernadette Dunne. (Running Time: 28800 sec.). (Daisy Dalrymple Mystery Ser.). 2006. 44.95 (978-0-7861-3789-3(4)); audio compact disk 55.00 (978-0-7861-7548-2(6)) Blckstn Audio.

Fall of a Philanderer. unabr. ed. Carola Dunn. Read by Bernadette Dunne. (Running Time: 28800 sec.). (Daisy Dalrymple Mystery Ser.). 2006. audio compact disk 29.95 (978-0-7861-7823-0(X)) Blckstn Audio.

***Fall of Candy Corn.** Zondervan. (Running Time: 5 hrs. 52 mins. 26 sec.). (Sweet Seasons Novel Ser.). (ENG.). (YA). 2010. 14.99 (978-0-310-86956-6(0)) Zondervan.

Fall of Che Guevara. unabr. ed. Henry Butterfield Ryan. Read by Richard McGonagle. (Running Time: 27000 sec.). 2006. 24.95 (978-0-7861-4855-4(1)); audio compact disk 24.95 (978-0-7861-6084-6(5)) Blckstn Audio.

Fall of Che Guevara: A Story of Soldiers, Spies, & Diplomats. unabr. ed. Henry Butterfield Ryan. Read by Richard McGonagle. 5 cass. (Running Time: 7 hrs.). 2000. 39.95 (978-0-7861-2632-3(9), 3238); audio compact disk 48.00 (978-0-7861-8742-3(5), 3238) Blckstn Audio.

Fall of Che Guevara: A Story of Soldiers, Spies, & Diplomats. unabr. ed. Henry Butterfield Ryan. Read by Richard McGonagle. (Running Time: 7 hrs.). (J). 2006. audio compact disk 29.95 (978-0-7861-8615-0(1), 3238) Blckstn Audio.

Fall of Constantinople. unabr. ed. Kenneth Bruce. 1 cass. (Running Time: 1 hr.). Dramatization. 12.50 Alpha Tape.

Fall of Fergal. Philip Ardagh. 2 cass. (Running Time: 2 hrs. 30 mins.). (Unlikely Exploits Ser.: Bk. 1). (J). (gr. 4 up). 2004. 19.55 (978-0-8072-2332-1(8), Listening Lib) Pub: Random Audio Pubg. Dist(s): NetLibrary CO

Fall of Frost. unabr. ed. Brian Hall. Narrated by Dick Hill. (Running Time: 13 hrs. 0 mins. 0 sec.). (ENG.). 2008. audio compact disk 24.99 (978-1-4001-5730-3(7)); audio compact disk 69.99 (978-1-4001-3730-5(6)) Pub: Tantor Media. Dist(s): IngramPubServ

Fall of Frost. unabr. ed. Brian Hall. Read by Dick Hill. (Running Time: 13 hrs. 0 mins. 0 sec.). (ENG.). 2008. audio compact disk 34.99 (978-1-4001-0730-8(X)) Pub: Tantor Media. Dist(s): IngramPubServ

***Fall of Giants.** Ken Follett. Bk. 1. 2010. audio compact disk 59.95 (978-0-14-242827-6(2), PengAudBks) Penguin Grp USA.

***Fall of Giants.** abr. ed. Ken Follett. Bk. 1. 2010. audio compact disk 29.95 (978-0-14-242828-3(0), PengAudBks) Penguin Grp USA.

Fall of Hyperion. unabr. ed. Dan Simmons. Read by Victor Bevine. (Running Time: 22 hrs.). (Hyperion Cantos Ser.). 2009. 44.97 (978-1-4233-8149-5(1), 9781423381495, BADLE); 44.97 (978-1-4233-8148-8(3), 9781423381488, Brlnc Audio MP3 Lib); 29.99 (978-1-4233-8147-1(5), 9781423381471, Brilliance MP3); audio compact disk 49.99 (978-1-4233-8145-7(9), 9781423381457, Bril Audio CD Unabri); audio compact disk 99.97 (978-1-4233-8146-4(7), 9781423381464, BriAudCD Unabrid) Brilliance Audio.

***Fall of Jericho, Joshua's Death, & the Story of Deborah.** unabr. ed. Zondervan. (Running Time: 0 hr. 13 mins. 55 sec.). (Best-Loved Stories of the Bible, NIrV Ser.). (ENG.). (J). 2010. 1.99 (978-0-310-86504-9(2)) Pub: Zondkidz. Dist(s): Zondervan

Fall of Paris: The Siege & the Commune 1870-1871. collector's ed. Alistair Horne. Read by Bill Kelsey. 15 hrs. (Running Time: 22 hrs. 30 min.). 2000. 120.00 (978-0-7366-4990-2(5), 5247) Books on Tape.
The collapse of France in 1870 had an overwhelming impact on Paris, on France & on the open-mouthed world. People everywhere saw Paris as the center of Europe & the hub of culture, fashion & invention. Suddenly France, not least to the disbelief of her own citizens, was in the vise of Prussian armies & forced to surrender on humiliating terms Politics & nature abhorring a vacuum, Paris was convulsed by the savagery of the Commune. In this brilliant study of the Siege & it's aftermath, Horne evokes the high drama of those ten fantastic months & the spiritual & physical agony which Paris & the Parisians suffered.

Fall of Reach. unabr. ed. Eric Nylund. Narrated by Todd McLaren. 9 CDs. (Running Time: 11 hrs. 0 mins. 0 sec.). (Halo Ser.). (ENG.). 2008. audio compact disk 69.99 (978-1-4001-3112-9(X)) Pub: Tantor Media. Dist(s): IngramPubServ

Fall of Reach. unabr. ed. Eric Nylund. Read by Todd McLaren. 9 CDs. (Running Time: 11 hrs. 0 mins. 0 sec.). (Halo Ser.). (ENG.). 2008. audio compact disk 34.99 (978-1-4001-0112-2(3)) Pub: Tantor Media. Dist(s): IngramPubServ

Fall of Reach. unabr. ed. Eric Nylund. Read by Todd McLaren. Narrated by Todd McLaren. 1 MP3-CD. (Running Time: 11 hrs. 0 mins. 0 sec.). (Halo Ser.). 2008. 19.99 (978-1-4001-5112-7(0)) Pub: Tantor Media. Dist(s): IngramPubServ

Fall of the House of Usher see Tales of Horror & Suspense

Fall of the House of Usher see Edgar Allan Poe

Fall of the House of Usher see Cask of Amontillado

Fall of the House of Usher see Mind of Poe

Fall of the House of Usher. (992) Spoken Arts.

Fall of the House of Usher: Abridged. (ENG.). 2007. (978-1-60339-009-5(X)); cd-rom & audio compact disk (978-1-60339-010-1(3)) Listenr Digest.

Fall of the House of Usher: The Pit & the Pendulum & Other Tales of Mystery & Imagination. Edgar Allan Poe. Read by William Roberts. 4 cass. (Running Time: 5 hrs.). 2003. 22.98 (978-962-634-783-6(X)); audio compact disk 28.98 (978-962-634-283-1(8), Naxos AudioBooks) Naxos.
The horrors of the Spanish Inquisition, with its dungeon of death, and the overhanging gloom on the House of Usher demonstrate unforgettably the unique imagination of Edgar Allan Poe. Unerringly, he touches upon some of our greatest nightmares - premature burial, ghostly transformation, words from beyond the grave. Written in the 1840s, they have retained their power to shock and frighten even now.

Fall of the House of Usher & Other Works. unabr. ed. Edgar Allan Poe. Perf. by Basil Rathbone. 1 cass. Incl. Bells. (CDL5 1195); Haunted Palace. (CDL5 1195); Telltale Heart. (CDL5 1195); (J). 1990. 9.95 (978-1-55994-099-3(9), CDL5 1195) HarperCollins Pubs.

Fall of the House of Usher & Other Writings see Invisible Man & Selected Short Stories of Edgar Allan Poe

Fall of the House of Usher & Other Writings. Edgar Allan Poe. 1 cass. (Running Time: 52 mins.). 1999. (978-0-7588-0009-1(6), Acme Record); audio compact disk (978-0-7588-0010-7(X), Acme Record) Goss Commns.

Fall of the House of Usher & Other Writings. Short Stories. Edgar Allan Poe. 1950. (DM-5120) Natl Recrd Co.

Fall of the House of Usher & Other Writings. unabr. ed. Edgar Allan Poe. Read by Lloyd Battista. Contrib. by Brad Hill. Intro. by Joyce Carol Oates & Peter Benchley. 1 cass. 11.95 (978-1-56268-000-8(5)); audio compact disk 14.95 Spencer Library.
Edgar Allan Poe's most famous story was the inspiration & cornerstone of the entire Spencer Library project. Roderick Usher's deteriorating state of mind, as well as his deteriorating estate of inheritance, are the basis & background of this horrifying tale that culminates in catastrophic justice.

Fall of the House of Usher & Other Writings. unabr. ed. Edgar Allan Poe. Read by Hurd Hatfield. 1 cass. (Running Time: 59 min.). 10.95 (978-0-8045-0992-3(1), SAC 992) Spoken Arts.
Two of Poe's classic stories! The tale of the ghostly ball which frolics while the plague rages; & the story of the house doomed by an unnatural death.

Fall of the House of Usher & Others. Edgar Allan Poe. Read by William Roberst. (Running Time: 5 hrs.). 2005. 28.95 (978-1-60083-734-0(4)) Iofy Corp.

Fall of the House of Usher & The Black Cat. Edgar Allan Poe. 1 cass. (Running Time: 1 hr.). (Radiobook Ser.). 1987. 4.98 (978-0-929541-14-3(6)) Radiola Co.
Two complete stories.

Fall of the House of Usher, the Pit & the Pendulum... & Other Tales of Mystery & Imagination: The Fall of the House of Usher; the Pit & the Pendulum; Ligeia; the Facts in the Case of M. Valdemar; the Tell-Tale Heart; the Black Cat; the Masque of the Red Death; the Cask of Amontillado; the Premature Burial. unabr. ed. Edgar Allan Poe. Read by William Roberts. (YA). 2007. 49.99 (978-1-60252-751-5(2)) Find a World.

***Fall of the House of Zeus: The Rise & Ruin of America's Most Powerful Trial Lawyer.** unabr. ed. Curtis Wilkie. Narrated by Sean Runnette. (Running Time: 11 hrs. 0 mins.). 2010. 34.99 (978-1-4001-9995-2(6)); 24.99 (978-1-4001-6995-5(X)); 17.99 (978-1-4001-8995-3(0)); audio compact disk 34.99 (978-1-4001-1995-0(2)); audio compact disk 83.99 (978-1-4001-4995-7(9)) Pub: Tantor Media. Dist(s): IngramPubServ

Fall of Troy. unabr. ed. Peter Ackroyd. Read by Michael Maloney. (YA). 2008. 59.99 (978-1-60514-574-7(2)) Find a World.

Fall on Your Knees. abr. ed. Ann-Marie MacDonald. Read by Nikki James. 8 CDs. (Running Time: 10 hrs.). (ENG.). 2002. audio compact disk 36.95 (978-1-56511-692-4(5), 1565116925) Pub: HighBridge. Dist(s): Workman Pub

Fall on Your Knees. abr. ed. Ann-Marie MacDonald. Read by Nikki James. (YA). 2006. 44.99 (978-1-59895-206-3(4)) Find a World.

Fall with Honor. unabr. ed. E. E. Knight. Read by Christian Rummel. (Running Time: 11 hrs.). (Vampire Earth Ser.: Bk. 7). 2009. 39.97 (978-1-4418-0848-6(5), 9781441808486, BADLE); audio compact disk 92.97 (978-1-4418-0845-5(0), 9781441808455, BriAudCD Unabrid) Brilliance Audio.

Fall with Honor. unabr. ed. Read by Christian Rummel. Ed. by E. E. Knight. (Running Time: 11 hrs.). (Vampire Earth Ser.: Bk. 7). 2009. 24.99 (978-1-4418-0846-2(9), 9781441808462, Brilliance MP3); 39.97 (978-1-4418-0847-9(7), 9781441808479, Brlnc Audio MP3 Lib); audio compact disk 29.99 (978-1-4418-0844-8(2), 9781441808448, Bril Audio CD Unabri) Brilliance Audio.

Fallacy of the "Stolen Concept" unabr. ed. Barbara Branden. 1 cass. (Running Time: 1 hr. 9 min.). (Principles of Efficient Thinking Ser.). 12.95 (709) J Norton Pubs.
The meaning of the stolen concept; common examples of the fallacy: "All property is theft;" "I think, therefore, I am;" "Who created the Universe?;" "The rights of the public supersede individual rights;" & "The acceptance of reason is an act of faith".

Fallen. abr. ed. T. Jefferson Parker. Read by David Colacci. (Running Time: 21600 sec.). 2006. audio compact disk 16.99 (978-1-59600-867-0(9), 9781596008670, BCD Value Price) Brilliance Audio.
Please enter a Synopsis.

Fallen. abr. unabr. ed. T. Jefferson Parker. Read by David Colacci. 5 CDs. (Running Time: 39600 sec.). 2006. audio compact disk 97.25 (978-1-59086-980-2(X), 9781590869802, BACDLib Ed) Brilliance Audio.
Robbie Brownlaw was an ordinary cop working fraud for the San Diego Police department. Until a push from a sixth floor hotel room changed everything. Beating the odds, he survived and became a hero. Rewarded with two quick promotions, he's now the youngest homicide detective on the SDPD. Then there's the matter of the little colored shapes he sees when people speak - a neurological condition known as synesthesia. Linked to the speaker's emotions, Robbie can use these shapes and colors as a primitive lie detector. Garrett Asplundh was also a cop on the SDPD - a sergeant in the Professional Standards Unit where he kept an eye on other cops. Until a personal tragedy changed everything, destroying his career and his marriage. These days Garrett is an investigator for the city's Ethics Authority Enforcement Unit, spending his days monitoring city officials. Just when it looks like Garrett is about to reconcile with his wife, he's found dead in his Ford Explorer. Heading up the case, Robbie is confident it's not a suicide. But discovering who killed Garrett might mean uncovering some of San Diego's nastiest secrets.

***Fallen.** unabr. ed. Lauren Kate. Narrated by Justine Eyre. 9 CDs. (Running Time: 10 hrs. 56 mins.). (YA). (gr. 8 up). 2009. audio compact disk 60.00 (978-0-307-70645-4(1), Listening Lib) Pub: Random Audio Pubg. Dist(s): Random

Fallen. unabr. ed. Lauren Kate. Read by Justine Eyre. (ENG.). (J). (gr. 7). 2009. audio compact disk 40.00 (978-0-307-70643-0(5)) Pub: RH Chldrns. Dist(s): Random

Fallen. unabr. ed. David Maine. Read by Simon Vance. (YA). 2007. 44.99 (978-1-60252-832-1(2)) Find a World.

Fallen. unabr. ed. David Maine. Narrated by Simon Vance. (Running Time: 8 hrs. 0 mins. 0 sec.). (ENG.). 2005. audio compact disk 19.99 (978-1-4001-5182-0(1)); audio compact disk 59.99 (978-1-4001-3182-2(0)) Pub: Tantor Media. Dist(s): IngramPubServ

Fallen. unabr. ed. David Maine. Read by Simon Vance. (Running Time: 8 hrs. 0 mins. 0 sec.). (ENG.). 2005. audio compact disk 29.99 (978-1-4001-0182-5(4)) Pub: Tantor Media. Dist(s): IngramPubServ

Fallen. unabr. ed. T. Jefferson Parker. Read by David Colacci. (Running Time: 11 hrs.). 2006. 39.25 (978-1-59710-942-0(8), 9781597109420, BADLE); 24.95 (978-1-59710-943-7(6), 9781597109437, BAD); 32.95 (978-1-59086-976-5(1), 9781590869765, BAU); 82.25 (978-1-59086-977-2(X), 9781590869772, BrilAudUnabridg); audio compact disk 36.95 (978-1-59086-979-6(6), 9781590869796, BACD); audio compact disk 24.95 (978-1-59335-695-8(1), 9781593356958, Brilliance MP3); audio compact disk 39.25 (978-1-59335-829-7(6), 9781593358297, Brlnc Audio MP3 Lib) Brilliance Audio.

Fallen. unabr. ed. T. Jefferson Parker. Read by David Colacci. (YA). 2008. 79.99 (978-1-60514-814-4(8)) Find a World.

Fallen Angel. unabr. ed. Don J. Snyder. Read by Ian Peakes. 5 cass. (Running Time: 7 hrs.). 2001. 27.95 (978-1-58788-774-1(6), 1587887746, BAU); 61.25 (978-1-58788-775-8(4), 1587887754, Unabridge Lib Edns) Brilliance Audio.
One night can change a life. For eight-year-old Terry McQuinn, it was a snowy Christmas Eve on the coast of Maine, when Terry glimpsed a world he'd never seen before - the "summer people's" world unknown to the son of a caretaker. Serenity Cottage was a place of beauty and privilege owned by the luminous Halworths - but in the blink of an eye a tragic accident left the family in ruins. Now thirty years later, Terry has spent his life putting distance between himself and his history. Determined not to follow in his father's footsteps, he became a high-flying Hollywood film agent - but has somehow lost himself along the way. Terry is finally called back to Maine by the death of his father - but in the workshop Terry comes across a note in his father's hand that stops him cold: Open Serenity for Christmas. No one has been in the house since that fateful night three decades earlier. Although Terry's first instinct is to leave it all behind, he soon discovers that Katherine Halworth, the girl from thirty years before, is the new owner. With her arrival imminent, Terry's past comes rushing back. In the hands of critically acclaimed author Don J. Snyder, Fallen Angel is a warm and unique Christmas tale, reminding us it's never too late to forgive - and never too late to love.

Fallen Angel. unabr. ed. Don J. Snyder. Read by Ian Peakes. (Running Time: 7 hrs.). 2004. 39.25 (978-1-59600-512-9(2), 1596005122, Brlnc Audio MP3 Lib); 24.95 (978-1-59600-511-2(4), 1596005114, Brilliance MP3); 39.25 (978-1-59600-514-3(9), 1596005149, BADLE); 24.95 (978-1-59600-513-6(0), 1596005130, BAD) Brilliance Audio.

Fallen Angels. Noel Coward. Read by Annette Bening et al. (Playaway Adult Fiction Ser.). (ENG.). 2009. 39.99 (978-1-60775-739-9(7)) Find a World.

Fallen Angels. Walter Dean Myers. Narrated by J. D. Jackson. 6 cass. (Running Time: 8 hrs. 15 mins.). (YA). 1988. 57.75 (978-1-4193-1633-3(8)) Recorded Bks.

Fallen Angels. unabr. ed. Noel Coward. Perf. by Annette Bening et al. 2 CDs. (Running Time: 1 hr. 32 mins.). Dramatization. (L. A. Theatre Works). 2001. audio compact disk 25.95 (978-1-58081-181-1(7), CDTPT38) Pub: L A Theatre. Dist(s): NetLibrary CO

Fallen Angels. unabr. ed. Noel Coward. Perf. by Annette Bening et al. 1 cass. (Running Time: 1 hr. 32 mins.). Dramatization. 2001. 20.95 (978-1-58081-025-8(X), TPT38) L A Theatre.
Two couples, Julia & Fred & Willy & Jane, are happilymarried & the best of friends until a postcard arrives with news of an imminent visit from Maurice, a handsome Frenchman carrying strong ties from the past.

***Fallen Blade.** unabr. ed. Jon Courtenay Grimwood. (Running Time: 12 hrs.). (Duke's Blade Ser.). 2011. 24.99 (978-1-4418-8761-0(X), 9781441887610, BAD); 39.97 (978-1-4418-8762-7(8), 9781441887627, BADLE); 24.99 (978-1-4418-8759-7(8), 9781441887597, Brilliance MP3); 39.97 (978-1-4418-8760-3(1), 9781441887603, Brlnc Audio MP3 Lib); audio compact disk 29.99 (978-1-4418-8757-3(1), 9781441887573, Bril Audio CD Unabri); audio compact disk 79.97 (978-1-4418-8758-0(X), 9781441887580, BriAudCD Unabrid) Brilliance Audio.

Fallen Gods. unabr. ed. Quintin Jardine. Read by James Bryce. 8 cass. (Running Time: 11 hrs. 37 mins.). (Isis Cassettes Ser.). (J). 2004. 69.95 (978-0-7531-1676-0(6)); audio compact disk 84.95 (978-0-7531-2250-1(2)) Pub: ISIS Lrg Prnt GBR. Dist(s): Ulverscroft US

Fallen Hearts. unabr. ed. V. C. Andrews. Read by Donada Peters. 8 cass. (Running Time: 12 hrs.). 1990. 64.00 (978-0-7366-1763-5(9), 2602) Books on Tape.
If the seeds of ambition take root in childhood, then Heaven Casteel's early years were fertile indeed. Tyrannized by a despotic father, brought up in squalor, she burned for all the good things in life. She grew into a lovely young woman, energetic, talented & loving. Then, with her new husband, she went back to her hometown, determined to reestablish the good name her family deserved. But things are seldom as simple as they seem, & in this third installment in the Casteel series, V. C. Andrews once more exercises her sure grasp, in character & circumstance as the players work out their destinies.

Fallen Hearts. unabr. ed. V. C. Andrews. Read by Laura Brook. 10 cass. (Running Time: 11 hrs. 45 min.). 1995. 84.95 (978-1-85695-870-7(1), 941108) Pub: ISIS Audio GBR. Dist(s): Ulverscroft US
Proud & beautiful, Heaven has come back to the hills as Logan's bride. Free from her father's clutches, she would live again as a respected teacher & cherished wife. Then she & Logan are invited to Farthinggale Manor, near Boston, & are persuaded to stay on, lured by her step-grandfather's guile to live amidst the Tatterton wealth & privilege. But the past cannot be kept dark, & its specters rise up, writhing around her fragile happiness & threatening her love.

Fallen Heroes. Voddie Baucham, Jr. (YA). 2002. audio compact disk 20.00 (978-0-633-09030-2(1)) LifeWay Christian.

Fallen Heroes. Dafydd ab Hugh. Read by Rene Auberjonois. (Running Time: 4 hrs.). 1998. 19.95 (978-1-60083-420-2(5), Audiofy Corp) Iofy Corp.

Fallen into the Pit. unabr. ed. Ellis Peters, pseud. Narrated by Simon Prebble. 8 cass. (Running Time: 10 hrs. 45 mins.). (Inspector George Felse Mystery Ser.: Vol. 1). 1991. 70.00 (978-1-55690-623-7(4), 91419E7) Recorded Bks.
Helmut Schauffler, a German living in England after World War II plays on the fears of the villagers who are his neighbors.

***Fallen Leaves.** Wilkie Collin. Read by Anais 9000. 2010. 27.95 (978-1-60112-246-9(2)) Babblebooks.

Fallen Man. Tony Hillerman. Narrated by George Guidall. 7 CDs. (Running Time: 7.5 hrs.). (Joe Leaphorn & Jim Chee Novel Ser.). audio compact disk 34.95 (978-1-4025-6285-3(3)) Recorded Bks.

Fallen Man. abr. ed. Tony Hillerman. Read by Gil Silverbird. (Joe Leaphorn & Jim Chee Novel Ser.). 2005. audio compact disk 14.95 (978-0-06-081504-2(3)) HarperCollins Pubs.

Fallen Man. unabr. ed. Tony Hillerman. Read by Jonathan Marosz. 7 cass. (Running Time: 7 hrs.). (Joe Leaphorn & Jim Chee Novel Ser.). 1997. 56.00 (978-0-913369-37-1(3), 4211) Books on Tape.
When hikers find a human skeleton on top of Ship Rock, a mountain sacred to Navajos, a 10 year-old missing person's case re-opens. Joe Leaphorn ends his retirement to take the case with Jim Chee. They set off across the high desert to mine clues from those who had known the "fallen man." What they find is a picture of a man who had everything & wasn't satisfied. His killers weren't either, for they begin murdering anew.

Fallen Man. unabr. ed. Tony Hillerman. Narrated by George Guidall. 6 cass. (Running Time: 7 hrs. 30 mins.). (Joe Leaphorn & Jim Chee Novel Ser.). 1997. 51.00 (978-0-7887-0907-4(0), 94961E7) Recorded Bks.
When a human skeleton is discovered on sacred Navajo land, the publicity surrounding the find sets off a vicious murder & widespread suspicion. After a Washington group hires Leaphorn to investigate "the fallen man," he joins Chee in unraveling the deadly intrigue.

Fallen Skies. unabr. ed. Philippa Gregory. Read by Marie McCarthy. 15 CDs. (Running Time: 17 hrs. 56 min.). (Isis Ser.). (J). 2003. audio compact disk 104.95 (978-0-7531-2225-9(1)) Pub: ISIS Lrg Prnt GBR. Dist(s): Ulverscroft US
Lily Valence wants to forget the war. She's determined to enjoy the 1920s. When she meets Captain Stephen Winters, she's drawn to his wealth and status. He sees in Lily his salvation from the past. But Lily has no intention of leaving her singing career. Stephen's nightmares merge even closer with reality and the truth of what took place in the mud and darkness brings him, and all who love him, to a terrible reckoning.

Fallen Skies. unabr. ed. Philippa Gregory & Marie McCarthy. 14 cass. (Running Time: 18 hrs.). (Isis Ser.). (J). 2002. 99.95 (978-0-7531-0925-0(5)) Pub: ISIS Lrg Prnt GBR. Dist(s): Ulverscroft US

Fallen Timbers. Donald Clayton Porter. Read by Lloyd James. 4 vols. No. 19. 2004. 25.00 (978-1-58807-235-1(5)); (978-1-58807-766-0(7)) Am Pubng Inc.

Fallen Tower of Siloam see Robert Graves Reads from His Poetry & the White Goddess

Fallibility of Teachers. unabr. ed. Sam Keen. 1 cass. (Running Time: 54 min.). 1973. 11.00 (05703) Big Sur Tapes.
As part of a conference on spiritual & therapeutic tyranny, Keen gives a pointed analysis of the ways in which power is misused by those who should know better.

Falling see James Dickey Reads His Poetry & Prose

Falling. E. J. Howard. 6 cass. (Running Time: 9 hrs.). 2001. (978-0-333-78007-7(8)) Macmillan UK GBR.

***Falling.** Created by Uncommon Sensing LLC. (ENG.). 1999. audio compact disk 60.00 (978-0-9826724-1-9(1)) Uncommon Sens.

Falling. abr. ed. Christopher Pike, pseud. Read by William Dufris. (Running Time: 21600 sec.). 2008. audio compact disk 14.99 (978-1-4233-3284-8(9), 9781423332848, BCD Value Price) Brilliance Audio.

Falling. unabr. ed. Elizabeth Jane Howard. Read by Diana Quick & Bates Alan. 12 cass. (Running Time: 45900 sec.). 2000. 96.95 (978-0-7540-0495-0(3), CAB1918) AudioGO.
Henry Kent is in late middle age, is almost without means & lives on a dank houseboat. He is not without charm, though. When Daily Langrish buys a cottage not far from where he moors his boat, Henry becomes interested in tending Daisy's garden, her daughter becomes suspicious; there's something not quite right about Henry.

Falling. unabr. ed. Elizabeth Jane Howard. Read by Alan Bates & Diana Quick. 12 CDs. (Running Time: 45900 sec.). 2000. 110.95 (978-0-7540-5381-1(4), CCD072) AudioGO.

Falling. unabr. ed. Christopher Pike, pseud. Read by William Dufris. (Running Time: 14 hrs.). 2007. 39.25 (978-1-4233-3282-4(2), 9781423332824, BADLE); 24.95 (978-1-4233-3281-7(4), 9781423332817, BAD); 92.25 (978-1-4233-3276-3(8), 9781423332763, BrilAudUnabridg); audio compact disk 112.25 (978-1-4233-3278-7(4), 9781423332787, BriAudCD Unabrid); audio compact disk 39.25 (978-1-4233-3280-0(6), 9781423332800, Brinc Audio MP3 Lib); audio compact disk 24.95 (978-1-4233-3279-4(2), 9781423332794, Brilliance MP3); audio compact disk 38.95 (978-1-4233-3277-0(6), 9781423332770, Bril Audio CD Unabri) Brilliance Audio.

Falling. unabr. ed. Colin Thubron. Read by Ian Craig. 5 cass. (Running Time: 5 hrs. 19 min.). 1993. 49.95 (978-1-85695-410-5(2), 92063) Pub: ISIS Audio GBR. Dist(s): Ulverscroft US
From the crowd below, a journalist watches as a circus-girl performs her strangely daring trapeze act, & is so captivated by her beauty, outrageous costumes & exotic make-up that he finds himself falling hopelessly in love with her.

Falling Angels. Tracy Chevalier. 6 cass. (Running Time: 8 hrs. 45 mins.). 69.00 (978-0-7887-9958-7(4)) Recorded Bks.

Falling Angels. unabr. ed. Tracy Chevalier. Read by Anne Twomey. (YA). 2007. 49.99 (978-1-60252-556-6(0)) Find a World.

Falling Angels. unabr. abr. ed. Tracy Chevalier. Read by Anne Twomey. 6 CDs. (Running Time: 7 hrs. 45 mins.). (ENG.). 2001. audio compact disk 36.95 (978-1-56511-508-8(2), 1565115082) Pub: HighBridge. Dist(s): Workman Pub

***Falling Apart in One Piece: One Optimist's Journey Through the Hell of Divorce.** unabr. ed. Stacy Morrison. (Running Time: 8 hrs. 30 mins.). 2010. 15.99 (978-1-4001-8552-8(1)); 19.99 (978-1-4001-6552-0(0)); audio compact disk 59.99 (978-1-4001-4552-2(X)); audio compact disk 29.99 (978-1-4001-1552-5(3)) Pub: Tantor Media. Dist(s): IngramPubServ

Falling Asleep over the Aeneid from "The Mills of the Kavanaughs" see Twentieth-Century Poetry in English, No. 32-33, Recordings of Poets Reading Their Own Poetry

Falling Awake. abr. ed. Jayne Ann Krentz. Read by Laural Merlington. (Running Time: 21600 sec.). 2004. audio compact disk 16.99 (978-1-59600-428-3(2), 9781596004283, BCD Value Price) Brilliance Audio.
A red scarf. A roller coaster. A tidal wave of blood. Isabel Wright spends her days at the Belvedere Center for Sleep Research analyzing the dreams of others. Dr. Martin Belvedere, a pioneer in the field, recognized her unique talent for what he calls Level Five lucid dreaming - and rescued her from a dead-end job at the psychic dreamer hotline. It's satisfying, lucrative work, but it can be emotionally draining at times. Especially when one of her anonymous subjects, known only as Client Number Two, captures her imagination through his compelling dream narratives. Secretly, she thinks of him as "dream man." Client Number Two's real name is Ellis Cutler. A loner who learned long ago not to let anyone get too close, he works for a highly classified government agency with an interest in the potential value of lucid dreaming. And he has just been ordered by his boss to make contact with Isabel, who's been fired after the sudden death of Dr. Belvedere. Heading to California, he pushes his own fantasies out of his mind, determined to maintain a professional relationship with the woman who reads his dreams, the mysterious figure he has come to think of as "Tango Dancer." But when they meet in the flesh, the dream becomes real enough to touch. And a waking nightmare begins - when a suspicious hit-and-run leads them into a perilous web of passion, betrayal and murder, and forces them to walk the razor-thin line between dreams and reality. . . .

Falling Awake. abr. ed. Jayne Ann Krentz. Read by Laural Merlington. (Running Time: 6 hrs.). 2009. audio compact disk 9.99 (978-1-4418-0822-6(1), 9781441808226, BCD Value Price) Brilliance Audio.

Falling Awake. unabr. ed. Jayne Ann Krentz. Read by Laural Merlington. (Running Time: 10 hrs.). 2004. 39.25 (978-1-59710-274-2(1), 1597102741, BADLE); 24.95 (978-1-59710-275-9(X), 159710275X, BAD); 39.25 (978-1-59335-837-2(7), 1593358377, Brinc Audio MP3 Lib); 24.95 (978-1-59335-703-0(6), 1593357036, Brilliance MP3); 32.95 (978-1-59355-150-6(9), 1593551509); 82.25 (978-1-59355-151-3(7), 1593551517, BAudLibEd); audio compact disk 36.95 (978-1-59355-153-7(3), 1593551533); audio compact disk 97.25 (978-1-59355-154-4(1), 1593551541, BACDLib Ed) Brilliance Audio.

***Falling Away.** unabr. ed. T. L. Hines. (ENG.). Narrated by Steve Cooper. (Running Time: 8 hrs. 22 mins. 51 sec.). (ENG.). 2010. 19.59 (978-1-60814-750-2(9)); audio compact disk 27.99 (978-1-59859-799-8(X)) Oasis Audio.

Falling Bodies. Andrew Mark. 2004. 14.95 (978-0-7435-4695-9(4)) Pub: S&S Audio. Dist(s): S and S Inc

Falling Bodies. unabr. collector's ed. Sue Kaufman. Read by Nancy Dannevik. 8 cass. (Running Time: 12 hrs.). 1981. 64.00 (978-0-7366-0278-5(X), 1268) Books on Tape.
After 14 years of marriage, Emma Sohier discovers some of her husband's decidedly irrational habits, & finds her son picking through New York City garbage pails.

Falling Bodies, Set. abr. ed. Andrew Mark. Read by Dylan Baker. 4 cass. 1999. 24.00 (FS9-43404) Highsmith.

Falling for a Dancer, Set. unabr. ed. Deirdre Purcell. Read by Maureen O'Brien. 16 cass. 1999. 124.95 (978-0-7540-0354-0(X), CAB1777) AudioGO.
Seduced by the raffish charm of George Gallagher, yet bound by the restrictions of pre-war Ireland, Elizabeth Sullivan is forced to marry another man. Trapped with him in the remote Beara peninsula, it is not long before her sexuality catapults her towards catastrophe & paradoxically freedom.

***Falling for Gracie.** unabr. ed. Susan Mallery. Read by Savannah Richards. (Running Time: 10 hrs.). 2010. 19.99 (978-1-4418-7608-9(1), 9781441876089, Brilliance MP3); 39.97 (978-1-4418-7609-6(X), 9781441876096, Brinc Audio MP3 Lib); 39.97 (978-1-4418-7610-2(3), 9781441876102, BADLE); audio compact disk 19.99 (978-1-4418-7606-5(5), 9781441876065, Bril Audio CD Unabri); audio compact disk 79.97 (978-1-4418-7607-2(3), 9781441876072, BriAudCD Unabrid) Brilliance Audio.

***Falling for Him.** Debbie Macomber. 2011. audio compact disk 9.99 (978-1-4418-5340-0(5)) Brilliance Audio.

***Falling for Him.** unabr. ed. Debbie Macomber. Read by Dan John Miller. (Running Time: 5 hrs.). 2010. 14.99 (978-1-4418-5338-7(3), 9781441853387, Brilliance MP3); 14.99 (978-1-4418-5339-4(1), 9781441853394, BAD); audio compact disk 14.99 (978-1-4418-5337-0(5), 9781441853370, Bril Audio CD Unabri) Brilliance Audio.

***Falling for Him; Ending in Marriage.** Debbie Macomber. Contrib. by Dan John Miller. (Midnight Sons Ser.: Vol. 3). 2010. 69.99 (978-1-4418-3763-9(9)) Find a World.

Falling for Him; Ending in Marriage; Midnight Sons & Daughters. unabr. ed. Debbie Macomber. Read by Dan John Miller. (Running Time: 12 hrs.). 2010. 24.99 (978-1-4418-1916-1(9), 9781441819161, Brilliance MP3); 24.99 (978-1-4418-1918-5(5), 9781441819185, BAD); audio compact disk 29.99 (978-1-4418-1914-7(2), 9781441819147, Bril Audio CD Unabri) Brilliance Audio.

Falling for Him; Ending in Marriage; Midnight Sons & Daughters. unabr. ed. Debbie Macomber. Read by Dan John Miller. (Running Time: 12 hrs.). (Midnight Sons Ser.: Vol. 3). 2010. 39.97 (978-1-4418-1919-2(3), 9781441819192, BADLE) Brilliance Audio.

Falling for Him; Ending in Marriage; Midnight Sons & Daughters, Vol. 3. unabr. ed. Debbie Macomber. Read by Dan John Miller. (Running Time: 12 hrs.). 2010. 39.97 (978-1-4418-1917-8(7), 9781441819178, Brinc Audio MP3 Lib); audio compact disk 97.97 (978-1-4418-1915-4(0), 9781441819154, BriAudCD Unabrid) Brilliance Audio.

Falling for You Again. unabr. ed. Gary Chapman. Narrated by Jill Shellabarger. (Seasons of Marriage Ser.). (ENG.). 2007. 17.49 (978-1-60814-196-8(9)) Oasis Audio.

Falling for You Again. unabr. ed. Gary Chapman & Catherine Palmer. Narrated by Jill Shellabarger. (Running Time: 36000 sec.). (Four Seasons Ser.). (ENG.). 2007. audio compact disk 24.99 (978-1-59859-283-2(1)) Oasis Audio.

***Falling Free.** unabr. ed. Lois McMaster Bujold. Read by Grover Gardner. (Running Time: 9 hrs. 0 mins.). 2010. 29.95 (978-1-4332-5087-3(X)); 59.95 (978-1-4332-5084-2(5)); audio compact disk 76.00 (978-1-4332-5085-9(3)) Blckstn Audio.

Falling Free. unabr. ed. Lois McMaster Bujold. 1 CD (MP3). (Running Time: 9 hrs.). (Vorkosigan Ser.). 1999. audio compact disk 24.95 (978-1-885585-17-2(9)) Readers Chair.

Falling Free. unabr. ed. Lois McMaster Bujold. Perf. by Michael Hanson & Carol Cowan. 7 cass. (Running Time: 9 hrs. 9 min.). (Vorkosigan Ser.). 1996. 42.00 Set. (978-0-9624010-9-1(9)) Readers Chair.
Engineering teacher Leo Graf is sent by his company to train a new breed of genetically manipulated space workers. What Leo encounters is a situation that forces him to examine the very meaning of freedom...for himself & for them.

Falling from Heaven: Holocaust Poems of a Jew & a Gentile. Louis Daniel Brodsky & William Heyen. 1991. pap. bk. 19.95 (978-1-877770-19-7(1)) Time Being Bks.

***Falling Glass.** unabr. ed. Adrian McKinty. Read by Gerard Doyle. (Running Time: 11 hrs. 5 mins.). (ENG.). 2011. 29.95 (978-1-4417-6969-5(2)); 72.95 (978-1-4417-6966-4(8)); audio compact disk 29.95 (978-1-4417-6968-8(4)); audio compact disk 105.00 (978-1-4417-6967-1(6)) Blckstn Audio.

***Falling Home.** Karen White. Read by Lyssa Browne. 2010. audio compact disk 29.95 (978-1-59316-565-9(X)) Listen & Live.

Falling in Love. Symphony Space Staff. (Selected Shorts Ser.). (ENG.). 2007. audio compact disk 28.00 (978-0-9719218-8-7(1)) Pub: Symphony Space. Dist(s): IPG Chicago

***Falling in Love: Audio CD.** Jeff Cooper. (Running Time: 78). (ENG.). 2010. 21.95 (978-0-9828811-2-5(6)) Jeff Cooper.

Falling in Love Again. Cathy Maxwell. Narrated by Vanessa Maroney. 8 cass. (Running Time: 10 hrs. 45 mins.). 72.00 (978-0-7887-9501-5(5)) Recorded Bks.

Falling in Love/Creating an Olympic Spirit. Marianne Williamson. Read by Marianne Williamson. 1 cass. (Running Time: 90 mins.). (Lectures on a Course in Miracles). 1999. 10.00 (978-1-56170-190-2(4), M718) Hay House.

Falling off Air. Catherine Sampson. Ed. by Kate Reading. 7 cass. (Running Time: 9 hrs.). 2004. 49.95 (978-0-7861-2824-2(0), 3307); audio compact disk 64.00 (978-0-7861-8439-2(6), 3307) Blckstn Audio.

Falling off Air. Catherine Simpson. Read by Kate Reading. (Running Time: 9 hrs.). 2004. 30.95 (978-1-59912-486-5(6)) Iofy Corp.

Falling off Air. unabr. ed. Catherine Sampson. 13 pieces. (Running Time: 9 hrs.). 2005. audio compact disk 24.95 (978-0-7861-8512-2(0), 3307); audio compact disk 39.95 (978-0-7861-8577-1(5), ZE3307); reel tape 32.95 (978-0-7861-2738-2(4), E3307) Blckstn Audio.
Robin Ballantyne's life is finally coming together. After learning she was pregnant with twins and being abandoned by her irresponsible boyfriend, Adam, she's settling into life as a singl mother. But one night, after putting the children to bed, she hears an argument and, suddenly, a body falls past her window. Running outside, she finds the body of Paula Carmichael, a renowned activist. When the police find Robin's name in Paula's diary and a connection through ex-boyfriend Adam, Robin becomes the prime suspect. She must figure out who killed Paula before she loses her freedom, her children, and her life.

Falling off the Map: Some Lonely Places of the World. unabr. collector's ed. Pico Iyer. Read by David Case. 7 cass. (Running Time: 7 hrs.). 1994. 42.00 (978-0-7366-2723-8(5), 3453) Books on Tape.
Showing the same sympathy & eye for the absurd that made his "Video Night in Kathmandu" such a delight, Pico Iyer now turns to places that most of us would make a point of avoiding. Places like Paraguay, Iceland, North Korea, Cuba, Vietnam & Bhutan.

Falling Stars. unabr. ed. V. C. Andrews. 9 cass. (Isis Ser.). (J). 2003. 76.95 (978-0-7531-1605-0(7)) Pub: ISIS Lrg Prnt GBR. Dist(s): Ulverscroft US

Falling Stars. unabr. ed. Read by Laurel Lefkow. 9 CDs. (Running Time: 36300 sec.). (Isis Ser.). 2003. audio compact disk 84.95 (978-0-7531-1728-6(2)) Pub: ISIS Lrg Prnt GBR. Dist(s): Ulverscroft US

Falling Tears, Awakening Heavens see Twentieth-Century Poetry in English, No. 10, Recordings of Poets Reading Their Own Poetry

***Falling While Running A Collection of Monologues.** Mia Alexander-Davis. Mia Alexander-Davis. (Running Time: 140). (ENG.). (C). 2009. audio compact disk 10.00 (978-0-615-34599-4(9)) Mia Alexander.

Fallout. James W. Huston. Read by Adams Morgan. 12 CDs. (Running Time: 14 hrs. 30 mins.). 2003. audio compact disk 96.00 (978-0-7861-9722-4(6), 2779) Blckstn Audio.

Fallout. James W. Huston. Read by Adams Morgan. 2001. 33.95 (978-1-59912-487-2(4)) Iofy Corp.

Fallout. unabr. ed. James W. Huston. Narrated by Adams Morgan. 12 CDs. (Running Time: 18 hrs.). 2001. audio compact disk 96.00 Blckstn Audio.
TOPGUN instructor Luke Henry quits the Navy to start a private aerial combat school in Nevada. A lucrative contract with the U.S. government brings him twenty Russian MiG-29 fighter planes with the condition that he train a group of Pakistani Air Force Pilots hand-picked by the Department of Defense. Luke is hesitant to train fighters from another country in the skills he learned at TOPGUN, but he cannot open the school without agreeing.

Fallout. unabr. ed. James W. Huston. Read by Adams Morgan. 10 cass. (Running Time: 14 hrs. 30 mins.). 2001. 69.95 (978-0-7861-2011-6(8), 2779); audio compact disk 24.95 (978-0-7861-9570-1(3), 2779) Blckstn Audio.

Fallout. unabr. ed. James W. Huston. Read by Adams Morgan. 10 pieces. 2004. reel tape 39.95 (978-0-7861-2227-1(7)) Blckstn Audio.

***Fallout.** unabr. ed. James W. Huston. Read by Adams Morgan. (Running Time: 13 hrs.). 2010. audio compact disk 29.95 (978-1-4417-3568-3(2)) Blckstn Audio.

Falls. unabr. ed. Read by Anna Fields. 11 cass. 89.95 (978-0-7927-3295-2(2)); audio compact disk 117.95 (978-0-7927-3296-9(0)) AudioGO.

Falls. unabr. ed. Joyce Carol Oates. Read by Anna Fields. 10 CDs. (Running Time: 15 hrs.). 2004. audio compact disk 39.95 (978-0-06-074188-4(0)) HarperCollins Pubs.

***Falls.** unabr. ed. Joyce Carol Oates. Read by Anna Fields. 2004. (978-0-06-081488-5(8), Harper Audio); (978-0-06-078656-4(6), Harper Audio) HarperCollins Pubs.

Falls: An Inspector Rebus Novel. Ian Rankin. Narrated by Samuel Gillies. 12 cass. (Running Time: 16 hrs.). 102.00 (978-1-84197-277-0(0)) Recorded Bks.

Falls: An Inspector Rebus Novel. unabr. ed. Ian Rankin. 2 vols. (Running Time: 2 hrs.). Dramatization. 2003. audio compact disk 29.95 (978-0-563-49678-6(9)) BBC Worldwide.

Falls in the Elderly. Kathy Shaw. 1 cass. (Running Time: 60 min.). 1997. bk. 20.00 (978-1-58111-003-6(0)) Contemporary Medical.
General information regarding occurrences of falls in the elderly population. Discusses risk factors & environmental hazards contributing to falls.

***Falls the Shadow.** abr. ed. William Lashner. Read by Don Leslie. (ENG.). 2005. (978-0-06-084559-7(7), Harper Audio); (978-0-06-084558-2(9), Harper Audio) HarperCollins Pubs.

Falls the Shadow. unabr. ed. William Lashner. Read by Jason Collins. 2 pieces. 2005. 49.95 (978-0-7927-3656-1(7), CMP 808); 79.95 (978-0-7927-3654-7(0), CSL 808); audio compact disk 110.95 (978-0-7927-3655-4(9), SLD 808) AudioGO.

False Accusations. abr. ed. Alan Jacobson. Read by Zeljko Ivanek. 4 cass. 1999. 23.00 (FS9-43373) Highsmith.

False Accusations. abr. ed. Alan Jacobson. 2004. 13.95 (978-0-7435-4699-7(7)) Pub: S&S Audio. Dist(s): S and S Inc

False Allegations. unabr. ed. Andrew Vachss. Read by Phil Gigante. (Running Time: 8 hrs.). (Burke Ser.). 2010. audio compact disk 79.97 (978-1-4418-2140-9(6), 9781441821409, BriAudCD Unabrid); audio compact disk 29.99 (978-1-4418-2139-3(2), 9781441821393, Bril Audio CD Unabri) Brilliance Audio.

***False Allegations.** unabr. ed. Andrew Vachss. Read by Phil Gigante. (Running Time: 8 hrs.). (Burke Ser.). 2010. 24.99 (978-1-4418-2141-6(4), 9781441821416, Brilliance MP3); 39.97 (978-1-4418-2144-7(9), 9781441821447, BADLE); 24.99 (978-1-4418-2143-0(0), 9781441821430, BAD); 39.97 (978-1-4418-2142-3(2), 9781441821423, Brinc Audio MP3 Lib) Brilliance Audio.

False Apparitions. Narrated by William Biersach & Charles A. Coulombe. 3 cass. (Running Time: 3 hrs. 30 mins.). 2000. 21.00 (20146) Cath Treas.
The first talk presents a general overview with instruction on how to discern genuine apparitions from the false. The second talk focuses specifically on the popular & alarmingly heretical spiritual smorgasbord known as The Kingdom of the Divine Will. A must if you have friends who chase apparitions.

False Colours. Judith Saxton. Read by Anne Cater. 4 cass. (Sound Ser.). (J). 2003. 44.95 (978-1-84283-223-3(9)) Pub: ISIS Lrg Prnt GBR. Dist(s): Ulverscroft US

False Dawn. unabr. ed. Edith Wharton. Read by Derek Jacobi. 2 cass. (Running Time: 2 hrs. 15 mins.). (gr. 9-12). 2000. 17.95 (978-1-57270-180-9(3), F21180u) Pub: Audio Partners. Dist(s): PerseuPGW
In the 1840's, Lewis Raycie's domineering father sends him to Europe to buy art. When he selects Italian primitives, not yet recognized as masterpieces, his appalled father disinherits him, only to discover, too late, the wisdom of his son's intuition.

***False Face.** Ernest Haycox. 2009. (978-1-60136-437-1(7)) Audio Holding.

False Face. Ernest Haycox. (Running Time: 0 hr. 36 mins.). 2000. 10.95 (978-1-60083-536-0(8)) Iofy Corp.

***False Friend.** unabr. ed. Myla Goldberg. Read by Myla Goldberg. (Running Time: 6 hrs. 30 mins.). 2010. audio compact disk 35.00 (978-0-307-75128-7(7), Random AudioBks) Pub: Random Audio Pubg. Dist(s): Random

False Gods, Real Men see Berrigan Raps

False Impression. Jeffrey Archer. 2006. 26.95 (978-1-59397-851-8(0)) Pub: Macmill Audio. Dist(s): Macmillan

False Impression. abr. ed. Jeffrey Archer. 2006. 17.95 (978-1-59397-850-1(2)) Pub: Macmill Audio. Dist(s): Macmillan

False Impression. abr. ed. Jeffrey Archer. Read by Byron Jennings. 5 CDs. (Running Time: 6 hrs. 0 mins. 0 sec.). 2006. audio compact disk 29.95 (978-1-59397-848-8(0)) Pub: Macmill Audio. Dist(s): Macmillan

***False Impression.** abr. ed. Jeffrey Archer. Read by Byron Jennings. (Running Time: 6 hrs. 0 mins. 0 sec.). (ENG.). 2011. audio compact disk 14.99 (978-1-4272-1193-4(0)) Pub: Macmill Audio. Dist(s): Macmillan

False Impression. unabr. ed. Jeffrey Archer. 1 MP3-CD. (Running Time: 8 hrs. 30 mins.). 2006. 29.95 (978-0-7927-3965-4(5), Chivers Sound Lib); 59.95 (978-0-7927-3904-3(3), Chivers Sound Lib); audio compact disk 94.95 (978-0-7927-3905-0(1), Chivers Sound Lib) AudioGO.

False Impression. unabr. ed. Jeffrey Archer. Read by Byron Jennings. 10 CDs. (Running Time: 11 hrs. 0 mins. 0 sec.). 2006. audio compact disk 44.95 (978-1-59397-849-5(9)) Pub: Macmill Audio. Dist(s): Macmillan

False Jewels see Great French & Russian Stories, Vol. 1, A Collection

False Jewels see Favorite Stories by Guy de Maupassant

False Memory. Dean Koontz. Read by Stephen Lang. 2000. 96.00 (978-0-7366-4834-9(8)) Books on Tape.

False Memory. unabr. ed. Dean Koontz. Read by Stephen Lang. 12 cass. (Running Time: 18 hrs.). 2000. 35.95 (5180) Books on Tape.
Four patients of the same therapist develop crippling fears, revealing the terrifying ability of the mind to torment & destroy.

False Memory. unabr. ed. Dean Koontz. Read by Stephen Lang. (Running Time: 77400 sec.). (Dean Koontz Ser.). (ENG.). 2007. audio compact disk 39.95 (978-0-7393-4146-9(4), Random AudioBks) Pub: Random Audio Pubg. Dist(s): Random

False Pretences. unabr. ed. Margaret Yorke. Read by Maureen O'Brien. 8 CDs. (Running Time: 12 hrs.). 2002. audio compact disk 79.95 (978-0-7540-5467-2(5), CCD 158) AudioGO.
When her goddaughter is arrested, Isabel Vernon is startled to discover that the child of her memory has become an overweight, shaven-headed environmentalist and that Isabel herself is now regarded as Emily Frost's next of kin. Emily is then released on bail to the Vernons in the village of Fordswick. But her presence in the Vernons' house proves troubling, and is deepening the tensions already within it.

False Pretences, Set. unabr. ed. Margaret Yorke. Read by Maureen O'Brien. 8 cass. (Running Time: 540 min.). 1999. 69.95 (978-0-7540-0304-5(3), CAB 1727) AudioGO.

False Pretenses. unabr. ed. Catherine Coulter. Read by Nicola Amos. 10 vols. (Running Time: 15 hrs.). 2000. bk. 84.95 (978-0-7927-2359-2(7), CSL 248, Chivers Sound Lib) AudioGO.
Elizabeth Carleton, a beautiful & dazzling concert pianist, is accused of her wealthy husband's murder. Not even a surprise acquittal in a cliffhanger trial can quiet the whispers of her guilt. Now three attractive men appear out of her past, offering to help & protect her. But whom can she trust when she alone knows that the real killer may now be stalking her.

False Pretenses. unabr. ed. Catherine Coulter. Read by Nicola Amos. 10 CDs. (Running Time: 15 hrs.). 2001. audio compact disk 94.95 (978-0-7927-9911-5(9), SLD 062, Chivers Sound Lib) AudioGO.

***False Princess.** unabr. ed. Eilis O'Neal. (ENG.). (J). 2011. audio compact disk 44.00 (978-0-307-87953-0(4), Listening Lib) Pub: Random Audio Pubg. Dist(s): Random

False Prophets of Our Day, I. Dan Corner. 1 cass. 3.00 (31) Evang Outreach.

False Prophets of Our Day, II. Dan Corner. 1 cass. 3.00 (32) Evang Outreach.

False Scent. unabr. ed. Ngaio Marsh. Read by James Saxon. 5 cass. (Running Time: 7 hrs. 20 mins.). 2001. 27.95 (978-1-57270-164-9(1), N51164u) Pub: Audio Partners. Dist(s): PerseuPGW
The festive event was her birthday party & aging actress Mary Bellamy reveled in the adoration of her family, friends & fans. That is, right up until one of them murdered her with a puff of deadly "perfume." When Inspector Roderick Alleyn arrives, he finds an entire collection of despicably fawning family & guests to sort through.

False Scent. unabr. ed. Ngaio Marsh. Read by James Saxon. 8 cass. (Running Time: 12 hrs.). (Inspector Alleyn Mystery Ser.). 2000. 59.95 (978-0-7451-6609-4(1), CAB 1225) Pub: Chivers Audio Bks GBR. Dist(s): AudioGO
Mary Bellamy, darling of the London stage, holds a 50th birthday party: a gala assembling everyone who loves her and fears her power. Then someone uses a deadly insect spray on Mary instead of the azaleas. As the suspects are all theatrically playing the part of mourners, Superintendent Alleyn must find out which one has played the part of murderer.

False Sense of Well Being. Jeanne Braselton. Narrated by Julia Gibson. 7 cass. (Running Time: 10 hrs. 15 mins.). 68.00 (978-0-7887-9645-6(3)) Recorded Bks.

False Testimony. Rose Connors. Read by Bernadette Dunne. (Running Time: 8 hrs.). 2005. reel tape 54.95 (978-0-7861-3526-4(3)) Blckstn Audio.

False Testimony. Rose Connors. Read by Bernadette Dunne. (Running Time: 36000 sec.). (Marty Nickerson Novels Ser.). 2005. audio compact disk 63.00 (978-0-7861-7825-4(6)); audio compact disk 29.95 (978-0-7861-8017-2(X)) Blckstn Audio.

False Witness. Patricia Hall. Read by Michael Tudor Barnes. 7 cass. 2009. 61.95 (978-1-84559-180-9(1)) Pub: Soundings Ltd GBR. Dist(s): Ulverscroft US

False Witness. abr. ed. Randy D. Singer. Narrated by Adam Verner. (ENG.). 2007. 17.49 (978-1-60814-197-5(7)); audio compact disk 24.99 (978-1-59859-226-9(2)) Oasis Audio.

Falsehood Is Prophetic. Neville Goddard. 1 cass. (Running Time: 62 min.). 1965. 8.00 (67) J & L Pubns.
Neville taught Imagination Creates Reality. He was a powerfully influential teacher of God as Consciousness.

Falsely Accused. Prod. by Laraim Associates. (Barclay Family Adventure Ser.). (J). 2005. audio compact disk (978-1-56254-990-9(1)) Saddleback Edu.

Falsely Accused. unabr. ed. Robert K. Tanenbaum. Read by Connor O'Brien. 7 cass. (Running Time: 10 hrs. 30 min.). (Butch Karp Mystery Ser.). 1998. 56.00 (978-0-7366-4026-8(6), 452511.95) Books on Tape.
Two terrified children from Central America refuse to divulge a secret. The murders of Guatemalan cab drivers by crooked cops go uninvestigated. Investigative reporter Ariadne Stupenagel is brutally beaten. Butch Karp & Marlene Ciampi delve into the mysteries & leave no one immune from suspicion.

Fame. abr. ed. Karen Kingsbury. Read by Sandra Burr. (Running Time: 4 hrs.). (Firstborn Ser.). 2005. 39.25 (978-1-59737-956-4(5), 9781597379564, BADLE); 9.99 (978-1-59737-955-7(7), 9781597379557, BAD); 19.95 (978-1-59600-193-0(3), 9781596001930); 49.25 (978-1-59600-194-7(1), 9781596001947, BAudLibEd); audio compact disk 21.95 (978-1-59600-195-4(X), 9781596001954, BACD); audio compact disk 69.25 (978-1-59600-196-1(8), 9781596001961, BACDLib Ed); audio compact disk 39.25 (978-1-59737-954-0(9), 9781597379540, Brilnc Audio MP3 Lib); audio compact disk 9.99 (978-1-59737-953-3(0), 9781597379533, Brilliance MP3) Brilliance Audio.
Karen Kingsbury brings listeners a new series that picks up where the Redemption series left off. The Firstborn series focuses on the surprise new member of the Baxter family: Dayne Matthews. As Dayne Matthews returns to Hollywood after his shocking discovery in Karen Kingsbury's bestselling novel Reunion, he faces the dangerous world of fame and paparazzi. Meanwhile, Katy Hart receives the offer of a lifetime - starring opposite Dayne in a Hollywood film. Dayne and Katy's choices will change their hearts and lives forever.

***Fame.** abr. ed. Karen Kingsbury. Read by Sandra Burr. (Running Time: 4 hrs.). (Firstborn Ser.). 2010. audio compact disk 9.99 (978-1-4418-7823-6(8), 9781441878236, BCD Value Price) Brilliance Audio.

Fame: Program from the Award Winning Public Radio Series. Hosted by Peter Kramer. Comment by John Hockenberry. 1 CD. (Running Time: 1 Hour). 2004. audio compact disk 21.99 (978-1-932479-46-1(5), LCM 319) Lichtenstein Creat.
Where does it come from, this burning need to be known? Guest host Dr. Peter Kramer, filling in for Dr. Fred Goodwin, speaks with those chasing fame, those who have achieved celebrity, and scientists who study it. They include: Howard Bloom, a Visiting Scholar at New York University, founder of the International Paleopsychology Project, and the author of "Global Brain: the Evolution of Mass Mind from the Big Bang to the 21st Century." Bloom has been called "the next Stephen Hawking" by Gear Magazine and "the Darwin, Einstein, Isaac Newton, and Sigmund Freud of the 21st Century" by Britain's Channel4 TV. His work with performers from Paul Simon to Kiss to The Talking Heads is part of his "20-year-long urban anthropology expedition to penetrate society's myth-making machinery, the inner sanctums of politics and the media." Simon Cowell the creator and unabashedly cynical judge on TV's mega-talent show, American Idol discusses the desire for fame, and developmental and psychological factors that he believes lead people to chase stardom; Sam Solovey, a contestant on the reality television series, The Apprentice, in which young people compete for a job with Donald Trump . . . and fame. Solovey was "fired" by Donald Trump for sleeping on the job, and says he wasn't interested in fame before he appeared on the show, but now he "craves it." comedian Lily Tomlin talks about fame, what it is . . . and isn't, and how she first found celebrity; singer songwriter Teddy Thompson, the son of folk rock duo Linda and Richard Thompson, talks about his search for celebrity and performs a song about the yearning for the spotlight; and psychologist Dr. Gene Ondrusek, who helped chose the first round of contestants on the original reality TV show, Survivor, discusses the price of fame and its addictive-like qualities.Plus, commentator John Hockenberry, with his biggest production number yet for The Infinite Mind, examines his own celebrity by way of "Biography," "Behind the Music," and "True Hollywood Story.".

Fame & Glory in Freedom, Georgia. unabr. ed. 2 cass. (Running Time: 2 hrs. 45 min.). 2004. 19.75 (978-1-4025-7049-0(X)) Recorded Bks.

Fame Island. Jonathan Lowe. Ed. by Kristoffer Tabori. 7 cass. (Running Time: 10 hrs.). 2004. 49.95 (978-0-7861-2870-9(4), 8360); audio compact disk 72.00 (978-0-7861-8346-3(2), 8360) Blckstn Audio.

Fame's Passionate Daughter. abr. ed. Helen Olian. 1 cass. (Running Time: 90 min.). (Listen to Love Ser.). 3.95 (907) Audio Bk.

Familia. Grover Bravo.Tr. of Family. (SPA.). 2009. audio compact disk 15.00 (978-1-935405-49-8(7)) Hombre Nuevo.

familia de Leon y Sus Aventuras en Mexico - the Leon Family & Their Adventures in Mexico: Read-along Bilingual Series for the Adult - Book #1. 2007. 24.95 (978-0-9793655-4-6(6)) R Language.

Familia Fuerte. 2004. audio compact disk 48.00 (978-1-57972-613-3(5)) Insight Living.

Familia Fuerte, Serie en. (SPA.). 2002. audio compact disk 45.50 (978-1-57972-477-1(9)) Insight Living.

Familia, se tu Misma. Mariano de Blas.Tr. of Family know Thyself. (SPA.). 2009. audio compact disk 25.00 (978-1-935405-16-0(0)) Hombre Nuevo.

Familia Silvestre Encuentra Hogar. Tr. of Make Way for Ducklings. (SPA.). 2004. 8.95 (978-0-7882-0252-0(9)) Weston Woods.

Familial Adenomatous Polyposis - A Bibliography & Dictionary for Physicians, Patients, & Genome Researchers. Compiled by Icon Group International, Inc. Staff. 2007. ring bd. 28.95 (978-0-497-11209-7(4)) Icon Grp.

Familial Dysautonomia - A Bibliography & Dictionary for Physicians, Patients, & Genome Researchers. Compiled by Icon Group International, Inc. Staff. 2007. ring bd. 28.95 (978-0-497-11210-3(8)) Icon Grp.

Familial Lipoprotein Lipase Deficiency - A Bibliography & Dictionary for Physicians, Patients, & Genome Researchers. Compiled by Icon Group International, Inc. Staff. 2007. ring bd. 28.95 (978-0-497-11211-0(6)) Icon Grp.

Familial Mediterranean Fever - A Bibliography & Dictionary for Physicians, Patients, & Genome Researchers. Compiled by Icon Group International, Inc. Staff. 2007. ring bd. 28.95 (978-0-497-11212-7(4)) Icon Grp.

Familiar see Classic Ghost Stories, Vol. 2, A Collection

Familiar Bird Songs of the Northwest. Contrib. by James L. Davis. 1988. 10.95 (978-0-931686-10-8(5)) Audubon Soc Portland.

Familiar Faces, Long Departed see Twentieth-Century Poetry in English, No. 25, Recordings of Poets Reading Their Own Poetry

Familiar Gregorian Chant. Ambrose Karels. 1 cass. (Running Time: 43 min.). 8.95 (AA0255) Credence Commun.
Remember when Gregorian chant was the music of your prayer? No? Then ask your parents. Chant is still beautiful, still prayerful. In this cassette the Marian antiphons are especially touching. Sung by the Kansas City-St. Joseph Diocese Men's Choir.

Familiar Passions. unabr. ed. Nina Bawden. Read by Sheila Mitchell. 6 cass. (Running Time: 9 hrs.). 1998. 49.95 (978-0-7540-0098-3(2), CAB 1521) Pub: Chivers Audio Bks GBR. Dist(s): AudioGO

Familiar Ring. Roger Terry. 3 cass. 2004. 14.95 (978-1-59156-262-7(7)); audio compact disk 15.95 (978-1-59156-263-4(5)) Covenant Comms.

Familiar Territory: Observations on American Life. unabr. ed. Joseph Epstein. Read by Michael Russotto. 8 cass. (Running Time: 8 hrs.). 1994. 48.00 (978-0-7366-2674-3(3), 3411) Books on Tape.
Fourteen essays on everyday life in the United States, by the editor of The American Scholar.

***Familiars.** unabr. ed. Adam Jay Epstein & Andrew Jacobson. Read by Lincoln Hoppe. (Familiars Ser.: Bk. 1). (ENG.). 2010. (978-0-06-199687-0(4)); (978-0-06-206370-0(7)) HarperCollins Pubs.

Families. Joanne Stover. 1 cass. 8.95 (334) Am Fed Astrologers.
Charts show how differently each member affected.

Families Are Forever: Boast or Complaint? Jack Marshall. 1 cass. 2004. 7.98 (978-1-55503-730-7(5), 069402) Covenant Comms.
Taking it one step at a time.

Families Have Rules: Early Explorers Emergent Set A Audio CD. Benchmark Education Staff. (J). 2006. audio compact disk 10.00 (978-1-4108-7593-8(8)) Benchmark Educ.

Families into Recovery. Pat McCaffrey. 2 cass. 18.00 set. (A0340-88) Sound Photosyn.
The most moving look at the problems of recovery, from CAMFTherapists Convention.

Families under Stress. Louis McBurney. 2 cass. 21.95 Self-Control Sys.
Stress arising outside of the family such as vocational demands, economic pressures, moral decay, society's erosion of traditional pattern of family & governmental involvement. Looks at stress coming from within the family unit which includes the tension created by each individual.

Famille: Level 1. H. Malo. (FRE.). bk. 14.95 (978-2-09-032978-0(5), CL9785E) Pub: Cle Intl FRA. Dist(s): Continental Bk

Family see Familia

Family. Mario Puzo & Carol Gino. Narrated by George Guidall. 10 cass. (Running Time: 14 hrs. 45 mins.). 2001. 88.00 (978-0-7887-9565-7(1), 96809) Recorded Bks.
The story of the most notorious crime families in history: the Borgias. In Puzo's hands, the story of the Borgias' affairs becomes a vivid 15th-century tapestry of pride, romance, jealousy and betrayal. The final triumph of a great storyteller.

Family. abr. ed. Karen Kingsbury. Read by Sandra Burr. (Running Time: 4 hrs.). (Firstborn Ser.). 2006. 39.25 (978-1-59737-960-1(3), 9781597379601, BADLE); 9.99 (978-1-59737-959-5(X), 9781597379595, BAD); 19.95 (978-1-59600-205-0(0), 9781596002050); audio compact disk 21.95 (978-1-59600-207-4(7), 9781596002074, BACD); 49.25 (978-1-59600-206-7(9), 9781596002067, BAudLibEd); audio compact disk 69.25 (978-1-59600-208-1(5), 9781596002081, BACDLib Ed); audio compact disk 39.25 (978-1-59737-958-8(1), 9781597379588, Brilnc Audio MP3 Lib); audio compact disk 9.99 (978-1-59737-957-1(3), 9781597379571, Brilliance MP3) Brilliance Audio.
Please enter a Synopsis.

***Family.** abr. ed. Karen Kingsbury. Read by Sandra Burr. (Running Time: 4 hrs.). (Firstborn Ser.). 2010. audio compact disk 9.99 (978-1-4418-7826-7(2), 9781441878267, BCD Value Price) Brilliance Audio.

***Family.** abr. ed. Mario Puzo. Read by Philip Bosco. (ENG.). 2004. (978-0-06-075231-6(9), Harper Audio) HarperCollins Pubs.

***Family.** abr. ed. Mario Puzo. Read by Philip Bosco. (ENG.). 2004. (978-0-06-081411-3(X), Harper Audio) HarperCollins Pubs.

Family. abr. unabr. ed. Read by Dick Cavett et al. 2008. audio compact disk 19.95 (978-0-06-164664-5(4), HarperChildAud) HarperCollins Pubs.

Family. unabr. ed. J. California Cooper. Read by J. California Cooper. Interview with Rebekah Presson. 1 cass. (Running Time: 29 min.). 1991. 10.00 (021591) New Letters.
Cooper has published three books of short stories, "Family" is her first novel. She talks about & reads a selection from the novel.

Family. unabr. ed. Laurence Houlgate. Read by Cliff Robertson. Ed. by John Lachs & Mike Hassell. 2 cass. (Running Time: 3 hrs.). Dramatization. (Morality in Our Age Ser.). 1994. 17.95 Set. (978-1-56823-023-8(0), 10502) Knowledge Prod.
For thousands of years, the family has been considered the cornerstone of civilized society. For a hundred years it has been in a crisis of changing expectations & attitudes. What really counts as family, & what obligations come with being married? Is divorce ever morally wrong? What constitutes abuse, & how will families be affected if minors can sue their parents? When parents become elderly, should they be cared for by their families or by the state?.

Family. unabr. ed. Mario Puzo. Read by Philip Bosco. 10 cass. (Running Time: 15 hrs.). 2001. Rental 13.95 (PH428); 39.95 (PH428, HarperCollinsT) Pub: HarperCollins Pubs. Dist(s): HarpCollins
Back to fifteenth-century Rome, reveals to us the extravagance and intrigue of the Vatican as surely as he once revealed the secrets of the Mafia. At the story's center is Rodrigo Borgia, Pope Alexander VI, a man whose lustful appetites were matched only by his consuming love of family. Surrounding him are his extraordinary children: simple, unloved Jofre; irascible, heartless Juan; beautiful, strong-willed Lucrezia; and passionate warrior Cesare, Machiavelli's friend and inspiration. Their stories constitute a symphony of human emotion and behavior, from pride to romance to jealousy to betrayal and murderous rage.

***Family.** unabr. ed. Mario Puzo. Read by George Guidall. (ENG.). 2004. (978-0-06-081412-0(8), Harper Audio) HarperCollins Pubs.

Family. unabr. ed. Mario Puzo & Carol Gino. Narrated by George Guidall. 12 CDs. (Running Time: 14 hrs. 45 mins.). 2001. audio compact disk 116.00 (978-1-4025-0914-8(6), C1582) Recorded Bks.
In Puzo's hands, the story of the Borgias' affairs becomes a vivid 15th century tapestry of pride, romance, jealousy, and betrayal. The final triumph of a great storyteller, The Family takes on an added power through George Guidall's narration.

Family. unabr. ed. Read by Cliff Robertson. (Running Time: 10800 sec.). (Morality in Our Age Ser.). 2006. audio compact disk 25.95 (978-0-7861-6491-2(3)) Pub: Blckstn Audio. Dist(s): NetLibrary CO

***Family.** unabr. ed. Jeff Sharlet. Read by Jeremy Guskin. (ENG.). 2009. (978-0-06-197731-2(4), Harper Audio); (978-0-06-197729-9(2), Harper Audio) HarperCollins Pubs.

Family: A Biblical & Systems View. Lou Bauer et al. 1986. 10.80 (0604) Assn Prof Chaplains.

Family: Basic Terms, Harris Winitz. Illus. by Sydney M. Baker. 2 cass. (All about Language Ser.). 1988. pap. bk. 32.00 (978-0-939990-53-5(9)) Intl Linguistics.

Family: Romans 8:15-17. Ed Young. 1984. 4.95 (978-0-7417-1377-3(2), 377) Win Walk.

Family: The Real Story of the Bush Dynasty. Kitty Kelley. 2004. audio compact disk 72.00 (978-1-4159-0326-1(3)) Books on Tape.

Family: The Real Story of the Bush Dynasty. unabr. ed. Kitty Kelley. 2004. 63.00 (978-1-4159-0325-4(5)) Books on Tape.

Family Advent Celebration. 1 cass. (978-1-55897-405-0(9), CSBK 5190 (USE CDBK 5190)) Brentwood Music.
This heartwarming collection of songs, stories, recipes, scriptures & activities will bring your family closer together as you share in the wonder of the Advent season.

Family Adventures! Children Learn to Speak & Understand Spanish with Dora & Diego. Pimsleur. (Running Time: 20 hrs. 0 mins. 0 sec.). (Speak Spanish with Dora & Diego Ser.). (ENG.). (J). 2009. audio compact disk 14.99 (978-0-7435-9978-8(0), Pimsleur) Pub: S&S Audio. Dist(s): S and S Inc

Family Affair. Perf. by Hezekiah Walker & Love Fellowship Crusade Choir. 1 cass. (Running Time: 1 hr. 14 mins.). 1999. (978-0-7601-3148-0(1)); audio compact disk (978-0-7601-3147-3(3)) Brentwood Music.
Recorded at The Hylton Memorial Chapel in Woodbridge, Virginia, exemplifies the extraordinary talents of Pastor Walker & his amazing chorale of choirs.

Family Affair. collector's ed. Rex Stout. Read by Michael Prichard. 4 cass. (Running Time: 6 hrs.). (Nero Wolfe Ser.). 2000. 32.00 (978-0-7366-5929-1(3)) Books on Tape.
Nero Wolfe's last recorded case.

Family Affair. unabr. ed. Maeve Haran. Read by Eve Matheson. 10 cass. (Running Time: 10 hrs.). 1997. 84.95 Set. (978-0-7451-6765-7(9), CAB 1381) AudioGO.
Charlotte Brandon built up Victoriana, her hugely successful clothing business in Dorset, from nothing, even though it meant putting the needs of the company before her two daughters, Connie & Lily. Connie has learned to live with her mother's disinterest, but the rebellious Lily has never accepted it. When Charlotte has a heart attack, needing her children for the first time in her life, it becomes a fight for survival not only for the family business, but also for the family itself.

***Family Affair.** unabr. ed. Debbie Macomber. (ENG.). 2011. (978-0-06-202720-7(4), Harper Audio) HarperCollins Pubs.

Family Affair. unabr. ed. Marcus Major. Read by Richard Allen. 6 cass. (Running Time: 9 hrs.). 2004. 54.95 (978-0-7927-3125-2(5), CSL 626,

Chivers Sound Lib); audio compact disk 74.95 (978-0-7927-3126-9(3), SLD 626, Chivers Sound Lib) AudioGO.

Family Affair. unabr. ed. Rex Stout. Read by Michael Prichard. (Running Time: 19980 sec.). (Nero Wolfe Ser.). 2005. 27.95 (978-1-57270-493-0(4)) Pub: Audio Partners. Dist(s): PerseuPGW
Published only a month before Rex Stout's death, this case is regarded as one of the author's truest. When Nero Wolfe's favorite waiter is murdered in an explosion just feet from him, the detective takes it as a personal affront and waives his trademark fee. As Wolfe and his sidekick Archie track down the culprit, a second murder is committed and Wolfe realizes that this case is a family affair.

Family Affair. unabr. ed. Rex Stout. Narrated by Michael Prichard. (Running Time: 19980 sec.). (Nero Wolfe Ser.). (ENG.). 2005. audio compact disk 27.95 (978-1-57270-494-7(2)) Pub: AudioGO. Dist(s): Perseus Dist

Family Affair II. Perf. by Hezekiah Walker. 2002. audio compact disk Provident Mus Dist.

Family Affairs. Sandra Kitt. Narrated by Kim Staunton. 6 cass. (Running Time: 9 hrs.). 1999. 57.00 (978-0-7887-4943-8(9), F0008L8) Recorded Bks.
Gayla owns a New York City art gallery & is happy with her life. But when she sees David Kanney, her past comes rushing back. Years ago, Gayla's mother rescued David from the streets of Harlem by taking him into her home. Gayla resented him then, but now that David has returned to her life, she may learn that this interloper is someone very special.

Family Affairs, Vol. 2. Cedering Fox. Read by Woodard Alfre. (WordTheatre Ser.). 2006. audio compact disk 9.95 (978-0-06-115422-5(9)) HarperCollins Pubs.

Family Album. 2002. 20.95 (978-1-57972-462-7(0)); audio compact disk 29.00 (978-1-57972-463-4(9)) Insight Living.

Family Album. unabr. ed. Penelope Lively. Narrated by Josephine Bailey. 1 MP3-CD. (Running Time: 8 hrs. 0 mins. 0 sec.). (ENG.). 2009. 24.99 (978-1-4001-6352-6(8)); audio compact disk 34.99 (978-1-4001-1352-1(0)); audio compact disk 69.99 (978-1-4001-4352-8(7)) Pub: Tantor Media. Dist(s): IngramPubServ

Family Album. unabr. ed. Charles R. Swindoll. 4 cass. (Running Time: 3 hrs. 45 mins.). 1998. 20.95 (978-1-57972-282-1(2)) Insight Living.

***Family Album: A Novel.** unabr. ed. Penelope Lively. Narrated by Josephine Bailey. (Running Time: 8 hrs. 0 mins.). 2009. 15.99 (978-1-4001-8352-4(9)) Tantor Media.

Family & Friends. unabr. ed. Anita Brookner. Read by Judith Whale. 6 cass. (Running Time: 6 hrs. 30 min.). 2001. 54.95 (978-1-85695-646-8(6), 931008) Pub: ISIS Audio GBR. Dist(s): Ulverscroft US

Family & Friends, Vol. 2. Tonja Evetts Weimer. Perf. by Tonja Evetts Weimer. 1 cass. (Running Time: 18 min.). (Fingerplays & Action Chants). (J). (ps-1). 1996. 8.95 (978-0-936823-03-4(8)) Pearce Evetts.
Award winning book & cassette. Features childrens folksongs, rhymes & chants about family & friends that use fingerplays & other actions to enrich the storyline. Designed for children to learn counting, story sequence & other pre-reading skills.

Family & Friends, Vol. 2. 2nd ed. Tonja Evetts Weimer. Illus. by Yvonne Kozlina. 1 cass. (Running Time: 18 min.). (Fingerplays & Action Chants). (J). (ps-1). 1995. pap. bk. 14.95 (978-0-936823-14-0(3)) Pearce Evetts.

Family & Medical Leave Act. 1993. bk. 99.00 (AC-827) PA Bar Inst.
Applies to all public & private employers who employ 50 or more employees & requires a total of 12 work weeks of unpaid leave during any 12-month period.

Family & Significant Losses. Myron Madden. 1986. 10.80 (0306) Assn Prof Chaplains.

Family Apart. Joan Lowery Nixon. Read by Barbara Caruso. 4 cass. (Running Time: 5 hrs.). (Orphan Train Adventures Ser.: Bk. 1). (YA). (gr. 5 up). 2000. pap. bk. 49.75 (978-0-7887-4331-3(7), 41126); 102.80 (978-0-7887-4432-7(1), 47123) Recorded Bks.
In 1860, life in New York City's slums is hard for Mrs. Kelly & her six children. In desperation, she sends her children west on an "orphan train" to families eager for help on their farms.

Family Apart. unabr. ed. Joan Lowery Nixon. Narrated by Barbara Caruso. 4 pieces. (Running Time: 5 hrs.). (Orphan Train Adventures Ser.: Bk. 1). (gr. 5 up). 2000. 37.00 (978-0-7887-4235-4(3), 96028E7) Recorded Bks.

Family Arrested. unabr. ed. Ann Edenfield. Read by Ann Edenfield. 4 vols. 2002. (978-1-58807-599-4(0)) Am Pubng Inc.

Family Arrested: How to Survive the Incarceration of a Loved One. unabr. abr. ed. Ann Edenfield. 3 vols. (Running Time: 4 hrs. 30 mins.). 2002. 22.00 (978-1-58807-099-9(9), 500) WngsPubng.
What do you do when a loved one is arrested? How do you make bail? What is a visit to a prison like, and what do you need to do before you can visit? What financial challenges will be encountered, and how do you overcome prison related social stigmas? This is a true story of survival, courage, and hope. Suddenly, Ann?s world came crashing down on her with the arrest of her husband and his 15-year prison sentence, leaving her to face a nightmare that no one could prepare her for. Ann discusses how to survive the prison system and shares a glimpse into this frightening and rarely discussed world. She guides the reader through stages of incarceration that anyone enduring the imprisonment of a loved one experiences. Her honesty and practical advice will benefit anyone trying to understand the confusing world of America?s prison system.This book is a must read for inmates, their spouses and family members, attorneys, employees of correctional institutions, law enforcement officials, clergy, prison chaplains, and caring people that span the globe.

Family Arsenal. unabr. ed. Paul Theroux. Read by Michael Prichard. 8 cass. (Running Time: 12 hrs.). 1986. 64.00 (978-0-7366-0925-8(3), 1868) Books on Tape.
Deptford is a seedy riverside district in London. Anonymously there lives a group that might pass for a family: Valentine Hood, ex-American consul; Mayo, a thief working with the IRA Provisionals; & two street-wise waifs - Murf, who makes bombs, & the girl Brodie, who plants them. Hood finds himself tangled up in murder & mayhem, learning that urban struggle is a family affair.

Family As a Path to Heaven. Peter Kreeft. Read by Peter Kreeft. 3 cass. 19.95 Set. (6803-C) Ignatius Pr.
Explains how the Church teaches us to embrace our family vocations, providing a bulwark of Catholic morality to protect our families from the surrounding chaos.

Family Atom: Earning. Ann Ree Colton. 1 cass. 7.95 A R Colton Fnd.

Family Baggage. Errol Strider & Lew Montgomery. 1 cass. 1989. (978-1-878868-00-8(4)) Strider Inner.

Family Bible Series: Adults. 2000. cass. & reel tape 12.40 (978-0-7673-5543-8(1)) LifeWay Christian.

Family Blessings. LaVyrle Spencer. Narrated by Barbara Rush. 11 cass. (Running Time: 15 hrs. 15 mins.). 92.00 (978-1-4025-2250-5(9)); audio compact disk 116.00 (978-1-4025-3075-3(7)) Recorded Bks.

Family Blessings. unabr. ed. Fern Michaels. Read by Laural Merlington. 2004. 15.95 (978-0-7435-4447-4(1)) Pub: S&S Audio. Dist(s): S and S Inc

Family Business. Basilio Balli Morales et al. Read by Basilio Balli et al. (Running Time: 1 hr.). (C). 2003. 14.95 (978-1-60083-300-7(4), Audiofy Corp) Iofy Corp.

Family Businesses. Glenn Swogger. Read by Glenn Swogger. Ed. by Patricia Magerkurth. 1 cass. (Running Time: 40 min.). (Management Ser.). 1992. 10.00 (978-1-56948-013-7(3)) Menninger Clinic.
There are several layers of emotional functioning at play when families are in business together. Glenn Swogger, MD discusses the subtle & not-so-subtle nuances that can affect family businesses. His insights will help those in a family business to better understand & define the overlapping issues related to work & family.

Family Bussiness see Los Negocios de Familia

Family-Centered Early Intervention for Children Who Are Deaf & Hard of Hearing. Mary Pat Mueller & Arlene Stredler-Brown. 1 cass. (Running Time: 1 hr.). 2000. pap. bk. 79.00 (978-1-58041-051-9(0), 0112256) Am Speech Lang Hearing.
Explore cutting-edge family-centered practices to involve family members in early decisions about treatment options for young children identified as hearing-impaired.

Family Christmas. abr. ed. Caroline Kennedy. Read by Tim Cain et al. (Playaway Adult Nonfiction Ser.). 2008. 54.99 (978-1-60640-510-9(1)) Find a World.

Family Christmas. unabr. ed. Read by Ensemble cast. Ed. by Caroline Kennedy. (ENG.). 2009. audio compact disk 9.99 (978-1-59887-869-1(7), 1598878697) Pub: HighBridge. Dist(s): Workman Pub

Family Christmas: A Child's Christmas in Wales/the Nutcracker/the Little Match Girl & Other Christmas Favourites. Read by Philip Madoc & Benjamin Zephaniah. 2. (Running Time: 9240 sec.). 2007. audio compact disk 17.98 (978-962-634-471-2(7), Naxos AudioBooks) Naxos.

Family Christmas Celebration. Charles R. Swindoll. 2007. audio compact disk 14.99 (978-1-57972-793-2(X)) Insight Living.

Family Comes of Age: An Unabridged Selection from with Ossie & Ruby. unabr. ed. Ruby Dee & Ossie Davis. Read by Ruby Dee & Ossie Davis. (Running Time: 5 hrs.). (ENG.). 2006. 14.98 (978-1-59483-492-9(X)) Pub: Hachet Audio. Dist(s): HachBkGrp

Family Communication & Growth. Virginia Satir. 1 cass. (Running Time: 60 min.). 1967. 11.00 (07801) Big Sur Tapes.
An early recording from Esalen in San Francisco, introducing & demonstrating family therapy techniques.

Family Communications. James McArthur. 1 cass. 3.95 (978-1-57734-391-2(3), 34441328) Covenant Comms.

Family Concert. Perf. by Barry Louis Polisar. 1 cass. (Running Time: 45 min.). 1990. bk. 9.95 (978-0-938663-12-6(7), 5161) Pub: Rainbow Morn. Dist(s): IPG Chicago
Family Concert presents the irreverent Barry Polisar in front of an audience of children & adults. Although most of the songs included on the cassette are on other Polisar recordings, his interaction with the audience makes this more than an additional purchase.

Family Concert. Barry Louis Polisar. Prod. by Ray Tilkens. 1 CD. (Running Time: 45 min.). (ENG.). (J). (gr. k-6). 1990. audio compact disk 14.95 (978-0-938663-44-7(5), 5161 CD) Pub: Rainbow Morn. Dist(s): IPG Chicago

Family Connections. Anna Jacobs. 2008. 69.95 (978-1-84559-858-7(X)); audio compact disk 79.95 (978-1-84559-859-4(8)) Pub: Soundings Ltd GBR. Dist(s): Ulverscroft US

Family Daughter. Maile Meloy. 8 CDs. (Isis (CDs) Ser.). 2006. audio compact disk 79.95 (978-0-7531-2590-8(0)) Pub: ISIS Lrg Prnt GBR. Dist(s): Ulverscroft US

Family Daughter. Maile Meloy. Read by Laurel Lefkow. 7 cass. (Running Time: 9 hrs.). (Isis Cassettes Ser.). 2006. 61.95 (978-0-7531-3619-5(8)) Pub: ISIS Lrg Prnt GBR. Dist(s): Ulverscroft US

Family Development in the Churches: Proceedings of 45th Annual Convention National Association of Evangelicals, Buffalo, New York. Read by Robert Fisher. 1 cass. (Running Time: 60 min.). 1987. 4.00 (316) Nat Assn Evan.

Family Dynamics & Schizophrenia. unabr. ed. Jerry Higgins. 1 cass. (Running Time: 18 min.). 12.95 (29037) J Norton Pubs.
Examines how family configuration is related to the schizophrenic & the differential development of the child contingent upon the type of family organization.

Family Economics - an Mp3 Audio Series. Prod. by Generations with Vision. 2009. 14.95 (978-0-9801910-7-3(6)) Gen With Vis.

***Family Economics Conference - Mp3.** Prod. by Generations with Vision. 2010. audio compact disk 34.95 (978-0-9826298-2-6(6)) Gen With Vis.

Family Effectiveness Training (F. E. T.) CD. Scripts. Narrated by Thomas Gordon. 1 CD. 1997. audio compact disk (978-0-9701895-3-0(2)) Gordon Training.

Family Finance Toolkit 2006. 2006th rev. ed. Peter Duckworth. 2006. audio compact disk 470.00 (978-1-84661-012-7(5)) Pub: Jordan Pubng GBR. Dist(s): Intl Spec Bk

Family First: Your Step-by-Step Plan for Creating a Phenomenal Family. abr. ed. Phil McGraw. Read by Phil McGraw. 6 CDs. (Running Time: 60 hrs. 0 mins. 0 sec.). (ENG.). 2004. audio compact disk 30.00 (978-0-7435-3831-2(5), Sound Ideas) Pub: S&S Audio. Dist(s): S and S Inc

Family First: Your Step-by-Step Plan for Creating a Phenomenal Family. abr. ed. Phil McGraw. Read by Phil McGraw. 2005. 15.95 (978-0-7435-5530-2(9)) Pub: S&S Audio. Dist(s): S and S Inc

Family-Focused Pediatrics for Primary Care. Contrib. by William L. Coleman et al. 1 cass. (Topics, Moderators, & Panelists Ser.: Vol. 19, No. 3). 1998. 20.00 Am Acad Pediat.

Family Folk Festival Sing-Along. Prod. by Leib Ostrow. 1 cass. 1990. 9.98 (978-1-877737-48-0(8), MLP 2105); audio compact disk 12.98 (978-1-877737-75-6(5), MLP D2105) MFLP CA.
Fifteen songs by leading artists to encourage families & children to sing together.

Family, Friends, & God: The Music & Preaching of Fr. Jim Marchionda, Op. Contrib. by Jim Marchionda. 2008. audio compact disk 17.00 (978-1-58459-346-1(6)) Wrld Lib Pubns.

Family Friendship Classics Memorable Songs from Film & Television. 1 cass. (Running Time: 30 min.). (J). (gr. k-6). 1998. 5.99 (978-1-56826-905-4(6)); 9.98 (978-1-56826-904-7(8)) Rhino Enter.
This collection of songs from various soundtracks is centered around a friendship theme.

Family from One End Street: And Some of Their Adventures. unabr. ed. Eve Garnett. Read by Julia Sands. 4 cass. (Running Time: 5 hrs. 8 mins.). (Isis Cassettes Ser.). (J). 2004. 44.95 (978-0-7531-1857-3(2)) Pub: ISIS Lrg Prnt GBR. Dist(s): Ulverscroft US

Family Frying Pan. unabr. ed. Bryce Courtenay. Read by Humphrey Bower. 5 cass. (Running Time: 8 hrs.). 2001. 40.00 (978-1-74030-439-9(X)) Pub: Bolinda Pubng AUS. Dist(s): Bolinda Pub Inc

Family Frying Pan. unabr. ed. Bryce Courtenay. Read by Melissa Eccleston. 7 CDs. (Running Time: 8 hrs.). 2003. audio compact disk 83.95 (978-1-74093-086-4(X)) Pub: Bolinda Pubng AUS. Dist(s): Bolinda Pub Inc

Family Fun Pack. Created by Radio Spirits. (Running Time: 10800 sec.). 2004. 9.98 (978-1-57019-723-9(7)); audio compact disk 19.98 (978-1-57019-722-2(9), OTR 27952) Pub: Radio Spirits. Dist(s): AudioGO

Family Fun Songs. 1 cass. (J). 1998. pap. bk. 7.95 (978-0-7601-2280-8(6)) Provident Mus Dist.
Treasured favorites from yesteryear, set to a contemporary beat for today's kids.

Family Garden. Perf. by John McCutcheon. 1 cass. (Running Time: 53 min.). (Family Ser.). (J). (ps-7). 1993. 9.98 (978-1-886767-22-5(X), 8026); audio compact disk 14.98 (978-1-886767-23-2(8), 8026) Rounder Records.
Features thirteen songs about growing up in a family - not "family" as it has been dictated to us - but a new definition of family.

Family Genealogy As It Impacts Mate Choice & Couple & Family Relationships. Read by Laura Dodson. 1 cass. (Running Time: 90 min.). 1988. 10.95 (978-0-7822-0054-6(0), 353) C G Jung IL.

Family Group see Paddington Dissapearing

Family Happiness. (9087) Books on Tape.

Family Happiness. Short Stories. 1982. (C-87) Jimcin Record.

Family Harmony. Barry Tesar. 1 cass. (Running Time: 1 hr.). (Subliminal Inspiration Ser.). 1992. 9.98 (978-1-56470-002-5(X)) Success Cass.
Subliminal program.

Family Harmony. unabr. ed. Judith L. Powell. Read by Judith L. Powell. 1 cass. (Running Time: 40 min.). (Successful Living Ser.). 1987. pap. bk. 12.95 (978-0-914295-25-9(X)) Top Mtn Pub.
Side A presents exercises designed to enrich family togetherness by improving inter-family relationships, support, strength & fun. Side B presents subliminal suggestions hidden in New Age Music.

Family Healing. David Freudberg. Perf. by Betty Ford & Lois Wilson. 1 cass. (Running Time: 1 hr.). (Thinking about Drinking Ser.). 1987. 10.95 (978-1-886373-02-0(7)) Human Media.
Children of alcoholics - description of the effects of growing up in dysfunctional homes from both adults & children.

Family History. unabr. ed. Dani Shapiro. 6 cass. (Running Time: 10 hrs. 30 mins.). 2004. 29.99 (978-1-4025-3685-4(2), 02684) Recorded Bks.
Intricate novel about the fragile bonds that hold families together?and the terrible secrets that can tear those bonds to shreds. Rachel is well on her way to establishing the perfect family when everything falls apart. Daughter Kate is trapped in a downward spiral that intensified when she accidentally dropped her baby brother. Is there more to this terrible accident than Kate admits?.

Family Honor. unabr. ed. Robert B. Parker. Read by Andrea Thompson. 6 cass. (Running Time: 7 hrs.). (Sunny Randall Ser.: No. 1). 2001. 32.00 (978-1-59040-000-5(3), Phoenix Audio) Pub: Amer Intl Pub. Dist(s): PerseuPGW
Young, smart and female, Sunny Randall, a former cop turned Boston P.I., is hired by a wealthy family as bodyguard for a difficult teenager who refuses to return to her family. The assignment leads to uncovering a criminal conspiracy that reaches to the top of the state government.

Family Honor. unabr. collector's ed. Robert B. Parker. Read by Andrea Thompson. 6 cass. (Running Time: 9 hrs.). (Sunny Randall Ser.: No. 1). 1999. 34.95 (978-0-7366-4782-3(1)) Books on Tape.
P.I. Sunny Randall must rescue a runaway from more than her pimp, the mob, & a criminal conspiracy within the state government.

Family Honor, Set. abr. ed. Robert B. Parker. Read by Andrea Thompson. 2 cass. (Sunny Randall Ser.: No. 1). 1999. 18.00 (FS9-51079) Highsmith.

Family in Relationship to the Dying Patient. John Campbell. 1986. 10.80 (0606) Assn Prof Chaplains.

Family Kit. bk. 12.95 (978-0-664-50054-2(4)) Pub: Presbyterian Pub. Dist(s): Westminster John Knox

Family Kit. 1998. bk. 10.95 (978-0-664-50055-9(2)) Pub: Presbyterian Pub. Dist(s): Westminster John Knox

Family know Thyself see Familia, se tu Misma

Family Law. Instructed by Marc Perlin. 4 cass. (Running Time: 4 hrs. 45 min.). (Outstanding Professors Ser.). 1995. 39.95 Set. (978-0-940366-74-9(6)) Sum & Substance.
Lecture given by a prominent American law school professor.

Family Law, 2nd ed. Marc Perlin. 4 cass. (Running Time: 4 hrs. 30 mins.). (Audio Tape Ser.). 1999. 40.00 (978-1-57793-043-3(6), 28473) Pub: Sum & Substance. Dist(s): West Pub

Family Law. 4th rev. ed. Marc G. Perlin. 57.00 (978-0-314-16921-1(0), West Lglwrks) West.

Family Law: Litigating to Win. 1991. 70.00 (AC-615) PA Bar Inst.

Family Law Litigation. Read by Peter J. McBrien et al. (Running Time: 6 hrs.). 1991. 115.00 Incl. Ethics: 15 min., & 114p. tape materials. (FA-55217) Cont Ed Bar-CA.
Explains key steps in a family law court proceeding from filing through appellate review & modifications. Covers filing, jurisdiction, types of proceedings; pretrial; trial; postjudgement proceedings; & appeal.

Family Law Practice: In Bucks, Chester, Delaware & Montgomery Counties. 1998. bk. 99.00 (ACS-2009) PA Bar Inst.
This looseleaf reference book gives you the help you need to improve your ability to handle divorce cases in Bucks, Chester, Delaware & Montgomery Counties. Streamlined & sustantially revised for 1998, this shows you how the family court system functions, how to work with key personnel, & how to get answers to the questions in your files. You'll learn about each county's procedures in the key areas of matrimonial practice: divorce, equitable distribution, alimony, support, custody, abuse, special relief & injunctions.

Family Law Practice: Recent Developments (1992) Read by Kenneth Black et al. (Running Time: 3 hrs. 30 min.). 1991. 89.00 Incl. 363p. tape materials. (FA-55231) Cont Ed Bar-CA.
Experts examine legislative & case law developments of the past year affecting family law practice. They cover support, custody, marital property, deferred compensation, attorney fees, & procedure.

Family Law Practice: Seven Strategies for Capturing Support. Prod. by Advantage Legal Seminars. (ENG.). 2008. 177.00 (978-0-9795737-1-2(8)) Anzman Publg.

Family Law Practice in Western Pennsylvania: Allegheny, Beaver, Butler, Washington & Westmoreland Counties. 1999. bk. 99.00 (ACS-2247) PA Bar Inst.
Have you ever taken a case in a neighboring county only to realize you were in a foreign procedural territory? Written by experienced family law practitioners from each county, they explain how each court system functions, how to navigate the local rules & how to work with court personnel.

Family Law Review for General Practitioners. Read by John C. Howett, Jr. 1 cass. 1990. 20.00 (AL-90) PA Bar Inst.

Family Law, 2002 ed. (Law School Legends Audio Series) 2005th rev. ed. Roger E. Schechter. (Law School Legends Audio Ser.). 2005. 52.00 (978-0-314-16096-6(5), gilbert); 47.95 (978-0-314-16095-9(7), gilbert) West.

Family Lawyer: Ethics & Avoiding Malpractice. Read by Max A. Goodman et al. (Running Time: 4 hrs.). 1992. 89.00 Incl. tape materials. (FA-56021) Cont Ed Bar-CA.
Expert practitioners & a family court bench officer explore, in a practical fashion, such issues as representing both spouses, conflicts of interest, fees, client control, the delicacy of client confidentiality when child abuse is alleged or evident, & the accuracy of income & expense declarations.

Family Life & Child-Raising. Michael N. Deranja et al. 1 cass. (Ananda Talks about Marriage Ser.). 9.95 (DM-6) Crystal Clarity.

Family Limited Partnerships. Jeffery Radowich. 1997. bk. 99.00 (ACS-1353) PA Bar Inst.
Get a sophisticated yet understandable review of the current issues in using family limited partnerships for your estate clients. The author highlights the key characteristics of a successful FLP & offers pragmatic advice on language to achieve those goals. While focusing on federal tax laws, this clarifies the Pennsylvania tax & corporate questions & points out the importance of non-tax, business rationales for an FLP.

Family Linen. unabr. ed. Lee Smith. Narrated by Linda Stephens. 7 cass. (Running Time: 10 hrs. 15 mins.). 1997. 60.00 (978-0-7887-0715-5(9), 94891E7) Recorded Bks.
When a polished, Southern woman goes to a hypnotist to discover the source of her blinding headaches, she cannot predict the loony mosaic of family history & mystery that will surface.

Family Love see amor en Familia

Family Love. unabr. ed. Joe Moriarty & Victor Vurpillat. Read by Joe Moriarty & Yamuna Van Gilder. 1 cass. Dramatization. 1989. 10.00 Crtv Source.
Subliminal with Music & Audio with music. Bonding & self-esteem for parent & children from birth to 5 years.

Family Madness. unabr. ed. Thomas Keneally. Read by Steve Hodson. 10 cass. (Running Time: 13 hrs. 45 min.). 1993. 84.95 (978-1-85089-675-3(5), 40491) Pub: ISIS Audio GBR. Dist(s): Ulverscroft US
"It's a brilliant book. More than any other contemporary writer, the author deals in moral concern." - The Guardian.

Family Man. Amanda Brookfield. Narrated by Gordon Griffin. 8 cass. (Running Time: 11 hrs.). 72.00 (978-1-84197-219-0(3)) Recorded Bks.

Family Man. unabr. ed. Amanda Brookfield. Narrated by Gordon Griffin. 10 CDs. (Running Time: 11 hrs.). 2001. audio compact disk 97.00 (978-1-4025-1014-4(4), C1592) Recorded Bks.
When Matt Webster gets a call from his wife asking him to pick up their son from the nursery, he doesn't realize that his wife has left him. When he eventually finds her two-line note, he is shocked with disbelief, especially since she has abandoned four-year-old Josh. Matt has been something of a hands-off parent prior to his wife's departure and has little experience of looking after Josh on a full-time basis. However, as the weeks stretch on, Matt finds that not only is he able to cope, he actually enjoys it.

Family Man. unabr. collector's ed. Jayne Ann Krentz. Read by Mary Peiffer. 8 cass. (Running Time: 12 hrs.). 1996. 64.00 (978-0-7366-3348-2(0), 3998) Books on Tape.
A decade of working for the Gilchrist empire has made Katy Wade tough as nails. Now she's got the deal of her career to close: persuading Luke Gilchrist, estranged heir, to save the floundering family business. Luke, a talented businessman, has sworn he'll never go home. All his life, the Gilchrists have alienated him, the product of his father's affair. But when Luke meets Katy, he thinks he might become a family man. It's not in her job description, but with one look into Luke's sexy green eyes she knows love is the bottom line.

Family Man: An Authorized Biography of Dr. James Dobson. Dale Buss. 24.99 (978-0-8423-8193-2(7)) Tyndale Hse.

Family Man: Ezekiel 18:2. Ed Young. 1991. 4.95 (978-0-7417-1863-1(4), 863) Win Walk.

Family Matinee Vol. 1: Let's Go to the Movies. 1 CD. (Running Time: 47 mins.). 2001. audio compact disk 15.98 MFLP CA.

Family Matinee Vol. 1: Let's Go to the Movies. 1 cass. (Running Time: 47 mins.). (J). 2001. 9.98 (978-1-56628-285-7(3)) MFLP CA.

Family Matters. Taffi L. Dollar. 15.00 (978-1-59089-029-5(9)) Pub: Creflo Dollar. Dist(s): STL Dist NA

Family Matters. Cathy Woodman. (Story Sound CD Ser.). 2007. audio compact disk 99.95 (978-1-84652-015-0(0)) Pub: Mgna Lrg Print GBR. Dist(s): Ulverscroft US

Family Matters. Cathy Woodman & Tanya Myers. (Story Sound Ser.). 2007. 76.95 (978-1-84652-014-3(2)) Pub: Mgna Lrg Print GBR. Dist(s): Ulverscroft US

Family Matters: A Celebration of the Short Story. Created by Symphony Space Staff. (Running Time: 3 hrs. 0 mins. 0 sec.). (Selected Shorts Ser.). (ENG.). 2007. audio compact disk 28.00 (978-1-934033-03-6(0)) Pub: Symphony Space. Dist(s): IPG Chicago

Family Matters: A Novel. unabr. ed. Rohinton Mistry. Read by Martin Jarvis. 12 cass. (Running Time: 12 hrs.). 2004. 45.00 (978-1-59007-273-8(1)) Pub: New Millenn Enter. Dist(s): PerseuPGW
A novel of familial pride, love and obligation. Set in Bombay in the 1990s, it defines the merging of personal and political corruption, the power of memory to keep truth alive, and the ultimate peril of memory denied. This is the story of a family in Bombay whose patriarch is ailing and needs constant care from his step-daughter. He lives under her thumb, except for his evening strolls. And, when he has an accident on an outing, he desire to pass him to her younger sister's house starts a chain of destruction that may never be repaired.

Family Matters: Discovering God's Plan for the Family. Kenneth Copeland & Creflo A. Dollar. 3 cass. (Running Time: 4 hrs. 30 min.). 1997. 15.00 (978-1-57562-197-5(5), TKC-197-5) K Copeland Pubns.

***Family Matters: Investing in the Things that Last.** Charles R. Swindoll. 2010. audio compact disk 30.00 (978-1-57972-875-5(8)) Insight Living.

***Family Meadow: A Selection from the John Updike Audio Collection.** unabr. ed. John Updike. Read by John Updike. (ENG.). 2009. (978-0-06-196235-6(X), Caedmon); (978-0-06-196236-3(8), Caedmon) HarperCollins Pubs.

Family Money Management: National Association of Evangelicals, 47th Annual Convention, Columbus, Ohio, March 7-9, 1989. Arvin Vaughan. 1 cass. (Workshops Ser.: No. 24-Wednesd). 1989. 4.00 ea. 1-8 tapes.; 4.35 ea. 9 tapes or more. Nat Assn Evan.

Family Music: Teach Yourself to Play Guitar & Harmonica. Ed. by Alfred Publishing. (ENG.). 2002. audio compact disk 29.95 (978-0-7390-2480-5(9)) Alfred Pub.

Family Music Party. Perf. by Trout Fishing in America Staff. 1 cass., 1 CD. (J). 1999. 7.98 (TRT 13); audio compact disk 12.78 CD Jewel box. (TRT 13) NewSound.

Family of the Empire. Sheelagh Kelly. Read by Nicolette McKenzie. 18 cass. (Sound Ser.). (J). 2002. 109.95 (978-1-84283-202-8(6)) Pub: ISIS Lrg Prnt GBR. Dist(s): Ulverscroft US

Family Patterns: Get Loose of Ties. Maritha Pottenger. 1 cass. 8.95 (284) Am Fed Astrologers.
Still trying to "prove" something to parents long gone?.

Family Planning. unabr. ed. Milton Diamond. 1 cass. (Running Time: 1 hr.). (Human Sexuality Ser.). 12.95 (34013) J Norton Pubs.

Family Planning in Thailand & Indonesia. Hosted by Nancy Pearlman. 1 cass. (Running Time: 31 min.). 10.00 (523) Educ Comm CA.

Family Portrait. Neville Goddard. 1 cass. (Running Time: 62 min.). 1970. 8.00 (105) J & L Pubns.
Neville taught Imagination Creates Reality. He was a powerfully influential teacher of God as Consciousness.

Family Possessed Audio Book. L. W. Stevenson. (ENG.). 2008. audio compact disk 17.95 (978-1-932278-45-3(1)) Pub: Mayhaven Pub. Dist(s): Baker Taylor

Family Practice Review, Vol. A182: Skills for the 21st Century. unabr. ed. 65 cass. 1995. 850.00 set. (978-1-57664-357-0(3)) CME Info Svcs.
Continuing medical education home-study. Complete package contains audiotapes, syllabus, self-assessment examination to earn CME Category 1 credit.

Family Radio. Garrison Keillor. 2 cass., 2 CD. (Running Time: 1 hr. 30 min.). 14.37 Set, blisterpack. (PHC 21022); audio compact disk 19.98 CD Set, Jewel box. (PHC 542971) NewSound.

Family Radio. abr. unabr. ed. Garrison Keillor. 2 CDs. (Running Time: 1 hr. 30 mins.). (ENG.). 1997. audio compact disk 24.95 (978-1-56511-208-7(3), 1565112083) Pub: HighBridge. Dist(s): Workman Pub

Family Relationships. Marianne Williamson. 4 cass. (Running Time: 4 hrs.). (ENG.). 1995. 30.00 (978-1-56170-300-5(1)) Hay House.
Lectures based on "A Course in Miracles" include: Not Judging Your Mother/Expectations (Tape 1); Criticism/Truth Cannot be Made a Lie (Incest) (Tape 2; Undoing Terrorism/Rebirth-Transformation (Tape 3); The Living Temple (Tape 4).

Family Roles: For 900 Professionals at "The Power of Laughter & Play Conference" Peter Alsop. Perf. by Peter Alsop. 1 cass. 11.00 Moose Schl Records.
A helpful tool for family therapists, drug counselors, anyone in recovery - parents/teahcers/teens.

***Family Secrets.** unabr. ed. Catherine Marshall. Adapted by C. Archer. Narrated by Jaimee Draper. (Catherine Marshall's Christy Ser.). (ENG.). 2010. 7.00 (978-1-60814-704-5(5), SpringWater) Oasis Audio.

Family Secrets: Lecture. unabr. ed. John Bradshaw. 2 cass. (Running Time: 3 hrs.). 1994. 18.00 Set. (978-1-57388-016-9(7)) J B Media.
This lecture pre-exists the PBS series & book by the same title exploring secrets in families, how they are created, how they influence us, & the risks we take exploring them.

Family Self-Esteem. unabr. ed. Jennifer James. Read by Jennifer James. 1 cass. (Running Time: 46 min.). 1984. 9.95 (978-0-915423-14-9(6)) Jennifer J.
Talks about the most important ingredients in our sense of self. Tells how to change behavior from one generation to the next, by building self-esteem in all family members & enrich family experiences.

Family Seminars for Caregiving: Helping Families Help (Facilitator's Manual) Ed. by Rhonda J. Montgomery. 1985. bk. 135.00 (978-0-295-72509-3(5)) U of Wash Pr.

Family Series. Brian Brodersen. 4 cassette. 2003. 24.99 (978-1-931667-66-1(7)) Calvar ChalPub.

Family Shadows, Set. unabr. ed. Rowena Summers. 11 cass. 1998. 103.95 (978-1-85903-153-7(6)) Pub: Magna Story GBR. Dist(s): Ulverscroft US

Family Snapshot. rev. ed. Simon Firth. 2000. 46.95 (978-1-873942-77-2(X)) Pub: P Chapman GBR. Dist(s): SAGE

Family Snapshots. 1 cass. (Running Time: 1 hr. 30 mins.). 2001. 9.95 (TINE002) Lodestone Catalog.

Family Snapshots. Scripts. Created by Conrad Bishop & Elizabeth Fuller. 1 CD. (Running Time: 78 min.). Dramatization. 2002. audio compact disk 14.95 (978-0-9745664-0-5(3)) WordWorkers.
Fifty-four 90-second micro-dramas about American family life today. Broadcast on more than 80 public stations, they range from the absurd to the unsettling - realistic audio cartoons based in the comedy of recognition.

Family Snapshots. Prod. by Independent Eye Staff. 1 cass. 12.95 (TINE002) Lodestone Catalog.

Family Songs & Stories from the North Carolina Mountains. Perf. by Doug Wallin & Jack Wallin. Anno. by Beverly Patterson & Daniel Patterson. Prod. by Wayne Martin. 1 cass. 1995. Incl. artist biographies, song notes, lyrics, bibliography, discography & photos. (0-9307-400130-9307-40013-2-5); audio compact disk (0-9307-40013-2-5) Smithsonian Folkways.
Brothers from Madison County, North Carolina, use fiddle, banjo & guitar accompaniment.

Family Spirituality. unabr. ed. Kathleen Chesto. Read by Kathleen Chesto. 1 cass. (Running Time: 29 min.). 1989. cass. & video 29.95 (978-0-89622-771-2(5), D-54) Twenty-Third.
Kathleen Chesto uses her own experience as a mother of three & as a family religious education consultant to bring encouragement & hope to parents. She helps them recognize the many ways that children can teach them about God.

Family Tax Planning. rev. ed. Cherie J. O'Neil & Diane W. Green. 2 cass. 119.00 set, incl. wkbk. (746401KQ) Am Inst CPA.
The American dream is to own a home & be able to send the kids to college. Here's a brand new course that deals exclusively with those goals. It shows you how to guide your clients to achieve them.

Family That Couldn't Sleep: A Medical Mystery. unabr. ed. Read by Grover Gardner. 7 CDs. (Running Time: 9 hrs. 0 mins. 0 sec.). (ENG.). 2006. audio compact disk 29.99 (978-1-4001-0289-1(8)) Pub: Tantor Media. Dist(s): IngramPubServ

Family That Couldn't Sleep: A Medical Mystery. unabr. ed. D. T. Max. Narrated by Grover Gardner. (Running Time: 9 hrs. 0 mins. 0 sec.). (ENG.). 2006. audio compact disk 59.99 (978-1-4001-3289-8(4)); audio compact disk 19.99 (978-1-4001-5289-6(5)) Pub: Tantor Media. Dist(s): IngramPubServ

***Family, the Low Price.** abr. ed. Mario Puzo. Read by Philip Bosco. (ENG.). 2004. (978-0-06-079804-8(1), Harper Audio) HarperCollins Pubs.

***Family Theater.** Perf. by Natalie Wood et al. 2010. audio compact disk 35.95 (978-1-57019-950-9(7)) Radio Spirits.

Family Theater, 1998th collector's ed. Perf. by Gregory Peck et al. 6 cass. (Running Time: 9 hrs.). 1998. bk. 17.49 (4029) Radio Spirits.
Some of the biggest names in radio and film appearing in 18 stories.

Family Theater: A Daddy for Christmas & Substitute Santa. 1 cass. (Running Time: 1 hr.). 2001. 6.98 (2214) Radio Spirits.

Family Therapy & Pastoral Care. Harold Nelson & Meg Nelson. 1986. 10.80 (0112) Assn Prof Chaplains.

Family Ties. Joanne Wickenburg. 1 cass. 8.95 (597) Am Fed Astrologers.
Derevative houses show hidden ties.

Family Ties. abr. ed. Danielle Steel. Read by Susan Ericksen. 5 CDs. (Running Time: 6 hrs.). 2010. audio compact disk 24.99 (978-1-4233-8854-8(2), 9781423388548, BACD) Brilliance Audio.

Family Ties. abr. ed. Danielle Steel. (Running Time: 6 hrs.). 2013. audio compact disk 14.99 (978-1-4233-8855-5(0), 9781423388555, BCD Value Price) Brilliance Audio.

Family Ties. unabr. ed. Danielle Steel. Read by Susan Ericksen. 1 MP3-CD. (Running Time: 10 hrs.). 2010. 39.97 (978-1-4233-8851-7(8), 9781423388517, Brlnc Audio MP3 Lib); 39.97 (978-1-4233-8853-1(4), 9781423388531, BADLE); 24.99 (978-1-4233-8850-0(X), 9781423388500, Brilliance MP3); 24.99 (978-1-4233-8852-4(6), 9781423388524, BAD); audio compact disk 92.97 (978-1-4233-8849-4(6), 9781423388494, BriAudCD Unabrid); audio compact disk 38.99 (978-1-4233-8848-7(8), 9781423388487, Bril Audio CD Unabri) Brilliance Audio.

***Family Ties.** unabr. ed. Danielle Steel. Read by Susan Ericksen. 1 Playaway. (Running Time: 10 hrs.). 2010. 39.99 (978-1-4418-6894-7(1)) Brilliance Audio.

Family Time with Henry & Mudge. Cynthia Rylant. Illus. by Suçie Stevenson. 44 vols. (Running Time: 37 mins.). 2002. pap. bk. 61.95 (978-0-87499-997-6(9)); pap. bk. 68.95 (978-1-59112-854-0(4)) Live Oak Media.

Family Tradition. (Family of God Ser.). 1997. 4.98; audio compact disk 7.98 Pub: Brentwood Music. Dist(s): Provident Mus Dist
Original versions of classic songs including "Just a Closer Walk with Thee" by the Speers, "Surely the Presence" by the Lanny Wolfe Trio & many more.

Family Travel Classics: Most Memorable Songs from Film & TV. 1 cass., 1 CD. (J). 4.78 (KID 75213); audio compact disk 7.98 CD. (KID 75213) NewSound.

Family Travel Classics: The Most Memorable Songs from Film & Television. 1 CD. 1998. audio compact disk 9.98 (978-1-56826-876-7(9)) Rhino Enter.

Family Travel Classics: The Most Memorable Songs from Film & Television. Rhino Records Staff. 1 cass. 1998. 5.98 (978-1-56826-874-3(2)) Rhino Enter.

Family Travel Tote, Set. 7 cass. 19.95 (978-1-57734-275-5(5), 0900168) Covenant Comms.
Seven talks & one book on tape to entertain the entire family.

Family Tree. Tom Chapin. Perf. by Tom Chapin. 1 cass. (Running Time: 30 min.). (J). 1992. 8.98 (978-1-56406-558-2(8)); 8.98 Incl. sleeve pack. (978-1-56406-584-1(7)); audio compact disk 13.98 CD. (978-1-56406-571-1(5)) Sony Music Ent.

Family Tree. unabr. ed. Katherine Ayres. Narrated by Carine Montbertrand. 3 pieces. (Running Time: 4 hrs.). (gr. 7 up). 2001. 28.00 (978-0-7887-5367-1(3)) Recorded Bks.
When Tyler Stoudt's sixth grade class is assigned research on their family tree, she must rely on her papa since her mom was killed in an automobile accident. She begins a painful journey of discovery about long-kept secrets on both sides of her parents' families as she tries to complete her assignment.

Family Tree. unabr. ed. Barbara Delinsky. Read by Karen White. 7 cass. (Running Time: 10 hrs. 45 mins.). 2007. 90.00 (978-1-4159-3750-1(8)); audio compact disk 110.00 (978-1-4159-3565-1(3)) Books on Tape.
Dana Clarke has always longed for the stability of home and family - her own childhood was not an easy one. Now she has married a man she adores and is about to give birth to their first child. But though her daughter is born beautiful and healthy, no one can help noticing the African American traits in her appearance. Dana's husband, to her great shock and dismay, begins to worry that people will think Dana has had an affair. The only way to repair the damage done is for Dana to track down the father she never knew. Dana's determination to discover the truth becomes a poignant journey back through her past that unearths secrets rooted in prejudice and fear.

Family Trip. Perf. by Barry Louis Polisar. 1 cass. (J). (gr. k-6). 1993. 9.95 (978-0-938663-19-5(4), 5171 CASS) Pub: Rainbow Morn. Dist(s): IPG Chicago
Polisar explores: being compared to the perfect child who lives next door; playing parents against each other; & having responsibility for a young sibling. The lyrics almost always speak to the reality of children's lives.

Family Trip. Barry Louis Polisar. 1 CD. (Running Time: 0 hr. 45 mins. 0 sec.). (ENG.). (J). (gr. k-6). 1996. audio compact disk 14.95 (978-0-938663-47-8(X), 5171 CD) Pub: Rainbow Morn. Dist(s): IPG Chicago

Family Vacation. Rosenshontz. Perf. by Gary Rosen & Bill Shontz. 1 cass. (Rosenshontz Ser.). (J). (ps-6). 1992. 8.98 (978-1-879496-59-0(3)); audio compact disk 13.98 CD. (978-1-56896-042-5(5)) Lightyear Entrtnmnt.
A two-man group singing delightful children's songs.

Family Vacation. Rosenshontz. Perf. by Gary Rosen & Bill Shontz. 1 cass. (Rosenshontz Ser.). (J). (ps-6). 1993. pap. bk. 8.98 Incl. long box. (978-1-879496-60-6(7)) Lightyear Entrtnmnt.

Family Values. unabr. ed. K. C. Constantine. Read by Lloyd James. 8 cass. (Running Time: 8 hrs.). (Mario Balzic Ser.: Vol. 13). 1998. 48.00 (978-0-7366-4035-0(5), 4534) Books on Tape.
Balzic comes out of retirement to investigate a trail of police corruption & brutality...even murder.

Family Values: Teaching by Example. Eknath Easwaran. 1 cass. (Running Time: 46 min.). 1992. 7.95 (978-1-58638-534-7(8), FVT) Nilgiri Pr.
Drawing on memories of his childhood & on the ancient wisdom of Hinduism, Easwaran describes how the family can transmit high ideals & nourish spiritual progress.

Family Vault. Charlotte MacLeod. Read by Mary Peiffer. 2000. 48.00 (978-0-7366-5082-3(2)) Books on Tape.

Family You've Always Wanted: Five Ways You Can Make It Happen. unabr. ed. Gary Chapman. Narrated by Chris Fabry. (Running Time: 6 hrs. 31 mins. 7 sec.). (ENG.). 2008. 19.59 (978-1-60814-198-2(5)) Oasis Audio.

Family You've Always Wanted: Five Ways You Can Make It Happen. unabr. ed. Gary Chapman. Read by Gary Chapman. Narrated by Chris Fabry. (Running Time: 6 hrs. 31 mins. 7 sec.). (ENG.). 2008. audio compact disk 27.99 (978-1-59859-432-4(X)) Oasis Audio.

FamilyLife Marriage Conference. abr. ed. Ed. by Keith Lynch. 16 cass. (Running Time: 16 hrs.). 1994. 59.95 Set. (978-1-57229-004-4(8)) FamilyLife.
Audio version of live marriage conference.

Famine of God's Word. unabr. ed. Warren W. Wiersbe. Read by Warren W. Wiersbe. 5 cass. (Running Time: 6 hrs.). 1989. 22.95 (978-0-8474-2358-3(1)) Back to Bible.
A study that helps identify & deal with those things that cause spiritual starvation in the believer's life.

Famine of Horses. unabr. ed. P. F. Chisholm. Read by Stephen Thorne. 7 cass. (Running Time: 10 hrs. 30 min.). (Isis Ser.). (J). 2004. 61.95 (978-0-7531-0035-6(5), 960601) Pub: ISIS Lrg Prnt GBR. Dist(s): Ulverscroft US

Famine of Horses: A Sir Robert Carey Mystery. unabr. ed. P. F. Chisholm. Read by Stephen Thorne. 7 cass. 1997. 61.95 Set. (960601) Eye Ear.
Paints a vivid picture of 16th century life in northern England, on Scotland's border. Sir Robert Carey has been dispatched to Carlisle - an area rife with warring clans, violence & corruption.

Famine Ships. unabr. ed. Edward Laxton. Read by Christopher Scott. 7 cass. (Running Time: 10 hrs. 30 mins.). 2001. 61.95 (23787) Pub: Soundings Ltd GBR. Dist(s): Ulverscroft US

Famous after Death. unabr. ed. Benjamin Cheever. Narrated by Johnny Heller. 6 cass. (Running Time: 7 hrs.). 1999. 49.00 (978-0-7887-3470-0(9), 95889E7) Recorded Bks.
Son of the esteemed writer John Cheever, Benjamin Cheever offers a darkly comic look at some of America's favorite obsessions. Noel Hammersmith is an overweight editor of diet books who yearns to be loved by beautiful women. When he is contacted by a visionary writer, Noel sees a brilliant way to attain thinness & adoration at the same time.

Famous Americans, Vol. 1. Short Stories. Arranged by Rich Herman. (J). 2004. audio compact disk 9.95 (978-0-9765630-0-6(2)) Family Bks N CDs.
Famous Americans Volume 1 - Contains six fun and exciting stories about: Louisa Alcott, Ben Franklin, George Washington, Kit Carson, Abraham Lincoln, and Thomas Jefferson. Your children will love these story CDs. Great patriotic music and voice talent make these stories come to life!http://www.FamilyBooksandCDs.com.

Famous Americans, Vol. 2. Arranged by Rich Herman. (J). 2004. audio compact disk 9.95 (978-0-9765630-1-3(0)) Family Bks N CDs.
Famous Americans Volume 2 - Contains six fun and exciting stories about Famous Americans. This selection contains two stories about George Washington, and stories about Thomas Jefferson, Paul Revere, Ben Franklin, and Andrew Jackson. Your children will love these story CDs. Great patriotic music and voice talent make these stories come to life!http://www.FamilyBooksandCDs.com.

Famous Americans in History. Barnaby Chesterman. Read by Kerry Shale & Lorelei King. (Classic Literature with Classical Music Ser.). (ENG.). (J). 2009. 39.99 (978-1-60775-748-1(6)) Find a World.

Famous Americans in History. Barnaby Chesterman. Read by Kerry Shale & Lorelei King. 2 cass. (Running Time: 2 hrs. 30 mins.). 2002. 13.98 (978-962-634-758-4(9), NA225814) Naxos.
This is the third title in the 'Famous People' series. Here are eight people who each left their mark upon American history through their achievements or through their own personality. They have been chosen to represent different areas of American life and background, showing the diversity of enterprise that has made the United States of America.

Famous Americans in History. unabr. ed. Barnaby Chesterman. Read by Kerry Shale & Lorelei King. 2 CDs. (Running Time: 2 hrs. 30 mins.). 2002. audio compact disk 17.98 (978-962-634-258-9(7), NA225812) Naxos.

Famous Banjo Pickin' Tunes. Janet Davis. 2000. pap. bk. 5.95 (978-0-7866-5074-3(5), 98530BCD) Mel Bay.

Famous Cases of Sherlock Holmes. unabr. ed. Arthur Conan Doyle. Read by John Brewster. 6 cass. (Running Time: 4 hrs. 31 min.). Incl. Case of the Five Orange Pips. Arthur Conan Doyle. (CXL512CX); Final Problem. (CXL512CX); Musgrave Ritual. (CXL512CX); Redheaded League. (CXL512CX); Scandal in Bohemia. Arthur Conan Doyle. (CXL512CX); Speckled Band. (CXL512CX); (Cassette Library). 1987. 44.98 (978-0-8072-2949-1(0), CXL512CX, Listening Lib) Random Audio Pubg.

Famous Cases of Sherlock Holmes, Set. unabr. ed. Arthur Conan Doyle. Read by John Brewster. 6 cass. 1999. 44.98 (LL 0026) AudioGO.

Famous Composers. Darren Henley. Read by Marin Alsop. (Running Time: 2 hrs. 30 mins.). (C). 2005. 20.95 (978-1-60083-736-4(0)) Iofy Corp.

Famous Composers. Darren Henley. Read by Marin Alsop. 2 CDs. (Running Time: 8246 sec.). (J). 2005. audio compact disk 17.98 (978-962-634-368-5(0)) Naxos UK GBR.

Famous Essays. Read by Marvin Miller. 6 cass. 35.70 (D-702) Audio Bk.
41 profound ocassionally funny & always provocative examples of the most civilized writings of the western world.

Famous Finales. (Running Time: 10 hrs.). 2004. 39.98 (978-1-57019-717-8(2)) Radio Spirits.

Famous Financial Fiascos, unabr. ed. John Train. Narrated by Nelson Runger. 3 cass. (Running Time: 3 hrs. 30 mins.). 1986. 26.00 (978-1-55690-173-7(9), 86390E7) Recorded Bks.
Anecdotal accounts of financial scams, embezzlements & crises throughout history.

Famous Firsts. (Running Time: 2 hrs.). 2004. 10.95 (978-1-57816-184-3(3)); audio compact disk 12.95 (978-1-57816-181-2(9)) Audio File.

Famous for Five Minutes. unabr. ed. Margaret Clark. Read by Peter Hardy. 3 cass. (Running Time: 3 hrs. 5 mins.). 2002. (978-1-74030-594-5(9)) Bolinda Pubng AUS.

Famous Gilson Bequest see Eyes of the Panther & Other Stories

Famous Gospel Favorites for Flatpicking Guitar QWIKGUIDE. William Bay. (ENG.). 2000. pap. bk. 5.95 (978-0-7866-5081-1(8), 98587BCD) Mel Bay.

Famous Greeks, Pts. I-II. Instructed by J. Rufus Fears. 12 cass. (Running Time: 12 hrs.). 54.95 (978-1-56585-076-7(9), 337) Teaching Co.

Famous Greeks, Pts. I-II. Instructed by J. Rufus Fears. 12 CDs. (Running Time: 12 hrs.). 2001. bk. 69.95 (978-1-56585-325-6(3), 337) Teaching Co.

Famous Greeks, Vol. 2. Instructed by J. Rufus Fears. 6 cass. (Running Time: 6 hrs.). 2001. 129.95 (978-1-56585-077-4(7)); audio compact disk 179.95 (978-1-56585-326-3(1)) Teaching Co.

Famous Jury Trials: Irene Miller Suspect & Wally Dent Stands Trial. 1 cass. (Running Time: 1 hr.). 2001. 6.98 (1868) Radio Spirits.

Famous "K" Talk. John Lilly & Toni Lilly. 1 cass. 10.00 (A0311-74) Sound Photosyn.
Aspen, Colorado, 8/11/74.

Famous Landmarks: Early Explorers Early Set B Audio CD. Mary Clare Goller. Adapted by Benchmark Education Staff. (J). 2007. audio compact disk 10.00 (978-1-4108-8223-3(3)) Benchmark Educ.

Famous Last Words, Talk on CD. Read by Sheri Dew. 2007. audio compact disk 13.95 (978-1-59038-737-5(6)) Desert Bks.

Famous Lasts. (Running Time: 2 hrs.). 2004. audio compact disk 12.95 (978-1-57816-185-0(1)) Audio File.

Famous People I Have Known. unabr. collector's ed. Ed McClanahan. Read by Walter Zimmerman. 6 cass. (Running Time: 6 hrs.). 1989. 36.00 (978-0-7366-1523-5(7), 2394) Books on Tape.
This is an autobiography by portraits.

Famous People in History. Nicolas Soames. Read by Trevor Nichols. (Running Time: 2 hrs. 30 mins.). (C). 2003. 20.95 (978-1-60083-737-1(9)) Iofy Corp.

Famous People in History, Set. abr. ed. Nicolas Soames. Read by Trevor Nichols. 2 cass. (Running Time: 2 hrs.). (J). (gr. 3-7). 1999. 16.85 Ulvrscrft Audio.
This lively history of 15 great personalities introduces a new series in the junior Classics range. Classical music that brings the periods to life.

Famous People in History, Vol. 1. Nicolas Soames. Read by Trevor Nichols. 2 cass. (Running Time: 2 hrs. 30 mins.). (J). (gr. 3-7). 1999. 13.98 (978-962-634-672-3(8), NA217214, Naxos AudioBooks) Naxos.
This lively history of 15 great personalities introduces children to those that changed the world in which they lived, including Alexander the Great, Abraham Lincoln, Christopher Columbus, William Shakespeare and others.

Famous People in History, Vol. 1. unabr. ed. Nicolas Soames. Read by Trevor Nichols. 2 CDs. (Running Time: 2 hrs. 30 mins.). (J). (gr. 3-7). 1999. audio compact disk 17.98 (978-962-634-172-8(6), NA217212, Naxos AudioBooks) Naxos.

Famous People in History, Vol. 2. Nicolas Soames. Read by Daniel Philpott et al. 2 cass. (Running Time: 2 hrs. 30 mins.). (J). (gr. 3-7). 2000. 13.98 (978-962-634-697-6(3), NA219714, Naxos AudioBooks); audio compact disk 17.98 (978-962-634-197-1(1), NA219712, Naxos AudioBooks) Naxos.
Recounts the stories of Alexander the Great, Joan of Arc, Leonardo da Vinci, Isaac Newton, Ludwig van Beethoven, Louis Pasteur, Marie Curie and Mahatma Gandhi.

Famous People in History: Christopher Columbus; Elizabeth I; William Shakespeare; Wolfgang Amadeus Mozart; Lord Nelson; Charles Darwin; Florence Nightingale; Abraham Lincoln; Anne Frank; Alexander the Great; Joan of Arc; Leonardo da Vinci; Isaac Newton; George Washington; Ludwig van Beethoven Louis Pasteur; Marie Curie. unabr. ed. Nicolas Soames. Read by Trevor Nichols et al. (J). 2006. 39.99 (978-1-59895-345-9(1)) Find a World.

Famous People in History (II) Nicolas Soames. Read by Daniel Philpott et al. (Running Time: 2 hrs. 45 mins.). (C). 2004. 20.95 (978-1-60083-738-8(7)) Iofy Corp.

Famous Personalities. John P. Fieg. 1988. 29.95 (978-0-933759-10-7(X)) Abaca Bks.

Famous Poems. unabr. ed. Christopher Marlowe et al. Read by Marvin Miller. 3 cass. 17.85 (E-601) Audio Bk.
80 of the world's best loved & known poems.

Famous Roadside Quickie: Radiant Embodiment. Executive Producer Sabine Grandke-Taft. 1. (Running Time: 7 .5 mins). 2005. audio compact disk 17.00 (978-1-59971-739-5(5)) AardGP.
7 1/2 minutes of fun partner energizing. You and your partner will connect in such a simple and joyful way.Radiant Embodiment - The Famous Roadside Quickie - This joyous 7 1/2 minute partner energizing exercise can be done on the roadside, in the office or at home. This session is a gift you can share with anyone. It awakens and clears the pathways for Life Force, restores energy and the ability to be present.

Famous Romans, Pts. I-II. Instructed by J. Rufus Fears. 12 CDs. (Running Time: 12 hrs.). 2001. bk. 69.95 (978-1-56585-331-7(8), 349); 54.95 (978-1-56585-082-8(3), 349) Teaching Co.

Famous Romans, Vol. 2. Instructed by J. Rufus Fears. 6 cass. (Running Time: 6 hrs.). 2001. 129.95 (978-1-56585-083-5(1)); audio compact disk 179.95 (978-1-56585-332-4(6)) Teaching Co.

Famous Story Poems. unabr. ed. Oscar Wilde. Read by Walter Zimmerman & Jack Benson. 1 cass. (Running Time: 76 min.). Dramatization. Incl. Annabel Lee. Edgar Allan Poe. 1979. (N-32); Ballad of Reading Gaol. Oscar Wilde. 1979. bk. (N-32); Belle Dame sans Merci. John Keats. 1979. (N-32); Gunga Din. Rudyard Kipling. 1979. (N-32); Highwayman. Alfred Noyes. 1979. (N-32); Hound of Heaven. Francis Thompson. 1979. (N-32); Kubla Khan. Samuel Taylor Coleridge. 1979. (N-32); My Last Duchess. Robert Browning. 1979. (N-32); Raven. Edgar Allan Poe. 1979. (N-32); 1979. 7.95 (N-32) Jimcin Record.

Famous Westerns. unabr. ed. Perf. by Brace Beemer et al. 10 vols. (Running Time: 10 hrs.). (10-Hour Collections). 2001. bk. 39.98 (978-1-57019-370-5(3), OTR4473) Pub: Radio Spirits. Dist(s): AudioGO
Return with us now to those thrilling days of yesteryear with radio's greatest cowboys, including Brace Beemer, John Dehner, Jimmy Stewart and William Conrad.

Famously Funny: A Collection of Beloved Stories & Poems. Short Stories. As told by Jim Weiss. Prod. by Greathall Productions Inc. 1 CD. (Running Time: 70 mins.). Dramatization. (Storyteller's Version Ser.). (J). 2004. audio compact disk 14.95 (978-1-882513-83-3(5)) Greathall Prods.
Prepare to laugh out loud! Jim Weiss has mixed together some of the funniest stories and poems from the world's wittiest authors for a recording that will delight the whole family. Meet an astounding array of characters: The Princess and the Pea, Emperor's New Clothes, Anansi, Father William,Jabberwocky, The yak, The Tiiger, The Brahman and Jackal.

Fan, Set. abr. ed. Peter Abrahams. Read by Joe Mantegna. 2 cass. (Running Time: 3 hrs.). 1995. 16.95 (978-1-879371-93-4(6), 392956) Pub Mills.
Two men. One is a baseball star. He has an ex-cheerleader for a wife & a girl in every big league town. The ball comes off his bat like a firecracker. Bobby Raybum isn't just a ballplayer. He's a god. The other has a wife who's left him. His bank balance slides towards zero while his child support & car payments soar through the roof. He hates his job & the product he pushes. But his license plate reads, "WNSX." Gil Renard isn't just a knife salesman, he's the fan. But what happens when the barrier between idolator & idol collapses? What happens when Gil Renard sacrifices everything he has left to raise the Sox from the depths & to rescue Bobby Raybum from what threatens to be an irreversible slump? What happens when Gil Renard crosses the white line & anoints himself a Player in the Game?.

Fan Club Favorites: Sex, Death, Peace, Love, Drugs & Computers. Perf. by Peter Alsop. 1 cass. 11.00; audio compact disk Moose Schl Records.

Fan-Tan. unabr. ed. Marlon Brando & Donald Cammell. Narrated by Simon Vance. (Running Time: 9 hrs. 30 mins. 0 sec.). (ENG.). 2005. audio compact disk 29.99 (978-1-4001-0190-0(5)); audio compact disk 19.99 (978-1-4001-5190-5(2)); audio compact disk 59.99 (978-1-4001-3190-7(1)) Pub: Tantor Media. Dist(s): IngramPubServ

Fanatic's Guide to Ear Training & Sight Singing. Bruce E. Arnold. (C). 1999. pap. bk. 31.50 (978-1-890944-19-3(X)) Muse Eek.

Fancies & Goodnights. abr. ed. John Collier. Read by Vincent Price. 1 cass. Incl. Evening Primrose. (SWC 1652); Touch of Nutmeg Makes It. (SWC 1652); 1989. 12.95 (978-0-89845-217-4(1), SWC 1652) HarperCollins Pubs.

Fancy Feet. unabr. ed. Patricia Reilly Giff. 1 cass. (Running Time: 49 min.). (New Kids at the Polk Street School Ser.). (J). (gr. 1-2). 1990. 15.98 incl. pap. bk. & guide. (978-0-8072-0184-8(7), FTR 142 SP, Listening Lib) Random Audio Pubg.

***Fancy Nancy.** abr. ed. Jane O'connor. Read by Isabel Keating. (ENG.). 2007. (978-0-06-133537-2(1)) HarperCollins Pubs.

***Fancy Nancy.** unabr. ed. Jane O'connor. Read by Isabel Keating. (ENG.). 2007. (978-0-06-146928-2(9)) HarperCollins Pubs.

***Fancy Nancy & the Boy from Paris.** Jane O'Connor. Illus. by Robin Preiss Glasser. (Fancy Nancy Ser.). (J). 2011. 9.99 (978-0-06-184055-5(6), HarperFestival) HarperCollins Pubs.

***Fancy Nancy & the Boy from Paris.** unabr. ed. Jane O'connor. Read by Isabel Keating. Illus. by Robin Preiss Glasser. (ENG.). 2010. (978-0-06-203454-0(5)) HarperCollins Pubs.

***Fancy Nancy & the Delectable Cupcakes.** unabr. ed. Jane O'connor. Illus. by Robin Preiss Glasser. (ENG.). 2010. (978-0-06-202698-9(4)) HarperCollins Pubs.

***Fancy Nancy & the Fabulous Fashion Boutique.** unabr. ed. Jane O'connor. Illus. by Robin Preiss Glasser. 2010. (978-0-06-199673-3(4)); (978-0-06-206374-8(X)) HarperCollins Pubs.

***Fancy Nancy & the Late, Late, LATE Night.** unabr. ed. Jane O'connor. Illus. by Robin Preiss Glasser. (ENG.). 2010. (978-0-06-203458-8(8), HarperFestival) HarperCollins Pubs.

***Fancy Nancy & the Posh Puppy.** abr. ed. Jane O'connor. (ENG.). 2007. (978-0-06-133536-5(3)) HarperCollins Pubs.

***Fancy Nancy & the Posh Puppy.** unabr. ed. Jane O'connor. (ENG.). 2007. (978-0-06-146929-9(7)) HarperCollins Pubs.

***Fancy Nancy & the Sensational Babysitter.** unabr. ed. Jane O'connor. Illus. by Robin Preiss Glasser. (ENG.). 2010. (978-0-06-203459-5(6), HarperFestival) HarperCollins Pubs.

***Fancy Nancy at the Museum.** unabr. ed. Jane O'connor. Read by Isabel Keating. Illus. by Robin Preiss Glasser. (ENG.). 2010. (978-0-06-203455-7(3)) HarperCollins Pubs.

***Fancy Nancy: Bonjour, Butterfly.** unabr. ed. Jane O'connor. Read by Isabel Keating. (ENG.). 2008. (978-0-06-157954-7(8)); (978-0-06-167370-2(6)) HarperCollins Pubs.

***Fancy Nancy: Every Day Is Earth Day.** unabr. ed. Jane O'connor. Illus. by Robin Preiss Glasser. (ENG.). 2010. (978-0-06-202699-6(2)) HarperCollins Pubs.

***Fancy Nancy: My Family History.** unabr. ed. Jane O'connor. Illus. by Robin Preiss Glasser. (ENG.). 2010. (978-0-06-202700-9(X)); (978-0-06-206375-5(8)) HarperCollins Pubs.

***Fancy Nancy: Pajama Day.** unabr. ed. Jane O'connor. Illus. by Robin Preiss Glasser. (ENG.). 2010. (978-0-06-202701-6(8)) HarperCollins Pubs.

***Fancy Nancy: Poison Ivy Expert.** unabr. ed. Jane O'connor. Read by Isabel Keating. Illus. by Robin Preiss Glasser. (ENG.). 2010. (978-0-06-203457-1(X)) HarperCollins Pubs.

***Fancy Nancy Sees Stars.** unabr. ed. Jane O'connor. Read by Isabel Keating. Illus. by Robin Preiss Glasser. (ENG.). 2010. (978-0-06-203456-4(1)) HarperCollins Pubs.

***Fancy Nancy Sees Stars Book & CD.** Jane O'Connor. Illus. by Robin Preiss Glasser. (I Can Read Book 1 Ser.). (J). 2011. 9.99 (978-0-06-188273-9(9), HarperFestival) HarperCollins Pubs.

***Fancy Nancy: Spectacular Spectacles.** unabr. ed. Jane O'connor. Illus. by Robin Preiss Glasser. (ENG.). 2010. (978-0-06-202702-3(6)) HarperCollins Pubs.

***Fancy Nancy: Splendiferous Christmas.** unabr. ed. Jane O'connor. Read by Isabel Keating. (ENG.). 2009. (978-0-06-180847-0(4)); (978-0-06-180848-7(2)) HarperCollins Pubs.

***Fancy Nancy: the Dazzling Book Report.** unabr. ed. Jane O'connor. Illus. by Robin Preiss Glasser. (ENG.). 2010. (978-0-06-202704-7(2)) HarperCollins Pubs.

***Fancy Nancy: the Show Must Go On.** unabr. ed. Jane O'connor. Illus. by Robin Preiss Glasser. (ENG.). 2010. (978-0-06-202705-4(0)) HarperCollins Pubs.

***Fancy Nancy: the 100th Day of School.** unabr. ed. Jane O'connor. Illus. by Robin Preiss Glasser. (ENG.). 2010. (978-0-06-202703-0(4)) HarperCollins Pubs.

Fancy Pants. unabr. collector's ed. Susan Elizabeth Phillips. Read by Anna Fields. 11 cass. (Running Time: 16 hrs. 30 min.). 1996. 88.00 (978-0-7366-3444-1(4), 4088) Books on Tape.
For Francesca Day, it's not the end of her world, but close to it. She's London-bred, wealthy & sophisticated, but fate leaves her flat broke & stranded on a back road in Texas. Now she's got to deal with reality without her rich girl props. How can she do it? In Dallas Beaudine, gritty & handsome, lies the answer. He stops his car to help Francesca, who needs a tune up on her life, as well as her car. Stopping could be the biggest mistake, or best time, ever.

Fandom of the Operator. unabr. ed. Robert Rankin. Narrated by Robert Rankin. 7 cass. (Running Time: 9 hrs. 30 mins.). 2001. 67.00 (978-1-84197-475-0(7)) Recorded Bks.

Fanfare Brillante: For Trombone Quartet. Composed by Nathan Farrell. 2007. pap. bk. 16.95 (978-90-431-2556-7(3), 9043125563) H Leonard.

Fanfare for Organ. Perf. by David Poulter. 1 cass. 1997. 11.95 (MoreHse Pubng); audio compact disk 16.95 CD. (MoreHse Pubng) Church Pub Inc.
Presents 22 contemporary pieces including "A Thornbury Fanfare," "Prelude on St. Botolph" & "Versets on a Choral Melody".

Fanfare 1: Cambridge Primary Music. Tim Cain. Contrib. by Tim Cain. (Running Time: 45 mins.). (Fanfare Ser.). (ENG.). 1997. audio compact disk 36.00 (978-0-521-45860-3(9)) Cambridge U Pr.

Fanfare 2: Cambridge Primary Music. Tim Cain. Contrib. by Tim Cain. (Running Time: 1 hr.). (Fanfare Ser.). (ENG.). 1997. audio compact disk 35.50 (978-0-521-45861-0(7)) Cambridge U Pr.

Fanfares of the Faith. Created by Hal Leonard Corporation Staff. 1995. audio compact disk 90.00 (978-0-00-512276-1(7), 75608286) Pub: Brentwood Music. Dist(s): H Leonard

Fanfares of the Faith. Created by Hal Leonard Corporation Staff. 1996. 11.98 (978-0-00-513536-5(2), 75608591); audio compact disk 90.00 (978-0-00-513535-8(4), 75608590) Pub: Brentwood Music. Dist(s): H Leonard

Fanfares of the Faith. Created by Hal Leonard Corporation Staff. 1996. audio compact disk 16.98 (978-0-00-513537-2(0), 75608589) Pub: Brentwood Music. Dist(s): H Leonard

Fanfares of the Faith, Vol. 2. Created by Hal Leonard Corporation Staff. 1996. 90.00 (978-0-00-513534-1(6), 75608592) Pub: Brentwood Music. Dist(s): H Leonard

Fanfou dans les Bayous: The Adventures of a Bilingual Elephant in Louisiana. Andre P. Perales. Illus. by Christian Jarlov. (J). (gr. 1-7). 1982. 11.95 (978-0-88289-410-2(2)) Pelican.

Fanfou dans les Bayous CD: Les aventures d'un elephant bilingue en Louisiane. Andre-Paul Perales. Narrated by Andre-Paul Perales. (Running Time: 30 mins.). (FRE.). (J). 2009. audio compact disk 15.95 (978-1-58980-740-2(5)) Pelican.

Fang. unabr. ed. James Patterson. Read by Jill Apple. (Running Time: 5 hrs. 30 mins.). (Maximum Ride Ser.). (ENG.). 2010. 15.98 (978-1-60024-790-3(3)); audio compact disk 22.98 (978-1-60024-789-7(X)) Pub: Hachet Audio. Dist(s): HachBkGrp

***Fang.** unabr. ed. James Patterson. Read by Jill Apple. (Running Time: 5 hrs. 30 mins.). (ENG.). 2011. audio compact disk 9.98 (978-1-60788-819-2(X)) Pub: Hachet Audio. Dist(s): HachBkGrp

***Fang: A Maximum Ride Novel.** unabr. ed. James Patterson. Narrated by Jill Apple. 1 MP3-CD. (Running Time: 5 hrs. 29 mins.). 2010. 34.99 (978-1-60788-450-7(X)) AudioGO.

***Fang: A Maximum Ride Novel.** unabr. ed. James Patterson. Narrated by Jill Apple. 5 CDs. (Running Time: 5 hrs. 29 mins.). 2010. audio compact disk 59.99 (978-1-60788-313-5(9)) Pub: Hachet Audio. Dist(s): HachBkGrp

Fanged Justice. unabr. ed. Patricia White. Read by Rusty Nelson. 6 cass. (Running Time: 7 hrs.). 2001. 39.95 (978-1-55686-761-3(1)) Books in Motion.

Mystery writer Albert Weston rescues two women after an auto accident. Hearing of their attempted murder, Weston befriends them and inherits a terrifying chase through the desert.

Fangland. unabr. ed. John Marks. Narrated by Ellen Archer et al. 10 CDs. (Running Time: 12 hrs. 30 mins. 0 sec.). (ENG.). 2007. audio compact disk 37.99 (978-1-4001-0359-1(2)); audio compact disk 24.99 (978-1-4001-5359-6(X)); audio compact disk 75.99 (978-1-4001-3359-8(9)) Pub: Tantor Media. Dist(s): IngramPubServ

FangZheng Chinese Fonts, 200 Simplified & Traditional. 2005. audio compact disk 149.00 (978-0-9715114-6-0(2)) TwinBridge.

Fanning Revival Fires, Set. As told by Frank Damazio. 3 Cass. 1998. 15.00 (978-1-886849-30-3(7)) CityChristian.

Fanning the Flames. Perf. by Maria Muldaur. 1 cass., 1 CD. 7.98 (TA 33394); 7.98 (TA 33394); audio compact disk 12.78 CD Jewel box. (TA 833394); audio compact disk 12.78 CD Jewel box. (TA 83394) NewSound.

Fanny Crosby. Doris Moose. (Running Time: 085 min.). (YA). (gr. 5 up). 2000. 9.95 (978-0-89084-910-1(2), 051169) BJUPr.

Fanny Crosby. abr. ed. Bernard Ruffin. 1 cass. (Running Time: 1 hrs. 30 min.). (Heroes of the Faith Ser.). (C). 4.97 (978-1-57748-089-1(9)) Barbour Pub.

Fanny Herself, Edna Ferber. Read by Flo Gibson. 7 cass. (Running Time: 10 hrs.). 1995. 25.95 (978-1-55685-377-7(7)) Audio Bk Con.

This somewhat autobiographical novel about the gifted Fanny Branbeis is sheer delight. From her childhood in Winnebago, with her kindly fiesty mother, who introduces her into the world of merchandising, we follow the young lady's development. Her achievements, talents, sensitivity & romance are explored with verve in the big cities of Chicago, New York & Paris & the wilds of Colorado.

Fanny Herself. abr. ed. Edna Ferber. 4 cass. 1999. 29.95 (978-1-893079-02-1(3), JCCAUDIOBOOKS) Jewish Contempry Classics.

Classic novel of a young Jewish girl's emergence toward liberation & fulfillment in the years before the first World War.

Fanny Hill. John Cleland. Read by Emma Fielding. (Running Time: 3 hrs. 45 mins.). 2002. 24.95 (978-1-60083-739-5(5)) Iofy Corp.

Fanny Hill: Or Memoirs of A Woman of Pleasure. abr. ed. John Cleland. Read by Connie Foster. Ed. by Beth Baxter. 2 cass. (Running Time: 3 hrs.). 1991. 12.95 (978-1-882071-24-1(7), 026) B-B Audio.

Fanny is more than sexually stimulating; shes a complex and believable character. In many ways, shes the ideal erotic companionuninhibited and capable of any variation of technique, yet genuinely tender, loving, discreet-every mans dream. Share her.

Fanny Hill: Or Memoirs of A Woman of Pleasure, unabr. ed. John Cleland. Narrated by Barbara McCulloh. 6 cass. (Running Time: 8 hrs. 30 mins.). 1986. 51.00 (978-1-55690-174-4(7), 86860E7) Recorded Bks.

The erotic adventures of an 18th Century "Lady of Pleasure".

Fanny Hill's Daughter. abr. ed. Read by Jill Daly. 3 cass. (Running Time: 3 hrs. 30 min.). 1992. 12.95 (978-1-882071-35-7(2)) B-B Audio.

Fanny Hill was as beautiful as she was bawdy. For two hundred years, readers have enjoyed learning of her exploits. Now Fanny is vividly reincarnated in the prodigal person of her only child, a young woman whose inherited skills of seduction made her th.

Fanny McBride. unabr. ed. Catherine Cookson. Read by Susan Jameson. 6 cass. (Running Time: 6 hrs.). 1993. 54.95 (978-0-7451-5849-5(8), CAB 212) AudioGO.

Fanny McBride. unabr. collector's ed. Catherine Cookson. Read by Mary Woods. 8 cass. (Running Time: 8 hrs.). 1984. 48.00 (978-0-7366-0941-8(5), 1884) Books on Tape.

No longer able to seek the protection of her husband, Fanny McBride now faces all of life's challenges alone.

Fanny Trollope. unabr. ed. Teresa Ransom. Narrated by Prunella Scales. 8 cass. (Running Time: 11 hrs.). 2001. 72.00 (978-1-84197-189-6(8), H1173E7) Recorded Bks.

The wealth & power of Fanny Trollope's writing has largely been forgotten today. If she is known at all, it is merely as Antony Trollope's mother. Yet in her time, her fame totally eclipsed her son. She was admired by such celebrities as Charles Dickens & Mark Twain for her wickedly accurate contemporary satires, & her style undoubtedly had a profound influence on her son. The importance of her contribution to contemporary literature is only now beginning to be recognized.

Fanny Witch & the Thunder Lizard. unabr. ed. Jeremy Strong. Read by Susan Sheridan. 2 cass. (Running Time: 3 hrs.). (J). 1997. 18.95 (CCA 3371, Chivers Child Audio) AudioGO.

Fanny Witch Goes Spikky Spoo. unabr. ed. Jeremy Strong. Read by Susan Sheridan. 2 cass. (Running Time: 2 hrs.). (J). 1997. 18.95 (CCA 3371, Chivers Child Audio) AudioGO.

Fantasia. 1 CD. (Running Time: 30 mins.). (J). (ps-3). 1999. audio compact disk 23.77 (978-0-7634-0593-9(0)) W Disney Records.

Fantasia, Vol. 2. 1 cass. (J). (ps-3). 1995. 14.37 (978-1-55723-162-8(1)) W Disney Records.

Fantasie Arabe. unabr. ed. 1 cass. 12.95 (7318) J Norton Pubs.

Fantasies: Short Story Masterpieces. unabr. ed. Ed. by Jackie Mallis. Narrated by Nelita B. Castillo & Amato Petale. 10 cass. (Running Time: 45 min. per cass.). (J). (gr. 5 up). 1984. bk. 156.74 (978-0-86617-052-9(9)) Multi Media TX.

Each story comes with a complete lesson plan plus a self-instructional student activity text & printed script for the tape. A teacher's guide accompanies each tape. 25 short stories from the great masters are included.

Fantasma de Canterville/Sherlock Holmes y el Sabueso de los Baskerville. Oscar Wilde & Arthur Conan Doyle. (Playaway Young Adult Ser.). (SPA.). 2009. 60.00 (978-1-60775-581-4(5)) Find a World.

Fantasma de la Opera. abr. ed. Gaston Leroux. Read by Fabio Camero. 3 CDs.Tr. of Phantom of the Opera. (SPA.). 2002. audio compact disk 17.00 (978-958-43-0183-3(7)) YoYoMusic.

Fantastic: The Life of Arnold Schwarzenegger. abr. ed. Laurence Leamer. Read by Mel Foster. (Running Time: 8 hrs.). 2005. 39.25 (978-1-59737-322-7(2), 9781597373227, BADLE); 24.95 (978-1-59737-321-0(4), 9781597373210, BAD); audio compact disk 87.25 (978-1-59737-318-0(4), 9781597373180, BACDLib Ed); 29.95 (978-1-59737-315-9(X), 9781597373159); cass. & DVD 74.25 (978-1-59737-316-6(8), 9781597373166, BAudLibEd); audio compact disk 39.25 (978-1-59737-320-3(6), 9781597373203, Brlnc Audio MP3 Lib); audio compact disk 24.95 (978-1-59737-319-7(2), 9781597373197, Brilliance MP3); audio compact disk 29.95 (978-1-59737-317-3(6), 9781597373173, BACD) Brilliance Audio.

The life of Arnold Schwarzenegger is one of the most extreordinary success stories of our time. An immigrant with a heavy accent from a village in Austria, he became the greatest bodybuilder in history, the number one movie star in the world, the Republican husband of a Kennedy princess, and the governor of the greatest of American states. Fantastic shows how and why this man of willful ambition and limitless drive achieved his unprecedented accomplishments. Leamer has had exclusive, intimate interviews with Govemor Schwarzenegger, his closest associates, including his elementary school friends in Austria, his mentors, bodybuilding competitors, lifelong friends, first serious girlfriend, political rivals, agents, publicists and producers, many of whom have never been interviewed before. Leamer captures the public and private Schwarzenegger, a political/cultural figure unlike any other, who could change the face of politics in our country. This intimate book is studded with news-making revelations: · The untold story of Arnold's traumatic relationship with his father · How Arnold's first mentor, a Jewish partisan in WW II, helped shape the youth · The intimate story of Arnold's first great love and the five years the couple lived together · Why Arnold married Maria Shriver and the startling story of their wedding day · The star who hated Arnold and tried to ruin his career · How Arnold overcame the sordid sexual revelations and prevailed politically · How Maria took over management of her husband's campaign · The game plan that may bring Arnold to the White House.

Fantastic Children Soundtrack. (YA). 2006. 14.98 (978-1-59409-612-9(0)) Bandai Ent.

Fantastic Firesides for Youth. Michael D. Christensen et al. 2 cass. 1998. 14.95 Set. (978-1-57008-545-1(5), Bkcraft Inc) Deseret Bk.

Fantastic Journey. Perf. by Erich Kunzel & Cincinnati Pops Orchestra. 1 cass., 1 CD. 7.98 (TA 30231); audio compact disk 12.78 CD Jewel box. (TA 80231) NewSound.

Fantastic Mr. Fox see Roald Dahl

Fantastic Mr. Fox. Roald Dahl. Read by Lionel Jeffries. 1 cass. (Running Time: 1 hr. 05 min.). (J). (gr. k-2). (CC/016) C to C Cassettes.

Farmers Boggis, Bunce & Bean try to stop Mr. Fox who is stealing their livestock.

Fantastic Mr. Fox. Roald Dahl. (Running Time: 54 min.). (J). 11.95 (HarperChildAud) HarperCollins Pubs.

Fantastic Mr. Fox. unabr. ed. Roald Dahl. Read by Lionel Jeffries. 1 cass. (Running Time: 1 hr. 5 mins.). 2002. (978-1-85549-732-0(8)) Cover To Cover GBR.

Boggis, Bunce and Bean are the nastiest farmers ever and are determined to catch Mr. Fox. But clever Mr. Fox has other plans.

***Fantastic Mr. Fox.** unabr. ed. Roald Dahl. Read by Roald Dahl. (ENG.). 2005. (978-0-06-089374-3(5)); (978-0-06-089373-6(7)) HarperCollins Pubs.

Fantastic Mr. Fox. unabr. ed. Roald Dahl. Read by Roald Dahl. (J). 2005. audio compact disk 9.99 (978-0-06-053627-5(6), HarperChildAud) HarperCollins Pubs.

Fantastic Reality. unabr. ed. Excerpts. Meatball Fulton & Thomas M. Lopez. 1 cass. (Running Time: 60 min.). 1977. 5.00 (978-1-881137-27-6(9)) ZBS Found.

Excerpts from ZBS stories.

Fantastic Rocks/Frogs & Toads. Steck-Vaughn Staff. 2002. (978-0-7398-5985-8(4)) SteckVau.

Fantastic Tales of Ray Bradbury. unabr. ed. Ray Bradbury. Read by Ray Bradbury. 6 cass. (Running Time: 4 hr. 40 min.). Incl. Crowd. 1979. (CXL 500CX); Dwarf. 1979. (CXL 500CX); Fever Dream. 1979. (CXL 500CX); Foghorn. 1979. (CXL 500CX); Illuminations. 1979. (CXL 500CX); Illustrated Man. 1979. (CXL 500CX); John Huff's Leavetaking (Short Story) 1979. (CXL 500CX); Lake. 1979. (CXL 500CX); Marionettes, Inc. 1979. (CXL 500CX); Pedestrian. 1979. (CXL 500CX); Smile. 1979. (CXL 500CX); Sound of Thunder. 1979. (CXL 500CX); There Will Come Soft Rains. 1979. (CXL 500CX); Veldt. Ray Bradbury. 1979. (CXL 500CX); (Cassette Library). 1979. 44.98 (978-0-8072-2900-2(8), CXL 500CX, Listening Lib); (Listening Lib) Random Audio Pubg.

Demonstrate why Ray Bradbury has been called "America's finest living fantasist. " Included in this collection are " The veldt"-children's futuristic nursery room holds exactly what meets the eye, & "There Will Come Soft Rains"-all the comforts of home, but nobody to enjoy them.

Fantastic Tales of Ray Bradbury, Set. unabr. ed. Ray Bradbury. Read by Ray Bradbury. 6 cass. 1999. 44.98 (SAB 013) AudioGO.

Fantastic Tales of Ray Bradbury, Set. unabr. ed. Short Stories. Ray Bradbury. Read by Ray Bradbury. 6 cass. (Running Time: 4 hrs. 37 mins.). 44.95 (L147) Blckstn Audio.

Includes: "The Lake," "The Smile," "The Foghorn," "The Veldt," "The Crowd," "John Huff's Leave-Taking" (from "Dandelion Wine"), "Illuminations," "The Illustrated Man," "Marionettes, Inc.," "The Pedestrian," "The Dwarf" & "Fever Dream.".

Fantasy see Twentieth-Century Poetry in English, No. 24, Recordings of Poets Reading Their Own Poetry

Fantasy: The Best of 2002. unabr. ed. Ed. by Robert A. Silverberg & Karen Haber. 6 cass. (Running Time: 10 hrs.). 2002. 32.00 (978-1-59040-554-3(4)) Audio Lit.

The present anthology is intended to show reach and range as it is demonstrated nowadays in the shorter forms of fiction. You will find very little that is formulaic here, although we have not ignored any of fantasy's great traditions.

Fantasy & Daydreaming, The Uses Of. unabr. ed. Jerome L. Singer. 1 cass. 12.95 (29306) J Norton Pubs.

Singer explains why fantasies & daydreams are so important to healthy development & how best to stimulate & use them.

Fantasy & Reality: Ray Bradbury Describes His World of Science Fiction. 1 cass. (Running Time: 27 min.). 14.95 (30121) MMI Corp.

Discusses the relationship between today's reality & fiction's fantasy.

Fantasy Bond Set: Freeing Yourself for Real Life Love. David Grudermeyer & Rebecca Grudermeyer. 2 cass. 18.95 INCL. HANDOUTS. (T-01) Willingness Wrks.

Fantasy Bond II Set: The Secret Source of Relationship Sabotage. David Grudermeyer & Rebecca Grudermeyer. 2 cass. 18.95 INCL. HANDOUTS. (T-22) Willingness Wrks.

Fantasy Bond III Set: Do You Love Your Partner or Your Fantasy? David Grudermeyer & Rebecca Grudermeyer. 2 cass. 18.95 INCL. HANDOUTS. (T-62) Willingness Wrks.

Fantasy in Death. abr. ed. J. D. Robb, pseud. Read by Susan Ericksen. 5 CDs. (Running Time: 6 hrs.). (In Death Ser.). 2010. audio compact disk 26.99 (978-1-4233-8374-1(5), 9781423383741, BACD) Brilliance Audio.

Fantasy in Death. abr. ed. J. D. Robb, pseud. Read by Susan Ericksen. (Running Time: 6 hrs.). (In Death Ser.). 2010. audio compact disk 14.99 (978-1-4233-8375-8(3), 9781423383758, BCD Value Price) Brilliance Audio.

Fantasy in Death. unabr. ed. J. D. Robb, pseud. Read by Susan Ericksen. 11 CDs. (Running Time: 12 hrs.). (In Death Ser.). 2010. audio compact disk 38.99 (978-1-4233-8368-0(0), 9781423383680, Bril Audio CD Unabri) Brilliance Audio.

***Fantasy in Death.** unabr. ed. J. D. Robb, pseud. Read by Susan Ericksen. (Running Time: 11 hrs.). (In Death Ser.). 2010. 24.99 (978-1-4233-8372-7(9), 9781423383727, BAD); 39.97 (978-1-4233-8371-0(0), 9781423383710, Brlnc Audio MP3 Lib); 39.97 (978-1-4233-8373-4(7), 9781423383734, BADLE); 24.99 (978-1-4233-8370-3(2), 9781423383703, Brilliance MP3); audio compact disk 92.97 (978-1-4233-8369-7(9), 9781423383697, BriAudCD Unabrid) Brilliance Audio.

Fantasy in Music. Prod. by Zobeida Perez. 1994. 17.00 (978-0-89898-794-2(6), BMR05080, Warner Bro) Alfred Pub.

***Fantasy Lover.** unabr. ed. Sherrilyn Kenyon. Narrated by Christine Louise Marshall. 1 Playaway. (Running Time: 10 hrs. 30 mins.). (Dark-Hunter Ser.). 2009. 89.95 (978-0-7927-6469-4(2)); audio compact disk 89.95 (978-0-7927-6468-7(4)) AudioGO.

Fantasy vs. Science Fiction. SERCON Panel. 1 cass. 9.00 (A0129-87) Sound Photosyn.

A discussion at the SF writers convention by Larry Niven, Goldstein, Douglas, & Lowentrout.

Fantomas, le Paravent Chinois, Set. Marcel Allain. Perf. by Cie de l'Escabeau. 2 cass. Dramatization. (FRE.). 1996. 28.95 (1843-LQP) Olivia & Hill.

Theatrical adaptation of one of the adventures of the famous crime fighter.

Fantome De l'Opera. Leroux. audio compact disk 12.95 (978-0-8219-3769-3(3)) EMC-Paradigm.

Fantome de l Opera. Gaston Leroux. pap. bk. 21.95 (978-88-7754-701-9(4)) Pub: Cideb ITA. Dist(s): Distribks Inc

Far As the Curse Is Found: Human Suffering & the Hope of the Gospel. Paul David Tripp et al. (ENG.). 2006. audio compact disk 42.95 (978-1-934885-66-6(5)) New Growth Pr.

Far As the Curse Is Found: Human Suffering & the Hope of the Gospel. unabr. ed. Joni Eareckson Tada et al. 6 cass. (Running Time: 5 hrs. 30 min.). 2003. 42.95 (978-1-930921-00-9(4)) Resources.

Far Away & Long Ago: A History of My Early Life. unabr. collector's ed. W. H. Hudson. Read by John MacDonald. 6 cass. (Running Time: 9 hrs.). 1991. 48.00 (978-0-7366-1884-7(8), 2713) Books on Tape.

William Henry Hudson was born more than 100 years ago in Argentina of an English father & an American mother. Hudson's parents encouraged his love of nature. Far Away & Long Ago, recalls this idyllic childhood. The Argentina of Hudson's boyhood was a poor & undeveloped wide open land where nature ruled.

Far Country. unabr. collector's ed. Nevil Shute. Read by Christopher Hurt. 8 cass. (Running Time: 12 hrs.). 1986. 64.00 (978-0-7366-1004-9(9), 1937) Books on Tape.

Jennifer fled the drab monotony of post-war London. When she landed in Australia, it was like coming home. She loved it & when she met Carl, she had every reason to stay. But the two came from different worlds, & this is the story of their building a life together.

Far Distant Place. unabr. ed. Danielle Thomas. Narrated by Liza Ross. 9 CDs. (Running Time: 10 hrs.). 2001. audio compact disk 89.00 (978-1-4025-1016-8(0), C1594) Recorded Bks.

The Iditarod, known as the Last Great Race, is the longest and most dangerous race in the world. In March each year, contestants face over 1000 miles of unforgiving winds from the North Pole and the mountainous wastelands of Alaska. Natu is a young native woman who is passionate about her ancestral land. She always dreamt of running the race, but has chosen to work with her fiance on the oilfields in the north. A family death forces her to reconsider her priorities, and she returns home to prepare. The Iditarod offers the ultimate triumph for those who succeed, but pain and tragedy for victims of the forbidding conditions.

Far Distant Place. unabr. ed. Danielle Thomas & Philip Hook. Narrated by Liza Ross & Christopher Kay. 7 cass. (Running Time: 10 hrs.). 2000. 64.00 (978-1-84197-223-7(1), H1210L8) Recorded Bks.

The Iditarod, known as the Last Great Race, is the longest & most dangerous race in the world. Contestants face over 1000 miles of unforgiving winds from the North Pole & the mountainous wastelands of Alaska. Natu, a young native woman, is passionate about her ancestral land & always dreamt of running the race. When a family death forces her to reconsider her priorities, she returns home to prepare.

Far from Home: I Want to Be Like You. Perf. by Far From Home. 1 cass. 1998. 10.98 (978-0-7601-2548-9(1)); audio compact disk 16.98 (978-0-7601-2549-6(X)) Provident Music.

Unite parents & youth through music that communicates their passionate commitment to Jesus Christ.

Far from Over. unabr. ed. Sheila O'Flanagan. Read by Kate Binchy. 12 cass. (Running Time: 18 hrs.). 2001. 96.95 (978-0-7540-0656-5(5), CAB 2078) Pub: Chivers Audio Bks GBR. Dist(s): AudioGO

Gemma Garvey's marriage has been over for ages. And it was Gemma's choice to end it, her decision to go it alone with two kids, rather than pretend her marriage to career-obsessed David was working. So why is she so upset when he marries that flame-haired bimbo, Orla O'Neill? Is it that Orla is nearer to Gemma's teenaged daughter's age, than to her own? For Orla, being wife number two isn't all she'd imagined. And the trouble has only just begun.

Far from the Madding Crowd. Thomas Hardy. Narrated by Flo Gibson. (ENG.). 2008. audio compact disk 36.95 (978-1-60646-017-7(X)) Audio Bk Con.

***Far from the Madding Crowd.** Thomas Hardy. Narrated by Nathaniel Parker. (Running Time: 14 hrs. 0 mins. 0 sec.). (Cover to Cover Ser.). (ENG.). 2010. audio compact disk 29.95 (978-1-60283-883-3(6)) Pub: AudioGO. Dist(s): Perseus Dist

Far from the Madding Crowd. Thomas Hardy. 2007. 16.95 (978-1-60112-016-8(8)) Babblebooks.

Far from the Madding Crowd. Thomas Hardy. Read by Nathaniel Parker. 12 vols. (Running Time: 18 hrs.). 2003. audio compact disk 110.95 (978-0-7540-8745-8(X)) Pub: Chivers Audio Bks GBR. Dist(s): AudioGO

Far from the Madding Crowd. Thomas Hardy. Read by John Lee. (Playaway Adult Nonfiction Ser.). (ENG.). 2009. 69.99 (978-1-60812-551-7(3)) Find a World.

Far from the Madding Crowd. Thomas Hardy. Read by Neville Jason. (Running Time: 4 hrs.). 1999. 24.95 (978-1-60083-740-1(9)) Iofy Corp.

Far from the Madding Crowd. Read by Neville Jason. Ed. by Thomas Hardy. 3 cass. (Running Time: 4 hrs.). 1998. 17.98 (978-962-634-636-5(1), NA313614, Naxos AudioBooks) Naxos.
The authors use of characters represent an elaborate weaving of styles in this literary creation, first published in 1874 to considerable acclaim.

Far from the Madding Crowd. Read by Jill Masters. Ed. by Thomas Hardy. 11 cass. (Running Time: 16 hrs.). 1989. 69.00 incl. album. (C-138) Jimcin Record.
Masterpiece of rural romance.

Far from the Madding Crowd. Read by Stephen Thorne. Ed. by Thomas Hardy. 11 cass. (Running Time: 14 hrs. 15 min.). 64.95 (CC/003) C to C Cassettes.
Gabriel Oak, Bathsheba Everdene & Sergeant Troy, a triangle violently broken by Farmer Boldwood.

Far from the Madding Crowd. Read by Stephen Thorne. Ed. by Thomas Hardy. 10 cass. (Running Time: 14 hrs. 15 min.). 1998. 44.95 Set. (13111FA) Filmic Archives.
Explores the conflicts between steady devotion & flaring passion. Though tragic, offers fine comic observation & presents a rich portrait of rustic, 19th-century British life.

Far from the Madding Crowd. Norman Vance. Ed. by Thomas Hardy. 2001. audio compact disk 21.45 (978-1-903342-12-1(0)) Wordsworth Educ GBR.

Far from the Madding Crowd. abr. ed. Thomas Hardy. (Running Time: 4 hrs.). 2009. audio compact disk 22.98 (978-962-634-970-0(0), Naxos AudioBooks) Naxos.

Far from the Madding Crowd. abr. ed. Read by Neville Jason. Ed. by Thomas Hardy. 3 CDs. (Running Time: 4 hrs.). 1997. audio compact disk 22.98 (978-962-634-136-0(X), NA313612, Naxos AudioBooks) Naxos.
The authors use of characters represent an elaborate weaving of styles in this literary creation, first published in 1874 to considerable acclaim.

Far from the Madding Crowd. unabr. ed. Thomas Hardy. Read by John Lee. Narrated by John Lee. (Running Time: 13 hrs. 30 mins. 0 sec.). (Tantor Unabridged Classics Ser.). (ENG.). 2008. 27.99 (978-1-4001-5698-6(X)); audio compact disk 72.99 (978-1-4001-3698-8(9)); audio compact disk 35.99 (978-1-4001-0698-1(2)) Pub: Tantor Media. Dist(s): IngramPubServ

Far from the Madding Crowd. unabr. ed. Read by Jill Masters. Ed. by Thomas Hardy. 12 cass. (Running Time: 17 hrs. 30 mins.). 1984. 83.95 (978-0-7861-0527-4(5), 2026) Blckstn Audio.
Thomas Hardy shows us the England of his youth - an England of traditional mannered society which exists no more. In this society lives a passionate but capricious young heroine for whom two men destroy their lives before she is at last married to her true love.

Far from the Madding Crowd. unabr. ed. Read by Nathaniel Parker. Ed. by Thomas Hardy. 12 cass. (Running Time: 90 mins. per cass.). 1998. 96.95 (978-0-7540-0125-6(3), CAB1548) AudioGO.
The mainspring of the story is Bathsheba Evans & her three suitors. In portraying her caprice & willfulness that is gradually crushed by bitter self-knowledge & rejection, Hardy makes his point about sexual love.

Far from the Madding Crowd. unabr. ed. Read by Nathaniel Parker. Ed. by Thomas Hardy. 12 cass. (Running Time: 18 hrs.). 2000. 79.95 (CAB 1548) Pub: Chivers Audio Bks GBR. Dist(s): AudioGO
The mainspring of the story is Bathsheba Evans and her three suitors. Bathsheba's caprice and willfulness is gradually crushed by bitter self-knowledge and rejection.

Far from the Madding Crowd. unabr. ed. Read by Stephen Thorne. Ed. by Thomas Hardy. 10 cass. (Running Time: 14 hrs. 15 mins.). (gr. 9-12). 2004. 39.95 (978-1-57270-066-6(1), F91066u) Pub: Audio Partners. Dist(s): PerseuPGW
Explores the conflicts between steady devotion & flaring passion. Presents a rich portrait of rustic, 19th-century British life.

Far from the Madding Crowd. unabr. collector's ed. Read by Jill Masters. Ed. by Thomas Hardy. 12 cass. (Running Time: 18 hrs.). 96.00 (978-0-7366-3905-7(5), 9138) Books on Tape.
Hardy brings us an England that once existed but is no more. Story of love & disillusionment where Hardy's heroine is torn between the three men in her life.

Far from the Madding Crowd, Set. unabr. ed. Thomas Hardy. Read by Flo Gibson. 9 cass. (Running Time: 13 hrs.). (gr. 6-12). 1997. 28.95 (978-1-55685-466-8(8), 466-8) Audio Bk Con.
Bathsheba Everdene's three wooers, the faithful Gabriel Oak, the passionate William Boldwood, & the adventurer Sergeant Troy, eventually cause madness & murder in this fatalistic novel, which is filled with beautiful descriptions & deep wisdom.

Far from the Tree. unabr. ed. Virginia DeBerry & Donna Grant. Read by Fran L. Washington. 8 cass. (Running Time: 12 hrs.). 2000. 35.95 (978-1-56740-381-7(6), 1567403816, BAU) Brilliance Audio.
Celeste English and Ronnie Frazier are sisters, but they couldn't be more different. Celeste is a doctor's wife, living a perfect and elegant façade. But secretly, her marriage is falling apart and her need to control people around her threatens to destroy them all. Ronnie is an actress, living in New York. But she has no money, she has no home, and her life is held together by "chewing gum, paper clips, and spit." When their father dies, the sisters inherit a house in Prosper, North Carolina. Their mother, Della, would rather they forget about going there and dredging up the past. Neither of them suspect that their trip to Prosper will uncover decades-old secrets, family betrayals, and tangled relationships - or that it will make these two strangers realize that they are, and always will be, sisters.

Far from the Tree. unabr. ed. Virginia DeBerry & Donna Grant. Read by Fran L. Washington. (Running Time: 12 hrs.). 2004. 24.95 (978-1-59600-515-0(7), 1596005157, Brilliance MP3); 39.25 (978-1-59600-518-1(1), 1596005181, BADLE); 24.95 (978-1-59600-517-4(3), 1596005173, BAD); 39.25 (978-1-59600-516-7(5), 1596005165, Brlnc Audio MP3 Lib) Brilliance Audio.

Far North, unabr. ed. William Hobbs. Narrated by Johnny Heller. 5 pieces. (Running Time: 6 hrs. 30 mins.). (gr. 5 up). 1998. 44.00 (978-0-7887-2522-7(X), 95541E7) Recorded Bks.
Trapped in a frozen world of moose, wolves & bears in northern Canada, two boys from vastly different cultures come to depend on each other for their very lives.

Far North: Class Set. unabr. ed. William Hobbs. Read by Johnny Heller. 5 cass., 10 bks. (Running Time: 6 hrs. 15 min.). (YA). (gr. 7). 1998. bk. 114.70 (978-0-7887-2563-0(7), 46733) Recorded Bks.
Trapped in a frozen world of moose, wolves & bears, two boys from vastly different cultures come to depend on each other for their very lives.

Far North: Homework Set. unabr. ed. William Hobbs. Read by Johnny Heller. 5 cass. (Running Time: 6 hrs. 15 min.). (J). 1998. pap. bk. 57.24 (978-0-7887-2565-4(3), 40801) Recorded Bks.

Far Pavilions, Vol. 1, Pt. 1. unabr. collector's ed. M. M. Kaye. Read by Kate Reading. 7 cass. (Running Time: 10 hrs. 30 min.). 1994. 56.00 (978-0-7366-2811-2(8), 3525A) Books on Tape.
A vast tapestry of love & war in British India spans 25 of the 19th century's most turbulent years.

Far Pavilions, Vol. 1, Pt. 2. collector's ed. M. M. Kaye. Read by Kate Reading. 10 cass. (Running Time: 15 hrs.). 1994. 80.00 (978-0-7366-2812-9(6), 3525-B) Books on Tape.
From the foothills of the Himalayas to the bone-strewn Khyber pass, a vast, rich & vibrant tapestry of love & war is told. Spanning 25 of the 19th century's most turbulent years, it is a story of hatred & bitter combat, of courage, cowardice & sacrifice of the star-crossed wedding of East & West & above all, of a love that transcends time & place.

Far Pavilions, Vol. 2, Pt. 1. unabr. collector's ed. M. M. Kaye. Read by Kate Reading. 8 cass. (Running Time: 12 hrs.). 1994. 64.00 (978-0-7366-2813-6(4), 3526-A) Books on Tape.
A vast tapestry of love & war in British India spans 25 of the 19th century's most turbulent years.

Far Pavilions, Vol. 2, Pt. 2. collector's ed. M. M. Kaye. Read by Kate Reading. 9 cass. (Running Time: 13 hrs. 30 min.). 1994. 72.00 (978-0-7366-2814-3(2), 3526-B) Books on Tape.
From the foothills of the Himalayas to the bone-strewn Khyber pass, a vast, rich & vibrant tapestry of love & war is told. Spanning 25 of the 19th century's most turbulent years, it is a story of hatred & bitter combat, of courage, cowardice & sacrifice of the star-crossed wedding of East & West & above all, of a love that transcends time & place.

Far Reaches. unabr. ed. Robert A. Monroe. Read by Robert A. Monroe. (Running Time: 45 min.). (Gateway Experience - Prospecting Ser.). 1984. 14.95 (978-1-56113-291-1(8)) Monroe Institute.
Dig deep. Soar high. You're beyond words.

Far Reaching Consequences of Unconditional Love. Carol Hemingway. 1 cass. 8.95 (417) Am Fed Astrologers.
Story of Cancer female & Leo lover.

Far Side of the Dollar. Ross MacDonald, pseud. Read by Tom Parker. 7 CDs. (Running Time: 8 hrs. 30 mins.). (Lew Archer Mystery Ser.). 2000. audio compact disk 56.00 (978-0-7861-9889-4(3), 1767) Blckstn Audio.
To reach the Barcelona Hotel you took Sunset & the coast highway. Once starlets & Navy boys had rubbed shoulders with tycoons & hustlers there, but for Lew Archer the old, closed-up palace held the key to a missing teenager & a hot murder. Archer knew that twenty years ago a handful of dreamers & losers had come together in the Barcelona. The only question now was what kind of deal had gone down there, & why a mixed-up rich kid & a beautiful blonde were the first to pay the price.

Far Side of the Dollar. unabr. ed. Ross MacDonald, pseud. Read by Tom Parker. 6 cass. (Running Time: 8 hrs. 30 mins.). (Lew Archer Mystery Ser.). 1996. 44.95 (978-0-7861-0990-6(4), 1767) Blckstn Audio.

Far Side of the World. (Running Time: 43200 sec.). (Aubrey-Maturin Ser.). 2005. 72.95 (978-0-7861-3779-4(7)); audio compact disk 90.00 (978-0-7861-7587-1(7)) Blckstn Audio.

Far Side of the World. Patrick O'Brian. Read by Patrick Tull. 9 Cass. (Running Time: 14.5 Hrs). (Aubrey-Maturin Ser.). 34.95 (978-1-4025-4091-2(4)) Recorded Bks.

Far Side of the World. Patrick O'Brian & Patrick Tull. 13 Cds. (Running Time: 14.5 Hrs). (Aubrey-Maturin Ser.). audio compact disk 49.95 (978-1-4025-4092-9(2)) Recorded Bks.

Far Side of the World. abr. unabr. ed. Patrick O'Brian. (Running Time: 43200 sec.). (Aubrey-Maturin Ser.). 2005. audio compact disk 29.95 (978-0-7861-7862-9(0)) Blckstn Audio.

Far Side of the World. abr. ed. Patrick O'Brian. Read by Simon Vance. 9 cass. (Running Time: 43200 sec.). (Aubrey-Maturin Ser.). 2006. 29.95 (978-0-7861-4471-6(8)); audio compact disk 29.95 (978-0-7861-7282-5(7)) Blckstn Audio.

Far Side of the World. unabr. ed. Patrick O'Brian. Read by Richard Brown. 10 cass. (Running Time: 15 hrs.). (Aubrey-Maturin Ser.). 1993. 80.00 (978-0-7366-2383-4(3), 3154) Books on Tape.
Jack Aubrey seeks out an American frigate sent to wreck Britain's whaling traade. Tenth in series.

Far Side of the World. unabr. ed. Patrick O'Brian. Narrated by Patrick Tull. 10 cass. (Running Time: 14 hrs. 30 mins.). (Aubrey-Maturin Ser.). 1994. 85.00 (978-0-7887-0095-8(2), 94336E7) Recorded Bks.
As the War of 1812 continues, Capt. Jack Aubrey sets a course for Cape Horn on a mission after his own heart: intercepting a powerful American frigate outward bound to play havoc with the British whaling trade.

Far Side of the World. unabr. ed. Patrick O'Brian. Read by Patrick Tull. 10 cass. (Running Time: 14 hrs. 30 min.). (Aubrey-Maturin Ser.). 1994. Rental 17.50 Set. (94336) Recorded Bks.

Far World, Book 1: Water Keep. Scott Savage. 2008. audio compact disk 39.95 (978-1-59038-978-2(6), Shadow Mount) Deseret Bk.

Faraway Land. Perf. by Ron Block. audio compact disk 17.98 Provident Mus Dist.

Farewell Celebration. Contrib. by Cathedrals. (Running Time: 2 hrs.). 2003. 19.98 (978-5-552-09204-8(X)) Spring House Music.

Farewell, I'm Bound to Leave You: Stories. unabr. ed. Fred Chappell. Narrated by Tom Stechschulte. 6 cass. (Running Time: 8 hrs.). 1997. 51.00 (978-0-7887-0718-6(3), 94894E7) Recorded Bks.
As an old woman lies dying in her Appalachian home, she recalls tales that provide her daughter, son-in-law & grandson with a rich legacy of oral history. These stories celebrate the people of the Southern mountains: their wisdom, their voices & their lives.

Farewell, My Friend, Adieu see Classical Russian Poetry

Farewell, My Lovely. unabr. ed. Raymond Chandler. Read by Elliott Gould. 5 cass. (Running Time: 7.5 hrs.). 2004. 29.95 (978-1-59007-091-8(7)); audio compact disk 45.00 (978-1-59007-092-5(5)) Pub: New Millenn Enter. Dist(s): PerseuPGW

Farewell, My Lovely & The Lady in the Lake. abr. ed. Raymond Chandler. 2 cass. (Running Time: 3 hrs.). 1999. 16.85 (978-0-563-55897-2(0)) BBC WrldWd GBR.
In "Farewell My Lovely" Moose Malloy was six feet five & dangerous & he wanted Marlowe to find his girl. Only trouble was, she had disappeared eight years ago. In "The Lady in the Lake" Crystal Kingsley was blonde, beautiful & wild. She often disappeared on flings - but this time she'd been gone too long & when a body appeared in an isolated mountain lake, it was time for Marlowe to start investigating.

Farewell, My Lunchbag. unabr. ed. Bruce Hale. Read by Jon Cryer. (Running Time: 1 hr. 30 mins.). (Chet Gecko Mystery Ser.: No. 3). (J). (gr. 3-6). 2004. pap. bk. 17.00 (978-0-8072-1708-5(5), S FTR 273 SP, Listening Lib) Random Audio Pubg.

Farewell, My Subaru: An Epic Adventure in Local Living. Doug Fine. Narrated by Doug Fine. (Running Time: 15300 sec.). (Recorded Books Unabridged Ser.). 2008. audio compact disk 29.99 (978-1-4281-9802-9(4)) Recorded Bks.

Farewell Performance. Tessa Barclay. Read by James Bryce. 6 cass. (Sound Ser.). (J). 2002. 54.95 (978-1-84283-198-4(4)) Pub: ISIS Lrg Prnt GBR. Dist(s): Ulverscroft US

Farewell Summer. unabr. ed. Ray Bradbury. Narrated by Robert Fass. 3 CDs. (Running Time: 12000 sec.). 2006. audio compact disk 39.95 (978-0-7927-4519-8(1), SLD 1049); audio compact disk 24.95 (978-0-7927-4565-5(5), CMP 1049) AudioGO.

Farewell Summer. unabr. ed. Ray Bradbury. Read by Robert Fass. 3 cass. (Running Time: 12000 sec.). 2006. 34.95 (978-0-7927-4542-6(6), CSL 1049) AudioGO.

Farewell Summer. unabr. ed. Ray Bradbury. Read by Robert Fass. (YA). 2007. 34.99 (978-1-60252-898-7(5)) Find a World.

Farewell the Trumpets: An Imperial Retreat, Pt. 2. collector's ed. Jan Morris. Read by David Case. 8 cass. (Running Time: 12 hrs.). 1996. 64.00 (978-0-7366-3412-0(6), 4058-B) Books on Tape.
This concluding volume follows the British Empire at the height of its vigor in 1897 to the death of Winston Churchill in 1965. Through superb studies of battles, ceremonies, landscapes & charcters runs a momentous historical theme: the decline of the greatest of nations.

Farewell the Trumpets Pt. 1: An Imperial Retreat. unabr. collector's ed. Jan Morris. Read by David Case. 8 cass. (Running Time: 12 hrs.). (Pax Britannica Trilogy: Vol. 3). 1996. 64.00 (978-0-7366-3411-3(8), 4058-A) Books on Tape.

Farewell! Thou Art Too Dear for My Possessing: Sonnet 87 see Palgrave's Golden Treasury of English Poetry

Farewell to Arms see Adios a las Armas

Farewell to Arms. Ed. by Ernest Hemingway. 2006. cd-rom 39.99 (978-1-59895-489-0(X)) Find a World.

Farewell to Arms. Ernest Hemingway. Read by Hernando Iván Cano. (Running Time: 3 hrs.). 2003. 16.95 (978-1-60083-280-2(6), Audiofy Corp) Iofy Corp.

Farewell to Arms. collector's unabr. ed. Ernest Hemingway. Read by Alexander Adams. 6 cass. (Running Time: 9 hrs.). 1990. 48.00 (978-0-7366-4528-7(4)) Books on Tape.
The unforgettable story of an American ambulance driver on the Italian front & his love for an English nurse. Hemingway's frank portrayal of the love between Frederic Henry & Catherine Barkley, caught in the inexorable sweep of war, glows with an intensity unrivaled in modern literature. A story of love & pain, of loyalty & desertion, of serene beauty amidst a world in chaos, Hemingway reaches a new level of romanticism.

Farewell to Arms. collector's unabr. ed. Ernest Hemingway. Read by Alexander Adams. 7 CDs. (Running Time: 8 hrs.). 2000. audio compact disk 34.95 (978-0-7366-5179-0(9)) Books on Tape.

Farewell to Arms. unabr. ed. Ernest Hemingway. Read by Alexander Adams. 6 cass. (Running Time: 9 hrs.). 1999. 29.95 (978-0-7366-4431-0(8)) Books on Tape.
The best American novel to emerge out of WW I, A Farewell to Arms is the unforgettable story of an American ambulance driver on the Italian front & his love for an English nurse. Hemingway's frank portrayal of the love between Frederic Henry & Catherine Barkley, caught in the inexorable sweep of war, glows with an intensity unrivaled in modern literature. A story of love & pain, of loyalty & desertion, of serene beauty amidst a world in chaos, Hemingway reaches a new level of romanticism.

Farewell to Arms. unabr. ed. Ernest Hemingway. Read by Alexander Adams. 7 CDs. (Running Time: 8 hrs.). 2001. audio compact disk 34.95 (978-0-7366-5698-6(7)) Books on Tape.
A story of love & war, set in Italy in WWI. Glows with an intensity unrivaled in modern literature.

Farewell to Arms. unabr. ed. Ernest Hemingway. Read by John Slattery. 8 cass. (Running Time: 8 hrs.). 2006. 37.75 (978-1-4281-1401-2(7), 98493); audio compact disk 49.75 (978-1-4281-1403-6(3), C3859) Recorded Bks.
This semi-autobiographical love story follows a young American soldier, Frederic Henry who falls in love with an English nurse while serving as an ambulance driver in Italy. Surrounded by the brutality of war, they find comfort in each other and Catherine soon becomes pregnant. But when Henry is ordered back to the front lines, he is unsure if he will ever see his lover again.

Farewell to Arms. unabr. ed. Ernest Hemingway. Read by John Slattery. 2006. 23.95 (978-0-7435-6510-3(X), Audioworks); audio compact disk 39.95 (978-0-7435-6437-3(5)) Pub: S&S Audio. Dist(s): S and S Inc

Farewell to Arms. unabr. ed. Ernest Hemingway & Wolfram Kandinsky. 6 cass. (Running Time: 9 hrs.). 1990. 48.00 (978-0-7366-1716-1(7), 2557) Books on Tape.
The best American novel to emerge out of WW I, A Farewell to Arms is the unforgettable story of an American ambulance driver on the Italian front & his love for an English nurse. Hemingway's frank portrayal of the love between Frederic Henry & Catherine Barkley, caught in the inexorable sweep of war, glows with an intensity unrivaled in modern literature. A story of love & pain, of loyalty & desertion, of serene beauty amidst a world in chaos, Hemingway reaches a new level of romanticism.

Farewell to Fairacre. unabr. ed. Miss Read. Read by Sian Phillips. 6 cass. (Running Time: 6 hrs.). (Fairacre Chronicles). 1995. 54.95 Set. (978-0-7451-4331-6(8), CAB 1014) AudioGO.
Having enjoyed good health through most of her career, Miss Read, the village schoolmistress at Fairacre, is looking forward to retirement in a few years. And when she's suddenly taken ill, she still refuses to give up her post at the school. But the memories of Miss Clare collapsing in front of the schoolchildren haunt her. Is it time to say farewell to Fairacre?.

Farewells. unabr. ed. Rose Boucheron. Read by Trudy Harris. 6 cass. (Storysound Ser.). (J). 2000. 54.95 (978-1-85903-358-6(X)) Pub: Mgna Lrg Print GBR. Dist(s): Ulverscroft US

Fargo. Hank Mitchum. Read by Charlie O'Dowd. 4 vols. No. 21. 2004. 25.00 (978-1-58807-204-7(5)); (978-1-58807-964-0(3)) Am Pubng Inc.

Fargo. Scripts. Hank Mitchum. 5 CDs. (Running Time: 6 hrs.). (Stagecoach Ser.: No. 21). 2005. 14.99 (978-1-58807-773-8(X)) Am Pubng Inc.
The stage company has hired Chance Dayton to push the stagecoach from Montana to Fargo. But it's more than a job with beautiful Polly Temple on board. He'll have to face Black Claw, Sioux renegade, and Dakota Smith, the lightning fast gun-slick. The trail to Fargo will be a trial of blood for Chance Dayton.

Farkle & Friends. Perf. by John Lithgow. 1 CD. (Running Time: 45 mins.). (J). 2002. audio compact disk 13.98 Rhino Enter.
A wonderful collection of original songs and familiar favorites for the whole family to enjoy. The album is highlighted by the story of Farkle McBride, a musical prodigy who learns how the different instruments in an orchestra can work together.

Farkle & Friends. Perf. by John Lithgow. 1 cass. (Running Time: 45 mins.). (J). (ps-3). 2002. 13.98 (978-0-7379-0249-5(3)) Rhino Enter.

***Farley Follows His Nose.** unabr. ed. Lynn Johnston. Read by Kathleen Mcinerney. (ENG.). 2009. (978-0-06-180597-4(1)); (978-0-06-177597-0(5)) HarperCollins Pubs.

Farm. Richard Benson. 7 CDs. (Isis (CDs) Ser.). 2006. audio compact disk 71.95 (978-0-7531-2606-6(0)) Pub: ISIS Lrg Prnt GBR. Dist(s): Ulverscroft US

Farm. Richard Benson. Read by Richard Stacey. 6 cass. (Running Time: 7 hrs. 15 mins.). (Isis Cassettes Ser.). 2006. 54.95 (978-0-7531-3635-5(X)) Pub: ISIS Lrg Prnt GBR. Dist(s): Ulverscroft US

Farm Animals. 1 cass. (Early Learning Ser.). (J). bk. (TWIN 418) NewSound.

Farm Animals. unabr. ed. Ed. by Linda Spizzirri. 48 cass. (Running Time: 15 min.). Dramatization. (Educational Coloring Book & cassette Package Ser.). (J). (gr. k-8). 1989. pap. bk. 6.95 (978-0-86545-154-4(0)) Spizzirri.
Features stock animals & working pets found on the American farm.

Farm City: The Education of an Urban Farmer. unabr. ed. Novella Carpenter. Narrated by Karen White. 1 MP3-CD. (Running Time: 10 hrs. 0 mins. 0 sec.). (ENG.). 2009. 24.99 (978-1-4001-6298-7(X)); audio compact disk 69.99 (978-1-4001-4298-9(9)); audio compact disk 34.99 (978-1-4001-1298-2(2)) Pub: Tantor Media. Dist(s): IngramPubServ

Farm Fatale: A Comedy of Country Manors. unabr. ed. Wendy Holden. Narrated by Phoebe James. 10 cass. Lib. Ed. (Running Time: 13 hrs.). 2004. 89.75 (978-1-4025-4009-7(4), RG434) Recorded Bks.

Farm Fatale: A Comedy of Country Manors. unabr. collector's ed. Wendy Holden. Narrated by Phoebe James. 10 cass. (Running Time: 13 hrs.). 2004. 39.95 (978-1-4025-4010-3(8), RG434) Recorded Bks.
City folk Rosie and her boyfriend have always dreamt of a countryside cottage. The nouveaux-riche Samantha and Guy are also seeking rural bliss: a mansion with a mile long drive and a team of gardeners. The village of Eight Mile Bottom seems the idyllic hide-away for them. But as dreams become reality, they soon realise that village life can be far from peaceful.

Farm on Nippersink Creek: Stories from a Midwestern Childhood. Jim May. Read by Jim May. 2 pieces. (Running Time: 2 hrs. 21 mins.). (American Storytelling Ser.). 1996. 18.00 (978-0-87483-419-2(8)) Pub: August Hse. Dist(s): Natl Bk Netwk
Stories from a midwestern childhood.

Farm Songs & the Sounds of Moo-sic! Book & CD. Alfred Publishing Staff. (ENG.). 2009. audio compact disk 14.95 (978-0-7390-6256-2(5)) Alfred Pub.

Farm Stand Mystery: Early Explorers Early Set A Audio CD. Benchmark Education Staff. (J). 2006. audio compact disk 10.00 (978-1-4108-7632-4(2)) Benchmark Educ.

Farm Women. Poems. Bertha Rogers. Read by Bertha Rogers. 1 cass., 1 CD. (Six Swans Sounds Ser.: Vol. 2). 1998. (978-1-893389-04-5(9)) Six Swans.

Farm Workers' Pesticides & an Anti-Hunting Activist. Hosted by Nancy Pearlman. 1 cass. (Running Time: 30 min.). 10.00 (411) Educ Comm CA.

Farmer see Wolf: A False Memoir

Farmer Boy. unabr. ed. Laura Ingalls Wilder. Read by Cherry Jones. 4 cass. (Running Time: 6 hr.). (J). 2004. 22.00 (978-0-06-056498-8(9)) HarperCollins Pubs.

Farmer Boy. unabr. abr. ed. Laura Ingalls Wilder. Read by Cherry Jones. 1 CD. (Running Time: 1 hr. 30 mins.). (J). 2004. audio compact disk 25.95 (978-0-06-056500-8(4)) HarperCollins Pubs.

***Farmer Cap.** Jill Kalz. Illus. by Sahin Erkocak. Contrib. by Dennis Spears. (Pfeffernut County Ser.). (ENG.). 2008. audio compact disk 11.93 (978-1-4048-5384-3(7)) CapstoneDig.

Farmer Dillo Paints His Barn. Jesse Adams. Illus. by Julie Speer & Christopher Owen Davis. (J). (ps-3). 2007. pap. bk. 12.95 (978-1-59166-808-4(5)) BJUPr.

Farmer Duck CD. unabr. ed. Martin Waddell. Perf. by Bill Oddie & Sophie Aldred. Music by Barry Gibson. Illus. by Helen Oxenbury. (Running Time: 1 hr. 7 mins.). (ENG.). (J). (ps-2). 2004. audio compact disk 7.99 (978-0-7636-2425-5(X)) Pub: Candlewick Pr. Dist(s): Random

Farmer Giles of Ham. J. R. R. Tolkien. 14.95 (978-0-00-105610-7(7)) Trafalgar.

Farmer in the Sky. Robert A. Heinlein. Read by Scott Brick. 2002. 48.00 (978-0-7366-8935-9(4)) Books on Tape.

Farmer Wants a Wife. Maeve Haran. (Isis (CDs) Ser.). 2006. audio compact disk 84.95 (978-0-7531-2569-4(2)) Pub: ISIS Lrg Prnt GBR. Dist(s): Ulverscroft US

Farmer Wants a Wife. unabr. ed. Maeve Haran. Read by Marie McCarthy. 12 cass. (Running Time: 13 hrs. 35 mins.). (Isis Ser.). (J). 2002. 94.95 (978-0-7531-1374-5(0)) Pub: ISIS Lrg Prnt GBR. Dist(s): Ulverscroft US
Flora Parker is sassy and stylish with a big mouth and a tendency to act before she things, which is how she ends up getting drunk and on the front of a newspaper in her Wonderbra. Filled with self-loathing, she retreats to her aunt's house in the country where she finds an overbearing uncle and a farm on the brink of bankruptcy. But instead of running away, she itches to put it right, especially when the farmer next door announces a bet: he will give his farm and glorious farmhouse to whichever of his handsome nephews finds a wife by Michaelmas. So Flo takes up the matchmaking.

***Farmers & Mercenaries: Book 1 of the Genesis of Oblivion Saga, vol. 1.** unabr. ed. Maxwell Alexander Drake. Ed. by Patrick LoBrutto. Narrated by Cameron Beierle. Illus. by Lars Grant-West. (Running Time: 1073). (Genesis of Oblivion Sage: 1). (ENG.). (YA). 2010. 24.95 (978-0-9819548-6-8(3)); 34.99 (978-0-9819548-5-1(5)) ImaginInterprises.

***Farmer's Daughter.** unabr. ed. Jim Harrison. (Running Time: 13 hrs. 0 mins.). 2010. 29.95 (978-1-4417-4223-0(9)); audio compact disk 32.95 (978-1-4417-4222-3(0)) Blckstn Audio.

***Farmer's Daughter.** unabr. ed. Jim Harrison. (Running Time: 13 hrs. 0 mins.). 2010. 72.95 (978-1-4417-4219-3(0)); audio compact disk 109.00 (978-1-4417-4220-9(4)) Blckstn Audio.

Farmers Huge Carrot. unabr. ed. Henry O. Tanner Elementary School Staff. 1 cass. (Running Time: 3 min.). (J). (ps-3). 1992. pap. bk. 13.90 (978-0-8045-6753-4(0), 6753) Spoken Arts.

Farmer's Market. Perf. by Timmy Abell. Prod. by Steven Heller. 1 cass. (Running Time: 39 min.). (J). (ps-4). 1989. 16.00 compact disc. (978-0-9665740-2-9(8), UP885) Upstream Prodns.
Original & traditional songs for children played on a variety of folk instruments. Includes "Mail Myself to You", "If I Were", "The Farmer's Market", "The Unicorn Song", "Hi Ho We're Rolling Home", "Jimmy Crack Corn" & "I Love You." Winner of American Library Assn. Notable Recording Award.

Farmer's Wife. unabr. ed. Rachel Moore. Contrib. by Emma Powell. 7 cass. (Story Sound Ser.). (J). 2006. 61.95 (978-1-85903-901-4(4)) Pub: Mgna Lrg Print GBR. Dist(s): Ulverscroft US

Farmer's Wife. unabr. ed. The Farmer's Wife Staff & Rachel Moore. 8 vols. (Story Sound CD Ser.). (J). 2006. audio compact disk 79.95 (978-1-85903-955-7(3)) Pub: Mgna Lrg Print GBR. Dist(s): Ulverscroft US

Farmer's Wife (La Esposa del Granjero) Idries Shah. Illus. by Rose Mary Santiago. 1 CD. (Running Time: 17 mins.). (ENG & SPA.). (J). (ps up). 2005. pap. bk. 18.95 (978-1-883536-70-1(7), FAWCB4, Hoopoe Books) ISHK.
The cumulative tale of a woman's efforts to retrieve an apple from a hole in the ground. Children will enjoy learning the highly predictable lines by heart. But when a surprise event changes the direction of the tale, their expectations will be jolted in a most amusing way, and they will have learned its valuable lessons about the nature of problem solving and discovery.

Farmhouse Crafts L. L. C. Seasons at the Olde Homestead. Diane Pryor. 2008. audio compact disk 10.00 (978-1-4276-3792-5(X)) AardGP.

Farming of Bones. collector's ed. Edwidge Danticat. Read by Rebecca Nicholas. 6 cass. (Running Time: 9 hrs.). 1999. 48.00 (978-0-7366-4891-2(7)) Books on Tape.
In 1937, Rafael Trujillo, President of Dominican Republic, decided to rid his country of the many Haitians who worked in the cane fields.

Farnsworth Score. abr. ed. Rex Burns. Read by Charlton Griffin. 2 vols. No. 1. 2003. (978-1-58807-665-6(2)) Am Pubng Inc.

Faro's Daughter. unabr. ed. Georgette Heyer. Read by Eve Matheson. 8 cass. (Running Time: 12 hrs.). 2000. 59.95 (978-0-7451-6507-3(9), CAB 1123) Pub: Chivers Audio Bks GBR. Dist(s): AudioGO
Max Ravenscar was handsome, a great fist-fighter, and one of the richest men in London. His visit to a gaming-house was strictly to rescue his cousin, Adrian, from Lady Bellingham, a well-known gold-digger. There, Ravenscar meets an overmatched opponent, leaving him unprepared. He is about to play for his highest stakes ever.

***Farraday Road.** Ace Collins. (Running Time: 10 hrs. 45 mins. 10 sec.). (Lije Evans Mysteries Ser.). (ENG.). 2009. 15.99 (978-0-310-77301-6(6)) Zondervan.

Farriers' Lane. Anne Perry. Read by Terrence Hardiman. 13 CDs. 2004. audio compact disk 56.95 (978-0-7927-3274-7(X), SLD 242, Chivers Sound Lib) AudioGO.

Farriers' Lane. unabr. ed. Anne Perry. Read by Terrence Hardiman. 12 vols. (Running Time: 18 Hrs.). (Thomas Pitt Ser.). 2000. bk. 96.95 (978-0-7927-2353-0(8), CSL 242, Chivers Sound Lib) AudioGO.
When Mr. Justice Stafford, a distinguished judge, falls ill & dies of opium poisoning, his shocking demise resurrects one of the most sensational cases ever to inflame England.

***Farseer: Assassin's Quest.** unabr. ed. Robin Hobb. Narrated by Paul Boehmer. (Running Time: 35 hrs. 0 mins.). (Farseer Ser.). 2010. 69.99 (978-1-4001-9436-0(9)) Tantor Media.

***Farseer: Assassin's Quest.** unabr. ed. Robin Hobb. Narrated by Paul Boehmer. (Running Time: 39 hrs. 0 mins. 0 sec.). (Farseer Ser.). (ENG.). 2010. audio compact disk 139.99 (978-1-4001-4436-5(1)) Pub: Tantor Media. Dist(s): IngramPubServ

***Farseer: Assassin's Quest.** unabr. ed. Robin Hobb. Narrated by Paul Boehmer. (Running Time: 35 hrs. 0 mins.). (Farseer Ser.). 2010. 34.99 (978-1-4001-8436-1(3)) Tantor Media.

***Farseer: Assassin's Quest.** unabr. ed. Robin Hobb. Narrated by Paul Boehmer. (Running Time: 39 hrs. 0 mins. 0 sec.). (Farseer Ser.). (ENG.). 2010. 49.99 (978-1-4001-6436-3(2)); audio compact disk 69.99 (978-1-4001-1436-8(5)) Pub: Tantor Media. Dist(s): IngramPubServ

***Farseer: Royal Assassin.** unabr. ed. Robin Hobb. Narrated by Paul Boehmer. (Running Time: 30 hrs. 0 mins. 0 sec.). (Farseer Ser.). (ENG.). 2010. 39.99 (978-1-4001-6435-6(4)); 27.99 (978-1-4001-8435-4(5)); audio compact disk 54.99 (978-1-4001-1435-1(7)) Pub: Tantor Media. Dist(s): IngramPubServ

Farsi: A Complete Course for Beginners. unabr. ed. Living Language Staff. 6 CDs. (Running Time: 6 hrs. 42 mins.). (World Languages Ser.). 2008. audio compact disk 72.00 (978-1-4000-2442-1(0), LivingLang) Pub: Random Info Grp. Dist(s): Random
Comprehensive self-study courses that meet the growing demands for new language offerings. Covering everything from grammar and vocabulary to cultural and practical information through the proven learning techniques from Living Language, the World Language Series will be a must-have. Includes 250+ page coursebook and a dictionary.

Farsi: Learn to Speak & Understand Farsi (Persian) with Pimsleur Language Programs. unabr. ed. Pimsleur Staff. 5 CDs. (Running Time: 5 hrs. 0 mins. 0 sec.). (Basic Ser.). (PEO & ENG.). 2005. audio compact disk 24.95 (978-0-7435-5124-3(9), Fireside) Pub: S and S. Dist(s): S and S Inc

Farsi: Learn to Speak & Understand Farsi (Persian) with Pimsleur Language Programs. unabr. ed. Pimsleur Staff. (Running Time: 160 hrs. 0 mins. 0 sec.). (Comprehensive Ser.). (ENG.). 2005. audio compact disk 345.00 (978-0-7435-4483-2(8), Pimsleur) Pub: S&S Audio. Dist(s): S and S Inc

Farsi (Persian), Conversational: Learn to Speak & Understand Farsi (Persian) with Pimsleur Language Programs. unabr. ed. Pimsleur Staff. 8 CDs. (Running Time: 80 hrs. 0 mins. 0 sec.). (Instant Conversation Ser.). (PEO & ENG.). 2005. audio compact disk 49.95 (978-0-7435-5118-2(4), Pimsleur) Pub: S&S Audio. Dist(s): S and S Inc

Farther. Perf. by Lori Wilke. 1 cass., 1 CD. (Running Time: 40 min.). 1998. 9.98 (978-1-891916-09-0(2)); 9.98 (978-1-891916-32-8(7)); audio compact disk 14.98 CD. (978-1-891916-10-6(6)) Spirit To Spirit.
Ministry to the lost.

Farther Afield. unabr. ed. Miss Read. Read by Sian Phillips. 6 cass. (Running Time: 9 hrs.). (Fairacre Chronicles). 2000. 49.95 (978-0-7451-4343-9(1), CAB 1026) Pub: Chivers Audio Bks GBR. Dist(s): AudioGO
Miss Read is looking foward to the peace of summer. But when she breaks her arm on the first day of vacation, her friend Amy whisks her away to the Island of Crete to recuperate. The change of scene gives the two women a chance to take a long look at the merits of single and married life.

Farther & Faster Audio CD. Adapted by Benchmark Education Company Staff. Based on a work by Katherine Scraper. (Early Explorers Set C Ser.). (J). (gr. 1). 2008. audio compact disk 10.00 (978-1-60437-529-9(9)) Benchmark Educ.

Farther Reaches of Human Nature. unabr. ed. Abraham H. Maslow. 2 cass. (Running Time: 3 hrs.). 1968. 18.00 Big Sur Tapes.

Farthest-Away Mountain. unabr. ed. Lynne Reid Banks. Read by Lynne Reid Banks. 3 cass. (Running Time: 3 hrs.). (YA). 1997. 23.98 (978-0-8072-7762-1(2), 395057, Listening Lib) Random Audio Pubg.
Dakin answers the calling of the beautiful farthest away mountain to discover the dark secrets that threaten to destroy the world.

Farthest-Away Mountain, Set. unabr. ed. Lynne Reid Banks. Read by Lynne Reid Banks. 3 cass. (YA). 1997. 28.98 (978-0-8072-7763-8(0), YA914SP, Listening Lib) Random Audio Pubg.

Farthest Shore. Ursula K. Le Guin. Read by Allison Green. 5 cass. (Running Time: 7 hrs. 30 min.). (Earthsea Ser.: Vol. 3). (J). 1993. 44.20 Set. (978-1-56544-028-9(5), 550009); Rental 7.80 30 day rental Set. (550009) Literate Ear.
Darkness has settled over Earthsea, & all the magic in the world is running out. Ged, the Dragonlord, sets out with a young prince to discover the source of this black power.

Farthest Shore. unabr. ed. Ursula K. Le Guin. Narrated by Rob Inglis. 6 cass. (Running Time: 8 hrs.). (Earthsea Ser.: Vol. 3). (gr. 6). 1995. 53.00 (978-0-7887-0181-8(9), 94406E7) Recorded Bks.
The great Dragonlord Ged must find the source of the dark shadow that is draining the magic from the wizards & mages of Earthsea.

Farthing Will Do. Lilian Harry. (Soundings Ser.). (J). 2005. 84.95 (978-1-84283-976-8(4)) Pub: ISIS Lrg Prnt GBR. Dist(s): Ulverscroft US

Farthing Will Do. unabr. ed. Lilian Harry & Hilary Neville. 10 CDs. (Running Time: 12 hrs. 30 mins.). (Soundings (CDs) Ser.). (J). 2005. audio compact disk 89.95 (978-1-84559-267-7(0)) Pub: ISIS Lrg Prnt GBR. Dist(s): Ulverscroft US

FASB 106: Accounting for Post-Retirement Benefits Other Than Pensions. Paul Munter & Thomas A. Ratcliffe. 3 cass. bk. 159.00 set. (CPE4070) Bisk Educ.
Learn the required way to account for the costs of healthcare, health insurance, life insurance, & all other nonpension benefits that are provided to retired employees.

FASB 109: Accounting for Income Taxes. Robert L. Monette & Thomas A. Ratcliffe. 6 cass. bk. 159.00 set. (CPE4220) Bisk Educ.
This program discusses the major implementation issues of FASB 109 which offers earnings gains to many corporations, the partial offset of OPEB liabilities, the recognition of deferred tax assets & NOL carryforwards & demonstrates the application of this new standard using real-world examples.

FASB 115: Accounting for Certain Investments in Debt & Equity Securities. Nathan M. Bisk & Robert L. Monette. 4 cass. 1995. bk. 129.00 set. (CPE4960) Bisk Educ.
A detailed discussion of what this pronouncement entails, its proper application, its far-reaching effects & more.

FASB 95: Statement of Cash Flows. Marilyn F. Hunt & Robert L. Monette. 6 cass. 159.00 set, incl. textbk. & quizzer. (978-0-88128-374-7(6), CPE2030) Bisk Educ.
Provides clear explanations of how cash receipts & disbursements must now be classified, how to disclose noncash investing & financing activities, & how to prepare statements under direct & indirect methods.

***Fascinate: Your 7 Triggers to Persuasion & Captivation.** unabr. ed. Sally Hogshead. Read by Sally Hogshead. (ENG.). 2010. (978-0-06-204245-3(9), Harper Audio); (978-0-06-206171-3(2), Harper Audio) HarperCollins Pubs.

Fascinating Loons: Alluring Sounds of the Common Loon. Stan Tekiela. 2006. cass., audio compact disk, audio compact disk 12.95 (978-1-59193-174-4(6)) Adventure Pubns.

Fascinating People: Intriguing Glimpses into Famous Lives. abr. ed. People. (Running Time: 35 mins.). (ENG.). 2006. 9.99 (978-1-59483-863-7(1)) Pub: Hachet Audio. Dist(s): HachBkGrp

Fascinating Stories of Forgotten Lives. 2006. 46.00 (978-1-57972-714-7(X)); audio compact disk 46.00 (978-1-57972-713-0(1)) Insight Living.

Fascinating Walt Disney: Hear How Walt Disney's Dreams Came True! Stephen Schochet. Read by Stephen Schochet. Prod. by Ivor Francis. 2 CDs. (Running Time: 1 hr. 39 mins.). (ENG.). 2003. audio compact disk 24.95 (978-0-9638972-1-3(7)) Pub: Hollywood Stories. Dist(s): Bk Clearing Hse
Tells the stories behind Disney's most famous creations, with music & sound effects. Fully orchestrated background music & sound effects.

Fascination of the Supernatural: Ghost Lore in Religion, Philosophy, & Psychology. Instructed by Manly P. Hall. 8.95 (978-0-89314-115-8(1), C800137) Philos Res.

Fascisme en France. Henri Guillemin. 1 cass. (FRE.). 1991. 22.95 (1204-VSL) Olivia & Hill.

Fascists & Fabians Communist. unabr. ed. Robert LeFevre. 1 cass. (Running Time: 1 hr. 52 min.). 12.95 (1012) J Norton Pubs.
Explores abolishment of property ownership & the sacrifice of the individual.

Fashion. Anne Schraff. Narrated by Larry A. McKeever. (Extreme Customs Ser.). (J). 2006. 10.95 (978-1-58659-129-8(0)); audio compact disk 14.95 (978-1-58659-363-6(3)) Artesian.

Fashion - Organic Clothes Plus Ecological Cosmetic & Hair Products. Hosted by Nancy Pearlman. 1 cass. (Running Time: 29 min.). 10.00 (1036) Educ Comm CA.

Fashion Designs. (Art Rom Create Your Own... Ser.). (J). 2004. pap. bk. 9.99 (978-1-84229-769-8(4)) Top That GBR.

Fashion in Shrouds. Margery Allingham. Read by Francis Matthews. 10 CDs. (Running Time: 15 hrs.). 2002. bk. 94.95 (978-0-7540-5536-5(1), CCD 227) Pub: Chivers Audio Bks GBR. Dist(s): AudioGO

Fashionable Address. unabr. ed. Pamela Evans. Read by Annie Aldington. 12 cass. (Running Time: 18 hrs.). 2001. 94.95 (978-1-86042-817-3(7)) Pub: Soundings Ltd GBR. Dist(s): Ulverscroft US
Kate's gambling father leaves her & her mother & sisters with crippling debts, yet she will build a successful millinery business & move up to a fashionable address.

Fashionable Vice. unabr. ed. Donal L. White. Read by Lynda Evans. 6 cass. (Running Time: 8 hrs.). 1998. 39.95 (978-1-55686-760-6(3)) Books in Motion.
A divorced woman becomes accustomed to living the high life when she finds herself romantically involved with a string of wealthy men.

Fashions in Music. 1994. 17.00 (978-0-7692-5006-9(8), Warner Bro) Alfred Pub.

Fast & Brutal Wing. unabr. ed. Kathleen Jeffrie Johnson. 5 cass. (Running Time: 6 hrs.). (YA). 2005. bk. 46.70 (978-1-4193-3247-0(3), 42029); 22.75 (978-1-4193-3245-6(7), 97997) Recorded Bks.
The books of Kathleen Jeffrie Johnson have been selected as Booklist Top Ten First Books for Youth, YALSA Quick Picks, ALA Best Book for Young Adults, and VOYA Top Ten Selections. A Fast and Brutal Wing is the fascinating story of a brother and sister who share the amazing power to change from human form to animal form and back. But do they really? Told through a series of letters, memos, and newspaper articles - interspersed with conventional chapters - this unique novel will captivate young adult listeners.

Fast & Easy: English for Spanish Speakers. 40 cass. (Running Time: 44 hrs.). Orig. Title: Ingles en Tres Meses. 2001. pap. bk. 515.00 (AFE390) J Norton Pubs.
Designed for the person who knows no English or has picked up only the most elementary vocabulary.

Fast & Easy Bk. 1: English for Spanish Speakers. Orig. Title: Ingles en Tres Meses. 2001. pap. bk. 165.00 (AFE375) J Norton Pubs.
All recorded instructions & drills have Spanish translations & provide over 600 vocabulary items with emphasis on the most commonly used verbs.

Fast & Easy Bk. 2: English for Spanish Speakers. 16 cass. (Running Time: 16 hrs.). Orig. Title: Ingles en Tres Meses. 2001. pap. bk. 215.00 (AFE380) J Norton Pubs.
Intended for the person who already speaks English at a basic level. It is essentially a course for refining one's English.

Fast & Easy Bk. 3: English for Spanish Speakers. 16 cass. (Running Time: 16 hrs.). Orig. Title: Ingles en Tres Meses. 2001. pap. bk. 215.00 (AFE385) J Norton Pubs.
Designed for the person who can hold a conversation in English but lacks the native feel for it.

Fast & the Furriest. unabr. ed. Andy Behrens. Read by Sean Runnette. (ENG.). (J). (gr. 3). 2010. 30.00 (978-0-307-70774-1(1), Listening Lib) Pub: Random Audio Pubg. Dist(s): Random

Fast Break. Eldon Taylor. Read by Eldon Taylor. 1 cass. (Running Time: 62 min.). (Neurophonics Ser.). 16.95 (978-1-55978-650-8(7), 1001) Progress Aware Res.
Sound patterns for Altered States of Consciousness with underlying subliminal affirmations & frequency response signals. Use with headphones only.

Fast Company: A Memoir of Life, Love, & Motorcycles in Italy. unabr. ed. David M. Gross. Read by Grover Gardner. (Running Time: 36000 sec.). 2007. 59.95 (978-0-7861-6857-6(9)); audio compact disk 72.00 (978-0-7861-6856-9(0)) Blckstn Audio.

Fast Company: A Memoir of Life, Love & Motorcycles in Italy. unabr. ed. David M. Gross & Blackstone Audio. (Running Time: 10 hrs. 8 mins.). (J). 2007. 29.95 (978-0-7861-4934-6(5)); audio compact disk 29.95 (978-0-7861-5888-1(3)) Blckstn Audio.

Fast Company: A Memoir of Life, Love & Motorcycles in Italy. unabr. ed. David M. Gross & Blackstone Audio. (Running Time: 10 mins.). (J). 2007. audio compact disk 29.95 (978-0-7861-7019-7(0)) Blckstn Audio.

Fast Flows the Stream. Connie Monk. 10 cass. (Running Time: 13 hrs. 15 mins.). (Story Sound Ser.). (J). 2005. 84.95 (978-1-85903-787-4(9)) Pub: Mgna Lrg Print GBR. Dist(s): Ulverscroft US

Fast Food Nation: The Dark Side of the All-American Meal. unabr. abr. ed. Eric Schlosser. Read by Rick Adamson. 8 CDs. (Running Time: 9 hrs.). (ENG.). 2004. audio compact disk 35.00 (978-0-7393-1250-6(2)) Pub: Random Audio Pubg. Dist(s): Random

***Fast Forward.** Carl Sommer. (Quest for Success Ser.). (ENG.). (YA). 2009. bk. 19.95 (978-1-57537-328-7(9)); pap. bk. 11.95 (978-1-57537-377-5(7)) Advance Pub.

Fast Forward: Blues Guitar. Ed. by Rikky Rocksby. Arranged by Rikky Rocksby. (Fast Forward Ser.). 1998. audio compact disk 15.95 (978-0-7119-7041-0(6), AM951160) Pub: Music Sales. Dist(s): H Leonard

Fast Forward: Boogie Woogie Piano. Bill Worrall. (Piano Ser.). 2004. audio compact disk 15.95 (978-0-7119-8197-3(3), AM958925) Pub: Music Sales. Dist(s): H Leonard

Fast Forward: Finger Picking Guitar. Ed. by Rikky Rooksby. Arranged by Rikky Rooksby. (Fast Forward Ser.). 1998. audio compact disk 15.95 (978-0-7119-7051-9(3), AM951159) Pub: Music Sales. Dist(s): H Leonard

Fast Forward: Funk Guitar. Rikky Rooksby. 2004. audio compact disk 15.95 (978-0-7119-8222-2(8), AM958529) Pub: Music Sales. Dist(s): H Leonard

Fast Forward: Hip Hop Drum Patterns. Dave Zubraski & Clive Jenner. 2004. audio compact disk 15.95 (978-0-7119-8398-4(4), AM966493) Pub: Music Sales. Dist(s): H Leonard

Fast Forward: Lead Guitar Solos. Ed. by Rikky Rooksby. Arranged by Rikky Rooksby. 1998. bk. 15.95 (978-0-7119-7064-9(5), AM950939) Pub: Music Sales. Dist(s): H Leonard

Fast Forward: Rock N Roll Piano. Bill Worrall. (Piano Ser.). 2004. audio compact disk 15.95 (978-0-7119-8129-4(9), AM963700) Pub: Music Sales. Dist(s): H Leonard

Fast Forward: String Bending. Rikky Rooksby. 2004. audio compact disk 15.95 (978-0-7119-8207-9(4), AM958947) Pub: Music Sales. Dist(s): H Leonard

***Fast Forward / Avance Acelarado.** ed. Carl Sommer. (Quest for Success Bilingual Ser.). (ENG & SPA.). (YA). 2009. bk. 21.95 (978-1-57537-427-7(7)) Advance Pub.

Fast Forward MBA in Financial Planning. abr. ed. Ed McCarthy. 2 cass. (Running Time: 6 hrs.). 2001. 18.00 (978-1-59040-125-5(5), Phoenix Audio) Pub: Amer Intl Pub. Dist(s): PerseuPGW

Fast Forward MBA in Technology. abr. ed. 2 cass. (Running Time: 3 hrs.). 2001. 18.00 (978-1-59040-173-6(5), Phoenix Audio) Pub: Amer Intl Pub. Dist(s): PerseuPGW

Fast Forward Metal Bass Styles. Phil Mulford. 1997. audio compact disk 15.95 (978-0-7119-4504-3(7)) Pub: Music Sales. Dist(s): H Leonard

Fast Greens, unabr. ed. Turk Pipkin. Read by Turk Pipkin. 2 cass. (Running Time: 3 hrs.). 1997. 17.95 (978-1-57453-108-4(5), 395015) Audio Lit.
Thirteen-year-old caddy Billy March learns about envy, jealousy, revenge, true love & the intersection between golf & life.

Fast Innovation: Achieve Superior Differentiation, Speeds to Market, & Increased Profitability. abr. ed. Michael L. George et al. Read by Dick Hill. (Running Time: 16200 sec.). 2007. audio compact disk 28.00 (978-1-933309-17-0(2)) Pub: A Media Intl. Dist(s): Natl Bk Netwk

Fast Men. unabr. ed. Tom McNab. Narrated by John Randolph Jones. 9 cass. (Running Time: 12 hrs. 45 mins.). 1989. 78.00 (978-1-55690-175-1(5), 89610E7) Recorded Bks.
Foot races in frontier towns draw big crowds & heavy bets. Buck Miller, one of the fastest, finds himself in a race for his life.

Fast mind, faster Mouth. Perf. by Groucho Marx & Chico Marx. 1 CD. (Running Time: 58 MIN.). 2005. audio compact disk 12.95 (978-1-57970-226-7(0), AF0486D) J Norton Pubs.

Fast Mind, Faster Mouth. unabr. ed. Perf. by Groucho Marx. 1 cass. (Running Time: 59 min.). 12.95 (#486) J Norton Pubs.
In the opening skit, Groucho & Chico are partners in the Square Deal Amusement Company, trying to make a go of being agents for actors. Another episode has Groucho embroiled in a confused & hilarious plot with guests Marilyn Maxwell & Harry von Zell. In a third sequence, Groucho has fantasies about life as a Marine Corps private. Finally there's an excerpt from "You Bet Your Life," with the usual banter between Groucho & his guest.

Fast Moving Consumer Goods (FMCG) in New Zealand: A Strategic Reference 2006. Compiled by Icon Group International, Inc. Staff. 2007. ring bd. 195.00 (978-0-497-82369-6(1)) Icon Grp.

Fast Shoes. unabr. ed. Michele Sobel Spirn. 1 cass. (Running Time: 7 min.). (Read It Alone Ser.). (J). (ps-2). 1985. 16.99 incl. hardcover. (978-0-87386-004-8(7)) Jan Prods.
Jim is a good runner. He thinks he is fast because of his shoes. Today is the big school race but Jim can't find his shoes.

Fast Show, No. 3. Read by Paul Whitehouse & Charlie Higson. 1 cass. (Running Time: 1 hr.). 1998. 11.25 (978-0-563-55845-3(8)) BBC WrldWd GBR.
Moments from The Fast Show.

Fast Track. Fern Michaels. Read by Laural Merlington. (Sisterhood Ser.: No. 10). 2009. 65.00 (978-1-60775-517-3(3)) Find a World.

Fast Track. abr. ed. Fern Michaels. Read by Laural Merlington. (Running Time: 3 hrs.). (Sisterhood Ser.: No. 10). 2008. audio compact disk 19.95 (978-1-4233-4501-5(0), 9781423345015, BACD) Brilliance Audio.

Fast Track. abr. ed. Fern Michaels. Read by Laural Merlington. (Running Time: 3 hrs.). (Sisterhood Ser.: No. 10). 2009. audio compact disk 14.99 (978-1-4233-4502-2(9), 9781423345022) Brilliance Audio.

Fast Track. unabr. ed. Fern Michaels. Read by Laural Merlington. (Running Time: 7 hrs.). (Sisterhood Ser.: No. 10). 2008. 39.25 (978-1-4233-4498-8(7), 9781423344988, Brinc Audio MP3 Lib); 39.25 (978-1-4233-4500-8(2), 9781423345008, BADLE); 24.95 (978-1-4233-4497-1(9), 9781423344971, Brilliance MP3); 24.95 (978-1-4233-4499-5(5), 9781423344995, BAD); audio compact disk 87.25 (978-1-4233-4496-4(0), 9781423344964, BriAudCD Unabrid); audio compact disk 29.95 (978-1-4233-4495-7(2), 9781423344957, Bril Audio CD Unabri) Brilliance Audio.

Fast-Track Czech, unabr. ed. Milan Fryscek et al. Contrib. by Peter Leimbigler. 6 cass. (Running Time: 6 hrs.). (Fast Track Ser.). (CZE.). 1996. pap. bk. 175.00 (978-0-88432-687-8(X), FTCZ20) J Norton Pubs.
Streamlined introductory course for the business person or traveler who wishes to acquire more knowledge & practice in using the language than provided in brief programs. Text contains 24 lessons based on everyday situations. A concise end-of-text grammar section is included.

Fast-Track Czech CDs & Text. 6 CDs. (Running Time: 6 hrs.). (CZE.). 2005. audio compact disk 175.00 (978-1-57970-112-3(4), AFCZ20D) J Norton Pubs.

Fast-Track Dutch, unabr. ed. Peter Leimbigler. 6 cass. (Running Time: 6 hrs.). (Fast Track Ser.). (DUT & ENG.). 1993. pap. bk. 175.00 (978-0-88432-685-4(3), FTDU20) J Norton Pubs.
Streamlined introductory language course for a business person or traveler. All dialogs, sentences & expressions are tied to concrete everyday situations. There are no isolated words or expressions to be memorized. Topics include travel, dining & business activities. Grammatical explanations are minimal & given only when necessary.

Fast-Track Dutch CDs & Text. 5 CDs. (Running Time: 6 hrs.). (Fast Track Ser.). (DUT.). 2005. audio compact disk 175.00 (978-1-57970-282-3(1), FTDU20D, Audio-For) J Norton Pubs.
A streamlined introductory course designed for the business person or traveler who wishes to acquire a confident and versatile command of modern spoken Dutch in a variety of practical situations. Both the audio and the accompanying text have been developed specifically for self-instruction. All dialogs, sentences, and expressions are tied to concrete everyday situations. There are no isolated words or expressions to be memorized. Topics covered include travel, dining, and business activities such as introducing oneself to colleagues, calling a meeting, credit-card dealings, leaving phone messages, etc. Grammar explanations are minimal and given only when necessary for the understanding of a specific text passage.

Fast-Track European Portuguese. Tr. by Leland Guyer. Contrib. by Peter Leimbigler. 6 cass. (Running Time: 5 hrs. 30 mins.). (ENG & POR., 1996. pap. bk. 155.00 (978-0-88432-935-0(6), FTPG20) J Norton Pubs.
A streamlined introductory course designed for the business person or traveler. All dialogs, sentences & expressions are tied to concrete everyday situations. Topics include travel, dining & business activities. No isolated words or expressions to be memorized. Grammatical explanations are kept to a minimum.

Fast-Track European Portuguese CDs & Text. 6 CDs. (Running Time: 5 hrs. 30 mins.). (Fast Track Ser.). (POR.). 2005. audio compact disk Rental 175.00 (978-1-57970-203-8(1), FTPG20D) J Norton Pubs.

Fast-Track European Spanish, unabr. ed. 6 cass. (Running Time: 4 hrs.). (Fast Track Ser.). (SPA.). (gr. 10-12). 1994. pap. bk. 175.00 (978-0-88432-786-8(8), FTSP10) J Norton Pubs.
Streamlined introductory course designed for the business person or traveler who wishes to acquire a confident & versatile command of modern spoken European Spanish in a variety of practical situations. All dialogs, sentences & expressions are tied to concrete everyday situations. No isolated words or expressions to be memorized. Topics covered include travel, dining & business activities. Grammatical explanations are kept to a minimum.

Fast-Track European Spanish CDs & Text. 6 CDs. (Running Time: 4 hrs.). (Fast Track Ser.). (SPA.). 2005. audio compact disk 175.00 (978-1-57970-211-3(2), FTSP10D) J Norton Pubs.

Fast Track French. Henry S. Raymond. 2 cass. (Running Time: 3 hrs.). (Fast Track Ser.). (FRE & ENG.). 1999. pap. bk. 19.95 (978-1-56015-567-6(1)) Penton Overseas.
A complete guide to business conversation & protocol. Designed to have one speaking & communicating in record time, while actually enjoying the learning experience! Created by renowned language experts, this program increases retention & comprehension. Includes pocket-sized Listening & Reference Guide & wallet-sized phrase guide.

Fast Track French. abr. ed. Nina Mattikow. 2 cass. (Running Time: 3 hrs.). Dramatization. (Language Ser.). 1992. 19.95 Set. (978-1-55569-554-5(X), 42002) Great Am Audio.
A language program designed to have you speaking & communicating in record time while you actually enjoy the learning experience.

Fast Track German. Henry S. Raymond et al. 2 cass. (Running Time: 3 hrs.). (Fast Track Ser.). (GER & ENG.). 1999. pap. bk. 19.95 (978-1-56015-566-9(3)) Penton Overseas.
A complete guide to business conversation & protocol. Designed to have one speaking & communicating in record time, while actually enjoying the learning experience! Created by renowned language experts, this program increases retention & comprehension. Includes pocket-sized Listening & Reference Guide & wallet-sized phrase guide.

Fast Track German. abr. ed. Nina Mattikow. 2 cass. (Running Time: 3 hrs.). Dramatization. (Language Ser.). 1992. 19.95 Set. (42003) Great Am Audio.
A language program designed to have you speaking & communicating in record time while you actually enjoy the learning experience.

Fast-Track German. unabr. ed. Peter Leimbigler. 6 cass. (Running Time: 6 hrs.). (J). (gr. 10-12). 1985. pap. bk. 175.00 (978-0-88432-123-1(1), FTG100) J Norton Pubs.
Streamlined introductory course designed for the business man or traveller who wishes to acquire more knowledge than provided in brief programs. Text includes 24 lesson units based on everyday situations including those encountered in business activities.

Fast Track Italian. Henry S. Raymond et al. 2 cass. (Running Time: 3 hrs.). (Fast Track Ser.). (ITA & ENG.). 1999. pap. bk. 19.95 (978-1-56015-570-6(1)) Penton Overseas.
A complete guide to business conversation & protocol. Designed to have one speaking & communicating in record time, while actually enjoying the learning experience! Created by renowned language experts, this program increases retention & comprehension. Includes pocket-sized Listening & Reference Guide & wallet-sized phrase guide.

Fast Track Japanese. Henry S. Raymond et al. 2 cass. (Running Time: 3 hrs.). (Fast Track Ser.). (JPN & ENG.). 1999. pap. bk. 19.95 (978-1-56015-569-0(8)) Penton Overseas.

Fast Track Japanese. abr. ed. Nina Mattikow. 2 cass. (Running Time: 3 hrs.). Dramatization. (Language Ser.). 1992. 19.95 Set. (978-1-55569-556-9(6), 42004) Great Am Audio.
A language program designed to have you speaking & communicating in record time while you actually enjoy the learning experience.

Fast-Track Japanese, unabr. ed. Peter Leimbigler. 6 cass. (Running Time: 6 hrs.). (JPN.). (J). (gr. 10-12). 1985. pap. bk. 175.00 (978-0-88432-121-7(5), FTJ210) J Norton Pubs.
Streamlined introductory course designed for the business man or traveller who wishes to acquire more knowledge than provided in brief programs. Text inculdes 24 lessons units based on everyday situations including those encountered in business activities.

Fast-Track Japanese CDs & Text. Peter Leimbigler. 6 CDs. (Running Time: 6 hrs.). (JPN.). 2006. audio compact disk 175.00 (978-1-57970-354-7(2), FTJ210D, Audio-For) J Norton Pubs.
A streamlined introductory course designed for the business person or traveler who wishes to acquire a confident and versatile command of modern spoken Japanese ina variety of practical situations. Both the audio recordings and the accompanying text have been developed specifically for self-instruction. All dialogs, sentences, and expressions are tied to concrete everyday situations. There are no isolated words or expressions to memorize. Topics covered include travel, dining, and business activities such as introducing oneself to colleagues, calling a meeting, credit-card dealings, leaving phone messages, etc. Grammar explanations are minimal and given only when necessary for the understanding of a specific text passage.

Fast Track Mandarin. unabr. ed. Peter Leimbigler. 6 cass. (Running Time: 6 hrs.). (YA). (gr. 10-12). 1986. pap. bk. 175.00 (978-0-88432-122-4(3), FTM520) J Norton Pubs.
Streamlined introductory course designed for the business man or traveller who wishes to acquire more knowledge than provided in brief programs. Text includes 24 lesson units based on everyday situations including those encountered in business activities. Extensive practice exercises for each lesson unit.

Fast Track Pack: Getting Started Training to Ensure Success in Network Marketing. Randy Gage. (ENG.). 2004. audio compact disk 37.00 (978-0-9762299-5-7(1)) Prime Concepts Grp.

Fast Track Phonics: For Young Adults & Adults. Kaye Wiley. (Fast Track Ser.). 2001. audio compact disk 43.00 (978-0-13-098741-9(7)) AddisonWesley.

Fast Track Spanish. abr. ed. Nina Mattikow. 2 cass. (Running Time: 3 hrs.). Dramatization. (Language Ser.). 1992. 19.95 Set. (978-1-55569-553-8(1), 42001) Great Am Audio.
A language program designed to have you speaking & communicating in record time while you actually enjoy the learning experience.

Fast Track Spanish. rev. ed. Henry S. Raymond. 2 cass. (Running Time: 3 hrs.). (Fast Track Ser.). (SPA & ENG.). 1999. 19.95 (978-1-56015-568-3(X)) Penton Overseas.
A complete guide to business conversation & protocol. Designed to have one speaking & communicating in record time, while actually enjoying the learning experience! Created by renowned language experts, this program increases retention & comprehension. Includes pocket-sized Listening & Reference Guide & wallet-sized phrase guide.

Fast Track Swahili. Sharifa M. Zawawi. 6 cass. (Running Time: 5 hrs. 30 mins.). (SWA & ENG.). 2001. pap. bk. 155.00 (FTSW10) J Norton Pubs.
Streamlined introductory course designed for the business person or traveler contains 24 lesson units based on everyday situations. Extensive practice exercises for each lesson unit.

Fast-Track Swahili. Sharifa M. Zawawi. 6 cass. (Running Time: 5 hrs. 30 mins.). (SWA., 1999. pap. bk. 175.00 (978-1-57970-077-5(2), FTSW10) J Norton Pubs.
Streamlined introductory course. 24 lesson units based on everyday situations.

Fast-Track Swahili CDs & Text. Sharifa Zawawi. 6 CDs. (Running Time: 5 hrs. 30 min.). (SWA.). 2005. audio compact disk 175.00 (978-1-57970-155-0(8), FTSW10D) J Norton Pubs.

Fast Track to Waste-Free Manufacturing: Straight Talk from a Plant Manager. John W. Davis. 2002. 39.95 (978-1-56327-278-3(4)) Pub: Product Pr. Dist(s): Taylor and Fran

Fast Track to Waste-Free Manufacturing: Straight Talk from a Plant Manager. John W. Davis. (Running Time: 17760 sec.). 2002. audio compact disk 39.95 (978-1-56327-279-0(2)) Pub: Product Pr. Dist(s): Taylor and Fran

Fast Women. unabr. ed. Jennifer Crusie, pseud. Read by Sandra Burr. (Running Time: 12 hrs.). 2004. 39.25 (978-1-59335-444-2(4), 1593354444, Brinc Audio MP3 Lib) Brilliance Audio.
New York Times and USA Today bestselling author Jennifer Crusie returns with her most hilarious, sizzling novel yet. Nell Dysart's in trouble. Her divorce is 18 months old, she's been sleepwalking through life, and the best job she can get is with a detective agency that specializes in relationship work. Determined to turn her life around, Nell flings herself into making McKenna Investigations a better place. On day one, she uncovers an embezzler. On day two, she turns up bribery. On day three, she has sex with the wrong man. On day four, she steals a dog. On day five, her boss tries to fire her . . . And fails miserably. Because even Gabe McKenna has to admit that no matter how much he hates the confusion she's brought into his life, Nell shares his passion for making things right. It's not long before they share another passion, one they can't ignore - even in the face of distractions like adultery, blackmail, arson, murder, and really bad business cards.

Fast Women. unabr. ed. Jennifer Crusie, pseud. Read by Sandra Burr. (Running Time: 12 hrs.). 2004. 49.97 (978-1-59710-277-3(6), 1597102776, BADLE); 24.95 (978-1-59710-276-6(8), 1597102768, BAD) Brilliance Audio.

***Fast Women.** unabr. ed. Jennifer Crusie, pseud. Read by Sandra Burr. (Running Time: 12 hrs.). 2010. audio compact disk 29.99 (978-1-4418-4071-4(0), 9781441840714, Bril Audio CD Unabri); audio compact disk 89.97 (978-1-4418-4072-1(9), 9781441840721, BriAudCD Unabrid) Brilliance Audio.

Fast Women. unabr. ed. Jennifer Crusie, pseud. Read by Sandra Burr. (Running Time: 12 hrs.). 2004. 24.95 (978-1-59335-081-9(3), 1593350813) Soulmate Audio Bks.

Faster! James Gleick. Narrated by John McDonough. 9 CDs. (Running Time: 10 hrs. 30 min.). 2000. audio compact disk 89.00 (C1245E7) Recorded Bks.
This considers our rapidly changing perception of time. From atomic clocks & instantaneous opinion polls to automatic dialing & elevator buttons, this is packed with fascinating information about the things that are speeding up our lives.

Faster: The Acceleration of Just about Everything. James Gleick. Narrated by John McDonough. 9 CDs. (Running Time: 10 hrs. 30 mins.). audio compact disk 89.00 (978-0-7887-4757-1(6)) Recorded Bks.

Faster: The Acceleration of Just about Everything. unabr. ed. James Gleick. Narrated by John McDonough. 8 cass. (Running Time: 10 hrs. 30 mins.). 1999. 70.00 (978-0-7887-4067-1(9), 96164E7) Recorded Bks.

***Faster Cheaper Better: The 9 Levers for Transforming How Work Gets Done.** unabr. ed. Michael Hammer & Lisa W. Hershman. (Running Time: 9 hrs. 0 mins.). 2010. 34.99 (978-1-4001-9859-7(3)); 15.99 (978-1-4001-8859-8(8)); 24.99 (978-1-4001-6859-0(7)); audio compact disk 34.99 (978-1-4001-1859-5(X)); audio compact disk 83.99 (978-1-4001-4859-2(6)) Pub: Tantor Media. Dist(s): IngramPubServ

Faster Reading. 1 cass. (Running Time: 45 min.). (Educational Ser.). 9.98 (978-1-55909-033-9(2), 38); 9.98 90 min. extended length stereo music. (978-1-55909-034-6(0), 38M) Randolph Tapes.
Improves comprehension & read faster. Subliminal messages are heard 3-5 minutes before becoming ocean sounds or music.

Faster Reading. Barrie Konicov. 1 cass. 11.98 (978-0-87082-298-8(5), 032) Potentials.
The average high school graduate reads under 300 words a minute. There are dozens of speed reading courses on the market that can increase speed & comprehension to thousands of words per minute. This tape contains the same techniques used in courses that cost up to $300 dollars & can produce the same results for substantially less money.

Faster Reading. Barrie Konicov. 1 CD. 2003. audio compact disk 16.98 (978-0-87082-974-1(2)) Potentials.
This program contains many of the same techniques used in courses that cost up to $500. Our program produces the same result, at a substantially lower investment. You will find the self-hypnosis on track 1 and the subliminal on track 2. The easy-listening music of the subliminal, together with the self-hypnosis, is the original format which most people love and with which they are most familiar.

Faster Than Light: Loopholes in Modern Physics. Ed. by Marco A. V. Bitetto. 1 cass. 2000. (978-1-58578-306-9(4)) Inst of Cybernetics.

Fasting. 4.95 (C3) Carothers.

Fasting. Derek Prince. 1 cass. 5.95 (066) Derek Prince.
God requires His people to humble themselves before Him, & has revealed a simple, practical way to accomplish this.

***Fasting: Opening the door to a deeper, more intimate, more powerful relationship with God.** unabr. ed. Jentezen Franklin. Narrated by Lloyd James. (ENG.). 2009. 12.98 (978-1-59644-744-8(3), christianSeed) christianaud.

Fasting: Opening the door to a deeper, more intimate, more powerful relationship with God. unabr. ed. Jentezen Franklin. Read by Lloyd James. (Running Time: 4 hrs. 30 mins. 0 sec.). (ENG.). 2009. audio compact disk 21.98 (978-1-59644-743-1(5), christianSeed) christianaud.

Fasting & Prayer. Kenneth Copeland. 4 cass. (Running Time: 4 hrs.). 1982. bk. 20.00 (978-0-938458-18-0(3), 01-1000) K Copeland Pubns.

Fasting for Spiritual Breakthrough. unabr. ed. Elmer L. Towns. Read by Michael Kramer. (Running Time: 6 hrs. 48 mins. 0 sec.). (ENG.). 2008. audio compact disk 24.98 (978-1-59644-555-0(6)) christianaud.

***Fasting for Spiritual Breakthrough: A Guide to Nine Biblical Fasts.** unabr. ed. Elmer Towns. Narrated by Michael Kramer. (ENG.). 2008. 14.98 (978-1-59644-556-7(4), Hovel Audio) christianaud.

***Fasting Made Easy.** abr. ed. Don Colbert. Narrated by Tim Lundeen. (ENG.). 2004. 10.49 (978-1-60814-733-5(9)) Oasis Audio.

Fasting Made Easy: Companion to Toxic Relief. abr. ed. Don Colbert. (Running Time: 6 hrs.). 2004. 11.99 (978-1-58926-729-9(X)) Oasis Audio.

Fasting Made Easy: Companion to Toxic Relief. abr. ed. Don Colbert. Narrated by Tim Lundeen. 2 CDs. (Running Time: 1 hr. 59 mins. 34 sec.). (ENG.). 2004. audio compact disk 14.99 (978-1-58926-730-5(3)) Oasis Audio.

Fasting Without Fear. C. S. Lovett. 1 cass. (Running Time: 50 min.). 6.95 Side 1, Theory; Side Two practical (day by day). (7032) Prsnl Christianity.

FastTrack Mini Harnonica Method - Book 1 with Hohner Blues Harmonica. Blake Neely & Doug Downing. (J). 2006. pap. bk. 12.95 (978-1-4234-1975-4(8), 1423419758) H Leonard.

Fastwalker. abr. ed. Jacques Vallee. Read by George Del Hoyo. 2 cass. (Running Time: 3 hrs.). 1996. bk. 18.95 (978-1-57453-068-1(2)) Audio Lit.
Cold warrior General Bushnell, alien abductee Rachel Rand, & Peter Keller, a lone reporter at the end of his professional ethics, all come together.

Fat see Nobody Said Anything

Fat Boy Swim. unabr. ed. Catherine Forde. Read by Gary Lewis. 4 cass. (Running Time: 4 hrs. 53 mins.). (YA). 2004. 32.00 (978-1-4000-9042-6(3), Listening Lib) Random Audio Pubg.
Fourteen Jimmy Kelly is Fat Boy Fat, the largest kid in his Scottish community, who is made to feel useless at everything. Only his family know?s he?s a whiz in the kitchen, and Jimmy?s determined to keep it that way. After all, what would people say if they discovered that Big Blob Kelly had one special talent and it involved food? So when GI Joe, the toughest coach at school, finds out his secret, Jimmy?s sure he?s doomed. But, Coach proposes a deal: If Jimmy helps him, Coach will help Jimmy . . . swim. With each stroke Coach teaches him, Jimmy feels like he?s getting closer to recognizing the Shadow Shape that?s been haunting his dreams. And closer to Ellie, whose chocolate brown curls look good enough to eat. Coach and Ellie know there?s more to Jimmy than meets the eye. Now it?s time for Jimmy to stop hiding and realize it himself.

***Fat Cat.** unabr. ed. Robin Brande. Read by Kirsten Potter. 7 CDs. (Running Time: 8 hrs. 22 mins.). (YA). (gr. 8 up). 2009. audio compact disk 55.00 (978-0-307-57992-8(1), Listening Lib) Pub: Random Audio Pubg. Dist(s): Random

Fat Cat. unabr. ed. Robin Brande. Read by Kirsten Potter. (ENG.). (J). (gr. 7). 2009. audio compact disk 37.00 (978-0-307-57990-4(5), Listening Lib) Pub: Random Audio Pubg. Dist(s): Random

Fat Cat. unabr. ed. Michele Sobel Spirn. 1 cass. (Running Time: 7 min.). (I Like to Read Ser.). (J). (ps-2). 1985. 16.99 incl. hardcover. (978-0-87386-000-0(4)) Jan Prods.
Jane has been getting her cat ready for the town pet show. She is sure Fat Cat will win a prize. But Fat Cat has eaten so much, he can't move.

Fat Cat & Friends. Perf. by Margaret Read MacDonald & Richard Sholtz. 1 CD. (Running Time: 1 hr. 5 mins.). 2002. audio compact disk 16.95 (978-0-87483-682-0(4)) Pub: August Hse. Dist(s): Natl Bk Netwk
When August House launched Fat Cat in picture book format a year ago, the media reaction was favorable both for the story and its inherent rhythms, but also for the vibrant artwork by Julie Paschis.

Fat Cat & Friends. unabr. ed. Margaret Read MacDonald. Read by Richard Scholtz. (J). 2007. 34.99 (978-1-59895-923-9(9)) Find a World.

***Fat Cat Sat on the Mat.** unabr. ed. Nurit Karlin. (ENG.). 2008. (978-0-06-169418-9(5)); (978-0-06-171004-9(0)) HarperCollins Pubs.

Fat Cats. 2 cass. (Running Time: 90 mins.). 2001. 17.00 (ZBSF035); audio compact disk 22.50 (ZBSF036) Lodestone Catalog.
A man's dream come true, until his shadowy past returns to haunt him & a car bomb blasts into the picture. Willie, hired to paint the immense living room, is an amateur sleuth who begins to hear in his head the voice of his favorite hardboiled detective.

Fat Charlie's Circus. unabr. ed. Marie-Louise Gay. 1 cass. (Running Time: 11 min.). (J). (gr. k-4). 1994. bk. 25.90 (978-0-8045-6816-6(2), 6816) Spoken Arts.

Fat, Fifty & Fed!** unabr. ed. Geoffrey McGeachin. Read by Peter Hosking. (Running Time: 6 hrs. 45 mins.). 2010. 43.95 (978-1-74214-666-9(X), 9781742146669) Pub: Bolinda Pubng AUS. Dist(s): Bolinda Pub Inc

Fat, Fifty & Fed!** unabr. ed. Geoffrey McGeachin. Read by Peter Hosking. (Running Time: 6 hrs. 45 mins.). 2010. audio compact disk 77.95 (978-1-74093-674-3(4)) Pub: Bolinda Pubng AUS. Dist(s): Bolinda Pub Inc

Fat Flush Plan. abr. ed. Ann Louise Gittleman. 3 cass. (Running Time: 4 hrs. 30 mins.). (McGraw Hill Audiobks.). 2003. 24.00 (978-0-9724462-5-9(7)); audio compact disk 28.00 (978-0-9724889-3-8(6)) Pub: A Media Intl. Dist(s): Natl Bk Netwk

Fat Int the Fire the Missing Links on Audio CD. Read by David Morrow. Based on a book by David Morrow. Prod. by Jet Productions. 2007. audio compact disk 12.95 (978-0-9799318-1-9(9)) David Morrow.

Fat Kid Rules the World. K. L. Going. Read by Mathew Lillard. 2004. audio compact disk (978-1-4000-9116-4(0)) Random Audio Pubg.

Fat Kid Rules the World. K. L. Going. 4 cass. (Running Time: 5 hrs. 43 mins.). (J). (gr. 7 up). 2004. 32.00 (978-0-8072-1695-8(X), Listening Lib) Pub: Random Audio Pubg. Dist(s): Random

***Fat Man: A Tale of North Pole Noir.** unabr. ed. Ken Harmon. (Running Time: 6 hrs. 0 mins.). 2010. 13.99 (978-1-4001-8986-1(1)); 19.99 (978-1-4001-6986-3(0)); audio compact disk 24.99 (978-1-4001-1986-8(3)) Pub: Tantor Media. Dist(s): IngramPubServ

Fat Man: Murder is the Medium. (MM6684) Natl Recrd Co.

Fat Man: Murder Plays the Horses & Murder Runs a Want Ad. Perf. by Jack Smart. 1 cass. (Running Time: 1 hr.). 2001. 6.98 (1888) Radio Spirits.

***Fat Man & Thin Man.** Perf. by J. Scott Smart & William Powell. 2009. audio compact disk 18.95 (978-1-57019-912-7(4)) Radio Spirits.

Fat Man from Colombia. James Pattinson. 2009. 44.95 (978-1-84559-945-4(4)); audio compact disk 51.95 (978-1-84559-946-1(2)) Pub: Soundings Ltd GBR. Dist(s): Ulverscroft US

Fat Man in the Mirror from "The Mills of Kavanaugh" see Twentieth-Century Poetry in English, No. 32-33, Recordings of Poets Reading Their Own Poetry

***Fat Man (Library Edition) A Tale of North Pole Noir.** unabr. ed. Ken Harmon. (Running Time: 6 hrs. 0 mins.). 2010. 24.99 (978-1-4001-9986-0(7)); audio compact disk 59.99 (978-1-4001-4986-5(X)) Pub: Tantor Media. Dist(s): IngramPubServ

Fat Ollie's Book. abr. ed. Ed McBain, pseud. Read by Ron McLarty. (87th Precinct Ser.: Bk. 52). 2004. 15.95 (978-0-7435-4700-0(4)) Pub: S&S Audio. Dist(s): S and S Inc

Fat Smash Diet: The Last Diet You'll Ever Need. unabr. ed. Ian K. Smith. Read by Ian K. Smith. (Running Time: 1 hr. 0 mins. 0 sec.). (ENG.). 2006. audio compact disk 12.95 (978-1-4272-0090-7(4)) Pub: Macmill Audio. Dist(s): Macmillan

Fat Tuesday. Sandra Brown. Narrated by Tom Stechschulte. 12 CDs. (Running Time: 15 hrs.). 2001. audio compact disk 116.00 (978-0-7887-5169-1(7), C1331E7) Recorded Bks.
A cop with nothing left to lose, Burke Basile is out to get revenge. Kidnapping Pinkie Duvall's trophy wife seems the perfect way to do just that. There's just one problem. He doesn't foresee the electric attraction he'll feel for this lonely, desperate woman from New Orelans.

Fat Tuesday. unabr. ed. Sandra Brown. Narrated by Tom Stechschulte. 10 cass. (Running Time: 15 hrs.). 1997. 91.00 (978-0-7887-3116-7(5), 95797E7) Recorded Bks.

***Fat Vampire.** unabr. ed. Adam Rex. Read by Kirby Heyborne. (ENG.). 2010. (978-0-06-205986-4(6)) HarperCollins Pubs.

***Fat Vampire: A Never Coming of Age Story.** unabr. ed. Adam Rex. Read by Kirby Heyborne. (ENG.). 2010. (978-0-06-199525-5(8)) HarperCollins Pubs.

Fatal. Michael Palmer. 9 cass. (Running Time: 13 hrs. 30 min.). 2002. 72.00 (978-0-7366-8588-7(X)) Books on Tape.
Dr. Matt Rutledge must find the links between an industrial polluter and a cluster of unexplained deaths before he winds up dead himself.

Fatal. unabr. ed. Michael Palmer. 2002. audio compact disk 88.00 (978-0-7366-8688-4(6)) Books on Tape.

Fatal Attachment. unabr. ed. Robert Barnard. Read by Frederick Davidson. 5 cass. (Running Time: 7 hrs.). 1995. 39.95 (978-0-7861-0879-4(7), 1537) Blckstn Audio.
A nationally known writer of popular biographies, Lydia Perceval lives a sterile, lonely existence in the tiny Yorkshire village of Bly. Her biographies of such men as Lord Nelson, Byron & Frederick the Great have brought recognition & affluence, but Lydia's personal life has been bleak since her two adored young nephews left town years ago. The special relationship began slowly as the boys grew to maturity, & gradually, Lydia had absorbed them into her sphere, imposing her cultural & class values, & alienating them from their parents. Once again, as with her nephews twenty years earlier, Lydia disrupts lives, forging ahead with a single-mindedness that is devoid of compassion & self-knowledge. Many people have reason to hate Lydia Perceval. One of them hates enough to kill.

Fatal Cipher see Classic Detective Stories, Vol. II, A Collection

Fatal Collection: Grave Secrets/Fatal Voyage/Bare Bones. abr. gif. unabr. ed. Kathy Reichs. Read by Katherine Borowitz & Michele Pawk. 15 CDs. (Running Time: 15 hrs. 30 mins. 0 sec.). (ENG.). 2006. audio compact disk 39.95 (978-0-7435-5469-5(8), Audioworks) Pub: S&S Audio. Dist(s): S and S Inc

Fatal Conceit. Richard Dortch. 1 cass. 1993. 12.95 (978-0-89221-246-0(2)) New Leaf.

Fatal Cure. unabr. ed. Robin Cook. Read by Michael McConnohie. 12 cass. (Running Time: 18 hrs.). 1994. 96.00 (978-0-7366-2774-0(X), 3493) Books on Tape.
Two doctors investigating several children's mysterious deaths from cystic fibrosis find their careers & lives at risk.

Fatal Cut. June Hampson. 2009. 69.95 (978-0-7531-4241-7(4)); audio compact disk 84.95 (978-0-7531-4242-4(2)) Pub: Isis Pubng Ltd GBR. Dist(s): Ulverscroft US

Fatal Cut. unabr. ed. Priscilla Masters. Narrated by Briony Sykes. 7 cass. (Running Time: 9 hrs. 45 mins.). 2000. 63.00 (978-1-84197-160-5(X), H1154E7) Recorded Bks.
Pathologist Karys Harper is puzzled by the nature of the body's injuries. The man died from strangulation, but found an incision that was made after he was dead & sewn up.

Fatal Deception: The Untold Story of Asbestos: Why it Is still legal & killing Us. abr. ed. Michael Bowker. Read by John Slattery. 2004. 15.95 (978-0-7435-4701-7(2)) Pub: S&S Audio. Dist(s): S and S Inc

***Fatal Error: A Novel.** unabr. ed. J. A. Jance. (Running Time: 10 hrs. 30 mins. 0 sec.). (ENG.). 2011. audio compact disk 39.99 (978-1-4423-3549-3(1)) Pub: S&S Audio. Dist(s): S and S Inc

***Fatal Flaw.** abr. ed. William Lashner. Read by Peter Francis James. (ENG.). 2004. (978-0-06-081405-2(5), Harper Audio); (978-0-06-079800-0(9), Harper Audio) HarperCollins Pubs.

Fatal Forecast: An Incredible True Story of Disaster & Survival at Sea. unabr. ed. Michael Tougias. Read by Jeff Cummings. (Running Time: 19800 sec.). 2007. audio compact disk 29.95 (978-1-4332-0054-0(6)) Blckstn Audio.

Fatal Forecast: An Incredible True Tale of Disaster & Survival at Sea. unabr. ed. Michael Tougias. Read by Jeff Cummings. (Running Time: 19800 sec.). 2007. 19.95 (978-1-4332-0052-6(X)); audio compact disk 19.95 (978-1-4332-0053-3(8)) Blckstn Audio.

Fatal Forecast: An Incredible True Tale of Disaster & Survival at Sea. unabr. ed. Michael Tougias. (Running Time: 19800 sec.). 2007. 34.95 (978-1-4332-0050-2(3)); audio compact disk 45.00 (978-1-4332-0051-9(1)) Blckstn Audio.

Fatal Glass of Beer. unabr. ed. Stuart M. Kaminsky. Narrated by George Guidall. 6 cass. (Running Time: 8 hrs. 30 mins.). (Toby Peters Mystery Ser.: No. 20). 1997. 51.00 (978-0-7887-0650-9(0), 94827E7) Recorded Bks.
Hollywood's funny man, W.C. Fields, stashed over a million dollars in banks around the country, & now a thief is emptying his accounts. Trying to save the boodle, Fields & the irasicble Toby dash through America's one-horse towns in hot pursuit of the scoundrel. But suddenly someone is shadowing them - & using them for target practice.

Fatal Glass of Beer, Set. unabr. ed. Stuart M. Kaminsky. Read by Tom Parker. 6 cass. (Toby Peters Mystery Ser.: No. 20). 1999. 44.95 (FS9-43273) Highsmith.

Fatal Grace. unabr. ed. Louise Penny. Read by Ralph Cosham. 11 CDs. (Running Time: 37800 sec.). (Chief Inspector Armand Gamache Ser.: Bk. 2). 2007. audio compact disk 29.95 (978-0-7861-5928-4(6)); 29.95 (978-0-7861-4918-6(3)) Blckstn Audio.
No one liked CC de Poitiers. Not her quiet, ineffectual husband. Not the pallid, spineless photographer she'd been cheating on him with. Not even her tremendously fat, silent eleven-year-old daughter Crie, dubbed "Brie" by her hateful classmates. And certainly none of the residents of Three Pines, a tiny village south of Montreal, each of whom CC had recently managed to offend with one callous and insensitive act or another. And therein lies the challenge for the brilliant inspector Armand Gamache of the Surete du Quebec, called once again from his headquarters in Montreal to investigate murder in this breathtaking hamlet. CC has been literally cooked alive in an apparent electrical accident on a local frozen lake, and everyone in town has a motive, even the inspector's good friends. The kind, compassionate, and whip-smart detective must employ all his talents, not least his ability to blend seamlessly into small-town life, to identify the calculating killer lurking within the pastoral landscape that is Three Pines.

Fatal Grace. unabr. ed. Louise Penny. Read by Ralph Cosham. (Running Time: 37800 sec.). (Chief Inspector Armand Gamache Ser.: Bk. 2). 2007. 79.95 (978-0-7861-6863-7(3)); audio compact disk 29.95 (978-0-7861-7054-8(9)); audio compact disk 99.00 (978-0-7861-6862-0(5)) Blckstn Audio.

Fatal Harvest. abr. ed. Catherine Palmer. Read by Kathy Garver. 2 cass. (Running Time: 3 hrs.). 2003. 17.95 (978-1-59086-920-8(6), 1590869206, Brill Audio); 44.25 (978-1-59086-921-5(4), 1590869214, BAudLibEd); audio compact disk 19.95 (978-1-59086-922-2(2), 1590869222, BACD); audio compact disk 62.25 (978-1-59086-923-9(0), 1590869230, BACDLib Ed) Brilliance Audio.
Teenager Matt Strong discovers a secret that could expose the indiscretions of the conglomerate who controls the world's food supply. Now he's been framed for murder and is on the run. Matt's father, Cole Strong, enlists the help of Matt's teacher Jill Pruitt to find the boy and save his life. Before long, the two are caught up in a dangerous quest with stakes much higher than either is prepared to face. Page-turning, contemporary, romantic suspense from bestselling author Catherine Palmer.

Fatal Harvest. abr. ed. Catherine Palmer. Read by Kathy Garver. (Running Time: 3 hrs.). 2006. 39.25 (978-1-4233-0360-2(1), 9781423303602, BADLE); 24.95 (978-1-4233-0359-6(8), 9781423303596, BAD); 39.25 (978-1-4233-0358-9(X), 9781423303589, Brlnc Audio MP3 Lib); audio compact disk 24.95 (978-1-4233-0357-2(1), 9781423303572, Brilliance MP3) Brilliance Audio.

Fatal Impact: The Invasion of the South Pacific. unabr. ed. Alan Moorehead. Read by Victor Rumbellow. 8 cass. (Running Time: 8 hrs.). 1980. 48.00 (978-0-7366-0220-4(8), 1218) Books on Tape.
Researching from primary source materials, Moorehead has created an account of the White Man's first contacts with natives in Tahiti, Australia, & Antarctica, from 1767 to 1840. It is not a pretty picture. Without editorializing, Moorehead shows how the wants, needs & whims of western man destroy native populations in previously unopened lands.

Fatal Inheritance. unabr. ed. Peter Cave. 4 cass. (Isis Ser.). (J). 2004. 44.95 (978-0-7531-0221-3(8)) Pub: ISIS Lrg Prnt GBR. Dist(s): Ulverscroft US

Fatal Inversion. unabr. ed. Barbara Vine, pseud. Read by William Gaminara. 8 cass. (Running Time: 12 hrs.). 2000. 11.50 (978-0-7451-6338-3(6), CAB 413) Pub: Chivers Audio Bks GBR. Dist(s): AudioGO
In 1976, Adam Verne-Smith gathers a group of people at Wyvis Hall. With the carelessness of youth, Adam, Rufus, Shiva, Vivien and Zosie scavenge, steal, pawn and sell the family heirlooms. Ten years later, two bodies are found in the animal cemetary. Adam and the others all have reasons to fear, as the events of 1976 unfold.

***Fatal Last Words.** Quintin Jardine. 2010. 84.95 (978-0-7531-4636-1(3)); audio compact disk 99.95 (978-0-7531-4637-8(1)) Pub: Isis Pubng Ltd GBR. Dist(s): Ulverscroft US

Fatal Light & The Wars of Heaven. Excerpts. Richard Currey. Read by Richard Currey. 1 cass. (Running Time: 1 hr.). 1991. 13.95 Am Audio Prose.

Fatal Majesty: A Novel of Mary, Queen of Scots. unabr. ed. Reay Tannahill. Read by Eve Karpf. 16 cass. (Running Time: 16 hrs.). 1998. 124.95 Set. (978-0-7540-0242-0(X), CAB1665) AudioGO.
Mary Queen of Scot's life as one of the most complex & violent political thrillers in the annals of British history.

Fatal Network. Trevor Scott. Ed. by Stefan Rudnicki. 5 cass. (Running Time: 7 hrs.). 2004. 49.95 (978-0-7861-2845-7(3), 3303) Blckstn Audio.

Fatal Network. Trevor Scott. Read by Stefan Rudnicki. (Running Time: 7 hrs.). 2004. 27.95 (978-1-59912-488-9(2)) Iofy Corp.

Fatal Network. abr. ed. Trevor Scott. Read by Bruce Watson. 4 vols. No. 1. 2002. (978-1-58807-551-2(6)) Am Pubng Inc.

Fatal Network. abr. ed. Trevor Scott. Read by Bruce Watson. 4 vols. (Running Time: 6 hrs.). (Jake Adams International Thriller Ser.: No. 1). 2002. 25.00 (978-1-58807-091-3(3)) Am Pubng Inc.
When a tech rep in charge of an avionics retrofit at a U.S. Air Base in Germany comes up missing, Jake Adams, a former Air Force intelligence and CIA officer, is hired to find him. Was the man selling out vital technology for the new Joint Strike Fighter? Back in a changed Europe, Adams struggles to survive in a world where profits are more important than past ideologies. Conspiracy, murder, espionage, and mystery lead Adams from an aircraft carrier off the coast of Italy to the chilly banks of the Rhine. Can Adams keep the technology away from the ruthless German and Hungarian agents? First he must save the woman he loves, and then stop the FATAL NETWORK.

Fatal Network. unabr. ed. Trevor Scott. Ed. by Stefan Rudnicki. 6 CDs. (Running Time: 7 hrs.). 2004. audio compact disk 64.00 (978-0-7861-8545-0(7), 3303) Blckstn Audio.

Fatal Network: The Jake Adams International Thriller Series #1. unabr. ed. Trevor Scott. Read by Christopher Lane. 6 CDs. (Running Time: 7 hrs.). (Jake Adams International Thriller Ser.). 2005. audio compact disk 29.95 (978-0-7861-8581-8(3), ZE3303); 29.95 (978-0-7861-2734-4(1), E3303) Blckstn Audio.

Fatal Remedies. Donna Leon. 2 cass. (Running Time: 3 hrs.). (Commissario Guido Brunetti Mystery Ser.: Bk. 8). 1999. 16.85 Set. (978-1-85686-631-6(9)) Ulvrscrft Audio.

Fatal Remedies. unabr. ed. Donna Leon. Read by Anna Fields. 5 cass. (Running Time: 7 hrs.). (Commissario Guido Brunetti Mystery Ser.: Bk. 8). 2001. 39.95 (978-0-7861-1983-7(7), 2753); audio compact disk 48.00 (978-0-7861-9741-5(2), 2753) Blckstn Audio.
A sudden act of vandalism had just been committed in the chilly Venetian dawn. But Commissario Guido Brunetti soon finds out that the perpetrator is no petty criminal. For the culprit waiting at the scene of the crime is none other than Paola Brunetti, his wife. With a crisis in the Brunetti household & Brunetti under increasing pressure at work: a daring robbery with Mafia connections is linked to a suspicious death & needs quick results. As his professional & personal lives clash, Brunetti's own career is under threat & the conspiracy which Paola had risked everything to expose draws him inexorably to the brink.

Fatal Remedies. unabr. ed. Donna Leon. Narrated by Samuel Gillies. 7 CDs. (Running Time: 8 hrs.). (Commissario Guido Brunetti Mystery Ser.: Bk. 8). 2001. audio compact disk 73.00 (978-1-84197-201-5(0), C1349E7) Recorded Bks.
Venetian Inspector Brunetti has his hands full. Even at home, there is no escape from his work. Commissario Guido Brunetti is living in a nightmare. He is called to investigate an act of mundane vandalism - a rock smashing a window in the silence of the Venetian dawn. Somewhat unusually, the vandal waited to be caught & the vandal is his wife, Paola Brunetti. In addition, the Mafia seems to be involved in an audacious robbery & an "accidental" death. Brunetti must find out how & why. Pressure from his superiors, pressure at home, has his life in turmoil, then there's the conspiracy his wife exposed in desperation.

Fatal Remedies. unabr. ed. Donna Leon. Narrated by Samuel Gillies. 6 cass. (Running Time: 8 hrs.). (Commissario Guido Brunetti Mystery Ser.: Bk. 8). 2001. 53.00 (978-1-84197-044-8(1), H1051E7) Recorded Bks.

Fatal Shore, Pt. 1. unabr. collector's ed. Robert Hughes. Read by Richard Brown. 11 cass. (Running Time: 16 hrs. 30 min.). 1987. 88.00 (978-0-7366-1217-3(3), 2136-A) Books on Tape.
A fascinating account of Australia's origins in the massive social experiment called "transport." A simple idea, transport called for the removal of criminals, thus the removal of crime. The first fleet carrying 736 convicts, arrived at Botany Bay in 1788. Eighty years & 100,000 convicts later, in 1868, the last ship dropped anchor. During this period the continent served as an enormous jail. But, against all odds, the inmates reformed themselves & Britain found she had on her hands not a jail, but a flourishing colony. How had it happened?.

Fatal Shore, Pt. 2. unabr. collector's ed. Robert Hughes. Read by Richard Brown. 10 cass. (Running Time: 15 hrs.). 1987. 80.00 (978-0-7366-1218-0(1), 2136-B) Books on Tape.

Fatal Strain: On the Trail of Avian Flu & the Coming Pandemic. unabr. ed. Alan Sipress. Narrated by George K. Wilson. (Running Time: 15 hrs. 30 mins. 0 sec.). (ENG.). 2009. 24.99 (978-1-4001-6415-8(X)); audio compact disk 75.99 (978-1-4001-4415-0(9)); audio compact disk 37.99 (978-1-4001-1415-3(2)) Pub: Tantor Media. Dist(s): IngramPubServ

***Fatal Strain: On the Trail of Avian Flu & the Coming Pandemic.** unabr. ed. Alan Sipress. Narrated by George K. Wilson. (Running Time: 15 hrs. 30 mins.). 2009. 20.99 (978-1-4001-8415-6(0)) Tantor Media.

Fatal Terrain. abr. ed. Dale Brown. Read by Joseph Campanella. 4 cass. (Running Time: 6 hrs.). 2004. 25.00 (978-1-59007-169-4(7)) Pub: New Millenn Enter. Dist(s): PerseuPGW
In Asia, all hell is breaking loose. Finally ready to flex its formidable muscle, the People's Republic of China has struck at Taiwan, and when the United States comes to Taiwan's aid, it is dealt a stunning setback.

Fatal Terrain. unabr. ed. Dale Brown. Read by Edward Lewis. 12 cass. (Running Time: 18 hrs.). 2000. 96.00 (978-0-7366-5511-8(5), 5351) Books on Tape.
All hell is breaking out in Asia. The Peoples Republic of China finally flexes its muscles, striking at Taiwan, and dealing the U.S. a stunning setback when she comes to Taiwan's aid. Emoldened, China begins to scoop up territory in Asia and sets in motion a plan to immobilize the United States. Patrick McLanahan, an aerial strike warfare expert, and John Masters, a genius aerospace engineer, have been working to develop the EB-52 Megafortress, but it's not quite ready, and they don't have enough of them. Now is not the time to hesitate. They must go with what they have.

Fatal Thaw. unabr. collector's ed. Dana Stabenow. Read by Marguerite Gavin. 5 cass. (Running Time: 7 hrs. 30 min.). (Kate Shugak Ser.). 1999. 40.00 (978-0-7366-4459-4(8), 4904) Books on Tape.
On the first day of spring a man went berserk, killing eight of his neighbors. Only there were nine bodies lying in the snow. The last victim was a golden blonde with a tarnished past & her killer was still at large. It's up to Kate Shugak, once the star investigator of the Anchorage D.A.'s office & her husky, Mutt, to track down the suspects before the murderer melts back into the snowscape. But the guilty party could be anyone, because in the Alaskan spring, old hatreds warm up quickly.

Fatal Tide. unabr. ed. Iris Johansen. Read by Bernadette Dunne. 6 cass. (Running Time: 9 hrs.). 2003. 64.80 (978-0-7366-9418-6(8)); audio compact disk 68.85 (978-0-7366-9526-8(5)) Pub: Books on Tape. Dist(s): NetLibrary CO
Pursued by deadly treasure hunters, a lone woman seeks a sunken Caribbean island.

***Fatal Undertaking: A Buryin' Barry Mystery.** unabr. ed. Mark de Castrique. (Running Time: 8 hrs. 30 mins.). 2010. 29.95 (978-1-4417-6537-6(9)); 54.95 (978-1-4417-6534-5(4)); audio compact disk 76.00 (978-1-4417-6535-2(2)) Blckstn Audio.

Fatal Voyage. Kathy Reichs. (Temperance Brennan Ser.: No. 4). 2004. 15.95 (978-0-7435-1862-8(4)) Pub: S&S Audio. Dist(s): S and S Inc

Fatal Voyage. abr. ed. Kathy Reichs. Read by Katherine Borowitz. 4 CDs. (Running Time: 50 hrs. 0 mins. 0 sec.). No. 4. (ENG.). 2001. audio compact disk 30.00 (978-0-7435-0463-8(1), Audioworks) Pub: S&S Audio. Dist(s): S and S Inc

Fatal Voyage. unabr. ed. Kathy Reichs. Read by Kate Harper. 10 vols. (Running Time: 15 hrs.). (Temperance Brennan Ser.: No. 4). 2002. bk. 84.95 (978-0-7927-2718-7(5), CSL 504, Chivers Sound Lib); audio compact disk 94.95 (978-0-7927-2747-7(9), SLD 504, Chivers Sound Lib) AudioGO.
When an Air TransSouth flight goes down in the mountains of western North Carolina, Temperance Brennan, a forensic anthropologist, rushes to the scene to assist in body recovery and identification. Many of the dead are members of a university soccer team. Is Tempe's daughter, Katy, among them? Frantic with worry, Tempe joins colleagues from the FBI, the NTSB, and other agencies to search for explanations. Was theplane brought down by a bomb or simple mechanical failure? And what about the prisoner on the plane who was being extradited to Canada?.

***Fatally Flaky.** unabr. ed. Diane Mott Davidson. Read by Barbara Rosenblat. (ENG.). 2009. (978-0-06-180557-8(2), Harper Audio); (978-0-06-180555-4(6), Harper Audio) HarperCollins Pubs.

Fatally Flaky. unabr. ed. Diane Mott Davidson. Read by Barbara Rosenblat. 9 CDs. (Running Time: 10 hrs. 30 mins.). (Goldy Schulz Culinary Mysteries Ser.: No. 15). 2009. audio compact disk 39.99 (978-0-06-171258-6(2), Harper Audio) HarperCollins Pubs.

Fatboy & the dancing Ladies. Michael Holman. Read by Jerome Pride. (Running Time: 7 hrs. 30 mins.). 2009. 69.99 (978-1-74214-178-7(1), 9781742141787) Pub: Bolinda Pubng AUS. Dist(s): Bolinda Pub Inc

Fatboy & the Dancing Ladies. unabr. ed. Michael Holman. Read by Jerome Pride. (Running Time: 27000 sec.). 2008. audio compact disk 77.95 (978-1-921415-04-3(5), 9781921415043) Pub: Bolinda Pubng AUS. Dist(s): Bolinda Pub Inc

Fatch Ali Khan Vol. 1: Patiala. 1 cass. (Gharana Ser.). 1994. (A94015) Multi-Cultural Bks.

Fatch Ali Khan Vol. 2: Patiala. 1 cass. (Gharana Ser.). 1994. (A94016) Multi-Cultural Bks.

Fate: Destiny or Karma. Ingrid Naiman. 2 cass. (Running Time: 3 hrs.). 20.00 (978-1-882834-97-6(6)) Seventh Ray.
The soul & subconscious as determinants of events & experiences.

Fate & Free Will. (130) Yoga Res Foun.

Fate & Free Will. Swami Jyotirmayananda. 1 cass. (Running Time: 1 hr.). 1990. 12.99 Yoga Res Foun.

Fate & Free Will. unabr. ed. Dane Rudhyar. 1 cass. (Running Time: 1 hr. 3 min.). 1970. 11.00 (10105) Big Sur Tapes.
Reconciling individual development & mystical self-realization with cosmic patterns & the intense desire of all cultures to maintain social order has been a focal point of Rudhyar's study. He contrasts the "great problems" of different cultures - "liberation" in India, "freedom of choice" in Europe, & "individual rights" in America - & maintains that "in a very real sense, they are all false problems," because they are meaningless unless defined by their opposites. The role of cosmic patterns, then, is not to determine events, but to provide a context for interpretation.

Fate & the Philosophy of Destiny. Instructed by Manly P. Hall. 8.95 (978-0-89314-473-9(8), C810712) Philos Res.

Fate Is the Hunter. unabr. collector's ed. Ernest K. Gann. Read by Dick Estell. 10 cass. (Running Time: 15 hrs.). 1987. 80.00 (978-0-7366-1094-0(4), 2020) Books on Tape.
An episodic log of some of the author's nearly ten thousand hours aloft in peace & (as a member of the Air Transport Command) in war.

Fate of Admiral Kolchak. unabr. collector's ed. Peter Fleming. Read by David Case. 6 cass. (Running Time: 9 hrs.). 1988. 48.00 (978-0-7366-1265-4(3), 2177) Books on Tape.
Kolchak, commander of Russia's Black Sea Fleet at the time of the Russian revolution, led a counter-revolution which was defeated by the Red Army. This book tells of his interrogation & subsequent fate.

Fate of Clowns, Nos. 16, 17 & 18. Carl Faber. 3 cass. (Running Time: 3 hrs. 40 min.). 1983. 28.50 (978-0-918026-39-2(3), SR 51-931) Perseus Pr.

Fate of the Earth. unabr. collector's ed. Jonathan Schell. Read by Michael Prichard. 7 cass. (Running Time: 10 hrs. 30 min.). 1982. 56.00 (978-0-7366-0634-9(3), 1595) Books on Tape.
Schell makes sure all of us know the horrendous possibilities of a nuclear exchange & all the reasons for bringing such possibilities to a halt - the question is, how do we get these monsters under control?.

Fate of the Stallion! Scripts. Ron Hevener. 4 cass. (Running Time: 4 hrs. 30 mins.). Dramatization. 2000. reel tape 24.95 (978-0-9679514-3-0(7), By title) Pennywood Pr.
A powerful Arabian racehorse stirs the battle for a child's love and the power of a father's haunting lullaby in a race to victory!.

Fate of the Universe. Read by George Steiner. 1 cass. (Running Time: 1 hr.). 14.95 (CBC864) MMI Corp.
Lecture on this subject & how it has affected our views of human fate.

***Fates Will Find Their Way: A Novel.** unabr. ed. Hannah Pittard. (ENG.). 2011. (978-0-06-204942-1(9), Harper Audio) HarperCollins Pubs.

Father. Short Stories. 1980. (N-50) Jimcin Record.

Father. Bjornson. (J). 1984. Multi Media TX.

Father & Daughter Discipleship Retreat. Douglas W. Phillips et al. 3 cass. (Running Time: 5 hrs.). 2001. 25.00 (978-0-9724173-6-5(2)); audio compact disk 30.00 (978-0-9724173-7-2(0)) Pub: Vision Forum. Dist(s): STL Dist NA

Father & His Family. E. W. Kenyon. Read by Stephen Sobozenski. 6 cassettes. (Running Time: 5 hrs. 45 mins.). 2004. 28.00 (978-1-57770-035-7(X)) Kenyons Gospel.
An outline of the plan of redemption. This book answers more vital questions about Christianity than any other book.

Father & Mother: Archetypal & Historical Realities. Luigi Zoja. 1 cass. (Running Time: 90 min.). 1990. 10.95 (978-0-7822-0342-4(6), 404) C G Jung IL.

Father & Son. Edmund Gosse. 2002. pap. bk. 84.95 (978-1-86015-005-0(5)) Ulverscroft US.

Father & Son. Edmund Gosse. Read by Peter Joyce. 2002. pap. bk. 61.95 (978-1-86015-474-4(3)) Ulverscroft US.

Father & Son. unabr. ed. Larry Brown. Narrated by Tom Stechschulte. 8 cass. (Running Time: 10 hrs. 45 mins.). 1996. 70.00 (978-0-7887-0661-5(6), 94838E7) Recorded Bks.
Glenn Davis is a bad seed - damaged, druken & dangerous.. When he returns to his rural Mississippi family, his path of destruction leads him to Sheriff Bobby Blanchard, who is everything Glenn is not.

Father Arseny, 1893-1973: Priest, Prisoner, Spiritual Father. Tr. by Vera Bouteneff & Peter Bouteneff. Narrated by Vera Bouteneff & Peter Bouteneff. 5 cass. (Running Time: 450 mins.). 2003. 22.95 (978-0-88141-243-7(0)) St Vladimirs.

Father Bear Comes Home. unabr. abr. ed. Else Holmelund Minarik. Read by Ann Bobby. Illus. by Maurice Sendak. 1 cass. (Running Time: 15 min.). (I Can Read Bks.). (J). (gr. k-3). 1995. 8.95 (978-0-694-70010-3(X)) HarperCollins Pubs.

***Father Brown Mysteries: Blue Cross, Secret Garden, Queer Feet, Arrow of Heaven.** G. K. Chesterton & M. J. Elliot. 2011. audio compact disk 9.99 (978-1-61106-474-2(0)) Brilliance Audio.

Father Brown Mysteries Volume 1. G. K. Chesterton. (ENG.). 2008. audio compact disk 9.95 (978-1-60245-171-1(0)) GDL Multimedia.

Father Brown Mysteries Volume 2. G. K. Chesterton. (ENG.). 2008. audio compact disk 9.95 (978-1-60245-172-8(9)) GDL Multimedia.

Father Brown Stories, Set. G. K. Chesterton. Read by Flo Gibson. 10 cass. (Running Time: 14 hrs. 30 min.). (Father Brown Mystery Ser.). 1992. 44.95 (978-1-55685-269-5(X)) Audio Bk Con.
These twelve tales from The Innocence of Father Brown & The Wisdom of Father Brown collections give a glorious sampling of the indomitable cleric's gentle expertise in ferreting out the guilty.

Father Brown Stories 1. unabr. ed. G. K. Chesteron. (Running Time: 5 hrs.). 2009. audio compact disk 28.98 (978-962-634-963-2(8), Naxos AudioBooks) Naxos.

Father Cares. Read by Basilea Schlink. 1 cass. (Running Time: 30 min.). 1985. (0271) Evang Sisterhood Mary.
Four watchwords that can help us to be victorious in the battle against our cares & worries; God's plan of salvation for His Chosen People & its relevance for our own lives.

Father Cares: The Last of Jonestown. Read by Robert J. Lifton et al. (Running Time: 3 hrs.). 26.50 teaching guide. (I0820B090, HarperThor) HarpC GBR.

***Father Centered Worldview.** John Eldredge. (ENG.). 2011. audio compact disk 28.99 (978-1-933207-46-9(9)) Ransomed Heart.

Father Coughlin & the Depression. 1 cass. (Running Time: 45 min. per cass.). 1985. 10.00 (HD424) Esstee Audios.
Radio program about the failures of the New Deal & how banks & interest rates had created the nation's shameful, intolerable blight.

***Father Fiction: Chapters for a Fatherless Generation.** unabr. ed. Donald Miller. Narrated by Kelly Ryan Dolan. (Running Time: 4 hrs. 46 mins. 24 sec.). (ENG.). 2010. 18.19 (978-1-60814-667-3(7)) Oasis Audio.

***Father Fiction: Chapters for a Fatherless Generation.** unabr. ed. Donald Miller. Narrated by Kelly Ryan Dolan. 5 CDs. (Running Time: 4 hrs. 46 mins. 24 sec.). (ENG.). 2010. audio compact disk 25.99 (978-1-59859-716-5(7)) Oasis Audio.

Father Gobbi Talks about Our Lady. Interview with Mother Angelica & Father Gobbi. 1 cass. (Running Time: 60 min.). (Mother Angelica Live Ser.). 1987. 10.00 (978-1-55794-090-2(8), T41) Eternal Wrd TV.

Father Goriot. Honoré de Balzac. Read by Guillermo Piedrahita. (Running Time: 3 hrs.). 2002. 16.95 (978-1-60083-198-0(2), Audiofy Corp) Iofy Corp.

Father Groeschel Speaks on the Present & Future Church. Benedict J. Groeschel. 1 cass. (Running Time: 1 hr. 26 min.). 1994. 8.95 (TAH309) Alba Hse Comns.
Father Groeschel analyzes recent church history & other cultural & intellectual movements in order to take an educated guess (not prophecy) as to where the church will be in the 21st century & how the church will get there.

Father Groeschel Speaks to Priests. Benedict J. Groeschel. 5 cass. (Running Time: 4 hrs. 41 min.). 1994. 40.95 Set. (TAH314) Alba Hse Comns.
Excellent meditation material for priests searching for discipleship. Filled with innumerable pastoral insights. Gives hope to the bogged down, the depressed, & the frustrated. Helps your understanding; helps your faith. Perfect listening for every priest.

Father Henson's Story of His Own Life see Black Pioneers in American History, Vol. 2, 19th - 20th Centuries

Father Hunger: Christ Church Ministerial Conference (2008) Tim Bayly et al. (ENG.). 2008. audio compact disk 28.00 (978-1-59128-381-2(7)) Canon Pr ID.

Father Hunt. Rex Stout. Read by Michael Prichard. (Nero Wolfe Ser.). 1999. audio compact disk 40.00 (978-0-7366-8287-9(2)) Books on Tape.

Father Hunt. collector's ed. Rex Stout. Read by Michael Prichard. 6 cass. (Running Time: 6 hrs.). (Nero Wolfe Ser.). 1999. 48.00 (978-0-7366-4786-1(4), 5133) Books on Tape.
Pretty Amy Denovo wants to find the father she has never seen, but she can't afford Nero Wolfe's outlandish fees... or can she?.

Father Hunt. unabr. ed. Rex Stout. Read by Michael Prichard. 4 cassettes. (Nero Wolfe Ser.). 2005. 27.95 (978-1-57270-458-9(6)) Pub: Audio Partners. Dist(s): PerseuPGW
Twenty-two-year-old Amy Denovo needs Nero Wolfe's help. She is determined to learn the identity of her father, a secret her mother scrupulously guarded - and took to her grave when struck by a hit-and-run driver. Now Wolfe and his sidekick, Archie, have just one clue to go on: a note from Amy's mother and a box with over $250,000. Seems every month since Amy's birth, her mother received $1,000 from an unknown source and saved it for Amy's future. It's easy enough for Amy to afford Wolfe's services, and he grudgingly agrees. But as the weeks go by, Wolfe realizes this may be one of his most challenging cases ever. Someone doesn't want Amy's pedigree discovered, and that someone appears to wield great power. It isn't long before Wolfe and Archie come to believe that Amy's mother was murdered - and that Amy could be next. Michael Prichard gives another of his masterful readings to this cleverly plotted tale.

Father Hunt. unabr. ed. Rex Stout. Narrated by Michael Prichard. 5 CDs. (Nero Wolfe Ser.). (ENG.). 2005. audio compact disk 27.95 (978-1-57270-459-6(4)) Pub: AudioGO. Dist(s): Perseus Dist

Father I Never Knew. Creflo A. Dollar. cass. & video 25.00 (978-1-59089-120-9(1)) Pub: Creflo Dollar. Dist(s): STL Dist NA

Father, I Trust You! 1985. (0233) Evang Sisterhood Mary.

Father Joe: A Hero's Journey. Jay O'Callahan. Perf. by Jay O'Callahan. 1 cass. (Running Time: 58 min.). Dramatization. (J). 1994. 10.00 (978-1-877954-50-4(0)) Pub: Artana Prodns. Dist(s): Yellow Moon
Father Joe was the Catholic Chaplain on board the aircraft carrier USS Franklin on March 19, 1945, 50 miles off the coast of Japan, when it was bombed by Japanese aircraft. 432 men were killed & 1000 were wounded.

In the midst of death & destruction Father Joe held onto his faith & rallied the dazed men. Amid smoke & Japanese strafing he administered to the dying, organized a team to flood the tons of explosives on board & started a human chain, passing hot bombs hand to hand, to jettison other lethal ammunition. Father Joe & the other heroes on board made the USS Franklin "the ship that wouldn't be sunk." When it limped into Pearl Harbor, it was the most damaged ship to ever reach port. Father Joe was the first Navy chaplain to receive the Congressional Medal of Honor.

Father Joe: A Hero's Journey. unabr. ed. Jay O'Callahan. Perf. by Jay O'Callahan. 1 CD. (Running Time: 58 mins.). 2000. audio compact disk 15.00 (978-1-877954-32-0(2)) Pub: Artana Prodns. Dist(s): High Windy Audio

On March 18, 1945, the aircraft carrier, the USS Franklin, was bombed by Japanese aircraft. Father Joe O'Callahan and the other heroes on board made the vessel "the ship that wouldn't be sunk".

Father Joe: The Man Who Saved My Soul. Tony Hendra. 9 CDs. (Running Time: 11 hrs.). 2004. audio compact disk 34.99 (978-1-4193-0607-5(3)) Recorded Bks.

Delivers a beautifully written, humorous, and profoundly moving memoir reminiscent of Tuesdays with Morrie. The New York Times says Father Joe ¿belongs in the first tier of spiritual memoirs ever written.

Father Knows Best. collector's ed. Perf. by Robert Young. 6 cass. (Running Time: 9 hrs.). 1999. bk. 34.98 (4187) Radio Spirits.

18 situation comedies depicting the lives of the Anderson family, an average American family living in an average American town.

Father Knows Best: Card Game & An Uncontrolled Dog. Perf. by Robert Young. 1 cass. (Running Time: 1 hr.). 2001. 6.98 (2237) Radio Spirits.

Father Knows Best: Father is Transferred to Chicago & Betty Announces Her Engagement. Perf. by Robert Young. 1 cass. (Running Time: 1 h r.). 2001. 6.98 (2136) Radio Spirits.

Father Knows Best: Father's Day Trip & A New Housekeeper. Perf. by Robert Young. 1 cass. (Running Time: 1 hr.). 2001. 6.98 (2279) Radio Spirits.

Father Knows Best: Gen. 2:7. Ed Young. 1991. 4.95 (978-0-7417-1838-9(3), 838) Win Walk.

Father Knows Best: Modernizing the Home & Banged up Fender. Perf. by Robert Young. 1 cass. (Running Time: 1 hr.). 2001. 6.98 (2097) Radio Spirits.

Father Knows Best: Thanksgiving Show & Too Many Rabbits. Perf. by Robert Young. 1 cass. (Running Time: 1 hr.). 2001. 6.98 (2436) Radio Spirits.

Father Knows Best: The Children Revolt & Father Gets Nothing for Christmas. Perf. by Robert Young. 1 cass. (Running Time: 1 hr.). 2001. 6.98 (2215) Radio Spirits.

Father Knows Best: The Golf Challenge & Betty's Screen Test. Perf. by Robert Young. 1 cass. (Running Time: 1 hr.). 2001. 6.98 (2256) Radio Spirits.

***Father Knows Best, Volume 1.** RadioArchives.com. (Running Time: 600). (ENG.). 2007. audio compact disk 29.98 (978-1-61081-103-3(8)) Radio Arch.

***Father Knows Best, Volume 2.** RadioArchives.com. (Running Time: 600). (ENG.). 2007. audio compact disk 29.98 (978-1-61081-119-4(4)) Radio Arch.

***Father Knows Best, Volume 3.** RadioArchives.com. (Running Time: 600). (ENG.). 2007. audio compact disk 29.98 (978-1-61081-120-0(8)) Radio Arch.

***Father Knows Best, Volume 4.** RadioArchives.com. (Running Time: 600). (ENG.). 2007. audio compact disk 29.98 (978-1-61081-121-7(6)) Radio Arch.

Father Knows Less, or Can I Cook My Sister? One Dad's Quest to Answer His Son's Most Baffling Questions. Wendell Jamieson. Read by Patrick G. Lawlor. (Playaway Adult Fiction Ser.). 2008. 59.99 (978-1-60640-978-7(6)) Find a World.

Father Knows Less, or: Can I Cook My Sister? One Dad's Quest to Answer His Son's Most Baffling Questions. unabr. ed. Wendell Jamieson. Read by Patrick G. Lawlor. (Running Time: 7 hrs. 30 mins. 0 sec.). (ENG.). 2007. audio compact disk 29.99 (978-1-4001-0558-8(7)); audio compact disk 59.99 (978-1-4001-3558-5(3)); audio compact disk 19.99 (978-1-4001-5558-3(4)) Pub: Tantor Media. Dist(s): IngramPubServ

Father of All Things: A Marine, His Son, & the Legacy of Vietnam. Tom Bissell. 2007. audio compact disk 39.99 (978-1-4281-3977-0(X)) Recorded Bks.

Father of Waters. Donald Clayton Porter. Read by Lloyd James. 4 vols. 2004. 25.00 (978-1-58807-234-4(7)) Am Pubng Inc.

Father of Waters. Donald Clayton Porter. Read by Lloyd James. 4 vols. No. 18. 2004. (978-1-58807-765-3(9)) Am Pubng Inc.

Father Pierre de Smet, S. J. Missionary & Hero 1801-1873. Perf. by John Vennari. 1 cass. (Running Time: 90 mins.). 7.00 (20208) Cath Treas.

The story of one of the most fascinating & inspirational American Missionaries of the 19th century. Father de Smet was the great "Apostle to the Rockies," evangelizing & Catholicizing tens of thousands of American Indians. He was thoroughly Catholic & deeply devoted to Our Blessed Mother.

Father Son & Company: My Life at IBM & Beyond. unabr. ed. Thomas J. Watson, Jr. & Peter Petre. Read by Jonathan Reese. 13 cass. (Running Time: 19 hrs. 30 min.). 1993. 104.00 (978-0-7366-2384-1(1), 3155) Books on Tape.

Story of the father & son team that, over the course of 60 years, built the colossus that is IBM.

Father, Spirit, Jesus. Richard Kingsmore. 2006. audio compact disk 24.99 (978-5-557-69945-7(7)) Lillenas.

Father Was a Wise Old Man. Donald Davis. 1 CD. (Running Time: 58 mins.). 2001. audio compact disk 14.95 (978-0-87483-610-3(7)) Pub: August Hse. Dist(s): Natl Bk Netwk

Father Was a Wise Old Man. unabr. ed. Donald Davis. 1 cass. (Running Time: 58 mins.). (American Storytelling Ser.). 2001. 12.00 (978-0-87483-611-0(5)) Pub: August Hse. Dist(s): Natl Bk Netwk

The five stories in Father was a Wise Old Man recall the wisdom of fathers with humor and rich detail: a visit to the Smithsonian inspires Father's memory; Father "cures" a boy's impulse to try cigarettes; Santa Claus learns an important lesson; someone plays a trick on a visiting preacher.

***Father Water, Mother Woods.** unabr. ed. Gary Paulsen. (Running Time: 3 hrs.). 2011. 39.97 (978-1-4558-0468-9(1), 9781455804689, Brinc Audio MP3 Lib); 39.97 (978-1-4558-0470-2(3), 9781455804702, BADLE); 12.99 (978-1-4558-0467-2(3), 9781455804672, Brilliance MP3); 12.99 (978-1-4558-0469-6(X), 9781455804696, BAD); audio compact disk 39.97 (978-1-4558-0466-5(5), 9781455804665, BriAudCD Unabrid); audio compact disk 12.99 (978-1-4558-0465-8(7), 9781455804658, Bril Audio CD Unabri) Brilliance Audio.

Father Who Keeps His Promises: God's Covenant Love in Scripture. Scott Hahn. Read by Paul Smith. 7 CDs. (Running Time: 30600 sec.). 2006. audio compact disk 41.95 (978-0-86716-786-3(6)) St Anthony Mess Pr.

In A Father Who Keeps His Promises, the popular Catholic apologist Scott Hahn focuses on the "big picture" of Scripture: God's plan in making and keeping covenants with us throughout salvation history-despite our faults and shortcomings-so that we might live as the family of God.

***Father Wounds.** Francis Anfuso. (ENG.). 2009. audio compact disk 10.00 (978-0-9824967-3-2(7)) Pilot Comm.

Fathered by God: Discover What Your Dad Could Never Teach You. unabr. ed. John Eldredge. Narrated by John Eldredge. (Running Time: 6 hrs. 23 mins. 12 sec.). (ENG.). 2009. 18.19 (978-1-60814-628-4(6)); audio compact disk 25.99 (978-1-59859-685-4(3)) Oasis Audio.

Fathered by God Live: Discover What Your Dad Could Never Teach You. Joshn Eldredge. 2009. audio compact disk 14.99 (978-1-933207-29-2(9)) Ransomed Heart.

Fatherhood. Derek Prince. 1 cass. 5.95 (004) Derek Prince.

Fatherhood is a man's highest achievement, combining the roles of prophet, priest & king.

Fathering. John E. Bradshaw. (Running Time: 3600 sec.). 2008. audio compact disk 50.00 (978-1-57388-235-4(6)) J B Media.

***Fatherless Generation: Redeeming the Story.** John A. Sowers. (Running Time: 3 hrs. 58 mins. 44 sec.). (ENG.). 2010. 14.99 (978-0-310-54800-3(4)) Zondervan.

Fathers. Kurt Bestor et al. 1 CD. 1998. bk. 24.95 (978-1-57008-440-9(8), Bkcraft Inc) Deseret Bk.

Fathers & Children. Ivan Turgueniev. Read by Hernando Iván Cano. (Running Time: 3 hrs.). 2002. 16.95 (978-1-60083-250-5(4), Audiofy Corp) Iofy Corp.

Fathers & Daughters. Anthea Fraser. Read by Margaret Tyzack. 8 vols. (Running Time: 12 hrs.). 2003. 69.95 (978-0-7540-8346-7(2)) Pub: Chivers Audio Bks GBR. Dist(s): AudioGO

Fathers & Sons. Ivan Turgenev. Narrated by Walter Zimmerman. (Running Time: 8 hrs.). 2006. 26.95 (978-1-59912-144-4(1)) Iofy Corp.

Fathers & Sons. abr. ed. Ivan Turgenev. Read by Tim Pigott-Smith. 2 cass. (Running Time: 3 hrs.). 2000. 7.95 (978-1-57815-120-2(1), 1082, Media Bks Audio) Media Bks NJ.

A powerful picture of the clash between generations & the spirit of rebellion within Russia.

Fathers & Sons. unabr. ed. Ivan Turgenev. Read by David Horovitch. 6 cass. (Running Time: 9 hrs.). 2004. 29.95 (978-1-57270-073-4(4), F61073u, Cvr to Cvr Classics) Pub: Audio Partners. Dist(s): PerseuPGW

Examines the conflict of generations & attitudes in mid-19th century Russia, as distant precursors of the revolution rumble through the rural landscape.

Fathers & Sons. unabr. ed. Ivan Turgenev. Read by Walter Zimmerman. 6 cass. (Running Time: 8 hrs. 30 mins.). 1981. 44.95 (978-0-7861-0512-0(7), 2012) Blckstn Audio.

One of the most controversial Russian novels ever written, "Fathers & Sons" incited protests from all branches of Russian society. Turgenev dramatized the volcanic issues that divided a Russia torn by the social unrest of conflict - peasants against masters, generations against generations & fathers against sons.

Fathers & Sons. unabr. ed. Ivan Turgenev. Read by Walter Zimmerman. 6 cass. (Running Time: 7 hrs.). 1981. 34.00 incl. album. (C-53) Jimcin Record.

One of the great Russian novels.

Fathers & Sons. unabr. ed. Ivan Turgenev. Narrated by George Guidall. 6 cass. (Running Time: 8 hrs. 15 mins.). 1994. 51.00 (978-0-7887-0092-7(8), 94333E7) Recorded Bks.

A university student returns home with his nihilist friend & confronts his father & uncle, liberal members of the landed gentry in 19th century Russia.

Fathers & Sons. unabr. collector's ed. Ivan Turgenev. Read by Walter Zimmerman. 8 cass. (Running Time: 8 hrs.). 1981. 48.00 (978-0-7366-3855-5(5), 9053) Books on Tape.

Deals with Russia in transition, from a formal & authoritarian society to one where all beliefs & relationships are questioned. Young people are at the intellectual throats of their parents, who of course fail to understand what is happening.

Fathers & Sons, Life & Death. 2006. audio compact disk 24.00 (978-1-890246-10-5(7)) B Katie Int Inc.

Father's Anima As a Clinical & Symbolic Problem. Read by John Beebe. 1 cass. (Running Time: 90 min.). 1984. 10.95 (978-0-7822-0012-6(5), 144) C G Jung IL.

Fathers Are Forever: A Co-Parenting Guide for the 21st Century. Steve Ashley. 5 CDs. 2003. audio compact disk 35.00 (978-0-9740714-0-4(4)) Divorced Fathers.

Audio CD version of the book Fathers Are Forever: A Co-Parenting Guide for the 21st Century.

Father's Biblical Objectives: Proverbs 8:35-36. Ed Young. 1989. 4.95 (978-0-7417-1738-2(7), 738) Win Walk.

Father's Boots. Baje Whitethorne, Sr. (Running Time: 60 mins.).Tr. of Azhe' e Bikenidoots' Osii. 2001. audio compact disk 10.95 (978-1-893354-30-2(X)) Pub: Salina Bkshelf. Dist(s): Natl Bk Netwk

Father's Care. audio compact disk 15.50 (978-1-57924-684-6(2)) BJUPr.

Father's Covenant. 2003. 30.00 (978-1-58602-141-2(9)); audio compact disk 50.00 (978-1-58602-142-9(7)) E L Long.

Fathers Cry, Too. Geneva Turner. 1995. 24.00 (978-1-882977-09-3(2)) Family Proj Pubs.

Father's Day. abr. ed. John Calvin Batchelor. Read by Bill Weideman. 2 cass. (Running Time: 3 hrs.). 2000. 7.95 (978-1-57815-007-6(8), 1037, Media Bks Audio) Media Bks NJ.

Add an incapacitated president & a ruthless vice president to the usual Washington stew of blind ambition, hardball politics & naked greed to make this political thriller.

***Father's Day: A Selection from Right Next Door.** unabr. ed. Debbie Macomber. Read by Angela Dawe. (Running Time: 5 hrs.). 2010. 14.99 (978-1-4418-6308-9(7), 9781441863089, BAD); 14.99 (978-1-4418-6307-2(9), 9781441863072, Brilliance MP3); audio compact disk 14.99 (978-1-4418-6306-5(0), 9781441863065, Bril Audio CD Unabri) Brilliance Audio.

Fathers Dilemma: Gen. 42:36-43:13. Ed Young. 1988. 4.95 (978-0-7417-1684-2(4), 684) Win Walk.

Father's Love. Perf. by Bob Carlisle. 1 CD. 1998. audio compact disk 8.98 (978-7-5132-6342-9(6), 751-326-3426) Brentwood Music.

Father's Love: Jesus came to show us the Father. Henry W. Wright. (ENG.). 2008. audio compact disk 17.95 (978-1-934680-30-8(3)) Be in Hlth.

Fathers Love Letter Spec. Adams Barry. 2004. DVD & audio compact disk 19.99 (978-1-894300-89-6(0)) Crown Video Dupl CAN.

Fathers Love Letter the Spoken. Adams Barry. 2004. audio compact disk 9.99 (978-1-894300-35-3(1)) Crown Video Dupl CAN.

Fathers Mandate: Deuteronomy 6:4-9. Ed Young. 1987. 4.95 (978-0-7417-1613-2(5), 613) Win Walk.

Fathers of Sci-Fi: 4-Crate. unabr. ed. 4 cass. (Running Time: 4 hrs.). 1989. 16.95 (978-1-55569-115-8(3), 5770-05) Great Am Audio.

Fathers' Race. Charles Jennings. Narrated by Charles Jennings. 7 cass. (Running Time: 10 hrs.). 63.00 (978-1-84197-297-8(5)) Recorded Bks.

Fathers, Sons & Golf: Lessons in Honor & Integrity. abr. ed. Andrew Shanley. Read by Bruce Joseph. (Running Time: 3 hrs.). 2009. 39.97 (978-1-4233-8643-8(4), 9781423386438, Brinc Audio MP3 Lib); 39.97 (978-1-4233-8645-2(0), 9781423386452, BADLE); 24.99 (978-1-4233-8642-1(6), 9781423386421, Brilliance MP3); 24.99 (978-1-4233-8644-5(2), 9781423386445, BAD) Brilliance Audio.

Father's Story. Short Stories. Read by Andre Dubus. 1 cass. (Running Time: 59 min.). 13.95 (978-1-55644-099-1(5), 4051) Am Audio Prose.

Father's Whiskers: Fabulously Fun Folk Songs for Folks of All Ages. Read by Pamela Ott. 1 cass. (Running Time: 45 min.). (Teaching Tunes Ser.). 14.95 (978-1-886655-08-9(1), 85084) Corwin Pr.

A collection of uniquely arranged folk songs that appeals to folks of all ages.

Father's Whiskers: Fabulously Fun Folk Songs for Folks of All Ages. Pamela Ott. 1 CD. (Teaching Tunes Ser.). 2000. audio compact disk 14.95 (978-0-8039-6876-9(0), 85083) Corwin Pr.

Fatima & America: National Fatima Symposium at Felician College. John A. Hardon et al. Read by John A. Hardon et al. 5 cass. (Running Time: 5 hrs.). 1991. 17.00 (978-1-56036-019-3(4), 361912) AMI Pr.

Talks presented during a National Fatima Symposium of the World Apostolate of Fatima, the Blue Army, at Felician College, Lodi, NJ. includes - Living the Fatima Message, Fatima & the Church in America, Fatima & the Church's Moral Teaching, Fatima & Modernism, & Speakers' panel questions from the audience.

Fatima & Communism. Alfred McBride. 1 cass. 1992. 2.50 (978-1-56036-048-3(8)) AMI Pr.

Fatima & Heroic Chastity. John A. Hardon. 1 cass. 1991. 2.50 (978-1-56036-061-2(5)) AMI Pr.

Fatima & Miracles of Conversion. John A. Hardon. 1 cass. 1991. 2.50 (978-1-56036-059-9(3)) AMI Pr.

Fatima & Modernism. Robert I. Bradley. 1 cass. 1991. 2.50 (978-1-56036-053-7(4)) AMI Pr.

Fatima & the Age of Martyrs. John A. Hardon. 1 cass. 1991. 2.50 (978-1-56036-062-9(3)) AMI Pr.

Fatima & the AntiChrist. Robert I. Bradley. 1 cass. 1992. 2.50 (978-1-56036-045-2(3)) AMI Pr.

Fatima & the Church's Moral Teaching. Anthony Mastroeni. 1 cass. 1991. 2.50 (978-1-56036-052-0(6)) AMI Pr.

Fatima & the Modern World. John A. Hardon. Read by John A. Hardon. 5 cass. (Running Time: 5 hrs.). 1992. 19.95 (978-1-56036-051-3(8), 362500) AMI Pr.

Tapes include: Fatima & Miracles of Conversion, Fatima & the Papal Primacy, Fatima & Heroic Chastity, Fatima & the Age of Martyrs, Fatima & the Pro-Life Movement. Recorded at Fatima, Portugal.

Fatima & the Papal Primacy. John A. Hardon. 1 cass. 1991. 2.50 (978-1-56036-060-5(7)) AMI Pr.

Fatima & the Pro-Life Movement. John A. Hardon. 1 cass. 1991. 2.50 (978-1-56036-063-6(1)) AMI Pr.

Fatima in Perspective: National Fatima Conference, 1992. 1 cass. 1992. 17.00 (978-1-56036-040-7(2)) AMI Pr.

Fatima Message. 1 cass. (Running Time: 60 min.). (Mother Angelica Live Ser.). 10.00 (978-1-55794-056-8(8), T7) Eternal Wrd TV.

Fatima Today! National Fatima Symposium at Catholic University of America. Frederick L. Miller et al. Read by Frederick L. Miller et al. 6 cass. (Running Time: 6 hrs.). 1990. 19.95 (978-1-56036-035-3(6), 361916) AMI Pr.

Tapes feature: The 1984 Consecration of Pope John Paul II, The Fatima Message in the Modern World, The Masonic Movement & the Fatima, Presenting the Fatima Message to Youth, Fatima & Recent Developments in Russia & Symposium Speakers answer questions from the audience.

Fatt Is a Four Letter Word. Gary Silverman. 1 cass. (Motivational Medicine Ser.: Vol. 1). 1994. (978-1-888202-00-7(9)) Motivat Med.

Medutainment - medical education that's entertaining.

Fattening for Gabon (A Story from Say You're One of Them) unabr. ed. Uwem Akpan. Read by Kevin Free. (Running Time: 4 hrs.). (ENG.). 2009. 7.98 (978-1-60788-493-4(3)) Pub: Hachet Audio. Dist(s): HachBkGrp

Fatty Batter. Michael Simkins. 2009. 69.95 (978-1-4079-0509-9(0)); audio compact disk 84.95 (978-1-4079-0510-5(4)) Pub: Soundings Ltd GBR. Dist(s): Ulverscroft US

Fault Line. Janet Tashjian. 4 cass. (Running Time: 6 hrs.). (J). (gr. 7 up). 2004. 32.00 (978-0-8072-2082-5(5), Listening Lib) Random Audio Pubg.

Fault Line. abr. ed. Barry Eisler. Read by Rob Shapiro. (ENG.). 2009. audio compact disk 29.95 (978-0-7393-8204-2(7), Random AudioBks) Pub: Random Audio Pubg. Dist(s): Random

***Fault Line.** unabr. ed. Barry Eisler. Read by Rob Shapiro. 8 CDs. (Running Time: 10 hrs. 15 mins.). 2009. audio compact disk 80.00 (978-1-4159-6083-7(6), BksonTape) Pub: Random Audio Pubg. Dist(s): Random

***Fault Lines.** abr. ed. Anne Rivers Siddons. Read by Kate Burton. (ENG.). 2005. (978-0-06-087927-3(0), Harper Audio); (978-0-06-087926-6(2), Harper Audio) HarperCollins Pubs.

***Fault Lines.** unabr. ed. Nancy Huston. Read by Edwina Wren. 8 CDs. (Running Time: 10 hrs. 15 mins.). 2010. audio compact disk 87.95 (978-1-74214-092-6(0), 9781742140926) Pub: Bolinda Pubng AUS. Dist(s): Bolinda Pub Inc

Fault Lines. unabr. ed. Anne Rivers Siddons. Read by Kate Reading. 9 cass. (Running Time: 13 hrs. 30 min.). 1996. 72.00 (978-0-7366-3212-6(3), 3875) Books on Tape.

Three women retreat to a remote lodge, set down in the Redwoods on California's northern coast. The women - a mother, her daughter & her sister, intimate all of their lives, but divided now - confront each other. They must decide, here in earthquake country, how they will cope when all of the fault lines converge - those buried deep in the hurt, no less than those fissures beneath the lodge.

Fault Lines. unabr. ed. Anne Rivers Siddons. Narrated by C. J. Critt. 11 cass. (Running Time: 15 hrs. 15 mins.). 1995. 91.00 (978-0-7887-0447-5(8), 94648E7) Recorded Bks.

Merritt Fowler jets to California where her teenaged daughter fled to find a glamorous aunt. Caught in an earthquake, each woman must rely on her strength to survive and escape.

Faultdancing see William Pitt Root

Faust, Set. Johann Wolfgang von Goethe. Read by Jacques Roland. 3 cass. 1996. 38.95 (1860-LQP) Olivia & Hill.

Faustina, or, Rock Roses see Twentieth-Century Poetry in English, No. 9, Recordings of Poets Reading Their Own Poetry

Fauteuil Haute, Set. Gaston Leroux. Read by Claude Lesko. 3 cass. (FRE.). 1991. 31.95 (1509-VSL) Olivia & Hill.
His predecessor, sitting in the same chair, had also died at the end of his acceptance speech after having received a mysterious letter.

Favorite African Folktales. Nelson Mandela. Compiled by Nelson Mandela. Read by LeVar Burton et al. 3 CDs. (Running Time: 3 hrs.). 2009. audio compact disk 16.98 (978-1-60024-666-1(4)) Pub: Hachet Audio. Dist(s): HachBkGrp

Favorite American Detectives. unabr. ed. Ed. by Martin Greenberg & Rosalind M. Greenberg. 4 cass. (Running Time: 6 hrs.). (Masters of Mystery Ser.). 1988. 21.95 Set, library case. (978-1-55656-122-1(9)) Dercum Audio.
Contains: By the Dawn's Early Light by Lawrence Block; The Leopold Locked Room by Edward Hoch; I'm in the Book by Loren D. Estleman; The Good Samaritan by Isaac Asimov; The Man Who Shot Lewis Vance by Stuart Kaminsky; Where Have You Gone, Sam Spade? by Bill Pronzini; The Riddle of the Twelve Amethysts by Stuart Palmer; The Adventure of Abraham Lincoln's Clue by Ellery Queen.

Favorite American Detectives, Vol. 1. unabr. ed. Lawrence Block et al. Ed. by Martin Greenberg & Rosalind M. Greenberg. 4 cass. (Running Time: 6 hrs.). (Mystery Library). 1998. pap. bk. 21.95 Set. (978-1-55656-251-8(9)) Dercum Audio.

Favorite American Poems. unabr. ed. Read by Ed Begley. 1 cass. Incl. Casey at the Bat: A Ballad of the Republic, Sung in the Year 1888. Ernest Lawrence Thayer. (SWC 1207); Face upon the Floor (The Face upon the Barroom Floor) H. Antoine D'Arcy. (SWC 1207); First Snowfall. James Russell Lowell. (SWC 1207); Grandfather's Clock. Henry C. Work. (SWC 1207); Home. (SWC 1207); Home, Sweet Home. John H. Payne. (SWC 1207); House by the Side of the Road. Sam W. Foss. (SWC 1207); I Remember, I Remember. Thomas Hood. (SWC 1207); In Flanders Fields. John McCrae. (SWC 1207); Invictus. William E. Henley. (SWC 1207); It Couldn't Be Done. Edgar A. Guest. (SWC 1207); Man with the Hoe. Edwin C. Markham. (SWC 1207); Old Oaken Bucket. Samuel Woodworth. (SWC 1207); Spell of the Yukon. Robert Service. (SWC 1207); Trees. Joyce Kilmer. (SWC 1207); Woodman, Spare That Tree. George P. Morris. (SWC 1207); 1970. 12.95 (978-0-694-50157-1(3), SWC 1207) HarperCollins Pubs.

Favorite Animal Songs. 1 cass. (Keepsake Collection). 9.95 (SCAS-8502-V); 13.00 Gift Box Set. (GBCA-8502-V) Coventry Mkting.

Favorite Author Collection: David McPhail. unabr. ed. David M. McPhail. 44 vols. (Running Time: 17 mins.). (J). (ps-3). 1999. pap. bk. 61.95 (978-0-87499-594-7(9)) Live Oak Media.
Includes: "The Bear's Bicycle," "The Bear's Toothache," "Emma's Pet," "Fix It" & "Pig Pig Grows Up.".

Favorite Author Collection: David Small & Sarah Stewart. unabr. ed. David Small & Sarah Stewart. 55 vols. (Running Time: 42 mins.). (J). 1999. pap. bk. 76.95 (978-0-87499-711-8(9)) Live Oak Media.
Includes: "The Gardener," "George Washington's Cows," "Imogene's Antlers," "The Library" & "Paper John.".

Favorite Author Collection: Don Freeman. unabr. ed. Don Freeman. 77 vols. (Running Time: 79 mins.). (J). (ps-3). 1999. pap. bk. 106.95 (978-0-87499-483-4(7)) Live Oak Media.
Includes: "Beady Bear," "Corduroy," "Dandelion," "Mop Top," "A Pocket for Corduroy" & "A Rainbow of My Own.".

Favorite Author Collection: Pat Hutchins. unabr. ed. Pat Hutchins. 3 vols. (J). (ps-3). 1999. pap. bk. 42.95 (978-0-87499-485-8(3)) Live Oak Media.
Includes: "Don't Forget the Bacon!," Happy Birthday, Sam" & "The Very Worst Monster.".

Favorite Childhood Tales. Virginia Cowsill. (J). 1990. 6.50 New Readers.

Favorite Children's Gospel Songs. Ed. by Marshall Toppo. 1 cass. (Running Time: 45 mins.). (J). (ps-5). 2003. 6.95 (978-0-9650258-2-9(9), Persnickety Pr) Pub: DBP & Assocs. Dist(s): Penton Overseas
Upbeat & fun collection of 12 children's gospel songs. Includes lyrics for singing along. Features such favorites as "This Little Light of Mine" & Kumbaya".

Favorite Children's Stories. unabr. collector's ed. 8 cass. (Running Time: 8 hrs.). (Jimcin Recording Ser.). (J). 1983. 48.00 (978-0-7366-3880-7(6), 9104) Books on Tape.
Among the 26 stories are: "Dick Whittington & His Cat," "Hok Lee & the Dwarfs," "The Magic Swan," "Childe Roland," "The Happy Prince," "The Remarkable Rocket" & "The Selfish Giant" among others.

Favorite Children's Stories, Vol. 1. unabr. ed. Short Stories. Silhouette Staff. 6 cass. (Running Time: 8 hrs. 30 mins.). (ps-3). 1983. 44.95 (978-0-7861-0544-1(5), 2039) Blckstn Audio.
A wonderful collection of 26 timeless stories.

Favorite Children's Stories: A Collection. unabr. ed. 8 cass. (Running Time: 1 hr. per cass.). Dramatization. Incl. Beginning of the Armadillos. Rudyard Kipling. (J). 1984. (C-103); Bremen Town Musicians. Jacob W. Grimm & Wilhelm K. Grimm. (J). 1984. (C-103); Cat That Walked by Himself. Rudyard Kipling. (J). 1984. (C-103); Childe Roland. (J). 1984. (C-103); Dick Whittington & His Cat. Oscar Wilde. (J). 1984. (C-103); Elephant's Child. Rudyard Kipling. (J). 1984. (C-103); Emperor's New Clothes. Hans Christian Andersen. (J). 1984. (C-103); Fisherman & His Wife. Jacob W. Grimm & Wilhelm K. Grimm. (J). 1984. (C-103); Gorgon's Head. Nathaniel Hawthorne. (J). 1984. (C-103); Happy Prince. Oscar Wilde. (J). 1984. (C-103); Hok Lee & the Dwarfs. (J). 1984. (C-103); How the Whale Got His Throat. Rudyard Kipling. (J). 1984. (C-103); King of the Golden River. John Ruskin. (J). 1984. (C-103); Magic Fishbone. Charles Dickens. (J). 1984. (C-103); Magic Swan. (J). 1984. (C-103); Remarkable Rocket. Oscar Wilde. (J). 1984. (C-103); Selfish Giant. Oscar Wilde. (J). 1984. (C-103); Six Servants. Jacob W. Grimm & Wilhelm K. Grimm. (J). 1984. (C-103); Six Sillies. (J). 1984. (C-103); Squirrel Nutkin. Helen Beatrix Potter. (J). 1984. (C-103); Story of the Three Bears. (J). 1984. (C-103); Tinder-Box. Hans Christian Andersen. (J). 1984. (C-103); Twelve Dancing Princesses. Jacob W. Grimm & Wilhelm K. Grimm. (J). 1984. (C-103); Ugly Duckling. Robert Van Nutt. Illus. by Robert Van Nutt. (J). 1984. (C-103); Well of the World's End. English Fairy Tale Staff. (J). 1984. (C-103); Wild Swans. Hans Christian Andersen. (J). 1984. (C-103); (J). 1984. 56.00 (C-103) Jimcin Record.
A collection of children's stories from around the world.

Favorite Children's Stories from England. unabr. ed. 6 cass. (Running Time: 2 hrs. 20 min.). Dramatization. (Magic Looking Glass Ser.). (J). (gr. 2-6). 1989. 9.95 set. (978-0-7810-0049-9(1), NIM-CW-131-C) NIMCO.
A series of folk tales of English heritage read by various readers. The stories are public domain.

Favorite Children's Stories from France. unabr. ed. 6 cass. (Running Time: 2 hrs.). Dramatization. (Magic Looking Glass Ser.). (J). (gr. 2-6). 1989. 9.95 set. (978-0-7810-0028-4(9), NIM-CW-128-C) NIMCO.
A collection of folk stories of French origin narrated by various readers.

Favorite Children's Stories from Germany. unabr. ed. 6 cass. (Running Time: 2 hrs. 20 min.). Dramatization. (Magic Looking Glass Ser.). (J). (gr. 2-6). 1989. 9.95 set. (978-0-7810-0021-5(1), NIM-CW-127-C) NIMCO.
A unit from the series which consists of 6 stories from Germany. The stories are public domain folk tales by various readers.

Favorite Children's Stories from Holland. unabr. ed. 6 cass. (Running Time: 1 hr. 20 min.). Dramatization. (Magic Looking Glass Ser.). (J). (gr. 2-6). 1989. 9.95 set. (978-0-7810-0035-2(1), NIM-CW-129-C) NIMCO.
A folk tale of Dutch descent.

Favorite Children's Stories from Ireland. unabr. ed. 6 cass. (Running Time: 2 hrs.). Dramatization. (Magic Looking Glass Ser.). (J). (gr. 2-6). 1989. 9.95 set. (978-0-7810-0014-7(9), NIM-CW-126-C) NIMCO.
Six audio cassettes, each cassette tells a story from the Land of Ireland. Public domain stories by various readers.

Favorite Children's Stories from Spain. unabr. ed. 6 cass. (Running Time: 1 hr. 20 min.). Dramatization. (Magic Looking Glass Ser.). (J). (gr. 2-6). 1989. 9.95 set. (978-0-7810-0043-7(2), NIM-CW-130-C) NIMCO.
A collection of Spanish folk tales recorded by various readers.

Favorite Classics Acoustic Guitar: Beginning to Intermediate Level. Ben Bolt. 1998. bk. 17.95 (978-0-7866-2497-3(3), 95102BCD) Mel Bay.

Favorite Collection, Set. unabr. ed. Evelyn Anthony et al. 62 cass. 423.38 AudioGO.
Includes: "The Tamarind Seed" by Evelyn Anthony, "Hotel du Lac" by Anita Brookner, "Waiting for Willa" by Dorothy Eden, "The Man with the Golden Gun" by Ian Fleming, "The Danger" by Dick Francis, "Luciano's Luck" by Jack Higgins, "Death in Zanzibar" by M.M. Kaye, "Puppet on a Chain" by Alistair MacLean, "Affairs at Thrush Green" by Miss Read, "Black Amber" by Phyllis A. Whitney.

Favorite Fairy Tales. abr. ed. Hans Christian Andersen et al. 2 cass. (Running Time: 1 hr. 46 min.). Dramatization. (J). (gr. 2-6). 1991. 12.95 set. (T-6) Jimcin Record.
Stories included are: "The Fisherman & His Wife," "The Twelve Dancing Princesses," "The Six Servants," "The Bremen Town Musicians," "The Emperor's New Clothes," "The Tinderbox," "The Wild Swans" & "The Ugly Duckling.".

Favorite Guitar Pickin Tunes. William Bay. 2000. pap. bk. 5.95 (978-0-7866-5084-2(2), 98591BCD) Mel Bay.

Favorite Holiday Songs. 1 cass. (Keepsake Collection). 9.95 (SCHS-8603-V); 13.00 Gift Box Set. (GBCH-8603-V) Coventry Mkting.

Favorite Holiday Stories. unabr. ed. Created by Radio Spirits. (Running Time: 10800 sec.). 2006. audio compact disk & audio compact disk 9.98 (978-1-57019-783-3(0)) Radio Spirits.

Favorite Hymns for Acoustic Guitar. Rick Foster. 1996. bk. 19.95 (978-0-7866-1414-1(5), 95438P); 10.98 (978-0-7866-1413-4(7), 95438C) Mel Bay.

Favorite Hymns for Piano Solo. Tim Price. 1 cass. pap. bk. 14.95 (93421P); 9.98 stereo. (93421C) Mel Bay.
Beautiful solo arrangements on hymns & sacred favorites. These arrangements feature beautiful harmonic treatment coupled with innovative voice leading. Selections include: "Breathe On Me Breath of God," "Come Thou Almighty King," "There Is A Balm in Gilead," "Let All Mortal Flesh Keep Silence," "Rock Of Ages," "True Happiness," & many more.

Favorite Hymns of Promise. 2004. 7.99 (978-0-8474-2515-0(0)); audio compact disk 9.99 (978-0-8474-1905-0(3)) Back to Bible.

Favorite Just So Stories. unabr. ed. Rudyard Kipling. 1 cass. (Running Time: 54 min.). Dramatization. Incl. Beginning of the Armadillos. Rudyard Kipling. (J). 1978. (G-4); Cat Who Walked by Himself. 1978. (G-4); Elephant's Child. Rudyard Kipling. 1978. (G-4); How the Whale Got His Throat. Rudyard Kipling. (J). 1978. (G-4); 1978. 7.95 (G-4) Jimcin Record.
Four stories from the "Just So" collection.

Favorite Locked Room Mysteries. unabr. ed. Ed. by Martin Greenberg & Rosalind M. Greenberg. 4 cass. (Masters of Mysteries Ser.). 1990. 21.95 Set, library case. (978-1-55656-149-8(0)) Dercum Audio.
Includes: The Exact Opposite by Erle Stanley Gardner; Vanishing Act by Bill Pronzini & Michael Kurland; The Problem of Cell 13 by Jacques Futrelle; His Heart Could Break by Craig Rice; The Long Way Down by Edward D. Hoch; The Man Who Read John Dickson Carr by William Brittain; The Doorndorf Mystery by Melville Davisson Post; The 51st Sealed Room or the MWA Murder by Robert Arthur.

Favorite Locked Room Mysteries, Vol. 1. unabr. ed. Bill Pronzini et al. Ed. by Martin Greenberg & Rosalind M. Greenberg. 4 cass. (Running Time: 6 hrs.). (Mystery Library). 1997. pap. bk. 21.95 (978-1-55656-197-9(0)) Pub: Dercum Audio. Dist(s): APG
The body's inside & the room is sealed! Who did it & how?.

Favorite Mystery Stories, Vol. 1. abr. ed. Nicholas Carter et al. 2 cass. (Running Time: 1 hr. 50 min.). Dramatization. (YA). (gr. 7-12). 1991. 12.95 set. (T-24A) Jimcin Record.
Stories included are: "The Mystery of Mrs. Dickenson," "The Purloined Letter," "The Stolen White Elephant" & "The Stolen Cigar Case.".

Favorite Mystery Stories, Vol. 2. unabr. ed. R. Austin Freeman & Jacques Futrelle. Read by Walter Covell & Walter Zimmerman. 2 cass. (Running Time: 2 hrs. 50 min.). (YA). (gr. 8-12). 1991. 12.95 set. (T-24B) Jimcin Record.
Stories included are: "The Problem of Cell 13" by Jacques Futrelle & "The Mandarin's Pearl" by R. Austin Freeman.

Favorite Mystery Stories, Vol. 3. unabr. ed. Arthur Morrison. Read by Walter Covell. 2 cass. (Running Time: 1 hr. 50 min.). (YA). (gr. 9-12). 1991. 12.95 set. (T-24C) Jimcin Record.
Stories included are: "The Lenton Croft Robberies" & "The Case of the Dixon Torpedo.".

Favorite Mystery Stories, Vol. 4. unabr. ed. Emmuska Orczy & R. Austin Freeman. Read by Walter Covell & Walter Zimmerman. 2 cass. (Running Time: 2 hrs. 30 min.). (J). (gr. 4 up). 1991. 12.95 set. (T-24D) Jimcin Record.
Stories included are: "The Glasgow Mystery," "The Dublin Mystery," & "The Aluminium Dagger.".

Favorite Nursery Songs. Nancy Chusid. 1 cass. (Sing along for Little Ones Ser.). (J). (ps-2). 1998. pap. bk. 6.95 (978-1-878624-05-5(9), McClanahan Book) Learn Horizon.

Favorite Poems: A Popular Anthology. unabr. ed. Poems. Read by Harold N. Cropp. Ed. by Dan Lyons. 8 cass. (Running Time: 11 hrs. 30 mins.). 1995. 56.95 (978-0-7861-0764-3(2), 1613) Blckstn Audio.
A former English teacher at Seattle University, Lyons enhanced his love for poetry by studying the great classical poets in the original Greek & Latin. This anthology is not just for connoisseurs. It is for everyone who enjoys poetry. The book is confined almost entirely to poems that rhyme. Of all our books, the fun & inspiration in these pages will probably boost your morale the most, & provide spiritual enrichment to your life. The poems are thrilling, as well as entertaining.

Favorite Russian Short Stories. unabr. ed. Alexander Pushkin et al. Read by Walter Zimmerman. 2 cass. (Running Time: 2 hrs. 50 min.). 1991. 12.95 set. (T-14) Jimcin Record.
Stories included are: "The Shot," "The Thief," "The Wedding," "The Long Exile" & "Where Love Is, There God Is Also".

Favorite Sacred Song - Holy. Anna Laura Page et al. 1 CD. (Running Time: 1 hr. 30 mins.). (ENG.). 2001. audio compact disk 29.95 (978-0-7390-1436-3(6), 19873) Alfred Pub.

Favorite Sacred Songs for Children. Composed by Anna Laura Page & Jean Anne Shafferman. 1 CD. (Running Time: 1 hr. 30 mins.). (ENG.). 2000. audio compact disk 29.95 (978-0-7390-0506-4(5), 19073) Alfred Pub.

Favorite Scandinavian Stories. unabr. ed. Selma Lagerlöf & Bjornstjerne Bjornson. Read by Walter Zimmerman. 2 cass. (Running Time: 2 hrs. 30 min.). (YA). (gr. 10-12). 1991. 12.95 set. (T-27) Jimcin Record.
Stories included are: "The Father," "Railroad & Churchyard," "The Outlaws" & "A Christmas Guest.".

Favorite Scary Stories of American Children. Perf. by Richard Alan Young & Judy Dockrey Young. Contrib. by Richard Alan Young & Judy Dockrey Young. (Running Time: 47 mins.). (gr. k-3). 1993. audio compact disk 14.95 (978-0-87483-743-8(X)) Pub: August Hse. Dist(s): Natl Bk Netwk

Favorite Scary Stories of American Children. Read by Richard Young & Judy D. Young. (Running Time: 1 hr.). (Roots of Modern Conflict Ser.). (gr. k-3). 1993. 12.00 (978-0-87483-148-1(2)) Pub: August Hse. Dist(s): Natl Bk Netwk

Favorite Scary Stories of American Children. unabr. ed. Read by Richard Young & Judy D. Young. 2 cass. (Running Time: 1 hr. per cass.). (J). 1991. 12.00 ea. August Hse.
Children aged 5-10 are the sources of these shivery stories. Two-part format, according to the "scariness level" of the stories.

Favorite Scary Stories of American Children. unabr. ed. Read by Richard Young & Judy D. Young. (Running Time: 1 hr.). (gr. 4-6). 1993. 12.00 (978-0-87483-175-7(X)) Pub: August Hse. Dist(s): Natl Bk Netwk

Favorite Scary Stories of American Children, Vol. 2. Perf. by Richard Alan Young & Judy Dockrey Young. Contrib. by Richard Alan Young & Judy Dockrey Young. (Running Time: 1 hr.). (gr. 4-6). 1993. audio compact disk 14.95 (978-0-87483-744-5(8)) Pub: August Hse. Dist(s): Natl Bk Netwk

Favorite Sherlock Holmes Mysteries, Vol. 1. abr. ed. Arthur Conan Doyle. 2 cass. (Running Time: 1 hr. 45 min.). Dramatization. (YA). (gr. 7-12). 1991. 12.95 set. (T-30A) Jimcin Record.
Stories included are: "A Scandal in Bohemia" & "The Adventure of the Speckled Band.".

Favorite Sherlock Holmes Mysteries, Vol. 2. abr. ed. Arthur Conan Doyle. 2 cass. (Running Time: 1 hr 50 min.). Dramatization. (YA). (gr. 9-12). 1991. 12.95 set. (T-30B) Jimcin Record.
Stories included are: "The Adventure of the Red-Headed League" & "The Adventure of the Noble Bachelor.".

Favorite Sherlock Holmes Mysteries, Vol. 3. unabr. ed. Arthur Conan Doyle. Read by Walter Zimmerman. 2 cass. (Running Time: 1 hr. 50 min.). (YA). (gr. 7-12). 1991. 12.95 set. (T-30C) Jimcin Record.
Stories included are: "The Adventure of the Empty House" & "The Adventure of the Six Napoleons.".

Favorite Sherlock Holmes Mysteries, Vol. 4. unabr. ed. Arthur Conan Doyle. Read by Walter Covell. 2 cass. (Running Time: 2 hrs. 20 min.). (YA). (gr. 7-12). 1991. 12.95 set. (T-30D) Jimcin Record.
Stories included are: "A Case of Identity," "The Solitary Cyclist" & "The Three Students.".

Favorite Sherlock Holmes Mysteries, Vol. 5. unabr. ed. Arthur Conan Doyle. Read by Walter Zimmerman & Jack Benson. 2 cass. (Running Time: 1 hr. 50 min.). (YA). (gr. 7-12). 1991. 12.95 set. (T-30E) Jimcin Record.
Stories included are: "The Adventure of Silver Blaze" & "The Adventure of the Musgrave Ritual.".

Favorite Sherlock Holmes Mysteries, Vol. 6. unabr. ed. Arthur Conan Doyle. Read by Walter Covell. 2 cass. (Running Time: 2 hrs. 30 min.). (YA). (gr. 7-12). 1991. 12.95 set. (T-30F) Jimcin Record.
Stories included are: "The Adventure of the Gloria Scott," "The Adventure of the Final Problem" & "The Adventure of the Naval Treaty.".

Favorite Sherlock Holmes Mysteries, Vol. 7. unabr. ed. Arthur Conan Doyle. Read by Walter Covell. 2 cass. (YA). (gr. 7-12). 1991. 12.95 set. (T-30G) Jimcin Record.
Stories included are: "The Adventure of the Blue Carbuncle" & "The Adventure of the Beryl Coronet.".

Favorite Sherlock Holmes Mysteries, Vol. 8. unabr. ed. Arthur Conan Doyle. Read by Walter Covell. 2 cass. (Running Time: 1 hr. 50 min.). (YA). (gr. 7-12). 1991. 12.95 set. (T-30H) Jimcin Record.
Stories included are: "The Boscombe Valley Mystery" & "The Adventure of the Norwood Builder.".

Favorite Sherlock Holmes Mysteries, Vol. 9. unabr. ed. Arthur Conan Doyle. Read by Walter Covell. 2 cass. (Running Time: 1 hr. 46 min.). (YA). (gr. 7-12). 1991. 12.95 set. (T-30I) Jimcin Record.
Stories included are: "The Adventure of the Priory School" & "The Adventure of the Copper Beeches.".

Favorite Sherlock Holmes Mysteries, Vol. 10. unabr. ed. Arthur Conan Doyle. Read by Walter Covell. 2 cass. (Running Time: 1 hr. 50 min.). (YA). (gr. 8-12). 1991. 12.95 set. (T-30J) Jimcin Record.
Stories included are: "The Adventure of the Golden Pince-Nez" & "The Adventure of the Second Stain.".

Favorite Sherlock Holmes Mysteries, Vol. 11. unabr. ed. Arthur Conan Doyle. Read by Walter Covell. 2 cass. (YA). (gr. 8-12). 1991. 12.95 set. (T-30K) Jimcin Record.
Stories included are: "The Adventure of the Dancing Men" & "The Adventure of Black Peter.".

Favorite Sherlock Holmes Mysteries, Vol. 12. unabr. ed. Arthur Conan Doyle. Read by Walter Covell. 2 cass. (Running Time: 1 hr. 45 min.). (YA). (gr. 8-12). 1991. 12.95 set. (T-30L) Jimcin Record.
Stories included are: "The Adventure of Charles Augustus Milverton" & "The Adventure of the Missing Three Quarter.".

Favorite Sherlock Holmes Mysteries, Vol. 13. unabr. ed. Arthur Conan Doyle. Read by Walter Covell. 2 cass. (Running Time: 2 hrs. 46 min.). (YA). (gr. 8-12). 1991. 12.95 set. (T-30M) Jimcin Record.
Stories included are: "The Man with the Twisted Lip," "The Adventure of the Engineer's Thumb" & "The Adventure of the Cardboard Box.".

Favorite Sherlock Holmes Mysteries, Vol. 14. unabr. ed. Arthur Conan Doyle. Read by Walter Covell. 2 cass. (Running Time: 2 hrs. 56 min.). (J). 1991. 12.95 set. (T-30N) Jimcin Record.
Stories included are: "The Adventure of the Yellow Face," "The Adventure of the Stockbroker's Clerk," "The Adventure of the Reigate Squire" & "The Adventure of the Greek Interpreter.".

Favorite Speeches of W. Cleon Skousen, Set, Vol. 1. unabr. ed. W. Cleon Skousen. 12 cass. (Running Time: 14 hrs.). 1990. 49.95 (978-0-910558-15-0(9)) Ensign Pub.

Favorite Speeches of W. Cleon Skousen, Set, Vol. 2. unabr. ed. W. Cleon Skousen. 12 cass. (Running Time: 16 hrs.). 1992. 49.95 (978-0-910558-16-7(7)) Ensign Pub.

Favorite Speeches of W. Cleon Skousen, Set, Vol. 3. unabr. ed. W. Cleon Skousen. 12 cass. (Running Time: 18 hrs.). 1998. 49.95 (978-0-910558-17-4(5)) Ensign Pub.

Favorite Stories. Short Stories. Nancy K. Duncan & Jean Giorno. As told by Nancy K. Duncan. Adapted by A. K. Ramanujan. (Running Time: 1 hr 8 mins). 2004. audio compact disk 15.00 (978-0-9719007-4-5(4)) STORY PERFORM.

Favorite Stories is Duncan's most recent CD, and includes six stories for adults. Road Kill (Duncan) and The Man Who Planted Trees (by John Giorno) are stories about the environment and originally appeared in her theatrical storytelling production Always/Never Coming Home, produced at the Lied Center of Performing Arts in Lincoln, NE in 1991. What Happens When You Really Listen, adapted from Folktales of India edited by A. K. Ramanujan, delineates the power of storytelling. Old Man and Old Woman is Duncan's version of a Blackfoot nation tale of how death came into the world. Losing & Getting is Nancy's story of her dance with breast cancer, and has been published in The Healing Heart: Families, New Society Publisher, edited by Alison Cox and David H. Albert, 2002. Nothing but the Truth is Nancy's account of a Halloween Carnival in Buford, GA in 1944.

Favorite Stories. abr. ed. Robert Louis Stevenson. 2 cass. (Running Time: 1 hr. 50 min.). Dramatization. 1991. 12.95 set. (T-21) Jimcin Record.

Stories included are: "The Sire de Maletroit's Door," "Markheim" & "The Body Snatchers.".

Favorite Stories. unabr. ed. Frank Richard Stockton. Read by Walter Zimmerman & Cindy Hardin. 2 cass. (Running Time: 2 hrs. 45 min.). (J). (gr. 4-8). 1991. 12.95 set. (T-19) Jimcin Record.

Stories included are: "The Lady or the Tiger," "The Discourager of Hesitancy," "Mr. Tolman," "The Griffon & the Minor Canon" & "Old Pypes & the Dryad.".

Favorite Stories by Ambrose Bierce. unabr. ed. Ambrose Bierce. Read by Jack Benson et al. 2 cass. (Running Time: 2 hrs. 36 min.). 1991. 12.95 set. (T-10) Jimcin Record.

Stories included are: "The Middle Toe of the Right Foot," "An Occurrence at Owl Creek Bridge," "The Boarded Window," "The Stranger" & "The Ways of Ghosts.".

Favorite Stories by Anton Chekov. unabr. ed. Anton Chekhov. Read by Walter Zimmerman & Jim Roberts. 2 cass. (Running Time: 1 hr. 45 min.). (YA). (gr. 8-12). 1991. 12.95 set. (T-15) Jimcin Record.

Stories included are: "The Bet," "A Work of Art," "The Lament," "The Slanderer," "The Kiss" & "The Lottery Ticket.".

Favorite Stories by Bret Harte. unabr. ed. Bret Harte. Read by Jack Benson. 2 cass. (Running Time: 2 hrs. 56 min.). (YA). (gr. 7-12). 1991. 12.95 set. (T-12) Jimcin Record.

Stories included are: "The Luck of Roaring Camp," "The Idyll of Red Gulch," "The Outcasts of Poker Flat," "Tennessee's Partner" & "Miss.".

Favorite Stories by Charles Dickens. abr. ed. Charles Dickens. 2 cass. (Running Time: 1 hr. 55 min.). Dramatization. (J). (gr. 4 up). 1991. 12.95 set. (T-25) Jimcin Record.

Stories included are: "A Christmas Carol," "The Signalman" & "The Trial for Murder.".

Favorite Stories by Edgar Allan Poe, Vol. 1. abr. ed. Edgar Allan Poe. 2 cass. (Running Time: 2 hrs. 40 min.). Dramatization. (YA). (gr. 8-12). 1991. 12.95 set. (T-5A) Jimcin Record.

Stories included are: "The Murders in the Rue Morgue," "The Purloined Letter," "The Cask of Amontillado," "Eiros & Charmion" & "The Fall of the House of Usher.".

Favorite Stories by Edgar Allan Poe, Vol. 2. unabr. ed. Edgar Allan Poe. 2 cass. (Running Time: 2 hrs. 30 min.). (YA). (gr. 8-12). 1991. 12.95 set. (T-5B) Jimcin Record.

Stories included are: "The Masque of the Red Death," "The Tell-Tale Heart," "William Wilson," "The Sphinx," "The Pit & the Pendulum" & "The Facts in the Case of M. Valdimar.".

Favorite Stories by Edith Wharton. unabr. ed. Edith Wharton. Read by Cindy Hardin & Walter Zimmerman. 2 cass. (Running Time: 1 hr. 56 min.). 1991. 12.95 set. (T-29) Jimcin Record.

Stories included are: "The Descent of Man" & "The Mission of Jane.".

Favorite Stories by Famous Women. abr. ed. Mary E. Wilkins Freeman et al. 3 cass. (Running Time: 4 hrs. 10 min.). Dramatization. 1991. 18.95 set. (C-231) Jimcin Record.

Short stories included are: "The Revolt of Mother," "A New England Nun," "Desiree's Baby," "A Winter Courtship," "The Mortal Immortal," "The White Heron," "The Other Two" & "The Story of an Hour.".

Favorite Stories by Guy de Maupassant. unabr. ed. Guy de Maupassant. Read by Cindy Hardin & Walter Zimmerman. 2 cass. (Running Time: 2 hrs. 40 min.). 1991. 12.95 set. (T-8) Jimcin Record.

Stories included are: "The Necklace," "Love's Awakening," "The False Jewels," "A Piece of String" & "Useless Beauty.".

Favorite Stories by Guy de Maupassant, Vol. 1. unabr. ed. Guy de Maupassant. Read by Cindy Hardin & Walter Zimmerman. 1 cass. (Running Time: 58 min.). Dramatization. Incl. False Jewels. 1977. (N-10); In the Moonlight. 1977. (N-10); Love's Awakening. 1977. (N-10); Necklace. 1977. (N-10); 1977. 8.95 (N-10) Jimcin Record.

Favorite Stories by Guy de Maupassant, Vol. 2. unabr. ed. Guy de Maupassant. Read by Walter Zimmerman & Cindy Hardin. 1 cass. (Running Time: 78 min.). Dramatization. Incl. Piece of String. 1977. (N-11); Useless Beauty. 1977. (N-11); 1977. 8.95 (N-11) Jimcin Record.

Favorite Stories by H. G. Wells. H. G. Wells. Read by Ivor Hugh & Walter Covell. 2 cass. (Running Time: 2 hrs. 45 min.). (YA). (gr. 9-12). 1991. 12.95 set. (T-7) Jimcin Record.

Stories included are: "The Man Who Could Work Miracles," "The Country of the Blind," "The Stolen Bacillus," "The Red Room" & "The Crystal Egg.".

Favorite Stories by Herman Melville. unabr. ed. Herman Melville. Read by Walter Covell. 2 cass. (Running Time: 2 hrs. 45 min.). (YA). (gr. 10-12). 1991. 12.95 set. (T-20) Jimcin Record.

Stories included are: "Bartelby, the Scrivner," "Jimmy Rose" & "The Fiddler.".

Favorite Stories by Jack London. unabr. ed. Jack London. Read by Walter Zimmerman & Jim Roberts. 2 cass. (Running Time: 2 hrs. 30 min.). (YA). (gr. 7-12). 1991. 12.95 set. (T-16) Jimcin Record.

Stories included are: "Love of Life," "The Law of Life," "The Man with the Gash," "The White Silence" & "In a Far Country.".

Favorite Stories by Joseph Conrad. unabr. ed. Joseph Conrad. Read by Walter Zimmerman. 2 cass. (Running Time: 2 hrs. 30 min.). 1991. 12.95 set. (T-28) Jimcin Record.

Stories included are: "The Lagoon," "An Outpost of Progress" & "The Idiots.".

Favorite Stories by Mark Twain, Vol. 1. unabr. ed. Mark Twain. Read by Walter Zimmerman & Jack Benson. 1 cass. (Running Time: 72 min.). Dramatization. Incl. Cannibalism in the Cars. (N-7); Celebrated Jumping Frog of Calavares County. (N-7); How I Edited an Agricultural Paper. (N-7); Story of the Bad Little Boy. (N-7); 8.95 (N-7) Jimcin Record.

Favorite Stories by Mark Twain, Vol. 1. unabr. ed. Mark Twain. Read by Walter Zimmerman & Jack Benson. 2 cass. (Running Time: 2 hrs. 30 min.). (YA). (gr. 8-12). 1991. 12.95 set. (T-4A) Jimcin Record.

Stories included are: "The Celebrated Jumping Frog of Calaveras County," "The Story of the Bad Little Boy," "Cannibalism in the Cars," "How I Edited an Agricultural Paper," "Journalism in Tennessee," "The Joke That Made Ed's Fortune," "The Man Who Put up at Gadsby's," & "Edward Mills & George Benton.".

Favorite Stories by Mark Twain, Vol. 2. unabr. ed. Mark Twain. Read by Walter Zimmerman & Jack Benson. 1 cass. (Running Time: 68 min.). Dramatization. Incl. Edward Mills & George Benton: A Tale. 1977. (N-8); Joke that Made Ed's Fortune. 1977. (N-8); Journalism in Tennessee. 1977. (N-8); Man that Put Up at Gadsby's. 1977. (N-8); 1977. 8.95 (N-8) Jimcin Record.

Favorite Stories by Mark Twain, Vol. 2. unabr. ed. Mark Twain. Read by Jack Benson & Walter Zimmerman. 2 cass. (Running Time: 2 hrs. 42 min.). (YA). (gr. 8-12). 1991. 12.95 set. (T-4B) Jimcin Record.

Stories included are: "The One Million Pound Bank Note," "The Story of the Good Little Boy," "The Californian's Tale," "The MacWilliams & the Burglar Alarm" & "The MacWilliams & the Lightning.".

Favorite Stories by Nathaniel Hawthorne, Vol. 1. unabr. ed. Nathaniel Hawthorne. Read by Walter Zimmerman et al. 2 cass. (Running Time: 2 hrs. 30 min.). (YA). (gr. 10-12). 1991. 12.95 set. (T-9A) Jimcin Record.

Short stories included are: "The Ambitious Guest," "Dr. Heidegger's Experiment," "The Minister's Black Veil" & "Young Goodman Brown.".

Favorite Stories by Nathaniel Hawthorne, Vol. 2. unabr. ed. Nathaniel Hawthorne. Read by Walter Covell & Walter Zimmerman. 2 cass. (Running Time: 2 hrs. 56 min.). (YA). (gr. 8-12). 1991. 12.95 set. (T-9B) Jimcin Record.

Stories included are: "The Great Stone Face," "My Kinsman, Major Molineux," "Mr. Higgonbothem's Catastrophe" & "The Birthmark.".

Favorite Stories by O. Henry, Vol. 1. unabr. ed. O. Henry. Read by Walter Zimmerman & Cindy Hardin. 1 cass. (Running Time: 56 min.). Dramatization. Incl. Cop & the Anthem. 1977. (N-5); Gift of the Magi. 1977. (N-5); Last Leaf. 1977. (N-5); Sound & Fury. 1977. (N-5); 1977. 8.95 (N-5) Jimcin Record.

Favorite Stories by O. Henry, Vol. 1. unabr. ed. O. Henry. Read by Walter Zimmerman et al. 2 cass. (Running Time: 2 hrs. 50 min.). (YA). (gr. 9-12). 1991. 12.95 set. (T-3A) Jimcin Record.

Stories included are: "The Gift of the Magi," "Sound & Fury," "The Last Leaf," "The Cop & the Anthem," "The Furnished Room," "After Twenty Years," "The Princess & the Puma" & "Mammon & the Archer.".

Favorite Stories by O. Henry, Vol. 2. unabr. ed. O. Henry. Read by Walter Zimmerman & Cindy Hardin. 1 cass. (Running Time: 66 min.). Dramatization. Incl. After Twenty Years. 1977. (N-6); Furnished Room. 1977. (N-6); Mammon & the Archer. 1977. (N-6); Princess & the Puma. 1977. (N-6); 1977. 8.95 (N-6) Jimcin Record.

Favorite Stories by O. Henry, Vol. 2. unabr. ed. O. Henry. Read by Walter Zimmerman et al. 2 cass. (Running Time: 2 hrs. 45 min.). (YA). (gr. 9-12). 1991. 12.95 set. (T-3B) Jimcin Record.

Stories included are: "Tobin's Palm," "A Cosmopolite in a Cafe," "The Skylight Room," "A Service of Love," "The Green Door," "Man about Town," "By Courier," "The Coming Out of Maggie," "The Love Philtre" & "Springtime a la Carte.".

Favorite Stories by O. Henry, Vol. 3. unabr. ed. O. Henry. Read by Walter Zimmerman & Cindy Hardin. 1 cass. (Running Time: 90 min.). Dramatization. Incl. Cosmopolite in a Cafe. 1977. (N-73); Green Door. 1977. (N-73); Service of Love. 1977. (N-73); Skylight Room. 1977. (N-73); Tobin's Palm. 1977. (N-73); 1977. 7.95 (N-73) Jimcin Record.

Favorite Stories by O. Henry, Vol. 3. unabr. ed. O. Henry. Read by Walter Covell et al. 2 cass. (Running Time: 1 hr. 47 min.). (YA). (gr. 9-12). 1991. 12.95 set. (T-3C) Jimcin Record.

Stories included are: "The Caliph, Cupid, & the Clock," "Sisters of the Golden Circle," "The Romance of a Busy Broker," "Lost on Dress Parade," "The Brief Debut of Tildy," "An Adjustment of Nature," "Memoirs of a Yellow Dog," "From the Cabby's Seat," "An Unfinished Story" & "Between Rounds.".

Favorite Stories by O. Henry, Vol. 4. unabr. ed. O. Henry. 1 cass. (Running Time: 90 min.). Dramatization. Incl. By Courier. 1981. (N-74); Coming Out of Maggie. 1981. (N-74); Love Philtre of Iky Schoenstein. 1981. (N-74); Man about Town. 1981. (N-74); Springtime a la Carte. 1981. (N-74); 1981. 8.95 (N-74) Jimcin Record.

Favorite Stories by O. Henry, Vol. 5. unabr. ed. O. Henry. Read by Jack Benson & Walter Covell. 1 cass. (Running Time: 90 min.). Dramatization. Incl. Adjustment of Nature. 1981. (N-75); Between Rounds. 1981. (N-75); From the Cabbie's Seat. 1981. (N-75); Memories of a Yellow Dog. 1981. (N-75); Unfinished Story. 1981. (N-75); 1981. 8.95 (N-75) Jimcin Record.

Favorite Stories by O. Henry, Vol. 6. unabr. ed. O. Henry. Read by Walter Zimmerman et al. 1 cass. (Running Time: 90 min.). Dramatization. Incl. Brief Debut of Tildy. 1981. (N-76); Caliph, Cupid & the Clock. 1981. (N-76); Lost on Dress Parade. 1981. (N-76); Romance of a Busy Broker. 1981. (N-76); Sisters of the Golden Circle. 1981. (N-76); 1981. 8.95 (N-76) Jimcin Record.

Favorite Stories by Oscar Wilde. unabr. ed. Oscar Wilde. Read by Walter Covell & Walter Zimmerman. 2 cass. (Running Time: 2 hrs. 30 min.). (YA). (gr. 8-12). 1991. 12.95 set. (T-26) Jimcin Record.

Stories included are: "The Canterville Ghost," "The Happy Prince," "The Remarkable Rocket" & "The Selfish Giant.".

Favorite Stories by Rudyard Kipling. abr. ed. Rudyard Kipling. 2 cass. (Running Time: 2 hrs. 50 min.). Dramatization. (J). (gr. 3-8). 1991. 12.95 set. (T-13) Jimcin Record.

Stories included are: "How the Whale Got Its Throat," "The Cat Who Walked by Himself," "The Elephant's Child," "The Beginning of the Armadillos," "Mowgli's Brothers" & "Riki-Tiki-Tavi.".

Favorite Stories by Stephen Crane. unabr. ed. Stephen Crane. Read by Jack Benson & Walter Zimmerman. 2 cass. (Running Time: 2 hrs. 50 min.). (YA). (gr. 8-12). 1991. 12.95 set. (T-11) Jimcin Record.

Stories included are: "The Blue Hotel," "The Bride Comes to Yellow Sky," "A Mystery of Heroism" & "The Open Boat.".

Favorite Stories by Washington Irving. abr. ed. Washington Irving. Read by Cindy Hardin & David Ely. 2 cass. 1991. 12.95 set. (T-22) Jimcin Record.

Stories included are: "The Legend of Sleepy Hollow," "The Mason's Tale," "The Stout Gentleman" & "The Phantom Island.".

Favorite Stories by Willa Cather. unabr. ed. Willa Cather. Read by Walter Zimmerman. 2 cass. (Running Time: 2 hrs. 40 min.). 1991. 12.95 set. (T-23) Jimcin Record.

Stories included are: "The Sculptor's Funeral," "Paul's Case," "A Wagner Matinee" & "Flavia & Her Artists.".

Favorite Stories of Christmas. Clement C. Moore et al. Read by Renee Raudman & Alan Sklar. (ENG.). 2007. audio compact disk 19.99 (978-1-4001-0570-0(6)) Pub: Tantor Media. Dist(s): IngramPubServ

Favorite Stories of Christmas Past. Clement C. Moore et al. Read by Renée Raudman & Alan Sklar. (Playaway Children Ser.). (J). 2008. 39.99 (978-1-60640-554-3(3)) Find a World.

Favorite Stories of Christmas Past. Clement C. Moore et al. Read by Renée Raudman & Alan Sklar. (Running Time: 18000 sec.). (ENG.). 2007. audio compact disk 39.99 (978-1-4001-3570-7(2)); audio compact disk 19.99 (978-1-4001-5570-5(3)) Pub: Tantor Media. Dist(s): IngramPubServ

Favorite Stories of Christmas Past. unabr. ed. Clement C. Moore et al. Narrated by Renée Raudman & Alan Sklar. (Running Time: 5 hrs. 0 mins. 0 sec.). (ENG.). 2008. 19.99 (978-1-4001-5916-1(4)); audio compact disk 19.99 (978-1-4001-0916-6(7)); audio compact disk 39.99 (978-1-4001-3916-3(3)) Pub: Tantor Media. Dist(s): IngramPubServ

Favorite Story: Vanity Fair & Mystery of Room. 1 cass. (Running Time: 1 hr.). 2001. 6.98 (1889) Radio Spirits.

Favorite Tales by Hans Christian Andersen. unabr. ed. Hans Christian Andersen. 1 cass. (Running Time: 56 min.). Dramatization. Incl. Emperor's New Clothes. (J). 1978. (G-2); Tinderbox. 1978. (G-2); Ugly Duckling. (J). (gr. k-6). 1978. (G-2); Wild Swans. 1978. (G-2); 1978. 9.95 incl. follow along script. (G-2); 8.95 incl. follow along script. Jimcin Record.

Favorite Tales by the Brothers Grimm. unabr. ed. Jacob W. Grimm & Wilhelm K. Grimm. 1 cass. (Running Time: 58 min.). Dramatization. Incl. Bremen Town Musicians. (J). 1978. (G-1); Fisherman & His Wife. (J). 1978. (G-1); Six Servants. (J). 1978. (G-1); Twelve Dancing Princesses. (J). 1978. (G-1); (J). 1978. 8.95 (G-1); 9.95 incl. follow-along script. Jimcin Record.

Favorite Tales for Children. Margaret Williams et al. (ENG.). (J). 2007. audio compact disk 5.99 (978-1-60339-168-9(1)) Listenr Digest.

Favorite Tales for Children. Margaret Williams et al. (ENG.). 2007. 5.99 (978-1-60339-167-2(3)) Listenr Digest.

Favorite Tales of Horror, Vol. 1. unabr. ed. Bram Stoker et al. Read by Walter Zimmerman & Jack Benson. 2 cass. (Running Time: 2 hrs. 30 min.). (YA). (gr. 10-12). 1991. 12.95 set. (T-17) Jimcin Record.

Stories included are: "Dracula's Guest," "The Judge's House," "The Upper Berth" & "The Apparition of Mrs. Veal.".

Favorite Tales of Horror, Vol. 2. unabr. ed. J. Sheridan Le Fanu et al. Read by Walter Covell et al. 2 cass. (Running Time: 2 hrs. 47 min.). 1991. 12.95 set. (T-18) Jimcin Record.

Stories included are: "A Terribly Strange Bed," "Sir Dominic Sarsfield," "The Dream Woman" & "What Was It?".

Favorite Texas Birds Vol. 1: Their Songs & Calls. Robert Benson & Karen Benson. 1 cass. (Louise Lindsey Merrick Natural Environment Ser.: No. 14). (ENG.). 1993. 10.95 (978-0-89096-549-8(8)) Tex AM Univ Pr.

The first in a series of recordings, provides the birder an interesting, informative, & convenient way to enjoy the songs of birds native to the state. This remarkable collection of vocalizations provides an easy means of learning & enjoying the distinctive songs & calls of Texas birds.

Favorite Texas Birds Vol. 1: Their Songs & Calls. Robert Benson & Karen Benson. 1 cass. (Louise Lindsey Merrick Natural Environment Ser.: No. 14). (ENG.). (gr. 7-12). 1993. 10.95 (978-0-89096-550-4(1)) Pub: Tex St Hist Assn. Dist(s): Tex AM Univ Pr

Favorite Toddler Tunes. 1 cass. (Running Time: 30 mins.). (J). 2002. 7.99 (978-1-894677-30-1(7)); audio compact disk 9.99 (978-1-894677-29-5(3)) Kidzup Prodns.

Favorite Wedding Classics, Med-Hi. Patrick Liebergen. (Favorite Classics for Solo Singers Ser.). (ENG.). 2001. audio compact disk 11.95 (978-0-7390-1570-4(2), 19899) Alfred Pub.

Favorite Wedding Classics, Med-Lo. Patrick Liebergen. (Favorite Classics for Solo Singers Ser.). (ENG.). 2001. audio compact disk 11.95 (978-0-7390-1573-5(7), 19902) Alfred Pub.

Favorites in the Key of Fun. Linda Arnold. 1 cass. (J). (ps-3). 1996. 9.98 Incl. lyrics. (978-1-889212-09-8(1), CAAR7); audio compact disk 14.98 CD Incl. lyrics. (978-1-889212-10-4(5), CDAR7) Ariel Recs.

A joyful compilation of children's songs plus five new selections. Twenty songs in all including 15 previously released.

Favoritism: James 2:1-13, 622. Ed Young. 1987. 4.95 (978-0-7417-1622-4(4), 622) Win Walk.

Favourite Essays: An Anthology. unabr. ed. Ed. by Montaigne et al. (Running Time: 5 hrs.). 2009. audio compact disk 28.98 (978-962-634-937-3(9), Naxos AudioBooks) Naxos.

Fawlty Towers, Vol. 1. John Cleese et al. Told to Andrew Sachs & Connie Booth. (Running Time: 7500 sec.). (BBC Radio Ser.). (ENG.). 2007. audio compact disk 14.95 (978-1-60283-349-4(4)) Pub: AudioGO. Dist(s): Perseus Dist

Fawn at Woodland Way. unabr. ed. Kathleen Weidner Zoehfeld. Read by Alexi Komisar. Illus. by Joel Snyder. Narrated by Alexi Komisar. 1 cass. Dramatization. (Smithsonian's Backyard Ser.). (J). (ps-2). 1994. 5.00 (978-1-56899-086-6(3), BC5003) Soundprints.

Cassette is read-a-long of the storybook, with authentic sound effects added. It consists of two sides - one with & one without page turning signals.

***Fawn Braun's Big City Blues.** Nicholas M. Healy. Illus. by Sahin Erkocak. Contrib. by Charity Jones. (Pfeffernut County Ser.). (ENG.). 2008. audio compact disk 11.93 (978-1-4048-5385-0(5)) CapstoneDig.

Fax on Demand. unabr. ed. Dan Poynter. Read by Dan Poynter. 1 cass. (Running Time: 1 hr.). 1996. 9.95 (978-1-56860-025-3(9), P-107) Para Pub.

One way to sell your information products while you sleep. For less than $1,000 you can set up an automated information retrieval system to sell your shorter reports as well as to display your brochures.

Fay. unabr. ed. Larry Brown. Narrated by Tom Stechschulte. 12 cass. (Running Time: 17 hrs. 30 mins.). 2000. 101.00 (978-0-7887-4369-6(4), 96251E7) Recorded Bks.

At 17, Fay Jones leaves her family's squalid home & heads for Biloxi. Beautiful & naive, Fay becomes the catalyst for desire & violence in the lives of those who befriend her.

Fay. unabr. ed. Larry Brown. Narrated by Tom Stechschulte. 15 CDs. (Running Time: 17 hrs. 30 mins.). 2001. audio compact disk 142.00 (978-0-7887-5175-2(1), C1337E7) Recorded Bks.

At 17, Fay Jones leaves her family's squalid home with $3 in her bra & ragged sneakers on her feet. As she heads for Biloxi, people befriend her - a policeman, his wife, a bouncer - but her impact on their lives is seductive & unpredictable. Beautiful & naive, Fay becomes the catalyst in a chain reaction of desire & violence. Her journey provides unflinching snapshots of the South, from beaches to bar rooms. Wherever she lands, though, Fay is fueled by a deep-rooted will to survive.

FBI: Inside the World's Most Powerful Law Enforcement Agency. unabr. ed. Ronald Kessler. Read by Jeff Riggenbach. 15 cass. (Running Time: 22 hrs.). 1996. 95.95 (978-0-7861-0949-4(1), 1728) Blckstn Audio.

It was vital evidence unearthed by award-winning journalist Ronald Kessler for "The FBI" - used by the Justice Department to launch its probe of abuses by FBA Director William S. Sessions - which ultimately resulted in his

dismissal by President Clinton. But the story behind William Session's dismissal - the first time in Bureau history a director has been fired - is only one of the fascinating revelations in "The FBI" that will change the way America perceives the once-sacrosanct Federal Bureau of Investigation.

FBI: Inside the World's Most Powerful Law Enforcement Agency. unabr. ed. Ronald Kessler. Read by Jeff Riggenbach. (Running Time: 21 hrs. 0 mins.). 2008. 44.95 (978-1-4332-4590-9(6)); cass. & audio compact disk 125.00 (978-1-4332-4589-3(2)) Blckstn Audio.

FBI in Peace & War: The Fence & Traveling Man. 1 cass. (Running Time: 1 hr.). 2001. 6.98 (1976) Radio Spirits.

FBS Adult. 2000. 12.40 (978-0-633-05129-7(2)) LifeWay Christian.

FBS Adult Audio. 2004. 13.30 (978-0-633-08079-2(9)) LifeWay Christian.

FBS Adult Audio. 2004. 13.30 (978-0-633-08581-0(2)) LifeWay Christian.

FBS Adult Audio. 2005. 13.30 (978-0-633-17575-7(7)) LifeWay Christian.

FBS Music for Babies 1s And 2s. 1999. audio compact disk 10.95 (978-0-7673-9750-6(9)) LifeWay Christian.

FBS Music for Babies 1s And 2s. 2000. 7.20 (978-0-7673-4520-0(7)) LifeWay Christian.

FBS Music for Babies 1s And 2s. 2003. 7.40 (978-0-633-07733-4(X)); audio compact disk 10.95 (978-0-633-07883-6(2)) LifeWay Christian.

FBS Music for Babies 1s And 2s. 2004. audio compact disk 11.40 (978-0-633-08255-0(4)) LifeWay Christian.

FBS Music for Babies 1s And 2s. 2004. 7.70 (978-0-633-08358-8(5)); audio compact disk 11.40 (978-0-633-08507-0(3)) LifeWay Christian.

FBS Music for Babies 1s And 2s. 2004. audio compact disk 11.40 (978-0-633-08757-9(2)) LifeWay Christian.

FBS Music for Babies 1s And 2s. 2004. 7.70 (978-0-633-17417-0(3)); audio compact disk 11.40 (978-0-633-17528-3(5)) LifeWay Christian.

FBS Music for Babies 1s And 2s. 2005. audio compact disk 11.40 (978-0-633-17726-3(1)) LifeWay Christian.

FBS Music for Babies 1s And 2s. 2005. 7.70 (978-0-633-17809-3(8)); audio compact disk 11.40 (978-0-633-17924-3(8)) LifeWay Christian.

FBS Music for Kindergarten. 1999. audio compact disk 10.95 (978-0-7673-9749-0(5)) LifeWay Christian.

FBS Music for Kindergarten. 2000. 7.20 (978-0-7673-4548-4(7)) LifeWay Christian.

FBS Music for Kindergarten. 2003. 7.40 (978-0-633-07735-8(6)); audio compact disk 10.95 (978-0-633-07882-9(4)) LifeWay Christian.

FBS Music for Kindergarten. 2004. audio compact disk 11.40 (978-0-633-08253-6(8)) LifeWay Christian.

FBS Music for Kindergarten. 2004. 7.70 (978-0-633-08360-1(7)); audio compact disk 11.40 (978-0-633-08506-3(5)) LifeWay Christian.

FBS Music for Kindergarten. 2004. audio compact disk 11.40 (978-0-633-08756-2(4)) LifeWay Christian.

FBS Music for Kindergarten. 2004. 7.70 (978-0-633-17419-4(X)); audio compact disk 11.40 (978-0-633-17527-6(7)) LifeWay Christian.

FBS Music for Kindergarten. 2005. audio compact disk 11.40 (978-0-633-17725-6(3)) LifeWay Christian.

FBS Music for Kindergarten. 2005. 7.70 (978-0-633-17811-6(X)); audio compact disk 11.40 (978-0-633-17923-6(X)) LifeWay Christian.

FBS Music for 3s-Pre K. 1999. audio compact disk 10.95 (978-0-7673-9769-8(X)) LifeWay Christian.

FBS Music for 3s-Pre K. 2003. audio compact disk 10.95 (978-0-633-07884-3(0)) LifeWay Christian.

FBS Music for 3s-Pre K. 2004. audio compact disk 11.40 (978-0-633-08256-7(2)) LifeWay Christian.

FBS Music for 3s-Pre K. 2004. audio compact disk 11.40 (978-0-633-08508-7(1)) LifeWay Christian.

FBS Music for 3s-Pre K. 2004. audio compact disk 11.40 (978-0-633-08758-6(0)) LifeWay Christian.

FBS Music for 3s-Pre K. 2004. audio compact disk 11.40 (978-0-633-17529-0(3)) LifeWay Christian.

FBS Music for 3s-Pre K. 2005. audio compact disk 11.40 (978-0-633-17727-0(X)) LifeWay Christian.

FBS Music for 3s-Pre K. 2005. audio compact disk 11.40 (978-0-633-17925-0(6)) LifeWay Christian.

FBS Music For 3s-Pre-K. 1999. 7.20 (978-0-7673-4534-7(7)) LifeWay Christian.

FBS Music For 3s-Pre-K. 2004. 7.70 (978-0-633-08106-5(X)) LifeWay Christian.

FBS Music For 3s-Pre-K. 2004. 7.70 (978-0-633-08608-4(8)) LifeWay Christian.

FBS Music For 3s-Pre-K. 2005. 7.40 (978-0-633-17612-9(5)) LifeWay Christian.

FBS Sound Truths Bible Studies On. 2000. reel tape 12.40 (978-0-633-05130-3(6)) LifeWay Christian.

FBS Sound Truths Bible Studies On. 2003. reel tape 12.75 (978-0-633-07707-5(0)) LifeWay Christian.

FBS Sound Truths Bible Studies On. 2004. reel tape 13.30 (978-0-633-08080-8(2)) LifeWay Christian.

FBS Sound Truths Bible Studies On. 2004. reel tape 13.30 (978-0-633-08332-8(1)) LifeWay Christian.

FBS Sound Truths Bible Studies On. 2004. reel tape 13.30 (978-0-633-17382-1(7)) LifeWay Christian.

FBS Sound Truths Bible Studies On. 2005. reel tape 13.30 (978-0-633-17576-4(5)) LifeWay Christian.

FBS Sound Truths Bible Studies On. 2005. reel tape 13.30 (978-0-633-17774-4(1)) LifeWay Christian.

FC GRE Take-Home Package. Annette Smith. Illus. by Richard Holt. 2005. pap. bk. 22.53 (978-1-4189-1486-8(X)) Rigby Educ.

FCYB Music CDs. Created by Gia Publications. 2008. audio compact disk 8.97 (978-1-55665-062-8(0)) GIA Pubns.

FDR. 2 cass. (Presidency Ser.). 10.00 Esstee Audios.
Examines Roosevelt's years in the White House.

Fdr. abr. ed. Jean Edward Smith. Read by Richard McGonagle. (ENG.). 2007. audio compact disk 34.95 (978-0-7393-4344-9(0), Random AudioBks) Pub: Random Audio Pubg. Dist(s): Random

Fdr: The First Hundred Days. unabr. ed. Anthony J. Badger. (Running Time: 6.5 hrs. 0 mins.). (ENG.). 2009. 29.95 (978-1-4332-7942-3(8)); audio compact disk 24.95 (978-1-4332-7941-6(X)) Blckstn Audio.

Fdr: The First Hundred Days. unabr. ed. Anthony J. Badger. Read by William Hughes. (Running Time: 6.5 hrs. 0 mins.). (ENG.). 2009. 44.95 (978-1-4332-7938-6(X)); audio compact disk 69.00 (978-1-4332-7939-3(8)) Blckstn Audio.

FDR, Fireside Chats Of, Set. unabr. ed. 3 cass. (Running Time: 2 hrs. 11 min.). 1994. 39.50 (S19550) J Norton Pubs.

FDR Remembered. 1 cass. (Running Time: 81 min.). 11.95 (F0210B090, HarperThor) HarpC GBR.

FDR's Folly: How Roosevelt & His New Deal Prolonged the Great Depression. unabr. ed. Jim Powell. (Running Time: 34200 sec.). 2008. audio compact disk 29.95 (978-1-4332-1342-7(7)); audio compact disk & audio compact disk 90.00 (978-1-4332-1341-0(9)) Blckstn Audio.

FDR's Folly: How Roosevelt & His New Deal Prolonged the Great Depression. unabr. ed. Jim Powell. Read by William Hughes. (Running Time: 12 hrs. 5 mins.). 2008. 72.95 (978-1-4332-1340-3(0)) Blckstn Audio.

Fe Explosiva (Audio Libro) Zondervan Publishing Staff & Edwin Santiago. (SPA.). 2007. audio compact disk 14.99 (978-0-8297-4901-4(2)) Pub: Vida Pubs. Dist(s): Zondervan

Fe Que Perdura. 2003. audio compact disk 23.00 (978-1-57972-550-1(3)) Insight Living.

Fe Sencilla. (SPA.). 2002. audio compact disk 36.50 (978-1-57972-467-2(1)) Insight Living.

Fear. 3 cass. 12.00 (S-1080) Faith Fellow Min.

Fear. 1 cass. (Running Time: 60 min.). 10.95 (008) Psych Res Inst.
Gain the confidence to eliminate needless fear & doubt through positive reinforcement.

***Fear.** 2010. audio compact disk (978-1-59171-170-4(3)) Falcon Picture.

Fear. L. Ron Hubbard. Read by Santiago Munevar. (Running Time: 3 hrs.). 2003. 16.95 (978-1-60083-281-9(4), Audiofy Corp) Iofy Corp.

Fear. J. Krishnamurti. 1 cass. (Running Time: 1 hr.). (Krishnamurti with Dr. Allan W. Anderson Ser.: No. 6). 8.50 (APA746) Krishnamurti.
These 1974 dialogues cover the entire spectrum of Krishnamurti's teaching in a series highly regarded for its depth of inquiry into each particular subject.

Fear. abr. ed. L. Ron Hubbard. Read by Roddy McDowall. 2 cass. (Running Time: 3 hrs.). 1991. 15.95 (978-0-88404-635-6(4)) Bridge Pubns Inc.

Fear. abr. ed. L. Ron Hubbard. Read by Roddy McDowall. 2 cass. 1995. 10.99 Set. (978-0-88404-938-8(8)) Bridge Pubns Inc.
Professor James Lowry didn't believe in spirits, or witches, or demons. Not until a gentle spring evening when his hat disappeared along with four hours of his life. Now Lowry is pursued by a dark, secret evil that is turning his whole world against him as he tries to remember - all the while hearing a warning from the shadows: "If you find your hat you'll find your four hours. If you find your four hours then you will die...".

Fear. abr. ed. L. Ron Hubbard. Read by Roddy McDowell. 2 cass. (Running Time: 3 hrs). 1991. 15.95 (978-1-59212-013-0(X)) Gala Pr LLC.

Fear. abr. ed. L. Ron Hubbard. Read by Roddy McDowall. 3 CDs. (Running Time: 10800 sec.). 2005. audio compact disk 19.95 (978-1-59212-167-0(5)) Gala Pr LLC.

Fear. unabr. ed. Terry Teykl. 8 cass. 1996. 30.00 Set. (978-1-57892-034-1(5)) Prayer Pt Pr.
Sermon/teaching on fear.

Fear. unabr. collector's ed. L. Ron Hubbard. Read by Michael Russotto. 5 cass. (Running Time: 5 hrs.). 1995. 30.00 (978-0-7366-3041-2(4), 3723) Books on Tape.
When a rationalist professor finds demonic possession, it nearly drives him around the bend. Powerful & imaginative.

Fear: The Toxic Emotion. Lois F. Timmins. 1 cass. (Running Time: 55 min.). 1986. 12.95 (978-0-931814-08-2(1)) Comn Studies.
Fear helps in recognizing danger, facilitating & energizing escape & self-protective moves; but it can also immobilize & hinder in experiencing any joy in living. Understanding fear gives insight into vulnerabilities.

***Fear: 13 Stories of Suspense & Horror.** unabr. ed. R. L. Stine. (Running Time: 7 hrs.). 2010. 19.99 (978-1-4418-8241-7(3), 9781441882417, Brilliance MP3); 39.97 (978-1-4418-8242-4(1), 9781441882424, Brlnc Audio MP3 Lib); 39.97 (978-1-4418-8243-1(X), 9781441882431, BADLE); audio compact disk 19.99 (978-1-4418-8239-4(1), 9781441882394, Bril Audio CD Unabri); audio compact disk 49.97 (978-1-4418-8240-0(5), 9781441882400, BriAudCD Unabrid) Brilliance Audio.

Fear & Fearlessness. Galek Rinpoche et al. 3 cass. 1991. 27.00 set. (OC280-62) Sound Horizons AV.

Fear & Loathing in Las Vegas. Hunter S. Thompson. Narrated by Ron McLarty. (Running Time: 22500 sec.). (Fear & Loathing Ser.). 2005. audio compact disk 19.99 (978-1-4193-5627-8(5)) Recorded Bks.

Fear & Loathing in Las Vegas: A Savage Journey to the Heart of the American Dream. unabr. ed. Hunter S. Thompson. Read by Ron McLarty. 5 CDs. (Running Time: 6 hrs.). (Fear & Loathing Ser.). 2005. audio compact disk 74.75 (978-1-4193-6338-2(7), C3461); 39.75 (978-1-4193-6336-8(0), 98218) Recorded Bks.
Maverick author Hunter S. Thompson introduced the world to "gonzo journalism" with this cult classic that shot back up the best-seller lists after Thompson's suicide in 2005. No book ever written has more perfectly captured the spirit of the 1960s counterculture. In Las Vegas to cover a motorcycle race, Raoul Duke (Thompson) and his attorney Dr. Gonzo (inspired by a friend of Thompson) are quickly diverted to search for the American dream. Their quest is fueled by nearly every drug imaginable and quickly becomes a surreal experience that blurs the line between reality and fantasy. But there is more to this hilarious tale than reckless behavior - for underneath the hallucinogenic facade is a stinging criticism of American greed and consumerism.

Fear & Other Uninvited Guests. abr. ed. Harriet Lerner. Read by Harriet Lerner. 1 CD. (Running Time: 1 hr. 30 mins.). 2004. audio compact disk 22.00 (978-0-06-072312-5(2)) HarperCollins Pubs.

***Fear & Other Uninvited Guests.** abr. ed. Harriet Lerner. Read by Harriet Lerner. (ENG.). 2004. (978-0-06-081361-1(X), Harper Audio) HarperCollins Pubs.

***Fear & Other Uninvited Guests: Tackling the Anxiety, Fear, & Shame That Keeps Us from Optimal Living & Loving.** abr. ed. Harriet Lerner. Read by Harriet Lerner. 2004. (978-0-06-077417-2(7), Harper Audio) HarperCollins Pubs.

Fear & Phobias: Conquer Them, Enjoy Life. Richard Jafolla & Mary-Alice Jafolla. Read by Richard Jafolla & Mary-Alice Jafolla. (Overcoming Ser.). 1986. 12.95 (140) Stppng Stones.
Motivational tapes that work on the subconscious mind (subliminal) & conscious mind to bring about self-improvement.

Fear & the Muse: The Story of Anna Akhmatova. Anna Andreevena Akhmatova. 1 cass. 1997. 10.95 (978-1-57523-178-5(6)) Unapix Enter.

Fear, Fear It's All Fear, Nos. 64, 65 & 66. Carl Faber. 3 cass. (Running Time: 3 hrs. 45 min.). 1987. 28.50 (978-0-918026-40-8(7), SR 85-968) Perseus Pr.

Fear Fighters. unabr. ed. Jentezen Franklin. (Running Time: 5 hrs. 30 mins. 0 sec.). (ENG.). 2009. audio compact disk 21.98 (978-1-59644-783-7(4), christianSeed) christianaud.

***Fear Fighters: How to Live by Faith in a World Driven by Fear.** unabr. ed. Jentezen Franklin. Narrated by Lloyd James. (ENG.). 2009. 12.98 (978-1-59644-784-4(2), christianSeed) christianaud.

Fear God: Exodus 20:1-6. Ed Young. 1999. 4.95 (978-0-7417-2219-5(4), A1219) Win Walk.

Fear is a Four Letter Word. Patricia O'Malley. Perf. by Barry Weiss. 1 cass. (Running Time: 50 min.). 1998. (978-1-892450-07-4(0), 135) Promo Music.
Guided imagery.

Fear Is the Key. unabr. ed. Alistair MacLean. Read by Francis Matthews. 8 cass. (Running Time: 10 hrs. 1 min.). (Audio Bks.). 1991. 69.95 set. (978-0-7451-6127-3(8), CAB 548) AudioGO.
Englishman John Montague Talbot, diamond & gold smuggler, & responsible for the death of a policeman in England, is now in Florida - wanted for jumping court, kidnapping a young woman & then killing a U. S. cop. What he doesn't know is that the hostage is the daughter of General Blair Ruthven, one of the richest oil magnates in Everglade country.

***Fear Itself.** unabr. ed. Andrew Clements. (Running Time: 3 hrs. 30 mins. 0 sec.). (Benjamin Pratt & the Keepers of the School Ser.). (ENG.). (J). 2011. audio compact disk 14.99 (978-1-4423-3425-0(8)) Pub: S&S Audio. Dist(s): S and S Inc

Fear Itself. unabr. ed. Walter Mosley. Read by Don Cheadle. (Fearless Jones Ser.: Bk. 2). (ENG.). 2005. 14.98 (978-1-59483-182-9(3)) Pub: Hachet Audio. Dist(s): HachBkGrp

Fear Itself. unabr. ed. Walter Mosley. Read by Don Cheadle. (Running Time: 7 hrs.). (ENG.). 2009. 54.98 (978-1-60024-974-7(4)) Pub: Hachet Audio. Dist(s): HachBkGrp

Fear Itself: The Origin & Nature of the Powerful Emotion That Shapes Our Lives & Our World, unabr. ed. Rush W. Dozier, Jr. Read by Patrick Cullen. 8 cass. (Running Time: 11 hrs. 30 mins.). 1999. 56.95 (978-0-7861-1611-9(0), 2439) Blckstn Audio.
A journey through the brain science & everyday reality of this most human emotion, fear.

Fear Itself: The Origin & Nature of the Powerful Emotion That Shapes Our Lives & Our World. unabr. ed. Rush W. Dozier, Jr. Read by Patrick Cullen. 10 CDs. (Running Time: 11 hrs. 30 mins.). 2000. audio compact disk 80.00 (978-0-7861-9801-6(X), 2439) Blckstn Audio.
Fear is the quintessential human emotion. Fear of disease, fear of injury, fear of poverty & a thousand other fears mold the most mundane aspects of our existence: what we eat, how we die, where we work. Yet fear is also behind the highest natures & the grandest tides of world history. By facing & overcoming our fears, we mature & fulfill our deepest human potential. Fear can start wars or end them. Fear can make us embrace or deny God.

Fear Less: Real Truth about Risk, Safety, & Security in a Time of Terrorism. unabr. ed. Gavin De Becker. Narrated by Tom Stechschulte. 4 cass. (Running Time: 6 hrs.). 2002. 42.00 (978-1-4025-1513-2(8)) Recorded Bks.
Addresses the concerns many have asked since the terrifying events of September 11, 2001. Is air travel safe? Are we at risk of chemical or biological weapons attacks? Can further acts be prevented by our government and military? How should parents discuss these concerns with their children? These and other vital questions are answered with expertise.

Fear No Evil: 2007 CCEF Annual Conference. Featuring Doug Green. (ENG.). 2007. audio compact disk 11.99 (978-1-934885-05-5(3)) New Growth Pr.

Fear No More: Exorcizing your Inner Public Speaking Demons. Narrated by T. J. Walker. 2003. audio compact disk 39.00 (978-1-932642-21-6(8)) Media Training.

Fear No More the Heat o' the Sun: From "Cymbeline" see Palgrave's Golden Treasury of English Poetry

Fear Not. Perf. by Wilmington Chester Mass Choir. 1 cass. 1997. audio compact disk 15.98 CD. (D2201) Diamante Music Grp.
One of the country's premier choral aggressions, members are from churches in New Jersey, Delaware & Pennsylvania.

Fear Not: The Creative Challenge of Crisis as a Catalyst for Positive Change, 1983. Read by Jack Schwarz. Contrib. by Will Noffke. 1983. 15.00 (#N2001) Aletheia Psycho.

Fear Not, Only Believe. Caryl Krueger. Read by Caryl Krueger. 2 cass. (Running Time: 3 hrs.). 2001. 17.00 Belleridge.
Hear these commands that heal physical and mental challenges and harmonize home and business. Learn the deeper meanings of these imperatives: Believe, fear not, rise up, go forth, be not troubled, love one another, rejoice!.

Fear Not Tomorrow, God Is Already There: Trusting Him in Uncertain Times. unabr. ed. Ruth Graham. Narrated by Ruth Graham. (Running Time: 8 hrs. 11 mins. 57 sec.). (ENG.). 2009. 20.99 (978-1-60814-520-1(4)); audio compact disk 29.99 (978-1-59859-581-9(4)) Oasis Audio.

Fear of Abandonment: Healing the Emotional Impact of Being Left, Set. David Grudermeyer & Rebecca Grudermeyer. 2 cass. 18.95 (T-23) Willingness Wrks.

Fear of Change: Cause of All Transformation & How to Respond. Read by Jack Schwarz. 1 cass. 1983. 12.00 Aletheia Psycho.
Lecture given at the Whole Life Expo in San Francisco.

Fear of Closed-In Places. Barrie Konicov. 1 cass. 11.98 (978-0-87082-305-3(1), 033) Potentials.
Konicov explains that when fears begin to control our minds we become a slave to them. Unlocks the chains that bind your mind & places you in a deep state of relaxation. Through sophisticated visualizations & imagination techniques, you systematically remove fear from your life.

Fear of Crowds. Barrie Konicov. 1 cass. (Fear Ser.). 11.98 (978-0-87082-306-0(X), 034) Potentials.
Explained that when fears begin to control our minds we become a slave to them. His Fear Series unlocks the chains that bind your mind & places you into a deep state of relaxation. Through sophisticated visualizations & imagination techniques, you systematically remove fear from your life.

Fear of Death. Barrie Konicov. 1 cass. 11.98 (978-0-87082-307-7(8), 035) Potentials.
Explains that when fears begin to control our minds, we become a slave to them. Unlocks the chains that bind your mind & places you into a deepstate of relaxation. Through sophisticated visualizations & imagination technique, you systematically remove fear from your life.

Fear of Driving. 2 CDs. 1981. audio compact disk 27.98 (978-1-56001-956-5(5)) Potentials.
Play this CD at your bedtime for a month and you'll learn to enjoy the convenience and joy of driving or being a passenger in a car.This 2-CD program from our Super Consciousness series is our newest, most powerful format. On the self-hypnosis CD, SC programs have the Subliminal Persuasion soundtrack added under Barrie?s voice. And the 17th Century Baroque music on the Subliminal CD has the same beat as your body's natural rhythm, thereby allowing the suggestions to enter deeply and effortlessly.

Fear of Driving. Barrie Konicov. 1 cass. (Fear Ser.). 11.98 (978-0-87082-308-4(6), 036) Potentials.
Explains that when fears begins to control our minds we become a slave to them. Unlocks the chains that bind your mind & places you into a deep state of relaxation. Through sophisticated visualizations & imagination techniques, you systematically remove fear from your life.

Fear of Driving. Barrie Konicov. 1 CD. 2004. audio compact disk 19.98 (978-1-56001-668-7(X)) Potentials.
You'll enjoy the convenience and joy of driving or being a passenger in a car. Just play this CD at your regular bedtime. You will find the self-hypnosis on track 1 and the subliminal on track 2. The easy-listening music of the subliminal, together with the self-hypnosis, is the original format which most people love and with which they are most familiar.

Fear of Dying. unabr. ed. Stanislov Grof & Christina Grof. 1 cass. (Running Time: 1 hr. 24 min.). 1975. 11.00 (00809) Big Sur Tapes.

Fear of Failure. 2 CDs. 1981. audio compact disk 27.98 (978-1-56001-957-2(3)) Potentials.
Do you have the desire to succeed, yet hold yourself back for fear of failure? With this 2-CD program you can become bold, adventurous, and confident of your success. This 2-CD program from our Super Consciousness series is our newest, most powerful format. On the self-hypnosis CD, SC programs have the Subliminal Persuasion soundtrack added under Barrie?s voice. And the 17th Century Baroque music on the Subliminal CD has the same beat as your body's natural rhythm, thereby allowing the suggestions to enter deeply and effortlessly.

Fear of Failure. Barrie Konicov. 1 cass. 11.98 (978-0-87082-429-6(5), 037) Potentials.
Explores & helps you overcome your fear of failure & emphasizes your desire to succeed.

Fear of Failure. Barrie Konicov. 1 CD. 2004. audio compact disk 19.98 (978-1-56001-672-4(8)) Potentials.
Do you have the desire to succeed, yet hold yourself back for fear of failure? With this program you can become bold, adventurous, and confident of your success. You will find the self-hypnosis on track 1 and the subliminal on track 2. The easy-listening music of the subliminal, together with the self-hypnosis, is the original format which most people love and with which they are most familiar.

Fear of Failure or Fear of Success? Theresa M. Danna. 1 cass. (Running Time: 27 min.). 2001. suppl. ed. 5.95 T M Danna.
Live self-help workshop defining fear of failure & fear of success, with exercises to help listeners overcome their fear & achieve their goals.

Fear of Flying. Erica Jong. Read by Erica Jong. 2 cass. (Running Time: 90 min. per cass.). 1990. 15.95 HarperCollins Pubs.

Fear of Flying. Barrie Konicov. 1 cass. 11.98 (978-0-87082-309-1(4), 038) Potentials.
Explains that when fears begin to control our minds we become a slave to them. His "Fear Series" unlocks the chains that bind your mind & places you into a deep state of relaxation. Through sophisticated visualizations & imagination techniques, you systematically remove fear from your life.

Fear of Flying. Barrie Konicov. 1 CD. 2004. audio compact disk 19.98 (978-1-56001-676-2(0)) Potentials.
Fear is a learned response, and perhaps your fear of flying was placed there by well-meaning friends or relatives, or by the media. The suggestions on this program may help. You will find the self-hypnosis on track 1 and the subliminal on track 2. The easy-listening music of the subliminal, together with the self-hypnosis, is the original format which most people love and with which they are most familiar.

Fear of Flying. Prod. by Learning Channel Staff. 1 cass. (Running Time: 60 min.). 10.95 (037) Psych Res Inst.
Removal of self imposed fears & barriers related to air travel.

Fear of Flying. unabr. ed. Erica Jong. Read by Hope Davis. (Running Time: 43200 sec.). 2006. audio compact disk 39.95 (978-0-06-114905-4(5)) HarperCollins Pubs.

***Fear of Flying.** unabr. ed. Erica Jong. Read by Hope Davis. (ENG.). 2006. (978-0-06-119066-7(7), Harper Audio); (978-0-06-119065-0(9), Harper Audio) HarperCollins Pubs.

Fear of Flying & Poems. abr. ed. Erica Jong. Read by Erica Jong. (Running Time: 45 min.). 10.95 (978-0-8045-1140-7(3), SAC 1140) Spoken Arts.
A poignant episode from "Fear of Flying" & several of her intimate poems.

Fear of God. Dan Corner. 1 cass. 3.00 (33) Evang Outreach.

Fear of Heights. 2 CDs. 1982. audio compact disk 27.98 (978-1-56001-958-9(1)) Potentials.
This fear has become a part of your life, a part of your psyche. Use this program and eliminate the fear of heights. This 2-CD program from our Super Consciousness series is our newest, most powerful format. On the self-hypnosis CD, SC programs have the Subliminal Persuasion soundtrack added under Barrie?s voice. And the 17th Century Baroque music on the Subliminal CD has the same beat as your body's natural rhythm, thereby allowing the suggestions to enter deeply and effortlessly.

Fear of Heights. Barrie Konicov. 1 cass. 11.98 (978-0-87082-310-7(8), 039) Potentials.
Explains that when fears begin to control our minds, we become a slave to them. Unlocks the chains that bind the mind & places the listener into a deep state of relaxation. Through sophisticated visualizations & imagination techniques, you can systematically remove fear from your life.

Fear of Heights. Barrie Konicov. 1 CD. 2004. audio compact disk 19.98 (978-1-56001-677-9(9)) Potentials.
This fear has become a part of your life, a part of your psyche. Use this program and eliminate the fear of heights. You will find the self-hypnosis on track 1 and the subliminal on track 2. The easy-listening music of the subliminal, together with the self-hypnosis, is the original format which most people love and with which they are most familiar.

Fear of Man. Dan Corner. 1 cass. 3.00 (34) Evang Outreach.

Fear of Masculinity & Femininity. unabr. ed. Nathaniel Branden. 1 cass. (Running Time: 1 hr. 12 min.). 12.95 (608) J Norton Pubs.
Discusses the following: selfishness & healthy sexuality; fear of one's sexual role; problems of a superior man or woman; the revolt against masculinity & femininity.

Fear of Monopoly & the Industrial Revolution. unabr. ed. Robert LeFevre. 1 cass. (Running Time: 1 hr. 52 min.). 12.95 (1007) J Norton Pubs.
Explores the effect of no government control & wealth distribution before & after the Revolution.

Fear of Rejection. 1 cass. (Running Time: 60 min.). 10.95 (033) Psych Res Inst.
Understand & overcome success related fear by increasing self confidence & assurance.

Fear of Success. Ben Bissell. 1 cass. (Running Time: 39 min.). 15.00 C Bissell.
People are often their own worst enemy in reaching their goals. Discusses ways in which people set themselves up for failure & how to avoid the traps that keep people from their goals.

Fear of Success. Barrie Konicov. 4 cass. 16.98 (978-1-56001-312-9(5), SC-II 040); 11.98 (978-0-87082-430-2(9), 040) Potentials.
A person with incredible talents goes just so far, & then falls flat on his face. The fear of success? A discussion & guide of the reasons for such fear & how to deal with them, to be a successs.

Fear of Success. Barrie Konicov. 1 CD. 2003. audio compact disk 16.98 (978-0-87082-982-6(3)) Potentials.
Why does a person with incredible talents go just so far, and then fall flat on his face? What is the problem? You can overcome barriers to success. You will find the self-hypnosis on track 1 and the subliminal on track 2. The easy-listening music of the subliminal, together with the self-hypnosis, is the original format which most people love and with which they are most familiar.

Fear of Success. Barrie Konicov. 2 CDs. 2003. audio compact disk 27.98 (978-1-56001-976-3(X)) Potentials.

Fear of Success. Created by Anne H. Spencer-Beacham. 1. 2003. audio compact disk (978-1-932163-41-4(7)) Infinity Inst.

Fear of Success/Surrender to God. Marianne Williamson. Read by Marianne Williamson. 1 cass. (Running Time: 90 mins.). (Lectures on a Course in Miracles). 1999. 10.00 (978-1-56170-192-6(0), M720) Hay House.

Fear of the Dark. unabr. ed. Eric Dalen. Read by Maynard Villers. 8 cass. (Running Time: 8 hrs. 30 min.). 1999. 49.95 (978-1-55686-909-9(6)) Books in Motion.
Neil Van Ness is an ordinary man who suddenly finds that his life is unraveling before his eyes. The first blow comes with the discovery of his wife's affair. The second comes from a news report from which he learns that he has become the target of a nationwide manhunt by the FBI for a murder that he didn't commit. The final blow comes when he discovers that the true killer is also on his trail.

Fear of the Dark. unabr. ed. Walter Mosley. 6 cass. (Running Time: 9 hrs.). (Fearless Jones Ser.: Bk. 3). 2006. 54.00 (978-1-4159-3462-3(2)) Books on Tape.

Fear of the Dark. unabr. ed. Walter Mosley. 8 CDs. (Running Time: 9 hrs.). (Fearless Jones Ser.: Bk. 3). 2006. audio compact disk 72.00 (978-1-4159-3463-0(0)) Books on Tape.

Fear of the Dark. unabr. ed. Walter Mosley. Read by Michael Boatman. (Running Time: 7 hrs.). (Fearless Jones Ser.: Bk. 3). (ENG.). 2006. 14.98 (978-1-59483-573-5(X)) Pub: Hachet Audio. Dist(s): HachBkGrp

Fear of the Dark. unabr. ed. Walter Mosley. Read by Michael Boatman. (Running Time: 7 hrs.). (ENG.). 2009. 49.98 (978-1-60788-147-6(0)) Pub: Hachet Audio. Dist(s): HachBkGrp

Fear of the Lord. Derek Prince. 1 cass. 5.95 (I-039) Derek Prince.
Seldom mentioned in contemporary Christianity, little understood by most Christians, this character aspect is essential for true success.

***Fear of the Lord: Discover the Key to Intimately Knowing God.** unabr. ed. John Bevere. (Running Time: 5 hrs. 30 mins. 0 sec.). (ENG.). 2011. audio compact disk 21.98 (978-1-61045-036-2(1)) christianaud.

***Fear of the Lord Life Message Series.** John Bevere. 2010. audio compact disk 0.00 (978-1-933185-61-3(9)) Messengr Intl.

Fear of the Lord 4 CD Series. 2007. audio compact disk 29.99 (978-1-933185-12-5(0)) Messengr Intl.

Fear of Water. Barrie Konicov. 1 cass. (YA). 11.98 (978-0-87082-311-4(6), 041) Potentials.
Explains that when fears begin to control our minds, we become a slave to them. His Fear Series unlocks the chains that bind the mind, & places you into a deep state of relaxation. Through sophisticated visualizations & imagination techniques, you systematically remove fear from your life.

Fear Place. unabr. ed. Phyllis Reynolds Naylor. Narrated by Ed Sala. 3 pieces. (Running Time: 3 hrs. 15 mins.). (gr. 3 up). 2001. 27.00 (978-0-7887-0592-2(X), 94769E7) Recorded Bks.

Fear Sign. unabr. ed. Margery Allingham. Read by Francis Matthews. 6 cass. (Running Time: 7 hrs. 30 mins.). (Albert Campion Ser.). 2000. 29.95 (978-1-57270-194-6(3), n61194u) Pub: Audio Partners. Dist(s): PerseuPGW

Fear, Stress & Physiology. Henry W. Wright. (ENG.). 2008. audio compact disk 24.95 (978-1-934680-44-5(3)) Be in Hlth.

Fear the Worst. abr. ed. Linwood Barclay. Read by Buck Schirner. (Running Time: 6 hrs.). 2010. audio compact disk 14.99 (978-1-4233-9844-8(0), 9781423398448, BCD Value Price) Brilliance Audio.

Fear the Worst. unabr. ed. Linwood Barclay. Read by Buck Schirner. (Running Time: 12 hrs.). 2009. 39.97 (978-1-4233-9841-7(6), 9781423398417, Brlnc Audio MP3 Lib); 24.99 (978-1-4233-9840-0(8), 9781423398400, Brilliance MP3); 24.99 (978-1-4233-9842-4(4), 9781423398424, BAD); 39.97 (978-1-4233-9843-1(2), 9781423398431, BADLE); audio compact disk 36.99 (978-1-4233-9838-7(6), 9781423398387); audio compact disk 92.97 (978-1-4233-9839-4(4), 9781423398394, BriAudCD Unabrid) Brilliance Audio.

Fear Will Do It, Set. unabr. ed. Sam Reaves. Read by Michael Hanson et al. 9 cass. (Running Time: 12 hrs. 23 mins.). (Cooper MacLeish Mystery Ser.: Vol. 2). 1994. 54.00 (978-0-9624010-8-4(0), 102665) Readers Chair.
Cooper's girlfriend Diana's past comes calling in the person of Tommy Thorne & the snake drops into Cooper's lakeside eden. In one terrifying moment, Diana loses control of her life & enters a world of professional killers. On her side, all she has is Cooper, & Cooper knows the stakes: win or lose - everything.

***Fearfully & Wonderfully Made.** Philip Yancey & Paul Brand. (Running Time: 6 hrs. 33 mins. 45 sec.). (ENG.). 2010. 12.99 (978-0-310-30444-9(X)) Zondervan.

Fearless. abr. ed. Diana Palmer. Read by Phil Gigante. (Running Time: 5 hrs.). 2010. audio compact disk 14.99 (978-1-4233-8255-3(2), 9781423382553, BCD Value Price) Brilliance Audio.

Fearless. unabr. ed. Diana Palmer. Read by Phil Gigante. 1 MP3-CD. (Running Time: 8 hrs.). (Long, Tall Texans Ser.). 2009. 24.99 (978-1-4233-8250-8(1), 9781423382508, Brilliance MP3); 39.97 (978-1-4233-8251-5(X), 9781423382515, Brlnc Audio MP3 Lib); 39.97 (978-1-4233-8253-9(6), 9781423382539, BADLE); 24.99 (978-1-4233-8252-2(8), 9781423382522, BAD); audio compact disk 87.97 (978-1-4233-8249-2(8), 9781423382492, BriAudCD Unabrid); audio compact disk 34.99 (978-1-4233-8248-5(X), 9781423382485) Brilliance Audio.

Fearless: Boundless Courage in Everyday Life. Barry Neil Kaufman. (ENG.). 2007. audio compact disk 29.50 (978-0-9798105-3-4(1)) Option Inst.

Fearless: Imagine Your Life Without Fear. abr. ed. Max Lucado. 2009. audio compact disk 24.99 (978-0-8499-6397-1(4)) Nelson.

Fearless Conversations: How to Speak to Anyone & Leave a Lasting Impression. Michael Chojnacki. (Running Time: 75 mins). (ENG.). 2007. audio compact disk (978-0-9786006-1-7(4)) Infinite Wisdm.

Fearless Flight Kit: The Remedy for the Fearful Flyer. Ron Nielsen & Jack L. Canfield. (Chicken Soup for the Soul Ser.). 2004. pap. bk. 24.95 (978-0-9722369-0-4(2)) ClearedfourTakeoff.

Fearless Flying: A Complete Program to Help You Overcome Your Fear of Flying. unabr. ed. Broadview Media, Inc. Staff. Arranged by Northwest Airlines. 2000. vinyl bd. 69.95 Album with Video, Audio, Book. (978-0-9679724-0-4(X)) Broadview Media.

Fearless Fourteen. abr. ed. Janet Evanovich. Read by Lorelei King. 3 CDs. (Running Time: 4 hrs. 0 mins. 0 sec.). (Stephanie Plum Ser.: No. 14). (ENG.). 2008. audio compact disk 19.95 (978-1-4272-0419-6(5)) Pub: Macmill Audio. Dist(s): Macmillan

Fearless Fourteen. unabr. ed. Janet Evanovich. Narrated by Lorelei King. 1 MP3-CD. (Running Time: 7 hrs.). (Stephanie Plum Ser.: No. 14). 2008. 49.95 (978-0-7927-5630-9(4)); audio compact disk 79.95 (978-0-7927-5457-2(3)) AudioGO.
The number one blockbuster selling phenomenon continues in the fourteenth Stephanie Plum adventure. America's favorite bounty hunter Stephanie Plum is back-and she's brought along her sidekicks Connie, Lula, and Grandma Mazur-for a non-stop action adventure that takes her throughout New Jersey, from Trenton, to the Jersey Shore, to Atlantic City, and beyond. Vice Captain Joe Morelli, Super Bounty Hunter, Ranger, and Bob the Dog are all along for the ride. There will be comic mayhem, hot sexual tension, plenty of junk food, exploding cars, pot roast with the Plum family, and a viewing at the Burg's premier funeral home.

Fearless Fourteen. unabr. ed. Janet Evanovich. Read by Lorelei King. 7 CDs. (Running Time: 7 hrs. 0 mins. 0 sec.). (Stephanie Plum Ser.: No. 14). (ENG.). 2008. audio compact disk 34.95 (978-1-4272-0417-2(9)) Pub: Macmill Audio. Dist(s): Macmillan

Fearless Heart: The Practice of Living with Courage & Compassion. unabr. ed. Pema Chödrön. (ENG.). 2010. audio compact disk 39.95 (978-1-59030-739-7(9)) Pub: Shambhala Pubns. Dist(s): Random

Fearless Jones. abr. ed. Walter Mosley. Read by Peter Francis James. (Fearless Jones Ser.: Bk. 1). (ENG.). 2005. 14.98 (978-1-59483-413-4(X)) Pub: Hachet Audio. Dist(s): HachBkGrp

Fearless Jones. unabr. ed. Walter Mosley. Read by William Andrew Quinn. 6 vols. (Running Time: 9 hrs.). (Fearless Jones Ser.: Bk. 1). 2001. bk. 54.95 (978-0-7927-2498-8(4), CSL 387, Chivers Sound Lib); audio compact disk 79.95 (978-0-7927-9927-6(5), SLD 078, Chivers Sound Lib) AudioGO.
Paris Minton is minding his own business when Elana Love walks in and asks a few questions. Within the next twenty-four hours, Paris has been beaten up, made love to, shot at, and robbed, and his bookstore has been burned to the ground. He's in so much trouble he has no choice but to get his friend Fearless Jones out of jail to help.

Fearless Life. Creflo A. Dollar. 2009. audio compact disk 28.00 (978-1-59944-770-4(3)) Creflo Dollar.

***Fearless Living.** Taffi L. Dollar. 2009. audio compact disk 14.00 (978-1-59944-780-3(0)) Creflo Dollar.

Fearless Love: The Answer to the Problem of Human Existence. Gary Renard. 2008. audio compact disk 19.95 (978-1-59179-669-5(5)) Sounds True.

Fearless Phil. Jill Eggleton. Illus. by Raymond McGrath. (Sails Literacy Ser.). (gr. 3 up). 10.00 (978-0-7578-6993-8(9)) Rigby Educ.

Fearless Speaking. Jeff Davidson. 2005. 13.95 (978-1-60729-227-2(0)) Breath Space Inst.

Fearless Speaking. Jeff Davidson. 2005. audio compact disk 14.95 (978-1-60729-118-3(5)) Breath Space Inst.

Fearlessness. (709) Yoga Res Foun.

Fearlessness. Swami Jyotirmayananda. 1 cass. (Running Time: 1 hr.). 1990. 12.99 Yoga Res Foun.

Fears & Phobias: Program from the Award Winning Public Radio Series. Hosted by Fred Goodwin. Comment by John Hockenberry. Contrib. by Jerilyn Ross et al. 1 cass. (Running Time: 1 hr.). (Infinite Mind Ser.). 1999. audio compact disk 21.95 (978-1-888064-14-8(5), LCM 61) Lichtenstein Creat.
Fear is normal. If we didn't have a fight or flight instinct, our species would have died out a long time ago. But some people are ruled by fear, by phobias that dictate where they go and what they do or, more commonly, where they don't go and what they don't do. This week on The Infinite Mind, you'll hear from people who have phobias and from doctors who treat them; about the difference between fears and phobias; about the regions and chemicals in the brain responsible for fear and anxiety; and about a virtual reality program used to treat fear of flying.

Fears & Phobias: To Improve Self-Confidence. unabr. ed. Robert B. Speigel. Read by Robert B. Speigel. 2 cass. (Running Time: 1 hr.). (Audio Suggestion Bedtime Story Tapes Ser.). (J). 1993. 16.95 set incl. coloring poster. (978-0-937977-04-0(7)) Speigel&Assoc.
Psychotherapist Robert B. Speigel tells a story from his own childhood & leads children through a series of relaxation & positive visualization exercises designed to help them gain confidence to overcome bad habits & negative thinking. A helpful "Parent Information" cassette is included that provides positive daytime techniques & facts about each problem compiled from current research.

Fears of Going Crazy, Orgasm & Death. unabr. ed. Osho Oshos. Read by Osho Oshos. 2 cass. (Running Time: 2 hrs.). (Last Testament Ser.). 15.95 set. (DLT-2016) Oshos.
A delightful talk shedding light on the source of each of these fears, & on therapy based in meditation - an essential ingredient.

Feast see Isaac Bashevis Singer Reader

Feast. (Sails Literacy Ser.). (gr. 2 up). 10.00 (978-0-7578-2669-6(5)) Rigby Educ.

Feast. Barbour Books Staff. 1999. bk. 9.97 (978-1-57748-580-3(7)) Barbour Pub.

***Feast for the Soul: Awakening.** Kathy Ziola. (Running Time: 50 mins.). (ENG.). 2010. audio compact disk 15.95 (978-0-9826130-0-9(8)) Feast Pubng.

Feast for 10. Cathryn Falwell. (Metro Reading Ser.). (J). (gr. k). 1996. 8.46 (978-1-58120-988-4(6)) Metro Teaching.

Feast of Carrion. Keith Mccarthy. 2009. 84.95 (978-0-7531-4237-0(6)); audio compact disk 99.95 (978-0-7531-4238-7(4)) Pub: Isis Pubng Ltd GBR. Dist(s): Ulverscroft US

Feast of Devotion. Read by Osel Tendzin. 5 cass. 1976. 54.00 (A057) Vajradhatu.
Five talks: 1) Doubt: The Gateway to Devotion; 2) The Discomfort of Surrender; 3) Devotion at the Hinayana level; 4) Surrendering to the Kalyanamitra; 5) The Love Affair.

Feast of Faith: The Transforming Power of the Eucharist. Marcellino D'Ambrosio. 2004. 12.95 (978-1-932927-21-4(2)); audio compact disk 19.95 (978-1-932927-20-7(4)) Ascensn Pr.

***Feast of Fools.** unabr. ed. Rachel Caine. Narrated by Cynthia Holloway. (Running Time: 8 hrs. 0 mins.). (Morganville Vampires Ser.). 2010. 15.99 (978-1-4001-8193-3(3)) Tantor Media.

Feast of Fools. unabr. ed. Rachel Caine. Narrated by Cynthia Holloway. (Running Time: 8 hrs. 0 mins. 0 sec.). (Morganville Vampires Ser.: BK. 4). (ENG.). (gr. 9-13). 2010. audio compact disk 29.99 (978-1-4001-1193-0(5)) Pub: Tantor Media. Dist(s): IngramPubServ

Feast of Fools. unabr. ed. Rachel Caine. Narrated by Cynthia Holloway. (Running Time: 8 hrs. 0 mins. 0 sec.). (Morganville Vampires Ser.: Bk. 4). (ENG.). (gr. 9-12). 2010. 19.99 (978-1-4001-6193-5(2)) Pub: Tantor Media. Dist(s): IngramPubServ

Feast of Fools. unabr. ed. Rachel Caine. Narrated by Cynthia Holloway. (Running Time: 8 hrs. 0 mins. 0 sec.). (Morganville Vampires Ser.: Bk. 4). (ENG.). (gr. 9-13). 2010. audio compact disk 59.99 (978-1-4001-4193-7(1)) Pub: Tantor Media. Dist(s): IngramPubServ

Feast of Life: Stories from the Gospel of Luke. Marty Haugen & Gary Daigle. 1 cass. 2000. 10.95 (CS-489); 10.95; audio compact disk 15.95 (CD-489); audio compact disk 15.95 (CD-489) GIA Pubns.

Feast of Love. unabr. ed. Charles Baxter. Read by Scott Brick & Amanda Karr. 6 cass. (Running Time: 12 hrs.). 2004. 29.95 (978-1-59007-502-9(1)) Pub: New Millenn Enter. Dist(s): PerseuPGW

Feast of Love. unabr. ed. Charles Baxter. Read by Scott Brick & Amanda Karr. 8 CDs. (Running Time: 12 hrs.). 2004. audio compact disk 49.95 (978-1-59007-503-6(X)) Pub: New Millenn Enter. Dist(s): PerseuPGW

Feast of Roses. Indu Sundaresan. Read by Sneha Mathan. (Running Time: 63000 sec.). 2007. 95.95 (978-1-4332-0073-1(2)); audio compact disk 120.00 (978-1-4332-0074-8(0)); audio compact disk 44.95 (978-1-4332-0075-5(9)) Blckstn Audio.

Feast of Tabernacles, Vol. I. Reuven Doron. 1 cass. (Running Time: 90 mins.). 2000. 5.00 (RD02-001) Morning NC.
With the insight of a completed Jew, Reuven details the Feast of Tabernacles & its significance to believers.

Feast of Tabernacles, Vol. II. Reuven Doron. 1 cass. (Running Time: 90 mins.). 2000. 5.00 (RD02-002) Morning NC.

Feast of Tabernacles, Vol. III. Reuven Doron. 1 cass. (Running Time: 90 mins.). 2000. 5.00 (RD02-003) Morning NC.

Feast of Tabernacles Series. Reuven Doron. 3 cass. (Running Time: 4 hrs. 30 mins.). 2000. 15.00 (RD02-000) Morning NC.

Feast of Words. unabr. ed. Cynthia G. Wolff. Read by Anna Fields. 14 cass. (Running Time: 20 hrs. 30 mins.). 1997. 89.95 (978-0-7861-1241-8(7), 1987) Blckstn Audio.
The mystery of how a wealthy New York socialite became a major American novelist.

Feast of Words: The Triumph of Edith Wharton. unabr. ed. Cynthia Griffin Wolff. Read by Anna Fields. (Running Time: 19 hrs. 30 mins.). 2010. 44.95 (978-1-4417-0604-1(6)); audio compact disk 123.00 (978-1-4417-0601-0(1)) Blckstn Audio.

Feasts of Israel. Chuck Missler. 2 cass. (Running Time: 3 hrs.). (Briefing Packages by Chuck Missler). 1993. 14.95 Incls. notes. (978-1-880532-86-7(7)) Koinonia Hse.
PassoverFeast of Unleavened Bread*Feast of First Fruits * Feast of PentecostFeast of Trumpets * Day of Atonement * Feast of Tabernacles * Do the Feasts of Moses predict the major milestones in God's plan? * Are the Feasts prophetic? * Has the Feast of Pentecost been completely fulfilled?* What are the New Testament implications?Set by God, these Feasts are not only commemorative in a historical context, but are also prophetic. The Feasts point to the Messiah's First and Second Coming and highlight the Church.In this briefing, Chuck Missler reveals the rich background of the Feasts with many surprises for the Bible believer, and yet only scratches the surface.*

Feasts of Our Lady. Monks of Solesmes Staff. 1 CD. 1985. audio compact disk 16.95 (978-1-55725-106-0(1), 930-065) Paraclete MA.

Feather & the Stone. Patricia Shaw. Read by Joy Mitchell. 13 cass. (Running Time: 19 hrs. 30 min.). 2001. (570624) Bolinda Pubng AUS.

Feather & the Stone. unabr. ed. Patricia Shaw. Read by Joy Mitchell. 13 cass. 1998. (978-1-86340-717-5(0), 570624) Bolinda Pubng AUS.
Tragically orphaned at sea, cast adrift in an alien land, Sibell applies for the post of secretary-companion to Charlotte Hamilton, & undertakes the arduous journey to Black Wattle Station in the Northern Territory to join her employer. The rigors of an isolated cattle station come as a tremendous shock to the gently brought-up English girl, & she is viewed with suspicion by Charlotte's sons.

Feather Boy. unabr. ed. Nicky Singer. 4 cass. (Running Time: 5 hrs. 27 mins.). (J). (gr. 5-9). 2004. 32.00 (978-0-8072-0725-3(X), Listening Lib) Random Audio Pubg.

Feather Moon. unabr. ed. 1 cass. (Running Time: 45 min.). (Kiowa, Star Lore Ser.). 14.95 (C19203) J Norton Pubs.
Native American myths.

Feather on the Moon, unabr. ed. Phyllis A. Whitney. Read by Anna Fields. 6 cass. (Running Time: 8 hrs. 30 mins.). 1999. 44.95 (978-0-7861-1658-4(7), 2486) Blckstn Audio.
Jennifer Blake could still vividly remember the day when, momentarily distracted by an odd young woman, she left her three-year-old daughter, Debbie, unattended in a grocery cart. When she turned back, the child had vanished. For seven years, there was no sign of Debbie - until the telephone call. Could it be true that she has found her daughter?.

Feather on the Moon. unabr. ed. Phyllis A. Whitney. Read by Anna Fields. 6 cass. (Running Time: 9 hrs.). 2001. 29.95 Pub: Blckstn Audio. Dist(s): Penton Overseas

Feather on the Moon. unabr. ed. Phyllis A. Whitney. Read by Anna Fields. (Running Time: 8.5 hrs. 0 mins.). (ENG.). 2009. 29.95 (978-1-4417-0318-7(7)); audio compact disk 76.00 (978-1-4417-0315-6(2)) Blckstn Audio.

Feathered Phonics! Barnyard Fun! 2004. 12.99 (978-0-9725854-3-9(5)) Pet Media.

Feathered Phonics! ESPANOL! 2004. audio compact disk 12.99 (978-0-9725854-8-4(6)) Pet Media.

Feathered Phonics International Edition! 8 Languages from around the World! 2005. audio compact disk 12.99 (978-0-9725854-5-3(1)) Pet Media.

Feathered Phonics Teach Your Bird to Talk 96 Words & Phrases. 1. 2001. audio compact disk 12.99 (978-0-9725854-1-5(9)) Pet Media.
Teach your Bird to Speak with Feathered Phonics. Volume 1 has 96 words and phrases.

Feathered Phonics! Teach your canary to Sing! 2004. audio compact disk 12.99 (978-0-9725854-7-7(8)) Pet Media.

Feathered Phonics! the Outback Edition! 2004. audio compact disk 12.99 (978-0-9725854-6-0(X)) Pet Media.

Feathered Phonics! University 101! 2004. audio compact disk 12.99 (978-0-9725854-9-1(4)) Pet Media.

Feathered Phonics! 96 More Words & Phrases to Teach Your Bird. George Ford. 2004. audio compact disk 12.99 (978-0-9725854-4-6(3)) Pet Media.

Feathered Phonics! 96 Songs & Rhymes! 2004. audio compact disk 12.99 (978-0-9725854-2-2(7)) Pet Media.

Feathered Serpent, Pt. 1, Vol. 3. Chris Heimerdinger. 5 CDs. (Tennis Shoes Adventure Ser.). 2004. audio compact disk 21.95 (978-1-59156-299-3(6)) Covenant Comms.

Feathered Serpent, Pt. 2, Vol. 4. Chris Heimerdinger. 5 CDs. (Tennis Shoes Adventure Ser.). 2004. audio compact disk 21.95 (978-1-59156-300-6(3)) Covenant Comms.

Feathered Serpent, Vol. 3, Pt. 1. Chris Heimerdinger. 4 cass. (Tennis Shoes Adventure Ser.). 2004. 19.95 (978-1-57734-488-9(X)) Covenant Comms.

Feathered Serpent, Vol. 4, Pt. 2. Chris Heimerdinger. 4 cass. (Tennis Shoes Adventure Ser.). 2004. 19.95 (978-1-57734-754-5(4)) Covenant Comms.

Featherless PArrot see Lorito Pelon

Feathers. Jacqueline Woodson. Read by Sisi Aisha Johnson. (Playaway Children Ser.). (J). 2008. 44.99 (978-1-60640-778-3(3)) Find a World.

Feathers. unabr. ed. Jacqueline Woodson. Read by Sisi Aisha Johnson. (Running Time: 3 hrs.). (J). 2008. audio compact disk 39.25 (978-1-4233-6567-9(4), 9781423365679, Brinc Audio MP3 Lib) Brilliance Audio.

Feathers. unabr. ed. Jacqueline Woodson. Read by Sisi Johnson. (Running Time: 3 hrs.). 2008. 39.25 (978-1-4233-6569-3(0), 9781423365693, BADLE) Brilliance Audio.

Feathers. unabr. ed. Jacqueline Woodson. Read by Sisi Aisha Johnson. (Running Time: 3 hrs.). 2008. 24.95 (978-1-4233-6568-6(2), 9781423365686, BAD) Brilliance Audio.

Feathers. unabr. ed. Jacqueline Woodson. Read by Sisi Aisha Johnson. 3 CDs. (Running Time: 3 hrs.). (J). (gr. 4). 2008. audio compact disk 19.95 (978-1-4233-6564-8(X), 9781423365648, Bril Audio CD Unabri); audio compact disk 24.95 (978-1-4233-6566-2(6), 9781423365662, Brilliance MP3) Brilliance Audio.

Feathers. unabr. ed. Jacqueline Woodson. Read by Sisi Aisha Johnson. 3 CDs. (Running Time: 3 hrs.). (J). (gr. 4-7). 2008. audio compact disk 62.25 (978-1-4233-6565-5(8), 9781423365655, BriAudCD Unabrid) Brilliance Audio.

Feathers & Other Stories. unabr. ed. Raymond Carver. Read by Tim Behrens. 2 cass. (Running Time: 2 hrs.). Dramatization. 1992. 16.95 (978-1-55686-460-5(4), 460) Books in Motion.
Three stories; Feathers, Menudo, & Vitamins. In Feathers, a childless, married couple is invited to dinner at the home of a co-worker. Upon arrival, they are confronted by a gregarious peacock who thinks he is human.

Feathers from My Nest: A Mother's Reflections. unabr. ed. Beth Moore. Narrated by Beth Moore. (ENG.). 2005. 12.59 (978-1-60814-199-9(3)); audio compact disk 17.99 (978-1-59859-016-6(2)) Oasis Audio.

Feathers in the Fire. unabr. ed. Catherine Cookson. Read by Susan Jameson. 8 cass. (Running Time: 8 hrs.). 1996. 69.95 set. (978-0-7451-6579-0(6), CAB1195) AudioGO.
Davie Armstrong watched, as his master Angus McBain, thrashed young Molly Geary for refusing to name the man who had dishonored her. And yet, not an hour later, Davie saw them alone in the malthouse, with Molly acting quite promiscuous. In a whirl of disbelieving rage, he overhears McBain's plan to have Davie take the blame & marry Molly. But it is the upcoming birth of McBain's legitimate son, Amos, who will bring disaster to all at Cock Shield Farm.

Feathers in the Fire. unabr. collector's ed. Catherine Cookson. Read by Mary Woods. 7 cass. (Running Time: 10 hrs. 30 min.). 1985. 56.00 (978-0-7366-0944-9(X), 1887) Books on Tape.
Davy Armstrong struggles hard for his place at Cock Shield Farm. He finds himself at odds with the owner, a man of mordant temper & villainous pride, whom the gods humble by sending him a son, born crippled. Davy's trials include the love of two women one he scorns, the other he marries.

Featured Flutist. Created by Boston Music Company. 2006. pap. bk. 9.95 (978-0-8256-3475-8(X), Boston Mus) Pub: Music Sales. Dist(s): H Leonard

Featured Flutist Made Easy. Created by Boston Music Company. 2006. pap. bk. 9.95 (978-0-8256-3476-5(8), Boston Mus) Pub: Music Sales. Dist(s): H Leonard

Featured Pianist. Created by Boston Music Company. 2006. pap. bk. 12.95 (978-0-8256-3477-2(6), Boston Mus) Pub: Music Sales. Dist(s): H Leonard

Featured Pianist Made Easy. Created by Boston Music Company. 2006. pap. bk. 12.95 (978-0-8256-3478-9(4), Boston Mus) Pub: Music Sales. Dist(s): H Leonard

Featured Violinist. Ed. by Rebecca Taylor. 2006. pap. bk. 9.95 (978-0-8256-3479-6(2), Boston Mus) Pub: Music Sales. Dist(s): H Leonard

Featured Violinist Made Easy! Ed. by Rebecca Taylor. 2006. pap. bk. 9.95 (978-0-8256-3480-2(6), Boston Mus) Pub: Music Sales. Dist(s): H Leonard

Featuring the Saint. unabr. ed. Leslie Charteris. Read by David Case. 5 cass. (Running Time: 5 hrs.). (Saint Ser.). 1990. 30.00 (978-0-7366-1823-6(6), 2659) Books on Tape.
Scene: the Calumet Club, where those in the know take a narrow flight of steps down into a basement room, dimly lighted, intimate, mysterious. One evening Simon Templar, aka the Saint, & always in the know, has a reason to visit the club. Sitting quietly by himself, he sees a man slip something into the drink of an exceptionally pretty young girl. Templar moves quickly, with results that startle the girl & give the man apoplexy.

Feaver see Love Poems of John Donne

Febrile Child - Respiratory Distress. Gary Fleisher & Joseph E. Simon. (Pediatric Emergencies: The National Conference for Practioners Ser.). 1986. 9.00 (978-0-932491-69-5(3)) Res Appl Inc.

Febrile Infant & Toddler. Contrib. by Margaret C. Fisher et al. 1 cass. (American Academy of Pediatrics UPDATE: Vol. 16, No. 9). 1998. 20.00 Am Acad Pediat.

***Fed Up! Our Fight to Save America from Washington.** unabr. ed. Rick Perry. Read by Ric Rietz. Frwd. by Newt Gingrich. (Running Time: 7 hrs.). (ENG.). 2010. 18.98 (978-1-60941-014-8(9)); audio compact disk 24.98 (978-1-60941-015-5(7)) Pub: Hachet Audio. Dist(s): HachBkGrp

Federal Appellate Practice. Contrib. by Leonard I. Garth. 3 cass. (Running Time: 4 hrs.). 1985. 80.00 incl. program handbook. NJ Inst CLE.
Assists attorneys in learning what is required to get an appeal validly documented, becoming sensitive to the emergency mechanism that can be utilized in federal appellate practice & understanding the new rules that impose sanctions for procedural defects.

Federal Budget Process: Capitol Learning Audio Course. Phil Joyce. Prod. by TheCapitol.Net. (ENG.). 2008. 47.00 (978-1-58733-083-4(0)) TheCapitol.

Federal BudgetObserver: Version 3. 0. Des. by George D. Krumbhaar. Created by Peter Cole. 2006. audio compact disk 34.50 (978-1-4276-0541-2(6)) AardGP.

Federal Civil Court Practice. (Running Time: 6 hrs.). 1995. 92.00 Incl. 349p. coursebk. (20561) NYS Bar.
Focuses on practice & procedure in the federal district court & is designed to familiarize the general practitioner, general litigator or other attorney who has not had extensive exposure to the federal court system with the theory, practice & tactics of litigating civil matters in federal court.

Federal Courts. 2nd rev. ed. John C. Jeffries, Jr. 3 cass. (Running Time: 3 hrs.). (Gilbert Law Summaries Ser.). (C). 2002. 39.95 (978-0-15-900372-5(5)) Barbri Grp.

Federal Courts, 2005 ed. (Law School Legends Audio Series) John C. Jeffries. (Law School Legends Audio Ser.). 2006. 52.00 (978-0-314-16098-0(1), gilbert); 46.95 (978-0-314-16097-3(3)) West.

Federal Estate & Gift Taxation. Stephen T. Galloway & Richard M. Feldheim. 6 cass. 159.00 set, incl. textbk. & quizzer. (CPE0550) Bisk Educ.
Provides proven, practical advice on how to take advantage of this area.

Federal Income Tax. Frank Doti. 4 cass. (Running Time: 3 hrs. 15 min.). (Outstanding Professor Ser.). 1996. 49.95 Set. (978-1-57793-017-4(7)) Sum & Substance.
Lecture by a prominent American law school professor.

Federal Income Tax 2d. 2nd rev. ed. Cheryl Block. 2002. 45.95 (978-0-15-900884-3(0)) West.

Federal Income Tax, 2005 ed. (Law School Legends Audio Series) Cheryl D. Block. (Law School Legends Audio Ser.). 2006. 52.00 (978-0-314-16100-0(7), gilbert); 51.95 (978-0-314-16099-7(X), gilbert) West.

Federal Personnel Guide on CD-ROM, 2005 Edition: Employment * Pay * Benefits * Civil Service * Postal Service. Ed. by Sandra M. Harris. 2005. audio compact disk 14.95 (978-1-881097-21-1(8)) Key Comm Grp.

Federal Regulatory Process: Piecing Together the Regulatory Puzzle (CD) Featuring Kenneth Ackerman. Prod. by TheCapitol.Net. 2006. 107.00 (978-1-58733-040-7(7)) TheCapitol.

Federal-State Workshop on Habeas Corpus Law. 3 cass. (Running Time: 13 hrs. 30 min.). 1999. Set; incl. 265p. study guide. Am Law Inst.
Third Circuit workshop designed for federal & state judges, prosecutors, & defense attorneys includes the changes effected by the Anti-Terrorism & Effective Death Penalty Act.

Federal Tax Advisor. Sidney Kess & Barbara Weltman. 6 cass. per year. 169.00 set. (9657) Toolkit Media.

Federal Tax Incentives for Historic Preservation. 1987. bk. 120.00; 75.00; 45.00 book only. PA Bar Inst.

Federal Tax Research. Gail L. Richmond. 3 cass. 1995. bk. 159.00 set. (CPE0065) Bisk Educ.
Gain an overall familiarity of the research process. Coverage includes an overview to tax research, primary legislative sources, primary administrative sources, primary judicial sources, citators, encyclopedias, form books, etc.

Federal Vision: Light or Dark. Read by Douglas Wilson & Rich Lusk. 2005. 8.00 (978-1-59128-484-0(8)) Canon Pr ID.

Federal Vision: Light or Dark. Read by Douglas Wilson & Lusk Rich. 2005. 6.00 (978-1-59128-482-6(1)) Canon Pr ID.

Federalism in the Third Century of the Constitution. American Bar Association, Urban, State and Local Government Law Section Staff. 2 cass. (Running Time: 2 hrs.). 1985. 22.95 (PC:533-0020-01) Amer Bar Assn.
Focuses on the concept of federalism.

Federalist Papers. Alexander Hamilton et al. Read by Jim Killavey. 6 cass. (Running Time: 6 hrs.). 1989. 42.00 (C-189); 47.00 incl. album. Jimcin Record.
In defense of the constitution.

Federalist Papers. George H. Smith. Read by Craig Deitschman. (Running Time: 9000 sec.). (Audio Classics Ser.). 2006. audio compact disk 25.95 (978-0-7861-7325-9(4)) Pub: Blckstn Audio. Dist(s): NetLibrary CO

***Federalist Papers.** unabr. ed. Alexander Hamilton. Read by Michael Edwards. (Running Time: 20 hrs. 30 mins.). 2010. 44.95 (978-1-4417-4115-8(1)); audio compact disk 123.00 (978-1-4417-4112-7(7)) Blckstn Audio.

Federalist Papers. unabr. ed. Alexander Hamilton et al. Read by Michael Edwards. 14 cass. (Running Time: 20 hrs. 30 mins.). 1989. 89.95 (978-0-7861-0035-4(4), 1034) Blckstn Audio.
These 85 letters in support of the Constitution have become recognized as the most important political science work ever written in the United States.

***Federalist Papers.** unabr. ed. Alexander Hamilton et al. Narrated by Arthur Morey. (Running Time: 23 hrs. 0 mins.). 2010. 25.99 (978-1-4526-7020-1(X)); 34.99 (978-1-4526-5020-3(9)); audio compact disk 45.99 (978-1-4526-0020-8(1)) Pub: Tantor Media. Dist(s): IngramPubServ

Federalist Papers. unabr. collector's ed. Alexander Hamilton et al. Read by Jim Killavey. 6 cass. (Running Time: 6 hrs.). 1988. 36.00 (978-0-7366-3944-6(6), 9189) Books on Tape.
Examines the series of popular essays that laid the intellectual & moral cornerstones for the American Revolution. Written by Alexander Hamilton, John Jay & James Madison these short pieces were widely circulated & generated extensive support for the independence movement.

Federalist Papers: Alexander Hamilton, James Madison, John Jay. abr. ed. George H. Smith & Wendy McElroy. Narrated by Craig Deitschman. 2 cass. (Running Time: 3 hrs.). Dramatization. (Giants of Political Thought Ser.: Vol. 9). 1986. 17.95 (978-0-938935-09-4(7), 390273) Pub: Knowledge Prod. Dist(s): APG
During the bitter debate over the ratification of the U.S. Constitution, this series of articles was published in various newspapers as a campaign to swing the pivotal state of New York. The presentation includes the essential ideas of this classic work, with a narrative explanation of the author's character, his times, the controversies he faced & the opinions of critics & supporters.

Federalist Papers Set: No. 1, 2, 3, 4, 5, 10, 15, 51 & U. S. Constitution. unabr. ed. Alexander Hamilton & James Madison. Read by Robert L. Halvorson. 2 cass. (Running Time: 180 min.). 14.95 (64) Halvorson Assocs.

***Federalist Papers (Library Edition)** unabr. ed. Alexander Hamilton et al. Narrated by Arthur Morey. (Running Time: 23 hrs. 0 mins.). 2010. 45.99 (978-1-4526-2020-6(2)); audio compact disk 109.99 (978-1-4526-3020-5(8)) Pub: Tantor Media. Dist(s): IngramPubServ

Federation. Scott Price. 1 CD. (Running Time: 1 hr. 30 mins.). 2000. audio compact disk 14.95 (978-0-7390-1505-6(2), 19766) Alfred Pub.

Federation. Judith Reeves-Stevens. (Star Trek Ser.). 2004. 10.95 (978-0-7435-4637-9(7)) Pub: S&S Audio. Dist(s): S and S Inc

Federigo & the Falcon see Piece of String

Feed. M. T. Anderson. Read by David Aaron Baker. 3 vols. (Running Time: 5 hrs. 2 mins.). (J). (gr. 7 up). 2004. pap. bk. 38.00 (978-1-4000-9022-8(9), Listening Lib) Random Audio Pubg.

Feed. abr. ed. M. T. Anderson. Read by David Aaron Baker et al. 3 cass. (Running Time: 5 hrs. 2 mins.). (J). (gr. 7 up). 2004. 30.00 (978-0-8072-1654-5(2), Listening Lib); audio compact disk 38.25 (978-0-8072-1773-3(5), Listening Lib) Pub: Random Audio Pubg. Dist(s): NetLibrary CO

Feed. unabr. ed. M. T. Anderson. Read by David Aaron Baker. (Running Time: 18600 sec.). (J). (gr. 7). 2008. audio compact disk 30.00 (978-0-7393-5620-3(8), Listening Lib) Pub: Random Audio Pubg. Dist(s): Random

***Feed.** unabr. ed. Mira Grant. Read by Jesse Bernstein & Paula Christensen. (Running Time: 15 hrs.). (Newsflesh Trilogy). (ENG.). 2010. 26.98 (978-1-60788-512-2(3)) Pub: Hachet Audio. Dist(s): HachBkGrp

Feed My Pig. Neville Goddard. 1 cass. (Running Time: 62 min.). 1963. 8.00 (27) J & L Pubns.
Neville taught Imagination Creates Reality. He was a powerfully influential teacher of God as Consciousness.

Feed My Sheep. unabr. ed. Read by Gayle D. Erwin. 1 cass. (Running Time: 1 hr.). 1992. 4.95 (978-1-56599-523-9(6), C-23) Yahshua Pub.
John 21: 1-19.

Feed the Tiger. James Tomasi. 3 cass. (Running Time: 3 hrs.). 2001. 19.95 (978-0-9709344-1-3(6)); audio compact disk 29.95 Internat Christian.
The autobiography of James Tomasi, President of J.C.S. It follows his life of greed, corruption & moral decay to meeting his Christ & a changed life style.

Feed Your Brain: Program from the Award Winning Public Radio Series. Hosted by Fred Goodwin. Comment by John Hockenberry. Contrib. by Andrew Weil & Lou Marinoff. 1 cass. (Running Time: 1 hr.). (Infinite Mind Ser.). 1998. audio compact disk 21.95 (978-1-888064-47-6(1), LCM 8) Lichtenstein Creat.
Top nutritional experts talk about eating for a healthy brain. With Dr. Andrew Weil, author of the best-selling books Spontaneous Healing and Eight Weeks To Optimum Health. With John Hockenberry and listener calls.

Feeding a Giant Audo CD. Read by Crisp Enterprises. 2009. audio compact disk 29.95 (978-1-892018-04-5(7)) R Crisp Ent.

Feeding Skinny Faith: Room for Doubt Series. Ben Young. 2000. 4.95 (978-0-7417-6206-1(4), B0206) Win Walk.

Feeding the Complete Person: Generally Overlooked Facts about Nutrition. Instructed by Manly P. Hall. 8.95 (978-0-89314-116-5(X), C800152) Philos Res.

Feeding the Demons. unabr. ed. Gabrielle Lord. Read by Nicki Paull. 9 cass. (Running Time: 11 hrs. 35 mins.). 2004. 72.00 (978-1-74030-590-7(6)) Pub: Bolinda Pubng AUS. Dist(s): Lndmrk Audiobks

Feeding the Hungry Heart. Geneen Roth. 4 CDs. (Running Time: 4 Hrs). 2005. audio compact disk 29.95 (978-1-59179-366-3(1), AW00261D) Sounds True.
On this live workshop, Geneen Roth shows you how to get off the diet/ binge roller coaster for good. For more than 25 years, her bestselling books and workshops have helped thousands of former dieters stop struggling - and start living. Why do we eat too much? To comfort ourselves and distance ourselves from painful feelings, says Roth. This is why diets are ineffective - and destructive. Here are the tools to transform your painful cravings into a love for food, your body, and your life.

Feeding the Mind with "Junk" Ideas. Instructed by Manly P. Hall. 8.95 (978-0-89314-117-2(8), C820523) Philos Res.

Feeding the Starved Marriage: 5 Keys to a Fat Happy Marriage. unabr. ed. Matt Townsend. (ENG.). 2006. 14.98 (978-1-59659-109-7(9), GildAudio) Pub: Gildan Media. Dist(s): HachBkGrp

Feeding Your Appetites. Stephen Arterburn & Debra Cherry. Ed. by Stephen Arterburn. 5 CDs. (Running Time: 6 hrs.). 2004. audio compact disk 40.00 (978-0-7861-8377-7(2), 3366) Blckstn Audio.

Feeding Your Appetites. unabr. ed. Arterburn Stephen. 4 cass. (Running Time: 6 hrs.). 2004. 25.99 (978-1-58926-701-5(X), 6701) Oasis Audio.

Feeding Your Appetites: Satisfy Your Wants, Needs & Desires Without Compromising Yourself. unabr. ed. Stephen Arterburn. Narrated by Stephen Arterburn. 5 CDs. (Running Time: 6 hrs.). (ENG.). 2004. audio compact disk 27.99 (978-1-58926-702-2(8), 6702) Oasis Audio.

Feeding Your Appetites: Satisfy Your Wants, Needs & Desires Without Compromising Yourself. unabr. ed. Stephen Arterburn. Narrated by Stephen Arterburn. (ENG.). 2004. 19.59 (978-1-60814-200-2(0)) Oasis Audio.

Feel: The Power of Listening to Your Heart. unabr. ed. Matthew Elliott. Narrated by Rob Lamont. (ENG.). 2008. 18.19 (978-1-60814-201-9(9)) Oasis Audio.

Feel: The Power of Listening to Your Heart. unabr. ed. Matthew Elliott. Read by Kelly Ryan Dolan. Narrated by Rob Lamont. (ENG.). 2008. audio compact disk 25.99 (978-1-59859-371-6(4)) Oasis Audio.

Feel Good Tape. Dick Sutphen. 1 cass. (Running Time: 1 hr.). (RX17 Ser.). 14.98 (978-0-87554-396-3(0), RX160) Valley Sun.

Feel Great, Be Beautiful over Forty: Inside Tips on How to Look Better, Be Healthier & Slow the Aging Process. abr. ed. Lillian Muller. Read by Lillian Muller. 2 cass. (Running Time: 3 hrs.). 1996. 16.95 (978-1-882071-67-8(0)) B-B Audio.
Lillian Muller, looks and feels better and is healthier and happier today at 43 years old and the mother of a three year old child, than when she was in her twenties as Playboys 1976 Playmate of the Year. Years of personal research have illuminated Lil.

Feel of Music. Perf. by Hap Palmer. 1 cass. (J). 11.95 (EA 556C); lp 11.95 (EA 556) Kimbo Educ.
Joy - Move & Rest - Soft & Loud - Good Old Fashioned Rock & Roll & more.

Feel Secure Now. Dick Sutphen. 1 cass. (Running Time: 1 hr.). (RX17 Ser.). 1986. 14.98 (978-0-87554-310-9(3), RX119) Valley Sun.
You feel safe, protected & secure. You are mentally fortified with inner strength. Every day in every way, you feel more confident of your ability to handle anything. You are a fortress of mental security. You are strong, stable & secure. You are at peace with yourself, the world & everyone in it.

Feel the Fear & Do It Anyway: Dynamic Techniques for Turning Fear, Indecision, & Anger into Power, Action, & Love. abr. ed. Susan Jeffers. Read by Susan Jeffers. 2 CDs. (Running Time: 10 hrs. 0 mins. 0 sec.). (ENG., 2001. audio compact disk 15.00 (978-0-7435-0918-3(8), Nightgale) Pub: S&S Audio. Dist(s): S and S Inc
Success can be yours with Susan Jeffers's Feel the Fear and Do it Anyway The world's foremost producer of personal development and motivational audio programs gives you the tools to face the fears that hold you back. We're all afraid of something: beginnings, endings, changing, getting stuck. But fear doesn't have to hold you back from happiness or success. You can change your relationship with fear - and in this dynamic, inspirational program, Susan Jeffers, Ph.D., teaches compassionate concepts and highly effective exercises that help you unravel the complexities and reverse the effects of fear. You'll learn: The five truths about fears How to weed negatives out of your words and thoughts How to develop goals that help extend your self-imposed limitations Don't be prisoner of you own insecurities. Career growth, personal harmony and financial rewards can by yours - when you learn to Feel the Fear and Do It Anyway.

Feel the Fear & Do It Anyway: Dynamic Techniques for Turning Fear, Indecision, & Anger into Power, Action, & Love. unabr. ed. Susan Jeffers. Read by Susan Jeffers. 4 cass. (Running Time: 6 hrs.). (ENG.). 1993. 25.00 (978-1-56170-057-8(6), 312) Hay House.
Dr. Susan Jeffers, bestselling author, reads her book & shows listeners concrete techniques to turn passivity into assertiveness & re-educate their minds to think more positively.

Feel the Fear & Do It Anyway Set: Dynamic Techniques for Turning Fear, Indecision, & Anger into Power, Action, & Love. Susan Jeffers. Read by Susan Jeffers. 8 CDs. 2007. audio compact disk 34.95 (978-1-4019-1970-2(7)) Hay House.

Feel the Fear Guide to Lasting Love. abr. ed. 3 CD's. (Running Time: 10800 sec.). 2005. audio compact disk 22.95 (978-0-9745776-6-1(9)) Pub: Jeffers Pr. Dist(s): Natl Bk Netwk
Author reading of an abridged version of the book with the same title. Using her own experiences and real-life stories, Susan Jeffers explains her perspective for creating a superb relationship for life. Learn her empowering techniques to help you transform your fears and anger into caring and appreciation so that your ability to love grows by leaps and bounds. Become empowered to replace destructive habits with positive thoughts and actions that will keep love vibrant and alive.

Feel the Music. Perf. by Parachute Express Staff. 1 cass., 1 CD. (J). 7.98 (TLR 1003); audio compact disk 11.18 CD Jewel box. (TLR 1003) NewSound.

Feel Yourself in Motion: Songs & Poems. unabr. ed. Judith Steinbergh & Victor Cockburn. Read by Judith Steinbergh & Victor Cockburn. 1 cass. (Running Time: 1 hr. 05 min.). (J). 1986. 10.00 (978-0-944941-10-2(9)) Talking Stone Pr.
Songs & poems about relationships & about the environment.

Feelin' at Home. Contrib. by Bill & Gloria Gaither and Their Homecoming Friends. (Gaither Gospel Ser.). 2006. 19.99 (978-5-558-40902-4(9)) Gaither Music Co.

Feelin' Good: Songs for Families to Share. Featuring Lisa Michaelis. Prod. by Laughing Pizza Productions Staff & Billy Schlosser. 1 CD. (Running Time: 60 mins.). 2002. audio compact disk 14.95 (978-0-9726038-2-9(4), Feelin Good) Laughing Pizza.
12 sing-a-long pop songs for families to share. Featuring Lisa Michaelis her husband Billy Schlosser and their daughter Emily.

Feeling - A Form of Prayer. Judith Barr. 1 cass. (Spoken Word on Behalf of the Feminine Ser.). 1994. 12.32 (978-1-886264-04-5(X)) Mysteries of Life.
Women's spirituality - psychology.

Feeling Bad about Feeling Bad. Ann Seagrave & Faison Covington. Read by Ann Seagrave & Faison Covington. (Anxiety Treatment Ser.). 15.50 CHAANGE.
Discusses one of life's important issues - that of responding productively & appropriately to the problems & distress that befall people.

Feeling Better: The Mind-Body Connection. Lloyd Glauberman. 2 cass. (Hypno-Peripheral Processing Tapes Ser.). 34.95 Set. (851PA-6M) Nightingale-Conant.
This breakthrough psychotechnology program combines the methods of hypnotherapy with the latest teachings of Neuro-Linguistic Programming. Each high-impact tape gently overloads your conscious mind with messages on two channels at once, creating a synergistic whole that unleashes both hemispheres of your brain.

Feeling Complete/God Doesn't Judge. Marianne Williamson. Read by Marianne Williamson. 1 cass. (Running Time: 90 mins.). (Lectures on a Course in Miracles). 1999. 10.00 (978-1-56170-193-3(9), M721) Hay House.

Feeling Fat: Touching Deep with Music. Howard Richman. 1 cass. (Running Time: 15 min.). (Entrainment Music Ser.). 1988. 15.95 (978-0-929060-59-0(8)) Sound Feelings.
Transformational music to help the emotional & physical symptoms of those who feel fat.

Feeling Fine Affirmations. Louise L. Hay. Read by Louise L. Hay. Music by Jai Josefs. 1 cass. (Running Time: 50 min.). 1990. 10.95 (978-0-937611-43-2(3), 215) Hay House.
Positive affirmations to establish a loving relationship with you & your body.

Feeling Fine Affirmations. Louise L. Hay. 1 CD. 2004. audio compact disk 10.95 (978-1-4019-0417-3(3)) Hay House.

Feeling Forgiveness: Guided Spiritual Meditations. unabr. ed. John D. Lentz. 1 CD. (Running Time: 30 min.). 2005. audio compact disk 14.95 (978-0-9740978-1-7(0)) Pub: Healing Words. Dist(s): STL Dist NA

Feeling Good: Four Guided Imagery Journeys for Healing Mind, Body & Spirit. Peggy Haymes & Susan Lautemann. 1. (Running Time: 80 minutes). 2004. audio compact disk 10.95 (978-0-9741775-1-9(2)) W Summit.

Feeling Good: The New Mood Therapy. abr. ed. David D. Burns. 1 cass. 2000. 17.95 (978-1-55935-333-5(3)) Soundelux.
Outlines his clinically proven drug-free treatment for depression.

Feeling Good about Yourself & Your Job. Ben Bissell. (Running Time: 40 min.). 15.00 C Bissell.
Captures the ingredients necessary for self-esteem. Recorded live, it gives you a sense of being there.

Feeling Good Now! New Rapid Recovery Techniques for Depression & Low Self-Esteem. Based on a work by David D. Burns. (ENG.). 2009. (978-0-9840694-0-8(2)) IAHB.

Feeling Good Together. David D. Burns. Read by Alan Sklar. (Playaway Adult Nonfiction Ser.). (ENG.). 2009. 64.99 (978-1-60812-545-6(9)) Find a World.

Feeling Good Together: The Secret to Making Troubled Relationships Work. unabr. ed. David Burns. Narrated by Alan Sklar. (Running Time: 8 hrs. 30 mins. 0 sec.). (ENG.). 2009. audio compact disk 34.99 (978-1-4001-0820-6(9)) Pub: Tantor Media. Dist(s): IngramPubServ

Feeling Good Together: The Secret to Making Troubled Relationships Work. unabr. ed. David D. Burns. Narrated by Paul Boehmer & Alan Sklar. (Running Time: 8 hrs. 30 mins. 0 sec.). (ENG.). 2009. audio compact disk 24.99 (978-1-4001-5820-1(6)) Pub: Tantor Media. Dist(s): IngramPubServ

Feeling Good Together: The Secret to Making Troubled Relationships Work. unabr. ed. David D. Burns. Narrated by Paul Boehmer. (Running Time: 8 hrs. 30 mins. 0 sec.). (ENG.). 2009. audio compact disk 69.99 (978-1-4001-3820-3(5)) Pub: Tantor Media. Dist(s): IngramPubServ

Feeling Great; Owning Joy. Eldon Taylor. 2 cass. 29.95 Set. (978-1-55978-747-5(3), 4412) Progress Aware Res.

Feeling of Power see Science Fiction Favorites of Isaac Asimov

Feeling of Power see Isaac Asimov Library

Feeling of What Happens: Body & Emotion in the Making of Consciousness. unabr. ed. Antonio Damasio. Narrated by George Guidall. 9 cass. (Running Time: 12 hrs. 30 mins.). 2000. 81.00 (978-0-7887-4407-5(0), 96185E7) Recorded Bks.
A distinguished professor & internationally renowned researcher in the field of neuroscience, the author makes the complex world of neurology both literary & accessible to the layman. He answers the age-old questions of how we develop a sense of self & how we know what we know.

Feeling Pain/Five Principles. Marianne Williamson. Read by Marianne Williamson. 1 cass. (Running Time: 90 mins.). (Lectures on a Course in Miracles). 1999. 10.00 (978-1-56170-310-4(9), M780) Hay House.

Feeling Safe & Secure. Created by Zoilita Grant. 2001. audio compact disk 15.95 (978-1-890575-27-4(5)) Zoilita Grant.

Feeling Sorry for Celia. Jaclyn Moriarty. Narrated by Anushka Carter. 5 cass. (Running Time: 6 hrs. 30 mins.). (YA). 2001. 58.75 (978-1-4193-0425-5(9)) Recorded Bks.

Feeling Stressed: Touching Deep with Music. Howard Richman. 1 cass. (Running Time: 22 min.). (Entrainment Music Ser.). 1988. 15.95 (978-0-929060-58-3(X)) Sound Feelings.
Transformational music to help release the deep long-term stress linked to pain, insomnia, addictions.

Feeling Weak? Logos September 19, 1999. Ben Young. 1999. 4.95 (978-0-7417-6148-4(3), B0148) Win Walk.

Feeling Without Limitation. abr. ed. Da Avabhasa. 1 cass. 1983. 11.95 (ATFWL) Dawn Horse Pr.

Feelings. Matthew Richardson. 1 cass. 1995. 7.95 (978-1-57008-095-1(X), Bkcraft Inc) Deseret Bk.

Feelings - Choice or Curse? Set: The Secret to Choosing How You Feel. David Grudermeyer & Rebecca Grudermeyer. 2 cass. 18.95 INCL. HANDOUTS. (T-31) Willingness Wrks.

Feelings Book. Todd Parr. 2000. audio compact disk 4.79 (978-1-58824-878-7(X)) ipicturebks LLC.

Feelings Bundle: Including - The Okay Book, It's Okay to Be Different, the Feelings Book, the Feel Good Book, Things That Make You Feel Good. unabr. ed. Todd Parr. (Running Time: 15 mins.). (ENG.). 2009. 10.98 (978-1-60788-362-3(7)) Pub: Hachet Audio. Dist(s): HachBkGrp

Feelings Buried Alive Never Die. Karol K. Truman. Read by Paul Kuhn & Mary Young. 6 cass. (Running Time: 9 hrs.). 1993. 35.00 (978-0-911207-01-9(5)) Olympus Distributing Corp.
Read word for word. Assists with resolving feelings to gain inner peace.

Feelings Buried Alive Never Die. Karol K. Truman. 2007. audio compact disk 39.95 (978-0-911207-07-1(4)) Olympus Distributing Corp.

Feelings Journey. Karol K. Truman. 6 cass. (Running Time: 8 hrs. 35 mins.). 1995. 35.00 (978-0-911207-05-7(8)) Olympus Distributing Corp.
Assists you with resolving some of the significant stumbling blocks to achieving inner peace. Uses principles & tools from the book "Feelings Buried Alive Never Die...".

Feelings 101: How to Distinguish Feelings from Thoughts. David Grudermeyer & Rebecca Grudermeyer. 2 cass. (Running Time: 3 hrs.). instr.'s hndbk. ed. 18.95 (T-05) Willingness Wrks.

Feelings 102: An Owner's Guide to the Skillful Use of Feelings. David Grudermeyer & Rebecca Grudermeyer. 2 cass. (Running Time: 3 hrs.). instr.'s hndbk. ed. 18.95 (T-09) Willingness Wrks.

***Feels Like Family.** unabr. ed. Sherryl Woods. (Running Time: 11 hrs.). (Sweet Magnolias Ser.). 2010. 19.99 (978-1-4418-6468-0(7), 9781441864680, BAD); 39.97 (978-1-4418-6469-7(5), 9781441864697, BADLE) Brilliance Audio.

***Feels Like Family.** unabr. ed. Sherryl Woods. Read by Janet Metzger. (Running Time: 11 hrs.). (Sweet Magnolias Ser.). 2010. 19.99 (978-1-4418-6466-6(0), 9781441864666, Brilliance MP3); 39.97 (978-1-4418-6467-3(9), 9781441864673, Brinc Audio MP3 Lib); audio compact disk 19.99 (978-1-4418-6464-2(4), 9781441864642, Bril Audio CD Unabri); audio compact disk 79.97 (978-1-4418-6465-9(2), 9781441864659, BriAudCD Unabrid) Brilliance Audio.

Fees (The Fairies) see Contes de Perrault

Feet of Clay. unabr. ed. Terry Pratchett. Read by Nigel Planer. 8 CDs. (Running Time: 10 hrs. 15 mins.). (Discworld Ser.). (J). 2000. audio compact disk 79.95 (978-0-7531-0744-7(9), 107449) Pub: ISIS Lrg Prnt GBR. Dist(s): Ulverscroft US

Feet of Clay. unabr. ed. Terry Pratchett. Read by Nigel Planer. 8 cass. (Running Time: 8 hrs.). (Discworld Ser.). (J). 2001. 69.95 (978-0-7531-0519-1(5), 990903) Pub: ISIS Lrg Prnt GBR. Dist(s): Ulverscroft US
Who's murdering harmless old men? Who's poisoning the Patrician? As autumn fogs hold Ankh-Morpork in their grip, the City Watch have to track down a murderer who can't be seen. Maybe the golems know something, but the solemn men of clay, who work all day & night & are never any trouble to anyone, have started to commit suicide. Whom can you trust when there are mobs on the street & plotters in the night & all the clues point the wrong way? In the gloom of the night, Watch Commander Sir Samuel Vimes finds that the truth may not be out there after all.

Feet of Clay: Logos 12/06/98. Ben Young. 1998. 4.95 (978-0-7417-6110-1(6), B0110) Win Walk.

Feet on the Street: Rambles Around New Orleans. unabr. ed. Roy Blount, Jr. Narrated by Paul Boehmer. 3 cass. (Running Time: 4 hrs.). 2005. 28.00 (978-1-4159-1569-1(5)); audio compact disk 36.00 (978-1-4159-1656-8(X)) Books on Tape.
Humorist Blount makes an attempt to present his observations about one of America's most eclectic cities, but this book probably won't get too many listeners packing their bags. The author's humor seems forced, whether he's talking about oysters, the backward-flowing Mississippi, or a mnemonic game for memorizing New Orleans's streets.

Felices Fiestas. Greg Skipper & Gail Skipper. (SPA.). 2001. 10.00 (978-0-311-48297-9(X)) Casa Bautista.

Felicia's Journey. unabr. ed. William Trevor. Narrated by Simon Prebble. 6 cass. (Running Time: 8 hrs. 30 mins.). 1999. 51.00 (978-0-7887-0323-2(4), 94515E7) Recorded Bks.
Felicia is young & pregnant, having stolen away from a small Irish town to search for her boyfriend in the industrial sprawl of the English Midlands. Fat, 50ish & unfailingly reasonable, Mr. Hilditch is looking for a new friend to join the five other girls he has "befriended." Under Trevor's master hand, both characters become startlingly sympathetic in their tragic dance from which only one of them will emerge victorious and alive.

Felicia's Journey. unabr. collector's ed. William Trevor. Read by David Hilder. 8 cass. (Running Time: 8 hrs.). 1995. 48.00 (978-0-7366-3120-4(8), 3796) Books on Tape.
Mr. Hilditch is fiftyish, neighborly, with a pleasant smile. But he's got a chilling pastime: killing women. Left lonely by the loss - or disappearance - of his five young women "friends," Mr. Hilditch looks for a new friend.

felicidad en tiempos de Crisis. Cesar Lozano. (SPA.). (YA). 2008. audio compact disk 16.95 (978-1-935405-84-9(5)) Hombre Nuevo.

Felicity: An American Girl. Valerie Tripp. Narrated by Carrie Hitchcock. (Running Time: 25200 sec.). (J). 2005. audio compact disk 19.99 (978-1-4193-6627-7(0)) Recorded Bks.

Felicity: An American Girl. unabr. ed. Valerie Tripp. Read by Carrie Hitchcock. 6 cass. (Running Time: 6 hrs. 45 mins.). (J). 2005. 59.75 (978-1-4193-5927-9(4), 98187) Recorded Bks.
Meet Felicity Merriman, a nine-year-old girl who's as spirited and independent as the American colonies she lives in. In 1774, Felicity's hometown of Williamsburg, Virginia, is buzzing with rumors: will the colonies soon break free from England's rule? Patriots like Felicity's father don't think it's fair to pay taxes to the King of England for things like tea that they buy in America. Loyalists like Felicity's grandfather and her best friend Elizabeth support the king. With fiercely conflicting loyalties dividing family and friends, something as simple as a cup of tea could change Felicity's world forever. Can she find the courage to stand strong for her own beliefs - even if it might mean losing her best friend? Six best-selling Felicity stories are included in this set: Meet Felicity, Felicity Learns a Lesson, Felicity's Surprise, Happy Birthday, Felicity!, Felicity Saves the Day, and Changes for Felicity.

Felix Holt, the Radical. unabr. ed. George Eliot. Read by Flo Gibson. 11 cass. (Running Time: 16 hrs.). 1998. 34.95 (978-1-55685-563-4(X)) Audio Bk Con.
Political electioneering, legal problems over inheritance, mystery concerning the heroine's birth, Felix Holt's ardent efforts to better the lot of the lower classes & rivalry for Esther's love make up the grand sweep of this novel.

Felix Holt, the Radical. unabr. ed. George Eliot. Read by Nadia May. 13 cass. (Running Time: 19 hrs.). 1999. 85.95 (978-0-7861-1727-7(3), 2519) Blckstn Audio.
Esther's "airs & graces," her proud & sensitive dreams of marrying into a life of refinement are transformed in the course of the novel, as she marks her choice between Harold Transome, who has returned to Treby Magna to claim his inheritance, Transome Court & to campaign in the wake of the 1832 Reform Act for a Radical seat in Parliament & Felix Holt, a young radical of a different kind.

Felix Holt, the Radical. unabr. ed. George Eliot. Read by Nadia May. (Running Time: 64800 sec.). 2006. audio compact disk 120.00 (978-0-7861-5938-3(3)); audio compact disk 44.95 (978-0-7861-7066-1(2)) Blckstn Audio.

Felix in the Underworld. unabr. ed. John Mortimer. Read by Martin Jarvis. 6 cass. (Running Time: 9 hrs.). 1998. 49.95 (978-0-7540-0127-0(X), CAB1550) Pub: Chivers Audio Bks GBR. Dist(s): AudioGO
Writer Felix Morsom no longer writes bestsellers. Then he hears about Gavin, a man destroyed by the Parental Rights & Obligations Department. They meet & he is introduced to Miriam who claims that Felix is the father of her son. He then finds himself the chief suspect in a murder case. Seeking the real murderer, Felix enters London's underworld, where he finds friendship, grace & hard times.

Feliz Cumpleanos. Lone Morton & Mary Risk. 1 cass. (Running Time: 20 min.). (I Can Read Bks.).Tr. of Happy Birthday. (ENG & SPA., (J). (ps up). 1998. 9.95 (978-0-7641-7192-5(5)) Barron.
Repeats every word of the bilingual text in both languages so that children can hear exactly how the words sound.

Feliz Mundo Nuevo. abr. ed. Aldous Huxley. 3 CDs.Tr. of Brave New World. (SPA.). 2006. audio compact disk 17.00 (978-958-8218-68-7(3)) YoYoMusic.

Fell. M. E. Kerr, pseud. Narrated by Jeff Woodman. 4 CDs. (Running Time: 4 hrs.). (YA). 1987. audio compact disk 39.75 (978-1-4025-7400-9(2)) Recorded Bks.

Fell. unabr. ed. David Clement-Davies. Read by Steven Crossley. 14 cass. (Running Time: 16 hrs. 50 mins.). (YA). (gr. 6 up). 2007. 102.75 (978-1-4281-3867-4(6)); audio compact disk 108.75 (978-1-4281-3872-8(2)) Recorded Bks.

Fell. unabr. ed. M. E. Kerr, pseud. Narrated by Jeff Woodman. 3 pieces. (Running Time: 4 hrs.). (gr. 7 up). 1994. 27.00 (978-0-7887-0015-6(4), 94214E7) Recorded Bks.
A working class teenager takes on a new identity as a rich student at an exclusive prep school. Will inspire thought-provoking discussions on class conflict & personal betrayal.

Fellini, Jung, & Yeats at the Movies. unabr. ed. Frank Barron. 1 cass. 1987. 9.00 (978-1-56964-474-4(8), A0009-87) Sound Photosyn.
A unique & clever comparison of works & personalities. This visit became the foundation of an Esalen workshop that is still warping the Akashic Records.

Fellowship. Derek Prince. 1 cass. (B-4012) Derek Prince.

Fellowship: The Distinguishing Mark of a Christian. Speeches. Creflo A. Dollar. 4 cass. (Running Time: 5 hrs.). 2001. 20.00 (978-1-59089-148-3(1)) Creflo Dollar.

Fellowship: The Lifestyle of a Christian. Speeches. Creflo A. Dollar. 5 cass. (Running Time: 6 hrs.). 2001. 25.00 (978-1-59089-150-6(3)) Creflo Dollar.

Fellowship of His Sufferings. Francis Frangipane. 1 cass. (Running Time: 90 mins.). (Disciples of the Cross Ser.: Vol. 1). 2000. 5.00 (FF01-001) Morning NC.
In this four-part series, Francis releases important information needed to clearly understand the principles of taking up the cross & following Christ.

Fellowship of the Burning Heart: A Collection of Sermons. A. W. Tozer. Contrib. by James L. Snyder. (Pure Gold Classics). (ENG., 2006. pap. bk. 13.99 (978-0-88270-219-3(X)) Bridge-Logos.

Fellowship of the Ring. unabr. ed. J. R. R. Tolkien. Narrated by Rob Inglis. 15 cass. (Running Time: 20 hrs. 30 mins.). (Lord of the Rings Ser.: Bk. 1). 2000. 120.00 (978-1-55690-321-2(9), 90014E7); audio compact disk 158.00 (978-0-7887-3957-6(3), C1112E7) Recorded Bks.
Inspired by The Hobbit, and begun in 1937, The Lord of the Rings is a trilogy that Tolkien created to provide "the necessary background of history for Elvish tongues." From these academic aspirations was born one of the most popular and imaginative works in English literature. The Fellowship of the Ring, the first volume in the trilogy, tells of the fateful power of the One Ring.

Fellowship of the Ring. unabr. ed. J. R. R. Tolkien. Narrated by Rob Inglis. 1 CD. (Lord of the Rings Ser.: Bk. 1). 1999. audio compact disk 158.00 (C1112) Recorded Bks.

Fellowship of the Ring. unabr. ed. J. R. R. Tolkien. Read by Rob Inglis. 12 cass. (Running Time: 20 hrs.). (Lord of the Rings Ser.: Bk. 1). (gr. 9-12). 2004. 34.99 (978-0-7887-8953-3(8), 00384); audio compact disk 49.99 (978-0-7887-8981-6(3), 00212) Recorded Bks.
Tells of the fateful power of the One Ring. It begins a magnificent tale of adventure that will plunge the members of the Fellowship of the Ring into a perilous quest and set the stage for the ultimate clash between powers of good and evil.

Fellowship of the Ring. unabr. ed. J. R. R. Tolkien. 8 cass. (Running Time: 12 hrs.). (Lord of the Rings Ser.: Bk. 1). 2002. (978-0-00-764608-1(9)) Zondervan.
In a sleepy village in the Shire, a young hobbit is entrusted with an immense task. He must make a perilous journey across Middle-earth to the Cracks of Doom, there to destroy the Ruling Ring of Power, the only think that prevents the Dark Lord's evil dominion.

Fellowship of the Ring. unabr. abr. ed. J. R. R. Tolkien. 3 CDs. (Running Time: 3 hrs. 30 mins.). Dramatization. Bk. 1. (ENG.). 2002. audio compact disk 19.95 (978-1-56511-667-2(4), 1565116674) Pub: HighBridge. Dist(s): Workman Pub

Fellowship of the Ring: Radio Dramatization. J. R. R. Tolkien. 4 CDs. (Running Time: 6 hrs.). (Lord of the Rings Ser.). (J). 2002. audio compact disk 49.95 (978-0-563-53055-8(3), BBCD 007) AudioGO.

Fellowship of the Son. Mark Chironna. 1 cass. 1992. 7.00 (978-1-56043-924-0(6)) Destiny Image Pubs.

Fellowship of Valor: The Battle History of the United States Marines. unabr. ed. Joseph H. Alexander et al. Narrated by Richard M. Davidson. 12 cass. (Running Time: 16 hrs. 30 mins.). 1998. 97.00 (978-0-7887-1884-7(3), 95306E7) Recorded Bks.
Col. Alexander's book celebrated the valiant accomplishments of the United States Marines from their first conflicts in 1776 to their diverse roles in today's troubled world.

Fellowship of Valor: The Battle History of the United States Marines. unabr. ed. Joseph H. Alexander et al. Narrated by Richard Davidson. 12 cass. (Running Time: 16 hrs. 30 mins.). 2002. 53.95 (RC935) Recorded Bks.
Packed with fascinating details and anecdotes, Col. Alexander's battle history celebrates the valiant accomplishments of the United States Marines from their first conflicts in 1776 to their diverse roles in today's troubled world. Backed with unerring accuracy and 10 years of careful research, this thrilling book is the basis for the documentary shown on The History Channel.

Fellrunner, Set. unabr. ed. Bob Langley. Read by Robbie MacNab. 7 cass. (Running Time: 9 hrs. 15 min.). 1999. 76.95 (978-1-85903-294-7(X)) Pub: Magna Story GBR. Dist(s): Ulverscroft US
By the time he was twenty-four, Lakeland shepherd Jonas Caudale had clocked up six fell-running records. When Jonas decided to run home to Buttermere across Nazi-occupied Europe, nobody knew he would become an international cause-celebre, but then no-one knew about the sinister mystery hidden within the Lakeland Peaks, or the secret torment eating at Jonas's soul. Why did the Official Secrets Act suppress the extraordinary story of Jonas Caudale's epic run for over fifty years?.

Female - Handle with Care. Peter Chambers. Read by Brian Rapkin. 4 cass. (Running Time: 6 hrs.). 1999. 44.95 (62981) Pub: Soundings Ltd GBR. Dist(s): Ulverscroft US

Female - Handle with Care. unabr. ed. Peter Chambers. 4 cass. (Sound Ser.). 2004. 44.95 (978-1-85496-298-0(1)) Pub: UlverLrgPrint GBR. Dist(s): Ulverscroft US

Female Authority: Clinical Applications of Animus Development. Read by Florence Wiedemann & Polly Young-Eisendrath. 3 cass. (Running Time: 4 hrs. 30 min.). 1988. 24.95 Set. (322) C G Jung IL.

Female Authority: Stages of Animus Development. Read by Florence Wiedemann & Polly Young-Eisendrath. 1 cass. (Running Time: 2 hrs.). 1988. 12.95 (978-0-7822-0324-0(8), 321) C G Jung IL.

Female of the Species. unabr. ed. Lionel Shriver. Read by Fred Stella. (Running Time: 14 hrs.). 2009. 24.99 (978-1-4233-9709-0(6), 9781423397090, Brilliance MP3); 24.99 (978-1-4233-9711-3(8), 9781423397113, BAD); 39.97 (978-1-4233-9710-6(X), 9781423397106, Brlnc Audio MP3 Lib); 39.97 (978-1-4233-9712-0(6), 9781423397120, BADLE); audio compact disk 36.99 (978-1-4233-9707-6(X), 9781423397076, Bril Audio CD Unabri); audio compact disk 97.97 (978-1-4233-9708-3(8), 9781423397083, BriAudCD Unabrid) Brilliance Audio.

Female Sexual Dysfunction. Bruce Goldberg. (ENG.). 2005. audio compact disk 17.00 (978-1-57968-046-6(1)) Pub: B Goldberg. Dist(s): Baker Taylor

Female Sexual Dysfunction. Bruce Goldberg. Read by Bruce Goldberg. 1 cass. (Running Time: 25 min.). (ENG.). 2005. 13.00 (978-1-885577-35-1(4)) Pub: B Goldberg. Dist(s): Baker Taylor
Overcome frigidity and increase sexual desire and enjoyment through self-hypnosis.

Female Sexuality. 1 cass. 10.00 (978-1-58506-023-8(2), 53) New Life Inst OR.
Sexual problems are a common concern for many people. These problems have been found to respond very well to subconscious suggestion. For sale only to adults.

Female Sexuality. Dick Sutphen. 1 cass. (Running Time: 1 hr.). (RX17 Ser.). 14.98 (978-0-87554-423-6(1), RX168) Valley Sun.

Female Sleuths. abr. ed. N. Hart Grafton. 4 cass. (Running Time: 6 hrs.). 1993. 25.95 (978-1-55935-117-1(9)) Soundelux.

Female Sleuths: Selections from a Woman's Eye. unabr. ed. Sara Paretsky et al. Read by Lorri Holt & Gina Leishman. 5 vols. (Great Mystery Ser.). 2001. audio compact disk 14.99 (978-1-57815-536-1(3), Media Bks Audio) Media Bks NJ.

Female Sleuths Set: Selections from a Woman's Eye. unabr. ed. Sue Grafton et al. Ed. by Sara Paretsky. 4 cass. (Running Time: 4 hrs.). 1994. vinyl bd. 21.95 (978-1-55935-149-2(7), 491985) Soundelux.
One of the hottest women mystery writers today has put together a collection of her favorite female sleuth authors.

Feminine Aggressiveness. Elizabeth Teissier. 1 cass. 8.95 (592) Am Fed Astrologers.
An AFA Convention workshop tape.

Feminine & Earth Spirituality. Zsuzsanna E. Budapest. 1 cass. 9.00 (A778-90) Sound Photosyn.
Neo-pagan rituals for the daily holiday.

Feminine As Hero. Read by Lois Khan. 1 cass. (Running Time: 2 hrs.). 1988. 12.95 (978-0-7822-0123-9(7), 332) C G Jung IL.

Feminine Consciousness. Marion Woodman. 2 cass. 18.00 (OC71L) Sound Horizons AV.

Feminine Factor in World Religions. Instructed by Manly P. Hall. 8.95 (978-0-89314-118-9(6), C850512) Philos Res.

Feminine Heart of Dharma. Swami Amar Jyoti. 1 cass. 1994. 9.95 (K-143) Truth Consciousness.
God the Father & Mother are One. Following the way of Dharma includes both law & compassion.

Feminine in Prayer. Vilma Seelaus. 1 cass. (Voices of John & Teresa Ser.). 1987. 7.95 (TAH175) Alba Hse Comns.
Explains how the feminine is a spirituality that grows from within & is affective as well as a revolutionary solidarity of women.

***Feminine Mistake CD.** abr. ed. Leslie Bennetts. Read by Leslie Bennetts. (ENG.). 2007. (978-0-06-143826-4(X), Harper Audio); (978-0-06-143825-7(1), Harper Audio) HarperCollins Pubs.

Feminine Modesty-mp3. Douglas Wilson. 2001. 9.50 (978-1-59128-236-5(5)) Canon Pr ID.

Feminine Modesty-tape. 4 cass. 2001. 12.00 (978-1-59128-238-9(1)) Canon Pr ID.

Feminine Muse: A Collection of Poetry & One Short Story. Karen Jean Matsko Hood. 2008. 29.95 (978-1-59649-032-1(2)); audio compact disk 24.95 (978-1-59649-031-4(4)) Whsprng Pine.

Feminine Mystique. unabr. ed. Betty Freidan. Read by Parker Posey. (Running Time: 16 hrs.). 2009. 24.99 (978-1-4233-9565-2(4), 9781423395652, Brilliance MP3); 39.97 (978-1-4233-9566-9(2), 9781423395669, Brlnc Audio MP3 Lib); 39.97 (978-1-4233-9567-6(0), 9781423395676, BADLE); audio compact disk 29.99 (978-1-4233-9563-8(8), 9781423395638, Bril Audio CD Unabri); audio compact disk 99.97 (978-1-4233-9564-5(6), 9781423395645, BriAudCD Unabrid) Brilliance Audio.

***Feminine Political Novel in Victorian England.** Barbara Leah Harman. (Victorian Literature & Culture Ser.). (ENG.). 27.50 (978-0-8139-2936-1(9)) U Pr of Va.

Feminine Principle. Vajracarya. Read by Chogyam Trungpa. 4 cass. 1975. 36.00 (A019) Vajradhatu.
Four talks: 1) Space & the Mother principle; 2) Concepts of Unborn, Unceasing, & Unoriginated; 3) Giving Birth to Reality; 4) The Dakini Principle.

Feminine Touch. Dan Cushman. (Running Time: 0 hr. 30 mins.). 1998. 10.95 (978-1-60083-483-7(3)) Iofy Corp.

Feminine Warrior: Balancing Love & Power. unabr. ed. Helaine Z. Harris. Read by Helaine Z. Harris. Contrib. by Pauline Moore. 1 cass. (Running Time: 56 min.). 1989. 11.00 (978-0-9652343-1-3(2)) An Awakening Encino.

***FeminineTouch.** Dan Cushman. 2009. (978-1-60136-472-2(5)) Audio Holding.

Femininity: Feminine Spirituality. Stuart Wilde. 1 cass. (Running Time: 1 hr.). (978-0-930603-43-4(5)) White Dove NM.
A woman's true warrior power lies deep within her. This subliminal tape reprograms your mind to remember that! The natural power & beauty within you is limitless. Realign & heal with the spiritual energy of Mother Earth.

Feminism & Pastoral Care: A Practical Approach. 1 cass. (Care Cassettes Ser.: Vol. 16, No. 1). 1989. 10.80 Assn Prof Chaplains.

Feminist Approaches to the Bible. Read by Phyllis Trible et al. Hosted by Hershel Shanks. 4 cass. (Running Time: 4 hrs. 30 min.). 1995. 32.95 set. (978-1-880317-43-3(5), 7HC4) Biblical Arch Soc.
Symposium at the Smithsonian Institution, September 24, 1994.

Feminist Fantasies. Phyllis Schlafly. (Running Time: 28800 sec.). 2005. audio compact disk 29.95 (978-0-7861-7860-5(4)) Blckstn Audio.

Feminist Fantasies. Phyllis Schlafly. Frwd. by Ann Coulter. (Running Time: 28800 sec.). 2005. 54.95 (978-0-7861-3781-7(9)); audio compact disk 63.00 (978-0-7861-7585-7(0)) Blckstn Audio.

Feminist Health Care Ethics. 1 cass. (Care Cassettes Ser.: Vol. 21, No. 4). 1994. 10.80 Assn Prof Chaplains.

Feminist Perspectives on Pastoral Care & Theology. 1 cass. (Care Cassettes Ser.: Vol. 16, No. 8). 1989. 10.80 Assn Prof Chaplains.

Feminist Poerty. Karen Jean Matsko Hood. 2010. audio compact disk 24.95 (978-1-59210-976-0(4)) Whsprng Pine.

Feminist Poetry: A Collection of Feminist Poems. Karen Jean Matsko Hood. 2005. 24.95 (978-1-59434-848-8(0)) Whsprng Pine.

Feminist Revolution: A Woman & Man Report from the Front. 9 cass. Incl. Feminist Revolution: An Introduction to the Series. Demaris Wehr & Patrick Henry. 1984.; Feminist Revolution: Conclusion: The Impact of Feminism on Our Lives, Relationships, & on the World. 1984.; Feminist Revolution: Feminism in Our Lives & in Academia. Elizabeth Gray & David D. Gray. 1984.; Feminist Revolution: Feminism in Our Lives & in the Church. Bob Ferguson & Peg Ferguson. 1984.; Feminist Revolution: My Personal Experience with Feminism. Patrick Henry & Demaris Wehr. 1984.; Feminist Revolution: The Feminist Revolution in Academia. Demaris Wehr & Patrick Henry. 1984.; Feminist Revolution: The Feminist Revolution in Religion. Demaris Wehr & Patrick Henry. 1984.; Feminist Revolution: The Feminist Revolution in Thought, Part I. Patrick Henry & Demaris Wehr. 1984.; Feminist Revolution: The Feminist Revolution in Thought, Part II. Patrick Henry & Demaris Wehr. 1984.; 1984. 28.00 Set.; 4.50 ea. Pendle Hill.

Feminist Revolution: An Introduction to the Series see Feminist Revolution: A Woman and Man Report from the Front

Feminist Revolution: Conclusion: The Impact of Feminism on Our Lives, Relationships, & on the World see Feminist Revolution: A Woman and Man Report from the Front

Feminist Revolution: Feminism in Our Lives & in Academia see Feminist Revolution: A Woman and Man Report from the Front

Feminist Revolution: Feminism in Our Lives & in the Church see Feminist Revolution: A Woman and Man Report from the Front

Feminist Revolution: My Personal Experience with Feminism see Feminist Revolution: A Woman and Man Report from the Front

Feminist Revolution: The Feminist Revolution in Academia see Feminist Revolution: A Woman and Man Report from the Front

Feminist Revolution: The Feminist Revolution in Religion see Feminist Revolution: A Woman and Man Report from the Front

Feminist Revolution: The Feminist Revolution in Thought, Part I see Feminist Revolution: A Woman and Man Report from the Front

Feminist Revolution: The Feminist Revolution in Thought, Part II see Feminist Revolution: A Woman and Man Report from the Front

Feminist Spirituality: Deepest & Most Significant Expression of the Women's Movement. Jean S. Bolen. 1 cass. 9.00 (A0279-89) Sound Photosyn.
Speaking at Stanford University, she is very convincing, & fills a short time with much information from the heart of the matter.

femme de Papier. unabr. ed. Francoise Rey. Read by Francoise Rey. (YA). 2007. 84.99 (978-2-35569-073-0(1)) Find a World.

Femme de Trente Ans, Set. abr. ed. Honoré de Balzac. Read by Pascal Monge. 2 cass. (FRE.). 1995. 26.95 (1749-KFP) Olivia & Hill.
The confessions of a young bride who married a goodlooking horseman & who is increasingly disappointed by the life she leads. An underlying brutality is ever present in a decor of luxury.

femme du Nil. unabr. ed. Brigitte Riebe. Read by Jean-Marie Galey. (YA). 2007. 79.99 (978-2-35569-005-1(7)) Find a World.

***Femme Fatale.** unabr. ed. Laura Lippman. Read by Linda Emond & Francois Battiste. 2008. (978-0-06-176300-7(4), Harper Audio); (978-0-06-176299-4(7), Harper Audio) HarperCollins Pubs.

femme Solaire. unabr. ed. Paule Salomon. Read by Paule Salomon. 2007. 69.99 (978-2-35569-087-7(1)) Find a World.

Femmes & le Pouvoir en France au XIIe. Georges Duby. 1 cass. (Running Time: 60 mins.). (College de France Lectures). (FRE.). 1996. 21.95 (1855) Olivia & Hill.

Femmes Savantes. Perf. by Mireille Perrey & Pierre Lecomte. (SAC 57-1) Spoken Arts.

Femmes Savantes, Set. Perf. by Francois Chaumette et al. Molière. 2 cass. (FRE.). 1991. 26.95 (1092-RF) Olivia & Hill.
In this comedy produced in 1672, Moliere ridicules the new vogue at the court of Louis XIV - the cult of grammar, philosophy & astronomy.

Fen-Phen Seventh Amendment Meeting Audiotape. Compiled by LexisNexis Staff. 2004. 399.00 (978-1-59579-477-2(8)) Pub: LexisNexis Mealey. Dist(s): LEXIS Pub

Fen Tiger. Catherine Cookson. Read by Anne Dover. 5 cass. (Running Time: 7 hrs. 30 mins.). 1999. 49.95 (64127) Pub: Soundings Ltd GBR. Dist(s): Ulverscroft US

***Fences Between Us: The Diary of Piper Davis.** Kirby Larson. (Dear America Ser.). (ENG.). 2010. audio compact disk 19.99 (978-0-545-24954-6(6)) Scholastic Inc.

***Fences Between Us: The Diary of Piper Davis.** unabr. ed. Kirby Larson. Read by Elaina Erika Davis. (Dear America Ser.). (J). 2010. audio compact disk 29.99 (978-0-545-24957-7(0)) Scholastic Inc.

Fencing Master. unabr. ed. Arturo Pérez-Reverte. Perf. by Michael York. 4 cass. (Running Time: 6 hrs.). 1999. 26.95 Set. (978-0-7871-1909-6(1)) S&S Audio.
Don Jaime de Astarloa is Spain's greatest fencing master. He lives an ordered & celibate life dedicated to his passion, the art of fencing. When a beautiful & mysterious woman destabilizes his existence, he is drawn into a violent web of corruption.

Feng Shui for Abundance. David Daniel Kennedy. (Running Time: 1 hr.). 2006. bk. 19.95 (978-1-59179-248-2(7), K896D) Sounds True.

Feng Shui Home Study Course. David Daniel Kennedy. 12 CDs. 2004. audio compact disk 129.00 (978-1-59179-103-4(0), AF00737D) Sounds True.

Feng Shui Now. L. Federici. 1 cass. (Running Time: 8 min.). On Move.

Fenimore Cooper to Membranous Croup. unabr. ed. Mark Twain. Read by Thomas Becker. 2 cass. (Running Time: 2 hrs. 10 min.). 1994. lib. bdg. 18.95 set incl. vinyl case with notes, author's picture & biography. (978-1-883049-32-4(6)) Sound Room.
A collection of ten stories & essays including: "Fenimore Cooper's Literary Offenses," "The Art of Authorship," "Punch-Brothers-Punch," "The Great Landslide Case," & "The Experience of the McWilliames with Membranous Croup.".

Fenimore Cooper to Membranous Croup, Set. unabr. ed. Short Stories. Mark Twain. Read by Thomas Becker. 2 cass. (Running Time: 2 hrs.). 1994. bk. 16.95 (978-1-883049-18-8(0), 390209, Commuters Library) Sound Room.
Collection includes: "Fenimore Cooper's Literary Offenses," "Punch-Brothers-Punch," "First Interview with Artemus Ward," "An Author's Soldiering," "To the California Pioneers," "The Great Landslide Case," "Political Economy," "Experience of the McWilliames with Membranous Croup," & "The McWilliames & the Burglar Alarm.".

Fenwick Houses. unabr. ed. Catherine Cookson. Read by Elizabeth Henry. 8 cass. (Running Time: 12 hrs.). (Sound Ser.). 2004. 69.95 (978-1-85496-052-8(0), 60520) Pub: UlverLrgPrint GBR. Dist(s): Ulverscroft US

Feodor Dostoevsky: The Grand Inquisitor. Excerpts. 2 cass. (Running Time: 1 hr. 40 mins.). (RUS.). bk. 39.50 (SRU210) J Norton Pubs.
A complete chapter from the novel "The Brothers Karamazov in which Ivan Karamazov narrates, as a "story within a story," an encounter between the Inquisitor & Christ, who has returned to the earth.

Fer-de-Lance. Rex Stout. Read by Michael Prichard. (Running Time: 8 hrs. 30 mins.). (Nero Wolfe Ser.). 2005. 27.95 (978-1-59912-386-8(X)) Iofy Corp.

Fer-de-Lance. unabr. ed. Rex Stout. Read by Michael Prichard. 6 cass. (Running Time: 8 hrs. 40 mins.). (Nero Wolfe Ser.). 2004. 29.95 (978-1-57270-035-2(1), N61035u) Pub: Audio Partners. Dist(s): PerseuPGW
The first Nero Wolfe mystery, this established the great detective in his New York brownstone with Archie as his assistant. They investigate the murders of an immigrant & a college president.

Fer-de-Lance. unabr. ed. Rex Stout. Narrated by Michael Prichard. 7 CDs. (Running Time: 8 hrs. 40 mins.). (Nero Wolfe Ser.). (ENG.). 2004. audio compact disk 29.95 (978-1-57270-388-9(1)) Pub: AudioGO. Dist(s): Perseus Dist

Fer-de-Lance. unabr. collector's ed. Rex Stout. Read by Michael Prichard. 6 cass. (Running Time: 9 hrs.). (Nero Wolfe Ser.). 1994. 48.00 (978-0-7366-2621-7(2), 3361) Books on Tape.
When someone makes a present of a fer-de-lance, the dreaded snake, to Nero Wolfe, Archie Goodwin knows he's close to solving two apparently unrelated murders. As for Wolfe, he's playing snake charmer in a case more deadly than a cobra - & whistling a seductive tune he hopes will catch a killer with poison in his heart.

Ferdinand Magellan: The First Voyage Around the World. unabr. ed. Betty Burnett. (Running Time: 2 hrs.). (Library of Explorers & Exploration Ser.). 2009. 39.97 (978-1-4233-9408-2(9), 9781423394082, Brinc Audio MP3 Lib); 39.97 (978-1-4233-9409-9(7), 9781423394099, BADLE); audio compact disk 39.97 (978-1-4233-9406-8(2), 9781423394068, BriAudCD Unabrid) Brilliance Audio.

Ferdinand Magellan: The First Voyage Around the World. unabr. ed. Betty Burnett. Read by Eileen Stevens. (Running Time: 2 hrs.). (Library of Explorers & Exploration Ser.). 2009. 19.99 (978-1-4233-9407-5(0), 9781423394075, Brilliance MP3); audio compact disk 19.99 (978-1-4233-9405-1(4), 9781423394051, Bril Audio CD Unabri) Brilliance Audio.

Ferdinando Carulli - Two Guitar Concerti (E Minor Op. 140 & A Major Op. 8a) Composed by Ferdinando Carulli. Christian Reichert. 2008. pap. bk. 34.98 (978-1-59615-761-3(5), 1596157615) Pub: Music Minus. Dist(s): H Leonard

Fereyel & Debbo the Witch see Spirits & Spooks for Halloween

Fergie: the United Years: The United Years. Tom Tyrrell. Read by Tom Tyrrell. (Running Time: 2 hrs.). 2006. 25.95 (978-1-59912-960-0(4)) Iofy Corp.

Fern Hill see Gathering of Great Poetry for Children

Fern Hill see Child's Christmas in Wales

Fern Hill see Dylan Thomas Reading His Poetry

Fern Hill see Caedmon Treasury of Modern Poets Reading Their Own Poetry

Fern Michaels: Fool Me Once; The Marriage Game; Up Close & Personal. abr. ed. Fern Michaels. Read by Laural Merlington. (Running Time: 18 hrs.). 2009. audio compact disk 34.99 (978-1-4233-7844-0(X), 9781423378440, BACD) Brilliance Audio.

***Fern Michaels: What You Wish For; Mr. & Miss Anonymous.** abr. ed. Fern Michaels. Read by Laural Merlington. (Running Time: 11 hrs.). 2010. audio compact disk 19.99 (978-1-4418-5038-6(4), 9781441850386, BACD) Brilliance Audio.

***Fern Michaels CD Collection 3: Vegas Rich, Vegas Heat, Vegas Sunrise.** abr. ed. Fern Michaels. Read by Laural Merlington. (Running Time: 9 hrs.). (Vegas Ser.). 2011. audio compact disk 29.99 (978-1-4418-7864-9(5), 9781441878649, BACD) Brilliance Audio.

Fern Michaels Collection: Listen to Your Heart; What You Wish For; Plain Jane. abr. ed. Fern Michaels. Read by Joyce Bean & Laural Merlington. (Running Time: 54000 sec.). 2005. 29.95 (978-1-59737-044-8(4), 9781597370448) Brilliance Audio.
Listen to Your Heart (Narrator: Joyce Bean, Director: Sandra Burr, Engineer: Melissa Coates): With her parents gone, her twin sister, Kitty, about to be married, and no hint of Mr. Right on the horizon, Josie Dupre is lonesome. Luckily, she has her booming New Orleans catering business, and her fluffy white dog, Rosie, to keep her company. Then, a jumbo-sized Boxer destroys Josie's flowering windowboxes, and in the process, brazenly captures petite Rosie's undying devotion. Josie finds herself an unwilling chaperone - and doing her best to avoid Zip's owner, the irritatingly appealing Paul Brouillette. What You Wish For (Narrator: Laural Merlington, Director: Laura Grafton, Engineer: Jill Sovis): If her abusive husband had not tried to kill her and her beloved dog, Helen Ward might never have left her million dollar home and run far away. When she meets college professor Sam Tolliver, she begins to believe fairy tales do come true. But the past is catching up with Helen - and her fear is growing. Soon, she'll have to face the biggest decision of her life. Plain Jane (Narrator: Laural Merlington, Director: Sandra Burr, Engineer: Jill Sovis): Back in college, plain Jane Lewis would have given anything to be like homecoming queen Connie Bryan. Today, a lovely and confident Dr. Jane Lewis has a thriving psychotherapy practice, her own radio talk show, a beautiful old Louisiana mansion, and her affectionate, nutty dog, Olive, to keep her company. But Jane has never forgotten Michael Sorenson, the boy she had admired from afar in college. She's also never forgotten the brutal, unsolved attack that ended Connie Bryan's life - and that haunts her still.

Fern Michaels Sisterhood CD Collection: Free Fall; Hide & Seek; Hokus Pokus. abr. ed. Fern Michaels. Read by Laural Merlington. (Running Time: 9 hrs.). (Sisterhood Ser.: Nos. 8-10). 2009. audio compact disk 29.99 (978-1-4418-1195-0(8), 9781441811950, BACD) Brilliance Audio.

Fern Michaels Sisterhood CD Collection: The Jury; Sweet Revenge; Lethal Justice. abr. ed. Fern Michaels. Read by Laural Merlington. (Running Time: 9 hrs.). (Sisterhood Ser.: Nos. 4-6). 2008. audio compact disk 29.95 (978-1-4233-5241-9(6), 9781423352419, BACD) Brilliance Audio.

Fern Michaels Sisterhood CD Collection: Weekend Warriors; Payback; Vendetta. abr. ed. Fern Michaels. Read by Laural Merlington. (Running Time: 18 hrs.). (Sisterhood Ser.). 2007. audio compact disk 34.95 (978-1-4233-2313-6(0), 9781423323136, Bril Audio CD Unabri) Brilliance Audio.

***Fern Michaels Sisterhood CD Collection 4: Fast Track, Collateral Damage, Final Justice.** abr. ed. Fern Michaels. Read by Laural Merlington. (Running Time: 9 hrs.). 2010. audio compact disk 29.99 (978-1-4418-5104-8(6), 9781441851048, BACD) Brilliance Audio.

Fern Michaels Texas Series CD Collection: Texas Rich; Texas Heat; Texas Fury; Texas Sunrise. abr. ed. Fern Michaels. Read by Laural Merlington. (Running Time: 24 hrs.). (Texas Ser.). 2007. audio compact disk 36.95 (978-1-4233-2311-2(4), 9781423323112, BACD) Brilliance Audio.

Fern Verdant & the Silver Rose. unabr. ed. Diana Leszczynski. (Running Time: 7 hrs. NaN mins.). 2008. 29.95 (978-1-4332-5382-9(8)); 54.95 (978-1-4332-5380-5(1)); audio compact disk 60.00 (978-1-4332-5381-2(X)) Blckstn Audio.

Fernandel. Interview with Jacques Chancel. 1 cass. (Radioscopie Ser.). (FRE.). 18.95 (1535-RF) Olivia & Hill.
Popular French comedian.

Fernando & Me. Based on a musical by Cathy Ellis. (ENG.). 2007. audio compact disk 22.95 (978-1-879542-60-0(9)) Ellis Family Mus.

Ferocious Beast with the Polka-Dot Hide: A Maggie & the Ferocious Beast Book. Betty Paraskevas. Narrated by John McDonough. 1 cass. (Running Time: 15 mins.). (ps up). 2001. 10.00 (978-0-7887-5352-7(5)) Recorded Bks.
When the ferocious beast with the polka-dot hide catches a piglet, he must decide whether to have him on whole wheat or rye brad. But the piglet saves his own life when he convinces the beast that the seams on his polka-dot hide are about to burst.

Ferris Beach. unabr. collector's ed. Jill McCorkle. Read by Donada Peters. 8 cass. (Running Time: 12 hrs.). 1991. 64.00 (978-0-7366-2005-5(2), 2822) Books on Tape.
Richly detailed & brimming with colorful small-town characters, this is the story of the changing South in the 1970s. Kate, daughter of Cleve & Alfred Tennyson Burns, is at a stage of life when everything is both wonderful & terrible. She's also caught in a kind of tug-of-war for her spirit, a contest between her prim & sensible mother & a beautiful & reckless cousin, Angela. Angela lives by the ocean, across the coastal plain, at a place called Ferris Beach. Angela is everything that Cleve Burns is not - imaginative & untethered as the wind. On one side Kate faces the pull of reason & safety & on the other the lure of romance, mystery & danger.

Fertigkeit Horen. Barbara Dahlhaus. 2 cass. (Running Time: 2 hrs. 40 mins.). (Fernstudienangebot Ser.: Vol. 5). (GER.). 2005. 15.95 (978-3-468-49671-4(0)) Langenscheidt.

Fertile Body Method: A Practicioner's Manual - The applications of Hypnosis in Mind-Body Approaches to Fertility. Sjanie Hugo. 2009. pap. bk. 49.95 (978-1-84590-096-0(0)) Crown Hse GBR.

Fertile Bodymind for Men. Susan A. Rothmann. Read by Susan A. Rothmann. Music by S. W. Mexcur. 1 cass. (Running Time: 1 hr.). (Fertile Imagination Ser.). 1998. 15.95 (978-0-9660540-5-7(9), F3003) Fertil Solns.
Guided imagery & affirmations designed for men in any part of the fertility process. Designed to support fertility & promote healing & wellness.

Fertile Rock. Contrib. by Chris Droney. (ENG.). 1995. audio compact disk 21.95 (978-0-8023-8110-1(3)) Pub: Clo Iar-Chonnachta IRL. Dist(s): Dufour

Fertile Rock. Contrib. by Chris Droney. (ENG.). 1995. 13.95 (978-0-8023-7110-2(8)) Pub: Clo Iar-Chonnachta IRL. Dist(s): Dufour

Fertility. unabr. ed. Garrison Keillor. Contrib. by Garrison Keillor. (ENG., 2008. audio compact disk 13.95 (978-1-59887-734-2(8), 1598877348) Pub: HighBridge. Dist(s): Workman Pub

Fertility Booster. Steven Gurgevich. (ENG.). 2002. audio compact disk 19.95 (978-1-932170-22-1(7), HWH) Tranceformation.

Fertility with Tina Taylor. Nick Kemp & Tina Taylor. (Running Time: 1 hr. 8 mins.). audio compact disk 24.95 (978-0-9545993-3-1(0)) Pub: Human Alchemy GBR. Dist(s): Crown Hse

Fesito Goes to Market: A Story from Nelson Mandela's Favorite African Folktales. Read by Don Cheadle. Compiled by Nelson Mandela. (Running Time: 16 mins.). (ENG.). 2009. 1.99 (978-1-60024-869-6(1)) Pub: Hachet Audio. Dist(s): HachBkGrp

Festival & Ritual Drumming: Rhythms of Spirit. Mishlen Linden & Louis Martinie. 1 cass. (Running Time: 1 hr.). 1993. 9.95 (978-0-89281-417-6(9), Destiny Audio Edits) Inner Tradit.

Festival of Gregorian Chants. Perf. by Monks of the Benedictine Abbey & L'Alumnat Boy's Choir. 1 cass. 5.98; audio compact disk 8.98 Lifedance.
Gregorian chants have a haunting, reverent quality to them that can be peaceful & serene. Male voices perform these liturgical pieces with one selection offering church bells in the background. Demo Cd or cassette available.

Festival of Lessons & Carols - ShowTrax. Arranged by John Leavitt. 1 CD. (Running Time: 30 mins.). 2000. audio compact disk 12.95 (08742431) H Leonard.
Based on the traditional English service held each year in King's College, Cambridge, this new work also holds enormous appeal to choirs looking to perform it in concert. Set for SATB choir with optional chamber orchestra, handbells & congregation, it is of the highest quality, yet crafted so that it will be successful with even medium-sized choirs from high school through adult. Includes: "As with Gladness Men of Old"; "Away in a Manger"; "Break Forth, O Beauteous Heavenly Light"; "Coventry Carol"; "Ding! Dong!" & more.

Festival of Lights. Perf. by New Troubadours. 1 cass. 9.98 (435); 12.98 Incl. songbook. (653) MFLP CA.
This joyous union of Father Christmas & Mother Earth inspired at Findhorn, Scotland celebrates the birth of light within each of us.

Festival of Lights: A Family Christmas Celebration. Contrib. by Tom Fettke. 2003. audio compact disk 90.00 (978-5-557-69326-4(2)) Lillenas.

Festival of Lights: A Family Christmas Celebration Arranged for Choirs of All Ages. Tom Fettke. 2003. 90.00 (978-5-557-69325-7(4)) Allegis.

Festivals. Jean Gilbert. 1998. 14.95 (978-0-19-321345-6(1)) OUP-CN CAN.

Festivals from Far Away. University of Iowa, CEEDE Staff. 3 cass. (VIE.). (YA). (gr. 7-12). 1988. 24.95 Set. (978-0-7836-1138-9(2), 8067); 24.95 Set. (978-0-7836-1133-4(1), 8066); 24.95 (978-0-7836-1129-7(3), 8065) Triumph Learn.
Stories about Indochinese ceremonies & customs for bilingual & ESL students.

Festivals from Far Away: Complete English Set. unabr. ed. University of Iowa, CEEDE Staff. 3 cass. 1988. 65.00 incl. student text, tchr's. guide & activity masters. (978-0-7836-0755-9(5), 8958) Triumph Learn.
Stories about Indochinese ceremonies & customs.

Festivals from Far Away: Complete Lao Set. unabr. ed. University of Iowa, CEEDE Staff. 4 cass. (LAO.). 1988. 65.00 incl. student text, tchr's. guide & activity masters. (978-0-7836-0756-6(3), 8959) Triumph Learn.

Festivals from Far Away: Complete Vietnamese Set. unabr. ed. University of Iowa, CEEDE Staff. 3 cass. (VIE.). 1988. 65.00 incl. student text, tchr's. guide & activity masters. (978-0-7836-0757-3(1), 8960) Triumph Learn.

***Festive Christmas: Upbeat Christmas Music for Your Holiday Gatherings - Featuring Gospel, Jazz, Panflute, & Other Styles.** Compiled by Barbour Publishing, Inc. (ENG.). 2010. audio compact disk 9.99 (978-1-61626-062-0(9), Barbour Bks) Barbour Pub.

Festivus: The Holiday for the Rest of Us. unabr. ed. Allen Salkin. Contrib. by Jerry Stiller. (Running Time: 2 hrs. 30 mins.). (ENG.). 2006. 14.98 (978-1-59483-647-3(7)) Pub: Hachet Audio. Dist(s): HachBkGrp

Festivus: The Holiday for the Rest of Us. unabr. ed. Allen Salkin. Contrib. by Jerry Stiller. (Running Time: 2 hrs. 30 mins.). (ENG.). 2009. 29.98 (978-1-60788-281-7(7)) Pub: Hachet Audio. Dist(s): HachBkGrp

Fetal Experimentation & the Human Genome Project. Steven Zielinski. 1 cass. 4.00 (95D) IRL Chicago.

***Fetch.** unabr. ed. Laura Whitcomb. Narrated by Jack Garrett. 10 cass. (Running Time: 11 hrs. 45 mins.). (YA). (gr. 6-10). 2009. 88.75 (978-1-4361-8774-9(5)); audio compact disk 108.75 (978-1-4361-8778-7(8)) Recorded Bks.

Fete de Celesteville. 1 cass. (FRE.). (J). (gr. 3 up). 1991. bk. 14.95 (1AD078) Olivia & Hill.
Babar invites all the animals to participate in the anniversary celebration of Celesteville, the city of elephants.

Fete Worse Than Death. Dolores Gordon-Smith. 2008. 69.95 (978-1-4079-0191-6(5)); audio compact disk 84.95 (978-1-4079-0192-3(3)) Pub: Soundings Ltd GBR. Dist(s): Ulverscroft US

Fetes Galantes. Poems. Paul Verlaine. Read by G. Bejean & J. Gouttenoire. 1 cass. (FRE.). 1991. 22.95 (1426-VSL) Olivia & Hill.
The poetry of this famous 19th-century lyric poet.

Fetish. Tara Moss. Read by Tara Moss. 2009. 74.99 (978-1-74214-270-8(2), 9781742142708) Pub: Bolinda Pubng AUS. Dist(s): Bolinda Pub Inc

Fetish. unabr. ed. Tara Moss. Read by Tara Moss. 6 cass. (Running Time: 7 hrs. 30 mins.). (Makedde Vanderwall Ser.: Bk. 1). 2004. 48.00 (978-1-74030-043-8(2), 500531); audio compact disk 83.95 (978-1-74093-079-6(7)) Pub: Bolinda Pubng AUS. Dist(s): Bolinda Pub Inc

***Fetish.** unabr. ed. Tara Moss. Read by Tara Moss. (Running Time: 7 hrs. 30 mins.). 2010. 43.95 (978-1-74214-579-2(5), 9781742145792) Pub: Bolinda Pubng AUS. Dist(s): Bolinda Pub Inc

Fettered for Life or Lord & Master, Set. unabr. ed. Lillie D. Blake. Read by Flo Gibson. 8 cass. (Running Time: 11 hrs.). 1998. bk. 26.95 (978-1-55685-539-9(7)) Audio Bk Con.
Written in 1874, this then-controversial novel takes up injustice to women with a vengence. Brutality in marriage, intolerance in the job market, general disrespect & no vote are among the issues with a romance intertwined.

Feu de Klo-ora, Set. Dan Dastier. Read by Yves Belluardo. 3 cass. (FRE.). 1995. 29.95 (1794-CO) Olivia & Hill.
Klo-Ora, the paradise planet which all space adventurers speak about & which perhaps exists only in dreams, is suddenly within the reach of Marcus. But at what price?.

Feud, unabr. collector's ed. Thomas Berger. Read by Christopher Hurt. 6 cass. (Running Time: 9 hrs.). 1989. 48.00 (978-0-7366-1524-2(5), 2395) Books on Tape.
The trouble begins when Dolf Beller, on an innocent mission for paint remover, chews an unfit cigar in Bud Bullard's hardware store, where no smoking is allowed. Within 24 hours the store burns down. Dolf's car blows up & the feud begins.

Feud That Sparked the Renaissance. unabr. ed. Paul Robert Walker. Read by Robert Whitfield. 8 CDs. (Running Time: 10 hrs.). 2003. audio compact disk 64.00 (978-0-7861-9180-2(5), 3097); 49.95 (978-0-7861-2462-6(8), 3097) Blckstn Audio.
Offers a glorious tour of fifteenth-century Florence, a bustling city on the verge of greatness, during a time of flourishing creativity.

***Fever.** 2010. audio compact disk (978-1-59171-192-6(4)) Falcon Picture.

Fever. Katherine Sutcliffe. Read by Anna Fields. 9 cass. (Running Time: 13 hrs. 30 mins.). 2001. 72.00 (978-0-7366-8079-0(9)) Books on Tape.
From the bayous of the American South comes a rush of steamy, lavish prose culminating in forbidden, passionate romance. A penniless orphan, Juliette Broussard is picked out of her isolated convent school by her godfather, Max Hollinsworth, to marry his lazy son Tylor - so that her family's run-down sugar cane plantation, BELLE JAROD, would be his. She is against marriage, until she falls in lust with her prospective husband. However, the plantation's overseer and Max's illegitimate son, Chantz Boudreaux, saves Juliette from the raging waters of the Mississippi and immediately falls in love with her. Together, they attempt to restore her ancestral estate, despite betrayal and plague.

Fever. unabr. ed. Robin Cook. Read by Donada Peters. 7 cass. (Running Time: 10 hrs. 30 min.). 1993. 56.00 (978-0-7366-2428-2(7), 3192) Books on Tape.
Cancer researcher blames chemical company for his daughter's battle with leukemia.

Fever. unabr. ed. Sean Rowe. Read by William Dufris. 5 cds. (Running Time: 5 hrs. 30 mins. 0 sec.). (ENG.). 2005. audio compact disk 24.99 (978-1-4001-0177-1(8)); audio compact disk 19.99 (978-1-4001-5177-6(5)); audio compact disk 49.99 (978-1-4001-3177-8(4)) Pub: Tantor Media. Dist(s): IngramPubServ

Fever. unabr. ed. Wallace Shawn. 2 CDs. (Running Time: 1 hr. 30 mins.). 2006. audio compact disk 11.98 (978-0-7389-3397-9(X)) Sony Music Ent.

Fever. unabr. ed. Katherine Sutcliffe. Read by Anna Fields. 9 cass. (Running Time: 13 hrs. 30 mins.). 2001. 54.00 Books on Tape.
A penniless orphan is slated to be married to her godfather's lazy son, but falls for the plantation overseer instead.

Fever: Twelve Stories. John Edgar Wideman. Read by John Edgar Wideman. (Running Time: 30 min.). 8.95 (AMF-234) Am Audio Prose.
Talks on creative interpretations of African-American history.

Fever - ShowTrax. Perf. by Peggy Lee. Arranged by Kirby Shaw. 1 CD. (Running Time: 5 mins.). 2000. audio compact disk 19.95 (08742344) H Leonard.
Peggy Lee's sizzling sound is adapted for SSA in a sensational setting.

***Fever Crumb - Audio.** Philip Reeve. Narrated by Philip Reeve. (ENG.). 2011. audio compact disk 34.99 (978-0-545-28279-6(9)) Scholastic Inc.

***Fever Crumb - Audio Library Edition.** Philip Reeve. (ENG.). 2011. audio compact disk 64.99 (978-0-545-28292-5(6)) Scholastic Inc.

Fever Dream see Fantastic Tales of Ray Bradbury

***Fever Dream.** Lincoln Child & Douglas Preston. Read by Rene Auberjonois. (Running Time: 7 hrs.). (ENG.). 2011. audio compact disk 14.98 (978-1-61113-815-3(9)) Pub: Hachet Audio. Dist(s): HachBkGrp

Fever Dream. abr. ed. Lincoln Child & Douglas Preston. (Running Time: 7 hrs.). 2010. 19.98 (978-1-60788-193-3(4)) Pub: Hachet Audio. Dist(s): HachBkGrp

Fever Dream. abr. ed. Lincoln Child & Douglas Preston. Read by Rene Auberjonois. 6 CDs. (Running Time: 7 hrs.). 2010. audio compact disk 29.98 (978-1-60788-192-6(6)) Pub: Hachet Audio. Dist(s): HachBkGrp

Fever Dream. unabr. ed. Lincoln Child & Douglas Preston. (Running Time: 14 hrs.). 2010. 29.98 (978-1-60788-195-7(0)) Pub: Hachet Audio. Dist(s): HachBkGrp

***Fever Dream.** unabr. ed. Lincoln Child & Douglas Preston. Narrated by Rene Auberjonois. 2 MP3-CDs. (Running Time: 14 hrs.). 2010. 69.99 (978-1-60788-532-0(8)); audio compact disk 114.99 (978-1-60788-531-3(X)) Pub: Hachet Audio. Dist(s): HachBkGrp

Fever Dream. unabr. ed. Lincoln Child & Douglas Preston. Read by Rene Auberjonois. 12 CDs. (Running Time: 14 hrs.). 2010. audio compact disk 44.98 (978-1-60788-194-0(2)) Pub: Hachet Audio. Dist(s): HachBkGrp

Fever Hill. unabr. ed. Michelle Paver. 12 cass. (Running Time: 14 hrs. 32 mins.). (Isis Cassettes Ser.). (J). 2004. 94.95 (978-0-7531-1612-8(X)); audio compact disk 104.95 (978-0-7531-2352-2(5)) Pub: ISIS Lrg Prnt GBR. Dist(s): Ulverscroft US

Fever of Unknown Origin. Read by Sheldon M. Wolff. 1 cass. (Running Time: 90 min.). 1986. 12.00 (C8639) Amer Coll Phys.

Fever Pitch, Set. unabr. ed. Nick Hornby. Read by Julian Rhind-Tutt. 8 cass. 1999. 69.95 (978-0-7540-0374-8(4), CAB1797) AudioGO.
Fever Pitch is the bitter-sweet autobiography which vividly recounts the elation & utter despair of a love affair with a particular football team. A phenomenal bestseller & William Hill Sports Book of the Year, this captures the truth & absurdities of the obsessed Arsenal fan's mind & whether you are interested in football or not, this is a sophisticated study of obsession, families, masculinity, class, identity, growing up, loyalty, depression & joy.

Fever Pitch, Set. unabr. ed. Nick Hornby. Read by Julian Rhind-Tutt. 8 CDs. (Running Time: 8 hrs.). 1999. audio compact disk 84.95 (978-0-7540-5317-0(2), CCD008) Pub: Chivers Audio Bks GBR. Dist(s): AudioGO

Fever 1793. unabr. ed. Laurie Halse Anderson. Read by Emily Bergl. 4 vols. (Running Time: 5 hrs. 45 mins.). (J). (gr. 5-9). 2004. pap. bk. 38.00 (978-0-8072-8719-4(9), LYA 246 SP, Listening Lib); 32.00 (978-0-8072-8718-7(0), Listening Lib) Random Audio Pubg.
Mattie Cook, a spirited 14-year-old girl, lives with her widowed mother who manages a coffee house during the late 1700's in Philadelphia, the nation's capital. During August of 1793, the yellow fever engulfs the city. Mattie must make decisions that affect herself, Eliza, a free black widow & friend, her grandfather & a orphaned girl, Nell.

Few: The American Knights of the Air Who Risked Everything to Fight in the Battle of Britain. Alex Kershaw. Read by Scott Brick. (Playaway Adult Nonfiction Ser.). 2008. 64.99 (978-1-60640-591-8(8)) Find a World.

Few: The American Knights of the Air Who Risked Everything to Fight in the Battle of Britain. abr. ed. Alex Kershaw. Read by Scott Brick. (Running Time: 21600 sec.). 2007. audio compact disk 14.99 (978-1-4233-1597-1(9), 9781423315971, BCD Value Price) Brilliance Audio.

Few: The American Knights of the Air Who Risked Everything to Fight in the Battle of Britain. unabr. ed. Alex Kershaw. Read by Scott Brick. (Running Time: 8 hrs.). 2006. 39.25 (978-1-4233-1595-7(2), 9781423315957, BADLE); 24.95 (978-1-4233-1594-0(4), 9781423315940, BAD); 39.25 (978-1-4233-1593-3(6), 9781423315933, Brlnc Audio MP3 Lib); 24.95 (978-1-4233-1592-6(8), 9781423315926, Brilliance MP3); 74.25 (978-1-4233-1589-6(8), 9781423315896, BrilAudUnabridg); audio compact disk 92.25 (978-1-4233-1591-9(X), 9781423315919, BriAudCD Unabrid); audio compact disk 34.95 (978-1-4233-1590-2(1), 9781423315902, Bril Audio CD Unabri) Brilliance Audio.
Optioned for a feature film by Tom Cruise and Michael Mann (Collateral, The Insider), The Few tells the story of a group of American Flyboys recruited by Winston Churchill to help in the fight against Nazi Germany. In the summer of 1940, World War II had been underway for nearly a year. Hitler was triumphant and the United States was neutral. But some Americans did not remain so. The worst days of the Battle of Britain - July 10 to September 15 - saw seven U.S. pilots fighting side by side with the English. They included ex-barnstormers, a farm-boy, and a millionaire playboy. Idealists, adventurers, and romantics, this motley crew of thrill-seekers cajoled their way into the Royal Air Force, defying the U.S. government to fly the remarkably lethal Spitfire and become the "knights of the air." They dueled with the brilliant Luftwaffe in the greatest man-on-man contest in the history of aviation. They also fell in love with England's finest "roses," shot down several of Herman Goering's aces, and were feted as national heroes. By October 1940, they had helped win the Battle of Britain, long before America entered WWII. In the mold of Stephen Ambrose, Kershaw is fast becoming the next great popular military historian.

Few Cents Worth. unabr. ed. Hushion House Staff. 1 cass. (Running Time: 90 min.). 2002. 9.95 (978-1-896617-07-7(7), SMA006) Stuffed Moose CAN.
Let some of the world's greatest humorists help you with life's little problems: how to raise chickens, how to serenade, how to stay in a gothic mansion.

Few Good Men Soundtrack. Prod. by Myattic Studio. (YA). 2000. audio compact disk 89.95 (978-0-7365-3277-8(3)) Films Media Grp.

Few Green Leaves. unabr. ed. Barbara Pym. Read by Jan Francis. 8 cass. (Running Time: 12 hrs.). 2000. 59.95 (SAB 005) Pub: Chivers Audio Bks GBR. Dist(s): AudioGO
Examines the quiet revolution of English village life as Emma Howick, a single anthropologist in her thirties, returns to her home town. Unexpectedly, an old flame now separated from his wife, moves into a nearby cottage.

Few Late Roses. Anne Doughty. 2008. 76.95 (978-1-4079-0162-6(1)); audio compact disk 84.95 (978-1-4079-0163-3(X)) Pub: Soundings Ltd GBR. Dist(s): Ulverscroft US

Few Loose Chapters 4 CD Audio Book. Thomas Henry Kelly. 4 CDs. 2007. audio compact disk 35.00 (978-1-56142-199-2(5)) T Kelly Inc.

Few More Pretty Good Jokes: A Prairie Home Companion. abr. unabr. ed. Garrison Keillor. 1 CD. (Running Time: 1 hr.). (ENG.). 2002. audio compact disk 14.95 (978-1-56511-729-7(8), 1565117298) Pub: HighBridge. Dist(s): Workman Pub

Few Seconds of Panic: A 5-Foot-8, 170-Pound, 43-Year-Old Sportswriter Plays in the NFL. Stefan Fatsis. Read by Stefan Fatsis. (Playaway Adult Nonfiction Ser.). 2008. 64.99 (978-1-60640-856-8(9)) Find a World.

Few Seconds of Panic: A 5-Foot-8, 170-Pound, 43-Year-Old Sportswriter Plays in the NFL. unabr. ed. Stefan Fatsis. (Running Time: 12 hrs. 0 mins. 0 sec.). (ENG.). 2008. audio compact disk 69.99 (978-1-4001-3767-1(5)) Pub: Tantor Media. Dist(s): IngramPubServ

Few Seconds of Panic: A 5-Foot-8, 170-Pound, 43-Year-Old Sportswriter Plays in the NFL. unabr. ed. Stefan Fatsis. Narrated by Stefan Fatsis. (Running Time: 12 hrs. 0 mins. 0 sec.). (ENG.). 2008. audio compact disk 24.99 (978-1-4001-5767-9(6)) Pub: Tantor Media. Dist(s): IngramPubServ

Few Seconds of Panic: A 5-Foot-8, 170-Pound, 43-Year-Old Sportswriter Plays in the NFL. unabr. ed. Stefan Fatsis. Read by Stefan Fatsis. (Running Time: 12 hrs. 0 mins. 0 sec.). (ENG.). 2008. audio compact disk 34.99 (978-1-4001-0767-4(9)) Pub: Tantor Media. Dist(s): IngramPubServ

Few Short Notes on Tropical Butterflies, Stories. John Murray. Read by Spinella Stephen. 1975. 14.95 (978-0-06-074372-7(7)) HarperCollins Pubs.

Few Words of a Kind see Dylan Thomas Reading On the Marriage of a Virgin, Over Sir John's Hill, In Country Sleep & Others

Feynman Lectures on Physics, Vols. 9 &10. Richard Phillips Feynman. 12 CDs. (Running Time: 43200 sec.). (ENG.). 1906. audio compact disk 69.95 (978-0-7382-0928-9(7)) Pub: Basic. Dist(s): Perseus Bks Grp

Feynman Lectures on Physics Pt. 2: Feynman on Electricity & Feynamn on Electromagnetis. Richard Phillips Feynman. (Running Time: 43200 sec.). (Feynman Lectures on Physics Ser.: Vols. 15 & 16). (ENG.). 1911. audio compact disk 69.95 (978-0-7382-0931-9(7)) Pub: Basic. Dist(s): Perseus Bks Grp

Feynman Lectures on Physics Vols. 1 & 2: Quantum Mechanics & Advanced Quantum Mechanics. Richard Phillips Feynman. (ENG.). 2003. audio compact disk 69.95 (978-0-7382-0924-1(4)) Pub: Basic. Dist(s): Perseus Bks Grp

Feynman Lectures on Physics Vols. 3 & 4: From Crystal Structure to Magnetism & Electrical & Magnetic Behavior. Richard Phillips Feynman. 12 CDs. (ENG.). 2004. audio compact disk 69.95 (978-0-7382-0925-8(2)) Pub: Basic. Dist(s): Perseus Bks Grp

Feynman Lectures on Physics Vols. 5 & 6: Commemorative Issue, Vol. 3. Richard Phillips Feynman. 1 cass. (Running Time: 1 hr.). 1999. 40.00 Basic.

Feynman Lectures on Physics Vols. 5 & 6: Energy & Motion; Kinetics & Heat. Richard Phillips Feynman. (ENG., (C). 2004. audio compact disk 59.95 (978-0-7382-0283-9(5)) Pub: Basic. Dist(s): Perseus Bks Grp

Feynman Lectures on Physics Vols. 7 & 8: Feynman on Mechanics & Feynman on Light. Richard Phillips Feynman. (Running Time: 43200 sec.). (ENG.). 2006. audio compact disk 59.95 (978-0-7382-0927-2(9)) Pub: Basic. Dist(s): Perseus Bks Grp

Feynman Lectures on Physics Vols. 11 & 12: Feynman on Science & Vision - Feynman on Sound. Richard Phillips Feynman. (Running Time: 43200 sec.). (Feynman Lectures on Physics). (ENG.). 1911. audio compact disk 69.95 (978-0-7382-0929-6(5)) Pub: Basic. Dist(s): Perseus Bks Grp

Feynman Lectures on Physics Vols. 13 & 14: Feynman on Fields - Feynman on Electricity & Magnetism, Part 1. Richard Phillips Feynman. Read by Richard Phillips Feynman. (Running Time: 43200 sec.). 1911. audio compact disk 69.95 (978-0-7382-0930-2(9)) Pub: Basic. Dist(s): Perseus Bks Grp

Feynman Lectures on Physics Vols. 17 & 18: Feynman on Electrodynamics & Feynman on Flow. Richard Phillips Feynman. (ENG.). 1911. audio compact disk 69.95 (978-0-7382-0932-6(5)) Pub: Basic. Dist(s): Perseus Bks Grp

Feynman Lectures on Physics Vols. 19&20: Quantum Mechanics & Electromagnetism. Richard Phillips Feynman. (ENG.). 1911. audio compact disk 65.00 (978-0-7382-0933-3(3)) Pub: Basic. Dist(s): Perseus Bks Grp

Feynman Tapes Vol. 1: Chief Research Chemist & Other Stories. Short Stories. Ed. by Ralph Leighton. As told by Richard Phillips Feynman. 1 audio CD. (Running Time: 57 mins). 2002. audio compact disk 14.95 (978-1-58490-018-4(0)) Scientific Consulting.

Fibber McGee & Molly. 1 cass. (Running Time: 60 min.). (Old Time Radio Classic Singles Ser.). 4.95 (978-1-57816-100-3(2), FM109) Audio File.
Includes: 1) Edgar Bergen & Charlie McCarthy visit Wistful Vista for the premier of "Look Who's Laughing." (11/11/41). 2) Molly's old boyfriend visits Wistful Vista. This was Jim Jordan's favorite program with Gale Gordon, Hal Peary. (12/26/39) Johnson's Wax.

Fibber McGee & Molly. 1 CD. (Running Time: 1 hr.). (Old-Time Radio Blockbusters Ser.). 2002. audio compact disk 4.98 (978-1-57019-393-4(2), OTR7704) Pub: Radio Spirits. Dist(s): AudioGO
Incl.: "Amusement Park," and "Off to Hollywood.".

Fibber Mcgee & Molly. Perf. by Jim Jordan & Marion Jordan. 2009. audio compact disk 35.95 (978-1-57019-890-8(X)) Radio Spirits.

Fibber McGee & Molly. Perf. by Charlie McCarthy et al. 1 cass. (Running Time: 60 min.). 7.95 (CC-7000) Natl Recrd Co.
The first sketch finds Fibber & Molly with Charley & Edgar at the airport, as they are all to attend the world premier of their new film. In the second sketch Fibber & Molly are at the train depot putting Uncle Sycamore on the train to Peoria when they meet Molly's old boyfriend; with Mel Blanc & Hal Peary.

***Fibber Mcgee & Molly.** RadioArchives.com. (Running Time: 360). (ENG.). 2010. audio compact disk 17.98 (978-1-61081-183-5(6)) Radio Arch.

Fibber McGee & Molly. collector's ed. Perf. by Bob Sweeney et al. 1 DVD. (Running Time: 3 hrs.). (TV from Yesteryear Ser.). 2001. bk. 9.98 (7802) Radio Spirits.
Contains three classic television shows and three complete old time radio shows.

Fibber McGee & Molly. unabr. ed. 1 cass. (Running Time: 58 min.). Incl. Fibber McGee & Molly: Fibber as a Dress Form. (#480); Fibber McGee & Molly: The Pipe Smoker. (#480); 12.95 (#480) J Norton Pubs.
The first broadcast has to do with Molly losing her opportunity to represent the Ladies' Club when the President of the Club walks in on Fibber who is posing in lieu of a dress form, with a cigar, hairy legs, & foul temper. The second episode concerns Fibber's giving up cigar smoking because he got a bargain in pipe tobacco, but since he can't light the pipe through the whole show, he goes back to his cigars.

Fibber McGee & Molly, Set. 2 cass. (Running Time: 2 hrs.). (Old Time Radio Classic Singles Ser.). vinyl bd. 10.95 (978-1-57816-051-8(0), FM2401) Audio File.
Includes: "March 5, 1940" Trying to find her misplaced dictionary, Molly decides to look in the hall closet. This is the first McGee show to use the now classic closet gag! "April 7, 1942" When Mrs. Uppington asks the McGees to contribute to the wartime scrap drive, Molly decides that it's time to clean out the hall closet. "March 21, 1944" Fibber has a frustrating time with his friends when he discovers his old mandolin in the hall closet. "January 7, 1947" When Fibber hears a radio news bulletin about some escaped criminals, he decides to defend himself & searches for his gun in the hall closet.

Fibber McGee & Molly, Vol. 1. collector's ed. Perf. by Jim Jordan & Marian Jordan. 6 cass. (Running Time: 9 hrs.). 1998. bk. 34.98 (4006) Radio Spirits.
It's back to 79 Wistful Vista & Fibber's famous "hall closet" of memories. 17 episodes.

Fibber McGee & Molly, Vol. 2. 1 cass. (Running Time: 60 min.). (Old Time Radio Classic Singles Ser.). 4.95 (978-1-57816-101-0(0), FM231) Audio File.
Includes: 1) Fibber wants to hear his Uncle Sycamore on the radio. (4/13/43). 2) Fibber tries to collect an old debt (2/24/48).

Fibber McGee & Molly, Vol. 2. (Running Time: 2 hrs.). 2004. 10.95 (978-1-57816-167-6(3)); audio compact disk 12.95 (978-1-57816-173-7(8)) Audio File.

Fibber McGee & Molly, Vol. 2. collector's ed. Perf. by Jim Jordan & Marian Jordan. 6 cass. (Running Time: 9 hrs.). 1998. bk. 34.98 (4042) Radio Spirits.
Includes Briefcase Bronson, Fibber, the Paper Boy, Working on Mrs. Carstairs' Lawnmower, Making Fudge, Cleaning the Hall Closet, McGee the Magician, Houseboat on Dugan's Lake, Fibber Teaches Molly to Drive, McGee's Car is Stolen and 9 more.

Fibber McGee & Molly, Vol. 3. collector's ed. Perf. by Jim Jordan et al. 6 cass. (Running Time: 9 hrs.). 1998. bk. 34.98 (4144) Radio Spirits.
Includes Molly Wants a Budget, Zither Lessons, Butler Gildersleeve, Borrows Gildy's Suit, StorkParrot Mix-Up, Escaped Convicts, Newspaper columnist, Fibber Too Ill to Do Housework, Jewelry Store Robbery, Package from Uncle Sycamore and 8 more.

Fibber McGee & Molly, Vol. 4. collector's ed. Perf. by Jim Jordan et al. 6 cass. (Running Time: 9 hrs.). 1999. bk. 34.98 (4175) Radio Spirits.
A nostalgic return to 79 Wistful Vista. Open this "hall closet" of 18 classic episodes.

Fibber McGee & Molly, Vol. 5. collector's ed. Perf. by Jim Jordan et al. 6 cass. (Running Time: 9 hrs.). 2001. bk. 34.98 (4686) Radio Spirits.
Eighteen classic shows.

Fibber McGee & Molly: Alice & Bert Stranded by Thunderstorm & Aunt Sarah Visits. Perf. by Jim Jordan & Marian Jordan. 1 cass. (Running Time: 1 hr.). 2001. 6.98 (1650) Radio Spirits.

Fibber McGee & Molly: Amusement Park & Off to Hollywood. 1 CD. (Running Time: 1 hr.). (Old-Time Radio Blockbusters Ser.). 2001. audio compact disk 4.98 (7004) Radio Spirits.

Fibber McGee & Molly: At the Carnival & Old Friend Thelma Visits. Perf. by Fibber McGee and Molly. 1 cass. (Running Time: 1 hr.). 2001. 6.98 (2576) Radio Spirits.

Fibber McGee & Molly: Best Kept Lawn & Handwriting Analysis. Perf. by Jim Jordan & Marian Jordan. 1 cass. (Running Time: 1 hr.). 2001. 6.98 (2238) Radio Spirits.

Fibber McGee & Molly: Broken Vacuum & Molly's Suit. Perf. by Jim Jordan & Marian Jordan. 1 cass. (Running Time: 1 hr.). 2001. 6.98 (1929) Radio Spirits.

Fibber McGee & Molly: Buckshot McGee & Kramer's Drugstore. Perf. by Jim Jordan & Marian Jordan. 1 cass. (Running Time: 1 hr.). 2001. 6.98 (2058) Radio Spirits.

Fibber McGee & Molly: Building a Kite & The Red Cross Drive. Perf. by Jim Jordan & Marian Jordan. 1 cass. (Running Time: 1 hr.). 2001. 6.98 (2369) Radio Spirits.

Fibber McGee & Molly: Catching Teeny's Cat & Rumors. Perf. by Jim Jordan & Marian Jordan. 1 cass. (Running Time: 1 hr.). 2001. 6.98 (2599) Radio Spirits.

Fibber McGee & Molly: Christmas Show of 1949. Perf. by Gale Gordon & Cliff Arquette. 1 cass. (Running Time: 60 min.). 7.95 (CC-9009) Natl Recrd Co.
In the "Fibber McGee & Molly" show the squire of Wistful Vista is decorating his house for the holidays as his regular visitors drop in: Mayor LaTrivia, Bessie, the Old Timer, & of course, Harlow Wilcox. On the "Burns & Allen" show, it is the night before Christmas & Gracie tells a bedtime story to her pet, Herman the Duck. She falls asleeps & dreams she is at the North Pole where Santa's bag of toys has been stolen by the Wicked Witch.

Fibber McGee & Molly: Circus in Town & Spaghetti Dinner. Perf. by Jim Jordan & Marian Jordan. 1 cass. (Running Time: 1 hr.). 2001. 6.98 (2362) Radio Spirits.

Fibber McGee & Molly: Citizen Test & Picnic at Dugan's Lake. Perf. by Jim Jordan & Marian Jordan. 1 cass. (Running Time: 1 hr.). 2001. 6.98 (1958) Radio Spirits.

Fibber McGee & Molly: Doc Gamble over for Dinner & Black-Market Meat. Perf. by Jim Jordan & Marian Jordan. 1 cass. (Running Time: 1 hr.). 2001. 6.98 (1848) Radio Spirits.

Fibber McGee & Molly: Early Golden Wedding Anniversary & McGee the Poet. Read by Jim Jordan & Marian Jordan. 1 cass. (Running Time: 1 hr.). 2001. 6.98 (1501) Radio Spirits.

Fibber McGee & Molly: Early to Bed & Bottle Collector. Perf. by Jim Jordan & Marian Jordan. 1 cass. (Running Time: 1 hr.). 2001. 6.98 (2196) Radio Spirits.

Fibber McGee & Molly: Election Day & Visiting Uncle Dennis. Perf. by Jim Jordan & Marian Jordan. 1 cass. (Running Time: 1 hr.). 2001. 6.98 (2366) Radio Spirits.

Fibber McGee & Molly: Fibber & Molly's Wedding Anniversary & Aviation Show. Perf. by Jim Jordan & Marian Jordan. 1 cass. (Running Time: 1 hr.). 2001. 6.98 (1655) Radio Spirits.

Fibber McGee & Molly: Fibber as a Dress Form see Fibber McGee & Molly

Fibber mcgee & Molly: Fibber as a dress form & the pipe Smoker. (ENG.). 2008. audio compact disk 12.95 (978-1-57970-515-2(4), Audio-For) J Norton Pubs.

Fibber McGee & Molly: Fibber Gives up Cigars & Missing Screwdriver. Perf. by Jim Jordan & Marian Jordan. 1 cass. (Running Time: 1 hr.). 2001. 6.98 (2364) Radio Spirits.

Fibber McGee & Molly: Fibber Makes a Radio Speech & Fibber's Old Mandolin. Perf. by Jim Jordan & Marian Jordan. 1 cass. (Running Time: 1 hr.). 2001. 6.98 (2257) Radio Spirits.

Fibber McGee & Molly: Fibber Manages Cannery & Fibber Thinks Neighbor Is Spy. Perf. by Jim Jordan & Marian Jordan. 1 cass. (Running Time: 1 hr.). 2001. 6.98 (1649) Radio Spirits.

Fibber McGee & Molly: Fibber Plans a Magic Act for the Elk's Club Smoker. Perf. by Gale Gordon et al. (CC-5121) Natl Recrd Co.

Fibber McGee & Molly: Fibber, the Piano Tuner? & Red Cross Collection. Perf. by Jim Jordan & Marian Jordan. 1 cass. (Running Time: 1 hr.). 2001. 6.98 (2280) Radio Spirits.

Fibber McGee & Molly: Fibber to Become a Songwriter & Government Drive. Perf. by Jim Jordan & Marian Jordan. 1 cass. (Running Time: 1 hr.). 2001. 6.98 (1890) Radio Spirits.

Fibber McGee & Molly: Fibber to Hire an Architect & Fibber Makes a Scene. Perf. by Jim Jordan & Marian Jordan. 1 cass. (Running Time: 1 hr.). 2001. 6.98 (2012) Radio Spirits.

Fibber McGee & Molly: Fibber to Prove His Manliness & Mileage Rationing. Perf. by Jim Jordan & Marian Jordan. 1 cass. (Running Time: 1 hr.). 2001. 6.98 (1870) Radio Spirits.

Fibber McGee & Molly: Fibber's Home Movies & The Suitcase. Perf. by Jim Jordan & Marian Jordan. 1 cass. (Running Time: 1 hr.). 2001. 6.98 (2077) Radio Spirits.

Fibber McGee & Molly: Fibber's Porch Swing & The Cattle Ranchers. Perf. by Jim Jordan & Marian Jordan. 1 cass. (Running Time: 1 hr.). 2001. 6.98 (1563) Radio Spirits.

Fibber McGee & Molly: Fixing Doc's Car & New Fire Alarm Box. Perf. by Jim Jordan & Marian Jordan. 1 cass. (Running Time: 1 hr.). 2001. 6.98 (1502) Radio Spirits.

Fibber McGee & Molly: Fixing Toys for the Needy & The Manhunt. Perf. by Jim Jordan & Marian Jordan. 1 cass. (Running Time: 1 hr.). 2001. 6.98 (2098) Radio Spirits.

Fibber McGee & Molly: Glidersleeve's Diary & Notre Dame vs. Army. Perf. by Jim Jordan & Marian Jordan. 1 cass. (Running Time: 1 hr.). 2001. 6.98 (2365) Radio Spirits.

Fibber McGee & Molly: Handmade Rug for the Elk's Club & Fibber Has to Answer to the I.R.S. Perf. by Jim Jordan & Marian Jordan. 1 cass. (Running Time: 1 hr.). 2001. 6.98 (2137) Radio Spirits.

Fibber McGee & Molly: Landscape Artist & Killer Davenport. Perf. by Jim Jordan & Marian Jordan. 1 cass. (Running Time: 1 hr.). 2001. 6.98 (2371) Radio Spirits.

Fibber McGee & Molly: Look Who's Laughing & Bergen & McCarthy. Perf. by Jim Marian et al. 1 cass. (Running Time: 1 hr.). 2001. 6.98 (1648) Radio Spirits.

Fibber McGee & Molly: Maple Syrup from the Tree & Search for Hip Boots. Perf. by Jim Jordan & Marian Jordan. 1 cass. (Running Time: 1 hr.). 2001. 6.98 (1652) Radio Spirits.

Fibber McGee & Molly: McGees Go to the Carnival & Molly's Old Friend Thelma Visits. Perf. by Jim Jordan & Marian Jordan. 1 cass. (Running Time: 1 hr.). 2001. 6.98 (2576) Radio Spirits.

Fibber McGee & Molly: Molly, Beulah Try to Clean & Neighbor Building Colonial Cabin. Perf. by Jim Jordan & Marian Jordan. 1 cass. (Running Time: 1 hr.). 2001. 6.98 (1810) Radio Spirits.

Fibber McGee & Molly: Molly Has a Twisted Ankle & The 1880 Quarter. Perf. by Jim Jordan & Marian Jordan. 1 cass. (Running Time: 1 hr.). 2001. 6.98 (1656) Radio Spirits.

Fibber McGee & Molly: New Suit for Doc & Cutting Firewood. Perf. by Jim Jordan & Marian Jordan. 1 cass. (Running Time: 1 hr.). 2001. 6.98 (2326) Radio Spirits.

Fibber McGee & Molly: Old Timer Hides Out & Duck Hunting with Mayor LaTrivia. Perf. by Jim Jordan & Marian Jordan. 1 cass. (Running Time: 1 hr.). 2001. 6.98 (2117) Radio Spirits.

Fibber McGee & Molly: Paints Christmas Tree White & Complains to the Post Office. Perf. by Jim Jordan & Marian Jordan. 1 cass. (Running Time: 1 hr.). 2001. 6.98 (1811) Radio Spirits.

Fibber McGee & Molly: Pancake Day Parade & Fixer-Upper McGee. Perf. by Jim Jordan & Marian Jordan. 1 cass. (Running Time: 1 hr.). 2001. 6.98 (2035) Radio Spirits.

Fibber McGee & Molly: Police Selling Banquet Tickets & Fishing with Doc Gamble. Perf. by Jim Jordan & Marian Jordan. 1 cass. (Running Time: 1 hr.). 2001. 6.98 (1651) Radio Spirits.

Fibber McGee & Molly: Preparing for Vacation & Returning from Vacation. Perf. by Jim Jordan & Marian Jordan. 1 cass. (Running Time: 1 hr.). 2001. 6.98 (2363) Radio Spirits.

Fibber McGee & Molly: Quits Smoking Again & Pirate of the Air Waves. Perf. by Jim Jordan & Marian Jordan. 1 cass. (Running Time: 1 hr.). 2001. 6.98 (2370) Radio Spirits.

Fibber McGee & Molly: Rummage Sale & Locked Out. Perf. by Jim Jordan & Marian Jordan. 1 cass. (Running Time: 1 hr.). 2001. 6.98 (2616) Radio Spirits.

Fibber McGee & Molly: Running Kramer's Drugstore & Trouble Paying Bills. Perf. by Jim Jordan & Marian Jordan. 1 cass. (Running Time: 1 hr.). 2001. 6.98 (1977) Radio Spirits.

***Fibber McGee & Molly: The Lost Episodes, Volume 1.** RadioArchives.com. (Running Time: 600). (ENG.). 2006. audio compact disk 29.98 (978-1-61081-050-0(3)) Radio Arch.

***Fibber McGee & Molly: The Lost Episodes, Volume 3.** RadioArchives.com. (Running Time: 600). (ENG.). 2007. audio compact disk 29.98 (978-1-61081-066-1(X)) Radio Arch.

***Fibber McGee & Molly: The Lost Episodes, Volume 4.** RadioArchives.com. (Running Time: 600). (ENG.). 2007. audio compact disk 29.98 (978-1-61081-069-2(4)) Radio Arch.

***Fibber Mcgee & Molly: The Lost Episodes, Volume 5.** RadioArchives.com. (Running Time: 600). (ENG.). 2008. audio compact disk 29.98 (978-1-61081-074-6(0)) Radio Arch.

***Fibber Mcgee & Molly: The Lost Episodes, Volume 6.** RadioArchives.com. (Running Time: 600). (ENG.). 2008. audio compact disk 29.98 (978-1-61081-081-4(3)) Radio Arch.

Fibber McGee & Molly: The Old Oak Tree & Big Talker McGee. Perf. by Jim Jordan & Marian Jordan. 1 cass. (Running Time: 1 hr.). 2001. 6.98 (1545) Radio Spirits.

Fibber McGee & Molly: The Pipe Smoker see Fibber McGee & Molly

Fibber McGee & Molly: Uncle Dennis Visits & 5 Tons of Coal. Perf. by Jim Jordan & Marian Jordan. 1 cass. (Running Time: 1 hr.). 2001. 6.98 (2367) Radio Spirits.

Fibber McGee & Molly: Unwelcome Mayor & Beauty Clay. Perf. by Jim Jordan & Marian Jordan. 1 cass. (Running Time: 1 hr.). 2001. 6.98 (2368) Radio Spirits.

Fibber McGee & Molly: War Bond & Diamond Ring & Craving For Ice Cream. Perf. by Jim Jordan & Marian Jordan. 1 cass. (Running Time: 1 hr.). 2001. 6.98 (1903) Radio Spirits.

Fibber McGee & Molly: 1944 Christmas Show & Diamond Stick Pin. Perf. by Jim Jordan & Marian Jordan. 1 cass. (Running Time: 1 hr.). 2001. 6.98 (1654) Radio Spirits.

Fibber McGee & Molly No. 2: Uncle Sycamore McGee & Collecting a Debt. unabr. ed. 1 cass. (Running Time: 60 min.). Dramatization. 7.95 Norelco box. (CC-8781) Natl Recrd Co.
Uncle Sycamore McGee: Fibber works hard to repair, & repair, & repair his radio so he can hear a radio program about Uncle Sycamore McGee. This is the first show of the McGees' 9th season on the air for sponsor Johnson's Wax, 1943. Collecting a Debt: Fibber gets a neighbor to contact Manila on his short-wave radio so he can collect a 7.00 dollar debt from an old friend. Fibber's famous Hall Closet is opened with a bang in this broadcast! Johnson's Wax, 1948.

Fibber McGee & Molly Pt. 1 & Pt. 2: A Rock, a Window, a Dream. Perf. by Jim Jordan & Marian Jordan. 1 cass. (Running Time: 1 hr.). 2001. 6.98 (1946) Radio Spirits.

Fibber McGee & Molly Vol. 3: Cleaning the Hall Closet; Trolley Car Prize. unabr. ed. 1 cass. (Running Time: 1 hr.). 4.95 (978-1-57816-102-7(9), FM341) Audio File.
Old time radio fun.

Fibber McGee & Molly, No. 3: Cleaning the Hall Closet & Trolley Car Suggestions. unabr. ed. 1 cass. (Running Time: 60 min.). Dramatization. 7.95 Norelco box. (CC-9806) Natl Recrd Co.
Cleaning the Hall Closet: Expecting a visit from wealthy Mrs. Carstairs, Molly insists that the hall closet be cleaned & organized. You'll hear the most famous sound effects in radio! Jim & Marion Jordan star, along with Alice Darling, Doc Gamble & Beulah, the maid. Johnson's Wax, 1945. Trolley Car Suggestions: The Wistful Vista Trolly Company offers a prize for the best idea to improve their business, & Fibber has an idea how to be the big winner! Trolly riders include Harlow Wilcox, Gale Gordon, Bill Thompson & Dick LeGrand. Johnson's Wax, 1949.

Fibber Mcgee Holiday Shows. (Running Time: 6 hrs.). 2004. audio compact disk 29.95 (978-1-57816-192-8(4)) Audio File.

Fiber McGee & Molly Holiday Shows, Set. unabr. ed. 6 cass. (Running Time: 6 hrs.). 24.95 (978-1-57816-007-5(3), FM601) Audio File.
Celebrate a year's worth of holidays with all the characters from Wistfull Vista.

Fibrodysplasia Ossificans Progressiva - A Bibliography & Dictionary for Physicians, Patients, & Genome Researchers. Compiled by Icon Group International, Inc. Staff. 2007. ring bd. 28.95 (978-0-497-11213-4(2)) Icon Grp.

Fibroid Healing. Steven Gurgevich. (ENG.). 2004. audio compact disk 19.95 (978-1-932170-24-5(3), HWH) Tranceformation.

Fibromyalgia & Chronic Fatigue Syndrome. Gary Silverman. 1 cass. (Motivational Medicine Ser.: Vol. 3). 1996. 12.00 (978-1-888202-02-1(5)) Motivat Med.
Motivational Medicine Medutainment Medical education that is entertaining Topic Interview information on fibromyalgia & CFS.

Fibrous Proteins: Muscle & Molecular Motors. John M. Squire & David A. D. Parry. (ENG., 2005. 156.00 (978-0-12-034271-6(5), Acad Press) Sci Tech Bks.

Fibs, Lies & Authenticity: Living a Lie-Free Life, Set. David Grudermeyer & Rebecca Grudermeyer. 2 cass. 18.95 (T-04) Willingness Wrks.

Ficelle see Treasury of Guy de Maupassant: Contes Choisis

Ficelle, Les Caresses, Le Lit. Short Stories. Guy de Maupassant. Read by Claude Beauclair. 1 cass. (FRE.). 1991. 13.95 (1255-OH) Olivia & Hill.
On market day in a small town, the stingy Normand Maitre Hauchecorne picks up a little piece of string only to be accused of having picked up a wallet which has been stolen that morning. In the second story, a young man sings the praises of physical love to a reluctant young woman.

Fiction to Fact Big Books Audio CD's. Compiled by Benchmark Education Staff. 2006. audio compact disk 99.00 (978-1-4108-6984-5(9)) Benchmark Educ.

Fiction Writers Are Liars & Thieves. Elmer Kelton. 1 cass. (Running Time: 45 min.). (ENG.). 1995. 12.95 (978-0-87565-148-4(8)) Pub: Tex Christian. Dist(s): Tex AM Univ Pr
Kelton's opening confession: "Someone has said that fiction by definition is a lie. By extension this means that fiction writers are liars. The author goes a step further to say that fiction writers are lars & thieves.

Fiction Writing. Ayn Rand. 21 cass. (Running Time: 23 hrs.). 1994. 275.00 Set. (978-1-56114-307-8(3), AR58D) Second Renaissance.
Course of study in Fiction Writing by the most compelling & influential 20th century writer.

Fiction Writing: Random Comments on the Business & the Art. unabr. ed. Jesse H. Ford. 1 cass. (Running Time: 58 min.). 1968. 12.95 (23005) J Norton Pubs.
A discussion of the creative process involved in fiction writing.

Fiddle & Bow see Robert Taylor Jr.

Fiddle Club. Contrib. by Calgary Fiddlers. (Fiddle Club Collection). 2001. audio compact disk 18.95 (978-0-7866-6043-8(0)) Mel Bay.

Fiddle Club: Collection 1. Contrib. by Calgary Fiddlers. (Fiddle Club Collection). 2001. audio compact disk 18.95 (978-0-7866-6042-1(2)) Mel Bay.

Fiddle Club: Collection 3. Contrib. by Calgary Fiddlers. (Fiddle Club Collection). 2001. audio compact disk 18.95 (978-0-7866-6044-5(9)) Mel Bay.

Fiddle Club Introductory Collection: Fiddle Tunes for the Beginning Violinist. Created by Mel Bay Publications Inc. 2003. audio compact disk 24.95 (978-0-7866-6995-0(0)) Mel Bay.

Fiddle Game. unabr. ed. Richard A. Thompson. Read by Robertson Dean. (Running Time: 28800 sec.). 2008. 44.95 (978-1-4332-1142-3(4)); audio compact disk & audio compact disk 29.95 (978-1-4332-1144-7(0)); audio compact disk & audio compact disk 60.00 (978-1-4332-1143-0(2)) Blckstn Audio.

Fiddle Music of Prince Edward Island. Ken Perlman. 1996. pap. bk. 37.95 (978-0-7866-1310-6(6), 95393CDP) Mel Bay.

Fiddle Music of the Scottish Highlands: Ceol Na Fidhle. Jonathan Pickow. 2 CDs. 2004. audio compact disk 32.95 (978-1-871931-53-2(3)) Pub: Taigh Teud GBR. Dist(s): Music Sales

Fiddle Tunes, Classic Rags & Cakewalks. Leo Wijnkamp, Jr. (Stefan Grossman's Guitar Workshop Ser.). 2007. pap. bk. 24.95 (978-0-7866-7763-4(5)) Mel Bay.

Fiddle Tunes for Beginning Viola. Stacy Phillips. 2001. bk. 17.95 (978-0-7866-4772-9(8)) Mel Bay.

Fiddler see Great American Short Stories, Vol. III, A Collection

Fiddler. 1985. (S-66) Jimcin Record.

Fiddler Dan & John J. Plenty. (J). (SAC 6692) Spoken Arts.

Fiddler of the Reels see Thomas Hardy: Selected Short Stories

Fiddler on the Make. Peter Kerr. 2009. 69.95 (978-1-4079-0535-8(X)); audio compact disk 79.95 (978-1-4079-0536-5(8)) Pub: Soundings Ltd GBR. Dist(s): Ulverscroft US

Fiddler on the Roof: Piano Play-along Volume 80. Composed by Jerry Bock. 2009. pap. bk. 14.99 (978-1-4234-7999-4(8), 1423479998) H Leonard.

Fiddlers: A Novel of the 87th Precinct. unabr. ed. Ed McBain, pseud. Read by Charles Stransky. 5 cds. (Running Time: 6 hrs.). Bk. 55. (ENG.). 2005. audio compact disk 26.95 (978-1-56511-989-5(4), 1565119894) Pub: HighBridge. Dist(s): Workman Pub

Fiddlers: A Novel of the 87th Precinct. unabr. ed. Ed McBain, pseud. Read by Charles Stransky. (YA). 2008. 54.99 (978-1-60252-960-1(4)) Find a World.

Fiddler's Almanac: A Wealth of Fiddling Lore & Illustrations. collector's ed. Ryan J. Thomson. 1985. lib. bdg. 29.95 (978-0-931877-00-1(8)) Captain Fiddle Pubns.

Fiddlers Philharmonic. Andrew Dabczynski & Robert H. Phillips. 1 CD. (Running Time: 1 hr.). (ENG.). 1996. audio compact disk 10.95 (978-0-7390-1931-3(7), 14038) Alfred Pub.

Fiddlers Philharmonic Encore! Andrew Dabczynski & Bob Phillips. (ENG.). 1999. audio compact disk 10.95 (978-0-7390-2128-6(1)) Alfred Pub.

Fiddler's Tale: How Hollywood & Vivaldi Discovered Me. unabr. ed. Louis Kaufman. Read by Annette Kaufman. 14 cds. 2005. audio compact disk 29.95 (978-0-299-21110-3(X)) Pub: U of Wis Pr. Dist(s): Chicago Distribution Ctr
Louis Kaufman (1905-1994) was probably the most-recorded violinist in history, with recordings of more than one hundred major concert works and hundreds of film soundtracks to his credit. Annette Kaufman, a pianist, shared Louis' passion for music, art, and theater as they traveled the globe on performance tours. Here she dramatically reads her husband's fascinating autobiography on fourteen CDs, with a fifteenth CD of musical selections inimitably played by one of the twentieth century's greatest violinists, Louis Kaufman.

Fiddlin' for Fun Acc. Patty Nicholas. (ENG.). 1998. audio compact disk 9.95 (978-0-87487-739-7(3), Warner Bro) Alfred Pub.

Fiddling for Beginners. Ryan J. Thomson. (Running Time: 60 mins.). (C). 1989. spiral bd. 14.95 (978-0-931877-08-7(3)) Captain Fiddle Pubns.

Fidel Castro: My Life - A Spoken Autobiography. unabr. ed. Fidel Castro & Ignacio Ramonet. Narrated by Todd McLaren & Patrick Lawlor. 3 MP3-CDs. (Running Time: 26 hrs. 30 mins. 0 sec.). (ENG.). 2008. 44.99 (978-1-4001-5592-7(4)); audio compact disk 59.99 (978-1-4001-0592-2(7)); audio compact disk 119.99 (978-1-4001-3592-9(3)) Pub: Tantor Media. Dist(s): IngramPubServ

Fidelio: An Introduction to Beethoven's Opera. Thomson Smillie. Read by David Timson. 1 CD. (Running Time: 1 hr. 39 min.). (Opera Explained Ser.). 2003. audio compact disk 8.99 (978-1-84379-085-3(8)) NaxMulti GBR.

Fidelity. unabr. ed. Thomas Perry. Narrated by Michael Kramer. 9 CDs. (Running Time: 11 hrs. 0 mins. 0 sec.). (ENG.). 2008. audio compact disk 69.99 (978-1-4001-3664-3(4)); audio compact disk 34.99 (978-1-4001-0664-6(8)) Pub: Tantor Media. Dist(s): IngramPubServ

Fidelity. unabr. ed. Thomas Perry. Read by Michael Kramer. 1 MP3-CD. (Running Time: 11 hrs. 0 mins. 0 sec.). (ENG.). 2008. audio compact disk 24.99 (978-1-4001-5664-1(5)) Pub: Tantor Media. Dist(s): IngramPubServ

Fidelity & Chastity. Linda Eyre & Richard Eyre. 2 cass. (Running Time: 3 hrs.). (Teaching Your Children Values Ser.). (J). (ps-7). 2000. bk. 16.95 (978-1-56015-791-5(7)) Penton Overseas.
Tape 1: a coaching, "how-to" program for parents; Tape 2: "Alexander's Amazing Adventures" program featuring stories, songs, sound effects & background music, that helps children ages 4-12 to develop social skills, communication skills & life skills. Includes activity cards.

Fidel's Last Days. unabr. ed. Roland Merullo. Read by Patrick Egan. 7 CDs. (Running Time: 8 hrs. 30 mins.). 2009. audio compact disk 100.00 (978-1-4159-6119-3(0), BksonTape) Pub: Random Audio Pubg. Dist(s): Random

Fiduciary Accounting: The Approval Process. 1991. 35.00 (AC-610) PA Bar Inst.

Fiduciary Accountings: The Approval Process. 1986. bk. 65.00; 40.00 PA Bar Inst.

Fiduciary Income Tax Course, 1996. Sidney Kess & Barbara Weltman. 3 cass. (Running Time: 3 hrs.). 1995. 105.00 Set. (0921) Toolkit Media.
Gives detailed, line-by-line instructions on how to prepare the fiduciary income tax return, Form 1041. Reviews the latest tax changes, the latest form changes, & recent cases, regulations & rulings. Includes study guide & quizzer for CPE credit.

Fiedler's Favorites for Children. Perf. by Boston Pops Orchestra & Arthur Fiedler. 1 cass. (J). (ps up). 7.98 (224) MFLP CA.
Familiar melodies arranged to be fun & inviting to children's ears. Includes: "Sabre Dance," "The Nutcracker," "Jamaican Rhumba," "Chim-Chim-Cher-ee," "Consider Yourself," "Masquerade," "Ritual Fire Dance," "Bahn Frei Polka," "Whistle While You Work.".

Fiefdom Syndrome. Robert J. Herbold. Read by Grover Gardner. (Running Time: 18000 sec.). 2005. audio compact disk 36.00 (978-0-7861-7794-3(2)) Blckstn Audio.

Fiefdom Syndrome. abr. ed. Robert J. Herbold. Read by Grover Gardner. 4 CDs. audio compact disk 25.99 (978-1-58926-930-9(6)) Oasis Audio.

Fiefdom Syndrome. abr. ed. Robert J. Herbold. Narrated by Grover Gardner. (ENG.). 2005. 13.99 (978-1-60814-202-6(7)) Oasis Audio.

Field: The Quest for the Secret Force of the Universe. Lynne McTaggart. 2 CDs. (Running Time: 8100 sec.). 2007. audio compact disk 19.95 (978-1-59179-562-9(1), AW01125D) Sounds True.

***Field Guide.** unabr. ed. Holly Black & Tony DiTerlizzi. Read by Mark Hamill. (Running Time: 1 hr. 5 mins.). (Spiderwick Chronicles: Bk. 1). (ENG.). (J). 2007. 7.50 (978-0-7393-6241-9(0), Listening Lib) Pub: Random Audio Pubg. Dist(s): Random

Field Guide. unabr. ed. Tony DiTerlizzi & Holly Black. 2 cass. (Running Time: 1 hr. 57 mins.). (Spiderwick Chronicles: Bk. 1). (J). (gr. 1-5). 2004. 23.00 (978-0-8072-1651-4(8), Listening Lib) Random Audio Pubg.

Field Guide & the Seeing Stone. Tony DiTerlizzi & Holly Black. Read by Mark Hamill. 2 CDs. (Running Time: 1 hr. 57 mins.). (Spiderwick Chronicles: Bks. 1-2). (J). (gr. 1-5). 2004. audio compact disk 24.00 (978-1-4000-8619-1(1), Listening Lib) Random Audio Pubg.

Field Guide to Bird Songs: Eastern & Central North America. Cornell Laboratory of Ornithology Staff. Ed. by Roger Tory Peterson. (Peterson Field Guides). (ENG., 2002. audio compact disk 20.00 (978-0-618-22594-1(3)) HM Harcourt.

Field Guide to the North American Wacko! unabr. ed. Tom Magliozzi & Ray Magliozzi. Contrib. by Tom Magliozzi & Ray Magliozzi. (Running Time: 12600 sec.). (ENG., 2008. audio compact disk 29.95 (978-1-59887-589-8(2), 1598875892) Pub: HighBridge. Dist(s): Workman Pub

Field Guide to Western Bird Songs: Western North America. Houghton Mifflin Company Staff et al. Contrib. by Roger Tory Peterson. 2 cass. (Peterson Field Guide Audio Ser.). (ENG., 1999. audio compact disk 30.00 (978-0-395-97519-0(0)) HM Harcourt.

***Field Guides: Fao Species Identification Sheets for Fishery Purposes.** Created by FAO. (ENG.). 2008. audio compact disk 24.00 (978-92-5-106037-7(1)) FAO ITA.

Field Notes: The Grace Note of the Canyon Wren. Barry Lopez. 2 cass. (Running Time: 3 hrs.). 1995. 16.95 (978-0-939643-65-3(0), NrthWrd Bks) TandN Child.

Field Notes from a Catastrophe: Man, Nature, & Climate Change. abr. ed. Elizabeth Kolbert. Read by Hope Davis. 2006. 17.95 (978-0-7435-6518-9(5)) Pub: S&S Audio. Dist(s): S and S Inc

Field of Darkness. abr. unabr. ed. Cornelia Read. Read by Hillary Huber. 6 cass. (Running Time: 39600 sec.). 2006. 29.95 (978-0-7861-4465-5(3)); audio compact disk 29.95 (978-0-7861-7287-0(8)); audio compact disk 29.95 (978-0-7861-7709-7(8)) Blckstn Audio.

Field of Darkness. unabr. ed. Cornelia Read. Read by Hillary Huber. (Running Time: 39600 sec.). 2006. 65.95 (978-0-7861-4662-8(1)); audio compact disk 81.00 (978-0-7861-6746-3(7)) Blckstn Audio.

Field of Dishonor. unabr. ed. David Weber. Read by Allyson Johnson. (Running Time: 13 hrs.). (Honor Harrington Ser.: Bk. 4). 2010. 24.99 (978-1-4233-9535-5(2), 9781423395355, Brilliance MP3); 39.97 (978-1-4233-9536-2(0), 9781423395362, Brlnc Audio MP3 Lib); 39.97 (978-1-4233-9537-9(9), 9781423395379, BADLE); audio compact disk 29.99 (978-1-4233-9533-1(6), 9781423395331, Bril Audio CD Unabri); audio compact disk 99.97 (978-1-4233-9534-8(4), 9781423395348, BriAudCD Unabrid) Brilliance Audio.

Field of Dreams. Ed Young. 1997. 4.95 (978-0-7417-2148-8(1), 1148) Win Walk.

Field of Peace. Marianne Williamson. Read by Marianne Williamson. 1 cass. (Running Time: 90 mins.). (Lectures on a Course in Miracles). (ENG.). 1998. 10.00 (978-1-56170-591-7(8), M865) Hay House.

Field of the Dogs. Katherine Paterson. Narrated by Johnny Heller. (Running Time: 1 hr. 15 mins.). (gr. 3 up). audio compact disk 12.00 (978-1-4025-0471-6(3)) Recorded Bks.

Field of the Dogs. unabr. ed. Katherine Paterson. Narrated by Johnny Heller. 1 cass. (Running Time: 1 hr. 15 mins.). (gr. 3 up). 2001. 10.00 (978-0-7887-5021-2(6)) Recorded Bks.

Field to Factory: Voices of the Great Migration (African American Spoken Word) Prod. by David Tarnow. Narrated by Spencer Crew. 1 cass. 1995. Incl. 18p. bklet. (0-9307-90005-4-5) Smithsonian Folkways.
Documentary about African Americans who migrated from the rural South to the urban North between 1915 & 1951. These Americans reminisce & tell their own stories.

Fields & Pastures New. unabr. ed. John McCormack. Read by Barrett Whitener. 7 cass. (Running Time: 10 hrs. 30 mins.). 1996. 56.00 (978-0-7366-3320-8(0), 3972) Books on Tape.
What James Herriot did for Yorkshire, Dr. McCormack does for the American South as he describes his "rookie" year as a country vet. The story begins in 1963 in Choctaw County, Alabama, the old South not yet entirely new. Mule-drawn wagons share the road with pickup trucks, the barber shares the day's news as reliably as any CNN reporter & a moonshiner shares his brew with his cow. In a world moving too fast, McCormack slows us down to experience the wonder. He shows us that treating an animal often means treating its owner.

Fields of Grace. abr. ed. Kim Vogel Sawyer. (Running Time: 7 hrs. 45 mins. 0 sec.). (ENG.). 2009. audio compact disk 24.98 (978-1-59644-773-8(7), christaudio) christianaud.

***Fields of Grace.** abr. ed. Kim Vogel-Sawyer. Narrated by Traci Svensgaard. (ENG.). 2009. 14.98 (978-1-59644-774-5(5), christaudio) christianaud.

Fields of Honor: Ruin Mist Chronicles, Book 3. unabr. ed. Robert Stanek, pseud. Narrated by Karl Fehr. (Running Time: 12 hrs. 2 mins.). (Ruin Mist Chronicles Ser.). 2008. audio compact disk 59.95 (978-1-57545-322-4(3), RP Audio Pubng) Reagent Press.

Fieldwork. unabr. ed. Mischa Berlinski. Read by William Dufris. (YA). 2007. 59.99 (978-1-60252-833-8(0)) Find a World.

Fieldwork. unabr. ed. Mischa Berlinski. (Running Time: 12 hrs. 0 mins. 0 sec.). (ENG.). 2007. audio compact disk 37.99 (978-1-4001-0364-5(9)) Pub: Tantor Media. Dist(s): IngramPubServ

Fieldwork. unabr. ed. Mischa Berlinski. (Running Time: 12 hrs. 0 mins. 0 sec.). (ENG.). 2007. audio compact disk 75.99 (978-1-4001-3364-2(5)); audio compact disk 24.99 (978-1-4001-5364-0(6)) Pub: Tantor Media. Dist(s): IngramPubServ

Fiendish Deeds. unabr. ed. P. J. Bracegirdle. Narrated by Katherine Kellgren. (Running Time: 6 hrs.). (Joy of Spooking Ser.: Bk. 1). (J). (gr. 4-6). 2008. 56.75; 41.75 (978-1-4361-3755-3(1)); audio compact disk 51.75 (978-1-4361-3760-7(8)) Recorded Bks.

Fiendish Deeds. unabr. collector's ed. P. J. Bracegirdle. Narrated by Katherine Kellgren. 5 CDs. (Running Time: 6 hrs.). (Joy of Spooking Ser.: Bk. 1). (J). (gr. 4-6). 2008. audio compact disk 39.95 (978-1-4361-3778-2(0)) Recorded Bks.

Fiennders Keepers. unabr. ed. Jean Marsh. Read by Jean Marsh. 10 cass. (Running Time: 10 hrs.). 1997. 84.95 (978-0-7540-0045-7(1)) AudioGO.
At Fiennders Abbey, the family had prospered for years. Anne Fiennders was proud of her sons, especially Richard, her eldest. Beyond the lawns, there were woods & beyond the trees was Keepers Cottage, where Mary lived with her brother, sister & parents. In the village, there was a school, a shop & a church. As the last century drew to a close, there was little to indicate that anything there could ever change. But change was just around the corner.

Fiera Dormida. abr. ed. Carlos Arniches. Perf. by Antonio Quijada & Lola del Dino. 1 cass. (Running Time: 50 min.). Dramatization. (Spanish Literature Ser.). (SPA.). 11.95 (978-0-8045-0844-5(5), SAC 49-6) Spoken Arts.

Fiera Dormida. unabr. ed. Carlos Arniches. Perf. by Radio Nacional de Espana Staff. 1 cass. (Running Time: 90 mins.). Dramatization. (SPA.). pap. bk. 16.95 (SSP390) J Norton Pubs.
Arniches is considered to be the best of the contemporary authors of one-act plays.

Fierce Conversations: Achieving Success at Work & in Life, One Conversation at a Time. abr. ed. Susan Scott. 2004. 15.95 (978-0-7435-4697-3(0)) Pub: S&S Audio. Dist(s): S and S Inc

Fierce Conversations: Achieving Success at Work & in Life, One Conversation at a Time. abr. ed. Susan Scott & Susan Craig Scott. Read by Susan Scott & Susan Craig Scott. 4 CDs. (Running Time: 50 hrs. 0 mins. 0 sec.). (ENG.). 2002. audio compact disk 30.00 (978-0-7435-2600-5(7), Sound Ideas) Pub: S&S Audio. Dist(s): S and S Inc
The author gives listeners the principles and tools to engage colleagues, customers, friends and family to provoke learning, tackle tough challenges and enrich relationships. They will master the courage and skills and, more importantly, enjoy the benefits of fierce conversations in every aspect of their lives.

Fierce Conversations: Achieving Success in Work & in Life, One Conversation at a Time. Susan Scott. Read by Bernadette Dunne. 2002. 64.00 (978-0-7366-8771-3(8)); audio compact disk 72.00 (978-0-7366-8832-1(3)) Books on Tape.

Fierce Invalids Home from Hot Climates. Tom Robbins. 10 cass. (Running Time: 15 hrs.). 2000. 44.95 (978-0-7366-5090-8(3), 5304) Books on Tape.
Switters is a contradiction for all seasons: an anarchist who works for the government, a pacifist who carries a gun, a vegetarian who sops up ham gravy, a cyber whiz who hates computers, a robust bon vivant who can be as squeamish as any fop, a man who, though obsessed with the preservations of innocence, is aching to deflower his high school age stepsister (only to become equally enamored of a nun ten years his senior shortly thereafter). As we follow Switter's strange journey through four continents, Robbins explores, challenges, mocks and celebrates virtually every major aspect of our mercurial era.

***Fierce Radiance: A Novel.** unabr. ed. Lauren Belfer. Read by Paula Christensen. (ENG.). 2010. (978-0-06-205969-7(6), Harper Audio); (978-0-06-204034-3(0), Harper Audio) HarperCollins Pubs.

Fierce Times Are Coming. Derek Prince. 1 cass. 5.95 (4399) Derek Prince.
In the last days, "fierce times" will come - this is not a possibility, but a certainty. When "men's hearts fail them" how will you respond?.

Fiery Cross. unabr. ed. Diana Gabaldon. Narrated by Davina Porter. 40 cass. (Running Time: 56 hrs.). (Outlander Ser.: Bk. 5). 2004. 248.00 (978-0-7887-9552-7(X)) Recorded Bks.
The year is 1771. Claire Randall is still an outlander, out of place and out of time. But now she is linked by love to her only anchor - Jamie Fraser. They have crossed oceans and centuries to build a life together in North Carolina. But tensions, both ancient and recent, threaten members of their clan. Knowing that his wife has the gift of prophecy, James must beleve Claire, though he would prefer not to. Claire has shared a dreadful truth - there will, without a doubt, be a war. Her knowledge of the oncoming revolution is a flickering torch that may light his way through perilous years ahead - or ignite a conflagaration that will leave their lives in ashes.

Fiery Furnace. unabr. ed. Timothy Mason. Perf. by L. D. Barrett et al. 1 cass. (Running Time: 1 hr. 20 min.). 1995. 19.95 (978-1-58081-080-7(2)) L A Theatre.
Around a family dining table deep in the Heartland, where Senator Joe McCarthy once sat & discussed his fondness for beets, nothing is as it seems. Gunnar, the family patriarch, is an upstanding farmer - or is he? Why is his favorite daughter so anxious to flee to Chicago? And why does her mother want to go too? Daughter Charity, a devoted wife & mother, is clearly frightened of something. Her husband, Jerry, hates anything un-American, but refuses to serve in Korea. As the mysteries multiply, author Timothy Mason solves them with wit & unrelenting suspense.

Fiery Peace in a Cold War: Bernard Schriever & the Ultimate Weapon. unabr. ed. Neil Sheehan. Read by Robertson Dean. 2009. audio compact disk 55.00 (978-0-307-57669-9(8), Random AudioBks) Pub: Random Audio Pubg. Dist(s): Random

Fiery Prophet: The Story of Elijah (From 1 & 2 Kings) Bert Polman. (Running Time: 40 mins.). (Scripture Alive Ser.). 1998. 15.95 (978-1-56212-331-4(9), 415103) FaithAliveChr.

***Fiery Trial: Abraham Lincoln & American Slavery.** unabr. ed. Eric Foner. (Running Time: 12 hrs. 30 mins.). 2010. 34.99 (978-1-4001-9960-0(3)); 24.99 (978-1-4001-6960-3(7)); 18.99 (978-1-4001-8960-1(8)); audio compact disk 83.99 (978-1-4001-4960-5(6)); audio compact disk 34.99 (978-1-4001-1960-8(X)) Pub: Tantor Media. Dist(s): IngramPubServ

Fiesta! Perf. by Erich Kunzel et al. 1 cass., 1 CD. 7.98 (TA 30235); audio compact disk 12.78 CD Jewel box. (TA 80235) NewSound.

Fiesta. Roy Tuckman. 1 cass. 10.00 (A0454-89) Sound Photosyn.
Music for Expanding Awareness whether in meditation or traffic...or both.

Fiesta. Ann Walker. 1 cass.; 1 CD. 1998. 9.98 (978-1-57330-630-0(4), 34443); audio compact disk 15.98 CD. (978-1-57330-629-4(0), 34443D) MFLP CA.

Fiesta! unabr. ed. Jennifer Reyes. Read by Jennifer Reyes. 1 cass. (Running Time: 40 min.). (Look, Listen & Learn - Spanish Club Ser.). (J). (ps-4). 1992. cass. & video 19.95 (978-0-9637984-1-1(3)) Peapod Prods.
Senora Reyes & the Spanish Club kids learn firsthand how to party through folk songs, games, & other activities.

Fiesta: Mexican & South American Favorites Alto Sax. James Curnow. 2009. pap. bk. 12.99 (978-1-4234-6780-9(9), 1423467809) H Leonard.

Fiesta: Mexican & South American Favorites Clarinet. James Curnow. 2009. pap. bk. 12.99 (978-1-4234-6779-3(5), 1423467795) H Leonard.

Fiesta: Mexican & South American Favorites E Flat Horn. James Curnow. 2009. pap. bk. 12.99 (978-1-4234-6784-7(1), 1423467841) H Leonard.

Fiesta: Mexican & South American Favorites Flute. James Curnow. 2009. pap. bk. 12.99 (978-1-4234-6776-2(0), 1423467760) H Leonard.

Fiesta: Mexican & South American Favorites Tenor Sax. James Curnow. 2009. pap. bk. 12.99 (978-1-4234-6781-6(7), 1423467817) H Leonard.

Fiesta: Mexican & South American Favorites Trombone/Baritone B. C. James Curnow. 2009. pap. bk. 12.99 (978-1-4234-6785-4(X), 142346785X) H Leonard.

Fiesta: Mexican & South American Favorites Trumpet/Baritone T. C. James Curnow. 2009. pap. bk. 12.99 (978-1-4234-6782-3(5), 1423467825) H Leonard.

***fiesta de cumpleaños Audio CD.** Francisco Blane. Adapted by Benchmark Education Company, LLC. (My First Reader's Theater Ser.). (SPA.). (J). 2009. audio compact disk 10.00 (978-1-935470-73-1(6)) Benchmark Educ.

Fiesta del Abecedario. Cecilia O. Avalos. (SPA.). 2001. (978-1-56801-381-7(7), SW4018) Sund Newbrdge.

Fiesta Latina. Created by Amnesty International Staff. (Think Global Ser.). 2008. audio compact disk 14.95 (978-1-906063-91-7(5)) Amnesty Intl Pubns GBR.

Fiesta Moon. unabr. ed. Linda Windsor. Read by Barbara McCulloh. 7 cass. (Running Time: 10.5 hrs.). 2005. 69.75 (978-1-4193-4843-3(4), K1173) Recorded Bks.
Christy finalist Linda Windsor's hilarious and uplifting Moonstruck series proves that higher powers are indeed at work when it comes to matchmaking. For playboy Mark Madison it seems like nothing could be further from the truth his first day on the construction site for a new orphanage in Mexico. A chilly reception from the beautiful social worker Corinne Diaz is the precursor to mayhem and disaster for Mark. But when a terrible curse threatens the completion of the project, the two must band together to find the culprit.

Fiesta Musical. 1 cass. (J). 1994. 9.98 (978-1-877737-21-3(6), MLP246/WB42525-4) MFLP CA.
Bilingual adventure through South America.

Fiesta Songs! 1 cass., 1 CD. (ENG & SPA.). (J). 7.98 (SME 63443); audio compact disk 11.18 CD Jewel box. (SME 63443) NewSound.
Collection of songs with the Sesame Street Characters.

Fiestas. Contrib. by Jose-Luis Orozco. Illus. by Elisa Kleven. (ENG & SPA.). (J). (gr. k-2). 12.00 (978-1-57417-017-7(1), AC1674) Pub: Arcoiris Recs. Dist(s): Lectorum Pubns

Fiestas: A Year of Latin American Songs of Celebration. unabr. ed. Tr. by Jose-Luis Orozco. 2 cass. (Running Time: 3 hrs.). 2002. audio compact disk 16.00 (978-1-57417-006-1(6)) Arcoiris Recs.

Fifi see Madeline & Other Bemelmans

Fifo en el Veterinario, EDL Level 18. (Fonolibros Ser.: Vol. 6). (SPA.). 2003. 11.50 (978-0-7652-1027-2(4)) Modern Curr.

Fifteen. unabr. ed. Beverly Cleary. 1 read-along cass. (Running Time: 85 min.). (Young Adult Cliffhangers Ser.). (J). (gr. 6 up). 1985. 15.98 (978-0-8072-1812-9(X), JRH 106 SP, Listening Lib); (Listening Lib) Random Audio Pubg.
Jane Purdy dreams of having a boyfriend just like Stan Crandall. He's everything she ever wanted & more, except for the little matter of his girlfriend back home.

Fifteen Keys to a Great Mission. Don J. Black. 1 cass. 1997. 9.98 (978-1-57734-107-9(4), 06005551) Covenant Comms.
Making the most of your mission.

Fifteen Minute Personal Growth: Initializing & Developing the Deeply Relaxed State, Vol. 1. unabr. ed. George H. Green. Read by George H. Green. 6 cass. 1996. 59.95 (978-1-890669-05-8(9), PCS-2) Biofeedback Ctr.
Six actual hypnosis sessions range from detailed directions through progressively less direction with increasingly subtle emotional experiences to stimulate personal growth or develop deeply relaxed self-actualization/self-help.

Fifteen Minute Revitalization. unabr. ed. Angelica Rose. 1 cass. (Running Time: 30 min.). 1995. 10.00 JLR Pub.
Guided meditation to help you relax your mind, calm your emotions, promote a positive attitude, stimulate joyful feelings, resolve your challenges.

Fifteen Minute Stress Relaxation. Patricia O'Malley. Perf. by Barry Weiss. 1 cass. (Running Time: 50 min.). 1998. (978-1-892450-01-2(1), 102) Promo Music.
Guided imagery.

Fifteen Minute Teacher Training: Age Two of Five. 1 cass. 1992. 14.99 (978-2-511-60340-6(3)) Gospel Lght.

Fifteen Minute Teacher Training Set: Grade One to Six. 2 cass. 1992. 14.99 (978-2-511-60341-3(1)) Gospel Lght.

Fifteen Streets. unabr. ed. Catherine Cookson. Read by Susan Jameson. 6 cass. (Running Time: 7 hrs. 17 min.). (Audio Bks.). 1992. 54.95 set. (978-0-7451-5860-0(9), CAB 135) AudioGO.
Life in the Fifteen streets was a continual struggle for survival against poverty. Some, like John O'Brien, fought grimly for a world they were only rarely allowed to glimpse, like on the day he met Mary Llewellyn. Mary lived well, dressed beautifully, & worked only because she wanted to. When John fell in love, he knew that nothing could bridge the gulf between their two separate worlds.

Fifteen Streets. unabr. collector's ed. Catherine Cookson. Read by Mary Woods. 8 cass. (Running Time: 8 hrs.). 1984. 48.00 (978-0-7366-0940-1(7), 1883) Books on Tape.
One man cuts the family's cycle of ignorance & want. He finds courage through the love of a very special woman, but must learn if such a love can survive in The Fifteen Streets.

Fifteen Traps for the Trial Lawyer & How to Avoid Them. 1 cass. (Running Time: 1 hr.). 1981. 15.00 PA Bar Inst.

Fifteen Volunteer, Professional & Organizational 1996 Chevron-Times Mirror Magazines Conservation Awards Recipients. Hosted by Nancy Pearlman. 1 cass. (Running Time: 29 min.). 10.00 (1421) Educ Comm CA.

Fifteen Ways to Master Change in Your Life Right Now! abr. ed. Vicki Field. 2006. audio compact disk (978-0-9785426-6-5(5)) Ultimate Wealth.

Fifteen Years of Music You Can Believe In. 1997. 12.98 (978-0-7601-1484-1(6), C10014); audio compact disk 17.98 CD. (978-0-7601-1485-8(4), CD10014) Brentwood Music.
Collection of thirty of the best Reunion Records music from the past fifteen years. Includes "Friends" by Michael Smith, "Awesome God" by Rich Mullins, "Everything Changes" by Kathy Troccoli, & many more.

***Fifth Agreement: A Practical Guide to Self-Mastery.** Don Miguel Ruiz & Don Jose Ruiz. Read by Peter Coyote. (Running Time: 4 hrs. 30 mins. 0 sec.). (ENG.). 2010. audio compact disk 23.95 (978-1-878424-59-4(9)) Pub: Amber-Allen Pub. Dist(s): Hay House

Fifth Angel. Tim Green. 2003. audio compact disk 99.00 (978-0-7366-9220-5(7)) Books on Tape.

Fifth Angel. abr. ed. Tim Green. Read by Tate Donovan. (ENG.). 2005. 14.98 (978-1-59483-349-6(4)) Pub: Hachet Audio. Dist(s): HachBkGrp

Fifth Angel. abr. ed. Tim Green. Read by Tate Donovan. (Running Time: 6 hrs.). (ENG.). 2009. 49.98 (978-1-60788-096-7(2)) Pub: Hachet Audio. Dist(s): HachBkGrp

Fifth Angel. unabr. ed. Tim Green. 6 cass. (Running Time: 9 hrs.). 2003. 81.00 (978-0-7366-9182-6(0)) Books on Tape.
A high-profile, successful lawyer can also be a serial murderer on the side.

Fifth Business. abr. ed. Robertson Davies. 4 cass. (Running Time: 3 hrs.). (Deptford Trilogy: Vol. 1). (gr. 9-12). 2005. bk. 24.95 (978-0-660-18654-2(3)) Canadian Broadcasting CAN.

Fifth Business. unabr. ed. Robertson Davies. Read by Dan Lazar. 10 cass. (Running Time: 10 hrs.). 60.00 (978-0-7366-0295-2(X), 1283) Books on Tape.
In writing his memoirs, Dunstan Ramsay reveals the unique role he played during his life, or rather, lives. For Ramsay is a man twice born, a man who returned from the trenches of World War I & was destined to live within the borderline between history & myth.

***Fifth Business.** unabr. ed. Robertson Davies. Read by Marc Vietor. (Running Time: 10 hrs.). 2010. 24.99 (978-1-4418-8588-3(9), 9781441885883, Brilliance MP3); 39.97 (978-1-4418-8589-0(7), 9781441885890, Brlnc Audio MP3 Lib); 39.97 (978-1-4418-8590-6(0), 9781441885906, BADLE); audio compact disk 29.99 (978-1-4418-8586-9(2), 9781441885869, Bril Audio CD Unabri); audio compact disk 69.97 (978-1-4418-8587-6(0), 9781441885876, BriAudCD Unabrid) Brilliance Audio.

Fifth Chakra: Key to Calmness & Keeness of Understanding. 1 cass. (Running Time: 90 min.). (Chakras Ser.). 9.95 (83F) Crystal Clarity.
Focuses on: the ether element in human consciousness; sweetness of voice as the result of harmonizing the vibrations of the throat chakra; how kundalini energy affects the chakras; contacting the chakras in deep sleep.

Fifth Child. unabr. ed. Doris Lessing. Read by Susan Fleetwood. 4 cass. (Running Time: 4 hrs. 45 min.). 1995. 44.95 (978-1-85695-667-3(9), 88112) Pub: ISIS Audio GBR. Dist(s): Ulverscroft US

Fifth Child. unabr. ed. Doris Lessing. Read by Susan Fleetwood. 5 CDs. (Running Time: 13 hrs. 23 mins.). (Isis Ser.). (J). 2002. audio compact disk 59.95 (978-0-7531-1483-4(6)) Pub: ISIS Lrg Prnt GBR. Dist(s): Ulverscroft US
Harriet and David, against the trends of the 1960s, favor fidelity, love, family life and a permanent home. They marry and begin their lives together in an old Victorian house; children fill the home and life is idyllic. It is only when Harriet becomes pregnant for the fifth time that problems occur. After a difficult pregnancy and birth, the strange-looking child develops fast and grows bigger; he is unloving and disliked by his brothers and sisters. Inexorably, his alien presence wrecks the dream of their happy family. Harriet's fear grows as she struggles to love and care for this "changeling" child.

Fifth Dimension Travel. Bruce Goldberg. (ENG.). 2005. audio compact disk 17.00 (978-1-57968-065-7(8)) Pub: B Goldberg. Dist(s): Baker Taylor

Fifth Dimension Travel. Bruce Goldberg. Read by Bruce Goldberg. 1 cass. (Running Time: 30 min.). (ENG.). 2006. 13.00 (978-1-57968-000-8(3)) Pub: B Goldberg. Dist(s): Baker Taylor
This self hypnosis tape guides you into hyperspace & the fifth dimension to explore the past, future, & parallel universe.

Fifth Discipline. abr. ed. Peter M. Senge. Read by Peter M. Senge. 4 CDs. (Running Time: 4 hrs.). (ENG.). 1999. audio compact disk 29.95 (978-0-553-45634-9(2)) Pub: Random Audio Pubg. Dist(s): Random
Peter Senge's groundbreaking ideas on building organizations have made him a household name amongst corporate managers. His theories help businesses to clarify their goals, to defy the odds, to more clearly understand threats, and to recognize new opportunities. He introduces managers to a new source of competitive advantage, and offers a marvelously empowering approach to work. Mastery of Senge's five disciplines enables managers to overcome their obstacles to growth and creates brave new futures for them and their companies. The five disciplines are drawn from science, spiritual wisdom, psychology, the cutting edge of management thought, and Senge's own work with top corporations that employ his methods. Listening to I The Fifth Discipline provides a searching personal experience and a dramatic professional shift of mind.

Fifth Discipline: The Art & Practice of the Learning Organization. unabr. ed. Peter M. Senge. 4 cass. 1996. 22.00 (47321) Books on Tape.
Peter Senge's ground-breaking ideas on building organizations have made him a household name amongst corporate managers. His theories help businesses to clarify their goals, to defy the odds, to more clearly understand threats & to recognize new opportunities. He introduces managers to a new source of competitive advantage, offering an empowering approach to work.

Fifth Discipline Challenge. abr. ed. Peter M. Senge. 4 cass.; 5 CDs. (Running Time: 6 hrs.). 1999. 25.00 (Random AudioBks); audio compact disk 29.95 (Random AudioBks) Random Audio Pubg.
Shows businesses how to use organizational change to keep producing results in a maelstrom of changing conditions - by successfully changing the very company itself.

Fifth Elephant. unabr. ed. Terry Pratchett. Read by Steven Briggs. 10 cass. (Running Time: 15 hrs.). (Discworld Ser.). 2001. 84.95 (978-0-7531-0839-0(9), 001205) Pub: ISIS Audio GBR. Dist(s): Ulverscroft US

Fifth Elephant. unabr. ed. Terry Pratchett. Read by Stephen Briggs. 10 CDs. (Running Time: 39000 sec.). (Discworld Ser.). 2001. audio compact disk 89.95 (978-0-7531-1132-1(2), 111322) Pub: ISIS Lrg Prnt GBR. Dist(s): Ulverscroft US
Everyone knows that the world is flat & supported on the backs of four elephants. But weren't there supposed to be five? Indeed there were & what happened to the fifth elephant is only one of the many perplexing mysteries solved in this new novel by today's most celebrated fantasy humorist. The Fifth Elephant begins, like so many of Pratchett's satirical inventions, with an invitation. This one is both royal & engraved, requiring that Commander Vimes of the Ankh-Morpork constabulary attends both detective & diplomat. The one role he relishes; the other, well requires ruby tights. Where cops (even those clad in tights) go, crime of course, follows & an attempted assassination & a theft soon lead to a desperate chase from the low halls of Discworld royalty to the legendary fat mines of Uberwald, where lard is found in underground seams along with tusks & teeth & other precious ivory artifacts. Vime's "elephant" adventure is as profound as it is hilarious, sending up every aspect of modern life from royalty (a British specialty) to bureaucrats (inescapable anywhere), from cops (especially those unusually dressed) to criminals (who, like fools, have their own guild), from fantasy to satire itself.

Fifth Horseman. unabr. ed. Larry Collins & Dominique Lapierre. Read by Christopher Hurt. 12 cass. (Running Time: 17 hrs. 30 mins.). 1992. 83.95 (978-0-7861-0201-3(2), 1177) Blckstn Audio.
Blending history & fact, the authors take the reader through a day & a half of suspenseful, anguished terror, from the White House to the streets of Brooklyn & Manhattan; from the elegant ministerial corridors of power in Paris to the pickpockets' dens, discotheques, fences' warehouses & dingy lofts where the New York Police Department & the FBI, in a race against the clock, are desperately searching for clues; from the vast desert of Libya, where Qaddafi waits to signal the destruction of the city, to the cabinet meeting room in Jerusalem, where the Israeli government must make a final, agonizing, life-or-death decision.

Fifth Life of the Catwoman, Set. unabr. ed. Kathleen Dexter. Read by Cindy Hollenberg. 6 cass. (Running Time: 9 Hrs.). 1999. 29.95 Set. (978-1-893530-12-6(4)) Arania Bks.
An allegory of prejudice, intolerance, second chances and the feline obsession with tuna. The catwoman hides out on her mirage, surrounded by 50 cats, just trying to survive her fifth of nine lives...until she begins to teach history not taught in textbooks!.

Fifth of March: A Story of the Boston Massacre. unabr. ed. Ann Rinaldi. 6 cass. (Running Time: 8 hrs.). (J). 2004. 39.95 (978-1-883332-97-6(4)); audio compact disk 49.95 (978-1-883332-98-3(2)) Audio Bkshelf.
14 yrs. old Rachel Marsh, nanny to John and Abigail Adams discovers her own strengths during the daysof the Boston Massacre.

Fifth Profession. abr. ed. David Morrell. Read by David McCullum. 2 cass. (Running Time: 3 hrs.). 2001. 18.00 (978-1-59040-126-2(3), Phoenix Audio) Pub: Amer Intl Pub. Dist(s): PerseuPGW

Fifth Profession. unabr. ed. David Morrell. (Running Time: 14 hrs.). 2006. 24.95 (978-1-59737-771-3(6), 9781597377713, BAD) Brilliance Audio.

Fifth Profession. unabr. ed. David Morrell. Read by Multivoice Production Staff. (Running Time: 14 hrs.). 2006. 39.25 (978-1-59737-772-0(4), 9781597377720, BADLE) Brilliance Audio.

Fifth Profession. unabr. ed. David Morrell. Read by Full Cast Production Staff. (Running Time: 50400 sec.). 2006. audio compact disk 39.25 (978-1-59737-770-6(8), 9781597377706, Brinc Audio MP3 Lib) Brilliance Audio.
Savage, a former Navy SEAL and American state-of-the-art security specialist. Akira, Japan's most brilliant executive protector and a master of the samurai arts. Their mission: the retrieval of Rachel Stone, a beautiful American woman whose ruthless billionaire husband is out to destroy her. But quickly Savage and Akira realize they are trapped in a mission more far-reaching than the protection of one person. For they are bound together in a common nightmare, a set of horrifying memories, a terrifying past that never happened, but is somehow inexplicably real. Only together can they confront the mystery. Yet when they do, an even more chilling scenario awaits them - one with the power to shatter not only their world but ours as well.

Fifth Profession. unabr. ed. David Morrell. Read by Multivoice Production Staff. (Running Time: 50400 sec.). 2006. audio compact disk 117.25 (978-1-59737-768-3(6), 9781597377683, BriAudCD Unabrid); audio compact disk 29.95 (978-1-59737-767-6(8), 9781597377676, Bril Audio CD Unabri); audio compact disk 24.95 (978-1-59737-769-0(4), 9781597377690, Brilliance MP3) Brilliance Audio.

Fifth Quarter. unabr. ed. Jennifer Allen. Read by Susie Breck. (Running Time: 9 hrs.). 2005. 39.25 (978-1-59600-526-6(2), 9781596005266, BADLE); 24.95 (978-1-59600-525-9(4), 9781596005259, BAD); 39.25 (978-1-59600-524-2(6), 9781596005242, Brinc Audio MP3 Lib); 24.95 (978-1-59600-523-5(8), 9781596005235, Brilliance MP3) Brilliance Audio.
Subtitled: The Scrimmage of a Football Coach's Daughter George Allen was a top-ranked NFL coach throughout the 1960s and 1970s, coaching in turn the Chicago Bears, the Los Angeles Rams, and the Washington Redskins. Raised in a home dominated by her three football obsessed older brothers and her father's relentless schedule, the author came of age in a cauldron of testosterone and a win-at-all-costs mentality. While the household was buffeted by the coach's tumultuous firings and hirings, which periodically propelled the family to a new city, Jennifer dreamed of being the first female quarterback in the NFL. But as she grew, she yearned mostly to be someone that her father would notice. In a world where only football mattered, what could she strive for, who could she become? Allen has written a memoir of the father she tried so hard to know, the family life that was wistfully sacrificed to his endless, fanatical pursuit of the Super Bowl. What emerges is a fascinating and singular behind-the-scenes look at professional football and a memorable, bittersweet portrait of a father and his daughter, told by an accomplished and assured writer.

Fifth Quarter: The Scrimmage of a Football Coach's Daughter. unabr. ed. Jennifer Allen. Read by Susie Breck. 6 cass. (Running Time: 9 hrs.). 2000. 29.95 (978-1-58788-154-1(3), 1587881543, BAU) Brilliance Audio.

Fifth Queen, Vol. 1. unabr. ed. Ford Madox Ford. Narrated by Flo Gibson. 5 cass. (Running Time: 7 hrs. 30 mins.). (YA). (gr. 8 up). 1997. 35.95 (978-1-55685-133-9(2)) Audio Bk Con.
Concerning the intrigues trials, tribulations & demise of Catherine Howard the wife of Henry VIII.

Fifth Queen, Vol. 231. unabr. ed. Ford Madox Ford. Read by Flo Gibson. 5 cass. (Running Time: 7 hrs. 30 min.). (gr. 8 up). 1997. 20.95 (978-1-55685-122-3(7)) Audio Bk Con.

Fifth Queen (Part 2), Vol. 2. unabr. ed. Ford Madox Ford. Narrated by Flo Gibson. (Running Time: 11 hrs. 24 mins.). 1989. 26.95 (978-1-55685-812-3(4)) Audio Bk Con.

Fifth Queen (Parts 1 And 2) unabr. ed. Ford Madox Ford. Narrated by Flo Gibson. (Running Time: 18 hrs. 41 mins.). 1989. 41.95 (978-1-55685-813-0(2)) Audio Bk Con.

Fifth Revenge. unabr. ed. Carl Burcham. Read by Gene Engene. 8 cass. (Running Time: 9 hrs. 48 min.). 2001. 49.95 (978-1-58116-085-7(2)); audio compact disk 58.50 (978-1-58116-120-5(4)) Books in Motion.
The spirit of the defeated Indian Nation arises in the form of the "Avenger," when the Secretary of the Interior is brutally murdered at the Washington Mall. As additional murders take place, D.C. Detective Quinn Shannon races to stop the Avenger, and find a rogue assassin before other innocents die.

Fifth Seal. unabr. ed. Bodie Thoene & Brock Thoene. Narrated by Sean Barrett. (Running Time: 11 hrs. 0 mins. 0 sec.). (A. D. Chronicles Ser.). (ENG.). 2009. audio compact disk 34.99 (978-1-59859-539-0(3)) Oasis Audio.

Fifth Sorceress, Pt. 1. unabr. ed. Robert Newcomb. 2002. 96.00 (978-0-7366-8756-0(4)) Books on Tape.
Three centuries ago, the unspeakable ravages of a devastating war nearly tore apart the kingdom of Eutracia. Those who masterminded the bloodshed - a quartet of powerful, conquest-hungry Sorceresses - were sentenced to exile, with return all but impossible, and death all but inevitable. Now a land of peace and plenty, protected and guided by a council of immortal wizards, Eutracia is about to crown a new king. But as the coronation approaches, an ancient evil nurtured over centuries of darkness will return with a vengeance - it's those Sorceresses again.

Fifth Sorceress, Pt. 2. unabr. ed. Robert Newcomb. 10 cass. (Running Time: 15 hrs.). 2002. 96.00 (978-0-7366-8806-2(4)) Books on Tape.

Fifth Step: Making Amends. Ed Young. 1998. 4.95 (978-0-7417-2201-0(1), 1201) Win Walk.

Fifth Summer. unabr. ed. Titia Sutherland. Read by Carole Boyd. 10 cass. (Running Time: 13 hrs. 30 mins.). (Isis Ser.). (J). 2000. 84.95 (978-0-7531-0452-1(0), 980904) Pub: ISIS Lrg Prnt GBR. Dist(s): Ulverscroft US
Every summer the Blair Family went to Italy, to the villa in The Garden, a lush wilderness of cypress trees & bougainvillea tumbling down to the sea. Phoebe, who owned the villa & lived close by, loved the Blairs, of all her summer guests they were the ones who gave meaning to her life. She was possessive, enigmatic, manipulative, but Will & Lorna never really minded, until the fifth summer. Something was wrong even before they arrived. There was a tension, a distance between them, something strange that Lorna could not quite define.

***Fifth Sun.** Nicholas A. Patricca. Music by The San Antonio Vocal Arts Ensemble & Xavier Quijas Yxaayotl. Directed By Elizabeth A. Peterson-Vita. Engineer James Vita. (ENG.). 2010. audio compact disk 13.99 (978-0-9817573-5-3(9)) Scene Unseen.

Fifth Vial. Michael Palmer. Read by J. Charles. (Playaway Adult Fiction Ser.). (ENG.). 2009. 75.00 (978-1-60775-540-1(8)) Find a World.

Fifth Vial. abr. ed. Michael Palmer. Read by J. Charles. (Running Time: 21600 sec.). 2007. audio compact disk 14.99 (978-1-4233-0648-1(1), 9781423306481, BCD Value Price) Brilliance Audio.

Fifth Vial. unabr. ed. Michael Palmer. Read by J. Charles. (Running Time: 12 hrs.). 2007. 39.25 (978-1-59737-059-2(2), 9781597370592, BADLE); 24.95 (978-1-59737-058-5(4), 9781597370585, BAD); 87.25 (978-1-59737-052-3(5), 9781597370523, BrilAudUnabridg); audio compact disk 39.25 (978-1-59737-057-8(6), 9781597370578, Brinc Audio MP3 Lib); audio compact disk 24.95 (978-1-59737-056-1(8), 9781597370561, Brilliance MP3); audio compact disk 102.25 (978-1-59737-055-4(X), 9781597370554, BriAudCD Unabrid); audio compact disk 38.95 (978-1-59737-054-7(1), 9781597370547, Bril Audio CD Unabri) Brilliance Audio.
Please enter a Synopsis.

***Fifth Witness.** abr. ed. Michael Connelly. (Running Time: 6 hrs.). (ENG.). 2011. 24.98 (978-1-60941-202-9(8)); audio compact disk & audio compact disk 29.98 (978-1-60941-201-2(X)) Pub: Hachet Audio. Dist(s): HachBkGrp

***Fifth Witness.** unabr. ed. Michael Connelly. (Running Time: 11 hrs.). (ENG.). 2011. 26.98 (978-1-60941-195-4(1)); audio compact disk & audio compact disk 39.98 (978-1-60024-722-4(9)) Pub: Hachet Audio. Dist(s): HachBkGrp

Fifth Woman. unabr. ed. Henning Mankell. Read by Dick Hill. Tr. by Steven T. Murray. (Running Time: 61200 sec.). (Kurt Wallander Ser.). 2007. 85.95 (978-1-4332-1117-1(3)); audio compact disk 99.00 (978-1-4332-1118-8(1)) Blckstn Audio.

Fifth Woman. unabr. ed. Henning Mankell & Dick Hill. Tr. by Steven T. Murray. (Running Time: 61200 sec.). (Kurt Wallander Ser.). 2007. audio compact disk 29.95 (978-1-4332-1119-5(X)) Blckstn Audio.

Fifty Acres & a Poodle. Jeanne Marie Laskas. Read by Karen White. 2000. 56.00 (978-0-7366-5651-1(0)) Books on Tape.

Fifty Acres & a Poodle. Jeanne Marie Laskas. 7 cass. (Running Time: 10 hrs.). 2000. 29.95 (978-0-7366-5831-7(9)) Books on Tape.
A story written with exhilarating wit and extraordinary wisdom about what happens when you follow your dream.

Fifty Cent Profile. unabr. ed. Craig Fraley. Read by Maynard Villers. 4 cass. (Running Time: 6 hrs.). (Kiahawk Ser.). 26.95 (978-1-55686-675-3(5)) Books in Motion.
Detective Greg Nolan uncovers a crime that changes history & unknowingly places his life in jeopardy when those in high government circles attempt to cover-up the discovery.

Fifty-Day Adventure Broadcast Tapes: Facing down Our Fears. unabr. ed. Chapel of the Air Ministries Staff et al. 7 cass. (Running Time: 10 hrs. 30 min.). (50-Day Spiritual Adventure Ser.). 1995. 19.99 Set. (978-1-879050-67-9(6)) Chapel of Air.
Duplication tapes from The Chapel of the Air radio programs for the 50-Day Spiritual Adventure.

Fifty-Day Spiritual Adventure Broadcast Tapes: Daring to Dream Again. Chapel of the Air Ministries Staff et al. 7 cass. (Running Time: 10 hrs. 30 min.). (50-Day Spiritual Adventure Ser.). 1994. 39.99 Set. (978-1-879050-42-6(0)) Chapel of Air.
Tapes of daily "Chapel of the Air" radio broadcasts related to the 1994 50-Day Spiritual Adventure.

Fifty Easy Classical Guitar Solos. Jerry Willard. 1 cass. 1990. pap. bk. 15.95 (978-0-8256-1153-7(9)) Music Sales.

Fifty Famous Fairy Tales. Rosemary Kingston. Narrated by Marguerite Gavin. (Running Time: 7 hrs.). (J). 2000. 27.95 (978-1-59912-489-6(0)) Iofy Corp.

Fifty Famous Fairy Tales. unabr. ed. Rosemary Kingston. Read by Marguerite Gavin. 6 CDs. (Running Time: 7 hrs.). 2001. audio compact disk 48.00 (978-0-7861-9701-9(3), 2812) Blckstn Audio.

Fifty Famous Fairy Tales. unabr. ed. Rosemary Kingston. Read by Marguerite Gavin. 5 cass. (Running Time: 7 hrs.). 2001. 39.95 (978-0-7861-2052-9(5), 2812) Blckstn Audio.
Tales in this collection include: "Puss in Boots," "Rumpelstiltskin," "The Frog Prince," "Cinderella and the Glass Slipper," "Jack and the Beanstalk," "The Wild Swans," "Snow White and Rose Red," "The Spirit in the Bottle," "Little Red Riding Hood," "The Three Bears," "The Musicians of Bremen," "The Fisherman and his Wife," and many others sure to be familiar to children and adults alike.

Fifty Famous Stories Retold. unabr. ed. James Baldwin. Read by Cliff Roles. (YA). 2007. 34.99 (978-1-60252-752-2(0)) Find a World.

Fifty, Female & Fabulous: A Holistic Guide to Love, Sex & Relationships. 619th unabr. ed. Barbara Griffin Moore. Illus. by Bob O'Brien. Interview with Bob O'Brien. 3 cass. (Running Time: 1 hr. 15 min.). 1998. pap. bk. & wbk. ed. 49.95 (978-0-9659346-9-5(1)) Mystic Moon NM.
Self-help for women over 50 based on spiritual, metaphysical & psychological concepts.

Fifty-Fifty Series: A Basic Course in Communicative English, Level 1. 2nd ed. Warren Wilson & Roger Barnard. 2002. 22.00 (978-0-13-920026-7(6)) Longman.

Fifty-Fifty Series: A Basic Course in Communicative English, Level 2. 2nd ed. Warren Wilson & Roger Barnard. 2002. 22.00 (978-0-13-920075-5(4)) Longman.

Fifty-Fifty Series: Introductory. 2nd ed. Warren Wilson & Roger Barnard. 2002. 22.00 (978-0-13-906984-0(4)) Longman.

Fifty-First Dragon. Heywood Hale Broun. 10.00 (LSS1122) Esstee Audios.

Fifty Grand see Stories of Ernest Hemingway

Fifty Grand. unabr. ed. Adrian McKinty. Read by Paula Christensen. (Running Time: 14 hrs. 0 mins.). (ENG.). 2009. 29.95 (978-1-4332-9249-1(1)); 65.95 (978-1-4332-9245-3(9)); audio compact disk 100.00 (978-1-4332-9246-0(7)) Blckstn Audio.

Fifty Most Romantic Things Ever Done. unabr. ed. Dini von Mueffling. Read by S. Patricia Bailey. 2 cass. (Running Time: 1 hr. 30 min. per cass.). 1997. Rental 7.95 Set, 30-day. (1870) Blckstn Audio.
The perfect gift book for Valentine's Day - & beyond! A delightful compendium of the most romantic things done by celebrities, famous figures from history, & ordinary people.

Fifty Poems of Emily Dickinson, Vol. 1. unabr. abr. ed. Emily Dickinson. Read by Stephanie Beacham et al. 11 cass. (Running Time: 1.5 hrs.). 2004. 15.00 (978-1-931056-80-9(3), N Millennium Audio) New Millenn Enter.

Fifty Poems of Emily Dickinson, Vol. 2. unabr. ed. Emily Dickinson. Read by Sharon Stone & Meryl Streep. 1 CD. (Running Time: 1 hr.). 2001. audio compact disk 15.00 (N Millennium Audio) New Millenn Enter.

Fifty Poems of Emily Dickinson, Vol. 2. unabr. ed. Emily Dickinson. Read by Jill Eikenberry et al. 21 cass. (Running Time: 1.5 hrs.). 2004. 15.00 (978-1-931056-81-6(1), N Millennium Audio) New Millenn Enter.

Fifty Poems of Emily Dickinson, Vol. 3. unabr. ed. Emily Dickinson. Read by Sharon Stone & Meryl Streep. 1 cass. (Running Time: 1 hr.). 2001. 15.00 (N Millennium Audio); audio compact disk 15.00 (N Millennium Audio) New Millenn Enter.

Fifty Poems of Emily Dickinson, Vol. 3. unabr. ed. Emily Dickinson. Read by Joan Allen et al. 31 CDs. (Running Time: 1.5 hrs.). 2004. audio compact disk 15.00 (978-1-931056-82-3(X), N Millennium Audio) New Millenn Enter.

Fifty Poems of Emily Dickinson, Volume I. abr. ed. Emily Dickinson. Read by Meryl Streep et al. (Running Time: 1800 sec.). 2007. audio compact disk 19.95 (978-1-4332-0702-0(8)) Blckstn Audio.

Fifty Poems of Emily Dickinson, Volume 1. unabr. abr. ed. Emily Dickinson. Read by Stephanie Beacham et al. (Running Time: 1800 sec.). 2007. audio compact disk & audio compact disk 17.00 (978-1-4332-1350-2(8)) Blckstn Audio.

Fifty Primary Universal Laws. 1 cass. (Condensed Books on Tape). 9.95 (978-0-87554-473-1(8), N117) Valley Sun.

***Fifty Reasons Why Jesus Came to Die.** unabr. ed. John Piper. Narrated by Robertson Dean. (ENG.). 2009. 5.98 (978-1-59644-625-0(0), Hovel Audio) christianaud.

Fifty Reasons Why Jesus Came to Die. unabr. ed. John Piper. Narrated by Robertson Dean. (Running Time: 3 hrs. 21 mins. 0 sec.). (ENG.). 2009. audio compact disk 5.98 (978-1-59644-624-3(2), Hovel Audio) christianaud.

Fifty Simple Things You Can Do to Save the Earth. Earthworks Group Staff. 1 cass. (Running Time: 1 hr.). 7.95 incl. bklt. (978-1-55569-445-6(4), 7211) Great Am Audio.

Fifty-Two Lesson Course in Chord Piano. Duane Shinn. Read by Duane Shinn. 5 cass. (Running Time: 5 hrs.). 199.95 set, incl. printed 52-lesson course in 3-ring binder. (CP-11) Duane Shinn.

Fifty-Two Offbeat Texas Stops: Traveling with Bob Phillips, Texas Country Reporter. Bob Phillips. Read by Bob Phillips. 2 cass. 1994. 19.95 set. (978-0-9636541-2-0(8)) Phillips Prods.
Fifty-two favorite stops of TV show (Texas Country Reporter) hosted by Bob Phillips.

Fifty Ways to Buy Country Property with Little or No Money Down. Read by B. K. Haynes. 2006. audio compact disk 19.95 (978-0-932586-09-4(0)) Greatland Pubng.

Fifty Ways to Fool Your Mother. Bill Harley. (J). 2000. audio compact disk 15.00 (978-1-878126-36-8(9)) Round Riv Prodns.
A great collection of original & traditional songs: Under One Sky; 50 Ways to Fool Your Mother; Mr. Spaceman; Nobody Knew; Somos el Barco/We Are the Boat; I'm On My Way; There Goes My Brother Again; Havin' A Party; My Dog Sam; When I First Came To This Land.

Fifty Ways to Fool Your Mother. unabr. ed. Bill Harley. Read by Bill Harley. 1 cass. (Running Time: 41 min.). (J). (gr. k-6). 1986. 10.00 (978-1-878126-01-6(6), RRR102) Round Riv Prodns.

Fifty Ways to Get Hired. Max Messmer. 4 cass. (Running Time: 6 hrs.). 1995. 19.95 (978-1-55977-320-1(0)) CareerTrack Pubns.

Fifty Ways to Get Hired: How to Open New Doors, Put Your Best Foot Forward & Lock up the Job You Want. Max Messmer. 4 cass. (Running Time: 3 hrs.). 1994. 49.95 Set. (V10164) CareerTrack Pubns.
This program gives you valuable hints & "how-tos" from job-placement luminary Max Messmer, chairman & CEO of Robert Half International, Inc. Listen, & you'll learn proven job-search strategies that give you an automatic lead over your competition.

Fifty Ways to Meet a Lover. Laura Des Jardins. 1 cass. 8.95 (851) Am Fed Astrologers.

Fifty Years after Fourteen August. Norman Corwin. Perf. by Charles Kuralt & Pat Carroll. Prod. by Mary Beth Kirchner. 1 cass. (Running Time: 30 min.). 1998. 12.95 (978-1-57677-023-8(0), CORW005) Radio Spirits.
Commemorates the anniversary of V-J Day.

Fifty Years of Silence: The Extraordinary Memoir of a War Rape Survivor. unabr. ed. Jan Ruff-O'Herne. Read by Beverley Dunn. (Running Time: 16800 sec.). 2008. audio compact disk 57.95 (978-1-921334-88-7(6), 9781921334887) Pub: Bolinda Pubng AUS. Dist(s): Bolinda Pub Inc

Fig Eater: A Novel. unabr. ed. Jody Shields. 2001. (978-1-58621-017-5(3)) Hachet Audio.

Fig Eater: A Novel. unabr. ed. Jody Shields. Read by Patricia Kilgarriff. (ENG.). 2005. 14.98 (978-1-59483-471-4(7)) Pub: Hachet Audio. Dist(s): HachBkGrp

Fig Pudding. Ralph J. Fletcher. Read by Jeff Woodman. 3 cass. (Running Time: 3 hrs. 30 mins.). (YA). 1999. stu. ed. 92.80 (978-0-7887-3227-0(7), 46883) Recorded Bks.
Eleven-year-old Cliff Abernathy isn't an ordinary elementary school kid. As the oldest in a family of six children, he has a lot of responsibilities & patience. Includes study guide.

Fig Pudding. unabr. ed. Ralph J. Fletcher. Narrated by Jeff Woodman. 3 cass. (Running Time: 3 hrs. 30 mins.). (YA). (gr. 5 up). 2000. pap. bk. 39.75 (978-0-7887-3181-5(5), 40916X4) Recorded Bks.

Fig Pudding, unabr. ed. Ralph J. Fletcher. Narrated by Jeff Woodman. 3 pieces. (Running Time: 3 hrs. 30 mins.). (gr. 5 up). 2000. 27.00 (978-0-7887-3197-6(1), 95756E7) Recorded Bks.

Figaro. Narrated by Jean-Pierre Cassell. 1 cass. (FRE.). (J). 1991. bk. 14.95 (1AD065) Olivia & Hill.

Fight: Are You Willing to Pick a Fight with Evil? Kenny Luck. (Running Time: 27000 sec.). (God's Man Ser.). (ENG.). 2008. audio compact disk 26.99 (978-1-934384-19-0(4)) Pub: Treasure Pub. Dist(s): STL Dist NA

Fight Back! Tackling Terrorism, Liddy Style. G. Gordon Liddy. Read by Stefan Rudnicki. (Running Time: 32400 sec.). 2006. audio compact disk 72.00 (978-0-7861-7334-1(3)) Blckstn Audio.

Fight Back: Tackling Terrorism, Liddy Style. G. Gordon Liddy. Read by Stefan Rudnicki. Told to James G. Liddy et al. (Running Time: 32400 sec.). 2006. 59.95 (978-0-7861-4449-5(1)) Blckstn Audio.

Fight Back! Tackling Terrorism, Liddy Style. unabr. ed. G. Gordon Liddy. 7 cass. (Running Time: 8 hrs.). (YA). 2006. 29.95 (978-0-7861-4392-4(4)) Blckstn Audio.

Fight Back! Tackling Terrorism, Liddy Style. unabr. ed. G. Gordon Liddy. Read by Stefan Rudnicki. 8 CDs. (Running Time: 32400 sec.). 2006. audio compact disk 29.95 (978-0-7861-7446-1(3)) Blckstn Audio.

***Fight Back & Win.** abr. ed. Gloria Allred. Read by Gloria Allred. (ENG.). 2006. (978-0-06-113191-2(1), Harper Audio); (978-0-06-113190-5(3), Harper Audio) HarperCollins Pubs.

Fight Back & Win: My Thirty-Year Fight Against Injustice - And How You Can Win Your Own Battles. abr. ed. Gloria Allred. Read by Gloria Allred. Told to Deborah Caulfield Rybak. (Running Time: 21600 sec.). 2006. audio compact disk 29.95 (978-0-06-087249-6(7)) HarperCollins Pubs.

Fight Cancer. Zoilita Grant. 2001. audio compact disk 15.95 (978-1-890575-30-4(5)) Zoilita Grant.

Fight Club. unabr. ed. Chuck Palahniuk. Narrated by James Colby. 5 cass. (Running Time: 5 hrs. 30 mins.). 2008. 61.75 (978-1-4281-5734-7(4)); audio compact disk 24.99 (978-1-4361-4960-0(6)); audio compact disk 72.75 (978-1-4281-5465-0(5)) Recorded Bks.

Fight for Competitive Advantage. Tom Peters & Richard Scase. 2005. audio compact disk 399.00 (978-0-273-70640-3(3), FT Pren) Pearson EducLt GBR.

Fight for Jerusalem. unabr. ed. Dore Gold. (Running Time: 9 hrs. 23 mins.). (J). 2007. 24.95 (978-0-7861-4790-8(3)) Blckstn Audio.

Fight for Jerusalem: Radical Islam, the West, & the Future of the Holy City. unabr. ed. Dore Gold. Read by Nadia May. (Running Time: 37800 sec.). 2007. 59.95 (978-0-7861-4784-7(9)); audio compact disk 29.95 (978-0-7861-7210-8(X)); audio compact disk 72.00 (978-0-7861-6277-2(5)) Blckstn Audio.

Fight for Jerusalem: Radical Islam, the West, & the Future of the Holy City. unabr. ed. Dore Gold. Read by Dore Gold. (Running Time: 37800 sec.). 2007. audio compact disk 24.95 (978-0-7861-6283-3(X)) Blckstn Audio.

Fight for Right. 2002. (978-0-7398-5125-8(X)) SteckVau.

Fight for Right Level 2. (J). 2002. audio compact disk (978-0-7398-5335-1(X)) SteckVau.

Fight for Your Life: The Story of Rubin Hurricane Carter. Godwin Chu. (Overcoming the Odds Sports Biographies Ser.). 2002. audio compact disk 18.95 (978-1-4105-0191-2(4)) D Johnston Inc.

Fight for Your Life: The Story of Rubin Hurricane Carter. Godwin Chu. Ed. by Jerry Stemach. 2002. audio compact disk 200.00 (978-1-58702-859-5(X)) D Johnston Inc.

Fight for Your Life: The Story of Rubin Hurricane Carter. Godwin Chu. Ed. by Jerry Stemach et al. Contrib. by Ted S. Hasselbring. (Start-to-Finish Books). (J). (gr. 2-3). 2002. 35.00 (978-1-58702-856-4(5)) D Johnston Inc.

Fight for Your Life: The Story of Rubin Hurricane Carter. unabr. ed. Godwin Chu. Ed. by Jerry Stemach et al. Contrib. by Ted S. Hasselbring. 2 cass. (Running Time: 3 hrs.). (Start-to-Finish Books). (J). (gr. 4-5). 2002. (978-1-58702-841-0(7), H10) D Johnston Inc.
In 1966, Rubin "Hurricane" Carter was one of the top ranked fighters in the sport of boxing. But after three people were murdered in a barroom in Paterson, New Jersey, Rubin and a friend named John Artis were arrested for the killings, and in 1967 they were convicted by an all-white jury for a crime they did not commit. While in prison, Carter researched his case, gathered compelling proof of his innocence, and published his story in The Sixteenth Round. The book helped Carter to gain the support of many people, including celebrities like Bob Dylan and Muhammad Ali.

Fight for Your Money: How to Stop Getting Ripped off & Save a Fortune. abr. ed. David Bach. Read by Oliver Wyman. (ENG.). 2009. audio compact disk 29.95 (978-0-7393-6885-5(0), Random AudioBks) Pub: Random Audio Pubg. Dist(s): Random

Fight of the Bumble Bee. unabr. ed. 2 CDs. (Running Time: 2 hrs.). 2000. audio compact disk 24.95 (978-0-9660392-6-9(2)) Pub: Radio Repertory. Dist(s): Timberwolf Pr
Featuring Marina Sirtis (Deanna Troi from Star Trek-TGN) as Nancy Coy, who tries to save both the Amalgamation & the man she has fallen in love with, Commander Kurk Manly.

Fight the Fear: Reducing Speaker Nervousness. Communication Development Associates Staff. 1 cass. (Running Time: 20 min.). 1991. 8.95 (978-0-9631301-0-5(2)) Comm Develop.
This program is designed to cure the butterflies, nervousness & anxiety individuals encounter when speaking in front of others.

Fight the Future. Chris Carter. 2 cass. (Running Time: 3 hrs.). (X-Files Ser.). 1998. 16.85 Set. (978-0-00-105542-1(9)) Zondervan.
The mysterious bombing of a Dallas office building & the secrets buried inside.

Fight Your Ticket. David W. Brown. 2 cass. 1994. 17.95 set. (978-1-885339-05-8(4)) Wolfpack Pub.
How to fight a traffic ticket.

***Fighter Pilot: The Memoirs of Legendary Ace Robin Olds.** unabr. ed. Robin Olds. (Running Time: 13 hrs. 0 mins.). 2010. 29.95 (978-1-4417-3698-7(0)); 79.95 (978-1-4417-3694-9(8)); audio compact disk 29.95 (978-1-4417-3697-0(2)); audio compact disk 105.00 (978-1-4417-3695-6(6)) Blckstn Audio.

Fighter Squadron at Guadalcanal. unabr. collector's ed. Max Brand. Read by Barrett Whitener. 6 cass. (Running Time: 6 hrs.). 1998. 36.00 (978-0-7366-4034-3(7), 4533) Books on Tape.
This personal & historical account arose from hundreds of hours of interviews with the flyers & ground crew caught in harm's way during World War II. Stories of air-to-air combat are recounted in the words of the men who were there.

Fighting Agents. W. E. B. Griffin. Read by Scott Brick. 2000. audio compact disk 88.00 (978-0-7366-8006-6(3)) Books on Tape.

Fighting Agents. unabr. ed. W. E. B. Griffin. Read by Scott Brick. 9 cass. (Running Time: 13 hrs. 30 mins.). 2000. 72.00 (978-0-7366-5509-5(3), 5349) Books on Tape.
In the Philippines, a ragtag American guerrilla army battles the Japanese under a most unusual commander. In Budapest, an agent must keep two key prisoners from being interrogated by the Gestapo, his only choices being to rescue them, or kill them. In Washington, an Army Air Corps captain suddenly finds himself assigned deep under the sea, his mission an improbably one of submarines, supplies, arms and gold. And in Cairo, an undistinguished pilot named Darmstadter wonders why the OSS is interested in his services, only to find out in the most dramatic way possible, and to become a hero in the process.

Fighting Back: A Guide for Self-Healing. Matthew Manning. Music by Enid. 1 cass. 11.95 (MM-101) White Dove NM.
Whether it be to relieve migraines, heal an ulcer or combat cancer, Fighting Back shows how you can help to accelerate your body's own healing processes. Matthew's "Fighting Back" idea grew from his successful treatment of patients with cancer.

Fighting Clowns. Perf. by Firesign Theatre. Text by Firesign Theatre. 1 CD. (Running Time: 39 mins). Dramatization. 2005. audio compact disk 15.95 (978-1-59938-022-3(6)) Lode Cat.
The Firesign Theatre faces the onslaught of the eighties, and the coming age of Reagan. And if they're going down, they're going down singing. Part song, part skit, this album was recorded live at the Roxy, early in 1980 before the election was decided. Remember Carter? Remember Reagan? Remember Afghanistan - the first time around? Hot tubs? Firesign manages to poke everyting and everyone in the eye - from German Cabaret to contemporary politics - with the usual full slathering of contemporary culture and intellectual mischief.

Fighting Clowns Ronald Reagan Assassination Show. 2 CDs. (Running Time: 2 hrs.). 2001. audio compact disk 24.95 Lodestone Catalog.
Life performance, recorded just hours after the attempt on Reagan's life on March 31, 1981 at the University of Maryland.

Fighting Disease. Compiled by Benchmark Education Staff. 2005. audio compact disk 10.00 (978-1-4108-5486-5(8)) Benchmark Educ.

Fighting Fair. John Bradshaw. 2 vols. (Running Time: 180 min.). 2000. 18.00 (978-1-57388-120-3(1)) J B Media.

Fighting Fair. John Bradshaw. (Running Time: 10800 sec.). 2008. audio compact disk 100.00 (978-1-57388-199-9(6)) J B Media.

Fighting Fire, unabr. ed. Caroline Paul. Narrated by Alyssa Bresnahan. 7 cass. (Running Time: 9 hrs.). 1998. 62.00 (978-0-7887-3125-9(4), 95674E7) Recorded Bks.
Caroline Paul astonished her friends & family by joining the San Francisco Fire Department a decade ago. She shares the moment when she first stepped into the male-dominated firehouse to the rigorous challenges of facing a fire blazing out of control.

Fighting for a Life: The Great Awakening. David Hadden. 2009. audio compact disk 37.99 (978-1-60696-819-2(X)) Tate Pubng.

Fighting for Air: The Battle to Control America's Media. unabr. ed. Eric Klinenberg. Read by Tom Weiner. (Running Time: 41400 sec.). 2008. 72.95 (978-1-4332-1331-1(1)); audio compact disk 29.95 (978-1-4332-1333-5(8)); audio compact disk & audio compact disk 90.00 (978-1-4332-1332-8(X)) Blckstn Audio.

Fighting for Flanders. Lance Auburn Everette. Read by Marguerite Gavin. 2 cass. (Running Time: 3 hrs.). 2005. 15.99 (978-1-58943-269-7(X)) Am Pubng Inc.
This is the first in a truly unique series of historical action-adventure novels: Michael. Sometimes, in history, things worked out for the best against all odds. Maybe Somebody intervened on the side of the correct path - even when we didn't know what that path was. But to intervene in the affairs of human beings without disrupting civilization completely is to wield human tools - and human weapons. So when the Archangels arrive to Change Things, watch out! In the early Middle Ages, Flanders was terribly vulnerable to invasion, from land or sea. How could it survive to become the most important commercial and intellectual centers of Europe, and not get conquered and plundered by every king around? Did Somebody help? Published for the first time ever by Americana Publishing. Michael: Spirituality - with an edge.

Fighting for Flanders. Lance Auburn Everette. Read by Marguerite Gavin. 3 CDs. (Running Time: 3 hrs.). 2005. audio compact disk 9.99 (978-1-58943-482-0(X)) Am Pubng Inc.

Fighting for the Hearts of Your Children. 1 CD. 2005. audio compact disk 9.99 (978-1-933207-08-7(6)) Ransomed Heart.

Fighting for Your Marriage: Positive Steps for Preventing Divorce & Preserving a Lasting Love. Howard Markman. 6 cass. 2001. cass. & cass. 39.95 (978-1-883886-25-7(2), Jossey-Bass) Wiley US.

Fighting France, from Dunkerque to Belfort, Set. unabr. ed. Edith Wharton. Read by Flo Gibson. 3 cass. (Running Time: 4 hr.). (gr. 8 up). 1991. 16.95 (978-1-55685-196-4(0)) Audio Bk Con.
Edith Wharton tours the length of the war front in France during World War I & describes in vivid detail the trenches, hospitals, villages, Paris' valiant struggles to preserve her values, & the esprit de corps of the gallant French.

Fighting Ground. unabr. ed. Avi. Read by Avi. 1 read-along cass. (Running Time: 68 min.). (Young Adult Cliffhangers Ser.). (YA). (gr. 4-6). 1986. 15.98 incl. bk. & guide. (978-0-8072-1844-0(8), JRH 124SP, Listening Lib) Random Audio Pubg.
The story of a 13 year-old boy caught up in the Revolutionary War. Jonathan is taken prisoner by the Hessians & in the turmoil that follows, begins to gain a new understanding of war & life.

Fighting Ground, unabr. ed. Avi. Narrated by George Guidall. 3 pieces. (Running Time: 3 hrs. 15 mins.). (gr. 4 up). 1994. 27.00 (978-0-7887-0009-5(X), 94208E7) Recorded Bks.
Thirteen year old Jonathan goes off to fight in the Revolutionary War & discovers the real war is being fought within himself.

Fighting Pattons. unabr. ed. Brian M. Sobel. Read by Adams Morgan. 10 cass. (Running Time: 14 hrs. 30 mins.). 2001. 69.95 (978-0-7861-2083-3(5), 2844) Blckstn Audio.
Maj. Gen. Patton's life and thoughts give us insight into his more famous father "I have seen many excellent studies of the legendary George Patton, ranging from The Fighting Pattons, The Fighting Pattons is personal, poignant and undeniable." "I fought in World War II under General Patton and young George fought under my command in Vietnam".

***Fighting Pattons.** unabr. ed. Brian M. Sobel. Read by Adams Morgan. (Running Time: 15 hrs. NaN mins.). (ENG.). 2011. 29.95 (978-1-4417-8386-8(5)); audio compact disk 118.00 (978-1-4417-8384-4(9)) Blckstn Audio.

Fighting Terrorism. unabr. ed. Benjamin Netanyahu. Read by Jeff Riggenbach. 4 CDs. 2004. audio compact disk 25.95 (978-0-7861-9483-4(9)) Blckstn Audio.

Fighting Terrorism: How Democracies Can Defeat Domestic & International Terrorism. unabr. ed. Benjamin Netanyahu. Narrated by Jeff Riggenbach. 4 cass. (Running Time: 5 hrs. 30 mins.). 2001. 32.95 (978-0-7861-2116-8(5), 2876); audio compact disk 32.00 (978-0-7861-9639-5(4), 2876); audio compact disk 24.95 (978-0-7861-9404-9(9), 2876) Blckstn Audio.
The spread of fundamentalist Islamic terrorism, coupled with the possibility that Iran will soon acquire nuclear weapons, poses a more frightening threat from an adversary less rational and therefore less controllable than was the Soviet Union. How democracies can defend themselves against this new threat concludes this innovative and concise new work.

Fighting Terrorism: How Democracies Can Defeat Domestic & International Terrorism. unabr. ed. Benjamin Netanyahu. Read by Jeff Riggenbach. 4 pieces. (Running Time: 19800 sec.). 2002. 25.95 (978-0-7861-2214-1(5)) Blckstn Audio.

Fighting the Cancer. Read by Mary Richards. 12.95 (505); 12.95 (630) Master Your Mind.
Discusses how to allow this critical illness to heighten spiritual growth & teach valuable lessons.

Fighting Words Vol. 1, Disc 3: Stories of My Life: Don't Live on Your Knees. Short Stories. Robert M. Katzman. 1. (Running Time: 1 hr. 8 mins.). 2004. audio compact disk 14.95 (978-0-9755279-3-1(2)) Fighting Words.

Fighting Words Vol. 1, Disc 4: Stories of My Life: Don't Live on Your Knees. Short Stories. Robert M. Katzman. 1. (Running Time: 1 hr. 3 mins.). 2004. audio compact disk 14.95 (978-0-9755279-4-8(0)) Fighting Words.

Fighting Words Vol. 1, Disc 5: Stories of My Life: Don't Live on Your Knees. Short Stories. Robert M. Katzman. 1. (Running Time: 1 hr. 9 mins.). 2004. audio compact disk 14.95 (978-0-9755279-5-5(9)) Fighting Words.
Announcement:11One Beating a Child 35:07Picked Last 34:05.

Fighting 69th: One Remarkable National Guard Unit's Journey from Ground Zero to Baghdad. unabr. ed. Sean Michael Flynn. Narrated by Erik Steele. (Running Time: 36000 sec.). (ENG.). 2007. audio compact disk 29.95 (978-1-60283-358-6(3)) Pub: AudioGO. Dist(s): Perseus Dist

Fighting 69th: One Remarkable National Guard Unit's Journey from Ground Zero to Baghdad. unabr. ed. Sean Michael Flynn. Read by Erik Steele. (YA). 2008. 74.99 (978-1-60514-884-7(9)) Find a World.

Fighting 69th: One Remarkable National Guard Unit's Journey from Ground Zero to Baghdad. unabr. ed. Sean Michael Rynn. Narrated by Erik Steele. 9 CDs. (Running Time: 11 hrs.). 2008. audio compact disk 89.95 (978-0-7927-5224-0(4)) AudioGO.
On the eve of September 11, 2001, New York City's famous National Guard regiment, the fighting 69th Infantry, was not fit for duty. Most of its soldiers were immigrant kids with no prior military experience, their uniforms were incomplete, and their equipment was derelict. The thought of deploying such a unit was laughable. Sean Flynn, himself a member of the 69th, memorably chronicles the transformation of this motley band of amateur soldiers into a battle-hardened troop at work in one of the most lethal quarters of Baghdad: the notorious Airport Road, a blood-soaked strand that grabbed headlines and became a bellwether for progress in post-invasion Iraq. At home on the concrete and asphalt like no other unit in the U.S. Army, Gotham's Fighting 69th brought justice to this lawless precinct by ignoring army discipline and turning to the street-fighting tactics they grew up with. The Fighting 69th is the story of how regular citizens come to grips with challenges far starker than what they.

Fights, Games & Debates. unabr. ed. Anatol Rapoport. 1 cass. (Running Time: 24 min.). 12.95 (27018) J Norton Pubs.
An analysis of the genesis & dynamics of conflict, with application of the components to the past & present global interactions.

***Figuras planas Audio CD.** April Barth. Adapted by Benchmark Education Co., LLC. (Content Connections Ser.). (SPA.). (J). 2010. audio compact disk 10.00 (978-1-61672-195-4(2)) Benchmark Educ.

***Figuras sólidas Audio CD.** April Barth. Adapted by Benchmark Education Co., LLC. (Content Connections Ser.). (SPA.). (J). 2010. audio compact disk 10.00 (978-1-61672-198-5(7)) Benchmark Educ.

***Figure in the Carpet & Other Stories.** Henry James. Narrated by William Coon. (ENG.). 2010. 12.95 (978-0-9830898-1-0(7)) Pub: Eloq Voice. Dist(s): OverDrive Inc

Figure of Eight. unabr. ed. Patrick Lynch. Read by Buck Schirner. (Running Time: 9 hrs.). 2007. 39.25 (978-1-4233-3598-6(8), 9781423335986,

BADLE); 24.95 (978-1-4233-3597-9(X), 9781423335979, BAD) Brilliance Audio.

Figure of Eight. unabr. ed. Patrick Lynch. Read by Buck Schirner. (Running Time: 32400 sec.). 2007. audio compact disk 24.95 (978-1-4233-3595-5(3), 9781423335955, Brilliance MP3); audio compact disk 39.25 (978-1-4233-3596-2(1), 9781423335962, Brlnc Audio MP3 Lib) Brilliance Audio.

***Figures in Silk.** unabr. ed. Vanora Bennett. Read by Katherine Kellgren. (ENG.). 2009. (978-0-06-180560-8(2), Harper Audio); (978-0-06-180561-5(0), Harper Audio) HarperCollins Pubs.

File & Forget see Thurber Country

File Under: Deceased. unabr. ed. Sarah Lacey. Read by Tessa Gallagher. 4 cass. (Running Time: 5 hrs. 15 min.). 1998. 57.95 Set. (978-1-85903-171-1(4)) Pub: Magna Story GBR. Dist(s): Ulverscroft US

Leah Hunter is twenty-five & single, which is not to say that she doesn't like men. But when a handsome stranger falls dead in her arms she feels the time has come to take an interest. As a tax inspector she has access to the dead man's file & it soon becomes clear that somebody thinks she knows more than she should. When her flat is broken into, & her car is burnt out, her Yorkshire town begins to seem a dangerous place to be.

File under Missing. unabr. ed. Sarah Lacey. Read by Tessa Gallagher. 5 cass. 1998. 63.95 (978-1-85903-176-6(5)) Pub: Magna Story GBR. Dist(s): Ulverscroft US

Filing: Syllabus. 2nd ed. Joanne Piper. (J). 1979. 105.25 (978-0-89420-146-2(8)) Natl Book.

Filíocht, Fiannaíocht agus sleachta as Leabhair see Legends of Fianna

Filipino Slang: Tagalog & Filipino Slang. Prod. by Ted Wiersma, III. 2 CDs. (TAG.). 2007. audio compact disk 29.95 (978-0-9771586-2-1(4)) Thirsty Rck.

Filipino (Tagalog) in 60 Minutes. (In 60 MINUTES Ser.). 2009. audio compact disk 9.95 (978-981-268-608-4(8)) Pub: Berlitz Pubng. Dist(s): Langenscheidt

Filipino (Tagalog) Phrase Book. Created by Berlitz. (Berlitz Phrase Books & CD Ser.). (ENG., 2007. audio compact disk 14.95 (978-981-268-197-3(3)) Pub: Berlitz Pubng. Dist(s): Langenscheidt

Filipino Word Book. Teresita V. Ramos & Josie Clausen. Read by Josie Clausen & Ruth Mabanglo. 1 cass. (Rainbow International Word Book Ser.). 1993. 7.95 Bess Pr.

A native speaker pronounces each word in the accompanying book twice.

Filipino Word Book. Teresita V. Ramos & Josie Clausen. Illus. by Jerri Asuncion & Boboy Betco. 2004. audio compact disk 14.95 (978-1-57306-194-0(8)) Bess Pr.

Fill It up Camp in a Can: Everything You Need to Kickstart Your Own Camp or Weekend Retreat. Kurt Johnston. 2007. audio compact disk 39.99 (978-5-557-78144-2(7)) Group Pub.

Fill My Cup. 1 cass., 1 CD. 10.98 (978-1-57908-327-4(7), 1397); audio compact disk 15.98 CD. (978-1-57908-326-7(9)) Platinm Enter.

Fill These Rooms: A Story of God's Faithfulness. Dotty Hash. 6 cass. 1998. 20.00 Set. (978-0-9664572-1-6(8)) Cadence Press.

fille aux yeux D'or. unabr. ed. Honoré de Balzac. Read by Martine Chide. (YA). 2007. 69.99 (978-2-35569-031-0(6)) Find a World.

Fille de l'Ecrivian. l.t. ed. Henri Troyat. (French Ser.). (FRE., 2001. bk. 30.99 (978-2-84011-438-3(0)) Pub: UlverLrgPrint GBR. Dist(s): Ulverscroft US

Fille du Feu. l.t. ed. Catherine Hermary-Vieille. (French Ser.). 2001. bk. 30.99 (978-2-84011-418-5(6)) Pub: UlverLrgPrint GBR. Dist(s): Ulverscroft US

Filled Pen. unabr. ed. P. K. Page. 1 CD. (Running Time: 1 hr.). 2004. audio compact disk 12.95 (978-1-895790-21-4(2)) Outlaw CAN.

Filling Your Love Cup: How Love Creates Love. 3 cass. (Running Time: 1 hr.). bk. 30.00 Set. (2002) Family Mtrs.

Have you ever yearned for some magic to turn your life around? Something to heal your aching heart, restore hope & confidence, spark creativity, movivate you to service, & somehow, transform the unloved into the beloved? This audio seminar can change your life. You'll find it not only instructive, but entertaining as well.

Film. unabr. ed. 1 cass. (Berkeley University Weekly Broadcasts Ser.). 12.95 (23703) J Norton Pubs.

"Shooting for Perfection," a personal interview with cinematographer James Wong Howe; "The Director's Chair," an interview with Joseph von Sternberg; "Movie History on Tape," with the actual voices of early stars; "The Disappearing Author" on the author of "Night Visitor".

Filmmaker John Huston see I'm Too Busy to Talk Now

Filo de la Navaja. abr. ed. Somerset Maugham. Read by Pedro Montoya. Tr. by Eliana Rojas. 3 CDs.Tr. of Razor's Edge. (SPA.). 2002. audio compact disk 17.00 (978-958-8161-15-0(0)) YoYoMusic.

Filth: The Unauthorized Biography of Cradle of Filth. Mark Crampton. (Maximum Ser.). (ENG.). 2001. audio compact disk 14.95 (978-1-84240-042-5(8)) Pub: Chrome Dreams GBR. Dist(s): IPG Chicago

Filthy Rich. unabr. ed. Dorothy J. Samuels. Read by Mary Peiffer. 4 cass. (Running Time: 6 hrs.). 2001. 32.00 (978-0-7366-8083-7(7)) Books on Tape.

takes up our national obsession with game shows and goes on to portray its wryly humorous effects on one Marcy Mallowitz, a thirty-something personal life trainer. Primed to be her orthodontist boyfriend's "lifeline" on WHO WANTS TO BE FILTHY RICH, she blows the question by giving him the wrong answer. In a fit of pique, he ends their engagement and their relationship on national television. Now, Marcy is set upon by the media; everyone wants to get her story as the victim of the "Big Brush-Off." She needs to rebuild her life, but her yenta mother is of little help. She must decide whether to retreat from the producers and paparazzi, or to expose herself completely to the world.

Final Account, Set. abr. ed. Peter Robinson. Read by John Rhys-Davies. 2 cass. (Running Time: 3 hrs.). (Inspector Banks Mystery Ser.). Orig. Title: Dry Bones That Dream. 1995. 17.00 (978-1-56876-045-2(0), 393291) Soundlines Ent.

The crime scene is almost surreal for Chief Inspector Banks, there are many avenues to pursue. Keith Rothwell was known as a financial wizard. His execution style murder hints that there may be powerful people involved. Rothwell was a mysterious man for all that Chief Banks can see, Rothwell was a businessman who made a murderous enemy along the way. But there could be more to this murder than strictly business.

Final Analysis. Keith Mccarthy. (Isis (CDs) Ser.). 2006. audio compact disk 99.95 (978-0-7531-2608-0(7)) Pub: ISIS Lrg Prnt GBR. Dist(s): Ulverscroft US

***Final Analysis.** abr. ed. Catherine Crier. Read by Catherine Crier. (ENG.). 2007. (978-0-06-122901-5(6), Harper Audio); (978-0-06-122900-8(8), Harper Audio) HarperCollins Pubs.

Final Analysis. unabr. ed. Keith McCarthy. Read by Sean Barrett. 10 cass. (Running Time: 12 hrs. 40 mins.). (Isis Cassettes Ser.). (J). 2006. 84.95 (978-0-7531-3522-8(1)) Pub: ISIS Lrg Prnt GBR. Dist(s): Ulverscroft US

Final Appeal. abr. ed. Lisa Scottoline. Read by Kate Burton. 2004. audio compact disk 14.95 (978-0-06-072636-2(9)) HarperCollins Pubs.

***Final Appeal.** abr. ed. Lisa Scottoline. Read by Kate Burton. (ENG.). 2004. (978-0-06-081809-8(3), Harper Audio); (978-0-06-081810-4(7), Harper Audio) HarperCollins Pubs.

Final Approach. unabr. ed. Rachel Brady. (Running Time: 1 hr. 0 mins.). (ENG.). 2009. 29.95 (978-1-4417-0130-5(3)); 54.95 (978-1-4417-0126-8(5)); audio compact disk 76.00 (978-1-4417-0127-5(3)) Blckstn Audio.

Final Argument. Clifford Irving. 2004. 10.95 (978-0-7435-4698-0(9)) Pub: S&S Audio. Dist(s): S and S Inc

Final Blackout. abr. ed. L. Ron Hubbard. Read by Roddy McDowall. 2 cass. (Running Time: 3 hrs.). 1991. 15.95 (978-0-88404-652-3(4)) Bridge Pubns Inc.

Final Blackout. abr. ed. L. Ron Hubbard. Read by Roddy McDowall. 2 cass. 1995. 10.99 Set. (978-0-88404-937-1(X)) Bridge Pubns Inc.

Incessant warfare has turned Europe into a hell - a battlefield torn by 30 years of explosive combat & biological warfare. A small band of soldiers & "The Lieutenant", their charismatic & brilliant leader, somehow survive the barren wasteland. Privation & violent, civilization-shattering war has filled The Lieutenant's life, yet nothing can prepare him to face the evil that caused it.

Final Blackout. abr. ed. L. Ron Hubbard. Read by Bruce Boxleitner. 2 cass. (Running Time: 3 hrs). 1996. 15.95 (978-1-59212-056-7(3)) Gala Pr LLC.

London 1975. As the great World War grinds to a halt, a force more sinister than Hitler's Nazis has seized control of Europe and is systematically destroying every adversary - except one. In the heart of France, a crack unit of British soldiers survives, overcoming all opposition under the leadership of a hardened military strategist highly trained in every method of combat and known only as "The Lieutenant." Ordered to return to British headquarters, the Lieutenant is torn between obeying the politicians in London or doing what he knows is right for his country, regardless of the price.

Final Blackout. abr. ed. L. Ron Hubbard. Read by Roddy McDowall. 3 CDs. (Running Time: 10800 sec.). 2005. audio compact disk 19.95 (978-1-59212-202-8(7)) Gala Pr LLC.

Final Candidate. unabr. ed. Alan Gold. Read by Stanley McGeagh. 10 cass. (Running Time: 13 hrs. 36 mins.). 2001. (978-1-74030-111-4(0), 500425) Bolinda Pubng AUS.

final confession of Mabel Stark. Robert Hough. Read by Betty Bobbitt. (Running Time: 15 hrs.). 2009. 99.99 (978-1-74214-246-3(X), 9781742142463) Pub: Bolinda Pubng AUS. Dist(s): Bolinda Pub Inc

Final Confession of Mabel Stark. unabr. ed. Robert Hough. Read by Betty Bobbit. 12 CDs. (Running Time: 15 hrs.). 2004. audio compact disk 108.95 (978-1-74093-370-4(2)) Pub: Bolinda Pubng AUS. Dist(s): Bolinda Pub Inc

Final Confession of Mabel Stark. unabr. ed. Robert Hough. Read by Betty Bobbitt. 11 cass. (Running Time: 15 hrs.). 2004. 88.00 (978-1-74093-289-9(7)) Pub: Bolinda Pubng AUS. Dist(s): Bolinda Pub Inc

Final Country. unabr. ed. James Crumley. Read by Barrett Whitener. 8 cass. (Running Time: 12 hrs.). 2001. 64.00 (978-0-7366-8321-0(6)) Books on Tape.

Milo Milodragovitch, a hard-boiled Texas P.I., must get himself out of a heap of trouble.

***Final Crisis: DC Comics.** Greg Cox. 2010. audio compact disk 19.99 (978-1-59950-706-4(4)) GraphicAudio.

Final Curtain. unabr. ed. Ngaio Marsh. Read by Nadia May. 7 cass. (Running Time: 10 hrs.). 1994. 49.95 (978-0-7861-0676-9(X), 1464) Blckstn Audio.

Beautiful Troy Alleyn, artist wife of the Inspector, had been warned about the famed old Shakespearean actor - & his eccentric household. But she was not prepared for their acts of malice & mischief. Now Sir Henry was dead, after a large & lethal birthday dinner of champagne & crayfish. Also, after changing his will in favor of his glamorous young fiancee. And Troy was suddenly star witness in one of her husband's most sensational cases to determine which of the flamboyant characters brought down the final curtain, & turned a drawing room farce into tragedy.

Final Cut. Paul Thomas. Read by David Tredinnick. 7 cass. (Running Time: 10 hrs.). 2000. (978-1-876584-99-3(8), 591212) Bolinda Pubng AUS.

Now James Alabaster, a man with a past but no future, ekes out a bare existence on the fringes of Sydney's glitzy, gaudy, cafe society. All that sustains him is his obsession with the beautiful but unobtainable Carla Sully, wife of one of Australia's richest men.

Final Cut: A Self-Help Program to Quit Cocaine. Trenna Daniells. Read by Trenna Daniells. 2 cass. (Running Time: 2 hrs.). bk. 39.95 Set. (FC01) Trenna Prods.

Final Dawn over Jerusalem. abr. ed. John Hagee. Read by John Hagee. 2 cass. (Running Time: 2 hrs.). 1998. 12.99 Set. (978-0-7852-7082-9(5), 70825) Nelson.

Discover what lies ahead through Bible prophecy & the secret meaning of Israel's seven feasts.

Final Days: The Last, Desperate Abuses of Power by the Clinton White House. unabr. ed. Barbara Olson. Read by Kimberly Schraf. 6 cass. (Running Time: 9 hrs.). 2002. 48.00 (978-0-7366-8549-8(9)); audio compact disk 56.00 (978-0-7366-8559-7(6)) Books on Tape.

Olson depicted the excesses and outright crimes she claims took place as the Clintons prepared to leave office. These include the granting of pardons to people of dubious legal status, such as the shadowy financier Marc Rich, and the last-minute signing into law of thousands of executive orders, a feat comparable only to John Adams's appointment of the "midnight judiciary." Olson's indignation knew no bounds when it came to the Clintons, and if you feel the same way, you'll relish every minute of this book.

Final Days of Socrates. unabr. ed. Plato. Narrated by Ray Atherton & Donal Donnelly. 4 cass. (Running Time: 6 hrs.). 1989. 35.00 (978-1-55690-176-8(3), 89683E7) Recorded Bks.

A re-creation of the trial & condemnation of the Greek philosopher, Socrates, composed by his pupil, Plato.

Final Deduction. Rex Stout. Narrated by Michael Prichard. (Running Time: 20160 sec.). (Nero Wolfe Ser.). (ENG.). 2006. audio compact disk 27.95 (978-1-57270-566-1(3)) Pub: AudioGO. Dist(s): Perseus Dist

Final Deduction. unabr. ed. Rex Stout. Read by Michael Prichard. 4 cass. (Running Time: 6 hrs.). (Nero Wolfe Ser.). 2001. 24.95 (978-1-57270-232-5(X), N41232u, Audio Edits Mystry) Pub: Audio Partners. Dist(s): PerseuPGW

As always, the appeal of the orchid-growing genius lies in his quirkiness & omniscience, combined with the humor & toughness of his wisecracking assistant Archie.

Final Deduction. unabr. collector's ed. Rex Stout. Read by Michael Prichard. 6 cass. (Running Time: 6 hrs.). (Nero Wolfe Ser.). 1996. 48.00 (978-0-7366-3413-7(4), 4059) Books on Tape.

Broadway can't match the real-life dramas of Manhattan's money set. Even Nero Wolfe tunes in when murder appears during the last act of a society romance.

Final Destination: Confronting the Reality of Hell, Comprehending the Wonder of Heaven. Mac Hammond. Read by Mac Hammond. 1996. 12.00 Album. (978-1-57399-054-7(X)) Mac Hammond.

The choice is ours in determining our final destination - heaven or hell.

Final Detail. Harlan Coben. Read by Jonathan Marosz. (Myron Bolitar Ser.: No. 6). 1999. audio compact disk 54.40 (978-0-7366-5193-6(4)) Pub: Books on Tape. Dist(s): NetLibrary CO

Final Detail. unabr. ed. Harlan Coben. Read by Jonathan Marosz. 7 cass. (Running Time: 10 hrs. 30 min.). (Myron Bolitar Ser.: No. 6). 1999. 56.00 (978-0-7366-4623-9(X), 5008) Books on Tape.

Myron Bolitar, sports agent & reluctant sleuth, is happily basking in the Caribbean sun with a beautiful woman he hardly knows. Interrupting this bliss, Win, his loyal but morally questionable sidekick, arrives to tell him that Esperanza, Myron's best friend & partner at MB SportsReps, has been arrested for the murder of a fallen baseball star. As he tries to unearth a killer amid a tangled trail of lies, Myron's own investigation points to only one other suspect: himself.

Final Detail. unabr. ed. Harlan Coben. Read by Jonathan Marosz. 8 CDs. (Running Time: 9 hrs. 25 mins.). (Myron Bolitar Ser.: No. 6). 2001. audio compact disk 64.00 Books on Tape.

Final Detail. unabr. ed. Harlan Coben. Read by Jonathan Marosz. (Running Time: 34200 sec.). (Myron Bolitar Ser.: No. 6). (ENG.). 2007. audio compact disk 19.99 (978-0-7393-4117-9(0), Random AudioBks) Pub: Random Audio Pubg. Dist(s): Random

Final Edition. unabr. ed. Val McDermid. Read by Vari Sylvester. 7 CDs. (Running Time: 7 hrs. 32 min.). (Isis (CDs) Ser.). (J). 2003. audio compact disk 71.95 (978-0-7531-2214-3(6)) Pub: ISIS Lrg Prnt GBR. Dist(s): Ulverscroft US

When she returns from a self-imposed exile in Italy, journalist Lindsay Gordon finds her world turned upside down. The lover she thought would wait for her has found a new partner; an ex-lover has been murdered; and a former colleague has been jailed for the crime.

Final Edition. unabr. ed. Val McDermid & Vari Sylvester. 6 cass. (Running Time: 7 hrs. 36 mins.). (Isis Ser.). (J). 2002. 54.95 (978-0-7531-1155-0(1)) Pub: ISIS Lrg Prnt GBR. Dist(s): Ulverscroft US

Final Episodes: The Story of the Messiah. 2005. audio compact disk 9.95 (978-0-9774447-0-0(8)) Sine Ministries.

Final Exam: Gen. 44:1-34. Ed Young. 1988. 4.95 (978-0-7417-1686-6(0), 686) Win Walk.

Final Flight. unabr. ed. Stephen Coonts. Read by Michael Prichard. 9 cass. (Running Time: 13 hrs. 30 mins.). (Jake Grafton Novel Ser.: Vol. 2). 1988. 72.00 (978-0-7366-1525-9(3), 2396) Books on Tape.

Jake Grafton, hero of Flight of the Intruder, now commands an air wing on the supercarrier USS United States, on patrol in the Med.

Final Frontier. Diane Carey. Read by Leonard Nimoy. (Star Trek Ser.). 2004. 7.95 (978-0-7435-4538-9(9)) Pub: S&S Audio. Dist(s): S and S Inc

Final Frontier. abr. ed. J. M. Dillard. Read by Leonard Nimoy & James Doohan. 1 cass. (Running Time: 60 min.). (Star Trek Ser.: No. 5). 7.95 S&S Audio.

Final Generation-Skipping Transfer Tax Regulations. 2 cass. (Running Time: 1 hr. 50 min.). 79.00 (YB77) Am Law Inst.

Discusses the most significant provisions of final regulations, including definitions, lifetime allocation of GST exemption, estate tax inclusion period, allocation of GST exemption after transferer's death, valuation, redetermination of applicable fraction, finality of inclusion ratio, separate shares & trusts, application of Chapter 13 to nonresident aliens, & effective dates.

Final Hour. abr. ed. Dave Carley & Glenda MacFarlane. (Running Time: 3600 sec.). 2005. audio compact disk 15.95 (978-0-660-19461-5(9)) Canadian Broadcasting CAN.

Final Hour: 1 John 2:18-29. Ed Young. 1984. 4.95 (978-0-7417-1374-2(8), 374) Win Walk.

Final Hours: A German Jet Pilot Plots Against Goering. unabr. ed. Johannes Steinhoff. Narrated by George Guidall. 6 cass. (Running Time: 8 hrs. 15 mins.). 1992. 51.00 (978-1-55690-667-1(6), 92115E7) Recorded Bks.

A German WWII pilot recounts his experiences, when in 1945, his ME-262 crashed on takeoff from the Munich-Riem Arifield. He spent the next two years in a hospital in Germany recuperating form burns that left his face badly disfigured.

Final Jeopardy. abr. ed. Linda Fairstein. (Alexandra Cooper Mysteries Ser.). 2004. 10.95 (978-0-7435-4702-4(0)) Pub: S&S Audio. Dist(s): S and S Inc

Final Jeopardy. unabr. ed. Linda Fairstein. Read by Bernadette Dunne. 8 cass. (Running Time: 12 hrs.). (Alexandra Cooper Mysteries Ser.). 1998. 64.00 (978-0-7366-4203-3(X), 4699) Books on Tape.

Final Judgement. unabr. ed. Daniel Easterman. Narrated by George Guidall. 8 cass. (Running Time: 11 hrs.). 2000. 72.00 (978-1-84197-149-0(9), H1143E7) Recorded Bks.

Kidnapping is a long-standing practice on Sardinia. So, when Aryeh Levin's son is snatched, it's seen as a routine misfortune. In growing fright & despair, Aryeh calls upon his estranged brother-in-law, Yosef, for help.

Final Judgement: Rev.20:1-10. Ed Young. 1987. 4.95 (978-0-7417-1582-1(1), 582) Win Walk.

Final Justice. abr. ed. Fern Michaels. Read by Laural Merlington. (Running Time: 3 hrs.). (Sisterhood Ser.: No. 12). 2009. audio compact disk 9.99 (978-1-4233-4520-6(7), 9781423345206, BCD Value Price) Brilliance Audio.

Final Justice. unabr. ed. Fern Michaels. Read by Laural Merlington. (Running Time: 7 hrs.). (Sisterhood Ser.: No. 12). 2009. 39.97 (978-1-4233-4518-3(5), 9781423345183, BADLE); 39.97 (978-1-4233-4516-9(9), 9781423345169, Brlnc Audio MP3 Lib); 24.99 (978-1-4233-4517-6(7), 9781423345176, BAD); 24.99 (978-1-4233-4515-2(0), 9781423345152, Brilliance MP3); audio compact disk 87.97 (978-1-4233-4514-5(2), 9781423345145, BriAudCD Unabrid); audio compact disk 29.99 (978-1-4233-4513-8(4), 9781423345138, Bril Audio CD Unabri) Brilliance Audio.

Final Move Beyond Iraq: The Final Solution While the World Sleeps. unabr. ed. Mike Evans. Narrated by Wayne Shepherd. (ENG.). 2008. 27.99 (978-1-60814-203-3(5)); audio compact disk 39.99 (978-1-59859-316-7(1)) Oasis Audio.

Final Pattern. unabr. ed. Tessa Barclay. Read by Lesley Mackie. 10 cass. (Running Time: 11 hrs.). (Sound Ser.). 2002. 84.95 (978-1-84283-121-2(6)) Pub: UlverLrgPrint GBR. Dist(s): Ulverscroft US

Jenny Armstrong, mistress of the thriving Corvill and Son weaving business, returns other native Scotland determined to achieve prosperity and comfort for her reunited family. But the death of her brother, Ned, brings disruption and harm. Once again, young Heather Armstrong is caught up in her widowed Aunt Lucy's machinations; Jenny's rekindled love affair with her husband, Ronald, is threatened, and strangers lurk in doorways to spy on the Armstrongs and their friends.

Final Problem see Memoirs of Sherlock Holmes

Final Problem see Famous Cases of Sherlock Holmes

Final Problem. 1983. (N-53) Jimcin Record.

Final Problem: A Sherlock Holmes Adventure. (ENG.). 2007. (978-1-60339-071-2(5)); cd-rom & audio compact disk (978-1-60339-072-9(3)) Listenr Digest.

Final Reckoning. Sam Bourne. 2009. 84.95 (978-0-7531-3926-4(X)); audio compact disk 99.95 (978-0-7531-3927-1(8)) Pub: Isis Pubng Ltd GBR. Dist(s): Ulverscroft US

Final Reckoning. unabr. ed. Robin Jarvis. Read by Roe Kendall. (Running Time: 36000 sec.). (Deptford Mice Ser.). (J). (gr. 4-7). 2007. 65.95 (978-1-4332-0574-3(2)); audio compact disk 29.95 (978-1-4332-0576-7(9)); audio compact disk 72.00 (978-1-4332-0575-0(0)) Blckstn Audio.

Final Reckoning & The Hunt. Perf. by Boris Karloff. 1 cass. (Running Time: 60 min.). Dramatization. (Creeps by Night Ser.). 1944. 6.00 Once Upon Rad.
Radio broadcasts - mystery & suspense.

Final Round. unabr. ed. William Bernhardt. 6 cass. (Running Time: 9 hrs.). 2002. 48.00 (978-0-7366-8631-0(2)) Books on Tape.
Maverick PGA golfer Connor Cross must clear his name of murder at the Masters tournament in Augusta.

Final Rounds: A Father, a Son, the Golf Journey of a Lifetime. unabr. ed. James Dodson. Narrated by Richard M. Davidson. 7 cass. (Running Time: 9 hrs. 30 mins.). 1997. 60.00 (978-0-7887-0847-3(3), 94993E7) Recorded Bks.
With the father given two months to live, he & his son set off for England & Scotland to fulfill a twenty-year-old promise & embrace the heartaches & joys of life together for the last time. More than just a golf story, it is also the story of a life's journey coming to an end & the enduring love that is passed from one generation to the next.

Final Salute: A Story of Unfinished Lives. unabr. ed. Jim Sheeler. Contrib. by Mark Deakins. (Running Time: 6 hrs.). (ENG.). (gr. 12 up). 2008. audio compact disk 29.95 (978-0-14-314325-3(5), PengAudBks) Penguin Grp USA.

Final Seconds. unabr. ed. John Lutz & David August. Read by Barrett Whitener. 10 cass. (Running Time: 14 hrs. 30 mins.). 1999. 69.95 (978-0-7861-1520-4(3), 2370) Blckstn Audio.
Will Harper, injured in the field & retired from the NYPD bomb squad, is in the process of fixing up his beaten-down brownstone, when his former partner is blown up, along with a paranoid bestselling author. Suddenly he's tracking a serial killer who is an expert in explosives as any terrorist.

Final Showdown under the Sun: You vs. Adversary. Robbin Wynn. (YA). 2005. per. 13.00 (978-0-9770682-0-3(X)) Inner Circle Pub.

Final Solution. Messenger Films Staff. 2004. DVD & audio compact disk 22.99 (978-1-894300-83-4(1)) Crown Video Dupl CAN.

Final Solution: A Story of Detection. unabr. ed. Michael Chabon. Read by Michael York. 2 cass. 2005. 24.95 (978-0-7927-3435-2(1), CSL 742); audio compact disk 39.95 (978-0-7927-3436-9(X), SLD 742) AudioGO.

Final Solution: A Story of Detection. unabr. ed. Michael Chabon. Read by Michael York. 2004. audio compact disk 22.00 (978-0-06-076571-2(2)) HarperCollins Pubs.

***Final Storm: A Novel of World War II in the Pacific.** unabr. ed. Jeff Shaara. (ENG.). 2011. audio compact disk 45.00 (978-0-307-91210-7(8), Random AudioBks) Pub: Random Audio Pubg. Dist(s): Random

***Final Storm: The Door Within Trilogy - Book Three.** unabr. ed. Wayne Thomas Batson. Narrated by Wayne Thomas Batson. (Running Time: 9 hrs. 0 mins. 0 sec.). (Door Within Trilogy). (ENG.). 2011. audio compact disk 27.99 (978-1-59859-882-7(1)) Oasis Audio.

***Final Summit: Audio Book on CD.** unabr. ed. Thomas Nelson. 2011. audio compact disk 24.99 (978-1-4003-1680-9(4)) Nelson.

Final Target. Iris Johansen. Narrated by Cristine McMurdo-Wallis. 9 CDs. (Running Time: 10 hrs.). audio compact disk 89.00 (978-1-4025-1586-6(3)) Recorded Bks.

Final Target. unabr. ed. Iris Johansen. Narrated by Cristine McMurdo-Wallis. 7 cass. (Running Time: 10 hrs.). 2001. 68.00 (978-0-7887-9005-8(6)) Recorded Bks.
The Wind Dancer, a priceless gold statue of Pegasus, has been in President Andreas' family for generations. While on a trip to Paris to loan the statue to a museum, the President's daughter survives a kidnapping attempt. Although she is rescued, she does not escape unscathed. The shock of seeing her nanny murdered has left her in a catatonic state. It will take a dedicated psychiatrist, the doctor's telepathic sister and an international information peddler to help the traumatized girl. Not only must they break her silence, they also find themselves in a dangerous game of cat and mouse with a psychotic art collector determined to find the girl and finish what he started.

Final Theory. abr. ed. Mark Alpert. Read by Adam Grupper. (Running Time: 6 hrs. 0 mins. 0 sec.). (ENG.). 2008. audio compact disk 29.95 (978-0-7435-7223-1(8)) Pub: S&S Audio. Dist(s): S and S Inc

Final Theory. unabr. ed. Mark Alpert. 2008. 49.95 (978-0-7435-7224-8(6)) Pub: S&S Audio. Dist(s): S and S Inc

***Final Theory: A Novel.** abr. ed. Mark Alpert. Read by Adam Grupper. (Running Time: 6 hrs. 0 mins. 0 sec.). (ENG.). 2011. audio compact disk 14.99 (978-1-4423-3815-9(6)) Pub: S&S Audio. Dist(s): S and S Inc

Final Truth. abr. unabr. ed. Mariah Stewart. Read by Anna Fields. 7 cass. (Running Time: 27000 sec.). 2006. 27.95 (978-0-7861-4478-5(5)) Blckstn Audio.

Final Truth. unabr. ed. Mariah Stewart. Read by Anna Fields. 8 CDs. (Running Time: 27000 sec.). 2006. audio compact disk 27.95 (978-0-7861-7276-4(2)); audio compact disk 29.95 (978-0-7861-7703-5(9)) Blckstn Audio.

Final Truth. unabr. ed. Mariah Stewart. Read by Anna Fields. (Running Time: 27000 sec.). 2006. 59.95 (978-0-7861-4701-4(6)); audio compact disk 72.00 (978-0-7861-6592-6(8)) Blckstn Audio.

Final Unfinished Voyage of Jack Aubrey. Patrick O'Brian. (Aubrey-Maturin Ser.). 2004. audio compact disk 19.99 (978-1-4193-0893-2(9)) Recorded Bks.

Final Verdict: Matthew 25:31-46. Ed Young. 1993. 4.95 (978-0-7417-1974-4(6), 974) Win Walk.

Final Verdict: The True Account of the Murder of John F. Kennedy. abr. ed. Vincent Bugliosi. 4 cass. (Running Time: 6 hrs. 00 min.). 2001. 25.00 (978-0-671-04377-3(3), Audioworks) S&S Audio.

***Final Voyage: A Story of Arctic Disaster & One Fateful Whaling Season.** unabr. ed. Peter Nichols. Narrated by Norman Dietz. (Running Time: 9 hrs. 30 mins.). 2009. 16.99 (978-1-4001-8254-1(9)) Tantor Media.

Final Voyage: A Story of Arctic Disaster & One Fateful Whaling Season. unabr. ed. Peter Nichols. Narrated by Norman Dietz. (Running Time: 9 hrs. 30 mins. 0 sec.). (ENG.). 2009. 24.99 (978-1-4001-6254-3(8)); audio compact disk 34.99 (978-1-4001-1254-8(0)); audio compact disk 69.99 (978-1-4001-4254-5(7)) Pub: Tantor Media. Dist(s): IngramPubServ

Final Warning. abr. ed. James Patterson. Read by Jill Apple. (Running Time: 5 hrs.). (Maximum Ride Ser.: No. 4). (ENG.). 2008. 9.98 (978-1-60024-156-7(5)) Pub: Little Brn Bks. Dist(s): HachBkGrp

Final Warning. abr. ed. James Patterson. Read by Jill Apple. 4 CDs. (Running Time: 5 hrs.). (Maximum Ride Ser.: No. 4). (ENG.). 2009. audio compact disk 9.98 (978-1-60024-445-2(9)) Pub: Little Brn Bks. Dist(s): HachBkGrp

Final Witness. unabr. ed. Simon Tolkien. Read by Simon Tolkien. 7 cass. (Running Time: 10 hrs.). 2002. 32.95 (978-1-59086-419-7(0), 1590864190, BAU); 82.25 (978-1-59086-420-3(4), 1590864204, CD Unabrid Lib Ed) Brilliance Audio.
One summer night, two men break into an isolated manor house and kill Lady Anne Robinson. Her son, Thomas, convinces the police that his father's beautiful personal assistant sent the killers, but Thomas is known for his overactive imagination, and he has reasons to lie. Thomas's father, Sir Peter Robinson, the British minister of defense, refuses to believe his son. Instead, he marries his assistant, Greta Grahame, and will be giving evidence for the defense at her trial. He will be the final witness. Author Simon Tolkien successfully combines legal suspense and psychological tension in this sharply etched portrait of four people whose lives are changed by a murder. Alternating between the trial in London's Central Criminal Court and private moments among the characters, Tolkien expertly describes the art of the trial, the clash between Britain's social classes, and, most notably, the complexity of family relations. Who is telling the truth - the new wife or the bereaved son? What will Sir Peter tell the court? With tantalizing ambiguity, Tolkien keeps readers guessing about the true motivations of these characters until the final witness..

Final Witness. unabr. ed. Simon Tolkien. Read by Simon Tolkien. (Running Time: 10 hrs.). 2004. 39.25 (978-1-59335-454-1(1), 1593354541, Brlnc Audio MP3 Lib) Brilliance Audio.

Final Witness. unabr. ed. Simon Tolkien. Read by Simon Tolkien. (Running Time: 10 hrs.). 2004. 39.25 (978-1-59710-281-0(4), 1597102814, BADLE); 24.95 (978-1-59710-280-3(6), 1597102806, BAD) Brilliance Audio.

***Final Witness.** unabr. ed. Simon Tolkien. Read by Simon Tolkien. (Running Time: 10 hrs.). 2010. audio compact disk 87.97 (978-1-4418-6102-3(5), 9781441861023, BriAudCD Unabrid); audio compact disk 29.99 (978-1-4418-6101-6(7), 9781441861016, Bril Audio CD Unabri) Brilliance Audio.

Final Witness. unabr. ed. Simon Tolkien. Read by Simon Tolkien. (Running Time: 10 hrs.). 2004. 24.95 (978-1-59335-083-3(X), 159335083X) Soulmate Audio Bks.

Final Word: John 14. Ed Young. 1983. 4.95 (978-0-7417-1322-3(5), 322) Win Walk.

Final Word from Attila the Hun: Neh. 13:10-31. Ed Young. 1990. 4.95 (978-0-7417-1822-8(7), 823) Win Walk.

Final Word on Who Is Blessed. Dan Corner. 1 cass. 3.00 (35) Evang Outreach.

Final Words (for Now) A Book by & about People. (23330) J Norton Pubs.

Final Wrath: Rev. 16:1-21. Ed Young. 1987. 4.95 (978-0-7417-1576-0(7), 576) Win Walk.

Final 2003. Ed. by On That Point Editors. (ENG.). (YA). 2006. audio compact disk 29.95 (978-1-932716-23-8(8)) Inter Debate.

Finalities (Part 6) see Twentieth-Century Poetry in English, No. 24, Recordings of Poets Reading Their Own Poetry

Finally. Perf. by Andrae Crouch. 1 cass. 4.98 (978-1-57908-460-8(5)); audio compact disk 5.98 (978-1-57908-459-2(1)) Platinm Enter.

***Finally Alive.** unabr. ed. John Piper. Narrated by Raymond Todd. (ENG.). 2009. 12.98 (978-1-59644-727-1(3), Hovel Audio) christianaud.

Finally Alive. unabr. ed. John Piper. Read by Raymond Todd. (Running Time: 5 hrs. 30 mins. 0 sec.). (ENG.). 2009. audio compact disk 21.98 (978-1-59644-726-4(5), Hovel Audio) christianaud.

Finally Home. Contrib. by MercyMe. (Inoriginal Performance Trax Ser.). 2007. audio compact disk 9.98 (978-5-557-49937-8(7)) Pt of Grace Ent.

Finance & Accounting for Nonfinancial Managers, Set. rev. ed. 6 cass. pap. bk. & wbk. ed. 165.00 (978-0-7612-0538-8(1), 80164) AMACOM.
Become fluent in the dollars & cents language of business.

Finance Your Business Dreams. Harold R. Lacy. 6 cass. 1996. 89.95 Set. (978-1-890439-00-2(2)) Money Inst.
Tips & techniques on how to locate & obtain funding for a small business.

Financial Accounting: A User's Perspective. 3rd ed. Hoskin. 2003. bk. 156.76 (978-0-470-83228-8(2)); bk. 28.76 (978-0-470-83229-5(0)) Wiley US.

Financial Accounting: Advanced Topics. Andrew B. Titen. 3 cass. bk. 129.00 set, incl. textbk. & quizzer. (CPE4604) Bisk Educ.
Here's an excellent reference guide for the accounting, recording, & financial statement presentation of many topics affecting financial accounting.

Financial Accounting: Balance Sheet. Andrew B. Titen. 3 cass. bk. 129.00 Set, incl. textbk. & quizzer. (CPE4584) Bisk Educ.
Arranged by topic, this program serves as a valuable reference guide for all aspects of the balance sheet.

Financial Accounting: Income Statement & Financial Analysis. Andrew B. Titen. 3 cass. bk. 129.00 set, incl. textbk. & quizzer. (CPE4594) Bisk Educ.
This program shows you how to apply the Generally Accepted Accounting Principles affecting most businesses, plus serves as a great working guide for the accounting, recording, & financial statement presentation of many financial accounting transactions.

***Financial Accounting by Michael P. Licata: First Accounting Course for Homeschool High School Students.** Michael Licata. Prod. by Professor In A Box LLC. (YA). 2008. audio compact disk 149.99 (978-0-578-04525-2(7)) ProfInABox.

Financial Accounting Report. Totaltape Editorial Board. 12 cass. 1995. bk. 225.00 set. (CPE5200) Bisk Educ.
Monthly subscription to help you keep up with industry news & trends in a time-saving manner.

*** Financial Acctg CD.** 5th ed. (C). 2003. audio compact disk 21.95 (978-0-324-18501-0(4)) Pub: South-West. Dist(s): CENGAGE Learn

Financial Analysis with Microsoft Excel. 2nd ed. Timothy R. Mayes & Todd M. Shank. (C). 2000. pap. bk. 47.95 (978-0-03-032621-9(4)) Dryden Pr.

Financial & Estate Planning Course. Sidney Kess. 6 cass. (Running Time: 4 hrs.). 1992. pap. bk. 150.00 (09151) Toolkit Media.
Includes the changes in the field of financial & estate planning brought about by recent tax changes; discusses both the opportunities & the problems presented to financial & estate planners by these recent law changes.

Financial & Political Picture for Nineteen Eighty-Four to Nineteen Eighty-Five. Grace K. Morris. 1 cass. 8.95 (245) Am Fed Astrologers.
Charts of Federal Reserve, NYSE & Potential presidential candidates.

Financial Astrology. David Williams. 1 cass. (Running Time: 90 min.). 1984. 8.95 (365) Am Fed Astrologers.

Financial Crises: Sensible Solutions. 2007. audio compact disk 17.99 (978-1-934570-05-0(2)) Lanphier Pr.

Financial English. unabr. ed. 2 cass. (Running Time: 1 hr. per cass.). 12.95 bk. only. (BEN118) J Norton Pubs.

Financial English. unabr. ed. British Broadcasting Corporation Staff. 2 cass. (Running Time: 1 hr. per cass.). pap. bk. 44.50 (978-0-88432-679-3(9), SEN225) J Norton Pubs.

Financial Fitness. Kevin Lust. 2 cass. (Running Time: 110 min.). 1998. 15.95 Set. (978-1-55977-749-0(4)) CareerTrack Pubns.
Topics: The key question to ask before you begin to budget; When it's OK to go into debt; A simple way to continuously refine your budget; Tactics to pay off your mortgage faster; The best ways to invest your savings; & How to dig out of debt - repayment strategies that work.

Financial Fitness. PUEI. 2006. audio compact disk 89.95 (978-1-933328-87-4(8), CareerTrack) P Univ E Inc.

Financial Forecast. Sam Crawford. 1 cass. 1992. 8.95 (1024) Am Fed Astrologers.

Financial Freedom. Bill Winston. 6 cass. (Running Time: 5hr.00min.). (C). 2001. 25.00 (978-1-931289-64-1(6)) Pub: B Winston Min. Dist(s): Anchor Distributors

Financial Freedom: Creating True Wealth Now. Suze Orman. 4 CDs. (ENG.). 2002. audio compact disk 23.95 (978-1-4019-0030-4(5)) Hay House.

Financial Freedom Investment Series. 6 cass. (Running Time: 60 min. per cass.). 1989. bk. 19.95 ea. Bonneville Media.

Financial Healing: Develop a Positive, Healthy Relationship to Money in Your Life. Mark Bancroft. Read by Mark Bancroft. 1 cass., bklet. (Running Time: 90 mins.). (General Self-Development/Improvement Ser.). 1999. instr.'s gde. ed. 12.95 (978-1-58522-032-8(9), 906, EnSpire Aud) EnSpire Pr.
Two complete sessions plus printed instruction manual/guidebook. With healing music soundtrack.

Financial Healing: Develop a Positive, Healthy Relationship to Money in Your Life. Mark Bancroft. Read by Mark Bancroft. 1 CD, bklet. (Running Time: 1 hr.). (General Self-Development/Improvement Ser.). 2006. audio compact disk 20.00 (978-1-58522-067-0(1)) EnSpire Pr.
Two complete sessions plus printed instructionmanual/guidebook. With healing music soundtrack.

Financial Health Emotional Wealth: Mastering the Economics of Emotion & Financial Wellness. William G. DeFoore. (ENG.). 2005. audio compact disk 29.99 (978-0-9814740-3-8(9)) Halcyon Life.

Financial Infidelity: Seven Steps to Conquering the #1 Relationship Wrecker. unabr. ed. Bonnie Eaker Weil. Read by Joyce Bean. (Running Time: 10 hrs.). 2008. 39.25 (978-1-4233-6350-7(7), 9781423363507, BADLE); 24.95 (978-1-4233-6349-1(3), 9781423363491, BAD); audio compact disk 39.25 (978-1-4233-6348-4(5), 9781423363484, Brinc Audio MP3 Lib); audio compact disk 24.95 (978-1-4233-6347-7(7), 9781423363477, Brilliance MP3); audio compact disk 34.95 (978-1-4233-6345-3(0), 9781423363453, Bril Audio CD Unabri); audio compact disk 92.25 (978-1-4233-6346-0(9), 9781423363460, BriAudCD Unabrid) Brilliance Audio.

***Financial Lives of the Poets.** unabr. ed. Jess Walter. Read by Jess Walter. (ENG.). 2009. (978-0-06-199311-4(5), Harper Audio); (978-0-06-198813-4(8), Harper Audio) HarperCollins Pubs.

***Financial Mistakes of New College Grads.** Joe Templin. Narrated by Kevin Readdean. (ENG.). (YA). 2010. 10.99 (978-1-936455-00-3(5)) Open Bk Aud.

Financial Peace Cash Flow Planning. Dave Ramsey. 1 cass. (Running Time: 90 mins.). 1993. 9.95 (978-0-9635712-8-1(1)) Lampo Inc.
Learn how to: stretch your money further; set up your own cash-flow system; live on a budget without hating it; have money left over at the end of the month; spend money without guilt; get control & keep control of your money.

Financial Peace Dumping Debt. Dave Ramsey. 1 cass. (Running Time: 90 mins.). 1993. 9.95 (978-0-9635712-7-4(3)) Lampo Inc.
Learn how to: get out of debt; stay out of debt;, save money; get control & keep control of your money; the snowball technique for dumping debt; set up an emergency fund.

Financial Peace, Jr. Cool Tools for Tomorrow's Millionaires. Dave Ramsey. 1 cass. (Running Time: 60 mins.). (J). (gr. k-6). 2000. 19.95 (978-0-9635712-2-9(2)) Lampo Inc.
Includes college planning CD, showing tuition rates & degrees offered at over 3000 colleges & universities.

Financial Picture for Nineteen Eighty-Seven to Nineteen Eighty-Eight. Grace K. Morris. 1 cass. 8.95 (568) Am Fed Astrologers.
Real estate, stock market, & MORE!.

Financial Planner As An Investment Strategist. Harold Gourgues, Jr. (Running Time: 40 min.). 25.00 Am Soc Chart.
Details rules of investing. Discusses selecting investment strategies.

Financial Planning. 1 cass. (Running Time: 45 min.). (Success Ser.). 9.98 (978-1-55909-064-3(2), 56) Randolph Tapes.
Tells you how to get the most from your earnings. Subliminal messages are heard for 3-5 minutes before becoming ocean sounds or music.

Financial Planning. David T. Demola. 2 cass. 8.00 (MS-016) Faith Fellow Min.

Financial Planning: A Basic Guide. Nathan M. Bisk & David Ness. 6 cass. 1995. bk. 199.00 set. (CPE5030) Bisk Educ.
The 550 page included guide contains the latest tools & techniques available to provide you & your clients safety of principal, consistent growth, & steady income.

Financial Planning & the Practice of Law. 1 cass. (Running Time: 50 min.). 1992. 95.00 Incl. study guide. (Y503) Am Law Inst.
Introduces the role of financial planning in various practices & addresses business, ethics, & regulatory concerns.

Financial Planning for Senior Executives I & II: Executive M. B. A. Seminar. abr. ed. Joseph F. Dunphy. 2 cass. (Running Time: 3 hrs. 15 min.). 1998. 29.95 digital. (978-1-892359-02-5(2)); 29.95 Set, Stereo Sound. (978-1-892359-00-1(6)) Mint Condtn Grph.
Helps individual executives manage money, job, & career issues differently from their predecessors. Highlights trends that have remained constant over 50 years, & how some have used them to attain a high level of achievement.

Financial Pot O'Goals. unabr. ed. Dorothy O'Donnell-Uhlman. Read by Leitha Christie. 1 cass., bklet. (Running Time: 22 mins.). (Success Ser.: Vol. 1). (C). 1996. pap. bk. 9.95 (978-0-9666062-0-1(5)) Uhlman Commns.
Enhanced health, well being, self-healing, self-talk affirmations. Book outlines true stories & success principles.

Financial Prosperity Series, Set. Elbert Willis. 4 cass. 13.00 Set. Fill the Gap.

Financial Pubic Relations 101: For Financial Service Professionals. (ENG.). 2006. audio compact disk 79.95 (978-1-932642-40-7(4)) Media Training.

Financial Reckoning Day Fallout: Surviving Today's Global Depression. unabr. ed. Addison Wiggin & William Bonner. Narrated by Mel Foster. (Running Time: 17 hrs. 0 mins. 0 sec.). (ENG.). 2009. 29.99 (978-1-4001-6369-4(2)); audio compact disk 79.99 (978-1-4001-4369-6(1)); audio compact disk 39.99 (978-1-4001-1369-9(5)) Pub: Tantor Media. Dist(s): IngramPubServ

***Financial Reckoning Day Fallout: Surviving Today's Global Depression.** unabr. ed. Addison Wiggin & William Bonner. Narrated by Mel Foster. (Running Time: 17 hrs. 0 mins.). 2009. 21.99 (978-1-4001-8369-2(3)) Tantor Media.

Financial Sales. (Specialized Sales Ser.). 1989. 14.98 (978-1-55909-222-7(X), 140P) Randolph Tapes.

Financial Statement Analysis: Basis for Management Advice. Wallace N. Davidson & James L. McDonald. 2 cass. (Running Time: 8 hrs.). 1995. bk. 119.00 set. (752202EZ) Am Inst CPA.
Whether you are an accountant in industry responsible for financial statement analysis or a public practitioner who helps client companies with business planning, this course will teach you how to evaluate financial performance. It presents financial statements as a set of dynamic instruments that provide accurate, relevant timely information on which to base financial decisions.

Financial Statement Analysis & Cash Flow Planning. Andrew B. Titen & Erich A. Helfert. 3 cass. bk. 129.00 set, incl. textbk. & quizzer. (CPE4520) Bisk Educ.
Learn how to use financial statement analysis to analyze the financial health of your - or your client's - operation, plus get proven techniques to help you identify & fix problem areas, evaluate proposals for profit potential, & improve the accuracy of your short- & long-term forecasting.

***Financial Statements.** Thomas R. Ittelson. 2011. audio compact disk 23.95 (978-1-59316-573-4(0)) Listen & Live.

Financial Stewardship. Created by AWMI. (ENG.). 2006. 35.00 (978-1-59548-068-2(4)); audio compact disk 35.00 (978-1-59548-067-5(6)) A Wommack.

Financial Strategies for VC Backed Companies Seminar - CFOs of Venture Capital Backed Companies on Management Team Strategies for Financial Tools, Controls & Growth Strategies Planning. Ed. by ReedLogic Staff. 2006. pap. bk. 499.95 (978-1-59701-079-5(0)) Aspatore Bks.

Financial Success. Read by Mary Richards. 12.95 (303) Master Your Mind.
Explains how to use the wisdom of ones deeper mind to draw to you the power & resources needed for financial independence.

Financial Success & Prosperity: Create & Experience Financial Success in Your Life. Mark Bancroft. Read by Mark Bancroft. 1 cass., bklet. (Running Time: 1 hrs.). (General Self-Development/Improvement Ser.). 1999. 12.95 (978-1-58522-031-1(0), 907, EnSpire Aud) EnSpire Pr.
Two complete sessions plus printed instruction manual/guidebook. With healing music soundtrack.

Financial Success & Prosperity: Create & Experience Financial Success in Your Life. Mark Bancroft. Read by Mark Bancroft. 1 CD, bklet. (Running Time: 1 hr.). (General Self-Development/Improvement Ser.). 2006. audio compact disk 20.00 (978-1-58522-045-8(0)) EnSpire Pr.
Two complete sessions plus printed instructionmanual.guidebook. With healing music soundtrack.

Financial Wisdom. Mac Hammond. 1 cass. (Running Time: 1 hour). 2005. 5.00 (978-1-57399-203-9(8)); audio compact disk 5.00 (978-1-57399-256-5(9)) Mac Hammond.

Financial Wisdom. Mac Hammond. 2008. audio compact disk 6.00 (978-1-57399-384-5(0)) Mac Hammond.

Financially Confident Woman. Mary Hunt. 1 cass. 1996. 17.99 (978-7-5135-4715-4(7)) BH Pubng Grp.

Financier. Theodore Dreiser. Read by Anais 9000. 2008. 33.95 (978-1-60112-158-5(X)) Babblebooks.

Financier. unabr. ed. Theodore Dreiser. Read by Flo Gibson. 14 cass. (Running Time: 19 hrs.). 1993. 42.95 (978-1-55685-288-6(6)) Audio Bk Con.
This powerful novel explores the dynamics of the financial world during the Civil War & after the stock market panic caused by the Chicago fire. Frank Cowperwood, a ruthlessly dominating broker & wheeler-dealer, climbs the ladder, goes to jail for illegal practices & returns to climb again, always with his loving mistress championing his every move.

Financing American Politics. unabr. ed. Herbert E. Alexander. 1 cass. (Running Time: 25 min.). 12.95 (27001) J Norton Pubs.
Lecture on the complexities of political finance in America. Where the money comes from & how much is available can affect many aspects of politics, even as to who will run for a particular office.

Find a Victim. unabr. ed. Ross MacDonald, pseud. Read by Tom Parker. 5 cass. (Running Time: 7 hrs.). (Lew Archer Mystery Ser.). 1999. 39.95 (978-0-7861-1493-1(2), 2344) Blckstn Audio.
After Lew Archer stops the car to help a boy who is dying of a gunshot wound, he is suspected by the law, hired by a target-shooting trucking magnate & propositioned by an adulterer's wife. A hijacked load of hooch & a band of sinners are on the loose in the hills & desert around this nice Southern California Town. So is this LA private eye, who keeps getting blood on his hands.

Find a Victim. unabr. ed. Ross MacDonald, pseud. Read by Tom Parker. 6 cass. (Running Time: 9 hrs.). 2001. 29.95 (978-0-7861-1920-2(9)) Pub: Blckstn Audio. Dist(s): Penton Overseas
The hitchhiker stumbles to his knees on the side of the road. When Archer stops the car and gets to him, he knows he is in for a ride - for the boy is dying of a gunshot wound.

Find a Victim. unabr. ed. Ross MacDonald, pseud & Ross MacDonald. (Running Time: 21600 sec.). 2007. audio compact disk 45.00 (978-0-7861-6285-7(6)) Blckstn Audio.

Find a Victim. unabr. ed. Ross MacDonald, pseud & Ross MacDonald. Read by Tom Parker. (Running Time: 21600 sec.). 2007. audio compact disk 29.95 (978-0-7861-7213-9(4)) Blckstn Audio.

Find a Victim, Set. unabr. ed. Ross MacDonald, pseud. Read by Tom Parker. 5 cass. (Lew Archer Mystery Ser.). 1999. 39.95 (FS9-50904) Highsmith.

Find Answers in Your Dreams. 1 cass. (Sleep Programming Tapes Ser.). 12.98 (978-0-87554-545-5(9), 1118) Valley Sun.

Find Happiness from Within. Dean A. Montalbano. 2 cds. (Running Time: 2.25 hrs). (Hypnotic Sensory Response Audio Ser.). 2004. audio compact disk 39.95 (978-1-932086-16-4(1)) L Lizards Pub Co.

Find Happiness from Within: A Self Hypnosis Tape Set. Dean A. Montalbano. (Hypnotic Sensory Response Audio Ser.). 2000. 39.95 (978-0-9708772-6-0(9)) L Lizards Pub Co.

Find Inner Peace. 17.95 (836AK) Nightingale-Conant.
Helps you rid yourself of bad habits you want to lose & develop the positive behavior patterns that will lead to a better, happier & more productive life.

Find It on the Wing. Perf. by Sandi Patti & Praise Hymn Sound Tracks Staff. 7.98 (PHT1059) Praise Hymn.

Find Love & Project Charisma. Dick Sutphen. 1 cass. (Running Time: 1 hr.). (Only Subliminals Ser.). 1990. 12.98 (978-0-87554-446-5(0), T206) Valley Sun.
One hour of soothing digitally mastered stereo music with positive subliminal suggestions phrased for maximum acceptance by your subconscious mind.

Find Me. unabr. ed. Carol O'Connell. 12 CDs. (Running Time: 57600 sec.). (Mallory Novels Ser.). 2007. audio compact disk 29.95 (978-1-59316-090-6(9)) Listen & Live.

Find Me. unabr. ed. Rosie O'Donnell. (ENG.). 2005. 14.98 (978-1-59483-372-4(9)) Pub: Hachet Audio. Dist(s): HachBkGrp

Find Me - A Mallory Novel. unabr. ed. Carol O'Connell. Read by Alyssa Bresnahan. (YA). 2007. 49.99 (978-1-60252-712-6(1)) Find a World.

***Find Out! The Dawning of Inner Freedom.** Mark Butler. (ENG.). 2009. 27.00 (978-0-9819832-0-2(0)) Eagle Lit Fnd.

***Find Out Who's Normal & Who's Not: Proven Techniques to Quickly Uncover Anyone's Degree of Emotional Stability.** unabr. ed. David J. Lieberman. Read by Sean Pratt. (Running Time: 5 hrs.). (ENG.). 2010. 19.98 (978-1-59659-538-5(8), GildAudio) Pub: Gildan Media. Dist(s): HachBkGrp

Find Out Who's Normal & Who's Not: Proven Techniques to Quickly Uncover Anyone's Degree of Emotional Stability. unabr. ed. David J. Lieberman. (Running Time: 5 hrs.). (ENG.). 2010. audio compact disk 24.98 (978-1-59659-360-2(1), GildAudio) Pub: Gildan Media. Dist(s): HachBkGrp

Find the Career of Your Dreams in 90 Days or Less. Speeches. Joan Hangarter. 1 CD. (Running Time: 39 mins.). 2004. audio compact disk 15.99 (978-0-9745590-3-2(2), 33-203) Mir Makers Cl.
Use your job loss as fuel to find the career of your choice. Teaching specific steps to success, Dr. Joan shows you how to find your purpose, commit, and create the career and the life of your dreams. She will help you unlock your hidden potential and overcome blocks to your success. Her approach and tenacity through it all show that stress and crisis can be managed when taking the proper approach.

Find the Job You Want... & Get It! unabr. ed. Pat Sladey. Read by Pat Sladey. 4 cass. (Running Time: 3 hrs.). 1986. pap. bk. 39.95 (SR 97 481) P Sladey.
Aimed at persons seeking positions at various levels in business & industry. Includes the Job Search, Researching the Hidden Job Market, Selling Yourself in the interview, preparing winning resumes & letters, staying motivated in thre job search.

Find This Woman. unabr. ed. Richard S. Prather. Read by Maynard Villers. 6 cass. (Running Time: 6 hrs. 36 min.). (Shell Scott Ser.: Bk. 4). 2001. 39.95 (978-1-55686-901-3(0)) Books in Motion.
When Harrison Bing hires an L.A. private eye to find his daughter in Las Vegas, the P.I. also evaporates. Shell Scott inherits the job, and finds men with guns, and more.

Find Those Missing Persons. Walta S. Jones. 1 cass. 8.95 (542) Am Fed Astrologers.
Horary, event & natal to locate.

Find Your Gifts, Follow Your Dreams. Anita Stansfield. 1 cass. 1999. 9.95 (978-1-57734-450-6(2), 06005934) Covenant Comms.
An inspirational talk about realizing your potential.

Find Your Hidden Reservoir of Healing Energy: A Gudied Meditation for Chronic Disease. Michael Mayer. 1 cass. (Running Time: 30 mins.). 2002. 11.95 (978-0-9704310-4-2(X)) Bodymind Heal.
*In this AudioTape Dr. Mayer will introduce you to tools to alleviate sufferingfor chronic diseases including:*Breathing Techniques derived from Qigong, a many thousand year-old method for cultivating the energy of life.*Visualizations and Self-hypnosis Methods to help you tap into the vital root system below the surface of your conscious mind*Self-touch Mehtods from Acupressure that soothe and revitalize.* Relaxing Music that will aid your inner journey.*

Find Your Hidden Reservoir of Healing Energy: A Guided Meditation for Cancer. 2002. 11.95 (978-0-9704310-3-5(1)) Bodymind Heal.
This tape is a valuable self -help tool that can help alleviate the suffering of those who are suffering from the effects of cancer. It contains breathing techniques, guided visualizations and self-touch methods with soothing music. It helps people activate their own healing resources and feel more energized and in control of their lives.

Find Your Ideal Relationship. Bruce Goldberg. (ENG.). 2005. audio compact disk 17.00 (978-1-57968-077-0(1)) Pub: B Goldberg. Dist(s): Baker Taylor

Find Your Ideal Relationship. Bruce Goldberg. Read by Bruce Goldberg. 1 cass. (Running Time: 25 min.). (ENG.). 2007. 13.00 (978-1-885577-44-3(3)) Pub: B Goldberg. Dist(s): Baker Taylor
Attract a soulmate through self-hypnosis.

Find Your Inner Guide. Created by Anne H. Spencer-Beacham. 1. 2003. audio compact disk (978-1-932163-43-8(3)) Infinity Inst.

Find Your Inner Happiness. Jack Boland. Read by Jack Boland. 1 cass. (Running Time: 59 min.). 8.95 Listen USA.

Find Your Karmic Purpose. Bruce Goldberg. (ENG.). 2005. audio compact disk 17.00 (978-1-57968-059-6(3)) Pub: B Goldberg. Dist(s): Baker Taylor

Find Your Karmic Purpose. Bruce Goldberg. Read by Bruce Goldberg. 1 cass. (Running Time: 25 min.). (ENG.). 2006. 13.00 (978-1-885577-67-2(2)) Pub: B Goldberg. Dist(s): Baker Taylor
Through self-hypnosis learn why one chose the current life & the goals to be accomplished.

Find Your Strongest Life: What the Happiest & Most Successful Women Do Differently. unabr. ed. Marcus Buckingham. Read by Marcus Buckingham. 1 MP3-CD. (Running Time: 7 hrs.). 2009. 24.99 (978-1-4418-0726-7(8), 9781441807267, Brilliance MP3); 39.97 (978-1-4418-0727-4(6), 9781441807274, Brlnc Audio MP3 Lib); 24.99 (978-1-4418-0728-1(4), 9781441807281, BAD); 39.97 (978-1-4418-0729-8(2), 9781441807298, BADLE); audio compact disk 29.99 (978-1-4418-0724-3(1), 9781441807243, Bril Audio CD Unabri); audio compact disk 87.97 (978-1-4418-0725-0(X), 9781441807250, BriAudCD Unabrid) Brilliance Audio.

Find Your Wings. Contrib. by Mark Harris. (Inoriginal Performance Trax Ser.). 2005. audio compact disk 9.98 (978-5-558-93084-9(5)) INO Rec.

Find Your Wings. Contrib. by Mark Harris. (Praise Hymn Soundtracks Ser.). 2006. audio compact disk 8.98 (978-5-558-32608-6(5)) Pt of Grace Ent.

Find Your Wings/I Believe I Can Fly. Contrib. by Johnathan Crumpton & Harold Ross. Prod. by Ed Kee. (ENG.). 2008. audio compact disk 24.99 (978-5-557-48402-2(7), Brentwood-Benson Music) Brentwood Music.

Finder. Greg Rucka. 1999. 60.00 (96082R4) Recorded Bks.

Finder. unabr. ed. Colin Harrison. Read by Jason Culp. (Running Time: 10 hrs.). 2008. 59.95 (978-0-7927-5318-6(6)); audio compact disk 94.95 (978-0-7927-5255-4(4)) AudioGO.

Finder. unabr. ed. Colin Harrison. Read by Jason Culp. 10 CDs. (Running Time: 12 hrs. 30 mins. 0 sec.). (ENG.). 2008. audio compact disk 39.95 (978-1-4272-0303-8(2)) Pub: Macmill Audio. Dist(s): Macmillan

Finder: An Atticus Kodiak Novel. unabr. ed. Greg Rucka. Narrated by George Wilson. 7 cass. (Running Time: 10 hrs. 15 mins.). 1999. 62.00 (978-0-7887-3994-1(8), 96082E7) Recorded Bks.
A story of suspense & danger immersed in a dark & violent world. Bodyguard Atticus Kodiac has been hired by a ruthless colonel to protect his 15-year-old daughter. Atticus quickly discovers that rogue assassins are after her & the stakes are much higher than the daughter's life.

Finders Keepers. 2004. 8.95 (978-1-56008-893-6(1)); cass. & flmstrp 30.00 (978-1-56008-666-6(1)) Weston Woods.

***Finders Keepers.** abr. ed. Fern Michaels. Read by Susan Ericksen. (Running Time: 3 hrs.). 2010. audio compact disk 9.99 (978-1-4418-6711-7(2), 9781441867117, BCD Value Price) Brilliance Audio.

Finders Keepers. unabr. ed. Fern Michaels. Read by Susan Ericksen. (Running Time: 15 hrs.). 2008. 24.95 (978-1-4233-5415-4(X), 9781423354154, Brilliance MP3); 24.95 (978-1-4233-5417-8(6), 9781423354178, BAD); 39.25 (978-1-4233-5416-1(8), 9781423354161, Brlnc Audio MP3 Lib); 39.25 (978-1-4233-5418-5(4), 9781423354185, Brlnc Audio MP3 Lib) Brilliance Audio.

***Finders Keepers.** unabr. ed. Fern Michaels. Read by Susan Ericksen. (Running Time: 13 hrs.). 2010. audio compact disk 89.97 (978-1-4418-4124-7(5), 9781441841247, BriAudCD Unabrid); audio compact disk 29.99 (978-1-4418-4123-0(7), 9781441841230, Bril Audio CD Unabri) Brilliance Audio.

Finders Keepers, Set. abr. ed. Fern Michaels. Read by Susan Ericksen. 2 cass. 1999. 17.95 (FS9-43226) Highsmith.

Finders Keepers, Set. unabr. ed. Fern Michaels. Read by Susan Ericksen. 10 cass. 1999. 89.25 (FS9-43178) Highsmith.

Finders Keepers: The Story of a Man Who Found $1 Million. unabr. ed. Mark Bowden. Read by Mark Bowden. 4 CDs. (Running Time: 6 hrs.). 2002. audio compact disk 49.95 (978-0-7927-2736-1(3), SLD 495, Chivers Sound Lib); bk. 29.95 (978-0-7927-2709-5(6), CSL 495, Chivers Sound Lib) AudioGO.
When Joey, a likeable longshoreman from the city's working class, happens upon $1.2 million in unmarked casino money on his way to score drugs, his life is turned upside down. He lives the week following the discovery in a whirlwind, plotting his future even as he grows anxious that he could be found out, captured, or even killed. The pulsing suspense never lets up as the entire city of Philadelphia is swept up in the hunt for the missing money and Joey struggles with an incredible moral dilemma.

Finders Keepers: The Story of a Man who found $1 Million. unabr. ed. Mark Bowden. 2004. 15.95 (978-0-7435-4703-1(9)) Pub: S&S Audio. Dist(s): S and S Inc

Finding a Girl in America: Ten Stories & a Novella. unabr. collector's ed. Andre Dubus. Read by Dan Lazar. 8 cass. (Running Time: 8 hrs.). 1982. 48.00 (978-0-7366-0465-9(0), 1437) Books on Tape.
Hank Allison whose life is overshadowed by a failed marriage, concern for his daughter & his need for new relationships. He emerges from his concerns as a man of healing insight & one who is capable of change, growth & affection.

Finding a Light in the Darkness. Read by Wayne Monbleau. 2 cass. 1994. 10.00 Set. (978-0-944648-34-6(7), LGT-1234) Loving Grace Pubns.
Religious.

Finding a Path to An Open Heart & Wisdom Has No Fear of Death. Comment by Ram Dass. (Running Time: 58 min.). 1987. Original Face.
Exploration of the awakening of a higher consciousness. Discusses the use of specific practices & teaches that death can be a vehicle for awakening.

Finding A Personal Place: A Step-by-Step Program for Learning to Relax Instantly. Created by David Bresler. (ENG.). 2007. audio compact disk 19.95 (978-1-887211-03-1(9), Imag Res) AlphaBks CA.

Finding Africa: Early Explorers Fluent Set B Audio CD. Jamie A. Schroeder. Adapted by Benchmark Education Staff. (J). 2007. audio compact disk 10.00 (978-1-4108-8250-9(0)) Benchmark Educ.

Finding An Ideal Mate. 1 cass. (Running Time: 60 min.). 10.95 (042) Psych Res Inst.

Finding & Keeping Love: An Imago-Based Program for Getting the Love You Want. Harville Hendrix. (ENG.). 2008. audio compact disk 69.95 (978-1-59179-660-2(1)) Sounds True.

Finding & Keeping Your Ideal Mate with Healing from the Body Level Up: A Two Tape Set. Created by Judith A. Swack. (ENG.). 2002. 25.00 (978-0-9786744-5-8(6)) HFTBLU.

Finding & Screening Prospective Church Planters: National Association of Evangelicals, 47th Annual Convention, Columbus, Ohio, March 7-9, 1989. Paul Taylor. 1 cass. (Workshops Ser.: No. 28-Thursda). 1989. 4.25 ea. 1-8 tapes.; 4.00 ea. 9 tapes or more. Nat Assn Evan.

Finding Beauty in a Broken World. Terry Tempest Williams. (Running Time: 2:00:00). 2009. audio compact disk 24.95 (978-1-59179-742-5(X)) Sounds True.

Finding Caruso. unabr. ed. Kim Barnes. 8 cass. (Running Time: 11 hrs.). 2003. 79.00 (978-1-4025-3973-2(8)) Recorded Bks.
An unforgettable story of two brothers and the complex ties that bind them. Alternately dark and violent, heartbreaking and tender, it is a coming-of-age tale that is both timeless and contemporary.

Finding Christ in the Old Testament. Scott Hahn. Read by Scott Hahn. 7 cass. 34.95 Set. (5267-C) Ignatius Pr.
Carefully examining the covenants, prophecies & promises in the Old Testament, Hahn shows how they all work together & point to the coming of Christ.

Finding Comfort in All Relationships: Instructions Included! J'en El. 2 CDs. (Running Time: 35 mins.). 2003. audio compact disk 19.95 (978-0-9722392-0-2(0)) Fortune's Gate Pubng Co.

Finding Davey. Jonathan Gash & Jonathan Gash. Contrib. by Jeff Harding. 10 cass. (Story Sound Ser.). 2006. 84.95 (978-1-85903-969-4(3)) Pub: Mgna Lrg Print GBR. Dist(s): Ulverscroft US

Finding Davey. unabr. ed. Jonathan Gash & Jonathan Gash. 6 CDs. (Running Time: 47700 sec.). (Story Sound CD Ser.). 2006. audio compact disk 99.95 (978-1-84652-033-4(9)) Pub: Mgna Lrg Print GBR. Dist(s): Ulverscroft US

Finding Ease of Mind; The Practice Path. H. E. Rinpoche. Read by Barry Spacks. 1 cass. (Running Time: 52 min.). (Mirror of Freedom Ser.: Nos. 2 & 3). 7.00 (PP-AVMF2) Padma Pub CA.

Finding Emotional Balance. Earnie Larsen. 1 cass. (Running Time: 1 hr.). 1989. 10.95 (978-1-56047-013-7(5), A117) E Larsen Enterprises.
Discusses the differences between painful emotions & correct emotions.

***Finding Faith: A Search for What Makes Sense.** Brian D. McLaren. (Running Time: 5 hrs. 19 mins. 58 sec.). (Finding Faith Ser.). (ENG.). 2010. 14.99 (978-0-310-30447-0(4)) Zondervan.

***Finding Faith - -A Search for What Is Real.** Brian D. McLaren. (Running Time: 5 hrs. 29 mins. 59 sec.). (Finding Faith Ser.). (ENG.). 2010. 14.99 (978-0-310-30446-3(6)) Zondervan.

Finding Faith in Difficult Times. Iyanla Vanzant. 1 CD. (Running Time: 1 hr.). 2006. audio compact disk 15.95 (978-1-59179-203-1(7), W848D) Sounds True.
Finding Faith in Difficult Times shares Vanzant's most cherished collection of insights, prayers, and meditations she developed to work through years of personal struggles. Here, listeners will learn how to cultivate faith and determination, build inner strength, and find lasting peace in even the darkest moments of life.

Finding Favor with the King: Preparing for Your Moment in His Presence. Tommy Tenney. 2003. 16.99 (978-0-7642-2860-5(9)) Pub: Bethany Hse. Dist(s): Baker Pub Grp

***Finding Fish.** abr. ed. Antwone Q. Fisher. Read by Alton Fitzgeral White. (ENG.). 2005. (978-0-06-112741-0(8), Harper Audio); (978-0-06-112742-7(6), Harper Audio) HarperCollins Pubs.

Finding Fish: A Memoir. unabr. ed. Antwone Quenton Fisher & Mim Eichler Rivas. Narrated by Tony Penny. 10 cass. (Running Time: 12 hrs. 15 mins.). 2001. 92.00 (978-0-7887-5269-8(3)) Recorded Bks.
Born in jail, Antwone Quenton Fisher was raised in abusive foster homes. When he hit rock bottom, he joined the Navy and found the strength to persevere, eventually becoming a top Hollywood producer and screenwriter.

Finding Freedom. Robert E. Lauder. 1 cass. 1998. 8.95 (978-5-559-65732-5(8), Resurrection Pr) Cathlic Bk Pub.

***Finding George Orwell in Burma.** unabr. ed. Emma Larkin. Narrated by Emily Durante. (Running Time: 8 hrs. 30 mins.). 2010. 29.99 (978-1-4001-9747-7(3)); 15.99 (978-1-4001-8747-8(8)) Tantor Media.

***Finding George Orwell in Burma.** unabr. ed. Emma Larkin. Narrated by Emily Durante. (Running Time: 8 hrs. 30 mins. 0 sec.). (ENG.). 2010. 19.99 (978-1-4001-6747-0(7)); audio compact disk 71.99 (978-1-4001-4747-2(6)); audio compact disk 29.99 (978-1-4001-1747-5(X)) Pub: Tantor Media. Dist(s): IngramPubServ

Finding God: Moving Through Your Problems Toward . abr. ed. Larry Crabb. (Running Time: 2 hrs. 0 mins. 0 sec.). (ENG.). 2003. 10.99 (978-0-310-26034-9(5)) Zondervan.

Finding God Beyond Harvard: The Quest for Veritas. unabr. ed. Kelly Kullberg. Narrated by Kate Reading. 8 CDs. (Running Time: 10 hrs. 15 mins. 0 sec.). (ENG.). 2006. audio compact disk 24.98 (978-1-59644-253-5(0), Hovel Audio) christianaud.
The quest for truth is an adventure into real life.In her book Finding God at Harvard, Kelly Monroe brought together the stories of thinking Christians whose search for truth led them to Veritas - -in the person of Jesus Christ. Now she tells the story of her own journey into wonder and discovery, which took her beyond the ivied walls of Harvard to universities across the country. In the midst of the arid skepticism of the academy, she found a vibrant, interdisciplinary community unafraid of facing life's toughest questions, embracing the quest for true knowledge with intellectual rigor, delight and joy. As The Veritas Forum grappled with the insights of the academy's brightest Christian scholars, Kelly came to realize that truth or Veritas is no mere abstract concept but the very light by which we see all things.Engaging narrative and provocative content come together in this mind-stretching and heart-challenging journey. Come with Kelly on an intellectual road trip as The Veritas Forum explores the deepest questions of the university world, and the culture at large. And discover for yourself that Veritas transcends philosophy or religion and instead brings true life.

***Finding God Beyond Harvard: The Quest for Veritas.** unabr. ed. Kelly Monroe Kullberg. Narrated by Kate Reading. (ENG.). 2006. 14.98 (978-1-59644-254-2(9), Hovel Audio) christianaud.

Finding God in Daily Life. Daya Mata. 1984. 6.50 (2116) Self Realization.
Speaks informally on family life, balancing work & meditation & other vital subjects including: the importance of positive thinking - to body, mind, & soul; guidance for raising children; communication among family members; how to attune our will with God's will.

Finding God in Hidden Places. unabr. ed. Joni Eareckson Tada. Narrated by Joni Eareckson Tada. (Running Time: 3 hrs. 4 mins. 8 sec.). (ENG.). 2010. 11.19 (978-1-60814-621-5(9)); audio compact disk 15.99 (978-1-59859-675-5(6)) Oasis Audio.

Finding God in Life & Prayer with the Help of Teresa's "Interior Castle" Keith J. Egan. Read by Keith J. Egan. 4 cass. 1986. 32.95 Incl. shelf-case. (TAH168) Alba Hse Comns.
Analyzes the guidelines set out by the Carmelite mystic for achieving union with God.

Finding God in Pain & Problems. unabr. ed. Thomas A. Jones. 1999. 16.99 (978-1-57782-123-6(8)) Discipleshp.

Finding God in the Audio Cass. Bruner & Ware. 2004. 17.99 (978-1-58926-300-0(6)) Domain Commns.

Finding God in the Audio Cd. Bruner & Ware. 2004. audio compact disk 19.99 (978-1-58926-301-7(4)) Domain Commns.

Finding God in the Lord of the Rings. unabr. ed. Kurt Bruner. 2 cass. (Running Time: 4 hrs. 30 min.). 2003. 17.99; audio compact disk 19.99 Oasis Audio.

Finding God in the Shack. unabr. ed. Roger E. Olson. Narrated by Roger Mueller. (Running Time: 4 hrs. 44 mins. 26 sec.). (ENG.). 2009. audio compact disk 22.99 (978-1-59859-563-5(6)) Oasis Audio.

Finding God in the Shack. unabr. ed. Roger E. Olson. Narrated by Roger Mueller. (Running Time: 4 hrs. 44 mins. 26 sec.). (ENG.). 2009. 16.09 (978-1-60814-481-5(X)) Oasis Audio.

Finding God in Unexpected Places. unabr. ed. Philip Yancey. Read by Mel Foster. (Running Time: 7 hrs.). 2005. 39.25 (978-1-59737-156-8(4), 9781597371568, BADLE); 24.95 (978-1-59737-155-1(6), 9781597371551, BAD) Brilliance Audio.

Finding God in Unexpected Places. unabr. ed. Philip Yancey. Read by Jim Bond & Mel Foster. (Running Time: 7 hrs.). 2005. 69.25 (978-1-59737-114-8(9), 9781597371148, BrilAudUnabridg); 26.95 (978-1-59737-113-1(0), 9781597371131, BAU); 39.25 (978-1-59737-154-4(8), 9781597371544, Brinc Audio MP3 Lib); 24.95 (978-1-59737-153-7(X), 9781597371537, Brilliance MP3); audio compact disk 82.25 (978-1-59737-116-2(5), 9781597371162, BriAudCD Unabrid); audio compact disk 29.95 (978-1-59737-115-5(7), 9781597371155, Bril Audio CD Unabri) Brilliance Audio.
An Atlanta slum. A pod of whales off the coast of Alaska. The prisons of Peru and Chile. The plays of Shakespeare. A health club in Chicago. For those with eyes to see, traces of God can be found in the most unexpected places. Yet many Christians have not only missed seeing God, they've overlooked opportunities to make him visible to those most in need of hope. In this enlightening book, author Philip Yancey serves as an insightful tour guide for those willing to look beyond the obvious, pointing out glimpses of the eternal where few might think to look. Whether finding God among the newspaper headlines, within the church, or on the job, Yancey delves deeply into the commonplace and surfaces with rich spiritual insight. Finding God in Unexpected Places takes listeners from Ground Zero to the Horn of Africa, and each stop along the way reveals footprints of God, touches of his truth, and grace that prompt listeners to search deeper within their own lives for glimpses of transcendence.

Finding God's Path Through Your Trials. unabr. ed. Elizabeth George. Narrated by Elizabeth George. (ENG.). 2008. 16.09 (978-1-60814-204-0(3)) Oasis Audio.

Finding God's Path Through Your Trials. unabr. ed. Elizabeth George & Elizabeth George. Narrated by Elizabeth George. (Running Time: 6 hrs. 57 mins. 2 sec.). (ENG.). 2008. audio compact disk 22.99 (978-1-59859-332-7(3)) Oasis Audio.

Finding Grace: A True Story about Losing Your Way in Life...and Finding It Again. unabr. ed. Donna VanLiere. Read by Donna VanLiere. Narrated by Renée Raudman. (Running Time: 4 hrs. 30 mins. 0 sec.). (ENG.). 2009. audio compact disk 49.99 (978-1-4001-4166-1(4)); audio compact disk 19.99 (978-1-4001-6166-9(5)); audio compact disk 24.99 (978-1-4001-1166-4(8)) Pub: Tantor Media. Dist(s): IngramPubServ

Finding Happiness. Emma Blair. Read by Vivien Heilbron. (Chivers Audio Bks.). 2003. 96.95 (978-0-7540-8410-5(8)) Pub: Chivers Audio Bks GBR. Dist(s): AudioGO

Finding Healing Through Forgiveness. 2004. audio compact disk 14.00 (978-1-57972-590-7(2)) Insight Living.

Finding Healing Through Forgiveness. Charles R. Swindoll. 2009. audio compact disk 14.00 (978-1-57972-839-7(1)) Insight Living.

Finding Help in the Mental Health Maze. Martha Thompson. Read by Neva Duyndam. 1 cass. 1989. 9.95 (978-1-878159-05-2(4)) Duvall Media.
Family members, caregivers & clients alike will learn where to locate groups that provide information & support.

Finding Home: An Imperfect Path to Faith & Family. unabr. ed. Jim Daly. Narrated by Jim Daly. (ENG.). 2007. 17.49 (978-1-60814-205-7(1)) Oasis Audio.

Finding Home: An Imperfect Path to Faith & Family. unabr. ed. Jim Daly. Narrated by Jim Daly. Told to Bob DeMoss. (Running Time: 5 hrs. 19 mins. 5 sec.). (ENG.). 2007. audio compact disk 24.99 (978-1-59859-238-2(6)) Oasis Audio.

Finding Hope- an Introduction on Spiritual Warfare for Women. Featuring John Eldredge. 2009. audio compact disk 12.99 (978-1-933207-38-4(8)) Ransomed Heart.

Finding Ideas for Articles That Sell. unabr. ed. Gordon Burgett. Read by Gordon Burgett. 1 cass. (Running Time: 1 hr.). 1992. 9.95 (978-0-910167-09-3(5)) Comm Unltd CA.
Explains where & how to find ideas that can be converted into salable articles.

Finding Inner Peace. Edd Anthony. 1 CD. (Running Time: 48 min.). 2003. audio compact disk 16.95 (978-1-881586-10-4(3)) Canticle Cass.

Finding Inner Peace. Edd Anthony. Read by Edd Anthony. Read by Tony Heim. 3 cass. (Running Time: 1 hr. 30 min.). 1992. 16.95 Set. (978-1-881586-01-2(4), FC-234) Canticle Cass.
Meditation & music (spoken word meditation).

Finding Investment Capital Made EZ: How to Prepare & Present a Venture Capital Request. Speeches. Mervin L. Evans & Lynette A. Bigelow. 2 Audio CD. (Running Time: 41 Minutes). 2004. 24.99 (978-0-914391-08-1(9)) Comm People Pr.

Finding Iris Chang: Friendship, Ambition, & the Loss of an Extraordinary Mind. unabr. ed. Paula Kamen. Read by Bernadette Dunne. (Running Time: 39600 sec.). 2007. 24.95 (978-1-4332-0518-7(1)); audio compact disk 24.95 (978-1-4332-0519-4(X)) Blckstn Audio.

Finding Iris Chang: Friendship, Amibition, & the Loss of an Extraordinary Mind. unabr. ed. Paula Kamen. Read by Bernadette Dunne. 1 MP3-CD. (Running Time: 11 hrs.). 2007. 29.95 (978-1-4332-0520-0(3)); audio compact disk 45.00 (978-1-4332-0517-0(3)) Blckstn Audio.

Finding Iris Chang: Friendship, Ambition, & the Loss of an Extraordinary Mind. unabr. ed. Paula Kamen & Bernadette Dunne. 4 cass. (Running Time: 11 hrs.). 2007. 34.95 (978-1-4332-0516-3(5)) Blckstn Audio.

Finding It: And Satisfying My Hunger for Life Without Opening the Fridge. abr. unabr. ed. Valerie Bertinelli. Read by Valerie Bertinelli. (Running Time: 6 hrs. 30 mins. 0 sec.). (ENG.). 2009. audio compact disk 29.99 (978-0-7435-9836-1(9)) Pub: S&S Audio. Dist(s): S and S Inc

Finding Little Sister. Yoriko Tsutsui. Illus. by Akiko Hayashi. 1913. bk. 12.95 (978-1-74126-039-7(6)) Pub: RICPub AUS. Dist(s): SCB Distributors

Finding Lost Things: Luke 15:1-7. Ed Young. (J). 1981. 4.95 (978-0-7417-1206-6(7), A0206) Win Walk.

Finding Love Online Freeway Guide: Click Your Way to Romance! Contrib. by Karin Anderson & Beth Roberts. (Playaway Adult Nonfiction Ser.). (ENG.). 2009. 39.99 (978-1-60847-838-5(6)) Find a World.

Finding Miracles. Julia Alvarez. 4 cass. (Running Time: 4:14 hrs.). 2004. 35.00 (978-1-4000-9048-8(2), Listening Lib) Random Audio Pubg.

Finding Miracles. unabr. ed. Julia Alvarez. 5 CDs. (Running Time: 4:14 hrs.). 2004. audio compact disk 50.00 (978-1-4000-9489-9(5), Listening Lib) Random Audio Pubg.

Finding Moon. abr. ed. Tony Hillerman. Read by Jay O. Sanders. 2005. audio compact disk 14.95 (978-0-06-081505-9(1)) HarperCollins Pubs.

Finding Moon. unabr. ed. Tony Hillerman. Read by Jonathan Marosz. 7 cass. (Running Time: 10 hrs. 30 min.). 1996. 56.00 (978-0-7366-3240-9(9), 3899) Books on Tape.
People counted on Moon Mathias to solve small problems. But when a telephone call delivers a problem as big as Southeast Asia, he finds himself in new territory.

Finding Moon. unabr. ed. Tony Hillerman. Narrated by George Guidall. 7 cass. (Running Time: 10 hrs.). 1996. 60.00 (978-0-7887-0456-7(7), 94649E7) Recorded Bks.
When a reporter learns that his brother fathered a child in south-east Asia before he died, the reporter is reluctantly pulled into an intense search.

Finding Mr Right. Emily Carmichael. Narrated by Barbara Rosenblat. 8 cass. (Running Time: 10 hrs. 15 mins.). 71.00 (978-1-4025-0948-3(0)); audio compact disk 89.00 (978-1-4025-2110-2(3)) Recorded Bks.

Finding My Family: Adoption Search & Reunion. Hosted by Mardie Caldwell. (ENG.). 2008. audio compact disk 19.95 (978-0-9705734-8-3(0)) Pub: Am Carrage Hse Pubng. Dist(s): STL Dist NA

Finding My Voice. Diane Rehm. Narrated by Diane Rehm. 7 cass. (Running Time: 10 hrs.). 65.00 (978-1-4025-1885-0(4)) Recorded Bks.

Finding My Way Home: Pathways to Life & the Spirit. Henri J. M. Nouwen. Read by Dan Anderson. (Running Time: 10800 sec.). (ENG.). 2007. audio compact disk 22.95 (978-0-86716-818-1(8)) St Anthony Mess Pr.

Finding Nevada, Bk. 3. unabr. ed. Frank Roderus. Read by Kevin Foley. 4 cass. (Running Time: 5 hrs.). 1995. 26.95 (978-1-55686-633-3(X)) Books in Motion.
Tenderfoot Harrison Wilke inherits a goldmine from his old friend John J. Trohoe, the man who taught Harrison how to be a bum. But a group of California investors claim they hold the title.

Finding Noel. abr. ed. Richard Paul Evans. Read by Richard Paul Evans. 2006. 17.95 (978-0-7435-6192-1(9)) Pub: S&S Audio. Dist(s): S and S Inc

Finding Noel. unabr. ed. Richard Paul Evans. Read by Richard Paul Evans. (Running Time: 5 hrs. 0 mins. 0 sec.). (ENG.). 2008. audio compact disk 14.99 (978-0-7435-7612-3(8)) Pub: S&S Audio. Dist(s): S and S Inc

***Finding of Jeremy.** Max Brand. 2009. (978-1-60136-407-4(5)) Audio Holding.

Finding Oneness of Life. Swami Amar Jyoti. 2 cass. 1979. 12.95 (M-7) Truth Consciousness.
Explores how we miss Oneness. Going beyond conceptions.

Finding Oprah's Roots: Finding Your Own. unabr. ed. Henry Louis Gates, Jr. Narrated by Dominic M. Hoffman. 5 CDs. (Running Time: 5 hrs.). 2007. audio compact disk 50.00 (978-1-4159-3914-7(4)) Random.

Finding Organic Church. unabr. ed. Frank Viola. (Running Time: 8 hrs. 30 mins. 0 sec.). (ENG.). 2009. audio compact disk 26.98 (978-1-59644-807-0(5), Hovel Audio) christianaud.

***Finding Organic Church: A Comprehensive Guide to Starting & Sustaining Authentic Christian Communities.** unabr. ed. Frank Viola. Narrated by Lloyd James. (ENG.). 2009. 16.98 (978-1-59644-808-7(3), Hovel Audio) christianaud.

Finding Our Own Path. Swami Amar Jyoti. 1 cass. 1981. 9.95 (M-16) Truth Consciousness.
Requirements on the Yoga paths. Couples on different paths.

Finding Our Right Space. Swami Amar Jyoti. 1 cass. 1980. 9.95 (K-37) Truth Consciousness.
Blessings of God & Guru are always there; how can we receive them? The answer told in the parable of the horse & the cart.

***Finding Our Way Again: The Return of the Ancient Practices.** unabr. ed. Brian McLaren. Narrated by Paul Michael. (ENG.). 2008. 14.98 (978-1-59644-597-0(1), Hovel Audio) christianaud.

Finding Our Way Again: The Return of the Ancient Practices. unabr. ed. Brian D. McLaren. Narrated by Paul Michael. (Running Time: 5 hrs. 0 mins. 0 sec.). (ENG.). 2008. audio compact disk 24.98 (978-1-59644-596-3(3), Hovel Audio) christianaud.

Finding Passion; Confessions of a Fifty Year Old Runaway on Audio. (ENG.). 2008. 9.99 (978-0-9800088-1-4(6)) C C Walker.

FINDING PEACE after the Loss of a Loved Animal Companion. Read by Diane Pomerance. (ENG.). 2006. audio compact disk 7.95 (978-0-9795218-1-2(5)) Pub: Polaire Pubna. Dist(s): Baker Taylor

Finding Peace & Harmony. Lexa Finley. Tammy Chi. 2009. audio compact disk 14.95 (978-0-9822494-0-6(3)) Journey Spirit.

Finding Peace in a Troubled Family. Benedict J. Groeschel. 1 cass. (Running Time: 75 min.). 7.95 (978-0-8198-2652-7(9)) Pauline Bks.

Finding Peace in the Midst of Chaos. (Running Time: 48 mins.). audio compact disk (978-1-59076-200-4(2)) DscvrHlpPubng.

Finding Peace of Mind. unabr. ed. Perf. by Eknath Easwaran. 1 cass. (Running Time: 1 hr.). 1989. 7.95 (978-1-58638-535-4(6)) Nilgiri Pr.

Finding Peggy. unabr. ed. Meg Henderson. Narrated by Dorothy Paul. 9 cass. (Running Time: 11 hrs.). 2000. 82.00 (978-1-84197-132-2(4), H1130E7) Recorded Bks.
Meg Henderson's childhood home was a 1950's Glasgow slum. Large families were squeezed into cramped quarters; relatives lived next door or in the same street. Meg's family was renowned for playing jokes on each other & her memory of Nan & Aunt Peggy is of them laughing so hard they had to hold each other for support.

***Finding Perfect.** unabr. ed. Susan Mallery. Read by Tanya Eby. (Running Time: 9 hrs.). (Fool's Gold Ser.). 2010. 19.99 (978-1-4418-4237-4(3), 9781441842374, Brilliance MP3); 39.97 (978-1-4418-4238-1(1), 9781441842381, Brinc Audio MP3 Lib); 39.97 (978-1-4418-4240-4(3), 9781441842404, BADLE); 19.99 (978-1-4418-4239-8(X), 9781441842398, BAD); audio compact disk 79.97 (978-1-4418-4236-7(5), 9781441842367, BriAudCD Unabrid); audio compact disk 19.99 (978-1-4418-4235-0(7), 9781441842350, Bril Audio CD Unabri) Brilliance Audio.

Finding Philippe. unabr. ed. Elizabeth Pewsey. 7 cass. (Isis Ser.). (J). 2002. 61.95 (978-0-7531-1369-1(4)) Pub: ISIS Lrg Prnt GBR. Dist(s): Ulverscroft US

Finding Purpose Beyond Our Pain: Uncover the Hidden Potential in Life's Most Common Struggles. unabr. ed. Paul Meier & David Livingstone Henderson. Narrated by Jon Gauger. (Running Time: 8 hrs. 57 mins. 0 sec.). (ENG.). 2009. 20.99 (978-1-60814-580-5(8)); audio compact disk 29.99 (978-1-59859-626-7(8)) Oasis Audio.

Finding Sandalwood Mountain. Greg & Fawn Andermann. (ENG.). 2007. (978-0-9777031-5-9(0)) Straube Ctrs.

Finding Serenity: Overcoming Dependence & Co-dependence. 2 cassettes. 1990. 19.45 (978-1-55841-208-8(5)) Emmett E Miller.
A warm, encouraging, illuminating and enjoyable heart-to-heart talk in which Dr. Miller helps you discover ways of growing through loss and letting go. Bonus: imagery and a song by Dr. Miller.

Finding Serenity: Overcoming Dependence & Co-dependence. 2 CDs. 1990. audio compact disk 25.50 (978-1-55841-133-3(X)) Emmett E Miller.

Finding Serenity in the Age of Anxiety. abr. ed. Robert Gerzon. Read by Robert Gerzon. 3 CDs. (Running Time: 3 hrs.). (ENG.). 2004. audio compact disk 22.95 (978-1-56511-933-8(9), 1565119339) Pub: HighBridge. Dist(s): Workman Pub

Finding Shapes & Solids: Early Explorers Fluent Set B Audio CD. Sophie Caribacas. Adapted by Benchmark Education Staff. (J). 2007. audio compact disk 10.00 (978-1-4108-8256-1(X)) Benchmark Educ.

Finding Start-Up Money, Vol. 42. 1 cass. (Running Time: 45 min.). (Business Opportunities Ser.). 1987. 7.95 B & H Comm.
Gives the six primary sources of start-up money & explains the first steps towards raising the money. Also discusses the important steps in a new business & how their financing needs differ.

Finding Stillness: Essential Knowledge, Skills, & Practice for Meditation. 1 CD. (Running Time: 80 mins.). 2003. audio compact disk 16.95 (978-0-9744663-0-9(1)) Matt Mind.

Finding strength & power Within: Regaining power & strength through creative Visualization. 2001. 12.95 (978-0-9720314-7-9(2)) Bagatto.

Finding Strength & Power Within: Regaining Power & Strength Through Creative Visualization. Elena Bussolino. Illus. by Albert Bussolino. Music by Rizwan Ahmad. Engineer Khalid Muhammad. Orig. Title: Original. 2000. 12.95 (978-0-9706743-2-6(5)) Bagatto.

Finding Strength in Weakness. Ben Young & Robert Huxley. 2000. 4.95 (978-0-7417-6175-0(0), B0175) Win Walk.

Finding Success in Gerontological Counseling: Complete Kit. Richard P. Johnson. Read by Richard P. Johnson. 8 cass. 124.00 Set. (74211) Am Coun Assn.
Richard Johnson illuminates the core competencies of gerontological counseling. He covers issues such as leisure & family counseling with older adults, dealing with depression & aging parent eldercare responsibilities, & elder abuse.

Finding the champion within: step-by-step plan reaching yr full potential Cst. Bruce Jenner. 2004. 9.95 (978-0-7435-4704-8(7)) Pub: S&S Audio. Dist(s): S and S Inc

Finding the Cross in Everday Life. John Sullivan. 1 cass. (Running Time: 56 min.). 8.95 I C S Pubns.
Fr. John Sullivan, O.C.D. comments on Edith Stein's thoughts about the daily burden that cannot be avoided.

Finding the Dream. abr. ed. Nora Roberts. Read by Sandra Burr. (Running Time: 3 hrs.). (Dream Trilogy: Bk. 3). 2009. audio compact disk 14.99 (978-1-4233-7904-1(7), 9781423379041) Brilliance Audio.

Finding the Dream. unabr. ed. Nora Roberts. Read by Sandra Burr. (Running Time: 11 hrs.). (Dream Trilogy: Bk. 3). 2008. 39.25 (978-1-4233-7881-5(4), 9781423378815, Brinc Audio MP3 Lib); 39.25 (978-1-4233-7883-9(0), 9781423378839, BADLE); 24.95 (978-1-4233-7880-8(6), 9781423378808, Brilliance MP3); 24.95 (978-1-4233-7882-2(2), 9781423378822, BAD); audio compact disk 102.25 (978-1-4233-7879-2(2), 9781423378792, BriAudCD Unabrid); audio compact disk 34.95 (978-1-4233-7878-5(4), 9781423378785, Bril Audio CD Unabri) Brilliance Audio.

Finding the God Within: The Message of Blessed Elizabeth of the Trinity. unabr. ed. Margaret Dorgan. 2 cass. (Running Time: 2 hrs. 47 min.). 1992. 18.95 set. (TAH276) Alba Hse Comns.
What does the Indwelling Trinity mean to you? Walk with Carmelite Blessed Elizabeth of the Trinity into new awareness of an Indwelling God who invites you to intimacy. She leads along a path of glory that shows how earthly life, rooted in the mystery of Jesus Christ, moves according to God's eternal design to give you already an anticipation of Heaven.

***Finding the Groove: Discovering the Gospel in Jazz.** Robert Gelinas. (Running Time: 5 hrs. 4 mins. 0 sec.). (ENG.). 2009. 14.99 (978-0-310-30237-7(4)) Zondervan.

Finding the Love of Your Life. Phyllis Light. 2 cass. (Running Time: 1 hr. 33 min.). (C). 1994. 19.95 (978-0-9648935-0-4(9)) Lght Unltd.
Focuses on helping people become whole within themselves so that they can best attract & sustain the healthiest, most loving relationship possible.

Finding the Magnificent in Lower Mundane. Bob Stromberg. 1 cass. (Running Time: 60 min.). 1994. 12.99 (978-0-310-40748-5(6)) Zondervan.
A fresh, new volume of humor, wisdom, & story from one of the CBA market's increasingly visible storytellers & humorists, based on the author's fictional hometown setting of Lower Mundane.

Finding the Peaceful Place Within: Relax into Healing Series (Spoken Audio CD & Booklet) Nancy Hopps. (Relax Into Healing Ser.). 2001. pap. bk. 19.95 (978-0-9663069-5-8(3)) Pub: Syner Systs. Dist(s): Baker Taylor

Finding the Perfect Job. Rick Jarow. 1 cass. 1993. 9.00 (OC328-70) Sound Horizons AV.

Finding the Perfect Master. Swami Amar Jyoti. 1 cass. 1976. 9.95 (N-17) Truth Consciousness.
Pitfalls of religious leadership. Work, discipline, art & Supreme Liberation. Finding a Guru; responsibilities of Gurus & disciple. Spirituality & civilization. Holocausts & cataclysms.

Finding the Real You. Zoilita Grant. 2001. audio compact disk 15.95 (978-1-890575-31-1(3)) Zoilita Grant.

Finding the Thread: The Psychology of Mourning & Renewal. Read by Peter Mudd. 2 cass. (Running Time: 4 hrs.). 1986. 21.95 Set. (978-0-7822-0209-0(8), 215) C G Jung IL.

Finding the Thrust of the Natal Chart. Chris McRae. 1 cass. (Running Time: 90 min.). 1988. 8.95 (630) Am Fed Astrologers.

Finding the Work You Love: Guided Visualizations. Astrid Berg. Read by Astrid Berg. 1 cass. (Running Time: 1 hr.). 1994. 11.95 ResPubnsCA.
Visualizations to help with decision-making, etc.

Finding Time to Love. unabr. ed. Perf. by Eknath Easwaran. 1 cass. (Running Time: 1 hr.). 1980. 7.95 (978-1-58638-536-1(4)) Nilgiri Pr.

Finding Walter. unabr. ed. Ann Warren Turner. Narrated by Barbara Caruso. 3 cass. (Running Time: 4 hrs. 30 mins.). (gr. 3 up). 1998. 27.00 (978-0-7887-2067-3(8), 95420E7) Recorded Bks.
When Emily & Rose begin to restore the old dollhouse in grandmother's attic, the dolls come to life & telepathically ask for help.

Finding Wine on Highway 29: A Shaun Andrews AudioTour. Shaun Andrews. Music by Shaun Andrews. Music by Kevin Holden. (ENG.). 2007. audio compact disk 15.00 (978-0-9794627-0-2(3)) WineFlight.

Finding Work That Matters. unabr. ed. Mark Albion. 3 CDs. (Running Time: 3 hrs.). 2002. audio compact disk 29.95 (978-1-56455-940-1(8), AW00580D) Sounds True.
Start answering the tough but necessary questions to become a "working visionary". What dreams have I andoned in order to "make a living"? What are my true skills, the ones that will bring me the most fulfillment while benefiting others?: How much will it actually cost to re-create my life? How did others do it? What lessons do their stories hold?.

***Finding Your Faith.** unabr. ed. Stephanie Perry Moore. Narrated by Robin Miles. (Running Time: 4 hrs. 18 mins. 0 sec.). (Yasmin Peace Ser.). (ENG.). 2010. 12.98 (978-1-61045-011-9(6), christaudio); audio compact disk 18.98 (978-1-61045-077-5(9), christaudio) christianaud.

***Finding Your Identity.** Ira Progoff. 2010. 15.00 (978-1-935859-08-6(0)) Dialogue Assoc.

Finding Your Inner Truth. 2005. audio compact disk (978-0-9762037-6-6(6)) Ctr Soulful.

Finding Your Life's Mission. Maxine Taylor. 1 cass. 8.95 (591) Am Fed Astrologers.
What are you doing here?.

Finding Your Life's Purpose: The Search for Meaning in Everyday Life, Set. David Grudermeyer & Rebecca Grudermeyer. 2 cass. 18.95 (T-13) Willingness Wrks.

Finding Your Literary Voice. abr. ed. Benjamin Alire Sáenz. Read by Benjamin Alire Sáenz. 1 cass. (Running Time: 90 mins.). 1995. 12.95 (978-1-880717-35-6(2)) Writers AudioShop.
Award-winning Chicano poet & novelist ("Carry Me Like Water"), Saenz examines the importance of language to the voice you choose as a writer, in this edited workshop for the Austin Writers' League. "Assume people don't care; make them care with language," says Saenz.

Finding Your Niche in Life. 1 cass. (Running Time: 60 min.). 10.95 (025) Psych Res Inst.
Use intuitive powers to lead to successful actions & situations.

Finding Your Own Mothering Style. unabr. ed. Susan Besze Wallace & Monica Reed. Narrated by Christian Taylor. (Running Time: 1 hr. 21 mins. 9 sec.). (New Moms' Guides). (ENG.). 2009. 9.09 (978-1-60814-489-1(5)) Oasis Audio.

Finding Your Own Mothering Style. unabr. ed. Susan Wallace & Monica Reed. Narrated by Christian Taylor. (Running Time: 1 hr. 21 mins. 9 sec.). (New Moms' Guides). (ENG.). 2009. audio compact disk 12.99 (978-1-59859-485-0(0)) Oasis Audio.

Finding Your Passion. Cheryl Richardson. 4 CDs. 2002. audio compact disk 23.95 (978-1-4019-0031-1(3)) Hay House.

Finding Your Perfect Work. Paul Edwards. 2 cass. 1997. 15.95 Set. (978-1-55977-705-6(2)) CareerTrack Pubns.

Finding Your Place. Derek Prince. 3 cass. 1986. 14.95 set. (I-FYP1) Derek Prince.
Your calling will determine your placement, your placement will release your special gifts.

Finding Your Sacred Contract Live Workshop. Caroline Myss. 4 CDs. 2003. audio compact disk 23.95 (978-1-4019-0204-9(9), 2049) Hay House.

Finding Your Spiritual Family. Kriyananda, pseud. 9.95 (ST-66) Crystal Clarity.
Topics include: What is a "spiritual family"?; why more & more people are seeking their spiritual families; how to go about finding your own; avoiding false identities.

Finding Your Teacher; Niscience & the Cosmos. Ann Ree Colton & Jonathan Murro. 1 cass. 7.95 A R Colton Fnd.

Finding Your True Self. Bernie S. Siegel. 1 CD. (Running Time: 7200 sec.). (Prescriptions for Living Ser.). 2006. audio compact disk 10.95 (978-1-4019-0666-5(4)) Hay House.

Finding Your Way Back Home. Michael D. Christensen. 1 cass. (Bountiful 84010 Ser.). 1996. 9.95 (978-1-57008-268-9(5), Bkcraft Inc) Deseret Bk.

Finding Your Way through Confusion. Elena Bussolino & Anna Florentis. 2000. 7.99 (978-0-9720314-3-1(X)) Bagatto.

Finding Your Way Through Confusion: Allowing Your Inner Self to Guide You on Your Path. Elena Bussolino. Illus. by Albert Bussolino. Music by Rizwan Ahmad. Engineer Khalid Muhammad. 2001. 12.95 (978-0-9706743-4-0(1)); audio compact disk 17.95 (978-0-9706743-6-4(8)) Bagatto.

Findings. unabr. ed. Mary Anna Evans. Read by Cassandra Campbell. (Running Time: 9.5 hrs. 0 mins.). (Faye Longchamp Mystery Ser.: Bk. 4). 2008. 29.95 (978-1-4332-3536-8(6)); 59.95 (978-1-4332-3532-0(3)); audio compact disk 80.00 (978-1-4332-3533-7(1)) Blckstn Audio.

Fine & Bitter Snow. unabr. ed. Dana Stabenow. 10 cass. (Running Time: 15 hrs.). (Kate Shugak Ser.). 2002. 40.00 (978-0-7366-8647-1(9)); audio compact disk 48.00 (978-0-7366-8648-8(7)) Books on Tape.
The possibility of drilling for oil in a wildlife preserve near the home of the dynamic Aleutian P.I. has battle lines drawn. Things heat up when a ranger at the preserve loses his job for political reasons, but when a passionate conservation spokesperson is found poisoned, the war begins in earnest. In a gripping story both entertaining and tense - not to mention timely - Dana Stabenow brings to life the beauty and danger of living - and dying - in Alaska. This could be the novel that catapults Stabenow into the forefront of crime fiction today.

***Fine & Private Place.** Peter S. Beagle. Read by Peter S. Beagle. Prod. by Connor Cochran & Jim Lively. Engineer Jim Lively. (ENG.). 2009. 30.00 (978-0-9706801-1-2(2)) Conlan Pr.

Fine Art of Small Talk: How to Start a Conversation, Keep It Going, Build Rapport & Leave a Positive Impression. Deborah Fine. 2 cass. (Running Time: 3 hrs.). 1995. 15.95 (978-1-55977-505-2(X)) CareerTrack Pubns.

Fine Art of Small Talk: How to Start a Conversation, Keep it Going, Build Rapport, & Leave a Positive Impression. Debra Fine. 2004. bk. 17.95 (978-0-9711322-3-8(2)) SmallTalk Pubng.

Fine Balance, Pt. 1. unabr. ed. Rohinton Mistry. Read by John Lee. 10 cass. (Running Time: 15 hs.). 2001. 80.00 (978-0-7366-8433-0(6)) Books on Tape.
Four people must survive the oppression, poverty, and mistreatment of Indira Gandhi's India of the mid 1970's.

Fine Balance, Pt. 2. unabr. ed. Rohinton Mistry. Read by John Lee. 17 cass. (Running Time: 25 hrs. 30 mins.). 2001. 56.00 (978-0-7366-8453-8(0)) Books on Tape.

Fine Balance, Pts. 1&2. unabr. ed. Rohinton Mistry. Read by John Lee. 17 cass. (Running Time: 25 hrs. 30 mins.). 2001. 160.00 (978-0-7366-8442-2(5)) Books on Tape.

Fine, Fine School. Sharon Creech. 11 vols. (Running Time: 13 mins.). 2003. bk. 25.95 (978-1-59112-221-0(X)) Live Oak Media.

Fine, Fine School. Sharon Creech. Illus. by Harry Bliss. 14 vols. (Running Time: 13 mins.). 2003. pap. bk. 37.95 (978-1-59112-222-7(8)); pap. bk. 39.95 (978-1-59112-555-6(3)); audio compact disk 12.95 (978-1-59112-495-5(6)) Live Oak Media.

Fine, Fine School. Sharon Creech. Read by Harry Bliss. 11 vols. (Running Time: 13 mins.). (Live Oak Readalong Ser.). (J). 2003. pap. bk. 16.95 (978-1-59112-220-3(1)) Pub: Live Oak Media. Dist(s): AudioGO

Fine Just the Way It Is. Annie Proulx. 2008. audio compact disk 29.95 (978-0-7435-7918-6(6)) Pub: S&S Audio. Dist(s): S and S Inc

***Fine Line: Re-Envisioning the Gap between Christ & Culture.** Kary Oberbrunner. (Running Time: 6 hrs. 5 mins. 0 sec.). (ENG.). 2009. 14.99 (978-0-310-30238-4(2)) Zondervan.

Fine Motor Dysfunction. Laura Levine. 1999. audio compact disk 99.00 (978-0-12-785030-6(9), Acad Press) Sci Tech Bks.

Fine Night for Dying. unabr. ed. Jack Higgins. Perf. by Nicholas Ball. 4 cass. (Running Time: 6 hrs.). 2004. 25.00 (978-1-59007-192-2(1)) New Millenn Enter.
Gangland boss Harvey Preston's body is dragged out of the English Channel & intelligence operative Paul Chavasse is on the case.

Fine Place for Death. unabr. ed. Ann Granger. Narrated by Judith Boyd. 9 cass. (Running Time: 9 hrs. 30 mins.). 1996. 79.75 (978-1-84197-976-2(7), H1631MC, Clipper Audio) Recorded Bks.

Fine Print, Set. Cheri Crane. 2 cass. 9.98 Set. (978-1-55503-838-0(7), 07001215) Covenant Comms.
A humorous & inspiring novel.

Fine Red Rain. unabr. ed. Stuart M. Kaminsky. Narrated by Mark Hammer. 6 cass. (Running Time: 8 hrs.). (Inspector Porfiry Rostnikov Mystery Ser.: No. 5). 1994. 51.00 (978-1-55690-982-5(9), 94121E7) Recorded Bks.
As Rostnikov watched, the drunken circus performer took a fatal leap off the statue in the park, hurling himself to his death on the pavement below. Shortly thereafter another trapeze artist meets with a fatal accident. Against the warnings of his superiors, Rostnikov casts aside what is politic & begins a full-scale investigation of the Moscow Circus. Is this a simple case of professional jealousy, or politically-motivated criminal activity that will once again put Rostnikov dangerously at odds with the KGB.

Fine Summer Knight. unabr. ed. Jan Mark. Read by Brigit Forsyth. 4 cass. (Running Time: 6 hrs.). (J). (gr. 1-8). 1999. 32.95 (CCA 3377, Chivers Child Audio) AudioGO.

Fine Tuning for Sports Performance. Jack Schwarz. 35.00 (402) Aletheia Psycho.

Fine-Tuning Your Business. Terrie Brill. 1 cass. 1992. 8.95 (1013) Am Fed Astrologers.

Fine White Dust. unabr. ed. Cynthia Rylant. Narrated by Jeff Woodman. 2 pieces. (Running Time: 2 hrs. 15 mins.). (gr. 6 up). 1997. 19.00 (978-0-7887-0998-2(4), 95220E7) Recorded Bks.
For 13-year old Peter Cassidy, summer is the time for mowing lawns & hanging around with his friends, until the Man comes to town. In a few short days, Pete leaves his secure, familiar world to follow this saver of souls. But is the stranger what he claims to be?.

Fine White Dust. unabr. ed. Cynthia Rylant. Read by Keith Nobbs. (Running Time: 2 hrs. 0 mins. 0 sec.). (ENG.). (J). 2009. audio compact disk 14.99 (978-0-7435-7252-1(1)) Pub: S&S Audio. Dist(s): S and S Inc

Finer End. Deborah Crombie. Narrated by Jenny Sterlin. 9 cass. (Running Time: 12 hrs. 15 mins.). (Duncan Kincaid/Gemma James Novel Ser.). 82.00 (978-1-84197-387-6(4)) Recorded Bks.

Finer Points of Sausage Dogs. Alexander McCall Smith. (von Igelfeld Ser.). 2004. audio compact disk 22.99 (978-1-4193-1698-2(2)) Recorded Bks.

Finer Points of Sausage Dogs. unabr. ed. Alexander McCall Smith. 3 cass. (Running Time: 4 hrs.). (von Igelfeld Ser.). 2004. 24.95 (978-1-4025-9052-8(0)) Recorded Bks.
The Finer Points of Sausage Dogs is a wonderfully entertaining showcase for Smith?s award-winning wit. Invited to lecture in America, von Igelfeld envisions a visit to California or New York. Instead, he finds himself surrounded by hogs.

Finger Cymbal Fantasies. Vicki Corona. 1 cass. 1990. 14.95 (978-1-58513-071-9(0), 1ME) Dance Fantasy.
Instruction on how to play Middle Eastern finger cymbals.

Finger Foods Are Fun! (J). 2005. audio compact disk (978-1-933796-09-3(X)) PC Treasures.

Finger Lickin' Fifteen. abr. ed. Janet Evanovich. Read by Lorelei King. 3 CDs. (Running Time: 4 hrs.). No. 15. 2009. audio compact disk 19.95 (978-1-4272-0664-0(3)) Pub: Macmill Audio. Dist(s): Macmillan

***Finger Lickin' Fifteen.** unabr. ed. Janet Evanovich. Read by Lorelei King. (Running Time: 6 hrs. 15 mins.). 2009. 44.95 (978-0-7927-6418-2(8)) AudioGO.

Finger Lickin' Fifteen. unabr. ed. Janet Evanovich. Narrated by Lorelei King. 7 CDs. (Running Time: 7 hrs.). (Stephanie Plum Ser.). 2009. audio compact disk 74.95 (978-0-7927-6377-2(7), Chivers Sound Lib) AudioGO.

Finger Lickin' Fifteen. unabr. ed. Janet Evanovich. Read by Lorelei King. (Running Time: 7 hrs.). (Stephanie Plum Ser.). 2009. 74.95 (978-0-7927-6486-1(2), Chivers Sound Lib); 44.95 (978-0-7927-6485-4(4), Chivers Sound Lib) AudioGO.

Finger Lickin' Fifteen. unabr. ed. Janet Evanovich. Read by Lorelei King. No. 15. (ENG.). 2009. audio compact disk 34.95 (978-1-4272-0662-6(7)) Pub: Macmill Audio. Dist(s): Macmillan

Finger Waving. Milady Publishing Company Staff. 1 cass. (Standard Ser.: Chapter 8). 1995. 8.95 (978-1-56253-280-2(4), Milady) Pub: Delmar. Dist(s): CENGAGE Learn

Fingerpicking Blues Solos. William Bay. 2000. pap. bk. 9.95 (978-0-7866-5070-5(2), 98634BCD) Mel Bay.

Fingerpicking Guitar Exercises & Hot Licks. Stefan Grossman. (Stefan Grossman's Guitar Workshop Ser.). 1999. pap. bk. 24.95 (978-0-7866-4901-3(1)) Mel Bay.

Fingerpicking Guitar Solos. Compiled by Stefan Grossman. 1996. bk. 17.95 (978-0-7866-2558-1(9), 94502BCD) Mel Bay.

Fingerpicking Guitar Solos. Gary Turner. 2004. pap. bk. 14.95 (978-1-86469-182-5(4)) Pub: Kolala Music SGP. Dist(s): Bookworld

Fingerpicking Hymns. Jeff Devine. 2003. pap. bk. 17.95 (978-0-7866-6844-1(X), 99969BCD) Mel Bay.

Fingerpicking Pattern Encyclopedia. Lou Manzi. (ENG.). 2000. audio compact disk 10.00 (978-0-7390-1093-8(X)) Alfred Pub.

Fingerplays & Footplays for Fun & Learning. Rosemary Hallum. (J). 1987. 11.95; audio compact disk 14.95 CD. Ed Activities.

Fingerprint. Patricia Wentworth. 2009. 61.95 (978-0-7531-3132-9(3)); audio compact disk 84.95 (978-0-7531-3133-6(1)) Pub: Isis Pubng Ltd GBR. Dist(s): Ulverscroft US

Fingerprints. Mary Hopkins. audio compact disk 14.95 (978-0-8198-2673-2(1), 332-093) Pauline Bks.

Fingerprints of God: The Search for the Science of Spirituality. unabr. ed. Barbara Bradley Hagerty. Narrated by Cassandra Campbell. (Running Time: 11 hrs. 0 mins. 0 sec.). (ENG.). 2009. audio compact disk 69.99 (978-1-4001-4210-1(5)) Pub: Tantor Media. Dist(s): IngramPubServ

Fingerprints of God: The Search for the Science of Spirituality. unabr. abr. ed. Barbara Bradley Hagerty. Narrated by Cassandra Campbell. (Running Time: 11 hrs. 0 mins. 0 sec.). (ENG.). 2009. audio compact disk 34.99 (978-1-4001-1210-4(9)); audio compact disk 24.99 (978-1-4001-6210-9(6)) Pub: Tantor Media. Dist(s): IngramPubServ

Fingerprints of the Gods. abr. ed. Graham Hancock. Read by Peter Reckell. 2 cass. (Running Time: 3 hrs.). (Alternative History Ser.). 1997. bk. 17.95 (978-1-57453-109-1(3)) Audio Lit.
Using tools as varied as archaeo-astronomy, geology & computer analysis of ancient myths, presents a compelling case to suggest that the story of mankind is far older than we have previously believed.

Fingersmith. unabr. ed. Sarah Waters. Narrated by Juanita McMahon. 17 cass. (Running Time: 23 hrs. 30 mins.). 2002. 99.75 (978-1-84197-469-9(2), H1401MC, Clipper Audio) Recorded Bks.

Fingerstyle Artistry. Contrib. by Richard Smith. (Running Time: 47 mins.). 2006. 24.95 (978-5-558-09066-6(9)) Mel Bay.

Fingerstyle Beginning. Workshop Arts Staff. (ENG.). 1996. audio compact disk 10.95 (978-0-7390-1784-5(5), 14825) Alfred Pub.

Fingerstyle Explorations. Jonas Mollberg. 2001. bk. 14.95 (978-0-7866-5353-9(1), 98642BCD) Mel Bay.

Fingerstyle Guitar Handbook. Tommy Flint. 1997. pap. bk. 9.95 (978-0-7866-2703-5(4), 94171BCD) Mel Bay.

Fingerstyle Guitar/New Dimensions & Exploration. Compiled by Stefan Grossman. 1995. spiral bd. 29.95 (978-0-7866-1263-5(0), 95328P) Mel Bay.

Fingerstyle Love Songs: 15 Romantic Classics Arranged for Solo Guitar. Created by Hal Leonard Corporation Staff. 2007. pap. bk. 17.95 (978-1-4234-2185-6(X), 142342185X) H Leonard.

Fingerstyle Mastering. Workshop Arts Staff. (ENG.). 1998. audio compact disk 10.95 (978-0-7390-1656-5(3), 17815) Alfred Pub.

Fingerstyle Noel: Selected Fingerstyle Guitar Transcriptions from Mark Hanson's Recording, "Yuletide Guitar" Mark Hanson. 1995. audio compact disk 21.95 (978-0-936799-12-4(9), AM 6044 BK) Pub: Accent Music. Dist(s): H Leonard

Fingerstyle Swing. Paul Lolax. 2003. pap. bk. 17.95 (978-0-7866-4968-6(2), 9830BCD) Mel Bay.

Fingertip Friends. rev. ed. Jane H. Stroschin. Illus. by Jane H. Stroschin. Contrib. by John Mooy & Harry Burkstaller. (J). (gr. 3 up). 1997. bk. 17.50 (978-1-883960-23-0(1)) Henry Quill.

***Finish Line for ELLs: English Proficiency Practice: Audio CD.** annot. ed. Continental Press Staff. 2009. audio compact disk 9.50 (978-0-8454-6098-6(6)); audio compact disk 9.50 (978-0-8454-6101-3(X)); audio compact disk 9.50 (978-0-8454-6097-9(8)); audio compact disk 9.50 (978-0-8454-6096-2(X)); audio compact disk 9.50 (978-0-8454-6095-5(1)); audio compact disk 9.50 (978-0-8454-6099-3(4)); audio compact disk 9.50 (978-0-8454-6094-8(3)); audio compact disk 9.50 (978-0-8454-6102-0(8)); audio compact disk 9.50 (978-0-8454-6100-6(1)) Continental Pr.

***Finish Line Math Strands: Assessment Links Package Level C.** Continental Press Staff. 2008. pap. bk. & stu. ed. 289.95 (978-0-8454-6029-0(3)) Continental Pr.

***Finish Line Math Strands: Assessment Links Package Level D.** Continental Press Staff. 2008. pap. bk. & stu. ed. 289.95 (978-0-8454-6030-6(7)) Continental Pr.

***Finish Line Math Strands: Assessment Links Package Level E.** Continental Press Staff. 2008. pap. bk. & stu. ed. 289.95 (978-0-8454-6031-3(5)) Continental Pr.

***Finish Line Math Strands: Assessment Links Package Level F.** Continental Press Staff. 2008. pap. bk. & stu. ed. 289.95 (978-0-8454-6032-0(3)) Continental Pr.

***Finish Line Math Strands: Assessment Links Package Level G.** Continental Press Staff. 2008. pap. bk. & stu. ed. 289.95 (978-0-8454-6033-7(1)) Continental Pr.

***Finish Line Math Strands: Assessment Links Package Level H.** Continental Press Staff. 2008. pap. bk. & stu. ed. 289.95 (978-0-8454-6034-4(X)) Continental Pr.

Finishing First. abr. ed. Barbara Pachter. Contrib. by Marjorie Brody. 4 cass. (Running Time: 4 hrs.). 1998. 39.95 Set; incl. wkbk. (978-1-929874-01-9(4), 11-0404) SkillPath Pubns.
Pachter & Brody know what it takes to make yourself stand out from the crowd, & they offer practical advice & lots of examples you can use immediately.

Finishing Karmas. Swami Amar Jyoti. 1 cass. 1978. 9.95 (G-3) Truth Consciousness.
Turning our bondages over to the Master. Being a Karma Yogi, doing all for God.

Finishing School. 2005. 24.95 (978-0-7861-3519-6(0)); audio compact disk 27.00 (978-0-7861-7832-2(9)) Blckstn Audio.

Finishing School. Michele Martinez. Read by Isabel Keating. 10 cass. (Running Time: 44640 sec.). (Sound Library). 2006. 84.95 (978-0-7927-3900-5(0), CSL 902); audio compact disk 94.95 (978-0-7927-3901-2(9), SLD 902) AudioGO.

***Finishing School.** abr. ed. Michele Martinez. Read by Anne Twomey. (ENG.). 2006. (978-0-06-087836-8(3), Harper Audio); (978-0-06-087835-1(5), Harper Audio) HarperCollins Pubs.

Finishing School. unabr. ed. Muriel Spark. Read by Nadia May. 2005. 29.95 (978-0-7861-8023-3(4)) Blckstn Audio.

Finishing Stroke. unabr. ed. Ellery Queen. Read by David Edwards. 6 vols. (Running Time: 26520 sec.). (Sound Library). 2000. 54.95 (978-0-7927-2341-7(4), CSL 230, Chivers Sound Lib) AudioGO.
Slow, deliberate murder, planned fantastically well. Ox, nail, monkey, hand, house. Tiny replicas of objects came during the first eleven nights after Christmas. On each night also came a warning of impending doom. Ellery & the police were there, but no one saw the messages come. Who was sending them? And who was the intended victim? Then came the twelfth night & the message: "On the twelfth night of Christmas, your true love sends to you, this fatal dagger, this jeweled knife, this finishing stroke to end your life." And when they found the corpse, the dagger was buried deep in its back.

Finishing Your Business with Mother. John E. Bradshaw. (Running Time: 23400 sec.). 2008. audio compact disk 199.00 (978-1-57388-146-3(5)) J B Media.

Finite & Infinite Games. James P. Carse. 2 cass. 18.00 (OC73) Sound Horizons AV.

Finn: A Novel. Jon Clinch. Narrated by Ed Sala. (Running Time: 40500 sec.). 2007. audio compact disk 34.99 (978-1-4281-2439-4(X)) Recorded Bks.

Finn: A Novel. Matthew Olshan. Read by Matthew Olshan. Ed. by Richard Roeder. Engineer Karen Goldberg. 3 cass. (Running Time: 4 hrs. 43 minutes). 2002. audio compact disk 29.95 (978-1-890862-20-6(7)) Pub: Bancroft MD. Dist(s): Baker Taylor
Modern retelling of Mark Twain's classic "Huck Finn," but with two teenage girls as the protaganists. Booklist magazine starred review (hardcover book), book featured twice on C-Span "About Books.".

Finn McCoul. Composed by Boys of the Lough Staff. Narrated by Catherine O'Hare. Contrib. by Henrik Drescher & Peter de Sève. (Running Time: 30 mins.). (Rabbit Ears Collection). (J). (gr. k-4). 1998. 9.95 (PRE942AC) Weston Woods.
The greatest champion in all of Ireland, gets a wee bit nervous when he discovers that the brutish giant Cucullin is after him. But with some ingenious culinary magic on the part of his clever wife, Finn manages to get out of the scrape with his dignity intact.

Finn McCoul. As told by Catherine O'Hara. Music by Boys of Lough. Illus. by Peter de Sève. 1 cass. (Running Time: 1 hr.). 9.95 Weston Woods.
The greatest champion in all of Ireland gets a wee bit nervous when he discovers that the brutish giant Cucullin is after him. But with some ingenious culinary magic on the part of his clever wife, Finn manages to get out of the scrape with his dignity intact.

***Finn Reeder, Flu Fighter: How I Survived a Worldwide Pandemic, the School Bu.** Eric Stevens. Illus. by Kay Fraser. (Finn Reeder Ser.). (ENG.). 2010. audio compact disk 14.60 (978-1-4342-2591-7(7)) CapstoneDig.

Finnegans Wake see James Joyce Soundbook

Finnegans Wake. James Joyce. Read by Patrick Bedford. (Running Time: 50 min.). 10.95 (978-0-8045-0854-4(2), SAC 45-3) Spoken Arts.
Poignant & pithy episodes from Joyce's great enigmatic work.

Finnegans Wake. unabr. ed. Scripts. James Joyce. Perf. by Gabriel Byrne. 12 cass. (Running Time: 18 hrs.). 2003. 50.00 (978-1-59007-003-1(8), N Millennium Audio) Pub: New Millenn Enter. Dist(s): PerseuPGW

Finnegans Wake & Anna Livia Plurabelle see James Joyce Reads James Joyce

Finnegan's Week. abr. ed. Joseph Wambaugh. Read by David Colacci. 2 cass. (Running Time: 3 hrs.). 2000. 7.95 (978-1-57815-008-3(6), 1009, Media Bks Audio) Media Bks NJ.
A police detective faces a deadly toxic chemical scheme in gripping, true-to-life police drama. He joins forces with two impressive female cops, one of which he has a past with, the other a possible future, if the killing can be stopped.

***Finnikin of the Rock.** unabr. ed. Melina Marchetta. Read by Jeffrey Cummings. 1 MP3-CD. (Running Time: 12 hrs.). 2010. 19.99 (978-1-4418-8872-3(1), 9781441888723, Brilliance MP3); 19.99 (978-1-4418-8874-7(8), 9781441888747, BAD); 39.97 (978-1-4418-8873-0(X), 9781441888730, Brinc Audio MP3 Lib); 39.97 (978-1-4418-8875-4(6), 9781441888754, BADLE); 74.99 (978-1-4418-9294-2(X), Candlewick Bril); audio compact disk 24.99 (978-1-4418-8870-9(5), 9781441888709, Bril Audio CD Unabri); audio compact disk 74.97 (978-1-4418-8871-6(3), 9781441888716, BriAudCD Unabrid) Brilliance Audio.

Finnish. (In 60 MINUTES Ser.). 2009. audio compact disk 9.95 (978-981-268-609-1(6)) Pub: Berlitz Pubng. Dist(s): Langenscheidt

Finnish. 2 cass. (Running Time: 80 min.). (Language - Thirty Library). bk. 16.95 set in vinyl album. Moonbeam Pubns.
Using the proven method based on the famous U.S. Military accelerated language learning program, Language/30 courses stress conversationally useful words & phrases.

Finnish. Ed. by Charles Berlitz. 2 cass. (Running Time: 1 hr. 30 mins.). (Language/30 Brief Course Ser.). 2001. pap. bk. 21.95 (AF1055) J Norton Pubs.
Quick, highly condensed introduction to the words & phrases you'll need to communicate effectively in the country you're visiting. Cassettes & phrase guide book are in a vinyl album.

Finnish: Language/30. rev. ed. Educational Services Corporation Staff. Intro. by Charles Berlitz. 2 cass. (FIN.). 1995. pap. bk. 21.95 (978-0-910542-84-5(8)) Educ Svcs DC.
Finnish self-teaching language course.

Finnish for Foreigners, Vol. 1. 10th ed. Maija-Hellikki Aaltio. 10 CDs. (Running Time: 8 hrs.). (FIN.). 2005. audio compact disk 225.00 (978-1-57970-283-0(X), AFFN01D, Audio-For) J Norton Pubs.
This introductory practical course in modern Finnish uses two books: one provides transcripts of the Finnish dialogs with idiomatic English translations, notes on structural patterns and explanations of essential points of grammar; the other provides a variety of exercises with instsructions in English. there is also a 78-page oral drills book.

Finnish Korva Tarkkana (Listen Attentively) unabr. ed. 1 cass. (Running Time: 1 hr.). J Norton Pubs.

Finnois sans Peine. 1 cass. (Running Time: 1 hr., 30 min.). (FIN & FRE.). 2000. bk. 75.00 (978-2-7005-1371-4(1)); bk. 95.00 (978-2-7005-2022-4(X)) Pub: Assimil FRA. Dist(s): Distribks Inc

Finny Finds Friends in the Forest: A Letter-Sound * Listen & Retell Adventure. Tini Sisters Staff. Illus. by Erin Marie Mauterer. 1 CD. (Running Time: 15 minutes). Dramatization. (Letter-Sound Listen & Retell Adventure Ser.). (J). 2002. bk. 18.95 (978-0-9678459-3-7(9)) Atori Pubng Inc.

Finster Frets. unabr. ed. Kent Baker. Illus. by H. Werner Zimmermann. (J). (ps-3). 1996. pap. bk. 15.95 (978-0-19-541055-6(6)) OUP.

Fiona Range. unabr. ed. Mary McGarry Morris. Read by Susie Breck. (Running Time: 14 hrs.). 2005. 39.25 (978-1-59600-552-5(1), 9781596005525, Brinc Audio MP3 Lib); 39.25 (978-1-59600-554-9(8), 9781596005549, BADLE); 24.95 (978-1-59600-553-2(X), 9781596005532, BAD); 24.95 (978-1-59600-551-8(3), 9781596005518, Brilliance MP3) Brilliance Audio.
Fiona Range's thirty years have been the battleground between her good upbringing and the innate recklessness she defiantly attributes to the beautiful Natalie, the young unwed mother who abandoned her in infancy. Most of Fiona's troubles seem to be kindled by a mix of the wrong men and the excesses of her kind heart. Finally rejected by the embarrassed and highly regarded Hollis family who raised her, Fiona has spent the last weeks of summer trying to get her life in order. But it takes only a single careless night to further condemn her in the eyes of the community. Finding herself even further estranged from relatives and friends, Fiona is drawn to the one man who wants nothing to do with her. He is her rumored father, Patrick Grady, so cruel and unstable that her Aunt Arlene and Uncle Charles Hollis fear for her safety. But, as always, Fiona will listen to no one. Determined to make Grady acknowledge their relationship, she pursues him in spite of his threats and increasingly erratic behavior. This is a deeply moving and hauntingly tragic tale of goodness undermined by guilt, of obsession, and of the twisted bond of betrayal committed in the name of love.

Fiona the Smart Ghost. Narrated by Lani Minella. (Running Time: 3060 sec.). (J). (gr. k-6). 2007. audio compact disk 12.95 (978-1-933781-06-8(8)) TallTales Aud.

Fiona's Bee. unabr. ed. Beverly Keller. 1 read-along cass. (Running Time: 16 min.). (Follow the Reader Ser.). (J). (gr. 1-2). 1981. 15.98 (978-0-8072-0002-5(6), FTR 52 SP, Listening Lib); (Listening Lib) Random Audio Pubg.
Fiona had no friends, but she did have a pet bee. When she decided to take it to the park, she was soon launched into fame & friendship.

Fir Tree. abr. ed. Hans Christian Andersen. (Running Time: 3600 sec.).Tr. of Grantraeet. 2005. audio compact disk 15.95 (978-0-660-19464-6(3)) Canadian Broadcasting CAN.

Fir Tree; The Little Match Girl. unabr. ed. Hans Christian Andersen. Narrated by Aurora Wetzel. 1 cass. (J). (ps up). 1991. 9.95 (978-1-887393-00-3(5)) Aurora Audio.
Christmas stories.

Fire. 1 CD. 2003. audio compact disk (978-1-932616-01-9(2)) Feng Shui Para.
If You are the Element Fire.....In Feng Shui you are the personal Trigram LI (pronounced "lee") and you represent the middle daughterWhen in balance, you are charismatic, lively, enthusiastic, charged, competitive, vivacious, quick to react and move, and very passionate about what you like and dislike. You exude energy.When you are not in balance, you can be excitable, combative, quick tempered, easily bored, over indulgent, exuberant in public and depressed when alone.The above is just a brief excerpt from the FIRE audio program. Discover the hidden mysteries of your life, recorded in China's ancient art, history and science. Learn about your lucky number and season, along with the kind of homes and offices that support you, and the types of locations that can deplete your business, health and finances. You will learn specific power directions to help you negotiate a sale, communicate with your friends and family, increase your wealth, improve your health, along with optimum directions to capitalize on to enhance love and good fortune in your life. This and more is available, today, on Suzee's audio program... FIRE.

Fire. Composed by Bhaskar Chandavarkar. 1 cass. (Elements Ser.: Vol. 3). 1995. (M95009); audio compact disk (CD M95009) Multi-Cultural Bks.
Flame, Invocation to Fire, Aurora, Fire in the Sky, Fireflies, The Fire Within, Quest for Fire, Forest Fire, Internal Combustion, Ode to Fire, Into the Light.

Fire. abr. ed. Sebastian Junger. Read by Sebastian Junger. Read by Kevin Conway. 4 cass. (Running Time: 6 hrs.). 2001. 18.95 (978-0-06-000059-2(7)) HarperCollins Pubs.
Prose brought to bear on the inner workings of a terrifying elemental force; a cast of characters risking everything in the effort to bring that force under control.

Fire. abr. ed. Sebastian Junger. Read by Sebastian Junger. 2002. 9.99 (978-0-06-052359-6(X)) HarperCollins Pubs.

***Fire.** abr. ed. Sebastian Junger. Read by Sebastian Junger. (ENG.). 2005. (978-0-06-088662-2(5), Harper Audio); (978-0-06-088661-5(7), Harper Audio) HarperCollins Pubs.

Fire. abr. ed. Katherine Neville. Read by Susan Denaker. 5 CDs. (Running Time: 5 hrs. 30 mins.). (ENG.). 2008. audio compact disk 29.95 (978-0-7393-5708-8(5), Random AudioBks) Pub: Random Audio Pubg. Dist(s): Random

Fire. abr. unabr. ed. Sebastian Junger. Read by Sebastian Junger. Read by Kevin Conway. 5 CDs. (Running Time: 6 hrs.). 2001. audio compact disk 39.95 (978-0-06-000061-5(9)) HarperCollins Pubs.

Fire. unabr. ed. Kristin Cashore. (Running Time: 13 hrs.). (ENG.). (gr. 12 up). 2009. audio compact disk 39.95 (978-0-14-314511-0(8), PengAudBks) Penguin Grp USA.

Fire. unabr. ed. Sebastian Junger. Read by Sebastian Junger. Read by Kevin Conway. 6 cass. (Running Time: 9 hrs.). 2001. 31.46 Books on Tape.
Junger's essays deal with the primal power of fire and with man's capacity for destruction.

***Fire.** unabr. ed. Sebastian Junger. Read by Kevin Conway. (ENG.). 2005. (978-0-06-115186-6(6), Harper Audio); (978-0-06-113970-3(X), Harper Audio) HarperCollins Pubs.

Fire. unabr. ed. Katherine Neville. Read by Susan Denaker. 15 CDs. (Running Time: 18 hrs. 15 mins.). 2008. audio compact disk 129.00 (978-1-4159-5663-2(4), BksonTape) Pub: Random Audio Pubg. Dist(s): Random

Fire: The Summer Season. Ann Bailey. Read by Ann Bailey. Read by Jon Bailey. 1 cass. (Running Time: 60 min.). (Wellness Through the Seasons Ser.). 1993. 12.00 incl. script. (978-1-889643-04-5(1)) SourcePoint.
Music, sounds & spoken word illustrate the connection between the summer season & health within body, mind & spirit.

Fire & Fog. Dianne Day. Read by Anna Fields. 2000. 48.00 (978-0-7366-4839-4(9)) Books on Tape.

Fire & Fog. unabr. ed. Dianne Day. Read by Anna Fields. 6 cass. (Running Time: 90 mins. per cass.). (Fremont Jones Mystery Ser.: 2). 2000. 36.00 (5186) Books on Tape.
Fremont Jones struggles to escape the chaos of the Great San Francisco Earthquake while investigating two murderous smugglers.

Fire & Ice see Robert Frost in Recital

Fire & Ice. Karen Jean Matsko Hood. 2009. audio compact disk 24.95 (978-1-59210-253-2(0)) Whsprng Pine.

Fire & Ice. abr. ed. Paul Garrison. Read by Michael Gross. 4 cass. (Running Time: 6 hrs.). 2001. 25.00 (978-1-59040-158-3(1), Phoenix Audio) Pub: Amer Intl Pub. Dist(s): PerseuPGW

Fire & Ice. unabr. ed. Julie Garwood. Read by Rebecca Lowman. 8 CDs. 2008. audio compact disk 100.00 (978-1-4159-5828-5(9), BksonTape) Pub: Random Audio Pubg. Dist(s): Random
Sophie Rose, a tough and determined newspaper reporter, is the daughter of Bobby Rose, a suave, charming, and handsome gentleman who also happens to be a notorious big-time thief sought by every law-enforcement agency in the country. When the major Chicago daily where she works insists she write an exposé about her roguish father, Sophie refuses, quits her job, and goes to work at a small newspaper. Far from her onetime high-powered crime beat, she now covers local personalities such as the quirky winner of several area 5K runs whose trademark is goofy red socks. Those red socks - with Sophie's business card neatly tucked inside - are practically all that's found after runner William Harrington's shredded corpse turns up in Prudhoe Bay, Alaska, the victim of a mysteriously dramatic death by polar bear. With an unerring nose for a good story, Sophie heads north to Alaska. What she doesn't realize is that her father's infamous reputation has spread even to the far reaches of Prudhoe Bay. Sophie's assigned a bodyguard - Jack MacAlister, a sexy FBI agent who grudgingly takes the assignment while recovering from an on-duty injury. But they will soon be fighting more than growing passion.

Fire & Ice. unabr. ed. Julie Garwood. Read by Rebecca Lowman. (ENG.). 2008. audio compact disk 39.95 (978-0-7393-5762-0(X), Random AudioBks) Pub: Random Audio Pubg. Dist(s): Random

***Fire & Ice.** unabr. ed. J. A. Jance. Read by Hillary Huber & Erik Davies. (ENG.). 2009. (978-0-06-190252-9(7), Harper Audio); (978-0-06-177667-0(X), Harper Audio) HarperCollins Pubs.

***Fire & Ice.** unabr. ed. J. A. Jance. Read by Hillary Huber & Erik Davies. 2010. audio compact disk 19.99 (978-0-06-201095-7(6), Harper Audio) HarperCollins Pubs.

Fire & Ice. unabr. collector's ed. Dana Stabenow. Read by Marguerite Gavin. 7 cass. (Running Time: 10 hrs. 30 min.). (Liam Campbell Mystery Ser.: Bk. 1). 1999. 56.00 (978-0-7366-4860-8(7), 5187) Books on Tape.
After losing his family and his career, Alaskan State Trooper Liam Campbell, finds himself on a plane to his new posting - a small native town far from Anchorage. And fate isn't finished with him yet. No sooner does he set foot off the plane than he is confronted with a dead body and the accusing glare of the only woman he'd ever truly loved . . . and lost.

Fire & Reign Director's Kit: A 10-Week Journey Into Spiritual Renewal. Jerry Sheveland. Contrib. by Linda Kotthoff. 1 CD, 1 DVD. 2005. spiral bd. 24.99 (978-0-935797-73-2(4)) Harvest IL.

Fire & Steam: A New History of the Railways in Britain. Christian Wolmar. 2009. 94.95 (978-1-4079-0506-8(6)); audio compact disk 99.95 (978-1-4079-0507-5(4)) Pub: Soundings Ltd GBR. Dist(s): Ulverscroft US

Fire at Sea: The Story of the Morro Castle. unabr. ed. Thomas Gallagher. Read by Justin Hecht. 6 cass. (Running Time: 6 hrs.). 1983. 36.00 (978-0-7366-0299-0(2), 1287) Books on Tape.
On a stormy September night in 1934, the luxury liner Morro Castle was plunging through heavy seas on its return voyage to New York from Havana. It was shortly after 2:00 a.m. & the ship was just few miles off the New Jersey shore. Most passengers were sleeping. Suddenly, spreading with tragic speed, sheets of flames engulfed the entire superstructure & within an hour hundreds were dead or floundering in the water.

Fire Away. 1 cass. (Running Time: 1 hr.). 2000. 15.95 Prof Pride.
Twenty brief questions. Creates some "heated" discussion. Fire basics.

Fire Baby. unabr. ed. Jim Kelly. Read by Ray Sawyer. 9 CDs. (Running Time: 10 hrs. 37 mins.). (Isis (CDs) Ser.). (J). 2006. audio compact disk 84.95 (978-0-7531-2499-4(8)) Pub: ISIS Lrg Prnt GBR. Dist(s): Ulverscroft US

Fire Baby. unabr. ed. Jim Kelly. Read by Ray Sawyer. 7 cass. (Running Time: 8 hrs. 30 mins.). (Isis Cassettes Ser.). (J). 2006. 61.95 (978-0-7531-3435-1(7)) Pub: ISIS Lrg Prnt GBR. Dist(s): Ulverscroft US

Fire, Baptism, & Division: Luke 12:49-53. Ed Young. 1986. 0.95 (978-0-7417-1548-7(1), 548) Win Walk.

Fire, Bed & Bone. unabr. ed. Henrietta Branford. Read by Eve Karpf. 2 cass. (J). (gr. 1-8). 1999. 18.95 (CCA 3485, Chivers Child Audio) AudioGO.

Fire, Bed & Bone. unabr. ed. Henrietta Branford. Read by Eve Karpf. 2 CDs. (Running Time: 3 hrs.). (J). 2002. audio compact disk 21.95 (978-0-7540-6504-3(9), CHCD 004, Chivers Child Audio) AudioGO.

Fire Burning in the Heart. Stephen Doyle. 2 cass. (Running Time: 2 hrs.). 2001. vinyl bd. 18.95 (A6600) St Anthony Mess Pr.
Examines the different approach to prophetic books in the Jewish faith and the role of a true prophet in the Hebrew Scriptures, the New Testament and the Church.

Fire by Night. unabr. ed. Lynn Austin. Narrated by Christina Moore. 11 cass. (Running Time: 15 hrs. 15 mins.). (Refiner's Fire Ser.: Vol. 2). 2003. 99.75 (978-1-4193-0999-1(4), K1117MC) Recorded Bks.

Fire Came By: The Riddle of the Great Siberian Explosion. unabr. collector's ed. John Baxter & Thomas Atkins. Read by Wolfram Kandinsky. 5

cass. (Running Time: 5 hrs.). 1979. 30.00 (978-0-7366-0199-3(6), 1199) Books on Tape.

Accidents of nature occurred in Siberia in 1908, when a fireball appeared over the horizon & slammed into a remote forest area of Siberia, creating shock waves which were felt half a world away. Explores not only what the Russian scientists have to say about the affair today, but also enlightened opinion from scientists worldwide, as well as on-the-scene reports & interviews.

Fire Dance at Spider Rock. abr. ed. Les Savage, Jr. Read by Buck Schirner. (Running Time: 3 hrs.). (Five Star Westerns Ser.). 2007. 39.25 (978-1-4233-3558-0(9), 9781423335580, BADLE); 24.95 (978-1-4233-3557-3(0), 9781423335573, BAD) Brilliance Audio.

Fire Dance at Spider Rock. unabr. ed. Les Savage, Jr. Read by Arthur Addison. 7 cass. (Running Time: 7 hrs.). 1997. 42.00 sale to libraries only. (978-0-7366-3812-8(1), 4480) Books on Tape.

Rim Fannin gets a job with a wagon train that moves freight at night, always under heavy guard, when indians attack & capture Fannin.

Fire Dance at Spider Rock: A Western Story. abr. ed. Les Savage, Jr. Read by Buck Schirner. (Running Time: 10800 sec.). (Five Star Westerns Ser.). 2007. audio compact disk 24.95 (978-1-4233-3555-9(4), 9781423335559, Brilliance MP3); audio compact disk 39.25 (978-1-4233-3556-6(2), 9781423335566, Brlnc Audio MP3 Lib) Brilliance Audio.

Fire down Below, Bk. 3. unabr. ed. William Golding. Read by William Golding. 8 cass. (Running Time: 7 hrs.). 2001. 69.95 (978-1-85089-765-1(4), 9008Y) Pub: ISIS Audio GBR. Dist(s): Ulverscroft US

William Golding's trilogy makes landfall at last.

Fire-Eaters. unabr. ed. David Almond. 2 cass. (Running Time: 3 hrs. 30 mins.). (J). (gr. 4 up). 2004. 23.00 (978-1-4000-8564-4(0), Listening Lib) Random Audio Pubg.

Fire Engine That Disappeared. unabr. ed. Maj Sjöwall & Per Wahlöö. Read by Tom Weiner. (Running Time: 7 hrs. 0 mins.). 2009. 29.95 (978-1-4332-6345-3(9)); 44.95 (978-1-4332-6341-5(6)); audio compact disk 69.00 (978-1-4332-6342-2(4)) Blckstn Audio.

Fire, Fire, Burning Bright. Richard Lewis. Incl. Fire, Fire, Burning Bright: Death. (J). (gr. 5-10). 1985.; Fire, Fire, Burning Bright: Dreams. (J). (gr. 5-10). 1985.; Fire, Fire, Burning Bright: Love. (J). (gr. 5-10). 1985.; Fire, Fire, Burning Bright: The Sea. (J). (gr. 5-10). 1985.; Fire, Fire, Burning Bright: The Sky. (J). (gr. 5-10). 1985.; Fire, Fire, Burning Bright: Time & Space. (J). (gr. 5-10). 1985.; (J). (gr. 5-10). 1985. 22.50 Set. Touchstone Ctr Pubns.

A series of six programs on the nature & origin of poetry.

Fire, Fire, Burning Bright: A Series of Six Programs on the Nature & Origin of Poetry. Richard Lewis. 3 cass. (Running Time: 90 min.). (YA). (gr. 5-12). 1985. 25.00 Set. Touchstone Ctr Pubns.

Each program is based on a particular theme: the sea, the sky, time, dreams, death, & love - & explores how these themes have been expressed through poetry by persons from a variety of world cultures & backgrounds.

Fire, Fire, Burning Bright: Death see Fire, Fire, Burning Bright

Fire, Fire, Burning Bright: Dreams see Fire, Fire, Burning Bright

Fire, Fire, Burning Bright: Love see Fire, Fire, Burning Bright

Fire, Fire, Burning Bright! Love & Death. Poems. 1 cass. (Running Time: 30 min.). (J). 9.95 (D008BB090, HarperThor) HarpC GBR.

Fire, Fire, Burning Bright: The Sea see Fire, Fire, Burning Bright

Fire, Fire, Burning Bright! The Sea & Sky. Poems. 1 cass. (Running Time: 30 min.). (J). 9.95 (D008CB090, HarperThor) HarpC GBR.

Fire, Fire, Burning Bright: The Sky see Fire, Fire, Burning Bright

Fire, Fire, Burning Bright: Time & Space see Fire, Fire, Burning Bright

Fire, Fire, Burning Bright! Time, Space & Dreams. Poems. 1 cass. (Running Time: 30 min.). (J). 9.95 (D008AB090, HarperThor) HarpC GBR.

Fire Fire Pants on Liar. Bil Lepp. (J). 2008. 12.95 (978-1-891852-62-6(0)) Pub: Quarrier Pr. Dist(s): WV Book Co

Fire Flight. unabr. ed. John J. Nance. Read by John J. Nance. 8 cass. (Running Time: 11 hrs.). 2003. 34.95 (978-1-59086-757-0(2), 1590867572, BAU); 87.25 (978-1-59086-758-7(0), 1590867580, BrilAudUnabridg) Brilliance Audio.

A pair of ferocious forest fires rages out of control, threatening to destroy two American national parks and incinerate thousands of homes and park buildings. As the desperate battle to squelch the global warming-induced fires before they "blow up" reaches a fever-pitch, a mysterious string of violent airborne accidents among the air tanker fleet produces a mounting body count. The air tankers - the old aircraft used by pilots to bomb the fires with fire retardant slurry - have been literally falling apart in midair. Clearly not designed for such punishing high-stakes flying, the flying museum pieces should have been grounded years ago. Veteran pilot Clark Maxwell thought his fire bombing days were well behind him. But when Jerry Stein, Maxwell's friend and air tanker fleet-owner, calls at the height of the fire season to beg him to reenter the war, he doesn't hesitate. As the wildfires spread, whipped by massive winds and the federal forces arrayed against the fires reach their limits, hysteria and potential evacuation threatens the local population. In the middle of this crisis, Clark Maxwell becomes convinced that a sinister cover-up is behind the rash of horrific air disasters. As he races to unravel a very real mystery and prevent a natural disaster of massive proportions, Maxwell's probe reaches the upper levels of government agencies charged with mounting the aerial fire fighting effort - a move that for wholly unexpected reasons just may cost him his life.

Fire Flight. unabr. ed. John J. Nance. Read by John J. Nance. (Running Time: 11 hrs.). 2004. 39.25 (978-1-59335-519-7(X), 159335519X, Brlnc Audio MP3 Lib) Brilliance Audio.

Fire Flight. unabr. ed. John J. Nance. Read by John J. Nance. (Running Time: 11 hrs.). 2004. 39.25 (978-1-59710-284-1(9), 1597102849, BADLE) Brilliance Audio.

Fire Flight. unabr. ed. John J. Nance. Read by John J. Nance. (Running Time: 11 hrs.). 2004. 24.95 (978-1-59335-248-6(4), 1593352484) Soulmate Audio Bks.

Fire Flight. unabr. ed. John J. Nance. Read by John J. Nance. (Running Time: 11 hrs.). 2004. 24.95 (978-1-59710-285-8(7), 1597102857, BAD) Brilliance Audio.

Fire from Heaven. unabr. ed. Mary Renault. Read by Ian Whitcomb. 11 cass. (Running Time: 16 hrs. 30 min.). (Alexander Trilogy). 1977. 88.00 (978-0-7366-0055-2(8), 1067) Books on Tape.

The story of Alexander the Great from childhood to age twenty.

Fire from Heaven: A Retreat for Men. Richard Rohr. 8 cass. (Running Time: 8 hrs.). 2001. vinyl bd. 64.95 (A6130) St Anthony Mess Pr.

Focuses on the yearning to rediscover passion in masculine identity and in the purpose of life.

Fire Hawk, Set. unabr. ed. Geoffrey Archer. Read by Christian Rodska. 12 cass. 1999. 96.95 (978-0-7540-0347-2(7), CAB1770) AudioGO.

Sam Parker was told to trust no one when he went to work for the Intelligence Service. Working undercover in Baghdad, he makes a shocking discovery: biological weapons have been smuggled out of Iraq for a devastating blow overseas. But moments later, Packer's cover is blown & he is captured. Suddenly freed, Packer can't forget that his arrest was because someone betrayed him.

Fire Ice. unabr. ed. Clive Cussler & Paul Kemprecos. (NUMA Files Ser.: No. 3). 2002. 90.00 (978-0-7366-8651-8(7)) Books on Tape.

Kurt Austin and the National Underwater and Marine Agency battle a Russian mining tycoon bent on overthrowing the Russian government.

Fire Ice. unabr. ed. Clive Cussler & Paul Kemprecos. 13 CDs. (Running Time: 15 hrs.). (NUMA Files Ser.: No. 3). 2002. audio compact disk 104.00 (978-0-7366-8652-5(5)) Books on Tape.

Kurt Austin is the leader of the National Underwater and Marine Agency's (NUMA's) Special Assignments Team. In previous encounters, they battled eco-extortionists and mad empire builders. Now they face an even deadlier threat. In the heart of the old Soviet Union, a mining tycoon has proclaimed himself czar of Russia. Claiming Romanov ancestry and backed by billions of dollars, he is determined to overthrow the already shaky Russian government - and U.S. opposition doesn't bother him one bit. A little crisis of their own should distract the Americans for awhile, and he knows just the thing.

Fire in Boomtown: The Story of the Great Chicago Fire. Amy Lowe & Megan Wells. 1 cass. (Running Time: 1 hr.). (J). 1997. 9.98 (978-0-9660947-2-5(7), EKCT5001); audio compact disk 14.98 (978-0-9660947-1-8(9), EKCD5001) Emphasis Ent.

Live performance using narrative & song - based on newspaper articles, letters, notes, photographs & actual testimonials from people/survivors of the great Chicago fire of 1871.

***Fire in Ember: A Novel.** Zondervan. (ENG.). 2011. 14.99 (978-0-310-41240-3(4)) Zondervan.

Fire in Her Soul. unabr. ed. Luella Dow. Read by Jami Belt. 4 cass. (Running Time: 6 hrs.). 2001. 26.95 (978-1-55686-754-5(9)) Books in Motion.

Washington Territory, circa 1880. Sarah Weatherby is faced with threats and subversive plot's by the town's power base when she leads the Women's Suffrage Movement.

Fire in November. unabr. ed. Roni S. Denholtz. 1 cass. (Running Time: 20 min.). (Fun to Read Ser.). (J). (gr. 3-6). 1983. bk. 16.99 (978-0-934898-39-3(1)); pap. bk. 9.95 (978-0-934898-27-0(8)) Jan Prods.

Arson plagues an old school in a multiethnic neighborhood. When the students wrongly suspect a new foreign student, it leads to a lesson about discrimination.

Fire in the Blood. unabr. ed. Irène Némirovsky. Read by Mark Bramhall. Tr. by Sandra Smith. 3 CDs. (Running Time: 3 hrs. 30 mins.). (ENG.). 2007. audio compact disk 27.95 (978-0-7393-5776-7(X), Random AudioBks) Pub: Random Audio Pubg. Dist(s): Random

***Fire in the East: Warrior of Rome Book I.** unabr. ed. Harry Sidebottom. Read by Stefan Rudnicki. (Running Time: 14 hrs. 30 mins.). (Warrior of Rome, Book I Ser.). 2010. 29.95 (978-1-4417-2808-1(2)); 79.95 (978-1-4417-2804-3(X)); audio compact disk 118.00 (978-1-4417-2805-0(8)) Blckstn Audio.

Fire in the Heart: A Spiritual Guide for Teens. unabr. ed. Deepak Chopra. 4 CDs. (Running Time: 5 hrs. 0 mins. 0 sec.). (ENG.). 2005. audio compact disk 24.95 (978-1-59397-671-2(2)) Pub: Macmill Audio. Dist(s): Macmillan

Fire in the Mind. John Lobell. 1 cass. (J. Campbell Symposium Ser.: No. 2). 9.00 Sound Horizons AV.

Fire in the Mind. David Miller. 1 cass. (J. Campbell Symposium Ser.: No. 3). 9.00 (OC292-64) Sound Horizons AV.

Fire in the Mind. Madeline Nold. 1 cass. (J. Campbell Symposium Ser.: No. 4). 9.00 (OC292-64) Sound Horizons AV.

Fire in the Mind. Robert Walker. 1 cass. (J. Campbell Symposium Ser.: No. 5). 9.00 (OC292-64) Sound Horizons AV.

Fire in the Mind: The Life of Joseph Campbell. Stephen C. Larsen & Robin Larsen. 1 cass. (J. Campbell Symposium Ser.: No. 1). 9.00 (OC292-64) Sound Horizons AV.

Fire Lover: A True Story. Joseph Wambaugh. Read by Ken Howard. 11 CDs. (Running Time: 13 hrs.). 2002. audio compact disk 88.00 (978-0-7861-9535-0(5), 2955) Blckstn Audio.

The incredible true story of John Orr who, as a young boy growing up in Los Angeles, watched with awe as firefighters scrambled to put out blazes with a seeming disregard for their own lives. Wanting to emulate his heroes, he later became a fireman with the Glendale Fire Department. An eccentric loner who made few friends, Orr moonlighted as a security guard, eventually becoming a fire captain and one of Southern California's most renowned serial arson investigators. Though he successfully helped apprehend a string of petty arsonists, there was one serial criminal Orr couldn't track down-one who was responsible for the deaths of four people. These perfectly executed blazes were set by a fire lover who used the same simple yet devastating device time after time. He went undiscovered until one day when he left a fingerprint, one clue investigators could match. When they did, they were stunned to discover that the print belonged to none other than John Orr.

Fire Lover: A True Story. unabr. ed. Joseph Wambaugh. Read by Ken Howard. 9 cass. (Running Time: 13 hrs.). 2002. 62.95 (978-0-7861-2231-8(5), 2955) Blckstn Audio.

As a young boy, John Orr watched with awe as firefighters scrambled to put out blazes with a seeming disregard for their own lives. Wanting to emulate his heroes, he later became a fireman with the Glendale Fire Department. An eccentric loner who made few friends, Orr moonlighted as a security guard, eventually becoming a fire captain and one of Southern California's most renowned serial arson investigators.

Fire Mass. unabr. ed. Perf. by Star-Scape Singers. Composed by Kenneth G. Mills & Christopher Dedrick. 1 cass. (Running Time: 84 min.). 1989. 21.98 2 CDs Set. (KGOC 26) Ken Mills Found.

A cappella masterwork! The Fire Mass is a 90-minute setting of the Ordinary of the Mass in Latin, & of the spontaneous poetry of Kenneth G. Mills in English. "This masterpiece provides the listener with an elevating & spiritual atmosphere".

Fire Next Time. unabr. ed. James Baldwin. Narrated by Jesse L. Martin. 2 CDs. (Running Time: 2 hrs.). (ENG.). 2008. audio compact disk 14.95 (978-1-60283-364-7(8)) Pub: AudioGO. Dist(s): Perseus Dist

Fire Next Time. unabr. ed. James Baldwin. Read by Jesse L. Martin. (YA). 2008. 34.99 (978-1-60514-958-5(6)) Find a World.

Fire of God. Jack Deere. 1 cass. (Running Time: 90 mins.). (Intimacy with God & the End-Time Church Ser.: Vol. 2). 2000. 5.00 (JD09-002) Morning NC.

Oneness with the Father is essential for every believer in these last days & the teaching in this six-tape series will impart a heartfelt hunger for intimate fellowship with Him.

Fire of Heaven. Bill Myers. Narrated by Richard Ferrone. 10 cass. (Running Time: 13 hrs. 45 mins.). 88.00 (978-1-4025-3253-5(9)) Recorded Bks.

Fire of Heaven. abr. ed. Bill Myers. (Running Time: 6 hrs. 0 mins. 0 sec.). (ENG.). 2003. 10.99 (978-0-310-26036-3(1)) Zondervan.

Fire of Heaven. unabr. ed. Bill Myers. 1999. 19.99 (978-0-310-23002-1(0)) Zondervan.

Fire of Love. Tim Valentine. 1 cass., 1 CD. 1998. 10.95 (CS-417); audio compact disk 15.95 (CD-417) GIA Pubns.

Fire of the Covenant. abr. ed. Gerald N. Lund. 2005. audio compact disk 39.95 (978-1-59038-412-1(1)) Deseret Bk.

***Fire of Truth.** Featuring Adyashanti. (ENG.). 2010. audio compact disk 65.00 (978-1-933986-84-5(0)) Open Gate Pub.

Fire Officer: Principles & Practice Instructor's ToolKit CD-ROM. IAFC. (C). 2006. audio compact disk 387.95 (978-0-7637-4518-9(9)) Jones Bartlett.

***Fire Officer's Handbook of Tactics, Third Edition - Audio Book.** John Norman. (ENG.). 2008. audio compact disk 79.00 (978-1-59370-172-7(1)) Pub: Fire Eng. Dist(s): PennWell Corp

Fire Officer's Handbook of Tactics Video Series #4: Hoseline Selection, Stretching & Placement. John Norman. (Fire Officer's Handbook of Tactics Video Ser.). 2008. 59.00 (978-1-59370-127-7(6), Fire Eng Bks & Vid) PennWell Corp.

Fire on Earth: Doomsday, Dinosaurs, & Humankind. unabr. ed. John Gribbin & Mary Gribbin. Narrated by Richard M. Davidson. 6 cass. (Running Time: 8 hrs. 45 mins.). 1997. 51.00 (978-0-7887-1171-8(7), 95123E7) Recorded Bks.

A riveting account of asteroids & comets on a collision course with Earth. Citing past destructive bombardments from the heavens & predicting future calamitous accidents, they offer an unsettling view of our fragile planet in peril.

Fire on the Altar. abr. ed. Duncan B. Campbell. 3 CDs. (Running Time: 3 hrs.). 2000. 19.99 (978-0-7684-0197-4(6)) Destiny Image Pubs.

***Fire on the Horizon: The Untold Story of the Explosion Aboard the Deepwater Horizon.** unabr. ed. Tom Shroder & John Konrad. (ENG.). 2011. (978-0-06-206437-0(1)); (978-0-06-206438-7(X)) HarperCollins Pubs.

Fire on the Mountain. John Maclean. 2004. 15.95 (978-0-7435-4729-1(2)) Pub: S&S Audio. Dist(s): S and S Inc

Fire on the Mountain, unabr. collector's ed. Edward Abbey. Read by Paul Shay. 7 cass. (Running Time: 7 hrs.). 1989. 42.00 (978-0-7366-1591-4(1), 2454) Books on Tape.

John Vogelin ranches the land adjoining White Sands Missile Range in New Mexico. When the Air Force tries to extend its holdings, Vogelin refuses to budge. Aided only by his 12-year-old grandson, Vogelin shows what one determined individual can do in the face of overwhelming legal & military power.

Fire on the Mountain-mp3. Read by Douglas Wilson. 1995. 32.00 (978-1-59128-263-1(2)) Canon Pr ID.

Fire on the Mountain-tape. Read by Douglas Wilson. 1995. 40.00 (978-1-59128-265-5(9)) Canon Pr ID.

Fire Plume: Legend of the American Indians. unabr. ed. Perf. by Jay Silverheels. Ed. by John Bierhorst. 1 cass. Incl. Fire Plume: The Broken Wing. (J). (CDL5 1451); Fire Plume: The Fire Plume. (J). (CDL5 1451); Fire Plume: The Red Swan. (J). (CDL5 1451); Fire Plume: Wawanosh. (J). (CDL5 1451); (J). 1973. 9.95 (978-0-89845-535-9(9), CDL5 1451) HarperCollins Pubs.

The four stories brought together in this collection are amongst the earliest tales recorded by the pioneer ethnographer Henry Rowe Schoolcraft.

Fire Plume: The Broken Wing see Fire Plume: Legend of the American Indians

Fire Plume: The Fire Plume see Fire Plume: Legend of the American Indians

Fire Plume: The Red Swan see Fire Plume: Legend of the American Indians

Fire Plume: Wawanosh see Fire Plume: Legend of the American Indians

Fire Sale. abr. ed. Sara Paretsky. Read by Sandra Burr. (Running Time: 21600 sec.). (V. I. Warshawski Ser.). 2006. audio compact disk 16.99 (978-1-59737-348-7(6), 9781597373487, BCD Value Price) Brilliance Audio.

V. I. Warshawski may have left her old South Chicago neighborhood, but she learns that she cannot escape it. When V. I. takes over coaching duties of the girls' basketball team at her former high school, she faces an ill-equipped, ragtag group of gangbangers, fundamentalists, and teenage moms, who inevitably draw the detective into their family woes. Through young Josie Dorrado, V. I. meets the girl's mother, who voices her worries about sabotage in the little flag manufacturing plant where she works. The biggest employer on the South Side, discount-store behemoth By-Smart, pays even less, and Ms. Dorrado doesn't know how she'll support her four children if the flag plant shuts down. The elder Dorrado's fears are realized when the plant explodes; V. I. is injured and the owner is killed. As V. I. begins to investigate, she finds herself confronting the Bysen family, who own the By-Smart company. Founder William "Buffalo Bill" Bysen, now in his eighties, has four sons who quarrel with each other and with him; the oldest, "Young Mr. William," is close to sixty and furious that his father doesn't cede more power to him. And then, there's "Billy the Kid," Young Mr. William's nineteen-year-old son, whose Christian idealism puts him on a collision course with his father, his grandfather, and the company as a whole. When Billy runs away with Josie Dorrado, V. I. is squeezed between the needs of two very different families. As she tries to find the errant teenagers, and to track down a particularly cruel murderer, her own life is almost forfeit in the swamps that lie under the city of Chicago.

Fire Sale. unabr. ed. Sara Paretsky. Read by Sandra Burr. (Running Time: 15 hrs.). (V. I. Warshawski Ser.). 2005. 39.25 (978-1-59710-918-5(5), 9781597109185, BADLE); 24.95 (978-1-59710-919-2(3), 9781597109192, BAD); 34.95 (978-1-58788-872-4(6), 9781587888724, BAU); 97.25 (978-1-58788-873-1(4), 9781587888731, BrilAudUnabridg); DVD & audio compact disk 24.95 (978-1-59335-672-9(2), 9781593356729, Brilliance MP3); audio compact disk 39.95 (978-1-58788-875-5(0), 9781587888755, Bril Audio CD Unabri); audio compact disk 112.25 (978-1-58788-876-2(9), 9781587888762, BriAudCD Unabrid); audio compact disk 39.25 (978-1-59335-806-8(7), 9781593358068, Brlnc Audio MP3 Lib) Brilliance Audio.

***Fire Season: Field Notes from a Wilderness Lookout.** unabr. ed. Philip Connors. Read by To be announced. (Running Time: 7 hrs. NaN mins.). (ENG.). 2011. 29.95 (978-1-4417-8214-4(1)) Blckstn Audio.

***Fire Season: Field Notes from a Wilderness Lookout.** unabr. ed. Philip Connors. Read by To be Announced. (Running Time: 7 hrs. NaN mins.). (ENG.). 2011. 44.95 (978-1-4417-8211-3(7)) Blckstn Audio.

***Fire Season: Field Notes from a Wilderness Lookout.** unabr. ed. Philip Connors. Read by To be announced. (Running Time: 7 hrs. NaN mins.). 2011. audio compact disk 24.95 (978-1-4417-8213-7(3)) Blckstn Audio.

***Fire Season: Field Notes from a Wilderness Lookout.** unabr. ed. Philip Connors. Read by To be Announced. (Running Time: 7 hrs. NaN mins.). (ENG.). 2011. audio compact disk 69.00 (978-1-4417-8212-0(5)) Blckstn Audio.

Fire So Big the Heavens Can See It. Contrib. by Search the City. 2008. audio compact disk 13.99 (978-5-557-47792-5(6)) Tooth & Nail.

Fire Stealer. 2004. 8.95 (978-1-56008-894-3(X)); cass. & flmstrp 30.00 (978-1-56008-667-3(X)) Weston Woods.

Fire Suppression DVD. International Association of Fire Chiefs Staff & National Fire Protection Association. 2005. 629.95 (978-0-7637-3611-8(2)) Jones Bartlett.

Fire, the Light & the Glory. Kenneth Copeland. Perf. by Kenneth Copeland. 7 cass. (Running Time: 7 hrs.). 1996. cass. & video 35.00 Set. (978-1-57562-131-9(2)) K Copeland Pubns.
Biblical teaching on the Glory of God.

Fire up Your Life! Living with Nothing to Prove, Nothing to Hide, & Nothing. Ken Davis. 1 cass. 1995. 12.99 (978-0-310-20021-5(0)) Zondervan.

Fire Wall. Andy McNab. Read by Clive Mantle. 12 vols. (Running Time: 18 hrs.). 2003. audio compact disk 110.95 (978-0-7540-8747-2(6)) Pub: Chivers Audio Bks GBR. Dist(s): AudioGO

***Fire Will Fall.** unabr. ed. Carol Plum-Ucci. (Running Time: 16 hrs.). 2011. 29.95 (978-1-4417-7137-7(9)); 89.95 (978-1-4417-7134-6(4)); audio compact disk 29.95 (978-1-4417-7136-0(0)); audio compact disk 118.00 (978-1-4417-7135-3(2)) Blckstn Audio.

Fire Your Inner Critic: Getting Free of Inner Shame & Outer Blame, Set. David Grudermeyer & Rebecca Grudermeyer. 2 cass. 18.95 (T-38) Willingness Wrks.

***Fire Your Therapist: Why Therapy Might Not Be Working for You & What You Can Do about It.** unabr. ed. Joe Siegler. (Running Time: 10 hrs. 30 mins.). (ENG.). 2010. 34.98 (978-1-59659-546-0(9), GildAudio) Pub: Gildan Media. Dist(s): HachBkGrp

Firearms: A Deadly American Love Affair. 2 cass. (Running Time: 2 hrs.). 14.95 set. (GO-040, HarperThor) HarpC GBR.

Firebird. abr. ed. Janice Graham. Read by Robert Foxworth. 4 cass. 1999. 25.00 (FS9-40047) Highsmith.

Firebird. unabr. ed. Keith Bilderbeck. Perf. by Penny Wiggins. 1 cass., 1 CD. (Running Time: 67min 45sec). (J). (ps-3). 1999. 8.00 (978-1-893721-05-0(1), BYR-10034) Baba Yaga.
Who is stealing the king's golden apples? The magical firebird thinks herself clever, until she falls into the clutches of Baba Yaga the Witch.

Firebird. unabr. ed. Keith Bilderbeck. Perf. by Penny Wiggins. 1 cass., 1 CD. (Running Time: 50 min.). (J). (gr. k-6). 2002. audio compact disk 12.00 CD. (978-1-893721-04-3(3), BYR-00032) Baba Yaga.

Firebird. unabr. ed. Janice Graham. Narrated by Richard Poe. 6 cass. (Running Time: 8 hrs. 15 mins.). 1999. 56.00 (978-0-7887-2912-6(8), 95705E7) Recorded Bks.
A love story that rises from the ashes of tragedy. Soon after Ethan, a Kansas lawyer, falls in love with an exotic visitor to his small town, he is forced to marry a local woman. But after his true love is killed in a fire, Ethan begins to notice mysterious changes in his wife.

Firebird. unabr. ed. Sophie Masson. Read by Richard Aspel. 7 CDs. (Running Time: 27600 sec.). (YA). (gr. 7-13). 2005. audio compact disk 83.95 (978-1-74093-602-6(7)) Pub: Bolinda Pubng AUS. Dist(s): Bolinda Pub Inc

Fireboat: The Heroic Adventure of the John J. Harvey. Maira Kalman. Illus. by Maira Kalman. (Running Time: 16 mins.). (J). 2004. 9.95 (978-1-59112-982-0(6)); audio compact disk 12.95 (978-1-59112-986-8(9)) Live Oak Media.

Fireboat: The Heroic Adventures of John J. Harvey. Maira Kalman. Read by Judd Hirsch. 11 vols. (Running Time: 16 mins.). (J). 2004. bk. 25.95 (978-1-59112-984-4(2)); bk. 28.95 (978-1-59112-988-2(5)) Pub: Live Oak Media. Dist(s): AudioGO

***Fireborn.** Nick Kyme. (ENG.). 2010. 17.00 (978-1-84416-929-0(4), Black Library) Pub: BL Pubng GBR. Dist(s): S and S Inc

Firebrand: The Life of Dostoevsky. unabr. collector's ed. Henri Troyat. Read by Wolfram Kandinsky. 12 cass. (Running Time: 18 hrs.). 1991. 96.00 (978-0-7366-1946-2(1), 2767) Books on Tape.
Fydor Mijkailovich Dostoevsky was born in Russia in 1821, the son of a Moscow military doctor who was murdered by his serfs. Raised to wealth but psychologically scarred by the death of his father, Fydor turned radical. Arrested, he was first imprisoned then exiled to Siberia for 10 years. These experiences, & especially his last-minute reprieve from execution, led him back to the church. But his radicalism remained, resulting in a tension that inspired some of the world's greatest novels, notably The Brothers Karamazov & Crime & Punishment.

Firebug. unabr. ed. David Harris. Read by Peter Hardy. 2 cass. (Running Time: 2 hrs. 30 mins.). 2002. 24.00 (978-1-74030-360-6(1)) Pub: Bolinda Pubng AUS. Dist(s): Lndmrk Audiobks

Fired! Tales of the Canned, Canceled, Downsized, & Dismissed. abr. ed. 3 CDs. (Running Time: 7020 sec.). 2005. audio compact disk 25.95 (978-1-58081-336-5(4), LA 066) Pub: L A Theatre. Dist(s): NetLibrary CO

Fired! Tales of the Canned, Canceled, Downsized, & Dismissed. unabr. ed. Annabelle Gurwitch. Read by A. Full Cast. (YA). 2008. 34.99 (978-1-60514-777-2(X)) Find a World.

Fired Again: Stories from the Book Fired! Tales of the Canned, Canceled, Downsized, & Dismissed. Annabelle Gurwitch. Contrib. by Tonya Pinkins et al. (Running Time: 8640 sec.). 2007. audio compact disk 25.95 (978-1-58081-355-6(0)) Pub: L A Theatre. Dist(s): NetLibrary CO

Fired Up. abr. ed. Jayne Ann Krentz. Read by Joyce Bean. (Running Time: 6 hrs.). (Arcane Society Ser.: Bk. 1). 2009. audio compact disk 26.99 (978-1-4233-2649-6(0), 9781423326496, BACD) Brilliance Audio.

Fired Up. abr. ed. Jayne Ann Krentz. Read by Joyce Bean. (Running Time: 6 hrs.). (Arcane Society Ser.: Bk. 1). 2011. audio compact disk 14.99 (978-1-4233-2650-2(4), 9781423326502, BCD Value Price) Brilliance Audio.

Fired Up. unabr. ed. Jayne Ann Krentz. Read by Joyce Bean. (Running Time: 10 hrs.). (Arcane Society Ser.: Bk. 1). 2009. 24.99 (978-1-4233-2645-8(8), 9781423326458, Brilliance MP3); 24.99 (978-1-4233-2647-2(4), 9781423326472, BAD); 39.97 (978-1-4233-2646-5(6), 9781423326465, Brlnc Audio MP3 Lib); 39.97 (978-1-4233-2648-9(2), 9781423326489, BADLE); audio compact disk 34.99 (978-1-4233-2643-4(1), 9781423326434, Bril Audio CD Unabri); audio compact disk 92.97 (978-1-4233-2644-1(X), 9781423326441, BriAudCD Unabrid) Brilliance Audio.

FiredUP Interviewing (audio Cd) Master the Secrets of Winning a New Job. Created by Winning Formula Studios. (ENG.). 2006. audio compact disk 24.95 (978-0-9779221-0-9(3)) Winning Formula.

FiredUP Interviewing New Grad Edition (audio Cd) Master the Secrets to Interview Success. Created by Winning Formula Studios. (ENG.). 2006. audio compact disk 24.95 (978-0-9779221-1-6(1)) Winning Formula.

Firefly. Peter T. Deutermann. Read by Dick Hill. (Playaway Adult Fiction Ser.). (ENG.). 2009. 54.99 (978-1-60775-671-2(4)) Find a World.

Firefly. abr. ed. P. T. Deutermann. Read by Dick Hill. 4 CDs. (Running Time: 6 hrs.). 2003. audio compact disk 74.25 (978-1-59086-868-3(4), 1590868684, BACDLib Ed) Brilliance Audio.
At midnight, in a secret medical clinic in Washington, D.C., two foreign doctors and their team are completing plastic surgery on an anonymous client who is changing the appearance of his face, among other things. After the procedure, the client begins to stir - and suddenly the operating room erupts in violence, and the clinic is ablaze. Washington police conduct an arson investigation, with inconclusive results. But one tantalizing fragment of evidence suggests that a terrorist bombing may be imminent. The presidential inauguration is quickly approaching, and Washington's police, fire, intelligence, military, federal, and White House security teams are making frantic preparations. Because of the strain on manpower, retired Secret Service agent Swamp Morgan is recalled to active duty. His task: investigate the incineration of the medical clinic as a "firefly" - Washington-speak for something that looks like a threat but isn't. As Swamp begins what he thinks is a routine check-and-dismiss, the clinic's missing client begins preparations for his mission: to launch an attack on the American government - a decapitation strike intended to wipe out both the outgoing and incoming administrations. As the crucial day approaches, Swamp, the only agent to take the firefly seriously, must operate alone as the clock clicks down to a breathtaking finale. Filled with brilliant twists and turns and heart-in-your-throat suspense, The Firefly offers first-class entertainment from beginning to end.

Firefly. abr. ed. P. T. Deutermann. Read by Dick Hill. (Running Time: 6 hrs.). 2005. audio compact disk 16.99 (978-1-59600-404-7(5), 9781596004047, BCD Value Price) Brilliance Audio.

Firefly. unabr. ed. P. T. Deutermann. Read by Dick Hill. 11 cass. (Running Time: 15 hrs.). 2003. 102.25 (978-1-59086-115-8(9), 1590861159, BrilAudUnabridg); 34.95 (978-1-59086-114-1(0), 1590861140, BAU) Brilliance Audio.

Firefly. unabr. ed. P. T. Deutermann. Read by Dick Hill. (Running Time: 15 hrs.). 2004. 39.25 (978-1-59335-557-9(2), 1593355572, Brlnc Audio MP3 Lib) Brilliance Audio.

Firefly. unabr. ed. P. T. Deutermann. Read by Dick Hill. (Running Time: 15 hrs.). 2004. 39.25 (978-1-59710-287-2(3), 1597102873, BADLE); 24.95 (978-1-59710-286-5(5), 1597102865, BAD) Brilliance Audio.

Firefly. unabr. ed. P. T. Deutermann. Read by Dick Hill. (Running Time: 15 hrs.). 2004. 24.95 (978-1-59335-257-8(3), 1593352573) Soulmate Audio Bks.

Firefly Beach. Luanne Rice. Narrated by Alexandra O'Karma. 12 CDs. (Running Time: 13 hrs. 30 mins.). audio compact disk 116.00 (978-1-4025-0479-2(9)) Recorded Bks.

Firefly Beach. Luanne Rice. Narrated by Alexandra O'Karma. 10 cass. (Running Time: 13 hrs. 30 mins.). 2001. 91.00 (978-0-7887-9927-3(4), L1033) Recorded Bks.
Reunite two childhood pen pals. years ago, Caroline and Joe were bound together by tragedy. Now, meeting as adults, they have a chance to heal that old wound. But what will be the emotional costs.

Firefly Cloak. unabr. ed. Sheri Reynolds. Read by Jenna Lamia. (YA). 2007. 44.99 (978-1-60252-500-9(5)) Find a World.

Firefly Cloak. unabr. ed. Sheri Reynolds. 7 CDs. (Running Time: 8 hrs.). (ENG.). 2006. audio compact disk 32.95 (978-1-59887-021-3(1), 1598870211) Pub: Penguin-HghBrdg. Dist(s): Penguin Grp USA

Firefly Fred Audio Book. Todd Porter. (ENG.). (J). 2007. audio compact disk 9.95 (978-1-932278-47-7(8)) Pub: Mayhaven Pub. Dist(s): Baker Taylor

Firefly Lane. Kristin Hannah. Read by Susan Ericksen. (Playaway Adult Fiction Ser.). (ENG.). 2009. 90.00 (978-1-60775-541-8(6)) Find a World.

Firefly Lane. abr. ed. Kristin Hannah. Read by Susan Ericksen. 5 CDs. (Running Time: 6 hrs.). 2008. audio compact disk 26.95 (978-1-4233-2507-9(9), 9781423325079, BACD) Brilliance Audio.

Firefly Lane. abr. ed. Kristin Hannah. Read by Susan Ericksen. (Running Time: 6 hrs.). 2009. audio compact disk 14.99 (978-1-4233-2508-6(7), 9781423325086, BCD Value Price) Brilliance Audio.

Firefly Lane. unabr. ed. Kristin Hannah. Read by Susan Ericksen. (Running Time: 18 hrs.). 2008. 44.25 (978-1-4233-2506-2(0), 9781423325062, BADLE); 29.95 (978-1-4233-2505-5(2), 9781423325055, BAD); 122.25 (978-1-4233-2500-0(1), 9781423325000, BrilAudUnabridg); audio compact disk 39.95 (978-1-4233-2501-7(X), 9781423325017, Bril Audio CD Unabri); audio compact disk 29.95 (978-1-4233-2503-1(6), 9781423325031, Brilliance MP3); audio compact disk 44.25 (978-1-4233-2504-8(4), 9781423325048, Brlnc Audio MP3 Lib); audio compact disk 127.25 (978-1-4233-2502-4(8), 9781423325024, BriAudCD Unabrid) Brilliance Audio.

Firefly Star: A Hispanic Folk Tale. unabr. ed. Sandra Robbins. 1 cass. (Running Time: 32 min.). (J). (gr. k-5). 1995. 5.50 (978-1-882601-24-0(6)) See-Mores Wrkshop.
A magical tale of El Dia de los Reyes (Three Kings Day). This non-religious story celebrates the Hispanic folk tradition.

Firefly Star: A Hispanic Tale (Three Kings Day) Adapted by Sandra Robbins. Music by Jeff Olmsted. 1 CD. (Running Time: 32 mins). (See-More's Stories Ser.). (J). 1995. pap. bk. 16.95 (978-1-882601-38-7(6)) See-Mores Wrkshop.

Firefly Summer: Full-Cast Radio Drama Starring David Soul. Maeve Binchy. (Running Time: 2 hrs. 55 mins. 0 sec.). (ENG.). 2009. audio compact disk 29.95 (978-1-60283-774-4(0)) Pub: AudioGO. Dist(s): Perseus Dist

Firegirl. unabr. ed. Tony Abbott. Read by Sean Kenim. 3 CDs. (Running Time: 2 hrs. 52 mins.). (J). (gr. 5-7). 2007. audio compact disk 30.00 (978-0-7393-4873-4(6), Listening Lib) Pub: Random Audio Pubg. Dist(s): Random

Firegirl. unabr. ed. Tony Abbott. Read by Sean Kenin. 3 CDs. (Running Time: 10320 sec.). (ENG.). (J). (gr. 5-7). 2007. audio compact disk 27.00 (978-0-7393-4880-2(9), Listening Lib) Pub: Random Audio Pubg. Dist(s): Random

Firehouse. unabr. ed. David Halberstam. Read by Mel Foster. 4 cass., Library ed. (Running Time: 5 hrs.). 2002. 62.25 (978-1-59086-344-2(5), 1590863445, Unabridge Lib Edns); audio compact disk 27.95 (978-1-59086-345-9(3), 1590863453, CD Unabridged); audio compact disk 69.25 (978-1-59086-346-6(1), 1590863461, CD Unabrid Lib Ed) Brilliance Audio.
"In the firehouse the men not only live and eat with each other, they play sports together, go off to drink together, help repair one another's houses and, most importantly, share terrifying risks; their loyalties to each other must, by the demands of the dangers they face, be instinctive and absolute." So writes David Halberstam, one of America's most distinguished reporters and historians in this stunning book about Engine 40, Ladder 35 - one of the firehouses hardest hit in the aftermath of the terrorist attack on the World Trade Towers. On the morning of September 11, 2001, two rigs carrying 13 men set out from this firehouse, located on the west side of Manhattan near Lincoln Center; twelve of the men would never return. Firehouse takes us to the very epicenter of the tragedy. We watch the day unfold, the men called to duty, while their families wait anxiously for news of them. In addition we come to understand the culture of the firehouse itself, why gifted men do this and why in so many instances they are anxious to follow in their fathers' footsteps and serve in so dangerous a profession - why more than anything else, it is not just a job, but a calling as well. Firehouse is journalism-as-history at its best. The story of what happens when one small institution gets caught in apocalyptic day, it is a book that will move readers as few others have in our time.

Firehouse. unabr. ed. David Halberstam. Read by Mel Foster. (Running Time: 5 hrs.). 2004. 39.25 (978-1-59335-351-3(0), 1593353510, Brlnc Audio MP3 Lib) Brilliance Audio.

Firehouse. unabr. ed. David Halberstam. Read by Mel Foster. (Running Time: 5 hrs.). 2004. 39.25 (978-1-59710-288-9(1), 1597102881, BADLE); 24.95 (978-1-59710-289-6(X), 159710289X, BAD) Brilliance Audio.

Firehouse. unabr. ed. David Halberstam. Read by Mel Foster. (Running Time: 5 hrs.). 2004. 24.95 (978-1-59335-011-6(2), 1593350112) Soulmate Audio Bks.

Firekeeper's Son. Linda Sue Park. Narrated by Norm Lee. (Running Time: 15 mins.). (J). 2004. audio compact disk 12.75 (978-1-4193-1761-3(X)) Recorded Bks.

Firelight Creative Music. (Firelight Ser.). 2004. audio compact disk 15.99 (978-0-8066-6404-0(5)) Augsburg Fortress.

Fireproof: Never Leave Your Partner. unabr. ed. Eric Wilson. Narrated by Greg Whalen. Sreenplay by Alex Kendrick & Stephen Kendrick. 6 CDs. (Running Time: 7 hrs. 35 mins. 44 sec.). (ENG.). 2008. audio compact disk 25.99 (978-1-59859-544-4(X)) Oasis Audio.

Fireproof: Never Leave Your Partner. unabr. ed. Eric Wilson. Narrated by Greg Whalen. (Running Time: 7 hrs. 35 mins. 44 sec.). (ENG.). 2009. 18.19 (978-1-60814-464-8(X)) Oasis Audio.

***Fireproof Your Life: Building a Faith That Survives the Flames.** unabr. ed. Michael Catt. Read by Tom Parks. (Running Time: 4 hrs.). 2010. 39.97 (978-1-4418-7229-6(9), 9781441872296, BADLE); 14.99 (978-1-4418-7228-9(0), 9781441872289, BAD); 14.99 (978-1-4418-7226-5(4), 9781441872265, Brilliance MP3); 39.97 (978-1-4418-7227-2(2), 9781441872272, Brlnc Audio MP3 Lib); audio compact disk 14.99 (978-1-4418-7224-1(8), 9781441872241, Bril Audio CD Unabri); audio compact disk 39.97 (978-1-4418-7225-8(6), 9781441872258, BriAudCD Unabrid) Brilliance Audio.

Fires of Heaven. abr. ed. Scripts. Robert Jordan. Perf. by Mark Rolston. 2 cass. (Running Time: 3 hrs.). (Wheel of Time Ser.: Bk. 5). 2004. 16.95 (978-1-59007-326-1(6)) Pub: New Millenn Enter. Dist(s): PerseuPGW

Fires of Heaven. abr. ed. Scripts. Robert Jordan. Read by Kate Reading. Perf. by Mark Rolston. 3 CDs. (Running Time: 3 hrs.). (Wheel of Time Ser.: Bk. 5). 2004. 20.95 (978-1-59007-327-8(4)) Pub: New Millenn Enter. Dist(s): PerseuPGW

Fires of Heaven. abr. ed. Robert Jordan. Read by Mark Rolston. 2 cass. (Running Time: 3 hrs.). (Wheel of Time Ser.: Bk. 5). 1993. 16.95 (978-1-879371-65-1(0)) Pub Mills.

Fires of Heaven. unabr. ed. Robert Jordan. Read by Kate Reading & Michael Kramer. 29 CDs. (Running Time: 38 hrs. 0 mins. 0 sec.). (Wheel of Time Ser.: Bk. 5). (ENG.). 2005. audio compact disk 74.95 (978-1-59397-606-4(2)) Pub: Macmill Audio. Dist(s): Macmillan

Fires of Heaven. unabr. ed. Scripts. Robert Jordan. Read by Michael Kramer & Kate Reading. 22 CDs. (Running Time: 27 hrs.). (Wheel of Time Ser.: Bk. 5). 2004. audio compact disk 69.95 (978-1-59007-393-3(2)); 49.95 (978-1-59007-392-6(4)) Pub: New Millenn Enter. Dist(s): PerseuPGW
With Dark One returning to the world and the Last Battle approaching, several reincarnated heroes join the quest to place the Dragon Reborn as the ruler of the world.

Fires of Heaven, Pt. 1. unabr. ed. Robert Jordan. Read by Kate Reading & Michael Kramer. 13 cass. (Running Time: 19 hrs. 30 min.). (Wheel of Time Ser.: Bk. 5). 1997. 104.00 (978-0-7366-3765-7(6), 4439-A) Books on Tape.
The Last Battle is approaching rapidly, for the seals of the Dark One's prison are beginning to crumble. Rand Al'thor, now fully realized as the Dragon Reborn, is closer to ruling the world.

Fires of Heaven, Pt. 2. unabr. ed. Robert Jordan. Read by Kate Reading & Michael Kramer. 13 cass. (Running Time: 19 hrs. 30 min.). (Wheel of Time Ser.: Bk. 5). 1997. 104.00 (978-0-7366-3766-4(4), 4439-B) Books on Tape.

Fires of Jubilee: Nat Turner's Fierce Rebellion. unabr. ed. Stephen B. Oates. Narrated by John McDonough. 6 cass. (Running Time: 7 hrs. 45 mins.). 1997. 51.00 (978-0-7887-0935-7(6), 95075E7) Recorded Bks.
A dramatic & insightful portrait of the charismatic visionary who led the bloody slave rebellion in Virginia in 1831. The author spent an idyllic childhood believing that he was destined for great things. At the age of 13, however, he was introduced to the brutality of slavery & became a prophet to his people.

Fires of Merlin. unabr. ed. T. A. Barron. Read by Kevin Isola. 5 cass. (Running Time: 8 hrs. 30 mins.). (Lost Years of Merlin Ser.: Bk. 3). (YA). 2004. 30.60 (978-0-8072-2070-2(1), Listening Lib) Pub: Random Audio Pubg. Dist(s): NetLibrary CO
Merlin must conquer an enchanted dragon in the third audiobook in this spellbinding series.

Fires of Spring. unabr. ed. James A. Michener. Read by Larry McKeever. 18 cass. (Running Time: 27 hrs.). 1994. 144.00 Set. (978-0-7366-2815-0(0), 3527A/B) Books on Tape.
David Harper learns about women & love in this bittersweet drama of a boy's perilous journey into manhood. A beautiful story.

Fires of Spring, Pt. 1. James A. Michener. Read by Larry McKeever. 9 cass. (Running Time: 13 hrs. 30 min.). 1994. 72.00 (3527-A) Books on Tape.

Fires of Spring, Pt. 2. James A. Michener. Read by Larry McKeever. 9 cass. (Running Time: 13 hrs. 30 min.). 1994. 72.00 (3527-B) Books on Tape.

Fireside. abr. ed. Susan Wiggs. Read by Joyce Bean. (Running Time: 6 hrs.). (Lakeshore Chronicles: Bk. 5). 2009. audio compact disk 14.99 (978-1-4233-9192-0(6), 9781423391920, BACD) Brilliance Audio.

Fireside. unabr. ed. Susan Wiggs. Read by Joyce Bean. (Running Time: 12 hrs.). (Lakeshore Chronicles: Bk. 5). 2009. 39.97 (978-1-4233-7597-5(1), 9781423375975, BADLE); 39.97 (978-1-4233-7595-1(5), 9781423375951, Brlnc Audio MP3 Lib); 24.99 (978-1-4233-7596-8(3), 9781423375968, BAD); 24.99 (978-1-4233-7594-4(7), 9781423375944, Brilliance MP3); audio compact disk 89.97 (978-1-4233-7593-7(9), 9781423375937, BriAudCD Unabrid); audio compact disk 38.99 (978-1-4233-7592-0(0), 9781423375920, Bril Audio CD Unabri) Brilliance Audio.

Fireside Al. Contrib. by Alan Maitland. 1 CD. (Running Time: 1 hr.). 2005. audio compact disk 15.95 (978-0-660-19042-6(7)) Pub: Canadian Broadcasting CAN. Dist(s): Georgetown Term
Alan Maitland, popularly known as Fireside Al and Front Porch Al, has delighted listeners across the country with his storytelling on the CBC radio program "As It Happens. His inimitable voice, charm, and skills as a storyteller have brought warmth and delight to generations of CBC radio listeners.

Fireside Al's Treasury of Christmas Stories. (ENG.). 2007. audio compact disk 15.95 (978-0-660-19732-6(4)) Canadian Broadcasting CAN.

Fireside Tales. unabr. ed. Mary S. Moore. Read by Mary S. Moore. Illus. by Cliff Clay. 1 cass. (J). (gr. 5-12). 1990. pap. bk. 10.00 (978-0-913678-19-0(8)) New Day Pr.
African-American folk-style tales.

Fireside Tales: More Lessons from the Animal People. Short Stories. Dovie Thomason Sickles. Music by Micky Sickles. 1 cass. (Running Time: 1 hr. 10 min.). (YA). 2001. 9.95 (978-0-938756-58-3(3)) Yellow Moon.
Sickles effectively stammers, snorts and clicks as she portrays the various animal characters in these seven appeal tales. In the Kiowa Apache-Lakota oral tradition, creatures boastful, mean, proud and dishonest receive their comeuppance from fellow beasts, serving as examples for human listeners. A good amount of humor keeps the tales flowing, assuring that the mood never gets too moralistic.

Fireside Tales: More Lessons from the Animal People. Short Stories. Dovie Thomason Sickles. Music by Micky Sickles. 1 CD. (Running Time: 1 hr. 10 min.). (J). (gr. k-6). 2001. audio compact disk 14.95 (978-0-938756-59-0(1)) Yellow Moon.

Firesign Theatre's Alternative Rose Parade. Perf. by Firesign Theatre Firesign Theatre Staff. 2 CDs. (Running Time: 2 hrs.). 2001. audio compact disk 24.95 Lodestone Catalog.
On New Year's Day, tune in the Rose Parade & turn off the sound..listen to this instead! Created live in 2000 fills.

Firesign Theatre's Pink Hotel Burns Down. Perf. by Firesign Theatre Firesign Theatre Staff. 1 cass. (Running Time: 1 hr.). 2001. 12.95; audio compact disk 15.95 Lodestone Catalog.
Unreleased & some barely-escaped. Hugely funny early recordings, live broadcasts from the legendary Magic Mushroom, an early version of Giant Rat.

***Firestarter.** unabr. ed. Stephen King. (Running Time: 15 hrs. 0 mins.). 2010. 29.95 (978-1-4417-3295-8(0)); 85.95 (978-1-4417-3291-0(8)); audio compact disk 75.00 (978-1-4417-3292-7(6)) Blckstn Audio.

Firestarter. unabr. ed. Stephen King. (Running Time: 15 hrs.). (ENG.). 2010. audio compact disk 49.95 (978-0-14-242784-2(5), PengAudBks) Penguin Grp USA.

Firestorm. David Klass. Read by Ramon de Ocampo. 9 cass. (Running Time: 10 hrs. 25 mins.). (Caretaker Trilogy: Bk. 1). (YA). (gr. 8 up). 2007. 67.75 (978-1-4281-3467-6(0)); audio compact disk 97.75 (978-1-4281-3472-0(7)) Recorded Bks.

Firestorm. abr. ed. Iris Johansen. Read by Kate Burton. 5 CDs. (Running Time: 5 hrs. 15 mins.). (ENG.). 2005. audio compact disk 14.99 (978-0-7393-1812-6(8)) Pub: Random Audio Pubg. Dist(s): Random

Firestorm. unabr. ed. Nevada Barr. Narrated by Barbara Rosenblat. 6 cass. (Running Time: 9 hrs. 15 mins.). (Anna Pigeon Ser.: No. 4). 1996. 53.00 (978-0-7887-3775-6(9), 95992E7) Recorded Bks.
Resourceful park ranger Anna Pigeon joins the forces battling a raging forest fire in California. After the inferno passes, she discovers a crew member didn't make it - but a knife, not the fire, killed him.

Firestorm: Allied Airpower & the Destruction of Dresden. unabr. ed. Marshall De Bruhl. Narrated by Michael Prichard. (Running Time: 13 hrs. 0 mins. 0 sec.). (ENG.). 2007. audio compact disk 69.99 (978-1-4001-3334-5(3)); audio compact disk 24.99 (978-1-4001-5334-3(4)) Pub: Tantor Media. Dist(s): IngramPubServ

Firestorm: Allied Airpower & the Destruction of Dresden. unabr. ed. Marshall De Bruhl. Read by Michael Prichard. 10 CDs. (Running Time: 13 hrs. 0 mins. 0 sec.). (ENG.). 2007. audio compact disk 34.99 (978-1-4001-0334-8(7)) Pub: Tantor Media. Dist(s): IngramPubServ
In Firestorm, Marshall De Bruhl re-creates the drama and horror of the Dresden bombing and offers the most cogent appraisal yet of the tactics, weapons, strategy, and rationale for the controversial attack. Using new research and contemporary reports, as well as eyewitness stories of the devastation, De Bruhl directly addresses many long-unresolved questions relating to the bombing: Why did the strike occur when the Allies' victory was seemingly so imminent? Was choosing a city choked with German refugees a punitive decision, intended to humiliate a nation? What, if any, strategic importance did Dresden have? How much did the desire to send a "message"-to Imperial Japan or the advancing Soviet armies-factor into the decision to firebomb the city?.

Firewalking. Larissa Villenskaya. 2 cass. 18.00 set. (A0147-85) Sound Photosyn.
ICSS '85.

Firewall. Andy McNab. Read by Clive Mantle. 12 cass. (Running Time: 18 hrs.). 2002. 96.95 (978-0-7540-0714-2(6), CAB 2136) AudioGO.

Firewall. unabr. ed. Henning Mankell. Read by Dick Hill. (Running Time: 13 hrs. 5 mins.). (Kurt Wallander Ser.). 2008. audio compact disk 79.95 (978-1-4332-2581-9(6)) Blckstn Audio.

Firewall. unabr. ed. Henning Mankell. Read by Dick Hill. Tr. by Ebba Segerberg from SWE. 13 CDs. (Running Time: 16 hrs.). (Kurt Wallander Ser.). 2008. audio compact disk 99.00 (978-1-4332-2582-6(4)) Blckstn Audio.

Firewall. unabr. ed. Henning Mankell. Read by Dick Hill. (Running Time: 13 hrs. 0 mins.). (Kurt Wallander Ser.). 2009. 29.95 (978-1-4332-2585-7(9)); audio compact disk 29.95 (978-1-4332-2584-0(0)) Blckstn Audio.

Fireweed. unabr. ed. Nellie B. Picken. Read by Gene Engene. 16 cass. (Running Time: 18 hrs. 30 min.). Dramatization. 1990. 74.95 (978-1-55686-338-7(1), 338) Books in Motion.
Recipient of the 1990 Governor's Writer Award. Ed McLaren who comes west in 1897 as a rebellious teenager, plays an active role in the development of the Oakanogan Valley of north central Washington. Drawn west by the lure of the gold fields, he finds a better life as a rancher.

Firework-Maker's Daughter. unabr. ed. Philip Pullman. Read by Nigel Lambert. 2 CDs. (Running Time: 3 hrs.). (J). 2002. audio compact disk 21.95 (978-0-7540-6523-4(5), CHCD 023, Chivers Child Audio) AudioGO.

Fireworks over Toccoa. unabr. ed. Jeffrey Stepakoff. Read by Kathleen McInerney. (Running Time: 6 hrs. 0 mins. 0 sec.). (ENG.). 2010. audio compact disk 29.99 (978-1-4272-0918-4(9)) Pub: Macmill Audio. Dist(s): Macmillan

Firing Offense. unabr. ed. David Ignatius. Narrated by Richard Ferrone. 10 cass. (Running Time: 13 hrs. 45 mins.). 1998. 85.00 (978-0-7887-2167-0(4), 95463E7) Recorded Bks.
Eric Truell is a star reporter at "The New York Mirror" when a maverick CIA agent begins passing him sensitive information. As Eric follows up the leaks, he is suddenly no longer sure of his role.

Firm. John Grisham. Read by Scott Brick. 2002. 88.00 (978-0-7366-8859-8(5)); audio compact disk 112.00 (978-0-7366-8860-4(9)) Books on Tape.

Firm. abr. ed. John Grisham. Read by D. W. Moffett. (Running Time: 3 hrs.). (John Grisham Ser.). (ENG.). 2003. audio compact disk 14.99 (978-0-7393-0375-7(9), Random AudioBks) Pub: Random Audio Pubg. Dist(s): Random

Firm, unabr. ed. John Grisham. Narrated by George Guidall. 10 cass. (Running Time: 14 hrs. 45 mins.). 1991. 85.00 (978-1-55690-177-5(1), 91227E7) Recorded Bks.
Mitchell McDeere's base salary at Bendini, Lambert & Locke was $80,000 the first year, accompanied by tempting benefits. But a number of suspicious deaths & some unnerving encounters with the FBI start McDeere wondering just how much the Firm might exact from its unsuspecting young associates in the end.

Firm Body. Eldon Taylor. 1 cass. (Running Time: 62 min.). (Inner Talk Ser.). 1997. 16.95 incl. script. (978-1-55978-128-2(9), 5363D) Progress Aware Res.
Soundtrack - Synthesized Moments with underlying subliminal affirmations.

Firm Body: Babbling Brook. Eldon Taylor. 1 cass. 16.95 (978-1-55978-750-5(3), 5363F) Progress Aware Res.

Firm Resolve. 1 cass. (Running Time: 1 hr.). 1981. 7.95 (978-1-58638-537-8(2)) Nilgiri Pr.
Harness determination in order to reach higher goals.

First Adams. (Presidency Ser.). 10.00 Esstee Audios.
Discusses the development of the two party system & the struggles within the administration.

First Adventure. Vanda N. McIntyre. 3 CDs. (Running Time: 3 hrs.). (Star Trek Ser.: 25). 2005. 25.00 (978-1-58807-888-9(4)) Am Pubng Inc.
James T. Kirk is the youngest man to be promoted to the rank of captain in Federation history. His crew consists of a first officer who finds him impetuous; a chief engineer who finds him arrogant; a chief medical officer who finds him trifling; and a helmsman who wants a transfer. But the young crew, quickly put aside their differences when a monstrous starship appears on their nascent flight path.

First Aid & CPR. 3rd ed. National Safety Council (NSC) Staff. (C). 1999. audio compact disk 244.95 (978-0-7637-0887-0(9), 0887-9) Jones Bartlett.

First Amendment Guarantee of Religious Liberty Resolved. The Wall of Separation Between Church & State Is in Jeopardy: Proceedings of the 45th Annual Convention National Association of Evangelicals Buffalo, New York. Read by John H. Buchanan & Forest D. Montgomery. 1 cass. (Running Time: 60 min.). 1987. 4.00 (303) Nat Assn Evan.

First American: The Life & Times of Benjamin Franklin. unabr. ed. H. W. Brands. Narrated by Nelson Runger. 25 cass. (Running Time: 36 hrs. 45 mins.). 2001. 149.00 (978-0-7887-8870-3(1)) Recorded Bks.
The first complete biography of Ben Franklin in over 60 years.

First American in Space, Pt. 2. 1 cass. (Running Time: 58 min.). 14.95 (18843) MMI Corp.
Commander Shephard returns to a hero's welcome. Covers summary of flight, press briefing, greeting by Pres. Kennedy & more.

First American in Space, Vol. 3. 1 cass. (Running Time: 55 min.). 14.95 (18845); 14.95 (18845) MMI Corp.
Discusses flight of Freedom 7, news conference in Washington with many humorous sidelights.

First American in Space: Alan Shephard's Historic Flight. (Running Time: 59 min.). 14.95 (18841) MMI Corp.
On-the-spot account of this flight, America's first attempt to send a man into space.

First among Equals. abr. ed. Jeffrey Archer. Narrated by Michael York. 2000. 15.95 (978-0-00-104764-8(7)) Pub: HarpC GBR. Dist(s): Trafalgar

First among Equals. abr. rev. ed. Jeffrey Archer. Read by Martin Jarvis. 3 CDs. (Running Time: 3 hrs. 45 mins. 0 sec.). (ENG.). 2004. audio compact disk 14.95 (978-1-59397-410-7(8)) Pub: Macmill Audio. Dist(s): Macmillan

First among Equals. unabr. ed. Jeffrey Archer. Read by Tony Britton. 10 cass. (Running Time: 15 hrs.). 2001. 69.95 (978-0-7451-6806-7(X), CAB 327) Pub: Chivers Audio Bks GBR. Dist(s): AudioGO
In the 1960's, four ambitious members of Parliament take their seats at Westminster. Over three decades, they share the turbulent race for power. As they become caught up in a dramatic game for the highest stakes of all, only one of them will reach the ultimate goal: the office of Prime Minister.

First among Equals. unabr. ed. Jeffrey Archer. Narrated by Simon Prebble. 11 cass. (Running Time: 15 hrs. 30 mins.). 1994. 91.00 (978-0-7887-0058-3(8), 94257E7) Recorded Bks.
Four young men of differing social backgrounds all share the dream of becoming Prime Minister of England, only one will be successful.

First Among Sequels. Jasper Fforde. Narrated by Emily Gray. (Running Time: 45900 sec.). (Thursday Next Ser.: No. 5). 2007. audio compact disk 34.99 (978-1-4281-5664-7(X)) Recorded Bks.

First Among Sequels. unabr. ed. Jasper Fforde. Narrated by Emily Gray. 11 CDs. (Running Time: 12 hrs. 45 mins.). (Thursday Next Ser.: No. 5). 2007. audio compact disk 123.75 (978-1-4281-5667-8(4)) Recorded Bks.

First Anniversary Celebration: Logos September 13, 1998. Ben Young. 1998. 4.95 (978-0-7417-6098-2(3), B0098) Win Walk.

First Annual TAT Symposium. unabr. ed. Tapas Fleming. Read by Stephanie Douglas et al. 4 cass. (Running Time: 4 hrs.). 2001. 40.00 (978-1-893412-08-8(3)) TAT Intl.
Experienced TAT practitioners describe how they use TAT in their healing practice to obtain better results.

First Arabic Handwriting Workbook. rev. ed. Lily Sayegh. (ARA.). 1999. pap. bk. 14.95 (978-0-86685-748-2(6)) Intl Bk Ctr.

First Assistant: A Continuing Tale from Behind the Hollywood Curtain. unabr. ed. Clare Naylor & Mimi Hare. Read by Shelly Frasier. (Running Time: 11 hrs. 0 mins. 0 sec.). (ENG.). 2006. audio compact disk 34.99 (978-1-4001-0284-6(7)); audio compact disk 24.99 (978-1-4001-5284-1(4)); audio compact disk 69.99 (978-1-4001-3284-3(3)) Pub: Tantor Media. Dist(s): IngramPubServ

First Be Then You Can Relate: On Love, Self-Knowing & Relationships. 1 cass. 1996. 12.95 (978-0-88050-002-9(6), SA-304) Oshos.

First Billion. unabr. ed. Christopher Reich. Read by James Daniels. 10 cass. (Running Time: 15 hrs.). 2002. 34.95 (978-1-59086-276-6(7), 1590862767, BAU); 97.25 (978-1-59086-277-3(5), 1590862775, Unabridge Lib Edns) Brilliance Audio.
The last thing Jett Gavallan would call himself was a hero. A fighter pilot in the Gulf War, he found himself in the wrong place at the wrong time. Now Gavallan lives with the memory and the blame for what happened. But he is determined not to let it destroy him. He has created Black Jet Securities, an international financial consulting firm, in order to use his expertise to create enough wealth to do some good in the world. It's a noble goal, but Black Jet Securities' latest and most ambitious deal could destroy everything that Gavallan has worked so hard to build. On the surface it seems like a perfectly lucrative and legitimate business venture: bring a Russian high-tech company to the U.S. Stock Exchange. But the company's owner turns out to be one of the most ruthless bosses in the Russian Mafia whose plans go far beyond the Stock Exchange. Suddenly Gavallan is dead center in a world where hired armies fight a secret war, alliances are made if the price is right - and deals are sealed with murder. To outwit Kirov and his assassins, Gavallan will need to summon all the raw courage and cunning of the combat pilot he once was and this time he cannot afford to fail.

First Billion. unabr. ed. Christopher Reich. Read by James Daniels. (Running Time: 15 hrs.). 2004. 39.25 (978-1-59335-369-8(3), 1593353693, Brlnc Audio MP3 Lib) Brilliance Audio.

First Billion. unabr. ed. Christopher Reich. Read by James Daniels. (Running Time: 15 hrs.). 2004. 39.25 (978-1-59710-290-2(3), 1597102903, BADLE); 24.95 (978-1-59710-291-9(1), 1597102911, BAD) Brilliance Audio.

First Billion. unabr. ed. Christopher Reich. Read by James Daniels. (Running Time: 54000 sec.). 2007. audio compact disk 117.25 (978-1-4233-3372-2(1), 9781423333722, BriAudCD Unabrid); audio compact disk 38.95 (978-1-4233-3371-5(3), 9781423333715, Bril Audio CD Unabri) Brilliance Audio.

First Billion. unabr. ed. Christopher Reich. Read by James Daniels. (Running Time: 15 hrs.). 2004. 24.95 (978-1-59335-039-0(2), 1593350392) Soulmate Audio Bks.

First Billion Is the Hardest: Reflections on a Life of Comebacks & America's Energy Future. abr. ed. T. Boone Pickens. Read by Arthur Morey. (ENG.). 2008. audio compact disk 29.95 (978-0-7393-6656-1(4), Random AudioBks) Pub: Random Audio Pubg. Dist(s): Random

First Bird Call. Bill Harley. 2008. audio compact disk 15.00 (978-1-878126-54-2(7)) Round Riv Prodns.

First Blood. unabr. ed. David Morrell. Read by Scott Brick. 6 cass. (Running Time: 9 hrs.). 2002. 32.00 (978-1-59040-228-3(6)) Audio Lit.
First came the man: a young wanderer in a fatigue coat and long hair. Then came the legend, as John Rambo sprang up from the pages of this book to take his place in the American cultural landscape. This remarkable novel pits a young Vietnam veteran against a small town cop who doesn't know whom he's dealing with, or how far Rambo will take him into a life-and-death struggle through the woods, hills and caves of rural Kentucky.

***First Blood.** unabr. ed. David Morrell. (Running Time: 12 hrs.). 2011. audio compact disk 19.99 (978-1-4558-0041-4(4), 9781455800414, Bril Audio CD Unabri) Brilliance Audio.

First Blood: The Story of Fort Sumter. unabr. collector's ed. W. A. Swanberg. Read by Jonathan Reese. 9 cass. (Running Time: 13 hrs. 30 min.). 1995. 72.00 (978-0-7366-3006-1(6), 3692) Books on Tape.
A dramatic chain of events triggers the Civil War's first battle & sets the tone for the nation's most tragic bloodletting. You'll think you were there.

First Book of Baritone Bass Solos, Vol. 2, Pt. 2. Ed. by Joan Frey Boytim. Created by Hal Leonard Corporation Staff. (Classroom Methods). (ENG.). 1997. audio compact disk 18.99 (978-0-7935-8646-2(1), 0793586461) H Leonard.

First Book of Baritone/Bass Solos. Ed. by Joan Frey Boytim. Compiled by G. Schirmer. Created by Hal Leonard Corporation Staff. 2 CDs. (Classroom Methods). (ENG.). 1997. audio compact disk 18.99 (978-0-7935-8642-4(9), 0793586429) H Leonard.

First Book of Broadway Solos: Baritone/Bass. Joan Frey Boytim. 2005. audio compact disk 12.95 (978-0-634-09496-5(3), 0634094963) H Leonard.

First Book of Broadway Solos: Mezzo-Soprano. Joan Frey Boytim. 2005. audio compact disk 12.95 (978-0-634-09494-1(7), 0634094947) H Leonard.

First Book of Broadway Solos: Soprano. Joan Frey Boytim. 2005. audio compact disk 12.95 (978-0-634-09493-4(9), 0634094939) H Leonard.

First Book of Broadway Solos: Tenor. Joan Frey Boytim. 2005. audio compact disk 12.95 (978-0-634-09495-8(5), 0634094955) H Leonard.

First Book of Mezzo-Soprano/Alto Solos. Ed. by Joan Frey Boytim. Compiled by G. Schirmer. Created by Hal Leonard Corporation Staff. (Classroom Methods). (ENG.). 1997. audio compact disk 18.99 (978-0-7935-8640-0(2), 0793586402) H Leonard.

First Book of Mezzo-Soprano/Alto Solos, Vol. 2, Pt. 2. Ed. by Joan Frey Boytim. Created by Hal Leonard Corporation Staff. 2 CDs. (Classroom Methods). (ENG.). 1997. audio compact disk 18.99 (978-0-7935-8644-8(5), 0793586445) H Leonard.

First Book of Soprano Solos. Ed. by Joan Frey Boytim. Compiled by G. Schirmer. Created by Hal Leonard Corporation Staff. 2 CDs. (Classroom Methods). (ENG.). 1997. audio compact disk 18.99 (978-0-7935-8638-7(0), 0793586380) H Leonard.

First Book of Soprano Solos, Vol. 2, Pt. 2. Ed. by Joan Frey Boytim. Created by Hal Leonard Corporation Staff. 2 CDs. (Classroom Methods). (ENG.). 1997. audio compact disk 18.99 (978-0-7935-8643-1(7), 0793586437) H Leonard.

First Book of Tenor Solos, Set. Ed. by Joan Frey Boytim. Compiled by G. Schirmer. Created by Hal Leonard Corporation Staff. 2 CDs. (Classroom Methods). (ENG.). 1997. audio compact disk 18.99 (978-0-7935-8641-7(0), 0793586410) H Leonard.

First Book of Tenor Solos, Vol. 2, Pt. 2. John Keene. Ed. by Joan Frey Boytim. Contrib. by G. Schirmer. Created by Hal Leonard Corporation Staff. (Classroom Methods). (ENG.). 1997. audio compact disk 18.99 (978-0-7935-8645-5(3), 0793586453) H Leonard.

First Boxer. unabr. ed. Christopher Ride. Read by Tyler Coppin. (Running Time: 17 hrs. 22 mins.). 2009. audio compact disk 118.95 (978-1-74214-520-4(5), 9781742145204) Pub: Bolinda Pubng AUS. Dist(s): Bolinda Pub Inc

***First Boxer.** unabr. ed. Christopher Ride. Read by Tyler Coppin. (Running Time: 17 hrs. 22 mins.). 2010. 43.95 (978-1-74214-594-5(9), 9781742145945) Pub: Bolinda Pubng AUS. Dist(s): Bolinda Pub Inc

First Boy. unabr. ed. Gary D. Schmidt. Read by Jesse Berns. 3 cass. (Running Time: 4 hrs. 47 mins.). (J). 2005. 30.00 (978-0-307-28342-9(9), BksonTape); audio compact disk 32.30 (978-0-307-28343-6(7), BksonTape) Pub: Random Audio Pubg. Dist(s): NetLibrary CO

First Break. 2 mono. cass. (Running Time: 20 min.). 1984. 12.95 FIDM Prods.
Guide for the teenager seeking part-time employment. The program presents four basic topics: your personal profile, getting ready for your job interview, how to complete your job application & how to keep your job.

First, Break All the Rules: What the World's Greatest Managers Do Differently. Marcus Buckingham & Curt Coffman. Narrated by Rick Rohan. 6 cass. (Running Time: 8 hrs. 30 mins.). 64.00 (978-0-7887-9454-4(X)); audio compact disk 69.00 (978-1-4025-2915-3(5)) Recorded Bks.

First, Break All the Rules: What the World's Greatest Managers Do Differently. abr. ed. Marcus Buckingham & Curt Coffman. Read by Marcus Buckingham. 3 CDs. (Running Time: 30 hrs. 0 mins. 0 sec.). (ENG.). 2000. audio compact disk 25.00 (978-0-7435-1011-0(9), Sound Ideas) Pub: S&S Audio. Dist(s): S and S Inc
Powered by the largest management study ever conducted, this reveals how the world's greatest managers challenge all the rules of conventional wisdom.

First Came the Law. Contrib. by Once Nothing. Prod. by Jamie King. 2008. audio compact disk 13.99 (978-5-557-50592-5(X)) Solid State MO.

First Cases: First Appearances of Classic Private Eyes. unabr. ed. Short Stories. Robert J. Randisi. 8 cass. (Running Time: 10 hrs. 30 mins.). 1996. 70.00 (978-0-7887-0462-8(1), 94655E7) Recorded Bks.
This collection reveals how 15 of America's favorite sleuths got started & how they've changed over the years. Introduces unforgettable characters such as Linda Barnes' Carlotta Carlyle, Lawrence Block's Matthew Scudder, Loren D. Estleman's Amos Walker, Sara Paretsky's V.I. Warshawski & Sue Grafton's Kinsey Milhone.

First Cases: First Appearances of Classic Private Eyes, Vol. 1. unabr. ed. Robert J. Randisi. Read by Richard Poe. 8 cass. (Running Time: 10 hrs. 30 min.). 1996. Rental 16.50 (94655) Recorded Bks.
Brings mystery buffs this collection of short stories to reveal how 15 of America's sleuths got started.

First Cases: The Private Eyes. unabr. ed. Read by Edward Lewis. 8 cass. (Running Time: 8 hrs.). 1997. 48.00 (978-0-7366-3605-6(6), 4259) Books on Tape.
Robert Randisi has assembled the first appearances in print of all the biggest names: Lawrence Block's Matthew Scudder, Sue Grafton's Kinsey Millhone, Sara Paretsky's V.I. Warshawski, Marcia Muller's Sharon McCone & Randisi's own Miles Jacoby, along with 10 others.

First Casualty. unabr. ed. Ben Elton. Read by Glen McCready. 9 cass. (Running Time: 12 hrs. 30 mins.). (Isis Cassettes Ser.). (J). 2006. 84.95 (978-0-7531-3514-3(0)); audio compact disk 99.95 (978-0-7531-2502-1(1)) Pub: ISIS Lrg Prnt GBR. Dist(s): Ulverscroft US

First Casualty. unabr. collector's ed. Phillip Knightey. Read by James Cunningham. 14 cass. (Running Time: 21 hrs.). 1978. 112.00 (978-0-7366-0118-4(X), 1125) Books on Tape.
An account of war correspondence in action for the past 120 years. It suggests that our attitudes toward history are molded by what we read in wartime & that what we read too often bears little resemblence to reality.

***First Certificate Trainer Audio CDs (3)** Peter May. (Running Time: 3 hrs. 44 mins.). (Authored Practice Tests Ser.). (ENG.). 2010. audio compact disk 50.00 (978-0-521-13547-4(8)) Cambridge U Pr.

First Chakra: Key to Loyalty, Discipline, & Focus. 1 cass. (Running Time: 90 min.). (Chakras Ser.). 9.95 (83M) Crystal Clarity.
Includes: The earth element in human consciousness; inflexibility & materialism as negative aspects of the earth element; the role of the chakras in our spiritual evolution; the relationship between astrology & the chakras.

First Christmas Tree: A Story of the Forest. Based on a story by Henry Van Dyke. (ENG.). 2007. 5.00 (978-1-60339-105-4(3)); audio compact disk 5.00 (978-1-60339-106-1(1)) Listenr Digest.

First Christmas Tree: The Mystery of the Seventh Wiseman. Eugene E. Whitworth. Read by Eugene E. Whitworth. Prod. by Arnold Gold & Terence Docherty. 2 cass. (Running Time: 2 hrs.). 1996. 19.95 Set. (978-0-944155-08-0(1)) Grt Western Univ.

First Church. Derek Prince. 1 cass. 5.95 (095) Derek Prince.
The church described in the New Testament remains our God-given standard. What was it like? What was its secret?.

First Class: English for Tourism. Trish Stott & Roger Holt. 1991. 17.50 (978-0-19-437604-4(4)) OUP.

First Class Passenger see Anton Chekhov

First-Class Temperament Pt. 1: The Emergence of Franklin D. Roosevelt. unabr. ed. Geoffrey Ward. Read by Grover Gardner. 11 cass. (Running Time: 16 hrs. 30 mins.). 1991. 88.00 (2798-A) Books on Tape.
The personal story of FDR, how he found within himself the strength to live with polio & then go on to master the two great crisis of our century.

First-Class Temperament Pt. 1 & 2: The Emergence of Franklin D. Roosevelt. unabr. ed. Geoffrey Ward. Read by Grover Gardner. 20 cass. (Running Time: 30 hrs.). 1991. 160.00 (978-0-7366-1980-6(1), 2798-A/B) Books on Tape.
This vivid, unsentimental account of FDR's emergence as a political force follows the author's portrait of the young Roosevelt in "Before the Trumpet." Beginning in 1905, with the Roosevelts' European honeymoon, "A First Class Temperament" traces FDR's career as a lawyer & follows him into politics. (He began as a New York State Senator, then moved to Washington during WW I where he served as Assistant Secretary of the Navy.) It also tells the personal story of FDR, how he found within himself the strength to live with polio & then went on to master the two great crises of our century...the Depression & WW II.

First-Class Temperament Pt. 2: The Emergence of Franklin D. Roosevelt. unabr. ed. Geoffrey Ward. Read by Grover Gardner. 9 cass. (Running Time: 13 hrs. 30 mins.). 1991. 72.00 (2798-B) Books on Tape.
The personal story of FDR, how he found within himself the strength to live with polio & then go on to master the two great crisis of our century.

***First Collier.** unabr. ed. Kathryn Lasky. Read by Pamela Garelick. (Running Time: 4.5 hrs. NaN mins.). (Guardians of Ga'Hoole Ser.). (ENG.). 2011. 19.95 (978-1-4417-7998-4(1)); 34.95 (978-1-4417-7995-3(7)); audio compact disk 19.95 (978-1-4417-7997-7(3)); audio compact disk 49.00 (978-1-4417-7996-0(5)) Blckstn Audio.

First Comes Love. Douglas Brinley & Mark Ogletree. 5 cass. 2004. 19.95 (978-1-57734-989-1(X)); audio compact disk 19.95 (978-1-59156-022-7(5)) Covenant Comms.

First Comes Love. Scott Hahn. 4 CDs. (Running Time: 4 hrs.). 2001. audio compact disk 26.95 (978-1-57058-370-4(6), 5618-cd) St Joseph Communs.
True to form, in First Comes Love, Dr. Hahn dives into the Gospels to show how "family terminology", words like brother, sister, mother, father and home, dominate the words of Our Lord and the writings of His first followers. It is these words that truly illuminate the central ideas of the Catholic Faith. As you explore such concepts as the fatherhood of God, the marriage of the Church to Christ, and the all-encompassing role of the Holy Spirit, Dr. Hahn will deepen your understanding of the Sacraments and teach you how to create a family life in the image of the Trinity. In chapter after chapter he demonstrates the ways in which the analogy of the family applies to every aspect of our Catholic Faith and its many practices, from the role of "Father" embodied by the ancient Patriarchs and contemporary parish priests, to the comfort and guidance offered by our brothers and sisters who comprise the Communion of Saints, to the nurturing embrace of the Blessed Virgin Mary, mother of all Christians.Real Life Examples Through real-life examples (both humorous and compassionate) and quotations drawn from the Scriptures and the Fathers and Doctors of the Church, Dr. Hahn makes it clear that no matter what sort of family you may come from, no matter what sort of "dysfunction" you may have experienced, you can find a family in the Church. Whether you're a recent convert, or a life-long Catholic, First Comes Love will provide you with an invitation to discover for yourself, a true home in the divine life of the Trinity. Order your copy (book, tapes or CDs) today and remember when you order either audio version of First Comes Love, you'll experience Scott Hahn's important theological work in a new way that goes beyond the words on the page. For the first time, the best selling author actually reads his latest book for you!IN THIS SERIES YOU WILL LEARN:The Oldest Story in the World Adam's Family Values The First Christian Revolution Life in the Trinity At Home in the Church The Sacred Hearth The Tribal Belt The Son also Rises God is One But Not Solitary Making Sense of the Story The Cross is a Trinitarian Event An Upward Fall There's No Place Like Rome And more!.

***First Comes Love, Then Comes Money.** unabr. ed. Bethany Palmer & Scott Palmer. Read by John Bedford Lloyd & Tory Wood. (ENG.). 2009. (978-0-06-187483-3(3), Harper Audio); (978-0-06-187481-9(7), Harper Audio) HarperCollins Pubs.

First Comes Marriage. unabr. ed. Mary Balogh. Read by Anne Flosnik. 1 MP3-CD. (Running Time: 11 hrs.). (Huxtable Quintet: Bk. 1). 2009. 39.97 (978-1-4233-8891-3(7), 9781423388913, Brinc Audio MP3 Lib); 39.97 (978-1-4233-8893-7(3), 9781423388937, BADLE); 24.99 (978-1-4233-8890-6(9), 9781423388906, Brilliance MP3); 24.99 (978-1-4233-8892-0(5), 9781423388920, BAD); audio compact disk 98.97 (978-1-4233-8889-0(5), 9781423388890, BriAudCD Unabrid); audio compact disk 28.99 (978-1-4233-8888-3(7), 9781423388883) Brilliance Audio.

***First Comes Marriage: A Selection from Married in Seattle.** unabr. ed. Debbie Macomber. Read by Angela Dawe. (Running Time: 4 hrs.). 2010. 14.99 (978-1-4418-6300-3(1), 9781441863003, BAD); 14.99 (978-1-4418-6299-0(4), 9781441862990, Brilliance MP3); audio compact disk 14.99 (978-1-4418-6298-3(6), 9781441862983, Bril Audio CD Unabri) Brilliance Audio.

First Command. Philip McCutchan. Read by Christopher Scott. 6 cass. (James Ogilvie Ser.). 2006. 54.95 (978-1-84283-756-6(7)) Pub: ISIS Lrg Prnt GBR. Dist(s): Ulverscroft US

First Commandment. abr. ed. Brad Thor. Read by Armand Schultz. (Running Time: 6 hrs. 0 mins. 0 sec.). (ENG.). 2009. audio compact disk 14.99 (978-0-7435-8298-8(5)) Pub: S&S Audio. Dist(s): S and S Inc

First Contact. J. M. Dillard. (Star Trek Ser.). 2004. 10.95 (978-0-7435-4635-5(0)) Pub: S&S Audio. Dist(s): S and S Inc

First Contact; Exploration Team. unabr. ed. Murray Leinster. 2 cass. (Running Time: 3 hrs.). (Science Fiction Library). 1997. pap. bk. 16.95 (978-1-55656-195-5(4)) Pub: Dercum Audio. Dist(s): APG
"Exploration Team" earned the Hugo award in the novella category. It chronicles a giant company's illegal colonization of a planet populated by a savage race of predators. In "First Contact" a solitary Earth ship & a solitary alien meet for the first time in a nebula remote from the home planet of each.

First Corinthians. (LifeLight Bible Studies: Course 20). 13.95 Set. (20-2552) Concordia.

First Counsel. Brad Meltzer. 2004. audio compact disk 24.98 (978-1-58621-124-0(2)) Hachet Audio.

First Counsel. abr. ed. Brad Meltzer. 2004. 24.98 (978-1-58621-123-3(4)) Hachet Audio.

First Counsel. abr. ed. Brad Meltzer. Read by D. B. Sweeney. (ENG.). 2005. 14.98 (978-1-59483-432-5(6)) Pub: Hachet Audio. Dist(s): HachBkGrp

First Counsel. unabr. ed. Brad Meltzer. 2004. 44.98 (978-1-58621-125-7(0)) Hachet Audio.

First Counsel. unabr. ed. Brad Meltzer. Read by Scott Brick. (ENG.). 2005. 16.98 (978-1-59483-433-2(4)) Pub: Hachet Audio. Dist(s): HachBkGrp

First Counsel. unabr. ed. Brad Meltzer. Read by Scott Brick. (Running Time: 15 hrs.). (ENG.). 2009. 69.98 (978-1-60788-097-4(0)) Pub: Hachet Audio. Dist(s): HachBkGrp

First Counsel. unabr. ed. Brad Meltzer. Narrated by Scott Brick. 11 cass. (Running Time: 15 hrs.). 2001. 88.00 (978-0-7887-4980-3(3), 96487E7) Recorded Bks.
Events happen at the White House that pull a young lawyer into a nightmare & his reputation & his life are at stake.

First Daughter. abr. ed. Eric Lustbader. Narrated by Richard Ferrone. (Running Time: 7 hrs. 0 mins. 0 sec.). (ENG.). 2008. audio compact disk 29.95 (978-1-4272-0534-6(5)) Pub: Macmill Audio. Dist(s): Macmillan

First Daughter. unabr. ed. Eric Lustbader. Narrated by Richard Ferrone. (Running Time: 12 hrs. 30 mins.). 2008. 59.95 (978-0-7927-5600-2(2), Chivers Sound Lib); audio compact disk 99.95 (978-0-7927-5499-2(9), Chivers Sound Lib) AudioGO.

First Daughter. unabr. ed. Eric Lustbader. Narrated by Richard Ferrone. 10 CDs. (Running Time: 12 hrs. 30 mins. 0 sec.). (ENG.). 2008. audio compact disk 39.95 (978-1-4272-0518-6(3)) Pub: Macmill Audio. Dist(s): Macmillan

First Day - the Armies Meet. 1 cass. Dramatization. (Voices of Gettysburg Ser.). 1991. 12.95 Heritage.
Dramatized reconstructions of Civil War-era voices.

First Day of School & Halloween Feud. Perf. by Fanny Brice. 1 cass. (Running Time: 60 min.). Dramatization. (Baby Snooks Ser.). 1946. 6.00 Once Upon Rad.
Radio broadcasts - humor.

First Day on a Strange New Planet. Dan Yaccarino. Narrated by L. J. Ganser. 1 cass. (Running Time: 15 mins.). (gr. k up). 2001. 10.00 (978-0-7887-5357-2(6)) Recorded Bks.
Blast Off Boy is headed to the planet Meep as an exchange students. Includes an interview with the author.

First Days see Poetry & Voice of James Wright

First Decade (Nineteen Eighty-Three - Nineteen Ninety-Three) Perf. by Michael W. Smith. 1 cass. 1993. audio compact disk Brentwood Music.
Showcasing the highlights of the first 10 years of a brilliant career, this gold-selling 15-song collection features the classics, Friends, Great is the Lord, Secret Ambition & 12 others.

First Degree. David Rosenfelt. Read by Grover Gardner. (Running Time: 28800 sec.). 2008. audio compact disk 29.95 (978-1-59316-127-9(1)) Listen & Live.

First Dog: And Other Chippewa-Cree Stories. unabr. ed. Read by Ron Evans. 1 cass. (Running Time: 60 min.). (Storytime Ser.). (J). (ps-5). 11.00 Parabola Bks.
Four stories, including Round-as-a-Ball Boy, The Girl Who Loved Colors.

***First Drop of Crimson.** unabr. ed. Jeaniene Frost. Read by Tavia Gilbert. (Running Time: 10 hrs.). (Night Huntress World Ser.). 2010. 29.95 (978-1-4417-6843-8(2)); 65.95 (978-1-4417-6840-7(8)); audio compact disk 32.95 (978-1-4417-6842-1(4)); audio compact disk 90.00 (978-1-4417-6841-4(6)) Blckstn Audio.

***First Drop of Rain: 0.** Leslie Parrott. (Running Time: 3 hrs. 8 mins. 0 sec.). (ENG.). 2009. 16.99 (978-0-310-30239-1(0)) Zondervan.

First Eagle. abr. ed. Tony Hillerman. Read by George Guidall. . (Running Time:). (Joe Leaphorn & Jim Chee Novel Ser.). 2005. audio compact disk 14.95 (978-0-06-076364-0(7)) HarperCollins Pubs.

First Eagle. unabr. ed. Tony Hillerman. Narrated by George Guidall. 7 CDs. (Running Time: 7 hrs. 30 mins.). (Joe Leaphorn & Jim Chee Novel Ser.). 1999. audio compact disk 58.00 (978-0-7887-3445-8(8), C1051E7) Recorded Bks.
As bubonic plague sweeps the Navajo reservation, someone is murdering the researchers who are struggling to control the disease. Lieutenant Chee & retired police officer Leaphorn must find the killer before it is too late.

First Eagle. unabr. ed. Tony Hillerman. Narrated by George Guidall. 6 cass. (Running Time: 7 hrs. 30 mins.). (Joe Leaphorn & Jim Chee Novel Ser.). 1998. 56.00 (978-0-7887-2160-1(7), 95456E7) Recorded Bks.

First Elizabeth. unabr. ed. Carolly Erickson. Narrated by Nelson Runger. 12 cass. (Running Time: 18 hrs. 30 mins.). 1986. 97.00 (978-1-55690-178-2(X), 86520E7) Recorded Bks.
Elizabeth was not just Queen, she was ruler. The life & history of Queen Elizabeth the First of England.

First Epistle of Clement to the Corinthians: Unabridged audio e-book CD. Narrated by Gerard VanHalsema. (ENG.). 2008. 14.00 (978-1-931848-12-1(2)) Christ Class Ethereal.

First Fair Wind, Set. unabr. ed. Agnes Short. Read by Pamela Donald. 8 cass. (Running Time: 10 hrs. 35 min.). 1999. 83.95 (978-1-85903-277-0(X)) Pub: Magna Story GBR. Dist(s): Ulverscroft US
The warm-hearted Christie family take in orphan Rachel & raise her as their own. Like the other fishermen Rachel gathers bait, wades into the icy sea at dawn to launch the boat, carries creels to market & dreams that one day she might have a house & family of her own. James, the handsome eldest Christie's son, longs for a different way of life, & dreams of building a fine ship that will carry him to trading ports around the world. But his ambitions bring him to a near disastrous conflict with a local merchant.

First Family. abr. ed. David Baldacci. Read by Ron McLarty. (Running Time: 6 hrs.). (Sean King & Michelle Maxwell Ser.: No. 4). (ENG.). 2009. 14.98 (978-1-60024-546-6(3)) Pub: Hachet Audio. Dist(s): HachBkGrp

First Family. abr. ed. David Baldacci. Read by Ron McLarty. (Running Time: 6 hrs.). (ENG.). 2010. audio compact disk 14.98 (978-1-60024-836-8(5)) Pub: Hachet Audio. Dist(s): HachBkGrp

First Family. unabr. ed. David Baldacci. Read by Ron McLarty. (Running Time: 14 hrs. 30 mins.). (Sean King & Michelle Maxwell Ser.: No. 4). (ENG.). 2009. 26.98 (978-1-60024-549-7(8)); audio compact disk 39.98 (978-1-60024-548-0(X)) Pub: Hachet Audio. Dist(s): HachBkGrp

***First Family: Abigail & John Adams.** unabr. ed. Joseph J. Ellis. Read by Kimberly Farr. 2010. audio compact disk 40.00 (978-0-7393-6874-9(5), Random AudioBks) Pub: Random Audio Pubg. Dist(s): Random

First Family: Terror, Extortion, Revenge, Murder, & the Birth of the American Mafia. unabr. ed. Mike Dash. Narrated by Lloyd James. (Running Time: 14 hrs. 0 mins. 0 sec.). (ENG.). 2009. 24.99 (978-1-4001-6364-9(1)); audio compact disk 75.99 (978-1-4001-4364-1(0)); audio compact disk 37.99 (978-1-4001-1364-4(4)) Pub: Tantor Media. Dist(s): IngramPubServ

First Few Words, Pt. I. unabr. ed. Gilbert Highet. 1 cass. (Running Time: 30 min.). (Gilbert Highet Ser.). 9.95 (23330) J Norton Pubs.
The first words of a book: why they are so important, & the last words of a book: why they are also so important.

First Few Words & the Final Words (audio CD) Gilbert Highet. (ENG.). 2006. audio compact disk 9.95 (978-1-57970-446-9(8), Audio-For) J Norton Pubs.

First Finds: A Yorkshire Childhood. unabr. ed. June Barraclough. Read by Anne Dover. 4 cass. (Running Time: 5 hrs. 16 mins.). (Isis Audio Reminiscence Ser.). (J). 2002. 44.95 (978-0-7531-1169-7(1)) Pub: ISIS Lrg Prnt GBR. Dist(s): Ulverscroft US
The exceptional story of Jill Brook's childhood in Yorkshire between two world wars. Firmly rooted in the West Riding of Yorkshire, this memorable story is an account of what it was like to grow up in the 1930s and 1940s.

First Five: The Genesis of Marques Vickers Visual Arts Career (1996-2001) Marques Vickers. 2002. cd-rom & audio compact disk 19.95 (978-0-9706530-4-8(2)) Marquis Pubng.

First Forest. John Gile. 1 cass. (Running Time: 14 min.). (J). (gr. 3 up). 1991. 10.95 (978-0-910941-04-4(1)) JGC.

First Four Years. unabr. ed. Laura Ingalls Wilder. Read by Cherry Jones. (Running Time: 10800 sec.). (Little House the Laura Years Ser.). (J). (gr. 4-7). 2006. 22.00 (978-0-06-056510-7(1)); audio compact disk 25.95 (978-0-06-056509-1(8)) HarperCollins Pubs.

First Fruits. Perf. by Byzantine Choir Staff. 1 cass., 1 CD. (ENG.). 11.95 (002818); audio compact disk 17.95 CD. (002817) Conciliar Pr.
Byzantine chants include Vespers & Matins, as well as Troparia & Kontakia for various feast days.

First Grade Stinks! Mary Ann Rodman. 1 cass. (Running Time: 11 mins.). (J). (ps-1). 2008. bk. 27.95 (978-0-8045-6970-5(3)); bk. 29.95 (978-0-8045-4195-4(7)) Spoken Arts.

First Grade Takes a Test. Miriam Cohen. 1 CD. (Running Time: 10 mins.). (J). (gr. k-2). 2008. bk. 29.95 (978-0-8045-4187-9(6)); bk. 27.95 (978-0-8045-6964-4(9)) Spoken Arts.
When the first grade class is given a test, they are troubled - for their proffered answers aren't exactly right. Fortunately, their teacher knows the things that are really important can't be graded. This is a great story to remind people that being smartest on a test is not the only thing that matters in a classroom.

***First Grave on the Right.** unabr. ed. Darynda Jones. (Running Time: 9 hrs. 30 mins. 0 sec.). (ENG.). 2011. audio compact disk 39.99 (978-1-4272-1130-9(2)) Pub: Macmill Audio. Dist(s): Macmillan

First Guitar Riffs. Music Sales Corporation Staff & Arthur Dick. (First Guitar Ser.). 2004. audio compact disk 12.95 (978-0-7119-7223-0(0)) Pub: Music Sales. Dist(s): H Leonard

First Guitar Scales. Music Sales Corporation Staff & Andy Jones. 1 CD. (Running Time: 1 hr.). (First Guitar Ser.). 2004. audio compact disk 14.95 (978-0-7119-7224-7(9), AM954195) Pub: Music Sales. Dist(s): H Leonard

First Half. unabr. ed. Toni Lamond. Narrated by Toni Lamond. 6 cass. (Running Time: 9 hrs.). 2004. 48.00 (978-1-74030-531-0(0)) Pub: Bolinda Pubng AUS. Dist(s): Lndmrk Audiobks

First Hebrew Primer Companion. Perf. by Reuven Trabin & Debby Graudenz. (HEB & ENG.). (C). 2004. audio compact disk 39.95 (978-0-939144-44-0(1)) EKS Pub Co.

First Hebrew Reader (Companion CD) (HEB & ENG.). 2002. audio compact disk 12.95 (978-0-939144-40-2(9)) EKS Pub Co.

First Heroes: The Extraordinary Story of the Doolittle Raid, America's First World War II Victory. Craig Nelson. Narrated by Raymond Todd. (Running Time: 19 hrs.). 2002. 50.95 (978-1-59912-660-9(5)) Iofy Corp.

First Heroes: The Extraordinary Story of the Doolittle Raid, America's First World War II Victory. unabr. ed. Craig Nelson. Read by Raymond Todd. 13 cass. (Running Time: 19 hrs.). 2003. 85.95 (978-0-7861-2342-1(7), 3044); audio compact disk 120.00 (978-0-7861-9342-4(5), 3044) Blckstn Audio.
Immediately after Japan's December 7, 1941, attack on Pearl Harbor, President Roosevelt sought to restore the honor of the United States with a dramatic act of vengeance: a retaliatory bombing raid on Tokyo itself. In those early days of World War II, America was ill prepared for any sort of warfare. But FDR was not to be dissuaded, and at his bidding a squadron of scarcely trained army fliers, led by the famous daredevil Jimmy Doolittle, set forth on what everyone regarded as a suicide mission.

First Horseman. unabr. ed. John Case. Read by Dick Hill. (Running Time: 10 hrs.). 2009. 24.99 (978-1-4233-9086-2(5), 9781423390862, Brilliance MP3); 39.97 (978-1-4233-9087-9(3), 9781423390879, Brinc Audio MP3 Lib); 24.99 (978-1-4233-9088-6(1), 9781423390886, BAD); 39.97 (978-1-4233-9089-3(X), 9781423390893, BADLE) Brilliance Audio.

First Human: The Race to Discover Our Earliest Ancestors. unabr. ed. Ann Gibbons. Read by Renée Raudman. 8 CDs. (Running Time: 10 hrs. 0 mins. 0 sec.). (ENG.). 2006. audio compact disk 34.99 (978-1-4001-0238-9(3)); audio compact disk 69.99 (978-1-4001-3238-6(X)); audio compact disk 24.99 (978-1-4001-5238-4(0)) Pub: Tantor Media. Dist(s): IngramPubServ

First Impact. Rod Ellis et al. 2002. (978-962-00-1157-3(0)) Longman.

First Impressions. abr. ed. Jude Deveraux. Read by Jennifer Wiltsie. 2005. 15.95 (978-0-7435-5468-8(X)) Pub: S&S Audio. Dist(s): S and S Inc

First Impressions. abr. ed. Jude Deveraux. Read by Jennifer Wiltsie. (Running Time: 4 hrs. 30 mins. 0 sec.). (ENG.). 2007. audio compact disk 14.99 (978-0-7435-6955-2(5)) Pub: S&S Audio. Dist(s): S and S Inc

First Impressions. unabr. ed. Nora Roberts. Read by Teri Clark Linden. (Running Time: 7 hrs.). 2010. audio compact disk 24.99 (978-1-4418-3813-1(9), 9781441838131, Bril Audio CD Unabri) Brilliance Audio.

***First Impressions.** unabr. ed. Nora Roberts. Read by Teri Clark Linden. (Running Time: 7 hrs.). 2010. 24.99 (978-1-4418-3815-5(5), 9781441838155, Brilliance MP3); 39.97 (978-1-4418-3816-2(3), 9781441838162, Brlnc Audio MP3 Lib); 39.97 (978-1-4418-3817-9(1), 9781441838179, BADLE); audio compact disk 79.97 (978-1-4418-3814-8(7), 9781441838148, BriAudCD Unabrid) Brilliance Audio.

First Impressions: Successfully Presenting Yourself. Janet G. Elsea. 1 cass. (Running Time: 1 hr.). (Listen & Learn U. S. A.! Ser.). 8.95 (978-0-88684-043-3(0)) Listen USA.
Outlines skills that are critical for business & personal success & for communicating first impressions that last.

First in His Class: The Biography of Bill Clinton. unabr. ed. David Maraniss. Read by Jeff Riggenbach. 16 cass. (Running Time: 23 hrs. 30 mins.). 1996. 99.95 (978-0-7861-0915-9(7), 1721) Blckstn Audio.
Who exactly is Bill Clinton & why was he, of all the brilliant & ambitious men in his generation, the first in his class to reach the White House? What explains the contradictory effects of his personality & character? Beginning with Clinton's youth & ending with his 1991 announcement that he would run for the nation's highest office, Maraniss presents a stunning, eye-opening portrait. He strips away the myths, many of them of Clinton's own making & gets beyond the narrow dimensions of a political world in which, increasingly, superficial judgments are being made.

First into Nagasaki: The Censored Eyewitness Dispatches on Post-Atomic Japan & Its Prisoners of War. unabr. ed. George Weller. Read by Stefan Rudnicki. Frwd. by Walter Cronkite. (Running Time: 41400 sec.). 2006. 29.95 (978-0-7861-4715-1(6)); audio compact disk 29.95 (978-0-7861-6581-0(2)) Blckstn Audio.

First into Nagasaki: The Censored Eyewitness Dispatches on Post-Atomic Japan & Its Prisoners of War. unabr. ed. George Weller. Read by Stefan Rudnicki. (Running Time: 14 mins.). (YA). 2007. audio compact disk 99.00 (978-0-7861-6130-0(2)) Blckstn Audio.

First into Nagasaki: The Censored Eyewitness Dispatches on Post-Atomic Japan & Its Prisoners of War. unabr. ed. George Weller. Read by Stefan Rudnicki. Ed. by Anthony Weller. Frwd. by Walter Cronkite. (Running Time: 41400 sec.). 2007. 79.95 (978-0-7861-4841-7(1)) Blckstn Audio.

First into Nagasaki: The Censored Eyewitness Dispatches on Post-Atomic Japan & Its Prisoners of War. unabr. ed. George Weller. Read by Stefan Rudnicki. Frwd. by Walter Cronkite. (Running Time: 41400 sec.). 2007. audio compact disk 29.95 (978-0-7861-7324-2(6)) Blckstn Audio.

First Jams: Banjo. Lee (Drew) Andrews. (ENG.). 2009. pap. bk. 14.95 (978-0-7866-7841-9(0)) Mel Bay.

First Jams: Dobro. Lee (Drew) Andrews. (ENG.). 2009. pap. bk. 14.99 (978-0-7866-7835-8(6)) Mel Bay.

***First Jams: Fiddle Book/CD Set.** Lee (Drew) Andrews. (ENG.). 2010. pap. bk. 14.99 (978-0-7866-8240-9(X)) Mel Bay.

First Jams: Flatpick Guitar. Lee (Drew) Andrews. (ENG.). 2009. pap. bk. 14.95 (978-0-7866-7843-3(7)) Mel Bay.

First Jams: Mandolin. Lee (Drew) Andrews. (ENG.). 2009. pap. bk. 14.95 (978-0-7866-7842-6(9)) Mel Bay.

First Jams: Mountain Dulcimer. Lee Drew Andrew. (ENG.). 2009. pap. bk. 14.99 (978-0-7866-7862-4(3)) Mel Bay.

First Jams: Ukulele. Lee (Drew) Andrews. (ENG.). 2009. pap. bk. 14.99 (978-0-7866-7844-0(5)) Mel Bay.

First Jesuit. Mary Purcell. 8 cass. 32.95 (733) Ignatius Pr.
Life of St. Ignatius Loyola, founder of the Jesuits.

First King of Shannara. abr. ed. Terry Brooks. (Shannara Ser.). 2003. audio compact disk 14.99 (978-0-7393-0432-7(1), Listening Lib) Pub: Random Audio Pubg. Dist(s): Random

First Kiss. Jonathan London. Read by John McDonough. 1 cass. (Running Time: 15 mins.). (YA). 2000. pap. bk. 97.30 (978-0-7887-4169-2(1), 47101); pap. bk. 97.30 (978-0-7887-4170-8(5), 47101) Recorded Bks.
The week before Valentine's Day a new girl joins Froggy's class. Frogilina is the cutest girl that Froggy's ever seen. Just looking at her makes his insides feel all wiggly. It must be love. But when she gives him a big kiss, smack, on the lips, he's not so sure.

First Kiss. unabr. ed. Jonathan London. Narrated by John McDonough. 1 cass. (Running Time: 15 mins.). (ps up). 2000. 10.00 (978-0-7887-4020-6(2), 96141E7) Recorded Bks.

First Knight Set: A Novel. abr. ed. Elizabeth Chadwick. Read by Ben Cross. Contrib. by William Nicholson. 2 cass. (Running Time: 3 hrs.). 1995. 17.00 (978-1-56876-041-4(8), 393155) Soundlines Ent.
In an epic retelling of the timeless & tragic love triangle, three lives converge in the golden city of Camelot. With no ties, no enemies & no fear, Lancelot is the perfect warrior. He comes to Camelot not for glory or knighthood, although he finds both, but for the love of one woman he cannot have, Lady Guinevere of Leonesse.

First Ladies: An Intimate Group Portrait of White House Wives. unabr. ed. Margaret Truman. Narrated by Barbara Caruso. 9 cass. (Running Time: 13 hrs.). 1996. 78.00 (978-0-7887-0614-1(4), 94794E7) Recorded Bks.
Paints a fascinating group portrait of the special women who have held "The World's Second Toughest Job".

First Lady. collector's ed. Susan Elizabeth Phillips. Read by Anna Fields. 8 cass. (Running Time: 12 hrs.). 2000. 64.00 (978-0-7366-5056-4(3)) Books on Tape.
The beautiful young widow of the President of the United States thought she was free of the White House, but circumstances have forced her back into the role of First Lady. She's made up her mind to escape, if only for a few days, so she can live the life of an ordinary person. An entire nations is searching for her but the First Lady is in the last place anyone would think to look, in the company of a seductive stranger whose charm & good looks are awakening the forgotten woman within. With two adorable little orphaned girls along for the ride, they're heading out across the heartland, chasing their own American Dream, on a wild journey of love, adventure & glorious rebirth.

First Lady. collector's ed. Susan Elizabeth Phillips. Read by Anna Fields. 9 CDs. (Running Time: 10 hrs. 36 min.). 2000. audio compact disk 72.00 (978-0-7366-5227-8(2)) Books on Tape.

First Lady. unabr. ed. Susan Elizabeth Phillips. Read by Anna Fields. 8 cass. (Running Time: 12 hrs.). 2000. 29.95 (978-0-7366-4763-2(5)) Books on Tape.

First Lady of Song: Ella Fitzgerald for the Record. unabr. ed. Geoffrey M. Fidelman. Read by Geoffrey M. Fidelman. 9 cass. (Running Time: 13 hrs. 30 min.). 1999. 62.95 (2413) Blckstn Audio.
Ella Fitzgerald, the artist who has been called a national treasure, has captivated an international audience for more than fifty years. A celebration of her life & work that includes memories of duets with Frank Sinatra, harmonizing with Dinah Shore, & solo triumphs at Carnegie Hall.

First Lady of Song: Ella Fitzgerald for the Record. unabr. ed. Geoffrey M. Fidelman. Read by Geoffrey M. Fidelman. 9 cass. (Running Time: 13 hrs.). 2001. 62.95 (978-0-7861-1584-6(X), 2413) Blckstn Audio.

First Law. abr. ed. John Lescroart. Read by Robert Lawrence. (Running Time: 6 hrs.). (Dismas Hardy Ser.: No. 9). 2006. audio compact disk 16.99 (978-1-4233-1948-1(6), 9781423319481, BCD Value Price) Brilliance Audio.
John Lescroart - author of the New York Times bestseller The Oath and a "master" of the modern thriller (People)- returns with a spellbinding novel about events that force defense attorney Dismas Hardy and Lieutenant Abe Glitsky outside the law and into a fight for their lives. Prodded by his father, Glitsky asks the new homicide lieutenant about the case, but the brass tells him in no uncertain terms to stay out of it. Guided by the Patrol Special - a private police force supervised by the SFPD that is a holdover from San Francisco's vigilante past - the police have already targeted their prime suspect: John Holiday, proprietor of a run-down local bar, and a friend and client of Dismas Hardy. While Dismas Hardy has built a solid legal practice and a happy family, John Holiday has not followed the same path. Despite this, Hardy has remained Holiday's attorney and confidant, and with Glitsky's help, Hardy finds ample reason to question Holiday's guilt. Hardy's case falls on hostile ears, however, and to avoid arrest, Holiday turns fugitive. The police now believe three things: that Hardy is a liar protecting Holiday, that Holiday is a cold-blooded killer, and that Glitsky is a bad cop on the wrong side of the law. As the suspense reaches fever pitch, Hardy, Glitsky, and even their families are caught in the crossfire and directly threatened. The police won't protect them. The justice system won't defend them. Shunned within the corridors of power, and increasingly isolated at every turn, Hardy and Glitsky face their darkest hour. For when the law forsakes them, they must look to another, more primal law in order to survive.

First Law. unabr. ed. John Lescroart. Read by Robert Lawrence. 9 cass. (Running Time: 13 hrs.). (Dismas Hardy Ser.: No. 9). 2003. 92.25 (978-1-59086-370-1(4), 1590863704); 34.95 (978-1-59086-369-5(0), 1590863690); audio compact disk 107.25 (978-1-59086-373-2(9), 1590863739); audio compact disk 42.95 (978-1-59086-372-5(0), 1590863720) Brilliance Audio.

First Law. unabr. ed. John Lescroart. Read by Robert Lawrence. 9 CDs. (Running Time: 13 hrs.). (Dismas Hardy Ser.: No. 9). 2004. 39.25 (978-1-59335-446-6(0), 1593354460, Brlnc Audio MP3 Lib) Brilliance Audio.

First Law. unabr. ed. John Lescroart. Read by Robert Lawrence. (Running Time: 13 hrs.). (Dismas Hardy Ser.: No. 9). 2004. 39.25 (978-1-59710-293-3(8), 1597102938, BADLE); 24.95 (978-1-59710-292-6(X), 159710292X, BAD) Brilliance Audio.

First Law. unabr. ed. John Lescroart. Read by Robert Lawrence. (Running Time: 13 hrs.). (Dismas Hardy Ser.: No. 9). 2004. 24.95 (978-1-59335-085-7(6), 1593350856) Soulmate Audio Bks.

First Lessons Accordion. Gary Dahl. 2002. bk. 7.95 (978-0-7866-6249-4(2), 99927bcd) Mel Bay.

First Lessons Banjo. Jack Hatfield. 2002. audio compact disk 7.95 (978-0-7866-2093-7(5)) Mel Bay.

First Lessons Bass. Jay Farmer. 2002. audio compact disk 7.95 (978-0-7866-6252-4(2)) Mel Bay.

First Lessons Beginning Guitar: Learning Chords/Playng Songs. William Bay. 2002. audio compact disk 7.95 (978-0-7866-5868-8(1)) Mel Bay.

First Lessons Beginning Guitar: Learning Notes/Playing Solos. William Bay. 2002. audio compact disk 7.95 (978-0-7866-6250-0(6)) Mel Bay.

First Lessons Blues Guitar. Corey Christiansen & Mike Christiansen. 2002. audio compact disk 7.95 (978-0-7866-2797-4(2)) Mel Bay.

First Lessons Drumset. Frank Briggs. 2002. audio compact disk 7.95 (978-0-7866-1827-9(2)) Mel Bay.

First Lessons Flatpicking Guitar. Joe Carr. 2002. audio compact disk 7.95 (978-0-7866-6254-8(9)) Mel Bay.

First Lessons Flute. Mizzy Mccaskill. 2002. audio compact disk 7.95 (978-0-7866-1828-6(0)) Mel Bay.

First Lessons Mandolin. Dix Bruce. 2002. bk. 7.95 (978-0-7866-6253-1(0), 99945BCD) Mel Bay.

First Lessons Piano. Per Danielsson. 2002. audio compact disk 7.95 (978-0-7866-6251-7(4)) Mel Bay.

First Lessons Rock Guitar. Mike Christiansen & Corey Christiansen. 2002. audio compact disk 7.95 (978-0-7866-6144-2(5)) Mel Bay.

First Lessons Violin. Craig Duncan. 2002. audio compact disk 7.95 (978-0-7866-1805-7(1)) Mel Bay.

First Letter & Insurance Fraud. Perf. by Alan Ladd. 1 cass. (Running Time: 60 min.). Dramatization. (Box Thirteen Ser.). 1948. 6.00 Once Upon Rad.
Radio broadcasts - mystery & suspense.

First Light. 1 cass. (Running Time: 43 min.). (Elements of Nature Ser.). 1994. audio compact disk 15.95 CD. (2804, Creativ Pub) Quayside.
Sunrise & awakening of the natural world. Delicate harmonies. Bruce Kurnow explores the shifting moods of dawn's early light.

First Light. 1 cass. (Running Time: 43 min.). (Elements of Nature Ser.). 1994. 9.95 (2802, NrthWrd Bks) TandN Child.

***First Light.** unabr. ed. Rebecca Stead. Narrated by David Ackroyd & Coleen Marlo. 6 CDs. (Running Time: 7 hrs. 6 mins.). (YA). (gr. 5-8). 2010. audio compact disk 50.00 (978-0-307-71067-3(X), Listening Lib) Pub: Random Audio Pubg. Dist(s): Random

First Light. unabr. ed. Rebecca Stead. Read by David Ackroyd & Coleen Marlo. (ENG.). (J). 2010. audio compact disk 34.00 (978-0-307-71065-9(3), Listening Lib) Pub: Random Audio Pubg. Dist(s): Random

First Light. unabr. ed. Bodie Thoene & Brock Thoene. Narrated by Sean Barrett. (Running Time: 15 hrs. 44 mins. 40 sec.). (A. D. Chronicles Ser.). (ENG.). 2008. audio compact disk 49.99 (978-1-59859-500-0(8)) Oasis Audio.

First Light. unabr. collector's ed. Peter Ackroyd. Read by David Case. 9 cass. (Running Time: 13 hrs. 30 min.). 1997. 72.00 (978-0-7366-4032-9(0), 4531) Books on Tape.
A neolithic grave is discovered, & a group of eccentrics descends on the site to discuss its economic implications.

First Line of Defense Against Adversity. Instructed by Manly P. Hall. 8.95 (978-0-89314-119-6(4), C840923) Philos Res.

First Lines from the Classics of the Future by Inventive Imposters. Ed. by Clive Priddle. Intro. by Geoff Nunberg. (ENG.). 2009. 9.95 (978-0-7867-4783-2(8)) Pub: PublicAffairs NY. Dist(s): Perseus Bks Grp

First Load Weaponry: Awesome Tools of Self-Defense. Campbell Sid. cass. & video 169.95 Gong Prods.
A complete programmed course in the use of common everyday items for practical self-defense.

First Lord's Fury. unabr. ed. Jim Butcher. Read by Kate Reading. (Running Time: 18 hrs.). Bk. 6. (ENG.). (gr. 12 up). 2009. audio compact disk 49.95 (978-0-14-314520-2(7), PengAudBks) Penguin Grp USA.

First Love. Scott Oliver. 1 cass. (Running Time: 1 hr.). 2000. 11.99 (978-0-9706112-4-6(2), Oligus Music); audio compact disk 17.99 (978-0-9706112-5-3(0), Oligus Music) Pt of Grace Ent.

First Love & Forever, Set. Anita Stansfield. 2 cass. 11.98 (978-1-55503-722-2(4), 079401) Covenant Comms.
A touching contemporary novel.

First Love, Second Chances, Set. Anita Stansfield. 2 cass. 11.98 (978-1-55503-789-5(5), 07001088) Covenant Comms.
A romantic sequel to "First Love & Forever".

First Man: The Life of Neil A. Armstrong. abr. ed. James R. Hansen. Read by Boyd Gaines. 2005. 21.95 (978-0-7435-5454-1(X)) Pub: S&S Audio. Dist(s): S and S Inc

First Man Called (Philip) John 1:43-46. Ed Young. 1985. 4.95 (978-0-7417-1469-5(8), 469) Win Walk.

First Man in Rome. Colleen McCullough. Read by Donada Peters. 12 cass. (Running Time: 18 hrs.). (Masters of Rome Ser.: No. 1). 1990. 96.00 (2688-B) Books on Tape.

First Man in Rome. Colleen McCullough. (Masters of Rome Ser.: No. 1). 2000. 15.99 (978-0-7435-0547-5(6), Audioworks) S&S Audio.

First Man in Rome. Colleen McCullough. (Masters of Rome Ser.: No. 1). 2004. 15.95 (978-0-7435-4896-0(5)) Pub: S&S Audio. Dist(s): S and S Inc

First Man in Rome. unabr. ed. Colleen McCullough. Read by Donada Peters. 12 cass. (Running Time: 18 hrs.). (Masters of Rome Ser.: No. 1). 1990. 96.00 (978-0-7366-1856-4(2), 2688A) Books on Tape.
The first of a projected five-volume series, The First Man in Rome is Colleen McCullough's most ambitious project. Set in 110 B.C., historically accurate & psychologically true, it pits two powerful men against each other in a struggle for supremacy within the state, literally to become "First Man in Rome." Each represents a type. Marius, middle-aged estate owner, shrewd & self-made, feels confident of success. Sulla, a youthful aristocrat, open to pleasure & indulgence, feels contempt for his adversary. Their contest is classic, as is the outcome, which seems pre-ordained.

First Man in Rome. unabr. ed. Colleen McCullough. Narrated by Jill Tanner. 30 cass. (Running Time: 40 hrs. 30 min.). (Masters of Rome Ser.: No. 1). 2004. 99.75 (978-1-4025-3561-1(9)) Recorded Bks.

First Man in Rome. unabr. collector's ed. Colleen McCullough. Narrated by Jill Tanner. 30 cass. (Running Time: 42 hrs. 30 min.). (Masters of Rome Ser.: No. 1). 2004. 99.95 (978-1-4025-3562-8(7), RG303) Recorded Bks.
Carries listeners into the pageantry and passion, politics and intrigue of ancient Rome. Cunning and ambition were prized in this vast and powerful empire, but what would it take to win its highest honor? To be First Man in Rome?.

First Man You Meet. unabr. ed. Debbie Macomber. Read by Kate Rudd. (Running Time: 2 hrs.). 2009. 14.99 (978-1-4418-4795-9(2), 9781441847959, Brilliance MP3); 14.99 (978-1-4418-4796-6(0), 9781441847966, BAD); audio compact disk 14.99 (978-1-4418-4794-2(4), 9781441847942, Bril Audio CD Unabri) Brilliance Audio.

First Meetings: In the Enderverse. unabr. rev. ed. Orson Scott Card. Read by Amanda Karr et al. 5 CDs. (Running Time: 5 hrs. 15 mins. 0 sec.). (ENG.). 2004. audio compact disk 29.95 (978-1-59397-472-5(8)) Pub: Macmill Audio. Dist(s): Macmillan

First Men in the Moon. H. G. Wells. Read by Anais 9000. 2008. 27.95 (978-1-60112-159-2(8)) Babblebooks.

First Men in the Moon. H. G. Wells. 2 cass. (Running Time: 2 hrs.). 2001. 17.95 (ALEN009); audio compact disk 19.95 (ALENO10) Lodestone Catalog.
Apollo 11 may have taken us to the moon in 1969, but H. G. Wells took us there first in 1902!.

First Men in the Moon. aut. ed. H. G. Wells. 2 cass. (Running Time: 2 hrs.). 2001. 75.00 (ALEN009a); audio compact disk 75.00 (ALEN10a) Lodestone Catalog.

First Moon: Passage to Womanhood. unabr. ed. Helynna Brooke & Ann Short. Read by Helynna Brooke & Ann Short. Perf. by Michael Fleming. 1 cass. (Running Time: 1 hr.). (YA). 1997. 14.95 (978-0-9660811-1-4(0), 73, First Moon) Brooke Co.
Spoken instructions, information & music for a ceremony celebrating the first menses of a young woman.

First Mountain Man 1. William W. Johnstone. (Running Time: 18000 sec.). (First Mountain Man Ser.: No. 1). 2007. audio compact disk 19.99 (978-1-59950-385-1(9)) GraphicAudio.

First Mountain Man 10: Preacher's Justice. Based on a novel by William W. Johnstone. (First Mountain Man Ser.: No. 10). 2008. audio compact disk 19.99 (978-1-59950-469-8(3)) GraphicAudio.

First Mountain Man 11: Preacher's Journey. William W. Johnstone. (First Mountain Man Ser.: No. 11). 2008. audio compact disk 19.99 (978-1-59950-493-3(6)) GraphicAudio.

First Mountain Man 12: Preacher's Fortune. William W. Johnstone. (First Mountain Man Ser.: No. 12). 2008. audio compact disk 19.99 (978-1-59950-502-2(9)) GraphicAudio.

First Mountain Man 13: Preacher's Quest. William W. Johnstone. (First Mountain Man Ser.: No. 13). 2008. audio compact disk 19.99 (978-1-59950-508-4(8)) GraphicAudio.

First Mountain Man 14: Preacher's Showdown. William W. Johnstone. (First Mountain Man Ser.: No. 14). 2009. audio compact disk 19.99 (978-1-59950-516-9(9)) GraphicAudio.

First Mountain Man 15: Preacher's Pursuit. William W. Johnstone. (First Mountain Man Ser.: No. 15). 2009. audio compact disk 19.99 (978-1-59950-534-3(7)) GraphicAudio.

First Mountain Man 16: Preacher's Fire. Based on a novel by William W. Johnstone. (First Mountain Man Ser.: No. 16). 2010. audio compact disk 19.99 (978-1-59950-642-5(4)) GraphicAudio.

***First Mountain Man 17: Preacher's Assault.** William W. Johnstone. 2011. audio compact disk 19.99 (978-1-59950-739-2(0)) GraphicAudio.

First Mountain Man 2: Blood on the Divide. abr. ed. William W. Johnstone. Read by Full Cast Production Staff. Directed By Bob Supan. (Running Time: 21600 sec.). (First Mountain Man Ser.: No. 2). 2007. audio compact disk 19.99 (978-1-59950-395-0(6)) GraphicAudio.

First Mountain Man 3: Absaroka Ambush. William W. Johnstone. (Running Time: 21600 sec.). (First Mountain Man Ser.: No. 3). 2008. audio compact disk 19.99 (978-1-59950-403-2(0)) GraphicAudio.

First Mountain Man 4: Forty Guns West. William W. Johnstone. (Running Time: 18000 sec.). (First Mountain Man Ser.: No. 4). 2008. audio compact disk 19.99 (978-1-59950-412-4(X)) GraphicAudio.

First Mountain Man 5: Cheyenne Challenge. William W. Johnstone. (First Mountain Man Ser.: No. 5). 2008. audio compact disk 19.99 (978-1-59950-420-9(0)) GraphicAudio.

First Mountain Man 6: Preacher & the Mt. Caesar. Directed By Bob Supan. Contrib. by Mort Shelby et al. (Running Time: 25200 sec.). (First Mountain Man Ser.). 2008. audio compact disk 19.99 (978-1-59950-440-7(5)) GraphicAudio.

First Mountain Man 7: Blackfoot Messiah. Based on a novel by William W. Johnstone. (First Mountain Man Ser.: No. 7). 2008. audio compact disk 19.99 (978-1-59950-447-6(2)) GraphicAudio.

First Mountain Man 8: Preacher. Based on a novel by William W. Johnstone. (First Mountain Man Ser.: No. 8). 2008. audio compact disk 19.99 (978-1-59950-454-4(5)) GraphicAudio.

First Mountain Man 9: Preacher's Peace. Based on a novel by William W. Johnstone. (First Mountain Man Ser.: No. 9). 2008. audio compact disk 19.99 (978-1-59950-461-2(8)) GraphicAudio.

First New Age Artist to Go Gold. Ray Lynch. 1 cass. (Running Time: 20 min.). (Roy Tuckman Interview Ser.). 9.00 (A0457-89) Sound Photosyn.
Twenty minutes on Something's Happening!.

First Nighter Program, Set. Perf. by Olan Soule et al. 2 cass. (Running Time: 2 hrs.). vinyl bd. 10.95 (978-1-57816-052-5(9), FN2401) Audio File.
Includes: "Three Who Faced Death" (10-25-40) An amnesia victim is followed by a criminal who insists he is her husband & she killed someone. "A Writer in the Family" (1-29-48) A writer meets a highway surveyor in a romantic comedy about hidden identity. "There's Something in the Air" (3-11-48) A romantic farce about some very special talents. "Drink for the Damned" (2-5-48) Romantic drama set in the time of King James' Court.

First Nighter Program: Chinese Gong & Wolf with Sheepskin. 1 cass. (Running Time: 1 hr.). 2001. 6.98 (1984) Radio Spirits.

First Noel. 1 CD. audio compact disk 10.98 (978-1-57908-390-8(0), 1663) Platinm Enter.

First Noel. Contrib. by Joe E. Parks. 1992. 39.98 (978-0-00-504498-8(7), 75607881); 11.98 (978-0-00-531215-5(9), 75607882) Pub: Brentwood Music. Dist(s): H Leonard

First Noel. Contrib. by Jaci Velasquez. Prod. by Chris Harris. (Studio Ser.). 2006. audio compact disk 9.98 (978-5-558-30758-0(7), Word Records) Word Enter.

First Offense, unabr. ed. Nancy Taylor Rosenberg. Narrated by C. J. Critt. 10 cass. (Running Time: 13 hrs. 30 mins.). 1995. 85.00 (978-0-7887-0149-8(5), 94371E7) Recorded Bks.
For probation officer Ann Carlisle, the terror begins when a bullet rips through her shoulder on her way home from a drug dealer's parole hearing. As Ann searches for clues to her assailant's identity, she exposes startling evidence that links the drug dealer, her own terror & a serial rape case she is investigating. The police claim they have the rapist in custody, but now Ann suspects he is still free.

First Parish. Helen Cannam. 5 cass. (Running Time: 7 hrs.). (Soundings Ser.). (J). 2004. 49.95 (978-1-84283-897-6(0)) Pub: ISIS Lrg Prnt GBR. Dist(s): Ulverscroft US

First Part Last. Angela Johnson. 2004. audio compact disk 20.40 (978-1-4000-9115-7(2), Listening Lib) Pub: Random Audio Pubg. Dist(s): NetLibrary CO

First Part Last. unabr. ed. Angela Johnson. 1 cass. (Running Time: 1 hr. 30 min.). 2004. 15.00 (978-1-4000-9066-2(0)) Pub: Random Audio Pubg. Dist(s): Random
Bobby is a typical urban New York City teenager - impulsive, eager, restless. For his sixteenth birthday he cuts school with his two best buddies, grabs a couple of slices at his favorite pizza joint, catches a flick at a nearby multiplex, and gets some news from his girlfriend, Nia, that changes his life forever: He's going to be a father. Suddenly things like school and house parties and fun times with friends are replaced by visits to Nia's pediatrician and countless social workers who all say that the only way for Nia and Bobby to lead a normal life is to put their baby up for adoption. Then tragedy strikes Nia, and Bobby finds himself in the role of single, teenage father. Because his child - their child - is all that remains of his lost love. With powerful language and keen insight, Johnson tells the story of a young man's struggle to figure out what the "right thing" is and then to do it. The result is a gripping portrayal of single teenage parenthood from the point of view of a youth on the threshold of becoming a man.

First Part Last. unabr. ed. Angela Johnson. Read by Khalipa Oldjohn. 2 CDs. (Running Time: 1 hr. 45 mins.). (ENG.). (J). 2004. audio compact disk 19.99 (978-1-4000-9065-5(2), Listening Lib) Pub: Random Audio Pubg. Dist(s): Random

First Partner: Hillary Rodham Clinton. abr. ed. Joyce Milton. Read by Sandra Burr. (Running Time: 6 hrs.). 2009. 39.97 (978-1-4233-7166-3(6), 9781423371663, BADLE); 39.97 (978-1-4233-7164-9(X), 9781423371649, Brlnc Audio MP3 Lib); 24.99 (978-1-4233-7163-2(1), 9781423371632, Brilliance MP3); 24.99 (978-1-4233-7165-6(8), 9781423371656, BAD) Brilliance Audio.

First Patient. abr. ed. Michael Palmer. Read by Phil Gigante. (Running Time: 6 hrs.). 2008. audio compact disk 14.99 (978-1-4233-0657-3(0), 9781423306573, BCD Value Price) Brilliance Audio.

First Patient. unabr. ed. Read by Phil Gigante. Ed. by Michael Palmer. (Running Time: 12 hrs.). 2008. 24.95 (978-1-59737-068-4(1), 9781597370684, BAD) Brilliance Audio.

First Patient. unabr. ed. Michael Palmer. Read by Phil Gigante. (Running Time: 12 hrs.). 2008. 39.25 (978-1-59737-069-1(X), 9781597370691, BADLE); 97.25 (978-1-59737-062-2(2), 9781597370622, BrilAudUnabridg); audio compact disk 102.25 (978-1-59737-065-3(7), 9781597370653, BriAudCD Unabrid); audio compact disk 39.25 (978-1-59737-067-7(3), 9781597370677, Brlnc Audio MP3 Lib); audio compact disk 24.95 (978-1-59737-066-0(5), 9781597370660, Brilliance MP3); audio compact disk 38.95 (978-1-59737-064-6(9), 9781597370646, Bril Audio CD Unabri) Brilliance Audio.
Please enter a Synopsis.

First Paul: Reclaiming the Radical Visionary Behind the Church's Conservative Icon. unabr. ed. Marcus J. Borg & John Dominic Crossan. Narrated by Mel Foster. (Running Time: 8 hrs. 0 mins. 0 sec.). (ENG.). 2009. audio compact disk 59.99 (978-1-4001-4256-9(3)); audio compact disk 29.99 (978-1-4001-1256-2(7)); audio compact disk 19.99 (978-1-4001-6256-7(4)) Pub: Tantor Media. Dist(s): IngramPubServ

First Person Rural & Second Person Rural. unabr. collector's ed. Noel Perrin. Read by Bob Erickson. 8 cass. (Running Time: 8 hrs.). 1984. 48.00 (978-0-7366-0462-8(6), 1434) Books on Tape.
Noel Perrin is a teacher, writer & farmer. Because he was transplanted from New York, Perrin has something to tell city folks about the transition & does it in a fresh way.

First Principles of Philosophy. Manly P. Hall. 5 cass. (Running Time: 150 min.). 1999. 40.00 Set. (978-0-89314-120-2(8)) Philos Res.
Includes: "The Four Aspects of Metaphysics;" "Logic & Ethics;" "Psychology & Epistemology;" "Esthetics & Theurgy;" & "The Symbolism of the Ten Bulls".

First Report on Arica Training in Chile. unabr. ed. John Lilly. 1 cass. (Running Time: 1 hr.). 1970. 11.00 (03907) Big Sur Tapes.
Speaks of his observations & experiences with Ichazo in Chile & relates particulars of the training. He also speaks of Ichazo's background & presence.

First Responder: Your First Response in Emergency Care. 2nd ed. AAOS Staff & National Safety Council (NSC) Staff. (C). 1999. tchr. ed. 123.75 (978-0-7637-1270-9(1), 1270-1) Jones Bartlett.

First Responder: Your First Response in Emergency Care. 4th rev. ed. David Schottke. Contrib. by American Academy of Orthopaedic Surgeons Staff. 2006. 69.95 (978-0-7637-4270-6(8)) Jones Bartlett.

First Rose. Megan McKenna. 2 cass. (Running Time: 2 hrs.). 1995. Set. (AA2926) Credence Commun.
McKenna told an audience at Loyola University in Chicago 5 stories - each story is about a facet of the Incarnation, each story reveals the mystery a little.

***First Rule.** Robert Crais. Contrib. by Robert Crais. (Joe Pike Ser.). 2010. 64.99 (978-1-4418-3783-7(3)) Find a World.

First Rule. abr. ed. Robert Crais. Read by Robert Crais. (Running Time: 5 hrs.). (Joe Pike Ser.). 2010. audio compact disk 24.99 (978-1-4233-7554-8(8), 9781423375548, BACD) Brilliance Audio.

First Rule. abr. ed. Robert Crais. Read by Robert Crais. (Running Time: 5 hrs.). (Joe Pike Ser.). 2010. audio compact disk 14.99 (978-1-4233-7555-5(6), 9781423375555, BCD Value Price) Brilliance Audio.

First Rule. unabr. ed. Robert Crais. Read by Robert Crais. (Running Time: 8 hrs.). (Joe Pike Ser.). 2010. 24.99 (978-1-4233-7550-0(5), 9781423375500, Brilliance MP3); 24.99 (978-1-4233-7552-4(1), 9781423375524, BAD); 39.97 (978-1-4233-7551-7(3), 9781423375517, Brlnc Audio MP3 Lib); 39.97 (978-1-4233-7553-1(X), 9781423375531, BADLE); audio compact disk 36.99 (978-1-4233-7548-7(3), 9781423375487, Bril Audio CD Unabri); audio compact disk 87.97 (978-1-4233-7549-4(1), 9781423375494, BriAudCD Unabrid) Brilliance Audio.

First Sacraments. unabr. ed. Inos Biffi. Read by Christopher Codol. 3 cass. (J). 14.95 set. (520) Ignatius Pr.
A companion tape to The Story of the Eucharist, this young person's introduction to the Sacraments is so enlightening & delightful that adults will not be able to resist listening in!.

First Salute. unabr. ed. Barbara W. Tuchman. Read by Grover Gardner. 9 cass. (Running Time: 13 hrs. 30 min.). 1989. 72.00 (978-0-7366-1638-6(1), 2493) Books on Tape.
On November 16, 1776, a ship carrying the flag of the Continental Congress entered port at St. Eustatius in the West Indies. Adhering to custom, the ship fired a salute & the guns of the fort returned their ritual response. But this act acknowledged the vessel & its country as legitimate. It was the first official salute to the United States of America. Taking this as her starting point, Barbara Tuchman illuminates the effect our revolution had not only on America & England, but Holland & France, & by extension, the entire Old World as well.

First Salute. unabr. ed. Barbara W. Tuchman. Narrated by Davina Porter. 10 cass. (Running Time: 14 hrs.). 1989. 85.00 (978-1-55690-179-9(8), 89700E7) Recorded Bks.
An account of the American Revolution from the first recognition of the flag of the Continental Congress by the Dutch on November 16, 1776.

First Salute: A View of the American Revolution. unabr. ed. Barbara W. Tuchman. Read by Nadia May. (Running Time: 13 hrs. 50 mins.). (ENG.). 2009. 29.95 (978-1-4332-1825-5(9)); 79.95 (978-1-4332-1821-7(6)); audio compact disk 99.00 (978-1-4332-1822-4(4)) Blckstn Audio.

First Sheriff. unabr. ed. Gary McCarthy. Read by Maynard Villers. 4 cass. (Running Time: 5 hrs. 30 min.). 1996. 26.95 (978-1-55686-725-5(5)) Books in Motion.
Glen Collins has the hands of a blacksmith, not a gunman. But he would have to be mighty quick to win the two things he wants most, the first sheriff's badge of San Diego, & Maria Silvas.

First Show & The First Date. Perf. by J. Carrol Naish. 1 cass. (Running Time: 60 min.). Dramatization. (Life with Luigi Ser.). 1949. 6.00 Once Upon Rad.
Radio broadcasts - humor.

First Sight. unabr. ed. Danielle Steel. (Running Time: 12 hrs.). 2012. 24.99 (978-1-4233-2054-8(9), 9781423320548, BAD); 39.97 (978-1-4233-2053-1(0), 9781423320531, Brlnc Audio MP3 Lib); 39.97 (978-1-4233-2055-5(7), 9781423320555, BADLE); audio compact disk 92.97 (978-1-4233-2051-7(4), 9781423320517, BriAudCD Unabrid) Brilliance Audio.

First Snowfall see Favorite American Poems

First Song see Gathering of Great Poetry for Children

First Stage Separation. unabr. ed. Robert A. Monroe. Read by Robert A. Monroe. (Running Time: 45 min.). (Gateway Experience - Freedom Ser.). 1983. 14.95 (978-1-56113-267-6(5)) Monroe Institute.
Learn to experience your consciousness apart from physical body.

First Step: Guitar for Kids. Matt Scharfglass. 2004. audio compact disk 9.95 (978-0-8256-1639-6(5), AM945296) Pub: Music Sales. Dist(s): H Leonard

First Step: Hitting Bottom: Gen. 3:1-3; Psalm 39:1-22. Ed Young. 1998. 4.95 (978-0-7417-2197-6(X), 1197) Win Walk.

First Step of Faith: Can You Really Trust God? Genesis 11:9-31. Ed Young. 1994. 4.95 (978-0-7417-2025-2(6), 1025) Win Walk.

First Step to Adopting a Child: Finding the Adoption Professional You Need. Hosted by Mardie Caldwell. (ENG.). 2008. audio compact disk 12.95 (978-1-935176-06-0(4)) Pub: Am Carrage Hse Pubng. Dist(s): STL Dist NA

First Step Toward Advanced Meditation. unabr. ed. Rama. Read by Rama. 1 cass. (Running Time: 30 mins.). 1990. 7.95 (978-0-89389-163-3(0), CS206MO) Himalayan Inst.
Swami Rama explains more subtle aspects of the inner world & presents a systematic method for the continuing meditator.

First Steps in English: English Language Teaching. (SPA.). 2005. stu. ed. (978-0-7428-0332-9(5)) CCLS Pubg Hse.

First Steps in Science: Measurements. Illa Podendorf. 1 cass. (First Steps in Science Ser.). (J). 12.00 (978-0-8442-6354-0(0), 6354-0, Natl Textbk Co) M-H Contemporary.
Helps children in grades 1-4 discover the process of scientific investigation. Part of the First Steps in Science Program.

First Steps in Synastry. Donna Van Toen. 1 cass. 8.95 (354) Am Fed Astrologers.

First Steps into the Light. Text by Linda N. Hackett. 2004. 19.95 (978-1-4276-3082-7(8)) AardGP.

First Steps to Excellence. Tom Peters. 1 cass. (Running Time: 60 min.). 8.95 (T25) Listen USA.
Learn how to break the barriers in the 8, priority areas of achieving corporate excellence by answering the question of corporate America, "How Do I Get Started?".

First Steps to Success in Outside Sales. Dave Kahle. 6 cass. 2000. ring bd. 275.00 (978-0-9647042-9-9(3)) DaCo.
How do you train your new salespeople? It's all about to change. Dave Kahle's new training kit, First Steps to Success in Outside Sales will: reduce the time you spend with new salespeoplemake them effective in half the timehelp them establish good habits before they have a change to develop bad ones I know, you have the best of intentions. But one thing leads to another, and you're never able to spend the kind of time of you'd like with your new salespeople. As a result, they are too often neglected and left to learn by doing. That's costly in a lot of ways: bad habits created, customers inappropriately handled, mistakes made, etc. Put an end to all of that with the training kit designed to free up your time and bring your new salespeople to profitability in half the time. Each kit contains 6 audio-cassettes and 161 pages of exercises, outlines, and worksheets designed to create good habits. Program Outline Lesson One: Introduction Lesson Two: Overview of the sales process. Understand that sales is a process, made up of several steps. Get an idea of what sales is all about. Recognizing the importance of relationships to sales. Lesson Three: Organizing your first few months. How to make the most of your first few months. Create relationships with inside people, learn product applications, become comfortable with your company's processes. Lesson Four: Making appointments How to prepare for voice mail, gatekeepers as well the decision-maker. Developing scripts. Positioning yourself before you call. Lesson Five: Making Your first sales call on a prospect - part 1 How to plan to create a relationship, gather information, educate the customer, and come to some agreement. Lesson Six: Making your first sales call on a prospect - part 2 Preparing an introduction, achieving rapport with the customer, understanding the customer. Lesson Seven: Making your first sales call on a prospect - part 3 Preparing a presentation. How to match your products/services to your customers' needs. Structuring a powerful offer. How to present your proposal in an attractive way. Lesson Eight: Making your first sales call on a prospect - part 4 Closing the sale, preparing to overcome objections, arriving at an agreement for the next step. Lesson Nine: Developing account strategies Categorizing the situation you find, developing effective strategies for every situation. Lesson Ten: Expanding the business with customers A.) How to handle new customers as well as inactive customers. B.) Finding additional opportunities. Lesson Eleven: Managing your territory. Creating goals for your key activities, working your territory effectively, planning each day, week and month. Lesson Twelve: Managing Yourself Working with integrity, maintaining a set of ethics, overcoming adversity and rejection.

First Strike. unabr. ed. Eric Nylund. Narrated by Todd McLaren. 10 CDs. (Running Time: 12 hrs. 0 mins. 0 sec.). (Halo Ser.). (ENG.). 2008. audio compact disk 69.99 (978-1-4001-3114-3(6)) Pub: Tantor Media. Dist(s): IngramPubServ

First Strike. unabr. ed. Eric Nylund. Read by Todd McLaren. Narrated by Todd McLaren. 1 MP3-CD. (Running Time: 12 hrs. 0 mins. 0 sec.). (Halo Ser.). (ENG.). 2008. 19.99 (978-1-4001-5114-1(7)); audio compact disk 34.99 (978-1-4001-0114-6(X)) Pub: Tantor Media. Dist(s): IngramPubServ

First Strike. unabr. ed. Douglas Terman. Read by Bob Erickson. 10 cass. (Running Time: 15 hrs.). 1983. 80.00 (978-0-7366-0526-7(6), 1500) Books on Tape.
At an underground factory in Siberia, the Russians have made a replica of a U.S. Navy warhead. In Moscow Soviet military planners carefully review the latest computer assessment of their chances to survive all-out nuclear war. And the KGB selects its target for high level political subversion...a vulnerable U.S. Senator with presidential ambitions. When these elements mesh in a series of improbable but possible combinations, the world stands on the brink of nuclear holocaust.

First Ten Thaat Raga Chalans: Chalan Practice Tapes. Ashwin Batish. 10 cass. (First Ten Thaat Raga Chalans Ser.). 1993. bk. Set. (978-1-882319-09-1(5)); 59.95 Set. (978-1-882319-36-7(2)) Batish Pubns.

First Test. unabr. ed. Tamora Pierce. Read by Bernadette Dunne. 5 CDs. (Running Time: 5 hrs. 46 mins.). (Protector of the Small Ser.: No. 1). (J). (gr. 4-7). 2007. audio compact disk 55.00 (978-0-7393-4910-6(4), Random AudioBks) Pub: Random Audio Pubg. Dist(s): Random

First Test. unabr. ed. Tamora Pierce. Read by Bernadette Dunne. (Running Time: 20760 sec.). (Protector of the Small Ser.: No. 1). (ENG.). (J). (gr. 5). 2007. audio compact disk 35.00 (978-0-7393-5649-4(6), Listening Lib) Pub: Random Audio Pubg. Dist(s): Random

First the Egg. Laura Vaccaro Seeger. Narrated by Elle Fanning. Music by Jack Sundrud & Rusty Young. 1 CD. (Running Time: 5 mins.). (J). (ps-1). 2009. bk. 29.95 (978-0-545-13454-5(4)); audio compact disk 12.95 (978-0-545-13444-6(7)) Weston Woods.

First Therapy Session: How to Interview Clients & Identify Problems Successfully. Jay Haley. Read by Jay Haley. 2 cass. (Running Time: 1 hr. 45 min.). (Psychology Ser.). 1989. 35.00 (978-1-55542-194-6(6), Jossey-Bass) Wiley US.

First Things First see Primero lo Primero

First Things First. Stephen R. Covey. 6 cass. 1999. 59.95 Set, incl. wkbk. (236-C47) Natl Seminars.
Do you know where you're going? Do you know how to get there? This program shows you how to take control of your life so you can accomplish your personal & professional goals & take the lead at home & work. "First Things First" will help you set your sights on success...by setting your compass for a rewarding personal journey. Covey's concepts cover self-management & self-motivation. After the seminar, you'll be ready to define & organize your priorities & accomplish more than you ever thought possible.

First Things First. Stephen R. Covey. 2002. audio compact disk 14.00 (978-0-7435-2767-5(4), Sound Ideas) S&S Audio.

First Things First. Stephen R. Covey et al. 6 cass. 59.95 Set incl. wkbk. (12640PAM) Nightingale-Conant.
Provides a model for principle-centered living that will give you a greater sense of purpose & direction...while meeting your basic need for mental, physical, spiritual & social fulfillment.

First Things First. abr. ed. Stephen R. Covey. 1 cass. 9.95 (86628) Books on Tape.
Offering a principle-centered approach & the wisdom & insight that made "The 7 Habits of Highly Effective People" a number 1 bestseller, "First Things First" empowers listeners to define what is truly important; to accomplish worthwhile goals; & to lead rich, rewarding & balanced lives.

First Things First. abr. ed. Stephen R. Covey. 2006. 17.95 (978-1-933976-13-6(6)) Pub: Franklin Covey. Dist(s): S and S Inc

First Things First. abr. ed. Stephen R. Covey et al. 3 CDs. (Running Time: 33 hrs. 0 mins. 0 sec.). (ENG.). 2002. audio compact disk 29.95 (978-1-929494-62-0(9)) Pub: Franklin Covey. Dist(s): S and S Inc

First Things First. abr. ed. Stephen R. Covey et al. Read by Stephen R. Covey. 1 CD. (Running Time: 11 hrs. 20 mins. 0 sec.). (ENG.). 1999. audio compact disk 14.00 (978-0-671-31556-6(0), Sound Ideas) Pub: S&S Audio. Dist(s): S and S Inc

First Things First. unabr. ed. Stephen R. Covey et al. Read by Stephen R. Covey. (YA). 2007. 39.99 (978-1-59895-938-3(7)) Find a World.

First Things First: The Rules of Being a Warner. unabr. ed. Kurt Warner & Brenda Warner. Told to Jennifer Schuchmann. 6 CDs. (ENG.). 2009. audio compact disk 26.99 (978-1-4143-3407-3(9)) Tyndale Hse.

First Things First: 1 Cor. 11:18-34. Ed Young. 1986. 4.95 (978-0-7417-1506-7(6), 506) Win Walk.

First Things First Every Day: Because Where You're Headed Is More Important Than How Fast You're Going. abr. ed. Stephen R. Covey et al. A. Roger Merrill. (Running Time: 7 hrs. 20 mins. 0 sec.). (ENG.). 2005. audio compact disk 14.00 (978-0-7435-5104-5(4)) Pub: S&S Audio. Dist(s): S and S Inc

FIRST THINGS FIRST EVERY DAY Because Where You're Headed is More Important Than How Fast You're Going STEVEN R. COVEY A. ROGER MERRILL AND REBECCA R. MERRILL A multiple-voice recording with an introduction by A. Roger Merrill FIRST THINGS FIRST HELPS YOU UNDERTAND WHAT'S MOST IMPORTANT EVERY DAY... Stephen R. Covey and the Merrills have shown millions of listeners how to balance the demands of a schedule with the desire for fulfillment. Now the principles they introduced in First Things First are distilled for everyday listening. Let First Things First Every Day be your guide to the rich relationships, the inner peace, and the confidence that come from knowing where you're headed, and why.

First Thought Best Thought. Allen Ginsberg et al. 4 CDs. 2004. audio compact disk 29.95 (978-1-59179-188-1(X), AW00823D) Sounds True.

First Thought, Best Thought: 108 Poems. Chogyam Trungpa. 1 cass. 1976. 12.50 (A092) Vajradhatu.

Chogyam Trungpa's unique combination of Tibetan poetics with contemporary Western techniques is presented.

First Three Minutes. Steven Weinberg. Narrated by Raymond Todd. (Running Time: 5 hrs. 30 mins.). 2000. 24.95 (978-1-59912-661-6(3)) Iofy Corp.

First Three Minutes: A Modern View of the Origin of the Universe. unabr. ed. Steven Weinberg. Narrated by Raymond Todd. 4 cass. (Running Time: 5 hrs. 30 mins.). 2001. 32.95 (978-0-7861-2120-5(3), 2880); audio compact disk 40.00 (978-0-7861-9636-4(X), 2880) Blckstn Audio.

Now updated with a major new afterword that incorporates the latest cosmological research, this classic of contemporary science writing by a Nobel prize-winning physicist explains to general readers what happened when the Universe began, and how we know.

***First Thrills: High-Octane Stories from the Hottest Thriller Authors.** unabr. ed. Lee Child & Steve Berry. (Running Time: 12 hrs.). 2010. 39.97 (978-1-4418-6451-2(2), 9781441864512, BADLE) Brilliance Audio.

***First Thrills: High-Octane Stories from the Hottest Thriller Authors.** unabr. ed. Lee Child & Steve Berry. Read by Multivoice Production Staff. (Running Time: 12 hrs.). 2010. 24.99 (978-1-4418-6448-2(2), 9781441864482, Brilliance MP3); 39.97 (978-1-4418-6449-9(0), 9781441864499, Brlnc Audio MP3 Lib); audio compact disk 99.97 (978-1-4418-6447-5(4), 9781441864475, BriAudCD Unabrid) Brilliance Audio.

***First Thrills: High-Octane Stories from the Hottest Thriller Authors.** unabr. ed. Lee Child & Steve Ber Child. (Running Time: 12 hrs.). 2010. 24.99 (978-1-4418-6450-5(4), 9781441864505, BAD) Brilliance Audio.

***First Thrills: High-Octane Stories from the Hottest Thriller Authors.** unabr. ed. Read by Multivoice Production Staff. Ed. by Lee Child. Afterword by Steve Berry. (Running Time: 12 hrs.). 2010. audio compact disk 39.99 (978-1-4418-6446-8(6), 9781441864468, Bril Audio CD Unabri) Brilliance Audio.

First-Time Homeowners: Maximize Your Investment & Enjoy Your New Home. rev. ed. Ilona Bray & Alayna Schroeder. (ENG.). 2009. audio compact disk 19.99 (978-1-4133-0962-1(3)) Nolo.

First-Time Manager. Joan Iaconetti & Patrick O'Hara. Narrated by Bob Askey. 6 cass. 89.95 set, incl. workbook. (C10012) CareerTrack Pubns.

If you want to get a head start as a new manager, the techniques you'll learn in this program are just what you need. You'll learn to take charge confidently. You'll get the information you need to avoid common errors. And you'll make a visible impact on your employees, boss & peers.

First Time Manager. 5th unabr. ed. Loren B. Belker & Gary S. Topchik. Read by Sean Pratt. (Running Time: 7 hrs.). (ENG.). 2008. 24.98 (978-1-59659-187-5(0), GildAudio); audio compact disk 29.98 (978-1-59659-170-7(6), GildAudio) Pub: Gildan Media. Dist(s): HachBkGrp

First to Fight. unabr. ed. Stephen Coonts. 4 cass. (Running Time: 6 hrs.). 2001. 25.00 (978-1-59040-149-1(2), Phoenix Audio) Pub: Amer Intl Pub. Dist(s): PerseuPGW

First to Land. unabr. ed. Douglas Reeman. Read by David Rintoul. 8 cass. (Running Time: 12 hrs.). 2002. 69.95 (978-0-7540-0844-6(4), CAB 2266) Pub: Chivers Pr GBR. Dist(s): AudioGO

First Touch. Perf. by Dominic Miller. 1 cass.; 1 CD. 1998. audio compact disk 15.98 CD. (978-1-56628-143-0(1), 72932D) MFLP CA.

***First Trip: Sex, Drugz, & Rock & Roll in The 70'z.** Cheryl Taylor. (Running Time: 258). (ENG.). (YA). 2010. audio compact disk 19.99 (978-0-615-36595-4(7)) Avenal Chimes.

***First Truth.** unabr. ed. Dawn Cook. Read by Marguerite Gavin. (Running Time: 12 hrs.). 2010. 29.95 (978-1-4417-5395-3(8)); audio compact disk 32.95 (978-1-4417-5394-6(X)) Blckstn Audio.

First Two Principles in Building. Rick Joyner. 1 cass. (Running Time: 90 mins.). (Foundation Ser.: Vol. 4). 2000. 5.00 (RJ05-004) Morning NC.

As an overview of God's plan for His church, this series contains essential truths for everyone who wants to see the church become all that she is called to be.

***First Tycoon: The Epic Life of Cornelius Vanderbilt.** unabr. ed. T. J. Stiles. Read by Mark Deakins. 23 CDs. (Running Time: 28 hrs. 45 mins.). 2009. audio compact disk 100.00 (978-1-4159-6591-7(9), BksonTape) Pub: Random Audio Pubg. Dist(s): Random

First Victim. abr. ed. Douglas MacKinnon. Read by Grover Gardner. 2 cass. (Running Time: 3 hrs.). 1999. 17.95 (978-1-882071-97-5(2), 395421) B-B Audio.

After years of being abused, Sabrina Ryan hopes and prays that the election of her husband Turner Ryan, as the next President of The United States, will take his mind off her, and onto the job of running the country. Sadly and tragically, it has the oppo.

First Victim. abr. ed. Ridley Pearson. Read by Scott Rosema. 3 CDs, Library ed. (Running Time: 3 hrs.). (Lou Boldt & Daphne Matthews Mystery Ser.: Vol. 6). 2003. audio compact disk 62.25 (978-1-59086-560-6(X), 159086560X, BAU) Brilliance Audio.

Lou Boldt is back and entering dark new territory in Ridley Pearson's gripping thriller. A shipping container washed ashore leads Seattle television news anchor Stevie McNeal and reporter friend Melissa on the trail of a scam involving the importation of illegal aliens. A career stepping-stone for McNeal, the investigation puts her at cross-purposes with the Seattle Police Department's Lou Boldt and Sergeant John LaMoia. When Melissa disappears, perhaps at the hands of the Chinese Triad, McNeal turns from foe to ally and teams up with the detectives on an investigation that takes them from Seattle's docklands to the offices of the INS. With a storyline that mirrors today's headlines, meticulous research, and fascinating forensic details, this thriller confirms Pearson's place at the top of the genre.

First Victim. unabr. ed. Douglas MacKinnon. Read by Michael Mitchell. 6 cass. (Running Time: 9 hrs.). 1997. 48.00 (978-0-7366-3839-5(3), 4559) Books on Tape.

President & First Lady Turner & Sabrina Ryan seem to be the ideal political couple, the "Ken & Barbie" of the political world. The truth is entirely different: Turner is a chronic wife-abuser.

First Victim. unabr. ed. Ridley Pearson. Read by Scott Rosema. 6 cass. (Running Time: 9 hrs.). (Lou Boldt/Daphne Matthews Ser.). 1999. 35.95 (978-1-56740-423-4(5), 1567404235, BAU); 57.25 (978-1-56740-649-8(1), 1567406491, Unabridge Lib Edns) Brilliance Audio.

Lou Boldt is back and entering dark new territory in Ridley Pearson's gripping new thriller. A shipping container washed ashore leads Seattle television news anchor Stevie McNeal and reporter friend Melissa on the trail of a scam involving the importation of illegal aliens. A career stepping-stone for McNeal, the investigation puts her at cross-purposes with the Seattle Police Department's Lou Boldt and Sergeant John LaMoia. When Melissa disappears, perhaps at the hands of the Chinese Triad, McNeal turns from foe to ally and teams up with the detectives on an investigation that takes them from Seattle's docklands to the offices of the INS. With a storyline that mirrors today's headlines, meticulous research, and fascinating forensic details, this latest thriller confirms Pearson's place at the top of the genre.

First Victim. unabr. ed. Ridley Pearson. Read by Scott Rosema. (Running Time: 9 hrs.). (Lou Boldt/Daphne Matthews Ser.). 2007. 39.25 (978-1-4233-1435-6(2), 9781423314356, BADLE); 24.95 (978-1-4233-1434-9(4), 9781423314349, BAD); audio compact disk 92.25 (978-1-4233-1431-8(X), 9781423314318, BriAudCD Unabrid); audio compact disk 39.25 (978-1-4233-1433-2(6), 9781423314332, Brlnc Audio MP3 Lib); audio compact disk 24.95 (978-1-4233-1432-5(8), 9781423314325, Brilliance MP3); audio compact disk 34.95 (978-1-4233-1430-1(1), 9781423314301, Bril Audio CD Unabri) Brilliance Audio.

First Victim, Set. abr. ed. Ridley Pearson. Read by Scott Rosema. 2 cass. 1999. 17.95 (FS9-50998) Highsmith.

First Vision. Paul Thomas Smith. 1 cass. 2004. 9.95 (978-1-57734-574-9(6), 06006159) Covenant Comms.

Little-known accounts of Joseph Smith's glorious vision.

First Voice. unabr. ed. David Attenborough. 1 cass. (Running Time: 54 min.). (Animal Language Ser.). 12.95 J Norton Pubs.

First Wedding see Little Women: With Good Wives

First Women over the Rockies, abr. ed. 3 cass. (Running Time: 4 hrs. 24 min.). 2001. 19.95 (978-1-889252-08-7(5)) Photosensitive.

First Words. abr. ed. Perf. by Spalding Gray et al. 1 cass. (Running Time: 1 hrs. 2 min.). 1996. 11.95 (978-1-57453-080-3(1)) Audio Lit.

Introduction to the pleasure of the contemporary monologue. Listen to some of the voices who are defining this new brand of entertainment for the nineties.

First Words Roos Bedtime. Laura Gates Galvin. 1 CD. (Running Time: 1 hr. 30 min.). (ENG., (J). 2004. 12.99 (978-1-59069-409-1(0), 1A108) Studio Mouse.

First World War. Ben Walsh. 2005. cd-rom 575.00 (978-0-7195-7973-8(2), HodderMurray) Pub: Hodder Edu GBR. Dist(s): Trans-Atl Phila

First World War. abr. ed. John Keegan. Read by Simon Prebble. 8 CDs. (Running Time: 9 hrs.). (ENG.). 2004. audio compact disk 38.00 (978-0-7393-1249-0(9)) Pub: Random Audio Pubg. Dist(s): Random

First Year: A Guide to Nurturing You & Your Baby. Katharine Kersey. 8 cass. 29.95 incl. study guide. (5015) SyberVision.

Covers every aspect of the child's first year, from establishing a new family routine to coping with colic, feeding, loving discipline & venturing out together for local & long distance travel by car or airplane.

First Year Program: Gilbert Law Summaries. Ed. by Gilbert Law Summaries. 2002. 195.00 (978-0-15-901110-2(8)) West.

First Year Program, 2006 (Law School Legends Audio Series) Gilbert Staff. audio compact disk 202.95 (978-0-314-16914-3(8)) West.

First Year Super Set: Civil Procedure, Contracts, Criminal Law, Property, Torts & Exam Skills - Essay Writing. unabr. ed. Arthur Raphael Miller et al. 24 cass. (Running Time: 41 hrs. 40 mins.). (Outstanding Professors Ser.). 199.95 (978-1-57793-029-7(0), 28441) Pub: Sum & Substance. Dist(s): West Pub

Lecture by prominent American law school professors. Encompasses five law school subjects: Civil Procedure, Contracts, Criminal, Real Property, Torts, Exam Skills: Essay Writing.

First Year Type 2 Diabetes: An Essential Guide for the Newly Diagnosed. abr. ed. Gretchen Becker. Narrated by Kate Reading. Frwd. by Allison B. Goldfine. (Running Time: 10800 sec.). 2001. audio compact disk 22.95 (978-1-933310-05-3(7)) STI Certified.

First! (14 Songs about Inventive, Interesting, & Innovative People) Composed by Sally K. Albrecht & Jay Althouse. (ENG.). 2006. audio compact disk 34.95 (978-0-7390-3956-4(3)) Alfred Pub.

First 30 Days: Your Guide to Any Change. unabr. ed. Ariane De Bonvoisin. Read by Ariane De Bonvoisin. (Running Time: 6 hrs. 0 mins. 0 sec.). (ENG.). 2008. audio compact disk 19.99 (978-1-4001-5780-8(3)) Pub: Tantor Media. Dist(s): IngramPubServ

First 30 Days: Your Guide to Any Change (and Loving Your Life More) Ariane de Bonvoisin. Read by Ariane de Bonvoisin. (Playaway Adult Nonfiction Ser.). 2008. 59.99 (978-1-60640-979-4(4)) Find a World.

First 30 Days: Your Guide to Any Change (and Loving Your Life More) unabr. ed. Ariane de Bonvoisin. Read by Ariane de Bonvoisin. (Running Time: 6 hrs. 0 mins. 0 sec.). (ENG.). 2008. audio compact disk 29.99 (978-1-4001-0780-3(6)) Pub: Tantor Media. Dist(s): IngramPubServ

First 30 Days: Your Guide to Any Change (And Loving Your Life More) unabr. ed. Ariane De Bonvoisin. Read by Ariane De Bonvoisin. (Running Time: 6 hrs. 0 mins. 0 sec.). (ENG.). 2008. audio compact disk 59.99 (978-1-4001-3780-0(2)) Pub: Tantor Media. Dist(s): IngramPubServ

First 48. abr. ed. Tim Green. Read by Stephen Lang. (ENG.). 2005. 14.98 (978-1-59483-323-6(0)) Pub: Hachet Audio. Dist(s): HachBkGrp

First 48. abr. ed. Tim Green. Read by Stephen Lang. (Running Time: 6 hrs.). (ENG.). 2009. 49.98 (978-1-60788-041-7(5)) Pub: Hachet Audio. Dist(s): HachBkGrp

First 90 Days: Critical Success Strategies for New Leaders at All Levels. unabr. ed. Lyndon Baines Johnson Library & Michael Watkins. Read by Kevin T. Norris. 6 CDs. (Running Time: 6 hrs.). (ENG.). 2006. audio compact disk 19.98 (978-1-59659-044-1(0), GildAudio) Pub: Gildan Media. Dist(s): HachBkGrp

Firstborn Advantage: Making Your Birth Order Work for You. Kevin Leman. 2008. audio compact disk 24.99 (978-0-8007-4439-7(X)) Pub: Revell. Dist(s): Baker Pub Grp

Fiscal & Income Policies. unabr. ed. G. Lowell Harris et al. 1 cass. (Running Time: 49 min.). 12.95 (288) J Norton Pubs.

***Fiscal Hangover: How to Profit from the New Global Economy.** unabr. ed. Keith Fitz-Gerald. Read by Sean Pratt. (Running Time: 11 hrs.). (ENG.). 2009. 29.98 (978-1-59659-506-4(X), GildAudio) Pub: Gildan Media. Dist(s): HachBkGrp

Fish see William Carlos Williams Reads His Poetry

Fish. L. S. Matthews. 2 cass. (Running Time: 3 hrs. 30 mins.). (J). (gr. 5 up). 2004. 23.00 (978-1-4000-8521-7(7), Listening Lib); audio compact disk 30.00 (978-1-4000-8988-8(3), Listening Lib) Random Audio Pubg.

My story starts the day that my parents told me we must leave our adopted home forever. Because of the soldiers and the drought we barely had enough to eat and we could no longer stay to help the people in our village. Right before we were leaving I saw a fish in a small brown puddle and I knew I had to take it with me. The journey would be hard to get across the mountains to the safety of the border and the people there who could help us.

Fish! A Remarkable Way to Boost Morale & Improve Results. Stephen C. Lundin. (FRE.). pap. bk. 18.95 (978-2-89558-099-7(5)) Pub: Coffragants CAN. Dist(s): Penton Overseas

Fish! A Remarkable Way to Boost Morale & Improve Results. unabr. ed. Stephen C. Lundin et al. Read by Mallory Kasdan. 2 CDs. (Running Time: 3 hrs.). (ENG.). 2001. audio compact disk 22.00 (978-0-553-52873-2(4), Random AudioBks) Pub: Random Audio Pubg. Dist(s): Random

A fictional manager is charged with the responsibility of turning a chronically unenthusiastic & unhelpful department into an effective team. Down the street is Seattle's very real Pike Place Fish, a world famous market that is wildly successful thanks to its fun, bustling, joyful atmosphere & great customer service. By applying ingeniously simple lessons learned from actual Pike Place fishmongers, our manager discovers how to energize those who report to her & effect an astonishing transformation in her workplace. Offers wisdom that is easy to grasp, instantly applicable & profound, the hallmarks of a true business classic.

Fish & Peter Rosa see Winter's Tales

Fish Bones. Poems. Don Wilsun. 1 cass. 1993. 5.00 (978-1-878888-16-7(1)) Nine Muses Books.

Cajun jazz poetry: spoken word with conga drums played Afro-Cuban style.

Fish Convention & Nine Other Stories. unabr. ed. Story Time Staff. Read by Alfreda C. Doyle. 2 cass. (Running Time: 1 hr. 30 min.). (J). (gr. 4-8). 1992. 17.95 set. (SRC 0026PLUS9) Sell Out Recordings.

Fish convention starts this tape collection with over 40 fish attending a convention. Other stories are educational, informative, inspirational & entertaining.

Fish Don't Swim in a Tree. unabr. ed. Marian L. Clish. Illus. by Lori Clish. 1 cass. (Running Time: 20 mins.). (J). (gr. k-3). 1999. pap. bk. 10.95 (978-1-928632-13-9(0)); pap. bk. 14.95 (978-1-928632-14-6(9)) Writers Mrktpl.

ABC book with characters, stories & poems. Parent reading guide at the end of the book.

Fish Face. unabr. ed. Patricia Reilly Giff. 1 cass. (Running Time: 1 hr. 17 mins.). (Follow the Reader Ser.). (J). (gr. 1-2). 1984. pap. bk. 17.00 incl. bk. & guide. (978-0-8072-0092-6(1), FTR101SP, Listening Lib) Random Audio Pubg.

Follows the kids in Ms. Rooney's second grae class as they learn & grow through an entire school year filled with fun & surprises. Corresponding month: October.

Fish Facts & Pumpkins in Fall. Steck-Vaughn Staff. (J). 2002. 10.00 (978-0-7398-5903-2(X)) SteckVau.

Fish! for Life: A Remarkable Way to Achieve Your Dreams. unabr. ed. Stephen C. Lundin et al. Read by Stephen C. Lundin et al. 2 cass. (Running Time: 3 hrs.). 2004. 18.98 (978-1-4013-9776-0(X), Hyperion Audio) Pub: Hyperion. Dist(s): HarperCollins Pubs

Fish-Hawk see Twentieth-Century Poetry in English, No. 25, Recordings of Poets Reading Their Own Poetry

Fish in Room 11. Heather Dyer. 2 CDs. 2006. audio compact disk 21.95 (978-0-7540-6730-6(0), Chivers Child Audio) AudioGO.

Fish in the Air. 2004. 8.95 (978-1-56008-895-0(8)); cass. & flmstrp 30.00 (978-1-56008-668-0(8)) Weston Woods.

Fish, Man, Control, Room. unabr. ed. John M. Bennett. Read by John M. Bennett. 1 cass. (Running Time: 60 min.). 1995. 6.00 (978-0-935350-61-6(6)) Luna Bisonte.

Set of avant-garde poems read by author in four different ways.

Fish Named Yum: A Mr. Pin Mystery. unabr. ed. Mary Elise Monsell. Narrated by John McDonough. 1 cass. (Running Time: 1 hr.). (gr. 2 up). 1998. 10.00 (978-0-7887-0954-8(2), 95080E7) Recorded Bks.

When water starts filling basements throughout Chicago, only Mr. Pin, the clever penguin detective from the South Pole, can save the city.

Fish or Cut Bait: Neh. 6:1-14. Ed Young. 1990. 4.95 (978-0-7417-1812-9(X), 812) Win Walk.

***Fish Out of Water.** Featuring Ravi Zacharias. 1993. audio compact disk 9.00 (978-1-61256-026-7(1)) Ravi Zach.

Fish! Sticks: A Remarkable Way to Adapt to Changing Times & Keep Your Work Fresh. unabr. abr. ed. Stephen C. Lundin et al. Read by Stephen C. Lundin et al. 2 cass. (Running Time: 3 hrs.). 2003. 18.98 (978-1-4013-9667-1(4)) Pub: Hyperion. Dist(s): HarperCollins Pubs

Fish Tales: Fish Stories from Here & Away. As told by Laura Simms. Music by Real Myth Ensemble. 1 CD. (Running Time: 52 min.). 2001. audio compact disk 16.95 Parabola Bks.

Features traditional stories from around the world, including "Spirit Dolphin and other Dreamtime Tales" from Australia, "The Fish Fairy" from Turkey, and "Eel Tale" from the Phillipines.

Fish That's a Song: Songs & Stories for Children. Perf. by Pete Seeger et al. 1 cass. (Running Time: 43 min.). (J). (ps-7). 1990. Incl. 38p. bklet. w/pictures & descriptions, lyrics in video-style bk. (0-9307-45037-4-4) Smithsonian Folkways.

Songs & stories related to folk art in the Hemphill Collection (National Museum of American Art).

Fish Trek: An Adventure in Articles. Thomas Cole. (C). 2000. bk. 34.50 (978-0-472-00299-3(6), 00299) U of Mich Pr.

Fishcastle: 9 Cassettes (unabridged) unabr. ed. Elizabeth Stead. 9 cass. (Running Time: 13 hrs.). 2004. 72.00 (978-1-74030-565-5(5)) Pub: Bolinda Pubng AUS. Dist(s): Lndmrk Audiobks

Fisher Boy. unabr. ed. Stephen Anable. Read by Paul Michael. (Running Time: 15 hrs. 50 mins.). 2008. 85.95 (978-1-4332-3504-7(8)); cass. & audio compact disk 110.00 (978-1-4332-3505-4(6)); audio compact disk 29.95 (978-1-4332-3508-5(0)) Blckstn Audio.

Fisher King. Paule Marshall. Narrated by Robin Miles. 5 cass. (Running Time: 6 hrs.). 48.00 (978-1-4025-2142-3(1)) Recorded Bks.

Fisherman see Twentieth-Century Poetry in English, No. 2, Recordings of Poets Reading Their Own Poetry

Fisherman & His Wife see Favorite Children's Stories: A Collection

Fisherman & His Wife see Favorite Tales by the Brothers Grimm

Fisherman & His Wife/The Ugly Duckling. Sue Arengo. (Classic Tales Ser.). 2001. 14.75 (978-0-19-422077-4(X)) OUP.

Fisherman's Bend. unabr. ed. Linda Greenlaw. Read by Sandra Burr. 1 MP3-CD. (Running Time: 7 hrs.). (Jane Bunker Ser.). 2008. 39.25 (978-1-4233-6180-0(6), 9781423361800, Brlnc Audio MP3 Lib); 39.25 (978-1-4233-6182-4(2), 9781423361824, BADLE) Brilliance Audio.

Fisherman's Bend. unabr. ed. Linda Greenlaw. Read by Sandra Burr & Jim Bond. 1 MP3-CD. (Running Time: 7 hrs.). (Jane Bunker Ser.). 2008. 24.95 (978-1-4233-6179-4(2), 9781423361794, Brilliance MP3) Brilliance Audio.

Fisherman's Bend. unabr. ed. Linda Greenlaw. Read by Sandra Burr. (Running Time: 7 hrs.). (Jane Bunker Ser.). 2008. 24.95 (978-1-4233-6181-7(4), 9781423361817, BAD); audio compact disk 87.25 (978-1-4233-6178-7(4), 9781423361787, BriAudCD Unabrid); audio compact disk 29.95 (978-1-4233-6177-0(6), 9781423361770, Bril Audio CD Unabri) Brilliance Audio.

***Fisherman's Testament.** César Vidal. (Running Time: 10 hrs. 45 mins. 10 sec.). (ENG.). 2009. 16.99 (978-0-310-77231-6(1)) Zondervan.

Fishers of Men. Gerald N. Lund. Read by Larry A. McKeever. (Running Time: 80100 sec.). (Kingdom & the Crown Ser.). 2008. audio compact disk 49.95 (978-1-59038-939-3(5), Shadow Mount) Deseret Bk.

Fishes of Hawaii. Contrib. by Andre P. Seale et al. (JPN.). 2004. audio compact disk 4.95 (978-1-57306-183-4(2)) Bess Pr.

Fishing for Stars. unabr. ed. Bryce Courtenay. Read by Humphrey Bower. (Running Time: 23 hrs.). 2008. audio compact disk 152.00 (978-1-74214-099-5(8), 9781742140995) Pub: Bolinda Pubng AUS. Dist(s): Bolinda Pub Inc

Fishing in the Air. Sharon Creech. Illus. by Chris Raschka. (Running Time: 10 mins.). 2003. pap. bk. 9.95 (978-1-59112-223-4(6)) Live Oak Media.

Fishing in the Air. Sharon Creech. Illus. by Chris Raschka. 11 vols. (Running Time: 10 mins.). (J). 2003. bk. 25.95 (978-1-59112-225-8(2)); pap. bk. 37.95 (978-1-59112-226-5(0)); pap. bk. 39.95 (978-1-59112-521-1(9)); audio compact disk 12.95 (978-1-59112-511-2(1)) Live Oak Media.

Fishing in the Air. Sharon Creech. Read by Jason Harris. 11 vols. (Running Time: 10 mins.). (Live Oak Readalong Ser.). (J). 2003. pap. bk. 16.95 (978-1-59112-224-1(4)) Pub: Live Oak Media. Dist(s): AudioGO

Fishing Lures & Fruitful Vines. (Power Tool Box Ser.: Vol. 2). (J). (gr. 1-6). 1998. ring bd. 164.99 (978-1-57405-044-8(3)) CharismaLife Pub.

Fishing the Manistique Lakes. unabr. ed. Bill Diem. 1 cass. (Running Time: 1 hr.). 1993. 14.95 (978-0-9629546-1-0(6)) Newberry News.
Seven local fishermen give advice on techniques, locations, & lore for fishing in the three Manistique Lakes in Michigan's Upper Peninsula.

Fish's Eye: Essays about Angling & the Outdoors. abr. ed. Ian Frazier. Narrated by Dick Hill. (Running Time: 16200 sec.). (Field & Stream Ser.). 2007. audio compact disk 28.00 (978-1-933309-12-5(1)) Pub: A Media Intl. Dist(s): Natl Bk Netwk

Fishy Riddles. pap. bk. 18.95 (978-1-59519-302-5(2)) Pub: Live Oak Media. Dist(s): AudioGO

Fishy Riddles. Katy Hall, pseud & Lisa Eisenberg. Illus. by Simms Taback. (Running Time: 8 mins.). 2000. 9.95 (978-1-59112-037-7(3)) Live Oak Media.

Fishy Riddles. unabr. ed. Katy Hall, pseud & Lisa Eisenberg. Read by Larry Robinson et al. Illus. by Simms Taback. 14 vols. (Running Time: 8 mins.). (J). (gr. 1). 2000. pap. bk. & stu. ed. 29.95 Reading Chest. (978-0-941078-71-9(X)) Live Oak Media.
What TV show do fish like best? Name That Tuna, of course. Forty-eight pages of piscine punch lines sure to hook any young reader with a sense of humor.

Fishy Riddles. unabr. ed. Katy Hall, pseud & Lisa Eisenberg. Read by Larry Robinson et al. Illus. by Simms Taback. 11 vols. (Running Time: 8 mins.). (J). (gr. 1-3). 2000. pap. bk. 16.95 (978-0-941078-70-2(1)) Live Oak Media.

Fist Load Weaponry: Awesome Tools of Self-Defense, Set. Sid Campbell. 2 cass. cass. & video 169.95 incl. 2 1-hr. audio cass. & 1 1-hr. video cass. Gong Prods.

Fist of God. unabr. ed. Frederick Forsyth. Read by David Case. 15 cass. (Running Time: 22 hrs. 30 min.). 1994. 120.00 (978-0-7366-2762-7(6), 3484) Books on Tape.
The Persian Gulf War turned into heart-stopping fiction: the story of what might have happened behind the headlines.

Fist of God, unabr. ed. Frederick Forsyth. Narrated by John Franklyn-Robbins. 16 cass. (Running Time: 23 hrs.). 1994. 128.00 (978-0-7887-0027-9(8), 94226E7) Recorded Bks.
What would have happened if Saddam Hussein's super-gun had been a key player in Operation Desert Storm? Combining fact with fiction as only he can, Forsyth creates a tale of suspense that will keep you on the edge until the last satisfying moment.

Fist Stick Knife Gun: A Personal History of Violence in America, unabr. ed. Geoffrey Canada & Jamar Nicholas. Narrated by Peter Francis James. 5 cass. (Running Time: 7 hrs.). 1996. 44.00 (978-0-7887-0624-0(1), 94798E7) Recorded Bks.
Accurately and vividly reveals a childhood world filled with drugs and violence. Drawing from the current inner-city realities & his own startling childhood memories, he offers a workable solution to this destructive cycle.

Fistful of Charms. unabr. ed. Kim Harrison. Read by Marguerite Gavin. (Hollows Ser.: Bk. 4). (YA). 2008. 84.99 (978-1-60514-635-5(8)) Find a World.

Fistful of Charms. unabr. ed. Kim Harrison. Read by Marguerite Gavin. 14 CDs. (Running Time: 17 hrs. 0 mins. 0 sec.). (Hollows Ser.: Bk. 4). (ENG.). 2008. audio compact disk 39.99 (978-1-4001-0474-1(2)); audio compact disk 29.99 (978-1-4001-5474-6(X)); audio compact disk 79.99 (978-1-4001-3474-8(9)) Pub: Tantor Media. Dist(s): IngramPubServ

***Fistful of Feathers: A Story from Guys Read: Funny Business.** unabr. ed. David Yoo. (ENG.). 2010. (978-0-06-206247-5(6)); (978-0-06-202765-8(4)) HarperCollins Pubs.

Fit & Athletic. Eldon Taylor. 2 cass. 29.95 Set. (978-1-55978-742-0(2), 4407) Progress Aware Res.

***Fit for a King.** unabr. ed. Diana Palmer. Read by Tanya Eby. (Running Time: 6 hrs.). 2010. 39.97 (978-1-4418-8082-6(8), 9781441880826, BADLE); 19.99 (978-1-4418-8080-2(1), 9781441880802, Brilliance MP3); 39.97 (978-1-4418-8081-9(X), 9781441880819, Brlnc Audio MP3 Lib); audio compact disk 19.99 (978-1-4418-8078-9(X), 9781441880789, Bril Audio CD Unabri); audio compact disk 69.97 (978-1-4418-8079-6(8), 9781441880796, BriAudCD Unabrid) Brilliance Audio.

Fit for a Princess: A Novel. Kylie Johnson. (YA). 2007. audio compact disk 24.99 (978-1-60247-666-0(7)) Tate Pubng.

Fit for the Kingdom CD Series. 2007. audio compact disk 44.99 (978-1-933185-18-7(X)) Messengr Intl.

***Fit to Be Tied.** Robin Lee Hatcher. (Running Time: 7 hrs. 32 mins. 0 sec.). (Sisters of Bethlehem Springs Ser.). (ENG.). 2009. 14.99 (978-0-310-77279-8(6)) Zondervan.

Fit to Live: The 5-Point Plan to Be Lean, Strong, & Fearless for Life. abr. ed. Pamela Peeke. Read by Pamela Peeke. 2007. audio compact disk 14.95 (978-1-4272-0171-3(4)) Pub: Macmill Audio. Dist(s): Macmillan

Fit to Live: The 5-Point Plan to Become Lean, Strong, & Fearless for Life. abr. ed. Pamela Peeke. Read by Pamela Peeke. (Running Time: 4 hrs. 0 mins. 0 sec.). (ENG.). 2007. audio compact disk 24.95 (978-1-4272-0170-6(6)) Pub: Macmill Audio. Dist(s): Macmillan

Fit to Travel Vol. 4: One Hundred One Tips to Stay Healthy & Stress Free on the Road or at Home. unabr. ed. David Essel. 1 cass. (Running Time: 1 hrs.). (David Essel's Dynamic Living Ser.). 1992. 9.95 (978-1-893074-02-6(1)) D Essel Inc.
While you travel: 1) Eat healthier, 2) Beat stress the esy way, 3) Sleep & Pack more productively, 4) Exercise in minutes a day, 5) Increase your productivity.

Fitcher's Bird: A Tale of Dismemberment & Wholeness. Judith Shaw. Read by Judith Shaw. 1 cass. (Running Time: 65 min.). 1992. 10.95 (978-0-7822-0396-7(5), 489) C G Jung IL.
In spite of our best intentions to seek wholeness as the goal of individuation, we inevitably find ourselves, at one time or another, trapped in negative behavior that leads into darkness. Despair, self-destructive impulses, & feelings of fragmentation are frequent companions in this necessary detour & must be reckoned with. Through a consideration of Grimm's tale, "Fitcher's Bird," this lecture examines forces of the shadow & negative animus & suggests the qualities that may prove decisive in coming to terms with these negative energies.

Fitness - Exercise. 1 cass. (Running Time: 45 min.). (Sports Ser.). 9.98 (978-1-55909-028-5(6), 35) Randolph Tapes.
To be used as background while doing your own exercise routine to your music, with your instructor, video tape, etc. Subliminal messages are heard 3-5 minutes before becoming ocean sounds or music.

Fitness & Exercise Motivation: Enhance Physical Health & Well-Being. Mark Bancroft. Read by Mark Bancroft. 1 cass., bklet. (Running Time: 1 hr.). (Health & Fitness Ser.). 1999. 12.95 (978-1-58522-013-7(2), 402) EnSpire Pr.
Two complete sessions plus printed instructionmanual/guidebook. With healing music soundtrack.

Fitness & Exercise Motivation: Enhance Physical Health & Well-Being. Mark Bancroft. Read by Mark Bancroft. 1 CD, 1 bklet. (Running Time: 1 hr.). (Health & Fitness Ser.). 2006. audio compact disk 20.00 (978-1-58522-056-4(6)) EnSpire Pr.

Fitness Equipment in Brazil: A Strategic Reference 2007. Compiled by Icon Group International, Inc. Staff. 2007. ring bd. 195.00 (978-0-497-35837-2(9)) Icon Grp.

Fitness First: Physical Exercises for All Ages. Grace Hill. Frwd. by Sidney Lyons. 1980. (978-0-318-52336-1(1)) G Hill.

Fitness fun Tunes. (J). 2004. audio compact disk (978-1-59250-157-1(5)) Gaiam Intl.

Fitness Walking. Great American Audio. 3 cass. (Running Time: 3 hrs.). 1990. 19.95 (978-1-55569-408-1(X), 7165) Great Am Audio.
Contains 3-60 minute digitally mastered cassettes.

Fitness Walking - Advanced. 1 cass. (Running Time: 60 min.). 1989. 9.95 (978-1-55569-308-4(3), FIW-7033) Great Am Audio.

Fitness Walking - Beginner. 1 cass. (Running Time: 60 min.). 1989. 9.95 (978-1-55569-306-0(7), FIW-7031) Great Am Audio.
Features a beat designed to walk one's way to fitness and increased energy.

Fitness Walking - Expert. 1 cass. (Running Time: 60 min.). (Fitness Walking Ser.). 1989. 9.95 (978-1-55569-309-1(1), FIW-7034) Great Am Audio.
Feature a beat designed to walk one's way to fitness and increased energy.

Fitness Walking - Intermediate. 1 cass. (Running Time: 60 min.). (Fitness Walking Ser.). 1989. 9.95 (978-1-55569-307-7(5), FIW-7032) Great Am Audio.
Features a beat designed to walk one's way to fitness and increased energy.

Fitting into a World of Bad, Rad, Outrageous & Awesome & Popularity. Jack Marshall. 1 cass. 7.98 (978-1-55503-250-0(8), 06004024) Covenant Comms.
Fitting in, without selling out.

Fitzgerald Ruse: A Sam Blackman Mystery. unabr. ed. Mark de Castrique. Read by William Dufris. (Running Time: 8.5 hrs. 0 mins.). (ENG.). 2009. 29.95 (978-1-4332-9031-2(6)); 54.95 (978-1-4332-9027-5(8)); audio compact disk 76.00 (978-1-4332-9028-2(6)) Blckstn Audio.

Fitzgerald Short Stories. unabr. ed. F. Scott Fitzgerald. Read by Alexander Scourby. 2 cass. Incl. Babylon Revisited. F. Scott Fitzgerald. (CB101CX); Bridal Party. (CB101CX); Lost Decade. (CB101CX); Three Hours between Planes. (CB101CX); (Cassette Bookshelf Ser.). 1987. 15.98 Set, Library ed. (978-0-8072-3403-7(6), CB101CX, Listening Lib) Random Audio Pubg.

Fitzgerald Short Stories, Set. unabr. ed. F. Scott Fitzgerald. Read by Alexander Scourby. 2 cass. (Cassette Bookshelf Ser.). 2000. 15.95 (978-0-8072-3498-3(2), CB 101 CXR, Listening Lib) Random Audio Pubg.

Fitzgerald's the Great Gatsby. Kate Maurer. (Cliffs Notes (Playaway) Ser.). 2007. 34.99 (978-1-60252-890-1(X)) Find a World.

***FitzOsbornes in Exile.** unabr. ed. Michelle Cooper. (Montmaray Journals). (ENG.). (J). 2011. audio compact disk 50.00 (978-0-307-74720-4(4), Listening Lib) Pub: Random Audio Pubg. Dist(s): Random

Five-BX Exercise Plan. unabr. ed. William Orban. 1 cass. 12.95 (1539) J Norton Pubs.
Keep fit, trim, & physically alert by regularly performing.

***Five Characters in Search of an Exit.** 2010. audio compact disk (978-1-59171-210-7(6)) Falcon Picture.

Five Children & IT. E. Nesbit. Read by Anna Bentinck. (Running Time: 2 hrs. 30 mins.). 2005. 20.95 (978-1-60083-741-8(7)) Iofy Corp.

Five Children & IT. abr. ed. E. Nesbit. 2 CDs. audio compact disk 17.98 (978-962-634-305-0(2), NA230512) Naxos.

Five Children & IT. unabr. ed. E. Nesbit. Read by Johanna Ward. 4 cass. (Running Time: 5 hrs. 30 mins.). 1994. 32.95 (978-0-7861-0779-7(0), 1507) Blckstn Audio.
Curious to see if people on the other side of the globe walk upside down, Robert, Anthea, Cyril, & Jane start digging a hole to Australia. They don't get too far, however, before they dig up a furry brown creature with bat's ears. It is a Psammead, an ancient Sand-fairy. The Sammyadd - as the children call it - grumpily tells them that he is obliged to grant their wishes, because making people's wishes come true is what Sand-fairies do. However, there is one catch: The wishes come undone at sunset. No matter how carefully the children plan, their wishes keep backfiring - like Robert's wish that everyone would love the Lamb, his baby brother, which leads to the Lamb's nearly being kidnapped.

Five Children & IT. unabr. ed. E. Nesbit. Narrated by Virginia Leishman. 4 pieces. (Running Time: 5 hrs. 45 mins.). (gr. 5 up). 2001. 39.00 (978-0-7887-4556-0(5), 96330E7) Recorded Bks.
On a summer holiday in the countryside of England, five children suddenly find themselves left alone with the housekeeper. They soon find more adventure than they can handle after digging up a sand fairy.

Five Children & IT. unabr. ed. E. Nesbit. Narrated by Virginia Leishman. 4 cass. (Running Time: 5 hrs. 45 mins.). (YA). 2001. pap. bk. & stu. ed. 53.24 Recorded Bks.

Five Children & It, Set. E. Nesbit. Narrated by Flo Gibson. 4 cass. (Running Time: 6 hrs.). (J). 1985. 19.95 (978-1-55685-053-0(0)) Audio Bk Con.
The world of Anthea, Cyril, Robert, Jane & "the lamb" is transformed by a Psammead, or sand fairy, who grants their wishes with unexpected results.

Five Chinese Brothers see Cinco Hermanos Chicos

Five Chinese Brothers. 2004. bk. 24.95 (978-0-89719-872-1(7)); pap. bk. 18.95 (978-1-55592-412-6(3)); pap. bk. 38.75 (978-1-55592-414-0(X)); pap. bk. 32.75 (978-1-55592-199-6(X)); pap. bk. 14.95 (978-1-56008-052-7(3)); 8.95 (978-1-56008-896-7(6)); 8.95 (978-1-56008-130-2(9)); cass. & flmstrp 30.00 (978-0-89719-591-1(4)); audio compact disk 12.95 (978-1-55592-910-7(9)) Weston Woods.

Five Chinese Brothers. Claire Huchet Bishop. Illus. by Kurt Wiese. 1 cass., 5 bks. (Running Time: 10 min.). (J). pap. bk. 32.75 Weston Woods.
Possession of a different supernatural quality saves each of five identical brothers when one is condemned to death.

Five Chinese Brothers. Claire Huchet Bishop. Illus. by Kurt Wiese. 1 cass. (Running Time: 10 min.). (J). (gr. k-4). bk. 24.95 (RAC018); pap. bk. 12.95 (RAC018) Weston Woods.

Five Conversations You Must Have with Your Daughter. unabr. ed. Vicki Courtney. Narrated by Pam Ward. (Running Time: 8 hrs. 12 mins. 54 sec.). (ENG.). 2010. 19.59 (978-1-60814-637-6(5)); audio compact disk 27.99 (978-1-59859-694-6(2)) Oasis Audio.

Five Crayons: French. Created by Berlitz Publishing. 1. (Running Time: 1 hr.). (Berlitz Adventures with Nicholas Ser.). (ENG & FRE., (ps-3). 2006. audio compact disk 9.95 (978-981-246-828-4(5)) Pub: Berlitz Pubng. Dist(s): Langenscheidt

Five Crayons French. Ed. by Berlitz Publishing Staff. 1. (Running Time: 30 mins.). (Berlitz Adventures with Nicholas Ser.). (ENG & FRE., 2005. audio compact disk 16.95 (978-981-246-751-5(3), 467513) Pub: Berlitz Pubng. Dist(s): Langenscheidt

Five Crayons: Italian. Created by Berlitz Publishing. 1. (Running Time: 1 hr.). (Berlitz Adventures with Nicholas Ser.). (ENG & ITA., (ps-3). 2006. audio compact disk 9.95 (978-981-246-830-7(7)) Pub: Berlitz Pubng. Dist(s): Langenscheidt

Five Crayons: Spanish. Created by Berlitz Publishing. 1. (Running Time: 1 hr.). (Berlitz Adventures with Nicholas Ser.). (ENG & SPA., (ps-3). 2006. audio compact disk 9.95 (978-981-246-831-4(5)) Pub: Berlitz Pubng. Dist(s): Langenscheidt

Five Crayons Spanish. Ed. by Berlitz Publishing Staff. 1. (Running Time: 30 mins.). (Berlitz Adventures with Nicholas Ser.). (ENG & SPA., 2005. audio compact disk 16.95 (978-981-246-752-2(1), 467521) Pub: Berlitz Pubng. Dist(s): Langenscheidt

Five Creatures. abr. ed. Emily Jenkins. 1 cass. (Running Time: 7 mins.). (J). 2004. bk. 24.95 (978-1-55592-147-7(7)); bk. 24.95 (978-1-55592-148-4(5)) Weston Woods.
Three people and two cats form a cozy quintet in the picture book based on a venn-diagram of the author's own family. It playfully charts comparisons between five family members' varied talents and tastes.

Five Creatures. abr. ed. Emily Jenkins. 1 cass. (Running Time: 7 mins.). (J). (ps-2). 2004. 8.95 (978-1-55592-827-8(7)); audio compact disk 12.95 (978-1-55592-894-0(3)) Weston Woods.

Five Days in London. unabr. ed. John Lukacs. Read by Geoffrey Howard. (Running Time: 6.5 hrs. 0 mins.). 2008. 29.95 (978-1-4332-4571-8(X)); audio compact disk & audio compact disk 60.00 (978-1-4332-4570-1(1)) Blckstn Audio.

Five Days in London: May 1940. John Lukacs. Narrated by Aelred Rosser. 6 CDs. (Running Time: 6 hrs. 30 mins.). audio compact disk 58.00 (978-0-7887-4752-6(5)) Recorded Bks.

Five Days in London: May 1940. John Lukacs. Narrated by Aelred Rosser. 6 CDs. (Running Time: 6 hrs. 30 mins.). 2000. audio compact disk 58.00 (C1240E7) Recorded Bks.
The course of history hung in the balance for five long days while Churchill's War Cabinet debated whether to negotiate with Hitler or continue opposing him. Transports you to London to listen in on the high level talks at 10 Downing Street & to observe the mood of the people on the street.

Five Days in London: May 1940. unabr. ed. John Lukacs. Read by Geoffrey Howard. 5 cass. (Running Time: 7 hrs. 30 min.). 2001. (978-0-7861-1921-9(7)) Blckstn Audio.
The days from May 24 to May 28, 1940, altered the course of history this century, as the members of the British War Cabinet debated whether to negotiate with Hitler or to continue the war.

Five Days in London: May 1940. unabr. ed. John Lukacs. Read by Geoffrey Howard. 5 cass. (Running Time: 8 hrs.). 2001. 27.95 Penton Overseas.

Five Days in London: May 1940. unabr. ed. John Lukacs. Narrated by Aelred Rosser. 5 cass. (Running Time: 6 hrs. 30 mins.). 2000. 46.00 (978-0-7887-4083-1(0), 96170E7) Recorded Bks.
The course of history hung in the balance for five long days while Churchill's War Cabinet debated whether to negotiate with Hitler or continue opposing him. Transports you to London to listen in on the high level talks at 10 Downing Street & to observe the mood of the people on the street.

Five Days in London, May 1940. unabr. ed. John Lukacs. Read by Geoffrey Howard. 5 cass. (Running Time: 7 hrs.). 2003. 39.95 (978-0-7861-1685-0(4), 2507) Blckstn Audio.
The days from May 24 to May 28, 1940 altered the course of history of this century, as the members of the British War Cabinet debated whether to negotiate with Hitler or to continue the war.

Five Directions. Neuro-Acoustic Laboratories Staff. 6 cass. (Running Time: 6 hrs.). 1996. 59.95 Set, incl. bklet. (14020PA) Nightingale-Conant.

Five Dysfunctions of a Team. unabr. ed. Patrick Lencioni. Intro. by Patrick Lencioni. Read by Charles Stransky. (Running Time: 13500 sec.). (ENG.). 2006. audio compact disk 30.00 (978-0-7393-3257-3(0), Random AudioBks) Pub: Random Audio Pubg. Dist(s): Random

Five Dysfunctions of a Team: A Leadership Fable. unabr. ed. Patrick Lencioni. Read by Charles Stransky. 3 CDs. (Running Time: 3 hrs.). 2006. audio compact disk 45.00 (978-1-4159-2977-3(7)); 36.00 (978-1-4159-2976-6(9)) Books on Tape.
After her first two weeks observing the problems at DecisionTech, Kathryn Petersen, its new CEO, had more than a few moments when she wondered is she should have taken the job. But Kathryn knew there was little chance she would have turned it down. After all, retirement had made her antsy, and

nothing excited her more than a challenge. What she could not have known when she accepted the job, however, was just how dysfunctional her team was, and how team members would challenge her in ways that no one ever had before.

Five Element Acupuncture: An Overview. Ann Bailey. Read by Ann Bailey. Read by Jon Bailey. 1 cass. (Running Time: 50 min.). (Wellness Through the Seasons Ser.). 1992. 12.00 incl. script. (978-1-889643-01-4(7)) SourcePoint.
Music, sounds & spoken word explain & illustrate acupuncture as a healthcare system.

Five Elements. Bruce Goldberg. Read by Bruce Goldberg. 1 cass. (Running Time: 25 min.). (ENG.). 2006. 13.00 (978-1-57968-005-3(4)) Pub: B Goldberg. Dist(s): Baker Taylor
Through self-hypnosis be introduced to your spirit guides that help strengthen the five elements of the soul.

Five Essentials of Communication. Mac Hammond. 2008. audio compact disk 6.00 (978-1-57399-379-1(4)) Mac Hammond.

Five Fabulous Folktales. Melea J. Brock. Illus. by Melea J. Brock. 1. (Running Time: 40 mins.). Dramatization. 1996. 10.00 (978-0-9667455-5-9(8)) Right-Side-Up.

Five Farthings. Susan Sallis. Read by Nicolette McKenzie. 10 CDs. (Soundings (CDs) Ser.). (J). 2005. audio compact disk 89.95 (978-1-84283-648-4(X)) Pub: ISIS Lrg Prnt GBR. Dist(s): Ulverscroft US

Five Farthings. unabr. ed. Susan Sallis. Narrated by Nicolette McKenzie. 10 cass. (Running Time: 14 hrs.). (Soundings Ser.). (J). 2005. 84.95 (978-1-84283-560-9(2)) Pub: ISIS Lrg Prnt GBR. Dist(s): Ulverscroft US

Five Fold Ministry & Help. David T. Demola. 1 cass. 4.00 (1-085) Faith Fellow Min.

Five-Fold Nature of the Self. Manly P. Hall. 5 cass. (Running Time: 150 min.). 1999. 40.00 set incl. album. (978-0-89314-121-9(6), S630522) Philos Res.

Five Forces of Wellness: The Ultraprevention System for Living an Active, Age-Defying, Disease-Free Life. unabr. ed. Mark Hyman. Read by Mark Hyman. (Running Time: 8 hrs. 0 mins. 0 sec.). (ENG.). 2006. audio compact disk 39.95 (978-0-7435-6140-2(6), Nightgale) Pub: S&S Audio. Dist(s): S and S Inc

***Five-Forty-Eight.** abr. ed. John Cheever. Read by Meryl Streep et al. (ENG.). 2009. (978-0-06-125290-7(5), Caedmon) HarperCollins Pubs.

***Five-Forty-Eight.** unabr. ed. John Cheever. Read by Meryl Streep et al. (ENG.). 2009. (978-0-06-196863-1(3), Caedmon) HarperCollins Pubs.

Five Frightening Biblical Facts: Matthew 7:21-23. Ed Young. 1983. 4.95 (978-0-7417-1323-0(3), 323) Win Walk.

Five from Commedia del Arte. S. Petch. 2 cass. (Running Time: 3 hrs.). 2005. audio compact disk 15.95 (978-0-660-18525-5(3)) Pub: Canadian Broadcasting CAN. Dist(s): Georgetown Term
Stroll the streets of Venice, and encounter some familiar favourites - Arlecchino and Isabella, il Dottore and il Capitano - and sometimes in deeply compromising positions! Pantolone's Dream brings together some of the best known and best loved comic plays of the last thousand years. Adapted for radio by Steve Petch and produced by Bill Lane - the same team that brought The Arabian Nights to CBC radio - this new production features hilarious performances from many of the same multi-talented performers.

Five Go off in a Caravan. unabr. ed. Enid Blyton. Read by Jan Francis. 4 cass. (Running Time: 6 hrs.). (Famous Five Adventure Ser.). (J). (gr. 1-8). 1999. 32.95 (CCA 3482, Chivers Child Audio) AudioGO.

Five Gods We Worship. 2007. audio compact disk 20.00 (978-1-58602-354-6(3)) E L Long.

Five Habits for Happiness: Create Joy in Your Everyday Life. Carl R. Nassar. Read by Carl R. Nassar. 1 CD. (Running Time: 46 mins.). 2001. audio compact disk 12.95 (978-0-9701595-0-2(1)) Miracle.

Five Habits for Happiness: Create Joy in Your Everyday Life. unabr. ed. Carl R. Nassar. Read by Carl R. Nassar. 1 cass. (Running Time: 45 mins.). 2001. 9.95 (978-0-9701595-1-9(X)) Miracle.
Dr. Carl R. Nassar, founder & director of the Miracle Center has not only invented a workable formula for creating happiness, but he packaged it.

Five Hans Christian Andersen Stories. unabr. ed. Hans Christian Andersen. Tr. by Erik Blegvad. Narrated by Aurora Wetzel. 1 cass. (J). (ps up). 1995. 9.95 (978-1-887393-10-2(2), 030) Aurora Audio.
Side A: The Shepherdess & the Chimney Sweep; The Sweethearts; The Pixie at the Grocer's. Side B: The Tinderbox; Twelve by Coach.

Five Horsemen of the Apocalypse. Chuck Missler. 1 CD-ROM. (Running Time: 10 hours). (Five Horsemen of the Apocalypse Ser.). 2000. 39.95 (978-1-57821-095-4(X)) Koinonia Hse.
In addition to the Four Horsemen of the Apocalypse depicted in Revelation Chapter 6, and their contemporary implications, Chuck Missler also explores some of the prevalent misunderstandings regarding the Ultimate Victor presented in Revelation Chapter 19 and unravels the controversies surrounding the Harpazo (or Rapture) which continues to cause confusion among many believers.

Five Keys to Emotional Balance. James Edward. 1 cass. (Running Time: 38 min.). (Think Plaid Ser.: No. 2). 1996. (978-0-9655823-0-8(2)) Keys to Opptnity.
Motivational material to help people live better lives & feel better about themselves.

Five Keys to High Performance: Juggle Your Way to Success. unabr. ed. Michael J. Gelb. Read by Michael J. Gelb. (Running Time: 4 hrs.). (ENG.). 2009. 19.98 (978-1-59659-434-0(9), GildAudio) Pub: Gildan Media. Dist(s): HachBkGrp

Five Key's to Living with Bipolar Disorder. Short Stories. Paul Edward Jones. (Running Time: 39mins). 2007. 14.95 (978-0-9758512-5-8(X)) ZassCo Pub.

Five Kingdoms: Life on Earth. Lynn Margulis & Karlene V. Schwartz. 1996. audio compact disk 96.00 (978-3-540-14501-1(X)) Spri.

Five Languages of Apology: How to Experience Healing in All Your Relationships. unabr. ed. Gary Chapman & Jennifer Thomas. Narrated by Gary Chapman & Jennifer Thomas. (ENG.). 2006. 16.09 (978-1-60814-206-4(X)) Oasis Audio.

Five Languages of Apology: How to Experience Healing in All Your Relationships. unabr. ed. Jennifer Thomas & Gary Chapman. Narrated by Jennifer Thomas & Gary Chapman. (Running Time: 23400 sec.). (ENG.). 2006. audio compact disk 22.99 (978-1-59859-149-1(5)) Oasis Audio.

Five Languages of Love. Taffi L. Dollar. 10.00 (978-1-59089-036-3(1)) Pub: Creflo Dollar. Dist(s): STL Dist NA

Five Lessons a Millionaire Taught Me about Life & Wealth. unabr. ed. Richard Paul Evans. Read by Richard Paul Evans. 2 CDs. (Running Time: 2 hrs. 0 mins. 0 sec.). (ENG.). 2005. audio compact disk 19.95 (978-0-7435-5236-3(9), Sound Ideas) Pub: S&S Audio. Dist(s): S and S Inc

Five Lessons a Millionaire Taught Me about Life & Wealth. unabr. ed. Richard Paul Evans. Read by Richard Paul Evans. 2006. 11.95 (978-0-7435-5587-6(2)) Pub: S&S Audio. Dist(s): S and S Inc

Five Lessons a Millionaire Taught Me for Women: About Life & Wealth. unabr. ed. Richard Paul Evans. Read by Richard Paul Evans. (Running Time: 3 hrs. 0 mins. 0 sec.). (ENG.). 2009. audio compact disk 19.99 (978-0-7435-9676-3(5)) Pub: S&S Audio. Dist(s): S and S Inc

Five Lessons I Didn't Learn from Breast Cancer (and One Big One I Did) Shelley Lewis. 2008. audio compact disk 23.95 (978-1-59316-139-2(5)) Listen & Live.

Five Lies That Ruin Relationships CD Series. 2005. audio compact disk 27.00 (978-1-59834-006-8(9)) Walk Thru the Bible.

Five Little Ladybugs: God Made Me to March & Sing. Karyn Henley. (ENG.). (J). 2006. audio compact disk 8.99 (978-1-933803-12-8(6)) Child Sens Comm.

Five Little Monkeys: Songs for Singing & Playing. 1 cass. (J). 2001. pap. bk. 10.95 (KIM 9155C); pap. bk. 14.95 (KIM 9155CD) Kimbo Educ.
Full of wiggles, giggles & fun! Kid-pleasing songs of old & new blend together for a lively musical mix.Full of wiggles, giggles & fun! Kid-pleasing songs of old & new blend together for a lively musical mix.You?ll want to keep this collection of classic singable songs handy. Kid-pleasing songs of old and new blend together for a lively musical mix. Includes extension activities and links to books. Timeless tunes include "Teddy Bear, Teddy Bear," "Down on Grandpa?s Farm," "It?s a Small World," "Wizard of Oz," "Dem Bones," "Mairsy Doats," a new jazzed up version of "Five Little Monkeys" & more. (Learning Fun, Early Childhood, Singable Songs) Includes guide with lyrics and activities.

Five Little Monkeys Jumping on the Bed Audiobook on CD. Eileen Christelow. (J). (gr. k-ps). 2005. audio compact disk 6.00 (978-0-618-70907-6(X), Clarion Bks) HM Harcourt.

Five Little Penguins Slipping on the Ice. Steve Metzger. Directed By Cheryl Smith. Illus. by Laura Bryant. Narrated by Fred Berman. Contrib. by Michael Abbott. (ENG.). (J). (ps-3). 2008. audio compact disk 18.95 (978-0-545-07408-7(8)) Scholastic Inc.

Five Little Peppers: And How They Grew. unabr. ed. Margaret Sidney. Read by Rebecca Burns. (J). 2007. 44.99 (978-1-59895-924-6(7)) Find a World.

Five Little Peppers & How They Grew. Margaret Sidney. Read by Rebecca C. Burns. (Running Time: 27000 sec.). (ENG.). (J). (ps-7). 2005. audio compact disk 59.99 (978-1-4001-3123-5(5)); audio compact disk 29.99 (978-1-4001-0123-8(9)); audio compact disk 19.99 (978-1-4001-5123-3(6)) Pub: Tantor Media. Dist(s): IngramPubServ

Five Little Peppers & How They Grew. unabr. ed. Margaret Sidney. Read by Grace Conlin. (Running Time: 25200 sec.). (J). (gr. 4-7). 2007. audio compact disk 29.95 (978-0-7861-7272-6(X)); audio compact disk 55.00 (978-0-7861-6195-9(7)) Blckstn Audio.

Five Little Peppers & How They Grew. unabr. ed. Margaret Sidney. Read by Flo Gibson. 5 cass. (Running Time: 7 hrs. 30 min.). (Classic Books on Cassette). (J). 1988. 20.95 (978-1-55685-103-2(0)) Audio Bk Con.
The homespun tale of Polly, Ben, Joel, Davie & Phronsie Pepper who grow up in a poor household that is rich in love, joy & laughter.

Five Little Peppers & How They Grew. unabr. ed. Margaret Sidney. Read by Grace Conlin. 5 cass. (Running Time: 7 hrs.). 1995. 39.95 (978-0-7861-0882-4(7), 1531) Blckstn Audio.
An adorable family of children growing up in a small town & cared for by their widowed mother. She is so poor that the pittance earned by her as the town seamstress fails to support or even sustain the family. The children are happy despite privation & the smallest pleasures cause delight & merriment in the little house. Everything happens to this brood while mother is away sewing, & no matter how dangerous the situation, they come out of it safe & smiling. Later on in the story, when the oldest girl faces a real chance to be adopted as a member of a rich family, she chooses to return to her poor old home. The author finds a way to make everybody happy.

Five Little Peppers & How They Grew, unabr. ed. Margaret Sidney. Narrated by Sally Darling. 6 cass. (Running Time: 8 hrs. 45 mins.). (gr. 4). 1997. 53.00 (978-0-7887-0528-1(8), 94723E7) Recorded Bks.
The five Pepper children have secret plans to surprise their mother on her birthday. But how can they make those plans come true without any money?.

Five Little Peppers & How They Grew. unabr. ed. Margaret Sidney. Narrated by Rebecca Burns. (Running Time: 7 hrs. 30 mins. 0 sec.). (ENG.). (J). 2009. audio compact disk 55.99 (978-1-4001-4127-2(3)) Pub: Tantor Media. Dist(s): IngramPubServ

Five Little Peppers & How They Grew. unabr. collector's ed. Margaret Sidney. Read by Rebecca C. Burns. 5 cass. (Running Time: 7 hrs. 30 mins.). (J). 1998. 40.00 (978-0-7366-4181-4(5), 4679) Books on Tape.
An adorable family of children growing up in a small town & cared for by their widowed mother.

Five Little Peppers & How They Grew, with EBook. unabr. ed. Margaret Sidney. Narrated by Rebecca Burns. (Running Time: 7 hrs. 30 mins. 0 sec.). (ENG.). (J). 2009. 19.99 (978-1-4001-6127-0(4)); audio compact disk 27.99 (978-1-4001-1127-5(7)) Pub: Tantor Media. Dist(s): IngramPubServ

***Five Little Peppers & How They Grew, with EBook.** unabr. ed. Margaret Sidney. Narrated by Rebecca Burns. (Running Time: 7 hrs. 30 mins.). (J). 2009. 27.99 (978-1-4001-9127-7(0)); 14.99 (978-1-4001-8127-8(5)) Tantor Media.

Five Little Pigs. unabr. ed. Agatha Christie. Read by Hugh Fraser. 5 cass. (Running Time: 6 hrs. 37 mins.). 2004. 27.95 (978-1-57270-407-7(1)) Pub: Audio Partners. Dist(s): PerseuPGW
A young woman named Carla Lemarchant needs Hercule Poirot's help. Sixteen years earlier, her father died from poison. Her mother was convicted of the crime and died after a year in prison. Carla fears that the man she is about to marry will always view her with suspicion unless her mother's name can be cleared. Poirot must delve deep into the past to find the real truth. Was it really murder? Suicide? Or, for sixteen years, has someone lived with the knowledge that he - or she - has committed the perfect crime?.

Five Little Pigs. unabr. ed. Agatha Christie. Narrated by Hugh Fraser. 6 CDs. (Mystery Masters Ser.). (ENG.). 2004. audio compact disk 29.95 (978-1-57270-408-4(X)) Pub: AudioGO. Dist(s): Perseus Dist

Five Little Pigs: A BBC Radio Full-Cast Dramatization. Agatha Christie. (Running Time: 1 hr. 30 mins. 0 sec.). (ENG.). 2009. audio compact disk 24.95 (978-1-60283-730-0(9)) Pub: AudioGO. Dist(s): Perseus Dist

Five Loaves for Levi. Bob Hartman & Michael McGuire. 1 cass. (J). (ps-3). 1994. 11.99 (3-0004) David C Cook.

Five Loaves for Levi. Bob Hartman & Mike McGuire. (What Was It Like Ser.). (J). 1994. 11.99 (3-0004) David C Cook.

Five Love Languages: How to Express Heartfelt Commitment to Your Mate. abr. ed. Gary Chapman. (ENG.). 2002. audio compact disk 16.99 (978-1-881273-37-0(7)) Pub: Northfield Pub. Dist(s): Moody
For partners seeking harmony, how we express ourselves is as important as what we say. This CD helps us figure out which words and actions our spouse interprets as loving and affirming, and which ones are indifferent and demeaning.Click here for the Study Guide for Spouse and Group Discussion.

Five Love Languages: How to Express Heartfelt Commitment to Your Mate. unabr. ed. Gary Chapman. Read by Gary Chapman. (Running Time: 18000 sec.). 2006. audio compact disk 45.00 (978-0-7861-6033-4(0)) Blckstn Audio.

Five Love Languages: How to Express Heartfelt Commitment to Your Mate. unabr. ed. Gary Chapman. Read by Gary Chapman. (YA). 2007. 44.99 (978-1-60252-720-1(2)) Find a World.

Five Love Languages: How to Express Heartfelt Commitment to Your Mate. unabr. ed. Gary Chapman. Narrated by Gary Chapman. (Running Time: 4 hrs. 46 mins. 52 sec.). (ENG.). 2005. 13.99 (978-1-60814-211-8(6)); audio compact disk 27.99 (978-1-58926-906-4(3)) Oasis Audio.

Five Love Languages: How to Express Heartfelt Commitment to Your Mate. unabr. ed. Gary Chapman. Narrated by Gary Chapman. (Running Time: 4 hrs. 59 mins. 27 sec.). (ENG.). 2005. audio compact disk 27.99 (978-1-59859-066-1(9)) Oasis Audio.

Five Love Languages: How to Express Heartfelt Commitment to Your Mate. unabr. ed. Gary Chapman. Narrated by Chris Fabry. (Running Time: 5 hrs. 51 mins. 58 sec.). (ENG.). 2009. audio compact disk 22.99 (978-1-59859-547-5(4)) Oasis Audio.

Five Love Languages: Men's Edition: How to Express Heartfelt Commitment to Your Mate. unabr. ed. Gary Chapman. Narrated by Gary Chapman. (Running Time: 4 hrs. 59 mins. 27 sec.). (ENG.). 2005. 19.59 (978-1-60814-212-5(4)) Oasis Audio.

Five Love Languages of Children. Gary Chapman & Ross Campbell. 2 cass. (Running Time: 90 min. per cass.). (ENG.). 1997. 14.99 (978-1-881273-11-0(3)) Pub: Northfield Pub. Dist(s): Moody

Five Love Languages of Children. abr. ed. Gary Chapman & Ross Campbell. 3 CDs. (Running Time: 2 hrs.45 mins.). (ENG.). 2005. audio compact disk 16.99 (978-1-881273-85-1(7)) Pub: Northfield Pub. Dist(s): Moody

Five Love Languages of Children. unabr. ed. Gary Chapman. Narrated by Chris Fabry. (ENG.). 2008. 13.99 (978-1-60814-208-8(6)) Oasis Audio.

Five Love Languages of Children. unabr. ed. Gary Chapman & Ross Campbell. Narrated by Chris Fabry. (ENG.). 2008. audio compact disk 19.99 (978-1-59859-394-5(3)) Oasis Audio.

Five Love Languages of Teenagers. abr. ed. Gary Chapman. 3 CDs. (Running Time: 3 hrs.15 mins.). (ENG.). 2005. audio compact disk 16.99 (978-1-881273-78-3(4)) Pub: Northfield Pub. Dist(s): Moody
Best-selling author of The Five Love Languages, Gary Chapman, narrates as you learn how to apply the love languages to your relationship with your teenagers. This audio compact disc is the perfect solution for those who are auditory learners, are sight-impaired, or who want to make best use of their time during a long commute or trip. Let the love languages transform your teenagers and you!.

Five Love Languages of Teenagers. unabr. ed. Gary Chapman. Narrated by Chris Fabry. (Running Time: 8 hrs. 33 mins. 6 sec.). (ENG.). 2008. 19.59 (978-1-60814-210-1(8)); audio compact disk 27.99 (978-1-59859-393-8(5)) Oasis Audio.

***Five Love Languages: Singles Edition.** unabr. ed. Gary Chapman. Narrated by Chris Fabry. (ENG.). 2009. 16.09 (978-1-60814-665-9(0)) Oasis Audio.

Five Main Ministries. Derek Prince. 6 cass. 29.95 (I-MM1) Derek Prince.

Five Megilloth, Set. Read by Tovah Feldshuh & Gregg Edelman. 5 pieces. (Running Time: 1 hr.). (Bible Titles Ser.). 2002. reel tape 49.95 (978-0-8276-0544-2(7)) JPS Phila.

Five Messages. unabr. ed. Robert A. Monroe. Read by Robert A. Monroe. (Running Time: 45 min.). (Gateway Experience - Adventure Ser.). 1984. 14.95 (978-1-56113-269-0(1)) Monroe Institute.
Gain insight into your total self.

Five Minds for the Future. unabr. ed. Howard Gardner. Read by Mark Adams. 5 CDs. (Running Time: 6 hrs. 15 mins.). (ENG.). 2008. audio compact disk 29.98 (978-1-59659-152-3(8), GildAudio) Pub: Gildan Media. Dist(s): HachBkGrp

Five-Minute Bible Stories. Lois Rock. Read by Clifford Norgate. 2 CDs. 2006. audio compact disk 21.95 (978-0-7540-6715-3(7), Chivers Child Audio) AudioGO.

Five-Minute Mysteries. unabr. ed. Jack Pachuta. Read by Jack Pachuta. 2 cass. (Running Time: 1 hr. 45 min.). Dramatization. 1995. 19.95 set. (978-1-888475-01-2(3)) Mangmt Stratgies.
Ten murder mystery scenarios, each five to six minutes in length. The mysteries are played, then the listeners attempt to solve the crimes. Solutions are then given to check logic.

Five Minutes a Day to Perfect Spelling. Kevin Trudeau & J. Mark Dufner. 6 cass. 69.95 (10010AX) Nightingale-Conant.
Kevin Trudeau & Mark Dufner - two highly successful authors & widely acknowledged experts on mind training - will teach you their proven approach to mastering spelling skills in just five minutes a day for 28 days. It's a program that will make you a "walking dictionary." And it works for adults & children. Includes workbook.

Five Minutes for Fitness. 1 cass. (Running Time: 1 hr.). (J). 2001. pap. bk. 5.95 (KIM 235C); 5.95 (KIM 235) Kimbo Educ.
Get fit in just five minutes every day! Vigorous activities for the entire body. Do fingertips to toes, trunk stretch propellers, jumping jacks. Includes guide.

Five Money-Making Ideas. unabr. ed. Howard Deutch et al. 2 cass. (Running Time: 1 hr. 27 min.). 12.50 (1325-1326) J Norton Pubs.
Covers ways to make high profits with negligible risks by investing in rolls of uncirculated coins, listed stock options, managed commodity programs, gemstones & U. S. commemorative stamps.

Five Most Important Questions: You Will Ever Ask about Your Organization. unabr. ed. Peter F. Drucker. Read by Erik Synnestvedt. (Running Time: 1 hr. 30 mins.). (ENG.). 2008. 14.98 (978-1-59659-304-6(0), GildAudio) Pub: Gildan Media. Dist(s): HachBkGrp

Five Needs Your Child Must Have Met at Home. abr. ed. Ron Hutchcraft. (Running Time: 2 hrs. 0 mins. 0 sec.). (ENG.). 2003. 7.99 (978-0-310-26039-4(6)) Zondervan.

Five Obstacles to Meditation. unabr. ed. Eknath Easwaran. Read by Eknath Easwaran. 1 cass. (Running Time: 56 mins.). 1989. 7.95 (978-1-58638-538-5(0)) Nilgiri Pr.
Easwaran identifies five obstacles that we will face in meditation and gives practical advice for overcoming them.

Five O'Clock Shadow see Sir John Betjeman Reading His Poetry

Five on a Treasure Island. unabr. ed. Enid Blyton. Read by Jan Francis. 3 cass. (Running Time: 4 hrs. 30 min.). (Famous Five Adventure Ser.). (J). 2001. 24.95 (CCA3417, Chivers Child Audio) AudioGO.

Five on Kirrin Island Again. unabr. ed. Enid Blyton. Read by Jan Francis. 4 cass. (Running Time: 6 hrs.). (Famous Five Adventure Ser.). (J). (gr. 1-8). 1999. 32.95 (CCA 3497, Chivers Child Audio) AudioGO.

Five One Act Plays. unabr. ed. W. B. Yeats. Perf. by Siobhan McKenna & Cyril Cusack. 3 cass. Dramatization. Incl. Cat & the Moon. (SWC 315); Only Jealousy of Emer. (SWC 315); Pot of Broth. (SWC 315); Purgatory. (SWC

315); Words upon a Windowpane. (SWC 315); 1988. 27.95 (978-0-694-50774-0(1), SWC 315) HarperCollins Pubs.
Cast includes: Marie Kean, Patrick Magee, Brian O'Higgins, Christopher Casson, Joyce Redman, Finuala O'Shannon, David Birch, James Caffrey, Colin Blakely, Barry Keegan, & Gillian Lind.

Five Past Midnight. unabr. ed. James Stewart Thayer. Read by David Brand. 10 vols. (Running Time: 15 hrs.). 2000. bk. 84.95 (978-0-7927-2226-7(4), CSL 115, Chivers Sound Lib) AudioGO.
Escaping from Colditz Castle as a prisoner of war, Jack Cray fights his way to Berlin in 1945, spreading a trail of terror and disinformation across Germany. The American army commando has just received orders to assassinate Hitler! But Otto Dietrich, a German detective with ties to the SS, will stop at nothing to get Cray.

Five Paths of Yoga. Manly P. Hall. 5 cass. (Running Time: 150 min.). 1999. 40.00 set incl. album. (978-0-89314-122-6(4), S800168) Philos Res.

Five People You Meet in Heaven see Cinco Personas Que Encontraras en el Cielo

Five People You Meet in Heaven. Mitch Albom. Read by Erik Singer. 5 cds. 2003. audio compact disk 40.00 (978-0-7366-9840-5(X)) Books on Tape.

Five People You Meet in Heaven. Read by Erik Singer. Ed. by Mitch Albom. 2005. 32.00 (978-0-7366-9721-7(7)) Books on Tape.

Five People You Meet in Heaven. unabr. ed. Mitch Albom. Read by Erik Singer. 4 cass. (Running Time: 6 hrs.). 2003. 25.98 (978-1-4013-9751-7(4)) Pub: Hyperion. Dist(s): HarperCollins Pubs

Five People You Meet in Heaven. unabr. ed. Mitch Albom. Read by Mitch Albom. (Running Time: 14400 sec.). 2008. audio compact disk 14.95 (978-1-4013-9134-8(6), Hyperion Audio) Pub: Hyperion. Dist(s): HarperCollins Pubs

Five Perspectives on the Problem of Evil. Read by John Sanford. 1 cass. (Running Time: 90 min.). 1981. 10.95 (978-0-7822-0244-1(6), 091) C G Jung IL.

Five Phases of Food. Annemarie Colbin. 2 cass. (Running Time: 2 hrs.). 1992. 16.95 set. (978-1-57124-004-0(7)) Creat Seminars.
Better health through better eating.

Five Principles for Christian Success. Frank Minirth & Paul Meier. Read by Frank Minirth & Paul Meier. 1 cass. (Running Time: 60 min.). (Minirth & Meier Home Counseling Audio Library). 1994. 9.95 (978-1-56707-040-8(X)) Dallas Christ Recs.
Keys that help us succeed.

Five Quarters of the Orange. unabr. ed. Joanne Harris. Read by Diana Bishop. 10 cass. (Running Time: 11 hrs.). (Sound Ser.). 2002. 84.95 (978-1-84283-084-0(8)); audio compact disk 89.95 (978-1-84283-178-6(X)) Pub: UlverLrgPrint GBR. Dist(s): Ulverscroft US
Beyond the main street of Les Laveuses runs the Loire,hiding a deadly undertow beneath its moving surface. This is where Framboise, a secretive widow named after a raspberry liqueur,piles her culinary trade at the creperie - and lets her memory play strange games. As the split blood of a tragic wartime childhood flow again, exposure beckons for Framboise, the widow with an invented past.

Five Questions. unabr. ed. Robert A. Monroe. Read by Robert A. Monroe. (Running Time: 45 min.). (Gateway Experience - Freedom Ser.). 1983. 14.95 (978-1-56113-265-2(9)) Monroe Institute.
Seek answers for a complete understanding of total self.

Five Red Herrings. unabr. ed. Dorothy L. Sayers. Read by Patrick Malahide. 10 cass. (Running Time: 15 hrs.). (Lord Peter Wimsey Mystery Ser.). 2000. 69.95 (978-0-7451-6259-1(2), CAB 607) Pub: Chivers Audio Bks GBR. Dist(s): AudioGO
With too much whiskey and some antagonism, a brawl at the McLellan Arms Pub was inevitable. And when one of the brawlers is found dead, many people found it just as inevitable. Six in particular. For Lord Peter Whimsey, the death was no accident. It wasn't the clue that convinced him, but the six undeniable suspects.

Five Relationships to God. unabr. ed. Perf. by Eknath Easwaran. 1 cass. (Running Time: 1 hr.). 1992. 7.95 Nilgiri Pr.

Five Ring Circus. unabr. ed. Jon Cleary. Read by David Tredinnick. 9 cass. (Running Time: 13 hrs. 30 mins.). 2001. (978-1-86442-364-8(1), 590270) Bolinda Pubng AUS.
As Sydney prepares for its grand role as host of the next Olympic Games. Scobie Malone is confronted with solving a scam that does nothing for the city's image. Lurking beneath the facade of respectability, illicit deals are being struck & money from Hong Kong is being banked in large quantities. But whose money is it & where is it really from? The people responsible will eliminate anyone who is a potential security risk, students & businessmen are being publicly & privately executed with the same sinister, systematic style. Meanwhile Scobie's investigation is frustrated at every turn by a wall of silence until he finds the cracks which will lead him to the unexpected truth.

Five Secrets You Must Discover Before You Die. unabr. ed. John Izzo. Narrated by John Izzo. (Running Time: 18000 sec.). (ENG.). 2007. audio compact disk 19.95 (978-1-60283-343-2(5)) Pub: AudioGO. Dist(s): Perseus Dist

Five Secrets You Must Discover Before You Die. unabr. ed. John Izzo. Read by John Izzo. 4 CDs. (Running Time: 5 hrs. 30 mins.). 2008. audio compact disk 49.95 (978-0-7927-5231-8(7)) AudioGO.
For this remarkable book and the upcoming companion TV program to be aired on PBS, Dr. John Izzo and his colleagues surveyed more than 200 people ages 60 to 106 identified by others as having lived happy lives and as having found purpose and contentment. Here he presents their valuable advice on what really matters in life, and how to put this cumulative wisdom into practice. The interviewees, ranging from aboriginal elders to town barbers, from Holocaust survivors to former CEOs, reflect back on their lives to identify the sources of happiness and meaning as well as lessons learned, regrets, and major crossroads. Based on these interviews, and Dr. Izzo's twenty years experience helping people find more spirit and purpose, the book explores the secrets to finding contentment and happiness.

Five Secrets You Must Discover Before You Die. unabr. ed. John Izzo. Read by John Izzo. (YA). 2008. 44.99 (978-1-60514-885-4(7)) Find a World.

Five Sisters. unabr. ed. Margaret Mahy. Narrated by Virginia Leishman. 2 pieces. (Running Time: 1 hr. 45 mins.). (gr. 3 up). 1998. 19.00 (978-0-7887-1914-1(9), 95335E7) Recorded Bks.
Sally's row of five paper dolls is snatched by a gust of wind & sent on a magical journey filled with adventure & laughter.

Five Skies. unabr. ed. Ron Carlson. 6 CDs. (Running Time: 7 hrs.). 2007. audio compact disk 80.00 (978-1-4159-4038-9(X)) Random.

Five Smooth Stones CD Series. 2004. audio compact disk 27.00 (978-1-59834-023-5(9)) Walk Thru the Bible.

Five Stages of Animus Development. Read by Diane Martin. 2 cass. (Running Time: 2 hrs.). 1989. 16.95 Set. (978-0-7822-0159-8(8), 374) C G Jung IL.

Five States of Mind, No. 1. Swami Jyotirmayananda. Read by Swami Jyotirmayananda. 1 cass. (Running Time: 45 min.). 10.00 (817) Yoga Res Foun.

Five States of Mind, No. 2. Swami Jyotirmayananda. 1 cass. (Running Time: 45 min.). 1990. 10.00 Yoga Res Foun.

Five States of Mind, No. 3. Swami Jyotirmayananda. Read by Swami Jyotirmayananda. 1 cass. (Running Time: 45 min.). 10.00 (818) Yoga Res Foun.

Five States of Mind, No. 4. Swami Jyotirmayananda. 1 cass. (Running Time: 45 min.). 1990. 10.00 Yoga Res Foun.

Five States of Mind, No. 5. Swami Jyotirmayananda. Read by Swami Jyotirmayananda. 1 cass. (Running Time: 45 min.). 10.00 (819) Yoga Res Foun.

Five Steps to Empowerment Set: Recognizing - Releasing - Victimization. David Grudermeyer & Rebecca Grudermeyer. 2 cass. 18.95 (T-03) Willingness Wrks.

Five Steps to Successful Selling. abr. ed. Zig Ziglar. Read by Zig Ziglar. 1 cass. (Running Time: 1 hr.). 1999. 16.85 (978-0-671-03348-4(4)) S and S Inc.
Sales career success stories result from study & observation rather than inborn talent.

Five-String Banjo. Earl Scruggs. 1968. 9.95 (978-0-317-00262-1(7), 60479-960) Peermusic Classical.

Five Tales from the Decameron. unabr. ed. Giovanni Boccaccio. Perf. by David McCallum & Carole Shelley. Tr. by Richard Aldington. 1 cass. 1984. 12.95 (978-0-694-50340-7(1), SWC 1650) HarperCollins Pubs.

Five Temptations of a CEO. Patrick Lencioni. 2004. 7.95 (978-0-7435-4730-7(6)) Pub: S&S Audio. Dist(s): S and S Inc

Five Temptations of a CEO. abr. ed. Patrick Lencioni. Read by Patrick Lencioni. Read by Boyd Gaines. (Running Time: 1 hr. 30 mins. 0 sec.). (ENG.). 2006. audio compact disk 19.95 (978-0-7435-6468-7(5), Sound Ideas) Pub: S&S Audio. Dist(s): S and S Inc

Five Tests of Maturity; God's Official Position on Sin. C. S. Lovett. 1 cass. 6.95 (7019) Prsnl Christianity.
Expands on teaching of the book, "Dynamic Truths".

Five Things I Wish I Had Learned in High School. Ben Bissell. 1 cass. (Running Time: 22 min.). 15.00 C Bissell.
Dr. Bissell's primary goal is to enhance the self-esteem of adolescents. The presentation is designed for high school students, but parents & teachers will also find it helpful.

Five Thousand Dollars in Cash & The Laundermat. 1 cass. (Running Time: 60 min.). Dramatization. (Fibber McGee & Molly Ser.). 1949. 6.00 Once Upon Rad.
Radio broadcasts - humor.

Five Truths about Truth: Retreat with Adyashanti - Fall 2005. Featuring Adyashanti. 10 CDs. (Running Time: 12 hrs.). 2006. audio compact disk 85.00 (978-1-933986-07-4(7), 2FTA) Open Gate Pub.
During this landmark retreat in the fall of 2005, Adyashanti distilled the essence of his teachings into five truths about the nature of ultimate reality. New students discovered a deep resonance with the profound simplicity, while advanced students found themselves riveted by the maturity, freshness, and radical directness of the teachings. These 10 CDs offer 12 hours of edited recordings from this powerfully transformative retreat. Included are:? A series of talks on the five truths about absolute truth? A stunning talk on the nature of karma? Insightful and engaging dialogues? A guided meditation on letting everything be as it is"You are going to lose your spiritual world if you take this far enough.".

Five Universal Shapes. unabr. ed. Angeles Arrien. 1 cass. (Running Time: 40 min.). 1987. 11.00 (AR002) Big Sur Tapes.
Guides us through the five universal shapes found in all art.

Five Ways of Loving: Psalm 45, 721. Ed Young. 1989. 4.95 (978-0-7417-1721-4(2), 721) Win Walk.

Five Ways to Chart a Location. Gail A. Guttman. 1 cass. 1992. 8.95 (1036) Am Fed Astrologers.

Five Wishes: How Answering One Simple Question Can Make Your Dreams Come True. unabr. ed. Gay Hendricks. 2 CDs. (Running Time: 2 hrs.). (ENG.). 2008. audio compact disk 17.95 (978-1-57731-639-8(8)) Pub: New Wrld Lib. Dist(s): PerseuPGW

Five Year Plan. Philip Kerr. 2004. 14.95 (978-0-7435-4731-4(4)) Pub: S&S Audio. Dist(s): S and S Inc

Five-Year Plan, unabr. collector's ed. Philip Kerr. Read by Geoffrey Howard. 7 cass. (Running Time: 10 hrs. 30 min.). 1999. 56.00 (978-0-7366-4286-6(2), 4784) Books on Tape.
Ex-con Dave Delano's scheme to hijack a yacht being used to smuggle money into Russian banks coincides with his five-year plan to put a million-five in his own pockets. Trouble is the Colombian drug cartel has also loaded the luxury yachts to the rafters with cocaine. When FBI agent Kate Fury crosses paths with Dave, the result is pure combustion.

Five Year Plan, Set. abr. ed. Philip Kerr. Read by Boyd Gaines. 4 cass. 1999. 24.00 (FS9-43196) Highsmith.

Fix-It. David M. McPhail. Illus. by David M. McPhail. 11 vols. (Running Time: 3 mins.). 1988. pap. bk. 18.95 (978-1-59519-254-7(9)); pap. bk. 35.95 (978-1-59519-255-4(7)); 9.95 (978-1-59112-038-4(1)); audio compact disk 12.95 (978-1-59519-253-0(0)) Live Oak Media.

Fix-It. David M. McPhail. Illus. by David M. McPhail. Read by Larry Robinson. 11 vols. (Running Time: 3 mins.). (J). (gr. k-3). 1988. pap. bk. 16.95 (978-0-87499-083-6(1)); pap. bk. & tchr. ed. 33.95 Reading Chest. (978-0-87499-085-0(8)) Live Oak Media.
When her father finally fixes the TV set after her extended display of tears, Emma no longer cares - she's discovered the joy of reading a good book.

Fix Like This. unabr. ed. K. C. Constantine. Read by Lloyd James. 8 cass. (Running Time: 12 hrs.). (Mario Balzic Ser.). 1997. 64.00 (978-0-7366-3693-3(5), 4372) Books on Tape.
Chief Mario Balzic is a man who likes things quiet & that's why he has an arrangement with Dom Muscotti, who keeps away prostitution, drugs & extortion.

Fix Your Eyes on Christ: Teresa of Avila's Way of Prayer. Daniel Chowning. 1 cass. (Running Time: 59 min.). 8.95 I C S Pubns.
Fr. Daniel Chowning, O.C.D. emphasizes Teresa's strong conviction about the humanity of Jesus in prayer.

Fixed Point: The Life & Death of Sherlock Holmes. David Stuart Davies. Contrib. by Meredith Granger. 1 cass. (Running Time: 30 min.). Dramatization. 1996. 7.95 (978-1-888728-03-3(5)) Clssic Spclties.
Sherlock Holmes is dead; Dr. Watson is in a home for the elderly. While giving an interview to a young reporter, Watson relives important life moments. Slipping in & out of consciousness, Watson interacts with the spirit of Holmes. The ending is a touching reunion of the famous pair.

Fixed Stars. Marilyn Muir. 1 cass. 8.95 (804) Am Fed Astrologers.

Fixer. unabr. collector's ed. Bernard Malamud. Read by Wolfram Kandinsky. 8 cass. (Running Time: 12 hrs.). 1986. 64.00 (978-0-7366-0890-9(7), 1834) Books on Tape.
Yakov Bok is an ordinary man accused of "ritual murder" & persecuted by agents of a remote & all-powerful state. But when he is pushed too far, he triumphs over incredible brutality & becomes a moral giant.

Fixer Upper. Mary Kay Andrews. Read by Isabel Keating. (ENG.). 2009. 64.99 (978-1-61574-927-0(6)) Find a World.

***Fixer Upper.** unabr. ed. Mary Kay Andrews. Read by Isabel Keating. (ENG.). 2009. (978-0-06-190227-7(6), Harper Audio); (978-0-06-190228-4(4), Harper Audio) HarperCollins Pubs.

Fixer Upper. unabr. ed. Mary Kay Andrews. Read by Isabel Keating. 2009. audio compact disk 39.99 (978-0-06-176804-0(9), Harper Audio) HarperCollins Pubs.

Fixing Hell: An Army Psychologist Confronts Abu Ghraib. abr. ed. Larry C. James. Read by Eric Kramer. Frwd. by Philip G. Zimbardo. Told to Gregory A. Freeman. (Running Time: 7 hrs.). (ENG.). 2008. 24.98 (978-1-60024-360-8(6)) Pub: Hachet Audio. Dist(s): HachBkGrp

Fl Prelic Key. 29th ed. Ed. by Kaplan Publishing Staff. 2005. cd-rom 34.88 (978-1-4195-2599-5(9)) Dearborn Financial.

Flabbergasted. unabr. ed. Ray Blackston. 6 cass. (Running Time: 9 hrs.). 2004. 29.99 (978-1-58926-331-4(6), 890619) Oasis Audio.

Flabbergasted. unabr. ed. Ray Blackston. Narrated by Andrew Peterson. (ENG.). 2003. 24.49 (978-1-60814-213-2(2)); audio compact disk 34.99 (978-1-58926-332-1(4), 100424, Oasis Kids) Oasis Audio.

Flag: Early Explorers Emergent Set B Audio CD. Katherine Scraper. Adapted by Benchmark Education Staff. (J). 2007. audio compact disk 10.00 (978-1-4108-8203-5(9)) Benchmark Educ.

Flag for Sunrise. (2141) Am Audio Prose.

***Flag in Exile.** unabr. ed. David Weber. Read by Allyson Johnson. (Running Time: 16 hrs.). (Honor Harrington Ser.). 2010. 29.99 (978-1-4418-6621-9(3), 9781441866219, Brilliance MP3); 44.97 (978-1-4418-6622-6(1), 9781441866226, Brinc Audio MP3 Lib); 44.97 (978-1-4418-6623-3(X), 9781441866233, BADLE) Brilliance Audio.

***Flag in Exile.** unabr. ed. David Weber. Read by Allyson Johnson. (Running Time: 17 hrs.). (Honor Harrington Ser.: Bk. 5). 2010. audio compact disk 29.99 (978-1-4418-6619-6(1), 9781441866196); audio compact disk 99.97 (978-1-4418-6620-2(5), 9781441866202, BriAudCD Unabrid) Brilliance Audio.

Flag of Truce. David Donachie. 2009. 76.95 (978-1-4079-0031-5(5)); audio compact disk 89.95 (978-1-4079-0032-2(3)) Pub: Soundings Ltd GBR. Dist(s): Ulverscroft US

Flags Around the World: Early Explorers Early Set B Audio CD. Edward Dixon. Adapted by Benchmark Education Staff. (J). 2007. audio compact disk 10.00 (978-1-4108-8234-9(9)) Benchmark Educ.

Flags of Our Fathers. abr. movie tie-in ed. James Bradley. Read by Barry Bostwick. 5 CDs. (Running Time: 23400 sec.). (ENG.). 2006. audio compact disk 14.99 (978-0-7393-3219-1(8), Random AudioBks) Pub: Random Audio Pubg. Dist(s): Random

Flak. unabr. ed. Michael Veitch. Read by Michael Veitch. (Running Time: 8 hrs. 50 mins.). 2007. audio compact disk 87.95 (978-1-74093-928-7(X), 9781740939287) Pub: Bolinda Pubng AUS. Dist(s): Bolinda Pub Inc

Flak. unabr. ed. Michael Veitch. Read by Michael Veitch. (Running Time: 8 hrs. 50 mins.). 2009. 43.95 (978-1-74214-141-1(2), 9781742141411) Pub: Bolinda Pubng AUS. Dist(s): Bolinda Pub Inc

Flambards. unabr. ed. K. M. Peyton. 5 cass. (Running Time: 5 hrs. 51 mins.). (Isis Cassettes Ser.). (J). 2004. 49.95 (978-0-7531-2010-1(0)) Pub: ISIS Lrg Prnt GBR. Dist(s): Ulverscroft US

Flame. unabr. ed. John Lutz. Read by Multivoice Production Staff. (Running Time: 6 hrs.). 2008. 24.95 (978-1-4233-5953-1(4), 9781423359531, BAD); 24.95 (978-1-4233-5951-7(8), 9781423359517, Brilliance MP3); 39.25 (978-1-4233-5952-4(6), 9781423359524, Brinc Audio MP3 Lib); 39.25 (978-1-4233-5954-8(2), 9781423359548, BADLE) Brilliance Audio.

Flame & the Flower. abr. ed. Kathleen E. Woodiwiss. Read by Jessica Arden. 1 cass. (Running Time: 90 min.). 1994. 5.99 (978-1-57096-018-5(6), RAZ 919) Romance Alive Audio.
After one night's mistake, Heather Simmons is plunged into marriage with Captain Brandon Birmingham. She embarks upon a voyage to the American colonies where her sweet & innocent seduction must woo her unwilling husband.

Flame in All of Us. Contrib. by Thousand Foot Krutch. Prod. by Ken Andrews. 2007. audio compact disk 17.99 (978-5-557-62795-5(2)) Tooth & Nail.

Flame in Your Heart / Life Is a Joy & Stress Is No More. Ormond McGill. 2005. audio compact disk (978-1-933332-38-3(7)) Hypnotherapy Train.

Flame in Your Heart / Life Is a Joy & Stress Is No More- 2 Sides. Ormond McGill. 1 cassette - 2 sides. 2000. (978-1-933332-04-8(2)) Hypnotherapy Train.

Flame Meditation. Instructed by Joe Powers. Music by Sammy Ibrahim. 1 CD. (Running Time: 24.47 Mins). 2004. audio compact disk 15.00 (978-0-9749458-1-1(1)) Soul Graffiti.

Flame of Pure Fire: Jack Dempsey & the Roaring '20s. unabr. ed. Roger Kahn. Read by Kevin Yon. (Running Time: 17 hrs.). 2009. 44.97 (978-1-4233-7783-2(4), 9781423377832, Brinc Audio MP3 Lib); 44.97 (978-1-4233-7785-6(0), 9781423377856, BADLE); 29.99 (978-1-4233-7782-5(6), 9781423377825, Brilliance MP3); 29.99 (978-1-4233-7784-9(2), 9781423377849, BAD); audio compact disk 99.97 (978-1-4233-7781-8(8), 9781423377818, BriAudCD Unabrid); audio compact disk 39.99 (978-1-4233-7780-1(X), 9781423377801, Bril Audio CD Unabri) Brilliance Audio.

Flame Out. unabr. ed. Keith Douglass. Read by David Hilder. 7 cass. (Running Time: 10 hrs.). (Carrier Ser.: No. 4). 2001. 29.95 (978-0-7366-6790-6(3)) Books on Tape.
Military hardliners resurrect the Soviet Union & launch a world takeover. It's up to Carrier Battle Group Fourteen to stop the Red march.

Flame Out. unabr. collector's ed. Keith Douglass. Read by David Hilder. 7 cass. (Running Time: 10 hrs. 30 mins.). (Carrier Ser.: No. 4). 1995. 56.00 (978-0-7366-3171-6(2), 3841) Books on Tape.
With the Cold War over, the world breathes easier. But then the unthinkable happens. Military hardliners resurrect the Soviet Union & a new Red machine strikes without warning. It crushes Norway & gobbles up Finland. The U.S. president knows where he can turn. He orders Carrier Battlegroup Fourteen to take out the Soviet amphibious force at all costs. Are Lt. Commander Tombstone Magruder & his crew a match for this relentless new aggressor?.

Flame Trees of Thika: Memories of an African Childhood. unabr. collector's ed. Elspeth Huxley. Read by Wanda McCaddon. 8 cass. (Running Time: 12 hrs.). 1984. 64.00 (978-0-7366-0832-9(X), 1783) Books on Tape.
Elspeth Huxley recreates for us a vanished Africa & shows it to us from the viewpoint of a perceptive child.

Flamedragon's Dance. unabr. ed. Gary Martin. Read by Gary Martin. 6 cass. (Running Time: 9 hrs.). 1996. 44.95 (978-0-7861-0616-5(6), 893861) Blckstn Audio.
In a world before recorded time, it was still possible for animals & strange mythical creatures to talk to humans - if they would take the time to listen. One human who did take the time, & thus had many animal friends, was Young Tom. Living in a peaceful little village, he could only dream of brave deeds & glorious guests. Then strange rumors of the rise of the "nasties" & the terrible Moloch began to reach the village. Soon Tom found himself on a heroic quest that was beyond even his imaginings - with the fate of his people in his hands.

Flamedragon's Dance, Set. unabr. ed. Gary Martin. Read by Gary Martin. 6 cass. (Running Time: 9 hrs.). (J). (gr. 6-12). 1994. 29.00 in vinyl album. (C-253) Jimcin Record.
A peaceful kingdom is threatened by "nasties." It takes young Tom, his forest friends & the Flamedragon to set things right again.

***Flamenco al Piano 2: Tangos: Metodo Progresivo: Aprendizaje, Interpretacion, Improvisacion, Composicion.** Lola Fernandez. (Flamenco: Didactica Ser.). (ENG & SPA.). 2009. audio compact disk 39.99 (978-84-936260-3-7(1)) AcordesCon ESP.

Flamenco, Body & Soul. Juan Serrano et al. 1 cass. 1989. bk. 26.95 (978-0-912201-20-7(7)); pap. bk. 16.95 (978-0-912201-21-4(5)) CSU Pr Fresno.

Flamenco Dreams. Perf. by Benedetti & Svoboda. 1 cass., 1 CD. 8.78 (DOMO 45601); audio compact disk 12.78 CD Jewel box. (DOMO 45601) NewSound.

Flamenco Guitar - Basic Techniques (Technicas Basicas) Juan Serrano. (ENG.). 1996. spiral bd. 24.95 (978-0-7866-2556-7(2), 93632BCD) Mel Bay.

Flaming Corsage. unabr. collector's ed. William Kennedy. Read by Michael Prichard. 8 cass. (Running Time: 8 hrs.). (Albany Cycle Ser.). 1996. 48.00 (978-0-7366-3405-2(3), 4051) Books on Tape.

Flaming Tree. unabr. ed. Phyllis A. Whitney. Read by Anna Fields. 6 cass. (Running Time: 7 hrs. 30 mins.). 1999. 44.95 (978-0-7861-1563-1(7), 2394) Blckstn Audio.
A compassionate woman haunted by her past. A mysterious man who leads her to love. And the dangerous secret that is stronger than both of them.

***Flaming Tree.** unabr. ed. Phyllis A. Whitney. Read by Anna Fields. (Running Time: 8 hrs.). 2010. 29.95 (978-1-4417-6708-0(8)); audio compact disk 76.00 (978-1-4417-6706-6(1)) Blckstn Audio.

Flaming Tree, Set. unabr. ed. Phyllis A. Whitney. Read by Anna Fields. 6 cass. 1999. 44.95 (FS9-50953) Highsmith.

Flaming Turkey. abr. ed. Robert H. Neill. Read by Robert H. Neill. 2 cass. (Running Time: 2 hrs. 30 min.). 1990. 15.95 set. (978-0-9617591-5-5(1)) MS River Pub.
A collection of stories about friendship, love of the out-of-doors, & turkey hunting. From the author's book.

Flamingo's Smile: Reflections in Natural History. unabr. collector's ed. Stephen Jay Gould. Read by Grover Gardner. 10 cass. (Running Time: 15 hrs.). 1987. 80.00 (978-0-7366-1187-9(8), 2107) Books on Tape.
Flamingos that feed upside down; flowers & snails that change from male to female; the probability that an errant asteroid sounded the death knell of the dinosaurs & ushered in the evolution of mankind...these are only a few of the things that open our eyes to the endless delights of Gould's subject.

Flanders' Fields: Canadian Voices from WWI. Interview. 3 DVDs. (Running Time: 17 hrs). 2006. audio compact disk 24.95 (978-0-660-19617-6(4), CBC Audio) Canadian Broadcasting CAN.

Flanimals. Ricky Gervais. 2006. audio compact disk (978-0-571-23193-5(4)) F F Ltd GBR.

Flap Your Wings. P. D. Eastman. (J). 1989. 8.97 (978-0-676-31541-7(0)) Glencoe.

Flappers & Philosophers. unabr. ed. Short Stories. F. Scott Fitzgerald. Read by William Dufris. 5 cass. (Running Time: 7 hrs.). 2000. 39.95 (978-0-7861-1789-5(3), 2588) Blckstn Audio.
Several of Fitzgerald's most beloved tales are represented in this classic collection of eight, including "Bernice Bobs Her Hair," "Head & Shoulders," "The Cut-Glass Bowl" & "The Offshore Pirate.".

Flappers & Philosophers. unabr. ed. Short Stories. F. Scott Fitzgerald. Read by William Dufris. 6 CDs. (Running Time: 25200 sec.). 2000. audio compact disk 48.00 (978-0-7861-9871-9(0), 2588) Blckstn Audio.

Flappers & Philosophers, Set. F. Scott Fitzgerald. Read by Flo Gibson. 5 cass. (Running Time: 7 hrs.). 1995. 20.95 (978-1-55685-369-2(6)) Audio Bk Con.
This remarkable & varied collection of stories includes: "The Offshore Pirate," "The Ice Palace," "Head & Shoulders," "The Cut-Glass Bowl," "Bernice Bobs Her Hair," "Benediction," "Dalrymple Goes Wrong," & "The Four Fists".

Flash. Jayne Ann Krentz. Read by Barbara Garrick. 2004. 10.95 (978-0-7435-4732-1(2)) Pub: S&S Audio. Dist(s): S and S Inc

Flash. unabr. ed. Jayne Ann Krentz. Read by Kate Fleming. 8 vols. (Running Time: 12 hrs.). 2000. bk. 69.95 (978-0-7927-2378-3(3), CSL 264, Chivers Sound Lib) AudioGO.
Olivia Chantry's Seattle-based company, Light Fantastic, creates the promotional flash her clients need. When she inherits 49 percent of Glow, Inc., her uncle's high-tech lighting firm, she finds herself butting heads with Jasper Sloan, who bagged the other 51 percent. From the start of their feisty business dealings, the partners nearly crash & burn & barely keep control of the sexual energy crackling between them. When they discover a blackmailer, intent on uncovering secrets & when extortion turns to murder, a union of their minds & hearts might be their only chance to stay alive.

Flash. unabr. ed. Jayne Ann Krentz. Read by Kate Fleming. 8 CDs. (Running Time: 12 hrs.). 2002. audio compact disk 79.95 (978-0-7927-9853-8(8), SLD 104, Chivers Sound Lib) AudioGO.
Olivia Chantry is a business dynamo: her company, Light Fantastic, provides the promotional flash her clients need. When she inherits 49 percent of Glow, Inc., she finds herself butting heads with Jasper Sloan, the interloper who bagged the other 51 percent. But when she and Sloan discover a blackmailer intent on uncovering secrets at Glow, Inc., and when extortion turns to murder, a union of their minds and hearts might be their only chance to stay alive.

Flash: Stop Motion. unabr. ed. Mark Schultz. Read by Richard Rohan. 6 CDs. (Running Time: 6 hrs.). (Justice League of America Ser.). 2009. audio compact disk 19.99 (978-1-59950-537-4(1)) GraphicAudio.

***Flash Burnout.** unabr. ed. L. K. Madigan. Read by MacLeod Andrews. (Running Time: 12 hrs.). 2010. 39.97 (978-1-4418-8247-9(2), 9781441882479, Brlnc Audio MP3 Lib); 24.99 (978-1-4418-8246-2(4), 9781441882462, Brilliance MP3); 39.97 (978-1-4418-8248-6(0), 9781441882486, BADLE); audio compact disk 59.97 (978-1-4418-8245-5(6), 9781441882455, BriAudCD Unabrid) Brilliance Audio.

***Flash Burnout.** unabr. ed. L. K. Madigan. Read by MacLeod Andrews. (Running Time: 8 hrs.). (YA). 2010. audio compact disk 24.99 (978-1-4418-8244-8(8), 9781441882448, Bril Audio CD Unabri) Brilliance Audio.

Flash Cards & Music CD Set. Weekly Reader Staff. (ps-k). 19.95 (978-0-8374-8256-9(9)) Wkly Read Corp.

Flash Fiction. (Running Time: 0 hr. 30 mins.). 2005. 16.95 (978-1-59912-926-6(4)) Iofy Corp.

Flash for Freedom! unabr. ed. George MacDonald Fraser. Read by David Case. 8 cass. (Running Time: 12 hrs.). (Flashman Ser.). 1994. 64.00 (978-0-7366-2724-5(3), 3454) Books on Tape.
A cad & scoundrel, Flashman takes a turn at running slaves. Funny & outrageous satire.

Flash Gordon. collector's ed. Perf. by Steve Holland et al. 1 DVD. (Running Time: 3 hrs.). (TV from Yesteryear Ser.). 2001. bk. 9.98 (7806) Radio Spirits.
Contains three classic television shows and three complete old time radio shows.

Flash Point. James W. Huston. Read by Adams Morgan. 2000. 43.95 (978-1-59912-490-2(4)) Iofy Corp.

Flash Point. unabr. ed. James W. Huston. Read by Adams Morgan. 14 cass. (Running Time: 20 hrs. 30 mins.). 2000. 89.95 (978-0-7861-1896-0(2), 2689); audio compact disk 136.00 (978-0-7861-9799-6(4), 2689) Blckstn Audio.
Sean Woods & Tony Vialli are F-14 pilots stationed aboard the USS George Washington in the Mediterranean. During a port call in Naples, Vialli falls for a beautiful woman who lures him out of the country to visit her. His lover's trip becomes a nightmare when Vialli & the woman are brutally attacked in what appears to be a terrorist action. When the United States refuses to retaliate against the man claiming responsibility, Woods joins a group of Israeli Air Force pilots, flying a section of F-14s with the Israelis, without the US Navy's knowledge. His flight turns into one of the biggest air battles since World War II. He must fight for his life, then fight to keep what he has done secret from the Navy & the rest of the world.

***Flash Point.** unabr. ed. James W. Huston. Read by Adams Morgan. (Running Time: 19 hrs. 30 mins.). 2010. audio compact disk 29.95 (978-1-4417-3576-8(3)) Blckstn Audio.

Flash Point. unabr. ed. James W. Huston. Narrated by George Guidall. 15 CDs. (Running Time: 16 hrs. 45 mins.). 2001. audio compact disk 142.00 (978-1-4025-0515-7(9), C1571) Recorded Bks.
Sean Woods, an F-14 pilot aboard the USS George Washington, is enraged when his roommate is killed in an apparent terrorist attack in Israel. Woods secretly participates in an epic air battle to take the terrorist out, but the mission fails. To Woods' great satisfaction, the United States declares war directly on the terrorist leader and unleashes the frightening power of the Navy. With a second chance to exact revenge, Woods intends to hit the mark. This action-packed novel could only be produced by someone with Huston's impressive credentials. A Top Gun graduate, he served as a flight officer in F-14s aboard the USS Nimitz, and worked in Naval intelligence.

Flash Point. unabr. ed. James W. Huston. Narrated by George Guidall. 12 cass. (Running Time: 16 hrs. 45 mins.). 2001. 98.00 (978-0-7887-4925-4(0), 96457E7) Recorded Bks.
A Top Gun graduate creates a story charged with explosive military action & political intrigue, when his roommate is murdered by terrorists & Sean Woods is out for revenge.

Flashback. Nevada Barr. 9 cass. (Running Time: 16 hrs.). (Anna Pigeon Ser.: No. 11). 2004. 34.99 (978-1-4025-3633-5(X), 02624) Recorded Bks.

Flashback. Created by Saddleback Educational Publishing. 1 cass. (Running Time: 4044 sec.). (PageTurner Science Fiction Ser.). (J). 2002. audio compact disk 10.95 (978-1-56254-487-4(X), SP 487X) Saddleback Edu.
Word-for-word read-along of Flashback.

***Flashback.** Jenny Siler. Read by Betty Bobbitt. (Running Time: 9 hrs.). 2009. 64.99 (978-1-74214-283-8(4), 9781742142838) Pub: Bolinda Pubng AUS. Dist(s): Bolinda Pub Inc

Flashback. abr. ed. Nevada Barr. Read by Joyce Bean. 4 cass. (Running Time: 6 hrs.). (Anna Pigeon Ser.: No. 11). 2003. 62.25 (978-1-59086-009-0(8), 1590860098); audio compact disk 74.25 (978-1-59086-007-6(1), 1590860071) Brilliance Audio.
Running from a proposal of marriage from Sheriff Paul Davidson, Anna Pigeon takes a post as a temporary supervisory ranger on remote Garden Key in Dry Tortugas National Park, a small grouping of tiny islands in a natural harbor seventy miles off Key West. This island paradise has secrets it would keep; not just in the present, but in shadows from its gritty past, when it served as a prison for the Lincoln conspirators during and after the Civil War. Here, on this last lick of the United States, in a giant crumbling fortress, Anna has little company except for an occasional sunburned tourist or unruly shrimper. When her sister, Molly, sends her a packet of letters from her great-great-aunt who lived at the fort with her husband, a career soldier, Anna's fantasy life is filled with visions of this long-ago time. When a mysterious boat explosion - and the discovery of unidentifiable body parts - keeps her anchored to the present, Anna finds crimes of past and present closing in on her. A tangled web that was woven before she arrived begins to threaten her sanity and her life. Cut off from the mainland by miles of water, poor phone service, and sketchy radio contact, and aided by one law-enforcement ranger, Anna must find answers or weather a storm to rival the hurricanes for which the islands are famous.

Flashback. abr. ed. Nevada Barr. Read by Joyce Bean. (Running Time: 21600 sec.). (Anna Pigeon Ser.: No. 11). 2005. audio compact disk 16.99 (978-1-59600-406-1(1), 9781596004061, BCD Value Price) Brilliance Audio.

Flashback. abr. ed. Nevada Barr. Read by Joyce Bean. (Running Time: 6 hrs.). (Anna Pigeon Ser.). 2006. 24.95 (978-1-4233-0067-0(X), 9781423300670, BAD) Brilliance Audio.

Flashback. abr. ed. Nevada Barr. Read by Joyce Bean. (Running Time: 6 hrs.). (Anna Pigeon Ser.: No. 11). 2006. 39.25 (978-1-4233-0068-7(8), 9781423300687, BADLE); audio compact disk 39.25 (978-1-4233-0066-3(1), 9781423300663, Brlnc Audio MP3 Lib); audio compact disk 24.95 (978-1-4233-0065-6(3), 9781423300656, Brilliance MP3) Brilliance Audio.

Flashback. unabr. ed. Nevada Barr. Narrated by Barbara Rosenblat. 11 cass. (Running Time: 16 hrs.). (Anna Pigeon Ser.: No. 11). 2003. 104.00 (978-1-4025-3850-6(2)) Recorded Bks.

Flashback. unabr. ed. Jenny Siler. Read by Betty Bobbitt. 8 x CDs. (Running Time: 32400 sec.). 2006. audio compact disk 49.95 (978-1-74094-904-0(8)); audio compact disk 87.95 (978-1-74093-700-9(7)) Pub: Bolinda Pubng AUS. Dist(s): Bolinda Pub Inc

***Flashback.** unabr. ed. Dan Simmons. (Running Time: 12 hrs.). (ENG.). 2011. 24.98 (978-1-60941-974-5(X)); audio compact disk & audio compact disk 34.98 (978-1-60941-972-1(3)) Pub: Hachet Audio. Dist(s): HachBkGrp

Flashback: A Dramatic Musical for Youth about the Faithfulness of God. Barny C. Robertson. 10 cass. (Running Time: 10 hrs.). (YA). 2001. bk. 54.99 (TA-9277PK); 12.99 (TA-9277C) Lillenas.
A youth musical that deals with some of the hard questions of life. Set in the 1970s, this new look at difficult questions shows that God's faithfulness never changes. The musical will provide your youth with an excellent opportunity for outreach & evangelism.

Flashback: A Dramatic Musical for Youth about the Faithfulness of God. Barry C. Robertson. 1 cass. (Running Time: 1 hr.). (J). 2001. 80.00 (MU-9277C); 80.00 (MU-9277T) Lillenas.
Meet Quasar, Venus & Polaris - "star" characters in this imaginative kids' musical. Along with Moon, their adult adviser, these heavenly characters interact with earth & relate their views of present-day Christmas & the original Christmas event. Original songs & an intriguing arrangement of "O Little Town of Bethlehem" combine with a highly creative, humorous script, giving solo & dramatic opportunities for lots of kids. The trax are especially fresh-sounding, utilizing "live" instruments. A strong, biblical message of God's love & concern for us is woven throughout, offering a uniquely evangelistic message from children. Accompaniment compact disc includes both split-channel & stereo trax mixes.

Flashback: The Amazing Adventures of a Film Horse. unabr. ed. Gillian Rubinstein. Read by Francis Greenslade. 2 CDs. (Running Time: 8100 sec.). (J). (gr. 3-8). 2005. audio compact disk 43.95 (978-1-74093-689-7(2)) Pub: Bolinda Pubng AUS. Dist(s): Bolinda Pub Inc

Flashcards on Tape: Civil Procedure. 2002. 22.95 (978-1-932440-40-9(2)) Flmngs Fdmntls Law.
Flashcards on tapes are interactive learning. An area of law is stated, then a 15 second delay, then the run of law is stated. Students are the say the rule of law and then repeat the rule.

Flashcards on Tape: Contracts 1. 1 cassette. (Running Time: 1 hour). 2002. 22.95 (978-1-932440-41-6(0)) Flmngs Fdmntls Law.

Flashcards on Tape: Contracts 2. 1 cassette. (Running Time: 1 hour). 2002. 22.95 (978-1-932440-42-3(9)) Flmngs Fdmntls Law.

Flashcards on Tape: Criminal Law 1. 1 audio tapes. (Running Time: 40 minutes). 2002. 22.95 (978-1-932440-37-9(2)) Flmngs Fdmntls Law.

Flashcards on Tape: Property 1. 1 CASSESTTE. (Running Time: 1 HOUR). 2002. 22.95 (978-1-932440-45-4(3)) Flmngs Fdmntls Law.

Flashcards on Tape: Torts 1. 1 cassette. (Running Time: 1 hour). 2002. 22.95 (978-1-932440-43-0(7)) Flmngs Fdmntls Law.

Flashcards on Tape: Torts 2. 1 cassette. (Running Time: 1 hours). 2002. 22.95 (978-1-932440-44-7(5)) Flmngs Fdmntls Law.

Flashcards on Tapes. 1 cassette. (Running Time: 1 hour). 2002. 22.95 (978-1-932440-46-1(1)) Flmngs Fdmntls Law.

Flashdance... What a Feeling - ShowTrax. Arranged by Kirby Shaw. 1 CD. (Running Time: 5 mins.). 2000. audio compact disk 19.95 (08201200) H Leonard.
This '80s classic has inspiring lyrics, a great hook & a powerful rock setting in this Kirby Shaw update.

Flashfire. unabr. ed. Richard Stark, pseud. 5 cass. (Running Time: 7 hrs. 30 mins.). 2001. 40.00 (978-0-7366-6206-2(5)) Books on Tape.
In a Midwestern city, Parker calmly tosses a firebomb through a plate-glass window, while some newfound partners in crime take down a nearby bank. Making their getaway, the bank robbers tell him that this heist was only seed money for a much gaudier one, & that Parker has to loan them his share of the take.

Flashforward. unabr. ed. Robert J. Sawyer. Read by Mark Deakins & Stefan Rudnicki. (Running Time: 10 hrs. 50 mins.). 2009. 29.95 (978-1-4332-5296-9(1)) Blckstn Audio.

Flashforward. unabr. ed. Robert J. Sawyer. Read by Mark Deakins. (Running Time: 10 hrs. 50 mins.). 2009. 65.95 (978-1-4332-5293-8(7)); audio compact disk 100.00 (978-1-4332-5294-5(5)) Blckstn Audio.

Flashforward. unabr. ed. Robert J. Sawyer. Read by Stefan Rudnicki. (Running Time: 10 hrs. 50 mins.). 2009. audio compact disk 29.95 (978-1-4332-5295-2(3)) Blckstn Audio.

Flashing Before My Eyes: 50 Years of Headlines, Deadlines & Punchlines. unabr. ed. Dick Schaap. Narrated by Dick Schaap. 8 cass. (Running Time: 10 hrs. 30 mins.). 2001. 74.00 (978-0-7887-9912-9(6)) Recorded Bks.
Longtime host of ESPN's The Sports Reporters recounts a charmed career in which he has met almost everyone and seen alomst everything.

Flashman. unabr. ed. George MacDonald Fraser. Read by David Case. 7 cass. (Running Time: 10 hrs. 30 min.). (Flashman Ser.). 1994. 56.00 (978-0-7366-2675-0(1), 3412) Books on Tape.
For starters, Harry Flashman is expelled from school as a drunken bully. After seducing his father's mistress, he begins a secret life that leads from the boudoirs & bordellos of Victorian England to the erotic frontiers of her exotic Empire. Along the way he lies, cheats, steals, fights fixed duels, betrays his country & proves a coward on the battlefield.

Flashman & the Angel of the Lord. unabr. ed. George MacDonald Fraser. Read by David Case. 10 cass. (Running Time: 15 hrs.). (Flashman Ser.). 1995. 80.00 (978-0-7366-3131-0(3), 3806) Books on Tape.
A hussy's pretty foot sends Flashy on hair-raising misadventures that shape America's Civil War period. Funny & accurate.

Flashman & the Dragon. unabr. ed. George MacDonald Fraser. Read by David Case. 9 cass. (Running Time: 13 hrs. 30 min.). (Flashman Ser.). 1995. 72.00 (978-0-7366-3053-5(8), 3735) Books on Tape.
Flashy rises to new lows in the ancient world. His most uninhibited, erotic adventure yet. Funny & educational.

Flashman & the Mountain of Light. unabr. ed. George MacDonald Fraser. Read by David Case. 10 cass. (Running Time: 15 hrs.). (Flashman Ser.). 1995. 80.00 (978-0-7366-3096-2(1), 3772) Books on Tape.
Good men are hard to find. But the British Empire wants a bad one, & they look no further than Harry Flashman. England seeks the brightest.

Flashman & the Redskins. unabr. ed. George MacDonald Fraser. Read by David Case. 12 cass. (Running Time: 18 hrs.). (Flashman Ser.). 1995. 96.00 (978-0-7366-3007-8(4), 3693) Books on Tape.
In the Old West, Flashy runs from danger, prospects cowboys & Indians for their women. Hilarious adventure.

Flashman & the Tiger. unabr. ed. George MacDonald Fraser. Read by David Case. 9 cass. (Running Time: 13 hrs. 30 mins.). 2000. 72.00 (978-0-7366-5575-0(1), 5389) Books on Tape.
The memoirs of Sir Harry Flashman, the celebrated Victorian soldier and scoundrel, are always full of adventures, related with verve, dash and meticulous historical detail. Now come three new episodes in the career of this eminent and disreputable adventurer. Flashy is once again at the center of pivotal historic events, the attempted assassination of Emperor Franz Joseph in the 1880s, the Tranby Croft gambling scandal involving the Price of Wales, and the aftermath of Rorke's Drift. Thrown into contact with assorted royalty, grand tarts, and political heavyweights, the author again observes the unvarnished early twentieth century.

Flashman & the Tiger. unabr. ed. George MacDonald Fraser. Read by David Case. 11 CDs. (Running Time: 13 hrs. 12 mins.). 2001. audio compact disk 88.00 Books on Tape.
Three new episodes in the career of this eminent & disreputable adventurer. Flashy is once again at the center of pivotal historic events - the attempted assassination of Emperor Franz Joseph in the 1880s, the Tranby Croft

gambling scandal involving the Prince of Wales & the aftermath of Rorke's Drift. Thrown into contact with assorted royalty, grand tarts & political heavyweights, including Bismarck, Flashman observes the uncensored truth about some of the twentieth century's greatest heroes & scoundrels.

Flashman & the Tiger. unabr. ed. George MacDonald Fraser. Read by David Case. 9 cass. (Running Time: 13 hrs. 30 mins.). 2000. 34.95 (978-0-7366-5688-7(X)) Books on Tape.

Flashman at the Charge. unabr. ed. George MacDonald Fraser. Read by David Case. 8 cass. (Running Time: 12 hrs.). (Flashman Ser.). 1994. 64.00 (978-0-7366-2775-7(8), 3494) Books on Tape.
With his usual courage, the world-class bounder Flashman runs away from Charge of the Light Brigade.

Flashman in the Great Game. unabr. collector's ed. George MacDonald Fraser. Read by Donada Peters. 9 cass. (Running Time: 13 hrs. 30 min.). (Flashman Ser.). 1995. 72.00 (978-0-7366-2908-9(4), 3605) Books on Tape.
Victorian England's swashbuckling scoundrel stumbles into the middle of an Indian mutiny as a secret agent extraordinaire.

Flashman's Lady. unabr. collector's ed. George MacDonald Fraser. Read by David Case. 9 cass. (Running Time: 13 hrs. 30 min.). (Flashman Ser.). 1995. 72.00 (978-0-7366-3008-5(2), 3694) Books on Tape.
Flashy takes a lecherous world tour. Don Juan would die with envy.

Flashpoint. Suzanne Brockmann. Read by Melanie Ewbank & Patrick G. Lawlor. (Troubleshooter Ser.: No. 7). 2008. 79.99 (978-1-60640-915-2(8)) Find a World.

Flashpoint. James W. Huston. Read by Adams Morgan. 1 cass. (Running Time: 1 hr. 30 min.). 2001. (2689); audio compact disk (z2689) Blckstn Audio.
Sean Woods and Tony Vialli are F-14 pilots stationed aboard the USS George Washington. During a port call in Naples, Vialli falls for a beautiful woman who lures him out of the country. Vialli submits false leave papers, swears Woods to secrecy and flies off to see her. His lover's trip becomes a nightmare when Vialli and the woman are brutally attacked in what appears to be a terrorist action.

Flashpoint. abr. ed. Suzanne Brockmann. Read by Melanie Ewbank & Patrick G. Lawlor. (Running Time: 21600 sec.). (Troubleshooter Ser.: No. 7). 2008. audio compact disk 14.99 (978-1-4233-6224-1(1), 9781423362241, BCD Value Price) Brilliance Audio.

Flashpoint. unabr. ed. Richard Aellen. Read by Bill Weideman. (Running Time: 8 hrs.). 2008. 39.25 (978-4-233-58565-7(X), 978423358565, Brlnc Audio MP3 Lib); 39.25 (978-4-233-58589-3(7), 978423358589, BADLE); 24.95 (978-4-233-58558-9(7), 978423358558, Brilliance MP3); 24.95 (978-4-233-58572-5(2), 978423358572, BAD) Brilliance Audio.

Flashpoint. unabr. ed. Richard Aellen. Read by Bill Weideman. (Running Time: 9 hrs.). 2008. 24.95 (978-1-4233-5857-2(0), 9781423358572, BAD); 39.25 (978-1-4233-5856-5(2), 9781423358565, Brlnc Audio MP3 Lib); 39.25 (978-1-4233-5858-9(9), 9781423358589, BADLE); 24.95 (978-1-4233-5855-8(4), 9781423358558, Brilliance MP3) Brilliance Audio.

Flashpoint. unabr. ed. Suzanne Brockmann. Read by Melanie Ewbank & Patrick G. Lawlor. 9 cass. (Running Time: 13 hrs.). (Troubleshooter Ser.: No. 7). 2004. 34.95 (978-1-59355-590-0(3), 1593555903) Brilliance Audio.
Jimmy Nash has already lived two lives - and he can't talk about either of them. Formerly an operative of a top secret government agency, he has found a new job with a shadowy company called SOS Inc. Created by a former Navy SEAL, SOS Inc. helps anyone in desperate need - which provides a perfect cover for its other, more perilous objective: covert special operations. Now Nash and a quickly assembled team of expert operators have come to the earthquake-ravaged country of Kazbekistan in the guise of relief workers. There, amid the dust and death, in a land of blood red sunsets and ancient blood feuds, they must track down a missing laptop computer that may hold secrets vital to national security. To get it done, Nash does what he does best: break every rule in the book and manipulate those who can help him get what he needs. But this time, Nash may have met his match in Tess Bailey, an SOS operative with all the right instincts - and zero field experience. The deep attraction between them is immediate . . . and potentially volatile, with risk at every turn.

Flashpoint. unabr. ed. Suzanne Brockmann. Read by Patrick G. Lawlor & Melanie Ewbank. (Running Time: 13 hrs.). (Troubleshooter Ser.: No. 7). 2004. audio compact disk 107.25 (978-1-59355-594-8(6), 1593555946) Brilliance Audio.

Flashpoint. unabr. ed. Suzanne Brockmann. Read by Melanie Ewbank & Patrick G. Lawlor. (Running Time: 13 hrs.). (Troubleshooter Ser.: No. 7). 2004. audio compact disk 38.95 (978-1-59355-593-1(8), 1593555938) Brilliance Audio.
Jimmy Nash has already lived two lives - and he can't talk about either of them. Formerly an operative of a top secret government agency, he has found a new job with a shadowy company called SOS Inc. Created by a former Navy SEAL, SOS Inc. helps anyone in desperate need - which provides a perfect cover for its other, more perilous objective: covert special operations. Now Nash and a quickly assembled team of expert operators have come to the earthquake-ravaged country of Kazbekistan in the guise of relief workers. There, amid the dust and death, in a land of blood red sunsets and ancient blood feuds, they must track down a missing laptop computer that may hold secrets vital to national security. To get it done, Nash does what he does best: break every rule in the book and manipulate those who can help him get what he needs. But this time, Nash may have met his match in Tess Bailey, an SOS operative with all the right instincts - and zero field experience. The deep attraction between them is immediate . . . and potentially volatile, with risk at every turn.

Flashpoint. unabr. ed. Suzanne Brockmann. Read by Melanie Ewbank & Patrick G. Lawlor. (Running Time: 13 hrs.). (Troubleshooter Ser.: No. 7). 2004. 39.25 (978-1-59335-532-6(7), 1593355327, Brlnc Audio MP3 Lib); 24.95 (978-1-59335-299-8(9), 1593352999, Brilliance MP3) Brilliance Audio.
Jimmy Nash has already lived two lives - and he can't talk about either of them. Formerly an operative of a top secret government agency, he has found a new job with a shadowy company called SOS Inc. Created by a former Navy SEAL, SOS Inc. helps anyone in desperate need - which provides a perfect cover for its other, more perilous objective: covert special operations. Now Nash and a quickly assembled team of expert operators have come to the earthquake-ravaged country of Kazbekistan in the guise of relief workers. There, amid the dust and death, in a land of blood red sunsets and ancient blood feuds, they must track down a missing laptop computer that may hold secrets vital to national security. To get it done, Nash does what he does best: break every rule in the book and manipulate those who can help him get what he needs. But this time, Nash may have met his match in Tess Bailey, an SOS operative with all the right instincts - and zero field experience. The deep attraction between them is immediate . . . and potentially volatile, with risk at every turn.

Flashpoint. unabr. ed. Suzanne Brockmann. Read by Patrick G. Lawlor & Melanie Ewbank. (Running Time: 13 hrs.). (Troubleshooter Ser.: No. 7). 2004. 39.25 (978-1-59710-294-0(6), 1597102946, BADLE); 24.95 (978-1-59710-295-7(4), 1597102954, BAD) Brilliance Audio.

Flashpoint. unabr. ed. Suzanne Brockmann et al. (Running Time: 13 hrs.). (Troubleshooter Ser.: No. 7). 2004. 92.25 (978-1-59355-591-7(1), 1593555911) Brilliance Audio.

Flat Edge of the Earth & Other Dramas. Harlan Ellison. Perf. by Harlan Ellison. Perf. by Nana Visitor et al. 2 cass. (Running Time: 3 hrs.). 2001. 19.95 (SEET001) Lodestone Catalog.

Flat Stanley. Jeff Brown. Read by David Healy. 1 cass. (Running Time: 30 min.). (J). (gr. k-2). (CC/011) C to C Cassettes.
A boy is flattened when his notice board falls on him. There are advantages however, when he goes to stay with a friend he can travel Air Mail.

Flat Stanley. unabr. ed. Jeff Brown. Read by David Healy. 2002. (978-1-85549-733-7(6)) Cover To Cover GBR.
Stanley is just a normal healthy boy, but since a large notice-board fell on him, he's been only half an inch thick.

Flat Stanley. unabr. ed. Jeff Brown. Read by Daniel M. Pinkwater. (Running Time: 10800 sec.). (J). 2006. audio compact disk 22.00 (978-0-06-089787-1(2)) HarperCollins Pubs.

***Flat Stanley Audio Collection.** unabr. ed. Jeff Brown. Read by Daniel M. Pinkwater. 2006. (978-0-06-122910-7(5)); (978-0-06-122909-1(1)) HarperCollins Pubs.

***Flatland: A Romance of Many Dimensions.** unabr. ed. Edwin A. Abbott. Narrated by James Langton. (Running Time: 3 hrs. 30 mins.). 2010. 11.99 (978-1-4001-8548-1(3)) Tantor Media.

***Flatland: A Romance of Many Dimensions.** unabr. ed. Abbott, Edwin A. Narrated by Langton, James. (Running Time: 3 hrs. 30 mins. 0 sec.). (ENG.). 2010. 19.99 (978-1-4001-6548-3(2)); audio compact disk 19.99 (978-1-4001-1548-8(5)); audio compact disk 39.99 (978-1-4001-4548-5(1)) Pub: Tantor Media. Dist(s): IngramPubServ

Flatpick Jam, Volume 1. Contrib. by Brad Davis. (Running Time: 2 hrs.). 2006. 24.95 (978-5-558-11113-2(5)) Mel Bay.

Flatpick Jam, Volume 3. Contrib. by Brad Davis. (Running Time: 2 hrs.). 2006. 24.95 (978-5-558-11111-8(9)) Mel Bay.

Flatpickin' the Gospels for Mandolin. Steve Kaufman. 1997. spiral bd. 23.95 (978-0-7866-3145-2(7), 95756P) Mel Bay.

***Flatpicking Bluegrass Guitar.** Lisle Crowley. (ENG.). 2010. pap. bk. 12.99 (978-1-4234-9769-1(4), 1423497694) H Leonard.

Flatpicking Collection Vol. 3: 20 Solos by Some of the World's Greatest Guitarists. Ed. by Dan Miller. 2002. bk. 19.95 (978-0-7866-6493-1(2), 20160BCD) Mel Bay.

Flatpicking Collection - 1997 Annual Edition. Ed. by Dan Miller. 1998. pap. bk. 19.95 (978-0-7866-3867-3(2), 97342BCD) Mel Bay.

***Flatpicking Guitar for the Complete Ignoramus!** Wayne Erbsen. 2010. pap. bk. 19.95 (978-1-883206-58-1(8)) Native Ground.

Flatpicking Guitar Masterpieces. Ed. by Scott Nygaard. (Acoustic Guitar Magazine's Private Lessons Ser.). 2000. pap. bk. 16.95 (978-1-890490-30-0(X)) String Letter.

Flatpicking Guitar Solos: 12 Bluegrass Standards. Created by Hal Leonard Corporation Staff. 2008. pap. bk. 16.99 (978-1-4234-3166-4(9), 1423431669) H Leonard.

Flatpicking Masters: 11 Legendary Flatpicking Solos. Transcribed by Dan Bowden. 1997. pap. bk. 19.95 (978-0-7866-3084-4(1), 96778BCD) Mel Bay.

Flatpicking the Gospels. Steve Kaufman. 1994. spiral bd. 21.95 (978-0-7866-1198-0(7), 95077P) Mel Bay.

***Flatpicking up the Neck Book/CD Set.** Jeff Troxel. 2010. pap. bk. 17.99 (978-0-7866-7938-6(7)) Mel Bay.

Flaubert: A Life. unabr. ed. Wall, Geoffrey Wall. Read by James Adams. (Running Time: 1 hr. 0 mins.). (ENG.). 2009. 29.95 (978-1-4332-1665-7(5)); 72.95 (978-1-4332-1661-9(2)); audio compact disk 105.00 (978-1-4332-1662-6(0)) Blckstn Audio.

Flautista de Hamelin. l.t. ed. Short Stories. Illus. by Graham Percy. 1 cass. (Running Time: 10 mins.). Dramatization.Tr. of Pied Piper of Hamelin. (SPA.). (J). (ps-3). 2001. 9.95 (978-84-86154-87-5(1)) Peralt Mont ESP.

Flavia & Her Artists see Troll Garden

Flavor of Fear: Seeing the Healing Hand of God. Shawna Brotherton. 2007. audio compact disk 19.99 (978-1-60247-948-7(8)) Tate Pubng.

***Flawed Dogs.** unabr. ed. Berkeley Breathed. Narrated by Johnny Heller. 1 Playaway. (Running Time: 3 hrs. 45 mins.). (J). (gr. 3-6). 2010. 54.75 (978-1-4407-7811-7(6)); 33.75 (978-1-4407-7800-1(0)); audio compact disk 46.75 (978-1-4407-7804-9(3)) Recorded Bks.

***Flawed Dogs.** unabr. collector's ed. Berkeley Breathed. Narrated by Johnny Heller. 4 CDs. (Running Time: 3 hrs. 45 mins.). (J). (gr. 3-6). 2010. audio compact disk 33.95 (978-1-4407-7808-7(6)) Recorded Bks.

Flawed Giant, Pt. 1. collector's ed. Robert Dallek. Read by Lloyd James. 12 cass. (Running Time: 18 hrs.). 2000. 96.00 (978-0-7366-5601-6(4)) Books on Tape.
In the final volume of his acclaimed biography, Dallek takes us through Lyndon Johnson's tumultuous years in the White House. We see Johnson as the visionary leader who worked his incredible will on Congress. We also see the depth of Johnson's private anguish as he became increasingly ensnared in Vietnam, a war that destroyed his hopes for The Great Society and a second term.

Flawed Giant, Pt. 2. collector's ed. Robert Dallek. Read by Lloyd James. 11 cass. (Running Time: 16 hrs. 30 min.). 2000. 88.00 (978-0-7366-5602-3(2)) Books on Tape.

***Flawless: Inside the Largest Diamond Heist in History.** unabr. ed. Scott Selby & Greg Campbell. Read by Don Hagen. (Running Time: 10 hrs.). (ENG.). 2010. 27.98 (978-1-59659-561-3(2), GildAudio) Pub: Gildan Media. Dist(s): HachBkGrp

Flawless Dog Showing Series. Created by Laura Boynton King. 5 CD's. 2002. audio compact disk 89.95 (978-0-9748885-7-6(5)) Summit Dynamics.
A 5 volume series of Self-Hypnosis CD's designed to help the dog handler become more relaxed while training and showing their dog.

Flea see Love Poems of John Donne

Flea. unabr. ed. 1 cass. (Running Time: 20 min.). Dramatization. (Magic Looking Glass Ser.). (J). (gr. 2-6). 1989. 9.95 (NIM-CW-130-1-C) NIMCO.
A Spanish folk tale.

Fleadh agus Feasta: The Songs of Colm de Bhailis. Contrib. by Colm de Bhailis. (ENG.). 1995. audio compact disk 21.95 (978-0-8023-8111-8(1)) Pub: Clo Iar-Chonnachta IRL. Dist(s): Dufour

Fleadh 'gus Feasta: The Songs of Colm de Bhailis. Contrib. by Colm de Bhailis. (ENG.). 1995. 13.95 (978-0-8023-7111-9(6)) Pub: Clo Iar-Chonnachta IRL. Dist(s): Dufour

Flecha Al Sol. Tr. of Arrow to the Sun. (SPA.). 2004. 8.95 (978-0-7882-0296-4(0)) Weston Woods.

Flecha al Sol. Gerald McDermott. Illus. by Gerald McDermott. 14 vols. (Running Time: 8 mins.). 1997. pap. bk. 39.95 (978-1-59519-164-9(X)); 9.95 (978-1-59112-039-1(X)); audio compact disk 12.95 (978-1-59519-162-5(3)) Live Oak Media.

Flecha al Sol. Gerald McDermott. Illus. by Gerald McDermott. 11 vols. (Running Time: 8 mins.). (SPA.). (J). 1997. pap. bk. 18.95 (978-1-59519-163-2(1)) Pub: Live Oak Media. Dist(s): AudioGO

Flecha al Sol: Un Cuento de los Indios Pueblo. Gerald McDermott. 1 cass. (Running Time: 35 min.).Tr. of Arrow to the Sun. (SPA., (J). 2001. 15.95 (XVS-44C) Kimbo Educ.

Flecha al Sol: Un Cuento de los Indios Pueblo. Gerald McDermott. Read by Angel Pineda. 11 vols. (Running Time: 8 mins.).Tr. of Arrow to the Sun. (SPA., 1997. pap. bk. & tchr. ed. 37.95 Reading Chest. (978-0-87499-413-1(6)) Live Oak Media.
A boy's transformation into an arrow that journeys between the sun & earth has been recognized for its unique cultural authenticity.

Flecha al Sol: Un Cuento de los Indios Pueblo. Gerald McDermott. 1 cass. (Running Time: 10 min.).Tr. of Arrow to the Sun. (SPA., (J). pap. bk. 15.95 (LM1027AC) Weston Woods.

Flecha al Sol: Un Cuento de los Indios Pueblo. unabr. ed. Gerald McDermott.Tr. of Arrow to the Sun. (ENG & SPA., (J). (gr. k-3). 1997. bk. 22.95 (978-0-87499-412-4(8)) Live Oak Media.

Flecha al Sol: Un Cuento de los Indios Pueblo. unabr. ed. Gerald McDermott. Read by Angel Pineda. 14 vols. (Running Time: 8 mins.).Tr. of Arrow to the Sun. (SPA.). (J). (gr. 3-5). 1997. pap. bk. 16.95 (978-0-87499-411-7(X), LK7305) Pub: Live Oak Media. Dist(s): AudioGO

Fledgling. Jane Langton. (YA). 2002. 17.99 (978-0-8072-0876-2(0), Listening Lib) Random Audio Pubg.

Fledgling. unabr. ed. Octavia E. Butler. Read by Tracey Leigh. 9 CDs. (Running Time: 12 hrs. 19 mins.). 2007. audio compact disk 94.95 (978-0-7927-4671-3(6)) AudioGO.

Fledgling. unabr. ed. Jane Langton. Read by Mary Beth Hurt. 3 vols. (Running Time: 4 hrs. 30 mins.). (J). (gr. 4-7). 2004. pap. bk. 36.00 (978-0-8072-8779-8(2), YA265SP, Listening Lib); 30.00 (978-0-8072-8778-1(4), Listening Lib) Random Audio Pubg.
Georgie lives in an unconventional household, but even her unusual family does not understand her belief that she can fly. Then a Canadian goose enters her life. His are the guiding wings that allow Georgie to fulfill her dream. However, where there are dreams there are always those who, lacking imagination, will seek to destroy them in the name of common sense. Georgie discovers this to her sorrow, yet learns that in opening the sky to her, her friend has truly given her the world.

Fleeced. Carol Higgins Clark. (Regan Reilly Mystery Ser.: No. 5). 2004. 15.95 (978-0-7435-4733-8(0)) Pub: S&S Audio. Dist(s): S and S Inc

Fleeced. abr. ed. Carol Higgins Clark. 2 cass. (Regan Reilly Mystery Ser.: No. 5). 1999. 17.98 (FS9-50996) Highsmith.

Fleeced. unabr. ed. Carol Higgins Clark. Read by Laura Hicks. 6 CDs. (Running Time: 6 hrs.). (Regan Reilly Mystery Ser.: No. 5). 2002. audio compact disk 54.95 (978-0-7927-2506-0(9), CSL 395, Chivers Sound Lib); audio compact disk 64.95 (978-0-7927-9946-7(1), SLD 097, Chivers Sound Lib) AudioGO.
When Regan Reilly arrives in New York City to attend a conference organized by her celebrity-author mother, the last thing she expects is to be plunged into a headline-making case. But that's just what happens when an old friend calls on Regan to investigate the murder of two fellow Settler's Club members, whose deaths have left the club in a financial bind and Regan's friend in an awful fix. Now, unless Regan can clear his name, her old friend just might find himself behind bars, if a ruthless killer doesn't get to him first.

Fleeced: How Barack Obama, Media Mockery of Terrorist Threats, Liberals Who Want to Kill Talk Radio, the Do-Nothing Congress, Companies That Help Iran, & Washington Lobbyists for Foreign Governments Are Scamming Us... & What to Do about It. Dick Morris & Eileen McGann. Read by Johnny Heller. (Playaway Adult Nonfiction Ser.). (ENG.). 2009. 65.00 (978-1-60775-621-7(8)) Find a World.

Fleeced: How Barack Obama, Media Mockery of Terrorist Threats, Liberals Who Want to Kill Talk Radio, the Do-Nothing Congress, Companies that Help Iran, & Washington Lobbyists for Foreign Governments Are Scamming Us... & What to Do about It. unabr. ed. Dick Morris & Eileen McGann. Read by Johnny Heller. 1 MP3-CD. (Running Time: 10 hrs. 30 mins. 0 sec.). (ENG.). 2008. audio compact disk 24.99 (978-1-4001-5729-7(3)); audio compact disk 69.99 (978-1-4001-3729-9(2)) Pub: Tantor Media. Dist(s): IngramPubServ

Fleeced: How Barack Obama, Media Mockery of Terrorist Threats, Liberals Who Want to Kill Talk Radio, the Do-Nothing Congress, Companies That Help Iran, & Washington Lobbyists for Foreign Governments Are Scamming Us... & What to Do about It. unabr. ed. Dick Morris & Eileen McGann. Read by Johnny Heller. 9 CDs. (Running Time: 10 hrs. 30 mins. 0 sec.). (ENG.). 2008. audio compact disk 34.99 (978-1-4001-0729-2(6)) Pub: Tantor Media. Dist(s): IngramPubServ

Fleet of Worlds. unabr. ed. Larry Niven & Edward M. Lerner. Read by Tom Weiner. (Running Time: 34200 sec.). 2008. 59.95 (978-1-4332-2941-1(2)); audio compact disk & audio compact disk 80.00 (978-1-4332-2942-8(0)); audio compact disk & audio compact disk 29.95 (978-1-4332-2945-9(5)) Blckstn Audio.

Fleming Brown: Appalachian Banjo Songs. 1 cass. 9.98 (C-4) Folk-Legacy.
Our first "Interpreter," a powerful Chicago artist.

Flesh & Blood. Michael Cunningham. 2004. 10.95 (978-0-7435-4734-5(9)) Pub: S&S Audio. Dist(s): S and S Inc

Flesh & Blood. Jonathan Kellerman. Read by John Rubinstein. (Alex Delaware Ser.: No. 15). 2001. 72.00 (978-0-7366-8314-2(3)) Books on Tape.

Flesh & Blood. unabr. ed. Thomas H. Cook. Narrated by George Guidall. 7 cass. (Running Time: 10 hrs. 30 mins.). (Frank Clemons Mystery Ser.: Vol. 2). 1993. 60.00 (978-1-55690-939-9(X), 93435E7) Recorded Bks.
Atlanta private eye Frank Clemons tackles a case in New York City.

Flesh & Blood. unabr. ed. John Harvey. Read by Gordon Griffin. 10 CDs. (Running Time: 12 hrs.). 2004. audio compact disk 109.75 (978-1-4025-9798-5(3), Clipper Audio) Recorded Bks.
Following his wife?s betrayal and his own retirement from the force, Detective Inspector Elder has fled as far as it is possible to go in England without running out of land. But he is haunted by the past and in particular by the unsolved disappearance of 16-year-old Susan Blacklock.

Flesh & Blood. unabr. ed. John Harvey. Read by Gordon Griffin. 11 cass. (Running Time: 12 hrs.). 2004. 99.75 (978-1-84505-016-0(9), H1639MC) Recorded Bks.

Flesh & Blood: Dark Desires; Erotic Tales of Crime & Passion. unabr. ed. Max Allan Collins & Gelb. 8 cass. (Running Time: 10 hrs.). 2001. 72.00 (978-0-7366-6833-0(0)) Books on Tape.
Sex and violence. They go together like greed and blackmail, and jealousy and murder. Now acclaimed masters and rising stars of today's crime and mystery fiction offer hard-hitting, emotionally riveting, hauntingly erotic tales of cops, private eyes, perps and average Joes and Janes swept up in the throes of urges too primal to be legal.

Flesh & Blood Vol. 1: Erotic Tales of Crime & Passion. unabr. ed. Ed. by Max Allan Collins & Jeff Gelb. 4 cass. (Running Time: 6 hrs.). 2001. 24.95 (978-0-7366-5846-1(7)) Books on Tape.
A saucy compendium of short stories written by the leading names in the mystery field.

Flesh & Blood Vol. 2: Dark Desires. Ed. by Max Allan Collins & Jeff Gelb. 2002. 56.00 (978-0-7366-8927-4(3)) Books on Tape.

Flesh & Blood Vol. 2: Erotic Tales of Crime & Passion. unabr. ed. Ed. by Max Allan Collins & Jeff Gelb. 4 cass. (Running Time: 6 hrs.). 2001. 24.95 (978-0-7366-5905-5(6)) Books on Tape.

***Flesh & Bone.** abr. ed. Jefferson Bass. Read by Erik Singer. (Body Farm Ser.). 2007. (978-0-06-126226-5(9), Harper Audio); (978-0-06-126227-2(7), Harper Audio) HarperCollins Pubs.

Flesh & Bone. abr. ed. Jefferson Bass. Read by Erik Singer. (Running Time: 21600 sec.). (Body Farm Ser.). 2007. audio compact disk 29.95 (978-0-06-122720-2(X)) HarperCollins Pubs.

Flesh & Fire. unabr. ed. Laura Anne Gilman. Narrated by Anne Flosnik. (Running Time: 15 hrs. 0 mins.). (Vineart War Ser.). 2009. 20.99 (978-1-4001-8523-8(8)); 29.99 (978-1-4001-6523-0(7)); audio compact disk 79.99 (978-1-4001-4523-2(6)); audio compact disk 39.99 (978-1-4001-1523-5(X)) Pub: Tantor Media. Dist(s): IngramPubServ

Flesh & Fire. unabr. ed. Laura Anne Gilman. Narrated by Anne Flosnik. (Running Time: 15 hrs. 0 mins.). (Vineart War Ser.: Bk. 1). 2009. 39.99 (978-1-4001-9523-7(3)) Tantor Media.

Flesh & Gold. unabr. ed. Phyllis Gotlieb. Read by Kate Harper. 8 cass. (Running Time: 12 hrs.). 2000. 59.95 (CSL 135) Pub: Chivers Audio Bks GBR. Dist(s): AudioGO
In Starry nova, Skerow, a telepathic alien judge, lonely and working far from her home planet, sees an amphibious human enslaved and displayed in a tank as an ad for a pleasure house. She resolves to investigate and do something about this illegal enslavement. But not long after her investigation begins, a fellow judge is found murdered. So begins a story of super science, slavery, murder and justice, in the distant future.

Flesh & Gold, Set. unabr. ed. Phyllis Gotlieb. Read by Kate Harper. 8 vols. (Running Time: 12 hrs.). (Chivers Sound Library American Collections). 1998. bk. 69.95 (978-0-7927-2246-5(9), CSL 135, Chivers Sound Lib) AudioGO.
In Starry Nova, a telepathic alien judge, lonely & working far from her home planet, sees an amphibious human enslaved & displayed in a tank as an ad for a pleasure house. She resolves to investigate & do something about this illegal enslavement. But not long after her investigation begins, a fellow judge is found murdered. So begins a story of super-science, slavery, murder & justice, in the distant future.

Flesh-Eating Machines: Maggots in the Food Chain. June Preszler. Contrib. by Patrick Olson & Charity Jones. (Extreme Life Ser.). (ENG.). (gr. 3-4). 2008. audio compact disk 12.99 (978-1-4296-3204-1(6)) CapstoneDig.

Flesh House. Stuart MacBride. Read by Kenny Blyth. (Running Time: 46800 sec.). (ENG.). 2008. audio compact disk 99.95 (978-0-7531-3996-7(0)) Isis Pubng Ltd GBR.

Flesh House. Stuart MacBride. 2008. 84.95 (978-0-7531-3293-7(1)); audio compact disk 99.95 (978-0-7531-3294-4(X)) Pub: Isis Pubng Ltd GBR. Dist(s): Ulverscroft US

Flesh of My Flesh. Contrib. by Leon Patillo. (Wedding Tracks Ser.). 2006. audio compact disk 8.98 (978-5-558-17520-2(6), Word Records) Word Enter.

Fleshmarket Alley. abr. ed. Ian Rankin. Read by James MacPherson. (Running Time: 28800 sec.). (Inspector Rebus Novel Ser.). 2006. audio compact disk 16.99 (978-1-59737-335-7(4), 9781597373357, BCD Value Price) Brilliance Audio.
Inspector John Rebus has confronted Edinburgh's most hardened criminals, its bloodiest crime scenes, and its most dangerous backstreets - but nothing could have prepared him for what he finds on Fleshmarket Alley. In the city's red-light district, men live out their sordid fantasies, and women with no other choice sell their bodies to make a buck. It's a neighborhood of lost inhibitions, forgotten scruples, and hopeless dreams. In its seediest clubs, refugees seeking asylum are subjected to the whims of the most ruthless characters in the crime world - men Rebus knows all too well.

***Fleshmarket Alley.** abr. ed. Ian Rankin. Read by James Macpherson. (Running Time: 7 hrs.). (Inspector Rebus Ser.). 2010. audio compact disk 9.99 (978-1-4418-7803-8(3), 9781441878038, BCD Value Price) Brilliance Audio.

Fleshmarket Alley. unabr. ed. Ian Rankin. Read by Michael Page. (Running Time: 14 hrs.). (Inspector Rebus Ser.). 2005. 39.25 (978-1-59710-297-1(0), 9781597102971, BADLE); 24.95 (978-1-59710-296-4(2), 9781597102964, BAD) Brilliance Audio.

Fleshmarket Alley. unabr. ed. Ian Rankin. Read by Michael Page. (Running Time: 14 hrs.). (Inspector Rebus Ser.). 2010. audio compact disk 29.99 (978-1-4418-3583-3(0), 9781441835833, Bril Audio CD Unabri); audio compact disk 89.97 (978-1-4418-3584-0(9), 9781441835840, BriAudCD Unabrid) Brilliance Audio.

Fleshmarket Alley: An Inspector Rebus Novel. abr. ed. Ian Rankin. Read by James MacPherson. 6 CDs. (Running Time: 7 hrs.). (Inspector Rebus Novel Ser.). 2005. audio compact disk 74.25 (978-1-59600-341-5(3), 9781596003415, CD Lib Edit) Brilliance Audio.
Please enter a Synopsis.

Fleshmarket Alley: An Inspector Rebus Novel. unabr. ed. Ian Rankin. Read by Michael Page. (Running Time: 14 hrs.). (Inspector Rebus Novel Ser.). 2005. 24.95 (978-1-59335-688-0(9), 9781593356880, Brilliance MP3); 39.25 (978-1-59335-822-8(9), 9781593358228, Brinc Audio MP3 Lib); 34.95 (978-1-59086-493-7(X), 9781590864937, BAU); 97.25 (978-1-59086-494-4(8), 9781590864944, BAudLibEd) Brilliance Audio.

Fletch. unabr. ed. Gregory Mcdonald. Read by Gardner Grover. 6 cass. (Running Time: 6 hrs.). (Fletch Ser.: No. 1). 1988. 36.00 (978-0-7366-1352-1(8), 2253) Books on Tape.
Fletch is risking his neck to bust a major drug dealer. Plus, he has a multi-millionaire mistaking him for a beach bum. It must be a fatal mistake...because the rich man asked Fletch to commit murder.

Fletch & the Man Who. unabr. ed. Gregory Mcdonald. Read by Grover Gardner. 7 cass. (Running Time: 7 hrs.). (Fletch Ser.: No. 6). 1988. 42.00 (978-0-7366-1380-4(3), 2273) Books on Tape.
Uncharacteristically, Fletch takes on PR chores for a presidential candidate. Characteristically, Fletch ends up in the soup.

Fletch & the Widow Bradley. unabr. ed. Gregory Mcdonald. Read by Grover Gardner. 6 cass. (Running Time: 6 hrs.). (Fletch Ser.: No. 4). 1988. 36.00 (978-0-7366-1418-4(4), 2304) Books on Tape.
An executive is dead in Switzerland. His ashes shipped home to prove it. Or do they? Job trouble - when Fletch's career is ruined for the mistake no reporter should make.

Fletch Reflected. unabr. ed. Gregory Mcdonald. Read by Grover Gardner. 6 cass. (Running Time: 6 hrs.). (Son of Fletch Ser.: No. 2). 1996. 36.00 (978-0-7366-3287-4(5), 3942) Books on Tape.
Helping a friend in need is one thing; being a sucker is another. Fletch's son, Jack, finds this out the hard way. He goes undercover to find out if someone wants to kill his ex-girlfriend's future father-in-law, Chester Radleigh.

Fletch, Too. unabr. ed. Gregory Mcdonald. Read by Grover Gardner. 6 cass. (Running Time: 6 hrs.). (Fletch Ser.: No. 9). 1989. 36.00 (978-0-7366-1492-4(3), 2368) Books on Tape.
Fletch is off for his honeymoon when he is diverted to Africa in search of his long-lost dad.

Fletch Won. unabr. ed. Read by William Dufris. (Running Time: 7 hrs. 0 mins. 0 sec.). (Fletch Ser.: No. 8). (ENG.). 2007. audio compact disk 29.99 (978-1-4001-0372-0(X)) Pub: Tantor Media. Dist(s): IngramPubServ

Fletch Won. unabr. ed. Gregory Mcdonald. Read by Grover Gardner. 7 cass. (Running Time: 7 hrs.). (Fletch Ser.: No. 8). 1988. 42.00 (978-0-7366-1452-8(4), 2334) Books on Tape.
This is Fletch's first case - the murder of Donald Malbeck, a wealthy criminal lawyer with a past that includes a roster of angry ex-clients, a certifiable crazy wife, a son confined to a monastery, & a daughter with an avant-garde Poet of Violence.

Fletch Won. unabr. ed. Gregory Mcdonald. Read by William Dufris. (Running Time: 7 hrs. 0 mins. 0 sec.). (Fletch Ser.: No. 8). (ENG.). 2007. audio compact disk 19.99 (978-1-4001-5372-5(7)); audio compact disk 59.99 (978-1-4001-3372-7(6)) Pub: Tantor Media. Dist(s): IngramPubServ

***Fletcher & the Falling Leaves.** Julia Rawlinson. Narrated by Katherine Kellgren. 1 CD. (Running Time: 10 mins.). (J). (ps-2). 2009. bk. 29.95 (978-0-545-19699-4(X)); pap. bk. 18.95 (978-0-545-19705-2(8)); audio compact disk 12.95 (978-0-545-19681-9(7)) Weston Woods.

Fletch's Fortune. unabr. ed. Gregory Mcdonald. Read by Grover Gardner. 6 cass. (Running Time: 6 hrs.). (Fletch Ser.: No. 3). 1988. 36.00 (978-0-7366-1398-9(6), 2287) Books on Tape.
Snatched from bliss on the Riveria, Fletch is whisked to the journalism convention with a suitcase full of bugging devices & a bizarre assignment: dig up juicy scandals on Walter March, newspaper tycoon. Then March is found dead - with a nasty pair of scissors stuck in his back.

Fletch's Moxie. unabr. ed. Gregory Mcdonald. Read by Grover Gardner. 7 cass. (Running Time: 7 hrs.). (Fletch Ser.: No. 5). 1988. 42.00 (978-0-7366-1442-9(7), 2325) Books on Tape.
Moxie's hot, a beautiful star. But her most surprising role features her in an on-camera murder. Can Fletch come to the rescue?.

Fleurs du Mal. Poems. Charles Baudelaire. Read by Claude Beauclair. 1 cass. (FRE.). 1991. 13.95 (1152-OH) Olivia & Hill.
Twenty-nine poems from "Les Fleurs du mal.".

Fleurs du Mal. unabr. ed. Charles Baudelaire. Perf. by Eva Le Gallienne & Louis Jourdan. 1 cass. (FRE.). 1984. 12.95 (SWC 1029) HarperCollins Pubs.

Flex-Ability Classics: For All Instruments. Alfred Publishing Staff. (Flex-Ability Ser.). (ENG.). 2009. audio compact disk 10.95 (978-0-7390-6042-1(2)) Alfred Pub.

Flex-Ability Holiday - Solo-Duet-Trio-Quartet with Optional Accompaniment: For All Instruments. Composed by Victor Lopez. (Flex-Ability Ser.). (ENG.). 2002. audio compact disk 10.95 (978-0-7579-0851-4(9)) Alfred Pub.

Flex-Ability More Pops: For All Instruments. Composed by Victor Lopez. (Flex-Ability Ser.). (ENG.). 2008. audio compact disk 10.95 (978-0-7390-5333-1(7)) Alfred Pub.

Flex-Ability Pops: All Instruments. Arranged by Victor Lopez. (Flex-Ability Ser.). (ENG.). 2002. audio compact disk 10.95 (978-0-7579-9202-5(1), 0638B, Warner Bro) Alfred Pub.

Flexibility/Inflexibility: Acts 21:27-40. Ben Young. 2000. 4.95 (978-0-7417-6174-3(2), B0174) Win Walk.

Flexible Sigmoidoscopy: Is Farther Better? 2 cass. (Colon & Rectal Surgery Ser.: C85-CR1). 15.00 (8555) Am Coll Surgeons.

***Flickering Pixels: How Technology Shapes Your Faith.** unabr. ed. Shane Hipps. (Running Time: 3 hrs. 59 mins. 0 sec.). (ENG.). 2009. 16.99 (978-0-310-77360-3(1)) Zondervan.

Flight see **Gladys Swan**

Flight. Shirley Ann Grau. Read by Shirley Ann Grau. 1 cass. 1989. 13.95 (978-1-55644-325-1(0), 9021) Am Audio Prose.
The author reads "Flight," a short story from her collection "nine women".

Flight. unabr. ed. Sherman Alexie. Read by Adam Beach. (Running Time: 16200 sec.). 2008. 34.95 (978-1-4332-0868-3(7)); audio compact disk 40.00 (978-1-4332-0869-0(5)) Blckstn Audio.

Flight. unabr. ed. Sherman Alexie. Read by Adam Beach. (Running Time: 16200 sec.). 2008. audio compact disk & audio compact disk 19.95 (978-1-4332-4642-5(2)) Blckstn Audio.

Flight. unabr. ed. Sherman Alexie & Paul M. Garcia. (Running Time: 4 mins. 30 sec.). 2007. audio compact disk 29.95 (978-1-4332-0870-6(9)) Blckstn Audio.

Flight. unabr. ed. Vanna Bonta. Read by Vanna Bonta. 17 CDs. (Running Time: 17 hrs.). 2007. audio compact disk 47.95 (978-0-912339-36-8(5)) Meridian Hse.

Flight. unabr. ed. Edmund Fuller. Read by Dan Lazar. 7 cass. (Running Time: 7 hrs.). 1980. 42.00 (978-0-7366-0262-4(3), 1257) Books on Tape.
With only a little more than a month to go until graduation, Greg Warren, to all appearances a normal 19-year-old, suddenly leaves his New England boys' school & decamps for Italy. His uncle, Samuel Tilden, a middle-aged widowed teacher at the same school, goes after him - wanting to help the boy & find some answers for himself.

Flight Attendant Well-Being. Shelley L. Stockwell. 1 cass. (Running Time: 60 min.). (Self-Hynosis Ser.). 1986. 10.00 (978-0-912559-05-6(5)) Creativity Unltd Pr.
Helps flight attendants face their passengers' feelings, positive, happy & relaxed.

Flight Fear. Pat Carroll. Read by Pat Carroll. Ed. by Tony Carroll. 1 cass. (Running Time: 30 min.). 10.00 Inner-Mind Concepts.
Discusses how to conquer fear of flying both in the air & on the ground.

Flight from Deathrow. Harry Hill. (Running Time: 2 hrs. 8 mins. 0 sec.). (ENG.). 2009. audio compact disk 22.95 (978-1-4055-0582-6(6)) Pub: Little BrownUK GBR. Dist(s): IPG Chicago

Flight from God. unabr. ed. Max Picard. Read by Robin Lawson. 4 cass. (Running Time: 5 hrs. 30 mins.). 1994. 32.95 (978-0-7861-0677-6(8), 1465) Blckstn Audio.
Picard argues that though the "flight from God" is not a phenomenon unique to this age, man has nevertheless put himself & society in an extremely dangerous situation with the progressive secularization of Western culture. Today, the world, not just the individual, is in flight & men must extricate themselves from modernity & make a deliberate decision to find & affirm Faith.

Flight from Stonewycke, Bk. 2. unabr. ed. Michael R. Phillips & Judith Pella. Narrated by Davina Porter. 8 cass. (Running Time: 11 hrs. 15 mins.). (Stonewycke Trilogy: Bk. 2). 1985. 68.00 (978-0-7887-5275-9(8), K0047L8) Recorded Bks.
After marrying against her father's wishes, Maggie Duncan plans to flee to America with her husband, Ian. But Ian is accused of murder, & honor requires him to stay in Scotland to face the charges. Alone, Maggie tries to set up a life for them in the New World, while Ian faces the horrors of prison. Thousands of miles apart, the two must learn to trust in God's greater will to reunite them.

Flight Lessons. abr. ed. Patricia Gaffney. Read by Jennifer Van Dyck. 1 CD. (Running Time: 1 hr. 30 mins.). 2004. audio compact disk 14.95 (978-0-06-074696-4(3)) HarperCollins Pubs.

***Flight Lessons.** abr. ed. Patricia Gaffney. Read by Jennifer Van Dyck. (ENG.). 2005. (978-0-06-083506-4(0), Harper Audio); (978-0-06-083505-7(2), Harper Audio) HarperCollins Pubs.

Flight of a Witch. unabr. ed. Ellis Peters, pseud. Read by Derek Hutchinson. 6 cass. (Running Time: 7 hrs.). (Inspector George Felse Mystery Ser.: Vol. 3). 1997. 54.95 (978-1-85695-993-3(7), 960509) Pub: ISIS Audio GBR. Dist(s): Ulverscroft US
When Annet disappears, the search takes two men along a trail of betrayal, robbery & murder to a deadly confrontation among the ancient stones of Hallowmount.

Flight of a Witch. unabr. ed. Ellis Peters, pseud. Read by Derek Hutchinson. 6 CDs. (Running Time: 9 hrs.). (Inspector George Felse Mystery Ser.: Vol. 3). 2001. audio compact disk 64.95 (978-0-7531-1248-9(5), 1248-5) Pub: ISIS Audio GBR. Dist(s): ISIS Pub
Annet Beck has the kind of breathtaking beauty that strikes people dumb & young teacher Tom Kenyon, a lodger in her parents' house, is no exception. When Annet disappears, last seen on the Hallowmount, an historic border site with an eerie reputation, Tom determines to find out where & why. Annet is adamant she's been away a mere two hours but there is irrefutable evidence that she has been gone for five days. Tom's amateur investigations get nowhere until Detective Inspector George Felse finds cause to connect those missing five days with his inquiry into a death. The subsequent search takes the two men along a trail of betrayal, robbery & murder to a deadly confrontation among the ancient stones of the Hallowmount.

Flight of Aurora Seven. 1 cass. (Running Time: 29 min.). 14.95 (8454) MMI Corp.
Live coverage of Scott Carpenter's exciting voyager. Discusses then current problems in space race.

Flight of Eagles. abr. ed. Jack Higgins. Perf. by Patrick Macnee. 4 cass. (Running Time: 6 hrs.). 2004. 25.00 (978-1-59007-058-1(5)) Pub: New Millenn Enter. Dist(s): PerseuPGW
In the early days of World War II, fate pits two brothers - both ace fighter pilots - against each other: Max Kelso with the German Luftwaffe, and Harry on Britain's RAF. Now, the machinery of war has set in motion an intrigue so devious, so filled with peril, that it will require them to question everything they hold most dear: their lives, their families, their loyalties. Against impossible odds, it is their courage alone that will decide the course of the war.

***Flight of Eagles.** unabr. ed. Jack Higgins. Read by Michael Page. (Running Time: 10 hrs.). (Dougal Munro/Jack Carter Ser.). 2010. 39.97 (978-1-4418-4418-7(X), 9781441844187, BADLE); 24.99 (978-1-4418-4415-6(5), 9781441844156, Brilliance MP3); 24.99 (978-1-4418-4417-0(1), 9781441844170, BAD); 39.97 (978-1-4418-4416-3(3), 9781441844163, Brinc Audio MP3 Lib); audio compact disk 87.97 (978-1-4418-4414-9(7), 9781441844149, BriAudCD Unabrid); audio compact disk 29.99 (978-1-4418-4413-2(9), 9781441844132, Bril Audio CD Unabri) Brilliance Audio.

Flight of Eagles. unabr. ed. Jack Higgins. Read by Patrick Macnee. (YA). 2008. 59.99 (978-1-60514-837-3(7)) Find a World.

Flight of Eagles, Set. unabr. ed. Jack Higgins. Read by Patrick Macnee. 8 cass. 1999. 40.00 (FS9-34514) Highsmith.

Flight of My Life: The Insyderz. Perf. by Insyderz, The. 1 cass., 1 CD. 10.98 (978-0-7601-2604-2(6)); audio compact disk 16.98 CD. (978-0-7601-2605-9(4)) Provident Mus Dist.
A project that shows their missionary intensity.

Flight of the Buffalo: Soaring to Excellence, Learning to Let Employees Lead. abr. ed. James A. Belasco & Ralph C. Stayer. 2 cass. (Running Time: 3 hrs.). 2004. 18.00 (978-1-931056-18-2(8), N Millennium Audio) New Millenn Enter.
The authors combine expertise, insight & passion to show how the nature of management must change if a company expects to survive in the white-knuckle world of modern business. They explain how to avoid being outmaneuvered by the competition; how to become more focused & flexible.

Flight of the Bumble Bee. 2 cass. (Running Time: 2 hrs.). 2001. 19.95 (RRCA005) Lodestone Catalog.

Flight of the Bumble Bee. unabr. ed. Read by Marina Sirtis. 2 cass. (Running Time: 2 hrs.). Dramatization. 1999. 19.95 (978-0-9660392-3-8(8)) Pub: Radio Repertory. Dist(s): Penton Overseas
Featuring Marina Sirtis (Deanna Troi from Star Trek-TGN) as Nancy Coy, who tries to save both the Amalgamation & the man she has fallen in love with, Commander Kurk Manly.

Flight of the Bumblebee, Set. 2 cass. 19.95 (RRCA005) Radio Repertory.

Flight of the Cormorants. unabr. ed. Mary Withall. Read by James Bryce. 12 cass. (Running Time: 16 hrs. 30 mins.). (Sound Ser.). 2002. 94.95 (978-1-84283-136-6(4)) Pub: UlverLrgPrint GBR. Dist(s): Ulverscroft US
Two Argyll villages are threatened with a take-over by developers. Will the promised influx of overseas investment bring prosperity to the islands, or destroy their unique character forever? Initially the proposals create division between friends, neighbors and even within families, but soon old adversaries bank together to undermine their scheming landlord.

Flight of the Falcon. unabr. ed. Daphne Du Maurier. Read by James B. Callis. 8 cass. (Running Time: 8 hrs.). 2000. 69.95 (978-0-7540-0479-0(1), CAB1902) AudioGO.
It is over 500 years since Duke Claudio the Falcon lived his brutal, twisted life in Ruffano, Italy. Now, the modern-day town has forgotten its violent history. Its university has a shiny new Commerce & Economics building; pointing to a golden future & flouting the dusty humanities & inhumanities of the past. But have things really changed?.

Flight of the Intruder. abr. ed. Stephen Coonts. Read by Frank Converse. 2 cass. (Running Time: 2 hrs. 48 mins.). (Jake Grafton Novel Ser.: Vol. 1). 1993. 9.95 (978-0-88690-314-5(9), A20203) Pub: Audio Partners. Dist(s): PerseuPGW
America's high-tech intruder attack planes described by a pilot who flew them in Vietnam.

Flight of the Intruder. abr. ed. Stephen Coonts. Read by Frank Converse. 2 cass. (Running Time: 3 hrs.). (Jake Grafton Novel Ser.: Vol. 1). 2000. 7.95

(978-1-57815-182-0(1), 1122, Media Bks Audio); audio compact disk 11.99 (978-1-57815-512-5(6), 1122 CD3, Media Bks Audio) Media Bks NJ.
About America's powerful high-tech intruder attack planes & the men who flew them in Vietnam.

Flight of the Intruder. unabr. ed. Stephen Coonts. Read by Multivoice Production Staff. (Running Time: 12 hrs.). (Jake Grafton Novel Ser.: Vol. 1). 2008. 39.25 (978-1-4233-5366-9(8), 9781423353669, BADLE); 39.25 (978-1-4233-5364-5(1), 9781423353645, Brinc Audio MP3 Lib); 24.95 (978-1-4233-5363-8(3), 9781423353638, Brilliance MP3); 24.95 (978-1-4233-5365-2(X), 9781423353652, BAD) Brilliance Audio.

***Flight of the Intruder.** unabr. ed. Stephen Coonts. Read by multivoice. (Running Time: 12 hrs.). 2010. audio compact disk 29.99 (978-1-4418-4115-5(6), 9781441841155, Bril Audio CD Unabri); audio compact disk 89.97 (978-1-4418-4116-2(4), 9781441841162, BriAudCD Unabrid) Brilliance Audio.

Flight of the Intruder. unabr. ed. Stephen Coonts. Narrated by Frank Muller. 8 cass. (Running Time: 11 hrs. 30 mins.). (Jake Grafton Novel Ser.: Vol. 1). 1986. 70.00 (978-1-55690-180-5(1), 86980E7) Recorded Bks.
A veteran A-6 Intruder aircraft carrier pilot wrote this riveting story of Navy flyers in Vietnam, putting the reader in the cockpit of an A-6 for a thrilling tale of air combat & into the hearts of the pilots & the psychological dilemmas of modern-day warfare.

Flight of the Intruder. unabr. collector's ed. Stephen Coonts. Read by Michael Prichard. 9 cass. (Running Time: 13 hrs. 30 min.). (Jake Grafton Novel Ser.: Vol. 1). 1987. 72.00 (978-0-7366-1175-6(4), 2097) Books on Tape.
Describes the lives of the airmen who flew the A-6 "Intruder" planes.

Flight of the Maidens. unabr. ed. Jane Gardam. Read by June Barrie. 8 cass. (Running Time: 12 hrs.). 2002. 69.95 (978-0-7540-0750-0(2), CAB 2172) AudioGO.
The delightful novel describes the post-war summer of 1946, and follows the growing-up of three young women in the months between leaving school and taking up their scholarships at university. Una Vane goes bicycling with Ray, the boy who delivers the fish and milk. Hetty Fallowes struggles to become independent of her possessive, loving, tactless mother. And Lieselotte Klein, who had arrived in 1939 on a train from Hamburg, uncovers tragedy in the past and magic in the present.

Flight of the Mind. Etzel Cardena. 1 cass. 9.00 (A0020-86) Sound Photosyn.
From ICSS 1987, Bill Leikem on the tape.

Flight of the Old Dog. abr. ed. Dale Brown. Read by Richard Allen. 4 cass. Library ed. (Running Time: 6 hrs.). 2003. 62.25 (978-1-59086-813-3(7), 1590868137, CD Lib Edit); audio compact disk 74.25 (978-1-59086-817-1(X), 159086817X, CD Lib Edit) Brilliance Audio.
Flight of the Old Dog is the runaway bestseller that launched the phenomenal career of Dale Brown. It is the riveting story of America's military superiority being surpassed as our greatest enemy masters space-to-Earth weapons technology-neutralizing the U.S. arsenal of nuclear missiles. America's only hope: The Old Dog Zero One, a battle-scarred bomber fully renovated with modern hardware-and equipped with the deadliest state-of-the-art armaments known to man.

Flight of the Old Dog. abr. ed. Dale Brown. Read by Richard Allen. (Running Time: 6 hrs.). 2005. audio compact disk 16.99 (978-1-59600-403-0(7), 9781596004030, BCD Value Price) Brilliance Audio.

Flight of the Old Dog. abr. ed. Dale Brown. Read by Richard Allen. (Running Time: 6 hrs.). 2006. 39.25 (978-1-4233-0072-4(6), 9781423300724, BADLE); audio compact disk 39.25 (978-1-4233-0070-0(X), 9781423300700, Brinc Audio MP3 Lib); audio compact disk 24.95 (978-1-4233-0069-4(6), 9781423300694, Brilliance MP3) Brilliance Audio.

Flight of the Old Dog. abr. ed. Dale Brown. Read by Richard Allen. (Running Time: 6 hrs.). 2006. 24.95 (978-1-4233-0071-7(8), 9781423300717, BAD) Brilliance Audio.

***Flight of the Old Dog.** abr. ed. Dale Brown. Read by Richard Allen. (Running Time: 6 hrs.). 2010. audio compact disk 9.99 (978-1-4418-5633-3(1), 9781441856333) Brilliance Audio.

Flight of the Omni. unabr. ed. C. S. Fuqua. Read by Kevin Foley. 8 cass. (Running Time: 9 hrs. 18 min.). (Deadlines Ser.: Bk. 3). 2001. 49.95 (978-1-55686-771-2(9)) Books in Motion.
Former reporter Dean Moore, now a public affairs writer for NASA, investigates two deaths linked to the liftoff of the space shuttle Omni.

Flight of the Phoenix. Elleston Trevor. Narrated by Grover Gardner. (Running Time: 7 hrs.). 2004. 27.95 (978-1-59912-662-3(1)) Iofy Corp.

Flight of the Phoenix. Elleston Trevor. Read by Grover Gardner. 5 cass. (Running Time: 7 hrs.). 2004. 44.95 (978-0-7861-2884-6(4), 3312); audio compact disk 55.00 (978-0-7861-8299-2(7), 3312) Blckstn Audio.

Flight of the Phoenix. unabr. ed. Elleston Trevor. Read by Grover Gardner. 6 CDs. (Running Time: 7 hrs.). 2004. audio compact disk 24.95 (978-0-7861-8507-8(4), 3312) Blckstn Audio.

Flight of the Phoenix. unabr. ed. Elleston Trevor. Read by Grover Gardner. 5 cass. (Running Time: 9 hrs.). 2004. reel tape 29.95 (978-0-7861-2743-6(0), E3312); audio compact disk 29.95 (978-0-7861-8547-4(3), ZE3312) Blckstn Audio.

Flight of the Phoenix. unabr. collector's ed. Elleston Trevor. Read by Richard Green. 7 cass. (Running Time: 7 hrs.). 1979. 42.00 (978-0-7366-0157-3(0), 1157) Books on Tape.
A cargo plane crash lands in the central Libyan desert during a violent sandstorm. Twelve men & a monkey survive to stare without hope into the desert sky; search planes will not seek their unscheduled flight. One man proposes the impossible - to build from the wreckage an aircraft capable of flying the 200 miles to the nearest oasis.

Flight of the Reindeer: The True Story of Santa Claus & His Christmas Mission. abr. ed. Robert Sullivan. Read by John Ritter. 2 cass. (Running Time: 3 hrs.). (J). 1996. 17.95 (978-1-57453-105-3(0)) Audio Lit.
Everyone believes in Christmas, but what about Santa Claus? Is it only the young who waits for that one special evening every year, when a jolly old elf harnesses eight tiny reindeer (plus one with a red nose) to a sleigh & flies them around the world to deliver presents to good children everywhere? Famed Arctic explorers have visited Santa's workshop at the North Pole; zoologists have confirmed the special breed of flying reindeer & during his administration, former President George Bush signed the Santa Claus Clause to clear airspace on Christmas Eve for Santa Claus's night flight. Yes, Virginia, there is a Santa Claus & now we have proof.

Flight of the White Horse. unabr. ed. Todd S. Moffett. Read by Patrick Treadway. 8 cass. (Running Time: 10 hrs.). Dramatization. (J). 1991. 44.95 Set. (978-1-55686-359-2(4), 359) Books in Motion.
Young Prince Tomlin departs on a quest to rescue a beautiful princess trapped in an amulet by an evil wizard.

Flight of the Witch. 1 CD. (Running Time: 1 hr.). 2004. audio compact disk 15.00 (978-0-9755843-2-3(4)) Dream Theater.

Flight of the Wizard. 1 CD. (Running Time: 1 hr.). 2004. audio compact disk 15.00 (978-0-9755843-3-0(2)) Dream Theater.

Flight Plan: The Real Secret of Success; How to Achieve More Faster Than You Ever Thought Possible. unabr. ed. Brian Tracy. Read by Brian Tracy. (Running Time: 3 hrs. 30 mins.). (ENG.). 2008. audio compact disk 19.98 (978-1-59659-203-2(6), GildAudio) Pub: Gildan Media. Dist(s): HachBkGrp

Flight Plan: The Secret of Success - How to Achieve More, Faster Than You Ever Dreamed Possible. unabr. ed. Brian Tracy. (Running Time: 3 hrs. 30 mins.). (ENG.). 2008. 14.95 (978-1-59659-195-0(1), GildAudio) Pub: Gildan Media. Dist(s): HachBkGrp

***Flight to Heaven: A Plane Crash... A Lone Survivor... A Journey to Heaven - and Back.** unabr. ed. Dale Black. Narrated by Dale Black. (Running Time: 6 hrs. 43 mins. 9 sec.). (ENG.). 2010. 16.09 (978-1-60814-692-5(8)); audio compact disk 22.99 (978-1-59859-744-8(2)) Oasis Audio.

Flight to Mons. Alexander Fullerton. 10 cass. (Running Time: 12 hrs.). (Soundings Ser.). (J). 2004. 84.95 (978-1-84283-677-4(3)) Pub: ISIS Lrg Prnt GBR. Dist(s): Ulverscroft US

Flight to Mons. Alexander Fullerton. Read by Peter Wickham. 11 CDs. (Soundings (CDs) Ser.). (J). 2005. audio compact disk 99.95 (978-1-84283-729-0(X)) Pub: ISIS Lrg Prnt GBR. Dist(s): Ulverscroft US

Flight with Angels. Patricia O'Malley. Perf. by Barry Weiss. 1 cass. (Running Time: 50 min.). 1998. (978-1-892450-29-6(1), 221) Promo Music.
Relaxation Music.

Flight #116 Is Down. unabr. ed. Caroline B. Cooney. Narrated by George Guidall. 4 pieces. (Running Time: 5 hrs. 15 mins.). (gr. 7 up). 35.00 (978-0-7887-0448-2(6), 94637E7) Recorded Bks.
When a 747 jumbo jet crashes in her backyard, 16-year-old Heidi Landseth must summon all her courage & strength to help local rescue workers save hundreds of injured & trapped passengers. Available to libraries only.

Flightpath. Perf. by Jonn Serrie. 1 cass. 9.98 (MPC2002); audio compact disk 14.98 CD. Miramar Images.
Serrie continues the voyage he began with And the Stars Go with You by taking the listener into the skies above.

Flights of Angels. unabr. collector's ed. Ellen Gilchrist. Read by Mary Peiffer. 7 cass. (Running Time: 10 hrs. 30 mins.). 1998. 56.00 (978-0-7366-4363-4(X), 4817) Books on Tape.
Whether exploring a Los Angeles medical clinic that caters solely to hypochondriacs or the machinations of a large southern family that has gathered to attend its patriarch's death.

Flights of Imagination, Vol. 16. Prod. by Focus on the Family Staff. Told to AIO Team Staff. 4 CDs. (Running Time: 6 hrs.). (Adventures in Odyssey Ser.: Vol. 16). (ENG.). (J). (gr. 3-7). 1993. audio compact disk 24.99 (978-1-56179-190-3(3)) Pub: Focus Family. Dist(s): Tyndale Hse

Flights of Passage. unabr. collector's ed. Samuel Hynes. Read by Christopher Hurt. 6 cass. (Running Time: 9 hrs.). 1988. 48.00 (978-0-7366-1419-1(2), 2305) Books on Tape.
In WW II Sam Hynes was a young Marine pilot. He flew more than a hundred missions. Now, some 40 years after those combat experiences, it is the mechanics of flying & warmaking that remain uppermost in his memory.

Flim-Flam! The Truth about Unicorns, Parapsychology & Other Delusions. abr. ed. James Randi. Read by James Randi. Intro. by Isaac Asimov. 2 pieces. (Running Time: 3 hrs.). (ENG.). 1995. 22.98 (978-1-57392-031-5(2)) Prometheus Bks.
Randi reads the book that helped expose dozens of outrageous deceptions widely promoted by the media.

Fling. John R. Erickson. (Hank the Cowdog Ser.: No. 38). 2001. 24.00 (978-0-7366-7535-2(3)) Books on Tape.
Hank gets trapped in a cattle trailer and ends up stranded in town where the real adventures begin.

Fling. unabr. ed. John R. Erickson. Read by John R. Erickson. 2 cass. (Running Time: 3 hrs.). (Hank the Cowdog Ser.: No. 38). (J). 2002. 17.99 (978-1-59188-338-8(5)) Maverick Bks.
It's bad enough when Hank accidentally gets trapped in a cattle trailer and ends up stranded in town. Then he gets picked up by the local dog catcher and locked in a cage. Just when it looks like things couldn't get any worse, Hank meets up with Dogpound Ralph and the two dogs break free and strike out on the adventure of a lifetime.

Fling. unabr. ed. John R. Erickson. Read by John R. Erickson. 3 CDs. (Running Time: Approx. 3 hours). (Hank the Cowdog Ser.: No. 38). (J). 2002. audio compact disk 19.99 (978-1-59188-638-9(4)) Maverick Bks.
When Hank the Cowdog accidentally hitches a ride into town on a cattle truck, he meets up with his old pal, Dogpound Ralph. Ralph convinces Hank to join him on a fling?dodging traffic, stealing meat from backyard barbecues, and hiding from the dogcatcher. It sounds like fun, but after a day of running from the law, Hank starts to long for the humble comforts of home. Can Hank survive his fling and make it back to the ranch in one piece?Hear two new songs, ?The Fling Song? and Buzzard Chant,? in this hilarious adventure for the whole family.

Fling. unabr. collector's ed. John R. Erickson. 2 cass. (Running Time: 2 hrs.). (Hank the Cowdog Ser.: No. 38). (J). 2001. 24.00 (978-0-7366-7534-5(5)) Books on Tape.
Hank gets trapped in a cattle trailer and ends up stranded in town where the real adventures begin.

Flint. Paul Eddy. Read by James Faulkner. 12 cass. (Running Time: 13 hrs. 23 min.). 2001. 45.95 (978-0-7540-0606-0(9)) AudioGO.
Undercover cop Grace Flint is cool & quick-thinking under pressure. One case goes badly wrong, however, & Grace almost loses her life. Her superiors fear that Grace won't be able to cope, especially when she starts to uncover the past.

Flint. unabr. ed. Paul Eddy. Read by Fiacre Douglas. 8 cass. (Running Time: 11 hrs.). 2000. 35.95 (978-1-58788-054-4(7), 1587880547) Brilliance Audio.

Flint. unabr. ed. Paul Eddy. Read by Fiacre Douglas. (Running Time: 11 hrs.). 2005. 39.25 (978-1-59600-791-8(5), 9781596007918, BADLE); 24.95 (978-1-59600-790-1(7), 9781596007901, BAD); audio compact disk 24.95 (978-1-59600-788-8(5), 9781596007888, Brilliance MP3); audio compact disk 39.25 (978-1-59600-789-5(3), 9781596007895, Brinc Audio MP3 Lib) Brilliance Audio.
An exceptionally talented undercover policewoman, Grace Flint nearly dies in a botched sting operation. Months later, physically healed but psychologically scarred, she gets an unexpected clue about her attacker, and disappears on a mission of revenge - unaware that she is about to pull the first string that will unravel a vastly complex web of international treachery, extortion, and murder. Pursuing her, using whatever clues he can find, is Harry Cohen, the former chief legal advisor to the British Security Services, who has been drawn back in as an impartial outsider because everybody is worried about Flint's safety. Or are they? Much to his surprise, he finds himself tugging on a string of his own that leads him high into governments on both sides of the Atlantic - and into a conspiracy with unexpected resonances, not only for him but for Flint. For there are many kinds of betrayal, and some of them are worse than others . .

Flint & Silver: A Prequel to Treasure Island. abr. ed. John Drake. Narrated by Tim Gregory. (Running Time: 11 hrs. 52 mins. 57 sec.). (ENG.). 2009. 25.89 (978-1-60814-556-0(5), SpringWater) Oasis Audio.

Flint & Silver: A Prequel to Treasure Island. abr. ed. John Drake. Read by Jon Gauger. Narrated by Tim Gregory. 10 CDs. (Running Time: 11 hrs. 52 mins. 57 sec.). (ENG.). 2009. audio compact disk 36.99 (978-1-59859-550-5(4), SpringWater) Oasis Audio.

Flint's Gift. unabr. ed. Richard S. Wheeler. Read by Patrick Cullen. 8 cass. (Running Time: 11 hrs. 30 mins.). (Sam Flint Novels Ser.: Bk. 1). 1999. 56.95 (978-0-7861-1355-2(3), 2258) Blckstn Audio.
The young community of Payday is a paradise of rolling meadows & balmy skies, with a quiet population of ranchers & merchants. Into this Eden comes a young editor Sam Flint, whose fledgling newspaper, "The Payday Pioneer," earns him friends within the town & trumpets Payday's glories throughout the West.

Flint's Gift. unabr. ed. Richard S. Wheeler. Narrated by Jonathan Hogan. 8 cass. (Running Time: 10 hrs. 45 mins.). (Sam Flint Novels Ser.: Bk. 1). 1998. 70.00 (978-0-7887-2280-6(8), 95449E7) Recorded Bks.
When Sam Flint moves to a remote frontier town to start a newspaper, he is pulled into a deadly fight for control - one that encompasses both the land & the future of the town.

Flint's Honor. unabr. ed. Richard S. Wheeler. Read by Patrick Cullen. 8 cass. (Running Time: 11 hrs. 30 mins.). (Sam Flint Novels Ser.: Bk. 3). 2000. 56.95 (978-0-7861-1780-2(X), 2579); audio compact disk 80.00 (978-0-7861-9875-7(3), 2579) Blckstn Audio.
The saga continues about Sam Flint, a dedicated frontier journalist whose only weapon is the truth. Sam feels an honest journalist has to take on "The Silver City Democrat" run by a corrupt editor, but how can he launch his own paper when the whole town is in his rival's pocket?.

Flint's Honor: The Sam Flint Series, Book 3. unabr. ed. Richard S. Wheeler. Read by Patrick Cullen. (Running Time: 11 hrs. 50 mins.). (ENG.). 2009. 29.95 (978-1-4332-9748-9(5)) Blckstn Audio.

Flint's Truth. unabr. ed. Richard S. Wheeler. Read by Patrick Cullen. 8 cass. (Running Time: 11 hrs. 30 mins.). (Sam Flint Novels Ser.: Bk. 2). 1998. 56.95 (978-0-7861-1373-6(1), 2280) Blckstn Audio.
Continues the popular series featuring frontier journalist Sam Flint, in a tale of corruption & cover-up set against the vibrant backdrop of the American West.

Flintstones Read Along. 1 cass. (Running Time: 30 mins.). (J). (ps-3). 2000. pap. bk. 6.98 (978-0-7634-0675-2(9)) W Disney Records.

Flinx Transcendent. unabr. ed. Alan Dean Foster. Read by Stefan Rudnicki. (Running Time: 15 hrs.). (Pip & Flinx Ser.: No. 14). 2009. 39.97 (978-1-4233-9319-1(8), 9781423393191, BADLE) Brilliance Audio.

Flinx Transcendent. unabr. ed. Alan Dean Foster & Alan Dean Foster. Read by Stefan Rudnicki. 2 MP3-CDs. (Running Time: 15 hrs.). (Pip & Flinx Ser.: No. 14). 2009. 24.99 (978-1-4233-9317-7(1), 9781423393177, Brilliance MP3); 39.97 (978-1-4233-9318-4(X), 9781423393184, Brinc Audio MP3 Lib); audio compact disk 32.99 (978-1-4233-9315-3(5), 9781423393153, Bril Audio CD Unabri); audio compact disk 117.97 (978-1-4233-9316-0(3), 9781423393160, BriAudCD Unabrid) Brilliance Audio.

Flip: How to Find, Fix, & Sell Houses for Profit Audio. Rick Villani & Clay Davis. Narrated by Cliff Haby. (ENG.). 2007. audio compact disk 59.00 (978-1-932649-08-6(5)) Relleck Pubng.

Flip: How to Find, Fix, & Sell Houses for Profit Digital Audio Book. Rick Villani & Clay Davis. Narrated by Cliff Haby. (ENG.). 2007. 59.00 (978-1-932649-10-9(7)) Relleck Pubng.

Flip: How to Turn Everything You Know on Its Head - -and Succeed Beyond Your Wildest Imaginings. unabr. ed. Peter Sheahan. Narrated by Simon Vance. (Running Time: 8 hrs. 0 mins. 0 sec.). (ENG.). 2008. audio compact disk 69.99 (978-1-4001-3718-3(7)); audio compact disk 34.99 (978-1-4001-0718-6(0)); audio compact disk 24.99 (978-1-4001-5718-1(8)) Pub: Tantor Media. Dist(s): IngramPubServ

Flip: How to Turn Everything You Know on Its Head-and Succeed Beyond Your Wildest Imaginings. Peter Sheahan. Read by Simon Vance. (Playaway Adult Nonfiction Ser.). (ENG.). 2009. 64.99 (978-1-60775-773-3(7)) Find a World.

Flip Flop & Hoot & a Possum in the Roses. Short Stories. 2. (Running Time: 2hrs 30 minutes). Dramatization. (Brown Bag Bedtime Bks.). (J). 2001. 10.00 (978-0-9704460-4-6(7)) Wrters Ink.

Flip-Flop Girl. unabr. ed. Katherine Paterson. Narrated by Alyssa Bresnahan. 3 pieces. (Running Time: 4 hrs. 15 mins.). (gr. 4 up). 1995. 27.00 (978-0-7887-0187-0(8), 94412E7) Recorded Bks.
A girl, still grieving after her father's death, has trouble making new friends when her family moves in with her grandmother in a small Virginia town.

Flip Side: Break Free of the Behaviors That Hold You Back. abr. ed. Flip Flippen. (Running Time: 3 hrs.). (ENG.). 2007. 14.98 (978-1-60024-194-9(8)); audio compact disk 16.98 (978-1-60024-184-0(0)) Pub: Hachet Audio. Dist(s): HachBkGrp

Flip Side of Sin. unabr. ed. Rosalyn McMillan. Narrated by Peter Jay Fernandez. 10 cass. (Running Time: 14 hrs. 45 mins.). 2001. 88.00 (978-0-7887-5225-4(1), F0026E7) Recorded Bks.
After twelve years behind bars, Isaac Coleman confronts the pressures of the modern world while attempting to reconcile with the friends & family he left on the outside.

***Flip the S. W. I. T. C. H. How to Turn on & Turn up Your Mindset.** P. J. McClure. (ENG.). 2010. audio compact disk 27.97 (978-0-9829833-2-4(8)) The MM LLC.

Flipped. unabr. ed. 5 cass. (Running Time: 7 hrs. 15 min.). (YA). (gr. 6-10). 2004. 46.75 (978-1-4025-7307-1(3)) Recorded Bks.
Julianna, one of those most unconventional innocents who forges ahead through life regardless of not fitting in, worships, her new good-looking and conventional neighbor, Bryce, from the day he moves in. The inauspicious beginning of their relationship at age seven is told and retold from the perspective of both in this audio version of the book by Wedneling Van Draanan.

Flirt. unabr. ed. Laurell K. Hamilton. (Running Time: 4 hrs.). (Anita Blake, Vampire Hunter Ser.: Bk. 18). (ENG.). 2010. audio compact disk 29.95 (978-0-14-242801-6(9), PengAudBks) Penguin Grp USA.

***Flirt.** unabr. ed. Laurell K. Hamilton. Read by Kimberly Alexis. 4 CDs. (Running Time: 3 hrs. 45 mins.). 2010. audio compact disk 40.00 (978-0-307-73700-7(4), BksonTape) Pub: Random Audio Pubg. Dist(s): Random

***Flirting with Disaster.** unabr. ed. Sherryl Woods. (Running Time: 11 hrs.). (Charleston Trilogy). 2011. 39.97 (978-1-4418-6486-4(5), 9781441864864, BADLE); 19.99 (978-1-4418-6485-7(7), 9781441864857, BAD); 39.97 (978-1-4418-6484-0(9), 9781441864840, Brinc Audio MP3 Lib); 19.99 (978-1-4418-6483-3(0), 9781441864833, Brilliance MP3); audio compact disk 79.97 (978-1-4418-6482-6(2), 9781441864826, BriAudCD Unabrid); audio compact disk 19.99 (978-1-4418-6481-9(4), 9781441864819, Bril Audio CD Unabri) Brilliance Audio.

Flirting with Pete. abr. ed. Barbara Delinsky. Read by Linda Emond. 2004. 15.95 (978-0-7435-4735-2(7)) Pub: S&S Audio. Dist(s): S and S Inc

***Flirting with the Truth.** Featuring Ravi Zacharias. 1992. audio compact disk 9.00 (978-1-61256-047-2(4)) Ravi Zach.

Flo Jo: The Story of Florence Griffith- Joyner. Alan Venable. (Overcoming the Odds Sports Biographies Ser.). 2000. audio compact disk 18.95 (978-1-4105-0144-8(2)) D Johnston Inc.

Flo Jo: The Story of Florence Griffith-Joyner. Alan Venable. Ed. by Jerry Stemach. 2000. audio compact disk 200.00 (978-1-58702-467-2(5)) D Johnston Inc.

Flo Jo: The Story of Florence Griffith-Joyner, Vol. 2. Alan Venable. Ed. by Jerry Stemach et al. Illus. by Jeff Ham. Narrated by Denise Jordan Walker. Contrib. by Ted S. Hasselbring. (Start-to-Finish Books). (J). (gr. 2-3). 2000. 35.00 (978-1-58702-468-9(3)) D Johnston Inc.

Flo Jo: The Story of Florence Griffith-Joyner, Vol. 2. unabr. ed. Alan Venable. Ed. by Jerry Stemach et al. Illus. by Jeff Ham. Narrated by Denise Jordan Walker. Contrib. by Ted S. Hasselbring. 1 cass. (Running Time: 1 hr.). (Start-to-Finish Books). (J). (gr. 2-3). 2000. (978-1-893376-56-4(7), F17) D Johnston Inc.
In 1988, Florence Griffith Joyner set two records in women's sprinting that still stood more than ten years later: a world record in the 100-meter dash that she set at the olympic trials i Indianapolis, and a world record in the 200 meters that she set at the Olympic games in Korea. Prior to that, "Flo Jo" (Dee Dee" as her family called her) had run well in world competitions but had never been the star As amazing as her times were her flamboyant outfits and stunning beauty.

Floatation Tanks. Glenn Perry & Lee Perry. 1 cass. 9.00 (A0101-87) Sound Photosyn.
A visit with the Samadhi Tank people, the first to produce John Lilly's invention.

Floating. unabr. ed. Robin Troy. Read by Karesa McElheny. 5 cass. (Running Time: 7 hrs. 30 mins.). 2000. 40.00 (978-0-7366-5426-5(7)); 24.95 (978-0-7366-4935-3(2)) Books on Tape.
For most people, Whitticker, Arizona, population 641, is just a rest stop on a highway to somewhere else, but for twenty-five year old Ruby Pearson there is nowhere else. With a husband in jail & an eight-year-old son at home, Ruby knows what she wants & what she doesn't & is determined to break free of a life going nowhere.

Floating Madhouse. unabr. ed. Alexander Fullerton. Read by Michael Tudor Barnes. 12 cass. (Running Time: 18 hrs.). 2001. 94.95 (978-1-86042-969-9(6), 2-969-6) Pub: Soundings Ltd GBR. Dist(s): Ulverscroft US
Michael Henderson, Lieutenant RN, has been caught in flagrante delicto with the young Princess Natasha Volodnyakov. The scandal breaks after a party to announce Tasha's engagement to a naval captain whom she doesn't like. Her great-uncle, General Igor Volodnyakov, is greatly concerned by Tasha's indiscretion with Michael. Having considerable influence at court, Igor is able to offer him a privilege he can't refuse - to sail as an observer with the Second Pacific Squadron.

Floating World. Cynthia Kadohata. Read by Cynthia Kadohata. Prod. by Moveable Feast Staff. 1 cass. (Running Time: 30 min.). 8.95 (AMF-224) Am Audio Prose.
Cynthia Kadohata reads from her acclaimed first novel "The Floating World" & talks about sexing chickens & the Japanese-American experience.

Floatplane Notebooks. unabr. ed. Clyde Edgerton. Narrated by Clyde Edgerton. Narrated by Norman Dietz & Sally Darling. 5 cass. (Running Time: 7 hrs. 30 mins.). 1993. 44.00 (978-1-55690-887-3(3), 93329E7) Recorded Bks.
The various members of a North Carolina family recount their lives & the lives of their forebears as they deal with the return of one of their members from the tragedy of Vietnam.

Floetic Heart of Rene Reyes: USA english Release, Vol. 2. 2nd ed. Voice by Rene Reyes. Rene Reyes.Tr. of O coração de floetic de Rene Reyes. 2007. pap. bk. 22.00 (978-0-9796282-0-7(2)) Sweet Verse.

Flood. unabr. ed. William Dietz. Narrated by Todd McLaren. 9 CDs. (Running Time: 11 hrs. 0 mins. 0 sec.). (Halo Ser.). (ENG.). 2008. audio compact disk 34.99 (978-1-4001-0113-9(1)) Pub: Tantor Media. Dist(s): IngramPubServ

Flood. unabr. ed. William C. Dietz. Narrated by Todd McLaren. 9 CDs. (Running Time: 11 hrs. 0 mins. 0 sec.). (Halo Ser.). (ENG.). 2008. audio compact disk 69.99 (978-1-4001-3113-6(8)) Pub: Tantor Media. Dist(s): IngramPubServ

Flood. unabr. ed. William C. Dietz. Read by Todd McLaren. Narrated by Todd McLaren. 1 MP3-CD. (Running Time: 11 hrs. 0 mins. 0 sec.). (Halo Ser.). (ENG.). 2008. 19.99 (978-1-4001-5113-4(9)) Pub: Tantor Media. Dist(s): IngramPubServ

Flood. unabr. ed. Andrew Vachss. Read by Christopher Lane. (Running Time: 12 hrs.). (Burke Ser.). 2009. 24.99 (978-1-4418-1706-8(9), 9781441817068, Brilliance MP3); 39.97 (978-1-4418-1707-5(7), 9781441817075, Brinc Audio MP3 Lib); 24.99 (978-1-4418-1708-2(5), 9781441817082, BAD); 39.97 (978-1-4418-1709-9(3), 9781441817099, BADLE); audio compact disk 29.99 (978-1-4418-1704-4(2), 9781441817044, Bril Audio CD Unabri); audio compact disk 79.97 (978-1-4418-1705-1(0), 9781441817051, BriAudCD Unabrid) Brilliance Audio.

Flood of Friends. Barbara Davoll & Dennis Hockerman. 1 cass. (Christopher Churchmouse Ser.). (J). (ps-2). 1990. bk. 11.99 (978-0-89693-137-4(4), 3-2137) David C Cook.

Flood of Noah. Chuck Missler. 2 cass. (Running Time: 2.5 hours +). (Briefing Packages by Chuck Missler). 1991. vinyl bd. 14.95 Incls. notes . (978-1-880532-76-8(X)) Koinonia Hse.
** Was there really a universal flood? * Could an ark contain all of the animals? * Just who were the "Nephilim?" * Why did God bring such a devastating judgment upon the Earth?* Why were only eight people saved?Discover the surprising answers to these questions and learn what Jesus meant when He said: "As the days of Noah were, so shall the days of the coming of the Son of Man be."Explore the amazing prophetic implications of the "Days of Noah" and the "Flood of Noah" in the Genesis account.*

Flood of Noah. Chuck Missler. 2 CD's. (Running Time: 120 mins.). (Briefing Packages by Chuck Missler). 1991. audio compact disk 19.95 (978-1-57821-303-0(7)) Koinonia Hse.
Was there really a universal flood? Could an ark contain all of the animals? Just who were the "Nephilim?" Why did God bring such a devastating judgment upon the Earth? Why were only eight people saved? Discover the surprising answers to these questions and learn what Jesus meant when He said: "As the days of Noah were, so shall the days of the coming of the Son of Man be."Explore the amazing prophetic implications of the "Days of Noah" and the "Flood of Noah" in the Genesis account.

Flood Tide. unabr. ed. Clive Cussler. Read by Michael Prichard. 15 cass. (Running Time: 22 hrs. 30 min.). (Dirk Pitt Ser.). 1998. 120.00 (978-0-7366-4066-4(5), 4577) Books on Tape.
The grand master of adventure returns & now Dirk Pitt is caught in a web of villainy on the high seas & the Mississippi river. A greedy Chinese smuggler is trading in human lives, trafficking Chinese immigrants into countries around the globe, including our own. Dirk Pitt tracks the man's nefarious activities from Washington State to Louisiana, where his quarry is busily constructing a huge shipping port in the middle of nowhere. The trail of misdeeds leads to the site of a mysterious treasure trove, filled with fifty-year-old booty from Chiang Kai-shek's regime. Pitt's opponent is as clever & dangerous as criminals come & the hero will be lucky if he can play him to a stalemate.

Floodgates. Prod. by Laraim Associates. (Barclay Family Adventure Ser.). (J). 2005. audio compact disk (978-1-56254-991-6(X)) Saddleback Edu.

Floodgates. unabr. ed. Mary Anna Evans. (Running Time: 7 hrs. 0 mins.). (ENG.). 2009. 29.95 (978-1-4332-9055-8(3)); 54.95 (978-1-4332-9051-0(0)); audio compact disk 69.00 (978-1-4332-9052-7(9)) Blckstn Audio.

Floodgates of the Annointing: Secrets to Releasing the Awesome Power of God in Your Life. Mac Hammond. 2 cass. (Running Time: 1 hr.). (Annointing Ser.: Vol. 5). 1998. 12.00 Set. (978-1-57399-069-1(8)) Mac Hammond.

Floodland. unabr. ed. Marcus Sedgwick. Read by Amanda Root. 2 vols. (Running Time: 3 hrs. 19 mins.). (Middle Grade Cassette Librariestm Ser.). (J). (gr. 4-7). 2004. pap. bk. 29.00 (978-0-8072-0976-0(1), S YA 282 SP, Listening Lib); 23.00 (978-0-8072-8864-1(0), Listening Lib) Random Audio Pubg.
Ten-year-old Zoe Black was left behind on Norwich by accident when her parents escaped in the last supply ship to visit the island. Zoe discovers a small rowboat & keeps it a secret until she can set out alone on the great sea to find her parents. She lands on tiny Eels Island, where she must survive in a nightmarish world run by wild children & their boy-leader, Dooby. Zoe & a boy called Munchkin escape & cross the sea to the mainland, to find not only Zoe's parents but a new family & a new world.

Floods, from Defence to Management. Alphen. 2006. audio compact disk (978-0-415-39123-8(7)) Taylor and Fran.

Floodtide. unabr. ed. Sally Stewart. Read by Julia Sands. 7 cass. (Running Time: 9 hrs. 15 mins.). 1999. 76.95 (978-1-85903-250-3(8)) Pub: Magna Story GBR. Dist(s): Ulverscroft US
Cressida Marlow leaves Derrycombe on the Devon coast for a career in London. Befriended by the glamorous Marguerite Credland, & dazzles by Colin, Marguerite's son, Cressy is still homesick for her family. Paris with Colin is exciting, but then, confronted with new knowledge about him that she cannot ignore, Cressy returns home, only to find tragedy in her own family. Alone & grief-stricken, it is only when natural disaster threatens Derrycombe's divided communities that Cressy discovers an unexpected ally.

Floor Display Unit. Kelly Howell. 2007. audio compact disk (978-1-881451-95-2(X)) Brain Sync.

Floppy Sleep Game. Patti Teel. Perf. by Patti Teel. 1 cass. (Running Time: 25 min.). (J). 1999. pap. bk. 9.95 (978-0-9656156-2-4(6)) Dream Flight Prods.
A perfect relaxation for bedtime. Teel's soothing voice accompanied by peaceful orchestrations, leads little ones through instructions for their bodies & minds, guiding them on their way to a restful sleep.

Floppy Sleep Game. Patti Teel. Perf. by Patti Teel. 1 CD. (Running Time: 25 min.). (J). (ps-7). 1999. pap. bk. 12.95 (978-0-9656156-3-1(4)); pap. bk. 9.95 (978-0-9656156-7-9(7)); audio compact disk 12.95 (978-0-9656156-8-6(5)) Pub: Dream Flight Prods. Dist(s): Penton Overseas

Florence Nightingale. Laura E. Richards. Narrated by Anna Fields. (Running Time: 4 hrs. 30 mins.). 2001. 22.95 (978-1-59912-491-9(2)) Iofy Corp.

Florence Nightingale. unabr. ed. Robert Hogrogian. 1 cass. (Running Time: 20 min.). (People to Remember Ser.: Set II). (J). (gr. 4-7). 1979. bk. 16.99 (978-0-934898-85-0(5)); pap. bk. 9.95 (978-0-934898-09-6(X)) Jan Prods.
The heart-warming story of a brave English nurse.

Florence Nightingale. unabr. ed. Laura Richards. Read by Anna Fields. 3 cass. (Running Time: 4 hrs.). 2001. 23.95 (978-0-7861-2094-9(0), 2856); audio compact disk 24.00 (978-0-7861-9679-1(3), 2856) Blckstn Audio.
This uplifting account of a noble life will inspire the entire family. The name of Florence Nightingale is a household word, but the exact nature and scope of her work, and the difficulties and discouragement under which it was accomplished, are unknown to many of today's youth. This is the story of that wonderful woman's life. The biography of this interesting and justly beloved woman, "the Angel of the Crimea," is written by one whose father was in part responsible for Miss Nightingale's decision to devote her life to nursing.

Florence Nightingale. unabr. collector's ed. Elspeth Huxley. Read by Donada Peters. 6 cass. (Running Time: 6 hrs.). 1989. 36.00 (978-0-7366-1660-7(8), 2510) Books on Tape.
The founder of modern nursing, Nightingale lived to be over 90 yet spent less than two years in the military hospitals at Scutari, where the image of the Lady of the Lamp was created. The "ministering angel" was in reality a tough, domineering & brilliant administrator, scholar & writer of government reports. She became the authority on hospital design & management &, without setting foot in India, so great an expert on Indian affairs that five viceroys came to seek her advice.

Florence Nightingale: Called to Serve with Buffalo Biff & Farley's Raiders. Jill G. Wood. Illus. by Brian T. Cox. (Time Traveler's Adventure Ser.). (J). 2006. bk. 13.50 (978-1-932332-29-2(4)) Toy Box Prods.

Florencewalks. Anne Holler. Narrated by Maria Tucci. Prod. by Carol Shapiro. 2 cass. (Running Time: 3 hrs.). (Walk Ser.: Vol. 5). 1999. 18.00 (978-1-890489-04-5(2)) Pub: Sound Trvl FRA. Dist(s): Penton Overseas
Takes you through Florence, a vivid & volatile city where rival churches & monastic orders, marble goddesses & 400 year old palaces greet you at every turn.

Florida. National Textbook Company Staff. 1 cass. (Discover America Ser.). 15.00 (978-0-8442-7497-3(6), Natl Textbk Co) M-H Contemporary.
Offers a fascinating introduction to key locations in the country. Especially designed for intermediate ESL students, combines language learning with American culture study.

Florida - Salesperson Prelicensing Key Point Review: Based on Florida Real Estate Principles, Practices & Law. 24th ed. 1 cass. (Running Time: 1 hr. 30 mins.). 2001. 31.95 (978-0-7931-4114-2(1), 16102024, Dearbrn Real Est Ed) Kaplan Pubng.

Florida Bird Songs. Donald J. Borror & Maurice L. Giltz. 2 cass. (Donald J. Borror Bird Song Library). 1989. pap. bk. 9.95 (978-0-486-99926-5(2)) Dover.

Florida Boys: The Ultimate Collection. Contrib. by Florida Boys. (Gospel Legacy Ser.). 2008. audio compact disk 13.99 (978-5-557-57358-0(5)) Pt of Grace Ent.

Florida Boys Greatest Hits. Perf. by Florida Boys. 1 cass. audio compact disk 15.99 CD. (D2022) Diamante Music Grp.

Florida Is Closed Today. unabr. ed. Jack D. Hunter. Read by Tom Weiner. (Running Time: 6 hrs. 30 mins.). 2010. 29.95 (978-1-4332-1961-0(1)); 44.95 (978-1-4332-1957-3(3)); audio compact disk 69.00 (978-1-4332-1958-0(1)) Blckstn Audio.

Florida Land Boom. 1 cass. (Running Time: 25 min.). 1980. 10.00 (HT413) Esstee Audios.
Describes the heroes & the dupes of this eastern land rush & the hopeful & the hopeless as they scrambled across the country in their Model-T Fords in a frantic effort to make prodigious profits from the land of palm trees & sun until a devastating hurricane & a general stockmarket decline burst the bubble.

Florida Sales Associate Prelicensing Key Point Review Audio CD's. Dearborn Real Estate Education Staff & Dearborn Real Estate Education. (ENG.). 2006. audio compact disk 35.23 (978-1-4277-6510-9(3)) Pub: Kaplan Pubng. Dist(s): S and S Inc

Florida Salesperson Prelicensing Key Point Review. 27th ed. Dearborn Real Estate. 2003. bk. 34.90 (978-0-7931-6075-4(8)) Kaplan Pubng.

Florida Salespersons. 25th ed. Contrib. by Dearborn Staff. 2001. audio compact disk 31.95 (978-0-7931-4835-6(9)) Kaplan Pubng.

***Florida Storytown, Grade 5.** Created by Harcourt School Publishers. (ENG.). (J). 2006. audio compact disk 76.20 (978-0-15-359730-5(5)) HM Schl Div.

Florida Straits, unabr. ed. Laurence Shames. Narrated by Richard Ferrone. 7 cass. (Running Time: 9 hrs. 30 mins.). 1997. 60.00 (978-0-7887-1751-2(0), 95229E7) Recorded Bks.
Top-notch suspense & killer comedy merge in this story filled with funky characters & inappropriately named "wise" guys. Ferrone brings every character to life, from bad guys in shiny blue suits to Steve the naked landlord.

Florida Straits. unabr. collector's ed. Laurence Shames. Read by Rob McQuay. 6 cass. (Running Time: 9 hrs.). 1998. 48.00 (978-0-7366-4079-4(7), 4588) Books on Tape.
A small-time wiseguy is looking for the big score when he's duped by another crook on the make.

Florida Workers' Compensation Practice, Sixth Edition. The Florida Bar Continuing Legal Education. 1905. audio compact disk 165.00 (978-0-327-15594-2(9)) Pub: FL Bar Legal Ed. Dist(s): LEXIS Pub

***Florida's Pocahontas: Milly Francis.** 2nd gif. ed. Red Fox Publishing. As told by Red Fox Publishing. (ENG.). (YA). 2010. 9.97 (978-0-9826047-4-8(2)) Red FoxLLC FL.

Flory: A Miraculous Story of Survival: Holocaust 1940-1945. unabr. ed. Flory Van Beek. Read by Kirsten Potter. (Running Time: 25200 sec.). 2008. 44.95 (978-1-4332-2541-3(7)) Blckstn Audio.

Flory: A Miraculous Story of Survival; Holocaust 1940-1945. unabr. ed. Flory A. Van Beek. Read by Kirsten Potter. (Running Time: 25200 sec.). 2008. audio compact disk & audio compact disk 60.00 (978-1-4332-2542-0(5)) Blckstn Audio.

Flory: A Miraculous Story of Survival: Holocaust 1940-1945. unabr. ed. Flory A. Van Beek. Read by Kirsten Potter. (Running Time: 25200 sec.). 2008. audio compact disk 29.95 (978-1-4332-2545-1(X)) Blckstn Audio.

Flossie & the Fox. 2004. 8.95 (978-1-56008-399-3(9)); cass. & flmstrp 30.00 (978-0-89719-607-9(4)); audio compact disk 12.95 (978-1-55592-872-8(2)) Weston Woods.

Flossie & the Fox. (J). 2004. pap. bk. 18.95 (978-1-55592-772-1(6)); pap. bk. 38.75 (978-1-55592-787-5(4)); pap. bk. 32.75 (978-1-55592-224-5(4)); pap. bk. 14.95 (978-1-55592-051-7(9)) Weston Woods.

Flossie & the Fox. Patricia C. McKissack. 1 cass., 5 bks. (Running Time: 13 min.). (J). pap. bk. 32.75 Weston Woods.
The story of Flossie who outfoxes a fox to protect a basket of eggs she must deliver to a nearby farm.

Flossie & the Fox. Patricia C. McKissack. Illus. by Rachel Isadora. 1 cass. (Running Time: 13 min.). (J). (gr. k-4). pap. bk. 12.95 Weston Woods.

Flossie & the Fox. Read by Patricia C. McKissack. 1 cass. (Running Time: 13 min.). (J). (gr. k-4). 1989. 8.95 (978-0-89719-991-9(X), RAC327) Weston Woods.

Flossie & the Fox. Read by Patricia C. McKissack. Illus. by Rachel Isadora. 1 cass. (Running Time: 13 min.). (J). (gr. k-4). 1989. bk. 24.95 (978-1-56008-009-1(4), HRA327) Weston Woods.

Flourishing Like a Palm Tree Pt. 1: Psalm 92. Ed Young. 1989. 4.95 (978-0-7417-1760-3(3), 760) Win Walk.

Flourishing Like a Palm Tree Pt. 2: Psalm 92. Ed Young. 1989. 4.95 (978-0-7417-1761-0(1), 761) Win Walk.

Flow. abr. ed. Phil Jackson. 4 cass. (Running Time: 6 hrs.). 2004. 25.95 (978-0-14-305704-8(9), PengAudBks) Penguin Grp USA.

Flow. unabr. ed. John Ortberg. Read by John Ortberg. 6 cass. (Running Time: 8 hrs.). 2004. 27.99 (978-1-58926-371-0(5)) Oasis Audio.

Flow. unabr. ed. John Ortberg. Narrated by John Ortberg. 8 CDs. (Running Time: 8 hrs.). (ENG.). 2004. audio compact disk 29.99 (978-1-58926-372-7(3)) Oasis Audio.

Flow: Living at the Peak of Your Abilities. Mihaly Csikszentmihalyi. 6 cass. 59.95 set. (10580AX) Nightingale-Conant.
Just as top achievers in Fortune 500 companies from Apple to Xerox do, you can use "it" to feel more alert, creative & able to live at the peak of your abilities. "It" is an experience called "flow" - a state of concentration in which activities are so spontaneous they become almost automatic. People in flow have better moods, motivation, concentration & control. In this series, you'll learn how to control the eight components of flow...master challenging tasks...banish limiting beliefs...make any job more likely to produce flow...generate higher levels of power, energy & concentration...even enjoy routine tasks. This revolutionary program also can give you a greater sense of meaning & purpose - even shape the way you look at your job & family relationships. Includes workbook.

Flow: The Psychology of Optimal Experience. abr. ed. Mihaly Csikszentmihalyi. Read by Mihaly Csikszentmihalyi. 1 CD. (Running Time: 20 hrs. 0 mins. 0 sec.). (ENG.). 2002. audio compact disk 19.95 (978-0-7435-2504-6(3), Nightgale) Pub: S&S Audio. Dist(s): S and S Inc
SUCCESS CAN BE YOURS WITH MIHALY CSIKSZENTMIHALYI'S FLOW The world's foremost producer of personal development and motivational audio programs gives you the tools to unleash the secret of peak performance. Remember the last time that you were so focused, so motivated that you felt at the absolute top of your form - alert, energized and free of self-consciousness? Chances are you were experiencing flow - an almost euphoric state of concentration and complete involvement. Now, esteemed psychologist Mihaly Csikszentmihalyi reveals how you can achieve this state of mind at will - and turn everyday experience into a moment by moment opportunity for joy and self-fulfillment. Drawing on over 30 years of breakthrough research into what makes people satisfied, he explains the key elements of the flow experience, including how to: Use flow to release yourself from anxiety and boredom Redirect your energy and take control Set clear goals Harmonize all the elements of your life

Flow My Tears, the Policeman Said. unabr. ed. Philip K. Dick. Read by Scott Brick. (Running Time: 32400 sec.). 2007. 59.95 (978-1-4332-1123-2(8)); audio compact disk 63.00 (978-1-4332-1124-9(6)) Blckstn Audio.

Flow My Tears, the Policeman Said. unabr. ed. Philip K. Dick & Scott Brick. (Running Time: 32400 sec.). 2007. audio compact disk 29.95 (978-1-4332-1125-6(4)) Blckstn Audio.

Flow of Grace: Invoke the Blessings & Empowerment of Hanuman with Sacred Chant from Krishna Das. Krishna Das. 2007. audio compact disk 19.98 (978-1-59179-549-0(4), M1110) Sounds True.

Flow of Life Exercise. Mark Earlix. 2000. 12.95 (978-0-9678058-3-2(X)) Art of Healing.

Flow of Naam: Developing Higher Power. Joseph Michael Levry. 2006. 19.00 (978-1-885562-14-2(4)) Root Light.

Flower Adornment Repentance. audio compact disk 15.00 (978-0-88139-711-6(3)) Buddhist Text.

Flower Essences I Workshop. 3 cass. (Running Time: 4 hrs. 30 mins.). 2004. 19.95 (978-0-927978-15-6(6), WT-105) Perelandra Ltd.

Flower Essences II Workshop. 4 cass. (Running Time: 6 hrs.). 2004. 23.95 (978-0-927978-16-3(4), WT-106) Perelandra Ltd.
A workshop by Machaelle for those who wish to include the more advanced processes in their flower essences use.

Flower Fairy Alphabet. 1 CD. (Running Time: 50:13 min.). (Famous Author Ser.). (J). 2003. audio compact disk 15.98 (978-1-56628-360-1(4)) MFLP CA.

Flower-Fed Buffaloes see Poetry of Vachel Lindsay

Flower-Fed Buffaloes see Gathering of Great Poetry for Children

Flower for Iggey. abr. ed. Beverly Hoffman & Sal J. Fiorilla. Perf. by Cliff Erickson. 1 cass. (Running Time: 50 min.). Dramatization. (J). (gr. k-4). 1994. bk. 6.95 Feather Fables.
12 children's songs with narration in between each number, both vocal versions & soundtrack version. Cliff Erickson stars as Iggey & Edgar Iguana with humor to teach children basic emotions & the fun of reading books.

Flower for Iggey: Iggey the Iguana. abr. ed. Beverly H. Erickson & Sal J. Fiorilla. Perf. by Cliff Erickson. Illus. by Beverly H. Erickson & Michael D. Robinson. 1 cass. (Running Time: 50 min.). Dramatization. (J). (gr. 3-6). 1993. bk. 12.95 (978-0-9634122-1-8(3)) Feather Fables.

Flower for My Papa. unabr. ed. Adele Z. Ames. Read by Eleanor Parent. Perf. by Pendleton St. School Students. 1 cass. (Running Time: 30 mins.). (J). (gr. 1-6). 1999. 5.00 (978-0-9677692-1-9(3)) Butterfly Pr ME.
The true story of the Rev. Timothy Zucchi's family coming to America from Switzerland in search of religious freedom in 1913.

Flower Girl. Elizabeth Lord. Read by Patricia Gallimore. 10 cass. (Running Time: 13 hrs. 45 mins.). (Isis Cassettes Ser.). (J). 2005. 84.95 (978-0-7531-3404-7(7)) Pub: ISIS Lrg Prnt GBR. Dist(s): Ulverscroft US

Flower in Season. Audrey Howard. Read by Carole Boyd. 12 vols. (Running Time: 18 hrs.). 2003. 96.95 (978-0-7540-8305-4(5)) Pub: Chivers Audio Bks GBR. Dist(s): AudioGO

Flower Net. unabr. ed. Lisa See. Read by Liza Ross. 10 CDs. (Running Time: 13 hrs.). (Red Princess Ser.: Bk. 1). 2000. audio compact disk 89.95 (978-0-7531-0903-8(4), 109034) Pub: ISIS Audio GBR. Dist(s): Ulverscroft US

Flower Net. unabr. ed. Lisa See. Read by Liza Ross. 10 cass. (Running Time: 13 hrs.). (Red Princess Ser.: Bk. 1). (J). 1999. 84.95 (978-0-7531-0443-9(1), 980905) Pub: ISIS Lrg Prnt GBR. Dist(s): Ulverscroft US
On a January morning in Beijing, a child skating on frozen lake finds the corpse of a white man under the ice. Liu Hulan, a female detective, is assigned to head what will be a delicate investigation, for the murder victim is the son of the American ambassador. David Stark, an assistant US attorney, boards a ship and finds the badly decomposed body of a "Red Prince:, the son of one of China's top officials. The murders appear to be unconnected until rare plant fibers are found coating the respiratory tracts of both victims & the Chinese & americans agree to work together.

Flower of Scotland. unabr. ed. Emma Blair. Read by Kara Wilson. 10 cass. (Running Time: 10 hrs.). 1998. 84.95 Set. (978-0-7540-0099-0(0), CAB1522) AudioGO.
The Drummond family has it all: Daughter Charlotte is in love & plans to marry. Peter, the eldest, is preparing to take over the family business. Fun loving Andrew is turning heads & hearts. The youngest, Nell, daydreams of a handsome Highlander. This is the idyllic scene in the summer of 1912. But World War I was to bring death, devastation, revenge, scandal & suicide to the Drummonds.

Flower That Shattered the Stone - ShowTrax. Perf. by John Denver. Arranged by Audrey Snyder. 1 CD. (Running Time: 5 mins.). 2000. audio compact disk 19.95 (08201191) H Leonard.
The beauty of the earth is celebrated in this gentle acoustic ballad. A wonderful, timeless message!.

Flowering Judas. unabr. ed. Elizabeth Palmer. Read by Judy Laister. 8 cass. (Running Time: 8 hrs.). 1997. 69.95 (978-0-7540-0058-7(3), CAB 1481) AudioGO.
Charmian has many married lovers, one for each day of the week. Weekends are spent with Giles in Sussex. It's a rewarding way of life, but when Giles falls in love with a neighbor, Charmian realizes it can't go on forever. When her brother is fired from his high-powered city job, Charmian resolves to exact revenge through her own contacts. But what she discovers is far more than she bargained for.

Flowering of Human Consciousness: Everyone's Life Purpose. Eckhart Tolle. 3 CDs. 2004. audio compact disk 24.95 (978-1-59179-168-3(5), AW00803D) Sounds True.
The bestselling author of The Power of Now reveals specific, powerful insights on how to be present in this very moment. Tolle teaches easy techniques for self-observation, how to stop the endless stream of thoughts that interrupt, and methods for breaking out of object consciousness by tapping into an intelligence that is greater than the personal mind.

Flowering of Human Nature. Swami Amar Jyoti. 1 cass. 1987. 9.95 (A-39) Truth Consciousness.
Inner refinement; winning our own victory. Living by the strength of virtue. Scriptures: beacon lights of education. The purpose & destiny of human nature.

Flowering Quince see Twentieth-Century Poetry in English, No. 27, Recordings of Poets Reading Their Own Poetry

Flowering the Fields fo Mars. unabr. ed. Tom Schwartz. Narrated by Ron Knowles. (Running Time: 2 hrs. 19 mins.). (ENG.). (J). 2006. 14.95 (978-1-57545-323-1(1), RP Audio Pubng) Pub: Reagent Press. Dist(s): OverDrive Inc

Flowering the Fields of Mars: How Mother Nature Flowered the Fields, Book 2. unabr. ed. Tom Schwartz. Read by Ron Knowles. (J). 2008. 34.99 (978-1-60514-636-2(6)) Find a World.

Flowering Wilderness. unabr. ed. John Galsworthy. Read by David Case. (Running Time: 28800 sec.). (Forsyte Chronicles Ser.). 2007. 54.95 (978-1-4332-0251-3(4)); audio compact disk 29.95 (978-1-4332-0253-7(0)); audio compact disk 63.00 (978-1-4332-0252-0(2)) Blckstn Audio.

Flowering Wilderness, unabr. collector's ed. John Galsworthy. Read by David Case. 6 cass. (Running Time: 9 hrs.). (End of Chapter Ser.: Vol. 2). 1999. 48.00 (978-0-7366-4383-2(4), 4849) Books on Tape.
Finds the Cherrells uneasy in a world of changing values.

Flowers by the Sea see William Carlos Williams Reads His Poetry

Flowers for Algernon. abr. ed. Daniel Keyes. Read by Brad Freggre. 4 cass. (Running Time: 6 hrs.). (J). 1995. 24.00 Set. (978-1-886392-04-5(8), Parrot Bks) Walberg Pubng.
A modern classic, this wildly acclaimed novel has been on "must read" lists since its original publicaiton. This fascinating tale of a daring human experiment has been described in glowing terms by many.

Flowers for Algernon, unabr. ed. Daniel Keyes. Narrated by Jeff Woodman. 6 pieces. (Running Time: 9 hrs.). (gr. 11 up). 1998. 53.00 (978-0-7887-2227-1(1), 95526E7) Recorded Bks.
As a mentally handicapped young man is transformed into a genius through surgery & medication, his pleasure is mixed with a growing fear that the experiment's effects may only be temporary.

Flowers for Algernon, Class Set. unabr. ed. Daniel Keyes. Read by Jeff Woodman. 6 cass., 10 bks. (Running Time: 9 hrs.). (YA). 1998. bk. 133.70 (978-0-7887-2549-4(1), 46719) Recorded Bks.

Flowers for Algernon, Homework Set. unabr. ed. Daniel Keyes. Read by Jeff Woodman. 6 cass. (Running Time: 9 hrs.). (YA). (gr. 7). 1998. bk. 67.24 (978-0-7887-2244-8(1), 40728) Recorded Bks.

Flowers for Algernon Soundtrack-on Cd. Prod. by Myattic Studio. (YA). 2000. audio compact disk 89.95 (978-0-7365-3276-1(5)) Films Media Grp.

Flowers for Healing: The Importance of Flower Essences on the Planet Today. unabr. ed. Interview with Bruce Stephen Holmes et al. 1 cass. (Running Time: 1 hr.). 1996. 5.55 Incl. bklet. (978-1-892457-01-1(6)) Laughng Star Pr.
An interview with flower essence makers.

Flowers for His Funeral. Ann Granger. Narrated by Judith Boyd. 7 cass. (Running Time: 10 hrs. 25 mins.). 2004. 69.75 (978-1-84197-975-5(9)); audio compact disk 99.75 (978-1-4025-8921-8(2)) Recorded Bks.

Flowers for the Judge. unabr. ed. Margery Allingham. Read by Francis Matthews. 8 cass. (Running Time: 12 hrs.). 2001. 59.95 (978-0-7451-4196-1(X), CAB 879) Pub: Chivers Audio Bks GBR. Dist(s): AudioGO
Nobody questioned the disappearance of the director of the publishing house of Barnabas... until his corpse was found in the firm's vault. Scandal spread, and Albert Campion set out to capture the murderer.

Flowers in the Attic. V. C. Andrews. Narrated by Alyssa Bresnahan. 14 CDs. (Running Time: 16 hrs. 45 mins.). audio compact disk 134.00 (978-0-7887-9888-7(X)) Recorded Bks.

Flowers in the Attic. unabr. ed. V. C. Andrews. Read by Donada Peters. 10 cass. (Running Time: 15 hrs.). 1988. 70.00 (978-0-7366-1326-2(9), 2230) Books on Tape.
When the father dies, the Dollanganger family is left destitute. The children's mother returns to her parents' estate for help. The grandmother locks the four children in a bedroom, with only an attic in which to roam. She whips them when they disobey her, and their mother seems to go along in hopes of inheriting her father's wealth.

Flowers in the Attic, unabr. ed. V. C. Andrews. Narrated by Alyssa Bresnahan. 12 cass. (Running Time: 16 hrs. 45 mins.). 1996. 97.00 (978-0-7887-0473-4(7), 94666E7) Recorded Bks.
In the first book of this series we meet the Dollangangers - a family haunted by a remorseless, demonic history.

Flowers in the Attic. unabr. ed. V. C. Andrews. Narrated by Alyssa Bresnahan. 12 /cds. (Running Time: 16 hrs. 45 min.). 2001. audio compact disk 142.00 (C1429) Recorded Bks.

Flowers in the Rain & Other Stories. unabr. ed. Rosamunde Pilcher. Read by Joanna David. 8 cass. (Running Time: 8 hrs.). 1993. 69.95 set. (978-0-7451-4172-5(2), CAB 855) AudioGO.
In this collection of heartwarming stories, Pilcher explores the hearts & minds of ordinary people with extraordinary perception. Through all of the characters, personal crises & triumphs are shown to be as important as the world's major events.

Flowers in the Rain & Other Stories. unabr. ed. Rosamunde Pilcher. Read by Penelope Dellaporta. 8 cass. (Running Time: 12 hrs.). 1995. 64.00 (978-0-7366-2977-5(7), 3668) Books on Tape.
Collection of vignettes shows how family bonds nurture & support. Lively characters, vivid settings.

Flowers in the Rain & Other Stories. unabr. ed. Short Stories. Rosamunde Pilcher. Narrated by Davina Porter. 7 cass. (Running Time: 10 hrs.). 1992. 60.00 (978-1-55690-624-4(2), 92101E7) Recorded Bks.
In this collection of short stories, Pilcher writes about the many faces of love, from a 12-year old boy who copes with his father's death, to a young couple who experience their first marital strife, to an elderly woman's renewed affirmation of life & marriage.

Flowers of Hawaii. Bess Press. (JPN.). 2004. audio compact disk 4.95 (978-1-57306-202-2(2)) Bess Pr.

Flowers of Joy. Pamela Warrick-Smith. 1994. 10.95 (317); audio compact disk 15.95 (317) GIA Pubns.

***Flowers on Main.** unabr. ed. Sherryl Woods. Read by Christina Traister. (Running Time: 11 hrs.). (Chesapeake Shores Ser.). 2010. 19.99 (978-1-4418-4995-3(5), 9781441849953, Brilliance MP3); 39.97 (978-1-4418-4996-0(3), 9781441849960, Brinc Audio MP3 Lib); 19.99 (978-1-4418-4997-7(1), 9781441849977, BAD); 39.97 (978-1-4418-4998-4(X), 9781441849984, BADLE); audio compact disk 19.99 (978-1-4418-4993-9(9), 9781441849939, Bril Audio CD Unabri); audio compact disk 79.97 (978-1-4418-4994-6(7), 9781441849946, BriAudCD Unabrid) Brilliance Audio.

Flowers on the Grass. unabr. ed. Monica Dickens. Read by Carole Boyd. 8 cass. (Running Time: 9 hrs. 33 min.). 2001. 69.95 (978-1-85695-440-2(4), 92096) Pub: ISIS Audio GBR. Dist(s): Ulverscroft US
Orphaned as a child, Daniel Brett could never settle down. After the tragic death of his beloved young wife, he abandons home & security, setting off to find the freedom he knew as a boy.

Flowers on the Mersey. unabr. ed. June Francis. Read by Marie McCarthy. 8 cass. (Running Time: 10 hrs. 35 min.). 1999. 83.95 (978-1-85903-255-8(9)) Pub: Magna Story GBR. Dist(s): Ulverscroft US
Happiness for Rebekah is threatened when her father decides to seek a new life for his family in America.

Flowing in the Anointing Vol. 1, Vol. 1. Speeches. Tim N. Enloe. 2 CDs. 1999. audio compact disk 17.99 (978-0-9749739-3-7(9)) E M Pubns.
Flowing In the Anointing: Volume One.Principles gleaned from biblical characters interacting with the anointing of the Holy Spirit. Disc one contains, "Learning from Elisha." Disk two contains, "Learning from Samson.".

Flowing in the Anointing Vol. 2, Vol. 2. Speeches. Tim N. Enloe. 2 CDs. 2000. audio compact disk 17.99 (978-0-9749739-1-3(2)) E M Pubns.
Flowing In the Anointing: Volume Two.Principles gleaned from biblical characters interacting with the anointing of the Holy Spirit. Disc one contains, "Learning from David." Disk two contains, "Learning from Saul.".

Flowing in Tune. Swami Amar Jyoti. 1 cass. 1980. 9.95 (J-36) Truth Consciousness.
Established personality is blocking the flow. Seeing everything as new & responding in a flowing manner. Space is our quality.

Flowing Water: Meditation for Well-Being. Voice by Catherine Sheeen. 2 CDs. (Running Time: Depends on the Track). 2005. audio compact disk 22.95 (978-0-9773381-3-9(4)) Reach In.
Flowing Water: Meditation for Well-Being is a meditation that promotes stress reduction and relaxation by using your breath and the musical sound of flowing water to help you focus and stay in the present. There are 2 CDs with 5, 10, 30 and 45 minute Flowing Water meditations and Preparation for Meditation and Instructions for Flowing Water Meditation tracks.

Floyd: The Unauthorized Biography of Pink Floyd. Martin Harper. 1 CD. (Running Time: 1 hr.). (Maximum Ser.). (ENG., 2001. audio compact disk 14.95 (978-1-84240-091-3(6)) Pub: Chrome Dreams GBR. Dist(s): IPG Chicago
One of Britains most successful rock bands of all times, Pink Floyd have grown into a multi-million dollar musical phenomenon. Musically unique and devoted to their audience, their extravagant stage shows have become legendary in the music business, as have their mammoth world tours. Maximum Floyd traces their thirty-five year career right up to the present day, following their rise to huge popularity and subsequent collapse under the pressure. With a second wind, they have risen to become even greater than before and continue to captivate with their rare mixture of blues, rock and psychedelia.

***FLSA Rules, Regulations, & Classification Standards.** PUEI. 2008. audio compact disk 199.00 (978-1-935041-04-7(5), CareerTrack) P Univ E Inc.

Flubber. 1 cass. (Play Packs Ser.). (J). bk. 14.99 (978-0-7634-0945-6(6)) W Disney Records.

Flubber. 1 cass. (Read-Along Ser.). (J). (ps-3). 1997. bk. 7.99 (978-0-7634-0365-2(2)) W Disney Records.

Flubber. (J). 1997. 13.99 (978-0-7634-0354-6(7)); 13.99 Norelco. (978-0-7634-0353-9(9)); audio compact disk 22.99 CD. (978-0-7634-0355-3(5)); audio compact disk 22.99 (978-0-7634-0356-0(3)) W Disney Records.
Soundtrack features remake of The Absent Minded Professor starring Robin Williams.

Flubber (Read-Along) Read by Robin Williams. 1 cass. (Disney Ser.). (J). 6.38 Blisterpack. (DISN 60304); 9.58 Soundtrack. (DISN 60952); audio compact disk 14.38 CD Jewel box, soundtrack. (DISN 60952) NewSound.
Professor Phillip Brainard, a man so lost in thought that he appears, at times, not to pay attention. Working away with his high-voltage, over-amorous flying robot assistant, Weebo, he creates a miraculous goo that, when applied to any object - cars, bowling balls...even people enables them to fly through the air at remarkable speeds. It defies gravity & looks like rubber.

Fluch der Mumie. Bottcher. pap. bk. 20.95 (978-88-7754-790-3(1)) Pub: Cideb ITA. Dist(s): Distribks Inc

Fluency Kit Audio CD - Levels F-M. ed. (J). 2004. audio compact disk (978-1-4108-2052-5(1)) Benchmark Educ.

Fluency Kit Audio CD - Levels N-U. ed. (J). 2004. audio compact disk (978-1-4108-2059-4(9)) Benchmark Educ.

Fluency Mini-Lessons. Newmark Learning, LLC. (Fluency Instruction Practice Ser.). (gr. 1). 2009. audio compact disk (978-1-60719-087-5(7)) Newmark Learn.

Fluency Mini-Lessons. Newmark Learning, LLC. (Fluency Instruction Practice Ser.). (gr. 2). 2009. audio compact disk (978-1-60719-088-2(5)) Newmark Learn.

Fluency Mini-Lessons. Newmark Learning, LLC. (Fluency Instruction Practice Ser.). (gr. 3). 2009. audio compact disk (978-1-60719-089-9(3)) Newmark Learn.

Fluent Chinese. Wang Xiaoning. (CHI & ENG.). 2005. bk. 11.95 (978-7-80187-814-4(0), FLCH1) Pub: New World Pr CHN. Dist(s): China Bks

Fluent Chinese, Vol. 2. Wang Xiaoning. (CHI & ENG.). 2005. bk. 11.95 (978-7-80187-815-1(9), FLCH2) Pub: New World Pr CHN. Dist(s): China Bks

Fluent Tibetan, 18 cass. (Running Time: 26 hrs.). 1993. pap. bk. 295.00 (978-0-88432-998-5(4), AFTB15) J Norton Pubs.
Proficiency-oriented learning system, beginning & intermediate levels.

Fluent Tibetan, Set. Foreign Service Institute Staff. 18 cass. (Running Time: 26 hrs.). bk. 255.00 (978-0-614-97144-6(6), AFTB15) J Norton Pubs.
A proficiency-oriented learning system, beginning & intermediate levels, developed by language experts & indigenous speakers. Three texts in fifteen units. Recorded by indigenous speakers. Glossary is both Tibetan-English & English-Tibetan.

Fluent Tibetan: The Vocabulary & Dialogues - A Proficiency-Oriented Learning System Novice & Intermediate Levels. William A. Magee. (TIB.). 1999. audio compact disk 45.00 (978-1-55939-111-5(1)) Pub: Snow Lion Pubns. Dist(s): Natl Bk Netwk

Fluenz French 1 + 2 Learning Suite. (ENG.). 2008. DVD & audio compact disk 357.00 (978-0-9821539-6-3(1)) Fluenz.

Fluenz French 1 + 2 Learning Suite for Mac OS X. (ENG.). 2008. DVD & audio compact disk 357.00 (978-0-9821539-9-4(6)) Fluenz.

Fluenz Italian 1. (ENG.). 2008. DVD & audio compact disk 218.00 (978-0-9821539-7-0(X)) Fluenz.

Fluenz Italian 1 + 2 Learning Suite. (ENG.). 2008. DVD & audio compact disk 357.00 (978-0-9821539-8-7(8)) Fluenz.

Fluenz Italian 1 + 2 Learning Suite for Mac OS X. (ENG.). 2008. DVD & audio compact disk 357.00 (978-0-9821539-1-8(0)) Fluenz.

Fluenz Mandarin 1 + 2 Learning Suite. 2008. DVD & audio compact disk 357.00 (978-0-9821539-2-5(9)) Fluenz.

Fluenz Mandarin 1 + 2 Learning Suite for Mac OS/X. 2008. DVD & audio compact disk 357.00 (978-0-9821539-5-6(3)) Fluenz.

Fluenz Spanish 1 + 2 Learning Suite. (ENG.). 2007. DVD & audio compact disk 357.00 (978-0-9821539-0-1(2)) Fluenz.

Fluenz Spanish 1 + 2 Learning Suite for Mac OS X. (ENG.). 2007. DVD & audio compact disk 357.00 (978-0-9821539-3-2(7)) Fluenz.

Fluffy told the Truth: Fluffy dijo la Verdad. (SPA., (J). 2006. 5.00 (978-0-9726946-2-9(5)) R Varas.

Fluid & Electrolyte Disturbances in the Critically Ill Patient. Read by Arnold Aberman. 1 cass. (Running Time: 90 min.). 1986. 12.00 (C8633) Amer Coll Phys.

Fluid Soloing - Book 1: Arpeggios for Lead Rock Guitar. Tim Quinn. (ENG.). 2008. spiral bd. 22.95 (978-0-7866-7275-2(7)) Mel Bay.

Fluids & Electrolytes Electronic Learning Program. 2nd ed. Joyce LeFever Kee et al. (ENG.). (C). 2009. audio compact disk 57.95 (978-1-4354-5369-2(7)) Pub: Delmar. Dist(s): CENGAGE Learn

Fluke. James Herbert. Read by Paul McGann. 3 CDs. (Running Time: 3 hrs. 0 mins. 0 sec.). (ENG.). 2008. audio compact disk 19.95 (978-0-230-70023-9(3)) Pub: Macmillan UK GBR. Dist(s): IPG Chicago

***Fluke.** unabr. ed. Christopher Moore. Read by Bill Irwin. (ENG.). 2005. (978-0-06-081842-5(5), Harper Audio); (978-0-06-081843-2(3), Harper Audio) HarperCollins Pubs.

Fluke: Or, I Know Why the Winged Whale Sings. unabr. ed. Christopher Moore. Read by Bill Irwin. (Running Time: 39600 sec.). 2007. audio compact disk 39.95 (978-0-06-123879-6(1)) HarperCollins Pubs.

Flumpa's World: Frogs, Rain Forests & More. 1 cass. (Running Time: 1 hr.). (J). (ps-4). 2001. 10.95 (ION 5123C); audio compact disk 14.95 (ION 5123CD) Kimbo Educ.
12 original tunes in various styles with catchy lyrics to help kids learn facts about frogs (amphibians), reptiles, the rain forest & other cool biological science facts. Reptile vs. Amphibian, Swamp Stompin', Habitats Rain Forest Rock, Voices of the Rainforest, The Future's In Our Hands & more.

Flumpa's World: Frogs, Rain Forests & Other Fun Facts. Music by Wendy Whitten & Rick Florian. 1 cass. (Running Time: 90 mins.). (J). 2000. 10.00 (978-1-886184-03-9(8), IIR5123-4) Ion Imagination.
Blends the best of science & environmental education with twelve original entertaining, sing-a-long songs about amphibians, reptiles, habitats & rain forests.

Flumpa's World: Frogs, Rain Forests & Other Fun Facts. Music by Wendy Whitten & Rick Florian. 1 CD. (Running Time: 90 mins.). (J). (ps-4). 2000. audio compact disk 14.00 (978-1-886184-04-6(6), IIR5123-4) Ion Imagination.

Flumpa's World: Out of This World! Wendy Whitten. (J). 2000. bk. 14.95 (978-1-886184-11-4(9)); audio compact disk 10.95 (978-1-886184-10-7(0)) Pub: Ion Imagination. Dist(s): Pi1casso Dist Srvcs

Flumpa's World: Out of This World! Wendy Whitten & Rick Florian. 1 cass. (Running Time: 30 mins.). (J). 2000. 10.00 Ion Imagination.
Flumpa the frog blasts into outer space to a soundtrack of tunes with factual, science-based lyrics. Songs include "Earth in Motion" & "Roy G Biv".

Flumpa's World: Out of This World! Wendy Whitten & Rick Florian. 1 CD. (Running Time: 90 mins.). (J). (ps-4). 2000. audio compact disk 14.00 Ion Imagination.

Flumpa(r)'s World: Water, Water Everywhere. (J). 2004. audio compact disk 15.00 (978-1-886184-13-8(5)) Ion Imagination.

Flunking of Joshua T. Bates. Susan Richards Shreve. Narrated by Johnny Heller. 2 cass. (Running Time: 2 hrs. 30 min.). (J). (gr. 5). 2001. 19.00 (95025E7) Recorded Bks.
What could be worse than having summer vacation end? For Joshua Bates it's coming home to find out he has to repeat third grade.

Flunking of Joshua T. Bates. unabr. ed. Susan Richards Shreve. Narrated by Johnny Heller. 2 pieces. (Running Time: 2 hrs. 30 mins.). (gr. 5 up). 1998. 10.00 (978-0-7887-1913-4(0), 95334) Recorded Bks.
The only thing worse for Joshua than having summer vacation end, is coming home to find out that he has to repeat the third grade.

Flunking of Joshua T. Bates. unabr. ed. Susan Richards Shreve. Read by Johnny Heller. 1 cass. (Running Time: 1 hr. 30 min.). (J). (gr. 4). 1998. 23.24 (978-0-7887-1941-7(6), 40648); 79.40 (978-0-7887-2891-4(1), 40648) Recorded Bks.
What can be worse than having summer vacation end? For Joshua Bates it's coming home to find out that he has to repeat the third grade.

Fluoridation, Laetrile & Cancer. unabr. ed. Dean Burk. 1 cass. (Running Time: 46 min.). 12.95 (940) J Norton Pubs.

Flush. collector's unabr. ed. Carl Hiaasen. Read by Michael Welch. 5 CDs. (Running Time: 6 hrs.). (J). (gr. 4-7). 2005. audio compact disk 68.85 (978-0-307-28290-3(2), Listening Lib); 35.00 (978-0-307-28289-7(9), Listening Lib) Pub: Random Audio Pubg. Dist(s): Random
You know it's going to be a rough summer when you spend Father's Day visiting your dad in the local lockup. Noah's dad is sure that the owner of the Coral Queen casino boat is flushing raw sewage into the harbor - which has made taking a dip at the local beach like swimming in a toilet. He can't prove it though, and so he decides that sinking the boat will make an effective statement. Right. The boat is pumped out and back in business within days and Noah's dad is stuck in the clink. Now Noah is determined to succeed where his dad failed. He will prove that the Coral Queen is dumping illegally... somehow. His allies may not add up to much - his sister Abbey, an unreformed childhood biter; Lice Peeking, a greedy sot with poor hygiene; Shelly, a bartender and a woman scorned; and a mysterious pirate - but Noah's got a plan to flush this crook out into the open. A plan that should sink the crooked little casino, once and for all.

Flush. unabr. ed. Carl Hiaasen. Read by Michael Welch. 6 CDs. (Running Time: 19380 sec.). (ENG.). (J). (gr. 7-12). 2005. audio compact disk 30.00 (978-0-307-28070-1(5), Listening Lib) Pub: Random Audio Pubg. Dist(s): Random

Flush. unabr. ed. Virginia Woolf. Read by Gretel Davis. 4 cass. (Running Time: 4 hrs. 43 min.). 1994. 44.95 (978-1-85695-541-6(9), 93033) Pub: ISIS Audio GBR. Dist(s): Ulverscroft US
This is the story of Flush, a dark brown cocker spaniel, with big hazel eyes & tasseled ears, who has a very good pedigree. The pet of Elizabeth Barrett Browning, he is an invaluable witness to the love between Elizabeth & Robert Browning. In this enchanting book we see life through Flush's eyes, based mainly on smell.

Flute Handbook. Mizzy McCaskill & Dona Gilliam. (Building Excellence Ser.). 1993. bk. 16.95 (978-0-87166-416-7(X), 94110P) Mel Bay.

Flute Method. Peter Gelling. (Progressive Ser.). 2004. pap. bk. 14.95 (978-1-86462-219-5(9), 256-069) Pub: Kolala Music SGP. Dist(s): Bookworld

Flute of God. Scripts. Paul Twitchell. 4 cass. (Running Time: 5 hrs. 48 mins.). (YA). 1989. 25.00 (978-1-57043-035-0(7), 160061) Eckankar.

Flute School. Alfred Publishing Staff. (ENG.). 1999. audio compact disk 15.95 (978-0-87487-460-0(2), Warner Bro) Alfred Pub.

Flute School, Vol. 12. Alfred Publishing Staff. (ENG.). 1999. audio compact disk 15.95 (978-0-87487-414-3(9), Warner Bro) Alfred Pub.

Flute School, Vol. 34. Alfred Publishing Staff. (ENG.). 1999. audio compact disk 15.95 (978-0-87487-459-4(9), Warner Bro) Alfred Pub.

Flute School, Vol. 345. rev. ed. Kenji Yamashita & Toshio Takahashi. (Suzuki Method Core Materials Ser.). (ENG.). 1997. audio compact disk 15.95 (978-0-87487-914-8(0), Warner Bro) Alfred Pub.

Flute Song: Easy familiar classics with Orchestra. Stuggart Festival Orchestra. 2005. pap. bk. 34.98 (978-1-59615-289-2(3), 586-008) Pub: Music Minus. Dist(s): Bookworld

Flute: the Blues Brothers. Blues Brothers. 2000. bk. 13.95 (978-1-85909-725-0(1), Warner Bro) Alfred Pub.

Flute with Piano Accompaniment. Perf. by David Pearl. Arranged by David Pearl. 1 CD. (Running Time: 1 hr.). (Solo Plus Ser.). 1999. pap. bk. 12.95 (978-0-8256-1677-8(8), AM947408, Amsco Music) Music Sales.

Fluted Girl. Paolo Bacigalupi. Narrated by Shondra Marie. (Great Science Fiction Stories Ser.). 2006. audio compact disk 10.99 (978-1-884612-36-7(9)) AudioText.

Flutes see Christmas with Ogden Nash

Flutes for Christmas: 20 Christmas Carols for One or Two Flutes. Created by Hal Leonard Corporation Staff. Barrie Carson Turner. (ENG.). 1999. pap. bk. 17.95 (978-1-84761-117-8(6), 1847611176) Pub: Schott Music Corp. Dist(s): H Leonard

Flutes of Interior Time. Perf. by Sarah Benson. 1 cass. 10.00 (MT017) White Dove NM.
This is healing music that in the musician's words "flows with that River of Time that has nothing to do with linear time, but weaves through the Earth & Universe connecting the Heart of the Earth & the Heart of the Universe." The music is perfect for meditation or body work.

Fly see Anthology of Poetry for Children

Fly. Michael Veitch. Read by Michael Veitch. (Running Time: 9 hrs. 15 mins.). 2009. 79.99 (978-1-74214-183-1(8), 9781742141831) Pub: Bolinda Pubng AUS. Dist(s): Bolinda Pub Inc

Fly. unabr. ed. Michael Veitch. Read by Michael Veitch. (Running Time: 9 hrs. 15 mins.). 2008. audio compact disk 87.95 (978-1-74214-028-5(9), 9781742140285) Pub: Bolinda Pubng AUS. Dist(s): Bolinda Pub Inc

***Fly.** unabr. ed. Michael Veitch. Read by Michael Veitch. (Running Time: 9 hrs. 15 mins.). 2010. 43.95 (978-1-74214-540-2(X), 9781742145402) Pub: Bolinda Pubng AUS. Dist(s): Bolinda Pub Inc

***Fly Away Home.** abr. ed. Jennifer Weiner. Read by Judith Light. (Running Time: 6 hrs. 0 mins. 0 sec.). 2010. audio compact disk 29.99 (978-1-4423-1684-3(5)) Pub: S and S. Dist(s): S and S Inc

Fly Away Home. unabr. ed. Jennifer Weiner. Read by Judith Light. 12 CDs. (Running Time: 14 hrs. 30 mins. 0 sec.). (ENG.). 2010. audio compact disk 39.99 (978-1-4423-1686-7(1)) Pub: S&S Audio. Dist(s): S and S Inc

Fly by Night. unabr. ed. Frances Hardinge. Read by Jill Tanner. 12 CDs. (Running Time: 13 hrs. 45 mins.). (YA). (gr. 5-9). 2006. audio compact disk 104.75 (978-1-4281-1063-2(1)); 85.75 (978-1-4281-1058-8(5)) Recorded Bks.
In the fractured realm, in a damp, backward village named Chough, there lives an unusual 12-year-old girl named Mosca. What makes her so unusual? Well, she has a feisty pet goose named Saracen, but that's not nearly as strange as the fact that she can read. This makes people deeply suspicious of her, as books are known to be extremely dangerous things.

***Fly by Wire: The Geese, the Glide, the Miracle on the Hudson.** William Langewiesche. Read by David Drummond. (Playaway Adult Nonfiction Ser.). (ENG.). 2010. 59.99 (978-1-61587-365-4(1)) Find a World.

Fly by Wire: The Geese, the Glide, the "Miracle" on the Hudson. unabr. ed. William Langewiesche. Narrated by David Drummond. (Running Time: 6 hrs. 0 mins. 0 sec.). (ENG.). 2009. 19.99 (978-1-4001-6546-9(6)); 13.99 (978-1-4001-8546-7(7)); 29.99 (978-1-4001-9546-6(2)); audio compact disk 59.99 (978-1-4001-4546-1(5)); audio compact disk 29.99 (978-1-4001-1546-4(9)) Pub: Tantor Media. Dist(s): IngramPubServ

Fly Fishin' Fool. abr. ed. James Babb. Narrated by Chris Ryan. (Running Time: 16200 sec.). 2006. audio compact disk 28.00 (978-1-933309-04-0(0)) Pub: A Media Intl. Dist(s): Natl Bk Netwk

Fly fishing for Sharks: An Angler's Journey Across America. Richard Louv. 2007. audio compact disk 28.00 (978-1-933309-63-7(6)) Pub: A Media Intl. Dist(s): Natl Bk Netwk

Fly Fishing Through the Midlife Crisis. abr. ed. Howell Raines. 2 cass. 1996. 13.99 set. (47328) Books on Tape.
This "New York Times" bestseller is part sporting autobiography & part guide to life's middle passage. Author Howell Raines blends humor & passion to describe his own experience. It will strike home for countless other men who wrestle with aging, divorce, new romances, growing children & death of loved ones.

Fly Free with the Enneagram: Break Through Internal Blocks. Speeches. Ben Saltzman. 3 CDs. (Running Time: 3 hrs.). 2002. audio compact disk 29.95 (978-0-9726460-1-7(9)) Lifestrides Pubg.
Ben Saltzman uses the Enneagram system of psychological and spiritual growth to help you enter new relationships, and work with new people without getting caught in the same old dysfunctional patterns.

Fly High. Music by ThunderBeat ThunderVision Records. 2008. (978-0-9814651-7-3(X)) ThunderVision.

***Fly Little Bird, Fly! & Beyond the Orphan Train: The True Story of Oliver Nordmark & America's Orphan Trains.** Donna Nordmark Aviles. 2009. 24.99 (978-1-61584-992-5(0)) Indep Pub IL.

Fly Me Like the Wind. Morningstar Inc. Staff. 1998. 10.99 (978-7-5124-0197-6(3)) Destiny Image Pubs.

Fly on the Wall. Tony Hillerman. Read by Tony Hillerman. 2 cass. (Running Time: 3 hrs.). 1990. 15.95 HarperCollins Pubs.

Fly on the Wall. unabr. ed. Tony Hillerman. Read by Jonathan Marosz. 7 cass. (Running Time: 7 hrs.). 1993. 56.00 (978-0-7366-2571-5(2), 3320) Books on Tape.
Death of a political reporter leads colleague to a corrupt candidate with his eye on the governorship.

Fly on the Wall. unabr. abr. ed. Tony Hillerman. Read by Tony Hillerman. 1 Cd. (Running Time: 1 hr. 30 min.). 2005. audio compact disk 14.95 (978-0-06-081513-4(2)) HarperCollins Pubs.

Fly on the Wall: How One Girl Saw Everything. unabr. ed. E. Lockhart. Read by Caitlin Greer. 3 cass. (Running Time: 4 hrs. 3 mins.). (YA). 2006. 30.00 (978-0-307-28578-2(2), Listening Lib); audio compact disk 38.00 (978-0-307-28579-9(0), Listening Lib) Pub: Random Audio Pubg. Dist(s): Random

Fly the Unfriendly Skies. abr. ed. Engle & Barnes. (Running Time: 2 hrs.). (Strange Matter Ser.). 2006. 9.95 (978-1-4233-0876-8(X), 9781423308768, BAD) Brilliance Audio.

Fly the Unfriendly Skies. abr. ed. Engle & Julian Barnes. Read by Multivoice Production Staff. (Running Time: 2 hrs.). (Strange Matter Ser.). 2006. 25.25 (978-1-4233-0877-5(8), 9781423308775, BADLE); audio compact disk 9.95 (978-1-4233-0874-4(3), 9781423308744, BACD) Brilliance Audio.
Terror in the aisles. Morgan Taylor was terrified of flying. Shocking visions of fatal falls and explosive crashes shook loose with each thump of the plane. The electrical storm didn't help much, nor did his sister Kelly. The thought of his father waiting at the boarding gate was the only thing pushing back his fear and swelling panic. Then a horrified scream brought Morgan's worst fears to life. Morgan and Kelly learn the horrible secret of an unseen war: a war being waged in our very bedrooms while we sleep. Invisible battles fought between dark and sinister visitors grappling to secure the survival of their race . . . And others who struggle desperately to bring us a grave warning before it's too late. Be aware . . . We are not alone.

Fly the Unfriendly Skies. abr. ed. Engle & Julian Barnes. Read by Multivoice Production Staff. 2 CDs. (Running Time: 2 hrs.). (Strange Matter Ser.). (J). (gr. 4-6). 2006. audio compact disk 25.25 (978-1-4233-0875-1(1), 9781423308751, BACDLib Ed) Brilliance Audio.

Fly Tier's Benchside Reference: To Techniques & Dressing Styles. Leesor & Schollmeyer. 2001. bk. 59.95 (978-1-57188-259-2(6)) F Amato Pubns.

Fly Went By. Mike McClintock. (J). 1987. 21.33 (978-0-394-01487-6(1)) McGraw.

Fly Without Fear: Guided Meditations for a Relaxing Flight. Krs Edstrom. 1 CD. (Running Time: 73 mins). 2002. audio compact disk 16.95 (978-1-886198-14-2(4)) Pub: Soft Stone Pub. Dist(s): Ingram Bk Co
"Fly Without Fear" is a powerful audio CD from stress expert KRS Edstrom which provides a unique and highly effective program to free you from your fear of flying. Accompanied by soothing music, Edstrom's guided meditations empower you to release the anxiety associated with flying and more... This exceptional "get results" CD includes calming meditations for boarding, take-off, in-flight and landing along with a desensitizing pre-flight "dress rehearsal" exercise. "Fly Without Fear" is a welcome new travel tool that can transform an anxious flight into a "Spa-in-the-Sky." Added bonus - this CD imparts skills that you can apply to any fear or phobia for the rest of your life!.

Fly Without Fear: Proven Breathing Techniques for in-Flight Relaxation. Gay Hendricks. 1 CD. (Running Time: 1 hr. 15 mins.). 2006. audio compact disk 15.95 (978-1-59179-138-6(3), W773D) Sounds True.

Flyboys: A True Story of Courage. abr. ed. James Bradley. (ENG.). 2005. 14.98 (978-1-59483-300-7(1)) Pub: Hachet Audio. Dist(s): HachBkGrp

Flyboys: A True Story of Courage. abr. ed. James Bradley. (Running Time: 6 hrs.). 2009. audio compact disk 14.98 (978-1-60024-466-7(1)) Pub: Hachet Audio. Dist(s): HachBkGrp

Flyboys: A True Story of Courage. unabr. ed. James Bradley. Read by James Bradley. (YA). 2007. 39.99 (978-1-60252-899-4(3)) Find a World.

Flyboys: A True Story of Courage. unabr. ed. James Bradley. (ENG.). 2005. 16.98 (978-1-59483-301-4(X)) Pub: Hachet Audio. Dist(s): HachBkGrp

Flyboys: A True Story of Courage. unabr. ed. James Bradley. (Running Time: 14 hrs.). (ENG.). 2009. 59.98 (978-1-60024-985-3(X)) Pub: Hachet Audio. Dist(s): HachBkGrp

Flyers 1: Examination Papers from University of Cambridge ESOL Examinations. 2nd rev. ed. Created by Cambridge University Press. (Running Time: 1 hr. 17 mins.). (ENG.). (J). (gr. 2-7). 2007. 24.15 (978-0-521-69346-2(2)) Cambridge U Pr.

Flyers 1: Examination Papers from University of Cambridge ESOL Examinations. 2nd rev. ed. Created by Cambridge University Press. (Running Time: 1 hr. 11 mins.). (ENG., (J). (gr. 2-7). 2007. audio compact disk 24.15 (978-0-521-69347-9(0)) Cambridge U Pr.

Flyers 3: Examination Papers from University of Cambridge ESOL Examinations. 2nd rev. ed. Created by Cambridge University Press. (Running Time: 1 hr. 13 mins.). (ENG., (J). (gr. 2-7). 2007. audio compact disk 15.00 (978-0-521-69396-7(9)) Cambridge U Pr.

Flyers 4: Examination Papers from University of Cambridge ESOL Examinations. 2nd rev. ed. Created by Cambridge University Press. (Running Time: 1 hr. 14 mins.). (ENG.). (J). (gr. 2-7). 2007. 15.75 (978-0-521-69407-0(8)) Cambridge U Pr.

Flyers 4: Examination Papers from University of Cambridge ESOL Examinations. 2nd rev. ed. Created by Cambridge University Press. (Running Time: 1 hr. 16 mins.). (ENG., (J). (gr. 2-7). 2007. audio compact disk 15.00 (978-0-521-69408-7(6)) Cambridge U Pr.

Flying Africans. Perf. by Alice McGill. 1 cass. (J). (gr. k up). 1989. 9.00 (978-1-886929-05-0(X), EW-C4913) Earwig.
Alice McGill considers herself a griot, in the West African tradition, a keeper of the tribal history, using storytelling to preserve & perpetuate the history of African-Americans. In her telling of the stories & singing of the songs on Flying Africans, Alice dramatically & humorously recreates the rich folklore of her cultural tradition. In The Monkey Takes a Ride & Please Don't Throw Me in the Briar Patch, the monkey & Brer Rabbit respectively outwit their scheming nemeses - the buzzard & the fox. Children suffer the consequences of failing to heed their parents' advice in the stories Old Man Bucket, Never Laugh in a Lion's Face on the Ground, & Little GirlBear. Ms. McGill uses her richly cultivated alto voice to enhance the old time southern feel of these stories, by interspersing children's songs & rhymes with the tales. She is ably accompanied by banjo, harmonica, & acoustic guitar on Uncle Jesse, I Smell My Mamma's Biscuits Burning.

Flying Closer to the Flame. 2003. 48.00 (978-1-57972-521-1(X)); audio compact disk 48.00 (978-1-57972-522-8(8)) Insight Living.

Flying Closer to the Flame: A Passion for the Holy Spirit, Set. Charles R. Swindoll. 7 cass. 1998. 34.95 (978-1-57972-143-5(5)) Insight Living.

Flying Cloud: Sail-Boat Crew's Storms. Vera Sharp. 1997. pap. bk. (978-0-9616987-2-0(1)) V Sharp.
Exciting escapades of crew on first class-sailboat from Bermuda Island up Atlantic into New York Harbor!!.

Flying Colors. unabr. ed. Tim Lefens. Read by Brian Emerson. 6 CDs. (Running Time: 7 hrs.). 2002. audio compact disk 48.00 (978-0-7861-9393-6(X), 3017); audio compact disk 24.95 (978-0-7861-9124-6(4), 3017) Blckstn Audio.

Flying Colors. unabr. ed. Tim Lefens. Read by Grover Gardner. (Running Time: 7 hrs.). 2002. audio compact disk 32.95 (978-0-7861-9344-8(1)) Blckstn Audio.

Flying Colors. unabr. ed. Tim Lefens. Read by Brian Emerson. 5 cass. (Running Time: 7 hrs.). 2002. 39.95 (978-0-7861-2358-2(3), 3017) Blckstn Audio.
When artist Tim Lefens visited the Matheny School and Hospital, a care facility for children and adults with cerebral palsy, he was overwhelmed by the intensity of the eyes that met his. Behind the twisted bodies, spastic muscles, and wheelchairs, Tim recognized huge spirits, bright, thinking individuals yearning to overcome their physical limitations. Tim devised a simple means for the students to achieve self-expression for the first time-a system of painting using their wheelchairs. From the initial class of four students, something magical began to happen.

Flying Colors. unabr. ed. Tim Lefens. Read by Grover Gardner. 5 pieces. (Running Time: 25200 sec.). 2007. 29.95 (978-0-7861-2336-0(2)) Blckstn Audio.

Flying Colours. C. S. Forester. Read by Ioan Gruffudd. 2 cass. (Running Time: 2 hrs.). 1999. 16.99 (978-1-85998-998-2(5)) Ulvrscrft Audio.
Facing a French firing squad, the terror of the Mediterranean makes a daring bid for freedom. The dramatic chase & naval skirmish that follow bring Captain Hornblower closer to England & liberty.

Flying Colours. unabr. ed. C. S. Forester. Read by Christian Rodska. 6 CDs. (Running Time: 9 hrs.). 2002. audio compact disk 64.95 (978-0-7540-5466-5(7), CCD 157) AudioGO.
In this riveting adventure, Hornblower becomes a national hero when he escapes a French firing squad. But the Terror of the Mediterranean becomes Europe's most wanted man, forced to fight alone for England, and liberty.

Flying Colours. unabr. collector's ed. C. S. Forester. Read by Bill Kelsey. 7 cass. (Running Time: 7 hrs.). (Hornblower Ser.: No. 7). 1989. 56.00 (978-0-7366-1493-1(1), 2369) Books on Tape.
It is an inauspicious beginning. Hornblower has lost the Sutherland, Bush his leg, & the two of them are prisoners of the French. Worse, they are to be tried for piracy.

Flying Cross. unabr. ed. Jack D. Hunter. Read by Tom Parker. 7 cass. (Running Time: 10 hrs.). 1996. 49.95 (978-0-7861-0944-9(0), 1699) Blckstn Audio.
Someone is murdering pilots of America's 107th Aero Squadron...diverting military funds to a secret place for an unknown reason...selling his country to the enemy for a price. Someone who looks, talks & acts like everyone else. Someone who must be stopped - fast. But there are those in high positions of trust & power who do not want the truth exposed - & are prepared to block the investigation, whatever the cost, because what is really happening is bigger & far more terrible than anyone has yet dared to imagine.

Flying Drunk: The True Story of a Northwest Airlines Flight, Three Drunk Pilots, & One Man's Fight for Redemption. unabr. ed. Joseph Balzer. Narrated by Joseph Balzer. (Running Time: 8 hrs. 12 mins. 4 sec.). (ENG.). 2009. 19.59 (978-1-60814-568-3(9), SpringWater); audio compact disk 27.99 (978-1-59859-511-6(3), SpringWater) Oasis Audio.

Flying Dutchman. abr. ed. Richard Wagner. Perf. by Douglas Fairbanks, Jr. 1 cass. Incl. Ghost Ship. More. (CDL5 1454); MS Found in a Bottle. Edgar Allan Poe. (CDL5 1454); Spectral Ship. Wilhelm Hauff. (CDL5 1454); 1975. 11.00 (978-0-89845-536-6(7), CDL5 1454) HarperCollins Pubs.

Flying Dutchman: An Introduction to Wagner's Opera. Thomson Smillie. Read by David Timson. 1 CD. (Running Time: 1 hr. 30 min.). (Opera Explained Ser.). 2003. audio compact disk 8.99 (978-1-84379-076-1(9)) NaxMulti GBR.

***Flying Feet.** unabr. ed. Patricia Reilly Giff. (Running Time: 1 hr. 30 mins.). (Zigzag Kids Ser.). (ENG.). (J). 2011. audio compact disk 20.00 (978-0-307-73871-4(X), Listening Lib) Pub: Random Audio Pubg. Dist(s): Random

Flying Finish. unabr. ed. Dick Francis. Read by David Case. 6 cass. (Running Time: 9 hrs.). 1994. 48.00 (978-0-7366-2676-7(X), 3413) Books on Tape.
Transporting racehorses around Europe by air gives blue-blooded Brit freedom - unless he ends up murdered.

Flying Finish. unabr. ed. Dick Francis. Read by Tony Britton. 6 cass. (Running Time: 9 hrs.). 2000. 49.95 (978-0-7451-6829-6(9), CAB 453) Pub: Chivers Audio Bks GBR. Dist(s): AudioGO
Amateur steeplechase jockey Henry Grey is a particularly reserved young man whose greatest problem is his mother's match-making plots. But on a sudden impulse, he throws away his respectable desk job to join a firm that transports racehorses all over the world. Yardman Transport proves to be Henry's passport to many things, it even brings him face to face with death.

Flying Finish. unabr. ed. Dick Francis. Narrated by Simon Prebble. 6 cass. (Running Time: 8 hrs. 45 mins.). 1997. 51.00 (978-0-7887-0252-5(1), 94461E7) Recorded Bks.
Henry Grey transports thoroughbred racehorses to exotic destinations. When he intercepts a cryptic message he learns that horses are not the only cargo.

Flying... Free. (Running Time: 40 min.). 1986. 9.95 (978-0-938925-03-3(2), U-105) U-Music.
Out of body travel is explored with the use of crystals.

Flying Free. unabr. ed. Robert A. Monroe. Read by Robert A. Monroe. 1 cass. (Running Time: 30 min.). (TimeOut Ser.). 1990. 14.95 (978-1-56102-804-7(5)) Inter Indus.
A delightfully liberating adventure that leads you into happy dreams.

Flying Hero Class. unabr. ed. Thomas Keneally. Narrated by Patrick Tull. 8 cass. (Running Time: 11 hrs. 30 mins.). 1991. 70.00 (978-1-55690-181-2(X), 91312E7) Recorded Bks.
Frank McCloud, a would-be novelist who manages a group of aborigine dancers, has been set up by a group of Palestinian hijackers. In coming to grips with his unsettling predicament, McCloud must grapple with some equally unsettling questions about himself. The time for circumspection is short-lived, however. McCloud's fate lies in the hands of his uncertain aborigine friends.

Flying High. 2 cass. 19.95 (BA16) Master Mind.
Based on Johnathan Livingston Seagull explores the dimension beyond. Listen very carefully to what Jonathan has to say & find that something deep inside your being & you will fly higher than you've ever flown before.

Flying Home. Lynn E. Taylor. Ed. by Theron Morgan. Illus. by Kate Sweeney. Intro. by Clair Stairrett. 1990. 9.95 (978-0-9627859-2-4(X)) Elliott Bay Pub.

Flying In, Walking Out. unabr. ed. Edward Sniders. Read by Peter Wickham. 6 cass. (Running Time: 6 hrs. 30 mins.). (Sound Ser.). 2002. 54.95 (978-1-86042-856-2(8)) Pub: UlverLrgPrint GBR. Dist(s): Ulverscroft US
Edward Sniders' experiences in the Second World War, as a Mosquito pilot, led a charmed life until his luck ran out in dramatic fashion. Hidden initially by the Resistance, he was betrayed and was lucky not to be shot "out of hand." Thereafter he became an irrepressible escaper.

Flying into Daybreak. Contrib. by Charlie Hall et al. Prod. by David Hodges. 2006. audio compact disk 16.99 (978-5-558-54363-6(9)) Pt of Grace Ent.

Flying Squadron. Richard Woodman. Read by Geoffrey Annis. 7 cass. (Running Time: 9 hrs. 15 mins.). (Nathaniel Drinkwater Ser.: Bk. 11). (J). 2004. 61.95 (978-1-85903-649-5(X)) Pub: Mgna Lrg Print GBR. Dist(s): Ulverscroft US

Flying Squirrel at Acorn Place. Barbara Gaines Winkelman. Read by Alexi Komisar. Illus. by Kristin Kest. Narrated by Alexi Komisar. 1 cass. (Smithsonian's Backyard Ser.: Vol. 16). (ENG.). (J). (ps-2). 1998. 19.95 (978-1-56899-671-4(3), BC5016) Soundprints.
Read-along story of a flying squirrel searching his home range for a new nest & storing food for the winter ahead.

Flying Through Midnight: A Pilot's Dramatic Story of His Secret Missions over Laos During the Vietnam War. abr. unabr. ed. John T. Halliday. Read by William Dufris. 13 CDs. (Running Time: 15 hrs. 30 mins. 0 sec.). (ENG.). 2005. audio compact disk 39.99 (978-1-4001-0186-3(7)) Pub: Tantor Media. Dist(s): IngramPubServ

Flying Through Midnight: A Pilot's Dramatic Story of His Secret Missions over Laos During the Vietnam War. unabr. ed. John T. Halliday. Read by William Dufris. (Running Time: 15 hrs. 30 mins. 0 sec.). (ENG.). 2005. audio compact disk 29.99 (978-1-4001-5186-8(4)); audio compact disk 79.99 (978-1-4001-3186-0(3)) Pub: Tantor Media. Dist(s): IngramPubServ

***Flying too High.** Kerry Greenwood. Read by Stephanie Daniel. (Running Time: 5 hrs. 10 mins.). (Phryne Fisher Mystery: Ser.). 2010. 64.99 (978-1-74214-612-6(0), 9781742146126) Pub: Bolinda Pubng AUS. Dist(s): Bolinda Pub Inc

Flying too High. unabr. ed. Kerry Greenwood. Read by Stephanie Daniel. (Running Time: 5 hrs. 10 mins.). (Phryne Fisher Mystery: Ser.). 2009. audio compact disk 63.95 (978-1-74214-454-2(3), 9781742144542) Pub: Bolinda Pubng AUS. Dist(s): Bolinda Pub Inc

Flying under Bridges. Sandi Toksvig. Narrated by Sandi Toksvig. 8 cass. (Running Time: 11 hrs.). 2001. 76.00 (978-1-84197-307-4(6)) Recorded Bks.

***Flying with Chinese.** Shuhan C. Wang. 2008. stu. ed. 6.95 (978-981-01-9964-7(3)); stu. ed. 6.95 (978-981-01-9972-2(4)); stu. ed. 6.95 (978-981-01-9962-3(7)); stu. ed. 6.95 (978-981-01-9968-5(6)); stu. ed. 6.95 (978-981-01-9960-9(0)); stu. ed. 6.95 (978-981-01-9966-1(X)); stu. ed. 6.95 (978-981-01-9958-6(9)) Cheng Tsui.

***Flying with Chinese.** Shuhan C. Wang. 2008. stu. ed. 6.95 (978-981-01-9970-8(8)) Cheng Tsui.

***Flying with Chinese.** Shuhan C. Wang. 2008. tchr. ed. 9.95 (978-981-01-9959-3(7)) Cheng Tsui.

***Flying with Chinese.** Shuhan C. Wang. 2008. tchr. ed. 9.95 (978-981-280-977-3(5)); tchr. ed. 9.95 (978-981-01-9963-0(5)); tchr. ed. 9.95 (978-981-01-9961-6(9)); tchr. ed. 9.95 (978-981-01-9965-4(1)); stu. ed. 6.95 (978-981-01-9974-6(0)) Cheng Tsui.

***Flying with Chinese.** Shuhan C. Wang. 2008. stu. ed. 9.95 (978-981-01-9986-9(4)); stu. ed. 9.95 (978-981-01-9978-4(3)); stu. ed. 9.95 (978-981-01-9984-5(8)) Cheng Tsui.

***Flying with Chinese.** Shuhan C. Wang. 2009. tchr. ed. 9.95 (978-981-01-9967-8(8)); tchr. ed. 9.95 (978-981-01-9973-9(2)) Cheng Tsui.

***Flying with Chinese.** Shuhan C. Wang. 2009. tchr. ed. 29.95 (978-981-280-958-2(9)) Cheng Tsui.

***Flying with Chinese.** Shuhan C. Wang. 2009. tchr. ed. 29.95 (978-981-280-272-9(X)); tchr. ed. 9.95 (978-981-01-9969-2(4)); stu. ed. 9.95 (978-981-01-9982-1(1)); stu. ed. 9.95 (978-981-01-9980-7(5)); stu. ed. 9.95 (978-981-01-9976-0(7)) Cheng Tsui.

***Flying with Chinese.** Shuhan C. Wang. 2009. tchr. ed. 9.95 (978-981-280-978-0(3)) Cheng Tsui.

Flynn. unabr. ed. Lesley Grant-Adamson. Read by Paddy Glynn. 8 cass. (Running Time: 12 hrs.). 2001. 69.95 (978-0-7531-1015-7(6), 001006) Pub: ISIS Audio GBR. Dist(s): Ulverscroft US

Flynn Flea Flicker Cassette. Stephen Cosgrove. 2004. 5.00 (978-1-58804-364-1(9)) PCI Educ.

***Flyovers.** Jeffrey Sweet. Contrib. by Amy Morton et al. (Running Time: 4800 sec.). (L. A. Theatre Works Audio Theatre Collections). (ENG.). 2010. audio compact disk (978-1-58081-783-7(1)) L A Theatre.

Flyte. unabr. ed. Angie Sage. Read by Gerard Doyle. 10 cass. (Running Time: 11 hrs. 30 mins.). (Septimus Heap Ser.: Bk. 2). (YA). (gr. 4 up). 2006. 85.75 (978-1-4193-9384-6(7), 98370); audio compact disk 104.75 (978-1-4193-9389-1(8), C3725) Recorded Bks.

Flywheel. Dave Christiano. 2004. DVD & audio compact disk 19.99 (978-0-9747369-0-7(2)) D Christiano Films.

Flyy Girl. Omar R. Tyree. Narrated by Sisi Johnson. 9 cass. (Running Time: 13 hrs. 30 mins.). 88.00 (978-0-7887-5329-9(0)); audio compact disk 124.00 (978-1-4025-0507-2(8)) Recorded Bks.

FM Atlas Catalog. 1 cass. 2.00 F M Atlas.
Updated annually. Contains most of the articles in the print catalog, including specially-modified FM radios to pick up the FM-SCA or subcarrier programs.

FM-DX Tape. 8.00 F M Atlas.
Hear how FM radio, sounded as received during periods when receiving conditions have been exceptionally good & picked up on stereo equipment. Includes an audio primer on how to experience the thrills of FM DX by Bruce F. Elving, the first person known to hve logged 1,000 different FM radio stations from one location.

FMEA Reference Toolkit: Essential Templates & Charts for Your Hospital. Kenneth R. Rohde. 2008. audio compact disk 129.00 (978-1-60146-223-7(9)) Opus Communs.

FMLA Complete Compliance: Master Leave Law & Train Managers. (ENG.). 2009. ring bd. 797.00 (978-1-60029-059-6(0)) M Lee Smith.

***FMLA Update 2009.** PUEI. 2009. audio compact disk 199.00 (978-1-935041-59-7(2), CareerTrack) P Univ E Inc.

Focal Point Alpha Meditation. Thomas Massari & Jan Massari. Read by Thomas Massari. 1 cass. (Running Time: 46 min.). 1989. 10.95 (978-1-56070-000-5(9)) TJM Prods.
Specially produced tones, waves & pulses will immediately take you into the alpha state of meditation.

Focal Point Inner Peace Meditation. Thomas Massari. 1CD. (Running Time: 46 mins). 1990. audio compact disk 15.00 (978-1-56070-126-2(9)) TJM Prods.
Enjoy powerful, deep meditation in minutes.A special structure of tones, pulses and waves is used to create an almost immediate state of deep meditation in which stress disappears, creativity is heightened, awareness is expanded, clarity of mind is achieved and health and vitality improve.

Focal Point Inner Peace Meditation. Thomas Massari. Read by Thomas Massari. 1 cass. (Running Time: 46 min.). 1990. 10.95 (978-1-56070-099-9(8)) TJM Prods.
A special structure of tones, waves & pulses are designed to produce an almost immediate state of alpha meditation. Side 1 contains music with no spoken words...Side 2 contains music with a guided meditation to produce inner peace.

Foch: The Man of Orleans. unabr. collector's ed. Basil H. Liddell-Hart. Read by Bill Kelsey. 13 cass. (Running Time: 19 hrs. 30 min.). 1987. 104.00 (978-0-7366-1170-1(3), 2093) Books on Tape.
Historical portrait of the man who led the allied armies in World War I. Part 1 of 2.

***Focus.** abr. ed. Al Ries. Read by Al Ries. (ENG.). 2005. (978-0-06-085996-1(2), Harper Audio); (978-0-06-085997-8(0), Harper Audio) HarperCollins Pubs.

Focus: A Guide to Clarity & Achievement. unabr. ed. Rich Fettke. 2 cass. (Running Time: 2 hrs. 30 min.). 1998. 19.95 Set. (978-0-9669803-0-1(1)) Fettke Grp.
A certified business & personal coach shares techniques & tools on how to get focused & stay focused on your success.

Focus: Achieving Your Highest Priorities. abr. ed. Stephen R. Covey. 2006. 17.95 (978-1-933976-14-3(4)) Pub: Franklin Covey. Dist(s): S and S Inc

Focus: Achieving Your Highest Priorities. abr. ed. Stephen R. Covey & Steve Jones. 3 CDs. (Running Time: 40 hrs. 0 mins. 0 sec.). (ENG.). 2004. audio compact disk 49.95 (978-1-929494-76-7(9), Audioworks) Pub: S&S Audio. Dist(s): S and S Inc

Focus: Achieving Your Highest Priorities. adpt. ed. Stephen R. Covey. Frwd. by Hyrum W. Smith. 4 Cds. (Running Time: 40 hrs. 0 mins. 0 sec.). (ENG.). 2003. audio compact disk 29.95 (978-1-929494-69-9(6)) Pub: Franklin Covey. Dist(s): S and S Inc
The Focus workshop presents an engaging and inspirational learning experience and will change your life in ways you never thought possible. With this audiobook, you will begin a process and journey to a new way of thinking about personal and professional focus and accomplishment. You'll learn how to identify - and focus - on the tasks and priorities that matter most so that you can deliver maximum results every day. You'll learn to turn the things you have to do into the things you want to do. Dr. Covey and master facilitator Steve Jones introduce you to the FranklinCovey workshop that has already helped 10 million people become more productive. With this audiobook, you'll also receive these valuable tools from FranklinCovey: A handy job-aid on Keeping Your Focus, designed to carry with you to remind you how to stay focused and achieve results A Resource CD-ROM packed with great tools such as teaching wizards to help you identify your values and mission and how to set goals A free 30-day trial of FranklinCovey's PlanPlus™ for Microsoft® Outlook® A screensaver of 200+inspirational quotes.

Focus: Achieving Your Highest Priorities. unabr. ed. Stephen R. Covey. Read by Stephen R. Covey. (YA). 2007. 39.99 (978-1-59895-925-3(5)) Find a World.

Focus - Relax - Peace. Sujantra G. McKeever. Read by Sujantra G. McKeever. Read by Gochan. 1 cass. (Running Time: 40 min.). 1995. 10.00 (978-1-885479-02-0(6)) McKeever Pubng.
Guides the listener through a 10 minute meditation/relaxation exercise.

Focus: Different Ways of Seeing. Created by Steck-Vaughn Staff. (Running Time: 3552 sec.). (Power up Extension Ser.). 2003. 10.40 (978-0-7398-8429-4(8)) SteckVau.

Focus for Success. Speeches. As told by Joan Koerber-Walker. 1 CD. (Running Time: 78 mins.). 2004. audio compact disk 19.95 (978-0-9747056-3-7(2)) CorePurpose.
Focus is key to taking your company from where you are...to where you want to be. Together we explore:" The Secrets of Great Companies " WHY we are in business" Where our greatest opportunities lie-Plus- " How to create and keep enthusiastic customers AND What it means to our business."What a great experience. By the end of the session I had new ideas I could put into action immediately."Kevin Dick - Edward Jones.

Focus Fulfilled Life CD Series: CD Series. Ed Turose. Ed. by Palm Tree Productions. Palm Tree Productions. (ENG.). 2007. audio compact disk (978-0-9799879-2-2(X)) Palm Tree.

Focus, Gateway to Freedom. Swami Amar Jyoti. 1 cass. 1990. 9.95 (I-17) Truth Consciousness.
Focus takes us beneath the surface & reveals Reality.

Focus, Intensity & Dedication. Swami Amar Jyoti. 1 cass. 1982. 9.95 (M-18) Truth Consciousness.
Facing our mind, keeping the eye on the Goal. If we are sincere, He deals with all our details.

Focus of Attention on Brain Waves. Jean Millay. 2 cass. 14.00 Set. (A0088-88) Sound Photosyn.

Focus on Children at Risk Pt. 1: Emotional Abuse. 1 cass. (Running Time: 1 hr.). 10.95 (D035AB090, HarperThor) HarpC GBR.

Focus on Children at Risk Pt. 3: Neglect. 1 cass. (Running Time: 1 hr. 30 min.). 11.95 (D035BB090, HarperThor) HarpC GBR.

Focus on Children at Risk Pt. 5: Child Abuse, Neglect, & Society. 1 cass. (Running Time: 1 hr. 30 min.). 11.95 (D035CB090, HarperThor) HarpC GBR.

Focus on Children at Risk Pt. 7: Parents & Sexual Abuse. 1 cass. (Running Time: 1 hr. 30 min.). 11.95 (D035DB090, HarperThor) HarpC GBR.

Focus on Environmental Education - Kimbark Elementary School. Hosted by Nancy Pearlman. 1 cass. (Running Time: 27 min.). 10.00 (513) Educ Comm CA.

Focus on Grammar: A Basic Course for Reference & Practice. 2nd ed. Irene E. Schoenberg. 2 cass. 2002. (978-0-201-67047-9(X)) AddisonWesley.

Focus on Grammar: A Basic Course for Reference & Practice. 2nd ed. Irene E. Schoenberg. 2001. 37.75 (978-0-201-34684-8(2)) Longman.

Focus on Grammar: A High-Intermediate Course for Reference & Practice. 2nd ed. Marjorie Fuchs & Margaret Bonner. 2 cass. 2002. (978-0-201-67046-2(1)) AddisonWesley.

Focus on Grammar: A High-Intermediate Course for Reference & Practice. 2nd ed. Marjorie Fuchs & Margaret Bonner. 2002. 37.75 (978-0-201-38304-1(7)) Longman.

Focus on Grammar: An Advanced Course for Reference & Practice. 2nd ed. Jay Maurer. 2 cass. 2002. (978-0-201-67045-5(3)) AddisonWesley.

Focus on Grammar: An Advanced Course for Reference & Practice. 2nd ed. Jay Maurer. 2002. 37.75 (978-0-201-38312-6(8)); audio compact disk 37.75 (978-0-201-68708-8(9)) Longman.

Focus on Grammar: An Intermediate Course for Reference & Practice. 2nd ed. Marjorie Fuchs et al. 2 cass. 2002. 37.75 (978-0-201-34675-6(3)); audio compact disk 37.75 (978-0-201-68707-1(0)) Longman.

Focus on Grammar: An Introductory Course for Reference & Practice. 2nd ed. Irene E. Schoenberg & Jay Maurer. 2 cass. 2001. 35.95 (978-0-13-087457-3(4)); audio compact disk 35.95 (978-0-13-087456-6(6)) Longman.

Focus on Pronunciation: Principles & Practice for Effective Communication, Set. Linda Lane. 1993. 72.77 (978-0-8013-0807-9(0), 78867) Pearson ESL.

Focus on Results. Brent Patmos. 1 CD. (Running Time: 74 mins.). 2003. audio compact disk (978-0-9748402-1-5(1)) Perpetual Devel.
This sales audio is designed to assist sales professionals in improving their process, income and results.

Focus on Robert Jastrow. Read by Robert Jeston. (Running Time: 57 min.). 14.95 (14705) MMI Corp.
Noted professor discusses future of space program. Fascinating 1969 interview covers many areas formerly in area of science fiction.

Focus on the Good Stuff: The Power of Appreciation. unabr. ed. Mike Robbins. Read by Mike Robbins. (Running Time: 4 hrs.). (ENG.). 2008. 24.98 (978-1-59659-230-8(3), GildAudio) Pub: Gildan Media. Dist(s): HachBkGrp

Focus on the Good Stuff: The Power of Appreciation. unabr. ed. Mike Robbins. Read by Mike Robbins. 6 CDs. (Running Time: 4 hrs.). (ENG.). 2009. audio compact disk 29.98 (978-1-59659-216-2(8), GildAudio) Pub: Gildan Media. Dist(s): HachBkGrp

Focus on the One Reality. Swami Amar Jyoti. 1 cass. 1988. 9.95 (M-92) Truth Consciousness.
Knowing the nature of illusion; the open door to Liberation. The essential solution for fulfillment of life. Our golden opportunities. Spiritual education is for everyone.

Focus Ten Free Flow. unabr. ed. Robert A. Monroe. Read by Robert A. Monroe. (Running Time: 45 min.). (Gateway Experience - Discovery Ser.). 1981. 14.95 (978-1-56113-255-3(1)) Monroe Institute.
An open exercise to use the imagination.

Focus Words. Charlene Bunas. 1 cass. (Running Time: 90 min.). 1992. (978-1-878385-08-6(9)) Media Bridge.

Focused Listening. Norma Shapiro et al. (Oxford Picture Dictionary Program Ser.). 2002. audio compact disk 54.95 (978-0-19-438403-2(9)) OUP.

Focused Listening Skills: How to Sharpen Your Concentration & Hear More of What People Are Saying. Instructed by Sally Scobey. 4 cass. (Running Time: 4 hrs. 55 min.). 59.95 Set, incl. wkbk., 39p. (Q10179) CareerTrack Pubns.
Master an important skill every professional needs to develop. If you're a manager...you'll connect better with your people if you're a receptive listener. If you're on a team - you can improve your on-the-job relationships with better listening skills. If you're a salesperson...you need to know how to talk & listen to make sales.

Focused Listening Skills: How to Sharpen Your Concentration & Hear More of What People Are Saying. Sally Scobey. 2 cass. (Running Time: 3 hrs.). 1996. 15.95 (978-1-55977-492-5(4)) CareerTrack Pubns.

Focused Mindstate: Maximizing Your Potential Through the Power of Concentration, Set. Joel Levey & Michelle Levey. 6 cass. 59.95 (683AX) Nightingale-Conant.
Focus your mind & overcome challenges - almost effortlessly. Based on research in neuropsychology, biofeedback & peak performance, here are the skills you need to focus your attentions & stay on target. Reach your "flow" state in which you feel most fully alive. Achieve a zone of concentration. Free yourself from mental dullness & agitation. Find a dynamic balance of flow & flexibility in your daily life! Includes guidebook & free bonus cassette.

Focusing: Complete Beginning Training Program. Rudy Noel. 1988. CN Video Creations.
Self help tape designed to get in touch with one's feeling & help problem solving & stress reduction.

Focusing: Complete Beginning Training Program. abr. ed. Rudy Noel. 1 cass. (Running Time: 90 mins.). (YA). 1988. (978-0-925332-01-1(1)) CN Video Creations.
Self help training audio designed to get in touch with one's feeling & help problem solving & stress reduction.

Focusing & Problem-Solving. unabr. ed. Barbara Branden. 1 cass. (Running Time: 1 hr. 35 min.). (Principles of Efficient Thinking Ser.). 12.95 (702) J Norton Pubs.
Explains: levels of mental focus; the state of full mental clarity; the motives & consequences of the failure to focus mentally; the role of purpose, specificity & question-asking in problem-solving.

Focusing Monographs, Set. Edwin M. McMahon & Peter A. Campbell. 1996. 139.95 (978-0-614-18806-6(7), SS7500, SheWard) Rowman.

Fog see Classic American Poetry

Fog. James Herbert. Read by Alex Jennings. (Running Time: 3 hrs. 0 mins. 0 sec.). (ENG., 2008. audio compact disk 19.95 (978-0-230-70000-0(4)) Pub: Macmillan UK GBR. Dist(s): IPG Chicago

Fog. Read by Alex Jennings. 2 cass. (Running Time: 3 hrs.). 2001. 16.99 (978-0-333-78009-1(4)) Pub: Macmillan UK GBR. Dist(s): Trafalgar

Fog. unabr. ed. James Herbert. Read by Gareth Armstrong. 9 CDs. (Running Time: 10 hrs. 4 mins.). (Isis (CDs) Ser.). (J). 2005. audio compact disk 84.95 (978-0-7531-2464-2(5)) Pub: ISIS Lrg Pmt GBR. Dist(s): Ulverscroft US

Fog. unabr. ed. James Herbert & Gareth Armstrong. 8 cass. (Isis Cassettes Ser.). (J). 2005. 69.95 (978-0-7531-0983-0(2)) Pub: ISIS Lrg Pmt GBR. Dist(s): Ulverscroft US

Fog. unabr. ed. Orville D. Johnson. Read by Rusty Nelson. 6 cass. (Running Time: 6 hrs.). 2001. 39.95 (978-1-55686-846-7(4)) Books in Motion.
After a lethal kamikaze attack, Merchant Marine John Gale attempts to get his ship back to Sydney, with stormy oceans, a questionable crew and a Japanese submarine in the way.

Foghorn see Fantastic Tales of Ray Bradbury

Fokus Deutsch: Beginning German 1. Annenberg. 1 cass. (Running Time: 1 hr.). (ENG.). (C). 1999. 16.88 (978-0-07-233449-4(5), 0072334495, Mc-H Human Soc) Pub: McGrw-H Hghr Educ. Dist(s): McGraw

Fokus Deutsch: Intermediate German: Kapitel 25-36. Created by McGraw-Hill Staff. 1 cass. (Running Time: 90 min.). (GER & ENG.). (C). 1999. 16.88 (978-0-07-233496-8(7), 0072334967, Mc-H Human Soc) Pub: McGrw-H Hghr Educ. Dist(s): McGraw

Folies Phoniques et Plus. abr. ed. Sara Jordan. Prod. by Sara Jordan. 1 CD. (Running Time: 30 min.). (Songs That Teach French Ser.). (FRE.). (J). (gr. 4-7). 1992. audio compact disk 13.95 (978-1-894262-07-1(7), JMP F03CD) Pub: S Jordan Publ. Dist(s): CrabtreePubCo

Folies phoniques et Plus: Initiation á la Lecture. Sara Jordan. Composed by Sara Jordan. Tr. by Michel Payen-Dumont. Engineer Mark Shannon. 1 cass. (Running Time: 29 min. 11 secs.). (FRE., (J). 1992. pap. bk. 14.95 (978-1-895523-14-0(1), JMP F03K) Jordan Music.
Students love to learn French with rap music. They'll learn about the alphabet, vowels, consonants, family members, parts of the body, days of the week, colors, fruit, opposites, and shapes.

Folk. Friedman-Fairfax and Sony Music Staff. 1 cass. (CD Ser.). 1994. pap. bk. 15.98 (978-1-56799-123-9(8), Friedman-Fairfax) M Friedman Pub Grp Inc.

Folk & Blues Harmonica. George Heaps-Nelson & Barbara Koehler. 1993. 10.98 (978-0-87166-758-8(4), 93371C) Mel Bay.

Folk & Blues Harmonica. George Heaps-Nelson & Barbara Koehler. 1976. pap. bk. 22.95 (978-0-7866-0917-8(6), 93371P) Mel Bay.

Folk Dance Fun. 1 CD. (Running Time: 1 hr.). (J). (ps-3). 2001. pap. bk. 14.95 CD Incl. guide. (7037CD) Kimbo Educ.
Popular folk songs & dances from many lands in an easy-to-learn style. Virginia Reel, Mexican Hat Dance, Greek Zorba Dance, German Clapping Dance, Irish Jig, Tarentella & more. Includes guide with lyrics & instructions. (Fitness and Dancing, Multicultural Themes).

Folk Dance Fun. 1 cass. (Running Time: 1 hr.). (J). (ps-6). 2001. pap. bk. 10.95 (KIM 7037C) Kimbo Educ.
Popular folk songs and dances from many lands in an easy-to-leam style. Virginia Reel, Mexican Hat Dance, Greek Zorba Dance, German Clapping Dance, Irish Jig, Tarentella & more. Guide with lyrics and instructions. Fitness and Dancing, Multicultural Themes).

Folk Dances of the Philippines Booklet w/Music CD. Vicki Corona. (Celebrate the Cultures Ser.: 6-10A). 2004. pap. bk. 24.95 (978-1-58513-115-0(6)) Dance Fantasy.

Folk Fables of Ancient Africa. unabr. ed. Perf. by Dylan Pritchett. 1 cass. (Running Time: 45 min.). Dramatization. (J). (gr. k up). 1989. 19.95 (978-1-56817-004-6(1)) Pepper Bird.
Authentic African folk fables with African musical instrument accompaniment.

Folk Fingerpicking Guitar: For Beginners. Brett Duncan. 2008. pap. bk. 24.95 (978-1-86469-375-1(4)) Kolala Music SGP.

Folk Guitar for Beginners. Paul Howard. (ENG.). 1998. audio compact disk 10.00 (978-0-7390-1802-6(7)) Alfred Pub.

Folk Humor of the Mormon Country. 1 cass. 9.98 (C-25) Folk-Legacy.
Surprisingly saucy stories collected in Utah.

Folk Keeper. unabr. ed. Franny Billingsley. 3 cass. (Running Time: 4 hrs., 30 min.). (YA). 2000. 30.00 (LL0210, Listening Lib) Random Audio Pubg.

Folk Keeper. unabr. ed. Franny Billingsley. Read by Marian Tomas Griffin. 3 vols. (Running Time: 4 hrs. 47 mins.). (J). (gr. 5-9). 2004. pap. bk. 36.00 (978-0-8072-0662-1(8), Listening Lib); 30.00 (978-0-8072-8421-6(1), LL 0210, Listening Lib) Random Audio Pubg.
Orphan Corinna disguises herself as a boy to pose as a Folk Keeper, one who keeps the Evil Folks at bay. When she is summoned to Cliffsend, which has miles of underground caverns populated by wild, especially savage Folk, she comes face to face with herself & the future she will need to choose.

Folk Masters: Great Performances. Contrib. by Nick Spitzer. 1 cass. or CD. 1993. (0-9307-400470-9307-40047-2-2); audio compact disk (0-9307-40047-2-2) Smithsonian Folkways.
Music & culture of contemporary European, African, Hispanic, & Native American Indian communities. Includes Dewey Balfa, The Johnson Mountain Boys, Cephas & Wiggins, The Texas Playboys, Boozoo Chavis, & others. Recorded live at the Barns of Wolf Trap in 1992.

Folk Music & Musical Instruments of the Punjab. Alka Pande. 1999. bk. 40.00 (978-1-890206-15-4(6)) Pub: Mapin Pubng IND. Dist(s): Antique Collect

Folk Music of India. 1 CD. (Running Time: 1 hr.). 1994. audio compact disk (CD F94012) Multi-Cultural Bks.

Folk Song see Twentieth-Century Poetry in English, No. 25, Recordings of Poets Reading Their Own Poetry

Folk Song Christmas. 1 CD. (Running Time: 54 mins.). (J). 2001. audio compact disk 13.50 (978-1-879305-31-1(3)) Am Melody.

Folk Song Lullabies. Perf. by Phil Rosenthal. 1 cass. (Running Time: 40 min.). (J). (gr. k-2). 1998. 9.98 (978-1-879305-29-8(1), AM-C-119) Am Melody.

Folk Song Lullabies. Perf. by Phil Rosenthal et al. 1 CD. (Running Time: 49 min. 15 sec.). (J). (gr. k-2). 1998. audio compact disk 13.50 (978-1-879305-30-4(5), AM-CD-5119) Am Melody.

Folk Songs: Easy Rhythm Guitar Series Volume 10. Created by Hal Leonard Corporation Staff. 2007. pap. bk. 14.99 (978-1-4234-1940-2(5), 1423419405) H Leonard.

***Folk Songs: Violin Play-along Volume 16.** Created by Hal Leonard Corp. (ENG.). 2010. pap. bk. 14.99 (978-1-4234-8649-7(8), 1423486498) H Leonard.

Folk Songs & Bluegrass. Perf. by Country Gentlemen. Anno. by Neil V. Rosenberg. 1 cass. (Running Time: 44 min.). 1991. (0-9307-400220-9307-40022-2-3); audio compact disk (0-9307-40022-2-3) Smithsonian Folkways.
Presents a sound & a repertoire now universally acclaimed as the definitive statement of modem bluegrass.

Folk Songs & Dances from the Balkans. Costel Puscoiu. 2008. pap. bk. 14.95 (978-0-7866-4916-7(X)) Mel Bay.

Folk Songs for Children. Tonja Evetts Weimer. Perf. by Tonja Evetts Weimer. 1 cass. (Running Time: 30 min.). (J). (ps-1). 1983. 9.98 (978-0-936823-05-8(4)) Pearce Evetts.
Features children's folksongs selected from the USA.

Folk Songs for Guitar. Adam Levy & Ron Manus. (ENG.). 1996. audio compact disk 9.95 (978-0-7390-2504-8(X)) Alfred Pub.

Folk Songs for Little Folks. Perf. by Sound Stage Orchestra. (J). (ps-3). 2000. audio compact disk 4.95 (978-1-878427-76-6(4)) Cimino Pub Grp.

Folk Songs for Schools & Camps. Jerry Silverman. 2002. per. 22.95 (978-0-7866-6535-8(1), 94558BCD) Mel Bay.

Folk Songs for Solo Singers: High Voice. Ed. by Jay Althouse. (For Solo Singers Ser.). (ENG.). 2003. audio compact disk 11.95 (978-0-7390-3306-7(9)) Alfred Pub.

Folk Songs for Solo Singers Bk. 1: Medium-Low Voice. Jay Althouse et al. 1 cass. 1993. pap. bk. 20.90 (978-0-88284-876-1(3), 4962) Alfred Pub.

Folk Songs for Solo Singers Bk.1: Medium-High Voice. Jay Althouse et al. 1 cass. 1993. pap. bk. 20.90 (978-0-88284-873-0(9), 4960) Alfred Pub.

Folk Songs for Young People. Perf. by Pete Seeger. 1 cass. (J). (ps-1). 1990. Incl. lyrics. (0-9307-45024-4-0) Smithsonian Folkways.
Includes "Skip to My Lou," "On Top of Old Smokey," "John Henry" & "Goodnight Irene".

Folk Songs in Old Wine in New Bottles. Gordon Jacob. Ed. by Robert J. Garofalo. Lyrics by Ralph Vaughan Williams. (Wind Band/Ensemble Anthology Ser.: Vol. 1). 2002. pap. bk. 21.50 (978-0-9798400-1-2(5)) Whirl Mus.

Folk Songs in Suite Française. Darius Milhaud. Ed. by Robert J. Garofalo. (Wind Band/Ensemble Anthology Ser.: Vol. 5). 2002. pap. bk. 21.50 (978-0-9798400-2-9(3)) Whirl Mus.

Folk Songs of Greenwich Village in the 1950's And 1960's. Ralph Lee Smith. 2008. pap. bk. 12.95 (978-0-7866-7176-2(9)) Mel Bay.

Folk Tales of the Tribes of Africa. unabr. ed. Read by Eartha Kitt. 1 cass. (J). 1984. 9.95 (978-0-89845-515-1(4), CDL5 1267) HarperCollins Pubs.

Folklore & Legends of the Akamba, Vol. 1. M. Norman Powell. As told by Victor Wooten. Music by Kai Eckhardt. 2003. audio compact disk 17.95 (978-1-57994-016-4(1)) Owlink.

Folklore of the Sea. Read by Horace Beck. 1 cass. (Running Time: 1 hr.). 10.95 (OP-76-12-30, HarperThor) HarpC GBR.

Folks Call Me Appleseed John, unabr. ed. Andrew Glass. Narrated by Tom Stechschulte. 1 cass. (Running Time: 15 mins.). (gr. k up). 1998. 12.00 (978-0-7887-2260-8(3), 95492E7) Recorded Bks.
Johnny Appleseed's city slicker brother came to live in a sycamore tree in the Pennsylvania wilderness to help care for Johnny's apple seedlings.

Folks Call Me Appleseed John, Class Set. unabr. ed. Andrew Glass. Read by Tom Stechschulte. 1 cass., 10 bks. (Running Time: 15 min.). (J). 1998. bk. 102.70 (978-0-7887-2552-4(1), 46722) Recorded Bks.

Folks Call Me Appleseed John, Homework. unabr. ed. Andrew Glass. Read by Tom Stechschulte. 1 cass. (Running Time: 15 min.). (J). 1998. bk. 27.24 (978-0-7887-2247-9(6), 40731) Recorded Bks.

Folks That Live on the Hill, unabr. collector's ed. Kingsley Amis. Read by David Case. 7 cass. (Running Time: 10 hrs. 30 min.). 1993. 56.00 (978-0-7366-2381-0(7), 3152) Books on Tape.
Harry Caldecote finds retirement promises anything but leisure. Instead, he feels responsible for everyone he knows.

Folksongs for Children. Perf. by Keith McNeil & Rusty McNeil. 1 cass. (J). 10.00 (102C) WEM Records.
Keith & Rusty's favorites for children of all ages.

Folksongs for Children. Perf. by Mike Seeger & Peggy Seeger. 3 cass. (J). (ps up). 19.98 Set. (2147); audio compact disk 24.98 (D2147) MFLP CA.
Collection of 94 tunes, by members of America's foremost folk family playing guitar, banjo, mandolin, pan pipes, concertina, fiddle & more. Book includes words & music to all these favorite folk songs, plus fun activities & interesting information.

Folksongs from the Beehive State: Early Field Recordings of Utah & Mormon Music. Elaine Thatcher & Randy Williams. 2008. audio compact disk 14.95 (978-0-87421-743-8(1)) Pub: Utah St U Pr. Dist(s): Chicago Distribution Ctr

Folktales. 1 cass. (Running Time: 40 min.). (Picture Book Parade Ser.). (J). (ps-4). 1981. 8.95 (978-0-89719-946-9(4), WW717C) Weston Woods.
Includes "A Story-A Story," "Suho & the White Horse," "Stone Soup," "Arrow to the Sun," & "The Great Big Enormous Turnip".

Folktales of Strong Women. Short Stories. Perf. by Doug Lipman. 1 cass. (Running Time: 1 hr.). (J). 1983. 9.95 (978-0-938756-11-8(7), 010) Yellow Moon.
Five tales of Woman from young girl, to crone, to immortal death. Included are: "The Chicken Woman," "The Clever Wife of Vietnam" & others. Each story presents a vital & entertaining image of a woman who takes command of her life. One side was recorded live in concert & the other live with friends in Doug's living room.

Folktales of Strong Women CD. As told by Doug Lipman. (ENG.). 2009. audio compact disk 14.95 (978-0-938756-73-6(7)) Yellow Moon.

Folktellers: Tales to Grow On. Read by Barbara Freeman & Connie Regan-Blake. 1 cass. (Running Time: 48 min.). (J). (gr. k-12). 1981. 8.95 (978-0-89719-943-8(X), WW711C) Weston Woods.
Folktales from the hills & "hollers" of Appalachia & the Deep South, including "Dark Dark Night," "Sody Sallyraytus," "Mama Mama Have You Heard," "The King at the Door," "Ghost Hunt," "Apples & Bananas" & "Wicked John & the Devil".

Folkways: The Original Vision. Perf. by Woody Guthrie & Lead Belly. Anno. by Alan Lomax. 1 cass. 1988. (0-9307-400010-9307-40001-2-0); audio compact disk (0-9307-40001-2-0) Smithsonian Folkways.
Includes "This Land Is Your Land," "Goodnight Irene" & "Midnight Special" with three previously unreleased selections.

Folkways Years 1944-1961. Perf. by Cisco Houston & Woody Guthrie. Anno. by Guy Logsdon. 1 cass. (0-9307-400590-9307-40059-2-7); audio compact disk (0-9307-40059-2-7) Smithsonian Folkways.
Twenty-nine songs featuring material Cisco learned while working & traveling across the country: cowboy songs, railroad songs, hobo songs, union songs, work songs, protest songs, children's songs & love songs. Includes "A Better World A Comin," "I Ain't Got No Home" & "Rambling, Gambling Man".

Folkways Years 1944-1963. Perf. by Sonny Terry. Anno. by Kip Lornell. 1 cass. 1991. (0-9307-400330-9307-40033-2-9); audio compact disk (0-9307-40033-2-9) Smithsonian Folkways.
Seventeen-song anthology illustrating the remarkable variety of styles in which this influential harmonica player performed blues, religious & folk material.

Folkways Years 1945-1959. Perf. by Brownie McGhee. Anno. by Kip Lornell. 1 cass. 1991. (0-9307-400340-9307-40034-2-8); audio compact disk (0-9307-40034-2-8) Smithsonian Folkways.
Eighteen-song compilation illustrating this stellar blues guitarist's remarkable musicianship & repertoire of older blues ballads & original compositions.

Folkways Years 1959-1961. Perf. by Dave Van Ronk. Anno. by Dave Van Ronk. Anno. by Kip Lornell. 1 cass. 1991. (0-9307-400410-9307-40041-2-8); audio compact disk (0-9307-40041-2-8) Smithsonian Folkways.
Twenty tracks representing Van Ronk's early material & revealing his original synthesis of jazz & folk. Includes "Willie the Weeper," "Come Back Baby" & "Yas, Yas, Yas".

Folkways Years 1959-1973. Perf. by Memphis Slim et al. 1 CD. (Running Time: 65 min.). 2000. audio compact disk 15.00 (SFWCD40128) Smithsonian Folkways.

Folle de Chaillot, Set. Jean Giraudoux. Perf. by Francois Chaumette & Gisele Casadesus. 2 cass. (FRE.). 1991. 26.95 (1052-RF) Olivia & Hill.
Giraudoux's satirical play portrays the conflicts in a society closely resembling our own, where money is God & the values of honesty, honor & love are affirmed only by madwomen.

Follow Bad Company - Trench-Town Days: Walk the Straight & Narrow. Ricardo A. Scott. 1 cass. (Ras Cardo Reggae Archives of Trench-Town Ser.: Vol. 1). 1999. pap. bk. (978-1-58470-007-4(6), RAS1999) Crnerstone GA.
The original Wailing Wailers: Cardo, Gartie, Junior Braithwaite Days in Trench-Town.

Follow Me Down. Shelby Foote. Narrated by Tom Parker. (Running Time: 10 hrs.). 2002. 30.95 (978-1-59912-492-6(0)) Iofy Corp.

Follow Me Down. unabr. ed. Shelby Foote. Read by Tom Parker. 8 CDs. (Running Time: 10 hrs.). 2002. audio compact disk 64.00 (978-0-7861-9527-5(4), 2950); 49.95 (978-0-7861-2189-2(0), 2950) Blckstn Audio.
The story of Luther Eustis, a respectably religious Mississippi farmer, who runs off to a deserted island with a young girl and brutally kills her after a three-week idyll. Why? And what was there about Eustis that attracted the young girl in the first place?.

Follow Me to America. unabr. ed. 8 cass. bk. 495.00 Set, incl. 8 bilingual texts, 8 wkbks., 8 video cass.; bk. 75.00 Set, incl. 2 bks., 1 video, 1 audio cass. (SV7351) J Norton Pubs.

Follow Me to Freedom: Leading as an Ordinary Radical. unabr. ed. John Perkins & Shane Claiborne. (Running Time: 8 hrs. 6 mins. 0 sec.). (ENG.). 2009. audio compact disk 18.98 (978-1-59644-763-9(X), Hovel Audio) christianaud.

***Follow Me to Freedom: Leading as an ordinary Radical.** unabr. ed. John Perkins & Shane Claiborne. Narrated by Valmont Thomas. (ENG.). 2009. 10.98 (978-1-59644-764-6(8), Hovel Audio) christianaud.

Follow That Car, Level 1. 1 cass. (Running Time: 1 hr. 30 min.). (J). 2002. (978-0-7398-5086-2(5)); audio compact disk (978-0-7398-5317-7(1)) SteckVau.

Follow That Dream. 1 cass. (Running Time: 1 hr.). 2001. 9.95 (LUDW001) Lodestone Catalog.

Follow That Dream - A Tribute to the King. Meredith Ludwig & Dan Coffey. Read by Meredith Ludwig & Dan Coffey. 1 cass. 9.95 (978-1-57677-004-7(4), LUDW001) Lodestone Catalog.

Follow That Star! Rebecca McKown Staton & Nylea L. Butler-Moore. 2004. bk. 12.00 (978-0-687-07976-6(4)); bk. 16.00 (978-0-687-07986-5(1)); bk. 50.00 (978-0-687-07996-4(9)); bk. 10.00 (978-0-687-08026-7(6)); bk. 12.00 (978-0-687-08036-6(3)); bk. 60.00 (978-0-687-08046-5(0)); bk. 40.00 (978-0-687-08056-4(8)) Abingdon.

Follow That Star! ldr.'s ed. Rebecca McKown Staton & Nylea L. Butler-Moore. 2004. bk. 26.00 (978-0-687-08016-8(9)) Abingdon.

Follow the Breath: Meditation for Well-Being. Voice by Catherine Sheen. 2 CDs. (Running Time: Depends on Track). 2005. audio compact disk 22.95 (978-0-9773381-2-2(6)) Reach In.
Follow the Breath: Meditation for Well-Being is a 2-CD meditation practice that promotes stress reduction and relaxation by using your breath to help you focus and stay in the present, emptying your mind of problems and worries. There are 5,10, 30 and 45 minute silent meditations and Preparation for Meditation and Instructions for Following the Breath Meditation tracks.

Follow the Drinking Gourd. unabr. ed. Rabbit Ears. Read by Morgan Freeman. (ENG.). (J). (ps). 2008. audio compact disk 11.95 (978-0-7393-3513-0(8), Listening Lib) Pub: Random Audio Pubg. Dist(s): Random

Follow the Drinking Gourd: A Story of the Under-Ground Railroad. As told by Morgan Freeman. Music by Taj Mahal. Illus. by Yvonne Buchanan. 1 cass. (Running Time: 1 hr.). 9.95 Weston Woods.
Based on the traditional American folksong, this compelling tale recounts the daring adventures of one family's escape from slavery via the underground railroad.

Follow the Drop; Before & After: Approaching Rain Storm followed by Bubbling, Running Water. Created by Thomas W. Gustin. 1 CD. (Running Time: 1 hr, 19 mins, 40 secs). 2004. audio compact disk 8.00 (978-0-9761848-3-6(4), EC3) Gustech.
Features 2 extremely high quality recordings made 9 Aug 03 & 10 Aug 03, at the barn & crick, respectively, here at The Emerald Cave. The coming storm & start of a heavy downpour will have you running for cover, while all your troubles will float away as you listen to the running water.

Follow the Leader. Instructed by Eugene H. Peterson. Hosted by Broadway Church, Vancouver, BC Staff. 2001. audio compact disk 28.50 (978-1-57383-602-9(8), Regent Audio) Regent College CAN.

Follow the Leader, Set. 7. 2005. audio compact disk 30.00 (978-1-932316-19-3(1)) Great C Pubng.

Follow the Money: How George W. Bush & the Texas Republicans Hog-Tied America. unabr. ed. John Anderson. Narrated by Dick Hill. 10 CDs. (Running Time: 11 hrs. 30 mins. 0 sec.). (ENG.). 2007. audio compact disk 69.99 (978-1-4001-3489-2(7)); audio compact disk 24.99 (978-1-4001-5489-0(8)) Pub: Tantor Media. Dist(s): IngramPubServ

Follow the Money: How George W. Bush & the Texas Republicans Hog-Tied America. unabr. ed. John Anderson. Read by Dick Hill. 10 CDs. (Running Time: 11 hrs. 30 mins. 0 sec.). (ENG.). 2007. audio compact disk 34.99 (978-1-4001-0489-5(0)) Pub: Tantor Media. Dist(s): IngramPubServ

Follow the Morning Star. Di Morrissey. Read by Natalie Bate. 12 cass. (Running Time: 18 hrs.). 2000. (978-1-876584-74-0(2), 591209) Bolinda Pubng AUS.
Queenie Hanlon is the mother of two adoring children, the wealthy owner of a thriving outback station & the lover of handsome bushman TR Hamilton. Then one day when TR is seriously injured in a riding accident, Queenie's perfect life suddenly comes crashing down.

Follow the Path of Christ, Krishna, & the Masters. Paramhansa Yogananda. (Running Time: 51 mins.). 2007. bk. 14.00 (978-0-87612-506-9(2)) Self Realization.

Follow the River. Sundance/Newbridge, LLC Staff. (Early Science Ser.). (gr. k-3). 2007. audio compact disk 12.00 (978-1-4007-6561-4(7)); audio compact disk 12.00 (978-1-4007-6562-1(5)); audio compact disk 12.00 (978-1-4007-6560-7(9)) Sund Newbrdge.

***Follow the River.** unabr. ed. James Alexander Thom. Narrated by David Drummond. (Running Time: 16 hrs. 30 mins. 0 sec.). 2010. 29.99 (978-1-4001-6997-9(6)); 21.99 (978-1-4001-8997-7(7)); audio compact disk 39.99 (978-1-4001-1997-4(9)); audio compact disk 95.99 (978-1-4001-4997-1(5)) Pub: Tantor Media. Dist(s): IngramPubServ

***Follow the River (Library Edition)** unabr. ed. James Alexander Thom. Narrated by David Drummond. (Running Time: 16 hrs. 30 mins.). 2010. 39.99 (978-1-4001-9997-6(2)) Tantor Media.

Follow the Ruler. Sue Lovett. 1 cass. 8.95 (215) Am Fed Astrologers.
Travel the chart by house for quick in-depth interpretation.

Follow the Star. Marshall Younger et al. Created by Focus on the Family Staff. (Adventures in Odyssey Audio Ser.). (ENG.). (J). 2008. audio compact disk 2.99 (978-1-58997-540-8(5), Tyndale Ent) Tyndale Hse.

***Follow the Stars Home.** abr. ed. Luanne Rice. Read by Susie Breck. (Running Time: 6 hrs.). 2010. audio compact disk 9.99 (978-1-4418-6701-8(5), 9781441867018, BCD Value Price) Brilliance Audio.

Follow the Stars Home. unabr. ed. Luanne Rice. Read by Susie Breck. (Running Time: 12 hrs.). 2005. 49.97 (978-1-59600-538-9(6), 9781596005389, BADLE); 24.95 (978-1-59600-537-2(8), 9781596005372, BAD); 39.25 (978-1-59600-536-5(X), 9781596005365, Brinc Audio MP3 Lib); 24.95 (978-1-59600-535-8(1), 9781596005358, Brilliance MP3) Brilliance Audio.
Being a good mother is never simple: each day brings new choices and challenges. For Diane Robbins, being a devoted single mother has resulted in her greatest joy and darkest sorrow. Weeks before her daughter was born, she and her husband, Tim McIntosh, received the news that every parent fears. Tim had not reckoned on their child being anything less than perfect, and abruptly fled to a solitary existence on the sea. Diane was left with a newborn - almost alone. It was Tim's brother, Alan, the town pediatrician, who stood by Diane and her exceptional daughter. Throughout years of waiting, watching, and caring, Alan hid his love for his brother's wife. But one of the many hard choices Diane has made is to close her heart toward any man - especially one named McIntosh. It will take a very special twelve-year-old to remind them all that love comes in many forms, and can be received with as much grace as it is given.

***Follow the Stars Home.** unabr. ed. Luanne Rice. Read by Susie Breck. (Running Time: 12 hrs.). 2010. audio compact disk 29.99 (978-1-4418-4099-8(0), 9781441840998, Bril Audio CD Unabri); audio compact disk 89.97 (978-1-4418-4100-1(8), 9781441841001, BriAudCD Unabrid) Brilliance Audio.

Follow the Wind. unabr. ed. Don Coldsmith. Read by Rusty Nelson. 6 cass. (Running Time: 6 hrs. 6 min.). 2001. 39.95 (978-1-58116-158-8(1)); audio compact disk 32.50 (978-1-58116-165-6(4)) Books in Motion.
Don Pedro Garcia listens to Captain Sanchez who says the Don's only son is still alive and living among the savages in the unchartered wilderness of new Spain. The Don makes Sanchez his guide on an expedition to find the young man. Lieutenant Cabeza, a soldier and friend to the Don, mistrusts Sanchez and his wild tales of a "hair face" living among the native peoples.

Follow This Path. abr. ed. Curt Coffman & Gabriel Gonzalez-Molina. Read by Benjamin King. (ENG.). 2005. 14.98 (978-1-59483-356-4(7)) Pub: Hachet Audio. Dist(s): HachBkGrp

Follow This Path: How the World's Greatest Organizations Drive Growth by Unleashing Human Potential. abr. ed. Curt Coffman & Gabriel Gonzalez-Molina. Read by Benjamin King. (Running Time: 3 hrs.). (ENG.). 2009. 39.98 (978-1-60788-079-0(2)) Pub: Hachet Audio. Dist(s): HachBkGrp

Follow Your Heart. unabr. ed. Susanna Tamaro. Narrated by Barbara Caruso. 4 cass. (Running Time: 5 hrs. 15 mins.). 1999. 35.00 (978-0-7887-0616-5(0), 94787E7) Recorded Bks.
With winter & death approaching, an elderly Italian woman spends a little over a month writing a long letter to her granddaughter in America. In the pages of this letter, the woman writes of her life, her love for the granddaughter, her lifelong secrets & her present need to follow her heart.

Follow Your North Star. Martha Beck. 4 CDs. (Running Time: 16200 sec.). 2005. audio compact disk 29.95 (978-1-59179-279-6(7), W926D) Sounds True.
Over two million readers a month look to Martha Beck for her advice in O: The Oprah Magazine. Now, here's the audio workshop her readers have been waiting for: her all-in-one guide for recognizing your life's purpose, staying on course, and reaching your fullest potential for happiness. On Follow Your North Star, Beck offers straightforward-yet-simple tools for "charting" your life path by following the unchangable "true north" markers of your life. "The terrain along the journey of life is spectacularly varied," teaches Martha Beck. "But the one thing that will never change is that your true nature will always urge you toward your destiny.".

Follower see Escape, No. 2

Followers. (Dovetales Ser.: Tape 16). pap. bk. 6.95 (978-0-944391-51-8(6)); 4.95 (978-0-944391-31-0(1)) DonWise Prodns.

Following Christ. 13.00 (978-1-59166-123-8(4)); audio compact disk 15.50 (978-1-59166-124-5(2)) BJUPr.

Following Christ: Experiencing Life in the Way It Was Meant to Be. abr. ed. Joseph M. Stowell. (Running Time: 2 hrs. 0 mins. 0 sec.). (ENG.). 2003. 9.99 (978-0-310-26042-4(6)) Zondervan.

Following Christ the Man of God. 2003. audio compact disk 48.00 (978-1-57972-531-0(7)) Insight Living.

Following Christ, the Man of God: John 6-14. unabr. ed. Charles R. Swindoll. 7 cass. (Running Time: 5 hrs. 45 mins.). 2000. 34.95 (978-1-57972-332-3(2)) Insight Living.

Following Divine Design. Lucile Johnson. 1 cass. 2004. 3.95 (978-1-57734-387-5(5), 34441263) Covenant Comms.

Following Divine Design; Is Anything Too Hard for the Lord? Lucile Johnson. 1 cass. 6.98 (978-1-55503-386-6(5), 06004423) Covenant Comms.
Warmth & humor.

Following God. Lynne Hammond. 1 cass. (Running Time: 1 hr.). 2005. 5.00 (978-1-57399-216-9(X)); audio compact disk 5.00 (978-1-57399-268-8(2)) Mac Hammond.

Following God with All Your Heart: Believing & Living God's Plan for You. unabr. ed. Elizabeth George. Narrated by Elizabeth George. (Running Time: 7 hrs. 22 mins. 21 sec.). (ENG.). 2008. 16.09 (978-1-60814-458-7(5)) Oasis Audio.

Following God with All Your Heart: Believing & Living God's Plan for You. unabr. ed. Elizabeth George & Elizabeth George. Read by Elizabeth George. Narrated by Elizabeth George. (Running Time: 7 hrs. 22 mins. 21 sec.). (ENG.). 2008. audio compact disk 22.99 (978-1-59859-364-8(1)) Oasis Audio.

Following Inspiration. Randall Bird. 2004. 9.95 (978-1-59156-266-5(X)); audio compact disk 11.95 (978-1-59156-267-2(8)) Covenant Comms.

Following is a Good Word. Dudley Hall. 1 cass. (Running Time: 90 mins.). (Keys to the Kingdom Ser.: Vol. 3). 2000. 5.00 (DH01-003) Morning NC.
These messages outline three essentials for successful Christian living.

Following Jesus: From Thought to Deed. Read by Mother Basilea Schlink. 1 cass. (Running Time: 30 min.). 1985. (0238) Evang Sisterhood Mary.
Includes: "If You Say So...," "Doesn't Anyone Sympathize?" & "The Most Beautiful Calling.".

***Following Jesus, the Servant King: A Biblical Theology of Covenantal Discipleship.** unabr. ed. Zondervan. (Biblical Theology for Life Ser.). (ENG.). 2010. 24.99 (978-0-310-41036-2(3)) Zondervan.

Following Kate, Set. Cheri Crane. 2 cass. 2004. 12.95 (978-1-57734-320-2(4), 07001894) Covenant Comms.
Meet Sabrina, Kate's younger sister. From the author of the best-selling "Kate's Turn" series.

Following Sound into Silence: Chanting Your Way Beyond Ego into Bliss. Kurt A. Bruder. Contrib. by Kailash. 1 CD. (ENG.). 2008. audio compact disk 15.00 (978-1-4019-1975-7(8)) Hay House.

Following the Blueprints: Neh. 8:1-18. Ed Young. 1990. 4.95 (978-0-7417-1817-4(0), 817) Win Walk.

Following the Divine Flow of God's Love. Short Stories. Joel Osteen. 1 Cass. (Running Time: 30 Mins.). (J). 2000. 6.00 (978-1-59349-071-3(2), JA0071) J Osteen.

***Following the Equator.** Mark Twain. Read by Alfred von Lecteur. 2009. 33.95 (978-1-60112-970-3(X)) Babblebooks.

Following the Equator: A Journey Around the World. unabr. ed. Mark Twain & Michael Kevin. (Running Time: 24 hrs. 5 mins.). 2008. 44.95 (978-1-4332-5280-8(5)); 109.95 (978-1-4332-5278-5(3)); audio compact disk 130.00 (978-1-4332-5279-2(1)) Blckstn Audio.

Following the Faith of Abraham. Kenneth Copeland. 6 cass. 1983. bk. 30.00 Set incl. study guide. (978-0-938458-28-9(0)) K Copeland Pubns.
Biblical teaching on faith & hope.

Following the Fire, Matters of the Heart: How to Fulfill Your Destiny by Cultivating Your Heart's Desire, Vol. 2. Mac Hammond. 4 cass. 2004. 20.00 (978-1-57399-126-1(0)) Mac Hammond.
If you have a hard time trusting your desires or feel ineffective in your pursuit of God's plan for your life, get this series by Mac Hammond and learn how to follow your heart's desire as it positions you to fulfill your destiny and become a person God can consistently bless.

Following the Fire, Matters of the Heart Vol. 2: How to Fulfill Your Destiny by Cultivating Your Heart's Desire. Mac Hammond. 4 CDs. 2004. audio compact disk 20.00 (978-1-57399-127-8(9)) Mac Hammond.

Following the Wisdom Tradition. Swami Amar Jyoti. 1 cass. 1977. 9.95 (Q-6) Truth Consciousness.
Details of Swamiji's approach. The living Saviour & the pure, eternal religion. Truth knows no compromise. Awakening Spirit within.

Following Your Dreams. Sarah Shapiro. 2000. 12.00 (978-0-9703366-1-3(6)) Chakra Healing.

Folly. Marion Chesney. Narrated by Jill Tanner. 4 cass. (Running Time: 6 hrs.). (Daughters of Mannerling Ser.: Vol. 4). 39.00 (978-1-4025-0974-2(X)) Recorded Bks.

Folly. Laurie R. King. Narrated by Frank Muller. 14 CDs. (Running Time: 16 hrs.). audio compact disk 134.00 (978-1-4025-1540-8(5)) Recorded Bks.

Folly. unabr. ed. Laurie R. King. Narrated by Frank Muller. 12 cass. (Running Time: 16 hrs.). 2001. 101.00 (978-0-7887-5237-7(5)) Recorded Bks.

***Folly Beach.** unabr. ed. Dorothea Benton Frank. Read by Tbd. 2011. audio compact disk 39.99 (978-0-06-207251-1(X), Harper Audio) HarperCollins Pubs.

Folly du Jour. Barbara Cleverly. (Detective Joe Sandilands Ser.). 2008. 84.95 (978-1-4079-0069-8(2)); audio compact disk 89.95 (978-1-4079-0070-4(6)) Pub: Soundings Ltd GBR. Dist(s): Ulverscroft US

Folly of Princes. unabr. ed. Nigel Tranter. Read by Joe Dunlop. 12 cass. (Running Time: 18 hrs.). (House of Stewart Trilogy: Bk. 2). (J). 1999. 94.95 (978-0-7531-0325-8(7), 971009) Pub: ISIS Lrg Prnt GBR. Dist(s): Ulverscroft US
In Scotland at the dawn of the 15th century, feeble Robert III still clung to the throne, his kingdom, rang with the sound of conflict as his son & brother grappled for power. Sir Jamie Douglas of Aberdour, married as he was to the king's illegitimate sister, had to tread a hazardous path through the warring factions. But having a conscience made life harder still.

Folly on Royal Street see Robert Penn Warren Reads Selected Poems

Fomentemos el amor y evitemos el Maltrato. Cesar Lozano. (SPA.). (YA). 2009. audio compact disk 16.95 (978-1-935405-79-5(9)) Hombre Nuevo.

Fond Du Lac Story: Alcoholism Intervention. 1 cass. (Care Cassettes Ser.: Vol. 10, No. 1). 1983. 10.80 Assn Prof Chaplains.

Fonética Funky. Sara Jordan. Composed by Sara Jordan. (Running Time: 1 hr. 1 mi). (Songs that Teach Spanish Ser.). (SPA.). (J). 2007. audio compact disk 13.95 (978-1-55386-079-2(9)) Pub: S Jordan Publ. Dist(s): CrabtreePubCo

Fonética Funky y algo Más: Aprende a Leer. Sara Jordan. Prod. by Sara Jordan. Tr. by Lorena Valdez & Sylvia Sotomayor. Engineer Mark Shannon. 1 cass. (Running Time: 27 min. 12 secs.). (SPA.). (J). 1993. 14.95 (978-1-895523-24-9(9), JMP S03K) Jordan Music.
Upbeat, toe-tapping songs in Spanish that teach the alphabet, vowels, consonants, time, days of the week, seasons, the environment and more.

Fonética Funky y algo Mas: Aprende a Leer. Sara Jordan. Prod. by Sara Jordan. Tr. by Lorena Valdez & Sylvia Sotomayor. Adapted by Ramiro Puerta. Engineer Mark Shannon. 1 CD. (Running Time: 27 min. 12 secs.). (SPA.). (J). (gr. k up). 1993. pap. bk. 16.10 (978-1-894262-14-9(X), JMP S03CDK) S Jordan Publ.
Songs in Spanish that teach the alphabet, vowels, consonants, time, days of the week, seasons, the environment and more.

Fong & the Indians. unabr. ed. Paul Theroux. Read by Michael Prichard. 7 cass. (Running Time: 7 hrs.). 1984. 42.00 (978-0-7366-0926-5(1), 1869) Books on Tape.
The Indians who plot against Fong are his rivals traders in a mythical East African country. Fong is a anti-hero. He survives, but it is always by the skin of his teeth & for the wrong reasons.

***Fonn le Fonn.** Tomas O. Ceannabhain. (ENG.). 1997. 11.95 (978-0-8023-7124-9(8)) Pub: Clo Iar-Chonnachta IRL. Dist(s): Dufour

Fonn le Fonn. Contrib. by Tomas O. Ceannabhain. (ENG.). 1998. audio compact disk 21.95 (978-0-8023-8124-8(3)) Pub: Clo Iar-Chonnachta IRL. Dist(s): Dufour

Fonolibros Collection. (Fonolibros Ser.). 2003. bk. 166.95 (978-0-7652-1020-3(7)) Modern Curr.

Fontica Funky. abr. ed. Prod. by Sara Jordan. Composed by Sara Jordan. 1 CD. (Running Time: 30 min.). (SPA.). (J). (gr. 4-7). 1993. audio compact disk 12.30 (978-1-894262-13-2(1), JMP S03CD) S Jordan Publ.

Foo Fighters: The Unauthorized Biography of the Foo Fighters. Andrea Thorn. (Maximum Ser.). (ENG.). 2001. audio compact disk 14.95 (978-1-84240-039-5(8)) Pub: Chrome Dreams GBR. Dist(s): IPG Chicago

Food. Anne Schraff. Narrated by Larry A. McKeever. (Extreme Customs Ser.). (J). 2006. 10.95 (978-1-58659-130-4(4)); audio compact disk 14.95 (978-1-58659-364-3(1)) Artesian.

Food: A Biblical Perspective & Common Sense Approach to God's Menu for Our Health: Friend or Foe? Speeches. John Schmitt. 5 cass. (Running Time: 5 hrs. 30 min.). 2002. 49.95 (978-0-9727334-0-3(X)) Triwell Min.
This set includes five audio cassettes recorded live from Dr. Schmitt's one day seminar. Also included are a booklet of notes for the same. God provides clear instructions on how to care for His temple through His perfect dietary plan. Join Dr. Schmitt as he discusses "Your Body Is A Temple; How Your Health Brecomes Compromised; Foods God Gave UsFor Our Well Being; How To Get Well and Stay Well.".

Food Additives: Student Syllabus. Ronald B. Froehlich. (J). 1978. 39.50 (978-0-89420-205-6(7), 16800O) Natl Book.

Food Allergy: Current Thoughts. Contrib. by Hugh A. Sampson et al. 1 cass. (American Academy of Pediatrics UPDATE: Vol. 16, No. 8). 1998. 20.00 Am Acad Pediat.

Food Almost Free or Cheap. Update Publicare Staff. 1 cass. (Running Time: 30 min.). 1992. 7.95 (37SOR301CT) Sell Out Recordings.
Possibilities for obtaining food almost free or cheap.

Food & Beverage Business Success Series. James Virgil. Ed. by Sonya L. Johnson. 1992. (978-0-9631121-3-2(9)) Lakewood Pub.

Food & Feelings 101. Deborah V. Gross. Contrib. by Marie Holloway. 5 cass. (Running Time: 1 hr. 30 min.). 1998. 59.95 Set. (978-0-9668210-0-0(9)) SeaStar Tools.
Self-help lecture series on emotional overeating.

Food & Mood: Program from the Award Winning Public Radio Series. Interview. Hosted by Peter Kramer. 1 CD. (Running Time: 1 hr.). 2005. audio compact disk 21.95 (978-1-932479-47-8(3), LCM 376) Lichtenstein Creat.
Just thinking about eating your favorite foods can make you feel good. Now, scientists are unearthing surprising links between the foods you eat and behavior. We'll hear about the latest research. Noted food critic and "Gourmet" magazine editor-in-chief Ruth Reichl starts the show with a reading about comfort food. Then, on a low carb diet? Feeling irritable or even blue? You are probably not alone. We'll speak with two M.I.T. researchers, On a low carb diet? Feeling irritable or even blue? You are probably not alone. Joining host Dr. Peter Kramer are two M.I.T. researchers, Richard Wurtman, MD and Judith Wurtman, Ph.D., who have investigated the possible links between serotonin and carbohydrate cravings, and explain why low carb diets might be making people crabby or even depressed. Also, Dr. Joseph Hibbeln, the National Institutes of Health researcher who helped first identify the link between Omega-3 fatty acids and depression, reveals new research indicating that eating fish may reduce violence in society. Plus, a visit to one of New York's hottest new restaurants, "Public," which has won awards for a mood that compliments the food. And we'll hear from Johns Hopkins anthropologist Dr. Sidney Mintz about the social role of food in cultures throughout the world, from "sinful" foods to why customers in Asia flock to McDonalds even though people may not like the food.

Food Detective. Judith Cutler. (Isis (CDs) Ser.). 2006. audio compact disk 79.95 (978-0-7531-2607-3(9)) Pub: ISIS Lrg Prnt GBR. Dist(s): Ulverscroft US

Food Detective. unabr. ed. Judith Cutler. Read by Diana Bishop. 7 cass. (Running Time: 8 hrs. 20 mins.). (Isis Cassettes Ser.). (J). 2006. 61.95 (978-0-7531-3448-1(9)) Pub: ISIS Lrg Prnt GBR. Dist(s): Ulverscroft US

Food Enzymes: Live Educational Seminar. Humbart Smokey Santillo. 1 cass. (Running Time: 1 hr.). 1996. audio compact disk 8.95 (978-0-934252-29-4(7)) Hohm Pr.
A "must" for anyone interested in optimal health. Complements the book "Food Enzymes: The Missing Link to Radiant Health".

Food Enzymes: The Missing Link to Radiant Health. unabr. ed. Humbart Smokey Santillo. Read by Steve Bell. 2 cass. (Running Time: 1 hr. 30 min.). 1992. 17.95 Set. (978-0-934252-11-9(4)) Hohm Pr.
Concise guide that explains why food enzymes are so important, how correct enzymes supplementations is beneficial, & how food enzymes funtion. Why we need food enzymes & which food enzymes are neccessary for a particular person's needs.

Food... Feeding Spirit & Body. Marianne Williamson. Read by Marianne Williamson. 1 cass. (Running Time: 90 mins.). (Lectures on a Course in Miracles). 1999. 10.00 (978-1-56170-194-0(7), M722) Hay House.

Food Fictions. unabr. ed. Created by Symphony Space Staff. 3 CDs. (Running Time: 10800 sec.). (Selected Shorts: A Celebration of the Short Story Ser.). (ENG.). (gr. 9 up). 2007. audio compact disk 28.00 (978-0-9719218-9-4(X)) Pub: Symphony Space. Dist(s): IPG Chicago

Food Fit for a King. (Sails Literacy Ser.). (gr. 2 up). 10.00 (978-0-7578-2670-2(9)) Rigby Educ.

Food for Life: A Retreat. Jose Hobday. Read by Jose Hobday. 10 cass. (Running Time: 11 hrs. 30 min.). 74.95 incl. vinyl album. (AA1888) Credence Commun.
In a retreat given to sisters the author talks about ordinary things - prayer, power, change, sex, words & flowers - but treats them in an extraordinary way.

Food for Specified Health Uses (FOSHU) in Japan: A Strategic Reference 2007. Compiled by Icon Group International, Inc. Staff. 2007. ring bd. 195.00 (978-0-497-82326-9(8)) Icon Grp.

Food for Thought. 2004. audio compact disk (978-0-9755937-0-7(6)) TheraScapes.

Food for Thought. Created by Ellen Chernoff Simon. 6. (Running Time: 35 minutes each). 2003. audio compact disk 58.00 (978-0-9765587-0-5(X)) Imadulation.
This audio set is a comprehensive weight management and lifestyle enhancement audio program that utilizes guided imagery and hypnosis to help address behaviors at the cuase level. The music is original and contains binaural beat tehcnology that entrains the brain to the alpha rhythm where we are most receptive to change.

Food in the Forest: Early Explorers Early Set B Audio CD. Jeanne Baca Schulte. Adapted by Benchmark Education Staff. (J). 2007. audio compact disk 10.00 (978-1-4108-8211-0(X)) Benchmark Educ.

Food in the Ocean: Early Explorers Early Set B Audio CD. Edward Dixon. Adapted by Benchmark Education Staff. (J). 2007. audio compact disk 10.00 (978-1-4108-8212-7(8)) Benchmark Educ.

Food Is Matter: Early Explorers Early Set B Audio CD. Danielle S. Hammelef. Adapted by Benchmark Education Staff. (J). 2007. audio compact disk 10.00 (978-1-4108-8221-9(7)) Benchmark Educ.

Food of a Younger Land: The WPA's Portrait of Food in Pre-World War II America. unabr. ed. Mark Kurlansky. Narrated by Stephen Hoye. 10 CDs. (Running Time: 11 hrs. 30 mins. 0 sec.). (ENG.). 2009. audio compact disk 69.99 (978-1-4001-4169-2(9)); audio compact disk 34.99 (978-1-4001-1169-5(2)); audio compact disk 24.99 (978-1-4001-6169-0(X)) Pub: Tantor Media. Dist(s): IngramPubServ

Food of Love: A Mouth Watering Romantic Comedy. unabr. ed. Anthony Capella. Narrated by Rocco Sisto. 8 cass. (Running Time: 10.75 hrs.). 2005. 79.75 (978-1-84505-251-5(X), H1765, Clipper Audio) Recorded Bks.
Laura Patterson is an American exchange student in Rome who, fed up with being inexpertly groped by her young Italian beaus, decides there's only one sure-fire way to find a sensual man: date a chef. Then she meets Tomasso, who's handsome, young - and cooks in the exclusive Templi restaurant. Perfect. Except, unbeknownst to Laura, Tomasso is in fact only a waiter at Templi - it's his shy friend Bruno who is the chef. But Tomasso is the one who knows how to get the girls, and when Laura comes to dinner he persuades Bruno to help him with the charade. It works: the meal is a sensual feast, Laura is utterly seduced and Tomasso falls in lust. But it is Bruno, the real chef who has secretly prepared every dish Laura has eaten, who falls deeply and unrequitedly in love. A delicious tale of Cyrano de Bergerac-style culinary seduction, but with sensual recipes instead of love poems.

Food of the Gods. unabr. ed. H. G. Wells. Read by Robert Whitfield. 5 cass. (Running Time: 7 hrs.). 2000. 39.95 (978-0-7861-1687-4(0), 2509) Blckstn Audio.
How could Mr. Bensington & Professor Redwood foresee that the new scientific wonder would escape their control - that rats would grow big enough to attack & kill a horse? How could they know that the stolen food would be fed to babies & that a new race of giants would one day smash the puny, pygmy world of men?.

Food of the Gods. unabr. ed. H. G. Wells. Read by Walter Covell. 6 cass. (Running Time: 9 hrs.). Dramatization. 1981. 35.00 incl. album. (C-79) Jimcin Record.
Giants walk the Earth! Professor Redwood invents a substance that products extraordinary growth in living matter. When it is leaked out into an unsuspecting world, the results are even more extraordinary.

Food of the Gods. unabr. collector's ed. H. G. Wells. Read by Walter Covell. 6 cass. (Running Time: 9 hrs.). 1983. 48.00 (978-0-7366-3871-5(7), 9079) Books on Tape.
It all began with the research of two scientists, Mr. Bensington & Professor Redwood, into the principles of growth in living matter. The fruit of their labors was a substance which they called "The Food of the Gods," because of its very special properties. Their tests produced a day-old chicken as big as a buzzard & when the substance was consumed by rats, they grew bigger than horses. Then they started feeding the "food" to babies.

Food or Famine: Common-Sense Survival Techniques. unabr. ed. Howard Ruff. 1 cass. (Running Time: 1 hr. 28 min.). 12.95 (399) J Norton Pubs.
Discusses the real possibility of food shortages, depression, violence & collapse of the cities.

Food Processing & Packaging Equipment in Ecuador: A Strategic Reference 2006. Compiled by Icon Group International, Inc. Staff. 2007. ring bd. 195.00 (978-0-497-35921-8(9)) Icon Grp.

Food Processing Equipment in Dominican Republic: A Strategic Reference 2007. Compiled by Icon Group International, Inc. Staff. 2007. ring bd. 195.00 (978-0-497-35915-7(4)) Icon Grp.

Food Processing Equipment in India: A Strategic Reference 2006. Compiled by Icon Group International, Inc. Staff. 2007. ring bd. 195.00 (978-0-497-36011-5(X)) Icon Grp.

Food Rules: An Eater's Manual. unabr. ed. Michael Pollan. 2009. audio compact disk 19.95 (978-0-14-314560-8(6)) Penguin Grp USA.

Food Supplements in Thailand: A Strategic Reference 2007. Compiled by Icon Group International, Inc. Staff. 2007. ring bd. 195.00 (978-0-497-82440-2(X)) Icon Grp.

Foodborne Illness. Contrib. by Michael Radetsky et al. 1 cass. (American Academy of Pediatrics UPDATE: Vol. 18, No. 8). 1998. 20.00 Am Acad Pediat.

Foods & Nutrition: Syllabus. Mary A. Plummer. (J). 1976. pap. bk. 58.10 (978-0-89420-147-9(6), 167040) Natl Book.

***Fool.** unabr. ed. Christopher Moore. Read by Euan Morton. 2010. audio compact disk 19.99 (978-0-06-200368-3(2), Harper Audio) HarperCollins Pubs.

Fool. unabr. ed. Christopher Moore. Narrated by Euan Morton. 7 cass. (Running Time: 8 hrs. 30 mins.). 2009. 82.75 (978-1-4361-7518-0(6)); audio compact disk 39.95 (978-1-4361-7520-3(8)); audio compact disk 123.75 (978-1-4361-7519-7(4)) Recorded Bks.

Fool. unabr. ed. Christopher Moore. Narrated by Euan Morton. (Running Time: 8 hrs. 30 mins.). 2009. 56.75 (978-1-4361-9248-4(X)) Recorded Bks.

***Fool.** unabr. ed. Christopher Moore. Read by Euan Morton. (ENG.). 2009. (978-0-06-176875-0(8), Harper Audio); (978-0-06-176868-2(5), Harper Audio) HarperCollins Pubs.

Fool & the Flying Ship. Composed by Klezmer Conservatory Band. As told by Robin Williams. (Running Time: 30 mins.). (Rabbit Ears Collection). (J). (gr. k-4). 1998. 9.95 (PRE942AC) Weston Woods.
A clever country bumpkin & his oddball crew of extraordinary friends build a flying ship to win the hand of the Tsar's daughter.

Fool & the Flying Ship. As told by Robin Williams. Music by Klezmer Conservatory Band. Illus. by Henrik Drescher. 1 cass. (Running Time: 1 hr.). 9.95 Weston Woods.

Fool Me Once. abr. ed. Fern Michaels. Read by Laural Merlington. (Running Time: 21600 sec.). 2007. audio compact disk 14.99 (978-1-4233-2777-6(2), 9781423327776, BCD Value Price) Brilliance Audio.

Fool Me Once. unabr. ed. Fern Michaels. Read by Laural Merlington. (Running Time: 11 hrs.). 2006. 39.25 (978-1-4233-2775-2(6), 9781423327752, BADLE); 24.95 (978-1-4233-2774-5(8), 9781423327745, BAD); 82.25 (978-1-4233-2769-1(1), 9781423327691, BrilAudUnabridg); audio compact disk 36.95 (978-1-4233-2770-7(5), 9781423327707, Bril Audio CD Unabri); audio compact disk 24.95 (978-1-4233-2772-1(1), 9781423327721, Brilliance MP3); audio compact disk 97.25 (978-1-4233-2771-4(3), 9781423327714, BriAudCD Unabrid); audio compact disk 39.25 (978-1-4233-2773-8(X), 9781423327738, Brlnc Audio MP3 Lib) Brilliance Audio.

Fool Moon. Jim Butcher. Narrated by James Marsters. 8 CDs. (Running Time: 10 hrs.). (Dresden Files Ser.: Bk. 2). 2003. audio compact disk 47.95 (978-0-9657255-2-1(9)) Buzzy Multimed.

Fool of the World & the Flying Ship. 2004. bk. 24.95 (978-0-7882-0557-6(9)); 8.95 (978-0-89719-902-5(2)); cass. & flmstrp 30.00 (978-0-89719-502-7(7)) Weston Woods.

Fooled by Randomness: The Hidden Role of Chance in Life & in the Markets. 2nd unabr. ed. Nassim Nicholas Taleb. Read by Sean Pratt. (Running Time: 10 hrs. 7 mins.). (ENG.). 2008. 29.98 (978-1-59659-184-4(6), GildAudio) Pub: Gildan Media. Dist(s): HachBkGrp

Fooled by Randomness: The Hidden Role of Chance in Life & in the Markets. 2nd unabr. ed. Nassim Nicholas Taleb. Read by Sean Pratt. 9 CDs. (Running Time: 10 hrs.). (ENG.). 2008. audio compact disk 39.98 (978-1-59659-201-8(X), GildAudio) Pub: Gildan Media. Dist(s): HachBkGrp

Fooling the Fox. Prescott Hill. 1 cass. (Running Time: 1 hr.). (Ten-Minute Thrillers Ser.). (YA). (gr. 6-12). 1995. pap. bk. 12.95 (978-0-7854-1077-5(5), 40810) Am Guidance.

Foolish about Windows see Carl Sandburg's Poems for Children

Foolish Frog. 2004. 8.95 (978-1-56008-897-4(4)); cass. & flmstrp 30.00 (978-1-56008-669-7(6)) Weston Woods.

Foolish Mother. Elbert Willis. 1 cass. (Tribute to Mothers Ser.). 4.00 Fill the Gap.

Foolish Promises to God: Ecc. 5:1-7. Ed Young. 1993. 4.95 (978-0-7417-1985-0(1), 985) Win Walk.

Foolish Rabbit's Big Mistake. Rafg Martin. (J). bk. 30.55 (978-0-676-31779-4(0)) SRA McGraw.

Foolish Virgin. unabr. ed. Margaret Penn. Read by Elizabeth Proud. 8 cass. (Running Time: 8 hrs. 35 min.). 2001. 69.95 (978-1-85089-812-2(X), 10192) Pub: ISIS Audio GBR. Dist(s): Ulverscroft US
The Foolish Virgin is an entertaining & humorous account of a young girl's reaction to being taken from a rural working class community & being plunged into the sophisticated & active life of a middle class professional family. This is the second book in the series of autobiographical novels written by Margaret Penn.

Foolishness to the Greeks: The Gospel & Western Culture. unabr. ed. Lesslie Newbigin. 5 CDs. (Running Time: 6 hrs. 0 mins. 0 sec.). (ENG.). 2005. audio compact disk 23.98 (978-1-59644-296-2(4), Hovel Audio) christianaud.
How can biblical authority be a reality for those shaped by the modern world? This book treats the First World as a mission field, offering a unique perspective on the relationship between the gospel and current society by presenting an outsider's view of contemporary Western culture.

***Foolishness to the Greeks: The Gospel & Western Culture.** unabr. ed. Lesslie Newbigin. Narrated by Simon Vance. (ENG.). 2005. 14.98 (978-1-59644-297-9(2), Hovel Audio) christianaud.

Foolproofing Your Life Audio Album Set: Wisdom for Untangling Your Most Difficult Relationships. unabr. ed. Jan Silvious. 6 cass. (YA). 1999. reel tape 29.95 (978-1-888655-70-4(4), 11820) Precept Ministries.
Companion audio series to the book with the same name: Learn new insights that can help you respond to those relationships that seem hard to untangle and make you feel "crazy".

Fool's Coach, Set. Richard S. Wheeler. Read by Thomas Vorce. 2 cass. (Running Time: 3 hrs.). (Spur Award Ser.). 1995. 16.95 (978-1-887546-00-3(6), 393116) Pegasus Aud.
Virginia City, 1863: A Wisconsin farmer, a gentleman gambler & a bordello madam are the targets of a gang of highway robbers.

Fool's Curtain. unabr. ed. Claire Lorrimer. Read by Judy Bennett. 12 cass. (Running Time: 18 hrs.). 2002. 96.95 (978-0-7540-0761-6(8), CAB 2183) AudioGO.
For three generations, Rochford Manor has dominated the lives of the women who live there. Willow Rochford became its chatelaine at seventeen. Her daughter, Lucy, taken from her mother and her home as an infant, fought long and hard to return to the life that should have been hers within its walls. For Zandra, Willow's young niece, the house became a place of sanctuary after the tragic death of her parents. But when the Rochford's family business falls victim to the Wall Street Crash, the future looks bleak and Rochford Manor itself is threatened.

Fools Die. Mario Puzo. Read by Grover Gardner. 1999. audio compact disk 128.00 (978-0-7366-8041-7(1)) Books on Tape.

***Fools Die.** unabr. ed. Mario Puzo. (Running Time: 20 hrs. 0 mins.). 2010. 44.95 (978-1-4417-1501-2(0)); 99.95 (978-1-4417-1497-8(9)); audio compact disk 123.00 (978-1-4417-1498-5(7)) Blckstn Audio.

***Fools Die.** unabr. ed. Mario Puzo. 2010. audio compact disk 34.95 (978-1-4417-1500-5(2)) Blckstn Audio.

Fools Die. unabr. collector's ed. Mario Puzo. Read by Grover Gardner. 13 cass. (Running Time: 19 hrs. 30 min.). 1999. 104.00 (978-0-7366-4389-4(3), 4852) Books on Tape.
Encompassing America's golden triangle of corruption - New York, Hollywood, Las Vegas. It plunges you into the electric excitement of luxurious gambling casinos - the heady arena for high rollers & big-time hustlers, scheming manipulators & fancy hookers - a world of greed, lust, violence & betrayal, where men ruthlessly use their power, where women ravenously use their sex, where only the strongest survive & fools die.

Fool's Gold. abr. ed. Johnny Quarles. Read by Michael Waugh. 4 cass. (Running Time: 6 hrs.). 1999. 24.95 (978-1-890990-17-6(5)) Otis Audio.
Retired outlaws Holt Flynn & Walker Krenz live a life full of regrets in the Oklahoma Panhandle. Then an old Cherokee chief offers them a proposition: If they'll take him home to die among his ancestors in the mountains of Georgia, he'll lead them to a hidden cave that sparkles with gold.

Fool's Gold: The Inside Story of J. P. Morgan & How Wall St. Greed Corrupted Its Bold Dream & Created a Financial Catastrophe. unabr. ed. Gillian Tett. Narrated by Stephen Hoye. 1 MP3-CD. (Running Time: 10 hrs. 0 mins. 0 sec.). (ENG.). 2009. 24.99 (978-1-4001-6283-3(1)); audio compact disk 34.99 (978-1-4001-1283-8(4)); audio compact disk 69.99 (978-1-4001-4283-5(0)) Pub: Tantor Media. Dist(s): IngramPubServ

Fool's Gold 1: The Skinners of Goldfield. Stephen Bly. Narrated by L. J. Ganser. 6 cass. (Running Time: 8 hrs. 30 mins.). 54.00 (978-0-7887-9894-8(4)); audio compact disk 69.00 (978-1-4025-2109-6(X)) Recorded Bks.

Fool's Paradise. Contrib. by Monday Morning. Prod. by Quinlan. Contrib. by Dino Elefante & John Elefante. 2005. audio compact disk 16.98 (978-5-558-84215-9(6)) Selectric Rec.

Fool's Song see Osbert Sitwell Reading His Poetry

Foot on the Head of the Serpent, Pt. 1. Kenneth Copeland. Perf. by Kenneth Copeland. 1 cass. (Spiritual Death of Jesus: The Great Plan Ser.: Tape 1). 1995. cass. & video 5.00 (978-1-57562-022-0(7)) K Copeland Pubns.
Biblical teaching on spiritual death of Jesus.

Football. Eldon Taylor. 1 cass. (Running Time: 62 min.). (Inner Talk Ser.). 16.95 incl. script. (978-1-55978-503-7(9), 5389F) Progress Aware Res.
Soundtrack - Brook with underlying subliminal affirmations.

Football: Music Theme. Eldon Taylor. 1 cass. 16.95 (978-0-940699-64-9(8), 5389C) Progress Aware Res.

Football: Rhythm. Eldon Taylor. Read by Eldon Taylor. Ed. by Leslie Brice. 1 cass. (Running Time: 1 hr.). 1992. 16.95 (978-1-56705-246-6(0)) Gateways Inst.
Self improvement.

Football: Stream. Eldon Taylor. Read by Eldon Taylor. Ed. by Leslie Brice. 1 cass. (Running Time: 1 hr.). 1992. 16.95 (978-1-56705-247-3(9)) Gateways Inst.

***Football Champ.** Tim Green. Read by Tim Green. (ENG.). 2010. audio compact disk 42.00 (978-1-934180-93-8(9)) Full Cast Audio.

Football Genius. Tim Green. Read by Tim Green. Read by Full Cast Production Staff. (Playaway Children Ser.). (J). 2008. 44.99 (978-1-60640-811-7(9)) Find a World.

Football Genius. unabr. ed. Tim Green. Narrated by Tim Green. 5 CDs. (Running Time: 5 hrs. 10 mins.). (J). (gr. 4-7). 2008. audio compact disk 38.00 (978-1-934180-40-2(8)) Full Cast Audio.

Football Hero. Tim Green. Read by Tim Green. 5 CDs. (Running Time: 5 hrs. 15 mins.). (YA). (gr. 5-8). 2009. audio compact disk 45.00 (978-1-934180-86-0(6)) Full Cast Audio.

football kings 1 - Antoine le roi du Drible. unabr. ed. Joachim Masamek. Read by Vincent Byrd Le Sage. (J). 2007. 79.99 (978-2-35569-009-9(X)) Find a World.

Football Mind. unabr. ed. Dave Meggyesy & Chip Oliver. 1 cass. (Running Time: 38 min.). 12.95 (35063) J Norton Pubs.

Football My Arse! The Funniest Football Book You'll Ever Read. unabr. ed. Ricky Tomlinson. 5 CDs. (Running Time: 3 hrs. 0 mins. 0 sec.). (ENG.). 2005. audio compact disk 14.95 (978-1-4055-0092-0(1)) Pub: Little BrownUK GBR. Dist(s): IPG Chicago

Footloose - ShowTrax. Arranged by Mark Brymer. 1 CD. (Running Time: 10 mins.). 2000. audio compact disk 49.95 (08621174) H Leonard.
Put on your dancing shoes & "cut footloose!" with this high-energy medley from the Broadway musical. Includes: "Almost Paradise," "Footloose," "The Girl Gets Around," "Holding Out for a Hero," "I'm Free (Heaven Helps the Man)" & "Let's Hear It for the Boy.".

Footloose in the Himalaya. unabr. ed. Mike Harding. Read by Mike Harding. 8 cass. (Running Time: 12 hrs.). 2000. 59.95 (978-0-7451-5995-9(8), CAB 679) Pub: Chivers Audio Bks GBR. Dist(s): AudioGO
This is Mike Hardin's humorous and personal account of his two journeys through the Kingdoms of Zanskar and Ladakh, and then to the foothills of Mt. Everest in the Himilayan country. Beginning in Delhi, Harding quickly escapes the crowds and enters the enchanting world of mountains and monasteries.

Footloose in the West of Ireland. unabr. ed. Mike Harding. Read by Mike Harding. 8 cass. (Running Time: 12 hrs.). 2000. 59.95 (978-0-7540-0037-2(0), CAB 1460) Pub: Chivers Audio Bks GBR. Dist(s): AudioGO
Mike Harding explores the mountains and hills of the west coast of Ireland. Over ten years in the making, this is more than just a travel guide: music, history, folklore and poetry thread the narrative which covers the counties of Cork and Kerry, Clare and Galway, Sligo, Mayo and Donegal.

Footnotes. Donald Lev. Ed. by Stanley H. Barkan. (Cross-Cultural Review Chapbook Ser.: No. 11). 1981. 10.00 (978-0-89304-835-8(6)) Cross-Cultrl NY.

Footprints: Songs along the Way. Edd Anthony. Read by Edd Anthony. 2007. audio compact disk 16.95 (978-1-881586-26-5(X)) Canticle Cass.

***Footprints in Butter.** Adapted by Siren Audio Studios. Prod. by Siren Audio Studios & Denise Dietz. Based on a novel by Denise Dietz. (ENG.). 2010. audio compact disk (978-0-9844180-7-7(5)) Siiren Audio.

Footprints of God. unabr. ed. Greg Iles. 9 CDs. Library ed. (Running Time: 12 hrs.). 2003. audio compact disk 107.25 (978-1-59086-595-8(2), 1590865952, BriAudCD Unabrid) Brilliance Audio.
In the heart of North Carolina's Research Triangle stands a corporate laboratory much like the others nearby. But behind its walls, America's top scientists work around the clock to attain the holy grail of the twenty-first century - a supercomputer that surpasses the power of the human mind. Appointed by the president as ethicist to Project Trinity, Dr. David Tennant finds himself in a pressure cooker of groundbreaking science and colossal ambition. When his friend and fellow scientist is murdered, David discovers that the genius who runs Project Trinity was responsible and that his own life is in danger. Unable to reach the president, and afraid to trust his colleagues, David turns to Rachel Weiss, the psychiatrist probing the nightmares that have plagued him during his work at Trinity. Rachel is skeptical of David's fears, but when an assassin strikes, the two doctors

must flee for their lives. Pursued across the globe by ruthless National Security Agency operatives, David and Rachel struggle to piece together the truth behind Project Trinity and the enormous power it could unleash upon the world. As constant danger deepens their intimacy, Rachel realizes the key to Trinity lies buried in David's disturbed mind. But Trinity's clock is ticking . . . Mankind is being held hostage by a machine that cannot be destroyed. Its only hope - a terrifying chess game between David and the Trinity computer, with the cities of the world as pawns. But what are the rules? How human is the machine? Can one man and woman change the course of history? Man's future hangs in the balance, and the price of failure is extinction.

Footprints of God. unabr. ed. Greg Iles. Read by Dick Hill. 8 cass. (Running Time: 12 hrs.). 2003. 32.95 (978-1-59086-592-7(8), 1590865928, BAU); 87.25 (978-1-59086-593-4(6), 1590865936, BAU); audio compact disk 38.95 (978-1-59086-594-1(4), 1590865944, Bril Audio CD Unabri) Brilliance Audio.

Footprints of God. unabr. ed. Greg Iles. Read by Dick Hill. 9 CDs. (Running Time: 12 hrs.). 2004. 39.25 (978-1-59335-612-5(9), 1593356129, Brinc Audio MP3 Lib) Brilliance Audio.
In the heart of North Carolina's Research Triangle stands a corporate laboratory much like the others nearby. But behind its walls, America's top scientists work around the clock to attain the holy grail of the twenty-first century - a supercomputer that surpasses the power of the human mind. Appointed by the president as ethicist to Project Trinity, Dr. David Tennant finds himself in a pressure cooker of groundbreaking science and colossal ambition. When his friend and fellow scientist is murdered, David discovers that the genius who runs Project Trinity was responsible and that his own life is in danger. Unable to reach the president, and afraid to trust his colleagues, David turns to Rachel Weiss, the psychiatrist probing the nightmares that have plagued him during his work at Trinity. Rachel is skeptical of David's fears, but when an assassin strikes, the two doctors must flee for their lives. Pursued across the globe by ruthless National Security Agency operatives, David and Rachel struggle to piece together the truth behind Project Trinity and the enormous power it could unleash upon the world. As constant danger deepens their intimacy, Rachel realizes the key to Trinity lies buried in David's disturbed mind. But Trinity's clock is ticking . . . Mankind is being held hostage by a machine that cannot be destroyed. Its only hope - a terrifying chess game between David and the Trinity computer, with the cities of the world as pawns. But what are the rules? How human is the machine? Can one man and woman change the course of history? Man's future hangs in the balance, and the price of failure is extinction.

Footprints of God. unabr. ed. Greg Iles. Read by Dick Hill. (Running Time: 12 hrs.). 2004. 39.25 (978-1-59710-298-8(9), 1597102989, BADLE); 24.95 (978-1-59710-299-5(7), 1597102997, BAD) Brilliance Audio.

Footprints of God. unabr. ed. Greg Iles. Read by Dick Hill. (Running Time: 12 hrs.). 2004. 24.95 (978-1-59335-222-6(0), 1593352220) Soulmate Audio Bks.
In the heart of North Carolina's Research Triangle stands a corporate laboratory much like the others nearby. But behind its walls, America's top scientists work around the clock to attain the holy grail of the twenty-first century - a supercomputer that surpasses the power of the human mind. Appointed by the president as ethicist to Project Trinity, Dr. David Tennant finds himself in a pressure cooker of groundbreaking science and colossal ambition. When his friend and fellow scientist is murdered, David discovers that the genius who runs Project Trinity was responsible and that his own life is in danger. Unable to reach the president, and afraid to trust his colleagues, David turns to Rachel Weiss, the psychiatrist probing the nightmares that have plagued him during his work at Trinity. Rachel is skeptical of David's fears, but when an assassin strikes, the two doctors must flee for their lives. Pursued across the globe by ruthless National Security Agency operatives, David and Rachel struggle to piece together the truth behind Project Trinity and the enormous power it could unleash upon the world. As constant danger deepens their intimacy, Rachel realizes the key to Trinity lies buried in David's disturbed mind. But Trinity's clock is ticking . . . Mankind is being held hostage by a machine that cannot be destroyed. Its only hope - a terrifying chess game between David and the Trinity computer, with the cities of the world as pawns. But what are the rules? How human is the machine? Can one man and woman change the course of history? Man's future hangs in the balance, and the price of failure is extinction.

Footprints of God-Abr. Greg Iles. 2010. audio compact disk 9.99 (978-1-4418-4189-6(X)) Brilliance Audio.

Footprints of the Messiah. Chuck Missler. 2 cass. (Running Time: 2.5 hours +). (Briefing Packages by Chuck Missler). 1991. vinyl bd. 14.95 Incls. notes. (978-1-880532-80-5(8)) Koinonia Hse.
What Old Testament Bible Study is mentioned twelve times in one book of the Bible, is given by seven different people and is almost never given today?That Jesus is the Messiah of Israel! How certain can we be that Jesus is the Messiah?Review some of the major passages in the Tanakh (the Old Testament) which predict and describe the Scriptural expectations to be fulfilled by the Messiah of Israel. This study will also take a mathematical analysis of a small sampling from the more than 300 predictions concerning the Jewish Messiah.

Footprints of the Messiah. Chuck Missler. 2 CD's. (Running Time: 120 mins.). (Briefing Packages by Chuck Missler). 1992. audio compact disk 19.95 (978-1-57821-297-2(9)) Koinonia Hse.

Footsteps: A Fireside Conversation on the Writer's Journey: A Writing Life. Speeches. Featuring David Whyte. 6 CDs. 2005. audio compact disk 60.00 (978-1-932887-16-7(4)) Pub: Many Rivers Pr. Dist(s): Partners-West

Footsteps in an Empty Room: 8 Cassettes (unabridged) unabr. ed. Lily Sommers. 8 cass. (Running Time: 13 hrs.). 2004. 64.00 (978-1-74030-592-1(2)) Pub: Bolinda Pubng AUS. Dist(s): Lndmrk Audiobks

Footsteps of Jesus. Greg Skipper. (SPA.). 1996. 10.98 (978-0-7673-0689-8(9)) LifeWay Christian.

Footsteps of Jesus. Greg Skipper & Stan Pethel. 1994. 11.98 (978-0-7673-0658-4(9)) LifeWay Christian.

Footsteps of Jesus Cassette Kit. Greg Skipper & Stan Pethel. 1994. 54.95 (978-0-7673-0144-2(7)) LifeWay Christian.

Footsteps of the Hawk. unabr. ed. Andrew Vachss. Read by Phil Gigante. (Running Time: 9 hrs.). (Burke Ser.). 2010. audio compact disk 29.99 (978-1-4418-2145-4(7), 9781441821454, Bril Audio CD Unabri) Brilliance Audio.

***Footsteps of the Hawk.** unabr. ed. Andrew Vachss. Read by Phil Gigante. (Running Time: 9 hrs.). (Burke Ser.). 2010. 39.97 (978-1-4418-2148-5(1), 9781441821485, Brinc Audio MP3 Lib); 39.97 (978-1-4418-2150-8(3), 9781441821508, BADLE); 24.99 (978-1-4418-2149-2(X), 9781441821492, BAD); 24.99 (978-1-4418-2147-8(3), 9781441821478, Brilliance MP3); audio compact disk 79.97 (978-1-4418-2146-1(5), 9781441821461, BriAudCD Unabrid) Brilliance Audio.

Footsteps of Worship (Stereo/Split Acc Cassette0. Greg Skipper & Stan Pethel. 1994. 40.00 (978-0-7673-0693-5(7)) LifeWay Christian.

For a Better Life. Steck-Vaughn Staff. 2003. (978-0-7398-8417-1(4)) SteckVau.

For a Few Demons More. unabr. ed. Kim Harrison. Read by Marguerite Gavin. (Hollows Ser.: Bk. 5). (YA). 2008. 84.99 (978-1-60252-962-5(0)) Find a World.

For a Few Demons More. unabr. ed. Kim Harrison. Read by Marguerite Gavin. 14 CDs. (Running Time: 17 hrs. 0 mins. 0 sec.). (Hollows Ser.: Bk. 5). (ENG.). 2007. audio compact disk 49.99 (978-1-4001-0453-6(X)); audio compact disk 34.99 (978-1-4001-5453-1(7)); audio compact disk 99.99 (978-1-4001-3453-3(6)) Pub: Tantor Media. Dist(s): IngramPubServ

For a Free Humanity: For Anarchy. Noam Chomsky. Read by Noam Chomsky. Music by Chumbawamba. 1 CD. (Running Time: 1 hr.). (AK Press Audio Ser.). (ENG.). 1997. audio compact disk 18.00 (978-1-873176-74-0(0)) Pub: AK Pr GBR. Dist(s): Consort Bk Sales

For a Lamb see Richard Eberhart Reading His Poetry

For a Poet see Poetry of Countee Cullen

For All but One. Stella March. Read by Margaret Holt. 5 cass. (Running Time: 7 hrs. 30 mins.). 1999. 49.95 (64119) Pub: Soundings Ltd GBR. Dist(s): Ulverscroft US

For All but One. Stella March. 5 cass. (Sound Ser.). 2004. 49.95 (978-1-85496-411-3(9)) Pub: UlverLrgPrint GBR. Dist(s): Ulverscroft US

For All Eternity. John Lund. 4 cass. 2004. 19.95 (978-1-59156-244-3(9)); audio compact disk 19.95 (978-1-59156-245-0(7)) Covenant Comms.

For All the Bright Promise. Elizabeth Lord. Read by Marie McCarthy. 11 CDs. (Running Time: 13 hrs. 5 mins.). (Isis (CDs) Ser.). (J). 2004. audio compact disk 99.95 (978-0-7531-2329-4(0)) Pub: ISIS Lrg Prnt GBR. Dist(s): Ulverscroft US

For All the Bright Promise. unabr. ed. Elizabeth Lord. Read by Marie McCarthy. 10 cass. (Running Time: 13 hrs. 5 mins.). (Isis Cassettes Ser.). (J). 2004. 84.95 (978-0-7531-1914-3(5)) Pub: ISIS Lrg Prnt GBR. Dist(s): Ulverscroft US

For All the Saints. 1 cass. 8.98 (120014) Covenant Comms.

***For All the Tea in China: How England Stole the World's Favorite Drink & Changed History.** unabr. ed. Sarah Rose. Narrated by Sarah Rose. (Running Time: 8 hrs. 0 mins.). 2010. 29.99 (978-1-4001-9537-4(3)); 19.99 (978-1-4001-6537-7(7)); 15.99 (978-1-4001-8537-5(8)); audio compact disk 29.99 (978-1-4001-1537-2(X)); audio compact disk 59.99 (978-1-4001-4537-9(6)) Pub: Tantor Media. Dist(s): IngramPubServ

For all who love the game lessons & teachings for Women: Lessons & Teachings for Women. Harvey Penick. 2004. 7.95 (978-0-7435-4736-9(5)) Pub: S&S Audio. Dist(s): S and S Inc

For Ann Gregory see Dylan Thomas Reads the Poetry of W. B. Yeats & Others

For Anyone Desiring Love in Their Lives: Finding True Love. Michele Blood & Asara Lovejoy. Illus. by Musivation International Staff. 2 cassettes. (Running Time: 90 mins). 2000. 19.95 (978-1-890679-15-6(1)) Micheles.
Michele Blood and Asara Lovejoy have combined their talents to produce a program that will forever change your LOVE LIFE and your ABILITY TO LOVE. In addition to hearing the answers that you seek, experience a deep release process combined with Michele?s affirmations and music which go directly to the heart of your mind to immediately bring you the love that you desire. You too can ?FIND TRUE LOVE?!!.

For A'That & A'That see Poetry of Robert Burns & Border Ballads

***For Better: The Science of a Good Marriage.** unabr. ed. Tara Parker-Pope. Read by Cassandra Campbell. (ENG.). 2010. audio compact disk 29.95 (978-1-61573-094-0(X), 161573094X) Pub: HighBridge. Dist(s): Workman Pub

For Better & for Worse. unabr. ed. Winston Smith. 3 CDs. (Running Time: 3 hrs.). 2003. audio compact disk 35.95 (978-1-930921-26-9(8)) Resources.

For Better & for Worse. unabr. ed. Winston Smith. 3 cass. (Running Time: 3 hrs.). 2003. 35.95 (978-1-930921-01-6(2)) Resources.

For Better, for Worse. Margaret Bacon & Margaret Sircom. 2008. 54.95 (978-1-84652-263-5(3)); audio compact disk 71.95 (978-1-84652-264-2(1)) Pub: Magna Story GBR. Dist(s): Ulverscroft US

For Better, for Worse. abr. ed. Carole Matthews. Read by Emilia Fox. 2003. 18.95 (978-0-06-055686-0(2)) HarperCollins Pubs.

For Cause & Comrades: Why Men Fought in the Civil War. unabr. collector's ed. James M. McPherson. Read by Dick Estell. 8 cass. (Running Time: 8 hrs.). 1997. 48.00 (978-0-7366-3695-7(1), 4374) Books on Tape.
An account of the Civil War, the author tries to answer the question of how Americans could fight against each other.

***For Colored Girls Who Have Considered Suicide, When the Rainbow Is Enuf.** unabr. ed. Ntozake Shange. (Running Time: 1 hr.). 2011. 39.97 (978-1-4418-8012-3(7), 9781441880123, BADLE); 39.97 (978-1-4418-8011-6(9), 9781441880116, Brinc Audio MP3 Lib); 9.99 (978-1-4418-8010-9(0), 9781441880109, Brilliance MP3); audio compact disk 39.97 (978-1-4418-8009-3(7), 9781441880093, BriAudCD Unabrid); audio compact disk 9.99 (978-1-4418-8008-6(9), 9781441880086, Bril Audio CD Unabri) Brilliance Audio.

***For Colored Girls Who Struggle & Pale Girls Who Juggle: For Colored Girls Who Struggle & Pale Girls Who Juggle poetry audiobook:poetic works for the daily celebration of Womanhood.** ed. Score by Henry Ashwood. Henry Ashwood. (Running Time: 72.00). (ENG.). 2010. 12.99 (978-0-9830867-0-3(2)) Poettreevines.

***For Crime Out Loud, Vol. 1.** Ed. by Robert J. Randisi. 2009. (978-1-60136-505-7(5)) Audio Holding.

***For Crime Out Loud, Vol. 2.** Ed. by Robert J. Randisi. 2009. (978-1-60136-506-4(3)) Audio Holding.

For Earth's Sake: The Life & Times of David Brower. David Brower. Read by David Brower. 2 cass. (Running Time: 3 hrs.). 1992. 16.95 (978-0-939643-40-0(5), NrthWrd Bks) TandN Child.
Part autobiography, part philosophy and part forward vision, re-examines the conservation battles that Brower counts as successes as well as those he counts as defeats. Above all, it is a call for all people to proceed wisely in their relationships to the planet.

For Eleanor & Bill Monahan see William Carlos Williams Reads His Poetry

For Elektra see Poetry & Voice of Marilyn Hacker

For Everyone Born: Global Songs for an Emerging Church. Ed. by Jorge Lockward & Christopher Heckert. Compiled by Jorge Lockward & Christopher Heckert. Carlton R. Young. 2008. audio compact disk 14.95 (978-1-933663-25-8(1), GBGMusik) Pub: Gnl Brd Glbl Minis. Dist(s): Cokesbury

For Freedom. Contrib. by Avalon. (Mastertrax Ser.). 2007. audio compact disk 9.98 (978-5-557-70335-2(7)) Pt of Grace Ent.

For Freedom: The Story of a French Spy. unabr. ed. 4 cass. (Running Time: 5 hrs.). 2003. bk. 38.00 (978-1-4025-6036-1(2)) Recorded Bks.

For Future Generations. Contrib. by Dennis Allen. 1994. 24.95 (978-0-00-508100-6(9), 75608170) Pub: Brentwood Music. Dist(s): H Leonard

For George Santayana from "Life Studies" see Twentieth-Century Poetry in English, No. 32-33, Recordings of Poets Reading Their Own Poetry

For God & Country: 12 Stories on Faith & American History. AIO Team Staff. Created by Tyndale House Publishers Staff. (Running Time: 14400 sec.). (Adventures in Odyssey Ser.). (ENG.). (J). (gr. 3-7). 2008. audio compact disk 24.99 (978-1-58997-474-6(3), Tyndale Ent) Tyndale Hse.

For God, Country & Coca-Cola: The Definitive History of the Great American Soft Drink & the Company That Makes It. unabr. collector's ed. Mark Pendergrast. Read by Jonathan Marosz. 15 cass. (Running Time: 22 hrs. 30 min.). 1994. 120.00 (978-0-7366-2867-9(3), 3573) Books on Tape.
How a patent medicine in post-Civil War Atlanta grew into an enterprise that changed the world. Provocative & entertaining.

For Hatching. Neville Goddard. 1 cass. (Running Time: 62 min.). 1964. 8.00 (65) J & L Pubns.
Neville taught Imagination Creates Reality. He was a powerfully influential teacher of God as Consciousness.

For I Have Touched the Sky. unabr. ed. Mike Resnick. Read by Pat Bottino. Ed. by Allan Kaster. 1 cass. (Running Time: 1 hr. 11 min.). (Great Science Fiction Stories Ser.). 1998. 11.99 (978-1-884612-25-1(3)) AudioText.
A young girl struggles for the right to read on the Kikuyu utopian world of Kirinyaga where women are not allowed to read.

For I was a Hungered. Michael Ballam. 2 cass. 13.98 (1100351) Covenant Comms.
Gives blueprints in word & song for a more Christlike life.

For I Was a Hungered, Set. Michael Ballam. 2 cass. 14.98 (978-1-55503-377-4(6), 1100351) Covenant Comms.
Gives blueprints in word & song for a more Christ-Like life.

For Just Such a Time. 10.00 Esstee Audios.
The story of Dorothea Dix & her fight to humanize social institutions in the U. S.

For Kicks. unabr. ed. Dick Francis. Read by David Case. 7 cass. (Running Time: 10 hrs. 30 min.). 1991. 56.00 (978-0-7366-1918-9(6), 2742) Books on Tape.
A man who calls himself "The Earl of October" offers Australian stud farm owner Daniel Roke $20,000 to pose as a common stable hand in order to investigate a horse-doping ring in England. Roke discovers physical & mental challenges - as well as danger.

For Kids & Just Plain Folks. Perf. by Pete Seeger. 1 cass., 1 CD. (Family Heritage Ser.). (J). 5.58 (SME 63424); audio compact disk 7.98 CD Jewel box. (SME 63424); 5.58 (SME 63424); audio compact disk 7.98 CD Jewel box. (SME 63424) NewSound.
Includes: "Michael Row the Boat Ashore," "This Land is Your Land," "If I Had a Hammer" & more.

For Kids Only. Lou DelBianco. Read by Lou DelBianco. 1 cass. (Running Time: 38 min.). Dramatization. (J). (ps-5). 1991. 10.00 (978-0-9642659-0-5(7), CL3386) Story Maker.
An audio cassette of folksongs & stories, as well as material from the author's childhood.

For King & Country. Annie Wilkinson & Colleen Predergast. 2008. 69.95 (978-1-84652-265-9(X)); audio compact disk 89.95 (978-1-84652-266-6(8)) Pub: Magna Story GBR. Dist(s): Ulverscroft US

For Kings & Planets: A Novel. unabr. ed. Ethan Canin. Read by Gregory Gorton. 10 vols. (Running Time: 15 hrs.). 1999. bk. 84.95 Set. (978-0-7927-2293-9(0), CSL 182, Chivers Sound Lib) AudioGO.
Story of Orno Tarcher, a man who thinks himself as moral, & who tests his character against power, deception & seduction.

For Laughing Out Loud: My Life & Good Times. abr. ed. Ed McMahon & David Fisher. (Running Time: 2 hrs.). (ENG.). 2006. 14.98 (978-1-59483-703-6(1)) Pub: Hachet Audio. Dist(s): HachBkGrp

For Liberty: A Story of the American Revolution. Godwin Chu. (Step into History Ser.). 2002. audio compact disk 18.95 (978-1-4105-0185-1(X)) D Johnston Inc.

For Liberty: A Story of the American Revolution. Godwin Chu. Ed. by Jerry Stemach. Illus. by Rick Clubb. 2002. audio compact disk 200.00 (978-1-58702-784-0(4)) D Johnston Inc.

For Liberty: A Story of the American Revolution. Godwin Chu. Ed. by Jerry Stemach et al. Illus. by Rick Clubb. Narrated by Joe Sikora. Contrib. by Ted S. Hasselbring. (Start-to-Finish Books). (J). (gr. 2-3). 2002. 35.00 (978-1-58702-781-9(X)) D Johnston Inc.

For Liberty: A Story of the American Revolution. unabr. ed. Godwin Chu. Ed. by Jerry Stemach et al. Illus. by Rick Clubb. Narrated by Joe Sikora. Contrib. by Ted S. Hasselbring. 1 cass. (Running Time: 1 hr.). (Start-to-Finish Books). (J). (gr. 2-3). 2002. 7.00 (978-1-58702-766-6(6), H04) D Johnston Inc.
From the Boston Tea Party, in 1773, to the British surrender at Yorktown, in 1781, For Liberty is a fictionalized journey through colonial America and the American Revolution. Follow our hero, David Brady a printer's apprentice in Boston who becomes a soldier in the continental Army as he shows readers what life was like during colonial times.Along the way, your students will experience famous historical events like The Shot Heard Around the World and the Battle of Bunker Hill.

For Liberty & Glory: Washington, Lafayette, & Their Revolutions. unabr. ed. James R. Gaines. Read by Norman Dietz. (YA). 2007. 74.99 (978-1-60252-900-7(0)) Find a World.

For Liberty & Glory: Washington, Lafayette, & Their Revolutions. unabr. ed. James R. Gaines. Read by Norman Dietz. 17 CDs. (Running Time: 21 hrs. 0 mins. 0 sec.). (ENG.). 2007. audio compact disk 49.99 (978-1-4001-0548-9(X)); audio compact disk 34.99 (978-1-4001-5548-4(7)); audio compact disk 99.99 (978-1-4001-3548-6(6)) Pub: Tantor Media. Dist(s): IngramPubServ

For Life. Music by Michael John Poirier. 1995. 11.00 (978-1-58459-118-4(8), 002669); audio compact disk 16.00 (978-1-58459-119-1(6), 002668) Wrld Lib Pubns.

For Love. abr. ed. Sue Miller. Read by Blair Brown. 2 cass. (Running Time: 3 hrs.). 2000. 7.95 (978-1-57815-055-7(8), 1038, Media Bks Audio) Media Bks NJ.
Had this summer been invented to teach her something?.

For Love. unabr. ed. Sue Miller. Read by Kate Reading. 10 cass. (Running Time: 15 hrs.). 1993. 80.00 (978-0-7366-2572-2(0), 3321) Books on Tape.
A return to childhood home causes woman to examine the consequences of what she's done, & will do, for love.

For Love Alone, Set. Anita Stansfield. 2 cass. 1999. 13.95 (978-1-57734-428-5(6), 07001991) Covenant Comms.
Novel about overcoming tragedy & discovering true love.

For Love & Glory. Janet MacLeod Trotter. (Story Sound CD Ser.). (J). 2002. audio compact disk 99.95 (978-1-85903-554-2(X)) Pub: Mgna Lrg Print GBR. Dist(s): Ulverscroft US

For Love & Zion, Set. Laurel Mouritsen. 2 cass. (Running Time: 3 hrs.). 1997. 11.98 Set. (978-1-57734-078-2(7), 07001487) Covenant Comms.
A riveting story of love & sacrifice in the early church.

For Love of Evil. unabr. ed. Piers Anthony. Narrated by Barbara Caruso. 11 CDs. (Running Time: 12 hrs. 30 mins.). (Incarnations of Immortality Ser.: Bk. 6). 2001. audio compact disk 111.00 (978-1-4025-1008-3(X), C1587) Recorded Bks.
Parry's promising life as a musician and apprentice in the arts of White Magic got thrown off track by the violent death of his beloved. Led down a path of depravity by a harlot demoness, Parry has lived a long, corrupt life that may finally be coming to an end, unless he can defeat Lucifer himself at the gates of Hell and become the new Incarnation of Evil. Completely accessible as a stand-alone book, For Love of Evil at the same time provides a fresh view of events from previous Incarnations of Immortality titles, such as Wielding a Red Sword and Being a Green Mother.

For Love of Evil. unabr. ed. Piers Anthony. Narrated by Barbara Caruso. 9 cass. (Running Time: 12 hrs. 30 mins.). (Incarnations of Immortality Ser.: Bk. 6). 2001. 81.00 (978-0-7887-5507-1(2), 96475x7) Recorded Bks.
Parry's promising life as a musician & apprentice in the arts of White Magic gets thrown violently off track by the violent death of his beloved. Led down a twisted path of wickedness & depravity by a harlot demoness, Parry lives a long life of complete corruption that will only end at his death - unless he can find a way to defeat Lucifer himself at the gates of Hell & become the new Incarnation of Evil.

For Love of Lily. Maggie Bennett. Contrib. by Tanya Myers. 12. 2007. 94.95 (978-1-84652-058-7(4)) Pub: ISIS Audio GBR. Dist(s): Ulverscroft US

For Love of Lily. Maggie Bennette. Read by Tanya Myers. 15. 2007. audio compact disk 104.95 (978-1-84652-059-4(2)) Pub: ISIS Audio GBR. Dist(s): Ulverscroft US

For Love of Mother-Not. unabr. ed. Alan Dean Foster. Read by Stefan Rudnicki. 1 MP3-CD. (Running Time: 8 hrs.). (Pip & Flinx Ser.: No. 5). 2009. 24.99 (978-1-4233-9545-4(X), 9781423395454, Brilliance MP3); 39.97 (978-1-4233-9546-1(8), 9781423395461, Brinc Audio MP3 Lib); 39.97 (978-1-4233-9547-8(6), 9781423395478, BADLE); audio compact disk 29.99 (978-1-4233-9543-0(3), 9781423395430, Bril Audio CD Unabri); audio compact disk 87.97 (978-1-4233-9544-7(1), 9781423395447, BriAudCD Unabrid) Brilliance Audio.

For Love of the Game. collector's ed. Michael Shaara. Read by Arthur Addison. 3 cass. (Running Time: 4 hrs. 30 min.). 1999. 28.00 (978-0-7366-4679-6(5), 5035) Books on Tape.
Baseball legend Billy Chapel has one last chance to prove who he is & what he can do.

For Love of the Game. collector's unabr. ed. Michael Shaara. Read by Arthur Addison. 4 CDs. (Running Time: 4 hrs. 48 mins.). 2000. audio compact disk 32.00 (978-0-7366-5195-0(0)) Books on Tape.

For Love of the Game, Set. abr. ed. Michael Shaara. Read by Jason Culp. 4 cass. 1999. 24.95 (FS9-51016) Highsmith.

For Love of the Game, Set. unabr. ed. Michael Shaara. Read by Jason Culp. 4 cass. 1999. 24.95 (FS9-51205) Highsmith.

For Matrimonial Purposes. unabr. ed. Kavita Daswani. Read by Anne Flosnik. 5 cass. (Running Time: 7 hrs.). 2003. 27.95 (978-1-59086-942-0(7), 1590869427, BAU); 69.25 (978-1-59086-943-7(5), 1590869435, Unabridge Lib Edns); audio compact disk 29.95 (978-1-59086-944-4(3), 1590869443, BriAudCD Unabrid); audio compact disk 82.25 (978-1-59086-945-1(1), 1590869451, BACDLib Ed) Brilliance Audio.
Unmarried at 24 - and with no prospects in sight - Anju is a great source of worry to her family. Despite the best efforts of relatives, fortune-tellers, and matchmakers to arrange a marriage, she can't seem to find a husband - or at least one she's willing to marry. Quickly becoming a spinster by her culture's standards, she is eager to escape the community that views her as a failure. After pleading with her parents for permission, she boards a plane bound for the United States and a dream of a career. And while husband-hunting isn't any easier in New York City, at least she's got company. In this sparkling debut, an unconventional heroine defies tradition by making a marriage between the strict customs of India and the wild freedoms of America to find her own happy ending. Hilarious and heart-warming, For Matrimonial Purposes proves that, while the search for love takes many forms, the heartbreak and exhilaration are universal.

For Matrimonial Purposes. unabr. ed. Kavita Daswani. Read by Anne Flosnik. (Running Time: 7 hrs.). 2004. 39.25 (978-1-59335-523-4(8), 1593355238, Brinc Audio MP3 Lib) Brilliance Audio.

For Matrimonial Purposes. unabr. ed. Kavita Daswani. Read by Anne Flosnik. (Running Time: 7 hrs.). 2004. 39.25 (978-1-59710-301-5(2), 1597103012, BADLE); 24.95 (978-1-59710-300-8(4), 1597103004, BAD) Brilliance Audio.

For Matrimonial Purposes. unabr. ed. Kavita Daswani. Read by Anne Flosnik. (Running Time: 7 hrs.). 2004. 24.95 (978-1-59335-196-0(8), 1593351968) Soulmate Audio Bks.

For Men Only. 2002. audio compact disk (978-1-931713-46-7(4)) Word For Today.

For Men Only. 2003. audio compact disk (978-1-931713-47-4(2)) Word For Today.

For Men Only: A Straightforward Guide to the Inner Lives of Women. unabr. ed. Shaunti Feldhahn & Jeff Feldhahn. Narrated by Nathan Larkin. (ENG.). 2006. 17.49 (978-1-60814-214-9(0)); audio compact disk 24.99 (978-1-59859-142-2(8)) Oasis Audio.

For Men Only: How to Love a Woman Without Losing Your Mind. unabr. ed. Joseph Angelo. Read by Danny Hizami. 1 cass. (Running Time: 1 hr. 30 mins.). (For Men Ser.). 1997. 12.95 (978-1-885408-09-9(9)) Listen & Live.
This book is for men who love women. It is for men who are tired of all the talk about how men should be, could be & will be when they become enlightened, tofued, refueled, & generally more like women.

For Men Only Tape Pack. 2002. (978-1-931713-39-9(1)) Word For Today.

For My Country's Freedom. unabr. ed. Alexander Kent, pseud. Read by Michael Jayston. 8 cass. (Running Time: 12 hrs.). (Richard Bolitho Ser.: Bk. 21). 2000. 59.95 (978-0-7451-6700-8(4), CAB 1316) Pub: Chivers Audio Bks GBR. Dist(s): AudioGO
It is 1811, and Bolitho is promoted to Admiral. But aware of his own vulnerability, Bolitho surrounds himself with men he can trust: the faithfull Allday, the withdrawn Avery, and James Tyacke. And when war erupts in America, Bolitho must fight an enemy not foreign but familiar: the freedom to leave the sea forever.

For My Good. Contrib. by Lashun Pace et al. 2007. audio compact disk 5.99 (978-5-557-67282-5(6)) Pt of Grace Ent.

For New Non-Smokers Weight Maintenance. Pat Carroll. Read by Pat Carroll. Ed. by Tony Carroll. 1 cass. (Running Time: 30 min.). 10.00 Inner-Mind Concepts.
Explains how to be slim & healthy without cigarettes.

For One More Day see Por un Día Más

For One More Day. unabr. ed. Mitch Albom. Read by Mitch Albom. 5 cass. 2006. (978-1-4159-3537-8(8)); audio compact disk (978-1-4159-3538-5(6)) Books on Tape.

For One More Day. unabr. ed. Mitch Albom. Read by Mitch Albom. (YA). 2007. 49.99 (978-1-59895-440-1(7)) Find a World.

For One More Day. unabr. ed. Mitch Albom. Read by Mitch Albom. 3 CDs. (Running Time: 12600 sec.). 2006. audio compact disk 26.98 (978-1-4013-8724-2(1), Hyperion Audio) Pub: Hyperion. Dist(s): HarperCollins Pubs

For Our Children. 10th ed. Perf. by Barbra Streisand et al. 1 cass. (Running Time: 1 hr.). (J). 2002. 10.98 (978-0-7379-0076-7(8), 75931); audio compact disk 16.98 (978-0-7379-0077-4(6), 75932) Rhino Enter.
The much requested reissue of the original, landmark For OUr Children album.

For Our Children: A Benefit for the Pediatric AIDS Foundation. 1 cass. (J). 9.98 (204); audio compact disk 16.98 (D204) MFLP CA.
In a tribute to the positive effect that music can have on people's lives, this exceptional recording was put together by concerned musicians wanting to help, Bob Dylan, Paul McCartney, Bruce Springsteen and many more.

For Our Children Too! To Benefit Pediatric AIDS Foundation. Perf. by Elton John et al. 1 cass. (Running Time: 1 hr.). (J). 2002. 10.98 (978-1-56826-723-4(1), 72493); 10.98 (978-1-56826-725-8(8), 72494); audio compact disk 16.98 (978-1-56826-722-7(3), 72493) Rhino Enter.
Today's biggest artists perform children's favorites for charity.

For Our Children Too! To Benefit Peiatric AIDS Foundation. Perf. by Elton John et al. 1 CD. (Running Time: 1 hr.). (J). 2002. audio compact disk 16.98 (978-1-56826-724-1(X), 72494) Rhino Enter.

For Parents Only: Getting Inside the Head of Your Kid. unabr. ed. Shaunti Feldhahn & Lisa A. Rice. Narrated by Shaunti Feldhahn. (Running Time: 4 hrs. 0 mins. 0 sec.). (ENG.). 2007. audio compact disk 17.99 (978-1-59859-284-9(X)) Oasis Audio.

For Parents Only: Getting Inside the Head of Your Kid. unabr. ed. Shaunti Feldhahn & Lisa Author Rice. Narrated by Shaunti Feldhahn. (ENG.). 2007. 12.59 (978-1-60814-215-6(9)) Oasis Audio.

For Pastors Only: A Pastor's Most Important Priority, Vol 1.3. George Pearsons. (ENG.). 2007. audio compact disk 5.00 (978-1-57562-953-7(4)) K Copeland Pubns.

For Pastors Only: Stop Comparing Yourself, Vol. 1.2. George Pearsons. (ENG.). 2007. audio compact disk 5.00 (978-1-57562-955-1(0)) K Copeland Pubns.

For Pastors Only: The Healthy Pastor Series, Vol. 2.1. George Pearsons. (ENG.). 2008. audio compact disk 10.00 (978-1-57562-963-6(1)) K Copeland Pubns.

For Pastors Only: When People Leave Your Church, Vol. 1.1. George Pearsons. (ENG.). 2007. audio compact disk 5.00 (978-1-57562-954-4(2)) K Copeland Pubns.

For Pastors Only: Why Do We Do What We Do?, Vol. 2.3. George Pearsons. (ENG.). 2008. audio compact disk 5.00 (978-1-57562-965-0(8)) K Copeland Pubns.

For Pastors Only; Refuse the Stress of Ministry, Vol. 2.2. George Pearson. (ENG.). 2008. audio compact disk 5.00 (978-1-57562-964-3(X)) K Copeland Pubns.

For Paul Laurence Dunbar see Poetry of Countee Cullen

For Sale or Swap. unabr. ed. Alyssa Brugman. Read by Alison Bell. (Running Time: 18600 sec.). (J). (gr. 3-7). 2006. audio compact disk 63.95 (978-1-74093-779-5(1)) Pub: Bolinda Pubng AUS. Dist(s): Bolinda Pub Inc

For Sale with Corpse. unabr. ed. J. M. Gregson. 4 cass. (Running Time: 6 hrs. 40 mins.). 2001. 32.00 (978-1-74030-543-3(4)) Pub: Bolinda Pubng AUS. Dist(s): Bolinda Pub Inc

For Somebody to Start Singing. unabr. ed. June Jordan. Perf. by Bernice Johnson Reagon. 1 cass. (Running Time: 59 min.). (Watershed Tapes of Contemporary Poetry). 1980. 12.95 (23642) J Norton Pubs.

For Such a Time. Elyse Larson. Ed. by Vanessa Benjamin. 10 cass. (Running Time: 14 hrs. 30 mins.). 2004. 69.95 (978-0-7861-2425-1(3), 3104) Blckstn Audio.
Giselle Munier and Jean Thornton are more like sisters than cousins, having spent many summers together while Giselle?s French father taught at the American university. But with the outbreak of World War II, both women?s lives take a dramatic turn. Jean joins the American Red Cross and is assigned to a sprawling military hospital in Wales. But Giselle, active in the French Resistance, has been betrayed and arrested by the Nazis. Though underground compatriots are able to rescue and hide her, Giselle remains in grave danger because she knows the identity of other Resistance leaders.

For Such a Time. unabr. ed. Elyse Larson. Ed. by Vanessa Benjamin. 11 CDs. (Running Time: 14 hrs. 30 mins.). 2004. audio compact disk 88.00 (978-0-7861-8831-4(6), 3104) Blckstn Audio.

For Such a Time As This: Ester 4:14. Ed Young. 1983. 4.95 (978-0-7417-1288-2(1), 288) Win Walk.

For Survivors of Abuse: Harmony. Eldon Taylor. Read by Eldon Taylor. Ed. by Leslie Brice. 1 cass. (Running Time: 1 hr.). 1992. 16.95 (978-1-56705-205-3(3)) Gateways Inst.
Self improvement.

For Survivors of Abuse: Ocean. Eldon Taylor. Read by Eldon Taylor. Ed. by Leslie Brice. 1 cass. (Running Time: 1 hr.). 1992. 16.95 (978-1-56705-206-0(1)) Gateways Inst.

For the Benefit of All Beings: A Commentary on the Way of the Bodhisattva. unabr. ed. Dalai Lama XIV. Read by James Gimian & Wulstan Fletcher. Tr. by Padmakara Translation Group Staff. 4 CDs. (Running Time: 5 hrs.). (ENG.). 2009. audio compact disk 24.95 (978-1-59030-707-6(0)) Pub: Shambhala Pubns. Dist(s): Random

For the Bride: Live Worship with the Body of Christ. Contrib. by Terry Macalmon. 2007. audio compact disk 16.99 (978-5-557-59870-5(7)) Maranatha Music.

For the Children's Sake. unabr. ed. Susan Schaeffer Macaulay. Read by Mary Woods. 4 cass. (Running Time: 5 hrs. 30 min.). 1999. 32.95 (2361) Blckstn Audio.
What education can be - for your child, in your home & in your school. Based on an understanding of what it means to be human - to be a child, a parent, a teacher & on the Christian meaning of life.

For the Children's Sake. unabr. ed. Susan Schaeffer Macaulay. Read by Mary Woods. 4 cass. (Running Time: 7 hrs.). 2006. 32.95 (978-0-7861-1511-2(4), 2361) Blckstn Audio.

For the Children's Sake: Foundations of Education for Home & School. unabr. ed. Susan Schaeffer Macaulay. Read by Mary Woods. (Running Time: 18000 sec.). 2007. audio compact disk 19.95 (978-0-7861-6201-7(5)) Blckstn Audio.

For the Children's Sake: Foundations of Education for Home & School. unabr. ed. Mary Woods & Susan Schaeffer Macaulay. (Running Time: 18000 sec.). 2007. audio compact disk & audio compact disk 36.00 (978-0-7861-6200-0(7)) Blckstn Audio.

For the Darkest Hours in Life. Read by Mother Basilea Schlink. 1 cass. (Running Time: 30 min.). 1985. (0243) Evang Sisterhood Mary.
Subjects discussed are: How to Deal with Serious Illness; When Loved Ones Are Taken Away; Against Despair.

For the Death of Me. Quintin Jardine. (Soundings (CDs) Ser.). 2006. audio compact disk 79.95 (978-1-84559-438-1(X)) Pub: ISIS Lrg Prnt GBR. Dist(s): Ulverscroft US

For the Death of Me. unabr. ed. Quintin Jardine. Read by Joe Dunlop. 8 cass. (Soundings Ser.). 2006. 69.95 (978-1-84559-400-8(2)) Pub: ISIS Lrg Prnt GBR. Dist(s): Ulverscroft US

For the Girl Buried in the Peat Bog & the Fourth Beast. Poems. Bertha Rogers. Read by Bertha Rogers. 1 cass. (Running Time: 55 min.). (Six Swans Sounds Ser.: Vol. 1). 1998. 6.95 (978-1-893389-02-1(2)) Six Swans.

***For the Good of the Service.** Tim Champlin. 2009. (978-1-60136-438-8(5)) Audio Holding.

For the Good of the Service. Tim Champlin. (Running Time: 0 hr. 24 mins.). 2000. 10.95 (978-1-60083-548-3(1)) Iofy Corp.

For the Greatest Good. unabr. ed. Andrew Cohen. 1 cass. (Running Time: 1 hr. 18 min.). 10.95 (978-1-883929-20-6(2)) Moksha Pr.
Reveals the sacred potential of human evolution - a deep & abiding care for the greatest good - that arises spontaneously when we are no longer governed by self-concern.

For the Health of America's Children. (Running Time: 46 min.). 1989. 12.95 (D0210B09, HarperThor) HarpC GBR.

For the Home. abr. ed. Nina Mattikow. 1 cass. Dramatization. (At the Sound of the Beep Ser.). 1992. 6.95 (978-1-55569-558-3(2), 41502) Great Am Audio.
Whether you're out running errands, unable to come to the telephone or just don't want to be disturbed, 20 prerecorded messages & sound effects have anticipated your every need.

***For the King: A Novel.** unabr. ed. Catherine Delors. (Running Time: 12 hrs. 0 mins.). 2010. 17.99 (978-1-4001-8774-4(5)) Tantor Media.

***For the King: A Novel.** unabr. ed. Catherine Delors. Narrated by Steven Crossley. (Running Time: 12 hrs. 0 mins. 0 sec.). (ENG.). 2010. 24.99 (978-1-4001-6774-6(4)); audio compact disk 34.99 (978-1-4001-1774-1(7)); audio compact disk 83.99 (978-1-4001-4774-8(3)) Pub: Tantor Media. Dist(s): IngramPubServ

For the Last Wolverine see James Dickey Reads His Poetry & Prose

For the Love of a Dog: Understanding Emotion in You & Your Best Friend. unabr. ed. Patricia McConnell. Read by Ellen Archer. (YA). 2008. 59.99 (978-1-60514-670-6(6)) Find a World.

For the Love of a Dog: Understanding Emotion in You & Your Best Friend. unabr. ed. Patricia B. McConnell. Read by Ellen Archer. (Running Time: 12 hrs. 30 mins. 0 sec.). (ENG.). 2006. audio compact disk 69.99 (978-1-4001-3300-0(9)) Pub: Tantor Media. Dist(s): IngramPubServ

For the Love of a Dog: Understanding Emotion in You & Your Best Friend. unabr. ed. Patricia B. McConnell. Read by Shelly Frasier. (Running Time: 12 hrs. 30 mins. 0 sec.). (ENG.). 2006. audio compact disk 24.99 (978-1-4001-5300-8(X)) Pub: Tantor Media. Dist(s): IngramPubServ

For the Love of a Dog: Understanding Emotion in You & Your Best Friend. unabr. ed. Patricia B. McConnell. Read by Ellen Archer. (Running Time: 12 hrs. 30 mins. 0 sec.). (ENG.). 2006. audio compact disk 34.99 (978-1-4001-0300-3(2)) Pub: Tantor Media. Dist(s): IngramPubServ

For the Love of Animals. unabr. ed. Cindy Rosenbaum et al. Perf. by Peter Thomas et al. Illus. by Anne Feiza. 1 cass. (J). (ps-4). 1992. pap. bk. 3.95 bk. (978-1-881567-00-4(1)) Happy Kids Prods.
Six personalized original songs for kids about animals. Songs about whales, panda bears, giraffes & much more. Plus a story about how the children save the animals. Child's name sung over 40 times.

For the Love of Country: Patriots & Countrymen, Vol. 3. Steve Bonta. Narrated by Bruce Miles. (YA). 2007. audio compact disk 9.95 (978-0-9815788-4-2(5)) Amer Two.

For the Love of Country: Revolutionary Women, Vol. 4. Steve Bonta. Narrated by Bruce Miles & Laura Durant. (ENG.). (YA). 2007. audio compact disk 9.95 (978-0-9815788-6-6(1)) Amer Two.

For the Love of Country: Struggle for the South, Vol. 4. Steve Bonta. Narrated by Bruce Miles. (ENG.). (YA). 2007. audio compact disk 9.95 (978-0-9815788-5-9(3)) Amer Two.

For the Love of Country: Tales of American Heroism, Vol. 1. Steve Bonta. Narrated by Bruce Miles. (ENG.). (YA). 2007. audio compact disk 9.95 (978-0-9815788-2-8(9)) Amer Two.

For the Love of Country: The Fringe of War, Vol. 2. Steve Bonta. Narrated by Bruce Miles. (ENG.). (YA). 2007. audio compact disk 9.95 (978-0-9815788-3-5(7)) Amer Two.

For the Love of Country: The Revolutionary Collection. Steve Bonta. Narrated by Bruce Miles & Laura Durant. (YA). 2008. audio compact disk 39.95 (978-0-9815788-7-3(X)) Amer Two.

For the Love of God. Jimmy Evans. 4 cass. (Running Time: 6 hrs.). 1996. 20.00 (978-0-00-519073-9(8)) HarperCollins Pubs.

***For the Love of Life: Companion CD.** Lindamichelle Baron. (Running Time: 50 mins.). 2004. audio compact disk 10.00 (978-0-940938-09-0(X)) Harlin Jacque.

For the Love of Money. unabr. ed. Omar R. Tyree. Narrated by Patricia R. Floyd. 12 cass. (Running Time: 17 hrs. 30 mins.). 2001. 98.00 (978-0-7887-5213-1(8), F0024E7, Griot Aud) Recorded Bks.
Tracy Ellison, twenty-eight years old & on the verge of superstardom as a screen writer & actress, is going back East to reconnect with family & friends.

For the Love of Teddi. adpt. ed. Esther Luttrell. Perf. by Jordan Nichole Sager & Rick Silanskis. 1 cass. (Running Time: 1 hr. 30 min.). Dramatization. (Starlight Theater/Angel). (J). (gr. k up). 1999. 12.95 (978-0-9667485-6-7(5)) Oak Shadow Pr.

For the Love of the Game. Contrib. by Pillar et al. Prod. by Travis Wyrick. 2008. audio compact disk 13.99 (978-5-557-48007-9(2)) Essential Recs.

For the Love of Turtles. (Greetings Ser.: Vol. 1). (gr. 2-3). 10.00 (978-0-7635-5870-3(2)) Rigby Educ.

For the Major, Set. Constance F. Woolson. Read by Flo Gibson. 3 cass. (Running Time: 4 hrs. 30 min.). 1991. 16.95 (978-1-55685-193-3(6)) Audio Bk Con.
The people & majestic scenery of a North Carolina mountain village serve as a finely drawn backdrop to the elderly Madam Carroll's secret effort to appear as young to her husband as he believes her to be. This, coupled with her caring for the Major through his growing senility, forms a story of true devotion.

For the Memories: A Special Collection. Perf. by Steve Hall. 1 cass., 1 CD. 7.98 (BANK 13); audio compact disk 12.78 CD Jewel box. (BANK 13) NewSound.

For the New Intellectual. unabr. ed. Ayn Rand. Read by Anna Fields. 6 cass. (Running Time: 8 hrs. 30 mins.). 2000. 44.95 (978-0-7861-1879-3(2), 2678) Blckstn Audio.

For the New Intellectual. unabr. ed. Ayn Rand. Read by Anna Fields. 6 cass. (Running Time: 9 hrs.). 2000. 44.95 (2678) Blckstn Audio.
A challenge to the prevalent philosophical doctrines of our time & the atmosphere of guilt, of panic, of despair, of boredom & of all-pervasive evasion that they create. One of the most controversial figures on the

intellectual scene, the author was the proponent of a moral philosophy-an ethic of rational self-interest, that stands in sharp opposition to the ethics of altruism & self-sacrifice.

For the New Intellectual. unabr. ed. Ayn Rand. Read by Anna Fields. 7 CDs. (Running Time: 8 hrs. 30 mins.). 2000. audio compact disk 56.00 (978-0-7861-9812-2(5), 2678) Blckstn Audio.
A challenge to the prevalent philosophical doctrines of our time & the atmosphere of guild, of panic, of despair, of boredom & of all-pervasive evasion that they create. One of the most controversial figures on the intellectual scene, the author was the proponent of a moral philosophy-an ethic of rational self-interest, that stands in sharp opposition to the ethics of altruism & self-sacrifice.

For the New Intellectual. unabr. ed. Ayn Rand. Read by Anna Fields. (Running Time: 8 hrs. NaN mins.). (ENG.). 2010. 24.95 (978-0-7861-9322-6(0), 2678) Blckstn Audio.

***For the New Intellectual.** unabr. ed. Ayn Rand. Read by Anna Fields. (Running Time: 8 hrs. NaN mins.). (ENG.). 2010. audio compact disk 24.95 (978-0-7861-9194-9(5)) Blckstn Audio.

For the Office. abr. ed. Nina Mattikow. 1 cass. Dramatization. (At the Sound of the Beep Ser.). 1992. 6.95 (978-1-55569-559-0(0), 41503) Great Am Audio.
When you're out of the office, make sure your calls are answered professionally. Sixteen prerecorded messages & four office sound effects.

For the People: American Populist Movements from the Revolution to The 1850s. Ronald P. Formisano. (ENG.). 2008. 36.95 (978-0-8078-8614-4(9)); audio compact disk 36.95 (978-0-8078-8616-8(5)) U of NC Pr.

For the Poets of Chile Who Died with Their Country see Philip Levine

For the Roses. Julie Garwood. Read by Megan Gallagher. (Clayborne Brides Ser.: Bk. 1). 2004. 10.95 (978-0-7435-4737-6(3)) Pub: S&S Audio. Dist(s): S and S Inc

For the Roses. unabr. ed. Julie Garwood. Read by Melissa Hughes. 2 CDs. (Running Time: 10 hrs.). (Clayborne Brides Ser.: Bk. 1). 2002. audio compact disk 49.95 (978-0-7927-2667-8(7), CMP 465, Chivers Sound Lib) AudioGO.
Of course, everyone in town knew better than to mess with the Claybornes. The brothers, four of the toughest hombres in the West, had once been a mismatched gang of street urchins. But they had found an abandoned baby girl in a new York City alley, named her mary Rose, headed West, and raised her to be a lady. Through the years the Claybornes had become a family, held together by loyalty and love if not by blood, when they suddenly faced the crisis that could tear them apart.

For the Sake of Elena. unabr. ed. Elizabeth George. Read by Donada Peters. 11 cass. (Running Time: 16 hrs. 30 min.). (Inspector Lynley Ser.). 1993. 88.00 (978-0-7366-2385-8(X), 3156) Books on Tape.
Scotland Yard's Thomas Lynley & Barbara Havers sift contradictory clues in Cambridge coed's murder.

For the Sake of Her Child. unabr. ed. Meg Hutchinson. Read by Marie McCarthy. 9 vols. (Running Time: 12 hr.). 1998. 90.95 (978-1-85903-194-0(3)) Pub: Magna Story GBR. Dist(s): Ulverscroft US
Anna Bradly knew she had to abandon her baby and make a new life if her son is to have a future. When fate leads her back to her roots, it is to a confrontation that could break- or mend-her heart.

For the Sake of the Children. unabr. ed. June Francis. Read by Margaret Sircom. 8 cass. (Running Time: 10 hrs. 35 mins.). (Story Sound Ser.). (J). 2004. 69.95 (978-1-85903-684-6(8)) Pub: Mgna Lrg Print GBR. Dist(s): Ulverscroft US

For the Seasons see Twentieth-Century Poetry in English, No. 10, Recordings of Poets Reading Their Own Poetry

For the Temple. Abr. by Jim Weiss. (ENG.). (YA). 2007. audio compact disk 32.95 (978-1-882513-91-8(6)) Pub: Greathall Prods. Dist(s): Allegro Dist

For the Temple: A Tale of the Fall of Jerusalem. G A Henty. Read by William Sutherland. (Running Time: 48600 sec.). (J). 2008. audio compact disk 29.95 (978-1-4332-0457-9(6)); audio compact disk 99.00 (978-1-4332-0456-2(8)) Blckstn Audio.

For the Temple: A Tale of the Fall of Jerusalem. unabr. ed. G. A. Henty. Read by William Sutherland. 10 cass. (Running Time: 13 hrs.). 2002. 69.95 (978-0-7861-2234-9(X), 2958) Blckstn Audio.
In this stirring tale of the last days of the temple at Jerusalem, robber bands and political infighting set the stage for the Roman destruction of the city in A.D. 70.

For the Temple: A Tale of the Fall of Jerusalem. unabr. ed. G. A. Henty. Read by Jim Hodges. 8 cass. (Running Time: 10 hrs.). (YA). (gr. 5 up). 2000. 35.00 (978-1-929756-03-2(8)) J Hodges.
Jerusalem and the Temple finally fall to Rome in A.D. 70.

For the Time Being. unabr. ed. Marie DesJardin. Read by Jerry Sciarrio. 12 cass. (Running Time: 18 hrs.). 2001. 64.95 (978-1-58116-191-5(3)) Books in Motion.
Ten graduate-level, MENSA-gifted misfits set out one night to explore a set of steam tunnels beneath their school and ended up being captured by aliens, and transported by space ship to another planet. Hoping to return home, the group secretly begins to build a time machine. When their scheme is discovered they find out they already promised the aliens in the past that they'd build a time machine to save their race from extinction 5000 years ago. Unraveling what they had done in the past, figuring out the future, and getting home while eluding two warring races becomes their dilemma.

For the Time Being, Set. unabr. ed. Dirk Bogarde. Read by Andrew Sachs. 8 cass. (Running Time: 12 hrs.). 1999. 69.95 (978-0-7540-0321-2(3), CAB1744) Pub: Chivers Audio Bks GBR. Dist(s): AudioGO
After two decades in France, the author returned to England to work for the "Daily Telegraph." Over the next eight years, Bogarde wrote much of the criticism, essays, obituaries, & fragments of autobiography which are collected in this volume: a body of work that offers fascinating insights into the mind & views of one of Britain's most admired authors & actors.

For the Tough Times: Reaching Toward Heaven for Hope. unabr. ed. Max Lucado. Narrated by Nathan Larkin. (ENG.). 2006. 9.09 (978-1-60814-216-3(7)); audio compact disk 12.99 (978-1-59859-167-5(3)) Oasis Audio.

For the Troops: Classic Radio for the Armed Forces. Created by Radio Spirits. (Running Time: 10800 sec.). 2004. 9.98 (978-1-57019-748-2(2)); audio compact disk 9.98 (978-1-57019-747-5(4)) Radio Spirits.

For the Union Dead from "For the Union Dead" see Twentieth-Century Poetry in English, No. 32-33, Recordings of Poets Reading Their Own Poetry

For the Win. unabr. ed. Cory Doctorow. Read by George Newbern. (ENG.). (J). 2010. audio compact disk 57.00 (978-0-307-71069-7(6), Listening Lib) Pub: Random Audio Pubg. Dist(s): Random

For the Working Artist see Art That Pays: The Emerging Artist's Guide to Making a Living

For the Young at Heart! Fitness for Seniors. 1 cass. (Running Time: 1 hr.). 2001. pap. bk. 10.95 (KIM 2047C); pap. bk. & pupil's gde. ed. 11.95 (KIM 2047) Kimbo Educ.
Tone, shape & strengthen your body with standing, seated & floor exercises. Warm-ups to loosen muscles & cool-downs to relax the body. New York, New York, Gentle on My Mind & more. Includes guide.

For They Have Come: An Ancient Hatred Becomes a Present Love. Kenneth Wapnick. 2008. 12.00 (978-1-59142-356-0(2)); audio compact disk 15.00 (978-1-59142-355-3(4)) Foun Miracles.

For Those in Fear & Suffering. Read by Mother Basilea Schlink. 1 cass. (Running Time: 30 min.). 1985. (0240) Evang Sisterhood Mary.
Includes: Treasure in the Cross; Emmaus-Sadness Transformed; Giving True Praise to God.

For Those Who Need a Comforter. Christine Wyrtzen et al. 1 cass. (50-Day Spiritual Adventure Ser.). 1994. 9.99 (978-1-879050-68-6(4)) Chapel of Air.
1995 50-Day Spiritual Adventures songs.

For Those Who Sleep in Church: Acts. 20:1-16. Ed Young. 2000. 4.95 (978-0-7417-2247-8(X), 1247) Win Walk.

For Time & All Eternity. Charles Beckert. 2004. audio compact disk 11.95 (978-1-57734-860-3(5)) Covenant Comms.

For Time & All Eternity. Charles B. Beckert. 2004. 9.95 (978-1-57734-846-7(X)) Covenant Comms.

For unto Us a Child Is Born. Read by Basilea Schlink. 1 cass. (Running Time: 30 min.). 1985. (0274) Evang Sisterhood Mary.
Jesus brings God's plan of salvation to its marvellous goal; Specially prepared messages for the Christmas season.

***For Us, the Living: A Comedy of Customs.** unabr. ed. Robert A. Heinlein. Read by Malcolm Hillgartner. (Running Time: 11 hrs. NaN mins.). (ENG.). 2011. 29.95 (978-1-4417-4340-4(5)); 44.95 (978-1-4417-4336-7(7)); audio compact disk 29.95 (978-1-4417-4339-8(1)) Blckstn Audio.

***For Us, the Living (Library Edition) A Comedy of Customs.** unabr. ed. Robert A. Heinlein. Read by Malcolm Hillgartner. (Running Time: 11 hrs. NaN mins.). 2011. audio compact disk 69.00 (978-1-4417-4337-4(5)) Blckstn Audio.

For Valour. Douglas Reeman. Read by David Rintoul. 2 cass. (Running Time: 3 hrs. 0 mins. 0 sec.). (ENG., 2000. (978-1-85686-542-5(8), Audiobks) Random GBR.

For Valour. unabr. ed. Douglas Reeman. Read by David Rintoul. 8 cass. (Running Time: 12 hrs.). 2001. 69.95 (978-0-7540-0682-4(4), CAB 2104) Pub: Chivers Audio Bks GBR. Dist(s): AudioGO

For What Earthly Reason. Contrib. by Lari Goss. 1997. 24.95 (978-0-7601-1804-7(3), 75600295) Pub: Brentwood Music. Dist(s): H Leonard

For What Earthly Reason. Contrib. by Janet Pascal. (Studio Tracks Plus Ser.). 2006. audio compact disk 9.98 (978-5-558-32153-1(9)) Sprg Hill Music Group.

For Whom the Bell Tolls see Por Quién Doblan Las Campanas

For Whom the Bell Tolls. Ernest Hemingway. Read by Alexander Adams. 1992. audio compact disk 104.00 (978-0-7366-7494-2(2)) Books on Tape.

For Whom the Bell Tolls. Ernest Hemingway. Read by Laura García. (Running Time: 3 hrs.). 2002. 16.95 (978-1-60083-251-2(2), Audiofy Corp) Iofy Corp.

For Whom the Bell Tolls. unabr. ed. Ernest Hemingway. Read by Alexander Adams. 11 cass. (Running Time: 16 hrs. 30 min.). 1999. 34.95 (978-0-7366-4429-7(6)) Books on Tape.
The story of Robert Jordan, an American fighting with anti-fascist guerrillas in the mountains of Spain. It tells of loyalty & courage, love & defeat, the tragic death of an ideal. It lives for us because of the great disillusionment that grew out of WWII, a war fought with such high hopes & concluded so cynically with a former ally gobbling up half of the Europe we hoped to liberate.

For Whom the Bell Tolls. unabr. ed. Ernest Hemingway. Read by Alexander Adams. 13 CDs. (Running Time: 16 hrs.). 2001. audio compact disk 39.95 (978-0-7366-5701-3(0)) Books on Tape.

For Whom the Bell Tolls. unabr. ed. Ernest Hemingway. Read by Campbell Scott. 2006. 29.95 (978-0-7435-6511-0(8), Audioworks); audio compact disk 49.95 (978-0-7435-6438-0(3)) Pub: S&S Audio. Dist(s): S and S Inc

For Whom the Bell Tolls. unabr. collector's ed. Ernest Hemingway. Read by Alexander Adams. 11 cass. (Running Time: 16 hrs. 30 min.). (J). 1992. 88.00 (978-0-7366-2145-8(8), 2943) Books on Tape.

For Women in Private. Michael R. Gach. 1 cass. (Running Time: 30 min.). (Greater Energy Ser.). 1988. 9.95 (978-0-945093-04-6(7)) Enhanced Aud Systs.
Explains how acupressure relieves tension & energizes the body.

For Women Only. 2003. (978-1-931713-57-3(X)); audio compact disk (978-1-931713-58-0(8)); audio compact disk (978-1-931713-79-5(0)) Word For Today.

For Women Only: Reducing Stress Is An Inside Job. Patricia J. Crane. Read by Patricia J. Crane. 3 cass. (Running Time: 3 hrs.). 1988. 30.00 Set. (978-1-893705-05-0(6)) Hlth Horiz.
Topics include communication, time management, positive affirmations, humor, & spiritual purpose.

For Women Only: Reducing Stress Is an Inside Job. Patricia J. Crane. 3 CDs. 2004. audio compact disk 29.95 (978-1-893705-18-0(8), Cranes Nest) Hlth Horiz.
Techniques for women to use in reducing stress. Relaxation exercises, changing thoughts, using humor, effective time management, and life purpose.

For Women Only: What You Need to Know about the Inner Lives of Men. unabr. ed. Shaunti Feldhahn. Narrated by Shaunti Feldhahn. (ENG.). 2006. 15.39 (978-1-60814-217-0(5)); audio compact disk 21.99 (978-1-59859-141-5(X)) Oasis Audio.

For You I Live. Contrib. by Resurrection Life Church. 2007. audio compact disk 13.99 (978-5-557-63538-7(6)) Integrity Music.

For Young Men Only: A Guys Guide to the Alien Gender. unabr. ed. Jeff Feldhahn & Eric Rice. Narrated by Kelly Ryan Dolan. (Running Time: 3 hrs. 44 mins. 28 sec.). (ENG.). (YA). 2008. 13.99 (978-1-60814-218-7(3)) Oasis Audio.

For Young Men Only: A Guys Guide to the Alien Gender. unabr. ed. Jeff Feldhahn & Eric Rice. Read by Jeff Feldhahn. Narrated by Kelly Ryan Dolan. (Running Time: 3 hrs. 44 mins. 28 sec.). (ENG.). (YA). 2008. audio compact disk 19.99 (978-1-59859-434-8(6)) Oasis Audio.

For Young Women Only: What You Need to Know about How Guys Think. unabr. ed. Shaunti Feldhahn & Lisa A. Rice. Narrated by Shaunti Feldhahn. (Running Time: 3 hrs. 48 mins. 0 sec.). (ENG.). (YA). (gr. 8-12). 2007. audio compact disk 14.99 (978-1-59859-285-6(8)) Oasis Audio.

For Young Women Only: What You Need to Know about How Guys Think. unabr. ed. Shaunti Feldhahn & Lisa Author Rice. Narrated by Shaunti Feldhahn. (ENG.). (YA). 2007. 10.49 (978-1-60814-219-4(1)) Oasis Audio.

For Younger I've Been. Perf. by Maggi Peirce. 1 cass. (Running Time: 80 min.). (J). (gr. 6 up). 1993. 9.95 (978-0-938756-46-0(X), 022) Yellow Moon.
A poignant journey into the world of Belfast, Northern Ireland, during the late 1930s & early 1940s. Combines humor, wisdom, & hindsight to call up the wondrous childhood in every listeners memory.

For Your Church: Stories of Love & Forgiveness. Melea J. Brock. Illus. by Melea J. Brock. 1. (Running Time: 1 Hr. 10 Mins.). Dramatization. 1998. 10.98 (978-0-9667455-7-3(4)) Right-Side-Up.

For Your Eyes Only. unabr. ed. Ian Fleming. Read by Robert Whitfield. 4 cass. (Running Time: 5 hrs. 30 mins.). 2001. 32.95 (978-0-7861-1984-4(5), 2754); audio compact disk 40.00 (978-0-7861-9740-8(4), 2754) Blckstn Audio.
Five short stories find James Bond facing danger from a variety of sources, all of which he escapes through fast thinking & even faster action. The action shifts from Paris to Venice to Bermuda to sudden death in Seychelles.

For Your Eyes Only. unabr. ed. Read by Simon Vance. Perf. by Ian Fleming. (Running Time: 5.5 hrs. 0 mins.). 2008. 29.95 (978-1-4332-7026-0(9)); audio compact disk 19.95 (978-1-4332-7025-3(0)) Blckstn Audio.

For Your Information. Sundance/Newbridge, LLC Staff. (Early Science Ser.). (gr. k-3). 2007. audio compact disk 12.00 (978-1-4007-6570-6(6)); audio compact disk 12.00 (978-1-4007-6571-3(4)); audio compact disk 12.00 (978-1-4007-6569-0(2)) Sund Newbrdge.

Forastero en el Camino a Emaús - Libro en Audio. (SPA.). 2004. audio compact disk (978-1-890082-44-4(9)) GS Intl CAN.

Forastero en el Camino a Emaús - Libro en Audio: Mp3. (SPA.). 2004. (978-1-890082-45-1(7)) GS Intl CAN.

Forbearance. Swami Jyotirmayananda. 1 cass. (Running Time: 1 hr.). 1990. 12.99 Yoga Res Foun.

Forbes for President. 1 cass. (Leonard Peikoff Show Ser.). 1996. 12.95 (LPXXC4) Second Renaissance.

Forbes Greatest Investing Stories. Richard Phalon. Read by Edward Lewis. (Running Time: 9 hrs.). 2003. 30.95 (978-1-59912-493-3(9)) Iofy Corp.

Forbes Greatest Investing Stories. unabr. ed. Richard Phalon. Read by David Hilder. 7 cass. (Running Time: 10 hrs.). 2003. 49.95 (978-0-7861-2418-3(0), 3084); audio compact disk 64.00 (978-0-7861-9243-4(7), 3084) Blckstn Audio.

Forbidden. abr. ed. Beverly Lewis. Narrated by Aimee Lilly. (Courtship of Nellie Fisher Ser.: Bk. 2). (ENG.). 2008. 16.09 (978-1-60814-220-0(5)); audio compact disk 22.99 (978-1-59859-386-0(2)) Oasis Audio.

Forbidden. abr. ed. Elizabeth Lowell. Read by Sarah Scott & Laural Merlington. (Running Time: 6 hrs.). (Medieval Ser.). 2009. audio compact disk 14.99 (978-1-4233-3233-6(4), 9781423332336, BCD Value Price) Brilliance Audio.

Forbidden. unabr. ed. Suzanne Brockmann. (Running Time: 18000 sec.). 2007. 34.95 (978-1-4332-1296-3(X)) Blckstn Audio.

Forbidden. unabr. ed. Suzanne Brockmann. Read by Traci Svendsgaard. (Running Time: 18000 sec.). 2007. audio compact disk 29.95 (978-1-4332-1298-7(6)); audio compact disk & audio compact disk 45.00 (978-1-4332-1297-0(8)) Blckstn Audio.

Forbidden. unabr. ed. Elizabeth Lowell. Read by Sarah Scott. 1 MP3-CD. (Running Time: 10 hrs.). (Medieval Ser.). 2008. 24.95 (978-1-4233-3228-2(8), 9781423332282, Brilliance MP3); 24.95 (978-1-4233-3230-5(X), 9781423332305, BAD); 39.25 (978-1-4233-3231-2(8), 9781423332312, BADLE); 39.25 (978-1-4233-3229-9(6), 9781423332299, Brinc Audio MP3 Lib); audio compact disk 36.95 (978-1-4233-3226-8(1), 9781423332268, Bril Audio CD Unabri); audio compact disk 97.25 (978-1-4233-3227-5(X), 9781423332275, BriAudCD Unabrid) Brilliance Audio.

Forbidden Affections. abr. ed. Jo Beverley. Read by Alexandra Thomas. 1 cass. (Running Time: 90 min.). 1996. 6.99 (978-1-57096-045-1(3), RAZ 946) Romance Alive Audio.
In Regency London, bubbly & vivacious Anna Featherstone discovers that her Gothic bedroom hides a secret connecting door that becomes a passageway to danger - & romance - & that crossing the threshold will lead her straight into the arms of the notorious & devilishly handsome Earl of Carn.

Forbidden Cancer Cures That Work: Eleven All-Natural Strategies That Could Save Your Life. Perf. by Clive Buchanan. 2 cass. (Running Time: 1 hr. 50 min.). (Wellness Audio Ser.). 1999. 16.95 Set. (978-1-56889-014-2(1), AW5232); 33.90 Set, incl. public performance rights for schools & libraries. Lghtwrks Aud & Vid.
Discover cancer answers in layman's terms from one of America's leading public speakers on herbology & preventative health care & author of "Herbal Knowledge, The Top Ten Power Supplements & More" & "Love, Money & Personal Power".

Forbidden Embrace. unabr. ed. Anna Jacobs. Read by Ruth Sillers. 6 cass. (Running Time: 8 hrs.). (Story Sound Ser.). (J). 2006. 54.95 (978-1-85903-874-1(3)) Pub: Mgna Lrg Print GBR. Dist(s): Ulverscroft US

Forbidden Feelings. unabr. ed. Una-Mary Parker. Read by Anita Wright. 14 CDs. (Running Time: 15 hrs. 53 min.). (Isis Ser.). (J). 2001. audio compact disk 104.95 (978-0-7531-1198-7(5)) Pub: ISIS Lrg Prnt GBR. Dist(s): Ulverscroft US
When strange events at her father's Scottish estate require investigation, Camilla Eaton is grateful for Philip's company and despite the difference in their ages, the couple embark on a heady love affair. Horrified by the unwelcome evidence of her mother's sexuality, Camilla's teenage daughter, Poppy, becomes involved with a group of militant political activists.

Forbidden Feelings. unabr. ed. Una-Mary Parker. Read by Anita Wright. 12 cass. (Running Time: 15 hrs. 52 min.). (Isis Ser.). (J). 2001. 94.95 (978-0-7531-1156-7(X)) Pub: ISIS Lrg Prnt GBR. Dist(s): Ulverscroft US

Forbidden Fruit. Paul Kurtz. Read by Paul Kurtz. 2 pieces. (Running Time: 3 hrs.). (ENG.). 1996. 24.98 (978-1-57392-100-8(9)) Prometheus Bks.
America's leading secular humanist philosopher affirms that morality without belief in God leads to a higher ethical level.

Forbidden Fruit: The Fall of Eve & Adam. unabr. ed. Judith Roberts Seto. 2 cass. (Running Time: 2 hrs.). 2001. 17.95 Penton Overseas.

Forbidden Fruit: The Fall of Eve & Adam. unabr. ed. Judith Roberts Seto. Read by Meghan Shea et al. Perf. by Clay Zambo. 2 cass. (Running Time: 1 hr. 48 mins.). 2000. 17.95 (978-0-9658148-1-2(5)) Scheherazade Audio.
A multi cast dramatic tapestry with a feminist motif, woven from five literary masterpieces about the Fall, with selections from the Bible, a medieval play & works by Milton Shaw & Twain. Changing depictions of Eve, reflect changing attitudes toward woman.

***Forbidden Game: The Hunter - The Chase - The Kill.** unabr. ed. L. J. Smith. (Running Time: 18 hrs.). (Forbidden Game Ser.: Bks. 1-3). 2010. 19.99 (978-1-4418-8087-1(9), 9781441880871, Brilliance MP3) Brilliance Audio.

***Forbidden Game: The Hunter - The Chase - The Kill.** unabr. ed. L. J. Smith. Read by Khristine Hvam. (Running Time: 18 hrs.). (Forbidden Game Ser.: Bks. 1-3). 2010. 39.97 (978-1-4418-8259-2(6), 9781441882592, Brinc Audio MP3 Lib); 39.97 (978-1-4418-8088-8(7), 9781441880888, BADLE) Brilliance Audio.

Force. Stuart Wilde. 2 CDs. 2007. audio compact disk 23.95 (978-1-4019-0675-7(3)) Hay House.

Force. unabr. ed. Stuart Wilde. Read by Stuart Wilde. 2 cass. (Running Time: 3 hrs.). 1996. 16.95 (978-1-56170-282-4(X), 389) Hay House.
The author emphasizes that there is nothing you cannot do when you have the Force in your life. Your heritage is to express a power for the benefit of yourself & others & by silently expressing that power, you allow a renaissance to come about!.

Force: How to Find, Hire, Train, Build, Pay, & Keep a First Class Team of Salespeople on FIRE! Created by Jeffrey Gitomer. 2007. 99.00 (978-0-9719468-5-9(X)) Lito Pr.

***Force & Motion.** Perf. by Millmark Education Staff. (ConceptLinks Ser.). 2007. audio compact disk 28.00 (978-1-4334-0033-9(2)) Millmark Educ.

***Force & Motion: CD add-on Set.** Perf. by Millmark Education Staff. (ConceptLinks Ser.). 2009. audio compact disk 50.00 (978-1-61618-354-7(3)) Millmark Educ.

***Force & Motion SB1 Audio CD Types of Forces.** Perf. by Millmark Education Staff. (Content Literacy Libraries Ser.). 2008. audio compact disk (978-1-4334-0396-5(X)) Millmark Educ.

***Force & Motion SB2 Audio CD Forces in Action.** Perf. by Millmark Education Staff. (Content Literacy Libraries Ser.). 2008. audio compact disk (978-1-4334-0397-2(8)) Millmark Educ.

***Force & Motion SB3 Audio CD Newton's Laws of Motion.** Perf. by Millmark Education Staff. (Content Literacy Libraries Ser.). 2008. audio compact disk (978-1-4334-0398-9(6)) Millmark Educ.

***Force & Motion SB4 Audio CD Applying Newton's Laws of Motion.** Perf. by Millmark Education Staff. (Content Literacy Libraries Ser.). 2008. audio compact disk (978-1-4334-0399-6(4)) Millmark Educ.

Force Fields: Science Fiction Poetry & Interview. Andrew Joron. 1 cass. 9.00 (A0048-87) Sound Photosyn.
Science fiction poetry & Faustin's interview which Brian records.

Force Heretic III: Reunion. abr. ed. Sean Williams & Shane Dix. Read by Jonathan Davis. 3 CDs. (Running Time: 3 hrs.). (Star Wars Ser.: Bk. 17). (ENG.). 2003. audio compact disk 19.95 (978-0-553-71366-4(3)) Pub: Random Audio Pubg. Dist(s): Random

Force of Disappointment. Mac Hammond. 1 cass. (Running Time: 1 hr.). 2005. 5.00 (978-1-57399-210-7(0)); audio compact disk 5.00 (978-1-57399-259-6(3)) Mac Hammond.

Force of Disappointment. Mac Hammond. 2008. audio compact disk 6.00 (978-1-57399-385-2(9)) Mac Hammond.

Force of Goodness. unabr. ed. Perf. by Eknath Easwaran. 1 cass. (Running Time: 1 hr.). 1977. 7.95 (978-1-58638-540-8(2)) Nilgiri Pr.

Force of Love. Kenneth Copeland. 1 cass. 1983. 5.00 (978-0-88114-026-2(0)) K Copeland Pubns.
Indepth biblical study on the human spirit.

Force of Nature. Suzanne Brockmann. Read by Patrick G. Lawlor & Melanie Ewbank. (Troubleshooter Ser.: No. 11). 2008. 84.99 (978-1-60640-802-5(X)) Find a World.

Force of Nature. abr. ed. Suzanne Brockmann. Read by Patrick G. Lawlor & Melanie Ewbank. (Running Time: 6 hrs.). (Troubleshooter Ser.: No. 11). 2008. audio compact disk 14.99 (978-1-59737-673-0(6), 9781597376730) Brilliance Audio.

Force of Nature. unabr. ed. Suzanne Brockmann. Read by Patrick G. Lawlor & Melanie Ewbank. (Running Time: 15 hrs.). (Troubleshooter Ser.: No. 11). 2007. 39.25 (978-1-59710-837-9(5), 9781597108379, BADLE); 24.95 (978-1-59710-836-2(7), 9781597108362, BAD); audio compact disk 24.95 (978-1-59335-950-8(0), 9781593359508, Brilliance MP3); 97.25 (978-1-59600-159-6(3), 9781596001596, BrilAudUnabridg); audio compact disk 38.95 (978-1-59600-160-2(7), 9781596001602, Bril Audio CD Unabri); audio compact disk 117.25 (978-1-59600-161-9(5), 9781596001619, BriAudCD Unabrid) Brilliance Audio.
Please enter a Synopsis.

Force of Nature. unabr. ed. Suzanne Brockmann. Read by Melanie Ewbank & Patrick G. Lawlor. 1 MP3-CD. (Running Time: 54000 sec.). (Troubleshooter Ser.: No. 11). 2007. audio compact disk 39.25 (978-1-59335-951-5(9), 9781593359515, Brinc Audio MP3 Lib) Brilliance Audio.

Force of Nature, Pt. 1. unabr. ed. Thomas Hager. Read by Jonathan Reese. 10 cass. (Running Time: 15 hrs.). 2001. 80.00 (978-0-7366-8303-6(8)) Books on Tape.
Today, Linus Pauling may be remembered only for his controversial statements that Vitamin C could help cure cancer. However, Linus Pauling was one of this country's most distinguished scientists. The winner of two unshared Nobel Prizes, one in Science and one in Peace, Pauling made fundamental contributions to the fields of chemistry, physics, biology, and medicine.

Force of Nature, Pt. 2. unabr. ed. Thomas Hager. Read by Jonathan Reese. 10 cass. (Running Time: 15 hrs.). 2001. 80.00 (978-0-7366-8304-3(6)) Books on Tape.
The life of Linus Pauling, distinguished scientist, committed activist, and dual Nobel Prize winner.

Force of Righteousness. Kenneth Copeland. 1 cass. 1983. 5.00 (978-0-88114-024-8(4)) K Copeland Pubns.
Indepth biblical study on the human spirit.

force qui nous Manque. unabr. ed. Eva Joly. Read by Eva Joly. Read by Nicole Vautier. (YA). 2007. 79.99 (978-2-35569-071-6(5)) Find a World.

Force Recon # 1. abr. ed. James Smith. 2 cass. (Running Time: 3 hrs.). 2003. 9.95 (978-1-931953-41-2(4)) Listen & Live.

Force Recon #2: Death Wind. abr. ed. James Smith. 2 cass. (Running Time: 3 hrs.). 2003. 9.95 (978-1-931953-42-9(2)) Listen & Live.

Force Recon #3: The Butcher's Bill. abr. ed. James Smith. 2 cass. (Running Time: 3 hrs.). 2003. 9.95 (978-1-931953-43-6(0)) Listen & Live.

Force Recon #4: Deep Strike. abr. ed. James Smith. 2 cass. (Running Time: 3 hrs.). 2003. 9.95 (978-1-931953-44-3(9)) Listen & Live.

Force Recon #5: Fatal Honor. abr. ed. James Smith. 2 cass. (Running Time: 3 hrs.). 2003. 9.95 (978-1-931953-45-0(7)) Listen & Live.

Force Recon #6: Stalking Tiger. abr. ed. James Smith. 2 cass. (Running Time: 3 hrs.). 2003. 9.95 (978-1-931953-46-7(5)) Listen & Live.

Force Unleashed. abr. ed. Sean Williams. Read by Jonathan Davis. (Star Wars Ser.). (ENG.). 2008. audio compact disk 29.95 (978-0-7393-5808-5(1), Random AudioBks) Pub: Random Audio Pubg. Dist(s): Random

***Force Unleashed II.** unabr. ed. Sean Williams. Read by Jonathan Davis. (Running Time: 10 hrs. 30 mins.). (Star Wars Ser.). 2010. audio compact disk 35.00 (978-0-307-75074-7(4), Random AudioBks) Pub: Random Audio Pubg. Dist(s): Random

Force 10 from Navarone. unabr. ed. Alistair MacLean. Read by Steven Pacey. 8 cass. (Running Time: 12 hrs.). 2000. 59.95 (CAB 865) Pub: Chivers Audio Bks GBR. Dist(s): AudioGO
Almost before the last echoes of guns have died away, three Navarone heroes parachute into war torn Yugoslavia to rescue a division of Partisans. It is a secret mission so deadly that it must be hidden from their own allies.

Forced Out. unabr. ed. Stephen Frey. (ENG.). 2008. audio compact disk 29.95 (978-1-60283-455-2(5)) Pub: AudioGO. Dist(s): Perseus Dist

Forces & Motion Audio CD Theme Set: Set of 6 Set A. Adapted by Benchmark Education Staff. (English Explorers Ser.). (J). (gr. 3-6). 2007. audio compact disk 60.00 (978-1-4108-9834-0(2)) Benchmark Educ.

Forces for Good: The Six Practices of High-Impact Non-Profits. unabr. ed. Leslie R. Crutchfield & Heather McLeod Grant. Read by Erik Synnestvedt. (Running Time: 9 hrs. 30 mins.). (ENG.). 2008. 24.98 (978-1-59659-242-1(7), GildAudio) Pub: Gildan Media. Dist(s): HachBkGrp

Forces of Fortune: The Rise of the New Muslim Middle Class & What It Will Mean for Our World. unabr. ed. Vali Nasr. Narrated by Arthur Morey. 1 MP3-CD. (Running Time: 11 hrs. 0 mins. 0 sec.). (ENG.). 2009. 24.99 (978-1-4001-6379-3(X)); audio compact disk 34.99 (978-1-4001-1379-8(2)); audio compact disk 69.99 (978-1-4001-4379-5(9)) Pub: Tantor Media. Dist(s): IngramPubServ

Forces of the Recreated Human Spirit. Kenneth Copeland. 8 cass. 1983. 40.00 Set incl. study guide. (978-0-938458-51-7(5)) K Copeland Pubns.
The recreated spirit of man.

Forcible Entry & Search & Rescue. International Association of Fire Chiefs Staff & National Fire Protection Association. 2005. 473.95 (978-0-7637-3608-8(2)) Jones Bartlett.

Ford: The Men & the Machine. unabr. ed. Robert Lacey. Read by Grover Gardner. 7 cass. (Running Time: 10 hrs. 30 mins.). 1989. 56.00 (978-0-7366-1541-9(5), 2410-A); 88.00 (978-0-7366-1540-2(7), 2410-B) Books on Tape.
Robert Lacey has captured the public achievements & the private tragedies, the feuds, affairs & personalities that make up this epic tale.

Ford & Carter: There Is a Difference. unabr. ed. James J. Kilpatrick. 1 cass. (Running Time: 56 min.). 12.95 (448) J Norton Pubs.

***Ford County.** unabr. ed. John Grisham. Read by John Grisham. 6 CDs. (Running Time: 7 hrs.). 2009. audio compact disk 60.00 (978-0-307-70212-8(X), BksonTape) Pub: Random Audio Pubg. Dist(s): Random

Ford County. unabr. ed. John Grisham. Read by John Grisham. (ENG.). 2009. audio compact disk 35.00 (978-0-307-70210-4(3), Random AudioBks) Pub: Random Audio Pubg. Dist(s): Random

Ford Madox Ford from "Life Studies" see Twentieth-Century Poetry in English, No. 32-33, Recordings of Poets Reading Their Own Poetry

Ford Theatre: A Connecticut Yankee in King Arthur's Court. 1 cass. (Running Time: 1 hr.). 2001. 6.98 (2059) Radio Spirits.

Ford Theatre: Double Indemnity. Perf. by Burt Lancaster & Joan Bennett. 1 cass. (Running Time: 1 hr.). 2001. 6.98 (2517) Radio Spirits.

Ford Theatre: The Horn Blows at Midnight. Perf. by Jack Benny. 1 cass. (Running Time: 1 hr.). 2001. 6.98 (1849) Radio Spirits.

Ford Theatre: The Man Who Played God. 1 cass. (Running Time: 1 hr.). 2001. 6.98 (2217) Radio Spirits.

Fords: An American Epic. unabr. ed. Peter Collier & David Horowitz. Read by Grover Gardner. 13 cass. (Running Time: 19 hrs.). 1989. 104.00 (978-0-7366-1482-5(6), 2358-A/B) Books on Tape.
Focuses on the generational conflict between fathers & sons, played out against the backdrop of a great industrial empire.

Fore! Play. abr. ed. Read by Bill Geist. 2 cass. (Running Time: 3 hrs.). 2002. 18.95 (978-1-58621-247-6(8)) Hachet Audio.
Bill Geist claims he's the only white man in North America over the age of 50 who hasn't been lured to the lush green grass of the golf course and he wants to know why. That's precisely the starting point for his exploration of America's infatuation with the game of golf.

Fore! Play: The Last American Male Takes up Golf! abr. ed. Bill Geist. (ENG.). 2005. 14.98 (978-1-59483-424-0(5)) Pub: Hachet Audio. Dist(s): HachBkGrp

Forebearance. (711) Yoga Res Foun.

Foreboding see Robert Graves Reads from His Poetry & the White Goddess

Forecast: A Journey to the Frontiers of Climate Change, from the Amazon to the Arctic, from Darfur to Napa Valley. unabr. ed. Stephan Faris. Read by Melisa Foster. (Running Time: 7 hrs. 0 mins. 0 sec.). (ENG.). 2009. audio compact disk 19.99 (978-1-4001-6058-7(8)); audio compact disk 59.99 (978-1-4001-4058-9(7)) Pub: Tantor Media. Dist(s): IngramPubServ

Forecast: A Journey to the Frontiers of Climate Change, from the Amazon to the Arctic, from Darfur to Napa Valley. unabr. ed. Stephan Faris. Read by Mel Foster. (Running Time: 7 hrs. 0 mins. 0 sec.). (ENG.). 2009. audio compact disk 29.99 (978-1-4001-1058-2(0)) Pub: Tantor Media. Dist(s): IngramPubServ

Forecasting Budgets: 25 Keys to Successful Planning. PH.D., Norman Moore. Read by Grover Gardner. (Running Time: 12600 sec.). (New York Times Pocket MBA Ser.). 2007. audio compact disk 19.95 (978-1-59316-095-1(X)) Listen & Live.

Forecasting Budgets: 25 Keys to Successful Planning. unabr. ed. Norman Moore. Read by Grover Gardner. 2 cass. (Running Time: 3 hrs.). (New York Times Pocket MBA Ser.). 2000. pap. bk. 27.95 Listen & Live.
Learn the 25 keys to the art of the budget in terms of forecasting costs, revenues & profits for short-term & long-term projections.

Forecasting Budgets: 25 Keys to Successful Planning. unabr. ed. Norman Moore. Read by Grover Gardner. 2 cass. (Running Time: 2 hrs. 30 mins.). (New York Times Pocket MBA Ser.). 2000. 16.95 (978-1-885408-41-9(2), LL034) Listen & Live.

Forecasting Change. Elayne J. Manago. 1 cass. 8.95 (694) Am Fed Astrologers.
An AFA Convention workshop tape.

Forecasting Exchange Rates. unabr. ed. James L. Burtle. 1 cass. (Running Time: 53 min.). 12.95 (295) J Norton Pubs.

Forecasting Techniques. Jeanne D. Lawlor. Read by Jeanne D. Lawlor. 1 cass. (Running Time: 90 min.). 1994. 8.95 (1169) Am Fed Astrologers.
Forecasting events using astrology.

Forecasting with Solar Eclipses. Vince Ploscik. Read by Vince Ploscik. 1 cass. (Running Time: 90 min.). 1994. 8.95 (1105) Am Fed Astrologers.
Using solar eclipses to forecast coming events.

Foreclosure Investing. abr. ed. Ralph R. Roberts & Joe Kraynak. Read by Brett Barry. 2008. audio compact disk 14.95 (978-0-06-167281-1(5), Harper Audio) HarperCollins Pubs.

Foreclosure Investing for Dummies. abr. ed. Read by Brett Barry & Ralph R. Roberts. Told to Joe Kraynak. (Playaway Adult Nonfiction Ser.). (ENG.). 2009. 59.99 (978-1-60812-581-4(5)) Find a World.

***Foreclosure Investing for Dummies.** abr. ed. Ralph R. Roberts & Joe Kraynak. Read by Brett Barry. (ENG.). 2008. (978-0-06-170730-8(9)); (978-0-06-170731-5(7)) HarperCollins Pubs.

Foreclosures & other Distressed Property Sales. 18th ed. Arranged by International Wealth Success. (ENG.). 2009. ring bd. 51.95 (978-1-56150-902-7(7)) Intl Wealth.

Foreign Body. unabr. ed. Robin Cook. Read by George Guidall. 10 CDs. (Running Time: 12 hrs.). No. 8. (ENG.). (gr. 8). 2008. audio compact disk 39.95 (978-0-14-314314-7(X), PengAudBks) Penguin Grp USA.

Foreign Body. unabr. ed. Robin Cook. Narrated by George Guidall. (Running Time: 12 hrs.). (Jack Stapleton Ser.: No. 8). 2008. 61.75 (978-1-4361-6487-0(7)); audio compact disk 123.75 (978-1-4361-3782-9(9)) Recorded Bks.
New York Times best-selling author Robin Cook is the master of the medical thriller. During a study break, UCLA medical student Jennifer Hernandez is shocked to learn that her grandmother died during surgery in New Delhi. Desperate to find out why, she uncovers several other unexplained deaths.

Foreign Correspondent. abr. ed. Alan Furst. Read by Alfred Molina. 2006. 17.95 (978-0-7435-6456-4(1), Audioworks) Pub: S&S Audio. Dist(s): S and S Inc

Foreign Devils on the Silk Road. unabr. collector's ed. Peter Hopkirk. Read by David Case. 7 cass. (Running Time: 10 hrs. 30 min.). 1990. 56.00 (978-0-7366-1764-2(7), 2603) Books on Tape.
The Silk Road, the great trans- Asian highway linking Imperial Rome & distant China, reached the height of its importance during the T'ang Dynasty. Along it travelled cargos of silk, gold, ivory, as well as new ideas, art & knowledge. But then, China lost control of the region & finally the towns disappeared under the sands. Local legends grew up of buried treasure. Almost 1000 years later the race for the treasures of the Silk Road began. Archaeologists carried off huge quantities of wall-paintings, sculptures, silks & early manuscripts, which are today scattered through museums worldwide. In piecing together this little-known chapter of Chinese history, Peter Hopkirk tells of the intrepid & determined men who led these archaeological raids & traces the fate of the artwork they removed. Little wonder that native governments resent this plunder & bear a grudge for the sack our great-grandfathers engineered.

Foreign Field. unabr. ed. Ben Macintyre. Narrated by Michael Wade. 7 cass. (Running Time: 9 hrs. 15 mins.). 2002. 64.00 (978-1-84197-369-2(6), RG205) Recorded Bks.
When Private Robert Digby and his men get trapped behind enemy lines during the First World War they are sheltered and fed by locals in a remote French village for 18 months. This is their true story. Constructed from letters, memories and real evidence, the account of their love, survival and ultimately their betrayal is truly amazing.

Foreign Influence. abr. ed. Brad Thor. Read by Armand Schultz. (Running Time: 6 hrs. 0 mins. 0 sec.). 2010. audio compact disk 29.99 (978-0-7435-7935-3(6)) Pub: S&S Audio. Dist(s): S and S Inc

Foreign Influence: A Thriller. unabr. ed. Brad Thor. Read by Armand Schultz. (Running Time: 11 hrs. 0 mins. 0 sec.). 2010. audio compact disk 39.99 (978-0-7435-7937-7(2)) Pub: S&S Audio. Dist(s): S and S Inc

Foreign Investment in the United States: A Practical Approach for the 1990s. 8 cass. (Running Time: 10 hrs. 30 min.). 1990. bk. 75.00 incl. 993-page course handbook. (T6-9145) PLI.

Foreign Land. unabr. collector's ed. Jonathan Raban. Read by David Case. 9 cass. (Running Time: 13 hrs. 30 min.). 1990. 72.00 (978-0-7366-1858-8(9), 2689) Books on Tape.
George Grey has been abroad for 40 years. He returns home nursing a vision of an England that has all but vanished. Everything seems cold & hostile. Moreover, George can't seem to make heads or tails of his only daughter, nor she him. Then George hatches his plan! He will escape - to the sea. Once embarked, George conjures up his earlier life - & the characters & events of the past become subtly, intricately interwoven with the demons & uncertainties of the present. These confused daydreams provide a counterpoint to his growing command of his boat & love of the sea.

***Foreign Language Teacher's Handbook in Spanish Version 2 & 3.** Lennon. (SPA.). 2009. tchr. ed. 37.95 (978-1-879279-35-3(5)) Proficiency Pr.

Foreign Language Teaching in the U. S. 1 cass. (Running Time: 1 hr.). 10.95 (G0430B09, HarperThor) HarpC GBR.

Foreign Policy: How Should America Be Defended? Read by David Friedman et al. 2 cass. (Running Time: 2 hrs.). (Cal Sate Univ., Long Beach Ser.). 1981. 18.00 (F127A & B) Freeland Pr.
Offers new ideas & practical solutions to this critical issue. Panel discussion.

Foreign Policy of a Mixed Economy: The Rebellion at Columbia University. Ayn Rand. Read by Ayn Rand. 1 cass. (Running Time: 60 min.). 12.95 (978-1-56114-012-1(0), AR23C) Second Renaissance.
Two presentations to college audiences: 1) How our program of foreign aid spreads the warfare of a mixed economy to an international battleground & who the actual profiteers are of this kind of global sacrifice. 2) The late 1960s saw mob rule at many of America's colleges. In this talk, Ayn Rand discusses the aims of the New Life movement & condemns the cowardly appeasement by the officials at Columbia.

Foreign Reserve Systems & Gold. unabr. ed. Robert Van Smit & Giuseppe Modiano. 1 cass. (Running Time: 1 hr. 27 min.). 12.95 (296) J Norton Pubs.

Foreign Rights Sales. Jeff Davidson. 1 CD. (Running Time: 60 min.). 2006. audio compact disk 23.95 (978-0-9771296-1-4(6)) Breath Space Inst.

Foreign Rights Sales for Your Book. Jeff Davidson. 2006. audio compact disk (978-1-60729-568-6(7)) Breath Space Inst.

Foreign Rights Sales for Your Book. Jeff Davidson. 2006. 22.95 (978-1-60729-342-2(0)) Breath Space Inst.

Foreign Service Institute (FSI) Courses, Pt. A. unabr. ed. 12 cass. (Running Time: 15 hrs.). (FRE.). 165.00 Set, incl. 194p. text. (F170) Books on Tape.

Foreign Service Institute (FSI) Courses, Pt. B. unabr. ed. 8 cass. (Running Time: 25 hrs.). (FRE.). 195.00 Set, incl. 290p. text. (F181) Books on Tape.

Foreign Service Institute (FSI) Courses, Vol. 1. unabr. ed. 10 cass. (Running Time: 13 hrs.). (GER.). 165.00 Set, incl. 161p. text. (G141); 165.00 Set, incl. 464p. text & manual. (S101) Books on Tape.
The basic concept is to learn a foreign language by hearing & imitating what is heard. Grammer rules are explained but the emphasis is on listening & repeating.

Foreign Student's Guide to Pronunciation: Using the Pronunciation Key of the American English Dictionary. Joan Ashkenas. 1 cass. 1986. 12.95 (978-0-943327-03-7(2)) JAG Pubns.
Follow the student text of the same title. Allows students to work individually or in small groups, learning to use the pronunciation key of the dictionary.

Forensic Chemistry. Compiled by Benchmark Education Staff. 2006. audio compact disk 10.00 (978-1-4108-6692-9(0)) Benchmark Educ.

Forensic Engineering: Diagnosing Failures & Solving Problems. Neale. 2005. audio compact disk (978-0-415-39525-0(9)) Taylor and Fran.

Forensic Science Experiments on File. Diagram Group. (gr. 6-12). 2005. audio compact disk 149.95 (978-0-8160-5814-3(8)) Facts On File.

Foreshortening & Other Stories. 1 cass. (Running Time: 60 min.). 1977. 10.00 (978-0-932360-29-8(7)) Archae Edns.
Rearranges eighty-four single-sentence-modules in systematically different ways, with two completely different readings-realizations of the text.

Forest. Edward Rutherfurd. Read by Lynn Redgrave. 3 cass. (Running Time: 5 hrs.). 2000. 25.00 (Random AudioBks) Random Audio Pubg.

Forest, Pt. 1. collector's ed. Edward Rutherfurd. Read by David Case. 10 cass. (Running Time: 15 hrs.). 2000. 80.00 (978-0-7366-4983-4(2), 5241-A) Books on Tape.
Edward Rutherfurd's new novel covers four centuries of British history, with the New Forest as background, culminating in a five family saga set in the days of Jane Austen. Few places in England are more resonant, more mysterious yet more friendly than the huge forest that lies by England's southern coast, that provided hunting for England's Saxon & Norman kings & whose ancient oaks were used to build Nelson's navy. It is against this rich backdrop that Rutherfurd tells a tale of woodsmen, monks, sailors, craftswomen & families who, in their evolution, developed what is known as the English character.

Forest, Pt. 2. collector's ed. Edward Rutherfurd. Read by David Case. 10 cass. (Running Time: 15 hrs.). 2000. 80.00 (978-0-7366-5055-7(5), 5241-B) Books on Tape.

Forest: A Dramatic Portrait of Life in the American Wild. unabr. ed. Roger A. Caras. Narrated by Sam Gray. 4 cass. (Running Time: 5 hrs. 15 mins.). 1993. 35.00 (978-1-55690-882-8(2), 93324E7) Recorded Bks.
Caras chooses the volatile, colorful life surrounding a 200-year-old regal hemlock as his milieu. He shows us life in the raw & the expediency of preserving the forest's invaluable cycles & rhythms.

Forest Fire. Prod. by Laraim Associates. (Barclay Family Adventure Ser.). (J). 2003. audio compact disk (978-1-56254-980-0(4)) Saddleback Edu.

Forest General Medical Center. 1997. 149.95 (978-0-8273-8180-3(8)) Delmar.

Forest House. abr. ed. Marion Zimmer Bradley. Read by Sue Carter. 2 cass. (Running Time: 3 hrs.). 2000. 7.95 (978-1-57815-009-0(4), 1062, Media Bks Audio) Media Bks NJ.
Tale of magic, romance & myth set in ancient Britain. Young Eilan, fate has predestined a struggle to the death for her land.

***Forest House.** unabr. ed. Marion Zimmer Bradley. Narrated by Rosalyn Landor. (Running Time: 18 hrs. 30 mins.). (Avalon Ser.). 2010. 22.99 (978-1-4001-8784-3(2)) Tantor Media.

***Forest House.** unabr. ed. Marion Zimmer Bradley. Narrated by Rosalyn Landor. (Running Time: 18 hrs. 0 mins. 0 sec.). (Avalon Ser.). (ENG.). 2010. 34.99 (978-1-4001-6784-5(1)); audio compact disk 119.99 (978-1-4001-4784-7(0)); audio compact disk 49.99 (978-1-4001-1784-0(4)) Pub: Tantor Media. Dist(s): IngramPubServ

Forest in the Rain. Read by Mary Richards. (Stress Reduction Ser.). 9.95 (096) Master Your Mind.

Forest in the Rain. Read by Mary Richards. 1 cass. (Running Time: 60 min.). (Energy Break Ser.). 2007. audio compact disk 19.95 (978-1-56136-156-4(9)) Master Your Mind.

***Forest Kingdom Saga 10: Beyond the Blue Moon (1 Of 2)** Simon R. Green. 2011. audio compact disk 19.99 (978-1-59950-741-5(2)) GraphicAudio.

***Forest Kingdom Saga 7: Hawk & Fisher 5: Guard Against Dishonor.** Simon R. Green. 2010. audio compact disk 19.99 (978-1-59950-718-7(8)) GraphicAudio.

***Forest Kingdom Saga 8: Hawk & Fisher Book 6:the Bones of Haven.** Simon R. Green. 2011. audio compact disk 19.99 (978-1-59950-723-1(4)) GraphicAudio.

***Forest Kingdom Saga 9: Down among the Dead Men.** Simon R. Green. 2011. audio compact disk 19.99 (978-1-59950-740-8(4)) GraphicAudio.

Forest Management or Mismanagement? Hosted by Nancy Pearlman. 1 cass. (Running Time: 28 min.). 10.00 (814) Educ Comm CA.

Forest of Eagles. unabr. ed. James Follett. 9 CDs. (Running Time: 38100 sec.). (Story Sound CD Ser.). 2006. audio compact disk 84.95 (978-1-85903-938-0(3)) Pub: Mgna Lrg Print GBR. Dist(s): Ulverscroft US

Forest of Eagles. unabr. ed. James Follett. Read by Glen McCready. 8 cass. (Story Sound Ser.). (J). 2006. 69.95 (978-1-85903-892-5(1)) Pub: Mgna Lrg Print GBR. Dist(s): Ulverscroft US

***Forest of Hands & Teeth.** unabr. ed. Carrie Ryan. Read by Vane Millon. 8 CDs. (Running Time: 9 hrs. 31 mins.). (YA). (gr. 9 up). 2009. audio compact disk 60.00 (978-0-7393-8536-4(4), Listening Lib) Pub: Random Audio Pubg. Dist(s): Random

Forest of Hands & Teeth. unabr. ed. Carrie Ryan. Read by Vane Millon. (J). (gr. 9). 2010. audio compact disk 40.00 (978-0-307-71031-4(9), Listening Lib) Pub: Random Audio Pubg. Dist(s): Random

Forest of Stars. unabr. ed. Kevin J. Anderson. 15 cass. (Running Time: 21 hrs.). (Saga of Seven Suns Ser.: Bk. 2). 2003. 99.75 (978-1-4025-3788-2(3)) Recorded Bks.

***Forest of Sure Things.** Megan Snyder-Camp. (ENG.). 2010. audio compact disk 12.00 (978-1-932195-98-9(X)) Tupelo Pr Inc.

Forest of the Pygmies. unabr. ed. Isabel Allende. Read by Blair Brown.Tr. of Bosque de los Pigmeos. (YA). 2005. audio compact disk 27.50 (978-0-06-078600-7(0), HarperChildAud) HarperCollins Pubs.

Forest Reflections. 2007. audio compact disk 19.95 (978-1-56136-401-5(0)) Master Your Mind.

Forest Song. Composed by L. A. Wendt. 1 cass. (Running Time: 60 min.). (Quiet Times Ser.). 1986. 9.98 (978-1-878328-01-4(8)) Realmusic.
Deep within a peaceful wood, a soft lyrical flute winds in counterpart with a gentle summer shower.

Forest Sounds. 1 cass. (Sounds of Nature Ser.). 10.98 (978-0-87554-255-3(7), M301) Valley Sun.
The Sounds of Nature are five beautiful releases that are wonderful aids for relaxation, meditation & visualization. It's all too easy to get caught up in the frantic pace of day-to-day living. Let the Sounds of Nature transport you to a special place.

Forest Warden & Champagne Safari. abr. ed. E. T. A. Hoffmann & Otto Lowy. 2 cass. (Running Time: 2 hrs.). (Mystery Theatre Ser.: Vol. 5). 2004. 18.99 (978-1-894003-23-0(3)) Pub: Scenario Prods CAN. Dist(s): PerseuPGW

Forests. Compiled by Benchmark Education Staff. 2005. audio compact disk 10.00 (978-1-4108-5493-3(0)) Benchmark Educ.

Forests of the Night. abr. ed. James W. Hall. Read by Laural Merlington. (Running Time: 6 hrs.). 2004. audio compact disk 74.25 (978-1-59600-321-7(9), 1596003219, BACDLib Ed) Brilliance Audio.
Patrol woman Charlotte Monroe has cop instincts. Scratch that. There isn't a name for the intuition she possesses, something that borders on psychic, an ability to read people's faces and body language like the morning headlines - to size up their intentions and act before they do. But none of that prepares her for the stranger who shows up on her doorstep with a chilling warning for her husband, a mysterious note scrawled in Cherokee hieroglyphics and a promise of things to come: "You're Next." The warning becomes more ominous as Charlotte and her husband, Parker, discover the complex truth about this man, including his position on the FBI Most Wanted list and his connection to their family. When Charlotte's deeply troubled teenage daughter runs away to join the charismatic outlaw, she follows them to the spectral mists of the Great Smoky Mountains - and to the beating heart of a 150-year-old blood feud that will endanger everything she loves and challenge everything she believes.

Forests of the Night. abr. ed. James W. Hall. Read by Laural Merlington. (Running Time: 21600 sec.). 2005. audio compact disk 16.99 (978-1-59737-664-8(7), 9781597376648, BCD Value Price) Brilliance Audio.

Forests of the Night. unabr. ed. James W. Hall. Read by Laural Merlington. (Running Time: 11 hrs.). 2004. 39.25 (978-1-59710-302-2(0), 1597103020, BADLE); 24.95 (978-1-59710-303-9(9), 1597103039, BAD); 24.95 (978-1-59600-322-4(7), 1596003227, Brilliance MP3); 39.25 (978-1-59600-323-1(5), 1596003235, Brlnc Audio MP3 Lib); 87.25 (978-1-59600-319-4(7), 1596003197, BrilAudUnabridg); 32.95 (978-1-59600-318-7(9), 1596003189, BAU) Brilliance Audio.

Forever. Kelly Caddell. 1 CD. (Running Time: 1 hr. 30 mins.). 1997. audio compact disk 5.99 (978-1-891020-16-2(1)) New Concepts.
Romance: They were lovers in another time & place. But evil threatens them.

Forever. abr. ed. Judith Gould. Read by Natalie West. 2 cass. (Running Time: 3 hrs.). 2000. 7.95 (978-1-57815-062-5(0), 1015, Media Bks Audio) Media Bks NJ.
A brutal murder catapults an investigative journalist into the mysterious & twisted world of a powerful, privileged family.

Forever. abr. ed. Judith Gould. Read by Natalie West. 3 vols. (YA). 2001. audio compact disk 11.99 (978-1-57815-518-7(5), Media Bks Audio) Media Bks NJ.

Forever. abr. ed. Judith Gould. Read by Natalie West. 2 cass. (Running Time: 3 hrs.). 1992. 15.95 Set. (978-1-879371-37-8(5), 40150) Pub Mills.
This is the latest action adventure romance from New York Times bestselling author Judith Gould. There is love & murder in the international jet-set from this ever popular storyteller.

Forever. abr. ed. Pete Hamill. Read by Stevie Ray Dallimore. 2006. 17.95 (978-0-7435-6130-3(9)) Pub: S&S Audio. Dist(s): S and S Inc

Forever. abr. ed. Karen Kingsbury. Read by Sandra Burr. (Running Time: 4 hrs.). (Firstborn Ser.). 2007. 39.25 (978-1-4233-0000-7(9), 9781423300007, BADLE); 9.99 (978-1-59737-999-1(9), 9781597379991, BAD); 49.25 (978-1-59737-656-3(6), 9781597376563, BAudLibEd); 19.95 (978-1-59737-655-6(8), 9781597376556); audio compact disk 69.25 (978-1-59737-658-7(2), 9781597376587, BACDLib Ed); audio compact disk 39.25 (978-1-59737-998-4(0), 9781597379984, Brlnc Audio MP3 Lib); audio compact disk 9.99 (978-1-59737-997-7(2), 9781597379977, Brilliance MP3); audio compact disk 21.95 (978-1-59737-657-0(4), 9781597376570, BACD) Brilliance Audio.

***Forever.** abr. ed. Karen Kingsbury. Read by Sandra Burr. (Running Time: 4 hrs.). (Firstborn Ser.). 2010. audio compact disk 9.99 (978-1-4418-7827-4(0), 9781441878274, BCD Value Price) Brilliance Audio.

Forever. unabr. ed. Pete Hamill. 17 cass. (Running Time: 24 hrs. 30 mins.). 2003. 135.00 (978-1-4025-4377-7(8)) Recorded Bks.

Forever. unabr. ed. Timmothy B. McCann. Narrated by Elizabeth Van Dyke. 12 cass. (Running Time: 16 hrs. 45 mins.). 2004. 98.00 (978-0-7887-9968-6(1)) Recorded Bks.

Forever Amber Brown. unabr. ed. Paula Danziger. Read by Dana Lubotsky. 1 cass. (Running Time: 1 hr. 6 mins.). (Amber Brown Ser.: No. 5). (J). (gr. 2-4). 1998. pap. bk. 17.00 (978-0-8072-0366-8(1), FTR185SP, Listening Lib) Random Audio Pubg.
Amber Brown is trying very hard to deal with the new changes in her life.

Forever & a Day. Contrib. by Easter Jeff & Sheri & Phil Johnson. Prod. by Michael Sykes. 2003. audio compact disk 16.98 (978-5-550-28227-4(5)) Sprg Hill Music Group.

Forever Blue: The True Story of Walter O'Malley, Baseball's Most Controversial Owner, & the Dodgers of Brooklyn & Los Angeles. unabr. ed. Michael D'Antonio. Read by Phil Gigante. 1 MP3-CD. (Running Time: 13 hrs.). 2009. 24.99 (978-1-4233-8416-8(4), 9781423384168, Brilliance MP3); 39.97 (978-1-4233-8417-5(2), 9781423384175, Brlnc Audio MP3 Lib); 39.97 (978-1-4233-8419-9(9), 9781423384199, BADLE); 24.99 (978-1-4233-8418-2(0), 9781423384182, BAD); audio compact disk 99.97 (978-1-4233-8415-1(6), 9781423384151, BriAudCD Unabrid); audio compact disk 34.99 (978-1-4233-8414-4(8), 9781423384144, Bril Audio CD Unabri) Brilliance Audio.

Forever Dog. Bill Cochran. 1 cass. (Running Time: 8 hrs. 30 mins.). 2007. pap. bk. 27.95 (978-0-89456-955-5(4)) Spoken Arts.

Forever Dog. Bill Cochran. 1 cass. (Running Time: 9 mins.). (J). (ps-2). 2007. bk. 27.95 (978-0-8045-6955-2(X)) Spoken Arts.

Forever Dog. unabr. ed. Bill Cochran. 1 CD. (Running Time: 9 mins.). (J). (ps-2). 2007. bk. 29.95 (978-0-8045-4177-0(9)) Spoken Arts.

Forever, for Now: Poems for a Later Love. Louis Daniel Brodsky. 1991. 12.95 (978-1-877770-31-9(0)) Time Being Bks.

Forever Free: Conquering Fear Once & for All. Creflo A. Dollar. (ENG.). 2006. 15.00 (978-1-59944-085-9(7)); audio compact disk 21.00 (978-1-59944-086-6(5)) Creflo Dollar.

Forever Free of Cigarettes: Classic. Eldon Taylor. Read by Eldon Taylor. Ed. by Leslie Brice. 1 cass. (Running Time: 1 hr.). 1992. 16.95 (978-1-56705-033-2(6)) Gateways Inst.
Self improvement.

Forever Free of Cigarettes: Easy. Eldon Taylor. Read by Eldon Taylor. Ed. by Leslie Brice. 1 cass. (Running Time: 1 hr.). 1992. 16.95 (978-1-56705-034-9(4)) Gateways Inst.

Forever Free of Cigarettes: Harmonies. Eldon Taylor. Read by Eldon Taylor. Ed. by Leslie Brice. 1 cass. (Running Time: 1 hr.). 1992. 16.95 (978-1-56705-035-6(2)) Gateways Inst.

Forever Free of Cigarettes: Ocean. Eldon Taylor. Read by Eldon Taylor. Ed. by Leslie Brice. 1 cass. (Running Time: 1 hr.). 1992. 16.95 (978-1-56705-036-3(0)) Gateways Inst.

Forever Free of Cigarettes: Soundtrack: Leisure Listening. Eldon Taylor. 1 cass. (Running Time: 62 min.). 16.95 (978-0-940699-05-2(2), 5301B) Progress Aware Res.
Musical soundtrack with underlying subliminal affirmations.

Forever Free of Cigarettes: Soundtrack: Musical Themes. Eldon Taylor. 1 cass. (Running Time: 62 min.). 16.95 incl. script. (978-0-940699-04-5(4), 5301C) Progress Aware Res.

Forever Free of Cigarettes: Soundtrack: Synthesized Moments. Eldon Taylor. 1 cass. (Running Time: 62 min.). 16.95 incl. script. (978-0-940699-72-4(9), 5301D) Progress Aware Res.

Forever Free of Cigarettes: Soundtrack: Tropical Lagoon. Eldon Taylor. 1 cass. (Running Time: 62 min.). 16.95 (978-0-940699-73-1(7), 5301A) Progress Aware Res.
Environmental soundtrack with underlying subliminal affirmations.

Forever Free of Cigarettes: Stream. Eldon Taylor. Read by Eldon Taylor. Ed. by Leslie Brice. 1 cass. (Running Time: 1 hr.). 1992. 16.95 (978-1-56705-037-0(9)) Gateways Inst.
Self improvement.

Forever Free of Cigarettes: Whisper. Eldon Taylor. Read by Eldon Taylor. Ed. by Leslie Brice. 1 cass. (Running Time: 1 hr.). 1992. 16.95 (978-1-56705-197-1(9)) Gateways Inst.

Forever Free of Nail Biting: Babbling Brook. Eldon Taylor. 1 cass. 16.95 (978-1-55978-477-1(6), 5343F) Progress Aware Res.

Forever Generation: 1 John 2:12-17. 1984. 4.95 (978-0-7417-1369-8(1), 369) Win Walk.

Forever I Do Vol. 2: With This Ring. audio compact disk 16.98 Provident Music.

Forever in Blue: The Fourth Summer of the Sisterhood. unabr. ed. Ann Brashares. Read by Angela Goethals. 7 CDs. (Running Time: 9 hrs. 3 mins.). (Sisterhood of the Traveling Pants Ser.: Bk. 4). (YA). 2007. audio compact disk 44.00 (978-0-7393-4845-1(0)) Books on Tape.

Forever in Blue: The Fourth Summer of the Sisterhood. unabr. ed. Ann Brashares. Read by Angela Goethals. (Running Time: 32580 sec.). (Sisterhood of the Traveling Pants Ser.: Bk. 4). (ENG.). (J). (gr. 7 up). 2007. audio compact disk 19.99 (978-1-4000-9859-0(9), Listening Lib) Pub: Random Audio Pubg. Dist(s): Random

Forever in My Heart. abr. ed. Jo Goodman. Read by Jessica Arden. 1 cass. (Running Time: 90 min.). 1995. 5.99 (978-1-57096-034-5(8), RAZ 934) Romance Alive Audio.
Injured & lost, naive heiress Mary Margaret Dennehy is thrown together with rakish Colorado rancher Connor Holiday for a night of lingering passion in a New York City bordello. Fate takes a hand when an arranged marriage between the two allows them to put aside the past & uncover a sweet, enduring love that they both have longed for in their hearts.

Forever in Your Embrace, Set. abr. ed. Kathleen E. Woodiwiss. 4 cass. 1999. 24.95 (FS9-51089) Highsmith.

Forever Kate, Set. Cheri Crane. 2 cass. 1999. 3.47 (978-1-57734-146-8(5), 07001584) Covenant Comms.
A story about friends, falling in love, & facing the future.

***Forever Mine: L-Book.** KD Williamson. 2009. 10.95 (978-1-934889-49-7(0)) Lbook Pub.

Forever Odd. unabr. ed. Dean Koontz. Read by David Aaron Baker. (Running Time: 30600 sec.). (Odd Thomas Ser.: No. 2). (ENG.). 2008. audio compact disk 19.99 (978-0-7393-6941-8(5), Random AudioBks) Pub: Random Audio Pubg. Dist(s): Random

Forever Odd. unabr. collector's ed. Dean Koontz. 7 cass. (Running Time: 10 hrs.). (Odd Thomas Ser.: No. 2). 2005. 63.00 (978-1-4159-2491-4(0)); audio compact disk 76.50 (978-1-4159-2492-1(9)) Pub: Books on Tape. Dist(s): NetLibrary CO

Forever Ours: Real Stories of Immortality & Living from a Forensic Pathologist. unabr. ed. Read by Janis Amatuzio. (Running Time: 4 hrs. 0 mins. 0 sec.). (ENG.). 2005. audio compact disk 24.95 (978-1-57731-520-9(0)) Pub: New Wrld Lib. Dist(s): PerseuPGW

Forever Peace. unabr. ed. Joe Haldeman. Narrated by George Wilson. 9 cass. (Running Time: 13 hrs.). 2000. 81.00 (978-0-7887-4887-5(4), 96418E7) Recorded Bks.
War in the 21st century is fought by remote-controlled mechanical monsters. As human soldiers hard-wire their brains together to form each military unit, their conflicts become a riveting portrayal of the effects of collective consciousness.

***Forever Princess.** unabr. ed. Meg Cabot. Narrated by Clea Lewis. 1 Playaway. (Running Time: 10 hrs. 15 mins.). (Princess Diaries: Bk. 10). (YA). (gr. 7-10). 2009. 59.75 (978-1-4407-0383-6(3)); 67.75 (978-1-4361-8754-1(0)); audio compact disk 97.75 (978-1-4361-8758-9(3)) Recorded Bks.

***Forever Princess.** unabr. collector's ed. Meg Cabot. Narrated by Clea Lewis. 9 CDs. (Running Time: 10 hrs. 15 mins.). (Princess Diaries: Bk. 10). (YA). (gr. 7-10). 2009. audio compact disk 46.95 (978-1-4361-8762-6(1)) Recorded Bks.

Forever Slim. Eldon Taylor. 2 cass. (Running Time: 62 min. per cass.). (Omniphonics Ser.). 29.95 incl. script Set. (978-1-55978-816-8(X), 4017) Progress Aware Res.
3-D soundtrack with underlying subliminal affirmations, night & day versions.

Forever Smoke Free: Stop Smoking Hypnosis. Trevor H. Scott. 2003. audio compact disk 39.95 (978-0-9763138-1-6(2)) Beverly Hills CA.

Forever Texas: Texas, the Way Those Who Lived it Wrote It. 8 cass. (Running Time: 11 hrs. 30 mins.). 73.00 (978-1-4025-3705-9(0)) Recorded Bks.

Forever the Victim... I Don't Think So, Set. T. D. Jakes. 3 cass. 1999. 15.00 (978-1-57855-324-2(5)) T D Jakes.

Forever Thin. Eldon Taylor. 1 cass. (Running Time: 62 min.). (Inner Talk Ser.). 16.95 incl. script. (978-1-55978-163-3(7), 53781C) Progress Aware Res.
Soundtrack - Musical Themes with underlying subliminal affirmations.

Forever Thin: Babbling Brook. Eldon Taylor. 1 cass. 16.95 (978-1-55978-499-3(7), 53781F) Progress Aware Res.

Forever Today. Deborah Wearing. (Soundings (CDs) Ser.). 2006. audio compact disk 99.95 (978-1-84559-447-3(9)) Pub: ISIS Lrg Prnt GBR. Dist(s): Ulverscroft US

Forever Today: A Memoir of Love & Amnesia. unabr. ed. Deborah Wearing. Read by Deborah Wearing. 10 cass. (Soundings Ser.). 2006. 84.95 (978-1-84559-395-7(2)) Pub: ISIS Lrg Prnt GBR. Dist(s): Ulverscroft US

Forever Trap: An Exclusive Audio Adventure. unabr. ed. Dan Abnett. Narrated by Catherine Tate. (Running Time: 1 hr. 30 mins. 0 sec.). (ENG.). 2010. audio compact disk 24.95 (978-1-60283-821-5(6)) Pub: AudioGO. Dist(s): Perseus Dist

Forever War. abr. ed. Dexter Filkins. Read by Dexter Filkins. 5 CDs. (Running Time: 6 hrs.). (ENG.). 2008. audio compact disk 29.95 (978-0-7393-7060-5(X), Random AudioBks) Pub: Random Audio Pubg. Dist(s): Random

Forever War. unabr. ed. Dexter Filkins. Read by Robertson Dean. 9 CDs. 2008. audio compact disk 110.00 (978-1-4159-5781-3(9), BksonTape) Pub: Random Audio Pubg. Dist(s): Random

Forever War. unabr. ed. Joe Haldeman. Narrated by George Wilson. 7 cass. (Running Time: 9 hrs. 30 mins.). 1999. 60.00 (978-0-7887-3773-2(2), 95990E7) Recorded Bks.
William Mandela is a soldier in Earth's elite brigade. But as the war against the Taurans sends him from galaxy to galaxy, the world he calls home is passing away.

Forever War. unabr. ed. Joe Haldeman. Narrated by George Wilson. 8 CDs. (Running Time: 9 hrs. 30 mins.). 2000. audio compact disk 75.00 (978-0-7887-3983-5(2), C1146E7) Recorded Bks.
William Mandella is a soldier in Earth's elite brigade. But as the war against the Taurans sends him from galaxy to galaxy, the world he calls home is passing away.

Forever Young. 2 CDs. audio compact disk 16.98 (978-1-57908-439-4(7)) Platinm Enter.

Forever Young. Created by Zoilita Grant. 2001. audio compact disk 15.95 (978-1-890575-34-2(8)) Zoilita Grant.

Forever Young: Harmonies. Eldon Taylor. Read by Eldon Taylor. Ed. by Leslie Brice. 1 cass. (Running Time: 1 hr.). 1992. 16.95 (978-1-56705-171-1(5)) Gateways Inst.
Self improvement.

Forever Young: My Friendship with John F Kennedy Jr. William S. Noonan. (Running Time: 30600 sec.). 2006. audio compact disk 34.99 (978-1-4281-1341-1(X)) Pub: Recorded Bks. Dist(s): NetLibrary CO

Forever Young: Ocean. Eldon Taylor. Read by Eldon Taylor. Ed. by Leslie Brice. 1 cass. (Running Time: 1 hr.). 1992. 16.95 (978-1-56705-172-8(3)) Gateways Inst.

Forever Young: Stream. Eldon Taylor. Read by Eldon Taylor. Ed. by Leslie Brice. 1 cass. (Running Time: 1 hr.). 1992. 16.95 (978-1-56705-173-5(1)) Gateways Inst.

Forever Young, Fit & Healthy. Eldon Taylor. Read by Eldon Taylor. 1 cass. (Running Time: 62 min.). (Inner Talk Ser.). 16.95 incl. script. (978-1-55978-374-3(5), 53808A) Progress Aware Res.
Soundtrack - Tropical Lagoon with underlying subliminal affirmations.

Forever Young, Fit & Healthy: Babbling Brook. Eldon Taylor. 1 cass. 16.95 (978-1-55978-523-5(3), 53808F) Progress Aware Res.

Forever Young, Fit & Healthy: Contemporary Moments. Eldon Taylor. 1 cass. 16.95 (978-1-55978-607-2(8), 53808N) Progress Aware Res.

Forever Yours Faithfully: My Love Story. Lorrie Morgan. 2000. 18.00 (978-0-7881-9187-9(X)) DIANE Pub.

Forevermore. abr. ed. Cathy Marie Hake. Narrated by Brooke Sanford. (ENG.). 2008. 16.09 (978-1-60814-221-7(3)); audio compact disk 22.99 (978-1-59859-318-1(8)) Oasis Audio.

Foreverness of Friends of a Feather, Set. Esther Hicks & Jerry Hicks. (Running Time: 10800 sec.). (Sara Ser.: Bk. 1). 2008. audio compact disk 17.95 (978-1-4019-2025-8(X)) Hay House.

***Foreword: I Think My Son Is A Catch: Selection from Things I've Learned from Women Who've Dumped Me.** abr. ed. Ben Karlin. (Running Time: 3 mins.). (ENG.). 2010. 1.98 (978-1-60788-802-4(5)) Pub: Hachet Audio. Dist(s): HachBkGrp

Forex Trading for Living: Strategy & Analyses. 2005. audio compact disk (978-0-9743923-4-9(0), GCC Pubs) Lib Soldiers.

Forfeit. unabr. ed. Dick Francis. Read by Richard Brown. 6 cass. (Running Time: 9 hrs.). 1991. 48.00 (978-0-7366-1885-4(6), 2714) Books on Tape.
James Tyrone, a racing reporter for a London scandal sheet, knows that fellow reporter Bert Chekov is a drunk, though always an honest one. But when Bert dies in an "accidental" fall, Tyrone suspects a clue to his death may be found in Bert's columns touting can't-lose horses. Somehow those horses always failed to show up on race day.

Forfeits see Twentieth-Century Poetry in English, No. 26, Recordings of Poets Reading Their Own Poetry

Forge. unabr. ed. Laurie Halse Anderson. Read by Tim Cain. (Running Time: 8 hrs.). (Chains Ser.). (YA). 2010. 24.99 (978-1-4233-6738-3(3), 9781423367383) Brilliance Audio.

***Forge.** unabr. ed. Laurie Halse Anderson. (Running Time: 7 hrs.). (Chains Ser.). (YA). 2010. 24.99 (978-1-4233-6740-6(5), 9781423367406, BAD); 39.97 (978-1-4233-6741-3(3), 9781423367413, BADLE) Brilliance Audio.

Forge. unabr. ed. Laurie Halse Anderson. Read by Tim Cain. (Running Time: 8 hrs.). (Chains Ser.). (YA). 2010. audio compact disk 29.99 (978-1-4233-6736-9(7), 9781423367369, Bril Audio CD Unabri) Brilliance Audio.

***Forge.** unabr. ed. Laurie Halse Anderson. Read by Tim Cain. (Running Time: 8 hrs.). (Chains Ser.). (YA). 2010. 39.97 (978-1-4233-6739-0(1), 9781423367390, Brinc Audio MP3 Lib); audio compact disk 74.97 (978-1-4233-6737-6(5), 9781423367376, BriAudCD Unabrid) Brilliance Audio.

Forge of Union, Anvil of Liberty. unabr. ed. Jeffrey St. John. Read by Jeff Riggenbach. 5 cass. (Running Time: 7 hrs.). 1999. 39.95 (978-0-7861-1627-0(7), 2455) Blckstn Audio.
Based on documented & newly-available sources, this is both a popular history & an important contribution to the study of the founding of the American Republic.

Forge of Union, Anvil of Liberty: A Correspondent's Report on the First Federal Elections, the First Federal Congress, & the Creation of the Bill of Rights. unabr. ed. Jeffrey St John. Read by Jeff Riggenbach. Frwd. by Warren E. Burger. (Running Time: 25200 sec.). 2007. audio compact disk 29.95 (978-0-7861-0131-3(8)) Blckstn Audio.

Forged by Fire. unabr. ed. Sharon M. Draper. Narrated by Thomas Penny. 3 pieces. (Running Time: 3 hrs. 45 mins.). (Hazelwood High Trilogy: Bk. 2). (gr. 7 up). 2002. 34.00 (978-1-4025-0892-9(1)) Recorded Bks.
Gerald is only three years old when his mama leaves him alone in the house while she visits her drug dealer. He finds the hot thing she uses to light her cigarettes and in no time, the house is ablaze. Mama is sent to prison, and Gerald goes to live with his Aunt Queen. When he turns nine, Gerald unhappily learns that his mama is being released from jail and wants her son back. Suddenly, he must switch from a loving home to a household dominated by his abusive stepfather. When Gerald learns a terrible secret about his stepfather and the half-sister he has grown to love, he'll have to find the courage to do what's right.

Forged by Honor. unabr. ed. Ronald Wanttaja. Read by Cameron Beierle. 6 cass. (Running Time: 6 hrs.). 2001. 39.95 (978-1-58116-052-9(6)) Books in Motion.
Young Nate Lawton's bravery in combat has earned him midshipman's rank. But he hides a shipment of neglect of duty and honor, an honor he is determined to regain aboard the USS Chesapeake when it squares off against the British blockage of Boston harbor.

***Forged in Faith: How Faith Shaped the Birth of the Nation 1607-1776.** unabr. ed. Rod Gragg. Narrated by Maurice England. (Running Time: 7 hrs. 16 mins. 0 sec.). (ENG.). 2010. 18.19 (978-1-60814-678-9(2)); audio compact disk 25.99 (978-1-59859-727-1(2)) Oasis Audio.

Forged in Honor. unabr. ed. Leonard B. Scott. Read by Edward Lewis. 10 cass. (Running Time: 14 hrs. 30 mins.). 1999. 69.95 (978-0-7861-1027-8(9), 1802) Blckstn Audio.
When retired Special Forces colonel Joshua Hawkins is recalled to active duty by order of the President, he must return to a past he could never lay to rest. Hawkins is called again to serve his country, to save his Shan friend Steven & to help the brave people he has never forgotten in their fight against a corrupt government & a ruthless heroin syndicate.

Forged in Steel: Steel Works Stories. Chuck Canty & Jeff Manes. Ed. by Chuck Canty. 1 CD. (Running Time: 1 hr.). 2002. audio compact disk 15.00 (978-0-9721641-0-8(3)) Osage Home.
A collection of stories and poems about life in a steel working environment. These writings are emotionally charged and bring together voices and vision of what it is like working in a heavy industrial job. A testament of a hard working class of people.

***Forged of Shadows: A Novel of the Marked Souls.** unabr. ed. Jessa Slade. (Running Time: 13 hrs. 30 mins.). 2010. audio compact disk 19.95 (978-1-4417-3468-6(6)) Blckstn Audio.

***Forged of Shadows: A Novel of the Marked Souls.** unabr. ed. Jessa Slade. Read by Renée Raudman. (Running Time: 13 hrs. 30 mins.). 2010. 29.95 (978-1-4417-3469-3(4)); 79.95 (978-1-4417-3465-5(1)); audio compact disk 109.00 (978-1-4417-3466-2(X)) Blckstn Audio.

Forgery of Venus. unabr. ed. Michael Gruber. Read by Eric Conger. 9 CDs. (Running Time: 11 hrs. 30 mins.). 2008. audio compact disk 39.95 (978-0-06-145304-5(8), Harper Audio) HarperCollins Pubs.

***Forgery of Venus.** unabr. ed. Michael Gruber. Read by Eric Conger. (ENG.). 2008. (978-0-06-163261-7(9)); (978-0-06-163262-4(7)) HarperCollins Pubs.

***Forget me Not.** Anne Cassidy. Read by Nicky Talacko. (Running Time: 6 hrs. 15 mins.). (YA). 2009. 64.99 (978-1-74214-548-8(5), 9781742145488) Pub: Bolinda Pubng AUS. Dist(s): Bolinda Pub Inc

Forget Me Not. abr. ed. Michele Ashman Bell. 4 CDs. (Running Time: 4 Hours, 30 Mins.). 2005. audio compact disk 15.95 (978-1-59156-731-8(9)) Covenant Comms.

Forget Me Not. abr. ed. Elizabeth Lowell. Read by Laural Merlington. (Running Time: 14400 sec.). 2008. audio compact disk 14.99 (978-1-4233-2398-3(X), 9781423323983, BCD Value Price) Brilliance Audio.

Forget-Me-Not. unabr. ed. Emma Blair. Read by Clare Higgins. 10 cass. (Running Time: 15 hrs.). 2002. 84.95 (978-0-7540-0735-7(9), CAB 2157) AudioGO.
Devon, 1912, and Tim Wilson cannot believe his luck. He has landed the job of his dreams as a newspaper reporter, and he is captivated by Katherine Coates Romance blossoms, but their happiness is short-lived, for Katherine's mother, Ruth, has her sights set much higher for her daughter's happiness. Tim is neither rich nor well connected enough for her liking and she breaks up the relationship by whisking Katherine off to the London scene to meet a suitable husband.

Forget-Me-Not. unabr. ed. Emma Blair. Read by Clare Higgins. 12 CDs. (Running Time: 18 hrs.). 2002. audio compact disk 110.95 (978-0-7540-5468-9(3), CCD 159) AudioGO.

***Forget Me Not.** unabr. ed. Anne Cassidy. Read by Nicky Talacko. 5 CDs. (Running Time: 6 hrs. 15 mins.). (YA). (gr. 9 up). 2009. audio compact disk 40.00 (978-1-74201-789-1(4), Bolinda Audio Bks) Bolinda Pub Inc.

Forget me Not. unabr. ed. Anne Cassidy. Read by Nicky Talacko. (Running Time: 6 hrs. 15 mins.). (YA). 2009. audio compact disk 63.95 (978-1-74214-113-8(7), 9781742141138) Pub: Bolinda Pubng AUS. Dist(s): Bolinda Pub Inc

Forget Me Not. unabr. ed. Elizabeth Lowell. Read by Laural Merlington. (Running Time: 8 hrs.). 2007. 39.25 (978-1-4233-2396-9(3), 9781423323969, BADLE); 24.95 (978-1-4233-2395-2(5), 9781423323952, BAD); 69.25 (978-1-4233-2390-7(4), 9781423323907, BrilAudUnabridg); audio compact disk 24.95 (978-1-4233-2393-8(9), 9781423323938, Brilliance MP3); audio compact disk 34.95 (978-1-4233-2391-4(2), 9781423323914, Bril Audio CD Unabri); audio compact disk 87.25 (978-1-4233-2392-1(0), 9781423323921, BriAudCD Unabrid); audio compact disk 39.25 (978-1-4233-2394-5(7), 9781423323945, Brinc Audio MP3 Lib) Brilliance Audio.

Forget the Price, Wrap It Up: Matthew 13:44-47. Ed Young. (J). 1981. 4.95 (978-0-7417-1196-0(6), A0196) Win Walk.

Forget What You Can't Remember. Teel McClanahan, 3rd. Narrated by Teel McClanahan, 3rd. 2009. 13.99 (978-1-934516-77-5(5)); audio compact disk 26.99 (978-1-934516-78-2(3)) Modern Evil.

Forgetful Fred. Created by Rigby Staff. 1993. 10.40 (978-0-435-05951-4(3), Rigby PEA) Pearson EdAUS AUS.

Forgetting Everything Else. Swami Amar Jyoti. 1 cass. 1982. 9.95 (M-29) Truth Consciousness.
Courage, faith & one-pointedness to transcend EVERYTHING, roses as well as thorns.

Forgetting Room. unabr. ed. Nick Bantock. 1 cass. (Running Time: 90 min.). 1997. 12.00 (978-0-694-51899-9(9), CPN 10124) HarperCollins Pubs.

Forging the System Vendor & Var Relationship: The Expectations: Selling Optical Systems. 1 cass. 1990. 8.50 Recorded Res.

Forgive & Forget. unabr. ed. Dee Williams. Read by Kim Hicks. 8 cass. (Running Time: 12 hrs.). 2002. 69.95 (978-0-7540-0745-6(6), CAB 2167) AudioGO.
As the Second World War enters its final year, Ruth Bentley feels that her life has dealt her more than her fair share of trials and tribulations. For the second time she has lost her home in a bomb attack on the Rotherhithe, and with her husband away fighting, her two daughters evacuated to Wales, and her mother killed and her father seriously injured in the attack, Ruth is left to face the devastation alone. But Ruth finds friendship with Lucy, and both women dream of the day when they'll be reunited with their loved ones.

Forgive & Release. Dick Sutphen. 1 cass. (Running Time: 1 hr.). (RX17 Ser.). 14.98 (978-0-87554-381-9(2), RX145) Valley Sun.

Forgive Me. abr. unabr. ed. Amanda Eyre Ward. Read by Ann Marie Lee. (Running Time: 27000 sec.). (ENG.). 2007. audio compact disk 29.95 (978-0-7393-4410-1(2), Random AudioBks) Pub: Random Audio Pubg. Dist(s): Random

Forgiven. abr. ed. Karen Kingsbury. Read by Sandra Burr. (Running Time: 4 hrs.). (Firstborn Ser.). 2005. 39.25 (978-1-59737-964-9(6), 9781597379649, BADLE); 9.99 (978-1-59737-963-2(8), 9781597379632, BAD); 49.25 (978-1-59600-198-5(4), 9781596001985, BAudLibEd); 19.95 (978-1-59600-197-8(6), 9781596001978); audio compact disk 21.95 (978-1-59600-199-2(2), 9781596001992, BACD); audio compact disk 69.25 (978-1-59600-200-5(X), 9781596002005, BACDLib Ed); audio compact disk 39.25 (978-1-59737-962-5(X), 9781597379625, Brinc Audio MP3 Lib); audio compact disk 9.99 (978-1-59737-961-8(1), 9781597379618, Brilliance MP3) Brilliance Audio.
A Deadly Accident The Christian Kids Theater group is devastated by a tragedy greater than any of them could've imagined. Now their director, Katy Hart, must find a way to walk the kids through their grief and give them a reason to believe again. But will hatred and revenge have the final word? An Aching Emptiness Dayne Matthews is at the top of the Hollywood list, working on what could be his best movie yet. Still, he is empty and unfocused, aching for real love and the family he'll never know. Then a friend tells him about a teaching center and a way to become like God. Is this the answer Dayne's been searching for? A Shocking Discovery John Baxter reconnects with an old friend and shares a buried secret, one that he and his wife shared all their married lives. Now - in his wife's honor - he decides to continue a very special search. But in the process he makes a critical mistake. What will happen when one of his daughters stumbles onto a letter she was never supposed to see? In this season for the Baxters, grace and redemption will play a greater role than ever before.

***Forgiven.** abr. ed. Karen Kingsbury. Read by Sandra Burr. (Running Time: 4 hrs.). (Firstborn Ser.). 2010. audio compact disk 9.99 (978-1-4418-7824-3(6), 9781441878243, BCD Value Price) Brilliance Audio.

***Forgiven.** unabr. ed. Shelley Shepard Gray. (Running Time: 9 hrs.). (Sisters of the Heart Ser.: Bk. 3). 2010. 29.95 (978-1-4417-7102-5(6)) Blckstn Audio.

Forgiven, Forgiving & Free. 2001. (978-0-940110-26-7(1)) Life Action Publishing.

***Forgiven (Library Edition) (Sisters of the Heart, Book 3)** unabr. ed. Shelley Shepard Gray. Read by Kirsten Potter. (Running Time: 9 hrs.). (Sisters of the Heart Ser.: Bk. 3). 2010. 34.95 (978-1-4417-7099-8(2)); audio compact disk 55.00 (978-1-4417-7100-1(X)) Blckstn Audio.

***Forgiven to Forgive - CD.** Theodore Kober et al. Narrated by Gene Walth. Jeff Hansen. 2010. audio compact disk 10.00 (978-0-9767874-5-7(8)) Ambassadors of Rec.

Forgiveness. Rick Brown. Read by Rick Brown. Ed. by John Quatro. 1 cass. (Running Time: 30 min.). (Subliminal - Easy Listening Ser.). 1993. 10.95 (978-1-57100-022-4(4), E155); 10.95 (978-1-57100-046-0(1), J155); 10.95 (978-1-57100-070-5(4), N155); 10.95 (978-1-57100-094-1(1), S155); 10.95 (978-1-57100-118-4(2), W155); 10.95 (978-1-57100-142-9(5), H155) Sublime Sftware.
Forgiveness is not forgetting. Teaches self-forgiveness.

Forgiveness. Kenneth Copeland. 1 cass. 1982. 5.00 (978-0-88114-000-2(7)) K Copeland Pubns.
Indepth biblical study on love.

Forgiveness. Perf. by Rhonda Gunn. Prod. by Bryan Lenox & Billy Smiley. 1 cass. audio compact disk (D8000) Diamante Music Grp.
Forgiveness brings a fresh musical & lyrical approach to songs of forgiveness, hope & healing.

Forgiveness. Contrib. by Lee Leferre. 1 cass. (Running Time: 38 min.). 1998. 6.00 (978-1-57838-123-4(1)) CrossLife Express.
Biblical perspectives on forgiveness.

Forgiveness. Interview with Mother Angelica & AnneMarie Schmidt. 1 cass. (Running Time: 60 min.). (Mother Angelica Live Ser.). 10.00 (978-1-55794-084-1(3), T35) Eternal Wrd TV.

Forgiveness. Derek Prince. 1 cass. 5.95 (056) Derek Prince.
Forgiveness centers in the cross - vertically from God to man, horizontally toward our fellow man.

Forgiveness: Key to Peace. Galexis. 2 cass. (Running Time: 3 hrs.). 1995. 17.95 Set. (978-1-56089-030-0(4)) Visionary FL.
Grand emotional healing, releasing the past, & creating a new foundation for joy. Incredibly powerful!. Includes meditation on Side 4.

Forgiveness: Mobilizing a Power Filled Life. Rick Joyner et al. 2005. audio compact disk 19.99 (978-1-929371-62-4(4)) Pub: Morning NC. Dist(s): Destiny Image Pubs

Forgiveness: Program from the Award Winning Public Radio Series. Hosted by Fred Goodwin. Comment by John Hockenberry. Contrib. by Robert Enright et al. 1 cass. (Running Time: 1 hr.). (Infinite Mind Ser.). 1998. audio compact disk 21.95 (978-1-888064-49-0(8), LCM 6) Lichtenstein Creat.
"As we forgive those who trespass against us" seems to have a basis in fact. New scientific research indicates that people who forgive are healthier and happier than those who hold a grudge - no matter how deep the wound. We'll be joined by leading forgiveness researcher, Dr. Robert Enright, plus those who have much to forgive - including former hostage Terry Anderson. Also - every generation thinks their kids are the most trouble ever - we'll examine if today's kids are the most violent. With John Hockenberry and listener calls.

Forgiveness: Release all Anger & Blame. Forgiveness for Self & Others. Heraty Eugenie. 2007. 16.98 (978-1-934332-01-6(1), Heal Voice) Inter Med Pub.

Forgiveness: Removing the Blocks to Peace. Read by Tara Singh. 1 cass. (Running Time: 60 min.). 1996. 10.95 (978-1-55531-279-4(9)) Life Action Pr.
We think that forgiving means pardoning a wrong. However, true forgiveness removes all judgments - introducing us to limitless peace.

Forgiveness: Returning to the Original Blessing. Paul Ferrini. Read by Paul Ferrini. Perf. by Michael Gray. 1 cass. (Running Time: 1 hr.). 1991. 10.00 (978-1-879159-12-9(0)) Heartways Pr.
This tape helps us learn from our mistakes, bringing our darkness to the light, dissolving anger, guilt & shame, & ending our ego-based search for perfection.

Forgiveness: The Greatest Healer of All, unabr. ed. Gerald G. Jampolsky. Read by Gerald G. Jampolsky. 2 cass. (Running Time: 3 hrs.). 2000. 18.00 (978-1-57453-378-1(9)) Audio Lit.
Concise & pertinent, it spells out why it is beneficial, even physically, to develop the willingness to forgive. This book describes what makes people hold on to grievances & how to let them go. Seasoned with uplifting stories, he inspires all who have suffered to open their hearts to love, harmony & health.

Forgiveness: The Only Approach to Problem-Solving. unabr. ed. 3 cass. (Running Time: 4 hrs.). 1994. 24.95 Set. (978-1-889642-04-8(5)) C Howe.
This set is for those who have "done it all" or think they must, & still find that lasting peace & happiness elude them. It "hits home" as we realize most attempts at problem-solving fail often leading to greater difficulties. Through this very humorous presentation, one discovers: The change of perception & attitude, rather than technique or strategy, which allows difficulties to melt away. The true meaning of forgiveness, through which feelings of safety, abundance, & contentment increase miraculously.

Forgiveness - Loving the Inner Child. Louise L. Hay. Read by Louise L. Hay. 1 cass. (Running Time: 56 min.). (Personal Power Through Imagery Ser.). 1989. 15.00 CD, 61 mins. (802) Hay House.
Helps you, through imagery, to forgive others who need forgiving & love your inner child.

Forgiveness - Loving the Inner Child. Louise L. Hay. Read by Louise L. Hay. 1 cass. (Running Time: 56 mins.). (Personal Power Through Imagery Ser.). 1989. 10.95 (978-0-937611-61-6(1), 222) Hay House.

Forgiveness - Releasing Hurts. Patricia O'Malley. Perf. by Barry Weiss. 1 cass. (Running Time: 50 min.). 1998. (978-1-892450-05-0(4), 110) Promo Music.
Guided imagery.

Forgiveness & the End of Time. Kenneth Wapnick. 4 CDs. 2005. audio compact disk 24.00 (978-1-59142-221-1(3), CD74) Foun Miracles.

Forgiveness As the Heart of Reconciliation. Martin Padovani. 2 cass. (Running Time: 1 hrs. 45 min.). 1998. 19.95 Set. (TAH393) Alba Hse Comns.
At the core of the Sacrament of Reconciliation is the need to be fully aware of our necessity to be forgiven, as well as our requirement to forgive. Forgiving is a tripartite process: intellectual, emotional & spiritual.

Forgiveness-Healing Meditation. Scripts. Created by Joan Marie Whelan. Voice by Joan Marie Whelan. 1 CD. (Running Time: 35 minutes). 2002. audio compact disk 15.95 (978-0-9718654-2-6(6)) Ser Hse.
This CD is in two parts. The First section shares insights on how one can achieve healing and forgiveness in his or her life. The second section is a beautiful and loving guided meditation on healing and forgiveness of self that will leave the listener feeling total love and oneness with the Universal Flow. Joan Marie states, "you can only grow as much as you are willing to let go." A dynamic and powerful speaker, she is gifted with the ability to

communicate with Angels, Spirit Guides and those who have passed to the other side.

Forgiveness Process. Read by Mary Richards. 12.95 (207) Master Your Mind.
Explores a process of letting go of grievances towards others & a process of forgiving yourself for any imagined wrongdoing.

Forgiveness Sets Me Free. Read by Mary Richards. (Course in Miracles Ser.). 12.95 (707) Master Your Mind.

Forgiveness Tape: Forgiving Yourself & Others. Ginger Chalford. 1 cass. (Metaphysical-Psychological Ser.). 1985. bk. 9.95 (978-1-56089-009-6(6)) Visionary FL.
Features an explanation of the forgiveness process. Two powerful guided visualizations included.

Forgiveness: the Mystery & Miracle: Finding Freedom & Peace at Last. Annette Stanwick. Read by Annette Stanwick. 2008. audio compact disk 29.95 (978-0-9783545-1-0(6)) H M Pubn CAN.

Forgiveness Therapy: A Christ Centered Approach. Ron Roth. 3 cass. (Running Time: 3 hrs.). 1994. 24.95 Set. (978-1-893869-06-6(7)) Celbrtng Life.
Ron leads in a creative meditation on how to forgive.

Forgiveness/Loving the Inner Child. Louise L. Hay. 1 CD. 2004. audio compact disk 10.95 (978-1-4019-0408-1(4)) Hay House.

Forgiving: What Is not There. Gary Arnold. (ENG.). 2009. audio compact disk 24.95 (978-1-57867-012-3(8)) Windhorse Corp.

Forgiving & Forgiven: Luke 23:34, 618. Ed Young. 1987. 495.00 (978-0-7417-1618-7(6), 618) Win Walk.

Forgiving & Forgiven: Luke 7:40-49. Ed Young. (J). 1981. 4.95 (978-0-7417-1200-4(8), A0200) Win Walk.

Forgiving & Letting Go. Eldon Taylor. 1 cass. (Running Time: 62 min.). (Inner Talk Ser.). 16.95 (978-1-55978-307-1(9), 5375A) Progress Aware Res.
Soundtrack - Tropical Lagoon with underlying subliminal affirmations.

Forgiving & Letting Go: Babbling Brook. Eldon Taylor. 1 cass. 16.95 (978-1-55978-495-5(4), 5375F) Progress Aware Res.

Forgiving & Letting Go: Harmonies. Eldon Taylor. Read by Eldon Taylor. Ed. by Leslie Brice. 1 cass. (Running Time: 1 hr.). 1992. 16.95 (978-1-56705-155-1(3)) Gateways Inst.
Self improvement.

Forgiving & Letting Go: Music Theme. Eldon Taylor. 1 cass. 16.95 (978-0-940699-54-0(0), 5375C) Progress Aware Res.

Forgiving & Letting Go: Ocean. Eldon Taylor. Read by Eldon Taylor. Ed. by Leslie Brice. 1 cass. (Running Time: 1 hr.). 1992. 16.95 (978-1-56705-156-8(1)) Gateways Inst.

Forgiving & Letting Go: Stream. Eldon Taylor. Read by Eldon Taylor. Ed. by Leslie Brice. 1 cass. (Running Time: 1 hr.). 1992. 16.95 (978-1-56705-157-5(X)) Gateways Inst.

Forgiving Jesus: Stranger on the Road. Kenneth Wapnick. 2CDs. 2004. audio compact disk 14.00 (978-1-59142-154-2(3), CD42) Foun Miracles.
The theme of this workshop is our need to forgive Jesus because he is right and we are wrong about who we truly are. This theme is discussed in the context of Helen Schucman's poem, "Stranger on the Road," which expresses her experiences of Jesus' crucifixion and resurrection, and reflects her conflict of despair and hope, death and life, fear and love, a conflict that virtually all students of A Course in Miracles share in developing a relationship with Jesus.

***Forgiving Jesus: Stranger on the Road.** Kenneth Wapnick. 2010. 11.00 (978-1-59142-482-6(8)) Foun Miracles.

Forgiving the Dead Man Walking. abr. ed. Debbie Morris. Told to Gregg Lewis. (Running Time: 3 hrs. 0 mins. 0 sec.). (ENG.). 2003. 9.99 (978-0-310-26043-1(4)) Zondervan.

Forgiving When It's Difficult/Illusions of Loss. Marianne Williamson. Read by Marianne Williamson. 1 cass. (Running Time: 90 mins.). (Lectures on a Course in Miracles). 1999. 10.00 (978-1-56170-195-7(5), M723) Hay House.

Forgiving Yourself & Others: Claiming Emotional Freedom & Unconditional Love. 1 cass. (Running Time: 1 hr. 30 mins.). 1999. 19.95 (978-1-893087-24-8(7)) Awaken Vis.

Forgotten. abr. ed. Faye Kellerman. (Peter Decker & Rina Lazarus Novel Ser.). 2006. 17.95 (978-0-7435-6131-0(7)) Pub: S&S Audio. Dist(s): S and S Inc

Forgotten. unabr. ed. Faye Kellerman. Read by Barrett Whitener. 10 vols. (Running Time: 13 hrs. 15 mins.). (Peter Decker & Rina Lazarus Novel Ser.). 2001. bk. 84.95 (978-0-7927-2482-7(8), CSL 371, Chivers Sound Lib); audio compact disk 110.95 (978-0-7927-9936-8(4), SLD 087, Chivers Sound Lib) AudioGO.
The unofficial caretaker of her small storefront synagogue, Rina is shocked when she receives a morning call from the police. The modest place of worship has been desecrated with anti-Semitic graffiti and grisly Nazi death-camp photographs. Rina's husband, Lt. Peter Decker, is also rocked by this outrage, which cuts close to the spiritual heart of his family, but he can't let his emotions get in the way of his duties.

***Forgotten.** unabr. ed. Cat Patrick. (ENG.). (J). 2011. audio compact disk 34.00 (978-0-307-71114-4(5), Listening Lib) Pub: Random Audio Pubg. Dist(s): Random

Forgotten. unabr. ed. Elie Wiesel. Narrated by George Guidall. 8 cass. (Running Time: 11 hrs. 30 mins.). 1992. 70.00 (978-1-55690-645-9(5), 92352E7) Recorded Bks.
A son returns to the small Romanian village where his father was born, in search of his aging father's memories. Malkiel Rosenbaum agrees begrudgingly to revisit the events of his father's wartime experiences in Romania fighting the Nazis & as a result, discovers another side to the stories & a truth his own generation is in danger of forgetting.

Forgotten among the Lilies: Learning to Love Beyond Our Fears. Ronald Rolheiser. Read by Jim Luken. 6 cass. (Running Time: 8 hrs. 30 mins.). 2005. 46.95 (978-0-86716-715-3(7)) St Anthony Mess Pr.

Forgotten by Man: Gen.39:20-40:23. Ed Young. 1988. 4.95 (978-0-7417-1680-4(1), 680) Win Walk.

Forgotten Dreams. Katie Flynn. 2008. 94.95 (978-1-84559-710-8(9)); audio compact disk 99.95 (978-1-84559-711-5(7)) Pub: Soundings Ltd GBR. Dist(s): Ulverscroft US

***Forgotten Garden.** Kate Morton. Read by Caroline Lee. (Running Time: 20 hrs. 40 mins.). 2009. 114.99 (978-1-74214-544-0(2), 9781742145440) Pub: Bolinda Pubng AUS. Dist(s): Bolinda Pub Inc

Forgotten Garden. unabr. ed. Kate Morton. Read by Caroline Lee. 16 CDs. (Running Time: 20 hrs. 40 mins.). 2009. audio compact disk 123.95 (978-1-921415-72-2(X), 9781921415722) Pub: Bolinda Pubng AUS. Dist(s): Bolinda Pub Inc

***Forgotten Garden.** unabr. ed. Kate Morton. Read by Caroline Lee. (Running Time: 20 hrs. 40 mins.). 2010. 54.95 (978-1-921415-77-7(0), 9781921415777) Pub: Bolinda Pubng AUS. Dist(s): Bolinda Pub Inc

Forgotten God: Reversing Our Tragic Neglect of the Holy Spirit. unabr. ed. Francis Chan. Narrated by Francis Chan. (Running Time: 4 hrs. 9 mins. 26 sec.). (ENG.). 2009. 12.59 (978-1-60814-515-7(8)); audio compact disk 17.99 (978-1-59859-576-5(8)) Oasis Audio.

Forgotten Hero. 1 cass. 10.00 Esstee Audios.
The story of the beginning of aerial warfare.

Forgotten Heroes: 35 Portraits. abr. ed. Kazin & Phillip Gould. 4 cass. (Running Time: 6 hrs.). 2001. 25.00 (978-1-59040-096-8(8), Phoenix Audio) Pub: Amer Intl Pub. Dist(s): PerseuPGW

Forgotten Journey. unabr. collector's ed. Peter Fleming. Read by David Case. 6 cass. (Running Time: 6 hrs.). 1988. 36.00 (978-0-7366-1374-3(9), 2269) Books on Tape.
Starting in Moscow & ending in Peking & points south, the author toured the Caucasus, Smarkand, Vladivostok & Mongolia, presenting snapshots of a world gone forever.

***Forgotten Man.** Robert Crais. 2010. audio compact disk 9.99 (978-1-4418-5693-7(5)) Brilliance Audio.

Forgotten Man. abr. ed. Robert Crais. Read by Robert Crais. (Running Time: 14400 sec.). (Elvis Cole Ser.). 2006. audio compact disk 14.99 (978-1-59600-832-8(6), 9781596008328, BCD Value Price) Brilliance Audio.
Los Angeles, 3:58 a.m.: Elvis Cole receives the phone call he's been waiting for since childhood. Responding to a gunshot, the LAPD has found an injured man in an alleyway. He has told the officer on the scene that he is looking for his son, Elvis Cole. Minutes later, the man is dead. Haunted throughout his life by a lack of knowledge about his father, Elvis turns to the one person who can help him navigate the minefield of his past - his longtime partner and confidant, Joe Pike. Together with hard-edged LAPD detective, Carol Starkey, they launch a feverish search for the dead man's identity - even as Elvis struggles between wanting to believe he's found his father at last, and allowing his suspicions to hold him back. With each long-buried clue they unearth, a frightening picture begins to emerge about who the dead man might have been, and the terrible secret he's been guarding. At the same time, Elvis has no way of knowing he has awakened a sleeping monster. The further he goes in his investigation, the closer he draws to a merciless killer who is violently connected to the unidentified man's past. This psychopath believes Cole is hunting him, and he goes on the attack to find Elvis before Elvis can find him.

Forgotten Man. unabr. ed. Robert Crais. Read by James Daniels. (Running Time: 8 hrs.). (Elvis Cole Ser.). 2005. 39.25 (978-1-59710-304-6(7), 9781597103046, BADLE); 24.95 (978-1-59710-305-3(5), 9781597103053, BAD); 24.95 (978-1-59335-698-9(6), 9781593356989, Brilliance MP3); 39.25 (978-1-59335-832-7(6), 9781593358327, Brlnc Audio MP3 Lib); 29.95 (978-1-59355-027-1(8), 9781593550271, BAU); 74.25 (978-1-59355-028-8(6), 9781593550288, BAudLibEd); audio compact disk 29.95 (978-1-59355-030-1(8), 9781593550301, Bril Audio CD Unabri); audio compact disk 87.25 (978-1-59355-031-8(6), 9781593550318, BACDLib Ed) Brilliance Audio.

***Forgotten Man: A New History.** unabr. ed. Amity Shlaes. Read by Terence Aselford. (ENG.). 2007. (978-0-06-147296-1(4), Harper Audio); (978-0-06-147295-4(6), Harper Audio) HarperCollins Pubs.

Forgotten Man: A New History of the Great Depression. unabr. ed. Amity Shlaes. Read by Terence Aselford. 2009. audio compact disk 19.99 (978-0-06-180729-9(X), Harper Audio) HarperCollins Pubs.

Forgotten Patriots: The Untold Story of American Prisoners During the Revolutionary War. Edwin G. Burrows. Read by Norman Dietz. (Playaway Adult Nonfiction Ser.). (ENG.). 2009. 64.99 (978-1-60812-546-3(7)) Find a World.

Forgotten Patriots: The Untold Story of American Prisoners During the Revolutionary War. unabr. ed. Edwin G. Burrows. Read by Norman Dietz. (Running Time: 10 hrs. 30 mins. 0 sec.). (ENG.). 2008. audio compact disk 34.99 (978-1-4001-0979-1(5)) Pub: Tantor Media. Dist(s): IngramPubServ

Forgotten Patriots: The Untold Story of American Prisoners During the Revolutionary War. unabr. ed. Edwin G. Burrows. Read by Norman D. Dietz. (Running Time: 10 hrs. 30 mins. 0 sec.). (ENG.). 2008. audio compact disk 24.99 (978-1-4001-5979-6(2)) Pub: Tantor Media. Dist(s): IngramPubServ

Forgotten Patriots: The Untold Story of American Prisoners During the Revolutionary War. unabr. ed. Edwin G. Burrows. Read by Norman Dietz. (Running Time: 10 hrs. 30 mins. 0 sec.). (ENG.). 2008. audio compact disk 69.99 (978-1-4001-3979-8(1)) Pub: Tantor Media. Dist(s): IngramPubServ

Forgotten Power of Rhythm: Taketina. Reinhard Flatischler. 1992. audio compact disk 16.95 (978-0-940795-13-6(2)) LifeRhythm.

Forgotten Story: Tales of Wise Jewish Men. Short Stories. Perf. by Doug Lipman. 1 cass. (Running Time: 60 min.). (J). 1988. 9.95 (978-0-938756-20-0(6), 012) Yellow Moon.
Here in these folktales & mystical stories are men who never lost the ability to feel, to reason, to sing, to dance, & to remedy injustice without need for violence. The stories are interspersed with singing & twelve-string guitar & will nourish the soul as well as the spirit.

***Forgotten Truth.** unabr. ed. Dawn Cook. Read by Marguerite Gavin. 1 Playaway. 2010. 64.99 (978-1-4417-5414-1(8)); 79.95 (978-1-4417-5407-3(5)) Blckstn Audio.

***Forgotten Truth.** unabr. ed. Dawn Cook. Read by Marguerite Gavin. 1 MP3-CD. (Running Time: 13 hrs.). (Truth Ser.). 2010. 29.95 (978-1-4417-5411-0(3)); audio compact disk 29.95 (978-1-4417-5410-3(5)) Blckstn Audio.

Forgotten Voices of the Great War: Interviews from the Imperial War Museum Archives. Max Arthur. 8 cass. (Running Time: 12 hrs. 0 mins. 0 sec.). (Brentford Trilogy). (ENG., 2003. 60.00 (978-1-85686-536-4(3), Audiobks) Pub: Random GBR. Dist(s): IPG Chicago

Forgotten Voices of the Great War: The Struggle to Victory - August 1917 - November 1918. Max Arthur. 2 cass. (Running Time: 3 hrs. 0 mins. 0 sec.). (Forgotten Voices Ser.). (ENG., 2003. 17.50 (978-1-85686-697-2(1), Audiobks) Pub: Random GBR. Dist(s): IPG Chicago

Forgotten Voices of the Second World War Set: Including Interviews from the Imperial War Museum Archives. Max Arthur. Ed. by Georgia Marnham. 8 cass. (Running Time: 12 hrs. 0 mins. 0 sec.). (Forgotten Voices Ser.). (ENG., 2004. 65.00 (978-1-85686-955-3(5), Audiobks) Pub: Random GBR. Dist(s): IPG Chicago

Forgotten Voices of the Second World War, Programme 4: June 1944 - May 1945. Imperial War Museum Staff & Max Arthur. Read by Timothy West. Narrated by Timothy West. 3 CDs. (Running Time: 3 hrs. 0 mins. 0 sec.). (Forgotten Voices Ser.). (ENG., 2004. audio compact disk 22.00 (978-1-85686-954-6(7), Audiobks) Pub: Random GBR. Dist(s): IPG Chicago

Forgotten Voices of WW2: War in the Mediterranean Audio. Imperial War Museum Staff & Max Arthur. Read by Timothy West. Narrated by Timothy West. 2 cass. (Running Time: 3 hrs. 0 mins. 0 sec.). (Forgotten Voices Ser.). (ENG., 2004. 17.50 (978-1-85686-948-5(2), Audiobks) Pub: Random GBR. Dist(s): IPG Chicago

Forgotten 500: The Untold Story of the Men Who Risked All for the Greatest Rescue Mission of World War II. unabr. ed. Gregory A. Freeman. Read by Patrick G. Lawlor. (Running Time: 11 hrs. 0 mins. 0 sec.). (ENG.). 2007. audio compact disk 34.99 (978-1-4001-0522-9(6)); audio compact disk 69.99 (978-1-4001-3522-6(2)); audio compact disk 24.99 (978-1-4001-5522-4(3)) Pub: Tantor Media. Dist(s): IngramPubServ

Forgotten 500: The Untold Story of the Men Who Risked All for the Greatest Rescue Mission of World War II. unabr. ed. Gregory A. Freeman. Read by Patrick G. Lawlor. (YA). 2008. 59.99 (978-1-60514-721-5(4)) Find a World.

Forgottenville, the Town that Arrested Santa Claus. unabr. ed. (Running Time: 39 min.). (Forgottenville Ser.). (J). (gr. k-8). 1983. 6.99 (978-0-941316-05-7(X)) TSM Books.
Dramatizes Santa's first visit to the town of "Forgottenville." Santa & the people of "Forgottenville" are almost tricked by Dr. S. Neak, but all ends well when a young child comes to Santa's rescue.

Forgottenville, the Town That Arrested Santa Claus. unabr. ed. Frank McQuilkin. Illus. by Doros Animations, Inc. Staff. (Running Time: 39 min.). (Forgottenville Ser.). (J). (ps-7). 1982. bk. 18.95 (978-0-941316-00-2(9)) TSM Books.

Form & Design. Roy Bennett. Contrib. by Roy Bennett. 1 cass. (Cambridge Assignments in Music Ser.). (ENG.). 1981. 38.99 (978-0-521-23662-1(2)) Cambridge U Pr.

Form & Design. Roy Bennett. Contrib. by Roy Bennett. (Cambridge Assignments in Music Ser.). (ENG.). 1985. 38.99 (978-0-521-26831-8(1)) Cambridge U Pr.

Form Line of Battle! Alexander Kent, pseud. Read by Michael Jayston. 10 cass. (Running Time: 15 hrs.). (Richard Bolitho Ser.: Bk. 9). 2002. 84.95 (978-0-7540-0913-9(0), CAB 2335) Pub: Chivers Audio Bks GBR. Dist(s): AudioGO

Form of Death. unabr. ed. Roy H. Lewis. Read by Jack Paulin. 5 cass. (Running Time: 13 hrs. 15 mins.). (Storysound Ser.). (J). 2002. 49.95 (978-1-85903-499-6(3)) Pub: Mgna Lrg Print GBR. Dist(s): Ulverscroft US

Form vs. Content: Sex & Money. Kenneth Wapnick. 4 CDs. 2005. audio compact disk 27.00 (978-1-59142-217-4(5), CD78) Foun Miracles.

Form vs. Content: Sex & Money. Kenneth Wapnick. 2009. 22.00 (978-1-59142-376-8(7)) Foun Miracles.

Form 1040: A Practical Guide. Nathan M. Bisk & Stephen T. Galloway. 6 cass. 199.00 set, incl. textbk. & quizzer. (978-0-88128-363-1(0), CPE1900) Bisk Educ.
Includes key tax changes, helpful tax saving tips, how to report & pay estimated tax, plus the impact of all recent tax acts on 1040 returns. A comprehensive case study includes filled-in sample forms, tables, & other reference materials.

Form 1120: A Practical Guide. Cris Van den Branden & Richard Feldheim. 3 cass. bk. 169.00 (978-0-88128-369-3(X), CPE2000) Bisk Educ.
This year-round tool features specific strategies for corporate tax planning & saving, full revisions reflecting all recent tax acts, & up-to-date information critical to all your corporate tax ventures. A comprehensive case study includes helpful filled-in forms.

Form 1120S: A Practical Guide. Nathan M. Bisk & Stephen T. Galloway. 6 cass. bk. 169.00 set. (CPE4120) Bisk Educ.
Get step-by-step filing guidance for Form 1120S returns, recent legislative, judicial, & regulatory changes, authoritative answers to tax return compliance questions, a realistic case study, & more.

Forma Efectiva de Resolver Conflictos Como Mejorar la Sociabilidad. unabr. ed. John F. Taylor. Read by Timothy Taylor. 1 cass. (Running Time: 25 min.). (Answers to ADD Ser.). (SPA.). 1994. 9.95 (978-1-883963-17-0(6)) ADD Plus.
Preventing "I Hate Him" burnout, increasing family harmony, improving negotiating skills, unearthing the roots of rivalry, increasing courtesy & generosity, avoiding the "be consistent" trap.

Formal Spoken Arabic: FAST Course with MP3 Files. Karin C. Ryding & Abdelnour Zaiback. 1 CD. (Georgetown Classics in Arabic Language & Linguistics Ser.). (ARA & ENG.). 2004. pap. bk. 39.95 (978-1-58901-106-9(6)) GeorgetownUPr.

Formation in the Fatima Message. Luciano Guerra & F. L. Miller. Read by Luciano Guerra & F. L. Miller. 4 cass. (Running Time: 4 hrs.). 17.00 (978-1-56036-007-0(0), 361572) AMI Pr.
Contains presentation on formation in the Fatima message, the catechetical truths of Fatima & Fatima Sanctuary Rector Msgr. Luciano Guerra answering questions about Fatima.

Formation of Conscience. Thomas Merton. 1 cass. (Running Time: 60 min.). (Humility Ser.). 4.50 (AA2107) Credence Commun.
Discussions on when humility begins & the growth of that trait.

Formative Causation. unabr. ed. Rupert Sheldrake. 1 cass. (Running Time: 1 hr. 23 min.). 1982. 11.00 (02303) Big Sur Tapes.
Sheldrake contends that there is another aspect of causation, the mystery of that order, the mystery of its form. The order or patterns we see in nature are not so much a reflection of eternal laws but depend on what has happened in the past.

Formative Living of Foundational Values in Today's World. Susan Muto. 3 cass. (Running Time: 3 hrs.). 1983. 24.95 incl. shelf-case. (TAH102) Alba Hse Comns.
Begins with a discussion of the terminology of Formative Spirituality & defines each of the words of the title so that there is no confusion as to the meaning.

Forme Equipos Trascendentes. Carlos Cuauhtemoc Sanchez. audio compact disk 15.95 (978-968-7277-61-5(0)) Pub: EdSelect MEX. Dist(s): Giron Bks

Formed by the Spirit. Carole Riley. 4 cass. (Running Time: 3 hrs. 30 min.). 1992. 33.95 set. (TAH272) Alba Hse Comns.
Sr. Riley, using her knowledge of psychology, spirituality & music, outlines a practical, joyful way to enter into God's presence.

Former & Latter Rain. Kenneth Copeland. 2 cass. 1985. 10.00 Set. (978-0-88114-758-2(3)) K Copeland Pubns.
Role of the Holy Spirit in the "last days".

Former Morehouse Students Remember Dr. Mays. Rex A. Barnett. (Running Time: 32 min.). (YA). 1990. 16.99 (978-0-924198-11-3(7)) Hist Video.
Past morehouse college students, now successful businessmen, recount the great student years with Dr. Mays.

Forming & Advising a New Business Entity. (Running Time: 5 hrs.). 1995. 92.00 Incl. 339p. coursebk. (20804) NYS Bar.
Basic-to-intermediate-level program helps counselors decide what would be the most advantageous form of business entity in a particular case given the client's situation, type of operation & goals & the current state of the law.

Forming & Advising the New York Not-for-Profit Organization. (Running Time: 5 hrs. 30 min.). 1993. 92.00 Incl. 293p. coursebk. (29350) NYS Bar.
This timely, basic-to-intermediate level series of presentations provides a practical assessment of the decisions & procedures necessary to form, obtain federal, state & local tax exemptions for, & advise a New York not-for-profit organization. The speakers discuss issues in such areas as organization options, formation or reorganization formalities, & operations, including fundraising, governance, programs & grantmaking issues.

Forming Pro-Life Principles According to the Mind of the Church & Questions & Answers of Panelists. William B. Smith. 1 cass. 4.00 (96C2) IRL Chicago.

***Formless Fabric of Reality.** Featuring Adyashanti. (ENG.). 2010. audio compact disk 40.00 (978-1-933986-74-6(3)) Open Gate Pub.

Forms & Mysteries: Morphogenic Fields & Psychedelic Experiences. Rupert Sheldrake & Terence McKenna. 2 cass. 18.00 set. (A0327-88) Sound Photosyn.
These two experts in their fields & experiences inspire each other to greater widths & heights.

Forms of Attachment. Swami Amar Jyoti. 1 cass. 1979. 9.95 (B-8) Truth Consciousness.
How attachment produces injustice & fragmentation.

Formula for Selling. unabr. ed. Robert E. Levinson. 1 cass. (Running Time: 24 min.). 12.95 (13002) J Norton Pubs.
An executive vice-president of the Steelcraft Manufacturing Co. talks about selling, the most important business today. His formula for producing the sales consists of K for the knowledge of one's product, customer's needs & oneself & D for the desire to do a good job, reach a goal & succeed for family & self.

Formula for Success. Jack Boland. 3 cass. 1983. 27.95 (978-0-88152-022-4(5)) Master Mind.
Maximize your performance! This winning formula will help you to gain control as it leads you to the success you desire. As a real performer you will be the executive director of your life.

Formula for Success. unabr. ed. L. Ron Hubbard. Read by L. Ron Hubbard. 1 cass. (Running Time: 1 hr. 15 min.). 9.95 (978-0-88404-867-1(5)) Bridge Pubns Inc.
A lecture by L. Ron Hubbard outlining five special conditions for personal & business success.

Formula One Maths, Yr. 8. Brian Seager & Mark Patmore. (Running Time: 2 hrs. 40 mins.). 2003. audio compact disk 229.50 (978-0-340-85661-1(0), HodderMurray) Pub: Hodder Edu GBR. Dist(s): Trans-Atl Phila

Formula One Maths: Medium Term Assessment Resource CD-ROM Version Year 7. Brian Seager & Mark Patmore. (Running Time: 2 hrs. 40 mins.). 2002. audio compact disk 229.50 (978-0-340-85660-4(2), HodderMurray) Pub: Hodder Edu GBR. Dist(s): Trans-Atl Phila

Forrest Gump. Winston Groom. Narrated by Mark Hammer. 8 CDs. (Running Time: 9.5 hrs.). audio compact disk 39.95 (978-0-7887-5443-2(2)) Recorded Bks.

Forrest Gump. Winston Groom. Read by Mark Hammer. 6 Cass. (Running Time: 9.5 Hrs). 2001. 29.95 (978-0-7887-5434-0(3)) Recorded Bks.

Forrest Gump. Winston Groom. 2004. 10.95 (978-0-7435-4738-3(1)) Pub: S&S Audio. Dist(s): S and S Inc

Forrest Gump. unabr. ed. Winston Groom. Read by Jonathan Marosz. 7 cass. (Running Time: 7 hrs.). 1995. 42.00 (978-0-7366-3025-2(2), 3708) Books on Tape.
Mental deficiency's no burden to this idiot. Born to succeed. Funny & inspiring.

Forrest Gump. unabr. ed. Winston Groom. Narrated by Mark Hammer. 6 cass. (Running Time: 9 hrs.). 1995. 51.00 (978-0-7887-0199-3(1), 94423E7) Recorded Bks.
When he is taken out of an institution at the age of 13 to play football, Forrest Gump enters the world of ordinary people & though he has only an IQ of 70, he has a lot to teach the world about life.

Forrestal Lecture at the U. S. Naval Academy. unabr. ed. Robert A. Heinlein. 1 cass. (Running Time: 1 hr. 13 min.). 12.95 (190) J Norton Pubs.
Discusses techniques of writing, science fiction, patriotism & the proud traditions of the naval service.

Forsaken by God? Matthew 27:46; Mark 15:34, 1210. Ed Young. 1999. 4.95 (978-0-7417-2210-2(0), 1210) Win Walk.

Forsaken Soul: A Medieval Mystery. unabr. ed. Priscilla Royal & Vanessa Benjamin. (Running Time: 7 hrs. NaN mins.). 2008. 29.95 (978-1-4332-3557-3(9)); 44.95 (978-1-4332-3553-5(6)); audio compact disk 60.00 (978-1-4332-3554-2(4)) Blckstn Audio.

Forsyte Saga. John Galsworthy. Narrated by Flo Gibson. 23 cass. (Running Time: 33 hrs. 49 mins.). 2007. 63.95 (978-1-55685-888-8(4)) Audio Bk Con.
Contains all three novels, ("A Man of Property", "In Chancery" and "To Let" as well as the interludes "Indian Summer of a Forsyte" and "The Awakening". Unabridged.

Forsyte Saga. John Galsworthy. Narrated by Fred Williams. (Running Time: 43 hrs.). 2005. 85.95 (978-1-59912-663-0(X)) Iofy Corp.

Forsyte Saga Vol. 1: The Man of Property. abr. ed. John Galsworthy. Narrated by Martin Jarvis. 4 CDs. (Running Time: 5 hrs.). (ENG.). 2009. audio compact disk 26.95 (978-1-934997-38-3(2)) Pub: CSAWord. Dist(s): PerseuPGW

Forsyte Saga Part 1 -Lib. John Galsworthy. Read by Fred Williams. 15 cass. (Running Time: 43 hrs.). 2005. 105.95 (978-0-7861-3026-9(1), 3435A,B); audio compact disk 120.00 (978-0-7861-8077-6(3), 3435A,B) Blckstn Audio.

Forsyte Saga Part 2 -Lib. John Galsworthy. Read by Fred Williams. 15 cass. (Running Time: 43 hrs.). 2005. 105.95 (978-0-7861-3027-6(X), 3435A,B); audio compact disk 120.00 (978-0-7861-8076-9(5), 3435A,B) Blckstn Audio.

Forsyte Saga Vol 1: The Man of Property. John Galsworthy. Read by Tbc Reader. (ENG.). 2009. audio compact disk 34.26 (978-1-906147-35-8(3), CSAW) CSA Telltapes GBR.

***Fort: A Novel of the Revolutionary War.** unabr. ed. Bernard Cornwell. Read by Robin Bowerman. 2010. (978-0-06-201917-2(1), Harper Audio); (978-0-06-204205-7(X), Harper Audio) HarperCollins Pubs.

Fort Island. unabr. ed. David Metzenthen. (J). 2002. audio compact disk 39.95 (978-1-74030-847-2(6)) Pub: Bolinda Pubng AUS. Dist(s): Bolinda Pub Inc

Fort Laramie: Playing Indian & Boredom. Perf. by Raymond Burr. 1 cass. (Running Time: 1 hr.). 2001. 6.98 (2456) Radio Spirits.

***Fort Laramie, Volume 1.** RadioArchives.com. (Running Time: 600). (ENG.). 2006. audio compact disk 29.98 (978-1-61081-047-0(3)) Radio Arch.

***Fort Laramie, Volume 2.** RadioArchives.com. (Running Time: 600). (ENG.). 2008. audio compact disk 29.98 (978-1-61081-078-4(3)) Radio Arch.

Fort Pillow: A Novel of the Civil War. unabr. ed. Harry Turtledove. Narrated by John Allen Nelson. (Running Time: 11 hrs. 0 mins. 0 sec.). (ENG.). 2009. audio compact disk 75.99 (978-1-4001-4139-5(7)); audio compact disk 37.99 (978-1-4001-1139-8(0)); audio compact disk 24.99 (978-1-4001-6139-3(8)) Pub: Tantor Media. Dist(s): IngramPubServ

Fort Sumter to Perryville. unabr. ed. Shelby Foote. Read by Grover Gardner. 3 pieces. (Running Time: 140400 sec.). (Civil War: A Narrative Ser.). 2000. audio compact disk 54.95 (978-0-7861-9103-1(1), 1102A,B) Blckstn Audio.

Fort-Vite. unabr. ed. Robert A. Monroe. Read by Roland Simon. 1 cass. (Running Time: 30 min.). (Human Plus Ser.). (FRE.). 1993. 14.95 (978-1-56102-101-7(6)) Inter Indus.
Gain instant muscular strength for short durations.

Fort Yuma. unabr. ed. Hank Mitchum. Read by Charlie O'Dowd. 4 vols. 2003. 25.00 (978-1-58807-191-0(X)) Am Pubng Inc.

Fort Yuma. unabr. ed. Hank Mitchum. Read by Charlie O'Dowd. 4 vols. No. 8. 2003. (978-1-58807-592-5(3)) Am Pubng Inc.

Fortaleza Digital. abr. ed. Scripts. Dan Brown. Read by Karl Hoffmann. 7 CDs. (Running Time: 480 sec.).Tr. of Digital Fortess. (SPA.). 2006. audio compact disk 29.95 (978-1-933499-26-0(5)) Fonolibro Inc.
Del mismo autor de los Bestsellers "El Codigo Da Vinci" y "Angeles y demonios," FonoLibro les trae una apasionante novela llena de claves secretas, mensajes ocultos, enga?os y crimenes. "Fortaleza Digital" los mantendra en suspenso y no podra dejar de escucharlo hasta que llegue al final. La supercomputadora de la Agencia de Seguridad Nacional se encuentra con un codigo el cual no puede descifrar. El subdirector de la agencia llama a la hermosa criptografa Susan Fletcher, La unica pista para romper ese codigo parece estar en el cadaver de un hombre fallecido en Espa?a, donde ha sido enviado el prometido de Susan, David Becker. Mientras David intenta hallar la clave y sobrevivir a la persecucion de un metodico e implacable asesino en las calles de Sevilla, Susan se enfrentara a su propio drama en las desoladas instalaciones de maxima seguridad de la Agencia, durante una larga noche en la que la mentira y el asesinato acechan tras cada puerta. A?ada a su coleccion "El Codigo Da Vinci" y "Angeles y demonios" de Dan Brown, en unas magnificas producciones con la reconocida e insuperable calidad de FonoLibro.

Fortissimo!, Set. Roy Bennett. 4 cass. (Running Time: 4 hrs.). (ENG., (YA). (gr. 9-11). 1996. audio compact disk 184.00 (978-0-521-56925-5(7)) Cambridge U Pr.

Fortitude. unabr. ed. Hugh Walpole. Read by Flo Gibson. 11 cass. (Running Time: 16 hrs.). 1994. 34.95 (978-1-55685-329-6(7)) Audio Bk Con.
In the best known work of Walpole's, Peter Westcott is sorely tested from childhood by a cruel father, the torments of boarding school, years as a struggling author, a troubled marriage & the loss of those he most deeply loved. This beautifully written book & Peter's courage are an inspiration to all.

Fortress. unabr. ed. David Harris. Read by Peter Hardy. 2 cass. (Running Time: 2 hrs. 30 mins.). 2002. 24.00 (978-1-74030-356-9(3)) Pub: Bolinda Pubng AUS. Dist(s): Lndmrk Audiobks

Fortress: A Diary of Anzio & After. unabr. ed. Raleigh Trevelyan. Read by David Case. 5 cass. (Running Time: 7 hrs. 30 min.). 1999. 40.00 (978-0-7366-4406-8(7), 4867) Books on Tape.
Early in 1944, Allied forces landed at Anzio in an attempt to outflank the Germans still desperately resisting in Italy, & to secure the road to Rome. It is said of the fighting for the beach-head that it most closely resembled that on the Western front during the Great War. The author was a twenty-year-old subaltern when he landed at Anzio, & was ordered to take his platoon into the dangerous sector known as "the Fortress.".

Fortress: Solo Track. Robert Nugent. Perf. by Christine Wyrtzen. 1 cass. (50-Day Spiritual Adventure Ser.). 1993. 9.99 (978-1-879050-27-3(7)) Chapel of Air.
Accompaniment track for solo singer.

Fortunate Lives. unabr. ed. Robb Forman Dew. Narrated by Alexandra O'Karma. 7 cass. (Running Time: 10 hrs.). 1992. 60.00 (978-1-55690-704-3(4), 92429E7) Recorded Bks.
The Howells family of Massachusetts, still coping with the death of their younger son, finds it hard to let go as their other child, David, seventeen, prepares to leave for college.

***Fortunate Pilgrim.** abr. ed. Mario Puzo. Read by John Kenneth. (Running Time: 3 hrs.). 2010. audio compact disk 9.99 (978-1-4418-6269-3(2), 9781441862693, BCD Value Price) Brilliance Audio.

Fortunate Pilgrim. abr. ed. Mario Puzo. Read by John Kenneth. 2 cass. (Running Time: 3 hrs.). 2000. 7.95 (978-1-57815-171-4(6), 1114, Media Bks Audio) Media Bks NJ.
A classic story about the loves, crimes & struggles confronted by one family of New York City immigrants living in Hell's Kitchen.

Fortunate Pilgrim. abr. ed. Mario Puzo. Read by John Kenneth. 3 CDs. (Running Time: 3 hrs.). (YA). 2000. audio compact disk 11.99 (978-1-57815-505-7(3), 1114 CD3, Media Bks Audio) Media Bks NJ.

Fortunate Pilgrim. unabr. ed. Mario Puzo. Read by John Kenneth. (Running Time: 10 hrs.). 2009. 24.99 (978-1-4233-9693-2(6), 9781423396932, Brilliance MP3); 24.99 (978-1-4233-9695-6(2), 9781423396956, BAD); 39.97 (978-1-4233-9694-9(4), 9781423396949, Brinc Audio MP3 Lib); 39.97 (978-1-4233-9696-3(0), 9781423396963, BADLE) Brilliance Audio.

***Fortunate Pilgrim.** unabr. ed. Mario Puzo. Read by John Kenneth. (Running Time: 10 hrs.). 2010. audio compact disk 89.97 (978-1-4418-4022-6(2), 9781441840226, BriAudCD Unabrid) Brilliance Audio.

***Fortunate Pilgrim.** unabr. ed. Mario Puzo. Read by John Kenneth. (Running Time: 10 hrs.). 2010. audio compact disk 29.99 (978-1-4418-4021-9(4), 9781441840219) Brilliance Audio.

Fortunate Son. abr. ed. Lewis B. Puller, Jr.. Read by Lewis B. Puller, Jr. 2 cass. (Running Time: 3 hrs.). 2000. 7.95 (978-1-57815-067-0(1), 1029, Media Bks Audio) Media Bks NJ.
A hero who overcame the enormous physical & psychological scars of the Vietnam war to find a courage & a victory of his own.

Fortunate Son. unabr. ed. Walter Mosley. 7 cass. (Running Time: 9 hrs.). 2006. 63.00 (978-1-4159-3000-7(7)); audio compact disk 81.00 (978-1-4159-3001-4(5)) Books on Tape.

Fortunate Son. unabr. ed. Walter Mosley. Read by Lorraine Toussaint. (Running Time: 10 hrs.). (ENG.). 2006. 14.98 (978-1-59483-508-7(X)) Pub: Hachet Audio. Dist(s): HachBkGrp

Fortunate Son. unabr. ed. Walter Mosley. Read by Lorraine Toussaint. (Running Time: 10 hrs.). (ENG.). 2009. 49.98 (978-1-60788-117-9(9)) Pub: Hachet Audio. Dist(s): HachBkGrp

Fortunate Son, Set. abr. ed. Lewis B. Puller, Jr.. Read by Lewis B. Puller, Jr. 2 cass. (Running Time: 3 hrs.). 1994. 16.95 (978-1-879371-85-9(5)) Pub Mills.
A wrenching yet inspiring look at a Vietnam war survivor's return home after a tragic injury & his struggle to cope with the changes - societal & personal - of the world after the war.

Fortune. unabr. ed. Robert Drewe. Read by David Tredinnick. 4 cass. (Running Time: 7 hrs.). 2004. 32.00 (978-1-74030-584-6(1)) Pub: Bolinda Pubng AUS. Dist(s): Lndmrk Audiobks

Fortune Branches Out. unabr. ed. Margaret Mahy. Read by Richard Mitchley. 2 cass. (Running Time: 3 hrs.). (Good Fortunes Gang Cousins Quartet Ser.: Vol. 3). (J). 1997. 18.95 (CCA3380, Chivers Child Audio) AudioGO.

***Fortune Cookie.** unabr. ed. Bryce Courtenay. 2010. audio compact disk 123.95 (978-1-74214-849-6(2), 9781742148496) Pub: Bolinda Pubng AUS. Dist(s): Bolinda Pub Inc

Fortune Favours the Merry. Peter\Horan & Peter\Horan. (ENG.). 2005. audio compact disk 23.95 (978-0-8023-8158-3(8)) Pub: Clo Iar-Chonnachta IRL. Dist(s): Dufour

Fortune for Mirabel see Twentieth-Century Poetry in English, No. 8, Recordings of Poets Reading Their Own Poetry

Fortune Hunters: Dazzling Women & the Men They Married. abr. ed. Charlotte Hays. (ENG.). 2007. audio compact disk 29.95 (978-1-4272-0206-2(0)) Pub: Macmill Audio. Dist(s): Macmillan

Fortune of Fear. L. Ron Hubbard. 2 cass. (Running Time: 3 hrs.). Dramatization. (Mission Earth Dekalogy Ser.: Vol. 5). 1991. 15.95 Set. (978-0-88404-689-9(3)) Bridge Pubns Inc.

Fortune of Fear. abr. ed. L. Ron Hubbard. (Mission Earth Ser.: Vol. 5). 2002. 15.95 (978-1-59212-061-1(X)) Gala Pr LLC.
Blazes an explosive trail from a secret Voltarian base in Turkey, across the Mediterranean, through Swiss banks, to the Mafia-controlled casinos of Atlantic City and the mean streets of New York.

Fortune of War. Patrick O'Brian. Read by Simon Vance. 8 cass. (Running Time: 11 hrs. 30 mins.). (Aubrey-Maturin Ser.). 2004. 65.95 (978-0-7861-2883-9(6), 3385); audio compact disk 81.00 (978-0-7861-8293-0(8), 3385) Blckstn Audio.

Fortune of War. Patrick O'Brian. Narrated by Simon Vance. (Running Time: 10 hrs. 30 mins.). (Aubrey-Maturin Ser.). 2004. 30.95 (978-1-59912-664-7(8)) Iofy Corp.

Fortune of War. Patrick O'Brian. Read by Patrick Tull. 8 Cass. (Running Time: 13 Hrs). (Aubrey-Maturin Ser.). 34.95 (978-1-4025-4093-6(0)) Recorded Bks.

Fortune of War. unabr. ed. Patrick O'Brian. Read by Simon Vance. 13 vols. (Running Time: 37800 sec.). (Aubrey-Maturin Ser.). 2004. audio compact disk 24.95 (978-0-7861-8353-1(5), 3385) Blckstn Audio.

Fortune of War. unabr. ed. Patrick O'Brian. Read by Simon Vance. 8 cass. (Running Time: 10 hrs. 30 mins.). (Aubrey-Maturin Ser.). 2005. 29.95 (978-0-7861-3444-1(5)) Blckstn Audio.

Fortune of War. unabr. ed. Patrick O'Brian. Read by Simon Vance. 9 CDs. (Running Time: 37800 sec.). (Aubrey-Maturin Ser.). 2005. audio compact disk 29.95 (978-0-7861-7994-7(5)) Blckstn Audio.

Fortune of War. unabr. ed. Patrick O'Brian. Read by Richard Brown. 9 cass. (Running Time: 13 hrs. 30 min.). (Aubrey-Maturin Ser.). 1992. 72.00 (978-0-7366-2276-9(4), 3064) Books on Tape.
The War of 1812 breaks out & Aubrey & Maturin, en route from the Dutch East Indies to England, are captured.

Fortune of War. unabr. ed. Patrick O'Brian. Read by John Lee. 8 cass. (Running Time: 11 hrs.). (Aubrey-Maturin Ser.). 2005. 72.00 (978-1-4159-2281-1(0)) Books on Tape.

Fortune of War. unabr. ed. Patrick O'Brian. Narrated by Patrick Tull. 9 cass. (Running Time: 13 hrs.). (Aubrey-Maturin Ser.: No. 6). 1993. 78.00 (978-1-55690-881-1(4), 93323E7) Recorded Bks.
Capt. Aubrey & Doctor Maturin end up prisoners-of-war in Boston during the War of 1812.

Fortune Teller. unabr. ed. Donald James. Read by Michael Tudor Barnes. 14 cass. (Running Time: 21 hrs.). 2001. 99.95 (978-0-7531-0690-7(6), 000812) Pub: ISIS Audio GBR. Dist(s): Ulverscroft US

Fortune Tellers: Inside Wall Street's Game of Money, Media, & Manipulation. Howard Kurtz. 2004. 15.95 (978-0-7435-1962-5(0)) Pub: S&S Audio. Dist(s): S and S Inc

Fortune's Child: A Portrait of the United States As Spendthrift Heir. unabr. collector's ed. Lewis H. Lapham. Read by Michael Prichard. 12 cass. (Running Time: 18 hrs.). 1981. 96.00 (978-0-7366-0598-4(3), 1565) Books on Tape.
A collection of 31 pieces by Lewis H. Lapham, editor of Harper's Magazine & one of the wittiest & most astute analysists of post-World War II America.

Fortune's Daughter. Elizabeth Lord. (Story Sound Ser.). (J). 2005. 44.95 (978-1-85903-734-8(8)) Pub: Mgna Lrg Print GBR. Dist(s): Ulverscroft US

Fortune's Favorites. Colleen McCullough. (Masters of Rome Ser.: No. 3). 2004. 15.95 (978-0-7435-4739-0(X)) Pub: S&S Audio. Dist(s): S and S Inc

Fortune's Favorites, Pt. 1. unabr. ed. Colleen McCullough. Read by Donada Peters. 14 cass. (Running Time: 21 hrs.). (Masters of Rome Ser.: No. 3). 1994. 112.00 (978-0-7366-2677-4(8), 3414A) Books on Tape.
Massive Roman epic featuring General Sulla & Pompey ("The Great"). Sequel to The First Man in Rome & The Grass Crown.

Fortune's Favorites, Pt. 2. Colleen McCullough. Read by Donada Peters. 12 cass. (Running Time: 18 hrs.). (Masters of Rome Ser.: No. 3). 1994. 96.00 (3414-B) Books on Tape.

Fortune's Hand. abr. ed. Belva Plain. 4 cass., 5 CDs. (Running Time: 6 hrs.). 1999. (Random AudioBks) Random Audio Pubg.
Compelling tale about two women who love the same man - the same man who almost destroys two families as he changes from an idealistic young lawyer into a man consumed by ambition.

Fortune's Hand. unabr. ed. Belva Plain. Read by Kate Harper. 8 cass. 2000. 69.95 (978-0-7540-0415-8(5), CAB 1838) Pub: Chivers Audio Bks GBR. Dist(s): AudioGO
Rob McDaniels, a schoolteacher with noble intentions, comes into a little money. This enables him to go to law school. Upon graduation, He goes to work for an honorable firm & marries the daughter of the senior partner, leaving behind his hometown sweetheart. But his dazzling career is about to take a shocking turn that will change his life forever.

Fortune's Hand, Set. abr. ed. Belva Plain. Read by Ken Howard. 4 cass. 1999. 25.00 (FS9-43421) Highsmith.

Fortune's Hand, Set. unabr. ed. Belva Plain. 10 CDs. (Running Time: 40620 sec.). (Jenny Cain Mysteries Ser.). 2000. audio compact disk 99.95 (978-0-7540-5324-8(5), CCD 015) Pub: Chivers Audio Bks GBR. Dist(s): AudioGO
It is 1939 & Caroline & Lore are young women living in Berlin amidst the madness engulfing Europe. With the death of their parents at the hands of the Nazis, the two flee to Switzerland. But when Caroline's young beau fails to join them there, Lore provides an explanation for his absence that will follow them & those around them, as they grasp for new hope & happiness in America.

Fortune's Journey. unabr. ed. Bruce Coville. Narrated by Christina Moore. 4 pieces. (Running Time: 5 hrs. 30 mins.). (gr. 5 up). 1995. 35.00 (978-0-7887-2624-8(2), 95628E7) Recorded Bks.
Set in the excitement of the gold rush era, this historical adventure is a creative take on early western expansion. As young Fortune Plunkett leads her late father's acting troupe west, she faces danger, romance & the unexpected. Her self-appointed mission, to fulfill his dream of reaching San Francisco, is an immense challenge for someone who is barely 16.

***Fortunes of Indigo Skye.** unabr. ed. Deb Caletti. Read by Ellen Grafton. (Running Time: 10 hrs.). 2010. 19.99 (978-1-4233-9661-1(8), 9781423396611, Brilliance MP3); 19.99 (978-1-4233-9663-5(4), 9781423396635, BAD); 39.97 (978-1-4233-9662-8(6), 9781423396628, Brinc Audio MP3 Lib); 39.97 (978-1-4233-9664-2(2), 9781423396642, BADLE); audio compact disk 54.97 (978-1-4233-9660-4(X), 9781423396604, BriAudCD Unabrid) Brilliance Audio.

***Fortunes of Indigo Skye.** unabr. ed. Deb Caletti. Read by Ellen Grafton. (Running Time: 10 hrs.). (YA). 2010. audio compact disk 19.99 (978-1-4233-9659-8(6), 9781423396598, Bril Audio CD Unabri) Brilliance Audio.

***Fortunes of Motie.** Anonymous. 2009. (978-1-60136-535-4(7)) Audio Holding.

Fortunes of War. Stephen Coonts. Read by Michael Prichard. 1998. audio compact disk 112.00 (978-0-7366-8040-0(3)) Books on Tape.

Fortunes of War. unabr. ed. Stephen Coonts. Read by Michael Prichard. 12 cass. (Running Time: 18 hrs.). 1998. 96.00 (978-0-7366-4207-1(2), 4704) Books on Tape.

Fortunes of War, Set. abr. ed. Stephen Coonts. Read by Richard Gilliland. 4 cass. 1999. 25.00 (FS9-43204) Highsmith.

Fortunes of War: The Great Fortune. abr. ed. Olivia Manning. Narrated by Emilia Fox. (Running Time: 5 hrs. 0 mins. 0 sec.). (ENG.). 2010. audio compact disk 26.95 (978-1-934997-54-3(4)) Pub: CSAWord. Dist(s): PerseuPGW

Fortune's Rocks, Anita Shreve. Read by Blair Brown. (Running Time: 5 hrs.). 2000. 29.95 (Random AudioBks) Random Audio Pubg.

Fortune's Rocks. unabr. ed. Anita Shreve. Read by Melissa Hughes. 12 vols. (Running Time: 50400 sec.). (Chivers Sound Library). 2000. 96.95 (978-0-7927-2351-6(1), CSL 240, Chivers Sound Lib) AudioGO.
It is 1900. Olympia Biddeford is the only child of a prominent Boston couple. Her summer at the family's vacation home in Fortune's Rocks is transformed by the arrival of a doctor whose new book about mill-town laborers has caused a sensation. She & the doctor, a married man, father & nearly three times her age, come together in an unthinkable affair, with cataclysmic results.

Fortune's Rocks. unabr. ed. Anita Shreve. Read by Melissa Hughes. 14 CDs. (Running Time: 21 hrs.). 2001. audio compact disk 115.95 (978-0-7927-9990-0(9), SLD 041, Chivers Sound Lib) AudioGO.

Fortuny Gown. unabr. ed. Rosalind Laker, pseud. Read by Lindsay Sandison. 10 cass. (Running Time: 13 hrs. 45 min.). 1996. 84.95 (978-1-85695-843-1(4), 950602) Pub: ISIS Audio GBR. Dist(s): Ulverscroft US

Forty Acres & Maybe a Mule. Harriette Gillem Robinet. Read by Andrea Johnson. 3 cass. (Running Time: 4 hrs. 15 mins.). (YA). 2000. 197.30 (978-0-7887-4433-4(X), 47124) Recorded Bks.
Twelve-year-old Pascal is thrilled to hear President Lincoln has freed the slaves & each slave family can have 40 acres of land. But Pascal still must hide from those who would return him to slavery. Will he ever know true freedom? The granddaughter of slaves on Robert E. Lee's Virginia estate, Harriette Gillem Robinet bases this story on research & oral stories of slavery.

Forty Acres & Maybe a Mule. Harriette Gillem Robinet. Read by Andrea Johnson. 3 cass. (Running Time: 4 hrs. 15 mins.). (YA). (gr. 3 up). 2000. pap. bk. 52.00 (978-0-7887-4332-0(5), 41127) Recorded Bks.

Forty Acres & Maybe a Mule. unabr. ed. Harriette Gillem Robinet. Narrated by Andrea Johnson. 3 pieces. (Running Time: 4 hrs. 15 mins.). (gr. 3 up). 2000. 29.00 (978-0-7887-4013-8(X), 95878E7) Recorded Bks.

Forty Acres of Thought Audio Book: Poems from Around the Bend. Roger Huisinga. (ENG.). 2007. audio compact disk 17.95 (978-1-932278-32-3(X)) Pub: Mayhaven Pub. Dist(s): Baker Taylor

Forty Days. Bob Simon. Read by Bob Simon. 2 cass. (Running Time: 3 hrs.). 1992. 15.95 Set. (978-1-879371-32-3(4), 20230) Pub Mills.
CBS News' Chief Middle Eastern correspondent Bob Simon recounts with chilling detail his ordeal at the hands of his Iraqi captors. This is an extraordinary journey through the mind of a highly sensitive, highly literate & resilient man who managed to survive through his own inner resources.

Forty-Five Degree Graphic Ephemeris. Pamela Rowe. 1 cass. (Running Time: 90 min.). 1990. 8.95 (808) Am Fed Astrologers.

Forty-five Degree Linear Diagram. Irene Goodale. 1 cass. 8.95 (857) Am Fed Astrologers.

Forty Four. Peter Sheridan. 2 cass. (Running Time: 3 hrs.). (ENG., 2001. (978-0-333-90278-3(5)) Macmillan UK GBR.

Forty Keys to Family Emergency Readiness. unabr. ed. Duane S. Crowther. Read by Duane S. Crowther. 1 cass. (Running Time: 60 min.). 1984. 13.98 (978-0-88290-248-7(2), 1810) Horizon Utah.
Offers a 40 point checklist to help the listener to identify his personal preparedness goals and to prepare a readiness plan with goals, schedule and budget.

***Forty Lashes Less One.** unabr. ed. Elmore Leonard. Read by Josh Clark. (ENG.). 2010. (978-0-06-199367-1(0), Harper Audio); (978-0-06-199751-8(X), Harper Audio) HarperCollins Pubs.

Forty Rules of Love. unabr. ed. Elif Shafak. Narrated by Laural Merlington. (Running Time: 12 hrs. 0 mins.). 2010. 17.99 (978-1-4001-8512-2(2)); 34.99 (978-1-4001-9512-1(8)) Tantor Media.

Forty Rules of Love. unabr. ed. Elif Shafak. Narrated by Laural Merlington. (Running Time: 12 hrs. 0 mins. 0 sec.). (ENG.). 2010. 24.99 (978-1-4001-6512-4(1)); audio compact disk 34.99 (978-1-4001-1512-9(4)); audio compact disk 69.99 (978-1-4001-4512-6(0)) Pub: Tantor Media. Dist(s): IngramPubServ

Forty-Two Stories. Douglas Post. Perf. by Fran Adams et al. 1 cass. (Running Time: 1 hr. 45 min.). 1998. 19.95 (978-1-58081-122-4(1), TPT103) L A Theatre.
Comedy about life inside a high-rise condominium building. A professional student from the University of Chicago is moonlighting as a janitor, a stressed-out apartment manager is at odds with residents & on the edge of a nervous breakdown, & a motley assortment of other staff members struggle with survival in the face of urban pandemonium & with the fact that one of them may be breaking into the units & stealing women's underware.

Forty Winks. Jessica Harper. 1 cass., 1 CD. (J). 7.98 (ALA 2008); audio compact disk 9.58 CD Jewel box. (ALA 2008); 7.98 (ALA 2008); audio compact disk 9.58 CD. (ALA 2008) NewSound.
Incorporate many genres including jazz, reggae & calpso into an upbeat style that's highlighted by sophisticated lyrics, lush arrangements & her creamy alto voice.

Forty Words for Sorrow. unabr. ed. Giles Blunt. Read by James Daniels. 7 cass. (Running Time: 10 hrs.). 2001. 32.95 (978-1-58788-585-3(9), 1587885859, BAU); 78.25 (978-1-58788-586-0(7), 1587885867, Unabridge Lib Edns) Brilliance Audio.
When the badly decomposed body of thirteen-year-old Katie Pine is found in an abandoned mine shaft, John Cardinal is vindicated. It was Cardinal who'd kept the Pine case open - insisting she was no mere runaway - and Cardinal had been demoted to the burglary squad for his excessive zeal. But Katie Pine isn't the only youngster to have gone missing in the rural town of Algonquin Bay, and Cardinal is now given the go-ahead to reopen the files on three other lost kids. When another youth is reported missing, he begins to see a pattern that screams "serial killer." Meanwhile, the brass have partnered him with Lisa Delorme, newly shifted to homicide from the Office of Special Investigations, and Cardinal can't help but wonder if she's been sent to keep tabs on him. A guilty conscience makes him think so. Superbly paced, with fully-fleshed characters and utterly convincing police detail, Forty Words for Sorrow is also a novel of place that transcends the genre. Blunt puts us in a small Canadian town in the dead of winter and makes us feel the cold, then turns the cold into a metaphor for the destruction of young lives. "Blunt has done for Canada's north what James Lee Burke did for Cajun Louisiana." - Margaret Cannon, Toronto Globe and Mail.

Forty Words for Sorrow. unabr. ed. Giles Blunt. Read by James Daniels. (Running Time: 10 hrs.). 2004. 39.25 (978-1-59335-368-1(5), 1593353685, Brlnc Audio MP3 Lib) Brilliance Audio.

Forty Words for Sorrow. unabr. ed. Giles Blunt. Read by James Daniels. (Running Time: 10 hrs.). 2004. 39.25 (978-1-59710-306-0(3), 1597103063, BADLE); 24.95 (978-1-59710-307-7(1), 1597103071, BAD) Brilliance Audio.

Forty Words for Sorrow. unabr. ed. Giles Blunt. Read by James Daniels. (Running Time: 10 hrs.). 2004. 24.95 (978-1-59335-038-3(4), 1593350384) Soulmate Audio Bks.

Forty's & Fifty's Walking One: (Beginner) Bruce Blackmon. 1 cass. (Running Time: 1 hr. 2 min.). 1991. 12.95 (978-1-56481-000-7(3)) Sports Music.
A one hour beginner level fitness walking program featuring well known songs from the 1940's & 1950's.

Forty's & Fifty's Walking Three: (Advanced) Bruce Blackmon. 1 cass. (Running Time: 1 hr. 2 min.). 1991. 12.95 Sports Music.
A one hour advanced level fitness walking program featuring well known songs from the 1940's & 1950's.

Forty's & Fifty's Walking Two: (Intermediate) Bruce Blackmon. 1 cass. (Running Time: 1 hr. 2 min.). 1991. 12.95 (978-1-56481-001-4(1)) Sports Music.
A one hour intermediate level fitness walking program featuring well known songs from the 1940's & 1950's.

Fortysomething: Women in Transition (Adjusting to Premenopause & Its Symptoms) unabr. ed. Mercedes Leidlich. Read by Mercedes Leidlich. 1 cass. (Running Time: 1 hr.). 1992. 10.95 in Norelco box. (978-1-882174-10-2(0), MLL-011) UFD Pub.
Spoken audio tape about the transitional decade of the forties, when a woman may begin to experience menopausal symptoms. The tape lists symptoms & how to cope with them, plus discusses the two hidden dangers that occur post-menopause of cardiovascular disease & osteoporosis.

Forward Intermediate. 2003. audio compact disk (978-1-903856-05-5(1), T & A.D Poyser) A and C Blk GBR.

Forward March. 1997. audio compact disk 12.95 (978-0-7692-1651-5(X), Warner Bro) Alfred Pub.

Forward Pre-Intermediate. 2003. audio compact disk (978-1-903856-02-4(7), T & A.D Poyser) A and C Blk GBR.

Forward the Foundation. unabr. ed. Isaac Asimov. Read by Larry McKeever. 12 cass. (Running Time: 18 hrs.). 1994. 96.00 (978-0-7366-2622-4(0), 3362) Books on Tape.
Hari Seldon sees the end is near for the Galactic Empire. If Hari can complete his revolutionary Theory of Psychohistory, it may ensure human survival! If not...destruction, death, disintegration.

Forwarding the Faith. Perf. by Men of Foundations Quartet. Prod. by Foundations Bible College. (Running Time: 61.43 min.). 2001. 7.95 (978-1-882542-33-8(9), 1882542339) Fndtns NC.

Forwarding the Faith: Sacred Hymns from the Whitefield Sanctuary. Perf. by Foundations Bible College & Men of Foundations Quartet. (Running Time: 61.43 min.). 2001. audio compact disk 13.95 (978-1-882542-32-1(0), 1882542320) Fndtns NC.

Fosdick & Faith. 10.00 Esstee Audios.
Sermon on whether religious people are fooling themselves.

Fossils Alive/Fossils - Pictures from the Past. Steck-Vaughn Staff. (J). 1999. (978-0-7398-0923-5(7)) SteckVau.

Fossils & Faith. Nathan Aviezer. Read by Michael Jarmus. Prod. by Alden Films Staff. (Running Time: 7 hrs. 9 mins. 0 sec.). (ENG.). 2010. audio compact disk 49.95 (978-1-877684-78-4(3)) Pub: Alden Films. Dist(s): Perseus Dist

Foster / MacDowell Companion CD. Compiled by Zeezok Publishing. (J). 2008. audio compact disk 7.95 (978-1-933573-22-9(8), 4843) Zeezok Pubng.

Foster Care: A Basic Introduction. 2005. 29.95 (978-1-59808-059-9(8)); audio compact disk 24.95 (978-1-59808-057-5(1)) Whsprng Pine.

Foster Parenting: A Basic Introduction. Karen Jean Matsko Hood. (Help a Child Ser.: 1). 2005. 24.95 (978-1-59210-028-6(7)) Whsprng Pine.

Fostering Minority Access & Achievement in Higher Education: The Role of Urban Community Colleges & Universities. Richard C. Richardson, Jr. & Louis W. Bender. (Higher & Adult Education Ser.). 1987. bk. 36.95 (978-1-55542-053-6(2), Jossey-Bass) Wiley US.

Fostering Religious Experiences. Vincent M. Walsh. Read by Maria Rosita. 3 cass. (Running Time: 3 hrs.). 10.00 Set. Key of David.

Fostering Vocations in Family Home. Sr. Troskowski. 1 cass. (National Meeting of the Institute, 1993 Ser.). 4.00 (93N5) IRL Chicago.

Foucault's Pendulum. unabr. ed. Umberto Eco. Read by Alexander Adams. 16 cass. (Running Time: 24 hr.). 1997. 128.00 (978-0-7366-3796-1(6), 4469-A\B) Books on Tape.
Three editors who have spent altogether too much time reviewing crackpot manuscripts on the occult, decide to have a little fun.

Foucault's Pendulum, Pt. 1. unabr. ed. Umberto Eco. Read by Alexander Adams. 8 cass. (Running Time: 12 hrs.). 1997. 64.00 (4469-A) Books on Tape.

Foucault's Pendulum, Pt. 2. unabr. ed. Umberto Eco. Read by Alexander Adams. 8 cass. (Running Time: 12 hrs.). 1997. 64.00 (4469-B) Books on Tape.

Foul Harvest. Hamsoken. Music by Nick Forte. Stacy Wakefield. Looming. 2009. audio compact disk 9.00 (978-0-9763355-2-8(2)) Evil Twin Pubns.

Foul Matter. unabr. ed. Martha Grimes. 8 cass. (Running Time: 12 hrs.). 2003. 90.00 (978-0-7366-9574-9(5)) Books on Tape.
An egotistical writer slashes his way through the cutthroat world of book publishing.

Foul Play. unabr. ed. Tori Carrington. Read by Rebecca Rogers. (Running Time: 28800 sec.). (Sofie Metropolis Novels Ser.). 2007. 59.95 (978-1-4332-1063-1(0)); audio compact disk 29.95 (978-1-4332-1065-5(7)); audio compact disk 72.00 (978-1-4332-1064-8(9)) Blckstn Audio.

Foul Play. unabr. ed. Janet Evanovich. Read by C. J. Critt. 2008. audio compact disk 14.95 (978-0-06-170304-1(4), Harper Audio) HarperCollins Pubs.

***Foul Play.** unabr. ed. Janet Evanovich. Read by C. J. Critt. (ENG.). 2008. (978-0-06-178976-2(3), Harper Audio); (978-0-06-178975-5(5), Harper Audio) HarperCollins Pubs.

Foul Shot. Molly Jackel. (Room 202 Ser.). 2005. pap. bk. 69.00 (978-1-4105-0614-6(2)); audio compact disk 18.95 (978-1-4105-0612-2(6)) D Johnston Inc.

Found. abr. ed. Karen Kingsbury. Read by Sandra Burr. (Running Time: 4 hrs.). (Firstborn Ser.). 2006. 39.25 (978-1-59737-968-7(9), 9781597379687, BADLE); 9.99 (978-1-59737-967-0(0), 9781597379670, BAD); 19.95 (978-1-59600-201-2(8), 9781596002012); 49.25 (978-1-59600-202-9(6), 9781596002029, BAudLibEd); audio compact disk 21.95 (978-1-59600-203-6(4), 9781596002036); audio compact disk 69.25 (978-1-59600-204-3(2), 9781596002043, BACDLib Ed); audio compact disk 39.25 (978-1-59737-966-3(2), 9781597379663, Brlnc Audio MP3 Lib); audio compact disk 9.99 (978-1-59737-965-6(4), 9781597379656, Brilliance MP3) Brilliance Audio.
Please enter a Synopsis.

***Found.** abr. ed. Karen Kingsbury. Read by Sandra Burr. (Running Time: 4 hrs.). (Firstborn Ser.). 2010. audio compact disk 9.99 (978-1-4418-7825-0(4), 9781441878250, BCD Value Price) Brilliance Audio.

Found. unabr. ed. Margaret Peterson Haddix. Narrated by Chris Sorensen. 6 cass. (Running Time: 7 hrs.). (Missing Ser.: Bk. 1). (J). (gr. 4-8). 2008. 61.75 (978-1-4361-0689-4(3)); audio compact disk 87.75 (978-1-4361-0694-8(X)) Recorded Bks.

Found Art: Discovering Beauty in Foreign Places. unabr. ed. Leeana Tankersley. (Running Time: 3 hrs. 56 mins. 0 sec.). (ENG.). 2009. 16.99 (978-0-310-77340-5(7)) Zondervan.

***Found: God's Will: Find the Direction & Purpose God Wants for Your Life.** John MacArthur. (Running Time: 1 hr. 25 mins. 0 sec.). (ENG.). 2011. audio compact disk 5.98 (978-1-61045-059-1(0)) christianaud.

Found Money, unabr. ed. James Grippando. Narrated by George Guidall. 8 cass. (Running Time: 11 hrs. 30 mins.). 1999. 75.00 (978-0-7887-3055-9(X), 95749E7) Recorded Bks.
It takes a former trial lawyer to understand the fine legal line between a blessing & a curse. When Ryan Duffy discovers a box of money in his dead father's attic, Duffy begins to wonder what other secrets his parent had.

Found Money. unabr. ed. James Grippando. Narrated by George Guidall. 8 cass. (Running Time: 11 hrs. 30 mins.). 2002. 39.95 (978-0-7887-8260-2(6), RD741) Recorded Bks.
The author's uses his experience as a trial lawyer and acclaimed storyteller to create a suspenseful thriller that draws and redraws the fine line between a blessing and a curse. Even as he mourns his father's recent, small town doctor Ryan Duffy is facing an expensive divorce. Suddenly, when he discovers millions of dollars in his father's attic, the baffled young man is faced with two questions. Where did a modest electrician get this much money? Can Ryan keep it? Several hundred miles away, Amy Parkens has received an unexpected fortune, too, from the same source. As Ryan and Amy are brought together by their search for answers, they learn that there are powerful people who will do anything to silence them and get the cash.

Found Money, Set. abr. ed. James Grippando. Read by Mark Blum. 2 cass. 1999. 18.00 (FS9-43312) Highsmith.

***Found Money Low Price.** abr. ed. James Grippando. Read by Mark Blum. (ENG.). 2004. (978-0-06-082398-6(4), Harper Audio); (978-0-06-082397-9(6), Harper Audio) HarperCollins Pubs.

Found Treasure. abr. ed. Grace Livingston Hill. Read by Aimee Lilly. 2 cass. (Running Time: 1 hr. 30 mins. per cass.). (Grace Livingston Hill Romances Ser.). 2004. 8.99 (978-1-886463-53-0(0)) Oasis Audio.
Effie Martin's act of heroism throws her into an extraordinary friendship that brings her faith - - and love. One cassette Over 1-1/2 hours Abridged.

Foundation. abr. ed. Isaac Asimov. Read by Larry McKeever. 6 cass. (Running Time: 6 cass.). 1983. 48.00 (978-0-7366-0865-7(6), 1816) Books on Tape.
The decline & fall of the Galactic Empire & the struggle of a scientific coterie to establish conditions for a new & better Empire.

Foundation. unabr. ed. Mercedes Lackey. (Running Time: 10 hrs.). (Valdemar Ser.). 2007. 24.95 (978-1-4233-0793-8(3), 9781423307938, Brilliance MP3); 39.25 (978-1-4233-0794-5(1), 9781423307945, Brlnc Audio MP3 Lib); audio compact disk 97.25 (978-1-4233-0792-1(5), 9781423307921, BriAudCD Unabrid) Brilliance Audio.

Foundation. unabr. ed. Mercedes Lackey. Read by Nick Podehl. (Running Time: 10 hrs.). (Valdemar Ser.). 2008. 24.95 (978-1-4233-0795-2(X), 9781423307952, BAD); 39.25 (978-1-4233-0796-9(8), 9781423307969, BADLE); audio compact disk 32.99 (978-1-4233-0757-0(7), 9781423307570, Bril Audio CD Unabri) Brilliance Audio.

Foundation, Set. Speeches. Eric J. Pepin. Prod. by Higher Balance Institute. 6 CDs. (Running Time: 5 hrs 50 mins). 2003. audio compact disk 149.00 (978-0-9759080-9-9(X)) Higher Bal.

Foundation: Acts 1:1-5. Ed Young. 1997. 4.95 (978-0-7417-2146-4(5), 1146) Win Walk.

Foundation: The Psychohistorians see SF Soundbook

Foundation & Earth. unabr. ed. Isaac Asimov. Read by Larry McKeever. 13 cass. (Running Time: 19 hrs. 30 min.). 1994. 104.00 (978-0-7366-2817-4(7), 3528) Books on Tape.
Centuries after the fall of the First Galactic Empire, mankind's descendants still search for humanity's legendary home, fabled Earth.

Foundation & Empire. Isaac Asimov. Read by Scott Brick. 2002. 64.00 (978-0-7366-8957-1(5)); audio compact disk 72.00 (978-0-7366-9238-0(X)) Books on Tape.

Foundation & Empire. unabr. ed. Isaac Asimov. Read by Dan Lazar. 8 cass. (Running Time: 8 hrs.). 1979. 48.00 (978-0-7366-0236-5(4), 1232) Books on Tape.
In this narrative, the Galactic Empire established in the previous episode is decaying- being consumed by its own immorality & scientific mismanagement. The Foundation is formed to counteract the Fall but soon gains equal, if not superior power to the disintegrating Empire.

Foundation for Living. Philip L. Hansen. 8 cass. 1986. 39.95 (6910) Hazelden.
In addition to the Twelve Steps of AA, Rev. Hansen discusses the enormity of alcoholism, symptoms & diagnosis, changes over the years, marriage & communication.

Foundation for Moral Purity: Teaching Your Children About Sexuality. Dennis Rainey & Barbara Rainey. 2003. 19.99 (978-1-57229-383-0(7)) FamilyLife.

Foundation of Consecration. Speeches. Creflo A. Dollar. 3 cass. (Running Time: 4 hrs.). 2003. 15.00 (978-1-59089-792-8(7)); audio compact disk 21.00 (978-1-59089-793-5(5)) Creflo Dollar.

Foundation of Covenant. Speeches. Creflo A. Dollar. 5 cass. (Running Time: 6 hrs.). 2003. 25.00 (978-1-59089-786-7(2)); audio compact disk 34.00 (978-1-59089-787-4(0)) Creflo Dollar.

Foundation of Esoteric Astrology. Beverly J. Farrell. 1 cass. 8.95 (113) Am Fed Astrologers.
Seven Rays, soul progress, energy and force, and more.

Foundation of Kingdom Addiction. Speeches. Creflo A. Dollar. 3 cass. (Running Time: 4 hrs.). 2003. 15.00 (978-1-59089-798-0(6)); audio compact disk Rental 21.00 (978-1-59089-799-7(4)) Creflo Dollar.

Foundation of Restoration. Rick Joyner. 1 cass. (Running Time: 90 mins.). (Apostolic Calling & Ministry Ser.: Vol. 1). 2000. 5.00 (RJ07-001) Morning NC.
This series gives a foundational understanding of the true apostolic authority that is being restored to the church.

Foundation of Spiritual Liberty. Rick Joyner. 1 cass. (Running Time: 90 mins.). (Foundation Ser.: Vol. 7). 2000. 5.00 (RJ04-007) Morning NC.
Firmly establishing basic Christian principles, these messages also illuminate some of the primary enemies of truth, such as legalism & the control spirit.

Foundation Series Part 1: Rock Solid Faith. Rick Joyner. 10 cass. (Running Time: 15 hrs.). 2000. 50.00 (RJ04-000) Morning NC.

Foundation Series Part II: The Dwelling Places of God. unabr. ed. Rick Joyner. 10 cass. (Running Time: 15 hrs.). 2000. 50.00 (RJ05-000) Morning NC.
As an overview of God's plan for His church, this series contains essential truths for everyone who wants to see the church become all that she is called to be.

Foundation Stones of the Ashram. Swami Amar Jyoti. 1 cass. 1975. 9.95 (M-61) Truth Consciousness.
The role & discipline of the ashram. Obligations of ashramite & householder disciples.

Foundation Truth. Frank Damazio. 13 cass. (Running Time: 19 hrs. 30 mins.). 2000. (978-1-886849-31-0(5)) CityChristian.

Foundational Doctrines of the Faith. Elmer L. Towns. 3 cass. 99.95 Set, incl. textbk., planning, teaching & promotional materials. (420) Chrch Grwth VA.
Helps christians know & understand basic foundational doctrines of the Christian faith.

Foundational Truths for Building Your Faith. Instructed by Lori Greenwood. 6 cass. (Running Time: 62 mins.). (YA). 2002. 25.00 (978-0-9747956-2-1(3)) Lori Greenwood Min.

Foundations. 2nd ed. Steven J. Molinsky & Bill Bliss. 2002. 61.20 (978-0-13-385139-7(7)) Longman.

Foundations & Fallacies. Steve Thompson. 1 cass. (Running Time: 90 mins.). (Prophetic Ministry Ser.: Vol. 1). 2000. 5.00 (ST01-001) Morning NC.
Now updated & expanded, this popular series combines insights from the Scriptures & personal experience to explain how we can more effectively hear from God & minister prophetically.

Foundation's Edge. unabr. ed. Isaac Asimov. Read by Larry McKeever. 9 cass. (Running Time: 13 hrs. 30 min.). 1983. 72.00 (978-0-7366-0866-4(4), 1817) Books on Tape.
It is 498 Years since the establishment of the first Foundation. Power struggles sweep the Foundations as each drives toward becoming the controlling nucleus in the planned second Galactic Empire. The destiny of humankind is at stake.

Foundations for Faith: Old Testament Survey. Speeches. Douglas Jacoby. 8 CDs. (Running Time: 8 hours). 2005. audio compact disk 32.00 (978-0-9767583-7-2(7)) Illumination MA.

Foundations for Fathers. Wilson Douglas. 6 CDs. (ENG.). 1990. audio compact disk 18.00 (978-1-59128-201-3(2)) Canon Pr ID.

Foundations for Fathers-tape. Douglas Wilson. 6 cass. 1990. 18.00 (978-1-59128-202-0(0)) Canon Pr ID.

Foundations for Reading & Writing, Bk. 1. J. N. Dale et al. Ed. by A. R. Evans. (Welcome to English Ser.). 1977. 12.00 (978-0-89285-044-0(2)) ELS Educ Servs.

Foundations for Reading & Writing, Bk. 2. J. N. Dale et al. Ed. by A. R. Evans. (Welcome to English Ser.). 1977. 12.00 (978-0-89285-045-7(0)) ELS Educ Servs.

Foundations for Reading & Writing, Bk. 3. J. N. Dale et al. Ed. by A. R. Evans. (Welcome to English Ser.). 1977. 12.00 (978-0-89285-046-4(9)) ELS Educ Servs.

Foundations for Reading & Writing, Bk. 4. J. N. Dale et al. Ed. by A. R. Evans. (Welcome to English Ser.). 1977. 12.00 (978-0-89285-047-1(7)) ELS Educ Servs.

Foundations in Elementary Education: Music Recordings. Music by Elizabeth B. Carlton & Phyllis S. Weikart. 1 CD. audio compact disk 15.95 (978-1-57379-001-7(X), E3201) High-Scope.
Thirty delightful songs based on important musical concepts. Each song is sung with simple accompaniment, so you can quickly join in. Designed to accompany the companion book: "Foundations in Elementary Education".

Foundations in Elementary Education: Music Recordings. Dagmar Stam. Tr. by Eric Van Deventer from DUT. Music by Phyllis S. Weikart. 1 cass. (J). 1995. bk. 10.95 (978-1-57379-025-3(7), K1008) High-Scope.

Foundations in Singing. 6th ed. Van A. Christy & John G. Paton. 1 cass. (Running Time: 1 hr. 30 mins.). 1996. 30.00 (978-0-697-35376-4(1), Mc-H Human Soc) Pub: McGrw-H Hghr Educ. Dist(s): McGraw

Foundations of American Government. unabr. ed. David Barton. Read by David Barton. 1 cass. (Running Time: 25 min.). 1994. 4.95 (978-0-925279-37-8(4), A12) Wallbuilders.
This presentation acquaints viewers with the truth that the current doctrine of "separation of church & state" is something never intended by the Founders.

Foundations of Dedication & Affection. Speeches. Creflo A. Dollar. 2 cass. (Running Time: 3 hrs.). 2003. 10.00 (978-1-59089-796-6(X)); audio compact disk 14.00 (978-1-59089-797-3(8)) Creflo Dollar.

Foundations of Economics: AP* Teacher Resource CD. 3rd ed. Bade & Parkin. 2006. audio compact disk 18.97 (978-0-13-173443-2(1)) PH School.

Foundations of Education for Blind & Visually Handicapped Children & Youth: Theory & Practice. unabr. ed. Read by Richard C. Dorf. Ed. by Geraldine T. Scholl. 6 cass. (Running Time: 34 hrs. 30 min.). 1986. 55.00 (978-0-89128-181-8(9)) Am Foun Blind.
Discusses current options in the education of blind & visually handicapped children, from preschool through high school.

Foundations of Ethics. unabr. ed. W. T. Stace. 1 cass. (Running Time: 23 min.). 12.95 (25025) J Norton Pubs.
A discussion of the origins of ethical behavior, with an examination of "religious" ethics as against "secular" or "naturalistic" ethics where morality is autonomous.

Foundations of Faith. Gary V. Whetstone. Instructed by June Austin. 9 cass. (Running Time: 13 hrs. 30 mins.). (Faith Ser.: F101). 1996. pap. bk. 170.00 (978-1-928774-48-8(2), BT 101 A00) Gary Whet Pub.
Emphasis on what faith is & what faith is not, where our faith comes from, how it causes us to grow according to the Word of God & how to apply the principles of faith.

Foundations of Low Vision: Clinical & Functional Perspectives. unabr. ed. Ed. by Anne L. Corn & Alan J. Koenig. 5 cass. (Running Time: 30 hrs.). 1996. 59.95 (978-0-89128-292-1(0)) Am Foun Blind.
Addresses both clinical & functional implications of low vision, their impact on the individual & the ways in which these implications are to be addressed by educators, rehabilitators & professionals. Not regular cassettes - 4 track 1-15/16 ips; special equipment to play.

Foundations of Nursing: An Integrated Approach - Classroom Manager. Lois White. 2000. audio compact disk 257.95 (978-0-7668-0828-7(9)) Delmar.

Foundations of Oracle CBT. Course Technology Staff. 2000. audio compact disk 53.95 (978-0-619-03414-6(9)) Course Tech.

Foundations of Rehabilitative Teaching: With Persons Who Are Blind or Visually Impaired. unabr. ed. Paul E. Ponchillia & Susan V. Ponchillia. 5 cass. (Running Time: 25 hrs. 20 min.). 1996. 59.95 (978-0-89128-291-4(2)) Am Foun Blind.
Comprehensive manual on profession of rehabilitative teaching. Details history & development of rehabilitative teaching & provides practical information & instructional strategies. Cannot be played in regular player - 4 track 1-15/16 ips - needs special equipment.

Foundations of Spiritual Visions. Rick Joyner. 1 cass. (Running Time: 90 mins.). (Foundation Ser.: Vol. 6). 2000. 5.00 (RJ04-006) Morning NC.
Firmly establishing basic Christian principles, these messages also illuminate some of the primary enemies of truth, such as legalism & the control spirit.

Foundations of Thai. 27 cass. 186.95 Set. U MI Lang Res.

Foundations of Tibetan Psychiatry. Mark Epstein. 2 cass. 18.00 (OC23L) Sound Horizons AV.

Foundations of Western Civilization, Parts I-IV. Instructed by Thomas Noble. 24 cass. (Running Time: 24 hrs.). 2002. bk. 99.95 (978-1-56585-532-8(9), 370); bk. 129.95 (978-1-56585-534-2(5), 370) Teaching Co.

Foundations of Western Civilization II: A History of the Modern Western World. Instructed by Robert Bucholz. 24 cass. (Running Time: 24 hrs.). 2006. 249.95 (978-1-59803-173-7(2)); audio compact disk 129.95 (978-1-59803-175-1(9)) Teaching Co.

Foundations, the Life of the Believer. Chuck Smith. (ENG.). 2001. audio compact disk 22.99 (978-1-932941-11-1(8)) Word For Today.

Founder: A Portrait of the First Rothschild & His Time. unabr. ed. Amos Elon. Read by Michael Prichard. 4 cass. (Running Time: 6 hrs.). 1999. 32.00 (978-0-7366-4418-1(0), 4879) Books on Tape.
An extraordinary portrait of the life & times of Meyer Amschel Rothschild.

Founders of Hilander in Orthodox Chant. Danica Petrovic. (ENG & SER., 1999. pap. bk. 99.50 (978-86-7025-287-5(2)) Pub: Srpska akad YUG. Dist(s): Coronet Bks

Founders of the Western World. unabr. ed. Michael Grant. Read by Nadia May. 7 cass. (Running Time: 10 hrs.). 1994. 49.95 Set. (978-0-7861-0826-8(6), 1544) Blckstn Audio.
Through in-depth analysis, Michael Grant introduces us to the political, military, cultural, social, economic, & religious life of the times that were the building blocks of what we now call the Western World. He creates a vivid panorama of the Greco-Roman world by bringing together the most dramatic events on record from its beginnings in 1,000 BC to the fall of the western Roman Empire in the fifth century AD.

Founders of Western Philosophy Vol. 1: Thales to Hume. Leonard Peikoff. 24 cass. (Running Time: 33 hrs.). (History of Philosophy Ser.). 1994. 295.00 Set. (978-1-56114-310-8(3), LP37D) Second Renaissance.
Presents the ideas that shaped Western Philosophy.

Founding. unabr. ed. Cynthia Harrod-Eagles. Read by Christopher Scott. 14 cass. (Running Time: 21 hrs.). (Morland Dynasty Ser.: No. 1). 2001. 99.95 (980106) Pub: ISIS Audio GBR. Dist(s): Ulverscroft US

Founding. unabr. ed. Cynthia Harrod-Eagles. Read by Christopher Scott. 14 cass. (Morland Dynasty Ser.: No. 1). (J). 2004. 99.95 (978-0-7531-0349-4(4)) Pub: ISIS Lrg Prnt GBR. Dist(s): Ulverscroft US

Founding Brothers: The Revolutionary Generation. Joseph J. Ellis. Narrated by Nelson Runger. 12 CDs. (Running Time: 13 hrs. 30 mins.). audio compact disk 118.00 (978-0-7887-9561-9(9)) Recorded Bks.

Founding Brothers: The Revolutionary Generation. unabr. ed. Joseph J. Ellis. Narrated by Nelson Runger. 10 cass. (Running Time: 13 hrs. 30 mins.). 2001. 81.00 (978-0-7887-5515-6(3), 95926) Recorded Bks.
Here are the stories behind the historical events that shaped America, such as the duel between Alexander Hamilton & Aaron Burr, & the secret dinner party that made Washington, D.C. the permanent national capitol.

Founding Brothers: The Revolutionary Generation. unabr. ed. Joseph J. Ellis. Read by Nelson Runger. 12 CDs. (Running Time: 13 hrs. 30 mins.). 2004. audio compact disk 39.95 (978-1-4025-0539-3(6), 00262) Recorded Bks.
With this New York Times best-seller, you'll discover the untold stories behind many of our most cherished historic events. Founding Brothers transports you back in time to witness exciting moments like the infamous duel between Alexander Hamilton and Aaron Burr, and the secret dinner party that determined the site for the national capital. Drawing on careful research, National Book Award winner Joseph J. Ellis crafts engaging portraits of Washington, Jefferson, Madison, and others who shaped our country.

Founding Communities of Prayer: Advice from Teresa of Avila. John Welch. Read by John Welch. 1 cass. (Running Time: 42 min.). 8.95 I C S Pubns.
Fr. John Welch, O. Carm. tells of Teresa's freeing her nuns to be friends with one another & with God.

Founding Documents. Larry Knapp & Big Radio Players Staff. (Running Time: 1 hr. 08 min.). 1996. 39.95 Compact Disc. (978-1-888928-01-3(8)) BIG RADIO.

Founding Faith: How Our Founding Fathers Forged a Radical New Approach to Religious Liberty. unabr. ed. Steven Waldman. Narrated by David Colacci. (Running Time: 35220 sec.). (ENG.). 2008. audio compact disk 29.95 (978-1-60283-377-7(X)) Pub: AudioGO. Dist(s): Perseus Dist

Founding Faith: How Our Founding Fathers Forged a Radical New Approach to Religious Liberty. unabr. ed. Steven Waldman. Read by David Colacci. 8 CDs. (Running Time: 7 hrs. 30 mins.). 2008. audio compact disk 79.95 (978-0-7927-5348-3(8)) AudioGO.
The culture wars have distorted the dramatic story of how Americans came to worship freely. Many activists on the right maintain that the United States was founded as a "Christian nation." Many on the left contend that the Founders were secular or Deist and that the First Amendment was designed to boldly separate church and state throughout the land. None of these claims are true, argues Beliefnet.com editor in chief Steven Waldman. With refreshing objectivity, Waldman narrates the real story of how our nation's Founders forged a new approach to religious liberty, a revolutionary formula that promoted faith . . . by leaving it alone. The spiritual custody battle over the Founding Fathers and the role of religion in America continues today. Waldman provocatively argues that neither side in the culture war has accurately depicted the true origins of the First Amendment. He sets the record straight, revealing the real history of religious freedom to be dramatic, unexpected, paradoxical, and inspiring.

Founding Father: Rediscovering George Washington. unabr. ed. Richard Brookhiser. Read by Dick Estell. 7 cass. (Running Time: 7 hrs.). 1996. 56.00 (978-0-7366-3414-4(2), 4060) Books on Tape.
George Washington was a monumental man, not a stone monument. His astounding career deserves fresh admiration.

Founding Fathers. unabr. ed. David Barton. Read by David Barton. 1 cass. (Running Time: 60 min.). 1992. 4.95 (978-0-925279-22-4(6)) Wallbuilders.
This tape highlights the accomplishments & noteable quotes of many of the more prominent & influential Founding Fathers, revealing their strong belief that Christian principles were vital to successful education & effective government.

Founding Fathers. unabr. ed. Ed. by Arthur M. Schlesinger, Jr. (Running Time: 20 hrs. 0 mins. 0 sec.). (American Presidents Ser.). 2008. audio compact disk 59.95 (978-1-4272-0550-6(7)) Pub: Macmill Audio. Dist(s): Macmillan

Founding Fathers: Architects of a Nation. Compiled by Encyclopaedia Britannica, Inc. 2009. audio compact disk 29.95; audio compact disk 29.95; audio compact disk 29.95; audio compact disk 29.95 Ency Brit Inc.

Founding Fathers - Architects of a Nation. unabr. ed. Encyclopedia Britannica. Read by Richard M. Davidson. (Listen & Learn Ser.). (YA). 2006. 44.99 (978-1-59895-465-4(2)) Find a World.

Founding Fathers: Architects of a Nation: Encyclopaedia Britannica's Listen & Learn Series. Compiled by Encyclopaedia Britannica, Inc. 2007. audio compact disk 34.95 (978-1-59339-542-1(6)) Ency Brit Inc.

Founding Fathers in Person. unabr. ed. Claude-Anne Lopez & Mary Jo Kline. 1 cass. (Running Time: 56 min.). 12.95 (40222) J Norton Pubs.
In an interview by Heywood Hale Broun, Lopez & Kline examine the many facets of Benjamin Franklin & John Adams - as statesmen, fathers, world travelers, & their private persons - destroying existing stereotypes.

Founding Fathers on Leadership: Classic Teamwork in Changing Times, unabr. ed. Donald T. Phillips. Narrated by Nelson Runger. 7 cass. (Running Time: 10 hrs.). 1997. 60.00 (978-0-7887-3780-0(5), 95997E7) Recorded Bks.
In the face of terrible odds, Washington, Paine, Jefferson & Madison achieved great success. Leadership expert Donald T. Phillips shows how the principles that worked for them translate into management practices that can be applied to today's business world. Exciting scenarios from history reveal our founding fathers' crucial decisions & the lessons they teach us.

Founding Fathers on Leadership: Classic Teamwork in Changing Times. unabr. ed. Donald T. Phillips. Narrated by Nelson Runger. 1 CD. 2000. audio compact disk 78.00 (C1189W5) Recorded Bks.

Founding Fathers on LeadershipTM: Classic Teamwork in Changing Times. Donald T. Phillips. Narrated by Nelson Runger. 8 CDs. (Running Time: 10 hrs.). audio compact disk 78.00 (978-0-7887-4487-7(9)) Recorded Bks.

Founding Fathers Uncommon Heroes. Steven W. Allen. 2004. audio compact disk 24.95 (978-1-879033-75-7(5)) Legal Awareness.
Learn what was in the minds and hearts of these amazing men as they shaped the Constitution.

Founding Fathers Uncommon Heroes: LDS Edition Audio Book on CD, LDS. Steven W. Allen. (ENG.). 2004. audio compact disk 24.95 (978-1-879033-74-0(7)) Legal Awareness.

Founding Freedom. Lance Auburn Everette. 2 cass. (Running Time: 3 hrs.). 2005. 15.99 (978-1-58943-272-7(X)) Am Pubng Inc.
This is the fourth book in a truly unique series of historical action-adventure novels: Michael. Sometimes, in history, things worked out for the best against all odds. Maybe Somebody intervened on the side of the correct path - even when we didn't know what that path was. But to intervene in the affairs of human beings without disrupting civilization completely is to wield human tools - and human weapons. So when the Archangels arrive to Change Things, watch out! In the remote valleys of the Alps, Swiss peasants and villagers have ruled themselves for centuries. Now, from greed and an arrogant lust for power, their nominal feudal overlords want to impose direct control by the sword. How could William Tell and his untrained, unarmed farmers and craftsmen resist knights in armor and professional men-at-arms?Did Somebody help? Published for the first time ever by Americana Publishing. Michael: Spirituality - with an edge.

Founding Freedom. Lance Auburn Everette. Read by Sherri Barth. 3 CDs. (Running Time: 3 hrs.). (Michael Ser.: No. 4). 2005. audio compact disk 9.99 (978-1-58943-485-1(4)) Am Pubng Inc.

***Founding Mothers.** unabr. ed. Cokie Roberts. Read by Cokie Roberts. (ENG.). 2004. (978-0-06-076421-0(X), Harper Audio); (978-0-06-081356-7(3), Harper Audio) HarperCollins Pubs.

Founding Mothers: The Women Who Raised Our Nation. abr. unabr. ed. Cokie Roberts. Read by Cokie Roberts. 4 cass. (Running Time: 6 hrs.). 2004. 25.95 (978-0-06-052788-4(9)) HarperCollins Pubs.

Founding Mothers: The Women Who Raised Our Nation. unabr. ed. Cokie Roberts. Read by Cokie Roberts. 2004. audio compact disk 29.95 (978-0-06-052787-7(0)) HarperCollins Pubs.

Founding of the Bar Harbor Mouse Bakery. unabr. ed. B. J. Morison. Read by Leitha Christie. 1 cass. (Running Time: 1 hr. 29 min.). (J). (gr. 5-8). 1994. 9.95 (978-1-889112-01-5(1)) Earbks.
A fable about "human" mice. Set in Maine.

Foundling see Poetry & Voice of Margaret Atwood

Foundling. unabr. ed. Humphrey Bower. Read by Humphrey Bower. 7 CDs. (Running Time: 8 hrs. 34 mins.). (Monster Blood Tattoo Ser.: Bk. 1). (J). (gr. 4-7). 2007. audio compact disk 55.00 (978-0-7393-5120-8(6), Random Hse Audible) Pub: Random Audio Pubg. Dist(s): Random

Foundling. unabr. ed. Georgette Heyer. Read by Phyllida Nash. 12 cass. (Running Time: 14 hrs. 28 min.). 2001. 96.95 (978-0-7540-0609-1(3), CAB2032) Pub: Chivers Audio Bks GBR. Dist(s): AudioGO
The shy young Duke of Sale has been brought up by an uncle & valet. His natural diffidence conceals a rebellious spirit & he enters into a dangerous world of intrigue, kidnap & adventure.

Fountain. unabr. ed. Emily Grayson. Narrated by Ruth Ann Phimister. 5 cass. (Running Time: 7 hrs.). 2002. 48.00 (978-1-4025-1338-1(0)) Recorded Bks.
Two days before Casey Becket is to throw an elaborate party celebrating her 20th wedding anniversary, Will Combray appears in her backyard. Will is Casey's first love. She has not seen him since he left her at the altar following a whirlwind romance. Jilted, Casey fell into the supportive arms of Michael, her best friend. They have enjoyed a pleasant marriage, but now Casey is at the crossroads of her life. Will wants her back, and she'll have to choose between passion and comfort.

Fountain Filled with Blood. Julia Spencer-Fleming. Read by Suzanne Toren. 8 cass. (Clare Fergusson/Russ Van Alstyne Mystery Ser.). 69.95 (978-0-7927-3315-7(0), CSL 692); audio compact disk 99.95 (978-0-7927-3316-4(9), SLD 692); audio compact disk 49.95 (978-0-7927-3317-1(7), CMP 692) AudioGO.

Fountain of Age. abr. ed. Betty Friedan. 2 cass. 1996. 13.95 set. (87585) Books on Tape.
The author of the "Feminine Mystique" now redefines how we think about ourselves as we grow older & how society thinks about aging. Drawing on a solid body of startling but little-known scientific evidence, she demolishes the constraining old myths & offers compelling alternatives for a different kind of aging. To her, it's an exuberant time for discovering new possibilities of intimacy, purpose & adventure.

Fountain of Grace. Perf. by Twila Paris. 1 cass. 1998. 7.98 HiLo Plus. (978-0-7601-2573-1(2)) Brentwood Music.

Fountain of Grace. Perf. by Twila Paris. 1 cass. 1999. (751-321-3674) Brentwood Music.

Fountain of Youth. Beverly J. Farrell. 1 cass. 8.95 (114) Am Fed Astrologers.
Avoid creating greater stress during the times we age the most.

Fountain of Youth. Ormond McGill. 1 cass. 2000. (978-1-933332-01-7(8)) Hypnotherapy Train.

Fountain of Youth. Ormond McGill. 2005. audio compact disk (978-1-933332-37-6(9)) Hypnotherapy Train.

Fountain of Youth. unabr. ed. Keith Bilderbeck. 1 cass. (Running Time: 1 hr. 30 mins.). (J). 2002. 9.95 (978-1-893721-07-4(8)); audio compact disk 14.95 (978-1-893721-06-7(X)) Baba Yaga.

Fountain of Youth: Using Your Mind to Rejuvenate Body. Richard Jafolla & Mary-Alice Jafolla. Read by Richard Jafolla & Mary-Alice Jafolla. (Health & Healing Ser.). 1986. 12.95 (320) Stppng Stones.
Motivational tapes that work on the subconscious mind (subliminal) & conscious mind to bring about self-improvement.

Fountain Society: A Novel. abr. ed. Wes Craven. Read by Campbell Scott. 2004. 15.95 (978-0-7435-4740-6(3)) Pub: S&S Audio. Dist(s): S and S Inc

Fountainhead. 24 cass. (Running Time: 1 hr. 30 min.). 141.90 Set. (AR97W) Second Renaissance.

Fountainhead. abr. unabr. ed. Ayn Rand. Read by Edward Herrmann. Contrib. by Edward Herrmann. (Running Time: 8 hrs. 30 mins.). (ENG.). 2003. audio compact disk 29.95 (978-1-56511-787-7(5), 1565117875) Pub: HighBridge. Dist(s): Workman Pub

Fountainhead. unabr. ed. Ayn Rand. Read by Christopher Lane. 3 CDs. (Running Time: 34 hrs.). 2001. audio compact disk 49.95 (978-0-7861-8965-6(7), 1518A, B) Blckstn Audio.

Fountainhead. unabr. ed. Ayn Rand. Read by Christopher Lane. 11 pieces. 2003. reel tape 44.95 (978-0-7861-2563-0(2)) Blckstn Audio.

Fountainhead. unabr. ed. Ayn Rand. Read by Christopher Lane. 24 pieces. 2004. reel tape 94.95 (978-0-7861-2562-3(4)) Blckstn Audio.

Fountainhead. unabr. ed. Ayn Rand. Read by Christopher Hurt. (Running Time: 115200 sec.). 2007. audio compact disk 44.95 (978-1-4332-0704-4(4)) Blckstn Audio.

Fountainhead, Pt. 1. unabr. ed. 13 cass. (Running Time: 90 min. per cass.). 85.95 Set. (AR95W) Second Renaissance.

Fountainhead, Pt. 1. unabr. ed. Ayn Rand. Read by Christopher Hurt. 13 cass. (Running Time: 34 hrs.). 1995. 85.95 (978-0-7861-0392-8(2), 1518A, B) Blckstn Audio.
An unprecedented phenomenon in modern literature. Arguably the century's most challenging novel of ideas, "The Fountainhead" is the story of a gifted young architect, his violent battle with conventional standards, & his explosive love affair with the beautiful woman who struggles to defeat him. In his fight for success, he first discovers, then rejects the seductive power of fame & money, finding that in the end, creative genius must triumph. His battle against mediocrity gives a gripping new dimension to the concept of evil.

Fountainhead, Pt. 1. unabr. collector's ed. Ayn Rand. Read by Kate Reading. 14 cass. (Running Time: 21 hrs.). 1995. 112.00 (978-0-7366-3026-9(0), 3709-A) Books on Tape.
A fiercely independent young architect grapples with standards of ho-hum, conventional design to pursue his own ideas. Part of his battle: a fiery love affair with a woman intent on destroying him.

Fountainhead, Pt. 2. 11 cass. (Running Time: 1 hr. 30 min.). 65.95 Set. (AR96W) Second Renaissance.

Fountainhead, Pt. 2. unabr. ed. Ayn Rand. Read by Christopher Hurt. 11 cass. (Running Time: 34 hrs.). 1995. 76.95 (978-0-7861-0878-7(9), 1518A, B) Blckstn Audio.
Story of a gifted young architect, his violent battle with conventional standards & his explosive love affair with the beautiful woman who struggles to defeat him. In his fight for success, he first discovers, then rejects the seductive power of fame & money, finding that in the end, creative genius must triumph. His battle against mediocrity gives a gripping new dimension to the concept of evil.

Fountainhead, Pt. 2. unabr. ed. Ayn Rand. Read by Kate Reading. 11 cass. (Running Time: 16 hrs. 30 mins.). 1995. 88.00 (978-0-7366-3027-6(9), 3709-B) Books on Tape.
A fiercely independent young architect grapples with standards of ho-hum, conventional design to pursue his own ideas. Part of his battle: a fiery love affair with a woman intent on destroying him.

Fountainhead Part A. unabr. ed. Ayn Rand. Read by Christopher Hurt. (Running Time: 15 hrs. 0 mins.). 2008. audio compact disk 110.00 (978-0-7861-6261-1(9)) Blckstn Audio.

Fountainhead Part B. unabr. ed. Ayn Rand. Read by Christopher Hurt. (Running Time: 17 hrs. 0 mins.). 2008. audio compact disk 120.00 (978-0-7861-6262-8(7)) Blckstn Audio.

Fountains of Aix see May Swenson

Fountains of Paradise see Arthur C. Clarke

Four Against the Arctic. David Roberts. Read by Robertson Dean. (Running Time: 10 hrs. 30 mins.). 2003. 30.95 (978-1-59912-494-0(7)) Iofy Corp.

Four Against the Arctic. unabr. ed. David Roberts. Read by Robertson Dean. 9 CDs. (Running Time: 11 hrs. 30 mins.). 2004. audio compact disk 72.00 (978-0-7861-9025-6(6), 3137) Blckstn Audio.

Four Against the Artic. David Roberts & Robertson Dean. 8 cass. (Running Time: 11 hrs. 30 mins.). 2002. 56.95 (978-0-7861-2503-6(9), 3137) Blckstn Audio.

Four Agreements: A Practical Guide to Personal Freedom. unabr. ed. Don Miguel Ruiz. Read by Peter Coyote. 2 cass. (Running Time: 2 hrs. 30 mins.). (Toltec Wisdom Ser.). 1999. 17.95 (978-1-878424-43-3(2)) Pub: Amber-Allen Pub. Dist(s): PerseuPGW

Four Agreements: A Practical Guide to Personal Freedom. unabr. ed. Don Miguel Ruiz. Read by Peter Coyote. 2 CDs. (Running Time: 2 hrs. 30 mins.). (ENG.). 2003. audio compact disk 18.95 (978-1-878424-77-8(7)) Amber-Allen Pub.

Four & Twenty Blackbirds Soaring. Louis Daniel Brodsky. 1989. pap. bk. 19.95 (978-1-877770-10-4(8)); 12.95 (978-1-877770-09-8(4)) Time Being Bks.

Four Aspects of Creation. George King. 2007. audio compact disk (978-0-937249-37-6(8)) Aetherius Soc.

Four Aspects of the Cross. Derek Prince. 2 cass. 11.90 Set. (4309-4310) Derek Prince.
These messages reveal four related aspects of the perfect sacrifice of Jesus. Through them God has supplied the total needs of humanity.

Four Baby Bumblebees: Classic Singable Songs. 1 cass. (Running Time: 34 min.). (J). (ps-1). 2001. pap. bk. & tchr. ed. 10.95 (KIM9161C); pap. bk. & tchr. ed. 14.95 (KIM9161CD) Kimbo Educ.
Collection of well-known songs, from traditional tunes such as "Skip to My Lou," to Broadway ditties such as "Bushel and a Peck," to songs from cartoons and films, including "The Wonderful Thing About Tiggers".

Four Basic Temperaments & How to Live with Them. Manly P. Hall. 1 cass. 8.95 (978-0-89314-123-3(2), C830403) Philos Res.

Four Blind Mice. abr. ed. James Patterson. 4 cass. (Running Time: 6 hrs.). (Alex Cross Ser.: No. 8). 2002. 26.98 (978-1-58621-402-9(0)) Hachet Audio.

Four Blind Mice. unabr. ed. James Patterson. Read by Peter Jay Fernandez & Michael Emerson. (Alex Cross Ser.: No. 8). (ENG.). 2005. 14.98 (978-1-59483-355-7(9)) Pub: Hachet Audio. Dist(s): HachBkGrp

Four Blind Mice. unabr. ed. James Patterson. Read by Peter Jay Fernandez & Michael Emerson. (Running Time: 7 hrs. 30 mins.). (Alex Cross Ser.: No. 8). (ENG.). 2009. 59.98 (978-1-60788-080-6(6)) Pub: Hachet Audio. Dist(s): HachBkGrp

Four by L'Amour: No Man's Man; Get Out of Town; McQueen of the Tumbling K; Booty for a Bad Man. abr. ed. Louis L'Amour. Read by Dramatization Staff. (Running Time: 14400 sec.). (Louis L'Amour Ser.). (ENG.). 2006. audio compact disk 22.00 (978-0-7393-4080-6(8), Random AudioBks) Pub: Random Audio Pubg. Dist(s): Random

Four-Card Draw; Desert Death Song; Trap of Gold. abr. ed. Louis L'Amour. 2 cass. (Running Time: 3 hrs.). (Louis L'Amour Collector Ser.:). 2000. 7.95 (978-1-57815-098-4(1), 1069, Media Bks Audio) Media Bks NJ.

Four-Card Draw; Desert Death Song; Trap of Gold; Keep Travelin' Rider. abr. ed. Louis L'Amour. 3 vols. (Louis L'Amour Collector Ser.). 2001. audio compact disk 11.99 (978-1-57815-528-6(2), Media Bks Audio) Media Bks NJ.

Four-Card Draw; Get Out of Town; One for the Pot. abr. ed. Louis L'Amour. (ENG.). 2009. audio compact disk 14.99 (978-0-7393-8315-5(9), Random AudioBks) Pub: Random Audio Pubg. Dist(s): Random

Four Champa Trees. unabr. ed. Alice Lucas. Read by Manh Phonboupha & Dorothea Bonneau. 1 cass. (Running Time: 46 min.). (Voices of Liberty Ser.). (ENG & LAO.). (J). (gr. 5-8). 1990. 7.00 (978-0-936434-52-0(X)) SF Study Ctr.
Traditional Laotian folktale told in English & Lao.

Four Corners of Night. unabr. ed. Craig Holden. Narrated by Tom Stechschulte. 9 cass. (Running Time: 11 hrs. 45 mins.). 2000. 80.00 (978-0-7887-3102-0(5), 95813E7) Recorded Bks.
To what lengths will we go to overlook what we don't want to see? The search for truth in a teenage girl's abduction case exposes the tattered heart of a midwestern city & throws the intertwined lives of two cops off balance.

Four Corners of Night, Set. abr. ed. Craig Holden. Read by Terrence Mann. 2 cass. 1999. 18.00 (FS9-43317) Highsmith.

Four Cornerstones of Networking Success. Speeches. Michael J. Hughes. 2 CDs. (Running Time: 114 mins). 2005. audio compact disk 59.00 (978-1-895186-38-3(2)) Multi-Media ON CAN.
This 2-CD set provides a concise and complete road map to create, manage, and leverage a networking strategy for more revenues, referrals, and meaningful relationships.Part One ? Get Everything You Want from a Networking GroupOptimize the potential of joining a group by tapping into the key leverage areas. This segment alone is worth the price.Part Two ? Managing the Networking ExperienceDiscover six networking phases that build rapport, develop trust, and identify opportunities for immediate networking results.Part Three ? Moving from Contact to ClientHow to develop and manage a fail-safe networking contact follow up program. Includes a step-by-step plan.Part Four ? Maximizing Networking RelationshipsA proven strategy to develop and leverage centers of influence to create advocates and on-going referral sources.Uncover the networking success secrets that will drive results and help you develop meaningful relationships. Guaranteed.

Four County Civil Practice: Bucks, Chester, Delaware & Montgomery Counties. 1998. bk. 129.00 (ACS-2064) PA Bar Inst.
Venturing into neighboring counties in a common occurrence for litigators in Bucks, Chester, Delaware & Montgomery counties. Yet, for the uninitiated, local practices can not only be confusing, but can place you at a considerable disadvantage over those having regular practices within the county. Each chapter highlights procedural & tactical methods for practicing within each county as well as comparisons to other counties.

Four Couples Within: The Structure of the Self & the Dynamics of Relationship. Read by Robert Moore. 3 cass. (Running Time: 4 hrs. 30 min.). 1989. 24.95 Set. (978-0-7822-0193-2(8), 388) C G Jung IL.
The four archetypal couples inherent in the Self - the King & Queen, the Warriors, the Magicians, the Lovers - create four distinct psychosocial environments within a relationship. The archetypal dynamics underlying both fulfillment & frustration in human relationships are examined, with particular focus on martial dynamics & sexual dysfunction.

Four Cultural Ecologies. William Thompson. 2 cass. 18.00 (OC17L) Sound Horizons AV.

Four Day Win: How to End the Diet Wars & Achieve Thinner Peace Four Days at a Time. abr. ed. Martha Beck. Read by Martha Beck. 2006. 17.95 (978-0-7435-6416-8(2), Sound Ideas) Pub: S&S Audio. Dist(s): S and S Inc

Four Days of Naples, unabr. ed. Aubrey Menen. Read by Nadia May. 8 cass. (Running Time: 11 hrs. 30 mins.). 1996. 56.95 (978-0-7861-0921-0(1), 1724) Blckstn Audio.
September 1943, Naples lay devastated by incessant bombardment from Allied planes. During the bombardment, the famed scugnizzi - the street boys - of Naples grew increasingly exasperated by the passiveness of their elders. Known for centuries for their daring, verve, & enterprise, the boys staged an incredible revolt against the occupying Germans on September 28, 1943. Dragging furniture into the roadways, they built barricades & shot at the enemy with stolen guns. Their courage inspired many adults & Italian army deserters to join their ranks. The fighting raged on for days, & hundreds of people died. But the valiant uprising was not in vain: On October 1, the Germans, having had their fill of Naples, left the city for good. Later that day the first of the Allied tanks rolled into Naples, to the cheers of the victorious scugnizzi.

Four Days of Naples. unabr. ed. Aubrey Menen. Read by Nadia May. (Running Time: 36000 sec.). 2007. audio compact disk 29.95 (978-0-7861-5852-2(2)); audio compact disk 72.00 (978-0-7861-6194-2(9)) Blckstn Audio.

Four Dharmas of Gampopa. Read by Chogyam Trungpa. 6 cass. 1975. 56.50 (A044) Vajradhatu.
A seminar on: Mind Following the Dharma; The Dharma of Knowing Oneself; Succeeding on the Path; Clarifying Confusion; Threefold Discipline; Fourth Dharma of Wisdom.

Four Directions: Guided Meditation. Yana L. Freeman. 1 CD. (Running Time: 30 mins.). (ENG.). 2007. audio compact disk 15.00 (978-0-9768728-2-5(X)) Sacred Path.

Four Disciplines of Execution. abr. ed. Stephen R. Covey. Told to Jennifer Colosimo. 2006. 17.95 (978-1-933976-16-7(0)) Pub: Franklin Covey. Dist(s): S and S Inc

Four Employee Benefits Reports, 1990-91 Series. Moderated by James P. Klein. 4 cass. 55.00 set. (T6-9103) PLI.

Four Essentials of Enduring Friendship CD. 1. 2002. audio compact disk 6.00 (978-1-932316-25-4(6)) Great C Pubng.

Four Faultless Felons, Set. unabr. ed. G. K. Chesterton. Read by Peter Joyce. 5 cass. 1999. 47.95 (978-1-86015-458-4(1)) T T Beeler.
A series of four mysterious novellas. "The Moderate Murderer" is set in the colonial district of Polybia, near Egypt, where the Viscount Tallboys has just arrived to announce an order that is certain to upset the natives. "The Honest Quack" tells of an artist's obsession with a mysterious tree. In "The Ecstatic Thief," a successful business man is cursed with three ungrateful sons. In "The Loyal Traitor," a fictional European state is threatened by an underground movement.

Four Feathers. A.E.W. Mason. Narrated by John Lee. (Running Time: 11 hrs.). 2003. 34.95 (978-1-59912-665-4(6)) Iofy Corp.

Four Feathers. unabr. ed. A. E. W. Mason. Read by John Lee. (Running Time: 39600 sec.). 2008. audio compact disk 19.95 (978-0-7861-8452-1(3)) Blckstn Audio.

Four Feathers. unabr. ed. A. E. W. Mason. Read by Ralph Cosham. (Running Time: 10 hrs. 0 mins.). 2009. 29.95 (978-1-4332-5959-3(1)); audio compact disk 59.95 (978-1-4332-5956-2(7)); audio compact disk 80.00 (978-1-4332-5957-9(5)) Blckstn Audio.

Four Feathers: Classic Collection. unabr. ed. A. E. W. Mason. Read by John Lee. (Running Time: 11 hrs. 50 mins.). 2008. audio compact disk & audio compact disk 19.95 (978-1-4332-4647-0(3)) Blckstn Audio.

Four Fires. Bryce Courtenay. Read by Humphrey Bower. (Running Time: 30 hrs.). 2009. 114.99 (978-1-74214-203-6(6), 9781742142036) Pub: Bolinda Pubng AUS. Dist(s): Bolinda Pub Inc

Four Fires. unabr. ed. Bryce Courtenay. Narrated by Humphrey Bower. 18 cass. (Running Time: 30 hrs.). 2002. 144.00 (978-1-74030-490-0(X)) Pub: Bolinda Pubng AUS. Dist(s): Bolinda Pub Inc
While there are many more fires that drive the human spirit, love being perhaps the brightest flame of all, it is these four that have moulded us most as Australian people. The four fires give us our sense of place and, for better or for worse, shape our national character.

Four Fires. unabr. ed. Bryce Courtenay. Read by Humphrey Bower. (Running Time: 30 hrs.). 2008. audio compact disk 123.95 (978-1-921415-92-0(4), 9781921415920) Pub: Bolinda Pubng AUS. Dist(s): Bolinda Pub Inc

Four Fires. unabr. ed. Bryce Courtenay. Read by Humphrey Bower. (Running Time: 30 hrs.). 2008. 54.95 (978-1-921415-28-9(2), 9781921415289) Pub: Bolinda Pubng AUS. Dist(s): Bolinda Pub Inc

***Four Fish: The Future of the Last Wild Food.** unabr. ed. Paul Greenberg. (Running Time: 8 hrs.). 2010. 39.97 (978-1-4418-7247-0(7), 9781441872470, BADLE); 24.99 (978-1-4418-7246-3(9), 9781441872463, BAD) Brilliance Audio.

***Four Fish: The Future of the Last Wild Food.** unabr. ed. Paul Greenberg. Read by Christopher Lane. (Running Time: 9 hrs.). 2010. 24.99 (978-1-4418-7244-9(2), 9781441872449, Brilliance MP3); 39.97 (978-1-4418-7245-6(0), 9781441872456, Brinc Audio MP3 Lib); audio compact disk 29.99 (978-1-4418-7242-5(6), 9781441872425, Bril Audio CD Unabri); audio compact disk 74.97 (978-1-4418-7243-2(4), 9781441872432, BriAudCD Unabrid) Brilliance Audio.

Four Friends see Istwa Tipoul

Four Friends - The Musical Donkey. Saeed Jaffrey. 1 cass. (Running Time: 048 min.). (Karadi Tales Ser.). (YA). (gr. 1 up). 1998. bk. 15.99 (978-81-86838-08-2(2)) APG.
Asian fairy tales & folklore.

Four Funny Folktales for Little Folk. unabr. ed. Joy Steiner. Perf. by Joy Steiner. 1 cass. (Running Time: 54 min.). (J). (ps-8). 1998. 10.00 (978-0-9654155-1-4(1), PJ-1002) Pickle Juice.
Playful collection of folktales & folksongs speaks to the heart of children, appealing to their youthful desires & concerns. Accompanied by delightful music, these unexpected heroes triumph through kindness & courage. Received Parent's Choice Honor 1998.

Four Giants of Philosophy. Andrew Bernstein. 4 cass. (Running Time: 4 hrs.). 1995. 49.95 Set. (978-1-56114-436-5(3), CB10D) Second Renaissance.
The moral & political philosophy of Plato, Aristotle, Kant & Ayn Rand.

Four Gifts of the Mind. Scripts. William Yabroff & Karen Keefer. 2 CDs. 2005. audio compact disk 39.95 (978-0-9771458-0-5(8)) Inn Image.
Four Gifts of the Mind is a set of two CDs with accompanying workbook for experiencing the Yabroff method of guided imagery. This imagery process, created by William Yabroff, Ph.D., allows an individual to elicit symbols for the four "gifts of the mind" first identified as basic mental functions by Carl Jung: Sensing, Intuition, Thinking and Feeling. The CDs provide an imagery journey for each gift plus a fifth journey to bring the images together to interact. The workbook contains journal pages for recording and interpreting one's imagery experiences, plus additional supporting information.

Four Gospels. Richard Rohr. 4 cass. (Running Time: 5 hrs. 30 min.). 39.95 Set. (AA2025) Credence Commun.
Rohr explains & preaches on main themes in each gospel recognized by contemporary scholarship.

Four Gospels: Revised Standard Version. Read by Joan Wagner. 8 cass. (Running Time: 9 hrs. 54 min.). 1984. 24.95 (TAH139) Alba Hse Comns.
A presentation of the Word which was first accepted into her life & later given to the world by a Woman.

Four Graham Greene Thrillers. Graham Greene. 9 CDs. (Running Time: 13 hrs. 30 mins.). 2002. audio compact disk 89.95 (978-0-563-53083-1(9), BBCD 010) BBC Worldwide.

Four Great Principles. Swami Amar Jyoti. 1 dolby cass. 1983. 9.95 (K-59) Truth Consciousness.
Prabhushri Swamiji's dialog with seekers clearly shows the way in which all our dealings should correlate with Principle. The four major eternal principles.

Four Greek Comedies: The Birds , the Frogs , the Clouds & the Peace. Aristophanes. Narrated by Flo Gibson. 2008. 20.95 (978-1-60646-070-2(6)) Audio Bk Con.

Four Greek Comedies: The Birds , the Frogs , the Clouds & the Peace. Aristophanes. Narrated by Flo Gibson. (ENG.). 2009. audio compact disk 27.95 (978-1-60646-120-4(6)) Audio Bk Con.

Four Guardians of La Grange see Luck of Roaring Camp & Other Stories

Four Guineas. unabr. collector's ed. Elspeth Huxley. Read by Donada Peters. 9 cass. (Running Time: 13 hrs. 30 mins.). 1991. 72.00 (978-0-7366-1919-6(4), 2743) Books on Tape.
This account of Elspeth Huxley's travels in the Gambia, Sierra Leone, the Gold Coast & Nigeria gilds the Dark Continent - not because she romanticizes it, but because she clarifies it...its history, superstitions & tribal ways, its beauty & power, its great contrasts & complexities.

Four Holy Sutras: (Prayerful Song to Praise & Bless the Holy Missioners, Nectarean Shower of Holy Doctrines, Song of the Angel, for Spiritual Healing) Masaharu Taniguchi. Voice by Bruce G. Mallery. Prod. by Seicho-No-Ie. 2008. audio compact disk 15.00 (978-0-9661797-3-6(0)) Seicho-No.

Four Horseman: Rev. 6:1-8. Ed Young. 1986. 4.95 (978-0-7417-1561-6(9), 561) Win Walk.

Four Horsemen of the Apocalypse. unabr. ed. Vicente Blasco Ibanez. Read by Frederick Davidson. (Running Time: 15 hrs. 0 mins.). 2009. 29.95 (978-1-4332-6732-1(2)); audio compact disk 110.00 (978-1-4332-6729-1(2)) Blckstn Audio.

Four Horsemen of the Apocalypse. unabr. ed. Vincente Blasco Ibáñez. Read by Frederick Davidson. 11 cass. (Running Time: 16 hrs.). 1999. 76.95 (978-0-7861-1562-4(9), 2393) Blckstn Audio.
Men & women who were inspired to attain unbelievable heights of courage, while degrading others in their lust for power.

***Four in Hand.** unabr. ed. Stephanie Laurens. Read by Ashford MacNab. (Running Time: 9 hrs.). 2011. audio compact disk 19.99 (978-1-4418-8385-8(1), 9781441883858, Bril Audio CD Unabri) Brilliance Audio.

Four Italian Poets see Osbert Sitwell Reading His Poetry

Four Just Men. Edgar Wallace. Read by Walter Covell. 5 cass. (Running Time: 5 hrs.). 1989. 28.00 incl. album. (C-169) Jimcin Record.
Justice outside the law.

Four Karmas. Read by Chogyam Trungpa. 1 cass. 1971. 12.50 (A101) Vajradhatu.

Four Keys to Staying Full of God. 1999. 25.00 (978-1-881541-68-4(1)) A Wommack.

Four Last Things. Ronald Lawler. 1 cass. (Inspiring Presentations from the National Rosary Congress Ser.). 2.50 (978-1-56036-093-3(3)) AMI Pr.

Four Last Things. unabr. ed. Andrew Taylor. Read by Ric Jerrom. 10 cass. (Running Time: 15 hrs.). 2003. 84.95 (978-0-7540-0932-0(7), CAB 2354) AudioGO.

Four Laws of Debt Free Prosperity: The Chequemate Story. unabr. ed. Blaine Harris & Charles A. Coonradt. Read by Robert Peterson. Ed. by Lee Nelson. Illus. by Michael Brian. 2 cass. (Running Time: 1 hr. 30 min.). 1996. 14.95 (978-0-9652874-1-8(6)) Chequemate.
Paul Smith is in debt. He doesn't see a way out. A woman, Mary Sessions, teaches Paul the Four Laws of Debt-free prosperity. The reader learns, along with Paul, how to live a debt-free & happy life without increasing income, just allocating money effectively.

Four Letters of Love. Niall Williams. Read by Stuart Langton. 6 cass. (Running Time: 9 hrs.). 2000. 29.95 (978-0-7366-4593-5(4)) Books on Tape.
This remarkable novel brings together two random Irish stories in a powerful portrait of the redemptive powers of love & fate.

Four Letters of Love. Niall Williams. 2 cass. (Running Time: 3 hrs.). (ENG., 2001. (978-0-333-78259-0(3)) Macmillan UK GBR.

Four Letters of Love. unabr. ed. Niall Williams. Read by Stuart Langton. 6 cass. (Running Time: 9 hrs.). 1998. 48.00 (978-0-7366-4148-7(3), 4651) Books on Tape.
Brings together two random Irish stories in a powerful portrait of the redemptive powers of love & fate.

Four Levels of Embodiment: Shirley Southerland. Interview. 1 CD. (Running Time: 41 minutes). 2004. audio compact disk 19.95 (978-0-9760403-0-9(1)) High Profile.
Take an inward journey of self-discovery to find a deeper identity and meaning to your life for spiritual and personal growth. Find new expressions that are fulfilling and healing for confronting old problems. Learn that while pain and suffering are unavoidable, feelings of anxiety, fear, depression, and guilt may not be. By redirecting the energies of the four bodies, we can experience comfort, acceptance, and increased self-esteem. Engage life with a fresh new outlook and an improved sense of well-being.

Four Little Foxes see Gathering of Great Poetry for Children

Four Lives: Program from the Award Winning Public Radio Series. Interview. Hosted by Fred Goodwin. 1 CD. (Running Time: 1 hr.). 2004. audio compact disk 21.95 (978-1-932479-48-5(1), LCM 317) Lichtenstein Creat.
The most gripping and insightful stories of mental illness are those of people who face it each day. They are the everyday heros who struggle to combat their illnesss, and work toward recovery. This week on The Infinite Mind, a special presentation, as we feature the remarkable stories of four people coping with mental illness, whose extraordinary lives and work offer hope and inspiration to all of us. Texas State Representative Garnet Coleman, former head of Ann Richard's campaign for governor, a nationally recognized leader in the fight for healthcare reform and better mental health services, who is living with manic-depressive illness; Meera Popkin, a star of Cats and Miss Saigon on Broadway and in London's West End, who was diagnosed with schizophrenia; and Twin sisters Pam and Carolyn Spiro, who have written a new book about Pam's struggle with schizoaffective disorder and how that has affected their relationship. Pam was a student at Brown University when she first became ill, and has since won an international poetry award. Carolyn works as a psychiatrist.

Four Lives Part 2 Of 2: Program from the Award-Winning Public Radio Series, 412. Interview. Hosted by Peter Kramer. 1 CD. (Running Time: 59 minutes). 2006. audio compact disk 21.95 (978-1-933644-28-8(1)) Lichtenstein Creat.
In the first episode, we hear two powerful tales of recovery from mental illness.First, the former First Lady of New Jersey, Mary Jo Codey, in one of the most remarkable interviews to air on The Infinite Mind, reveals her courageous battle to overcome the postpartum depression that caused her to constantly think of killing herself and her newborn son. After her husband was elected governor and a radio "shock jock" made her private struggle the brunt of a public joke ? foreshadowing a similar, acrid exchange between Tom Cruise and Brooke Shields - Ms. Codey realized she had a cause worth fighting for. She joins The Infinite Mind?s Mary Carmichael for a startlingly candid discussion.Next, renowned TV newscaster Jane Pauley tells The Infinite Mind?s Bill Lichtenstein how steroids and anti-depressants, intended to treat a case of hives, instead sent her spiraling into depression and mild mania, unmasking a hidden vulnerability to bipolar disorder. When she started thinking about suicide, her doctor sent her to the hospital, and in the process, she re-evaluated who she was ? emerging as an advocate for people with living with bipolar disorder and mental illnesses.

Four Loves. C. S. Lewis. 2 CDs. (Running Time: 2 hrs.). 2002. audio compact disk (978-0-7861-8929-8(0)) Blckstn Audio.

Four Loves. abr. ed. C. S. Lewis. 2 CDs. (Running Time: 2 hrs. 15 mins.). 2004. audio compact disk 24.99 (978-0-8499-6372-8(9)) Nelson.
In his classic book The Four Loves, Lewis describes the four basic kinds of human love_affection, friendship, erotic love, and the love of God. Since this is the only commercial recording of C. S. Lewis that is available today, fans of his writing will desire to add this impressive recording to their collection. While Lewis's writings have impacted more evangelical Christians than perhaps any other writer, this audio product of the author_s reading of this classic book will undoubtedly expand the theological understanding of the nature of love to a much wider audience. He explores the love between parents and children, the love of friends, the love of men and women for each other, and the love of God that may enrich all love. He also goes in-depth into questions of sex, possessiveness, jealousy, pride, false sentimentality, manners in loving, and the need for more laughter between lovers. Lewis_s wise and candid reflections on the virtues and dangers of love draw on sources from Jane Austen to Saint Augustine. This recording features a new audio introduction and commentary by Chuck Colson. The CD will also include a study guide - perfect for individual or group use.

Four Million. unabr. ed. O. Henry. Read by Walter Zimmerman et al. 4 cass. (Running Time: 6 hrs.). 1979. 27.00 incl. album. (C-26) Jimcin Record.
Consists of: "Tobin's Palm," "The Gift of the Magi," "A Cosmopolite in a Cafe," "Between Rounds," "The Skylight Room," "A Service of Love," "The Coming-Out of Maggie," "The Cop & the Anthem," "An Adjustment of Nature," "Memoirs of a Yellow Dog," "The Love Philtre of Ikey Schoenstein," "Mammon & the Archer," "Springtime a la Carte," "The Green Door," "From the Cabby's Seat," "An Unfinished Story," "The Caliph, Cupid & the Clock," "Sisters of the Golden Circle," "The Romance of a Busy Broker," "After Twenty Years," & "Lost on Dress Parade," etc.

Four Million. unabr. collector's ed. O. Henry. 6 cass. (Running Time: 6 hrs.). (J). 1982. 36.00 (978-0-7366-3850-0(4), 9026) Books on Tape.
Inspired by the then population of New York of 1906. The promise of a new century energizes everyone from Eastside tenement dwellers to the denizens of Fifth Avenue.

***Four O'Clock.** 2010. audio compact disk (978-1-59171-168-1(1)) Falcon Picture.

***Four of Us Are Dying.** 2010. audio compact disk (978-1-59171-292-3(0)) Falcon Picture.

Four Oscar Wilde Plays: Radio Dramatization. unabr. ed. Oscar Wilde. 6 CDs. (Running Time: 9 hrs.). 2003. audio compact disk 64.95 (978-0-563-49586-4(3), BBCD 013) BBC Worldwide.

Four Part Harmony. Marcie Brown. 5 CDs. (Running Time: 366 min). Dramatization. 2005. audio compact disk 27.95 (978-1-889409-27-6(8), Signature CDs) LadybugPr CA.

Four Past Midnight: The Sun Dog. Stephen King. Read by Tim Sample. (Playaway Adult Fiction Ser.). 2009. 45.00 (978-1-60775-559-3(9)) Find a World.

Four Past Midnight: The Sun Dog. unabr. ed. Stephen King. Read by Stephen King. Read by Tim Sample. (ENG., 2008. audio compact disk 29.95 (978-1-59887-750-2(X), 159887750X) Pub: HighBridge. Dist(s): Workman Pub

Four Pathways to Success: Succeed in Life Using Discipline, Wisdom, Unconditional Love, & Surrender. Wayne W. Dyer. 2 CDs. 2004. audio compact disk 18.95 (978-1-4019-0431-9(9)) Hay House.

Four Pillars of a Seeker. Swami Amar Jyoti. 1 cass. 1980. 9.95 (P-37) Truth Consciousness.
Seasoned formulas & ingredients for the seeker on the path to liberation.

Four Pillars of Investing: Lessons for Building a Winning Portfolio. William Bernstein. 3 CDs. (Running Time: 4 hrs. 30 min.). 2003. audio compact disk 28.00 (978-1-932378-01-6(4)); 24.00 (978-0-9724889-8-3(7)) Pub: A Media Intl. Dist(s): Natl Bk Netwk
This book presents an easy to follow step-by-step program for achieving long-term investing success.

***Four Pillars of Parenting: Audio CD Program.** Lori Barr. (Running Time: 107). (ENG.). 2010. audio compact disk 14.95 (978-0-9829746-3-6(9)) MindTamers.

Four Point Listening & Speaking 2, Advanced. Betsy Parrish. Ed. by Keith S. Folse. (Four Point Ser.). 2009. pap. bk. 28.50 (978-0-472-03185-6(6)) U of Mich Pr.

Four Powers for Greatness Personal Learning Course: Listening, Reading, Speaking, Writing. unabr. ed. J. Michael Bennett & Paul R. Scheele. Read by J. Michael Bennett & Paul R. Scheele. 6 cass. (Running Time: 4 hrs.). 1998. 129.95 Set. (978-0-925480-63-7(0)) Learn Strategies.
Professor Bennett condensed 320 hours of college instruction to help develop the skills of a powerful communicator.

Four Preludes on Playthings of the Wind see Carl Sandburg Reading Cool Tombs & Other Poems

Four Quartets. abr. ed. T. S. Eliot. Perf. by T. S. Eliot. 1 cass. 1984. 8.98 (CDL5 1403) HarperCollins Pubs.

Four Queens: The Provencal Sisters Who Ruled Europe. Nancy Goldstone. Read by Josephine Bailey. (ENG.). 2009. 64.99 (978-1-60812-800-6(8)) Find a World.

Four Queens: The Provencal Sisters Who Ruled Europe. unabr. ed. Nancy Goldstone. Narrated by Josephine Bailey. (Running Time: 11 hrs. 30 mins. 0 sec.). (ENG.). 2007. audio compact disk 34.99 (978-1-4001-0384-3(3)); audio compact disk 24.99 (978-1-4001-5384-8(0)); audio compact disk 69.99 (978-1-4001-3384-0(X)) Pub: Tantor Media. Dist(s): IngramPubServ

Four Questions in Church History. 1. 2005. audio compact disk (978-0-9718128-3-3(7)) Bridegroom.

Four Riders of the Apocalypse see Cuatro Jinetes del Apocalipsis

Four Saints for Now. Truman G. Madsen. 2 cass. 1995. 13.95 Set. (978-1-57008-195-8(6), Bkcraft Inc) Deseret Bk.

Four Scottish Sonatas: For Violin & Keyboard, with optional Cello - Score & Parts. Ed. by David Johnson. 2007. pap. bk. 22.95 (978-1-902455-33-4(9), 1902455339) Pub: Schott Music Corp. Dist(s): H Leonard

Four Seasons see Las cuatro Estaciones

Four Seasons. Bruce Goldberg. Read by Bruce Goldberg. 1 cass. (Running Time: 25 min.). 2006. 13.00 (978-1-57968-008-4(9)) Pub: B Goldberg. Dist(s): Baker Taylor
Through self-hypnosis you are trained to remove negativity, gather, expand and connect to your soul's energy.

Four Seasons. Sundance/Newbridge, LLC Staff. (Early Science Ser.). (gr. k-3). 2007. audio compact disk 12.00 (978-1-4007-6146-3(8)); audio compact disk 12.00 (978-1-4007-6145-6(X)); audio compact disk 12.00 (978-1-4007-6147-0(6)) Sund Newbrdge.

Four Seasons. Perf. by Antonio Vivaldi. 1 cass.; 1 CD. 1998. 10.98 (978-1-56628-076-1(1), 42584); audio compact disk 15.98 CD. (978-1-56628-075-4(3), 42584D) MFLP CA.

***Four Seasons.** unabr. ed. Mary Alice Monroe. (Running Time: 13 hrs.). 2010. 24.99 (978-1-4418-5288-5(3), 9781441852885, BAD) Brilliance Audio.

***Four Seasons.** unabr. ed. Mary Alice Monroe. Read by Sandra Burr. (Running Time: 13 hrs.). 2010. 39.97 (978-1-4418-5289-2(1), 9781441852892, BADLE); 24.99 (978-1-4418-5284-7(0), 9781441852847, Brilliance MP3); 39.97 (978-1-4418-5286-1(7), 9781441852861, Brlnc Audio MP3 Lib); audio compact disk 29.99 (978-1-4418-5280-9(8), 9781441852809, Bril Audio CD Unabri); audio compact disk 79.97 (978-1-4418-5282-3(4), 9781441852823, BriAudCD Unabrid) Brilliance Audio.

Four Seasons of Marriage. unabr. ed. Gary Chapman. 5 CDs. (Running Time: 5 hrs. 30 mins.). (ENG.). 2005. audio compact disk 24.99 (978-1-4143-0022-1(0)) Tyndale Hse.

Four Sermons to Save the Black Family. Jawanza Kunjufu. 1 cass. (Running Time: 60 mins.). 1999. 19.95 (AT17) African Am Imag.

Four Short Stories. Arthur Conan Doyle. Read by Carl Rigg. (Running Time: 2 hrs. 30 mins.). 1999. 20.95 (978-1-60083-742-5(5)) Iofy Corp.

Four Short Stories. unabr. ed. Short Stories. Elizabeth Gaskell. Read by Judith Whale. 5 cass. (Running Time: 5 hrs.). 2001. 44.95 (89085) Pub: ISIS Audio GBR. Dist(s): Ulverscroft US
"The Manchester Marriage" is about a woman in her second marriage, & a story in which there is an exploration of a dynamic interaction between the sexes in which the man stands to gain. "Lizzie Leigh" involves Lizzie, an unmarried mother who is classed as a "fallen" woman driven into the world of prostitution so that she is capable of supporting her daughter. "The Well of Pen-Morfa" is the story of the strong bond between mother & daughter. Eleanor's patience, courage & endurance help Nest when she finds herself deserted by her lover after she becomes physically handicapped. "The Eras of Libbie Marsh" is also about the life of an unmarried mother with a small child, who works hard as a seamstress in the working class district of Manchester. Here is a story of women who survive without men & why.

Four Short Stories: The Horror of the Heights; The Terror of Blue John Gap; Lot No. 249; The Sealed Room. Short Stories. Arthur Conan Doyle. Read by Carl Rigg. 2 cass. (Running Time: 2 hrs. 30 mins.). (Sherlock Holmes Stories). 1996. 13.98 (978-962-634-550-4(0), NA205014, Naxos AudioBooks) Naxos.

Four Somali Folktales Read in Somali & English: Sheekoy, Sheeko, Sheeko Xariira. abr. ed. Created by Minnesota Humanities Commission. 2008. audio compact disk 15.95 (978-1-931016-20-9(8)) MN Humanities.

Four Souls: A Novel. Louise Erdrich. Read by Anna Fields. 6 vols. 2004. audio compact disk 32.95 (978-0-7927-3289-1(8), SLD 681, Chivers Sound Lib) AudioGO.

***Four Souls/Tracks.** unabr. ed. Louise Erdrich. Read by Anna Fields. (ENG.). 2004. (978-0-06-082450-1(6), Harper Audio); (978-0-06-082449-5(2), Harper Audio) HarperCollins Pubs.

Four Spiritual Laws of Prosperity: A Simple Guide to Unlimited Abundance. unabr. ed. Edwene Gaines. (Running Time: 6 hrs.). (ENG.). 2006. audio compact disk 19.98 (978-1-59659-072-4(6), GildAudio) Pub: Gildan Media. Dist(s): HachBkGrp

Four Splits of Separation Revisited. Kenneth Wapnick. 1 CD. (Running Time: 4 hrs. 24 mins.). 2006. 21.00 (978-1-59142-241-9(8), 3m122); audio compact disk 26.00 (978-1-59142-235-8(3), CD122) Foun Miracles.

Four Spokes of Destiny. (ENG.). 2008. 15.00 (978-0-9708648-1-9(7)) Self Enquiry.

Four Stages in Spiritual Development. Eknath Easwaran. 1 cass. (Running Time: 38 min.). 1992. 7.95 (978-1-58638-541-5(0), FSS) Nilgiri Pr.
Picks up the story (from "Family Values") of Easwaran leaving his village to strike out into the world. Describes the four traditional stages in spiritual development, illustrated through Easwaran's own life & experience.

Four Stages of Desire. unabr. ed. Perf. by Eknath Easwaran. 1 cass. (Running Time: 1 hr.). 1990. 7.95 (978-1-58638-542-2(9)) Nilgiri Pr.

Four Star Playhouse: The Hunted & Anna Lee. 1 cass. (Running Time: 1 hr.). 2001. 6.98 (2099) Radio Spirits.

FOUR STEPS to a LEANER, HEALTHIER YOU: A Simple Regimen for Detoxification, Weight Loss & Disease Prevention. (ENG.). 2009. 14.95 (978-0-9842720-0-6(3)) Prom Pub FL.

Four Steps to Enjoying a Healthy, Balanced Life. 2007. audio compact disk (978-0-9796135-5-5(8)) Curing the Cause.

Four Steps to Responsibility: Techniques to Lead Children to Responsible Decision Making. Jim Fay. Read by Jim Fay. Ed. by Bert Gurule Mizke. 1 cass. (Running Time: 1 hr. 30 mins.). 1994. 11.95 (978-0-944634-05-9(2)) Pub: Love Logic. Dist(s): Penton Overseas

Four Steps to Responsibility: Techniques to Lead Children to Responsible Decision Making. unabr. ed. Jim Fay. Read by Jim Fay. 1 CD . (Running Time: 1 hr. 20 mins.). 2000. audio compact disk 13.95 (978-1-930429-07-9(X)) Pub: Love Logic. Dist(s): Penton Overseas
Jim Fay shares the secret about why parents who are not afraid to allow their children to fail, raise young people who are independent, responsible decision-makers with high self-concepts.

Four Steps to Turn Any Problem into a Pleasant Surprise. Guy Finley. (ENG.). 2006. 7.49 (978-1-929320-56-1(6)) Life of Learn.

Four Stories by Franz Kafka: A Hunger Artist, a Report to the Academy, a Country Doctor, a Little Woman. unabr. ed. Franz Kafka. 1 CD. (Running Time: 3600 sec.). 2006. audio compact disk 15.95 (978-0-660-19550-6(X), CBC Audio) Canadian Broadcasting CAN.

Four-Story Mistake. Elizabeth Enright. Read by Pamela Dillman. (Running Time: 5 hrs.). 2005. 19.95 (978-1-59912-900-6(0)) Iofy Corp.

Four-Story Mistake. unabr. ed. Elizabeth Enright. 4 CDs. (Running Time: 5 hrs.). (What's New Ser.). (J). 2004. audio compact disk 27.95 (978-1-59316-021-0(6), LL113) Listen & Live.

Four Story Mistake. unabr. ed. Elizabeth Enright. Read by Pamela Dillman. (J). 2007. 34.99 (978-1-59895-981-9(6)) Find a World.

Four Streams: How Christ Heals Our Hearts. Short Stories. John Eldredge. 4 CDs. (Running Time: 3 hrs. 50 mins.). 2004. audio compact disk 35.00 (978-1-933207-01-8(9)) Ransomed Heart.
Christ wants to do more for us than simply forgive. He wants to restore us. If you will look again at the ways in which Christ ransoms people, the means by which he makes a man or woman come fully alive, you'll find he offers his life to us through the Four Streams: Discipleship, Warfare, Counseling, and Healing. To discover for yourself that the glory of God is man fully alive, you must drink deeply from the Four Streams.

Four Swans. unabr. ed. Winston Graham. Read by Tony Britton. 14 cass. (Running Time: 21 hrs.). (Poldark Ser.: Bk. 6). 2000. 89.95 (CAB 1547) Pub: Chivers Audio Bks GBR. Dist(s): AudioGO
For Ross Poldark, secure in his hard-won prosperity, new dilemmas are on the horizon. All four women, the four swans whose lives have touched Ross, face a crisis in the coming years. For his wife Demelza, his old love Elizabeth, his friend's wife Caroline and the unhappy Morwenna Chynoweth, the worst of times are yet to come.

Four Temperaments. 1 cass. (Running Time: 60 min.). (Mother Angelica Live Ser.). 1986. 10.00 (978-1-55794-071-1(1), T22) Eternal Wrd TV.

Four Temperaments. Eugene Schwartz. 2 cass. 18.00 (OC141) Sound Horizons AV.

Four Testimonies about Earnest Prayer. Read by Mother Basilea Schlink. 1 cass. (Running Time: 30 min.). 1985. (0256) Evang Sisterhood Mary.
Includes: Prayer-Foolishness or Reality?; God's Promises Come True; God Wants to Be Taken at His Word; God's Fatherly Love.

Four Tests in the Life of Joseph. unabr. ed. Theodore H. Epp. Read by Theodore H. Epp. 2 cass. (Running Time: 2 hrs. 30 min.). 1989. 9.95 (978-0-8474-2357-6(3)) Back to Bible.
Messages on Joseph & Elijah, teaching that God works all things in the life according to His will.

Four Tickets to Christmas: A Dramatic Musical. Contrib. by Deborah Craig-Claar & Mark Hayes. (ENG.). 1996. audio compact disk 90.00 (978-0-00-515116-7(3)); audio compact disk 16.00 (978-0-00-515614-8(9)) Allegis.

Four to Score. Janet Evanovich. Read by C. J. Critt. 6 Cass. (Running Time: 9.75 Hrs). (Stephanie Plum Ser.: No. 4). 29.95 (978-1-4025-6288-4(8)) Recorded Bks.

Four to Score. Janet Evanovich. Narrated by C. J. Critt. 9 CDs. (Running Time: 9 hrs. 30 mins.). (Stephanie Plum Ser.: No. 4). 2000. audio compact disk 89.00 (978-0-7887-4749-6(5), C1235E7) Recorded Bks.
Bounty Hunter Stephanie Plum is hot on the trail of Maxine Nowicki, a waitress-gone-bad.

Four to Score. abr. ed. Janet Evanovich. (Stephanie Plum Ser.: No. 4). 2001. audio compact disk 11.99 (978-1-57815-544-6(4), 1111) Media Bks NJ.

Four to Score. abr. ed. Janet Evanovich. (Stephanie Plum Ser.: No. 4). 2001. 7.95 (978-1-57815-263-6(1)) Media Bks NJ.

Four to Score. abr. ed. Janet Evanovich. 2 cass. (Running Time: 3 hrs.). (Stephanie Plum Ser.: No. 4). 1998. 15.00 (978-0-333-74772-8(0)) Ulvrscrft Audio.
A rollercoaster comic thriller starring bounty hunter Stephanie Plum.

Four to Score. abr. ed. Janet Evanovich & Debi Mazar. 3 CDs. (Running Time: 3 hrs. 0 mins. 0 sec.). (Stephanie Plum Ser.: No. 4). (ENG.). 2005. audio compact disk 19.95 (978-1-55927-963-5(X)) Pub: Macmill Audio. Dist(s): Macmillan

Four to Score. unabr. ed. Janet Evanovich. Read by C. J. Critt. 9 CDs. (Running Time: 10 hrs. 0 mins. 0 sec.). (Stephanie Plum Ser.: No. 4). (ENG.). 2005. audio compact disk 39.95 (978-1-59397-749-8(2)) Pub: Macmill Audio. Dist(s): Macmillan

Four to Score. unabr. ed. Janet Evanovich. Narrated by C. J. Critt. 8 CDs. (Running Time: 9.75 hrs.). (Stephanie Plum Ser.: No. 4). audio compact disk 39.95 (978-1-4025-6289-1(6)) Recorded Bks.

Four to Score. unabr. ed. Janet Evanovich. Narrated by C. J. Critt. 7 cass. (Running Time: 9 hrs. 30 mins.). (Stephanie Plum Ser.: No. 4). 1999. 66.00 (978-0-7887-2593-7(9), 95613E7) Recorded Bks.
Bounty Hunter Stephanie Plum is hot on the trail of Maxine Nowicki, a waitress-gone-bad.

Four Tots: Mostly Motown: Soulful Songs Arranged & Performed for the Very Young. Floyd Domino. (J). 1990. bk. 12.95 (978-0-938971-49-8(2)) JTG Nashville.

Four Watchwords for Times of Trouble. 1985. (0219) Evang Sisterhood Mary.

Four-Way Mental Communication & Emotional Sharing. abr. ed. Jackie Woods. 2001. audio compact disk 19.95 (978-0-9659665-4-2(2)) Adawehi Pr.

Four Ways to the Center. 4 cass. 45.00 set. (1111) MEA A Watts Cass.

Four Windows of Knowing. Eligio Stephen Gallegos. 2 cass. 1992. 18.00 set. (OC290-64) Sound Horizons AV.

***Four Years, Five Seasons.** Peter S. Beagle. Read by Peter S. Beagle. Prod. by Connor Cochran & Jim Lively. Engineer Jim Lively. (ENG.). 2010. 20.00 (978-0-9706801-2-9(0)) Conlan Pr.

Fourberies de Scapin. Molière. Perf. by Andre Roussin. 1 CD. (FRE.). 1991. audio compact disk 24.95 (1689) Olivia & Hill.
Scapin, a resourceful valet, comes to the aid of two young men, Octave & Leandre, who have fallen in love while their fathers are away.

Fourfold Gospel: Jesus as Savior, Sanctifier, Healer & Coming King Audio Excerpts CD. Albert B. Simpson. (Pure Gold Classics). 2007. pap. bk. 14.99 (978-0-88270-336-7(6)) Bridge-Logos.

Fourfold Gospels. Neville Goddard. 1 cass. (Running Time: 62 min.). 1963. 8.00 (29) J & L Pubns.
Neville taught Imagination Creates Reality. He was a powerfully influential teacher of God as Consciousness.

Fourier Transform NMR Spectroscopy. Instructed by Edwin D. Becker. 6 cass. (Running Time: 4 hrs. 18 min.). 365.00 incl. 90pp. manual. (71) Am Chemical.
Examines the development & the widespread adoption of Fourier transform methods.

Fourmis, Set. Bernard Werber. Read by Francois Berland & Claude Berman. 6 cass. (FRE.). 1996. 46.95 (1803-LV) Olivia & Hill.
This fascinating thriller taking place simultaneously in the world of men & of ants has become an international bestseller.

Fourteen American Masterpieces. abr. ed. 2 cass. (Running Time: 3 hrs. 4 min.). Incl. Casey at the Bat. (803); Congressional Record. (803); Episode of War. (803); Furnished Room. (803); Haircut. (803); Interview with a Lemming. (803); Ladies Wild. (803); Occurrence at Owl Creek Bridge. (803); Old Country Advice to the American Traveler. (803); On the English Language. (803); Outcasts of Poker Flat. (803); Swallowing an Oyster Alive. (803); Uncle Remus Tales. (J). (803); 12.95 (978-0-89926-115-7(9), 803) Audio Bk.

Fourteen Contemporary Styles. Andrew D. Gordon. 1 cass. 1992. 20.00 (978-1-882146-11-6(5)) A D G Prods.

Fourteen Days to Higher SAT Scores. 3rd ed. Samuel C. Brownstein et al. 2 cass. (Running Time: 3 hrs.). 1994. bk. 16.95 Set, incl. bklt., 64p. (978-0-8120-8164-0(1)) Barron.

Fourteen Rats & a Rat-Catcher. 2004. 8.95 (978-1-56008-898-1(2)); cass. & flmstrp 30.00 (978-1-56008-670-3(X)) Weston Woods.

Fourteen Rats & a Rat-Catcher. (J). 2004. bk. 24.95 (978-1-56008-200-2(3)) Weston Woods.

Fourteen Rats & a Rat-Catcher; Trip, the; John Brown, Rose & the Midnight Cat; Bedtime! 2004. (978-0-89719-846-2(8)); cass. & flmstrp (978-0-89719-702-1(X)) Weston Woods.

Fourteen Things Witches Hope Parents Never Find Out. David Benoit. 1994. 19.95 (978-1-879366-76-3(2)) Hearthstone OK.

Fourteenth Annual Federal Securities Institute. 8 cass. (Running Time: 11 hrs. 30 min.). 1996. 345.00 Set; incl. study guide 597p. (MA28) Am Law Inst.
Designed to benefit anyone engaged in the practice of securities law, as well as handling corporate matters for public companies, empasizes recent developments.

Fourth Ace. unabr. ed. Bernie Kite. Read by Gene Engene. 8 cass. (Running Time: 9 hrs.). Dramatization. 1992. 49.95 (978-1-55686-379-0(9), 379) Books in Motion.
A desperate need for supplies in a starving mining camp forces four people to face incredible dangers while crossing the Cascade Mountains in the dead of winter.

Fourth Annual Criminal Law Symposium: Recent Cases-Juvenile Law-Sentencing-Ethics-Accident Reconstruction-Sexual Abuse. 1987. bk. 150.00; 100.00 PA Bar Inst.

Fourth Bear. unabr. ed. Jasper Fforde. Read by Simon Vance. 7 cass. (Running Time: 11 hrs.). (Nursery Crime Ser.: No. 2). 2006. 63.00 (978-1-4159-2983-4(1)); audio compact disk 81.00 (978-1-4159-2984-1(X)) Books on Tape.

Fourth Bear. unabr. ed. Jasper Fforde. Read by Simon Vance. (Running Time: 11 hrs.). No. 2. (ENG.). (gr. 12 up). 2006. audio compact disk 39.95 (978-0-14-305874-8(6), PengAudBks) Penguin Grp USA.

Fourth Chakra: Key to Love & Expansiveness. 1 cass. (Running Time: 90 min.). (Chakras Ser.). 9.95 (83TH) Crystal Clarity.
Presents: The air element in human conciousness; the importance of the heart (love) to spiritual advacement; why we need to be warmly loving; devotion as the source of the strength needed to overcome faults.

Fourth Comings. abr. ed. Megan McCafferty. Read by Renée Raudman. (Running Time: 6 hrs.). (Jessica Darling Ser.: No. 4). 2008. audio compact disk 14.99 (978-1-4233-4455-1(3), 9781423344551, BCD Value Price) Brilliance Audio.

Fourth Comings. unabr. ed. Megan McCafferty. Read by Renée Raudman. (Running Time: 11 hrs.). (Jessica Darling Ser.: No. 4). 2007. 39.25 (978-1-4233-4453-7(7), 9781423344537, BADLE); 24.95 (978-1-4233-4452-0(9), 9781423344520, BAD); 82.25 (978-1-4233-4447-6(2), 9781423344476, BrilAudUnabridg); audio compact disk 34.95 (978-1-4233-4448-3(0), 9781423344483); audio compact disk 24.95 (978-1-4233-4450-6(2), 9781423344506, Brilliance MP3); audio compact disk 39.25 (978-1-4233-4451-3(0), 9781423344513, Brlnc Audio MP3 Lib); audio compact disk 97.25 (978-1-4233-4449-0(9), 9781423344490, BriAudCD Unabrid) Brilliance Audio.

Fourth Company. Rifat Ilgaz. 2 cass. (Running Time: 2 hrs.). 2001. 11.95 (978-1-84059-305-1(9)) Pub: Milet Pub. Dist(s): Tuttle Pubng

Fourth Company. Rifat Ilgaz. 2 cass. (Running Time: 2 hrs.). (TUR.). (YA). 2001. bk. 11.95 (978-1-84059-304-4(0)) Pub: Milet Pub. Dist(s): Tuttle Pubng

Fourth Dawn. unabr. ed. Bodie Thoene & Brock Thoene. Narrated by Sean Barrett. (Running Time: 8 hrs. 43 mins. 6 sec.). (A. D. Chronicles Ser.). (ENG.). 2008. audio compact disk 29.99 (978-1-59859-503-1(2)) Oasis Audio.

Fourth Degree of Humility. Thomas Merton. 1 cass. (Running Time: 60 min.). (Humility Ser.). 4.50 (AA2108) Credence Commun.
Discussions on when humility begins & the growth of that trait.

Fourth, Eighth & Twelfth Houses. Joanne Wickenburg. Read by Joanne Wickenburg. 1 cass. (Running Time: 90 min.). 1994. 8.95 (1144) Am Fed Astrologers.
Discussion of the water houses - 4, 8, 12 - of the horoscope.

Fourth Empire. abr. ed. Mack Maloney. Read by Charlton Griffin. 2 vols. No. 3. 2003. (978-1-58807-550-5(8)) Am Pubng Inc.

Fourth Empire. abr. ed. Mack Maloney. Read by Charlton Griffin. 4 cass. (Running Time: 6 hrs.). (Starhawk Ser.: No. 3). 2003. 25.00 (978-1-58807-138-5(3)) Am Pubng Inc.
The year is 7200 A.D. The Specials have controlled the galaxy with near-immortal power and savage brutality. At the soul of the empire is the militaristic state of Earthand one man with the courage to destroy the will of the inhuman oppressors...For thousands of years, the great forces of the United Planets have been held captive in a barbaric galactic prisonuntil liberation by rogue pilot Hawk Hunter and the crew of the starship America. Now only on thing controls the band of brothers: the need for total war against the mysterious forces behind the Fourth Empire.Hunters ingenious scheme for guerrilla combat? Strike the Imperial Solar Guard when and where they least expect it. Now, planet by planet, the avenging freedom fighters are bringing the war closer to the Emperors doorstepand closer to bringing the Emperor to his knees. But thats only the beginning. An even greater impasse awaits Hunter and his crew: a billion-year-old secret about the galaxy that the Specials will do anything to protect.

Fourth Estate. unabr. ed. Jeffrey Archer. Narrated by Simon Prebble. 14 cass. (Running Time: 20 hrs.). 112.00 (978-0-7887-0608-0(X), 94804E7) Recorded Bks.
Two men who lust for power strive to become the first to create a global media empire. Available to libraries only.

Fourth Hand. John Irving. 2001. 56.00 (978-0-7366-7044-9(0)) Books on Tape.

Fourth Hand. unabr. ed. John Irving. Read by Jason Culp. 7 cass. (Running Time: 7 hrs.). 2001. 39.95 (H954) Blckstn Audio.
A miracle of medicine involving a donor, a recipient, a surgeon, a particular Green Bay Packer fan and the remarkable left hand that brings them together.

Fourth Horseman: One Man's Mission to Wage the Great War in America. Robert Koenig. Read by Normand Dietz. (Playaway Adult Nonfiction Ser.). (ENG.). 2009. 70.00 (978-1-60775-647-7(1)) Find a World.

Fourth Horseman: One Man's Mission to Wage the Great War in America. unabr. ed. Robert Koenig. Read by Norman Dietz. (Running Time: 15 hrs. 0 mins. 0 sec.). (ENG.). 2007. audio compact disk 37.99 (978-1-4001-0350-8(9)) Pub: Tantor Media. Dist(s): IngramPubServ

Fourth Horseman: The Tragedy of Anton Dilger & the Birth of Biological Terrorism. unabr. ed. Robert Koenig. (Running Time: 15 hrs. 0 mins. 0 sec.). (ENG.). 2007. audio compact disk 24.99 (978-1-4001-5350-3(6)); audio compact disk 75.99 (978-1-4001-3350-5(5)) Pub: Tantor Media. Dist(s): IngramPubServ

Fourth K. unabr. collector's ed. Mario Puzo. Read by Grover Gardner. 8 cass. (Running Time: 12 hrs.). 1991. 64.00 (978-0-7366-1947-9(X), 2768) Books on Tape.
President Francis Xavier Kennedy is elected to office, thanks largely to the legacy of his forebears - good looks, privilege, wealth. He is the very embodiment of youthful political optimism. But the political process gets to him &, unbelievably for intimates & the public alike, he suffers something very like a personality change. When a terrorist targets his daughter, Kennedy responds with bloody decision. Not for nothing has he studied the killings of his two famous uncles.

Fourth Little Pig. Teresa Celsi. (Metro Reading Ser.). (J). (gr. k). 2000. 8.46 (978-1-58120-986-0(X)) Metro Teaching.

***Fourth Nephite.** Jeffrey S. Savage. 2010. audio compact disk 24.99 (978-1-60908-009-9(2)) Deseret.

***Fourth Order: Unabridged Value-Priced Edition.** Stephen Frey. Narrated by Holter Graham. (Running Time: 11 hrs. 0 mins. 0 sec.). (ENG.). 2010. audio compact disk 14.95 (978-1-60283-999-1(9)) Pub: AudioGO. Dist(s): Perseus Dist

Fourth Perimeter. abr. ed. Tim Green. Read by Ron Perlman. (ENG.). 2005. 14.98 (978-1-59483-381-6(8)) Pub: Hachet Audio. Dist(s): HachBkGrp

Fourth Perimeter. unabr. ed. Tim Green. Read by Nick Sullivan. 6 vols. (Running Time: 9 hrs.). 2002. bk. 54.95 (978-0-7927-2720-0(7), CSL 506, Chivers Sound Lib); audio compact disk 79.95 (978-0-7927-2748-4(7), SLD 506, Chivers Sound Lib) AudioGO.
Kurt Ford, a former Secret Service agent, is determined to prove that his son, assigned to guard the U. S. president, did not commit suicide. When he discovers that several young agents have also died after witnessing a strange, secret meeting involving the president, Ford becomes obsessed with finding the truth.

Fourth Protocol. unabr. ed. Frederick Forsyth. Read by Rupert Keenlyside. 10 cass. (Running Time: 15 hrs.). 1985. 80.00 (978-0-7366-0819-0(2), 1768) Books on Tape.
A million dollar robbery in London, flawlessly conceived & meticulously executed, sets the tone for this story. Not for money alone, it masks a more sinister plot. The game is to stage an "accident" that will change the face of British politics & shatter the Western Alliance. John Peston, special agent, suspects treachery among the Queen's most trusted advisors & closes in on his elusive & deadly foe.

Fourth Quarter: Romans 8:5-18. Ed Young. 1984. 4.95 (978-0-7417-1376-6(4), 376) Win Walk.

Fourth Reich Death Squad. abr. ed. Axel Kilgore. Read by Charlton Griffin. 2 vols. No. 3. 2003. (978-1-58807-650-2(4)) Am Pubng Inc.

Fourth Reich Death Squad. abr. ed. Axel Kilgore. Read by Charlton Griffin. 2 vols. (Running Time: 3 hrs.). (Mercenary Ser.: No. 3). 2003. 18.00 (978-1-58807-159-0(6)) Am Pubng Inc.
"Every forty-eight hours, until ten million dollars in diamonds is paid, we'll send back a piece of professor Balsam." That message and a bloody finger are all Hank Frost finds after he loses his prize charge to terrorist kidnappers. And to get Balsam back, the fast-talking, fast-shooting, one-eyed mercenary captain has to gut his way through a sadistic torture team, neo-Nazi gunmen, and a vastly powerful Fourth Reich conspiracy. To add to the already harrowing situation, the French police, Israeli Intelligence, and Marita, a beautiful Mossad agent claiming to be Balsam's daughter, are all after him for one reason or another.

Fourth Reich Death Squad. abr. ed. Axel Kilgore. Read by Carol Eason. 3 CDs. (Running Time: 3 hrs.). (Mercenary Ser.: No. 3). 2004. audio compact disk 25.00 (978-1-58807-327-3(0)) Am Pubng Inc.
EVERY FORTY-EIGHT HOURS, UNTIL TEN MILLION DOLLARS IN DIAMONDS IS PAID, WE'LL SEND BACK A PIECE OF PROFESSOR BALSAM... That message and a bloody finger are all Hank Frost finds after he loses his prize charge to terrorist kidnappers. And to get Balsam back, the fast-talking, fast-shooting, one-eyed mercenary captain has to gut his way through a sadistic torture team, neo-Nazi gunmen, and a vastly powerful Fourth Reich conspiracy. To add to the already harrowing situation, the French police, Israeli Intelligence, and Marita, a beautiful Mossad agent claiming to be Balsam's daughter, are all after him for one reason or another. From Chicago to Paris to the Bavarian Alps, from terrorist assaults to torture sessions, Hank Frost is in trouble - up to his eye patch.

Fourth Reich Rising. unabr. ed. Tom Schwartz. Narrated by Ron Knowles. (Running Time: 4 hrs. 30 mins.). 2009. audio compact disk 24.95 (978-1-57545-324-8(X), RP Audio Pubng) Pub: Reagent Press. Dist(s): OverDrive Inc

***Fourth Stall.** unabr. ed. Chris Rylander. (ENG.). 2011. (978-0-06-203649-0(1)) HarperCollins Pubs.

Fourth Star: Four Generals & the Epic Struggle for the Future of the United States Army. abr. ed. Greg Jaffe & David Cloud. Read by Richard McGonagle. (ENG.). 2009. audio compact disk 32.00 (978-0-7393-8508-1(9), Random AudioBks) Pub: Random Audio Pubg. Dist(s): Random

Fourth Step. unabr. ed. Carl Burcham. Read by Gene Engene. 8 cass. (Running Time: 10 hrs. 12 min.). 2001. 49.95 (978-1-55686-982-2(7)) Books in Motion.
Detective Quinn Shannon and Washington Press reporter Katie St. Clair are in a race against time to learn the truth behind a conspiracy of death and destruction in the Washington D.C. political arena.

Fourth Step: A Moral Check List: Luke 12:1-6; Prov. 5:1-6. Ed Young. 1998. 4.95 (978-0-7417-2200-3(3), 1200) Win Walk.

Fourth Street East. abr. ed. Jerome Weidman. Narrated by Sam Guncler. 5 CDs. (Running Time: 6 hrs.). 2002. audio compact disk 44.95 (978-1-893079-11-3(2), JCCAUDIOBOOKS) Jewish Contempry Classics.
From the author of "Fiorello" & "I Can Get It for You Wholesale" comes an unforgettable collection of stories & characters from an hilarious boyhood.

Fourth Suspect. unabr. ed. Betty Rowlands. Read by Diana Bishop. 6 cass. (Running Time: 8 hrs.). (Sound Ser.). 2002. 54.95 (978-1-84283-150-2(X)) Pub: UlverLrgPrint GBR. Dist(s): Ulverscroft US
Cotswold-based crime writer, Melissa Craig, has acquired a reputation for solving real mysteries. But when her estranged father is found murdered in his own workshop, events come chillingly close to home. To Melissa's horror, fingerprints found on the murder weapon prove to be those of the mother with whom she has had no contact for almost thirty years. Determined to prove her mother's innocence, Melissa starts her own investigation with the help of her literary agent, Joe Martin.

Fourth Tower of Inverness. 5 cass. (Running Time: 7 hrs.). 2001. 35.00 (ZBS009); audio compact disk 45.00 (ZBSF010) Lodestone Catalog.
Jack Flanders, encounters strange happenings at an old Victorian mansion.

Fourth Tower of Inverness. unabr. ed. Meatball Fulton. Read by Meatball Fulton. Read by Robert Lorick et al. 5 cass. (Running Time: 7 hrs. 30 min.). 1972. 35.00 set. (978-1-881137-09-2(0)); audio compact disk 50.00 (978-1-881137-95-5(3), ZBSF010) ZBS Found.
Jack Flanders engages in adventures of the mind & body in these stories of discovery & drama. A young Jack travels to a mysterious old mansion. Although only three towers are visible, Jack is certain he's seen a fourth & the search begins.

Fourth Tower of Inverness, Set. Meatball Fulton. Read by Meatball Fulton. Read by Robert Lorick et al. 5 cass. (Running Time: 7 hr.). 35.00 (ZBSF009) ZBS Ind.

Fourth Way: Gurdjieff, Ouspensky & Nicoll. unabr. ed. Stephan Hoeller. 1 cass. (Running Time: 1 hr. 30 min.). 1980. 11.00 (40007) Big Sur Tapes.
Speaks of the major features of the Fourth Way movement & its greatest contributors.

Fox, unabr. ed. D. H. Lawrence. Narrated by Sheri Blair. 2 cass. (Running Time: 3 hrs.). 1999. 18.00 (978-1-55690-185-0(2), 83052E7) Recorded Bks.
Two girls set up house in a farm in Cornwall, England. Then, a young man arrives & their domestic order is threatened.

Fox & His Friends. unabr. ed. James Marshall & Edward Marshall. 1 cass. (Running Time: 15 mins.). (Follow the Reader Ser.). (J). (gr. k-3). 1985. pap. bk. 17.00 incl. bk. & guide. (978-0-8072-0074-2(3), FTR92SP, Listening Lib) Random Audio Pubg.
All Fox wants to do is play with his friends, but Mom insists he baby-sit for little sister Louise, who is nothing but trouble.

Fox & the Hound. 1 cass. (Read-Along Ser.). (J). bk. 7.99 (978-1-55723-019-5(6)) W Disney Records.

Fox at School. unabr. ed. James Marshall & Edward Marshall. 1 cass. (Running Time: 14 mins.). (Follow the Reader Ser.). (J). (gr. k-3). 1985. pap. bk. 17.00 (978-0-8072-0072-8(7), FTR91SP, Listening Lib) Random Audio Pubg.
Fox just can't believe his luck. He is going to be the handsome prince in the school play. But Fox doesn't realize that being a star means hard work, so he loses the lead role; Fox will not retreat however, he continues to pursue stardom.

Fox Busters. unabr. ed. Dick King-Smith. Read by Nigel Lambert. 2 cass. (Running Time: 2 hrs.). (J). 1993. 18.95 (978-0-7451-8582-8(7), CCA 3022, Chivers Child Audio) AudioGO.

fox called Sorrow. Isobelle Carmody. Read by Isobelle Carmody. (Running Time: 4 hrs. 50 mins.). (Legend of Little Fur Ser.). (J). 2009. 59.99 (978-1-74214-367-5(9), 9781742143675) Pub: Bolinda Pubng AUS. Dist(s): Bolinda Pub Inc

Fox Called Sorrow: The Legend of Little Fur. unabr. ed. Isobelle Carmody. Read by Isobelle Carmody. (Running Time: 17400 sec.). (Legend of Little Fur Ser.). (J). (gr. 1-7). 2006. audio compact disk 57.95 (978-1-74093-815-0(1)) Pub: Bolinda Pubng AUS. Dist(s): Bolinda Pub Inc

Fox Evil. unabr. ed. Minette Walters. 9 cass. (Running Time: 13 hrs. 30 min.). 2003. 87.00 (978-1-4025-5654-8(3)) Recorded Bks.

Fox, Fin & Feather. Bart Jacobs & Henry W. Hooker. 2002. audio compact disk 25.00 (978-1-58667-090-0(5)) Pub: Derrydale Pr. Dist(s): Natl Bk Netwk

Fox in Love. unabr. ed. James Marshall & Edward Marshall. 1 cass. (Running Time: 14 mins.). (Follow the Reader Ser.). (J). (gr. k-3). 1984. pap. bk. 17.00 (978-0-8072-0078-0(6), FTR94SP, Listening Lib) Random Audio Pubg.
Fox never had any interest in taking his sister Louise to the park until he spots Raisin, who Fox thinks looks just like a movie star.

Fox in Socks. Dr. Seuss. (J). 1976. bk. 30.65 (978-0-394-03651-9(4)) SRA McGraw.

Fox in the Forest: Early Explorers Emergent Set A Audio CD. Benchmark Education Staff. (J). 2006. audio compact disk 10.00 (978-1-4108-7588-4(1)) Benchmark Educ.

Fox on Wheels. unabr. ed. Edward Marshall & James Marshall. 1 cass. (Running Time: 13 mins.). (Follow the Reader Ser.). (J). (gr. k-3). 1985. pap. bk. 17.00 (978-0-8072-0080-3(8), FTR95SP, Listening Lib) Random Audio Pubg.
Fox & his sister Louise & the rest of the gang are back for another adventure.

Fox Trot see Osbert Sitwell Reading His Poetry

Fox Went Out on a Chilly Night. 2004. bk. 24.95 (978-1-56008-240-8(2)); pap. bk. 14.95 (978-1-56008-201-9(1)); 8.95 (978-1-56008-899-8(0)); cass. & flmstrp 30.00 (978-0-89719-618-5(X)) Weston Woods.

Fox Went Out on a Chilly Night. unabr. ed. Illus. by Peter Spier. Narrated by Tom Chapin. 1 cass. (Running Time: 9 mins.). (J). (ps-3). 2006. pap. bk. 16.95 (978-1-59112-440-5(9)); pap. bk. 18.95 (978-1-59112-441-2(7)) Live Oak Media.

Fox Went Out on a Chilly Night, Set. unabr. ed. Illus. by Peter Spier. Narrated by Tom Chapin. 1 cass. (Running Time: 9 mins.). (J). (ps-3). 2006. pap. bk. 37.95 (978-1-59112-442-9(5)); pap. bk. 39.95 (978-1-59112-443-6(3)) Live Oak Media.

Foxe's Book of Martyrs. John Foxe. Narrated by Robin Lawson. (Running Time: 13 hrs.). 1993. 41.95 (978-1-59912-495-7(5)) Iofy Corp.

Foxe's Book of Martyrs. John Foxe. Frwd. by Gwen Shamblin. 2001. pap. bk. 13.95 (978-1-892729-76-7(8)) Weigh Down Work.

Foxe's Book of Martyrs. unabr. ed. John Foxe. Read by Robin Lawson. 9 cass. (Running Time: 13 hrs.). 1994. 62.95 (978-0-7861-0494-9(5), 1445) Blckstn Audio.
After the Bible itself, no book so profoundly influenced early Protestant sentiment as the Book of Martyrs. Even in our time it is still a living force. It is more than a record of persecution. It is an arsenal of controversy, a storehouse of romance, as well as a source of edification.

Foxe's Book of Martyrs. unabr. ed. John Foxe. Ed. by William Byron Forbush. Narrated by Nadia May. (Running Time: 17 hrs. 30 mins. 0 sec.). (ENG.). 2008. audio compact disk 34.98 (978-1-59644-606-9(4), Hovel Audio) christianaud.

***Foxe's Book of Martyrs.** unabr. ed. John Foxe. Narrated by Nadia May. (ENG.). 2008. 19.98 (978-1-59644-607-6(2), Hovel Audio) christianaud.

Foxe's Book of Martyrs. unabr. ed. John Foxe. Ed. by William Byron Forbush. Narrated by Nadia May. (Running Time: 17 hrs. 30 mins. 0 sec.). (ENG.). 2008. lp 19.98 (978-1-59644-621-2(8), Hovel Audio) christianaud.

Foxe's Christian Martyrs of the World. John Foxe. 1998. 4.97 (978-1-57748-207-9(7)) Barbour Pub.

Foxes of Harrow. unabr. ed. Frank Yerby. Read by Dan Lazar. 12 cass. (Running Time: 18 hrs.). 1982. 96.00 (978-0-7366-0431-4(6), 1403) Books on Tape.
Stephen Fox arrived in New Orleans in 1825 on a pig boat, with a ten-dollar gold piece, a pearl stick-pin & a dream. Stephen Fox saw his chance & took it - took it from indolent, slave-ridden, castebound people, with the skill & daring of the card-sharp he was. He gambled & won & built "Harrow" the greatest manor house & plantation in Louisiana.

Foxglove Tree. Elizabeth Gill. Read by Trudy Harris. 6. 2007. 54.95 (978-1-84652-121-8(1)); audio compact disk 71.95 (978-1-84652-122-5(X)) Pub: Magna Story GBR. Dist(s): Ulverscroft US

Foxman. unabr. ed. Gary Paulsen. Narrated by Johnny Heller. 2 pieces. (Running Time: 3 hrs.). (gr. 4 up). 2001. 19.00 (978-0-7887-0328-7(5), 94520E7) Recorded Bks.
Explores the similar psychological effects of war & domestic abuse. Traces the growth of an unusual friendship between an emotionally fragile 15-year-old & a hideously deformed war veteran.

Fox's Earth. unabr. ed. Anne Rivers Siddons. Narrated by Sally Darling. 14 cass. (Running Time: 19 hrs. 30 mins.). 1995. 112.00 (978-0-7887-0316-4(1), 94508E7) Recorded Bks.
Beautiful, dirt-poor Ruth Yancey rises to become the mistress of Sparta, Georgia's finest mansion. For three generations, she rules the mansion through evil manipulation until one woman decides to match her madness.

Foxtails: The Adventures of Freddie Fox. Short Stories. Robert Hanrott. Narrated by Robert Hanrott. Music by Martha Horsley. 1. (Running Time: 60 mins). (J). 2004. audio compact disk 14.95 (978-0-9721035-6-5(2)) ByD Pr.
Children's audio CD of stories with music. Set in the English countryside, Freddie's adventures, told in rhymed verse, can be enjoyed on several levels. For adults and children 6 and up. Educational, glossary included.

Foxy Fox see Let's Read Together

Foxy Fox. Created by Kane Press. (Let's Read Together Ser.). 2005. audio compact disk 4.25 (978-1-57565-173-6(4)) Pub: Kane Pr. Dist(s): Lerner Pub

Fr. Rutler on Christianity in Modern World & Award to Sr. Assumpta. 1 cass. (National Meeting of the Institute, 1993 Ser.). 4.00 (93N3) IRL Chicago.

Fra Lippo Lippi see Poetry of Robert Browning

Fra Lippo Lippi see Treasury of Robert Browning

Fractal Mode. unabr. ed. Piers Anthony. Read by Mark Winston. (Running Time: 11 hrs.). (Mode Ser.). 2008. 39.25 (978-1-4233-5334-8(X), 9781423353348, BADLE); 24.95 (978-1-4233-5333-1(1), 9781423353331, BAD) Brilliance Audio.

Fractal Mode. unabr. ed. Piers Anthony & Piers Anthony. Read by Mark Winston. (Running Time: 11 hrs.). (Mode Ser.). 2008. audio compact disk 39.25 (978-1-4233-5332-4(3), 9781423353324, Brlnc Audio MP3 Lib); audio compact disk 24.95 (978-1-4233-5331-7(5), 9781423353317, Brilliance MP3) Brilliance Audio.

Fractal Time: The Secret of 2012 & a New World Age. Gregg Braden. 4 CDs. 2009. audio compact disk 23.95 (978-1-4019-2066-1(7), 606) Hay House.

Fractions & Equivalent Fractions Audio CD Theme Set. Based on a work by 04. (Math Explorers Ser.). (J). (gr. 3-8). 2008. audio compact disk 75.00 (978-1-60437-476-4(3)) Benchmark Educ.

Fractions as a Tool: An Individualized, Self-Directing, Self-Correcting Program. John Blackwood & Elizabeth Alden. 5 cass. 79.00 incl. activity worksheets, individualized education prescription, progress chart, guide. (978-0-89525-212-8(0), AMC 353) Ed Activities.
Uses the ruler to enable students to visualize, conceptualize & work with fractions, such as covering inches & feet, using halves, quarter, eighths & sixteenth of an inch, adding & subtracting with like & unlike denominators, multiplying & dividing fractions, solving problems involving fractions, decimals, percentages & mixed numbers in real-life situations.

Fractions at the Pet Shop. Based on a book by Barbara Andrews. (J). 2008. audio compact disk 10.00 (978-1-4108-8071-0(0)) Benchmark Educ.

Fractions at the Pet Shop E-Book: Set A. Benchmark Education Staff. Ed. by Barbara Andrews. (Math Explorers Ser.). (J). 2008. audio compact disk 15.00 (978-1-60437-153-6(6)) Benchmark Educ.

Fractions at Work. Based on a book by Brett Kelly. (J). 2008. audio compact disk 10.00 (978-1-4108-8075-8(3)) Benchmark Educ.

Fractions at Work E-Book: Set A. Benchmark Education Staff. Ed. by Brett Kelly. (Math Explorers Ser.). (J). 2008. audio compact disk 15.00 (978-1-60437-157-4(9)) Benchmark Educ.

Fractions in Sports. Based on a book by Barbara Andrews. (J). 2008. audio compact disk 10.00 (978-1-4108-8072-7(9)) Benchmark Educ.

Fractions in Sports E-Book: Set A. Benchmark Education Staff. Ed. by Barbara Andrews. (Math Explorers Ser.). (J). 2008. audio compact disk 15.00 (978-1-60437-154-3(4)) Benchmark Educ.

Fractions in the Garden. Based on a book by Tara Funk. (J). 2008. audio compact disk 10.00 (978-1-4108-8074-1(5)) Benchmark Educ.

Fractions in the Garden E-Book: Set A. Benchmark Education Staff. Ed. by Tara Funk. (Math Explorers Ser.). (J). 2008. audio compact disk 15.00 (978-1-60437-156-7(0)) Benchmark Educ.

Fractions in the Kitchen. Based on a book by Tara Funk. (J). 2008. audio compact disk 10.00 (978-1-4108-8076-5(1)) Benchmark Educ.

Fractions in the Kitchen E-Book: Set A. Benchmark Education Staff. Ed. by Tara Funk. (Math Explorers Ser.). (J). 2008. audio compact disk 15.00 (978-1-60437-158-1(7)) Benchmark Educ.

Fractions with Friends. Based on a book by Barbara Andrews. (J). 2008. audio compact disk 10.00 (978-1-4108-8070-3(2)) Benchmark Educ.

Fractions with Friends E-Book: Set A. Benchmark Education Staff. Ed. by Barbara Andrews. (Math Explorers Ser.). (J). 2008. audio compact disk 15.00 (978-1-60437-152-9(8)) Benchmark Educ.

Fracture Zone: A Return to the Balkans. unabr. ed. Simon Winchester. Narrated by Steven Crossley. 7 CDs. (Running Time: 8 hrs. 30 mins.). 2001. audio compact disk 78.00 (978-1-4025-1050-2(0), C1596) Recorded Bks.
Unrest in the Balkans has gone on for centuries. A seasoned reporter, Winchester visited the region twenty years ago. When Kosovo reached crisis level in 1997, Winchester thought a return visit to the beleaguered area would help to make sense out of the awful violence. He decided to use Vienna and Istanbul, two great cities whose rivalries helped create the dynamics at work today, as the beginning and end points of his trip. Not specifically a book about war, it is more a portrait of a place and its people in turmoil.

Fracture Zone: A Return to the Balkans. unabr. ed. Simon Winchester. Narrated by Steven Crossley. 6 cass. (Running Time: 8 hrs. 30 mins.). 2001. 57.00 (978-0-7887-4864-6(5), 96378x7) Recorded Bks.
Combining history & interviews with the people who live there, Winchester offers a fascinating glimpse into the complex issues at work in this chaotic region.

Fractured. abr. ed. Karin Slaughter. Read by Phil Gigante. 5 CDs. (Running Time: 6 hrs.). (Will Trent Ser.: No. 2). 2008. audio compact disk 24.99 (978-1-4233-4227-4(5), 9781423342274, BACD) Brilliance Audio.

Fractured. abr. ed. Karin Slaughter. (Running Time: 6 hrs.). (Will Trent Ser.: No. 2). 2009. audio compact disk 14.99 (978-1-4233-4228-1(3), 9781423342281) Brilliance Audio.

Fractured. unabr. ed. Karin Slaughter. Read by Phil Gigante. 1 MP3-CD. (Running Time: 13 hrs.). (Will Trent Ser.: No. 2). 2008. 24.95 (978-1-4233-4223-6(2), 9781423342236, Brilliance MP3); 39.25 (978-1-4233-4224-3(0), 9781423342243, Brlnc Audio MP3 Lib); 39.25 (978-1-4233-4226-7(7), 9781423342267, BADLE); 24.95 (978-1-4233-4225-0(9), 9781423342250, BAD); audio compact disk 32.99 (978-1-4233-4221-2(6), 9781423342212, Bril Audio CD Unabri); audio compact disk 117.25 (978-1-4233-4222-9(4), 9781423342229, BriAudCD Unabrid) Brilliance Audio.

Fractured Classics Theme: Reader's Theater Classics Set A Read Aloud Think Aloud CD Rom. Compiled by Benchmark Education Staff. 2007. audio compact disk 10.00 (978-1-4108-8557-9(7)) Benchmark Educ.

Fractured Fairy Tales. Jay Ward. Read by Full Cast Production Staff. (Running Time: 5400 sec.). 2007. 15.95 (978-1-4332-0161-5(5)); audio compact disk 24.00 (978-1-4332-0162-2(3)); audio compact disk 19.95 (978-1-4332-0163-9(1)) Blckstn Audio.

Fractured Land, Healing Nations: A Contextual Analysis of the Role of Religious Faith Sodalities Towards Peace-Building in Bosnia-Herzegovina. Stephen R. Goodwin. Vol. 139. 2006. pap. bk. 62.95 (978-3-631-55306-0(4)) P Lang Pubng.

Fractured Mind. Robert B. Oxnam. Read by William Dufris. (Running Time: 9 hrs. 30 mins.). 2005. 19.95 (978-1-59912-918-1(3)) Iofy Corp.

Fractured Mind: My Life with Multiple Personality Disorder. Robert B. Oxnam. Read by William Dufris. 8 CDs. (Running Time: 34200 sec.). 2005. audio compact disk 34.95 (978-1-59316-070-8(4), LL162) Listen & Live.

Frag Box. unabr. ed. Richard Thompson. (Running Time: 8.5 hrs. 0 mins.). (ENG.). 2009. 29.95 (978-1-4417-0291-3(1)); 54.95 (978-1-4417-0287-6(3)); audio compact disk 76.00 (978-1-4417-0288-3(1)) Blckstn Audio.

***Fragile Beasts.** unabr. ed. Tawni O'Dell. Narrated by Paul Boehmer & Laural Merlington. 13 CDs. (Running Time: 16 hrs. 30 mins. 0 sec.). 2010. audio compact disk 99.99 (978-1-4001-4696-3(8)) Pub: Tantor Media. Dist(s): IngramPubServ

***Fragile Beasts: A Novel.** unabr. ed. Tawni O'Dell. Narrated by Paul Boehmer & Laural Merlington. (Running Time: 18 hrs. 0 mins.). 2010. 22.99 (978-1-4001-8696-9(X)) Tantor Media.

***Fragile Beasts: A Novel.** unabr. ed. Tawni O'Dell. Narrated by Paul Boehmer & Laural Merlington. 2 MP3-CDs. (Running Time: 16 hrs. 30 mins. 0 sec.). 2010. 34.99 (978-1-4001-6696-1(9)); audio compact disk 49.99 (978-1-4001-1696-6(1)) Pub: Tantor Media. Dist(s): IngramPubServ

***Fragile Eternity.** unabr. ed. Melissa Marr. Read by Nick Landrum. (ENG.). 2009. (978-0-06-177892-6(3)); (978-0-06-180594-3(7)) HarperCollins Pubs.

***Fragile Eternity.** unabr. ed. Melissa Marr. Narrated by Nick Landrum. 1 Playaway. (Running Time: 11 hrs. 15 mins.). (YA). (gr. 9 up). 2009. 64.75 (978-1-4407-3045-0(8)); 67.75 (978-1-4407-3035-1(0)); audio compact disk 97.75 (978-1-4407-3039-9(3)) Recorded Bks.

***Fragile Eternity.** unabr. collector's ed. Melissa Marr. Narrated by Nick Landrum. 11 CDs. (Running Time: 11 hrs. 15 mins.). (YA). (gr. 9 up). 2009. audio compact disk 51.95 (978-1-4407-3043-6(1)) Recorded Bks.

Fragile: Handle with Care! 11 Cor. 4:7-12. Ed Young. 1990. 4.95 (978-0-7417-1781-8(6), 781) Win Walk.

Fragile Paradise. unabr. ed. Glynn Christian. Read by Glynn Christian. 10 cass. (Running Time: 12 hrs. 30 mins.). 2004. 80.00 (978-1-74030-093-3(9), 500219) Pub: Bolinda Pubng AUS. Dist(s): Bolinda Pub Inc

Fragile Species. unabr. ed. Lewis Thomas. Narrated by George Guidall. 6 cass. (Running Time: 8 hrs.). 1992. 51.00 (978-1-55690-670-1(6), 92222E7) Recorded Bks.
Essays on contemporary concerns from AIDS to ozone depletion, revealing the author's clear thinking & his ability to cut through the fog of modern problems.

***Fragile Stone Audio Book: The Emotional Life of Simon Peter.** abr. ed. Michael Card. (ENG.). 2009. 16.00 (978-0-8308-5563-6(7), IVP Bks) InterVarsity.

***Fragile Things.** unabr. ed. Neil Gaiman. Read by Neil Gaiman. 2006. (978-0-06-122996-1(2), Harper Audio); (978-0-06-122995-4(4), Harper Audio) HarperCollins Pubs.

***Fragile Things: A Study in Emerald.** abr. ed. Neil Gaiman. Read by Neil Gaiman. 2007. (978-0-06-136733-5(8), Harper Audio) HarperCollins Pubs.

Fragile Things: Short Fictions & Wonders. unabr. ed. Neil Gaiman. 13 cass. 2006. 104.95 (978-0-7927-4538-9(8), CSL 1056) AudioGO.

Fragile Things: Short Fictions & Wonders. unabr. ed. Neil Gaiman. 16 CDs. (Running Time: 38820 sec.). 2006. audio compact disk 119.95 (978-0-7927-4526-6(4), SLD 1056) AudioGO.

Fragile Things: Short Fictions & Wonders. unabr. ed. Neil Gaiman. Narrated by Neil Gaiman. 2 CDs. (Running Time: 38820 sec.). 2006. audio compact disk 74.95 (978-0-7927-4561-7(2), CMP 1056) AudioGO.

***Fragile Things: Short Fictions & Wonders.** unabr. ed. Neil Gaiman. Read by Neil Gaiman. 2010. audio compact disk 19.99 (978-0-06-200367-6(4), Harper Audio) HarperCollins Pubs.

Fragile Treasures: The Spiritual Teachings of St. Paul. Ronald Witherup. 1 cass. (Running Time: 1 hr. 13 mins.). 2001. 8.95 (A8041) St Anthony Mess Pr.

Fragile X Syndrome: Medical & Educational Approaches to Treatment. unabr. ed. Perf. by Randy Hagerman. Interview with Lois E. Hickman & Tracy Stackhouse. 1 cass. (Running Time: 1 hr. 20 min.). (Belle Curve Information Ser.). 1993. 15.00 (978-1-893601-25-3(0), BCIS-1) Sensory Res.
Important features are discussed, along with treatment options.

Fragile X Syndrome - A Bibliography & Dictionary for Physicians, Patients, & Genome Researchers. Compiled by Icon Group International, Inc. Staff. 2007. ring bd. 28.95 (978-0-497-11214-1(0)) Icon Grp.

Fragments see Poetry of Ralph Waldo Emerson

***Fragments: Poems, Intimate Notes, Letters.** abr. ed. Marilyn Monroe. Read by Isabel Keating. Ed. by Stanley Buchthal & Bernard Comment. 2 CDs. (Running Time: 3 hrs.). 2010. audio compact disk 19.99 (978-1-4272-1167-5(1)) Pub: Macmill Audio. Dist(s): Macmillan

Fragments of Isabella. unabr. ed. Isabella Leitner. Read by Isabella Leitner. 1 cass. 1986. 9.95 (978-0-89845-645-5(2), A 1800) HarperCollins Pubs.
Distilled memories of Auschwitz experienced by the author.

Fragments of My Life: A Memoir. abr. ed. Catherine Doherty. Read by Helen Porthouse. 4 cass. (Running Time: 5 hrs. 30 mins.). 24.95 (978-0-921440-58-1(8)) Madonna Hse CAN.
A journey into Catherine's life, disclosing the mysteries of world events that shaped her life; the mysteries of her leadership; the mysteries of her marriage; and, most of all, the mysteries of God's love. Catherine tells in her own words how she was born to wealth in pre-revolutionary Russia, raised among Arab children and pashas in Egypt, French students in Paris, and Russian peasants and aristocrats on her family estate. She shares how she dodged bullets as a nurse during World War I, barely survived the Russian Revolution, encountered poverty as a refugee and returned from her rags to riches in North America. Then finally, how she gave everything away to serve the poor on the streets of Toronto and Harlem. She tells of her adventures as a magazine correspondent in pre-World War II Europe, as a leader in the U.S. Civil Rights movement, and as an internationally-renowned speaker and writer who dodged rotten eggs and tomatoes, calling for racial and economic justice, ecumenism, and an active role for lay people in the Church. Finally, she explains how she fell in love with and married Eddie Doherty, the famed Irish-American newspaperman, and how they together founded Madonna House.

Fragments of the Ark. unabr. ed. Louise Meriwether. Read by John H. McCants Jr. (Running Time: 13 hrs.). 2008. 39.25 (978-1-4233-5784-1(1), 9781423357841, Brlnc Audio MP3 Lib); 39.25 (978-1-4233-5786-5(8), 9781423357865, BADLE); 24.95 (978-1-4233-5785-8(X), 9781423357858, BAD); 24.95 (978-1-4233-5783-4(3), 9781423357834, Brilliance MP3) Brilliance Audio.

Frailing the Five-String Banjo. Eric Muller & Barbara Koehler. 1993. bk. 18.95 (978-0-7866-0913-0(3), 93335P); 9.98 (978-0-87166-756-4(8), 93335C) Mel Bay.

Framed. unabr. ed. Frank Cottrell Boyce. Read by Jason Hughes. 6 CDs. (Running Time: 25200 sec.). (J). (gr. 5-9). 2006. audio compact disk 25.95 (978-0-06-114043-3(0), HarperChildAud) HarperCollins Pubs.

***Framed.** unabr. ed. Frank Cottrell Boyce. Read by Jason Hughes. (ENG.). 2006. (978-0-06-122934-3(2), KTegenBooks); (978-0-06-122937-4(7), KTegenBooks) HarperCollins Pubs.

Framed. unabr. ed. Carolyn Keene. Read by Rebecca Rogers. (Running Time: 10800 sec.). (Nancy Drew: Girl Detective Ser.). (J). (gr. 3-7). 2007. audio compact disk 29.95 (978-1-4332-0034-2(1)) Blckstn Audio.

Framed. unabr. ed. Carolyn Keene. Read by Rebecca Rogers. (Running Time: 10800 sec.). (Nancy Drew: Girl Detective Ser.). (J). (gr. 4-7). 2007. 24.95 (978-1-4332-0030-4(9)); audio compact disk 27.00 (978-1-4332-0031-1(7)) Blckstn Audio.

Framed for Love, Set. Rachel Ann Nunes. 2 cass. 1999. 13.95 (978-1-57734-475-9(8), 07002092) Covenant Comms.
Sequel to "Love to the Highest Bidder.".

Framed in Cornwall. Janie Bolitho. 6 cass. (Running Time: 7 hrs. 30 min.). (Soundings Ser.). 2007. 54.95 (978-1-84283-895-2(4)) Pub: Soundings Ltd GBR. Dist(s): Ulverscroft US

Framely Parsonage. unabr. ed. Anthony Trollope. Read by David Case. 15 cass. (Running Time: 22 hrs. 30 min.). 1993. 120.00 set. (3193) Books on Tape.
Captures the essence of Victorian England where property, status, family & convention are paramount.

Frames of Mind-Comp 21 Cd-Stan. (C). 2004. audio compact disk 41.95 (978-1-4130-1305-4(8)) Pub: Heinle. Dist(s): CENGAGE Learn

Framework for Death. unabr. ed. Aileen Schumacher. Read by Stephanie Brush. 12 cass. (Running Time: 12 hrs. 12 min.). (Tory Travers Mystery Ser.: Bk. 2). 2001. 64.95 (978-1-55686-983-9(5)) Books in Motion.
The structural collapse of a residence reveals a concealed room containing two bodies, one of which comes complete with three sets of ID's. Tory Travers and Detective Alvarez attempt to find the builder, currently involved with the drug underworld.

Framework for Understanding Poverty. Ruby K. Payne. Orig. Title: Poverty - A Framework for Understanding & Working with Students & Adults from Poverty. 2004. audio compact disk 35.00 (978-1-929229-05-5(4)) aha Process.

Framework for Understanding Poverty. Ruby K. Payne et al. 1997. audio compact disk 225.00 (978-1-929229-56-7(9)) aha Process.

Framley Parsonage. unabr. ed. Anthony Trollope. Read by Simon Vance. (Running Time: 68400 sec.). 2007. 95.95 (978-1-4332-0119-6(4)); audio compact disk 44.95 (978-1-4332-0121-9(6)); audio compact disk 120.00 (978-1-4332-0120-2(8)) Blckstn Audio.

Framley Parsonage. unabr. collector's ed. Anthony Trollope. Read by David Case. 15 cass. (Running Time: 22 hrs. 30 mins.). (Barsetshire Chronicles: No. 4). 1993. 120.00 (978-0-7366-2429-9(5), 3193) Books on Tape.
Captures the essence of Victorian England where property, status, family & convention are paramount.

Framley Parsonage, Set. Anthony Trollope. Read by Flo Gibson. 15 cass. (Running Time: 20 hrs.). 1995. 43.95 (978-1-55685-360-9(2)) Audio Bk Con.
The lives & loves of Lucy Robarts & Lord Lufton, Griselda Grantly & Lord Dumbello, Olivia Proudie & Mr. Tickler, & Miss Dunstable & Dr. Thorne are depicted with warmth & humor; & we witness the callousness & greed of such characters as Mrs. Proudie, Mr. Sowerby & Tom Tozer.

Fran Lebowitz. Fran Lebowitz. Read by Fran Lebowitz. Prod. by Moveable Feast Staff. 1 cass. (Running Time: 30 min.). 8.95 (AMF-22) Am Audio Prose.
Witty reading from "Metropolitan Life" & "Social Studies." Lebowitz talks about wit & style in the 1980s.

Fran Lebowitz. Interview. Interview with Fran Lebowitz. 1 cass. (Running Time: 25 min.). 1980. 11.95 (L043) TFR.
Lebowitz talks about the pleasures & perils as described in her book Metropolitan Life. She discusses her other work, Social Studies, in which she came out of the closet as a Republican. Mannes talks about her autobiography, Out Of My Time, in which she asserts that she never liked the age she was born in, her ideas were way ahead of her time & "I Hit it too Soon".

Francais Depart Arrivee. 3rd ed. John Rassias. 1992. pap. bk. 44.95 (978-0-470-00248-3(4), JWiley) Wiley US.

Francais pour Arabophones. 1 cass. (Running Time: 1 hr. 30 min.).Tr. of French for Arabic Speakers. (ARA & FRE., 1997. pap. bk. 75.00 (978-2-7005-1361-5(4)) Pub: Assimil FRA. Dist(s): Distribks Inc

Francais pour Debutants. Sara Jordan. Prod. by Sara Jordan. Illus. by Hector Obando. Engineer Mark Shannon. 1 cass. (Running Time: 44 min. 50 sec.). (FRE.). (J). 2001. pap. bk. 14.95 (978-1-895523-44-7(3), JMP F05K) Jordan Music.
Great for beginners. Songs that teach the alphabet, farm animals, counting, family members, parts of the body, days of the week, colors, fruit, opposites and shapes in French. A complement of instrumental accompaniment tracks allows students to become performers, boosting literacy skills, karaoke style, and making performances fun. Packaged with an activity/lyrics book.

Francais pour Debutants. abr. ed. Sara Jordan. Prod. by Sara Jordan. 1 CD. (Running Time: 30 min.). (Songs That Teach French Ser.). (FRE.). (J). (gr. 4-7). 1993. audio compact disk 13.95 (978-1-894262-05-7(0), JMP F05CD) Pub: S Jordan Publ. Dist(s): CrabtreePubCo

Francais Sous l'Occupation Set: La Rupture Du Pacte Germano-Sovietique. Henri Amouroux. 2 cass. (World War II Ser.). (FRE.). 1995. 26.95 (1230-RF) Olivia & Hill.
The story of France during the Occupation, illustrated with original recordings. Sabotage, hostages & antisemitism.

France. 1 cass. (Passport's Travel Paks Ser.). 29.95 (Natl Textbk Co) M-H Contemporary.
Presents a language & control cassette to help prepare for a trip to France.

France: Paris - A Traveler's Companion. 1 cass. (Running Time: 60 min.). 11.95 (CC401) Comp Comms Inc.
Tells you where to find outdoor street markets, historic book stalls & shops where the greatest French chefs buy their own ladies, from the Left Bank to the Louvre to Rue du Faubourg St. Honore.

France: Paris - Your Personal Guide (Walking Tour) 2 cass. (Running Time: 2 hrs.). 16.95 (CC403) Comp Comms Inc.
Covers La Cite, Right Bank, Marais, Montmarte, also gives a brief introduction to Paris & then takes the visitor on 4 walks.

France & The Third Republic. 10.00 (HE822) Esstee Audios.
Discusses why a great democracy failed.

France, Echos De. unabr. ed. 1 cass. 1994. bk. 14.95 (978-0-88432-465-2(6), SFR155) J Norton Pubs.
Literary classics.

France en Poche. 18.95 (978-88-536-0930-4(3)) EMC-Paradigm.

France Explores the Americas. Compiled by Benchmark Education Staff. 2005. audio compact disk 10.00 (978-1-4108-5481-0(7)) Benchmark Educ.

France Smarts by Dancing Beetle. Perf. by Eugene Ely. 1 cass. (Running Time: 85 min.). (J). 1995. 10.00 Erthviibz.
France, science, myth, ecology & nature sounds come together when Ms. Oyster & the spunky musical humans read & sing with Dancing Beetle.

Frances. unabr. ed. Russell Hoban. 1 cass. (Running Time: 1 hr. 30 mins.). 2003. 7.99 (978-0-06-058440-5(8)) Pub: HarperCollins Pubs. Dist(s): HarpCollins

Frances. unabr. ed. Russell Hoban. Read by Glynis Johns. (Running Time: 2700 sec.). (J). (ps-3). 2006. audio compact disk 14.99 (978-0-06-085281-8(X), HarperChildAud) HarperCollins Pubs.

Frances. unabr. abr. ed. Russell Hoban. Illus. by Glynis Johns. 1 cass. (Running Time: 45 min.). Incl. Frances: A Baby for Frances. (J). (ps-3). 1989. (CPN 1546); Frances: A Birthday for Frances. (J). (ps-3). 1989. (CPN 1546); Frances: Bedtime for Frances. (J). (ps-3). 1989. (CPN 1546); Frances: Bread & Jam for Frances. (J). (ps-3). 1989. (CPN 1546); (Stand Alone Ser.). (J). (ps-3). 1989. 12.00 (978-0-89845-871-8(4), CPN 1546) HarperCollins Pubs.

Frances: A Baby for Frances see Frances

Frances: A Birthday for Frances see Frances

Frances: Bedtime for Frances see Frances

Frances: Bread & Jam for Frances see Frances

Frances de cada Dia. (SPA.). 2002. bk. 8.90 (978-84-494-2380-2(5), 1402) Oceano Grupo ESP.

Frances Fitzgerald. Interview with Frances FitzGerald. 1 cass. (Running Time: 1 hr.). 1972. 12.95 (L024) TFR.
Fitzgerald talks about Fire in the Lake, her book about Vietnamese culture & the effects of U. S. intervention.

Frances Perfeccionamiento. 1 cass. (Running Time: 1 hr. 30 min.).Tr. of Using French. (FRE & SPA.). 2000. bk. 75.00 (978-2-7005-1305-9(3)) Pub: Assimil FRA. Dist(s): Distribks Inc

Frances Sherwood. unabr. ed. Ed. by Jim McKinley. Prod. by Rebekah Presson. 1 cass. (Running Time: 29 min.). (New Letters on the Air Ser.). 1994. 10.00 New Letters.
Sherwood's novel, "Vindication" is a fictionalized biography of the mother of Mary Shelley, Mary Wollstonecraft. Wollstonecraft was an 18th century feminist who wrote "A Vindication of the Rights of Women" & Sherwood wrote about her "to make every woman in America know about her" & to popularize her. Sherwood's book has been called "startling & unforgettable".

Francesca's Party. Patricia Scanlan. Read by Trudy Harris. 13 CDs. (Running Time: 15 hrs. 22 mins.). (Isis (CDs) Ser.). (J). 2005. audio compact disk 99.95 (978-0-7531-2428-4(9)) Pub: ISIS Lrg Prnt GBR. Dist(s): Ulverscroft US

Francesca's Party. unabr. ed. Patricia Scanlan. 12 cass. (Running Time: 15 hrs. 22 mins.). (Isis Cassettes Ser.). (J). 2005. 94.95 (978-0-7531-1313-4(9)) Pub: ISIS Lrg Prnt GBR. Dist(s): Ulverscroft US

Francesco Layolle & Music of the Florentine Renaissance. unabr. ed. 1 cass. 11.95 (C11223) J Norton Pubs.

Franchise Affair. unabr. ed. Josephine Tey. Read by Carole Boyd. 8 cass. (Running Time: 12 hrs.). (Inspector Grant Mystery Ser.: Bk. 3). 2000. 59.95 (978-0-7451-6324-6(6), CAB 578) Pub: Chivers Audio Bks GBR. Dist(s): AudioGO
The Franchise is the name of a large country house where Marion Sharpe and her mother live. The affair concerns the accusation by a 15-year-old schoolgirl that these two apparently respectable ladies kept her locked in their attic for a month, beat her and starved her. In this version of a notorious case in the 18th century, it is the task of Inspector Grant and Robert Blair to unravel the case.

Franchises, Dealerships & Distributorships. 1986. bk. 65.00 incl. book.; 35.00 cass. only.; 35.00 book only. PA Bar Inst.

Franchising in Brazil: A Strategic Reference 2006. Compiled by Icon Group International, Inc. Staff. 2007. ring bd. 195.00 (978-0-497-35838-9(7)) Icon Grp.

Franchising in Ecuador: A Strategic Reference 2007. Compiled by Icon Group International, Inc. Staff. 2007. ring bd. 195.00 (978-0-497-35922-5(7)) Icon Grp.

Franchising in Egypt: A Strategic Reference 2007. Compiled by Icon Group International, Inc. Staff. 2007. ring bd. 195.00 (978-0-497-35929-4(4)) Icon Grp.

Franchising in Finland: A Strategic Reference 2006. Compiled by Icon Group International, Inc. Staff. 2007. ring bd. 195.00 (978-0-497-35937-9(5)) Icon Grp.

Franchising in Indonesia: A Strategic Reference 2007. Compiled by Icon Group International, Inc. Staff. 2007. ring bd. 195.00 (978-0-497-36029-0(2)) Icon Grp.

Franchising in Mexico: A Strategic Reference 2007. Compiled by Icon Group International, Inc. Staff. 2007. ring bd. 195.00 (978-0-497-82354-2(3)) Icon Grp.

Franchising in Norway: A Strategic Reference 2006. Compiled by Icon Group International, Inc. Staff. 2007. ring bd. 195.00 (978-0-497-82376-4(4)) Icon Grp.

Franchising in Thailand: A Strategic Reference 2007. Compiled by Icon Group International, Inc. Staff. 2007. ring bd. 195.00 (978-0-497-82441-9(8)) Icon Grp.

Franchising in Turkey: A Strategic Reference 2007. Compiled by Icon Group International, Inc. Staff. 2007. ring bd. 195.00 (978-0-497-82444-0(2)) Icon Grp.

Franchising in Uruguay: A Strategic Reference 2007. Compiled by Icon Group International, Inc. Staff. 2007. ring bd. 195.00 (978-0-497-82464-8(7)) Icon Grp.

Franchising in Vietnam: A Strategic Reference 2006. Compiled by Icon Group International, Inc. Staff. 2007. ring bd. 195.00 (978-0-497-82473-0(6)) Icon Grp.

Franchising 1989: Business Strategies & Legal Compliance. unabr. ed. David J. Kaufmann. 4 cass. (Running Time: 5 hrs. 30 min.). 1989. 50.00 course handbk. (T7-9252) PLI.
In this recording of PLI's November 1989 satellite program, the panel, consisting of franchising experts & government & regulatory officials, discusses: structuring the franchise relationship, federal & state regulation of franchising: registration, disclosure & "relationship" laws, the spread of international franchising, what special concerns arise in the course of franchise-related mergers, acquisitions & leveraged buyouts, business & legal aspects of the relationship between franchisors & franchisees.

Francie. unabr. ed. Karen English. Narrated by Sisi Johnson. 4 pieces. (Running Time: 4 hrs. 30 mins.). (gr. 5 up). 2002. 37.00 (978-1-4025-2131-7(6)) Recorded Bks.
Whenever she gets a break from her endless chores, 12-year-old Francie Weaver heads to a hilltop where she can wave at the train that will soon take her away from Noble, Alabama, to live with her Daddy in the North. Meanwhile, Francie faces the everyday prejudice and discrimination of her small community.

Francie. unabr. ed. Joe Robinson. Read by Elizabeth Henry. 12 cass. (Running Time: 14 hrs. 30 min.). (Sound Ser.). (J). 2003. 94.95 (978-1-84283-420-6(7)) Pub: ISIS Lrg Prnt GBR. Dist(s): Ulverscroft US

Francine, Believe It or Not! unabr. ed. Marc Brown. Text by Stephen Krensky. 1 cass. (Running Time: 40 mins.). (Arthur Chapter Bks.: Bk. 14). (J). (gr. 2-4). 2004. pap. bk. 17.00 (978-0-8072-0345-3(9), Listening Lib) Random Audio Pubg.

Francis: Model of Discipleship. Michael Crosby. 5 cass. (Running Time: 6 hrs.). 1993. 39.95 set. (AA2647) Credence Commun.
Crosby's genius in presenting Francis is that he present him in tension with his church & even more so with his culture. When you hear this approach to Francis you will be both enchanted & challenged by this most popular saint.

Francis: The Journey & the Dream. abr. ed. Murray Bodo. Read by Murray Bodo. 4 CDs. (Running Time: 18000 sec.). 2006. audio compact disk 29.95 (978-0-86716-819-8(6)) St Anthony Mess Pr.
In his 50 years as a Franciscan, which include many summers in Assisi leading pilgrims in the steps of Francis and Clare, Murray Bodo has been able to drink in the spirit of Francis. With the imagination and vision of a poet, he invites all who will listen to heed their dreams and accept the challenge of journeying with Francis.?Murray Bodo is a poet and he has used his poet?s vision to present a Francis of Assisi who is alive and appealing to the contemporary reader. But he?s done much more than that. There is wisdom here, and there are insights into many situations that fret us all today. It?s a book to use for meditation and one that every follower of the gospel life will want to have on hand for the journey.??Naomi Burton, literary agent and close friend of Thomas Merton.

Francis, Babette & Charles, Population Myth - U. N. Rights of the Child. 1 cass. 4.00 (93Y) IRL Chicago.

Francis Jammes: A Prayer to Go to Paradise with the Donkeys see Twentieth-Century Poetry in English, No. 29, Recordings of Poets Reading Their Own Poetry

Francis Marion. unabr. ed. Robert Hogrogian. 1 cass. (Running Time: 20 min.). (People to Remember Ser.: Set II). (J). (gr. 4-7). 1979. bk. 16.99 (978-0-934898-87-4(1)); pap. bk. 9.95 (978-0-934898-13-3(8)) Jan Prods.
The exciting account of the Swamp Fox of the Revolutionary War.

Francis of Assisi. Instructed by William Cook & Ronald Herzman. 6 cass. (Running Time: 6 hrs.). 29.95 (978-1-56585-167-2(6)) Teaching Co.

Francis of Assisi. Instructed by William Cook & Ronald Herzman. 6 CDs. (Running Time: 6 hrs.). 2000. audio compact disk 134.95 (978-1-56585-361-4(X)) Teaching Co.

Francis, Theroux, Howarth, Set. unabr. ed. Contrib. by Dick Francis. 3 cass. (Running Time: 4 hrs. 30 min.). (Author Talks Ser.). 1998. 26.00 (92432) Recorded Bks.
Features: Dick Francis - best-selling author of beloved equestrian mysteries; Paul Theroux - novelist & celebrated travel writer; & David Howarth - author of popular histories.

Franciscan Conspiracy. unabr. ed. John Sack. Read by Geoffrey Blaisdell. (Running Time: 55800 sec.). 2008. 85.95 (978-1-4332-2893-3(9)); audio compact disk & audio compact disk 29.95 (978-1-4332-2897-1(1)); audio compact disk & audio compact disk 110.00 (978-1-4332-2894-0(7)) Blckstn Audio.

Franciscan Crown: A Rosary of Joy. Curt Johnson. Read by Curt Johnson. 1 CD. (Running Time: 30 min.). 2003. audio compact disk 14.95 (978-1-881586-12-8(X)) Canticle Cass.
Historical and contemporary reflection on the crown (Rosary) with meditation and music.

Franco, Pt. 1. unabr. collector's ed. Paul Preston. Read by David Case. 15 cass. (Running Time: 22 hrs. 30 min.). 1996. 120.00 (978-0-7366-3389-5(8), 4039A) Books on Tape.
Francisco Franco, Spain's Caudillo for five decades, won the civil war, kept Spain neutral during WWII, modernized his country, orchestrated its economic boom & selected his own successor.

Franco, Pt. 2. unabr. collector's ed. Paul Preston. Read by David Case. 14 cass. (Running Time: 21 hrs.). 1996. 112.00 (978-0-7366-3390-1(1), 4039-B) Books on Tape.

Franco Corelli: Un Uomo, Una Voce see Corelli: The Man, the Voice

Francois le Champi, Set. abr. ed. George Sand. Read by Nathalie Adam. 2 cass. (FRE.). 1995. 26.95 (1751-KFP) Olivia & Hill.
The touching tale of an abandoned child who is taken in by a poor peasant woman has brought tears to many readers throughout the years.

Francois Truffaut. Jacques Chancel. 1 cass. (Radioscopie Ser.). 1991. 16.95 (1177-RF) Olivia & Hill.
Filmmaker of the "cinema verite.".

Francoise Sagan. Jacques Chancel. 1 cass. (Radioscopie Ser.). 1991. 16.95 (1026-RF) Olivia & Hill.
Author of "Bonjour Tristesse.".

***Frank: The Voice, 1915-1954.** unabr. ed. James Kaplan. Read by Rob Shapiro. (Running Time: 22 hrs.). (ENG.). 2010. audio compact disk 50.00 (978-0-307-74848-5(0), Random AudioBks) Pub: Random Audio Pubg. Dist(s): Random

Frank A. Barbera: Sector Rotation - New Ideas for Market Timing Industry Groups. Frank A. Barbera. 1 cass. 30.00 Dow Jones Telerate.
This workshop will begin by reviewing some of the classic techniques used to identify changes in market leadership, & will then demonstrate how to construct & use certain traditional market timing tools; Breadth, Sentiment, Momentum & Volume, to improve timing of specific industry groups. Indicators which will be discussed include: Breadth - Advance-Decline Oscillators, Sentiment - Put/Call Volume & Premium Ratios, Volume - The ARMS Index & Up/Down Money Flow.

Frank & Jesse James. unabr. ed. Wyman Windsor & Janet Windsor. Narrated by Bennie Shipley. Prod. by Joe Loesch. 1 cass. (Running Time: 64 mins.). (Wild West Ser.). (YA). 1999. 12.95 (978-1-887729-69-7(0)) Toy Box Prods.
Times were hard in the no-man's land of Missouri during the last days of the Civil War. Union soldiers foraged, pillaged & terrorized anyone they suspected of helping the southern cause. So begins a terrifying chapter in American history. The saga of Frank & Jesse James is rooted in the smoldering fires of a southern cause that had burned itself out.

Frank Bertel's Lively Talking Book: Study Tapes Off 100 Recent Coast to Coast Appearances on Male Liberation Seminars. Frank Bertels. 1 cass. 1982. 10.00 Brun Pr.

Frank Carlucci: The East-West Dialogue. 1 cass. (Running Time: 1 hr.). 10.95 (NP-88-06-27, HarperThor) HarpC GBR.

Frank Chin. unabr. ed. Ed. by Jim McKinley. Prod. by Rebekah Presson. 1 cass. (Running Time: 29 min.). (New Letters on the Air Ser.). 1994. 10.00 (031993) New Letters.
The author of "The Chinaman Pacific & Frisco R.R. Co." & "Donald Duk" is at the center of a raging controversy over the use ofChinese mythology in literature. Chin charges popular writers Amy Tan & & Maxine Hong Kingston with promoting racist stereotypes by misusing traditional stories & he in turn has been termed a misogynist & a literary fascist. Chin offers no-holds-barred opinions & reads from "Donald Duk".

Frank Gambale Bk. 1: Technique. Frank Gambale. Ed. by Gene Dinkins. Illus. by Jon Morgan. 1 cass. pap. bk. 24.95 (BD017) DCI Music Video.
Looks at solos over chordal harmonies. Chordal harmonies covered are Minor 7, Dorian & Aeolian, Major 7 & Lydian, unaltered dominant 7 super Locrian harmonies. A must for learning modes & chord-patterns.

Frank Gambale Bk. 2: Technique. Frank Gambale. Ed. by Wayne King. Illus. by Iain Scott. 1 cass. pap. bk. 24.95 (BD060) DCI Music Video.
Looks at soloing over chordal harmonies. Chordal harmonies covered are altered dominant 7 diminished 1/2-whole & Phygian, Minor 7 ocrian, Aeolian & Locrian, diminished & super Locrian. A must for learning modes & chord patterns.

Frank Knight & the Chicago School. unabr. ed. Arthur Diamond. Ed. by Israel M. Kirzner & Mike Hassell. Narrated by Louis Rukeyser. 2 cass. (Running Time: 80 min. per cass.). Dramatization. (Great Economic Thinkers Ser.). (YA). (gr. 10 up). 1988. 17.95 (978-0-938935-39-1(9), 10209) Knowledge Prod.
At the University of Chicago circa World War II, Frank Knight was an abstract theorist who emphasized the importance of uninsurable uncertainty in economic affairs. The followers of this school have been repeatedly honored by the Nobel Committee.

Frank Knight & the Chicago School: The Role of Economic Uncertainty. abr. ed. Arthur Diamond. Read by Louis Rukeyser. (Running Time: 10800 sec.). (Great Economic Thinkers Ser.). 2006. audio compact disk 25.95 (978-0-7861-6948-1(6)) Pub: Blckstn Audio. Dist(s): NetLibrary CO

Frank Leahy's Christmas Jubilee: Played on Don Messer's Violin. Perf. by Frank Leahy et al. Contrib. by Chad Irschick at Inception Sound staff. Prod. by Frank Leahy & Tom Szczesniak. Contrib. by Tom Szczesniak. (Running Time: 30 mins.). 2006. audio compact disk 15.95 (978-0-660-19515-5(1), CBC Audio) Canadian Broadcasting CAN.

Frank Lloyd Wright. Read by Edgar Taffell. 1 cass. (Running Time: 60 min.). 10.95 (OP-78-04-12, HarperThor) HarpC GBR.

Frank Lloyd Wright. unabr. ed. Ada Louise Huxtable. Read by Carrington MacDuffie. 5 cass. (Running Time: 7 hrs.. 30 min.). 2004. 54.00 (978-1-4159-0320-9(4)); audio compact disk 63.00 (978-1-4159-0321-6(2)) Books on Tape.
From the Pulitzer Prize-winning architecture critic for the New York Times comes an intimate, behind-the-scenes portrait of the world-renowned architect Frank Lloyd Wright. Huxtable looks at the architect and the man, exploring the sources of his tumultuous and troubled life and his long career as a master builder as well as his search for lasting, true love.

Frank Lloyd Wright: His Living Voice. Frank Lloyd Wright. Comment by Bruce B. Pfieffer. 1 cass. 1987. pap. bk. 17.95 (978-0-912201-14-6(2)) CSU Pr Fresno.

Frank Lloyd Wright Speaking. unabr. ed. Frank Lloyd Wright. 1 cass. 1984. 12.95 (978-0-694-50051-2(8), SWC 1064) HarperCollins Pubs.

Frank Muir at the Beeb. Frank Muir. 2 cass. 1999. 16.85 Set. (978-0-563-55858-3(X)) BBC WrldWd GBR.

Frank Proffitt: The Memorial Album. 1 cass. 9.98 (C-36) Folk-Legacy.
The last tapes of an important artist & great friend.

Frank Proffitt of Reese, NC. 1 cass. 9.98 (C-1) Folk-Legacy.
Traditional ballads & songs sung with fretless banjo.

Frank Sinatra: The Man, the Music. Ross Porter & Tom Anniko. Narrated by Ross Porter. 4 CDs. (Running Time: 14400 sec.). (After Hours Ser.). 2006. audio compact disk 29.95 (978-0-660-19553-7(4), CBC Audio) Canadian Broadcasting CAN.

Frank Sinatra Set: The Voice... the Music. Perf. by Frank Sinatra. Music by RRSO Orchestra. 2 CDs. 1998. audio compact disk 13.98 Lifedance.
The first CD has Ol' Blue Eyes singing many of his classics from the '40s & '50s. The second CD offers nicely orchestrated, versions from his later years.

Frank Sinatra - Hallmark Christmas Show of 1946 & The Amos 'N Andy Christmas Show of 1950. unabr. ed. 1 cass. (Running Time: 60 min.). Dramatization. 7.95 Norelco box. (DC-4127) Natl Recrd Co.
Frank Sinatra: A True Story..."Room for a Stranger." It's a Reader's Digest narrative of a Navy flier just back from overseas duty. He is on leave for Christmas, but then receives orders to report for duty before he gets to see his best girl. It shows the friendly Christmas spirit of people in a small midwestern town. One of the finest & most sentimental stories of the season. Amos 'N Andy: The funniest, warmest & most famous Amos 'N Andy radio broadcast. It's Christmas Eve, & Andy wants to get a doll for Amos' daughter, Arbadella. He gets himself a job as a department store Santa Claus to earn one for her. Later, Amos recites the Lord's Prayer to his daughter as she learns the true meaning of Christmas. A touching sentimental program, sponsored by Rinso.

Frank Sinatra Show on Light up Time: Shows 76-79. Perf. by Frank Sinatra. 1 cass. (Running Time: 1 hr.). 2001. 6.98 (2158) Radio Spirits.

Frank Sinatra Story. John Garton. (ENG., 2001. audio compact disk 24.95 (978-1-84240-007-4(X)) Pub: Chrome Dreams GBR. Dist(s): IPG Chicago

Frank Sinatra Visits & Robert Taylor Visits. Perf. by Jack Benny. 1 cass. (Running Time: 60 min.). Dramatization. (Jack Benny Show Ser.). 1948. 6.00 Once Upon Rad.
Radio broadcasts - humor.

Frank Waters. Interview. Interview with Frank Waters & Kay Bonetti. 1 cass. (Running Time: 1 hr. 09 min.). 13.95 (978-1-55644-086-1(3), 3132) Am Audio Prose.
Waters' unusual viewpoint on the implications of nuclear energy & its development within the heart of American Indian Culture, plus a wide range of issues surrounding his long life & career, including his Jungian perspective & the whole question of the relation between his biography & the themes & subject matter of his nine novels.

Frank Waters. unabr. ed. Frank Waters. Read by Frank Waters. 1 cass. (Running Time: 29 min.). 1990. 10.00 (041390) New Letters.
One of the greatest of all the southwestern writers, Waters has been nominated twice for the Nobel Prize in literature. This interview was recorded in the writer's home in Tucson, Arizona.

Frankenstein. John Bergez. Mary Wollstonecraft Shelley. (Classic Literature Ser.). 2000. audio compact disk 18.95 (978-1-4105-0159-2(0)) D Johnston Inc.

Frankenstein. Perf. by Stacy Harris et al. 1 CD. (Running Time: 1 hr.). Dramatization. (Halloween at Radio Spirits Ser.). 2002. audio compact disk 4.98 (978-1-57019-388-0(6), OTR7029) Pub: Radio Spirits. Dist(s): AudioGO

***Frankenstein.** Margrete Lamond. Read by Colin Moody. (Running Time: 5 hrs. 25 mins.). (J). 2009. 64.99 (978-1-74214-562-4(0), 9781742145624) Pub: Bolinda Pubng AUS. Dist(s): Bolinda Pub Inc

Frankenstein. Perf. by Quicksilver Radio Theatre. 1 cass. (Running Time: 1 hr.). 2001. 12.95 (QUSL002); 34.95 (QUSL126) Lodestone Catalog.
A skilled, straightforward adaptation, with the focus on the relationship between Viktor & his monstrous creation.

Frankenstein. Perf. by Arthur D. Vinton. 1 cass. (Running Time: 1 hr.). Dramatization. (Adventures in Old-Time Radio Ser.). 2002. 4.98 (978-1-57019-387-3(8), OTR7028) Pub: Radio Spirits. Dist(s): AudioGO

Frankenstein. abr. ed. Mary Wollstonecraft Shelley. Perf. by St. Charles Players. 2 cass. (Running Time: 2 hrs.). Dramatization. (Mystery Theatre Ser.). 1999. 16.95 (978-1-56994-513-1(6), 348844, Monterey SoundWorks) Monterey Media Inc.
Lightning strikes the pole sending electric waves racing across dark castle walls into the laboratory & the lifeless body stitched together by a scientist called "mad" because he wants to create life in a lifeless creature. He dreams of a son, a companion, an incredible recreation of life, anything but...a monster. Lightning flashes...It's alive.

Frankenstein. unabr. ed. Read by Ralph Cosham. 8 CDs. (Running Time: 11 hrs.). 2002. audio compact disk 79.00 (978-1-58472-174-1(X), Commuters Library) Sound Room.
This immortal horror story, which has implications for modern science and genetic engineering, has captured the imagination of countless generations.

Frankenstein. unabr. ed. Margrete Lamond. Read by Colin Moody. (Running Time: 5 hrs. 25 mins.). (J). 2009. audio compact disk 63.95 (978-1-74214-088-9(2), 9781742140889) Pub: Bolinda Pubng AUS. Dist(s): Bolinda Pub Inc

Frankenstein: A Classic Pop-Up Tale. Mary Wollstonecraft Shelley. Narrated by Flo Gibson. (ENG.). 2007. audio compact disk 27.95 (978-1-55685-946-5(5)) Audio Bk Con.

Frankenstein: A Classic Pop-Up Tale. Mary Wollstonecraft Shelley. Narrated by Ralph Cosham. (Running Time: 25860 sec.). (Unabridged Classics in MP3 Ser.). (ENG.). 2008. audio compact disk 24.00 (978-1-58472-511-4(7), In Aud) Sound Room.

Frankenstein: A Classic Pop-Up Tale. abr. adpt. ed. Mary Wollstonecraft Shelley. (Bring the Classics to Life: Level 3 Ser.). 2008. audio compact disk 12.95 (978-1-55576-589-7(0)) EDCON Pubng.

Frankenstein: A Classic Pop-Up Tale. unabr. ed. Mary Wollstonecraft Shelley. Read by Ralph Cosham. (YA). 2006. 64.99 (978-1-59895-167-7(X)) Find a World.

Frankenstein: A Classic Pop-Up Tale, Set. unabr. ed. Mary Wollstonecraft Shelley & Mary Wollstonecraft Shelley. Read by Flo Gibson. 5 cass. (Running Time: 7 hrs. 30 min.). 1998. 20.95 (978-1-55685-552-8(4)) Audio Bk Con.
As the result of Victor Frankenstein's creation of a monster out of the remains of human corpses, a series of horrifying events occur.

Frankenstein: Abridged. (ENG.). 2007. (978-1-60339-011-8(1)); cd-rom & audio compact disk (978-1-60339-012-5(X)) Listenr Digest.

Frankenstein: An A+ Audio Study Guide. unabr. ed. Mary Wollstonecraft Shelley. Read by Julian Sands. (Running Time: 1 hr.). (ENG.). 2006. 5.98 (978-1-59483-553-7(5)) Pub: Hachet Audio. Dist(s): HachBkGrp

Frankenstein: An A+ Audio Study Guide. unabr. ed. Mary Wollstonecraft Shelley. Read by Julian Sands. (Running Time: 1 hr.). (ENG.). 2009. 14.98 (978-1-60788-262-6(0)) Pub: Hachet Audio. Dist(s): HachBkGrp

***Frankenstein: Bring the Classics to Life.** adpt. ed. Mary Wollstonecraft Shelley. (Bring the Classics to Life Ser.). 2008. pap. bk. 21.95 (978-1-55576-600-9(5)) EDCON Pubng.

Frankenstein: Classic Radio Sci-Fi. Mary Wollstonecraft Shelley. (Running Time: 2 hrs. 0 mins. 0 sec.). (ENG.). 2009. audio compact disk 24.95 (978-1-60283-780-5(5)) Pub: AudioGO. Dist(s): Perseus Dist

Frankenstein: Or the Modern Prometheus. Mary Wollstonecraft Shelley & Mary Wollstonecraft Shelley. 4 cass. 26.95 (978-1-885546-03-6(3)) Big Ben Audio.

Frankenstein: Or the Modern Prometheus. Mary Wollstonecraft Shelley & Mary Wollstonecraft Shelley. Ed. by Jerry Stemach. Retold by John Bergez. Narrated by Nick Sandys. 2000. audio compact disk 200.00 (978-1-58702-512-9(4)) D Johnston Inc.

Frankenstein: Or the Modern Prometheus. Mary Wollstonecraft Shelley & Mary Wollstonecraft Shelley. Prod. by Spoken Arts Staff. 1 cass. (Running Time: 50 min.). 9.95 (FO-100, HarperThor) HarpC GBR.

Frankenstein: Or the Modern Prometheus. Mary Wollstonecraft Shelley & Mary Wollstonecraft Shelley. (Running Time: 2 hrs. 30 mins.). 1998. 20.95 (978-1-60083-743-2(3)) Iofy Corp.

Frankenstein: Or the Modern Prometheus. Mary Wollstonecraft Shelley & Mary Wollstonecraft Shelley. Read by Fabio Camero. (Running Time: 3 hrs.). 2001. 16.95 (978-1-60083-157-7(5), Audiofy Corp) Iofy Corp.

Frankenstein: Or the Modern Prometheus. Mary Wollstonecraft Shelley & Mary Wollstonecraft Shelley. Read by Ralph Cosham. (Running Time: 7 hrs.). 2002. 26.95 (978-1-59912-064-5(X), Audiofy Corp) Iofy Corp.

Frankenstein: Or the Modern Prometheus. Mary Wollstonecraft Shelley & Mary Wollstonecraft Shelley. Read by Daniel Philpott et al. 2 cass. (Running Time: 2 hrs. 30 mins.). 1996. 28.98 (978-962-634-503-0(9), NA200314, Naxos AudioBooks) Naxos.
The gothic tale of Frankenstein & his construction of a human being which runs amok has, with the help of numerous films, become one of the most vivid horror stories.

Frankenstein: Or the Modern Prometheus. Mary Wollstonecraft Shelley & Mary Wollstonecraft Shelley. Narrated by George Guidall. 9 CDs. (Running Time: 9 hrs. 30 mins.). audio compact disk 89.00 (978-1-4025-2101-0(4)) Recorded Bks.

Frankenstein: Or the Modern Prometheus. Mary Wollstonecraft Shelley & Mary Wollstonecraft Shelley. 2006. cd-rom 34.95 (978-1-4281-0113-5(6)) Recorded Bks.

Frankenstein: Or the Modern Prometheus. Mary Wollstonecraft Shelley & Mary Wollstonecraft Shelley. 2004. 10.95 (978-0-7435-4741-3(1)) Pub: S&S Audio. Dist(s): S and S Inc

Frankenstein: Or the Modern Prometheus. abr. ed. Mary Wollstonecraft Shelley & Mary Wollstonecraft Shelley. Read by Julie Harris. (Running Time: 10800 sec.). 2008. audio compact disk 19.95 (978-1-4332-0957-4(8)); audio compact disk & audio compact disk 33.00 (978-1-4332-1356-4(7)) Blckstn Audio.

Frankenstein: Or the Modern Prometheus. abr. ed. Mary Wollstonecraft Shelley & Mary Wollstonecraft Shelley. Perf. by James Mason. 1 cass. (J). 1984. 9.95 (978-0-89845-882-4(X), CP 1541) HarperCollins Pubs.

Frankenstein: Or the Modern Prometheus. abr. ed. Mary Wollstonecraft Shelley & Mary Wollstonecraft Shelley. Read by Kenneth Branagh. 2 cass. (Running Time: 3 hrs.). 2000. 13.99 (978-1-84032-441-9(4), HoddrStoughton) Pub: Hodder General GBR. Dist(s): Trafalgar
Victor Frankenstein, a man so obsessed with conquering death, decides to create life.

Frankenstein: Or the Modern Prometheus. abr. ed. Mary Wollstonecraft Shelley & Mary Wollstonecraft Shelley. Read by Daniel Philpott et al. 2 CDs. (Running Time: 2 hrs. 30 mins.). (J). (gr. 9-12). 1994. audio compact disk 17.98 (978-962-634-003-5(7), NA200312) Naxos.
The gothic tale of Frankenstein & his construction of a human being which runs amok has, with the help of numerous films, become one of the most vivid horror stories.

Frankenstein: Or the Modern Prometheus. abr. ed. Mary Wollstonecraft Shelley & Mary Wollstonecraft Shelley. (Running Time: 2 hrs. 30 mins.). 2009. audio compact disk 17.98 (978-962-634-965-6(4), Naxos AudioBooks) Naxos.

Frankenstein: Or the Modern Prometheus. abr. ed. Mary Wollstonecraft Shelley & Mary Wollstonecraft Shelley. Read by Julie Harris. 2 cass. (Running Time: 3 hrs.). 2004. 18.00 (978-1-59007-009-3(7)) Pub: New Millenn Enter. Dist(s): PerseuPGW
The most famous & compelling horror story of all time.

Frankenstein: Or the Modern Prometheus. abr. ed. Mary Wollstonecraft Shelley & Mary Wollstonecraft Shelley. (Running Time: 50 min.). Dramatization. 10.95 (978-0-8045-1088-2(1), SAC 1088) Spoken Arts.
The original classic, presented with intellect & atmosphere.

Frankenstein: Or the Modern Prometheus. abr. ed. Mary Wollstonecraft Shelley & Mary Wollstonecraft Shelley. Read by Fabio Camero. 3 CDs. (SPA.). 2001. audio compact disk 17.00 (978-958-9494-43-1(9)) YoYoMusic.

Frankenstein: Or the Modern Prometheus. abr. ed. Mary Wollstonecraft Shelley et al. (Running Time: 3 hrs.). (ENG.). (gr. 12 up). 2005. audio compact disk 14.95 (978-0-14-305813-7(4), PengAudBks) Penguin Grp USA.

Frankenstein: Or, the Modern Prometheus. unabr. ed. Mary Wollstonecraft Shelley. Read by Edward French. 5 cass. (Running Time: 7 hrs. 15 min.). 1991. 40.00 Set. (978-0-9631737-0-6(7)) E French Inc.

Frankenstein: Or the Modern Prometheus. unabr. ed. Mary Wollstonecraft Shelley & Mary Wollstonecraft Shelley. (Barnes & Noble Audio Ser.). 2003. audio compact disk 34.95 (978-0-7607-3476-6(3)) Barnes & Noble Inc.

Frankenstein: Or the Modern Prometheus. unabr. ed. Mary Wollstonecraft Shelley & Mary Wollstonecraft Shelley. Read by David Case et al. 7 cass. (Running Time: 10 hrs.). (gr. 9-12). 2000. 49.95 (978-0-7861-0877-0(0), 1540) Blckstn Audio.
Victor Frankenstein discovers the secret of creating life & fashions an eight-foot monster, only to bring danger & destruction to the lives of those he loves.

Frankenstein: Or the Modern Prometheus. unabr. ed. Mary Wollstonecraft Shelley & Mary Wollstonecraft Shelley. Read by Dan Lazar. 8 cass. (Running Time: 12 hrs.). 2001. 29.95 (978-0-7366-6817-0(9)) Books on Tape.
The famous tale of Dr. Frankenstein, who creates a monster in his laboratory who comes to life, escapes & is beyond control.

Frankenstein: Or the Modern Prometheus. unabr. ed. Mary Wollstonecraft Shelley & Mary Wollstonecraft Shelley. Read by Dan Lazar. 7 cass. (Running Time: 10 hrs. 30 mins.). 2002. 56.00 (978-0-7366-8470-5(0)); audio compact disk 72.00 (978-0-7366-8598-6(7)) Books on Tape.
At 166 plus, FRANKENSTEIN is still going strong. This king of the monster stories is all the more remarkable because it was written by a young woman, the 21-year-old bride of Percy Bysshe Shelley.

Frankenstein: Or the Modern Prometheus. unabr. ed. Mary Wollstonecraft Shelley & Mary Wollstonecraft Shelley. Read by Tom Casaletto. 6 cass. (Running Time: 8 hrs.). 2002. 29.95 (978-1-59086-281-0(3), 1590862813, BAU) Brilliance Audio.
Dr. Frankenstein learns the secret of imparting life to inanimate matter. To test his theories, he collects bones from the charnel-houses to construct a "human" being, and then gives it life. The creature, endowed with supernatural size and strength, is revolting to look at, and frightens all who see it. Lonely and miserable, it comes to hate its creator. The monster murders Frankenstein's brother and his bride, and flees. The doctor pursues his creation in order to destroy it, but dies himself in the attempt. The story of Frankenstein was first written as a ghost story to be told as part of a contest between Mary Shelley, her husband, and Lord Byron. This tale of terror has been a world favorite since it was first published in 1818, and has been made into countless movies.

Frankenstein: Or the Modern Prometheus. unabr. ed. Mary Wollstonecraft Shelley & Mary Wollstonecraft Shelley. Read by Tom Casaletto. (Running Time: 8 hrs.). 2004. 39.25 (978-1-59335-522-7(X), 159335522X, Brlnc Audio MP3 Lib) Brilliance Audio.

Frankenstein: Or the Modern Prometheus. unabr. ed. Mary Wollstonecraft Shelley & Mary Wollstonecraft Shelley. Read by Tom Casaletto. (Running Time: 8 hrs.). 2004. 39.25 (978-1-59710-308-4(X), 159710308X, BADLE); 24.95 (978-1-59710-309-1(8), 1597103098, BAD) Brilliance Audio.

Frankenstein: Or the Modern Prometheus. unabr. ed. Mary Wollstonecraft Shelley & Mary Wollstonecraft Shelley. Read by Tom Casaletto. 7 CDs. (Running Time: 28800 sec.). (Classic Collection (Brilliance Audio) Ser.). 2005. audio compact disk 97.25 (978-1-59737-130-8(0), 9781597371308, BriAudCD Unabrid); audio compact disk 32.95 (978-1-59737-129-2(7), 9781597371292, Bril Audio CD Unabri) Brilliance Audio.

Frankenstein: Or the Modern Prometheus. unabr. ed. Mary Wollstonecraft Shelley & Mary Wollstonecraft Shelley. Read by Cindy Hardy et al. 6 cass. (Running Time: 8 hrs. 30 min.). 1980. 42.00 incl. album. (C-45) Jimcin Record.
The most famous monster of all stalks the earth. This story is all the more remarkable, because it was written by 21 year old Mary Shelly, the wife of poet Percy Bysshe Shelly & was her first attempt at fiction.

Frankenstein: Or the Modern Prometheus. unabr. ed. Mary Wollstonecraft Shelley & Mary Wollstonecraft Shelley. Narrated by George Guidall. 6 cass. (Running Time: 9.5 hrs.). 19.95 (978-1-4025-1146-2(9)) Recorded Bks.

Frankenstein: Or the Modern Prometheus, unabr. ed. Mary Wollstonecraft Shelley & Mary Wollstonecraft Shelley. Narrated by George Guidall. 7 cass. (Running Time: 9 hrs. 30 mins.). 1993. 60.00 (978-1-55690-771-5(0), 93108E7) Recorded Bks.
A doctor creates a monster & chases him around the globe.

Frankenstein: Or the Modern Prometheus. unabr. ed. Mary Wollstonecraft Shelley & Mary Wollstonecraft Shelley. Read by Tom Casaletto. (Running Time: 8 hrs.). 2004. 24.95 (978-1-59335-194-6(1), 1593351941) Soulmate Audio Bks.
Dr. Frankenstein learns the secret of imparting life to inanimate matter. To test his theories, he collects bones from the charnel-houses to construct a "human" being, and then gives it life. The creature, endowed with supernatural size and strength, is revolting to look at, and frightens all who see it. Lonely and miserable, it comes to hate its creator. The monster murders Frankenstein's brother and his bride, and flees. The doctor pursues his creation in order to destroy it, but dies himself in the attempt. The story of Frankenstein was first written as a ghost story to be told as part of a contest between Mary Shelley, her husband, and Lord Byron. This tale of terror has been a world favorite since it was first published in 1818, and has been made into countless movies.

Frankenstein: Or the Modern Prometheus. unabr. ed. Mary Wollstonecraft Shelley & Mary Wollstonecraft Shelley. Read by Ralph Cosham. 6 cds. (Running Time: 7 hrs 11 mins). 2002. audio compact disk 33.95 (978-1-58472-252-6(5), 091, In Aud) Pub: Sound Room. Dist(s): Baker Taylor
This immortal horror story, which has implications for modern science and genetic engineering, has captured the imagination of countless generations.

Frankenstein: Or the Modern Prometheus. unabr. ed. Mary Wollstonecraft Shelley & Mary Wollstonecraft Shelley. Read by Ralph Cosham. 1 cd. (Running Time: 7 hrs 11 mins). 2002. audio compact disk 18.95 (978-1-58472-387-5(4), In Aud) Pub: Sound Room. Dist(s): Baker Taylor
MP3 format.

Frankenstein: Or the Modern Prometheus. unabr. collector's ed. Mary Wollstonecraft Shelley & Mary Wollstonecraft Shelley. Read by Dan Lazar. 8

cass. (Running Time: 8 hrs.). (J). 1980. 48.00 (978-0-7366-0314-0(X), 1301) Books on Tape.
The famous tale of Dr. Frankenstein who creates a monster in his laboratory who comes to life, escapes & is beyond control.

Frankenstein: Or the Modern Prometheus, Pt. 1. Mary Wollstonecraft Shelley & Mary Wollstonecraft Shelley. 1 cass. (Running Time: 1 hr.). (Radiobook Ser.). 1987. 4.98 (978-0-929541-16-7(2)) Radiola Co.

Frankenstein: Or the Modern Prometheus, Pt. 2. Mary Wollstonecraft Shelley & Mary Wollstonecraft Shelley. 1 cass. (Running Time: 1 hr.). (Radiobook Ser.). 1987. 4.98 (978-0-929541-17-4(0)) Radiola Co.

Frankenstein: Or the Modern Prometheus, Set. Mary Wollstonecraft Shelley & Mary Wollstonecraft Shelley. Read by Jacques Roland. 4 cass. 1992. 48.95 (1624-LQP) Olivia & Hill.
The powerful tale of Gothic horror first published in 1818. The story of an ambitious young scientist, Victor Frankenstein, who creates a monstrous creature.

Frankenstein: Or the Modern Prometheus, Vol. 5. Mary Wollstonecraft Shelley & Mary Wollstonecraft Shelley. Ed. by Jerry Stemach et al. Retold by John Bergez. Illus. by Jeff Ham. Narrated by Nick Sandys. Contrib. by Ted S. Hasselbring. (Start-to-Finish Books). (J). (gr. 2-3). 2000. 35.00 (978-1-58702-513-6(2)) D Johnston Inc.

Frankenstein: Or the Modern Prometheus, Vol. 5. Mary Wollstonecraft Shelley & Mary Wollstonecraft Shelley. Ed. by Jerry Stemach & Gail Portnuff Venable. Retold by John Bergez. Illus. by Jeff Ham. Narrated by Nick Sandys. (Start-to-Finish Books). 2002. 100.00 (978-1-58702-950-9(2)) D Johnston Inc.

Frankenstein: Or the Modern Prometheus, Vol. 5. abr. ed. Mary Wollstonecraft Shelley & Mary Wollstonecraft Shelley. Ed. by Jerry Stemach et al. Retold by John Bergez. Illus. by Jeff Ham. Contrib. by Ted S. Hasselbring. 1 cass. (Running Time: 1 hr.). (Start-to-Finish Books). (J). (gr. 2-3). 2000. (978-1-58702-372-9(5), F32K2) D Johnston Inc.
Scientist Viktor Frankenstein has always dreamed of discovering the secret of life. Then one day, after weeks of exacting research and gory work, he succeeds. But his creature, which seemed beautiful on the operating table, is monstrous when it opens its yellow eyes. Frankenstein flees the creature in terror, leaving him alone to first experience the world. As the creature wanders in search of the man who made him, he comes to hate men for their cruelty.

Frankenstein: The Creator. Mary Wollstonecraft Shelley. 1 cass. (Running Time: 60 min.). 7.95 (MM-5790) Natl Recrd Co.
A radio dramatization of Shelley's classic novel, "Frankenstein," is the story of Victor Frankenstein who has a dream of creating the perfect man, but his expperiment results in creating a monster. "The Lodger" is about a killer who became the scourge of London in the year 1888.

***Frankenstein: The Modern Prometheus.** Mary Wollstonecraft Shelley. Narrated by Matt Armstrong. (ENG.). (YA). 2010. 6.95 (978-1-936455-01-0(3)) Open Bk Aud.

Frankenstein Factory. A. J. Butcher. Read by Richard Aspel. (Running Time: 6 hrs. 45 mins.). (Spy High Ser.). (YA). 2009. 69.99 (978-1-74214-301-9(6), 9781742143019) Pub: Bolinda Pubng AUS. Dist(s): Bolinda Pub Inc

Frankenstein Factory. unabr. ed. Aj Butcher. Read by Richard Aspel. (Running Time: 24300 sec.). (Spy High Ser.). (J). 2007. audio compact disk 77.95 (978-1-74093-704-7(X)) Pub: Bolinda Pubng AUS. Dist(s): Bolinda Pub Inc

Frankenstein, or the Modern Prometheus. unabr. ed. Mary Wollstonecraft Shelley. Read by Simon Templeman et al. (Running Time: 30600 sec.). 2008. audio compact disk 19.95 (978-1-4332-1564-3(0)) Blckstn Audio.

Frankenstein, or the Modern Prometheus. unabr. ed. Mary Wollstonecraft Shelley. Read by Anthony Heald et al. (Running Time: 30600 sec.). 2008. 59.95 (978-1-4332-1562-9(4)); audio compact disk 29.95 (978-1-4332-1565-0(9)); audio compact disk & audio compact disk 70.00 (978-1-4332-1563-6(2)) Blckstn Audio.

Frankenstein, or the Modern Prometheus. unabr. ed. Mary Wollstonecraft Shelley. Narrated by Simon Vance. (Running Time: 8 hrs. 30 mins. 0 sec.). (ENG.). 2008. audio compact disk 19.99 (978-1-4001-5634-4(3)); audio compact disk 59.99 (978-1-4001-3634-6(2)); audio compact disk 29.99 (978-1-4001-0634-9(6)) Pub: Tantor Media. Dist(s): IngramPubServ

Frankie, Peaches & Me: Stella, Etc. Karen McCombie. Read by Jenny Bryce. (Running Time: 17400 sec.). (J). 2001. audio compact disk 29.95 (978-0-7540-6764-1(5)) AudioGo GBR.

Frankie's Place. Jim Sterba. Read by Christopher Lane. (Running Time: 10 hrs.). 2003. 30.95 (978-1-59912-496-4(3)) Iofy Corp.

Frankies Place. Jim Sterba & Christopher Lane. 7 cass. (Running Time: 9 hrs. 30 mins.). 2002. 49.95 (978-0-7861-2605-7(1), 3201) Blckstn Audio.

Frankie's Place: A Love Story. unabr. ed. Jim Sterba. Read by Christopher Lane. (Running Time: 9 hrs. 30 mins.). 2003. 24.95 (978-0-7861-8764-5(6), 3201) Blckstn Audio.

Frankie's Place: A Love Story. unabr. ed. Jim Sterba. Read by Christopher Lane. 8 CDs. (Running Time: 9 hrs. 30 mins.). 2004. audio compact disk 64.00 (978-0-7861-8933-5(9), 3201) Blckstn Audio.

Franklin: A Biography. unabr. ed. David F. Hawke. Narrated by Nelson Runger. 12 cass. (Running Time: 16 hrs. 15 mins.). 1988. 97.00 (978-1-55690-186-7(0), 88810E7) Recorded Bks.
The life of America's first diplomat & foremost politician through the signing of the Declaration of Independence in 1776.

Franklin & Lucy: President Roosevelt, Mrs. Rutherfurd, & the Other Remarkable Women in His Life. abr. ed. Joseph E. Persico. Read by Len Cariou. 5 CDs. (Running Time: 6 hrs. 30 mins.). (ENG.). 2008. audio compact disk 29.95 (978-0-7393-6841-1(9), Random AudioBks) Pub: Random Audio Pubg. Dist(s): Random

Franklin & the Tooth Fairy. Paulette Bourgeois. Read by Paulette Bourgeois. Illus. by Brenda Clark. Music by Bruce Cockburn. (Franklin Ser.). (ENG.). (J). (ps-3). 1999. 9.95 (978-1-55074-793-5(2)) Kids Can Pr CAN.

Franklin & Winston: An Intimate Portrait of an Epic Friendship. abr. ed. Jon Meacham. Read by Len Cariou. (Running Time: 9 hrs.). (ENG.). 2003. audio compact disk 37.95 (978-0-7393-0677-2(4)) Pub: Random Audio Pubg. Dist(s): Random

Franklin Delano Roosevelt. abr. rev. ed. Roy Jenkins. Read by Richard Rohan. Arthur M. Schlesinger. 3 CDs. (Running Time: 3 hrs. 30 mins. 0 sec.). (American Presidents Ser.). (ENG., 2003. audio compact disk 19.95 (978-1-55927-962-8(1)) Pub: Macmill Audio. Dist(s): Macmillan

Franklin Delano Roosevelt: Letters from a Mill Town Girl. Elizabeth Winthrop. Illus. by Elizabeth Winthrop. 2003. 9.95 (978-1-59112-209-8(0)); 9.95 (978-1-59112-210-4(4)) Live Oak Media.

Franklin Delano Roosevelt: Letters from a Mill Town Girl. unabr. ed. Elizabeth Winthrop. Illus. by Elizabeth Winthrop. 2 vols. (Running Time: 2 hrs. 30 mins.). (J). (gr. 4-7). 2003. bk. 25.95 (978-1-59112-213-5(9)) Live Oak Media.

Franklin Fibs. Paulette Bourgeois. Read by Paulette Bourgeois. Illus. by Brenda Clark. Music by Bruce Cockburn. (Franklin Ser.). (ENG.). (J). (ps-3). 1999. 9.95 (978-1-55074-668-6(5)) Kids Can Pr CAN.

Franklin Has a Sleepover. Paulette Bourgeois. Read by Paulette Bourgeois. Illus. by Brenda Clark. Music by Bruce Cockburn. (Franklin Ser.). (ENG.). (J). (ps-3). 1999. 9.95 (978-1-55074-664-8(2)) Kids Can Pr CAN.

Franklin Is Lost. Paulette Bourgeois. Read by Paulette Bourgeois. Illus. by Brenda Clark. Music by Bruce Cockburn. (Franklin Ser.). (ENG.). (J). (ps-3). 1999. 9.95 (978-1-55074-670-9(7)) Kids Can Pr CAN.

Franklin Is Messy. Paulette Bourgeois. Read by Paulette Bourgeois. Illus. by Brenda Clark. Music by Bruce Cockburn. (Franklin Ser.). (ENG.). (J). (ps-3). 1999. 9.95 (978-1-55074-678-5(2)) Kids Can Pr CAN.

Franklin Manor Christmas. Paul Willcott. Read by Paul Willcott. (Franklin Manor Ser.: Vol. 1). 2008. 28.95 (978-0-9816716-2-8(4)) Pub: Wordstruck. Dist(s): AtlasBooks

Franklin Roosevelt: Before the Trumpet. unabr. ed. Geoffrey Ward. Read by Grover Gardner. 10 cass. (Running Time: 15 hrs.). 1991. 80.00 (2761) Books on Tape.
An intimate portrait of the early years & the private world of the man who was to become FDR, 32nd President of the United States.

Franklin Roosevelt, Jr.: A Third Party see Buckley's Firing Line

Franklin Wants a Pet. Paulette Bourgeois. Read by Paulette Bourgeois. Illus. by Brenda Clark. Music by Bruce Cockburn. (Franklin Ser.). (ENG.). (J). (ps-3). 2000. 9.95 (978-1-55074-795-9(9)) Kids Can Pr CAN.

***Franklins.** The Franklins. (ENG.). 2009. audio compact disk 14.95 (978-0-9778908-4-2(8)) Pub: Tylis Pubng. Dist(s): STL Dist NA

Franklin's Blanket. Paulette Bourgeois. Read by Paulette Bourgeois. Illus. by Brenda Clark. Music by Bruce Cockburn. (Franklin Ser.). (ENG.). (J). (ps-3). 2000. 9.95 (978-1-55074-686-0(3)) Kids Can Pr CAN.

Franklin's New Friend. Paulette Bourgeois. Created by Paulette Bourgeois. Illus. by Brenda Clark. Music by Bruce Cockburn. (Franklin Ser.). (ENG.). (J). (ps-3). 1999. 9.95 (978-1-55074-797-3(5)) Kids Can Pr CAN.

Franklin's Secret Club. Paulette Bourgeois. Read by Paulette Bourgeois. Illus. by Brenda Clark. Music by Bruce Cockburn. (Franklin Ser.). (ENG.). (J). (ps-3). 1999. 9.95 (978-1-55074-672-3(3)) Kids Can Pr CAN.

Frannie in Pieces. unabr. ed. Danielle Ferland. Narrated by Danielle Ferland. 7 cass. (Running Time: 7 hrs. 45 mins.). (YA). (gr. 7-10). 2007. 51.75 (978-1-4281-7266-1(1)); audio compact disk 66.75 (978-1-4281-7271-5(8)) Recorded Bks.

Frantastic Days. Elmer L. Towns & Bill Bryan. 4 cass. 1986. bk. 89.95 (978-0-941005-22-7(4)) Chrch Grwth VA.

Frantic. unabr. ed. Katherine Howell. Read by Caroline Lee. (Running Time: 39060 sec.). 2007. audio compact disk 93.95 (978-1-74093-993-5(X), 9781740939935) Pub: Bolinda Pubng AUS. Dist(s): Bolinda Pub Inc

Franz & Dennis Country Home. 2002. audio compact disk (978-0-89610-903-2(8)) Island Heritage.

Franz Liszt. Narrated by Jeremy Siepmann & Neville Jason. 2 CDs. (Running Time: 2 hrs. 30 mins.). 2002. pap. bk. 17.99 (978-1-930838-15-4(8), 8.558005-06) Naxos.
Narrated biography illustrated with extensive examples of musical works, companion booklet including word-for-word transcript of spoken text and detailed historical background, graded listening plan and more.

Franz Liszt. Read by Jeremy Siepmann & Neville Jason. 2 CDs. (Running Time: 2 hrs. 35 min.). (Life & Works Ser.). 2003. pap. bk. 17.99 (978-1-84379-090-7(4)) Naxos.

Franz Schubert: Die Schone Mullerin. UW Sch of Music. Contrib. by Paul Rowe & Martha Fischer. 2007. audio compact disk 15.00 (978-1-931569-13-2(4)) Pub: U of Wis Pr. Dist(s): Chicago Distribution Ctr

Franz Schubert: Die Schone Mullerin. Contrib. by Paul Rowe & Martha Fischer. 2006. audio compact disk 25.00 (978-1-931569-12-5(6)) Pub: U of Wis Pr. Dist(s): Chicago Distribution Ctr

Franzmann Commentary. 1 cd. 1999. audio compact disk 119.99 Northwest Pub.

Franzmann Commentary. Werner H. Franzmann. 1998. audio compact disk 119.99 (978-0-8100-0895-3(5)) Northwest Pub.

Franzosisch Ohne Muhe Heute. 1 cass. (Running Time: 1 hr. 30 min.).Tr. of French with Ease. (ENG & GER., 1997. pap. bk. 75.00 (978-2-7005-1009-6(7)) Pub: Assimil FRA. Dist(s): Distribks Inc

Franzosisch Ohne Muhe Heute. 1 CD. (Running Time: 1 hr. 30 min.).Tr. of French with Ease. (FRE & GER.). 2000. bk. 95.00 (978-2-7005-1054-6(2)) Pub: Assimil FRA. Dist(s): Distribks Inc

Fraternity of the Stone. unabr. ed. David Morrell. (Running Time: 11 hrs.). 2006. 24.95 (978-1-59737-759-1(7), 9781597377591, BAD); audio compact disk 29.95 (978-1-59737-755-3(4), 9781597377553); audio compact disk 102.25 (978-1-59737-756-0(2), 9781597377560, BriAudCD Unabrid); audio compact disk 24.95 (978-1-59737-757-7(0), 9781597377577, Brilliance MP3) Brilliance Audio.
Drew Maclane was a star agent - until the day the killing had to stop. He withdrew and for six years lived the life of a hermit in a monastery. But someone has tracked him down, leaving a trail of corpses. Someone who knows all about him, who knows how to draw him back into that electrifying world where no one is as he seems, and where life's most horrifying and harrowing game is played.

Fraternity of the Stone. unabr. ed. David Morrell. Read by Multivoice Production Staff. (Running Time: 11 hrs.). 2006. 39.25 (978-1-59737-760-7(0), 9781597377607, BADLE); audio compact disk 39.25 (978-1-59737-758-4(9), 9781597377584, Brinc Audio MP3 Lib) Brilliance Audio.

Frau Holle. Jacob W. Grimm & Wilhelm K. Grimm. 1 cass. (Running Time: 60 min.). (Bruder Grimm Kinder & Hausmarchen Ser.). (GER.). 1996. pap. bk. 19.50 (978-1-58085-217-3(3), GR-12) Interlingua VA.

Freak the Mighty. unabr. ed. Rodman Philbrick. Read by Elden Henson. 2 cass. (Running Time: 3 hrs.). (J). (gr. 1-8). 1999. 23.00 (LL 0117, Chivers Child Audio) AudioGO.

Freak the Mighty. unabr. ed. Rodman Philbrick. Read by Elden Henson. 2 vols. (Running Time: 3 hrs. 16 mins.). (J). (gr. 7 up). 1998. pap. bk. 29.00 (978-0-8072-7982-3(X), YA959SP, Listening Lib); 23.00 (978-0-8072-7981-6(1), YA959CX, Listening Lib) Random Audio Pubg.
"I never had a brain until Freak came along..." That's what Max thought. All his life he'd been called stupid, dumb, slow. It didn't help that his body was growing faster than his mind, & that people were afraid of him. So Max learned to be alone. At least until Freak came along. Freak was weird too. He had a little body & a really big brain. Together, Max & Freak were unstoppable. Together, they were "Freak the Mighty!".

Freak the Mighty. unabr. ed. Rodman Philbrick. Read by Eldon Henson. (Running Time: 11760 sec.). (ENG.). (J). (gr. 5-7). 2008. audio compact disk 27.00 (978-0-7393-6310-2(7), Listening Lib) Pub: Random Audio Pubg. Dist(s): Random

Freak the Mighty. unabr. ed. W. R. Philbrick. Read by Elden Henson. 2 cass. (YA). 1999. 16.98 (FS9-34451) Highsmith.

Freaked! A Gotee Tribute to dcTalk's Jesus Freak. Contrib. by Toby McKeehan & Joey Elwood. 2006. audio compact disk 13.99 (978-5-558-40878-2(2)) Gotee Records.

Freakonomics: A Rogue Economist Explores the Hidden Side of Everything. rev. unabr. ed. Steven D. Levitt & Stephen J. Dubner. Read by Stephen J. Dubner. 7 CDs. (Running Time: 28800 sec.). 2006. audio compact disk 34.99 (978-0-06-123853-6(8)) HarperCollins Pubs.

***Freakonomics: A Rogue Economist Explores the Hidden Side of Everything.** unabr. ed. Steven D. Levitt & Stephen J. Dubner. Read by Stephen J. Dubner. (ENG.). 2005. (978-0-06-084296-3(2), Harper Audio); (978-0-06-084295-6(4), Harper Audio) HarperCollins Pubs.

Freakonomics: A Rogue Economist Explores the Hidden Side of Everything. unabr. ed. Steven D. Levitt & Stephen J. Dubner. Read by Stephen J. Dubner. 6 Cds . (Running Time: 7 Hrs). 2005. audio compact disk 29.95 (978-0-06-077613-8(7)) HarperCollins Pubs.

***Freakonomics: And Other Riddles of Modern Life.** unabr. rev. ed. Steven D. Levitt & Stephen J. Dubner. Read by Stephen J. Dubner. 2007. (978-0-06-125469-7(X), Harper Audio); (978-0-06-125468-0(1), Harper Audio) HarperCollins Pubs.

Freaks: Alive on the Inside. unabr. ed. Annette Curtis Klause. Read by Ramon de Ocampo. 9 CDs. (Running Time: 10 hrs. 15 mins.). (YA). 2006. audio compact disk 94.75 (978-1-4193-7143-1(6), C3549); 65.75 (978-1-4193-7138-7(X), 98274) Recorded Bks.
In this unique fantasy tale set in 1899, teenaged Abel Dandy lives with his parents in Faeryland, a community of human oddities. Abel, who is normal, runs away. But when he gets mixed up with the wicked Dr. Mink and his traveling freak show, dark and dangerous secrets emerge that change Abel's life forever.

Freaks of Mayfair. unabr. ed. Edward F. Benson. Read by Flo Gibson. 3 cass. (Running Time: 4 hrs. 4 mins.). 2001. vinyl bd. 16.95 (978-1-55685-670-9(9)) Audio Bk Con.
An amusing look at snobs, hypocondriacs, faddists, psychics & social climbers.

Freaky Deaky. Elmore Leonard. Narrated by Frank Muller. 5 cas. (Running Time: 8.75 hrs.). 24.95 (978-1-4025-5842-9(2)) Recorded Bks.

***Freaky Deaky.** unabr. ed. Elmore Leonard. Read by Frank Muller. (ENG.). 2010. (978-0-06-199379-4(4), Harper Audio); (978-0-06-206268-0(9), Harper Audio) HarperCollins Pubs.

Freaky Deaky. unabr. ed. Elmore Leonard. Narrated by Frank Muller. 6 cass. (Running Time: 8 hrs. 45 mins.). 1995. 51.00 (978-0-7887-0324-9(2), 94516E7) Recorded Bks.
Robin and Skip are lovers from the 60s who dynamite a federal building. Reunited in Detroit after years in prison, they've decided to light the fuse of revolution with a wild bombing spree. Before long Robin & Skip have taken more than one explosively wrong turn.

Freaky Deaky. unabr. collector's ed. Elmore Leonard. Read by Alexander Adams. 6 cass. (Running Time: 9 hrs.). 1997. 48.00 (978-0-7366-3606-3(4), 4260) Books on Tape.
A contemporary classic from the reigning king of the hard-boiled crime novel.

Freaky Friday. Mary Rodgers. Read by Susannah Fellows. 2 cass. (Running Time: 3 hrs. 20 mins.). (J). 2000. 18.00 (978-0-7366-9103-1(0)) Books on Tape.
Thirteen years old Annabel sometimes wishes that she was someone else. That wish comes true one Friday morning when Annabel suddenly finds herself in her mother's body.

Freaky Friday. unabr. ed. Read by Susannah Fellows. Ed. by Mary Rodgers. 2 vols. (Running Time: 3 hrs. 21 mins.). (J). (gr. 5-9). 1995. pap. bk. 29.00 (978-0-8072-7591-7(3), YA886SP, Listening Lib) Random Audio Pubg.
One morning, Annabel Adams awakens to discover that she has turned into her mother, & that her mother has taken over Annabel's own body. In A Billion for Boris (1974, 1976), a television set that broadcasts tomorrow's programs gives Annabel the urge to do good deeds, but inspires her friend Boris to make a fortune at the racetrack. In "Summer Switch" (1982), Annabel's brother, Ben, inadvertently trades bodies with his father while Ben is at summer camp & his father is on a business trip in Hollywood. Outstanding Quality.

Freaky Friday. unabr. ed. Mary Rodgers. 1 read-along cass. (Running Time: 23 min.). (Soundways to Reading Ser.). (J). (gr. 4-6). 1980. 15.98 incl. bk. & guide. (978-0-8072-1074-1(9), SWR 16 SP, Listening Lib) Random Audio Pubg.
A story about a girl who awakens one morning in her mother's body, & who sees herself as others see her & faces her problems squarely.

Freaky Friday. unabr. ed. Mary Rodgers. Read by Susannah Fellows. 2 cass. (Running Time: 3 hrs. 21 mins.). (J). (gr. 5-9). 1996. 23.00 (978-0-8072-7590-0(5), YA886CX, Listening Lib) Random Audio Pubg.
Annabel woke up to the ultimate surprise. It was the curlers in her hair that tipped her off! She had turned into her mother! Follow the events of a hilarious day in the life of Annabel as she develops a healthy respect for her mother & a new angle on her own life!.

Freaky Friday. unabr. ed. Mary Rodgers. Read by Susannah Fellows. (Running Time: 12060 sec.). (ENG.). (J). (gr. 4-7). 2007. audio compact disk 14.99 (978-0-7393-4891-8(4), Listening Lib) Pub: Random Audio Pubg. Dist(s): Random

Freaky Friday, Set. unabr. ed. Mary Rodgers. Read by Susannah Fellows. 2 cass. (YA). 1999. 16.98 (FS9-26768) Highsmith.

Freaky Green Eyes. unabr. ed. 5 cass. (Running Time: 6 hrs. 15 min.). (J). 2004. 45.75 (978-1-4025-8453-4(9)) Recorded Bks.

***Freaky Monday.** unabr. ed. Mary Rodgers. Read by Jennifer Stone. (ENG.). 2009. (978-0-06-190173-7(3), KTegenBooks); (978-0-06-190174-4(1), KTegenBooks) HarperCollins Pubs.

Freaky Monday. unabr. ed. Mary Rodgers. Read by Jennifer Stone. 3 CDs. (Running Time: 4 hrs.). (J). (gr. 5-8). 2009. audio compact disk 17.99 (978-0-06-176008-2(0), HarperChildAud) HarperCollins Pubs.

Freckle Juice. Judy Blume. 1 cass. (Running Time: 35 min.). (J). (ps-4). 2001. bk. 15.98 (LL-64C) Kimbo Educ.
Presents Andrew who wishes he had loads of freckles to hide his dirty neck. He purchases a secret freckle juice formula & is in for a surprise. Includes read along book.

Freckle Juice. unabr. ed. Judy Blume. Read by Lionel Wilson. 1 cass. (Running Time: 31 mins.). (Follow the Reader Ser.). (J). (gr. 2-4). 1982. pap. bk. 17.00 (978-0-8072-0018-6(2), FTR 64 SP, Listening Lib) Random Audio Pubg.
Andrew wishes he had loads of freckles to hide his dirty neck. When the class know-it-all sells him a secret freckle juice formula for fifty cents, Andrew is in for some dotty surprises.

Freckle Juice & the One in the Middle is the Green Kangaroo. unabr. ed. 1 cass. (Running Time: 1:30 hrs.). 2004. 15.00 (978-1-4000-9892-7(0), Listening Lib) Random Audio Pubg.

***Freckle Juice & the One in the Middle Is the Green Kangaroo.** unabr. ed. Judy Blume. Read by Laura Hamilton. (ENG.). (J). 2011. audio compact disk 15.00 (978-0-307-74567-5(8), Listening Lib) Pub: Random Audio Pubg. Dist(s): Random

Frederick Douglass: Adventures in Literacy. Gwendolyn J. Crenshaw & Aesop Enterprise Inc. Staff. 1 cass. (Heroes & Sheroes Ser.). (J). (gr. 3-12). 1991. (978-1-880771-03-7(9)) AESOP Enter.

Frederick Douglass: Freedom's Force. Time-Life Books Editors. (YA). (gr. 5-9). 1999. bk. 69.95 (978-0-7835-5436-5(2)) Time-Life Educ.

Frederick Douglass: From Slave to Statesman. unabr. ed. Alice Fleming. Read by Roscoe Orman. 1 MP3-CD. (Running Time: 2 hrs.). (Library of American Lives & Times Ser.). 2009. 19.99 (978-1-4233-8210-2(2), 9781423382102, Brilliance MP3); 39.97 (978-1-4233-8211-9(0), 9781423382119, Brlnc Audio MP3 Lib); 39.97 (978-1-4233-8212-6(9), 9781423382126, BADLE); audio compact disk 39.97 (978-1-4233-8209-6(9), 9781423382096, BriAudCD Unabrid); audio compact disk 19.99 (978-1-4233-8208-9(0), 9781423382089, Bril Audio CD Unabri) Brilliance Audio.

Frederick Douglass: His Life & Analysis of His Greatness. 1 cass. (Running Time: 60 mins.). 1999. 12.95 (SPA-738) African Am Imag.

Frederick Douglass: Narrative of an American Slave. Frederick Douglass. 2006. audio compact disk 19.95 (978-0-9779883-2-7(5)) Legacy Audio Bks.

Frederick Douglass: A Hero for All Times. Devorah Major. Ed. by Jerry Stemach et al. Illus. by Jack Nichols. Narrated by Denise Jordan Walker & Bernard Mixon. Contrib. by Ted S. Hasselbring. (Start-to-Finish Books: Vol. 2). 2000. 35.00 (978-1-58702-450-4(0)) D Johnston Inc.

Frederick Douglass African American Campaigner for Human Rights & Freedom from Slavery: An Epic Story of the Superiority of Character to Circumstances & Environment. Charles Chesnut. Ed. by Ross M. Armetta. Narrated by Ross M. Armetta. 1 CD. (Running Time: Approx. 50 Mins.). 2005. audio compact disk 11.99 (978-1-59733-501-0(0), Antecdent Wisdom) InfoFount.

This 1 CD audiobook is a ?short and sweet? biography of the life, times, and achievement of Frederick Douglas (approximately 50 minutes long).If it be no small task for a man of the most favored circumstances and the most fortunate surroundings to rise above mediocrity in a great nation, it is surely a more remarkable achievement for a man of the very humblest origin possible to humanity in any country in any age of the world, in the face of obstacles seemingly insurmountable, to win high honors and rewards, to retain for more than a generation the respect of good men in many lands, and to be deemed worthy of enrolment among his country's great men. Such a man was Frederick Douglass, and the example of one who thus rose to eminence by sheer force of character and talents that neither slavery nor caste proscription could crush must ever remain as a shining illustration of the essential superiority of charachter to environment.Circumstances made Frederick Douglass a slave, but they could not prevent him from becoming a freeman and a leader among mankind.This is a story that people of all races will enjoy and benefit from hearing. It shows how a man overcame seemingly impossible circumstances, to become "master" of his owndestiny and an example of excellence, morality, and a champion of strength for others.No matter what the circumstances were this man would never let his mind and spirit be enslaved. Born of mixed black and white parentage, he became a uniter and healer of thought, heart, and race.From the night of slavery Douglass emerged, passed through the limbo of prejudice which he encountered as a freeman, and took his place in history. "As few of the world's great men have ever had so checkered and diversified a career," says Henry Wilson, "so it may at least be plausibly claimed that no man represents in himself more conflicting ideas and interests. His life is, in itself, an epic which finds fewto equal it in the realms of either romance or reality." It was, after all, no misfortune for humanity that Frederick Douglass felt the iron hand of slavery; for his genius changed the drawbacks of color and condition into levers by which he raised himself and his people.

Frederick (Fritz) Perls: Ten Programs for Public Radio. Featuring Frederick (Fritz) Perls. 5 CDs. (Running Time: 5 hrs.). 1984. audio compact disk 45.00 (978-0-939266-61-6(X)) Gestalt Journal.

Fredericksburg, Comfort, & a Railroad. 2 CDs. 2005. audio compact disk 24.95 (978-0-9668839-3-0(4)) TX Daytripper.

Fredericksburg Expedition Guide: The Complete Guide to the Battlefield of Fredericksburg. 2002. cd-rom & audio compact disk 24.95 (978-0-9705809-7-9(5), 949 951-3223) TravelBrains.

Fredericksburg to Meridian. unabr. ed. Shelby Foote. Read by Grover Gardner. 3 pieces. (Running Time: 169200 sec.). (Civil War: A Narrative Ser.). 2009. audio compact disk 54.95 (978-0-7861-9102-4(3), 1103A,B) Blckstn Audio.

Frederik Pohl. unabr. ed. Read by Frederik Pohl. 1 cass. (Running Time: 29 min.). 1985. 10.00 New Letters.

Science fiction writer Frederik Pohl reads two stories: "Day Million" & "Punch".

Fredman's Epistles & Songs: A Selection in English with A Short Introduction by Paul Britten Austin. Carl Michael Bellman. Tr. by Paul Britten Austin from SWE. 1999. bk. 34.50 (978-92-3-103608-8(4)) Pub: UNESCO FRA. Dist(s): Renouf Publ

Free Agent Nation. abr. ed. Contrib. by Daniel H. Pink. 2 cass. (Running Time: 3 hrs.). 2002. 18.98 (978-1-58621-248-3(6)) Hachet Audio.

There are 25 million free agents, entrepreneurs, independent contractors, free lancers, and temps. In this landmark book, trend-watcher Daniel H. Pink shows why those numbers are growing exponentially.

Free Agent Nation: How America's New Independent Workers Are Transforming the Way We Live. abr. ed. Daniel H. Pink. (ENG.). 2005. 14.98 (978-1-59483-423-3(7)) Pub: Hachet Audio. Dist(s): HachBkGrp

Free Air. unabr. ed. Sinclair Lewis. Read by Barrett Whitener. 6 cass. (Running Time: 9 hrs.). 1997. 44.95 (978-0-7861-1146-6(1), 1913) Blckstn Audio.

Free & Equal Blues. Composed by Josh White. 1 CD. audio compact disk Smithsonian Folkways.

Free & Happy Children. unabr. ed. Hosted by Peter Breggin. 1 cass. (Famous Authorities Talk about Children Ser.). 12.95 (AF0390) J Norton Pubs.

Free & Other Stories. unabr. ed. Theodore Dreiser. Read by Flo Gibson. 3 cass. (Running Time: 3 hrs. 23 min.). (YA). 2003. 24.95 (978-1-55685-577-1(X)) Audio Bk Con.

Includes "The Second Choice," "The Lost Phoebe," & "Marriage." Delves into the ups & downs of relationships & death.

Free As a Running Fox. unabr. ed. T. D. Calnan. Read by Dan Lazar. 8 cass. (Running Time: 12 hrs.). 1981. 64.00 (978-0-7366-0359-1(X), 1345) Books on Tape.

The account of World War II R.A.F. fighter pilot T.D. Calnan. Shot down on a routine reconnaissance flight, badly burned, more dead than alive when captured, Calnan was hospitalized, then sent to the first of many prison camps he would occupy until the end of the war.

Free at Last. unabr. ed. Daniel Greenberg. 4. (Running Time: 6 hrs). 2002. 20.00 (978-1-888947-61-8(6)) Sudbury Valley.

Free at Last! Free at Last! His Truth Is Marching On. 1 cass. (Running Time: 60 mins.). (J). (gr. 4 up). 1999. 12.95 African Am Imag.

Free at Last (Revised Edition with Study Guide & CD Insert) Removing the Past from Your Future. 2nd rev. ed. Larry Huch. Frwd. by Benny Hinn. 2004. bk. & stu. ed. 14.99 (978-0-88368-428-3(4), 774284) Pub: Whitaker Hse. Dist(s): Anchor Distributors

Free Book. unabr. ed. Brian Tome. Narrated by Brian Tome. (Running Time: 6 hrs. 1 mins. 23 sec.). (ENG.). 2010. 18.19 (978-1-60814-640-6(5)); audio compact disk 25.99 (978-1-59859-697-7(7)) Oasis Audio.

Free Byrd: The Power of the Liberated Life. unabr. ed. Paul Byrd. Narrated by Tim Gregory. (Running Time: 8 hrs. 30 mins. 0 sec.). (ENG.). 2008. 19.59 (978-1-60814-222-4(1), SpringWater) Oasis Audio.

Free Byrd: The Power of the Liberated Life. unabr. ed. Paul Byrd. Read by Paul Byrd. Narrated by Tim Gregory. (Running Time: 8 hrs. 30 mins. 0 sec.). (ENG.). 2008. audio compact disk 27.99 (978-1-59859-355-6(2)) Oasis Audio.

Free Cowboy Hats. Poems. Perf. by Willie Smith et al. 1 cass. 5.00 (978-1-878888-34-1(X)) Nine Muses Books.

Poetry backed up by music.

***Free Dirt.** 2010. audio compact disk (978-1-59171-284-8(X)) Falcon Picture.

Free Energy. Bruce Depalma. 2 cass. (Roy Tuckman Interview Ser.). 18.00 Set. (A0185-87) Sound Photosyn.

Free Enterprise. unabr. ed. H. Edward Rowe. 1 cass. (Running Time: 55 min.). 12.95 (728) J Norton Pubs.

Explains the origins of our economic system & tells how it is being threatened with destruction today.

Free Enterprise System: 11 Cor. 9:6-15. Ed Young. 1990. 4.95 (978-0-7417-1785-6(9), 785) Win Walk.

Free Fall. Prod. by Laraim Associates. (Barclay Family Adventure Ser.). (J). 2005. audio compact disk (978-1-56254-992-3(8)) Saddleback Edu.

Free Fall. Fern Michaels. Read by Laural Merlington. (Sisterhood Ser.: No. 7). 2008. 64.99 (978-1-60640-787-5(2)) Find a World.

Free Fall. Kyle Mills. Read by Michael Kramer. 2000. audio compact disk 96.00 (978-0-7366-6071-6(2)) Books on Tape.

Free Fall. abr. ed. Robert Crais. Read by James Daniels. 4 cass. (Running Time: 6 hrs.). (Elvis Cole Ser.). 2002. 44.25 (978-1-58788-513-6(1), 1587885131, Lib Edit) Brilliance Audio.

Elvis Cole is just a detective who can't say no, especially to a girl in a terrible fix. And Jennifer Sheridan qualifies: Her fiance, Mark Thurman, is a decorated LA cop with an elite plainclothes unit, but Jennifer's sure he's in trouble - the kind of serious trouble that only Elvis Cole can help him out of. Five minutes after his new client leaves his office, Elvis and his partner, the enigmatic Joe Pike, are hip-deep in a deadly situation as they plummet into a world of South Central gangs, corrupt cops, and conspiracies of silence. And before the case is through, every cop in the LAPD will be gunning for a pair of escaped armed-and-dangerous killers - Elvis Cole and Joe Pike. "Elvis lives, and he's on his way to being crowned the king of detectives." - Booklist.

Free Fall. abr. ed. Robert Crais. Read by James Daniels. (Running Time: 6 hrs.). (Elvis Cole Ser.). 2006. 24.95 (978-1-4233-0075-5(0), 9781423300755, BAD) Brilliance Audio.

Free Fall. abr. ed. Fern Michaels. Read by Laural Merlington. (Running Time: 3 hrs.). (Sisterhood Ser.: No. 7). 2009. audio compact disk 9.99 (978-1-4418-3658-8(6), 9781441836588, BCD Value Price) Brilliance Audio.

Free Fall. unabr. ed. Robert Crais. Read by Mel Foster. (Running Time: 9 hrs.). (Elvis Cole Ser.). 2008. 39.25 (978-1-4233-5656-1(X), 9781423356561, BADLE); 39.25 (978-1-4233-5654-7(3), 9781423356547, Brlnc Audio MP3 Lib); 24.95 (978-1-4233-5655-4(1), 9781423356554, BAD); audio compact disk 92.25 (978-1-4233-5652-3(7), 9781423356523, BriAudCD Unabrid); audio compact disk 34.95 (978-1-4233-5651-6(9), 9781423356516, Bril Audio CD Unabri); audio compact disk 24.95 (978-1-4233-5653-0(5), 9781423356530, Brilliance MP3) Brilliance Audio.

Free Fall. unabr. ed. Fern Michaels. Read by Laural Merlington. 1 MP3-CD. (Running Time: 25200 sec.). (Sisterhood Ser.: Bk. 7). 2007. audio compact disk 39.25 (978-1-59737-595-5(0), 9781597375955, Brlnc Audio MP3 Lib) Brilliance Audio.

Please enter a Synopsis.

Free Fall. unabr. ed. Fern Michaels. Read by Laural Merlington. (Running Time: 7 hrs.). (Sisterhood Ser.: No. 7). 2007. 39.25 (978-1-59737-597-9(7), 9781597375979, BADLE); 24.95 (978-1-59737-596-2(9), 9781597375962, BAD); audio compact disk 29.95 (978-1-59737-592-4(6), 9781597375924, Bril Audio CD Unabri); audio compact disk 24.95 (978-1-59737-594-8(2), 9781597375948, Brilliance MP3); 69.25 (978-1-59737-591-7(8), 9781597375917, BrilAudUnabridg); audio compact disk 87.25 (978-1-59737-593-1(4), 9781597375931, BriAudCD Unabrid) Brilliance Audio.

Free Fall. unabr. ed. Kyle Mills. Read by Michael Kramer. 10 cass. (Running Time: 15 hrs.). 2001. 80.00 (978-0-7366-5449-4(6)); audio compact disk 96.00 Books on Tape.

A suspended FBI agent must find an elusive woman & a top secret file in order to save himself & his country.

Free Fall, unabr. ed. Joyce Sweeney. Narrated by Ed Sala. 5 pieces. (Running Time: 6 hrs. 15 mins.). (gr. 6 up). 1997. 44.00 (978-0-7887-0734-6(5), 94911E7) Recorded Bks.

When four teenaged boys explore a cave hidden deep in the Ocala National Forest, they forget they are alone & no one knows where they are.

Free Fall in Crimson. unabr. collector's ed. John D. MacDonald. Read by Michael Prichard. 8 cass. (Running Time: 8 hrs.). (Travis McGee Ser.: Vol. 19). 1981. 48.00 (978-0-7366-0632-5(7), 1593) Books on Tape.

This is the story of an inherited fortune & an unsolved murder. It ranges from Florida to California & involves Travis McGee in everything from motorcycles to movies to hot air balloons. As the pace quickens, McGee moves with increasing assurance & in the book's turbulent climax is fully restored as our reigning folk hero.

Free Fall of Webster Cummings, the - the American Odyssey Collection. abr. ed. Tom Bodett. Read by Tom Bodett. (Running Time: 15 hrs.). (Odyssey Ser.). 2009. 39.97 (978-1-4233-8555-4(1), 9781423385554, Brlnc Audio MP3 Lib); 39.97 (978-1-4233-8557-8(8), 9781423385578, BADLE); 24.99 (978-1-4233-8554-7(3), 9781423385547, Brilliance MP3); 24.99 (978-1-4233-8556-1(X), 9781423385561, BAD) Brilliance Audio.

Free Falling. Red Grammer & Kathy Grammer. 1 cass. (J). 1991. 10.00 (978-1-886146-05-1(5)); audio compact disk 15.00 CD. (978-1-886146-08-2(X)) Red Note Recs.

Free Fire. unabr. ed. C. J. Box. Read by David Chandler. 10 cass. (Running Time: 10 hrs. 45 mins.). (Joe Pickett Ser.: No. 7). 2007. 82.75 (978-1-4281-5748-4(4)); audio compact disk 123.75 (978-1-4281-5750-7(6)) Recorded Bks.

Free Flight. unabr. ed. Douglas Terman. Read by Bob Erickson. 8 cass. (Running Time: 12 hrs.). 1983. 64.00 (978-0-7366-0686-8(6), 1646) Books on Tape.

The Russians have won World War III with a brief, horrifying nuclear stroke. The year is 1987. Greg Mallen, American Air Force officer, is one of the survivors of the war. Driven by his recollections of the formerly free America, Mallen sets up an irrevocable kill-or-be-killed attempt to save what is left of humanity.

Free Flow 12. unabr. ed. Robert A. Monroe. Read by Robert A. Monroe. (Running Time: 45 min.). (Gateway Experience - Adventure Ser.). 1983. 14.95 (978-1-56113-270-6(5)) Monroe Institute.

Provide a unique & unparalleled background for your exploration.

Free Food for Millionaires. Min Jin Lee. Read by Shelly Frasier. (Playaway Adult Fiction Ser.). (ENG.). 2008. 99.99 (978-1-60640-717-2(1)) Find a World.

Free Food for Millionaires. unabr. ed. Min Jin Lee. Read by Shelly Frasier. 16 CDs. (Running Time: 20 hrs. 30 mins. 0 sec.). (ENG.). 2007. audio compact disk 109.99 (978-1-4001-3460-1(9)); audio compact disk 39.99 (978-1-4001-5460-9(X)); audio compact disk 54.99 (978-1-4001-0460-4(2)) Pub: Tantor Media. Dist(s): IngramPubServ

Casey Han's parents, who live in Queens, are Korean immigrants working in a dry cleaner, desperately trying to hold on to their culture and their identity. Their daughter, on the other hand, has entered into rarified American society via scholarships. Free Food for Millionaires offers up a fresh exploration of the complex layers we inhabit both in society and within ourselves and examines maintaining one's identity within changing communities.

Free from the Spirit of Unbelief. Kingsley Fletcher. 1 cass. 1992. 7.00 (978-0-938612-91-9(3)) Destiny Image Pubs.

Free Gift. Contrib. by Pam Andrews. 1996. 11.98 (978-0-7601-0893-2(5), 75602067); 85.00 (978-0-7601-0896-3(X), 75606292) Pub: Brentwood Music. Dist(s): H Leonard

Free in Christ. Lance Howerton. 2001. 11.98 (978-0-633-01525-1(3)); audio compact disk 85.00 (978-0-633-01534-3(2)); audio compact disk 16.98 (978-0-633-01530-5(X)) LifeWay Christian.

Free in Christ (Stereo/Split Acc Cassette. Lance Howerton. 2001. 75.00 (978-0-633-01520-6(2)) LifeWay Christian.

Free Independent Travel in Malaysia: A Strategic Reference 2006. Compiled by Icon Group International, Inc. Staff. 2007. ring bd. 195.00 (978-0-497-82343-6(8)) Icon Grp.

Free Life. unabr. ed. Ha Jin. Narrated by Jason Ma. 2 MP3-CDs. (Running Time: 22 hrs.). 2007. 124.95 (978-0-7927-5082-6(9)); audio compact disk 124.95 (978-0-7927-5043-7(8)) AudioGO.

Introducing the Wu family - father Nan, mother Pingping, and son Taotao. We meet them as they arrange to fully sever ties with China in the aftermath of the 1989 massacre at Tiananmen Square, and to begin a new, free life in the United States. At first, their future seems well-assured. Nan's graduate work in political science at Brandeis University ensures him a teaching position. But after the fallout from Tiananmen, his disillusionment turns him toward his first love, poetry. Leaving his studies, he takes on a variety of menial jobs as Pingping works for a wealthy widow as a cook and housekeeper. As Nan struggles to adapt to a new language and culture, his love of poetry and literature sustains him through difficult, lean years. As Pingping and Taotao slowly adjust to American life, Nan still feels a strange attachment to his homeland, though he violently disagrees with Communist policy. But severing all ties - including his love for a woman who rejected him in his youth - proves to be more difficult than he could have ever imagined.

Free Life. unabr. ed. Ha Jin. Read by Jason Ma. (YA). 2008. 109.99 (978-1-60514-575-4(0)) Find a World.

***Free Life: Unabridged Value-Priced Edition.** Ha Jin. Narrated by Jason Ma. (Running Time: 21 hrs. 51 mins. 0 sec.). (ENG.). 2010. audio compact disk 14.95 (978-1-60283-988-5(3)) Pub: AudioGO. Dist(s): Perseus Dist

Free-market Economics. unabr. ed. Instructed by Murray Newton Rothbard. 18 cass. (Running Time: 22 hrs.). 99.00 (978-0-88432-218-4(1), S00301) J Norton Pubs.

The course consists of sixteen lectures on basic free-market economics presented by one of the leading economic philosophers of this century.

Free Market Fantasies: Capitalism in the Real World. Noam Chomsky. (AK Press Audio Ser.). (ENG.). 1999. audio compact disk 13.98 (978-1-873176-79-5(1)) Pub: AK Pr GBR. Dist(s): Consort Bk Sales

Free Money for Everyone: How to Get Government Grants for the Whole Family! Matthew Lesko. Told to Mary Ann Martello. 2005. 19.95 (978-1-878346-84-1(9)) Info USA.

Free of Anxiety & Stress: Power Imaging. Eldon Taylor. Read by Eldon Taylor. Ed. by Leslie Brice. 1 cass. (Running Time: 1 hr.). 1992. 12.95 (978-1-56705-023-3(9)) Gateways Inst.

Self improvement.

Free of Depression. Eldon Taylor. 1 cass. (Running Time: 62 min.). (Inner Talk Ser.). 16.95 incl. script. (978-1-55978-485-6(7), 5356F) Progress Aware Res.

Soundtrack - Brook with underlying subliminal affirmations.

Free of Depression: Classic. Eldon Taylor. Read by Eldon Taylor. Ed. by Leslie Brice. 1 cass. (Running Time: 1 hr.). 1992. 16.95 (978-1-56705-134-6(0)) Gateways Inst.

Self improvement.

Free of Depression: Easy. Eldon Taylor. Read by Eldon Taylor. Ed. by Leslie Brice. 1 cass. (Running Time: 1 hr.). 1992. 16.95 (978-1-56705-135-3(9)) Gateways Inst.

Free of Depression: Harmonies. Eldon Taylor. Read by Eldon Taylor. Ed. by Leslie Brice. 1 cass. (Running Time: 1 hr.). 1992. 16.95 (978-1-56705-136-0(7)) Gateways Inst.

Free of Depression: Music Theme. Eldon Taylor. 1 cass. 16.95 (978-1-55978-431-3(8), 5356M) Progress Aware Res.

Free of Depression: Ocean. Eldon Taylor. Read by Eldon Taylor. Ed. by Leslie Brice. 1 cass. (Running Time: 1 hr.). 1992. 16.95 (978-1-56705-137-7(5)) Gateways Inst.

Free of Depression: Rhythm. Eldon Taylor. Read by Eldon Taylor. Ed. by Leslie Brice. 1 cass. (Running Time: 1 hr.). 1992. 16.95 (978-1-56705-138-4(3)) Gateways Inst.

Free of Depression: Stream. Eldon Taylor. Read by Eldon Taylor. Ed. by Leslie Brice. 1 cass. (Running Time: 1 hr.). 1992. 16.95 (978-1-56705-139-1(1)) Gateways Inst.

Free of Depression: The Geometry of Being - Geometry in Motion. Eldon Taylor. Directed By Eldon Taylor. 1 cass. (Running Time: 30 min.). (Sacred Geometry Ser.). 1997. cass. & video 29.95 (978-1-55978-698-0(1), V105) Progress Aware Res.

Geometry in motion developing from fractals, forming mandalas, absolutely mesmerizing with tones & frequencies.

Free of Fear (Subliminal & Hypnosis), Vol. 40. Jayne Helle. 1 cass. (Running Time: 56 min. per cass.). 1998. 15.00 (978-1-891826-39-9(5)) Introspect.

Stop cowering from fear. Helps one come from strength & become the person one wants to be.

Free or Slave? Neville Goddard. 1 cass. (Running Time: 62 min.). 1967. 8.00 (47) J & L Pubns.

Neville taught Imagination Creates Reality. He was a powerfully influential teacher of God as Consciousness.

Free Prize Inside! The Next Big Marketing Idea. unabr. ed. Seth Godin. Read by Seth Godin. (Running Time: 3 hrs.). (ENG.). 2009. 9.98 (978-1-59659-390-9(3), GildAudio) Pub: Gildan Media. Dist(s): HachBkGrp

Free Range Lanning. unabr. collector's ed. Max Brand. Read by Jonathan Marosz. 7 cass. (Running Time: 7 hrs.). 1995. 42.00 (978-0-7366-2909-6(2), 3606) Books on Tape.
Andy Lanning is suddenly famous. Whoever brings him in - dead or alive - gets 5000 dollars!.

Free-Release Method. the Golf Audio Book: Story, Path, Technique & Background. Frank Drollinger. Prod. by United Golfers GmbH.Tr. of Free-Release Methode. das Golf Hörbuch. (ENG.). 2007. audio compact disk 14.95 (978-3-940556-04-2(1)) United Golfers DEU.

Free-Release Methode. das Golf Hörbuch see Free-Release Method. the Golf Audio Book: Story, Path, Technique & Background

Free Samples. Troy Dunn. 2004. 9.95 (978-1-57734-777-4(3)); audio compact disk 10.95 (978-1-57734-778-1(1)) Covenant Comms.

Free Spirit. Contrib. by Martin Donohoe. (ENG.). 1993. 13.95 (978-0-8023-7089-1(6)) Pub: Clo Iar-Chonnachta IRL. Dist(s): Dufour

Free Spirit. Contrib. by Martin Donohue. (ENG.). 1993. audio compact disk 21.95 (978-0-8023-8089-0(1)) Pub: Clo Iar-Chonnachta IRL. Dist(s): Dufour

Free the Captives. Read by Tim Gray et al. 2001. 22.95 (978-1-931018-03-6(0)) Emmaus Rd Pubng.

Free the Horses. Michael Popkin. 1 cass. (Running Time: 40 min.). 1991. 8.95 (K5070) Active Parenting.
Based on concepts from Free the Horses: A Self-Esteem Adventure Video program. 11 original songs.

Free the Trees. Kathleen Gibson. Read by Kathleen Gibson. Illus. by Jo Dose. 1 cass. (Running Time: 20 min.). (Rainbow Readers Ser.). (J). (ps-5). 1996. pap. bk. 12.50 (978-1-888862-01-0(7), RR6201) Rainbow Rdrs.
An innocently wise plea for conscious use of our forests & natural resources. Beginning reader storybook & musical read-along cassette includes activities for creativity, conservation awartness, art & literacy.

Free to Be Me-Power Words. unabr. ed. Mary Richards. Music by Charles Alberts. 1 cass. (Running Time: 50 min.). (Power Words Ser.). 2007. audio compact disk 19.95 (978-1-56136-207-3(7)) Master Your Mind.
Short guided relaxation with awareness exercises plus audible power words. Excellent 12 step support.

Free to Be Well: Using Food & Supplements to Prevent Illness, Set unabr. ed. Usha Honeyman. Read by Usha Honeyman. 6 cass. (Running Time: 6 hr.). 1998. bk. 110.00 (978-0-9673767-2-1(6), T-F2B); audio compact disk 119.95 (978-0-9673767-3-8(4), TB-F2B) Oos Pubg.
Information about using diet & nutritional supplements to prevent disease 7 improve health. Explains common sources of toxins & how to avoid them.

Free to Be... You & Me. Marlo Thomas. Perf. by Alan Alda et al. 1 cass. (J). (ps-4). 9.98 (229) MFLP CA.
Marlo Thomas has brought us one of the most unique & exciting projects ever produced. Touching on real issues with music & skits, the audio provokes thought & heartfelt laughter.

Free to Choose. unabr. ed. Milton Friedman & Rose Friedman. Read by James Adams. (Running Time: 45000 sec.). 2007. 29.95 (978-1-4332-0016-8(3)); audio compact disk 29.95 (978-1-4332-0017-5(1)); audio compact disk 29.95 (978-1-4332-0019-9(8)) Blckstn Audio.

Free to Choose. unabr. ed. Milton Friedman & Rose D. Friedman. Read by Daniel Laurence. 9 cass. (Running Time: 13 hrs.). 1988. 62.95 (978-0-7861-0021-7(4), 1021) Blckstn Audio.
Freedom has been eroded & prosperity undermined through the rapid growth of governmental agencies, laws & regulations.

Free to Choose: A Personal Statement. unabr. ed. Milton Friedman. (Running Time: 45000 sec.). 2007. 62.95 (978-1-4332-0631-3(5)); audio compact disk 99.00 (978-1-4332-0015-1(5)) Blckstn Audio.

Free to Worship: Live at the Potter's House. Contrib. by Fred Hammond. (Running Time: 1 hr. 30 mins.). 2007. 19.98 (978-5-558-11377-8(4), Verity) Brentwood Music.

Free Verse, Affirmations & Haiku for Women Survivors. unabr. ed. Mercedes Leidlich. Read by Mercedes Leidlich. 1 cass. (Running Time: 1 hr.). 1992. 10.95 in Norelco box. (978-1-882174-06-5(2), MLL-007) UFD Pub.
This tape has been specifically designed for women who are recovering from life traumas, such as physical, mental, verbal, or sexual abuse, addiction to alcohol, drugs, food, sex, gambling, or who are recovering from grief or another type of major loss. This tape contains nurturing, healing verse & affirmations meant to help the listener to reflect & cleanse the mind of busy thoughts.

Free Will. unabr. ed. Nathaniel Branden. 1 cass. (Running Time: 1 hr. 26 min.). (Basic Principles of Objectiveness Ser.). 12.95 (565) J Norton Pubs.
Discusses the meaning & nature of volition; the fallacy of psychological determination; free will as the choice to think or not to think.

Free Will & Genetics. unabr. ed. Nathaniel Branden. 1 cass. (Running Time: 37 min.). 12.95 (811) J Norton Pubs.
To be free is to challenge beliefs of other people & to come to your own conclusions. Most people are capable of working at a more abstract level & a higher one than they normally do. Consciousness considered as the organ of survival.

Free Will Baptist Doctrine - Charismatic Confusion, Set. Robert E. Picirilli. Ed. by Sound Impressions Staff. 2 cass. 1992. 9.95 (978-0-89265-659-2(X), 28057) Randall Hse.

Free Woman. unabr. ed. Libby Purves. 8 cass. (Isis Ser.). (J). 2002. 69.95 (978-0-7531-1390-5(2)) Pub: ISIS Lrg Prnt GBR. Dist(s): Ulverscroft US

Free Your Creativity! Liah Kraft-Kristaine. Read by Liah Kraft-Kristaine. 1 cass. (Running Time: 62 min.). 1989. 9.95 (978-1-878095-03-9(X)) LMI Prodns.
Techniques in brain synch, relaxation & imagery to activate creative potential.

Free Your Finances. George Bloomer. 3. audio compact disk Whitaker Hse.

Free Your Finances. George Bloomer. 3 CDs. (Running Time: 4 hrs.). 2004. audio compact disk 39.99 (978-0-88368-618-8(X)) Whitaker Hse.
Do you desire to build a firm financial foundation in your life? Do you want to practice biblical stewardship in regard to all that God gives you? If so, then let Bishop George Bloomer teach you scriptural principles that will keep you from falling into one financial strait after another. With wisdom and insights gleaned from God's Word, Bishop Bloomer will set you on a path to financial stability and freedom!.

Free Yourself from Tension & Other Topics. Daya Mata. 1984. 6.50 (2118) Self Realization.
Discusses ways in addition to meditation by which we can reduce or completely eliminate the accumulated stress of modern living & thus feel more deeply the peace of God's presence in our lives.

Freebooters. unabr. collector's ed. Elleston Trevor. Read by Christopher Hurt. 8 cass. (Running Time: 8 hrs.). 1986. 48.00 (978-0-7366-0838-1(9), 1789) Books on Tape.
In the middle of a hundred thousand square miles of East African bush, a British regiment stands within a ring of barbed wire. Ordered not to respond to provocation, it holds its ground & its fire while terrorist drums sound through the night, sentries are speared in the dark, peaceful farmers & missionaries are slaughtered in their beds. This is a story of fighting men who give up because they are not allowed to fight, a story of mutiny, desertion & escape through hostile territory.

Freed see Bible in Living Sound: Life and Times of the Old Testament; Life and Times of Jesus; Life and Times of Paul

Freedman's Story see Black Pioneers in American History, Vol. 2, 19th - 20th Centuries

***Freedom.** unabr. ed. Jonathan Franzen. Read by David LeDoux. 19 CDs. (Running Time: 25 hrs.). (ENG., 2010. audio compact disk 59.99 (978-1-4272-1049-4(7)) Pub: Macmill Audio. Dist(s): Macmillan

Freedom: A Novel of Abraham Lincoln & the Civil War. unabr. ed. William Safire & Jeff Riggenbach. (Running Time: 21 hrs. NaN mins.). 2008. 69.95 (978-1-4332-5408-6(5)); audio compact disk 125.00 (978-1-4332-5405-5(0)); audio compact disk 125.00 (978-1-4332-5407-9(7)) Blckstn Audio.

Freedom: Expanding Personal Freedom. Instructed by Stuart Wilde. 2 cass. (Self-Help Tape Ser.). 19.95 set. (978-0-930603-23-6(0)) White Dove NM.
Stuart at his very best - powerful & witty - teaches that the only way to reach fulfillment & absolute safety in the coming years is to completely detach from the weakness inherent in the aspirations of man & to develop a vise-like grip on your own self-improvement. If you are ready, & you are dedicated to yourself, this tape is for you.

Freedom: The Key to Ending Poverty. unabr. ed. Dean Russell. 1 cass. (Running Time: 29 min.). 12.95 (108) J Norton Pubs.

Freedom: The Philosophy of Liberation. Instructed by Dennis Dalton. 4 cass. (Running Time: 6 hrs.). 1994. 39.95 (978-1-56585-117-7(X)) Teaching Co.

Freedom: The Philosophy of Liberation. Instructed by Dennis Dalton. 2008. audio compact disk 54.95 (978-1-59803-456-1(1)) Teaching Co.

Freedom: The Story of My Second Life. Malika Oufkir. 2007. 24.98 (978-1-4013-8501-9(X)) Pub: Hyperion. Dist(s): HarperCollins Pubs

Freedom: The Story of My Second Life. abr. ed. Malika Oufkir. Read by Edita Brychta. (Running Time: 10800 sec.). 2006. audio compact disk 24.98 (978-1-4013-8487-6(0)) Pub: Miramax Bks. Dist(s): HarperCollins Pubs

Freedom Pt. 1: A Novel of Abraham Lincoln & the Civil War. unabr. ed. William Safire. Read by Jeff Riggenbach. 15 cass. (Running Time: 44 hrs.). 1994. 95.95 (978-0-7861-0463-5(5), 1415A,B) Blckstn Audio.
Plunges the listener into the reality & drama of the American Civil War, the most critical period in the life of our nation. Based on the real people who struggled & bled for what Southerners hailed as independence, & Northerners condemned as disunion, William Safier's novel explores the first two years of this war - years that posed the question that reverberates today: How much freedom must be denied each American to protect & extend the freedom of all? Safire's towering Lincoln looms as a figure of controversy as he approaches the moment of emancipation. This unforgettable Lincoln - far-seeing, grimly humorous, harsh & devious when necessary, tortured, & above all intensely purposeful - will surprise many of his countrymen who revere the myth without understanding the man.

Freedom Pt. 2: A Novel of Abraham Lincoln & the Civil War. unabr. ed. William Safire. Read by Jeff Riggenbach. 15 cass. (Running Time: 44 hrs.). 1994. 95.95 (978-0-7861-0735-3(9), 1415A,B) Blckstn Audio.

Freedom Album. Robert A. Monroe. Read by Robert A. Monroe. (Running Time: 45 min.). (Gateway Experience - Freedom Ser.). 1989. 72.00 (978-1-56113-282-9(9)) Monroe Institute.
Freedom album for 6 cassettes.

Freedom & Bondage. unabr. ed. Read by Gayle D. Erwin. 1 cass. (Running Time: 1 hr.). 1992. 4.95 (978-1-56599-526-0(0), C-26) Yahshua Pub.

Freedom & Free Agency. Jake Garn. 6.98 (978-1-56236-708-4(0)) Pub: Aspen Bks. Dist(s): Origin Bk Sales

Freedom & Joy, Our Natural State. Swami Amar Jyoti. 1 cass. 1997. 9.95 (A-56) Truth Consciousness.
The way to Freedom & Joy, our natural inheritance. Relaxation & humility. Loving the Lord, living for Him.

Freedom & the Sacred. J. Krishnamurti. 1 cass. (Running Time: 1 hr.). (Ojai Public Talks - 1983 Ser.: No. 4). 8.50 (AJT834) Krishnamurti.
In the idyllic setting of the oak grove in Ojai, California, Krishnamurti began giving talks in 1922. Over the years, hundreds of thousands of people have heard Krishnamurti explore every aspect of our lives, his language & expression constantly changing, as he strove to communicate to each successive generation those profound truths which he had come upon, & which he maintained were accessible to all.

Freedom & Wilderness. unabr. ed. Edward Abbey. Read by Edward Abbey. 2 cass. (Running Time: 2 hrs. 52 min.). 1987. 16.95 (978-0-939643-12-7(X), NrthWrd Bks) TandN Child.
Selections from the author's books; "Desert Solitaire", "The Journey Home," "Abbey's Road," & "Down the River".

***Freedom at Midnight.** unabr. ed. Larry Collins. Read by Frederick Davidson. (Running Time: 23 hrs. 30 mins.). 2010. 44.95 (978-1-4417-4638-2(2)); audio compact disk 123.00 (978-1-4417-4635-1(8)) Blckstn Audio.

Freedom at Midnight. unabr. ed. Larry Collins & Dominique Lapierre. Read by Frederick Davidson. 16 cass. (Running Time: 23 hrs. 30 mins.). 1993. 99.95 set. (978-0-7861-0409-3(0), 1361) Blckstn Audio.
The subject of this book is the eclipse of the British Raj & the birth of an independent India & Pakistan; the violent transformation of that fabled India - the land of maharajas with their palaces, vices, jewels & harems, their gold-caparisoned elephants & their glittering private armies; the India of Kipling's army, with its centuries of legendary heroism, its skirmishes along the Khyber Pass & the Northwest Frontier against the fiercest warriors on the globe, the Pathans, its young British officers commanding troops of a dozen races & religions & castes; the India of tiger hunts & pigsticking, of polo & memsahibs, of dazzling balls & luxurious clubs; the India of astrologers & sadhus, holy men & strange customs; the India that was the heart & soul of an empire - into the new India of Gandhi & Nehru, precursor of the Third World.

Freedom Exercises. Lee Harris & Story Waters. 2007. audio compact disk (978-1-60546-001-7(X)) Limitlessness.

Freedom Files. 2001. audio compact disk 995.00 (978-0-9716335-4-4(1)) Intl Bus Systms.

Freedom Flight: The Origins of Mental Power. Lanny Bassham. 2 CDs. (Running Time: 2 hrs). 2003. 30.00 (978-1-934324-01-1(9)) Mental Mgmnt.

Freedom for Mothers Audio CD Set. Denise Glenn. Ed. by Delynn Halloran. Des. by Christena Ray. (ENG.). 2009. audio compact disk 29.99 (978-0-9825183-6-6(6)) Kardo Intl Min.

Freedom from Acne. Barrie Konicov. 1 cass. (YA). 11.98 (978-0-87082-320-6(5), 042) Potentials.
Explores & discusses how to eliminate waste products of the body through the organs of elimination, rather than through the pores of the skin which causes acne.

Freedom from Addiction. Read by Mary Richards. (Subliminal - Self Hypnosis Ser.). 12.95 (811) Master Your Mind.

Freedom from Addiction. Read by Mary Richards. 1 cass. (Running Time: 76 min.). (Series Two Thousand). 2007. audio compact disk 19.95 (978-1-56136-101-4(1)) Master Your Mind.

Freedom from Addiction (Hypnosis), Vol. 41. Jayne Helle. 1 cass. (Running Time: 28 min.). 1998. 15.00 (978-1-891826-40-5(9)) Introspect.
Enables one to take control of one's life, in order to regain life purpose & happiness.

Freedom from Alcohol. 1 cass. (Running Time: 60 min.). 10.95 (055) Psych Res Inst.
Eliminate alcohol use completely.

Freedom from Alcohol. Norman J. Caldwell. Read by Norman J. Caldwell. Ed. by Achieve Now Institute Staff. 1 cass. (Running Time: 20 min.). (Better Health Ser.). 1988. 9.97 (978-1-56273-049-9(5)) My Mothers Pub.
Enjoy new freedom, being your own best friend. Relax & feel good about yourself: set yourself free now!.

Freedom from Alcohol. Eldon Taylor. 1 cass. (Running Time: 62 min.). (Inner Talk Ser.). 16.95 incl. script. (978-1-55978-147-3(5), 5369C); 16.95 incl. script. (978-1-55978-244-9(7), 5369E); 16.95 incl. script. (978-1-55978-491-7(1), 5369F) Progress Aware Res.
Soundtrack - Brook with underlying subliminal affirmations.

Freedom from All Belief. abr. ed. Jiddu Krishnamurti. 1 CD. (Running Time: 1 hr. 5 mins.). (Living Life Without Conflict Ser.: Vol. 4). 2008. audio compact disk 16.95 (978-1-888004-61-8(4)) Pub: K Publications GBR. Dist(s): SCB Distributors
First of all, authority in so-called spiritual matters is really nonspiritual. I think that must be clear and must be understood deeply. There is no authority in man's endeavor to find out if there is that ultimate truth.

Freedom from Allergies. Barrie Konicov. 1 cass. (YA). 11.98 (978-0-87082-321-3(3), 043) Potentials.
Demonstrates how you can change your mind & free your body of all allergies.

Freedom from Allergies. Eldon Taylor. 1 cass. (Running Time: 62 min.). (Inner Talk Ser.). 16.95 incl. script. (978-1-55978-352-1(4), 5351A) Progress Aware Res.
Soundtrack - Tropical Lagoon with underlying subliminal affirmations.

Freedom from Allergies: Harmonies. Eldon Taylor. Read by Eldon Taylor. Ed. by Leslie Brice. 1 cass. (Running Time: 1 hr.). 1992. 16.95 (978-1-56705-207-7(X)) Gateways Inst.
Self improvement.

Freedom from Allergies: Ocean. Eldon T[illegible]r. Read by Eldon Taylor. Ed. by Leslie Brice. 1 cass. (Running Time: 1 [illegible] 992. 16.95 (978-1-56705-208-4(8)) Gateways Ins[illegible]

Freedom from Allergies: Pastoral Themes. Eldon Taylor. 1 cass. 16.95 (978-1-55978-577-8(2), 5351M) Progress Aware Res.

Freedom from Arthritis. Eldon Taylor. 1 cass. (Running Time: 62 min.). (Inner Talk Ser.). 16.95 (978-1-55978-317-0(6), 5377A) Progress Aware Res.
Ocean with underlying subliminal affirmations.

Freedom from Arthritis: Babbling Brook. Eldon Taylor. 1 cass. 16.95 (978-1-55978-497-9(0), 5377F) Progress Aware Res.

Freedom from Arthritis: Music Theme. Eldon Taylor. 1 cass. 16.95 (978-0-940699-16-8(8), 5377C) Progress Aware Res.

Freedom from Back Pain. Eldon Taylor. 1 CD. (Running Time: 52 min.). (Whole Brain Innertalk Ser.). 1998. audio compact disk (978-1-55978-863-2(1)) Progress Aware Res.

Freedom from Back Pain. Eldon Taylor. 1 CD. (Running Time: 52 min.). (Whole Brain Innertalk Ser.). 1999. audio compact disk (978-1-55978-911-0(5)); audio compact disk (978-1-55978-910-3(7)) Progress Aware Res.

Freedom from Back Pain: The Mensendieck System. Karen A. Perlroth. 1 cass. (Running Time: 55 min.). 10.95 (978-1-880688-05-2(0)) New Life Opt.

Freedom from Bedwetting: Soundtrack: Leisure Listening. Eldon Taylor. 1 cass. (Running Time: 62 min.). 16.95 (978-0-940699-34-2(6), 5323B) Progress Aware Res.
Musical soundtrack with underlying subliminal affirmations.

Freedom from Bedwetting: Soundtrack: Musical Themes. Eldon Taylor. 1 cass. (Running Time: 62 min.). 16.95 incl. script. (978-0-940699-35-9(4), 5323C) Progress Aware Res.

Freedom from Bedwetting: Soundtrack: Synthesized Moments. Eldon Taylor. 1 cass. (Running Time: 62 min.). 16.95 (978-0-940699-66-3(4), 5323D) Progress Aware Res.

Freedom from Burnout: Babbling Brook. Eldon Taylor. 1 cass. 16.95 (978-1-55978-466-5(0), 5317F) Progress Aware Res.

Freedom from Burnout: Classic. Eldon Taylor. Read by Eldon Taylor. Ed. by Leslie Brice. 1 cass. (Running Time: 1 hr.). 1992. 16.95 (978-1-56705-209-1(6)) Gateways Inst.
Self improvement.

Freedom from Burnout: Harmonies. Eldon Taylor. Read by Eldon Taylor. Ed. by Leslie Brice. 1 cass. (Running Time: 1 hr.). 1992. 16.95 (978-1-56705-210-7(X)) Gateways Inst.

Freedom from Burnout: Ocean. Eldon Taylor. Read by Eldon Taylor. Ed. by Leslie Brice. 1 cass. (Running Time: 1 hr.). 1992. 16.95 (978-1-56705-305-0(X)) Gateways Inst.

Freedom from Burnout: Soundtrack: Leisure Listening. Eldon Taylor. 1 cass. (Running Time: 62 min.). 16.95 (978-0-940699-48-9(6), 5317B) Progress Aware Res.
Musical soundtrack with underlying subliminal affirmations.

Freedom from Burnout: Soundtrack: Musical Themes. Eldon Taylor. 1 cass. (Running Time: 62 min.). 16.95 incl. script. (978-0-940699-49-6(4), 5317C) Progress Aware Res.

Freedom from Burnout: Soundtrack: Synthesized Moments. Eldon Taylor. 1 cass. (Running Time: 62 min.). 16.95 (978-0-940699-68-7(0), 5317D) Progress Aware Res.

Freedom from Burnout: Soundtrack: Tropical Lagoon. Eldon Taylor. 1 cass. (Running Time: 62 min.). 16.95 (978-0-940699-69-4(9), 5317A) Progress Aware Res.
Environmental soundtrack with underlying subliminal affirmations.

Freedom from Burnout: Stream. Eldon Taylor. Read by Eldon Taylor. Ed. by Leslie Brice. 1 cass. (Running Time: 1 hr.). 1992. 16.95 (978-1-56705-211-4(8)) Gateways Inst.
Self improvement.

Freedom from Chronic Pain. Michael P. Kelly. 1 cass. 1992. 14.95 (978-1-883700-11-9(6)) ThoughtForms.
Self help.

Freedom from Co-Dependence: Echotech. Eldon Taylor. Read by Eldon Taylor. Ed. by Leslie Brice. 1 cass. (Running Time: 1 hr.). 1992. 19.95 (978-1-56705-000-4(X)) Gateways Inst.
Self improvement.

Freedom from Codependency - How to Make the Best Choices. Robert E. Griswold. Read by Robert E. Griswold. 1 cass. (Super Strength Ser.). 1996. 10.95 (978-1-55848-321-7(7)) EffectiveMN.
Side One: The program will benefit both you & your loved ones by helping you to let go, take care of yourself, & enjoy a happier, more fulfilling life. Side Two: You'll gain self-esteem & the confidence needed for better personal & business decisions with the step-by-step instructions on this relaxing program.

Freedom from Dental Anxiety. unabr. ed. Leonard G. Horowitz. Read by Leonard G. Horowitz. 2 cass. (Running Time: 2 hrs. 45 min.). (Freedom from Ser.). 1988. pap. bk. 19.95; 19.95 Tetrahedron Pub.
This package contains all you need to conquer chronic, intense & debilitating dental fears at an extremely affordable price.

Freedom from Dental Anxiety: The Geometry of Being - Geometry in Motion. Eldon Taylor. Directed By Eldon Taylor. 1 cass. (Running Time: 60 min.). (Sacred Geometry Ser.). 1997. cass. & video 39.95 (978-1-55978-669-0(8), V107) Progress Aware Res.
Geometry in motion developing from fractals, forming mandalas, absolutely mesmerizing with tones & frequencies.

Freedom from Desk Job Stress. Leonard G. Horowitz & Mary Lynn Pulley. 1 cass. (Running Time: 90 min.). 1989. 14.95 incl. bklt. Tetrahedron Pub.
Provides vital information & training to improve the total health & safety of people who earn a living operating computers & other desktop technologies.

Freedom from Drugs: Eliminate Addiction. Barrie Konicov. 1 cass. 11.98 (978-0-87082-322-0(1), 044) Potentials.
Reveals how hypnosis can free you from the physical, mental & emotional dependency on drugs.

Freedom from Fear. 2002. 24.95 (978-1-58557-047-8(8)) Dynamic Growth.

Freedom from Fear. Kenneth Copeland. 4 cass. 1982. bk. 20.00 Set incl. study guide. (978-0-938458-34-0(5)) K Copeland Pubns.
How to overcome fear.

Freedom from Fear. Swami Amar Jyoti. 1 cass. 1984. 9.95 (R-63) Truth Consciousness.
The Ghost of fear. Confronting mental limitations, crossing over fear. What do we know about God?.

Freedom from Fear: Meditation Scriptures on the Biblical Promises for Freedom from Fear. Excerpts. Compiled by Steven B. Stevens. Voice by Steven B. Stevens. Engineer Thomas A. Webb. Executive Producer Thomas A. Webb. 1 CD. (Running Time: 32 mins). (Promises for Life Ser.). 2005. audio compact disk 14.95 (978-0-9726363-3-9(1), CD-113, Promises for Life) Brite Bks.
Selected meditation scriptures focused on Bible Promises for Freedom From Fear. Un-unabridged, non-commentary, non-denominational audio reading of like topic bible promises from multiple translations all on the subject of Freedom From Fear.

***Freedom from Fear: The American People in Depression & War, 1929-1945.** unabr. ed. David M. Kennedy. Read by Tom Weiner. (Running Time: 33 hrs. 30 mins.). 2010. 59.95 (978-1-4417-6162-0(4)); 89.95 (978-1-4417-0079-7(X)); 89.95 (978-1-4417-6159-0(4)); audio compact disk 160.00 (978-1-4417-6160-6(8)) Blckstn Audio.

Freedom from Fear: 11 Cor. 3:17. Ed Young. (J). 1980. 4.95 (978-0-7417-1126-7(5), A0126) Win Walk.

Freedom from Fear & Anger: The Geometry of Being - Geometry in Motion. Eldon Taylor. Directed By Eldon Taylor. 1 cass. (Running Time: 30 min.). (Sacred Geometry Ser.). 1997. cass. & video 29.95 (978-1-55978-694-2(9), V101) Progress Aware Res.
Geometry in motion developing from fractals, forming mandalas, absolutely mesmerizing with tones & frequencies.

Freedom from Fears: Babbling Brook. Eldon Taylor. 1 cass. 16.95 (978-1-55978-465-8(2), 5316F) Progress Aware Res.

Freedom from Fears: Classic. Eldon Taylor. Read by Eldon Taylor. Ed. by Leslie Brice. 1 cass. (Running Time: 1 hr.). 1992. 16.95 (978-1-56705-094-3(8)) Gateways Inst.
Self improvement.

Freedom from Fears: Easy. Eldon Taylor. Read by Eldon Taylor. Ed. by Leslie Brice. 1 cass. (Running Time: 1 hr.). 1992. 16.95 (978-1-56705-095-0(6)) Gateways Inst.

Freedom from Fears: Harmonies. Eldon Taylor. Read by Eldon Taylor. Ed. by Leslie Brice. 1 cass. (Running Time: 1 hr.). 1992. 16.95 (978-1-56705-096-7(4)) Gateways Inst.

Freedom from Fears: Ocean. Eldon Taylor. Read by Eldon Taylor. Ed. by Leslie Brice. 1 cass. (Running Time: 1 hr.). 1992. 16.95 (978-1-56705-097-4(2)) Gateways Inst.

Freedom from Fears: Soundtrack: Leisure Listening. Eldon Taylor. 1 cass. (Running Time: 62 min.). 16.95 (978-0-940699-26-7(5), 5316B) Progress Aware Res.
Musical soundtrack with underlying subliminal affirmations.

Freedom from Fears: Soundtrack: Musical Themes. Eldon Taylor. 1 cass. (Running Time: 62 min.). 16.95 incl. script. (978-0-940699-27-4(3), 5316C) Progress Aware Res.

Freedom from Fears: Soundtrack: Synthesized Moments. Eldon Taylor. 1 cass. (Running Time: 62 min.). 16.95 (978-0-940699-78-6(8), 5316D) Progress Aware Res.

Freedom from Fears: Soundtrack: Tropical Lagoon. Eldon Taylor. 1 cass. (Running Time: 62 min.). 16.95 (978-0-940699-79-3(6), 5316A) Progress Aware Res.
Environmental soundtrack with underlying subliminal affirmations.

Freedom from Fears: Stream. Eldon Taylor. Read by Eldon Taylor. Ed. by Leslie Brice. 1 cass. (Running Time: 1 hr.). 1992. 16.95 (978-1-56705-098-1(0)) Gateways Inst.
Self improvement.

Freedom from Gambling: Music Theme. Eldon Taylor. 1 cass. 16.95 (978-0-940699-56-4(7), 5332C) Progress Aware Res.

Freedom from Guilt. 1 CD. 1980. audio compact disk 19.98 (978-1-56001-700-4(7)) Potentials.
Worry is unproductive and quite unnecessary. This program will teach you how to turn your mind toward peaceful, harmonious thoughts.The self-hypnosis is on track 1 and the subliminal is on track 2. The easy-listening music of the subliminal, together with the self-hypnosis, is the original format which most people love and with which they are most familiar.

Freedom from Guilt. Barrie Konicov. 1 cass. 11.98 (978-0-87082-323-7(X), 045) Potentials.
Discusses how guilt can influence every part of your life & how it will remain until you willingly release it.

Freedom from Hair Loss. Eldon Taylor. 1 cass. (Running Time: 62 min.). (Inner Talk Ser.). 16.95 (978-1-55978-158-9(0), 5384N) Progress Aware Res.
Soundtrack - Contemporary Moments with underlying subliminal affirmations.

Freedom from Hair Loss: Ocean. Eldon Taylor. Read by Eldon Taylor. Ed. by Leslie Brice. 1 cass. (Running Time: 1 hr.). 1992. 16.95 (978-1-56705-306-7(8)) Gateways Inst.
Self improvement.

Freedom from Hangups. Swami Amar Jyoti. 1 cass. 1979. 9.95 (C-19) Truth Consciousness.
Clearing our psychological hang-ups & joyfully giving up to God.

Freedom from Headaches. unabr. ed. Leonard G. Horowitz. Read by Leonard G. Horowitz. 1 cass. (Running Time: 1 hr. 30 min.). (Freedom from Ser.). 1988. bk. 14.95 (978-0-9609386-4-3(8)) Tetrahedron Pub.
Provides a complete selfcare program to help diagnose, treat, & prevent migraine & tension headaches using a multidisciplinary approach.

Freedom from Insecurity & Inferiority. Gary V. Whetstone. 6 cass. (Running Time: 9 hrs.). (Freedom Ser.). 1993. pap. bk. 50.00 (978-1-58866-214-9(4), VROO4A) Gary Whet Pub.
Do you struggle with insecurities & feelings of inferiority? Do the memories of your past seem to limit your future potential?.

Freedom from Insomnia - Overcoming Worry. Robert E. Griswold. Read by Robert E. Griswold. 1 cass. (Super Strength Ser.). 1993. 10.95 (978-1-55848-312-5(8)) EffectiveMN.
Two complete non-subliminal programs to help let go of worries & fall asleep effortless.

Freedom from Jealousy (Subliminal & Hypnosis), Vol. 39. Jayne Helle. 1 cass. (Running Time: 56 min. per cass.). 1998. 15.00 (978-1-891826-38-2(7)) Introspect.
Have faith from fear, learn to trust, you have chosen someone who is kind & sensitive to your needs.

Freedom from Junk Food. Eldon Taylor. 1 cass. (Running Time: 62 min.). (Inner Talk Ser.). 16.95 incl. script. (978-1-55978-470-2(9), 5325F) Progress Aware Res.
Soundtrack - Book with underlying subliminal affirma tions.

Freedom from Junk Food: Classic. Eldon Taylor. Read by Eldon Taylor. Ed. by Leslie Brice. 1 cass. (Running Time: 1 hr.). 1992. 16.95 (978-1-56705-105-6(7)) Gateways Inst.
Self improvement.

Freedom from Junk Food: Easy. Eldon Taylor. Read by Eldon Taylor. Ed. by Leslie Brice. 1 cass. (Running Time: 1 hr.). 1992. 16.95 (978-1-56705-106-3(5)) Gateways Inst.

Freedom from Junk Food: Harmonies. Eldon Taylor. Read by Eldon Taylor. Ed. by Leslie Brice. 1 cass. (Running Time: 1 hr.). 1992. 16.95 (978-1-56705-107-0(3)) Gateways Inst.

Freedom from Junk Food: Music Theme. Eldon Taylor. 1 cass. 16.95 (978-1-55978-111-4(4), 5325C) Progress Aware Res.

Freedom from Junk Food: Ocean. Eldon Taylor. Read by Eldon Taylor. Ed. by Leslie Brice. 1 cass. (Running Time: 1 hr.). 1992. 16.95 (978-1-56705-108-7(1)) Gateways Inst.

Freedom from Junk Food: Stream. Eldon Taylor. Read by Eldon Taylor. Ed. by Leslie Brice. 1 cass. (Running Time: 1 hr.). 1992. 16.95 (978-1-56705-109-4(X)) Gateways Inst.

Freedom from Legalism. Speeches. Joel Osteen. 1 Cass. (Running Time: 30 Mins.). 2002. 6.00 (978-1-59349-155-0(7), Ja0155) J Osteen.

Freedom from Manipulation. Speeches. Tim N. Enloe. 2 CDs. 2004. audio compact disk 17.99 (978-0-9749739-7-5(1)) E M Pubns.
Practical teaching on how to become free from manipulation; living free from the control of Satan, others and yourself. Disc one contains, "I Bug Me." Disc two contains, "Freedom from Manipulation.".

Freedom from Nail Biting. Eldon Taylor. 1 cass. (Running Time: 62 min.). (Inner Talk Ser.). 16.95 incl. script. (978-1-55978-077-3(0), 5343C) Progress Aware Res.
Soundtrack - Musical Themes with underlying subliminal affirmations.

Freedom from Nausea: Music Theme. Eldon Taylor. 1 cass. 16.95 (978-0-940699-08-3(7), 5359C) Progress Aware Res.

Freedom from Need Domination Through Purpose Motivation. Gary V. Whetstone. 4 cass. (Running Time: 6 hrs.). (Finance Ser.). 1993. pap. bk. 35.00 (978-1-58866-235-4(7), VIOO2A) Gary Whet Pub.
All things in life are pre-programmed to work for us through His purposes. Most have recognized the pressure of needs; need has been a major motivator.

Freedom from Pain: Eliminating Tension Headaches - Eliminating Migraine Headaches. Diana Keck. Read by Diana Keck. 1 cass. 1985. 9.95 (978-0-929653-03-7(3), TAPE 201) Mntn Spirit Tapes.

Freedom from Pain: Free Yourself from Pain - Breathing Away Pain. Diana Keck. Read by Diana Keck. 1 cass. 9.95 (978-0-929653-02-0(5), TAPE 200) Mntn Spirit Tapes.

Freedom from Pain: How to Use Pain to Transform Your Life. unabr. ed. Inna Segal. Read by Inna Segal. (Running Time: 1 hr.). (ENG.). 2008. 12.98 (978-1-59659-263-6(X), GildAudio) Pub: Gildan Media. Dist(s): HachBkGrp

Freedom from Phobias. Eldon Taylor. 1 cass. (Running Time: 62 min.). (Inner Talk Ser.). 16.95 incl. script. (978-1-55978-187-9(4), 53804C) Progress Aware Res.
Soundtrack - Musical Themes with underlying subliminal affirmations.

Freedom from Phobias: Babbling Brook. Eldon Taylor. 1 cass. 16.95 (978-1-55978-520-4(9), 53804F) Progress Aware Res.

Freedom from Phobias: Ocean. Eldon Taylor. Read by Eldon Taylor. Ed. by Leslie Brice. 1 cass. (Running Time: 1 hr.). 1992. 16.95 (978-1-56705-189-6(8)) Gateways Inst.
Self improvement.

Freedom from Phobias: Stream. Eldon Taylor. Read by Eldon Taylor. Ed. by Leslie Brice. 1 cass. (Running Time: 1 hr.). 1992. 16.95 (978-1-56705-190-2(1)) Gateways Inst.

Freedom from Profanity. Eldon Taylor. 1 cass. (Running Time: 62 min.). (Inner Talk Ser.). 16.95 incl. script. (978-1-55978-075-9(4), 5339C) Progress Aware Res.
Soundtrack - Musical Themes with underlying subliminal affirmations.

Freedom from Salt. Eldon Taylor. 1 cass. (Running Time: 62 min.). (Inner Talk Ser.). 16.95 incl. script. (978-1-55978-121-3(1), 5330B) Progress Aware Res.
Soundtrack - Leisure Listening with underlying subliminal affirmations.

Freedom from Salt: Ocean. Eldon Taylor. Read by Eldon Taylor. Ed. by Leslie Brice. 1 cass. (Running Time: 1 hr.). 1992. 16.95 (978-1-56705-307-4(6)) Gateways Inst.
Self improvement.

Freedom from Sexual Guilt. Barrie Konicov. 1 cass. 11.98 (978-0-87082-324-4(8), 046) Potentials.
Until you stop tormenting yourself for past sexual conduct, the author says you will not allow yourself to enjoy the pleasures of the moment. It is time to rid yourself of past sexual guilt & go on with your life.

Freedom from Sin, Vol. 1; Romans 6. John MacArthur, Jr. 5 cass. 16.95 (20153, HarperThor) HarpC GBR.

Freedom from Sin, Vol. 2; Romans 7. John MacArthur, Jr. 4 cass. 13.95 (20157, HarperThor) HarpC GBR.

Freedom from Smoking: Live a Smoke-Free, Healthy Life. Mark Bancroft. Read by Mark Bancroft. 1 cass., bklet. (Running Time: 1 hr.). (Health & Fitness Ser.). 1999. 12.95 (978-1-58522-004-5(3), 401) EnSpire Pr.
Two complete sessions plus printed instructionmanual/guidebook. With healing music soundtrack.

Freedom from Smoking: Live a Smoke-Free, Healthy Life. Mark Bancroft. Read by Mark Bancroft. 1 CD. (Running Time: 1 hr.). (Health & Fitness Ser.). 2006. audio compact disk 20.00 CD & bklet. (978-1-58522-005-2(1)) EnSpire Pr.

Freedom from Snoring. Eldon Taylor. 1 cass. (Running Time: 62 min.). (Inner Talk Ser.). 16.95 incl. script. (978-1-55978-476-4(8), 5341F) Progress Aware Res.
Soundtrack - Babbling Brook with underlying subliminal affirmations.

Freedom from Snoring: Music Theme. Eldon Taylor. 1 cass. 16.95 (978-1-55978-074-2(6), 5341C) Progress Aware Res.

Freedom from Snoring: Stream. Eldon Taylor. Read by Eldon Taylor. Ed. by Leslie Brice. 1 cass. (Running Time: 1 hr.). 1992. 16.95 (978-1-56705-308-1(4)) Gateways Inst.
Self improvement.

Freedom from Stress. Eldon Taylor. 2 cass. (Running Time: 62 min.). (Inner Talk Ser.). 16.95 (978-0-940699-92-2(3), 5307D) Progress Aware Res.
Soundtrack - Synthesized Moments with underlying subliminal affirmations.

Freedom from Stress. Eldon Taylor. 1 CD. (Running Time: 52 min.). (Whole Brain Innertalk Ser.). 1998. audio compact disk (978-1-55978-868-7(2)) Progress Aware Res.

Freedom from Stress. Eldon Taylor. 1 CD. (Running Time: 52 min.). (Whole Brain Innertalk Ser.). 1999. audio compact disk (978-1-55978-949-3(2)) Progress Aware Res.

Freedom from Stress: Babbling Brook. Eldon Taylor. 1 cass. 16.95 (978-1-55978-456-6(3), 5307F) Progress Aware Res.

Freedom from Stress: Classic. Eldon Taylor. Read by Eldon Taylor. Ed. by Leslie Brice. 1 cass. (Running Time: 1 hr.). 1992. 16.95 (978-1-56705-057-8(3)) Gateways Inst.
Self improvement.

Freedom from Stress: Easy. Eldon Taylor. Read by Eldon Taylor. Ed. by Leslie Brice. 1 cass. (Running Time: 1 hr.). 1992. 16.95 (978-1-56705-058-5(1)) Gateways Inst.

Freedom from Stress: Ocean. Eldon Taylor. Read by Eldon Taylor. Ed. by Leslie Brice. 1 cass. (Running Time: 1 hr.). 1992. 16.95 (978-1-56705-059-2(X)) Gateways Inst.

Freedom from Stress: Soundtrack: Leisure Listening. Eldon Taylor. 1 cass. (Running Time: 62 min.). 16.95 (978-0-940699-14-4(1), 5307B) Progress Aware Res.
Musical soundtrack with underlying subliminal affirmations.

Freedom from Stress: Soundtrack: Musical Themes. Eldon Taylor. 1 cass. (Running Time: 62 min.). 16.95 incl. script. (978-0-940699-15-1(X), 5307C) Progress Aware Res.

Freedom from Stress: Stream. Eldon Taylor. Read by Eldon Taylor. Ed. by Leslie Brice. 1 cass. (Running Time: 1 hr.). 1992. 16.95 (978-1-56705-060-8(3)) Gateways Inst.
Self improvement.

Freedom from Stress: Whisper. Eldon Taylor. Read by Eldon Taylor. Ed. by Leslie Brice. 1 cass. (Running Time: 1 hr.). 1992. 16.95 (978-1-56705-204-6(5)) Gateways Inst.

Freedom from Stress & Anxiety: The Geometry of Being - Geometry in Motion. Eldon Taylor. Directed By Eldon Taylor. 1 cass. (Running Time: 30 min.). (Sacred Geometry Ser.). 1997. cass. & video 29.95 (978-1-55978-695-9(7), V102) Progress Aware Res.
Geometry in motion developing from fractals, forming mandalas, absolutely mesmerizing with tones & frequencies.

Freedom from Stress, Musical Hypnotherapy. 1000th ed. Arranged by Walter Hnot, 3rd. Compiled by Walter Hnot, Jr. 2007. 19.99 (978-0-9788297-0-4(0)) Marble Mount.

Freedom from Stuttering. Eldon Taylor. 1 cass. (Running Time: 62 min.). (Inner Talk Ser.). 16.95 incl. script. (978-1-55978-073-5(8), 5340C) Progress Aware Res.
Soundtrack - Musical Themes with underlying subliminal affirmations.

Freedom from Stuttering: Babbling Brook. Eldon Taylor. 1 cass. 16.95 (978-1-55978-475-7(X), 5340F) Progress Aware Res.

Freedom from Stuttering: Ocean. Eldon Taylor. Read by Eldon Taylor. Ed. by Leslie Brice. 1 cass. (Running Time: 1 hr.). 1992. 16.95 (978-1-56705-309-8(2)) Gateways Inst.
Self improvement.

Freedom from Substance Abuse. Eldon Taylor. 1 cass. (Running Time: 62 min.). (Inner Talk Ser.). 16.95 incl. script. (978-1-55978-469-6(5), 5324F) Progress Aware Res.
Soundtrack - Babbling Brook with underlying subliminal affirmations.

Freedom from Substance Abuse: Easy. Eldon Taylor. Read by Eldon Taylor. Ed. by Leslie Brice. 1 cass. (Running Time: 1 hr.). 1992. 16.95 (978-1-56705-102-5(2)) Gateways Inst.
Self improvement.

Freedom from Substance Abuse: Music Theme. Eldon Taylor. 1 cass. 16.95 (978-1-55978-066-7(5), 5324C) Progress Aware Res.

Freedom from Substance Abuse: Ocean. Eldon Taylor. Read by Eldon Taylor. Ed. by Leslie Brice. 1 cass. (Running Time: 1 hr.). 1992. 16.95 (978-1-56705-103-2(0)) Gateways Inst.

Freedom from Substance Abuse: Stream. Eldon Taylor. Read by Eldon Taylor. Ed. by Leslie Brice. 1 cass. (Running Time: 1 hr.). 1992. 16.95 (978-1-56705-104-9(9)) Gateways Inst.

Freedom from Sugar. Eldon Taylor. 1 cass. (Running Time: 62 min.). (Inner Talk Ser.). 16.95 incl. script. (978-1-55978-122-0(X), 5331C) Progress Aware Res.
Soundtrack - Musical Themes with underlying subliminal affirmations.

Freedom from Sugar: Ocean. Eldon Taylor. Read by Eldon Taylor. Ed. by Leslie Brice. 1 cass. (Running Time: 1 hr.). 1992. 16.95 (978-1-56705-310-4(6)) Gateways Inst.
Self improvement.

Freedom from Technophobia. Eldon Taylor. 1 CD. (Running Time: 52 min.). (Whole Brain Innertalk Ser.). 1998. audio compact disk (978-1-55978-860-1(7)) Progress Aware Res.

Freedom from Teeth Clenching & Night Grinding. Leonard G. Horowitz. 1 cass. (Running Time: 60 min.). (Freedom from Ser.). 1989. pap. bk. 14.95 incl. bklt. (978-0-9609386-8-1(0)) Tetrahedron Pub.
Designed to put you to sleep fast & work while you sleep to help stop the noisy, annoying & unhealthy habit of night grinding.

Freedom from Television. Eldon Taylor. 1 CD. (Running Time: 52 min.). (Whole Brain Innertalk Ser.). 1999. audio compact disk (978-1-55978-913-4(1)) Progress Aware Res.

Freedom from Television Addiction. Eldon Taylor. 1 CD. (Running Time: 52 min.). (Whole Brain Innertalk Ser.). 1998. audio compact disk (978-1-55978-861-8(5)) Progress Aware Res.

Freedom from the Bondage of Habit. unabr. ed. Swami Amar Jyoti. 1 cass. (Satsangs of Swami Amar Jyoti). 1997. 9.95 (978-0-933572-23-2(9), J-59) Truth Consciousness.
The Yoga paths help us in facing, admitting & clearing self-imposed habits. Fearlessness & unfoldment.

Freedom from the Known: Uranus Factor. Jeff Green. 1 cass. 8.95 (527) Am Fed Astrologers.

Freedom from the Past. John Gray. 2 cass. 1996. 17.95 Set. (978-1-886095-11-3(6)) Genesis Media Grp.

Freedom from the Past. Read by Wayne Monbleau. 3 cass. (Running Time: 4 hrs.). 1993. 15.00 Set. (978-0-944648-18-6(5), LGT-1197) Loving Grace Pubns.
Religious.

Freedom from the Self. J. Krishnamurti. 1 cass. (Running Time: 75 min.). (Brockwood Park Talks, 1983 Ser.: No. 3). 8.50 (ABT833) Krishnamurti.
Subjects examined: Is the movement from what is to what should be the psychological process of time, one of the causes of fear? Realizing that possibility, even intellectually, is it possible to end fear? Sorrow is part of the continuity of memory. Can that memory, not only of my sorrow but of mankind's sorrow, memory which is sorrow, come to an end? Can we, while living, without any cause or hope for the future, end something? If you go beyond time, is there anything to experience? Can the self, the "me", the ego, all the self-centered activity, which is the movement of memory, end?.

Freedom from Thumb Sucking. Eldon Taylor. Interview with XProgress Aware Staff & Progress Aware Staff. 1 cass. (Running Time: 62 min.). (Inner Talk Ser.). 16.95 incl. script. (978-0-940699-55-7(9), 5337C) Progress Aware Res.
Soundtrack - Musical Themes with underlying subliminal affirmations.

Freedom from TMJ. Scripts. Denise Lynch. Voice by Denise Lynch. 1 CD. 2003. audio compact disk 25.00 (978-0-9772925-9-2(2)) Clear Mind.
Audio process for the relief of symptoms associated with TMJ.

Freedom from TMJ Pain Syndrome. unabr. ed. Leonard G. Horowitz. Read by Leonard G. Horowitz. 1 cass. (Running Time: 1 hr. 30 min.). (Freedom from Ser.). 1988. bk. 29.95 (978-0-9609386-3-6(X)) Tetrahedron Pub.
Powerful awareness exercises designed to prevent pain without using drugs, & motivate lifestyle changes for lasting pain relief.

Freedom from Tooth Decay & Gum Disease: Use Your Imagination to Achieve Better Oral Hygiene & Dental Health. unabr. ed. Leonard G. Horowitz. Read by Leonard G. Horowitz. 1 cass. (Running Time: 60 min.). Dramatization. (Freedom from Ser.). 1988. 9.95 (978-0-9609386-6-7(4)) Tetrahedron Pub.

Freedom from Within. Emmett Miller. Katherine Morgenstein. (ENG.). 2009. audio compact disk 25.50 (978-1-55841-001-5(5)) Emmett E Miller.

Freedom from Worry. 2 CDs. 1982. audio compact disk 27.98 (978-1-56001-959-6(X)) Potentials.
Worry is unproductive and quite unnecessary. This program will teach you how to turn your mind toward peaceful, harmonious thoughts.This 2-CD program from our Super Consciousness series is our newest, most powerful format. On the self-hypnosis CD, SC programs have the Subliminal Persuasion soundtrack added under Barrie?s voice. And the 17th Century Baroque music on the Subliminal CD has the same beat as your body's natural rhythm, thereby allowing the suggestions to enter deeply and effortlessly.

Freedom from Worry. Shad Helmstetter. 1 cass. (Self-Talk Cassettes Ser.). 10.95 (978-0-937065-23-5(4)) Grindle Pr.

Freedom from Worry. Richard Jafolla & Mary-Alice Jafolla. Read by Richard Jafolla & Mary-Alice Jafolla. (Overcoming Ser.). 1986. 12.95 (160) Stppng Stones.
Motivational tapes that work on the subconscious mind (subliminal) & conscious mind to bring about self-improvement.

Freedom from Worry. Barrie Konicov. 1 cass. 11.98 (978-0-87082-325-1(6), 047) Potentials.
Teaches how to turn your mind to peaceful, harmonious thoughts & to forget worrying which is unproductive, unnecessary & totally useless.

Freedom from Worry. Barrie Konicov. 1 CD. 2004. audio compact disk 19.98 (978-1-56001-665-6(5)) Potentials.
Worry is unproductive and quite unnecessary. This program will teach you how to turn your mind toward peaceful, harmonious thoughts.You will find the self-hypnosis on track 1 and the subliminal on track 2. The easy-listening music of the subliminal, together with the self-hypnosis, is the original format which most people love and with which they are most familiar.

Freedom... from Your Erroneous Zones. Jack Boland. 4 cass. 1977. 34.95 (978-0-88152-004-0(7)) Master Mind.
A blending of Dr. Wayne Dyer's psychology & Jack Boland's truth principles that will show you what your mind can do to get rid of self-defeating thoughts & feelings.

Freedom from Your Past. 12 cass. (Running Time: 18 hrs.). 1998. 120.00 (978-0-00-525743-2(3)) Majestic Mda.

Freedom Highway. unabr. ed. Nigel Krauth. Read by Noel Hodda. 9 cass. (Running Time: 13 hrs. 40 mins.). 2004. 72.00 (978-1-74030-562-4(0)) Pub: Bolinda Pubng AUS. Dist(s): Lndmrk Audiobks

Freedom in Christ. Featuring Bill Winston. 3 CDs. (ENG.). 2003. audio compact disk 24.00 (978-1-59544-002-0(X)) B Winston Min.
You have a right to enjoy all of the privileges of kingdom citizenship in this life on earth. Learn your rights as a citizen of heaven and break free from oppression, depression, lack, poverty, and sickness.

Freedom in Constitutional Contract. James Buchanan. 1 cass. (Running Time: 30 min.). 1987. 9.95 (978-0-945999-11-9(9)) Independent Inst.
The Basis of Freedom under Constitutional Law, Showing That Such a System Cannot Preserve Freedom When Government Power Is Centralized.

Freedom in Romance/Power of the Feminine. Marianne Williamson. Read by Marianne Williamson. 1 cass. (Running Time: 90 mins.). (Lectures on a Course in Miracles). 1999. 10.00 (978-1-56170-196-4(3), M724) Hay House.

Freedom Is Found. unabr. ed. Kenneth G. Mills. 1 cass. (Running Time: 1 hr.). 1991. pap. bk. 10.95 (978-0-919842-12-0(7), KG0C30) Ken Mills Found.
Cassette & 36 page transcription booklet of a spontaneous lecture by philosopher, poet, musician Kenneth George Mills. The author states in the lecture "Freedom is in the ability to question what you think".

Freedom is Worth Fighting For. Tony Evans. (America Responds Ser.). 8.99 (978-1-58926-021-4(X)) Oasis Audio.

Freedom Movement. unabr. ed. Coretta Scott King. 1 cass. 1984. 12.95 (978-0-694-50248-6(0), SWC 1406) HarperCollins Pubs.

Freedom Observed. unabr. ed. Gwyn Griffin. Read by Wolfram Kandinsky. 9 cass. (Running Time: 1 hr. 30 min. per cass.). 1979. 72.00 (978-0-7366-0171-9(6), 1173) Books on Tape.
Sebangerisque is a former French colony in West Africa. It is busily imposing upon itself a domestic rule considerably more brutal than that from which it has recently escaped. We join a small group of whites traveling from one part of the country to another.

Freedom of Being Good. 2002. audio compact disk 11.95 (978-0-911203-55-4(9)) New Life.

Freedom of Consciousness. Swami Amar Jyoti. 1 cass. 1982. 9.95 (K-51) Truth Consciousness.
The way to true freedom. Conscious relaxation, simplification of life. Spiritual education, changing just one person.

***Freedom of Simplicity.** unabr. ed. Richard J. Foster. Narrated by Lloyd James. (ENG.). 2007. 14.98 (978-1-59644-522-2(X), Hovel Audio) christianaud.

Freedom of Simplicity: Finding Harmony in a Complex World. unabr. ed. Richard J. Foster. Read by Lloyd James. (Running Time: 8 hrs. 15 mins. 0 sec.). (ENG.). 2007. audio compact disk 26.98 (978-1-59644-521-5(1), Hovel Audio) christianaud.

Freedom of the Soul. Swami Amar Jyoti. 2 cass. 1979. 12.95 (Q-11) Truth Consciousness.
Increasing intensity to find freedom. The Middle Path. Temporary & eternal laws. How dogma is born. Religion in its purest form.

Freedom Riders: John Lewis & Jim Zwerg on the Front Lines of the Civil Rights Movement. unabr. ed. Ann Bausum. 2 cass. (Running Time: 1 hrs. 30 mins.). (YA). (gr. 5-9). 2008. 25.75 (978-1-4281-8683-5(2)); audio compact disk 25.75 (978-1-4281-8688-0(3)) Recorded Bks.

Freedom Road. unabr. ed. Howard Fast. Narrated by Norman Dietz. 7 cass. (Running Time: 9 hrs. 45 mins.). 1988. 60.00 (978-1-55690-188-1(7), 88350E7) Recorded Bks.
A novelistic re-creation of life in the period of reconstruction following the Civil War.

***Freedom Summer: The Savage Season That Made Mississippi Burn & Made America a Democracy.** unabr. ed. Bruce Watson. (Running Time: 13 hrs. 30 mins.). 2010. 18.99 (978-1-4001-8748-5(6)); 37.99 (978-1-4001-9748-4(1)); audio compact disk 90.99 (978-1-4001-4748-9(4)) Pub: Tantor Media. Dist(s): IngramPubServ

***Freedom Summer: The Savage Season That Made Mississippi Burn & Made America a Democracy.** unabr. ed. Bruce Watson. Narrated by David Drummond. (Running Time: 14 hrs. 30 mins. 0 sec.). 2010. 24.99 (978-1-4001-6748-7(5)); audio compact disk 37.99 (978-1-4001-1748-2(8)) Pub: Tantor Media. Dist(s): IngramPubServ

Freedom Through Higher Awareness. Wayne W. Dyer. 6 cass. (Running Time: 6 hrs.). 1994. 59.95 Set. (11230A); 59.95 incl. quote bk. (978-1-55525-040-9(8), 11230A) Nightingale-Conant.
In this enlightening program, Dr. Dyer shows you how to leave the constraints of daily awareness & realize a limitless vision. He teaches you to discard old beliefs & opinions that clutter your reality & to make space for a vibrant new energy - one that's genuinely enlightened, fully functioning & anxiety-free.

Freedom to Fly Presents: Inflight Relaxation Exercise. unabr. ed. Ralph Tassinari. Read by Ralph Tassinari. 1 cass. (Running Time: 22 min.). (In Flight Relief Ser.). 1991. 9.95 (978-1-879928-11-4(6)) Freedom to Fly.
Guided routine to bring about a relaxation response.

Freedom to Fly Presents: Inflight Relief for the Fearful Flyer. unabr. ed. Ralph Tassinari. Read by Ralph Tassinari. 2 cass. (Running Time: 47 min.). (In Flight Relief Ser.). 1991. 15.95 set. (978-1-879928-12-1(4)) Freedom to Fly.
Educational/psychological tape to help fearful flyers overcome their fear. Second tape is guided routine to bring about a relaxation response.

Freedom to Forgive: The Power to Put the Past Behind You. Guy Finley. (ENG.). 2006. 7.49 (978-1-929320-57-8(4)) Life of Learn.

Freedom to Love. Christopher West. 2005. audio compact disk 14.95 (978-1-932927-35-1(2)) Ascensn Pr.

Freedom to Love: The Role of Negation in St. John of the Cross. Daniel Chowning. 1 cass. (Running Time: 56 min.). 8.95 I C S Pubns.
Fr. Daniel Chowning, O.C.D. sets forth the constructive significance of the Carmelite Doctor's teaching on detachment & the 'nada' based on the radical call to love.

Freedom to Succeed with the Six Steps to EQ Mastery: Turn the Things You Have to Do into the Things You Love to Do. Timothy A. R. Clark. 9 CD's. (Running Time: 11 hrs. 51 mins.). 2002. audio compact disk 39.99 (978-0-9638625-3-2(7)) Mind Power.

Freedomnomics: Why the Free Market Works & Other Half-Baked Theories Don't. unabr. ed. John R. Lott, Jr. Read by Brian Emerson. (Running Time: 25200 sec.). 2007. 29.95 (978-0-7861-4950-6(7)); 54.95 (978-0-7861-6814-9(5)); audio compact disk 29.95 (978-0-7861-7005-0(0)) Blckstn Audio.

Freedomnomics: Why the Free Market Works & Other Half-Baked Theories Don't. unabr. ed. John R. Lott, Jr. Read by Brain Emerson. (Running Time: 25200 sec.). 2007. audio compact disk 29.95 (978-0-7861-5843-0(3)) Blckstn Audio.

Freedomnomics: Why the Free Market Works & Other Half-Baked Theories Don't. unabr. ed. John R. Lott, Jr. Read by Brian Emerson. (Running Time: 25200 sec.). 2007. audio compact disk 63.00 (978-0-7861-6813-2(7)) Blckstn Audio.

***Freedom's Challenge.** abr. ed. Anne McCaffrey. Read by Susie Breck & Dick Hill. (Running Time: 3 hrs.). (Freedom Ser.). 2010. audio compact disk 9.99 (978-1-4418-6271-6(4), 9781441862716, BCD Value Price) Brilliance Audio.

Freedom's Challenge. unabr. ed. Anne McCaffrey. Read by Multivoice Production Staff. 6 cass. (Running Time: 9 hrs.). (Freedom Ser.). 1998. 57.25 (978-1-56740-575-0(4), 1567405754, Unabridge Lib Edns) Brilliance Audio.
Kris Bjornsen has come a long way since alien slave ships scooped her up in Denver with thousands of others. Dropped of an apparently uninhabited world with the rest, she has fallen in love with Zainal, a renegade Catteni, and made a comfortable life for herself and her new family. But she feels a soldier's duty to escape Botany and rejoin the struggle for freedom. As the Eosi overlords continue to drop captives on Botany, the colonists learn that there are freedom fighters on every captured world, and Earth is full of pockets of resistance. There are even rebels among the warlike Catteni. Now the colonists have the technology they need to go back to war with the deadly Eosi - with a surprise strike at the enslaved planet Earth itself!.

Freedom's Challenge. unabr. ed. Anne McCaffrey. Read by Susie Breck & Dick Hill. (Running Time: 9 hrs.). (Freedom Ser.). 2007. 39.25 (978-1-4233-3016-5(1), 9781423330165, BADLE); 24.95 (978-1-4233-3015-8(3), 9781423330158, BAD); audio compact disk 39.25 (978-1-4233-3014-1(5), 9781423330141, Brlnc Audio MP3 Lib); audio compact disk 24.95 (978-1-4233-3013-4(7), 9781423330134, Brilliance MP3) Brilliance Audio.

***Freedom's Challenge.** unabr. ed. Anne McCaffrey. Read by Dick Hill & Susie Breck. (Running Time: 9 hrs.). (Freedom Ser.). 2010. audio compact disk 29.99 (978-1-4418-4031-8(1), 9781441840318) Brilliance Audio.

***Freedom's Challenge.** unabr. ed. Anne McCaffrey. Read by Susie Breck & Dick Hill. (Running Time: 9 hrs.). (Freedom Ser.). 2010. audio compact disk 89.97 (978-1-4418-4032-5(X), 9781441840325, BriAudCD Unabrid) Brilliance Audio.

Freedom's Challenge, Set. abr. ed. Anne McCaffrey. 2 cass. 1999. 17.95 (FS9-34620) Highsmith.

Freedom's Challenge, Set. unabr. ed. Anne McCaffrey. 6 cass. 1999. 73.25 (FS9-43218) Highsmith.

***Freedom's Choice.** abr. ed. Anne McCaffrey. Read by Dick Hill & Susie Breck. (Running Time: 3 hrs.). (Freedom Ser.). 2010. audio compact disk 9.99 (978-1-4418-6272-3(2), 9781441862723, BCD Value Price) Brilliance Audio.

Freedom's Choice. unabr. ed. Anne McCaffrey. Read by Susie Breck et al. 8 cass. (Running Time: 10 hrs.). (Freedom Ser.). 1997. 73.25 (978-1-56100-816-2(8), 1561008168, Unabridge Lib Edns) Brilliance Audio.
Anne McCaffrey captured the interest and hearts of many with "Freedom's Landing" as Catteni slaves unexpectedly became settlers establishing a new colony on Botany, presumably an uninhabited M-type planet. In "Freedom's Choice" the saga progresses to an extraordinary level. The shipments of Catteni slaves continue, but they find that they are enjoyably reinventing the creature comforts of home, and searching for the origin of the Farmers who were the original occupants of Botany, all under the keen eyes of two very different observers. When scouts for the Emassi come to retrieve Zainal, shanghaied in the original shipment of slaves, Botany changes irrevocably. Listeners will delight in this continued adventure of survival, romance, and ingenuity.

Freedom's Choice. unabr. ed. Anne McCaffrey. Read by Susie Breck & Dick Hill. (Running Time: 10 hrs.). (Freedom Ser.). 2007. 39.25 (978-1-4233-3020-2(X), 9781423330202, BADLE); 24.95 (978-1-4233-3019-6(6), 9781423330196, BAD); audio compact disk 39.25 (978-1-4233-3018-9(8), 9781423330189, Brlnc Audio MP3 Lib); audio compact disk 24.95 (978-1-4233-3017-2(X), 9781423330172, Brilliance MP3) Brilliance Audio.

***Freedom's Choice.** unabr. ed. Anne McCaffrey. Read by Susie Breck & Dick Hill. (Running Time: 10 hrs.). (Freedom Ser.). 2010. audio compact disk 29.99 (978-1-4418-4033-2(8), 9781441840332); audio compact disk 89.97 (978-1-4418-4034-9(6), 9781441840349, BriAudCD Unabrid) Brilliance Audio.

***Freedom's Landing.** abr. ed. Anne McCaffrey. Read by Susie Breck. (Running Time: 3 hrs.). (Freedom Ser.). 2010. audio compact disk 9.99 (978-1-4418-6273-0(0), 9781441862730, BCD Value Price) Brilliance Audio.

Freedom's Landing. unabr. ed. Anne McCaffrey. Read by Susie Breck. 8 cass. (Running Time: 11 hrs.). (Freedom Ser.). 1995. 73.25 (978-1-56100-265-8(8), 1561002658, Unabridge Lib Edns) Brilliance Audio.
It's the dawning of a new age for mankind when the Catteni descend to Earth and easily overcome the Earth's population. Thousands are herded onto slave ships headed for the intergalactic auction block. Kris Bjornsen is captured in Denver on her way to her college classes and wakes up on the primitive planet Barevi. Courageous and resourceful, she manages a single-woman escape from the Catteni and is living in the wilds of the planet when she comes to the aid of a Catteni soldier pursued by his own ranks. Recaptured together, they join forces with other slaves to outwit their captors and a hostile planetary environment. Listeners will delight in this "against-the-odds" story of survival, ingenuity and romance. As her audience has come to expect of McCaffrey, she delivers a rich and intricate science fiction adventure in "Freedom's Landing", sure to win over even more listeners and add to her legions of fans.

Freedom's Landing. unabr. ed. Anne McCaffrey. Read by Susie Breck. (Running Time: 11 hrs.). (Freedom Ser.). 2007. 39.25 (978-1-4233-3024-0(2), 9781423330240, BADLE); 24.95 (978-1-4233-3023-3(4), 9781423330233, BAD); audio compact disk 39.25 (978-1-4233-3022-6(6), 9781423330226, Brlnc Audio MP3 Lib); audio compact disk 24.95 (978-1-4233-3021-9(8), 9781423330219, Brilliance MP3) Brilliance Audio.

***Freedom's Landing.** unabr. ed. Anne McCaffrey. Read by Susie Breck. (Running Time: 11 hrs.). (Freedom Ser.). 2010. audio compact disk 29.99 (978-1-4418-4035-6(4), 9781441840356) Brilliance Audio.

***Freedom's Landing.** unabr. ed. Anne McCaffrey. Read by Susie Breck. (Running Time: 11 hrs.). (Freedom Ser.). 2010. audio compact disk 89.97 (978-1-4418-4036-3(2), 9781441840363, BriAudCD Unabrid) Brilliance Audio.

***Freedom's Ransom.** abr. ed. Anne McCaffrey. Read by Dick Hill. (Running Time: 5 hrs.). (Freedom Ser.). 2010. audio compact disk 9.99 (978-1-4418-6721-6(X), 9781441867216) Brilliance Audio.

Freedom's Ransom. unabr. ed. Anne McCaffrey. Read by Dick Hill. 6 cass. (Running Time: 8 hrs.). (Freedom Ser.: Vol. 4). 2002. 74.25 (978-1-58788-889-2(0), 1587888890, Unabridge Lib Edns); 29.95 (978-1-58788-888-5(2), 1587888882, BAU) Brilliance Audio.
When Kris Bjornsen and her fellow slaves were dumped on an uninhabited planet by the alien overlords called Catteni, there was no guarantee they would survive. Without the help of Zainal, a renegade Catteni exiled by his own people, they might all have been food for the predators of the new world. But they did survive, building a civilization and a home on the planet they named Botany. In time they were instrumental in driving the Catteni away from Earth and neighboring planets. Botany is free now, and so is the devastated Earth. The survivalist days are over, and the time has come for Botany to find its place in the power struggles of the newly configured universe. As an agricultural planet, rich in resources, Botany has more to offer than the colonists may have thought. A trip to Earth shows Kris and Zainal very dramatically how weakened the home planet is after years of Catteni domination, and how much Earth needs what Botany can give. Other worlds too have had their wealth skimmed away by the Catteni: the nearby planet of Barevi is little more than a corrupt bazaar, where bits and pieces of Earth's once powerful technology can be traded for grain and mineral ores. Earth needs food, and the resources to rebuild. Botany needs technology - from solar satellite panels to simple batteries - and, some say, the will to protect itself from being overrun by refugees who may or may not have strength and skills. As alien influence fades, the people of Botany must decide what kind of world they will become.

Freedom's Ransom. unabr. ed. Anne McCaffrey. Read by Dick Hill. 7 CDs. (Running Time: 8 hrs.). (Freedom Ser.). 2004. 39.25 (978-1-59335-450-3(9), 1593354509, Brlnc Audio MP3 Lib) Brilliance Audio.

Freedom's Ransom. unabr. ed. Anne McCaffrey. Read by Dick Hill. (Running Time: 8 hrs.). (Freedom Ser.). 2004. 39.25 (978-1-59710-310-7(1), 1597103101, BADLE); 24.95 (978-1-59710-311-4(X), 159710311X, BAD) Brilliance Audio.

***Freedom's Ransom.** unabr. ed. Anne McCaffrey. Read by Dick Hill. (Running Time: 8 hrs.). (Freedom Ser.). 2010. audio compact disk 29.99 (978-1-4418-4037-0(0), 9781441840370) Brilliance Audio.

Freedom's Ransom. unabr. ed. Anne McCaffrey. Read by Dick Hill. (Running Time: 8 hrs.). (Freedom Ser.). 2004. 24.95 (978-1-59335-098-7(8), 1593350988) Soulmate Audio Bks.

***Freedom's Ransom.** unabr. ed. Anne McCaffrey. Read by Dick Hill. (Running Time: 8 hrs.). (Freedom Ser.). 2010. audio compact disk 89.97 (978-1-4418-4038-7(9), 9781441840387, BriAudCD Unabrid) Brilliance Audio.

***Freefall.** unabr. ed. Ariela Anhalt. Read by Fred Berman. (Running Time: 7 hrs.). 2010. 39.97 (978-1-4418-8344-5(4), 9781441883445, Brlnc Audio MP3 Lib); 19.99 (978-1-4418-8343-8(6), 9781441883438, Brilliance MP3); 39.97 (978-1-4418-8345-2(2), 9781441883452, BADLE) Brilliance Audio.

***Freefall.** unabr. ed. Ariela Anhalt. Read by Fred Berman. (Running Time: 7 hrs.). (YA). 2010. audio compact disk 49.97 (978-1-4418-8342-1(8), 9781441883421, BriAudCD Unabrid); audio compact disk 19.99 (978-1-4418-8341-4(X), 9781441883414, Bril Audio CD Unabri) Brilliance Audio.

Freefall: A Sea Turtle Falls from the Sky. Lyn Littlefield Hoopes. Read by Tom Chapin. 1 cass. (Running Time: 12 min.). (Humane Society of the United States Animal Tales Ser.). (J). (gr. 1-4). 1998. pap. bk. 19.95 Incl. plush animal. (978-1-58021-043-0(0)) Benefactory.
A hungry seagull drops a newly-hatched loggerhead turtle on to the hood of a car. The hatchling, Freefall, is brought to the museum of Discovery & Science in Fort Lauderdale to heal & grow until she can be released.

Freefall: A Sea Turtle Falls from the Sky. Lyn Littlefield Hoopes & Lyn L. Hoppes. Read by Tom Chapin. 1 cass. (Running Time: 12 min.). (Humane Society of the United States Animal Tales Ser.). (J). (gr. 1-4). 1999. pap. bk. 9.95 (978-1-58021-041-6(4)) Benefactory.

***Freefall: America, Free Markets, & the Sinking of the World Economy.** unabr. ed. Joseph E. Stiglitz. Narrated by Dick Hill. (Running Time: 13 hrs. 30 mins.). 2010. 18.99 (978-1-4001-8536-8(X)); 24.99 (978-1-4001-6536-0(9)); audio compact disk 34.99 (978-1-4001-1536-5(1)); audio compact disk 69.99 (978-1-4001-4536-2(8)) Pub: Tantor Media. Dist(s): IngramPubServ

Freeing America's Farmers: The Heritage Plan for Rural Prosperity. John Frydenlund. 1995. 9.95 (978-0-614-95842-3(3)) Heritage Found.

Freeing the Female Orgasm: Awakening the Goddess. Charles Muir & Caroline Muir. 2 cass. (Running Time: 2 hrs. 20 min.). bk. 29.95 (A5764) Lghtwrks Aud & Vid.
Essential information for women, & the men who love them, on how to clear the emotional & energetic "scars" caused by Western society's negative conditioning about sexual love. The Muirs share techniques that have helped thousands of women open to their ability to have powerful, instantaneous & extended orgasms. The practices described in this audio set & accompanying 32-page illustrated book empower, youth & awaken consciousness in the woman while creating a magical bond that enables a couple to grow in love.

Freeing the Writer Within. abr. ed. Natalie Goldberg. Read by Natalie Goldberg. 1 cass. (Running Time: 90 mins.). 1988. 12.95 (978-1-880717-16-5(6)) Writers AudioShop.
The best-selling author of "Writing down the Bones" & "Wild Mind" offers a series of uniquely effective exercises for gaining real confidence in your own ability to write. With roots in Zen meditative practice, Natalie's method skips the academic & helps the writer get to the essentials.

Freeing Your Inner Child & Adolescent Selves. Ginger Chalford. 2 cass. (Metaphysical-Psychological Ser.). 1988. bk. 17.95 (978-1-56089-010-2(X)) Visionary FL.
Identify childhood & adolescent emotional patterns. In visualizations, "visiting" the past, developing a warm relationship with the inner child & adolescent self & releasing his or her problems & limiting beliefs.

Freeing Yourself from Fear. 3 CDs. 1981. audio compact disk 39.95 (978-1-55841-138-8(0)) Emmett E Miller.
Three easy-to-use cassettes to systemically desensitize fears. Awaken your own internal antidote to fears and phobias through deep relaxation, guided imagery, affirmations and breathing techniques.

Freeing Yourself from Negative Forces. Galexis. 2 cass. (Running Time: 3 hrs.). 1994. 17.95 Set. Visionary FL.
Learn to identify & handle psychic obstacles. Change course before sabotages occur. Includes meditation on Side 4.

Freeway Guide to Spicing up Your Sex Life (for Her) From Routine to Racy! Lora Somoza. Ed. by Jared Patrick. (Freeway Guides: Practical Audio for People on the Go Ser.). 2008. audio compact disk 18.95 (978-1-933754-62-8(1)) Pub: Waterside Pub CA. Dist(s): Perseus Dist

Freeway System Training: Your Road to Success Presents. Joseph Cutler. Perf. by Preston R. Scott. 2 cass. (Running Time: 2 hrs. 30 mins.). 2000. 29.00 (978-0-9702311-3-0(X)); audio compact disk 29.00 (978-0-9702311-2-3(1)) Freeway Bus Sys.
Retail sales training for services and/or products. Designed for the home business. This is done on 2 compact discs.

Freewheeling Through Ireland: Travels with My Bicycle. unabr. ed. Edward Enfield. 6 cass. (Running Time: 6 hrs. 30 mins.). 2006. 41.75 (978-1-84632-504-5(8), Clipper Audio) Recorded Bks.

Freeze Frame. Sandra D. Bricker. Narrated by Larry A. McKeever. (Mystery Ser.). (J). 2000. audio compact disk 14.95 (978-1-58659-279-0(3)) Artesian.

Freeze Frame. unabr. ed. Sandra D. Bricker. Narrated by Larry A. McKeever. 1 cass. (Running Time: 40 min.). (Take Ten Ser.). (J). 2000. 10.95 (978-1-58659-010-9(3), 54105) Artesian.

Freeze Frame. unabr. ed. Peter May. Read by Simon Vance. (Running Time: 13 hrs. 30 mins.). 2010. 29.95 (978-1-4417-2708-4(6)); 54.95 (978-1-4417-2704-6(3)); audio compact disk 76.00 (978-1-4417-2705-3(1)) Blckstn Audio.

Freight Train & Other North Carolina Folk Songs & Tunes. Perf. by Elizabeth Cotten. Anno. by Mike Seeger. 1 cass. (Running Time: 34 min.). 1989. (0-9307-400090-9307-40009-2-2); audio compact disk CD. (0-9307-40009-2-2) Smithsonian Folkways.
Includes "Oh Babe It Ain't No Lie".

French. Ed. by Berlitz Publishing Staff. (Running Time: 1 hr.). (Berlitz Rush Hour Express Ser.). (FRE & ENG.). 2004. audio compact disk 9.95 (978-981-246-594-8(4), 465944) Pub: APA Pubns Serv SGP. Dist(s): IngramPubServ

French. Created by Berlitz Publishing Staff. (Berlitz Guaranteed Ser.). (FRE & ENG., 2007. audio compact disk 19.95 (978-981-268-230-7(9)) Pub: APA Pubns Serv SGP. Dist(s): IngramPubServ

French. Ed. by Berlitz Publishing Staff. (Berlitz iPhrase Ser.). (ENG.). 2008. audio compact disk 12.95 (978-981-268-485-1(9)) Pub: APA Pubns Serv SGP. Dist(s): IngramPubServ

French. Berlitz Publishing Staff. (Berlitz for Your Trip Ser.). 2007. audio compact disk 9.95 (978-981-268-044-0(6)) Pub: Berlitz Pubng. Dist(s): Langenscheidt

French. Ed. by Berlitz Publishing Staff. 3 CDs. (ADVANCED Ser.). 2008. audio compact disk 34.95 (978-981-268-320-5(8)) Pub: Berlitz Pubng. Dist(s): Langenscheidt

French. Gaelle Graham. 1 cass. (Running Time: 60 min.). (Language Complete Course Packs Ser.). 1993. 17.95 (Passport Bks) McGraw-Hill Trade.

***French.** Kristine K. Kershul. ([i]10 minutes a day[/i][sup]R[/sup] AUDIO CD Ser.). (ENG.). 2007. audio compact disk 42.95 (978-1-931873-25-3(9)) Pub: Bilingual Bks. Dist(s): Midpt Trade

French. Rosi McNab & Collins UK Staff. Contrib. by Rosi McNab. (Running Time: 3 hrs. 0 mins. 0 sec.). (Collins Easy Learning Audio Course Ser.). (ENG.). 2009. audio compact disk 13.95 (978-0-00-727173-3(5)) Pub: HarpC GBR. Dist(s): IPG Chicago

French. Pimsleur Staff. 16 cass. (FRE.). 2000. 295.00 (978-0-671-31600-6(1), Pimsleur) S&S Audio.

French. Kim Mitzo Thompson & Karen Mitzo Hilderbrand. Arranged by Hal Wright. 1 cass. (Running Time: 90 min.). (J). 1994. pap. bk. 13.99 (978-1-57583-325-5(5), Twin 410CD); audio compact disk 12.99 (978-1-57583-302-6(6), Twin 110CD) Twin Sisters.

French. unabr. ed. Ed. by Charles Berlitz. 2 cass. (Running Time: 1 hr. 30 mins.). (Language/30 Brief Course Ser.). pap. bk. 21.95 (AF1022) J Norton Pubs.
Quick, highly condensed introduction to the words & phrases you'll need to communicate effectively in the country you're visiting. Cassettes & phrase guide book are in a vinyl album.

French. unabr. ed. Linguistics Team. Narrated by Linguistics Team. Created by Oasis Audio Staff. (Running Time: 2 hrs. 24 mins. 44 sec.). (Complete Idiot's Guide Ser.). (ENG.). 2005. audio compact disk 19.99 (978-1-59859-055-5(3)) Oasis Audio.

French. unabr. ed. Linguistics Team. Narrated by Linguistics Team. Created by Oasis Audio Staff. 2 cass. (Running Time: 3 hrs.). (Complete Idiot's Guide to Languages Ser.). (ENG & FRE.). 2005. audio compact disk 9.99 (978-1-59859-118-7(5)) Oasis Audio.

French. unabr. ed. Oasis Audio Staff & Linguistics Team. Narrated by Linguistics Team. (Complete Idiot's Guides). (ENG.). 2005. audio compact disk 39.99 (978-1-59859-061-6(8)) Oasis Audio.

French. unabr. ed. Harold Stearns. 4 cass. (Running Time: 6 hrs.). (Accent English Ser.). (FRE & ENG.). 1991. bk. 89.50 set, incl. visual aids cards. J Norton Pubs.
English as a second language instructional program.

French. 2nd ed. Rosi McNab & Collins Educational Staff. Contrib. by Rosi McNab. (Running Time: 3 hrs. 0 mins. 0 sec.). (Collins Easy Learning Audio Course Ser.). (FRE & ENG.). 2009. audio compact disk 17.95 (978-0-00-728753-6(4)) Pub: HarpC GBR. Dist(s): IPG Chicago

French. 2nd rev. ed. Howard Beckerman. Created by Langenscheidt Publishers Staff. 3 CDs. (Running Time: 1 hr.). (Rush Hour Ser.). (FRE.). 2003. audio compact disk 24.95 (978-981-246-272-5(4), 462724) Pub: Berlitz Pubng. Dist(s): Langenscheidt

French. 2nd rev. ed. Created by Berlitz Guides. (Berlitz Deluxe Language Pack Ser.). (FRE & ENG., 2008. audio compact disk 79.95 (978-981-268-404-2(2)) Pub: Berlitz Pubng. Dist(s): Langenscheidt

French. 3rd rev. ed. Created by Berlitz Publishing Staff. 3 CDs. (Berlitz Intermediate Ser.). 2008. audio compact disk 29.95 (978-981-268-407-3(7)) Pub: Berlitz Pubng. Dist(s): Langenscheidt

French, Pack. deluxe ed. Created by Berlitz Guides Staff. 12. (Berlitz Deluxe Language Ser.). (ENG & FRE., 2005. audio compact disk 79.95 (978-981-246-705-8(X), 46705X) Pub: Berlitz Pubng. Dist(s): Langenscheidt

***French, Set.** Rosi McNab. Contrib. by Rosi McNab. (Running Time: 6 hrs. 45 mins.). (Collins Easy Learning Audio Course Ser.). (FRE & ENG.). 2010. audio compact disk 24.95 (978-0-00-734777-3(4)) Pub: HarpC GBR. Dist(s): IPG Chicago

French, Vol. 1. unabr. ed. Brad Caudle & Richard Caudle. 1 cass. (Running Time: 55 min.). (Rock 'N Learn Ser.). (J). (gr. 1 up). 1993. pap. bk. 12.99 (978-1-878489-26-5(7), RL926) Rock N Learn.
Original, pop/rock music with a French Flair & educational lyrics teaches beginning French. Covers counting, colors, parts of the body, survival\travel phrases, & more. Includes Illustrated book.

French: All the French You Need to Get Started in a Simple Audio-Only Program. unabr. l.t. ed. Living Language Staff. (Living Language Ser.). (ENG.). 2008. audio compact disk 15.95 (978-1-4000-2463-6(3), LivingLang) Pub: Random Info Grp. Dist(s): Random

French: Beginning, Intermediate, Advanced. Learning Curve Series Staff. 3 cass. (Running Time: 1 hr. 16 min. per cass.). (Learning Curve). (ENG & FRE.). pap. bk. 19.99 incl. study guide. (978-0-88676-145-5(X), 49782) Metacom Inc.
Provides a way to learn the language quickly & easily. Ideal for busy people, lessons can be worked on at the individual's own pace.

French: Language 30. Educational Services Corporation Staff. 2004. audio compact disk 21.95 (978-1-931850-02-5(X)) Educ Svcs DC.

French: Language/30. rev. ed. Educational Services Corporation Staff. Intro. by Charles Berlitz. 2 cass. (FRE.). 1992. pap. bk. 21.95 (978-0-910542-59-3(7)) Educ Svcs DC.
French self-teaching language course.

French: Learn to Speak & Understand French with Pimsleur Language Programs. 2nd unabr. ed. Pimsleur. Created by Simon and Schuster Staff. 5 CDs. (Running Time: 50 hrs. 0 mins. 0 sec.). (Basic Ser.). (FRE & ENG.). 2005. audio compact disk 24.95 (978-0-7435-5067-3(6), Pimsleur) Pub: S&S Audio. Dist(s): S and S Inc

French: Speak & Read the Pimsleur Way. Pimsleur Staff. (Running Time: 7 hrs. 30 mins. 0 sec.). (Go Ser.). (ENG.). 2009. audio compact disk 29.99 (978-0-7435-9654-1(4), Pimsleur) Pub: S&S Audio. Dist(s): S and S Inc

French: Travel Pack. 2nd ed. Berlitz Publishing Staff. 1 CD. (Running Time: 1 hr. 10 mins.). (CD Pack Ser.). (FRE & ENG., 2002. pap. bk. 19.95 (978-2-8315-7847-7(7), 578477) Pub: Berlitz Pubng. Dist(s): Langenscheidt

French Level 1: Basic. 4 cass. (Learn While You Drive Ser.). (FRE.). 1995. bk. 47.95 (1513-AMR) Olivia & Hill.
Language course designed specifically for use in your car. The sentence in the foreign language is always followed by an English translation. Subjects covered: travel, shopping, ordering meals, placing telephone calls, telling time, counting money, using postal system, sightseeing, theater, arranging & attending business meetings & above all, making friends. Recorded with voices from Paris & the provinces.

French Level 2: Basic. 4 cass. (Learn While You Drive Ser.). (FRE.). 1995. bk. 44.95 (1514-AMR) Olivia & Hill.

French No. 1: Learn to Speak & Understand French with Pimsleur Language Programs. 2nd ed. Pimsleur Staff & Pimsleur. (Running Time: 400 hrs. 0 mins. NaN sec.). (Quick & Simple Ser.). (FRE, ITA & ENG.). 2002. audio compact disk 19.95 (978-0-7435-0951-0(X), Pimsleur) Pub: S&S Audio. Dist(s): S and S Inc

French Vol. 3: Advanced. 4 cass. (Learn While You Drive Ser.). (FRE.). 1995. bk. 47.95 (1515-AMR) Olivia & Hill.
Language course designed specifically for use in your car. The sentence in the foreign language is always followed by an English translation. Assumes a basic knowledge of the language. Complex sentence structure & grammar are taught within the context of practical everyday situations: conversations, newspapers, the day's events, medical problems, shopping, politics, schools, social occasions, etc.

French Vol. 4: Advanced. 4 cass. (Learn While You Drive Ser.). (FRE.). 1995. bk. 44.95 (1516-AMR) Olivia & Hill.

French - Chinese, Level 1. 1 cass. (VocabuLearn Ser.). (FRE & CHI.). 1995. pap. bk. 15.95 (978-957-9330-79-4(4)) Penton Overseas.

French Admiral. unabr. ed. Dewey Lambdin. 11 cass. (Running Time: 16 hrs. 30 min.). (Alan Lewrie Naval Adventures Ser.). 2001. 88.00 (978-0-7366-7622-9(8)) Books on Tape.

French Admiral. unabr. ed. Dewey Lambdin. 1 CD. (Running Time: 1 hr. 30 mins.). (Alan Lewrie Naval Adventures Ser.). 2001. audio compact disk 104.00 (978-0-7366-8011-0(X)) Books on Tape.

French, Alexandre Dumas Vol. 1: La Dame Aux Camelias. unabr. ed. 3 cass. 1994. 34.95 Set. (SFR420) J Norton Pubs.
Literary classic.

French, Alexandre Dumas Vol. 2: La Dame Aux Camelias. unabr. ed. 3 cass. 1994. 34.95 Set. (SFR425) J Norton Pubs.

French & Spanish Testing Kit. unabr. ed. Foreign Service Institute Staff. 1 cass. 1981. 95.00 (978-0-88432-202-3(5)) J Norton Pubs.

French Ars Antiqua. unabr. ed. 1 cass. 11.95 (C11221) J Norton Pubs.
The long-forgotten art of the Notre Dame epoch comes alive in this recording of conductus & motet.

French Basic Course Advanced Level Part A CDs & Text. 34 CDs. (Running Time: 27 hrs.). (Foreign Service Institute Basic Course Ser.). (FRE.). 2005. audio compact disk 275.00 (978-1-57970-183-3(3), AFF260D) J Norton Pubs.

French Basic Course Advanced Part B FSI CDs & Text. 23 CDs. (Running Time: 22 hrs.). (FRE.). 2005. audio compact disk 275.00 (978-1-57970-114-7(0), AFF290B) J Norton Pubs.

French Basic Course Part A FSI CDs & Text. 22 CDs. (Running Time: 15 hrs.). (FRE.). 2005. audio compact disk 225.00 (978-1-57970-113-0(2), AFF170D) J Norton Pubs.

French Basic Course Part B CDs & Text. 35 CDs. (Running Time: 25 hrs.). (Foreign Service Institute Basic Course Ser.). (FRE.). 2005. audio compact disk 245.00 (978-1-57970-185-7(X), AFF181D) J Norton Pubs.

French Bible - Genesis. Read by Charles Guillot. 4 cass. (Running Time: 6 hrs.). 1996. 12.97 (978-1-58968-048-7(0), 3020A) Chrstn Dup Intl.

French Bible - Isaiah. Read by Charles Guillot. 4 cass. (Running Time: 6 hrs.). 1996. 12.97 (978-1-58968-049-4(9), 3025A) Chrstn Dup Intl.

French Bible - Proverbs. 2nd ed. Read by Charles Guillot. 2 cass. 1996. 8.97 (978-1-58968-051-7(0), 3030A) Chrstn Dup Intl.

French Bible - Psalms. 2nd ed. Read by Charles Guillot. 4 cass. 1996. 12.97 (978-1-58968-050-0(2), 3010A) Chrstn Dup Intl.

French Blend: Celtic Music's France Odyssey. 1 cass., 1 CD. 1998. 9.98; audio compact disk 15.98 CD. Lifedance.

French Business Situations: A Spoken Language Guide. Stuart Williams & Nathalie McAndrew Cazorla. 4 cass. (Running Time: 6 hrs.). (Languages for Business Ser.). 1995. 34.95 (978-0-415-12850-6(1)) Pub: Routledge. Dist(s): Taylor and Fran
A handy reference and learning text for all those who use or need spoken French for business. It is suitable for self-study or class use.

French, Conversational: Learn to Speak & Understand French with Pimsleur Language Programs. 2nd unabr. ed. Pimsleur Staff & Pimsleur. Created by Simon and Schuster Staff. 8 CDs. (Running Time: 80 hrs. 0 mins. 0 sec.). (Instant Conversation Ser.). (FRE & ENG.). 2005. audio compact disk 49.95 (978-0-7435-5042-0(0), Pimsleur) Pub: S&S Audio. Dist(s): S and S Inc

French Culture Capsules. unabr. ed. 1 cass. (Running Time: 1 hr.). 12.95 (978-0-88432-504-8(0), CCFR01) J Norton Pubs.
The brief culture capsules recorded in English at the end of each lesson unit of the introductory courses are available as separate cassettes.

French Dirt: A Story of a Garden in the South of France. unabr. ed. Richard Goodman. Read by George Dunn. 5 CD's. (Running Time: 5 hrs. 12 mins.). 2005. audio compact disk 28.95 (978-0-9767847-0-8(X), AudioExped) Pemaquid Audio.
French Dirt by Richard Goodman is a gentle narrative about the sublime joys of gardening, and about the friendships the author developed over the course of a year in a small community in the south of France. Armchair travelers, francophiles, and gardeners alike will enjoy this memoir.

French Executioner. C. C. Humphreys. Read by C. C. Humphreys. 14 CDs. (Running Time: 14 hrs. 48 mins.). (Isis (CDs) Ser.). (J). 2004. audio compact disk 104.95 (978-0-7531-2280-8(4)) Pub: ISIS Lrg Prnt GBR. Dist(s): Ulverscroft US

French Executioner. unabr. ed. C. C. Humphreys. Read by C. C. Humphreys. 12 cass. (Running Time: 14 hrs. 50 mins.). (Isis Cassettes Ser.). (J). 2004. 94.95 (978-0-7531-1938-9(2)) Pub: ISIS Lrg Prnt GBR. Dist(s): Ulverscroft US

French Experience Kit: A Self-Guided Course of Beginners Learning. Marie-Therese Bougard et al. 4 cass. (Running Time: 300 min.). (Self - Guided Language... Ser.). (FRE.). 2003. pap. bk. 49.95 (978-0-8442-1759-8(X), 1759X, Contemporary) Pub: McGraw-Hill Trade. Dist(s): McGraw

French Folk Songs. unabr. ed. Colette Crosnier. 2 cass. (Running Time: 35 mins. per cass.). (FRE & ENG.). 1992. pap. bk. 29.95 set incl. 64p. bklet. (978-0-88432-493-5(1), SFR305) J Norton Pubs.
Songs have always been a traditional part of French culture: "En France, tout finit par des chansons." Twenty-eight unusual folk songs have been recorded in this unique, new collection. There are songs from the provinces, rounds, canons, marching songs, sea chanteys, satirical tunes, & love ballads that recount happy or sad stories. The booklet contains historical notes, French lyrics & English translations.

French Folk Songs: CDs & Book. Perf. by Colette Crosnier. Compiled by Colette Crosnier. 2 CDs. (Running Time: 72 mins.). (FRE.). 2006. audio compact disk 29.95 (978-1-57970-383-7(6), SFR305D, Audio-For) J Norton Pubs.
28 folk songs have been recorded: rounds, canons, marching songs, sea chanteys, satirical tunes, and love ballads.

French for Arabic Speakers see Francais pour Arabophones

French for Beginners: Passport's Language Guides. Passport Books Staff. (Passport's Languages for Beginners Ser.). (J). 1999. pap. bk. 12.95 (978-0-8442-1624-9(0), 16240, Passport Bks) McGraw-Hill Trade.

French for Business. unabr. ed. Anita Linke. 8 cass. (Running Time: 6 hrs.). 1989. pap. bk. 225.00 (978-0-88432-267-2(X), SFR225) J Norton Pubs.
Low-intermediate level program designed to teach those who plan to do business in France the most necessary words, phrases & concepts such as negotiating a deal, marketing & advertising, visiting a subsidiary, making phone calls, responding to customer letters, etc.

French for Dummies. unabr. ed. Zoe Erotopoulos. Read by Becky Wilmes & Marcel Theboul. (YA). 2008. 34.99 (978-1-60514-576-1(9)) Find a World.

French for Dummies, Set. Zoe Erotopoulos. (FRE & ENG.). 2007. audio compact disk 19.99 (978-0-470-09587-4(3), For Dummies) Wiley US.

French for Kids: And the Whole Family. Pamela Rand. Perf. by Christians Lelaure. Illus. by Lynn M. Coleman. Intro. by Ivan Barzakov. 2 cass. (Running Time: 1 hr.). Orig. Title: French for Tots. (J). (ps-6). 1988. pap. bk., act. bk. ed., instr.'s planning gde. ed. 19.95 (978-1-878245-02-1(3)) OptimaLearning.
Original songs & lively conversations by native speakers. Based on renown OptimaLearning method. Course is highly motivational for children & whole family.

French for Speakers of English: Level 1. rev. ed. 16 cass. (Running Time: 15 hrs.). (Pimsleur Tapes Ser.). (FRE.). 1996. 345.00 set. (18105, Pimsleur) S&S Audio.
Spoken foreign-language proficiency training. Thirty, half-hour, intensive, spoken-language lesson units to be completed at the rate of one lesson per day for 30 days. By achieving eighty-percent correct answers to the questions in each unit, the Pimsleur Spoken Language Programmed Instructional Method will enable the learner to achieve the ACTFL Intermediate-Low Spoken Proficiency Levle.

French for Speakers of English: Level 2. 2nd ed. 16 cass. (Running Time: 15 hrs.). (Pimsleur Tapes Ser.). (FRE.). 1996. 345.00 set. (18126, Pimsleur) S&S Audio.
An additional thirty-lesson unit program, accomplished at the same rate as a Pimsleur I. Will enable the learner to achieve the ACTFL Intermediate-Mid Spoken Proficiency Level.

French for Speakers of English: Level 3. unabr. ed. 16 cass. (Running Time: 15 hrs.). (Pimsleur Tapes Ser.). (FRE.). 1995. 345.00 set. (18175, Pimsleur) S&S Audio.
An additional thirty-lesson-unit program, for a total of ninety lesson units. Will allow the learner to achieve the ACTFL Intermediate-High Spoken Proficiency Level.

French for Starters. Edith Baer et al. 2 cass. (ENG.). 1986. 53.00 (978-0-521-24883-9(3)) Cambridge U Pr.

French for Tots see French for Kids: And the Whole Family

French Fries: II Cor 9:6-15. Ed Young. 1992. 4.95 (978-0-7417-1910-2(X), 910) Win Walk.

French Genesis. Catherine Guillot. 4 cass. (Running Time: 6 hrs.). (FRE.). 1994. 12.98 (978-7-902032-80-3(8)) Chrstn Dup Intl.

French, George Sand: LaPetite Fadette. unabr. ed. 4 cass. 1994. 39.95 (SFR410) J Norton Pubs.
Literary classic.

French, Gustave Flaubert Vol. 1: Madame Bovary. unabr. ed. 4 cass. 1994. 39.95 Set. (SFR430) J Norton Pubs.

French, Gustave Flaubert Vol. 2: Madame Bovary. unabr. ed. 4 cass. 1994. 39.95 Set. (SFR435) J Norton Pubs.

French, Guy de Maupassant: Le Horla. unabr. ed. 1 cass. 1994. 15.95 (SFR400) J Norton Pubs.

French I, Set. Paul Pimsleur. 16 cass. (Pimsleur Language Learning Ser.). 1996. pap. bk. & stu. ed. 345.00 Incl. study guide. (0671-52153-5) SyberVision.

French I: Learn to Speak & Understand French with Pimsleur Language Programs. 2nd rev. ed. Pimsleur Staff. 16 CDs. (Running Time: 160 hrs. 0 mins. 0 sec.). (Comprehensive Ser.). (ENG.). 2002. audio compact disk 345.00 (978-0-7435-1834-5(9), Pimsleur) Pub: S&S Audio. Dist(s): S and S Inc

French I Basic. Paul Pimsleur. 8 lessons on 4 cass. (Pimsleur Language Learning Ser.). 1995. 29.95 (52162-1) SyberVision.

French II. unabr. ed. 16 cass. 2001. 295.00 (978-0-7435-0023-4(7), Pimsleur) S&S Audio.

French II, Set. Paul Pimsleur. 16 cass. (Pimsleur Language Learning Ser.). 1996. pap. bk. & stu. ed. 345.00 (0671-57072-2) SyberVision.

French II: Learn to Speak & Understand French with Pimsleur Language Programs. 3rd ed. Pimsleur Staff & Pimsleur. 30 Cass. (Running Time: 160 hrs. 0 mins. 0 sec.). (Comprehensive Ser.). (ENG.). 2004. audio compact disk 345.00 (978-0-7435-0621-2(9), Pimsleur) Pub: S&S Audio. Dist(s): S and S Inc

French III, Set. Paul Pimsleur. 16 cass. (Pimsleur Language Learning Ser.). 1996. pap. bk. & stu. ed. 345.00 (0671-57922-3) SyberVision.

French III: Learn to Speak & Understand French with Pimsleur Language Programs. 2nd unabr. ed. Pimsleur Staff. (Running Time: 160 hrs. 0 mins. 0 sec.). (Comprehensive Ser.). (ENG.). 2004. audio compact disk 345.00 (978-0-7435-2875-7(1), Pimsleur) Pub: S&S Audio. Dist(s): S and S Inc

French in a Minute. Cimino. 1 cass. (Language in a Minute Cassette Ser.). 1990. 5.95 (978-0-943351-14-8(6), XC1001) Cimino Pub Grp.
Feel at home in any foreign country with these 101 esssential words & phrases. Hear each word introduced in English, hear them pronounced by a Voice of America instructor. Practice at your own pace, you can check yourself with the wallet sized dictionary included.

French in Action Pt. 1: A Beginning Course in Language & Culture. 2nd ed. Pierre J. Capretz. (ENG.). 2003. audio compact disk 210.00 (978-0-300-10136-2(8)) Yale U Pr.

French in 30 Days. 2nd rev. abr. ed. Created by Berlitz Guides. (Berlitz in 30 Days Ser.). 2007. audio compact disk 19.95 (978-981-268-219-2(8)) Pub: APA Pubns Serv SGP. Dist(s): Langenscheidt

French Indispensables. unabr. ed. 1 cass. (Running Time: 25 min.). 1996. 11.95 (978-0-88432-948-0(8), CFR104) J Norton Pubs.
50 useful phrases for foreign travel.

French Isaiah. Catherine Guillot. 4 cass. (Running Time: 6 hrs.). (FRE.). 1994. 12.98 (978-7-902032-87-2(5)) Chrstn Dup Intl.

French Language. 2005. 44.99 (978-1-59895-001-4(0)) Find a World.

***French Lessons: A Novel.** unabr. ed. Ellen Sussman. (Running Time: 6 hrs.). (ENG.). 2011. audio compact disk 30.00 (978-0-307-93227-3(3), Random AudioBks) Pub: Random Audio Pubg. Dist(s): Random

French Lessons: Adventures with Knife, Fork & Corkscrew. unabr. ed. Peter Mayle. 4 cass. (Running Time: 6 hrs.). 2001. 32.00 (978-0-7366-6827-9(6)) Books on Tape.
A joyous exploration and celebration of the infinite gastronomic pleasure of France.

***French Lieutenant's Woman.** John Fowles. Narrated by Paul Shelley. (Running Time: 17 hrs. 0 mins. 0 sec.). (ENG.). 2011. audio compact disk 29.95 (978-1-60998-190-7(1)) Pub: AudioGO. Dist(s): Perseus Dist

French Lieutenant's Woman. abr. ed. John Fowles. Read by Jeremy Irons. 2 cass. (Running Time: 3 hrs.). 2000. 15.95 (978-0-945353-20-1(0), M20320) Pub: Audio Partners. Dist(s): PerseuPGW
A tale set in Victorian times with Victorian morality & the devastation of a woman who is marked.

French Lieutenant's Woman. unabr. ed. John Fowles. Read by Paul Shelley. 14 CDs. (Running Time: 21 hrs.). 2002. audio compact disk 115.95 (978-0-7540-5465-8(9), CCD 156) AudioGO.
At Lyme Regis on the Dorset coast, a young Victorian amateur paleontologist, Charles Smithson, is struck by a solitary figure standing at the far end of the Cobb, staring out to sea. It is Sarah Woodruff, known to the locals as "poor tragedy" because of her apparent liaison with a French sailor who has since deserted her. Although Charles is already engaged to a young heiress, he is immediately beguiled and eventually infatuated by Sarah.

French Music for Guitar. Bill Piburn. 1999. pap. bk. 24.95 (978-0-7866-3824-6(9), 97064BCD) Mel Bay.

French New Testament. Narrated by Charles Guillot. 16 cass. (Running Time: 24 hrs.). (FRE.). 1994. 39.98 (978-7-902032-66-7(2)) Chrstn Dup Intl.

French New Testament Bible on Cassette (Spoken Word) Segond Version, 16 Cassettes. Read by Charles Guillot. 16 cass. 1996. 39.97 (978-1-58968-047-0(2), 3001A) Chrstn Dup Intl.

French Now. Christopher Kendris. 1997. 19.95 Barron.

French on the Go. 2nd unabr. ed. Annie Heminway. 2 CDs. (Running Time: 3 hrs.). (On the Go Ser.). 2001. 14.95 (978-0-7641-7348-6(0)) Barron.
Foreign language-learning series features updated dialogue that closely reflect the contemporary scene in France and French-speaking countries. Programs use cassette tapes to emphasize emementary speaking and listening comprehension in target language.

French on the Go, Set. Tessa Krailing. 2 cass. (Languages on the Go Ser.). (FRE.). 1992. bk. 14.95 (978-0-8120-7832-9(2)) Barron.

French on the Go: A Level One Language Program. 3rd ed. Anne Heminway. (On the Go/Level 1 Ser.). (ENG & FRE., 2004. bk. 16.95 (978-0-7641-7755-2(9)) Barron.

French on the Move: The Lively Audio Language Program for Busy People. rev. ed. Jane Wightwick. (ENG & FRE.). 2003. 16.95 (978-0-07-141347-3(2), 0071413472) McGraw.

French on the Road: Level 2. Annie Heminway. 2 cass. (Running Time: 3 hrs.). (Languages on the Road Ser.). (ENG & FRE.). 1992. bk. 11.95 incl. script set. (978-0-8120-7939-5(6)) Barron.
Designed for busy people who possess basic language skills, here are lively, interesting conversations on tape with practically no English coaching at all. Each package offers a twin track stereo system on tape. One track presents the language without English interruptions, while the other track features an English narrator to help students. Timed pauses let listeners repeat what they've heard. The spoken word is stressed without the use of a textbook, so listeners can learn in the car or while doing chores.

French Phonology Audio Cassettes & Text. unabr. ed. Foreign Service Institute Staff. 8 cass. (Running Time: 10 hrs.). (FRE.). (YA). (gr. 10-12). 1967. pap. bk. 195.00 (978-0-88432-032-6(4), AFF250) J Norton Pubs.
Designed to help you sound as much as possible like a native-born speaker of the language. Although this program may be used at any stage of learning, it is especially valuable for those who already have a technical mastery of the language. Includes manual.

French Phonology FSI CDs, text & Manual. 12 CDs. (Running Time: 10 hrs.). (FRE.). 2005. audio compact disk 195.00 (978-1-57970-115-4(9), AFF250D) J Norton Pubs.

French Phrase Book Pack. Collins Publishers Staff. (ENG & FRE.). 2003. pap. bk. 13.99 (978-0-00-765100-9(7)) Pub: HarpC GBR. Dist(s): Trafalgar

French Phrasebook & Dictionary Tape Pack. 16.99 (978-0-00-472141-5(1), HarperSport) Pub: HarpC GBR. Dist(s): Trafalgar

French Plus: Learn to Speak & Understand French with Pimsleur Language Programs. Pimsleur Staff & Pimsleur. Created by Simon and Schuster Audio Staff. (Running Time: 5 hrs. 0 mins. 0 sec.). (Compact Ser.). (ENG.). 2008. audio compact disk 115.00 (978-0-7435-7163-0(0), Pimsleur) Pub: S&S Audio. Dist(s): S and S Inc

French Powder Mystery. unabr. ed. Ellery Queen. Read by Scott Harrison. 8 cass. (Running Time: 11 hrs. 30 mins.). 1999. 56.95 (978-0-7861-1285-2(9), 2182) Blckstn Audio.
French's department store was famous for the rare merchandise it offered its elite clientele. But no one there could be proud of its latest exclusive window display: the blood-stained corpse of the owner's wife. Ellery Queen & his father would soon discover a viper's nest of fear & hatred.

French Proverbs. Catherine Guillot. 2 cass. (Running Time: 3 hrs.). (FRE.). 1994. 8.98 (978-7-902032-94-0(8)) Chrstn Dup Intl.

French Psalms. Catherine Guillot. 4 cass. (Running Time: 6 hrs.). (FRE.). 1994. 12.98 (978-7-902032-73-5(5)) Chrstn Dup Intl.

French Quarter. Perf. by NPR Playhouse. 7 cass. (Running Time: 6 hrs.). 2001. 44.95 (MEBT001) Lodestone Catalog.
Visit America's most infamous & misunderstood neighborhood, as seen by the people who live there. From cops to bartenders, shopkeepers to professors, the Quarter comes to life with mystery, murder, comedy & crime.

French Radio Commercials. 1 cass. (Running Time: 1 hr.). pap. bk. & wbk. ed. 24.95 (SFR231) J Norton Pubs.
Listening-comprehension program features actual commercials covering topics & situations of daily living. Hear French as it is currently spoken by children, teenagers & adults. Songs & jingles assist in the learning of idiomatic expressions.

French Revolution see Cambridge Treasury of English Prose: Austen to Bronte

French Revolution. Thomas Carlyle. Read by Anais 9000. 2008. 33.95 (978-1-60112-127-1(X)) Babblebooks.

French Revolution. unabr. ed. 1 cass. 12.95 (C19702) J Norton Pubs.

French Revolution, Vols. I & II. Kenneth Bruce. 2 cass. (Running Time: 2 hrs. 15 min.). Dramatization. (Excursions in History Ser.). 12.50 Set. Alpha Tape.
Exciting, accurate portrayal of the French Revolution.

French Revolution: Kings, Queens & Guillotines. Compiled by Encyclopaedia Britannica, Inc. 2009. audio compact disk 29.95; audio compact disk 29.95; audio compact disk 29.95; audio compact disk 29.95 Ency Brit Inc.

French Revolution - Kings, Queens & Guillotines. unabr. ed. Encyclopedia Britannica. Read by Peter Johnson. (Listen & Learn Ser.). (YA). 2006. 44.99 (978-1-59895-467-8(9)) Find a World.

French Rush Hour Express Cd Berlitz. (RUSH HOUR EXPRESS Ser.). 2008. audio compact disk 9.95 (978-981-268-235-2(X)) Pub: Berlitz Pubng. Dist(s): Langenscheidt

French Sans Tears. unabr. ed. 1 cass. 1992. 19.95 (978-0-88432-467-6(2), SFR150) J Norton Pubs.
Basic rules of pronunciation are explained in English for those who know some French. Also includes 150 expressions & idioms.

French Savvy Traveler, Business CDs & Booklet. 2 CDs. (Running Time: 110 mins.). (FRE.). 2005. audio compact disk 21.95 (978-1-57970-116-1(7), SFR575D) J Norton Pubs.

French Savvy Traveler, Food & Dining 2 CDs & Booklet. 2 CDs. (Running Time: 99 mins.). (FRE.). 2005. audio compact disk 21.95 (978-1-57970-117-8(5), SFR580) J Norton Pubs.

French Savvy Traveler, Shopping CD & Booklet. 1 CD. (Running Time: 66 mins.). (FRE.). 2005. audio compact disk 14.95 (978-1-57970-118-5(3), SFR585) J Norton Pubs.

French Savvy Traveler, Travel CD & Booklet. 1 CD. (Running Time: 48 mins.). (FRE.). 2005. audio compact disk 14.95 (978-1-57970-119-2(1), SFR590) J Norton Pubs.

French Savvy Traveler 4-vol. set CDs & Booklets. 6 CDs. (Running Time: 5 hrs. 30 min.). (FRE.). 2005. audio compact disk 59.95 (978-1-57970-148-2(5), SFR600D) J Norton Pubs.

French Silk. abr. ed. Sandra Brown. Read by Natalie Ross & Renée Raudman. (Running Time: 6 hrs.). 2010. audio compact disk 14.99 (978-1-4418-1389-3(6), 9781441813893, BACD) Brilliance Audio.

***French Silk.** abr. ed. Sandra Brown. Read by Renée Raudman. (Running Time: 6 hrs.). 2010. 9.99 (978-1-4418-9393-2(8), 9781441893932, BAD) Brilliance Audio.

French Silk. abr. ed. Sandra Brown. (Running Time: 6 hrs.). 2011. audio compact disk 9.99 (978-1-4418-1390-9(X), 9781441813909, BCD Value Price) Brilliance Audio.

French Silk. unabr. ed. Sandra Brown. Read by Natalie Ross & Renée Raudman. (Running Time: 16 hrs.). 2010. audio compact disk 29.99 (978-1-4418-1383-1(7), 9781441813831, Bril Audio CD Unabri) Brilliance Audio.

***French Silk.** unabr. ed. Sandra Brown. Read by Renée Raudman. (Running Time: 16 hrs.). 2010. 24.99 (978-1-4418-1385-5(3), 9781441813855, Brilliance MP3); 39.97 (978-1-4418-1386-2(1), 9781441813862, Brlnc Audio MP3 Lib); 24.99 (978-1-4418-1387-9(X), 9781441813879, BAD); 39.97 (978-1-4418-1388-6(8), 9781441813886, BADLE) Brilliance Audio.

***French Silk.** unabr. ed. Sandra Brown. Read by Natalie Ross & Renée Raudman. (Running Time: 16 hrs.). 2010. audio compact disk 92.97 (978-1-4418-1384-8(5), 9781441813848, BriAudCD Unabrid) Brilliance Audio.

French Slang. Jacqueline Morton. 1 cass. (Running Time: 1 hr. 30 mins.). (FRE.). 1995. pap. bk. 9.95 (978-0-934034-27-2(3)) Olivia & Hill.
French slang equivalent of over 200 common French words. French words are read by French natives individually & in sentence followed by English translation.

French Slang: The Key to Spoken French. 1 cass. (Running Time: 90 min.). (FRE.). 1996. 2.95 Olivia & Hill.
French slang, known as "l'argot," is a rich aspect of the French language. It is used daily by French people from all walks of life. While in English there are some slang words such as "dough" for "money," in French there is an extensive parallel vocabulary, even for the most common words. If you wish to understand spoken French, understanding slang is essential.

French Slang: The Key to Spoken French. Jacqueline Morton. 1 cass., bklet. (Running Time: 90 mins.). (FRE.). 1996. 9.95 (978-0-934034-26-5(5)) Olivia & Hill.

French Songs for Beginners. 1 cass. (Running Time: 1 hr.). 15.95 J Norton Pubs.
Twelve original, easy-to-follow songs introduce French to beginners of any age. Lyric sheet in French included. "Alexander the Clown" & a variety of musical instruments & back-up voices animate the catchy, humorous tunes, whose titles include "In My Garden, "At the Zoo" & "A Fruit Salad.".

French Songs for Beginners: Une Salade de Fruits. Paul Langel. a cass. (Running Time: 60 mins.). (FRE.). 1996. 15.95 (978-1-57970-095-9(0), CFR101) J Norton Pubs.

French Songs for Beginners CD: Une Salade de Fruits. ed. Paul Langel. 1 CD. (Running Time: 40 mins.). (FRE.). 2005. audio compact disk 15.95 (978-1-57970-344-8(5), CFR101D, Audio-For) J Norton Pubs.
12 original, easy-to-follow songs introduce French to beginners of any age. Contemporary music styles and basic language content make these songs fun to listen to, and encourage singing along. "Alexander the Clown" and a variety of musical instruments and back-up voices animate the catchy, humourous tunes, whose titles include "In My Garden," "At the Zoo," and "A Fruit Salad." Lyric sheet in French included.

French Songs for Children. 1 cass. (J). (gr. 3 up). 1991. bk. 16.95 (1179-SA) Olivia & Hill.
Professional group of French children, aged 7 to 13, sings traditional songs.

French Speakers: Learning the Sounds of American English. unabr. ed. 4 cass. (Accent English Ser.). bk. 89.50 incl. 144-pg bk, 42 visual aid cards, mirror. (SEN165) J Norton Pubs.

French Talk One. Symonds. 1989. pap. bk. 22.61 (978-0-582-20657-1(X), 70814) Longman.

French Talk Two. Symonds. 1988. pap. bk. 22.61 (978-0-582-20658-8(8), 70815) Longman.

French Tangos for Guitar. Ole Halen. 1998. pap. bk. 17.95 (978-0-7866-0804-1(8), 96928BCD) Mel Bay.

French Toast. Harriet Welty Rochefort. Read by Anna Fields. 4 CDs. (Running Time: 4 hrs.). 2000. audio compact disk 32.00 (978-0-7861-9944-0(X), 2475) Blckstn Audio.
Harriet demystifies the French. She makes sense of their ever-so-French thought on food, money, sex, love, marriage, manners, schools, style & much more. Her first-person account offers both a helpful reality-check & a lot of very funny moments.

French Toast, unabr. ed. Harriet Welty Rochefort. Read by Anna Fields. 3 cass. (Running Time: 4 hrs.). 1999. 23.95 (978-0-7861-1647-8(1), 2475) Blckstn Audio.

French Vocabulary, Set. 4 cass. (Learn While You Drive Ser.). 1995. bk. 47.95 (1517-AMR) Olivia & Hill.
A wealth of words not covered in the basic courses (2000 words). Specifically designed to increase vocabulary without opening a book.

French Vocabulary, Set. AMR Staff. 4 cass. (Running Time: 0 hr. 60 min.). (Foreign Language Vocabulary Builder Ser.). 1980. 43.95; 43.95 (978-1-55536-152-5(8)) Oasis Audio.
Vocabulary words presented in alphabetical order. Teaches approximately 500 words per cassette. Words not covered in the basic or advanced courses.

***French Winko Teddy Bear Flash Cards & Cd.** Compiled by Audio-Forum. (ENG & FRE.). (J). 2005. 34.95 (978-1-57970-414-8(X), Audio-For) J Norton Pubs.

French with Ease see Nuevo Frances sin Esfuerzo

French with Ease see Franzosisch Ohne Muhe Heute

French with Ease see Nuovo Francese Senza Sforzo

French with Ease see Nuevo Frances sin Esfuerzo

French with Ease see Franzosisch Ohne Muhe Heute

French with Ease see Nuevo Frances Sin Esfuerzo

French with Ease see Nuovo Francese Senza Sforzo

French with Ease. Assimil Staff. (Assimil Ser.). (ENG & FRE.). 1997. pap. bk. 69.95 (978-2-7005-1069-0(0)) Pub: Assimil FRA. Dist(s): Distribks Inc

French with Michel Thomas. (Delux Language Ser.). 2000. 69.95 (978-0-658-00797-2(1), 007971) M-H Contemporary.

French Women Don't Get Fat: The Secret of Eating for Pleasure. abr. ed. Mireille Guiliano. Read by Mireille Guiliano. (Running Time: 10800 sec.). (ENG.). 2007. audio compact disk 14.99 (978-0-7393-5872-6(3), Random AudioBks) Pub: Random Audio Pubg. Dist(s): Random

French Women for All Seasons: A Year of Secrets, Recipes, & Pleasure. abr. ed. Mireille Guiliano. Read by Mireille Guiliano. (Running Time: 7200 sec.). (ENG.). 2006. audio compact disk 22.00 (978-0-7393-4059-2(X), Random AudioBks) Pub: Random Audio Pubg. Dist(s): Random

French Year 2 Ultimate Course with Book. Alpha Omega. 2004. audio compact disk 129.95 (978-1-58204-236-7(5)) Power-Glide.

French 1. 9. 1991. 75.50 (978-1-57924-163-6(8)) BJUPr.

French 2. 75.50 (978-1-59166-100-9(5)) BJUPr.

French/Chinese Level I. Vocabuleam. 1 cass. (VocabuLearn Ser.). (FRE & CHI.). 1995. pap. bk. 15.95 (978-957-9330-77-0(8)) Penton Overseas.

French/Chinese Level II. Vocabuleam. 1 cass. (VocabuLearn Ser.). (FRE & CHI.). 1995. pap. bk. 15.95 (978-957-9330-78-7(6)) Penton Overseas.

Frenchman's Creek. Daphne Du Maurier. Read by John Castle. 6 cass. (Running Time: 8 hrs. 50 min.). 44.95 (CC/021) C to C Cassettes.
The daring Frenchman who plunders the Cornish shores is pursued by the local gentry but he has already captured the heart of the beautiful Lady Dona St Columb.

Frenchman's Creek. unabr. ed. Daphne Du Maurier. Read by John Castle. 6 cass. (Running Time: 8 hrs. 45 mins.). (Germany & the United States of America Ser.). (gr. 9-12). 1999. 29.95 (978-1-57270-098-7(X), F61098u) Pub: Audio Partners. Dist(s): PerseuPGW
Bored with a frivolous life, the captivating Lady Dona St. Columb retires to her country estate where she becomes involved with a French philosopher-pirate.

Frenchman's Creek. unabr. ed. Daphne Du Maurier. Read by Wanda McCaddon. 7 cass. (Running Time: 10 hrs. 30 mins.). 56.00 (978-0-7366-0938-8(5), 1881) Books on Tape.
England during the Restoration provides the setting for this tale of a titled lady & a daring pirate.

Frenchman's Creek. unabr. ed. Daphne Du Maurier. Narrated by Davina Porter. 6 cass. (Running Time: 8 hrs. 45 mins.). 1988. 51.00 (978-1-55690-189-8(5), 88886E7) Recorded Bks.
Lady Dona stumbles across a French privateer anchored near her Cornish home. When she boards the boat her life's adventure begins.

Frenchtown Summer. unabr. ed. Robert Cormier. Read by Rene Auberjonois. 2 vols. (Running Time: 1 hr. 42 mins.). (J). (gr. 7 up). 2004. pap. bk. 29.00 (978-0-8072-0663-8(6), Listening Lib); 23.00 (978-0-8072-8422-3(X), LL0211, Listening Lib) Random Audio Pubg.
In the summer of his first paper route, as he walks the tenement canyons of his hometown, 13-year-old Eugene begins his journey of self-awareness. It is the summer of his first love, of expeditions with his boisterous cousins, of exciting encounters with friends & bitter ones with enemies. But it is most especially the summer of the airplane & the bond it creates between Eugene & the distant, enigmatic father he adores.

***Frenzy.** unabr. ed. Robert Liparulo. Read by Joshua Swanson. (Running Time: 11 hrs. NaN mins.). (Dreamhouse Kings Ser.). (ENG.). 2011. 29.95 (978-1-4417-8277-9(X)); 65.95 (978-1-4417-8274-8(5)); audio compact disk 100.00 (978-1-4417-8275-5(3)) Blckstn Audio.

Frequency Vol. 3: Audio Anthology. Short Stories. Kenneth Brady et al. Read by Carel Struykcen & Tadao Tomomatsu. Ed. by Jeremy Bloom. 1 CD. (Running Time: 72 mins). 2002. audio compact disk 9.95 (978-0-9707056-3-1(8), 56-3) Frquency Pubng.
A short story collection - science fiction, fantasy and horror, read by talented actors.

Frequency Audio, Vol. 2. Short Stories. Bruce Holland Rogers et al. Read by Tadao Tomomatsu & William Foss. Ed. by Jeremy Bloom & Jaq Greenspon. 1 CD. (Running Time: 72 mins). 2001. audio compact disk 9.95 (978-0-9707056-2-4(X), 56-2) Frquency Pubng.
A short story collection - science fiction, fantasy and horror. Authors include winners of the prestigeous Nebula and Hugo awards.

Frequency Audio Anthology. Short Stories. Ray Vukcevich et al. Read by Peter Dillard. Ed. by Jaq Greenspon & Jeremy S. Bloom. 1 CD. (Running Time: 72 mins). 2000. audio compact disk 9.95 (978-0-9707056-1-7(1), 56-1) Frquency Pubng.

Frequency Audio Anthology: The Hugo Nominees 2000. Short Stories. Michael Swanwick et al. Read by Patrick Stinson et al. Ed. by Jeremy Bloom & Jaq Greenspon. 2 Cds. (Running Time: 2 hrs 24 mins). 2000. audio compact disk 9.95 (978-0-9707056-0-0(3)) Frquency Pubng.

Frequent Flyer, 1. unabr. ed. Raymond Elias & Greg McPhee. Read by Raymond Elias. (YA). 2007. 59.99 (978-1-60252-940-3(X)) Find a World.

Frequent Flyer, 2. unabr. ed. Raymond Elias & McPhee Greg. Read by Raymond Elias. (YA). 2007. 59.99 (978-1-60252-941-0(8)) Find a World.

Frequently Asked Questions in Quantitative Finance. unabr. ed. Paul Wilmott. Read by Paul Wilmott. (YA). 2008. 54.99 (978-1-60514-637-9(4)) Find a World.

Frere Jacques. 1 cass. (Running Time: 1 hr., 30 mins.). (Musicontes Ser.). (FRE.). (J). 2000. bk. 24.95 (978-2-09-230365-8(1)) Pub: F Nathan FRA. Dist(s): Distribks Inc

Fresh Air: Calvin Trillin, Humorist-Reporter & John Cage, Composer-Philosopher. Perf. by Terry Gross. 1 cass. (Running Time: 60 min.). 10.95 (FA-85-08-27, HarperThor) HarpC GBR.

Fresh Air: Faith, Reason & Doubt. abr. ed. Terry Gross. 3 CDs. (Running Time: 5 hrs. 50 mins.). (ENG., 2008. audio compact disk 24.95 (978-1-59887-533-1(7), 1598875337) Pub: HighBridge. Dist(s): Workman Pub

Fresh Air: Fred Rogers on Childhood & Studs Terkel, Author-Radio Host. Perf. by Terry Gross. Prod. by WHYY Staff. 1 cass. (Running Time: 60 min.). 10.95 (FA-85-04-16, HarperThor) HarpC GBR.

Fresh Air: Joe Piscopo, Comedian & Frank Stella, Painter. Perf. by Terry Gross. Prod. by WHYY Staff. 1 cass. (Running Time: 60 min.). 10.95 (FA-85-04-02, HarperThor) HarpC GBR.

Fresh Air: John Waters, Filmmaker & Mary Gordon, Novelist. Perf. by Terry Gross. Prod. by WHYY Staff. 1 cass. (Running Time: 60 min.). 9.00 (FA-85-07-09, HarperThor) HarpC GBR.

Fresh Air: Laughs. unabr. ed. Terry Gross. 3 CDs. (Running Time: 3 hrs. 30 mins.). (ENG.). 2004. audio compact disk 22.95 (978-1-56511-919-2(3), 1565119193) Pub: HighBridge. Dist(s): Workman Pub

Fresh Air: Laughs with Terry Gross. Interview. Interview with Terry Gross. Hosted by Terry Gross. Prod. by WHYY Staff. Executive Producer Danny Miller. 3 CD's. (Running Time: 3 hrs. 30 mins.). 2003. audio compact disk 21.95 (978-0-9718412-6-0(8)) WHYY Inc.
Fresh Air explores laughter and comedy with this updated CD set. Six new interviews are added to the 14 interviews on the previous audiocassette set, over three and one half hours of content on 3 discs, in a triple jewel case. Terry brings out of these funny people more than humor and a cheap chuckle. It can sometimes be serious business walking that fine line between funny and way outta hand that makes for an exciting audio collection showcasing thebest of public radio.

Fresh Air: Roger Ebert, Film Critic & Pete Seeger, Folksinger. Perf. by Terry Gross. Prod. by WHYY Staff. 1 cass. (Running Time: 60 min.). 10.95 (FA-85-05-14, HarperThor) HarpC GBR.

Fresh Air: Terry Gross Interviews Stars of Stage & Screen. unabr. ed. Terry Gross. 2 CDs. (Running Time: 2 hrs.). (ENG.). 2007. audio compact disk 22.95 (978-1-59887-069-5(6), 1598870696) Pub: HighBridge. Dist(s): Workman Pub

Fresh Air: The Best of Stage & Screen. abr. unabr. ed. Terry Gross. (Running Time: 3 hrs.). (ENG.). 2005. audio compact disk 22.95 (978-1-56511-981-9(9), 1565119819) Pub: Penguin-HghBrdg. Dist(s): Penguin Grp USA

Fresh Air: Writers Speak. unabr. ed. Terry Gross. 3 CDs. (Running Time: 3 hrs. 30 mins.). (ENG.). 2004. audio compact disk 22.95 (978-1-56511-918-5(5), 1565119185) Pub: HighBridge. Dist(s): Workman Pub

Fresh-Air Fiend, 1985-2000. unabr. ed. Paul Theroux. Narrated by Norman Dietz. 16 cass. (Running Time: 23 hrs.). 2000. 99.75 (978-1-4025-1601-6(0), 97411MC, Griot Aud) Recorded Bks.

Fresh Air on Stage & Screen, Vol. 1. Interview. Interview with Terry Gross. Hosted by Terry Gross. Prod. by WHYY Staff. 2 Cass. (Running Time: 3 hrs). 1998. 16.95 (978-0-9664605-1-3(0)) WHYY Inc.

Fresh Air on Stage & Screen, Vol. 2. Interview. Interview with Terry Gross. Hosted by Terry Gross. Prod. by WHYY Staff. 3 CDs. (Running Time: 3 hrs 10mins). 2000. audio compact disk 19.95 (978-0-9664605-3-7(7)) WHYY Inc.

Fresh Air with Terry Gross: Alec Guinness on Being Funny. Interview with Alec Guinness & Terry Gross. 1 cass. (Running Time: 30 min.). 9.95 (A0270B090, HarperThor) HarpC GBR.

Fresh Air with Terry Gross: Art Spiegelman: Why "Maus"? Interview with Terry Gross & Art Spiegelman. 1 cass. (Running Time: 30 min.). 9.95 (A0600B090, HarperThor) HarpC GBR.

Fresh Air with Terry Gross: Athol Fugard, White South African Playwright. Interview with Athol Fugard & Terry Gross. 1 cass. (Running Time: 30 min.). 9.95 (A0400B090, HarperThor) HarpC GBR.

Fresh Air with Terry Gross: Chaim Potok, Novelist. Interview with Chaim Potok & Terry Gross. 1 cass. (Running Time: 30 min.). 9.95 (A0570B090, HarperThor) HarpC GBR.

Fresh Air with Terry Gross: Dennis Brutus, Exiled Black South African Poet. Interview with Dennis Brutus & Terry Gross. 1 cass. (Running Time: 30 min.). 9.95 (A0410B090, HarperThor) HarpC GBR.

Fresh Air with Terry Gross: Ellie Greenwich - Hit Songwriter of the '60s. Interview with Ellie Greenwich & Terry Gross. 1 cass. (Running Time: 30 min.). 9.95 (FA-86-06-10, HarperThor) HarpC GBR.

Fresh Air with Terry Gross: Gail Lumet Buckley - A Sense of Belonging. Interview with Gail Lumet Buckley & Terry Gross. 1 cass. (Running Time: 30 min.). 8.00 (A0290B090, HarperThor) HarpC GBR.

Fresh Air with Terry Gross: Kurt Vonnegut. Interview with Kurt Vonnegut & Terry Gross. 1 cass. (Running Time: 30 min.). 9.95 (A0260B090, HarperThor) HarpC GBR.

Fresh Air with Terry Gross: Leonard Cohen, Singer Songwriter. Interview with Leonard Cohen & Terry Gross. 1 cass. (Running Time: 30 min.). 9.95 (A0450B090, HarperThor) HarpC GBR.

Fresh Air with Terry Gross: Linda Ellerbee, Broadcast Journalist. Interview with Linda Ellerbee & Terry Gross. 1 cass. (Running Time: 30 min.). 9.95 (A0280B090, HarperThor) HarpC GBR.

Fresh Air with Terry Gross: Michael Bennett, Choreographer & Director. Interview with Michael Bennett & Terry Gross. 1 cass. (Running Time: 30 min.). 9.95 (A0380B090, HarperThor) HarpC GBR.

Fresh Air with Terry Gross: Pat Conroy - On Discipline & Power. Interview with Pat Conroy & Terry Gross. 1 cass. (Running Time: 30 min.). 9.95 (A0610B090, HarperThor) HarpC GBR.

Fresh Air with Terry Gross: Pauline Kael, Film Critic. Interview with Pauline Kael & Terry Gross. 1 cass. (Running Time: 30 min.). 9.95 (A0240B090, HarperThor) HarpC GBR.

Fresh Air with Terry Gross: Phyllis Diller - In a Man's World. Interview with Phyllis Diller & Terry Gross. 1 cass. (Running Time: 30 min.). 9.95 (A0500B090, HarperThor) HarpC GBR.

Fresh Air with Terry Gross: Quentin Crisp, Gay Author. Interview with Quentin Crisp & Terry Gross. 1 cass. (Running Time: 30 min.). 9.95 (A0390B090, HarperThor) HarpC GBR.

Fresh Air with Terry Gross: Red Grooms - The Comedy of Cities. Interview with Red Grooms & Terry Gross. 1 cass. (Running Time: 30 min.). 9.95 (FA-86-05-20, HarperThor) HarpC GBR.

Fresh Air with Terry Gross: Robert Bauman - Admitting Homosexuality. Interview with Robert Bauman & Terry Gross. 1 cass. (Running Time: 30 min.). 9.95 (FA-86-12-02, HarperThor) HarpC GBR.

Fresh Air with Terry Gross: Robert Jay Lifton, Psychiatrist - On Modern Holocausts. Interview with Robert J. Lifton & Terry Gross. 1 cass. (Running Time: 30 min.). 9.95 (A0490B090, HarperThor) HarpC GBR.

Fresh Air with Terry Gross: Robert MacNeil - To Be a TV Newsman. Interview with Terry Gross & Robert MacNeil. 1 cass. (Running Time: 30 min.). 9.95 (A0330B090, HarperThor) HarpC GBR.

Fresh Air with Terry Gross: Steve Reich, Composer. Interview with Steve Reich & Terry Gross. 1 cass. (Running Time: 30 min.). 9.95 (A0430B090, HarperThor) HarpC GBR.

Fresh Air with Terry Gross: The Reverend William Sloane Coffin, Peace Activist. Interview with Terry Gross & William S. Coffin. 1 cass. (Running Time: 30 min.). 9.95 (A0440B090, HarperThor) HarpC GBR.

Fresh Air with Terry Gross: Vito Russo: Gays in Film. Interview with Vito Russo & Terry Gross. 1 cass. (Running Time: 30 min.). 8.00 (A0250B090, HarperThor) HarpC GBR.

Fresh Air with Terry Gross: Woody Herman, Big Band Man. Interview with Woody Herman & Terry Gross. 1 cass. (Running Time: 30 min.). 9.95 (A0580B090, HarperThor) HarpC GBR.

Fresh As the Rain. Read by Laura Simms. Music by Steve Gorn. 1 cass. (Running Time: 45 mins.). (J). 2000. 9.95 Yellow Moon.

Fresh Beginning: Genesis 35:1. Ed Young. 1982. 4.95 (978-0-7417-1271-4(7), 271) Win Walk.

Fresh Customer Service. Michael D. Brown. (Running Time: 14400 sec.). (ENG.). 2007. audio compact disk 29.95 (978-0-9799949-5-1(0)) Pub: Acanthus Pubg. Dist(s): AtlasBooks

Fresh Customer Service: Executive Summary Audio Book. Michael D. Brown. (Running Time: 4500 sec.). 2008. audio compact disk 9.95 (978-0-9799949-1-3(8)) Pub: Acanthus Pubg. Dist(s): AtlasBooks

Fresh Disasters. Stuart Woods. Read by Tony Roberts. (Running Time: 8 hrs.). No. 13. (ENG.). (gr. 8). 2007. audio compact disk 19.95 (978-0-14-314266-9(6), PengAudBks) Penguin Grp USA.

Fresh Disasters. unabr. ed. Stuart Woods. Read by Tony Roberts. 6 CDs. (Running Time: 8 hrs.). No. 13. (ENG.). (gr. 8). 2007. audio compact disk 29.95 (978-0-14-314192-1(9), PengAudBks) Penguin Grp USA.

Fresh Faith. unabr. ed. Zondervan Publishing Staff & Jim Cymbala. Told to Dean Merrill. (Running Time: 7 hrs. 0 mins. 0 sec.). (ENG.). 2004. 13.99 (978-0-310-26149-0(X)) Zondervan.

Fresh Faith: What Happens When Real Faith Ignites God's People. abr. ed. Jim Cymbala. Told to Dean Merrill. (Running Time: 1 hr. 50 mins. 0 sec.). (ENG.). 2003. 10.99 (978-0-310-26235-0(6)) Zondervan.

Fresh Fire - Sion Alford. Contrib. by Sion Alford. 1997. audio compact disk 85.00 (978-0-7601-1334-9(3), 75606309) Pub: Brentwood Music. Dist(s): H Leonard

Fresh from the Country. unabr. ed. Miss Read. Read by Gwen Watford. 6 cass. (Running Time: 6 hrs. 21 min.). (Audio Bks.). 1992. 54.95 set. (978-0-7451-6168-6(5), CAB 683) AudioGO.
Miss Read draws us magically into the world of the primary school in this humorous & charming story. Anna Lacey, a young country girl, is given her first job in greater London. As she learns to cope with the challenges of her new life, we share with her the delights & pleasures of teaching those dear, devilish, infuriating, exhausting, yet delightful creatures, which are her young pupils.

Fresh Glimpse of the Dove. T. D. Jakes. 1 cass. 1997. 40.00 (978-1-57855-014-2(9)) T D Jakes.

Fresh Manna, Fresh Bread. 2003. audio compact disk (978-1-59024-120-2(7)) B Hinn Min.

Fresh Outlook. Swami Amar Jyoti. 1 cass. 1979. 9.95 (I-9) Truth Consciousness.
A fresh approach to meditation. Finding the perennial joy & beauty of life.

Fresh Power. unabr. ed. Zondervan Publishing Staff & Jim Cymbala. Told to Dean Merrill. (Running Time: 7 hrs. 0 mins. 0 sec.). (ENG.). 2004. 13.99 (978-0-310-26150-6(3)) Zondervan.

Fresh Power: Experiencing the Vast Resources of the Spirit of God. abr. ed. Jim Cymbala. 2 cass. (Running Time: 2 hrs.). 2001. 17.99 (978-0-310-23476-0(X)) Zondervan.
Basis for this study as Cymbala delves into what it was like for Christians back in the first century - and what it can be like for them today. He explains how the same life in Christ that the first-century Christians professed through the power of the Holy Spirit is available in the present for those who are longing for revival.

Fresh Power: Experiencing the Vast Resources of the Spirit of God. abr. ed. Jim Cymbala. (Running Time: 2 hrs. 0 mins. 0 sec.). (ENG.). 2003. 10.99 (978-0-310-26044-8(2)) Zondervan.

Fresh Power: Experiencing the Vast Resources of the Spirit of God. unabr. ed. Jim Cymbala & Dean Merrill. 2001. audio compact disk 34.99 (978-0-310-24200-0(2)) Zondervan.

Fresh Spring see Hearing Great Poetry: From Chaucer to Milton

Fresh Start: God's Invitation to a Great Life. unabr. ed. Doug Fields. Narrated by Doug Fields. (Running Time: 9 hrs. 30 mins. 0 sec.). (ENG.). 2009. 16.09 (978-0-60814-581-2(6)); audio compact disk 22.99 (978-1-59859-627-4(6)) Oasis Audio.

Fresh View of Things. unabr. ed. Ord L. Morrow. Read by Ord L. Morrow. 1 cass. (Running Time: 1 hr. 15 min.). 1989. 4.95 (978-0-8474-2361-3(1)) Back to Bible.
A challenge to examine one's beliefs & to verify that they are biblical.

***Fresh Wind, Fresh Fire.** abr. ed. Carol Cymbala. (Running Time: 2 hrs. 0 mins. 0 sec.). (ENG.). 2004. 10.99 (978-0-310-26236-7(4)) Pub: Zondervan Bks. Dist(s): Zondervan

Fresh Wind, Fresh Fire. unabr. ed. Jim Cymbala. Contrib. by Dean Merrill. 1997. 17.99 (978-0-310-21199-0(9)) Zondervan.

Fresh Wind, Fresh Fire. unabr. ed. Zondervan Publishing Staff & Jim Cymbala. Told to Dean Merrill. (Running Time: 7 hrs. 0 mins. 0 sec.). (ENG.). 2004. 13.99 (978-0-310-26152-0(X)) Zondervan.

Fretboard Basics for Guitar: Scales, Arpeggios, Modes & Exercises. Steven Wohlrab. 2002. per. 19.95 (978-0-7866-5935-7(1), 99315BCD) Mel Bay.

Freud. Anthony Storr. Read by Neville Jason. (Running Time: 4 hrs.). (C). 2005. 24.95 (978-1-60083-744-9(1)) Iofy Corp.

Freud. Anthony Storr. Read by Neville Jason. 2003. pap. bk. 22.98 (978-962-634-297-8(8)) Naxos.

Freud Pt. 1: A Life for Our Time. unabr. collector's ed. Peter Gay. Read by Walter Zimmerman. 14 cass. (Running Time: 21 hrs.). 1991. 112.00 (978-0-7366-1886-1(4), 2715A-B) Books on Tape.
Enter the world of Sigmund Freud: his family, his city, his professional struggles, his long, fruitful & embattled life. We see him at work in times of declining liberalism, devastating war, uneasy peace, the rise of Hitler & the fall of Austria. We watch him devising & revising his epoch-making theories, struggling toward his discoveries, quarreling with his disciples.

Freud Pt. 2: A Life for Our Time. unabr. collector's ed. Peter Gay. Read by Walter Zimmerman. 12 cass. (Running Time: 18 hrs.). 1991. 96.00 (978-0-7366-1887-8(2), 2715B) Books on Tape.

Freudian Astrology. Elizabeth Greenwood. 1 cass. 8.95 (830) Am Fed Astrologers.

Freudian Fallacy. unabr. ed. E. M. Thornton. Read by Nadia May. 9 cass. (Running Time: 13 hrs.). 1992. 62.95 (978-0-7861-0208-2(X), 1183) Blckstn Audio.
This book makes the claims that Freud's central postulate, the unconscious mind, does not exist; that his theories were based on pathological phenomena; & that Freud himself, when formulating these theories was under the influence of a highly toxic drug.

Freud's "Friends" Program from the Award Winning Public Radio Series. Perf. by Robert Klein. Hosted by Fred Goodwin. Comment by John Hockenberry. Contrib. by Jonathan Katz et al. 1 cass. (Running Time: 1 hr.). (Infinite Mind Ser.). 1999. audio compact disk 21.95 (978-1-888064-24-7(2), LCM 46) Lichtenstein Creat.
It's been nearly 100 years since Sigmund Freud published his first work on psychoanalysis. Since then, he's become a household name - overshadowing other pioneering investigators of the mind. We hear Freud's own words, as read by Robert Klein, and learn about Freud's teacher Jean-Martin Charcot and contemporaries such as Pierre Janet and Sandor

Ferenczi. Jonathan Katz, the alter ego of Comedy Central's Dr. Katz, professional therapist, answers common questions about therapy. Plus a visit with contemporary analysts, the lastest news from Psychology Today, and commentary on rage and impulse control from John Hockenberry.

Freud's Introduction to Psychoanalysis, Vol. I unabr. collector's ed. Sigmund Freud. Read by Jonathan Reese. 6 cass. (Running Time: 6 hrs.). 1996. 36.00 (978-0-7366-3492-2(4)) Books on Tape.
According to Freud, all dreams are wish fulfillments. Interpreting them can result in more meaningful living.

Freud's Introduction to Psychoanalysis, Vol. II. collector's ed. Sigmund Freud. Read by Jonathan Reese. 6 cass. (Running Time: 6 hrs.). 1996. 36.00 Books on Tape.

Friction. E. R. Frank. 3 cass. (Running Time: 4 hrs. 13 mins.). (J). (gr. 6-9). 2004. 30.00 (978-0-8072-1648-4(8), Listening Lib) Random Audio Pubg.

Friction & Facilitation: Intimate Relationship As a Container for Individuation. Kenneth James. Read by Kenneth James. 3 cass. (Running Time: 3 hrs. 30 min.). 1992. 24.95 set. (978-0-7822-0400-1(7), 491) C G Jung IL.
In the first part of the series The Questions & Meanings of Intimate Relationship, Kenneth James explores how the intimate relationship may facilitate the individuation process. He also introduces the concepts of projection & complex formation, & describes the roles they play in both individuation & relationship.

Frida: A Biography of Frida Kahlo. Hayden Herrera. Read by Kimberly Schraf. 2002. audio compact disk 112.00 (978-0-7366-8801-7(3)) Books on Tape.

Frida: A Biography of Frida Kahlo. abr. ed. Hayden Herrera. 4 cass. (Running Time: 6 hrs.). 2002. 24.95 (978-1-57511-118-6(7), Audio Sel) Pub: Pub Mills. Dist(s): TransVend
Drawing on firsthand sources including collectors, friends, and fellow artists, Herrera has produced an exhaustive study of the Mexican painter's life, loves, and artistry.

Friday. unabr. ed. Robert A. Heinlein. Read by Robert McQuay. 9 cass. (Running Time: 13 hrs. 30 mins.). 1997. 62.95 (978-0-7861-1084-1(8), 115028) Blckstn Audio.
Friday is a secret courier. She is employed by a man known to her only as "Boss." Operating from & over a near-future Earth, in which North America has become Balkanized into dozens of independent states, where culture has become bizarrely vulgarized & chaos is the happy norm, she finds herself on shuttlecock assignment at Boss' seemingly whimsical beheste. From one to another of the new states of America's disunion, she keeps her balance nimbly with quick, expeditious solutions to one calamity & scrape after another.

Friday. unabr. ed. Robert A. Heinlein. Read by Hillary Huber. (Running Time: 50400 sec.). 2008. 72.95 (978-1-4332-4559-6(0)); audio compact disk 29.95 (978-1-4332-4561-9(2)); audio compact disk & audio compact disk 90.00 (978-1-4332-4560-2(4)) Blckstn Audio.

***Friday Night Bites.** unabr. ed. Chloe Neill. Narrated by Cynthia Holloway. (Running Time: 12 hrs. 0 mins.). (Chicagoland Vampires Ser.). 2010. 17.99 (978-1-4001-8937-3(3)); 24.99 (978-1-4001-6937-5(2)); audio compact disk 34.99 (978-1-4001-1937-0(5)) Pub: Tantor Media. Dist(s): IngramPubServ

***Friday Night Bites (Library Edition)** unabr. ed. Chloe Neill. Narrated by Cynthia Holloway. (Running Time: 12 hrs. 0 mins.). (Chicagoland Vampires Ser.). 2010. 34.99 (978-1-4001-9937-2(9)); audio compact disk 83.99 (978-1-4001-4937-7(1)) Pub: Tantor Media. Dist(s): IngramPubServ

Friday Night Class. Stephen Gaskin. 2 cass. 18.00 set. (A0635-90) Sound Photosyn.
A public gathering in Los Angeles with Stephen articulating the manifestation of idealistic principals in the real world.

Friday Night Knitting Club. unabr. ed. Kate Jacobs. (Running Time: 45000 sec.). (Friday Night Knitting Club Ser.). 2007. 72.95 (978-1-4332-0290-2(5)) Blckstn Audio.

Friday Night Knitting Club. unabr. ed. Kate Jacobs. Read by Carrington MacDuffie. (Running Time: 45000 sec.). (Friday Night Knitting Club Ser.). 2007. audio compact disk 90.00 (978-1-4332-0291-9(3)); audio compact disk 29.95 (978-1-4332-0182-0(8)) Blckstn Audio.

Friday Night Knitting Club. unabr. ed. Kate Jacobs. Read by Carrington MacDuffie. (Running Time: 45000 sec.). (Friday Night Knitting Club Ser.). 2007. 29.95 (978-1-4332-0180-6(1)); audio compact disk 29.95 (978-1-4332-0181-3(X)) Blckstn Audio.

Friday Night Lights: A Town, a Team, & a Dream. H. G. Bissinger. Read by Alex Karras. 2 cass. (Running Time: 3 hrs.). 1991. 15.95 set. (978-0-9627187-9-3(3), 20050) Pub Mills.
This bestselling book is the true story of how high school football in Odessa, Texas infuses the entire town with a sense of worth & esteem, but takes its toll on the young players by resting the responsibility for those feelings on their shoulders.

Friday Night Lights: A Town, a Team, & a Dream. unabr. ed. H. G. Bissinger. Read by John MacDonald. 8 cass. (Running Time: 12 hrs.). 1991. 64.00 (978-0-7366-1948-6(8), 2769) Books on Tape.
Odessa, Texas. Closed-up movie theatres, empty storefronts, for-sale signs everywhere. Although it has seen better days, Odessa still has a dream. And that dream comes to life once a week every fall when the Permian High Panthers take to the football field under the Friday night lights.

Friday the Rabbi Slept Late. unabr. ed. Harry Kemelman. Narrated by George Guidall. 5 cass. (Running Time: 6 hrs. 30 mins.). (Rabbi Small Mystery Ser.). 2000. 49.00 (978-0-7887-1300-2(0), 95135E7) Recorded Bks.
Rabbi Small is quietly leading the Jewish Community at Barnard's Crossing when the body of a young woman is discovered near the temple. Suddenly he must find the killer, or lose more than his reputation.

Friday's Child. unabr. ed. Georgette Heyer. Read by Eve Matheson. 12 CDs. (Running Time: 18 hrs.). 2002. audio compact disk 110.95 (978-0-7540-5444-3(6), CCD 135) AudioGO.
Young Lord Sheringham, rejected by the woman he deeply loved, could not gain his inheritance until he married. On a passionate impulse, he vowed to marry the next woman he saw. Enter Hero Wantage, the adorable life-long friend who has secretly loved Sheringham her entire life. Regency Romance reissue.

Friday's Child, Set. unabr. ed. Georgette Heyer. Read by Eve Matheson. 10 cass. 1999. 84.95 (978-0-7540-0366-3(3), CAB1789) AudioGO.
Rejected by Miss. Milborne, Lord Sheringham is bent on avenging fate & coming into his fortune. But the very first woman he meets is Hero Wantage, the young & charmingly unsophisticated girl who has loved him since childhood.

Fried Green Tomatoes at the Whistle Stop Cafe. abr. ed. Fannie Flagg. Read by Fannie Flagg. (Running Time: 7200 sec.). (ENG.). 2007. audio compact disk 14.99 (978-0-7393-4353-1(X), Random AudioBks) Pub: Random Audio Pubg. Dist(s): Random

Friedreich Ataxia - A Bibliography & Dictionary for Physicians, Patients, & Genome Researchers. Compiled by Icon Group International, Inc. Staff. 2007. ring bd. 28.95 (978-0-497-11215-8(9)) Icon Grp.

Friedrich Durrenmatt: Der Richter und Sein Henker. unabr. ed. 3 cass. (Running Time: 3 hrs.). 34.95 (SGE340) J Norton Pubs.
A policeman's killer is caught & punished in a novel manner in this gripping tale.

Friedrich Durrenmatt: Grieche Sucht Griechin. unabr. ed. 3 cass. (Running Time: 3 hrs.). (GER.). 34.95 (SGE335) J Norton Pubs.
A Naive young Greek advertises for a bride & is skyrocketed to sudden prominence & riches.

Friedrich Nietzsche: Germany (1844-1900) abr. ed. Narrated by Charlton Heston. (Running Time: 8062 sec.). (Audio Classics: the Giants of Philosophy Ser.). 2006. audio compact disk 25.95 (978-0-7861-6937-5(0)) Pub: Blckstn Audio. Dist(s): NetLibrary CO

Friedrich Nietzsche: Germany (1844-1900), unabr. ed. Read by Charlton Heston. 2 cass. (Running Time: 3 hrs.). (Giants of Philosophy Ser.). 17.95 (K127) Blckstn Audio.
See how one of the world's most important philosophers created a complete system of thought, including his views on ethics, metaphysics, politics & aesthetics. Learn about his epistemology - how we know what we know.

Friend, a Laugh, a Walk in the Woods. Dan Crow. Perf. by Dan Crow. 1 cass. (Running Time: 30 min.). (J). 1992. 8.98 (978-1-56406-549-0(9)); 8.98 Incl. sleeve pack. (978-1-56406-578-0(2)); audio compact disk 13.98 CD. (978-1-56406-565-0(0)) Sony Music Ent.

Friend Day, Resource Packet. rev. ed. Elmer L. Towns. Ed. by Cindy G. Spear. 4 cass. 1983. bk. 99.95 Set, incl. resource pkt. & 2 bklets. (978-1-57052-008-2(9)) Chrch Grwth VA.
A unique comprehensive evangelistic attendance campaign & outreach program that involves every member of your church in the task of reaching their friends for Christ.

Friend of God. Contrib. by Phillips Craig & Dean. (Praise Hymn Soundtracks Ser.). 2005. audio compact disk 8.98 (978-5-558-80662-5(1)) Pt of Grace Ent.

Friend of Kafka see Isaac Bashevis Singer Reader

Friend of Kafka. unabr. ed. Isaac Bashevis Singer. Read by Wolfram Kandinsky. 8 cass. (Running Time: 12 hrs.). 1986. 64.00 (978-0-7366-0390-4(5), 1367) Books on Tape.
A collection of 21 short stories. Singer's people are the dispossessed of the modern world, European Jews who have fled their homelands & taken up new lives in cities from Buenos Aires to New York.

Friend of My Youth. unabr. ed. Alice Munro. Read by Beth Fowler. 8 vols. (Running Time: 12 hrs.). 2000. bk. 69.95 (978-0-7927-2390-5(2), CSL 279, Chivers Sound Lib) AudioGO.
A woman haunted by dreams of her dead mother. An adulterous couple stepping over the line where the initial excitement ends & the pain begins. A widow visiting a Scottish village in search of her husband's past & instead discovering unsettling truths about a total stranger. The ten stories in this collection convey the unspoken mysteries at the heart of all human experience.

***Friend of the Devil.** unabr. ed. Peter Robinson. Read by Simon Prebble. (Inspector Banks Mystery Ser.). (ENG.). 2008. (978-0-06-157958-5(0)); (978-0-06-157959-2(9)) HarperCollins Pubs.

Friend of the Devil. unabr. ed. Peter Robinson. Read by Simon Prebble. 11 CDs. (Running Time: 13 hrs. 30 mins.). (Inspector Banks Mystery Ser.). 2008. audio compact disk 44.95 (978-0-06-145753-1(1), Harper Audio) HarperCollins Pubs.

Friend of the Devil. unabr. ed. Peter Robinson. Read by Simon Prebble. 8 cass. (Running Time: 13 hrs. 15 mins.). (Inspector Banks Mystery Ser.). 2008. 110.00 (978-1-4159-4874-3(7), BksonTape); audio compact disk 110.00 (978-1-4159-4849-1(6), BksonTape) Pub: Random Audio Pubg. Dist(s): Random
One morning in March, on the edge of a cliff overlooking the sea, a woman named Karen Drew is found in her wheelchair with her throat slit. Back in Eastvale on that same morning, in a tangle of narrow alleys behind a market square, the body of Hayley Daniels is found raped and strangled. Two murders . . . two towns. . . On loan to a sister precinct, Detective Inspector Annie Cabbot draws the first case. Karen Drew seems to have lived a quiet and nearly invisible life for the past seven years. Try as she might, Annie turns up nothing in the woman's past that might have promoted someone to help her out to the sea and to her death. Meanwhile, in the Hayley Daniels murder, Chief Inspector Alan Banks has suspects galore. Everywhere she went, the nineteen-year-old student attracted attention. Anyone could have followed her on the night she was out drinking with her friends, making sure she never made it back home. Then a breakthrough spins Annie's case in a shocking and surprising new direction, straight toward Banks. Coincidence? Not in Eastvale, Banks and Annie are searching for two killers who might strike again at any moment with bloody fury.

Friend of the Earth. T. C. Boyle. Read by Scott Brick. 2000. audio compact disk 80.00 (978-0-7366-7505-5(1)) Books on Tape.

Friend of the Earth. collector's unabr. ed. T. C. Boyle. Read by Scott Brick. 9 cass. (Running Time: 13 hrs. 30 min.). 2000. 72.00 (978-0-7366-5580-4(8)) Books on Tape.
A former ecoterrorist & his wife rediscover each other in a bleak world of biosphere collapse.

Friend of the Earth. unabr. ed. T. C. Boyle. Read by Scott Brick. 9 cass. (Running Time: 12 hrs.). 2001. 34.95 (978-0-7366-5681-8(2)) Books on Tape.

Friend of the Family. Lisa Jewell. Read by Tim Bruce. 10 CDs. (Running Time: 11 hrs. 33 mins.). (Isis (CDs) Ser.). (J). 2005. audio compact disk 89.95 (978-0-7531-2433-8(5)) Pub: ISIS Lrg Prnt GBR. Dist(s): Ulverscroft US

Friend of the Family. unabr. ed. Lauren Grodstein. Read by Rick Adamson. 8 CDs. (Running Time: 8 hrs.). 2009. audio compact disk 34.95 (978-1-59887-943-8(X), 159887943X) Pub: HighBridge. Dist(s): Workman Pub

Friend of the Family. unabr. ed. Lisa Jewell. Read by Tim Bruce. 8 cass. (Running Time: 11 hrs. 33 mins.). (Isis Cassettes Ser.). (J). 2004. 69.95 (978-0-7531-1892-4(0)) Pub: ISIS Lrg Prnt GBR. Dist(s): Ulverscroft US

Friend of the Family. unabr. ed. Nicola Thorne. Read by Joanna David. 6 cass. (Running Time: 9 hrs.). 2003. 54.95 (978-0-7540-0919-1(X), CAB 2321) AudioGO.

Friend of the Flock: Tales of a Country Veterinarian, unabr. ed. John McCormack. Read by Barrett Whitener. 7 cass. (Running Time: 10 hrs. 30 mins.). 1998. 56.00 (978-0-7366-4100-5(9), 896005) Books on Tape.
McCormack captures every comical & heartwarming detail of a rural Southern life in this account of putting down roots, traveling the dirt roads & becoming a trusted member of a community as the local country veterinarian in Butler, Alabama.

Friend or Fiend? with the Pain & the Great One: With the Pain & the Great One. unabr. ed. Judy Blume. Read by Judy Blume. Read by Kathleen McInerney. (ENG.). (J). (gr. 1). 2009. audio compact disk 14.95 (978-0-7393-8059-8(1), Listening Lib) Pub: Random Audio Pubg. Dist(s): Random

***Friendly Dialogue Between an Atheist & a Christian.** Luis Palau & Zhao Qizheng. (Running Time: 2 hrs. 27 mins. 0 sec.). (ENG.). 2009. 14.99 (978-0-310-77239-2(7)) Zondervan.

Friendly Letters: A Collection of 10 Piano Solo Pieces. Composed by Carla K. Bartlett. 2008. pap. bk. 15.95 (978-1-57424-232-4(6), 1574242326) Pub: Centerstream Pub. Dist(s): H Leonard

Friendly Persuasion. unabr. ed. Jessamyn West. Read by Roses Prichard. 8 cass. (Running Time: 8 hrs.). 1979. 48.00 (978-0-7366-0166-5(X), 1168) Books on Tape.
The story of the Birdwell family of Indiana - pious Quakers with an inexhaustible relish for life. The eight Birdwells live according to the dictates of William Penn - but the Civil War interrupts their tranquil existence & tests their strength & faith.

Friends see Amigos

Friends. 1986. (6101) Am Audio Prose.

Friends. (Dovetales Ser.: Tape 13). pap. bk. 6.95 (978-0-944391-48-8(6)); 4.95 (978-0-944391-28-0(1)) DonWise Prodns.

Friends. Alma Flor Ada. Illus. by Viví Escrivá. (Stories for the Telling Ser.). (J). (gr. k-3). 4.95 (978-1-58105-324-1(X)) Santillana.

Friends. Barbour Books Staff. 1999. bk. 9.97 (978-1-57748-579-7(3)) Barbour Pub.

Friends. Crazy Curt. Perf. by Crazy Curt and the Fireballs. 1 CD. (Running Time: 33 min.). (J). (gr. 1-5). 2000. audio compact disk 14.98 (978-1-893967-14-4(X), EK5012) Emphasis Ent.
Crazy Curt writes music that is honest, respectful & fun. With this third release, Curt continues his tradition in building a musical bridge between children & adults.

Friends. Nelson Gill. 1 cass. (J). 2001. 10.95 (KNG 3106C); audio compact disk 14.95 (KNG 3106CD) Kimbo Educ.
These upbeat songs are filled with positive messages. Tick-Tock, Power to Be Me, Dance Punta, Soca Rock & more. Some songs in English & Spanish.

Friends. Ed. by Robert A. Monroe. 1 cass. (Running Time: 30 min.). (Meta Music Ser.). 1986. 12.95 (978-1-56102-210-6(1)) Inter Indus.
Experience the comfort, the love & support, the presence, if one desires - of our nonphysical friends who are always with us to support us in our life journeys.

Friends, unabr. ed. Kazumi Yumoto. Narrated by Jeff Woodman. 4 pieces. (Running Time: 5 hrs.). (gr. 5 up). 1997. 35.00 (978-0-7887-0886-2(4), 95024E7) Recorded Bks.
Kiyama & his friends become obsessed with the desire to see what a dead person looks like. Thinking an old man who lives alone will die soon, they begin spying on him. The old man, however, is no fool.

Friends. unabr. ed. Kazumi Yumoto. Read by Jeff Woodman. 4 cass. (Running Time: 3 hrs.). (J). (gr. 5 up). 1997. bk. 55.50 (978-0-7887-1134-3(2), 40483); Rental 11.50 Recorded Bks.

Friends & Family. Perf. by Nancy Raven. 1 cass. (Running Time: 40 min.). (J). (ps-6). 1992. 10.00 (978-1-885292-04-9(X)) Lizards Rock.
Folk music for children, families & teachers.

Friends & Heroes. unabr. ed. Olivia Manning. Read by Harriet Walter. 10 cass. (Running Time: 15 hrs.). (Balkan Ser.: Bk. 3). 2000. 69.95 (SAB 082) Pub: Chivers Audio Bks GBR. Dist(s): AudioGO
Bucharest has fallen as Harriet and Guy Pringle escape to Athens where acquaintances await them. But Athens becomes a very dangerous place when Greece is threatened by the Axis Powers.

Friends & Lovers. abr. ed. Eric Jerome Dickey. Read by Eric Jerome Dickey. 4 cass. (Running Time: 6 hrs.). 2002. 24.95 (978-1-57511-106-3(3)) Pub Mills.
When Debra meets Leonard, she makes it clear that if he wants her love, he'll have to produce a ring. Leonard must face that moment when he has to decide what matters most and whether he's ready for the love of a good woman. A wise and witty look at the human condition.

Friends & Lovers. unabr. ed. Eric Jerome Dickey. 10 cass. (Running Time: 13 hrs. 45 mins.). 1997. 88.00 (978-0-7887-6033-4(5), F0045L8) Recorded Bks.
The story of two couples looking for lasting love. As each pair searches for the key to happiness, they just might discover that the answer lies in the journey instead of the destination.

Friends & Lovers. unabr. ed. Eric Jerome Dickey. 2001. (978-0-7887-3466-3(0), F0045x7) Recorded Bks.
A story of two couples looking for lasting love. As each pair searches for the key to happiness, they just might discover that the answer lies in the process, not the goal. Sassy & sexy, Friends & Lovers explores all the angles of big-city love & romance.

Friends & Lovers. unabr. ed. Helen MacInnes. Read by Christine Dawe. 8 cass. (Running Time: 12 hrs.). 2001. 69.95 (978-1-85496-142-6(X), 6142X) Pub: Soundings Ltd GBR. Dist(s): Ulverscroft US
David Bosworth is a penniless undergraduate at Oxford, with a head full of dreams. Penelope Lorrimer is the pretty daughter of a wealthy Edinburgh family. They have plans for her, but their ambitions do not match hers. When Penelope & David fall in love, the odds are against them, which only draws them closer than a love more easily won. The bond between them is stronger & more durable than the one between mere friends & lovers.

Friends & Neighbours. unabr. ed. Rose Boucheron. Read by Julia Sands. 6 cass. (Running Time: 8 hrs.). 1999. 69.95 (978-1-85903-259-6(1)) Pub: Magna Story GBR. Dist(s): Ulverscroft US
Minna is passionate & demanding. Beth is more reserved, less flamboyant, a hardworking helpmate to her doctor husband & happy with the quieter pace of her small village, Chantry Green. To Beth's surprise, Minna declares she & her husband Jimmy are ready to settle down to peace & stability. Although Minna is her best friend, Beth sometimes secretly envied her, but with Minna's move to Chantry Green the two friends are brought into closer proximity & Beth learns that, amazingly, she herself possesses the one thing her glamorous, have-it-all friend has always yearned for.

Friends & Relations. unabr. ed. Margaret Bacon. Read by Frances Brown. 5 cass. (Running Time: 6 hrs 35 min.). 1998. 63.95 Set. (978-1-85903-178-0(1)) Pub: Magna Story GBR. Dist(s): Ulverscroft US
Kate & Betty had once been inseparable, growing up together in the rough beauty of North Yorkshire, in league against the adult world. Betty became a successful London lawyer & married an ambitious Tory party candidate, whilst Kate opted for a more domestic life & motherhood, but despite the differences in their lives, they kept in touch. To help her friend, Kate suggests that Claire, the daughter of another childhood friend, might be suitable for the position as secretary to Betty's MP husband - a suggestion that is to have a devastating impact on all their lives.

***Friends & Romans.** John Miller. 2010. 71.95 (978-1-4079-1121-2(X)); audio compact disk 71.95 (978-1-4079-1122-9(8)) Pub: Soundings Ltd GBR. Dist(s): Ulverscroft US

Friends at Thrush Green. unabr. ed. Miss Read. Read by Gwen Watford. 8 cass. (Running Time: 12 hrs.). (Thrush Green Chronicles). 2000. 59.95

(978-0-7451-6216-4(9), CAB 605) Pub: Chivers Audio Bks GBR. Dist(s): AudioGO
The Cotswold village of Thrush Green is a particularly close-knit community, where most of the inhabitants have known one another since childhood. The visit of retired schoolteachers Miss Watson and Miss Fogerty gives great pleasure to all. The new headmaster, Alan Lester, is cautiously approved; while the behavior of farmer Percy Hodge is also a cause of local speculation.

Friends Come Back & That's a Good Thing. Read by Donald Davis. 1 CD. (Running Time: 59 mins.). 2002. audio compact disk 14.95 (978-0-87483-683-7(2)) Pub: August Hse. Dist(s): Natl Bk Netwk
The best friend of our youth has no replacement, ever. Though we may start out as "two peas in a pod," we often lose touch with one another. In this affecting tale of two adults who reclaim their childhood bond after thirty years apart, the comforts of friendship are affirmed with humor and wit. The second story, "The Frog Jumped Twice," recalls a childhood lesson, learned at no small cost, that comes to full flower in adulthood. As usual, Davis deftly disguises a realization of enduring values in the guise of humor and remembrance.

Friends Don't Quit - Audio Book. Scripts. Arthur Rathburn. Read by Arthur Rathburn. Read by Ursula Rathburn. 6 CDs. (Running Time: 7 hrs, 30 mins). 2006. 32.95 (978-0-9779516-3-5(4)) Fort Dane.
A true story of love and loyalty in wartime Germany.The captivating biography of three women courageously struggling to survive the turbulence of wartime Berlin.Based on live interviews, personal documents, and thorough historical research.One professional reviewer called it "The most loving, compassionate story of friendship and devotion ever.".

Friends, Enemies & Allies Episode 2. unabr. abr. ed. Simon R. Green. Narrated by Richard Rohan & Nanette Savard. 2 cass. (Running Time: 3 hrs.). (Deathstalker Ser.). 2002. 9.95 (978-1-931953-19-1(8)) Listen & Live.
The imperial Majesty Lionstone XIV ruled the human Empire with fear. When Owen Deathstalker, unwilling head of his clan, sought to avoid the perils of the Empire's warring factions, he unexpectedly found a price on his head. He fled to Mistworld, where he began to build an unlikely force to topple the thrown. With the help of his crew, Deathstalker took the first step on a far more dangerous journey to claim the role for which he'd been destined since before his birth.

Friends, Family & Countrymen. AIO Team Staff. Created by Focus on the Family Staff. 4 CDs. (Running Time: 6 hrs.). (Adventures in Odyssey Ser.: Vol. 39). (ENG.). (J). 2004. audio compact disk 24.99 (978-1-58997-046-5(2)) Pub: Focus Family. Dist(s): Tyndale Hse

Friends for Always see Be Kind, Be Friendly, Be Thankful: The Adventures of Brisky Bear & Trooper Dog

Friends for Life. unabr. ed. 1 cass., 1 CD. (Running Time: 39 min.). 9.98 (978-1-56896-158-3(8), 54179-4); 15.98 CD. (978-1-56896-157-6(X), 54179-2) Lightyear Entrtnmnt.
An album to benefit The Save the Children Foundation, which contains a wonderfully diverse blend of music & artists gathered together to celebrate the gifts of love & friendship. Incl. Boyz II Men, Wynonna, Lorrie Morgan, Marty Morgan, Los Lobos, Ziggy, Marley & The Melody Makers, Al Jarreau, Brenda Russell, The Monkees, Richard Marx, Tuck & Patti, & Catch V.

Friends Forever. Perf. by Solas. 1 cass., 1 CD. (Winnie the Pool Ser.). (J). 9.58 (DISN 60963); audio compact disk 14.38 CD Jewel box. (DISN 60963) NewSound.
Features the original Solas instrumental track.

Friends in High Places. 2007. audio compact disk (978-1-933919-08-9(6)) Catholic Answers.

Friends in High Places. unabr. ed. Donna Leon. Read by Anna Fields. 6 cass. (Running Time: 8 hrs. 30 mins.). (Commissario Guido Brunetti Mystery Ser.: Bk. 9). 2001. 44.95 (978-0-7861-2103-8(3), 2865); audio compact disk 56.00 (978-0-7861-9646-3(7), 2865) Blckstn Audio.
When Commissario Guide Brunetti is visited by a young bureaucrat concerned with investigating the lack of official approval for the building of Brunetti's apartment years before, his first reaction like any other Venetian, even a cop, is to think of whom he knows who might bring pressure to bear on the relevant local government department.

Friends in High Places. unabr. ed. Donna Leon. Narrated by Gordon Griffin. 7 cass. (Running Time: 9 hrs. 15 mins.). (Commissario Guido Brunetti Mystery Ser.: Bk. 9). 2000. 64.00 (978-1-84197-211-4(8), H1208L8) Recorded Bks.
When a young bureaucrat phones Commissero Guido Brunetti at work regarding the building plans for his apartment, the man is clearly scared by some information he plans to give Guido. When the young bureaucrat is found dead under some scaffolding, something is unmistakably going on that is greater than the fate of Guido's own apartment.

Friends, Lovers, Chocolate. Alexander McCall Smith. Narrated by Davina Porter. (Running Time: 30600 sec.). (Isabel Dalhousie Ser.: No. 2). 2005. 24.99 (978-1-4193-4330-8(0)); audio compact disk 29.99 (978-1-4193-4329-2(7)) Recorded Bks.

Friends, Lovers, Chocolate. unabr. ed. Alexander McCall Smith. Narrated by Davina Porter. 7 CDs. (Running Time: 8 hrs.). (Isabel Dalhousie Ser.: No. 2). 2005. audio compact disk 89.75 (978-1-4193-4894-5(9), C3365); 59.75 (978-1-4193-4892-1(2), 98091) Recorded Bks.
From New York Times best-selling author Alexander McCall Smith, creator of the sensationally popular No. 1 Ladies' Detective Agency series, comes the second mystery starring the ever-ethical and undeniably charming Isabel Dalhousie. Working at her niece's deli, Isabel notices a customer named Ian, who is avoiding chocolate - doctors says it's bad for the new heart he recently received. Ian is haunted by memories he can't place. Could his new heart be the cause?.

Friends of Eddie Coyle: A Novel. unabr. ed. George V. Higgins. Narrated by Mark Hammer. 4 cass. (Running Time: 5 hrs. 30 mins.). 1996. 35.00 (978-0-7887-0643-1(8), 94820E7) Recorded Bks.
This intriguing tale of cops, robbers, and big-city life will keep you on the edge of your seat.

Friends of Eddie Coyle: A Novel. unabr. ed. George V. Higgins. Read by Mark Hammer. 4 cass. (Running Time: 5 hrs. 30 min.). 1996. Rental 11.50 (94820) Recorded Bks.

Friends of Eddie Coyle: A Novel. unabr. collector's ed. George V. Higgins. Read by Walter Zimmerman. 6 cass. (Running Time: 6 hrs.). 1990. 36.00 (978-0-7366-1859-5(7), 2690) Books on Tape.
Eddie works for Jimmy Scalsi, supplying guns for bank jobs from gun-dealing Jackie. A cop named Foley is leaning on Eddie to finger Scalsi while Dillon, a full-time bartender & a part-time contract killer, is pretending to be Eddie's friend. These are the people who make up the world of Eddie Coyle. Hoods, gunmen, thieves & other unsavory characters. Looking at his "friends," Eddie knows that he has a problem - who to sell out to avoid being sent up the river - or worse.

Friends of Freeland, Pt. 1. unabr. collector's ed. Brad Leithauser. Read by Michael Prichard. 9 cass. (Running Time: 13 hrs. 30 min.). 1997. 72.00 (978-0-7366-4003-9(7), 4502-A) Books on Tape.
Political machinations & modern social problems come to an island-country in the North Atlantic. A poignant, but pointed social satire.

Friends of Freeland, Pt. 2. unabr. collector's ed. Brad Leithauser. Read by Michael Prichard. 7 cass. (Running Time: 10 hrs. 30 min.). 1997. 56.00 (978-0-7366-4004-6(5), 4502-B) Books on Tape.

Friends of Sabio & Prudente, Songs see Club de amiguitos de sabio y prudente, Canciones

Friends, Robots, Countrymen: Asimov's All Time Favorite Robot Stories. unabr. ed. Isaac Asimov. 4 cass. (Running Time: 6 hrs.). 26.95 (978-1-55656-121-4(0)) Pub: Dercum Audio. Dist(s): APG

Friends, Robots, Countrymen Vol. 1: Asimov's All Time Favorite Robot Stories. unabr. ed. Ed. by Robert Bloch et al. 4 cass. (Running Time: 6 hrs.). (Science Fiction Library). 1997. pap. bk. 21.95 Set. (978-1-55656-256-3(X)) Dercum Audio.

Friends We Keep: A Woman's Quest for the Soul of Friendship. unabr. ed. Sarah Zacharias Davis. 4 CDs. (Running Time: 4 hrs. 10 mins. 51 sec.). (ENG.). 2009. audio compact disk 19.99 (978-1-59859-573-4(3)) Oasis Audio.

Friends We Keep: A Woman's Quest for the Soul of Friendship. unabr. ed. Sarah Zacharias Davis. (Running Time: 4 hrs. 10 mins. 51 sec.). (ENG.). 2009. 13.99 (978-1-60814-512-6(3)) Oasis Audio.

Friendship see Custom

Friendship. Focus on the Family Staff. 3 cass. (Running Time: 3 hrs.). (Adventures in Odyssey Ser.). (J). (gr. 1-7). 2001. 9.99 (978-1-58997-023-6(3)) Pub: Focus Family. Dist(s): Tommy Nelson

Friendship. Running Press Staff. 3 cass. (Running Time: 3 hrs.). (Adventures in Odyssey). (J). (gr. k-4). 2001. 12.99 Pub: Focus Family. Dist(s): Tommy Nelson
Adventures in Odyssey stories packaged by theme.

Friendship. Barry Tesar. 1 cass. (Running Time: 1 hr.). (Subliminal Inspiration Ser.). 1992. 9.98 (978-1-56470-013-1(5)) Success Cass.
Subliminal program.

Friendship, Vol. 8. AIO Team Staff. Created by Focus on the Family Staff. (Running Time: 1 hr. 10 mins. 0 sec.). (Adventures in Odyssey Life Lessons Ser.). (ENG.). (J). 2005. audio compact disk 5.99 (978-1-58997-225-4(2)) Pub: Focus Family. Dist(s): Tyndale Hse

Friendship: Another Myself. 1999. 39.00 (978-0-9666941-1-6(2)) Pub: Medio Media Pubng. Dist(s): Continuum

Friendship: Dynamic Duos. Michael D. Christensen & Vickey Pahnke. 1 cass. 1998. 9.95 (978-1-57008-425-6(4), Bkcraft Inc) Deseret Bk.

***Friendship According to Humphrey.** unabr. ed. Betty Birney. (Running Time: 4 hrs.). 2010. audio compact disk 39.97 (978-1-4418-5850-4(4), 9781441858504, BriAudCD Unabrid) Brilliance Audio.

***Friendship According to Humphrey.** unabr. ed. Betty G. Birney. Read by Hal Hollings. (Running Time: 3 hrs.). (YA). 2010. 39.97 (978-1-4418-5852-8(0), 9781441858528, Brinc Audio MP3 Lib) Brilliance Audio.

***Friendship According to Humphrey.** unabr. ed. Betty G. Birney. Read by Hal Hollings. (Running Time: 3 hrs.). (YA). 2010. audio compact disk 19.99 (978-1-4418-5849-8(0), 9781441858498, Bril Audio CD Unabri) Brilliance Audio.

Friendship Between Men & the Transcendent Function. Read by Murray Stein. 1 cass. (Running Time: 90 min.). 1988. 10.95 (978-0-7822-0282-3(9), 355) C G Jung IL.

***Friendship Bread: A Novel.** unabr. ed. Darien Gee. (ENG.). 2011. audio compact disk 40.00 (978-0-307-91442-2(9), Random AudioBks) Pub: Random Audio Pubg. Dist(s): Random

Friendship, Love & Sex. Asha Praver et al. 2 cass. (Ananda Talks about Marriage Ser.). 14.95 (DM-2) Crystal Clarity.
Topics include: why friendship is the key to a successful marriage; understanding the power of love; sex & the single person; birth control; unwanted pregnancies & abortion.

Friendship Song. Karen Blomgren & Clarence Thomson. 1 cass. (Running Time: 13 min.). (J). 1993. 6.95 (AA2645) Credence Commun.
An enchanting children's story & song about a little Meadowlark who couldn't learn to sing...until she found a friend.

Friendship Songs: Year 1. 1 cass. (Running Time: 1 hr. 30 mins.). 9.95 (978-1-56212-748-0(9), 300610) FaithAliveChr.

Friendship Songs: Year 2. 1 cass. (Running Time: 1 hr. 30 mins.). 9.95 (978-1-56212-749-7(7), 300620) FaithAliveChr.

Friendship Songs: Year 3. 1 cass. (Running Time: 1 hr. 30 mins.). 9.95 (978-1-56212-750-3(0), 300630) FaithAliveChr.

Friendship Stew: Songs from Here, There, & Around the World. Perf. by Pam Donkin & Greta Pedersen. 1 cass. (Running Time: 50m). (J). 2001. 9.95 (978-1-58467-012-4(6), GW1062); audio compact disk 14.95 (978-1-58467-013-1(4)) Gentle Wind.

Friendship, The Nature Of. unabr. ed. Nathaniel Branden. 1 cass. (Running Time: 44 min.). 12.95 (837) J Norton Pubs.
A discussion about different kinds of friends that exist; the differentiation between friends & acquaintances; & the involvement of intimacy & sex with friends.

Friendship the Year of the Friend: Proverbs 18:24. Ed Young. 1994. 4.95 (978-0-7417-1993-5(2), 993) Win Walk.

Friendship with God: An Uncommon Dialogue. unabr. ed. Neale Donald Walsch. Read by Neale Donald Walsch. Read by Edward Asner & Ellen Burstyn. 6 cass. (Running Time: 9 hrs.). 1999. 34.95 (978-1-57453-332-3(0)) Audio Lit.
Walsch continues his extraordinary dialogue, asking how the wisdom in "Conversations with God" can be applied to every day situations & what we can do to have a working friendship with God.

Friendships: You Can Take Them with You. Lucile Johnson. 1 cass. 1996. 9.98 (978-1-57734-100-0(7), 06005519) Covenant Comms.
Enjoy the sweet rewards of friendship.

Frieze of Doctors' Wives: Mrs. Humbleby, Mrs. Grandestin, Mrs. Frossart, Mrs. Chivers see Osbert Sitwell Reading His Poetry

Fright Before Christmas, unabr. ed. Tom B. Stone. Narrated by Jeff Woodman. 2 cass. (Running Time: 2 hrs. 15 mins.). (Graveyard School Ser.: No. 15). (gr. 3-7). 19.00 (978-0-7887-1093-3(1), 95124E7) Recorded Bks.
An adventure of spooky danger & grisly humor centers around a school so weird that its students are dying to go to class. Available to libraries only.

Frightful's Daughter. Jean Craighead George. Narrated by Jeff Woodman. (Running Time: 15 mins.). 2002. 10.00 (978-1-4025-4099-8(X)) Recorded Bks.

Frightful's Mountain. unabr. ed. Jean Craighead George. Narrated by Jeff Woodman. 5 cass. (Running Time: 6 hrs. 20 mins.). (YA). 2001. pap. bk. & stu. ed. 75.99 Recorded Bks.
Frightful, the peregrine falcon, is back. Freed from captors, she soars into unfamiliar woodlands & finds a mate. But construction crews, bird poachers & even a bald eagle threaten her new family.

Frightful's Mountain. unabr. ed. Jean Craighead George. Narrated by Jeff Woodman. 5 pieces. (Running Time: 6 hrs. 15 mins.). (gr. 5 up). 2001. 52.00 (978-0-7887-4553-9(0), 96327E7) Recorded Bks.

Frightful's Mountain. unabr. ed. Jean Craighead George. Narrated by Jeff Woodman. 6 CDs. (Running Time: 6 hrs. 15 mins.). (gr. 5 up). 2001. audio compact disk 58.00 (978-0-7887-5218-6(9), C1366E7) Recorded Bks.
Freed from captors, Frightful soars into unfamiliar woodlands & finds a mate. But construction crews, bird poachers & even a bald eagle threaten her family.

Frindle. Andrew Clements. Read by John Fleming. 8 cass. (Running Time: 1 hrs. 40 mins.). (J). 2000. 64.00 (978-0-7366-9134-5(0)) Books on Tape.
Nicholas Allen is not a troublemaker, but he likes to live things up at Lincoln Elementary (who can forget the time he turned his classroom into a tropical island). But nobody gets away with anything in Mrs. Granger's fifth grade language arts class; plus she is a fanatic about the dictionary. Nick has the greatest plan yet, he invents a new word. From now on a pen will be called a frindle.

Frindle. unabr. ed. Andrew Clements. Read by John Fleming. 2 cass. (Running Time: 3 hrs.). (J). (gr. 1-8). 1999. 23.00 (LL 0126, Chivers Child Audio) AudioGO.

Frindle. unabr. ed. Andrew Clements. Read by John Fleming. 2 cass. (Running Time: 1 hr. 39 mins.). (J). (gr. 3-7). 1998. 23.00 (978-0-8072-7993-9(5), YA961CX, Listening Lib) Random Audio Pubg.
Nick is not a troublemaker, but he livens things up at Lincoln Elementary. He invents a word - frindle - and it becomes a new word for pen.

Frindle. unabr. ed. Andrew Clements. 2 CDs. (Running Time: 1 hr. 39 mins.). (Middle Grade Cassette Librariestm Ser.). (J). (gr. 3-7). 2004. audio compact disk 20.40 (978-0-8072-1160-1(5), S YA 961 CD, Listening Lib) Pub: Random Audio Pubg. Dist(s): NetLibrary CO
"Nicholas Allen likes to liven things up at school and he has his best plan yet for Mrs. Granger's fifth grade language arts class-he invents a new word. From now on a pen will be called a frindle, and it doesn't take long to catch on and spread beyond the school.".

Frindle. unabr. ed. Andrew Clements. Read by John Fleming. 2 vols. (Running Time: 1 hr. 39 mins.). (Middle Grade Cassette Librariestm Ser.). (J). (gr. 3-7). 2004. pap. bk. 29.00 (978-0-8072-7994-6(3), S YA 961 SP, Listening Lib) Random Audio Pubg.

Frindle. unabr. ed. Andrew Clements. Read by John Fleming. 2 CDs. (Running Time: 1 hr. 39 mins.). (ENG.). (J). (gr. 3). 2004. audio compact disk 19.99 (978-1-4000-9505-6(0), Listening Lib) Pub: Random Audio Pubg. Dist(s): Random

Frindle. unabr. ed. Andrew Clements. Read by Keith Nobbs. (Running Time: 1 hr. 40 mins. 0 sec.). (ENG.). (J). 2009. audio compact disk 14.99 (978-0-7435-8170-7(9)) Pub: S&S Audio. Dist(s): S and S Inc

Frindle, Set. unabr. ed. Andrew Clements. Read by John Fleming. 2 cass. (YA). 1999. 16.98 (FS9-43236) Highsmith.

Frisbee: Official Soundtrack: the Life & Death of a Hippie Preacher. 2007. audio compact disk 15.99 (978-0-9790740-4-2(5)) D DiSabatino.

Fritz Perls - Gestalt Therapy. Robert Stone. 1 cass. 1983. 10.00 (978-0-938137-02-3(6)) Listen & Learn.
Includes: definition of gestalt; foreground-background; here & now orientation; neurotic mechanisms; content vs. process; rules & games; topdog vs. underdog; inborn wisdom of the organism; nonverbal behavior; dream interpretation & integration.

Frog & Toad. unabr. ed. Arnold Lobel. Read by Arnold Lobel. 2 CDs. (Running Time: 3 hrs.). (J). 2004. audio compact disk 17.95 (978-0-06-074053-5(1), HarperChildAud) HarperCollins Pubs.

Frog & Toad All Year. Arnold Lobel & Donna Addison. (I Can Read It All by Myself Ser.). (J). (gr. 1-3). 1982. bk. 33.26 (978-0-394-69358-3(2)) Random.

Frog & Toad All Year. abr. ed. Arnold Lobel. Illus. by Arnold Lobel. (I Can Read Bks.). (J). (gr. k-3). 2005. 9.99 (978-0-06-078698-4(1), HarperFestival) HarperCollins Pubs.

***Frog & Toad All Year.** abr. ed. Arnold Lobel. Read by Arnold Lobel. (ENG.). 2006. (978-0-06-123223-7(8)) HarperCollins Pubs.

***Frog & Toad All Year.** unabr. ed. Arnold Lobel. Read by Arnold Lobel. (ENG.). 2008. (978-0-06-171232-6(9)) HarperCollins Pubs.

Frog & Toad All Year. unabr. abr. ed. Arnold Lobel. Illus. by Arnold Lobel. 1 cass. (I Can Read Bks.). (J). (ps-3). 1990. 8.99 (978-1-55994-228-7(2)) HarperCollins Pubs.

***Frog & Toad Are Friends.** abr. ed. Arnold Lobel. Read by Arnold Lobel. (ENG.). 2006. (978-0-06-123222-0(X)) HarperCollins Pubs.

***Frog & Toad Are Friends.** unabr. ed. Arnold Lobel. Read by Arnold Lobel. (ENG.). 2008. (978-0-06-171230-2(2)) HarperCollins Pubs.

Frog & Toad Are Friends. unabr. abr. ed. Arnold Lobel. Illus. by Arnold Lobel. 1 cass. (I Can Read Bks.). (J). (ps-3). 1990. 8.99 (978-1-55994-229-4(0)) HarperCollins Pubs.

Frog & Toad Are Friends. unabr. abr. ed. Arnold Lobel. Illus. by Arnold Lobel. (I Can Read Bks.). (J). (ps-3). 2005. 9.99 (978-0-06-074106-8(6), HarperFestival) HarperCollins Pubs.

***Frog & Toad Audio Collection.** unabr. ed. Arnold Lobel. Read by Arnold Lobel. (ENG.). 2004. (978-0-06-081796-1(8)); (978-0-06-081795-4(X)) HarperCollins Pubs.

Frog & Toad Calls of the Pacific Coast. Carlos Davidson. 1 cass. (Running Time: 1 hr. 05 min.). 1996. 11.95 (978-0-938027-14-0(X)); audio compact disk 14.95 CD. (978-0-938027-15-7(8)) Crows Nest Bird.
Field guide for 25 species of frogs & toads that occur in the Pacific Coast states.

Frog & Toad Calls of the Rocky Mountains. Carlos Davidson. 1 cass. (Running Time: 1 hr. 07 min.). 1995. 12.95 (978-0-938027-29-4(8)); audio compact disk 15.95 CD. (978-0-938027-30-0(1)) Crows Nest Bird.
Thirty-eight species of frogs & toads that occur in the Rocky Mountains & Southern United States & Canadian provinces. Includes a 28-page booklet of descriptions of calls, breeding season & habitats.

Frog & Toad Collection. unabr. ed. Arnold Lobel. 1 cass. (Running Time: 1 hr. 30 mins.). 2003. 7.99 (978-0-06-058445-0(9)) HarperCollins Pubs.

Frog & Toad Together. Arnold Lobel. Read by Arnold Lobel. 1 read-along cass. (Running Time: 15 min.). (I Can Read Bks.). (J). (gr. 1-3). 1973. HarperCollins Pubs.
Features a turn-te-page beep signal on one side & uninterrupted narration for more experienced readers on the other.

***Frog & Toad Together.** abr. ed. Arnold Lobel. Read by Arnold Lobel. (ENG.). 2006. (978-0-06-123216-9(5)) HarperCollins Pubs.

Frog & Toad Together. abr. ed. Arnold Lobel. Illus. by Arnold Lobel. (I Can Read Bks.). (J). (ps-3). 2007. 9.99 (978-0-06-124773-6(1), HarperFestival) HarperCollins Pubs.

***Frog & Toad Together.** unabr. ed. Arnold Lobel. Read by Arnold Lobel. (ENG.). 2008. (978-0-06-171218-0(3)) HarperCollins Pubs.

Frog & Toad Together. unabr. abr. ed. Arnold Lobel. Illus. by Arnold Lobel. 1 cass. (I Can Read Bks.). (J). (ps-3). 1990. pap. bk. 8.99 (978-1-55994-230-0(4)) HarperCollins Pubs.

Frog in the Kitchen Sink. Lyrics by Jim Post. Moderated by Jim Post & Janet Smith Post. (J). 2001. audio compact disk 10.00 (978-0-9702826-0-6(5)) BTSBRBE.

Frog in the Meadow: Music, Now I'm Two! John M. Feierabend & Luann Saunders. 1 cass. (First Steps in Music Ser.). (ENG., (J). (ps). 2000. 9.95 (978-1-57999-089-3(4)); audio compact disk 12.95 (978-1-57999-085-5(1)) Pub: GIA Pubns. Dist(s): IPG Chicago
Geared toward two-year-olds, this CD is a compilation of songs & rhymes from all five of the First Steps in Music Books. There are 67 songs & rhymes, such as "Trot, Trot to Boston," "Wee Wiggie," "The Mulberry Bush," "All the Pretty Little Horses" & "Peas Porridge Hot".

Frog in the Throat. unabr. ed. Elizabeth Ferrars. Read by Diana Bishop. 6 cass. (Running Time: 6 hrs. 15 min.). (Isis Ser.). (J). 1998. 54.95 (978-0-7531-0239-8(0), 980209) Pub: ISIS Lrg Prnt GBR. Dist(s): Ulverscroft US
Virginia Freer & her husband, Felix, attend a party celebrating the engagement of a local poet & a best-selling historical novelist. The novelist's sister turns up, distraught with the news that she has found her sister shot dead. Virginia, Felix & their friends, the Bostcotts accompany her - & find circumstances drastically & shockingly changed.

Frog on a Log. (Song Box Ser.). (gr. 1-2). 8.50 (978-0-7802-2257-1(1)) Wright Group.

Frog on a Log: 1 Big Book, 6 Each of 1 Student Book, & 1 Cassette. (Song Box Ser.). (gr. 1-2). 68.95 (978-0-7802-3204-4(6)) Wright Group.

***Frog Prince.** Anonymous. 2009. (978-1-60136-531-6(4)) Audio Holding.

Frog Prince. Jan Callner. 1 cass. (Running Time: 47 min.). Dramatization. (J). (ps-4). 1998. 10.95 (978-1-928851-01-1(0)); audio compact disk 14.95 (978-1-928851-00-4(2)) Mike & Me.
Musical play with dialogue & 7 songs, with 6 characters.

Frog Prince. Perf. by Jan Callner. 1 cass. Dramatization. (J). 1999. 9.98; audio compact disk 14.98 Penton Overseas.
In this new version a prince & royal companion find themselves hopping all over the place. The upbeat music is catchy & the voices of the six characters are enchanting.

Frog Prince. Based on a story by Wilhelm K. Grimm & Jacob W. Grimm. 1 cass. (Running Time: 45 mins.). (J). 2001. 12.95 (MMPR003) Lodestone Catalog.

Frog Prince. Robert Guillaume. (J). 1992. 9.95 (978-1-882179-02-2(1)) Confetti Ent.

Frog Prince. Read by Julie Harris. 1 read-along cass. (Running Time: 9 min.). Dramatization. (World of Words Ser.). (J). (gr. k-3). bk. 15.00 (SAC 6500E) Spoken Arts.

Frog Prince. unabr. ed. Naomi Fox. Illus. by Neal Fox. Narrated by Robert Guillaume. 1 cass. (Running Time: 15 min.). Dramatization. (Confetti Company Proudly Presents Ser.). (J). (ps-1). 1992. bk. 9.95 (978-1-882179-11-4(0)) Confetti Ent.
The Confetti Company, a cast of children, reenact the classic fairy tale with a modern upbeat tempo.

Frog Prince: A Fairy Tale for Consenting Adults, unabr. ed. Stephen Mitchell. Read by Stephen Mitchell. 2 cass. (Running Time: 3 hrs.). 1999. 17.95 (978-1-57453-345-3(2)) Audio Lit.
Tells the story of a meditative frog's love for a rebellious princess, how she came to love him in spite of herself & how her refusal to compromise helped him become who he truly was. This is a magical tale that moves (amphibiously) from story to meditation & back, from the outrageous to the sublime.

Frog Prince: Theatre Package. unabr. ed. 1 cass. (Running Time: 45 mins.). Dramatization. (J). (ps-4). 2001. 14.95 (978-1-928851-08-0(8)) Mike & Me.
Musical play with dialogue & 7 songs, with 6 characters. Feature Broadway actors & recording artists. Tales are based on the Brothers Grimm stories. Includes puppet theatre and puppet.

Frog Prince: Theatre Package. unabr. ed. Jan Callner. 1 CD. (Running Time: 45 mins.). Dramatization. (J). (ps-4). 2001. audio compact disk 19.95 (978-1-928851-06-6(1)) Mike & Me.

Frog Prince, Continued. Jon Scieszka. Read by Patrick G. Lawlor. 1 cass. (Running Time: 10:40 min.). (Live Oak Readalong Ser.). (J). 2003. pap. bk. 37.95 (978-1-59112-230-2(9)) Live Oak Media.

Frog Prince, Continued. Jon Scieszka. Illus. by Steve Johnson. 14 vols. (Running Time: 11 mins.). 2003. pap. bk. 39.95 (978-1-59112-522-8(7)) Live Oak Media.

Frog Prince, Continued. Jon Scieszka. Illus. by Steve Johnson. (Running Time: 11 mins.). (J). 2003. 9.95 (978-1-59112-227-2(9)); audio compact disk 12.95 (978-1-59112-489-4(1)) Live Oak Media.

Frog Prince, Continued. Jon Scieszka. Read by Patrick G. Lawlor. 11 vols. (Running Time: 11 mins.). (Live Oak Readalong Ser.). (J). 2003. bk. 25.95 (978-1-59112-229-6(5)); bk. 28.95 (978-1-59112-515-0(4)); pap. bk. 16.95 (978-1-59112-228-9(7)); pap. bk. 18.95 (978-1-59112-490-0(5)) Pub: Live Oak Media. Dist(s): AudioGO

Frog Princess. unabr. ed. E. D. Baker. Read by Katherine Kellgren. 4 cass. (Running Time: 5 hrs. 30 mins.). (J). 2005. 39.75 (978-1-4193-2953-1(7), 97971) Recorded Bks.
Princess Emma will do just about anything to get out of marrying the selfcentered Prince Jorge. So when she meets a frog named Eadric who claims - of course - to be a prince, she decides to give him a kiss and see what happens. Bad idea. The frog stays a frog, and worse still, Emma turns into a frog herself. It turns out only the person who cast the spell can break it, so Emma and Eadric are soon hopping along trying to find the witch who can make them human again. This clever twist on the classic fairy tale is full of good-natured fun and romance.

Frog Someday: Early Explorers Early Set A Audio CD. Benchmark Education Staff. (J). 2006. audio compact disk 10.00 (978-1-4108-7610-2(1)) Benchmark Educ.

Frog Talk. 1 cass. (Running Time: 60 min.). 1994. audio compact disk 15.95 CD. (0247, Creativ Pub) Quayside.
Wood frogs, leopard frogs, & spring peepers.

Frog Talk. 1 cass. (Running Time: 60 min.). 1994. 9.95 (0243, NrthWrd Bks) TandN Child.

Frog Town Band. Lyrics by Janet Smith Post. Music by Jim Post. 1. (J). 2000. audio compact disk 20.00 (978-0-9702826-2-0(1)) BTSBRBE.

Frog Went a Courtin. (J). 2004. pap. bk. 14.95 (978-0-7882-0506-4(4)) Weston Woods.

Frog Went A-Courtin' 2004. pap. bk. 14.95 (978-1-56008-053-4(1)); 8.95 (978-1-56008-900-1(8)); 8.95 (978-1-56008-131-9(7)); cass. & flmstrp 30.00 (978-0-89719-602-4(3)) Weston Woods.

Frog Went A-Courtin' (J). 2004. bk. 24.95 (978-0-89719-874-5(3)); pap. bk. 32.75 (978-1-55592-225-2(2)); pap. bk. 32.75 (978-1-55592-226-9(0)) Weston Woods.

Frog Went A-Courtin' John Langstaff. Illus. by Feodor Rojankovsky. 1 cass., 5 bks. (Running Time: 13 min.). (J). pap. bk. 32.75 Weston Woods.
John Langstaff sings & narrated this 400 year old ballad about the courtship of Mr. Frog & Miss Mouse.

Frog Went A-Courtin' John Langstaff. Read by John Langstaff. 1 cass. (Running Time: 13 min.). (J). (ps-3). 8.95 (RAC028) Weston Woods.
John Langstaff sings & narrates this 400-year-old ballad about the courtship of Mr. Frog & Miss Mouse.

Frog Went A-Courtin' John Langstaff. Illus. by Feodor Rojankovsky. 1 cass. (Running Time: 13 min.). (J). (ps-3). bk. 24.95 Weston Woods.

Frog Went A-Courtin' John Langstaff. Read by John Langstaff. Illus. by Feodor Rojankovsky. 1 cass. (Running Time: 13 min.). (J). (ps-3). pap. bk. 12.95 (PRA028) Weston Woods.

Froggie Went A-Courting. Marjorie Priceman. Perf. by Dee Hoty. 1 cass. (Running Time: 8 min.). (J). (gr. k-3). 2001. bk. 26.90 (978-0-8045-6879-1(0), 6879) Spoken Arts.
With a wedding gown from Chinatown, a cake with as many layers as the Empire State Building and a party atop the Statue of Liberty, this is one wedding celebration no one will want to miss!.

Froggie Who Flunked Jumping School. Louie Swift. Read by Barry McAlister. 4 cass. (Running Time: 2 hrs.). Dramatization. (J). (ps-3). 2000. lib. bdg. 19.95 (978-0-9675577-2-4(0)) Puddleduck Pubg.
The complete set of the Froggie stories, thirty-one songs, stories & poems for children with music, character voices & sound effect.

Froggie Who Flunked Jumping School, Vol. 1. Louie Swift. Read by Barry McAlister. 6 cass. (Running Time: 30 min.). Dramatization. (Froggie's Tales: Vol. 1). (J). (ps-3). 2001. 12.95 (978-0-9675577-3-1(9)) Puddleduck Pubg.
Eighteen songs, stories & poems for children. Little Froggie narrates the stories, along with 20 character voices, music & sound effects to produce an exceptional hour of entertainment. Stories, songs & poems include the "The Froggie Who Flunked Jumping School", "Get up, Little Horsie", "The Goo-Run From Poo-Ruu", "The Little Dutch Hound", "The Crow's Tall Tree" & many more.

Froggy Eats Out. unabr. ed. Jonathan London. Narrated by John McDonough. 1 cass. (Running Time: 15 mins.). (ps up). 2001. 10.00 (978-0-7887-5498-2(X), 96626) Recorded Bks.
Froggy is going out to dinner with his parents for their anniversary. He's hoping for burgers and flies, but Froggy's mother tells him Chez Yum is a very fancy restaurant. Froggy puts on his best clothes. He even has to wash. At the restaurant, Froggy's mother warns him to "be neat, be quiet, and don't put your feet on the table." It's just too much to ask of a lively little frog. Froggy can't help himself, he sucks on ice and sugar, he slurps spaghetti and flies and he flops and sings. When he sees Frogilina, a cute girl frog from his school, across the room, he's so embarrassed he crawls under the table. Then the real fun begins.

Froggy Gets Dressed. unabr. ed. Jonathan London. Narrated by John McDonough. 1 cass. (Running Time: 15 mins.). (ps up). 1998. 10.00 (978-0-7887-1904-2(1), 95325E7) Recorded Bks.
Froggy can't wait to play in the snow, but will he be able to pull together mittens, boots & all those chilly weather layers?.

Froggy Gets Dressed. unabr. ed. Jonathan London. Read by John McDonough. 1 cass. (Running Time: 15 min.). (J). (gr. 1). 1998. 79.40 CLASS SET . (978-0-7887-3555-4(1), 46209); 23.24 HMWK SET . (978-0-7887-1932-5(7), 40639) Recorded Bks.
Froggy can't wait to play in the snow, but will he be able to pull together mittens, boots, & all those chilly weather layers?.

Froggy Goes to School. Jonathan London. Narrated by John McDonough. (Running Time: 15 mins.). (J). 1998. 10.75 (978-1-4193-1601-2(X)) Recorded Bks.

Froggy goes to the Doctor. Jonathan London. Narrated by John McDonough. (Running Time: 15 mins.). (ps up). 10.00 (978-1-4025-3420-1(5)) Recorded Bks.

Froggy Plays in the Band. Jonathan London. Narrated by John McDonough. (Running Time: 15 mins.). 2002. 10.00 (978-1-4025-3984-8(3)) Recorded Bks.

Froggy Plays Soccer. unabr. ed. Jonathan London. Narrated by John McDonough. 1 cass. (Running Time: 20 mins.). (J). 2001. pap. bk. & stu. ed. 32.99 Recorded Bks.
Froggy is so excited he can't get to sleep. But morning comes & he's ready to go. If the Dream Team beats the Wild Things, they win the City Cup.

Froggy Plays Soccer. unabr. ed. Jonathan London. Read by John McDonough. 1 cass. (Running Time: 15 mins.). (ps up). 2001. 10.00 (978-0-7887-4716-8(9), 96390E7) Recorded Bks.

Frogs & French Kisses. unabr. ed. Sarah Mlynowski. Read by Ariadne Meyers. 7 CDs. (Running Time: 8 hrs. 14 mins.). (YA). (gr. 6-9). 2008. audio compact disk 55.00 (978-0-7393-7943-1(7), Listening Lib) Pub: Random Audio Pubg. Dist(s): Random

Frogs & Their Monster. Gurumayi Chidvilasananda. 1 CD. (Running Time: 19 mins.). (J). 1999. audio compact disk 9.95 (978-0-911307-94-8(X), 106203, Siddha Yoga Pubs) SYDA Found.
"If only something would happen," the frogs wished. They were bored. Then with a great crash! something did happen. In the end, through the help of a wise friend, the frogs learned how to cherish the peacefulness of their lovely marsh.

Frogs & Their Monster. Gurumayi Chidvilasananda. Read by Gurumayi Chidvilasananda. 1 cass. (Running Time: 19 mins.). (J). 1999. (978-0-911307-93-1(1), Siddha Yoga Pubs) SYDA Found.

***Frogs & Toads All Sang.** unabr. ed. Arnold Lobel. Read by Mark Linn-baker. Illus. by Adrianne Lobel. (ENG.). 2009. (978-0-06-196704-7(1)); (978-0-06-190164-5(4)) HarperCollins Pubs.

Frogs of the Great Lakes Region. Compiled by Jim McGrath. Narrated by Jim McGrath. 2000. audio compact disk 14.00 (978-0-9779615-0-4(8)) Nature Dis.

Frog's Party. Mary Lu Walker. 1 cass. (Running Time: 40 min.). (J). (ps-3). 1989. 9.95 (978-0-939065-48-6(7), GW1052) Gentle Wind.
Mary Lu Walker writes entertaining songs for preschoolers that are sweet, simple & meaningful. These cute songs about animals, birthdays & mittens are also about self-esteem, peace & appreciating our wonderful earth.

Frog's Party. Mary Lu Walker. (J). 1999. audio compact disk 14.95 (978-0-939065-89-9(4)) Gentle Wind.

Frogs Wore Red Suspenders. unabr. ed. Jack Prelutsky. Read by Jack Prelutsky. 1 cass. (Running Time: 1 hr. 30 mins.). 2003. 7.99 (978-0-06-058456-6(4)) HarperCollins Pubs.
Poet laureate of the preposterous, Jack Preslutsky has a new partner in rhyme - Petra Mathers - and the result is a stupendous spree of twenty-eight exuberant poems. In this collection there are tongue-twisting (but real) places to visit, such as Tuscaloosa and Winnemucca. There are remarkable sights, such as an elephant perched in a sycamore tree. And there are unforgettable characters, including Granny Gooding, Sarah Small, and Barnaby Boone, all of whose poems are guaranteed to make you smile. Young, sweet, and simply silly, you can bet your boots that this book will have everyone seeing red - suspenders, that is!.

Frogs Wore Red Suspenders. unabr. ed. Jack Prelutsky. Read by Jack Prelutsky. 2 CDs. (Running Time: 2 hrs.). (J). 2005. 13.95 (978-0-06-075836-3(8), HarperChildAud) HarperCollins Pubs.

***Frogs Wore Red Suspenders.** unabr. ed. Jack Prelutsky. Read by Jack Prelutsky. (ENG.). 2005. (978-0-06-083998-7(8), GreenwillowBks); (978-0-06-083999-4(6), GreenwillowBks) HarperCollins Pubs.

Frogspawn & Floor Polish. Mary Mackie. Read by Diana Bishop. 5 cass. (Running Time: 6 hrs. 30 mins.). (Soundings Ser.). (J). 2004. 49.95 (978-1-84283-623-1(4)); audio compact disk 64.95 (978-1-84283-650-7(1)) Pub: ISIS Lrg Prnt GBR. Dist(s): Ulverscroft US

Frohliche Weihnachten: Sing along & Learn Carols in German. (Teach Me Ser.). (GER.). (J). (ps-13). 2007. audio compact disk 14.99 (978-1-59972-903-9(2), Tch Me) Teach Me.

Froissart's Chronicles - Excerpts: From the Great Wars of England & France. unabr. ed. Excerpts. Jean Froissart. Narrated by John Horton. 3 cass. (Running Time: 3 hrs.). 1990. 26.00 (978-1-55690-190-4(9), 90051E7) Recorded Bks.
Jean Froissart (1337-1410) was the world's first great war correspondent, covering the great age of the Hundred Years War. Documentary accounts by the 14th Century chronicler, Froissart, of some of the major events of his day.

From a Buick 8. unabr. ed. Stephen King. 9 cass. (Running Time: 13 hrs. 30 mins.). 2004. 93.00 (978-1-4025-1886-7(2)) Recorded Bks.

From a Buick 8. unabr. ed. Stephen King. 9 cass. (Running Time: 11 hrs. 15 mins.). 2002. 49.95 (2C370) Recorded Bks.
For 20 years, an abandoned Buick Roadmaster has been stored in a shed behind a police barracks in rural Pennsylvania. It is a continual source of the strange and supernatural: weird flowers grow in it, temperatures drop, alien beings creep out. Written at the time the NYT best-selling author was almost killed by a car, this novel examines the horrors that lurk in the dark and the consequences of trying too hard to explain them.

From a Buick 8. unabr. ed. Stephen King. 12 CDs. (Running Time: 13 hrs. 30 mins.). 2002. audio compact disk 124.00 (978-1-4025-2975-7(9), C1860) Recorded Bks.

From a Buick 8. unabr. ed. Stephen King. Read by Stephen Tobolowsky et al. 10 CDs. (Running Time: 133 hrs. 0 mins. 0 sec.). (ENG., 2002. audio compact disk 49.95 (978-0-7435-2096-6(3), Audioworks) Pub: S&S Audio. Dist(s): S and S Inc
The state police of Troop D in rural Pennsylvania have kept a secret in Shed B out back of the barracks ever since 1979, when Troopers Ennis Rafferty and Curtis Wilcox answered a call from a gas station just down the road and came back with an abandoned Buick Roadmaster. Curt Wilcox knew old cars, and he knew immediately that this one was...wrong, just wrong. A few hours later, when Rafferty vanished, Wilcox and his fellow troopers knew the car was worse than dangerous. Curt's avid curiosity took the lead, and they investigated as best they could, as much as they dared. Over the years, the troop absorbed the mystery as part of the background to their work, the Buick 8 sitting out there like a still-life painting that breathes - inhaling a little bit of this world, exhaling a little bit of what world it came from. In the fall of 2001, a few months after Curt Wilcox is killed in a gruesome auto accident, his eighteen-year-old boy, Ned, starts coming by the barracks. Sandy Dearborn, Sergeant Commanding, knows it's the boy's way of holding onto his father, and Ned is allowed to become part of the Troop D family. One day he looks in the window of Shed B and discovers family secret. Like his father, Ned wants answers... From a Buick 8 is an audiobook about our fascination with deadly things, about our insistence on answers when there are none, about terror and courage in the face of the unknowable.

From a Buick 8. unabr. ed. Stephen King. Read by James Rebhorn et al. 2006. 29.95 (978-0-7435-6333-8(6), Audioworks) Pub: S&S Audio. Dist(s): S and S Inc

From a Buick 8. unabr. ed. Stephen King. Read by James Rebhorn et al. (Running Time: 133 hrs. 0 mins. 0 sec.). (ENG.). 2008. audio compact disk 21.99 (978-0-7435-8161-5(X)) Pub: S&S Audio. Dist(s): S and S Inc

From a Poem see Poetry of Pasternak

From A Small Place near You. Fresh Air Production. (Running Time: 1 hr.). 2005. 16.95 (978-1-59912-927-3(2)) Iofy Corp.

From a World at War to the Triumph of Freedom, Vol. 2. unabr. ed. William J. Bennett. Narrated by Jon Gauger. (America: the Last Best Hope Ser.). (ENG.). 2007. 34.99 (978-1-60814-032-9(6)) Oasis Audio.

From a World at War to the Triumph of Freedom, 1914-1989, Vol. 2. unabr. ed. William J. Bennett. Narrated by Jon Gauger. (Running Time: 20 hrs. 28 mins. 58 sec.). (America: the Last Best Hope Ser.). (ENG.). 2007. audio compact disk 49.99 (978-1-59859-208-5(4)) Oasis Audio.

From Africa to the Americas: African-American Hymns. Read by Claude J. Johnson. 1 cass. (Running Time: 30 min.). (Horizon Ser.). 9.95 (HO-88-02-23, HarperThor) HarpC GBR.

From Africa to the Americas: Brazilian Samba. Read by Taj Mahal. 1 cass. (Running Time: 30 min.). (Horizon Ser.). 9.95 (HO-88-02-16, HarperThor) HarpC GBR.

***From Agnes with Love.** 2010. audio compact disk (978-1-59171-232-9(7)) Falcon Picture.

From Alienation to Cynicism: Effects of Watergate on the Voter see Campaigning, Innovative: Four Case Studies

From Ambition to Meaning. Wayne W. Dyer. 4 CDs. 2009. audio compact disk 23.95 (978-1-4019-1188-1(9)); audio compact disk 23.95 (978-1-4019-1827-9(1)) Hay House.

From Anger to Forgiveness. Earnie Larsen & Carol Larsen Hegarty. 1 cass. (Running Time: 60 min.). 1992. pap. bk. 10.00 (978-0-89486-835-1(7)) Hazelden.
Earnie Larsen delivers a one-to-one explanation of the life-enhancing power of forgiveness.

From Anger to Intimacy: How Forgiveness Can Transform a Marriage. unabr. ed. Gary Smalley. Narrated by Lloyd James. (Running Time: 7 hrs. 30 mins. 0 sec.). (ENG.). 2008. audio compact disk 21.98 (978-1-59644-666-3(8), christianSeed) christianaud.

***from Anger to Intimacy: How Forgiveness Can Transform a Marriage.** unabr. ed. Greg Smalley & Ted Cunningham. Narrated by Lloyd James. (ENG.). 2008. 12.98 (978-1-59644-667-0(6), christianSeed) christianaud.

From Ashes to Ash, Dust to Stardust: The Ins & Outs, Ups & Downs of Alchemical Soul. Beverley Zabriskie. 1 cass. (Running Time: 1 hr. 12 min.). 1995. 10.95 (978-0-7822-0504-6(6), 579) C G Jung IL.
Jungian analyst Beverley Zabriskie guides the listener through Jung's understanding of alchemical soul.

From Baghdad to America: Life Lessons from a Dog Named Lava. Jay Kopelman. Read by Christopher Lane. (Playaway Adult Nonfiction Ser.). (ENG.). 2009. 49.99 (978-1-60812-531-9(9)) Find a World.

From Baghdad to America: Life Lessons from a Dog Named Lava. unabr. ed. Jay Kopelman. Read by Christopher Lane. (Running Time: 3 hrs. 30 mins. 0 sec.). (ENG.). 2008. audio compact disk 19.99 (978-1-4001-5875-1(3)); audio compact disk 49.99 (978-1-4001-3875-3(2)) Pub: Tantor Media. Dist(s): IngramPubServ

From Baghdad to America: Life Lessons from a Dog Named Lava. unabr. ed. Jay Kopelman. Read by Christopher Lane. Frwd. by Wayne Pacelle. (Running Time: 3 hrs. 30 mins. 0 sec.). (ENG.). 2008. audio compact disk 24.99 (978-1-4001-0875-6(6)) Pub: Tantor Media. Dist(s): IngramPubServ

From Baghdad with Love. unabr. ed. Read by Michael Kramer. (Running Time: 3 hrs. 59 mins.). (ENG.). 2006. 15.00 (978-0-7393-4298-5(3), Random AudioBks) Pub: Random Audio Pubg. Dist(s): Random

From Battle to Victory. Kenneth Copeland. 4 cass. 1992. 20.00 Set. (978-0-88114-915-9(2)) K Copeland Pubns.
Biblical teaching on overcoming power.

From Bauhaus to Our House. unabr. ed. Tom Wolfe. Read by Dennis McKee. 3 cass. (Running Time: 4 hrs.). 1999. 23.95 (978-0-7861-1620-1(X), 2448) Blckstn Audio.
This sequel to "The Painted Word" shows how social & intellectual fashions have determined aesthetic form in our time, & how willingly the creators have abandoned personal vision & originality in order to work a la mode.

From Bauhaus to Our House. unabr. collector's ed. Tom Wolfe. Read by Ken Ohst. 4 cass. (Running Time: 4 hrs.). 1984. 24.00 (978-0-7366-0892-3(3), 1836) Books on Tape.
Walter Groppius, a.k.a. the Silver Prince, the slender, meticulously groomed & irresistibly urbane granddaddy of steel & glass, conceived his architectural vision in the rubble of World War I & the decadence of Weimar in the decade after. His doctrine found fertile soil in America, where it was time to adopt a clearly defined & suitable representative architecture. Groppius & his disciples taught that every element of design was to be a statement against bourgeois taste.

***From Behind the Veil: A Hijabi's Journey to Happiness.** unabr. ed. Farheen Khan. (Running Time: 2 hrs. 30 mins.). (ENG.). 2010. 24.98 (978-1-59659-607-8(4), GildAudio) Pub: Gildan Media. Dist(s): HachBkGrp

From Beirut to Jerusalem. abr. ed. Thomas L. Friedman. Read by Thomas L. Friedman. 2006. audio compact disk 22.95 (978-0-06-128425-0(4), Harper Audio) HarperCollins Pubs.

***From Beirut to Jerusalem.** abr. ed. Thomas L. Friedman. Read by Thomas L. Friedman. (ENG.). 2006. (978-0-06-125915-9(2), Harper Audio); (978-0-06-134157-1(6), Harper Audio) HarperCollins Pubs.

From Belgium to Boston. unabr. ed. Elisabeth Elliot. Read by Elisabeth Elliot. 1 cass. (Running Time: 1 hr.). 1989. 4.95 (978-0-8474-1971-5(1)) Back to Bible.
Elisabeth's life story from her birth in Belgium to her present home in Boston.

From Bitter to Better. Patricia Livingston. 1 cass. (Running Time: 1 hr.). 2001. 9.95 (A6411) St Anthony Mess Pr.
Explores divine compassion and reveals the sacred in the ordinary.

From Bourbon Street to Paradise. Contrib. by Henri Albers et al. 1 cass. 1998. 16.99 (VAIA1153) VAI Audio.
A survey of the French Opera House of New Orleans & its singers, 1859-1919.

From Bow to Bond Street. Elizabeth Lord. Read by Patricia Gallimore. 12 CDs. (Running Time: 14 hrs. 23 mins.). (Isis (CDs) Ser.). (J). 2004. audio compact disk 99.95 (978-0-7531-2287-7(1)) Pub: ISIS Lrg Pmt GBR. Dist(s): Ulverscroft US

From Bow to Bond Street. unabr. ed. Elizabeth Lord. Read by Patricia Gallimore. 12 cass. (Running Time: 15 hrs.). (Isis Ser.). (J). 2003. 94.95 (978-0-7531-1686-9(3)) Pub: ISIS Lrg Pmt GBR. Dist(s): Ulverscroft US
With the Armistice only a few months past, times are hard for most people in the East End, and the Glover family with their cramped terraced house in Bow are no exception. But eighteen-year-old Geraldine Glover, slim and pretty, daydreams of a glamorous West End existence - even though, as a machinist at Rubins clothing factory, her chances of living in the lap of luxury seem remote.

From Bridge to Boardwalk: An Audio Journey Across Maryland's Eastern Shore. 2nd ed. Interview. Prod. by Tatiana Irvine. Featuring Louis Kelly et al. Contrib. by Lora Bottinelli et al. 2 CDs. (Running Time: 1 hr. 50 mins.). 2004. audio compact disk 24.95 (978-0-9727796-3-0(9)) Mid Atlantic Arts.
From Bridge to Boardwalk: An Audio Journey Across Maryland?s Eastern Shore features 2 CD?s with over two hours of interviews with Shore personalities, historical recordings, music, and ambient sound. The accompanying 76-page book includes a pull-out map, essays, photographs, and tips to finding local arts and cultural treasures. The audio portion of the product features twelve interviews highlighting the culture of the Shore including: the building of the Bay Bridge; watermen; skipjacks; the poultry industry; muskrat skinning; crab picking; Scorchy Tawes; master decoy carvers, the Ward Brothers; Smith Island; gospel music; hunting and duck calling; and the Ocean City Beach Patrol. The concealed spiral bound book includes a map and essays by community scholars and folklorists highlighting the soul of the Shore by exploring the food, communities, agricultural ties, and tourism that shaped the region into what it is today. Photographs ? both historic and recent ? illustrate the changes taking place in the region. A resource section rounds out From Bridge to Boardwalk with tips on festivals and events, links to park information, cultural contacts, and places to visit. From Bridge to Boardwalk is sure to please everyone who has ever had the pleasure of crossing the Bridge ? and those who are new to Maryland?s shores.

From Buddy to Boss: Effective Fire Service Leadership. Chase Sargent. Narrated by Jack Shook. 2008. audio compact disk 59.00 (978-1-59370-153-6(5), Fire Eng Bks & Vid) PennWell Corp.

***From Buddy to Boss: Effective Fire Service Leadership - Audio Book.** Chase Sargent. (ENG.). 2008. audio compact disk 59.00 (978-1-59370-170-3(5)) Pub: Fire Eng. Dist(s): PennWell Corp

From Canyons to Rocks in Los Angeles County Parks. Hosted by Nancy Pearlman. 1 cass. (Running Time: 28 min.). 10.00 (521) Educ Comm CA.

From Chaos to Coherence: The Power to Change Performance. Doc Lew Childre & Barry Cryer. 2000. audio compact disk 49.95 (978-1-879052-45-1(8)) HeartMath.

From Chaos to Cosmos: Creation Myths & the Quest for Centered Self. Robert Moore. Read by Robert Moore. 3 cass. (Running Time: 3 hrs. 30 min.). 1991. 24.95 set. (978-0-7822-0359-2(0), 457) C G Jung IL.
This seminar focuses on the psychological significance of the mythology of creation with emphasis on understanding its relationship to the process of forming & consolidating a centered & cohesive self.

From Chocolate to Morphine: Everything You Need to Know about Mind-Altering Drugs. unabr. ed. Andrew Weil. 2 cass. 1993. 18.00 set. (OC344-72) Sound Horizons AV.

From Coach to Coach & Business to Business: Real World Wisdom from the Athletic Industry's Finest. Sam K. Shriver. Illus. by George High. Frwd. by Ken Blanchard. 6 cass. 60.00 Fulcourt Pr.

From Conflict to Intimacy & Beyond. Jordan Paul & Margaret Paul. 6 cass. 1985. 25.00 (978-0-912389-02-8(8)) Evolving Pubns.
How to improve relationships using the intent to learn as described in "Do I Have to Give Up Me to Be Loved By You?".

From Confusion to Surrender. Swami Amar Jyoti. 1 cass. 1976. 9.95 (C-4) Truth Consciousness.
Dealing with the root cause of confusion. How is true surrender born?.

From Curse to Blessing, Pt. 1. Derek Prince. 1 cass. (Running Time: 60 min.). (I-138) Derek Prince.

From Curse to Blessing, Pt. 2. Derek Prince. 1 cass. (Running Time: 60 min.). (I-139) Derek Prince.

From Darkness to Grace. Featuring Sai Maa Lakshmi Devi & Marianne Williamson. 2004. audio compact disk 16.00 (978-1-933488-07-3(7)) HIU Pr.
A multi-cultural, interfaith audience gathered in St. James' Church, the centerpiece of London's Piccadilly Square. They had chosen to join renowned NY Times #1 Best Selling Author Marianne Williamson and Spiritual Master, Sai Maa Lakshmi Devi for an evening described as "an extraordinary moment in history." With electrifying presentation and powerful presence, these two speakers spoke in tandem about the "new global conversation for spiritual evolution" and the possibilities that reside in each of us to "be who we authentically are, rather than being what we are not." This live recording will inspire, transform and awaken you in Self-Mastery and service to the world.

From Darkness to Light. P Ferrini. audio compact disk 16.95 (978-1-879159-54-9(6)) Heartways Pr.

From Darkness to Light. Kenneth Wapnick. 1 CD. (Running Time: 3 hrs. 43 mins. 57 secs.). 2005. 18.00 (978-1-59142-266-2(3), 3m63) Foun Miracles.

From Darkness to Light. Kenneth Wapnick. 4 CDs. 2006. audio compact disk 22.00 (978-1-59142-257-0(4), CD63) Foun Miracles.

From Darkness to Light: A Healing Path Through Grief, Set. unabr. ed. Terence P. Curley. 2 cass. (Running Time: 1 hrs. 55 min.). 1998. 19.95 (TAH400) Alba Hse Comns.
Father Curley presents an overview to grief, explaining the symptoms & helping the bereaved to place the experiences into the context of faith. A rich resource for spiritual development, especially during critical times.

From Dawn to Decadence: 1500 to the Present: 500 Years of Western Cultural Life. unabr. ed. Jacques Barzun. Read by Edward Lewis. 4 pieces. (Running Time: 153000 sec.). 2008. audio compact disk 69.95 (978-0-7861-9073-7(6), 2722A,B) Blckstn Audio.

From Dawn to Decadence Pt. 1: 500 Years of Western Cultural Life, 1500 to the Present. unabr. ed. Jacques Barzun. Read by Edward Lewis. 16 cass. (Running Time: 42 hrs. 30 mins.). 2001. 99.95 (978-0-7861-1951-6(9), 2722A,B) Blckstn Audio.
The triumphs & defeats of five hundred years from an inspiring saga that modifies the current impression of one long tale of oppression by white European males. Women & their deeds are prominent & freedom (even in sexual matters) is not an invention of the last decades.

From Dawn to Decadence Pt. 2: 500 Years of Western Cultural Life, 1500 to the Present. unabr. ed. Jacques Barzun. Read by Edward Lewis. 13 CDs. (Running Time: 42 hrs. 30 mins.). 2001. audio compact disk 85.95 (978-0-7861-2009-3(6), 2722A,B) Blckstn Audio.
The triumphs & defeats of five hundred years from an inspiring saga that modifies the current impression of one long tale of oppression by white European males. Women & their deeds are prominent & freedom (even in sexual matters) is not an invention of the last decades.

From Dawn to Decadence, Part I: 1500 to the Present. unabr. ed. Jacques Barzun. Read by Edward Lewis. (Running Time: 77400 sec.). 2008. audio compact disk & audio compact disk 125.00 (978-1-4332-4520-6(5)) Blckstn Audio.

From Dawn to Decadence: 1500 to the Present: Part II: 500 Years of Western Cultural Life. unabr. ed. Jacques Barzun. Read by Edward Lewis. (Running Time: 66600 sec.). 2008. audio compact disk & audio compact disk 120.00 (978-1-4332-4521-3(3)) Blckstn Audio.

From Dead to Worse. unabr. ed. Charlaine Harris. Read by Johanna Parker. 9 cass. (Running Time: 10 hrs. 15 mins.). (Sookie Stackhouse Ser.: Bk. 8). 2008. 72.75 (978-1-4361-0520-0(X)); audio compact disk 102.75 (978-1-4361-0522-4(6)) Recorded Bks.

From Dead to Worse. unabr. ed. Charlaine Harris. Narrated by Johanna Parker. 1 Playaway. (Running Time: 10 hrs. 15 mins.). (Sookie Stackhouse Ser.: Bk. 8). 2009. 56.75 (978-1-4361-3257-2(6)) Recorded Bks.

From Dead to Worse. unabr. ed. Charlaine Harris. Read by Johanna Parker. 9 CDs. (Running Time: 10 hrs.). (Sookie Stackhouse Ser.: Bk. 8). 2008. audio compact disk 34.99 (978-1-4361-0519-4(6)) Recorded Bks.

From Death: The Last Taboo. Cheri Quincy & Tom Pinkson. 1 cass. 9.00 (A0732-90) Sound Photosyn.
Cheri: "Social, Political, & Biological Death"; Tom: "Teachings from Children with Life Threatening Illnesses".

From Death to Birth: Understanding Karma & Reincarnation. unabr. ed. Pandit Rajmani Tigunait. Read by D. C. Rao. 5 cass. (Running Time: 7 hrs. 30 mins.). 2007. audio compact disk 29.95 (978-0-89389-173-2(8), AB602MO) Pub: Himalayan Inst. Dist(s): Natl Bk Netwk

From Death to Morning. unabr. collector's ed. Thomas Wolfe. Read by John Edwardson. 8 cass. (Running Time: 12 hrs.). 1997. 64.00 (978-0-7366-3671-1(4), 4348) Books on Tape.
A collection of 14 stories by one of twentieth-century America's greatest & most influential authors.

From Death to Victory. Read by Basilea Schlink. 1 cass. (Running Time: 30 min.). 1985. (0211) Evang Sisterhood Mary.
Gives an Easter message that will change sadness into joy, discusses the power of the Holy Spirit at work today.

From Doon with Death. unabr. ed. Ruth Rendell. Read by Michael Bryant. 4 cass. (Running Time: 6 hrs.). (Inspector Wexford Mystery Ser.: Bk. 1). 2000. 34.95 (978-0-7451-4202-9(8), CAB 885) Pub: Chivers Audio Bks GBR. Dist(s): AudioGO
Margaret Parsons was dead. The Police knew all about her life, and by the look of it, it was very dull. Margaret was a good person, she was religious, respectable and old-fashioned. Her life had been as spotless and ordinary as her home, but it was not her life that interested Chief Wexford. It was her death: passionate, violent and unfathomable.

From Eros to Gaia. abr. ed. Freeman J. Dyson. 2 cass. (Running Time: 3 hrs.). 1993. 16.95 (978-0-939643-52-3(9), NrthWrd Bks) TandN Child.
Philosophy, social aspects.

From Eternity to Here: Rediscovering the Ageless Purpose of God. unabr. ed. Frank Viola. (Running Time: 8 hrs. 30 mins. 0 sec.). (ENG.). 2009. audio compact disk 26.98 (978-1-59644-724-0(9), Hovel Audio) christianaud.

***From Eternity to Here: Rediscovering the Ageless Purpose of God.** unabr. ed. Frank Viola. Narrated by Lloyd James. (ENG.). 2009. 16.98 (978-1-59644-725-7(7), Hovel Audio) christianaud.

***From Eternity to Here: The Quest for the Ultimate Theory of Time.** unabr. ed. Sean Carroll. Narrated by Erik Synnestvedt. (Running Time: 16 hrs. 30 mins.). 2010. 21.99 (978-1-4001-8565-8(3)) Tantor Media.

***From Eternity to Here: The Quest for the Ultimate Theory of Time.** unabr. ed. Sean Carroll. Narrated by Erik Synnestvedt. (Running Time: 16 hrs. 30 mins. 0 sec.). (ENG.). 2010. 29.99 (978-1-4001-6565-0(2)); audio compact disk 39.99 (978-1-4001-1565-5(5)); audio compact disk 79.99 (978-1-4001-4565-2(1)) Pub: Tantor Media. Dist(s): IngramPubServ

***From Facts to Faith: Evidences in Defense of the Faith.** Douglas Jacoby. 2009. 10.00 (978-0-9745342-9-9(3)) Illumination MA.

From Faith to Results. Creflo A. Dollar. 2008. audio compact disk 50.00 (978-1-59944-727-8(4)) Creflo Dollar.

From Fantasy to Fate: The Tranformative Power of Imagination. Jean S. Bolen et al. 4 cass. (Running Time: 6 hrs.). 1997. 31.95 (978-0-7822-0536-7(4)) C G Jung IL.
This symposium aims to confront the participant with the puzzles & enigmas of the imagination as well as the challenge to act that the imagination poses.

From Farm to Table: Early Explorers Early Set B Audio CD. Mary Butenhoff. Adapted by Benchmark Education Staff. (J). 2007. audio compact disk 10.00 (978-1-4108-8232-5(2)) Benchmark Educ.

From Father to Son. (Greetings Ser.: Vol. 1). (gr. 3-5). 10.00 (978-0-7635-1749-6(6)) Rigby Educ.

From Fear to Fearlessness. unabr. ed. Pema Chödrön. 2 CDs. (Running Time: 2 hrs. 30 mins.). 2003. audio compact disk 24.95 (978-1-59179-108-9(1), W742D) Sounds True.
From Fear to Fearlessness brings us into the company of beloved teacher Pema Chödrön to discover and cultivate these four immeasurables maitri (loving-kindness), compassion, joy, and equanimity. They are our greatest antidote to fear, teaches Ani Pema. By practicing them, we begin to experience a supreme steadfastness and peace independent of conditions.

From First Draft to First Edition: A Step-by-Step Guide to Self Publishing. unabr. ed. Duane S. Crowther. Read by Duane S. Crowther. 1 cass. (Running Time: 60 min.). 1986. 13.98 (978-0-88290-376-7(4), 1821) Horizon Utah.
The author tells the would-be author how to go about publishing from start to finish. The technical aspects of printing are explained, and the tape tells how to work with typesetters, printers, and others in the industry so as to obtain the best quality possible at an affordable price.

From Fixation to Freedom. Eli Jaxon-Bear. 2008. audio compact disk 69.95 (978-1-59179-593-3(1)) Sounds True.

From Freedom to Slavery: The Rebirth of Tyranny in America. unabr. ed. Gerry Spence. Read by John MacDonald. 6 cass. (Running Time: 6 hrs.). 1994. 36.00 (978-0-7366-2776-4(6), 3495) Books on Tape.
This book says that freedom's dead, that the corporate & governmental conglomerate controls.

From Freewill to Freedom. George King. 2009. audio compact disk (978-0-937249-19-2(X)) Aetherius Soc.

From Freud to Jung & Beyond: Turning Points in Psychoanalytic & Religious Thought. Murray Stein & James Wyly. Read by Murray Stein & James Wyly. 2 cass. (Running Time: 1 hr. 45 min.). 1992. 16.95 set. (978-0-7822-0386-8(8), 484) C G Jung IL.
Jungian analyst & author Murray Stein presents his view on human spirituality & religious experience - areas of study that have been largely taboo or pathologized by psychoanalysis, but which are now open to wider investigation because of the Jungian revolution. His talk focuses primarily on the interrelationship between instinct & archetype. James Wyly's response frames these turning points in a cultural & historical perspective, & explores the implications of Jung's theory of individuation with regard to the collective experience of religion.

From Fullness to Overflow. Kenneth Copeland. 5 cass. 2006. (978-1-57562-820-2(1)); audio compact disk (978-1-57562-821-9(X)) K Copeland Pubns.

From Futility to Happiness: Sisyphus as Everyman. Kenneth Wapnick. 4CDs. 2005. audio compact disk 24.00 (978-1-59142-199-3(3), CD114) Foun Miracles.

***From Futility to Happiness: Sisyphus as Everyman.** Kenneth Wapnick. 2009. 19.00 (978-1-59142-467-3(4)) Foun Miracles.

From Generation to Generation: A Legacy of Lullabies. unabr. ed. Perf. by Tanja Solnik. 1 cass. (Running Time: 36 min.). (J). 1993. 10.00 (978-0-9638749-0-0(X), DS 101) DreamSong Recs.
Traditional folk songs & stories (lullabies) for children in Yiddish, Hebrew & Ladino. 1994 ALA Notable Children's Recording.

From Genesis; Manic-Depressive Lincoln, National Hero see Twentieth-Century Poetry in English, No. 9, Recordings of Poets Reading Their Own Poetry

From Ghetto to Guerrilla: Memior of a Jewish Resistance Fighter. Interview. Samuel Lato. Sir Martin Gilbert. Jim Johnston/ ImageBlast. 1. (Running Time: 45 ,ims). 2006. audio compact disk 39.95 (978-0-9777621-9-4(X)) Preeminent.

***From Girlz II Women: A Journey Through the 6 Essentials for Transforming Girlz into Phenomenal Women, vol. 1.** Velvet Steel Publishing. (ENG.). (J). 2010. audio compact disk 9.95 (978-0-9788461-1-4(7)) Velvet Steel.

From Golden Mycenae. Diana Gainer. Read by Kevin Foley. 12 cass. (Running Time: 12 hrs. 48 min.). (Bronze Age Ser.). 1994. 59.95 Set. (978-1-55686-525-1(2)) Books in Motion.
Here is a highly-researched, story of Helen, the Spartan queen kidnapped by the Trojan Prince, Paris. A thousand Greek ships were launched to rescue Helen.

From Grief to Glory. Caryl Krueger. Read by Caryl Krueger. 2 cass. (Running Time: 3 hrs.). 2001. 17.00 Belleridge.
When someone passes from our sight, what kind of thoughts flood our consciousness? Are we overcome with grief or do we consider the glory of everlasting life? The Bible gives us many helpful ideas, ones that are both comforting and inspiring.

From "Heart's Needle": Child of My Winter; Late April & You Are Three; The Vicious Winter Finally Yields see Twentieth-Century Poetry in English, No. 29, Recordings of Poets Reading Their Own Poetry

From Heaven Lake. unabr. collector's ed. Vikram Seth. Read by Michael Prichard. 5 cass. (Running Time: 7 hrs. 30 mins.). 1985. 40.00 (978-0-7366-0283-9(6), 1273) Books on Tape.
Account of Seth's travels from the arid wastes of China's far west to the Potala Palace in Lhasa. He endures bureaucratic delay, climatic extremes & the protracted discomforts of long-distance lorries with equal aplomb.

From Here to Alternity Workshop. John Lilly. 1 cass. 10.00 (A0184-89) Sound Photosyn.
Up to date, fresh & pithy at the L.A. Whole Life Expo.

***From Here to Eternity.** Chuck Missler. (ENG.). 2009. audio compact disk 19.95 (978-1-57821-451-8(3)) Koinonia Hse.

From Here to Eternity: The Physics of Immortality. Chuck Missler. 2 cass. (Running Time: 3 hours). (Briefing Packages by Chuck Missler). 1995. vinyl bd. 14.95 Incls. notes. (978-1-880532-54-6(9)) Koinonia Hse.
How can a decomposed body be resurrected?How can we reconcile the resurrection with the laws of science?What insights can we get from Jurassic Park?If Jesus' Second Coming is preceded by seven years of events, how can we expect Him at any moment?Study the Apostle Paul's famous "Resurrection Chapter" (I Corinthians 15) and explore why the resurrection is essential to the faith.The very idea that an ancient living animal can be recreated from its genetic history encoded in a single DNA molecule should give us a provocative insight into the potential technology of immortality and the resurrection!Review the physics of immortality, the geometry of eternity, and the real nature of our true selves.

From I to J: Isabel Coixet/John Berger. Created by Actar. 2009. bk. 29.95 (978-84-96954-85-4(4)) Actar ESP.

From in the Dream. Helga Sandburg. 1 cass. (Running Time: 1 hr.). 2001. 12.95 (FCWW300) Lodestone Catalog.

From Innocence to Entitlement. 2005. (978-1-930429-85-7(1)) Love Logic.

From Inside the Tree. Bryce Milligan. Illus. by Jim Harter. 1 cass. (Running Time: 1 hr.). (YA). 1990. 8.00 (978-0-913983-09-6(8)) M & A Edns.
Poetry & songs from book, "Litany Sung at Hell's Gate.".

From Jesus to Christ: The First Christians. 1 cass. 1998. 11.95 WGBH Boston.

From Jesus to Constantine: A History of Early Christianity, Parts I-II. Instructed by Bart D. Ehrman. 12 cass. (Running Time: 12 hrs.). 2004. bk. 54.95 (978-1-56585-843-5(3), 6577); bk. 69.95 (978-1-56585-845-9(X), 6577) Teaching Co.

From Jumpstreet: A Story of Black Music. 1 cass. (Running Time: 1 hr.). Incl. Pt. 1. From Jumpstreet: West African Heritage. (C071DB090); Pt. 2. From Jumpstreet: Gospel & Spirituals. (C071DB090); 11.50 (C071DB090, HarperThor) HarpC GBR.

From Jumpstreet: A Story of Black Music. Perf. by Pearl Bailey & L. O. Sloane. 1 cass. (Running Time: 1 hr.). Incl. Pt. 9. From Jumpstreet: Black Music in Theatre & Film. (HO-82-01-08); Pt. 10. From Jumpstreet: Black Influence in the Recording Industry. (HO-82-01-08); 11.50 (HO-82-01-08, HarperThor) HarpC GBR.

From Jumpstreet: A Story of Black Music. Perf. by Bo Didley & Chuck Berry. 1 cass. (Running Time: 1 hr.). Incl. Pt. 5. From Jumpstreet: Rhythm & Blues. (C071AB090); Pt. 6. From Jumpstreet: Early Jazz. Perf. by Eubie Blake & Jelly Roll Morton. (C071AB090); 11.50 (C071AB090, HarperThor) HarpC GBR.

From Jumpstreet: A Story of Black Music. Perf. by Aretha Franklin & Stevie Wonder. 1 cass. (Running Time: 1 hr.). Incl. Pt. 3. From Jumpstreet: Soul. (C071EB090); Pt. 4. From Jumpstreet: Blues: Country Meets City. Perf. by Brownie McGhee & Sonny Terry. (C071EB090); 11.50 (C071EB090, HarperThor) HarpC GBR.

From Jumpstreet: A Story of Black Music. Perf. by Billie Holiday & Al Jarreau. 1 cass. (Running Time: 1 hr.). Incl. Pt. 7. From Jumpstreet: The Jazz Vocalist. (C071BB090); Pt. 8. From Jumpstreet: Jazz People. Perf. by Thelonious Monk, Jr. & Oscar Peterson. (C071BB090); 11.50 (C071BB090, HarperThor) HarpC GBR.

From Jumpstreet: Black Influence in the Recording Industry see From Jumpstreet: A Story of Black Music

From Jumpstreet: Black Music in Theatre & Film see From Jumpstreet: A Story of Black Music

From Jumpstreet: Blues: Country Meets City see From Jumpstreet: A Story of Black Music

From Jumpstreet: Early Jazz see From Jumpstreet: A Story of Black Music

From Jumpstreet: Gospel & Spirituals see From Jumpstreet: A Story of Black Music

From Jumpstreet: Jazz People see From Jumpstreet: A Story of Black Music

From Jumpstreet: Rhythm & Blues see From Jumpstreet: A Story of Black Music

From Jumpstreet: Soul see From Jumpstreet: A Story of Black Music

From Jumpstreet: The Jazz Vocalist see From Jumpstreet: A Story of Black Music

From Jumpstreet: West African Heritage see From Jumpstreet: A Story of Black Music

From Liturgy to Worship: The Gift of Presence. Richard Fragomeni. 1 cass. (Running Time: 1 hr. 4 mins.). 2001. 8.95 (A8021) St Anthony Mess Pr.
True worship of God is God's gift flowing through us for each other.

From Liverpool to Abbey Road: A Beginning Guitar Method Featuring 33 Songs of Lennon & McCartney. Ron Manus & L. C. Harnsberger. 1 CD. (ENG., 1999. pap. bk. 24.95 (978-0-7390-0251-3(1), 19322) Alfred Pub.

From Liverpool to Abbey Road: A Beginning Guitar Method Featuring 33 Songs of Lennon & McCartney. Ron Manus & L. C. Harnsberger. (ENG.). 2000. audio compact disk 10.00 (978-0-7390-0252-0(X), 19323) Alfred Pub.

From Magical Child to Magical Adult. Joseph C. Pearce. 5 cass. 1991. 45.00 set. (OC278-62) Sound Horizons AV.

From Main Street to Madison Avenue. unabr. ed. Louis Kronenberger. 1 cass. (Running Time: 44 min.). 12.95 (35030) J Norton Pubs.
Traces our social order & cultural directions from Babbitt to Big Business.

From Mao to Mozart to Survival. Ralph Alan Dale. Read by Ralph Alan Dale. 1 cass. (Running Time: 90 min.). 1982. 9.00 (10) Dialectic Pubng.
A program for human liberation.

From Midnight to Dawn: The Last Tracks of the Underground Railroad. unabr. ed. Jacqueline Tobin. Read by Richard Allen. Told to Hettie Jones. (Running Time: 10 hrs. 0 mins. 0 sec.). (ENG.). 2007. audio compact disk 24.99 (978-1-4001-5354-1(9)); audio compact disk 69.99 (978-1-4001-3354-3(8)) Pub: Tantor Media. Dist(s): IngramPubServ

From Midnight to Dawn: The Last Tracks of the Underground Railroad. unabr. ed. Jacqueline L. Tobin. Read by Richard Allen. Told to Hettie Jones. (Running Time: 10 hrs. 0 mins. 0 sec.). (ENG.). 2007. audio compact disk 34.99 (978-1-4001-0354-6(1)) Pub: Tantor Media. Dist(s): IngramPubServ

From Mind to Market: Reinventing the Retail Supply Chain. unabr. ed. Roger D. Blackwell. Read by Dennis McKee. 6 cass. (Running Time: 8 hrs. 30 mins.). 1999. 44.95 (978-0-7861-1485-6(1), 2337) Blckstn Audio.
When companies like Wal-Mart, Kinko's, & Service Corp. International adopted active, consumer-driven marketing strategies, they became more profitable & market leaders as well. Explores what it means to be a mind-to-market leader & how any company can beat its competition by employing visionary leadership strategies.

From Missouri. unabr. ed. Zane Grey. Read by Tom Weiner. (Running Time: 1 hr. 0 mins.). 2009. 19.95 (978-1-4332-2385-3(6)); 15.95 (978-1-4332-2381-5(3)); audio compact disk 20.00 (978-1-4332-2382-2(1)) Blckstn Audio.

From Mystery to Mysticism in the Gnosis. Stephan Hoeller. 1 cass. 1994. 11.00 (40030) Big Sur Tapes.
1994 Los Angeles.

From Organic Gardens to the Table. Hosted by Nancy Pearlman. 1 cass. (Running Time: 29 min.). 10.00 (317) Educ Comm CA.

From Paella to Porridge. Peter Kerr. (Soundings (CDs) Ser.). 2007. audio compact disk 84.95 (978-1-84559-581-4(5)) Pub: ISIS Lrg Prnt GBR. Dist(s): Ulverscroft US

From Paella to Porridge. Peter Kerr. Read by James Bryce. 8 cass. (Soundings Ser.). 2007. 69.95 (978-1-84559-556-2(4)) Pub: ISIS Lrg Prnt GBR. Dist(s): Ulverscroft US

From Pain to Passion: Building a Truly Great Relationship. Adele Britton. Narrated by Adele Britton. (Running Time: 3hrs. 45 min.). 2003. audio compact disk 29.00 (978-0-9745488-0-7(4)) Lighthrt Pr.
Stories of eighteen couples in conflict over common relationship pitfalls. Nine of which struggle and cannot break through their difficulties. Nine couples come through the conflict triumphantly.

From Panic to Power. abr. ed. Lucinda Bassett. Read by Lucinda Bassett. 2 cass. (Running Time: 3 hrs.). 1995. 18.95 (978-0-694-51595-0(7), CPN 2511, Harper Audio) HarperCollins Pubs.

From Panic to Power: Proven Techniques to Calm Your Anxieties, Conquer Your Fears, & Put You in Control of Your Life. unabr. abr. ed. Lucinda Bassett. Read by Lucinda Bassett. (Running Time: 7200 sec.). 2008. audio compact disk 14.95 (978-0-06-144185-1(6), Harper Audio) HarperCollins Pubs.

From Patent to Profit: Secrets & Strategies for Success. Bob DeMatteis. Read by Bob DeMatties. 4 cass. (Running Time: 4 hrs.). 1997. pap. bk. 39.95 Set. (978-0-9660455-1-2(3)) Inventions Co.
Includes: All about Patents; Writing Patents & Mkt'g. Strategies; Finding Mfg. & Mkt'g. Partners; & All about Licensing.

From Peanuts to Peanut Butter. Sundance/Newbridge, LLC Staff. (Early Science Ser.). (gr. k-3). 2007. audio compact disk 12.00 (978-1-4007-6174-6(3)); audio compact disk 12.00 (978-1-4007-6172-2(7)); audio compact disk 12.00 (978-1-4007-6173-9(5)) Sund Newbrdge.

From Pebbles to Rock (Peter) John 1:42. Ed Young. 1985. 4.95 (978-0-7417-1465-7(5), 465) Win Walk.

From Pieces to Weight: Once upon a Time in Southside Queens. abr. ed. 50 Cent. Read by J. D. Williams. Told to Kris Ex. 2005. 13.95 (978-0-7435-5225-7(3)) Pub: S&S Audio. Dist(s): S and S Inc

From Pieces to Weight: Once upon a Time in Southside Queens. abr. ed. 50 Cent. Read by J. D. Williams. Told to Kris Ex. 2005. 9.95 (978-0-7435-5489-3(2)) Pub: S&S Audio. Dist(s): S and S Inc

From Plato to Post-Modernism, Pts. I-II. Instructed by Louis Markos. 12 CDs. (Running Time: 12 hrs.). 1999. audio compact disk 179.95 (978-1-56585-314-0(8)) Teaching Co.

From Plato to Post-Modernism, Vol. 1, Pts. I-II. Instructed by Louis Markos. 12 cass. (Running Time: 12 hrs.). 1999. 129.95 (978-1-56585-062-0(9)) Teaching Co.

From Plato to Post-Modernism Vol. 2: Understanding the Essence of Literature & the Role of the Author. Instructed by Louis Markos. 6 cass. (Running Time: 6 hrs.). 1999. 129.95 (978-1-56585-063-7(7)) Teaching Co.

From Plato to Post-Modernism Vol. 2: Understanding the Essense of Literature & the Role of the Author. Instructed by Louis Markos. 6 CDs. (Running Time: 6 hrs.). 1999. audio compact disk 179.95 (978-1-56585-315-7(6)) Teaching Co.

From Possibility to Profitability: 10 P's to Grow Your Business Successfully. Franne McNeal. 2007. 15.00 (978-0-9791643-4-7(6)) Significant Bus.

From Potter's Field. Patricia Cornwell. (Kay Scarpetta Ser.: No. 6). 2000. 15.99 (978-0-7435-0568-0(9), Audioworks) S&S Audio.

From Potter's Field. abr. ed. Patricia Cornwell. (Running Time: 43 hrs. 0 mins. 0 sec.). No. 6. (ENG.). 2002. audio compact disk 14.95 (978-0-7435-3760-5(2), S&S Encore) Pub: S&S Audio. Dist(s): S and S Inc
PATRICIA CORNWELL'S BLOCKBUSTER BESTSELLER AT A NEW LOW PRICE! FROM POTTER'S FIELD Read by Blair Brown IT'S CHRISTMAS EVE IN NEW YORK AND A SADISTIC KILLER IS ABOUT TO DISTURB THE PEACE!?? An unidentified nude female sits propped against a fountain in Central Park. There are no signs of struggle. When Dr. Kay Scarpetta and her colleagues Benton Wesley and Pete Marino arrive on the scene, they instantly recognize the signature of serial killer Temple Brooks Gault. Only Scarpetta can interpret the forensic hieroglyphics at the New York City morgue and give a name to the nameless. As she sifts through conflicting clues, Gault strikes again - moving terrifyingly close to Scarpetta herself. From Potter's Field is a stunning achievement from a bestselling author at the peak of her powers.

From Potter's Field. unabr. ed. Patricia Cornwell. Read by Donada Peters. 7 cass. (Running Time: 10 hrs. 30 min.). (Kay Scarpetta Ser.: No. 6). 1996. 56.00 (978-0-7366-3241-6(7), 3900) Books on Tape.
The sadistic killer washes his bloody hands in the snow of New York's Central Park, then disappears into the City's fetid subway tunnels, leaving his bald & naked female victim propped against a frozen fountain. For Dr. Kay Scarpetta, chief medical examiner for Virginia & consultant to the FBI, it's the return of her worst nightmare.

From Provision to Prosperity, Confessions. Robb Thompson. audio compact disk 10.00 (978-1-889723-48-8(7)) Pub: Family Harvest. Dist(s): Harrison Hse

From Psychedelics to Cybernetics. Featuring Timothy Leary. 1994. 9.95 (978-1-59157-009-7(3)) Assn for Cons.

From Rag's to Records. (YA). 2008. pap. bk. (978-0-578-00009-1(1)) Mbudnik.

From Reason to Faith. Swami Amar Jyoti. 1 cass. 1979. 9.95 (J-30) Truth Consciousness.
Mind's reaction to our seeking. The role of reason. Aim of true religion & awakened faith. Death as seen from the fourth dimension.

From Rejection to Acceptance. Derek Prince. 1 cass. (Running Time: 60 min.). 5.95 (B-4038) Derek Prince.

From Rice Paddies & Temple Yards: Traditional Music of Vietnam. Phong Nguyen & Patricia S. Campbell. Perf. by Phong Nguyen. 1996. pap. bk. 20.95 (978-0-937203-73-6(4)) World Music Pr.

From Rice Paddies & Temple Yards: Traditional Music of Vietnam, Set. Phong Nguyen & Patricia S. Campbell. Perf. by Nguyen, Phong, Ensemble & Vietnamese Musicians Residing in the U. S. 1 cass. (Running Time: 40 min.). (J). (gr. 3 up). 1990. pap. bk. 16.95 (978-0-937203-34-7(3)) World Music Pr.
Features an examination of the traditional music of Vietnam & its place in the society, presented in English. Includes history, cultural information, information about each piece, translations, pronunciation, numerous photos of the country & instruments, bibliography, index, & information for teachers on how to work with the pieces in the classroom. Designated "Best Folk Recording of 1990." Folk Life Center Library of Congress.

From Russia with Love. unabr. ed. Ian Fleming. (Running Time: 8 hrs. 30 mins.). (James Bond Ser.). 2005. audio compact disk 24.95 (978-0-7861-9315-8(8), 2644) Blckstn Audio.

From Russia with Love. unabr. ed. Ian Fleming. Read by Robert Whitfield. 6 cass. (Running Time: 8 hrs. 30 mins.). (James Bond Ser.). 2000. 44.95 (978-0-7861-1845-8(8), 2644); audio compact disk 56.00 (978-0-7861-9829-0(X), 2644) Blckstn Audio.
The light nudge at his ankle wakes Bond. He doesn't move. His senses come to life like an animal's. What has woken him? "Sorry to disturb you, old man, I feel in the mood for a talk." Bond puts his feet softly down to the floor. He sits up straighter. Danger, like a third man, is standing in the room. S.M.E.R.S.H is the Soviet organ of vengeance: of interrogation, torture & death & James Bond is dedicated to the destruction of its agents wherever he finds them.

From Russia with Love. unabr. ed. Ian Fleming. Read by Robert Whitfield. 6 cass. (Running Time: 9 hrs.). (James Bond Ser.). 2001. (978-0-7861-1919-6(5)) Blckstn Audio.
James Bond confronts SMERSH - the Soviet organ of vengeance, interrogation, torture and death.

From Russia with Love. unabr. ed. Ian Fleming. Read by Robert Whitfield. 6 pieces. (James Bond Ser.). 2004. reel tape 29.95 (978-0-7861-2225-7(0)) Blckstn Audio.

From Russia with Love. unabr. ed. Ian Fleming. Read by Simon Vance. (Running Time: 8.5 hrs. 0 mins.). 2009. audio compact disk 19.95 (978-1-4332-5856-5(0)) Blckstn Audio.

From Russia with Love & Moonraker. unabr. ed. Ian Fleming. Read by Simon Vance. 13 CDs. (Running Time: 52200 sec.). 2006. audio compact disk 24.95 (978-0-7861-6891-0(9)); audio compact disk 29.95 (978-0-7861-7473-7(0)) Blckstn Audio.

From San Francisco to Wine Country: A Listen As You Drive Tour from the Golden Gate Through the Historic Napa & Sonoma Valleys. unabr. ed. 1 cass. (Running Time: 1 hr.). (Listen As You Drive Ser.). 12.95 incl. map. (978-0-944857-03-8(5), 12001) Matthew Media.
Designed for use in car, from the Golden Gate Bridge into the wine country of the Napa & Sonoma Valleys.

From Saul to Paul: Identity Change at Midlife. Read by Murray Stein. 1 cass. (Running Time: 90 min.). (Patterns of Divinity Ser.: No. 6). 1988. 10.95 (978-0-7822-0279-3(9), 306) C G Jung IL.

From School to Work. J. J. Littrell et al. (gr. 9-12). tchr. ed. 200.00 (978-1-56637-973-1(3)) Goodheart.

From Sea to Shining Sea: Monterey's Path of History, a Walking Tour. David K. Wittrock. 1 cass. (Running Time: 90 min.). 1993. 10.95 (978-0-9640315-0-0(7)) DKW Prods-AudioTours.

***From Sea to Shining Sea Audio Book.** Peter J. Marshall. 1996. audio compact disk (978-0-9771811-9-3(7)) Pet Mars Mini.

From Self-Doubt to Self-Acceptance. Tom Rusk. Read by Tom Rusk. 1 cass. (Running Time: 55 min.). 1991. 10.95 (978-1-56170-027-1(4), 254N) Hay House.
Helps you analyze childhood experiences to pinpoint sources of self-doubt, hurt, & rejection.

From Shadows to Spotlights: How to Get the Media Talking & People Listening to What You Have to Offer. (ENG.). 2008. ring bd. 149.00 (978-0-615-23224-9(8)) AMO EMPLOYER S.

From Shadows to Sunlight: Praying As a Growth in Glory. Margaret Dorgan. 5 cass. 34.95 Set. (AA2400) Credence Commun.
Discussion on the process of glorification from Ruth onward.

From Shakespeare - With Love: The Best of the Sonnets. unabr. ed. William Shakespeare. Read by David Tennant et al. 1 CD. (Running Time: 1 hr. 15 mins.). (Great Poets Ser.). 2009. audio compact disk 14.98 (978-962-634-956-4(5), Naxos AudioBooks) Naxos.

From Sicily to Syria: The Growth of Trade & Colonization. Teaching Co.

From Sister to Sister One Last Gift: One Sister's Gift after Death Leads Another Sister on A Spiritual Journey. Read by Yana L. Freeman. 5 CDs. (Running Time: 6 hrs.12 mins.). 2006. audio compact disk 25.00 (978-0-9768728-1-8(1), 72811) Sacred Path.

From Skyline to Shoreline San Francisco-Santa Cruz: A Listen As You Drive Tour of California's Scenic Coast & Magnificent Redwood Forests. unabr. ed. Roadrunner Audio Staff. 1 cass. (Running Time: 1 hr.). (Listen As You Drive Ser.). 12.95 incl. map. (978-0-944857-04-5(3), 12002) Matthew Media.
Designed for use in car, from San Francisco to Santa Cruz & back. Includes History, culture, Geology & Biology.

From Song of Myself (A Poem from the Poets' Corner) The One-and-Only Poetry Book for the Whole Family. unabr. ed. Walt Whitman & John Lithgow. Read by John Lithgow. (Running Time: 10 mins.). (ENG.). 2008. 0.99 (978-1-60024-328-8(2)) Pub: Hachet Audio. Dist(s): HachBkGrp

From Sound to Sentence: Basic Literacy & Spelling, Phonics & Sight Words. Raymond C. Clark. 2 CD'S. 2007. audio compact disk 20.00 (978-0-86647-253-1(3)) Pro Lingua.

From Sound to Sentence: Basic Literacy & Spelling, Phonics & Sight Words. Raymond C. Clark. 2 CD'S. 2007. pap. bk. 32.00 (978-0-86647-255-5(X)) Pro Lingua.

From Sound to Symbol, Set. rev. ed. Ruth Schoening. 1975. pap. bk. 15.00 (978-0-913191-14-9(0)) AGEI Pub.

From Sound to Symbol, Set. rev. ed. Ruth Schoening. 1976. pap. bk. 15.00 (978-0-913191-15-6(9)) AGEI Pub.

From Sound to Symbol, Set. rev. ed. Ruth Schoening. 1977. pap. bk. 15.00 (978-0-913191-17-0(5)); pap. bk. 15.00 (978-0-913191-18-7(3)) AGEI Pub.

From Spanish to Brazilian Portuguese. Foreign Service Institute Staff. 2 cass. (Running Time: 2 hrs.). (POR & SPA.). (J). (gr. 10-12). 1980. pap. bk. 45.00 (978-0-88432-059-3(6), AFSP50) J Norton Pubs.
Designed for those who already have a good command of Spanish & want to learn Brazilian Portuguese. Focuses on pronunciation, grammar & vocabulary which have similar but not always identical counterparts in Spanish.

From Spanish to Brazilian Portuguese (FSI) 2 CDs. (Running Time: 2 hrs.). (Foreign Service Institute Language Ser.). (POR.). 2005. audio compact disk 45.00 (978-1-57970-210-6(4), AFSP50D) J Norton Pubs.

From Steep Ilios. Diana Gainer. Read by Kevin Foley. 12 cass. (Running Time: 12 hrs. 30 min.). (Bronze Age Ser.: No. 2). 1994. 59.95 Set. (978-1-55686-531-2(7)) Books in Motion.
The siege of Troy continues. Agamemnon & Menelaus struggle to keep the Grecian Army together & focused on battling Troy.

From Strength to Strength. Lyrics by Julie Silver. Music by Julie Silver. (Running Time: 40 min.). (ENG & HEB.). 1997. audio compact disk 15.95 (978-1-890161-30-9(6)) Sounds Write.

From Stress to Success. unabr. ed. Michael A. Podolinsky. 2 cass. (Smart Tapes Ser.). 1995. pap. bk. 19.99 Set, incl. pocket guide. (978-1-55678-055-4(9), 3265) Oasis Audio.
Learn to use your stress productively, increase your stress tolerance & use risk to your advantage.

From Stress to Success. unabr. ed. Michael A. Podolinsky. 2 CDs. (Smart Tapes Ser.). 2004. audio compact disk 19.99 (978-1-58926-050-4(3)) Oasis Audio.

*__From Success to Significance: When the Pursuit of Success Isnâ€(tm)t Enough.__ Lloyd Reeb. (Running Time: 5 hrs. 27 mins. 0 sec.). (ENG.). 2009. 16.99 (978-0-310-30448-7(2)) Zondervan.

From Tadpole to Frog. Wendy Pfeffer. Read by Peter Lerangis. Illus. by Holly Keller. (Running Time: 15 min.). (J). 7.95 (HarperChildAud) HarperCollins Pubs.

From Tadpole to Frog. abr. ed. Wendy Pfeffer. Read by Peter Lerangis. Illus. by Holly Keller. (Let's-Read-and-Find-Out Science Ser.). (J). (ps-1). 1996. 8.99 (978-0-694-70046-2(0)) HarperCollins Pubs.

From the Abundance of the Heart: Inspirational Poetry. abr. ed. Deborah Mitchell. Perf. by John Lawrence. 1 CD. (Running Time: 55 min.). 1999. audio compact disk 15.00 (978-0-9650828-3-9(0)) All Things.
Inspirational poetry set to music. Something of interest for all age levels. Upbeat, uplifting, self-esteem building poetry set to contemporary jazz.

From the Age of Discovery to a World at War, Vol. 1. unabr. ed. William J. Bennett. Narrated by Wayne Shepherd. (America: the Last Best Hope Ser.). (ENG.). 2006. 34.99 (978-1-60814-031-2(8)) Oasis Audio.

From the Age of Discovery to a World at War, Vol. 1. unabr. ed. William J. Bennett. Read by William J. Bennett. Narrated by Wayne Shepherd. 18 CDs. (Running Time: 19 hrs. 31 mins. 0 sec.). (America: the Last Best Hope Ser.). (ENG.). 2006. audio compact disk 49.99 (978-1-59859-131-6(2)) Oasis Audio.

From the Ashes: A Spiritual Response to the Attack on America. Read by Richard Davidson & Alison Fraser. Contrib. by Billy Graham et al. (ENG.). 2009. 44.99 (978-1-60775-726-9(5)) Find a World.

From the Back of the Bus. Bill Harley. Read by Bill Harley. 1 cass. (Running Time: 1 hr. 5 mins.). (gr. 3-7). 1995. 12.00 (978-0-87483-441-3(4)) Pub: August Hse. Dist(s): Natl Bk Netwk
The schoolbus isn't school - & it isn't home; it's a daily neverland where (to the horror of many a bus driver) children rule. It is from the back of the bus that the strongest intimations of childhood are emitted. The taunters, sassers, & singers of song parodies seem to be drawn to the back of the bus.

From the Back of the Bus. Bill Harley. (J). 2003. audio compact disk 15.00 (978-1-878126-42-9(3)) Round Riv Prodns.
Humorous stories about growing up - bridging the gap between childhood & adulthood. Included on the tracks are: In the Back of the Bus; Bottlecaps; & Mr. Anderson.

From the Back of the Bus: Completely True Stories. unabr. ed. Bill Harley. Read by Bill Harley. 1 cass. (Running Time: 1 hr. 2 min.). (J). (gr. 4-8). 1995. 10.00 (978-1-878126-16-0(4), RRR109) Round Riv Prodns.

From the Bancroft Library: History of Early California: Hispanicization of California; California Gold Rush; Mark Twain in the West. Comment by James J. Rawls et al. 3 cass. 2000. 20.00 (978-1-893663-06-0(X)) Bancroftd Lib.

From the Bell Curve to the Mountain: A New Vision for Leadership & Achievement. Douglas B. Reeves. 2003. video & audio compact disk 14.00 (978-0-9709455-1-8(5)) LeadplusLrn.
Presents three tell-tale signs of a Bell Curve school. Four reasons the Bell Curve is inaccurate and dangerous. Five traits of a Mountain leader. Six steps to move any school from the bell Curve to the Mountain.

From the Bell Curve to the Mountain: A New Vision for Leadership & Achievement. Douglas B. Reeves. 2002. audio compact disk 15.00 (978-0-9709455-6-3(6)) LeadplusLrn.

From the Cabbie's Seat see O. Henry Favorites

From the Cabbie's Seat see Best of O. Henry

From the Cabbie's Seat see O. Henry Library

From the Cabbie's Seat see Favorite Stories by O. Henry

From the Corner of His Eye. Dean Koontz. Read by Stephen Lang. 2001. 104.00 (978-0-7366-6035-8(6)) Books on Tape.

From the Corner of His Eye. unabr. ed. Dean Koontz. Read by Stephen Lang. (Dean Koontz Ser.). (ENG.). 2007. audio compact disk 39.95 (978-0-7393-4148-3(0), Random AudioBks) Pub: Random Audio Pubg. Dist(s): Random

From the Corporate Front Line: The Impact of Coaching on Today's Leaders. Interview with Judi Craig. 4 cass. (Running Time: 2 hrs. 48 mins.). 2000. 40.00 (978-0-9705648-0-1(5)) J Craig.

From the Courage of Commitment. Vivienne Verdon-Roe. 1 cass. (Running Time: 20 min.). 7.00 (A0269-88) Sound Photosyn.
Twenty minutes of passionate elegance.

From the Dance. James Edwards. 1998. pap. bk. 17.95 (978-0-7866-0551-4(0), 95487BCD) Mel Bay.

From the Dark Side of the Moon Giving: National Association of Evangelicals, 47th Annual Convention, Columbus, Ohio. March 7-9, 1989. Andy Miller. 1 cass. (Luncheons Ser.: No. 113-Thursd). 1989. 4.00 ea. 1-8 tapes.; 4.25 ea. 9 tapes or more. Nat Assn Evan.

From the Dust Returned. unabr. ed. Ray Bradbury. Read by Michael Prichard. 4 cass. (Running Time: 6 hrs.). 2001. 32.00 (978-0-7366-8489-7(1)) Books on Tape.
Ray Bradbury brings together the family of spooks he once wrote about to celebrate All-Hallows Eve.

*__From the Dust Returned.__ unabr. ed. Ray Bradbury. Read by John Glover. (ENG.). 2005. (978-0-06-085507-9(X), Harper Audio); (978-0-06-085505-5(3), Harper Audio) HarperCollins Pubs.

From the Earth to the Moon. abr. adpt. ed. Jules Verne. (Bring the Classics to Life: Level 4 Ser.). (ENG.). 2008. audio compact disk 12.95 (978-1-55576-575-0(0)) EDCON Pubng.

From the Earth to the Moon. unabr. ed. Jules Verne. Read by Bernard Mayes. 4 cass. (Running Time: 5 hrs. 30 mins.). 2000. 32.95 (978-0-7861-1766-6(4), 2569) Blckstn Audio.
The war of the Rebellion is over, & the members of the American Gun Club, bored with inactivity, look around for a new project. At last they have it: "We will build the greatest projectile the world has ever seen, & make the moon our thirty-eighth state!".

From the Earth to the Moon. unabr. ed. Jules Verne. Read by Jim Killavey. 3 cass. (Running Time: 4 hrs. 30 min.). 1980. 21.00 incl. album. (C-20) Jimcin Record.
Although writing in the 1860's, Verne was in many ways accurate about the speeds & times involved in space flight. In addition, this is a compelling human drama & good-natured satire of popular myths about America.

*__From the Earth to the Moon: Bring the Classics to Life.__ adpt. ed. Jules Verne. (Bring the Classics to Life Ser.). 2008. pap. bk. 21.95 (978-1-55576-616-0(1)) EDCON Pubng.

From the End of Heaven. Read by Chris Stewart. (Great & Terrible Ser.: Vol. 5). 2008. audio compact disk 35.95 (978-1-59038-883-9(6)) Deseret Bk.

From the Eye of the Cat. Susannah Brin. Narrated by Larry A. McKeever. (Horror Ser.). (J). 2001. 10.95 (978-1-58659-079-6(0)); audio compact disk 14.95 (978-1-58659-339-1(0)) Artesian.

From the Eye of the Cat. Dwayne Epstein. Narrated by Larry A. McKeever. (Horror Ser.). (J). 2001. 10.95 (978-1-58659-076-5(6)); audio compact disk 14.95 (978-1-58659-336-0(6)) Artesian.

From the Father's Heart. Charles Slagle & Paula Slagle. 1 cass. 1993. 10.99 (978-1-56043-936-3(X)) Destiny Image Pubs.

From the Goddess. Perf. by Robert Gass & On Wings of Song. 1 cass. (Running Time: 1 hr.). 9.98 (SA230) White Dove NM.
A joyous & powerful celebration of the Divine Feminine. The chanting has many wonderful variations.

From the Ground Up: Poems of One Southerner's Passage to Adulthood. Robert Hamblin. 1992. 12.95 (978-1-877770-67-8(1)) Time Being Bks.

From the Heart: Eight Rules to Live By. abr. ed. Robin Roberts. (ENG.). 2007. 12.99 (978-1-4013-8729-7(2)) Pub: Hyperion. Dist(s): HarperCollins Pubs

From the Heart: Eight Rules to Live By. abr. ed. Robin Roberts. Read by Robin Roberts. 2 CDs. (Running Time: 2 hrs. 30 mins.). 2007. audio compact disk 19.98 (978-1-4013-8727-3(6)) Pub: Hyperion. Dist(s): HarperCollins Pubs

From the Heart: Luke 11. Ed Young. 1992. 4.95 (978-0-7417-1924-9(X), 924) Win Walk.

From the Heart of God. Speeches. Creflo A. Dollar. 1 cass. (Running Time: 1 hr. 20 mins.). 2000. 11.00 (978-1-59089-720-1(X)); audio compact disk 15.00 (978-1-59089-136-0(8)) Creflo Dollar.

From the Heavens. Contrib. by Meha Shamayim & Leonardo Bella. Prod. by Leonardo Bella. 2007. audio compact disk 16.98 (978-5-557-72181-3(9)) Pt of Grace Ent.

From the Inaugural Celebration: The Center for Studies in Science & Spirituality. Edie Hartshorne. 1 cass. 9.00 (A0606-90) Sound Photosyn.
The music & other talks from the event.

From the Lotus of the Heart. Speeches. Sai Ma Lakshmi Devi. 1. 2005. audio compact disk 16.00 (978-0-9766664-3-1(X)) HIU Pr.

From the Mixed-up Files of Mrs. Basil E. Frankweiler. E. L. Konigsburg. Read by Jan Miner. 2 cass. (Running Time: 3 hrs. 40 mins.). (J). 2000. 18.00 (978-0-7366-9098-0(0)) Books on Tape.
Claudia must solve a mystery as she stages a unique form of demonstration: a secret live-in at New York's Metropolitan Museum of Art.

From the Mixed-up Files of Mrs. Basil E. Frankweiler. E. L. Konigsburg. Read by Jan Miner. 3 CDs. (Running Time: 3 hrs. 39 mins.). (J). (gr. 3-7). 2004. audio compact disk 25.50 (978-0-8072-1784-9(0), Listening Lib) Pub: Random Audio Pubg. Dist(s): NetLibrary CO

From the Mixed-up Files of Mrs. Basil E. Frankweiler. unabr. ed. E. L. Konigsburg. Read by Jan Miner. 2 vols. (Running Time: 3 hrs. 39 mins.). (J). (gr. 3-7). 1989. pap. bk. 29.00 (978-0-8072-8538-1(2), LB 5SP, Listening Lib); 23.00 (978-0-8072-8515-2(3), LB 5 CX, Listening Lib) Random Audio Pubg.
For Claudia & Jaimie, running away seemed like the perfect solution & the Metropolitan Museum of Art was the perfect place to hide. But after they realized that running away wasn't the answer, Claudia still had to solve a mystery.

From the Mixed-up Files of Mrs. Basil E. Frankweiler. unabr. ed. E. L. Konigsburg. Read by Jan Miner. 2 cass. (Running Time: 3 hrs.). (J). 1995. 30.00 (978-0-8072-8531-2(5), LL 0042, Listening Lib) Random Audio Pubg.
Claudia Kincaid is almost twelve, the oldest of four children who live in Connecticut. But Claudia is restless & wants to do something exciting. So when she decides to run away, she goes to New York's Metropolitan Museum of Art, & takes her brother Jamie with her! What happens to Claudia & Jamie, & the changes that come about, prove greater than either had bargained for.

From the Mixed-up Files of Mrs. Basil E. Frankweiler. unabr. ed. E. L. Konigsburg. Read by Jill Clayburgh. (Running Time: 3 hrs. 30 mins. 0 sec.). (ENG.). (J). 2009. audio compact disk 19.99 (978-0-7435-9715-9(X)) Pub: S&S Audio. Dist(s): S and S Inc

From the Mixed-up Files of Mrs. Basil E. Frankweiler. unabr. ed. E. L. Konigsburg. Narrated by Jan Miner. 2 cass. (Running Time: 2 hrs.). (J). pap. bk. 23.00 (LL1032AC) Weston Woods.

From the Mixed-up Files of Mrs. Basil E. Frankweiler, Set. unabr. ed. E. L. Konigsburg. Read by Jan Miner. 3 cass. (YA). 1999. 16.98 (FS9-34152) Highsmith.

From the Past to the Future. Perf. by Pima Express Staff. 1 cass., 1 CD. 7.98 (CANR 8109) NewSound.
Performs a combination of Chicken Scratch (Waila) & country music.

From the Rising of the Sun. Contrib. by Kathy Shooster. Prod. by Margaret Becker. 2007. audio compact disk 16.98 (978-5-557-58537-8(0)) Pt of Grace Ent.

From the River to the Ends of Earth-mp3. Read by Douglas Wilson. 1997. 20.00 (978-1-59128-305-8(1)) Canon Pr ID.

From the River to the Ends of Earth-tape. Read by Douglas Wilson. 8 cass. 1997. 24.00 (978-1-59128-307-2(8)) Canon Pr ID.

From the Rock Untombed see Savagery of Love: Brother Antoninus Reads His Poetry

From the Shadows, Pt. 1. unabr. ed. Robert M. Gates. Read by Jonathan Reese. 9 cass. (Running Time: 13 hrs. 30 min.). 1997. 72.00 (4407-A) Books on Tape.
Robert M. Gates is the only man to rise from entry level analyst to Director of the CIA & to serve on the White House staffs of four Presidents.

From the Shadows, Pt. 2. Robert M. Gates. Read by Jonathan Reese. 8 cass. (Running Time: 12 hrs.). 1997. 64.00 (978-0-7366-3726-8(5), 4407-B) Books on Tape.
The ex-director of the CIA lays bare thirty years of covert actions against the USSR. A fascinating & frightening look inside the world.

From the Sixties to the Nineties. Stephen Gaskin. 1 cass. 9.00 (A0611-90) Sound Photosyn.
How it was & how it is - the warp & the woof from this great yarn spinner!.

From the Start: Beginning Listening. J. Huizenga. (J). (gr. 1-9). 1988. 40.88 (978-0-582-90726-3(8)) AddisonWesley.

From the Start: Beginning Listening. J. Huizenga. (J). (gr. 1-9). 1988. 51.11 (978-0-8013-0020-2(7)) Longman.

From This Beloved Hour. unabr. ed. Willa Lambert. Read by Denise S. Utter. 8 cass. (Running Time: 10 hrs. 24 min.). 1994. 49.95 (978-1-55686-546-6(5)) Books in Motion.
Jenny Mowry's archaeological assignment in Egypt becomes complicated when she is pursued by a powerful sheikh & a handsome Englishman.

*__From This Day.__ unabr. ed. Nora Roberts. (Running Time: 7 hrs.). 2010. 24.99 (978-1-4418-5407-0(X), 9781441854070, Brilliance MP3); 39.97 (978-1-4418-5408-7(8), 9781441854087, Brinc Audio MP3 Lib); 39.97 (978-1-4418-5409-4(6), 9781441854094, BADLE); audio compact disk 24.99 (978-1-4418-5405-6(3), 9781441854056, Bril Audio CD Unabri); audio compact disk 79.97 (978-1-4418-5406-3(1), 9781441854063, BriAudCD Unabrid) Brilliance Audio.

*__From This Day Forth.__ Janet Woods. 2010. 69.95 (978-1-84559-624-8(2)) Pub: Soundings Ltd GBR. Dist(s): Ulverscroft US

*__From Those Wonderful Folks Who Gave You Pearl Harbor: Front-Line Dispatches from the Advertising War.__ unabr. ed. Jerry Della Femina & Charles Sopkin. Narrated by Peter Berkrot. (Running Time: 7 hrs. 30 mins. 0 sec.). 2010. 19.99 (978-1-4001-6989-4(5)); 14.99 (978-1-4001-8989-2(6)); audio compact disk 29.99 (978-1-4001-1989-9(8)); audio compact disk 71.99 (978-1-4001-4989-6(4)) Pub: Tantor Media. Dist(s): IngramPubServ

*__From Those Wonderful Folks Who Gave You Pearl Harbor (Library Edition) Front-Line Dispatches from the Advertising War.__ unabr. ed. Jerry Della Femina & Charles Sopkin. Narrated by Peter Berkrot. (Running Time: 7 hrs. 30 mins.). 2010. 29.99 (978-1-4001-9989-1(1)) Tantor Media.

From Time Immemorial: The Origins of the Arab-Jewish Conflict over Palestine. unabr. ed. Joan Peters. Read by Mary Woods. 14 cass. (Running Time: 21 hrs.). 1986. 112.00 Set. (978-0-7366-1065-0(0), 1992) Books on Tape.
Unfolds an historical record that shatters the widely-held belief that Arabs & Jews co-existed for centuries in the Arab World. The fact that Jews, along with other non-Muslims, were second-class citizens oppressed for more than a millenium. This continuing hostility continues to underlie every Arab action toward the State of Israel.

From Time to Eternity. Derek Prince. 1 cass. 5.95 (124) Derek Prince.
God weans us from the temporal that we may find ultimate satisfaction in the eternal.

From Time to Time. abr. ed. Jack Finney. 4 cass. (Running Time: 6 hrs). 2000. 15.99 (978-0-7435-0551-2(4), Audioworks) S&S Audio.

From Time to Time. unabr. ed. Jack Finney. Narrated by Paul Hecht. 8 cass. (Running Time: 11 hrs.). 1995. 70.00 (978-0-7887-0338-6(2), 94530E7) Recorded Bks.
In this sequel to "Time & Again," when Ruben Prien discovers a way to prevent the outbreak of World War I & therefore alter the course of history, he calls Simon Morley back from the 1880s.

From Time to Time: The Sequel to Time & Again. Jack Finney. 2004. 13.95 (978-0-7435-4742-0(X)) Pub: S&S Audio. Dist(s): S and S Inc

From Time to Timelessness. Kenneth Wapnick. 2 CDs. 2007. audio compact disk 11.00 (978-1-59142-312-6(0), CD48) Foun Miracles.

From Time to Timelessness. Kenneth Wapnick. 1 CD. (Running Time: 1 hr. 54 mins. 55 secs.). 2007. 9.00 (978-1-59142-313-3(9), 3m48) Foun Miracles.

From "To a Little Girl, One Year Old in a Ruined Fortress": Gull's Cry; The Child Next Door see Twentieth-Century Poetry in English, No. 29, Recordings of Poets Reading Their Own Poetry

From Tragedy to Grace: Stages in the Process of Dying & the Experience of Dying: A Guided Meditation. Johanna Luther. Comment by Stephen Levine. (Running Time: 51 min.). 1987. Original Face.
Includes the classic stages of dying & the mind states that come & go as death approaches.

From Turmoil to Tranquility: Eliminate Fear, Phobias, Anger & Depression Forever. unabr. ed. Cynthia Cooke. Ed. by Cynthia Cooke. 5 cass. (Running Time: 3 hrs.). 2001. 49.95 (978-0-9714346-0-8(3)) Therapist Within.
Eliminate anxiety, depression, obsessive thoughts forever. Why talk therapy and medication don't work. Based on the latest brain research regarding the mind/body/spirit connection.

From Turmoil to Tranquility Vol. 1: Eliminate Fear, Phobias, Anger & Depression Forever. unabr. ed. Cynthia Cooke. Ed. by Cynthia Cooke. 5 CDs. (Running Time: 3 hrs.). 2001. audio compact disk 49.95 (978-0-9714346-3-9(8)) Therapist Within.
Eliminate anxiety, depression, obsessive thoughts forever. Why talk therapy and medication don't work. Based on the latest brain research regarding the mind/body/spirit connection.

From Ulster to the Carolinas: Irish Church Records - Church of Ireland, Presbyterian, & Catholic, No. 4. David E. Rencher. (ENG.). 2008. 12.00 (978-0-936370-18-7(1)) N C Genealogical.

From Ulster to the Carolinas: Irish Immigration - the Sources in Ireland, No. 2. David E. Rencher. (ENG.). 2008. 12.00 (978-0-936370-16-3(5)) N C Genealogical.

From Ulster to the Carolinas: Irish Jurisdictions & Reference Works, No. 1. David E. Rencher. 2008. 12.00 (978-0-936370-15-6(7)) N C Genealogical.

From Ulster to the Carolinas: The Scots-Irish in North Carolina, No. 3. David E. Rencher. (ENG.). 2008. 12.00 (978-0-936370-17-0(3)) N C Genealogical.

From Unexpected Places. Edd Anthony. Read by Edd Anthony. 2007. audio compact disk 16.95 (978-1-881586-23-4(5)) Canticle Cass.

From WBEZ Chicago - Lies, Sissies & Fiascoes: The Best of This American Life. Rhino Records Staff. 2 CDs. (Running Time: 3 hrs.). 1999. audio compact disk 17.98 (978-0-7379-0034-7(2), R75705) Rhino Enter.

From WBEZ Chicago - Lies, Sissies & Fiascoes: The Best of This American Life. Rhino Records Staff. 2 cass. (Running Time: 3 hrs.). 1999. 10.98 (978-0-7379-0035-4(0), R4 75705) Rhino Enter.

From What to How's: Living Mindfulness with Marsha M. Linehan, Ph. D., ABPP, Seattle Intensive 2004-2005, Day 2. Executive Producer Shree A. Vigil. Prod. by Behavioral Tech. 2005. audio compact disk 15.95 (978-0-9745002-8-7(3)) Behavioral Tech.

*__From Whence the Power? How Do We Live in Such Demanding Times?__ Featuring Arun Andrews. 2009. audio compact disk 9.00 (978-1-61256-001-4(6)) Ravi Zach.

From Worry to Worship. Warren W. Wiersbe. Read by Warren W. Wiersbe. 3 cass. 14.95 (978-0-8474-2232-6(1)) Back to Bible.
These 12 messages from Habakkuk show how God's people can go from worry to worship, in spite of world conditions without & fears within.

From Yao to Mao: 5000 Years of Chinese History, Vol. I-III. Instructed by Kenneth Hammond. 18 CDs. (Running Time: 18 hrs.). 2004. bk. 99.95 (978-1-56585-867-1(0), 8320) Teaching Co.

From Yao to Mao Vol. I-III: 5000 Years of Chinese History. Instructed by Kenneth Hammond. 18 cass. (Running Time: 18 hrs.). 2004. bk. 79.95 (978-1-56585-865-7(4), 8320) Teaching Co.

From Zeus to Aliens. 2002. 10.00 (978-0-7398-5197-5(7)) SteckVau.

From Zeus to Aliens. Steck-Vaughn Staff. 2002. pap. bk. 41.60 (978-0-7398-6982-6(5)) SteckVau.

From Zeus to Aliens Level 4. (J). 2002. audio compact disk (978-0-7398-5353-5(8)) SteckVau.

Frommer's(r) Best of Paris Audio Tour & Paris's Montmartre Audio Walking Tour. unabr. ed. Myka Del Barrio. Read by Pauline Frommer. (YA). 2008. 34.99 (978-1-60514-578-5(5)) Find a World.

Frommer's(r) Best of Rome Audio Tour & Rome's Trastevere Audio Walking Tour. unabr. ed. A. Lipsitz Flippin. Read by Pauline Frommer. (YA). 2008. 34.99 (978-1-60514-577-8(7)) Find a World.

Frommer's(r) New York City's Lower Eastside & Chinatown Audio Walking Tour. unabr. ed. A. Lipsitz Flippin. Read by Pauline Frommer. (YA). 2008. 34.99 (978-1-60252-966-3(3)) Find a World.

***Front & Center.** unabr. ed. Catherine Gilbert Murdock. Narrated by Natalie Moore. 5 CDs. (Running Time: 5 hrs. 55 mins.). (YA). (gr. 8-11). 2010. audio compact disk 45.00 (978-0-307-58324-6(4), Listening Lib) Pub: Random Audio Pubg. Dist(s): Random

Front Men of the Illuminati. Ed. by Alan H. Peterson. As told by Doc Marquis. (American Focus on Satanic Crime Ser.: Vol. 11). 2000. 49.95 (978-1-877858-11-6(0)) Amer Focus Pub.

Front Page see Theatre Highlights

Front Page. Perf. by Pat O'Brien & Adolphe Menjou. 1 cass. (Running Time: 60 min.). 1946. 7.95 (DD-8405) Natl Recrd Co.

In the story "Front Page", Editor Menjou wants crack newspaper man O'Brien to cover a hanging at the state prison. However, O'Brien is about to get married & is not about to cover the story, but Menjou is not to be denied, even if he has to stop the marriage. The story "Shadow of a doubt" is a gripping suspense play in the typical Alfred Hitchcock style. A niece suspects her favorite Uncle Charlie of being the Merry Widow Murderer. Both shows were aired originally on Academy Award Theater.

Front Porch Favorites: Nineteenth Century American Classics. Perf. by Wayne Erbsen. 1 cass. (Running Time: 55 min.). 1993. 9.95 (978-1-883206-00-0(6), NG007); audio compact disk 14.95 CD. (978-1-883206-14-7(6), NG-CD-007) Native Ground.

Seventeen historic American melodies that traveled along with the pioneers in covered wagons, through the Civil War period & up to today.

Front Porch Gospel: 36 Smoky Mountain Gospel Favorites. Contrib. by Rick Brown & Tom Calvani. Created by Hendrickson Worship. 2007. audio compact disk 19.95 (978-1-59856-262-0(2)) Hendrickson MA.

Front Porch Music. Perf. by Tillery, Linda and the CHC. 1 cass.; 1 CD. 1998. 10.98 (978-1-56628-139-3(3), 72881); audio compact disk 15.98 CD. (978-1-56628-138-6(5), 72881D) MFLP CA.

Front Porch Old-Time Songbook. Wayne Erbsen. 1993. pap. bk. 24.95 (978-0-7866-0635-1(5), 95034CDP) Mel Bay.

Front-Porch Rocking Chairs. Kathryn Tucker Windham. (What Makes Us Southerners Ser.: Vol. 3). 2002. 12.00 (978-0-87483-657-8(3)); audio compact disk 14.95 (978-0-87483-658-5(1)) Pub: August Hse. Dist(s): Natl Bk Netwk

Front Porch Songbook. 1995. 10.98 (978-1-56222-978-8(8), 95034C) Mel Bay.

Front Porch Songbook. Wayne Erbsen. 1995. audio compact disk 15.98 (978-0-7866-0634-4(7), 95034CD) Mel Bay.

Front Porch Songbook. Wayne Erbsen. 1993. bk. 19.95 (978-0-7866-1183-6(9), 95034P) Mel Bay.

Front Row at the White House: My Life & Times. abr. ed. Helen Thomas. Read by Judith Cummings. 4 cass. (Running Time: 6 hrs.). 2001. 25.00 (978-1-59040-013-5(5), Phoenix Audio) Pub: Amer Intl Pub. Dist(s): PerseuPGW

A unique glimpse into the White House from the woman who has reported on every president from Kennedy to Clinton.

Front Row Center. Steve Amerson. 1998. 10.98 (978-7-83491-562-5(2)) Pub: Amerson Mus Min. Dist(s): STL Dist NA

Front Row Center: Audio Version Mp3 192kbps. Cynthia B. Ainsworthe. 2008. (978-0-9802459-3-6(1)) C B Ainsworthe.

Front Row Center: Audio Version Mp3 96kbps. Cynthia B. Ainsworthe. (ENG.). 2008. (978-0-9802459-2-9(3)) C B Ainsworthe.

Front Row Center: Audio Version Wma 20kbps. Cynthia B. Ainsworthe. (ENG.). 2008. audio compact disk (978-0-9802459-1-2(5)) C B Ainsworthe.

Front Row Center: Audio Version 36 CD Set. Cynthia B. Ainsworthe. (ENG.). 2008. audio compact disk (978-0-9802459-4-3(X)) C B Ainsworthe.

Front Row Center: Inspiring Songs from State to Screen. Steve Amerson. (Running Time: .25 mins.). (ENG.). 2006. audio compact disk 15.98 (978-5-551-66535-9(6)) Pub: Amerson Mus Min. Dist(s): STL Dist NA

***Front Row Center Ii (cd)** Steve Amerson. (ENG.). 2006. audio compact disk 15.98 (978-5-558-62651-3(8)) Pub: Amerson Mus Min. Dist(s): STL Dist NA

Frontal Attack - Touch All Bases - The Fait Accomplice & 81 Others. Richard Buskirk. Read by Richard Buskirk. 6 cass. 1992. 59.95 set. (878A) Nightingale-Conant.

Whether it's called politics, game-playing or "just the way things are" tactics are used all around you everyday. R. Buskirk shows you how to recognize them, counter them & use them to your advantage.

Frontal Sinus Mucoceles - Diagnosis & Treatment. 2 cass. (Otorhinolaryngology Ser.: C85-OT6). 1985. 15.00 (8578) Am Coll Surgeons.

Frontier Freedom Fighter: The Story of Clarina Nichols. abr. ed. Excerpts. Diane Eickhoff. Read by Diane Eickhoff. 1 CD. (Running Time: 4500 sec.). 2006. audio compact disk 14.95 (978-0-9764434-7-6(3)) Quindaro Pr.

Clarina Nichols (1810-1885) devoted her life to improving the lives of women. In the 1850s she joined a small group to launch the women's rights movement in America. She left the comforts of her native Vermont and moved her family to rugged Kansas Territory, joining John Brown to stop the spread of slavery. But her real passion was women's rights. Frontier Freedom Fighter tells how Clarina Nichols overcame personal hardships and heartbreaks to become one of the country's earliest champions of women. Written for readers of all ages and read by the author in a powerful CD audio presentation.

Frontier Gentleman. Perf. by John Dehner. (ENG.). 2008. audio compact disk 31.95 (978-1-57019-855-7(1)) Radio Spirits.

Frontier Gentleman, collector's ed. Perf. by John Dehner. 6 cass. (Running Time: 9 hrs.). 1998. bk. 17.49 (4147) Radio Spirits.

J.B. Kendall, reporter for the London Times, writes colorful and unusual accounts of life and death in the lawless and early West. But as a man with a gun, he lived and became a part of the violent years in the new territories. 18 episodes of this 1958 series.

***Frontier Gentleman: Life & Death.** Perf. by John Dehner & Harry Bartell. 2010. audio compact disk 31.95 (978-1-57019-917-2(5)) Radio Spirits.

Frontier Gentleman: The Preacher & The Rainmaker. Perf. by John Dehner. 1 cass. 2001. 6.98 (2600) Radio Spirits.

Frontier Stories. unabr. ed. Jack London. Read by Randall James Stanton. 2 cass. (Running Time: 2 hrs.). 1993. 12.95 (978-1-882071-30-2(1)) B-B Audio.

Only the toughest survive in this pair of short stories from the great author of Call of The Wild. A prospectors dream comes true in All Gold Canyon, but can he make the dream last? A northern tracker in Love of Life, slowly becomes a part of the w.

***Frontier Town.** RadioArchives.com. (Running Time: 600). (ENG.). 2004. audio compact disk 29.98 (978-1-61081-016-6(3)) Radio Arch.

Frontiers Set: An Active Introduction to English Grammar. John Schmidt & Terry Simon. 2002. 50.20 (978-0-201-14992-0(3)) AddisonWesley.

Frontline Leaders Vol. 1: Service Managers Who Make a Difference. 2 cass. (Running Time: 29 min. per cass.). 1990. 27.95 Resource Direction.

Frontpage 2002 for Educators W/CD: An Introduction to Web Design for Educators & Trainers. Albert L. Ingram & Ruth A. Watson. 2003. per. 59.00 (978-1-933403-11-3(X)) Crown Custom.

Frontrunner. John Lilly. 1 cass. 1983. 10.00 (978-1-56964-624-3(4), A0066-83) Sound Photosyn.

An inspired talk, discussing his future & amid the galaxies, & other topics.

Frost at Christmas. unabr. ed. R. D. Wingfield. Read by Stephen Thorne. 8 cass. (Running Time: 9 hrs.). (Jack Frost Ser.: Bk. 1). 1997. 69.95 (961210) Pub: ISIS Audio GBR. Dist(s): Ulverscroft US

Rude, crude & insubordinate - that's Jack Frost. Wingfield's sloppiest English detective is scruffy & chaotic, & with a healthy disregard for rules, he attracts trouble like a magnet. Frost is assigned to the disappearance of a prostitute's daughter. When they unearth an ancient skeleton & the fresh corpse of a bank employee, he is also drawn into an unsolved bank robbery from the almost forgotten past. His method - to first risk his career, & then his life.

Frost at Christmas. unabr. ed. R. D. Wingfield. Read by Stephen Thorne. 8 CDs. (Running Time: 8 hrs. 48 min.). (Jack Frost Ser.: Bk. 1). (J). 2001. audio compact disk 79.95 (978-0-7531-1199-4(3)) Pub: ISIS Lrg Prnt GBR. Dist(s): Ulverscroft US

Frost, assisted and annoyed by his new sidekick, is assigned to the disappearance of a prostitute's daughter and with characteristic rashness he launches into the case. But when they unearth an ancient skeleton and the fresh corpse of a bank employee turns up, Frost is also drawn into an unsolved bank robbery from the almost forgotten past. His method - to risk first his career, and then his life.

Frost at Christmas. unabr. ed. R. D. Wingfield. Read by Stephen Thorne. 8 cass. (Jack Frost Ser.: Bk. 1). (J). 2004. 69.95 (978-0-7531-0101-8(7)) Pub: ISIS Lrg Prnt GBR. Dist(s): Ulverscroft US

Frost at Midnight see Poetry of Coleridge

Frost at Midnight see Rime of the Ancient Mariner

Frost at Midnight. unabr. ed. Elizabeth Falconer. Narrated by Virginia Leishman. 8 cass. (Running Time: 10 hrs. 45 mins.). 2000. 72.00 (978-1-84197-107-0(3), H1112E7) Recorded Bks.

Misha ben Bella was happy with her career & her lover. Then she met his girlfriend & child. Only her colleague Paul sees her misery, but as concern breeds affection, Paul must think again. Old enough to be Misha's father, he doesn't want to take advantage of her. Elsewhere, Olivia is an impasse. Her older husband wants a baby, but she refuses. As their paths collide, each brings the others a different perspective - but for better or worse remains to be seen.

***Frost Child.** unabr. ed. Eoin McNamee. Read by Kirby Heyborne. 7 CDs. (Running Time: 8 hrs. 50 mins.). (Navigator Trilogy: Bk. 3). (YA). (gr. 5-8). 2009. audio compact disk 55.00 (978-0-7393-8040-6(0), Listening Lib) Pub: Random Audio Pubg. Dist(s): Random

Frost Child. unabr. ed. Eoin McNamee. Read by Kirby Heyborne. (Navigator Trilogy). (ENG.). (J). (gr. 4). 2009. audio compact disk 45.00 (978-0-7393-8038-3(9), Listening Lib) Pub: Random Audio Pubg. Dist(s): Random

Frost Fair. unabr. ed. Elizabeth Hawksley. Read by Diana Bishop. 7 cass. (Running Time: 8 hrs.). (Sound Ser.). (J). 2002. 61.95 (978-1-84283-284-4(0)); audio compact disk 71.95 (978-1-84283-408-4(8)) Pub: ISIS Lrg Prnt GBR. Dist(s): Ulverscroft US

Frost Fair. unabr. ed. Edward Marston. Narrated by Glen McCready. 10 cass. (Running Time: 11 hrs.). 2004. 89.75 (978-1-84505-215-7(3), H1760MC, Clipper Audio) Recorded Bks.

Frost in May. unabr. ed. Antonia White. Read by Gretel Davis. 7 cass. (Running Time: 7 hrs. 30 min.). 1993. 61.95 (978-1-85089-843-6(X), 10292) Pub: ISIS Audio GBR. Dist(s): Ulverscroft US

It is 1908 & nine-year-old Nanda Gray is sent to the Convent of the Five Wounds on the outskirts of London, where she will spend the next five years of her life. Her quick wit, resilience & enthusiasm soon become repressed in this closed world where her desires & passions have to be only those the church permits. In this intense atmosphere girls are taught to endure, to bear obedience only to the highest goal.

Frost of Spring Green: A Collection of Poetry. Karen Jean Matsko Hood. 2008. 29.95 (978-1-930948-98-3(0)) Whsprng Pine.

Frost of Spring Green: A Collection of Poetry. Karen Jean Matsko Hood. 2010. audio compact disk 24.95 (978-1-59210-154-2(2)) Whsprng Pine.

Frost of Spring Green - English/German Bilingual Translation: A Collection of Poetry. Karen Jean Matsko Hood. (GER.). 2005. 24.95 (978-1-59649-931-7(1)) Whsprng Pine.

Frost of Spring Green - English/Hindu Bilingual Translation: A Collection of Poetry. Karen Jean Matsko Hood. (HIN.). 2005. 24.95 (978-1-59649-937-9(0)) Whsprng Pine.

Frost of Spring Green - English/Korean Bilingual Translation: A Collection of Poetry. Karen Jean Matsko Hood. (KOR.). 2005. 24.95 (978-1-59649-943-0(5)) Whsprng Pine.

Frost of Spring Green - English/Russian Bilingual Translation: A Collection of Poetry. Karen Jean Matsko Hood. (RUS.). 2005. 24.95 (978-1-59649-949-2(4)) Whsprng Pine.

Frost of Spring Green - English/Spanish Bilingual Translation: A Collection of Poetry. Karen Jean Matsko Hood. (SPA.). 2005. 24.95 (978-1-59649-955-3(9)) Whsprng Pine.

Frost of Spring Green, Catholic Edition. Karen Jean Matsko Hood. 2010. audio compact disk 24.95 (978-1-59210-297-6(2)) Whsprng Pine.

Frost of Spring Green, Christian Edition. Karen Jean Matsko Hood. 2010. audio compact disk 24.95 (978-1-59210-337-9(5)) Whsprng Pine.

Frost on My Moustache: The Arctic Exploits of a Lord & a Loafer. unabr. ed. Tim Moore. Narrated by Richard Greenwood. 8 cass. (Running Time: 11 hrs.). 2000. 72.00 (978-1-84197-124-7(3), H1121E7) Recorded Bks.

Unknown to most people, a certain successful Lord Dufferin made an epic voyage to Iceland in 1856, travelling all round the island. To emulate his achievement well over a century later seemed like a good idea to Tim Moore. However, he soon discovered that following in such famous footsteps is not a task for the fainthearted.

Frost on My Moustache: The Arctic Exploits of a Lord & a Loafer. unabr. ed. Tim Moore. Narrated by Richard Greenwood. 10 CDs. (Running Time: 11 hrs.). 2001. audio compact disk 101.00 (978-1-84197-165-0(0), C1283E7) Recorded Bks.

Frost the Fiddler. unabr. ed. Janice Weber. Read by Sandra Burr. (Running Time: 14 hrs.). 2009. 39.97 (978-1-4233-8563-9(2), 9781423385639, Brinc Audio MP3 Lib); 39.97 (978-1-4233-8565-3(9), 9781423385653, BADLE); 24.99 (978-1-4233-8562-2(4), 9781423385622, Brilliance MP3); 24.99 (978-1-4233-8564-6(0), 9781423385646, BAD) Brilliance Audio.

Frostbite: A Werewolf Tale. unabr. ed. David Wellington. Read by Tai Sammons. (Running Time: 9 hrs. 0 mins.). 2010. 29.95 (978-1-4417-2502-8(4)); 54.95 (978-1-4417-2498-4(2)); audio compact disk 76.00 (978-1-4417-2499-1(0)) Blckstn Audio.

***Frostbitten: A Women of the Otherworld Novel.** Kelley Armstrong. Narrated by Jen Taylor. (Running Time: 10 hrs. 34 mins. 0 sec.). (ENG.). 2011. audio compact disk 29.95 (978-1-60998-192-1(8)) Pub: AudioGO. Dist(s): Perseus Dist

***Frost/Nixon: Behind the Scenes of the Nixon Interview.** abr. ed. David Frost. (ENG.). 2008. (978-0-06-156059-0(6)); (978-0-06-156083-5(9)) HarperCollins Pubs.

Frosty: A Raccoon to Remember & Indomitable. unabr. collector's ed. Harriet E. Weaver. Read by Roses Prichard. 5 cass. (Running Time: 7 hrs. 30 min.). (J). (gr. 4-7). 1986. 40.00 (978-0-7366-0470-3(7), 1445) Books on Tape.

A month-old coon kit, brought to Harriet Weaver by a boy who rescued it after its family was accidentally killed, became her boisterous charge for the next 9 months. Indomitable was a salmon - a member of Prairie Creek Hatchery's Class of '64 . Then the entire class vanished from the watershed. Their disappearance remained a mystery until a morning of utter amazement two months later.

Frosty the Snow Man - ShowTrax. Arranged by Kirby Shaw. 1 CD. (Running Time: 5 mins.). 2000. audio compact disk 19.95 (08742186) H Leonard.

Frosty & friends come thumpity-thumping right down to town, but with a little bit of a rock 'n' roll update for the year 2000.

Frosty the Snowman. Perf. by Jimmy Durante. 1 cass. (J). 3.98 Clamshell. (978-1-55886-150-3(5), BB/PT 457) Smarty Pants.

Frozen: My Journey into the World of Cryonics, Deception, & Death. unabr. ed. Larry Johnson & Scott Baldyga. Narrated by William Dufris. (Running Time: 15 hrs. 0 mins.). 2009. 20.99 (978-1-4001-8527-6(0)); 39.99 (978-1-4001-9527-5(6)); 29.99 (978-1-4001-6527-8(X)); audio compact disk 79.99 (978-1-4001-4527-0(9)); audio compact disk 39.99 (978-1-4001-1527-3(2)) Pub: Tantor Media. Dist(s): IngramPubServ

Frozen Assets Workshop: A How-To Workshop. abr. ed. Speeches. Deborah Taylor-Hough. 1 cassette. (Running Time: 1 hr.). 2000. (978-1-891400-39-1(8)) Sourcebks.

Deborah Taylor-Hough talks listeners through the methodology behind her revolutionary cooking methods, which allow home chefs to cook just one day, yet prepare enough meals for 30 days. Listeners will learn indise tips, hints, preparation ideas and planning strategies.

Frozen Deep. Wilkie Collins. 2005. pap. bk. 34.95 (978-1-86015-477-5(8)) Ulverscroft US.

Frozen Dinners. abr. ed. Engle & Barnes. Read by Full Cast Production Staff. Directed By Sandra Bovee. (Running Time: 7200 sec.). (Strange Matter Ser.). (J). (gr. 4-7). 2006. audio compact disk 9.95 (978-1-4233-0870-6(0), 9781423308706, BACD) Brilliance Audio.

Don't go outside. Max is trapped. A freak snowstorm has him sealed in his uncle's mountain cabin, along with his brother Mark and sister Teresa. But Uncle Shoe is missing, and no one's co[illegible] to rescue them. Should they take their chances and hike down the [illegible]ain to safety? Max doesn't think so, especially not since he found those [illegible] tracks in the snow. Then there's that inhuman howling coming from the woods. Now barricaded behind the cabin door, Max thinks he knows what it might be. He's found some old reports that the Abominable Snowman, the yeti, was sighted there fifty years earlier. Has it returned? The kids aren't taking any chances. They've boarded up the cabin, because as much as they want to get out . . . Something else wants in.

Frozen Dinners. abr. ed. Engle & Barnes. (Running Time: 2 hrs.). (Strange Matter Ser.). 2006. 9.95 (978-1-4233-0872-0(7), 9781423308720, BAD) Brilliance Audio.

Frozen Dinners. abr. ed. Engle & Julian Barnes. Read by Multivoice Production Staff. (Running Time: 2 hrs.). (Strange Matter Ser.). 2006. 25.25 (978-1-4233-0873-7(5), 9781423308737, BADLE) Brilliance Audio.

Frozen Dinners. abr. ed. Marion Engle & Johnny Ray Barnes, Jr. (Running Time: 7200 sec.). (Strange Matter Ser.). (J). (gr. 4-7). 2006. audio compact disk 25.25 (978-1-4233-0871-3(9), 9781423308713, BACDLib Ed) Brilliance Audio.

Frozen Fire. unabr. ed. Bill Evans & Marianna Jameson. (Running Time: 14 hrs.). 2009. 59.95 (978-0-7927-6413-7(7), Chivers Sound Lib) AudioGO.

Frozen Fire. unabr. ed. Bill Evans & Marianna Jameson. Read by Peter Larkin. 11 CDs. (Running Time: 14 hrs. 0 mins. 0 sec.). (ENG.). 2009. audio compact disk 39.95 (978-1-4272-0750-0(X)) Pub: Macmill Audio. Dist(s): Macmillan

Frozen Pizza & Other Slices of Life: Level 6. Antoinette Moses. Contrib. by Philip Prowse. (Running Time: 3 hrs. 13 mins.). (Cambridge English Readers Ser.). (ENG.). 2002. 17.85 (978-0-521-75079-0(2)) Cambridge U Pr.

Frozen Ship & Others. unabr. ed. Short Stories. James Oliver Curwood. Read by Jack Sondericker. 2 cass. (Running Time: 2 hrs. 30 min.). Dramatization. 1991. 16.95 (978-1-55686-389-9(6), 389) Books in Motion.

Four short stories are included: The Frozen Ship, The Law of the Lakes, The Amateur Pirates, Captain Kidd of the Underground.

Frozen Terror. abr. ed. Read by Gary Alexander & Phil Tonken. 1 cass. (Running Time: 1 hr.). (Outdoor Life; Classic Stories of the Great Outdoors Ser.: Vol. 2). 1998. 9.95 (978-1-886463-43-1(3)) Oasis Audio.

Fruit & Gifts of the Spirit. 2003. (978-1-59024-167-7(3)); audio compact disk (978-1-59024-168-4(1)) B Hinn Min.

Fruit Hunters: A Story of Nature, Adventure, Commerce & Obsession. unabr. ed. Adam Leith Gollner. Read by Stephen Hoye. (Running Time: 11 hrs. 0 mins. 0 sec.). (ENG.). 2008. audio compact disk 34.99 (978-1-4001-0745-2(8)) Pub: Tantor Media. Dist(s): IngramPubServ

Fruit Hunters: A Story of Nature, Adventure, Commerce & Obsession. unabr. ed. Adam Leith Gollner. Read by Stephen Hoye. Narrated by Stephen Hoye. (Running Time: 11 hrs. 0 mins. 0 sec.). (ENG.). 2008. audio compact disk 69.99 (978-1-4001-3745-9(4)); audio compact disk 24.99 (978-1-4001-5745-7(5)) Pub: Tantor Media. Dist(s): IngramPubServ

Fruit of Her Hands. Nancy Wilson. Read by Ellen Helsel. 4 cass. 1998. 20.00 (978-1-59128-544-1(5)) Canon Pr ID.

Fruit of Her Hands: Audio Book-mp3. Nancy Wilson. Read by Ellen Helsel. 1998. 20.00 (978-1-59128-542-7(9)) Canon Pr ID.

Fruit of Her Hands AudioBook: Respect & the Christian Woman. Nancy Wilson. Read by Ellen Helsel. 4 CDs. (ENG.). 1998. audio compact disk 20.00 (978-1-59128-543-4(7)) Canon Pr ID.

Fruit of the Spirit. 1 cass. (Music Machine Ser.). (J). 9.95 (AMMF) Brdgstn Multimed Grp.
From the same award winning musical writers of "Bullfrogs & Butterflies" comes the original "Music Machine" tape, a certified platinum album.

Fruit of the Spirit. Bridgestone Staff. 2004. audio compact disk 7.98 (978-1-56371-022-3(6)) Brdgstn Multimed Grp.

Fruit of the Spirit. Gloria Copeland. 5 cass. 1988. 25.00 Set. (978-0-88114-824-4(5)) K Copeland Pubns.
How to walk in the Holy Spirit.

Fruit of the Spirit. Mark Crow. 9 cass. (Running Time: 9 hrs.). 2001. (978-1-931537-21-6(6)) Vision Comm Creat.

Fruit of the Spirit. Derek Prince. 2 cass. 11.90 Set. (009-010) Derek Prince.
Fruit of the Spirit, just like natural fruit, needs to be cultivated with skill & hard work.

Fruit of the Spirit. Dale Von Seggen et al. 1 cass. (Running Time: 30 min.). Dramatization. 1980. 15.00 incl. script. (978-1-58302-026-5(8), STP-05) One Way St.
Nine puppet plays, each five to six minutes long, all based on Galatians 5:22-23. Each script can be performed by a minimum of two puppeteers (five characters in all).

Fruit of the Spirit. Dale Liz VonSeggen & Randy Benefield. Prod. by Dale Liz VonSeggen. 2001. audio compact disk 15.00 (978-1-58302-180-4(9)) One Way St.
Contains all nine puppet plays pre-recorded.

Fruit of the Spirit. Warren W. Wiersbe. Read by Warren W. Wiersbe. 3 cass. (Running Time: 3 hrs. 45 min.). 1986. 14.95 (978-0-8474-2291-3(7)) Back to Bible.
Features messages from Galatians 5: 22-26, exhorting Christians to surrender to the Spirit to bring forth fruit in the life.

Fruit of the Spirit. unabr. ed. Keith A. Butler. 6 cass. (Running Time: 9 hrs.). 2001. 30.00 (A128) Word Faith Pubng.

Fruit of the Spirit: Enemies of Love. Gloria Copeland. 8 cass. 2006. 20.00 (978-1-57562-853-0(8)); audio compact disk 20.00 (978-1-57562-854-7(6)) K Copeland Pubns.

Fruit of the Spirit - Tu see Fruit of the Spirit Teaching Unit

Fruit of the Spirit Teaching Unit. Scripts. Dale VonSeggen & Liz VonSeggen. Prod. by One Way Street Staff. Illus. by Jere Cannon. Orig. Title: Fruit of the Spirit - Tu. (J). 2002. audio compact disk 35.00 (978-1-58302-215-3(5)) One Way St.
The ten-lesson teaching unit focuses on each of the nine fruit of the Spirit in Galatians 5:22-23, plus a summary review lesson. Each lesson includes two puppet plays, a story, an object lesson, music suggections, and scripture memory activities, plus a spiritual challenge. this NEW CD includes a puppet play for each week plus theme songs.

Fruit of the Tree, Set. Edith Wharton. Read by Flo Gibson. 10 cass. (Running Time: 14 hrs. 30 min.). 1990. 44.95 (978-1-55685-176-6(6)) Audio Bk Con.
John Amherst & Justine Brent crusade for a better world. Labor & management conflicts & euthanasia are a part of this remarkable novel which could have been written today.

Fruit, the Life of the Believer. Chuck Smith. (ENG.). 2001. audio compact disk 22.99 (978-1-932941-14-2(2)) Word For Today.

Fruitcake. Contrib. by Johnathan Crumpton & Don Marsh. Prod. by Craig Adams. (ENG.). 2008. audio compact disk 24.99 (978-5-557-38260-1(7), Brentwood-Benson Music) Brentwood Music.

Fruitcake: A Mystery. unabr. ed. Jane Rubino. Read by Stephanie Brush. 8 cass. (Running Time: 11 hrs. 48 min.). 2001. 49.95 (978-1-58116-155-7(7)) Books in Motion.
Reporter Cat Austin reluctantly takes on a fluff piece feature on the "Party of the Year" gala at an Atlantic City casino. But "fluff" turns to murder when Cat escapes a speeding car, and finds a recently deposited corpse in the parking garage.

Fruitcake Special & Other Stories, Set, Level 4. Frank Brennan. Contrib. by Philip Prowse. (Running Time: 2 hrs. 27 mins.). (Cambridge English Readers Ser.). (ENG.). 2000. 15.00 (978-0-521-78366-8(6)) Cambridge U Pr.

Fruitful Mother. Elbert Willis. 1 cass. (Tribute to Mothers Ser.). 4.00 Fill the Gap.

Fruits & Gifts of the Spirit. 2001. (978-1-59024-027-4(8)); audio compact disk (978-1-59024-028-1(6)) B Hinn Min.

Fruits & Vegetables: The Basis of Health. Humbart Smokey Santillo. 1 cass. (Running Time: 37 min.). 1995. cass. & audio compact disk 8.95 (978-0-934252-65-2(3)) Hohm Pr.
Everything you need to know about fruits & vegetables.

Fruits d'Or, Set. Nathalie Sarraute. Read by Nathalie Sarraute. 4 cass. (FRE.). 1991. 34.95 (1289-AV) Olivia & Hill.
What is the fate of a book once it is published? That is the theme of this novel which appeared in 1963 & won the International Prize for Literature.

Fruits of Faithfulness: Reaping the Rewards of Living True to What You Believe. 3 cass. (Running Time: 3 hrs.). 2003. 15.00 (978-1-57399-165-0(1)); audio compact disk 15.00 (978-1-57399-166-7(X)) Mac Hammond.
Why do most Christians not experience the level of success and victory they ought? The answer lies in one word-faithfulness. Take a giant step toward abundant blessing and learn how to live true to what you believe by applying the powerful principles revealed in this practical series.

Frumious Bandersnatch. Ed McBain, pseud. Read by Ron McLarty. (87th Precinct Ser.: Bk. 53). 2004. 15.95 (978-0-7435-3922-7(2)) Pub: S&S Audio. Dist(s): S and S Inc

Fruto del Espiritu: Mensajes para Ninos. Daniel Klenovsky & Edith Cabala. (SPA., (J). 2008. pap. bk. 19.99 (978-0-7586-1459-9(4)) Concordia.

Fry's English Delight. Read by Stephen Fry. (Running Time: 2 hrs. 0 mins. 0 sec.). (ENG.). 2009. audio compact disk 24.95 (978-1-60283-747-8(3)) Pub: AudioGO. Dist(s): Perseus Dist

***Fry's English Delight: Series Three.** Read by Stephen Fry. (Running Time: 2 hrs. 0 mins. 0 sec.). (ENG.). 2010. audio compact disk 24.95 (978-1-4084-6749-7(6)) Pub: AudioGO. Dist(s): Perseus Dist

***Fry's English Delight: Series Two.** Read by Stephen Fry. (Running Time: 2 hrs. 0 mins. 0 sec.). (ENG.). 2010. audio compact disk 24.95 (978-1-4084-2743-9(5)) Pub: AudioGO. Dist(s): Perseus Dist

FSH, Vol. 1. Dick Jonas. 1 cass. or CD. 10.00; audio compact disk 15.00 EROSONIC.
Includes: "Tales That I Can Tell," "The Ballad of Robin Olds," "Little Town up North," "Son of Satan's Angels," "Thud Pilot," "Tchepone," "Yankee Air Pirate," "Will There Be a Tomorrow," "Banana Valley," "Downtown," "The MiG-21," & "A Fighter Pilot's Christmas".

FSH, Vol. 2. Dick Jonas. 1 cass. or CD. 15.00 EROSONIC.
Includes: "Battle Hymn of the Red River Rats," "Wolfpack's Houseboy", "Blue Four", "Pine Cones & Oak Leaves," "Normandy's Sand," "Old Weird Harold," "Uncle's Nephews," I Druther Be An F-4 Jock," "Short Timing Sailor Boy," "Love Angel," "I've Been Everywhere," & "Machete Flight".

FSI Amharic Basic Course: Multilingual Books Language Course. Sergie Obolensky et al. 26. (Intensive Cassette Ser.). (AMH.). (C). 1998. spiral bd. 270.00 (978-1-58214-006-3(5)) Language Assocs.

FSI Amharic Basic Course Reader Glossary Level 2: Multilingual Books Language Course. Sergie Obolensky et al. 5 Cass. (Multilingual Books Intensive Cassette Foreign Language Ser.). (AMH.). 1964. spiral bd. 100.00 (978-1-58214-050-6(2)) Language Assocs.

FSI Amharic Basic Course Vol. 2, CDs & Text. ed. Serge Obolensky et al. 3 CDs. (Running Time: 3 hrs.). (Foreign Service Institute Basic Course Ser.). (AMH.). 2007. audio compact disk 99.50 (978-1-57970-457-5(3), AFAM15D, Audio-For) J Norton Pubs.

FSI Bulgarian Basic Course Level 2: Multilingual Books Language Course. Carleton T. Hodge. 11. (Multilingual Books Intensive Cassette Foreign Language Ser.). 1961. spiral bd. 199.00 (978-1-58214-157-2(6)) Language Assocs.

FSI Bulgarian Basic Course Levels 1 & 2. Carleton T. Hodge. 34. (Multilingual Books Intensive Cassette Foreign Language Ser.). (C). 1961. spiral bd. 395.00 (978-1-58214-057-5(X)) Language Assocs.

FSI Bulgarian Intensive Course: Multilingual Books Language Course. Carleton T. Hodge. 23. (BUL.). 1998. spiral bd. 239.00 (978-1-58214-005-6(7)) Language Assocs.

FSI Cambodian Level 2: Multilingual Books Language Course. Someth Suos. 29 Cass. (Multilingual Books Intensive Language Courses). (CAM.). (C). 2004. per. 285.00 (978-1-58214-190-9(8)) Language Assocs.

FSI Cantonese, Level 1. E. Doyle & & Assoc Delbridge. 15 CD's. (Multilingual Books Intensive Language Courses). (CHI.). (C). 2004. per. 229.00 (978-1-58214-370-5(6)) Language Assocs.

FSI Cantonese Basic Course Level 1: Multilingual. E. Doyle & Delbridge and Associates Staff. 15. (Multilingual Books Intensive Cassette Foreign Language Ser.). 1970. spiral bd. 225.00 (978-1-58214-158-9(4)) Language Assocs.

FSI Cantonese Basic Course Level 2: Multilingual Books Language Course. Elisabeth L. Boyle & Delbridge and Associates Staff. 14. (Multilingual Books Intensive Cassette Foreign Language Ser.). (C). 1970. spiral bd. 285.00 (978-1-58214-015-5(4)) Language Assocs.

FSI Cantonese Basic Course Levels 1 & 2: Multilingual Books Language Course. 29. (Multilingual Books Intensive Cassette Foreign Language Ser.). 1970. spiral bd. 445.00 (978-1-58214-068-1(5)) Language Assocs.

FSI Cantonese Intensive Cassette Course: Multilingual Books Language Course. Elisabeth L. Boyle. 15. (C). 1997. spiral bd. 225.00 (978-0-9631518-1-0(9)) Language Assocs.

FSI Cantonese Level 2: Multilingual Books Foreign Language Course. Elizabeth Boyle & & Assoc Delbridge. 14 CD's. (Multilingual Books Intensive Language Courses). 2004. per. 229.00 (978-1-58214-371-2(4)) Language Assocs.

FSI Chinese Module One: Multilingual Books Language Course. FSI Staff. 9 cass. (Multilingual Books Intensive Cassette Foreign Language Ser.). (CHI.). (C). 2003. per. 199.00 (978-1-58214-069-8(3)) Language Assocs.

FSI Chinyanja Basic Course: Multilingual Books Language Course. Told to FSI Staff. (Multilingual Books Intensive Cassette Foreign Language Ser.). 2000. spiral bd. 225.00 (978-1-58214-060-5(X)) Language Assocs.

FSI Conversational Finnish: Multilingual Books Language Course. Suomea Keskustellen. 15 cass. (Multilingual Books Intensive Cassette Foreign Language Ser.). (C). 1999. pap. bk. 225.00 (978-1-58214-016-2(2)) Language Assocs.

FSI Estonian Basic Course: Multilingual Books Language Course. Felix J. Oinas. (Multilingual Books Intensive Cassette Foreign Language Ser.). (C). 1993. spiral bd. 295.00 (978-1-58214-161-9(4)) Language Assocs.

FSI Fast Course Spanish (Remastered) (ENG.). 2006. 49.95 (978-0-9786090-1-6(8)) Learn Craz Inc.

FSI Fast Czech: Multilingual Books Language Course. Radovan Pletka. 10. (Intensive Cassette Ser.). (CZE.). (C). 1998. spiral bd. 225.00 (978-1-58214-011-7(1)) Language Assocs.

FSI Fast Polish: Multilingual Books Language Course. Krystyna Stypolkowska-Smith & Krystyna Sadlowsko. 5 cass. (Intensive Cassette Ser.). (POL.). (C). 1998. per. 139.00 (978-1-58214-013-1(8)) Language Assocs.

FSI French Basic Course Level 1: Multilingual Books Language Course. Monique Cossard. 15 cass. (Multilingual Books Intensive Cassette Foreign Language Ser.). (FRE.). (C). 1999. per. 199.00 (978-1-58214-018-6(9)) Language Assocs.

FSI French Basic Course Level 2: Multilingual Books Language Course. Monique Cossard. 29 cass. (Multilingual Books Intensive Cassette Foreign Language Ser.). (C). 1999. pap. bk. 225.00 (978-1-58214-019-3(7)) Language Assocs.

FSI French Basic Course Level 2: Multilingual Books Language Course. FSI Staff. 29 CD's. (Multilingual Books Intensive Language Courses). (C). 2003. per. 269.00 (978-1-58214-196-1(7)) Language Assocs.

FSI French Basic Course Level 3: Multilingual Books Language Course. Monique Cossard. 29 cass. (Multilingual Books Intensive Cassette Foreign Language Ser.). (FRE.). (C). 1999. per. 285.00 (978-1-58214-020-9(0)) Language Assocs.

FSI French FSI Basic Course Level 4: Multilingual Books Language Course. Monique Cossard & Robert Salazar. 24 cass. (Multilingual Books Intensive Language Courses). (FRE.). (C). 2001. per. 285.00 (978-1-58214-199-2(1)) Language Assocs.

FSI French Level 1 Level 4: Multilingual Books Language Course. Monique Cossard & Robert Salazar. 15 CD's. (Multilingual Books Intensive Cassette Foreign Language Ser.). (FRE.). (C). 1946. per. 239.00 (978-1-58214-021-6(9)) Language Assocs.

FSI French Level 3: Multilingual Books Language Course. Monique Cossard & Robert Salazar. 24 CD's. (Multilingual Books Intensive Language Courses). (FRE.). 2004. per. 299.00 (978-1-58214-363-7(3)) Language Assocs.

FSI French Level 4 CD: Multilingual Books Language Course. Monique Cossard & Robert Salazar. 24 CD's. (Multilingual Books Intensive Language Courses). (FRE.). (C). 2004. per. 269.00 (978-1-58214-138-1(X)) Language Assocs.

FSI German Basic Course Level 1: Multilingual Books Language Course. FSI Staff. 11 CD's. (Multilingual Books Intensive Language Courses). (GER.). (C). 2003. per. 199.00 (978-1-58214-135-0(5)) Language Assocs.
Units one to seven of basic course.

FSI German Basic Course Levels 1-2: Multilingual Books Language Course. FSI Staff. 30 cass. (Multilingual Books Intensive Cassette Foreign Language Ser.). (GER.). (C). 1999. spiral bd. 405.00 (978-1-58214-073-5(1)) Language Assocs.

FSI German Basic Course Level 1: Multilingual Books Language Course. FSI Staff. 12 cass. (Multilingual Books Intensive Cassette Foreign Language Ser.). (GER.). (C). 1946. spiral bd. 225.00 (978-1-58214-071-1(5), 942) Language Assocs.

FSI German Basic Course Level 2: Multilingual Books Language Course. FSI Staff. 18 cass. (Multilingual Books Intensive Cassette Foreign Language Ser.). (GER.). (C). 1946. spiral bd. 225.00 (978-1-58214-072-8(3)) Language Assocs.

FSI Greek Intensive Course Level 1. FSI Staff. 16 CDs. (Multilingual Books Intensive Language Courses). (GRE.). 2005. per. 225.00 (978-1-58214-335-4(8)) Language Assocs.

FSI Hebrew Basic Course: Modern Spoken Hebrew. Joseph Reif & Hanna Levinson. 24 cass. (Multilingual Books Intensive Cassette Foreign Language Ser.). (HEB.). (C). 1965. spiral bd. 285.00 (978-1-58214-200-5(9)) Language Assocs.

FSI Hebrew Course: Multilingual Books Language Course. Joseph A. Reif & Hanna Levinson. 24 CD's. (Multilingual Books Intensive Language Courses). (HEB.). (C). 2004. per. 269.00 (978-1-58214-139-8(8)) Language Assocs.

FSI Hungarian Basic Course: Multilingual Books Language Course. FSI Staff. 12 cass. (Multilingual Books Intensive Cassette Foreign Language Ser.). (HUN.). (C). 1999. spiral bd. 225.00 (978-1-58214-178-7(9)) Language Assocs.

FSI Hungarian Basic Course: Multilingual Books Language Course. August A. Koski & Ilona Mihalyfy. 12 cass. (Multilingual Books Intensive Cassette Foreign Language Ser.). (HUN.). (C). 1997. 225.00 (978-0-9631518-3-4(5)) Language Assocs.

FSI Hungarian Basic Course Level 2: Multilingual Books Language Course. Ilona Mihalyfy et al. 26 cass. (Multilingual Books Intensive Cassette Foreign Language Ser.). (HUN.). (C). 1999. spiral bd. 285.00 (978-1-58214-033-9(2)) Language Assocs.

FSI Hungarian Basic Course Level 1: Multilingual Books Language Course. FSI Staff. 12 cass. (Multilingual Books Intensive Cassette Foreign Language Ser.). (HUN.). (C). 1946. per. 225.00 (978-1-58214-162-6(2)) Language Assocs.

FSI Hungarian Basic Course Level 2 on CD. FSI Staff. 26 CDs. (Multilingual Books Intensive Language Courses). (HUN.). 2006. per. 285.00 (978-1-58214-333-0(1)) Language Assocs.

FSI Hungarian Basic Course Levels 1 & 2: Multilingual Books Language Course. FSI Staff. 30. (Multilingual Books Intensive Cassette Foreign Language Ser.). (HUN.). (C). 1946. spiral bd. 395.00 (978-1-58214-090-2(1)) Language Assocs.

FSI Hungarian Basic Course on CD: Language Associates Course. FSI Staff. 24 CDs. (Multilingual Books Intensive Language Courses). (HUN.). 2006. per. 299.00 (978-1-58214-332-3(3)) Language Assocs.

FSI Igbo Basic Course: Multilingual Books Language Course. FSI Staff. 12. (Multilingual Books Intensive Cassette Foreign Language Ser.). (IBO.). (C). 1970. per. 199.00 (978-1-58214-034-6(0)) Language Assocs.

FSI Intensive Serbian-Croatian Cassette Course Level 1: Multilingual Books Language Course. 22 cass. (Multilingual Books Intensive Cassette Foreign Language Ser.). (SBC.). (C). 1997. spiral bd. 225.00 (978-0-9631518-7-2(8)) Language Assocs.

FSI Kirundi Basic Course: Multilingual Books Language Course. Raymond Setukuru et al. 19 cass. (Multilingual Books Intensive Cassette Foreign Language Ser.). (C). 1999. per. 225.00 (978-1-58214-065-0(0)) Language Assocs.

FSI Kituba Course: Multilingual Books Language Course, L. B. Swifa & E. W. Zola. 18 cass. (Multilingual Books Intensive Language Courses). (C). 1999. spiral bd. 225.00 (978-1-58214-154-1(1)) Language Assocs.

FSI Korean Basic Course Level 1: Multilingual Books Language Course. Foreign Institute Staff. 18 cass. (Multilingual Books Intensive Cassette Foreign Language Ser.). (KOR.). (C). 1999. 225.00 (978-1-58214-038-4(3)) Language Assocs.

FSI Korean Level: Multilingual Books Language Course. FSI Staff. 18 CD's. (Multilingual Books Intensive Language Courses). (KOR.). (C). 2003. per. 239.00 (978-1-58214-359-0(5)) Language Assocs.

FSI Korean Level 2: Multilingual Books Language Course. FSI Staff. 16 CD's. (Multilingual Books Intensive Language Courses). (KOR.). 2005. per. 295.00 (978-1-58214-347-7(1)) Language Assocs.

FSI Levantine Arabic Pronunciation: Multilingual Books Language Course, James Snow. 10 cass. (Multilingual Books Interactive Language Courses Ser.). (ARA.). (C). 1999. 199.00 (978-1-58214-051-3(0)) Language Assocs.

FSI Luganda Basic Course: Multilingual Books Language Course. F. Kamoga & E. Stevick. 10 cass. (Multilingual Books Intensive Cassette Foreign Language Ser.). (LUG.). (C). 1968. spiral bd. 150.00 (978-1-58214-040-7(5)) Language Assocs.

FSI Modern Written Arabic Level 1: Multilingual Books Language Course. FSI Staff. 24 cass. (Multilingual Books Intensive Cassette Foreign Language Ser.). (ARA.). (C). 2002. per. Rental 275.00 (978-1-58214-188-6(6)) Language Assocs.

FSI Modern Written Arabic Level 2: Multilingual Books Language Course. FSI Staff. 8 cass. (Multilingual Books Intensive Cassette Foreign Language Ser.). (ARA.). (C). 2002. per. 175.00 (978-1-58214-189-3(4)) Language Assocs.

FSI More' Basic Course: Multilingual Books Language Course. M. Lehrer et al. 29 cass. (Multilingual Books Intensive Cassette Foreign Language Ser.). (C). 1966. spiral bd. 285.00 (978-1-58214-165-7(7)) Language Assocs.

FSI Platiquemos Spanish Levels 1 - 8: Multilingual Books Language Course. Don Casteel. 54 CDs. (Running Time: 60 min ea avg.). (Multilingual Books Intensive Language Courses). (SPA.). (C). 2002. per. 669.00 (978-1-58214-285-2(8)) Language Assocs.

FSI Portuguese Level 1: Multilingual Books Language Course. Jack Lee Ulsh. 15 CD's. (Multilingual Books Intensive Language Courses). (POR.). (C). 1999. per. 239.00 (978-1-58214-092-6(8)) Language Assocs.

FSI Portuguese Level 2: Multilingual Books Language Course. FSI Staff. 22 CD's. (Multilingual Books Intensive Language Courses). (POR.). 2005. per. 285.00 (978-1-58214-348-4(X)) Language Assocs.

FSI Portuguese Programmatic Course Level 1: Multilingual Books Language Course. Jack Ulsh and Associates Staff. 23 CDs. (Multilingual Books Intensive Cassette Foreign Language Ser.). (POR.). (C). 1946. spiral bd. 239.00 (978-1-58214-066-7(9)) Language Assocs.

FSI Portuguese Programmatic Course Level 1: Multilingual Books Language Course. Jack Ulsh and Associates Staff. 22 cass. (Multilingual Books Intensive Cassette Foreign Language Ser.). (POR.). (C). 1946. spiral bd. 285.00 (978-1-58214-058-2(8)) Language Assocs.

FSI Portuguese Programmatic Level 1: Multilingual Books Language Course, Vol. 2. Jack Ulsh and Associates Staff. 22 cass. (Intensive Cassette Ser.). (POR.). (C). 1998. spiral bd. 225.00 (978-1-58214-003-2(0)) Language Assocs.

FSI Programmatic Portuguese Level 2. FSI Staff. 22 CDs. (Multilingual Books Intensive Language Courses). (POR.). 2005. per. 285.00 (978-1-58214-336-1(6)) Language Assocs.

FSI Programmatic Spanish, Level 1 (Re-Mastered) Learning Like Crazy. (ENG.). 2007. 97.00 (978-0-9766661-5-8(4)) Learn Craz Inc.

FSI Programmatic Spanish, Level 2 (Re-Mastered) Learning Like Crazy. (ENG.). 2007. 92.15 (978-0-9766661-8-9(9)) Learn Craz Inc.

FSI Saudi Arab Intensive Course: Language Associates Course. Margaret Omar & FSI Staff. 1 CD. (Multilingual Books Intensive Language Courses). (ARA.). 2006. 99.00 (978-1-58214-326-2(9)) Language Assocs.
Saudi Arabic of the Urban Hajazi Dialect, the most widely used on the Arabian peninsula. This disc contains the complete course book and audio.

FSI Saudi Arabic Basic Course: Multilingual Books Language Course. Margaret Omar. 15 CD's. (Multilingual Books Intensive Language Courses). (ARA.). (C). 2001. per. 239.00 (978-1-58214-184-8(3)) Language Assocs.

FSI Saudi Arabic Intensive Course: Multilingual Books Language Course. FSI Staff. 15 CDs. (Multilingual Books Intensive Language Courses). (ARA.). (C). 1998. per. 239.00 (978-1-58214-181-7(9)) Language Assocs.

FSI Saudi Arabic Intensive Course: Multilingual Books Language Course. Maryaret K. Omar. 15 cass. (Intensive Cassette Ser.). (ARA.). (C). 1998. spiral bd. 199.00 (978-1-58214-004-9(9)) Language Assocs.

FSI Serbo Croatian Basic Course Level 1: Multilingual Books Language Course. Hodge et al. 22 cass. (Multilingual Books Intensive Cassette Foreign Language Ser.). (SBC.). (C). 1965. spiral bd. 225.00 (978-1-58214-166-4(5)) Language Assocs.

FSI Serbo Croatian Basic Course Level 2. Hodge et al. 24 cass. (Multilingual Books Intensive Cassette Foreign Language Ser.). (SBC.). (C). 1968. spiral bd. 285.00 (978-1-58214-044-5(8)) Language Assocs.

FSI Shona Basic Course: Multilingual Books Language Course. Matthew Mataranyika. Ed. by E. Stevick. 10 cass. (Multilingual Books Intensive Cassette Foreign Language Ser.). (SHO.). (C). 1965. spiral bd. 225.00 (978-1-58214-043-8(X)) Language Assocs.

FSI Sinhalese Basic Course: Multilingual Books Language Course. FSI Staff. 10 cass. (Multilingual Books Intensive Cassette Foreign Language Ser.). (SNH.). (C). 1965. spiral bd. 285.00 (978-1-58214-168-8(1)) Language Assocs.

FSI Spanish Basic Course Level I: Multilingual Books Language Course. David Trease & Jack Ulsh and Associates Staff. 24 CDs. (Running Time: 18 hrs.). (Multilingual Books Intensive Cassette Foreign Language Ser.). (SPA.). (C). 1999. per. 239.00 (978-1-58214-054-4(5)) Language Assocs.

FSI Spanish Basic Course 3: Multilingual Books Language Course. W. A. Swift. 15 cass. (Multilingual Books Interactive Language Courses Ser.). (SPA.). (C). 1999. spiral bd. 199.00 (978-1-58214-053-7(7)) Language Assocs.

FSI Spanish Course Levels 1-4: Multilingual Books Language Course. Vicente Arbelaez Camacho et al. 73 cass. (Multilingual Books Intensive Cassette Foreign Language Ser.). (SPA.). (C). 1970. spiral bd. 595.00 (978-1-58214-171-8(1)) Language Assocs.

FSI Spanish Programmatic Course Levels 1 & 2: Multilingual Books Language Course. Vicente Arbelaez Camacho et al. 40 cass. (Multilingual Books Intensive Cassette Foreign Language Ser.). (SPA.). 1970. spiral bd. 395.00 (978-1-58214-170-1(3)) Language Assocs.

FSI Spanish Programmatic Level 1: Multilingual Books Language Course. Harris. 24 cass. (Multilingual Books Intensive Cassette Foreign Language Ser.). (SPA.). (C). 2004. 225.00 (978-1-58214-169-5(X)) Language Assocs.

FSI Spanish to Portuguese: Multilingual Books Language Course. Jack Lee Ulsh. Ed. by FSI Staff. 2 CD's. (Multilingual Books Intensive Language Courses). (SPA & POR.). (C). 2000. per. 59.00 (978-1-58214-180-0(0)) Language Assocs.

FSI Standard Chinese Module 1 on CD: Multilingual Books Language Course. FSI Staff. 9 CD's. (Multilingual Books Intensive Language Courses). (CHI.). (C). 2003. per. 239.00 (978-1-58214-197-8(5)) Language Assocs.

FSI Standard Chinese Module 2: Multilingual Books Language Course. FSI Staff. 9 CD's. (Multilingual Books Intensive Language Courses). (CHI.). (C). 2004. per. 269.00 (978-1-58214-369-9(2)) Language Assocs.

FSI Standard Chinese Module 3: Language Associates Course. FSI Staff. 17 Cass. (Multilingual Books Intensive Language Courses). (CHI.). 2005. per. 199.00 (978-1-58214-074-2(X)); per. 199.00 (978-1-58214-337-8(4)) Language Assocs.
This Module covers Money. It should be used in conjuction with Module 1-Orientation.

FSI Swahil Intensive Course Part 2: Multilingual Books Foreign Language Course. C. W. Saevick et al. 12 Cass. (Multilingual Books Intensive Cassette Foreign Language Ser.). (SWA.). 2004. per. 149.00 (978-1-58214-365-1(X)) Language Assocs.

FSI Swahili Course Part 1: Multilingual Books Foreign Language Course. C. W. Saevick et al. 12 Cass. (Multilingual Books Intensive Cassette Foreign Language Ser.). (SWA.). 2004. per. 149.00 (978-1-58214-364-4(1)) Language Assocs.

FSI Swahili Intensive Course: Multilingual Books Language Course. C. W. Saevick et al. Ed. by Carlton Lodge. 24 cass. (Multilingual Books Intensive Cassette Foreign Language Ser.). (SWA.). (C). 1999. spiral bd. 285.00 (978-1-58214-056-8(1)) Language Assocs.

FSI Swedish Basic Course: Multilingual Books Language Course. 15 cass. (Multilingual Books Intensive Cassette Foreign Language Ser.). (SWE.). (C). 1997. spiral bd. 199.00 (978-0-9631518-5-8(1)) Language Assocs.

FSI Swedish Basic Course: Multilingual Books Language Course. FSI Staff. 15 cass. (Multilingual Books Intensive Cassette Foreign Language Ser.). (SWE.). (C). 1946. spiral bd. 199.00 (978-1-58214-173-2(8)) Language Assocs.

FSI Swedish Course: Multilingual Books Language Course. FSI Staff. 15 cass. (Multilingual Books Intensive Language Courses). (SWE.). (C). 2003. per. 239.00 (978-1-58214-137-4(1)) Language Assocs.

FSI Thai Basic Course Level 1: Multilingual Books Foreign Service Institute Language Course. Warren G. Yates & Tyron Absorn. 19 CD's. (Multilingual Books Intensive Language Courses). (THA.). (C). 1999. per. 239.00 (978-1-58214-263-0(7)) Language Assocs.

FSI Thai Basic Course Level 1: Multilingual Books Language Course. Warren G. Yates & Absorn Tryon. 19 cass. (Intensive Cassette Ser.). (THA.). (C). 1998. spiral bd. 225.00 (978-1-58214-002-5(2)) Language Assocs.

FSI Thai Basic Course Levels 1 & 2: Multilingual Books Language Course. Warren G. Yates & Tryon Asborn. 38 cass. (Multilingual Books Intensive Cassette Foreign Language Ser.). (THA.). (C). 1946. per. 375.00 (978-1-58214-175-6(4)) Language Assocs.

FSI Thai Level 2. FSI Staff. 12 CDs. (Multilingual Books Intensive Language Courses). (THA.). 2005. per. 245.00 (978-1-58214-334-7(X)) Language Assocs.

FSI Turkish Basic Course. FSI Staff. 14 CDs. (Multilingual Books Intensive Language Courses). (TUR.). 2006. per. 239.00 (978-1-58214-328-6(5)) Language Assocs.

FSI Turkish Basic Course. 2nd ed. Lloyd B. Swift & Selman Agrali. 14 cass. (Intensive Cassette Ser.). (TUR.). 1997. per. 225.00 (978-1-58214-007-0(3)) Language Assocs.

FSI Turkish Basic Course Level 2: Multilingual Books Language Course. Lloyd B. Swift & Selman Agrali. 13 cass. (Multilingual Books Intensive Cassette Foreign Language Ser.). (TUR.). (C). 1999. spiral bd. 225.00 (978-1-58214-046-9(4)) Language Assocs.

FSI Twi Basic Course Level 1: Multilingual Books Language Course. Kenneth R. Redden & OWUSU Staff. 9 cass. (Multilingual Books Intensive Cassette Foreign Language Ser.). (TWI.). (C). 1963. spiral bd. 225.00 (978-1-58214-047-6(2)) Language Assocs.

FSI TWI Intensive Course: Multilingual Books Language Course. J. E. Redden & N. Owusu. 9 cass. (TWI.). (C). 1997. spiral bd. 225.00 (978-0-9631518-4-1(3)) Language Assocs.

FSI Vietnamese: FSI Audio Course, Level 1. FSI Staff. 22 cass. (Multilingual Books Intensive Cassette Foreign Language Ser.). (VIE.). (C). 1999. spiral bd. 225.00 (978-1-58214-176-3(2)) Language Assocs.

FSI Vietnamese Basic Course, Level 2. Eleanor Jordan et al. 10 cass. (Intensive Cassette Ser.). (VIE.). (C). 1998. spiral bd. 199.00 (978-1-58214-012-4(X)) Language Assocs.

FSI Yoruba Basic Course. Earl W. Stevick & Olaleye Aremv. 36 cass. (Intensive Cassette Ser.). (YOR.). (C). 1998. spiral bd. 295.00 (978-1-58214-009-4(X)) Language Assocs.

Fuck It: The Ulitmate Spiritual Way. unabr. ed. John Parkin. 2009. audio compact disk (978-1-84850-123-2(4), 1056) Hay Hse GBR.

Fudge-a-Mania. Judy Blume. 2 cass. (Running Time: 3 hrs.). (Fudge Ser.). (J). 2000. 18.00 (978-0-7366-9078-2(6)) Books on Tape.

Fudge-a-Mania. unabr. ed. Judy Blume. 2 cass. (Running Time: 2 hrs.). (Fudge Ser.). (J). 1997. 23.00 (LL 3232, Chivers Child Audio) AudioGO.

Fudge-a-Mania. unabr. ed. Judy Blume. 2 cass. (Running Time: 2 hrs. 49 mins.). Dramatization. (Fudge Ser.). (J). (gr. 3-7). 1992. 23.00 (978-0-8072-7377-7(5), YA 841 CX, Listening Lib) Random Audio Pubg.

Fudge-a-Mania. unabr. ed. Judy Blume. 2 vols. (Running Time: 2 hrs. 49 mins.). Dramatization. (Fudge Ser.). (J). (gr. 3-7). 1992. pap. bk. 29.00 (978-0-8072-7378-4(3), YA 841 SP, Listening Lib) Random Audio Pubg.

Fudge-a-Mania. unabr. ed. Judy Blume. 2 CDs. (Running Time: 2 hrs. 49 mins.). (Fudge Ser.). (J). (gr. 3-7). 2004. audio compact disk 35.00 (978-0-8072-1165-6(6), S YA 841 CD, Listening Lib) Random Audio Pubg.

Fudge-a-Mania. unabr. ed. Judy Blume. Read by Judy Blume. (Running Time: 9780 sec.). (Fudge Ser.). (ENG.). (J). (gr. 3-7). 2007. audio compact disk 19.95 (978-0-7393-5627-2(5), Listening Lib) Pub: Random Audio Pubg. Dist(s): Random

Fudge-a-Mania, Set. unabr. ed. Judy Blume. 2 cass. (YA). 1999. 16.98 (FS9-24953) Highsmith.

Fudge Cupcake Murder. Joanne Fluke. Narrated by Suzanne Toren. 7 cass. (Running Time: 9 hrs.). (Hannah Swensen Mystery Ser.: No. 5). 2004. 55.80 (978-1-4025-7254-8(9)); audio compact disk 71.80 (978-1-4025-8703-0(1)) Recorded Bks.

Fudge Series. unabr. ed. Judy Blume. Read by Judy Blume. 8 cass. (Running Time: 12 hrs.). (J). (ps-3). 1997. 52.00 (978-0-7366-3659-9(5), 4333) Books on Tape.
Speaks openly to children & young adults without condescension.

Fuego Angelical: Magia, Leyendas y Tradiciones. Dona Carolina da Silva. Narrated by Wanda Arriaga. 4 cass. (Running Time: 5 hrs. 30 mins.).Tr. of Angelic Fire. 58.00 (978-0-7887-9970-9(3)) Recorded Bks.

Fuel Cells Durability & Performance. 4th ed. Ed. by Knowledge Press Staff. 2009. pap. bk. 499.00 (978-1-59430-187-2(5)) Knowledge Pr MA.

Fuel Cells Durability & Performance 2nd Edition Proceedings: Real World Solutions to the Most Significant Challenge Facing Fuel Cell Commercialization. 2007. per. 399.00 (978-1-59430-124-7(7)) Knowledge Pr MA.

Fueling Great Relationships. Mark Crow. 6 cass. (Running Time: 6 hrs.). 2001. (978-1-931537-05-6(4)) Vision Comm Creat.

Fuente Ovejuna (It Serves Them Right) unabr. ed. Lope de Vega. Perf. by Christine Avila et al. 1 cass. (Running Time: 1 hr. 45 min.). 1993. 19.95 (978-1-58081-092-0(6)) L A Theatre.
A story of honor & revenge in 17th Century Spain.

Fuerte Reproche para una Iglesia Escandalosa. (SPA.). 2006. audio compact disk 42.00 (978-1-57972-699-7(2)) Insight Living.

Fuerzas para Seguir. unabr. ed. Imperial Banda & Zondervan Publishing Staff. (SPA.). 2002. 7.99 (978-0-8297-4154-4(2)) Pub: Vida Pubs. Dist(s): Zondervan

Fuga di Bach. Regina Assini. pap. bk. 20.95 (978-88-7754-902-0(5)) Pub: Cideb ITA. Dist(s): Distribks Inc

***Fugitive.** 2010. audio compact disk (978-1-59171-238-1(6)) Falcon Picture.

Fugitive. Marcel Proust. Read by Neville Jason. (Running Time: 3 hrs. 30 mins.). 2005. 24.95 (978-1-60083-745-6(X)) Iofy Corp.

Fugitive. Marcel Proust. Read by Neville Jason. 3 cass. (Running Time: 3 hrs. 30 min.). (Remembrance of Things Past Ser.: Vol. XI). 2001. 17.98 (978-962-634-711-9(2), NA321114, Naxos AudioBooks); audio compact disk 22.98 (978-962-634-211-4(0), NA321112, Naxos AudioBooks) Naxos.

Fugitive. unabr. ed. Phillip Margolin. Read by Jonathan Davis. 2009. audio compact disk 39.99 (978-0-06-176795-1(6), Harper Audio) HarperCollins Pubs.

***Fugitive.** unabr. ed. Phillip Margolin. Read by Jonathan Davis. (ENG.). 2009. (978-0-06-190195-9(4), Harper Audio); (978-0-06-190196-6(2), Harper Audio) HarperCollins Pubs.

Fugitive Pieces. abr. ed. Anne Michaels. Narrated by Neil Munro & Diego Matamoros. 3 CDs. (Running Time: 4 hrs.). (ENG.). (gr. 3-6). 2001. audio compact disk 19.95 (978-0-86492-249-6(3)) Pub: BTC Audiobks CAN. Dist(s): U Toronto Pr
In 1940, seven-year-old Jakob Beer is rescued from hiding in Poland by a Greek geologist. Decades later he revisits the past through an encounter with a young professor. The dual narration of Neil Munro and Diego Matamoros imparts a deep sense of truth to this critically acclaimed first novel, which won the Orange Prize for Fiction.

Fugitive Pieces. abr. ed. Anne Michaels. Narrated by Diego Matamoros & Neil Munroe. Prod. by CBC Radio Staff. 3 cass. (Running Time: 4 hrs.). (ENG.). 2001. 19.95 (978-0-86492-247-2(7)) Pub: BTC Audiobks CAN. Dist(s): U Toronto Pr

Fugitive Pieces. unabr. ed. Anne Michaels. Read by Peter Marinker. 8 cass. (Running Time: 12 hrs.). 2000. 59.95 (978-0-7540-0134-8(2), CAB 1557) Pub: Chivers Audio Bks GBR. Dist(s): AudioGO
Young Jakob Beer is rescued from Poland during World War II and taken to Greece by scientist and humanist, Athos Roussos. They spend the last years of the war in the house of Athos, a precarious refuge of poetry and art. After the war, Athos leaves for a position in the University of Toronto's new Geography department. But for Jakob, the war has not yet ended; for he is unaware of his sister's fate.

Fugitive Pigeon. unabr. ed. Donald E. Westlake. Read by Nick Sullivan. 4 cass. (Running Time: 4 hrs. 47 min.). 2001. 24.95 (978-1-57270-217-2(6), N41217u, Audio Edits Mystry) Pub: Audio Partners. Dist(s): PerseuPGW
Charlie Poole has a serious case of ennui. Stuck tending bar at his gangster uncle's Brooklyn saloon, he awakens from his slumber only when two hit men threaten to kill him. While on the lam, Charlie has to handle his Mafia uncle, stand up for himself & come to terms with the beautiful woman who saves his life.

Fugitive Pigeon, unabr. ed. Donald E. Westlake. Read by Nick Sullivan. 4 vols. (Running Time: 5 hrs. 30 mins.). 1999. bk. 39.95 (978-0-7927-2290-8(6), CSL 179, Chivers Sound Lib) AudioGO.
When two hitmen come after Charlie Poole, a Canarsie bartender, couch potato & one of the biggest nebbishes in Brooklyn, he's totally baffled & suddenly on the run. Now Charlie has to learn how to handle his Mafia Uncle Al: Point with a gun, not a finger & threaten to tell Aunt Florence everything! He has to learn how to deal with a beautiful woman who saves his life & must do the very thing he has been avoiding all his life: Stand up for himself.

Fugitive Pigeon. unabr. ed. Donald E. Westlake. Read by Nick Sullivan. 6 CDs. (Running Time: 9 hrs.). 2001. audio compact disk 64.95 (978-0-7927-9988-7(7), SLD 039, Chivers Sound Lib) AudioGO.

Fugitive Trail, Set. unabr. ed. Zane Grey. Read by William Dufris. 5 cass. (Sagebrush Western Ser.). (J). 1999. 49.95 (978-1-57490-230-3(X)) Pub: ISIS Lrg Prnt GBR. Dist(s): Ulverscroft US

Fugitive's Fire. unabr. collector's ed. Max Brand. Read by Jonathan Marosz. 6 cass. (Running Time: 6 hrs.). 1995. 36.00 (978-0-7366-3097-9(X), 3773) Books on Tape.
Among his Cheyenne captors, Paul Torridon is known as an instrument of the spirits, sent by the Sky People to cure the sick & bring victory to the warriors of the tribe. Christened "White Thunder," he is a prisoner, pampered, yet viewed with fear, awe & suspicion.

Fugue De Bach. Boutegege & Longo. audio compact disk 12.95 (978-0-8219-3787-7(1)) EMC-Paradigm.

Fugue in Hell's Kitchen. Hal Glatzer. 6. (Running Time: 7 hrs. 11 min.). Dramatization. 2004. audio compact disk 50.00 (978-0-9702147-2-0(3)) Audio Play.

Fuhrer's Reserve. unabr. ed. Paul Lindsay. Read by Bill Weideman. (Running Time: 12 hrs.). 2007. 39.25 (978-1-4233-3610-5(0), 9781423336105, BADLE); 24.95 (978-1-4233-3609-9(7), 9781423336099, BAD) Brilliance Audio.

Fuhrer's Reserve. unabr. ed. Paul Lindsay. Read by Bill Weideman. (Running Time: 43200 sec.). 2007. audio compact disk 24.95 (978-1-4233-3607-5(0), 9781423336075, Brilliance MP3); audio compact disk 39.25 (978-1-4233-3608-2(9), 9781423336082, Brlnc Audio MP3 Lib) Brilliance Audio.

***Fuiste Creado para Trabajar No para Tener un Trabajo.** Tr. of You Were Created to Work, Not Have A Job. (SPA.). 2006. audio compact disk 24.00 (978-0-944129-27-2(7)) High Praise.

Fujiyama. Akira Jimbo. (ENG, JPN & SPA.). 2004. audio compact disk 19.95 (978-0-8258-5010-3(X)) Fischer Inc NY.

Fula. unabr. ed. Foreign Service Institute Staff. 29 cass. (Running Time: 20 hrs.). (YA). (gr. 10-12). pap. bk. 295.00 (978-0-88432-291-7(2), AFFU10) J Norton Pubs.
Fula (also known as Peul, Fulani) is spoken principally in northern Nigeria. The Sene-Gambian dialect of Fula is represented in the text. Glossary is Fula-English.

Fula Basic Course - FSI - Audio CDs & Text. Lloyd B. Swift et al. 24 CDs. (Running Time: 20 hrs.). (Foreign Service Institute Basic Course Ser.). 2006. audio compact disk 295.00 (978-1-57970-356-1(9), AFFU10D, Audio-For) J Norton Pubs.
U.S. State Department Foreign Service Institute Basic Course in Fula. The sene-Gambian dialect of Fula (Fulani) is represented in the text.

Fulfill Your Destiny: Discover Your Bliss. Rhea Powers. Read by Rhea Powers. 1 cass. (Running Time: 60 min.). 1997. (978-1-881451-62-4(3)) Brain Sync.
Empowers you to connect with your higher guidance to discover your true purpose for existence.

Fulfill Your Earthly Purpose. unabr. ed. Dick Sutphen. Read by Dick Sutphen. 1 cass. (Running Time: 1 hr.). (Spirit Guide Meditations). 1999. 14.98 (978-0-87554-638-4(2), SG111) Valley Sun.

Fulfilled Family. 8 cass. 24.95 (2052, HarperThor) HarpC GBR.

Fulfilled Life: A Key to Personal & Professional Success. Timothy Hedrick. Narrated by Andrea Eaton & Dave Giorgio. (ENG.). 2009. audio compact disk 14.95 (978-1-60031-062-1(1)) Spoken Books.

Fulfilling Career: Creative Visualizations for Creating a New Reality. Created by Stanley Haluska. 1 CD. (Running Time: 70 mins). 2004. audio compact disk 15.00 (978-0-9668872-7-3(1), AP112) Awakening Pubns Inc.

Fulfilling Career: Creative Visualizations into Self Empowerment & Spiritual Identity. (ENG.). 2009. 15.95 (978-0-9758866-7-0(3)) Awakening Pubns Inc.

Fulfilling Life's Needs. unabr. ed. Jack Boland. Read by Jack Boland. 2 cass. (Running Time: 2 hrs.). 19.95 set. (978-0-88152-059-0(4), BA287) Master Mind.

Fulfilling My Mission Impossible. Frank Damazio. 6 cass. (Running Time: 9 hrs.). 2000. 30.00 (978-1-886849-71-6(4)) CityChristian.

Fulfilling the Promise of Children's Services: Why Primary Prevention Efforts Fail & How They Can Succeed. David G. Blumenkrantz. Frwd. by Seymour B. Sarason. (Social & Behavioral Science Ser.). 1992. bk. 40.00 (978-1-55542-450-3(3), Jossey-Bass) Wiley US.

Fulfilling the Soul's Longing. Featuring Sai Maa Lakshmi Devi. 2003. audio compact disk 16.00 (978-1-933488-08-0(5)) HIU Pr.
This recording of a highly acclaimed conference call with Sai Maa Lakshmi Devi captures Sai Maa's profound, yet practical teachings and the palpable power of Her Shakti.Be Victorious in Love - 9:51 The Soul's Longing - 2:11 Pure Thoughts & Good Action - 2:08 Samskaras & Past Impressions - 4:20 Power of Forgiveness - 5:24 Purifying the Soul - 12:20 Empowering the Soul - 10:00 Dialogue with the I AM - 4:20.

Fulfillment of Desire. unabr. ed. Perf. by Eknath Easwaran. 1 cass. (Running Time: 1 hr.). 1986. 7.95 (978-1-58638-543-9(7)) Nilgiri Pr.

Fulfillment of Oneness. Swami Amar Jyoti. 1 cass. 1975. 9.95 (R-71) Truth Consciousness.
How to attain balance of the three gunas (qualities of mind). Shining truths from the Vedic Upanishads & Puranas.

***Full: A Life Without Dieting.** unabr. ed. Michael, , Michael Snyder. Read by Michael, , Michael Snyder. (Running Time: 8 hrs. 0 mins. 0 sec.). (ENG.). 2010. audio compact disk 29.99 (978-1-4423-4109-8(2)) Pub: S&S Audio. Dist(s): S and S Inc

Full Blast. Janet Evanovich & Charlotte Hughes. (Janet Evanovich's Full Ser.: Bk. 4). 2004. 215.40 (978-1-59397-559-3(7)) Pub: Macmill Audio. Dist(s): Macmillan

Full Blast. Janet Evanovich & Charlotte Hughes. Read by Lorelei King. (Janet Evanovich's Full Ser.: Bk. 4). 2004. 17.95 (978-1-59397-390-2(X)) Pub: Macmill Audio. Dist(s): Macmillan

Full Blast. abr. ed. Janet Evanovich & Charlotte Hughes. Read by Lorelei King. (Janet Evanovich's Full Ser.: Bk. 4). 2004. 10.95 (978-1-59397-389-6(6)) Pub: Macmill Audio. Dist(s): Macmillan

Full Blast. unabr. ed. Janet Evanovich & Charlotte Hughes. Read by Lorelei King. 5 cass. (Janet Evanovich's Full Ser.: Bk. 4). 2005. pap. bk. 49.95 (978-0-7927-3188-7(3), CSL 644); pap. bk. 54.95 (978-0-7927-3189-4(1), SLD 644); pap. bk. 29.95 (978-0-7927-3190-0(5), CMP 644) AudioGO.

Full Blast. unabr. ed. Janet Evanovich & Charlotte Hughes. Read by Lorelei King. (Janet Evanovich's Full Ser.: Bk. 4). (YA). 2007. 59.99 (978-1-60252-834-5(9)) Find a World.

Full Blast. unabr. rev. ed. Janet Evanovich & Charlotte Hughes. Read by Lorelei King. 6 CDs. (Running Time: 7 hrs. 30 mins. 0 sec.). (Janet Evanovich's Full Ser.: Bk. 4). (ENG.). 2004. audio compact disk 34.95 (978-1-55927-977-2(X)) Pub: Macmill Audio. Dist(s): Macmillan

Full Bloom. abr. ed. Janet Evanovich & Charlotte Hughes. Read by Lorelei King. (Running Time: 14400 sec.). (Janet Evanovich's Full Ser.: Bk. 5). 2006. audio compact disk 14.99 (978-1-59600-838-0(5), 9781596008380, BCD Value Price) Brilliance Audio.
Dear Reader, The temperature's on "sizzle" again in Beaumont, South Carolina, where peach trees are in season and ripe for the picking. So is its newest entrepreneur, Annie Fortenberry, who has inherited her grandmother's B&B (and its eccentric handyman Erdle Thomey). According to a local psychic she also inherited a spirit from its glory days as a brothel - not the kind of publicity the Peach Tree Bed & Breakfast needs if it's hosting millionaire Max Holt's upcoming wedding! If rumors of a naughty, prank-playing ghost aren't stressful enough, a mysterious man has arrived with an eye on Annie and her master suite. Wes Bridges is all leather and denim, sporting a two-day beard, straddling a Harley, and sending the B&B's testosterone level through the roof. Annie's cool demeanor may be dropping as fast as Wes's jeans, but leave it to her missing ex-husband to dampen the passion! Turns out someone has done him in, and all evidence points to Annie! Wrapped up in a murder plot, Annie must find the killer, save her own neck, and get back to where she was - wrapped up in Wes's strong loving arms... We guarantee that you're going to have as much fun listening to Full Bloom as we had writing it! (Even if we were surprised by the ending!) And you won't want to miss the hair-raising shenanigans when Fleas, the hound dog, meets the most cantankerous, snooty, bad-tempered, twenty-two-pound orange cat... Janet & Charlotte.

Full Bloom. abr. ed. Janet Evanovich & Charlotte Hughes. Read by Lorelei King. (Running Time: 4 hrs.). (Janet Evanovich's Full Ser.: Bk. 5). 2009. audio compact disk 9.99 (978-1-4418-0821-9(3), 9781441808219, BCD Value Price) Brilliance Audio.

Full Bloom. unabr. ed. Janet Evanovich & Charlotte Hughes. Read by Lorelei King. (Running Time: 8 hrs.). (Janet Evanovich's Full Ser.: Bk. 5). 2005. 39.25 (978-1-59710-873-7(1), 9781597108737, BADLE); 24.95 (978-1-59710-872-0(3), 9781597108720, BAD); 24.95 (978-1-59335-942-3(X), 9781593359423, Brilliance MP3); 39.25 (978-1-59335-943-0(8), 9781593359430, Brinc Audio MP3 Lib); 29.95 (978-1-59600-136-7(4), 9781596001367, BAU); 74.25 (978-1-59600-137-4(2), 9781596001374, BrilAudUnabridg); audio compact disk 31.95 (978-1-59600-139-8(9), 9781596001398, Bril Audio CD Unabri); audio compact disk 87.25 (978-1-59600-140-4(2), 9781596001404, BriAudCD Unabrid) Brilliance Audio.
Please enter a Synopsis.

Full Body Blessing: Praying with Movement. J. Michael Sparough et al. 2 cass. (Running Time: 2 hrs.). 2001. vinyl bd. 18.95 (A5990) St Anthony Mess Pr.
Can be used by individuals and groups for liturgical prayer and meditation. Presents liturgical movement as a way to better appreciate our senses and bodies as doors to the mystery of God.

Full Box Set: Full House - Full Tilt - Full Speed - Full Blast. abr. gif. ed. Janet Evanovich & Charlotte Hughes. Read by Lorelei King. 12 CDs. (Running Time: 12 hrs. 0 mins. 0 sec.). (Janet Evanovich's Full Ser.: Bks. 1-4). (ENG.). 2006. audio compact disk 49.95 (978-1-59397-926-3(6)) Pub: Macmill Audio. Dist(s): Macmillan

***Full Brain Marketing for the Small Business: Merging Traditional, Digital & Social Media.** unabr. ed. D. J. Heckes. (Running Time: 7 hrs.). (ENG.). 2010. 24.98 (978-1-59659-560-6(4), GildAudio) Pub: Gildan Media. Dist(s): HachBkGrp

Full Catastrophe Living: Using the Wisdom of Your Body & Mind to Face Stress, Pain, & Illness. abr. ed. Jon Kabat-Zinn. Read by Jon Kabat-Zinn. (Running Time: 21600 sec.). (ENG.). 2008. audio compact disk 29.95 (978-0-7393-5858-0(8), Random AudioBks) Pub: Random Audio Pubg. Dist(s): Random

***Full Circle.** David L. Cisco. 2010. 0.00 (978-0-615-36341-7(5)) D L C Enterpris.

Full Circle. unabr. ed. Davis Bunn. Narrated by Greg Whalen. (ENG.). 2008. 20.99 (978-1-60814-223-1(X)) Oasis Audio.

Full Circle. unabr. ed. Gary Chapman & Davis Bunn. Narrated by Greg Whalen. (ENG.). 2008. audio compact disk 29.99 (978-1-59859-382-2(X)) Oasis Audio.

Full Circle. unabr. ed. Michael Palin. Narrated by Michael Palin. (Running Time: 6 hrs. 0 mins. 0 sec.). (ENG.). 2010. audio compact disk 49.95 (978-1-60283-836-9(4)) Pub: AudioGO. Dist(s): Perseus Dist

Full Circle. unabr. ed. Michael Palin. Read by Michael Palin. 10 cass. (Running Time: 15 hrs.). 1998. 69.95 (978-0-7540-0214-7(4), CAB 1637) Pub: Chivers Audio Bks GBR. Dist(s): AudioGO
Adventures of Michael Palin as he negotiates mountains, gorges, glaciers & icebergs that stretches around the Pacific Ocean.

Full Circle. unabr. collector's ed. J. E. Johnson. Read by Gary Martin. 7 cass. (Running Time: 10 hrs. 30 min.). 1987. 56.00 (978-0-7366-1138-1(X), 2063) Books on Tape.
This narrative chronicles the achievements of great fighter leaders of both World Wars.

Full Circle of Meditation: Healing, Prosperity & Peace. unabr. ed. Ruth Lee. Read by Ruth Lee. Perf. by John Hasinger & Ray Hasinger. 1 cass. (Running Time: 40 min.). (Meditate with Ruth Lee Ser.: Vol. I). 1994. 9.95 (978-1-888988-03-1(7)) LeeWay.
Meditation class each side. (1) Learn Yoga way to breathe in order to revitalize you & heal. (2) Learn to chant ancient Tibetan Mantra "Om, Mani Padmi, Hum" for peace & prosperity.

Full Contact Rules for the Christian Manager - Audio Book: How a 3,000 Year Old Book Can Help You Manage Your Business. (ENG.). 2008. 29.95 (978-0-9801973-8-9(4)) Newgate Inc.

Full Court Press. abr. ed. Mike Lupica. Read by Stephanie Knox. 5 CDs. (Running Time: 6 hrs.). 2001. audio compact disk 29.95 (978-1-58788-881-6(5), 1587888815, CD); audio compact disk 69.25 (978-1-58788-882-3(3), 1587888823, CD Lib Edit) Brilliance Audio.
This is what happens when the desperate golden-boy owner of the worst pro-basketball team in the world and his equally desperate golden-boy coach do the unthinkable: sign the first woman ever to play in the NBA. Her name is Dee Gerard, the daughter of a New York playground legend and the product of God having an exceptionally good day. A star in Europe, but weary of bad arenas, she retires - until the day a scout for the hapless New York Knights calls his boss: "I found you a point guard who is perfect, except for one thing." What, no heart? "It's not the heart, exactly. But you're close." The league doesn't want a circus. The other players don't want her. The owner wants fannies in the seats. The sportswriters just want their column inches. What she wants . . . is to play in the best game there is. How she gets there, the hilarious and sobering things that happen to her, the personal and professional entanglements that spring up everywhere, the pitfalls of remaining old-school when all about her are tattooed, self-indulgent, young millionaires - this is a smart, funny, outrageous, wonderful story of Full Court Press.

Full Court Press. unabr. ed. Mike Lupica. Read by Stephanie Knox. 7 cass. (Running Time: 10 hrs.). 2001. 32.95 (978-1-58788-878-6(5), 1587888785, BAU); 78.25 (978-1-58788-879-3(3), 1587888793, Unabridge Lib Edns) Brilliance Audio.

Full Court Press. unabr. ed. Mike Lupica. Read by Stephanie Knox. (Running Time: 10 hrs.). 2004. 39.25 (978-1-59335-365-0(0), 1593353650, Brinc Audio MP3 Lib) Brilliance Audio.

Full Court Press. unabr. ed. Mike Lupica. Read by Stephanie Knox. (Running Time: 10 hrs.). 2004. 49.97 (978-1-59710-313-8(6), 1597103136, BADLE); 24.95 (978-1-59710-312-1(8), 1597103128, BAD) Brilliance Audio.

Full Court Press. unabr. ed. Mike Lupica. Read by Stephanie Knox. (Running Time: 10 hrs.). 2004. 24.95 (978-1-59335-037-6(6), 1593350376) Soulmate Audio Bks.

Full Cry. Rita Mae Brown. Narrated by Rita Mae Brown. 6 cass. (Running Time: 10 hrs. 45 mins.). (Foxhunting Mysteries Ser.). 2004. 29.99 (978-1-4025-6357-7(4), 03774) Recorded Bks.

Full Cry. unabr. ed. Rita Mae Brown. 8 cass. (Running Time: 10.75 min). (Foxhunting Mysteries Ser.). 2004. 82.00 (978-1-4025-6376-8(0)) Recorded Bks.

***Full Cup: Sir Thomas Lipton's Extraordinary Life & His Quest for the America's Cup.** unabr. ed. Michael D'Antonio. (Running Time: 12 hrs. 0 mins. 0 sec.). (ENG.). 2010. 24.99 (978-1-4001-6591-9(1)); 17.99 (978-1-4001-8591-7(2)); audio compact disk 69.99 (978-1-4001-4591-1(0)); audio compact disk 34.99 (978-1-4001-1591-4(4)) Pub: Tantor Media. Dist(s): IngramPubServ

Full Cupboard of Life. unabr. ed. Alexander McCall Smith. 6 cassettes. (Running Time: 7.75 hrs). (No. 1 Ladies' Detective Agency Ser.: No. 5). 2004. 59.75 (978-1-4025-5072-0(3)) Recorded Bks.

Full Cupboard of Life. unabr. ed. Alexander McCall Smith. Narrated by Lisette Lecat. 5 cass. (Running Time: 7 hrs. 45 mins.). (No. 1 Ladies' Detective Agency Ser.: No. 5). 2004. 24.99 (978-1-4025-6987-6(4), 03904); audio compact disk 29.99 (978-1-4025-6988-3(2), 01362) Recorded Bks.

***Full Dark, No Stars.** unabr. ed. Stephen King. Read by Jessica Hecht & Craig Wasson. 12 CDs. (Running Time: 14 hrs.). 2010. audio compact disk 39.99 (978-1-4423-3576-9(9)) Pub: S&S Audio. Dist(s): S and S Inc

Full Dress Gray. unabr. ed. Lucian K. Truscott IV. Read by Robert Lawrence. (Running Time: 11 hrs.). 2009. 39.97 (978-1-4233-8917-0(4), 9781423389170, Brinc Audio MP3 Lib); 39.97 (978-1-4233-8919-4(0), 9781423389194, BADLE); 24.99 (978-1-4233-8916-3(6), 9781423389163, Brilliance MP3); 24.99 (978-1-4233-8918-7(2), 9781423389187, BAD) Brilliance Audio.

***Full Exposure.** abr. ed. Susie Bright. Read by Susie Bright. (ENG.). 2005. (978-0-06-085297-9(6), Harper Audio); (978-0-06-085298-6(4), Harper Audio) HarperCollins Pubs.

Full Exposure: Opening up to Sexual Creativity & Erotic Expression. unabr. ed. Susie Bright. Read by Susie Bright. 2 cass. (Running Time: 3 hrs.). 1999. 18.00 (978-0-694-52230-9(9), Harper Audio) HarperCollins Pubs.
Reveals the ways in which sexual expression has the power to transform all aspects of our lives.

Full Faith in the Ultimate. Swami Amar Jyoti. 2 cass. 1983. 12.95 (D-9) Truth Consciousness.
Founding life on the bedrock of Truth. How faith is born.

Full Forgiveness Set: Choosing to Leave the Painful Past Behind. David Grudermeyer & Rebecca Grudermeyer. 2 cass. 18.95 INCL. HANDOUTS. (T-20) Willingness Wrks.

Full House. unabr. ed. Janet Evanovich & Charlotte Hughes. Read by Lorelei King. 6 vols. (Running Time: 9 hrs.). (Janet Evanovich's Full Ser.: Bk. 1). 2002. 54.95 (978-0-7927-2705-7(3), CSL 491, Chivers Sound Lib); audio compact disk 79.95 (978-0-7927-2730-9(4), SLD 491, Chivers Sound Lib); audio compact disk 29.95 (978-0-7927-2760-6(6), CMP 491, Chivers Sound Lib) AudioGO.
Polo instructor Nicholas Kaharchek senses danger the minute he sees Billie Pearce, a divorced mother of two. She represents everything he's so artfully avoided: a happy home life, parenthood, stability. To his horror, Nick is fascinated - and irresistibly attracted. When Billie offers to share her home with Nick's crazy cousin Deedee, Nick finds himself visiting - often. But as the sparks begin to fly, Billie and Nick don't realize that danger is lurking where they least expect it, and that a killer is closing in on them . . .

Full House. unabr. rev. ed. Janet Evanovich & Charlotte Hughes. Read by Lorelei King. 7 CDs. (Running Time: 9 hrs. 0 mins. 0 sec.). (Janet Evanovich's Full Ser.: Bk. 1). (ENG., 2002. audio compact disk 40.00 (978-1-55927-779-2(3)) Pub: Macmill Audio. Dist(s): Macmillan

Full House; Full Tilt. Janet Evanovich & Charlotte Hughes. (Janet Evanovich's Full Ser.: Bks. 1-2). 2003. 431.40 (978-1-55927-924-6(9)); audio compact disk 480.00 (978-1-55927-925-3(7)) Pub: Macmill Audio. Dist(s): Macmillan

Full House; Full Tilt. abr. ed. Janet Evanovich & Charlotte Hughes. (Janet Evanovich's Full Ser.: Bks. 1-2). 2003. 215.40 (978-1-55927-923-9(0)) Pub: Macmill Audio. Dist(s): Macmillan

Full House in Death Cards. unabr. ed. Bernie Kite. Read by Gene Engene. 6 cass. (Running Time: 8 hrs. 30 min.). 1994. 39.95 (978-1-55686-513-8(9)) Books in Motion.
Sequel to "The Fourth Ace." Mountain man Bear Walker is mystified at the rash of untimely deaths occuring among local prospectors in N. Central Washington.

Full-Length Diagnostic Form CD1. Contemporary. (Assessment Program for the Ged Ser.). 22.25 (978-0-07-282212-0(0)) M-H Contemporary.

Full-Length Diagnostic Form CD2. Contemporary. (Assessment Program for the Ged Ser.). 22.25 (978-0-07-282214-4(7)) M-H Contemporary.

Full Moon, Flood Moon. unabr. ed. Theodore Enslin. Read by Theodore Enslin. 1 cass. (Running Time: 53 min.). (Watershed Tapes of Contemporary Poetry). 1979. 12.95 (23621) J Norton Pubs.
Based on Ruminations, meditations & exhortations.

Full of Grace. Dorothea Benton Frank. 2006. audio compact disk 39.95 (978-0-06-112223-1(8)) HarperCollins Pubs.

***Full of Grace.** abr. ed. Dorothea Benton Frank. Read by Susan Bennett. (ENG.). 2006. (978-0-06-113513-2(5), Harper Audio); (978-0-06-113512-5(7), Harper Audio) HarperCollins Pubs.

Full of Grace. abr. ed. Dorothea Benton Frank. Read by Susan Bennett. 2008. audio compact disk 14.95 (978-0-06-157120-6(2), Harper Audio) HarperCollins Pubs.

Full Opening to Perfection. Swami Amar Jyoti. 1 cass. 1989. 9.95 (R-97) Truth Consciousness.
Well-being of body & mind, immunity to outer conditions. Coming back to fundamental, true Being. Direct comunication from Guru to disciple.

Full "Peace" Lecture. unabr. ed. Myrtle Smith. Prod. by David Keyston. 1 cass. (Running Time: 1 hrs. 8 min.). (Myrtle Smyth Audiotapes Ser.). 1998. , CD. (978-1-893107-15-1(9), M15, Cross & Crown) Healing Unltd.

Full Quivers & Empty Pockets: 1 Cor. 13:11. Ed Young. 1992. 4.95 (978-0-7417-2015-3(9), 1015) Win Walk.

Full Salvation & How to Enter In. Derek Prince. 2 cass. (B-2007, 8) Derek Prince.

Full Scoop. abr. ed. Janet Evanovich & Charlotte Hughes. Read by Lorelei King. (Running Time: 4 hrs.). (Janet Evanovich's Full Ser.: Bk. 6). 2007. audio compact disk 14.99 (978-1-59737-692-1(2), 9781597376921, BCD Value Price) Brilliance Audio.

Full Scoop. unabr. ed. Janet Evanovich & Charlotte Hughes. Read by Lorelei King. (Running Time: 8 hrs.). (Janet Evanovich's Full Ser.: Bk. 6). 2006. 39.25 (978-1-59710-874-4(X), 9781597108744, BADLE); 24.95 (978-1-59710-875-1(8), 9781597108751, BAD); 29.95 (978-1-59600-142-8(9), 9781596001428, BAU); 69.25 (978-1-59600-143-5(7), 9781596001435, BrilAudUnabridg); audio compact disk 31.95 (978-1-59600-145-9(3), 9781596001459, Bril Audio CD Unabri); audio compact disk 87.25 (978-1-59600-146-6(1), 9781596001466, BriAudCD Unabrid); audio compact disk 24.95 (978-1-59335-944-7(6), 9781593359447, Brilliance MP3); audio compact disk 39.25 (978-1-59335-945-4(4), 9781593359454, Brinc Audio MP3 Lib) Brilliance Audio.
Please enter a Synopsis.

Full Scoop-ABR. Janet Evanovich & Charlotte Hughes. 2010. audio compact disk 9.99 (978-1-4418-4182-7(2)) Brilliance Audio.

***Full Set Quick60 Alphabet Books - audio (26 Files)** (ENG.). (J). 2009. 55.00 (978-1-77540-235-0(5)) Iversen NZL.

Full Speed. unabr. ed. Janet Evanovich & Charlotte Hughes. Read by Lorelei King. (Janet Evanovich's Full Ser.: Bk. 3). (YA). 2007. 59.99 (978-1-60252-901-4(9)) Find a World.

Full Speed. unabr. rev. ed. Janet Evanovich & Charlotte Hughes. Read by Lorelei King. 6 CDs. (Running Time: 7 hrs. 30 mins. 0 sec.). (Janet Evanovich's Full Ser.: Bk. 3). (ENG., 2003. audio compact disk 34.95 (978-1-55927-930-7(3)) Pub: Macmill Audio. Dist(s): Macmillan

Full Steam Ahead! Unleash the Power of Vision in Your Company & Your Life. unabr. ed. Ken Blanchard & Jesse Stoner. Read by Michele Pawk. 2004. 15.95 (978-0-7435-4743-7(8)) Pub: S&S Audio. Dist(s): S and S Inc

Full Throttle: The Life & Fast Times of NASCAR Legend Curtis Turner. unabr. ed. Robert Edelstein. Read by Rex Linn. (Running Time: 43200 sec.). 2007. 19.95 (978-0-7861-4927-8(2)); audio compact disk 29.95 (978-0-7861-7020-3(4)); audio compact disk 19.95 (978-0-7861-5894-2(8)) Blckstn Audio.

Full Throttle: The Life & the Fast Times of NASCAR Legend Curtis Turner. unabr. ed. Robert Edelstein. Read by Rex Linn. (Running Time: 43200 sec.). 2006. 65.95 (978-0-7861-4891-2(8)); audio compact disk 81.00 (978-0-7861-5989-5(8)) Blckstn Audio.

Full Tilt. unabr. rev. ed. Janet Evanovich & Charlotte Hughes. Read by Lorelei King. 6 CDs. (Running Time: 7 hrs. 30 mins. 0 sec.). (Janet Evanovich's Full Ser.: Bk. 2). (ENG., 2003. audio compact disk 29.95 (978-1-55927-864-5(1)) Pub: Macmill Audio. Dist(s): Macmillan

Full Tilt: How to reclaim your life inspite of living with a chronic Illness! Sheila Dereka Shaw. 2007. audio compact disk 19.95 (978-1-4276-1444-5(X)) AardGP.

Full Tilt: Ireland to India with a Bicycle, Set. unabr. ed. Dervla Murphy. Read by Kate Binchy. 6 cass. (Running Time: 9 hrs.). 1989. 49.00 (978-1-55690-191-1(7), 89200) Recorded Bks.
An account of the author's journey from Ireland to India by bicycle.

Full-Time Professional, No. II. Wendy Hawks. 1 cass. 1992. 8.95 (1043) Am Fed Astrologers.

Fuller Life (Male) 1 cass. (Relationship Ser.). 12.98 (99) Randolph Tapes.
Let go of the past. Enjoy Health, Success, Happiness, Better Relationships with this dynamic tape (for men only).

Fullness from Fullness, Set. Sister Ishpriya. Read by Sister Ishpriya. 4 cass. (Running Time: 4 hrs. 23 min.). 1993. 29.95 (978-7-900786-59-3(7), AA2659) Credence Commun.
Drawing from both Christian & Hindu wells of tradition, Ishpriya explains & unfolds the sacred Hindu scriptures, the Isi Upanisads.

Fullness of Grace. Derek Prince. 1 cass. (B-2023) Derek Prince.

Fullness of the Cross, Album 1. Derek Prince. 6 cass. (Running Time: 60 min.). 29.95 (I-FC1) Derek Prince.

Fullness of the Cross, Album 2. Derek Prince. 6 cass. (Running Time: 60 min.). 29.95 (I-FC2) Derek Prince.

Fullness of the Cross, Album 3. Derek Prince. 6 cass. (Running Time: 60 min.). 29.95 (I-FC3) Derek Prince.

Fullness of the Cross, Album 4. Derek Prince. 6 cass. (Running Time: 60 min.). 29.95 (I-FC4) Derek Prince.

Fullness of Time. Norman Pittenger. 1 cass. 9.00 (A0383-89) Sound Photosyn.
An amusing & touching keynote address by the revolutionary gay Episcopalian leader at the Integrity Convention.

Fullness of Time: Recognizing & Responding to your Divine Destiny. Mac Hammond. 6 cass. (Running Time: 5 hrs). 2005. 30.00 (978-1-57399-225-1(9)) Mac Hammond.
In this series, you'll gain insight on how to recognize God's plan for your family, vocation, and personal life as well as establish the goals necessary to fulfill that plan.

Fully Alive from 9 to 5! Creating Work Environments That Invite Health, Humor, Compassion & Truth. Louise LeBrun. 1999. 21.95 (978-0-9685566-7-2(1)) Par3tners Renewal CAN.

Fully Open Heart. Swami Amar Jyoti. 1 cass. 1982. 9.95 (K-53) Truth Consciousness.
Full love, an inexhaustible treasure, needs a fully open heart. What happens when our hearts close & how to open them again.

Fully Persuaded... Totally Blessed: Discovering the Faith-Building Power of the Blood Covenant, 2. Mac Hammond. 3 cass. (Running Time: 3 hrs.). 2005. 7.50 (978-1-57399-190-2(2)) Mac Hammond.
When you're "fully persuaded" concerning a promise in God's Word, it's yours. But how do you get there? Find out how in this powerful teaching on Abraham and the principles of the blood covenant.

Fully Persuaded... Totally Blessed: Discovering the Faith-Building Power of the Blood Covenant, 2 of Faith Series. Mac Hammond. 3 cds. (Running Time: 3 hrs). 2005. audio compact disk 15.00 (978-1-57399-191-9(0)) Mac Hammond.

***Fully Present: The Science, Art, & Practice of Mindfulness.** unabr. ed. Susan L. Smalley & Diana Winston. Read by Elizabeth London. (Running Time: 8 hrs. 30 mins.). (ENG.). 2010. 29.98 (978-1-59659-619-1(8), GildAudio) Pub: Gildan Media. Dist(s): HachBkGrp

Fulo Bone Sandhya. Nazrul Islam. Voice by Sheema Mohit. 1 cd. 1999. audio compact disk 10.00 (978-0-9647672-9-4(5)) Beacon Hse IN.

Fun-a-Rooey. unabr. ed. Dave Kinnoin. 1 cass., 1 CD. (Running Time: 28 min.). (J). (gr. k-1). 1987. 9.98 (978-1-881304-00-5(0), SW101-4); audio compact disk 12.98 CD. (978-1-881304-10-4(8), SW101-2) Song Wizard Recs.
Fun & inspiring original songs, sung by Dave Kinnoin.

Fun Activities for Perceptual Motor Skills. 1 cass. (J). 10.95 Incl. manual. (KIM 9071C) Kimbo Educ.
Everyone's favorite! Aids in motor skill development with simple rhythm games including clapping, hand shakes, easy dance steps & finger exercises. Sneaky Snake, Ukulele Man & more.

Fun Activities for Toddlers. 1 cass. (Running Time: 1 hr.). (J). 2001. pap. bk. 10.95 (KIM 2017C); pap. bk. & stu. ed. 11.95 (KIM 2017) Kimbo Educ.
Upbeat activity songs & exercises. Favorites include Zip-A-Dee Doo Dah, You Are My Sunshine, Wake Up Your Muscles, Be My shadow, Small People, Be a Bubble & More. Manual included.

Fun Activities Perceptual Motor Skills. 1 CD. (Running Time: 1 hr.). (J). 2001. audio compact disk 10.95 (KIM 9071C) Kimbo Educ.
Everyone's favorite! Aids in motor skill development with simple rhythm games including clapping, hand shakes, easy dance steps & finger exercises. Sneaky Snake, Ukulele Man, One, Melody of Love, Ease on Down the Road & more. Includes manual.

Fun Activities Perceptual Motor Skills: Actividades Divertidas de las Habilidades de la Percepcion Motor. Georgiana Stewart. 1 cass. (Running Time: 35 min.). (SPA & ENG.). (J). (ps-3). 2001. pap. bk. 10.95 (KMS 9071C); pap. bk. 11.95 (KMS 9071) Kimbo Educ.
Simple rhythm games, everyone's favorite! Side A - English translation. Side B - Spanish narration. Manual in English with narration script in Spanish.

Fun Activity Songs. Penton Overseas, Inc. Staff. 1 CD. (Running Time: 1 hr.). (Ready-Set-Sing Collection). (ENG.). (J). (ps-7). 2003. audio compact disk 4.99 (978-1-56015-234-7(6)) Penton Overseas.
These four new collections of kids favorite sing-along songs include fun activity songs to get everyone up, moving & having great fun.

Fun & Easy Easter Pageant. Paul N. Lessard. 1 CD. 1997. pap. bk. 24.99 (978-1-55945-499-5(7)) Group Pub.

Fun & Games. Perf. by Greg Scelsa & Steve Millang. Composed by Greg Scelsa & Steve Millang. (J). 2001. 13.99 (978-1-57471-837-9(1), YM 018-CN) Creat Teach Pr.

Fun & Praise. 2000. 35.00 (978-0-633-00612-9(2)); 11.98 (978-0-633-00610-5(6)); audio compact disk 45.00 (978-0-633-00613-6(0)); audio compact disk 16.98 (978-0-633-00611-2(4)) LifeWay Christian.

Fun As Psychotherapy. Albert Ellis. 1 cass. (Running Time: 42 min.). 9.95 (C005) A Ellis Institute.
The peerless Ellis wit & style are applied to helping combat perfectionism, anger, & anxiety - in sum, to helping people not take themselves so seriously! Includes Ellis singing two of his rational humorous songs.

Fun As Psychotherapy. Albert Ellis. 1 cass. 9.95 (C005) Inst Rational-Emotive.

Fun at the Beach: Early Explorers Emergent Set A Audio CD. Benchmark Education Staff. (J). 2006. audio compact disk 10.00 (978-1-4108-7586-0(5)) Benchmark Educ.

Fun Bus. (Sails Literacy Ser.). (gr. 1 up). 10.00 (978-0-7578-2660-3(1)) Rigby Educ.

Fun Dances for Children. 1 LP. (J). stu. ed. 11.95 (KEA 1134); 10.95 incl. manual. (KEA 1134C) Kimbo Educ.
The Twist, Monkey, Swim, Freddy & other dances of the 60's. Dances are cued, taught & instrumentals provided.

Fun, Foolery & Folktales. Short Stories. As told by Donna L. Washington. 1 CD. (Running Time: 63 min 46 sec). (J). 2004. audio compact disk 15.00 (978-0-9769396-1-0(4)) DLW Storyteller.
Review:A collection of energizing participatory tales for all youngsters, Donna Washington subtly pulls the audience into her story world of pleasure and fun, beginning with her African American version of Epaminandus. Listeners joining in the numerous repetitive lines of this story will be challenged to mimic the interesting vocal sound effects. Her adaptation of Sody Saluradus also entices participants to repeat phrases and sing the jingles as she is telling the story, and her variants of two popular tongue twisters (Peter Piper... and Betty Boughta...) beckon listeners to tickle and train their vocal palates. Washingtona??s versions of Rumplestiltskin and Why Mosquitoes Buzz in Peoplea??s Ears add mystery, delight, and intrigue to these traditional English and African folktales.Dr. Flora Joy A?2004 Parents' Choice.

Fun for Flyers. Anne Robinson. (Running Time: 1 hr. 29 mins.). (ENG.). 2006. 23.00 (978-0-521-61368-2(X)) Cambridge U Pr.

Fun for Flyers Audio CDs (2) 2nd ed. Anne Robinson & Karen Saxby. (Running Time: 2 hrs. 34 mins.). (ENG.). 2010. audio compact disk 42.00 (978-0-521-74859-9(3)) Cambridge U Pr.

Fun for Movers. Anne Robinson. (Running Time: 1 hr. 19 mins.). (ENG.). 2006. 24.15 (978-0-521-61364-4(7)) Cambridge U Pr.

Fun for Movers Audio CD. 2nd ed. Anne Robinson & Karen Saxby. (Running Time: 1 hr. 18 mins.). (ENG.). 2010. audio compact disk 24.00 (978-0-521-74831-5(3)) Cambridge U Pr.

Fun for Starters Audio CD. 2nd ed. Anne Robinson & Karen Saxby. (Running Time: 1 hr. 19 mins.). (ENG.). 2010. audio compact disk 24.00 (978-0-521-74863-6(1)) Cambridge U Pr.

Fun French for Kids. Beth Manners. 1 cass. (FRE.). (J). 7.98 (FBC 1); (FBC 1); 7.98 (FBC1) NewSound.
Stresses comprehension of French with a system of short segments & songs.

Fun Learning Songs. Prod. by Twin Sisters Productions Staff. 1 CD. (Running Time: 30 mins). (J). 2005. audio compact disk 4.99 (978-1-57583-802-1(8)) Twin Sisters.
Learning is fun and easy with this collection of classic children's songs and new learning songs! Mixed with traditional children favorites, young kids will also sing and learn about colors, shapes, letters, numbers, and counting. Perfect for home and travel, preschool and kindergarten, and childcare programs. BONUS! Includes 50 fun things to do with kids!.

Fun 'n Friendly Songs: More Positively Singable Songs. Perf. by Ronno. 1 LP. (J). pupil's gde. ed. 11.95 (KIM 9138) Kimbo Educ.

Fun 'n Friendly Songs: More Positively Singable Songs. Perf. by Ronno. 1 cass. (Running Time: 35 min.). (J). 2000. pap. bk. 10.95 (KIM 9138C); pap. bk. 14.95 (KIM 9138CD) Kimbo Educ.

Fun New Way to Learn the Multiplication Facts: Uncle Wilton Singing & Rapping the Facts from 1 - 12. Wilton Banks. Illus. by Harvey Shaw & Bill Looney. Contrib. by Gary Wooten. Photos by Kevin Bowens. (Uncle Wilton Singing & Rapping the Facts Ser.). (J). (gr. 3-6). 1988. bk. & wbk. ed. 9.95 (978-1-892549-00-6(X)) Uncle Wltons.

Fun Phonics: Continents. (J). 1993. 10.98 Creat Teach Pr.

Fun Phrases in French. 2 cass. (Running Time: 2 hrs.). pap. bk. 24.95 J Norton Pubs.
Two native French speakers introduce you to French terms that you might wish to use as they guide you through a variety of scenes & situations such as dining, meeting people, visiting Paris & writing a love letter.

Fun Songs for Tadpoles to Frogs. Terry Grosvenor et al. 1 cass. (Running Time: 45 min.). (J). (gr. k-7). 1994. 9.95 (978-0-9644433-0-3(9)) R&T Grosvenor.
This cassette contains 14 selections - 12 selections are based on classic children's poetry including works of Edward Lear, Eugene Field, Laura Richards, Mildred Meigs, Aileen Fisher, Lewis Carroll, Rose Fyleman, James Whitcomb Riley, George Cooper. 2 selections contain original lyrics written by Richard, Terry & Amanda Grosvenor. All the music is composed, arranged & performed by Terry Grosvenor. The music has a contemporary style.

Fun Spanish for Kids. Beth Manners. 1 cass. (SPA.). (J). (FBC 2) NewSound.

Fun They Had see Best of Isaac Asimov

Fun-to-Sing: A Songbook for Balance-Control Karaoke. Mark Johnson. Illus. by Mark Johnson. (Sing-along Fun Ser.). (J). (gr. k-12). 1993. pap. bk. 8.99 (978-1-883988-01-2(2)) RSV Prods.

Fun to Sing Series. Esther Nelson & Bruce Haack. 5 cass. (J). (ps-3). 49.75 Set, incl. hang up bag. (978-0-945110-13-2(8)) Granny Pr.
This celebrated series of interactive cassettes is a treasury of infectious jump-rope chants, rounds, nonsense ditties, songs that won't end, clapping songs, yukky songs, old favorites, songs for the campfire or the car, & more.

Fun-to-Sing Songbook. Esther Nelson & Bruce Haack. 1 cass. (Running Time: 1 hr. 30 mins.). (J). (ps-4). 1987. 9.95 (978-0-945110-02-6(2), D411) Granny Pr.
Instructs children to follow directions given to music, with the goal of intensifying the listeners imagination & creativity through body movement.

Fun Tunes for Strings: For Violin, Viola & Cello/Bass. Bud Caputo. 2004. audio compact disk 9.95 (978-0-8258-5269-5(2)); audio compact disk 9.95 (978-0-8258-5270-1(6)); audio compact disk 9.95 (978-0-8258-5271-8(4)) Fischer Inc NY.

Fun While It Lasted: My Rise & Fall in the Land of Fame & Fortune. unabr. ed. Bruce McNall & Michael D'Antonio. Read by Bruce McNall. 8 CDs. (Running Time: 9 hrs.). 2004. audio compact disk 49.95 (978-1-59007-507-4(2)); 29.95 (978-1-59007-506-7(4)) Pub: New Millenn Enter. Dist(s): PerseuPGW
In the tradition of Catch Me If You Can, here is a wildly entertaining account by one of America's high stakes players-who lost it all when he was indicted for fraud. "The first thing everyone wants to know is how I did it. How had I turned my intelligence, nerve, and a bit of fraud, into a business worth hundreds of millions of dollars. And how had I hidden the truth, while enjoying a jet setting public life for so many years." Bruce McNall became obsessed with coin collecting at the age of ten. At sixteen, his collection was worth $60,000. During college, he traveled the world buying coins stolen from ancient sites and tombs. McNall's first major sale was to Sy Weintraub, the head of Panavision, who bought $500,000 worth of coins in one sitting. Soon, McNall branched out into horse racing, movie making (The Fabulous Baker Boys), and owning the L.A. Kings hockey team. But in the 1990s, his house of cards collapsed, and McNall was sent to prison for defrauding investors. Fun While It Lasted is his whirlwind story of life as a player, including: How he convinced Wayne Gretzky to leave the Edmonton Oilers to play for his L.A. Kings How he helped Merrill Lynch start a coin fund which eventually lost millions of dollars How he and movie producer David Begelman played fast and loose with other people's money.

Fun with Astrology. Arthur Young. 1 cass. 9.00 (A0264-87) Sound Photosyn.

Fun with Bongos. Trevor Salloum. 1999. pap. bk. 21.95 (978-0-7866-4740-8(X), 98284CDP) Mel Bay.

Fun with Bongos Cd. Trevor Salloum. 1999. audio compact disk 9.98 (978-0-7866-4739-2(6)) Mel Bay.

Fun with Fives: Early Explorers Early Set A Audio CD. Benchmark Education Staff. (J). 2006. audio compact disk 10.00 (978-1-4108-7627-0(6)) Benchmark Educ.

Fun with Folk & Alternative Rock: Alto Sax. Composed by John Hosay. 2005. pap. bk. 12.95 (978-90-431-2155-2(X), 904312155X) H Leonard.

Fun with Folk & Alternative Rock: Clarinet. Composed by John Hosay. 2005. pap. bk. 12.95 (978-90-431-2154-5(1), 9043121541) H Leonard.

Fun with Folk & Alternative Rock: Flute. Composed by John Hosay. 2005. pap. bk. 12.95 (978-90-431-2153-8(3), 9043121533) H Leonard.

Fun with Folk & Alternative Rock: Trombone. Composed by John Hosay. 2005. pap. bk. 12.95 (978-90-431-2157-6(6), 9043121576) H Leonard.

Fun with Folk & Alternative Rock: Trumpet. Composed by John Hosay. 2005. pap. bk. 12.95 (978-90-431-2156-9(8), 9043121568) H Leonard.

Fun with Numbers. Ed. by Publications International Staff. 2004. bk. & wbk. ed. 12.98 (978-0-7853-8957-6(1)) Pubns Intl Ltd.

***Fun with Problems.** unabr. ed. Robert Stone. Narrated by David Colacci. (Running Time: 7 hrs. 0 mins.). 2010. 24.99 (978-1-4001-9597-8(7)); 19.99 (978-1-4001-6597-1(0)); 14.99 (978-1-4001-8597-9(1)); audio compact disk 49.99 (978-1-4001-4597-3(X)); audio compact disk 24.99 (978-1-4001-1597-6(3)) Pub: Tantor Media. Dist(s): IngramPubServ

Fun with the Banjo. Composed by Mel Bay. 1998. audio compact disk 9.98 (978-0-7866-4654-8(3)) Mel Bay.

Fun with the Banjo. Bay, Mel, Publications, Inc. Staff. (Fun Bks.). 1986. 9.98 (978-0-87166-433-4(X), 93268C) Mel Bay.

Fun with the Banjo. Mel Bay Staff et al. 1998. pap. bk. 19.95 (978-0-7866-4655-5(1), 93268CDP) Mel Bay.

Fun with the Baritone Uke. Mel Bay. 1998. audio compact disk 9.98 (978-0-7866-4511-4(3)) Mel Bay.

Fun with the Baritone Uke. Mel Bay Staff. 1998. pap. bk. 19.95 (978-0-7866-4512-1(1), 93266CDP) Mel Bay.

Fun with the Fife. Mizzy McCaskill & Dona Gilliam. 1998. pap. bk. 19.95 (978-0-7866-4284-7(X), 94811CDP) Mel Bay.

Fun with the Fife. Mizzy McCaskill & Dona Gilliam. 2001. bk. 14.95 (978-0-7866-6137-4(2), 94811BCD) Mel Bay.

Fun with the Guitar. Mel Bay Staff. (Fun Bks.). 1986. 9.98 (978-0-87166-446-4(1), 93262C) Mel Bay.

Fun with the Guitar. Mel Bay Staff. 1998. pap. bk. 19.95 (978-0-7866-4659-3(4), 93262CDP) Mel Bay.

Fun with the Mandolin. Contrib. by Mel Bay. 1998. audio compact disk 9.98 (978-0-7866-4656-2(X)) Mel Bay.

Fun with the Mandolin. Mel Bay Staff. (Fun Bks.). 1986. 9.98 (978-0-87166-451-8(8), 93258C) Mel Bay.

Fun with the Mandolin. Mel Bay Staff. 1998. pap. bk. 19.95 (978-0-7866-4657-9(8), 93258CDP) Mel Bay.

Fun with the Melody Flute. Mizzy McCaskill & Dona Gilliam. (Fun Bks.). 1993. bk. 13.95 (978-0-7866-1117-1(0), 94812P) Mel Bay.

Fun with the Melody Flute. Mizzy McCaskill & Dona Gilliam. (Fun Bks.). 1992. 9.98 (978-1-56222-451-6(4), 94812C) Mel Bay.

Fun with the Pan Flute: Beginning Level. Kristopher Faubion. 1997. bk. 15.95 (978-0-7866-2306-8(3), 94838BCP) Mel Bay.

Fun with the Tenor Banjo. Mel Bay Staff. Contrib. by Joe Carr. 1998. pap. bk. 19.95 (978-0-7866-4510-7(5), 93260CDP) Mel Bay.

Fun with the Tin Whistle. William Bay. (Fun Bks.). 1990. bk. 13.95 (978-0-7866-1054-9(9), 94526P); 9.98 (978-1-56222-073-0(X), 94526C) Mel Bay.

Fun with the Ukulele. Mel Bay Staff. 1998. pap. bk. 19.95 (978-0-7866-4653-1(5), 93270CDP) Mel Bay.

Funambule: L'Enfant Criminel. Jean Genet. Read by Marie Trintignant. 1 cass. (FRE.). 1991. 22.95 (1352-EF) Olivia & Hill.
For Jean Genet writing is a matter of love & hate: love for the criminals & hate for the guardians of morality.

Function & Meaning of Dreams. unabr. ed. Calvin S. Hall. 1 cass. 12.95 (29291) J Norton Pubs.
Talks about common themes in dreams, dream symbolism & age & sex differences in dream contents. He also gives pointers on how to better recall & record these valuable inner messages.

Function of Blizzard see Robert Penn Warren Reads Selected Poems

***Functional Endocrinology 36 Hour Certification Program.** Patrick Garrett. 2009. audio compact disk 720.00 (978-0-578-04639-6(3)) Nat Med Sem.

Functional Family. Jimmy Evans. 6 cass. 1996. 30.00 Set. (978-0-00-519060-9(6)) Majestic Mda.

Functional Microbial Genomics, Vol. 33. Brendan Wren & Nick Dorrell. (Methods in Microbiology Ser.). 2003. 67.95 (978-0-12-787766-2(5), Acad Press) Sci Tech Bks.

Functional Phonetics Workbook. Mary Lou Cancio & Sadanand Singh. (C). 2007. spiral bd. 45.00 (978-1-59756-094-8(4)) Plural Pub Inc.

Functional Relationships/Applying the Principle. Marianne Williamson. Read by Marianne Williamson. 1 cass. (Running Time: 90 mins.). (Lectures on a Course in Miracles). 1999. 10.00 (978-1-56170-197-1(1), M725) Hay House.

Functions of American English: Communication Activities for the Classroom. Leo Jones & C. Von Baeyer. 1 cass. (Running Time: 1 hr. 15 mins.). (ENG.). 1983. 23.00 (978-0-521-24211-0(8)) Cambridge U Pr.

Functions of American English: Communication Activities for the Classroom. Leo Jones & C. Von Baeyer. 1 cass. 19.95 Midwest European Pubns.
For intermediate & advanced levels who need to learn to communicate effectively with the English they have already acquired.

Functions of Prices. John Robbins. 1 cass. (Introduction to Economics Ser.: No. 8). 5.00 Trinity Found.

Fundamental Analysis, Value Investing & Growth Investing. Narrated by Louis Rukeyser. Contrib. by Janet C. Lowe & Roger Lowenstein. 2 cass. (Secrets of the Great Investors Ser.: Vol. 4). 17.95 Set. (978-1-56823-056-6(7)) Knowledge Prod.
Benjamin Graham developed "value investing," a style adopted by Warren Buffett, one of history's most successful investors; it is based on "fundamental analysis," which quantitatively compares a company's stock price to various measures of financial strength & promise. "Growth investing" is a fundamentally different style that seeks to identify tomorrow's great business successes. Learn the ins & outs, & the pros & cons, of these basic investment styles.

Fundamental Analysis, Value Investing & Growth Investing. unabr. ed. Roger Lowenstein & Janet C. Lowe. Read by Louis Rukeyser. (Running Time: 9000 sec.). (Secrets of the Great Investors Ser.). 2006. audio compact disk 25.95 (978-0-7861-6487-5(5)) Pub: Blckstn Audio. Dist(s): NetLibrary CO

Fundamental Cause of Fear. unabr. ed. Swami Amar Jyoti. 1 cass. (Running Time: 1 hr.). 2000. 9.95 (978-0-933572-59-1(X), K-170) Truth Consciousness.
Fear blocks joy and freedom. The root cause is within us. How we lost the image of God.

Fundamental Sacramental Theology. Fr. Hardon. 10 cass. 40.00 Set. (92S) IRL Chicago.

Fundamentals. 1 CD. (Running Time: 25 mins, 30 secs). (J). 1995. audio compact disk 15.99 (978-0-9678416-2-5(3)) Suite A.

Fundamentals. Jeanie Eller. Read by Jeanie Eller. 6 cass. (Running Time: 10 hrs. 45 mins.). 2000. (978-1-928606-18-5(0)) Action Readg.
Systematic lean to read program.

Fundamentals: Puns, Parables & Perilous Predicaments. unabr. ed. AIO Team Staff. Created by Focus on the Family Staff. 4 CDs. (Running Time: 6 hrs.). (Adventures in Odyssey Ser.: Vol. 4). (ENG.). (J). 2005. audio compact disk 24.99 (978-1-58997-073-1(X)) Pub: Focus Family. Dist(s): Tyndale Hse

Fundamentals: 8 Plays for Winning the Games of Business & Life. Isiah Thomas. Narrated by Tony Penny. 5 cass. (Running Time: 7 hrs.). 45.00 (978-0-7887-9564-0(3)) Recorded Bks.

Fundamentals Foundation Training for Every Dog. Brenda Aloff. (Running Time: 6960 sec.). 2005. DVD, audio compact disk, audio compact disk 34.95 (978-1-929242-28-3(X)) Dogwise Pubng.

Fundamentals in Ministry. Kenneth W. Hagin, Jr. 5 cass. 20.00 (10J) Faith Lib Pubns.

Fundamentals Manual. Harvey Jackins. 1 cass. 10.00 (978-1-885357-96-0(6)) Rational Isl.
Manual for beginning classes in re-evaluation counseling.

Fundamentals of Bankruptcy Law, Set. 14 cass. (Running Time: 17 hrs.). 1998. 275.00 Incl. course materials. (MC32) Am Law Inst.
Designed to introduce bankruptcy & business reorganization law to general practitioners covering all the basic areas of bankruptcy liquidation & rehabilitation, both the substantive & procedural law.

Fundamentals of Bankruptcy Practice. Read by Thomas E. Carlson et al. (Running Time: 18 hrs.). 1989. 220.00 Incl. 252p. tape materials. (BU-53112) Cont Ed Bar-CA.

Fundamentals of Biochemistry. unabr. ed. Read by LeRoy Kuehl. 12 cass. (Running Time: 10 hrs. 50 min.). 655.00 Set, incl. 417p. manual. (76) Am Chemical.

Fundamentals of Chapter 11 Business Reorganization, Set. 11 cass. (Running Time: 15 hrs.). 1995. stu. ed. 172.50 (MA46) Am Law Inst.
Basic course examines how financially distressed companies should plan for a Chapter 11 filing & how lawyers can assist their clients in organizing for a dramatic change in which a business must conduct itself under court supervision.

Fundamentals of Civil Depositions. 1985. bk. 65.00 incl. book.; 40.00 cass. only.; 25.00 book only. PA Bar Inst.

Fundamentals of Drama Therapy Level 1: A Beginner's Guide to Drama Therapy & Narrative Approaches. Pam B. Dunne. 3 cass. (Running Time: 55 min. per cass.). 1993. Set. (978-1-888657-07-4(3)) Drama Thrpy Inst.
Includes: (1) Drama Therapy Theory; (2) Psychodramatic & Projective Techniques; & (3) Externalizing Techniques.

Fundamentals of Employee Benefits Law. 11 cass. (Running Time: 16 hrs. 30 min.). 1999. 345.00 Set; incl. study guide 870p. (MD81) Am Law Inst.
Familiarizes nonspecialists, & those who would be specialists, with the basic laws & regulations governing employee pension & welfare benefit plans. Beneficial for lawyers, accountants, actuaries, & consultants, the course covers both qualified & nonqualified plans covered by ERISA.

Fundamentals of Estate Administration. 1997. bk. 99.00 (ACS-1354); bk. 99.00 (ACS-1354) PA Bar Inst.
Like a personal mentor, this guides the inexperienced practitioner through each stage of an estate administration. Learn the steps to take, the pitfalls to avoid, & the tactical decisions to make which save your clients taxes, time & expense.

Fundamentals of Estate Administration. 1990. 40.00 (AC-585) PA Bar Inst.

Fundamentals of Estate Planning. 1998. bk. 99.00 (ACS-1459); bk. 99.00 (ACS-1459) PA Bar Inst.
You get a pragmatic overview of the issues that every estate planner must address. The experienced authors guide you through the opportunities & pitfalls you encounter.

Fundamentals of Estate Planning. 1991. 40.00 PA Bar Inst.

Fundamentals of Experimental Design. Stanley N. Deming & Stephen L. Morgan. 4 cass. (Running Time: 4 hrs.). 465.00 incl. manual. (978-0-8412-1048-6(9), 88); 36.00 manual. (978-0-8412-1049-3(7)) Am Chemical.
Significantly improve the quality & efficiency of your R & D effort by properly designing your experiments. Examines the strengths & limitations of popular experimental design techniques.

Fundamentals of Family Interviewing. unabr. ed. Walter Kempler. 2 cass. 22.95 Kempler Inst.
Answers key questions on family counseling: How to find the working point promptly, how to track it efficiently, how to create impact, & what to do when an impasse occurs.

Fundamentals of Family Law. unabr. ed. 8 cass. (Running Time: 12 hrs.). 1998. bk. 99.00 (ACS-1464); bk. 99.00 (ACS-1464) PA Bar Inst.
Explores the state of the law in every area of family practice. Lawyers with little or no experience are exposed to every major topic you are likely to encounter, with up-to-date developments. This provides in-depth coverage of family law & offers sample clauses for marital settlement agreements.

Fundamentals of Family Law. unabr. ed. 6 cass. (Running Time: 9 hrs). 1991. 45.00 (AC-606) PA Bar Inst.

Fundamentals of Fire Fighter Skills. National Fire Protection Association Staff. (C). 2004. stu. ed. 40.95 (978-0-7637-2558-7(7), 0763725587) Jones Bartlett.

Fundamentals of Fire Fighter Skills. National Fire Protection Association Staff. 2005. tchr. ed. 1750.95 (978-0-7637-2557-0(9)) Jones Bartlett.

Fundamentals of Group Dynamics. unabr. ed. Michael Grinder. 3 cass. (Running Time: 3 hrs. 40 mins.). 1998. 59.95 (978-0-9705492-1-1(0)) N L P Comp.
Fine tune your non-verbal behavior in order to effectively direct group dynamics.

Fundamentals of International Business Transactions. 13 cass. 1997. 345.00 Incl. course materials. (MCO5) Am Law Inst.
Annual ALI-ABA Course of Study, November 6-8, 1997, Washington, D.C. (Loews L'Enfant Plaza Hotel). Introductory discussion of the basics of international law & researching skills, covers international sales of goods; regulation of imports & exports; contracting with agents & distributors; intellectual property rights & licensing; environmental law considerations; foreign investment, including foreign law restrictions & insurance; joint ventures; & dispute resolution. Also included are issues of immigration law & ethics & professional responsibility. Throughout, the tax aspects of the transactions discussed are considered.

Fundamentals of Investment Real Estate. unabr. ed. Tom Lundstedt. Read by Tom Lundstedt. 2 cass. (Running Time: 3 hrs.). 1998. 49.95 set, incl. study guide. (978-1-881049-02-9(7)) Winding Brook.
A step-by-step guide to understanding & analyzing the benefits of investing in real estate.

Fundamentals of Microbiology. 6th ed. I. Edward Alcamo. (C). 2000. audio compact disk 199.00 (978-0-7637-1394-2(5), 1394-5) Jones Bartlett.

Fundamentals of Municipal Borrowing. 1988. bk. 170.00; 85.00 PA Bar Inst.

Fundamentals of Nursing: A Multimedia Lecture Series. Mary Jane Hopkins & Maria Seidel. 2. (C). 2004. audio compact disk 49.95 (978-0-9745098-3-9(3)) Pioneer River.
Fundamentals of nursing focuses on the basic needs of individuals and the nurse's role in meeeting these needs. This course includes the history and trends in nursing, legal, and ethica responsibilities, geriatric, oncologic, and perioperative concepts, and basic technical and professional skills. The nursing process is the starting point for the Nursing curriculum and is designed to prepare the learner to develop both academic and practical skills essential for success in subsequent courses. Minimum system requirements: Windows 98 or better, Pentium III Processor, Sound Card, 12X CD Rom drie, and 128 MB RAM.

Fundamentals of Nursing: Standards & Practice - Student Study Guide. Sue C. DeLaune & Marilyn Stapleton. (C). 1998. stu. ed. 39.95 (978-0-7668-0192-9(6)) Pub: Delmar. Dist(s): CENGAGE Learn

Fundamentals of Nursing (Audio version Only) A Multimedia Lecture Series. Mary Jane Hopkins & Maria Seidel. 2. (C). 2004. audio compact disk 59.95 (978-0-9745098-2-2(5)) Pioneer River.

Fundamentals of Patent Law & Practice. 6 cass. (Running Time: 8 hrs. 30 min.). 1993. pap. bk. 260.00 Set; incl. bk. 156p. (M962) Am Law Inst.

Fundamentals of Pennsylvania Civil Practice & Procedure. 1991. 45.00 (AC-619) PA Bar Inst.

Fundamentals of Pennsylvania Civil Practice & Procedure. 1999. bk. 99.00 (ACS-2249) PA Bar Inst.
Covers the procedural issues arising at every step of a civil case. Peruse this manual to catch up on the latest case law, statute & rule changes in cases through the court system.

Fundamentals of Pennsylvania Securities Law. 1990. 35.00 (AC-581) PA Bar Inst.

Fundamentals of Phonetics: A Practical Guide for Students. Larry H. Small. (Running Time:). 2001. (978-0-205-27332-4(7)) Allyn.

Fundamentals of Phonetics: A Practical Guide for Students. 2nd ed. Larry H. Small. 2004. audio compact disk 38.40 (978-0-205-41911-1(9)) Allyn.

Fundamentals of Play. unabr. ed. Caitlin Macy. Read by James Daniels. (Running Time: 9 hrs.). 2005. 39.25 (978-1-59600-556-3(4), 9781596005563, Brlnc Audio MP3 Lib); 24.95 (978-1-59600-555-6(6), 9781596005556, Brilliance MP3); 39.25 (978-1-59600-558-7(0), 9781596005587, BADLE); 24.95 (978-1-59600-557-0(2), 9781596005570, BAD) Brilliance Audio.

Fundamentals of Preparing the Fiduciary & the Decedent's Final Income Tax Returns. (Running Time: 4 hrs.). 1999. bk. 99.00 (ACS-2221) PA Bar Inst.
Do you fully comprehend each line of the fiduciary & decedent final income tax returns? Although tax forms often look innocuous on their face, pitfalls lie hidden in them for the unwary. The authors walk you through the Pennsylvania & federal fiduciary & decedent's final income tax forms along with their accompanying schedules.

Fundamentals of Real Estate Exchanging. Tom Lundstedt. Read by Tom Lundstedt. 2 cass. (Running Time: 1 hr. 10 min.). 1998. 49.95 set, incl. study guide. (978-1-881049-01-2(9)) Winding Brook.
A practical guide to understanding & analyzing tax-free exchanges of like-kind property.

Fundamentals of Spiritual Alchemy. Caroline Myss. (Fundaments of Spiritual Alchemy). 2000. 55.00 (978-1-893869-58-5(X)) Celbrtng Life.

Fundamentals of Spiritual Alchemy Live Workshop. unabr. ed. Caroline Myss. 4 CDs. (Running Time: 4 hrs.). 2003. audio compact disk 23.95 (978-1-4019-0205-6(7), 2057) Hay House.

Fundamentals of Spiritual Warfare. Francis Frangipane. 2006. audio compact disk 29.99 (978-1-59933-009-9(1)) Pub: Morning NC. Dist(s): Destiny Image Pubs

***Fundamentals of Teaching English to Speakers of Other Languages in K-12 Mainstream Classrooms Cd.** 2nd rev. ed. Ariza. (ENG.). 2010. audio compact disk 78.39 (978-0-7575-4204-6(2)) Kendall-Hunt.

Fundamentals of the Faith - Inerrancy of the Scriptures, Set. Robert E. Picirilli et al. Ed. by Sound Impressions Staff. 2 cass. 1992. 9.95 (978-0-89265-671-4(9), 28035) Randall Hse.

Fundamentals of Voice & Articulation. Lyle V. Mayer. (C). 1995. (978-0-697-27068-9(8)) Brown & Benchmark.

Fundamentals of Voice & Diction. 10th ed. Lyle V. Mayer. (C). 1993. (978-0-697-13934-4(4)) Brown & Benchmark.

Fundamentals of Workers' Compensation. 1997. bk. 99.00 (ACS-1424) PA Bar Inst.
The experienced authors review the current law & procedure of workers' compensation & occupational disease in Pennsylvania. They guide you through every aspect of handling a case & offer practical tips - for both sides-as well as the perspective of a workers' compensation judge. This is designed for new attorneys as well as more experienced practitioners who want a refresher course or who are considering expanding their practices to include workers' compensation cases.

Fundamentals of Workers' Compensation. 1989. 45.00 (AC-516) PA Bar Inst.

Fundamentals of Worker's Compensation. 1997. bk. 99.00 (ACS-1424) PA Bar Inst.

Fundamentals of Your Feminine Voice. Lynn Skinner & Kathe Perez. 1 CD. (Running Time: 47:23). 2004. audio compact disk 25.00 (978-0-9705402-2-5(1)) Except Voice Inc.
Voice Training For TG Women.

***Fundamentals of 5-String Banjo Book/CD/DVD Set.** Ross Nickerson. 2010. pap. bk. 29.99 (978-0-7866-8252-2(3)) Mel Bay.

Fundamentals Prime Time with God Leaders Guide. Pam Brown. (J). (gr. 1-6). 2002. audio compact disk 24.95 (978-0-7673-9319-5(8)) LifeWay Christian.

Fundamentos de la Relacion. Ronald Hubbard. 2007. audio compact disk 17.00 (978-958-8318-00-4(9)) Centro de Literatura COL.

Fundraising with the Corporate Letter Request. unabr. ed. Beverly A. Browning. Read by Beverly A. Browning. 1 cass. (Running Time: 30 min.). 1999. 19.95 (978-0-9671073-2-5(6)) Bev Browning.
Quick tips on writing a successful corporate letter request to raise funds for your project.

Funeral see Love Poems of John Donne

Funeral Games. unabr. ed. Mary Renault. Read by Christopher Hurt. 8 cass. (Running Time: 12 hrs.). (Alexander Trilogy). 1985. 64.00 (978-0-7366-0873-2(7), 1823) Books on Tape.
Alexander the Great lies dying & his only heirs are his unborn child & his simpleton half-brother. He slips into a coma without having named his successor. When Homer's heroes fell, their fellow warriors held funeral games, racing & wrestling for rich prizes to honor the dead. Now Alexander's generals, no longer united by his magnetic presence, begin their struggle for the glittering prize of his vast dominions.

Funeral in Berlin. unabr. collector's ed. Len Deighton. Read by Paul Daneman. 8 cass. (Running Time: 8 hrs.). 1991. 48.00 (978-0-7366-1949-3(6), 2770) Books on Tape.
A spellbinding tale of espionage & its counter in which double & triple crosses are common. Berlin with its infamous wall symbolized the Cold War as did no other place. It was like theater, but for real.

Funeral in Blue. abr. ed. Anne Perry. Read by David Colacci. 5 CDs. (Running Time: 6 hrs.). (William Monk Novel Ser.). 2001. audio compact disk 69.25 (978-1-58788-743-7(6), 1587887436, CD Lib Edit) Brilliance Audio.
The headlines were gruesome: two beautiful women found strangled in the studio of a well-known London artist. To investigator William Monk and his wife Hester, the murders are a nightmare. One of the victims is an obscure artist's model. The other is the wife of Hester's cherished colleague, distinguished surgeon Dr. Kristian Beck, a Viennese emigre who swiftly becomes the principal suspect. With an intensity born of desperation, Hester, Monk, and their dear friend Lady Callandra Daviot, who cannot hide her deep love for the accused, seek evidence that will save Kristian from the hangman - hoping to penetrate not only the mystery of Elissa Beck's death... but the riddle of her life.

***Funeral in Blue.** abr. ed. Anne Perry. Read by David Colacci. (Running Time: 6 hrs.). 2011. audio compact disk 9.99 (978-1-4418-6702-5(3), 9781441867025, BCD Value Price) Brilliance Audio.

Funeral in Blue. unabr. ed. Anne Perry. Narrated by David Colacci. 8 cass. (Running Time: 11 hrs.). (William Monk Novel Ser.). 2001. 89.25 (978-1-58788-740-6(1), 1587887401, Unabridge Lib Edns) Brilliance Audio.

Funeral in Blue. unabr. ed. Anne Perry. Read by David Colacci. (Running Time: 39600 sec.). (William Monk Novel Ser.). 2004. audio compact disk 39.25 (978-1-59335-367-4(7), 1593353677, Brlnc Audio MP3 Lib) Brilliance Audio.

Funeral in Blue. unabr. ed. Anne Perry. Read by David Colacci. (Running Time: 11 hrs.). (William Monk Ser.). 2004. 39.25 (978-1-59710-314-5(4), 1597103144, BADLE); 24.95 (978-1-59710-315-2(2), 1597103152, BAD) Brilliance Audio.

Funeral in Blue. unabr. ed. Anne Perry. Read by David Colacci. (Running Time: 11 hrs.). (William Monk Novel Ser.). 2004. 24.95 (978-1-59335-036-9(8), 1593350368) Soulmate Audio Bks.

***Funeral in Blue.** unabr. ed. Anne Perry. Read by David Colacci. (Running Time: 12 hrs.). (William Monk Ser.). 2011. audio compact disk 19.99 (978-1-4418-4091-2(5), 9781441840912, Bril Audio CD Unabri); audio compact disk 59.97 (978-1-4418-4092-9(3), 9781441840929, BriAudCD Unabrid) Brilliance Audio.

Funeral Music see Poetry of Geoffrey

Funeral Music. unabr. ed. Morag Joss. 8 cass. (Isis Ser.). (J). 2002. 69.95 (978-0-7531-1353-0(8)) Pub: ISIS Lrg Prnt GBR. Dist(s): Ulverscroft US

Funk & R & B Guitar Method. Peter Gelling. (Progressive Ser.). 2004. pap. bk. 23.95 (978-1-875690-72-5(7), 256-064) Pub: Kolala Music SGP. Dist(s): Bookworld

Funk & R & B Keyboard Method. Peter Gelling. (Progressive Ser.). 2004. pap. bk. 19.95 (978-1-875690-62-6(X), 256-065) Pub: Kolala Music SGP. Dist(s): Bookworld

Funk Bass. Stephan Richter. (Progressive Ser.). 2004. pap. bk. 19.95 (978-1-86469-179-5(4), 256-060) Kolala Music SGP.

Funk Drumming. Jim Payne. 1999. spiral bd. 29.95 (978-0-7866-4814-6(7), 93892CDP) Mel Bay.

Funk Piano Method. Peter Gelling. (Progressive Ser.). 2004. pap. bk. 19.95 (978-1-86469-080-4(1), 256-067) Kolala Music SGP.

Funkdawgs - Jazz Fusion Unleashed: Drum Play Along. Funkdawgs. 2006. pap. bk. 24.98 (978-1-59615-710-1(0), 1596157100) Pub: Music Minus. Dist(s): H Leonard

Funky. unabr. ed. 1 cass. (Running Time: 1 hr. 30 min.). (SPA.). 2004. (978-0-8297-3994-7(7)) Vida Pubs.
Based on Christian life themes,Funky attempts to motivate the listener with his catchy rhythms that include a fusion of a variety of well known sounds that range from pop and rock to merengue, salsa and praise and worship, all fused with the rap style that characterizes funky.

Funky Beats & Breaks. Frank Biggs. 1998. pap. bk. (978-0-7866-3272-5(0), 97061BCD) Mel Bay.

Funky Phonics. abr. ed. Sara Jordan. Prod. by Sara Jordan. 1 CD. (Running Time: 30 min.). (Songs that Teach Language Arts Ser.). (ENG.). (J). (gr. 4-7). 1992. audio compact disk 13.95 (978-1-894262-18-7(2), JMP 103CD) Pub: S Jordan Publ. Dist(s): CrabtreePubCo

Funky Phonics: Reading Readiness. 1 CD. (Running Time: 1 hr.). (J). (gr. k-3). 2001. pap. bk. 16.95 (RT 101CD) Kimbo Educ.
Kids learn to sequence the alphabet, time, money, the continents & oceans, days of the week, months of the year & the season through "funky" motivation songs. Includes book.

Funky Phonics: Reading Readiness. Sara Jordan. 1 cass. (Running Time: 1 hr.). (J). (gr. k-3). 2001. pap. bk. 14.95 (RT 101C) Kimbo Educ.

Funky Phonics & More Vol. 1: Reading Readiness. Sara Jordan. Narrated by Sara Jordan. Engineer Mark Shannon. 1 cass. (Running Time: 27 min. 2 secs.). (J). (gr. k-3). 1992. pap. bk. 14.95 (978-1-895523-08-9(7), JMP103K) Jordan Music.
A great introduction to Reading! Uses both phonetic and whole language approaches. Learn about the alphabet, vowels, consonants (C and G), telling time, days of the week, seasons, the environment and more.

Funkytown. unabr. ed. Funky & Luis Marrero. (SPA.). 2002. 9.99 (978-0-8297-3714-1(6)) Pub: Vida Pubs. Dist(s): Zondervan

Funnt File. 3 CDs. (Running Time: 3 hrs.). 2001. audio compact disk 39.95 (THAR126) Lodestone Catalog.
A former starship captain who has fallen from grace, down to a janitor, accidentally lands at the helm of the freighter Excelsior & caroms around space in search of his destiny. All 6 episodes.

Funnt File Vol. 2: The Big Shave, Phantom of the Excelsior. 1 CD. (Running Time: 1 hr.). 2001. audio compact disk 15.95 (THAR004) Lodestone Catalog.
A former starship captain who has fallen from grace, down to a janitor, accidentally lands, at the helm of the freighter Excelsior & caroms around space in search of his destiny.

Funnt File Vol. 3: What Hal Says, Ballad of the Space Brains. 1 CD. (Running Time: 1 hr.). 2001. audio compact disk 15.95 (THAR006) Lodestone Catalog.
A former starship captain who has fallen from grace, down to a janitor, accidentally lands, at the helm of the freighter Excelsior & caroms around space in search of his destin.

Funny Bone Boulevard. Michael Medina. (J). 2007. audio compact disk 14.99 (978-1-60247-703-2(5)) Tate Pubng.

Funny Bone Poems Read-Alongs, Set. unabr. ed. Poems. Othello Bach. Read by Sandy Duncan. 4 cass. Incl. Funny Bone Poems Read-Alongs: Does My Room Come Alive at Night. (J).; Funny Bone Poems Read-Alongs: Jake Snake's Race. (J).; Funny Bone Poems Read-Alongs: The Man with Big Ears. (J).; (J). 1986. 9.95 HarperCollins Pubs.

Funny Bone Poems Read-Alongs: Does My Room Come Alive at Night see Funny Bone Poems Read-Alongs

Funny Bone Poems Read-Alongs: Jake Snake's Race see Funny Bone Poems Read-Alongs

Funny Bone Poems Read-Alongs: The Man with Big Ears see Funny Bone Poems Read-Alongs

Funny Boy. abr. ed. Shyam Selvadurai. Narrated by Sugith Varughese. Prod. by CBC Radio Staff. 2 cass. (Running Time: 2 hrs. 30 mins.). (Between the Covers Collection). (ENG.). 1998. 16.95 (978-0-86492-262-5(0)) Goose Ln Eds CAN.
"When his father realizes that Arjie prefers playing ""bride-bride"" to batting balls with the boys, he sends him away to a Dickensian boarding school. Set in Sri Lanka, Shyam Selvadurai's award-winning ""novel in six stories"" describes a Tamil boy's bittersweet discovery of his homosexuality amid the social unrest that led to the anti-Tamil riots of 1983.".

Funny Boys. Warren Adler. Read by Tom Weiner. (Playaway Adult Fiction Ser.). 2008. 79.99 (978-1-60640-758-5(9)) Find a World.

Funny Boys. unabr. ed. Warren Adler. (Running Time: 12 hrs. 30 mins.). 2008. 29.95 (978-1-4332-1000-6(2)) Blckstn Audio.

Funny Boys. unabr. ed. Warren Adler. Read by Tom Weiner. (Running Time: 28800 sec.). 2008. 72.95 (978-1-4332-0998-7(5)); audio compact disk 29.95

(978-1-4332-1001-3(0)); audio compact disk & audio compact disk 29.95 (978-1-4332-1002-0(9)); audio compact disk & audio compact disk 90.00 (978-1-4332-0999-4(3)) Blckstn Audio.

Funny Business: The Best of Uproar Comedy. Perf. by Brian Regan et al. 2000. audio compact disk 9.98 (978-1-929243-09-9(X)) Uproar Ent.

Funny Cide: How a Horse, a Trainer, a Jockey, & a Bunch of High School Buddies Took on the Sheiks & Blue Bloods ... & Won. Funny Cide Team Staff & Sally Jenkins. Read by Dan Cashman. 2004. audio compact disk 81.00 (978-1-4159-0251-6(8)) Books on Tape.

Funny Farm. Jackie Moffat. (Story Sound Ser.). (J). 2005. 61.95 (978-1-85903-776-8(3)) Pub: Mgna Lrg Print GBR. Dist(s): Ulverscroft US

Funny Food Songs. 1 cass. (Classic Collections). (J). 7.99 (978-1-55723-608-1(9)); 7.99 Norelco. (978-1-55723-607-4(0)); audio compact disk 13.99 CD. (978-1-55723-609-8(7)); audio compact disk 13.99 (978-1-55723-610-4(0)) W Disney Records.

Funny Little Woman. 2004. bk. 24.95 (978-0-89719-875-2(1)); pap. bk. 18.95 (978-1-55592-415-7(8)); pap. bk. 38.75 (978-1-55592-416-4(6)); pap. bk. 32.75 (978-1-55592-227-6(9)); pap. bk. 14.95 (978-1-56008-054-1(X)); 8.95 (978-1-56008-901-8(6)); 8.95 (978-1-56008-132-6(5)); cass. & flmstrp 30.00 (978-1-56008-671-0(8)); audio compact disk 12.95 (978-1-55592-911-4(7)) Weston Woods.

Funny Little Woman. Arlene Mosel. 1 cass. (Running Time: 9 min.). (J). (gr. k-4). 8.95 (RAC162) Weston Woods.

In this story of old Japan, a little woman who loves to cook rice dumplings & loves to laugh is taken captive by the wicked one. Caldecott Medal Book.

Funny Little Woman. Arlene Mosel. Illus. by Blair Lent. 1 cass. (Running Time: 9 min.). (J). (gr. k-4). pap. bk. 12.95 (PRA162) Weston Woods.

Funny Little Woman. Retold by Arlene Mosel. Illus. by Blair Lent. 1 cass., 5 bks. (Running Time: 30 min.). (J). (gr. k-4). pap. bk. 32.75 Weston Woods.

Funny Papers. unabr. ed. Elaine Scott. Narrated by Norman Dietz. 2 cass. (Running Time: 2 hrs. 15 mins.). (gr. 2 up). 1997. 19.00 (978-0-7887-0696-7(9), 94870E7) Recorded Bks.

See how cartoon superstars like Garfield, Mother Goose & Grimm, Blondie & all their friends make their journey from the cartoonists' drawing board to your breakfast table.

Funny Songbook. Esther Nelson & Bruce Haack. 1 cass. (Running Time: 60 min.). (J). (ps-4). 1986. 9.95 (978-0-945110-01-9(4), D311) Dragonhawk Pub.

Instructs children to follow directions given to music, with the goal of intensifying the listeners imagination & creativity through body movement.

Funny Stuff: Off-beat Observational Comedy. unabr. ed. 1 cass. (Running Time: 45 mins.). 1999. (978-0-9700349-9-1(7)) Mayfield Present.

Funny Stuff You Can Do on the Piano. Duane Shinn. 1 cass. 19.95 (NS-8) Duane Shinn.

Presents 14 different things to do to create a laugh whenever the occasion calls for it.

Funny Thing Happened on My Way to Perfection. Jack Marshall. 2004. audio compact disk 10.95 (978-1-57734-656-2(4)); 9.95 (978-1-57734-353-0(0), 06005861) Covenant Comms.

An entertaining talk about avoiding the potholes of life.

***Funny Thing Happened on the Way to the Future.** Michael J. Fox. (ENG.). 2010. 14.99 (978-1-4013-9517-9(1)) Pub: Hyperion. Dist(s): HarperCollins Pubs

***Funny Thing Happened on the Way to the Future: Twists & Turns & Lessons Learned.** unabr. ed. Michael J. Fox. Read by Michael J. Fox. 1 CD. (Running Time: 2 hrs.). 2010. audio compact disk 18.99 (978-1-4013-9518-6(X), Hyperion Audio) Pub: Hyperion. Dist(s): HarperCollins Pubs

Funny Thing Happened on the Way to the White House: Humor, Blunders, & Other Oddities from the Presidential Campaign Trail. Charles Osgood. Read by Norman Dietz. (Playaway Adult Nonfiction Ser.). (ENG.). 2009. 49.99 (978-1-60812-532-6(7)) Find a World.

Funny Thing Happened on the Way to the White House: Humor, Blunders, & Other Oddities from the Presidential Campaign Trail. unabr. ed. Charles Osgood. Narrated by Norman Dietz. (Running Time: 5 hrs. 30 mins. 0 sec.). (ENG.). 2008. audio compact disk 49.99 (978-1-4001-3752-7(7)) Pub: Tantor Media. Dist(s): IngramPubServ

Funny Thing Happened on the Way to the White House: Humor, Blunders, & Other Oddities from the Presidential Campaign Trail. unabr. ed. Charles Osgood. Read by Norman Dietz. (Running Time: 5 hrs. 30 mins. 0 sec.). (ENG.). 2008. audio compact disk 19.99 (978-1-4001-5752-5(8)) Pub: Tantor Media. Dist(s): IngramPubServ

Funny Thing Happened on the Way to the White House: Humor, Blunders, & Other Oddities from the Presidential Campaign Trail. unabr. ed. Charles Osgood. Read by Norman Dietz. (Running Time: 5 hrs. 30 mins. 0 sec.). (ENG.). 2008. audio compact disk 24.99 (978-1-4001-0752-0(0)) Pub: Tantor Media. Dist(s): IngramPubServ

Funny Thing Is. unabr. ed. Ellen DeGeneres. Read by Ellen DeGeneres. 4 CDs. (Running Time: 40 hrs. 0 mins. 0 sec.). (ENG.). 2003. audio compact disk 30.00 (978-0-7435-3362-1(3), Audioworks) Pub: S&S Audio. Dist(s): S and S Inc

Funny, You Don't Look Like a Grandmother. unabr. ed. Lois Wyse. Read by Lois Wyse. 2 cass. (Running Time: 2 hrs. 5 min.). 1990. 15.95 set. (978-0-9627187-0-0(X), 20000) Pub Mills.

This bestselling book is a humorous, touching & insightful look at modern grandmotherhood & its many facets. Witty, engaging & sure to be a perennial favorite.

Funtime Tales. Perf. by Barney Staff. 1 cass. (J). (ps-3). 1996. 7.95 (978-1-57064-139-8(0)) Lyrick Studios.

Fur Coat, No Knickers. unabr. ed. Anna King. Read by Diana Bishop. 12 cass. (Running Time: 13 hrs. 30 mins.). (Sound Ser.). 2002. 94.95 (978-1-86042-801-2(0)) Pub: UlverLrgPrint GBR. Dist(s): Ulverscroft US

***Fur, Fortune, & Empire: The Epic History of the Fur Trade in America.** unabr. ed. Eric Jay Dolin. (Running Time: 14 hrs.). 2010. 29.95 (978-1-4417-6063-0(6)); audio compact disk 32.95 (978-1-4417-6062-3(8)) Blckstn Audio.

Furies. abr. ed. John Jakes. Read by Bruce Watson. 4 cass. (Running Time: 6 hrs.). (Kent Family Chronicles: No. 4). 2000. 12.99 (978-1-57815-163-9(5), 4412, Media Bks Audio) Media Bks NJ.

Furies. unabr. collector's ed. John Jakes. Read by Michael Kramer. 11 cass. (Running Time: 16 hrs. 30 min.). (Kent Family Chronicles: No. 4). 1993. 88.00 (978-0-7366-2430-5(9), 3194) Books on Tape.

Kent family saga continues as the nation girds for civil war. Follows The Seekers.

Furies of Calderon. unabr. ed. Jim Butcher. (Running Time: 20 hrs.). Bk. 1. (ENG.). (gr. 8). 2008. audio compact disk 49.95 (978-0-14-314376-5(X), PengAudBks) Penguin Grp USA.

Furious Longing of God. unabr. ed. Brennan Manning. (Running Time: 2 hrs. 0 mins. 0 sec.). (ENG.). 2009. audio compact disk 12.98 (978-1-59644-720-2(6), Hovel Audio) christianaud.

***Furious Longing of God.** unabr. ed. Brennan Manning. Narrated by Dan Cashman. (ENG.). 2009. 8.98 (978-1-59644-721-9(4), Hovel Audio) christianaud.

***Furious Love: Elizabeth Taylor, Richard Burton, & the Marriage of the Century.** unabr. ed. Sam Kashner & Nancy Schoenberger. Read by Paul Boehmer. (ENG.). 2010. (978-0-06-198880-6(4), Harper Audio) HarperCollins Pubs.

***Furious Love: The Love Affair of Elizabeth & Richard.** unabr. ed. Sam Kashner & Nancy Schoenberger. Read by Paul Boehmer. (ENG.). 2010. (978-0-06-199744-0(7), Harper Audio) HarperCollins Pubs.

Furnace of Creation, Cradle of Destruction: A Journey to the Birthplace of Earthquakes, Volcanoes, & Tsunamis. abr. ed. Roy Chester. Read by Bill Weideman. 1 MP3-CD. (Running Time: 7 hrs.). 2008. 39.25 (978-1-4233-6403-0(1), 9781423364030, Brinc Audio MP3 Lib); 24.95 (978-1-4233-6402-3(3), 9781423364023, Brilliance MP3); audio compact disk 29.95 (978-1-4233-6400-9(7), 9781423364009, Bril Audio CD Unabri); audio compact disk 82.25 (978-1-4233-6401-6(5), 9781423364016, BriAudCD Unabrid) Brilliance Audio.

Furnace of Creation, Cradle of Destruction: A Journey to the Birthplace of Earthquakes, Volcanoes, & Tsunamis. unabr. abr. ed. Roy Chester. Read by Bill Weideman. (Running Time: 7 hrs.). 2008. 24.95 (978-1-4233-6404-7(X), 9781423364047, BAD); 39.25 (978-1-4233-6405-4(8), 9781423364054, BADLE) Brilliance Audio.

Furnished Room see O. Henry Favorites

Furnished Room see Great American Short Stories

Furnished Room see Fourteen American Masterpieces

Furnished Room see Classic Ghost Stories, Vol. 1, A Collection

Furnished Room see Favorite Stories by O. Henry

Furnished Room: Mark 14:12-16. Ed Young. (J). 1982. 4.95 (978-0-7417-1252-3(0), 252) Win Walk.

Furniture in Italy: A Strategic Reference 2006. Compiled by Icon Group International, Inc. Staff. 2007. ring bd. 195.00 (978-0-497-36038-2(1)) Icon Grp.

Furrtails. Shandi Finnessey. Narrated by Sharon Eisenhour. 1 CD. (Running Time: 9 mins., 41 secs.). 2006. audio compact disk 9.95 (978-1-60031-003-4(6)) Spoken Books.

Written by Miss USA, 2004 (and current co-host of the game show, LINGO) this is a story of the Furrtails; a family of rabbits, who live in their burrow next to Mr. Villman's farm. Sammy, is not as quick and smart as his younger brother, and soon finds himself stuck in a cage and unable to get out. Each rabbit must use his or her "special" gifts to help free Sammy from the trap. This story is intended to teach children that each of us have special talents, and that when we work together, even the little ones, we can all pull together and make great things happen.

Furrtails See & Listen Version. Shandi Finnessey. Narrated by Sharon Eisenhour. 1 CD. (Running Time: 0:09:59). (ENG.). (J). 2006. audio compact disk 18.95 (978-1-60031-007-2(9)) Spoken Books.

Further Adventures of Hank the Cowdog. John R. Erickson. Read by John R. Erickson. 2 cass. (Running Time: 2 hr. 30 min.). (Hank the Cowdog Ser.: No. 2). (J). (gr. 2-5). 1989. 16.95 (978-0-87719-122-3(0), AF196R) Lone Star Bks.

Tricked & abandoned to a terrible fate, poor Hank is in double trouble this time when he is stricken with "Eye-Crosserosis" & has the fight of his life with Rufus, a Doberman, over the affections of Beaulah, a beautiful collie.

Further Adventures of Hank the Cowdog. unabr. ed. John R. Erickson. 2 cass. (Running Time: 3 hrs.). (Hank the Cowdog Ser.: No. 2). (J). (gr. 2-5). 2001. (978-0-7366-6137-9(9)) Books on Tape.

Hank defends the ranch against the attack of a Silver Monster Bird. Later, suffering from the dreaded Eye-Crosserosis, Hank visits the cave of a witchy little owl named Madame Moonshine. He also tries to win the heart of Beulah, the collie of his dreams, and to squelch his rival, Plato the bird dog.

Further Adventures of Hank the Cowdog. unabr. ed. John R. Erickson. Read by John R. Erickson. 2 cass. (Running Time: 3 hrs.). (Hank the Cowdog Ser.: No. 2). (J). (gr. 2-5). 2001. 16.95 (978-0-7366-6891-0(8)) Books on Tape.

Despite suffering from Eye-Crosserosis, Hank tries to win the heart of Beulah, the collie of his dreams & to squelch his rival, Plato the bird dog.

Further Adventures of Hank the Cowdog. unabr. ed. John R. Erickson. Read by John R. Erickson. Illus. by Gerald L. Holmes. 2 cass. (Hank the Cowdog Ser.: No. 2). (J). (gr. 2-5). 1983. bk. 13.95 (978-0-916941-02-4(7)) Maverick Bks.

Further Adventures of Hank the Cowdog. unabr. ed. John R. Erickson. Read by John R. Erickson. 2 cassettes. (Running Time: approx. 3 hours). (Hank the Cowdog Ser.: No. 2). (J). 2002. 17.99 (978-1-59188-302-9(4)) Maverick Bks.

Further Adventures of Hank the Cowdog. unabr. ed. John R. Erickson. Read by John R. Erickson. 3 CDs. (Running Time: Aprrox. 3 hours). (Hank the Cowdog Ser.: No. 2). (J). 2002. audio compact disk 19.99 (978-1-59188-602-0(3)) Maverick Bks.

It starts as a routine morning on the ranch for Hank the Cowdog?sweeps and patrols, defense maneuvers against an attacking silver monster bird, and the usual flak from Pete the Barncat. But the day takes a surprising turn when Hank is stricken with a terrible case of ?Eye Crosserosis.? Unless he can find a cure for this dangerous condition, his position as Head of Ranch Security is at stake. Only the mysterious Madame Moonshine may be able to help him?but to reach her Hank must endure a perilous journey from which few have returned alive!Madame Moonshine sings ?I Am a Witch? in this hilarious adventure for the whole family.

Further Adventures of Hank the Cowdog. unabr. ed. John R. Erickson. Read by John R. Erickson. 2 cass. (Running Time: 2 hrs. 30 mins.). (Hank the Cowdog Ser.: No. 2). (J). (gr. 2-5). 2000. 18.00 (978-0-8072-8251-9(0), Listening Lib) Random Audio Pubg.

Further Adventures of Hank the Cowdog. unabr. ed. John R. Erickson. 2 cass. (Hank the Cowdog Ser.: No. 2). (J). (gr. 2-5). 1998. 17.00 (21630) Recorded Bks.

Further Adventures of Hank the Cowdog. unabr. collector's ed. John R. Erickson. 3 CDs. (Running Time: 4 hrs. 30 mins.). (Hank the Cowdog Ser.: No. 2). (J). (gr. 2-5). 2001. audio compact disk 28.00 Books on Tape.

Hank defends the ranch against the attack of a Silver Monster Bird. Later, suffering from the dreaded Eye-Crosserosis, Hank visits the cave of a witchy little owl named Madame Moonshine. He also tries to win the heart of Beulah, the collie of his dreams, and to squelch his rival, Plato the bird dog.

Further Adventures of Robinson Crusoe. Daniel Defoe. Read by Alfred von Lecteur. 2009. 27.95 (978-1-60112-975-8(0)) Babblebooks.

***Further Adventures of Sherlock Holmes, Vol. 3.** Bert Coules. Narrated by Clive Merrison et al. (Running Time: 4 hrs. 0 mins. 0 sec.). (ENG.). 2010. audio compact disk 34.95 (978-1-84607-084-6(8)) Pub: AudioGO. Dist(s): Perseus Dist

Further Adventures of Sherlock Holmes: A BBC Radio Full-Cast Dramatization. Bert Coules. (Running Time: 2 hrs. 55 mins. 0 sec.). (ENG.). 2009. audio compact disk 34.95 (978-1-60283-754-6(6)) Pub: AudioGO. Dist(s): Perseus Dist

Further Adventures of Sherlock Holmes: Inspired by the Original Stories of Sir Arhur Conan Doyle. unabr. ed. Bert Coules. Narrated by Full Cast. (Running Time: 5 hrs. 0 mins. 0 sec.). (ENG.). 2010. audio compact disk 34.95 (978-1-60283-852-9(6)) Pub: AudioGO. Dist(s): Perseus Dist

Further Adventures of Sherlock Holmes Complete Collection Volume 1. Jim French. (ENG.). 2008. audio compact disk 39.95 (978-1-60245-088-2(9)) GDL Multimedia.

***Further Adventures of Sherlock Holmes, Vol. 4: Three BBC Radio Full-Cast Radio Dramas.** Bert Coules. Narrated by Clive Merrison et al. (Running Time: 3 hrs. 0 mins. 0 sec.). (ENG.). 2010. audio compact disk 34.95 (978-1-4084-2732-3(X)) Pub: AudioGO. Dist(s): Perseus Dist

Further Adventures of Sherlock Holmes Volume 1. (ENG.). 2008. audio compact disk 9.95 (978-1-60245-117-9(6)) GDL Multimedia.

Further Adventures of Sherlock Holmes Volume 2. Jim French. (ENG.). 2008. audio compact disk 9.95 (978-1-60245-143-8(5)) GDL Multimedia.

Further Adventures of Sherlock Holmes Volume 3. Jim French. (ENG.). 2008. audio compact disk 9.95 (978-1-60245-144-5(3)) GDL Multimedia.

Further Adventures of Sherlock Holmes Volume 4. Jim French. (ENG.). 2008. audio compact disk 9.95 (978-1-60245-145-2(1)) GDL Multimedia.

Further Adventures of Sherlock Holmes Volume 5. Jim French. (ENG.). 2008. audio compact disk Rental 9.95 (978-1-60245-146-9(X)) GDL Multimedia.

Further Adventures of Sherlock Holmes Volume 6. Jim French. (ENG.). 2008. audio compact disk 9.95 (978-1-60245-147-6(8)) GDL Multimedia.

Further Ahead: Learner's Book. Sarah Jones-Macziola & Greg White. (Running Time: hrs. mins.). (ENG.). 1998. 24.00 (978-0-521-59785-2(4)) Cambridge U Pr.

Further Ahead: Learner's Book. Sarah Jones-Macziola & Greg White. (Running Time: hrs. mins.). (ENG.). 1998. audio compact disk 25.20 (978-0-521-63928-6(X)) Cambridge U Pr.

Further Ahead Home: A Communication Skills Course for Business English. Sarah Jones-Macziola. (Running Time: 55 mins.). (ENG.). 1999. stu. ed. 24.00 (978-0-521-59782-1(X)) Cambridge U Pr.

Further Ahead Home Study: A Communication Skills Course for Business English. Sarah Jones-Macziola. (Running Time: 55 mins.). (ENG.). 1999. stu. ed. 25.20 (978-0-521-63929-3(8)) Cambridge U Pr.

Further along the Road Less Traveled: Self Love V. Self-Esteem. M. Scott Peck. 2004. 7.95 (978-0-7435-4746-8(2)) Pub: S&S Audio. Dist(s): S and S Inc

Further along the Road Less Traveled: Sexuality & Spirituality. M. Scott Peck. 2004. 7.95 (978-0-7435-4748-2(9)) Pub: S&S Audio. Dist(s): S and S Inc

Further along the Road Less Traveled: The Unending Journey Toward Spiritual Growth. M. Scott Peck. 6 cass. (Running Time: 6 hrs.). 1995. bk. 59.95 Set. (12950AS) Nightingale-Conant.

Delivers the spiritual & philosophical tools you can use to learn & grow from difficult transitions. You will aslo discover the deeper meaning in life that will bring you that inner joy & happiness.

Further along the road less traveled: a tast for mystery Cst: The Taste for Mystery. M. Scott Peck. 2004. 7.95 (978-0-7435-4752-9(7)) Pub: S&S Audio. Dist(s): S and S Inc

Further along the road less traveled addiction Th: Addiction, the Sacred Disease. M. Scott Peck. 2004. 7.95 (978-0-7435-4745-1(4)) Pub: S&S Audio. Dist(s): S and S Inc

Further along the road less traveled giong to omaha the issue of death & Mean: Going to Omaha - the Issue of Death & Meaning. M. Scott Peck. 2004. 7.95 (978-0-7435-4749-9(7)) Pub: S&S Audio. Dist(s): S and S Inc

Further along the road less traveled growing Up: Growing up Painfully: Consciousness & the Problem of Pain. M. Scott Peck. 2004. 7.95 (978-0-7435-4750-5(0)) Pub: S&S Audio. Dist(s): S and S Inc

Further along the road less traveled mythology & human Nature. M. Scott Peck. 2004. 7.95 (978-0-7435-4751-2(9)) Pub: S&S Audio. Dist(s): S and S Inc

Further along the road less traveled the new age movement what in god's or Satan: The New Age Movement: What in God's or Satan's Name Is It? M. Scott Peck. 2004. 7.95 (978-0-7435-4747-5(0)) Pub: S&S Audio. Dist(s): S and S Inc

Further along the road less traveled the Unending: The Unending Journey Toward Spiritual Growth. M. Scott Peck. 2004. 12.95 (978-0-7435-4744-4(6)) Pub: S&S Audio. Dist(s): S and S Inc

Further Chronicles of Avonlea. unabr. ed. L. M. Montgomery. Read by Grace Conlin. 5 cass. (Running Time: 7 hrs.). (Avonlea Ser.: No. 7). (gr. 3-8). 1996. 39.95 (978-0-7861-1004-9(X), 1781) Blckstn Audio.

When Miss Montgomery conjured up the lovely character of Anne Shirley, the heroine of her first novel "Anne of Green Gables" & surrounded Anne with her beloved Prince Edward Island, she created one of the favorite heroines in all modern fiction. In this volume of heartwarming tales a Persian cat plays an amazing role in a marriage proposal, a young girl risks losing her mother in her quest to find her father, & a foolish lie threatens to make an unattached woman the town's laughingstock. These fifteen short stories present piquant & fascinating pictures of life in the villages & country surrounding Avonlea.

Further Chronicles of Avonlea. unabr. ed. L. M. Montgomery. Read by Grace Conlin. (Running Time: 7.5 hrs. NaN mins.). 2009. 29.95 (978-1-4332-6740-6(3)); audio compact disk 60.00 (978-1-4332-6737-6(3)) Blckstn Audio.

Further Chronicles of Conan. abr. ed. Robert Jordan. 1 cass. 1999. 22.95 (978-1-55935-328-1(7)) Soundelux.

Three classic novels telling stories of Conan the Barbarian.

Further Fables for Our Time. (1637) Books on Tape.

***Further Tales of the City.** abr. ed. Armistead Maupin. Read by Armistead Maupin. (ENG.). 2009. (978-0-06-197735-0(7), Harper Audio); (978-0-06-197734-3(9), Harper Audio) HarperCollins Pubs.

Further Tales of the City. unabr. ed. Armistead Maupin. Narrated by Barbara Rosenblat. 8 cass. (Running Time: 10 hrs. 45 mins.). (Tales of the City Ser.: Vol. 3). 1995. 70.00 (978-0-7887-0254-9(8), 94463E7) Recorded Bks.

The calamity-prone residents of 28 Barbary Lane are at it again in this dark story of romance & betrayal.

Further Tales of Uncle Remus: The Misadventures of Brer Rabbit, Brer Fox, Brer Wolf, the Doodang, & Other Creatures. unabr. ed. Julius Lester. Narrated by Julius Lester. 3 pieces. (Running Time: 3 hrs. 45 mins.). 2003. 28.00 (978-0-7887-9049-2(8)) Recorded Bks.

Further up the Organization. Robert Townsend. Intro. by A. E. Whyte. 1 cass. (Running Time: 60 min.). (Listen & Learn USA! Ser.). 8.95 (978-0-88684-051-8(1)) Listen USA.

Offers advice on solving the corporate leadership gap.

Furthermore: The Live Sessions & from the Studio. Perf. by Jars of Clay. 2 CDs. (Running Time: 3 hrs.). 2003. audio compact disk Essential Recs.

Fury. abr. ed. Robert K. Tanenbaum. Read by Lee Sellars. 2005. 15.95 (978-0-7435-5217-2(2)) Pub: S&S Audio. Dist(s): S and S Inc

Fury: A Novel. Salman Rushdie. Narrated by Salman Rushdie. 8 CDs. (Running Time: 9 hrs. 15 mins.). audio compact disk 78.00 (978-1-4025-0888-2(3)) Recorded Bks.

Fury: A Novel. Salman Rushdie. Narrated by Salman Rushdie. 7 cass. (Running Time: 9 hrs. 15 mins.). 2001. 65.00 (978-1-4025-0685-7(6), 96922) Recorded Bks.
Fifty-five year old Malik Solanka leaves his family behind in England to escape the "furies" that have taken hold of him. In New York City, Solanka attempts to overcome his rage and melancholy, falling in love with a beautiful Neela along the way.

Fury: A Novel. Salman Rushdie. 6 cass. (Running Time: 9 hrs. 15 mins.). 2004. 29.99 (978-1-4025-0176-0(5), 00614) Recorded Bks.

Fury from the Deep. Lou Wakefield & Carole Hayman. 2 CDs. (Running Time: 2 hrs. 15 mins.). 2003. audio compact disk 29.95 (978-0-563-52410-6(3)) AudioGO.

Fury of Aerial Bombardment see Richard Eberhart Reading His Poetry

Fury of Aerial Bombardment see Twentieth-Century Poetry in English, No. 1, Recordings of Poets Reading Their Own Poetry

Fusion. Roberto Orellana. 2003. 2.00 (978-0-8297-3895-7(9)); audio compact disk 3.60 (978-0-8297-3893-3(2)) Zondervan.

Fusion Drum Styles. James Morton. 1997. audio compact disk 19.95 (978-0-7866-3313-5(1)) Mel Bay.

Fussin', Fightin', & Feudin' Genesis 1: 1-18. Ed Young. 1986. 4.95 (978-0-7417-1535-7(X), 535) Win Walk.

Futility of Ego. Swami Amar Jyoti. 1 dolby cass. 1983. 9.95 (M-41) Truth Consciousness.
Strong words on the losing game of preserving ego. A class in wisdom.

Futrtools: Power Tools for Your Mind: A Simple, Fun, Audio System for Planning Your Future. unabr. ed. Mary J. Michael. 4 cass. (Running Time: 2 hrs.). (Virtual Gym Ser.: Vol. 1). 1997. 39.95 Set. (978-0-9651947-1-6(X)) MXM Inc.
Fully-structured, audio software program for putting your intuition & creativity to work for you.

Futur de nos Terres: Faire Face au Defi. (ITA.). 2001. cd-rom 40.00 (978-92-5-204496-7(7)) Pub: FAO ITA. Dist(s): Bernan Associates

Future. Contrib. by Del. Prod. by Noize et al. Contrib. by Delmar Lawrence. 2005. audio compact disk 11.98 (978-5-558-92016-1(5)) Pt of Grace Ent.

Future Challenges to Individual Happiness. unabr. ed. Nathaniel Branden. 1 cass. (Running Time: 1 hr. 3 min.). 12.95 (558) J Norton Pubs.
A consideration of individualism & individual happiness in the years ahead. Branden discusses alienation, the fear of choice, progress, the decline of religion & tradition, masculinity & femininity, leisure, art & related subjects,.

Future Doc ADD/ADHD Alternatives. 2008. audio compact disk (978-1-935457-01-5(2)) Future Doc.

Future Doc Allergy Alternatives. 2008. audio compact disk (978-1-935457-03-9(9)) Future Doc.

Future Doc Andropause Alternatives. 2007. audio compact disk (978-1-935457-05-3(5)) Future Doc.

Future Doc Arthritis Alternatives. 2008. audio compact disk (978-1-935457-07-7(1)) Future Doc.

Future Doc Autism Alternatives. 2008. audio compact disk (978-1-935457-09-1(8)) Future Doc.

Future Doc Breast Health Naturally. 2007. audio compact disk (978-1-935457-11-4(X)) Future Doc.

Future Doc Diabetes Alternatives. 2007. audio compact disk (978-1-935457-13-8(6)) Future Doc.

Future Doc Female Hormones Naturally. 2007. audio compact disk (978-1-935457-15-2(2)) Future Doc.

Future Doc Fibromyalgia Alternatives. 2008. audio compact disk (978-1-935457-17-6(9)) Future Doc.

Future Doc Heart Disease Alternatives. 2007. audio compact disk (978-1-935457-21-3(7)) Future Doc.

Future Doc Heavy Metal Toxicities. 2008. audio compact disk (978-1-935457-23-7(3)) Future Doc.

Future Doc Hyberbaric Oxygen Therapy. 2008. audio compact disk (978-1-935457-19-0(5)) Future Doc.

Future Doc in Defense of Medical Heresy. 2007. audio compact disk (978-1-935457-25-1(X)) Future Doc.

Future Doc Osteoporosis Alternatives. 2007. audio compact disk (978-1-935457-27-5(6)) Future Doc.

Future Doc Sustainable Nutrition. 2007. audio compact disk (978-1-935457-29-9(2)) Future Doc.

Future Has a Past. J. California Cooper. 7 cass. (Running Time: 9 hrs. 30 mins.). 64.00 (978-0-7887-5477-7(7)) Recorded Bks.

Future Interests, 2005 ed. (Law School Legends Audio Series) 2005th rev. ed. Catherine L. Carpenter. 2005. 36.95 (978-0-314-16101-7(5)); audio compact disk 36.95 (978-0-314-16102-4(3)) West.

Future Is Electronic Payment Systems. 1 cass. (America's Supermarket Showcase '96 Ser.). 1996. 11.00 (NGA96-025) Sound Images.

Future Life Progression. Bruce Goldberg. (ENG.). 2005. audio compact disk 17.00 (978-1-57968-032-9(1)) Pub: B Goldberg. Dist(s): Baker Taylor

Future Life Progression. Bruce Goldberg. 1 cass. (Hypnotic Time Travel Ser.). (ENG.). 2006. 13.00 (978-1-885577-04-7(4)) Pub: B Goldberg. Dist(s): Baker Taylor
Self hypnosis program that guides you forward in your current life or into future lifetimes.

Future Medicine. abr. ed. Interview with Daniel Goleman & Michael Toms. 2 cass. (Running Time: 1 hr. 30 min.). (New Dimensions Ser.). 1997. 15.95 (978-1-56170-416-3(4), 334) Hay House.
Leading edge of medicine today is discovering how the mind & the emotions influence medical conditions. Goleman describes how many formerly "alternative" therapies are now being accepted into orthodox science.

Future of Book Publishing. unabr. ed. Dan Poynter. Read by Dan Poynter. 1 cass. (Running Time: 1 hr. 10 min.). 1993. 9.95 (978-1-56860-007-9(0), P-106) Para Pub.
Learn how the Information Highway will affect book publishing. Find out why smaller publishers are in a better position to move into electronic books. Dan Poynter describes what is happening & shows you how to profit from the changes. The Information Highway is being built. Make sure you are part of the steamroller, not part of the road. Cash in now.

Future of Capitalism: How Today's Economic Forces Shape Tomorrow's World. abr. ed. Lester C. Thurow. 2 cass. (Running Time: 4 hrs.). 1999. 24.95 (978-0-9660180-3-5(6)) Scholarly Audio.
Provides a productive look at the changing structure of the global economy & what it will take for individuals, firms & nations to succeed at the end of the century.

Future of Christian Music, Vol. 1. Diamante Staff. 2004. audio compact disk 5.99 (978-5-550-13784-0(4)) Nairi ARM.

Future of Civilization. unabr. ed. Karl Hess. 1 cass. (Running Time: 1 hr. 3 min.). 12.95 (969) J Norton Pubs.
Hess postulates that although impossible to predict anything due to many variables, our future rests in taking prudential actions today to situate ourselves for long survival; ideology does not move society, but organization does; people practicing civility is vital for the future of civilization.

Future of Communicating. 4 cass. 45.00 set. (9811) MEA A Watts Cass.

Future of Corporations. unabr. ed. Robert Bleiberg & Irving Kristol. 1 cass. (Running Time: 1 hr. 49 min.). 12.95 (279) J Norton Pubs.

Future of Electronic Benefits Transfer. 1 cass. (America's Supermarket Showcase '96 Ser.). 1996. 11.00 (NGA96-006) Sound Images.

Future of Freedom: Illiberal Democracy at Home & Abroad. Fareed Zakaria. 7 cass. (Running Time: 13 hrs. 30 min.). 2003. 49.95 (978-0-7861-2536-4(5)) Blckstn Audio.

Future of Freedom: Illiberal Democracy at Home & Abroad. Fareed Zakaria. Read by Ned Schmidtke. (Running Time: 10 hrs.). (C). 2003. 30.95 (978-1-59912-666-1(4)) Iofy Corp.

Future of Freedom: Illiberal Democracy at Home & Abroad. unabr. ed. Fareed Zakaria. Read by Ned Schmidtke. 8 CDs. (Running Time: 10 hrs.). 2003. audio compact disk 64.00 (978-0-7861-9039-3(6), 3165); audio compact disk 24.95 (978-0-7861-8863-5(4), 3165); 49.95 (978-0-7861-2564-7(0), 3165) Blckstn Audio.
Points out that the American form of democracy is one of the least democratic in use today.

Future of Freedom: Illiberal Democracy at Home & Abroad. unabr. ed. Fareed Zakaria. Read by Ned Schmidtke. 8 CDs. 2004. audio compact disk 35.95 (978-0-7861-9087-4(6)); reel tape 29.95 (978-0-7861-2565-4(9)) Blckstn Audio.
American democracy is, in many people's minds, the model for the rest of the world. Fareed Zakaria points out that the American form of democracy is one of the least democratic in use today. Members of the Supreme Court and the Federal Reserve, institutions that fundamentally shape our lives, are appointed, not elected. The Bill of Rights enumerates a set of privileges to which citizens are entitled, no matter what the majority says. By restricting our democracy, we enhance our freedom.

Future of Freedom: Illiberal Democracy at Home & Abroad. unabr. ed. Fareed Zakaria. Read by Ned Schmidtke. (Running Time: 36000 sec.). 2008. audio compact disk 19.95 (978-1-4332-1044-0(4)) Blckstn Audio.

Future of Great Britain. unabr. ed. Margaret Thatcher. 1 cass. (Running Time: 1 hr. 1 min.). 12.95 (388) J Norton Pubs.

Future of Humankind CD: Letters from the Field. Interview. Margaret Mead. Interview with Heywood Hale Broun, Jr. 1 CD. (Running Time: 51 mins.). (Heywood Hale Broun Ser.). 2006. audio compact disk 12.95 (978-1-57970-413-1(1), C40319D, Audio-For) J Norton Pubs.

Future of Justification: A Response to N. T. Wright. unabr. ed. John Piper. Narrated by Robertson Dean. (Running Time: 6 hrs. 0 mins. 0 sec.). (ENG.). 2007. lp 19.98 (978-1-59644-573-4(4)) christianaud.

***Future of Justification: A Response to N. T. Wright.** unabr. ed. John Piper. Narrated by Robertson Dean. (ENG.). 2008. 16.98 (978-1-59644-552-9(1), Hovel Audio) christianaud.

Future of Justification: A Response to N. T. Wright. unabr. ed. John Piper. Read by Robertson Dean. (Running Time: 6 hrs. 0 mins. 0 sec.). (ENG.). 2008. audio compact disk 26.98 (978-1-59644-551-2(3)) christianaud.

Future of Libertarianism. unabr. ed. Murray Newton Rothbard. 1 cass. (Running Time: 1 hr. 25 min.). 12.95 (216) J Norton Pubs.
Analyzes where the Libertarian movement is headed in the face of rising statism.

Future of Liberty & Alternative Lifestyles. Read by Bob McGinley & Linda Abrams. (Running Time: 60 min.). (Cypress College Ser.). 1980. 9.00 (F113) Freeland Pr.
Describes the direction of personal relationships & how society influences the structures of these relationship; Linda Abrams adds insights into the legal aspects of seeking alternative lifestyles when you wish to exclude the state. Panel discussion.

Future of Life. abr. ed. Edward O. Wilson. Read by Ed Begley, Jr. 6 CDs. (Running Time: 7.5 hrs.). 2004. audio compact disk 34.95 (978-1-59007-084-0(4)) Pub: New Millenn Enter. Dist(s): PerseuPGW
From one of the world's most influential scientists (and two-time Pulitzer Prize-winning author) comes his most timely and important book yet: an impassioned call for quick and decisive action to save Earth's biological heritage, and a plan to achieve that rescue.

Future of Life. unabr. ed. Edward O. Wilson. Read by Ed Begley, Jr. 6 cass. (Running Time: 9 hrs.). 2004. 34.95 (978-1-59007-083-3(6)) New Millenn Enter.

Future of Management. unabr. ed. Gary Hamel. Read by Sean Pratt. (Running Time: 8 hrs.). (ENG.). 2008. 24.98 (978-1-59659-189-9(7), GildAudio) Pub: Gildan Media. Dist(s): HachBkGrp

Future of Management. unabr. ed. Gary Hamel. Read by Gary Hamel. Read by Sean Pratt. Told to Bill Breen. 7 CDs. (Running Time: 8 hrs.). (ENG.). 2008. audio compact disk 29.98 (978-1-59659-161-5(7), GildAudio) Pub: Gildan Media. Dist(s): HachBkGrp

Future of Planet Earth Seminar Proceedings. Ed. by Jean Gilbertson. Des. by Kevan Rayne. (ENG.). 2009. pap. bk. (978-0-9794081-5-1(6)) Fndt for the Future.

Future of Politics. 4 cass. 45.00 set. (9911) MEA A Watts Cass.

Future of Religion. 4 cass. 45.00 set. (9611) MEA A Watts Cass.

Future of Scientific Research. unabr. ed. Abdus Salam. 1 cass. 1990. 12.95 (ECN097-A) J Norton Pubs.

***Future of Scientology & the Western Civilization.** L. Ron Hubbard. (ENG.). 2002. audio compact disk 15.00 (978-1-4031-1136-4(7)) Bridge Pubns Inc.

Future of Selling. Robert Krulwich. 1 cass. (Running Time: 35 min.). 9.95 (ME-82-08-16, HarperThor) HarpC GBR.

Future of the Dollar: Inflation vs. Deflation. unabr. ed. Julian Snyder. 1 cass. (Running Time: 28 min.). 12.95 (1113) J Norton Pubs.
Snyder attacks the Carter administration for depreciation of the dollar & the continued future inflation. He predicts the slaughter of international dollar holders as the first step toward the eventual economic death of the planet.

Future of the Economy: Alternatives & Methods for Economic Survival. Read by John Pugsley & Anthony Harris. (Running Time: 60 min.). (Cypress College Ser.). 1980. 9.00 (F108) Freeland Pr.
A discussion on alternate economic futures & ways to achieve the ultimate free market solutions. Panel discussion.

Future of the Family. John E. Bradshaw. (Running Time: 10800 sec.). 2008. audio compact disk 100.00 (978-1-57388-064-0(7)) J B Media.

Future of the Family: Returning the Family to Emotional Health. abr. ed. John Bradshaw. 2 cass. (Running Time: 3 hrs.). 1997. 18.00 (978-1-57388-063-3(9)) J B Media.
Author has turned to recent family research & recovery materials to explore the individual in both a family & societal setting. He concentrates on developing goodness & character.

Future of the Federal Reserve Board, Vol. 36. Tracy Herrick. 1 cass. (Running Time: 45 min.). (Money Talk Ser.). 1986. 7.95 B & H Comm.
Describes how the Federal Reserve Board became the nation's most powerful non-elected branch of the government & why it will be increasingly in the news.

Future of the Nixon Administration. unabr. ed. Herbert Klein. 1 cass. (Running Time: 37 min.). 12.95 (AFO177) J Norton Pubs.

Future of Warfare. Ed. by Marco A. V. Bitetto. 1 cass. 2000. (978-1-58578-334-2(X)) Inst of Cybernetics.

Future Planning. abr. ed. Linda L. McNeil. Read by Linda L. McNeil. 2 cass. (Running Time: 1 hrs. 20 min.). 1996. pap. bk. 49.95 Set; incl. computer disk. (978-1-891446-08-5(8)) Open Mind.
Leads user through the process of business planning & marketing strategy in a one day do-it-yourself format. Includes the 10 keys for successful planning. Specifically for small businesses.

Future Sounds. Ronald Gariboldi. 1 cass. 1990. 14.95 Alfred Pub.

Future Stakes: American Memory, Pt. 4. Charles Blitzer & Lynne V. Cheney. 1 cass. (400) Natl Humanities.

Future Tools of Perception. Alexander Shulgin. 1 cass. 9.00 (A0133-83) Sound Photosyn.
An urgent, heartfelt & impassioned plea from the synthesiser of MDMA. From the 1983 Psychedelic Conference, with Terence McKenna on tape.

Future Within Reach 2008: Regional Partnerships for the Millennium Developments Goals in Asia & the Pacific (Folder set includes book, overview booklet, CD-ROM & Delivering as One: Asia-Pacific Regional MDG Road Map 2008-2015) United Nations. 2009. pap. bk. 75.00 (978-92-1-120547-3(6)) Untd Nat Pubns.

Future World Oil Market. Cecil B. Thompson. (453) J Norton Pubs.

Futurehit. dna: How the digital revolution Is changing Top 10 Songs. Jay Frank. (ENG.). 2009. 24.95 (978-0-615-28570-2(8)) Futurehit.

Futureland: Nine Stories of an Imminent World. unabr. ed. Walter Mosley. Read by Richard Allen. 7 cass. (Running Time: 10 hrs.). 2001. 78.25 (978-1-58788-986-8(2), 1587889862, Unabridge Lib Edns); 32.95 (978-1-58788-985-1(4), 1587889854, BAU) Brilliance Audio.
Life in America a generation from now isn't much different from today: The drugs are better, the daily grind is worse. The gap between the rich and the poor has widened to a chasm. You can store the world's legal knowledge on a chip in your little finger, while the Supreme Court has decreed that constitutional rights don't apply to any individual who challenges the system. Justice is swiftly delivered by automated courts, so the prison industry is booming. And while the media declare racism is dead, word on the street is that even in a colorless society, it's a crime to be black. But the world still turns and folks still have to get by with the hands they're dealt, folks such as: Ptolemy "Popo" Bent: This gentle backwoods child has a genius I.Q.- and a soul so pure that officials want him locked up forever... Folio Johnson: A hardboiled, cyber-augmented private eye who can see beneath the dark poetry of the metropolis, he will need an even greater edge than that to find out who's systematically murdering rich, young Nazis... Fera Jones: She's the boxing Queen of the Ring who must still fight all comers to save her dad, preserve her identity, and protect the fans who believe in her... Dr. Ivan Kismet: The world's richest man, Macrocode's CEO is a tycoon, tyrant, and messiah who is evidently more powerful than God. So it's too bad for everyone that Dr. Kismet is utterly insane... Walter Mosley brings to life the celebs, working stiffs, leaders, victims, technocrats, crooks, oppressors, and revolutionaries who inhabit a glorious all-American nightmare that's just around the corner. Welcome to FUTURELAND.

Futureland: Nine Stories of an Imminent World. unabr. ed. Walter Mosley. Read by Richard Allen. (Running Time: 10 hrs.). 2004. 39.25 (978-1-59335-447-3(9), 1593354479, Brinc Audio MP3 Lib) Brilliance Audio.

Futureland: Nine Stories of an Imminent World. unabr. ed. Walter Mosley. Read by Richard Allen. (Running Time: 10 hrs.). 2004. 39.25 (978-1-59710-316-9(0), 1597103160, BADLE); 24.95 (978-1-59710-317-6(9), 1597103179, BAD) Brilliance Audio.

Futureland: Nine Stories of an Imminent World. unabr. ed. Walter Mosley. Read by Richard Allen. (Running Time: 10 hrs.). 2004. 24.95 (978-1-59335-086-4(4), 1593350864) Soulmate Audio Bks.

Futures, Elections. Tyrone Williams. (ENG.). 2005. 10.00 (978-1-933675-02-2(0)) Dos Madres Pr.

Futureshaping. Richard A. Zarro. 14 cass. (Running Time: 21 hrs.). Incl. Becoming a Transformer. (Running Time: 3 hrs.). 1987. (978-0-944812-06-8(6)); Gaia & the Omega Point. (Running Time: 3 hrs.). 1987. (978-0-944812-00-6(7)); Lucid Dreaming & Dream Programming. (Running Time: 3 hrs.). 1987. (978-0-944812-05-1(8)); New Age of Mind & Consciousness. (Running Time: 3 hrs.). 1987. (978-0-944812-01-3(5)); Visualization Programming of the Human Bio-Computer. (Running Time: 3 hrs.). 1987. (978-0-944812-02-0(3)); 1987. 19.00 ea.; 95.00 Set. Trans Tech NY.

Futurist. Marco A. V. Bitetto. Read by Marco A. V. Bitetto. 1 cass. 2000. (978-1-58578-020-4(0)) Inst of Cybernetics.

Futurist. unabr. ed. James P. Othmer. Read by William Dufris. (Running Time: 10 hrs. 0 mins. 0 sec.). (ENG.). 2006. audio compact disk 24.99 (978-1-4001-5248-3(8)); audio compact disk 69.99 (978-1-4001-3248-5(7)); audio compact disk 34.99 (978-1-4001-0248-8(0)) Pub: Tantor Media. Dist(s): IngramPubServ
Yates is a Futurist. Which is to say he makes a very good living flying around the world dispensing premonitory wisdom, aka prepackaged bull, to world governments, corporations, and global leadership conferences. He is an optimist by trade and a cynic by choice. He's the kind of man who can give a lecture on successive days to a leading pesticide manufacturer and the Organic Farmers of America, and receive standing ovations at both. But just as the American Empire is beginning to fray around the edges, so too is Yates's carefully scripted existence. On the way to the Futureworld Conference in Johannesburg, he opens a handwritten note from his girlfriend, saying she's left him for a sixth-grade history teacher. Then he witnesses a soccer riot in which a number of South Africans are killed, to the chagrin of the South African PR people at Futureworld. Sparked by a heroic devastation of his minibar and inspired by the rookie hooker sent to his hotel room courtesy of his hosts, Yates delivers a spectacularly career-ending speech at Futureworld, which leads to a sound beating, a meeting with some quasi-governmental creeps, and a hazy mission to go around the world answering the question: Why does everyone hate us?.

Fuzz. unabr. ed. Ed McBain, pseud. Read by Jonathan Marosz. 7 cass. (Running Time: 7 hrs.). (87th Precinct Ser.: Bk. 22). 1997. 42.00 (978-0-7366-3637-7(4), 4298) Books on Tape.
The death threats are the work of a crank - or so the detectives at the 87th Precinct believe.

Fuzzy Navel. abr. ed. J. A. Konrath. (Running Time: 3 hrs.). (Jacqueline "Jack" Daniels Mystery Ser.). 2009. audio compact disk 14.99 (978-1-4233-1260-4(0), 9781423312604, BCD Value Price) Brilliance Audio.

Fuzzy Navel. unabr. ed. J. A. Konrath. Read by Susie Breck & Dick Hill. (Running Time: 7 hrs.). (Jacqueline "Jack" Daniels Mystery Ser.). 2008. 24.95 (978-1-4233-1255-0(4), 9781423312550, Brilliance MP3); 24.95 (978-1-4233-1257-4(0), 9781423312574, BAD); audio compact disk 29.95 (978-1-4233-1253-6(8), 9781423312536, Bril Audio CD Unabri) Brilliance Audio.

Fuzzy Navel. unabr. ed. J. A. Konrath et al. (Running Time: 7 hrs.). (Jacqueline "Jack" Daniels Mystery Ser.). 2008. 39.25 (978-1-4233-1256-7(2), 9781423312567, Brinc Audio MP3 Lib); 39.25 (978-1-4233-1258-1(9), 9781423312581, BADLE); audio compact disk 82.25 (978-1-4233-1254-3(6), 9781423312543, BriAudCD Unabrid) Brilliance Audio.

Fuzzy Thinking: The New Science of Fuzzy Logic. abr. ed. Bart Kosko. Read by Michael Toms. 2 cass. (Running Time: 3 hrs.). 1995. 16.95 (978-0-944993-97-2(4)) Audio Lit.
Shows us how fuzzy thinking can lead us out of the rigid system of binary logic to a world view reflecting the ancient truths of the East. Fuzzy logic like the great Tao embraces both yin & yong & opens our minds to the ambiguity of existence.

Fynn, My Fiery Friend. Colleen Beckwith. (ENG.). (J). 2007. (978-0-9799957-0-5(1)) Beck & Blue.

F2f the ultimate thriller of high-tech Terror: The Ultimate Thriller of High-Tech Terror. Phillip Finch. 2004. 10.95 (978-0-7435-4694-2(6)) Pub: S&S Audio. Dist(s): S and S Inc

G

G. A. Henty Short Story Collection Vol.1: Featuring Surly Joe & the Frontier Girl. Read by Jim Weis. (YA). 2004. audio compact disk Rental 14.99 (978-1-931587-38-9(8)) PrestonSpeed.

G. A. Henty Short Story Collection, Vol. 1. Short Stories. Read by Jim Weiss. Prod. by Greathall Productions. 1 CD. (Running Time: 70 Minutes). Dramatization. (YA). 2004. audio compact disk 14.95 (978-1-882513-98-7(3)) Greathall Prods.
Fans of GA Henty may be familiar with the beloved author's more than seventy historical novels, which offer vivid, accurate protraits of three thousand years of human history-here are two short stories: Frontier Girl and Surly Joe.In Frontier Girl, a fifteen year old girl on the Ohio frontier must employ her wits and all her physical skills to save her parents and herself during a native uprising. In Surly Joe, an English sailor of the late 1800s reveals his own story of honor, sacrifice, despair and personal redemption. Both stories reflect henty's code of courage and moral uplift.

G. B. Shaw on War. George Bernard Shaw. Read by George Bernard Shaw. 10.00 (HE819) Esstee Audios.
In a 1937 BBC broadcast, the playwright gives his views on the violence of war.

G. E. Murray. unabr. ed. Interview with G. E. Murray. 1 cass. (Running Time: 29 min.). 1985. 10.00 New Letters.
One of a weekly half-hour radio program with authors talking & presenting their own works. Chicago poet G.E. Murray here reads from Repairs.

G. I. JOURNAL: Mel Blanc, Arthur Treacher & Loraine Day, Ranson Sherman. Perf. by Mel Blanc et al. 1 cass. (Running Time: 1 hr.). 2001. 6.98 (1658) Radio Spirits.

"G" Is for Grafton. unabr. ed. N. Kaufman & C. Kay. Read by Bernadette Dunne. 10 cass. (Running Time: 15 hrs.). (Kinsey Millhone Mystery Ser.). 1998. 80.00 (978-0-7366-4085-5(1), 4594) Books on Tape.
This lively book is a "biography" of Sue Grafton's detective, Kinsey Millhone. A fascinating picture of an author & her creation.

G Is for Gumshoe. unabr. collector's ed. Sue Grafton. Read by Mary Peiffer. 6 cass. (Running Time: 9 hrs.). (Kinsey Millhone Mystery Ser.). 1994. 48.00 (978-0-7366-2679-8(4), 3415) Books on Tape.
For Kinsey's 33rd birthday, she received the top slot on Tyrone Patty's hit list. Obviously, it would turn out to be a birthday to remember. Once again, she's on a case at the heart of which is a long-buried betrayal.

G-Man's Life: The FBI, Being 'Deep Throat, ' & the Struggle for Honor in Washington. unabr. ed. Mark Felt & John O'Connor. Narrated by Michael Prichard. (Running Time: 13 hrs. 0 mins. 0 sec.). (ENG.). 2006. audio compact disk 75.99 (978-1-4001-3229-4(0)) Pub: Tantor Media. Dist(s): IngramPubServ

G-Man's Life: The FBI, Being 'Deep Throat, ' & the Struggle for Honor in Washington. unabr. ed. Mark Felt & John O'Connor. Read by Michael Prichard. (Running Time: 13 hrs. 0 mins. 0 sec.). (ENG.). 2006. audio compact disk 24.99 (978-1-4001-5229-2(1)) Pub: Tantor Media. Dist(s): IngramPubServ

G-Man's Life: The FBI, Being Deep Throat, & the Struggle for Honor in Washington. Mark Felt & John O'Connor. Read by Michael Prichard. (Playaway Adult Nonfiction Ser.). (ENG.). 2009. 69.99 (978-1-60847-906-1(4)) Find a World.

G-Man's Life: The FBI, Being Deep Throat, & the Struggle for Honor in Washington. unabr. ed. Mark Felt & John O'Connor. Narrated by Michael Prichard. (Running Time: 13 hrs. 0 mins. 0 sec.). (ENG.). 2006. audio compact disk 37.99 (978-1-4001-0229-7(4)) Pub: Tantor Media. Dist(s): IngramPubServ

G. S. Sharat Chandra. unabr. ed. Read by G. S. Chandra. 1 cass. (Running Time: 29 min.). 1985. 10.00 New Letters.
A poet from India who has lived in the U. S. for many years reads poems about both countries.

GAAP Guide Level A. Jan R. Williams & Joseph V. Carcello. 2007. audio compact disk 169.00 (978-0-8080-9129-5(8)) Toolkit Media.

GAAP Guide Level A on CD-ROM, 2007 (Standalone CD) 2007th rev. ed. Jan R. Williams & Joseph V. Carcello. 2006. audio compact disk 159.00 (978-0-8080-9061-8(5)) Toolkit Media.

Gable Faces East, Set. Anita Stansfield. 5 cass. 2004. 19.95 (978-1-57734-526-8(6), 07002173) Covenant Comms.

Gables Against the Sky. Anita Stansfield. 5 cass. 2004. 19.95 (978-1-57734-608-1(4)) Covenant Comms.

Gables of Legacy: The Guardian. Anita Stansfield. 3 cass. 2004. 14.95 (978-1-59156-082-1(9)) Covenant Comms.

Gables of Legacy Vol. 2: A Guiding Star. Anita Stansfield. 3 cass. 2004. 14.95 (978-1-59156-112-5(4)) Covenant Comms.

Gables of Legacy Vol. 3: The Silver Linings. Anita Stansfield. 3 cass. 2004. 14.95 (978-1-59156-169-9(8)) Covenant Comms.

Gables of Legacy Vol. 4: An Eternal Bond. Anita Stansfield. 3 cass. 2004. 14.95 (978-1-59156-295-5(3)); audio compact disk 15.95 (978-1-59156-318-1(6)) Covenant Comms.

Gables of Legacy Vol. 5: The Miracle. Anita Stansfield. 3 cass. 2004. 14.95 (978-1-59156-322-8(4)); audio compact disk 15.95 (978-1-59156-323-5(2)) Covenant Comms.

***Gabriel Allon: Moscow Rules, the Defector.** abr. ed. Daniel Silva. Read by Phil Gigante. (Running Time: 12 hrs.). (Gabriel Allon Ser.: Nos. 8-9). 2010. audio compact disk 19.99 (978-1-4418-6168-9(8), 9781441861689, BACD) Brilliance Audio.

Gabriel en Espana. NTC/Contemporary Publishing Group Staff. (Gabriel, the Happy Ghost Ser.). (J). 59.95 (978-0-8442-7342-6(2), Natl Textbk Co) M-H Contemporary.
Presents a series of adventure fantasies in Spanish & English featuring Gabriel Ghost.

Gabriel en Puerto Rico. NTC Publishing Group Staff. 1 cass. (Gabriel, the Happy Ghost Ser.). 59.95 (978-0-8442-7341-9(4), Natl Textbk Co) M-H Contemporary.
Presents a series of adventures in Spanish & English featuring Gabriel the Ghost.

Gabriel Hounds, unabr. ed. Mary Stewart. Narrated by Davina Porter. 8 cass. (Running Time: 11 hrs. 15 mins.). 1991. 70.00 (978-1-55690-192-8(5), 91202E7) Recorded Bks.
A young woman pays a visit to her mysterious Great Aunt Harriet in Dar Ibrahim, a palace atop a hill in Lebanon's Adonis Valley. Though her family has told of her aunt's many eccentricities, Christabel is unprepared for what lurks behind Dar Ibrahim's walls.

Gabriole O'Annonzio from Terra Vergine: Multilingual Books Literature. Excerpts. Ed. by Maurizio Falyhera & Cristina Giocometti. 1 CD. (Running Time: 90 mins.). (Audio Anthology of Italian Literature Ser.: 12). (ITA.). 1999. audio compact disk 29.95 (978-1-58214-123-7(1)) Language Assocs.

Gabriole O'Annonzio from Terra Vergine Vol. 12: Multilingual Books Literature. Excerpts. Ed. by Maurizio Falyhera & Cristina Giocometti. 1 cass. (Running Time: 90 mins.). (Audio Anthology of Italian Literature Ser.: 12). (ITA.). 1999. spiral bd. 19.95 (978-1-58214-122-0(3)) Language Assocs.

Gadiantons & the Silver Sword, Set. Chris Heimerdinger. 2 cass. 11.98 (978-1-55503-350-7(4), 071934) Covenant Comms.
Fiction at its best-adventurous "Tennis Shoes" sequel.

Gadiantons & the Silver Sword, Vol. 2. Chris Heimerdinger. 4 cass. (Tennis Shoes Adventure Ser.). 2004. 19.95 (978-1-57734-470-4(7), 07002319); audio compact disk 21.95 (978-1-59156-066-1(7)) Covenant Comms.

Gael Force. 1 cass., 1 CD. 11.18 (GRV 210); audio compact disk 15.18 CD Jewel box. (GRV 210) NewSound.

Gaelcheol Tire Phlearaca Chonamara. (ENG.). 1994. 13.95 (978-0-8023-7108-9(6)); audio compact disk 21.95 (978-0-8023-8108-8(1)) Pub: Clo Iar-Chonnachta IRL. Dist(s): Dufour

Gaelic Made Easy, Set. John M. Paterson. 4 cass., 4 bklets. (Running Time: 4 hrs.). (GAE & ENG.). 1992. pap. bk. 89.95 (978-0-88432-443-0(5), AFSG20) J Norton Pubs.
Foreign Language Instruction. An introductory, full-length course developed in Glasgow. Forty-three lesson units include an interesting section of "do's & don'ts" of grammatical usage with examples that begins each lesson, which includes vocabulary & readings in Gaelic. English translations given at the end of each lesson unit.

Gaelic Made Easy 4 CDs & 4 Booklets. John Paterson. 4 CDs. (Running Time: 4 hrs.). (GAE.). 2005. audio compact disk 89.95 (978-1-57970-124-6(8), AFSG20D) J Norton Pubs.

Gaelic Songs & Legends. Perf. by Ann Moray. 1 cass. (Running Time: 60 mins.). (GAE & ENG.). 2001. 14.95 (C11322) J Norton Pubs.
Songs (in Gaelic) of love & longing for family, lullabies, the sea & the world of fairies plus a few uncanny stories in English.

Gaelic Songs & Legends CDg. Perf. by Ann Moray. 1 CD. (Running Time: 50 mins.). (GAE.). 2006. audio compact disk 14.95 (978-1-57970-388-2(7), C11322D, Audio-For) J Norton Pubs.
Songs in Gaelic of love and longing for family, lullabies, the sea, and the world of fairies. Sung by Ann Moray, who also tells a few uncanny stories in English.

Gafni on Advocacy in Non-Jury Trials. 1992. bk. 99.00 (AC-762) PA Bar Inst.
No judge in Philadelphia can offer more pragmatic tips on how to handle a case in this forum. Learn what distinguishes jury & bench trials. Find out how you can make it easier for the judge to hold for your client. Get insights on how to ensure that your judge reaches a timely decision.

Gahan Megher Chaya. A. Mohit. Voice by Sheema Mohit. 1 cd. 1999. audio compact disk 10.00 (978-0-9647672-6-3(0)) Beacon Hse IN.

Gahan Wilson, Cartoonist: Childhood Fears. Gahan Wilson. Read by Gahan Wilson. 1 cass. (Running Time: 30 min.). (A0420B090, HarperThor) HarpC GBR.

Gai-Jin Pt. 1: A Novel of Japan. unabr. collector's ed. James Clavell. Read by John Lee. 11 cass. (Running Time: 16 hrs. 30 min.). 2000. 88.00 (978-0-7366-5912-3(9)) Books on Tape.
Malcolm Stuan, the heir to the Noble House, meets a young French woman who will after his destiny & his family's entire legacy.

Gai-Jin Pt. 2: A Novel of Japan. unabr. collector's ed. James Clavell. Read by John Lee. 13 cass. (Running Time: 19 hrs. 30 min.). 2000. 104.00 (978-0-7366-5974-1(9)) Books on Tape.

Gai-Jin Pt. 3: A Novel of Japan. unabr. collector's ed. James Clavell. Read by John Lee. 11 cass. (Running Time: 16 hrs. 30 min.). 2000. 88.00 (978-0-7366-5975-8(7)) Books on Tape.

Gaia & the Omega Point see Futureshaping

Gaia Consciousness. Ralph Metzner. 1 cass. 9.00 (A0429-88) Sound Photosyn.

Gaia's Children. Theosophical Society Staff. 1 cass. (Running Time: 60 min.). 1989. 8.95 (978-0-8356-1902-8(0)) Theos Pub Hse.
Feminism & respect for nature.

Gaia's Ovation: Mother Nature's Ongoing Clapping. Prod. by Thomas W. Gustin. 2 CDs. (Running Time: 2hrs. 38mins., 49secs). 2005. audio compact disk 16.00 (978-0-9761848-7-4(7), GO1) Gustech.
Gaia's Ovation (Mother Nature's Clapping) is a compilation of 316 (all different) back-to-back "Thunder Thingy's"; all recorded live here at the Emerald Cave; from 15 different storms over several years; claps & rolls; some with rain and/or birds' some roll over a minute. These are the new definition of "Reality CDs," a true "Concert for all Seasons." Like the Emerald Cave Recordings, these are 99.9% pure Nature Sounds, a "Must-Hear-to-Believe" Audio Treat.

Gaidhlig Blasad (A Taste of Gaelic) unabr. ed. Donald MacLennan. 1 cass. (gr. 10-12). pap. bk. 21.95 (978-0-88432-615-1(2), AFSG10) J Norton Pubs.
Essential words & phrases of everyday conversation.

Gail E Haley: Wood & Linoleum Illustration. 2004. 8.95 (978-1-56008-902-5(4)); cass. & flmstrp 30.00 (978-1-56008-672-7(6)) Weston Woods.

Gail E Haley: Wood & Linoleum Illustration; Go Away, Stay Away. 2004. cass. & flmstrp 30.00 (978-1-56008-808-0(7)) Weston Woods.

Gail Gibbons' Creatures Great & Small Series. Gail Gibbons. Illus. by Gail Gibbons. 55 vols. (Running Time: 78 mins.). (J). (gr. 1-6). 2000. pap. bk. 76.95 (978-0-87499-579-4(5)) Live Oak Media.
Includes: "Sea Turtles," "Sharks," "Spiders," "Whales" & "Wolves.".

Gail Godwin Interview with Kay Bonetti. Interview. Interview with Gail Godwin & Kay Bonetti. 1 cass. 1986. 13.95 (978-1-55644-160-8(6), 6072) Am Audio Prose.
Discusses the recurring themes & aesthetic concerns which inform her novels & short fiction.

Gain Control over Health Problems. 1998. 24.95 (978-1-58557-014-0(1)) Dynamic Growth.

Gain More Through Goal Setting. unabr. ed. Tom Hopkins. Read by Tom Hopkins. 1 cass. (Self-Help Ser.). 1986. 9.95 (978-0-07-030370-6(3), TDM 1081) HarperCollins Pubs.
Designed to help the listener focus on a particular area of his or her personal or professional life & learn how to deal with it better, achieving more, succeeding more often & finding greater happiness & satisfaction on a day-to-day basis. In this program, Hopkins lays out a plan for greater achievement through effective goal setting, showing what real goals are & why they are essential.

Gain the Confidence to Overcome Fear in Public Speaking. unabr. ed. Ed Foreman. 2 cass. (Running Time: 1 hr. 50 min.). 1989. 29.95 Set. (978-1-893603-05-9(9)) Exec Dev Syst.
Step-by-step approach to becoming an effective communicator: one-on-one or to any size audience.

Gaining a Fresh Perspective. 2002. 20.95 (978-1-57972-511-2(2)); audio compact disk 29.00 (978-1-57972-512-9(0)) Insight Living.

Gaining Competitive Advantage. Bill Caskey. 1 CD. (Running Time: 66 mins). 2003. audio compact disk 39.95 (978-0-9722587-3-9(6)) Caskey Ach Strat.

Gaining Control of Your Future: Staying Younger Longer. unabr. ed. Jerry V. Teplitz. 4 cass. (Running Time: 4 hrs.). 50.00 (118) Happiness Unltd.
Begins by focusing in our mind. It shows the listener how completely powerful we really are. You can try the techniques & prove it yourself. The Longevity Factors part of the album focuses on the three key factors involved in living longer healthfully. Those factors are nutrition, exercise & attitude. Listeners will understand the many things they can do in their own lives to live longer. By listening to the album you will be able to choose the quality of your life experience. It will put you back in charge.

Gaining Control of Your Mind. Charles R. Swindoll. 2009. audio compact disk 12.00 (978-1-57972-840-3(5)) Insight Living.

Gaining Employment. Bill Wells. Read by Paul Linnman & Nancy Schifferdecker. Ed. by Dan Clark & Bill Berry. 1 cass. (Running Time: 55 min.). 1993. 9.95 (978-1-881884-02-6(3), MC101) Berry Music.
Includes excerpts from over 10 hours of interviews with personnel officers & human resources professionals speaking about what they look for in a job applicant, how to dress, resumes, eye contact, etc.

Gaining Proficiency in English. Avis Agin & Johanna P. Prather. 8 cass. (YA). 89.00 incl. 150 activity masters, guide. (978-0-89525-260-9(0), AKC 223) Ed Activities.
A course in understanding & correct usage of the basic elements of the English language. Emphasizes functional & practical application of grammar in the classroom & in on-the-job situations & includes correct usage of nouns, verbs, clauses, pronouns, prepositions, conjuctions, interjections.

Gaining the Edge: Building Business in the 21st Century: Audio Book. John De Puy. Ed. by Palm Tree Productons. Told to David T. Walters. (ENG.). 2008. audio compact disk (978-0-9799879-5-3(4)) Palm Tree.

Gaining Thinness. Dean A. Montalbano. 2 cds. (Running Time: 2.25 hrs). (Hypnotic Sensory Response Audio Ser.). 2004. audio compact disk 39.95 (978-1-932086-17-1(X)) L Lizards Pub Co.

Gaining Thinness Self Hypnosis Set. Dean A. Montalbano. (Hypnotic Sensory Response Audio Ser.). 1999. 39.95 (978-0-9708772-8-4(5)) L Lizards Pub Co.

Gaining Through Losing. 1 cass. (Running Time: 1 hr.). 10.95 (OP-80-05-14, HarperThor) HarpC GBR.

Gaining Weight. Bruce Goldberg. Read by Bruce Goldberg. 1 cass. (Running Time: 25 min.). (ENG.). 2006. 13.00 (978-1-885577-53-5(2)) Pub: B Goldberg. Dist(s): Baker Taylor
Self-hypnosis.

Gaither Vocal Band & Ernie Haase & Signature Sound... Together. Contrib. by Gaither Vocal Band et al. Prod. by Bill Gaither. Contrib. by Barry Jennings. Prod. by Ernie Haase. (Running Time: 2 hrs.). (Gaither Gospel Ser.). 2007. 19.99 (978-5-557-57350-4(X)) Gaither Music Co.

Gaither Vocal Band & Ernie Haase & Signature Sound... Together. Contrib. by Gaither Vocal Band et al. Prod. by Bill Gaither et al. (Gaither Gospel Ser.). 2007. audio compact disk 13.99 (978-5-557-57348-1(8)) Gaither Music Co.

Gal: A True Life. abr. ed. Ruthie M. Bolton. Read by Cch Pounder. 2 cass. (Running Time: 3 hrs.). 1995. 16.95 (978-0-944993-92-7(3)) Audio Lit.
In the midst of poverty in the rural South, Bolton's life demonstrates the capacity of the human spirit to overcome seemingly impossible odds.

Galactic Club. unabr. collector's ed. Ronald N. Bracewell. Read by Michael Prichard. 5 cass. (Running Time: 5 hrs.). (Portable Stanford Ser.). 1984. 30.00 (978-0-7366-0972-2(5), 1914) Books on Tape.
A scholastic examination of the possibility that life exists beyond our universe.

Galactic Conquest. Contrib. by Eleventyseven. 2007. audio compact disk 11.99 (978-5-557-60939-5(3)) Flicker.

Galactic Distances. 1 cass. (Running Time: 29 min.). 14.95 (23578) MMI Corp.
Astronomers discuss distance in astronomy, measuring distance, is there an end to the universe?.

Galactic North. unabr. ed. Alastair Reynolds. (Running Time: 12 hrs. 30 mins. 0 sec.). (ENG.). 2009. 29.99 (978-1-4001-6054-9(5)); audio compact disk 79.99 (978-1-4001-4054-1(4)); audio compact disk 39.99 (978-1-4001-1054-4(8)) Pub: Tantor Media. Dist(s): IngramPubServ

Galactic Pot-Healer. unabr. ed. Philip K. Dick. Read by Tom Parker. 4 cass. (Running Time: 6 hrs.). 1998. 32.95 (978-0-7861-1349-1(9), 2252) Blckstn Audio.
Combining quixotic adventure, horror & deliriously paranoid theology, this is a uniquely Dickian voyage to alternate worlds of the imagination. If the Glimming is a god, is it positive or malign?.

Galactosemia - A Bibliography & Dictionary for Physicians, Patients, & Genome Researchers. Compiled by Icon Group International, Inc. Staff. 2007. ring bd. 28.95 (978-0-497-11216-5(7)) Icon Grp.

Galante's Venture Capital & Private Equity Directory: 2000 Edition. Ed. by Steven P. Galante & Keith W. Moore. 2000. audio compact disk 395.00 (978-1-893648-05-0(2)) Dow JonesCo.

Galapagos Galore. Daniel Polin. Photos by Sis Polin. Contrib. by Susana Struve. 1 CD. (Running Time: 90 mins.). (ENG & SPA., 1999. pap. bk. 29.95 (978-0-9645795-2-1(9)) Light Words & Music.

Galatea 2.2. unabr. collector's ed. Richard Powers. Read by Michael Kramer. 9 cass. (Running Time: 13 hrs. 30 min.). 1996. 72.00 (978-0-7366-3349-9(9), 3999) Books on Tape.
A novelist programs a computer to pass English literature exams, & it comforts him when he loses faith. A modern-day Pygmalion story.

Galatians: A Letter of Liberation. unabr. ed. Charles R. Swindoll. 10 cass. (Running Time: 8 hrs.). 1998. 48.95 (978-1-57972-113-8(3)) Insight Living.

Galatians - Biblical Studies. Douglas Wilson. (ENG.). 2003. audio compact disk 84.00 (978-1-59128-368-3(X)) Canon Pr ID.

Galatians - Philippians - Colossians. (LifeLight Ser.). audio compact disk 15.00 (978-0-570-07856-2(3), 20-3318) Concordia.

Galatians Commentary. Chuck Missler. 8 CD's. (Running Time: 8 hours aprox). (Chuck Missler Commentaries). 2008. audio compact disk 44.95 (978-1-57821-408-2(4)) Koinonia Hse.

Galatians Commentary: Verse-by-Verse with Chuck Missler. Chuck Missler. 1 CD Rom. (Running Time: 10 hrs.). 2000. cd-rom 29.95 (978-1-57821-117-3(4)) Koinonia Hse.
The Book of Galatians is regarded as one of the greatest and most important of Paul's epistles. Galatians, more than any other single book, became the manifesto of freedom and revival of Biblical truth in the Reformation Era. It stands as a challenge to all who would seek to take away the joy and freedom of the Gospel of Grace.

Galatians-mp3-Vol. 1: Lessons from Antioch. Read by Douglas Wilson. 8. 2003. 22.00 (978-1-59128-455-0(4)) Canon Pr ID.

Galatians-mp3-Vol. 2: Abraham, Sarah & Hagar. Read by Douglas Wilson. 8. 2004. 22.00 (978-1-59128-461-1(9)) Canon Pr ID.

Galatians-mp3-Vol. 3: Liberty & Love. Read by Douglas Wilson. 5. 2004. 13.00 (978-1-59128-464-2(3)) Canon Pr ID.

Galatians-tape-Vol. 1: Lessons from Antioch. Read by Douglas Wilson. 8 cass. 2003. 28.00 (978-1-59128-457-4(0)) Canon Pr ID.

Galatians-tape-Vol. 2: Liberty & Love. Read by Douglas Wilson. 5 cass. 2004. 17.00 (978-1-59128-466-6(X)) Canon Pr ID.

Galatians-tape-Vol. 3: Abraham, Sarah & Hagar. Read by Douglas Wilson. 8 cass. 2004. 28.00 (978-1-59128-463-5(5)) Canon Pr ID.

Galaxy. Douglas Adams. 2005. 34.99 (978-1-59895-039-7(8)) Find a World.

Galaxy. unabr. ed. Douglas Adams. (ENG.). 2008. audio compact disk 24.95 (978-1-60283-511-5(X)) Pub: AudioGO. Dist(s): Perseus Dist

Galaxy. unabr. ed. Douglas Adams. Read by Alexander Adams. 5 cass. (Running Time: 5 hrs.). (Hitchhiker's Guide to the Galaxy Ser.). 1994. 30.00 (978-0-7366-2681-1(6), 3417) Books on Tape.
Mild-mannered, out-to-lunch earthling Arthur Dent is plucked from his planet by his friend Ford Prefect seconds before it is demolished to make way for a hyperspace bypass.

Galaxy. unabr. ed. Douglas Adams. Read by Stephen Fry. 5 CDs. (Running Time: 6 hrs.). (ENG.). 2005. audio compact disk 27.95 (978-0-7393-2220-8(6), Random AudioBks) Pub: Random Audio Pubg. Dist(s): Random

Galaxy, Vol. 4. unabr. ed. Douglas Adams. Read by Douglas Adams. 4 cass. (Running Time: 6 hrs.). 2004. 25.00 (978-1-59007-256-1(1)) Pub: New Millenn Enter. Dist(s): PerseuPGW

Galaxy Trilogy: Star Ways, Druid's World, & the Day the World Stopped. unabr. ed. Poul Anderson et al. Read by Tom Weiner. (Running Time: 48600 sec.). 2007. 89.95 (978-1-4332-0224-7(7)) Blckstn Audio.

Galaxy Trilogy: Star Ways/Druid's World/the Day the World Stopped. unabr. ed. Poul Anderson et al. Read by Tom Weiner. (Running Time: 48600 sec.). 2007. audio compact disk 99.00 (978-1-4332-0225-4(5)); audio compact disk 29.95 (978-1-4332-0226-1(3)) Blckstn Audio.

Galaxy Trilogy, Vol. 3: Giants from Eternity, Lords of Atlantis, & City on the Moon. unabr. ed. Manly Wade Wellman et al. Read by Tom Weiner. (Running Time: 13 hrs. 50 mins.). (ENG.). 2009. 29.95 (978-1-4332-9281-1(5)); 79.95 (978-1-4332-9277-4(7)); audio compact disk 109.00 (978-1-4332-9278-1(5)) Blckstn Audio.

Galaxy Trilogy, Vol. 4: (Across Time, Mission to a Star, the Rim of Space) unabr. ed. Belknap Grinnell & Chandler. Read by Tom Weiner. (Running Time: 1 hr. 0 mins.). (ENG.). 2009. 29.95 (978-1-4417-0020-9(X)); 72.95 (978-1-4417-0016-2(1)); audio compact disk 105.00 (978-1-4417-0017-9(X)) Blckstn Audio.

Galaxy Trilogy, Volume 2: A Collection of Tales from the Early Days of Science Fiction. unabr. ed. Various Authors. Read by Tom Weiner. (Running Time: 13 hrs. 50 mins.). (ENG.). 2009. 29.95 (978-1-4332-9111-1(8)); 79.95 (978-1-4332-9107-4(X)); audio compact disk 99.00 (978-1-4332-9108-1(8)) Blckstn Audio.

Galaxy 3000. unabr. ed. Roni S. Denholtz. 1 cass. (Running Time: 20 min.). (Fun to Read Ser.). (J). (gr. 3-6). 1983. bk. 16.99 (978-0-934898-42-3(1)); pap. bk. 9.95 (978-0-934898-30-0(8)) Jan Prods.
It is the year 3000. Cylia & Gregg Ryan, along with their parents, are forced to land their interstellar spaceship on a mysterious planet complete with an out-of-this-world amusement park. It seems like fun, until strange things begin to happen.

Galaxy 4, Vol. 4. Read by Peter Purves. 2 CDs. (Running Time: 1 hr. 40 mins.). 2001. audio compact disk 15.99 (978-0-563-47700-6(8)) London Brdge.

Gale Force. unabr. collector's ed. Elleston Trevor. Read by Rupert Keenlyside. 6 cass. (Running Time: 9 hrs.). 1984. 48.00 (978-0-7366-0599-1(1), 1566) Books on Tape.
Captain Carlsen was finally rescued from the Flying Enterprise after days alone aboard his doomed ship, many people must have thought. What a tale Conrad would have made of this. Elleston Trevor has done it. Gale Force transforms an epic of our own time into a novel of the sea with a dramatic grip & haunting descriptive power which irresistibly reminds the reader of Typhoon.

Gale Force Winds: Acts 4:23-31. Ed Young. 1997. 4.95 (978-0-7417-2154-9(6), A1154) Win Walk.

Galilee. unabr. ed. Clive Barker. Narrated by Paul Hecht. 17 cass. (Running Time: 23 hrs. 45 mins.). 1999. 141.00 (978-0-7887-2485-5(1), 95560E7) Recorded Bks.
An intriguing saga of two families bound by a shared history of murder, insanity & adultery. This takes listeners to the realm of the supernatural. When Rachel Geary & Galilee, the seductive prince of the Barbaross clan, fall in love, they unleash powerful forces that could destroy both dynasties.

Galileo. unabr. ed. James Reston, Jr. Read by Jeff Riggenbach. 9 cass. (Running Time: 13 hrs.). 1995. 62.95 (978-0-7861-0889-3(4), 1677) Blckstn Audio.
For the last four hundred years, Galileo has fascinated & inspired writers, theologians, playwrights, historians, & scientists. As the founder of modern science & the embodiment of the conflict between science & faith, Galileo remains the most fascinating figure of his age. Here James Reston, Jr., writes a lively, dramatic life of Galileo, one that not only takes us to the heart of this passionate, embattled, prickly, vain, arrogant, & brilliant man, but also paints a vivid picture of Renaissance Italy, of its unparalleled cultural richness & political & religious intrigues. At the center of the story, of course, is Galileo's discovery of the telescope, which revolutionized astronomy but put Galileo into conflict with the Catholic church until 1633, when the Inquisition denounced him, banishing him for the last nine years of his life.

Galileo & the Stargazers. Short Stories. As told by Jim Weiss. 1 cass. (Running Time: 1 hr.). Dramatization. (J). (gr. 2 up). 2001. 10.95 (978-1-882513-21-5(5), 1124-21); audio compact disk 14.95 (978-1-882513-46-8(0), 1124-021) Greathall Prods.
Swashbuckling heroes and quiet scholars, kings and seekers of scientific knowledge spring to life in some of the exciting true stories of all time. Includes "Archimedes and the Golden Crown," "Ptolemy vs. Copernicus," "Tycho Brahe Scans the Skies," "Kepler and Galileo," "The Trial of Galileo" and "Isaac Newton".

Galileo's Daughter. abr. ed. Dava Sobel. Read by Fritz Weaver. 5 CDs. (Running Time: 18900 sec.). (ENG.). 2005. audio compact disk 14.99 (978-0-7393-2290-1(7), Random AudioBks) Pub: Random Audio Pubg. Dist(s): Random

Galileo's Daughter: A Historical Memoir of Science, Faith & Love. unabr. ed. Dava Sobel. Read by George Guidall. 7 cass. (Running Time: 10 hrs.). 1999. 56.00 (978-0-7366-4801-1(1)) Books on Tape.
Portrait of the man whose clash with Catholic doctrine divided science & religion.

Galileo's Daughter: A Historical Memoir of Science, Faith & Love, Set. unabr. ed. Dava Sobel. 5 CDs. (Running Time: 12 hr.). 1999. audio compact disk 29.95 SET, CD. (978-0-375-40939-4(4), Random AudioBks) Random Audio Pubg.
Narrative of one of science's greatest figures & his eldest daughter.

***Galileo's Leaning Tower Experiment.** Wendy Macdonald. Narrated by Matthew Arkin. 1 cass. (Running Time: 16 mins.). (J). (gr. 2-4). 2009. 27.95 (978-0-8045-6983-5(5)); audio compact disk 29.95 (978-0-8045-4208-1(2)) Spoken Arts.

Galimoto. unabr. ed. Karen Lynn Williams. Illus. by Catherine Stock. 1 cass. (Running Time: 15 min.). (J). (gr. k-3). 2001. pap. bk. 16.90 (978-0-8045-6845-6(6), 6845) Spoken Arts.
Kondi is a young African boy searching for scraps of wire to build a "galimoto", a toy vehicle. This is a fine lesson: that dreams fueled by steadfastness make success attainable.

Gallachers. unabr. ed. Margaret Thomson Davis. Narrated by Jean Simmons. 10 cass. (Running Time: 13 hrs. 45 mins.). 2000. 89.00 (978-1-84197-060-8(3), H1062E7) Recorded Bks.
Kate Gallacher knows what she wants in life. A dream husband, an ideal home & adorable kids are high on her list. They also seem to be within her grasp. Her parents are horrified when Kate insists on marrying Pete Brodie, but after all, Kate is pregnant with his child. Delighted her stubbornness has paid off, Kate eagerly awaits the wedding. She is soon disillusioned. Pete doesn't love her, misery is part of daily life & her only joy is her baby. Yet Kate won't give up. She sets her brother up in the ice cream business, making the ice cream herself. Prudently, Kate puts her share of money into a secret account. Somehow she knows how crucial the money will become.

Gallagher. unabr. ed. Jeffrey Poston. Read by Rusty Nelson. 6 cass. (Running Time: 6 hrs.). 2001. 39.95 (978-1-55686-950-1(9)) Books in Motion.
Black gunfighter and ex-outlaw Jason Peares has to defend his town against the Strange Scalpers Gang, a marauding group terrorizing SW Colorado. After their fight, Jason comes face to face with the famous Marshall Gallagher, who is tracking the gang, and also Jason's past.

Gallant Lady. Don Keith & Ken Henry. Ed. by Alan Sklar. 11 cass. (Running Time: 14 hrs. 30 mins.). 2004. 76.95 (978-0-7861-2826-6(7), 3304); audio compact disk 96.00 (978-0-7861-8393-7(4), 3304) Blckstn Audio.

Gallant Lady. unabr. ed. Don Keith & Ken Henry. Ed. by Alan Sklar. 13 pieces. (Running Time: 14 hrs. 30 mins.). 2004. audio compact disk 24.95 (978-0-7861-8515-3(5), 3304) Blckstn Audio.

Gallant Lady: The Biography of the USS Archerfish. unabr. ed. Ken Henry & Don Keith. Read by Alan Sklar. 11 CDs. (Running Time: 14 hrs. 30 mins.). 2005. audio compact disk 39.95 (978-0-7861-8580-1(5), ZE3304); reel tape 32.95 (978-0-7861-2735-1(X), E3304) Blckstn Audio.
The Archerfish, a diesel powered Balao-class submarine crafted in the 1940s, won a unique, heroic place in military history and the memories of her crew members. Here is her story: from her assembly in New England and her dedication at the hand of Eleanor Roosevelt, to her service in World War II, where she broke the back of the Japanese Navy, and her critical role in the Cold War. Here too, is the story of her crew, who waited years to serve on the Archerfish. In their own words, these men tell how, against all odds, they sent a Japanese aircraft carrier to the ocean floor. Heroic actions, exotic ports, B-girls, perilous shore leaves, and the fascinating details of life aboard a sub-it's all here. An extraordinary real-life odyssey, Gallant Lady is a vivid, unforgettable portrait of a submariner's life.

Gallant Tailor. unabr. ed. 1 cass. (Running Time: 20 min.). Dramatization. (Magic Looking Glass Ser.). (J). (gr. 2-6). 1989. 9.95 (978-0-7810-0025-3(4), NIM-CW-127-4-C) NIMCO.
A folk tale of German descent.

Gallery of Light. Billy Lamont. 1993. 11.95 (978-0-9632881-2-7(1)) Natl Post Modern.

Gallery Whispers. unabr. ed. Quintin Jardine. Read by James Bryce. 8 cass. (Running Time: 10 hrs. 10 mins.). (Isis Ser.). (J). 2002. 69.95 (978-0-7531-1114-7(4)); audio compact disk 99.95 (978-0-7531-1398-1(8)) Pub: ISIS Lrg Prnt GBR. Dist(s): Ulverscroft US
One of the world's most ruthless terrorists is on his way to Edingurgh, and he can only have one thing on his mind: the forthcoming conference of world Heads of Government. If Skinner doesn't pick up his trail fast, he could have a global disaster in his backyard. While all eyes are focused on the terrorist threat, a terminally ill woman is found dead, an apparent suicide. But a policewoman sees the subtle marks of an assisted death, and therefore, according to the law, murder. it is the beginning of an ominous pattern.

Gallinita Roja. Tr. of Little Red Hen. (SPA.). 2004. 8.95 (978-0-7882-0291-9(X)) Weston Woods.

gallinita Roja. (SPA.). (gr. k-1). 10.00 (978-0-7635-6267-0(X)) Rigby Educ.

***gallinita roja / the Litte Red Hen.** Christianne C. Jones. Tr. by Patricia Abello. Illus. by Natalie Magnuson. (Read-it! Readers en Español). (SPA.). 2008. audio compact disk 9.27 (978-1-4048-4467-4(8)) CapstoneDig.

gallinita roja Audio CD. Benchmark Education Company. Based on a work by Brenda Parkes. (Shared Reading Classics Ser.). (J). (gr. k-2). 2009. audio compact disk 10.00 (978-1-60634-980-9(5)) Benchmark Educ.

Gallipoli. unabr. collector's ed. Alan Moorehead. Read by Bill Kelsey. 9 cass. (Running Time: 13 hrs. 30 min.). 1987. 72.00 (978-0-7366-1062-9(6), 1989) Books on Tape.
The author describes the great amphibious campaign of WWI. Winston Churchill, then First Lord of the Admiralty, was its strongest proponent . He was blamed for the fiasco that followed: a plan so admirable in concept yet so abominable in its execution. The idea was to relieve pressure on the Western front. But the idea stalled in planning & was delayed in execution. Results were disastrous. Turkish artillery & machine guns scythed down British troops. The failure cost Churchill his post: he served the remainder of the was an an officer in the trenches in France.

***Gallipoli: Our last man Standing.** unabr. ed. Jonathon King. Read by Peter Byrne. 2010. audio compact disk 83.95 (978-1-74214-427-6(6), 9781742144276) Pub: Bolinda Pubng AUS. Dist(s): Bolinda Pub Inc

Galloway. unabr. ed. Louis L'Amour. Read by Jason Culp. (Running Time: 18000 sec.). (Sacketts Ser.). (ENG.). 2007. audio compact disk 25.95 (978-0-7393-2118-8(8), Random AudioBks) Pub: Random Audio Pubg. Dist(s): Random

Gallows Gamble. Max Brand. (Running Time: 1 hr. 12 mins.). 2000. 10.95 (978-1-60083-531-5(7)) Iofy Corp.

***Gallows Gamble.** Max Brand. 2009. (978-1-60136-396-1(6)) Audio Holding.

***Gallows Thief.** abr. ed. Bernard Cornwell. Read by James Frain. (ENG.). 2005. (978-0-06-083887-4(6), Harper Audio); (978-0-06-078451-5(2), Harper Audio) HarperCollins Pubs.

Gallows Thief. unabr. ed. Bernard Cornwell. Read by Sean Barrett. 6 cass. (Running Time: 9 hrs.). 2002. 54.95 (978-0-7540-0850-7(9), CAB 2272) Pub: Chivers Pr GBR. Dist(s): AudioGO

Gallows View. unabr. ed. Peter Robinson. (Running Time: 8 hrs. 30 mins. 0 sec.). (Inspector Banks Mystery Ser.). (ENG.). 2009. 24.99 (978-1-4001-6269-7(6)) Pub: Tantor Media. Dist(s): IngramPubServ

Gallows View. unabr. ed. Peter Robinson. Narrated by Mark Honan. 7 CDs. (Running Time: 8 hrs. 30 mins. 0 sec.). (Inspector Banks Mystery Ser.). 2009. audio compact disk 34.99 (978-1-4001-1269-2(9)); audio compact disk 69.99 (978-1-4001-4269-9(5)) Pub: Tantor Media. Dist(s): IngramPubServ

Gallows Waiting. Matthew S. Hart. Read by Charlton Griffin. 2 vols. No. 10. 2004. 18.00 (978-1-58807-252-8(5)); (978-1-58807-747-9(0)) Am Pubng Inc.

***Galton Case.** unabr. ed. Ross Macdonald. Read by Grover Gardner. (Running Time: 6 hrs. 30 mins.). 2010. 29.95 (978-1-4332-7853-2(7)); 44.95 (978-1-4332-7849-5(9)); audio compact disk 69.00 (978-1-4332-7850-1(2)) Blckstn Audio.

***Galveston: A Novel.** unabr. ed. Nic Pizzolatto. (Running Time: 7 hrs. 0 mins.). 2010. 29.99 (978-1-4001-9756-9(2)); 14.99 (978-1-4001-8756-0(7)) Tantor Media.

***Galveston: A Novel.** unabr. ed. Nic Pizzolatto. Narrated by Michael Kramer. (Running Time: 7 hrs. 30 mins. 0 sec.). 2010. 19.99 (978-1-4001-6756-2(6)); audio compact disk 29.99 (978-1-4001-1756-7(9)); audio compact disk 71.99 (978-1-4001-4756-4(5)) Pub: Tantor Media. Dist(s): IngramPubServ

Galway Kinnell. unabr. ed. Galway Kinnell. Read by Galway Kinnell. 1 cass. (Running Time: 29 min.). 1991. 10.00 (022682) New Letters.

Galway Kinnell: A Reading. 1 cass. 1992. 9.00 (OC314-68) Sound Horizons AV.

Gaman: A Generation in Hawaii. unabr. ed. Sharon K. Simmons. 1 cass. (Running Time: 01 hr. 26 min.). 1997. (978-1-891956-00-3(0)); audio compact disk (978-1-891956-01-0(9)) Aloha Audio Bks.

Gambara. Honoré de Balzac. Read by Francoise Malettra. 1 cass. (FRE.). 1991. 24.95 (1312-EF) Olivia & Hill.
The story of Signore Paolo Gambara, a poor musician who dreams about writing a great opera, Mahomet. Extracts from this story about the problems of creativity.

Gambit. unabr. ed. Rex Stout. Read by Michael Prichard. (Nero Wolfe Ser.). 2005. 24.95 (978-1-57270-440-4(3)) Pub: Audio Partners. Dist(s): PerseuPGW
Miss Sarah Blount, better known as Sally, has come to Wolfe to plead for his help with her father's case. Matthew Blount is charged with poisoning a man to death at the Gambit Club, and all evidence points to his guilt. Sally knows that her father is innocent, but doesn't trust his lawyer, who seems too interested in her mother. Despite the lack of cooperation by Matthew Blount or the lawyer, Wolfe takes the case, trumping the police with a list of four suspects. But when one of those suspects turns up dead, Wolfe is forced to retrench, so unnerved that he forgoes a fabulous lunch and ignores his treasured orchids. Sally's increasing interest in Wolfe is only one of many trials he faces in this witty, cleverly plotted tale.Rex Stout's literary creation, Nero Wolfe, is one of the greatest fictional detectives of all time. And, as always, Archie's assistance as the perennial wise guy and legman complements Wolfe's devotion to orchids, gourmet meals, and his specially constructed brown leather chair. Together, Archie and Wolfe make an entertaining odd couple.

Gambit. unabr. ed. Rex Stout. Narrated by Michael Prichard. (Nero Wolfe Ser.). (ENG.). 2004. audio compact disk 27.95 (978-1-57270-441-1(1)) Pub: AudioGO. Dist(s): Perseus Dist

Gambit. unabr. collector's ed. Rex Stout. Read by Michael Prichard. 6 cass. (Running Time: 6 hrs.). (Nero Wolfe Ser.). 1996. 48.00 (978-0-7366-3415-1(0), 4061) Books on Tape.
Nero Wolfe helps a pawn accused of murder at a private chess club. Can he checkmate the real killer?.

Gamble: General David Petraeus & the American Military Adventure in Iraq, 2006-2008. Thomas E. Ricks. Contrib. by James Lurie. (Running Time: 10 hrs.). (ENG.). (gr. 12 up). 2009. audio compact disk 39.95 (978-0-14-314410-6(3), PengAudBks) Penguin Grp USA.

Gambler. Fyodor Dostoyevsky. Read by Hernando Iván Cano. (Running Time: 3 hrs.). 2002. 16.95 (978-1-60083-219-2(9), Audiofy Corp) Iofy Corp.

Gambler. unabr. ed. Fyodor Dostoyevsky. Read by Simon Prebble. (Running Time: 6 hrs. 0 mins.). 2010. 29.95 (978-1-4417-1715-3(3)); 44.95 (978-1-4417-1711-5(0)); audio compact disk 55.00 (978-1-4417-1712-2(9)) Blckstn Audio.

Gambler. unabr. ed. Fyodor Dostoyevsky. Read by Walter Zimmerman. 7 cass. (Running Time: 8 hrs. 30 min.). 1989. 39.00 incl. album. (C-136) Jimcin Record.
Study of an addiction.

Gambler. unabr. collector's ed. Fyodor Dostoyevsky. Read by Walter Zimmerman. 7 cass. (Running Time: 7 hrs.). 1998. 42.00 (978-0-7366-3903-3(9), 9136) Books on Tape.
The author writes from the point of view of an addict about his own addiction.

Gambler, the Nun & the Radio see Stories of Ernest Hemingway

***Gambler's Woman.** unabr. ed. Jayne Ann Krentz. Read by Alyson Silverman. (Running Time: 6 hrs.). 2010. 39.97 (978-1-4418-8477-0(7), 9781441884770, BADLE); 19.99 (978-1-4418-8475-6(0), 9781441884756, Brilliance MP3); 39.97 (978-1-4418-8476-3(9), 9781441884763, Brlnc Audio MP3 Lib); audio compact disk 19.99 (978-1-4418-8473-2(4), 9781441884732, Bril Audio CD Unabri); audio compact disk 69.97 (978-1-4418-8474-9(2), 9781441884749, BriAudCD Unabrid) Brilliance Audio.

Gambling: Program from the Award Winning Public Radio Series. Interview. Hosted by Fred Goodwin. Comment by John Hockenberry. 1 CD. (Running Time: 1hr.). (Infinite Mind Ser.). 2002. audio compact disk 21.95 (978-1-888064-71-1(4), LCM 207) Lichtenstein Creat.
In this hour, we explore Gambling. Why can some people walk away from the casino, and others just can't quit? Guests include Dr. Eric Hollander, Professor of Psychiatry and Director of the Compulsive, Impulsive, and Anxiety Disorders Program at Mount Sinai School of Medicine in New York City; Keith Whyte, Executive Director of the National Council on Problem Gambling; sociologist Dr. Gerda Reith, author of The Age of Chance: Gambling in Western Culture; and Joanna Franklin, chief trainer for the Institute for Problem Gambling. Plus commentary by John Hockenberry.

Gambling Man. unabr. ed. Catherine Cookson. Read by Gordon Griffin. 9 cass. (Running Time: 13 hrs. 30 mins.). (Sound Ser.). 2004. 76.95 (978-1-85496-427-4(5), 64275) Pub: UlverLrgPrint GBR. Dist(s): Ulverscroft US

***Game.** abr. ed. Neil Strauss. Read by Neil Strauss. (ENG.). 2009. (978-0-06-190099-0(0), Harper Audio); (978-0-06-186687-6(3), Harper Audio) HarperCollins Pubs.

Game. unabr. ed. A. S. Byatt. Read by Nadia May. 7 cass. (Running Time: 10 hrs.). 1994. 49.95 (978-0-7861-0469-7(4), 1421) Blckstn Audio.
When they were little girls, Cassandra & Julia played a game in which they entered an alternate world modeled on the landscapes of Arthurian romance. Now the sisters are hostile strangers - until a figure from their past, a man they once both loved & suffered over re-enters their lives.

Game. unabr. ed. Laurie R. King. Narrated by Jenny Sterlin. 10 cass. Library ed. (Running Time: 13 hrs. 30 min.). (Mary Russell Mystery Ser.: Vol. 7). 2004. 89.75 (978-1-4025-7492-4(4), M1001); audio compact disk 109.75 (978-1-4025-7494-8(0), CM001) Recorded Bks.

Game. unabr. collector's ed. Laurie R. King. Narrated by Jenny Sterlin. (Mary Russell Mystery Ser.: Vol. 7). 2004. audio compact disk 39.95 (978-1-4025-7752-9(4), CC048) Recorded Bks.

Game. unabr. collector's ed. Laurie R. King. Narrated by Jenny Sterlin. 8 cass. (Running Time: 13 hrs. 30 mins.). (Mary Russell Mystery Ser.: Vol. 7). 2004. 34.99 (978-1-4025-7274-6(3), 03964) Recorded Bks.
Winner of the Edgar, Macavity, Nero Wolfe and John Creasey Awards, Laurie R. King is highly acclaimed for her stunning mysteries featuring Mary Russell and her iconic husband/partner Sherlock Holmes. The Game is a cleverly plotted and richly atmospheric masterpiece. English spy Kimball O'Hara-who inspired Rudyard Kipling's famous title character in Kim-has gone missing and is feared either kidnapped or killed. Russell and Holmes, a secret friend of Kim, make for India to take up the search. During their passage, danger seems to lurk in every shadow. And when they do arrive, they quickly learn that no one in this faraway place can be trusted.

Game, Set. unabr. ed. A. S. Byatt. Read by Nadia May. 7 cass. 1999. 49.95 (FS9-51124) Highsmith.

Game: Penetrating the Secret Society of Pickup Artists. abr. ed. Neil Strauss. Read by Neil Strauss. 2010. audio compact disk 34.99 (978-0-06-199532-3(0), Harper Audio) HarperCollins Pubs.

Game after Supper see Poetry & Voice of Margaret Atwood

Game & the Glory. Michelle Akers & Gregg Lewis. 2000. 16.99 (978-0-310-23557-6(X)) Zondervan.

Game & the Glory: An Autobiography. abr. ed. Michelle Akers. (Running Time: 2 hrs. 0 mins. 0 sec.). (ENG.). (J). 2003. 9.99 (978-0-310-26046-2(9)) Zondervan.

***Game As Old As Empire: Unabridged Value-Priced Edition.** Steven Hiatt. Narrated by Erik Synnestvedt. (Running Time: 7 hrs. 0 mins. 0 sec.). (ENG.). 2010. audio compact disk 14.95 (978-1-60998-002-3(6)) Pub: AudioGO. Dist(s): Perseus Dist

***Game Change: Obama & the Clintons, McCain & Palin, & the Race of a Lifetime.** unabr. ed. John Heilemann & Mark Halperin. Read by Dennis Boutsikaris. 2010. (978-0-06-195373-6(3), Harper Audio); (978-0-06-196752-8(1), Harper Audio) HarperCollins Pubs.

***Game Change: Obama & the Clintons, McCain & Palin, & the Race of a Lifetime.** unabr. ed. John Heilemann & Mark Halperin. Read by Dennis Boutsikaris. 2010. audio compact disk 39.99 (978-0-06-200563-2(4), Harper Audio) HarperCollins Pubs.

***Game Change: Obama & the Clintons, McCain & Palin, & the Race of a Lifetime.** unabr. ed. John Heilemann & Mark Halperin. 2010. audio compact disk 19.99 (978-0-06-207323-5(0), Harper Audio) HarperCollins Pubs.

Game Control. unabr. ed. Lionel Shriver. Narrated by Laural Merlington. 9 CDs. (Running Time: 11 hrs.). 2008. audio compact disk 97.25 (978-1-4233-6086-5(9), 9781423360865, BriAudCD Unabrid) Brilliance Audio.

Game Control. unabr. ed. Lionel Shriver. Read by Laural Merlington. (Running Time: 11 hrs.). 2008. 24.95 (978-1-4233-6089-6(3), 9781423360896, BAD); 39.25 (978-1-4233-6088-9(5), 9781423360889, Brlnc Audio MP3 Lib); 24.95 (978-1-4233-6087-2(7), 9781423360872, Brilliance MP3); 39.25 (978-1-4233-6090-2(7), 9781423360902, BADLE); audio compact disk 29.99 (978-1-4233-6085-8(0), 9781423360858, Bril Audio CD Unabri) Brilliance Audio.

Game Development. Heather Maxwell Chandler. 2009. 49.95 (978-0-7637-7635-0(1)) Jones Bartlett.

Game for a Lifetime: More Lessons & Teachings. Harvey Penick. 2004. 7.95 (978-0-7435-4753-6(5)) Pub: S&S Audio. Dist(s): S and S Inc

Game for Heroes. abr. ed. Jack Higgins. Perf. by Christopher Lee. 2 cass. (Running Time: 2 hrs.). 2004. 18.00 (978-1-59007-055-0(0)) Pub: New Millenn Enter. Dist(s): PerseuPGW
The end of the doomed Third Reich means little to an isolated island in the English Channel, where Nazi invaders have vowed to fight to the death. Their brilliant and ruthless SS commander has turned the peaceful outpost into an impregnable fortress - even if it becomes the last remnant of National Socialism in the world. It's up to Owen Morgan, British soldier of fortune, spy and daredevil, to lead a ruffian band of commandos in a bold move to destroy the enemy. The mission means certain death for Morgan and his men - but it may be the island's only hope for survival.

Game for Heroes. unabr. ed. Scripts. Jack Higgins. Read by Christian Rodska. 6 cass. (Running Time: 9 hrs.). 2004. 29.95 (978-1-59007-375-9(4)) Pub: New Millenn Enter. Dist(s): PerseuPGW

***Game of Character: A Family Journey from Chicago's Southside to the Ivy League & Beyond.** Craig Robinson. 2010. audio compact disk 34.99 (978-1-4498-2354-2(8)) Recorded Bks.

Game of Ego. Swami Amar Jyoti. 1 cass. 1980. 9.95 (J-29) Truth Consciousness.
Habits & self-preservation games of the mind are ego's securities. Keeping our bondage or breaking the habits. Cleaning the inside first.

Game of Kings. unabr. ed. Dorothy Dunnett. Narrated by Samuel Gillies. 18 cass. (Running Time: 25 hrs.). (Lymond Chronicles: Bk. 1). 1961. 149.00 (978-0-7887-4378-8(3), 96317E7) Recorded Bks.
Transports you to 1547 Scotland where four-year-old Queen Mary "rules" & unrest grips the land. Notorious outlaw Francis Crawford of Lymond has set fire to his brother's castle. As Edinburgh tongues wag over this latest outrage, the rebellious "Lymond" sets in motion his own agenda of violence that rocks the balance of power in Europe.

Game of Life: And How to Play It. Excerpts. Florence Scovel Shinn. 1 CD. (Running Time: 65 minutes). 2005. audio compact disk 15.95 (978-0-87516-817-3(5), Devorss Pubns) DeVorss.

Game of Life & How to Play It see Jeu de la Vie

Game of Life & How to Play It see Jeu de la vie

Game of Love. unabr. ed. Margaret McDonagh. Read by Maggie Mash. 4 cass. (Running Time: 3 hrs.). (Sound Ser.). (J). 2003. 44.95 (978-1-84283-555-5(6)) Pub: ISIS Lrg Prnt GBR. Dist(s): Ulverscroft US

Game of Negotiating: Caring... But Not That Much. unabr. ed. Herb Cohen. 3 CDs. (Running Time: 3.5 hrs.). 2004. audio compact disk 25.00 (978-1-59007-159-5(X)) Pub: New Millenn Enter. Dist(s): PerseuPGW
This book is a sequel to Herb's twenty years of speeches, seminars, and personal experiences. This bok covers relationships between husband and wife, child-rearing, and employer/employee dealings. With his trademark humor and irreverent style, Herb uses stories, metaphors and real-life examples to inspire, teach and demonstrate how negotiation is a need of life.

Game of Negotiating: Caring... But Not That Much. unabr. abr. ed. Herb Cohen. 2 cass. 2004. 18.00 (978-1-59007-158-8(1)) Pub: New Millenn Enter. Dist(s): PerseuPGW

***Game of Pool.** 2010. audio compact disk (978-1-59171-282-4(3)) Falcon Picture.

Game of Scandal. Kathryn Smith. Narrated by Vanessa Maroney. 10 cass. (Running Time: 14 hrs. 15 mins.). 71.00 (978-1-4025-2258-1(4)) Recorded Bks.

Game of Shadows: Barry Bonds, BALCO, & the Steroids Scandal That Rocked Professional Sports. unabr. ed. Mark Fainaru-Wada & Lance Williams. Read by Scott Brick. 9 CDs. (Running Time: 10 hrs. 30 mins.). 2006. audio compact disk 84.15 (978-1-4159-2906-3(8)) Pub: Books on Tape. Dist(s): NetLibrary CO

Game of Shadows: Barry Bonds, BALCO, & the Steroids Scandal That Rocked Professional Sports. unabr. ed. Mark Fainaru-Wada & Lance Williams. Read by Scott Brick. 9 cass. (Running Time: 10 hrs. 30 mins.). 2006. 81.00 (978-1-4159-2905-6(X), BksonTape) Pub: Random Audio Pubg. Dist(s): Random

Game of Silence. unabr. ed. Louise Erdrich. Read by Nicolle Littrell. 5 CDs. (Running Time: 6 hrs.). 2002. audio compact disk 44.95 (978-1-883332-83-9(4), CD6-02) Audio Bkshelf.
This is a vital and dramatic novel of a year in the life of a young Ojibwa girl in the mid 1800s.

Game of Silence. unabr. ed. Louise Erdrich. Read by Nicolle Littrell. 4 cass. (Running Time: 6 hrs.). (YA). (gr. 7 up). 2002. 34.95 (978-1-883332-79-2(6), 6-02) Audio Bkshelf.
The compelling classic of a boy's coming of age during the Civil War is based on stories the author's grandfather told her about his own life.

Game of Silence. unabr. ed. Louise Erdrich. Read by Anna Fields. (J). 2008. 54.99 (978-1-60514-824-3(5)) Find a World.

Game of Silence. unabr. ed. Louise Erdrich. Read by Anna Fields. 5 CDs. (Running Time: 21600 sec.). (J). (gr. 4-7). 2005. audio compact disk 27.95 (978-0-06-075839-4(2), HarperChildAud) HarperCollins Pubs.

***Game of Silence.** unabr. ed. Louise Erdrich. Read by Anna Fields. (ENG.). 2005. (978-0-06-084591-9(0)) HarperCollins Pubs.

***Game of Silence.** unabr. ed. Louise Erdrich. Read by Anna Fields. (ENG.). 2005. (978-0-06-079687-7(1)) HarperCollins Pubs.

Game of Sunken Places. unabr. ed. M. T. Anderson. Read by Marc Cashman. 5 cass. (Running Time: 6 hrs. 53 mins.). 2005. 40.00 (978-0-307-28220-0(1), Listening Lib); audio compact disk 50.00 (978-0-307-28221-7(X), Listening Lib) Pub: Random Audio Pubg. Dist(s): Random

Game of the Foxes, Pt. 1. unabr. collector's ed. Ladislas Farago. Read by Wolfram Kandinsky. 12 cass. (Running Time: 18 hrs.). 1983. 96.00 (978-0-7366-0748-3(X), 1703-A/B) Books on Tape.
German Espionage in the US & Great Britain during WW II.

Game of the Foxes, Pt. 2. collector's ed. Ladislas Farago. Read by Wolfram Kandinsky. 11 cass. (Running Time: 16 hrs. 30 min.). 1983. 88.00 (978-0-7366-0749-0(8)) Books on Tape.
German espionage in the U. S. & Great Britain during WW II.

Game of the Goose. unabr. ed. Ursula Dubosarsky. Read by Francis Greenslade. 2 cass. (Running Time: 2 hrs. 45 mins.). 2002. (978-1-74030-574-7(4)) Bolinda Pubng AUS.

Game of the Goose. unabr. ed. Ursula Dubosarsky. Read by Francis Greenslade. (Running Time: 2 hrs. 45 mins.). (YA). 2007. audio compact disk 43.95 (978-1-74093-920-1(4), 9781740939201) Pub: Bolinda Pubng AUS. Dist(s): Bolinda Pub Inc

Game of Thirty. unabr. ed. William Kotzwinkle. Narrated by Frank Muller. 6 cass. (Running Time: 7 hrs. 45 mins.). 1995. 51.00 (978-0-7887-0155-9(X), 94377E7) Recorded Bks.
A private eye pursuing a murderer among the rich & influential art & antiques dealers of New York City uncovers the seedy secrets of a child pornography ring.

***Game of Thrones: A Song of Ice & Fire, Book 1.** unabr. ed. George R. R. Martin. Read by Roy Dotrice. (ENG.). 2011. audio compact disk 45.00 (978-0-307-91309-8(0), Random AudioBks) Pub: Random Audio Pubg. Dist(s): Random

Game Over. Cynthia Harrod-Eagles. 2009. 61.95 (978-1-4079-0438-2(8)); audio compact disk 79.95 (978-1-4079-0439-9(6)) Pub: Soundings Ltd GBR. Dist(s): Ulverscroft US

***Game Over.** abr. ed. Fern Michaels. Read by Laural Merlington. 3 CDs. (Running Time: 3 hrs.). (Sisterhood Ser.). 2010. audio compact disk 14.99 (978-1-4418-1692-4(5), 9781441816924, BACD) Brilliance Audio.

***Game Over.** unabr. ed. Fern Michaels. Read by Laural Merlington. (Running Time: 8 hrs.). (Sisterhood Ser.). 2010. 24.99 (978-1-4233-8000-9(2), 9781423380009, BAD); 24.99 (978-1-4233-7998-0(5), 9781423379980, Brilliance MP3); 39.97 (978-1-4233-8001-6(0), 9781423380016, BADLE); 39.97 (978-1-4233-7999-7(3), 9781423379997, Brlnc Audio MP3 Lib); audio compact disk 29.99 (978-1-4233-7996-6(9), 9781423379966, Bril Audio CD Unabri); audio compact disk 87.97 (978-1-4233-7997-3(7), 9781423379973, BriAudCD Unabrid) Brilliance Audio.

Game Over: How Nintendo Zapped an American Industry, Captured Your Dollars, & Enslaved Your Children. unabr. collector's ed. David Sheff. Read by Michael Russotto. 13 cass. (Running Time: 19 hrs. 30 mins.). 1995. 104.00 (978-0-7366-2910-2(6), 3607) Books on Tape.
The story of how Nintendo, one of the world's most influential corporations, dominated a $6 billion dollar industry.

***Game Plan: Winning Strategies for the Second Half of Your Life.** unabr. ed. Bob Buford. (Running Time: 4 hrs. 24 mins. 0 sec.). (ENG.). 2009. 14.99 (978-0-310-77135-7(8)) Zondervan.

Game Plan for Life: Your Personal Playbook for Success. abr. ed. Joe Gibbs. Read by Todd Busteed. Told to Jerry B. Jenkins. 6 CDs. (ENG.). 2009. audio compact disk 26.99 (978-1-4143-2981-9(4)) Tyndale Hse.

***Game Plan for Life Small Group Leader Kit, Volume 1, Group Edition.** Joe Gibbs & Derwin L. Gray. (ENG.). 2010. bk. & pap. bk. (978-1-4158-7038-9(1)) LifeWay Christian.

Game Plans: Sport Strategies for Business. Robert Keidel. 1 cass. 8.95 (978-0-88684-083-9(X)) Listen USA.
Shows how to apply game strategies to business.

Game That Makes Kids Smart. unabr. ed. Christina Clement. Read by Thomas Amshay. 1 cass. (Running Time: 1 hr.). 1986. 5.00 (978-0-939401-11-6(8)) RFTS Prod.
Teaching kids that life is a game & if one plays by the rules one will win.

Game to Miss Cowan. Frances Paige. Read by Lesley Mackie. 7 cass. (Sound Ser.). (J). 2002. 61.95 (978-1-84283-221-9(2)) Pub: ISIS Lrg Prnt GBR. Dist(s): Ulverscroft US

Game 1. unabr. ed. Phil Bildner. (Barnstormers Ser.). (J). 2007. 10.99 (978-0-7435-6112-9(0)) Pub: S&S Audio. Dist(s): S and S Inc

***Games.** L. Ron Hubbard. (POR.). 2010. audio compact disk 15.00 (978-1-4031-7359-1(1)); audio compact disk 15.00 (978-1-4031-7351-5(6)); audio compact disk 15.00 (978-1-4031-7349-2(4)); audio compact disk 15.00 (978-1-4031-1152-4(9)); audio compact disk 15.00 (978-1-4031-7361-4(3)); audio compact disk 15.00 (978-1-4031-7356-0(7)); audio compact disk 15.00 (978-1-4031-7357-7(5)); audio compact disk 15.00 (978-1-4031-7360-7(5)); audio compact disk 15.00 (978-1-4031-7362-1(1)); audio compact disk 15.00 (978-1-4031-7350-8(8)); audio compact disk 15.00 (978-1-4031-7363-8(X)); audio compact disk 15.00 (978-1-4031-7364-5(8)); audio compact disk 15.00 (978-1-4031-7352-2(4)); audio compact disk 15.00 (978-1-4031-7358-4(3)); audio compact disk 15.00 (978-1-4031-7355-3(9)); audio compact disk 15.00 (978-1-4031-7353-9(2)); audio compact disk 15.00 (978-1-4031-7354-6(0)) Bridge Pubns Inc.

Games & Songs see Juegos/Canciones

Games for a Rainy Day. unabr. ed. 1 cass. (Running Time: 40 min.). (J). (gr. k up). 8.95 (C23944) J Norton Pubs.

Games for a Rainy Day, Games for the Birthday Party & Games for Sick Days. unabr. ed. 3 cass. (Running Time: 40 min. per cass.). (J). 24.50 Set. (SGAMES) J Norton Pubs.

Games for Birthday Parties. Deborah Valentine. Read by Deborah Valentine. Read by Verne Critz & Dana Critz. 1 cass. (Running Time: 40 min.). (J). (gr. 3-9). 1991. 5.99 incl. coloring-activity book & crayons. (978-1-878963-13-0(9)) Northstar Ent.
Games & activity plans for entire family for birthday parties.

Games for Rainy Days. Deborah Valentine. Read by Deborah Valentine. Read by Verne Critz & Dana Critz. 1 cass. (Running Time: 40 min.). (J). (gr. 3-9). 1991. 5.99 incl. coloring-activity book & crayons. (978-1-878963-11-6(2)) Northstar Ent.
Activities for rainy days, travel & summer vacation.

Games for Sick Days. Deborah Valentine. Read by Deborah Valentine. Read by Verne Critz & Dana Critz. 1 cass. (Running Time: 40 min.). (J). (gr. 3-9). 1991. 5.99 incl. coloring-activity book & crayons. (978-1-878963-12-3(0)) Northstar Ent.
Games for home enjoyment when sick or in hospital or shut in.

Games for Sick Days. unabr. ed. 1 cass. (Running Time: 40 min.). (J). 8.95 (C23945) J Norton Pubs.

Games for the Birthday Party. unabr. ed. 1 cass. (Running Time: 40 min.). (J). 8.95 (C23946) J Norton Pubs.

Games for the Road. Deborah Valentine. Read by Deborah Valentine. Read by Verne Critz & Dana Critz. 1 cass. (Running Time: 40 min.). (J). (gr. 3-9). 1990. 5.99 incl. coloring-activity book & crayons. (978-1-878963-10-9(4)) Northstar Ent.
Fun & games for entire family while traveling.

Games for the Road. unabr. ed. 1 cass. (J). 14.95 incl. bklt. (S23943) J Norton Pubs.
Twenty-three games, designed to strengthen skills in language arts, math, social studies & science, range in difficulty so that pre-schoolers can enjoy some, older children will be challenged by others. The booklet describes each game & rates its difficulty.

Games, Games, Games. Perf. by Wee Sing Staff. 1 cass., 1 CD. (J). bk. 7.98 Blisterpack. (PSS 7404); audio compact disk 10.38 CD Longbox, incl. bk. (PSS 7402) NewSound.
Collection of musical & non-musical games features both old favorites & some newer ones too.

Games to Keep the Dark Away. unabr. ed. Marcia Muller. Read by Kathleen O'Malley. 6 cass. (Running Time: 6 hrs.). (Sharon McCone Mystery Ser.: No. 4). 1997. 36.00 (978-0-7366-3566-0(1), 4212) Books on Tape.
When a missing person McCone is tracking turns up dead, McCone must get past the locals in a small town to find answers.

GameWay to Phonics & Reading. l.t. ed. Ellen G. Dana. 2 cass. 1994. 24.00 Includes Flashcards. (978-0-9706545-2-6(9)) Caring Comm.

Gami Akij Story. Rebekah Joy Anast. 1 cassette. (YA). 1997. (978-1-892112-58-3(2)) No Greater Joy.

Gaming Industry: Current, Legal, Regulatory, & Social Issues. 9 cass. (Running Time: 12 hrs. 30 min.). 1998. 345.00 Set; incl. study guide 529p. (MC91) Am Law Inst.
New advanced course covers the most important & controversial areas of gaming, enabling experienced governmental, regulatory, private, & in-house counsel in the field to keep on top of the latest trends.

Gamma Meditation System. unabr. ed. Jeffrey Thompson. (Running Time: 2:00:00). 2006. audio compact disk 19.98 (978-1-55961-747-5(0)) Sounds True.

Gammage Cup. Carol Kendall. Read by Christina Moore. 4 cass. (Running Time: 5 hrs. 45 mins.). (YA). 2000. pap. bk. 51.25 (978-0-7887-4333-7(3), 41128); 117.80 (978-0-7887-4434-1(8), 47125) Recorded Bks.
In a far away land, a few brave Minnipins must leave their comfortable homes for the mountains. There, they will discover a horrible foe: the Mushroom People.

Gammage Cup. unabr. ed. Carol Kendall. Narrated by Christina Moore. 4 pieces. (Running Time: 5 hrs. 45 mins.). (gr. 3 up). 2000. 37.00 (978-0-7887-4249-1(3), 96217E7) Recorded Bks.

Gampopa. Vajracarya. Read by Chogyam Trungpa. 1 cass. 1970. 12.50 (A043) Vajradhatu.
The development of Gampopa from an ordinary monk to the founder fo the Kagyu Lineage.

Gandhi. unabr. collector's ed. William L. Shirer. Read by Larry McKeever. 7 cass. (Running Time: 10 hrs. 30 min.). 1988. 56.00 (978-0-7366-1286-9(6), 2194) Books on Tape.
Gandhi was a man, not a saint. The author shows him in all his complexity...& he was complex!.

Gandhi: A Personal Encounter. 1 cass. (Running Time: 1 hr.). 7.95 (978-1-58638-545-3(3)) Nilgiri Pr.
A visit to Gandhi's ashram.

Gandhi: Taking His Message Home. 1 cass. (Running Time: 1 hr.). 1983. 7.95 (978-1-58638-546-0(1)) Nilgiri Pr.
Discusses what Gandhi's life means to ones lives.

Gandhi & Nonviolence. Ernest Yaniger. Read by Tim O'Connor. 1 cass. (Running Time: 32 min. per cass.). 1982. 10.00 (HT344) Esstee Audios.
Mahatma Gandhi, a man born of an upperclass Indian family, took upon himself the burden of freeing India from English rule, giving up his wealth & family to devote himself completely to the political & social good of his land.

***Gandhi CEO: 14 Principles to Guide & Inspire Modern Leaders.** unabr. ed. Alan Axelrod. Read by Don Hagen. (Running Time: 5 hrs. 30 mins.). (ENG.). 2010. 27.98 (978-1-59659-574-3(4), GildAudio) Pub: Gildan Media. Dist(s): HachBkGrp

Gandhi M/C: Wrestles with Dogs. Ira D. Parnes. Des. by Zephyr Wazallann. Illus. by Zephyr Wazallann. Arranged by Swante J. Music by Bill Horist. (ENG.). 2008. audio compact disk 10.00 (978-0-9800368-1-7(X)) Spankstra Pr.

Gandhi on Faith. unabr. ed. Perf. by Eknath Easwaran. 1 cass. (Running Time: 1 hr.). 1989. 7.95 (978-1-58638-544-6(5)) Nilgiri Pr.

Gandhi-Peaceful Fighter. unabr. ed. Elizabeth R. Montgomery. Read by Susan Smith. 3 cass. (Running Time: 3 hrs. 30 min.). 21.95 (978-1-55686-182-6(6), 182) Books in Motion.

Ganesh, Vol. 1. Music by Shruti Sadolikar et al. 1 cass. (Bhaktimala Ser.). 1992. (C92071) Multi-Cultural Bks.

Ganesh, Vol. 2. Music by Ashwini Bhide & Veena Sahasrabudhe. 1 cass. (Bhaktimala Ser.). 1992. (D92002); audio compact disk (CD D92002) Multi-Cultural Bks.

Ganesh-Rama, Vol. 1. Music by Ashwini Bhide & Veena Sahasrabuddhe. 1 cass. (Bhaktimala Ser.). 1992. (D92015); audio compact disk (CD D92015) Multi-Cultural Bks.

Gang Busters. collector's ed. Perf. by Mandel Kramer et al. Created by Phillips H. Lord. 6 cass. (Running Time: 9 hrs.). 1999. bk. 34.98 (4135) Radio Spirits.
18 episodes.

Gang Busters. collector's ed. Perf. by Jay Novello et al. 1 DVD. (Running Time: 3 hrs.). (TV from Yesteryear Ser.). 2001. bk. 9.98 (7805) Radio Spirits.
Contains three classic television shows and three complete old time radio shows.

Gang Busters: Cases of Crime. Perf. by Original Cast. 2009. audio compact disk 39.98 (978-1-57019-880-9(2)) Radio Spirits.

Gang Busters: Counterfeit Combine & Triple Threat Bandits. 1 cass. (Running Time: 1 hr.). 2001. 6.98 (2258) Radio Spirits.

***Gang Busters: Crime Wave.** Perf. by Broadcasts Original Radio. 2010. audio compact disk 31.95 (978-1-57019-933-2(7)) Radio Spirits.

Gang Busters: Sledge Hammer Handicap & High School Hot Shots. 1 cass. (Running Time: 1 hr.). 2001. 6.98 (2013) Radio Spirits.

Gang Busters: The Case of the Cumberland Safecracker & The Case of the Broadway Bandits. 1 cass. (Running Time: 1 hr.). 2001. 6.98 (2239) Radio Spirits.

Gang Busters: The Case of the Quincy Killers & The Case of the Kidnapped Paymaster. 1 cass. (Running Time: 1 hr.). 2001. 6.98 (2457) Radio Spirits.

Gang Busters: The Dakota Badman & The Case of Medos-Carter-Henderson. 1 cass. (Running Time: 1 hr.). 2001. 6.98 (2197) Radio Spirits.

Gang Busters & Mr. District Attorney: A Prizefighter Called "The Soldier" & Deported Narcotics Gangster Re-Enters the U. S. unabr. ed. 1 cass. (Running Time: 60 min.). Dramatization. 7.95 Norelco box. (MM712) Natl Recrd Co.
Gang Busters: Criminals start spending stolen money taken from a tool company robbery, & soon one ends up very dead. Detectives from the New York City Homicide Detail take over, & solve this robbery & murder. Mr. District Attorney: Champion of the people, defender of truth, guardian of our fundamental rights to life, liberty & the pursuit of happiness. Starring Jay Jostyn in the title role, with Glenn Doyle as Harrington & Vicki Bolla as Miss Miller.

***Gang Leader for a Day.** unabr. ed. Sudhir Venkatesh. Read by Reg Rogers & Stephen J. Dubner. (ENG.). 2008. (978-0-06-162922-8(7)); (978-0-06-162923-5(5)) HarperCollins Pubs.

Gang Leader for a Day. unabr. ed. Sudhir Alladi Venkatesh. Read by Reg Rogers & Stephen J. Dubner. 7 CDs. (Running Time: 8 hrs. 30 mins.). 2008. audio compact disk 34.95 (978-0-06-157113-8(X), Harper Audio) HarperCollins Pubs.

Gangaji on the Holy River Ganga: The End of Suffering. unabr. ed. Gangaji Foundation Staff. Read by Gangaji Foundation Staff. 3 cass. (Running Time: 3 hrs.). 1993. 24.00 set. (978-0-9632194-9-7(9)) The Gangaji Fnd.
Gangaji reveals the secret for direct self-realization & ending egoic suffering.

Gangbusters. 2 cass. (Running Time: 2 hrs.). vinyl bd. 10.95 (978-1-57816-053-2(7), GB2401) Audio File.
Includes: "Park Avenue Pilferers" (1946) The story of the burglar king & queen who looted New York City's most luxurious apartments. "Case of the Tennessee Trigger Men" (1947) The tale of two couples who were skilled at kidnapping & bank robbery. "Hitch-Hikers' Murder Victim" (1953) On the way home from vacation a carpenter picks up a pair of hitch-hikers. "Burglary Ring" (1952) Good undercover work & a wire tap on a public phone break up a burglary ring.

Gangbusters. 6 cass. 24.98 Set. Moonbeam Pubns.

Gangbusters. 1 cass. (Running Time: 60 min.). Incl. Gangbusters: The Athletic Bandit. (MM-5130); Gangbusters: The Death Mask Killer. (MM-5130); 7.95 (MM-5130) Natl Recrd Co.
In "The Death Mask Killer", Bowers & a friend hold up five taverns in 48 hours, kill a State Trooper & are arrested by police; Bowers is sent to prison where he makes a death mask to fool the guards. "The Athletic Bandit" is about a college athlete turned killer. He plays golf so well he is accepted by high society & invited to wealthy parties where he robs the guests.

Gangbusters. Read by Mandell Kramer et al. (Running Time: 32400 sec.). 1997. 48.58 (978-1-57019-115-2(8)) Radio Spirits.

Gangbusters: The Athletic Bandit see Gangbusters

Gangbusters: The Death Mask Killer see Gangbusters

Gangbusters: The Destruction of America's Last Great Mafia Dynasty, unabr. ed. Ernest Volkman. Narrated by Richard M. Davidson. 11 cass. (Running Time: 15 hrs.). 1998. 91.00 (978-0-7887-2602-6(1), 95599E7) Recorded Bks.
Volkman delves deeply into the infrastructure of organized crime & the secrets that protected one of the Mafia's most influential families.

Gangland: How the FBI Broke the Mob. Howard Blum. 2004. 10.95 (978-0-7435-4754-3(3)) Pub: S&S Audio. Dist(s): S and S Inc

Ganglands. unabr. ed. Maureen McCarthy. 6 cass. (Running Time: 6 hrs. 43 mins.). 2002. 32.00 (978-1-74030-791-8(7)) Pub: Bolinda Pubng AUS. Dist(s): Bolinda Pub Inc

Ganins Pit. abr. ed. Allan Folsom. Perf. by Michael York. 6 cass. (Running Time: 9 hrs.). 2002. 29.95 (978-1-59007-073-4(9), N Millennium Audio); audio compact disk 39.95 (978-1-59007-074-1(7), N Millennium Audio) Pub: New Millenn Enter. Dist(s): PerseuPGW

***Gannet Has Landed.** Peter Kerr. 2010. 69.95 (978-1-4079-0944-8(4)); audio compact disk 84.95 (978-1-4079-0945-5(2)) Pub: Soundings Ltd GBR. Dist(s): Ulverscroft US

Ganz Ohr: Horanlasse und Arbeitsblatter fur Anfanger und Fortgeschrittene. Graziella Ghisla et al. 1 cass. (Running Time: 90 mins.). (GER.). 1996. 23.95 (978-3-468-49559-5(5)) Langenscheidt.

Gap Creek. abr. ed. Robert Morgan. Read by Jill Hill. (YA). 2006. 44.99 (978-1-59895-538-5(1)) Find a World.

Gap Creek: The Story of a Marriage. abr. ed. Robert Morgan et al. Read by Jill Hill. 4 CDs. (Running Time: 5 hrs.). (ENG.). 2000. audio compact disk 34.00 (978-1-56511-387-9(X), 156511387X) Pub: HighBridge. Dist(s): Workman Pub

Gap Creek: The Story of a Marriage. unabr. ed. Robert Morgan. Narrated by Kate Forbes. 11 CDs. (Running Time: 11 hrs. 15 mins.). 2000. audio compact disk 97.00 (978-0-7887-4891-2(2), C1266E7) Recorded Bks.
A story of a young woman's struggles in early 20th century Appalachia. Julie Harmon is a hard worker living a hard life. Only a teenager, she has already witnessed the death of her brother & father when she loses herself in the work of a new marriage. The trials she faces from fires & floods to nearly unbearable hunger, gradually build into a wonderful examination of the ways the human spirit can triumph over adversity.

Gap Creek: The Story of a Marriage. unabr. ed. Robert Morgan. Narrated by Kate Forbes. 9 cass. (Running Time: 11 hrs. 15 mins.). 2000. 76.00 (96276K8) Recorded Bks.
Starkly naturalistic story of a young woman's life in early 20th-century Appalachia.

Gap Standing & Hedge Building. Frank Damazio. 12 cass. (Running Time: 18 hrs.). 2000. (978-1-886849-34-1(X)) CityChristian.

Garage Band Method: How the Rest of Us Can Learn to Play. William D. Hargrove & Robert D. Ratcliff. 1997. audio compact disk 14.95 CD. (978-1-889975-02-3(8)) Camels Back Pr.
A new method for learning to play blues, rock & other improvised music by ear, based on the writer's experience learning to play blues saxophone at age 42.

Garage Band Method: How the Rest of Us Can Learn to Play. William D. Hargrove & Robert D. Ratcliff. 1997. pap. bk. 24.95 (978-1-889975-01-6(X)) Camels Back Pr.

Garbage Monster from Outer Space. unabr. ed. John R. Erickson. Read by John R. Erickson. 2 cass. (Running Time: 1 hr.). (Hank the Cowdog Ser.: No. 32). (J). (gr. 5-7). 2001. 24.00 (978-0-7366-6247-5(2)) Books on Tape.
Someone has been raiding Sally May's garbage barrels! Hank knows the crime is the work of the notorious gang of raccoons. However, in a tragic case of mistaken identity, the Head of Ranch Security is himself forced to take the heat. More trouble lies ahead. Rip and Snort, the good-for-nothing coyote brothers are planning to pull an even bigger job. Not only is Hank powerless to stop them, he's compelled to fight on the side of evil and comes face to face with terrifyng forces.

Garbage Monster from Outer Space. unabr. ed. John R. Erickson. Read by John R. Erickson. 3 CDs. (Running Time: 3 hrs. 36 mins.). (Hank the Cowdog Ser.: No. 32). (J). (gr. 4-7). 2001. audio compact disk 14.95 Books on Tape.
Hank is forced to take the blame when a notorious gang of raccoons raids Sally May's garbage barrels.

Garbage Monster from Outer Space. unabr. ed. John R. Erickson. Read by John R. Erickson. 3 CDs. (Running Time: 1 hr. 12 mins.). (Hank the Cowdog Ser.: No. 32). (J). (gr. 4-7). 2001. audio compact disk 24.00 (978-0-7366-7554-3(X)) Books on Tape.
Someone has been raiding Sally May's garbage barrels! Hank knows the crime is the work of the notorious gang of raccoons. However, in a tragic case of mistaken identity, the Head of Ranch Security is himself forced to take the heat. More trouble lies ahead. Rip and Snort, the good-for-nothing coyote brothers are planning to pull an even bigger job. Not only is Hank powerless to stop them, he's compelled to fight on the side of evil and comes face to face with terrifyng forces.

Garbage Monster from Outer Space. unabr. ed. John R. Erickson. Read by John R. Erickson. 2 cass. (Running Time: 3 hrs.). (Hank the Cowdog Ser.: No. 32). (J). 2002. 17.99 (978-1-59188-332-6(6)) Maverick Bks.

Garbage Monster from Outer Space. unabr. ed. John R. Erickson. Read by John R. Erickson. 3 CDs. (Running Time: Approx. 3 hours). (Hank the Cowdog Ser.: No. 32). (J). 2002. audio compact disk 19.99 (978-1-59188-632-7(5)) Maverick Bks.
Someone has been raiding Sally May?s garbage barrels! Hank knows the crime is the work of a notorious gang of raccoons, but in a tragic case of mistaken identity, the Head of Ranch Security is himself forced to take the heat. More trouble lies ahead. Rip and Snort, the good-for-nothing coyote brothers, are planning to pull an even bigger job. Not only is Hank powerless to stop them, he?s compelled to fight on the side of evil?and comes face to face with terrifying forces!Rip and Snort sing ?Oh Boy!? and Hank sings ?If I?d Been Your Ma? to Alfred in this hilarious adventure for the whole family.

Garbo. unabr. ed. Barry Paris. Read by Anna Fields. 15 cass. (Running Time: 22 hrs.). 1997. 95.95 (978-0-7861-1135-0(6), 1902) Blckstn Audio.
Supplants the legend of Garbo the "enigma" with a revelation of the real woman, whose grip on our imagination remains as powerful today as it was almost seventy years ago when she dazzled the world in "Flesh and the Devil.".

Garcia Marquez in 90 Minutes. Paul Strathern. Read by Robert Whitfield. (Running Time: 7200 sec.). 2005. 22.95 (978-0-7861-3035-1(0)); audio compact disk 24.00 (978-0-7861-7939-8(2)) Blckstn Audio.

Garcia Marquez in 90 Minutes. unabr. ed. Paul Strathern. Read by Robert Whitfield. 2 cass. (Running Time: 1 hr. 30 mins.). 2005. 16.95 (978-0-7861-3431-1(3)); audio compact disk 16.95 (978-0-7861-7981-7(3)) Blckstn Audio.

Garden Behind the Moon-A Real Story of the Moon Angel. Howard Pyle. Narrated by Bobbie Frohman. Music by David Thorn. Engineer Scott Weiser. B. J. Bedford. (ENG.). (J). 2009. audio compact disk (978-0-9821853-9-2(2)) Alcazar AudioWorks.

Garden Circus. (J). 2003. audio compact disk 17.99 (978-0-9740847-6-3(X)) GiGi Bks.
What's bugging you? Listeners will love this adorable poem about some personable bugs that decide to host a circus in a child's garden. Complete with an illustrated picture book that will capture your child's attention with each exciting turn of the page. The audio story brings the bugs to life as they "act out" each scene. The audio story concludes with a toe tapping song for your young child to enjoy.

Garden Lodge see Troll Garden

Garden Lunch: Early Explorers Emergent Set A Audio CD. Benchmark Education Staff. (J). 2006. audio compact disk 10.00 (978-1-4108-7592-1(X)) Benchmark Educ.

Garden Meditation. Read by Mary Richards. 1 cass. (Running Time: 60 min.). (Energy Break Ser.). 2007. audio compact disk 19.95 (978-1-56136-155-7(0), 094) Master Your Mind.

Garden of Abdul Gasazi. (J). 1982. bk. 38.59 SRA McGraw.

Garden of Beasts: A Novel of Berlin 1936. abr. ed. Jeffery Deaver. Read by Jefferson Mays. 2005. 15.95 (978-0-7435-5170-0(2)) Pub: S&S Audio. Dist(s): S and S Inc

Garden of Beasts: A Novel of Berlin 1936. abr. ed. Jeffery Deaver. Read by Jefferson Mays. (Running Time: 6 hrs. 0 mins. 0 sec.). 2007. audio compact disk 14.99 (978-0-7435-6957-6(1)) Pub: S&S Audio. Dist(s): S and S Inc

Garden of Beasts: A Novel of Berlin 1936. unabr. ed. Jeffery Deaver. Narrated by Jefferson Mays. 9 cassettes. (Running Time: 13.50 hrs). 2005. 79.75 (978-1-4193-0892-5(0)) Recorded Bks.

Garden of Eden see Jardin del Eden

Garden of Eden. unabr. ed. Ernest Hemingway. Read by Alexander Adams. 8 cass. (Running Time: 11 hrs.). 2001. 29.95 (978-0-7366-5674-0(X)) Books on Tape.
A late Hemingway story of a love triangle in a Mediterranean setting.

Garden of Eden. unabr. ed. Ernest Hemingway. Read by Patrick Wilson. 2006. 17.95 (978-0-7435-6350-5(6), Audioworks); audio compact disk 29.95 (978-0-7435-6448-9(0)) Pub: S&S Audio. Dist(s): S and S Inc

Garden of Eden. unabr. collector's ed. Max Brand. Read by Jonathan Marosz. 7 cass. (Running Time: 7 hrs.). 1995. 42.00 (978-0-7366-2938-6(6), 3634) Books on Tape.
Race track gambler Ben Connor knows horses. The day he first saw an Eden Gray run, he knew it was fast enough to earn a lot of money. So why not find the reclusive deaf mute who owns the Eden Grays, buy one, enter it in races & watch his fortune grow?.

Garden of Eden. unabr. collector's ed. Ernest Hemingway. Read by Wolfram Kandinsky. 8 cass. (Running Time: 8 hrs.). 1990. 48.00 (978-0-7366-1822-9(8), 2658) Books on Tape.
David Bourne, a young American writer, finds his Mediteranean honeymoon interrupted by a flood of good notices about his second novel. Catherine, his wife, encourages him in his work, or does she? Does Catherine resent the time that he spends at his desk? Is he crazy, or has she put a younger, more exotic woman in his path? All David knows is that this is a dangerous game.

Garden of Eden & Other Criminal Delights. abr. ed. Faye Kellerman. Read by Dennis Boutsikaris et al. (Running Time: 6 hrs.). (ENG.). 2006. 14.98 (978-1-59483-528-5(4)) Pub: Hachet Audio. Dist(s): HachBkGrp

Garden of Eden & Other Criminal Delights. abr. ed. Faye Kellerman. Read by Dennis Boutsikaris et al. (Running Time: 6 hrs.). (ENG.). 2009. 44.98 (978-1-60788-139-1(X)) Pub: Hachet Audio. Dist(s): HachBkGrp

Garden of Eden & Other Criminal Delights. unabr. ed. Faye Kellerman. 8 cass. (Running Time: 9 hrs. 30 mins.). 2006. 79.75 (978-1-4281-0553-9(0)); audio compact disk 119.75 (978-1-4281-0555-3(7)) Recorded Bks.

Garden of Eve. unabr. ed. K. L. Going. Read by Allyson Ryan. 4 CDs. (Running Time: 4 hrs. 42 mins.). (YA). (gr. 5-8). 2007. audio compact disk 38.00 (978-0-7393-6142-9(2), Listening Lib) Pub: Random Audio Pubg. Dist(s): Random
Without Mom, there are no more bedtime stories, no more answers carried on the wind, and no more magic gardens. Evie doesn't believe in magic now. After all, if magic were real, her mom would still be alive. But when Evie moves to Beaumont, New York, where her father has bought a withered apple orchard that the townspeople whisper is cursed, she learns about a lost girl, receives a mysterious seed, and meets a boy who claims to be dead. Before long, Evie finds herself in the middle of a fairy tale. And this one is real.

Garden of Eve. unabr. ed. K. L. Going. Read by Allyson Ryan. (Running Time: 16920 sec.). (J). (gr. 5-9). 2007. audio compact disk 28.00 (978-0-7393-5959-4(2), Listening Lib) Pub: Random Audio Pubg. Dist(s): Random

Garden of Evil. unabr. ed. Edna Buchanan. Narrated by Barbara Caruso. 7 cass. (Running Time: 9 hrs. 15 mins.). (Britt Montero Mystery Ser.). 2000. 65.00 (978-0-7887-4420-4(8), 96128E7) Recorded Bks.
The "Kiss-Me Killer" is loose in Florida, leaving a trail of gruesome slain bodies in her wake. Journalist Britt Montero is cultivating a dangerous fascination with the killer & the feeling is mutual.

Garden of Evil. unabr. ed. Edna Buchanan. Narrated by Barbara Caruso. 8 CDs. (Running Time: 9 hrs. 15 mins.). (Britt Montero Mystery Ser.). 2001. audio compact disk 78.00 (978-0-7887-5195-0(6), C1352E7) Recorded Bks.
The "Kiss-Me-Killer" is loose in Florida, leaving a trail of gruesomely slain bodies in her wake. Journalist Britt Montero is cultivating a dangerous fascination with the killer & the feeling is mutual.

Garden of Evil. unabr. collector's ed. Edna Buchanan. Read by Anna Fields. 6 cass. (Running Time: 9 hrs.). (Britt Montero Mystery Ser.). 1999. 48.00 (978-0-7366-4840-0(2)) Books on Tape.
Reporter Britt Montero tracks a beautiful serial murderer who is decimating Miami's hard partying South Beach scene.

Garden of Evil, Set. abr. ed. Edna Buchanan. 2 cass. (Britt Montero Mystery Ser.). 1999. 17.95 (FS9-51091) Highsmith.

Garden of Evil, Set. unabr. ed. Edna Buchanan. Read by Sandra Burr. 6 cass. (Britt Montero Mystery Ser.). 1999. 57.25 (FS9-51030) Highsmith.

Garden of Faith. Lynne Hinton. Narrated by Julia Gibson. 6 CDs. (Running Time: 6 hrs. 15 mins.). audio compact disk 58.00 (978-1-4025-2126-3(X)) Recorded Bks.

Garden of Faith. unabr. ed. Lynne Hinton. Narrated by Julia Gibson. 5 cass. (Running Time: 6 hrs. 25 mins.). 2002. 32.95 (978-1-4025-2127-0(8), RF984) Recorded Bks.
By the time five women from the Hope Springs Community Church have finished their Women's Guild Cookbook, they share strong bonds of community and faith. But when one of them becomes seriously ill, their friendship is put to the test.

Garden of Giving. unabr. ed. Lisa M. Nelson. 1 cass. (Running Time: 44 min.). (Positive Music for Today's Kids! Ser.). (J). (gr. k-6). 1991. 9.95 (978-0-9627863-3-4(0)) Brght Ideas CA.
Songs of self-esteem for children ages 5-11. Original songs by various artists.

Garden of Last Days. unabr. ed. Andre Dubus, III. Read by Dan John Miller. (Running Time: 15 hrs.). 2008. 24.95 (978-1-4233-6661-4(1), 9781423366614, BAD); 39.25 (978-1-4233-6662-1(X), 9781423366621, BADLE); audio compact disk 38.95 (978-1-4233-6657-7(3), 9781423366577, Bril Audio CD Unabri); audio compact disk 24.95 (978-1-4233-6659-1(X), 9781423366591, Brilliance MP3); audio compact disk 39.25 (978-1-4233-6660-7(3), 9781423366607, Brlnc Audio MP3 Lib); audio compact disk 122.25 (978-1-4233-6658-4(1), 9781423366584, BriAudCD Unabrid) Brilliance Audio.

Garden of Lies. abr. ed. Eileen Goudge. Read by Tovah Feldshuh. 2 cass. (Running Time: 3 hrs.). 2000. 7.95 (978-1-57815-053-3(1), 1018, Media Bks Audio) Media Bks NJ.
A woman's shame & deceit gave birth to a secret too shocking to tell - until destiny collided with the greatest lie of all.

Garden of Lies. unabr. ed. Eileen Goudge. Read by Donada Peters. 14 cass. (Running Time: 21 hrs.). 1990. 112.00 (978-0-7366-1687-4(X), 2533) Books on Tape.
A desperate mother's gamble to swap babies works, but with fateful consequences.

Garden of Shadows. unabr. ed. V. C. Andrews. Read by Donada Peters. 8 cass. (Running Time: 12 hrs.). 1990. 64.00 (978-0-7366-1717-8(5), 2558) Books on Tape.
Prequel to the Dollanganger series. Sets the stage for FLOWERS IN THE ATTIC & its tale of incest & perversion.

Garden of Shadows, unabr. ed. V. C. Andrews. Narrated by Sally Darling. 9 cass. (Running Time: 12 hrs. 45 mins.). 1996. 78.00 (978-0-7887-0491-8(5), 94683E7) Recorded Bks.
The curse of Foxworth Hall has fascinated millions of readers & this is where it all begins - in this prequel to "Flowers in the Attic".

Garden Part. unabr. ed. Maeve Binchy. Read by Stella McCusker et al. 1 CD. (ENG.). 2009. audio compact disk 14.95 (978-1-60283-556-6(X)) Pub: AudioGO. Dist(s): Perseus Dist

Garden Party. Katherine Mansfield. Read by Dame Peggy Ashcroft. 2 cass. (Running Time: 2 hrs. 5 min.). Incl. Daughters of the Late Colonel. (CC/004); Her First Ball. (CC/004); Singing Lesson. (CC/004); Stranger. (CC/004); 15.95 (CC/004) C to C Cassettes.
Reveals the profound ironies of life - both comic & tragic. The Garden Party was the last collection to be published in Mansfield's lifetime.

Garden Party. unabr. ed. Katherine Mansfield. Read by Marguerite Gavin. 5 cass. (Running Time: 7 hrs. 30 min.). 1999. 39.95 (978-0-7861-1510-5(6), 2360) Blckstn Audio.
Demonstrates the genius of a woman who, in her short life, was compared to Chekhov.

Garden Rubbish. unabr. ed. W. C. Sellar & R. J. Yeatman. Read by Peter Joyce. 2 cass. (Running Time: 2 hrs. 30 min.). 1998. 27.95 Set. (978-1-86015-455-3(7)) T T Beeler.
Light hearted satire on the "joys" of country living.

Garden Show. Scripts. 1 cass. or 1 CD. (Running Time: 25 mins.). (J). (gr. 2-6). 2000. pap. bk. & tchr. ed. 29.95 Bad Wolf Pr.
Students learn about soil, photosynthesis, pollination & lots of creatures in the garden from a wild bunch of characters - dive-bombing bees, aliens from planet Chlorophyll & a singing compost pile. Sheet music available.

Garden Spells. abr. ed. Sarah Addison Allen. Read by Susan Ericksen. (Running Time: 5 hrs.). 2008. audio compact disk 14.99 (978-1-4233-3338-8(1), 9781423333388, BCD Value Price) Brilliance Audio.

Garden Spells. unabr. ed. Sarah Addison Allen. Read by Susan Ericksen. (Running Time: 8 hrs.). 2007. 39.25 (978-1-4233-3336-4(5), 9781423333364, BADLE); 24.95 (978-1-4233-3335-7(7), 9781423333357, BAD); 74.25 (978-1-4233-3330-2(6), 9781423333302, BrilAudUnabridg); audio compact disk 34.95 (978-1-4233-3331-9(4), 9781423333319, Bril Audio CD Unabri); audio compact disk 24.95 (978-1-4233-3333-3(0), 9781423333333, Brilliance MP3); audio compact disk 87.25 (978-1-4233-3332-6(2), 9781423333326, BriAudCD Unabrid); audio compact disk 39.25 (978-1-4233-3334-0(9), 9781423333340, Brlnc Audio MP3 Lib) Brilliance Audio.

Garden Spells. unabr. ed. Sarah Addison Allen. Read by Susan Ericksen. (YA). 2008. 69.99 (978-1-60514-815-1(6)) Find a World.

Garden Wedding: Genesis 2:19-24. Ed Young. 1986. 4.95 (978-0-7417-1531-9(7), 531) Win Walk.

Gardener see Twentieth-Century Poetry in English, No. 25, Recordings of Poets Reading Their Own Poetry

Gardener. 1 cass. (Running Time: 35 min.). (J). (gr. k-3). 2001. bk. 15.95 (VX-532C) Kimbo Educ.
A young girl is sent to live with her Uncle Jim in the city. Includes book.

Gardener. 1 cass. (Running Time: 60 mins.). (J). 2000. bk. 65.98 (T 6609S, Listening Lib); 9.98 (T 6562CX, Listening Lib) Random Audio Pubg.
Lydia Grace arrives at the home of her Uncle Jim, a contankerous baker, with a suitcase full of seeds & a passion for gardening. Gradually she transforms the bakery to a blossoming place, bringing smiles to all the customers & even Uncle Jim.

Gardener. Sarah Stewart. Read by Bonnie Kelly-Young. Illus. by David Small. 1 cass. (J). 2000. pap. bk. 19.97 (978-0-7366-9203-8(7)) Books on Tape.
Depression-era story of a young girl sent to live with her uncle Jim in the city has a sweet, wistful quality.

Gardener. Sarah Stewart. Illus. by David Small. 9.95 (978-1-59112-306-4(2)) Live Oak Media.

Gardener. Sarah Stewart. Illus. by David Small. 14 vols. (Running Time: 11 mins.). 1998. pap. bk. 39.95 (978-1-59112-530-3(8)); audio compact disk 12.95 (978-1-59112-311-8(9)) Live Oak Media.

Gardener. Sarah Stewart. Perf. by Bonnie K. Young. 1 cass. (Running Time: 11 mins.). (J). (gr. k-4). 1998. 9.95 (978-0-87499-428-5(4)) Live Oak Media.
Lydia Grace Finch brings a suitcase full of seeds, plenty of stationery, & a passion for gardening to the big gray city, where she chose to stay with her Uncle Jim. There she initiates a gradual transformation, brightening the baker & bringing smiles to customers' faces with the flowers she grows. In a secret place Lydia Grace works on her masterpiece, which she hopes will be powerful enough to make even Uncle Jim smile.

Gardener. Sarah Stewart. Read by Bonnie Kelly-Young. Illus. by David Small. 11 vols. (Running Time: 11 mins.). (J). (gr. k-3). 1999. pap. bk. 16.95 (978-0-87499-431-5(4)) Pub: Live Oak Media. Dist(s): AudioGO
Story of a young girl sent to live with her Uncle Jim in the city.

Gardener. unabr. ed. S. A. Bodeen. (Running Time: 6 hrs.). 2010. 39.97 (978-1-4233-8485-4(7), 9781423384854, BADLE); 22.99 (978-1-4233-8484-7(9), 9781423384847, BAD) Brilliance Audio.

Gardener. unabr. ed. S. A. Bodeen. Read by Luke Daniels. 1 MP3-CD. (Running Time: 6 hrs.). 2010. 39.97 (978-1-4233-8483-0(0), 9781423384830, Brlnc Audio MP3 Lib); 22.99 (978-1-4233-8482-3(2), 9781423384823, Brilliance MP3); audio compact disk 54.97 (978-1-4233-8481-6(4), 9781423384816, BriAudCD Unabrid); audio compact disk 22.99 (978-1-4233-8480-9(6), 9781423384809, Bril Audio CD Unabri) Brilliance Audio.

Gardener. unabr. ed. Sarah Stewart. Read by Bonnie Kelly-Young. Illus. by David Small. 11 vols. (Running Time: 11 mins.). (J). (gr. k-3). 1998. bk. 25.95 (978-0-87499-430-8(6)) Live Oak Media.
Lydia Grace Finch brings a suitcase full of seeds, plenty of stationery, & a passion for gardening to the big gray city, where she chose to stay with her Uncle Jim. There she initiates a gradual transformation, brightening the baker & bringing smiles to customers' faces with the flowers she grows. In a secret place Lydia Grace works on her masterpiece, which she hopes will be powerful enough to make even Uncle Jim smile.

Gardener. unabr. ed. Sarah Stewart. Read by Bonnie Kelly-Young. Illus. by David Small. 14 vols. (Running Time: 11 mins.). (J). (gr. k-3). 1999. pap. bk. & tchr. ed. 37.95 Reading Chest. (978-0-87499-432-2(2)) Live Oak Media.

Gardening Equipment, Tools & Hardware in Slovakia: A Strategic Reference 2006. Compiled by Icon Group International, Inc. Staff. 2007. ring bd. 195.00 (978-0-497-82420-4(5)) Icon Grp.

Gardening Story Rhymes. unabr. ed. Alfreda C. Doyle. Read by Alfreda C. Doyle. 1 cass. (Running Time: 35 min.). (Alfreda's Radio Ser.: Vol. 9). (J). (gr. 5-9). 1998. 16.95 (978-1-56820-313-3(6)) Story Time.
Stories that educate, entertain, inform & rhyme.

Gardening the Soul. Michael Toms. Read by Michael Toms. Interview with Alice Walker. 2 cass. (Running Time: 2 hrs.). (New Dimensions Ser.). 2000. 16.95 (978-1-56170-701-0(5), 4036) Hay House.
Alice Walker & Michael Toms discuss how to celebrate human life in all its moments.

Gardens at Rainbow Farm. O. J. Youngberg. 2005. audio compact disk 19.95 (978-0-9766994-0-8(0)) RainbowFarm.

Gardens of Water. unabr. ed. Alan Drew. Read by Mark Bramhall. (Running Time: 41400 sec.). 2008. audio compact disk 34.95 (978-0-7393-5881-8(2), Random AudioBks) Pub: Random Audio Pubg. Dist(s): Random

Gardner's Chemical Synonyms & Trade Names. Michael Ash & Irene Ash. 1994. audio compact disk 250.00 (978-0-566-07557-5(1), Gower Pubng); audio compact disk 250.00 (978-0-566-07559-9(8), Gower Pubng) Pub: Ashgate Pub GBR. Dist(s): Ashgate Pub

Garfield Assassination. (Presidency Ser.). 10.00 Esstee Audios.

Garfield Mini Totebook It's All about Colors Shapes & Time vol. 1 Ages 4-5 (KINDERGARTEN) Prod. by PC Treasures Staff. (J). 2006. audio compact disk (978-1-933796-77-2(4)) PC Treasures.

Garfield Mini Totebook It's All about Colors Shapes & Time vol. 2 Ages 4-5 (KINDERGARTEN) Prod. by PC Treasures Staff. (J). 2006. audio compact disk (978-1-933796-78-9(2)) PC Treasures.

Garfield Mini Totebook It's All About Letters & Words, vol. 2. Prod. by PC Treasures Staff. (J). 2006. audio compact disk (978-1-933796-74-1(X)) PC Treasures.

Garfield Mini Totebook It's All about Math Readiness vol. 1 Ages 4-5 (KINDERGARTEN) Prod. by PC Treasures Staff. (J). 2006. audio compact disk (978-1-933796-81-9(2)) PC Treasures.

Garfield Mini Totebook It's All about Math Readiness vol. 2 Ages 4-5 (KINDERGARTEN) Prod. by PC Treasures Staff. (J). 2006. audio compact disk (978-1-933796-82-6(0)) PC Treasures.

Garfield Mini Totebook It's All about Math vol. 1 Ages 5-6 (GRADE 1) Prod. by PC Treasures Staff. (J). 2006. audio compact disk (978-1-933796-91-8(X)) PC Treasures.

Garfield Mini Totebook It's All about Math vol. 1 Ages 6-7 (GRADE 2) Prod. by PC Treasures Staff. (J). 2006. audio compact disk (978-1-60072-001-7(3)) PC Treasures.

Garfield Mini Totebook It's All about Math vol. 1 Ages 7-8 (GRADE 3) Prod. by PC Treasures Staff. (J). 2006. audio compact disk (978-1-60072-011-6(0)) PC Treasures.

Garfield Mini Totebook It's All about Math vol. 2 Ages 5-6 (GRADE 1) Prod. by PC Treasures Staff. (J). 2006. audio compact disk (978-1-933796-92-5(8)) PC Treasures.

Garfield Mini Totebook It's All about Math vol. 2 Ages 6-7 (GRADE 2) Prod. by PC Treasures Staff. (J). 2006. audio compact disk (978-1-60072-002-4(1)) PC Treasures.

Garfield Mini Totebook It's All about Math vol. 2 Ages 7-8 (GRADE 3) Prod. by PC Treasures Staff. (J). 2006. audio compact disk (978-1-60072-012-3(9)) PC Treasures.

Garfield Mini Totebook It's All about Numbers & Counting vol. 1 Ages 3-4 (PRESCHOOL) Prod. by PC Treasures Staff. (J). 2006. audio compact disk (978-1-933796-71-0(5)) PC Treasures.

Garfield Mini Totebook It's All about Numbers & Counting vol. 2 Ages 3-4 (PRESCHOOL) Prod. by PC Treasures Staff. (J). 2006. audio compact disk (978-1-933796-72-7(3)); audio compact disk (978-1-933796-73-4(1)) PC Treasures.

Garfield Mini Totebook It's All about Phonics vol. 1 Ages 3-4 (PRESCHOOL) Prod. by PC Treasures Staff. (J). 2006. audio compact disk (978-1-933796-75-8(8)) PC Treasures.

Garfield Mini Totebook It's All about Phonics vol. 2 Ages 3-4 (PRESCHOOL) Prod. by PC Treasures Staff. (J). 2006. audio compact disk (978-1-933796-76-5(6)) PC Treasures.

Garfield Mini Totebook It's All about Reading & Phonics vol. 1 Ages 5-6 (GRADE 1) Prod. by PC Treasures Staff. (J). 2006. audio compact disk (978-1-933796-85-7(5)) PC Treasures.

Garfield Mini Totebook It's All about Reading & Phonics vol. 1 Ages 6-7 (GRADE 2) Prod. by PC Treasures Staff. (J). 2006. audio compact disk (978-1-933796-95-6(2)) PC Treasures.

Garfield Mini Totebook It's All about Reading & Phonics vol. 1 Ages 7-8 (GRADE 3) Prod. by PC Treasures Staff. (J). 2006. audio compact disk (978-1-60072-005-5(6)) PC Treasures.

Garfield Mini Totebook It's All about Reading & Phonics vol. 2 Ages 5-6 (GRADE 1) Prod. by PC Treasures Staff. (J). 2006. audio compact disk (978-1-933796-86-4(3)) PC Treasures.

Garfield Mini Totebook It's All about Reading & Phonics vol. 2 Ages 6-7 (GRADE 2) Prod. by PC Treasures Staff. (J). 2006. audio compact disk (978-1-933796-96-3(0)) PC Treasures.

Garfield Mini Totebook It's All about Reading & Phonics vol. 2 Ages 7-8 (GRADE 3) Prod. by PC Treasures Staff. (J). 2006. audio compact disk (978-1-60072-006-2(4)) PC Treasures.

Garfield Mini Totebook It's All about Science vol. 1 Ages 4-5 (KINDERGARTEN) Prod. by PC Treasures Staff. (J). 2006. audio compact disk (978-1-933796-83-3(9)) PC Treasures.

Garfield Mini Totebook It's All about Science vol. 1 Ages 5-6 (GRADE 1) Prod. by PC Treasures Staff. (J). 2006. audio compact disk (978-1-933796-93-2(6)) PC Treasures.

Garfield Mini Totebook It's All about Science vol. 1 Ages 6-7 (GRADE 2) Prod. by PC Treasures Staff. (J). 2006. audio compact disk (978-1-60072-003-1(X)) PC Treasures.

Garfield Mini Totebook It's All about Science vol. 1 Ages 7-8 (GRADE 3) Prod. by PC Treasures Staff. (J). 2006. audio compact disk (978-1-60072-013-0(7)) PC Treasures.

Garfield Mini Totebook It's All about Science vol. 2 Ages 4-5 (KINDERGARTEN) Prod. by PC Treasures Staff. (J). 2006. audio compact disk (978-1-933796-84-0(7)) PC Treasures.

Garfield Mini Totebook It's All about Science vol. 2 Ages 5-6 (GRADE 1) Prod. by PC Treasures Staff. (J). 2006. audio compact disk (978-1-933796-94-9(4)) PC Treasures.

Garfield Mini Totebook It's All about Science vol. 2 Ages 6-7 (GRADE 2) Prod. by PC Treasures Staff. (J). 2006. audio compact disk (978-1-60072-004-8(8)) PC Treasures.

Garfield Mini Totebook It's All about Science vol. 2 Ages 7-8 (GRADE 3) Prod. by PC Treasures Staff. (J). 2006. audio compact disk (978-1-60072-014-7(5)) PC Treasures.

Garfield Mini Totebook Its All about Spelling & Vocabulary vol. 1 Ages 5-6 (GRADE 1) Prod. by PC Treasures Staff. (J). 2006. audio compact disk (978-1-933796-89-5(8)) PC Treasures.

Garfield Mini Totebook Its All about Spelling & Vocabulary vol. 1 Ages 6-7 (GRADE 2) Prod. by PC Treasures Staff. (J). 2006. audio compact disk (978-1-933796-99-4(5)) PC Treasures.

Garfield Mini Totebook Its All about Spelling & Vocabulary vol. 1 Ages 7-8 (GRADE 3) Prod. by PC Treasures Staff. (J). 2006. audio compact disk (978-1-60072-009-3(9)) PC Treasures.

Garfield Mini Totebook Its All about Spelling & Vocabulary vol. 2 Ages 5-6 (GRADE 1) Prod. by PC Treasures Staff. (J). 2006. audio compact disk (978-1-933796-90-1(1)) PC Treasures.

Garfield Mini Totebook Its All about Spelling & Vocabulary vol. 2 Ages 6-7 (GRADE 2) Prod. by PC Treasures Staff. (J). 2006. audio compact disk (978-1-60072-000-0(5)) PC Treasures.

Garfield Mini Totebook It's All about Spelling & Vocabulary vol. 2 Ages 7-8 (GRADE 3) Prod. by PC Treasures Staff. (J). 2006. audio compact disk (978-1-60072-010-9(2)) PC Treasures.

Garfield Mini Totebook It's All about Thinking Skills vol. 1 Ages 4-5 (KINDERGARTEN) Prod. by PC Treasures Staff. (J). 2006. audio compact disk (978-1-933796-79-6(0)) PC Treasures.

Garfield Mini Totebook It's All about Thinking Skills vol. 2 Ages 4-5 (KINDERGARTEN) Prod. by PC Treasures Staff. (J). 2006. audio compact disk (978-1-933796-80-2(4)) PC Treasures.

Garfield Mini Totebook It's All about Writing & Grammar vol. 1 Ages 5-6 (GRADE 1) Prod. by PC Treasures Staff. (J). 2006. audio compact disk (978-1-933796-87-1(1)) PC Treasures.

Garfield Mini Totebook It's All about Writing & Grammar vol. 1 Ages 6-7 (GRADE 2) Prod. by PC Treasures Staff. (J). 2006. audio compact disk (978-1-933796-97-0(9)) PC Treasures.

Garfield Mini Totebook It's All about Writing & Grammar vol. 1 Ages 7-8 (GRADE 3) Prod. by PC Treasures Staff. (J). 2006. audio compact disk (978-1-60072-007-9(2)) PC Treasures.

Garfield Mini Totebook It's All about Writing & Grammar vol. 2 Ages 5-6 (GRADE 1) Prod. by PC Treasures Staff. (J). 2006. audio compact disk (978-1-933796-88-8(X)) PC Treasures.

Garfield Mini Totebook It's All about Writing & Grammar vol. 2 Ages 6-7 (GRADE 2) Prod. by PC Treasures Staff. (J). 2006. audio compact disk (978-1-933796-98-7(7)) PC Treasures.

Garfield Mini Totebook It's All about Writing & Grammar vol. 2 Ages 7-8 (GRADE 3) Prod. by PC Treasures Staff. (J). 2006. audio compact disk (978-1-60072-008-6(0)) PC Treasures.

Garfield Phonics Activity Totebook (Ag[illegible] Volume 1. (J). 2005. audio compact disk (978-1-933796-48-2(0)) [illegible]easures.

Garfield Totebook It's All about Color Shapes & Time Ages 4-5 (KINDERGARTEN) (J). 2006. audio compact disk (978-1-933796-52-9(9)) PC Treasures.

Garfield Totebook It's All about Letters & Words Ages 3-4 (PRESCHOOL) (J). 2006. audio compact disk (978-1-933796-50-5(2)) PC Treasures.

Garfield Totebook It's All about Math Ages 5-6 (GRADE 1) (J). 2006. audio compact disk (978-1-933796-59-8(6)) PC Treasures.

Garfield Totebook It's All about Math Ages 6-7 (GRADE 2) Prod. by PC Treasures Staff. (J). 2006. audio compact disk (978-1-933796-64-2(2)) PC Treasures.

Garfield Totebook It's All about Math Ages 7-8 (GRADE 3) Prod. by PC Treasures Staff. (J). 2006. audio compact disk (978-1-933796-69-7(3)) PC Treasures.

Garfield Totebook It's All about Math Readiness Ages 4-5 (KINDERGARTEN) (J). 2006. audio compact disk (978-1-933796-54-3(5)) PC Treasures.

Garfield Totebook It's All about Numbers & Counting Ages 3-4 (PRESCHOOL) (J). 2006. audio compact disk (978-1-933796-49-9(9)) PC Treasures.

Garfield Totebook It's All about Phonics Ages 3-4 (PRESCHOOL) (J). 2006. audio compact disk (978-1-933796-51-2(0)) PC Treasures.

Garfield Totebook It's All about Reading & Phonics Ages 5-6 (GRADE 1) (J). 2006. audio compact disk (978-1-933796-56-7(1)) PC Treasures.

Garfield Totebook It's All about Reading & Phonics Ages 6-7 (GRADE 2) Prod. by PC Treasures Staff. (J). 2006. audio compact disk (978-1-933796-61-1(8)) PC Treasures.

Garfield Totebook It's All about Reading & Phonics Ages 7-8 (GRADE 3) Prod. by PC Treasures Staff. (J). 2006. audio compact disk (978-1-933796-66-6(9)) PC Treasures.

Garfield Totebook It's All about Science Ages 4-5 (KINDERGARTEN) (J). 2006. audio compact disk (978-1-933796-55-0(3)) PC Treasures.

Garfield Totebook It's All about Science Ages 5-6 (GRADE 1) (J). 2006. audio compact disk (978-1-933796-60-4(X)) PC Treasures.

Garfield Totebook It's All about Science Ages 6-7 (GRADE 2) Prod. by PC Treasures Staff. (J). 2006. audio compact disk (978-1-933796-65-9(0)) PC Treasures.

Garfield Totebook It's All about Science Ages 7-8 (GRADE 3) Prod. by PC Treasures Staff. (J). 2006. audio compact disk (978-1-933796-70-3(7)) PC Treasures.

Garfield Totebook It's All about Spelling & Vocabulary Ages 5-6 (GRADE 1) (J). 2006. audio compact disk (978-1-933796-58-1(8)) PC Treasures.

Garfield Totebook It's All about Spelling & Vocabulary Ages 6-7 (GRADE 2) Prod. by PC Treasures Staff. (J). 2006. audio compact disk (978-1-933796-63-5(4)) PC Treasures.

Garfield Totebook It's All about Spelling & Vocabulary Ages 7-8 (GRADE 3) Prod. by PC Treasures Staff. (J). 2006. audio compact disk (978-1-933796-68-0(5)) PC Treasures.

Garfield Totebook It's All about Thinking Skills Ages 4-5 (KINDERGARTEN) (J). 2006. audio compact disk (978-1-933796-53-6(7)) PC Treasures.

Garfield Totebook It's All about Writing & Grammar Ages 5-6 (GRADE 1) (J). 2006. audio compact disk (978-1-933796-57-4(X)) PC Treasures.

Garfield Totebook It's All about Writing & Grammar Ages 6-7 (GRADE 2) Prod. by PC Treasures Staff. (J). 2006. audio compact disk (978-1-933796-62-8(6)) PC Treasures.

Garfield Totebook It's All about Writing & Grammar Ages 7-8 (GRADE 3) Prod. by PC Treasures Staff. (J). 2006. audio compact disk (978-1-933796-67-3(7)) PC Treasures.

Gargoyle. unabr. ed. Andrew Davidson. Read by Lincoln Hoppe. 11 cass. 2008. 120.00 (978-1-4159-5929-9(3), BksonTape); audio compact disk 120.00 (978-1-4159-5688-5(X), BksonTape) Pub: Random Audio Pubg. Dist(s): Random

The narrator of The Gargoyle is a very contemporary cynic, physically beautiful and sexually adept, who dwells in the moral vacuum that is modern life. As the book opens, he is driving along a dark road when he is distracted by what seems to be a flight of arrows. He crashes into a ravine and suffers horrible burns over much of his body. As he recovers in a burn ward, undergoing the tortures of the damned, he awaits the day when he can leave the hospital and commit carefully planned suicide - for he is now a monster in appearance as well as in soul. A beautiful and compelling, but clearly unhinged, sculptress of gargoyles by the name of Marianne Engel appears at the foot of his bed and insists that they were once lovers in medieval Germany. In her telling, he was a badly injured mercenary and she was a nun and scribe in the famed monastery of Engelthal who nursed him back to health. As she spins their tale in Scheherazade fashion and relates equally mesmerizing stories of deathless love in Japan, Iceland, Italy, and England, he finds himself drawn back to life - and, finally, in love. He is released into Marianne's care and takes up residence in her huge stone house. But all is not well. For one thing, the pull of his past sins becomes ever more powerful as the morphine he is prescribed becomes ever more addictive. For another, Marianne receives word from God that she has only twenty-seven sculptures left to complete - and her time on earth will be finished.

Gargoyle. unabr. ed. Andrew Davidson. Read by Lincoln Hoppe. (Running Time: 19 hrs. 30 mins.). (ENG.). 2008. 27.50 (978-0-7393-2896-5(4), BksonTape); audio compact disk 49.95 (978-0-7393-2895-8(6), Random AudioBks) Pub: Random Audio Pubg. Dist(s): Random

Garland for a Dead Maiden. Nicholas Rhea. Read by Graham Padden. 7 cass. (Running Time: 9 hrs. 15 mins.). (Story Sound Ser.). (J). 2004. 61.95 (978-1-85903-662-4(7)); audio compact disk 79.95 (978-1-85903-690-7(2)) Pub: Mgna Lrg Print GBR. Dist(s): Ulverscroft US

Garland for Girls. unabr. ed. Louisa May Alcott. Read by C. M. Herbert. 5 cass. (Running Time: 7 hrs.). (gr. 4-7). 2000. 39.95 (978-0-7861-1802-1(4), 2601) Blckstn Audio.

Rich girls, poor girls, haughty girls, timid girls, clever girls & silly girls, all the sorts of girls who make a world-float through these pages & before you have finished you will feel that you have known each one, almost as well as your own best friends.

***Garland for Girls.** unabr. ed. Louisa May Alcott. Read by C. M. Hebert. (Running Time: 7 hrs. 0 mins.). 2010. 29.95 (978-1-4417-5566-7(7)); audio compact disk 69.00 (978-1-4417-5563-6(2)) Blckstn Audio.

Garland of Moksha Mantras. abr. ed. Yogi Hari. 2002. audio compact disk 14.95 (978-1-57777-038-1(2), 407-017) Pub: Nada Prodns. Dist(s): Bookworld

Garland of Rational Songs. Albert Ellis. 1 cass. (Running Time: 32 min.). bk. 13.00 (C057); 9.95 (C006) A Ellis Institute.

Albert Ellis lyrics, sung to popular tunes. Humorous songs sung by the lyricist himself in his inimitable baritone. It's entertaining, therapeutic, & makes a great gift.

Garland of Rational Songs. Albert Ellis. 1 cass. (Running Time: 32 min.). 9.95 (C006); 13.00 Incl. songbk. (C057) Inst Rational-Emotive.

***Garlands of Gold.** Rosalind Laker, pseud. 2010. 76.95 (978-1-4079-0894-6(4)); audio compact disk 89.95 (978-1-4079-0895-3(2)) Pub: Soundings Ltd GBR. Dist(s): Ulverscroft US

Garlic & Sapphires: The Secret Life of a Critic in Disguise. unabr. ed. Ruth Reichl. Read by Bernadette Dunne. 9 CDs. (Running Time: 11 hrs.). 2005. audio compact disk 68.85 (978-1-4159-1675-9(6)); 63.00 (978-1-4159-1591-2(1)) Books on Tape.

Just as eating in restaurants is about more than food, being a reviewer involves more than writing. These principles are illustrated constantly in Reichl's account of her six years as a restaurant critic for The New York Times. She devotes much of the book to how she hid her identity by creating disguises and accompanying personalities when dining out and the effects these had on her family and friends. The jealousies and infighting at the Times, an unpleasant place to work according to the author, are yet another problem. Nevertheless, her tale is the most entertaining of her three memoirs because of her enthusiasm for good food and her love of the diversity and romance of her native city.

Garment. unabr. ed. Catherine Cookson. Read by Elizabeth Henry. 8 cass. (Running Time: 12 hrs.). 2001. 69.95 (978-1-85496-053-5(9), 60539) Pub: Soundings Ltd GBR. Dist(s): Ulverscroft US

It took her two years to recognize that her marriage was a hollow shell. In the restricted society of the North Country village, affection soon turned to bitterness & sympathy to passion.

Garment of Priase - Size 6: How God Blessed Me to Lose 130 + Pounds. unabr. ed. Mary Frances Cable. Read by Mary Frances Cable. 3 cass. (Running Time: 4 hrs. 8 mins.). 2002. 25.95 (978-0-9722331-1-8(3)) Capstone Pubns.

Testimony of how the Lord spared my life following a total of three strokes, as well as how He enabled me to lose 130+ pounds, healed me of diabetes, etc. Practical guidelines concerning diet and lifestyle changes.

Garnet Hill. unabr. ed. Denise Mina. Read by Katy Anderson. 10 cass. (Isis Cassettes Ser.). (J). 2005. 84.95 (978-0-7531-1798-9(3)) Pub: ISIS Lrg Prnt GBR. Dist(s): Ulverscroft US

Garnethill. Denise Mina. (Isis (CDs) Ser.). (J). 2005. audio compact disk 89.95 (978-0-7531-2401-7(7)) Pub: ISIS Lrg Prnt GBR. Dist(s): Ulverscroft US

Garrison Hospital. unabr. ed. Alex Stuart. 5 cass. (Sound Ser.). 2004. 49.95 (978-1-85496-339-0(2)) Pub: UlverLrgPrint GBR. Dist(s): Ulverscroft US

Garrison Keillor: A Life in Comedy. abr. unabr. ed. Garrison Keillor. Contrib. by Garrison Keillor. 2 CDs. (Running Time: 2 hrs. 30 mins.). (ENG.). 2003. audio compact disk 22.95 (978-1-56511-696-2(8), 1565116968) Pub: HighBridge. Dist(s): Workman Pub

Garrison Keillor Comedy Gift Pack. abr. unabr. ed. Garrison Keillor. 5 CDs. (Running Time: 5 hrs.). (ENG.). 1998. audio compact disk 49.95 (978-1-56511-290-2(3), 1565112903) Pub: HighBridge. Dist(s): Workman Pub

***Garrison Retreat Weekend.** Featuring Adyashanti. 2010. audio compact disk 65.00 (978-1-933986-76-0(X)) Open Gate Pub.

***Garro: Oath of the Moment.** James Swallow. (ENG.). 2010. 17.00 (978-1-84416-845-3(X), Black Library) Pub: BL Pubng GBR. Dist(s): S and S Inc

Garson Kerbs Private Eye. unabr. ed. National Public Radio Staff. 4 cass. (Running Time: 4 hrs.). 1999. 24.95 (978-0-9660392-2-1(X)) Pub: Radio Repertory. Dist(s): Penton Overseas

A tongue-in-cheek private detective with all the answers & all the problems. A detective comedy-adventure with a real film noir feel.

Garson Krebs: Private Detective. Perf. by Radio Repertory Company Staff. 4 cass. (Running Time: 4 hrs.). 2001. 24.95 (RRCA003) Lodestone Catalog.

A combination of the best of old time radio acting with modern sound effects, music & technology. With eight zany half-hour episodes.

Garson Krebs Private Eye. (Nostalgia Classics Ser.). 24.99 Moonbeam Pubns.

Includes "Man with a Past;" "The Lottery;" "The Diva;" "Portrait of a Lady;" "The Prime Minister's Daughter;" "The Device;" "Double Exposure;" "The Chocolate Passion;" "Club of Fear;" "The Case of the Missing Husband".

Gary Burton. Read by Gary Burton. 1 cass. (Running Time: 60 min.). (Marian McPartland's Piano Jazz Ser.). 13.95 (MM-87-04-23, HarperThor) HarpC GBR.

Gary Faith Crusade. Featuring Bill Winston. 3 CDs. 2004. audio compact disk 24.00 (978-1-59544-194-2(8)) Pub: B Winston Min. Dist(s): Anchor Distributors

Gary Fith Crusade. Featuring Bill Winston. 3 cass. 2004. 24.00 (978-1-59544-193-5(X)) Pub: B Winston Min. Dist(s): Anchor Distributors

Gary Gildner I: "Letters from Vicksburg" unabr. ed. Read by Gary Gildner. 1 cass. (Running Time: 29 min.). 1986. 10.00 New Letters.

Reads a sonnet sequence based on letters written by a Civil War soldier.

Gary Gildner II: "Childhood" unabr. ed. Read by Gary Gildner. 1 cass. (Running Time: 29 min.). 1986. 10.00 New Letters.

Iowa poet reads poems reflecting his childhood memories.

Gary Gilmore: Shot in the Heart. unabr. ed. Mikal Gilmore. Read by Michael Prichard. 14 cass. (Running Time: 21 hrs.). 1994. 112.00 (3653) Books on Tape.

After Gary Gilmore was convicted of killing two men in cold blood, he campaigned for his own death by firing squad. But he may have died spiritually long before the State of Utah executed him. Abused often by his father, Gary had a history of criminal acts, suicide attempts & substance abuse long witnessed by his younger brother Mikal. But Mikal escaped his family before Gary's bitterness exploded into murder. His eloquent portrait of Gary's life & of his own shows how a desperate family creates a killer. In the hands of his brother Mikal, Gary Gilmore's story calls up pity to witness a tragedy unfolding.

Gary Hudson: Freeports of Earth: The Case for Floating Islands. (Running Time: 60 min.). (Freeland Ser.: No. I). 1983. 9.00 (FL3) Freeland Pr.

Cites several exlamples of the mechanics of such "islands" & presents ideas which can be implemented now.

Gary Hudson: Liberty from the Pacific Rim to Space. (Running Time: 40 min.). (Freeland Ser.: No. II). 1984. 9.00 (FL11) Freeland Pr.

Takes us through time, from China & Japans's influence on our present culture to space, as the ultimate & unlimited frontier.

Gary Hudson: The Privatization of Space. (Running Time: 60 min.). (Cal State Univ., Long Beach). 1982. 9.00 (F133) Freeland Pr.

The author discusses his prior 13 years experience in privitizing space & his approaches to various corporations regarding their participation in this endeavor.

Gary Null's Perfect Health System. Gary Null. Read by Gary Null. (Running Time: 8 hrs.). (C). 2005. 42.95 (978-1-59912-162-8(X)) Iofy Corp.

Gary Null's Ultimate Anti-Aging Program, Set. abr. ed. Gary Null. Read by Robert Deyan. 4 cass. (Running Time: 6 hrs.). 1999. 24.95 (978-1-55935-310-6(4)) Soundelux.

Four part program based on the most recent scientific findings.

Gary S. Wagner: Incredible Insights Derived from Candlestick Charting. Read by Gary S. Wagner. 1 cass. 30.00 Dow Jones Telerate.

Traders worldwide now want the wealth of knowledge that only this elusive technique can generate. Japanese candlesticks blend perfectly with nearly all of the common Western technical analysis methods & will increase your understanding of any commodity or stock issue as well as provide incredible insight into any markets future price moves. Our technologically advanced era provides the necessary tools (computers & software) to simplify the candlestick technique & make it available to anyone interested in using this enhanced technical analysis method.

Gary Snyder see Inner Ear

Gary Soto. unabr. ed. Poems. Gary Soto. Ed. by James McKinley. Prod. by Rebeah Presson. 1 cass. (Running Time: 29 min.). (On the Air Ser.). 1992. 10.00 New Letters.

University of California at Berkeley Professor Soto reads his poems about his childhood as a migrant worker, & talks about the upsurge in Chicano literature.

Gary Soto. unabr. ed. Read by Gary Soto & Rebekah Presson. Ed. by James McKinley. 2 cass. (Running Time: 29 min.). (New Letters on the Air Ser.). 1992. 10.00 set. (040982); 18.00 2-sided cass. (011092) New Letters.

Soto is interviewed by Rebekah Presson & reads from his work.

Gary Soto II. unabr. ed. Gary Soto. 1 cass. (Running Time: 29 min.). (New Letters on the Air Ser.). 1992. 10.00 (011092) New Letters.

Soto reads poems & talks about the recent rise in Chicano literature.

Gary the G-Man. Vernon Brobst. Read by Brad Venable. Prod. by Dreamervision Studios. (ENG.). 2008. 19.95 (978-1-934965-01-6(4)) Dreamervision Pub.

Gary the G-Man. Vernon Brobst. Read by Venable Brad. Prod. by Dreamervision Studios. (ENG.). 2008. audio compact disk 29.95 (978-1-934965-00-9(6)) Dreamervision Pub.

Gas Chromatography - Mass Spectrometry. Instructed by J. T. Watson. 5 cass. (Running Time: 5 hrs.). 435.00 incl. 134pp. manual. (77) Am Chemical.

An introduction to the operating principles & applications of Gas Chromatography & Mass Spectrometry.

Gas City. unabr. ed. Loren D. Estleman. Read by Mel Foster. (YA). 2008. 59.99 (978-1-60514-863-2(6)) Find a World.

Gas City. unabr. ed. Loren D. Estleman. Read by Mel Foster. 1 MP3-CD. (Running Time: 10 hrs. 30 mins. 0 sec.). (ENG.). 2008. 24.99 (978-1-4001-5620-7(3)); audio compact disk 34.99 (978-1-4001-0620-2(6)); audio compact disk 69.99 (978-1-4001-3620-9(2)) Pub: Tantor Media. Dist(s): IngramPubServ

Gas Giants. Read by Isaac Asimov. 1 cass. (Running Time: 26 min.). 14.95 (CBC1031) MMI Corp.

Guided tour of Jupiter, Saturn & other planets. Asimov, Pohl & others discuss how knowledge of Jupiter can help us to understand our own planet.

Gasp! Zapt! Splat! unabr. ed. Terry Denton. Read by Stig Wemyss. (Running Time: 2400 sec.). (J). (gr. k-5). 2006. audio compact disk 39.95 (978-1-74093-819-8(4)) Pub: Bolinda Pubng AUS. Dist(s): Bolinda Pub Inc

Gaspard de la Nuit, Set. Aloysius Bertrand. Read by J. Gouttenoire & Claude Lesko. 2 cass. (FRE.). 1991. 26.95 (1431-VSL) Olivia & Hill.

A collection of fantasies, forming a succession of scintillating, often grotesque images, written in ornate & rhythmical language by this precursor of the Symbolists & Surrealists.

Gasparine. l.t. ed. Jean-Michel Thibaux. (French Ser.). 2001. bk. 30.99 (978-2-84011-422-2(4)) Pub: UlverLrgPrint GBR. Dist(s): Ulverscroft US

Gasping for Airtime: Two Years in the Trenches at Saturday Night Live. Jay Mohr. Read by Jay Mohr. 6 vols. 2004. bk. 32.95 (978-0-7927-3249-5(9), SLD 666, Chivers Sound Lib) AudioGO.

Gaspipe: Confessions of a Mafia Boss. Philip Carlo. Read by Alan Sklar. (Playaway Adult Nonfiction Ser.). (ENG.). 2009. 64.99 (978-1-60775-774-0(5)) Find a World.

Gaspipe: Confessions of a Mafia Boss. unabr. ed. Philip Carlo. Read by Alan Sklar. Narrated by Alan Sklar. (Running Time: 12 hrs. 30 mins. 0 sec.). (ENG.). 2008. audio compact disk 34.99 (978-1-4001-0711-7(3)); audio compact disk 69.99 (978-1-4001-3711-4(X)); audio compact disk 24.99 (978-1-4001-5711-2(0)) Pub: Tantor Media. Dist(s): IngramPubServ

Gastrointestinal Cancer. Moderated by Harold J. Wanebo. (Postgraduate Courses Ser.). 1986. 115.00 (8620(C86-PG10)) Am Coll Surgeons.

Provides the surgeon with an update regarding current concepts & the most recent advances regarding gastrointestinal cancer.

Gastrointestinal Disease. (Postgraduate Programs Ser.: C85-PG2). 85.00 (8512) Am Coll Surgeons.

Updates the practicing surgeon on recent advances in gastrointestinal surgery.

Gastrointestinal Disease. (Postgraduate Programs Ser.: C84-PG2). 1984. 85.00 (8482) Am Coll Surgeons.

Provides surgical residents & practicing surgeons information concerning various gastrointestinal conditions.

Gastrointestinal Disease. Moderated by David Fromm. (Postgraduate Courses Ser.: C86-PG2). 1986. 115.00 (8612) Am Coll Surgeons.

Provides advances in gastrointestinal surgery & reviews pitfalls of several operative procedures.

Gastrointestinal Motility Disorders: Preoperative & Postoperative. 2 cass. (General Sessions Ser.: C84-GS5). 1984. 15.00 (8409) Am Coll Surgeons.

Gastrointestinal Surgery: Step by Step Management. Rao. 2005. audio compact disk 75.00 (978-81-8061-429-3(8)) Jaypee Brothers IND.

Gastrostomy Care: A Guide to Practice. Scripts. Ed. by Catherine Barrett. 2 CDs. (Running Time: 2 hrs.). (Ausmed Guide to Practice Ser.). 2004. pap. bk. 59.95 (978-0-9751585-2-4(X)) Pub: Ausmed AUS. Dist(s): MPHC

Two one hour audio CDs spoken in a neutral female voice. Very easy to listening. Each chapter of the book is reduced to a seven minute mini lecture of the content. An ideal teaching tool or fast learning system for busy professionals.

***Gate at the Stairs.** unabr. ed. Lorrie Moore. Narrated by Mia Barron. 1 Playaway. (Running Time: 12 hrs.). 2009. 94.95 (978-0-7927-6841-8(8)); audio compact disk 94.95 (978-0-7927-6838-8(8)) AudioGO.

Gate at the Stairs. unabr. ed. Lorrie Moore. Read by Mia Barron. 10 CDs. (Running Time: 11 hrs. 0 mins. 0 sec.). (ENG.). 2009. audio compact disk 29.95 (978-1-60283-716-4(3)) Pub: AudioGO. Dist(s): Perseus Dist

Gate House. abr. ed. Nelson DeMille. Read by Christian Rummel. (Running Time: 9 hrs. 30 mins.). (ENG.). 2008. 19.98 (978-1-60024-407-0(6)) Pub: Hachet Audio. Dist(s): HachBkGrp

Gate House. abr. ed. Nelson DeMille. Read by Christian Rummel. (Running Time: 9 hrs. 30 mins.). (ENG.). 2009. audio compact disk 19.98 (978-1-60024-828-3(4)) Pub: Hachet Audio. Dist(s): HachBkGrp

Gate House. unabr. ed. Nelson DeMille. Read by Christian Rummel. (Running Time: 22 hrs.). (ENG.). 2008. 32.98 (978-1-60024-409-4(2)); audio compact disk 49.98 (978-1-60024-410-0(6)) Pub: Hachet Audio. Dist(s): HachBkGrp

Gate House. unabr. ed. Nelson DeMille. Read by Christian Rummel. 19 CDs. 2008. audio compact disk 129.00 (978-1-4159-6069-1(0), BksonTape); 129.00 (978-1-4159-6090-5(9), BksonTape) Pub: Random Audio Pubg. Dist(s): Random

After John Sutter's aristocratic wife killed her Mafia don lover, John left America and set out in his sailboat on a three-year journey around the world, eventually settling in London. Now, ten years later, he has come home to the Gold Coast of Long Island - that stretch of land that once held the greatest concentration of wealth and power in America - to attend the imminent funeral of an old family servant. Taking up residence in the gatehouse of Stanhope Hall, the family home of his ex-wife, Susan Stanhope Sutter, John finds himself living only a quarter of a mile from Susan, who has also returned to Long Island after living in Hilton Head for the past decade. But Susan isn't the only person from John's past who has resurfaced. Though Frank Bellarosa, infamous Mafia don and Susan's ex-lover, is long dead, his son, Anthony, is alive and intent on two missions: drawing John back into the violent world of the Bellarosa family, and exacting revenge on his father's murderer - Susan Sutter. At the same time, John and Susan's mutual attraction reawakens and old passions begin to reignite - and John finds himself being pulled deeper and deeper into a web of seduction and betrayal.

Gate in the Wall. unabr. ed. Ellen Howard. Narrated by Jenny Sterlin. 3 cass. (Running Time: 4 hrs. 30 mins.). (YA). 2000. pap. bk. & stu. ed. 53.00 (41061X4) Recorded Bks.

Ten-year-old Emma works long hours in a Victorian England textile mill. One day, she notices a gate swinging in the high wall alongside the road. As she steps through the opening, she enters a strange world of canals & boats. A vivid picture of the canal system England used for two centuries & the boat folk who navigated it.

Gate in the Wall. unabr. ed. Ellen Howard. Narrated by Jenny Sterlin. 3 pieces. (Running Time: 4 hrs. 30 mins.). (gr. 4 up). 2000. 30.00 (978-0-7887-3891-3(7), 96075E7) Recorded Bks.

Gate in the Wall, Class Set. Ellen Howard. Read by Jenny Sterlin. 3 cass. (Running Time: 4 hrs. 30 mins.). (YA). 1999. pap. bk. & stu. ed. 198.30 (978-0-7887-3989-7(1), 47055) Recorded Bks.

Gate of Angels. unabr. ed. Penelope Fitzgerald. Read by Nadia May. 4 cass,. (Running Time: 5 hrs.). 2000. 32.95 (978-0-7861-1691-1(9), 2514) Blckstn Audio.

It is 1912 & at Cambridge University the modem age is knocking at the gate. In lecture halls & laboratories, the model of a universe governed by the Mind of God is at last giving way to something wholly rational, a universe

governed by the Laws of Physics. This comes as a great comfort to Fred Fairly, a junior at the college of St Angelicus. Science, he is certain will soon explain everything. Mystery will be routed by reason & the demands of the soul will be seen for that they are, a distraction & an illusion.

Gate of Heaven, Set. Matthew B. Brown. 2 cass. 2004. 13.95 (978-1-57734-512-1(6), 07002149) Covenant Comms.

Gate of Heaven Part I: A Collection of Catholic Hymnody. Mary Oberle Hubley. Ed. by Mary Oberle Hubley. (ENG.). 2007. audio compact disk 17.00 (978-0-9819212-0-4(5)) Nic Maria.

Gate of Heaven, Part II: A Collection of Catholic Hymns. Mary Oberle Hubley. Ed. by Mary Oberle Hubley. (ENG.). 2007. audio compact disk 17.00 (978-0-9819212-1-1(3)) Nic Maria.

Gate of Heaven, Part III: A Collection of Catholic Hymns. Mary Oberle Hubley. Ed. by Mary Oberle Hubley. (ENG.). 2008. audio compact disk 17.00 (978-0-9819212-2-8(1)) Nic Maria.

Gate of His Enemies. unabr. ed. Gilbert Morris. Read by Maynard Villers. 8 cass. (Running Time: 11 hrs. 30 min.). (Appomattox Ser.: Bk. 2). 1998. 49.95 (978-1-55686-833-7(2)) Books in Motion.
The Civil War has left a chasm between North & South, turning friends & brothers into bitter enemies. Deborah Steele is torn between her belief in the Union & her love for a dashing Confederate officer.

Gate of No Return Audio Book. Rooster Morris. Read by Rooster Morris. Read by Jody Logsdon. (J). 2004. audio compact disk 15.95 (978-0-9755895-3-3(9)) Axle Pubng Co.

Gate of No Return Song CD. Rooster Morris. (J). 2004. audio compact disk 7.95 (978-0-9755895-2-6(0)) Axle Pubng Co.

Gate of the Temple. Richard Rohr. Read by Richard Rohr. 3 cass. (Running Time: 3 hrs.). 1991. 24.95 Set. (978-7-900782-91-5(5), AA2443) Credence Commun.
How sexuality can be integrated into a healthy spirituality.

Gate 12 & Its Lines. Ra Uru Hu. 1 CD. (Running Time: 34 mins.). (Commentaries). 2000. audio compact disk (978-1-931164-04-7(5)) zc design.

Gate 15 & Its Lines. Ra Uru Hu. (Commentaries). 2000. audio compact disk 15.00 (978-1-931164-05-4(3)) zc design.

Gate 16 & Its Lines. Ra Uru Hu. 1 CD. (Running Time: 39 mins.). (Commentaries). 2000. audio compact disk (978-1-931164-01-6(0)) zc design.

Gate 2 & Its Lines. Ra Uru Hu. 1 CD. (Running Time: 32 mins.). (Commentaries). 2000. audio compact disk (978-0-9671115-5-1(2)) zc design.

Gate 20 & Its Lines. Ra Uru Hu. 1 CD. (Running Time: 39 mins.). (Commentaries). 2000. audio compact disk (978-0-9671115-8-2(7)) zc design.

Gate 23 & Its Lines. Ra Uru Hu. 1 CD. (Running Time: 32 mins.). (Commentaries). 2000. audio compact disk (978-0-9671115-6-8(0)) zc design.

Gate 24 & Its Lines. Ra Uru Hu. 1 CD. (Running Time: 41 mins.). (Commentaries). 2000. audio compact disk (978-0-9671115-4-4(4)) zc design.
Lecture on Hexagram/Gate 27 of the Rave I'Ching.

Gate 27 & Its Lines. Ra Uru Hu. 1 CD. (Running Time: 38 mins.). (Commentaries). 2000. audio compact disk (978-0-9671115-3-7(6)) zc design.

Gate 35 & Its Lines. Ra Uru Hu. 1 CD. (Running Time: 37 mins.). (Commentaries). 2000. audio compact disk (978-1-931164-02-3(9)) zc design.

Gate 39 & Its Lines. Ra Uru Hu. (Commentaries). 2000. audio compact disk 15.00 (978-1-931164-07-8(X)) zc design.

Gate 45 & Its Lines. Ra Uru Hu. 1 CD. (Running Time: 30 mins.). (Commentaries). 2000. audio compact disk (978-1-931164-03-0(7)) zc design.

Gate 52 & Its Lines. Ra Uru Hu. (Commentaries). 2000. audio compact disk 15.00 (978-1-931164-06-1(1)) zc design.

Gate 53 & Its Lines. Ra Uru Hu. (Commentaries). 2000. audio compact disk 15.00 (978-1-931164-08-5(8)) zc design.

Gate 56 & Its Lines. Ra Uru Hu. (Commentaries). 2000. audio compact disk 15.00 (978-1-931164-13-9(4)) zc design.

Gate 62 & Its Lines. Ra Uru Hu. (Commentaries). 2000. audio compact disk 15.00 (978-1-931164-09-2(6)) zc design.

Gate 8 & Its Lines. Ra Uru Hu. 1 CD. (Running Time: 30 mins.). (Commentaries). 2000. audio compact disk (978-0-9671115-7-5(9)) zc design.

Gatecrasher. unabr. ed. Madeleine Wickham. Read by Katherine Kellgren. 7 CDs. (Running Time: 9 hrs. 0 mins. 0 sec.). (ENG.). 2009. audio compact disk 29.99 (978-1-4272-0437-0(3)) Pub: Macmill Audio. Dist(s): Macmillan

Gatecrashers. unabr. ed. Alexander Fullerton. Read by Terry Wale. 12 cass. (Running Time: 18 hrs.). 2001. 94.95 (978-1-86042-880-7(0)) Pub: Soundings Ltd GBR. Dist(s): Ulverscroft US
As "The Gatecrashers" draws to its thunderous climax, father & son will face their final, most searching test... These are the most meticulously researched of war novels.

Gatecrashers. unabr. ed. Alexander Fullerton. Read by Terry Wale. 12 CDs. (Running Time: 14 hrs. 41 mins.). (Sound Ser.). 2002. audio compact disk 99.95 (978-1-86042-947-7(5)) Pub: UlverLrgPrint GBR. Dist(s): Ulverscroft US

Gatekeeper. Philip Shelby. 2004. 10.95 (978-0-7435-4755-0(1)) Pub: S&S Audio. Dist(s): S and S Inc

***Gatekeepers.** unabr. ed. Robert Liparulo. Read by Joshua Swanson. (Running Time: 10 hrs. NaN mins.). (Dreamhouse Kings Ser.). (ENG.). 2011. 29.95 (978-1-4417-7745-4(8)); 59.95 (978-1-4417-7742-3(3)); audio compact disk 90.00 (978-1-4417-7743-0(1)) Blckstn Audio.

Gates. unabr. ed. John Connolly. Read by Jonathan Cake. 6 CDs. (Running Time: 7 hrs. 0 mins. 0 sec.). (ENG.). 2009. audio compact disk 29.99 (978-1-4423-0060-6(4)) Pub: S&S Audio. Dist(s): S and S Inc

Gates of Angels, unabr. ed. Penelope Fitzgerald. Read by Nadia May. 4 cass. (Running Time: 6 hrs.). 2000. 32.95 (2514) Blckstn Audio.
It is 1912 & at Cambridge University the modern age is knocking at the gate. Science, Fred Fairly is certain, will soon explain everything. Mystery will be routed by reason & the demands of the soul will be seen for what they are - a distraction & an illusion. Into Fred's orderly life comes Daisy, with a bang - literally. Fellow cyclists on a dark country road; the next, they are casualties of a freakish accident. Is she a manifestation of Chaos, or is she a sign of another kind of Order?.

Gates of Eden. Ethan Coen. 4 cass. (Running Time: 4 hrs.). 1999. 24.35 (978-0-671-03357-6(3)) S and S Inc.
Features characters struggling to comprehend their place in the world & trying to understand the situations fate has placed in front of them.

Gates of Fire: An Epic Novel of the Battle of Thermopylae. abr. ed. Steven Pressfield. Read by Derek Jacobi. 4 cass. 1999. 23.95 (FS9-43323) Highsmith.

Gates of Fire: An Epic Novel of the Battle of Thermopylae. unabr. ed. Steven Pressfield. Narrated by George Guidall. 11 cass. (Running Time: 15 hrs.). 1999. 93.00 (978-0-7887-3771-8(6), 95988E7) Recorded Bks.
Puts you at the side of the valiant Spartan warriors in 480 BC for the glorious, climactic battle at Thermopylae, where a handful of Sparta's finest held back the invading Persian army.

Gates of Greenham. unabr. ed. Tony Biggin. Perf. by Eiddwen Harrhy et al. Narrated by Sheila Hancock & Barry Wilsher. Contrib. by John Hywel. 2 cass. (Running Time: 2 hrs. 30 min.). 1986. 16.00 incl. libretto. Pendle Hill.
Inspired by the story of the first three years of the women's encampment at Greenham Common (American Air Force Base) near Newbury in Berkshire, England, which was being developed to house cruise missles. Drawn from writings, poetry, attitudes, news reports & individual campaigner's experiences.

Gates of Hell. Francis Frangipane. 1 cass. (Running Time: 90 mins.). (Strategies for our Cities Ser.: Vol. 6). 2000. 5.00 (FF06-006) Morning NC.
This series provides practical, biblical solutions that have been tested & have born fruit for those with a vision for their cities.

Gates of Hell. Mac Hammond. 2 cass. (Running Time: 2 hrs). 2005. 10.00 (978-1-57399-238-1(0)) Mac Hammond.
Jesus told us "the gates of hell shall not prevail" against the Church. But what does that mean to you personally? Find out in this teaching designed to make you invincible to the attacks of the enemy.

Gates of Hell. T. D. Jakes. 1 cass. 1997. 20.00 (978-1-57855-000-5(9)) T D Jakes.

Gates of Hell. unabr. ed. Paul C. Doherty. Read by Terry Wale. 10 cass. (Soundings Ser.). 2006. 84.95 (978-1-84559-195-3(X)) Pub: ISIS Lrg Prnt GBR. Dist(s): Ulverscroft US

Gates of Holiness. 2006. audio compact disk 14.95 (978-0-9663210-5-0(7), CV013) Pub: Cistercian Pubns. Dist(s): Liturgical Pr

Gates of Midnight. unabr. ed. Jessica Stirling. Read by Sheila Steafel. 8 cass. (Running Time: 8 hrs.). (Beckman Trilogy: Vol. 3). 1997. 69.95 Set. (978-0-7451-6761-9(6), CAB 1377) AudioGO.
Holly Beckman & her family move into the dark years of World War II. Recently widowed, Holly has lost interest in her antique business with the outbreak of the war, & her life is now overshadowed by the fears for her son, an RAF fighter pilot. When Holly's first lover, David Aspinall, returns home, it seems she may again fall under the spell of his fatal charm. Holly's brother Ritchie watches his lucrative art business crumble as the Germans advance on Paris.

Gates of Paradise see Poetry of William Blake

Gates of Paradise. Beryl Kingston & Laurence Kennedy. (Story Sound Ser.). 2007. 54.95 (978-1-84652-022-8(3)); audio compact disk 71.95 (978-1-84652-023-5(1)) Pub: Mgna Lrg Print GBR. Dist(s): Ulverscroft US

Gates of Paradise. unabr. ed. V. C. Andrews. Read by Donada Peters. 9 cass. (Running Time: 1 hr. 30 min. per cass.). 1991. 72.00 (978-0-7366-1888-5(0), 2716) Books on Tape.
The fourth titles in the Casteel series finds Heaven orphaned & in the clutches of the possessive Tony Tatterton.

Gates of Paradise. unabr. ed. V. C. Andrews. Read by Lorelei King. 12 cass. (Running Time: 14 hrs. 15 min.). 1996. 94.95 (978-1-85695-731-1(4), 940206) Pub: ISIS Audio GBR. Dist(s): Ulverscroft US
Heaven's daughter Annie has grown up in the happy home that always seemed out of her mother's reach as a child. But a terrible, tragic car accident changes everthing.

***Gates of Rome: Book I of the Emperor Series.** Conn Iggulden. Narrated by Robert Glenister. (Running Time: 13 hrs. 11 mins. 0 sec.). (ENG.). 2010. audio compact disk 29.95 (978-1-60998-098-6(0)) Pub: AudioGO. Dist(s): Perseus Dist

Gates of Splendor. Elisabeth Elliot. Read by Elisabeth Elliot. 4 cass. (Running Time: 4 hrs.). 1989. 18.95 (978-0-8474-2004-9(3)) Back to Bible.
Discusses the story of Jim Elliot's mission to the Auca Indians, along with four other men.

Gates of the Alamo. unabr. ed. Stephen Harrigan. Narrated by George Guidall. 17 cass. (Running Time: 23 hrs. 15 mins.). 2000. 138.00 (978-0-7887-5319-0(3), 96566K8) Recorded Bks.
Brings one of the pivotal battles in American history to life.

Gates of the Alamo, Set. abr. ed. Stephen Harrigan. 5 CDs. (Running Time: 6 hrs.). 2000. audio compact disk 29.95 (978-0-375-41560-9(2), Random AudioBks) Random Audio Pubg.

Gates of Zion. unabr. ed. Bodie Thoene. Des. by Brock Thoene. Narrated by Suzanne Toren. 10 cass. (Running Time: 14 hrs. 30 mins.). (Zion Chronicles: Bk. 1). 2000. 93.00 (978-0-7887-4842-4(4), K0004E7) Recorded Bks.
An historical novel filled with vivid settings & finely crafted characters. A portrayal of a young woman searching for identity & purpose amidst the chaos of post-World War II Jerusalem. When American photojournalist Ellie Warne takes pictures of an ancient scroll in Jerusalem, she finds herself a pawn in a political chess game where danger lurks around every corner.

Gates of Zion. unabr. ed. Bodie Thoene & Brock Thoene. Read by Susan O'Malley. 11 cass. (Running Time: 16 hrs.). (Zion Chronicles: Bk. 1). 2001. 76.95 (978-0-7861-1943-1(8), 2714); audio compact disk 104.00 (978-0-7861-9776-7(5), 2714) Blckstn Audio.
Ellie Warne, a young American photojournalist, finds herself in the Jerusalem of 1947. She unwittingly becomes a pawn in a political chess game when she photographs some ancient scrolls discovered by Bedouins. Who would guess that a few innocent photos could entangle her in such a desperate web of intrigue and peril? David Meyer seems to love her dearly, but Moshe Sachar has a purpose and commitment in life that intrigues her more than she can say. Through it all, Ellie discovers a people, a spirit and a person who profoundly change the direction of her life.

Gates to Buddhist Practice. H. E. Rinpoche. Read by Yontan Gonpo. 5 cass. 39.00 Set. (PP-AVGBP) Padma Pub CA.
Book on Tibetan Buddhism.

Gates to Buddhist Practice, Set. Chagdud Tulku. Read by Yontan Gonpo. 5 cass. 1995. pap. bk. 28.00 (978-1-881847-23-6(3)) Padma Pub CA.
This collection of oral teachings presents traditional Tibetan Buddhist wisdom to Western readers in Tulku's uniquely accessible style, including stories from his native Tibet & step-by-step exploration of the foundation & essence of Vajrayana Buddhism.

Gateway Experience Album Discovery. unabr. ed. Robert A. Monroe. Read by Robert A. Monroe. (Running Time: 45 min.). (Gateway Experience - Discovery Ser.). 1989. 72.00 (978-1-56113-280-5(2)) Monroe Institute.
Album containing the six cassettes.

Gateway to Chinese Language & Culture: A Complete Interactive Course. Xueying Wang et al. 2 CDs. (C). 2005. stu. ed. 48.95 (978-0-88727-455-8(2)) Cheng Tsui.

Gateway to German Lieder: An Anthology of Songs - High Voice. John Glenn Paton. Perf. by Joan Thompson. 1 CD. (Gateway Ser.). (GER.). 2000. audio compact disk 19.95 (978-0-7390-0108-0(6), 17614) Alfred Pub.

Gateway to German Lieder: Low Voice, 2 CDs. John Glenn Paton. Ed. by John Glenn Paton. 1 CD. (Gateway Ser.). (GER.). 2000. audio compact disk 14.95 (978-0-7390-0275-9(9), 17620) Alfred Pub.

Gateway to Italian Songs & Arias: High Voice, 2 CDs. John G. Paton. Ed. by John Glenn Paton. 1 cass. (Gateway Ser.). (ITA.). 2005. audio compact disk 14.95 (978-0-7390-0030-4(6)) Alfred Pub.

Gateway to Italian Songs & Arias: Low Voice. Ed. by John Glenn Paton. (Gateway Ser.). (ITA.). 2005. audio compact disk 14.95 (978-0-7390-3654-9(8)) Alfred Pub.

Gateway to the Chinese Classics: A Practical Guide to Literary Chinese. Jeannette L. Faurot. Date not set. 9.95 (978-0-8351-2632-8(3), GACHCT) China Bks.

Gateway to the Chinese Classics: A Practical Guide to Literary Chinese. Jeannette L. Faurot. 1998. reel tape 24.95 (978-0-8351-2633-5(1), GACHBT) China Bks.

***Gateway to the Heavens: Meditations.** K. L. French. Music by Harry Price. (ENG.). 2008. audio compact disk 16.00 (978-0-9557256-2-3(3)) Pub: ygb Pubng GBR. Dist(s): IPG Chicago

Gateway to Wholeness - House of Selves. Michael P. Marshall. Read by Michael P. Marshall. Ed. by Jonathan C. Renaud. Music by Ted Crook. 1 cass. (Running Time: 52 min.). 1995. 9.00 (978-0-912403-05-2(5)) Prod Renaud.
Explores the different levels of personality & personal responsibility. The guided meditation explores wholeness integration & "being true to the self".

Gateways to Now. Eckhart Tolle. 2004. 11.95 (978-0-7435-4866-3(3)) Pub: S&S Audio. Dist(s): S and S Inc

Gateways to Now. abr. unabr. ed. Eckhart Tolle. Read by Eckhart Tolle. (Running Time: 20 hrs. 0 mins. 0 sec.). (ENG.). 2003. audio compact disk 19.95 (978-0-7435-3547-2(2), Sound Ideas) Pub: S&S Audio. Dist(s): S and S Inc

Gather No Moss. unabr. ed. Sarah A. Shears. Read by Tanya Myers. 6 cass. (Running Time: 8 hrs.). 1998. 69.95 (978-1-85903-244-2(3)) Pub: Magna Story GBR. Dist(s): Ulverscroft US
Second volume of Sarah Shears' autobiography. She's off to Holland as a nanny, & then to Switzerland.

Gather 'Round & Sing: 6 Rounds for 2-Part & 3-Part Children's Choirs. Composed by Ruth Elaine Schram & Tim Hayden. (ENG.). 2008. audio compact disk 29.95 (978-0-7390-5036-1(2)) Alfred Pub.

Gather 'Round the Fire: Joining in Stories from Around the World. Barry Marshall & Jeri Burns. 1 cass. (Running Time: 50 min.). 1998. 9.95 Storycraft.
The Storycrafters share five tales which invite audience participation.

Gather the Leftover... There Is Life in Them. Rita Twiggs. 1 cass. (Running Time: 60 mins.). 2001. 5.99 (978-0-88368-743-7(7), 777437) Pub: Whitaker Hse. Dist(s): Anchor Distributors

Gather Together in My Name. unabr. ed. Maya Angelou. Narrated by Lynne Thigpen. 5 cass. (Running Time: 6 hrs. 30 mins.). 1994. 46.00 (978-0-7887-0046-0(4), 94245E7) Recorded Bks.
Maya Angelou's memoir of adolescence & early adulthood as a single mother & aspiring performer.

Gather Ye Rose-Buds While Ye May see Palgrave's Golden Treasury of English Poetry

Gather Your Dreams. Dana Cohenour. 1 cass. (Running Time: 40 min.). (J). 1994. 9.95 UPC 7-06891-01014-1. (978-1-889449-00-5(8), RMFK 101C); audio compact disk 14.95 CD UPC 7-06891-01012-7. (978-1-889449-03-6(2), RMFK 101J) Real Music Kidz.
National Parenting Publications Gold Award. (NAPPA) 1994. 12 original lullabies & morning songs by Award-Winning recording artist, Dana. Pop-folk style, appropriate for all ages newborn to five.

***Gathering.** Isobelle Carmody. Read by Peter Hardy. (Running Time: 5 hrs.). (YA). 2009. 59.99 (978-1-74214-306-4(7), 9781742143064) Pub: Bolinda Pubng AUS. Dist(s): Bolinda Pub Inc

Gathering. unabr. ed. Isobelle Carmody. Read by Peter Hardy. 6 cass. (Running Time: 8 hrs.). 2002. (978-1-74030-058-2(0), 591218) Bolinda Pubng AUS.
Outside the wind was blowing the wrong way & the world was filled with the smell of death, something is wrong with Chesthunt. Nathaniel feels it the moment he arrives.

Gathering. unabr. ed. Isobelle Carmody. Read by Peter Hardy. (Running Time: 8 hrs.). (YA). 2007. audio compact disk 83.95 (978-1-74093-411-4(3), 9781740934114) Pub: Bolinda Pubng AUS. Dist(s): Bolinda Pub Inc

Gathering. unabr. ed. William X. Kienzle. 7 cass. (Running Time: 10 hrs. 30 min.). (Father Koesler Mystery Ser.: No. 24). 2002. 56.00 (978-0-7366-8630-3(4)) Books on Tape.
Father Koesler must solve a murder among a group of men and women who have chosen a vocation in the Catholic Church.

Gathering & Proving Medical Evidence. Read by Lawrence Kern et al. (Running Time: 3 hrs.). 1991. 89.00 Incl. 94p. tape materials. (TO-55224) Cont Ed Bar-CA.

Gathering & Scattering: Themes in Luke's Gospel. Gil Bailie. 12 cass. (Running Time: 12 hrs.). 69.95 Set. (AA2932) Credence Commun.
Bailie talks in plain language to people without a theological or anthropology background & still he brings out themes in Luke you've never heard developed like this. He's simple, he makes his points vividly, sometimes from several points of view & everybody gets it.

Gathering Blue. unabr. ed. Lois Lowry. Read by Katherine Borowitz. 4 vols. (Running Time: 5 hrs. 27 mins.). (Middle Grade Cassette Librariestm Ser.). (J). (gr. 5-9). 2004. pap. bk. 38.00 (978-0-8072-0989-9(9), S YA 250 SP, Listening Lib); 32.00 (978-0-8072-8731-6(8), YA250CX, Listening Lib) Random Audio Pubg.
Left orphaned & physically flawed, young Kira faces a frightening, uncertain future. Blessed with an almost magical talent that keeps her alive, she struggles with ever broadening responsibilities in her quest for truth, discovering things that will change her life forever.

Gathering Darkness. unabr. ed. Thomas Gallagher. Read by John MacDonald. 7 cass. (Running Time: 10 hrs. 30 mins.). 56.00 (978-0-7366-1043-8(X), 1973) Books on Tape.
It is 1929 & the market is already wobbly. When John McPeek plays it, he loses more than money; he loses his family & nearly his life.

Gathering Energy. unabr. ed. Gary Arnold. 1 cass. (Running Time: 1 hr.). 1997. pap. bk. 12.95 (978-1-57867-258-5(9)) Windhorse Corp.
Maximizing personal energy.

Gathering in the Memory of Alan Watts. Joanna Watts et al. 1 cass. 1999. 11.00 (02512) Big Sur Tapes.
1974 Malibu.

Gathering Medicine. Angeles Arrien. 2 CDs. (Running Time: 2 Hrs 30 Mins). 2006. audio compact disk 19.95 (978-1-59179-485-1(4), AW00237D) Sounds True.
What lessons can the modern seeker of truth gain from the shaman's way? Join respected anthropologist and folklorist Angeles Arrien as she bridges the past with the present to find powerful methods based on the shamanic tradition for gaining clarity and direction in your life. The shaman's way, offers Angeles Arrien, is to gather medicine by reconnecting with yourself on the deepest internal level. This soul work utilizes imagery, reflective questioning, dream work, and storytelling to help you integrate inner and outer experiences. Thus you travel the fourfold path of the ancients to find your personal truth, the way back home. Gathering Medicine contains stories, spiritual teachings, and ideas for using timeless shamanic principles in your own modern-day life. Topics include: your body's inner wisdom; the shape-shifter; the four rivers (inspiration, challenge, surprise, and love); three types of vocal energy; Rainbow Hoop and Medicine Wheel meditations; and much more.

Gathering of Days: A New England Girl's Journal 1830-32, unabr. ed. Joan W. Blos. Narrated by Madeleine Potter. 3 pieces. (Running Time: 3 hrs. 45 mins.). (gr. 5 up). 1992. 27.00 (978-1-55690-646-6(3), 92353E7) Recorded Bks.
Catherine Cabot Hall's journal of her life growing up in 19th century New Hampshire. Records hardships of pioneer life, the death of her mother & her father's remarriage as well as many other joys & sorrows.

Gathering of Great Poetry for Children, Vol. 1. unabr. ed. Read by Julie Harris et al. Ed. by Richard Lewis. 1 cass. Incl. Anonymous: How Do You Do? Edward Lear. (J). (gr. k up). (CDL5 1235); Cradle Song. Thomas Dekker. (J). (gr. k up). (CDL5 1235); Doors. Carl Sandburg. (J). (gr. k up). (CDL5 1235); Hush Little Baby. Edward Lear. (J). (gr. k up). (CDL5 1235); I Fell into a Box of Eggs. Edward Lear. (J). (gr. k up). (CDL5 1235); If All the Seas Were One Sea. Edward Lear. (J). (gr. k up). (CDL5 1235); If You Should Meet a Crocodile. Edward Lear. (J). (gr. k up). (CDL5 1235); Kangaroo. Edward Lear. (J). (gr. k up). (CDL5 1235); Lavender's Blue. Edward Lear. (J). (gr. k up). (CDL5 1235); Little Mouse. Padraic Colum. (J). (gr. k up). (CDL5 1235); Little Turtle. Vachel Lindsay. (J). (gr. k up). (CDL5 1235); Madame Mouse Trots. Edith Sitwell. (J). (gr. k up). (CDL5 1235); Magical Mouse. Kenneth Patchen. (J). (gr. k up). (CDL5 1235); Milk-White Moon. Carl Sandburg. (J). (gr. k up). (CDL5 1235); Old Woman. Edward Lear. (J). (gr. k up). (CDL5 1235); Owl & the Pussycat. Edward Lear. (J). (gr. k up). (CDL5 1235); Poem. William Carlos Williams. (J). (gr. k up). (CDL5 1235); Spring Thunder. Mark Van Doren. (J). (gr. k up). (CDL5 1235); (J). (gr. k up). 1985. 8.98 (CDL5 1235) HarperCollins Pubs.

Gathering of Great Poetry for Children, Vol. 2. unabr. ed. Read by Julie Harris et al. Ed. by Richard Lewis. 1 cass. (YA). (gr. 3 up). 1985. 8.98 (CDL5 1237) HarperCollins Pubs.

Gathering of Great Poetry for Children, Vol. 3. unabr. ed. Read by Julie Harris et al. Ed. by Richard Lewis. Incl. Auction. John Holmes. (J). (CDL5 1237); Boy in the Barn. Herbert Read. (J). (CDL5 1237); Centaurs. James Stephens. (J). (CDL5 1237); Easy Decision. Kenneth Patchen. (J). (CDL5 1237); First Song. Galway Kinnell. (J). (CDL5 1237); Flower-Fed Buffaloes. Vachel Lindsay. (J). (CDL5 1237); Haughty Snail-King. Vachel Lindsay. (J). (CDL5 1237); How to Eat a Poem. Eve Merriam. (J). (CDL5 1237); I Know Some Lonely Houses Off the Road. Emily Dickinson. (J). (CDL5 1237); I Remember. Thomas Hood. (J). (CDL5 1237); I'll Sail upon the Dog-star. Thomas Durfey. (J). (CDL5 1237); In the Orchard. James Stephens. (J). (CDL5 1237); Lake Isle of Innisfree. W. B. Yeats. (J). (CDL5 1237); Legs. Robert Graves. (J). (CDL5 1237); Lighthearted William. William Carlos Williams. (J). (CDL5 1237); Mid-Country Blow. Theodore Roethke. (J). (CDL5 1237); Midsummer Night's Dream. William Shakespeare. (J). (CDL5 1237); Night Bells. Carl Sandburg. Perf. by Carl Sandburg. (J). (CDL5 1237); On Easter Knoll. John Masefield. (J). (CDL5 1237); Parrots. Wilfred Gibson. (J). (CDL5 1237); Pied Beauty. Gerard Manley Hopkins. (J). (CDL5 1237); Preludes I. T. S. Eliot. Perf. by T. S. Eliot. (J). (CDL5 1237); Rainy Summer. Alice Meynell. (J). (CDL5 1237); Song in the Wood. John Fletcher. (J). (CDL5 1237); Story-Teller. Mark Van Doren. (J). (CDL5 1237); There Was Once a King of York. (J). (CDL5 1237); Tree-Sleeping. Robert P. Tristam Coffin. (J). (CDL5 1237); Tyger. William Blake. (J). (CDL5 1237); Windy Day. Andrew Young. (J). (CDL5 1237); (YA). (gr. 3 up). 1970. 9.95 (978-0-89845-511-3(1), CDL5 1237) HarperCollins Pubs.

Gathering of Great Poetry for Children, Vol. 4. abr. ed. Poems. Richard Lewis. Read by Julie Harris et al. 1 cass. Incl. Acquainted with the Night. Robert Frost. Perf. by Robert Frost. (J). (CDL5 1238); Bete Humaine. Francis Brett Young. (J). (CDL5 1238); Bird Came Down the Walk. Emily Dickinson. (J). (CDL5 1238); Fern Hill. Dylan Thomas. Read by Dylan Thomas. (J). (CDL5 1238); Four Little Foxes. Lew Sarett. (J). (CDL5 1238); Heron. Theodore Roethke. (J). (CDL5 1238); I Could Not Sleep for Thinking of the Sky. John Masefield. (J). (CDL5 1238); I Know Where I'm Going, I Will Give My Love an Apple. (J). (CDL5 1238); I Like What I Like When I Do Not Worry. Gertrude Stein. (J). (CDL5 1238); I Loved My Friend. Langston Hughes. (J). (CDL5 1238); I Thank You God for Most This Amazing. e e cummings. Read by e e cummings. (J). (CDL5 1238); I'll Tell You How the Sun Rose. Emily Dickinson. (J). (CDL5 1238); Little Things. James Stephens. (J). (CDL5 1238); Lyrebirds. Judith Wright. (J). (CDL5 1238); Miracles. Walt Whitman. (J). (CDL5 1238); Out of School. Hal Summers. (J). (CDL5 1238); Rescue. Hal Summers. (J). (CDL5 1238); Song of Wandering Aengus. W. B. Yeats. (J). (CDL5 1238); Warning to Children. Robert Graves. Read by Robert Graves. (J). (CDL5 1238); Young Girl: Annam. Padraic Colum. (J). (CDL5 1238); (YA). (gr. 4 up). 1984. 9.95 (978-0-89845-512-0(X), CDL5 1238) HarperCollins Pubs.

Gathering of Men. Robert Bly & Bill Moyers. 1 cass. (Running Time: 88 min.). 10.95 (978-1-56176-148-7(6)) Mystic Fire.
Interviews & conversations examining the psychology & nature of masculinity in modern times (from the PBS series).

Gathering of Old Men. Ernest J. Gaines. Read by Ernest J. Gaines. 1 cass. 1986. 13.95 (978-1-55644-155-4(X), 6051) Am Audio Prose.

Gathering of Old Men, unabr. ed. Ernest J. Gaines. 6 cass. (Running Time: 7 hrs. 45 mins.). 2001. 51.00 (978-0-7887-0399-7(4), 94591E7) Recorded Bks.
Powerfully describes the racial tensions in 1970s Louisiana.

Gathering of Old Men. unabr. collector's ed. Ernest J. Gaines. Read by Ron Shoop. 7 cass. (Running Time: 7 hrs.). 1987. 42.00 (978-0-7366-1184-8(3), 2104) Books on Tape.
Beau Boutan, a Cajun farmer, is shot dead. Candy Marshall, the headstrong young plantation owner, tells everyone that she killed Beau. But when the sheriff arrives, he finds a dozen aging black men in turn claiming to have done the deed.

Gathering of Spies. unabr. ed. John Altman. Read by Michael Page. (Running Time: 8 hrs.). 2005. 39.25 (978-1-59600-578-5(5), 9781596005785, BADLE); 24.95 (978-1-59600-577-8(7), 9781596005778, BAD); 39.25 (978-1-59600-576-1(9), 9781596005761, Brinc Audio MP3 Lib); 24.95 (978-1-59600-575-4(0), 9781596005754, Brilliance MP3) Brilliance Audio.
In 1943, America thought it had rounded up all the German spies on its soil. Now Germany's greatest weapon - a woman with special talents, both for tradecraft and for death - is headed home with critical information about the still-developing atomic bomb, and the Allies chief hope for stopping her is a British agent with agendas of his own. Originally recruited into MI5 to pose as a double agent, he's been telling Germans that he'd do anything to free his wife, a prisoneer of a Polish concentration camp. This happens to be true. The question is: how much would he really do to set her free? Where are his loyalties exactly? As the two spies play cat-and-mouse across three countries, the ambiguities deepen, each figure showing new sides, each action providing new twists, until at last both agents are swept into a series of climaxes as breathtakingly unpredictable as they are inevitable.

Gathering or Scattering: 1 John 2:15-17. Ed Young. 1984. 4.95 (978-0-7417-1371-1(3), 371) Win Walk.

Gathering Personal Power. Michael P. Marshall. 1 cass. (Running Time: 52 min.). 1995. 9.00 (978-0-912403-04-5(7)) Prod Renaud.
How to create your life anew & positive in every moment of sacred time. Includes a 20 minute, guided meditation that reveals the source of personal creativity.

Gathering Power. unabr. ed. Gary Arnold. 1 cass. (Running Time: 1 hr.). 1997. pap. bk. 12.95 (978-1-57867-101-4(9)) Windhorse Corp.
Experience the power of recreating your life.

Gathering Storm. unabr. ed. Robert Jordan & Brandon Sanderson. Read by Michael Kramer & Kate Reading. (Running Time: 34 hrs. 30 mins. 0 sec.). (Wheel of Time Ser.: Bk. 12). (ENG.). 2009. audio compact disk 69.99 (978-1-59397-767-2(0)) Pub: Macmill Audio. Dist(s): Macmillan

***Gathering Storm.** unabr. ed. Bodie Thoene & Brock Thoene. Narrated by Bodie Thoene. (Running Time: 13 hrs. 0 mins. 0 sec.). (Zion Diaries). (ENG.). 2010. audio compact disk 34.99 (978-1-59859-773-8(6)) Oasis Audio.

Gathering the Sun: Spanish Songs. Poems. 1 CD. Dramatization. (SPA.). (J). 2001. audio compact disk 15.95 (978-1-58186-209-6(1)) Del Sol Pub.
A CD companion to Gathering the Sun: An ABC in Spanish and English.

Gathering to Nauvoo. Fred E. Woods. 2 cass. 2004. 5.98 (978-1-59156-033-3(0)) Covenant Comms.

Gathering to Nauvoo. abr. ed. Fred E. Woods. 2 Cass. 2002. 14.95 (978-1-59156-034-0(9)) Covenant Comms.

Gato Bandido. unabr. ed. Abuelo Historias Del. (SPA.). 2007. audio compact disk 13.00 (978-958-8318-10-3(6)) Pub: Yoyo Music COL. Dist(s): YoYoMusic

Gato con Botas. Charles Perrault. 1 cass. (Running Time: 1 hr. 30 min.).Tr. of Puss in Boots. (SPA., (J). 2000. 12.95 (978-84-207-6730-7(1)) Pub: Grupo Anaya ESP. Dist(s): Distribks Inc

Gato con Botas. l.t. ed. Short Stories. Illus. by Graham Percy. 1 CD. (Running Time: 10 mins.). Dramatization.Tr. of Puss in Boots. (SPA.). (ps-3). 2001. 11.90 (978-84-8214-034-6(5), 1620) Peralt Mont ESP.

Gato Que Rompio las Reglas, EDL Level 18. (Fonolibros Ser.: Vol. 7). (SPA.). 2003. 11.50 (978-0-7652-1028-9(2)) Modern Curr.

Gatomaquia. Lope de Vega. (SPA & ESP.). 2005. audio compact disk 21.95 (978-84-7039-409-6(6)) Fondo CA.

***Gator A-Go-Go: A Novel.** unabr. ed. Tim Dorsey. Read by Oliver Wyman. (ENG.). 2010. (978-0-06-195368-2(7), Harper Audio); (978-0-06-196753-5(X), Harper Audio) HarperCollins Pubs.

Gator Kill. unabr. ed. Bill Crider. Read by Jim Kille. Ed. by Richard Haywood. 2 cass. (Running Time: 3 hrs.). (Truman Smith Ser.). 1995. 17.00 Set. (978-1-883268-27-5(3)) Spellbinders.
PI, Truman Smith, is hired by Fred Benton to solve a mystery; who shot Benton's alligator? All too soon Tru gets caught up in...something worth killing for...& the killing has begun.

***Gator on the Loose! Vol. 1: Special Delivery!** unabr. ed. Sue Stauffacher. Read by Harlie Vaughn. (Animal Rescue Team Ser.: Nos. 1-2). (ENG.). (J). 2010. audio compact disk 34.00 (978-0-307-73838-7(8), Listening Lib) Pub: Random Audio Pubg. Dist(s): Random

***Gatos Black on Halloween.** Marisa Montes. Narrated by Maria Conchita Alonso. 1 CD. (Running Time: 8 mins.). (J). (ps-3). 2009. bk. 29.95 (978-0-545-19701-4(5)); audio compact disk 12.95 (978-0-545-19689-5(2)) Weston Woods.

Gaucher Disease - A Bibliography & Dictionary for Physicians, Patients, & Genome Researchers. Compiled by Icon Group International, Inc. Staff. 2007. ring bd. 28.95 (978-0-497-11220-2(5)) Icon Grp.

Gaucho Martin Fierro. (SPA.). 2001. 16.95 (SSP230) J Norton Pubs.
For the advanced listener. Includes notes.

***Gaudy Night.** Dorothy L. Sayers. Narrated by Ian Carmichael & Full Cast Production Staff. 2 CDs. (Running Time: 2 hrs. 0 mins. 0 sec.). (ENG., 2010. audio compact disk 24.95 (978-0-563-49409-6(3)) Pub: AudioGO. Dist(s): Perseus Dist

Gaudy Night. unabr. ed. Dorothy L. Sayers. Read by Ian Carmichael. 10 cass. (Running Time: 15 hrs. 31 mins.). (Lord Peter Wimsey Mystery Ser.). 2004. 39.95 (978-1-57270-401-5(2)) Pub: Audio Partners. Dist(s): PerseuPGW
Lord Peter Wimsey continues to ply Harriet Vane with marriage proposals, but she has other things in mind a reunion at her alma mater, Oxford. The normally staid academic setting suffers a rash of bizarre pranks: scrawled obscenities, burnt effigies, and poison-pen letters - including one that says, "Ask your boyfriend with the title if he likes arsenic in his soup." Some of the notes threaten murder, all are perfectly ghastly, and all are impeccably worded. Harriet finds herself ensnared in a nightmare of romance and terror, with few clues to challenge her powers of detection and those of her sometime boyfriend, Lord Peter.

Gaudy Night. unabr. ed. Dorothy L. Sayers. Narrated by Ian Carmichael. (Running Time: 56340 sec.). (Lord Peter Wimsey Mystery Ser.). (ENG.). 2005. audio compact disk 47.95 (978-1-57270-499-2(3)) Pub: AudioGO. Dist(s): Perseus Dist
When Harriet Vane attends her Oxford reunion, known as the Gaudy, the prim academic setting is haunted by a rash of bizarre pranks: scrawled obscenities, burnt effigies, and poison-pen letters, including one that says, Ask your boyfriend with the title if he likes arsenic in his soup. Some of the notes threaten murder - and all are dreadful concoctions of a sick mind - yet in spite of their deplorable, criminal nature, the letters are perfectly worded. Soon, Harriet finds herself ensnared in a nightmare of romance and terror, with only the tiniest shreds of clues to challenge her powers of detection, and those of her paramour, Lord Peter Wimsey.

Gaudy Night. unabr. ed. Dorothy L. Sayers. Read by Ian Carmichael. 12 cass. (Running Time: 18 hrs.). (Lord Peter Wimsey Mystery Ser.). 1993. 79.95 (978-0-7451-4106-0(4), CAB 789) Pub: Chivers Audio Bks GBR. Dist(s): AudioGO
Returning to Oxford for a college reunion, Harriet Vane encounters hostility. A newspaper labels her a murderess, referring to the time in her past when Harriet was on trial, wrongly accused of murdering her lover. Lord Peter Wimsey had saved her from the gallows then. Again, he must do everything in his power to protect her.

Gauntlet: A Western Trio. Max Brand. 2009. (978-1-60136-321-3(4)) Audio Holding.

Gauranga Bhajana. 1 cass.; 1 CD. 4.95 (CD-13); audio compact disk 14.95 CD. Bhaktivedanta.

Gay & Unhappy. Barrie Konicov. 1 cass. (Emotional Health Ser.). 11.98 (978-0-87082-635-1(2), 152) Potentials.
Designed for who wish to change their sexual orientation.

Gay Artists in Modern American Culture: An Imagined Conspiracy. Michael S. Sherry. (ENG., 2007. 29.95 (978-0-8078-8607-6(6)); audio compact disk 34.95 (978-0-8078-8609-0(2)) U of NC Pr.

Gay Children, Straight Parents: A Plan for Family Healing. Richard Cohen. 2008. 49.95 (978-0-9637058-8-4(1)) Intl Healing.

Gay Comedy Jam. Perf. by Scott Kennedy et al. 2000. audio compact disk 16.98 (978-1-929243-16-7(2)) Uproar Ent.

Gay Old Dog. (SWC 1719) HarperCollins Pubs.

Gay Sex, Gay Love. unabr. ed. Peter Breggin. 2 cass. (Running Time: 1 hr. 40 min.). 19.95 (S29450) J Norton Pubs.
A discussion about monogamy & other issues with a Gay Rap Group. Breggin concludes that straights & gays have many similar problems, & that everyone should be anything they want - as long as they remain free & are able to love.

Gay Talese. Interview with Gay Talese. 1 cass. (Running Time: 1 hr.). 12.95 (L074) TFR.
In separate interviews, the author talks about "The New York Times" as seen in his book, "The Kingdom & the Power" & about modern sexuality in "Thy Neighbor's Wife".

Gayatri Mantra Meditations: Long Form including 1000 Names of Gayatri. Voice by Thomas Ashley-Farrand. Thomas Ashley-Farrand. Saraswati Publications. (ENG.). 2004. audio compact disk 25.00 (978-0-9825238-1-0(5)) SaraswaPubns.

Gayatri Upasana. Swami Jyotirmayananda. 1 cass. (Running Time: 1 hr.). 1990. 12.99 Yoga Res Foun.

Gayle Pemberton. unabr. ed. Read by Gayle Pemberton & Rebekah Presson. Ed. by James McKinley. 1 cass. (Running Time: 29 min.). (New Letters on the Air Ser.). 1992. 10.00 (103089); 18.00 2-sided cass. (103092) New Letters.
Pemberton is interviewed by Rebekah Presson & reads from her book of personal essays, The Hottest Water in Chicago.

Gaza Station. unabr. ed. Joel C. Rosenberg. (Running Time: 13 hrs.). 2003. audio compact disk 112.25 (978-1-59355-087-5(1), 1593550871, BriAudCD Unabrid) Brilliance Audio.
Osama bin Laden is dead. Saddam Hussein is buried. Baghdad lies in ruins. Now the eyes of the world are on Jerusalem as Jon Bennett - a Wall Street strategist turned senior White House advisor - his beautiful CIA partner Erin McCoy, and the U.S. Secretary of State arrive in the Middle East to meet with Palestinian leader Yasser Arafat. On the table: a dramatic and potentially historic Arab-Israeli peace plan, of which Bennett is the chief architect. At the heart of the proposed treaty is the discovery of black gold deep underneath the Mediterranean - a vast and spectacular tract of oil and natural gas that could offer unprecedented riches for every Muslim, Christian, and Jew in Israel and Palestine. But in the shadows lie men whose hearts are filled with evil - men who do not relish a post-Saddam era, men for whom the prospect of a Palestinian peace accord with Israel goes against everything for which their fathers have fought and died. Such men - and the countries that finance them - are ready to do anything necessary to slaughter those who stand in their way. The clock is ticking. Can Bennett, McCoy, and the American president make peace before the Middle East once again erupts in war?.

Gazebo. Emily Grayson. Narrated by Linda Stephens. 5 cass. (Running Time: 6 hrs. 30 mins.). 2000. 48.00 (978-0-7887-4406-8(2), 96187E7) Recorded Bks.
A man offers a newspaper editor his personal memories of a 50-year love affair & the story forces the editor to rethink her own choices in life.

Gazebo. Emily Grayson. Narrated by Linda Stephens. 6 CDs. (Running Time: 6 hrs. 30 mins.). 2000. audio compact disk 58.00 (978-0-7887-4906-3(4), C1281E7) Recorded Bks.

Gazzetta Veneta. Gasparo Gozzi. Read by Elsa Proverbio. 1 cass. (Running Time: 1 hrs.). (Letterati, Memorialisti E Viaggiatori Del 700 Ser.). (ITA.). 1996. pap. bk. 19.50 (978-1-58085-459-7(1)) Interlingua VA.

GBS Versus GKC - Shaw Festival. Jean Morpungo. 1 CD. (Running Time: 1 hr. 30 mins.). 2005. audio compact disk 12.95 (978-0-660-18812-6(0)) Pub: Canadian Broadcasting CAN. Dist(s): Georgetown Term

Gcse Business Studies. Neil Denby & Peter Thomas. 2005. audio compact disk (978-0-340-88785-1(0)) Hodder General GBR.

Gcse Modern World History 4 - International Relations, 1945-1990. Ben Walsh. 4 pieces. 2005. cd-rom 575.00 (978-0-7195-7975-2(9), HodderMurray) Pub: Hodder Edu GBR. Dist(s): Trans-Atl Phila

GE Reflux. Contrib. by David Dudgeon et al. 1 cass. (American Academy of Pediatrics UPDATE: Vol. 19, No. 4). 1998. 20.00 Am Acad Pediat.

Gear: Left of Center of the Universe: Left of Center of the Universe. The Gear. (YA). 2009. audio compact disk 12.99 (978-1-60706-143-4(0)) Pub: Image Comics. Dist(s): Diamond Book Dists

Gear: Left of Center of the Universe - Limited Signed Edition: Left of Center of the Universe - Limited Signed Edition. The Gear. (YA). 2009. audio compact disk 24.99 (978-1-60706-144-1(9)) Pub: Image Comics. Dist(s): Diamond Book Dists

***Gears of War: Anvil Gate.** unabr. ed. Karen Traviss. Narrated by David Colacci. (Running Time: 15 hrs. 0 mins. 0 sec.). (Gears of War Ser.). 2010. 29.99 (978-1-4001-6472-1(9)); 20.99 (978-1-4001-8472-9(X)); audio compact disk 39.99 (978-1-4001-1472-6(1)) Pub: Tantor Media. Dist(s): IngramPubServ

***Gears of War: Anvil Gate (Library Edition)** unabr. ed. Karen Traviss. Narrated by David Colacci. (Running Time: 15 hrs. 0 mins.). (Gears of War Ser.). 2010. 39.99 (978-1-4001-9472-8(5)); audio compact disk 95.99 (978-1-4001-4472-3(8)) Pub: Tantor Media. Dist(s): IngramPubServ

***Gears of War: Jacinto's Remnant.** unabr. ed. Karen Traviss. Narrated by David Colacci. (Running Time: 16 hrs. 0 mins.). (Gears of War Ser.). 2010. 20.99 (978-1-4001-8471-2(1)) Tantor Media.

***Gears of War: Jacinto's Remnant.** unabr. ed. Karen Traviss. Narrated by David Colacci. (Running Time: 16 hrs. 0 mins. 0 sec.). (Gears of War Ser.). (ENG.). 2010. 29.99 (978-1-4001-6471-4(0)); audio compact disk 39.99 (978-1-4001-1471-9(3)) Pub: Tantor Media. Dist(s): IngramPubServ

GED Fast Track to Work Vol. 1: Activity Journal Instructions. Helen K. Cleminshaw & Dee Siegferth. 1 cass. (Running Time: 30 min.). (YA). 1998. 6.95 (978-1-893679-36-8(5)) Int Fam.
Introduction & assessment of video training system.

GED Fast Track to Work Vol. 2: Reading. Helen K. Cleminshaw & Dee Siegferth. 1 cass. (Running Time: 30 min.). (YA). 1998. 6.95 (978-1-893679-37-5(3)) Int Fam.
Review of basic reading skills before using video training system.

GED 2002 Teaching Strategies. Created by Steck Vaughan. 2002. tchr. ed. (978-0-7398-6940-6(X)) SteckVau.

Gee Whiz Years. Arthur Young & Ruth Young. 1 cass. 9.00 (A0380-89) Sound Photosyn.
The search that took the inventor of the Bell helicopter & the founder of the Peace Academy on an international adventure that culminated in the beginning of the Institute for the Study of Consciousness.

Geek Love: A Novel. unabr. ed. Katherine Dunn. Narrated by Christina Moore. 11 cass. (Running Time: 15 hrs. 30 mins.). 1983. 93.00 (978-0-7887-3107-5(6), 95818E7) Recorded Bks.
In order to save her family's carnival from bankruptcy, the pregnant Mrs. Binewski ingests radioisotopes & insecticides to make her babies "special." Not for the squeamish or faint of heart, its evocative prose is guaranteed to amaze.

GEF (Global Environment Facility) - Dr. Gary Herbertson on the Rio Earth Summit & Financing the Environment. Hosted by Nancy Pearlman. 1 cass. (Running Time: 30 min.). 10.00 (1018) Educ Comm CA.

Gefahrliche Wege. 7 cass. (Running Time: 7 hrs.). (Mystery Thrillers in German Ser.). (GER.). 2001. pap. bk. 89.95 (SGE260) J Norton Pubs.
Recorded by native professional actors in a radio-play format, these short-episode thrillers on an intermediate level were especially created to develop listening comprehension skills. Book provides a transcripts of the recording, exercises & vocabulary.

Gefahrliche Wege. Emile De Harven. 95.95 (978-0-8219-3633-7(6)) EMC-Paradigm.

Geheime Mission. Hans J. Konig. 95.95 (978-0-8219-3630-6(1)) EMC-Paradigm.

Gehen: German Verbs of Walk. Sigrid S. Hildebrand & Eckart Hildebrand. Ed. by Josef Rohrer. Illus. by Sydney M. Baker. Intro. by Harris Winitz. (GER.). (YA). (gr. 7 up). 1990. bk. 25.00 (978-0-939990-64-1(4)) Intl Linguistics.

Gem Italian Phrase-Finder. (ITA & ENG.). 1999. 12.00 (978-0-00-371092-2(0)) Zondervan.

Gem Portuguese Phrase Book. rev. ed. Collins Publishers Staff. (POR & ENG.). 2003. pap. bk. 13.99 (978-0-00-765096-5(5)) Pub: HarpC GBR. Dist(s): Trafalgar

Gem Portuguese Phrase-Finder. (POR & ENG.). 1996. 12.00 (978-0-00-371122-6(6)) Pub: HarpC GBR. Dist(s): Trafalgar

Gem Spanish Phrase Book. rev. ed. (ENG & SPA.). 2003. pap. bk. 13.99 (978-0-00-765095-8(7)) Pub: HarpC GBR. Dist(s): Trafalgar

Gemagick. unabr. ed. Mary Leonesio. Read by Mary Leonesio. Perf. by Russ Schiedler. 1 cass. (Running Time: 45 min.). 1991. 9.95 (978-0-87542-398-2(1), L-398) Llewellyn Pubns.
Author gives a lecture on the basics of crystal, gemstone & jewelry magick, along with specific rituals & spells to perform.

Gemeinwirtschaft see Socialism

Gemini. Narrated by Patricia G. Finlayson. Music by Mike Cantwell. Contrib. by Marie De Seta & TMY Communications Staff. 1 cass. (Running Time: 30 min.). (Astrologer's Guide to the Personality Ser.: Vol. 3). 1994. 7.99 (978-1-878535-14-6(5)) De Seta-Finlayson.
Astrological description of the sign of Gemini; individually customized, covering love, money, career, relationships & more.

Gemini: May Twenty-One - June Twenty. Barrie Konicov. 4 cass. 16.98 (978-1-56001-552-9(7), SC-II HA048); 11.98 (978-0-87082-093-9(1), 048) Potentials.
Explains how each sign of the Zodiac has its positive & negative aspects & that as individuals, in order to master our own destiny, we must enhance our positive traits.

Gemini: Unleash the Power of Your True Self. 1 cass. (Running Time: 1 hr.). 1999. 9.99 (978-1-928996-02-6(7)) MonAge.

Gemini: Your Relationship with the Energy of the Universe. Loy Young. 1993. 9.95 (978-1-882888-15-3(4)) Aquarius Hse.

Gemini Contenders. unabr. collector's ed. Robert Ludlum. Read by Michael Prichard. 10 cass. (Running Time: 15 hrs.). 1984. 80.00 (978-0-7366-0806-0(0), 1756) Books on Tape.
December 9, 1939, Salonika, Greece. Five trucks enter the guarded encampment of the Order of Xenope, a harsh monastic brotherhood. All instructions & schedules have been meticulously planned. The objective: to deliver a small iron vault into the hands of one Savarone Fontini-Christi, a wealthy & influential padrone of Northern Italy. The vault has been buried for over 15 centuries. What are its contents & why is there such desperate urgency?.

Gemorah Classroom - Every Child Can Learn; a Lesson in Individualized Instruction. Nochem Kaplan. 1 cass. (Running Time: 90 mins.). 1999. 6.00 (V60FZ) Torah Umesorah.

Gemorah; Presentation of Incremental Learning in Action. Ephraim Kletenik. 1 cass. (Running Time: 90 mins.). 1999. 6.00 (V60SH) Torah Umesorah.

Gems & Stones: The Ring of Fire. unabr. ed. Maia C. Shamayyim. Read by Maia C. M. Shamayyim. 1 cass. (Running Time: 32 min.). (Blue Stone Ser.: Vol. 5). 1980. 8.50 Spirit Hrt Sanc.
Information & visualizations with gems & stones for healing self & others.

Gen Deithch: Animating Strega Nonna. 2004. 8.95 (978-1-56008-904-9(0)) Weston Woods.

Gender & Dialogue: Mature Dependence in Couple Relationship. Read by Polly Young-Eisendrath. 1 cass. (Running Time: 90 min.). 1988. 10.95 (978-0-7822-0338-7(8), 350) C G Jung IL.

Gender & Drama. Ed. by Lizbeth Goodman. (Approaching Literature Ser.). 1998. 41.95 (978-0-415-14657-9(7)) Pub: Routledge. Dist(s): Taylor and Fran

Gender in the Workplace. Murray Stein. Read by Murray Stein. 1 cass. (Running Time: 98 min.). 1993. 10.95 (978-0-7822-0459-9(7), 536) C G Jung IL.
Gender dynamics in the workplace encompass far more than blatant sexual harassment & "office romance." They are often so subtle as to be nearly undetectable, yet their power can transform the workplace into a place of explosive tension & anxiety. These gender-related energies play a central role in evaluation, promotion, & communication, & they impact the whole range of office politics. Jungian analyst Murray Stein leads a seminar exploring anima/animus dynamics, & attempting to open gender workplace issues to greater understanding.

Gene Deitch: Animating Picture Books. 2004. 8.95 (978-1-56008-903-2(2)); cass. & flmstrp 30.00 (978-0-89719-585-0(X)) Weston Woods.

Gene Deitch: Animating Strega Nonna. 2004. cass. & flmstrp 30.00 (978-0-89719-586-7(8)) Weston Woods.

Gene Deitch: Animating Strega Nonna; Strega Nonna. 2004. cass. & flmstrp 30.00 (978-1-56008-809-7(5)) Weston Woods.

Gene Frumkin. unabr. ed. Read by Gene Frumkin. 1 cass. (Running Time: 29 min.). 1985. 10.00 New Letters.
Gene Franklin of New Mexico reads from "Clouds & Red Earth".

***Gene of Isis.** unabr. ed. Traci Harding. (Running Time: 19 hrs. 3 mins.). (Mystique Ser.). 2010. audio compact disk 123.95 (978-1-74214-724-6(0), 9781742147246) Pub: Bolinda Pubng AUS. Dist(s): Bolinda Pub Inc

Gene Wolfe. Interview. Interview with Gene Wolfe & Chris Merrick. 1 cass. (Running Time: 1 hr.). 13.95 (978-1-55644-120-2(7), 4152) Am Audio Prose.
Explores beliefs in legend & superstition & gives a compassionate but worried look at the future of the human race.

Generacion de Josue. Enrique Bremer. 6 cass. (SPA.). 2003. 29.99 (978-0-89985-402-1(8)); audio compact disk 35.00 (978-0-89985-421-2(4)) Christ for the Nations.

Generaciones. Greenia. (C). 1997. bk., wbk. ed., lab manual ed. 35.50 (978-0-15-503386-3(7)) Harcourt.

General. abr. ed. Robert A. Monroe. Read by Robert A. Monroe. 6 cass. 1983. 69.00 Set. (978-1-56102-706-4(5)) Inter Indus.
Facilitate general healing.

General. unabr. ed. Patrick A. Davis. Read by Jim Bond. (Running Time: 10 hrs.). 2009. 24.99 (978-1-4233-9154-8(3), 9781423391548, Brilliance MP3); 24.99 (978-1-4233-9156-2(X), 9781423391562, BAD); 39.97 (978-1-4233-9155-5(1), 9781423391555, Brinc Audio MP3 Lib); 39.97 (978-1-4233-9157-9(8), 9781423391579, BADLE) Brilliance Audio.

General. unabr. collector's ed. C. S. Forester. Read by Richard Brown. 7 cass. (Running Time: 10 hrs. 30 min.). 1991. 56.00 (978-0-7366-2045-1(1), 2859) Books on Tape.
Herbert Curzon is a former cavalry officer who earned fortuitous distinction in the Boer War. He knew little then; he has learned nothing since. But the army, desperate for officers in the opening months of WW I, hands Curzon a new division to train. A few months later his formations dissolve at the Somme, hosed down by German machine guns. Uninstructed, Curzon still thinks himself a leader. When a German offensive threatens his remaining troops, he gallops suicidally into the fighting. He prefers death to self-knowledge.

General A. P. Hill: The Story of a Confederate Warrior. unabr. collector's ed. James I. Robertson, Jr. Read by Dick Estell. 10 cass. (Running Time: 15 hrs.). 1989. 80.00 (978-0-7366-1592-1(X), 2455) Books on Tape.
"Lee's forgotten general," Hill was one of the ablest & most combative soldiers of the South.

General American: An Accent Training Resource for Actors. Gwyneth Strong & Penny Dyer. (ENG., 2008. audio compact disk 29.95 (978-0-7136-8509-1(3)) Pub: A and C Blk GBR. Dist(s): Macmillan

General Athletics. abr. ed. Roger W. Bretemitz. 1 cass. (Running Time: 45 min.). 1985. pap. bk. 9.95 (978-1-893417-23-6(9)) Vector Studios.
Hypnosis: Side A introduction has suggestions to improve athletic performance, food to eat, sleep, etc. Side B hypnosis implants suggestions to change belief system to being a winner, & being victorious.

General Aviation Equipment & Services in Venezuela: A Strategic Reference 2007. Compiled by Icon Group International, Inc. Staff. 2007. ring bd. 195.00 (978-0-497-82468-6(X)) Icon Grp.

General Biology Resource Disk: Resouces for College Level General Biology. 2001. audio compact disk (978-0-929941-34-9(9)) Wood River Assocs.

General Chemistry. 3rd rev. ed. William J. Vining et al. (C). 2002. audio compact disk 37.95 (978-0-03-035319-2(X)) Pub: Brooks-Cole. Dist(s): CENGAGE Learn

General Chemistry, Set. 2nd ed. Rodney Schreiner et al. (C). 1981. bk. 613.50 (978-0-03-058169-4(9)) SCP.

General Class Audio Theory Course: FCC Element 3 License Preparation. 6th ed. Gordon West. 4 CDs. (Running Time: 5 hrs. 9 mins.). 2004. audio compact disk 24.95 (978-0-945053-39-2(8)) Pub: Master Pub Inc. Dist(s): W5YI Group
Audio Theory course for Element 3 FCC Amateur Radio License for exams valid 7/1/2004 thru 6/30/2008. Course recorded by Gordon West is "book on tape" for exam study.

General Douglas MacArthur. abr. ed. Ed. by Carl Betz. 2 cass. (Running Time: 1 hr. 46 min.). Dramatization. 12.95 (978-0-89926-172-0(8), 854) Audio Bk.

General Douglas MacArthur: Soldier. unabr. ed. Read by Douglas MacArthur. 1 CD. (Running Time: 90 mins.). 1999. audio compact disk 15.95 Jerden Recs.
Live speeches given by General McArthur.

General Dwight D. Eisenhower. unabr. ed. 1 cass. (Running Time: 20 min.). 12.95 (#19563) J Norton Pubs.
Speech before Congress of June 18, 1945 where he asks that a lasting peace be obtained & ensured after the unconditional surrender of Germany & the victory over Nazism.

General from America. unabr. ed. Richard Nelson. Perf. by Richard Dreyfuss et al. 1 cass. (Running Time: 1 hrs. 32 min.). 1998. 19.95 (978-1-58081-111-8(6), TPT108) L A Theatre.
An intimate portrait of the American Revolution, from occupied New York to the squalor of Philadelphia. When Alexander Hamilton arrives to question General Benedict Arnold about wartime profiteering, the stage is set for high treason.

General George Washington: A Military Life. unabr. ed. Edward G. Lengel. 2005. audio compact disk 39.99 (978-1-4193-4328-5(9)) Recorded Bks.

General Illness. 1 cass. (Running Time: 1 hr.). 2001. 9.95 (CA601) Pub: VisnQst Vid Aud. Dist(s): TMW Media
Keep focused and maintain a positive attitude as you change your emotions that result in changing physical symptoms to promote healing from any illness.

General Interviewing Techniques: A Self-Instructional Workbook for Telephone & Personal Interviewer Training. Pamela J. Guenzel et al. (C). 1983. 15.00 (978-0-685-07792-4(6)) Inst Soc Res.

General James Longstreet. unabr. ed. Jeffrey Wert. Read by Jonathan Reese. 13 cass. (Running Time: 19 hrs. 30 min.). 1995. 104.00 (3736) Books on Tape.
Longstreet: Confederate hero or goat? Author says "Old Pete" was the best commander on either side, despite his post-war coziness with Union. Comprehensive & convincing.

General James Longstreet: The Confederacy's Most Controversial Soldier. Jeffry D. Wert. Read by Jonathan Reese. 1995. 104.00 (978-0-7366-3054-2(6)) Books on Tape.

General Lee's Army: From Victory to Collapse. Joseph T. Glatthaar. Read by Robertson Dean. (Playaway Adult Nonfiction Ser.). (ENG.). 2008. 129.99 (978-1-60640-759-2(7)) Find a World.

General Lee's Army: From Victory to Collapse. unabr. ed. Joseph T. Glatthaar. Read by Robertson Dean. (Running Time: 91800 sec.). 2008. audio compact disk 34.95 (978-1-4332-1015-0(0)); audio compact disk 44.95 (978-1-4332-1016-7(9)); audio compact disk & audio compact disk 140.00 (978-1-4332-1014-3(2)) Blckstn Audio.

General Lee's Army, Part I: From Victory to Collapse. unabr. ed. Joseph T. Glatthaar. Read by Robertson Dean. (Running Time: 46800 sec.). 2008. 72.95 (978-1-4332-1013-6(4)) Blckstn Audio.

General Lee's Army, Part II: From Victory to Collapse. unabr. ed. Joseph T. Glatthaar. Read by Robertson Dean. (Running Time: 45000 sec.). 2008. 72.95 (978-1-4332-4615-9(5)) Blckstn Audio.

General Mathematics: Syllabus. 2nd ed. Al Gray & Clifford H. Matousek. (J). 1972. 103.55 (978-0-89420-148-6(4)) Natl Book.

General Meditation. Bruce Goldberg. (ENG.). 2005. audio compact disk 17.00 (978-1-57968-037-4(2)) Pub: B Goldberg. Dist(s): Baker Taylor

General Meditation. Bruce Goldberg. Read by Bruce Goldberg. 1 cass. (Running Time: 25 min.). (ENG.). 2006. 13.00 (978-1-885577-23-8(0)) Pub: B Goldberg. Dist(s): Baker Taylor
A guide into relaxing meditation, and conditioning for the before and after death meditation programs.

General Motors Mid-Size & Large Cars, 1982-2000. Chilton Automotive Editorial Staff. (Chilton Total Car Care Ser.). 2004. audio compact disk 19.95 (978-1-4018-8052-1(5)) Pub: Delmar. Dist(s): CENGAGE Learn

General Musicianship. Roy Bennett. Contrib. by Roy Bennett. (Cambridge Assignments in Music Ser.). (ENG.). 1984. 38.99 (978-0-521-24316-2(5)) Cambridge U Pr.

General of the Army: George C. Marshall, Soldier & Statesman. unabr. collector's ed. Ed Cray. Read by Dick Estell. 13 cass. (Running Time: 19 hrs. 30 min.). 1991. 104.00 (978-0-7366-2046-8(X), 2860-A/B); 104.00 (978-0-7366-2047-5(8), 2860-B) Books on Tape.
As chief of staff of the United States Army during WW II, George Marshall helped shape the defeat of Nazi Germany & Imperial Japan. He was an active, often decisive, influence in the conferences between Roosevelt, Churchill & Stalin. Secretary of State under Truman, Marshall engineered the European Recovery Act (Marshall Plan) to rebuild a war-ravaged continent. At the conclusion of his long career, Marshall was given the Nobel Peace Prize - the first & only military man to be so honored.

General Practitioners' Update. 1999. bk. 99.00 (ACS-2282) PA Bar Inst.
This is an up-to-the-minute review of developments in six fields of law. Designed specifically for the generalist who represents clients in many different areas of the law, this offers a review of case law & legislative developments in the past year. Two experienced practitioners in each field highlight the most important changes in the law & offer their insights on how these developments impact the files on your desk.

General Principles for Planning Children's Liturgies. Voice by Elaine Rendler. 1 cass. 1994. 7.95 (9913) OR Catholic.
Topics of this lecture include: an overview of official liturgical books, the "Ten Vital Points" to remember when planning a children's liturgy, etc.

General Prologue & the Physician's Tale: In Middle English & in Modern Verse Translation. unabr. ed. Geoffrey Chaucer. Read by Richard Bebb et al. 2 CDs. (Running Time: 8309 sec.). 2006. audio compact disk 17.98 (978-962-634-400-2(8), Naxos AudioBooks) Naxos.

General Relaxation. abr. ed. Roger W. Bretemitz. 1 cass. (Running Time: 45 min.). 1985. pap. bk. 9.95 (978-1-893417-17-5(4)) Vector Studios.
Hypnosis: Teaches the necessary steps to deep relaxation, how to go even deeper, achieve benefits of 8 hours of sleep in 1 hour & awake fully refreshed & "Powered Up.".

General Session: Beyond the Fee Freeze-Strategies for Reforming Medicare's Physician Payment System. Allen Dobson et al. 2 cass. Incl. General Session: The Congressional Perspective on Changing Physician Reimbursement. (3A/3B); 15.00 (3A/3B) Recorded Res.

General Session: Gramm-Rudman-Hollings: Focus on the Future. Warren B. Rudman & Robert J. Saner, II. Incl. General Session: Legislative Briefing - Nineteen Eighty-Six Political Climate & Preparation for Capitol Hill Visits. (TAPE 5); 9.00 per cass. (TAPE 5) Recorded Res.

General Session: Legislative Briefing - Nineteen Eighty-Six Political Climate & Preparation for Capitol Hill Visits see General Session: Gramm-Rudman-Hollings: Focus on the Future

General Session: Malpractice Reform at the Federal Level. Richard E. Merritt & Robert J. Saner, II. Moderated by James B. Cobb. Incl. General Session: State Efforts to Tackle the Malpractice Problem. (TAPE 14); 9.00 per cass. (TAPE 14) Recorded Res.

General Session: State Efforts to Tackle the Malpractice Problem see General Session: Malpractice Reform at the Federal Level

General Session: The Congressional Perspective on Changing Physician Reimbursement see General Session: Beyond the Fee Freeze-Strategies for Reforming Medicare's Physician Payment System

General Sherman's Christmas: Savannah 1864. unabr. ed. Stanley Weintraub. Narrated by Ed Sala. (Running Time: 8 hrs. 0 mins. 0 sec.). (ENG.). 2009. 19.99 (978-1-4001-6391-5(9)); audio compact disk 59.99 (978-1-4001-4391-7(8)); audio compact disk 29.99 (978-1-4001-1391-0(1)) Pub: Tantor Media. Dist(s): IngramPubServ

***General Sherman's Christmas: Savannah 1864.** unabr. ed. Stanley Weintraub. Narrated by Ed Sala. (Running Time: 8 hrs. 0 mins.). 2009. 15.99 (978-1-4001-8391-3(X)) Tantor Media.

General Structures Mock Exam. Ed. by Architectural License Seminars Staff. 2004. audio compact disk 45.00 (978-0-7931-9398-1(2)) Kaplan Pubng.

General Structures 2 & Lateral Forces. Robert Marks. 2004. 59.00 (978-0-7931-9378-3(8), Kaplan Trade) Kaplan Pubng.

General Surgery Module. 2nd ed. Ed. by American Association for Medical Transcription Staff. Intro. by Claudia Tessier. 6 cass. (Running Time: 3 hrs.). (Exploring Transcription Practices Ser.). (C). 1996. bk. & wbk. ed. 225.00 (978-0-935229-29-5(9)) Am Assoc Med.
Operative dictation. Contains six 30 minute cassettes with accompanying materials.

General Wellness. 2000. audio compact disk Hlth Jrnys.

Generally Speaking. abr. ed. Claudia J. Kennedy & Malcolm McConnell. (ENG.). 2005. 14.98 (978-1-59483-402-8(4)) Pub: Hachet Audio. Dist(s): HachBkGrp

Generals. W. E. B. Griffin. Read by Michael Russotto. 9 cass. (Running Time: 13 hrs. 30 min.). (Brotherhood of War Ser.: No. 6). 1995. 72.00 (3710) Books on Tape.
Their bold decisions changed the outcome of battles & often the fate of a country. The Generals earned their stars in Normandy's spectacular landing, in grueling South Pacific campaigns, on Korea's icy slopes & in the wastelands of Vietnam. It was there they commanded their troops against an unyielding & implacable foe. In a new kind of war, the Generals forged a new kind of army, resillient, tough & unafraid.

Generals. unabr. collector's ed. W. E. B. Griffin. Read by Michael Russotto. 9 cass. (Running Time: 13 hrs. 30 min.). (Brotherhood of War Ser.: No. 6). 1995. 72.00 (978-0-7366-3028-3(7), 3710) Books on Tape.
W.E.B. Griffin brilliantly captures the realism & grit of military adventure.

General's Daughter. collector's ed. Nelson DeMille. Read by John MacDonald. 12 CDs. (Running Time: 10 hrs.). 2000. audio compact disk 96.00 (978-0-7366-5133-2(0)) Books on Tape.
Paul Brenner, one of the army's elite undercover agents, has authority to arrest any military person anywhere in the world. He's always wondered how far he could push it . . .now he's about to find out. When troops find Captain Ann Campbell, a general's daughter, raped & murdered on the firing range, Brenner's instincts tell him to avoid the case. It can only mean trouble.

General's Daughter. unabr. ed. Nelson DeMille. Read by Scott Brick. (Running Time: 19 hrs.). (ENG.). 2009. 24.98 (978-1-60024-902-0(7)) Pub: Hachet Audio. Dist(s): HachBkGrp

General's Daughter. unabr. collector's ed. Nelson DeMille. Read by John MacDonald. 10 cass. (Running Time: 15 hrs.). 1999. 80.00 (978-0-7366-2573-9(9), 3322) Books on Tape.

Generals in Bronze: Interviewing the Commanders of the Civil War. unabr. ed. Read by Patrick Cullen. (Running Time: 54000 sec.). 2008. 85.95 (978-1-4332-1325-0(7)); audio compact disk 29.95 (978-1-4332-1327-4(3)) Blckstn Audio.

Generals in Bronze: Interviewing the Commanders of the Civil War. unabr. ed. William B. Styple. Read by Patrick Cullen. (Running Time: 54000 sec.). 2008. audio compact disk & audio compact disk 99.00 (978-1-4332-1326-7(5)) Blckstn Audio.

Generating a Positive Environment. 1 cass. (Meeting the Challenge of Living in the World Ser.). 9.95 (ST-64) Crystal Clarity.
Includes: what is negativity?; why we should avoid negative people; the importance of basing positive thinking on non-egoic motives; specific ways to improve your vibrational environment.

Generating Never-Ending Motivation. Ratanjit. Contrib. by Raymond C Somich Sr. (Running Time: 3295 sec.). (Stress-Free Living Ser.). 2007. audio compact disk 17.90 (978-1-59076-258-5(4)) DscvrHlpPubng.

Generating Service Sales: ASP-SA-CD-361-00. Aspire Staff. 2000. audio compact disk 149.00 (978-1-4018-0738-2(0)) Delmar.

Generating Trust: The Genius of Selling Professional Services. Jerry Sears. Narrated by Jesse Pearlman. 3 CDs. (Running Time: 4 hours 15min). 2005. audio compact disk 95.00 (978-1-887597-02-9(6)) Assocs Pubs.

Generation Blend: Managing Across the Technology Age Gap. abr. ed. Rob Salkowitz. Read by Bill Weideman. 1 MP3-CD. (Running Time: 7 hrs.). 2008. 24.95 (978-1-4233-6003-2(6), 9781423360032, Brilliance MP3); audio compact disk 39.25 (978-1-4233-6004-9(4), 9781423360049, Brlnc Audio MP3 Lib); audio compact disk 82.25 (978-1-4233-6002-5(8), 9781423360025, BriAudCD Unabrid); audio compact disk 29.95 (978-1-4233-6001-8(X), 9781423360018, Bril Audio CD Unabri) Brilliance Audio.

Generation Blend: Managing across the Technology Age Gap. unabr. abr. ed. Rob Salkowitz. Read by Bill Weideman. (Running Time: 7 hrs.). 2008. 39.25 (978-1-4233-6006-3(0), 9781423360063, BADLE); 24.95 (978-1-4233-6005-6(2), 9781423360056, BAD) Brilliance Audio.

Generation Ex: Adult Children of Divorce & the Healing of Our Pain. abr. ed. Jen Abbas. Read by Sandra Burr. 2 cass. (Running Time: 3 hrs.). 2004. 17.95 (978-1-59355-817-8(1), 1593558171); 44.25 (978-1-59355-818-5(X), 159355818X); audio compact disk 19.95 (978-1-59355-819-2(8), 1593558198); audio compact disk 62.25 (978-1-59355-820-8(1), 1593558201) Brilliance Audio.
One of the hardest truths about divorce is that every split - no matter when it occurs - will have lifelong effects on the children caught in the crossfire. While most people acknowledge our pain during our parents' parting, few of us realize that our most significant insecurities, questions, and doubts may not show up for years, when we seek our own intimate relationships as adults. In fact, millions of adult children of divorce feel lost, displaced, or unwanted years after the ink has dried on their parents' divorce decree. Like them, you may fear abandonment, betrayal, or failure in your own marriage. Despite outward successes, you may doubt your emotional abilities. You may notice that your parents' divorce affects you more each year, not less. You are not alone. Through research, interviews, and personal stories, Generation Ex will help you understand the effect of your parents' divorce on your identity, faith, and relationships, and will give you the tools you need to create a dramatically different legacy.

Generation Ex: Adult Children of Divorce & the Healing of Our Pain. abr. ed. Jen Abbas. Read by Sandra Burr. (Running Time: 3 hrs.). 2006. 39.25 (978-1-4233-0304-6(0), 9781423303046, BADLE); 24.95 (978-1-4233-0303-9(2), 9781423303039, BAD); 39.25 (978-1-4233-0302-2(4), 9781423303022, Brlnc Audio MP3 Lib); 24.95 (978-1-4233-0301-5(6), 9781423303015, Brilliance MP3) Brilliance Audio.

Generation Kill: Devil Dogs, Iceman, Captain America, & the New Face of American War. Evan Wright. Read by Patrick G. Lawlor. (Playaway Adult Nonfiction Ser.). (ENG.). 2009. 70.00 (978-1-60775-622-4(6)) Find a World.

Generation Kill: Devil Dogs, Iceman, Captain America, & the New Face of American War. unabr. ed. Evan Wright. 2 MP3-CDs. (Running Time: 13 hrs. 30 mins. 0 sec.). (ENG.). 2008. 29.99 (978-1-4001-5974-1(1)); audio compact disk 79.99 (978-1-4001-3974-3(0)) Pub: Tantor Media. Dist(s): IngramPubServ

Generation Kill: Devil Dogs, Iceman, Captain America, & the New Face of American War. unabr. ed. Evan Wright. Read by Patrick G. Lawlor. 11 CDs. (Running Time: 13 hrs. 30 mins. 0 sec.). (ENG.). 2008. audio compact disk 39.99 (978-1-4001-0974-6(4)) Pub: Tantor Media. Dist(s): IngramPubServ

Generation Next: Winning the Spiritual Battle for Your Teens & Preteens. unabr. ed. Wyndham Shaw et al. 4 cass. (Running Time: 4 hrs.). 1998. 21.99 Set. (978-1-57782-063-5(0)) Discipleshp.
There is a spiritual battle raging for the minds & souls of preteens & teens. In the midst of all the world's influences, the greatest influence in a child's life is his or her parents & their spirituality. These messages contain practical solutions & answers that make winning the battle possible.

Generation Next CD Series. 2003. audio compact disk 32.00 (978-1-59834-061-7(1)) Walk Thru the Bible.

Generation of Vipers. unabr. collector's ed. Philip Wylie. Read by Ron Shoop. 8 cass. (Running Time: 12 hrs.). 1983. 64.00 (978-0-7366-0546-5(0), 1520) Books on Tape.
Wylie pleads for a more rational society, one that is based on sound psychological principles. For those who agree with him, his book is a reaffirmation. For those who don't, it stimulates the circulation.

Generation-Skipping Transfer Tax Exemption Allocation: Tax Returns & Administration Issues. American Law Institute-American Bar Association, Committee on Continuing Professional Education Staff. Instructed by Paul N. Frimmer et al. 1 cass. (Running Time: 58 min.). 1995. 75.00 incl. study materials. (M229) Am Law Inst.
Concentrates on the technical aspects of allocating the $1 million GST exemption, with attention to U.S. tax forms 706 & 709 & relevant schedules. Topics include: automatic allocation, mechanics of allocating, formula severance & formula allocation, filing returns, valuation rules, marital deduction funding, postmortem repair.

Generation-Skipping Transfer Tax Planning & Drafting. American Law Institute-American Bar Association, Committee on Continuing Professional Education Staff. Instructed by Paul N. Frimmer et al. 2 cass. (Running Time: 1 hr. 53 min.). 1995. 125.00 Set, incl. study materials. (M228) Am Law Inst.
Offers intermediate-level instruction for those who are ready for more savvy planning & drafting strategies & techniques, especially in connection with the $1 million dollar exemption. Topics include: the inclusion ratio, drafting trusts to keep them exempt, best uses of the $1 million exemption, opting in or out of GST tax, planning with powers of appointment.

Generation Skipping Transfer Tax Series. 7 cass. (Running Time: 6 hrs. 36 min.). 359.00 Set, incl. study materials. (YB79); , individual cass. Am Law Inst.

Generation-Skipping Transfers in Estate Planning. Read by Jon Gallo & Jerry A. Kasner. (Running Time: 2 hrs. 45 min.). 1991. 70.00 Incl. 241p. tape materials. (ES-54148) Cont Ed Bar-CA.

Generation Skipping Transfers under the New Law. 1988. bk. 55.00; 55.00 PA Bar Inst.

Generation Skipping Transfers under the New Law. 1988. 45.00 (AC-422) PA Bar Inst.

Generation Text: Raising Well-Adjusted Kids in an Age of Instant Everything. unabr. ed. Michael Osit. Read by Dan John Miller. 1 MP3-CD. (Running Time: 11 hrs.). 2008. 39.25 (978-1-4233-6417-7(1), 9781423364177, Brlnc Audio MP3 Lib); 39.25 (978-1-4233-6419-1(8), 9781423364191, BADLE); 24.95 (978-1-4233-6418-4(X), 9781423364184, BAD); 24.95 (978-1-4233-6416-0(3), 9781423364160, Brilliance MP3); audio compact disk 29.95 (978-1-4233-6414-6(7), 9781423364146, Bril Audio CD Unabri); audio compact disk 82.25 (978-1-4233-6415-3(5), 9781423364153, BriAudCD Unabrid) Brilliance Audio.

Generation to Generation: A Legacy of Love & Wisdom. Gerard Smith. 8 cassettes. (Running Time: 12 hours). 2004. 59.95 (978-0-9625616-3-4(0)) Pub: Lght The Fire Within. Dist(s): STL Dist NA
The Generation to Generation Audio Journal comes with guidelines, questions and suggested interview techniques that will help you talk comfortably with your loved ones. The audio journal comes in a beautiful dark blue linen-covered and embossed audio case to keep the completed tapes safe. Each of the 8 90-minute audioapes are imprinted with titles for each chapter of a person's life.

Generation Unleashed. Created by Maranatha! Music. 2008. audio compact disk 12.99 (978-5-557-49734-3(X)) Maranatha Music.

Generation X Celebration. Perf. by Walt Walt Whitman and the Soul Children of Chicago. 1 cass. 10.98 (978-1-57908-434-9(6)); audio compact disk 16.98 (978-1-57908-433-2(8)) Platinm Enter.

Generational Sins. Michael Pearl. 1 CD. 2003. audio compact disk (978-1-892112-52-1(3)) No Greater Joy.

Generational Transfer. 2008. audio compact disk 30.00 (978-1-58602-384-3(5)) Pub: E L Long. Dist(s): Anchor Distributors

Generations. 2004. 25.99 (978-7-5124-0239-3(2)) Mrning Str.

Generations. J. M. Dillard. (Star Trek Ser.). 2004. 10.95 (978-0-7435-4634-8(2)) Pub: S&S Audio. Dist(s): S and S Inc

Generations. Don Nori. 6 cass. 35.00 Set. (978-1-56043-386-6(8)) Destiny Image Pubs.

Generations: Tough Guys. Concept by Andrew Speight. 2008. audio compact disk 15.00 (978-1-4276-3197-8(2)) AardGP.

Generations & the Kingdom. Stephen Mansfield. 1 cass. (Running Time: 90 mins.). (Studies in Church History Ser.: Vol. 9). 2000. 5.00 (SM02-009) Morning NC.
An in-depth look at different philosophies that have influenced church history, this series provides excellent keys for understanding how to effectively confront the important issues of our times.

Generations of the Heart. Viqui Litman. Narrated by Cynthia Darlow. 8 cass. (Running Time: 11 hrs. 15 mins.). 72.00 (978-1-4025-1618-4(5)) Recorded Bks.

Generations of the Heart. unabr. ed. Viqui Litman. Narrated by Cynthia Darlow. 8 cass. (Running Time: 11 hrs. 15 mins.). 2002. 39.95 (978-1-4025-1622-1(3), RF863) Recorded Bks.
A tale of mothers, daughters, and modern maternity When Rita's beautiful blonde daughter moves back to The Ladies Farm, she soon has everyone abuzz with her plans to be a surrogate mother.

***Generations Unite in Prayer: The Divine Mercy Chaplet in Song.** Short Trish. (ENG.). 2007. audio compact disk 20.00 (978-1-59614-175-9(1)) Pub: Marian Pr. Dist(s): STL Dist NA

***Generations Unite in Prayer (CD Version) The Divine Mercy Chaplet in Song.** Short Trish. (ENG.). 2008. audio compact disk 15.95 (978-1-59614-176-6(X)) Pub: Marian Pr. Dist(s): STL Dist NA

Generative Personality: Enjoying the Present & Building the Future. John Grinder & Steven Gilligan. Read by John Grinder & Steven Gilligan. 7 cass. (Running Time: 10 hrs. 30 min.). (Syntax of Behavior Two Ser.: Vol. II). 1989. 89.95 set. Metamorphous Pr.
Conflict resolution, relationship negotiation, skill mastery & future orientation are addressed in the 10-hour program. Topics explored include prerequisites for creativity, the functions & varieties of attention, dissolving fixed patterns, integrating opposites, claiming inner & outer resources, & envisioning & creating desired outcomes.

Generic Cowboy Poetry. Poems. Baxter Black. 1 cass. 1985. 9.99 (978-0-939343-28-7(2)) Coyote Cowboy.
Recorded live at Bax's camp in Colorado complete with crackling fire, crickets & cowboy friends. Join them as Baxter does "The Oyster," "Why Do the Trees All Lean in Wyoming?," "The Spur" & 15 more.

Generic Pharmaceuticals in Belgium: A Strategic Reference 2006. Compiled by Icon Group International, Inc. Staff. 2007. ring bd. 195.00 (978-0-497-35826-6(3)) Icon Grp.

Generica. Will Ferguson. Narrated by Ron Halder. Abr. by Emil Sher. 3 cass.,. (Running Time: 3 hrs. 45 mins). (ENG.). 2001. 19.95 (978-0-86492-326-4(0)) Pub: BTC Audiobks CAN. Dist(s): U Toronto Pr

Generosidad Hilarante. Charles R. Swindoll.Tr. of Hilarious Generosity. 2009. audio compact disk 19.00 (978-1-57972-806-9(5)) Insight Living.

Generosity: An Enhancement. unabr. ed. Richard Powers. Read by David Pittu. (Running Time: 12 hrs. 0 mins. 0 sec.). (ENG.). 2009. audio compact disk 39.99 (978-1-4272-0767-8(4)) Pub: Macmill Audio. Dist(s): Macmillan

Generosity Factor: Discover the Joy of Giving Your Time, Talent, & Treasure. unabr. ed. Ken Blanchard & S. Truett Cathy. 2002. 19.99 (978-0-310-24797-5(7)); audio compact disk 19.99 (978-0-310-24796-8(9)) Zondervan.

***Generosity Factorâ„¢: Discover the Joy of Giving Your Time, Talent, & Treasure.** unabr. ed. Ken Blanchard & S. Truett Cathy. (Running Time: 2 hrs. 0 mins. 0 sec.). (ENG.). 2003. 11.99 (978-0-310-26153-7(8)) Zondervan.

Generous Gardener. Trisha Ashley. 9 cass. (Running Time: 11 hrs. 45 mins.). (Isis Cassettes Ser.). 2006. 76.95 (978-0-7531-3601-0(5)) Pub: ISIS Lrg Prnt GBR. Dist(s): Ulverscroft US

***Generous Justice: How God's Grace Makes Us Just.** unabr. ed. Timothy Keller. Read by Tom Parks. 1 MP3-CD. (Running Time: 5 hrs.). 2010. 19.99 (978-1-4418-3083-8(9), 9781441830838, Brilliance MP3); 39.97 (978-1-4418-3084-5(7), 9781441830845, Brlnc Audio MP3 Lib); 19.99 (978-1-4418-3085-2(5), 9781441830852, BAD); 39.97 (978-1-4418-3086-9(3), 9781441830869, BADLE); audio compact disk 19.99 (978-1-4418-3081-4(2), 9781441830814, Bril Audio CD Unabri); audio compact disk 69.97 (978-1-4418-3082-1(0), 9781441830821, BriAudCD Unabrid) Brilliance Audio.

Generous Orthodoxy. abr. ed. Brian D. McLaren. (Running Time: 3 hrs. 59 mins. 0 sec.). (ENG.). 2006. 12.99 (978-0-310-26925-0(3)) Zondervan.

***Generous Orthodoxy.** unabr. ed. Brian D. McLaren. (Running Time: 8 hrs. 0 mins. 0 sec.). (ENG.). 2009. 14.99 (978-0-310-77151-7(X)) Zondervan.

Generous Orthodoxy. unabr. abr. ed. Brian D. McLaren. Read by Brian D. McLaren. (Running Time: 2 hrs. 40 mins. 0 sec.). (ENG.). 2006. audio compact disk 19.99 (978-0-310-26924-3(5)) Zondervan.

Genes & the Brain: Program from the Award Winning Public Radio Series. Interview. Hosted by Fred Goodwin. 1 CD. (Running Time: 1 hr.). 2004. audio compact disk 21.95 (978-1-932479-49-2(X), LCM 340) Lichtenstein Creat.
Now that we've mapped the human genome, what clues is this stunning scientific feat providing about how the brain works and why, sometimes, it doesn't? Guests include Dr. Eric Kandel, professor of physiology and psychiatry at Columbia University and the first psychiatrist to win the Nobel Prize in more than 70 years; Dr. Christopher Walsh, professor of neurology at Harvard Medical School and the chief of neurogenetics at Beth Israel Deaconess Medical Center; Dr. Jenae Neiderhiser, associate professor of psychiatry and behavioral sciences at George Washington University; and Dr. Michael Kaplitt, assistant professor of neurosurgery and director of the Center for Stereotactic and Molecular Neurosurgery at the Weill Medical College of Cornell University.

Gene's Boot Camp: Selling Prepaid Services. Gene Retske. 7 CDs. (Running Time: 6 hrs.). 2003. audio compact disk 197.00 (978-0-9745500-1-5(9)) Solvox Inc.
Gene's Boot Camp Kit for Prepaid. Includes 6 audio CDs, Resource Cd and Boot Camp Manual.

Genesis see Poetry of Geoffrey

Genesis. 4 cass. (Running Time: 360 mins.). (SPA.). 9.98 Set. (2007A) Chrstn Dup Intl.
Part of the 1909 Antigua Reina-Valera Revision, the classic edition of the Spanish Bible.

Genesis. Read by Wendy Jensen. 1 CD. (Running Time: 1 hr. 30 mins.). 2001. audio compact disk 19.95 (978-0-9709286-6-5(1)) Brave New.

Genesis. Narrated by Samuel Montoya. 4 cass. (SPA.). 1994. 12.98 Set. (978-7-902032-52-0(2)) Chrstn Dup Intl.

Genesis. Contrib. by Joy Williams. Prod. by Matt Bronlewee. Contrib. by Jason McArthur et al. 2005. audio compact disk 13.97 (978-5-559-08295-0(3)) Pt of Grace Ent.

Genesis. deluxe ed. Chuck Missler. 32 cass. (Running Time: 48 hrs.). (Heirloom Edition Ser.). 1996. im. lthr. 34.95 Incl. notes. (978-1-880532-19-5(0)) Koinonia Hse.
Pulling back the veil of prehistory, Chuck will take you on a journey into the very nature of our universe, exploring the mechanics of creation, time and space, the physics of eternity and the intricate design of God's wonderful plan for our salvationThis foundational study begins where any true adventure does..."In the Beginning".

Genesis. unabr. ed. Bernard Beckett. Read by Becky A. Wright. (Running Time: 4 hrs.). 2009. 39.97 (978-1-4233-8155-6(6), 9781423381556, BADLE) Brilliance Audio.

Genesis. unabr. ed. Bernard Beckett. Read by Becky Wright. 1 MP3-CD. (Running Time: 4 hrs.). 2009. 39.97 (978-1-4233-8153-2(X), 9781423381532, Brlnc Audio MP3 Lib); 24.99 (978-1-4233-8152-5(1), 9781423381525, Brilliance MP3); 24.99 (978-1-4233-8154-9(8), 9781423381549, BAD); audio compact disk 48.97 (978-1-4233-8151-8(3), 9781423381518, BriAudCD Unabrid); audio compact disk 24.99 (978-1-4233-8150-1(5), 9781423381501, Bril Audio CD Unabri) Brilliance Audio.

Genesis. unabr. ed. Read by Peter Coyote. Tr. by Robert Alter from HEB. Contrib. by Thomas Moore & Michael Toms. 3 cass. (Running Time: 4 hr. 30 min.). 1998. 21.95 (978-1-57453-101-5(8)) Audio Lit.
Recovers the eloquence of the ancient Hebrew & conveys it in striking literary English.

Genesis. unabr. ed. Read by Edward Herrmann. 4 cass. 2004. 24.95 (978-1-59007-476-3(9)); audio compact disk 29.95 (978-1-59007-477-0(7)) Pub: New Millenn Enter. Dist(s): PerseuPGW

Genesis, Pt. 1. (LifeLight Ser.). 2000. audio compact disk 15.00 (978-0-570-07859-3(8), 20-3324) Concordia.

Genesis, Pt. 2. 2001. audio compact disk 15.00 (978-0-570-07862-3(8), 20-3330) Concordia.

Genesis: A Biblical Interpretation. Concept by Ermance Rejebian. (ENG.). 2007. 5.99 (978-1-60339-137-5(1)); audio compact disk 5.99 (978-1-60339-138-2(X)) Listenr Digest.

Genesis: A Classical Christian Educators Conference. Mitch Stokes. (ENG.). 2008. audio compact disk 16.00 (978-1-59128-401-7(5)) Canon Pr ID.

Genesis: A New Translation of the Classic Bible Stories. Stephen Mitchell. 2 cass. 1996. 18.00 Set. (978-0-694-51653-7(8)) HarperCollins Pubs.

Genesis: A Story from Wolf Willow. unabr. ed. Wallace Stegner. Read by Page Stegner. 3 cass. (Running Time: 3 hrs. 45 min.). Dramatization. 1994. 24.95 (978-0-939643-54-7(5), 3576, NrthWrd Bks) TandN Child.
This is a dramatic story of a young man's coming-of-age as he helps his cowboy heroes round up cattle during a bleak, bitter winter on the Saskatchewan plains.

Genesis: Digging Deeper into the Beginnings. abr. ed. Narrated by Kailey Bell & Todd Busteed. (Running Time: 7200 sec.). (Kidz Rock Ser.). (ENG.). (J). 2008. audio compact disk 8.99 (978-1-59859-324-2(2)) Oasis Audio.

Genesis: King James Version, unabr. ed. Narrated by Norman Dietz. 3 cass. (Running Time: 4 hrs. 30 mins.). 1990. 26.00 (978-1-55690-193-5(3), 90086E7) Recorded Bks.
A word-for-word reading of the Creation Story. Includes Genesis, Exodus, leviticus, numbers, Deuteronomy & Joshua.

Genesis: The Creation & Noah. abr. ed. Perf. by Judith Anderson. 1 cass. 1984. 12.95 (978-0-694-50075-8(5), SWC 1096) HarperCollins Pubs.

Genesis Set: A New Translation & Study. abr. ed. Stephen Mitchell. 2 cass. (Running Time: 3 hrs.). 1996. 18.00 (978-1-55994-953-8(8), 391813, Harper Audio) HarperCollins Pubs.
Emphasizes what the Biblical stories can still teach us - & their relevance to modern life. Not only considered one of the best translators of ancient texts today, Mitchell moves beyond a fine rendering of this Old Testament landmark to provide us with a scholarly & insightful interpretation.

***Genesis According to Yabit (Part One)** Read by Veronica Weymouth. (ENG.). 2009. audio compact disk 27.95 (978-0-9841881-2-3(6)) Audrey L.

Genesis & the Big Bang. Chuck Missler. 2 CD's. (Running Time: 120 min. aprox.). (Briefing Packages by Chuck Missler). 1991. audio compact disk 19.95 (978-1-57821-300-9(2)) Koinonia Hse.

Genesis & the Big Bang. Chuck Missler. 2 cass. (Running Time: 2.5 hours +). (Briefing Packages by Chuck Missler). 1991. vinyl bd. 14.95 Incls. notes. (978-1-880532-75-1(1)) Koinonia Hse.

Genesis Code. unabr. ed. John Case. Read by Dick Hill. (Running Time: 17 hrs.). 2009. 29.99 (978-1-4233-9082-4(2), 9781423390824, Brilliance MP3); 44.97 (978-1-4233-9083-1(0), 9781423390831, Brlnc Audio MP3 Lib); 29.99 (978-1-4233-9084-8(9), 9781423390848, BAD); 44.97 (978-1-4233-9085-5(7), 9781423390855, BADLE) Brilliance Audio.

Genesis Commentary. Chuck Missler. 24 CD's. (Running Time: 24 hours). (Chuck Missler Commentaries). 2004. audio compact disk 89.95 (978-1-57821-257-6(X)) Koinonia Hse.
*Recent breakthroughs in the fields of physics, technology and biology led Chuck Missler to update and re-record this wonderful study in Genesis. With over 24 hours of teaching, this verse-by-verse study of the book of Genesis has been one of our most sought-after and best-selling series in the history of Koinonia House.Pulling back the veil of prehistory, Chuck will take you on a journey into the very nature of our universe, exploring the mechanics of creation, time and space, the physics of eternity and the intricate design of God's wonderful plan for our salvationThis foundational study begins where any true adventure does..."In the Beginning".This MP3 CD-ROM (compatible with both Windows and Macintosh operating systems) is self-contained and includes: * Over 24 hours of Verse-by-Verse audio teaching through the book of Genesis as MP3 files. * 24 individual slideshow presentations. * Extensive searchable study notes as PDF files. * Listings of other MP3 resources. * Real ? Player and Real ? Juke Box. This program will play MP3 audio files. * Adobe Acrobat? Reader.This program will read the PDF notes.*

Genesis Enigma. unabr. ed. Andrew Parker. (Running Time: 10 hrs. 30 mins. 0 sec.). (ENG.). 2009. audio compact disk 26.98 (978-1-59644-809-4(1), Hovel Audio) christianaud.

***Genesis Enigma: Why the Bible Is Scientifically Accurate.** unabr. ed. Andrew Parker. Narrated by James Adams. (ENG.). 2009. 16.98 (978-1-59644-810-0(5), Hovel Audio) christianaud.

Genesis Face. Kelley Varner. 1 cass. 7.00 (978-1-56043-972-1(6)) Destiny Image Pubs.

Genesis: First - Twenty-Second: The Covenant. Scott Hahn. 7 cass. 34.95 Set. (5279-C) Ignatius Pr.
Once you really grasp what God is saying in the familiar but rarely understood Genesis stories, you will realize what is at stake in the history of Israel, & in Christ's sacrifice on the Cross.

Genesis I. (LifeLight Bible Studies: Course 3). 13.95 Set. (20-2260) Concordia.

Genesis of Justice: Ten Stories of Biblical Injustice That Led to the Ten Commandments & Modern Law. Alan M. Dershowitz. 6 cass. (Running Time: 9 hrs.). 2000. 35.00 (978-1-57453-381-1(9)) Audio Lit.

Genesis of Justice: Ten Stories of Biblical Injustice That Led to the Ten Commandments & Modern Morality & Law. Alan M. Dershowitz. Read by Alan M. Dershowitz. 2 cass. (Running Time: 3 hrs.). 2001. 17.98 (978-1-58621-103-5(X)) Hachet Audio.
Cain murders his brother & walks, God gets angry - millions die in flood, Jacob robs brother & gets away with it. In this probing, fascinating & entertaining book, America's leading lawyer looks at the Bible & in particular at the Book of Genesis - as a tale of justice done, justice undone & justice in the eyes of the beholder.

Genesis of Justice: Ten Stories of Biblical Injustice That Led to the Ten Commandments & Modern Morality & Law. unabr. ed. Alan M. Dershowitz. (ENG.). 2005. 14.98 (978-1-59483-436-3(9)) Pub: Hachet Audio. Dist(s): HachBkGrp

Genesis of Love: Relationship Magic in Heaven & on Earth. Guy Finley. (ENG.). 2006. 24.95 (978-1-929320-45-5(0)); 34.95 (978-1-929320-28-8(0)); audio compact disk 34.95 (978-1-929320-29-5(9)) Life of Learn.
This powerful audio program, recorded live by best-selling self-realization author Guy Finley, helps listeners form a lasting relationship with genuine love. Includes ways to awaken the sweetness and magic in all relationships, communicate with clarity and compassion, uncover the boldness and daring audacity of one's True Self, and learn the one great secret to a success with no down side!.

Genesis of the New Catechism. Michael Wrenn. 1 cass. (Inspiring Presentations from the National Rosary Congress Ser.). 2.50 (978-1-56036-096-4(8)) AMI Pr.

Genesis of Vedanta. Swami Amar Jyoti. 1 dolby cass. 1984. 9.95 (R-56) Truth Consciousness.
The highest philosophy, direct Truth; the simplest way possible, yet the most misused. On the imparting of Vedanta. What is Reality?.

Genesis Through Joshua Bible. Ty Fischer & Emily Fischer. Perf. by Steve Scheffler. 1998. 6.95 (978-1-930710-85-6(2)) Veritas Pr PA.

Genesis Wave, Bk. 1. John Vornholt. Read by Tim Russ. 2004. 10.95 (978-0-7435-5096-3(X)); 10.95 (978-0-7435-4638-6(5)) Pub: S&S Audio. Dist(s): S and S Inc

Genesis Wave, Bk. 2. John Vornholt. 3 CDs. (Running Time: 3 hrs.). 2001. audio compact disk 23.50 S&S Audio.

Genesis Wave, Bk. 2. John Vornholt. Read by Tim Russ. 2004. 10.95 (978-0-7435-4658-4(X)) Pub: S&S Audio. Dist(s): S and S Inc

Genesis Wave, Bk. 3. John Vornholt. 2004. 10.95 (978-0-7435-4659-1(8)) Pub: S&S Audio. Dist(s): S and S Inc

Genesis 2. (LifeLight Bible Studies: Course 4). bk. 5.50 (978-0-570-09262-9(0), 20-2259) Concordia.

Genetic Counseling & Testing in Gynecologic Patients. Contrib. by Susan J. Gross et al. 1 cass. (Topics, Moderators, & Panelists Ser.: Vol. 24, No. 8). 1998. 20.00 Am Coll Obstetric.

Genetic Engineering: Who Decides? 1 cass. (Running Time: 30 min.). 8.00 (G0640B090, HarperThor) HarpC GBR.

Genetically Modified Products in Brazil: A Strategic Reference 2007. Compiled by Icon Group International, Inc. Staff. 2007. ring bd. 195.00 (978-0-497-35839-6(5)) Icon Grp.

Genetics: Analysis of Genes & Genomes. 5th ed. Daniel Hartl & Elizabeth Jones. (C). 2001. audio compact disk 99.00 (978-0-7637-1605-9(7), 1605-7) Jones Bartlett.

Genetics & Cell Biology on File. rev. ed. Diagram Group. (gr. 9). 2005. audio compact disk 149.95 (978-0-8160-5404-6(5)) Facts On File.

Genetics, Diversity, & the Biosphere. Denson McLain. Read by Amy Bruce & Brian Hill. 3 CDs. (Running Time: 3 hrs.). 2005. audio compact disk 19.99 (978-1-884612-50-3(4)) AudioText.

Genetics, Diversity, & the Biosphere. unabr. ed. Denson K. McLain. Read by Amy Bruce & Brian Hill. Ed. by Allan G. Kaster. 2 cass. (Running Time: 3 hrs.). (Biology-on-Tape Ser.). 1994. 19.99 set. (978-1-884612-02-2(4)) AudioText.
A study guide of biology covering cellular division, chromosomes, inheritance, recombinant technology, populations, adaptation, the evolution of life, kingdoms, global climate, levels of organization, predation & competition.

Genetics in Pediatric Practice. Contrib. by Larry Shapiro et al. 1 cass. (American Academy of Pediatrics UPDATE: Vol. 16, No. 1). 1998. 20.00 Am Acad Pediat.

Geneva Mystery. unabr. ed. Francis Durbridge. Read by Michael Tudor Barnes. 3 cass. (Running Time: 4 hrs. 45 mins.). (Isis Cassettes Ser.). (J). 2004. 34.95 (978-0-7531-1890-0(4)) Pub: ISIS Lrg Prnt GBR. Dist(s): Ulverscroft US

Geneva Mystery. unabr. ed. Francis Durbridge. Read by Michael Tudor Barnes. 4 CDs. (Running Time: 4 hrs. 45 mins.). (Isis (CDs) Ser.). (J). 2004. audio compact disk 51.95 (978-0-7531-2257-0(X)) Pub: ISIS Lrg Prnt GBR. Dist(s): Ulverscroft US

Genevieve. unabr. ed. Eric Jerome Dickey. Read by Richard Allen. (Running Time: 8 hrs.). 2005. 39.25 (978-1-59710-866-9(9), 9781597108669, BADLE); 24.95 (978-1-59710-867-6(7), 9781597108676, BAD); 24.95 (978-1-59335-778-8(8), 9781593357788, Brilliance MP3); 39.25 (978-1-59335-912-6(8), 9781593359126, Brlnc Audio MP3 Lib); 29.95 (978-1-59355-998-4(4), 9781593559984, BAU); 74.25 (978-1-59355-999-1(2), 9781593559991, BrilAudUnabridg); audio compact disk 32.95 (978-1-59600-001-8(5), 9781596000018, Bril Audio CD Unabri); audio compact disk 87.25 (978-1-59600-002-5(3), 9781596000025, BriAudCD Unabrid) Brilliance Audio.
Please enter a Synopsis.

Genevox inner Circle Gmg Cd Plan. 1998. audio compact disk (978-0-7673-9412-3(7)) LifeWay Christian.

Genghis: Birth of an Empire. unabr. ed. Conn Iggulden. Read by Stefan Rudnicki. 1 CD. (Running Time: 14 hrs. 0 mins.). 2008. 29.95 (978-1-4332-1533-9(0)); 79.95 (978-1-4332-1529-2(2)); audio compact disk 99.00 (978-1-4332-1530-8(6)) Blckstn Audio.

Genghis: Birth of an Empire. unabr. ed. Conn Iggulden. Read by Stefan Rudnicki. (Running Time: 14 hrs. 0 mins.). 2008. 32.95 (978-1-4332-1531-5(4)); audio compact disk 32.95 (978-1-4332-1532-2(2)) Blckstn Audio.

Genghis: Bones of the Hills. unabr. ed. Conn Iggulden. Narrated by Richard Ferrone. 14 cass. (Running Time: 17 hrs. 15 mins.). (Conqueror Ser.: No. 3). 2009. 113.75 (978-1-4361-7459-6(7)); audio compact disk 123.75 (978-1-4361-7460-2(0)) Recorded Bks.

Genghis: Bones of the Hills. unabr. ed. Conn Iggulden. Narrated by Richard Ferrone. 14 CDs. (Running Time: 17 hrs. 15 mins.). (Conqueror Ser.: No. 3). 2009. audio compact disk 74.95 (978-1-4361-7461-9(9)) Recorded Bks.

Genghis: Bones of the Hills. unabr. ed. Conn Iggulden. Narrated by Richard Ferrone. (Running Time: 17 hrs. 15 mins.). (Conqueror Ser.: No. 3). 2009. 61.75 (978-1-4361-9256-9(0)) Recorded Bks.

***Genghis Khan & the Making of the Modern World.** unabr. ed. Jack Weatherford. (Running Time: 16 hrs.). 2010. 39.97 (978-1-4418-4528-3(3), 9781441845283, BADLE) Brilliance Audio.

***Genghis Khan & the Making of the Modern World.** unabr. ed. Jack Weatherford. Read by Jonathan Davis. (Running Time: 14 hrs.). 2010. 39.97 (978-1-4418-4520-7(8), 9781441845207, Brlnc Audio MP3 Lib); 24.99 (978-1-4418-4511-5(9), 9781441845115, Brilliance MP3); audio compact disk 89.97 (978-1-4418-4503-0(8), 9781441845030, BriAudCD Unabrid) Brilliance Audio.

***Genghis Khan & the Making of the Modern World.** unabr. ed. Jack Weatherford & History. Read by Jonathan Davis. (Running Time: 15 hrs.). 2010. audio compact disk 29.99 (978-1-4418-4489-7(9), 9781441844897) Brilliance Audio.

Gengrative Hypnosis. unabr. ed. Stephen G. Gilligan. 3 cass. (Running Time: 4 hrs.). 1998. 39.95 (978-0-9705492-0-4(2)) N L P Comp.
Introduction to Ericksonian Hypnosis.

Genie Within. Chris Douglass. 1 cass. (Running Time: 1 hr.). 1997. 9.98 (978-1-882786-38-1(6)) New Dawn NY.

Genie Within - Audio CD. Chris Douglass. 2007. audio compact disk 14.95 (978-1-4276-2036-1(9)) AardGP.

Génitrix, Set. Francois Mauriac. Ed. by John Porter Houston & Mona Tobin Houston. 2 cass. (Masterpieces of French Literature Ser.). (FRE.). 1991. 26.95 (1368-LV) Olivia & Hill.
Fernand, at 50, still lives with his mother who has reduced him to a state of childish dependence. In a last attempt to assert himself, he marries Mathilde, a pathetic young woman in search of security. She becomes a pawn in the claustrophobic battle between mother & son.

Genius: Program from the Award Winning Public Radio Series. Interview. Hosted by Fred Goodwin. Comment by John Hockenberyy. 1 CD. (Running Time: 1 hr.). 2004. audio compact disk 21.95 (978-1-932479-50-8(3), LCM 310) Lichtenstein Creat.
We see it in figures as different - and distant - as Leonardo da Vinci and Albert Einstein: a rare combination of unusual intelligence, remarkable insight, and amazing inventiveness. It's called genius, and most of us, at one point or another, wish we had it. But what is genius, and where does it come from? Are there many types of genius? And is there any real connection between genius and madness?Joining host Dr. Fred Goodwin are Dr. Dean Keith Simonton, professor of psychology at the University of California, Davis, and the author of "Genius and Creativity" and "Greatness: Who Makes History and Why"; Dr. Ellen Winner, professor psychology at Boston College, who studies artistic genius; Dr. Darold Treffert, professor of psychiatry at the University of Wisconsin Medical School, and a world leading expert on Savant Syndrome, the unusual combination of severe mental disability and intellectual giftedness; and Dr. Harold Bloom, eminent literary and cultural critic, Sterling Professor of Humanities at Yale University, and the author of Genius: A Mosaic of One Hundred Exemplary Minds. Plus commentary by John Hockenberry.

Genius: The Life & Science of Richard Feynman, unabr. ed. James Gleick. Read by Dick Estell. 14 cass. (Running Time: 21 hrs.). 1996. 112.00 (978-0-7366-3493-9(2), 4133) Books on Tape.
It's said that a genius performs magic, does things nobody else can do. To his scientific colleagues, Richard Feynman was a magician of the highest caliber. Architect of quantum theories, "enfant terrible" of the atomic bomb project, critic of the space shuttle commission, winner of the Nobel Prize for his work in particle physics, he left his mark on just about every area of modern physics.

***Genius Files: Mission Unstoppable.** unabr. ed. Dan Gutman. (ENG.). 2011. (978-0-06-201254-8(1)) HarperCollins Pubs.

Genius for War. Read by Jack Perkins. 1 cass. (Running Time: 90 min.). (Biography Ser.). 1997. 9.95 (978-0-7670-0003-1(X)) A & E Home.
Each biography offers a careful examination of the subject's life as well as a historical account of the times during which each person lived.

Genius Formula. Tony Buzan & Raymond Keene. 6 cass. 59.95 Set. (12390PAM) Nightingale-Conant.
Once you understand The Genius Formula, you'll generate more creative ideas, more often. You'll expand your mental capabilities so you can think more quickly, accomplish more & make smarter decisions. And you'll understand how you, too, can function at the genius level.

Genius in All of Us: Why Everything You've Been Told about Genetics, Talent & IQ Is Wrong. unabr. ed. David Shenk. Read by Mark Deakins. (ENG.). 2010. audio compact disk 30.00 (978-0-307-70444-3(0), Random AudioBks) Pub: Random Audio Pubg. Dist(s): Random

Genius Network: Joe Polish Interviews Tim Ferriss (#1 New York Times Best Seller the 4-Hour Work Week) Interview with Joe Polish. 2007. 24.99 (978-0-9817804-0-5(7)) Piranha Market.

Genius of Alexander the Great. unabr. ed. Nicholas G. Hammond. Narrated by Nelson Runger. 8 cass. (Running Time: 10 hrs. 30 mins.). 1997. 70.00 (978-0-7887-1319-4(1), 95177E7) Recorded Bks.
Written for the layman & based on accounts of Alexander's contemporaries.

Genius of Arab Civilization. unabr. ed. 1 cass. 12.95 (C40228) J Norton Pubs.
Heywood Hale Broun interviews two members of the NYU Dept. of Near Eastern History who discuss the contributions of the medieval Arab world in the development of mathematics, medicine, technology, urbanization, & more.

Genius of Generosity CD Series. 2005. audio compact disk 29.95 (978-1-59834-029-7(8)) Walk Thru the Bible.

Genius of James Joyce & W. B. Yeats: A Light & Enlightening Lecture, Featuring Elliot Engel. 2001. bk. 15.00 (978-1-890123-49-9(8)) Media Cnslts.

Genius of Mark Twain: A Light & Enlightening Lecture, Featuring Elliot Engel. 2000. bk. 15.00 (978-1-890123-22-2(6)) Media Cnslts.

Genius of Matthew, Set. Eugene LaVerdiere. Read by Eugene LaVerdiere. 2 cass. (Running Time: 1 hr. 45 min.). 1994. 17.95 (978-7-900787-14-9(3), AA2696) Credence Commun.
Explanation of who Matthew really was & what he was trying to accomplish. Matthew's mingling of tradition & innovation, Gentile & Jew, history & faith are remarkably good models for our own struggles.

Genius of Mentoring: Youth, Mentors & Elders. 2001. 11.00 (978-0-9716011-1-6(9)); audio compact disk 13.00 (978-0-9716011-0-9(0)) Mosaic Multicult Found.

Genius of Milton Erickson. John Bradshaw. (Running Time: 7200 sec.). 2008. audio compact disk 70.00 (978-1-57388-242-2(9)) J B Media.

Genius of Orson Welles. collector's ed. Perf. by Orson Welles. 6 cass. (Running Time: 9 hrs.). 2001. bk. 34.98 (4099) Radio Spirits.
Sixteen episodes, including: "The Cavalcade of America," "The Jack Benny Program," "The Rudy Vallee Program," "The Mercury Theatre on the Air," "Orson Welles Almanac," "The Gulf Screen Guild Theatre," "Suspense," "War Bond Show".

Genius of Orson Welles, Set. Perf. by Orson Welles. 6 cass. (Running Time: 1 hr. 30 mins. per cass.). 34.98 (Q107) Blckstn Audio.
Gleaned from a wide range of radio theater projects Welles graced with his talent.

Genius Power. Eldon Taylor. 1 CD. (Running Time: 52 min.). (Whole Brain Innertalk Ser.). 1998. audio compact disk (978-1-55978-867-0(4)) Progress Aware Res.

Genius Power. Eldon Taylor. 1 CD. (Running Time: 52 min.). (Whole Brain Innertalk Ser.). 1999. audio compact disk (978-1-55978-907-3(7)) Progress Aware Res.

Genius Skills I. Speeches. Edward Strachar. 1 cass. (Running Time: 45 mins.). 2002. 14.95 (978-0-9723168-2-8(5)) InGenius Inc.

Genius Skills II. Speeches. Edward Strachar. 6 cass. (Running Time: 4 hrs. 50 mins.). 2002. 59.95 (978-0-9723168-5-9(X)) InGenius Inc.

Genius Squad. unabr. ed. Catherine Jinks. Read by Justine Eyre. 13 CDs. (Running Time: 15 hrs. 45 mins.). (YA). (gr. 7 up). 2008. audio compact disk 75.00 (978-0-7393-7126-8(6), Listening Lib) Pub: Random Audio Pubg. Dist(s): Random

Genius Within You. 2002. audio compact disk 14.95 (978-0-9728185-6-8(1)) InGenius Inc.

Genius Within You. Alexander Everett. 1990. 59.95 (978-0-9717185-0-0(4)) InGenius Inc.

Genius Within You. Alexander Everett. Read by Alexander Everett. 6 cass. 1990. 59.95 set. (893A) Nightingale-Conant.
Use your own mental strengths & your mind's hidden mental capabilities. By using "The Rainbow Process" you'll discover insights concerning career choices, emotional make-up & life decisions.

Genius Within You. abr. ed. Speeches. Edward Strachar. 1 cass. (Running Time: 60 mins.). 2002. 14.95 (978-0-9719358-7-7(4)) InGenius Inc.

GenKeeper Photo Index System: Save the Stories Behind Your Family Photos for Future Generations. Kevin S. Yorke. 1 cass. (Running Time: 45 min.). 1996. 9.95 Incl. bk. & decal system. (978-1-890958-06-0(9)) Gen Keeper.

GenKeeper System: GenKeeper Basic System. unabr. ed. Kevin S. Yorke. 1996. pap. bk. 49.95 (978-1-890958-03-9(4)) Gen Keeper.

GenKeeper System: How it Works. abr. ed. Kevin S. Yorke. 1 cass. (Running Time: 25 min.). 1996. 9.95 Incl. 3-ring binder & bk. (978-1-890958-01-5(8)) Gen Keeper.
A step-by-step lesson how to create family wisdom that can be passed down to future generations.

GenKeeper System: "The Book on Tape" abr. ed. Kevin S. Yorke. 1 cass. (Running Time: 1 hr. 30 min.). 1997. 17.95 (978-1-890958-02-2(6)) Gen Keeper.
Explains how to create a living history of a loved one.

Genki 1. Banno. 2004. stu. ed. 31.95 (978-4-7890-1162-4(3)) Pub: Japan Times JPN. Dist(s): Cheng Tsui

Genki 1, Set. Banno. 6 CDs. 2004. audio compact disk 225.00 (978-4-7890-0986-7(6)) Pub: Japan Times JPN. Dist(s): Cheng Tsui

Genki 2. Banno. 2004. stu. ed. 31.95 (978-4-7890-1163-1(1)) Pub: Japan Times JPN. Dist(s): Cheng Tsui

Genki 2. Eri Banno et al. 2004. wbk. ed. 225.00 (978-4-7890-0987-4(4)) Pub: Japan Times JPN. Dist(s): Cheng Tsui

Genome: The Autobiography of a Species in 23 Chapters. unabr. ed. Matt Ridley & Elizabeth Berg. Narrated by Paul Matthews & Suzanne Toren. 11 cass. (Running Time: 15 hrs.). 2001. 98.00 (978-0-7887-5961-1(2), 96663x7) Recorded Bks.
Focusing on newly discovered genes from each of 23 different human chromosomes, the author highlights some of the most recent scientific breakthroughs toward decoding the human genome, the book found in each of our cells that tells the story of who we are.

GenoType Diet: Change Your Genetic Destiny to Live the Longest, Fullest, & Healthiest Life Possible. unabr. ed. Read by Patrick G. Lawlor. Told to Catherine Whitney. (Running Time: 9 hrs. 30 mins. 0 sec.). (ENG.). 2008.

audio compact disk 24.99 (978-1-4001-5586-6(X)); audio compact disk 69.99 (978-1-4001-3586-8(9)) Pub: Tantor Media. Dist(s): IngramPubServ

GenoType Diet: Change Your Genetic Destiny to Live the Longest, Fullest & Healthiest Life Possible. unabr. ed. Catherine Whitney & Peter J. D'Adamo. Read by Patrick G. Lawlor. (Running Time: 9 hrs. 30 mins. 0 sec.). (ENG.). 2008. audio compact disk 34.99 (978-1-4001-0586-1(2)) Pub: Tantor Media. Dist(s): IngramPubServ

Genotype Diet: Change Your Genetic Destiny to Live the Longest, Fullest & Healthiest Life Possible. unabr. ed. Catherine Whitney & Peter J. D'Adamo. Read by Patrick G. Lawlor. (YA). 2008. 59.99 (978-1-60514-864-9(4)) Find a World.

Gente: Curso Comunicativo Basado en el Enfoque por Tareas. Ernesto Martin Peris & Neus Sans Baulenas. Ed. by Olga Juan Lazaro. 2 vols. (Running Time: 1 hr. 15 min.). (SPA., 2001. stu. ed. 39.95 (978-84-89344-38-9(8), DIF4388E) Pub: Difusion Centro Inv ESP. Dist(s): Continental Bk
"Gente es el primer curso de espanol basado en el enfoque por tareas. Las secuencias didacticas, disenadas en torno a un tema, tienen como eje la realizacion de una tarea final. Los alumnos gestionan en grupo la preparacion de las tareas y, partiendo de la".

Gente: Curso Comunicativo Basado en el Enfoque por Tareas. Ernesto Martin Peris et al. Ed. by Eduard Sancho Rutllant. 2 vols. (Running Time: 3 hrs.). (SPA., 2001. 39.95 (978-84-89344-44-0(2), DIF4442E) Pub: Difusion Centro Inv ESP. Dist(s): Continental Bk

Gente: Curso Comunicativo Basado en el Enfoque por Tareas, Level 2. Ernesto Martin Peris & Neus Sans Baulenas. 2 vols. (Running Time: 3 hrs.). (SPA., 2001. stu. ed. 39.95 (978-84-89344-45-7(0), DIF4450E) Pub: Difusion Centro Inv ESP. Dist(s): Continental Bk

Gente: Edicion Norteamericana. 2nd ed. Created by Pearson/Prentice Hall. 2006. audio compact disk 21.60 (978-0-13-194419-0(3)) Pearson Educ CAN CAN.

Gente Nueva: Casetes Para Comunidades de Fe. 2 cass. (Running Time: 090 min.). (SPA.). 2000. 19.95 (978-0-88177-260-9(7)) Discipleship Res.

Gente Nueva: Songs for Communities of Faith. 2001. audio compact disk 24.95 (978-0-88177-360-6(3)) Discipleship Res.

Gentle Axe. unabr. ed. R. N. Morris. Narrated by Simon Vance. (Running Time: 10 hrs. 0 mins. 0 sec.). (ENG.). 2007. audio compact disk 24.99 (978-1-4001-5333-6(6)); audio compact disk 69.99 (978-1-4001-3333-8(5)) Pub: Tantor Media. Dist(s): IngramPubServ

Gentle Axe. unabr. ed. R. N. Morris. Narrated by Simon Vance. 10 CDs. (Running Time: 10 hrs. 0 mins. 0 sec.). (ENG.). 2007. audio compact disk 34.99 (978-1-4001-0333-1(9)) Pub: Tantor Media. Dist(s): IngramPubServ

Gentle Dream Live. Poems. London Pain. Ed. by London Pain. 1. (Running Time: 40). (ENG.). 2005. audio compact disk 13.99 (978-0-9722025-4-1(4)) Share & Care Society.

Gentle Folk. unabr. ed. Alexander Baron. 6 CDs. (Running Time: 5 hrs. 30 min.). (Sound Ser.). (J). 2003. audio compact disk 64.95 (978-1-84283-697-2(8)) Pub: ISIS Lrg Prnt GBR. Dist(s): Ulverscroft US

Gentle Folk. unabr. ed. Alexander Baron. Read by Robin Welch. 4 cass. (Running Time: 5 hrs. 30 min.). (Sound Ser.). (J). 2003. 44.95 (978-1-84283-578-4(5)) Pub: ISIS Lrg Prnt GBR. Dist(s): Ulverscroft US

Gentle Giving. abr. ed. Dorothy Garlock. Read by Victoria Pryne. 1 cass. (Running Time: 90 min.). 1993. 5.99 (978-1-57096-000-0(3), RAZ 901) Romance Alive Audio.
Willa Hammer clashes with drunken brawler Smith Bowman when she hires him to escort her & two orphaned children through the rugged West. She soon comes to realize that he is a man with a wounded soul & that she is just the woman to heal him.

Gentle Halloween. Valerie Leonhart Smalkin. Read by Valerie Leonhart Smalkin. 1 cass. (J). (ps-3). 1995. 10.00 (978-1-887882-04-0(9)) Small Kin Music.
Non-scary children's Halloween songs for 3 to 10 year olds.

Gentle Joy. 1 cass. (Running Time: 40 min.). 1999. 12.00 (978-1-884479-10-6(3)); audio compact disk 16.00 (978-1-884479-11-3(1)) Spirit Song.
Gentle, prayerful Christmas songs.

Gentle, Passionate Art of Not-Knowing: Mindfulness Meditation & the Heart of Zen. Scott Morrison. 1 cass. 1998. 7.50 (978-1-882496-01-3(9)) Twnty Frst Cntry Ren.
Zen Buddhist meditation.

Gentle Rain. Great American Audio. Composed by Steven Gruskin. Contrib. by Kathen Cowan. 1 cass. (Running Time: 1 hr.). (Interludes Music Ser.). 1991. 9.95 (978-1-55569-467-8(5), 3809) Great Am Audio.
You are in tune with nature, refreshed & rejuvenated. This is your own private interlude, which you may visit in solitude or share with someone special. Soothing sounds of nature & music.

Gentle Rogue. abr. ed. Johanna Lindsey. Read by Alana Windsor. 1 cass. (Running Time: 90 min.). (Malory Ser.). 1995. 5.99 (978-1-57096-037-6(2), RAZ 937) Romance Alive Audio.
In this, the third novel in the masterful Malory saga, Georgina Anderson disguises herself as a boy & hires on board Captain James Malory's ship crossing the Atlantic. The irrepressible rake plays along with the feisty temptress as the pirate & the high-spirited beauty are thrown into a whirlwind of smoldering desire that threatens to overwhelm them.

Gentle Rogue. unabr. ed. Johanna Lindsey. Read by Laural Merlington. (Running Time: 11 hrs.). (Malory Ser.). 2008. 24.95 (978-1-4233-5103-0(7), 9781423351030, Brilliance MP3); 39.25 (978-1-4233-5104-7(5), 9781423351047, Brinc Audio MP3 Lib); 39.25 (978-1-4233-5106-1(1), 9781423351061, BADLE); 24.95 (978-1-4233-5105-4(3), 9781423351054, BAD); audio compact disk 97.25 (978-1-4233-5102-3(9), 9781423351023, BriAudCD Unabrid); audio compact disk 36.95 (978-1-4233-5101-6(0), 9781423351016, Bril Audio CD Unabri) Brilliance Audio.

Gentle Savior. Contrib. by David Phelps. (Studio Ser.). 2005. audio compact disk 9.98 (978-5-558-71895-9(1), Word Records) Word Enter.

Gentle Shall Inherit the Earth. unabr. ed. Perf. by Eknath Easwaran. 1 cass. (Running Time: 1 hr.). 1986. 7.95 (978-1-58638-547-7(X)) Nilgiri Pr.

Gentle Solution: 7 Steps to the Horse You've Always Wanted. Frank Bell. Prod. by Rick Lamb. 1 cass. (Running Time: 1 hr. 30 min.). 2000. 14.95 (978-0-9679487-7-5(0)) Horse Show.
Popular clinician Frank Bell introduces his 7-Step Safety System, a versatile tool for preparing any horse to be ridden, whether it is a young horse, a problem horse or a seasoned campaigner.

Gentle Sounds. Contrib. by Carey Landry. 2005. audio compact disk 17.00 (978-0-00-672815-3(4)) OR Catholic.

Gentle Spears. Arthur Dobrin. Ed. by Stanley H. Barkan. (Cross-Cultural Review Chapbook Ser.: No. 3: American Poetry 2). 1980. 10.00 (978-0-89304-827-3(5)) Cross-Cultrl NY.

Gentle Warrior. abr. ed. Julie Garwood. Read by Anne Flosnik. (Running Time: 6 hrs.). 2010. audio compact disk 14.99 (978-1-4418-1218-6(0), 9781441812186, BACD) Brilliance Audio.

Gentle Warrior. unabr. ed. Julie Garwood. Read by Anne Flosnik. (Running Time: 11 hrs.). 2010. 24.99 (978-1-4418-1214-8(8), 9781441812148, Brilliance MP3); 24.99 (978-1-4418-1216-2(4), 9781441812162, BAD); 39.97 (978-1-4418-1215-5(6), 9781441812155, Brinc Audio MP3 Lib); 39.97 (978-1-4418-1217-9(2), 9781441812179, BADLE); audio compact disk 29.99 (978-1-4418-1212-4(1), 9781441812124, Bril Audio CD Unabri); audio compact disk 87.97 (978-1-4418-1213-1(X), 9781441812131, BriAudCD Unabrid) Brilliance Audio.

Gentlehands, unabr. ed. M. E. Kerr, pseud. Narrated by Jeff Woodman. 3 pieces. (Running Time: 4 hrs. 15 mins.). (gr. 7 up). 27.00 (978-0-7887-0371-3(4), 94459E7) Recorded Bks.
A working class teenager spends a summer falling in love with a rich girl & fending off accusations that his grandfather is a Nazi war criminal. Available to libraries only.

Gentleman Called. unabr. ed. Dorothy Salisbury Davis. Narrated by George Guidall. 5 cass. (Running Time: 6 hrs.). 1998. 44.00 (978-0-7887-2041-3(4), 95405E7) Recorded Bks.
Serves up a tantalizing mystery laced with warm humor & top-notch suspense.

Gentleman Drunk - the Truth about Alcoholism. Scripts. Jeffrey Taylor. 2. (Running Time: 3:00). Dramatization. 2005. audio compact disk 17.95 (978-0-9727047-2-4(8)) Jeffrey Taylor.
A Gentleman Drunk (AUDIO CD) is a dramatization of the book A Gentleman Drunk by Jeffrey Taylor. The audio recounts the difficulties Jeffrey encountered in his first year in an alcoholic recovery program.

Gentleman from San-Francisco see Gospodin Iz San-Francisco

Gentleman Is Cold see Middle-Aged Man on the Flying Trapeze

Gentleman Jim. Perf. by Errol Flynn & Alexis Smith. 1 cass. (Running Time: 60 min.). 1944. 7.95 (DD-5090) Natl Recrd Co.
In the story "Gentleman Jim", James J. Corbett fights John L. Sullivan for 21 rounds before knocking him out for the Championship."China Seas" is a stirring romantic tale of adventure in the Far East. A freighter running between Singapore & Hong Kong with a few women passengers is attacked by pirates.

Gentleman of Leisure. unabr. ed. P. G. Wodehouse. Read by Frederick Davidson. 5 cass. (Running Time: 7 hrs.). 1994. 39.95 (978-0-7861-0451-2(1), 1403) Blckstn Audio.
When Jimmy Pitt bets an actor friend that any fool could burgle a house, a feat which he offers to demonstrate that very night, he puts his reputation on the line. Although he hires the services of a professional burglar, the difficulty is raised when he has the misfortune to select Police-Captain McEachern's house. And imagine Jimmy's consternation when he learns that McEachern's daughter is none other than the beautiful Molly, whom he has worshipped from afar for quite some time.

Gentleman Rogue. abr. ed. Matt Braun. Read by Jim Gough. 2002. 25.00 (978-1-59183-003-0(6)) Pub: Otis Audio. Dist(s): Lndmrk Audiobks

Gentlemen & Players. Joanne Harris. Read by Steven Pacey. 2 CDs. 2006. audio compact disk 49.95 (978-0-7927-3964-7(7), CMP 903) AudioGO.

Gentlemen & Players. Joanne Harris. Read by Steven Pacey. 9 cass. (Running Time: 44880 sec.). 2006. 79.95 (978-0-7927-3902-9(7), CSL 903) AudioGO.

Gentlemen & Players. unabr. ed. Joanne Harris. Read by Steven Pacey. 11 CDs. (Running Time: 44880 sec.). (Sound Library). 2006. audio compact disk 99.95 (978-0-7927-3903-6(5), SLD 903, Chivers Sound Lib) AudioGO.

Gentlemen & Players. unabr. ed. Joanne Harris. Read by Steven Pacey. 11 CDs. (Running Time: 13.5 hrs). 2006. audio compact disk 39.95 (978-0-06-112328-3(5)) HarperCollins Pubs.

***Gentlemen & Players.** unabr. ed. Joanne Harris. Read by Steven Pacey. (ENG.). 2005. (978-0-06-113453-1(8), Harper Audio) HarperCollins Pubs.

***Gentlemen & Players.** unabr. ed. Joanne Harris. Read by Steven Pacey. (ENG.). 2006. (978-0-06-113454-8(6), Harper Audio) HarperCollins Pubs.

Gentlemen, Be Seated see SF Soundbook

***Gentlemen, Be Seated.** (ENG.). 2010. audio compact disk (978-1-59171-257-2(2)) Falcon Picture.

Gentlemen in England. unabr. ed. A. N. Wilson. Read by Michael Tudor Barnes. 12 cass. (Running Time: 14 hrs. 5 min.). (Isis Ser.). (J). 1990. 94.95 (978-1-85089-712-5(3), 90016) Pub: ISIS Lrg Prnt GBR. Dist(s): Ulverscroft US

Gentlemen of the Road: A Tale of Adventure. unabr. ed. Michael Chabon. Afterword by Michael Chabon. Read by Andre Braugher. 4 CDs. (Running Time: 4 hrs.). (ENG.). 2007. audio compact disk 24.95 (978-0-7393-5789-7(1), Random AudioBks) Pub: Random Audio Pubg. Dist(s): Random

Gentlemen Prefer Blondes. unabr. ed. Anita Loos. Read by Flo Gibson. 3 cass. (Running Time: 3 hrs. 25 mins.). 2001. vinyl bd. 16.95 (978-1-55685-669-3(5)) Audio Bk Con.
The humorous diary of a not-too-bright beauty tells of her many suitors, insatiable appetite for shopping & travels in Europe.

Gentlemen Prefer Blondes. unabr. ed. Anita Loos. Read by Marni Webb. 3 cass. (Running Time: 4 hrs.). 1998. 21.95 (978-1-57270-060-4(2), C31060u) Pub: Audio Partners. Dist(s): PerseuPGW
Brilliant satire of the Jazz Age, featuring the funniest bad blonde in American literature. Glamorous Lorelei Lee always gets what she wants, & these immortal diaries reveal how she does it. As she sets about acquiring a diamond tiara & developing a film career, she never forgets her ultimate goal: finding the richest man.

Gentleness: The Soul's Language. Elbert Willis. 1 cass. (Gentleness & Goodness Ser.). 4.00 Fill the Gap.

Gentleness & Goodness Series, Set. Elbert Willis. 4 cass. 13.00 Set. Fill the Gap.

Gentleness Within: Finding the Willingness to Accept Ourselves. Stephen R. Schwartz. 2 cass. 20.00 Set. Riverrun Piermont.

Gentle's Holler. unabr. ed. Kerry Madden. Read by Kate Forbes. 4 cass. (Running Time: 5 hrs. 45 mins.). 2006. 39.75 (978-1-4193-7128-8(2), 98273) Recorded Bks.
Kerry Madden earned starred reviews from for this tale of humor and pathos set in the 1960s Great Smoky Mountains. One of eight kids, Livy is angry with her brother for wanting to run off. But she's even more concerned about her sister Gentle's eyes. Experiencing great joys and deep sorrows, this loving family is poor in what money buys but rich in what really matters.

Gentling Giant China. Lance Auburn Eveerett. 3 CDs. (Running Time: 3 hrs.). (Michael Ser.). 2005. 25.00 (978-1-58943-055-6(7)) Am Pubng Inc.

Gently into Music. Mary York. (Running Time: 25 mins.). (ENG.). 1988. 39.99 (978-0-521-56896-8(X)) Cambridge U Pr.

Gently with the Millions. unabr. ed. Alan Hunter. Read by Frank Duncan. 5 cass. (Running Time: 5 hrs. 50 min.). 2001. 49.95 (978-1-85695-472-3(2), 92104) Pub: ISIS Audio GBR. Dist(s): Ulverscroft US
Charles Reason, once Managing Director of a respected City firm, is now a disgraced man, living in reduced circumstances. But when a locked room in the ex-tycoon's flat is discovered to contain a battery of computer screens & six telephones, suspicions are aroused.

Genuine Chaos. unabr. ed. Lou Lipsitz. Read by Lou Lipsitz. 1 cass. (Running Time: 45 min.). (Watershed Tapes of Contemporary Poetry). 1979. 12.95 (23645) J Norton Pubs.
Signature series from this master of political & psychological dissection.

Genuserwerb Bei Griechischen Lernern des Deutschen: Eine Empirische Untersuchung und Didaktische Implikationen. Polichronia Thomoglou. Vol. 277. (GER., 2004. bk. 47.95 (978-3-631-53452-6(3)) P Lang Pubng.

GEO Principle: God in Every Occupation means purpose for every job ¿ even Yours! 2009. audio compact disk (978-0-9754134-5-6(7)) NFR Comm Inc.

Geochron World Watch ScreenSaver CD. (World CD-ROM Products Ser.). audio compact disk 54.95 (978-0-7834-2800-0(6)) Map Link.

Geodetic Charts. Inga Lohse. 1 cass. 8.95 (554) Am Fed Astrologers.
An AFA Convention workshop tape.

Geodetics. Chris McRae. 1 cass. 1992. 8.95 (1065) Am Fed Astrologers.

Geoff Kaufman: Fair Stood with Wind. 1 cass. 9.98 (C-525) Folk-Legacy.
Sea songs & shanties from a Mystic shantyman.

Geoff Kaufman: Tree of Life. 1 cass., 1 CD. 9.98 (C-526); audio compact disk 14.98 CD. (CD-526) Folk-Legacy.
Songs of Celebration & Concern for Life on Earth.

Geoffrey Chaucer: A Light & Enlightening Lecture, Featuring Elliot Engel. 2000. bk. 15.00 (978-1-890123-32-1(3)) Media Cnslts.

Geoffrey Chaucer: In Middle English. abr. ed. Geoffrey Chaucer. Read by Nevill Coghill & Norman Davis. 1 cass. (Running Time: 32 min.). 11.95 Incl. text. (978-0-8045-0919-0(0), SAC 919) Spoken Arts.
Readings of The Prologue & The Pardoner's Tale; also includes a biography of Chaucer and a treatise on pronunciation.

Geoffrey Wolff: The Final Club. unabr. ed. Geoffrey Wolff. Read by Geoffrey Wolff. Prod. by Rebekah Presson. 1 cass. (Running Time: 29 min.). 1990. 10.00 (091490) New Letters.
This program coincided with the publication of Wolff's seventh book, a novel titled "The Final Club".

Geographer (for Luther Thomas Cupp, 1947-1974) see Poetry & Voice of Marilyn Hacker

Geographic Energy Chakras. Donald Keyes. 1 cass. 9.00 (A0415-89) Sound Photosyn.

***Geography: CD add-on Set.** Perf. by Millmark Education Staff. (ConceptLinks Ser.). 2009. audio compact disk 50.00 (978-1-61618-361-5(6)) Millmark Educ.

***Geography Audio CD.** Perf. by Millmark Education Staff. (ConceptLinks Ser.). 2009. audio compact disk 28.00 (978-1-4334-0642-3(X)) Millmark Educ.

***Geography Audio CD: Asking Geographic Questions.** Perf. by Millmark Education Staff. (Content Literacy Libraries Ser.). 2009. audio compact disk (978-1-61618-142-0(7)) Millmark Educ.

***Geography Audio CD: Earth's Resources.** Perf. by Millmark Education Staff. (Content Literacy Libraries Ser.). 2009. audio compact disk (978-1-61618-138-3(9)) Millmark Educ.

***Geography Audio CD: How Places Change.** Perf. by Millmark Education Staff. (Content Literacy Libraries Ser.). 2009. audio compact disk (978-1-61618-134-5(6)) Millmark Educ.

***Geography Audio CD: Places & Regions.** Perf. by Millmark Education Staff. (Content Literacy Libraries Ser.). 2009. audio compact disk (978-1-61618-130-7(3)) Millmark Educ.

Geography of Bliss: One Grump's Search for the Happiest Places in the World. unabr. ed. Eric Weiner. (Running Time: 12 hrs.). (ENG.). 2008. 14.98 (978-1-60024-259-5(6), Twelve) Pub: GrandCentral. Dist(s): HachBkGrp

Geography of Bliss: One Grump's Search for the Happiest Places in the World. unabr. ed. Eric Weiner. Read by Eric Weiner. (Running Time: 12 hrs.). (ENG.). 2009. audio compact disk 14.98 (978-1-60024-434-6(3), Twelve) Pub: GrandCentral. Dist(s): HachBkGrp

Geography on File. (gr. 6-12). 2005. audio compact disk 149.95 (978-0-8160-5838-9(5)) Facts On File.

Geography Songs. 2004. audio compact disk 22.95 (978-1-883028-13-8(2)) Audio Memory.

Geography Songs. Audio. 1 cass. (Running Time: 1 hr.). pap. bk. & tchr. ed. 19.95 (978-1-883028-04-6(3), 2) Audio Memory.
Contains 18 songs on cassette, 25" x 36" map of the world to label & color, 96 page workbook with song lyrics, maps, crossword puzzles & matching pictures.

Geography Songs: Sing Around the World. 1 CD. (Running Time: 1 hr.). 2000. pap. bk., tchr. ed., wbk. ed. 22.95 (2CD) Audio Memory.
Features 27 songs which teach the countries of the world by region plus continents, oceans and solar system. Includes 25"x36" black and white map to label and color.

***Geology of National Parks Cd.** 6th rev. ed. Harris. (ENG.). 2010. audio compact disk 75.56 (978-0-7575-0578-2(3)) Kendall-Hunt.

Geometry of Sisters. abr. ed. Luanne Rice. Read by Blair Brown & Caitlin Greer. (ENG.). 2009. audio compact disk 29.95 (978-0-7393-4364-7(5), Random AudioBks) Pub: Random Audio Pubg. Dist(s): Random

Geopolitics of Emotion: How Cultures of Fear, Humiliation, & Hope Are Reshaping the World. unabr. ed. Dominique Moisi. Read by Scott Peterson. (Running Time: 6 hrs.). (ENG.). 2009. 24.98 (978-1-59659-403-6(9), GildAudio) Pub: Gildan Media. Dist(s): HachBkGrp

Georg Wilhelm Friedrich Hegel: Germany (1770-1831) abr. ed. Narrated by Charlton Heston. (Running Time: 7595 sec.). (Audio Classics: the Giants of Philosophy Ser.). 2006. audio compact disk 25.95 (978-0-7861-6936-8(2)) Pub: Blckstn Audio. Dist(s): NetLibrary CO

Georg Wilhelm Friedrich Hegel: Germany (1770-1831), Set. unabr. ed. Read by Charlton Heston. 2 cass. (Giants of Philosophy Ser.). 17.95 (K124) Blckstn Audio.

George & dick the CD. Illus. by Barbara Pikus. Prod. by Electronic Garage Productions. Another Jones Graphics. Voice by Sharon Streeter. Afterword by Dave Lee. Lyrics by Sharon Streeter. (ENG.). 2007. audio compact disk 12.95 (978-0-9765948-4-0(6)) Dio S Bks.

George & Elizabeth: A Royal Marriage. unabr. ed. David Duff. Read by Frances Jeater. 8 cass. (Running Time: 8 hrs. 45 min.). 2001. 69.95 (978-1-85089-720-0(4), 88012) Pub: ISIS Audio GBR. Dist(s): Ulverscroft US
George & Elizabeth is the story of a reign & a marriage, a story of shared love & support. David Duff tells the private story behind the public events & argues that the political influence of the royal couple should not be underestimated.

George B. McClellan: The Young Napoleon. unabr. collector's ed. Stephen W. Sears. Read by Dick Estell. 12 cass. (Running Time: 18 hrs.). 1989. 96.00 (978-0-7366-1639-3(X), 2494) Books on Tape.
Stephen Sears posits that "General McClellan's importance in shaping the course of the Union during the Civil War was matched only by that of President Lincoln & Generals Grant & Sherman".

***George Bailey - It's a Wonderful Life.** Arranged by Polishing the Pulpit. 2010. audio compact disk 25.00 (978-1-60644-118-3(3)) Heart Heart.

***George Bailey - the God I Love.** Arranged by Polishing the Pulpit. 2010. audio compact disk 25.00 (978-1-60644-119-0(1)) Heart Heart.

George Barker: The Spoken Word. British Library Staff & Vrej Nersessian. (British Library - British Library Sound Archive Ser.). 2009. audio compact disk 15.00 (978-0-7123-0540-2(8)) Pub: Britis Library GBR. Dist(s): Chicago Distribution Ctr

George Bernard Shaw Package, Set. George Bernard Shaw. 5 cass. 75.00 L A Theatre.
Includes: "Candida," "The Devil's Disciple," "Mrs. Warren's Profession," & "Pygmalion".

George Burns: One Hundred Years, One Hundred Stories. George Burns. Read by John Bynere & Milton Berle. 1 cass. (Running Time: 90 min.). 1996. 10.95 (978-1-57511-018-9(0)) Pub Mills.
George Burns' career spanned the history of modern show business: he starred in big-time vaudeville; on radio, television, the movies, & the recording industry: & on the nightclub stage. This collection of the beloved centenarian's favorite & funniest stories come directly from his private stock. From recollections of events in his past to tales about friends & performers who have crossed his path - including Al Jolson, Groucho Marx, Jack Benny, Bob Hope, Ann-Margaret, & Goldie Hawn.

George Burns: One Hundred Years, One Hundred Stories. As told by John Byner. Intro. by Milton Berle. 2000. audio compact disk 16.98 (978-1-929243-19-8(7)) Uproar Ent.

George Burns & Friends. 6 cass. 24.98 Set. Moonbeam Pubns.

George Burns & the Hundred Yard Dash. unabr. ed. Martin Gottfried. Read by Jonathan Reese. 7 cass. (Running Time: 10 hrs. 30 min.). 1996. 44.80 (4213) Books on Tape.
The image of George Burns, smiling, squinting through his black-framed glasses, puffing his Corona, is one of a man who could handle anything.

George Bush: The Pursuit of Peace & Freedom. Read by George H. W. Bush. 1 cass. (Running Time: 60 min.). (National Press Club Ser.). 10.95 (NP-88-01-05, HarperThor) HarpC GBR.

George Cables. 1 cass. (Running Time: 1 hr.). (Marian McPartland's Piano Jazz Ser.). 13.95 (MM-88-06-11, HarperThor) HarpC GBR.

George Carlin Reads to You. George Carlin. Read by George Carlin. (ENG.). 2009. 79.99 (978-1-60812-739-9(7)) Find a World.

George Carlin Reads to You: Brain Droppings, Napalm & Silly Putty, & More Napalm & Silly Putty. unabr. ed. George Carlin. Contrib. by George Carlin. (ENG.). 2009. audio compact disk 39.95 (978-1-59887-924-7(3), 1598879243) Pub: HighBridge. Dist(s): Workman Pub

George Eliot: The Last Victorian. unabr. ed. Kathryn Hughes. Read by Nadia May. 15 cass. (Running Time: 22 hrs.). 2001. 95.95 (978-0-7861-1958-5(6), 2729) Blckstn Audio.
The daughter of a self-made businessman of impeccable respectability, the middle-aged Eliot was cast into social exile when she began a scandalous liaison with the married writer & scientist George Henry Lewes. Only her burgeoning literary success allowed her to overcome society's disapproval & eventually take her proper place at the heart of London's literary elite. The territory of her novels comprised nothing less than the entire span of Victorian society. Although years of rigorous reading had given Eliot an unparalleled understanding of the intellectual debates of her day, she preferred to champion a pragmatic middle ground, where idealism is tempered by love, habit & history.

***George Eliot: The Last Victorian.** unabr. ed. Kathryn Hughes. Read by Nadia May. (Running Time: 21 hrs. 30 mins.). 2010. 44.95 (978-1-4417-1901-0(6)); audio compact disk 123.00 (978-1-4417-1898-3(2)) Blckstn Audio.

George Freibott: The Inventor. unabr. ed. Nikola Tesla et al. 1 cass. 1983. 11.00 (08501) Big Sur Tapes.
Freibott & Grof discuss Tesla, his ideas, & his many inventions, particularly in alternative energy, which were ahead of his time.

George Garrett. Interview. Interview with George P. Garrett & Kay Bonetti. 1 cass. (Running Time: 1 hr. 20 min.). 13.95 (978-1-55644-102-8(9), 4062) Am Audio Prose.
Includes anecdotes for which Garrett is famous, plus a good discussion of his craft.

George Garrett. unabr. ed. George P. Garrett. Read by Tim Richards. 1 cass. (Running Time: 29 min.). 1989. 10.00 New Letters.
Garrett is interviewed & a chapter from his novel-in-progress is read.

George Gershwin: His Life Story. 1 cass. (Running Time: 1 hr.). 7.95 (DD8840) Natl Recrd Co.

George Gurley: "Cures" unabr. ed. Read by George Gurley et al. 1 cass. (Running Time: 29 min.). 1986. 10.00 New Letters.
Gurley is interviewed & his play is presented by various actors.

George Gurley & Michael Paul Novak. unabr. ed. Read by George Gurley & Michael P. Novak. 1 cass. (Running Time: 29 min.). 1986. 10.00 New Letters.
Two Kansas poets read their works.

George Harrison. abr. ed. Alan Clayson. Read by Mike Read. 3 CDs. (Running Time: 3 hrs. 36 mins.). 2003. audio compact disk (978-1-86074-536-2(9)) Sanctuary Pubng GBR.
George Harrison's recent death marked the loss of a subtle but prodigious talent. Expert Alan Clayson tracks Harrison's progress in all the arenas of his life in the chaotic world of Beatledom. The internecine warfare with his fellow Beatles, the legal wrangles with a former film partner, the death threats - all are here, along with the sometimes unexpected musical triumphs and personal successes.

George Harrison: The Unauthorized Biography of George Harrison. Keith Rodway. (Maximum Ser.). (ENG., 2003. audio compact disk 14.95 (978-1-84240-177-4(7)) Pub: Chrome Dreams GBR. Dist(s): IPG Chicago

George Hitchcock. unabr. ed. Read by George Hitchcock. 1 cass. (Running Time: 29 min.). 1985. 10.00 New Letters.
California poet & editor of "Kayak" magazine reads poems & talks about his work.

George III: A Personal History. unabr. ed. Christopher Hibbert. Narrated by Simon Prebble. 11 cass. (Running Time: 15 hrs. 30 mins.). 1998. 97.00 (978-0-7887-4675-8(8), 96383E7) Recorded Bks.
Portrait of one of England's most misunderstood monarchs. He is most often remembered as the tyrant who taxed America into a revolution or from film as a madman running through the palace halls. Neither view captures the life of a man who held the throne during a time when the absolute right of a ruler was being called into question.

George London: Of Gods & Demons. Nora London. (Great Voices Ser.: Vol. 9). 2005. bk. 39.95 (978-1-880909-74-4(X)) Pub: Baskerville. Dist(s): Hushion Hse

George Lucas. Dana White. Read by Robert Abia. 1 cass. (Running Time: 1 hr. 30 min.). (YA). (gr. 5-12). 2000. 9.95 (978-0-7366-4710-6(4), 5271-C) Books on Tape.
When he was young, he didn't take school or anything else seriously. But when he enrolled in film school, it was clear he'd found his calling.

George Lucas. abr. collector's ed. Dana White. Read by Robert Abia. 1 cass. (Running Time: 1 hr. 30 min.). (Biography Ser.). (YA). (gr. 5-12). 2000. 9.95 (978-0-7366-5057-1(1), 5271) Books on Tape.

George Lucas. collector's ed. Dana White. Read by Robert Abia. 2 CDs. (Running Time: 2 hrs. 24 mins.). (YA). 2000. audio compact disk 12.95 (978-0-7366-5233-9(7), 5271-b) Books on Tape.

George MacDonald: His Life & Works. unabr. ed. Rolland Hein. Read by Kate Reading. 1 CD. (Running Time: 1 hr. 12 mins. 0 sec.). (ENG.). 2005. audio compact disk 12.98 (978-1-59644-100-2(3), Hovel Audio) christianaud.

***George MacDonald: His Life & Works: A Short Biography by Roland Hein.** unabr. ed. Rolland Hein. Narrated by Jonathan Marosz. (ENG.). 2005. 8.98 (978-1-59644-098-2(8), Hovel Audio) christianaud.

George Muller: Man of Faith & Miracles. unabr. ed. Basil Miller. Read by Lloyd James. (Running Time: 5 mins.). 2007. 23.95 (978-0-7861-2428-2(8)); audio compact disk 32.00 (978-0-7861-8825-3(1)) Blckstn Audio.

George of the Jungle. 1 cass. (J). 13.99 (978-0-7634-0237-2(0)); 13.99 Norelco. (978-0-7634-0236-5(2)); audio compact disk 22.99 CD. (978-0-7634-0238-9(9)); audio compact disk 22.99 (978-0-7634-0239-6(7)) W Disney Records.

George Orwell. unabr. ed. Gordon Bowker. Read by Christopher Kay. 17 cass. (Running Time: 25 hrs.). 2004. 109.75 (978-1-84197-937-3(6), Clipper Audio) Recorded Bks.
One of the greatest writers of the 20th century, George Orwell left an enduring mark on our language and culture, with concepts such as Big Brother, Room 101, and Newspeak. His reputation rests not only on his political shrewdness and his sharp satires, but also on his clear writing style and his essays. Gordon Bowker?s biography, written to coincide with Orwell?s centenary, includes material which brings the writer?s life into unfamiliar focus, revealing Orwell?s family background; his superstitious streak and his chaotic and reckless sex life.

George Orwell: A Portrait in Sound, Set unabr. ed. George Orwell. Read by George Rose. 6 cass. 1999. 44.98 (LL 0049) AudioGO.

George Orwell Pt. 1: A Life. unabr. collector's ed. Bernard Crick. Read by Rupert Keenlyside. 9 cass. (Running Time: 13 hrs. 30 min.). 1984. 72.00 (978-0-7366-0635-6(1), 1596A/B) Books on Tape.
Puts into perspective the many forces that shaped Orwell. As an outgrowth of this fear, orwell dissected propaganda & exposes the many ways in which language can be made a tool of tyranny.

George Orwell Pt. 2: A Life. unabr. collector's ed. Bernard Crick. Read by Rupert Keenlyside. 8 cass. (Running Time: 12 hrs.). 1984. 64.00 (978-0-7366-0636-3(X), 1596-B) Books on Tape.

George Orwell Boxed Set: 1984; Animal Farm. unabr. ed. George Orwell. Read by Simon Prebble & Ralph Cosham. (Running Time: 52200 sec.). 2007. 32.95 (978-1-4332-0325-1(1)); audio compact disk 29.95 (978-1-4332-0327-5(8)) Blckstn Audio.

George Orwell Boxed Set: 1984; Animal Farm. unabr. ed. George Orwell. Read by Simon Prebble & Ralph Cosham. 12 CDs. (Running Time: 14 hrs. 45 mins.). (J). 2007. audio compact disk 32.95 (978-1-4332-0326-8(X)) Blckstn Audio.

George Orwell Society with Karl Hess & Richard Deyo: Why Reagan Is the Biggest Fascist since FDR & the Art of Non-Voting. (Running Time: 120 min.). (Workshop Speeches). 1983. 18.00 (FW601) Freeland Pr.
Reminds the audience that "this is 1984!".

George Passant. unabr. ed. C. P. Snow. Read by Robert Mundy. 8 cass. (Running Time: 1 hr. 30 min. per cass.). Orig. Title: Strangers & Brothers. 64.00 Set. (1411) Books on Tape.
The story is set in an English provincial town where Lewis Eliot, the narrator, is training in law. George Passant is his friend & mentor, an idealistic lawyer & a man of principle & courage. Passant exerts a strong influence on the young people around him as he assists them in their careers - often at considerable personal sacrifice. But Passant's future is shattered at a time when he is charged with fraud.

George Roberts on Astronomy & Peruvian Antiquities & a Look at IMAX's "Destiny in Space" Hosted by Nancy Pearlman. 1 cass. (Running Time: 30 min.). 10.00 (1309) Educ Comm CA.

George Rogers Clark: Boy of the Northwest Frontier. Katharine E. Wilkie. Read by Patrick G. Lawlor. (Running Time: 7200 sec.). (Young Patriots Ser.). (J). (gr. 3-7). 2007. 22.95 (978-1-4332-0157-8(7)); audio compact disk 24.00 (978-1-4332-0158-5(5)) Blckstn Audio.

George Rogers Clark: Boy of the Northwestern Frontier. unabr. ed. Katharine E. Wilkie. Read by Patrick G. Lawlor. (Young Patriots Ser.). (J). 2007. 34.99 (978-1-60252-637-2(0)) Find a World.

George Sanders: The Memoirs of a Professional Cad. unabr. ed. George Sanders. Read by Tony Thomas. 4 cass. (Running Time: 6 hrs.). 1991. 24.95 Set. (978-0-936939-03-2(6)) Cambria Records.
George Sanders recreates his life - that of the cultural Cad. In 1972, he took his life & left a note saying he was bored with life & wished us all good luck.

George Seferis. abr. ed. George Seferis. Perf. by George Seferis. Perf. by Edmund Keeley. 1 cass. Incl. Crickets. (SWC 1277); Details on Cyprus. (SWC 1277); Helen. (SWC 1277); In the Goddess' Name, I Summon You. (SWC 1277); Memory I. (SWC 1277); Spring A. D. (SWC 1277); Thrush. (SWC 1277); Pts. IV & V. Erotikos Logos. (SWC 1277); 1977. 14.00 (978-0-694-50191-5(3), SWC 1277) HarperCollins Pubs.

George Shearing. Perf. by George Shearing. 1 cass. (Running Time: 60 min.). (Marian McPartland's Piano Jazz Ser.). 13.95 (MM-87-02-12, HarperThor) HarpC GBR.

George Sheehan on Running. George Sheehan. Intro. by A. E. Whyte. 1 cass. (Running Time: 50 min.). (Listen & Learn USA! Ser.). 8.95 (978-0-88684-021-1(X)) Listen USA.
Provides practical how-to's on running.

George Smith: Does Public Education Educate? (Running Time: 90 min.). (Remanent Tapes). 1978. 10.00 (R300) Freeland Pr.
Gives a libertarian analysis of state education & argues for the end to government's role in education. Also examines the history of state education, noting that U.S. politicians in the 1830s argued for government controlled education in an effort to make better citizens of students, & not to increase literacy, since that was already considered high.

George Tirebiter Collection #1: Live from the Islands. Perf. by David Ossman. Text by David Ossman. 1 CD. (Running Time: 57 mins.). Dramatization. 2005. audio compact disk 15.95 (978-1-59938-045-2(5)) Lode Cat.

George Tirebiter Collection #2: Radio Follies. Perf. by David Ossman. Text by David Ossman. 1 CD. (Running Time: 71 mins.). Dramatization. 2005. audio compact disk 15.95 (978-1-59938-046-9(3)) Lode Cat.

George Tirebiter Collection #3: Hollywood Madhouse & Radio Daze. Perf. by David Ossman. Text by David Ossman. 1 CD. (Running Time: 58 mins.). Dramatization. 2005. audio compact disk 15.95 (978-1-59938-047-6(1)) Lode Cat.

George Tirebiter Collection #4: Another Christmas Carol. Perf. by David Ossman. Text by David Ossman. 1 CD. (Running Time: 56 mins.). Dramatization. 2005. audio compact disk 15.95 (978-1-59938-048-3(X)) Lode Cat.

George Tirebiter's Radio Follies. 1 CD. audio compact disk 15.95 (978-1-57677-098-6(2), OWME007) Lodestone Catalog.

George V. Higgins. Interview with George V. Higgins. 1 cass. (Running Time: 45 min.). 13.95 (L036) TFR.
Higgins talks about "A City on a Hill", his novel about the people behind Washington politicians & in a separate interview, about "The Friends of Eddie Coyle", a novel told almost entirely in dialogue about gun running in Boston.

George Wallace: The Wallace Crusade see Buckley's Firing Line

George Washington. Ron Sinclair. Read by Ron Sinclair. 1 cass. (Running Time: 1 hr.). (Uncle Sam Says Ser.). (J). 1996. bk. 11.95 (978-1-889992-00-6(3)) R Sinclair Pub.
True stories about George Washington told in a home/fireside climate.

George Washington. unabr. ed. Berg, Ivan Association Staff. 1 cass. (Running Time: 58 min.). (History Maker Ser.). 12.95 (41026) J Norton Pubs.
The courageous convictions of this dedicated man raised the beliefs & principles of freedom to unknown heights. His life, his awesome sense of purpose & his devotion to liberty & the unity of America is covered.

George Washington. unabr. ed. Calista McCabe Courtenay. Read by Wahoo Jacobs. (J). 2007. 34.99 (978-1-60252-754-6(7)) Find a World.

George Washington. unabr. ed. Robert Hogrogian. (Running Time: 15 min.). (People to Remember Ser.: Set I). (J). (gr. 4-7). 1979. bk. 16.99 (978-0-934898-44-7(8)); pap. bk. 9.95 (978-0-934898-00-3(6)) Jan Prods.
The story about the first president of the United States of America.

George Washington. unabr. ed. Ingri Parin D'Aulaire & Edgar Parin D'Aulaire. 1 cass. (Running Time: 6 min.). (J). (gr. 3-5). 1989. pap. bk. 10.00 (6512-E) Spoken Arts.
Find out about the young Washington, who enjoyed several careers before becoming the first President.

George Washington. unabr. ed. Ingri Parin D'Aulaire & Edgar Parin D'Aulaire. 1 cass. (Running Time: 15 min.). (J). (gr. 3-5). 2001. pap. bk. 20.00 (978-0-8045-6717-6(4), 65125E/6) Spoken Arts.
Find out about the young Washington, who enjoyed several careers before becoming the first President. Includes 6 books.

George Washington. unabr. ed. Willard S. Randall. Read by Jonathan Reese. 9 cass. (Running Time: 13 hrs. 30 mins.). 1998. 72.00 (4649-B) Books on Tape.

George Washington. unabr. ed. Willard S. Randall. Read by Jonathan Reese. 18 cass. (Running Time: 27 hrs.). 1998. 144.00 (978-0-7366-4145-6(9), 4649 A&B); 72.00 (978-0-7366-4146-3(7), 4649-A) Books on Tape.
George Washington's early career is the main focus of this biography, all-too-human story of courage, ambition, rebellion & public service.

George Washington: A Biography. unabr. ed. John R. Alden. Read by Grover Gardner. 8 cass. (Running Time: 11 hrs. 30 mins.). 1989. 56.95 (978-0-7861-0034-7(6), 1033) Blckstn Audio.
Ambitious in scope, Alden's sweeping account chronicles the ideas, events & personalities that surrounded Washington, from his younger years in Virginia to his heroic days in battle & eventually through his Presidency & famed farewell address.

George Washington: Anguish & Farewell 1793-1799. unabr. ed. James T. Flexner. Read by Wolfram Kandinsky. 2 pts. on 16 cass. (Running Time: 1 hr. 30 min. per cass.). 1969. 128.00 set. (978-0-7366-2220-2(9), 3011A/B) Books on Tape.
Washington's hope for a private life was extinguished during his second presidential term. A beautiful tribute & farewell.

George Washington: His Visions of the Future & His Published Prayers. Scripts. Glenn Kimball. Perf. by Dana Harper & Lori Curtis. 1 CD. (Running Time: 00:58:39). 2005. audio compact disk 15.00 (978-1-59772-045-8(3), Your Own Wrld Bks) Your Own Wrld.
George Washington had an amazing experience during Dec. 1777, where he saw the vision of a being who taught him about the future. George Washington was not a mere ?Deist.? Contained within this CD is the published proof of his deepest feelings and his most private beliefs.David Parry, who had fought alongside Washington in two wars, said that when Washington came out of the tent after his vision, Washington expressed that ?the eleventh of September will be a ?most dreadfull and fearful day.? Capt. David Parry published this in his book, Reflection of an Old Soldier, before 1830.

George Washington: Leader of a New Nation. unabr. ed. Daniel C. Gedacht. Read by Benjamin Becker. (Running Time: 2 hrs.). (Library of American Lives & Times Ser.). 2009. 39.97 (978-1-4233-8202-7(1), 9781423382027, BADLE); 39.97 (978-1-4233-8201-0(3), 9781423382010, Brinc Audio MP3 Lib); 19.99 (978-1-4233-8200-3(5), 9781423382003, Brilliance MP3); audio compact disk 19.99 (978-1-4233-8198-3(X), 9781423381983, Bril Audio CD Unabri) Brilliance Audio.

George Washington: Leader of a New Nation. unabr. ed. Daniel C. Gedacht. Read by Benjamin Becker. 2 CDs. (Running Time: 2 hrs.). (Library of American Lives & Times Ser.). (J). (gr. 4-8). 2009. audio compact disk 39.97 (978-1-4233-8199-0(8), 9781423381990, BriAudCD Unabrid) Brilliance Audio.

George Washington: Leading a New Nation. Matt Doeden. Illus. by Cynthia Martin. (Graphic Biographies Ser.). (ENG.). (gr. 3-4). 2007. audio compact disk 6.95 (978-1-4296-1469-6(2)) CapstoneDig.

George Washington: The Man Who Would Not Be King. Stephen Krensky. Read by Nelson Runger. 2 cass. (Running Time: 2 hrs. 30 mins.). (YA). 1999. pap. bk. 32.75 (978-0-7887-3186-0(6), 40921); 76.80 (978-0-7887-3232-4(3), 46888) Recorded Bks.
The Revolution was over. Many Americans wanted to crown their leader king, but rather than allow his fellow patriots to live under a monarchy such as the one they had just defeated, General Washington refused. See our famous American hero as a man who set noble standards for the young country to follow.

George Washington: The Man Who Would Not Be King. unabr. ed. Stephen Krensky. Narrated by Nelson Runger. 2 pieces. (Running Time: 2 hrs. 30 mins.). (gr. 5 up). 1999. 21.00 (978-0-7887-3164-8(5), 95837E7) Recorded Bks.

George Washington: The Pennsylvania Rebellion. 1 cass. (Running Time: 1 hr.). 7.95 (CC7940) Natl Recrd Co.

George Washington: Young Leader. unabr. ed. Augusta Stevenson. Read by Lloyd James. 4 cass. (Running Time: 5 hrs. 30 mins.). (Childhood of

Famous Americans Ser.). (gr. 1-3). 2001. pap. bk. 35.95 (978-0-7861-2031-4(2), K2796) Blckstn Audio.
As a child growing up on his parent's tobacco plantation, George had already begun to exhibit leadership qualities. The boys looked up to him for his strength, skills, intelligence & honesty. But his love of pranks occasionally plunged him into trouble, like the time he stole his headmaster's wig.

George Washington Pt. 1: A Biography. unabr. collector's ed. Washington Irving. Read by Dick Estell. Ed. by Charles Neider. 10 cass. (Running Time: 15 hrs.). 1995. 80.00 (978-0-7366-3014-6(7), 3699-A) Books on Tape.
An elegant abridgment of Washington Irving's masterpiece. Intimate detail, fresh & absorbing.

George Washington Pt. 2: A Biography. unabr. collector's ed. Washington Irving. Read by Dick Estell. Ed. by Charles Neider. 12 cass. (Running Time: 18 hrs.). 1995. 96.00 (978-0-7366-3015-3(5), 3699B) Books on Tape.

George Washington Vol. 1: The Forge of Experience 1732-1775. unabr. ed. James T. Flexner. Read by Wolfram Kandinsky. 10 cass. (Running Time: 15 hrs.). 1991. 80.00 (978-0-7366-2006-2(0), 2823) Books on Tape.
George Washington suffered a hero's fate: two centuries of veneration. Everything interesting & remotely human about him took a back seat to the symbol. But Flexner revives him. Washington was a solid & durable youth, well connected in the Virginia aristocracy, but also with a habit of independent mind. He was intelligent & reliable rather than brilliant.

George Washington Vol. 2: In the American Revolution 1775-1783. unabr. ed. James T. Flexner. Read by Wolfram Kandinsky. 9 cass. (Running Time: 13 hrs. 30 mins.). 1991. 72.00 (2861-A); 72.00 (2861B) Books on Tape.
War & fortune travel hand in hand, & it was the Revolutionary War that catapulted Washington into command of the Continental Army. Though seasoned in frontier combat, Washington had never directed large forces. Not surprisingly, in the early years he was outgeneraled. But because Washington turned setbacks to his advantage, he became stronger with each mistake. His enemies, at the end of a long supply line, lacked his stamina. Washington's sense of purpose never deserted him, with historic consequences that he could never have foreseen.

George Washington Vol. 3: And the New Nation (1783-1793) unabr. ed. James T. Flexner. Read by Wolfram Kandinsky. 13 cass. (Running Time: 19 hrs. 30 mins.). 1993. 104.00 (2972) Books on Tape.
Volume III of Flexner's study of George Washington begins with his return to Mount Vernon. Soon Washington is called to lead the Continental Congress. It is a short step to the presidency.

George Washington & the AMER Revolution. Compiled by Benchmark Education Staff. 2005. audio compact disk 10.00 (978-1-4108-5510-7(4)) Benchmark Educ.

George Washington & the Founding of a Nation. Albert Marrin. Narrated by Pat Bettino. 7 pieces. (Running Time: 9 hrs. 30 mins.). 2001. 61.00 (978-1-4025-4097-4(3)) Recorded Bks.

George Washington & the General's Dog. Frank Murphy. Narrated by Johnny Heller. (Running Time: 15 mins.). 2002. 10.00 (978-1-4025-3792-9(1)) Recorded Bks.

George Washington Carver. unabr. ed. Robert Hogrogian. 1 cass. (Running Time: 20 min.). (People to Remember Ser.: Set II). (J). (gr. 4-7). 1979. bk. 16.99 (978-0-934898-58-4(8)); pap. bk. 9.95 (978-0-934898-08-9(1)) Jan Prods.
The fascinating narrative of one of the nation's most productive scientists.

George Washington Carver: The Great Peanut Adventure. Joe Loesch. Ed. by Cheryl J. Hutchinson. Illus. by Brian T. Cox. 1 cass. (Running Time: 1 hr. 30 mins.). (Backyard Adventure Ser.). (J). (gr. k-5). 2002. pap. bk. 14.95 (978-1-887729-87-1(9)); pap. bk. 16.95 (978-1-887729-88-8(7)) Toy Box Prods.
Buffalo Biff and Farley's Raiders journey in time to meet George Washington Carver, one of the nation's greatest educators, inventors and agricultural researchers. George was a student of life and a scholar, excelling in art and music. As an African American, he faced great challenges during his life time. Join the Raiders as they meet "The Plant Doctor" and learn about his adventures with the peanut.

***George Washington Carver: The Life of the Great American Agriculturalist.** unabr. ed. Linda McMurry Edwards. Read by Roscoe Orman. (Running Time: 2 hrs.). (J). 2011. audio compact disk 24.99 (978-1-4558-0185-5(2), 9781455801855, Bril Audio CD Unabri); audio compact disk 29.97 (978-1-61106-486-5(4), 9781611064865, BriAudCD Unabrid) Brilliance Audio.

George Washington Carver: What Do You See? Janet Benge. Illus. by Kennon James. 1 cass. Dramatization. (Another Great Achiever Ser.). (J). 2003. lib. bdg. 23.95 (978-1-57537-792-6(6)); 16.95 (978-1-57537-592-2(3)) Advance Pub.

George Washington (INK Audiocassette) Leading a Nation. (Graphic Library Biographies I Ser.). (ENG.). 2006. audio compact disk 5.95 (978-0-7368-7451-9(8)) CapstoneDig.

George Washington on Leadership. unabr. ed. Richard Brookhiser. Narrated by Patrick G. Lawlor. (Running Time: 8 hrs. 30 mins. 0 sec.). (ENG.). 2008. audio compact disk 29.99 (978-1-4001-0707-0(5)) Pub: Tantor Media. Dist(s): IngramPubServ

George Washington on Leadership. unabr. ed. Richard Brookhiser. Read by Patrick G. Lawlor. Narrated by Patrick G. Lawlor. (Running Time: 8 hrs. 30 mins. 0 sec.). (ENG.). 2008. audio compact disk 59.99 (978-1-4001-3707-7(1)); audio compact disk 19.99 (978-1-4001-5707-5(2)) Pub: Tantor Media. Dist(s): IngramPubServ

George Washington, Spymaster: How the Americans Outspied the British & Won the Revolutionary War. unabr. ed. Narrated by Brian Keeler. 2 cass. (Running Time: 2 hrs. 45 mins.). (J). 2005. 19.75 (978-1-4193-2959-3(6), 97972) Recorded Bks.
To beat the British forces, George Washington needed more than soldiers. He needed information about the enemy's plans. Historian Thomas B. Allen creates a colorful account of Washington's activities as a master spy. He also shows young listeners how to use codes to decipher the secret identities of those who changed America's history.

George Washington's Cows. David Small. 1 cass. (Running Time: 35 min.). (J). (ps-4). 2001. pap. bk. 15.95 (VX-56C) Kimbo Educ.
A gentleman farmer is forced to cope with fussy cows, dandified pigs & intellectually superior sheep. Includes read along book.

George Washington's Cows. David Small. Read by Peter Fernandez. 14 vols. (Running Time: 6 mins.). 1997. pap. bk. & tchr. ed. 37.95 (978-0-87499-407-0(1)) Live Oak Media.
As George Washington is forced to cope with fussy cows, dandified pigs, & intellectually superior sheep, it soon becomes apparent that the man is simply not cut out for country living & he jumps at the chance to make a career change into politics.

George Washington's Cows. David Small. Illus. by David Small. 11 vols. (Running Time: 6 mins.). 1997. bk. 28.95 (978-1-59519-035-2(X)); pap. bk. 39.95 (978-1-59519-034-5(1)); 9.95 (978-1-59112-040-7(3)); audio compact disk 12.95 (978-1-59519-032-1(5)) Live Oak Media.

George Washington's Cows. David Small. Illus. by David Small. 11 vols. (Running Time: 6 mins.). (J). 1997. pap. bk. 18.95 (978-1-59519-033-8(3)) Pub: Live Oak Media. Dist(s): AudioGO

George Washington's Cows. unabr. ed. David Small. Read by Peter Fernandez. 11 vols. (Running Time: 6 mins.). (J). (gr. k-3). 1997. pap. bk. 16.95 (978-0-87499-405-6(5)) AudioGO.

George Washington's Cows. unabr. ed. David Small. Read by Peter Fernandez. 11 vols. (Running Time: 6 mins.). (J). (gr. k-3). 1997. bk. 25.95 (978-0-87499-406-3(3)) Live Oak Media.

George Washington's Mother. 2004. 8.95 (978-1-55592-991-6(5)) Weston Woods.

George Washington's Mother. (J). 2004. pap. bk. 32.75 (978-1-55592-351-8(8)) Weston Woods.

George Washington's Mother. Jean Fritz. Illus. by DyAnne DiSalvo-Ryan. Narrated by B. J. Ward, Jr. 1 cass., 5 bks. (Running Time: 20 min.). (J). pap. bk. 32.75 Weston Woods.
This is the true story of Mary Washington. When she wasn't worrying about being poor, she was poking her nose in George's business, baking ginergread & smoking a pipe.

George Washington's Mother. Jean Fritz. Illus. by DyAnne DiSalvo-Ryan. Narrated by B. J. Ward. Music by Bruce Zimmerman. 1 cass. (Running Time: 22 min.). (J). (gr. k-5). 2000. pap. bk. 12.95 (978-1-55592-065-4(9), QPRA433) Weston Woods.
This is the true story of Mary Washington. When she wasn't worrying about being poor, she was poking her nose in George's business, baking gingerbread & smoking a pipe.

***George Washington's Mother.** Weston Woods Staff. (YA). audio compact disk 12.95 (978-0-439-72283-4(7)) Weston Woods.

George Washington's Socks. Elvira Woodruff. Read by Johnny Heller. 3 cass. (Running Time: 3 hrs. 45 mins.). (YA). 1999. pap. bk. 40.75 (978-0-7887-2995-9(0), 40877); 93.80 (978-0-7887-3025-2(8), 46842) Recorded Bks.
Fifth-grader Matthew & his friends find camping in the backyard boring, especially with Matt's little sister along. Looking for some excitement, they take a moonlight hike around Lake Levart. But when they step into a mysterious rowboat, they find themselves in the midst of the Revolutionary War.

George Washington's Socks, unabr. ed. Elvira Woodruff. Narrated by Johnny Heller. 3 pieces. (Running Time: 3 hrs. 45 mins.). (gr. 4 up). 1999. 28.00 (978-0-7887-2965-2(9), 95739E7) Recorded Bks.

Georges Brassens. Georges Brassens. Interview with Paul Nemo. 1 cass. (FRE.). 1991. 22.95 (1433-LQP) Olivia & Hill.
During this 90-minute interview on French radio in the 1980s Brassens talks about music, songs, talent, love, morality, power & commitment.

George's Cosmic Treasure Hunt. unabr. ed. Lucy Hawking & Stephen W. Hawking. Read by Hugh Dancy. (Running Time: 6 hrs. 0 mins. 0 sec.). (ENG.). (J). 2009. audio compact disk 29.99 (978-0-7435-8370-1(1)) Pub: S&S Audio. Dist(s): S and S Inc

Georges Courteline: La Paix Chex Soi & La Peur des Coups. unabr. ed. 1 cass. (FRE.). bk. 16.95 (SFR465) J Norton Pubs.

***George's Marvelous Medicine.** unabr. ed. Roald Dahl. Read by Richard E. Grant. (ENG.). 2005. (978-0-06-084067-9(6)); (978-0-06-084066-2(8)) HarperCollins Pubs.

George's Marvelous Medicine. unabr. ed. Roald Dahl. Read by Richard E. Grant. (J). 2005. audio compact disk 17.95 (978-0-06-075832-5(5), HarperChildAud) HarperCollins Pubs.

George's Secret Key to the Universe. Stephen W. Hawking & Lucy Hawking. (Playaway Children Ser.). (J). (gr. 3-7). 2009. 60.00 (978-1-60775-614-9(5)) Find a World.

George's Secret Key to the Universe. unabr. ed. Stephen W. Hawking & Lucy Hawking. Read by Hugh Dancy. (Running Time: 6 hrs. 0 mins. 0 sec.). (ENG.). (J). (gr. 3). 2007. audio compact disk 29.95 (978-0-7435-7161-6(4)) Pub: S&S Audio. Dist(s): S and S Inc

Georgia O'Keeffe. Carole Marsh. 1 cass. (Running Time: 35 min.). 10.95 (PT-87-11-16, HarperThor) HarpC GBR.

Georgia Savage: The House Tibet. unabr. ed. Georgia Savage. Read by Georgia Savage. Interview with Rebekah Presson. 1 cass. (Running Time: 29 min.). 1991. 10.00 (051091) New Letters.
Savage is highly-regarded in her home country, Australia. Her new novel, "The House Tibet", is her first to be published in the United States. In the novel, Savage tells of the saga of a young woman who travels the country after being raped by her father.

Georgian: A Reading Grammar. Howard I. Aronson. 4 cass. (Running Time: 3 hrs. 30 mins.). (GEO & ENG.). pap. bk. 99.50 (SGG150) J Norton Pubs.
Specially designed to teach how to read Georgian literature. Intended for beginners & starts by teaching the unique Georgian alphabet & basic pronunciation. The reading & translation passages have been selected from both classical & modern publications & are on the tapes.

Georgian Newspaper Reader, Set. Ketevan Gabounia & John D. Murphy. 2 cass. (Running Time: 1 hr. 30 min. per cass.). (GEO & ENG.). 1995. 19.00 (3124) Dunwoody Pr.
Includes forty selections which appeared in the Georgian press in 1993 & 1994. Subjects covered include a broad variety of themes, including national & international affairs, theater, literature, etc. English translations are provided.

Georgiana, Duchess of Devonshire. unabr. ed. Amanda Foreman. Narrated by Virginia Leishman. 13 cass. (Running Time: 18 hrs.). 2001. 98.00 (978-0-7887-4870-7(X), 96440E7) Recorded Bks.
A portrait of late 18th-century British aristocracy & its leader, Lady Georgiana Spencer an ancestor of Diana, Princess of Wales & how her personal life was marked with problems.

Georgie see Jorgito

Georgie. 2004. 8.95 (978-1-56008-905-6(9)); cass. & flmstrp 30.00 (978-0-89719-531-7(0)) Weston Woods.

Georgie; Red Carpet, the; Stone Soup; Story about Ping. 2004. (978-0-89719-801-1(8)); cass. & flmstrp (978-0-89719-710-6(0)) Weston Woods.

Geostatistical Case Studies. Ed. by G. Matheron & M. Armstrong. (Quantitative Geology & Geostatistics Ser.). (C). 1987. 160.00 (978-1-55608-019-7(0)) Spri.

Gepetto Soundtrack. (J). (ps-3). 2000. 16.98 (978-0-7634-0670-7(8)) W Disney Records.

Gerald & Elizabeth. D. E. Stevenson. Read by Gordon Griffin. 7 cass. 2005. 61.95 (978-1-84559-112-0(7)) Pub: UlverLrgPrint GBR. Dist(s): Ulverscroft US

Gerald Barrax. unabr. ed. Gerald Barrax. Read by Gerald Barrax. 1 cass. (Running Time: 29 min.). 1989. 10.00 New Letters.
Barrax reads from The Death of Animals & Lesser Gods & is interviewed.

Gerald Early: Tuxedo Junction. unabr. ed. Gerald Early. Read by Gerald Early. 1 cass. (Running Time: 29 min.). 1990. 10.00 (022390) New Letters.
Early has written extensively on the subject of jazz & African-American popular culture. He reads from a new book, "Tuxedo Junction" & talks about his work.

Gerald Feinberg on Science & Creation. Read by Gerald Feinberg. 1 cass. (Running Time: 30 min.). 1990. 14.95 (CBC596) MMI Corp.
Covers basic nature of cosmos, How did it begin?, current theories, work of Einstein.

Gerald Feinberg on Science & Creation. Gerald Feinberg. Read by Gerald Feinberg. 1 cass. (Running Time: 30 min.). 1992. 14.95 (CBC 596) MMI Corp.

Gerald Ford: Gambling with America's Budget. 1 cass. (Running Time: 1 hr.). 10.95 (NP-88-06-06, HarperThor) HarpC GBR.

Gerald Hausman. unabr. ed. Gerald Hausman. Read by Gerald Hausman. Interview with Rebekah Presson. 1 cass. (Running Time: 29 min.). 1990. 10.00 (030290) New Letters.
Hausman lives in Santa Fe, New Mexico, where he is editor of Lotus Press. Hausman is also the author of many books of poetry & fiction, a large number of which recount his experience with Native American culture.

Gerald Heard: Guide of Souls. Stephan Hoeller. 1 cass. 1999. 11.00 (40026) Big Sur Tapes.
1996 Los Angeles.

Gerald McBoing Boing & Other Stories. Perf. by Adam Stem. Narrated by Carl Reiner & Werner Klemperer. Based on a story by Dr. Seuss. 1 cass. (Running Time: 49 min.). (J). (ps-5). 9.98 (344); audio compact disk 15.98 (D344) MFLP CA.
This fun-tastic tape combines the joys of classical music with imaginative stories. Richly varied classical ensembles conducted by Adam Stem plus dramatic narrations by Carl Reiner & Werner Klemperer.

Gerald Stern. unabr. ed. Read by Gerald Stern. 1 cass. (Running Time: 29 min.). 1985. 10.00 New Letters.
Gerald Stern's poetry books include Lucky Life & The Red Coal.

Gerald Stern II. unabr. ed. Gerald Stern. 1 cass. (Running Time: 29 min.). (New Letters on the Air Ser.). 1992. 10.00 (030692) New Letters.
For this program, Stem reads from "Bread Without Sugar.".

Gerald Vizenor. unabr. ed. Read by Gerald R. Vizenor & Rebekah Presson. Ed. by James McKinley. 1 cass. (Running Time: 29 min.). (New Letters on the Air Ser.). 1992. 10.00 (102392); 18.00 2-sided cass. New Letters.
Vizenor is interviewed by Rebekah Presson & reads from his work.

Geraldi Trail. Max Brand. Read by Gough Jim. 7 CDs. (Running Time: 8 hrs. 30 mins.). 2004. audio compact disk 56.00 (978-0-7861-8647-1(X), 3283) Blckstn Audio.
James Geraldi is one of the most legendary thieves in the West. But he is not an ordinary thief, preying on the unwitting and defenseless. James Geraldi is a very exclusive thief, stealing only from other thieves. From the largest towns to the loneliest outposts of the desert his name is known, but few could identify him¿although many an honest rancher or townsman has become a loyal friend when Geraldi rescued their savings, and many a bandit has been conned or bested by him.

Geraldi Trail. unabr. ed. Max Brand. Read by Gough Jim. 6 cass. (Running Time: 8 hrs. 30 mins.). 2004. 44.95 (978-0-7861-2724-5(4), 3283) Blckstn Audio.

Gerald's Game. unabr. ed. Stephen King. Read by Lindsay Crouse. (ENG., 2008. audio compact disk 36.95 (978-1-59887-764-9(X), 159887764X) Pub: HighBridge. Dist(s): Workman Pub

Gerard de Nerval a Paris et dans le Valois, Set. Gérard de Nerval. 3 cass. (FRE.). 1991. 32.95 (1478-RF) Olivia & Hill.
The Nervalian itinerary starts with the roots of his childhood & ends with a tentative diagnosis of his mental sickness through the meanders of his poetic world.

Gerard Manley Hopkins: The Wreck of the Deutschland. unabr. ed. Read by Paul Scofield. 1 cass. 12.95 (ECN 138) J Norton Pubs.
Reflects on the nature of God & how through suffering man recognises grace. Includes Sir Ralph Richardson presenting his favourite Marvell's verse & talks with understanding & affection. Also Odes search for inner truth & the essence of things.

Geriatric Gynecology. Contrib. by Anne M. Weber et al. 1 cass. (American College of Obstetrics & Gynecologists UPDATE: Vol. 21, No. 6). 1998. 20.00 Am Coll Obstetric.

Germain Vol 2 Earworms. (EARWORMS Ser.). 2009. audio compact disk 24.95 (978-0-8416-1069-9(X)) Pub: Berlitz Pubng. Dist(s): Langenscheidt

German. Ed. by Berlitz Publishing Staff. (Running Time: 1 hr.). (Berlitz Rush Hour Express Ser.). (GER & ENG.). 2004. audio compact disk 9.95 (978-981-246-595-5(2), 465952) Pub: APA Pubns Serv SGP. Dist(s): IngramPubServ

German. Ed. by Berlitz Publishing Staff. (Berlitz iPhrase Ser.). (ENG.). 2008. audio compact disk 12.95 (978-981-268-487-5(5)) Pub: APA Pubns Serv SGP. Dist(s): IngramPubServ

German. Paul Coggle. 1 cass. (Running Time: 60 min.). (Language Complete Course Packs Ser.). 1993. 17.95 (Passport Bks) McGraw-Hill Trade.

***German.** Kristine K. Kershul. ([i]10 minutes a day[/i][sup]R[/sup] AUDIO CD Ser.). (ENG.). 2007. audio compact disk 42.95 (978-1-931873-26-0(7)) Pub: Bilingual Bks. Dist(s): Midpt Trade

German. Rosi McNab & Collins UK Staff. Contrib. by Rosi McNab. (Running Time: 3 hrs. 0 mins. 0 sec.). (Collins Easy Learning Audio Course Ser.). (GER & ENG.). 2009. audio compact disk 19.95 (978-0-00-731383-9(7)) Pub: HarpC GBR. Dist(s): IPG Chicago

German. Pimsleur Staff. 16 cass. 2000. 295.00 (978-0-671-31601-3(X), Pimsleur) S&S Audio.

German. rev. ed. Berlitz Editors. 1 cass. (Running Time: 090 min.). (CD Pack Ser.). (GER & ENG., 1998. pap. bk. 19.95 (978-2-8315-6343-5(7)) Berlitz Intl Inc.

German. unabr. ed. Ed. by Charles Berlitz. 2 cass. (Running Time: 1 hr. 30 mins.). (Language/30 Brief Course Ser.). pap. bk. 21.95 (1023) J Norton Pubs.
Quick, highly condensed introduction to the words & phrases you'll need to communicate effectively in the country you're visiting. Cassettes & phrase guide book are in a vinyl album.

German. unabr. ed. Berlitz Editors. 1 cass. (Running Time: 1 hr. 30 min.). (Cassette Packs Ser.). (GER., 1998. pap. bk. 17.95 (978-2-8315-6331-2(3)) Pub: Berlitz Intl Inc. Dist(s): Globe Pequot
For travelers.

German. unabr. ed. Linguistics Staff. Created by Oasis Audio Staff. 2 cass. (Running Time: 3 hrs.). (Complete Idiot's Guide to Languages Ser.). (ENG & GER.). 2005. audio compact disk 9.99 (978-1-59859-119-4(3)) Oasis Audio.

German. unabr. ed. Linguistics Team. Narrated by Linguistics Team. Created by Oasis Audio Staff. (Complete Idiot's Guide Ser.). (ENG.). 2005. audio compact disk 19.99 (978-1-59859-056-2(1)) Oasis Audio.

German. unabr. ed. Oasis Audio Staff & Linguistics Staff. Narrated by Linguistics Staff. (Complete Idiot's Guides). (ENG.). 2005. audio compact disk 39.99 (978-1-59859-062-3(6)) Oasis Audio.

German. 2nd ed. Ed. by Ruth Fach. 3 cass. (Running Time: 3 hrs. 30 min.). (Just Listen N' Learn Ser.). 1993. audio compact disk 39.95 CD. M-H Contemporary.

German. 2nd ed. Ed. by Ruth Fach. 3 cass. (Running Time: 3 hrs. 30 min.). (Just Listen N' Learn Ser.). 1993. 29.95 set. (Passport Bks) McGraw-Hill Trade.

German. 2nd rev. ed. Howard S. Beckerman. Created by Langenscheidt Publishers Staff. 3 CDs. (Running Time: 1 hr.). (Rush Hour Ser.). (GER.). 2003. audio compact disk 24.95 (978-981-246-274-9(0), 462740) Pub: Berlitz Pubng. Dist(s): Langenscheidt

German. 3rd rev. abr. ed. Created by Berlitz Publishing Staff. 3 CDs. (Berlitz Intermediate Ser.). 2008. audio compact disk 29.95 (978-981-268-408-0(5)) Pub: Berlitz Pubng. Dist(s): Langenscheidt

***German, Set.** Ed. by Collins. 2008. cd-rom 250.00 (978-0-340-96859-8(1)) Pub: Hodder Edu GBR. Dist(s): Trans-Atl Phila

German, Set. Edward Swick. (Running Time: 10800 sec.). (For Dummies Ser.). (GER & ENG., 2008. audio compact disk 19.99 (978-0-470-22256-0(5), For Dummies) Wiley US.

German, Vol. 1. Foreign Service Institute Staff. (GER.). 1978. bk. 185.00 (978-0-88432-017-3(0)) J Norton Pubs.

German: Language 30. Educational Services Corporation Staff. 2004. audio compact disk 21.95 (978-1-931850-03-2(8)) Educ Svcs DC.

German: Language/30. rev. ed. Educational Services Corporation Staff. 2 cass. (Running Time: 1 hr. 30 min.). (GER.). 1992. pap. bk. 21.95 incl. phrase bk. (978-0-910542-58-6(9)) Educ Svcs DC.
Guided practice including greetings, introduction, & questions at hotels, restaurants, places of business & entertainment. Phrases spoken in target language & English, so tapes can be used while driving or exercising. Ideal for the business traveler, tourist, or as a refresher course.

German: Learn to Speak & Understand German with Pimsleur Language Programs. Pimsleur Staff & Pimsleur. 1 CD. (Running Time: 11 hrs. 50 mins. 0 sec.). (Express Ser.). (ENG.). 2003. audio compact disk 11.95 (978-0-7435-3392-8(5), Pimsleur) Pub: S&S Audio. Dist(s): S and S Inc

German: Speak & Read the Pimsleur Way. Pimsleur Staff. (Running Time: 7 hrs. 30 mins. 0 sec.). (Go Ser.). (ENG.). 2009. audio compact disk 29.99 (978-0-7435-9656-5(0), Pimsleur) Pub: S&S Audio. Dist(s): S and S Inc

German: The All-Audio Beginner's Course. Created by Berlitz Publishing Staff. (Berlitz Guaranteed Ser.). (ENG.). 2007. audio compact disk 19.95 (978-981-268-231-4(7)) Pub: APA Pubns Serv SGP. Dist(s): IngramPubServ

German Level 3: Advanced. 4 cass. (Learn While You Drive Ser.). bk. 47.95 (3177-AMR) Olivia & Hill.
Language course designed specifically for use in your car. The sentence in the foreign language is always followed by an English translation. Assumes a basic knowledge of the language. Complex sentence structure & grammar are taught within the context of practical everyday situations: conversations, newspapers, the day's events, medical problems, shopping, politics, schools, social occasions, etc.

German Level 4: Advanced. 4 cass. (Learn While You Drive Ser.). 1995. bk. 44.95 (3178-AMR) Olivia & Hill.

German No. 1: Learn to Speak & Understand German with Pimsleur Language Programs. 2nd rev. ed. Pimsleur Staff & Pimsleur. (Running Time: 400 hrs. 0 mins. NaN sec.). (Quick & Simple Ser.). (ITA & ENG.). 2002. audio compact disk 19.95 (978-0-7435-0953-4(6), Pimsleur) Pub: S&S Audio. Dist(s): S and S Inc

German Set: Basic 1, 4 cass. (Learn While You Drive Ser.). 1995. bk. 47.95 (3175-AMR) Olivia & Hill.
Language course designed specifically for use in your car. The sentence in the foreign language is always followed by an English translation. Subjects covered: travel, shopping, ordering meals, placing telephone calls, telling time, counting money, using postal system, sightseeing, theater, arranging & attending business meetings & above all, making friends. Recorded in high German.

German Set: Basic 2, 4 cass. (Learn While You Drive Ser.). 1995. bk. 44.95 (3176-AMR) Olivia & Hill.

German Set: Traveler's Edition. unabr. ed. Pimsleur Staff. 8 cass. 59.95 S&S Audio.
Provides language skills needed to navigate foreign countries & helpful add-ins to make the trip go smoothly. Also includes phrase cards, 2 luggage tags, mail-in offer for Pimsleur duffel bag, international phone card, Pimsleur World Language Map, & post cards.

German - Chinese Level 1: Includes Wordlist. Vocabulearn. 2 cass. (Running Time: 90 min. ea.). (VocabuLearn Ser.). (GER & CHI.). 1995. 15.95 (978-957-9330-80-0(8)) Penton Overseas.

German - Chinese Level 2: Includes Wordlist. Vocabulearn. 1 cass. (VocabuLearn Ser.). (GER & CHI.). 1995. 15.95 (978-957-9330-81-7(6)) Penton Overseas.

German - Chinese Level 3: Includes Wordlist, Level 3. Vocabulearn. 2 cass. (Running Time: 90 min. ea.). (VocabuLearn Ser.). (GER & CHI.). 1995. 15.95 (978-957-9330-82-4(4)) Penton Overseas.

German - English. 1 cass. (Lyric Language Ser.). (GER & ENG.). (J). 7.98 Blisterpack. (POI 502) NewSound.

German - English, Level 2. Vocabulearn. 2 cass. (Running Time: 90 min. per cass.). (VocabuLearn Ser.). (ENG & GER.). 1987. 15.95 (978-0-939001-58-3(6)) Penton Overseas.

German - English, Level III. Vocabulearn. 2 cass. (Running Time: 90 min. per cass.). (VocabuLearn Ser.). (ENG & GER.). 1997. 15.95 (978-0-939001-28-6(4)) Penton Overseas.

German Audio Vocabulary Builder. unabr. ed. 1 cass. 12.95 (SGE010) J Norton Pubs.
Provides 101 essential words & phrases for the traveler.

German Basic Course Vol. I: Beginner Level, unabr. ed. Foreign Service Institute Staff. 10 cass. (Running Time: 9 hrs. 30 mins.). (GER.). 1971. pap. bk. 225.00 (978-0-88432-441-6(9), SGE500) J Norton Pubs.
Learn by listening & repeating & repeating again. The cassette player becomes your "tireless tutor." Native voices provide models of correct pronunciation. Each lesson begins with a presentation of new sounds & structures to be featured in that unit, followed by a dialog presented in a sentence-by-sentence "build-up" that makes it easy to understand & pronounce correctly. Brief culture capsules in English follow each lesson unit & provide insight into German customs & language usage.

German Basic Course Vol. II: Intermediate Level, unabr. ed. Foreign Service Institute Staff. 8 cass. (Running Time: 8 hrs.). (GER.). (YA). 1965. pap. bk. 175.00 (978-0-88432-018-0(9), AFG151) J Norton Pubs.
Intermediate program provides additional vocabulary & training in more complex language structures. Material for a greater understanding of the written language is also provided. Contains narratives designed to develop reading skills & conversation exercises for perfecting grammatical usage.

German Basic Course Vol. III: Advanced Level, unabr. ed. Foreign Service Institute Staff. 18 cass. (Running Time: 17 hrs. 30 mins.). (GER.). 1965. pap. bk. 275.00 (978-0-88432-043-2(X), AFG160) J Norton Pubs.
Advanced level program provides additional vocabulary & training in more complex language structures. Material for a greater understanding of the written language is also provided. Contains narratives designed to develop reading skills & conversation exercises for perfecting grammatical usage.

German Basic Course (FSI), Vol. 2. 9 CDs. (Running Time: 8 hrs.). (GER.). 2005. audio compact disk 175.00 (978-1-57970-126-0(4), AFG151D, Audio-For) J Norton Pubs.

German Basic Course (FSI) & Text, Vol. 1. 11. (Running Time: 9 hrs. 30 min.). (GER.). 2005. audio compact disk 225.00 (978-1-57970-125-3(6), SGE500D, Audio-For) J Norton Pubs.

German Bible - New Testament: Luther Edition. Read by Edwin Achenbach. 24 cass. 1996. 49.97 (978-1-58968-053-1(7), 5001A) Chrstn Dup Intl.

German Bible - Psalms: Luther Edition. Read by Edwin Achenbach. 5 cass. 1996. 15.97 (978-1-58968-054-8(5), 5010A) Chrstn Dup Intl.

German Business Situations: A Spoken Language Guide. Paul Hartley et al. (Languages for Business Ser.). 1995. 45.00 (978-0-415-12851-3(X)) Pub: Routledge. Dist(s): Taylor and Fran

German, Conversational: Learn to Speak & Understand German with Pimsleur Language Programs. 2nd unabr. ed. Pimsleur Staff. 8 CDs. (Running Time: 80 hrs. 0 mins. 0 sec.). (Instant Conversation Ser.). (GER & ENG.). 2005. audio compact disk 49.95 (978-0-7435-5047-5(1), Pimsleur) Pub: S&S Audio. Dist(s): S and S Inc

German Culture Capsules. unabr. ed. 1 cass. (Running Time: 1 hr.). 12.95 (978-0-88432-505-5(9), CCGE01) J Norton Pubs.
The brief culture capsules recorded in English at the end of each lesson unit of the introductory courses are available as separate cassettes.

German Empire: 1870-1918. Michael Sturmer. Narrated by Paul Hecht. 3 cass. (Running Time: 4 hrs. 30 mins.). 36.00 (978-1-4025-1356-5(9)) Recorded Bks.

German for Beginners, Set. Ilona Davydova. 8 cass. (Running Time: 8 hr.). 1996. 179.00 (978-0-9675296-3-9(8)) Express Method.

German for Beginners: Passport's Language Guide. Angela Wilkes. 1 cass. (Running Time: 1 hr.). (Passport's Languages for Beginners Ser.). 1999. pap. bk. 14.95 (978-0-8442-1477-1(9), 14779, Passport Bks) McGraw-Hill Trade.

German for Business & Economics Vol. 1: Die Volks - und Welwirtschaft (Economics) 2nd ed. Patricia Ryan Paulsell et al. 1 cass. (GER.). 2000. audio compact disk 15.00 (978-0-87013-554-5(6)) Mich St U Pr.

German for Business & Economics Vol. 1: Die Volks-und Welwirtschaft (Economics) 2nd rev. ed. Patricia Ryan Paulsell et al. 2 Vols. (GER & ENG., (C). 2000. cass. & cd-rom 50.00 (978-0-87013-538-5(4)) Mich St U Pr.

German for Business & Economics Vol. 2: Die Betriebs-Wirtschaft (Business) 2nd rev. ed. Patricia Ryan Paulsell et al. (GER & ENG., (C). 2000. cass. & cd-rom 50.00 (978-0-87013-539-2(2)) Mich St U Pr.

German for Business & Economics Vol. 2: Die Betriegswirtschaft (Business) 2nd ed. Patricia Ryan Paulsell et al. 1 cass. (GER.). 2000. audio compact disk 15.00 (978-0-87013-555-2(4)) Mich St U Pr.

German for Dummies. unabr. ed. Edward Swick. Read by Becky Wilmes & Marc Falkenberg. (YA). 2008. 34.99 (978-1-60514-681-2(1)) Find a World.

German for French Speakers see Nouvel Allemand sans Peine

German for Speakers of English: Level 1. 2nd ed. 16 cass. (Running Time: 15 hrs.). (Pimsleur Tapes Ser.). (GER.). 1995. 345.00 set. (18457, Pimsleur) S&S Audio.
Spoken foreign-language proficiency training. Thirty, half-hour, intensive, spoken-language lesson units to be completed at the rate of one lesson per day for 30 days. By achieving eighty-percent correct answers to the questions in each unit, the Pimsleur Spoken Language Programmed Instructional Method will enable the learner to achieve the ACTFL Intermediate-Low Spoken Proficiency Level.

German for Speakers of English: Level 2. 2nd ed. 16 cass. (Running Time: 15 hrs.). (Pimsleur Tapes Ser.). (GER.). 1995. 345.00 set. (18460, Pimsleur) S&S Audio.
An additional thirty-lesson unit program accomplished at the same rate as a Pimsleur I. Will enable the learner to achieve the ACTFL Intermediate-Mid Spoken Proficiency Level.

German for Speakers of English: Level 3. unabr. ed. 16 cass. (Running Time: 15 hrs.). (Pimsleur Tapes Ser.). (GER.). 1994. 345.00 set. (18459, Pimsleur) S&S Audio.
An additional thirty-lesson-unit program, for a total of ninety lesson units. Will allow the learner to achieve the ACTFL Intermediate-High Spoken Proficiency Level.

German for Starters, Set. Diane Collett & Michael Spencer. 4 cass. (ENG.). 1998. 53.00 (978-0-521-59747-0(1)) Cambridge U Pr.

German for Your Trip. Berlitz Publishing Staff. (Berlitz for Your Trip Ser.). 2007. audio compact disk 9.95 (978-981-268-045-7(4)) Pub: Berlitz Pubng. Dist(s): Langenscheidt

German Generals Talk. unabr. collector's ed. Basil H. Liddell-Hart. Read by Justin Hecht. 7 cass. (Running Time: 10 hrs. 30 min.). 1983. 56.00 (978-0-7366-0479-6(0), 1454) Books on Tape.
Like many of his brother officers, Liddell Hart served in both World Wars. Many German generals were junior officers on the Western front in that first encounter, master planners in the second.

German Historical School of Economics. unabr. ed. Nicholas Balabkins. Ed. by Israel M. Kirzner & Mike Hassell. Narrated by Louis Rukeyser. 2 cass. (Running Time: 80 min. per cass.). Dramatization. (Great Economic Thinkers Ser.). (YA). (gr. 10 up). 1988. 17.95 (978-0-938935-35-3(6), 10205) Knowledge Prod.
To a group of late 19th-century German professors, classical economic theories only expressed what happens in a simplified world, not the real world. To solve pressing problems, they enthusiastically supported government intervention in the economy through social welfare legislation.

German Historical School of Economics: Welfare Capitalism Begins. abr. ed. Nicholas Balabkins. Read by Louis Rukeyser. (Running Time: 9000 sec.). (Great Economic Thinkers Ser.). 2006. audio compact disk 25.95 (978-0-7861-6949-8(4)) Pub: Blckstn Audio. Dist(s): NetLibrary CO

German I, Set. Paul Pimsleur. 16 cass. (Pimsleur Language Learning Ser.). 1995. pap. bk. & stu. ed. 345.00 (0671-52154-3) SyberVision.

German I: Learn to Speak & Understand German with Pimsleur Language Programs. 2nd rev. ed. Pimsleur Staff. 16 CDs. (Running Time: 160 hrs. 0 mins. 0 sec.). (Comprehensive Ser.). (ENG.). 2002. audio compact disk 345.00 (978-0-7435-1836-9(5), Pimsleur) Pub: S&S Audio. Dist(s): S and S Inc

German I Basic. Paul Pimsleur. 8 lessons on 4 cass. (Pimsleur Language Learning Ser.). 1995. 29.95 (52163-1) SyberVision.

German Idealism & the Jew: The Inner Anti-Semitism of Philosophy & German Je. Michael Mack. Read by Michael Jarmus. Prod. by Alden Films Staff. (Running Time: 9 hrs. 8 mins. 0 sec.). (ENG.). 2010. audio compact disk 49.95 (978-1-877684-84-5(8)) Pub: Alden Films. Dist(s): Perseus Dist

German II. Paul Pimsleur. 16 cass. (Pimsleur Language Learning Ser.). 1995. pap. bk. & stu. ed. 345.00 (0671-57073-0) SyberVision.

German II: Learn to Speak & Understand German with Pimsleur Language Programs. 3rd ed. Pimsleur Staff. 30 CDs. (Running Time: 160 hrs. 0 mins. 0 sec.). (Comprehensive Ser.). (ENG.). 2003. audio compact disk 345.00 (978-0-7435-2349-3(0), Pimsleur) Pub: S&S Audio. Dist(s): S and S Inc

German III, Set. Paul Pimsleur. 16 cass. (Pimsleur Language Learning Ser.). 1994. pap. bk. & stu. ed. 345.00 (0671-57926-6) SyberVision.

German III: Learn to Speak & Understand German with Pimsleur Language Programs. 2nd ed. Pimsleur Staff & Pimsleur. (Running Time: 160 hrs. 0 mins. 0 sec.). (Comprehensive Ser.). (ENG.). 2006. audio compact disk 345.00 (978-0-7435-2877-1(8), Pimsleur) Pub: S&S Audio. Dist(s): S and S Inc

German Illustrated Phrasebook & Travel Information. Kate Corney et al. 2 cass. (Destination Ser.). (GER., (gr. 4-7). 1995. pap. bk. 15.95 (978-0-8442-9424-7(1)) M-H Contemporary.

German in a Minute. 1 cass. (Language in a Minute Cassette Ser.). 5.95 (978-0-943351-25-4(1), XC1009) Cimino Pub Grp.
Feel at home in any foreign country with these 101 esssential words & phrases. Hear each word introduced in English, hear them pronounced by a Voice of America instructor. Practice at your own pace, you can check yourself with the wallet sized dictionary included.

German in 30 Days. 2nd rev. abr. ed. Created by Berlitz Guides. (Berlitz in 30 Days Ser.). (ENG.). 2007. 19.95 (978-981-268-220-8(1)) Pub: APA Pubns Serv SGP. Dist(s): IngramPubServ

German in 30 Days/Deutsch in 30 Tagen see Deutsch in 30 Tagen

German in 30 Days/Deutsch in 30 Tagen Text with Cassette. Angelika G. Beck. (GER.). 1998. 28.95 (978-3-581-68767-9(4)) Langenscheidt.

German Intermediate Level. unabr. ed. Foreign Service Institute Staff. 8 cass. (Running Time: 8 hr.). bk. 245.00 Set; Vol. III (advanced), incl. 18 audio cass.; 375 p. text. (AFG160) J Norton Pubs.

German Language. 2005. 44.99 (978-1-59895-003-8(7)) Find a World.

German Lyric Poetry. unabr. ed. Poems. Perf. by Lotte Lehmann. 1 cass. Incl. German Lyric Poetry: Als Ich auf dem Euphrat Schiffte. Johann Wolfgang von Goethe. 1984.; German Lyric Poetry: Begegnung. Eduard Morike. 1984.; German Lyric Poetry: Der Genesene an die Hoffnung. Eduard Morike. 1984.; German Lyric Poetry: Der Rosenkavalier: Monologues from Act I. Hugo von Hofmannsthal. 1984.; German Lyric Poetry: Dichterliebe. Heinrich Heine. 1984.; German Lyric Poetry: Ganymed. Johann Wolfgang von Goethe. 1984.; German Lyric Poetry: Gebet. Eduard Morike. (SWC 1072); German Lyric Poetry: Geheimes. Johann Wolfgang von Goethe. 1984.; German Lyric Poetry: Ich Lebe Mein Leben in Wachsenden Ringen. Rainer Maria Rilke. 1984.; German Lyric Poetry: Im Fruhling. Eduard Morike. 1984.; German Lyric Poetry: Mignon. Johann Wolfgang von Goethe. 1984.; German Lyric Poetry: Nimmersatte Liebe. Eduard Morike. 1984.; German Lyric Poetry: Peregrina I. Eduard Morike. 1984.; German Lyric Poetry: Verborgenheit. Eduard Morike. 1984.; German Lyric Poetry: Wanderers Nachtlied. Johann Wolfgang von Goethe. 1984.; German Lyric Poetry: Winterreise. Wilheim Muller. 1984.; (GER.). 1970. 14.00 (978-0-694-50059-8(3), SWC 1072) HarperCollins Pubs.

German Lyric Poetry: Als Ich auf dem Euphrat Schiffte see German Lyric Poetry

German Lyric Poetry: Begegnung see German Lyric Poetry

German Lyric Poetry: Der Genesene an die Hoffnung see German Lyric Poetry

German Lyric Poetry: Der Rosenkavalier: Monologues from Act I see German Lyric Poetry

German Lyric Poetry: Dichterliebe see German Lyric Poetry

German Lyric Poetry: Ganymed see German Lyric Poetry

German Lyric Poetry: Gebet see German Lyric Poetry

German Lyric Poetry: Geheimes see German Lyric Poetry

German Lyric Poetry: Ich Lebe Mein Leben in Wachsenden Ringen see German Lyric Poetry

German Lyric Poetry: Im Fruhling see German Lyric Poetry

German Lyric Poetry: Mignon see German Lyric Poetry

German Lyric Poetry: Nimmersatte Liebe see German Lyric Poetry

German Lyric Poetry: Peregrina I see German Lyric Poetry

German Lyric Poetry: Verborgenheit see German Lyric Poetry

German Lyric Poetry: Wanderers Nachtlied see German Lyric Poetry

German Lyric Poetry: Winterreise see German Lyric Poetry

German Music. Kim Mitzo Thompson & Karen Mitzo Hilderbrand. Arranged by Hal Wright. (J). 1994. audio compact disk 12.99 (978-1-57583-303-3(4), Twin 111CD) Twin Sisters.

German Music. Kim Mitzo Thompson & Karen Mitzo Hilderbrand. Composed by Hal Wright. (J). 1994. pap. bk. 13.99 (978-1-57583-326-2(3), TWIN 411CD) Twin Sisters.

German New Testament. Narrated by Edwin Achenbach. 1 cass. (GER.). 1994. 49.98 Set. (978-7-902033-08-4(1)) Chrstn Dup Intl.
Bible.

German on the Go. 2 cass. (Running Time: 3 hrs.). (On the Go Ser.). (GER.). 1992. spiral bd. 14.95 (978-0-8120-7830-5(6)) Barron.

German on the Road, Level 2. Hiller. 2 cass. (Running Time: 3 hrs.). (Languages on the Road Ser.). (ENG & GER.). 1992. pap. bk. 11.95 incl. script set. (978-0-8120-7938-8(8)) Barron.
Designed for busy people who possess basic language skills, here are lively, interesting conversations on tape with practically no English coaching at all. Each package offers a twin track stereo system on tape. One track presents the language without English interruptions, while the other track features an English narrator to help students. Timed pauses let listeners repeat what they've heard. The spoken word is stressed without the use of a textbook, so listeners can learn in the car or while doing chores.

German Oom-Pah-Pah Dances w/Companion Audio CD. 2nd ed. Vicki Corona. (Celebrate the Cultures Ser.). 1990. pap. bk. 14.95 (978-1-58513-136-5(9)) Dance Fantasy.

German Phrase Book Pack. rev. ed. Collins Publishers Staff. (ENG & GER.). 2003. pap. bk. 13.99 (978-0-00-765099-6(X)) Pub: HarpC GBR. Dist(s): Trafalgar

German Plus: Learn to Speak & Understand German with Pimsleur Language Programs, 10 units. Pimsleur Staff. 5 CDs. (Running Time: 500 hrs. 0 mins. NaN sec.). (Compact Ser.). (ENG.). 2001. audio compact disk 115.00 (978-0-7435-0022-7(9), Pimsleur) Pub: S&S Audio. Dist(s): S and S Inc

German Psalms. Narrated by Edwin Achenbach. 5 cass. (GER.). 1994. 15.98 Set. (978-7-902033-15-2(4)) Chrstn Dup Intl.
Bible.

German Requiem: Poems of the War & the Atonement of a Third Reich Child. Ted Hirschfield. 1993. 12.95 (978-1-877770-88-3(4)) Time Being Bks.

German Rush Hour Express Cd Berlitz. (RUSH HOUR EXPRESS Ser.). 2008. audio compact disk 9.95 (978-981-268-236-9(8)) Pub: Berlitz Pubng. Dist(s): Langenscheidt

German Songs for Beginners. unabr. ed. 1 cass. 15.95 (CGE101) J Norton Pubs.

German Survival Guide: The Language & Culture You Need to Travel with Confidence in Germany & Austria. Elizabeth Bingham. 2001. pap. bk. 39.95 (978-0-9703734-3-4(0)) World Prospect.

German (Swiss) Learn to Speak & Understand Swiss German with Pimsleur Language Programs. unabr. ed. Pimsleur Staff. 5 cass. (Running Time: 500 hrs. 0 mins. NaN sec.). (Pimsleur Language Program Ser.). (GER & ENG.). 1997. 95.00 (978-0-671-57953-1(3), Pimsleur) Pub: S&S Audio. Dist(s): S and S Inc

With Pimsleur Language Programs you don't just study a language, you learn it - the same way you mastered English! And because the technique relies on interactive spoken language training, the Pimsleur Language Programs are totally audio - no book is needed! The Pimsleur programs provide a method of self-practice with an expert teacher and native speakers in lessons specially designed to work with the way the mind naturally acquires language information. The various components of language - vocabulary, pronunciation and grammar - are all learned together without rote memorization and drills. Using a unique method of memory recall developed by renowned linguist, Dr. Paul Pimsleur, the programs teach listeners to combine words and phrases to express themselves the way native speakers do. By listening and responding to thirty minute recorded lessons, students easily and effectively achieve spoken proficiency. No other language program or school is as quick, convenient, and effective as the Pimsleur Language Programs. The Comprehensive Program is the ultimate in spoken language learning. For those who want to become proficient in the language of their choice, the Comprehensive programs go beyond the Basic Programs to offer spoken-language fluency. Using the same simple method of interactive self-practice with native speakers, these comprehensive programs provide a complete language learning course. The Comprehensive Program is available in a wide variety of languages and runs through three levels (thirty lessons each) in French, German, Italian, Japanese, Russian and Spanish. At the end of a full Comprehensive Program listeners will be conducting complete conversations and be well on their way to mastering the language. The Comprehensive Programs are all available on cassettes and are also on CD in the six languages in which we offer the Basic Program on CD.

German Technical DICT. Routledge Staff. 1996. audio compact disk 295.00 (978-0-415-16067-4(7)) Pub: Routledge. Dist(s): Taylor and Fran

German Technical Dictionary. Routledge Staff. (Routledge Bilingual Specialist Dictionaries Ser.). 1997. cd-rom 820.00 (978-0-415-13360-9(2)) Pub: Routledge. Dist(s): Taylor and Fran

German Vocabulary, Set. 4 cass. (Learn While You Drive Ser.). (GER.). 1995. 47.95 (3179-AMR) Olivia & Hill.

A wealth of words not covered in the basic courses (2000 words). Specifically designed to increase vocabulary without opening a book.

***German Winko Teddy Bear Flash Cards & Cd.** Compiled by Audio-Forum. (ENG & GER.). (J). 2005. 34.95 (978-1-57970-552-7(9), Audio-For) J Norton Pubs.

German with Ease see O Novo Alemao Sem Custo

German with Ease see Nuevo Aleman sin Esfuerzo

German with Ease see O Novo Alemao Sem Custo

German with Ease: German for English Speakers. 1 cass. (Running Time: 1 hr.). (ENG & GER.). 1997. cass., audio compact disk, audio compact disk 69.95 (978-2-7005-1050-8(X)) Pub: Assimil FRA. Dist(s): Distribks Inc

German with Michel Thomas. (Delux Language Ser.). 2000. 69.95 (978-0-658-00745-3(9), 007459) M-H Contemporary.

German, Wolfgang Altendorf: Eskimomaedchen, Set. unabr. ed. 2 cass. 1994. 19.95 (SGE360) J Norton Pubs.

Novel.

German Woman. unabr. ed. Paul Griner. Read by Anne Flosnik & Michael Page. 1 MP3-CD. (Running Time: 12 hrs.). 2009. 24.99 (978-1-4233-9201-9(9), 9781423392019, Brilliance MP3); 24.99 (978-1-4233-9203-3(5), 9781423392033, BAD); 39.97 (978-1-4233-9202-6(7), 9781423392026, Brinc Audio MP3 Lib); 39.97 (978-1-4233-9204-0(3), 9781423392040, BADLE); audio compact disk 29.99 (978-1-4233-9199-9(3), 9781423391999, Bril Audio CD Unabri); audio compact disk 99.97 (978-1-4233-9200-2(0), 9781423392002, BriAudCD Unabrid) Brilliance Audio.

Germanicus Mosaic. unabr. ed. Rosemary Rowe. Read by Ric Jerrom. 6 cass. (Running Time: 9 hrs.). 2002. 54.95 (978-0-7540-0744-9(8), CAB 2166) AudioGO.

It is 186 AD. Britain is a province of the Roman Empire. The inland tribes have settled into peace, the island is crisscrossed by military roads, and Roman law prevails. In Glevem lives Libertus, a freedman. For years he has been searching for his wife and has just heard of a possible sighting when his patron asks for his help on a murder case. A body has been found in a nearby villa. A slave is missing and the solution to the mystery seems obvious. But nothing is as it appears.

Germany. Robert S. Kane. 1 cass. (Passport's Travel Paks Ser.). bk. & pap. bk. 29.95 incl. vinyl case & map. (978-0-8442-9232-8(X), Passport Bks) McGraw-Hill Trade.

An introduction to the country's culture & customs, plus brief language orientation of common words, phrases & expressions.

Germany. unabr. ed. Ralph Raico. Read by Harry Reasoner et al. 2 cass. (Running Time: 3 hrs.). (World's Political Hot Spots Ser.). 1991. 17.95 Set. (978-0-938935-89-6(5), 10354) Knowledge Prod.

Germany is historically one of the most important of all nations. Since emerging from its days as a Roman province, Germany has had a central role in European affairs.

Germany: Knowledge Products. unabr. ed. Raico Ralph. Read by Reasoner Harry. 2006. audio compact disk 25.95 (978-0-7861-6696-1(7)) Pub: Blckstn Audio. Dist(s): NetLibrary CO

Germany Smarts by Dancing Beetle. Perf. by Eugene Ely. 1 cass. (Running Time: 73 min.). (J). 1994. 10.00 Erthviibz.

German science, myth, ecology & nature sounds come together when Ms. Earthworm & the spunky musical humans read & sing with Dancing Beetle.

Germinal. unabr. ed. Emile Zola. Read by Frederick Davidson. Tr. by Havelock Ellis. 13 cass. (Running Time: 70200 sec.). 1997. 85.95 (978-0-7861-0955-5(6), 1732) Blckstn Audio.

With flawless construction & impeccable detail, Zola chronicles the conflicts, lusts, & deprivation of life in the coal fields of nineteenth-century France. One family, the Maheus, is typical of those in the mining settlements. Father & three of seven children work brutal hours to extract coal 700 meters beneath the earth. Hazards include landslides, fire, & poisoned air. Workers are subject to anemia, black bronchitis, & asthma: their skin is tattooed with coal dust. Despite their toil, the Maheus barely make enough money for food. When their lodger, Etienne, shares ideas of a workers' revolt, the family gradually embraces his plans. Soon the settlement is aflame with resolve to strike for better wages & working conditions.

Germinal. unabr. ed. Emile Zola. Read by Frederick Davidson. (Running Time: 19 mins.). 2007. audio compact disk 120.00 (978-0-7861-5806-5(9)) Blckstn Audio.

Germinal. unabr. ed. Emile Zola. Tr. by Havelock Ellis. (Running Time: 63000 sec.). 2007. audio compact disk 44.95 (978-0-7861-5807-2(7)) Blckstn Audio.

Germinal. unabr. ed. Emile Zola. Read by Frederick Davidson. (YA). 2008. 104.99 (978-1-60514-722-2(2)) Find a World.

Germinal, Pt. 1, Set. Emile Zola. 3 cass. (FRE.). 1995. 31.95 (1709-VSL) Olivia & Hill.

Etienne Lantier, a machinist, is dismissed from his employment for his political views. He finds work in a mining district where workers struggle to survive on starvation wages. Read by a cast of actors.

Germinal, Pt. 2, Set. Emile Zola. 4 cass. (FRE.). 1995. 34.95 (1710-VSL) Olivia & Hill.

Germinal, Pt. 3, Set. Emile Zola. 4 cass. (FRE.). 1995. 34.95 (1711-VSL) Olivia & Hill.

Germinal, Pt. 4, Set. Emile Zola. 3 cass. (FRE.). 1995. 31.95 (1712-VSL) Olivia & Hill.

Germinal, Pts. 1-4, Set. Emile Zola. 14 cass. (FRE.). 1995. 119.95 (1709/12-VSL) Olivia & Hill.

Germinal, Set. unabr. ed. Emile Zola. Read by Frederick Davidson. 13 cass. (Running Time: 1 hr. 30 mins. per cass.). 1996. 85.95 (1732) Blckstn Audio.

With flawless construction & impeccable detail, Zola chronicles the conflicts, lusts, & deprivation of life in the coal fields of nineteenth-century France. One family, the Maheus, is typical of those in the mining settlements. Father & three of seven children work brutal hours to extract coal 700 meters beneath the earth. Hazards include landslides, fire, & poisoned air. Workers are subject to anemia, black bronchitis, & asthma: their skin is tattooed with coal dust. Despite their toil, the Maheus barely make enough money for food. When their lodger, Etienne, shares ideas of a workers' revolt, the family gradually embraces his plans. Soon the settlement is aflame with resolve to strike for better wages & working conditions.

Germs: Biological Weapons & America's Secret War. abr. ed. Judith Miller. 2004. 15.95 (978-0-7435-4756-7(X)) Pub: S&S Audio. Dist(s): S and S Inc

Germs: Biological Weapons & America's Secret War. abr. ed. Judith Miller et al. 1 CD. audio compact disk 30.00 S&S Audio.

Geronimo. unabr. ed. Alexander B. Adams. Narrated by Richard Poe. 8 cass. (Running Time: 11 hrs.). 1999. 70.00 (978-1-55690-848-4(2), 93216E7) Recorded Bks.

Biography of the Apache chieftain who came to national attention in 1885 for leading his people against the white man.

Geronimo, Level 1. 2 cass. (Running Time: 1 hr. 30 mins.). (SmartReader Ser.). (J). 1999. pap. bk. & tchr. ed. 19.95 (978-0-7887-0764-3(7), 79348T3) Recorded Bks.

As a fearless champion of his Native American people, Geronimo became a legend through his courage & determination.

Geronimo, Level 2. 2 cass. (Running Time: 1 hr. 30 mins.). (SmartReader Ser.). (J). 1999. pap. bk. & tchr. ed. 19.95 (978-0-7887-0127-6(4), 79315T3) Recorded Bks.

Geronimo: His Own Story. unabr. ed. S. M. Barrett. Read by Pat Bottino. 3 cass. (Running Time: 4 hrs.). 1999. 23.95 (978-0-7861-1659-1(5), 2487) Blckstn Audio.

Contains the authentic testament of a remarkable "war shaman" who for several years held off both Mexico & the U. S. in fierce defense of Apache lands. During 1905 & 1906, Geronimo, the legendary Apache warrior & honorary war chief, dictated his story through a native interpreter to S. M. Barrett.

Geronimo: His Own Story. unabr. ed. S. M. Barrett. Read by Pat Bottino. (Running Time: 12600 sec.). 2008. audio compact disk & audio compact disk 33.00 (978-1-4332-3442-2(4)) Blckstn Audio.

Geronimo: His Own Story: The Autobiography of a Great Patriot Warrior. unabr. ed. Read by Pat Bottino. Ed. by S. M. Barrett. (Running Time: 12600 sec.). 2008. audio compact disk & audio compact disk 19.95 (978-1-4332-3443-9(2)) Blckstn Audio.

Geronimo Stilton, Bks. 17 & 18. Geronimo Stilton. Narrated by Bill Lobley. (Geronimo Stilton Ser.). (ENG.). (J). (gr. 2-5). 2009. audio compact disk 19.95 (978-0-545-13863-5(9)) Scholastic Inc.

Geronimo Stilton, Nos. 11-12. Geronimo Stilton. Narrated by Billy J. Lobley. (ENG.). (J). (gr. 2-5). 2008. audio compact disk 19.99 (978-0-545-02879-0(5)) Scholastic Inc.

***Geronimo Stilton, Nos. 20 & 21.** Geronimo Stilton. (ENG.). 2010. audio compact disk 29.99 (978-0-545-20310-4(4)) Scholastic Inc.

***Geronimo Stilton, Nos. 20 & 21.** Geronimo Stilton. Narrated by Bill Lobley. (ENG.). 2010. audio compact disk 19.99 (978-0-545-20309-8(0)) Scholastic Inc.

Geronimo Stilton: Lost Treasure of the Emerald Eye, The Curse of the Cheese Pyramid & Cat & Mouse in a Haunted House, Bks. 1-3. Geronimo Stilton. Read by Edward Herrmann. 2 cass. (J). 2004. 23.00 (978-1-4000-9121-8(7), Listening Lib); audio compact disk 25.50 (978-1-4000-9488-2(7), Listening Lib) Pub: Random Audio Pubg. Dist(s): NetLibrary CO

Geronimo Stilton: Lost Treasure of the Emerald Eye, The Curse of the Cheese Pyramid & Cat & Mouse in a Haunted House, Bks. 1-3. unabr. ed. Geronimo Stilton. Read by Edward Herrmann. 3 CDs. (Running Time: 3 hrs.). (ENG.). (J). (gr. 1). 2004. audio compact disk 25.00 (978-0-307-20691-6(2), ImaginStudio) Pub: Random Audio Pubg. Dist(s): Random

Originally released in Italy, the Geronimo Stilton books have been translated into 35 languages, and the rights have been sold in over 175 countries. In less than three years, the books have become the most popular children's books in Italy, with over 1.6 million copies in print. Book #1 - LOST TREASURE OF THE EMERALD EYE It all started when my sister, Thea, discovered an old, mysterious map . . . Book #2 - THE CURSE OF THE CHEESE PYRAMID It was a dream come true - I was off to Egypt to interview a famous archaeologist! A crabby old camel took me across the desert to the Cheese Pyramid . . . Book #3 - CAT AND MOUSE IN A HAUNTED HOUSE Lost in a dark, spooky forest, I quickly discovered that it was haunted - by cats! And in this case, curiosity almost killed the mouse . . . Book #4 - I'M TOO FOND OF MY FUR When my old friend Professor von Volt called to ask for help, I trekked halfway around the world to Mouse Everest and then was kidnapped by a yeti!.

Geronimo Stilton: Red Pizzas for a Blue Count; Attack of the Bandit Cats; A Fabumouse Vacation for Geronimo, Bks. 7-9. unabr. ed. Geronimo Stilton. Read by Edward Herrmann. 2 cass. (Running Time: 3 hrs. 2 mins.). (J). (gr. 2-4). 2005. 23.00 (978-0-307-24572-4(1)); audio compact disk 30.00 (978-0-307-24573-1(X)) Books on Tape.

Geronimo Stilton: The Phantom of the Subway - The Temple of the Ruby of Fire. unabr. ed. Geronimo Stilton. Read by Bill Lobley. 2 CDs. (Running Time: 2 hrs. 25 mins.). (Geronimo Stilton Ser.: Nos. 13-14). (ENG.). (J). (gr. 2-5). 2007. audio compact disk 19.99 (978-0-545-02880-6(9)) Scholastic Inc.

Geronimo Stilton: #4: I'm Too Fond of My Fur; #5: Four Mice Deep in the Jungle; #6: Paws Off, Cheddarface!, Bks. 4-6. unabr. ed. Geronimo Stilton. Read by Edward Herrmann. 3 CDs. (Running Time: 3 hrs.). (J). (ps-3). 2005. audio compact disk 19.55 (978-0-307-20687-9(4)); 23.00 (978-1-4000-9870-5(X)) Books on Tape.

Book #4 I'M TOO FOND OF MY FUR! When my old friend Professor von Volt called to ask for help, I agreed immediately - even though it meant trekking halfway around the world to Mouse Everest! The trip was long and dangerous. I almost froze my tail off along the way. And then I was kidnapped by a yeti! Yes, it was truly an amazing adventure . . . Book #5 FOUR MICE DEEP IN THE JUNGLE I have never been a brave mouse . . . but lately, my fears were taking over my life! So Thea and Trap decided to cure me. They dragged me away on an airplane (I'm afraid of flying!) all the way to the jungle. There I was forced to eat bug soup, climb trees as tall as skyscrapers, swim in raging rivers, and even wrangle snakes. How would a 'fraidy mouse like me every survive? Book #6 PAWS OFF, CHEDDARFACE! Holey cheese, it was strange! Rodents kept telling me I'd done things I had not memory of. Was I going crazy? Had the cheese finally slipped off my cracker? No, I soon discovered the truth: There was a Geronimo look-a-like going around, pretending to be me! Worst of all, he was trying to take of The Rodent's Gazette! I had to get that greedy impostor's paws off my newspaper, but how? From the Cassette edition.

Geronimo Stilton Bks. 7-9: Red Pizzas for a Blue Count, Attack of the Bandit Cats, a Fabumouse Vacation for Gernimo. unabr. ed. Geronimo Stilton. Read by Edward Herrmann. 3 CDs. (Running Time: 10920 sec.). (ENG.). (J). (gr. 1-5). 2005. audio compact disk 25.00 (978-0-307-24521-2(7), ImaginStudio) Pub: Random Audio Pubg. Dist(s): Random

Geronimo Stilton Books 13 And 14: The Phantom of the Subway/the Temple of the Ruby of Fire. Geronimo Stilton. Read by Bill Lobley. (Running Time: 8700 sec.). (Geronimo Stilton Ser.: Nos. 13-14). (ENG.). (J). (gr. 2-5). 2007. audio compact disk 29.95 (978-0-545-02883-7(3)) Scholastic Inc.

Geronimo Stilton #11-12. Geronimo Stilton. (ENG.). (J). (gr. 2-5). 2008. audio compact disk 29.95 (978-0-545-03326-8(8)) Scholastic Inc.

Geronimo Stilton #11-12 - It's Halloween, You 'Fraidy Mouse!/ Merry Christmas, Geronimo! It's Halloween, You 'Fraidy Mouse!; Merry Christmas, Geronimo! unabr. ed. Geronimo Stilton. Read by Bill Lobley. (J). 2008. 34.99 (978-1-60514-723-9(0)) Find a World.

Geronimo Stilton #13-#14 - the Phantom of the Subway/ the Temple of the Ruby Fire. unabr. ed. Geronimo Stilton. Read by Bill Lobley. (J). 2007. 34.99 (978-1-60252-902-1(7)) Find a World.

Gerry Mulligan. Read by Gerry Mulligan. 1 cass. (Running Time: 60 min.). (Marian McPartland's Piano Jazz Ser.). 13.95 (MM-87-04-09, HarperThor) HarpC GBR.

Gershwin CD Collection. Perf. by Fred Astaire. 2 CDs. (Running Time: 8 hrs. 45 mins.). 1999. audio compact disk 25.98 (E6690) Video Collection.

Features selections never before offered.

Gertrude Mccluck, Chicken in Charge: The Missing Eggs. Cyndi Gernhart. Read by Cyndi Gernhart. Illus. by Carlie Gernhart. 1. (Running Time: 25 mins.). (J). 2006. 10.00 (978-0-9778240-5-2(5)) Prairie Winds Pub.

Gertrude McFuzz see Dr. Seuss Audio Collection

Gertrude Stein Reads. abr. ed. Gertrude Stein. Read by Gertrude Stein. 1 cass. (Running Time: 50 min.). 1996. 12.00 (978-0-694-51761-9(5), CPN 1050) HarperCollins Pubs.

Gertrude Stein Reads from Her Works. unabr. ed. Gertrude Stein. Read by Gertrude Stein. 1 cass. Incl. If I Told Him: A Completed Portrait of Picasso. (V 1050); Madame Recamier: An Opera. (V 1050); Making of Americans: Pts. I & II. (V 1050); Matisse. (V 1050); Valentine to Sherwood Anderson. (V 1050); (J). 1984. 11.95 (978-1-55994-104-4(9), V 1050) HarperCollins Pubs.

Gesamtwerk in Sieben Baende: Band 1: Gedichte, Band 2: Gedichte, Band 3: Dramen, Band 4: Erzaehlungen, Band 5: Vermischte Prosa, Band 6: Mein Leben bis zum Kriege, Band 7: Als Mariner im Krieg, Set. Joachim Ringelnatz. (GER.). 1994. (978-3-257-06040-9(8)) Diogenes Verlag CHE.

Gestalt & Pastoral Care. 1 cass. (Care Cassettes Ser.: Vol. 10, No. 1). 1983. 10.80 Assn Prof Chaplains.

Gestalt Therapy: Lecture - Demonstration. unabr. ed. James Simkin. 1 cass. (Running Time: 59 min.). 1971. 11.00 (04403) Big Sur Tapes.

Drawing on his own experiences, Simkin gives an introduction to Gestalt therapy & then goes on to demonstrate Gestalt awareness training by working directly with some individuals.

Gestalt Therapy: Working Through Negative Feelings. Claudio Naranjo. 1 cass. 1999. 11.00 (04208) Big Sur Tapes.

Esalen Institute.

Gestalt Therapy & How It Works. Frederick Perls. 1 cass. (Running Time: 60 min.). 1966. 11.00 Big Sur Tapes.

Gestalt Training: The Psychology of Self-Regulating Success. Bruce Aaron. 6 cass. (Running Time: 6 hrs.). 1992. 59.95 set. (299A) Nightingale-Conant.

Gestalt Workshop: Contact & Support. unabr. ed. Laura Perls. 1 cass. 1973. 11.00 (07501) Big Sur Tapes.

The exploration of the value of sympathetic support in a group environment.

Gestapo Crows: Holocaust Poems. Louis Daniel Brodsky. 1993. 19.95 (978-1-877770-78-4(7)) Time Being Bks.

Gestiefelte Kater und Das. Schneiderlein. pap. bk. 20.95 (978-88-7754-962-4(9)) Pub: Cideb ITA. Dist(s): Distribks Inc

Gestures of Love Deck & Disc. 2002. pap. bk. 14.95 (978-1-931918-03-9(1)) Compass Labs.

***Gesturing.** unabr. ed. John Updike. Read by John Updike. (ENG.). 2009. (978-0-06-196240-6(0), Caedmon) HarperCollins Pubs.

***Gesturing: A Selection from the John Updike Audio Collection.** unabr. ed. John Updike. Read by John Updike. (ENG.). 2009. (978-0-06-196239-4(2), Caedmon) HarperCollins Pubs.

Gesundheit! Bringing Good Health to You, the Medical System & Society Through Physician Service, Complementary Therapies, Humor & Joy. unabr. ed. Patch Adams & Maureen Mylander. Read by Arte Johnson. 4 cass. (Running Time: 6 hrs.). 1999. 24.95 (978-1-57453-315-6(0)) Audio Lit.

In 1971, Patch Adams challenged the foundations of modern medicine by establishing the Gesundheit Institute in West Virginia, dedicated to the belief that medical care should be personal, humane, fun & free.

Get a Brand or Die a Generic: How to achieve Exponential Personal & Professional Success. Michael Brown. (ENG.). 2009. 14.95 (978-0-9818958-7-1(5)) Pub: Acanthus Pubg. Dist(s): AtlasBooks

Get a Clue. Matthew Richardson. 1 cass. 1996. 9.95 (978-1-57008-241-2(3), Bkcraft Inc) Deseret Bk.

Get a financial Life. Beth Kobliner. 2004. 7.95 (978-0-7435-4757-4(8)) Pub: S&S Audio. Dist(s): S and S Inc

Get a Good Start. Georgiana Liccione Stewart. 1 cass. (J). 2001. pap. bk. 10.95 (KIM 7054C); pap. bk. 14.95 (KIM 7054CD); pap. bk. & stu. ed. 11.95 (KIM 7054) Kimbo Educ.
What better way to start your children's day than with fun & simple aerobic activities ideal for the very young. Short & easy exercises develop kids physically as they naturally respond to music & movement. Help kids "get a good start" with favorites like Warm Up Tim, I Can Do More, Jumping Jack, Bendable, Stretchable, Simon Says Jog Along, Ready, Set, Go, Angels in the Snow & more. Includes guide.

Get-a-Job Book. 2nd abr. ed. Dawn Rosenburg McKay. Narrated by Michael Coon. (Running Time: 18000 sec.). (Everything Bks.). (ENG.). 2007. audio compact disk 19.99 (978-1-59859-192-7(4)) Oasis Audio.

Get A Job... NOW!!! Handbook for the Job Seeker AUDIO EDITION. Speeches. 1. (Running Time: 2 hrs. 18 mins). Dramatization. 2006. Rental 19.95 (978-0-9767888-1-2(0)) So Pub.
Get A Job...NOW!!! Handbook For The Job Seeker give you the tools necessary to find a job quickly and never be without a job again. This audio book covers the three biggest biggest challanges the unemployed have: How to use the Phone, How to Interview and How to Network.

Get a Life. Jeff Davidson. (ENG.). 2004. audio compact disk 19.95 (978-1-60729-115-2(0)) Breath Space Inst.

Get a Life: Live & Work at a Comfortable Pace. Jeff Davidson. 1999. 17.95 (978-1-60729-216-6(5)) Breath Space Inst.

Get a Life! Living & Working at a Comfortable Pace in a High-Speed World. Jeff Davidson. 2 cass. (Smart Tapes Ser.). (gr. 10 up). 1997. pap. bk. 19.99 (978-1-55678-066-0(4), 3290) Oasis Audio.

Get a Raise in 7 Days. abr. ed. Caryl Krannich & Ron Krannich. 2 cass. (Running Time: 3 hrs.). 2002. 16.95 (978-1-885408-78-5(1)) Listen & Live.
Step-by-step audiobook that outlines exactly what to do and say in order to get raises and promotions.

Get Acquainted with God. Kenneth W. Hagin, Jr. 1 cass. 4.95 (SJ01) Faith Lib Pubns.

Get an Edge: Be the Clear Choice of Employers. 5 CD's. (Running Time: 4 Hrs. 30 Mins). 2001. audio compact disk 64.99 (978-0-9716280-0-7(9)) Keenan Enterp.
Complete with workbook and sample marketing documents.

Get Anyone to Do Anything. abr. ed. David J. Lieberman. 2 CDs. (Running Time: 13 hrs. 0 mins. 0 sec.). (ENG.). 2002. audio compact disk 19.95 (978-0-7435-2285-4(0), Sound Ideas) Pub: S&S Audio. Dist(s): S and S Inc
Explains how to see through people, how to avoid being manipulated and how to get the upper hand in every situation.

Get Anything You Want. Michael P. Kelly. 1 cass. 1992. 14.95 (978-1-883700-13-3(2)) ThoughtForms.
Self help.

Get Around to It. Paul R. Scheele. 1 cass. (Running Time: 40 min.). (Paraliminal Tapes Ser.). 24.95 (978-0-925480-09-5(6)) Learn Strategies.
Guides to eliminate procrastination as one realigns priorities.

Get BIG Results from your small Ad Budget: More Bang for Your Marketing Buck. Clay Campbell. 2007. audio compact disk 12.95 (978-1-932226-59-1(1)) Wizard Acdmy.

Get by in French. 2 cass. (YA). 1991. pap. bk. & stu. ed. 79.95 (978-1-55980-478-3(5)) Ambrose Video.
Quick learning system for travelers uses sight, sound & exercises to help you leam French.

Get by in German. 2 cass. (YA). 1991. pap. bk. & stu. ed. 79.95 (978-1-55980-475-2(0)) Ambrose Video.
Quick learning system for travelers uses sight, sound & exercises to help you leam German.

Get by in Italian. 2 cass. (YA). 1991. pap. bk. & stu. ed. 79.95 (978-1-55980-477-6(7)) Ambrose Video.
Quick learning system for travelers uses sight, sound & exercises to help you leam Italian.

Get by in Spanish. 2 cass. (YA). 1991. pap. bk. & stu. ed. 79.95 (978-1-55980-476-9(9)) Ambrose Video.
Quick learning system for travelers uses sight, sound & exercises to help you leam Spanish.

***Get Capone: The Secret Plot That Captured America's Most Wanted Gangster.** unabr. ed. Jonathan Eig. (Running Time: 16 hrs. 0 mins.). 2010. 20.99 (978-1-4001-8531-3(9)); 39.99 (978-1-4001-9531-2(4)) Tantor Media.

***Get Capone: The Secret Plot That Captured America's Most Wanted Gangster.** unabr. ed. Jonathan Eig. Narrated by Dick Hill. (Running Time: 17 hrs. 30 mins. 0 sec.). (ENG.). 2010. 29.99 (978-1-4001-6531-5(8)); audio compact disk 79.99 (978-1-4001-4531-7(7)); audio compact disk 39.99 (978-1-4001-1531-0(0)) Pub: Tantor Media. Dist(s): IngramPubServ

Get Dumped Before it Matters (an Essay from Things I've Learned from Women Who've Dumped Me) abr. ed. David Rees. Read by David Rees. Ed. by Ben Karlin. (Running Time: 15 mins.). (ENG.). 2008. 1.98 (978-1-60024-351-6(7)) Pub: Hachet Audio. Dist(s): HachBkGrp

Get Everything You Want from a Networking Group... & More! Speeches. Michael J. Hughes. 1 CD. (Running Time: 27 mins). 2005. audio compact disk 18.47 (978-1-895186-33-8(1)) Multi-Media ON CAN.
In this first installment from the Four Cornerstones of Networking Success, author Michael J. Hughes, known as Canada?s Networking Guru, shows you how to choose the perfect networking group for you, and then how to maximize your involvement to achieve results. In this recording, the author shares his most useful information, insights, and patented networking strategies.The success of your involvement with any group is based on the ability to tum your investment into results. Discover networking group success strategies that lead to immediate and long-term payoffs. Guaranteed.

Get Going. 1 cass. 1985. 6.50 Set. (978-0-88684-033-4(3)) Listen USA.

Get Healthy Now! Set: A Complete Guide to Prevention, Treatment & Healthy Living. abr. ed. Gary Null. Read by Robert Deyan. 4 cass. (Running Time: 6 hrs.). 1999. 24.95 (978-1-55935-311-3(2), 698852) Soundelux.
Comprehensive guide to alternative health, offering an encyclopedic education on detoxification, prevention, basic & enhanced nutrition, & treatment options. All information is up-to-date, & contains special sections for men, women & seniors.

Get Hooked on the Spirit! (Running Time: 40 min.). Dramatization. 1998. 9.50 (978-0-9669491-1-7(0)) C Ulrich.
Motivational speech given to church groups, recovery groups & chronic pain groups.

Get in the Game. abr. ed. Vanessa Summers. 2 cass. (Running Time: 2 hrs. 30 min.). (Smart Audio Ser.). 2004. 19.99 (978-1-58926-089-4(9), B62L-010D) Oasis Audio.
As a mentor to her peer group and speaking from her own experience, author Vanessa Summers is well equipped to help young women develop a sense of confidence and competence about their money matters.

Get in the Game. unabr. ed. Vanessa Summers. 2 CDs. (Running Time: 2 hrs. 30 min.). (Smart Audio Ser.). 2003. audio compact disk 19.99 (978-1-58926-090-0(2), B62L-010D) Oasis Audio.

Get Lost in Jerusalem. unabr. ed. Ted A. Hildebrandt. 2000. audio compact disk 29.99 (978-0-310-23789-1(0)) Zondervan.

Get More Joy Out of Sex: Female. Barrie Konicov. 1 cass. 11.98 (978-0-87082-326-8(4), 049) Potentials.
Explains why many of us are so uptight & confused that we cannot fully & freely enjoy the giving & receiving of sexual pleasure, & then shows how sex life is a beautiful facet of a fullfilling life.

Get More Joy Out of Sex: Male. Barrie Konicov. 1 cass. 11.98 (978-0-87082-327-5(2), 050) Potentials.
Explains why many of us are so uptight & confused that we cannot fully enjoy the giving & receiving of sexual pleasure. He then shows how sex life is a beautiful facet of a fulfilling life.

Get Motivated! 17.95 (826AK) Nightingale-Conant.
Helps you rid yourself of bad habits you want to lose & develop the positive behavior patterns that will lead to a better, happier & more productive life.

Get Motivated! Overcome Any Obstacle, Achieve Any Goal & Accelerate Your Success with Motivational DNA. abr. unabr. ed. Tamara Lowe. Read by Tamara Lowe. (ENG.). 2009. audio compact disk 29.95 (978-0-7393-8339-1(6), Random AudioBks) Pub: Random Audio Pubg. Dist(s): Random

Get off the Bench. Matthew Richardson. 1 cass. 1997. 9.95 (Bkcraft Inc) Deseret Bk.

Get off the Phone & Drive. unabr. ed. Dan Chopin. 1 cass. 6.95; audio compact disk 10.95 Wildstone Media.
Comedy songs & standup from one of the country's most popular comics. Titles included "Get off the Phone & Drive F," "Mobile Home Man," "Surfing With A Woody" & more.

Get off the Porch: 31 Daily Reminders to Get Motivated to Prosper. Michael A. Phillips. (ENG., 2007. pap. bk. 11.95 (978-1-934746-00-4(2)) New Des.

Get off Your But: How to End Self-Sabotage & Stand up for Yourself. unabr. ed. Sean Stephenson. Read by Sean Stephenson. (Running Time: 5 hrs.). (ENG.). 2009. 24.98 (978-1-59659-418-0(7), GildAudio) Pub: Gildan Media. Dist(s): HachBkGrp

Get on Board, Children. Arranged by Otis Skillings. Lyrics by Janette Smart. Music by Terry Camsey. 1 cass. (Running Time: 25 min.). (J). 1976. 12.99 (TA-7137C) Lillenas.
A classic children's musical that is still as fun, singable & relevant as it was at its premiere. Charming & imaginative work depicting life on Noah's ark, with unison/optional 2-part arrangements. A cast of six, plus choir & narrator, presents a biblical lesson on faith.

Get on Board, Children. Arranged by Otis Skillings. Music by Terry Camsey. Lyrics by Janette Smart. 1 cass. (Running Time: 25 min.). (J). 1986. 80.00 (MU-7137C) Lillenas.
A classic children's musical that is still as fun, singable & relevant as it was at its premiere. A charming & imaginative work depicting life on Noah's are, with unison/optional 2-part arrangements. A cast of six, plus choir & narrator, presents a biblical lesson on faith.

Get on the Bus Pt. 1: Acts 16:9. Ed Young. 1998. 4.95 (978-0-7417-2178-5(3), A1178) Win Walk.

Get on the Rock & Roll over Music CD. Perf. by Ken Norberg. 2005. audio compact disk 14.99 (978-0-9771318-8-4(2)) Pub: Hope Harvest Pub. Dist(s): Baker Taylor

Get on with It: Live. Chumbawamba. (Running Time: 0 hr. 53 mins. 0 sec.). (PM Audio Ser.). (ENG.). 2008. audio compact disk 14.99 (978-1-60486-001-6(4)) Pub: Pm Pre. Dist(s): IPG Chicago

Get Organized. unabr. ed. Matthew Parvis. Read by Matthew Parvis. 1 cass. (Self-Help Ser.). 1986. bk. 9.95 (978-0-07-048701-7(4), TDM 1103) HarperCollins Pubs.
Improving organizational skills can lead a more effective & less stressful personal & professional life & in this program Parvis details exactly what the benefits of strong organization are, outlines the steps to take & the techinques to master in order to achieve an effective level of organization.

Get Organized the Clear & Simple Way: Reclaim Your Home, Your Office, Your Life. unabr. rev. ed. Marla Dee. Read by Marla Dee. (Running Time: 8 hrs.). (ENG.). 2007. audio compact disk 29.98 (978-1-59659-077-9(7), GildAudio) Pub: Gildan Media. Dist(s): HachBkGrp

Get Out of Debt. Ed. by Socrates Media Editors. 2005. audio compact disk 29.95 (978-1-59546-100-1(0)) Pub: Socrates Med LLC. Dist(s): Midpt Trade

Get Out of My Life, but First Could You Drive Me & Cheryl to the Mall. 2nd abr. ed. Anthony E. Wolf. Read by Anthony E. Wolf. 2 CDs. (Running Time: 2 hrs. 30 mins. 0 sec.). (ENG.). 2008. audio compact disk 14.95 (978-1-4272-0657-2(0)) Pub: Macmill Audio. Dist(s): Macmillan

Get Out of My Life, but First Could You Drive Me & Cheryl to the Mall? A Parent's Guide to the New Teenager, unabr. ed. Anthony E. Wolf. Narrated by George Guidall. 4 cass. (Running Time: 6 hrs.). 1996. 35.00 (978-0-7887-0672-1(1), 94849E7) Recorded Bks.
Focuses on the legendary tasks all parents must face: raising teenagers. Not only defines the physical & mental changes of growing up, but also illustrates ways to effectively deal with problems ranging from intermittent defiance to drug use & suicide.

Get Out of That Pit: Straight Talk about God's Deliverance. unabr. ed. Beth Moore. Read by Beth Moore. (Running Time: 16800 sec.). 2007. audio compact disk 26.99 (978-1-59145-581-3(2)) Nelson.

Get Out of Town: Acts 23:12-35. Ed Young. 2000. 4.95 (978-0-7417-2250-8(X), 1250) Win Walk.

Get over It: 12 Sure-Fire Ways to Earn Less, Stress More & Get Left Behind the Global Economy. Karl G. Schoemer. Read by Gary Applegate. 1 cass. (Running Time: 31 mins.). 1998. (978-1-929037-07-0(4)) KGS Inc.
Eliminating excuses & taking personal responsibility.

Get Paid More & Promoted Faster: 21 Great Ways to Get Ahead in Your Career. unabr. ed. Brian Tracy. (Running Time: 1 hr.). (ENG.). 2008. 9.98 (978-1-59659-222-3(2), GildAudio) Pub: Gildan Media. Dist(s): HachBkGrp

Get Ready for Boston! Exploring Boston & Its Neighborhoods in Songs, Poems, & Stories. Created by Judith W. Steinbergh. Selected by Judith W. Steinbergh & Victor Cockburn. Prod. by Victor Cockburn. Teresa Flavin. (ENG., (J). 2002. pap. bk. 29.95 (978-0-944941-09-6(5)) Talking Stone Pr.

Get Ready for Company: How to Welcome Guests to Your Church & Develop a Follow-Up Program to Keep Them Coming Back. Gary McIntosh. Ed. by Cindy G. Spear. 1997. pap. bk. 54.95 (978-1-57052-070-9(4)) Chrch Grwth VA.

Get Ready for Miracles. As told by Markus Bishop. 3 cass. (Running Time: 1 hr. 30 mins.). 2000. 15.00 (978-0-9628301-5-0(1)) M Bishop Minis.

Get Ready for Second Grade, Amber Brown. Paula Danzinger. Illus. by Tony Ross. 14 vols. (Running Time: 14 mins.). 2003. pap. bk. 31.95 (978-1-59112-562-4(6)) Live Oak Media.

Get Ready for Second Grade, Amber Brown. Paula Danzinger. Illus. by Tony Ross. 11 vols. (Running Time: 14 mins.). (Readalongs for Beginning Readers Ser.). (J). 2003. bk. 25.95 (978-1-59112-234-0(1)); pap. bk. 16.95 (978-1-59112-233-3(3)); pap. bk. 29.95 (978-1-59112-235-7(X)); 9.95 (978-1-59112-232-6(5)) Live Oak Media.

Get Ready for Second Grade, Amber Brown. Paula Danzinger. Illus. by Tony Ross. (Running Time: 14 mins.). (J). (gr. k-3). 2003. 12.95 (978-1-59112-363-7(1)) Live Oak Media.

Get Ready... Get Set... Date! Michael W. Allred. 1 cass. 7.98 (978-1-55503-784-0(4), 06004989) Covenant Comms.
Insights on whos, whys & hows of dating.

Get Ready, Get Set, Sing! Songs for Early Childhood. Sarah Barchas. Illus. by David Hoffman & Elizabeth Gething. (Running Time: 52 min.). (J). (ps-3). 1994. pap. bk. 12.95 (978-0-9632621-1-0(4)); pap. bk. 15.98 (978-0-9632621-2-7(2)) High Haven Mus.

Get Ready to Square Dance. 1 cass. (J). (gr. k-6). 2001. pap. bk. 11.95 (EA 68C); pap. bk. 14.95 (EA 68CD) Kimbo Educ.
8 easy song & movement games teach beginning square dance patterns. Cotton-Eyed Joe, Oh Belinda, Shoo Fly, Turkey in the Straw, Comin' Round the Mountain & more. Includes guide.

Get Real. unabr. ed. Donald E. Westlake. Read by William Dufris. 6 CDs. (Running Time: 7 hrs.). 2009. audio compact disk 69.95 (978-0-7927-6389-5(0)) AudioGO.

Get Real, Get Rich: Conquer the 7 Lies Blocking You from Success. Farrah Gray. Read by Farrah Gray. (Playaway Adult Nonfiction Ser.). 2008. 74.99 (978-1-60640-897-1(6)) Find a World.

Get Real, Get Rich: Conquer the 7 Lies Blocking You from Success. unabr. ed. Farrah Gray. (Running Time: 7 hrs.). 2007. 39.25 (978-1-4233-5155-9(X), 9781423351559, BADLE) Brilliance Audio.

Get Real, Get Rich: Conquer the 7 Lies Blocking You from Success. unabr. ed. Farrah Gray. Read by Farrah Gray. 1 MP3-CD. (Running Time: 7 hrs.). 2007. 39.25 (978-1-4233-5153-5(3), 9781423351535, Brinc Audio MP3 Lib); 24.95 (978-1-4233-5154-2(1), 9781423351542, BAD); 74.25 (978-1-4233-5149-8(5), 9781423351498, BrilAudUnabridg); audio compact disk 82.25 (978-1-4233-5151-1(7), 9781423351511, BriAudCD Unabrid); audio compact disk 24.95 (978-1-4233-5152-8(5), 9781423351528, Brilliance MP3); audio compact disk 29.95 (978-1-4233-5150-4(9), 9781423351504, Bril Audio CD Unabri) Brilliance Audio.

***Get Rich Quick Club.** unabr. ed. Dan Gutman. Read by Angela Goethals. (ENG.). 2005. (978-0-06-083501-9(X), Harper Audio); (978-0-06-083502-6(8), Harper Audio) HarperCollins Pubs.

Get Rid of Guilt. 1 cass. 10.00 (978-1-58506-016-0(X), 43) New Life Inst OR.
Smash your guilty feelings that imprison you & enjoy life.

Get Rid of the Performance Review! How Companies Can Stop Intimidating, Start Managing - And Focus on What Really Matters. unabr. ed. Samuel A. Culbert. Told to Lawrence Rout. (Running Time: 7 hrs.). (ENG.). 2010. audio compact disk 26.98 (978-1-60788-175-9(6)) Pub: Hachet Audio. Dist(s): HachBkGrp

Get Rid of the Performance Review! How Companies Can Stop Intimidating, Start Managing - and Focus on What Really Matters. unabr. ed. Samuel A. Culbert. Read by Samuel A. Culbert. Told to Lawrence Rout. (Running Time: 7 hrs.). (ENG.). 2010. 18.98 (978-1-60788-176-6(4)) Pub: Hachet Audio. Dist(s): HachBkGrp

Get Rid of Time-off Ted, Attitude Alice, & Slacker Sam: How to Legally Terminate Employees. PUEI. 2007. audio compact disk 199.00 (978-1-934147-18-4(4), CareerTrack) P Univ E Inc.

Get Set for School Sing Along. Lyrics by Jan Z. Olsen. Music by Emily Knapton. Emily Knapton. Voice by Cathy Fink & Marcy Marxer. Lyrics by Bill Wellington. Music by Bill Wellington. 2003. stu. ed. 12.95 (978-1-891627-42-2(2)) Handwriting.

Get Shorty. unabr. ed. Elmore Leonard. Read by Alexander Adams. 8 cass. (Running Time: 8 hrs.). 1992. 64.00 (978-0-7366-2222-6(5), 3012) Books on Tape.
Hollywood producer is into Miami loan shark Chili Palmer big time. They form an uneasy partnership launching Chili into the movie biz. The only problem is someone wants Chili dead.

Get Smart about Investing. Greg McGraime. 2007. audio compact disk 59.95 (978-0-9795255-9-9(4)) Now You Know.

Get Started on Guitar. Chet Atkins & John Knowles. (Stefan Grossman's Guitar Workshop Ser.). 2006. pap. bk. 24.95 (978-0-7866-7484-8(9)) Mel Bay.

***Get Syked Success4Life x 6 CD Series - Shelley Sykes: Get Syked for Life.** 21st ed. 2008. 99.00 (978-0-9775258-6-7(4)) Beautiful AUS.

Get That Job. Betty L. Randolph. (Running Time: 45 min.). (Success Ser.). 1989. bk. 9.98 (978-1-55909-095-7(2) [illegible] Randolph Tapes.

Get the Board Out of Your Eye. 2 cass. [illegible] 2-14, HarperThor) HarpC GBR.

Get the Ring: How to Find & Keep the Right One for Life. Interview. Rosie Einhorn et al. Compiled by David Levine. 6 CDs. (Running Time: 5 hrs. 20 mins.). 2003. audio compact disk 59.00 (978-0-9726215-0-2(4)) Warm Wisdom Pr.

Get the Ring: How to Find & Keep the Right One for Life. Speeches. Rosie Einhorn et al. Compiled by David Levine. 6 cassettes. (Running Time: 5hrs. 20 mins.). 2003. 59.00 (978-0-9726215-1-9(2)); audio compact disk 44.00 (978-0-9726215-2-6(0)) Warm Wisdom Pr.
Greetings. Your search is ending! Now there's no more excuse to put off meeting - and winning - your own soul mate! No more miserable dates! No more broken promises and broken dreams! Finding a loving, lasting relationship just got easier! In this box is all the help you need to avoid making the tragic mistakes that have brought nothing but misery to so many of your friends. Here you will discover the same techniques for finding a mate that have resulted in the most successful marriages... and the lowest divorce rate... in the world! Get The Ring brings together the best advice from seven of today's top counselors and speakers on dating and marriage. It is practical, clear information that can transform your life and help you not only find the Right One, but also build a lasting and loving relationship.

***Get Those Big Dogs off Our Roof!** Sam Johnston & Julie Cook. (Dudley & Beanz Ser.). (ENG., (J). 2009. pap. bk. 16.99 (978-0-9791432-2-9(5)) DudleyCat.

Get to the Concept. Eastern Michigan Gospel Choir. (Running Time: 30 min.). 2003. 11.98 (978-5-553-07929-1(2)) Pub: Pt of Grace Ent. Dist(s): STL Dist NA

Get to the Concert. Eastern Michigan Gospel Choir. (Running Time: 1 hr.). 2003. audio compact disk 16.98 (978-5-553-44845-5(X)) Pub: Pt of Grace Ent. Dist(s): STL Dist NA

Get Together. 2nd ed. Ed. by Oxford Staff. (Get Together Ser.). 2007. audio compact disk 24.50 (978-0-19-451612-9(1)) OUP.

Get Together. 3rd ed. David McKeegan & Susan Iannuzzi. 2003. 22.75 (978-0-19-437498-9(X)) OUP.

Get Together 2. 2nd ed. Ed. by Oxford Staff. (Get Together Ser.). 2007. audio compact disk 24.50 (978-0-19-451613-6(X)) OUP.

Get Unstuck! the Simple Guide to Restart Your Life: Audio Book. Speeches. John Seeley. 1. (Running Time: 1 Hr 9 Min.). 2004. 16.95 (978-0-9749177-6-4(1)) A New Day.

Get Up. Perf. by Oslo Gospel Choir. 1 cass. 1995. audio compact disk Brentwood Music.
Hailing from Oslo, Norway, this choir achieved platinum sales internationally. Co-produced by Andre Crouch, features the popular song, He Will Never Stop Lovin' Me, which they performed on the worldwide televised Billy Graham Crusade.

Get Up & Bar the Door see Poetry of Robert Burns & Border Ballads

Get up & Grow Songs: Feeling Good about Ourselves. Music by Jill Gallina & Michael Gallina. 1 cass. (Running Time: 1 hr.). (J). (ps). 2001. pap. bk. 10.95 (KIM 9135C); pap. bk. & pupil's gde. ed. 11.95 (KIM 9135) Kimbo Educ.

Get Well. 1 cass. 12.98 (978-0-87554-510-3(6), 1108) Valley Sun.
Positive affirmations support healing acceleration. You focus the unlimited power of your mind upon healing your body. Every cell in your body is filled with Divine healing light. Perfect health is your Divine right. Every breath you take contains positive healing energy. The blue healing ray of the Universal light is entering your crown chakra & healing your body and mind. Much, much more.

Get Well Soon. unabr. ed. Julie Halpern. Narrated by Mandy Siegfried. 4 CDs. (Running Time: 5 hrs. 6 mins.). (YA). (gr. 8 up). 2008. audio compact disk 38.00 (978-0-7393-6512-0(6), Listening Lib) Pub: Random Audio Pubg. Dist(s): Random

Get What You Want! Patrick Wanis. Read by Patrick Wanis. (ENG.). 2006. audio compact disk 29.95 (978-0-9779192-4-6(2)) WOW Prods.

Get with the Program! Getting Real about Your Weight, Health, & Emotional Well-Being. abr. ed. Bob Greene. 2004. 11.95 (978-0-7435-4758-1(6)) Pub: S&S Audio. Dist(s): S and S Inc

Get Your Book Published. Jeff Davidson. 1987. 11.95 (978-1-60729-356-9(0)) Breath Space Inst.

***Get Your Dream Job! Job Hunting & Career Success Skills.** unabr. ed. Made for Success. Read by Larry; Hansen, Mark Victor, Bob; Iverson Proctor. (Made for Success Ser.). 2010. audio compact disk 34.95 (978-1-4417-6791-2(6)) Blckstn Audio.

***Get Your Dream Job! (Library Edition) Job Hunting & Career Success Skills.** unabr. ed. Made for Success. Read by Larry; Hansen Proctor. (Running Time: 5 hrs. 30 mins.). (Made for Success Ser.). 2010. audio compact disk 105.00 (978-1-4417-6790-5(8)) Blckstn Audio.

Get Your First Fifty Clients: Fill Your Coaching Practice Without Selling! David Wood. (ENG.). 2002. 39.00 (978-0-9817647-0-2(3)) SolBox.

Get Your Power Back: Find & Remove the Underlying Conditions That Destroy Love & Sabotage Your Life. Bill Ferguson. (Running Time: 9480 sec.). 2008. audio compact disk 21.95 (978-1-878410-42-9(3)) Return Heart.

Getaways, No. 16. 1 cass. (Running Time: 44 min.). (Daydreams Ser.: No. 1). 11.95 (978-0-938586-78-4(5), DD1) Whole Person.
Five guided tours to peaceful places inside the mind. Accompanied by Halpern sounds. Cabin Retreat evokes the solitude & serenity of a mountain hideaway. Night Sky explores the awe & wonder of the infinite expanse of stars. Hot Spring enfolds the listener in the cleansing warmth of bubbling water. Mountain View brings alive the sights & sounds of majestic mountains. Superior Sail refreshes the listener with an invigorating aquatic adventure.

Gets a Little Stranger. collector's ed. Louis Sachar. Read by Louis Sachar. 2 cass. (Running Time: 3 hrs.). (J). 2000. 18.00 (978-0-7366-9007-2(7)) Books on Tape.
It took 243 days to get rid of all the cows & now the wackiest school is open again! But anything can still happen.

Gets a Little Stranger. unabr. ed. Louis Sachar. Read by Louis Sachar. 2 cass. (Running Time: 3 hrs.). (J). (gr. 1-8). 1999. 23.00 (LL 0151, Chivers Child Audio) AudioGO.

Gets a Little Stranger. unabr. ed. Louis Sachar. Read by Louis Sachar. 2 vols. (Running Time: 2 hrs. 58 mins.). (Middle Grade Cassette Librariestm Ser.). (J). (gr. 3-7). 2004. pap. bk. 29.00 (978-0-8072-8141-3(7), S YA 116 SP, Listening Lib); 23.00 (978-0-8072-8140-6(9), BWYA116CX, Listening Lib) Random Audio Pubg.
Well, all the cows are gone & now wacky Wayside School is open again! That may explain the coffee pots, potatoes & pencil sharpeners flying out of the windows of Mrs. Drazil's class. Or the dogs, cats & skunks causing an uproar on the thirtieth floor. After all, this is a place where you can expect anything to happen.

Gets His Man. unabr. ed. Donald J. Sobol. Narrated by Greg Steinbruner. 1 cass. (Running Time: 1 hr. 15 mins.). (J). (gr. 3-6). 2008. 15.75 (978-1-4281-8242-4(X)); audio compact disk 15.75 (978-1-4281-8247-9(0)) Recorded Bks.
For decades, Donald J. Sobol's kid detective Encyclopedia Brown has thrilled amateur sleuths of all ages with his uncanny knack for solving the most difficult mysteries. Sobol was even honored with a special Edgar Award for this timeless series. Ten-year-old Encyclopedia, the son of Idaville's police chief, investigates all sorts of curious cases for kids around the neighborhood - all for 25 cents a day, plus expenses.

***GETTIN' LOOSE with MOTHER GOOSE & Some of Her Silly Friends!** Created by Storytellin' Time. (Running Time: 53 minutes). (ENG.). (J). 2010. audio compact disk 15.00 (978-0-9722213-0-6(1)) Storytellin Time.

Gettin' Old Ain't for Wimps: Inspirations & Stories to Warm Your Heart & Tickle Your Funny Bone. unabr. ed. Karen O'Connor. Narrated by Karen O'Connor. (ENG.). 2007. 13.99 (978-1-60814-224-8(8)); audio compact disk 19.99 (978-1-59859-278-8(5)) Oasis Audio.

Gettin' Ready for the Miracle: A Christmas Musical for Young Voices. Music by Tom Fettke. Lyrics by Linda Rebuck. 1 cass. (Running Time: 35 min.). (J). 1986. 12.99 (TA-9071C) Lillenas.
What an enjoyable way for kids to celebrate the Christmas event! A musical which combines humor, new songs & traditional carols. Using both contemporary & biblical settings, it brings home the great value of God's Christmas gift to us - His Son. Arranged for unison/optional 2-part choir.

Getting. Paul R. Scheele. 1 cass. (Running Time: 40 min.). (Personal Celebration Ser.). 1992. 9.95 (978-0-925480-78-1(9)) Learn Strategies.
Helps you get whatever you need to succeed.

Getting a Church Started. Elmer L. Towns. 5 cass. 54.95 Set, incl. printed outline of seminar & manual 164p. (350) Chrch Grwth VA.
The Biblical basis of Church planting.

Getting a Good Night's Sleep. John Selby. 2004. 11.95 (978-0-7435-3920-3(6)) Pub: S&S Audio. Dist(s): S and S Inc

Getting a Job: An Easy, Smart Guide to Getting the Right Job. Janet Garber. (B & N Basics Ser.). 2003. audio compact disk 9.98 (978-0-7607-3769-9(X), Silver Lini) M Friedman Pub Grp Inc.

Getting a New Orientation. Swami Amar Jyoti. 1 cass. 1981. 9.95 (C-30) Truth Consciousness.
Are we gratifying our desires in His name? Turning from ego's willfulness to freedom of the soul.

Getting a New, True Perspective. Lynn Scoresby. 1 cass. 2004. 3.95 (978-1-57734-375-2(1), 34441131) Covenant Comms.

Getting Ahead Home: A Communication Skills Course for Business English. 2nd ed. Sarah Jones-Macziola. (Running Time: 1 hr. 9 mins.). (ENG.). 2000. stu. ed. 24.00 (978-0-521-65404-3(1)) Cambridge U Pr.

Getting Ahead Home: A Communication Skills Course for Business English. 2nd ed. Sarah Jones-Macziola. (Running Time: hrs. mins.). (ENG.). 2000. stu. ed. 24.00 (978-0-521-65403-6(3)) Cambridge U Pr.

Getting Ahead Learner's Book: A Communication Skills Course for Business English. 2nd rev. ed. Sarah Jones-Macziola. (Running Time: 5940 sec.). (ENG.). 2000. audio compact disk 25.20 (978-0-521-65402-9(5)) Cambridge U Pr.

Getting Ahead Learner's Book: A Communication Skills Course for Business English. 2nd rev. ed. Sarah Jones-Macziola & Greg White. (Running Time: 1 hr. 40 mins.). (ENG.). 2000. 25.20 (978-0-521-65401-2(7)) Cambridge U Pr.

Getting Along. Kendall F. Haven. Music by Rita Abrams. 1 cass. (J). 1999. bk. 18.95 (30324) Courage-to-Change.
Lessons of sharing, accepting others, being kind, taking care of our things & much more.

Getting Along: A Fun-Filled Set of Stories, Songs & Activities to Help Kids Work & Play Together. Parker Page. Illus. by Mitchell Rose. (Running Time: 60 min.). (J). (ps-5). 1989. bk. 18.95 (978-0-929831-00-8(4)) Childrens TV Resource.

Getting Along: Stories, Songs & Activities to Help Kids Work & Play Together. 1 cass. (Running Time: 60 min.). (J). (ps-5). bk. 14.98 (617) MFLP CA.
These songs offer sympathetic, practical & appropriate alternatives to help kids become more self-confident in their relationships with siblings, classmates & friends.

Getting along in Spanish. Ana C. Jarvis. 2003. (978-0-395-96306-7(0)) CENGAGE Learn.

Getting along with Our Partner. Swami Amar Jyoti. 1 cass. 1978. 9.95 (L-6) Truth Consciousness.
Tackling our problems; starting with ourselves. Learning to forgive. Selfless Karma Yoga & freedom of worship in the family.

Getting & Giving: 1 Cor. 8:1-12. Ed Young. 1986. 4.95 (978-0-7417-1510-4(4), 510) Win Walk.

Getting Articles Published. Jeff Davidson. 1 CD. (Running Time: 57 min.). 2006. audio compact disk 23.95 (978-0-9771296-3-8(2)); audio compact disk (978-1-60729-566-2(0)) Breath Space Inst.

Getting Articles Published. Jeff Davidson. 2006. 22.95 (978-1-60729-340-8(4)) Breath Space Inst.

Getting at the Root of the Matter. 1 cass. (Running Time: 30 min.). 1985. (0261) Evang Sisterhood Mary.
Covers: The Well of Truth; I'm Interested in Everything; Why Can't I Do Anything Right?; Jesus,the Prince of Victory.

Getting Back Brahms. unabr. ed. Mavis Cheek. Read by Kim Hicks. 6 cass. (Running Time: 9 hrs.). 2002. 54.95 (978-0-7540-0837-8(1), CAB 2259) Pub: Chivers Pr GBR. Dist(s): AudioGO

Getting Back to Even. abr. ed. James J. Cramer. Read by James J. Cramer. (Running Time: 6 hrs. 0 mins. 0 sec.). 2009. audio compact disk 29.99 (978-0-7435-9841-5(5)) Pub: S&S Audio. Dist(s): S and S Inc

Getting Back Together: How to Create a New, Loving Relationship & Make It Last. Bettie B. Youngs & Masa Goetz. 6 cass. 29.95 (5012) SyberVision.
Step-by-step program, to help you understand what went wrong, what you really want & how to renew your bond-or prepare you to end your relationship with insight & mutual compassion.

Getting Beyond "Hello" Miss Mingle's Guide to Social Success. abr. ed. Jeanne Martinet. Read by Jeanne Martinet. 2 cass. (Running Time: 2 hrs. 15 min.). 2004. 17.95 (978-1-57270-046-8(7), L21046) Pub: Audio Partners. Dist(s): PerseuPGW
Amusing, proven strategies for social success. Miss Mingle offers answers to actual letters from perplexed inquirers.

Getting Beyond the Party Line, Pt. 1. Ben Young. 1997. 4.95 (978-0-7417-6043-2(6), B0043) Win Walk.

Getting Beyond the Party Line, Pt. 2. Ben Young. 1997. 4.95 (978-0-7417-6044-9(4), B0044) Win Walk.

Getting Bigger. unabr. ed. Perf. by Dave Kinnon. 1 cass., 1 CD. (Running Time: 40 min.). (J). (gr. 1-6). 1997. 9.98 (978-1-881304-03-6(5), SW104-4); audio compact disk 12.98 CD. (978-1-881304-04-3(3), SW104-2) Song Wizard Recs.
Contains background effects that add to the stories which include "Turtle on a Stick," "The Three Spinners," "The Oak & the Linden," "A Drop of Honey," "The Archer," & "The Golden Key".

Getting Business to Come to You, Set. Paul Edwards & Sarah Edwards. 6 cass. 1994. 59.95 (11070PAX) Nightingale-Conant.
In this program, you'll learn how to quickly & effortlessly attract a steady flow of repeat customers without spending time selling or cold calling. It teaches you how to successfully market, advertise, publicize & promote your small or home-based business step-by-step. Ideal for anyone who's self-employed or would like to be, this series gives you hundreds of proven techniques - tactics that have been used profitably by America's most successful small businesses.

Getting by in English: Japanese Language Edition. Pamela J. Sharpe. 2 cass. (Getting by in...Ser.). (JPN & ENG.). 1983. pap. bk. 20.95 (978-0-8120-7155-9(7), BA1557) Pub: Barron. Dist(s): Continental Bk

Getting by in Greek. David Hardy & John Pavlides. 2 cass. (Getting by in...Ser.). 1983. pap. bk. 18.95 (978-0-8120-7153-5(0)) Barron.

Getting by in Italian: A Quick Beginner's Course for Tourists & Business People. 2nd ed. Emmanuela Tandello. 2 cass. 1996. Barron.

Getting by in Turkish: A Quick Beginner's Course in Spoken Turkish for Tourists & Businesspeople. rev. ed. Bengisu Rona. Prod. by Alan Wilding. (Barron's Educational Ser.). 1996. pap. bk. 18.95 (978-0-8120-8454-2(3)) Barron.

Getting Credit & Getting Credit Back. Dennis F. Regan. Read by Dennis F. Regan. 1 cass. (Running Time: 45 min.). 1992. 12.95 incl. guide bklt. (978-1-882991-01-3(X)) Mainst Pubs.
Offers help in obtaining new credit & in restoring credit when faced with financial difficulties. Who to contact & how to go about it.

Getting 'Culture Smart' Mastering the Basics. Sondra Thiederman. Read by Sondra Thiederman. 1 cass. (Running Time: 67 min.). 1995. 9.95 (978-0-9644977-1-9(9)) Cross-Cult Comms.
Designed to teach the basic skills of communicating with those who are different from yourself. Content includes practical tips for overcoming stereotypical thinking & learning about your own culture so as to avoid projecting that culture onto others.

Getting Details Right: A Writer's Primer. Featuring Ken Rand. (ANG.). 2005. (978-1-933846-04-0(6)) Med Man.

Getting down to Business with Your Home Based Business, Vol. 1. unabr. ed. Ilene L. Meckley. 1 cass. (Running Time: 55 min.). 1997. 12.00 (978-1-892464-02-6(0)) Meckley Pubng Co.
How to be successful in a home-based network marketing business.

Getting Even with Dad, Set. abr. ed. Elizabeth Faucher. Read by Saul Rubinek. 2 cass. (Running Time: 3 hrs.). 1994. 16.95 (978-1-56876-026-1(4)) Soundlines Ent.
Ex-convict, Ray Gleason & his accomplices have just committed the perfect crime. They've just stolen a million dollars worth of rare coins. Unfortunately, they picked the wrong week to do it. Eleven-year old Tim Gleason has just dropped in on his dad, & after a life time of being ignored he's finally found a way of getting even. The men think they can outsmart Timmy, but he's got a few tricks up his sleeve.

***Getting Fired for the Glory of God: Collected Words of Mike Yaconelli for Youth Workers.** Mike Yaconelli. (Running Time: 2 hrs. 34 mins. 0 sec.). (ENG.). 2008. 16.99 (978-0-310-30240-7(4)) Zondervan.

Getting Fit. (For Your Information Ser.). 1993. 16.00 (978-1-56420-024-2(8)) New Readers.

Getting Fit Before, During & after Pregnancy. Shapprell L. Dallas. Read by Shapprell L. Dallas. Ed. by Patrick Dallas. Photos by Patrick Dallas. 2 cass. (Running Time: 2 hrs.). 2002. 19.95 (978-0-9718839-0-1(4)) Top Bodies Fitness.
Fitness and nutrition tips for getting healthy before, during and after childbirth. A motivational and inspirational book for all women.

Getting Funded ! Making a Successful Business. Speeches. Mervin Evans & Lynette Bigelow. 2 CD-Audio. (Running Time: 100 M). 2007. audio compact disk 99.99 (978-0-914391-65-4(8)) Comm People Pr.

Getting Funded Made Easy - The Business Owner Version: How to Find $$$ for Your New Business. Speeches. Mervin L. Evans. 8 Audiocassettes. (Running Time: 10 Hours). 2002. 149.99 (978-0-914391-01-2(1)) Comm People Pr.

Getting God's Attention CD Series. 2007. audio compact disk 29.99 (978-1-933185-17-0(1)) Messengr Intl.

***Getting God's Attention Life Message Series.** John Bevere. 2010. audio compact disk 0.00 (978-1-933185-62-0(7)) Messengr Intl.

Getting Green Done: Hard Truths from the Frontlines of Sustainability Revolution. unabr. ed. Auden Schendler. Read by Walter Dixon. (Running Time: 6 hrs. 30 mins.). (ENG.). 2009. 24.98 (978-1-59659-419-7(5), GildAudio) Pub: Gildan Media. Dist(s): HachBkGrp

***Getting Hip.** Created by Uncommon Sensing LLC. (ENG.). 2006. audio compact disk 60.00 (978-0-9826724-7-1(0)) Uncommon Sens.

Getting in Shape: An Easy, Smart Guide to Getting in Shape. Carol Leonetti Dannhauser. (B & N Basics Ser.). 2003. audio compact disk 9.98 (978-0-7607-3768-2(1), Silver Lini) M Friedman Pub Grp Inc.

Getting in Touch with Your Higher Self. Joyce Morris. 1 cass. (Running Time: 45 min.). (978-1-888196-03-0(3)) Ctr Bkstore.
Beginning with a Reiki attunement, Morris takes you on a guided visualization through field & forest to mountain top for a meeting with your Higher Self. Beautifully detailed & accompanied by gentle music composed by Will Morris. Side two contains a subliminal version of side one, along with music.

Getting into Gift Baskets. Shirley Frazier. (Running Time: 53 minutes). 2003. 15.00 (978-0-9653408-4-7(8)) Sweet Survival.
Shirley Frazier, author of How to Start a Home-Based Gift Basket, reveals what it's like to own a gift basket business at home or in a retail store. Products, storage, daily activities, anecdotal stories, pricing, marketing and more are covered. At the end, you'll know if this popular business or hobby is right for you.

Getting into Hammered Dulcimer. Linda G. Thomas. (ENG.). 2009. lib. bdg. 19.99 (978-0-7866-7940-9(9)) Mel Bay.

Getting into Jazz Mandolin. Ted Eschliman. (ENG.). 2008. lib. bdg. 19.95 (978-0-7866-7642-2(6)) Mel Bay.

Getting into Your Customer's Head: The Eight Roles of Customer-Focused Selling. abr. ed. Kevin Davis. 4 cass. (Running Time: 3 hrs. 50 min.). 1998. bk. 34.95 (978-0-9648829-2-8(2)) Wyncom.
Eight steps that customers go through in making decisions, the buy-learning process, matched with eight roles of selling, that get you the results you want. Increases sales & repeat business with more business.

Getting It All Together: Matthew 6:10. Ed Young. (J). 1979. 4.95 (978-0-7417-1079-6(X), A0079) Win Walk.

Getting It Done Set: How to Lead When You're Not in Charge. abr. ed. Roger Fisher & Alan Sharp. Read by Mario Machado. 2 cass. (Running Time: 3 hrs.). 1999. 17.95 (978-1-57453-344-6(4)) Audio Lit.
In a world of teams, matrix management, & horizontal organizations, knowing how to lead laterally enables managers to achieve the ultimate goal of successful collaboration. Shows groups how to formulate a clear vision of desired results, offer ideas that will be heard, & influence the actions of others.

Getting It Right. William F. Buckley, Jr. Read by Patrick Cullen. (Running Time: 570 hrs. NaN mins.). 2006. 59.95 (978-0-7861-4504-1(8)); audio compact disk 72.00 (978-0-7861-7225-2(8)) Blckstn Audio.

Getting It Right. unabr. ed. William F. Buckley, Jr. Read by Patrick Cullen. (Running Time: 34200 sec.). 2006. audio compact disk 29.95 (978-0-7861-7659-5(8)) Blckstn Audio.

Getting It Right. unabr. ed. Elizabeth Jane Howard. Read by Eleanor Bron. 10 cass. (Running Time: 90 mins. per cass.). 1982. 84.95 Set, Dolby Sound. (978-0-7540-0173-7(3), CAB 1596) AudioGO.
Getting it right was not Gavin Lamb's forte, at least where human relationships were concerned. In the hairdressing salon, he was an expert with the tools of his trade. But back at home with his mother, it was quite a different matter. He didn't know how to deal with women since he was a prototype late developer. But after Joan's party, he would never be the same again.

Getting It Right Set: A Self-Directed Program for Engaged Couples. Earnie Larsen. 3 cass. (Running Time: 180 min.). 1996. vinyl bd. 19.95 Incl. worksheets. (978-0-87946-151-5(9), 302) ACTA Pubns.

Getting Married. Short Stories. James B. Hall. Read by James B. Hall. 1 cass. (Running Time: 1 hr. 26 min.). 13.95 (978-1-55644-014-4(6), 1081) Am Audio Prose.
Covers a "story of manners" & an "extreme fiction".

Getting Married: A Complete Guide to Planning Your Special Day. Andrea Rotondo Hospidor. (B & N Basics Ser.). 2003. audio compact disk 9.98 (978-0-7607-3773-6(8), Silver Lini) M Friedman Pub Grp Inc.

Getting Money Right: The Psychology of Wealth. Fred Lehrman. 6 cass. 50.00 (FL 3) Sound Horizons AV.
Helps you build a sound philosophical context within which you can handle money in an enlightened way. Explores basic ideas that are necessary if you wish to maintain a clear and stable personal economy, where love and money, spirituality and materialism are in harmony and alignment.

***Getting More: How to Negotiate to Achieve Your Goals in the Real World.** unabr. ed. Stuart Diamond. Read by Stuart Diamond. Read by Marc Cashman. (ENG.). 2010. audio compact disk 45.00 (978-0-307-74912-3(6), Random AudioBks) Pub: Random Audio Pubg. Dist(s): Random

Getting More Done in Less Time. Shad Helmstetter. 1 cass. (Self-Talk Cassettes Ser.). 10.95 (978-0-937065-26-6(9)) Grindle Pr.

Getting More Out of the Mass. Marcellino D'Ambrosio. 2004. 7.95 (978-1-932927-08-5(5)); audio compact disk 7.95 (978-1-932927-09-2(3)) Ascensn Pr.

Getting Mother's Body. unabr. ed. Suzan-Lori Parks. 6 CDs. (Running Time: 7 hrs. 30 mins.). 2003. audio compact disk 40.00 (978-0-7366-9329-5(7)) Books on Tape.

Getting My Awareness into Alignment with Reality. unabr. ed. Lilburn S. Barksdale. Read by Mark Denis. 1 cass. (Running Time: 1 hr. 07 min.). 1980. 9.95 (978-0-918588-31-9(6), 165) NCADD.
Realizations, affirmations & action statements are given for replacing judgmental, stress-producing thoughts with acceptance of self, others & reality.

Getting Naked: A Business Fable about Shedding the Three Fears That Sabotage Client Loyalty. unabr. ed. Patrick Lencioni. Read by Dan Woren. (ENG.). 2010. 30.00 (978-0-7393-4422-4(6), Random AudioBks) Pub: Random Audio Pubg. Dist(s): Random

Getting near to Baby. unabr. ed. Audrey Couloumbis. Read by Mischa Barton. 3 vols. (Running Time: 3 hrs. 54 mins.). (J). (gr. 5-9). 2004. pap. bk. 36.00 (978-0-8072-8876-4(4), LYA 287 SP, Listening Lib); 30.00 (978-0-8072-8875-7(6), Listening Lib) Random Audio Pubg.
Willa Jo is up on the roof at Aunt Patty's house. She went up to see the sunrise & Little Sister followed her, like she always does. But by mid-morning, Willa Jo is still up on that roof & she knows it wasn't just the sunrise that brought her there. Audrey Couloumbis has perfectly captured the pervasive feelings that can take hold when tragedy strikes the slow, subtle revelations that come when one can finally get near to the source.

Getting New Clients. Jeff Davidson. 1989. audio compact disk (978-1-60729-569-3(5)) Breath Space Inst.

Getting New Clients. Jeff Davidson. 1989. 20.95 (978-1-60729-344-6(7)) Breath Space Inst.

Getting of Wisdom. unabr. ed. Henry Handel Richardson. Read by Shaela Connor. 6 cass. (Running Time: 7 hrs. 42 min.). Dramatization. 1992. 39.95 (978-1-55686-451-3(5), 451) Books in Motion.
Larua Tweedle Rambotham, the spoiled eldest daughter of a provincial poor, but genteel family finds herself at the bottom of her school's social ladder. Her efforts to improve her standing are ingenious & always unique.

Getting on in Arabic. unabr. ed. British Broadcasting Corporation Staff. 2 cass. (ARA.). bk. 44.50 Set, incl. text, 300p. (978-0-88432-666-3(7), S325AR) J Norton Pubs.

Getting on in French. unabr. ed. 2 cass. 29.00 text only. (B1GOIRF) J Norton Pubs.

Getting on with It Set: How to Conquer Procrastination. David Grudermeyer & Rebecca Grudermeyer. 2 cass. 18.95 (T-39) Willingness Wrks.

Getting Organized. Shad Helmstetter. 1 cass. (Self-Talk Cassettes Ser.). 10.95 (978-0-937065-25-9(0)) Grindle Pr.

Getting Organized. Barry Tesar & Roxanne Tesar. 1 cass. 9.98 (978-1-56470-003-2(8)) Success Cass.
Would you like to accomplish more? Procrastinate less? Eliminate clutter? Add efficiency to your day? If so, "Getting Organized" will help you get a handle on your life. Play this cassette at home, or office, & amaze yourself at how quickly & efficiently things get done. The positive & supportive affirmations will inspire you to take charge. Create your life the way you want it to be. Start now!.

Getting Organized. Stephanie Winston. 2004. 7.95 (978-0-7435-4759-8(4)) Pub: S&S Audio. Dist(s): S and S Inc

Getting Organized. unabr. collector's ed. Stephanie Winston. Read by Penelope Dellaporta. 7 cass. (Running Time: 7 hrs.). 1986. 42.00 (978-0-7366-0955-5(5), 1899) Books on Tape.
Learn how to maximize your storage space, expand your studio apartment, make the most of your new house or your office, reduce your shopping time & increase your efficiency - even organize the spouse & kids.

Getting Organized in the Google Era: How to Get Stuff Out of Your Head, Find It When You Need It, & Get It Done Right. unabr. ed. Douglas Merrill & James A. Martin. Read by Douglas Merrill. (ENG.). 2010. audio compact disk 30.00 (978-0-307-71246-2(X), Random AudioBks) Pub: Random Audio Pubg. Dist(s): Random

Getting Out from Under. Stephanie Winston. Read by Stephanie Winston. 1 cass. (Running Time: 1 hr. 30 min.). 1999. 16.85 (978-0-671-03364-4(6)) S and S Inc.
Winston provides listeners with specific strategies for staying sane in today's stressful, sometimes over-whelming times of stress & commitment.

Getting out from Under. Stephanie Winston. 2004. 7.95 (978-0-7435-4760-4(8)) Pub: S&S Audio. Dist(s): S and S Inc

Getting Out of Debt. Elbert Willis. 1 cass. (Grace of Giving Ser.). 4.00 Fill the Gap.

Getting Out of Power Struggles. Martha B. Beveridge. 1 cass. (Running Time: 60 min.). 1994. 9.95 (978-1-889237-33-6(7)) Options Now.
Learn to get past the ABC's (attack, blame, criticism) of painful power struggles through conscious acts of intentional love.

***Getting over Mr Right.** Chrissie Manby. 2010. 71.95 (978-1-4450-0101-2(2)); audio compact disk 79.95 (978-1-4450-0102-9(0)) Pub: Isis Pubng Ltd GBR. Dist(s): Ulverscroft US

Getting over the Hump. C. S. Lovett. Read by C. S. Lovett. 1 cass. (Running Time: 60 min.). 6.95 (544) Prsnl Christianity.
Gives you instruction as you prepare your body for a big change in your eating routine. To be used with the "Help Lord" book.

Getting Paid. Emmet L. Robinson. Read by Emmet L. Robinson. 1 cass. (Running Time: 39 min.). 1991. 13.95 King Street.
How to collect the money you earn.

Getting Past No: Negotiating with Difficult People. abr. ed. William L. Ury. Read by William L. Ury. 2 CDs. (Running Time: 2 hrs.). (ENG.). 2002. audio compact disk 21.95 (978-0-553-75558-9(7)) Pub: Random Audio Pubg. Dist(s): Random

Getting Past Smoking. 1 cass. 12.95 (978-1-884305-64-1(4)) Changeworks.
This tape will work whether you want to reduce & control your smoking habit or quit completely. It will help you identify "stress triggers" & psychological factors behind smoking & develop healthier substitutes.

Getting Published - 3 CD Series. Jeff Davidson. 3 CDs. (Running Time: 176 min.). 2006. audio compact disk 48.95 (978-0-9771296-4-5(0)) Breath Space Inst.

Getting Published Series. Jeff Davidson. 2006. 54.95 (978-1-60729-217-3(3)); audio compact disk 54.95 (978-1-60729-353-8(6)) Breath Space Inst.

Getting Ready. Bernie S. Siegel. 1 CD. 2004. audio compact disk 10.95 (978-1-4019-0398-5(3)) Hay House.

Getting Ready: Preparing for Surgery, Chemotherapy & Other Treatments. Bernie S. Siegel. 1 cass. (Running Time: 1 hr.). 1999. 10.95 (978-1-56170-649-5(3), 482) Hay House.
A lecture on how to prepare for medical procedure.

Getting Ready for School Audio CD. Adapted by Benchmark Education Company Staff. Based on a work by Katherine Scraper. (Early Explorers Set C Ser.). (J). (gr. 1). 2008. audio compact disk 10.00 (978-1-60437-531-2(0)) Benchmark Educ.

Getting Real Program: Measurable Functional Academics for IEPs. 2005. spiral bd. 69.00 (978-1-57861-533-9(X), IEP Res) Attainment.

Getting Results! Michael LeBoeuf. 6 cass. (Running Time: 6 hrs.). 1993. 49.95 Set. (1491AM) Nightingale-Conant.
Why do some organizations run like clockwork? Because they adhere to the "Greatest Management Principle" presented in this groundbreaking program. According to Michael LeBoeuf, ineffective or unproductive behavior is too often rewarded, while productive behavior is frequently punished. Getting Results! gives you solid strategies for putting the timeless principle of behavior & reward to work to stimulate creativity, increase productivity & encourage cooperation in your organization.

Getting Results. Tommy Newberry. Read by Tommy Newberry. 1 cass. (Running Time: 55 min.). 1995. 15.00 (978-1-886669-06-2(6)) One Percent Club.
Discover the seven elements that influence your results in life & what you can do beginning immediately, to stack the deck in your favor.

Getting Rich in America. Brian S. Tracy. 6 cass. 59.95 Set. (5401AM) Nightingale-Conant.
This perennially popular program - based on an in-depth study of self-made millionaries - gives you all the strategies & tactics you need to multiply your income & enjoy luxuries beyond the reach of others. Learn the secret to smart investing, the 10 rules for investing to win & the five ways to become a millionaire. Discover how to put your career on the fast track...become a "money magnet"... & much more.

***Getting Rid of Bradley.** unabr. ed. Jennifer Crusie, pseud. Read by Elenna Stauffer. (Running Time: 6 hrs.). 2010. 39.97 (978-1-4418-8071-0(2), 9781441880710, BADLE); 19.99 (978-1-4418-8069-7(0), 9781441880697, Brilliance MP3); 39.97 (978-1-4418-8070-3(4), 9781441880703, Brinc Audio MP3 Lib); audio compact disk 19.99 (978-1-4418-8067-3(4), 9781441880673, Bril Audio CD Unabri); audio compact disk 69.97 (978-1-4418-8068-0(2), 9781441880680, BriAudCD Unabrid) Brilliance Audio.

Getting Serious about Getting Married AudioBook. Debbie Maken. Read by Gentry Rench. (ENG.). 2008. audio compact disk 20.00 (978-1-59128-402-4(3)) Canon Pr ID.

***Getting Staretd Series.** Chuck Missler. 2009. audio compact disk 49.95 (978-1-57821-447-1(5)) Koinonia Hse.

Getting Started. Elbert Willis. 1 cass. (Controlling Your Mind Guidelines Ser.). 4.00 Fill the Gap.

Getting Started & Staying with It. Shad Helmstetter. 1 cass. (Self-Talk Ser.). 10.95 (978-0-937065-45-7(5)) Grindle Pr.
Companion Self-Talk Cassettes as mentioned in the book, "What To Say When You Talk To Your Self".

Getting Started in Signing. unabr. ed. Elaine Costello. 2 cass. (Running Time: 3 hrs.). 2000. pap. bk. 15.95 (LivingLang) Random Info Grp.

Getting Started or Changing Over-mp3. Read by Tom Garfield. 1994. 8.00 (978-1-59128-317-1(5)) Canon Pr ID.

Getting Started or Changing Over-tape. Read by Tom Garfield. 2 CDs. 1998. 10.00 (978-1-59128-319-5(1)) Canon Pr ID.

Getting Stoned with Savages: A Trip Through the Islands of Fiji & Vanuatu. unabr. ed. J. Maarten Troost. (Running Time: 27000 sec.). 2007. 59.95 (978-1-4332-0288-9(3)); audio compact disk 63.00 (978-1-4332-0289-6(1)) Blckstn Audio.

Getting Stoned with Savages: A Trip Through the Islands of Fiji & Vanuatu. unabr. ed. J. Maarten Troost. Read by Simon Vance. (Running Time: 27000 sec.). 2007. 29.95 (978-1-4332-0177-6(1)); audio compact disk 29.95 (978-1-4332-0178-3(X)); audio compact disk 29.95 (978-1-4332-0179-0(8)) Blckstn Audio.

Getting the Answers & Ten Ways to Make Your Kids Feel Great. Diane Bills. 1 cass. 7.98 (978-1-55503-419-1(5), 06004547) Covenant Comms.

Getting the Information You Need: Freedom of Information Act (CD) Featuring Scott Hodes. Prod. by TheCapitol.Net. 2006. 107.00 (978-1-58733-049-0(0)) TheCapitol.

Getting the Love You Want: A Guide for Couples. abr. rev. ed. Read by Harville Hendrix. Ed. by Joe McNeely. 2 CDs. (Running Time: 2 hrs. 0 mins. 0 sec.). 2004. audio compact disk 17.95 (978-1-59397-447-3(7)) Pub: Macmill Audio. Dist(s): Macmillan

Getting the Love You Want: A Guide for Couples. 20th unabr. anniv. ed. Harville Hendrix. Read by Jack Garrett. Frwd. by Helen LaKelly Hunt. (Running Time: 12 hrs. 30 mins. 0 sec.). (ENG.). 2007. audio compact disk 44.95 (978-1-4272-0240-6(0)) Pub: Macmill Audio. Dist(s): Macmillan

Getting the Love You Want Audio Companion: The New Couples' Study Guide. abr. ed. Harville Hendrix & Helen Hunt. Read by Harville Hendrix. 2 CD. (Running Time: 23 hrs. 0 mins. 0 sec.). (ENG.). 2004. audio compact disk 20.00 (978-0-7435-3808-4(0)) Pub: S&S Audio. Dist(s): S and S Inc

Getting the Love You Want Audio Companion: The New Couples' Study Guide. abr. ed. Harville Hendrix & Helen Hunt. 2004. 12.95 (978-0-7435-4901-1(5)) Pub: S&S Audio. Dist(s): S and S Inc

Getting the Message 1: A Reading Course for Schools. Dermot Murphy & Janelle Cooper. (Running Time: hrs. mins.). (ENG.). 1995. 24.15 (978-0-521-42299-4(X)) Cambridge U Pr.

Getting the Most from Your People. Arthur R. Pell. 1990. (978-0-318-67224-3(3)) P-H.

Getting the Most Out of Your Job & Your Organization. Harold McAlindon. 1 cass. 10.00 (SP100046) SMI Intl.
Your work brings you more than money. As a source of self-fulfillment, it allows you to express who you are. Listen & discover how to use your abilities to get your job done by developing an effective team.

***Getting the Pretty Back.** unabr. ed. Molly Ringwald. Read by Molly Ringwald. (ENG.). 2010. (978-0-06-198806-6(5), Harper Audio) HarperCollins Pubs.

***Getting the Pretty Back: Friendship, Family, & Finding the Perfect Lipstick.** unabr. ed. Molly Ringwald. Read by Molly Ringwald. (ENG.). 2010. (978-0-06-198805-9(7), Harper Audio) HarperCollins Pubs.

Getting the Pretty Back: Friendships, Family & Finding the Perfect Lipstick. abr. unabr. ed. Molly Ringwald. Read by Molly Ringwald. 2010. audio compact disk 29.99 (978-0-06-183671-8(0), Harper Audio) HarperCollins Pubs.

Getting the Raise You Deserve. Barrie Konicov. 1 cass. 11.98 (978-0-87082-431-9(7), 051) Potentials.
You deserve a raise, but you are uncertain about how to ask for it. How much should you ask for & what to do if you are turned down are covered in this program.

Getting There. unabr. ed. Gilda O'Neill. Read by Judy Bennett. 10 cass. (Running Time: 15 hrs.). 2002. 84.95 (978-0-7540-0857-6(6), CAB 2279) Pub: Chivers Pr GBR. Dist(s): AudioGO

Getting There: EFL for Native Speakers of Spanish, Levels 1-2. (Getting There). (J). (gr. 5-9). 2000. 8.99 (978-1-928882-92-3(7)) CCLS Pubg Hse.

Getting There from Here Vol. 17. abr. ed. David Schickler et al. 3 CDs. (Running Time: 3 Hours). (Selected Shorts Ser.). (ENG.). 2004. audio compact disk 28.00 (978-0-9719218-1-8(4)) Pub: Symphony Space. Dist(s): IPG Chicago

***Getting There 1 - CD De Áudio.** (ENG.). 2005. audio compact disk (978-0-7428-1700-5(8)) CCLS Pubg Hse.

***Getting There 2 - CD De Áudio.** (ENG.). 2005. audio compact disk (978-0-7428-1701-2(6)) CCLS Pubg Hse.

***Getting There 3 - CD De Áudio.** (ENG.). 2005. audio compact disk (978-0-7428-1702-9(4)) CCLS Pubg Hse.

***Getting There 4 - CD De Áudio.** 2005. audio compact disk (978-0-7428-1703-6(2)) CCLS Pubg Hse.

Getting Things Done. Edwin C. Bliss. 4 cass. (Running Time: 2 hrs. 59 min.). 49.95 CareerTrack Pubns.
Presents a course on personal productivity, covering topics such as the psychology behind effective self-management, productivity "habits", concentration & creativity, overcoming interruptions & delegation.

Getting Things Done. unabr. ed. Edwin C. Bliss. Read by Edwin C. Bliss. 2 cass. (Running Time: 2 hrs. 80 min.). 1995. 15.95 (978-1-55977-031-6(7)) CareerTrack Pubns.

Getting Things Done: Keys to a Successful Business. Contrib. by Gabriela Cora. (ENG., 2007. pap. bk. 37.00 (978-1-933437-14-9(6)) Exe H & W Inc.

Getting Things Done: The Art of Stress Free Productivity. 2005. 34.99 (978-1-59895-032-8(0)) Find a World.

Getting Things Done: The Art of Stress-Free Productivity. abr. ed. David Allen. Read by David Allen. 2002. 13.95 (978-0-7435-6132-7(5)); audio compact disk 25.00 (978-0-7435-2034-8(3), Sound Ideas) Pub: S&S Audio. Dist(s): S and S Inc

Getting Things Done: The Art of Stress-Free Productivity. unabr. ed. David Allen. Read by David Allen. (Running Time: 8 hrs. 0 mins. 0 sec.). (ENG.). 2008. audio compact disk 39.95 (978-0-7435-7165-4(7)) Pub: S&S Audio. Dist(s): S and S Inc

Getting Through: Cold Calling Techniques to Get Your Foot in the Door. abr. ed. Stephan Schiffman. Read by Stephan Schiffman. (Running Time: 13 hrs. 0 mins. 0 sec.). (ENG.). 1999. audio compact disk 19.95 (978-0-7435-2021-8(1), Sound Ideas) Pub: S&S Audio. Dist(s): S and S Inc

Getting Through: Cold Calling Techniques to Get Your Foot in the Door. abr. ed. Stephan Schiffman. 2004. 7.95 (978-0-7435-4761-1(6)) Pub: S&S Audio. Dist(s): S and S Inc

Getting Through the Day. unabr. ed. Nancy J. Napier. Read by Nancy J. Napier. 4 cass. (Running Time: 4 hrs.). 1996. 45.95 Set. (978-0-9658191-1-4(6)) Lotus Blossom.
Guided meditations & exercises.

Getting Through the Tough Stuff see Cuado se Atraviesa Tiempos Dificiles

Getting Through the Tough Stuff. 2004. 48.00 (978-1-57972-624-9(0)) Insight Living.

Getting Through the Tough Stuff. 2005. audio compact disk 48.00 (978-1-57972-623-2(2)) Insight Living.

***Getting to Happy.** Terry McMillan. Contrib. by LaChanze et al. (Running Time: 12 hrs.). (ENG.). 2010. audio compact disk 39.95 (978-0-14-242841-2(8), PengAudBks) Penguin Grp USA.

Getting to Joy: A Western Householder's Spiritual Journey with Mata Amritanandamayi. 2nd ed. Karuna Poole. 6. (Running Time: 6 hrs 10 minutes). 2002. 23.00 (978-0-9643629-4-9(5)) K Poole.
The personal and vulnerable story of Karuna's wonderful journey into the mystery of Divinity through the Guru-Disciple relationship. She is able to weave together her extensive training as a psychotherapist with in-depth exposure to the Christian revivalism of the Deep South and the Hindu mysticism of India without sidestepping around apparent contradictions and inconsistencies.

Getting to Know ArcGIS Desktop: Basics of ArcView, Arceditor, & Arcinfo. 2nd ed. Tim Ormsby et al. (Getting to Know Ser.). (ENG., 2008. 79.95 (978-1-58948-210-4(7), ESRI Pr) Pub: ESRI. Dist(s): IngramPubServ

Getting to Know Jesus. George MacDonald. Read by Lloyd James. 4 cass. (Running Time: 5 hrs.). 2004. 34.95 (978-0-7861-2827-3(5), 3309); audio compact disk 45.00 (978-0-7861-8387-6(X), 3309) Blckstn Audio.

Getting to Know Jesus. unabr. ed. George MacDonald. Read by Rob Gregory. 6 cass. (Running Time: 9 hrs.). 1987. 44.95 (978-0-7861-0140-5(7), 1125) Blckstn Audio.
MacDonald provides fresh glimpses into the life of Jesus. It will help you know Him better.

Getting to Know Jesus. unabr. ed. George MacDonald. Read by Lloyd James. 13 vols. (Running Time: 5 hrs.). 2005. audio compact disk 24.95 (978-0-7861-8510-8(4), 3309); audio compact disk 29.95 (978-0-7861-8575-7(9), ZE3309); reel tape 29.95 (978-0-7861-2740-5(6), E3309) Blckstn Audio.
In this inspirational collection of twelve sermons, George MacDonald offers compelling insight into the life of Jesus Christ. MacDonald stressed the necessity of salvation and the importance of combining Christian faith with obedience to Jesus' teachings. He also believed that God's universal grace would eventually save everyone. Though written in the midnineteenth century, these sermons, including "Mirrors of Christ," "Glorified through Trouble, "Salvation from Sin," and "The Giver of Rest," continue to provide contemporary followers with the spiritual guidance they seek. For those who wish to know Jesus better, this is a book you will want to hear.

Getting to Know Labradors: A Guide to Choosing & Owning a Labrador. Cathy Lambert. Ed. by Diana Andersen. (ENG., 2008. audio compact disk 19.99 (978-1-921537-00-4(0)) Animalinfo AUS.

Getting to Know Myself. Perf. by Hap Palmer. 1 cass. (Running Time: 1 hr.). (J). 2001. pap. bk. 11.95 (EA 543C); pap. bk. 14.95 (EA543CD) Kimbo Educ.
Feelings - Sammy - Touch - Shake Something - Be My Friend, Left & Right, The Circle & more. Includes guide.

Getting to Know Myself. Hap Palmer. 1 cass., 1 CD. (J). 7.58 (AC 543); audio compact disk 11.98 CD Jewel box. (AC 543) NewSound.
Includes: "Sammy," "Feelings," "Touch," "Shake Something," "The Circle," "Turn" & more.

Getting to Know Poodles: A Guide to Choosing & Owning a Poodle. Cathy Lambert. Ed. by Diana Andersen. (ENG., 2008. audio compact disk 19.99 (978-1-921537-02-8(7)) Animalinfo AUS.

Getting to Know Snakes, Lizards & Frogs. Hosted by Nancy Pearlman. 1 cass. (Running Time: 28 min.). 10.00 (215) Educ Comm CA.

Getting to Know the General. unabr. ed. Graham Greene. Read by Jonathan Oliver. 6 cass. (Running Time: 7 hrs. 20 min.). 2001. 54.95 (978-1-85089-713-2(1), 90021) Pub: ISIS Audio GBR. Dist(s): Ulverscroft US
Mr. Greene came to know Omar Torrijos, the ruler of Panama (1969-1981), during a vital period in the history of that country. He also came to know the bizarre & beautiful country.

Getting to Know the Holy Spirit. Ben Young. 2000. 4.95 (978-0-7417-6221-4(8), B0221) Win Walk.

Getting to Know William Shakespeare: A Dramatic Life. unabr. ed. Joy Wake. Read by Fred Childs. 1 cass. (Running Time: 1 hr. 14 min.). Dramatization. (Road Scholar Ser.). 2001. 13.95 (978-1-883605-02-5(4)); audio compact disk 14.95 (978-1-883605-05-6(9)) Pub: Echo Peak Prods. Dist(s): Bookpeople
An entertaining audio presentation on the life of William Shakespeare featuring music, film clips and insights from scholars and actors in their own words.

Getting to Know You Better, Tape 1. Jill Daniels. 1 cass. 8.95 (393) Am Fed Astrologers.
An AFA Convention workshop tape.

Getting to Know You Better, Tape 2. Jill Daniels. 1 cass. 8.95 (394) Am Fed Astrologers.

Getting to Sleep. Shad Helmstetter. 1 cass. (Self-Talk Ser.). 10.95 (978-0-937065-49-5(8)) Grindle Pr.
Companion Self-Talk Cassettes as mentioned in the book, "What To Say When You Talk To Your Self".

Getting to the Economic Buying Influence. unabr. ed. Stephen E. Heiman. Interview with Diane Sanchez. 2 cass. (Running Time: 1 hr. 36 min.). (Strategic Selling Advanced Ser.: Vol. 1). 1994. 19.95 Set. (978-0-9619073-4-1(7)); audio compact disk (978-1-889888-00-2(1)) Miller Heiman.
Based on a concept from Miller Heiman's Strategic Selling Program, these two tapes contain extensive information about how to get to the Economic Buying Influence, as explained by selling experts Diane Sanchez, President & CEO, & Stephen E. Heiman, co-founder, Miller Heiman, Inc.

Getting to the Source of Everything. Swami Amar Jyoti. 1 cass. 1982. 9.95 (M-19) Truth Consciousness.
Transcending thinking, flowing with abandonment in Love, the Origin, the Zero Point. How a true seeker acts in the world.

Getting to Yes. 2005. 34.99 (978-1-59895-030-4(4)) Find a World.

Getting to Yes. Roger Fisher. 2006. 34.99 (978-1-59895-479-1(2)) Find a World.

***Getting to Yes: How to Negotiate Agreement Without Giving In.** unabr. ed. Roger Fisher & William Ury. Read by Murphy Guyer. (Running Time: 6 hrs. 0 mins. 0 sec.). (ENG.). 2011. audio compact disk 29.99 (978-1-4423-3952-1(7)) Pub: S&S Audio. Dist(s): S and S Inc

Getting to Yes: Negotiating Agreement Without Giving In. unabr. ed. Roger Fisher & William Ury. Read by Robert Fisher. 6 cass. (Running Time: 4 hrs. 30 min.). 1987. 59.95 (978-0-671-63486-5(0), 0004) S&S Audio.
You'll learn to take control of negotiation right from the start, wrap your argument in irrefutable logic, & create alternative solutions that satisfy both sides.

Getting to Yes: Negotiating Agreement Without Giving In. unabr. ed. Roger Fisher et al. Read by Murphy Guyer. 2004. 17.95 (978-0-7435-4762-8(4)) Pub: S&S Audio. Dist(s): S and S Inc

Getting to Yes: Negotiating Agreement Without Giving In. unabr. rev. ed. Roger Fisher et al. Read by Murphy Guyer. 6 CDs. (Running Time: 60 hrs. 0 mins. 0 sec.). (ENG.). 2003. audio compact disk 29.95 (978-0-7435-2693-7(7), Sound Ideas) Pub: S&S Audio. Dist(s): S and S Inc
Getting to Yes is a straightforward, universally applicable method for negotiating personal and professional disputes without getting taken - and without getting angry. It offers a concise, step-by-step, proven strategy for coming to mutually acceptable agreements in every sort of conflict - whether it involves parents and children, neighbors, bosses and employees, customers or corporations, tenants or diplomats. Based on the work of Harvard Negotiation Project, a group that deal continually with all levels of negotiations and conflict resolutions from domestic to business to international, Getting to Yes tells you how to: separate the people from the problem; Focus on interests, not positions; Work together to create opinions that will satisfy both parties; negotiate successfully with people who are more powerful, refuse to play by the rules, or resort to "dirty tricks"

Getting Together: Building Relationships As We Negotiate. unabr. ed. Roger Fisher. Read by Jim Bond. (Running Time: 7 hrs.). 2009. 39.97 (978-1-4233-9984-1(6), 9781423399841, BADLE) Brilliance Audio.

Getting Together: Building Relationships As We Negotiate. unabr. ed. Roger Fisher & Scott Brown. Read by Jim Bond. (Running Time: 7 hrs.). 2009. 39.97 (978-1-4233-9982-7(X), 9781423399827, Brinc Audio MP3 Lib); 24.99 (978-1-4233-9983-4(8), 9781423399834, BAD); audio compact disk 82.97 (978-1-4233-9980-3(3), 9781423399803, BriAudCD Unabrid) Brilliance Audio.

Getting Together: Building Relationships As We Negotiate. unabr. ed. Roger Fisher & Brown Scott. Read by Jim Bond. (Running Time: 7 hrs.). 2009. 24.99 (978-1-4233-9981-0(1), 9781423399810, Brilliance MP3) Brilliance Audio.

Getting Together: Building Relationships As We Negotiate. unabr. ed. Fisher Roger & Scott B. Brown. Read by Jim Bond. (Running Time: 7 hrs.). 2009. audio compact disk 24.99 (978-1-4233-9979-7(X), 9781423399797) Brilliance Audio.

Getting Unstuck. Pema Chödrön. 3 CDs. (Running Time: 3 hrs. 30 mins.). 2006. audio compact disk 24.95 (978-1-59179-238-3(X), W886D) Sounds True.

Getting Unstuck: How Dead Ends Become New Paths. unabr. ed. Timothy Butler. Read by Erik Synnestvedt. (Running Time: 5 hrs.). (ENG.). 2007. 24.98 (978-1-59659-191-2(9), GildAudio) Pub: Gildan Media. Dist(s): HachBkGrp

Getting up to Speak! pap. bk. & wbk. ed. 30.00 (978-0-7612-0597-5(7), 80157) AMACOM.
You'll learn how to: Organize your ideas into attention-getting, convincing presentations; Conquer your fear & dread of public speaking by following 10 simple rules; Grab your audience's attention; Use gestures & body language; Win commitment for your ideas & projects with persuasive language; Stay in control of your question-&-answer period.

Getting up to Speak!, Set. 6 cass. pap. bk. & wbk. ed. 155.00 (978-0-7612-0596-8(9), 80156) AMACOM.

Getting What You Want. Emmet L. Robinson. Read by Emmet L. Robinson. 1 cass. (Running Time: 32 min.). 1991. 9.95 King Street.
How to take charge of your life & achieve your dreams.

Getting What You Want: How to Reach Agreement & Resolve Conflict Every Time. Read by Kare Anderson. Ed. by Carl Birkmeyer. 1 cass. 1993. bk. 30.00; bk. 115.00 incl. video.; 12.00 (978-1-56641-010-6(X)) Library Video.
Communications expert Kare Anderson offers tips & techniques for winning at negotiations. Simple & effective methods for winning agreement & speaking memorably are presented in the audiotape.

Getting You & Your Baby off to a Good Start: A Book of Operating Instructions. unabr. ed. Read by Katy Abel. 1 cass. (Running Time: 45 mins.). 1996. 5.00 (978-0-9704925-1-7(0)) MA Soc.
Answers to parents' most frequently asked questions on sleeping, eating & crying. All delivered in a friendly useful way meant to build parents' confidence.

Getting Your Baby to Sleep: Tips for Parents... A Lullaby for Baby. Vicki Lansky. 1 cass. (Running Time: 1 hr.). 1990. 9.98 (978-0-916773-61-8(2)) Pub: Book Peddlers. Dist(s): PerseuPGW
For thirty minutes the author reads tips from her book "Getting Your Child to Sleep"; Wordless music comprises the remaining thirty minutes.

Getting Your Baby to Sleep (And Back to Sleep) unabr. ed. Vicki Lansky. Read by Vicki Lansky. 1 cass. (Running Time: 55 min.). 1990. 9.98 (978-0-942303-06-3(7), HW1208C) High Windy Audio.
"Family Circle" columnist & parenting expert, Vicki Lansky, gives parents practical, easy-to-follow tips on getting baby to sleep. Side two features "Suite for Baby" a lullaby with heartbeat & womb sounds.

Getting Your Priorities in Order. Gary F. Hutchison. Read by Gary F. Hutchison. 1 cass. (Running Time: 1 hr. 30 min.). (YA). (gr. 8 up). 1995. 7.50 (978-1-885631-10-7(3)) G F Hutchison.
Helps listener sort through & arrange his values in the most useful order.

Getting Your Public Relations Story on TV & Radio: An Audio Adaptation. Tracy St. John. 1 cass. (Running Time: 30 min.). 1988. 9.95 Reeder Pr.
Shows how to get products and services on radio & TV talk shows, news, public affairs, etc.

Getting Your Work Done. Dora C. Fowler. 1 cass. (Running Time: 60 min.). 1993. 9.95 (978-1-57323-025-4(1)) Natl Inst Child Mgmt.
Staff training material for child care.

Gettysburg. James Reasoner. Read by Lloyd James. 8 cass. (Running Time: 12 hrs.). (Civil War Battle Ser.: Bk. 6). 2005. 65.95 (978-0-7861-2945-4(X), 3417); audio compact disk 90.00 (978-0-7861-8138-4(9), 3417) Blckstn Audio.

Gettysburg. Jerry Robbins. Perf. by Colonial Radio Theatre Staff. 3 cass. (Running Time: 4 hrs.). 2000. 24.99 Penton Overseas.

Gettysburg. Stephen W. Sears. 14 cass. (Running Time: 23 hrs. 30 mins.). 2004. 39.99 (978-1-4025-5599-2(7), 03214) Recorded Bks.

Gettysburg. Time-Life Books Editors. 1999. (978-1-57042-721-3(6)) Hachet Audio.

Gettysburg. 5th anniv. ed. 1 cass., 1 CD. 17.58 Soundtrack, double. (MLN 35847); audio compact disk 27.98 CD Soundtrack, double. (MLN 35847) NewSound.

Gettysburg: A Novel of the Civil War. unabr. ed. Newt Gingrich & William R. Forstchen. Narrated by Tom Stechschulte. 12 cass. Library ed. (Running Time: 17 hrs. 15 min.). 2004. 99.75 (978-1-4025-6737-7(5)); audio compact disk 39.99 (978-1-4025-7705-5(2), 01652) Recorded Bks.

Gettysburg: A Novel of the Civil War. unabr. ed. Newt Gingrich & William R. Forstchen. Narrated by Tom Stechschulte. 15 CDs. (Running Time: 17 hrs. 15 mins.). 2004. audio compact disk 39.99 (978-1-4025-8364-3(8), 01652) Recorded Bks.

Gettysburg: A Novel of the Civil War. unabr. collector's ed. Newt Gingrich & William R. Forstchen. Narrated by Tom Stechschulte. 12 cass. (Running Time: 17 hrs. 15 min.). 2004. 39.95 (978-1-4025-6738-4(3), RG888) Recorded Bks.
Former Speaker of the House Newt Gingrich and veteran author William R. Forstchen combine their talents in Gettysburg, a powerful alternate history of the most legendary Civil War battle. Instead of attacking on the third day, General Lee flanks the Federals, cutting them off from Washington, D.C. and their supplies. Staring at the face of disaster, the Federals are forced into a desperate fight to survive.

Gettysburg: Circle Tour. 1 cass. incl. map. (Running Time: 90 min.). (Guided Auto Tape Tour). 12.95 (E2) Comp Comms Inc.

Gettysburg: Missing in Action. William Reeder. (Step into History Ser.). 2006. pap. bk. 69.00 (978-1-4105-0560-6(X)); audio compact disk 18.95 (978-1-4105-0558-3(8)) D Johnston Inc.

Gettysburg: The Complete Radio Drama. Perf. by Colonial Radio Theatre Staff. 3 cass. (Running Time: 3 hrs.). 2001. 25.95 (COLR009) Lodestone Catalog.
Whether you favor the Blue or the Grey, Gettysburg will have your heart pounding with suspense.

Gettysburg: The Complete Radio Drama. Jerry Robbins. Perf. by Colonial Radio Theatre Staff. Prod. by Mark Vander Berg. Music by Jeffrey Gage. 3 cass. (Running Time: 3 hrs. 30 mins.). Dramatization. (J). 2000. 24.99 (978-1-929244-08-9(8)) Pub: Colonial Radio. Dist(s): Penton Overseas
Features top-notch actors & special effects for Civil War buffs & students.

Gettysburg Address in Translation: What It Really Means. Kay Melchisedech Olson. Contrib. by Scott Combs & Miles Tagmeyer. (Kids' Translations Ser.). (ENG.). (gr. 3-4). 2008. audio compact disk 17.32 (978-1-4296-3224-9(0)) CapstoneDig.

Gettysburg & Other Ghost Stories. Short Stories. Nancy K. Duncan & William A. Logan. Read by Nancy K. Duncan. 1. (Running Time: 1 hr., 2 mins). (J). 2002. audio compact disk 15.00 (978-0-9719007-2-1(8)) STORY PERFORM.
Storyteller Nancy Duncan tells her original story, Gettysburg, about a father's rich friendship with his son and how the details of the father's death determine his son's future. Also on this CD are Duncan's story of her friendship with the poet Robert Frost, Duncan's rendition of a traditional ghost story from North Carolina, and a poem by William Logan - The Man on the Bed.

Gettysburg, Day Three. Jeffry D. Wert. Read by Barrett Whitener. 2001. 80.00 (978-0-7366-7643-4(0)) Books on Tape.

***Gettysburg Expedition Guide.** 2nd rev. ed. 2010. spiral bd. 29.95 (978-1-933763-02-6(7)) TravelBrains.

Gettysburg Field Guide: A Self-Guided Audio Tour & Companion Guidebook to the Battle of Gettysburg. 2000. bk. & per. 19.95 (978-0-9705809-3-1(2)); per. 19.95 (978-0-9705809-1-7(6)) TravelBrains.

Gettysburg Gospel: The Lincoln Speech That Nobody Knows. unabr. ed. Gabor Boritt. Read by Michael Kramer. (Running Time: 10 hrs. 0 mins. 0 sec.). (ENG.). 2006. audio compact disk 34.99 (978-1-4001-0351-5(7)); audio compact disk 69.99 (978-1-4001-3351-2(3)); audio compact disk 24.99 (978-1-4001-5351-0(4)) Pub: Tantor Media. Dist(s): IngramPubServ

Gettysburg National Military Park (PA) 1 cass. 12.95 (978-1-55606-000-7(9), CCI306) Comp Comms Inc.
Gettysburg was fought one of the most violent & controversial battles of the Civil War on July 1, 2, & 3, 1863. As the events of the 3-day battle unfold, some may well characterize it as a study of military daring & genius - handicapped by human frailties.

Getzel the Monkey see Isaac Bashevis Singer Reader

Ghetto Health. Bluetilful Blue. (ENG.). 2008. audio compact disk 10.00 (978-0-9799611-5-1(7), GreenParrot) Salty Cove Pr.

Ghetto Roses. 2000. 12.95 (978-0-9666484-5-4(5)) Dimby Co Inc.

Ghost. abr. movie tie-in ed. Robert Harris. Read by Roger Rees. (Running Time: 6 hrs. 0 mins. 0 sec.). (ENG.). 2010. audio compact disk 14.99 (978-0-7435-8304-6(3)) Pub: S&S Audio. Dist(s): S and S Inc

Ghost. unabr. ed. Robert Harris. Read by Roger Rees. (Running Time: 10 hrs. 0 mins. 0 sec.). (ENG.). 2007. audio compact disk 39.95 (978-0-7435-6962-0(8)) Pub: S&S Audio. Dist(s): S and S Inc

Ghost. unabr. ed. Alan Lightman. Read by Christopher Price. (YA). 2008. 59.99 (978-1-60514-579-2(3)) Find a World.

Ghost: Confessions of a Counterterrorism Agent. unabr. ed. Fred Burton. Read by Tom Weiner. (Running Time: 9.5 hrs. 0 mins.). 2008. 59.95 (978-1-4332-4717-0(8)); audio compact disk 80.00 (978-1-4332-4718-7(6)); audio compact disk & audio compact disk 29.95 (978-1-4332-4719-4(4)) Blckstn Audio.

Ghost: Confessions of a Counterterrorism Agent. unabr. ed. Fred Burton & Tom Weiner. (Running Time: 34200 sec.). 2008. audio compact disk 29.95 (978-1-4332-4720-0(8)) Blckstn Audio.

Ghost & Flesh, Water & Dirt. Short Stories. William Goyen. Read by William Goyen. 1 cass. (Running Time: 1 hr. 13 min.). 1990. 13.95 (978-1-55644-044-1(8), 2061) Am Audio Prose.

Ghost & Horror. unabr. ed. 6 cass. (Running Time: 9 hrs.). 1990. 35.70 (C-420) Audio Bk.
Tales of things that go bump in the night, including dozens of spine tingling classics.

Ghost & Horror Stories. abr. ed. Algernon Blackwood et al. 2 cass. (Running Time: 2 hrs. 4 min.). 12.95 (978-0-89926-174-4(4), 858) Audio Bk.

Ghost & Mrs. Hobbs. unabr. ed. Cynthia C. DeFelice. Narrated by Christina Moore. 3 pieces. (Running Time: 3 hrs. 45 mins.). (gr. 6 up). 2002. 28.00 (978-1-4025-1427-2(1)) Recorded Bks.
Allie Nicholas is a sixth grader with the ability to see ghosts. A few weeks after helping the ghost of a young girl solve a murder, Allie is approached by another spirit to do the same for him. Allie's class is doing a project for Elder's Day that involves interviewing an older person. The ghost encourages her to pick Mrs. Hobbs, a woman who works in the school cafeteria, as the subject of her project. Although every child in the school is afraid of Mrs. Hobbs, Allie agrees to do it if it will help lay the ghost to rest. Soon, everywhere Allie goes, fires start suspiciously. This new ghost appears to be a handsome young man in need of help, but Allie learns that ghosts are not always what they seem to be.

Ghost Belonged to Me. Richard Peck. (J). 1991. 15.95 Live Oak Media.

Ghost Biker. Anne Schraff. Narrated by Larry A. McKeever. (Standing Tall 1 Mystery Ser.). (J). 2000. audio compact disk 14.95 (978-1-58659-265-3(3)) Artesian.

Ghost Biker. unabr. ed. Anne Schraff. Narrated by Larry A. McKeever. 1 cass. (Running Time: 40 min.). (Standing Tall 1 Mystery Ser.). (J). 2000. 10.95 (978-1-58659-092-5(8), 54132) Artesian.

Ghost Boy. unabr. ed. Iain Lawrence. Narrated by George Guidall. 7 pieces. (Running Time: 9 hrs.). (gr. 7 up). 2001. 64.00 (978-0-7887-9406-3(X)) Recorded Bks.

Ghost Bull of the Mavericks. J. Frank Dobie. Read by J. Frank Dobie. 1 cass. 1992. TX Bks & Tapes.
A collection of folk tales.

Ghost Canoe. William Hobbs. Read by Boyd Gaines. 4 cass. (Running Time: 5 hrs. 10 mins.). (J). 2000. 30.00 (978-0-7366-9129-1(4)) Books on Tape.
From the moment 14-year-old Nathan arrives on the Washington coastline to help his father tend the lighthouse, he realizes something is amiss.

Ghost Canoe. William Hobbs. Read by Boyd Gaines. 4 vols. (Running Time: 5 hrs. 10 mins.). (J). (gr. 5-9). 2004. pap. bk. 38.00 (978-0-8072-0450-4(1), Listening Lib) Random Audio Pubg.

Ghost Canoe. unabr. ed. William Hobbs. Read by Boyd Gaines. 4 cass. (Running Time: 5 hrs. 10 mins.). (J). (gr. 5-9). 2004. 32.00 (978-0-8072-0449-8(8), Listening Lib) Random Audio Pubg.
After a sailing ship breaks up on the rocks off Washington's storm-tossed Cape Flattery, Nathan MacAllister, the fourteen-year-old son of the lighthouse keeper, refuses to believe the authorities, who say there were no survivors. Unexplained footprints on a desolate beach, a theft at the trading post, and glimpses of a wild "hairy man" convince Nathan that someone is hiding in the remote sea caves along the coast.

Ghost Country. abr. ed. Sara Paretsky. Read by Jean Smart. 4 cass. (Running Time: 6 hrs.). 2002. 40.00 (978-1-59040-234-4(0)) Audio Lit.
They came from different worlds and met in a time of crisis for each of them: Luisa, a former diva brought low by alcohol and delusion, Mara, a furious nineteen-year-old searching for her mother and her truths. Madeleine, a homeless woman who sees the blood of the Virgin Mary seeping through concrete under a luxury Chicago hotel. Hector, an idealistic young doctor struggling to give hope to the city's dispossessed. They are the men and women of Ghost Country.

***Ghost Country.** unabr. ed. Patrick Lee. (ENG.). 2010. (978-0-06-206277-2(8), Harper Audio); (978-0-06-206164-5(X), Harper Audio) HarperCollins Pubs.

Ghost Dancer. abr. ed. John Case. Read by Dick Hill. (Running Time: 21600 sec.). 2007. audio compact disk 14.99 (978-1-59737-359-3(1), 9781597373593, BCD Value Price) Brilliance Audio.
Please enter a Synopsis.

Ghost Dancer. abr. unabr. ed. John Case. Read by Dick Hill. (Running Time: 46800 sec.). 2006. audio compact disk 107.25 (978-1-59355-452-1(4), 9781593554521, BACDLib Ed) Brilliance Audio.
From the New York Times bestselling author of The Genesis Code, a quintessential John Case novel - an international thriller (Baalbek, Belgrade, Transdniester, Switzerland, and Hawaii) that's driven by a charismatic villain hell-bent on the destruction of Western civilization, which he refers to as "the great leveling." Jack Wilson has just been released from a maximum

security federal prison, and now that he's a free man, he is fixated on a "return to Paradise." A Native American by birth, Wilson is a brilliant mathematician obsessed with the secret notebooks of Nicola Tesla, a turn-of-the-century genius who claimed that he had discovered a weapon of unparalleled destructiveness, one that used harmonic resonance to dismantle the molecular structure of any target. Jack Wilson sets that diabolical scheme in motion.

Ghost Dancer. unabr. ed. John Case. Read by Dick Hill. (Running Time: 46800 sec.). 2006. 92.25 (978-1-59355-449-1(4), 9781593554491, BrilAudUnabridg); audio compact disk 24.95 (978-1-59335-723-8(0), 9781593357238, Brilliance MP3); audio compact disk 39.25 (978-1-59335-857-0(1), 9781593358570, Brinc Audio MP3 Lib) Brilliance Audio.

Ghost Dancer. unabr. ed. John Case. Read by Dick Hill. (Running Time: 13 hrs.). 2006. 39.25 (978-1-59710-894-2(4), 9781597108942, BADLE); audio compact disk 39.95 (978-1-4233-0617-7(1), 9781423306177, Bril Audio CD Unabri) Brilliance Audio.
Photojournalist Mike Burke carried his camera into every war zone and hellhole on earth - and came back with the pictures (and battle scars) to prove it. He was flying high until, quite suddenly, he wasn't. When Burke's helicopter crashed and burned in Africa, he came away with his life but lost his heart to the beautiful woman who saved him. That's when he decided it was time to stop dancing with the devil. But a wicked twist of fate puts an end to Burke's dreams, leaving him adrift in Dublin with bittersweet memories . . . and no appetite for danger. But neither danger - nor the devil - is done with him yet. An ocean away, Jack Wilson leaves prison burning for revenge. Like Mike Burke, Jack has had something taken from him. And he, too, dreams of starting life over. Only Jack's dream is the rest of the world's nightmare. Driven by his obsession with a Native American visionary, and guided by the secret notebooks of Nikola Tesla, the man who is said to have "invented the twentieth century," Wilson dreams of the Apocalypse - and plans to make it happen. As a terrifying worldwide chain reaction is set in motion, one thing stands between Jack Wilson and the time of reckoning he is calling forth: Mike Burke. With nothing left to lose, and little understanding of precisely whom and what he's facing, Burke tracks Wilson from a terrorist arsenal in the Transdneister to the diamond fields of the Congo, risking everything, one last time, in a battle of wits with an enemy who knows no fear . . . and shows no mercy.

Ghost Dancer: A Novel. unabr. ed. John Case. Read by Dick Hill. (Running Time: 13 hrs.). 2006. 24.95 (978-1-59710-895-9(2), 9781597108959, BAD) Brilliance Audio.

Ghost Dancers. (Running Time: 60 mins.). 2002. audio compact disk 15.99 (978-1-904972-21-1(7)) Global Jrny GBR GBR.

Ghost Followed Us Home. unabr. ed. Peg Kehret. Narrated by Carine Montbertrand. 2 cass. (Running Time: 2 hrs. 45 mins.). (Frightmares Ser.: No. 5). (gr. 5 up). 1997. 19.00 (978-0-7887-0832-9(5), 94977E7) Recorded Bks.
Sixth-graders Kayo & Rosie hear strange music & sounds coming from a locked glass case in the Oakwood Doll Museum. Could it be a ghost?.

Ghost for Maggie. Emily Carmichael. Narrated by Cristine McMurdo-Wallis. 8 cass. (Running Time: 11 hrs.). 72.00 (978-1-4025-0950-6(2)) Recorded Bks.

Ghost for Maggie. Emily Carmichael. Narrated by Cristine McMurdo-Wallis. 10 CDs. (Running Time: 11 hrs. 30 mins.). 1999. audio compact disk 97.00 (978-1-4025-3820-9(0)) Recorded Bks.

Ghost Force. Patrick Robinson. Narrated by Erik Steele. 14 CDs. (Running Time: 54540 sec.). (Sound Library). 2006. audio compact disk 115.95 (978-0-7927-4048-3(3), SLD 954); audio compact disk & audio compact disk 49.95 (978-0-7927-4225-8(7), CMP 954) AudioGO.

Ghost Gallery. CMH Records Staff. 1996. 7.98 (978-1-885505-09-5(4)); 9.98 (978-1-885505-10-1(8)) CMH Records.

***Ghost House.** Stephen Cole. Narrated by Elisabeth Sladen. (Running Time: 1 hr. 0 mins. 0 sec.). (ENG.). 2011. audio compact disk 24.95 (978-1-4084-0059-3(6)) Pub: AudioGO. Dist(s): Perseus Dist

Ghost House. Perf. by Daniel Sjerven. Created by Daniel Sjerven. Prod. by Braun Media. (ENG.). 2008. (978-1-59987-668-9(X)) Braun Media.

Ghost Hunter. abr. ed. Jayne Castle, pseud. Read by Laural Merlington. (Running Time: 4 hrs.). (Harmony Ser.: No. 4). 2010. audio compact disk 9.99 (978-1-4418-0823-3(X), 9781441808233, BCD Value Price) Brilliance Audio.

Ghost Hunter. unabr. ed. Jayne Castle, pseud. Read by Laural Merlington. (Running Time: 9 hrs.). (Harmony Ser.: No. 4). 2006. 39.25 (978-1-4233-0823-2(9), 9781423308232, BADLE); 24.95 (978-1-4233-0822-5(0), 9781423308225, BAD); 74.25 (978-1-4233-0817-1(4), 9781423308171, BrilAudUnabridg); audio compact disk 92.25 (978-1-4233-0819-5(0), 9781423308195, BriAudCD Unabrid); audio compact disk 39.25 (978-1-4233-0821-8(2), 9781423308218, Brinc Audio MP3 Lib); audio compact disk 34.95 (978-1-4233-0818-8(2), 9781423308188, Bril Audio CD Unabri); audio compact disk 24.95 (978-1-4233-0820-1(4), 9781423308201, Brilliance MP3) Brilliance Audio.
Please enter a Synopsis.

Ghost Hunters: William James & the Search for Scientific Proof of Life after Death. unabr. ed. Deborah Blum. Narrated by George K. Wilson. 11 CDs. (Running Time: 52980 sec.). 2006. audio compact disk 99.95 (978-0-7927-4511-2(6), SLD 1041); audio compact disk 59.95 (978-0-7927-4558-7(2), CMP 1041) AudioGO.

Ghost Image. unabr. ed. Joshua Gilder. Read by Patrick G. Lawlor. (Running Time: 11 hrs.). 2004. 39.25 (978-1-59335-366-7(9), 1593353669, Brinc Audio MP3 Lib) Brilliance Audio.
The last thing plastic surgeon Jackson Maebry wants after a long day in the operating room is a call to the ER. When he gets there, he discovers a trauma case as horrific as he has ever seen: a young woman, beaten and burned almost beyond recognition. What Jackson's colleagues don't know is that the victim, Allie Sorosh, is Jackson's lover. With Allie in a coma, Jackson keeps their relationship quiet and takes part in her reconstruction, a complicated set of procedures only the most skilled specialists can perform. But as he and the other doctors struggle to put her back together, the fractures in Jackson's own life begin to break apart dramatically. When the San Francisco Police's investigation of the attack leads to his door, Jackson knows the truth can no longer be suppressed.

Ghost Image. unabr. ed. Joshua Gilder. Read by Patrick G. Lawlor. (Running Time: 11 hrs.). 2004. 39.25 (978-1-59710-318-3(7), 1597103187, BADLE); 24.95 (978-1-59710-319-0(5), 1597103195, BAD) Brilliance Audio.

Ghost Image. unabr. ed. Joshua Gilder. Read by Patrick G. Lawlor. (Running Time: 11 hrs.). 2004. 24.95 (978-1-59335-035-2(X), 159335035X) Soulmate Audio Bks.

Ghost Image: A Novel. unabr. ed. Joshua Gilder. Read by Patrick G. Lawlor. 8 cass. (Running Time: 11 hrs.). 2002. 34.95 (978-1-59086-440-1(9), 1590864409, BAU); 87.25 (978-1-59086-441-8(7), 1590864417, Unabridge Lib Edns) Brilliance Audio.

Ghost in Love. unabr. ed. Jonathan Carroll. (Running Time: 10 hrs. NaN mins.). 2008. 29.95 (978-1-4332-4871-9(9)); 65.95 (978-1-4332-4868-9(9)) Blckstn Audio.

Ghost in Love. unabr. ed. Jonathan Carroll. Read by Ray Porter. 8 CDs. (Running Time: 9 hrs.). 2008. audio compact disk 80.00 (978-1-4332-4869-6(7)) Blckstn Audio.

Ghost in Love. unabr. ed. Jonathan Carroll. Read by Ray Porter. 8 CDs. (Running Time: 9 hrs.). 2008. audio compact disk 29.95 (978-1-4332-4870-2(0)) Blckstn Audio.

Ghost in the Big Brass Bed. unabr. ed. Bruce Coville. Narrated by Christina Moore. 4 pieces. (Running Time: 4 hrs. 45 mins.). (gr. 5 up). 35.00 (978-0-7887-0591-5(1), 94768E7) Recorded Bks.
Sixth-grader Nine Tanleven knows that old Mrs. Watson's house is haunted. She feels the ghost as soon as she walks toward the faded porch. But when Nine climbs the stairs to look for an antique wardrobe in the tower room, she has to wonder what else the spooky mansion is hiding. Available to libraries only.

Ghost in the Desert. Susannah Brin. Narrated by Larry A. McKeever. (Chillers Ser.). (J). 2001. audio compact disk 14.95 (978-1-58659-296-7(3)) Artesian.

Ghost in the Desert. unabr. ed. Susannah Brin. Narrated by Larry A. McKeever. 1 cass. (Running Time: 40 min.). (Take Ten Ser.). (J). (gr. 3-12). 2001. 10.95 (978-1-58659-057-4(X), 54127) Artesian.

Ghost in the Machine. Perf. by John Thaw. 2 cass. (Running Time: 1 hr. 50 min.). (Inspector Morse Mystery Ser.). 1998. 14.95 (978-1-56938-256-1(5), AMP-2565) Acorn Inc.
Paintings, valuable & erotic, are stolen & the wealthy owner mysteriously disappears. Inspector Morse probes the motives & morals of the aristocracy in an attempt to solve this baffling crime.

Ghost in the Mirror. unabr. ed. John Bellairs & Brad Strickland. Narrated by George Guidall. 3 cass. (Running Time: 4 hrs. 15 mins.). (Lewis Barnavelt Ser.: Bk. 4). (gr. 5 up). 1994. 27.00 (978-0-7887-0138-2(X), 94363E7) Recorded Bks.
A young girl & a witch travel back in time to confront the power of an evil sorcerer.

Ghost in the New House. unabr. ed. Roni S. Denholtz. Illus. by Nelsy Fontalvo. 1 cass. (Running Time: 7 min.). (Friends & Neighbors Ser.). (J). (gr. k-2). 1986. lib. bdg. 16.99 incl. hardcover. (978-0-87386-017-8(9)) Jan Prods.
When Melissa & her friends peek in the window of a house that's for sale, they think they see a ghost.

Ghost in the Noonday Sun. unabr. ed. Sid Fleischman. Narrated by Spike McClure. 3 pieces. (Running Time: 4 hrs. 15 mins.). (gr. 6 up). 1993. 27.00 (978-1-55690-773-9(7), 93136E7) Recorded Bks.
Twelve year old Oliver Finch is kidnapped by pirates who carry him off on a search for buried treasure.

Ghost in the Shell Stand Alone Complex Soundtrack. (YA). 2003. audio compact disk (978-1-59409-336-4(9)) Bandai Ent.

Ghost in the Shell 2: Innocence le w/ CD. (YA). 2009. DVD 29.98 (978-1-59409-971-7(5)) Bandai Ent.

Ghost in the Third Row. unabr. ed. Bruce Coville. Narrated by Christina Moore. 3 pieces. (Running Time: 3 hrs. 15 mins.). (gr. 5 up). 27.00 (978-0-7887-0531-1(8), 94726E7) Recorded Bks.
For sixth-grader Nine Tanleven, nothing is scarier than auditioning for a play at the famous old Grand Theater. But Nine changes her mind when she climbs on stage to audition & sees a ghost sitting in the audience. Available to libraries only.

***Ghost Light.** Joseph O'Connor. (Running Time: 8 hrs. 0 mins. 0 sec.). (ENG.). 2011. audio compact disk 29.95 (978-1-60998-146-4(4)) Pub: AudioGO. Dist(s): Perseus Dist

Ghost Light: A Memoir. abr. ed. Frank Rich. Read by Frank Rich. 4 cass. (Running Time: 6 hrs.). 2004. 25.00 (978-1-931056-06-9(4), N Millennium Audio) New Millenn Enter.
Ghost light, in theatre parlance, is that single light left burning at center stage after the audience, actors & musicians have gone home. Superstition says that without it, a ghost will take up residence in the dark theatre. The author tells how the theatre itself became his ghost light, a beacon of security for a child finding his way while struggling with his parents' divorce & the trials of childhood.

Ghost Map: The Story of London's Most Terrifying Epidemic - and How It Changed Science, Cities, & the Modern World. unabr. ed. Steven Johnson. Narrated by Alan Sklar. 7 CDs. (Running Time: 8 hrs. 30 mins. 0 sec.). (ENG.). 2006. audio compact disk 34.99 (978-1-4001-0298-3(7)); audio compact disk 24.99 (978-1-4001-5298-8(4)); audio compact disk 69.99 (978-1-4001-3298-0(3)) Pub: Tantor Media. Dist(s): IngramPubServ

Ghost Medicine. unabr. ed. Andrew Smith. Read by Mike Chamberlain. (ENG.). (J). (gr. 9). 2008. audio compact disk 44.00 (978-0-7393-7243-2(2), Listening Lib) Pub: Random Audio Pubg. Dist(s): Random

***Ghost Moon.** abr. ed. Heather Graham. (Running Time: 6 hrs.). (Bone Island Trilogy). 2010. 14.99 (978-1-4418-8187-8(5), 9781441881878, BAD) Brilliance Audio.

***Ghost Moon.** abr. ed. Heather Graham. Read by Angela Dawe. (Running Time: 5 hrs.). (Bone Island Trilogy). 2010. audio compact disk 14.99 (978-1-4418-8185-4(9), 9781441881854, BACD) Brilliance Audio.

***Ghost Moon.** unabr. ed. Heather Graham. Read by Angela Dawe. (Running Time: 10 hrs.). (Bone Island Trilogy). 2010. 24.99 (978-1-4418-8000-0(3), 9781441880000, BAD); 39.97 (978-1-4418-7999-8(4), 9781441879998, Brinc Audio MP3 Lib); 39.97 (978-1-4418-8001-7(1), 9781441880017, BADLE); 24.99 (978-1-4418-7998-1(6), 9781441879981, Brilliance MP3); audio compact disk 84.97 (978-1-4418-7997-4(8), 9781441879974, BriAudCD Unabrid); audio compact disk 29.99 (978-1-4418-7996-7(X), 9781441879967, Bril Audio CD Unabri) Brilliance Audio.

Ghost Mountain Boys: Their Epic March & the Terrifying Battle for New Guinea - -the Forgotten War of the South Pacific. unabr. ed. James Campbell. Read by Stephen Hoye. (YA). 2008. 59.99 (978-1-60514-865-6(2)) Find a World.

Ghost Mountain Boys: Their Epic March & the Terrifying Battle for New Guinea - -the Forgotten War of the South Pacific. unabr. ed. James Campbell. Read by Stephen Hoye. 9 CDs. (Running Time: 10 hrs. 30 mins. 0 sec.). (ENG.). 2007. audio compact disk 34.99 (978-1-4001-0576-2(5)); audio compact disk 69.99 (978-1-4001-3576-9(1)); audio compact disk 24.99 (978-1-4001-5576-7(2)) Pub: Tantor Media. Dist(s): IngramPubServ

***Ghost Night.** abr. ed. Heather Graham. (Running Time: 6 hrs.). (Bone Island Trilogy). 2010. audio compact disk 14.99 (978-1-4418-2551-3(7), 9781441825513, BACD) Brilliance Audio.

***Ghost Night.** unabr. ed. Heather Graham. (Running Time: 10 hrs.). (Bone Island Trilogy). 2010. audio compact disk 97.97 (978-1-4233-9884-4(X), 9781423398844, BriAudCD Unabrid) Brilliance Audio.

***Ghost Night.** unabr. ed. Heather Graham. Read by Angela Dawe. (Running Time: 10 hrs.). (Bone Island Trilogy). 2010. 24.99 (978-1-4233-9887-5(4), 9781423398875, BAD); 24.99 (978-1-4233-9885-1(8), 9781423398851, Brilliance MP3); 39.97 (978-1-4233-9888-2(2), 9781423398882, BADLE); 39.97 (978-1-4233-9886-8(6), 9781423398868, Brinc Audio MP3 Lib); audio compact disk 29.99 (978-1-4233-9883-7(1), 9781423398837, Bril Audio CD Unabri) Brilliance Audio.

Ghost of a Chance. Susan Hepburn & Maggie Mash. 2008. 69.95 (978-1-84652-287-1(0)); audio compact disk 84.95 (978-1-84652-288-8(9)) Pub: Magna Story GBR. Dist(s): Ulverscroft US

***Ghost of a Chance.** unabr. ed. Jayne Ann Krentz. (Running Time: 6 hrs.). 2011. audio compact disk 19.99 (978-1-4418-8478-7(5), 9781441884787, Bril Audio CD Unabri) Brilliance Audio.

Ghost of a Flea: A Lew Griffin Mystery. unabr. ed. James Sallis. (Running Time: 9 hrs. 0 mins.). (ENG.). 2009. 29.95 (978-1-4332-3025-7(9)); 59.95 (978-1-4332-3021-9(6)); audio compact disk 76.00 (978-1-4332-3022-6(4)) Blckstn Audio.

Ghost of Able Mabel & the Spectre of Hairy Hector. Read by Richard Mitchley. (Running Time: 4920 sec.). (J). 2001. audio compact disk 21.95 (978-0-7540-6752-8(1)) AudioGo GBR.

Ghost of Buckskin Run. abr. ed. Louis L'Amour. 1 cass. (Running Time: 60 min.). Dramatization. 2000. 9.99 (978-0-553-52530-4(1), Random AudioBks) Random Audio Pubg.
Classic western tale with original music & western sound effects.

Ghost of Caesar: Guilt's Shadow. Kenneth Wapnick. 4 CDs. 2004. audio compact disk 24.00 (978-1-59142-159-7(4), CD102) Foun Miracles.

***Ghost of Crutchfield Hall.** unabr. ed. Mary Downing Hahn. (Running Time: 3 hrs.). 2011. 24.99 (978-1-61106-102-4(4), 9781611061024, BAD); 24.99 (978-1-61106-100-0(8), 9781611061000, Brilliance MP3); 39.97 (978-1-61106-103-1(2), 9781611061031, BADLE); 39.97 (978-1-61106-101-7(6), 9781611061017, Brinc Audio MP3 Lib); audio compact disk 24.99 (978-1-61106-098-0(2), 9781611060980, Bril Audio CD Unabri); audio compact disk 54.97 (978-1-61106-099-7(0), 9781611060997, BriAudCD Unabrid) Brilliance Audio.

Ghost of Fossil Glen. Cynthia C. DeFelice. 3 cass. (Running Time: 3 hrs. 30 mins.). (YA). (gr. 6 up). 2000. pap. bk. 52.00 (978-0-7887-4334-4(1), 41129) Recorded Bks.
After sixth-grader Allie Nichols gets trapped on a ledge while rock climbing, a soothing voice guides her to safety. When Allie shares her experience, her best friends call her a liar. But Allie knows the voice was real. Could it have been a ghost?.

Ghost of Fossil Glen. Cynthia C. DeFelice. Read by Christina Moore. 3 cass. (Running Time: 3 hrs. 30 mins.). (YA). 2000. 197.30 (978-0-7887-4435-8(6), 47126) Recorded Bks.

Ghost of Fossil Glen. unabr. ed. Cynthia C. DeFelice. Narrated by Christina Moore. 3 pieces. (Running Time: 3 hrs. 30 mins.). (gr. 6 up). 2000. 29.00 (978-0-7887-4247-7(7), 96215E7) Recorded Bks.

Ghost of Free Will. unabr. ed. James E. Royce. 1 cass. (Running Time: 19 min.). 12.95 (25024) J Norton Pubs.
Tells About the conflict which has developed in psychology & philosophy between causation & determinism & between causation & predictability.

Ghost of Guir House. unabr. ed. Charles W. Beale. Read by Jim Killavey. 4 cass. (Running Time: 5 hrs.). 1982. 21.00 incl. album. (C-89) Jimcin Record.

Ghost of Napoleon. unabr. collector's ed. Basil H. Liddell-Hart. Read by Bill Kelsey. 5 cass. (Running Time: 5 hrs.). 1987. 30.00 (978-0-7366-1204-3(1), 2122) Books on Tape.
Concentrates on two intellections, each of which vitally affected the course of history in the last two centuries. One was responsible for the triumphs of Revolutionary France & for Napoleon's empire; the other W. W. I.

Ghost of Nebraska Wesleyan. Duane Hutchinson. Read by Duane Hutchinson. 1 cass. (Running Time: 1 hrs.). 1997. 9.95 (978-0-934988-39-1(0)) Foun Bks.
Story of former music teacher, Clara Urania Mills.

Ghost of Raven Hill. unabr. ed. Emily Rodda. Read by Rebecca Macauley. 3 CDs. (Running Time: 12300 sec.). (Raven Hill Mysteries #1: Ser.). (J). (gr. 3-8). 2005. audio compact disk 54.95 (978-1-74093-621-7(3)) Pub: Bolinda Pubng AUS. Dist(s): Bolinda Pub Inc

Ghost of Slow Sam. unabr. ed. Allan Zullo. Read by John Ratzenberger. 2008. 1.37 (978-1-4233-8073-3(8), 9781423380733, BAD) Brilliance Audio.

Ghost of Spirit Bear. unabr. ed. Ben Mikaelsen. Read by Jason Harris. 3 CDs. (Running Time: 3 hrs. 42 mins.). (YA). (gr. 6-10). 2008. audio compact disk 39.00 (978-0-7393-7262-3(9), Listening Lib) Pub: Random Audio Pubg. Dist(s): Random

Ghost of Spirit Bear. unabr. ed. Ben Mikaelsen. Read by Jason Harris. (ENG.). (J). (gr. 7). 2008. audio compact disk 27.00 (978-0-7393-7260-9(2), Listening Lib) Pub: Random Audio Pubg. Dist(s): Random

Ghost of the Bar-H. unabr. ed. M. Lehman. Read by Gene Engene. 4 cass. (Running Time: 5 hrs. 42 min.). 1994. 26.95 (978-1-55686-505-3(8)) Books in Motion.
Cynthia & Abigail inherit their brothers Wyoming ranch which according to local gossip is "hexed." Ghost or no ghost, the ladies from New England are determined to move in.

Ghost of the Chattering Bones. Gertrude Chandler Warner. (Running Time: 5400 sec.). (Boxcar Children Ser.: No. 102). (J). 2005. audio compact disk 14.95 (978-0-7861-7484-3(6)) Blckstn Audio.

Ghost of the Chattering Bones. unabr. ed. Gertrude Chandler Warner. Read by Joyce Bean. 2 pieces. (Boxcar Children Ser.: No. 102). 12.99 (978-1-58926-889-0(X)); audio compact disk 14.99 (978-1-58926-890-6(3)) Oasis Audio.

Ghost of the Sierras see Luck of Roaring Camp & Other Stories

Ghost on the Haunted Ship. unabr. ed. Esther Luttrell. Perf. by Sean Krohune & Buddy Reaves. 1 cass. (Running Time: 30 min.). (J). (gr. 3-6). 1999. 7.95 (978-0-9667485-8-1(1)) Oak Shadow Pr.

Ghost Orchid. Carol Goodman. 9 cass. (Running Time: 42840 sec.). 2006. 79.95 (978-0-7927-3916-6(7), CSL 910); audio compact disk 94.95 (978-0-7927-3917-3(5), SLD 910) AudioGO.

Ghost Orchid. Carol Goodman. Read by Jen Taylor. 2006. audio compact disk 29.95 (978-0-7927-3969-2(8), CMP 910) AudioGO.

***Ghost Radio.** unabr. ed. Leopoldo Gout. Read by Pedro Pascal. (ENG.). 2008. (978-0-06-171340-8(6)); (978-0-06-171345-3(7)) HarperCollins Pubs.

Ghost Radio. unabr. ed. Leopoldo Gout. Read by Pedro Pascal. 2008. audio compact disk 34.95 (978-0-06-166157-0(0), Harper Audio) HarperCollins Pubs.

Ghost Rider. unabr. ed. Max Brand. Read by Ian Esmo. 6 cass. (Running Time: 9 hrs.). 1999. 44.95 (897456) Blckstn Audio.
The misadventures of a man who fits in nowhere because he comes from two races in collision, paints a picture of the violent Southwest filled with the culture classes fueled by Mexican & American homesteaders & outlaws, & Chinese gamblers who see life & death with different eyes.

Ghost Rider, Set. unabr. ed. Max Brand. Read by Ian Esmo. 6 cass. 1999. 44.95 (FS9-50903) Highsmith.

Ghost Riders. unabr. ed. Sharyn McCrumb. Read by Dick Hill & Susie Breck. 8 cass. (Running Time: 11 hrs.). (Ballad Ser.: No. 7). 2003. 32.95

(978-1-59086-788-4(2), 1590867882, BAU); 82.25 (978-1-59086-789-1(0), 1590867890, Lib Edit) Brilliance Audio.
In 1861 the Civil War reached the mountainous South - where the enemy was your neighbor, the victims were your friends, and the wrong army was whichever one you joined. When Malinda Blalock's husband, Keith, joined the army, she dressed as a boy and went with him. They spent the war close to home in the North Carolina mountains, acting as Union guerilla fighters, raiding the farms of Confederate sympathizers and making as much trouble as they could locally. As hard riding, deadly out-laws, Keith and Malinda avenged Confederate raids on their kin and neighbors. McCrumb also brings to her story the larger-than-life narrative of the historical political figure Zebulon Vance, a self-made man and Confederate governor, who was from the mountains and fought for the interests of Appalachia within the hierarchy of the Confederacy. Linking the forces of historical unrest with the present-day stories of mountain wisefolk Rattler and Nora Bonesteel, McCrumb weaves two overlapping narratives. It is up to Nora Bonesteel and Rattler to calm the Civil War ghosts who are still wandering the mountains, and prevent a clash between the living and the dead.

Ghost Riders. unabr. ed. Sharyn McCrumb. Read by Dick Hill & Susie Breck. (Running Time: 11 hrs.). (Ballad Ser.: No. 7). 2004. 39.25 (978-1-59335-524-1(6), 1593355246, Brlnc Audio MP3 Lib) Brilliance Audio.

Ghost Riders. unabr. ed. Sharyn McCrumb. Read by Dick Hill & Susie Breck. (Running Time: 11 hrs.). (Ballad Ser.). 2004. 39.25 (978-1-59710-320-6(9), 1597103209, BADLE) Brilliance Audio.

Ghost Riders. unabr. ed. Sharyn McCrumb. Read by Dick Hill & Susie Breck. 1 MP3-CD. (Running Time: 11 hrs.). (Ballad Ser.: No. 7). 2004. 24.95 (978-1-59335-197-7(6), 1593351976) Soulmate Audio Bks.

Ghost Riders. unabr. ed. Sharyn McCrumb. Read by Dick Hill & Susie Breck. (Running Time: 11 hrs.). (Ballad Ser.). 2004. 24.95 (978-1-59710-321-3(7), 1597103217, BAD) Brilliance Audio.

Ghost Road. unabr. ed. Pat Barker. Narrated by Steven Crossley. 6 cass. (Running Time: 7 hrs. 30 mins.). 1996. 51.00 (978-0-7887-0583-0(0), 94761E7) Recorded Bks.
Individual stories of triumph & tragedy as World War I enters its final phase in 1918.

***Ghost Shadow.** abr. ed. Heather Graham. Read by Angela Dawe. (Running Time: 5 hrs.). (Bone Island Trilogy). 2010. audio compact disk 14.99 (978-1-4418-2604-6(1), 9781441826046, BACD) Brilliance Audio.

***Ghost Shadow.** unabr. ed. Heather Graham. (Running Time: 9 hrs.). (Bone Island Trilogy). 2010. 24.99 (978-1-4233-9879-0(3), 9781423398790, Brilliance MP3); 24.99 (978-1-4233-9881-3(5), 9781423398813, BAD); 39.97 (978-1-4233-9880-6(7), 9781423398806, Brlnc Audio MP3 Lib); 39.97 (978-1-4233-9882-0(3), 9781423398820, BADLE) Brilliance Audio.

***Ghost Shadow.** unabr. ed. Heather Graham. Read by Angela Dawe. (Running Time: 10 hrs.). (Bone Island Trilogy). 2010. audio compact disk 92.97 (978-1-4233-9878-3(5), 9781423398783, BriAudCD Unabrid); audio compact disk 29.99 (978-1-4233-9877-6(7), 9781423398776, Bril Audio CD Unabri) Brilliance Audio.

Ghost Ship see Flying Dutchman

Ghost Ship. unabr. ed. Dietlof Reiche. Read by Marguerite Gavin. 4 cass. (Running Time: 21600 sec.). (J). 2005. 34.95 (978-0-7861-3794-7(0)); audio compact disk 45.00 (978-0-7861-7578-9(8)); audio compact disk 29.95 (978-0-7861-7853-7(1)) Blckstn Audio.

Ghost Ship. unabr. ed. Dietlof Reiche. Read by Marguerite Gavin. (J). 2007. 44.99 (978-1-60252-501-6(3)) Find a World.

Ghost Ship Mystery. Gertrude Chandler Warner. (Running Time: 5400 sec.). (Boxcar Children Ser.: No. 39). (J). 2005. audio compact disk 14.95 (978-0-7861-7488-1(9)) Blckstn Audio.

Ghost Ship Mystery. unabr. ed. Gertrude Chandler Warner. 2 cass. (Running Time: 1 hr. 50 min.). (Boxcar Children Ser.: No. 39). (J). 2003. 12.99 (978-1-58926-288-1(3), Oasis Kids) Oasis Audio.

Ghost Ship Mystery. unabr. ed. Gertrude Chandler Warner. Narrated by Aimee Lilly. (Boxcar Children Ser.). (ENG.). (J). 2003. 10.49 (978-1-60814-094-7(6)) Oasis Audio.

Ghost Ship Mystery. unabr. ed. Gertrude Chandler Warner. Narrated by Aimee Lilly. 2 CDs. (Running Time: 1 hr. 50 min.). (Boxcar Children Ser.: No. 39). (ENG.). (J). 2003. audio compact disk 14.99 (978-1-58926-289-8(1), Oasis Kids) Oasis Audio.

Ghost Soldiers: The Forgotten Epic Story of World War II's Most Dramatic Mission. Hampton Sides. Read by Michael Prichard. 2001. 80.00 (978-0-7366-7584-0(1)); audio compact disk 96.00 (978-0-7366-8300-5(3)) Books on Tape.

Ghost Soldiers: The Forgotten Epic Story of World War II's Most Dramatic Mission. abr. ed. Hampton Sides. Read by James Naughton. (Running Time: 21600 sec.). (ENG.). 2006. audio compact disk 19.99 (978-0-7393-4176-6(6), Random AudioBks) Pub: Random Audio Pubg. Dist(s): Random

Ghost Soldiers: The Forgotten Epic Story of World War II's Most Dramatic Mission. unabr. collector's ed. Hampton Sides. Read by Michael Prichard. 10 cass. (Running Time: 15 hrs.). 2001. 80.00 Books on Tape.
On January 28, 1945, 121 hand-selected troops from the elite U.S. 6th Ranger Battalion slipped behind enemy lines in the Philippines. Their mission: march thirty miles in an attempt to rescue 513 American and British POWs who had spent three years in a hellish camp near the city of Cabanatuan. The prisoners included the last survivors of the Bataan Death March left in the camp, and their extraordinary will to live might soon count for nothing. As the Rangers stealthily moved through enemy-occupied territory, they learned that Cabanatuan had become a major transshipment point for the Japanese retreat, and instead of facing the few dozen prison guards, they could possibly confront as many as 8,000 battle-hardened enemy troops.

Ghost Squad: Operation Stingray. unabr. ed. Bob Casemore. Read by Jerry Sciarrio. 6 cass. (Running Time: 7 hrs. 6 min.). 2001. 39.95 (978-1-58116-011-6(9)) Books in Motion.
The Ghost Squad is a combat-hardened special force trained to operate behind enemy lines. Its mission is to find a renegade American who is sending information via short-wave to the Japanese regarding American troop movements.

Ghost Stories. abr. ed. Charles Dickens. Perf. by Paul Scofield. 4 cass. (Running Time: 6 hrs.). (Ultimate Classics Ser.). 2004. 25.00 (978-1-931056-55-7(2), N Millennium Audio) New Millenn Enter.
Beguiled in early childhood by his nursemaid's stories of giants & demons, ghosts & monsters, Charles Dickens harbored all his life a fascination with ghosts, apparitions & chilling coincidence. Here are some of the eeriest tales from the greatest storyteller of them all.

Ghost Stories. abr. ed. Charles Dickens. Read by Paul Scofield. 5 CDs. (Running Time: 6 hrs.). 2004. audio compact disk 34.95 (978-1-59007-572-2(2)) Pub: New Millenn Enter. Dist(s): PerseuPGW

***Ghost Stories, Vol. 1.** M. R. James. Narrated by Derek Jacobi. (Running Time: 2 hrs. 30 mins. 0 sec.). (ENG.). 2010. audio compact disk 24.95 (978-1-4056-7814-8(3)) Pub: AudioGO. Dist(s): Perseus Dist

Ghost Stories from the American Southwest. unabr. ed. Richard Young & Judy D. Young. 1 cass. (Running Time: 45 min.). (gr. 6-12). 1993. 12.00 (978-0-87483-149-8(0)) Pub: August Hse. Dist(s): Natl Bk Netwk
For adults & children. Chilling tales collected from people all over the southwest, in the oral tradition, reflecting the rich cultural diversity of the region.

Ghost Stories of an Antiquary. unabr. ed. M. R. James. Read by Nigel Lambert. 3 cass. (Running Time: 3 hrs. 36 min.). 2001. 34.95 (978-1-85695-467-9(6), 92125) Pub: ISIS Audio GBR. Dist(s): Ulverscroft US
Apparitions, spooks & nameless terrors haunt this marvelous collection of ghost stories. They are all, like Arthur Conan Doyle's detective stories or Edgar Allan Poe's tales of mystery, unbeatable period classics of the genre.

Ghost Stories of an Antiquary. unabr. ed. M. R. James. Read by Walter Covell. 4 cass. (Running Time: 6 hrs.). 1981. 28.00 incl. album. (C-52) Jimcin Record.
Consists of: "Canon Alberti's Scrapbook," "The Mezzotint," "The Ash Tree," "Number 13," "Count Magnus," "Oh Whistle, & I'll Come to You, My Lad," "Lost Hearts," "The Treasure of Abbot Thomas".

Ghost Stories Series. Betty Ren Wright. Illus. by Betty Ren Wright. 5 cass. (Running Time: 5 hrs. 57 mins.). 2002. 40.95 (978-0-87499-994-5(4)) Live Oak Media.

Ghost Stories World-Wide by Dancing Beetle. Perf. by Eugene Ely. 1 cass. (Running Time: 74 min.). (J). 1991. 10.00 Erthviibz.
Ghost stories, ecology & nature sounds come together when Ms. Fox-Bat & the spunky musical humans read & sing with Dancing Beetle.

Ghost Story see Classic Ghost Stories, Vol. 2, A Collection

Ghost Story see Classic Ghost Stories, Vol. 2, A Collection

Ghost Story. abr. ed. Peter Straub. 2004. 10.95 (978-0-7435-4763-5(2)) Pub: S&S Audio. Dist(s): S and S Inc

***Ghost Story.** unabr. ed. Jim Butcher. Read by James Marsters. (Running Time: 16 hrs.). (Dresden Files Ser.: Bk. 13). (ENG.). 2011. audio compact disk 49.95 (978-0-14-242906-8(6), PengAudBks) Penguin Grp USA.

Ghost, the Gallant, the Gael, & the Goblin see Classic Ghost Stories, Vol. 3, A Collection

***Ghost Town.** unabr. ed. Rachel Caine. Narrated by Cynthia Holloway. (Running Time: 9 hrs. 0 mins. 0 sec.). (Morganville Vampires Ser.). 2010. 24.99 (978-1-4001-6535-3(0)); 15.99 (978-1-4001-8535-1(1)); audio compact disk 34.99 (978-1-4001-1535-8(3)) Pub: Tantor Media. Dist(s): IngramPubServ

Ghost Town. unabr. ed. J. R. Roberts, pseud. Narrated by Randall James Stanton. 2 cass. (Running Time: 3 hrs.). (Gunsmith Ser.: No. 127). 1996. 12.95 set. (978-1-882071-41-8(7)) B-B Audio.
Chasing the trail of a suspicious unsigned letter, the Gunsmith winds up in a dusty eyesore known as Patience, Oklahoma. This faceless enemy from the Gunsmiths past wants Clint scared stiff first-and stone dead second.

Ghost Town at Sundown. unabr. ed. Mary Pope Osborne. 1 cass. (Running Time: 50 mins.). (Magic Tree House Ser.: No. 10). (J). (gr. k-3). 2004. pap. bk. 17.00 (978-0-8072-0535-8(4), Listening Lib) Random Audio Pubg.

***Ghost Town (Library Edition)** unabr. ed. Rachel Caine. Narrated by Cynthia Holloway. (Running Time: 9 hrs. 0 mins.). (Morganville Vampires Ser.). 2010. 34.99 (978-1-4001-9535-0(7)); audio compact disk 83.99 (978-1-4001-4535-5(X)) Pub: Tantor Media. Dist(s): IngramPubServ

Ghost Tracker. R. G. Hilson. Narrated by Paul Strikwerda. (ENG.). 2008. audio compact disk 15.95 (978-1-60031-036-2(2)) Spoken Books.

Ghost Tracker II. R. G. Hilson. Narrated by Paul Strikwerda. 2008. audio compact disk 15.95 (978-1-60031-045-4(1)) Spoken Books.

Ghost Twisters. ed. (ENG.). (J). 2006. 17.95 (978-0-9787519-0-6(6)) Edge of Imag.

Ghost Walker. unabr. ed. Margaret Coel. Read by Stephanie Brush. 6 cass. (Running Time: 6 hrs. 54 min.). (Wind River Ser.). 1999. 39.95 (978-1-55686-865-8(0)) Books in Motion.
Father John discovers a frozen body in the Arapaho Reservation. a corpse that later disappears.

Ghost War. abr. ed. Mack Maloney. 2 cass. (Running Time: 3 hrs.). (Wingman Ser.: Vol. 10). 2002. 9.95 (978-1-931953-03-0(1)) Listen & Live.

Ghost War. unabr. ed. Alex Berenson. Read by George Guidall. (Running Time: 12 hrs.). (ENG.). (gr. 8). 2008. audio compact disk 39.95 (978-0-14-314285-0(2), PengAudBks) Penguin Grp USA.

Ghost Watcher. Stuart Manning. 2009. audio compact disk 15.95 (978-1-84435-372-9(9)) Pub: Big Finish GBR. Dist(s): Natl Bk Netwk

Ghost Wore Gray. unabr. ed. Bruce Coville. Narrated by Christina Moore. 3 pieces. (Running Time: 4 hrs.). (gr. 6 up). 1993. 27.00 (978-1-55690-776-0(1), 93137E7) Recorded Bks.
Young listeners will be captivated by this light-hearted story of two best friends who meet the ghost of a Confederate soldier & they'll also learn a great deal about the history of the Underground Railroad.

Ghost Writer. Philip Roth. Narrated by George Guidall. 4 cass. (Running Time: 5 hrs.). 42.00 (978-1-4025-2559-9(1)) Recorded Bks.

***Ghostgirl.** unabr. ed. Tonya Hurley. Read by Parker Posey. 1 Playaway. (Running Time: 6 hrs.). (YA). (gr. 7 up). 2009. 59.75 (978-1-4407-3096-2(2)); 41.75 (978-1-4407-3086-3(5)); audio compact disk 51.75 (978-1-4407-3090-0(3)) Recorded Bks.

***Ghostgirl.** unabr. collector's ed. Tonya Hurley. Narrated by Parker Posey. 5 CDs. (Running Time: 6 hrs.). (YA). (gr. 7 up). 2009. audio compact disk 46.95 (978-1-4407-3094-8(6)) Recorded Bks.

Ghosthunters & the Gruesome Invincible Lightning Ghost! unabr. ed. Cornelia Funke. Read by John Beach. 2 cass. (Running Time: 1 hr. 54 mins.). (Ghosthunters Ser.: No. 2). (J). (gr. 3-5). 2006. 23.00 (978-0-7393-3825-4(0), Listening Lib); audio compact disk 25.50 (978-0-7393-3797-4(1), Listening Lib) Pub: Random Audio Pubg. Dist(s): NetLibrary CO

Ghosthunters & the Gruesome Invincible Lightning Ghost! unabr. ed. Cornelia Funke. Read by John Beach. (Running Time: 6840 sec.). (Ghosthunters Ser.: No. 2). (ENG.). (J). (gr. 1-5). 2006. audio compact disk 19.95 (978-0-7393-3105-7(1), Listening Lib) Pub: Random Audio Pubg. Dist(s): Random

Ghosthunters & the Muddy Monster of Doom! unabr. ed. Cornelia Funke. Read by John Beach. 3 CDs. (Running Time: 2 hrs. 41 mins.). (Ghosthunters Ser.: No. 4). (J). (ps-3). 2007. audio compact disk 30.00 (978-0-7393-5126-0(5), Random Hse Audible) Pub: Random Audio Pubg. Dist(s): Random

Ghosthunters & the Muddy Monster of Doom! unabr. ed. Cornelia Funke. Read by John Beach. (Running Time: 9660 sec.). (Ghosthunters Ser.: No. 4). (ENG.). (J). (gr. 1-5). 2007. audio compact disk 25.00 (978-0-7393-5048-5(X), Listening Lib) Pub: Random Audio Pubg. Dist(s): Random

Ghosthunters & the Totally Moldy Baroness! unabr. ed. Cornelia Funke. Read by John Beach. 1 CD. (Running Time: 1 hr. 50 mins.). (Ghosthunters Ser.: No. 3). (J). (gr. 3-5). 2007. audio compact disk 24.00 (978-0-7393-4867-3(1), Random AudioBks) Pub: Random Audio Pubg. Dist(s): Random

Ghosthunters & the Totally Moldy Baroness! unabr. ed. Cornelia Funke. Read by John Beach. (Running Time: 6600 sec.). (Ghosthunters Ser.: No. 3). (ENG.). (J). (gr. 1). 2007. audio compact disk 19.95 (978-0-7393-3881-0(1), Listening Lib) Pub: Random Audio Pubg. Dist(s): Random

Ghostly Companions. unabr. ed. Vivien Alcock. Read by Kenneth Shanley. 3 cass. (Running Time: 4 hrs., 30 min.). (J). (gr. 1-8). 1999. 30.00 (LL 3042, Chivers Child Audio) AudioGO.

Ghostly Companions, Set. unabr. ed. Vivien Alcock. Read by Kenneth Shanley. 3 cass. (J). 1996. 23.98 (978-0-8072-7200-8(0), YA802CX, Listening Lib) Random Audio Pubg.

Ghostly Experiences at Gettysburg. Patti O'Day. Read by John Darren Kamp. 1 cass. (Running Time: 40 min.). 1997. 10.95 (978-1-890541-98-9(2)) Americana Souvenirs & Gifts.

Ghostly Hand of Spital House see Graveyard of Ghost Tales

Ghostly Kiss see Great American Short Stories, Vol. III, A Collection

Ghostly Rental see Classic Ghost Stories, Vol. 3, A Collection

Ghostly Songs & Stories. (J). 1997. 6.00 (978-1-57375-548-1(6)) Audioscope.

***Ghostly Tales: A Collection of Spine-Tingling Short Stories.** Various Authors. Read by Andrew Sachs. (Running Time: 2 hrs. 0 mins. 0 sec.). (ENG.). 2010. audio compact disk 24.95 (978-1-4084-6672-8(4)) Pub: AudioGO. Dist(s): Perseus Dist

Ghostly Tales of Japan. Short Stories. Rafe Martin. 1 cass. (Running Time: 60 min.). (J). (gr. 3 up). 1989. 9.95 (978-0-938756-23-1(0), 025) Yellow Moon.
Traditional & original ghost stories from Japan. "Rafe Martin's convincing delivery & excellent timing cast listeners under the spell of Japan..." - Booklist.

Ghosts. 1 cass. (Running Time: 28 min.). 12.00 (L360) MEA A Watts Cass.

Ghosts. Henrik Ibsen. Narrated by Flo Gibson. (ENG.). 2009. audio compact disk 16.95 (978-1-60646-094-8(3)) Audio Bk Con.

Ghosts. unabr. ed. Ed McBain, pseud. Read by Jonathan Marosz. 6 cass. (Running Time: 6 hrs.). (87th Precinct Ser.: Bk. 34). 1998. 36.00 (978-0-7366-4109-8(2), 4614) Books on Tape.
A famous author of supernatural tales has been murdered & Steve Carella must enter the frightening world of the occult.

Ghosts. unabr. ed. Adrian Plass. 2003. 29.99 (978-0-310-25215-3(6)) Zondervan.

Ghosts, Set. unabr. ed. Henrik Ibsen. Narrated by Henrik Ibsen. Read by Flo Gibson. 2 cass. (Running Time: 2 hrs. 30 min.). 1993. 14.95 (978-1-55685-274-9(6)) Audio Bk Con.
Haunting memories of the sins of the father & Oswald's heredity are the moving themes of this drama.

Ghosts! Ghostly Tales from Folklore. unabr. abr. ed. Alvin Schwartz. Illus. by Victoria Chess. 1 cass. (Running Time: 15 min.). (I Can Read Bks.). (J). (ps-3). 1995. 8.99 (978-0-694-70026-4(6)) HarperCollins Pubs.

Ghosts: The Story of a Reunion. unabr. ed. Zondervan Publishing Staff & Adrian Plass. (Running Time: 6 hrs. 22 mins. 0 sec.). (ENG.). 2003. 10.99 (978-0-310-26154-4(6)) Zondervan.

Ghosts among Us. James Van Praagh. Narrated by Lloyd James. (Playaway Adult Nonfiction Ser.). 2008. 54.99 (978-1-60640-556-7(X)) Find a World.

Ghosts among Us: Uncovering the Truth about the Other Side. unabr. ed. James Van Praagh. Narrated by Lloyd James. (Running Time: 7 hrs. 0 mins. 0 sec.). (ENG.). 2008. audio compact disk 19.99 (978-1-4001-5728-0(5)) Pub: Tantor Media. Dist(s): IngramPubServ

Ghosts among Us: Uncovering the Truth about the Other Side. unabr. ed. James Van Praagh. Read by Lloyd James. (Running Time: 7 hrs. 0 mins. 0 sec.). (ENG.). 2008. audio compact disk 29.99 (978-1-4001-0728-5(8)) Pub: Tantor Media. Dist(s): IngramPubServ

Ghosts among Us: Uncovering the Truth about the Other Side. unabr. ed. James Van Praagh. Read by Lloyd James. Narrated by Lloyd James. (Running Time: 7 hrs. 0 mins. 0 sec.). (ENG.). 2008. audio compact disk 59.99 (978-1-4001-3728-2(4)) Pub: Tantor Media. Dist(s): IngramPubServ

***Ghosts & Lightning.** unabr. ed. Trevor Byrne. Narrated by John Lee. (Running Time: 7 hrs. 30 mins.). 2010. 14.99 (978-1-4001-8555-9(6)); 34.99 (978-1-4001-9555-8(1)); 24.99 (978-1-4001-6555-1(5)); audio compact disk 69.99 (978-1-4001-4555-3(4)); audio compact disk 34.99 (978-1-4001-1555-6(8)) Pub: Tantor Media. Dist(s): IngramPubServ

ghost's Child. Sonya Hartnett. Read by Caroline Lee. (Running Time: 4 hrs. 20 mins.). (J). 2009. 59.99 (978-1-74214-395-8(4), 9781742143958) Pub: Bolinda Pubng AUS. Dist(s): Bolinda Pub Inc

Ghost's Child. unabr. ed. Sonya Hartnett. Read by Caroline Lee. 4 CDs. (Running Time: 4 hrs. 20 mins.). (YA). (gr. 8 up). 2008. audio compact disk 57.95 (978-1-921334-68-9(1), 9781921334689) Pub: Bolinda Pubng AUS. Dist(s): Bolinda Pub Inc

Ghosts, Coast to Coast. Compiled by Kalyomi. 2008. audio compact disk 18.95 (978-1-4276-3512-9(9)) AardGP.

Ghosts Coast to Coast. Kalyomi. 2008. 23.99 (978-1-4276-3586-0(2)) AardGP.

Ghosts in the Gallery: My Life with Carlos Castaneda. Barbara Brooks Wallace. Narrated by Christina Moore. 4 CDs. (Running Time: 4 hrs. 30 mins.). (gr. 3 up). audio compact disk 39.00 (978-1-4025-1962-8(1)) Recorded Bks.

Ghosts in the Gallery: My Life with Carlos Castaneda. unabr. ed. Barbara Brooks Wallace. Narrated by Christina Moore. 4 pieces. (Running Time: 4 hrs. 30 mins.). (gr. 3 up). 2001. 36.00 (978-0-7887-5024-3(0), 96377E7) Recorded Bks.
Even though her family is poor, 11-year-old Jenny loves her life in China. But after her stepfather dies & her mother falls ill, Jenny finds herself on a long ocean voyage to America - to live with a grandfather she has never seen.

***Ghosts of Cannae: Hannibal & the Darkest Hour of the Roman Republic.** unabr. ed. Robert L. O'Connell. (Running Time: 14 hrs. 0 mins.). 2010. 19.99 (978-1-4001-8722-5(2)) Tantor Media.

***Ghosts of Cannae: Hannibal & the Darkest Hour of the Roman Republic.** unabr. ed. Robert L. O'Connell. Narrated by Alan Sklar. (Running Time: 13 hrs. 30 mins. 0 sec.). 2010. 29.99 (978-1-4001-6722-7(1)); audio compact disk 79.99 (978-1-4001-4722-9(0)); audio compact disk 39.99 (978-1-4001-1722-2(4)) Pub: Tantor Media. Dist(s): IngramPubServ

Ghosts of Everest: The Search for Mallory & Irvine. collector's ed. Jochen Hemmleb et al. Read by Arthur Addison. 5 cass. (Running Time: 7 hrs. 30 min.). 1999. 40.00 (978-0-7366-4856-1(9)) Books on Tape.
One of the most puzzling & compelling adventure mysteries of all time. On June 6, 1924, George Leigh Mallory & Andrew Comyn Irvine were only a few hundred feet short of becoming the first men to reach the highest spot on earth when they simply walked into the mist, never to be seen again. Did they reach the summit of Mount Everest, nearly three decades before

Edmunt Hillary & Tenzing Norgay? This is the meticulous report of both the 1924 British Expedition & the 1999 Mallory & Irvine Research Expedition which found George Mallory's body & answers to the questions that have plagued historians & mountaineers alike. Did they make it & if they did, what happened to them?.

Ghosts of Everest: The Search for Mallory & Irvine. collector's unabr. ed. Jochen Hemmleb et al. Read by Arthur Addison. 6 CDs. (Running Time: 7 hrs. 12 mins.). 2000. audio compact disk 48.00 (978-0-7366-5209-4(4)) Books on Tape.

Ghosts of Everest: The Search for Mallory & Irvine. unabr. ed. Jochen Hemmleb & Larry A. Johnson. Read by Arthur Addison. 5 cass. (Running Time: 7 hrs. 30 mins.). 2000. 30.00 (5164) Books on Tape.
The complete story of two of the most highly publicized Mount Everest expeditions of the century.

Ghosts of Everest: The Search for Mallory & Irvine. unabr. ed. Jochen Hemmleb et al. Read by Arthur Addison. 6 CDs. (Running Time: 7 hrs. 30 mins.). 2000. audio compact disk 34.95 (978-0-7366-5047-2(4)) Books on Tape.
One of the most puzzling & compelling adventure mysteries of all tiem. On June 6, 1924, George Leigh Mallory & Andrew Comyn Irvine were only a few hundred feet short of becoming the first men to reach the highest spot on earth when they simply walked into the mist, never to be seen again. did they reach the summit of Mount Everest, nearly three decades before Edmunt Hillary & Tenzing Norgay? This is the meticulous report of both the 1924 British Expedition & the 1999 Mallory & Irvine Research Expedition which found George Mallory's body & answers to the questions that have plagued historians & mountaineers alike. Did they make it & if they did, what happened to them.

Ghosts of Everest: The Search for Mallory & Irvine. unabr. ed. Jochen Hemmleb et al. 5 cass. (Running Time: 7 hrs. 30 mins.). 2000. 24.95 (978-0-7366-4932-2(8)) Books on Tape.
The complete story of two of the most highly publicized Mount Everest expeditions of the century.

Ghosts of Fear Street, Vols. 1-2, set. abr. ed. R. L. Stine. 2 cass. (Running Time: 2 hrs.). (Ghosts of Fear Street Ser.: Nos. 1-2). (YA). (gr. 7 up). (395157) S&S Audio.
In "Three Little Wishes" Hannah's younger brother opens the bottle she found in Fear Lake, in spite of the warning label. He lets loose a genie with evil plans. In "The Creature From Club Lagoona." Tad's family vacation at a water resort seems like it will be nothing but fun, but Tad's afraid of the water & he should be.

***Ghosts of Kerfol.** unabr. ed. Deborah Noyes. (Running Time: 4 hrs.). 2010. 39.97 (978-1-4418-8969-0(8), 9781441889690, Candlewick Bril); 14.99 (978-1-4418-8968-3(X), 9781441889683, Candlewick Bril); audio compact disk 14.99 (978-1-4418-8966-9(3), 9781441889669, Candlewick Bril); audio compact disk 39.97 (978-1-4418-8967-6(1), 9781441889676, Candlewick Bril) Brilliance Audio.

***Ghosts of Kerfol.** unabr. ed. Deborah Noyes. Read by Justine Eyre. (Running Time: 4 hrs.). 2010. audio compact disk 14.99 (978-1-4418-8964-5(7), 9781441889645, Candlewick Bril); audio compact disk 44.97 (978-1-4418-8965-2(5), 9781441889652, Candlewick Bril) Brilliance Audio.

Ghosts of N-Space. Doctor Who. 3 CDs. (Running Time: 2 hrs. 45 mins.). 2001. audio compact disk 13.99 (978-0-563-47701-3(6)) London Brdge.

Ghosts of Onyx. unabr. ed. Eric S. Nylund & Eric Nylund. Read by Jonathan Davis. 8 CDs. (Running Time: 11 hrs. 0 mins. 0 sec.). (Halo Ser.). (ENG.). 2007. audio compact disk 29.95 (978-1-59397-983-6(5)) Pub: Macmill Audio. Dist(s): Macmillan

Ghosts of Rathburn Park. unabr. ed. Zilpha Keatley Snyder. Narrated by Ramon de Ocampo. 4 pieces. (Running Time: 4 hrs. 45 mins.). 2002. 39.00 (978-1-4025-3943-5(6)) Recorded Bks.

Ghosts of Sleath. James Herbert. (Isis Cassettes Ser.). 1997. 94.95 (978-1-85695-927-8(9)) Pub: ISIS Lrg Prnt GBR. Dist(s): Ulverscroft US

Ghosts of Sleath. unabr. ed. James Herbert. Read by Edmund Dehn. 12 cass. (Running Time: 15 hrs. 45 min.). 1997. 94.95 (978-1-85695-917-9(1), 951006) Pub: ISIS Audio GBR. Dist(s): Ulverscroft US
A small village hidden away in the Chiltern Hills, where little disturbs the centuries-old tranquility until the ghosts begin to appear & frighteningly bizarre events start to occur.

Ghosts of Sleath. unabr. ed. James Herbert. Read by Edmund Dehn. 14 CDs. (Running Time: 21 hrs.). 2001. audio compact disk 104.95 (1244-4) Pub: ISIS Audio GBR. Dist(s): ISIS Pub
Psychic investigator David Ash, a man burdened by the dark secret of his own past, is sent to Sleath to investigate the phenomena & his discoveries there drive him to the very edge of his own sanity. The incidents grow worse until, in the final night of horror, awesome & malign forces are unleashed in a supernatural storm that threatens to consume the village itself. For Sleath is not what it seems. And the Dead have returned for a reason.

Ghosts of the Buffaloes see Poetry of Vachel Lindsay

***Ghosts of War.** unabr. ed. Ryan Smithson. Read by Ryan Smithson. (ENG.). 2009. (978-0-06-189649-1(7)) HarperCollins Pubs.

***Ghosts of War: The True Story of a 19-Year-Old GI.** unabr. ed. Ryan Smithson. Read by Ryan Smithson. (ENG.). 2009. (978-0-06-180952-1(7)) HarperCollins Pubs.

Ghosts of Yesteryear. unabr. ed. Kathleen Dayus. Read by Diana Bishop. 4 cass. (Running Time: 6 hrs. 3 min.). (Isis Ser.). (J). 2001. 44.95 (978-0-7531-0880-2(1)) Pub: ISIS Lrg Prnt GBR. Dist(s): Ulverscroft US
Looking back with warmth, wit an honesty, Kathleen Dayus returns to her childhood years in a Birmingham slum and life before marriage. Now in her nineties, the author recalls the support and affection of her father and elder sister, Mary; the rivalries and friendships of her schooldays; her early working experiences and romantic encounters - memories that remain as sharp and evocative as ever.

Ghostway. Tony Hillerman. Read by Nelson Runger. 6 cass. (Running Time: 7 hrs. 30 min.). (Joe Leaphorn & Jim Chee Novel Ser.). 1993. 47.20 Set. (978-1-56544-040-1(4), 250033); Rental 8.50 30 day rental Set. (250033) Literate Ear.
Old Joseph Joe witnessed the shooting at the Shiprock laundromat. The killer drove off, but Old Joe saw the Polaroid of the man he was looking for. Enter Sergeant Jim Chee.

Ghostway. unabr. ed. Tony Hillerman. Read by Jonathan Marosz. 7 cass. (Running Time: 7 hrs.). (Joe Leaphorn & Jim Chee Novel Ser.). 1994. 56.00 (978-0-7366-2748-1(0), 3473) Books on Tape.
Jim Chee follows his leads where they take him...even after the FBI warns him off.

Ghostway. unabr. ed. Tony Hillerman. Read by George Guidall. 4 Cass. (Running Time: 7.25). (Joe Leaphorn & Jim Chee Novel Ser.). 19.95 (978-1-4025-3711-0(5)); audio compact disk 29.95 (978-1-4025-3712-7(3)) Recorded Bks.

Ghostway. unabr. ed. Tony Hillerman. Narrated by George Guidall. 5 cass. (Running Time: 7 hrs. 15 mins.). (Joe Leaphorn & Jim Chee Novel Ser.). 1990. 44.00 (978-1-55690-194-2(1), 90098E7) Recorded Bks.
An old man's hazy memory & a Polaroid snapshot are all Chee has to go on, but they are enough to send him deep into an underworld of murder & revenge.

Ghostway. unabr. abr. ed. Tony Hillerman. Read by Gil Silverbird. (Joe Leaphorn & Jim Chee Novel Ser.). 2005. audio compact disk 14.95 (978-0-06-081508-0(6)) HarperCollins Pubs.

***Ghostwriter Secret.** unabr. ed. Mac Barnett. Read by Arte Johnson. (Running Time: 3 hrs. 20 mins.). (Brixton Brothers Ser.: Bk. 2). (ENG.). (J). 2010. audio compact disk 25.00 (978-0-307-71044-4(0), Listening Lib) Pub: Random Audio Pubg. Dist(s): Random

Ghostwriting: The Ultimate Guide to Creating a Bestseller (2007 Edition) Joel Hochman & Larry Leichman. 2009. 9.95 (978-0-9841992-0-4(9)) Arbor Bks NY.

Giant. unabr. collector's ed. Edna Ferber. Read by Flo Gibson. 10 cass. (Running Time: 15 hrs.). 1984. 80.00 (978-0-7366-0667-7(X), 1629) Books on Tape.
Leslie Lynnton, beautiful & spirited, leaves the peaceful charm & gracious pace of her Virginia home to meet the challenges of the wide open spaces of Texas with her husband, Bick Benedict, owner of the Reata Ranch Empire.

Giant, Set. unabr. ed. Edna Ferber. Read by Flo Gibson. 10 cass. (Running Time: 15 hrs.). (Classic Books on Cassettes Coll.). 1998. 80.00 Audio Bk Con.
A novel of Texas & its inhabitants, all larger than life.

Giant & the Rabbit: Six Bilingual Folktales from Hispanic Culture. Ed. by Sarah Barchas. Adapted by Sarah Barchas. Illus. by Elizabeth Gething. (Running Time: 70 min.). (ENG & SPA.). (J). (gr. k-5). 1996. pap. bk. 12.95 (978-0-9632621-6-5(5)) High Haven Mus.
Folktales reflecting the richness & diversity of Hispanic culture.

Giant Axonal Neuropathy - A Bibliography & Dictionary for Physicians, Patients, & Genome Researchers. Compiled by Icon Group International, Inc. Staff. 2007. ring bd. 28.95 (978-0-497-11221-9(3)) Icon Grp.

Giant Bones. Peter S. Beagle. Narrated by Peter S. Beagle. (Running Time: 10 hrs.). (J). 2002. 30.95 (978-1-59912-497-1(1)) Iofy Corp.

Giant Book of Poetry: Complete Audio Library. unabr. ed. Ed. by William Roetzheim. 19 CDs. 2008. audio compact disk 29.95 (978-1-933769-40-0(8)) Pub: Level Four Pr. Dist(s): Midpt Trade

Giant Book of Poetry: Poems of Loss & Sorrow. Ed. by William Roetzheim. 2007. audio compact disk 9.95 (978-1-933769-01-1(7)) Pub: Level Four Pr. Dist(s): Midpt Trade

Giant Book of Poetry: Poems of Working. Ed. by William Roetzheim. 2007. audio compact disk 9.95 (978-1-933769-04-2(1)) Pub: Level Four Pr. Dist(s): Midpt Trade

Giant Book of Poetry: Poems That Make a Statement. Poems. Ed. by William Roetzheim. 2 CDs. Dramatization. 2007. audio compact disk 9.95 (978-1-933769-05-9(X)) Pub: Level Four Pr. Dist(s): Midpt Trade

Giant Book of Poetry: Poets Look at War & Peace. Ed. by William Roetzheim. 2007. audio compact disk 9.95 (978-1-933769-07-3(6)) Pub: Level Four Pr. Dist(s): Midpt Trade

Giant Book of Poetry - Audio Edition V. 1: Poems of Romance. unabr. ed. Poems. Ed. by William Roetzheim. Prod. by Robert Masson. Directed By Joel Castellaw. Dramatization. 2006. audio compact disk 9.95 (978-0-9768001-4-9(4)) Pub: Level Four Pr. Dist(s): Midpt Trade
Professionally performed and produced audio CD containing Poems of Romance from "The Giant Book of Poetry." Contains forty-eight poems grouped by courting, unrequited love, beauty, love, seperation, redemption, and commitment. Disk 1 of a 15 disk set covering all genres from "The Giant Book of Poetry." Additional disks will be released monthly.

Giant Book of Poetry Audio Edition: Case of 100 assorted Titles. 2006. audio compact disk 995.00 (978-1-933769-11-0(4)) Pub: Level Four Pr. Dist(s): Baker Taylor

Giant Book of Poetry Audio Edition: Poems for Children of all Ages, Vol. 6. Ed. by William Roetzheim. 2007. audio compact disk 9.95 (978-0-9768001-9-4(5)) Pub: Level Four Pr. Dist(s): Midpt Trade

Giant Book of Poetry Audio Edition: Poems of Ghosts, Evil, & Superstition. Poems. Ed. by William Roetzheim. 2 CDs. Dramatization. 2007. audio compact disk 9.95 (978-1-933769-00-4(9)) Pub: Level Four Pr. Dist(s): Midpt Trade

Giant Book of Poetry Audio Edition: Poems of Nature. Ed. by William Roetzheim. 2007. audio compact disk 9.95 (978-1-933769-02-8(5)) Pub: Level Four Pr. Dist(s): Midpt Trade

Giant Book of Poetry Audio Edition: Poems of the Human Condition. Ed. by William Roetzheim. 2007. audio compact disk 9.95 (978-1-933769-03-5(3)) Pub: Level Four Pr. Dist(s): Midpt Trade

Giant Book of Poetry Audio Edition: Poets Look at Choices in Life. Ed. by William Roetzheim. 2007. audio compact disk 9.95 (978-1-933769-06-6(8)) Pub: Level Four Pr. Dist(s): Midpt Trade

Giant Book of Poetry Audio Edition: Poets Look at Writing, Art, & Poetry. Ed. by William Roetzheim. 2007. audio compact disk 9.95 (978-1-933769-08-0(4)) Pub: Level Four Pr. Dist(s): Midpt Trade

Giant Book of Poetry Audio Edition, V. 2: Poets Look at Growing up & Growing Old. Poems. Ed. by William Roetzheim. Prod. by Robert Masson. Directed By Joel Castellaw. Dramatization. 2006. audio compact disk 9.95 (978-0-9768001-5-6(2)) Pub: Level Four Pr. Dist(s): Midpt Trade
Professionally performed and produced audio CD containing poems dealing with "growing up and growing old" from The Giant Book of Poetry. Poems are collected by generations, purberty, middle-age, looking back, aging, waiting for death, and mortal illness. More than 50 poems. Second in a series of fifteen disks that will be released monthly.

Giant Book of Poetry Audio Edition V. 3: Poems of Inspiration & Faith, 3. unabr. ed. Poems. Ed. by William Roetzheim. Dramatization. 2006. audio compact disk 9.95 (978-0-9768001-6-3(0)) Pub: Level Four Pr. Dist(s): Midpt Trade
Professionally performed and produced audio disk containing 39 poems of inspiration from The Giant Book of Poetry. Poems are grouped by western religion, pagan religion, eastern religion, questioning religion, and inspiration. Third in a series of fifteen audio poetry disks that will be released monthly.

Giant Book of Poetry Audio Edition V. 4: Poets Look at Lust, Betrayal, & Lost Love, Poems. Ed. by William Roetzheim. Dramatization. 2006. audio compact disk 9.95 (978-0-9768001-7-0(9)) Pub: Level Four Pr. Dist(s): Midpt Trade
Professionally performed and produced audio CD containing 45 poems of lust, betrayal and lost love from The Giant Book of Poetry. Poems are grouped by lust, philandering, betrayal, battle of the sexes, failed relationships, and moving on. This is disk four of a fifteen disk release, with disks released one per month.

Giant Book of Poetry Audio Edition V. 5: Poets Look at Eternity, Poems. Ed. by William Roetzheim. Dramatization. 2006. audio compact disk 9.95 (978-0-9768001-8-7(7)) Pub: Level Four Pr. Dist(s): Midpt Trade
Professionally performed and produced audio CD containing poems 49 about eternity from The Giant Book of Poetry. Poems are grouped by priorities; the march of time; dust unto dust; a passageway; heaven, hell, and purgatory; immortality; and the end of the world. This is disk five of a fifteen disk set containing poems from The Giant Book of Poetry. Disks are released monthly.

Giant Devil-Dingo. 2004. bk. 24.95 (978-1-56008-202-6(X)); 8.95 (978-1-56008-906-3(7)); cass. & flmstrp 30.00 (978-1-56008-673-4(4)) Weston Woods.

Giant Jim & the Hurricane. unabr. ed. Jeremy Strong. Read by Tony Robinson. 1 cass. (Running Time: 42 mins). 2002. (978-1-85549-173-1(7)) Cover To Cover GBR.
Jim is so big that the people of the town tell him he has to leave, even though the children love him. But when a terrible hurricane strikes, Giant Jim is the only one who can help.

***Giant John.** Arnold Lobel. Narrated by Jim Brownold. 1 CD. (Running Time: 10 mins.). (J). (gr. 1-4). 2009. bk. 29.95 (978-0-8045-4203-6(1)); bk. 27.95 (978-0-8045-6978-1(9)) Spoken Arts.

Giant Killer: A Heart Like David. Perf. by Dennis Jernigan. 2002. audio compact disk Provident Mus Dist.

Giant of Ginger Hill. (Sails Literacy Ser.). (gr. 2 up). 10.00 (978-0-7578-2671-9(7)) Rigby Educ.

Giant of the Sea: A Story of a Sperm Whale. Courtney Granet Raff. (ENG.). (J). (ps-2). 2005. 8.95 (978-1-59249-068-4(9), SC4023) Soundprints.

Giant Problem. Holly Black & Tony DiTerlizzi. Read by Andrew McCarthy. (Beyond the Spiderwick Chronicles: Bk. 2). (J). 2008. 39.99 (978-1-60640-957-2(3)) Find a World.

Giant Problem. unabr. ed. Holly Black & Tony DiTerlizzi. Read by Andrew McCarthy. (Running Time: 2 hrs. 0 mins. 0 sec.). (Beyond the Spiderwick Chronicles: Bk. 2). (ENG.). (J). 2008. audio compact disk 17.99 (978-0-7435-7469-3(9)) Pub: S&S Audio. Dist(s): S and S Inc

Giant Steps: Small Changes to Make a Big Difference. abr. ed. Anthony Robbins. Read by Anthony Robbins. 2 Cds. (Running Time: 20 hrs. 0 mins. 0 sec.). (ENG.). 2003. audio compact disk 19.95 (978-0-7435-2901-3(4), Sound Ideas) Pub: S&S Audio. Dist(s): S and S Inc

Giants! A Colossal Collection of Tales & Tunes. Short Stories. As told by Jim Weiss. 1 CD. (Running Time: 1 hr.). Dramatization. (Storyteller's Version Ser.). (J). (gr. k up). 1996. audio compact disk 14.95 (978-1-882513-42-0(8), 1124-017) Greathall Prods.
A rollicking and colorful collection of classics and folktales with musical accompaniment about giants and ogres that will leave a giant grin on every listener's face. Includes "Jack and the Beanstalk," "The Selfish Giant (includes song: "In the Garden"), "The Giant of Grabbist," Song: "If I Were a Giant" and "The "Fantastical Tale of Finn MacCoul".

Giants! A Colossal Collection of Tales & Tunes. Short Stories. As told by Jim Weiss. 1 cass. (Running Time: 1 hr.). Dramatization. (Storyteller's Version Ser.). (J). (gr. k up). 1996. 10.95 (978-1-882513-17-8(7), 1124-17) Greathall Prods.

Giants! A Colossal Collection of Tales & Tunes. Jim Weiss. 1 cass., 1 CD. (J). 7.98 (GHP 17); audio compact disk 11.98 CD. NewSound.
A collection of classics & folktales with musical accompaniment about giants & ogres.

Giants & Birds. unabr. ed. Gioia Timpanelli. 1 cass. 1983. 9.00 (978-1-56964-817-9(4), A0144-83) Sound Photosyn.
An enthusiastic & exceptional storyteller for all ages.

Giants & the Dwarfs. unabr. ed. 1 cass. (Running Time: 20 min.). Dramatization. (Magic Looking Glass Ser.). (J). (gr. 2-6). 1989. 9.95 (978-0-7810-0041-3(6), NIM-CW-129-6-C) NIMCO.
A Dutch folk tale.

Giants & the Joneses. unabr. ed. Julie Donaldson. Read by Patricia Conolly. 3 CDs. (Running Time: 3 hrs. 30 mins.). (J). 2006. audio compact disk 29.75 (978-1-4193-7103-5(7), C3545); 29.75 (978-1-4193-7098-4(7), 98270) Recorded Bks.
British author and Smarties Book Prize recipient Julia Donaldson has written over 50 books for children. She pens a delightful twist to an old fairy tale. Jumbeelia plants her own bimblestonk (beanstalk) and makes a daring trip down to the land of the iggly plops (little people). The humans don¿t believe in giants, so they are in for a big surprise when Jumbeelia comes looking for souvenirs!.

Giant's Cauldron: Viking Myths of Adventure. unabr. rev. ed. Odds Bodkin Storytelling Library Staff. 1 cass. (Running Time: 1 hr. 6 mins.). Dramatization. (Odds Bodkin Musical Story Collection). (gr. 3-7). 2003. 9.95 (978-1-882412-03-7(6)) Pub: Rivertree. Dist(s): Penton Overseas
Includes: "Thor Against the Frost Giants" & "The Mead of Poetry." Performed on twelve-string guitars.

Giants, Ghosts & Goblins: Traditional Tales from Around the World. John Matthews & John Matthews. Read by Jerry Nelson. 2 CDs. (Running Time: 2 mins. 55 sec.). (ENG., (J). (gr. 1-5). 2001. audio compact disk 19.99 (978-1-84148-421-1(0)) BarefootBksMA.
Tales from around the world, full of ghosts, ghouls and demons.

Giant's Ice Cream. Jill Eggleton. Illus. by Kelvin Hawley. (Sails Literacy Ser.). (gr. k up). 10.00 (978-0-7578-2647-4(4)) Rigby Educ.

Giants of Philosophy, Set. Charlton Heston. 26 cass. (Audio Classics Ser.). 1991. 194.00 (978-0-938935-16-2(X), 10325) Knowledge Prod.
These cassettes describe & explain the views of the most influential philosophers in history. Assuming no prior knowledge of the listener, each pair of cassettes presents the concerns, questions, interests, & overall world view of a great philosopher. A special emphasis is placed on making each idea both clear & relevant to modern listeners, to gain a new arsenal of insights to help us live better lives.

Giants of Philosophy Boxed Set. unabr. ed. Berel Lang et al. Read by Charlton Heston. (Running Time: 93600 sec.). (Audio Classics Ser.). 2008. audio compact disk 99.95 (978-0-7861-5893-5(X)) Blckstn Audio.

Giants of Political Thought. Narrated by Craig Deitschmann. 24 cass. (Audio Classics Ser.). 1987. 179.00 Set. (978-0-938935-00-1(3), 10125) Knowledge Prod.
Government & politics have a daily influence on our lives. The authority & responsibilities given to government affect not only our social customs but our prosperity & our freedom. These cassettes present the most important ideas in political history. Includes Paine, Jefferson, Thoreau, William Lloyd Garrison, Adam Smith, J.S. Mill, Wollstonecraft, Machiavelli, Boetie, Marx & Engels, Rousseau, Burke, Paine, Hamilton, Madison & Jay, Hobbes, Locke, Tocqueville.

Giants of Political Thought Boxed Set. unabr. ed. Thomas Paine et al. Read by Craig Deitschmann. (Running Time: 113400 sec.). (Audio Classics Ser.). 2008. audio compact disk 99.95 (978-0-7861-5891-1(3)) Blckstn Audio.

Giants of the Faith. John A. O'Brien. Read by Al Covaia. 9 cass. (Running Time: 31 hrs.). 1987. 39.95 (761) Ignatius Pr.
Studies of St. Paul, St. Augustine, John Henry Newman, G.K. Chesterton, Orestes Brownson. Issac Hecker.

Giants of the Frost. unabr. ed. Kim Wilkins. Read by Edwina Wren. (Running Time: 55080 sec.). 2007. audio compact disk 113.95 (978-1-74093-967-6(0), 9781740939676) Pub: Bolinda Pubng AUS. Dist(s): Bolinda Pub Inc

***Giants of the Frost.** unabr. ed. Kim Wilkins. Read by Edwina Wren. (Running Time: 15 hrs. 20 mins.). 2010. 43.95 (978-1-74214-583-9(3), 9781742145839) Pub: Bolinda Pubng AUS. Dist(s): Bolinda Pub Inc

Giapponese Senza Sforzo. Tr. of Japanese with Ease. (ITA & JPN., 1997. pap. bk. 75.00 (978-2-7005-1357-8(6)) Pub: Assimil FRA. Dist(s): Distribks Inc

Gib & the Gray Ghost. Zilpha Keatley Snyder. Narrated by Ed Sala. 5 CDs. (Running Time: 5 hrs. 45 mins.). (gr. 5 up). audio compact disk 48.00 (978-1-4025-0472-3(1)) Recorded Bks.

Gib & the Gray Ghost. unabr. ed. Zilpha Keatley Snyder. Narrated by Ed Sala. 4 pieces. (Running Time: 5 hrs. 45 mins.). (gr. 5 up). 2001. 38.00 (978-0-7887-5500-2(5)) Recorded Bks.
Once again, Gib is living on the Thornton's ranch, feeling like an outsider, but hoping to be adopted. A beautiful gray horse appears from nowhere. Gib has no idea how much helping the "Gray Ghost" will change his own life.

Gib Rides Home. Zilpha Keatley Snyder. Read by Ed Sala. 5 cass. (Running Time: 6 hrs.). (YA). 1999. 122.80 (978-0-7887-3023-8(1), 46840) Recorded Bks.
In all his 11 years, orphaned Gib has longed for a place to call home. Being adopted in the early 1900s means being farmed out to work, so he wonders if he will ever have a family to call his own.

Gib Rides Home. Zilpha Keatley Snyder. Read by Ed Sala. 5 cass. (Running Time: 6 hrs.). (YA). (gr. 5 up). 1999. pap. bk. 59.75 (978-0-7887-2993-5(4), 40875) Recorded Bks.

Gib Rides Home. unabr. ed. Zilpha Keatley Snyder. Narrated by Ed Sala. 5 pieces. (Running Time: 6 hrs.). (gr. 4 up). 1999. 47.00 (978-0-7887-2963-8(2), 95737E7) Recorded Bks.

Gibbons. abr. ed. Kaye Gibbons. (ENG.). 2012. audio compact disk 29.95 (978-0-7393-2193-5(5), Random AudioBks) Pub: Random Audio Pubg. Dist(s): Random

Gibraltar: The History of a Fortress. unabr. collector's ed. Ernle Bradford. Read by Walter Zimmerman. 7 cass. (Running Time: 7 hrs.). 1991. 42.00 (978-0-7366-2050-5(8), 2862) Books on Tape.
Gibraltar has been a major landmark ever since the first galleys ventured into the Atlantic. To Greeks & Romans it was one of the two pillars of Hercules - the end of the known world & the beginning of the "Stream of Ocean." Gibraltar's location dictated that it would become a fortress. Over the ages it has served different masters...Roman, Arab, Spanish, English. Today, despite all the technology the 20th century can muster, Gibraltar remains as strategically vital as ever.

Gibraltar Passage. unabr. ed. T. Davis Bunn. Read by Ron Varela. 4 cass. (Running Time: 4 hrs. 48 mins.). (Destiny Ser.: Bk. 2). 1999. 26.95 (978-1-55686-964-8(9)) Books in Motion.
When Pierre Servais learns from a refugee that his twin brother, Patrique, might be alive, a search begins that leads Pierre & his friend Jake Burnes from France through Gibraltar to Morocco.

Gibson Electric Guitar Basics. 1999. bk. 3.70 (978-0-7692-6882-8(X), Warner Bro) Alfred Pub.

Giddy-Up! Sing, Dance & Read with Me. Susan James. 1 CD. (Running Time: 1 hr). (J). (ps-3). 2000. pap. bk. 29.95 (978-1-931127-46-2(8), 986-003) Kindermusik Intl.
This softcover whimsical, rhythmical book features an imaginative rendition of the childhood favorite activity of giddy-upping. A cassette contains three readings of the story, two with page - turn signals.

Gideon. unabr. ed. Russell Andrews. Read by James Daniels. (Running Time: 14 hrs.). 2008. 39.25 (978-1-4233-3992-2(4), 9781423339922, BADLE); 39.25 (978-1-4233-3990-8(8), 9781423339908, Brlnc Audio MP3 Lib); 24.95 (978-1-4233-3989-2(4), 9781423339892, Brilliance MP3); 24.95 (978-1-4233-3991-5(6), 9781423339915, BAD) Brilliance Audio.

Gideon, Set. abr. ed. Russell Andrews. Read by James Daniels. 2 cass. 1999. 17.95 (FS9-50940) Highsmith.

Gideon, Set. unabr. ed. Russell Andrews. Read by James Daniels. 9 cass. 1999. 39.95 (FS9-50933) Highsmith.

Gideon the Cutpurse, Pt. 1. unabr. ed. Linda Buckley-Archer. Read by Gerard Doyle. 10 CDs. (Running Time: 12 hrs. 0 mins. 0 sec.). (ENG.). (J). (gr. 4-7). 2006. audio compact disk 39.95 (978-0-7435-5558-6(9)) Pub: SandS Childrens. Dist(s): S and S Inc

Gideon the Cutpurse: Being the First Part of the Gideon Trilogy. unabr. ed. Linda Buckley-Archer. Read by Gerard Doyle. 10 cass. (Running Time: 12 hrs.). (YA). (gr. 5-8). 2006. 71.75 (978-1-4281-1068-7(2)); audio compact disk 108.75 (978-1-4281-1073-1(9)) Recorded Bks.

Gideon the Cutpurse: Being the First Part of the Gideon Trilogy. unabr. ed. Linda Buckley-Archer. Read by Gerard Doyle. (J). 2006. 23.95 (978-0-7435-6425-0(1)) Pub: S&S Audio. Dist(s): S and S Inc

Gideon's Gift. Karen Kingsbury. Narrated by John McDonough. 3 cass. (Running Time: 3 hrs. 30 mins.). 2002. 28.00 (978-1-4025-4406-4(5)) Recorded Bks.

Gideon's Spies. abr. ed. Gordon Thomas. Read by Theodore Bikel. 4 cass. (Running Time: 6 hrs.). 2001. 25.00 (978-1-59040-122-4(0), Phoenix Audio) Pub: Amer Intl Pub. Dist(s): PerseuPGW

***Gideon's Sword.** unabr. ed. Douglas Preston & Lincoln Child. Read by John Glover. (Running Time: 14 hrs.). (ENG.). 2011. 26.98 (978-1-60024-996-9(5)); audio compact disk 39.98 (978-1-60024-997-6(3)) Pub: Hachet Audio. Dist(s): HachBkGrp

Gifford Lectures. Prod. by Michael Ignatieff. Hosted by Michael Ignatieff. 5 CDs. (Running Time: 5 hrs.). 2005. audio compact disk 39.95 (978-0-660-19226-0(8)) Pub: Canadian Broadcasting CAN. Dist(s): Georgetown Term

***Gift.** (ENG.). 2010. audio compact disk (978-1-59171-256-5(4)) Falcon Picture.

Gift. (Paws & Tales Ser.: Vol. 27). (J). 2002. audio compact disk 5.99 (978-1-57972-437-5(X)) Insight Living.

Gift. (Paws & Tales Ser.: Vol. 27). (J). 2002. 3.99 (978-1-57972-436-8(1)) Insight Living.

Gift. Max Brand. (Running Time: 2 hrs. 24 mins.). 1999. 10.95 (978-1-60083-484-4(1)) Iofy Corp.

***Gift.** Max Brand. 2009. (978-1-60136-408-1(3)) Audio Holding.

***Gift.** unabr. ed. Cecelia Ahern. Read by Kevin Kearns. (ENG.). 2009. (978-0-06-196706-1(8), Harper Audio); (978-0-06-184560-4(4), Harper Audio) HarperCollins Pubs.

Gift. unabr. ed. Richard Paul Evans. Read by John Dossett. (Running Time: 5 hrs. 0 mins. 0 sec.). (ENG.). 2007. audio compact disk 29.95 (978-0-7435-6887-6(7)) Pub: S&S Audio. Dist(s): S and S Inc

***Gift.** unabr. ed. Richard Paul Evans. Read by John Dossett. (Running Time: 5 hrs. 0 mins. 0 sec.). (ENG.). 2010. audio compact disk 14.99 (978-1-4423-3552-3(1)) Pub: S&S Audio. Dist(s): S and S Inc

Gift. unabr. ed. James Patterson & Gabrielle Charbonnet. Read by Spencer Locke & Elijah Wood. (Running Time: 5 hrs.). (ENG.). 2009. 9.98 (978-1-60024-773-6(3)) Pub: Hachet Audio. Dist(s): HachBkGrp

***Gift.** unabr. ed. James Patterson & Gabrielle Charbonnet. Read by Spencer Locke & Elijah Wood. (Running Time: 5 hrs.). (ENG.). 2010. audio compact disk 9.98 (978-1-60788-818-5(1)) Pub: Hachet Audio. Dist(s): HachBkGrp

***Gift.** unabr. ed. James Patterson & Ned Rust. Read by Spencer Locke et al. (Running Time: 7 hrs.). (ENG.). 2010. 15.98 (978-1-60788-675-4(8)) Pub: Hachet Audio. Dist(s): HachBkGrp

***Gift.** unabr. gif. ed. James Patterson & Ned Rust. Read by Peter Giles et al. (Running Time: 7 hrs.). (ENG.). 2010. audio compact disk 22.98 (978-1-60788-674-7(X)) Pub: Hachet Audio. Dist(s): HachBkGrp

Gift: A treasury of mental techniques strategies to empower your Riding. Frwd. by Lynn Palm, Sr. (ENG.). 2008. audio compact disk (978-0-9662585-2-3(5)) Ctr For Equestrian.

Gift: Audio Program MP3 Files. Created by Henry A. Penix. (ENG.). 2007. 29.95 (978-0-9795672-0-9(3)) PFC Inc.

Gift: Compete Audio Program. Created by Henry A. Penix. (ENG.). 2007. audio compact disk 49.95 (978-0-9795672-1-6(1)) PFC Inc.

Gift: Poems by Hafiz, the Great Sufi Master. unabr. ed. Hafiz. Read by Daniel Ladinsky. 4 cass. (Running Time: 6 hrs.). 2001. 25.00 (978-1-57453-384-2(3)) Audio Lit.

Gift Bag Chronicles. Hilary De Vries. Read by Laura Hamilton. (Running Time: 6 hrs.). 2005. 21.95 (978-1-60083-326-7(8)) Iofy Corp.

Gift Bag Chronicles. abr. ed. Hilary De Vries. Read by Laura Hamilton. 5 CDs. (Running Time: 21600 sec.). 2005. audio compact disk 29.95 (978-1-59316-055-5(0), LL147) Listen & Live.
The Gift Bag Chronicles continues the outrageous misadventures of Hollywood girl-about-town Alex Davidson, who has moved up the ladder at her firm - formerly a mere publicist, she's now the head of 'event planning' division, which means she's a party planner. And what goes on behind the scenes while the real stars (and the plastic-surgeons who want to be treated like real stars) sip champagne, makes for the funniest, zingiest, sexiest story yet.

Gift Basket Business: Your Guide to Ideas & Possibilities. 1 cass. (Running Time: 23 min.). 35.95 (CFSS/CS28) Ctr Self Suff.

Gift Basket Idea Dialogue. Alfreda C. Doyle. Read by Sell Out Recordings Staff. 1 cass. (Running Time: 15 min.). 1991. 19.00 (S.O.R. 4003) Sell Out Recordings.
Ideas for gift baskets.

Gift Box Set. Created by Henry A. Penix. 2007. audio compact disk 316.84 (978-0-9772969-8-9(9)) PFC Inc.

Gift for All People: Thoughts on God's Great Grace. unabr. ed. Max Lucado. Narrated by Mark Warner. (ENG.). 2005. 13.99 (978-1-60814-225-5(6)); 17.99 (978-1-58926-919-4(5)) Oasis Audio.

Gift for Dusty. unabr. ed. Glen E. Guy. Read by Danny Taylor. 1 cass. (Running Time: 45 min.). Dramatization. (Adventures of Dusty Sourdough Ser.). (J). 1994. pap. bk. 14.95 (978-0-9644491-2-1(9)); 5.00; Rental 9.95 (978-0-9644491-1-4(0)) Old Alaska.
Story of Alaska in the 1800s based on historical fact.

Gift for the King: Piano arrangement of old Christmas favorites. gif. ed. Perf. by Joshua Harris. Arranged by Joshua Harris. (ENG.). (YA). 2006. audio compact disk 10.00 (978-1-930547-75-9(7)) Deeper Roots.

Gift from the Sea. 50th unabr. anniv. ed. Anne M. Lindbergh. Read by Claudette Colbert & Reeve Lindbergh. 2 CDs. (Running Time: 2 hrs. 30 mins.). (ENG.). 2005. audio compact disk 16.00 (978-0-7393-1801-0(2), Random AudioBks) Pub: Random Audio Pubg. Dist(s): Random
Over a quarter of a century after its first publication, the great and simple wisdom in this book continues to influence women's lives. From the Hardcover edition.

Gift Keepers. Julia Rose Martinez. (J). 2007. audio compact disk 19.99 (978-1-60247-953-1(4)) Tate Pubng.

Gift of an Ordinary Day: A Mother's Memoir. unabr. ed. Katrina Kenison. Read by Katrina Kenison. (Running Time: 10 hrs.). (ENG.). 2009. 24.98 (978-1-60024-734-7(2)); audio compact disk 29.98 (978-1-60024-733-0(4)) Pub: Hachet Audio. Dist(s): HachBkGrp

***Gift of Change.** abr. ed. Marianne Williamson. Read by Marianne Williamson. (ENG.). 2004. (978-0-06-081818-0(2), Harper Audio); (978-0-06-081817-3(4), Harper Audio) HarperCollins Pubs.

Gift of Change: Spiritual Guidance for a Radically New Life. abr. ed. Marianne Williamson. Read by Marianne Williamson. 2004. audio compact disk 29.95 (978-0-06-073845-7(6)) HarperCollins Pubs.

***Gift of Church: How God Designed the Local Church to Meet Our Needs As Christians.** unabr. ed. Jim Samra. (Running Time: 4 hrs. 56 mins. 35 sec.). (ENG.). 2010. 14.99 (978-0-310-40579-5(3)) Zondervan.

Gift of Dogfood. Blaine Yorgason & Brenton Yorgason. Read by Marvin Payne. 1 cass. (Gospel Power Ser.). 6.95 (978-0-929985-50-3(8)) Jackman Pubng.
A father's letter to his son concerning loving our neighborhood.

Gift of Dyslexia: Why Some of the Smartest People Can't Read & How They Can Learn. Ronald D. Davis. Ed. by Eldon M. Braun. Intro. by Joan M. Smith. 3 cass. 1994. bk. 34.95 (978-0-929551-24-1(9)) Ability Workshop Pr.

Gift of Dyslexia: Why Some of the Smartest People Can't Read & How They Can Learn. Ronald D. Davis. 3 cass. (Running Time: 90 min. per cass.). 34.95 Set, incl. bk. (RD110) OptimaLearning.
Based on 12 years of research, reveals why the same perceptual abilities that produce genius can also cause Dyslexia, ADD, & other learning problems. Corrective procedures are explained step-by-step.

Gift of Dyxlexia: Why Some of the Smartest People Can't Read & How They Can Learn, Set. unabr. ed. Ronald D. Davis & Eldon M. Braun. 4 CDs. (Running Time: 4 hrs. 28 mins.). 2000. audio compact disk 39.95 Jewel case. DDAI.

Gift of Fear: Survival Signals That Protect Us from Violence. Gavin De Becker. Narrated by Tom Stechschulte. 11 CDs. (Running Time: 12 hrs. 45 mins.). 2000. audio compact disk 111.00 (978-0-7887-4755-7(X), C1243E7) Recorded Bks.
Course in survival that could save your life. Learn how a predator chooses his victim. Acquire a comprehensive set of crucial questions for your child's school & in the process, understand & become empowered by your own natural gift for survival.

Gift of Fear: Survival Signals That Protect Us from Violence, abr. ed. Gavin De Becker. Read by Gavin De Becker. 2 cass. (Running Time: 3 hrs.). 1997. 17.95 (978-1-57453-208-1(1), 395426) Audio Lit.
Drawing on case histories, academic studies & personal experience, de Becker shows how the combination of intuitive knowledge & rational principles can enable us to predict & thereby avoid personal violence.

Gift of Fear: Survival Signals That Protect Us from Violence. unabr. ed. Gavin De Becker. Narrated by Tom Stechschulte. 9 cass. (Running Time: 12 hrs. 45 mins.). 1999. 83.00 (978-0-7887-4039-8(3), 96090E7) Recorded Bks.
Course in survival that could save your life. Learn how a predator chooses his victim. Acquire a comprehensive set of crucial questions for your child's school & in the process, understand & become empowered by your own natural gift for survival.

Gift of Fire. unabr. ed. Jayne Ann Krentz. Read by Wendy Petersen. (Running Time: 9 hrs.). 2009. 39.97 (978-1-4233-8708-4(2), 9781423387084, Brlnc Audio MP3 Lib); 24.99 (978-1-4233-8707-7(4), 9781423387077, Brilliance MP3); 39.97 (978-1-4233-8710-7(4), 9781423387107, BADLE); 24.99 (978-1-4233-8709-1(0), 9781423387091, BAD); audio compact disk 29.99 (978-1-4233-8705-3(8), 9781423387053, Bril Audio CD Unabri); audio compact disk 82.97 (978-1-4233-8706-0(6), 9781423387060, BriAudCD Unabrid) Brilliance Audio.

Gift of Fire. unabr. ed. Michele Sobel Spirn. 1 cass. (Running Time: 20 min.). (Time Traveler Ser.). (J). (gr. 3-6). 1984. bk. 16.99 (978-0-934898-60-7(X)); pap. bk. 9.95 (978-0-934898-72-0(3)) Jan Prods.
Diana & Tom Morris, twin brother & sister, discover a magic that allows them to return to earlier ages. In their first adventure, they travel back to cave days to bring the gift of fire to cave people.

Gift of Friendship. Edd Anthony. Read by Edd Anthony. 2007. audio compact disk 16.95 (978-1-881586-15-9(4)) Canticle Cass.

Gift of God: His Christmas Story (Listner's Bible) Narrated by Max E. McLean. 2004. audio compact disk 7.95 (978-1-931047-37-1(5)) Fellow Perform Arts.

Gift of Gold. unabr. collector's ed. Jayne Ann Krentz. Read by Mary Peiffer. 9 cass. (Running Time: 13 hrs. 30 min.). 1996. 72.00 (978-0-7366-3445-8(2), 4089) Books on Tape.
Jonas Quarrel knows Verity Ames holds the key to a secret from his past. Will he break her heart to find the truth.

***Gift of Grace.** Amy Clipston. (Running Time: 7 hrs. 56 mins. 0 sec.). (Kauffman Amish Bakery Ser.). (ENG.). 2009. 10.99 (978-0-310-77331-3(8)) Zondervan.

Gift of Heaven. Camp Kirkland. 2001. 75.00 (978-0-633-01637-1(3)); 11.98 (978-0-633-01635-7(7)); audio compact disk 85.00 (978-0-633-01638-8(1)); audio compact disk 16.98 (978-0-633-01636-4(5)) LifeWay Christian.

Gift of Jazzy. unabr. ed. Scripts. Cindy Adams. Read by Cindy Adams. 4 cass. (Running Time: 6 hrs.). 2004. 25.00 (978-1-59007-306-3(1)); 39.95 (978-1-59007-307-0(X)) Pub: New Millenn Enter. Dist(s): PerseuPGW

Gift of Legends. unabr. ed. Michael Ayrton. Read by Yehudi Menuhin. 1 cass. (Running Time: 43 min.). 1973. 12.95 (11018) J Norton Pubs.
The sculptor talks to the musician about mazes, symbols & the power of legend.

Gift of Love. Michael Ballam. 1 cass. 9.95 (1100858); audio compact disk 14.95 (1100831) Covenant Comms.
A beautiful Christmas album with ten unique Christmas songs.

Gift of Love: Loss of a Loved One. Eldon Taylor. 1 cass. (Running Time: 62 min.). (Inner Talk Ser.). 16.95 incl. script. (978-1-55978-161-9(0), 5387C) Progress Aware Res.
Soundtrack - Musical Themes with underlying subliminal affirmations.

Gift of Love: Loss of a Loved One: Babbling Brook. Eldon Taylor. 1 cass. 16.95 (978-1-55978-751-2(1), 5387F) Progress Aware Res.

Gift of Make-Believe. (J). 1999. 12.99 Laughing Sun.
Collection of classic children's literature set to music with accompanying booklet of lyrics & illustrations.

Gift of Make-Believe. Ginger Sands. Illus. by Geoffrey Brittingham et al. 1 CD. (Running Time: 54 min.). (J). (ps). 1999. pap. bk. 15.99 (978-0-9674849-0-7(1), 061496) Laughing Sun.
Collection of classic children's literature set to music with accompanying booklet of lyrics & illustrations.

Gift of Music. unabr. ed. Yehudi Menuhin & Michael Ayrton. 1 cass. (Running Time: 38 min.). 1973. 12.95 (11019) J Norton Pubs.
Yehudi Menuhin tells Michael Ayrton of his own relationship to his art.

Gift of Peace. abr. ed. Joseph Louis Bernardin. Read by Kenneth Velo. 2 cass. 1998. 17.95 Set. (978-1-55935-266-6(3)) Soundelux.
A mission to share personal reflections & insights in the final two months of life using the previous three years as a framework.

Gift of Priesthood. Father Michael et al. 1 cass. (Running Time: 60 min.). 1988. 10.00 (T63) Eternal Wrd TV.
Discusses the nature of priesthood & the gift it is to the Catholic Church.

Gift of Sanctuary. Candace Robb. Read by Stephen Thorne. 8 cass. (Running Time: 12 hrs.). (Owen Archer Mystery Ser.). 2001. 69.95 (991011); audio compact disk 79.95 (109026) Pub: ISIS Audio GBR. Dist(s): Ulverscroft US

Gift of Santuary, Set. unabr. ed. Candace Robb. Read by Frances Jeater. 8 cass. (Running Time: 10 hrs. 30 mins.). (Sixth Owen Archer Mystery Ser.). 2000. 69.95 (978-0-7531-0671-6(X), 991011) Ulverscroft US.
Owen Archer, sometime spy, joins a pilgrimage to Wales in order to recruit archers for the Duke of Lancaster's forthcoming expedition to France. Joined by Geoffrey Chaucer, reporting on the King's defenses, the two men suspect the royal steward is betraying his King to the Welsh rebels. Dragged into investigating brutal murders, tension in the steward's household & theft, Owen must investigate charges of infidelity & homicide, whilst all the while working to prevent further deaths.

Gift of Santuary, Set. unabr. ed. Candace Robb. Read by Stephen Thorne. 8 CDs. (Running Time: 10 hrs. 30 mins.). 2000. audio compact disk 79.95 (978-0-7531-0902-1(6), 109026) Ulverscroft US.

Gift of Sexual Morality & the Catechism. Thomas Morrow. 1 cass. (Inspiring Presentations from the National Rosary Congress Ser.). 2.50 (978-1-56036-094-0(1)) AMI Pr.

Gift of Story. Clarissa Pinkola Estes. 2005. audio compact disk 14.95 (978-1-59179-440-0(4)) Sounds True.

Gift of the Angel's-Music. 2007. audio compact disk 16.95 (978-1-56136-434-3(7)) Master Your Mind.

Gift of the Eagle. 1 CD. (Running Time: 40 min.). (J). (gr. 2-5). 2000. tchr. ed. 16.99 (DCD264) Summit Records.
This is the story of black cat Katrina who is guided through time and history by wise eagle Alistair. Kat is not sure what she wants to do with her life and Alistair encourages her to do something she loves. She explores sound and music throughout time and in the end decides to be a musician.

Gift of the Ego, Fear; the Gift of God, Love: A Commentary on the Gifts of God Prose Poem Scribed by Helen Schucman. Kenneth Wapnick. 10 CDs. 2004. audio compact disk 60.00 (978-1-59142-144-3(6), CD55) Foun Miracles.
The prose poem, "The Gifts of God," Helen Schucman's last scribing from Jesus, summarizes the core teachings of the Course. Its primary emphasis is on allowing Jesus to help us with our fear, which we mistakenly connect with something in the world. This commentary explains the cause of all fear in the context of our dreaming that we have separated from God, believing we deserve to be punished as a result. The ego's gift of fear is undone by our accepting Jesus' gift of love, which leads us out of the dream and back to God.

Gift of the Gab. unabr. ed. Morris Gleitzman. Read by Mary-Anne Fahey. 3 CDs. (Running Time: 3 hrs.). (J). (gr. 5-7). 2007. audio compact disk 54.95 (978-1-74093-841-9(0)) Pub: Bolinda Pubng AUS. Dist(s): Bolinda Pub Inc

Gift of the Jews: How a Tribe of Desert Nomads Changed the Way Everyone Thinks & Feels. unabr. ed. Thomas Cahill. Narrated by Richard M. Davidson. 5 cass. (Running Time: 7 hrs. 30 mins.). 1998. 49.00 (978-0-7887-1978-3(5), 95365E7) Recorded Bks.
Be transported to the distant past to rub elbows with such renowned biblical characters as Sarah, Moses, Job, & Ruth.

Gift of the Magi see Your Own World

Gift of the Magi see O. Henry Favorites

Gift of the Magi see Great American Short Stories

Gift of the Magi see Best of O. Henry

Gift of the Magi see Ten All Time Favorite Stories

Gift of the Magi see O. Henry Library

Gift of the Magi see Favorite Stories by O. Henry

Gift of the Magi. 1 cass. (Running Time: 1 hr. 30 mins.). (SmartReader Ser.). (J). 1999. pap. bk. & tchr. ed. 19.95 (978-0-7887-2854-9(7), 79671T3) Recorded Bks.
Della Young only has one dollar & eighty-seven cents to buy her husband a Christmas present. Join the Youngs in New York City 100 years ago & learn how they celebrate this memorable holiday.

Gift of the Magi. O. Henry. Ed. by Walter Pauk & Raymond Harris. Illus. by Robert J. Pailthorpe. (Classics Ser.). (YA). (gr. 6-12). 1980. pap. bk. 17.96 (978-0-89061-187-6(4), 402) Jamestown.

Gift of the Magi. O. Henry. Perf. by St. Charles Players. 2 cass. (Running Time: 3 hrs.). 2000. 16.95 (Monterey SoundWorks) Monterey Media Inc.

Gift of the Magi. O. Henry. Read by Paula Parker. 1 cass. (Running Time: 21 mins.). (Creative Short Story Audio Library Ser.). 1999. 11.00 (978-0-8072-6122-4(X), Y CS 907 CX, Listening Lib) Random Audio Pubg.
Christmas story of poor Della, who sells her hair to buy a present for her loving husband, Jim.

Gift of the Magi. abr. ed. O. Henry. Perf. by St. Charles Players. 2 cass. (Running Time: 73 mins.). 2000. 16.95 (978-1-56994-530-8(6), 314114) Monterey Media Inc.
Once three wise men came bearing gifts. Now a light dust of snow quieted the city streets. Christmas was upon a young couple whose sharing of lives together had just begun. A gift was needed & only a dollar & eighty-seven cents had been saved. Can the joy, the dreams, the hope for the future, the lovely burning flame of love, be adequately expressed with a dollar & eighty-seven cents?.

Gift of the Magi. unabr. ed. O. Henry. 1 cass. (Running Time: 21 min.). (Creative Short Story Audio Library Ser.). (YA). (gr. 7-12). 1995. 9.98 (978-0-8072-6121-7(1), CS907CX, Listening Lib) Random Audio Pubg.

Gift of the Magi. unabr. ed. O. Henry. Read by Robert Ryan. (Running Time: 32 min.). 10.95 (978-0-8045-1006-6(7), SAC 1006) Spoken Arts.

Gift of the Magi: And The Little Match Girl. O. Henry & Hans Christian Andersen. Read by Michael York & Robby Benson. 1 cass. (Running Time: 30 min.). (J). 1992. 8.95 incl. puzzle keepsake. Olive Brnch.

Gift of the Magi & Other Short Stories by O. Henry. O. Henry. Retold by Noe Venable. (Classic Literature Ser.). 2005. pap. bk. 69.00 (978-1-4105-0068-7(3)); audio compact disk 18.95 (978-1-4105-0069-4(1)) D Johnston Inc.

Gift of the Present. Louise L. Hay. Read by Louise L. Hay. Music by Joshua Leeds. 1 cass. (Running Time: 1 hr. 22 min.). (Songs of Affirmations Ser.: Vol. II). 1988. 10.95 (978-0-937611-40-1(9), 208) Hay House.
A combination of meditations & affirmative songs about the power of the present moment, prospering & deserving good, & loving ourselves unconditionally.

Gift of the Red Bird: The Story of a Divine Encounter. Paula D'Arcy. 3 CDs. (Running Time: 3 hrs. 30 mins.). 2005. audio compact disk 24.95 (978-0-86716-771-9(8)) St Anthony Mess Pr.
?A powerful testimony of how the Divine woos the soul into a sacred embrace.??Joyce Rupp, author of Your Sorrow is My Sorrow and Praying Our Goodbyes?I was deeply moved by this beautiful true story, and you will be too.?Madeleine L?Engle?A story full of hope, reminding us not only of our need to learn and relearn certain basic truths, but of God?s patience in guiding us.??Spiritual Book News.

Gift of the Tortoise. Perf. by Ladysmith Black Mambazo. 1 cass. (J). 1994. 9.98 (978-1-56628-027-3(3), MLP2231/WB42553-4) MFLP CA.
This imaginative adventure is guided by Fudugazi, a wise, old tortoise, who shares his love of music & magical stories from his native South Africa.

Gift of Time. Barbara Murphy. 7 cass. (Running Time: 9 hrs. 15 mins.). (Story Sound Ser.). (J). 2004. 61.95 (978-1-85903-694-5(5)) Pub: Mgna Lrg Print GBR. Dist(s): Ulverscroft US

Gift of Tongues. Instructed by Dan Hayden. 6 CDs. (Running Time: 4 hrs. 11 mins). 2003. audio compact disk 24.95 (978-0-9726331-4-7(6)) Pub: Sola Scriptura. Dist(s): STL Dist NA
"Many charismatic Christians say that every believer should speak in tongues as evidence that they have received the fullness of the Holy Spirit. Is that true? Understanding the original purpose for tongues speaking is essential when seeking to evaluate the current phenomenon. In The Gift of Tongues, Dr. Dan Hayden reminds us that God's Word is the final authority in our search for truth-including the truth concerning tongues speaking. Dan leads us through an enlightening study that looks at various biblical texts, lays out the way this gift was used in Bible times, and demonstrates that what is being practiced today is not at all what the early church knew as ""the gift of tongues.""".

Gift of Valor: A War Story. Michael M. Phillips. 2005. 45.00 (978-1-4159-2002-2(8)); audio compact disk 54.00 (978-1-4159-2134-0(2)) Books on Tape.

Gift of Woman Spirit. Susan Muto. 2 cass. (Running Time: 2 hrs. 9 min.). 1995. 17.95 Set. (TAH328) Alba Hse Comns.
Learn the five stages of radiating Christ so clearly illustrated by the annunciation, visitation, incarnation, presentation of Jesus & the finding of Jesus in the temple. Learn also the building blocks of a Christian woman's life & how to put all together & revitalize your faith.

Gift Outright see Robert Frost in Recital

Gift Outright see Twentieth-Century Poetry in English, No. 6, Recordings of Poets Reading Their Own Poetry

Gift That Wasn't Perfect. unabr. ed. Roni S. Denholtz. 1 cass. (Running Time: 7 min.). (Holidays Are Fun Ser.). (J). (ps-2). 1985. 16.99 incl. hardcover. (978-0-87386-009-3(8)) Jan Prods.
Adam's first grade class is making gifts for Mother's Day. Adam's gift isn't quite as neat as Billy's, but Adam learns that gifts don't have to be perfect to be appreciated.

Gift to My Children: A Father's Lessons for Life & Investing. unabr. ed. Jim Rogers. Narrated by Johnny Heller. 2 CDs. (Running Time: 1 hr. 30 mins. 0 sec.). (ENG.). 2009. audio compact disk 39.99 (978-1-4001-4150-0(8)); audio compact disk 19.99 (978-1-4001-1150-3(1)); audio compact disk 19.99 (978-1-4001-6150-8(9)) Pub: Tantor Media. Dist(s): IngramPubServ

Gift to Share/Gifts to Make. Steck-Vaughn Staff. 1997. (978-0-8172-7373-6(5)) SteckVau.

Gift Too Wonderful for Words: Luke 2:8-14. Ed Young. 1998. 4.95 (978-0-7417-2203-4(8), 1203) Win Walk.

Gifted. unabr. ed. Nikita Lalwani. Read by Sneha Mathan. (Running Time: 10 hrs. 0 mins.). 2010. 29.95 (978-1-4332-2929-9(3)); 59.95 (978-1-4332-2925-1(0)); audio compact disk 90.00 (978-1-4332-2926-8(9)) Blckstn Audio.

Gifted: Season One. Contrib. by Johnny Wright et al. Prod. by Russell Hall & Philip McIntyre. (Running Time: 3 hrs.). 2007. 19.99 (978-5-558-00290-4(5)) Pt of Grace Ent.

Gifted by God: Leading, Loving, & Teaching with Your Life. Laura Savage et al. 2 cass. (Running Time: 60 min. per cass.). bk. 16.95 (N974104) NwHopePub.
Christian women everywhere will benefit from the insights offered in this audio.

Gifted Children: Ocean. Eldon Taylor. Read by Eldon Taylor. Ed. by Leslie Brice. 1 cass. (Running Time: 1 hr.). 1992. 16.95 (978-1-56705-312-8(2)) Gateways Inst.
Self improvement.

Gifted Children, Working with Creatively. unabr. ed. Hosted by E. Paul Torrance. 1 cass. (Famous Authorities Talk about Children Ser.). 12.95 (C17006) J Norton Pubs.

Gifted Gregory Learns to Make Friends. Pamela M. Goldberg & Stephanie N. Lemelin. Illus. by Jimmy Boring. Narrated by Kaitlin Doubleday. (J). 2008. pap. bk. (978-0-9778941-0-9(X)) Camp MakeBelieve.

Gifted Hands: The Ben Carson Story. Ben Carson & Cecil Murphey. 2 cass. (Running Time: 60 min.). 1992. 14.99 Set. (978-0-310-54658-0(3)) Zondervan.
Condensed version of the book.

Gifted Hands: The Ben Carson Story. abr. ed. Ben Carson. (Running Time: 2 hrs. 4 mins. 0 sec.). (ENG.). 2003. 10.99 (978-0-310-26047-9(7)) Zondervan.

Gifted Kids Have Feelings Too. Sylvia Rimm. Read by Sylvia Rimm. 2 cass. (Running Time: 2 hrs. 40 min.). (J). (gr. 6-12). 1990. 20.00 Set. (978-0-937891-08-7(8), SR202) Apple Pub Wisc.
Dr. Sylvia Rimm reads stories from her book, Gifted Kids Have Feelings Too, & shares some discussion questions & activities from Exploring Feelings.

***Gifted to Lead: The Art of Leading as a Woman in the Church.** Nancy Beach. (Running Time: 4 hrs. 25 mins. 0 sec.). (ENG.). 2008. 16.99 (978-0-310-30241-4(2)) Zondervan.

Gifts. Ursula K. Le Guin. Narrated by Jim Colby. 5 cass. (Running Time: 6 hrs.). (Chronicles of the Western Shore Ser.: No. 1). (YA). 2004. 58.75 (978-1-4193-0860-4(2)) Recorded Bks.

Gifts: 1 Cor. 12:7-11. Ed Young. 1986. 4.95 (978-0-7417-1508-1(2), 508) Win Walk.

Gifts & Tools of the New Age. Kryon. Read by Lee Carroll. 1 cass. (Running Time: 53 min.). 1996. 10.00 (978-1-888053-03-6(8)) Kryon Writings.
Recording of live event. Channeling of spiritual information.

Gifts for the Church. Instructed by Dan Hayden. 12 CDs. (Running Time: 8hrs. 46 mins.). 2003. audio compact disk 34.95 (978-0-9726331-2-3(X)) Pub: Sola Scriptura. Dist(s): STL Dist NA
"When Jesus Christ sent the Holy Spirit to represent Him, He also gave spiritual gifts through the Spirit to the church. These gifts are special abilities that enable believers to function as a spiritual force in the world. Here is a study to help you understand the meaning and purpose of the gifts as a means of discovering your unique place in the Body of Christ. It is a practical exposition of two key passages on the subject of spiritual gifts-Ephesians 4 and Romans 12.".

Gifts from Above: Conferences on Accepting God's Help. Benedict J. Groeschel. Read by Benedict J. Groeschel. 6 cass. (Running Time: 5 hrs. 40 min.). 49.95 incl. vinyl album. Credence Commun.
Explains the gifts of the Holy Spirit & how they support & direct striving for personal growth.

Gifts from the Master: Spiritual Exercises; The Six Sounds of the Organs of the Body. unabr. ed. Ann Ree Colton. 1 cass. (Running Time: 1 hr. 30 min.). 1984. 15.95 Set. (978-0-917189-27-2(2)) A R Colton Fnd.
Meditation & visualization exercises, Lecture from the tradition of the T'ao.

Gifts from the Soul: 360 Ways to Enter the Dream. Connie Kaplan. 1 CD. 2006. audio compact disk 18.95 (978-0-9786239-5-1(9)) Generosity Inc.

Gifts from the Soul 4 Book Set & Gifts form the Soul Meditation CD. Connie Kaplan. Read by Connie Kaplan. 2006. audio compact disk 69.95 (978-0-9786239-4-4(0)) Generosity Inc.

Gifts I: 1 Cor 12:1-3. Ed Young. (J). 1980. 4.95 (978-0-7417-1099-4(4), A099) Win Walk.

Gifts II: 1 Cor 12:1-7. Ed Young. (J). 1980. 4.95 (978-0-7417-1101-4(X), A0101) Win Walk.

Gifts III: 1 Cor.12. Ed Young. (J). 1980. 4.95 (978-0-7417-1103-8(6), A0103) Win Walk.

Gifts in Action. Dawn E. Clark. 1 cass. (Running Time: 90 mins.). 2000. (978-1-928532-04-0(7)) Aarron Pubg.

Gifts IV: 1 Cor. 12. Ed Young. (J). 1980. 4.95 (978-0-7417-1104-5(4), A0104); 4.95 (978-0-7417-1106-9(0), A0106) Win Walk.

Gifts IX (Gift of Giving) 1 Cor. 12. Ed Youth. (J). 1980. 4.95 (978-0-7417-1109-0(5), A0109) Win Walk.

Gifts of God: The Poetry of Helen Schucman. Kenneth Wapnick. 2007. 25.00 (978-1-59142-333-1(3)); audio compact disk 31.00 (978-1-59142-332-4(5)) Foun Miracles.

Gifts of Life. Black Bear. 1 cass. (Running Time: 1 hr. 30 mins.). 1998. 15.00 (978-0-9700042-3-9(0), DI008) Divine Ideas.
Teaching, told in the form of a story, which shows how to honor the sacred gift of life given to us, the two leggeds.

Gifts of Revelation Vol. 2: Understanding the Word of Knowledge, the Word of Wisdom & Other Extraordinary Gifts. Mac Hammond. 4 cass. (Running Time: 1 hr.). (Annointing Ser.: Vol. 2). 1998. 24.00 Set. (978-1-57399-065-3(5)) Mac Hammond.

Gifts of the Angels. Music by Steven Halpern. 1 cass. 9.95 (LA126); audio compact disk 14.95 (LA126D) Lghtwrks Aud & Vid.
Showcases the luminous quality of sound - & the source of inspiration - that has always been the hallmark of Steven Halpern's music. This timely collection presents the sounds of an angelic choir in concert with piano, harp & other evocative electronic instruments. Never before available in such a complete, unified collection, "Gifts of Angels" creates a sonic ambiance that enhances any environment.

Gifts of the Body. unabr. ed. Rebecca Brown. Read by Rebecca Brown. 3 cass. (Running Time: 3 hrs. 30 min.). 1996. 19.95 Set. (978-1-888348-02-6(X), HCB103) Hall Closet.
Award winning story about dying & death as told by the home-care worker assisting people with AIDS. The narrator is a person driven by the need to honor the people she cares for, in all their dignity, all their frailty, all their humanity.

Gifts of the Holy Spirit. 2003. audio compact disk (978-1-931713-86-3(3)) Calvar ChalPub.

Gifts of the Holy Spirit. Gospel Light Publications Staff. 1 cass. 1997. 6.99 (978-7-5116-0037-0(9)) Gospel Lght.
Pentacostalism.

Gifts of the Holy Spirit. Lester Sumrall. 15 cass. (Running Time: 22 hrs. 30 mins.). 1999. 48.00 (978-1-58568-048-1(6)) Sumrall Pubng.

Gifts of the Jews: How A Tribe of Desert Nomads Changed the Way Everyone Thinks & Feels. Thomas Cahill. Read by Claire Bloom. 2004. 13.95 (978-0-7435-2007-2(6)) Pub: S&S Audio. Dist(s): S and S Inc

Gifts of the Jews: How a Tribe of Desert Nomads Changed the Way Everyone Thinks & Feels. unabr. ed. Thomas Cahill. Narrated by Richard M. Davidson. 6 CDs. (Running Time: 7 hrs. 30 mins.). (Hinges of History Ser.: Vol. 2). 2001. audio compact disk 58.00 (978-0-7887-7176-7(0), C1426) Recorded Bks.
An accessible portrait of an ancient society & their vision that would later inspire the concept of individual worth. Until the third millennium, it was a widely-held belief that people were pawns in an endless cycle of birth & death, with no hope of altering their fate. But when Abraham followed God's command in ancient Sumer to go forth into the wilderness, a remarkable shift in thought emerged. As Abraham led his tribe through strange lands, these people called Jews began to view time as having starting ending points & holding the possibility of a better tomorrow.

Gifts of the Phoenix: Poetry & Prose. unabr. ed. Poems. Michael A. Williams. Read by Michael A. Williams. 1 cass. (Running Time: 90 min.). 7.00 (978-1-878527-18-9(5)) Black Phoenix Pr.
This live recording presents an entire public reading program & open discussion from the Martin Luther King Memorial Library (Washington, DC) featuring works by the author. Included are 30 minutes of poetry from "The Last Phoenix: The End of Freedom" & 30 minutes of prose from "The Inheritance of Fathers: A Black Man's Meditations on the Sacred Meaning of Marriage".

Gifts of the Spirit. Kenneth Copeland. 6 cass. 1982. bk. 30.00 Set incl. study guide. (978-0-938458-39-5(6)) K Copeland Pubns.
Teaching on biblical gifts of the spirit.

***Gifts of the Spirit.** Kenneth Copeland. (ENG.). 2010. audio compact disk 30.00 (978-1-60463-081-7(7)) K Copeland Pubns.

Gifts of the Spirit. Derek Prince. 2 cass. 11.90 Set. (007-008) Derek Prince.
Tools, not toys, gifts of the Spirit are part of God's equipment for every believer.

Gifts of the Spirit. unabr. ed. Terry Teykl. 6 cass. 1996. 25.00 Set. (978-1-57892-032-7(9)) Prayer Pt Pr.
Sermon/teaching on Gift of Spirit.

Gifts of Tongues & Prophecy. Contrib. by Gospel Light Publications Staff. 1 cass. 1997. 6.99 (978-7-5116-0038-7(7)) Gospel Lght.
Pentacostalism.

Gifts V: 1 Cor. 12; Acts 6:1-4. Ed Young. (J). 1980. 4.95 (978-0-7417-1105-2(2), A0105) Win Walk.

Gifts VII (Tongues) 1 Cor.12. Ed Young. (J). 1980. 4.95 (978-0-7417-1107-6(9), A0107) Win Walk.

Gifts VIII (Greater Than the Gifts) 1 Cor. 13. Ed Young. (J). 1980. 4.95 (978-0-7417-1108-3(7), A0108) Win Walk.

Gigantic Ants: And Other Cases. unabr. ed. Seymour Simon. Narrated by Johnny Heller. 1 cass. (Running Time: 1 hr.). (Einstein Anderson, Science Detective Ser.). (gr. 3 up). 2001. 10.00 (978-0-7887-4711-3(8), 96294E7) Recorded Bks.
He can solve mysteries involving giant ants, hurricane machine & anything else that seems a little fishy.

Gigantic Ants & Other Stories. unabr. ed. Seymour Simon. Narrated by Johnny Heller. 1 cass. (Running Time: 1 hr.). (J). 2001. pap. bk. & stu. ed. 23.24 Recorded Bks.
He can solve mysteries involving giant ants, hurricane machine & anything else that seems a little fishy.

Giggle, Giggle, Quack see Jaja, Jiji, Cuac

Giggle, Giggle Quack. 2004. audio compact disk 12.95 (978-1-55592-550-5(2)) Weston Woods.

Giggle, Giggle Quack. (J). 2004. bk. 24.95 (978-1-55592-691-5(6)) Weston Woods.

Giggle, Giggle, Quack. 2004. 8.95 (978-1-55592-543-7(X)) Weston Woods.

Giggle, Giggle, Quack. (J). 2004. pap. bk. 18.95 (978-1-55592-684-7(3)); pap. bk. 38.75 (978-1-55592-686-1(X)); pap. bk. 32.75 (978-1-55592-685-4(1)); pap. bk. 14.95 (978-1-55592-683-0(5)) Weston Woods.

Gigi & the Cat. unabr. ed. Sidonie-Gabrielle Colette. Read by Leslie Caron. 2 cass. (Running Time: 2 hrs. 5 mins.). Dramatization. (Well-Spoken Companions Ser.). 1996. 16.95 (978-1-57270-030-7(0), M21030u) Pub: Audio Partners. Dist(s): PerseuPGW
Colette's best-known, best-loved novella is read by the actress who starred in the film & the only one available in English.

Gigolo & Gigolette. (SWC 1721) HarperCollins Pubs.

Gil Blas de Santillana. Ed. by William T. Tardy. (Dos Novelas Picarescas Ser.). 15.00 (978-0-8442-7104-0(7), Natl Textbk Co) M-H Contemporary.
Features an introduction to spanish literature.

Gila. unabr. ed. Gary McCarthy. Read by Gene Engene. 12 cass. (Running Time: 11 hrs. 54 min.). (Rivers West Ser.: Bk. 6). 1997. 64.95 (978-1-55686-736-1(0)) Books in Motion.
Where the Gila River flowed through the Sonoran Desert, conflict raged between Pima farmers & fierce Apaches. Then came Spaniards & whites.

Gila Bend Showdown. unabr. ed. Steve Hailes. Read by Maynard Villers. 4 cass. (Running Time: 6 hrs.). 1996. 39.95 (978-1-55686-735-4(2)) Books in Motion.
The Cavanah gang was a bunch of mean Missourians who beat up Mormons & blacks, stole from Mexicans for fun & killed when it suited them. Jackson Gilbert intends to stop them.

Gilbert & Sullivan: The D'Oyly Carte Opera Company. unabr. ed. Gilbert & Sullivan. 2 cass. ea. set. Incl. H. M. S. Pinafore; Mikado; Patience; Pirates of Penzance; 16.95 ea. Set. HarperCollins Pubs.
Recordings of the original London productions with libretto.

Gilbert & Sullivan & Their Victorian World. collector's ed. Christopher Hibbert. Read by David Case. 7 cass. (Running Time: 10 hrs. 30 min.). 2000. 56.00 (978-0-7366-4976-6(X)) Books on Tape.
The dramas written by the most popular playwright of the Victorian era & the music of that era's most honored composer are largely unknown today yet join these two together & you get Gilbert & Sullivan who together revolutionized the world of musical comedy in the late 1800s. However, behind their enormously popular collaboration, they simply did not get along. It was success after success that forced the team to stay together for fifteen glorious years. The start of the second century of Gilbert & Sullivan's popularity provides a fine occasion to look again at the story behind these brilliant men & their amazing comic operas.

Gilbert & Sullivan Set Me Free. unabr. ed. Kathleen Karr. Read by Full Cast Production Staff. (J). 2007. 39.99 (978-1-60252-557-3(9)) Find a World.

Gilbert Grosvenor: Geographic Illiteracy. 1 cass. (Running Time: 1 hr.). 10.95 (NP-88-07-27, HarperThor) HarpC GBR.

Gilbert Law Legends Corpration. 3rd rev. ed. Gilbert. 2002. 45.95 (978-0-15-901122-5(1)) West.

Gilberto & the Wind. 2004. 8.95 (978-1-56008-907-0(5)); cass. & flmstrp 30.00 (978-1-56008-674-1(2)) Weston Woods.

Gilberto & the Wind. (J). 2004. bk. 24.95 (978-1-56008-203-3(8)) Weston Woods.

Gilberto & the Wind. Marie Hall Ets. Illus. by Marie Hall Ets. (Running Time: 8 mins.). 1983. audio compact disk 12.95 (978-1-59112-836-6(6)) Live Oak Media.

Gilberto & the Wind. unabr. ed. Marie Hall Ets. Read by Jenna Whidden. 11 vols. (Running Time: 8 mins.). (J). (gr. k-3). 1974. bk. 24.95 (978-0-670-34030-9(8)); pap. bk. 16.95 (978-0-670-34033-0(2)); pap. bk. & tchr. ed. 33.95 Reading Chest. (978-0-670-34027-9(8)) Live Oak Media.
The story of a small Mexican boy & his discovery of the wind.

Gilberto & the Wind. unabr. ed. Marie Hall Ets. Illus. by Marie Hall Ets. 22 vols. (Running Time: 17 mins.). (ENG & SPA.). (J). (gr. k-3). 1999. pap. bk. 33.95 (978-0-87499-568-8(X)) Live Oak Media.

Gilberto & the Wind cassette LC-754CS. Contrib. by Marie Hall Ets. 9.95 (978-1-59112-501-3(4)) Live Oak Media.

Gilberto y el Viento. Marie Hall Ets. 1 cass. (Running Time: 1 hr.). (SPA.). (J). 2001. 15.95 (VXS-39C) Kimbo Educ.

Gilberto y el Viento. Marie Hall Ets. Illus. by Marie Hall Ets. 11 vols. (Running Time: 10 mins.). 1996. bk. 28.95 (978-1-59519-168-7(2)); pap. bk. 35.95 (978-1-59519-167-0(4)); 9.95 (978-1-59112-042-1(X)); audio compact disk 12.95 (978-1-59519-165-6(8)) Live Oak Media.

Gilberto y el Viento. Marie Hall Ets. Illus. by Marie Hall Ets. 11 vols. (Running Time: 10 mins.). (SPA.). (J). 1996. pap. bk. 18.95 (978-1-59519-166-3(6)) Pub: Live Oak Media. Dist(s): AudioGO

Gilberto y el Viento. Marie Hall Ets. (SPA.). 2004. 8.95 (978-0-7882-0280-3(4)) Weston Woods.

Gilberto y el Viento. unabr. ed. Marie Hall Ets. Illus. by Marie Hall Ets. Read by Susan Rybin. 11 vols. (Running Time: 10 mins.). (SPA.). (J). (gr. k-3). 1996. bk. 25.95 (978-0-87499-363-9(6)); pap. bk. & tchr. ed. 33.95 Reading Chest. (978-0-87499-364-6(4)) Live Oak Media.
The story of a small Mexican boy & his discovery of the wind. The pictures are very effective & the short text is exactly perfect to underscore the action of the pictures.

Gilberto y el Viento. unabr. ed. Marie Hall Ets. Illus. by Marie Hall Ets. Read by Susan Rybin. 11 vols. (Running Time: 10 mins.). (SPA.). (J). (gr. k-3). 2005. pap. bk. 16.95 (978-0-87499-362-2(8), LK1058) Pub: Live Oak Media. Dist(s): AudioGO

Gilda Joyce: Psychic Investigator. unabr. ed. Jennifer Allison. Narrated by Jessica Almasy. 7 CDs. (Running Time: 8 hrs.). 2005. audio compact disk 69.75 (978-1-4193-6769-4(2), C3505); 54.75 (978-1-4193-4311-7(4), 98048) Recorded Bks.
This debut novel from high school teacher Jennifer Allison has earned glowing critical praise for its blend of humor, substance, and scares. In a starred review, Booklist says, "Allison pulls off something special here." Gilda Joyce is a zany, 13-year-old psychic who's always trying to contact her dead father. But while visiting relatives in San Francisco, she encounters a different ghost.

***Gilda Joyce: The Dead Drop.** unabr. ed. Jennifer Allison. Narrated by Jessica Almasy. 1 Playaway. (Running Time: 7 hrs. 15 mins.). (YA). (gr. 5-8). 2009. 59.75 (978-1-4407-0779-7(0)); 56.75 (978-1-4407-0770-4(7)); audio compact disk 77.75 (978-1-4407-0774-2(X)) Recorded Bks.

***Gilda Joyce: The Dead Drop.** unabr. collector's ed. Jennifer Allison. Narrated by Jessica Almasy. 6 CDs. (Running Time: 7 hrs. 15 mins.). (YA). (gr. 5-8). 2009. audio compact disk 44.95 (978-1-4407-2556-2(X)) Recorded Bks.

Gilda Joyce: The Ghost Sonata. unabr. ed. Jennifer Allison. Narrated by Jessica Almasy. 7 cass. (Running Time: 9 hrs. 5 mins.). (Gilda Joyce Ser.: Bk. 3). (YA). (gr. 5-10). 2007. 56.75 (978-1-4281-7206-7(8)) Recorded Bks.
When best friend Wendy Choy gets an invitation to compete in a piano competition in Oxford, England, Gilda Joyce manages to secure a position as Wendy's page turner. They will sip tea, flirt with English boys, and bask in the warm glow of applause. But when Wendy seems set to become the next victim of a local ghost, the Psychic Investigator goes to work.

Gilda Joyce: The Ghost Sonata. unabr. ed. Jennifer Allison. Narrated by Jessica Almasy. 8 CDs. (Running Time: 9 hrs. 5 mins.). (Gilda Joyce Ser.: Bk. 3). (YA). (gr. 5-8). 2007. audio compact disk 77.75 (978-1-4281-8144-1(X)) Recorded Bks.

Gilda Joyce: The Ladies of the Lake. unabr. ed. Jennifer Allison. Read by Jessica Almasy. 7 CDs. (Running Time: 8 hrs.). (YA). (gr. 6-9). 2006. audio compact disk 74.75 (978-1-4193-9047-0(3)); 49.75 (978-1-4193-9042-5(2)) Recorded Bks.
In this sequel, 13-year-old psychic investigator Gilda is not happy about the scholarship she won to attend Our Lady of Sorrows private school. Time to wear a uniform and hang out with a bunch of debutantes, she figures. But then Gilda learns a drowned student's ghost may be haunting the grounds. Now it's time to investigate!.

***Gilded Age.** unabr. ed. Mark Twain. Read by Anthony Heald. (Running Time: 14 hrs. 5 mins.). (ENG.). 2011. 29.95 (978-1-4417-8200-7(1)); 85.95 (978-1-4417-8197-0(8)); audio compact disk 32.95 (978-1-4417-8199-4(4)); audio compact disk 118.00 (978-1-4417-8198-7(6)) Blckstn Audio.

Gilded Age, Pts. 1-2. Giles Gunn & Robert Ter Horst. 2 cass. Set. (187, 188) Natl Humanities.

Gilded Cage. abr. ed. Josephine Cox. Read by Carole Boyd. 2 cass. (Running Time: 3 hrs.). (ENG., 1999. 16.99 (978-1-84032-137-1(7), HoddrStoughton) Pub: Hodder General GBR. Dist(s): IPG Chicago
Leonard Carstairs is a powerful, ruthless man. Once his eldest daughter tastes a "new world" she knows she cannot remain in the old one.

Gilded Cage, Set. unabr. ed. Josephine Cox. Read by Carole Boyd. 8 cass. 2000. 69.95 (978-0-7540-0422-6(8), CAB 1845) Pub: Chivers Audio Bks GBR. Dist(s): AudioGO
Leonard Mears is a powerful businessman with a hard heart. Ruthlessly presiding over his wife & children, he shuts them away from the outside world. He is also a man with a dark secret: many years ago he forced his sister & her husband to raise his illegitimate daughter. Now a young woman, she has discovered the truth about her father.

Gilead. unabr. ed. Marilynne Robinson. Read by Tim Jerome. 6 cass. 2005. 54.95 (978-0-7927-3433-8(5), CSL 741); audio compact disk 74.95 (978-0-7927-3434-5(3), SLD 741) AudioGO.

Gilead. unabr. ed. Marilynne Robinson. Read by Tim Jerome. 7 CDs. (Running Time: 9 hrs. 0 mins. 0 sec.). (ENG.). 2005. audio compact disk 34.95 (978-1-59397-822-8(7)) Pub: Macmill Audio. Dist(s): Macmillan

Gilgamesh. Joan London. Read by Deidre Rubenstein. (Running Time: 9 hrs. 5 mins.). 2009. 79.99 (978-1-74214-258-6(3), 9781742142586) Pub: Bolinda Pubng AUS. Dist(s): Bolinda Pub Inc

Gilgamesh. unabr. ed. Joan London. 6 cass. (Running Time: 9 hrs. 5 mins.). 2004. 48.00 (978-1-74030-865-6(4)) Pub: Bolinda Pubng AUS. Dist(s): Bolinda Pub Inc

Gilgamesh. unabr. ed. Joan London. Read by Deidre Rubenstein. 8 CDs. (Running Time: 9 hrs. 5 mins.). 2004. audio compact disk 87.95 (978-1-74093-109-0(2)) Pub: Bolinda Pubng AUS. Dist(s): Bolinda Pub Inc

Gilgamesh. unabr. ed. Tr. by Stephen Mitchell. 5 CDs. (Running Time: 5 hrs. 15 mins.). 2004. audio compact disk 24.99 (978-1-4025-9766-4(5), 01832) Recorded Bks.
The story of literature?s first hero, an historical king of Uruk in Babylonia, and his journey of self-discovery. Along the way, Gilgamesh discovers that friendship can bring peace to a whole city and that wisdom can be found only when the quest for it is abandoned.

Gilgamesh: A New English Version. unabr. ed. Stephen Mitchell. Narrated by George Guidall. 3 cass. (Running Time: 4 hrs. 15 mins.). 2004. 29.75 (978-1-4193-0538-2(7), 97852MC) Recorded Bks.

Gilgamesh - A Verse Play. Based on a play by Yusef Komunyakaa & Chad Gracia. Music by Rahim ALHaj. (ENG.). 2008. audio compact disk 14.99 (978-0-9817573-0-8(8)) Scene Unseen.

***Gilgamesh the King.** Robert Silverberg. Narrated by William Coon. (Running Time: 802). (ENG.). 2010. 24.95 (978-0-9844138-9-8(8)) Pub: Eloq Voice. Dist(s): OverDrive Inc

Gillyvors. unabr. ed. Catherine Cookson. Read by Susan Jameson. 8 cass. (Running Time: 9 hrs. 38 min.). (Audio Bks.). 1991. 69.95 set. (978-0-7451-5861-7(7), CAB 564) AudioGO.
A century or so ago there lived at Heap Hollow in County Durham a man & a woman & their six children. To an outsider they would have suggested a close & loving family group, endowed with the domestic virtues. Yet across this happy facade lay a shadow that had lengthened & darkened with passing years.

Gilman & London, Set. unabr. ed. Charlotte Perkins Gilman & Jack London. Read by Claudette Sutherland & George Gonneau. Hosted by Peter Benchley & Joyce Carol Oates. 2 cass. (Running Time: 2 hr.). (Spencer Audio Theater Ser.). 1995. 20.95 library ed. (978-1-883049-63-8(6)) Sound Room.
Musically scored dramatic readings of two classic stories: "The Yellow Wallpaper," & "To Build a Fire".

Gi'me Elbow Room: Folk Songs from a Scottish Childhood. Poems. Bonnie Rideout. Perf. by Rod Cameron. 1 cass., 1 CD. (J). 7.98 (MMS 219); audio compact disk 11.98 CD. (MMS 219) NewSound.
Introduces Scottish culture music with its joyful stepdances, lilting poetry in easy-to-hear dialect, & intriguing instruments like the bagpipes & clarsach (harp). Poetry of Robert Louis Stevenson.

Gimme a Call. unabr. ed. Sarah Mlynowski. (ENG.). (J). 2010. audio compact disk 37.00 (978-0-307-71150-2(1), Listening Lib) Pub: Random Audio Pubg. Dist(s): Random

Gimme Five. David Freudberg. Perf. by Phil Hartman et al. 1 cass. (Running Time: 30 min.). 1993. 9.95 (978-0-9640914-1-2(0)) Human Media.
Fast-paced, humorous adventure showing quick & easy ways to increase your consumption of healthy fruits & vegetables.

Gimme More. unabr. ed. Liza Cody. 9 cass. (Isis Ser.). (J). 2002. 76.95 (978-0-7531-1357-8(0)) Pub: ISIS Lrg Prnt GBR. Dist(s): Ulverscroft US

Gimme My Money Back: Your Guide to Beating the Financial Crisis. unabr. ed. Ali Velshi. Narrated by Ali Velshi. 3 CDs. (Running Time: 2 hrs. 53 mins. 10 sec.). (ENG.). 2009. audio compact disk 17.99 (978-1-59859-567-3(9)) Oasis Audio.

Gimme My Money Back: Your Guide to Beating the Financial Crisis. unabr. ed. Ali Velshi. Narrated by Ali Velshi. (Running Time: 2 hrs. 53 mins. 10 sec.). (ENG.). 2009. 12.59 (978-1-60814-484-6(4)) Oasis Audio.

Gimnasia Mental. unabr. ed. Carlos González. Ed. by Dina Gonzalez. 16 cass. (Running Time: 9 hrs. 50 min.). (SPA.). 1993. 189.00 (978-1-56491-060-8(1)) Imagine Pubs.
A complete exercise for the mind.

Gimnasia Mental. 2nd rev. ed. Carlos Gonzalez. 8 CDs. (Running Time: 8 hrs.). (SPA.). 2004. audio compact disk 149.00 (978-1-56491-119-3(5)) Imagine Pubs.

***Gimp.** abr. ed. Mark Zupan. Read by Mark Zupan. (ENG.). 2006. (978-0-06-123048-6(0), Harper Audio); (978-0-06-123047-9(2), Harper Audio) HarperCollins Pubs.

Gimpel the Fool & Other Stories see Isaac Bashevis Singer Reader

Gimpel the Fool & Other Stories see Isaac Bashevis Singer

Gimpel the Fool & Other Stories. Isaac Bashevis Singer. Narrated by Theodore Bikel. (Audio Editions Ser.). (ENG.). 2007. audio compact disk 19.95 (978-1-57270-729-0(1)) Pub: AudioGO. Dist(s): Perseus Dist

Gimpel the Fool & Other Stories. unabr. ed. Short Stories. Isaac Bashevis Singer. Read by Theodore Bikel. 2 cass. (Running Time: 2 hrs. 30 min.). 2004. 15.95 (978-0-88690-129-5(4), M20027u) Pub: Audio Partners. Dist(s): PerseuPGW
Four wise & funny tales by Singer in classic Yiddish storyteller cadence.

Gin Game. unabr. ed. D. L. Coburn. Perf. by Katherine Helmond & Harris Yulin. 1 cass. (Running Time: 1 hr. 3 mins.). 1996. 20.95 (978-1-58081-059-3(4), WTA2) L A Theatre.
The quiet front porch of a rest home for the aged explodes with emotion when prim Fonsia Dorsey sits down to play gin rummy with the cynical Weller Martin, in this serious & funny Pulitzer Prize-winning drama.

Gin Palace. unabr. ed. Emile Zola. Read by Frederick Davidson. 5 cass. (Running Time: 7 hrs.). 1999. 39.95 (978-0-7861-1636-2(6), 2464) Blckstn Audio.
When Gervaise gazes beyond the gray & interminable wall she sees a great light, a golden mist waving & shimmering with the dawn of a new Parisian day. But it is to the Barriere Poissonniers that her eyes persistently return - watching dully the uninterrupted flow of men & cattle, wagons & sheep which come down from Montmarte & from la Chapelle.

Gina d'd Kids Club, Vol. 1. Music by J. B. DiFrancesco. (J). 2002. audio compact disk 12.95 (978-0-9717916-2-6(7), GDCDV1) Raven MoonEnt.

Gina d's Christmas Music CD. Joey DiFrancesco. 2003. audio compact disk 9.99 (978-0-9727850-7-5(8)) Raven MoonEnt.

Gina D's Dance Party. Joey DiFrancesco & Bernadette DiFrancesco. Perf. by Gina D. 2003. audio compact disk 12.99 (978-0-9727850-8-2(6)) Raven MoonEnt.

Gina d's Kids Club Music, Vol. 2. Music by J. B. DiFrancesco. (J). 2002. audio compact disk 12.95 (978-0-9717916-9-5(4)) Raven MoonEnt.

Ginger. unabr. ed. Christobel Mattingley. (Aussie Bites Ser.). (YA). 2003. audio compact disk 39.95 (978-1-74030-960-8(X)) Pub: Bolinda Pubng AUS. Dist(s): Bolinda Pub Inc

Ginger Pye. Eleanor Estes. Read by Kate Forbes. 5 cass. (Running Time: 6 hrs.). (YA). 1999. stu. ed. 223.30 (978-0-7887-3225-6(0), 46881) Recorded Bks.
Ten-year-old Jerry Pye wants a puppy more than anything. But when he finally gets the one he wants, strange things start to happen. A sneaky stranger in a yellow hat starts following them everywhere. Then Ginger disappears. Finally, after months of fruitless searching, their determination is rewarded by a stroke of good luck & a gust of wind. Includes study guide.

Ginger Pye. Eleanor Estes. Narrated by Kate Forbes. 5 CDs. (Running Time: 6 hrs.). (J). 1979. audio compact disk 58.75 (978-1-4025-5348-6(X)) Recorded Bks.

Ginger Pye. Eleanor Estes. (J). 1979. 21.33 (978-0-394-76816-8(7)) SRA McGraw.

Ginger Pye. unabr. ed. Eleanor Estes. Narrated by Kate Forbes. 5 cass. (Running Time: 6 hrs.). (YA). 2000. pap. bk. 69.00 (978-0-7887-3179-2(3), 40914X4) Recorded Bks.

Ginger Pye. unabr. ed. Eleanor Estes. Narrated by Kate Forbes. 5 pieces. (Running Time: 6 hrs.). (gr. 4 up). 2000. 45.00 (978-0-7887-3160-0(2), 95833E7) Recorded Bks.

Ginger Pye. unabr. ed. Eleanor Estes. 2004. audio compact disk 24.99 (978-1-4193-0609-9(X)) Recorded Bks.
Ten-year-old Jerry Pye wants a dog more than anything. And not just any dog. He has a puppy all picked out. But someone else wants him, too. So Jerry and his sister must hurry to earn enough money to buy him. When they get Ginger home, strange things start to happen. A sneaky stranger in a yellow hat starts following them everywhere. When their precious Ginger disappears on Thanksgiving Day, they start looking for the man in the yellow hat. If they find him, they¿ll probably find their pup. Finally, after months of fruitless searching, their determination is rewarded by a stroke of good luck and a gust of wind.

Ginger Tree, Set. unabr. ed. Oswald Wynd. Read by Jill Tanner. 9 cass. (Running Time: 12 hrs. 30 min.). 1999. 75.00 (978-0-7887-0370-6(6), 94562) Recorded Bks.
Betrothed to a military attache in China, a twenty year old Mary MacKenzie sets sail for China in 1903.

Gingerbread. unabr. ed. Rachel Cohn. Narrated by Carine Montbertrand. 4 cass. (Running Time: 6 hrs.). (YA). (gr. 9 up). 2005. 37.75 (978-1-4193-5133-4(8), RH950) Recorded Bks.
Rachel Cohn's acclaimed debut novel Gingerbread, both an ALA Best Book for Young Adults and an ALA Quick Pick, is also a School Library Journal Best Book. After being expelled from boarding school, teenaged Cyd Charisse is coping with her life circumstances as best she can. She even has a new boyfriend named Shrimp. But her mother is disturbed by Cyd's rebellious behavior and sends her away from San Francisco to live with her biological father in New York City.

Gingerbread. unabr. ed. Rachel Cohn. Read by Carine Montbertrand. 4 cass. (Running Time: 6 hrs.). (YA). (gr. 9 up). 2005. audio compact disk 51.75 (978-1-4193-3032-2(2)) Recorded Bks.

Gingerbread Baby. Jan Brett. 1 cass. (Running Time: 15 min.). (J). (gr. k-3). 2001. bk. 28.00 (978-0-8045-6870-8(7), 6870) Spoken Arts.
It all begins when Matti opens the oven too soon and out jumps a cheeky little Gingerbread Baby. A merry chase through a charming Swiss village leads to a surprise ending.

Gingerbread Baby. Jan Brett. Read by Frances Sternhagen. 1 cass. (Running Time: 15 min.). (J). (ps-2). 2001. bk. 27.95 (SAC6870) Spoken Arts.
When young Mattie fails to follow the directions in his cookbook while making a gingerbread boy, the Gingerbread Baby escapes. He leads Mattie's parents, several animals & some villagers on the familiar chase, until Mattie's creativity catches him in the end.

Gingerbread Boy. Read by Peter Kovner. (J). (gr. k-3). 2005. audio compact disk 6.00 (978-0-618-70903-8(7), Clarion Bks) HM Harcourt.

Gingerbread Boy & Other First Tales. Melody Warnick. Read by Tavia Gilbert. (Running Time: 0 hr. 47 mins. 0 sec.). (PlainTales First Tales Ser.). (ENG.). (J). (gr. k-k). 2009. audio compact disk 12.95 (978-0-9820282-2-3(9)) Pub: PlainTales. Dist(s): IPG Chicago

Gingerbread Girl. Sheila Newberry & Julia Franklin. 2009. 54.95 (978-1-84652-511-7(X)); audio compact disk 71.95 (978-1-84652-512-4(8)) Pub: Magna Story GBR. Dist(s): Ulverscroft US

Gingerbread Girl. unabr. ed. Stephen King. Read by Mare Winningham. 2 CDs. (Running Time: 2 hrs. 0 mins. 0 sec.). (ENG.). 2008. audio compact disk 19.95 (978-0-7435-7118-0(5)) Pub: S&S Audio. Dist(s): S and S Inc

Gingerbread Man see Hombrecito de Mazapan

Gingerbread Man. 1 cass. (Running Time: 35 min.). (J). (ps-3). 2001. pap. bk. 15.95 (VX-49C) Kimbo Educ.
The classic tale of the freshly-baked gingerbread man who's convinced he can outrun any danger. Includes read along book.

Gingerbread Man. 1 cass. (Easy-to-Read Folktales Ser.). (J). (ps-2). 1985. pap. bk. 5.95 (978-0-590-63066-5(0)) Scholastic Inc.

Gingerbread Man. Arlene Capriola & Rigmor Swenson. Ed. by Cherisse Mastry. Illus. by Kathy Burns. 1 cass. (Once upon a Time Ser.). (J). (gr. k-2). 1998. 6.95 (978-1-57022-162-0(6), ECS1626) ECS Lrn Systs.

Gingerbread Man. Arlene Capriola & Rigmor Swenson. Ed. by Cherisse Mastry. Illus. by Kathy Burns. 1 cass. (Once upon a Time Ser.). (J). (gr. k-2). 1998. pap. bk. & wbk. ed. 12.95 (978-1-57022-173-6(1)) ECS Lrn Systs.

Gingerbread Man. Eric A. Kimmel. Illus. by Megan Lloyd. (Running Time: 9 mins.). (J). (ps-3). 1994. 9.95 (978-1-59112-043-8(8)); audio compact disk 12.95 (978-1-59112-784-0(X)) Live Oak Media.

Gingerbread Man. Eric A. Kimmel. Read by Larry Robinson. 11 vols. (Running Time: 9 mins.). (J). 2004. pap. bk. 18.95 (978-1-59112-785-7(8)) Pub: Live Oak Media. Dist(s): AudioGO

Gingerbread Man. Charles Mead. Composed by Charles Mead. Illus. by Steve Neale & Bill Schwartz. 1 cass. (Running Time: 15 mins.). (HandClaps & FingerSnaps Ser.: Vol. 1). (J). (ps up). 1995. bk. 17.95 (978-0-918812-84-1(4), SE0259) MMB Music.

Gingerbread Man. Read by Larry Robinson. Retold by Eric A. Kimmel. Illus. by Megan Lloyd. 11 vols. (Running Time: 9 mins.). (J). (gr. k-3). 1994. bk. 25.95

(978-0-87499-319-6(9)); pap. bk. 37.95 Reading Chest. (978-0-87499-320-2(2)) Live Oak Media.
The classic tale of the freshly-baked gingerbread man who sets out to make his way in the world. Convinced that he can outrun any danger that may confront him, he fails to appreciate that a very fast runner is no match for a very sly fox.

Gingerbread Man. Read by Larry Robinson. Retold by Eric A. Kimmel. Illus. by Megan Lloyd. 11 vols. (Running Time: 9 mins.). (J). (gr. k-3). 2004. pap. bk. 16.95 (978-0-87499-318-9(0)) Pub: Live Oak Media. Dist(s): AudioGO
Convinced that he can outrun any danger, the freshly-baked gingerbread man fails to appreciate that a very fast runner is no match for a very sly fox.

Gingerbread Man. Retold by Karen Schmidt. 1 CD. (Running Time: 6 mins.). (J). (ps-2). 2007. pap. bk. 9.95 (978-0-545-01773-2(4)) Scholastic Inc.

Gingerbread Man. l.t. ed. Short Stories. Illus. by Graham Percy. 1 cass. (Running Time: 10 mins.). Dramatization. (J). (ps-3). 2001. bk. 8.99 (978-84-86154-40-0(5)) Pub: Peralt Mont ESP. Dist(s): imaJen

Gingerbread Man & Other Children's Favorites. (J). 2005. audio compact disk (978-1-933796-37-6(5)) PC Treasures.

Gingerbread Man Audio CD. Benchmark Education Company. Based on a work by Brenda Parkes. (Shared Reading Classics Ser.). (J). (gr. k-2). 2009. audio compact disk 10.00 (978-1-60634-765-2(9)) Benchmark Educ.

Gingerbread Man Classic Read along Audio Book. Prod. by PC Treasures Staff. (J). 2007. (978-1-60072-057-4(9)) PC Treasures.

Gingerbread Man/the Town Mouse & the Country Mouse Sue Arengo. (Classic Tales Ser.). 1999. 14.75 (978-0-19-422032-3(X)) OUP.

Giocomo Leopardi: Multilingual Books Literature. Excerpts. Ed. by Maurizio Falyhera & Cristina Giocometti. 1 CD. (Running Time: 90 mins.). (Audio Anthology of Italian Literature Ser.). (ITA.). 1999. spiral bd. 29.95 (978-1-58214-115-2(0)) Language Assocs.

Giocomo Leopardi Vol. 8: Multilingual Books Literature. Excerpts. Ed. by Maurizio Falyhera & Cristina Giocometti. 1 cass. (Running Time: 90 mins.). (Audio Anthology of Italian Literature Ser.: 8). (ITA.). 1999. spiral bd. 19.95 (978-1-58214-114-5(2)) Language Assocs.

Giovanni Boccaccio from Decameron - Selected Tales: Multilingual Books Literature. Excerpts. Ed. by Maurizio Falyhera & Cristina Giocometti. 1 CD. (Running Time: 90). (Audio Anthology of Italian Literature Ser.: 3). (ITA.). 1999. spiral bd. 29.95 (978-1-58214-105-3(3)) Language Assocs.

Giovanni Boccaccio from Decameron - Selected Tales Vol. 3: Multilingual Books Literature. Ed. by Maurizio Falyhera & Cristina Giocometti. 1 cass. (Running Time: 90). (Audio Anthology of Italian Literature Ser.: 3). (ITA.). 1999. spiral bd. 19.95 (978-1-58214-104-6(5)) Language Assocs.

Giovanni Hidalgo (Slick) Giovanni Hidalgo. 1995. 1.00 (978-0-7692-9099-7(X), Warner Bro) Alfred Pub.

Giovanni Pierluigi da Palestrina. Gloriae Dei Cantores. 1 CD. 1999. audio compact disk 16.95 (978-1-55725-240-1(8), GDCD106) Paraclete MA.

Giovanni's Gift. unabr. ed. Bradford Morrow. Read by Jonathan Marosz. 8 cass. (Running Time: 12 hrs.). 1998. 64.00 (978-0-7366-4077-0(0), 4586) Books on Tape.
A man sets out to avenge the murder of a family friend & discovers a host of unwelcome secrets.

Giovanni's Gift, Set. abr. ed. Bradford Morrow. Read by Frank Muller. 4 cass. (Running Time: 6 hrs.). 1997. 24.95 (978-1-57511-023-3(7), 695316) Pub Mills.
Morrow's mystery relies on a sustained mood of strangeness & disquite. This tale is about a murder & the secrets it reveals is set in the rural Rockies. Giovanni Trentas, a caretaker has been slain & mutilated on the farm of a respected couple. Their nephew Grant travels in from Rome to come to their aid. Grant has been given a cigar box containing Giovanni's personal effects. The items serve as an ongoing map of clues for Grant.

Gipsy Moth Circles the World. unabr. collector's ed. Francis Chichester. Read by Rodney Lay. 7 cass. (Running Time: 10 hrs. 30 mins.). 1986. 56.00 (978-0-7366-0963-0(6), 1905) Books on Tape.
Francis Chichester mapped new air routes, flew uncharted skies & pioneered solo in his plane. In his 60s he set himself the ultimate sailing challenge... to circle the world alone.

Giraffe see Your Own World

***Giraffe, the Pelly & Me.** unabr. ed. Roald Dahl. Read by Richard E. Grant. (ENG.). 2006. (978-0-06-087841-2(X)); (978-0-06-087842-9(8)) HarperCollins Pubs.

Giraffe, the Pelly & Me. unabr. ed. Roald Dahl. Read by Richard E. Grant. (Running Time: 2400 sec.). (J). (gr. 4-7). 2006. audio compact disk 13.95 (978-0-06-085275-7(5), HarperChildAud) HarperCollins Pubs.

Giraffe Who Lost Its Spots. unabr. ed. Roger W. Bretemitz. 1 cass. (Running Time: 20 min.). Dramatization. (Take-along-Stories Ser.: Vol. 1). (J). (gr. k-5). 1997. 8.95 (978-1-893417-03-8(4), 003) Vector Studios.
A baby giraffe gets separated from its parents in Africa, mysteriously loses it spots, then regains them when the rain washes off the dust caused by a helicopter.

Giraffes Can't Dance. Giles Andreae. Illus. by Billy Dee Williams. (Running Time: 8 hrs.). 2007. audio compact disk 12.95 (978-0-439-02729-8(2)) Scholastic Inc.

Giraffes Can't Dance. Giles Andreae. Read by Billy Dee Williams. (Running Time: 8 hrs.). 2007. 8.95 (978-0-439-02730-4(6)) Scholastic Inc.

Giraffes Can't Dance. unabr. ed. Giles Andreae. Read by Billy Dee Williams. Illus. by Guy Parker-Rees. 1 CD. (Running Time: 7 mins.). (J). (ps-1). 2007. bk. 29.95 (978-0-439-02734-2(9)); bk. 24.95 (978-0-439-02733-5(0)) Scholastic Inc.

Girish Ghosh - audio CD: A Lecture by Christopher Isherwood. Speeches. Christopher Isherwood. 1 CD. (Running Time: 50 mins). 2006. audio compact disk 9.95 (978-0-87481-953-3(9)) Vedanta Pr.

Girl. unabr. collector's ed. Catherine Cookson. Read by Mary Woods. 7 cass. (Running Time: 10 hrs. 30 min.). 1985. 56.00 (978-0-7366-0948-7(2), 1891) Books on Tape.
Hannah Boyle, at eight, trudged 23 miles with her dying mother from Newcastle to Hexham. Her mother lived long enough to deliver Hannah to the man she claimed was Hannah's father & to entrust to the church a letter to be delivered to Hannah on her wedding day.

Girl & Horse, 1928 see Poetry & Voice of Margaret Atwood

Girl Beyond the Waves. Michael Mish. 1 CD. (Running Time: 48 mins.). 1999. audio compact disk 12.00 (978-1-888311-00-6(2)) Mish Mash Music.
grief of a loved one.

Girl Called Al. unabr. ed. Constance C. Greene. 1 read-along cass. (Running Time: 59 min.). (Children's Cliffhangers Ser.). (J). (gr. 4-6). 1984. 15.98 incl. bk. & guide. (978-0-8072-1120-5(6), SWR41SP, Listening Lib) Random Audio Pubg.
Rather fat & wearing pigtails & glasses, Al (Alexandra) becomes friends with the girl down the hall. This story is about developing friendship...both the humorous & sober aspects of it.

***Girl Called Rosie.** Anne Doughty. 2010. 76.95 (978-1-4079-0801-4(4)); audio compact disk 89.95 (978-1-4079-0802-1(2)) Pub: Soundings Ltd GBR. Dist(s): Ulverscroft US

Girl Crazy. Perf. by Mickey Rooney & Judy Garland. 1 cass. (Sandy Hook Release Ser.: No. 114). 1989. 7.98 (CSH-2114) Radiola Co.
Original soundtrack recording, music by George & Ira Gershwin, with Tommy Dorsey & his Orchestra.

Girl from Barefoot House. unabr. ed. Maureen Lee. Read by Clare Higgins. 12 cass. (Running Time: 12 hrs.). 2001. 96.95 (978-0-7540-0626-8(3), CAB2049) Pub: Chivers Audio Bks GBR. Dist(s): AudioGO
Little Josie Flynn is sitting at the top of the stairs outside her attic room in Liverpool when her journey through life is turned into heartbreak, when Josie is sent to live with her miserable Aunt Ivy. She later takes on job as a paid companion to an elderly, cantankerous woman & it seemed to promise a life-long happiness when she meets handsome, Jack Coltrane in New York. But life never turns out quite the way you want.

Girl from Ipanema. Vinicius De Moraes. Ed. by Stanley H. Barkan. Tr. by Gregory Rabassa. Compiled by Ray Cravzow. (Review Chapbook Ser.: No. 34: Brazillian Poetry 1). (POR & ENG.). 1989. 10.00 (978-0-89304-883-9(6)) Cross-Cultrl NY.

Girl from Penvarris. Rosemary Aitken. Read by June Barrie. 12 vols. (Running Time: 18 hrs.). 2003. 96.95 (978-0-7540-8303-0(9)) Pub: Chivers Audio Bks GBR. Dist(s): AudioGO

Girl from Seaforth Sands. Katie Flynn. Read by Anne Dover. 12 cass. (Running Time: 52200 sec.). (Soundings Ser.). 2005. 94.95 (978-1-84283-141-0(0)) Pub: ISIS Lrg Prnt GBR. Dist(s): Ulverscroft US

Girl from Seaforth Sands. unabr. ed. Katie Flynn. Read by Anne Dover. 12 CDs. (Running Time: 14 hrs.). (Soundings (CDs) Ser.). (J). 2005. audio compact disk 99.95 (978-1-84559-236-3(0)) Pub: ISIS Lrg Prnt GBR. Dist(s): Ulverscroft US

Girl from the South. Joanna Trollope. Read by Lorelei King. 8 cass. (Running Time: 12 hrs.). 2002. 69.95 (978-0-7540-0874-3(6), CAB 2296); audio compact disk 79.95 (978-0-7540-5533-4(7)) Pub: Chivers Audio Bks GBR. Dist(s): AudioGO

Girl from Wish Lane. Anne Douglas. 2009. 94.95 (978-1-4079-0494-8(9)); audio compact disk 99.95 (978-1-4079-0495-5(7)) Pub: Soundings Ltd GBR. Dist(s): Ulverscroft US

Girl Help see Twentieth-Century Poetry in English, No. 12, Recordings of Poets Reading Their Own Poetry

Girl I Wanted to Be. unabr. ed. Sarah Grace McCandless. Read by Marguerite Gavin. (Running Time: 18000 sec.). 2007. 34.95 (978-1-4332-0218-6(2)); audio compact disk 36.00 (978-1-4332-0219-3(0)); audio compact disk 19.95 (978-1-4332-0220-9(4)) Blckstn Audio.

Girl in Hyacinth Blue. Susan Vreeland. Read by Ensemble Cast. 2009. 44.99 (978-1-60775-727-6(3)) Find a World.

Girl in Hyacinth Blue. Susan Vreeland. Read by Maxwell Caulfield & Juliet Mills. 4 cass. (Running Time: 6 hrs.). 2001. 24.95 (978-1-57511-082-0(2)) Pub Mills.
Story begins when a professor invites a colleague to his home to see a painting that he swears is a Vermeer. But why has the professor hidden this important work for so long? The reasons unfold in a series of events that trace the ownership of the painting back to Amsterdam during World War II, & still further back to the moment of the work's inspiration. As the painting's history is revealed, poignant moments in each of its owner's lives are quietly brought to the surface. Ultimately, each individual's love of this painting reveals how beauty transforms the spirit.

Girl in Hyacinth Blue. unabr. ed. Susan Vreeland. Read by Maxwell Caulfield & Juliet Mills. 4 cass. (Running Time: 6 hrs.). 2000. 24.95 Pub Mills.

Girl in Hyacinth Blue. unabr. abr. ed. Sheryl Bernstein et al. Read by Loren Lester. 4 CDs. (Running Time: 5 hrs.). (ENG.). 2001. audio compact disk 26.95 (978-1-56511-544-6(9), 1565115449) Pub: HighBridge. Dist(s): Workman Pub

Girl in Red. unabr. ed. Gaye Hicyilmaz. Read by Richard Aspel. 4 cass. (Running Time: 5 hrs. 50 mins.). 2004. 32.00 (978-1-74030-576-1(0)); audio compact disk 63.95 (978-1-74030-880-9(8)) Pub: Bolinda Pubng AUS. Dist(s): Bolinda Pub Inc

Girl in the Case. unabr. ed. Lesley Grant-Adamson. Read by Anita Wright. 6 cass. (Running Time: 8 hrs. 15 min.). 1998. 54.95 (978-0-7531-0264-0(1), 971206) Pub: ISIS Audio GBR. Dist(s): Ulverscroft US
Maddy Knewton thinks there is nowhere she'd rather be than her Cotswold village in spring. But then a woman's body is discovered & the stream of gossip touches the lives of Maddy, her friends & feckless lover, but never tells the whole truth. By the time she faces stark reality, it is too late. This portrait of a village under pressure is a masterpiece of suspense.

***Girl in the Garden.** unabr. ed. Kamala Nair. (Running Time: 9 hrs.). (ENG.). 2011. 24.98 (978-1-60941-222-7(2)); audio compact disk & audio compact disk 29.98 (978-1-60941-221-0(4)) Pub: Hachet Audio. Dist(s): HachBkGrp

Girl in the Green Glass Mirror. unabr. ed. Elizabeth McGregor. Read by Clare Wille & Martyn Read. 8 CDs. (Running Time: 34500 sec.). (Isis (CDs) Ser.). 2006. audio compact disk 79.95 (978-0-7531-2496-3(3)) Pub: ISIS Lrg Prnt GBR. Dist(s): Ulverscroft US

Girl in the Green Glass Mirror. unabr. ed. Elizabeth McGregor & Elizabeth Mcgregor. Read by Clare Wille & Martyn Read. 8 cass. (Running Time: 9 hrs. 50 mins.). (Isis Cassettes Ser.). (J). 2006. 69.95 (978-0-7531-3418-4(7)) Pub: ISIS Lrg Prnt GBR. Dist(s): Ulverscroft US

***Girl in the Green Raincoat.** unabr. ed. Laura Lippman. (ENG.). 2011. (978-0-06-202722-1(0), Harper Audio) HarperCollins Pubs.

***Girl in the Mirror.** unabr. ed. Mary Alice Monroe. (Running Time: 13 hrs.). 2011. audio compact disk 19.99 (978-1-4418-5296-0(4), 9781441852960, Bril Audio CD Unabri) Brilliance Audio.

***Girl in the Mirror.** unabr. ed. Mary Alice Monroe. Read by Sandra Burr. (Running Time: 13 hrs.). 2011. 24.99 (978-1-4418-5300-4(6), 9781441853004, Brilliance MP3); 39.97 (978-1-4418-5302-8(2), 9781441853028, Brlnc Audio MP3 Lib); audio compact disk 59.97 (978-1-4418-5297-7(2), 9781441852977, BriAudCD Unabrid) Brilliance Audio.

Girl in the Picture. unabr. ed. Denise Chong. Read by Denise Chong. 10 cass. (Running Time: 15 hrs.). 2000. 80.00 Books on Tape.
The story behind a photograph of the Vietnam War, a little girl screaming in pain & terror after being burned by napalm.

Girl in the Picture: The Story of Kim Phuc. unabr. collector's ed. Read by Denise Chong. 10 cass. (Running Time: 15 hrs.). 2001. 34.95 (978-0-7366-5667-2(7)) Books on Tape.
The story behind a photograph of the Vietnam War: a little girl screaming in pain and terror after being burned by napalm.

Girl in the Plain Brown Wrapper: A Travis Mcgee Novel. unabr. collector's ed. John D. MacDonald. Read by Michael Prichard. 7 cass. (Running Time: 10 hrs. 30 min.). (Travis McGee Ser.: Vol. 10). 1984. 56.00 (978-0-7366-0704-9(8), 1667) Books on Tape.
While making good his promise to prevent a young girl from committing suicide, Travis McGee encounters an entirely new string of problems of his own.

Girl in the Sun see Twentieth-Century Poetry in English, No. 1, Recordings of Poets Reading Their Own Poetry

***Girl in the Yellow Bikini.** unabr. ed. Phillip Margolin. Read by Austin Cooper. (ENG.). 2008. (978-0-06-136547-8(5), Harper Audio); (978-0-06-172670-5(2)) HarperCollins Pubs.

***Girl in Translation.** unabr. ed. Jean Kwok. (Running Time: 9 hrs.). (ENG.). 2010. audio compact disk 39.95 (978-0-14-242799-6(3), PengAudBks) Penguin Grp USA.

***Girl in Translation.** unabr. ed. Jean Kwok. Narrated by Grayce Wey. 8 CDs. (Running Time: 9 hrs.). 2010. audio compact disk 39.95 (978-0-307-73618-5(0), BksonTape) Pub: Random Audio Pubg. Dist(s): Random

Girl Missing. abr. ed. Tess Gerritsen. Read by Susan Ericksen. (Running Time: 5 hrs.). 2009. audio compact disk 14.99 (978-1-4418-1792-1(1), 9781441817921, BACD) Brilliance Audio.

Girl Missing. unabr. ed. Tess Gerritsen. Read by Susan Ericksen. (Running Time: 8 hrs.). 2009. 24.99 (978-1-4418-1788-4(3), 9781441817884, Brilliance MP3); 39.97 (978-1-4418-1789-1(1), 9781441817891, Brlnc Audio MP3 Lib); 24.99 (978-1-4418-1790-7(5), 9781441817907, BAD); 39.97 (978-1-4418-1791-4(3), 9781441817914, BADLE); audio compact disk 97.97 (978-1-4418-1787-7(5), 9781441817877, BriAudCD Unabrid); audio compact disk 29.99 (978-1-4418-1786-0(7), 9781441817860, Bril Audio CD Unabri) Brilliance Audio.

Girl Named Disaster. Nancy Farmer. (J). audio compact disk 111.75 (978-1-4025-5080-5(4)) Recorded Bks.

Girl Named Disaster. unabr. ed. Nancy Farmer. Narrated by Lisette Lecat. 9 pieces. (Running Time: 12 hrs. 15 mins.). (J). (gr. 9 up). 1997. 77.75 (978-0-7887-1342-2(6), 95191E7) Recorded Bks.
Eleven-year old Nhamo is running for her life. To escape an arranged marriage to a cruel man she embarks upon a lonely & dangerous journey that evolves into a rich & luminous spiritual experience.

Girl Named Disaster. unabr. ed. Nancy Farmer. Read by Lisette Lecat. 9 cass. (Running Time: 12 hrs. 15 min.). (YA). (gr. 2). 1997. bk. 101.70 (978-0-7887-1722-2(7), 40590); Rental 17.50 Recorded Bks.

***Girl Named Mister.** Nikki Grimes. (Running Time: 2 hrs. 15 mins. 33 sec.). (ENG.). (YA). 2010. 15.99 (978-0-310-39960-5(2)) Zondervan.

Girl Named Zippy. unabr. ed. Haven Kimmel. Read by Haven Kimmel. (YA). 2006. 44.99 (978-1-59895-209-4(9)) Find a World.

Girl Named Zippy: Growing up Small in Mooreland, Indiana. unabr. ed. Haven Kimmel. Read by Haven Kimmel. 5 CDs. (Running Time: 6 hrs.). (ENG.). 2005. audio compact disk 26.95 (978-1-59887-010-7(6), 1598870106) Pub: Penguin-HghBrdg. Dist(s): Penguin Grp USA

Girl Now Leaving. unabr. ed. Betty Burton. Read by Nicolette McKenzie. 12 cass. (Running Time: 15 hrs.). (Soundings Ser.). (J). 2006. 94.95 (978-1-84559-211-0(5)) Pub: ISIS Lrg Prnt GBR. Dist(s): Ulverscroft US

Girl of His Dreams. unabr. ed. Donna Leon. Narrated by David Colacci. 1 MP3-CD. (Running Time: 9 hrs. 8 mins.). (Commissario Guido Brunetti Mystery Ser.: Bk. 17). 2008. 54.95 (978-0-7927-5515-9(4)); audio compact disk 79.95 (978-0-7927-5489-3(1)) AudioGO.
On a rainy morning, not long after the funeral of his mother, Commissario Brunetti and Ispettore Vianello respond to a 911 call reporting a body floating near the steps in one of Venice's side canals. Reaching down to pull it out, Brunetti's wrist is caught by the silkiness of golden hair, and he sees a small foot - together he and Vianello lift a dead girl from the water. But, inconceivably, no one has reported a missing child, nor the theft of the gold jewelry that she carries. So Brunetti is drawn into a search not only for the cause of her death but also for her identity, her family, and for the secrets that people will keep in order to protect their children - be they innocent or guilty. The investigation takes Brunetti from the canals and palazzos of Venice to a Gypsy encampment on the mainland, through quicksands of connections and relationships both known and concealed, as he struggles with both institutional prejudice and entrenched criminality to try to unravel the fate of the dead child.

Girl of His Dreams. unabr. ed. Donna Leon. Narrated by David Colacci. (Commissario Guido Brunetti Mystery Ser.: Bk. 17). (ENG.). 2008. audio compact disk 29.95 (978-1-60283-404-0(0)) Pub: AudioGO. Dist(s): Perseus Dist

Girl of Kosovo. Alice Mead. Narrated by Julie Dretzin. 2 pieces. (Running Time: 2 hrs. 45 mins.). (gr. 5 up). 19.00 (978-1-4025-1719-8(X)) Recorded Bks.

Girl of Lost Things. unabr. ed. Ann Brashares. 4 cass. (Running Time: 6 hrs.). 2006. 36.00 (978-1-4159-2102-9(4)); audio compact disk 54.00 (978-1-4159-2103-6(2)) Books on Tape.

Girl of Lost Things. unabr. ed. Ann Brashares. (YA). 2006. audio compact disk 29.95 (978-0-14-305871-7(1), PengAudBks) Penguin Grp USA.

Girl of the Bitterlost, Vol. 2. unabr. ed. Chief Little Summer. Interview with Warm Night Rain. 2 CDs. (J). (gr. 6-12). 1999. audio compact disk 14.95 CD Set. (978-1-880440-15-5(6)) Piqua Pr.
Eleven year old girl from Venus is found in the Bitter Lost by the Indian twins who take her home to school.

Girl of the Limberlost. unabr. ed. Gene Stratton-Porter. Narrated by Flo Gibson. 8 cass. (Running Time: 12 hrs.). (gr. 6 up). 2002. 26.95 (978-1-55685-681-5(4),) Audio Bk Con.
In the face of adversity, sweet-tempered Elnora takes comfort in the natural world around her and discovers a unique way to further her formal education.

Girl of the Limberlost. unabr. ed. Gene Stratton-Porter. Read by Mary Starkey. 8 cass. (Running Time: 11 hrs.). 1985. 49.95 (978-1-55686-226-7(1), 226) Books in Motion.
Sequel to Freckles. A moving & richly human story of a young girl whose own kindness & wholesome philosophy enables her to brighten the lives of her many friends.

Girl of the Limberlost. unabr. ed. Gene Stratton-Porter. Narrated by Christina Moore. 9 pieces. (Running Time: 12 hrs.). (gr. 9 up). 2001. 78.00 (978-0-7887-5106-6(9)) Recorded Bks.
Elnora Comstock is energetic, resourceful, and cheerful despite the fact that her mother is embittered by personal tragedy and financial hardships.

***Girl on a Motorcycle: 250 Headwords.** Ed. by Oxford University Press Staff. (Oxford Bookworms ELT Ser.). 2008. audio compact disk 6.75 (978-0-19-423404-7(5)) Pub: OUP-CN CAN. Dist(s): OUP

Girl on Legare Street. Karen White. Read by Aimee Bruneau. (Tradd Street Ser.: No. 2). 2009. audio compact disk 29.95 (978-1-59316-470-6(X)) Listen & Live.

Girl on the Boat. unabr. ed. P. G. Wodehouse. Read by Frederick Davidson. 5 cass. (Running Time: 7 hrs.). 1998. 39.95 (978-0-7861-1437-5(1), 2323) Blckstn Audio.
Wilhelmina "Billie" Bennett is to marry Eustace Hignett, the weak, poetry-writing son of Mrs. Horace Hignett, the famous English writer on theosophy. Enter Sam Marlowe, Eustace's cousin & Jane Hubbard, & another romp unfolds.

Girl on the Boat, Set. unabr. ed. P. G. Wodehouse. Read by Frederick Davidson. 5 cass. 1999. 39.95 (FS9-50907) Highsmith.

***Girl Parts.** unabr. ed. John Cusick. Read by Chris Patton. (Running Time: 5 hrs.). 2010. 19.99 (978-1-4418-5842-9(3), 9781441858429, BAD); 39.97 (978-1-4418-5843-6(1), 9781441858436, BADLE) Brilliance Audio.

***Girl Parts.** unabr. ed. John M. Cusick. Read by Chris Patton. (Running Time: 5 hrs.). 2010. 39.97 (978-1-4418-5841-2(5), 9781441858412, Brlnc Audio MP3 Lib); audio compact disk 54.97 (978-1-4418-5839-9(3), 9781441858399, BriAudCD Unabrid) Brilliance Audio.

***Girl Parts.** unabr. ed. John M. Cusick. Read by Chris Patton. (Running Time: 5 hrs.). 2010. 19.99 (978-1-4418-5840-5(7), 9781441858405, Brilliance MP3) Brilliance Audio.

***Girl Parts.** unabr. ed. John M. Cusick. Read by Chris Patton. (Running Time: 6 hrs.). (YA). 2010. audio compact disk 24.99 (978-1-4418-5838-2(5), 9781441858382, Bril Audio CD Unabri) Brilliance Audio.

Girl Reporter Blows Lid off Town. unabr. ed. Linda Ellerbee. Narrated by Carine Montbertrand. 3 pieces. (Running Time: 4 hrs. 30 mins.). (Get Real Ser.). (gr. 3 up). 2001. 28.00 (978-0-7887-5023-6(2)) Recorded Bks.
Casey Smith, girl reporter, is desperate to break a serious water pollution story for the school paper. But Megan wants to fill the paper with reports on the latest school fashions, horoscopes and birthday wishes.

Girl Reporter Sinks School. Linda Ellerbee. Narrated by Carine Montbertrand. 3 pieces. (Running Time: 3 hrs. 45 mins.). (Get Real Ser.: Vol. 2). (gr. 3 up). 28.00 (978-0-7887-9372-1(1)) Recorded Bks.

Girl to Come Home To. abr. ed. Grace Livingston Hill. Read by Aimee Lilly. 2 cass. (Running Time: 1 hr. 30 mins. per cass.). (Grace Livingston Hill Romances Ser.). 2004. 8.99 (978-1-886463-54-7(9)) Oasis Audio.
A courageous officer is caught up in a desperate espionage plot - - until a gentle young girl helps him find the strength to overcome. One cassette Over 1-1/2 hours Abridged.

Girl Underground. Morris Gleitzman. Read by Mary-Anne Fahey. (Running Time: 3 hrs. 30 mins.). (J). 2009. 54.99 (978-1-74214-382-8(2), 9781742143828) Pub: Bolinda Pubng AUS. Dist(s): Bolinda Pub Inc

Girl Underground. unabr. ed. Morris Gleitzman. Read by Morris Gleitzman. Read by Mary-Anne Fahey. 3 CDs. (Running Time: 3 hrs. 30 mins.). (YA). 2004. audio compact disk 54.95 (978-1-74093-526-5(8)) Pub: Bolinda Pubng AUS. Dist(s): Bolinda Pub Inc

***Girl Who Chased the Moon.** unabr. ed. Sarah Addison Allen. Narrated by Rebecca Lowman. 6 CDs. (Running Time: 7 hrs.). 2010. audio compact disk 90.00 (978-1-4159-6219-0(7), BksonTape) Pub: Random Audio Pubg. Dist(s): Random

***Girl Who Circumnavigated Fairyland in a Ship of Her Own Making.** unabr. ed. Catherynne M. Valente. Read by Catherynne Valente. (Running Time: 8 hrs.). 2011. 39.97 (978-1-4418-7763-5(0), 9781441877635, Brlnc Audio MP3 Lib); 39.97 (978-1-4418-7765-9(7), 9781441877659, BADLE); 24.99 (978-1-4418-7764-2(9), 9781441877642, BAD); audio compact disk 79.97 (978-1-4418-7761-1(4), 9781441877611, BriAudCD Unabrid) Brilliance Audio.

***Girl Who Circumnavigated Fairyland in a Ship of Her Own Making.** unabr. ed. Catherynne Valente & Catherynne M. Valente. Read by Catherynne Valente. (Running Time: 8 hrs.). 2011. 24.99 (978-1-4418-7762-8(2), 9781441877628, Brilliance MP3); audio compact disk 29.99 (978-1-4418-7760-4(6), 9781441877604, Bril Audio CD Unabri) Brilliance Audio.

Girl Who Creid Flowers & Other Tales. 2004. 8.95 (978-0-89719-927-8(8)) Weston Woods.

Girl Who Fell from the Sky. unabr. ed. Heidi W. Durrow. Read by Karen Murray et al. 6 CDs. (Running Time: 7 hrs.). 2010. audio compact disk 29.95 (978-1-59887-923-0(5), 1598879235) Pub: HighBridge. Dist(s): Workman Pub

Girl Who Had Everything. Janice Greene. (Running Time: 4354 sec.). (Pageturners Ser.). (J). 2004. 10.95 (978-1-56254-711-0(9)) Saddleback Edu.

Girl Who Heard Dragons. unabr. ed. Anne McCaffrey. Read by Constance Towers. 8 CDs. (Running Time: 9 hrs.). 2002. audio compact disk 42.50 (978-1-59040-557-4(9)) Audio Lit.

***Girl Who Kicked the Hornet's Nest.** unabr. ed. Stieg Larsson. Read by Simon Vance. (Running Time: 20 hrs. 30 mins.). (ENG.). 2010. 20.00 (978-0-7393-8420-6(1), Random AudioBks) Pub: Random Audio Pubg. Dist(s): Random

Girl Who Kicked the Hornet's Nest. unabr. ed. Stieg Larsson. Read by Simon Vance. Tr. by Reg Keeland from SWE. 16 CDs. (Running Time: 20 hrs. 30 mins.). (Millennium Trilogy: No. 3). (ENG.). 2010. audio compact disk 40.00 (978-0-7393-8419-0(8), Random AudioBks) Pub: Random Audio Pubg. Dist(s): Random

***Girl Who Kicked the Hornet's Nest.** unabr. ed. Stieg Larsson & Reg Keeland. Narrated by Simon Vance. 13 CDs. 2010. audio compact disk 40.00 (978-0-307-73501-0(X), BksonTape) Pub: Random Audio Pubg. Dist(s): Random

Girl Who Loved Horses. Paul Goble. Illus. by Paul Goble. 11 vols. (Running Time: 13 mins.). (J). 2001. pap. bk. 18.95 (978-1-59112-314-9(3)) Pub: Live Oak Media. Dist(s): AudioGO

Girl Who Loved Tom Gordon. Stephen King. Narrated by Anne Heche. 6 cass. (Running Time: 6 hrs. 30 mins.). 2001. 48.00 (96604E7) Recorded Bks.
What if the woods were full of them? And of course they were, the woods are full of everything you don't like, everything you are afraid of! While hiking the Appalachian trail, nine-year-old Trisa tires of the constant bickering between her mother & brother & decides to wander off. Lost in the forest, she draws comfort from tuning her radio to Boston Red Socks broadcasts & following her hero, relief pitcher Tom Gordon. She imagines Tom is with her & is her key to surviving.

Girl Who Loved Tom Gordon. Stephen King. Narrated by Anne Heche. 6 CDs. (Running Time: 6 hrs. 30 mins.). 2001. audio compact disk 58.00 (978-0-7887-5153-0(0), C1316E7) Recorded Bks.

Girl Who Loved Tom Gordon. unabr. ed. Stephen King. Read by Anne Heche. 6 cass. 1999. 29.95 (FS9-43416) Highsmith.

Girl Who Loved Tom Gordon. unabr. ed. Stephen King. Narrated by Anne Heche. 6 cass. (Running Time: 6 hrs. 30 mins.). 2001. 48.00 (978-0-7887-5469-2(6), 96604x7) Recorded Bks.
A gripping tale of a young girl's frightening adventure deep into the New England wilderness. Lost off the Appalachian Trail, Trisha is comforted by Boston Red Sox radio broadcasts involving her hero, relief pitcher Tom Gordon. He gives her the strength to survive the unseen enemy leaving slaughtered animals & mangled trees in its wake.

Girl Who Loved Tom Gordon. unabr. ed. Stephen King. Read by Anne Heche. 2006. 18.95 (978-0-7435-6339-0(5), Audioworks) Pub: S&S Audio. Dist(s): S and S Inc

Girl Who Loved Tom Gordon. unabr. ed. Stephen King. Read by Anne Heche. (Running Time: 63 hrs. 0 mins. 0 sec.). (ENG.). 2008. audio compact disk 14.99 (978-0-7435-7818-9(X)) Pub: S&S Audio. Dist(s): S and S Inc

Girl Who Loved Wild Horses. Paul Goble. Illus. by Paul Goble. 14 vols. (Running Time: 13 mins.). 2001. pap. bk. 39.95 (978-1-59112-534-1(0)); audio compact disk 12.95 (978-1-59112-313-2(5)) Live Oak Media.

Girl Who Loved Wild Horses. Paul Goble. Illus. by Paul Goble. (Running Time: 13 mins.). (J). (gr. k-3). 2001. 9.95 (978-0-87499-761-3(5)) Live Oak Media.

Girl Who Loved Wild Horses. Paul Goble. (J). 1985. 18.66 (978-0-394-66015-8(3)) SRA McGraw.

Girl Who Loved Wild Horses. abr. ed. Paul Goble. 14 vols. (Running Time: 13 mins.). (J). (ps-2). 2001. pap. bk. 37.95 (978-0-87499-764-4(X)) Live Oak Media.
It is the tale of a Native American girl whose tribe follows the buffalo. She tends the horses and grows to love them so much that eventually she joins them. Accompanied by Native American music. One side of the tape includes page-turn signals, while the other does not.

Girl Who Loved Wild Horses. abr. ed. Paul Goble. Read by Lance White Magpie. 11 vols. (Running Time: 13 mins.). (J). (ps-2). 2001. bk. 25.95 (978-0-87499-763-7(1)) Live Oak Media.

Girl Who Loved Wild Horses. unabr. ed. Paul Goble. 11 vols. (Running Time: 13 mins.). (J). (ps-2). 2001. pap. bk. 16.95 (978-0-87499-762-0(3)) Pub: Live Oak Media. Dist(s): AudioGO
The story of an Indian girl who feels such kinhsip with the wild horses grazing near her village that she eventually becomes one of them.

Girl Who Married a Lion: And Other Tales from Africa. Ed. by Alexander McCall Smith. 2004. 24.99 (978-1-4025-9427-4(5), 04124); audio compact disk 29.99 (978-1-4025-9428-1(3), 01792) Recorded Bks.

Girl Who Married a Lion: And Other Tales from Africa. unabr. ed. Ed. by Alexander McCall Smith. 3 cass. (Running Time: 4 hrs. 30 mins.). 2004. 49.75 (978-1-4193-0589-4(1), 97861MC) Recorded Bks.

Girl Who Married a Lion: And Other Tales from Africa. unabr. ed. Ed. by Alexander McCall Smith. 2004. audio compact disk 69.75 (978-1-4193-0753-9(3)) Recorded Bks.

Girl Who Owned a City. unabr. ed. O. T. Nelson. Narrated by Julie Dretzin. (J). (gr. 7). 1998. bk. 50.75 (978-0-7887-2664-4(1), 40824) Recorded Bks.
A horrible plague has swept across the earth, killing everyone over the age of 12. Fierce gangs of wild children roam the streets making life miserable & dangerous for everyone. The children of Grand Avenue have a better life than most. Lisa, their 10-year-old leader, has gained control & found a way to keep them safe, for now.

Girl Who Owned a City, unabr. ed. O. T. Nelson. Narrated by Julie Dretzin. 4 pieces. (Running Time: 5 hrs. 45 mins.). (gr. 4 up). 1998. 38.00 (978-0-7887-2634-7(X), 95637E7) Recorded Bks.

***Girl Who Played with Fire.** unabr. ed. Stieg Larsson. Read by Simon Vance. 15 CDs. (Running Time: 18 hrs. 30 mins.). (Millennium Trilogy: Bk. 2). 2009. audio compact disk 100.00 (978-1-4159-6436-1(X), BksonTape) Pub: Random Audio Pubg. Dist(s): Random

Girl Who Played with Fire. unabr. ed. Stieg Larsson. Read by Simon Vance. (Millennium Trilogy: No. 2). (ENG.). 2009. audio compact disk 39.95 (978-0-7393-8417-6(1), Random AudioBks) Pub: Random Audio Pubg. Dist(s): Random

Girl Who Ran off with Daddy. unabr. ed. David Handler. Narrated by Tom Stechschulte. 7 cass. (Running Time: 9 hrs. 45 mins.). (Stewart Hoag Mystery Ser.: Vol. 7). 2000. 62.00 (978-0-7887-0848-0(1), 94994E7) Recorded Bks.
Join the dapper ghost writer, Hoagy Hoag, on his most bizarre case yet. An old friend, Thor Gibbs, 71-year-old macho-man author, has roared up to Hoagy's doorstep with the latest love of his life, his 17-year-old stepdaughter. In the turmoil that follows, deception & murder join the scandal surrounding Thor's life.

Girl Who Stopped Swimming. unabr. ed. Joshilyn Jackson. (Running Time: 9 hrs. 30 mins.). (ENG.). 2008. 19.98 (978-1-59483-923-8(9)) Pub: Hachet Audio. Dist(s): HachBkGrp

Girl with a Pearl Earring. Tracy Chevalier. Narrated by Ruth Ann Phimister. 7 CDs. (Running Time: 8 hrs.). audio compact disk 69.00 (978-1-4025-3485-0(X)) Recorded Bks.

Girl with a Pearl Earring. Tracy Chevalier. 2004. audio compact disk 24.95 (978-1-4193-1176-5(X)) Recorded Bks.

Girl with a Pearl Earring. abr. ed. Tracy Chevalier. Read by Jenna Lamia. 4 vols. (Running Time: 4 hrs. 45 mins.). (ENG.). 2001. audio compact disk 26.95 (978-1-56511-497-5(3), 1565114973) Pub: HighBridge. Dist(s): Workman Pub

Girl with a Pearl Earring. unabr. ed. Tracy Chevalier. Narrated by Ruth Ann Phimister. 6 cass. (Running Time: 8 hrs.). 2000. 59.00 (978-0-7887-4355-9(4)) Recorded Bks.
Set in 17th century Delft, historical novel intertwines the art of Johannes Vermeer with his life and that of a maiden servat in his household.

Girl with a Pearl Earring. unabr. ed. Tracy Chevalier. Read by Ruth Ann Phimister. 5 cass. (Running Time: 8 hrs.). 2004. 25.95 (978-0-7887-6044-0(0), 00304) Recorded Bks.
Best-selling author Tracy Chevalier re-creates the 17th-century world of Johannes Vermeer in Girl with a Pearl Earring, a haunting work of historical fiction. In 1664, 16-year-old Griet enters the Vermeer household as a servant. Daughter of a Delft tile maker, she has a natural eye for color and design. As she cleans the master's studio, Griet learns how Vermeer sees the people he paints. And as his attention focuses on her, she realizes that she, too, is becoming one of his subjects. Tracy Chevalier fills this unusual love story with the shades, sounds, and textures of everyday life in Holland.

***Girl with Curious Hair: Stories.** unabr. ed. David Foster Wallace. Read by Robert Petkoff. (Running Time: 10 hrs.). (ENG.). 2010. 24.98 (978-1-60788-558-0(1)) Pub: Hachet Audio. Dist(s): HachBkGrp

***Girl with No Shadow.** unabr. ed. Joanne Harris. Read by Susanna Burney. (ENG.). 2008. (978-0-06-167272-9(6)); (978-0-06-167273-6(4)) HarperCollins Pubs.

Girl with No Shadow. unabr. ed. Joanne Harris. Read by Susanna Burney. 12 CDs. (Running Time: 14 hrs. 30 mins.). 2008. audio compact disk 39.95 (978-0-06-155764-4(1), Harper Audio) HarperCollins Pubs.

Girl with the Botticelli Eyes. unabr. ed. Herbert Lieberman. Narrated by George Guidall. 9 cass. (Running Time: 11 hrs. 45 mins.). 1997. 78.00 (978-0-7887-0789-6(2), 94932E7) Recorded Bks.
A curator of the Metropolitan Museum in New York is working on a show of Botticelli's work. He meets a woman who is a direct decendant of the Primavera model. But a madman is working to destroy both the woman & the priceless canvases.

Girl with the Broken Wing. unabr. ed. Heather Dyer. Read by Alison Reid. 2 CDs. (Running Time: 2 hrs. 2 mins.). (J). (gr. 2-4). 2008. audio compact disk 21.95 (978-1-4056-5819-5(3), Chivers Child Audio) AudioGO.

Girl with the Creel. unabr. ed. Doris Davidson. Read by Lesley Mackie. 16 cass. (Running Time: 21 hrs. 30 mins.). 1999. 104.95 (978-1-86042-533-2(X), 2533X) Pub: Soundings Ltd GBR. Dist(s): Ulverscroft US
Lizann Jappy is the daughter of a fisherman from the close community of Buckie, Scotland. Having led a sheltered girlhood, her life is turned upside-down when it is discovered that the man she loves is married - for divorce is an unthinkable disgrace & her family lives by the traditions that have guided the local folk for generations. But Lizann finds that, when the need arises, she can be every bit as proud & resourceful as the people of her home town. Forced to flee by a series of misunderstandings & tragedies, she must leave behind almost everything. Yet as long as she can carry her creel on her back, she hopes she will not starve. Against the background of the herring fleets & the bombing of Aberdeen in the Second World War, this heartwarming tale brims with adventure, humor & passion.

Girl with the Dragon Tattoo. abr. ed. Stieg Larsson. Read by Martin A. Wenner. Tr. by Reg Keeland from SWE. 6 CDs. (Running Time: 7 hrs. 30 mins.). (Millennium Trilogy: No. 1).Tr. of Män Som Hatar Kvinnor. (ENG.). 2008. audio compact disk 29.95 (978-0-7393-7064-3(2), Random AudioBks) Pub: Random Audio Pubg. Dist(s): Random

Girl with the Dragon Tattoo. unabr. ed. Stieg Larsson. Read by Simon Vance. (Millennium Trilogy: No. 1).Tr. of Män Som Hatar Kvinnor. (ENG.). 2009. audio compact disk 35.00 (978-0-307-57758-0(9), Random AudioBks) Pub: Random Audio Pubg. Dist(s): Random

***Girl with the Dragon Wing Eyes.** Jack Bates. Read by Bruce Reizen. (ENG.). 2010. audio compact disk 2.99 (978-0-9825278-7-0(X)) Mind Wings Aud.

***Girl with the Dragon Wing Eyes: A Harry Landers Episode.** Jack Bates. Read by Bruce Reizen. (Running Time: 55). (ENG.). 2010. 2.99 (978-1-61114-017-0(X)) Mind Wings Aud.

Girl with the Incredible Feeling. unabr. ed. Elizabeth Swados. Perf. by Elizabeth Swados. 1 cass. (J). (ps-6). 1988. 9.95 (978-0-89845-787-2(4), CPN 1830) HarperCollins Pubs.

Girl with the Long Green Heart. Lawrence Block. Read by Alan Sklar. 4 cass. 39.95 (978-0-7927-3794-0(6), CSL 863); audio compact disk 59.95 (978-0-7927-3795-7(4), SLD 863); audio compact disk 29.95 (978-0-7927-3846-6(2), CMP 863) AudioGO.

***Girl with the Mermaid Hair.** unabr. ed. Delia Ephron. Read by Sarah Drew. (ENG.). 2010. (978-0-06-193829-0(7)); (978-0-06-196754-2(8)) HarperCollins Pubs.

Girl, 15, Charming but Insane. Sue Limb. 4 cassettes. (Running Time: 6:23 hrs). (Girl, 15 Ser.). (YA). (gr. 7-10). 2005. 32.00 (978-1-4000-9110-2(1), Listening Lib); audio compact disk 38.25 (978-1-4000-9482-0(8), Listening Lib) Pub: Random Audio Pubg. Dist(s): NetLibrary CO

Girl, 20. unabr. collector's ed. Kingsley Amis. Read by Richard Green. 8 cass. (Running Time: 8 cass.). 1978. 48.00 (978-0-7366-0092-7(2), 1100) Books on Tape.
The plight of an aging conductor: Husband in an unsatisfactory marriage, father to an unhappy brood. When a young woman responds to his overtures, he breaks the marriage & bursts the family.

Girlfriends: Invisible Bonds, Enduring Ties, abr. ed. Carmen Renee Berry & Tamara Traeder. Read by Cindy Williams et al. 2 cass. (Running Time: 3 hrs.). 1997. 17.95 (978-1-57453-209-8(X)) Audio Lit.
Inspiring & revealing tales tell of friendships old & new. Explores acceptance, forgiveness, loyalty & many other aspects of women's friendships.

Girlfriend's Guide to Football: How to Talk His Language. unabr. ed. Paula Duffy. (ENG.). 2006. 3.99 (978-1-59659-065-6(3), GildAudio) Pub: Gildan Media. Dist(s): HachBkGrp

Girlfriends Talk about Men: Sharing Secrets for a Great Relationship, abr. ed. Carmen Renee Berry & Tamara Traeder. Read by Cindy Williams et al. 2 cass. (Running Time: 3 hrs.). 1997. 17.95 (978-1-57453-210-4(3)) Audio Lit.
Real life stories share advice & anecdotes on how to meet the right man & when to become intimate, how to divide up household chores & surviving infidelity.

Girlfriendship. 2005. audio compact disk 14.99 (978-0-88368-891-5(3)) Whitaker Hse.

Girls. Amy Goldman Koss. 2 cass. . (Running Time: 3 hrs). 2002. lib. bdg. 20.00 (978-1-932076-06-6(9)) Full Cast Audio.

Girls. unabr. ed. Edna Ferber. Read by Flo Gibson. 5 cass. (Running Time: 7 hrs. 30 min.). 1998. 20.95 (978-1-55685-510-8(9)) Audio Bk Con.
A great-aunt, domineering mother & mature daughter live together through trying circumstances. Two World Wars, spinsterhood, three brief romances & illegitimacy are death with.

Girls. unabr. ed. Amy Goldman Koss. Read by Full Cast Production Staff. (J). 2007. 34.99 (978-1-60252-558-0(7)) Find a World.

Girls: A Novel. abr. ed. Lori Lansens. Read by Stephanie Zimbalist & Lolita Davidovitch. (Running Time: 6 hrs.). (ENG.). 2006. 14.98 (978-1-59483-518-6(7)) Pub: Hachet Audio. Dist(s): HachBkGrp

Girls Acting Catty. unabr. ed. Leslie Margolis. Read by Ellen Grafton. (Running Time: 4 hrs.). 2009. 39.97 (978-1-4418-2497-4(9), 9781441824974, Brlnc Audio MP3 Lib); 39.97 (978-1-4418-2499-8(5), 9781441824998, BADLE); 24.99 (978-1-4418-2496-7(0), 9781441824967, Brilliance MP3); 24.99 (978-1-4418-2498-1(7), 9781441824981, BAD); audio compact disk 24.99 (978-1-4418-2494-3(4), 9781441824943, Bril Audio CD Unabri) Brilliance Audio.

Girls Acting Catty. unabr. ed. Leslie Margolis. Read by Ellen Grafton. 4 CDs. (Running Time: 4 hrs.). (J). (gr. 5-7). 2009. audio compact disk 48.97 (978-1-4418-2495-0(2), 9781441824950, BriAudCD Unabrid) Brilliance Audio.

Girls & Boys Come Out to Play. Perf. by Barolk Folk Staff & Madeline MacNeil. 1 cass. (Running Time: 45 min.). (J). (gr. 3 up). 1991. 9.98 (978-1-877737-74-9(7), MLP 2275) MFLP CA.
Familiar rhymes from Mother Goose, sung to traditional tunes & paired with joyous dances. Hammered dulcimer, treble viol, recorder, guitar & piano.

Girls & Boys, Come Out to Play! Traditional Nursery Songs & Dances. Perf. by Madeline MacNeil & Barbara Hess. 1 cass. (Running Time: 45 min.). (J). (ps-2). 9.98 (2275); audio compact disk 12.98 (D2275) MFLP CA.
Beginning with a Mother Goose rhyme sung to its original tune, each of these 20 traditional songs transitions to a lively folk dance instrumental, perfect accompaniment to creative movement for children.

Girls at Play. unabr. ed. Paul Theroux. Read by Michael Prichard. 8 cass. (Running Time: 8 hrs.). 1984. 48.00 (978-0-7366-0920-3(2), 1863) Books on Tape.
Story concerns the ambitions of three women, teachers at a remote girls' school. They are the only white women in the region & each is in her own way doomed.

Girls Don't Make Passes at Boys with Fat Asses (an Essay from Things I've Learned from Women Who've Dumped Me) abr. ed. Andy Richter. Read by Andy Richter. Ed. by Ben Karlin. (Running Time: 15 mins.). (ENG.). 2008. 1.98 (978-1-60024-330-1(4)) Pub: Hachet Audio. Dist(s): HachBkGrp

Girl's Garden (From Through the Eyes of a Child) - ShowTrax. Music by John Leavitt. 1 CD. (Running Time: 1 hr. 30 mins.). 2000. audio compact disk 49.95 (08742483) H Leonard.
The familiar Robert Frost poem in a delightful & whimsical concert setting. Other movements from this choral suite (available separately) include: "The Bells," "Between Two Hills," "Polly Wolly Doodle." All four movements available.

Girls' Guide to Hunting & Fishing. unabr. ed. Melissa Bank. Ed. by Melissa Bank. Read by Lorelei King. 6 vols. (Running Time: 9 hrs.). (Chivers Sound Library American Collections). 1999. bk. 54.95 (978-0-7927-2331-8(7), CSL 220, Chivers Sound Lib) AudioGO.
Maps the progress of Jane Rosenal as she sets out on a personal & spirited expedition through the perilous terrain of sex, love & relationships. After several relationships that have gone in the wrong direction, one with an older man & a few come & go boyfriends, Jane learns not only when to fish & when to cut bait, but who really makes the rules.

Girls' Guide to Hunting & Fishing. unabr. ed. Melissa Bank. Ed. by Melissa Bank. Read by Lorelei King. 6 CDs. (Running Time: 9 hrs.). 2000. audio compact disk 64.95 (978-0-7540-5328-6(8), CCD 019) Pub: Chivers Audio Bks GBR. Dist(s): AudioGO
Jane Rosenal sets out on a personal expedition through the perilous terrain of sex, love & relationships. After several relationships that have gone wrong, Jane learns not only when to fish & when to cut bait, but who really makes the rules.

Girls' Guide to Hunting & Fishing. unabr. ed. Melissa Bank. Read by Lorelei King. 6 CDs. (Running Time: 9 hrs.). 2002. audio compact disk 64.95 (978-0-7927-9860-6(0), SLD 111, Chivers Sound Lib) AudioGO.

Girls Have Style .... at School! A Glam Girl's Guide to Taking on the Day with Grace & Style. Read by Elaine Swann. (YA). 2006. audio compact disk 10.95 (978-0-9773520-2-9(1)) W S Pubng.

Girls Have Style... at School! A Glam Girl's Guide to Taking on the Day with Grace & Style. Read by Elaine Swann. (YA). 2006. 4.95 (978-0-9773520-1-2(3)) W S Pubng.

Girls He Adored. unabr. ed. Jonathan Nasaw. Narrated by Tom Stechschulte. 11 CDs. (Running Time: 12 hrs.). 2001. audio compact disk 111.00 (978-1-4025-1054-0(3), C1600) Recorded Bks.
When a man pulled over for a routine traffic stop commits two gruesome acts of violence, the FBI suspects he may be the psychopath who has kidnapped at least a dozen strawberry blond women across the country. Court-appointed psychiatrist Irene Cogan is fascinated by the multiple identities struggling for control of his mind, but it's only when he stages a stunning jailbreak and takes Irene hostage that she begins to understand the minefield of his mental state. Held prisoner beyond the hope of rescue, Irene finds herself at the mercy of a man who can't decide whether she's just another victim - or his one chance for salvation.

Girls He Adored. unabr. ed. Jonathan Nasaw. Narrated by Tom Stechschulte. 9 cass. (Running Time: 12 hrs.). 2001. 84.00 (978-0-7887-8863-5(9)) Recorded Bks.
Trapped in a secluded house with an escaped convict, psychologist Irene Cogan must navigate through her captor's various personalities to survive a seductive killer who sees her as both a prisoner - and his last chance at salvation.

Girls He Adored: A Novel. Jonathan Nasaw. Read by Lee Sellars. 2004. 15.95 (978-0-7435-4897-7(3)) Pub: S&S Audio. Dist(s): S and S Inc

Girls in Love. unabr. ed. Jacqueline Wilson. Read by Brigit Forsyth. 3 cass. (Running Time: 3 hrs.). (J). (gr. 1-8). 1999. 24.95 (CCA 3498, Chivers Child Audio) AudioGO.

Girls in Pants: The Third Summer of the Sisterhood. unabr. ed. Ann Brashares. Read by Angela Goethals. 6 CDs. (Running Time: 7 hrs. 17 mins.). (Sisterhood of the Traveling Pants Ser.: Bk. 3). (ENG.). (YA). (gr. 7 up). 2005. audio compact disk 19.99 (978-1-4000-9943-6(9), Listening Lib) Pub: Random Audio Pubg. Dist(s): Random

Girls in the Velvet Frame. unabr. ed. Adele Geras. 1 cass. (Running Time: 90 min.). (J). 2002. (978-0-00-714115-9(7)) Zondervan.
Five sisters in Jerusalem, 1913 try to find their lost brother in New York with the help of a photograph.

Girls in Trucks. unabr. ed. Katie Crouch. (Running Time: 7 hrs. 30 mins.). (ENG.). 2008. 24.98 (978-1-60024-273-1(1)) Pub: Hachet Audio. Dist(s): HachBkGrp

Girls Like Us: Carole King, Joni Mitchell, Carly Simon - and the Journey of a Generation. unabr. ed. Sheila Weller. Read by Susan Ericksen. (YA). 2008. 84.99 (978-1-60514-866-3(0)) Find a World.

Girls Like Us: Carole King, Joni Mitchell, Carly Simon - and the Journey of a Generation. unabr. ed. Sheila Weller. 2 MP3-CDs. (Running Time: 23 hrs. 30 mins. 0 sec.). (ENG.). 2008. audio compact disk 34.99 (978-1-4001-5649-8(1)) Pub: Tantor Media. Dist(s): IngramPubServ

Girls Like Us: Carole King, Joni Mitchell, Carly Simon - and the Journey of a Generation. unabr. ed. Sheila Weller. Read by Susan Ericksen. 19 CDs. (Running Time: 23 hrs. 30 mins. 0 sec.). (ENG.). 2008. audio compact disk 99.99 (978-1-4001-3649-0(0)); audio compact disk 49.99 (978-1-4001-0649-3(4)) Pub: Tantor Media. Dist(s): IngramPubServ

Girls Next Door. Cheri Crane. 3 cass. 2004. 14.95 (978-1-59156-073-9(X)) Covenant Comms.

***Girls of Murder City: Fame, Lust, & the Beautiful Killers Who Inspired Chicago.** unabr. ed. Douglas Perry. (Running Time: 10 hrs. 0 mins.). 2010. 34.99 (978-1-4001-9769-9(4)); 16.99 (978-1-4001-8769-0(9)) Tantor Media.

***Girls of Murder City: Fame, Lust, & the Beautiful Killers Who Inspired Chicago.** unabr. ed. Douglas Perry. Narrated by Peter Berkrot. (Running Time: 10 hrs. 30 mins. 0 sec.). 2010. 24.99 (978-1-4001-6769-2(8)); audio compact disk 83.99 (978-1-4001-4769-4(7)); audio compact disk 34.99 (978-1-4001-1769-7(0)) Pub: Tantor Media. Dist(s): IngramPubServ

Girls of Slender Means. unabr. ed. Muriel Spark. (Running Time: 4.5 hrs. NaN mins.). (J). 2008. 34.95 (978-1-4332-2013-5(X)) Blckstn Audio.

Girls of Slender Means. unabr. ed. Muriel Spark. (Running Time: 4.5 hrs. NaN mins.). 2008. 19.95 (978-1-4332-2017-3(2)); audio compact disk 40.00 (978-1-4332-2014-2(8)) Blckstn Audio.

Girls of Tender Age: A Memoir. abr. ed. Mary-Ann Tirone Smith. Read by Mary-Ann Tirone Smith. 2006. 17.95 (978-0-7435-5417-6(5)) Pub: S&S Audio. Dist(s): S and S Inc

***Girls on the Edge: The Four Factors Driving the New Crisis for Girls.** unabr. ed. Leonard Sax. (Running Time: 9 hrs. 30 mins.). 2010. 29.95 (978-1-4417-4348-0(0)); 59.95 (978-1-4417-4344-2(8)); audio compact disk 32.95 (978-1-4417-4347-3(2)); audio compact disk 90.00 (978-1-4417-4345-9(6)) Blckstn Audio.

***Girls Only! Volume 1, Books 1-4.** unabr. ed. Beverly Lewis. Narrated by Renée Raudman. (Running Time: 10 hrs. 0 mins. 0 sec.). (ENG.). 2010. audio compact disk 24.98 (978-1-59644-853-7(9), christaudio) christianaud.

***Girls Only! Volume 2, Books 5-8.** unabr. ed. Beverly Lewis. Narrated by Renée Raudman. (Running Time: 10 hrs. 0 mins. 0 sec.). (ENG.). 2010. audio compact disk 24.98 (978-1-59644-855-1(5), christaudio) christianaud.

Girl's Song see Poetry of William Butler Yeats

***Girls with Games of Blood.** unabr. ed. Alex Bledsoe. Read by Stefan Rudnicki. (Running Time: 10 hrs. 30 mins.). 2010. 29.95 (978-1-4417-3437-2(6)); 65.95 (978-1-4417-3433-4(3)); audio compact disk 100.00 (978-1-4417-3434-1(1)) Blckstn Audio.

***Girlz Want to Know: Answers to Real-Life Questions.** Susie Shellenberger. (Running Time: 2 hrs. 32 mins. 0 sec.). (ENG.). (J). 2009. 7.99 (978-0-310-77246-0(X)) Pub: Zondkidz. Dist(s): Zondervan

Gita: A Key to Mystical Consciousness. John Algeo. (Running Time: 75 min.). 1986. 8.95 (978-0-8356-2002-4(6)) Pub: Theos Pub Hse. Dist(s): Natl Bk Netwk
The Bhagavad Gita as a guide to higher consciousness.

Gitanilla. Cervantes. audio compact disk 12.95 (978-0-8219-3820-1(7)) EMC-Paradigm.

Gitanjali: A Collection of Indian Poems by the Nobel Laureate. Rabindranath Tagore. Read by Deepak Chopra. 2 cass. 16.95 set. (978-1-879323-10-0(9)) Sound Horizons AV.

Gits: SAC OST2 Soundtrack (CD #3) (YA). 2005. 14.98 (978-1-59409-417-0(9)) Bandai Ent.

Gits: SAC Soundtrack OST3 (CD#4) (YA). 2006. 14.98 (978-1-59409-719-5(4)) Bandai Ent.

Giuliani - Guitar Concerto No. 1 in A Major, Op. 30: 2-CD Set. Composed by Mauro Giuliani. 2006. pap. bk. 34.98 (978-1-59615-382-0(2), 1596153822) Pub: Music Minus. Dist(s): H Leonard

Giulio Cesare: Highlights. Perf. by Beverly Sills & Norman Treigle. Composed by George Frideric Handel. Contrib. by Karl Richter. 1 CD. 1968. audio compact disk 16.99 (VAIA 1184) VAI Audio.
Live from the Teatro Colon, Buenos Aires, features the singers at the peak of their careers.

Giuseppe Verdi. Read by Jeremy Siepmann & Freddie Jones. 4 CDs. (Running Time: 4 hrs. 50 min.). (Life & Works Ser.). 2003. pap. bk. 35.99 (978-1-84379-077-8(7)) Naxos.

Give a Boy a Gun. Todd Strasser. Narrated by Todd Strasser. 3 CDs. (Running Time: 3 hrs. 30 mins.). (gr. 9 up). audio compact disk 32.00 (978-1-4025-1966-6(4)) Recorded Bks.

Give a Boy a Gun. unabr. ed. Todd Strasser. Narrated by Todd Strasser. 3 pieces. (Running Time: 3 hrs. 30 mins.). (gr. 9 up). 2000. 28.00 (978-0-7887-9376-9(4), 96739) Recorded Bks.
A heartbreaking novel that offers no easy answers, Give a Boy a Gun addresses the growing problem of school violence. Although it is a work of fiction, it could tragically be the leading nightly news story in any community. After a high school shooting at her alma mater, a college journalism student returns home to interview students, teachers, parents, and friends of the suspects. Intermingled with her interviews are journal entries written by the two troubled boys responsible for the shooting. Their journals chronicle years of systematic abuse at the hands of their classmates and follow the boys' frustration and pain as they turn to rage.

Give a Corpse a Bad Name. unabr. ed. E. X. Ferrars. Read by Christopher Scott. 6 cass. (Running Time: 9 hrs.). (Isis Ser.). (J). 2000. 54.95 (978-0-7531-0536-8(5), 000106) Pub: ISIS Lrg Prnt GBR. Dist(s): Ulverscroft US
Toby Dyke, in conjunction with the local police, investigates the curious circumstances surrounding the death of a middle-aged stranger who is run over by a car one winter's night while lying drunk in a lane.

Give a Corpse a Bad Name. unabr. ed. Elizabeth Ferrars. Read by Christopher Scott. 6 CDs. (Running Time: 9 hrs.). (Isis Ser.). (J). 2000. audio compact disk 64.95 (978-0-7531-1281-6(7), 1281-7) Pub: ISIS Lrg Prnt GBR. Dist(s): Ulverscroft US
Ex-reporter Toby Dyke, with the local police, investigates the death of a middle-aged stranger who is run over by a car one winter's night while lying drunk in the lane. Driving the car is Anna Milne, an attractive widow from South Africa. But is it merely coincidence that the dead man also comes from South Africa & has Anna's address in his pocket?.

Give a Dog a Name. Gerald Hammond. Read by Donald Douglas. 4 cass. (Running Time: 6 hrs.). 2001. 44.95 (990510) Pub: ISIS Audio GBR. Dist(s): Ulverscroft US

Give a Dog a Name. unabr. ed. Gerald Hammond. Read by Donald Douglas. 4 cass. (Running Time: 5 hrs.). 1999. 44.95 (978-0-7531-0480-4(6), 990510) Pub: ISIS Audio GBR. Dist(s): ISIS Pub
John & Beth Cunningham own the Three Oaks Kennel in Fife, Scotland & when a rich businessman brings in his wounded springer spaniel, Horace, for treatment, it is all part of a day's work. The spaniel was shot & Cunningham begins to suspect that someone wants the dog killed. Accusations of cruelty, frame-ups & theft follow, but before Cunningham can expose the sham, he must discover the motives behind it. Someone is desperate to compromise his professional reputation.

Give A Gift Worth Giving see Da un Regalo Util

Give All to Love see Poetry of Ralph Waldo Emerson

Give & Take: The Complete Guide to Negotiating Strategies & Tactics. unabr. ed. Chester L. Karrass. Read by Thomas Andrews. 6 cass. (Running Time: 8 hrs. 30 mins.). 1989. 44.95 (978-0-7861-0041-5(9), 1040) Blckstn Audio.
Designed to help people in business & personal negotiations. This practical guide describes over 200 strategies & tactics, explains how & why they work & teaches how to defend yourself against them.

Give 'Em Hell, Harry! 1 cass. (Running Time: 1 hr.). 10.95 (F0570B090, HarperThor) HarpC GBR.

Give 'Em Hell, Harry. 1 cass. (Running Time: 1 hr.). 10.95 (OP-76-10-13, HarperThor) HarpC GBR.

Give Glory: New English Hymns from Czech Tunes (77) Anita Smisek & Joel Blahnik. Illus. by Dennis Dvorak. 1 cass. (Running Time: 2 hrs. 15 min.). (CZE & ENG.). 1991. 6.95 (978-1-878158-03-1(1), AP-119) Alliance Pubns.
Vocal book of hymnal, 2-part (77 folk hymns) (12 have a 4-pt setting); all have English text from Czech sources. 24 have Czech verses also. Detailed indexes & Czech pronunciation guide.

Give Glory, Earth & Heaven: Anthology of Czech Religious Folk Hymns (47) Ed. by Anita Smisek. Tr. by Anita Smisek. 1 cass. (Running Time: 94 min.). (CZE & ENG.). 1990. 15.00 (978-1-878158-00-0(7), AP-004) Alliance Pubns.
Recording, both vocal & instrumental, 47 selections, from the hymnal, Give Glory.

Give Him Praise. Darrell Pitts & Chosen. (Running Time: 30 min.). 2003. 11.98 (978-5-550-14856-3(0)) Pub: Pt of Grace Ent. Dist(s): STL Dist NA

Give Him Praise. Prod. by Shawn McLemore. Contrib. by Herman Burroughs & Darrell Pitts & Chosen. (Running Time: 60 min.). 2003. audio compact disk 16.98 (978-5-550-14857-0(9)) Pub: Pt of Grace Ent. Dist(s): STL Dist NA

Give It a Guess! Sundance/Newbridge, LLC Staff. (Early Math Ser.). (gr. k-1). 2000. 12.00 (978-1-58273-989-2(7)) Sund Newbrdge.

Give It a Rest! Your 20 Minute Mind/Body Stress Buster. Jean Hammer. 1. (Running Time: 22 mins, 13 Sec.). 2003. audio compact disk 17.99 (978-0-9747940-0-6(7)) Uniquely Kneaded.
Give It A Rest! Your 20 Minute Mind/Body Stress Buster was designed to relax, replenish and ignite your energy level so you can regain mental clarity in only minutes.

Give It All EP. 1 CD. 2003. audio compact disk 8.99 (978-1-893716-10-0(4)) Church Rk.

Give It Away. Contrib. by Gaither Vocal Band. (Gaither Homecoming Trax Ser.). 2006. audio compact disk 9.98 (978-5-558-11568-0(8)) Gaither Music Co.

Give It Away. Contrib. by Gaithers. (Christian World Soundtraks Ser.). 2007. audio compact disk 8.99 (978-5-557-60861-9(3)) Christian Wrld.

***Give Me a Break.** abr. ed. John Stossel. Read by John Stossel. (ENG.). 2005. (978-0-06-085605-2(X), Harper Audio); (978-0-06-085606-9(8), Harper Audio) HarperCollins Pubs.

Give Me a Break: How I Exposed Hucksters, Cheats, & Scam Artists & Became the Scourge of the Liberal Media. abr. ed. John Stossel. Read by John Stossel. 5 CDs. (Running Time: 6 Hours). 2004. audio compact disk 29.95 (978-0-06-058567-9(6)) HarperCollins Pubs.

Give Me Back My Credit. Denise Richards. Narrated by Marilyn Russel. 6 discs. (Running Time: 7:27:15). 2006. audio compact disk 24.95 (978-1-60031-011-9(7)) Spoken Books.
This is an amazing and powerful first hand accounting of credit identity theft, and is a vital tool towards understanding what we are all up against in our current age of data collection and unchecked usage. The author, Denise Richardson, paid a little extra on her mortgage each month, hoping to shorten the length of her mortgage and pay less interest charges. That simple, recommended practice catapulted her into a decade of epic David vs. Goliath battles, stealing her true credit identity and 10 years of her life. After reclaiming her good name-briefly, she realized others were shredding her credit, thus stealing another five years of her life. Denise paints a human face on the insidious effects of Identity theft, inaccurate credit reporting and loan servicing fraud while offering chapter lessons that provide knowledgeable tips to help prevent becoming a victim of a system gone terribly wrong. This book will show you the errors and dangers of certain conventional wisdoms, allowing you to steer clear of gut wrenching financial problems.

Give Me Back My Heart. Denise Robins. Read by Jacqueline King. 6 cass. (Running Time: 9 hrs.). 1999. 54.95 (67819) Pub: Soundings Ltd GBR. Dist(s): Ulverscroft US

Give Me Back My Heart. unabr. ed. Denise Robins. Read by Jacqueline King. 6 cass. 1993. 54.95 (978-1-85496-781-7(9)) Pub: UlverLrgPrint GBR. Dist(s): Ulverscroft US

Give Me Back My Legions! A Novel of Ancient Rome. unabr. ed. Harry Turtledove. Narrated by Simon Vance. 9 CDs. (Running Time: 12 hrs. 0 mins. 0 sec.). (ENG.). 2009. audio compact disk 34.99 (978-1-4001-1138-1(2)); audio compact disk 69.99 (978-1-4001-4138-8(9)); audio compact disk 24.99 (978-1-4001-6138-6(X)) Pub: Tantor Media. Dist(s): IngramPubServ

Give Me Immortality or Give Me Death. Perf. by Firesign Theatre Firesign Theatre Staff. 1 CD. (Running Time: 1 hr.). 2001. audio compact disk 15.95 Lodestone Catalog.
It's RadioNOW on New Year's Eve! Firesign's first album in seventeen years landed a Grammy nomination & is the PERFECT gift this year.

Give Me Immortality or Give Me Death. Perf. by Firesign Theatre Firesign Theatre Staff. 1 CD. (Running Time: 1 hr.). 1998. audio compact disk 16.98 (978-1-56826-978-8(1), R2 75509) Rhino Enter.

Give Me Immortality or Give Me Death. aut. ed. Perf. by Firesign Theatre Firesign Theatre Staff. 1 CD. (Running Time: 1 hr.). 2001. audio compact disk 55.00 Lodestone Catalog.
It's RadioNOW on New Year's Eve! Firesign's first new album in seventeen landed a Grammy nomination & is the Perfect holiday gift.

Give Me Jesus. 2000. 11.98 (978-0-633-02964-7(5)); 40.00 (978-0-633-00787-4(0)); audio compact disk 16.98 (978-0-633-02959-3(9)); audio compact disk 45.00 (978-0-633-00855-0(9)) LifeWay Christian.

Give Me Jesus. Contrib. by Jeremy Camp. (Praise Hymn Soundtracks Ser.). 2007. audio compact disk 8.98 (978-5-557-63292-8(1)) Pt of Grace Ent.

Give Me Jesus. Contrib. by Jeremy Camp. (Ultimate Tracks (Word Tracks) Ser.). 2007. audio compact disk 8.99 (978-5-557-78389-7(X), Word Records) Word Enter.

Give Me Liberty: A Handbook for American Revolutionaries. unabr. ed. Naomi Wolf. (Running Time: 11 hrs. 0 mins. 0 sec.). (ENG.). 2009. audio compact disk 69.99 (978-1-4001-4072-5(2)); audio compact disk 34.99 (978-1-4001-1072-8(6)); audio compact disk 24.99 (978-1-4001-6072-3(3)) Pub: Tantor Media. Dist(s): IngramPubServ

Give Me Liberty: Freeing Ourselves in th[illegible] Twenty-First Century. unabr. ed. Gerry Spence. Read by Jonathan Mar[illegible] cass. (Running Time: 13 hrs. 30 min.). 1999. 72.00 (4910) Books on [illegible]
Examining America both from a historica[illegible] well as a contemporary point of view, the author proclaims that we are no longer a democracy, but a society of "New American Slaves," shackled to the corporate behemoths that control the airwaves, our buying habits & our jobs. Yet far from being the voice of doom, the author offers many political, economic & social reforms designed to restore power to the people. Filled with controversial, even outrageous ideas.

Give Me My Money, Please! abr. ed. Glenn Shepard. Read by Mike Robbins. Ed. by Tim White. 2 cass. (Running Time: 2 hrs.). 1994. 19.95 Set. (978-1-887126-94-6(5)) Natl Bus Bur.
A comprehensive program for businesses which do their own collections in-house. Includes sample phone conversations, legalities, prevention & sample letters.

Give Me My Money, Please! unabr. ed. Glenn Shepard. Read by Mike Robbins. Ed. by Tim White. 6 cass. (Running Time: 3 hrs.). 1994. 99.95 Set. (978-1-887126-96-0(1)) Natl Bus Bur.

Give Me This Mountain, Set. Michael Ballam. 2 cass. 2004. 14.98 (978-1-55503-751-2(8), 1100564) Covenant Comms.

Give Me Tomorrow. Elizabeth Lord. 11 cass. (Running Time: 13 hrs. 50 mins.). (Isis Cassettes Ser.). 2007. 89.95 (978-0-7531-3643-0(0)) Pub: ISIS Lrg Prnt GBR. Dist(s): Ulverscroft US

***Give Me Tomorrow: The Korean War's Greatest Untold Story: the Epic Stand of the Marines of George Company.** unabr. ed. Patrick K. O'Donnell. Read by Lloyd James. (Running Time: 10 hrs. 30 mins.). 2010. audio compact disk 24.95 (978-1-4417-7275-6(8)) Blckstn Audio.

***Give Me Tomorrow: The Korean War's Greatest Untold Story¿the Epic Stand of the Marines of George Company.** unabr. ed. Patrick K. O'Donnell. (Running Time: 10 hrs. 30 mins.). 2010. 29.95 (978-1-4417-7276-3(6)) Blckstn Audio.

***Give Me Tomorrow (Library Edition) The Korean War's Greatest Untold Story: the Epic Stand of the Marines of George Company.** unabr. ed. Patrick K. O' Donnell. Read by Lloyd James. (Running Time: 10 hrs. 30 mins.). 2010. 44.95 (978-1-4417-7273-2(1)); audio compact disk 55.00 (978-1-4417-7274-9(X)) Blckstn Audio.

Give Me Your Eyes. Contrib. by Brandon Heath. (Mastertrax Ser.). 2008. audio compact disk 9.98 (978-5-557-38663-0(7)) Pt of Grace Ent.

***Give Me Your Heart: Tales of Mystery & Suspense.** Joyce Carol Oates. (Running Time: 7 hrs. 0 mins. 0 sec.). (ENG.). 2011. audio compact disk 29.95 (978-1-60998-145-7(6)) Pub: AudioGO. Dist(s): Perseus Dist

Give Me Your Heart, My Son. As told by Doug Phillips et al. 8 CDs. 2003. audio compact disk 35.00 (978-1-929241-84-2(4)) Vsn Forum.

Give Me Your Heart, My Son. Featuring Douglas W. Phillips et al. 8 cass. (Running Time: 9 hrs.). 2001. 30.00 (978-1-929241-44-6(5)) Vsn Forum.

Give My Regards. Michael Ballam. 2 CDs. audio compact disk 24.95 (3333191) Covenant Comms.
A collection of Broadway musical favorites.

Give of Encouragement: 1 Samuel 30:6. Ed Young. 1979. 4.95 (978-0-7417-1038-3(2)) Win Walk.

***Give peas a Chance.** Morris Gleitzman. Read by Morris Gleitzman. Read by Ruth Schoenheimer. (Running Time: 3 hrs. 50 mins.). (J). 2009. 39.99 (978-1-74214-388-0(1), 9781742143880) Pub: Bolinda Pubng AUS. Dist(s): Bolinda Pub Inc

Give Peas a Chance: And Other Funny Stories. unabr. ed. Morris Gleitzman. Read by Morris Gleitzman. Read by Ruther Schoenheimer. 3 CDs. (Running Time: 3 hrs. 50 mins.). (J). (gr. 4-7). 2007. audio compact disk 54.95 (978-1-921334-02-3(9), 9781921334023) Pub: Bolinda Pubng AUS. Dist(s): Bolinda Pub Inc

Give Thanks unto the Lord, Vol. 1. unabr. ed. Ralph McCoy. Read by Ralph McCoy et al. Read by Donna McCoy. 1 cass. (Running Time: 60 min.). 1994. pap. bk. 10.95; 7.95 (978-1-885819-02-4(1)) His Songs.
Scripture songs for adults.

Give Thanks unto the Lord, Vol. 2. unabr. ed. Ralph McCoy. Read by Ralph McCoy et al. Read by Donna McCoy. 1 cass. (Running Time: 60 min.). 1994. pap. bk. 10.95; 7.95 (978-1-885819-03-1(X)) His Songs.

Give the Boys a Great Big Hand. unabr. ed. Ed McBain, pseud. Read by Paul Shay. 6 cass. (Running Time: 6 hrs.). (87th Precinct Ser.: Bk. 11). 1992. 36.00 (978-0-7366-2251-6(9), 3040) Books on Tape.
Severed hands are showing up all over town. But where are the bodies? Steve Carella must first find the victims.

Give the Daughters Their Inheritance. 2001. audio compact disk (978-1-58602-095-8(1)) E L Long.

Give the Daughters Their Inheritance. 2002. 9.99 (978-1-58602-109-2(5)) E L Long.

Give up Your Likes & Dislikes: Volume 3, Vol. 3. Speeches. Bhagat Singh Thind. Clark Walker. (Running Time: 60 mins). (ENG.). 2003. audio compact disk 12.00 (978-1-932630-04-6(X)) Pub: Dr Bhagat Sin. Dist(s): Baker Taylor

Give up Your Likes & Dislikes: Volume 3, Vol. 3. Speeches. As told by Bhagatr Singh Thind. (Running Time: 60 mins.). (ENG., 2003. 6.50 (978-1-932630-27-5(9)) Pub: Dr Bhagat Sin. Dist(s): Baker Taylor

***Give Us Liberty: A Tea Party Manifesto.** unabr. ed. Dick Armey & Matt Kibbe. Read by Pete Larkin. 2010. (978-0-06-206206-2(9), Harper Audio); (978-0-06-206205-5(0), Harper Audio) HarperCollins Pubs.

***Give Us Liberty: A Tea Party Manifesto.** unabr. ed. Dick Armey & Matt Kibbe. Read by Pete Larkin. 2010. audio compact disk 34.99 (978-0-06-202713-9(1), Harper Audio) HarperCollins Pubs.

Give Us Peace. unabr. ed. Paul F. Secord. 1 cass. (Running Time: 90 mins.). 2001. audio compact disk 7.99 (978-0-88368-716-1(X)) Pub: Whitaker Hse. Dist(s): Anchor Distributors
The inspiration for this work on Tuesday, September 11, following the terrorisat attacks on the World Trade Center and the Pentagon. Overwrought with concern and confusion, Paul sat down at his piano to search for the answers to the questions everyone has been asking. Why? Howcould this be happening here? How do we heal? Give UsPeace is the beginning of the journey.

Give Us Peace: With Accompaniment Trax. Paul Secord. audio compact disk Whitaker Hse.

Give Us This Day, Pt. 1. unabr. collector's ed. R. F. Delderfield. Read by Stuart Courtney. 10 cass. (Running Time: 15 hrs.). 1988. 80.00 (978-0-7366-1266-1(1), 2178-A) Books on Tape.
Covers the historical saga of upper-class life in Victorian England; sequel to "God is an Englishman" & "Theirs Was the Kingdom".

Give Us This Day, Pt. 2. unabr. collector's ed. R. F. Delderfield. Read by Stuart Courtney. 10 cass. (Running Time: 15 hrs.). 1988. 80.00 (978-0-7366-1267-8(X), 2178B) Books on Tape.

Give You Glory. Contrib. by Jeremy Camp. (Christian World Soundtraks Ser.). 2007. audio compact disk 8.99 (978-5-557-60868-8(0)) Christian Wrld.

Give Your Child an Advantage (audio) A Witty Exposé on the Formative Years. Sharon Reed. 2008. audio compact disk 27.99 (978-1-60696-781-2(9)) Tate Pubng.

Give Your Gifts: The Basics. Gary Daigle. Contrib. by Kate Cuddy & Robert W. Piercy. 1 cass., 1 CD. 1999. 19.95 (CS-452); audio compact disk 24.95 (CD-452) GIA Pubns.

Give Your Gifts: The Songs. Gary Daigle. Contrib. by Kate Cuddy & Robert W. Piercy. 1 cass., 1 CD. 1999. 10.95 (CS-454); audio compact disk 15.95 (CD-454) GIA Pubns.

Give Yourself Away. Contrib. by Robbie Seay Band. Prod. by Tedd T & Robbie Seay. 2007. audio compact disk 13.99 (978-5-557-67269-6(9)) Pt of Grace Ent.

Given Day. unabr. ed. Dennis Lehane. Read by Michael Boatman. 20 CDs. (Running Time: 24 hrs.). 2008. audio compact disk 75.00 (978-0-06-166151-8(1), Harper Audio) HarperCollins Pubs.

***Given Day.** unabr. ed. Dennis Lehane. Read by Michael Boatman. (ENG.). 2008. (978-0-06-180280-5(8), Harper Audio); (978-0-06-180278-2(6), Harper Audio) HarperCollins Pubs.

Given NAE's Commitment to the Pro-life Position, When Is Civil Disobedience Appropriate? National Association of Evangelicals 47th Annual Convention, Columbus, Ohio March 7-9, 1989. 1 cass. (Leadership Sessions Ser.: No. 7-Tuesday). 1989. 4.25 ea. 1-8 tapes.; 4.00 ea. 9 or more tapes. Nat Assn Evan.

Giver. unabr. ed. Lois Lowry. Read by Ron Rifkin. 4 cass. (Running Time: 5 hrs.). (J). 2000. 30.00 (978-0-7366-9042-3(5)) Books on Tape.
When Jonas turns 12, he is singled out to receive special training from The Giver, who alone holds memories of pain & pleasure in life. Now there can be no turning back from the truth.

Giver. unabr. ed. Lois Lowry. Read by Ron Rifkin. 4 CDs. (Running Time: 6 hrs.). 2001. audio compact disk 33.00 Books on Tape.

Giver. unabr. ed. Lois Lowry. Read by Ron Rifkin. (J). 2006. 39.99 (978-0-7393-7479-5(6)) Find a World.

Giver. unabr. ed. Lois Lowry. Read by Ron Rifkin. 4 CDs. (Running Time: 4 hrs. 57 mins.). (ENG.). (YA). (gr. 6-8). 2001. audio compact disk 28.00 (978-0-8072-6203-0(X), Listening Lib) Pub: Random Audio Pubg. Dist(s): Random

Giver. unabr. ed. Lois Lowry. Read by Ron Rifkin. 4 vols. (Running Time: 4 hrs. 48 mins.). (J). (gr. 5 up). 2004. pap. bk. 38.00 (978-0-8072-8313-4(4), YA159SP, Listening Lib); 32.00 (978-0-8072-8312-7(6), LL0175, Listening Lib); audio compact disk 32.30 (978-0-8072-8609-8(5), S YA 159 CD, Listening Lib) Pub: Random Audio Pubg. Dist(s): NetLibrary CO
"This 1994 Newbery Medal winner tells the spellbinding story of a seemingly utopian lifestyle in a futuristic world where there are no choices. When Jonas turns 12, he is singled out to receive special training from The Giver-who alone holds memories of pain and pleasure in life. Now there can be no turning back from the truth.".

Giver. unabr. ed. Lois Lowry. Narrated by Ron Rifkin. 4 cass. (Running Time: 4 hrs.). (J). pap. bk. 35.00 (LL1033AC) Weston Woods.

Giving: How Each of Us Can Change the World. unabr. ed. Bill Clinton. Read by Bill Clinton. (YA). 2007. 49.99 (978-0-7393-7481-8(8)) Find a World.

Giving: How Each of Us Can Change the World. unabr. ed. Bill Clinton. Read by Bill Clinton. 5 CDs. (Running Time: 21600 sec.). (ENG.). 2007. audio compact disk 29.95 (978-0-7393-6806-0(0), Random AudioBks) Pub: Random Audio Pubg. Dist(s): Random

Giving: Index of Character. Elbert Willis. 1 cass. (Grace of Giving Ser.). 4.00 Fill the Gap.

Giving: Quality or Quantity. Elbert Willis. 1 cass. (Prosperity Insights Ser.). 4.00 Fill the Gap.

Giving: The Secrets of a Blessed Man. 2003. 6.00 (978-1-58602-175-7(3)); audio compact disk 10.00 (978-1-58602-176-4(1)) E L Long.

Giving a Good Speech: The Art of Conversation. unabr. ed. Read by Sharon Parish & Frank Farrelly. 1 cass. 12.95 (1568) J Norton Pubs.
Teaches you how to make a good speech & the ingredients which go into it. Learn the five keys to good conversation.

Giving a Presentation. Jude Westerfield. (B & N Basics Ser.). 2003. audio compact disk 9.98 (978-0-7607-3771-2(1), Silver Lini) M Friedman Pub Grp Inc.

Giving & Getting Crticism. Arleen LaBella. 1986. 9.75 (978-0-932491-35-0(9)) Res Appl Inc.
Learn how to handle giving & receiving criticism.

Giving & Receiving. 1 cass. (Running Time: 60 min.). 1999. 10.00 (978-1-930455-17-7(8)) E P Inc Pubng Co.
Everyone should know that giving and receiving are the same.

Giving & Receiving Love. John Gray. Read by John Gray. 2 cass. (Running Time: 2 hrs.). (Secrets of Successful Relationships Ser.). 1994. 17.95 (978-1-886095-03-8(5)) Genesis Media Grp.
A seminar series helping people understand the opposite sex.

Giving Angels Something to Work With. Nathaniel Holcomb. 2 cass. (Running Time: 3 hrs.). 1998. (978-1-930918-23-8(2)) Its All About Him.

Giving Better Presentations. Jeff Davidson. 2005. audio compact disk 12.95 (978-1-60729-126-8(6)) Breath Space Inst.

Giving Better Presentations. Jeff Davidson. 2005. 11.95 (978-1-60729-358-3(7)) Breath Space Inst.

Giving God Your Whole Heart. Kenneth Copeland. 1 CD. 2006. audio compact disk (978-1-57562-763-2(9)) K Copeland Pubns.

Giving Good Weight. unabr. ed. John McPhee. Read by Walter Zimmerman. 7 cass. (Running Time: 10 hrs. 30 min.). 1990. 56.00 Set. (978-0-7366-1792-5(2), 2629) Books on Tape.
The five pieces in this collection, written in the late '70s, are beautiful examples of McPhee at his best. The first, "Giving Good Weight," is a story of farmers selling their produce in the Greenmarkets of New York City, while "The Atlantic Generating Station" describes a plan to build floating nuclear power plants. "The Pinball Philosophy" pits two grandmasters of pinball against each other, & contrasts nicely with "The Keep of Lake Dickey," where a journey down a wild Maine river ends in the shadow of a huge projected dam. Finally, "Brigade de Cuisine" introduces an extraordinary but anonymous chef who seeks kudos for his profession rather than his personality.

Giving Guidelines. Elbert Willis. 1 cass. (Grace of Giving Ser.). 4.00 Fill the Gap.

Giving in Versus Holding Out Set: How to Break Free of Power Struggles. David Grudermeyer & Rebecca Grudermeyer. 2 cass. 18.95 (T-10) Willingness Wrks.

Giving Love Away. 211th ed. Scripts. Robert Shahidi. 1 CD. (Running Time: 50 mins.). 2002. audio compact disk 15.98 (978-1-57654-241-5(6), GLA0211, Creative Core) Creat Core.
Self Help | Inspiration | Expressing Love.

Giving Nuggets: God's Principles, Purpose, & Pathway to Prosperity. Mac Hammond. 2 CDs. (Running Time: 2 hours). 2005. audio compact disk 15.00 (978-1-57399-278-7(X)) Mac Hammond.
This two-CD volume by Mac Hammond is a compilation of more than 30 offering messages that will help reveal the pathway to becoming the cheerful giver God has called you to be.

Giving Our Hearts to God. Swami Amar Jyoti. 1 cass. 1976. 9.95 (C-39) Truth Consciousness.
Giving our total hearts to Him, we are totally reborn.

Giving Plans. Elbert Willis. 1 cass. (Grace of Giving Ser.). 4.00 Fill the Gap.

Giving Receiving & Prospering. Frank Damazio. 10 cass. (Running Time: 15 hrs.). 2000. (978-1-886849-36-5(6)) CityChristian.

Giving Sorrow Words. rev. ed. Steven Killick & Stuart Lindeman. 1999. 74.95 (978-1-873942-72-7(9)) Pub: P Chapman GBR. Dist(s): SAGE

Giving Thanks. 2004. pap. bk. 32.75 (978-1-55592-228-3(7)); pap. bk. 32.75 (978-1-55592-229-0(5)); pap. bk. 14.95 (978-1-55592-656-4(8)) Weston Woods.

Giving Thanks. Jake Swamp. Illus. by Erwin Printup, Jr. 1 cass., 5 bks. (Running Time: 8 min.). (J). pap. bk. 32.75 Weston Woods.
Known as the "Thanksgiving Address," this good morning message believes the natural world is precious. Narrated in English & Mohawk.

Giving Thanks. unabr. ed. Poems. 1 cass. (Running Time: 29 min.). 1991. 10.00 (111684) New Letters.
Various authors & readers celebrating Thanksgiving through poetry.

Giving Thanks. unabr. ed. Chief Jake Swamp. Illus. by Erwin Printup, Jr. 1 cass. (Running Time: 8 min.). (ENG & MIS.). (J). (ps-4). 1997. bk. 24.95 (978-0-7882-0670-2(2), HRA367); pap. bk. 14.95 (978-0-7882-0681-8(8), PRA367) Weston Woods.
Known as the "Thanksgiving Address," this good morning message believes the natural world is precious. Narrated in English & Mohawk.

Giving Thanks. unabr. ed. Jake Swamp. 1 cass. (Running Time: 8 min.). (ENG & MIS.). (J). (ps-4). 1997. 8.95 (978-1-56008-816-5(8), RAC367) Weston Woods.

Giving Thanks: Teachings & Meditations for Cultivating a Gratitude-Filled Heart. Iyanla Vanzant. 1 CD. (Running Time: 4500 sec.). (Inner Vision (Sounds True) Ser.). 2005. audio compact disk 15.95 (978-1-59179-249-9(5), W897D) Sounds True.

Giving Thanks to God & Guru. Swami Amar Jyoti. 1 cass. 1980. 9.95 (F-7) Truth Consciousness.
The Law of Karma & the role of the Guru.

Giving the love that Heals: A Guide for Parents. Harville Hendrix. 2004. 10.95 (978-0-7435-4784-0(5)) Pub: S&S Audio. Dist(s): S and S Inc

Giving Them a Name. Richard Grossinger. 1 cass. (AA & A Symposium Ser.). 9.00 (A0257-87) Sound Photosyn.

Giving to Yourself. Iyanla Vanzant. 1 CD. (Running Time: 1 hr. 15 mins.). 2006. audio compact disk 15.95 (978-1-59179-196-6(0), W831D) Sounds True.

Giving up Control/Purity. Marianne Williamson. Read by Marianne Williamson. 1 cass. (Running Time: 90 mins.). (Lectures on a Course in Miracles). 1999. 10.00 (978-1-56170-198-8(X), M726) Hay House.

Giving up Specialness/Releasing the Past. Marianne Williamson. Read by Marianne Williamson. 1 cass. (Running Time: 90 mins.). (Lectures on a Course in Miracles). 1999. 10.00 (978-1-56170-199-5(8), M727) Hay House.

Giving up the Mind. Swami Amar Jyoti. 1 cass. 1981. 9.95 (J-40) Truth Consciousness.
Our consciousness is trapped in the pigeonholes of mind. Myth of "peace of Mind." Deciding to let mind go & freeing the soul.

Giving Voice & Finding Form: Expressing the Symbolic. Mary Dougherty. 1 cass. (Running Time: 40 min.). (Language & Life of Symbols Ser.). 1995. 8.95 (978-0-7822-0495-7(3), 571) C G Jung IL.
Art therapist Mary Dougherty guides the listener through several journalling & art exercises designed to facilitate personal expression.

Giving Your Life to God: A Retreat. Speeches. Perf. by Catherine Doherty. Hosted by Emile Briere. 2 cass. (Running Time: 2 hrs.). 2001. 13.95 (978-0-921440-72-7(3)) Madonna Hse CAN.
Take part in an intimate conversation with Catherine Doherty-in her cabin on the Madawaska river in Combermere-where she speaks to a group of men and women preparing to commit their lives to the service of the Gospel in poverty, chastity, and obedience. Whatever your vocation, you will find encouragement and joy in listening. Divided into four sections, this makes an excellent addition to a two- or four-day spiritual retreat.

Gizmo. unabr. ed. Paul Jennings. (Running Time: 40 mins.). 2002. (978-1-74030-343-9(1)) Bolinda Pubng AUS.

Gizmo. unabr. ed. Paul Jennings. 1 CD. (Running Time: 40 mins.). (Gizmo Ser.). 2002. audio compact disk 18.00 (978-1-74030-603-4(1)) Pub: Bolinda Pubng AUS. Dist(s): Bolinda Pub Inc

Gizmo Again. unabr. ed. Paul Jennings. Read by Francis Greenslade. (Running Time: 50 mins.). (J). 2002. (978-1-74030-350-7(4)) Bolinda Pubng AUS.

Gizmo Again. unabr. ed. Paul Jennings. Read by Francis Greenslade. 1 CD. (Running Time: 50 mins.). (Gizmo Ser.). 2002. audio compact disk 18.00 (978-1-74030-750-5(X)) Pub: Bolinda Pubng AUS. Dist(s): Bolinda Pub Inc

Glace Bay Miners' Museum. abr. ed. Sheldon Currie. Narrated by Mary Colin Chisholm. 1 CD. (Running Time: 1 hr. 30 mins.). (ENG.). 2001. audio compact disk 12.95 (978-0-86492-261-8(2)) Pub: BTC Audiobks CAN. Dist(s): U Toronto Pr
The novel behind the acclaimed movie Margaret's Museum tells the heart-wrenching story of Margaret MacNeil, a miner's wife who takes her own macabre revenge on the pits. Cape Breton actress Mary Colin Chisholm starred in the stage version of this startling work of fiction.

Glace Bay Miners' Museum. abr. ed. Sheldon Currie. Read by Mary Colin Chisholm. 1 cass. (Running Time: 1 hr. 30 mins.). (ENG.). 2001. 12.95 (978-0-86492-259-5(0)) Pub: BTC Audiobks CAN. Dist(s): U Toronto Pr
Margaret MacNeil swears she won?t marry a coal miner, but she reckons without Neil Currie, a big-hearted bagpiper stalked by fate. The narrator, a native-born Cape Bretoner, tells the hilarious and tragic story of their love and Margaret?s macabre defiance when disaster strikes. The inspiration for the Helena Bonham Carter film Margaret?s Museum.

Glace Bay Miners' Museum. abr. collector's ed. Sheldon Currie. Narrated by Mary C. Chisolm. 1 cass. (Running Time: 1 hr. 30 mins.). (Between the Covers Collection). (ENG.). (gr. 3-6). 1997. 12.95 (978-0-86492-215-1(9)) Pub: BTC Audiobks CAN. Dist(s): U Toronto Pr
The novel behind the acclaimed movie Margaret's Museum tells the heart-wrenching story of Margaret MacNeil, a miner's wife who takes her own macabre revenge on the pits. Cape Breton actress Mary Colin Chisholm starred in the stage version of this startling work of fiction.

Glace Bay Miners' Museum. abr. collector's ed. Sheldon Currie. Narrated by Mary Colin Chisholm. 1 CD. (Running Time: 1 hr. 30 mins.). (Between the Covers Collection). (ENG.). (gr. 3-6). 1997. audio compact disk 12.95 (978-0-86492-213-7(2)) Pub: BTC Audiobks CAN. Dist(s): U Toronto Pr

Glacier National Park: St. Mary to West Glacier. 1 cass. (Running Time: 90 min.). (Guided Auto Tape Tour). 12.95 (P4) Comp Comms Inc.

Glacier National Park Poems. Karen Jean Matsko Hood. 2010. audio compact disk 24.95 (978-1-59210-969-2(1)) Whsprng Pine.

Glaciers. Compiled by Benchmark Education Staff. 2005. audio compact disk 10.00 (978-1-4108-5484-1(1)) Benchmark Educ.

Glaciers, Icebergs & People: Bone-Chilling Facts & Heart-Warming Stories. Short Stories. Tim Hostiuck. Read by Tim Hostiuck. 2 cass. (Running Time: 3 hrs. 8 min.). (J). 1998. 20.00 (978-1-928952-01-5(1)) Misty Peaks.
Forty adventurous stories reveal glacial secrets entwined with human history, including the iceberg's view of "Titanic," the Exxon Valdez debacle, things stuck in Greenland & Antarctic glaciers, & gold-lusting prospectors trekking across Alaskan glaciers. Sides 1,2 & 3 for age 12 & up, side 4 for ages 7-11.

Glad Acapella: Worship & Praise. Perf. by Glad. Prod. by Ed Nalle & George King. Contrib. by Bob Kauflin. 1 cass., 1 CD. 1998. 10.98; audio compact disk 16.98 CD. Provident Mus Dist.
Great worship songs in the heroic acapella style.

Glad Collector's Series. Perf. by Glad. 2 cass., 2 CD. 1998. 16.99 Boxed set.; 16.99; audio compact disk 19.99 CD.; audio compact disk 19.99 CD. Provident Mus Dist.

Glad That You Asked. Nancy Tucker. 1 cass. (Running Time: 40 min.). (J). (gr. k-7). 1988. 9.95 (978-0-939065-41-7(X), GW 1045) Gentle Wind.
Clever puns & word plays in songs for children.

Glad That You Asked. Nancy Tucker. (J). 1999. audio compact disk 14.95 (978-0-939065-77-6(0)) Gentle Wind.

Glad Tidings. Perf. by Ray Boltz. 1 cass. 1999. Provident Music.

Glad Tidings of Great Joy. Read by Bob Ravenscroft. 1 cass. 1996. 7.95 (978-1-889387-00-0(2)); audio compact disk 9.95 CD. (978-1-889387-01-7(0)) Crtve Commns MO.
Music of the Christmas season interpreted on synthesizer.

Glad to Be Who I Am. Perf. by Judith Black. 1 cass. (Running Time: 60 min.). (J). 1988. 9.95 (978-0-938756-18-7(4), 035) Yellow Moon.
Winner of the 1988 Parent's Choice Gold Award, her first tape for kids is full of stories that will be sure to tempt, entice, tease & soothe your child's fears, woes & joys as only Judith can.

Glad You Made It. Perf. by Parkway Staff. 1 CD. (Running Time: 30 mins.). 2000. audio compact disk (978-0-7601-2913-5(4)) Brentwood Music.
Songs include: "Found Me Out," "Your Love Surrounds Me," "Don't Do It," "Are You Bored?" & more.

Glade Manor Murder. Elizabeth Lemarchard. Read by Gordon Griffin. 5 cass. (Running Time: 7 hrs. 30 mins.). 1999. 49.95 (6884X) Pub: Soundings Ltd GBR. Dist(s): Ulverscroft US

***Gladiator.** Simon Scarrow. Read by Sherman Howard. (Running Time: 4 hrs.). (ENG.). 2009. audio compact disk 26.95 (978-1-4055-0757-8(8)) Pub: Little BrownUK GBR. Dist(s): IPG Chicago

Gladiators from Capua. Caroline Lawrence. Read by Michael Praed. (Running Time: 3 hrs. 0 mins. 0 sec.). (Roman Mysteries Ser.). (ENG.). (J). (gr. 7-9). 2004. audio compact disk 24.99 (978-0-7528-6693-2(1)) Pub: OrnChdrns Bks GBR. Dist(s): IPG Chicago

Gladly the Cross-Eyed Bear. unabr. ed. Ed McBain, pseud. Read by Michael Prichard. 6 cass. (Running Time: 9 hrs.). (Matthew Hope Mystery Ser.: No. 12). 1997. 48.00 (978-0-913369-38-8(1), 4214) Books on Tape.
Gladly, a cuddly cross-eyed teddy bear, is the brainchild of Lainie Cummins, beautiful & a bit cross-eyed herself. In a trademark dispute with Brett Toland, toy tycoon, Lainie calls on Matthew Hope.

Gladstone Bag. Charlotte MacLeod. 6 cass. (Running Time: 9 hrs.). 2001. 48.00 (978-0-7366-6203-1(0)) Books on Tape.
Sarah Kelling's Aunt Emma leaps at the chance to stay at her old friend Adelaide's summer place, enjoying a quiet time repairing some stage jewelry while keeping an eye on the artists & writers who'll be occupying Adelaide's six guest cottages.

Gladys Swan. unabr. ed. Read by Gladys Swan. 1 cass. (Running Time: 29 min.). Incl. Flight; 1987. 10.00 New Letters.

Glamorama see Glamorama

Glamorama. Bret Easton Ellis. 2 cass. (Running Time: 3 hrs.).Tr. of Glamorama. 2001. (978-0-333-78165-4(1)) Macmillan UK GBR.

Glamorama. unabr. ed. Bret Easton Ellis. Read by Jonathan Davis. (Running Time: 21 hrs.).Tr. of Glamorama. 2010. 29.99 (978-1-4418-0636-9(9), 9781441806369, Brilliance MP3); 44.97 (978-1-4418-0637-6(7), 9781441806376, Brlnc Audio MP3 Lib); 44.97 (978-1-4418-0638-3(5), 9781441806383, BADLE); audio compact disk 29.99 (978-1-4418-0634-5(2), 9781441806345, Bril Audio CD Unabri); audio compact disk 89.97 (978-1-4418-0635-2(0), 9781441806352, BriAudCD Unabrid) Brilliance Audio.

Glamorous Powers. unabr. ed. Susan Howatch. Read by Dermot Crowley. 16 cass. (Running Time: 24 hrs.). (Church of England Ser.: Bk. 2). 2000. 99.95 (978-0-7451-6042-9(5), CAB 644) Pub: Chivers Audio Bks GBR. Dist(s): AudioGO
Jon Darrow has been a shady faith-healer, naval chaplain, passionate husband, awkward father, tormented widower, and Anglo-Catholic monk. In 1940, he returns to the world beyond the cloister. As he continues to serve God as a priest, he flounders amidst potentially disastrous temptations.

***Glamour of Grammar Uab.** Roy Clark. 2010. audio compact disk 29.98 (978-1-59659-522-4(1)) Pub: Gildan Media. Dist(s): HachBkGrp

Glasgow Belle. unabr. ed. Margaret Thomson Davis. Narrated by Jean Simmons. 6 cass. (Running Time: 8 hrs.). 2000. 56.00 (978-1-84197-115-5(4), H1111E7) Recorded Bks.
Isla Anderson is amazed at her luck. She has always dreamed of leaving Glasgow's slums. A chance encounter with the old Earl of Kirklee, to whose long dead daughter Isla bears an uncanny resemblance, makes her fantasy reality.

Glasgow Mystery see Classic Detective Stories, Vol. I, A Collection

Glasgow Mystery. unabr. ed. Emmuska Orczy. Read by Walter Covell & Cindy Hardin. (Running Time: 52 min.). Dramatization. 1981. 7.95 (N-79) Jimcin Record.
Covers best of the famous "Old Man in the Corner" stories.

Glass. (Materials Ser.). (ENG.). 2009. audio compact disk 5.95 (978-1-4329-3249-7(7), AcornHR) Heinemann Rai.

Glass. unabr. ed. Ellen Hopkins. Read by Laura M. Flanagan. 6 CDs. (Running Time: 7 hrs. 15 mins.). (ENG., 2008. audio compact disk 26.95 (978-1-59887-762-5(3), 1598877623) Pub: HighBridge. Dist(s): Workman Pub

Glass Bead Game. unabr. ed. Hermann Hesse. Read by David Colacci. 17 CDs. (Running Time: 17 hrs.). 2009. audio compact disk 39.99 (978-0-7927-5608-8(8)) AudioGO.

Glass Bead Game. unabr. ed. Hermann Hesse. (ENG.). 2008. audio compact disk 29.95 (978-1-60283-491-0(1)) AudioGO.

Glass Blowers. unabr. ed. Daphne Du Maurier. Read by Donada Peters. 9 cass. (Running Time: 13 hrs. 30 mins.). 1985. 72.00 (978-0-7366-0937-1(7), 1880) Books on Tape.
A historical romance without the romance, the story follows the fortunes of a large family of merchant craftsmen 200 years ago in revolution-torn France.

Glass Books of the Dream Eaters. abr. ed. Gordon Dahlquist. Read by Alfred Molina. 2006. 29.95 (978-0-7435-6189-1(9)) Pub: S&S Audio. Dist(s): S and S Inc

Glass Castle: A Memoir. Jeannette Walls. Narrated by Julia Gibson. 2005. audio compact disk 34.99 (978-1-4193-3979-0(6)) Recorded Bks.

Glass Castle: A Memoir. unabr. ed. Jeannette Walls. Narrated by Julia Gibson. 10 CDs. (Running Time: 11 hrs. 15 mins.). 2005. audio compact disk 119.75 (978-1-4193-4104-5(9), 02792); 79.75 (978-1-4193-4102-1(2), 98044) Recorded Bks.
This extraordinary memoir from Jeannette Walls is a stirring and distinctive story that has won tremendous critical acclaim. In a starred review, Publishers Weekly applauds the author's "fantastic storytelling knack," saying, "Walls doesn't pull her punches... in this excellent, unusual book." With an alcoholic father and a distracted mother, the author and her siblings had to fend for themselves. This is a striking testament to the power of human determination, and will long resonate in the minds of all who read it.

***Glass Castle: A Memoir.** unabr. ed. Jeannette Walls. Read by Jeannette Walls. (Running Time: 9 hrs. 0 mins. 0 sec.). (ENG.). 2010. audio compact disk 34.99 (978-1-4423-3970-5(5)) Pub: S&S Audio. Dist(s): S and S Inc

Glass Dog & the Capture of Father Time. (J). 2005. audio compact disk (978-1-933796-40-6(5)) PC Treasures.

Glass Highway. abr. ed. Loren D. Estleman. Read by Alan Zimmerman. 4 cass. (Running Time: 360 min.). (Amos Walker Ser.). 2000. 25.00 (978-1-58807-047-0(6)) Am Pubng Inc.
Amos Walker undertakes an assignment that brings him up against Detroit drug dealers in the midst of a power struggle. Walker starts out working for a television newscaster who is in search of his son, Bud. Walker finds Paula, the South American beauty Bud is protecting, and Fern, the silver-eyed seductress and then finds Bud himself.

Glass House Sonnets. Perf. by Marcia Roberts. Created by Marcia Roberts. Prod. by Sounds in Mind Staff. (ESP.). 2002. audio compact disk 10.00 (978-0-9701556-4-1(6)) Open Field.

Glass Houses. Sandra Howard. 2007. 84.95 (978-0-7531-3752-9(6)); audio compact disk 99.95 (978-0-7531-2720-9(2)) Pub: ISIS Audio GBR. Dist(s): Ulverscroft US

Glass Houses. unabr. ed. Rachel Caine. Narrated by Cynthia Holloway. 7 CDs. (Running Time: 8 hrs. 30 mins. 0 sec.). (Morganville Vampires Ser.: Bk. 1). (ENG.). 2009. audio compact disk 59.99 (978-1-4001-4190-6(7)); audio compact disk 19.99 (978-1-4001-6190-4(8)); audio compact disk 29.99 (978-1-4001-1190-9(0)) Pub: Tantor Media. Dist(s): IngramPubServ

Glass Key. unabr. ed. Dashiell Hammett. Read by Michael Prichard. 8 cass. (Running Time: 8 hrs.). 1998. 64.00 (978-0-7366-4039-8(8), 4538) Books on Tape.
Sam Spade is hired out as a gumshoe in a plot that leads from theft to murder.

Glass Key. unabr. ed. Dashiell Hammett. Read by William Dufris. 6 cass. (Running Time: 6 hrs.). (Isis Ser.). (J). 2001. 54.95 (978-1-85695-712-0(8), 940413); audio compact disk 64.95 (978-0-7531-0901-4(8), 109018) Pub: ISIS Lrg Prnt GBR. Dist(s): Ulverscroft US
Ned Beaumont is thrust into the center of a violent & puzzling situation. He must track down a killer & in doing so he breaks up a bootlegging operation & finds himself embroiled in a bitter power struggle.

Glass Lake. unabr. ed. Maeve Binchy. Read by Kate Binchy. 16 cass. (Running Time: 24 hrs.). 2000. 99.95 (978-0-7451-6541-7(9), CAB 1157) Pub: Chivers Audio Bks GBR. Dist(s): AudioGO
Kit McMahon and her mother were living in the lakeside village of Lough when her mother disappeared. Despite her mother's absence, Kit grows up determined to make something of her life, which is what her mother would have wanted.

Glass Lake, unabr. ed. Maeve Binchy. Narrated by Barbara Caruso. 18 cass. (Running Time: 25 hrs. 30 mins.). 1995. 144.00 (978-0-7887-0269-3(6), 94478K8) Recorded Bks.
Lough Glass is the lake at the heart of the small Irish town that bears its name. Serene and dark, its waters harbor secrets as deep and unfathomable as the woman who roams the shores.

Glass Lake. unabr. ed. Maeve Binchy. Read by Barbara Caruso. 18 cass. (Running Time: 25 hrs. 30 mins.). 1995. Rental 23.50 (94478) Recorded Bks.

Glass Menagerie. abr. ed. Tennessee Williams. Read by Jessica Tandy. 3 cass. (Running Time: 4 hrs. 30 mins.). 2000. 24.00 (978-0-694-52375-7(5)) HarperCollins Pubs.

Glass Menagerie. unabr. ed. Tennessee Williams. Narrated by Montgomery Clift et al. 1 cass. 1999. 21.00 (21672) Recorded Bks.

Glass Menagerie Soundtrack. Prod. by Myattic Studio. (YA). 2000. audio compact disk 89.95 (978-0-7365-3271-6(4)) Films Media Grp.

Glass of Beer see Evening with Dylan Thomas

Glass of Time. Michael Cox. Read by Josephine Bailey. (Playaway Adult Fiction Ser.). (ENG.). 2009. 89.99 (978-1-60812-560-9(2)) Find a World.

Glass of Time. unabr. ed. Michael Cox. Narrated by Josephine Bailey. (Running Time: 18 hrs. 0 mins. 0 sec.). (ENG.). 2008. audio compact disk 99.99 (978-1-4001-3976-7(7)); audio compact disk 49.99 (978-1-4001-0976-0(0)); audio compact disk 34.99 (978-1-4001-5976-5(8)) Pub: Tantor Media. Dist(s): IngramPubServ

Glass Palace. unabr. ed. Amitav Ghosh. Read by Simon Vance. (Running Time: 20 hrs.). 2010. 29.99 (978-1-4418-3492-8(3), 9781441834928, BAD); 44.97 (978-1-4418-3491-1(5), 9781441834911, Brlnc Audio MP3 Lib); 29.99 (978-1-4418-3490-4(7), 9781441834904, Brilliance MP3); 44.97 (978-1-4418-3493-5(1), 9781441834935, BADLE); audio compact disk 34.99 (978-1-4418-3488-1(5), 9781441834881, Bril Audio CD Unabri); audio compact disk 99.97 (978-1-4418-3489-8(3), 9781441834898, BriAudCD Unabrid) Brilliance Audio.

Glass Rainbow. abr. ed. James Lee Burke. Read by Will Patton. (Running Time: 7 hrs. 0 mins. 0 sec.). (Dave Robicheaux Ser.). 2010. audio compact disk 29.99 (978-1-4423-0429-1(4)) Pub: S&S Audio. Dist(s): S and S Inc

Glass Rainbow. unabr. ed. James Lee Burke. Read by Will Patton. 14 CDs. (Running Time: 16 hrs.). (Dave Robicheaux Ser.). 2010. audio compact disk 49.99 (978-1-4423-0431-4(6)) Pub: S&S Audio. Dist(s): S and S Inc

Glass Rose. unabr. ed. MiChelle A. Butler. 4 cass. (Running Time: 6 hrs.). 2002. 20.00 (A163) Word Faith Pubng.

Glass Virgin. unabr. ed. Catherine Cookson. Read by Elizabeth Henry. 10 cass. (Running Time: 13 hrs. 30 min.). (Sound Ser.). 2004. 84.95 (978-1-85496-580-6(8), 65808) Pub: UlverLrgPrint GBR. Dist(s): Ulverscroft US
In 19th century England the starvation conditions of the village children were accepted even though the cellars of Redford Hall held food in abundance. From her happy childhood to womanhood, Annabella was to know wealth, misfortune & poverty.

Glastonbury to Wye Valley in Wales to Stratford-upon-Avon. 1 cass. (Running Time: 1 hr. 30 min.). 12.95 (978-1-55606-026-7(2), CCI-422) Comp Comms Inc.
Features a tour through the Mendip Hills describing Cheddar Gorge & the cheese that made it famous, Bath, the resting place of the Romans, & Wye Valley in Wales.

***Glee: Piano Play-along Volume 102.** Created by Hal Leonard Corp. (ENG.). 2010. pap. bk. 14.99 (978-1-4234-9632-8(9), 1423496329) H Leonard.

***Glee: Pro Vocal Male/Female Edition Volume 8.** Created by Hal Leonard Corp. (ENG.). 2010. pap. bk. 14.99 (978-1-4234-9852-0(6), 1423498526) H Leonard.

***Glee: the Beginning: An Original Novel.** unabr. ed. Sophia Lowell. Read by Emma Galvin. (Running Time: 5 hrs.). (ENG.). (YA). 2010. 13.98 (978-1-60788-979-3(X)) Pub: Hachet Audio. Dist(s): HachBkGrp

Glempses of Power: Luke 5:1-26. Ed Young. 1996. 4.95 (978-0-7417-2089-4(2), 1089) Win Walk.

Glen Miller. Conducted by Glen Miller. 1945. audio compact disk 12.95 (978-1-57970-500-8(6), Audio-For) J Norton Pubs.

Glen Miller & His Orchestra. Glenn Miller. 4 cass. 1993. 16.95 Set. (978-0-929541-62-4(6)) Radiola Co.

Glencoe: The Story of the Massacre. unabr. ed. John Prebble. Narrated by Donal Donnelly. 7 cass. (Running Time: 10 hrs. 30 mins.). 1986. 60.00 (978-1-55690-196-6(8), 86830E7) Recorded Bks.
On February 15, 1692, a band of Argyll Campbells put their MacDonald hosts to the sword. Their act of violence had deep roots & weighty consequences.

Glencoe Medical Terminology Study Tapes: Language for Health Care. Created by McGraw-Hill Staff. 2001. 41.25 (978-0-02-801291-9(7)) McGraw.

Glenda's Story. 1994. 14.99 (978-0-8474-5056-5(2)) Back to Bible.

Glengarth. Alexandra Jones. 15 cass. (Running Time: 20 hrs. 30 mins.). (Soundings Ser.). (J). 2004. 104.95 (978-1-84283-913-3(6)) Pub: ISIS Lrg Prnt GBR. Dist(s): Ulverscroft US

Glenn Luck: Logos December 28, 1997. Ben Young. 1997. 7.45 (978-0-7417-6062-3(2), B0062) Win Walk.

***Glenn McGrath: Line & Strength - the Complete Story.** unabr. ed. Glenn McGrath & Daniel Lane. Read by Shane McNamara. (Running Time: 12 hrs. 35 mins.). 2010. 43.95 (978-1-74214-529-7(9), 9781742145297) Pub: Bolinda Pubng AUS. Dist(s): Bolinda Pub Inc

Glenn Miller. unabr. ed. Perf. by Glenn Miller. 1 cass. (Running Time: 55 min.). 12.95 (#479) J Norton Pubs.
Recording of one of Glenn Miller's famous shows with the great songs from the war era: Moonlight Serenade, Holiday for Strings, Alexander's Ragtime Band, Walls of Jericho & Hot Time in the Town of Berlin.

Glenn Savan: Interview with Glenn Savan & Kay Bonetti. unabr. ed. 1 cass. 1989. 13.95 (978-1-55644-332-9(3), 9042) Am Audio Prose.

Glenrannoch. unabr. ed. Rona Randall. Read by Margaret Sircom. 6 cass. (Running Time: 8 hrs.). 1998. 69.95 (978-1-85903-228-2(1)) Pub: Magna Story GBR. Dist(s): Ulverscroft US
When fate calls Lavinia to be mistress of Glenrannoch, she learns of the legend of the "Midnight Walker" who brings death to her family.

Glimmer Palace. unabr. ed. Beatrice Colin. Read by Justine Eyre. 12 CDs. (Running Time: 14 hrs. 30 mins.). 2008. audio compact disk 100.00 (978-1-4159-5490-4(9), BksonTape) Pub: Random Audio Pubg. Dist(s): Random

Glimmerwing. unabr. ed. Ted Dickey. Read by Lynda Evans. 6 cass. (Running Time: 7 hrs. 24 min.). 2001. 39.95 (978-1-55686-776-7(X)) Books in Motion.
When a young pilot steals the chalice that protects a remote Pacific Ocean island, home to a population of fairies, a female fairie Glimmerwing is assigned the task to retrieve it.

Glimpse of Glory. Perf. by Greenes. 2003. audio compact disk Provident Mus Dist.

Glimpse of Sion's Glory. unabr. ed. Isabel Colegate. Read by Judith Whale. 4 cass. (Running Time: 5 hrs. 45 min.). (Isis Ser.). (J). 2004. 44.95 (978-1-85089-742-2(5), 9009X) Pub: ISIS Lrg Prnt GBR. Dist(s): Ulverscroft US

Glimpses. Contrib. by Anne Herring. Prod. by Buck Herring. 1996. audio compact disk 16.98 (978-7-474-00146-7(2)) Sprg Hill Music Group.

Glimpses of Bengal. l.t. ed. Rabindranath Tagore. 1985. audio compact disk 5.50 (978-0-333-90352-0(8)) Asia Bk Corp.

Glimpses of Grace: A Family Struggles with Alzheimer's. abr. ed. Rosemary J. Upton. Read by Rosemary J. Upton. 2 cass. (Running Time: 3 hrs.). 1998. 16.95 Set. (978-0-9648046-2-3(X), LH-G98) Liv Hist Pub.
"You will cry & you might laugh, but one thing is sure - God's love shines forth as a beacon".

Glimpses of Heaven: True Stories of Hope & Peace at the End of Life's Journey. Trudy Harris. (Running Time: 4 hrs. 56 mins.). 2009. audio compact disk 19.99 (978-0-8007-4455-7(1)) Pub: Revell. Dist(s): Baker Pub Grp

Glimpses of the Great. unabr. ed. A. L. Rowse. Read by Bill Kelsey. 7 cass. (Running Time: 10 hrs. 30 mins.). 1989. 56.00 (978-0-7366-1443-6(5), 2326) Books on Tape.
"Glimpses of the Great" offers not only glimpses but insights into a remarkable range of characters. Bertrand Russell, Maynard Keyes, Clement Attlee, Ernest Bevin, Evelyn Waugh, Cyril Connolly & John Betjeman were all contemporaries of Rowse, as were John Buchan ("The Thirty-Nine Steps"), Rebecca West, H.G. Wells, C.S. Lewis & Elizabeth Bowen.

***Glimpses of the Moon.** Edith Wharton. Read by Amy von Lecteur. 2010. 27.95 (978-1-60112-958-1(0)) Babblebooks.

Glimpses of the Moon, abr. ed. Edith Wharton. Read by Mari Devon. 2 cass. (Running Time: 3 hrs.). 2000. 7.95 (978-1-57815-150-9(3), 1109, Media Bks Audio) Media Bks NJ.
About the romantic misadventures of Nick Lansing & Susy Branch, a couple with the right connections but not much in the way of funds.

Glimpses of the Moon, unabr. ed. Edith Wharton. Read by Anna Fields. 7 cass. (Running Time: 10 hrs.). 1999. 49.95 (978-0-7861-1264-7(6), 2189) Blckstn Audio.
Details the romantic misadventures of Nick Lansing & Susy Branch, a couple with the right connections but not much in the way of funds. They devise a shrewd bargain: they'll marry & spend a year or so sponging off their wealthy friends, honeymooning in their mansions & villas. How their plan unfolds is a comedy of Eros that will charm all.

Glimpses of the Moon. unabr. ed. Edith Wharton. Read by Anna Fields. (Running Time: 32400 sec.). 2007. audio compact disk 29.95 (978-0-7861-5952-9(9)); audio compact disk 63.00 (978-0-7861-5951-2(0)) Blckstn Audio.

Glimpses of the Moon. unabr. ed. Edith Wharton. Read by Mari Devon. 7 cass. (Running Time: 10 hrs. 30 mins.). 1995. 56.00 (978-0-7366-2911-9(4), 3608) Books on Tape.
Set in the 1920s, this novel details the romantic misadventures of Nick & Susy, a couple with the right social connections & the wrong financial statement. A marriage of convenience, their adventure takes them far, including to the one destination they'd not banked on, falling in love with one another.

Glimpses of the Moon, Set. Edith Wharton. Read by Flo Gibson. 6 cass. (Running Time: 8 hrs.). 1999. 24.95 (978-1-55685-395-1(5)) Audio Bk Con.
In a society where extra-marital affairs hardly raise an eyebrow, a one-year marriage contract may not seem surprising. However, when they fall in love, behavior & the changing of the rules bears examination.

Glimpses of Truth: The Wycliffe Translation. unabr. ed. Jack Cavanaugh. Narrated by Virginia Leishman. 8 cass. (Running Time: 11 hrs. 30 mins.). (Book of Books Ser.). 2001. 68.00 (978-0-7887-5482-1(3), K0066E7) Recorded Bks.
Life holds great promise for 14th-century intellectual Thomas Torr, chosen by the illustrious John Wycliffe to help translate the Latin Vulgate into English. But the Roman Church punishes possession of an English Bible

with death, & Thomas soon faces a baptism of fire that takes him from the British hinterlands to the catacombs of Rome.

Glinda of Oz, Set. L. Frank Baum. Read by Flo Gibson. 3 cass. (Running Time: 3 hrs. 30 min.). (Oz Ser.). (YA). (gr. 5-8). 1997. 16.95 (978-1-55685-483-5(8)) Audio Bk Con.
Glinda the Good, Princess Ozma, the Wizard, Dorothy & many other favorite characters strive for peace between the Skeevers & the flatheads, which results in many adventures.

Glissandos, Tremolos, Trills, Grace Notes, Turns & Various Other Embellishments. Duane Shinn. 1 cass. 19.95 (NS-6) Duane Shinn.
Covers all those little moves that are not written in the music. A sprinkling of these will make your playing sound very professional.

Glister: A Novel. unabr. ed. John Burnside. (Running Time: 8 hrs. NaN mins.). 2009. 29.95 (978-1-4332-6409-2(9)); audio compact disk 24.95 (978-1-4332-6408-5(0)); audio compact disk 70.00 (978-1-4332-6406-1(4)); audio compact disk 54.95 (978-1-4332-6405-4(6)) Blckstn Audio.

Glitch in Sleep. John Hulme & Michael Wexler. Read by Oliver Wyman. (Running Time: 23040 sec.). (Seems Ser.). (ENG.). (J). (gr. 4-7). 2007. audio compact disk 54.95 (978-0-545-02753-3(5)) Scholastic Inc.

Glitch in Sleep. unabr. ed. John Hulme & Michael Wexler. Narrated by Oliver Wyman. 5 CDs. (Running Time: 6 hrs. 24 mins.). (Seems Ser.). (ENG.). (J). (gr. 4-8). 2007. audio compact disk 29.95 (978-0-545-02752-6(7)) Scholastic Inc.

***Glitter Baby.** unabr. ed. Susan Elizabeth Phillips. Read by Julia Gibson. (ENG.). 2008. (978-0-06-176938-2(X), Harper Audio); (978-0-06-176942-9(8), Harper Audio) HarperCollins Pubs.

Glitter Baby. unabr. ed. Susan Elizabeth Phillips & Susan E. Phillips. Read by Julia Gibson. 2009. audio compact disk 39.99 (978-0-06-176505-6(8), Harper Audio) HarperCollins Pubs.

Glitter Baby. unabr. collector's ed. Susan Elizabeth Phillips. Read by Anna Fields. 10 cass. (Running Time: 15 hrs.). 1996. 80.00 (978-0-7366-3446-5(0), 4090) Books on Tape.
Fluer Savager stares out from the covers of the world's most glamorous magazines. Hollywood loves her, men adore her. So why does she leave it all behind?.

Glitter Girls & the Great Fake-Out. Meg Cabot. Contrib. by Scholastic, Inc. Staff. (Running Time: 4 hrs.). (Allie Finkle's Rules for Girls Ser.). (ENG.). (J). (gr. 3-7). 2010. audio compact disk 49.95 (978-0-545-21252-6(9)) Scholastic Inc.

Glitter Girls & the Great Fake Out. Meg Cabot. Narrated by Tara Sands. (Running Time: 4 hrs.). (Allie Finkle's Rules for Girls Ser.). (ENG.). (J). (gr. 3-7). 2010. audio compact disk 19.99 (978-0-545-20961-8(7)) Scholastic Inc.

***Glitz.** unabr. ed. Elmore Leonard. 2010. (978-0-06-206257-4(3), Harper Audio); (978-0-06-206271-0(9), Harper Audio) HarperCollins Pubs.

Global Access: Complete Language Course - Advanced. 4 cass. (Running Time: 90 min. per cass.). 34.95 ea. Set. Penton Overseas.
Penton Overseas has combined its two best-selling language learning programs - "Learn in Your Car" & "VocabuLearn" - into one complete fast, effective, & truly easy-to-use foreign language course. Includes two complete text Listening Guides with helpful notes & explantions. Convenience of learning while driving in your car, walking or doing things around the home of office.

Global Access: Complete Language Course - Beginning. 4 cass. (Running Time: 90 min. per cass.). 34.95 ea. Set. Penton Overseas.

Global Access: Complete Language Course - Intermediate. 4 cass. (Running Time: 90 min. per cass.). 34.95 ea. Set. Penton Overseas.

Global Access: Export Success Program. Jimmie Yianilos. . cass. & video 895.00 Set, incl. video & computerized support services. (978-0-9621142-1-2(9)) La Jolla Bk Pub.

Global Access French Advanced, Set. Penton Overseas, Inc. Staff & Henry N. Raymond. 4 cass. (Running Time: 6 hrs.). (Global Access Ser.). (FRE.). 1994. pap. bk. 34.95 (978-1-56015-505-8(1)) Penton Overseas.
Two best-selling language learning programs, Learn in Your Car & VocabuLearn, together as one complete, fast, effective & truly easy-to-use foreign language course. Includes two complete text Listening Guides with helpful notes & explanations. Learn while driving in your car, walking, or doing things around the home or office.

Global Access French Beginning. Penton Overseas, Inc. Staff & Henry N. Raymond. 4 cass. (Running Time: 6 hrs.). (Global Access Ser.). (FRE.). 1994. pap. bk. 34.95 (978-1-56015-503-4(5)) Penton Overseas.

Global Access French Intermediate. Penton Overseas, Inc. Staff & Henry N. Raymond. 4 cass. (Running Time: 6 hrs.). (Global Access Ser.). (FRE.). 1994. pap. bk. 34.95 (978-1-56015-504-1(3)) Penton Overseas.

Global Access German Advanced, Set. Penton Overseas, Inc. Staff & Henry N. Raymond. 4 cass. (Running Time: 6 hrs.). (Global Access Ser.). (GER.). 1994. pap. bk. 34.95 (978-1-56015-508-9(6)) Penton Overseas.

Global Access German Beginning. Penton Overseas, Inc. Staff & Henry N. Raymond. 4 cass. (Running Time: 6 hrs.). (Global Access Ser.). (GER.). 1994. pap. bk. 34.95 (978-1-56015-506-5(X)) Penton Overseas.

Global Access German Intermediate. Penton Overseas, Inc. Staff & Henry N. Raymond. 4 cass. (Running Time: 6 hrs.). (Global Access Ser.). (GER.). 1994. pap. bk. 34.95 (978-1-56015-507-2(8)) Penton Overseas.

Global Access Italian Advanced. Penton Overseas, Inc. Staff & Henry N. Raymond. 4 cass. (Running Time: 6 hrs.). (Global Access Ser.). (ITA.). 1994. pap. bk. 34.95 (978-1-56015-511-9(6)) Penton Overseas.
Two language learning programs, Learn in Your Car & VocabuLearn, together as one complete, fast, effective & truly easy-to-use foreign language course. Includes two complete text Listening Guides with helpful notes & explanations. Learn while driving in your car, walking, or doing things around the home or office.

Global Access Italian Beginning. Penton Overseas, Inc. Staff & Henry N. Raymond. 4 cass. (Running Time: 6 hrs.). (Global Access Ser.). (ITA.). 1994. pap. bk. 34.95 (978-1-56015-509-6(4)) Penton Overseas.
Two best-selling language learning programs, Learn in Your Car & VocabuLearn, together as one complete, fast, effective & truly easy-to-use foreign language course. Includes two complete text Listening Guides with helpful notes & explanations. Also Free Lonely Planet Phrasebook/Dictionary. Learn while driving in your car, walking, or doing things around the home or office.

Global Access Italian Intermediate. Penton Overseas, Inc. Staff & Henry N. Raymond. 4 cass. (Running Time: 6 hrs.). (Global Access Ser.). (ITA.). 1994. pap. bk. 34.95 (978-1-56015-510-2(8)) Penton Overseas.

Global Access Japanese Advanced. Penton Overseas, Inc. Staff & Henry N. Raymond. 4 cass. (Running Time: 6 hrs.). (Global Access Ser.). (JPN.). 1994. pap. bk. 34.95 (978-1-56015-514-0(0)) Penton Overseas.
Two language learning programs, Learn in Your Car & VocabuLearn, together as one complete, fast, effective & truly easy-to-use foreign language course. Includes two complete text Listening Guides with helpful notes & explanations. Learn while driving in your car, walking, or doing things around the home or office.

Global Access Japanese Beginning. Penton Overseas, Inc. Staff & Henry N. Raymond. 4 cass. (Running Time: 6 hrs.). (Global Access Ser.). (JPN & ENG.). 1994. pap. bk. 34.95 (978-1-56015-512-6(4)) Penton Overseas.

Global Access Japanese Intermediate. Penton Overseas, Inc. Staff & Henry N. Raymond. 4 cass. (Running Time: 6 hrs.). (Global Access Ser.). (JPN.). 1994. pap. bk. 34.95 (978-1-56015-513-3(2)) Penton Overseas.

Global Access Russian Advanced. Penton Overseas, Inc. Staff & Henry N. Raymond. 4 cass. (Running Time: 6 hrs.). (Global Access Ser.). (RUS.). 1994. pap. bk. 34.95 (978-1-56015-517-1(5)) Penton Overseas.

Global Access Russian Beginning. rev. ed. Penton Overseas, Inc. Staff & Henry N. Raymond. 4 cass. (Running Time: 6 hrs.). (Global Access Ser.). (RUS & ENG.). 1994. 34.95 (978-1-56015-515-7(9)) Penton Overseas.

Global Access Russian Intermediate. Penton Overseas, Inc. Staff & Henry N. Raymond. 4 cass. (Running Time: 6 hrs.). (Global Access Ser.). (RUS.). 1994. pap. bk. 34.95 (978-1-56015-516-4(7)) Penton Overseas.

Global Access Spanish Advanced. Penton Overseas, Inc. Staff & Henry N. Raymond. 4 cass. (Running Time: 6 hrs.). (Global Access Ser.). (ENG & SPA.). 1994. pap. bk. 34.95 (978-1-56015-502-7(7)) Penton Overseas.
Two best-selling language learning programs, Learn in Your Car & VocabuLearn, together as one complete, fast, effective & truly easy-to-use foreign language course. Includes two complete text Listening Guides with helpful notes & explanations. Learn while driving in your car, walking, or doing things around the home or office.

Global Access Spanish Beginning. rev. ed. Penton Overseas, Inc. Staff & Henry N. Raymond. 4 cass. (Running Time: 6 hrs.). (Global Access Ser.). (SPA.). 1994. pap. bk. 34.95 (978-1-56015-500-3(0)) Penton Overseas.

Global Access Spanish Intermediate. Penton Overseas, Inc. Staff & Henry N. Raymond. 4 cass. (Running Time: 6 hrs.). (Global Access Ser.). (SPA.). 1994. pap. bk. 34.95 (978-1-56015-501-0(9)) Penton Overseas.

***Global Adventures for Fingerstyle Guitarists Book/Cd Set.** Steve Eckels. 2010. pap. bk. 22.99 (978-0-7866-7674-3(4)) Mel Bay.

Global Balkanization. Ayn Rand. Read by Ayn Rand. 1 cass. (Running Time: 80 min.). 12.95 (978-1-56114-077-0(5), AR17C) Second Renaissance.
A probing examination of "ethnicity" & the rise of modern tribalism in the West. Identifies "ethnicity" as an anti-concept used to disguise the word "racism." Reveals the premises of irrationalism & collectivism from which "ethnicity," as manifest in the growing number of "separatist" political movements in the West, springs.

Global Balkanization. Comment by Ayn Rand. 1 cass. (Running Time: 80 min.). (Ford Hall Forum Ser.). 1977. 12.95 (AR17C) Second Renaissance.
Examination of the rise of modern tribalism in the West. Identifies the irrationalism from which the anti-concept "ethnicity" springs. Includes Q&A.

Global Business Navigator: Doing Business in Brazil. 2000. audio compact disk 399.00 (978-0-9703429-2-8(6)) AcrossFrontiers.

Global Business Navigator: Doing Business in Germany. 2000. audio compact disk 399.00 (978-0-9703429-3-5(4)) AcrossFrontiers.

Global Business Navigator: Doing Business in Japan. 2000. audio compact disk 399.00 (978-0-9703429-0-4(X)) AcrossFrontiers.

Global Business Navigator: Doing Business in Mexico. 2000. audio compact disk 399.00 (978-0-9703429-1-1(8)) AcrossFrontiers.

Global Business Navigator: Doing Business in Singapore. 2000. audio compact disk 399.00 (978-0-9703429-4-2(2)) AcrossFrontiers.

Global Celebration. 4 cass. 1993. 29.95 Set. (978-1-55961-224-1(X)); audio compact disk 44.95 (978-1-55961-225-8(8)) Relaxtn Co.

Global Deal: Climate Change & the Creation of a New Era of Progress & Prosperity. unabr. ed. Nicholas Stern. (Running Time: 11 hrs. 0 mins.). 2009. audio compact disk 29.95 (978-1-4332-6538-9(9)) Blckstn Audio.

Global Deal: Climate Change & the Creation of a New Era of Progress & Prosperity. unabr. ed. Nicholas Stern. (Running Time: 8 hrs. 0 mins.). (ENG.). 2009. 29.95 (978-1-4332-6539-6(7)); 65.95 (978-1-4332-6535-8(4)); audio compact disk 90.00 (978-1-4332-6536-5(2)) Blckstn Audio.

Global Economy & Digital Society. Ed. by Erik Bohlin et al. Contrib. by International Telecommunications Society, Conference Staff. 2004. 173.95 (978-0-444-51335-9(3)) Pub: E G Pubng GBR. Dist(s): TurpinDistUSA

Global Jihad: Understanding September 11. Quintan Wiktorowicz. Narrated by Grover Gardner. (Running Time: 6600 sec.). (ENG.). 2008. audio compact disk 24.00 (978-1-58472-624-1(5), In Aud) Sound Room.

Global Jihad: Understanding September 11. unabr. ed. Quintan Wiktorowicz. 2 CDs. (Running Time: 3 hrs.). 2002. audio compact disk 30.00 (978-1-58472-269-4(X)) Sound Room.
Thought-provoking, challenging work will enlighten many and show that there is indeed, a light at the end of the seemingly endless tunnell constructed of terrorism, hatred, and turmoil.

Global Jihad: Understanding September 11th. Quintan Wiktorowicz. Read by Grover Gardner. (Playaway Adult Nonfiction Ser.). 2008. 44.99 (978-1-60640-835-3(6)) Find a World.

Global Links: False Beginning, Level 1. Keith Adams & Rafael Dovale. 2002. audio compact disk 24.00 (978-0-13-088385-8(9)) Pearson ESL.

Global Links: Low-Intermediate, Level 2. Angela Blackwell. 2002. audio compact disk 24.00 (978-0-13-088382-7(4)) Longman.

Global Links Level 1: False Beginning. Keith Adams & Rafael Dovale. 2002. 24.00 (978-0-13-089363-5(3)) Pearson ESL.

Global Links Level 2: Low-Intermediate. Angela Blackwell. 2002. 24.00 (978-0-13-089364-2(1)) Longman.

Global Links Level 3: Intermediate. Keith Adams & Rafael Dovale. 2002. 24.00 (978-0-13-089365-9(X)) Longman.

Global Meditation. 4 cass. 1992. 29.95 Set. (978-1-55961-170-1(7)) Relaxtn Co.

Global Monetary Policy: Implications for the U. S. Dollar & Gold. unabr. ed. Arthur Laffer. 1 cass. (Running Time: 20 min.). 12.95 (1109) J Norton Pubs.

Global Music. bk. 10.00 (978-0-687-04926-4(1)) Abingdon.

Global Perspectives & Psychedelic Poetics, Set. Terence McKenna. 2 cass. 1994. 16.95 (978-1-879323-26-1(5)) Sound Horizons AV.
Students of shamanism, psychedelics & the English Language will relate to this presentation by the author of "The Food of the Gods" & "History Ends in Green". Terence McKenna brings his considerable talents to bear on the meltdown of values of Western Civilization & the future of the human species. Provocative, stimulating & entertaining.

Global Pharmaceuticals in the 21st Century: Introductory Historical Overview of Pharmaceutical Marketing & the Drivers of the Pharmaceutical Industry Around the World. 21st ed. M. Daniel Farb. Ed. by Daniel Farb. 2004. audio compact disk 49.95 (978-1-59491-103-3(7)) Pub: UnivofHealth. Dist(s): AtlasBooks

Global Relaxation: Soothing Traditional Music. Erica K. Azim. 4 cass. (Running Time: 4 hrs.). 1996. 29.95 (978-1-55961-357-6(2)) Relaxtn Co.

Global Relaxation; Soothing Music from Around the World. Erica K. Azim. 4 CDs. (Running Time: 4 hrs.). 1996. audio compact disk 34.95 (978-1-55961-356-9(4)) Relaxtn Co.

***Global Soccer Mom: How I Learned I Could Change the World.** unabr. ed. Zondervan. (ENG.). 2011. 14.99 (978-0-310-32559-8(5)) Zondervan.

Global Solutions for Urban Drainage: Proceedings of the International Conference on Urban Drainage (9th: 2002: Portland, Oregon) Ed. by Eric W. Strecker & Wayne C. Huber. 2002. audio compact disk 198.00 (978-0-7844-0644-1(8), 40644) Am Soc Civil Eng.

Global Songs. Bread for the Journey Staff. 2004. audio compact disk 16.98 (978-0-8066-5021-0(4)) Augsburg Fortress.

Global Songs, Vol. 3. Bread for the Journey Staff. 2004. audio compact disk 16.98 (978-0-8066-5020-3(6)) Augsburg Fortress.

Global Songs 2: Bread for the Journey. 2004. audio compact disk 16.98 (978-0-8006-5673-7(3), Fortress Pr) Augsburg Fortress.
Hear the voices, the stories and the struggles of fellow Christians world-wide in the new songs that speak from a theology of justice, nonviolence, and care of creation. Performed by singers and musicians dedicated to building community through song.

Global Warning: Are We on the Brink of World War III? abr. unabr. ed. Tim LaHaye. Narrated by Edward E. Hindson. (Running Time: 21600 sec.). (ENG.). 2007. audio compact disk 25.99 (978-1-59859-286-3(6)) Oasis Audio.

Global Warning: Are We on the Brink of World War III? unabr. ed. Tim LaHaye. Narrated by Ed Hindson. (ENG.). 2007. 18.19 (978-1-60814-226-2(4)) Oasis Audio.

Globality: Competing with Everyone from Everywhere for Everything. abr. ed. Jim Hemerling et al. Read by Christian Rummel. Told to John Butman. (Running Time: 3 hrs. 15 mins.). (ENG.). 2009. audio compact disk 14.98 (978-1-60024-612-8(5)) Pub: Hachet Audio. Dist(s): HachBkGrp

Globality: Competing with Everyone from Everywhere for Everything. abr. ed. Harold L. Sirkin et al. Read by Christian Rummel. Told to John Butman. (Running Time: 5 hrs. 15 mins.). (ENG.). 2008. 22.98 (978-1-60024-177-2(8)) Pub: Hachet Audio. Dist(s): HachBkGrp

***Globalization: CD add-on Set.** Perf. by Millmark Education Staff. (ConceptLinks Ser.). 2009. audio compact disk 50.00 (978-1-61618-360-8(8)) Millmark Educ.

Globalization: N. the Irrational Fear That Someone in China Will Take Your Job. unabr. ed. Bruce C. Greenwald & Judd Kahn. Read by Michael Page. (Running Time: 5 hrs.). 2008. 39.25 (978-1-4233-6048-3(6), 9781423360483, BADLE); 39.25 (978-1-4233-6046-9(X), 9781423360469, Brinc Audio MP3 Lib); 24.95 (978-1-4233-6045-2(1), 9781423360452, Brilliance MP3); 24.95 (978-1-4233-6047-6(8), 9781423360476, BAD); audio compact disk 82.25 (978-1-4233-6044-5(3), 9781423360445, BriAudCD Unabrid); audio compact disk 29.99 (978-1-4233-6043-8(5), 9781423360438, Bril Audio CD Unabri) Brilliance Audio.

***Globalization Audio CD.** Perf. by Millmark Education Staff. (ConceptLinks Ser.). 2009. audio compact disk 28.00 (978-1-4334-0678-2(0)) Millmark Educ.

***Globalization Audio CD: A Changing World.** Perf. by Millmark Education Staff. (Content Literacy Libraries Ser.). 2009. audio compact disk (978-1-61618-131-4(1)) Millmark Educ.

***Globalization Audio CD: Challenges & Opportunities.** Perf. by Millmark Education Staff. (Content Literacy Libraries Ser.). 2009. audio compact disk (978-1-61618-139-0(7)) Millmark Educ.

***Globalization Audio CD: Cooperation & Conflict.** Perf. by Millmark Education Staff. (Content Literacy Libraries Ser.). 2009. audio compact disk (978-1-61618-143-7(5)) Millmark Educ.

***Globalization Audio CD: Our Global Connections.** Perf. by Millmark Education Staff. (Content Literacy Libraries Ser.). 2009. audio compact disk (978-1-61618-135-2(4)) Millmark Educ.

Globalullabies. Perf. by Freyda Epstein. 1 cass.; 1 CD. 1998. 9.98 (978-1-56628-062-4(1), 42571); audio compact disk 15.98 CD. (978-1-56628-061-7(3), 42571D) MFLP CA.

***Globish: How the English Language Became the World's Language.** unabr. ed. Robert McCrum. (Running Time: 10 hrs. 0 mins. 0 sec.). (ENG.). 2010. audio compact disk 83.99 (978-1-4001-4743-4(3)) Pub: Tantor Media. Dist(s): IngramPubServ

***Globish: How the English Language Became the World's Language.** unabr. ed. Robert McCrum. Narrated by James Langton. (Running Time: 10 hrs. 0 mins. 0 sec.). (ENG.). 2010. 24.99 (978-1-4001-6743-2(4)); audio compact disk 34.99 (978-1-4001-1743-7(7)) Pub: Tantor Media. Dist(s): IngramPubServ

***Globish: How the English Language Became the World¿s Language.** unabr. ed. Robert McCrum. (Running Time: 12 hrs. 0 mins.). 2010. 17.99 (978-1-4001-8743-0(5)); 34.99 (978-1-4001-9743-9(0)) Tantor Media.

***Glocalization: How Followers of Jesus Engage a Flat World.** unabr. ed. Bob Roberts Jr. (Running Time: 7 hrs. 47 mins. 0 sec.). (ENG.). 2009. 18.99 (978-0-310-77177-7(3)) Zondervan.

Gloom, Laughter, Humor. unabr. ed. Fulton J. Sheen. 7 cass. (Running Time: 30 min.). (Life Is Worth Living Ser.: 0003). 1985. 29.95 F Sheen Comm.
The late Bishop Sheen explains how the amount of humor anyone gets out of the world depends upon the size of the world in which they live.

Glor Mhaigh Eo. (ENG.). 1997. 13.95 (978-0-8023-7125-6(6)); audio compact disk 21.95 (978-0-8023-8125-5(1)) Pub: Clo Iar-Chonnachta IRL. Dist(s): Dufour

Gloria: A Christmas Festival of Praise. Contrib. by Doug Holck. (ENG.). 1988. 12.00 (978-0-00-504632-6(7)) Lillenas.

Gloria! Eb Alto Saxophone - Grade 2-3. Stephen Bulla. 2001. pap. bk. 12.95 (978-90-431-1118-8(X), 904311118X) H Leonard.

Gloria! F Horn - Grade 2-3. Stephen Bulla. 2001. pap. bk. 12.95 (978-90-431-1120-1(1), 9043111201) H Leonard.

Gloria! Trombone/Euphonium - Grade 2-3. Stephen Bulla. 2001. pap. bk. 12.95 (978-90-431-1119-5(8), 9043111198) H Leonard.

Gloria: A Christmas Celebration. Prod. by Charlie Peacock & Scott Dente. Contrib. by Don Donahue. 2005. audio compact disk 17.98 (978-5-559-46494-7(5)) Rocket.

Gloria Estefan. Michael Benson. Read by Marita DeLeon. 1 cass. (Running Time: 1 hr. 30 min.). 2000. 9.95 (978-0-7366-4705-2(8)) Books on Tape.
The year she graduated from high school, Gloria began college, met her future husband & started the journey to become the most popular Cuban-American entertainer in the world. Discover the woman behind the microphone.

Gloria Estefan. collector's unabr. ed. Michael Benson. Read by Marita DeLeon. 2 CDs. (Running Time: 2 hrs. 12 mins.). 2000. audio compact disk 12.95 (978-0-7366-5235-3(3)) Books on Tape.

Gloria Estefan. unabr. collector's ed. Michael Benson. Read by Marita DeLeon. 1 cass. (Running Time: 1 hr. 30 mins.). (Biography Ser.). (YA). (gr. 5-12). 2000. 9.95 (978-0-7366-5059-5(8), 5273) Books on Tape.

Gloria Estefan, Level 1. 2 cass. (Running Time: 1 hr. 30 mins.). (SmartReader Ser.). (J). 1999. pap. bk. & tchr. ed. 19.95 (978-0-7887-1032-2(X), 79338T3) Recorded Bks.
Once Latin music & salsa appealed to only a small audience. Now, thanks to the talents of Gloria Estefan, this music is popular across the country. Learn about this remarkable woman's journey to stardom.

Gloria Estefan, Level 2. 2 cass. (Running Time: 1 hr. 30 mins.). (SmartReader Ser.). (J). 1999. pap. bk. & tchr. ed. 19.95 (978-0-7887-1036-0(2), 79339T3) Recorded Bks.

Gloria Fuertes Os Cuenta Cuentos de Animales. (SPA.). 2003. 8.76 (978-84-305-8647-9(4), SU4861) Susaeta Ed ESP.

Gloria in Excelsis Deo. Contrib. by Tom Fettke. (ENG.). 1998. audio compact disk 90.00 (978-5-559-27364-8(3)) Lillenas.

Gloria Naylor: Interview with Kay Bonetti. Gloria Naylor. 1 cass. (Running Time: 77 min.). 1988. 13.95 (978-1-55644-305-3(6), 8082) Am Audio Prose.
In this animated discussion, National Book Award-winner Naylor talks about her struggle to complete her first novel, & to cultivate & sustain her own sense of self-approval & self-definition necessary to maintain her focus & discipline for the hard work of writing.

Gloria Naylor Reads: The Women of Brewster Place & Mama Day. Gloria Naylor. Read by Gloria Naylor. 1 cass. (Running Time: 57 min.). 1988. 13.95 (978-1-55644-304-6(8), 8081) Am Audio Prose.
Reads selections from two of her novels, taking us into their crowded & interconnected worlds, exploring the rich diversity of African-American experience.

Gloria Scott see Memoirs of Sherlock Holmes

Gloria Scott. unabr. ed. Arthur Conan Doyle. Read by Walter Covell. 1 cass. (Running Time: 82 min.). Dramatization. 1983. 7.95 (N-53) Jimcin Record.

Gloria Steinem. Interview with Gloria Steinem. 1 cass. (Running Time: 25 min.). 12.95 (L070) TFR.
The author of "Outrageous Acts & Everyday Rebellions" talks in separate interviews about the the evolution of her philosophy & in describing the sexism of food, reveals that she is a sugar junkie.

Gloria Steinem: Live from New York! 2 cass. (Running Time: 2 hrs.). 1993. 16.95 set. Sound Horizons AV.
Live talk on the subject of self-esteem.

Gloria Vando. unabr. ed. Ed. by Jim McKinley. Prod. by Rebekah Presson. 1 cass. (Running Time: 29 min.). (New Letters on the Air Ser.). 1994. 10.00 (052893) New Letters.
Vando's poems often deal with her heritage, growing up Puerto Rican in New York, the daughter of well-known night club performer. Vando, who was the publisher of the elegant literary magazine of women's writing & art, "Helicon Nine," reads from her first collection of poetry, "Promesas: Geography of the Impossible".

Gloriana. Joanna Dessau. 5 cass. (Running Time: 7 hrs.). (Soundings Ser.). (J). 2004. 49.95 (978-1-84283-748-1(6)) Pub: ISIS Lrg Prnt GBR. Dist(s): Ulverscroft US

Glorify Thy Name. Perf. by Crystal Gayle. 2006. audio compact disk 12.95 (978-1-59987-414-2(8)) Braun Media.

Glorious. Contrib. by Dave Williamson. Created by Chris Tomlin & Jesse Reeves. 2007. audio compact disk 24.98 (978-5-557-53096-5(7), Word Music) Word Enter.

Glorious Appearing: The End of Days. Tim LaHaye & Jerry B. Jenkins. Narrated by Richard Ferrone. 7 cass. (Running Time: 11 hrs. 15 mins.). (Left Behind Ser.: Bk. 12). 2004. 29.95 (978-1-4025-7042-1(2), 03914) Recorded Bks.

Glorious Appearing: The End of Days. abr. ed. Tim LaHaye & Jerry B. Jenkins. 3 CDs. (Left Behind Ser.: Bk. 12). (ENG., 2004. audio compact disk 19.99 (978-0-8423-3973-5(6)) Tyndale Hse.

Glorious Appearing: The End of Days. unabr. ed. Tim LaHaye & Jerry B. Jenkins. Narrated by Richard Ferrone. 10 CDs Lib. Ed. (Running Time: 11 hrs.). (Left Behind Ser.: Bk. 12). 2004. 109.75 (978-1-4025-7463-4(0), C2503); 79.75 (978-1-4025-7142-8(9), 01372) Recorded Bks.

Glorious Appearing: The End of Days. unabr. ed. Tim LaHaye & Jerry B. Jenkins. Narrated by Richard Ferrone. 10 CDs. (Running Time: 11 hrs. 15 mins.). (Left Behind Ser.: Bk. 12). 2004. audio compact disk 39.95 (978-1-4025-7043-8(0), 01372) Recorded Bks.
Beginning with the global smash hit title novel, the Left Behind(r) series quickly became the best-selling inspirational fiction series in the history of publishing. Now the incredible saga reaches its extraordinary conclusion. Armageddon, the cosmic battle of the ages, has concluded, and not all the members of the Tribulation Force have survived. As foretold in the Bible's Book of Revelation, it is time for the Lord God to make His Glorious Appearing in a world shattered by the apocalypse.

Glorious Cause Pt. A: A Novel of the American Revolution. unabr. ed. Jeff Shaara. 12 cass. (Running Time: 27 hrs.). 2002. 120.00 (978-0-7366-8851-2(X)) Books on Tape.
History buffs will rejoice at Jeff Shaara's latest foray into the glorious days of America's founding. This dramatic sequel to his Rise to Rebellion chronicle the key characters of the American Revolution and animates some of the most compelling scenes in America's history: Washington's harrowing winter at Valley Forge, Benedict Arnold's tragic downfall, and the fiercely-fought battles at Trenton, Brandywine Creek, and Yorktown.

Glorious Cause Pt. A: The American Revolution 1763-1789. unabr. collector's ed. Robert Middlekauff. Read by Dick Estell. 12 cass. (Running Time: 18 hrs.). 1991. 96.00 (978-0-7366-2051-2(6), 2863-A) Books on Tape.
Over 20 years in the making, The Oxford History of the United States historical writing of our generation. The series consists of nine volumes. Each recounts the story of a particular period or era. The first, The Glorious Cause, recalls the struggle for independence. It's not hard to imagine, a king who felt he could dictate to us, his local bureaucracy putting on the squeeze. It united us, & when you remember our regional differences, it was a miracle. An equal miracle is the way the author captures the times with their conflict, glory, opportunity & choices.

Glorious Cause Pt. B: A Novel of the American Revolution. unabr. ed. Jeff Shaara. Read by Grover Gardner. 20 CDs. (Running Time: 27 hrs.). 2002. audio compact disk 160.00 (978-0-7366-8852-9(8)) Books on Tape.

Glorious Cause Pt. B: The American Revolution 1763-1789. unabr. collector's ed. Robert Middlekauff. Read by Dick Estell. 9 cass. (Running Time: 13 hrs. 30 min.). 1991. 72.00 (978-0-7366-2052-9(4), 2863-B) Books on Tape.

Glorious Church Without Spot or Blemish. Joyce Meyer. 5 cass. (Running Time: 5 hrs.). 2001. 26.00 (TJM-137) Harrison Hse.
The Glory is Here (tape 1) - God's glory is all around us. A new realm of His glory is coming into the lives of believers, He wants us to have the best of everything. Don't let Satan steal the glory from you! From Glory to Glory (tape 2) - God is changing us from glory to glory, but He cannot promote us to the next level of glory until He has finished His work in us where we are. Persecution and God's Glory (tape 3) - There is a right and wrong way to handle persecution. Handled the right way, the spirit of glory rests on us. Learn to endure! The Glory of Obedience (tape 4) - We will have joy unspeakable and full of glory when we learn to obey what He tells us, when He tells us. A Glorious Church (tape 5) - The glorious church for which Jesus is returning to earth refers to what is going on inside each of us. Allow Him to do a deep work in your secret hidden places!.

Glorious Day: A Modern Day Worship Choir Collection: Bass. Contrib. by Johnathan Crumpton. Prod. by Johnathan Crumpton & Travis Cottrell. Prod. by Travis Cottrell. (ENG.). 2008. audio compact disk 5.00 (978-5-557-42358-8(3), Brentwood-Benson Music) Brentwood Music.

Glorious Day: A Modern Day Worship Choir Collection: Guitar. Contrib. by Johnathan Crumpton & Travis Cottrell. Prod. by Travis Cottrell & David Moffitt. (ENG.). 2008. audio compact disk 7.00 (978-5-557-42355-7(9), Brentwood-Benson Music) Brentwood Music.

Glorious Day: A Modern Worship Choir Collection. Contrib. by Travis Cottrell. Created by Travis Cottrell. Created by David Moffitt & Sue C. Smith. 2008. audio compact disk 10.00 (978-5-557-42394-6(X), Brentwood-Benson Music) Brentwood Music.

Glorious Day: A Modern Worship Choir Collection: Alto. Contrib. by Johnathan Crumpton. Prod. by Johnathan Crumpton & Travis Cottrell. Prod. by Travis Cottrell. (ENG.). 2008. audio compact disk 5.00 (978-5-557-42392-2(3), Brentwood-Benson Music) Brentwood Music.

Glorious Day: A Modern Worship Choir Collection: Bass Guitar. Contrib. by Johnathan Crumpton & Travis Cottrell. Prod. by Travis Cottrell & David Moffitt. (ENG.). 2008. audio compact disk 7.00 (978-5-557-42356-4(7), Brentwood-Benson Music) Brentwood Music.

Glorious Day: A Modern Worship Choir Collection: Drums. Contrib. by Johnathan Crumpton & Travis Cottrell. Prod. by Travis Cottrell & David Moffitt. (ENG.). 2008. audio compact disk 7.00 (978-5-557-42357-1(5), Brentwood-Benson Music) Brentwood Music.

Glorious Day: A Modern Worship Choir Collection: Keyboard. Contrib. by Johnathan Crumpton & Travis Cottrell. Prod. by Travis Cottrell & David Moffitt. (ENG.). 2008. audio compact disk 7.00 (978-5-557-42354-0(0), Brentwood-Benson Music) Brentwood Music.

Glorious Day: A Modern Worship Choir Collection: Soprano. Contrib. by Johnathan Crumpton. Prod. by Johnathan Crumpton & Travis Cottrell. Prod. by Travis Cottrell. (ENG.). 2008. audio compact disk 5.00 (978-5-557-42393-9(1), Brentwood-Benson Music) Brentwood Music.

Glorious Day: A Modern Worship Choir Collection: Tenor. Contrib. by Johnathan Crumpton. Prod. by Johnathan Crumpton & Travis Cottrell. Prod. by Travis Cottrell. (ENG.). 2008. audio compact disk 5.00 (978-5-557-42359-5(1), Brentwood-Benson Music) Brentwood Music.

Glorious Day: A Modern Worship Collection. Contrib. by Johnathan Crumpton & Travis Cottrell. Prod. by Travis Cottrell. Created by David Moffitt & Sue C. Smith. (ENG.). 2008. audio compact disk 90.00 (978-5-557-42395-3(8), Brentwood-Benson Music) Brentwood Music.

Glorious Discovery. Read by Mother Basilea Schlink. 1 cass. (Running Time: 30 min.). 1985. (0263) Evang Sisterhood Mary.
Topics are: Bible Verses Happen; The Daring Prayer of Faith; Prayer Moves God's Arm.

Glorious Fight. Alice Provenson & Martin Provenson. Illus. by Alice Provenson & Martin Provenson. 14 vols. (Running Time: 8 mins.). 1999. pap. bk. 39.95 (978-1-59519-038-3(4)) Live Oak Media.

Glorious Fight. Alice Provenson & Martin Provenson. Illus. by Alice Provenson & Martin Provenson. 11 vols. (Running Time: 8 mins.). (J). 1999. pap. bk. 18.95 (978-1-59519-037-6(6)) Pub: Live Oak Media. Dist(s): AudioGO

Glorious Fight. Alice Provenson & Martin Provenson. Illus. by Alice Provenson & Martin Provenson. (Running Time: 8 mins.). (J). (gr. k-3). 1999. audio compact disk 12.95 (978-1-59519-036-9(8)) Live Oak Media.

Glorious Flight. Alice Provenson & Martin Provenson. Illus. by Alice Provenson & Martin Provenson. (Running Time: 8 mins.). 1998. 9.95 (978-1-59112-044-5(6)) Live Oak Media.

Glorious Flight. unabr. ed. Alice Provensen & Martin Provensen. Read by Peter Fernandez. 1 cass., 4 bks. (Running Time: 8 min.). (J). (gr. 4-6). 1998. pap. bk. 37.95 reading chest Incl. 4 pap. bks., cass. & guide. Live Oak Media.
A dramatic retelling of the historic & heroic efforts of Louis Bleriot & the strong support of his family- in becoming the first person to fly across the English Channel.

Glorious Flight. unabr. ed. Alice Provensen & Martin Provensen. Read by Peter Fernandez. 1 cass. (Running Time: 8 mins.). (J). (gr. k-3). 1999. pap. bk. 15.95 Live Oak Media.

Glorious Flight: Across the Channel with Louis Bleriot. unabr. ed. Alice Provensen & Martin Provensen. Read by Peter Fernandez. 11 vols. (Running Time: 8 mins.). (J). (gr. 1-6). 1987. pap. bk. 16.95 (978-0-87499-061-4(0)) AudioGO.
A dramatic retelling of the historic & heroic flight across the English Channel by aviation pioneer Louis Bleriot, a flight made possible by his persistent efforts & his family's loving support.

Glorious Flight: Across the Channel with Louis Bleriot. unabr. ed. Alice Provensen & Martin Provensen. 1 cass. (Running Time: 25 mins.). (J). (gr. 4-6). 1987. bk. 22.95 (978-0-87499-062-1(9)) Live Oak Media.

Glorious Flight, Grades 1-6: Across the Channel with Louis Bleriot. Alice Provensen & Martin Provensen. Read by Peter Fernandez. 14 vols. (Running Time: 8 mins.). (J). 1987. pap. bk. & tchr. ed. 37.95 Reading Chest. (978-0-87499-063-8(7)) Live Oak Media.

Glorious Gospel Songs Cassette Promo Pak. Greg Skipper. 1997. 8.00 (978-0-7673-3029-9(3)) LifeWay Christian.

Glorious Gospel Songs Choir. Greg Skipper. 1997. 11.98 (978-0-7673-3026-8(9)) LifeWay Christian.

Glorious Gospel Songs Stereo/Split Acc. Greg Skipper. 1997. 40.00 (978-0-7673-3027-5(7)) LifeWay Christian.

Glorious Impossible. Contrib. by Gaither Vocal Band. (Daywind Soundtracks Ser.). 2006. audio compact disk 9.98 (978-5-558-11576-5(9)) Gaither Music Co.

Glorious Intruder: God's Presence in Life's Chaos. abr. ed. Joni Eareckson Tada. Read by Joni Eareckson Tada. 2 cass. (Running Time: 2 hrs.). (Selec-Sounds Ser.). 1989. 13.95 (978-0-88070-319-2(9), Mltnmah) Doubday Relig.
From the time God created the world to the time He entered it as a baby in the manger, God has shown His willingness to "intrude" into the affairs of humankind. Contrary to those who say God sits back and watches history with folded hands, the author insists He is involved with the tiniest details of our lives.

Glorious Is Thy Name. Stephen Neilson & O. V. Young. 1999. audio compact disk 16.98 (978-0-633-00293-0(3)) LifeWay Christian.

Glorious Is Thy Name. Nielson & Cynthia Y. Young. 1999. 11.98 (978-0-633-00292-3(5)) LifeWay Christian.

Glorious Mysteries / Misterios Gloriosos: The Holy Rosary Audio CD / el Santo Rosario Audio CD, Vol. 4. Kenneth L. Davison, Jr.. Kenneth L. Davison, Jr. Prod. by Brian Shields. Music by William Straub. (ENG & SPA.). (J). 2008. audio compact disk 15.00 (978-0-9801121-3-9(3)) Holy Heroes.

Glorious Mysteries of the Rosary. unabr. ed. Perf. by Benedictine Sisters of Erie Staff. 1 cass. (Running Time: 30 min.). 1998. 7.00 (978-1-890890-33-9(2)) Benetvision.
Contemporary & creative presentation of the rosary includes meditations & musical accompaniments.

Glorious Qur'an: Meaning & the Message. Compiled by Akram Zahoor. 2002. audio compact disk 69.00 (978-0-9702389-2-4(4)) ZMD.

Glorious Rider: Rev.19:11-21. Ed Young. 1987. 4.95 (978-0-7417-1581-4(3), 581) Win Walk.

Glory. Contrib. by Manafest. Prod. by Adam Messinger. 2006. audio compact disk 16.99 (978-5-558-21030-9(3)) BEC Recordings.

Glory. Contrib. by Selah & Nichole Nordeman. (Praise Hymn Soundtracks Ser.). 2007. audio compact disk 8.98 (978-5-557-92879-3(0)) Pt of Grace Ent.

Glory. Perf. by Jaci Velasquez. 1 cass. 1998. 7.98 HiLo Plus. (978-0-7601-2570-0(8)) Brentwood Music.

Glory. Perf. by Jaci Velasquez. 1 cass. 1999. (751-321-3666) Brentwood Music.

***Glory.** unabr. ed. Vladimir Nabokov. (Running Time: 7 hrs.). 2011. 39.97 (978-1-4418-7308-8(2), 9781441873088, BADLE); 24.99 (978-1-4418-7307-1(4), 9781441873071, BAD); 24.99 (978-1-4418-7305-7(8), 9781441873057, Brilliance MP3); 39.97 (978-1-4418-7306-4(6), 9781441873064, Brinc Audio MP3 Lib); audio compact disk 29.99 (978-1-4418-7303-3(1), 9781441873033, Bril Audio CD Unabri); audio compact disk 74.97 (978-1-4418-7304-0(X), 9781441873040, BriAudCD Unabrid) Brilliance Audio.

Glory, Pt. 1. unabr. ed. Herman Wouk. Read by Theodore Bikel. 9 cass. (Running Time: 13 hrs. 30 min.). 1995. 72.00 (978-0-7366-2983-6(1), 3674-A) Books on Tape.
Potent sequel to "The Hope" chronicles Israel's trials & triumphs since 1967 Six-Day War. Lively characters, brilliant portraits of world figures.

Glory, Pt. 2. unabr. ed. Herman Wouk. Read by Theodore Bikel. 8 cass. (Running Time: 12 hrs.). 1995. 64.00 (3674-B) Books on Tape.

Glory & Praise Be to the Lamb. 1985. (0288) Evang Sisterhood Mary.

Glory & Promise. unabr. ed. Kim Murphy. Read by Dianna Dorman. (Running Time: 11 hrs. 0 mins.). (ENG.). 2009. 29.95 (978-1-4332-2441-6(0)); 65.95 (978-1-4332-2437-9(2)); audio compact disk 100.00 (978-1-4332-2438-6(0)) Blckstn Audio.

Glory & the Dream. unabr. ed. William Manchester. 1 cass. (Running Time: 56 min.). 12.95 (40088) J Norton Pubs.
Heywood Hale Broun & Manchester talk about "The Glory & the Dream," a dramatic work that spans four decades & virtually every aspect of the American way of life from 1932 to 1972.

Glory & the Dream, Pt. 1. collector's ed. William Manchester. Read by Grover Gardner. 10 cass. (Running Time: 15 hrs.). 1984. 80.00 (978-0-7366-0718-6(8), 1680-A) Books on Tape.
A narrative history of America 1932-1972 is history at its most detailed & finest. It covers an incredible array of the major events, sensational happenings & news-making personalities from the Great Depression through the second inauguration of Richard M. Nixon. By no means, a stark, dry collection, Manchester breathes life into the great periods of America's growth.

Glory & the Dream, Pt. 1. unabr. ed. William Manchester. Read by Jeff Riggenbach. 13 cass. (Running Time: 60 hrs.). 1994. 85.95 (978-0-7861-0693-6(X), 1478A,B,C) Blckstn Audio.
Chronicles the progress of life in the United States from the time William Manchester & his generation reached the beginning of awareness in the desperate summer of '32 to President Nixon's Second Inaugural Address - & the opening scenes of Watergate. Masterfully compressing four crowded decades of our history, Manchester relives the epic or significant or just memorable events that befell the generation of Americans whose lives pivoted between the America before & the America after the Second World War.

Glory & the Dream, Pt. 2. collector's ed. William Manchester. Read by Grover Gardner. 11 cass. (Running Time: 16 hrs. 30 min.). 1984. 88.00 (978-0-7366-0719-3(6), 1680-B) Books on Tape.
A narrative history of America 1932-1972 is history at its most detailed & finest. It covers an incredible array of the major events, sensational happenings & news-making personalities from the Great Depression through the second inauguration of Richard M. Nixon. By no means, a stark, dry collection, Manchester breathes life into the great periods of America's growth.

Glory & the Dream, Pt. 2. unabr. ed. William Manchester. Read by Jeff Riggenbach. 13 cass. (Running Time: 60 hrs.). 1994. 85.95 (978-0-7861-0694-3(8), 1478A,B,C) Blckstn Audio.

Glory & the Dream, Pt. 3. collector's ed. William Manchester. Read by Grover Gardner. 12 cass. (Running Time: 18 hrs.). 1984. 96.00 (978-0-7366-0720-9(X), 1680-C) Books on Tape.

Glory & the Dream, Pt. 3. unabr. ed. William Manchester. Read by Jeff Riggenbach. 15 cass. (Running Time: 60 hrs.). 1994. 95.95 (978-0-7861-0695-0(6), 1478A,B,C) Blckstn Audio.

Glory & the Dream, Pt. 4. collector's ed. William Manchester. Read by Grover Gardner. 11 cass. (Running Time: 16 hrs. 30 min.). 1984. 88.00 (978-0-7366-0721-6(8), 1680-D) Books on Tape.

Glory & the Dream, Pt. 5. collector's ed. William Manchester. Read by Grover Gardner. 6 cass. (Running Time: 9 hrs.). 1984. 48.00 (978-0-7366-0722-3(6), 1680-E) Books on Tape.

Glory & the Dream: A Narrative History of America, 1932-1972. unabr. ed. William Manchester. Read by Jeff Riggenbach. (Running Time: 57 hrs. 50 mins.). 2008. 69.95 (978-1-4332-5024-8(1)) Blckstn Audio.

Glory & the Dream- Part A: A Narrative History of America, 1932-1972. unabr. ed. William Manchester. Read by Jeff Riggenbach. (Running Time: 30 hrs. 0 mins.). 2008. audio compact disk 160.00 (978-1-4332-5022-4(5)) Blckstn Audio.

Glory & the Dream- Part B: A Narrative History of America, 1932-1972. unabr. ed. William Manchester. Read by Jeff Riggenbach. (Running Time: 27 hrs. 50 mins.). 2008. audio compact disk 140.00 (978-1-4332-5023-1(3)) Blckstn Audio.

Glory & the Dream (audio CD) William Manchester. Interview with Heywood Hale Broun, Jr. (ENG.). 2007. audio compact disk 12.95 (978-1-57970-474-2(3), Audio-For) J Norton Pubs.

Glory Boys, Set. unabr. ed. Gerald Seymour. Read by Christian Rodska. 8 cass. (Running Time: 8 hrs.). 1993. bk. 69.95 (978-0-7451-6268-3(1)) AudioGO.

Glory Bugs: All Fired Up! Mike Wright & Michael McCullough. (Running Time: 1860 sec.). (J). 2007. audio compact disk 9.99 (978-1-60462-132-7(X)) Tate Pubng.

Glory Bugs: Twas Not a Silent Night. Michael McCullough & Mike Wright. Illus. by Kevin Spear. Contrib. by Nathan Ashton. (Running Time: 1620 sec.). (J). 2007. audio compact disk 9.99 (978-1-60462-131-0(1)) Tate Pubng.

Glory Cass. 2004. 10.99 (978-7-5124-0155-6(8)) Mrning Str.

Glory Day: David Haas & Friends in Concert. David Haas. 1997. 18.95 (390); audio compact disk 24.95 (390) GIA Pubns.

Glory Days Convention. 2002. (978-1-59024-038-0(3)) B Hinn Min.

Glory Defined: the Best of Building 429. Contrib. by Building 429. Prod. by Jim Cooper. 2008. audio compact disk 13.99 (978-5-557-42171-3(8), Word Records) Word Enter.

Glory Denied: The Saga of Jim Thompson, America's Longest-Held Prisoner of War. Tom Philpott. Read by Michael Prichard. 2001. 104.00 (978-0-7366-7621-2(X)) Books on Tape.

Glory Divine Name, No. 1. Swami Jyotirmayananda. Read by Swami Jyotirmayananda. 1 cass. (Running Time: 45 min.). 10.00 (807) Yoga Res Foun.

Glory Divine Name, No. 2. Swami Jyotirmayananda. 1 cass. (Running Time: 45 min.). 1990. 10.00 Yoga Res Foun.

Glory (From the Civil War) - ShowTrax. Perf. by Will Smith. Arranged by Mark Brymer. 1 CD. (Running Time: 90 mins.). 2000. audio compact disk 19.95 (08201121) H Leonard.

This cool dance number from the blockbuster movie is sure to be a hit with singers & audiences. Featured rap solo.

Glory Honor & Praise. Mark Hayes. 2001. 11.98 (978-0-633-01522-0(9)) LifeWay Christian.

Glory Honor Praise (Listening Cd0. Mark Hayes. 2001. audio compact disk 16.98 (978-0-633-01527-5(X)) LifeWay Christian.

Glory in Death. J. D. Robb, pseud. Narrated by Cristine McMurdo-Wallis. 9 CDs. (Running Time: 11 hrs.). (In Death Ser.). 2001. audio compact disk 89.00 (978-0-7887-5168-4(9), C1330) Recorded Bks.

When two beautiful highly successful women are found murdered, police lieutenant Eve Dallas has a long list of suspects. The two glamorous women rubbed elbows with a number of wealthy, powerful men, including her own lover, Roarke.

Glory in Death. abr. ed. J. D. Robb, pseud. Read by Susan Ericksen. 4 cass. (Running Time: 6 hrs.). (In Death Ser.). 2001. 53.25 (978-1-58788-197-8(7), 1587881977, Lib Edit) Brilliance Audio.

In a time when technology can reveal the darkest of secrets, there's only one place to hide a crime of passion - in the heart. . . The first victim was found lying on a sidewalk in the rain. The second was murdered in her own apartment building. Police lieutenant Eve Dallas had no problem finding connections between the two crimes. Both victims were beautiful and highly successful women. Their glamorous lives and loves were the talk of the city. And their intimate relations with men of great power and wealth provided Eve with a long list of suspects - including her own lover, Roarke. As a woman, Eve was compelled to trust the man who shared her bed. But as a cop, it was her job to follow every lead . . .to investigate every scandalous rumor . . .to explore every secret passion, no matter how dark. Or how dangerous.

Glory in Death. abr. ed. J. D. Robb, pseud. Read by Susan Ericksen. (Running Time: 6 hrs.). (In Death Ser.). 2007. audio compact disk 14.99 (978-1-4233-3658-7(5), 9781423336587, BCD Value Price) Brilliance Audio.

***Glory in Death.** abr. ed. J. D. Robb, pseud. 2010. audio compact disk 9.99 (978-1-4418-5634-0(X)) Brilliance Audio.

Glory in Death. unabr. ed. J. D. Robb, pseud. Read by Susan Ericksen. 1 MP3-CD. (Running Time: 9 hrs.). (In Death Ser.). 2004. 24.95 (978-1-59335-326-1(X), 159335326X, Brilliance MP3); 39.25 (978-1-59335-481-7(9), 1593354819, Brlnc Audio MP3 Lib); 29.95 (978-1-59355-829-1(5), 1593558295, BAU); 74.25 (978-1-59355-830-7(9), 1593558309, BrilAudUnabridg); audio compact disk 33.95 (978-1-59355-831-4(7), 1593558317, Bril Audio CD Unabri); audio compact disk 82.25 (978-1-59355-832-1(5), 1593558325, BriAudCD Unabrid) Brilliance Audio.

Glory in Death. unabr. ed. J. D. Robb, pseud. Read by Susan Ericksen. (Running Time: 9 hrs.). (In Death Ser.). 2004. 39.25 (978-1-59710-323-7(3), 1597103233, BADLE); 24.95 (978-1-59710-322-0(5), 1597103225, BAD) Brilliance Audio.

Glory in Death. unabr. ed. J. D. Robb, pseud. Narrated by Cristine McMurdo-Wallis. 8 cass. (Running Time: 11 hrs.). (In Death Ser.). 1995. 74.00 (978-0-7887-4374-0(0), 96127E7) Recorded Bks.

When two highly successful women are found murdered, Lt. Eve Dallas has a long list of suspects. The two glamorous women rubbed elbows with a number of wealthy, powerful men, including Eve's own lover.

***Glory Light of Jesus Heals Your Soul.** Katie Souza. (ENG.). 2011. audio compact disk 25.00 (978-0-7684-0267-4(0)) Pub: Expected End. Dist(s): Destiny Image Pubs

Glory of Baroque. Perf. by Terence Charlston. 1 cass. 1997. 11.95 (MoreHse Pubng); audio compact disk 16.95 CD. (MoreHse Pubng) Church Pub Inc.

Celebrated organist at Douai Abbey draws from works by Bach, Boyvin, Gigault, Frescobaldi & Muffat.

Glory of Christmas - Jesus Christ our Lord. 2005. 15.00 (978-1-933561-05-9(X)) BFM Books.

Glory of God. Kenneth E. Hagin. 1 cass. 4.95 (SH10) Faith Lib Pubns.

Glory of Good-Association, No. 3. Swami Jyotirmayananda. 1 cass. (Running Time: 1 hr.). 1990. 12.99 Yoga Res Foun.

Glory of Lord Shiva. Swami Amar Jyoti. 1 cass. 1990. 9.95 (K-120) Truth Consciousness.

Lord Shiva, destroyer & transformer, the Beautiful Auspicious One. Churning of ocean by gods & demons.

Glory of Satsanga. 1 cass. (Running Time: 1 hr.). 12.99 (105) Yoga Res Foun.

Glory of Satsanga II. (167) Yoga Res Foun.

Glory of Sexual Purity. Jack Deere. 1 cass. (Running Time: 90 mins.). (Sexual Purity & Marital Fidelity Ser.: Vol. 2). 2000. 5.00 (JD07-002) Morning NC.

Marriages are under attack, but God has ordained spiritual principles that will enable us to stand strong.

Glory of the Conquered. unabr. ed. Susan Glaspell. Narrated by Flo Gibson. 6 cass. (Running Time: 8 hrs. 52 mins.). 2003. 24.95 (978-1-55685-659-4(8)) Audio Bk Con.

A glorious story! Love, compassion and courage take the reader through adjustments to sudden blindness by a brilliant scientist, pursuing a cure for cancer while being supported by his adoring, artistic wife.

Glory of the Holy Name. Swami Amar Jyoti. 2 cass. 1987. 12.95 (H-7) Truth Consciousness.

The science of sound; going back the way we came.

Glory of Their Times: The Story of the Early Days of Baseball Told by the Men Who Played It. unabr. ed. Lawrence S. Ritter. (ENG.). 2008. audio compact disk 29.95 (978-1-59887-592-8(2), 1598875922) Pub: HighBridge. Dist(s): Workman Pub

Glory of Your Name. Contrib. by Watermark. (Mastertrax Ser.). 2004. audio compact disk 9.98 (978-5-559-51674-5(0)) Pt of Grace Ent.

Glory Songs Accompaniment. 2003. 25.00 (978-0-633-07714-3(3)) LifeWay Christian.

Glory Songs Accompaniment. 2004. 25.00 (978-0-633-08086-0(1)) LifeWay Christian.

Glory Songs Accompaniment. 2004. 25.00 (978-0-633-08338-0(0)) LifeWay Christian.

Glory Songs Accompaniment. 2004. 25.00 (978-0-633-08588-9(X)) LifeWay Christian.

Glory Songs Accompaniment. 2004. 25.00 (978-0-633-17402-6(5)) LifeWay Christian.

Glory Songs Accompaniment. 2005. 25.00 (978-0-633-17596-2(X)) LifeWay Christian.

Glory Songs Accompaniment. 2005. 25.00 (978-0-633-17794-2(6)) LifeWay Christian.

Glory Songs Ttrack Master. 1999. 25.00 (978-0-7673-3953-7(3)) LifeWay Christian.

Glory Stories Vol. 1: The Stories of Blessed Imelda Lambertini & Saint Juan Diego. Kenneth Davison, Jr. & Jim Morlino. Music by Jim Morlino. Veronica Charles & Caroline Clifford. (ENG & SPA.). 2003. audio compact disk 13.00 (978-0-9765180-3-7(1)) Cat Wrld Miss.

Glory Stories Vol. 2: The Stories of St. Therese of Lisieux & the Courageous Saints of the Knights of Columbus. Kenneth Davison, Jr. et al. Narrated by Jim Morlino. Music by Jose DeJesus. Narrated by Brian Shields. Prod. by Brian Shields. (ENG & SPA.). (J). 2004. audio compact disk 13.00 (978-0-9765180-7-5(4)) Cat Wrld Miss.

Glory Stories Vol. III: The Story of St. Joseph & the Story of St. Katherine Drexel. Shana Buck. 1. (Running Time: 60 mins.). (J). 2004. audio compact disk 13.00 (978-0-9747571-3-1(6)) Cat Wrld Miss.

Glory Stories Vol. IV: The Story of Blessed Mother Teresa & the Story of St. Faustina Kowalska. James Morlino & Kenneth Davison, Jr. 1. (Running Time: 60 mins.). (J). 2004. audio compact disk 13.00 (978-0-9747571-4-8(4)) Cat Wrld Miss.

Glory Stories Vol. V: The stories of Blessed Kateri Tekakwitha & St. Cecelia. Jim Morlino. 1. (Running Time: 27 Mins.). Dramatization. (J). 2004. audio compact disk 9.50 (978-0-9747571-5-5(2)) Cat Wrld Miss.

Glory Stories Vol. VI: The Story of Saint Joan of Arc & the Story of Saint Anthony. Shane M. Buck & Madeline Pecora Nugent. Prod. by Jim Morlino. Music by Jim Morlino. 1. (Running Time: 55 mins.). (J). 2004. audio compact disk 9.50 (978-0-9747571-6-2(0)) Cat Wrld Miss.

Glory Stories Vol. 9: The Story of Blessed Jose Sanchez. Kenneth Davison, Jr. Tr. by Ignacio Bono. Illus. by Caroline Clifford. (ENG & SPA.). (J). 2005. audio compact disk 13.00 (978-0-9765180-5-1(8)) Cat Wrld Miss.

Glory Stories Volume VII: The Story of St. Martin de Porres & the Story of St. Clare. Short Stories. Kenneth Davison, Jr. et al. Music by Jose DeJesus. Prod. by Jim Morlino & Brian Shields. 1 CD. (Running Time: 1 hr.). Dramatization. (J). 2005. audio compact disk 13.00 (978-0-9747571-9-3(5)) Cat Wrld Miss.

Glory Stories Volume VIII: The Passion for Chldren. Kara Turton. Prod. by Jim Morlino. (ENG & SPA.). (J). 2005. audio compact disk 13.00 (978-0-9765180-4-4(X)) Cat Wrld Miss.

Glory Stories Volume X: The Stories of St. Maximilian Kolbe & St. Rose of Lima. Carlos Briceno & Kenneth Davison, Jr. Narrated by Jim Morlino. Prod. by Jim Morlino. Music by Eric Genuis. (ENG & SPA.). (J). 2005. audio compact disk 13.00 (978-0-9765180-6-8(6)) Cat Wrld Miss.

Glory to Come. Lynne Hammond. 1 cass. (Running Time: 1 hr.). 2005. 5.00 (978-1-57399-251-0(8)) Mac Hammond.

Glory to God in the Highest: A Simple Christmas Musical for Kids. Created by Luke Gambill. (Running Time: 1200 sec.). (J). (gr. 4-7). 2008. audio compact disk 12.98 (978-5-557-40894-3(0), Brentwood-Benson Music) Brentwood Music.

Glory to God in the Highest: Unison. Contrib. by Johnathan Crumpton. Created by Luke Gambill. Prod. by Luke Gambill. (J). (gr. 4-7). 2008. audio compact disk 59.95 (978-5-557-40893-6(2), Brentwood-Benson Music) Brentwood Music.

Glory to God in the Highest: Unison. Created by Luke Gambill. 2008. audio compact disk 10.00 (978-5-557-40892-9(4), Brentwood-Benson Music) Brentwood Music.

Glory to the Lamb. Grace World Outreach Center. 1984. 7.00 (978-0-933643-21-5(7)) Grace Ch-St Louis.

Glossary of Sanskrit Terms & Key to Their Correct Pronunciation. Geoffrey A. Barborka. 1972. cass. & audio compact disk 7.00 (978-0-913004-89-0(8)) Point Loma Pub.

Glove Anesthesia. Bruce Goldberg. Read by Bruce Goldberg. 1 cass. (Running Time: 25 min.). (ENG.). 2007. 13.00 (978-1-885577-82-5(6)) Pub: B Goldberg. Dist(s): Baker Taylor

Through self-hypnosis learn to block pain from minor physical ailments.

Glove Anesthesia: A Step-by-Step Program for Learning to Relax Instantly. Created by David Bresler. (ENG.). 2007. audio compact disk 19.95 (978-1-887211-02-4(0), Imag Res) AlphaBks CA.

Glow of the Season. unabr. ed. Perf. by Bettine Clemen & Ray Dretske. Ed. by Charles Beres. 1 cass. (Running Time: 47 min.). 1996. 9.98 (978-1-883152-12-3(7), AD107); audio compact disk 14.98 CD. (978-1-883152-13-0(5)) Amirra Pr.

Synthesizer orchestra & flutes. Instrumental versions of Christmas carols to reflect the excitement & the stillness of the season.

Glowing Ball of Death. unabr. ed. Allan Zullo. Read by John Ratzenberger. 2008. 1.37 (978-1-4233-8083-2(5), 9781423380832, BAD) Brilliance Audio.

Glucose-6-Phosphate Dehydrogenase Deficiency - A Bibliography & Dictionary for Physicians, Patients, & Genome Researchers. Compiled by Icon Group International, Inc. Staff. 2007. ring bd. 28.95 (978-0-497-11222-6(1)) Icon Grp.

Gluskabe Stories. abr. ed. Short Stories. Joe Bruchac. 1 cass. (Running Time: 4800 sec.). (J). (gr. 3 up). 1990. 9.95 (978-0-938756-26-2(5), 006) Yellow Moon.

Collection of 10 stories from the Abenaki tribe of New England. Winner of the 1990 Choice Magazine Audio Award.

Glutaric Acidemia Type I - A Bibliography & Dictionary for Physicians, Patients, & Genome Researchers. Compiled by Icon Group International, Inc. Staff. 2007. ring bd. 28.95 (978-0-497-11223-3(X)) Icon Grp.

Glutaric Acidemia Type II - A Bibliography & Dictionary for Physicians, Patients, & Genome Researchers. Compiled by Icon Group International, Inc. Staff. 2007. ring bd. 28.95 (978-0-497-11224-0(8)) Icon Grp.

G'Morning Johann. Perf. by Ric Louchard. 1 cass. 1991. 9.98 (978-1-877737-77-0(1), MLP 2266); audio compact disk 12.98 (978-1-877737-78-7(X), MLP D2266) MFLP CA.

Classical acoustic piano recorded live in Chapel of Notre Dame. Bach, Beethoven, Mozart, Scarlatti, & S. Joplin.

GMP Training Package. Daniel Farb et al. 2004. audio compact disk 449.95 (978-1-932634-58-7(4)) Pub: UnivofHealth. Dist(s): AtlasBooks

GMWA Live: Thirty Years in the Spirit. 1 cass. 10.98 (978-1-57908-253-6(X), 1348); audio compact disk 15.98 CD. (978-1-57908-252-9(1), 1348) Platinm Enter.

GMWA Men of Promise. 1 cass. 10.98 (978-1-57908-307-6(2), 1358); audio compact disk 15.98 CD. (978-1-57908-306-9(4), 1358) Platinm Enter.

G'Night Wolfgang. Perf. by Ric Louchard. 1 cass. (Running Time: 45 min.). 1990. 9.98 (978-1-877737-64-0(X), MLP 2108); 12.98 compact disc. (978-1-877737-63-3(1), MLP D2108) MFLP CA.

Natural lullabies, eight familiar classical piano pieces written by Mozart, create serene bedtime atmosphere & nourish appreciation for the classics.

Gnosis, Set. Houston Smith. 3 cass. 1999. 26.00 (02404) Big Sur Tapes.

Gnosis Mysteries Today. Stephan Hoeller. 1 cass. 1999. 11.00 (40029) Big Sur Tapes.

1988 Los Angeles.

Gnostic Critique, Past & Present. Murray Stein. Read by Murray Stein. 1 cass. (Running Time: 70 min.). 1993. 10.95 (978-0-7822-0427-8(9), 510) C G Jung IL.

Like the Gnostics, Jung experienced a radical revision of the consciousness that had taken shape in the two millennia since the time of Jesus. Author & analyst Murray Stein discusses how modern depth psychology, based on the perception of deep structures of relatedness united everything that exists, forces us to confront our ego-determined insistence upon dominance & progress.

Gnostic Gospels. unabr. ed. Elaine Pagels. Read by Lorna Raver. 6 CDs. (Running Time: 25200 sec.). (ENG.). 2006. audio compact disk 25.00 (978-0-7393-3317-4(8), Random AudioBks) Pub: Random Audio Pubg. Dist(s): Random

Gnostic Vision in Jung's Psychology: Panel Discussion (June Singer, Robert Segal, Murray Stein, Robert Moore, & Peter Mudd) 1 cass. (Running Time: 50 min.). 1993. 9.95 (978-0-7822-0429-2(5), 512) C G Jung IL.

GO-A Command to Every Believer. Alfred D. Harvey, Jr. 8 cass. 2003. 40.00 (978-1-932508-36-9(8)) Doers Pub.

Go & Catch a Falling Star see Palgrave's Golden Treasury of English Poetry

Go Ask Alice, unabr. ed. Narrated by Christina Moore. 4 pieces. (Running Time: 5 hrs.). (gr. 8 up). 1997. 35.00 (978-0-7887-0690-5(X), 94864E7) Recorded Bks.

Based on the actual diary of a fifteen-year-old drug user, this is the heartbreaking, intimate account of one girl's journey through the world of addiction.

***Go Away, Dog.** unabr. ed. Joan L. Nodset. (ENG.). 2008. (978-0-06-169422-5(3)); (978-0-06-172143-4(3)) HarperCollins Pubs.

Go Away, I Need You: 2007 CCEF Annual Conference. Featuring Winston Smith. (ENG.). 2007. audio compact disk 11.99 (978-1-934885-11-6(8)) New Growth Pr.

Go Away, Stay Away. 2004. 8.95 (978-1-56008-908-7(3)); cass. & flmstrp 30.00 (978-0-89719-622-2(8)) Weston Woods.

Go Beyond Guilt & Regret to Realize a New You. Guy Finley. (ENG.). 2006. 7.49 (978-1-929320-58-5(2)) Life of Learn.

Go Directly to the Creation. abr. ed. Walt Whitman. Read by Lyn Dalebout. 1 cass. (Running Time: 1 hr.). Dramatization. (Poetry of Nature Ser.). 1994. 10.95 (978-0-939643-63-9(4), 3602, NrthWrd Bks) TandN Child.

Whitman's ecstatic and passionate use of language is full of joy and love for this earth.

Go down, Moses. unabr. ed. Short Stories. William Faulkner. Narrated by Mark Hammer. 10 cass. (Running Time: 13 hrs. 45 mins.). 1995. 85.00 (978-0-7887-0217-4(3), 94442E7) Recorded Bks.

A compilation of William Faulkners most famous short stories, lovingly and expertly reshaped into a novel that has become one of the most popular in the author's canon.

Go! Exercise with the Teletubbies. (J). 2002. pap. bk. 7.98 (978-0-7379-0170-2(5), 76716) Rhino Enter.

Tinky Winky, Dipsy, Laa-Laa, and Po invite your preschooler to read along and listen to the Teletubbies' first book and audiotape release. Children can play along with the Teletubbies in a series of activities such as stretching, running, jumping and hopping.

Go-Fers Christmas. Lyrics by Grace Hawthorne. Music by Larry Mayfield. 1 cass. (Running Time: 1 hr.). (J). (gr. 3-6). 1987. 12.99 (TA-9080C) Lillenas.

Children & senior adults combine to present this fun & attractive musical on "the gift of giving": God gave us His own Son & we have the chance to give of ourselves. Both the drama & the music feature children & senior adults, with new & traditional songs included. One selection has optional parts for handbell choir. Complete accompaniement tapes are provided in a split-channel format, with voices on one channel & instruments on the other for easy learning.

Go-Fers Christmas: A Musical for Kids & Senior Adults. Lyrics by Grace Hawthorne. Music by Larry Mayfield. 1 cass. (Running Time: 40 min.). (J). (gr. 3-6). 1987. 80.00 (MU-9080C) Lillenas.

Children & senior adults combine to present this fun & attractive musical on "the gift of giving": God gave us His own Son & we have teh chance to give of ourselves. Both the drama & the music feature children & senior adults, with new & traditional songs included. One selection has optonal parts for handbell choir. Complete accompaniement tapes are provided in a split-channel format, with voices on one channel & instruments on the other for easy learning.

***Go for It!, BK. 1.** 2nd ed. David Nunan. (C). 2004. 50.95 (978-1-4130-0038-2(X)) Pub: Heinle. Dist(s): CENGAGE Learn

***Go for It, Bk. 3.** 2nd ed. Nunan. (ENG.). (C). 2005. 68.95 (978-1-4130-0022-1(3)) Pub: Heinle. Dist(s): CENGAGE Learn

Go for It, Bks. 1-4. David Nunan. 8.95 (978-0-8384-6403-8(3)) Heinle.

Go for It! How to Win at Love, Work, & Play. Irene C. Kassorla. (Listen & Learn USA! Ser.). 8.95 (978-0-88684-028-0(7)) Listen USA.

Shows how to start & how to identify what it takes to put a smile on your face & go for it.

Go for It Bk. 1: Tests & Games. David Nunan. bk. (978-0-8384-0178-1(3)) Heinle.

Go for It Bk. 2: Tests & Games. David Nunan. bk. (978-0-8384-0180-4(5)) Heinle.

Go for It Bk. 3: Tests & Games. David Nunan. 2002. bk. (978-0-8384-0183-5(X)) Heinle.

This integrated, four-level program motivates young learners to communicate accurately and creatively through a step-by-step series of language-building activities.

Go for It Bk. 4: Test & Games. David Nunan. 1 cass. bk. (978-0-8384-0188-0(0)) Heinle.

***Go for It Bk 2 2e-Aud Tps.** 2nd ed. David Nunan. (ENG.). (C). 2004. 50.95 (978-1-4130-0017-7(7)) Pub: Heinle. Dist(s): CENGAGE Learn

***Go for It Book 1/2-Wall Charts.** 2nd ed. Nunan. (C). 2004. audio compact disk 189.95 (978-1-4130-0034-4(7)) Pub: Heinle. Dist(s): CENGAGE Learn

Go for the Gold. Denis E. Waitley. Intro. by A. E. Whyte. 1 cass. (Running Time: 57 min.). (Listen & Learn USA! Ser.). 8.95 (978-0-88684-054-9(6)) Listen USA.

Apply the motto of champions to win in every aspect of life.

Go for Your Goals. unabr. ed. Michael A. Podolinsky. 2 cass. (Running Time: 3 hrs.). (Smart Tapes Ser.). 1995. pap. bk. 19.99 Set, incl. pocket guide. (978-1-55678-056-1(7), 3255) Oasis Audio.

Learn to keep a winners attitude by deciding exactly what you want, keeping your motivation high & by doubling your productive time.

Go for Your Goals. unabr. ed. Michael A. Podolinsky. 2 CDs. (Smart Tapes Ser.). 2004. audio compact disk 19.99 (978-1-58926-052-8(X)) Oasis Audio.

Go Forth with Faith. 1 cass. 9.95 (10001247); audio compact disk 14.95 (2800896) Covenant Comms.

Go-Getter: A Story That Tells You How to Be One. unabr. rev. ed. Peter B. Kyne et al. Read by Arthur Morey. 2 CDs. (Running Time: 1 hr. 30 mins. 0 sec.). (ENG.). 2003. audio compact disk 20.00 (978-1-55927-840-9(4)) Pub: Macmill Audio. Dist(s): Macmillan

Go! Gilgamesh! Go!; Prometheus Rebound. 1 CD. 1998. audio compact disk 15.95 (978-1-57677-113-6(X), HEAD002) Lodestone Catalog.

Go-Giver: A Little Story about a Powerful Business Idea. unabr. ed. Bob Burg & John David Mann. (Running Time: 2 hrs. 30 mins.). (ENG.). 2008. 14.98 (978-1-59659-199-8(4), GildAudio) Pub: Gildan Media. Dist(s): HachBkGrp

Go-Giver: A Little Story about a Powerful Business Idea. unabr. ed. Bob Burg & John David Mann. Read by Bob Burg & John David Mann. 2 CDs. (Running Time: 2 hrs. 30 mins.). (ENG.). 2008. audio compact disk 19.98 (978-1-59659-200-1(1), GildAudio) Pub: Gildan Media. Dist(s): HachBkGrp

***Go-Givers Sell More: Unleashing the Power of Generosity.** unabr. ed. Bob Burg & John David Mann. (Running Time: 3 hrs. 30 mins.). (ENG.). 2010. 17.98 (978-1-59659-536-1(1), GildAudio) Pub: Gildan Media. Dist(s): HachBkGrp

Go-Givers Sell More: Unleashing the Power of Generosity. unabr. ed. Bob Burg & John David Mann. (Running Time: 4 hrs.). (ENG.). 2010. audio compact disk 19.98 (978-1-59659-449-4(7), GildAudio) Pub: Gildan Media. Dist(s): HachBkGrp

Go! Go! Go! 2001. 8.00 (978-1-931262-14-9(4)) Rose Leibund.

Go Go Jonah. Kathie Hill. 1993. 75.00 (978-0-7673-1275-2(9)) LifeWay Christian.

Go, Go Jonah. Kathie Hill. 1993. 11.98 (978-0-7673-1317-9(8)) LifeWay Christian.

Go Grab Your Shoes. 2004. audio compact disk (978-0-9755937-8-3(1)) TheraScapes.

Go Green, Live Rich: 50 Simple Ways to Save the Earth & Get Rich Trying. abr. unabr. ed. David Bach & Hillary Rosner. Read by David Bach & Oliver Wyman. (Running Time: 10800 sec.). (ENG.). 2008. audio compact disk 21.00 (978-0-7393-6852-7(4), Random AudioBks) Pub: Random Audio Pubg. Dist(s): Random

Go I Know Not Whither, Bring Back I Know Not What. Read by Lois Khan. 1 cass. (Running Time: 90 min.). (Fairytales Ser.: No. 1). 1987. 10.95 (978-0-7822-0114-7(8), 227) C G Jung IL.

Go in Peace Vol. 4: The Eucharist As Mystagogy. Text by Ed Foley. 2001. audio compact disk (978-1-58459-086-6(0)) Wrld Lib Pubns.

Go Long! unabr. ed. Jerry Rice. Read by Mirron Willis. (Running Time: 7 hrs. 37 mins.). (J). 2007. 19.95 (978-0-7861-4788-5(1)); audio compact disk 19.95 (978-0-7861-6281-9(3)) Blckstn Audio.

Go Long! unabr. ed. Jerry Rice. Read by Mirron Willis. (Running Time: 6 mins.). (YA). 2007. audio compact disk 29.95 (978-0-7861-7208-5(8)) Blckstn Audio.

Go Long! My Journey Beyond the Game & the Fame. unabr. ed. Jerry Rice. Read by Mirron Willis. Told to Brian Curtis. (Running Time: 19800 sec.). 2007. audio compact disk 45.00 (978-0-7861-6275-8(9)) Blckstn Audio.

Go Long! My Journey Beyond the Game & the Fame. unabr. ed. Jerry Rice & Brian Curtis. Read by Jerry Rice. (Running Time: 19800 sec.). 2007. 44.95 (978-0-7861-4782-3(2)) Blckstn Audio.

Go, Lovely Rose see Palgrave's Golden Treasury of English Poetry

***Go, Mutants! A Novel.** unabr. ed. Larry Doyle. (ENG.). 2011. (978-0-06-206791-3(5), Harper Audio); (978-0-06-206792-0(3), Harper Audio) HarperCollins Pubs.

Go on Vacation: The Bugville Critters. unabr. ed. Robert Stanek, pseud. Narrated by Victoria Charters. (Running Time: 14 mins.). (ENG.). (J). 2008. 4.95 (978-1-57545-325-5(8), RP Audio Pubng) Pub: Reagent Press. Dist(s): OverDrive Inc

Go Phonics Songs for Learning to Read: Songbook. Davison Sylvia. (gr. k-2). 2002. pap. bk. 10.00 (978-0-9726479-2-2(9)) Foundations Learn.

Go Put Your Strengths to Work: 6 Powerful Steps to Achieve Outstanding Performance. unabr. ed. Marcus Buckingham. Read by Marcus Buckingham. 6 CDs. (Running Time: 6 hrs. 30 mins. 0 sec.). (ENG.). 2007. audio compact disk 29.95 (978-0-7435-6669-8(6)) Pub: S&S Audio. Dist(s): S and S Inc

Go Team! Take Your Team to the Next Level 3 Steps to Great Results. unabr. ed. Ken Blanchard et al. Read by Jonathan Marosz. (Running Time: 3 hrs.). (ENG.). 2007. 14.98 (978-1-59659-178-3(1), GildAudio) Pub: Gildan Media. Dist(s): HachBkGrp

Go Team! Take Your Team to the Next Level 3 Steps to Great Results. unabr. ed. Ken Blanchard et al. Read by Jonathan Marosz. 3 CDs. (Running Time: 3 hrs.). (ENG.). 2008. audio compact disk 19.98 (978-1-59659-171-4(4), GildAudio) Pub: Gildan Media. Dist(s): HachBkGrp

Go Tell It! A Spirit Filled Christmas. Perf. by Tramaine Hawkins et al. 1 cass. audio compact disk 15.99 CD. (D2030) Diamante Music Grp.
Also includes The Voices of Binghampton.

Go Tell It on the Mountain - ShowTrax. Arranged by Roger Emerson. 1 CD. (Running Time: 5 mins.). 2000. audio compact disk 19.95 (08742345) H Leonard.
A striking contemporary arrangement of the traditional spiritual! Exciting vocal textures & interesting harmonies make this an appealing choice for developing choirs.

Go the Distance. Terry Franklin & Barbi Franklin. 2002. 9.95 (978-7-901442-45-0(X)) Pub: Tylis Music. Dist(s): STL Dist NA

Go the Distance. Terry Franklin & Barbi Franklin. (ENG.). 2007. audio compact disk 14.95 (978-7-901442-52-8(2)) Pub: Tylis Pubng. Dist(s): STL Dist NA

Go Through the Gates. Perf. by Barry Segal & Batya Segal. 2002. audio compact disk 16.98 Provident Mus Dist.

Go to School: The Bugville Critters. unabr. ed. Robert Stanek, pseud. Narrated by Victoria Charters. (Running Time: 12 mins.). (ENG.). (J). 2008. 4.95 (978-1-57545-326-2(6), RP Audio Pubng) Pub: Reagent Press. Dist(s): OverDrive Inc

Go to Sleep Little One. Silvia Silk. 1980. (978-0-938861-11-9(5)) Jasmine Texts.

Go to Sleep Quickly. 1 cass. (Sleep Programming Tapes Ser.). 12.98 (978-0-87554-550-9(5), 1123) Valley Sun.

Go to the Ant. Music by Judy Rogers. 1 cass. (Running Time: 1 hr.). (J). (gr. k-8). 2002. 8.50 (JR00001) Christian Liberty.
These 10 songs capture the great wisdom of God from Proverbs.This collection covers teachings on responsibility, laziness, the use of the tongue, one's attitude toward learning, lying and more.

Go to the Ant. Judy Rogers. 1 CD. (Running Time: 1 hr.). 2001. audio compact disk (978-5-550-02908-4(1)) Nairi ARM.

Go to the Shrine That's on a Tree see Richard Eberhart Reading His Poetry

Go West Young Man. Perf. by Michael W. Smith. 1 cass. 1990. audio compact disk Brentwood Music.
The near platinum selling release features the top 5 mainstream radio hit, Place in This World.

Go Wild! Survival Skills for Business & Life. PUEI. 2006. audio compact disk 89.95 (978-1-933328-53-9(3), CareerTrack) P Univ E Inc.

Go with the Flow: Acts 2:1-21. Ed Young. 1982. 4.95 (978-0-7417-1225-7(3), 225) Win Walk.

Go Within Feel the Love. unabr. ed. Poems. Carolyn Ann O'Riley. 1 cass. (Running Time: 45 mins.). 2000. 10.00 (978-1-891870-13-2(0)) Archangels Pen.
Archangel Michael divinely inspired poetry, uplifting & self empowering. It leads to discovery of one's angels & their own path.

Goal. unabr. ed. Eliyahu M. Goldratt. 8 cass. (Running Time: 10 hrs.). 2000. 24.95; audio compact disk 29.95 HighBridge.

Goal, Vol. 1. Dos Santos. 1996. 25.00 (978-0-07-018156-4(X)) Pub: McGrw-H Hghr Educ. Dist(s): McGraw

Goal, Vol. 2. Dos Santos. 1996. 25.00 (978-0-07-018160-1(8)) Pub: McGrw-H Hghr Educ. Dist(s): McGraw

Goal, Vol. 3. 1996. 25.00 (978-0-07-018164-9(0)) Pub: McGrw-H Hghr Educ. Dist(s): McGraw

Goal, Vol. 4. 1996. 25.00 (978-0-07-018168-7(3)) Pub: McGrw-H Hghr Educ. Dist(s): McGraw

Goal: A Process of Ongoing Improvement. 3rd ed. Eliyahu M. Goldratt & Jeff Cox. Narrated by Ensemble Cast & Eric Conger. (Playaway Adult Nonfiction Ser.). 2008. 54.99 (978-1-60640-511-6(X)) Find a World.

Goal: A Process of Ongoing Improvement. 3rd unabr. rev. ed. Eliyahu M. Goldratt. Read by Ensemble Cast Staff. Told to Jeff Cox. (Running Time: 43200 sec.). 2006. audio compact disk 39.95 (978-1-59887-064-0(5), 1598870645) Pub: HighBridge. Dist(s): Workman Pub

Goal Acceleration. Tommy Newberry. Read by Tommy Newberry. 1 cass. (Running Time: 28 min.). 1994. 12.00 (978-1-886669-00-0(7)) One Percent Club.
This highly innovative & effective audio tape will accelerate your goal achievement through the use of specially worded audible affirmations, super-retention classical music, & soothing ocean sounds. Replace destructive thought patterns with positive beliefs & expectations.

Goal Achievement. Read by Mary Richards. 12.95 (106); 12.95 (605) Master Your Mind.
Argues that by drawing upon the intuitive & rational mind, one can create positive changes, so that life is a series of successes.

Goal Creation. Liah Kraft-Kristaine. Read by Liah Kraft-Kristaine. 2 cass. (Running Time: 2 hrs. 4 min.). 1988. 17.95 set. (978-1-878095-19-0(6)) LMI Prodns.
Techniques on clearing unconscious barriers, focusing, gaining control & intensifying determination.

Goal for Joaquin. Jerry McGinley. Perf. by The High Sierra Players. Narrated by Poppy Hill. Score by David Fabrizio. Directed By David Fabrizio. 2 CDs. (Running Time: 1 hr. 30 mins.). Dramatization. (YA). (gr. 1). 2004. audio compact disk 16.95 (978-1-58124-004-7(X)) Pub: Fiction Works. Dist(s): Brodart

Goal of All Seeking. Swami Amar Jyoti. 1 cass. 1982. 9.95 (M-36) Truth Consciousness.
The Ultimate Goal, the only end to seeking spiritually or materially. Guidance of the Master. Prayer & meditation.

Goal of Christian Living. Derek Prince. 2 cass. 11.90 Set. Derek Prince.
Being saved is merely the first step that should lead us into intimate fellowship with Christ. Do you know Him, or only know about Him? Are you ready, like Paul, to attain the goal of the first resurrection?.

Goal of Life. 1 cass. (Running Time: 1 hr.). 12.99 (187) Yoga Res Foun.

Goal of Our Life. Swami Amar Jyoti. 1 cass. 1988. 9.95 (M-93) Truth Consciousness.
Being & doing good is a must, but it is not the end. Going deeper, seeking the ultimate fulfillment. The meaning of freedom.

Goal of Worship: Touching God. Read by Wayne Monbleau. 4 cass. (Running Time: 5 hrs.). 1993. 20.00 Set. (978-0-944648-26-1(6), LGT-1210) Loving Grace Pubns.
Religious.

Goal Power. Eldon Taylor. 1 cass. (Running Time: 62 min.). (Inner Talk Ser.). 16.95 incl. script. (978-1-55978-105-3(X), 5322A) Progress Aware Res.
Soundtrack - Tropical Lagoon with underlying subliminal affirmations.

Goal Power: Classic. Eldon Taylor. Read by Eldon Taylor. Ed. by Leslie Brice. 1 cass. (Running Time: 1 hr.). 1992. 16.95 (978-1-56705-313-5(0)) Gateways Inst.
Self improvement.

Goal Power: Music Theme. Eldon Taylor. 1 cass. 16.95 (978-1-55978-107-7(6), 5322C) Progress Aware Res.

Goal Power: Ocean. Eldon Taylor. Read by Eldon Taylor. Ed. by Leslie Brice. 1 cass. (Running Time: 1 hr.). 1992. 16.95 (978-1-56705-314-2(9)) Gateways Inst.

Goal Setting. Charles L. Hughes. 9.95 () AMACOM.
Discusses hows & whys of mapping strategy, communicating action plans, setting performance standards, anticipating problems & evaluating results.

Goal Setting. Barrie Konicov. 1 cass. (YA). 11.98 (978-0-87082-432-6(5), 052) Potentials.
Whatever goal you set for yourself, you can achieve. There are no limitations, there are no unobtainable goals. Organize your present goals, create new goals, & develop them in your life.

Goal Setting. Barrie Konicov. 2 CDs. 2003. audio compact disk 27.98 (978-1-56001-977-0(8)) Potentials.
Organize your present goals, create new ones and develop them in your life. Without setting goals, you stagnate. Remember: there are no limitations, no unobtainable goals. You will find the self-hypnosis on track 1 and the subliminal on track 2. The easy-listening music of the subliminal, together with the self-hypnosis, is the original format which most people love and with which they are most familiar.

Goal Setting. Barrie Konicov. 1 CD. 2004. audio compact disk 19.98 (978-1-56001-671-7(X)) Potentials.

Goal Setting. Betty L. Randolph. 1 stereo cass. (Running Time: 45 min.). (Self-Hypnosis Ser.). 9.98 (811) Randolph Tapes.
Learn how to achieve goals using Mind Power!.

Goal Setting: How to Create an Action Plan & Achieve Your Goals. abr. ed. Susan B. Wilson & Michael S. Dobson. Read by Jim Bond. (Running Time: 3 hrs.). (WorkSmart Ser.). 2008. 24.95 (978-1-4233-6397-2(3), 9781423363972, BAD); 39.25 (978-1-4233-6398-9(1), 9781423363989, BADLE); audio compact disk 24.95 (978-1-4233-6395-8(7), 9781423363958, Brilliance MP3) Brilliance Audio.

Goal Setting: How to Create an Action Plan & Achieve Your Goals. 2nd abr. ed. Susan B. Wilson & Michael S. Dobson. Read by Jim Bond. (Running Time: 10800 sec.). (WorkSmart Ser.). 2008. audio compact disk 19.95 (978-1-4233-6393-4(0), 9781423363934, BACD); audio compact disk 39.25 (978-1-4233-6396-5(5), 9781423363965, Brlnc Audio MP3 Lib); audio compact disk 62.25 (978-1-4233-6394-1(9), 9781423363941, BACDLib Ed) Brilliance Audio.

Goal Setting: Hypnotic & Subliminal Learning. David Illig. 2000. 14.99 (978-0-86580-012-0(X)) Success World.

Goal Setting & Achievement. Earnie Larsen. 1 cass. (Running Time: 1 hr.). 1989. 10.95 (978-1-56047-016-8(X), A120) E Larsen Enterprises.
Discusses why goals are important - the power of goal setting.

Goal Setting & Moral Values. Hyrum Smith. 1 cass. 9.95 (978-1-55503-198-5(6), 06004032) Covenant Comms.
An entertaining, direct, enlightening talk for youth.

Goalie, unabr. ed. Susan Richards Shreve. Narrated by Alyssa Bresnahan. 2 cass. (Running Time: 2 hrs. 30 mins.). (gr. 5 up). 1997. 19.00 (978-0-7887-0887-9(2), 95025E7) Recorded Bks.
Julie MacNeil's only wish is to be a goalie of her school's soccer team. But when her father falls in love with the mother of her only rival for goalie, she suddenly feels competition at home & on the field.

Goals! How to Get Everything You Want - Faster Than You Ever Thought Possible. abr. ed. Brian Tracy. Read by Brian Tracy. 3 CDs. (Running Time: 3 hrs. 21 mins.). (ENG.). 2003. audio compact disk 24.95 (978-1-57270-358-2(X)) Pub: AudioGO. Dist(s): Perseus Dist

Goals! How to Get Everything You Want - Faster Than You Ever Thought Possible. abr. ed. Brian S. Tracy. Read by Brian S. Tracy. 3 cass. (Running Time: 3 hrs. 45 mins.). 2003. 21.95 (978-1-57270-357-5(1)) Pub: Audio Partners. Dist(s): PerseuPGW
Drawing on two decades of research into the dynamics of personal achievement, Brian Tracy has developed his own inspiring, goal-oriented system for success. People in every walk of life can follow it to take charge of their futures and move swiftly in the direction they want to go. Drawing on his experience as a professional speaker, Tracy puts the listener in a positive, can-do frame of mind. He explains why goals are necessary for future happiness, outlines ways to set goals that reflect one's true self, gives tips on overcoming obstacles, and tells how to persist until objectives are fully met. Other topics include clarifying values, associating with the best people to further personal aims, making a plan of action, visualizing, remaining flexible, and discovering inner creativity.

Goals: How to Set Them, How to Reach Them. Zig Ziglar. Read by Zig Ziglar. 6 cass. (Running Time: 6 hrs.). 1989. 59.95 (978-1-55525-042-3(4), 483A) Nightingale-Conant.
Schedule yourself for success.

Goals: Setting & Achieving Them on Schedule. unabr. abr. ed. Zig Ziglar. Read by Zig Ziglar. 2 CDs. (Running Time: 20 hrs. 0 mins. 0 sec.). (ENG.). 2002. audio compact disk 19.95 (978-0-7435-2507-7(8), Nightgale) Pub: S&S Audio. Dist(s): S and S Inc
SUCCESS CAN BE YOURS WITH ZIG ZIGLAR'S GOALS IF YOU HAVE DREAMS, THEN YOU NEED GOAL In Goals, bestselling author Zig Ziglar presents his dynamic seven-step formula for clearly defining your immediate and long-term goals...and then realizing your dreams. This step by step program is filled with inspiring stories from sports, business and science that demonstrate how to: Begin with a set of specific written goals Understand the reasons behind your ambitions Identify the resources you need to achieve success Develop a scheduled plan of action You'll learn how to work around obstacles and change your strategies without changing your vision; how to become a team player, how to master your time; and how to set goals for everything you want in life. Goals create motivation; motivation creates energy; energy helps make your dreams a reality. Take the first step toward reaching your aspirations and set your goals today!.

Goals for Living: Managing Your Resources. Nancy Wehlage & Mary Larson-Kennedy. (gr. 9-12). 2001. tchr. ed. 52.00 (978-1-56637-763-8(3)) Goodheart.

Goals of a Romantic Relationship. unabr. ed. Nathaniel Branden. 1 cass. (Running Time: 1 hr. 17 min.). 12.95 (609) J Norton Pubs.
The characteristics of a good romantic relationship are explored, including communication & psychological visibility.

Goals of Faith. 1 cass. (Running Time: 30 min.). 1985. (0259) Evang Sisterhood Mary.
Shattering iron portals; more than just a ray of hope.

Goals Program, Set. unabr. ed. Zig Ziglar. Read by Zig Ziglar. Ed. by Bert Newman. 6 cass. (Running Time: 6 hrs.). (How to Stay Motivated Ser.). 1993. 69.95 (978-1-56207-234-6(X)) Zig Ziglar Corp.
The Goals Program helps eliminate the 4 obstacles that stand between most people & their goals. Utilize Zig's 7-step methodology to set goals & practice Zig's 11 step formula to reach your goals.

Goat: A Memoir. Brad Land. Narrated by Nick Landrum. 6 CDs. (Running Time: 6 hrs. 15 mins.). 2004. audio compact disk 24.99 (978-1-4025-7367-5(7), 01472) Recorded Bks.

Goat: A Memoir. unabr. ed. Brad Land. Narrated by Nick Landrum. 4 cass. (Running Time: 6 hrs. 15 mins.). 2004. 24.99 (978-1-4025-7200-5(X), 03934) Recorded Bks.
At turns shockingly fierce and surprisingly tender, Goat is a shattering memoir that graphically portrays the scarred emotional landscape of young men. Author Brad Land's story is one of heartbreak and loneliness, but also of bravery and hope in an increasingly brutal world. Brad is driving two strangers home from a party when he realizes they are leading him to the middle of nowhere. Viciously beaten and left in the middle of the road, Brad survives. But as his physical injuries heal, his psychological wounds worsen.

Goat Song. unabr. ed. Frank Yerby. Read by Dan Lazar. 11 cass. (Running Time: 16 hrs. 30 min.). 1982. 88.00 (978-0-7366-0432-1(4), 1404) Books on Tape.
The principal character is Ariston, a well-born young Spartan, whose series of adventures mature him physically & psychologically.

Goats, unabr. ed. Brock Cole. Narrated by Ed Sala. 4 pieces. (Running Time: 4 hrs. 45 mins.). (gr. 9 up). 1997. 35.00 (978-0-7887-1786-4(3), 95257E7) Recorded Bks.
At summer camp, Howie & Laura are the misfits. One night, the other kids strip them & strand them on a nearby island. But these two Goats are resourceful, smart & stubborn.

Gobble, Quack, Moon. Matthew Gollub. Perf. by Matthew Gollub. Illus. by Judy Love. Composed by Dennis Hysom. (J). (ps-3). 2002. bk. 18.95 (978-1-889910-20-8(1)) Tortuga Pr.

Gobible Traveler, King James Version: Narrated by Alexander Scourby. Concept by L. L. C. The GoBible. As told by Alexander Scourby. 2009. 59.95 (978-1-4276-3929-5(9)) AardGP.

Gobible Traveler, New International Version: Narrated by Charles Taylor. Arranged by L. L. C. The GoBible. Narrated by Chris Taylor. 2009. 59.95 (978-1-4276-3930-1(2)) AardGP.

Gobible Traveler, Nueva Version Internacional see Gobible Viajero, Nueva Version Internacional: Narrated by Rafael Cruz

Gobible Viajero, Nueva Version Internacional: Narrated by Rafael Cruz. Arranged by The GoBible LLC. Narrated by Rafael Cruz.Tr. of Gobible Traveler, Nueva Version Internacional. (SPA.). 2009. 59.95 (978-1-4276-3931-8(0)) AardGP.

Gobible Voyager: Narrated by Charles Taylor. The GoBible LLC. 2009. audio compact disk 99.95 (978-1-4276-4210-3(9)) AardGP.

Gobible Voyager: Narrated by Stephen Johnston. The GoBible LLC. 2009. audio compact disk 99.95 (978-1-4276-4211-0(7)) AardGP.

Gobible Voyager- King James Version: Narrated by Alexander Scourby. Created by The GoBible LLC. 2009. audio compact disk 99.95 (978-1-4276-4209-7(5)) AardGP.

Goblin Tales: Spectacles. unabr. ed. Ann Beattie. Read by Ann Beattie. 1 cass. 1986. 8.98 (978-0-89845-545-8(6), CP 1786) HarperCollins Pubs.

Goblin Tales: The Temptation of Wilfred Malachey. unabr. ed. William F. Buckley, Jr.. Read by William F. Buckley, Jr. 1 cass. 1986. 8.98 (978-0-89845-546-5(4), CP 1787) HarperCollins Pubs.

Goblins Will Be Seen: When it's time for Halloween. Frances Donnell. Ed. by Catherine Hebert. Illus. by Donna Merchant. Arranged by Catherine Hebert & Bill and John Storch. 1 CD. (Running Time: 8 mins). (J). 2005. per. 16.95 (978-0-9770893-0-7(4)) 2 Do Bks.

***GoChinese: Speak & Learn the Pimsleur Way.** Pimsleur & goPimsleur. (Running Time: 7 hrs. 30 mins. 0 sec.). (Go Pimsleur Ser.). (ENG.). 2010. audio compact disk 29.99 (978-1-4423-3455-7(X), Pimsleur) Pub: S&S Audio. Dist(s): S and S Inc

God: A Biography. unabr. ed. Jack Miles. Read by Michael Prichard. 14 cass. (Running Time: 21 hrs.). 1996. 112.00 (978-0-7366-3213-3(1), 3876) Books on Tape.
God: just who or what is he? What is his life story? For answers, Jack Miles looks with a literary eye at the Old Testament. God emerges as the epic hero, from his first appearance as the creator to his last as the enduring Ancient of Days. A god-warrior, he fights his greatest battle with himself. Through his relationship with man, made in his image, God wrestles with his own conflicting urges. He is tender & ruthless, creative & destructive, omniscient & blind...wondrously mysterious.

God: A Course in World Religions & Spiritual Paths 14 CD Set. Steven S. Sadleir. (ENG.). 2009. audio compact disk 167.00 (978-1-883544-14-0(9)) Pub: Self Awareness. Dist(s): New Leaf Dist

God, a Woman, & the Way. M. Raymond. 8 cass. 32.95 (912) Ignatius Pr.
Meditations on the Seven Sorrows of Mary.

God Adventure. unabr. ed. Terry Meeuwsen. Read by Terry Meeuwsen. 4 CDs. audio compact disk 24.99 (978-1-58926-922-4(5)) Oasis Audio.

God Adventure. unabr. ed. Terry Meeuwsen. Narrated by Terry Meeuwsen. (ENG.). 2005. 17.49 (978-1-60814-227-9(2)) Oasis Audio.

***God & Career.** unabr. ed. Marianne Williamson. 2010. audio compact disk (978-1-61544-100-6(X)) Better Listen.

***God & Football: Faith & Fanaticism in the Southeastern Conference.** Chad Gibbs. (Running Time: 5 hrs. 6 mins. 22 sec.). (ENG.). 2010. 13.99 (978-0-310-58986-0(X)) Zondervan.

God & Hillary Clinton CD: A Spiritual Life. abr. ed. Paul Kengor. 2007. audio compact disk 29.95 (978-0-06-136713-7(3), Harper Audio) HarperCollins Pubs.

God & His People. 13.00 (978-1-59166-136-8(6)); audio compact disk 15.50 (978-1-57924-339-5(8)) BJUPr.

God & Man. 10.00 (RJ121) Esstee Audios.

God & Man at Yale: The Superstitions of Academic Freedom. unabr. ed. William F. Buckley, Jr. Read by Michael Edwards. 5 cass. (Running Time: 7 hrs.). 1988. 39.95 (978-0-7861-0008-8(7), 1007) Blckstn Audio.
As a young recent Yale graduate, Buckley took on Yale's professional & administrative staffs, citing their hypocritical diversion from the tenets on which the institution was built.

God & Mankind: Comparative Religions. Instructed by Robert Oden. 4 pieces. (Running Time: 6 hrs.). (C). bk. 29.95 (978-1-56585-168-9(4), 616) Teaching Co.

God & Mankind: Comparative Religions. Instructed by Robert Oden. 8 CDs. (Running Time: 6 hrs). audio compact disk 39.95 (978-1-59803-105-8(8)) Teaching Co.

God & Mankind: Comparative Religions, Course 616. Robert A. Oden, Jr. 4 cass. (Running Time: 6 hrs.). 19.95 (616) Teaching Co.
Eight lectures approach religious belief & ritual as a group of answers to mankind's most difficult & enduring questions. Underscores both the unity & the diversity of religious approaches to life in a sweeping conceptual grasp.

God & Money - Effortless Accomplishment. Marianne Williamson. Read by Marianne Williamson. 1 cass. (Running Time: 90 mins.). (Lectures on a Course in Miracles). 1999. 10.00 (978-1-56170-225-1(0), M728) Hay House.

God & Mr. Gomez. 2005. 44.95 (978-0-7861-3514-1(X)) Blckstn Audio.

God & Mr. Gomez. Jack Smith. Read by William Dufris. (Running Time: 25200 sec.). 2005. audio compact disk 55.00 (978-0-7861-7837-7(X)) Blckstn Audio.

God & Mr. Gomez. unabr. ed. Jack Smith. Read by William Dufries. 2005. 29.95 (978-0-7861-8052-3(8)) Blckstn Audio.

God & Mr. Gomez. unabr. collector's ed. Jack Smith. Read by Michael Prichard. 7 cass. (Running Time: 7 hrs.). 1983. 42.00 (978-0-7366-0918-0(0), 1861) Books on Tape.
An account of the building of a dream house in Baja California.

***God & Remembrance.** Featuring Ravi Zacharias. 2004. audio compact disk 9.00 (978-1-61256-062-5(8)) Ravi Zach.

***God & Sex: What the Bible Really Says.** unabr. ed. Michael Coogan. (Running Time: 8 hrs.). (ENG.). 2010. 24.98 (978-1-60788-720-1(7)) Pub: Hachet Audio. Dist(s): HachBkGrp

God & the Big Bang: Discovering Harmony Between Science & Spirituality. abr. ed. Daniel Chanan Matt. Read by Daniel Chanan Matt. 2 cass. (Running Time: 3 hrs.). 1997. bk. 17.95 (978-1-57453-150-3(6)) Audio Lit.
Drawing on the insights of physics & Jewish mysticism, Matt uncovers the sense of wonder & oneness that connects us with the universe & God.

God & the Brain: The Physiology of Spiritual Experience. abr. ed. Andrew Newberg. 2008. audio compact disk 24.95 (978-1-59179-802-6(7)) Sounds True.

God & the Evolving Universe. unabr. abr. ed. James Redfield et al. Read by Chris Ryan. 6 CDs. (Running Time: 7 hrs.). (ENG.). 2001. audio compact disk 34.95 (978-1-56511-642-9(9), 1565116429) Pub: HighBridge. Dist(s): Workman Pub

God As He Longs for You to See Him CD Series. 2005. audio compact disk 39.95 (978-1-59834-021-1(2)) Walk Thru the Bible.

God Bless America. Contrib. by Sandi Patty. (Inoriginal Performance Trax Ser.). 2004. audio compact disk 9.98 (978-5-559-38083-4(0)) INO Rec.

God Bless America, Level 1. (Yamaha Clavinova Connection Ser.). 2004. disk 1.04 (978-0-634-09582-5(X)) H Leonard.

God Bless America: Live from Carnegie Hall. Contrib. by Gaither, Bill & Gloria & Their Homecoming Friends. (Running Time: 1 hr. 50 mins.). (Gaither Gospel Ser.). 2002. 19.98 (978-5-550-14846-4(3)) Spring House Music.

God Bless Our Cozy Cottage. Read by Clair LeBear. Perf. by Clair LeBear. 1 CD. (Running Time: 1 hr.). (Clair's Cozy Cottage Music Ser.). 2000. audio compact disk 14.95 (978-0-9706321-5-9(0), CC003) Cozy Cottage.
A variety of children's songs.

God Bless the Sick & Afflicted. Elaine Cannon. 2 cass. 1989. 11.95 Set. (Bkcraft Inc) Deseret Bk.

God Bless the U. S. A. 1 cass. 9.95 (1000659); audio compact disk 14.95 (109113) Covenant Comms.

God Bless the U. S. A. 1986. audio compact disk 22.95 (978-0-634-09195-7(6)) H Leonard.

God Bless the U. S. A. Lee Greenwood. 1998. audio compact disk 22.95 (978-0-634-09107-0(7)) H Leonard.

God Bless the USA. Contrib. by Various Artists. 2008. audio compact disk 18.99 (978-5-557-44626-6(5), Word Records) Word Enter.

God Bless the USA: A Patriotic Musical. Contrib. by Johnathan Crumpton & Russell Mauldin. Created by Russell Mauldin et al. (ENG.). 2008. audio compact disk 90.00 (978-5-557-46537-3(5), Brentwood-Benson Music) Brentwood Music.

God Bless the USA: A Patriotic Musical. Contrib. by Russell Mauldin. Created by Russell Mauldin. Created by Joel Lindsey & Sue C. Smith. (ENG.). 2008. audio compact disk 16.99 (978-5-557-46538-0(3), Brentwood-Benson Music) Brentwood Music.

God Bless the USA: A Ready to Sing Patriotic Musical: Alto. Contrib. by Johnathan Crumpton & Russell Mauldin. Created by Russell Mauldin et al. (ENG.). 2008. audio compact disk 5.00 (978-5-557-46533-5(2), Brentwood-Benson Music) Brentwood Music.

God Bless the USA: A Ready to Sing Patriotic Musical: Bass. Contrib. by Johnathan Crumpton & Russell Mauldin. Created by Russell Mauldin et al. (ENG.). 2008. audio compact disk 5.00 (978-5-557-46531-1(6), Brentwood-Benson Music) Brentwood Music.

God Bless the USA: A Ready to Sing Patriotic Musical: Soprano. Contrib. by Johnathan Crumpton & Russell Mauldin. Created by Russell Mauldin et al. (ENG.). 2008. audio compact disk 5.00 (978-5-557-46534-2(0), Brentwood-Benson Music) Brentwood Music.

God Bless the USA: A Ready to Sing Patriotic Musical: Tenor. Contrib. by Johnathan Crumpton & Russell Mauldin. Prod. by Russell Mauldin. (ENG.). 2008. audio compact disk 5.00 (978-5-557-46532-8(4), Brentwood-Benson Music) Brentwood Music.

God Bless You, Dr. Kevorkian. collector's ed. Kurt Vonnegut. Read by Scott Brick. 1 cass. (Running Time: 1 hr.). 2000. 10.95 (978-0-7366-5458-6(5)) Books on Tape.
Only Vonnegut could make death & our aversion to it, a comic adventure. Here he skips back & forth between life & the afterlife as if the difference between them were slight. In thirty-some interviews with Isaac Newton, Clarence Darrow, Eugene Debs, John Brown, Adolf Hitler, William Shakespeare & among others, a nonentity who died while rescuing his schnauzer from a pit bull, Vonnegut trips down the "blue tunnel to the pearly gates" in the guise of a roving reporter for public radio. All the qualities that make Vonnegut an inimitable voice, his irreverence, humor, love of humanity & power to make readers stop & think, permeate this book of vignettes.

God Bless You, Dr. Kevorkian. collector's ed. unabr. ed. Kurt Vonnegut. Read by Scott Brick. 1 CD. (Running Time: 1 hr. 12 mins.). 2000. audio compact disk 9.95 (978-0-7366-5562-0(X)) Books on Tape.

God Bless You, Dr. Kevorkian. unabr. ed. Kurt Vonnegut. Read by Scott Brick. 1 cass. (Running Time: 1 hrs. 30 mins.). 2000. 10.95 (978-0-7366-5490-6(9)) Books on Tape.
Thirty-some vignettes that dance between life & the afterlife with dazzling humor & disturbing insight.

God Bless You, Dr. Kevorkian. unabr. ed. Kurt Vonnegut. Read by Scott Brick. 1 CD. (Running Time: 1 hr. 12 mins.). 2000. audio compact disk 14.95 (978-0-7366-5489-0(5)) Books on Tape.
Only Vonnegut could make death & our aversion to it, a comic adventure. Here he skips back & forth between life & the afterlife as if the difference between them were slight. In thirty-some interviews with Isaac Newton, Clarence Darrow, Eugene Debs, John Brown, Adolf Hitler, William Shakespeare & among others, a nonentity who died while rescuing his schnauzer from a pit bull, Vonnegut trips down the "blue tunnel to the pearly gates" in the guise of a roving reporter for public radio. All the qualities that make Vonnegut an inimitable voice, his irreverence, humor, love of humanity & power to make readers stop & think, permeate this book of vignettes.

God Built: Shaped by God... in the Bad & Good of Life. unabr. ed. Steve Farrar. Narrated by Jim Sanders. (Running Time: 6 hrs. 8 mins. 40 sec.). (Bold Men of God Ser.). (ENG.). 2008. 16.09 (978-1-60814-228-6(0)) Oasis Audio.

God Built: Shaped by God... in the Bad & Good of Life. unabr. ed. Steve Farrar. Read by Steve Farrar. Narrated by Jim Sanders. (Running Time: 6 hrs. 8 mins. 40 sec.). (Bold Men of God Ser.). (ENG.). 2008. audio compact disk 22.99 (978-1-59859-435-5(4)) Oasis Audio.

God, Butterflies & Miracles: Cool Songs & Awesome Activites for Kids. abr. ed. Created by Pauline Books Media & Music. (J). 2005. audio compact disk 14.95 (978-0-8198-3104-0(2), 332-446) Pub: Pauline Bks. Dist(s): Bookworld

God Calls You to Intimacy. George Maloney. 4 cass. 1984. 32.95 incl. shelf-case. (TAH152) Alba Hse Comns.
Discusses how each of us is a theophany - a visible manifestation of the presence of God.

God Came Near: Max Lucado with Jeff Nelson. Perf. by Max Lucado et al. 1 cass. 1998. 9.99 (978-1-58229-004-1(0)); audio compact disk 13.99 (978-1-58229-003-4(2)) Provident Mus Dist.
Songs of praise & words of inspiration.

God Can. Mary M. Morrissey. Read by Mary M. Morrissey. 1 cass. (Running Time: 60 min.). 9.95 (978-1-886491-18-2(6)) Tiger Mtn Pr.
Interweaves Morrissey's own dramatic story with the spiritual principles of how God Can.

God Can Do Anything. 4.95 (C6) Carothers.

God Can Turn It Around. Gloria Copeland. Perf. by Gloria Copeland. 4 cass. 1994. cass. & video 20.00 Set. (978-1-57562-073-2(1)) K Copeland Pubns.
Biblical teaching on God intervening.

God Can Turn It Around, Vol. 1. Gloria Copeland. Perf. by Gloria Copeland. 1 cass. 1994. cass. & video 5.00 (978-1-57562-074-9(X)) K Copeland Pubns.

God Can Turn It Around, Vol. 2. Gloria Copeland. Perf. by Gloria Copeland. 1 cass. 1994. cass. & video 5.00 (978-1-57562-075-6(8)) K Copeland Pubns.

God Can Turn It Around, Vol. 3. Gloria Copeland. Perf. by Gloria Copeland. 1 cass. 1994. cass. & video 5.00 (978-1-57562-076-3(6)) K Copeland Pubns.

God Can Turn It Around, Vol. 4. Gloria Copeland. Perf. by Gloria Copeland. 1 cass. 1994. cass. & video 5.00 (978-1-57562-077-0(4)) K Copeland Pubns.

God Cares but Waits. Short Stories. (1081) Am Audio Prose.

God Chasers: My Soul Follows Hard after Thee. Tommy Tenney. 3 cass. (Running Time: 4 hrs. 30 mins.). 1999. 19.99 (978-0-7684-2042-5(3)) Destiny Image Pubs.

God Chasers Set: My Soul Follows Hard after Thee. Tommy Tenney. Read by Tommy Tenney. 6 cass. 1999. 39.99 (978-0-7684-0186-8(0)) Destiny Image Pubs.

God Chasers Series. Tommy Tenney. 6 CDs. (Running Time: 9 hrs.). 1999. audio compact disk 49.99 (978-0-7684-0194-3(1)) Destiny Image Pubs.

God Class. Featuring Bill Winston. 3. 2004. audio compact disk 24.00 (978-1-59544-027-3(5)) Pub: B Winston Min. Dist(s): Anchor Distributors
In order to function in this earth, you must know who you areand what you are capable of achieving. Once this new identityis revealed, you will never be the same.

God-Class Living. Creflo A. Dollar. 20.00 (978-1-59089-197-1(X)) Pub: Creflo Dollar. Dist(s): STL Dist NA

God Comes to Us. Peter Eide. 1 CD. (Running Time: 1 hr.). (Firelight Ser.). 2004. audio compact disk 5.99 (978-0-8066-6444-6(4)) Augsburg Fortress.

God-Core Chronicles, Vol. 1. 1 CD. audio compact disk 15.98 (978-1-57908-301-4(3), 1366) Platinm Enter.

God-Core Chronicles, Vol. 2. 1 cass. 10.98 (978-1-57908-304-5(8), 1367); audio compact disk 15.98 CD. (978-1-57908-303-8(X), 1367) Platinm Enter.

God Delusion. unabr. ed. Richard Dawkins. Read by Richard Dawkins. Read by Lalla Ward. (YA). 2007. 64.99 (978-1-60252-609-9(5)) Find a World.

God Delusion. unabr. ed. Richard Dawkins. Read by Richard Dawkins. Read by Lalla Ward. (Running Time: 14 hrs. 0 mins. 0 sec.). (ENG.). 2007. audio compact disk 39.99 (978-1-4001-0378-2(9)); audio compact disk 79.99 (978-1-4001-3378-9(5)); audio compact disk 29.99 (978-1-4001-5378-7(6)) Pub: Tantor Media. Dist(s): IngramPubServ

God Discover His Character Audio: Discover His Character. Bill Bright. 2 cass. (Running Time: 240 min.). 2000. 14.99 (978-1-56399-139-4(X), NewLifePub) CampCrus.

God Does Hear & Answer Prayers. JoAnn Hibbert Hamilton. 1 cass. 7.98 (978-1-55503-813-7(1), 06005152) Covenant Comms.
An inspiring story of triumph over adversity.

God Don't Like Ugly. Mary Monroe. Narrated by Denise Burse. 10 cass. (Running Time: 14 hrs. 45 mins.). 88.00 (978-1-4025-0603-1(1)); audio compact disk 124.00 (978-1-4025-2105-8(7)) Recorded Bks.

God Emperor of Dune. unabr. ed. Frank Herbert & Frank Herbert. 14 CDs. (Running Time: 16 hrs. 0 mins. 0 sec.). (ENG.). 2008. audio compact disk 49.95 (978-1-4272-0315-1(6)) Pub: Macmill Audio. Dist(s): Macmillan

God Emperor of Dune, unabr. collector's ed. Frank Herbert. Read by Connor O'Brien. 10 cass. (Running Time: 15 hrs.). (Dune Chronicles). 1999. 80.00 (978-0-7366-4422-8(9), 4839) Books on Tape.
Opens to find centuries have passed on Dune itself, & the planet is green with life. Leto, the son of Dune's savior, is still alive but far from human, & the fate of all humanity hangs on his awesome sacrifice.

God Encounters: Stories of His Involvement in Life's Greatest Moments. unabr. ed. James S. Bell. (Running Time: 6 hrs. 18 mins. 19 sec.). (ENG.). 2009. 18.19 (978-1-60814-598-0(0)); audio compact disk 25.99 (978-1-59859-646-5(2)) Oasis Audio.

***God Engines.** unabr. ed. John Scalzi. (Running Time: 3 hrs.). 2010. 19.99 (978-1-4418-9083-2(1), 9781441890832, BAD); 39.97 (978-1-4418-9084-9(X), 9781441890849, BADLE) Brilliance Audio.

***God Engines.** unabr. ed. John Scalzi. Read by Christopher Lane. (Running Time: 3 hrs.). 2010. 19.99 (978-1-4418-9081-8(5), 9781441890818, Brilliance MP3); 39.97 (978-1-4418-9082-5(3), 9781441890825, Brlnc Audio MP3 Lib); audio compact disk 19.99 (978-1-4418-9079-5(3), 9781441890795, Bril Audio CD Unabri); audio compact disk 49.97 (978-1-4418-9080-1(7), 9781441890801, BriAudCD Unabrid) Brilliance Audio.

God Factor. Marcus Hester. Prod. by Agape Media. Narrated by Dick Murdock. 4 CDs. (Running Time: 4 hrs. 45 mins.). 2004. audio compact disk (978-0-9755537-0-1(4)) Agape Media Grp.
What is God up to these days? It's a question on many hearts, as believers must cope with increasing change and uncertainty, both in the church and in the world at large.The God Factor is a compelling book that will answer this and many other probing questions on the work of God in the workplace. Not only does he answer the what, but - like a good journalist for Jesus - Hester informs us about the why's, the how's, the where's, and the when's.

God Faithful & True. 1 CD. (Running Time: 36 mins.). 2002. audio compact disk 6.99 (978-1-57583-527-3(4), 3000CD) Twin Sisters.
God is the Creator, the Rock, the Redeemer! He is compassionate and gracious, faithful to His promises. And above all, God is love. Kids and adults, too, will bow down to God giving Him the praise only He deserves as they sing these great new contemporary praise and worship songs.

God Feeds Us: Lost & Found. 1 CD. (Running Time: 1 hr.). 2004. audio compact disk 5.99 (978-0-8066-6427-9(4)) Augsburg Fortress.

God First. Daya Mata. 1984. 6.50 (2104) Self Realization.
The author testifies to the inestimable joy of God-centered living & points out how each of us can achieve this state. Discussion includes: Enjoying life with spiritual consciousness; Practicing the presence of God; The value of silence; Paramahansa Yogananda's guidance for solving problems; The Mother aspect of God.

God Forgets: Jeremiah 31:34. Ed Young. (J). 1981. 4.95 (978-0-7417-1187-8(7), A0817) Win Walk.

God, Freedom & Immortality: A Critical Analysis. Antony G. Flew. (ENG.). 1984. audio compact disk 24.98 (978-0-87975-251-4(3)) Prometheus Bks.

God Gave Us This Country: Tekamthi & the First American Civil War. unabr. ed. Bill Gilbert. Narrated by Nelson Runger. 12 cass. (Running Time: 16 hrs. 45 mins.). 1999. 97.00 (978-1-55690-197-3(6), 91114E7) Recorded Bks.
Shows how the Shawnee outwitted their white foes & became adept at beating them at their own game.

God Has a Dream: A Vision of Hope for Our Time. unabr. rev. ed. Desmond Tutu & Doug Abrams. Read by Desmond Tutu. Intro. by James Jacobson. 4 CDs. (Running Time: 4 hrs. 30 mins.). 2004. audio compact disk (978-0-9752631-0-5(2)) Maui Media.
This award-winning audiobook written and read by Desmond Tutu offers an extremely personal and liberating message of hope and light in dark times. In it, the Archbishop shows how important it is that even as we face the harsh realities of our individual lives and global conditions, we remember the importance of hope and dreams - for it is on hope and dreams that a better future will be built, and that God's dream for us will be fulfilled. And Tutu also demonstrates how to bring these dreams to fruition in very practical terms, for example in learning how to love; ridding ourselves of our prejudices; opposing injustice; promoting the qualities of forgiveness, humility and generosity in ourselves; taking time to be still and quiet; and in being patient.

God Has a Dream for Your Life. unabr. ed. Sheila Walsh. Narrated by Sheila Walsh. (Running Time: 5 hrs. 5 mins. 25 sec.). (ENG.). 2009. audio compact disk 25.99 (978-1-59859-554-3(7)) Oasis Audio.

God Has A Dream for Your Life. unabr. ed. Sheila Walsh. Narrated by Sheila Walsh. (Running Time: 5 hrs. 5 mins. 25 sec.). (ENG.). 2009. 18.19 (978-1-60814-472-3(0)) Oasis Audio.

God Has a Plan. 1 cass. (Running Time: 30 min.). 1985. (0233) Evang Sisterhood Mary.
A ray of hope in a chaotic world; a lifeline for today & tomorrow.

God Has a Purpose. Neville Goddard. 1 cass. (Running Time: 62 min.). 1964. 8.00 (39) J & L Pubns.
Neville taught Imagination Creates Reality. He was a powerfully influential teacher of God as Consciousness.

God Has Become All This. unabr. ed. Swami Amar Jyoti. 1 cass. (Running Time: 1 hr.). (Satsangs of Swami Amar Jyoti Ser.). 2000. 9.95 (978-0-933572-53-9(0), R-121) Truth Consciousness.
When we raise our consciousness we see that God has become all this. Appreciating infinite variety.

God Has Done Marvelous Things. David Haas & Leon C. Roberts. 1997. 10.95 (398); audio compact disk 15.95 (398) GIA Pubns.

God Has Plans for You. unabr. ed. Keith A. Butler, II. 1 cass. (Running Time: 1 hr. 30 mins.). 2001. 5.00 (A182) Word Faith Pubng.

***God Hater.** unabr. ed. Bill Myers. (ENG.). 2010. 14.98 (978-1-59644-929-9(2), christaudio); audio compact disk 24.98 (978-1-59644-928-2(4), christaudio) christianaud.

God Hates Sinners. Michael Pearl. 1 CD. 2005. audio compact disk (978-1-892112-74-3(4)) No Greater Joy.

God He Reigns: Live Worship from Hillsong Church. Contrib. by Hillsong. 2005. audio compact disk 17.98 (978-5-558-81617-4(1)) Hillsong Pubng AUS.

God Help Us. Perf. by Miserable Offenders. 1 cass. 1996. 11.95 (MoreHse Pubng); audio compact disk 15.95 CD. (MoreHse Pubng) Church Pub Inc.
Familiar songs & hymns presented in an innnovative fashion. Closely harmonized & intricately arranged.

God I Am: From Tragic to Magic. unabr. ed. Peter O. Erbe. Read by Richard Bienvenu. 7 cass. (Running Time: 9 hrs. 30 min.). 1999. bk. 49.95 Set. (978-1-928839-00-2(2)) New Resonance.
Learn of True Perception & the ego's efforts to reverse True Perception. Learn of the God I Am that we all are.

***God I Don't Understand: Reflections on Tough Questions of Faith.** unabr. ed. Christopher J. H. Wright. (Running Time: 10 hrs. 58 mins. 0 sec.). (ENG.). 2008. 19.99 (978-0-310-30056-4(8)) Zondervan.

God I Love: A Lifetime of Walking with Jesus. unabr. ed. Joni Eareckson Tada. 2003. audio compact disk 44.99 (978-0-310-25315-0(2)) Zondervan.

God I Love: A Lifetime of Walking with Jesus. unabr. ed. Joni Eareckson Tada & Adrian Plass. 9 cass. (Running Time: 14 hrs.). 2003. 39.99 (978-0-310-25314-3(4)) Zondervan.

God I Love: A Lifetime of Walking with Jesus. unabr. ed. Zondervan Publishing Staff & Joni Eareckson Tada. (Running Time: 14 hrs. 0 mins. 0 sec.). (ENG.). 2003. 26.99 (978-0-310-26155-1(4)) Zondervan.

God in Me. Contrib. by Daniel Doss. (Mastertrax Ser.). 2008. audio compact disk 9.98 (978-5-557-46112-2(4)) Pt of Grace Ent.

***God in Ruins.** abr. ed. Leon Uris. Read by Stephen Lang. (ENG.). 2005. (978-0-06-085603-8(3), Harper Audio); (978-0-06-085604-5(1), Harper Audio) HarperCollins Pubs.

God in Ruins. unabr. ed. Leon Uris. Read by Christian Noble. 10 cass. (Running Time: 15 hrs.). 1999. 80.00 (5001) Books on Tape.
Spanning the decades from WWII to the 2008 presidential campaign. This is an unforgettable story of Quinn Patrick O'Connell. A principled & courageous man, he is on the brink of becoming the second Irish Catholic President of the United States. But Quinn is a man with an explosive secret that can shatter his political ambitions & threaten his life, a secret that even he does not know. Through the years Quinn has made some powerful enemies, including presidential incumbent Thornton Tomtree, a right-wing pragmatist who will court the most dangerous & deadly elements of society & risk most America's safety to achieve his own ambitions.

God in Sandals -Lib. Margaret Montreuil. Read by Mark Rosenwinkel. 9 cass. (Running Time: 12 hrs.). 2005. 72.95 (978-0-7861-3015-3(6), 3424); audio compact disk 90.00 (978-0-7861-8082-0(X), 3424) Blckstn Audio.

God in the Dock. unabr. ed. Read by Ralph Cosham. (Running Time: 39600 sec.). 2007. 65.95 (978-1-4332-1287-1(0)); audio compact disk 29.95 (978-1-4332-1289-5(7)) Blckstn Audio.

God in the Dock: Essays on Theology & Ethics. unabr. ed. Read by Ralph Cosham. (Running Time: 39600 sec.). 2007. audio compact disk & audio compact disk 72.00 (978-1-4332-1288-8(9)) Blckstn Audio.

God in the Foxhole: Inspiring True Stories of Miracles on the Battlefield. unabr. ed. Charles Sasser. Narrated by Wes Bleed. (Running Time: 9 hrs. 57 mins. 50 sec.). (ENG.). 2008. audio compact disk 29.99 (978-1-59859-467-6(2), SpringWater) Oasis Audio.

God in the Foxhole: Inspiring True Stories of Miracles on the Battlefield. unabr. ed. Charles W. Sasser. Narrated by Wes Bleed. (Running Time: 9 hrs. 57 mins. 50 sec.). (ENG.). 2008. 20.99 (978-1-60814-460-0(7), SpringWater) Oasis Audio.

God in the Human Story: Through the Eyes of Therese of Lisieux. Vilma Seelaus. 2 cass. (Running Time: 3 hrs. 20 mins.). 35.95 Set. (TAH369) Alba Hse Comns.
This series makes alive the presence of God in the human story. Though the context of her life is limited, we see Therese expand in spirit. She is not diminished by suffering, & in her human fragility she meets God's merciful love. Themes such as: "Therese & Her Family Relationships;" "Growth Through Suffering;" "A Spirituality of Imperfection;" & "Therese & the Maternal Face of God" are explored through the prism of contemporary spiritual & psychological insights. As we see Therese break through the narrow confines of her life to spiritual depths, we find meaning for our own lives beyond human success or failure.

God in the Marketplace: 45 Questions Fortune 500 Executives Ask about Faith, Life, & Business. unabr. ed. Henry Blackaby & Richard Blackaby. Narrated by Wayne Shepherd. (ENG.). 2008. audio compact disk 22.99 (978-1-59859-397-6(8)) Oasis Audio.

God in the Marketplace: 45 Questions Fortune 500 Executives Ask about Faith, Life, & Business. unabr. ed. Henry T. Blackaby & Richard Blackaby. Narrated by Wayne Shepherd. (ENG.). 2008. 16.09 (978-1-60814-229-3(9)) Oasis Audio.

God Is. Guest John. 2004. 34.99 (978-1-58926-373-4(1)); audio compact disk 24.99 (978-1-58926-374-1(X)) Domain Commns.

God Is a Big God. Taffi L. Dollar. 2 cass. (Running Time: 3 hrs.). 2000. 10.00 (978-1-931172-42-4(0), TS242, Kidz Faith) Pub: Creflo Dollar. Dist(s): STL Dist NA

God Is a God of Restoration. Speeches. Joel Osteen. 1 Cass. (Running Time: 30 Mins.). 2001. 6.00 (978-1-59349-107-9(7), JA0107) J Osteen.

God Is a Good God. Gloria Copeland. 2 cass. 1987. 10.00 Set. (978-0-88114-775-9(3)) K Copeland Pubns.
Biblical teaching on God's goodness.

God Is a Matchmaker. Derek Prince. 2 cass. 11.90 Set. Derek Prince.
The Bible, which begins & ends with a wedding, reveals the unique importance which God Himself attaches to marriage.

God Is a Salesman: Learn from the Master. unabr. ed. Mark Stevens. (Running Time: 3 hrs. 30 mins.). (ENG.). 2008. 14.98 (978-1-60024-140-6(5)) Pub: Hachet Audio. Dist(s): HachBkGrp

God Is a Surprise. unabr. ed. Read by Mr. Harry. Prod. by Phyllis U. Hiller. 1 cass. (Running Time: 25 min.). (J). (gr. 4-12). 1990. 10.95 (978-1-884877-14-8(1), 199219CS) Creat Mats Lib.
Accompanies the song book of the same title.

God Is after Himself. 2003. 6.00 (978-1-58602-150-4(8)) E L Long.

God Is after Himself. 2003. audio compact disk 10.00 (978-1-58602-151-1(6)) E L Long.

God Is an Englishman, Pt. 1. unabr. collector's ed. R. F. Delderfield. Read by Ian Whitcomb. 13 cass. (Running Time: 19 hrs. 30 min.). 1983. 104.00 (978-0-7366-0487-1(1), 1462-A) Books on Tape.
Adam Swann, scion of an army family, returns home in 1858 after service with her Majesty's Army in Crimea & India, determined to build his fortune in the dog-eat-dog world of Victorian commerce. Swann is captivated by Henrietta, the high-spirited daughter of a local mill owner. The two share adventures, reversal & fortune.

God Is an Englishman, Pt. 2. unabr. collector's ed. R. F. Delderfield. Read by Ian Whitcomb. 9 cass. (Running Time: 13 hrs. 30 min.). 1983. 72.00 (978-0-7366-0488-8(X), 1462-B) Books on Tape.

God Is Closer Than You Think: If God Is Always with Us, Why Is He So Hard to Find? unabr. ed. John Ortberg. (Running Time: 60 hrs. 0 mins. 0 sec.). (ENG.). 2005. audio compact disk 24.99 (978-0-310-26379-1(4)) Zondervan.

God Is Closer Than You Think: If God Is Always with Us, Why Is He So Hard to Find? unabr. ed. John Ortberg. (Running Time: 4 hrs. 37 mins. 0 sec.). (ENG.). 2005. 12.99 (978-0-310-26700-3(5)) Zondervan.

God Is Dead. Ron Currie, Jr. Read by Gabriel Baron. (ENG.). 2007. 44.99 (978-1-60252-835-2(7)) Find a World.

God Is Dead. unabr. ed. Ron Currie, Jr. Read by Gabriel Baron. 5 CDs. (Running Time: 21600 sec.). 2007. audio compact disk 29.95 (978-1-59316-100-2(X)) Listen & Live.

God Is for Every Day(r) - Stories & Songs for Children: Teach-A-Child Companion Book/Cassette Tape Set, Vol. 1. Short Stories. Valerie Spickler. Pref. by Lois Monson. Music by Lois Monson. Lyrics by Carol Loperena. Music by Carol Loperena. Featuring Rudy. 1 cassette. (Running Time: 1 hour). Dramatization. (J). 2002. bk. 21.99 (978-0-9727786-2-6(4), 978-0-9727786-2-6) JoySoul Corp.
The God Is For Every Day(r) cassette tape includes 49 tracks and comes in the original jewel case. It contains all of the material presented in the book. It is packaged with the book and midi disc inside the plastic tie-string envelope. The first part of the recording introduces the children to 8 themes, such as the "Lord, I'm So Grumpy" theme. Each theme includes a story and song, and each story and song has its own short introduction. The introductions are recorded with the voice of Dr. Rudy. The 8 stories are read by Angelika, who reads as a first person child. All eight songs are sung by Angelika also.

God Is for Every Day(r) - Stories & Songs for Children: Teach-a-Child Companion Book/Compact Disc Set, Vol. 1. Short Stories. Valerie Spickler. Pref. by Lois Monson. Music by Lois Monson. Lyrics by Carol Loperena. Music by Carol Loperena. Featuring Rudy. 1 CD. (Running Time: 1 hr). Dramatization. (J). 2002. bk. 24.99 (978-0-9727786-1-9(6), 978-0-9727786-1-9) JoySoul Corp.
The God Is For Every Day(r) CD includes 49 tracks and comes in the original jewel case. It contains all of the material presented in the book. It is packaged with the book and midi disc inside the plastic tie-string envelope. CD makes playing specific stories or songs easy for the teacher. Each story and song has its own track. The first part of the recording introduces the children to 8 themes, such as the "Lord, I'm So Grumpy" theme. Each theme includes a story and song, and each story and song has its own short introduction. The introductions are recorded with the voice of Dr. Rudy. The 8 stories are read by Angelika, who reads as a first person child. The eight songs are sung by Angelika also.

God Is Great. 1 cass. (Bullfrogs & Butterflies Ser.). (J). 9.95 (AAGG) Brdgstn Multimed Grp.
Punny the Butterfly & her pal Floydd Frogg sing about the greatest metamorphosis of all - not from caterpillar to butterfly or polywog to bullfrog - but the spiritual change that comes with knowing such a Great God!.

God Is Great. Bridgestone Staff. 2004. audio compact disk 7.98 (978-1-56371-036-0(6)) Brdgstn Multimed Grp.

God Is Hope Anthem. Anna Mullin & Nylea L. Butler-Moore. 1998. 5.00 (978-0-687-02388-2(2)) Abingdon.

God Is in Control. Arranged by Nan Allen & Dennis Allen. 10 cass. (Running Time: 10 hrs.). (YA). 1995. bk. 54.99 (TA-9190PK); 12.99 (TA-9190C) Lillenas.
Incredible musical to help today's youth learn about God's sovereignty, authority, provision, promise, people, power & grace. The music is an exciting mix of contemporary styles made popular by some of today's best-known artists, including Steven Curtis Chapman, Twila Paris, Point of Grace, Scott Wesley Brown, Kim Boyce, Clay Crosse & Rich Mullins. Perform as an entire musical, use the songs & dramatic sketches as thematic packages, or use as a collection of individual songs. What a poignant message for teens & adults alike - God is in control.

God Is in Control. Kenneth Copeland. 4 cass. 1983. 20.00 Set incl. study guide. (978-0-938458-61-6(2)) K Copeland Pubns.
Biblical presence of God in people's lives.

God Is in Control: Walking in the Confidence of God During Troubled Times. Kenneth Copeland. (ENG.). 2008. audio compact disk 20.00 (978-1-57562-966-7(6)) K Copeland Pubns.

***God Is in the Pancakes.** unabr. ed. Robin Epstein. Read by Cassandra Morris. (ENG.). (J). 2010. audio compact disk 37.00 (978-0-307-73822-6(1), Listening Lib) Pub: Random Audio Pubg. Dist(s): Random

God Is My Friend. 1 cass. (Bullfrogs & Butterflies Ser.). (J). 9.95 (AAGF) Brdgstn Multimed Grp.
Welcome to Agapeland - wonderland of love. The lively tunes on this original "Bullfrogs & Butterflies" tape are guaranteed to get kids excited about praising the Lord. Glorious fun for all.

God Is Not Great: How Religion Poisons Everything. unabr. ed. Christopher Hitchens. (Running Time: 9 hrs.). (ENG.). 2007. 14.98 (978-1-60024-010-2(0), Twelve) Pub: GrandCentral. Dist(s): HachBkGrp

God Is Not Great: How Religion Poisons Everything. unabr. ed. Christopher Hitchens. Read by Christopher Hitchens. (Running Time: 9 hrs.). (ENG.). 2009. audio compact disk 19.98 (978-1-60024-557-2(9)) Pub: Hachet Audio. Dist(s): HachBkGrp

God Is Not Impressed with Intelligence. Jack Deere. 1 cass. (Running Time: 90 mins.). (Receiving Spiritual Gifts Ser.: Vol. 3). 2000. 5.00 (JD03-003) Morning NC.
This is a powerful debunking of aguments against the use of spiritual gifts & reveals major hindrances to believers walking in the power of God.

***God Is Not One: The Eight Rival Religions That Run the World & Why Their Differences Matter.** unabr. ed. Stephen R. Prothero. Read by Paul Boehmer. 2010. (978-0-06-198867-7(7), Harper Audio); (978-0-06-201602-7(4), Harper Audio) HarperCollins Pubs.

God Is Number One: Exodus 20:2-3. Ed Young. 1985. 4.95 (978-0-7417-1428-2(0), 428) Win Walk.

God Is Our Help: Comfort in Scripture & Song. Music by Karla Carey. 1 cass. (Running Time: 60 min.). (Inspiration in Words & Music Ser.). 1988. 10.00 (978-1-55768-535-3(5)) LC Pub.
Brings spiritual readings from the King James version of the Bible that fortifies the listener with courage.

God Is Still Speaking. Jack Deere. 1 cass. (Running Time: 90 mins.). (Hearing God's Voice Ser.: Vol. 1). 2000. 5.00 (JD04-001) Morning NC.
These messages are an outstanding collection that lay a solid & practical foundation for discerning God's voice.

God Is Still Speaking. Read by Basilea Schlink. 1 cass. (Running Time: 30 min.). Incl. God Is Still Speaking: Practical Steps for Living Out God's Word. 1985. (0285); 1985. (0285) Evang Sisterhood Mary.
The "Commandments of Love"-strength to overcome in this troubled age. Includes: The Greatest of These; You Will Never Be Put To Shame; The Way To Real Life; Sing Unto The Lord; The Battle of Faith;Is Jesus Your First Love?; The Way is Prepared.

God Is Still Speaking: Practical Steps for Living Out God's Word see God Is Still Speaking

God Is the Cure/Release in Relationships. Marianne Williamson. Read by Marianne Williamson. 1 cass. (Running Time: 90 mins.). (Lectures on a Course in Miracles). 1999. 10.00 (978-1-56170-226-8(9), M729) Hay House.

God Is the Gospel: Meditations of God's Love As the Gift of Himself. unabr. ed. John Piper. Narrated by Michael Kramer. 1 MP3CD. (Running Time: 5 hrs. 30 mins. 0 sec.). (ENG.). 2006. lp 19.98 (978-1-59644-371-6(5), Hovel Audio) christianaud.
God, who said, "Let light shine out of darkness," has shone in our hearts to give the light of the knowledge of the glory of God in the face of Jesus Christ.2 Corinthians 4:6This book is a cry from the heart of John Piper. He is pleading that God himself, as revealed in Christ?s death and resurrection, is the ultimate and greatest gift of the gospel.None of Christ's gospel deeds and none of our gospel blessings are good news except as means of seeing and savoring the glory of Christ. Forgiveness is good news because it opens the way to the enjoyment of God himself. Justification is good news because it wins access to the presence and pleasures of God himself. Eternal life is good news because it becomes the everlasting enjoyment of Christ.All God's gifts are loving only to the degree that they lead us to God himself. That is what God's love is: his commitment to do everything necessary (most painfully the death of his only Son) to enthrall us with what is most deeply and durably satisfying - namely, himself.Saturated with Scripture, centered on the cross, and seriously joyful, this book leads us to satisfaction for the deep hungers of the soul. It touches us at the root of life where practical transformation gets its daily power. It awakens our longing for Christ and opens our eyes to his beauty.Piper writes for the soul-thirsty who have turned away empty and in desperation from the mirage of methodology. He invites us to slow down and drink from a deeper spring. "This is eternal life," Jesus said, "that they know you the only true God, and Jesus Christ whom you have sent." This is what makes the gospel - and this book?good news.

God Is the Gospel: Meditations on God's Love as the Gift of Himself. unabr. ed. John Piper. 5 CDs. (Running Time: 5 hrs. 30 mins. 0 sec.). (ENG.). 2006. audio compact disk 23.98 (978-1-59644-369-3(3), Hovel Audio) christianaud.

***God Is the Gospel: Meditations on God's Love As the Gift of Himself.** unabr. ed. John Piper. Narrated by Michael Kramer. (ENG.). 2006. 14.98 (978-1-59644-370-9(7), Hovel Audio) christianaud.

God Is the Judge. Jack Deere. 1 cass. (Running Time: 90 mins.). (Sexual Purity & Marital Fidelity Ser.: Vol. 1). 2000. 5.00 (JD07-001) Morning NC.
Marriages are under attack, but God has ordained spiritual principles that will enable us to stand strong.

God Is the Treasure. Frederick Ransom Gray. 2007. audio compact disk 37.99 (978-1-60247-639-4(X)) Tate Pubng.

God Is Truth. Swami Amar Jyoti. 2 cass. 1982. 12.95 (Q-18) Truth Consciousness.
Taking the shelter of truth. Shaking off the conception of being "just religious." The inner becoming process.

***God Is with Us.** Directed By Gregory Solak. (ENG.). 2010. audio compact disk 18.00 (978-0-913836-53-8(2)) St Vladimirs.

God Is with Us: Chants for Christmas with Carols from Poland & Ukraine. Illus. by J. Michael Thompson. 1 CD. audio compact disk 16.00 (978-0-937690-61-1(9), 4032) Wrld Lib Pubns.

God Is Your Constant Companion. Swami Chidvilasananda. 1 CD. (Running Time: 54 mins.). 2001. audio compact disk 15.95 (108120, Siddha Yoga Pubs) SYDA Found.
When sincere longing to be with God every moment arises in a seeker's heart, the assurance does come that God is very present. This longing and knowledge of God's presence is priceless, the fruit of many lifetimes. "When you experience such closeness to God, such an affinity with God, then you are able to experience all of creation as your support, as your greatest teacher, and your loving protector.

God-Kind of Faith. Kenneth E. Hagin. 1 cass. 4.95 (SH04) Faith Lib Pubns.

God-Kind of Faith. Bill Winston. 6 cass. (Running Time: 5hr.14min.). (C). 1999. 25.00 (978-1-931289-57-3(3)) Pub: B Winston Min. Dist(s): Anchor Distributors

God Kind of Love. Featuring Bill Winston. 3 cass. 2006. 15.00 (978-1-59544-165-2(4)); audio compact disk 24.00 (978-1-59544-166-9(2)) Pub: B Winston Min. Dist(s): Anchor Distributors

God-Kind of Love Series. Kenneth W. Hagin, Jr. 4 cass. 1994. 16.00 Set. (30J) Faith Lib Pubns.

God Kingdom. (K. I. D. S. Church Ser.: Vol. 3). (J). (gr. 1-6). 1998. ring bd. 119.99 (978-1-57405-037-0(0)) CharismaLife Pub.

God Knows No Generation Gap. Derek Prince. 1 cass. 5.95 (4410) Derek Prince.
God's standards for Christians are the same for all age groups. His conditions for success never vary. A question & answer session follows with frank answers to frank questions from today's young people.

God Knows You're Amazing: How Young Women Can Discover God's Plan for Them, Talk on CD. Read by Laurel Christensen. 2006. audio compact disk 13.95 (978-1-59038-730-6(9)) Desert Bks.

God Lives! 1 cass. (Running Time: 30 min.). Incl. God Lives! When God Examines Us. 1985. (0253); 1985. (0253) Evang Sisterhood Mary.
Discusses an undeniable certainty in an atheistic world & God's truth-my greatest opportunity.

God Lives!: When God Examines Us see God Lives!

God Loves America. ed. Imani Bradford. (J). 2005. audio compact disk (978-0-9671796-1-2(0)) Segue Pubs.

God Loves Country Music! 12 Country Inspirational Favorites. 2007. audio compact disk 9.98 (978-5-557-73289-5(6)) Maranatha Music.

God Loves Fun. 1 cass. (Bullfrogs & Butterflies Ser.). (J). 9.95 (AGLF) Brdgstn Multimed Grp.
Indeed He does - That's why children will enjoy more of the same exciting musical fun & praise in the tradition of the original.

God Loves Fun. Bridgestone Staff. 2004. audio compact disk 7.98 (978-1-56371-035-3(8)) Brdgstn Multimed Grp.

God Loves You - Even You! Gloria Copeland. 3 cass. 1992. 15.00 Set. (978-0-88114-870-1(9)) K Copeland Pubns.
Biblical teaching God's love for you.

God-Made Millionaire Audio Compact Disc: Personal & Business Finance God's Way. (ENG.). 2008. audio compact disk 9.99 (978-0-9818691-0-0(6)) Changing Point.

God-Made Millionaire Audio Compact Disc & Author's Notes Companion DVD: Personal & Business Finance God's Way. (ENG.). 2008. DVD & audio compact disk 10.99 (978-0-9818691-2-4(2)) Changing Point.

God Made You Special. Contrib. by VeggieTales. 2007. audio compact disk 10.99 (978-5-557-67270-2(2)) Big Idea.

God Makes the Rivers to Flow. Read by Eknath Easwaran. 4 cass. bk. 45.00 incl. binder.; pap. bk. 35.00; 25.00 incl. binder. Nilgiri Pr.
Presents selections from the scriptures, saints & mystics of religious traditions, East & West. Suited for meditation.

***God Moments in Time.** Thomas Brewer. Narrated by Eric Smith. (ENG.). 2010. 26.99 (978-0-9723261-3-1(8)) ProActFaith.

God Never Blinks: 50 Lessons for Life's Little Detours. unabr. ed. Regina Brett. Read by Regina Brett. (Running Time: 6 hrs.). (ENG.). 2010. 16.98 (978-1-60788-169-8(1)); audio compact disk 24.98 (978-1-60788-168-1(3)) Pub: Hachet Audio. Dist(s): HachBkGrp

God Never Sleeps: Songs from the Iona Community. John L. Bell. Perf. by Cathedral Singers. 1995. 10.95 (348); audio compact disk 15.95 (348) GIA Pubns.

God of All Comfort. Hannah Whitall Smith & Susan O'Malley. Orig. Title: Living Confidently in God's Love. 2002. 44.95 (978-0-7861-1690-4(0)) Blckstn Audio.

God of All Comfort. unabr. ed. Hannah Whitall Smith. Read by Susan O'Malley. 6 cass. (Running Time: 9 hrs.). Orig. Title: Living Confidently in God's Love. 2000. 44.95 (2513) Blckstn Audio.
Smith shares with you her wisdom & understanding of the great rewards awaiting those who accept God's love.

***God of All Comfort.** unabr. ed. Hannah Whitall Smith. Narrated by Marguerite Gavin. Orig. Title: Living Confidently in God's Love. (ENG.). 2007. 16.98 (978-1-59644-469-0(X), Hovel Audio) christianaud.

God of All Comfort. unabr. ed. Hannah Whitall Smith. Read by Susan O'Malley. (Running Time: 8 hrs. 30 mins. 0 sec.). Orig. Title: Living Confidently in God's Love. (ENG.). 2007. audio compact disk 26.98 (978-1-59644-468-3(1)) christianaud.

***God of All Comfort: Finding Your Way into His Arms.** unabr. ed. Dee Brestin. (Running Time: 5 hrs. 55 mins. 0 sec.). (ENG.). 2009. 16.99 (978-0-310-77369-6(5)) Zondervan.

God of Animals. unabr. ed. Aryn Kyle. Read by Lillian Rabe. 10 cass. (Running Time: 11 hrs.). 2007. 82.75 (978-1-4281-4233-6(9)); audio compact disk 123.75 (978-1-4281-4235-0(5)) Recorded Bks.

God of Animals: A Novel. abr. ed. Aryn Kyle. 2007. 17.95 (978-0-7435-6155-6(4)) Pub: S&S Audio. Dist(s): S and S Inc

God of Animals: A Novel. unabr. ed. Aryn Kyle. 2007. 29.95 (978-0-7435-6156-3(2)) Pub: S&S Audio. Dist(s): S and S Inc

God of Death. abr. ed. Barry Sadler. Read by Bruce Watson. 2 vols. (Casca Ser.: No. 2). 2002. (978-1-58807-507-9(9)) Am Pubng Inc.

God of Death. abr. ed. Barry Sadler. Read by Bruce Watson. 2 vols. (Running Time: 3 hrs.). (Casca Ser.: No. 2). 2002. 18.00 (978-1-58807-102-6(2)) Am Pubng Inc.
Casca is cursed by Jesus on Golgotha and condemned to the immortal and brutal life of a soldier. His travels lead him to the land of the Vikings, where he gathers allies, and then west to Mexico, where he encounters love, danger, and mystical religions. After being captured by the Teotec Indians, he finds himself atop a great pyramid about to be sacrificed by a priest. CASCA deems himself an almighty God, the Teotec's Quetza, but can he survive the vicious torture and unbearable pain of having a knife plunged into his chest and his heart wrenched out of his body?.

God of Death. abr. ed. Barry Sadler. Read by Bruce Watson. 2 vols. (Casca Ser.: No. 2). 2003. audio compact disk 25.00 (978-1-58807-276-4(2)); audio compact disk (978-1-58807-707-3(1)) Am Pubng Inc.

God of Heaven. Composed by Heather Sorenson. (ENG.). 2009. audio compact disk 26.99 (978-1-4234-8680-0(3), 1423486803) Pub: Shawnee Pr. Dist(s): H Leonard

God of His Fathers. Jack London. Read by John Chatty. 4 cass. (Running Time: 5 hrs. 30 min.). 1989. 24.00 incl. album. (C-98) Jimcin Record.
Tales of the frozen Northland.

God of His Fathers. unabr. ed. Jack London. 4 cass. (Running Time: 5 hrs. 30 min.). 28.00 (C-98) Jimcin Record.

God of Life. Contrib. by John Michael Talbot. Prod. by Phil Perkins. 1995. audio compact disk 6.99 (978-0-00-507746-7(X)) Pt of Grace Ent.

God of New Beginings CD Set. 4. 2004. audio compact disk 20.00 (978-1-932316-20-9(5)) Great C Pubng.

God of Our Praise. Cindy Berry. 1993. 15.98 (978-0-7673-1272-1(4)) LifeWay Christian.

God of Second Chances. unabr. ed. Don Baker. Read by Raymond Todd. 3 cass. (Running Time: 4 hrs.). 2002. 23.95 (978-0-7861-2370-4(2), 3029); audio compact disk 24.00 (978-0-7861-9382-0(4), 3029) Blckstn Audio.

God of Small Things. Arundhati Roy. Read by Donada Peters. 1998. audio compact disk 64.00 (978-0-7366-8536-8(7)) Books on Tape.

God of Small Things. unabr. ed. Arundhati Roy. Read by Donada Peters. 8 cass. (Running Time: 12 hrs.). 1998. 64.00 (978-0-7366-4162-3(9), 4665) Books on Tape.
Southern India, 1969. In the state of Kerala, twins Rahel & Esthappen fashion a childhood for themselves out of the wreckage that serves them as a family, divorced mother, live-in grandmother, brilliant but conflicted uncle. When their English cousin, Sophie Mol, comes to visit for Christmas, Rahel & Estha learn that lives can change in an instant. Tragic yet filled with hope & infinite joy, the lives of the twins echo that of their country.

God of War. unabr. ed. Marisa Silver. (Running Time: 7 hrs. 30 mins.). 2008. 24.95 (978-1-4332-1226-0(9)) Blckstn Audio.

God of War. unabr. ed. Marisa Silver. Read by Scott Brick. 6 CDs. (Running Time: 7 hrs. 30 mins.). 2008. audio compact disk 24.95 (978-1-4332-1227-7(7)) Blckstn Audio.

God of War. unabr. ed. Marisa Silver. Read by Scott Brick. (Running Time: 25200 sec.). 2008. 54.95 (978-1-4332-1224-6(2)); audio compact disk 29.95 (978-1-4332-1228-4(5)); audio compact disk & audio compact disk 60.00 (978-1-4332-1225-3(0)) Blckstn Audio.

***God of War.** unabr. ed. Matthew Stover & Robert E. Vardeman. (Running Time: 12 hrs. 0 mins.). 2010. 17.99 (978-1-4001-8721-8(4)) Tantor Media.

***God of War.** unabr. ed. Matthew Stover & Robert E. Vardeman. Narrated by Stephen Hoye. (Running Time: 10 hrs. 0 mins. 0 sec.). (ENG.). 2010. 24.99 (978-1-4001-6721-0(3)); audio compact disk 34.99 (978-1-4001-1721-5(6)); audio compact disk 69.99 (978-1-4001-4721-2(2)) Pub: Tantor Media. Dist(s): IngramPubServ

God of Weakness: How God Works Through the Weak Things of the World. John Timmer. 1996. stu. ed. 10.95 (978-1-56212-175-4(8), 150480) FaithAliveChr.

God on a Harley: A Spiritual Fable. unabr. ed. Joan Brady. 2004. 10.95 (978-0-7435-4785-7(3)) Pub: S&S Audio. Dist(s): S and S Inc

God Out of Control. Don Nori. 1 cass. 25.00 (978-1-56043-859-5(2)) Destiny Image Pubs.

God Plays All the Parts. Neville Goddard. 1 cass. (Running Time: 62 min.). 1967. 8.00 (26) J & L Pubns.
Neville taught Imagination Creates Reality. He was a powerfully influential teacher of God as Consciousness.

God Project. abr. ed. John Saul. Read by Mel Foster. 5 CDs, library ed. (Running Time: 6 hrs.). 2003. audio compact disk 74.25 (978-1-59086-878-2(1), 1590868781, BACDLib Ed); 62.25 (978-1-59086-876-8(5), 1590868765, BAudLibEd) Brilliance Audio.
Something is happening to the children of Eastbury, Massachusetts... Something that causes healthy babies to turn cold in their cribs. Something that strikes at the heart of every parent's darkest fears. Something unexplained that is taking the children, one by one. Sally Montgomery has just lost her beautiful little baby girl. Lucy and Jim Corliss, bitterly divorced, have been reunited by the sudden disappearance of their son. An entire town waits on the edge of panic for the next child to be taken. They all know there must be a reason for the terror. But no one ever expected...The God Project.

God Project. abr. ed. John Saul. Read by Mel Foster. (Running Time: 6 hrs.). 2006. audio compact disk 16.99 (978-1-4233-1569-8(3), 9781423315698, BCD Value Price) Brilliance Audio.

God Project. abr. ed. John Saul. Read by Mel Foster. (Running Time: 6 hrs.). 2006. 39.25 (978-1-4233-0080-9(7), 9781423300809, BADLE); 24.95 (978-1-4233-0079-3(3), 9781423300793, BAD); 39.25 (978-1-4233-0078-6(5), 9781423300786, Brlnc Audio MP3 Lib); audio compact disk 24.95 (978-1-4233-0077-9(7), 9781423300779, Brilliance MP3) Brilliance Audio.

God Project, Nathaniel, & Perfect Nightmare. abr. ed. John Saul. Read by Mel Foster et al. (Running Time: 18 hrs.). 2007. audio compact disk 34.95 (978-1-4233-1683-1(5), 9781423316831, BACD) Brilliance Audio.

God Rest Ye Merry Gentlemen. Contrib. by Juanita Bynum. (Soundtraks Ser.). 2007. audio compact disk 8.99 (978-5-557-56219-5(2)) Christian Wrld.

God Rest Ye Merry Gentlemen. Perf. by Praise Hymn Sound Tracks Staff. 1 cass. 1999. Provident Music.

God Rest Ye Merry Soldiers: A True Civil War Christmas Story. unabr. ed. James McIvor. (Running Time: 3 hrs. 30 mins. 0 sec.). (ENG.). 2005. audio compact disk 39.99 (978-1-4001-3173-0(1)) Pub: Tantor Media. Dist(s): IngramPubServ

God Rest Ye Merry Soldiers: A True Civil War Christmas Story. unabr. ed. James McIvor. Narrated by Michael Prichard. (Running Time: 3 hrs. 30 mins. 0 sec.). (ENG.). 2005. audio compact disk 19.99 (978-1-4001-0173-3(5)) Pub: Tantor Media. Dist(s): IngramPubServ

God Rest Ye Merry Soldiers: A True Civil War Christmas Story. unabr. ed. James McIvor. Read by Michael Prichard. 1 MP3-CE. (Running Time: 3 hrs. 30 mins. 0 sec.). (ENG.). 2005. audio compact disk 16.99 (978-1-4001-5173-8(2)) Pub: Tantor Media. Dist(s): IngramPubServ

God Revealed in His Names. Derek Prince. 2 cass. 5.95 ea. Derek Prince.
The names of God reveal the various aspects of His nature, just like the many facets of a gem.

God Save the Child. unabr. collector's ed. Robert B. Parker. Read by Michael Prichard. 6 cass. (Running Time: 6 hrs.). (Spenser Ser.). 1988. 48.00 (978-0-7366-1381-1(1), 2274) Books on Tape.
Appie Knoll is the kind of suburb where kids grow up right. But something is wrong. Fourteen year old Kevin Bartlett disappears. Everyone thinks he's run away - until the comic strip ransom note arrives. It doesn't take Spenser long to get the picture, an affluent family seething with rage, a desperate boy making strange friends, friends like Vic Harroway, body builder. Mr. Muscle is Spenser's only lead & he isn't talking, except with his fists. But when push comes to shove, when a boy's life is on the line, spenser can speak that language too.

God Save the Sweet Potato Queens. Jill Conner Browne. 2003. audio compact disk 40.00 (978-0-7366-9283-0(5)) Books on Tape.

God, Sex & the Meaning of Life. 2003. 6.95 (978-1-932631-02-9(X)); audio compact disk 6.95 (978-1-932631-05-0(4)) Ascensn Pr.

God Shines on You: Music for Young Peoples' Worship & Celebration. Mark Friedman & Janet Vogt. Read by Mark Friedman & Janet Vogt. 1 cass. (J). (gr. k-12). 1995. 11.95 (10113); audio compact disk 19.95 (10904) OR Catholic.
Readings, songs and dramatic stories for use at worship or in the classroom.

***God-Sized Vision: Revival Stories that Stretch & Stir.** Collin Hansen & John D. Woodbridge. (Running Time: 5 hrs. 41 mins. 25 sec.). (ENG.). 2010. 16.99 (978-0-310-55870-5(0)) Zondervan.

***God So Loved, He Gave: Entering the Movement of Divine Generosity.** unabr. ed. Kelly M. Kapic. Told to Justin L. Borger. (Running Time: 8 hrs. 26 mins. 10 sec.). (ENG.). 2010. 19.99 (978-0-310-39227-9(6)) Zondervan.

God So Loved the World. Camp Kirkland. 1993. audio compact disk 16.98 (978-0-7673-1286-8(4)) LifeWay Christian.

God So Loved the World. Camp Kirkland. 1993. 11.98 (978-0-7673-1315-5(1)) LifeWay Christian.

God So Loves the World. Camp Kirkland. 1993. 75.00 (978-0-7673-1271-4(6)) LifeWay Christian.

God Speaking. Contrib. by Johnathan Crumpton & J. Daniel Smith. Prod. by Ed Kee. (ENG.). 2008. audio compact disk 24.99 (978-5-557-46530-4(8), Brentwood-Benson Music) Brentwood Music.

God Speaks, Creation Listens: The Story of Beginnings. Bert Polman. (Running Time: 40 mins.). (Scripture Alive Ser.). 2000. 15.95 (978-1-56212-364-2(5), 415112) FaithAliveChr.

God Speaks Through Prophets Today. unabr. ed. Duane S. Crowther. Read by Duane S. Crowther. 1 cass. (Running Time: 60 min.). 1982. 13.98 (978-0-88290-398-9(5), 1807) Horizon Utah.
Shows how God ministered to His people through Old and New Testament times. It tells hos the Bible prophecied of future Prophets who will minister in the last days.

God Speaks Your Love Language: How to Feel & Reflect God's Love. unabr. ed. Gary Chapman. Narrated by Chris Fabry. (Running Time: 5 hrs. 58 mins. 17 sec.). (ENG.). 2009. 16.09 (978-1-60814-477-8(1)); audio compact disk 22.99 (978-1-59859-559-8(8)) Oasis Audio.

***God Strong: Exploring Spiritual Truths Every Military Wife Needs to Know.** unabr. ed. Sara Horn. (Running Time: 6 hrs. 28 mins. 55 sec.). (ENG.). 2010. 14.99 (978-0-310-77372-6(5)) Zondervan.

God Struck America-mp3. Read by Douglas Wilson et al. 2001. 15.00 (978-1-59128-371-3(X)) Canon Pr ID.

God Struck America-tape. Read by Douglas Wilson et al. 5 cass. 2001. 15.00 (978-1-59128-373-7(6)) Canon Pr ID.

God the Builder. (ENG.). (J). 2007. audio compact disk 15.00 (978-0-9769666-8-5(9)) Concord I Minis.

God the Mother. Swami Amar Jyoti. 1 cass. 1991. 9.95 (K-133) Truth Consciousness.
Divine Mother, the point from which creation happens. Awareness of our own creation. Invoking Her strength to help us.

God Wants a Powerful People. Read by Sheri Dew. 2007. audio compact disk 24.95 (978-1-59038-821-1(6)) Deseret Bk.

God Wants to Meet Your Wants. David T. Demola. 6 cass. 24.00 (S-1045) Faith Fellow Min.

God Wants You to Walk in Divine Health. David T. Demola. 4 cass. 16.00 (S-1085) Faith Fellow Min.

God Wants You Well. 4 cass. 2002. 20.00 (978-1-881541-78-3(9)) A Wommack.

God Wants You Well. Created by AWMI. 2004. audio compact disk 25.00 (978-1-59548-040-8(4)) A Wommack.

God Wants You Well. Gloria Copeland. 2 cass. (Running Time: 2 hrs.). 1994. 10.00 (978-0-88114-961-6(6), TKC-10) K Copeland Pubns.
Biblical teaching on healing.

God Wants Your Body: Discovering God's Will for Your Life. Ken Davis. 1 cass. (Running Time: 1 hr. 30 min.). 2000. 9.99 (978-1-886463-90-5(5)) Oasis Audio.
Does it seem that God is playing games, leaving you to guess what He wants out of you? With humor & insight.

God Was Just Practicing When He Made Men. Kathryn Tucker Windham. (What Makes Us Southerners Ser.: Vol. 5). 2002. 12.00 (978-0-87483-661-5(1)); audio compact disk 16.95 (978-0-87483-662-2(X)) Pub: August Hse. Dist(s): Natl Bk Netwk

God Who Hung on the Cross: How God Uses Ordinary People to Build His Church. unabr. ed. Dois I. Rosser & Ellen Vaughn. Read by Grover, Pam and Gardner Ward. (Running Time: 5.5 hrs. 0 mins.). 2008. audio compact disk 19.95 (978-1-4332-7062-8(5)) Blckstn Audio.

God Who Hung on the Cross: How God Uses Ordinary People to Build His Church. unabr. ed. Dois I. Rosser, Jr. & Ellen Vaughn. (Running Time: 7 hrs. NaN mins.). 2008. 44.95 (978-1-4332-5454-3(9)); audio compact disk 60.00 (978-1-4332-5455-0(7)) Blckstn Audio.

God Who Hung on the Cross: How God Uses Ordinary People to Build His Church. unabr. ed. Dois I. Rosser, Jr. & Ellen Vaughn. (Running Time: 5.5 hrs. 0 mins.). 2008. 29.95 (978-1-4332-5456-7(5)) Blckstn Audio.

God Who Is More Than Enough. Mac Hammond. 1 cass. 1996. 12.00 (978-1-57399-033-2(7)) Mac Hammond.
Teaching on God supplying your needs.

God Who Truly Is/Love Is How I Got to Here, Vol. 1. Adi Da Samraj. 2001. audio compact disk 24.95 (978-1-57097-119-8(6)) Dawn Horse Pr.

God Will Do the Rest: 7 Keys to the Desires of Your Heart. unabr. ed. Catherine Galasso-Vigorito. Read by Catherine Galasso-Vigorito. (Running Time: 8 hrs. 5 mins.). (ENG.). 2009. 27.98 (978-1-59659-463-0(2), GildAudio) Pub: Gildan Media. Dist(s): HachBkGrp

God Will Do the Rest: 7 Keys to the Desires of Your Heart. unabr. ed. Catherine Galasso-Vigorito. Read by Catherine Galasso-Vigorito. (Running Time: 8 hrs.). (ENG.). 2009. audio compact disk 29.98 (978-1-59659-341-1(5), GildAudio) Pub: Gildan Media. Dist(s): HachBkGrp

God Will Make a Way. Henry Cloud & John Townsend.Tr. of Dios lo Hara. 2004. audio compact disk 17.99 (978-1-59145-101-3(9)) Nelson.

God Will Make a Way. Contrib. by Don Moen. (iWorship Ser.). 2003. audio compact disk 9.98 (978-5-550-25970-2(2)) Integrity Music.

God Will Make a Way Personal Discovery Guide: What to Do When You Don't Know What to Do. unabr. ed. Henry Cloud & John Townsend. 2 cass. (Running Time: 2 hrs.). (Songs 4 Worship Ser.). 2002. 17.99 (978-1-59145-025-2(X)) Nelson.

God Will Show Up. Steve Thompson. 1 cass. (Running Time: 90 mins.). (He Still Heals Ser.: Vol. 1). 2000. 5.00 (SAO1-001) Morning NC.
Learn about the healing power of God that is available to believers today.

God with the Wind. (Paws & Tales Ser.: Vol. 9). (J). 2001. 3.99 (978-1-57972-402-3(7)); audio compact disk 5.99 (978-1-57972-403-0(5)) Insight Living.

God with Us. Contrib. by MercyMe. (Sound Performance Soundtracks Ser.). 2007. audio compact disk 5.98 (978-5-557-51417-0(1)); audio compact disk 9.98 (978-5-557-49939-2(3)) Pt of Grace Ent.

God with Us: The Christmas Message from the Gospels. Bert Polman. (Running Time: 1 hr.). (Scripture Alive Ser.). 1998. 15.95 (978-1-56212-363-5(7), 415108) FaithAliveChr.

God Wrote Your Scenario. Derek Prince. 1 cass. (B-4131) Derek Prince.

God You Worship: Logos June 20, 1999. Ben Young. 1999. 4.95 (978-0-7417-6138-5(6), B0138) Win Walk.

God You're Looking For. Bill Hybels. 1997. bk. 15.99 (978-0-7852-7157-4(0)) Nelson.
An audio for those who hunger for a loving God. Listeners will be shown the fulfilling relationship between God & the committed follower.

Goddess & the Moon. Shirley Chenoweth. 1 cass. 1992. 8.95 (1019) Am Fed Astrologers.

Goddess & the Skylark: Dancing through the Word Labyrinth. Nordette Adams & Aberjhani. Perf. by Nordette Adams & Aberjhani. Music by Mark "Rahkyt" Rockeymoore. Mark "Rahkyt" Rockeymoore. (ENG.). 2008. audio compact disk 11.95 (978-0-9662356-3-0(0)) Black Skylark.

Goddess in My Shoes. Rickie Moore. 2 cass. (Running Time: 2 hrs.). 17.95 (978-0-89334-124-4(X)) Humanics Pub Grp.

Goddess of Yesterday. unabr. ed. Caroline B. Cooney. Read by Christina Moore. 6 cass. (Running Time: 9 hrs.). 2003. 54.00 (978-1-4025-4669-3(6)) Recorded Bks.

Goddess Spirituality. 1 cass. (Running Time: 29 min.). 9.95 (IO-170, HarperThor) HarpC GBR.

Goddess Trilogy, Vol. 7. Jane Williams & Northwestern University Staff. Ed. by Michael Buritt. Tr. by Gail Williams. 1998. audio compact disk 18.00 (978-0-8101-3708-0(9)) Pub: Northwestern U Pr. Dist(s): Chicago Distribution Ctr

Goddesses & Angels: Awakening Your Inner High-Priestess & Source-Eress. abr. ed. Doreen Virtue. Read by Doreen Virtue. 4 CDs. 2006. audio compact disk 23.95 (978-1-4019-1070-9(X)) Hay House.

Goddesses & Gods in Every Artist. Jean S. Bolen. 1 cass. 9.00 (A0338-88) Sound Photosyn.
A Jungian therapist's interpretation, presented at the Embodying the Spiritual in the Art of the Future symposium.

Goddesses & Gods of Ancient Europe. Marija Gimbutas. 1 cass. 9.00 (A0334-88) Sound Photosyn.
With slides, at the Embodying the Spiritual in the Art of the Future Symposium, Gimbutas concisely runs through her groundbreaking work relating to the period of 6500 B.C. to 2500 B.C.

Goddesses As Feminine Personifications of the Self. Read by Caroline Stevens. 1 cass. (Running Time: 90 min.). 1984. 10.95 (978-0-7822-0301-1(9), 149) C G Jung IL.

Goddesses in Everywoman. Read by Jean Shinoda Bolen. 3 cass. (Running Time: 4 hrs.). 1985. 24.95 Set. (978-0-7822-0021-8(4), 161) C G Jung IL.

Godfather. abr. ed. Mario Puzo. Narrated by Joe Mantegna. 4 cass. (Running Time: 6 hrs.). 1998. 24.95 Set. (978-1-882071-84-5(0)) B-B Audio.

Godfather. abr. ed. Mario Puzo. 1 CD MP3. (Running Time: 8 hrs.). 2001. audio compact disk 39.95 (978-0-929071-79-4(4)) B-B Audio.
The Godfather is a supercharged account of a family that uses guns, axes, and the psychology of fear to achieve dominance over the whole Mafia network in the United States. The Godfather is Don Vito Corleone, a Sicilian-American patriarch, already one.

Godfather. abr. ed. Mario Puzo. Narrated by Joe Mantegna. 7 CDs. (Running Time: 8 hrs.). 2001. audio compact disk 39.95 (978-0-929071-69-5(7)) B-B Audio.

Godfather. unabr. ed. Mario Puzo. Read by Multivoice Production Staff. 10 cass. (Running Time: 14 hrs.). 2001. 29.95 (978-1-58788-772-7(X), 158788772X, BAU) Brilliance Audio.
The Godfather is an extraordinary novel which has become a modern day classic. Puzo pulls us inside the violent society of the Mafia and its gang wars. The leader, Vito Corleone, is the Godfather. He is a benevolent despot who stops at nothing to gain and hold power. His command post is a fortress on Long Island from which he presides over a vast underground empire that includes the rackets, gambling, bookmaking, and unions. His influence runs through all levels of American society, from the cop on the beat to the nation's mighty. Mario Puzo, a master storyteller, introduces us to unforgettable characters, and the elements of this world explode to life in this violent and impassioned chronicle.

Godfather. unabr. ed. Mario Puzo. Read by Full Cast Production Staff. (Running Time: 50400 sec.). 2004. audio compact disk 39.25 (978-1-59335-345-2(6), 1593353456, Brlnc Audio MP3 Lib) Brilliance Audio.

Godfather. unabr. ed. Mario Puzo. (Running Time: 14 hrs.). 2004. 24.95 (978-1-59710-325-1(X), 159710325X, BAD) Brilliance Audio.

Godfather. unabr. ed. Mario Puzo. Read by Multivoice Production Staff. (Running Time: 14 hrs.). 2004. 39.25 (978-1-59710-324-4(1), 1597103241, BADLE) Brilliance Audio.

Godfather. unabr. ed. Mario Puzo. 12 CDs. (Running Time: 14 hrs.). 2004. audio compact disk 39.95 (978-1-59600-243-2(3), 1596002433) Brilliance Audio.

Godfather. unabr. ed. Mario Puzo. Read by Multivoice Production Staff. (Running Time: 14 hrs.). 2004. audio compact disk 112.25 (978-1-59600-244-9(1), 1596002441, BriAudCD Unabrid) Brilliance Audio.

Godfather. unabr. ed. Mario Puzo. 1 MP3-CD. (Running Time: 14 hrs.). 2004. 24.95 (978-1-59335-005-5(8), 1593350058) Soulmate Audio Bks.

Godfather. unabr. collector's ed. Mario Puzo. Read by Grover Gardner. 11 cass. (Running Time: 16 hrs. 30 min.). 1993. 88.00 (978-0-7366-2386-5(8), 3157) Books on Tape.
The deadliest Mafioso rules a vast empire of extortion, gambling & unions without ever touching a gun.

Godfather Pack: The Godfather & Frank Sinatra: An American Legend. unabr. abr. ed. Mario Puzo & Nancy Sinatra. Read by Nancy Sinatra & Joe Mantegna. 2 cass. (Running Time: 3 hrs.). 2001. 34.95 (978-0-929071-26-8(3)) B-B Audio.
Plugn Play Travelpaks contain everything your customers will need for many hours of audiobook listening. 2 Fantastic Audiobooks with1 Portable Cassette Player plus1 Comfortable Headset plus 2 Batteriers GODFATHER PAK: 11 HoursTHE GODFATHER By Mari.

Godfather Returns: The Saga of the Family Corleone. unabr. ed. Mark Winegardner. 12 cass. (Running Time: 18 hrs.). 2004. 96.00 (978-1-4159-0364-3(6)); audio compact disk 115.60 (978-1-4159-0496-1(0)) Pub: Books on Tape. Dist(s): NetLibrary CO
The Godfater Returns begins in 1955, with the story of the "year of delicate political maneuvering" that ended Mario Puzo's the Godfather. Winegardner vividly brings to life the missing chapters in the story of the Family Corleone by describing the event.

Godfather's Revenge. unabr. ed. Mark Winegardner. Read by Scott Brick. 8 cass. (Running Time: 12 hrs.). 2006. 72.00 (978-1-4159-3458-6(4)); audio compact disk 90.00 (978-1-4159-3459-3(2)) Books on Tape.

***Godforsaken: Bad Things Happen. Is there a God who cares? Yes. Here's Proof.** unabr. ed. Dinesh D'Souza. (ENG.). 2011. 14.98 (978-1-61045-056-0(6)); audio compact disk 26.98 (978-1-61045-055-3(8)) christianaud.

Godkinz. Contrib. by Godkinz. 2007. audio compact disk 13.98 (978-5-557-52314-1(6)) Syntax AUS.

Godless: The Church of Liberalism. abr. ed. Ann Coulter. Read by Ann Coulter. (Running Time: 21600 sec.). (ENG.). 2007. audio compact disk 14.99 (978-0-7393-4310-4(6), Random AudioBks) Pub: Random Audio Pubg. Dist(s): Random

Godless Man. unabr. ed. Paul C. Doherty. Read by Terry Wale. 10 cass. (Soundings Ser.). 2006. 84.95 (978-1-84559-196-0(8)) Pub: ISIS Lrg Prnt GBR. Dist(s): Ulverscroft US

Godly Leadership. Speeches. Joel Osteen. 10 audio cass. (J). 2001. 40.00 (978-1-931877-12-1(2)); audio compact disk 40.00 (978-1-931877-29-9(7)) J Osteen.

Godly Man or Peter Pan. Speeches. 1 CD, 1 Cass. (Running Time: 1 hrs., 65 mins.). (SPA.). 2003. audio compact disk (978-0-9746329-1-9(0)) J Molina.
The instructions for developing Godly character is the foundation of this series. Godly Man or Peter Pan is a message directed at a grave dilema facing men all over the world. Upon hearing this selection men will have the foundation pattern and model to follow in order to achieve a true Godly Character.

Godly Mother: Provl 31; 11 Sam. 21. Ed Young. 1993. 4.95 (978-0-7417-1968-3(1), 968) Win Walk.

Godly Mother: 1 Samuel 2:1-2. Ed Young. (J). 1983. 4.95 (978-0-7417-1298-1(9), 298) Win Walk.

Godly Woman or Wicked Witch. 2003. audio compact disk (978-0-9746329-2-6(9)) J Molina.

Godplayer. unabr. ed. Robin Cook. Read by Donada Peters. 6 cass. (Running Time: 9 hrs.). 1993. 48.00 (978-0-7366-2387-2(6), 3158) Books on Tape.
Boston doctor suspects hospital staffer is behind a series of mysterious deaths. Could it be her husband.

God's Abundance. Derek Prince. 4 cass. 23.80 Set. (087-088-089-090) Derek Prince.
How my we appropriate God's abundance for every area of our lives - & then use it for purposes He has intended?.

Gods & Generals. abr. ed. Jeff Shaara. 4 cass. (Running Time: 4 hrs). 2000. 23.50 (978-0-375-45188-1(9), Random AudioBks) Random Audio Pubg.

Gods & Generals. unabr. collector's ed. Read by Dick Estell. Photos by Jeff Shaara. 13 cass. (Running Time: 19 hrs. 30 min.). 1988. 104.00 (978-0-7366-4240-8(4), 4741) Books on Tape.
The men who led the fight at the Battle of Gettysburg.

Gods Answer Is You. Rita Twiggs. 1 cass. (Running Time: 60 mins.). 2001. 5.99 (978-0-88368-246-3(X), 77246X) Pub: Whitaker Hse. Dist(s): Anchor Distributors

God's Answer to Anxiety. David T. Demola. 4 cass. 16.00 (S-1064) Faith Fellow Min.

God's Answers to Man's Questions. unabr. ed. William MacDonald. Read by William MacDonald. 1 cass. (Running Time: 1 hr. 13 min.). (Upward Call Ser.: Vol. 2). 1995. 8.95 (978-0-9629152-5-3(4)) Lumen Prodns.
Biblical answers to 190 questions most frequently asked by people seeking God.

Gods Are Athirst. Anatole France. Read by Laura García. (Running Time: 3 hrs.). 2002. 16.95 (978-1-60083-231-4(8), Audiofy Corp) Iofy Corp.

Gods Are Athirst, unabr. ed. Anatole France. Read by Flo Gibson. 5 cass. (Running Time: 7 hrs. 30 min.). (gr. 6-12). 1997. 20.95 (978-1-55685-475-0(7), 475-7) Audio Bk Con.
The lives of artists, nobles, commoners & members of the Revolutionary Tribunal during the Reign of Terror in Paris, with the guillotine playing a major role, are dealt with vividly to reveal the author's world.

God's Armorbearer, Vol. 1 & 2 Audio Seminar. Terry Nance. 2009. audio compact disk 34.99 (978-0-7684-2761-5(4)) Destiny Image Pubs.

God's Armorbearer, Vol. 3 Audio Seminar. Terry Nance. 2009. audio compact disk 34.99 (978-0-7684-2762-2(2)) Destiny Image Pubs.

God's Army. Jack Deere. 1 cass. (Running Time: 90 mins.). (Loving God & Hating Evil Ser.: Vol. 2). 2000. 5.00 (JD05-002) Morning NC.
The teaching contained in this miniseries can change your life & strengthen your relationship with God.

God's Army: Fit Through Few. 1979. 4.95 (978-0-7417-1004-8(8)) Win Walk.

God's Battalions: The Case for the Crusades. unabr. ed. Rodney Stark. Narrated by David Drummond. (Running Time: 8 hrs. 0 mins. 0 sec.). (ENG.). 2009. 19.99 (978-1-4001-6470-7(2)); audio compact disk 29.99 (978-1-4001-1470-2(5)); audio compact disk 59.99 (978-1-4001-4470-9(1)) Pub: Tantor Media. Dist(s): IngramPubServ

***God's Battalions: The Case for the Crusades.** unabr. ed. Rodney Stark. Narrated by David Drummond. (Running Time: 8 hrs. 0 mins.). 2009. 29.99 (978-1-4001-9470-4(9)); 15.99 (978-1-4001-8470-5(3)) Tantor Media.

God's Been Good! Contrib. by Theola Booker & Greater St Matthew Choir. Prod. by Marty Harvey. Contrib. by Assured Blessings Ministry & Herman Burroughs. (Running Time: 60 min.). 2002. audio compact disk 16.98 (978-5-550-14855-6(2)) Pub: Pt of Grace Ent. Dist(s): STL Dist NA

Gods Behaving Badly. abr. ed. Marie Phillips. Read by Tom Sellwood. (Running Time: 6 hrs.). (ENG.). 2007. 24.98 (978-1-60024-073-7(9)) Pub: Hachet Audio. Dist(s): HachBkGrp

God's Big Idea. Myles Munroe. Read by Carey Conley. (ENG.). 2008. 24.99 (978-1-4245-0867-9(3)) Tre Med Inc.

God's Big Idea Audio Book: Reclaiming God's Original Purpose for Your Life. Myles Munroe. 2008. 34.99 (978-0-7684-2731-8(2)) Destiny Image Pubs.

God's Blueprint for Your Life: Knowing God's Will Series. Ben Young. 2000. 4.95 (978-0-7417-6200-9(5), B0200) Win Walk.

God's Boundaries for Abundant Living CD Series. 2005. audio compact disk 48.00 (978-1-59834-047-1(6)) Walk Thru the Bible.

God's Call to Fast. George Maloney. Read by George Maloney. 1 cass. (Running Time: 68 min.). 8.95 Credence Commun.
Discusses an approach to fasting as a total experience - physical, psychic & spiritual.

***God's Choice.** abr. ed. George Weigel. Read by George Weigel. (ENG.). 2005. (978-0-06-111732-9(3), Harper Audio); (978-0-06-111731-2(5), Harper Audio) HarperCollins Pubs.

God's Choice: Pope Benedict XVI & the Future of the Catholic Church. abr. ed. George Weigel. Read by George Weigel. (Running Time: 27000 sec.). 2005. audio compact disk 29.95 (978-0-06-088195-5(X)) HarperCollins Pubs.

God's Comfort: Bible Passages Which Bring Strength & Hope in Times of Suffering. abr. ed. 2006. 5.95 (978-0-7435-5573-9(2), Sound Ideas) Pub: S&S Audio. Dist(s): S and S Inc

God's Comfort: Bible Passages Which Bring Strength & Hope in Times of Suffering. abr. ed. Created by Simon and Schuster Staff. (Running Time: 1 hr. 0 mins. 0 sec.). (ENG.). 2006. audio compact disk 7.95 (978-0-7435-5450-3(7)) Pub: S&S Audio. Dist(s): S and S Inc

God's Complete Plan. Elbert Willis. 1 cass. (Because of Calvary Ser.). 4.00 Fill the Gap.

God's Country & the Woman. unabr. ed. James Oliver Curwood. Read by Laurie Klein. 6 cass. (Running Time: 7 hrs. 18 min.). Dramatization. 1992. 39.95 (978-1-55686-433-9(7), 433) Books in Motion.
Deep in the Canadian wilderness, Philip Weyman agrees to help a beautiful woman in her fight against a band of outlaws & cutthroats who are trying to take her land.

God's Covenant of Exchange. Creflo A. Dollar. 4 cass. (Running Time: 6 hrs.). 2000. 20.00 (978-1-931172-62-2(5), TS275, Kidz Faith) Pub: Creflo Dollar. Dist(s): STL Dist NA

God's Covenant with Your Family. Gary V. Whetstone. 4 cass. (Running Time: 6 hrs.). (Family & Relationships Ser.). 1997. bk. 35.00 (978-1-58866-227-9(6), VA007A) Gary Whet Pub.
Did you know that God's covenant with us has both blessings & curses that not only affect you, but also your family? This series details all the benefits & influences.

God's Creative Power Gift Collection. gif. ed. Narrated by Charles Capps. 3 CDs. (Running Time: 3 hrs. 45 mins). 2006. audio compact disk 19.95 (978-0-9747513-5-1(9)) Capps Pubng.

God's Crucible: Islam & the Making of Europe, 570-1215. David Levering Lewis. Read by Richard Allen. (Playaway Adult Nonfiction Ser.). 2008. 69.99 (978-1-60640-869-8(0)) Find a World.

God's Debris: A Thought Experiment. (ENG., (C). 2009. 5.95 (978-0-615-31710-6(3)) SAdams.

God's Dilemma. Ben Young. 2000. 4.95 (978-0-7417-6185-9(8), B0185) Win Walk.

God's Disguises. Derek Prince. 1 cass. 5.95 (I-045) Derek Prince.
God usually approaches man in forms which cloak His divinity. It is important to penetrate his disguises.

God's Divine Favor. Speeches. Joel Osteen. 1 Cass. (Running Time: 30 Mins.). (J). 2000. 6.00 (978-1-59349-068-3(2), JA0068) J Osteen.

God's Divine Favor, Pt. 2. Short Stories. Joel Osteen. 1 Cass. (Running Time: 30 Mins.). (J). 2000. 6.00 (978-1-59349-069-0(0), JA0069) J Osteen.

God's Dream for Man. Gloria Copeland. 2 cass. 1987. 10.00 Set. (978-0-88114-927-2(6)) K Copeland Pubns.
Biblical teaching on God's will for man.

God's Dream for Your Life. Speeches. Joel Osteen. 1 Cass. (Running Time: 30 Mins.). (J). 2000. 6.00 (978-1-59349-066-9(6), JA0066) J Osteen.

God's Dwelling Place. Kelley Varner. 8 cass. 1992. 42.00 Set. (978-0-938612-76-6(X)) Destiny Image Pubs.

***God's Economy: Redefining the Health & Wealth Gospel.** unabr. ed. Jonathan Wilson-Hartgrove. (Running Time: 4 hrs. 39 mins. 0 sec.). (ENG.). 2009. 14.99 (978-0-310-77365-8(2)) Zondervan.

God's Eternal Plan of Salvation. unabr. ed. Duane S. Crowther. Read by Duane S. Crowther. 1 cass. (Running Time: 60 min.). 1982. 13.98 (978-0-88290-397-2(7), 1806) Horizon Utah.
Draws from the Bible to answer such questions as Did I live before birth? What is the purpose of mortal life? What happens when I die? What are my eternal possibilities if I am righteous?.

God's Eternal Program. Michael Pearl. 1 CD. (ENG.). 2006. audio compact disk 6.95 (978-1-892112-54-5(X)) Pub: No Greater Joy. Dist(s): STL Dist NA

God's Family: Logos 11/29/98. Ben Young. 1998. 4.95 (978-0-7417-6109-5(2), B0109) Win Walk.

God's Favorite Word: Revelation 22:17. Ed Young. 1980. 4.95 (978-0-7417-1137-3(0), A0137) Win Walk.

God's Financial Harvest Plan. Gary V. Whetstone. 5 cass. (Running Time: 7 hrs. 30 mins.). (Finance Ser.). 1998. 40.00 (978-1-58866-237-8(3), V1010A) Gary Whet Pub.
God has a plan to bless your finances, but it is conditional upon your faith in & obedience to His Word.

Gods Fought Above Troy & Are Still Fighting. Manly P. Hall. 8.95 (978-0-89314-125-7(9), C880605) Philos Res.
Explains philosophy & religion.

God's Future Dealings With Man: Lessons 37-52. 10 cass. (Running Time: 10 hrs.). 2000. 42.99 (978-1-55829-155-3(5)) Dake Publishing.
Two future world empires, the beast with seven heads & ten horns heaven & the resurrections, rapture & the second advent, Where are the dead? - immortality, seven judgments, hell, Daniel expounded,110 prophetic future earthly wonders, Armageddon, the millennium, the new heavens & new earth &much more.

God's Gift to Our Generation. Kingsley Fletcher. 2 cass. 1992. 12.00 Set. (978-0-938612-87-2(5)) Destiny Image Pubs.

God's Glory. (Dovetales Ser.: Tape 9). pap. bk. 6.95 (978-0-944391-44-0(3)); 4.95 (978-0-944391-24-2(9)) DonWise Prodns.

God's Grace. Interview with Mother Angelica. Contrib. by Kenneth Roberts. 1 cass. (Running Time: 60 min.). (Mother Angelica Live Ser.). 10.00 (978-1-55794-058-2(4), T9) Eternal Wrd TV.

God's Grace: His Remarkable Gift to Those Who Lean on Him, Set. Mac Hammond. 7 cass. (Running Time: 7 hrs.). 2000. (978-1-57399-098-1(1)) Mac Hammond.
The message of scripture is clear. God's grace, His supernatural favor, is more than enough to take you through any trouble you might face in life.

God's Grace from Ground Zero. unabr. ed. Jim Cymbala. 2002. audio compact disk 19.99 (978-0-310-24733-3(0)) Zondervan.

God's Grace from Ground Zero. unabr. ed. Jim Cymbala & Sorenson. 2 cass. (Running Time: 2 hrs.). 2002. 17.99 (978-0-310-24686-2(5)) Zondervan.
In the face of unspeakable tragedy, God is reaching out to the heart of a grieving city, to the people of a wounded nation, and to a world that fears what the future may hold. Cymbala urges us that in the midst of our grief, our fear, and our lack of answers for things that make no sense, it is time to worship God with all our hearts and trust him like never before.

God's Great Love. Contrib. by Lari Goss. 1996. 24.95 (978-0-00-513349-1(1), 75608526) Pub: Brentwood Music. Dist(s): H Leonard

God's Great Love for You. Caryl Krueger. Read by Caryl Krueger. 2 cass. (Running Time: 3 hrs.). 2001. 17.00 Belleridge.
You are God's beloved, never for a moment separated from His care. Hear of God's love from the time of early history, through examples from the Old and New Testaments, right up to present stories of those who feel God's love in action.

God's Greatest Blessing to Man. Kenneth Copeland. 8 cass. 1982. bk. 40.00 Set incl. study guide. (978-0-938458-22-7(1)) K Copeland Pubns.
Discovering God's greatest blessing.

God's Greatest Requirement - Obedience. Kingsley Fletcher. 1 cass. 1992. 7.00 (978-0-938612-92-6(1)) Destiny Image Pubs.

***God's Guest List: Welcoming Those Who Influence Our Lives.** unabr. ed. Debbie Macomber. (Running Time: 5 hrs. 0 mins. 0 sec.). (ENG.). 2010. audio compact disk 24.99 (978-1-4423-3802-9(4)) Pub: S&S Audio. Dist(s): S and S Inc

God's Harvard: A Christian College on a Mission to Save America. unabr. ed. Hanna Rosin. (Running Time: 34200 sec.). 2007. 65.95 (978-1-4332-0360-2(X)); audio compact disk 81.00 (978-1-4332-0361-9(8)) Blckstn Audio.

God's Harvard: A Christian College on a Mission to Save America. unabr. ed. Hanna Rosin. Read by Bernadette Dunne. (Running Time: 34200 sec.). 2007. 29.95 (978-1-4332-0362-6(6)); audio compact disk 29.95 (978-1-4332-0363-3(4)); audio compact disk 29.95 (978-1-4332-0364-0(2)) Blckstn Audio.

God's Healing Love. unabr. ed. Swami Amar Jyoti. 1 cass. (Running Time: 1 hr. 30 min.). (Satsangs of Swami Amar Jyoti Ser.). 1998. 9.95 (978-0-933572-36-2(0), K164) Truth Consciousness.
God's Love purifies & saves us, solves all problems, gives peace, relaxation & healing. Loving, rather than wanting to be loved.

Gods Healing Word. Creflo A. Dollar. (ENG.). 2002. 5.00 (978-1-59089-133-9(3)) Pub: Creflo Dollar. Dist(s): STL Dist NA

God's Healing Word. Speeches. Creflo A. Dollar. 1 cass. (Running Time: 1 hr. 20 mins.). 1994. audio compact disk 7.00 (978-1-59089-134-6(1)) Creflo Dollar.

God's Health Care Plan. Chuck Schiappacasse. 3 cass. (Running Time: 3 hrs. 30 min.). 1995. 15.95 Set. (978-0-9635913-2-6(0)) C Schiappacasse.

God's Heart for Healing. Steve Thompson. 1 cass. (Running Time: 90 mins.). (Power of Suffering Ser.: Vol. 1). 2000. 5.00 (ST04-001) Morning NC.
Steve's messages offer helpful instruction on an often misunderstood pathway which can release spiritual power in our lives.

God's High Calling for Women. John MacArthur, Jr. 4 cass. 15.95 (20152, HarperThor) HarpC GBR.

God's Historical Dealings with Man Pt. II: Lessons 9-18. 10 cass. (Running Time: 10 hrs.). 2000. 42.99 (978-1-55829-153-9(9)) Dake Publishing.
The Ante-Diluvian Age - its two dispensations, God's plan for the needs of man & why it is not realized, the Post-Diluvian Age - its four dispensations, giants before & after the flood of Noah also divine healing & divine health-asking & receiving, the times of the Gentiles-eight world empires & law & grace & the old Testament Church.

***God's Ideal Marriage.** 2010. audio compact disk (978-0-9826360-2-2(4)) Mid A Bks & Tapes.

Gods in Alabama. unabr. ed. Joshilyn Jackson. Read by Catherine Taber. (ENG.). 2005. 14.98 (978-1-59483-161-4(0)) Pub: Hachet Audio. Dist(s): HachBkGrp

Gods in Alabama. unabr. ed. Joshilyn Jackson. Read by Catherine Taber. (Running Time: 7 hrs.). (ENG.). 2009. 49.98 (978-1-60788-039-4(3)) Pub: Hachet Audio. Dist(s): HachBkGrp

Gods in Everyman. Read by Jean Shinoda Bolen. 5 cass. (Running Time: 6 hrs.). 1987. 37.95 Set. (978-0-7822-0022-5(2), 298) C G Jung IL.

Gods in Everyman. unabr. ed. Jean Shinoda Bolen. Read by Jean Shinoda Bolen. 6 cass. (Running Time: 7 hrs. 55 min.). 1987. 56.00 Set. (11601) Big Sur Tapes.
Topics include the Greek gods - Zeus, Poseidon, Apollo, Hermes Dionysus & others - whose myths provide insights into patterns that occur in everyone, which are most prominent in the lives of men.

God's Invisible Army. Dan Corner. 1 cass. 3.00 (36) Evang Outreach.

God's Kids Worship: Green/Blue. Bob Singleton. 2 CDs. (Running Time: 2 hrs.). (J). 2003. audio compact disk 19.99 (978-1-4003-0231-4(5)) Nelson.
A collection of today's top Praise and Worship recording produced for and sung by kids 8-14 years old.

God's Kids Worship: Orange/Red. Bob Singleton. 2 CDs. (Running Time: 2 hrs.). (J). 2003. audio compact disk 19.99 (978-1-4003-0232-1(3)) Nelson.
A collection of today's top Praise and Worship recordings produced for and sung by kids 8-14 years old.

God's Kids Worship Blue. unabr. ed. Created by Bob Singleton. (Running Time: 45 mins.). 2002. audio compact disk 10.99 (978-1-4003-0048-8(7)) Nelson.
God_s Kids Worship is a new collection of today_s top Praise & Worship recordings produced for and sung by kids 8-14 years old. Each all-new recording of God_s Kids Worship: Blue, Green, Red, and Orange will feature the most popular songs kids are already singing in church today. Included on these recordings are all of the top 25 and most of the top 100 of today_s most popular Praise & Worship songs as established by Christian Copyright Licensing International. Each recording also includes at least six hymns and traditional songs. Perfect for at home listening or sing-alongs at Sunday School, children_s church, small group, and backyard Bible clubs. Produced by four-time Children_s Album Dove nominee and multi-platinum Grammy nominee, Bob Singleton. Songs included on God_s Kids Worship: Blue 1. He Has Made Me Glad 2. Shout to the Lord 3. Blessed Assurance 4. His Eye is on the Sparrow 5. Rejoice in the Lord Always 6. King of Kings 7. Majesty 8. He Who Began a Good Work in You 9. Thou Art Worthy 10. Down in My Heart 11. Oh, For a Thousand Tongues 12. Cast Your Burden 13. I Could Sing of Your Love Forever 14. Give Me Jesus 15. Holy, Holy, Holy 16. Cry of My Heart 17. Bless His Holy Name 18. Come, Christians, Join to Sing 19. From the Rising of the Sun 20. Blessed Be the Name of the Lord.

God's Kids Worship Green. unabr. ed. Created by Bob Singleton. (Running Time: 45 mins.). (J). 2002. audio compact disk 10.99 (978-1-4003-0049-5(5)) Nelson.

God's Kids Worship Red. unabr. ed. Created by Bob Singleton. (Running Time: 45 mins.). (J). 2002. audio compact disk 10.99 (978-1-4003-0050-1(9)) Nelson.

God's Kind of Love. Andrew Wommack. 3 cass. (Running Time: 4 hrs. 30 min.). set. (978-1-881541-16-5(9), 1015) A Wommack.
Before we can love others, we have to have a true revelation of God's love for us. We can't give what we haven't received. This tape series will help you receive a deeper revelation of God's unconditional love for you.

God's Kind of Love: The Cure for What Ails Ya! Andrew Wommack. 3. 2004. audio compact disk 21.00 (978-1-881541-88-2(6)) A Wommack.

God's Kind of Love Through You. Created by Awmi. (ENG.). 2008. audio compact disk 60.00 (978-1-59548-110-8(9)) A Wommack.

God's Kind of Love to You. Created by AWMI. (ENG.). 2007. audio compact disk 30.00 (978-1-59548-108-5(7)) A Wommack.

God's Kiss: Mrs. Seebo's Classics. Donna Seebo. Read by Donna Seebo. 1 cass. (Running Time: 15 min.). (J). (ps-6). 1993. 9.95 (978-1-883164-02-7(8)) Delphi Intl.
A story about a child's dream journey to a valley where children & animals from all over the world have gathered for a very special happening called "God's Kiss".

God's Kiss: Mrs. Seebo's Classics. Donna D. Seebo. Read by Donna D. Seebo. Illus. by Ed Gedrose. 1 cass. (Running Time: 15 min.). (J). (gr. k-6). 1993. bk. 19.95 (978-1-883164-03-4(6)) Delphi Intl.

God's Last Word: An Exposition of Hebrews, Album 1. Derek Prince. 6 cass. 29.95 (A-GLW1) Derek Prince.

God's Last Word: An Exposition of Hebrews, Album 2. Derek Prince. 6 cass. 29.95 (A-GLW2) Derek Prince.

God's Last Word: An Exposition of Hebrews, Album 3. Derek Prince. 6 cass. 29.95 (A-GLW3) Derek Prince.

God's Last Word: An Exposition of Hebrews, Album 4. Derek Prince. 5 cass. 24.95 (A-GLW4) Derek Prince.

God's Latest Scribe? Neale Donald Walsch. 2009. audio compact disk 19.95 (978-1-4019-2585-7(5), 1068) Hay House.

God's Law (Love) Redeems & Restores; It Does Not Condemn. unabr. ed. Myrtle Smith. Prod. by David Keyston. 1 cass. (Running Time: 1 hrs. 32 min.). (Myrtle Smyth Audiotapes Ser.). 1998. , CD. (978-1-893107-11-3(6), M11, Cross & Crown) Healing Unltd.

God's Little Acre. unabr. ed. Erskine Caldwell. Read by John MacDonald. 5 cass. (Running Time: 7 hrs. 30 min.). 1996. 39.95 (978-0-7861-0926-5(2), 1681) Blckstn Audio.
Chronicles the final decline of a white family in rural Georgia. Exhorted by their patriarch Ty Ty, the Waldens ruin their land by digging it up in search of gold. Complex sexual entanglements & betrayals lead to a murder within the family that completes its dissolution. Juxtaposed against the Waldens' obsessive search is the story of Ty Ty's son-in-law, a cotton mill worker in a nearby town who is killed during a strike.

God's Little Acre, unabr. ed. Erskine Caldwell. Narrated by Mark Hammer. 6 cass. (Running Time: 7 hrs. 45 mins.). 1995. 51.00 (978-0-7887-0420-8(6), 94612E7) Recorded Bks.
A classic story of a poor white Southern family caught between dreams & despair.

God's Little Acre, Set. unabr. ed. Erskine Caldwell. Read by John MacDonald. 5 cass. 1999. 39.95 (FS9-51103) Highsmith.

God's Little Mountain see Poetry of Geoffrey

God's Little Princess Lullabies: Soothing Scriptures, Peaceful Prayers, & Gentle Blessings. unabr. ed. Sheila Walsh. (Gigi, God's Little Princess Ser.). (J). 2009. audio compact disk 10.99 (978-1-4003-1451-5(8)) Nelson.

God's Love. Edd Anthony. Read by Edd Anthony. 2007. audio compact disk 16.95 (978-1-881586-16-6(2)) Canticle Cass.

God's Love. Swami Amar Jyoti. 1 cass. 1976. 9.95 (K-4) Truth Consciousness.
Love is the full method for realization. Creation is His play in Love. Love is within us, are we applying it?.

God's Love - Bottom Line. John Arnott. 1 cass. 1996. 7.00 (978-0-7684-0029-8(5)) Destiny Image Pubs.

God's Love for a Lost World. unabr. ed. David P. Jeremiah. Read by David P. Jeremiah. 1 cass. (Running Time: 1 hr. 30 min.). 1989. 4.95 (978-0-8474-2330-9(1)) Back to Bible.
The biblical basis for missions - God's love for the lost & the needs in missions today.

God's Love for You. Read by Tim Greenwood. 1 cass. (Running Time: 60 mins.). 1999. (978-0-9666689-6-4(0)) TGMinist.

God's Man in Today's World. Richard D. Dobbins. 6 cass. 29.95 Set. (978-1-890329-56-3(8)) Totally Alive.
Learning how to be God's man in the church, home & on the job.

God's Man Plays the Fool Again: 11 Samuel 24. Ed Young. 1982. 4.95 (978-0-7417-1248-6(2), 248) Win Walk.

God's Master Plan for Your Life. unabr. ed. Gloria Copeland. Read by Gloria Copeland. (Running Time: 5 hrs.). (ENG.). (gr. 8). 2008. audio compact disk 29.95 (978-0-14-314320-8(4), PengAudBks) Penguin Grp USA.

God's Masterwork. Charles Sevindoll. 1 cass. 1997. 15.99 (978-0-8499-6276-9(5)) Nelson.

God's Masterwork Vol. 1: Genesis Through Second Chronicles, Charles R. Swindoll. 7 cass. (Running Time: 15 hrs.). (Concerto in Sixty-Six Movements Ser.: Vol. 1). 1997. 34.95 (978-1-57972-015-5(3)) Insight Living.
Book-by-book study of the Bible.

God's Masterwork Vol. 2: Ezra Through Daniel, Charles R. Swindoll. 7 cass. (Running Time: 15 hrs.). (Concerto in Sixty-Six Movements Ser.: Vol. 2). 1997. 34.95 (978-1-57972-001-8(3)) Insight Living.

God's Masterwork Vol. 3: Hosea through Malachi, Charles R. Swindoll. 6 cass. (Running Time: 11 hrs.). (Concerto in Sixty-Six Movements Ser.: Vol. 3). 1997. 30.95 (978-1-57972-016-2(1)) Insight Living.
In the Minor Prophets of the Bible, stern-minded men proclaimed God's displeasure over sin, announced His Judgement, offered His mercy & forgiveness & reminded people that God would keep His covenants with them.

God's Masterwork Vol. 4, Set: Matthew through First Thessaionians. Charles R. Swindoll. 7 cass. (Running Time: 12 hrs.). (God's Masterwork Ser.: Vol. 4). 1997. 34.95 (978-1-57972-071-1(4)) Insight Living.
Book-by-book study of the Bible.

God's Masterwork Vol. 5, Set: Second Thessalonians through Revelation. Charles R. Swindoll. 7 cass. (Running Time: 12 hrs. 30 min.). (God's Masterwork Ser.: Vol. 5). 1998. 34.95 (978-1-57972-017-9(9)) Insight Living.

God's Masterwork Vol 1 see Obra Maestra de Dios Vol 1

God's Masterwork Vol 2 see Obra Maestra de Dios Vol 2

God's Masterwork Vol 3 see Obra Maestra de Dios Vol 3

God's Masterwork Vol 4 see Obra Maestra de Dios Vol 4

God's Masterwork Vol 5 see Obra Maestra de Dios Vol 5

God's Medicine. Kenneth E. Hagin. 4 cass. (Running Time: 4 hrs.). 2000. 16.00 (TKH63H) Faith Lib Pubns.

God's Medicine Bottle. Derek Prince. 1 cass. 5.95 (093) Derek Prince.
For those willing to follow its directions, God's "medicine bottle" contains healing & health for all our flesh.

God's Meiman-Marcus Attire: 1 Peter 5:1-5. Ed Young. 1983. 4.95 (978-0-7417-1297-4(0), 297) Win Walk.

God's Menu: Exodus 16:17. Ed Young. 1984. 4.95 (978-0-7417-1424-4(8), 424) Win Walk.

God's Mission, God's Song CD. Compiled by GBGMusik. Executive Producer S. T. Kimbrough, Jr. (ENG.). 2006. audio compact disk 12.95 (978-1-933663-09-8(X), GBGMusik) Pub: Gnl Brd Glbl Minis. Dist(s): Mission Res

God's Name. Swami Amar Jyoti. 1 cass. 1976. 9.95 (H-3) Truth Consciousness.
The sweetness of repeating His name. The science & efficacy of mantra.

God's New Community: Logos April 30, 2000. Ben Young. 2000. 4.95 (978-0-7417-6181-1(5), B0181) Win Walk.

God's Not Through with You! unabr. ed. Kerry Miller. Perf. by Stan Paget. 1 cass. (Running Time: 1hr. 20 min.). 1999. 4.95 (978-1-929168-25-5(X), HC-C0906) Lasting Impr KS.
The author shares with a live audience his personal pilgrimage from abandoning his family & God & living in rebellious sin to embracing God's plan for his life & living victoriously, showing how his congregation played a pivotal role in that process. An inspiring & motivational story of God's persistence in redemption.

***Gods of Greenwich: A Novel.** unabr. ed. Norb Vonnegut. (Running Time: 9 hrs. 30 mins. 0 sec.). 2011. 24.99 (978-1-4526-5043-2(8)); 16.99 (978-1-4526-7043-0(9)); audio compact disk 34.99 (978-1-4526-0043-7(0)) Pub: Tantor Media. Dist(s): IngramPubServ

***Gods of Greenwich (Library Edition) A Novel.** unabr. ed. Norb Vonnegut. (Running Time: 9 hrs. 30 mins.). 2011. 34.99 (978-1-4526-2043-5(1)); audio compact disk 83.99 (978-1-4526-3043-4(7)) Pub: Tantor Media. Dist(s): IngramPubServ

Gods of Mars. Edgar Rice Burroughs. Read by John Bolen. (Martian Tales of Edgar Rice Burroughs Ser.). (ENG.). 2001. audio compact disk 78.00 (978-1-4001-3020-7(4)) Pub: Tantor Media. Dist(s): IngramPubServ

Gods of Mars. Edgar Rice Burroughs. Narrated by Jim Killavey. (Running Time: 8 hrs.). 1989. 27.95 (978-1-59912-822-1(5)) Iofy Corp.

Gods of Mars. Edgar Rice Burroughs. Read by John Bolen. (Running Time: 8 hrs. 30 mins.). 2001. 27.95 (978-1-60083-592-6(9), Audiofy Corp) Iofy Corp.

Gods of Mars, abr. ed. Edgar Rice Burroughs. Read by Grover Gardner. 2 cass. (Running Time: 3 hrs.). (Mars Ser.). 1999. 16.95 (978-1-882071-77-7(8), 394313) B-B Audio.
After a long exile on Earth, John Carter finally returned to his beloved Mars. But beautiful Dejah Thoris, the woman he loved, had vanished. Now he was trapped in the legendary Eden of Mars - an Eden from which none ever escaped alive.The other a.

Gods of Mars. unabr. ed. Edgar Rice Burroughs. Narrated by John Bolen. (Running Time: 8 hrs. 30 mins. 0 sec.). (Barsoom Ser.). (ENG.). 2009. audio compact disk 19.99 (978-1-4001-5934-5(2)); audio compact disk 55.99 (978-1-4001-3934-7(1)) Pub: Tantor Media. Dist(s): IngramPubServ

Gods of Mars. unabr. ed. Edgar Rice Burroughs. Read by John Bolen. Narrated by John Bolen. (Running Time: 8 hrs. 30 mins. 0 sec.). (Barsoom Ser.). (ENG.). 2009. audio compact disk 27.99 (978-1-4001-0934-0(5)) Pub: Tantor Media. Dist(s): IngramPubServ

Gods of Mars. unabr. ed. Edgar Rice Burroughs. Read by Gene Engene. 8 cass. (Running Time: 8 hrs. 54 min.). (Mars Ser.: Bk. 2). 2001. 49.95 (978-1-55686-947-1(9)) Books in Motion.
After the long exile on Earth, John Carter finally returns to his beloved Mars. But beautiful Dejah Thoris, the woman he loves, has vanished. Now he is trapped in the legendary Eden of Mars - and Eden from which none have ever escaped alive.

Gods of Mars. unabr. ed. Edgar Rice Burroughs. Read by John Bolen. 1 CD. (Running Time: 8 hrs. 30 mins.). 2001. audio compact disk 25.00; audio compact disk 57.00 Books on Tape.

Gods of Mars. unabr. ed. Edgar Rice Burroughs. Read by John Bolen. 7 CDs. (Running Time: 8 hrs. 23 mins.). (Martian Ser.: Vol. 2). (ENG.). 2001. audio compact disk 39.00 (978-1-4001-0020-0(8)); audio compact disk 20.00 (978-1-4001-5020-5(5)) Pub: Tantor Media. Dist(s): IngramPubServ
John Carter returns to the red planet ten years after his Martian death in search of his wife, Princess Dejah Thoris. He joins forces with old comrades and forms new lifetime alliances as he battles hostile enemies, previously unknown to his people of Barsoom. His adventures reveal the truth about the Gods of Mars.

***Gods of Mars.** unabr. ed. Edgar Rice Burroughs. Read by William Dufris. (Running Time: 9 hrs. NaN mins.). (Martian Ser.). (ENG.). 2011. 29.95 (978-1-4417-7462-0(9)); 59.95 (978-1-4417-7459-0(9)); audio compact disk 24.95 (978-1-4417-7461-3(0)); audio compact disk 76.00 (978-1-4417-7460-6(2)) Blckstn Audio.

Gods of Newport. abr. ed. John Jakes. John Jakes. Read by Edward Herrmann. 2006. 17.95 (978-0-7435-6521-9(5), Audioworks) Pub: S&S Audio. Dist(s): S and S Inc

God's One Perfect Way. Swami Amar Jyoti. 2 cass. 1983. 12.95 (M-39) Truth Consciousness.
Earth's most golden opportunity. How can God's ways be known?.

God's other Son. Don Imus. 2004. 9.95 (978-0-7435-4786-4(1)) Pub: S&S Audio. Dist(s): S and S Inc

God's Outrageous Claims. Lee Strobel. 1997. 14.99 (978-0-310-21194-5(8)) Zondervan.

God's Outrageous Claims: Discover What They Mean for You. abr. ed. Lee Strobel. (Running Time: 2 hrs. 30 mins. 0 sec.). (ENG.). 2005. 12.99 (978-0-310-26888-8(5)) Zondervan.

God's Outrageous Claims: Thirteen Discoveries That Can Revolutionize Your Life. abr. ed. Lee Strobel. (Running Time: 2 hrs. 30 mins. 0 sec.). (ENG.). 2003. 10.99 (978-0-310-26048-6(5)) Zondervan.

God's Patience Runs Out: I Kings 21:1-29. Ed Young. 1987. 4.95 (978-0-7417-1603-3(8), 603) Win Walk.

God's Peace Confessions. Robb Thompson. audio compact disk 10.00 (978-1-889723-46-4(0)) Pub: Family Harvest. Dist(s): Harrison Hse

God's Place for You. Speeches. Joel Osteen. 1 Cass. (Running Time: 30 Mins.). (J). 2000. 6.00 (978-1-59349-067-6(4), JA0067) J Osteen.

God's Plan for a Joy-Filled Marriage: A Marriage Preparation Supplement Designed to Help Couples Understand & Embrace. Christopher West. 2006. audio compact disk 44.95 (978-1-932927-49-8(2)) Ascensn Pr.

God's Plan for Childbearing. Donna Wright et al. (ENG.). 2007. audio compact disk 17.95 (978-1-934680-36-0(2)) Be in Hlth.

God's Plan for Giving. 6 cass. 19.95 (20123, HarperThor) HarpC GBR.

God's Plan for Man. 2 CDs. 2003. audio compact disk 39.99 (978-1-55829-099-0(0)) Dake Publishing.

God's Plan for Man. Gloria Copeland. 6 cass. 1983. 30.00 Set incl. study guide. (978-0-938458-65-4(5)) K Copeland Pubns.
God's plan for man.

God's Plan for Man. Gloria Copeland. (ENG.). 2007. audio compact disk 30.00 (978-1-57562-939-1(9)) K Copeland Pubns.

God's Plan for Man Tape Series. Finis J. Dake, Sr. 48.95 (978-1-55829-043-3(5)) Dake Publishing.
Bible study.

God's Plan for Your Body. Derek Prince. 1 cass. (Running Time: 60 min.). 5.95 (I-4260) Derek Prince.

God's Plan for Your Life. 2007. audio compact disk (978-0-9789883-8-8(8)) TSEA.

God's Plan for Your Money. Derek Prince. 2 cass. 11.90 Set. (117-118) Derek Prince.
Your attitude to money reveals your attitude to God. The right attitude produces the right results.

God's Play. Swami Amar Jyoti. 1 cass. 1975. 9.95 (K-71) Truth Consciousness.
Relationships with God. Seeing His hand in everything.

God's Poet Recital. Poems. Thomas H. Stephens. 1 cass. 1997. 5.00 (978-1-890556-06-8(8)) T Stephens Pub.
Religious poetry recital.

***God's Politics.** abr. ed. Jim Wallis. Read by Jim Wallis. Read by Sam Freed. (ENG.). 2005. (978-0-06-085663-2(7), Harper Audio); (978-0-06-085662-5(9), Harper Audio) HarperCollins Pubs.

God's Politics: Why the Right Gets It Wrong & the Left Doesn't Get It. abr. ed. Jim Wallis. Read by Jim Wallis. Read by Sam Freed. 2005. audio compact disk 29.95 (978-0-06-083832-4(9)) HarperCollins Pubs.

God's Power to Change Your Life. Rick Warren. (Running Time: 4 hrs. 49 mins. 41 sec.). (Living with Purpose Ser.). (ENG.). 2006. audio compact disk 19.99 (978-0-310-27553-4(9)) Zondervan.

God's Power with Your Legal Right to Use It. Gary V. Whetstone. 4 cass. (Running Time: 6 hrs.). (Theology Ser.: TH102). 1996. 80.00 (978-1-58866-084-8(2), BT 102 A00) Gary Whet Pub.
Authority is the governing word in God's Kingdom, in government, in business, in family & in our personal life.

God's Prescription for Contentment: Exodus 20:17. Ed Young. 1999. 4.95 (978-0-7417-2227-0(5), 1227) Win Walk.

God's Presence on Our Path. Swami Amar Jyoti. 1 cass. 1991. 9.95 (M-86) Truth Consciousness.
Feeling the Presence everywhere, at each moment. How our path is determined; how to walk it rightly.

God's Present Dealings with Man Pt. III: Lessons 19-36. 13 cass. (Running Time: 13 hrs.). 2000. 55.99 (978-1-55829-154-6(7)) Dake Publishing.
The New Testament program for the Modern Church, all about grace, the deity, names & attributes of Jesus, a Christian's power of attorney, the biblical doctrine of sin, a study of the Divine Trinity, spirit baptism & much more.

***God's Principles for Operating a Business.** 2004. 60.00 (978-1-56427-099-3(8)) Crown Fin Min Inc.

God's Principles for Operating a Business. Larry Burkett. 11 cass. (Running Time: 16 hrs. 30 mins.). 1988. 39.99 (978-1-56427-100-6(5), GP305) Crown Fin Min Inc.

***God's Problem.** unabr. ed. Bart D. Ehrman. Read by L. J. Ganser. (ENG.). 2008. (978-0-06-162969-3(3)); (978-0-06-162970-9(7)) HarperCollins Pubs.

God's Problem: How the Bible Fails to Answer Our Most Important Question - Why We Suffer. unabr. ed. Bart D. Ehrman. Read by L. J. Ganser. 8 CDs. (Running Time: 10 hrs.). 2008. audio compact disk 39.95 (978-0-06-145642-8(X), Harper Audio) HarperCollins Pubs.

God's Promises. Cherie Larkin. Read by Michael Moran. 1999. 10.95 (978-0-87159-856-1(6)) Unity Schl Christ.

God's Promises to You. Caryl Krueger. Read by Caryl Krueger. 2 cass. (Running Time: 3 hrs.). 2001. 17.00 Belleridge.
Here are Bible promises to bless every aspect of your life: financial, health, safety, work, family relationships, and most importantly: the promise of eternal life. Many true stories of those blessed by these promises.

God's Protection: It's for Today. Gloria Copeland. 1 cass. 1986. 5.00 (978-0-88114-741-4(9)) K Copeland Pubns.
A teaching on Psalm 91 - Your Safety Zone.

***God's Pursuit of Man: The Divine Conquest of the Human Heart.** unabr. ed. A. w. Tozer. Narrated by Grover Gardner. (ENG.). 2006. 12.98 (978-1-59644-420-1(7), Hovel Audio) christianaud.

God's Pursuit of Man: Tozer's Profound Prequel to the Pursuit of God. unabr. ed. A. W. Tozer. 3 CDs. (Running Time: 3 hrs. 0 mins. 0 sec.). (ENG.). 2006. audio compact disk 21.98 (978-1-59644-419-5(3), Hovel Audio) christianaud.

God's Remnant: Romans 11:1-11. Ed Young. 1997. 4.95 (978-0-7417-2137-2(6), 1137) Win Walk.

God's Rose: A Testimony of God's Love. Darlene Ballard. 2 cass. (Running Time: 2 hrs.). 1999. bk. Set. (978-0-9670536-1-5(7)) Teen Chall GA.
A powerful testimony of how we can help others through our own experiences of abuse, suffering & pain.

God's Secrets to Unanswered Prayers. Sandra Aleman Ponce. 2007. audio compact disk 14.99 (978-1-60247-712-4(4)) Tate Pubng.

God's Seven Gifts. 2005. 39.95 (978-1-888992-69-4(7)); audio compact disk 39.95 (978-1-888992-70-0(0)) Catholic Answers.

God's Shadow of Protection. Creflo Taffi. 2008. audio compact disk 14.00 (978-1-59944-703-2(7)) Creflo Dollar.

God's Smuggler. abr. ed. Brother Andrew. 4 cass. (Running Time: 6 hrs. 30 min.). (Life of Glory Ser.). 2003. 25.99; audio compact disk 25.99 Oasis Audio.

***God's Smuggler.** unabr. ed. Brother Andrew & John Sherill. Narrated by Simon Vance. (ENG.). 2008. 16.98 (978-1-59644-654-0(4), Hovel Audio) christianaud.

God's Smuggler. unabr. ed. Brother Andrew et al. Read by Robert Whitfield. 6 cass. (Running Time: 8 hrs. 30 mins.). 2001. 44.95 (978-0-7861-1408-5(8), 2285) Blckstn Audio.

God's Smuggler. unabr. ed. Brother Andrew et al. Narrated by Simon Vance. (Running Time: 9 hrs. 0 mins. 0 sec.). (ENG.). 2008. lp 19.98 (978-1-59644-653-3(6), Hovel Audio); audio compact disk 26.98 (978-1-59644-652-6(8), Hovel Audio) christianaud.

God's Smuggler. unabr. ed. Read by Robert Whitfield. Featuring Brother Andrew. 8 CDs. (Running Time: 8 hrs. 30 mins.). 2000. audio compact disk 64.00 (978-0-7861-9930-3(X), 2285) Blckstn Audio.
Brother Andrew prayed & the guards passed his car bulging with Bibles across the Yugoslav border in 1957. He began his mission to bring the Word to worshipers cut off from their religion. It was a mission fraught with peril & pathos, financed by faith, supported by miracles.

God's Story: From Creation to Eternity. David Minazian et al. Read by Dan Shattuck. Perf. by Drews Minazian. Narrated by Dean Jones. Music by Dan Shattuck. 1 cass. (Running Time: 73 min.). Dramatization. 1995. 9.95 (978-1-878993-85-4(2)); audio compact disk 11.95 (978-1-878993-84-7(4)) Jeremiah Films.
Story & soundtrack from Jeremiah Music.

God's Story (as Told by John) unabr. ed. Read by Scott Brick & Michelle Gomez. (Running Time: 3 hrs. 36 mins. 0 sec.). (ENG.). 2007. audio compact disk 12.98 (978-1-59644-417-1(7)) christianaud.

God's System vs the World System. Creflo A. Dollar et al. 45.00 (978-1-59089-007-3(8)) Pub: Creflo Dollar. Dist(s): STL Dist NA

God's Three End Time Purposes. Derek Prince. 1 cass. 5.95 (4379) Derek Prince.
"Thy kingdom come, Thy will be done..." - familiar words to all of us. But do we know what God's will really is?" Are we prepared to play our part?.

God's Timetable: Daniel 9:20-27. Ed Young. 1995. 4.95 (978-0-7417-2079-5(5), 1079) Win Walk.

God's Timing for Me: Esther 4:14. Ed Young. 1983. 4.95 (978-0-7417-1294-3(6), 294) Win Walk.

God's Top Ten. Contrib. by Genie Nilson & Troy Nilson. 1996. 85.00 (978-0-7601-1138-3(3), 75606302) Pub: Brentwood Music. Dist(s): H Leonard

God's Treasure Chest. Created by Gospel Gospel Vision Staff. (J). 2003. audio compact disk 13.95 (978-0-910683-90-6(5)) Townsnd-Pr.

God's Treasure Chest. Created by Gospel Gospel Vision Staff. 2003. 7.50 (978-0-910683-91-3(3)) Townsnd-Pr.

God's Triple A Church. Nathaniel Holcomb. 3 cass. (Running Time: 4 hrs. 30 mins.). 1998. (978-1-930918-18-4(6)) Its All About Him.

God's Trombones. Gloriae Dei Cantores. 1 CD. 1995. audio compact disk 16.95 (978-1-55725-133-6(9), 930-083) Paraclete MA.

God's Trombones: Seven Negro Sermons in Verse. unabr. ed. James Weldon Johnson. Contrib. by Ensemble Cast Staff. 1 CD. (Running Time: 1 hr. 11 mins.). (ENG.). 2009. audio compact disk 14.95 (978-1-59887-868-4(9), 1598878689) Pub: Penguin-HghBrdg. Dist(s): Workman Pub

God's Unchanging Love. Interview with Mother Angelica. Contrib. by John T. Catoir. 1 cass. (Running Time: 60 min.). (Mother Angelica Live Ser.). 10.00 (978-1-55794-059-9(2), T10) Eternal Wrd TV.

God's Vision for Our Generation. Ben Young. 2000. 4.95 (978-0-7417-6190-3(4), B0190) Win Walk.

God's Wacky Animals. 1 cass. (Running Time: 30 mins.). (J). 1997. 12.99 (978-0-7601-1157-4(X), V80001) Pub: Brentwood Music. Dist(s): Provident Mus Dist
Kids love animals & music. This fun-filled adventure includes "super-cool" music & songs that remind kids of God's awesome world that He has created.

God's Waiting Room: The Time Between Revelation & Manifestation, Set. Mac Hammond. 5 cass. (Running Time: 5 hrs.). 2000. (978-1-57399-097-4(3)) Mac Hammond.

***God's Waiting Room: Understanding & Embracing the Process of Preparation.** Mac Hammond. 2010. audio compact disk 30.00 (978-1-57399-458-3(8)) Mac Hammond.

God's Wake up Call Tape Pack. 2001. (978-1-931713-06-1(5)) Word For Today.

God's Way Works: Exodus 4:18-31. Ed Young. 1984. 4.95 (978-0-7417-1419-0(1), 419) Win Walk.

God's Way=My Way. ldr.'s ed. (J). (gr. 1-6). 1999. audio compact disk 69.95 (978-0-7673-9425-3(9)) LifeWay Christian.

God's Will for You. Read by Rose Leibundguth. 1 cass. (Running Time: 1 hr. 2 mins.). 2001. 6.00 (978-1-931262-12-5(8)) Rose Leibund.

God's Will Is Prosperity. unabr. ed. Keith A. Butler. 5 cass. (Running Time: 7 hrs. 30 mins.). 2001. 25.00 (A138) Word Faith Pubng.

God's Wisdom: Bible Passages Exploring God's Guidance for Our Lives. abr. ed. 2006. 5.95 (978-0-7435-5574-6(0), Sound Ideas) Pub: S&S Audio. Dist(s): S and S Inc

God's Wisdom: Bible Passages Exploring God's Guidance for Our Lives. abr. ed. Created by Simon and Schuster Audio Staff. (Running Time: 1 hr. 0 mins. 0 sec.). (ENG.). 2006. audio compact disk 7.95 (978-0-7435-5448-0(5)) Pub: S&S Audio. Dist(s): S and S Inc

God's Word: Your Inexhaustible Resource. Derek Prince. 2 cass. (Running Time: 1 hr. per cass.). 1991. 5.95 ea. Derek Prince.
Are the promises of God missing from your life? Discover what His word will do for you in every area of your life - & how to apply it.

God's Word - Final Authority: God's Word Should Be the Alpha & Omega Word in Your Life. Kenneth Copeland. (ENG.). 2008. audio compact disk 10.00 (978-1-57562-969-8(0)) K Copeland Pubns.

God's Word Final Authority: God's Word Should Be the Alpha & Omega. Kenneth Copeland. 2 cass. 1987. 10.00 Set. (978-0-88114-917-3(9)) K Copeland Pubns.
Study on authority of God's Word.

God's Word, God's World & You: A Fresh Look at Evangelism, Set. Charles R. Swindoll. 5 cass. (Running Time: 8 hrs. 45 mins.). 1997. 25.95 (978-1-57972-056-8(0)) Insight Living.
Understanding God's plan for evangelism & how you fit into it.

God's Word, His World, & You CD see Palabra de Dios, el Mundo de Dios y Usted

God's Word Is Our Joy: Easter Sunday & Second Sunday of Easter, Cycle A. Lucien Deiss. 1 cass. 1999. 11.00 (978-0-937690-78-9(3), 2768) Wrld Lib Pubns.
Reflections on biblical scripture.

God's Word Is Our Joy: Fifth & Sixth Sundays of Easter, Cycle A. Lucien Deiss. 1 cass. 1999. 11.00 (978-0-937690-80-2(5), 2772) Wrld Lib Pubns.

God's Word Is Our Joy: Seventh Sunday of Easter, Ascension, Pentecost Sunday, Cycle A. Lucien Deiss. 1 cass. 1999. 11.00 (978-0-937690-81-9(3), 2774) Wrld Lib Pubns.

God's Word Is Our Joy: Third & Fourth Sundays of Easter, Cycle A. Lucien Deiss. 1 cass. 1999. 11.00 (978-0-937690-79-6(1), 2770) Wrld Lib Pubns.

God's Word New Testament. Narrated by Stephen Johnston. 12 cass. 1997. 21.99 (978-0-529-10639-1(6), WBC-96BL) Nelson.
Accurate & easy-to-understand God's Word. Narrator is an Emmy Winner.

God's Word on Anger: Uncovering Causes/Rooting It Out. Read by Joshua Daniels. 1 cass. (Running Time: 60 min.). (Foundation Stones Scripture Meditations Ser.). 1998. (978-1-58526-000-3(2)) Broken Wall Pubg.
Twenty-four Scriptures, repeated constantly, that root out anger at its sources & expose the hidden causes so they can be resolved.

God's Word on Believers' Authority. Read by Joshua Daniels. 1 cass. (Running Time: 60 min.). (Foundation Stones Scripture Meditations Ser.). 1998. (978-1-58526-001-0(0)) Broken Wall Pubg.
Twenty-four selected Scriptures, repeated constantly, to get one rooted & grounded in one's authority in Christ.

God's Word on Deliverance. Read by Joshua Daniels. 1 cass. (Running Time: 60 min.). (Foundation Stones Scripture Meditations Ser.). 1998. (978-1-58526-002-7(9)) Broken Wall Pubg.
Twenty-four Scriptures, repeated constantly, that build the faith to bring about & maintain deliverance.

God's Word on Fear. Read by Joshua Daniels. 1 cass. (Running Time: 60 min.). (Foundation Stones Scripture Meditations Ser.). 1998. (978-1-58526-003-4(7)) Broken Wall Pubg.
Twenty-four selected Scriptures, repeated constantly, that calm & heal fear permanently, addressing & destroying all its roots.

God's Word on Food. Read by Joshua Daniels. 1 cass. (Running Time: 60 min.). (Foundation Stones Scripture Meditations Ser.). 1998. (978-1-58526-004-1(5)) Broken Wall Pubg.
Twenty-four Scriptures, repeated constantly, that soothe & lay to rest all food issues - Anorexia, Bulimia, etc.

God's Word on Guidance. Read by Joshua Daniels. 1 cass. (Running Time: 60 min.). (Foundation Stones Scripture Meditations Ser.). 1998. (978-1-58526-005-8(3)) Broken Wall Pubg.
Twenty-four selected Scriptures, constantly repeated, that clarify the voice of God in the listener's heart.

God's Word on Healing. Read by Joshua Daniels. 1 cass. (Running Time: 60 min.). (Foundation Stones Scripture Meditations Ser.). 1998. (978-1-58526-006-5(1)) Broken Wall Pubg.
Twenty-four selected Scriptures, constantly repeated, that build faith to receive & give the healing that the Scriptures say follow those who believe.

God's Word on Holiness. Read by Joshua Daniels. 1 cass. (Running Time: 60 min.). (Foundation Stones Scripture Meditations Ser.). 1998. (978-1-58526-007-2(X)) Broken Wall Pubg.
Twenty-four selected Scriptures, repeated constantly, that draw the heart to holiness & drive out baseness.

God's Word on Peace. Read by Joshua Daniels. 1 cass. (Running Time: 60 min.). (Foundation Stones Scripture Meditations Ser.). 1998. (978-1-58526-009-6(6)) Broken Wall Pubg.
Twenty-four Scriptures, constantly repeated, that quiet the anxious heart, emotions & mind.

God's Word on Prosperity. Read by Joshua Daniels. 1 cass. (Running Time: 60 min.). (Foundation Stones Scripture Meditations Ser.). 1998. (978-1-58526-010-2(X)) Broken Wall Pubg.
Twenty-four Scriptures, repeated constantly, that build the faith to lay hold of the prosperity God wants one to have.

God's Word on Purity. Read by Joshua Daniels. 1 cass. (Running Time: 60 min.). (Foundation Stones Scripture Meditations Ser.). 1998. (978-1-58526-011-9(8)) Broken Wall Pubg.
Twenty-four selected Scriptures, repeated constantly, that root out impurity & cleanse the contaminated heart.

God's Word on Righteousness. Read by Joshua Daniels. 1 cass. (Running Time: 60 min.). (Foundation Stones Scripture Meditations Ser.). 1998. (978-1-58526-012-6(6)) Broken Wall Pubg.
Twenty four selected Scriptures, repeated constantly, that bring repentence & build righteousness in the heart & mind of the believer.

God's Word on Shame. Read by Joshua Daniels. 1 cass. (Running Time: 60 min.). (Foundation Stones Scripture Meditations Ser.). 1998. (978-1-58526-013-3(4)) Broken Wall Pubg.
Twenty-four selected Scriptures, repeated constantly, that alter the shame-based heart to know its value & worth.

God's Word on Who You Are. Read by Joshua Daniels. 1 cass. (Running Time: 60 min.). (Foundation Stones Scripture Meditations Ser.). 1998. (978-1-58526-008-9(8)) Broken Wall Pubg.
Twenty-four Scriptures, repeated constantly, that teach your heart who God sees you as, & who you should see yourself as.

God's Word to an Ungodly Society. 2 cass. 7.95 (22-6, HarperThor) HarpC GBR.

God's Words to Inspire the Angel in You. Speeches. I. Am. (Running Time: 62 mins). 2003. audio compact disk 9.95 (978-1-892177-26-1(9)) Angel Food Bks.
I AM is an American lady author, whom God has directed to come in His Name. She hears God?s Words directly and speaks them verbatim to audiences and individuals. She first achieved the ability to hear God?s Voice in 1991. Now, at His request, she has published God?s Words for the New Millennium in four exquisite volumes richly adorned in Angel Art. Now available in Audio, I AM is accompanied by the celestial golden harp of Carmen Dragon. This CD contains 1/3 of the book.

God's World. 1 cass. (Wee Sing Ser.). (J). bk. 7.98 Blisterpack. (PSS 7852) NewSound.

God's World Reloaded. R. A. Beisner. 2007. audio compact disk 19.99 (978-1-60247-209-9(2)) Tate Pubng.

Godseed: The Journey of Christ. Jean Houston. Read by Jean Houston. 2 cass. (Running Time: 2 hrs. 17 min.). 1995. 10.95 (978-0-8356-2096-3(4), Quest) Pub: Theos Pub Hse. Dist(s): Natl Bk Netwk

Godsmack: The Unauthorized Biography of Godsmack. Michael Sumsion. (Maximum Ser.). (ENG.). 2001. audio compact disk 14.95 (978-1-84240-104-0(1)) Pub: Chrome Dreams GBR. Dist(s): IPG Chicago

Godspeed & Happy Landings: Becoming the Pilot in Command of Your Goals. Monica Ballard. 2007. audio compact disk 12.95 (978-1-932226-58-4(3)) Wizard Acdmy.

Godwulf Manuscript. unabr. collector's ed. Robert B. Parker. Read by Michael Prichard. 6 cass. (Running Time: 6 hrs.). (Spenser Ser.). 1988. 48.00 (978-0-7366-1353-8(6), 2254) Books on Tape.
Spenser is hired to recover a valuable & irreplaceable manuscript.

Goes Around Comes Around. 1 cass. 1999. 10.98 (978-0-7601-2876-3(6)); audio compact disk 16.98 Provident Music.

Goethe: His Personality & Work. Albert Schweitzer. Tr. by Thornton Wilder. 1 CD. (Running Time: 78 mins.). (GER.). 2006. audio compact disk 12.95 (978-1-57970-365-3(8), C23140D, Audio-For) J Norton Pubs.
Thornton Wilder translations the speech given by Albert Schweitzer, in German, on Goethe. Recorded outdoors without sophisticated sound equipment, it is nevertheless valuable for hearing both great men, Schweitzer and Wilder, at what is probably the only occasion they both spoke together and were recorded.

Goethe: His Personality & Work. unabr. ed. Albert Schweitzer. 1 cass. (Running Time: 1 hr. 23 min.). 12.95 (23140) J Norton Pubs.
The only speech the great humanitarian & scholar ever made in the U.S. Thornton Wilder alternates sentence by sentence with Schweitzer to provide English translation.

Goethe Set: Master Poet. abr. ed. Thomas Carlyle. Read by Robert L. Halvorson. 2 cass. (Running Time: 180 min.). 14.95 (23) Halvorson Assocs.

Goggles! see Anteojos!

Goggles! 2004. 8.95 (978-1-56008-909-4(1)); 8.95 (978-1-56008-137-1(6)); cass. & flmstrp 30.00 (978-1-56008-675-8(0)); audio compact disk 12.95 (978-1-55592-912-1(5)) Weston Woods.

Goggles! (J). 2004. pap. bk. 18.95 (978-1-55592-417-1(4)); pap. bk. 38.75 (978-1-55592-418-8(2)); pap. bk. 32.75 (978-1-55592-232-0(5)); pap. bk. 14.95 (978-1-56008-084-8(1)) Weston Woods.

Goggles. Ezra Jack Keats. 1 read-along cass. (Running Time: 6 min.). (J). 8.95 (RAC152) Weston Woods.
One side with page turn signals, one side without.

Goggles. Ezra Jack Keats. Narrated by Geoffrey Holder. 1 cass., 5 bks. (Running Time: 6 min.). (J). 32.75 Weston Woods.

Goggles. Ezra Jack Keats. Narrated by Geoffrey Holder. 1 read-along cass. (Running Time: 6 min.). (J). (gr. k-4). 2000. pap. bk. 12.95 (PRA152) Weston Woods.

Goggles!; Little Red Hen, the; Bill's Balloon Ride; Harold's Fairy Tale. 2004. (978-0-89719-836-3(0)); cass. & flmstrp (978-0-89719-744-1(5)) Weston Woods.

Goin' Down: It's like riding a nuclear bomb... except you'll probably survive This. 2007. 19.95 (978-0-9793080-1-7(1)) S Narged.

Goin Quackers. 1 cass. (Retro Mickey Ser.). (J). 7.99 Norelco. (978-1-55723-947-1(9)); audio compact disk 13.99 CD. (978-1-55723-948-8(7)) W Disney Records.

Goin' to the Chapel: Dreams of Love & Realities of Marriage. abr. ed. Charlotte Mayerson. Read by Ellen Burstyn. 2 cass. (Running Time: 3 hrs.). 1996. 18.95 (978-1-57453-074-2(7)) Audio Lit.
Writer & poet Mayerson traveled across the country interviewing women about their girlhood dreams of marriage & how those dreams were realized in their lives. Their tales are touching, articulate & recognizable.

Goin' to the Zoo. Tom Paxton. 1 cass. (Running Time: 36 mins.). (J). 1997. 9.98 (978-1-57940-013-2(2)); audio compact disk 14.98 (978-1-57940-010-1(8)) Rounder Records.
A collection of 15 musical songs ideal for young children.

Going after Cacciato. unabr. ed. Tim O'Brien. Read by John MacDonald. 7 cass. (Running Time: 10 hrs. 30 min.). 1985. 56.00 (978-0-7366-0898-5(2), 1842) Books on Tape.
Cacciato is one dumb soldier. He walks away from the Vietnam War. Across mountains, deserts & swamps, he plans to hike 8600 miles from Vietnam to Paris. He's after peace & freedom. A squad of his buddies goes after him & they're told to bring him back or else.

Going after the Glory. Voice by Eddie Lo[illegible]NG.). 2008. audio compact disk 32.00 (978-1-58602-368-3(3)) Pub[illegible] Long. Dist(s): Anchor Distributors

Going All the Way. abr. ed. Dan Wakefield. Read by Ben Affleck. 2 cass. (Running Time: 3 hrs.). 1997. 17.95 (978-1-57453-127-5(1)) Audio Lit.
Chronicles the beginnings of the sexual revolution in 1950s America: the drive-ins, lovers' lanes, living room couches & phrases like "making out" & "going all the way".

Going Back to Bisbee. Richard Shelton. Read by Jack Bannon. 12 cass. (Running Time: 14 hrs.). 1995. 59.95 set. (978-1-55686-599-2(6)) Books in Motion.
Originally published by the University of Arizona press, this is a marvelous & ultra-entertaining group of historic & current, socially significant tales of the Arizona desert & its national importance.

Going Berserk. Timothy Chandler. 1 cass. 1999. bk. 26.95 (978-1-929409-06-8(0)); 32.95 (978-1-929409-07-5(9)) Blade Pubg.
Weight loss program for those willing to "go berserk" to quick results. Author dropped a total of 150 lbs. on this program.

Going Beyond Form & Name. Swami Amar Jyoti. 1 cass. 1988. 9.95 (R-92) Truth Consciousness.
On the astral, fourth dimension, we clearly see the Oneness beneath all forms & names. Fulfilling our mission in life.

***Going Bovine.** unabr. ed. Libba Bray. Read by Erik Davies. 12 CDs. (Running Time: 15 hrs. 9 mins.). (YA). (gr. 9 up). 2009. audio compact disk 75.00 (978-0-7393-8559-3(3), BksonTape) Pub: Random Audio Pubg. Dist(s): Random

Going Bovine. unabr. ed. Libba Bray. Read by Erik Davies. (J). (gr. 9). 2009. audio compact disk 50.00 (978-0-7393-8557-9(7), Listening Lib) Pub: Random Audio Pubg. Dist(s): Random

Going Bugs! James Hillman. 2004. 12.95 (978-1-879816-00-8(8)) Pub: Spring Pubns. Dist(s): Natl Bk Netwk

Going down the Tube: Television & the Family. Bruce A. Baldwin. Read by Bruce A. Baldwin. 1 cass. (Running Time: 40 min.). 1986. 7.95 (978-0-933583-04-7(4), PDC#874) Direction Dynamics.
Book on Tape: Chapter from "Beyond the Cornucopia Kids." Outlines the psychological effects of abusive television habits on parents; Discusses structural impact problems of television that compromise learning necessary life skills in children; Suggests a dozen television guidelines for a healthy family life.

Going Faster Audio CD. Adapted by Benchmark Education Company Staff. Based on a work by Cynthia Swain. (Early Explorers Set C Ser.). (J). (gr. k-1). 2008. audio compact disk 10.00 (978-1-60437-519-0(1)) Benchmark Educ.

Going for the Good Life. Jack Boland. 4 cass. 1980. 34.95 (978-0-88152-021-7(7)) Master Mind.
You can do, be, achieve all that your heart desires. Take a giant step forward in this adventure called your life & let Jack Boland lead you through these steps that will transform your dreams into reality.

Going for the Green: Selling in the 21st Century. Doug Peterson. 2004. audio compact disk 29.95 (978-0-9706909-8-2(3)) L T I Pubng.
Designed to motivate business professionals to outperform their competition. Simple steps are carefully outlined explaining the essential tools, skills and processes that will transform the sales game from a discussion on product and price to one of helping the customer achieve their business goals.

Going Global: Are You a Global Company? Do You even WANT to Be? Speeches. As told by Joan Koerber-Walker. 1 CD. (Running Time: 42 mins.). 2004. audio compact disk 19.95 (978-0-9747056-5-1(9)) CorePurpose.
In 1993, I worked for a company that was "going global". North American based, it started to buy up companies around the world. Ten years later, it had operations in 63 countries. But - were they global? In the midst of a global economy, common sense tells us that to be competitive we have to be global too - right? "Going Global?" looks at the challenges of creating a global company from its most important aspect - People. This live audio session looks at the following key questions: ? What is a "global" company? ? Who are they - are there any? ? If you are going global - how does it affect the people that really matter - Your Employees, Your Customers, and Your Shareholders?.

Going Global: 25 Keys to International Operations. unabr. ed. Jeffrey H. Bergstrand. Read by Jeff Woodman. 2 cass. (Running Time: 3 hrs.). (New York Times Pocket MBA Ser.). 2000. pap. bk. 27.95 Listen & Live.
Learn the 25 keys to doing business on an international scale, including foreign exchange risks & import/export duties.

Going Global: 25 Keys to International Operations. unabr. ed. Jeffrey H. Bergstrand. Read by Jeff Woodman. 2 cass. (Running Time: 2 hrs. 30 mins.). (New York Times Pocket MBA Ser.). 2000. 16.95 (978-1-885408-46-4(3), LL039) Listen & Live.

Going, Going, Gone! Music & Memories from Broadcast Baseball. Friedman-Fairfax and Sony Music Staff et al. 1 cass. (CD Ser.). 1994. pap. bk. 15.98 (978-1-56799-078-2(9), Friedman-Fairfax) M Friedman Pub Grp Inc.

Going, Going, Gone! with the Pain & the Great One. unabr. ed. Judy Blume. Read by Kathleen McInerney. 2 CDs. (Running Time: 1 hrs. 24 mins.). (J). (gr. 1-3). 2008. audio compact disk 20.00 (978-0-7393-7150-3(9), Listening Lib) Pub: Random Audio Pubg. Dist(s): Random

Going, Going, Gone! with the Pain & the Great One. unabr. ed. Judy Blume. Read by Kathleen McInerney. (ENG.). (J). (gr. 1). 2008. audio compact disk 16.95 (978-0-7393-7148-0(7), Listening Lib) Pub: Random Audio Pubg. Dist(s): Random

Going Home. unabr. ed. Robert A. Monroe. Read by Robert A. Monroe. Read by Elisabeth Kubler-Ross & Charles Tart. 12 cass. (Life Span Learning Ser.). 1994. 188.00 Set. (978-1-56113-650-6(6)) Monroe Institute.
Set of learning exercises to help people in the process of dying (& their loved ones) release the fears associated with death; & let go of emotions, guilt & obligations.

Going Home. unabr. ed. Valerie Wood. Read by Kim Hicks. 2002. 69.95 (978-0-7540-0860-6(6), CAB 2282) Pub: Chivers Pr GBR. Dist(s): AudioGO

Going Home: Jesus & Buddha as Brothers. Thich Nhat Hanh. Read by Michael York. 2004. 10.95 (978-0-7435-4787-1(X)) Pub: S&S Audio. Dist(s): S and S Inc

Going Home from the Party see Twentieth-Century Poetry in English, No. 12, Recordings of Poets Reading Their Own Poetry

***Going Home to Glory: A Memoir of Life with Dwight D. Eisenhower, 1961-1969.** unabr. ed. David Eisenhower & Julie Nixon Eisenhower. (Running Time: 13 hrs. 30 mins. 0 sec.). 2010. 24.99 (978-1-4001-6956-6(9)); 18.99 (978-1-4001-8956-4(X)); audio compact disk 37.99 (978-1-4001-1956-1(1)) Pub: Tantor Media. Dist(s): IngramPubServ

***Going Home to Glory (Library Edition) A Memoir of Life with Dwight D. Eisenhower, 1961-1969.** unabr. ed. David Eisenhower & Julie Nixon Eisenhower. (Running Time: 13 hrs. 30 mins.). 2010. 37.99 (978-1-4001-9956-3(5)); audio compact disk 90.99 (978-1-4001-4956-8(8)) Pub: Tantor Media. Dist(s): IngramPubServ

Going Home to Liverpool. unabr. ed. June Francis. Read by Margaret Sircom. 8 cass. (Running Time: 10 hrs. 35 mins.). 1999. 83.95 (978-1-85903-256-5(7)) Pub: Magna Story GBR. Dist(s): Ulverscroft US
Elizabeth Knight is surprised to receive a visitor at her quiet convent school, & outraged when the young woman introduces herself as Phyllis Knight, her new stepmother. But the girl's anger dissolves when Elizabeth is orphaned. Accepting Phyllis suggestion, Elizabeth moves into the boisterous household of her parents house in Liverpool. Crowded into an old terraced house & rechristened Lizzie by the family, Elizabeth finds that she must rapidly adapt to her new life & its unfamiliar surroundings.

Going International, Set. 14 cass. 149.95 (439PAX) Nightingale-Conant.
With Going International, you'll learn how to: successfully market & advertise products & services overseas; select & work with foreign agents & representatives; train & transfer skills to local workers; win in foreign negotiations; set up overseas operations; conduct meetings & negotiations tactfully & skillfully; manage your personal & family life overseas; & much more.

Going International: Fundamentals of International Business Transactions. 13 cass. (Running Time: 18 hrs.). 1997. 345.00 Incl. bk. (MC05) Am Law Inst.
Course orients & updates lawyers beginning to counsel business clients who enter the international arena.

Going International: Fundamentals of International Business Transactions. 1 cass. (Running Time: 28 hrs. 30 min.). 1999. 495.00 Incl. bk. (AE06) Am Law Inst.

Going Lean: How the Best Companies Apply Lean Manufacturing Principles to Shatter Uncertainty, Drive Innovation, & Maximize Profits. unabr. abr. ed. Stephen A. Ruffa. Read by Jim Bond. (Running Time: 7 hrs.). 2008. 39.25 (978-1-4233-6461-0(9), 9781423364610, BADLE); 24.95 (978-1-4233-6460-3(0), 9781423364603, BAD); 24.95 (978-1-4233-6458-0(9), 9781423364580, Brilliance MP3); 39.25 (978-1-4233-6459-7(7), 9781423364597, Brlnc Audio MP3 Lib); audio compact disk 29.95 (978-1-4233-6456-6(2), 9781423364566, Bril Audio CD Unabri); audio compact disk 82.25 (978-1-4233-6457-3(0), 9781423364573, BriAudCD Unabrid) Brilliance Audio.

Going Low: How to Break Your Individual Golf Scoring Barrier by Thinking Like a Pro. abr. ed. Patrick Cohn. Read by Lloyd James. (Running Time: 16200 sec.). 2007. audio compact disk 28.00 (978-1-933309-19-4(9)) Pub: A Media Intl. Dist(s): Natl Bk Netwk

***Going Mutant: the Bat Boy Exposed: The Bat Boy Exposed.** unabr. ed. Barry H. Leeds & Weekly World News Editors. Read by Patrick Lawlor. (Running Time: 5 hrs.). 2010. 39.97 (978-1-4418-9071-9(8), 9781441890719, BADLE) Brilliance Audio.

***Going Mutant: the Bat Boy Exposed: The Bat Boy Exposed.** unabr. ed. Barry Leed McGinness & Weekly World News Editors. Read by Patrick Lawlor. (Running Time: 6 hrs.). 2010. 19.99 (978-1-4418-9068-9(8), 9781441890689, Brilliance MP3); 39.97 (978-1-4418-9069-6(6), 9781441890696, Brlnc Audio MP3 Lib); audio compact disk 19.99 (978-1-4418-9066-5(1), 9781441890665, Bril Audio CD Unabri); audio compact disk 49.97 (978-1-4418-9067-2(X), 9781441890672, BriAudCD Unabrid) Brilliance Audio.

***Going Mutant: the Bat Boy Exposed: The Bat Boy Exposed.** unabr. ed. Weekly World News Editors. Read by Patrick Lawlor. (Running Time: 5 hrs.). 2010. 19.99 (978-1-4418-9070-2(X), 9781441890702, BAD) Brilliance Audio.

Going Nowhere Fast. abr. ed. Gar Anthony Haywood. Read by Fran L. Washington. 2 cass. (Running Time: 3 hrs.). 2000. 7.95 (978-1-57815-010-6(8), 1063, Media Bks Audio) Media Bks NJ.
A police officer & his wife, happily on a road trip to the Grand Canyon, return to find their yougest son with a gun & a dead man nearby.

Going on to Perfection. Rick Joyner. 1 cass. (Running Time: 90 mins.). (Walking in Truth Ser.: Vol. 1). 2000. 5.00 (RJ02-001) Morning NC.
Rick reinforces our calling to walk in truth & integrity while pursuing God's perfect will for our lives.

Going Places. Nelson Gill. 1 cass. (SPA & ENG.). (J). 2001. 10.95 (KNG 3105C); audio compact disk 14.95 (KNG 3105CD) Kimbo Educ.
Help prepare little ones for elementary school with 10 Little Ducks, Big Farm, Play the Game, Dance Merengue & more. Some songs in English & Spanish.

Going Places Reader: 96 Lessons Focus on USA Destinations. (gr. 7-12). 2005. spiral bd. 49.00 (978-1-57861-547-6(X), IEP Res) Attainment.

Going Postal. unabr. ed. Terry Pratchett. Read by Stephen Briggs. Ed. by Olga Vezeris. (Discworld Ser.). 2004. audio compact disk 39.95 (978-0-06-074088-7(4)) HarperCollins Pubs.

***Going Postal.** unabr. ed. Terry Pratchett. Read by Stephen Briggs. (ENG.). 2005. (978-0-06-082469-3(7), Harper Audio); (978-0-06-082468-6(9), Harper Audio) HarperCollins Pubs.

Going Public As a Professional Astrologer. Sue Lovett. 1 cass. (Running Time: 90 min.). 1994. 8.95 (216) Am Fed Astrologers.

Going Public with Your Faith. abr. unabr. ed. William Carr Peel & Larimore Walt. 2003. 24.99 (978-0-310-24618-3(0)) Zondervan.

Going Public with Your Faith: Becoming a Spiritual Influence at Work. abr. ed. William Carr Peel & Larimore Walt. (Running Time: 4 hrs. 0 mins. 0 sec.). (ENG.). 2003. 17.99 (978-0-310-26049-3(3)) Zondervan.

Going Public with Your Faith CD Series. 2005. audio compact disk 27.00 (978-1-59834-020-4(4)) Walk Thru the Bible.

***Going Rogue: An American Life.** abr. ed. Sarah Palin. Read by Sarah Palin. (ENG.). 2009. (978-0-06-199098-4(1), Harper Audio); (978-0-06-199074-8(4), Harper Audio) HarperCollins Pubs.

***Going Rogue: An American Life.** abr. ed. Sarah Palin. Read by Sarah Palin. 2010. audio compact disk 19.99 (978-0-06-202775-7(1), Harper Audio) HarperCollins Pubs.

***Going Solo.** abr. ed. Roald Dahl. Read by Derek Jacobi. (ENG.). 2005. (978-0-06-089566-2(7)); (978-0-06-089565-5(9)) HarperCollins Pubs.

Going Solo. unabr. ed. Roald Dahl. Read by Andrew Sachs. 4 cass. (Running Time: 5 hrs. 4 min.). 2001. 25.95 (978-0-7540-0592-6(5), CAB2015) Pub: Chivers Audio Bks GBR. Dist(s): AudioGO
The second part of Roald Dahl's autobiography, in which he creates a world as bizarre & unnerving as any you will find. In Africa, our hero, more or less single-handed, rounds up a convoy of Germans leaving Dar-es-Salaam at the beginning of the Second World War.Then he becomes a fighter pilot, crashing a plane into no man's land in the Western Desert & then does yeoman service in Hurricanes during the last hopeless days in Greece before he is grounded.

Going Solo. unabr. ed. Roald Dahl. Read by Andrew Sachs. 4 CDs. (Running Time: 18240 sec.). (J). (gr. 3-7). 2001. 29.95 (978-0-7540-5407-8(1), CCD 098) Pub: Chivers Audio Bks GBR. Dist(s): AudioGO
The author creates a world as bizarre & unnerving as any you find. Starting in Africa, our hero rounds up a convoy of Germans leaving Dar-es-Salaam at the beginning of the Second World War. Then he becomes a fighter pilot, crashing a plane into no man's land in the Western Desert & finally does yeoman service in Hurricanes during the last hopeless days in Greece before he is grounded.

Going Some. unabr. ed. Rex Ellingwood Beach. Read by David Sharp. 4 cass. (Running Time: 5 hrs.). 1995. 26.95 (978-1-55686-578-7(3)) Books in Motion.
Light-hearted competition exists between two southwest ranches over which ranch has the fastest foot racer. The victory cup is an Echo phonograph, one of the few in that locale.

Going the Whole Hog. Erica Adams. 10 cass. (Running Time: 11 hrs. 30 mins.). (Soundings Ser.). (J). 2004. 84.95 (978-1-84283-879-2(2)) Pub: ISIS Lrg Prnt GBR. Dist(s): Ulverscroft US

Going Through Depression: Ecc. 2:12-26. Ed Young. 1993. 4.95 (978-0-7417-1979-9(7), 979) Win Walk.

Going to Bend. unabr. ed. Diane Hammond. Read by Hillary Huber. 8 cass. (Running Time: 11 hrs. 30 mins.). 2004. 56.95 (978-0-7861-2618-7(3), 3208) Blckstn Audio.

Going to Bend. unabr. ed. Diane Hammond. Read by Hillary Huber. 6 CDs. (Running Time: 7 hrs.). 2005. audio compact disk 55.00 (978-0-7861-8895-6(2), 1451) Blckstn Audio.

Going to College: Learning to Write. 1 cass. (Running Time: 30 min.). 9.95 (OE-81-09-08, HarperThor) HarpC GBR.

Going to Grandma's. Read by Donald Davis. (Running Time: 45 mins.). 2002. audio compact disk 14.95 (978-0-87483-685-1(9)) Pub: August Hse. Dist(s): Natl Bk Netwk

Going to Grandma's: Sing, Color'n Say. Phillip Siadi & Lenore Paxton. Read by Phillip Siadi & Lenore Paxton. 1 cass. (Running Time: 46 min.). (World of Language Activity Pack Ser.). (J). (ps-3). 1992. 5.95 (978-1-880449-01-1(3)) Wrldkids Pr.
Song, music, language lesson, related "facts" about each country & teaches children to say "I love you, Grandma," & "Grandpa" in ten different languages, fun facts about each of 10 countries. Companion coloring book included.

Going to Grandma's: Sing, Color'n Say. 2nd ed. Lenore Paxton & Phillip Siadi. Read by Lenore Paxton & Phillip Siadi. 1 cass. (Running Time: 46 min.). (World of Language Activity Pack Ser.). (J). (ps up). 1994. pap. bk. 7.95 (978-1-880449-08-0(0)) Wrldkids Pr.

Going to Grandma's (Around the World) Lenore Paxton & Phillip Siadi. Read by Lenore Paxton & Phillip Siadi. Contrib. by Paul Henderson. 1 cass. (Running Time: 20 min.). (J). (ps-5). 1998. cass. & video 14.95 (978-1-880449-21-9(8), WKV1) Wrldkids Pr.
Children's introduction to foreign languages & countries. They learn "I Love You Grandma" & "Grandpa" in ten languages while visiting 10 countries. Color video is computer animated.

Going to Ground: Simple Life on a Georgia Pond. Narrated by Amy Blackmarr. Music by Chase Anderson & Chase Anderson. (ENG.). 2007. audio compact disk 19.95 (978-0-9773173-1-8(5)) Willa Pub Co.

Going to the Chapel. unabr. ed. Rebecca Kelly. Narrated by Sherri Berger. (Running Time: 6 hrs. 22 mins. 2 sec.). (Grace Chapel Inn Ser.). (ENG.). 2009. 18.19 (978-1-60814-505-8(0)) Oasis Audio.

Going to the Chapel. unabr. ed. Rebecca Kelly. Read by Brooke Sanford. Narrated by Sherri Berger. (Running Time: 6 hrs. 22 mins. 2 sec.). (Grace Chapel Inn Ser.). (ENG.). 2009. audio compact disk 25.99 (978-1-59859-480-5(X)) Oasis Audio.

Going with the Flow. Bruce Scofield. 1 cass. 8.95 (307) Am Fed Astrologers.
Make better decisions, cope with problems using Astrology.

Going Within. Rhegina Sinozich. 2008. audio compact disk 14.95 (978-0-9706297-4-6(5)) Abrezia Pr.

Going Wrong. unabr. ed. Ruth Rendell. Read by Dermot Crowley. 8 cass. (Running Time: 12 hrs.). 2000. 59.95 (978-0-7451-6233-1(9), CAB 684) Pub: Chivers Audio Bks GBR. Dist(s): AudioGO
Guy still believed that Leonora loved him, as she had when she was younger when he was the leader of a London street gang. Guy's family lived in a block of council flats, while Leonora lived out in Holland Park. Guy's obsession with Leonora increased as the years passed. He always believed she would come back to him. But life was not a romantic fantasy and Guy could not accept the truth. It created in him a murderous madness.

Going Wrong. unabr. collector's ed. Ruth Rendell. Read by Donada Peters. 6 cass. (Running Time: 9 hrs.). 1991. 48.00 (978-0-7366-1920-2(8), 2744) Books on Tape.
Once Guy & Leonora were lovers. Now it's over but Guy can't forget...or forgive. Every day he calls Leo with fantasies about their love & their future. All she wants is him out of her life. But Guy isn't about to oblige. Then Leo announces her engagement & she finds out just how sick he is. But when Guy tries to kill two members of her family, she finally realizes the peril in which she stands.

***GoJapanese: Speak & Read the Pimsleur Way.** Pimsleur & goPimsleur. (Running Time: 7 hrs. 30 mins. 0 sec.). (Go Pimsleur Ser.). (ENG.). 2010. audio compact disk 29.99 (978-1-4423-3456-4(8), Pimsleur) Pub: S&S Audio. Dist(s): S and S Inc

Gold & International Finance: An Emphasis on Timing. unabr. ed. James E. Sinclair. 1 cass. (Running Time: 54 min.). 12.95 (370) J Norton Pubs.

Gold & the Equity & Bond Markets. unabr. ed. Thomas J. Holt. 1 cass. (Running Time: 34 min.). 12.95 (1117) J Norton Pubs.
Holt presents his flow of funds analysis & stresses the requirements of successful investment: logic, common sense & self-confidence. He discusses how politics influences the South African gem & gold values & predicts institutions will put more money into bonds in the future because of higher yield than stocks.

Gold & the Sand. Contrib. by Corey Crowder. Prod. by Aaron Sprinkle. 2008. audio compact disk 9.99 (978-5-557-47522-8(2)) Tooth & Nail.

Gold Bug see Great American Short Stories, Vol. III, A Collection

Gold Bug see Best of Edgar Allan Poe

Gold Bug see Edgar Allan Poe

Gold Bug. Edgar Allan Poe. Ed. by Raymond Harris. Illus. by Robert J. Pailthorpe. (Classics Ser.). (YA). (gr. 6-12). 1982. pap. bk. 17.96 (978-0-89061-270-5(6), 480) Jamestown.

Gold Bug. unabr. ed. Edgar Allan Poe. Perf. by Walter Covell. 1 cass. (Running Time: 82 min.). Dramatization. 1985. 7.95 (S-68) Jimcin Record.

Gold Chromosome. unabr. ed. Harley L. Sachs. 6 cass. (Running Time: 6 hrs.). 2000. 25.00 (978-0-9705390-3-8(7)) I D E V C O.

Gold City: Collection, Set. Perf. by Gold City. 2 CDs. 1998. audio compact disk 19.99 (978-0-7601-2093-4(5)) Provident Music.
Thirty-six of Gold City's most popular songs.

Gold City Set: Collection. Perf. by Gold City. 2 cass. 1998. 16.99 (978-0-7601-2092-7(7)) Provident Music.

Gold Coast. Nelson DeMille. 2 cass. (Running Time: 3 hrs. 28 mins.). (J). 2000. 18.00 (978-0-7366-9091-1(3)) Books on Tape.

Gold Coast. Elmore Leonard. Read by Frank Muller. audio compact disk 29.95 (978-1-4025-6298-3(5)) Recorded Bks.

Gold Coast. unabr. ed. Nelson DeMille. Read by Christian Rummel. (Running Time: 21 hrs.). (ENG.). 2008. 29.98 (978-1-60024-511-4(0)); audio compact disk 44.98 (978-1-60024-510-7(2)) Pub: Hachet Audio. Dist(s): HachBkGrp

***Gold Coast.** unabr. ed. Elmore Leonard. Read by Frank Muller. (ENG.). 2010. (978-0-06-199373-2(5), Harper Audio); (978-0-06-199752-5(8), Harper Audio) HarperCollins Pubs.

Gold Coast. unabr. ed. Elmore Leonard. Narrated by Frank Muller. 4 cass. (Running Time: 6.5 hrs.). 19.95 (978-1-4025-6297-6(7)) Recorded Bks.

Gold Coast, unabr. ed. Elmore Leonard. Narrated by Frank Muller. 5 cass. (Running Time: 6 hrs. 30 mins.). 1995. 44.00 (978-0-7887-0257-0(2), 94466E7) Recorded Bks.

Karen DiCilia reads her Mafia husband's will and finds he has left millions to her. Of course, she'll lose everything the minute she sleeps with another man. But Karen's husband didn't count on a sexy dolphin trainer with a scam to get Karen & her money.

Gold Coast. unabr. collector's ed. Elmore Leonard. Read by Alexander Adams. 7 cass. (Running Time: 7 hrs.). 1995. 42.00 (978-0-7366-3160-0(7), 3831) Books on Tape.

A con-man's scam could send a mobster's wife down easy street, or six feet under. Hard-boiled suspense from a master.

Gold Dog. Lev Ustinov. Read by Max Showalter. Music by Max Showalter & Peter Walker. 1 cass. (Running Time: 1 hr. 2 min.). (J). (gr. 1-7). 1991. 9.98 (978-1-879305-11-3(9), AM-C-110) Am Melody.

Two fairy tales by Soviet children's author Lev Ustinov, narrated & with original music & songs by actor Max Showalter (lyrics by Peter Walker).

Gold Dust or Bust. Scripts. 1 cass. or 1 CD. (Running Time: 30 mins.). (J). (gr. 2-6). 2000. pap. bk. & tchr. ed. 29.95 Bad Wolf Pr.

Presents the highlights of the great stampede of forty-niners to the California goldfields. From Sutter's Mill to Mad Mule Gulch, Sacramento to Fiddletown, the land's gone nuts with Gold Fever. Guiding the tour is Luzena Wilson - wife, professional cook, innkeeper, commodities gambler, banker & founder of a city. Sheet music available.

Gold from Gemini. unabr. ed. Jonathan Gash. Narrated by Christopher Kay. 7 CDs. (Running Time: 7 hrs. 45 mins.). (Lovejoy Mystery Ser.). 1999. audio compact disk 59.00 (978-1-84197-090-5(5), C1126E7) Recorded Bks.

An old man dies leaving two rough diaries & a sketch. Are they the clues to a possible Roman hoard? When an antique dealer is knocked down in a "hit & run" & Lovejoy himself is threatened, things turn nasty.

Gold from Gemini. unabr. ed. Jonathan Gash. Narrated by Christopher Kay. 6 cass. (Running Time: 7 hrs. 45 mins.). (Lovejoy Mystery Ser.). 1999. 53.00 (978-1-84197-020-2(4), H1020E7) Recorded Bks.

An old man dies leaving two rough diaries & a sketch. Are they the clues to a possible Roman board? When an antique dealer is knocked down in a "hit & run" & Lovejoy himself is threatened, things turn nasty. Can Lovejoy solve the clues & did the Roman Gemini Legion invade the Isle of Man?.

Gold from Gemini, Set. unabr. ed. Jonathan Gash. Narrated by Christopher Kay. 6 cass. 1999. 53.00 (H1020K4, Clipper Audio) Recorded Bks.

Gold, Hard Money, & Financial Gurus. Narrated by Louis Rukeyser. 2 cass. (Running Time: 2 hrs. 30 mins.). (Secrets of the Great Investors Ser.: Vol. 7). 2003. 17.95 (978-1-56823-059-7(1)) Pub: Knowledge Prod. Dist(s): APG

Learn about the timeless strategies, tactics, judgments, & principles that have produced great wealth. Hear history's great figures & personalities - in their own words - describe their techniques & achievements in finance & investing. Now you can listen to these great lessons while commuting, traveling, walking...anytime your hands are busy, but your mind is not.

Gold, Hard Money, & Financial Gurus. unabr. ed. Michael Ketcher. Read by Louis Rukeyser. (Running Time: 10800 sec.). (Secrets of the Great Investors Ser.). 2006. audio compact disk 25.95 (978-0-7861-6529-2(4)) Pub: Blckstn Audio. Dist(s): NetLibrary CO

Gold Hunters. unabr. ed. James Oliver Curwood. Read by Maynard Villers. 6 cass. (Running Time: 6 hrs. 12 min.). 1996. 39.95 (978-1-55686-723-1(9)) Books in Motion.

Here is the sequel to The Wolf Hunters with Rod, Wabi & Mukoki now in possession of the secret to a great fortune. Romance, adventure, discovery await them in the North country.

Gold in Dark Places: Shadow Work in the Struggle for Selfhood Conference, 1991. 7 cass. (Running Time: 10 hrs.). 1991. 64.95 set. (978-0-7822-0354-7(X), SHADOW) C G Jung IL.

In his countless descriptions of the individuation process, Jung always pointed to the inevitability of collision with the shadow. This painful, disillusioning encounter confronts us with our disowned, exiled parts, but it also offers a point of entry into a fuller, more human self. That which was once considered "other" & kept segregated & suppressed demands inclusion, & that inclusion demands intense work. The reward for this effort is the aurum non vulgi, the uncommon gold, of a deeper relation to the self & the world. This conference looks deeply into the nature & dynamics of the shadow as it confronts us & challenges us to enter & endure the work of transformation. Includes the following tapes: Schwartz-Salant No. 462, Giannini No. 463, McAfee No. 464, Van Eenwyk No. 465, Bolen No. 466, Engelsman No. 467, & Samuels No. 468.

Gold Is a Game of Confidence. abr. ed. Bob Rotella. Read by Bob Rotella. 2 CD. (Running Time: 13 hrs. 0 mins. 0 sec.). (ENG.). 2001. audio compact disk 18.00 (978-0-7435-0810-0(6), Audioworks) Pub: S&S Audio. Dist(s): S and S Inc

Dr. Bob Rotella, whose clients include Nick Price, Davis Love III, Tom Kite and Pat Bradley, is firmly established as the premier performance enhancement specialist in the golf world. In Golf is a Game Of Confidence, "Doc" Rotella focuses on the most important skill a golfer can have: the ability to think confidently. Confidence, or "playing with your eyes," can be the difference between making par and a bogey, one-putting and three-putting, winning and losing. To help listeners revolutionize their own course management and mental game, Rotella relates stories of the game's legendary figures, and allows the listener not only to get inside the ropes but also to get inside the heads of the game's greatest players in their most important moments. Filled with lore about the great players, great courses, and great tournaments, Golf Of Confidence inspires golfers to reach new heights in their games and their lives.

***Gold Madness.** T. V. Olsen. 2009. (978-1-60136-524-8(1)) Audio Holding.

Gold Mine. Wilbur Smith. Read by David Rintoul. 2 cass. (Running Time: 3 hrs.). (ENG., 2001. 16.99 (978-0-333-78262-0(3)) Pub: Macmillan UK GBR. Dist(s): Trafalgar

Gold Mine. unabr. ed. Wilbur Smith. Read by Roy Marsden. 6 cass. (Running Time: 9 hrs.). (Ballantyne Novel Ser.). 2000. 49.95 (978-0-7451-6292-8(4), CAB 084) Pub: Chivers Audio Bks GBR. Dist(s): AudioGO

Mining expert Rod Ironside is promoted to general manager of the Sonder Ditch Gold Mine. However, Manfred Steyner, owner of the mine, staunchly demands his unquestioning obedience. And when Manfred discovers that Rod is deeply involved in an affair with his wife, icy dislike turns to mortal hatred.

Gold Mine. unabr. collector's ed. Wilbur Smith. Read by Richard Brown. 8 cass. (Running Time: 8 hrs.). (Ballantyne Novels Ser.). 1988. 48.00 (978-0-7366-1444-3(3), 2327) Books on Tape.

How the game of great mineral wealth is played in South Africa.

***Gold Mine: A Novel of Lean Turnaround.** Based on a book by Freddy Balle & Michael Balle. 2010. (978-0-9763152-9-2(7)) Lean Enter Inst.

Gold Mining. unabr. ed. Gail Taylor. Read by Gail Taylor. Ed. by James B. Kirgan. 1 cass. (Running Time: 1 hr. 30 min.). (Essence of Nature Ser.: Vol. 6). (J). 1989. 12.99 stereo. (978-1-878362-06-3(2)) Emerald Ent.

On this tape Thumper, the adventure dog, joins a gold mining expedition as they explore the South Dakota Black Hills. This tape includes the actual sounds of nature from the South Dakota Black Hills & Custer State Park.

Gold of Exodus: The Discovery of the Real Mount Sinai. Howard Blum. 2004. 15.95 (978-0-7435-4788-8(8)) Pub: S&S Audio. Dist(s): S and S Inc

Gold of Kings. unabr. ed. Davis Bunn. Read by Phil Gigante. 1 MP3-CD. (Running Time: 11 hrs.). 2009. 24.99 (978-1-4233-9599-7(9), 9781423395997, Brilliance MP3); 24.99 (978-1-4233-9601-7(4), 9781423396017, BAD); 39.97 (978-1-4233-9600-0(6), 9781423396000, Brlnc Audio MP3 Lib); 39.97 (978-1-4233-9602-4(2), 9781423396024, BADLE); audio compact disk 89.97 (978-1-4233-9598-0(0), 9781423395980, BriAudCD Unabrid); audio compact disk 29.99 (978-1-4233-9597-3(2), 9781423395973, Bril Audio CD Unabri) Brilliance Audio.

Gold Refining & Recycling. James M. McDonald. 2004. audio compact disk (978-0-9703194-0-1(1), GEB1a) TCS Sales.

Gold Rush. Steck-Vaughn Staff. 2002. (978-0-7398-6220-9(0)) SteckVau.

Gold Rush Community: San Francisco. Compiled by Benchmark Education Staff. 2006. audio compact disk 10.00 (978-1-4108-6620-2(3)) Benchmark Educ.

Gold Seeker. unabr. ed. Charles R. Lee. Read by Cameron Beierle. 12 cass. (Running Time: 14 hrs. 36 min.). 2001. 64.95 (978-1-55686-960-0(6)) Books in Motion.

A man named Jim Turner relates how he started out in Montana and became sole owner of a large, multi-national corporation. Turner is not an intellectual giant. Forever in trouble with the law, always one step removed from a noose, he is cursed with a silly sense of humor, a violent temper, homicidal instincts and a knack for attracting bad company.

Gold Standard: Building a World-Class Team. unabr. ed. Mike Krzyzewski. Read by Jamie K. Spatola. Told to Jamie K. Spatola. (Running Time: 7 hrs.). (ENG.). 2009. 24.98 (978-1-60024-678-4(8)); audio compact disk 29.98 (978-1-60024-677-7(X)) Pub: Hachet Audio. Dist(s): HachBkGrp

Gold Standard Diet; How to Live to Be One Hundred. Charles R. Attwood. 2 cass. 1996. 17.95 Set. (978-1-56823-050-4(8)) Knowledge Prod.

Gold Standard of Interviewing: What the winners know & you Don't. DGS Consulting LLC. Tr. by Castro Maria. Transcribed by Casillas Maria. (SPA.). 2007. audio compact disk 17.99 (978-0-9797897-6-2(1)) DGS Con.

Gold Standard of Interviewing - Cantonese: What the winners Know. DGS Consulting LLC. Tr. by Jonathan Choy. Transcribed by Cynthia Liu. (CHI.). 2007. audio compact disk 17.99 (978-0-9797897-8-6(8)) DGS Con.

Gold Standard of Interviewing - Mandarin: What winners Know. DGS Consulting LLC. Tr. by Jonathan Choy. Transcribed by Cynthia Liu. (CHI.). 2007. audio compact disk 17.99 (978-0-9797897-7-9(X)) DGS Con.

Gold Standard of Public Speaking & Presentation Techniques: Talk your way to the top in America. DGS Consulting LLC. Tr. by Rhee Joanne. Transcribed by Rhee Joanne. (KOR.). 2007. audio compact disk 18.25 (978-0-9797897-4-8(5)) DGS Con.

Gold Standard of Public Speaking & Presentation Techniques: What we know Works. DGS Consulting LLC. (ENG.). 2007. audio compact disk 18.25 (978-0-9797897-0-0(2)) DGS Con.

Gold Standard of Public Speaking & Presentation Techniques: What we know Works. DGS Consulting LLC. Tr. by Maria Castro. Transcribed by Casillas Maria. (SPA.). 2007. audio compact disk 18.25 (978-0-9797897-1-7(0)) DGS Con.

Gold Standard of Public Speaking & Presentation Techniques- Catonese: Talk your way to the top in America. DGS Consulting LLC. Tr. by Jonathan Choy. Transcribed by Cynthia Liu. (CHI.). 2007. audio compact disk 17.99 (978-0-9797897-3-1(7)) DGS Con.

Gold Standard of Public Speaking & Presentation Techniques- Mandarin: Talk your way to the top in America. DGS Consulting LLC. Tr. by Jonathan Choy. Transcribed by Cynthia Liu. (CHI.). 2007. audio compact disk 17.99 (978-0-9797897-2-4(9)) DGS Con.

Gold Standard Trade & Banking. unabr. ed. Raymond Kendall. 1 cass. (Running Time: 25 min.). 12.95 (317) J Norton Pubs.

This is a discussion by an electronic expert & financial consultant about how computer technology can facilitate money flows in a gold-backed monetary system.

Goldbergs see Great Soap Operas: Selected Episodes

Golden. unabr. ed. Jennifer Lynn Barnes. Read by Jenna Lamia. (Running Time: 6 hrs.). 2006. 39.25 (978-1-4233-1192-8(2), 9781423311928, BADLE); 24.95 (978-1-4233-1191-1(4), 9781423311911, BAD) Brilliance Audio.

Golden. unabr. ed. Jennifer Lynn Barnes. Read by Jenna Lamia. (Running Time: 21600 sec.). (YA). (gr. 7-12). 2006. audio compact disk 74.25 (978-1-4233-1188-1(4), 9781423311881, BriAudCD Unabrid) Brilliance Audio.

Please enter a Synopsis.

Golden. unabr. ed. Jennifer Lynn Barnes & Jenna Lamia. (Running Time: 21600 sec.). (YA). (gr. 7-12). 2006. 62.25 (978-1-4233-1186-7(8), 9781423311867, BrilAudUnabridg); audio compact disk 39.25 (978-1-4233-1190-4(6), 9781423311904, Brlnc Audio MP3 Lib); audio compact disk 26.95 (978-1-4233-1187-4(6), 9781423311874, Bril Audio CD Unabri); audio compact disk 24.95 (978-1-4233-1189-8(2), 9781423311898, Brilliance MP3) Brilliance Audio.

Golden Afternoon Vol. 2: The Autobiography of M. M. Kaye. collector's ed. M. M. Kaye. Read by Kate Reading. 12 cass. (Running Time: 18 hrs.). 2000. 96.00 (978-0-7366-5438-8(0)) Books on Tape.

The second volume of Kaye's autobiography. It is 1927 & after studying in England, nineteen year old Mollie Kaye is reunited with India, the country where she spent her early years. As an awkward girl with a vivacious & intrepid mother, Kaye seeks comfort in her early years. As an awkward girl with a vivacious & intrepid mother, Kaye seeks comfort in her Indian friends, her sister & father, her talent for watercolors & her ongoing love affair with India itself. She vividly recreates all the richness of the Raj, the complex ceremonies of high-caste Indian life & the beauty of a kahmir spring.

***Golden Age.** unabr. ed. Tahmima Anam. Read by Madhur Jaffrey. (ENG.). 2007. (978-0-06-158002-4(3)) HarperCollins Pubs.

Golden Age. unabr. ed. Tahmima Anam. Read by Madhur Jaffrey. 8 CDs. (Running Time: 9 hrs.). 2008. audio compact disk 34.95 (978-0-06-153788-2(8), Harper Audio) HarperCollins Pubs.

***Golden Age.** unabr. ed. Tahmima Anam. Read by Madhur Jaffrey. (ENG.). 2008. (978-0-06-158006-2(6)) HarperCollins Pubs.

Golden Age, Set. unabr. ed. Kenneth Grahame. Narrated by Flo Gibson. 3 cass. (Running Time: 4 hrs. 30 min.). (J). 1985. 16.95 (978-1-55685-054-7(9)) Audio Bk Con.

The magic & mischief of childhood is played out with vivid imagination by children who view the adults who people their world as the "Olympians".

Golden Age: The Golden Age of Radio. Martha Wickham. Illus. by Dan Brown. 1 cass. Dramatization. (Smithsonian Odyssey Ser.). (ENG.). (J). (gr. 2-5). 1996. 7.95 (978-1-56899-378-2(1), C6004) Soundprints.

Moving to the beat of her Walkman through the Smithsonian's National Museum of American History, Emma finds the old radios in the Information Age exhibit vaguely familiar. They remind her of something she has seen in her Grandma's living room. Emma finds a spot to sit down. She closes her eyes & listens to her favorite song through her headphones. Big Band music is playing. She opens her eyes to find herself sitting in the middle of an unfamiliar living room with a strange family. There is no TV or stereo, only a radio - just like the one in Grandma's living room - announcing news about World War II!.

***Golden Age of Atlantis.** Diana Cooper. Andrew Brel. (Running Time: 1 hr. 10 mins. 0 sec.). (Information & Meditation Ser.). (ENG.). 2010. audio compact disk 14.95 (978-1-84409-521-6(5)) Pub: Findhorn Pr GBR. Dist(s): IPG Chicago

***Golden Age of Bbc Radio Comedy: Hancock's Half Ho.** Ray Galton & Alan Simpson. (Running Time: 2 hrs. 0 mins. 0 sec.). (ENG.). 2011. audio compact disk 24.95 (978-1-4084-6763-3(1)) Pub: AudioGO. Dist(s): Perseus Dist

Golden Age of Clipper Ships. Kenneth Bruce. 1 cass. (Running Time: 1 hr.). Dramatization. (Excursions in History Ser.). 12.50 Alpha Tape.

Golden Age of Comedy. unabr. ed. 2 cass. (Running Time: 1 hr.). (Double Value Pack Ser.). 1990. 9.95 (978-1-55569-364-0(4), 7097) Great Am Audio.

A narrated trip including radio's greatest comedians & most memorable comedy performances.

Golden Age of Comedy, Vol. 2. 6 CDs. (Running Time: 6 hrs.). 2004. audio compact disk 29.95 (978-1-57816-210-9(6)) Audio File.

Golden Age of Detectives, Vol. 2. 6 CDs. (Running Time: 6 hrs.). 2004. audio compact disk 29.95 (978-1-57816-211-6(4)) Audio File.

Golden Age of Hollywood, Set. 3 cass. 1998. 35.94 (978-1-56826-972-6(2)) Rhino Enter.

Golden Age of Mystery, Vol. 2. 6 CDs. (Running Time: 6 hrs.). 2004. audio compact disk 29.95 (978-1-57816-209-3(2)) Audio File.

Golden Age of Radio. 10.00 (HD421) Esstee Audios.

Golden Age of the Movies. Read by Paul Berman. 1 cass. (Running Time: 24 min. per cass.). 1979. 10.00 (HD413) Esstee Audios.

Discusses the personalities of the post-World War I era, the rise of the studio, the establishment of male & female leads, the standardizing of the feature film length, the advent of sound, the appearance of more screen personalities, & the characteristic productions of the major studios.

Golden Altar Worship. Freddy & Rebekah Hayler. 2007. audio compact disk 19.99 (978-0-903770-03-3(2)) Destiny Image Pubs.

***Golden Apples of the Sun.** unabr. ed. Ray Bradbury. Narrated by Michael Prichard. (Running Time: 13 hrs. 0 mins. 0 sec.). (ENG.). 2010. 24.99 (978-1-4001-6821-7(X)); 18.99 (978-1-4001-8821-5(0)); audio compact disk 37.99 (978-1-4001-1821-2(2)) Pub: Tantor Media. Dist(s): IngramPubServ

Golden Apples of the Sun, unabr. collector's ed. Ray Bradbury. Read by Michael Prichard. 7 cass. (Running Time: 7 hrs.). 1988. 42.00 (978-0-7366-1327-9(7), 2231) Books on Tape.

Only Ray Bradbury could make plausible a deep sea monster's infatuation with a flirtatious foghorn, or a misunderstood man with a perfectly reasonable explanation for murdering his house, or a nubile young witch who works out an ingenious method for experiencing human love, or a spaceship captain determined to gather a cupful of the sun, or...18 other bizarre & wonderful tales.

***Golden Apples of the Sun (Library Edition)** unabr. ed. Ray Bradbury. Narrated by Michael Prichard. (Running Time: 13 hrs. 0 mins.). 2010. 37.99 (978-1-4001-9821-4(6)); audio compact disk 90.99 (978-1-4001-4821-9(9)) Pub: Tantor Media. Dist(s): IngramPubServ

Golden Arm see Great Ghost Stories - Volume 1

Golden Arrows. unabr. ed. Craig Fraley. Read by Kevin Foley. 8 cass. (Running Time: 10 hrs.). (Kiahawk Ser.: Bk. 3). 1995. 49.95 (978-1-55686-611-1(9)) Books in Motion.

Treacherous Lake Shanoha townspeople uncover gold on the Kiahawk reservation & inadvertently unleash a deadly spirit that feasts on human flesh.

Golden Bowl. Henry James. Perf. by St. Charles Players. 2 cass. (Running Time: 3 hrs.). Dramatization. 2000. 16.95 (Monterey SoundWorks) Monterey Media Inc.

Golden Bowl. abr. ed. Henry James. Read by Christopher Casenove. 4 cass. (Running Time: 6 hrs.). (Ultimate Classics Ser.). 2004. 25.00 (978-1-931056-08-3(0), N Millennium Audio) New Millenn Enter.

The Golden Bowl portrays a couple before & after an adulterous affair. The story is told in such a subtle, nuanced way that the reader is kept guessing whether Maggie Verver is really aware of her husband's faithless behavior.

Golden Bowl. unabr. ed. Henry James. Perf. by St. Charles Players. 2 cass. (Running Time: 2 hrs. 30 min.). 2001. 16.95 (978-1-56994-527-8(6), Monterey SoundWorks) Monterey Media Inc.

Golden Bowl. unabr. ed. Henry James. Read by Christopher Casenove. 12 cass. (Running Time: 18 hrs.). (Ultimate Classics Ser.). 2004. 39.95 (978-1-931056-07-6(2), N Millennium Audio) New Millenn Enter.

Golden Bowl, Set. unabr. ed. Henry James. Read by Flo Gibson. 14 cass. (Running Time: 20 hrs. 30 min.). 1991. 42.95 (978-1-55685-206-0(1)) Audio Bk Con.

Here the Dean of Innuendo weaves a tale of a complex quandrangle when a wealthy collector of objects d'art & his daughter innocently marry a pair of lovers, the beautiful Charlotte & a charming Italian Prince.

Golden Bridge: The Meditation CD that elevates your Soul. Cainan Ashton. Gus Dwi. (ENG.). 2007. audio compact disk 15.00 (978-1-921370-73-1(4)) Red Truck AUS.

Golden Bullet. unabr. ed. M. Lehman. Read by Gene Engene. 4 cass. (Running Time: 5 hrs. 15 min.). Dramatization. 1992. 26.95 (978-1-55686-435-3(3), 435) Books in Motion.

Young Jim Moseby & Matt Rossiter find a fortune in gold. To commemorate their good fortune, Matt makes a bullet out of the gold ... a bullet which fulfills a deadly destiny.

Golden Butterfly. Anita Burgh. Read by Anne Dover. 18 cass. (Sound Ser.). (J). 2003. 109.95 (978-1-84283-253-0(0)) Pub: ISIS Lrg Prnt GBR. Dist(s): Ulverscroft US

Golden Cage. Alma Flor Ada. (Stories for the Year 'Round Ser.). (J). (gr. k-3). 4.95 (978-1-58105-317-3(7)) Santillana.

Golden Chain of Homer That Binds Heaven & Earth. Instructed by Manly P. Hall. 8.95 (978-0-89314-126-4(7), C810913) Philos Res.

Golden Chance. unabr. ed. Jayne Ann Krentz. Read by Patrick G. Lawlor & Patrick G. Franette Liebow. 1 MP3-CD. (Running Time: 11 hrs.). 2009. 39.97 (978-1-4233-8702-2(3), 9781423387022, Brinc Audio MP3 Lib) Brilliance Audio.

Golden Chance. unabr. ed. Jayne Ann Krentz. Read by Patrick G. Lawlor & Franette Liebow. 1 MP3-CD. (Running Time: 11 hrs.). 2009. 24.99 (978-1-4233-8701-5(5), 9781423387015, Brilliance MP3) Brilliance Audio.

Golden Chance. unabr. ed. Jayne Ann Krentz. Read by Patrick G. Lawlor & Patrick G. Franette Liebow. (Running Time: 11 hrs.). 2009. 39.97 (978-1-4233-8704-6(X), 9781423387046, BADLE) Brilliance Audio.

Golden Chance. unabr. ed. Jayne Ann Krentz. Read by Patrick G. Lawlor & Franette Liebow. (Running Time: 11 hrs.). 2009. 24.99 (978-1-4233-8703-9(1), 9781423387039, BAD) Brilliance Audio.

Golden Chance. unabr. ed. Jayne Ann Krentz. Read by Patrick G. Lawlor & Patrick G. Franette Liebow. 9 CDs. (Running Time: 11 hrs.). 2009. audio compact disk 82.97 (978-1-4233-8700-8(7), 9781423387008, BriAudCD Unabrid) Brilliance Audio.

Golden Chance. unabr. ed. Jayne Ann Krentz. Read by Patrick G. Lawlor & Franette Liebow. 9 CDs. (Running Time: 11 hrs.). 2009. audio compact disk 29.99 (978-1-4233-8699-5(X), 9781423386995) Brilliance Audio.

Golden Chord. Fernand Moutet. Ed. by Stanley H. Barkan. Tr. by Nancy Festinger. (Review Chapbook Ser.: No. 17: Provencal Poetry 1). 1981. 10.00 (978-0-89304-841-9(0)) Cross-Cultrl NY.

Golden Compass. Philip Pullman. 9 cass. (Running Time: 649 min.). (His Dark Materials Ser.: Bk. 1). (YA). (gr. 7-12). 2001. audio compact disk 55.00 (978-0-8072-0504-4(4), Listening Lib) Random Audio Pubg.

Golden Compass. unabr. ed. Philip Pullman. Read by Full Cast Production Staff. 8 cass. (Running Time: 12 hrs.). (His Dark Materials Ser.: Bk. 1). (YA). (gr. 7-12). 1999. 50.00 (LL 0135, Chivers Child Audio) AudioGO.

Golden Compass. unabr. ed. Philip Pullman. Read by Philip Pullman. 8 cass. (Running Time: 11hrs. 30 mins.). (His Dark Materials Ser.: Bk. 1). (YA). (gr. 7-12). 2000. 50.00 (978-0-7366-9001-0(8)) Books on Tape.
Accompanied by her demon, Lyra Belaqua sets out to prevent her best friend & other kidnapped children from becoming the subjects of gruesome experiments in the far north. This tale of adventure & fantasy crosses all ages & intertwines mythology & legends.

Golden Compass. unabr. ed. Philip Pullman. Read by Full Cast Production Staff. (YA). 2007. 59.99 (978-0-7393-7483-2(4)) Find a World.

Golden Compass. unabr. ed. Philip Pullman. 8 cass. (His Dark Materials Ser.: Bk. 1). (YA). (gr. 7-12). 1999. 59.98 (FS9-50915) Highsmith.

Golden Compass. unabr. ed. Philip Pullman. 1 cass. (His Dark Materials Ser.: Bk. 1). (YA). (gr. 7-12). 1999. (Listening Lib) Random Audio Pubg.

Golden Compass. unabr. ed. Philip Pullman. 8 vols. (Running Time: 10 hrs. 49 mins.). (His Dark Materials Ser.: Bk. 1). (J). (gr. 7 up). 1999. pap. bk. 58.00 (978-0-8072-8063-8(1), S YA 001 SP, Listening Lib) Random Audio Pubg.
Accompanied by her daemon, Lyra Belacqua sets out to prevent her best friend & other kidnapped children from becoming the subjects of gruesome experiments in the far north. This tale of adventure & fantasy crosses all ages & intertwines mythology & legends.

Golden Compass. unabr. ed. Philip Pullman. Read by Full Cast Production Staff. 3 cass. (Vol. 1). (His Dark Materials Ser.: Bk. 1). (YA). (gr. 7-12). 1999. 19.95 (978-0-8072-8093-5(3), YA102CXR, Listening Lib) Random Audio Pubg.
Accompanied by her daemon, Lyra Belacque sets out to prevent her best friend & other kidnapped children from being used in gruesome experiments in the far north.

Golden Compass. unabr. ed. Philip Pullman. Read by Philip Pullman. Read by WTW Repertory Company. 8 cass. (Running Time: 10 hrs. 49 mins.). (His Dark Materials Ser.: Bk. 1). (J). (gr. 7 up). 1999. 50.00 (978-0-8072-8062-1(3), S YA 991 CX, Listening Lib) Random Audio Pubg.
Accompanied by her daemon, Lyra Belacqua sets out to prevent her best friend & other kidnapped children from becoming the subjects of gruesome experiments in the far north. This tale of adventure & fantasy crosses all ages & intertwines mythology & legends.

Golden Compass. unabr. ed. Philip Pullman. 3 cass. (His Dark Materials Ser.: Bk. 1). (YA). (gr. 7-12). 1999. 19.95 Set; trade pkg. (978-0-8072-8143-7(3), BWYA114CXR, Listening Lib) Random Audio Pubg.
Accompanied by her daemon, Lyra Belacqua sets out tp prevent her best friend & other kidnapped children from being the subjects of gruesome experiments in the far north. Intertwines mythology & legends.

Golden Compass. unabr. ed. Philip Pullman. Perf. by Philip Pullman. Prod. by Words Take WingTM Production Staff. 9 CDs. (Running Time: 10 hrs. 49 mins.). (His Dark Materials Ser.: Bk. 1). (YA). (gr. 7 up). 2004. audio compact disk 60.00 (978-0-8072-1049-9(8), S YA 991 CD, Listening Lib) Random Audio Pubg.

Golden Compass. unabr. ed. Philip Pullman. Read by Philip Pullman. Read by Full Cast Production Staff. 9 CDs. (Running Time: 10 hrs. 49 mins.). (His Dark Materials Ser.: Bk. 1). (ENG.). (J). (gr. 5-12). 2004. audio compact disk 30.00 (978-0-8072-0471-9(4), Listening Lib) Pub: Random Audio Pubg. Dist(s): Random

Golden Compass. unabr. collector's ed. Philip Pullman. Read by David Case. 8 cass. (Running Time: 12 hrs.). (His Dark Materials Ser.: Bk. 1). (YA). (gr. 7-12). 1997. 64.00 (978-0-7366-3682-7(X), 4361) Books on Tape.
Lyra Belacqua just may hold the future of the universe in her hands. It all begins when her uncle, Lord Asriel, returns to England with tales of mystery & danger.

Golden Compass. 10th unabr. anniv. ed. Philip Pullman. Read by Philip Pullman. Read by Full Cast Production Staff. (Running Time: 10 hrs. 49 mins.). (His Dark Materials Ser.: Bk. 1). (J). (gr. 7-12). 2006. audio compact disk 44.00 (978-0-7393-3704-2(1), Listening Lib) Pub: Random Audio Pubg. Dist(s): Random

*__Golden Crab.__ Anonymous. 2009. (978-1-60136-577-4(2)) Audio Holding.

Golden Cradle: Daily Bread see Golden Cradle: Immigrant Women in the United States

Golden Cradle: Education see Golden Cradle: Immigrant Women in the United States

Golden Cradle: Identity - the New American Woman see Golden Cradle: Immigrant Women in the United States

Golden Cradle: Immigrant Women in the United States. 1 cass. (Running Time: 1 hr.). Incl. Golden Cradle Pt. 3: Neighborhoods. (G035BB090); Golden Cradle Pt. 4: Industrial Work. (G035BB090); 10.95 (G035BB090, HarperThor); 10.95 (G035CB090, HarperThor); 10.95 (G035DB090, HarperThor); 10.95 (G035EB090, HarperThor) HarpC GBR.

Golden Cradle: Immigrant Women in the United States. Read by Liv Ullmann. 1 cass. (Running Time: 1 hr.). Incl. Golden Cradle Pt. 1: The Journey. (G035AB090); Golden Cradle Pt. 2: The Arrival. (G035AB090); 10.95 (G035AB090, HarperThor) HarpC GBR.

Golden Cradle, Pt. 1, The Journey see Golden Cradle: Immigrant Women in the United States

Golden Cradle, Pt. 2, The Arrival see Golden Cradle: Immigrant Women in the United States

Golden Cradle, Pt. 3, Neighborhoods see Golden Cradle: Immigrant Women in the United States

Golden Cradle, Pt. 4, Industrial Work see Golden Cradle: Immigrant Women in the United States

Golden Cradle, Pt. 5, Three Portraits see Golden Cradle: Immigrant Women in the United States

Golden Cradle, Pt. 8, Networking see Golden Cradle: Immigrant Women in the United States

Golden Cradle, Pt. 9, Tapestries - Women's Stories, Woman's Songs see Golden Cradle: Immigrant Women in the United States

Golden Crown, Vol. 7. Chris Heimerdinger. 4 cass. (Tennis Shoes Adventure Ser.). 2004. 19.95 (978-1-57734-499-5(5), 07002270) Covenant Comms.

Golden Dawn Vol. 1: The Banishing Ritual of the Pentagram; Awareness & Relaxation. Israel Regardie. Music by Zehm Aloim. 2001. audio compact disk 31.00 (978-1-56184-201-8(X)) New Falcon Pubns.

Golden Dawn Vol. 2: Mantram & Breathing; the Middle Pillar Ritual. Israel Regardie. 2001. audio compact disk 31.00 (978-1-56184-203-2(6)) New Falcon Pubns.

Golden Dawn Vol. 3: Banishing; Relaxation/Awareness; Mantram/Breathing; Middle Pillar; Practice Presence of God/HGA; Rose Cross. Speeches. Israel Regardie. 6 CDs. 2001. audio compact disk 93.00 (978-1-56184-207-0(9)) New Falcon Pubns.

Golden Dawn Vol. 4: The Knowledge Lectures. Israel Regardie. 2001. audio compact disk 31.00 (978-1-56184-208-7(7)) New Falcon Pubns.

*__Golden Days.__ D. E. Stevenson. 2010. 54.95 (978-1-4079-0994-3(0)); audio compact disk 64.95 (978-1-4079-0995-0(9)) Pub: Soundings Ltd GBR. Dist(s): Ulverscroft US

Golden Dreams-Music. 2007. audio compact disk 16.95 (978-1-56136-420-6(7)) Master Your Mind.

Golden Drum. 1 cass. (Running Time: 56 min.). (J). (ps up). 9.98 (314) MFLP CA.
Empowering tale about a young girl who uses courage, wisdom & wit to pursue her dreams.

Golden Drum. Jay O'Callahan. Perf. by Jay O'Callahan. 1 CD. (Running Time: 46 min. 12 sec.). (YA). 2003. audio compact disk 15.00 (978-1-877954-44-3(6)) Pub: Artana Prodns. Dist(s): Yellow Moon
Ororingy, an extraordinary woman, uses wit and courage in her quest for the magic drum that will save the enchanted land of Artana.

Golden Drum. Jay O'Callahan. Perf. by Jay O'Callahan. 1 cass. (Running Time: 46 min.). (YA). (gr. 2 up). 1994. 10.00 (978-1-877954-04-7(7)) Artana Prodns.
Ororingy uses wit and courage in her quest for the magic drum that will save the enchanted land of Artana.

Golden Earth. unabr. collector's ed. Norman Lewis. Read by Richard Brown. 8 cass. (Running Time: 12 hrs.). 1991. 64.00 (978-0-7366-1889-2(9), 2717) Books on Tape.
The second of Norman Lewis' travel books, Golden Earth describes his journeys in Burma at a time when the Far East was passing out of reach for the ordinary traveler. Lewis was determined to see the Far East while it was still possible. He was just in time. Burma, China, North Korea, Vietnam...all were soon to fall behind a bamboo curtain nearly impossible for Westerners to penetrate.

Golden Flame Meditation. Scripts. Created by Joan Marie Whelan. Narrated by Joan Marie Whelan. 1 CD. (Running Time: 60 mins). 2002. audio compact disk 17.95 (978-0-9718654-4-0(2)) Ser Hse.
The purpose of "The Golden Flame" meditation is to allow you to own your heart's desire at a much deeper level; thus facilitating you to create your life's destiny in the present moment. Many people utilize their mind to create goals and lists they wish to accomplish, but seldom reach their true life's purpose. This meditation will assist in accomplishing this end. By repetitively listening to this meditation and teaching and giving yourself permission to relax and let go of the outcome, you will be shown how to help your mind, body and energy level within by going to a much deeper level of attraction, thus reaching your ultimate goal.

Golden Fleece see Tanglewood Tales

Golden Fleece. (147) Books in Motion.

Golden Fleece. unabr. ed. Nathaniel Hawthorne. Read by Walter Zimmerman. 1 cass. (Running Time: 78 min.). Dramatization. 7.95 (S-26) Jimcin Record.
Hawthorne's version of the story of Jason & his famous ghost.

Golden Fleece & the Heroes Who Lived Before Achilles. Padraic Colum. Read by Fred Williams. (Running Time: 9 hrs.). 2002. 30.95 (978-1-59912-667-8(2)) Iofy Corp.

Golden Fleece & the Heroes Who Lived Before Achilles. unabr. ed. Padraic Colum. Read by Fred Williams. 7 cass. (Running Time: 10 hrs.). 2002. 49.95 (978-0-7861-2196-0(3), 2943); audio compact disk 64.00 (978-0-7861-9533-6(9), 2943) Blckstn Audio.
The story of Jason, the Argonauts, and their quest for the Golden Fleece.

Golden Fox. unabr. ed. Wilbur Smith. Read by Richard Brown. 15 cass. (Running Time: 22 hrs. 30 min.). (Courtney Novels). 1993. 120.00 (978-0-7366-2524-1(0), 3277) Books on Tape.
The Courtney's rally to free their daughter from a terrorist's clutches.

Golden Fox. unabr. ed. Wilbur Smith. Read by Christian Rodska. 14 cass. (Running Time: 21 hrs.). (Sean Courtney Adventure Ser.). 2000. 89.95 (978-0-7451-4160-2(9), CAB 843) Pub: Chivers Audio Bks GBR. Dist(s): AudioGO
In Africa, two decades of bitter dynastic conflict explode with terrifying ferocity. To Garry and Sean Courtney it is a struggle to the end; brother against brother as they are dragged unwittingly into the lair of international terrorists. Only Isabella Courtney can prevent their mutual destruction. She is the link to "Golden Fox," a man who hides a deadly secret.

Golden Ghetto: The Psychology of Affluence. unabr. ed. Jessie H. O'Neill. 7 cass. (Running Time: 8 hrs. 23 mins.). 2001. 45.00 (978-0-9678554-1-7(1)); audio compact disk 55.00 (978-0-9678554-2-4(X)) Affluenza Proj.
First hand account of growing up in affluence & provides a look at why attaining wealth proves to be a hollow achievement for many. A description on understanding & treating the problems of those who have amassed great wealth.

Golden Girls. unabr. ed. Elvi Rhodes. Read by Jacqueline King. 7 cass. (Running Time: 10 hrs.). 2001. 61.95 (978-1-86042-559-2(3), 25593) Pub: Soundings Ltd GBR. Dist(s): Ulverscroft US
Eleanor Heaton was twenty-three when her husband died, leaving her with three small daughters & nothing else. She was reduced to going to Akersfield market & asking Dick Fletcher for help. It was to take many years & all the tragedy of the 1914 war before Eleanor was able to repay Dick Fletcher the great debt she owed him.

*__Golden Goose.__ Anonymous. 2009. (978-1-60136-608-5(6)) Audio Holding.

Golden Goose. Susan Saunders. Read by Madelon Thomas et al. Illus. by Isadore Seltzer. 1 cass. (Running Time: 20 min.). (J). (ps-3). 1988. bk. 5.95 Scholastic Inc.

Golden Goose. unabr. ed. Read by Julie Harris. 1 read-along cass. (Running Time: 10 min.). (World of Words Ser.). (J). (gr. k-3). bk. 15.00 (SAC 6500L) Spoken Arts.

Golden Hawk. unabr. ed. Will C. Knott. Read by Maynard Villers. 4 cass. (Running Time: 4 hrs. 12 min.). (Golden Hawk Ser.: Bk. 1). 1995. 26.95 (978-1-55686-638-8(0)) Books in Motion.
Raised by the Comanches who killed his parents & took him into their tribe, Jed Thompson, now full grown, faces the choice of which world to live in.

*__Golden Hell.__ unabr. ed. L. Ron Hubbard. Read by Owen Sun et al. Narrated by R. F. Daley. 2 CDs. (Running Time: 2 hrs.). (Stories from the Golden Age Ser.). 2010. audio compact disk 9.95 (978-1-59212-253-0(1)) Gala Pr LLC.

Golden Hour. unabr. ed. 5 cass. (Running Time: 7:30 hrs). (YA). (gr. 5-8). 2005. 45.75 (978-1-4193-0378-4(3)) Recorded Bks.

*__Golden Hustla.__ unabr. ed. Wahida Clark. (Running Time: 11 hrs.). 2010. 29.95 (978-1-4417-6407-2(0)); 65.95 (978-1-4417-6404-1(6)); audio compact disk 29.95 (978-1-4417-6406-5(2)); audio compact disk 100.00 (978-1-4417-6405-8(4)) Blckstn Audio.

Golden Key. abr. ed. George MacDonald. Read by Michael Zebulon. 1 cass. (Running Time: 1 hr. 30 min.). 1995. 10.95 (978-0-944993-23-1(0)) Audio Lit.
Our favorite fairytale by the master of fantasy, in which you can regain through the magical world the wonder & innocence of childhood.

Golden Key. unabr. ed. George MacDonald. 1 CD. (Running Time: 1 hr. 0 mins. 0 sec.). (Fairy Tale (Hovel Audio) Ser.). (ENG.). (J). (gr. 4-7). 2004. audio compact disk 12.98 (978-1-59644-013-5(9), Hovel Audio) christianaud.
Join the children Tangle and Mossy as they embark on a journey of faith, spiritual maturity and sanctification. Richly imaginative and sparkling with mythic qualities, this story communicates the joy of entering into faith as a child, traveling through life with a loving companion, and longing for the heavenly country. Poignant and beautifully written, The Golden Key will nourish both faith and imagination in the listener. C.S. Lewis delighted in the cleansing ability of reading George MacDonald, and The Golden Key certainly represents that quality.

*__Golden Key.__ unabr. ed. George MacDonald. Narrated by Paul Eggington. (Running Time: 1 hr. 0 mins. 0 sec.). (ENG.). 2004. 8.98 (978-1-59644-011-1(2), Hovel Audio) christianaud.

Golden Key to Reading: The Paula Di Intensive Phonics Method of Reading-Writing-Spelling, Set. 2nd ed. Pauline G. DiGiovanni. 1985. pap. bk. 124.99 (978-0-936543-11-6(6)) Paula Di Ed.

Golden Lies. unabr. ed. Barbara Freethy. Narrated by Julia Gibson. 9 cass. (Running Time: 13 hrs. 30 mins.). 2004. 79.75 (978-1-4193-1193-2(X), L1132MC) Recorded Bks.

Golden Lilies: Letters by Kwei Li. unabr. ed. Eileen Goudge. Read by Donada Peters. 5 cass. (Running Time: 5 hrs.). 1994. 30.00 (978-0-7366-2623-1(9), 3363) Books on Tape.
An intimate portrait of Chinese life, Golden Lilies derives from a series of long-lost letters. They take us inside a world foreign in time & place, where women played a surprisingly important role.

Golden Lion of Granpere. Anthony Trollope. Narrated by Flo Gibson. 2008. 20.95 (978-1-60646-022-1(6)) Audio Bk Con.

Golden Mean: In Which the Extraordinary Correspondence of Griffin & Sabine Concludes. unabr. ed. Nick Bantock. Read by Maxwell Caufield et al. 1 cass. (Running Time: 40 min.). (Griffin & Sabine Trilogy). 1993. 10.95 (978-1-879371-49-1(9)) Pub Mills.
The powerful conclusion of The Griffin & Sabine trilogy which follows the rare & brilliant relationship of two lovers through their extraordinary correspondence.

Golden Mermaid. unabr. ed. 1 cass. (Running Time: 20 min.). Dramatization. (Magic Looking Glass Ser.). (J). (gr. 2-6). 1989. 9.95 (978-0-7810-0026-0(2), NIM-CW-127-5-C) NIMCO.
A folk tale of German descent.

Golden Mountain. Irene Kai. Read by Anna Fields. (Running Time: 11 hrs.). 2005. 34.95 (978-1-59912-668-5(0)) Iofy Corp.

Golden Mountain: Beyond the American Dream. unabr. ed. Irene Kai. Read by Anna Fields. 9 CDs. (Running Time: 39600 sec.). 2006. audio compact disk 34.95 (978-0-9744890-1-8(8)) Pub: Silver Lght Pubns. Dist(s): PerseuPGW

Golden Mountain -Lib. Irene Kai. Read by Anna Fields. 9 cass. (Running Time: 12 hrs.). 2005. 72.95 (978-0-7861-2946-1(8), 3418); audio compact disk 90.00 (978-0-7861-8137-7(0), 3418) Blckstn Audio.

Golden Nuggets: From Sir John Templeton. John Templeton. 1 CD. (Running Time: 45 Minutes). 2005. audio compact disk 12.95 (978-1-932031-81-2(2)) Pub: Templeton Pr. Dist(s): Chicago Distribution Ctr

Golden Nuggets from Forgotten Places: Selected Studies from Kings & Chronicles, Charles R. Swindoll. 5 cass. (Running Time: 8 hrs.). 1996. 25.95 (978-1-57972-024-7(2)) Insight Living.
Bible study on the lesser-known kings of Israel & Judah.

Golden Ocean. unabr. ed. Patrick O'Brian. Read by David Case. 7 cass. (Running Time: 10 hrs. 30 min.). 1995. 56.00 (978-0-7366-2912-6(2), 3609) Books on Tape.
Patrick O'Brian's first novel of the sea, a precursor to the acclaimed Aubrey/Maturin series.

Golden Ocean. unabr. ed. Patrick O'Brian. Narrated by John Franklyn-Robbins. 8 cass. (Running Time: 11 hrs.). 1995. 70.00 (978-0-7887-0388-1(9), 94579E7) Recorded Bks.
In 1740, two young Irishman - lifelong friends Peter & Sean - join Commodore Anson & his crew on their quest for fortune & fame in the golden ocean.

Golden Ocean. unabr. ed. Patrick O'Brian. Narrated by John Franklyn-Robbins. 10 CDs. (Running Time: 11 hrs.). 2000. audio compact disk 97.00 (978-0-7887-4469-3(0), C1166W5) Recorded Bks.
In 1740, two young Irishman, lifelong friends Peter & Sean, join Commodore Anson & his crew on their quest for fortune & fame in the golden ocean.

*__Golden One.__ abr. ed. Elizabeth Peters. Read by Barbara Rosenblat. (ENG.). 2005. (978-0-06-084282-6(2), Harper Audio); (978-0-06-084283-3(0), Harper Audio) HarperCollins Pubs.

Golden One. abr. ed. Elizabeth Peters, pseud. Read by Barbara Rosenblat. (Amelia Peabody Ser.: No. 14). 2005. audio compact disk 14.95 (978-0-06-076362-6(0)) HarperCollins Pubs.

Golden One: A Novel of Suspense. unabr. ed. Elizabeth Peters, pseud. Narrated by Barbara Rosenblat. 13 cass. (Running Time: 18 hrs.). (Amelia Peabody Ser.: No. 14). 2002. 106.00 (978-1-4025-2401-1(3)) Recorded Bks.
Egyptologist and millionaire Amelia Peabody Emerson is back in Egypt hunting down tomb robbers, uncovering antiquities fraud, and meddling in the life of her son Ramses. In 1917, with the war looming in the distance, Amelia and her family return to Egypt for an extensive archaeological dig after learning of another tomb that was desecrated by thieves. Hot on their trail, Amelia's family is thrown into disarray when her son, Ramses, is called

away by the British government for a covert operation in Gaza, the gateway to the Holy Land.

Golden Pince-Nez see Return of Sherlock Holmes

Golden Ring. Perf. by Surkhai Askerov. 1 cass. (Running Time: 32 min.). 1996. 5.95 (17795-11114-1) Azerbaijan Intl.
Surkhai Askerov, 14 year old lad (soprano) sings Azerbaijan & European classics accompanied by the Azerbaijan State Chamber Orchestra with Yashar Imanov directing.

Golden Ring: A Gathering of Friends for Making Music. George Armstrong et al. 1 cass., 1 CD. 9.98 (C-16); audio compact disk 14.98 CD. (CD-16) Folk-Legacy.
The joy of sharing music with friends.

Golden Road. unabr. ed. L. M. Montgomery. Read by Grace Conlin. 6 cass. (Running Time: 8 hrs. 30 mins.). 1999. 44.95 (978-0-7861-1489-4(4), 2340) Blckstn Audio.
Sara Stanley is the Story Girl. When she returns to Carlisle to spend the winter with the King family, she comes up with the idea of publishing a magazine. "Our Magazine" quickly becomes the most entertaining publication anyone has ever read. But nothing is forever.

Golden Road, Set. unabr. ed. L. M. Montgomery. Read by Grace Conlin. 6 cass. (J). 1999. 44.95 (FS9-43390) Highsmith.

Golden Rule. Ilene Cooper. Illus. by Gabi Swiatkowska. (J). 2007. bk. 29.95 (978-0-8045-4191-6(4)) Spoken Arts.

Golden Rule. Ilene Cooper. Illus. by Gabi Swiatkowska. 1 cass. (Running Time: 8 mins.). (J). (gr. k-4). 2008. bk. 27.95 (978-0-8045-6968-2(1)) Spoken Arts.

Golden Rule of Schmoozing. Aye Jay. Read by Penn Jillette. (Running Time: 3 hrs.). (C). 2005. 19.95 (978-1-59912-907-5(8)) Iofy Corp.

Golden Rule of Schmoozing. Aye Jay. Read by Penn Jillette. 3 CDs. (Running Time: 3 hrs. 30 mins.). 2004. audio compact disk 19.95 (978-1-59316-037-1(2)) Listen & Live.
So what is schmoozing? According to Webster's unabridged dictionary, schmoozing is a Yiddish word that means to chat or to converse idly. But today there is a common misconception that the word has come to suggest a con or trickery. It's not.Schmoozing is the Golden Rule at full throttle. It's a thrill and an art form that encourages people to say, "you've made my day" instead of demanding "make my day". It's a technique for turning others on, not taking others on. A schmoozer is someone who talks to people as if they really mattered-and they do!Read by Penn Jillette, who has been called the most wired magician on this planet, and is the more gregarious half of Penn & Teller?the world?s most famous magic duo.

Golden Rule of Schmoozing. abr. ed. Aye Jay. Read by Penn Jillette. 2 cass. (Running Time: 3 hrs.). 2000. pap. bk. 27.95 Listen & Live.
Jaye, a professional performer & clown, has applied the Yiddish term "schmoozing," or "chatting," to all aspects of life: business dealings, romance strategies & child-rearing. He says he taught himself this art as a way of coping with being a "functional illiterate" at loose in the world.

Golden Rule of Schmoozing. abr. ed. Aye Jaye. Read by Penn Jillette. (YA). 2008. 34.99 (978-1-60514-690-4(0)) Find a World.

Golden Scorpion. Sax Rohmer, pseud. Read by John Bolen. (Running Time: 6 hrs. 45 mins.). 2001. 27.95 (978-1-60083-586-5(4), Audiofy Corp) Iofy Corp.

Golden Scorpion. Sax Rohmer, pseud. (Gaston Max Ser.). (ENG.). 2005. audio compact disk 72.00 (978-1-4001-3013-9(1)) Pub: Tantor Media. Dist(s): IngramPubServ

Golden Scorpion. unabr. ed. Sax Rohmer, pseud. Narrated by John Bolen. 6 CDs. (Running Time: 6 hrs. 44 mins.). (Gaston Max: Vol. 2). (ENG.). 2001. audio compact disk 36.00 (978-1-4001-0013-2(5)) Pub: Tantor Media. Dist(s): IngramPubServ

Golden Scorpion. unabr. ed. Sax Rohmer, pseud. Narrated by John Bolen. 1 CD (MP3). (Running Time: 6 hrs. 44 mins.). (Gaston Max: Vol. 2). (ENG.). 2001. audio compact disk 20.00 (978-1-4001-5013-7(2)) Pub: Tantor Media. Dist(s): IngramPubServ

Golden Scorpion. unabr. ed. Sax Rohmer, pseud. Narrated by John Bolen. (Running Time: 6 hrs. 30 mins. 0 sec.). (ENG.). 2009. audio compact disk 55.99 (978-1-4001-4095-4(1)); audio compact disk 19.99 (978-1-4001-6095-2(2)); audio compact disk 27.99 (978-1-4001-1095-7(5)) Pub: Tantor Media. Dist(s): IngramPubServ

Golden Sheaves, Black Horses. unabr. ed. Fred Archer. 4 cass. (Isis Cassettes Ser.). 2006. 44.95 (978-0-7531-2041-5(0)) Pub: ISIS Lrg Prnt GBR. Dist(s): Ulverscroft US

Golden Shoe Goalie. Shaun Gayle & Pat Owsley. Illus. by Pat Owsley. 1 cass. (Shaun Gayle's Sports Tales Ser.). (J). (gr. 5-9). 1995. pap. bk. 8.99 (978-1-56476-463-8(X), 6-3463) David C Cook.

Golden Shrine: A Tale of War at the Dawn of Time. unabr. ed. Harry Turtledove. Narrated by William Dufris. (Running Time: 14 hrs. 0 mins. 0 sec.). (Opening of the World Ser.). (ENG.). 2009. 24.99 (978-1-4001-5785-3(4)); audio compact disk 37.99 (978-1-4001-0785-8(7)); audio compact disk 75.99 (978-1-4001-3785-5(3)) Pub: Tantor Media. Dist(s): IngramPubServ

***Golden Shrine: A Tale of War at the Dawn of Time.** unabr. ed. Harry Turtledove. Narrated by William Dufris. (Running Time: 14 hrs. 0 mins.). (Opening of the World Ser.). 2009. 19.99 (978-1-4001-7785-1(5)) Tantor Media.

Golden Skylark. unabr. collector's ed. Elizabeth Goudge. Read by Donada Peters. 7 cass. (Running Time: 10 hrs. 30 min.). 1992. 56.00 (978-0-7366-2146-5(6), 2944) Books on Tape.
Short stories to help us escape. Beautifully written.

Golden Slumbers: Lullabies from Far & Near. Music by Pete Seeger & Oscar Brand. (Running Time: 25 min.). (J). 11.95 (HarperChildAud) HarperCollins Pubs.

Golden Soak. unabr. collector's ed. Hammond Innes. Read by H. H. Cornell. 7 cass. (Running Time: 10 hrs. 30 min.). 1984. 56.00 (978-0-7366-0858-9(3), 1809) Books on Tape.
Innes re-creates the virgin Australian wilderness in this novel of greed & corruption within the mining industry.

Golden Spiders. Rex Stout. Narrated by Michael Prichard. (Running Time: 21840 sec.). (Nero Wolfe Ser.). (ENG.). 2007. audio compact disk 27.95 (978-1-57270-845-7(X)) Pub: AudioGO. Dist(s): Perseus Dist

Golden Spiders. unabr. ed. Rex Stout. Read by Michael Prichard. 6 cass. (Running Time: 6 hrs. 4 min.). (Nero Wolfe Ser.). 2004. 29.95 (978-1-57270-038-3(6), N61038u) Pub: Audio Partners. Dist(s): PerseuPGW
When a young lad who is seeking the woman with the golden spider earrings is murdered, his dying wish is that all of his money - $4.30 - be used to retain Wolfe to find the woman, whom he thought was in danger.

Golden Spiders. unabr. collector's ed. Rex Stout. Read by Michael Prichard. 7 cass. (Running Time: 7 hrs.). (Nero Wolfe Ser.). 1995. 56.00 (978-0-7366-3132-7(1), 3807) Books on Tape.
Why does Nero Wolfe take a case for $4.30? What do gold earrings have to do with two murders? Wolfe will find out.

***Golden Spirit.** unabr. ed. Stephanie Perry Moore. Narrated by Debora Raell. (Running Time: 2 hrs. 30 mins. 0 sec.). (Carmen Browne Ser.). (ENG.). 2010. audio compact disk 12.98 (978-1-61045-084-3(1), christaudio) christianaud.

Golden Steed. Jeffrey Lord. Read by Lloyd James. 2 vols. No. 13. 2004. 18.00 (978-1-58807-368-6(8)); (978-1-58807-786-8(1)) Am Pubng Inc.

Golden Straw. unabr. ed. Catherine Cookson. Read by Susan Jameson. 14 cass. (Running Time: 14 hrs.). 1994. 110.95 Set. (978-0-7451-4320-0(2), CAB 1003) AudioGO.
It all began with the golden straw hat that Mabel Arkwright gave to her friend, Emily Pearson. Upon Mabel's death, Emily takes a vacation in Southern France to recuperate. There, the young woman in the golden straw hat attracts the gaze of Paul Steerman. But Paul is not at all what he seems to be, & he will bring nothing but hardship to Emily.

***Golden Thirteen: Recollections of the First Black Naval Officers.** unabr. ed. Paul Stillwell. Narrated by Alan Bomar Jones. (Running Time: 9 hrs. 0 mins.). 2010. 34.99 (978-1-4001-9907-5(7)); 24.99 (978-1-4001-6907-8(0)); 15.99 (978-1-4001-8907-6(1)); audio compact disk 34.99 (978-1-4001-1907-3(3)); audio compact disk 83.99 (978-1-4001-4907-0(X)) Pub: Tantor Media. Dist(s): IngramPubServ

Golden Treasury of Catholic Verse. Read by Leo Brady. 10.95 (978-0-8045-0712-7(0), SAC 712) Spoken Arts.

Golden Treasury of French Drama. 1 cass. pap. bk. 16.95 (SFR145) J Norton Pubs.
Jean-Louis Barrault & Madeleine Renaud, the French theater couple, interpret scenes from the repertoire of Moliere.

Golden Treasury of French Drama. Read by Jean-Louis Barrault & Madeleine Renaud. 1 cass. (Running Time: 50 min.). Dramatization. (FRE.). 11.95 (978-0-8045-0715-8(5), SAC 48-6) Spoken Arts.
Scenes from: Moliere (Le Misanthrope II,i; Amphitryon- Prologue); Marivaux (Le Fausses Confidences II, 13, 15); Beaumarchais (Le Mariage de Figaro I, i; V, 3); Musset (Les Caprices de Marianne II, i).

Golden Treasury of French Drama. unabr. ed. Read by Jean-Louis Barrault & Madeleine Renaud. 1 cass. 1992. pap. bk. 16.95 (978-0-88432-466-9(4), SFR145) J Norton Pubs.
Foreign Language Instruction. Jean-Louis Barraudt & Madeleine Renaud interpret scenes from the repertoire of Moliere.

Golden Treasury of French Verse. Read by Jean Vilar. Ed. by Kenneth Cornell. 1 cass. (Running Time: 50 min.). (FRE.). 11.95 (978-0-8045-0711-0(2), SAC 48-1) Spoken Arts.
Contains representative poetry from the famous literary figures of France as Charles d'Orleans, Ronsard & Apollinaire.

Golden Treasury of French Verse. unabr. ed. 1 cass. 1992. pap. bk. 16.95 (978-0-88432-472-0(9), SFR140) J Norton Pubs.
Foreign Language Instruction. Representative poems from French literature ranging from Charles d'Orleans & Roussard to Apollinaire.

Golden Treasury of Greek Poetry & Prose. unabr. ed. Poems. Mimnermus et al. Perf. by Pearl Wilson. 1 cass. (GEC.). 1984. 12.95 (978-0-694-50028-4(3), SWC 1034) HarperCollins Pubs.

Golden Treasury of Irish Verse. unabr. ed. Read by Padraic Colum. 1 cass. (Running Time: 50 min.). 10.95 (978-0-8045-0706-6(6), SAC 45-2) Spoken Arts.
Poems by James Mangan, Thomas Moore, Jonathan Swift, John P. Curran, James Stephens, James Joyce & others.

Golden Treasury of Italian Verse. unabr. ed. 1 cass., bklet. (Running Time: 1 hr.). 1992. pap. bk. 16.95 (978-0-88432-474-4(5), SIT110) J Norton Pubs.
A broad anthology by fourteen of the major poets such as San Francesco, Dante, Petrarca, Ariosto, Michelangelo, Tasso & d'Annunzio. Complete with text in Italian with English translation.

Golden Treasury of James Stephens. unabr. ed. James Stephens. Read by James Stephens. 1 cass. (Running Time: 50 min.). 10.95 (978-0-8045-0744-8(9), SAC 45-6) Spoken Arts.

Golden Treasury of Spanish Prose. abr. ed. Read by Manuel Duran. (Running Time: 50 min.). (Spanish Literature Ser.). (SPA.). 11.95 (978-0-8045-0831-5(3), SAC 49-5) Spoken Arts.
Twelve selections by authors from the Sixteenth Century to the Present. Includes Cervantes, Quevedo, Feijoo, Valera, Pereda, Ganivet & Galdos, with critical analysis.

Golden Treasury of Spanish Prose. unabr. ed. 1 cass. (Running Time: 60 mins.). (SPA.). 1992. pap. bk. 16.95 (978-0-88432-478-2(8), SSP210) J Norton Pubs.
Foreign Language Instruction. Twelve selections by authors from the 16th Century to the present. Includes Cervantes, Quevado, Feijoo, Valera, Pereda, Ganivet & Galdos.

Golden Treasury of Spanish Verse. Valdes et al. Read by Ricardo Florit. (SPA.). 11.95 (978-0-8045-0829-2(1), SAC 49-3); Spoken Arts.
Spanish lyric poetry from the 15th through 19th centuries.

Golden Triangle. unabr. ed. Bertil Lintner. Read by Richard C. Hottelet. (Running Time: 10800 sec.). (World's Political Hot Spots Ser.). 2006. audio compact disk 25.95 (978-0-7861-6442-4(5)) Pub: Blckstn Audio. Dist(s): NetLibrary CO

Golden Triangle. unabr. ed. Bertil Lintner. Read by Richard C. Hottlet. Ed. by Wendy McElroy. 2 cass. (Running Time: 3 hrs.). Dramatization. (World's Political Hot Spots Ser.). (YA). (gr. 11 up). 1992. 17.95 (978-0-938935-63-6(1), 10368) Knowledge Prod.
Thailand, Laos & Burma have been known as the "Golden Triangle" because of their historically prominent role in the drug trade. For centuries, these countries have produced the opium that has attracted traders from Europe & elsewhere.

Golden Unicorn. unabr. ed. Phyllis A. Whitney. Read by Liza Ross. 10 cass. (Running Time: 15 hrs.). 1998. 69.95 (978-0-7540-0120-1(2), CAB1543) Pub: Chivers Audio Bks GBR. Dist(s): AudioGO
Devastated by the sudden death of her adoptive parents, writer Courtney Marsh decides to look for her natural parents to fill the gap left behind. Her only clue is a tiny golden unicorn that was found hanging on a chain from her neck when she was adopted at just two months of age. As Courtney searches the past, she comes face to face with the murderer her real mother has not yet escaped.

Golden Valkyrie. unabr. ed. Iris Johansen. Read by Angela Brazil. 5 CDs. (Running Time: 5 hrs. 25 mins.). (Loveswept Romance Ser.). (ENG.). 2008. audio compact disk 19.95 (978-1-60283-422-4(9)) Pub: AudioGO. Dist(s): Perseus Dist

Golden Verses of Pythagoras. Instructed by Manly P. Hall. 8.95 (978-0-89314-127-1(5), C571110) Philos Res.

Golden Web. unabr. ed. Simon Gandolfi. Read by Garard Green. 6 cass. (Running Time: 8 hrs.). (Isis Ser.). (J). 1995. 54.95 (978-1-85695-897-4(3), 950104) Pub: ISIS Lrg Prnt GBR. Dist(s): Ulverscroft US

Golden Willow: The Story of a Lifetime of Love. unabr. ed. Harry Bernstein. Narrated by Mike Kellogg. (Running Time: 5 hrs. 45 mins. 45 sec.). (ENG.). 2009. 18.19 (978-1-60814-555-3(7), SpringWater); audio compact disk 25.99 (978-1-59859-549-9(0), SpringWater) Oasis Audio.

Golden World. unabr. ed. Robert Johnson. 6 CDs. (Running Time: 6 Hrs). 2007. audio compact disk 69.95 (978-1-59179-622-0(9), AF01188D) Sounds True.

Golden Years? Mental Health & the Elderly: Program from the award winning public radio Series. Interview. Hosted by Fred Goodwin. 1 CD. (Running Time: 1hr). (Infinite Mind Ser.). 2002. audio compact disk 21.95 (978-1-888064-79-7(X), LCM 219) Lichtenstein Creat.
In this hour, we explore The Golden Years? Mental Health and the Elderly. Guests include Dr. Ira Katz, director of the geriatric psychiatry program at the University of Pennsylvania; Dr. Mildred Reynolds, a retired psychiatric social worker who has, herself, been diagnosed with depression and is now on the board of the National Depressive and Manic-Depressive Association and an advocate for elderly people with mental illness; Dr. Ellen Langer, a professor of psychology at Harvard University and the author of Mindfulness and The Power of Mindful Learning; and English professor and writer Carolyn Heilbrun, author of The Last Gift of Time: Life Beyond Sixty.

Golden Years Ain't for Wimps: Humorous Stories for Your Senior Moments. unabr. ed. Karen O'Connor. Narrated by Karen O'Connor. (ENG.). 2008. 13.99 (978-1-60814-230-9(2)); audio compact disk 19.99 (978-1-59859-342-6(0)) Oasis Audio.

Goldengrove. unabr. ed. Francine Prose. Read by Mamie Gummer. 7 CDs. (Running Time: 8 hrs.). 2008. audio compact disk 39.95 (978-0-06-166458-8(8), Harper Audio) HarperCollins Pubs.

Goldengrove. unabr. ed. Francine Prose. Read by Mamie Gummer. 7 CDs. (Running Time: 8 hrs.). 2008. audio compact disk 92.75 (978-1-4361-5845-9(1)) Recorded Bks.

Goldfinger. Ian Fleming. Read by Robert Whitfield. 1 CD. (Running Time: 8 hrs. 30 mins.). 2001. audio compact disk 19.95 (2743) Blckstn Audio.
A friendly game of two-handed canasta that turns out thoroughly crooked. And a beautiful golden girl who ends up thoroughly dead.... In Bond's first encounter with the world's cleverest, cruelest criminal, useful lessons are learned. Soon the game will change & the stakes will rise... to 15 billion dollars' worth of U. S. government bullion. 007 knows that Auric Goldfinger's rules remain brutally simple - heads I win, tails you die.

Goldfinger. unabr. ed. Ian Fleming. Read by Robert Whitfield. 6 cass. (Running Time: 8 hrs. 30 mins.). 2001. 44.95 (978-0-7861-1973-8(X), 2743); audio compact disk 64.00 (978-0-7861-9752-1(8), 2743) Blckstn Audio.
A friendly game of two-handed canasta that turns out thoroughly crooked. And a beautiful golden girl who ends up thoroughly dead. . . Bond's first encounter with Auric Goldfinger, the world's cleverest, cruelest criminal, teaches him useful lessons. Soon the game will change and the stakes will rise. . . to fifteen billion dollars worth of U.S. gold bullion reserves. But 007 knows that Goldfinger's rules remain brutally simple - "Heads I win, tails you die.".

Goldfinger. unabr. ed. Ian Fleming. Read by Robert Whitfield. 7 pieces. 2004. reel tape 29.95 (978-0-7861-2226-4(9)) Blckstn Audio.

Goldfinger. unabr. ed. Ian Fleming. Read by Simon Vance. 8 CDs. (Running Time: 8 hrs. 30 mins.). 2009. audio compact disk 19.95 (978-1-4332-5858-9(7)) Blckstn Audio.

Goldfish. Raymond Chandler. Perf. by Harris Yulin & Harry Anderson. 1 cass. 12.95 (978-1-57677-000-9(1), OWME004) Lodestone Catalog.

Goldfish. Raymond Chandler. 1 CD. audio compact disk 15.95 (OWME008) Otherworld Ent.

***Goldilicious.** unabr. ed. Victoria Kann. Read by Kathleen Mcinerney. (ENG.). 2009. (978-0-06-190197-3(0)); (978-0-06-177621-2(1)) HarperCollins Pubs.

Goldilocks see Boucle d'Or et les Trois Ours

Goldilocks. (J). 2004. pap. bk. 14.95 (978-0-7882-0688-7(5)) Weston Woods.

Goldilocks. unabr. ed. Ed McBain, pseud. Read by Michael Prichard. 6 cass. (Running Time: 6 hrs.). (Matthew Hope Mystery Ser.: No. 1). 1985. 36.00 (978-0-7366-1032-2(4), 1962) Books on Tape.
A woman & her two little girls have been brutally murdered & none of the alibis add up. The one person who couldn't possibly have a motive for the crime is the only one confessing to it & he insists on Matthew Hope for his defense. Hope finds himself unravelling three heartless killings in which every half-sister, stepson & first wife seemed to have have had a hand.

Goldilocks & the Three Bears see Boucles d'Or et les Trois Ours

Goldilocks & the Three Bears. 1 cass. (Running Time: 12 min.). (Talking Bear Tapes Ser.). (J). 1986. 4.95 (978-0-89926-203-1(1), 916D) Audio Bk.

Goldilocks & the Three Bears. Scripts. 1 cass. or 1 CD. (Running Time: 15 mins.). (J). (gr. k-3). 2000. pap. bk. & tchr. ed. 29.95 Bad Wolf Pr.
A perfect introduction to musical theater. The entire class sings the story, interrupted by several enthusiastic students who repeatedly try to introduce characters from other favorite children's tales. Sheet music available.

Goldilocks & the Three Bears. (Ladybird Bks.). (ARA., (J). bk. 12.95 (978-0-86685-254-8(9), LDL109C) Intl Bk Ctr.

Goldilocks & the Three Bears. 2004. bk. 24.95 (978-0-89719-876-9(X)); bk. 24.95 (978-0-89719-877-6(8)); pap. bk. 32.75 (978-1-55592-230-6(9)); pap. bk. 32.75 (978-1-55592-231-3(7)); pap. bk. 14.95 (978-0-7882-0396-1(7)); 8.95 (978-0-89719-911-7(1)); 8.95 (978-1-56008-910-0(5)); 8.95 (978-1-56008-138-8(4)); 8.95 (978-1-56008-139-5(2)); cass. & flmstrp 30.00 (978-0-89719-511-9(6)); cass. & flmstrp 30.00 (978-0-89719-632-1(5)) Weston Woods.

Goldilocks & the Three Bears. Read by Dorothee Berryman. Illus. by Annabel Malak. 1 cass. (Running Time: 15 mins.). (Classic Stories Ser.). (J). cass. & audio compact disk 9.95 (978-2-921997-84-3(3)) Coffragants CAN.
This is the story of an amazing encounter between a curious little girl & three grumpy bears which turns into a beautiful friendship.

Goldilocks & the Three Bears. James Marshall. 1 cass., 5 bks. (Running Time: 8 min.). (J). pap. bk. 32.75 Weston Woods.
Goldilocks disobediently takes a short cut through the woods to the home of the three bears.

Goldilocks & the Three Bears. James Marshall. 1 cass. (Running Time: 10 min.). (J). (ps-3). pap. bk. 12.95 (RAC342) Weston Woods.
Three bears come home from a bicycling trip through the woods to find a little girl "all nice & cozy & fast asleep" in Baby Bear's bed.

Goldilocks & the Three Bears. James Marshall. 1 cass. (Running Time: 8 min.). (J). (ps-4). pap. bk. 12.95 (PRA342) Weston Woods.
Goldilocks disobediently takes a short cut through the woods to the home of the three bears.

Goldilocks & the Three Bears. James Marshall. 1 cass. (Running Time: 8 min.). (J). (ps-4). bk. 24.95 (HRA342) Weston Woods.

Goldilocks & the Three Bears. Narrated by Pam Tillis. Illus. by Margitta Hanff. 1 cass. (Running Time: 30 min.). (Froggy's Country Storybook Ser.: Vol. 1). (J). (gr. k-3). 1997. pap. bk. 12.98 Incl. full color follow-along bk. & autographed photo of narrator with Froggy, the host. (978-1-890818-70-8(4)) Virginia Recs.
Classic children's story told with a country adaptation with excerpts of hit country songs.

***Goldilocks & the Three Bears.** Weston Woods Staff. (J). audio compact disk 12.95 (978-0-439-72256-8(X)) Weston Woods.

Goldilocks & the Three Bears. l.t. ed. Short Stories. Illus. by Graham Percy. 1 cass. (Running Time: 10 mins.). Dramatization. (J). (ps-3). 2001. bk. 8.99 (978-84-86154-91-2(X)) Pub: Peralt Mont ESP. Dist(s): imaJen

Goldilocks & the Three Bears & Other Children's Favorites. (J). 2005. audio compact disk (978-1-933796-33-8(2)) PC Treasures.

Goldilocks & the Three Bears & Other Stories. unabr. ed. Robert Southey. Read by Claire Bloom. 1 cass. Incl. Babes in the Wood. (J). (CDL5 1392); Brave Little Tailor. (J). (CDL5 1392); Little One Eye, Little Two Eyes & Little Three Eyes. (J). (CDL5 1392); (J). 1984. 9.95 (978-0-694-50897-6(7), CDL5 1392) HarperCollins Pubs.

Goldilocks & the Three Bears Classic Read along Audio Book. Prod. by PC Treasures Staff. (J). 2007. (978-1-60072-053-6(6)) PC Treasures.

Goldilocks & the Three Bears; Dawn; Good-Night Owl!; Who's in Rabbit's House? 2004. (978-0-89719-852-3(2)); cass. & flmstrp (978-0-89719-708-3(9)) Weston Woods.

Goldilocks Comes Back. Steck-Vaughn Staff. 1996. (978-0-8172-6461-1(2)) SteckVau.

Goldilocks (English to Italian - Level 2) Learn ITALIAN Through Fairy Tales. David Burke. (Learn Italian Through Fairy Tales Ser.). (ENG & ITA.,(J). 2007. per. 14.95 (978-1-891888-82-3(X)) Slangman Pubng.

Goldilocks, Grandiosity & the Power Complex. Nancy Dougherty. Read by Nancy Dougherty. 1 cass. (Running Time: 1 hrs. 10 min.). 1996. 10.95 (978-0-7822-0523-7(2), 590) C G Jung IL.
Illustrates the soul's reconnection to the psyche & the body. Explores the unconscious power complex & speculates about its potential transformation & integration.

GOLDILOCKS (Japanese to English - Level 2) Learn ENGLISH Through Fairy Tales. David Burke. (JPN & ENG.). (J). 2007. per. 14.95 (978-1-891888-04-5(8)) Slangman Pubng.

GOLDILOCKS (Korean to English - Level 2) Learn ENGLISH Through Fairy Tales. David Burke. (KOR & ENG.). (J). 2007. per. 14.95 (978-1-891888-10-6(2)) Slangman Pubng.

Goldilocks Returns. Lisa Campbell Ernst. Narrated by Dee Hoty. 1 cass. (Running Time: 15 min.). (J). (gr. k-3). 2001. bk. 26.95 (978-0-8045-6874-6(X), 6874) Spoken Arts.
The grown-up Goldilocks is so wracked with guilt over breaking into the three bears' house that she shortens her name, pins up her curls and opens a lock shop. But that isn't enough to make her feel better, so she goes back to the bears' house to make amends. Once again she arrives when no one is home, but this time she stocks the pantry, fixes the furniture and installs a lock on the front door. She's delighted with the results. As for the bears, they'll need another fifty years to recover.

GOLDILOCKS (Spanish to English - Level 2) Learn ENGLISH Through Fairy Tales. David Burke. (SPA & ENG.). (J). 2007. per. 14.95 (978-1-891888-96-0(X)) Slangman Pubng.

Goldin Boys. unabr. ed. Joseph Epstein. Read by Michael Russotto. 6 cass. (Running Time: 9 hrs.). 1994. 48.00 (978-0-7366-2818-1(5), 3529) Books on Tape.
Highly original stories, an assortment of colorful characters, a sure winner from the editors of "The American Scholar," famous for his essays.

Goldkeeper. Sally Prue. 6 CDs. 2006. audio compact disk 59.95 (978-0-7540-6721-4(1), Chivers Child Audio) AudioGO.

Goldman's Anatomy. abr. ed. Glenn Savan. Read by Barry Williams. 2 cass. (Running Time: 3 hrs.). 1994. 16.95 Set. (978-1-879371-57-6(X), 40240) Pub Mills.
Arnie Goldman hasn't seen his high school buddy for quite some time. Now at twenty-five, he has crippling rheumatoid arthritis & depends on a pair of aluminum crutches for mobility. When Redso Wolff re-enters his life, he brings with him earthy Billy Rubin, who, until recently, has led a sheltered life controlled by her eccentric rabbi father. A love triangle of obsession & lust develops & Billy is forced to choose between them.

Goldmine's Promo Record & CD Price Guide. Fred Heggeness. 1995. pap. bk. 24.95 (978-0-87341-411-1(X), PRC01) Krause.

Goldwyn: A Biography. abr. ed. A. Scott Berg. Read by Roddy McDowell. 3 CDs. (Running Time: 3 hrs.). 2004. audio compact disk 25.00 (978-1-59007-518-0(8)) Pub: New Millenn Enter. Dist(s): PerseuPGW

Goldwyn: A Biography. abr. ed. A. Scott Berg. Read by Roddy McDowall. 2 cass. (Running Time: 3 hrs.). 2004. 18.00 (978-1-59007-167-0(0)) Pub: New Millenn Enter. Dist(s): PerseuPGW
In an adventure that would have played well in one of his own films, Schmuel Goldfisz left the Warsaw ghetto in 1895. He walked 300 miles to the Oder River, where he paid someone to row him across, smuggling him out of the Russian empire into Germany, past border patrols to another long walk to Hamburg. The gleam in his eye was America, "a far-away country, a vision of paradise." Schmuel Goldfisz became Samuel Goldwyn, one of the producers who created the Hollywood film industry. His pictures, notably Stella Dallas, Wuthering Heights, and The Best Years of Our Lives, were famous for "the Goldwyn touch.".

Goldwyn Pt. 1: A Biography. unabr. collector's ed. A. Scott Berg. Read by Wolfram Kandinsky. 10 cass. (Running Time: 15 hrs.). 1990. 80.00 (978-0-7366-1793-2(0), 2630A) Books on Tape.
Samuel Goldwyn, Hollywood's greatest pioneer film producer, the man responsible for classics like "The Best Years of Our Lives," & "Wuthering Heights," started life as Schmuel Gelbfisz in Poland in 1879. How he worked his way to America, how he got to Hollywood, how he produced the first full-length movie there, is the stuff movies are made of. Through Goldwyn's central role in movie-making for over five decades, A. Scott Berg examines the innovations & incidents that defined Hollywood - the advent of sound, the "passing fad" of Technicolor, the studio system.

Goldwyn Pt. 2: A Biography. collector's ed. A. Scott Berg. Read by Wolfram Kandinsky. 10 cass. (Running Time: 15 hrs.). 1990. 80.00 (978-0-7366-1794-9(9), 2630 - B) Books on Tape.

Golem. 2004. 8.95 (978-1-56008-911-7(3)); cass. & flmstrp 30.00 (978-1-56008-676-5(9)) Weston Woods.

Golem's Eye. rev. unabr. ed. Jonathan Stroud. Read by Simon Jones. 10 cass. (Bartimaeus Trilogy: Bk. 2). 2004. 65.00 (978-0-8072-1979-9(7), Listening Lib) Random Audio Pubg.

Golem's Eye. unabr. ed. Jonathan Stroud. Read by Simon Jones. 14 CDs. (Bartimaeus Trilogy: Bk. 2). (YA). 2005. audio compact disk 72.25 (978-0-307-24568-7(3)) Pub: Random Audio Pubg. Dist(s): NetLibrary CO

Golem's Eye. unabr. ed. Jonathan Stroud. Read by Simon Jones. (Bartimaeus Trilogy: Bk. 2). (ENG.). (J). (gr. 7). 2009. audio compact disk 57.00 (978-0-7393-7135-0(5), Listening Lib) Pub: Random Audio Pubg. Dist(s): Random

Golf. 1 cass. (Running Time: 60 min.). 10.95 (SP4) Psych Res Inst.
Mental sport conditioning.

Golf. 1 cass. (Running Time: 45 min.). (Sports Ser.). 9.98 (978-1-55909-087-2(1), 73); 9.98 90 min. extended length stereo music. (978-1-55909-088-9(X), 73M) Randolph Tapes.
Works on your swing & stance. Subliminal messages are heard before becoming ocean sounds or music.

Golf. Paul Kennedy. 1 CD. (Running Time: 1 hr. 30 mins.). 2005. audio compact disk 12.95 (978-0-660-18915-4(1)) Pub: Canadian Broadcasting CAN. Dist(s): Georgetown Term

Golf. Eldon Taylor. 1 cass. (Running Time: 62 min.). (Inner Talk Ser.). 16.95 incl. script. (978-1-55978-506-8(3), 5392F) Progress Aware Res.
Soundtrack - Brook with underlying subliminal affirmations.

Golf: Music Theme. Eldon Taylor. 1 cass. 16.95 (978-0-940699-61-8(3), 5392C) Progress Aware Res.

Golf: Rhythm. Eldon Taylor. Read by Eldon Taylor. Ed. by Leslie Brice. 1 cass. (Running Time: 1 hr.). 1992. 16.95 (978-1-56705-252-7(5)) Gateways Inst.
Self improvement.

Golf: Stream. Eldon Taylor. Read by Eldon Taylor. Ed. by Leslie Brice. 1 cass. (Running Time: 1 hr.). 1992. 16.95 (978-1-56705-253-4(3)) Gateways Inst.

Golf: The Cure for the Grumpy Old Man. Peter Alliss. (Running Time: 2 hrs. 30 mins. 0 sec.). (ENG.). 2008. audio compact disk 24.95 (978-1-84456-786-7(9), HoddrStoughton) Pub: Hodder General GBR. Dist(s): IPG Chicago

Golf - Improve & Win. Norman J. Caldwell. Read by Norman J. Caldwell. Ed. by Achieve Now Institute Staff. 1 cass. (Running Time: 20 min.). (Sports Achievement Ser.). 1988. 9.97 (978-1-56273-083-3(5)) My Mothers Pub.
Improve your swing & stance.

Golf & Athletic Success. Dean A. Montalbano. 2 cds. (Running Time: 2.25 hrs). 2004. audio compact disk 39.95 (978-1-932086-18-8(8)) L Lizards Pub Co.

Golf & Athletic Success: A Self Hypnotic Tape Set. Narrated by Dean A. Montalbano. (Hypnotic Sensory Response Audio Ser.). 2001. 39.95 (978-0-9708772-3-9(4)) L Lizards Pub Co.

Golf & the Spirit: Lessons for the Journey. M. Scott Peck. Read by Michael Kramer. 1999. audio compact disk 80.00 (978-0-7366-6295-6(2)) Books on Tape.

Golf & the Spirit: Lessons for the Journey. abr. ed. M. Scott Peck. Read by M. Scott Peck. 4 cass., 6 CD. 1999. 39.95 CD. Macmill Audio.

Golf & the Spirit: Lessons for the Journey. unabr. ed. M. Scott Peck. Read by Michael Kramer. 8 cass. (Running Time: 12 hrs.). 1999. 64.00 (978-0-7366-4575-1(6), 4982) Books on Tape.
Reveals how the game of golf has taught him - & can teach us all - some of life's most important lessons.

Golf & the Spirit: Lessons for the Journey. unabr. ed. M. Scott Peck. Read by Michael Kramer. 10 CDs. (Running Time: 15 hrs.). 2001. audio compact disk 80.00 Books on Tape.

Golf Confidence for Women. Kathryn C. Wilder et al. 1 cass. (Running Time: 90 mins.). 2000. 17.98 (978-0-9676628-0-0(X)) K C Wilder.

Golf Course Construction/Renovation & Grow-In. 2006. audio compact disk 40.00 (978-0-89118-559-8(3)) Am Soc Agron.

Golf Empowerment (Hypnosis), Vol. 1. Jayne Helle. 1 cass. (Running Time: 56 min.). 1997. 15.00 (978-1-891826-00-9(X)) Introspect.
Dynamic self-hypnosis program to improve the mental game of golf.

Golf for Enlightenment: The Seven Lessons for the Game of Life. Deepak Chopra. 2003. audio compact disk 32.00 (978-0-7366-9282-3(7)) Books on Tape.

Golf for Enlightenment: The Seven Lessons for the Game of Life. unabr. ed. Deepak Chopra. 3 cass. (Running Time: 4 hrs. 30 mins.). 2003. 28.00 (978-0-7366-8966-3(4)) Books on Tape.
Golf is a no-nonsense sport. You've got your balls, your clubs, and your course. So what is this Indian spiritualist doctor doing barging into the middle of it with his mystical theories of life? Well, as Harvey Penick once observed, golf is life. And if there's a way to improve your life, it will probably improve your golf. This is where Dr. Chopra comes in, because he's a keen observer and diagnostician of life and golf.

Golf in the Zone: Achieving Peak Performance in the Mental Game of Gold. unabr. ed. Marcia Reynolds. Narrated by Marcia Reynolds. 2 CDs. (Running Time: 3 hrs.). (Smart Audio Ser.). (ENG.). 2003. audio compact disk 19.99 (978-1-58926-132-7(1), R22J-334D) Oasis Audio.

Golf in the Zone: Achieving Peak Performance in the Mental Game of Gold. unabr. ed. Marcia Reynolds. 2 cass. (Running Time: 3 hrs.). (Smart Tapes Ser.). (gr. 10 up). 2003. pap. bk. 19.99 (978-1-55678-065-3(6), R22J-334D) Oasis Audio.
Achieving peak performance in the mental game of golf.

Golf Is A Game of Confidence. Bob Rotella. 2004. 7.95 (978-0-7435-2025-6(4)) Pub: S&S Audio. Dist(s): S and S Inc

Golf Is Not A Game of Perfect. Bob Rotella. 2004. 7.95 (978-0-7435-2024-9(6)) Pub: S&S Audio. Dist(s): S and S Inc

Golf Is Not a Game of Perfect. abr. ed. Bob Rotella. Read by Bob Rotella. 2 CDs. (Running Time: 13 hrs. 0 mins. 0 secs.). (ENG., 2001. audio compact disk 18.00 (978-0-7435-0809-4(2), Audioworks) Pub: S&S Audio. Dist(s): S and S Inc

Golf My Own Damn Way. unabr. ed. John Daly. Read by Glen Waggoner. (YA). 2008. 34.99 (978-1-60514-580-8(7)) Find a World.

Golf My Own Damn Way: A Real Guy's Guide to Chopping Ten Strokes off Your Score. unabr. ed. John Daly. 3 CDs. (Running Time: 3 hrs. 0 mins. 0 sec.). (ENG.). 2007. audio compact disk 39.99 (978-1-4001-3518-9(4)); audio compact disk 19.99 (978-1-4001-5518-7(5)) Pub: Tantor Media. Dist(s): IngramPubServ

Golf My Own Damn Way: A Real Guy's Guide to Chopping Ten Strokes off Your Score. unabr. ed. John Daly. Read by William Dufris. 3 CDs. (Running Time: 3 hrs. 0 mins. 0 sec.). (ENG.). 2007. audio compact disk 19.99 (978-1-4001-0518-2(8)) Pub: Tantor Media. Dist(s): IngramPubServ

Golf of Your Dreams. abr. ed. Bob Rotella. 2004. 7.95 (978-0-7435-4789-5(6)) Pub: S&S Audio. Dist(s): S and S Inc

Golf Rules & Etiquette: The Cheat Sheets of Culture. Ted Sheftic & Michael Spease. Read by Ken Boynton. 1 cass. (Running Time: 1 hr.). (Instant Genius Ser.). (C). 1999. 12.00 (978-1-891115-17-2(0)) Good Think.
Brief but comprehensive introduction to the rules & the etiquette of golf written by renowned PGA professionals.

Golf with Patty Sheehan. 4 cass. 49.95 (1018) SyberVision.
After winning more than a dozen national championship titles - & the LPGA Player of the Year Award - Patty Sheehan is recognized as one of the finest woman golfers on tour today. Topics covered: The Driver, Fairway Woods, Short Irons, Chipping, The Sand Wedge, Long Irons, Pitching, Putting. Includes video & training guide.

Golfer's Education. Darren Kilfara. Narrated by Scott Shina. 8 cass. (Running Time: 11 hrs.). 76.00 (978-1-4025-0943-8(X)) Recorded Bks.

Golfer's Life. abr. ed. Arnold Palmer. Read by Arnold Palmer. 4 cass. (Running Time: 4 hrs.). 1999. 24.35 Set. (978-1-85686-641-5(6)) Ulvrscrft Audio.
The first-hand account of how a boy from a modest background became not only 'the best-loved man ever to play the game,' but also a multi-Major winning champion & one of golf's first superstars.

Golfer's Mind: Play to Play Great. Bob Rotella. Told to Bob Cullen. 2004. 8.95 (978-0-7435-4497-9(8)) Pub: S&S Audio. Dist(s): S and S Inc

Golfer's Mind: Play to Play Great. abr. ed. Bob Rotella. Read by Bob Rotella. Told to Bob Cullen. 2 CDs. (Running Time: 112 hrs. 0 mins. NaN sec.). (ENG.). 2004. audio compact disk 14.00 (978-0-7435-3977-7(X), Audioworks) Pub: S&S Audio. Dist(s): S and S Inc

Golfing Out of Your Mind. unabr. ed. Robert J. Rotella & Richard Coop. 3 cass. (Running Time: 90 min.). 1985. 39.95 incl. bk. Creative Mgmt.
Teaches golfer to confidence, concentration, & compuser. Techniques for overcoming two major problems, negative thinking & "going to sleep" on a shot, are also provided explains, "the better the player, the more important the mental aspect of the game". Coop describes how to take a grooved swing from the practice tee to the course.

Golf's Greatest Championship: The 1960 U. S. Open. unabr. ed. Julian I. Graubart. Read by Tom Parker. 7 cass. (Running Time: 10 hrs.). 1998. 49.95 (978-0-7861-1376-7(6), 2260) Blckstn Audio.
Brings alive a near-mythic moment in modern golf, with interviews with the players & observations by reporters covering the tournament.

***Golf's Greatest Championship: The 1960 U. S. Open.** unabr. ed. Julian I. Graubart. Read by Tom Parker. (Running Time: 9 hrs. 0 mins.). 2010. 29.95 (978-1-4417-6236-8(1)); audio compact disk 90.00 (978-1-4417-6234-4(5)) Blckstn Audio.

Golf's Sacred Journey: Seven Days at the Links of Utopia. David L. Cook. (ENG.). 2008. audio compact disk 29.95 (978-0-9818051-1-5(6)) Sacred Story.

Golf's Sacred Journey: Seven Days at the Links of Utopia. unabr. ed. David Cook. (Running Time: 4 hrs. 18 mins. 0 sec.). (ENG.). 2009. audio compact disk 21.99 (978-0-310-32065-4(8)) Zondervan.

***Golf's Sacred Journey: Seven Days at the Links of Utopia.** unabr. ed. Zondervan Publishing Staff & David L. Cook. (Running Time: 4 hrs. 16 mins. 0 sec.). (ENG.). 2010. 16.99 (978-0-310-41583-1(7)) Zondervan.

Goliath. (Paws & Tales Ser.: Vol. 28). (J). 2002. 3.99 (978-1-57972-457-3(4)); audio compact disk 5.99 (978-1-57972-458-0(2)) Insight Living.

Goliath Bird-Eating Spiders & Other Extreme Bugs. Deirdre A. Prischmann. Contrib. by Patrick Olson & Charity Jones. (Extreme Life Ser.). (ENG.). (gr. 3-4). 2008. audio compact disk 12.99 (978-1-4296-3206-5(2)) CapstoneDig.

Goliath Bone. unabr. ed. Mickey Spillane. (Running Time: 7 hrs. NaN mins.). 2008. 29.95 (978-1-4332-4830-6(1)); 44.95 (978-1-4332-4827-6(1)); audio compact disk 60.00 (978-1-4332-4828-3(X)) Blckstn Audio.

Goliath Bone. unabr. ed. Mickey Spillane & Max Allan Collins. Read by Stacy Keach. 6 CDs. (Running Time: 8 hrs.). 2008. audio compact disk 24.95 (978-1-4332-4829-0(8)) Blckstn Audio.

Golly Sisters Go West. Betsy Byars. Read by C. J. Critt. 1 cass. (Running Time: 15 mins.). (YA). 2000. pap. bk. 23.20 (978-0-7887-4335-1(X), 41130); wbk. ed. 71.30 (978-0-7887-4436-5(4), 47127) Recorded Bks.
Heading West in their wagon, the Golly Sisters get into many zany situations while stopping to perform their colorful song & dance routine.

Golly Sisters Go West. unabr. ed. Betsy Byars. Narrated by C. J. Critt. 1 cass. (Running Time: 15 mins.). (gr. 2 up). 2000. 11.00 (978-0-7887-4226-2(4), 96204E7) Recorded Bks.

Golly Sisters Go West. unabr. abr. ed. Betsy Byars. Read by Kathryn Grody. Illus. by Sue Truesdell. 1 cass. (Running Time: 15 min.). (I Can Read Bks.). (J). (ps-3). 1995. 8.99 (978-0-694-70027-1(4)) HarperCollins Pubs.

Golly Sisters Ride Again: An I Can Read Book. unabr. ed. Betsy Byars. Narrated by C. J. Critt. 1 cass. (Running Time: 30 mins.). (I Can Read Bks.). (gr. 1 up). 1997. 10.00 (978-0-7887-1114-5(8), 95108E7) Recorded Bks.
Wacky Rose & May-May meet up with a pesky goat & a talking rock as they sing & dance their way through the old West in five laugh-out-loud adventures.

Golosa: A Basic Course in Russian: Book 1. 4th ed. Created by Pearson/Prentice Hall. 2006. audio compact disk 32.00 (978-0-13-227140-0(0)) Pearson Educ CAN CAN.

Golosa Bk. 2: A Basic Course in Russian. 2nd ed. Kathryn Henry & Joanna Robin. 1998. 33.33 (978-0-13-895137-5(3)) PH School.

Golosa: A Basic Course in Russian, Book 1. 4th ed. Richard Robin et al. 2007. bk. & pap. bk. 139.60 (978-0-13-514772-6(7)) P-H.

Goloso Pulpo Gris/the Greedy Gray Octopus. Created by Rigby Staff. (J). 1993. 10.40 (978-0-435-05943-9(2), Rigby PEA) Pearson EdAUS AUS.

Gom on Windy Mountain. unabr. ed. Grace Chetwin. Narrated by Grace Chetwin. 5 cass. (Running Time: 7 hrs. 30 mins.). 1991. 46.00 (978-1-55690-198-0(4), 91126E7) Recorded Bks.
The first in a fantasy series featuring boy-wizard. When Gom, a woodcutter's son, discovers that he possesses magical powers, he begins a quest for a place to put his powers to use - a quest that leads to an evil wizard & a mountain filled with dark, endless tunnels.

Gombinski's Colors in Spanish, French, & German. Scripts. Harris Winitz et al. Illus. by Syd Baker & Rita Gombinski. 1 CD. (Running Time: 45 mins.). (J). 2004. audio compact disk 14.95 (978-1-887371-92-6(3), 328C) Intl Linguistics.

Gomorrah: A Personal Journey into the Violent International Empire of Naples' Organized Crime System. unabr. ed. Roberto Saviano. Read by Michael Kramer. (YA). 2008. 59.99 (978-1-60514-639-3(0)) Find a World.

Gomorrah: A Personal Journey into the Violent International Empire of Naples' Organized Crime System. unabr. ed. Roberto Saviano. Read by Michael Kramer. (Running Time: 11 hrs. 30 mins. 0 sec.). (ENG.). 2007. audio compact disk 34.99 (978-1-4001-0557-1(9)); audio compact disk 69.99 (978-1-4001-3557-8(5)) Pub: Tantor Media. Dist(s): IngramPubServ

Gomorrah: A Personal Journey into the Violent International Empire of Naples' Organized Crime System. unabr. ed. Roberto Saviano. Read by Michael Kramer. Tr. by Virginia Jewiss from ITA. (Running Time: 11 hrs. 30 mins. 0 sec.). (ENG.). 2007. audio compact disk 24.99 (978-1-4001-5557-6(6)) Pub: Tantor Media. Dist(s): IngramPubServ

Gone. RiverRain Publishing Staff. 2004. DVD & audio compact disk 16.99 (978-0-9727792-0-3(5)) RiverRain.

Gone. abr. ed. Lisa Gardner. Read by Kirsten Kairos. 5 CDs. (Running Time: 21600 sec.). (ENG.). 2006. audio compact disk 14.99 (978-0-7393-4159-9(6), Random AudioBks) Pub: Random Audio Pubg. Dist(s): Random

Gone. abr. ed. Jonathan Kellerman. Read by John Rubinstein. 5 CDs. (Running Time: 21600 sec.). (Alex Delaware Ser.: No. 20). (ENG.). 2007. audio compact disk 14.99 (978-0-7393-5707-1(7), Random AudioBks) Pub: Random Audio Pubg. Dist(s): Random

Gone. unabr. ed. Lisa Gardner. Read by Julia Gibson & Richard Ferrone. 11 CDs. (Running Time: 10 hrs.). 2006. audio compact disk 61.20 (978-1-4159-2738-0(3)) Pub: Books on Tape. Dist(s): NetLibrary CO

Gone. unabr. ed. Lisa Gardner. Read by Anna Fields. 7 cass. (Running Time: 10 hrs.). 2006. 81.00 (978-1-4159-2737-3(5)) Books on Tape.
When someone you love vanishes without a trace, how far would you go to get them back? For ex-FBI profiler Pierce Quincy, it's the beginning of his worst nightmare: a car abandoned on a desolate stretch of Oregon highway, engine running, purse on the driver's seat. And his estranged wife, Rainie Conner, gone, leaving no clue to her fate. Did one of the ghosts from Rainie's troubled past finally catch up with her? Or could her disappearance be the result of one of the cases they'd been working - a particularly vicious double homicide or the possible abuse of a deeply disturbed child Rainie took too close to heart? Together with his daughter, FBI agent Kimberly Quincy, Pierce is battling the local authorities, racing against time, and frantically searching for answers to all the questions he's been afraid to ask. One man knows what happened that night. Adopting the alias of a killer caught eighty years before, he has already contacted the press. His terms are clear: he wants money, he wants power, he wants celebrity. And if he doesn't get what he wants, Rainie will be gone for good.

Gone. unabr. ed. Jonathan Kellerman. Read by John Rubinstein. 8 CDs. (Running Time: 9 hrs.). (Alex Delaware Ser.: No. 20). 2006. audio compact disk 61.20 (978-1-4159-2712-0(X)); 54.00 (978-1-4159-2711-3(1)) Books on Tape.
Dylan Meserve and Michaela Brand, young lovers and fellow acting students, vanish on the way home from a rehearsal. Three days later, the two of them are found in the remote mountains of Malibu -battered and terrified after a harrowing ordeal at the hands of a sadistic abductor. The details of the nightmarish event are shocking and brutal: The couple was carjacked at gunpoint by a masked assailant and subjected to a horrific regimen of confinement, starvation and assault. But before long, doubts arise about the couple's story, and as forensic details unfold, the abduction is exposed as a hoax. Charged as criminals themselves, the aspiring actors claim emotional problems, and the court orders psychological evaluation for both. Michaela is examined by Alex Delaware, who finds that her claims of depression and stress ring true enough. But they don't explain her lies, and Alex is certain that there are hidden layers in this sordid psychodrama that even he hasn't been able to penetrate. Nevertheless, the case is closed - only to be violently reopened when Michaela is savagely murdered. When the police look for Dylan, they find that he's gone. Is he the killer or a victim himself? Casting their dragnet into the murkiest corners of L.A., Delaware and Sturgis unearth more questions than answers = including a host of eerily identical killings. What really happened to the couple who cried wolf? And what bizarre and brutal epidemic is infecting the city with terror, madness, and sudden, twisted death?.

Gone. unabr. ed. Jonathan Kellerman. Read by John Rubinstein. (Alex Delaware Ser.: No. 20). (YA). 2007. 59.99 (978-0-7393-7485-6(0)) Find a World.

Gone. unabr. ed. Lisa McMann. Read by Ellen Grafton. (Running Time: 5 hrs.). (Wake Trilogy: Bk. 3). 2010. 19.99 (978-1-4418-1997-0(5), 9781441819970, Brilliance MP3); 19.99 (978-1-4418-1999-4(1), 9781441819994, BAD); 39.97 (978-1-4418-1998-7(3), 9781441819987, Brlnc Audio MP3 Lib); 39.97 (978-1-4418-2000-6(0), 9781441820006, BADLE); audio compact disk 19.99 (978-1-4418-1995-6(9), 9781441819956, Bril Audio CD Unabri); audio compact disk 44.97 (978-1-4418-1996-3(7), 9781441819963, BriAudCD Unabrid) Brilliance Audio.

Gone-Away Lake. Elizabeth Enright. Read by Colleen Delany. (Running Time: 21600 sec.). (J). (gr. 3-7). 2008. audio compact disk 27.95 (978-1-59316-133-0(6)) Listen & Live.

Gone-Away Lake. unabr. ed. Elizabeth Enright. Read by Colleen Delaney. (J). 2007. 34.99 (978-1-59895-926-0(3)) Find a World.

Gone-Away Lake. unabr. ed. Elizabeth Enright. Read by Colleen Delany. 4 cass. (Running Time: 6 hrs.). (Elizabeth Enright Ser.). (J). (gr. 4-7). 2003. 25.95 (978-1-59316-000-5(3)) Listen & Live.
Enjoy the adventures of eleven year-old Portia, who together with her younger brother, Foster, spend a summer with their cousin, Julian, engaged in more than the usual summer pastimes of sun, fun and games. The three intrepid children soon discover a fascinating abandoned summer resort, consisting of deserted crumbling Victorian summer homes surrounding a vanished lake, which is now a swamp. But, best of all, they discover and befriend an elderly eccentric brother and sister who tell them the story of Gone-Away Lake.

***Gone, but Not Forgotten.** unabr. ed. Phillip Margolin. (Running Time: 11 hrs.). 2011. 39.97 (978-1-61106-207-6(1), 9781611062076, BADLE); 14.99 (978-1-61106-206-9(3), 9781611062069, BAD); 39.97 (978-1-61106-205-2(5), 9781611062052, Brlnc Audio MP3 Lib); 14.99 (978-1-61106-204-5(7), 9781611062045, Brilliance MP3); audio compact disk 69.97 (978-1-61106-203-8(9), 9781611062038, BriAudCD Unabrid); audio compact disk 19.99 (978-1-61106-202-1(0), 9781611062021, Bril Audio CD Unabri) Brilliance Audio.

Gone, but Not Forgotten. unabr. ed. Read by Michael Russotto. Ed. by Phillip Margolin. 8 cass. (Running Time: 12 hrs.). 1994. 64.00 (978-0-7366-2726-9(X), 3456) Books on Tape.
In Portland, Oregon, rich women disappear leaving only a black rose & a cryptic note. A detective arrives to tell of a similar series of disappearances she investigated 10 years ago. Who's killing these women & why?.

Gone Fishin' Walter Mosley. Narrated by Paul Winfield. 2 cass. (Running Time: 3 hrs.). (Easy Rawlins Mystery Ser.). 19.00 (978-1-4025-2260-4(6)); audio compact disk 29.00 (978-1-4025-2470-7(6)) Recorded Bks.

Gone Fishin' abr. ed. Walter Mosley. Read by Paul Winfield. 2 cass. (Running Time: 3 hrs.). 2001. 18.00 (978-1-59040-073-9(9), Phoenix Audio) Pub: Amer Intl Pub. Dist(s): PerseuPGW

Gone Fishin' abr. ed. Walter Mosley. Contrib. by Paul Winfield. (Playaway Adult Fiction Ser.). 2008. 39.99 (978-1-60640-662-5(0)) Find a World.

Gone Fishin' abr. ed. Walter Mosley. Read by Paul Winfield. 2 cass. (Running Time: 3 hrs.). (Easy Rawlins Mystery Ser.). 2004. 18.00 (978-1-59007-203-5(0)) New Millenn Enter.
The travel adventure of Easy Rawlings and Mouse Alexander to Pariah, Texas. About to marry Etta mae, Mouse is in need of money from his stepfather. But Easy has known Etta Mae, and his fear of Mouse's reaction leads to the crux of the matter. Sex, voodoo, and death are center stage in this mysterious bayou world.

Gone Fishin' Portfolio: Get Wise, Get Wealthy... & Get on with Your Life. unabr. ed. Steve Alexander & Sjuggerud Green. Read by Erik Synnestvedt. (Running Time: 5 hrs. 30 mins.). (ENG.). 2008. 24.98 (978-1-59659-302-2(4), GildAudio) Pub: Gildan Media. Dist(s): HachBkGrp

Gone for Good. abr. ed. Harlan Coben. Read by Dylan Baker. (Running Time: 5 hrs.). (ENG.). 2005. audio compact disk 14.99 (978-0-7393-2212-3(5), Random AudioBks) Pub: Random Audio Pubg. Dist(s): Random
Gone For Good As a boy, Will Klein had a hero: his older brother, Ken. Then, on a warm suburban night in the Kleins’ affluent New Jersey neighborhood, a young woman - a girl Will had once loved - was found brutally murdered in her family’s basement. The prime suspect: Ken Klein. With the evidence against him overwhelming, Ken simply vanished. And when his shattered family never heard from Ken again, they were sure he was gone for good. Now eleven years have passed. Will has found proof that Ken is alive. And this is just the first in a series of stunning revelations as Will is forced to confront startling truths about his brother, and even himself. As a violent mystery unwinds around him, Will knows he must press his search all the way to the end. Because the most powerful surprises are yet to come. From the Paperback edition.

Gone for Good. unabr. ed. Harlan Coben. 8 cass. (Running Time: 12 hrs.). 2002. 64.00 (978-0-7366-8551-1(0)); audio compact disk 80.00 (978-0-7366-8694-5(0)) Books on Tape.
Will Klein must get to the truth about his vanished brother and his vanished girlfriend.

Gone for Soldiers: A Novel of the Mexican War. unabr. ed. Jeff Shaara. Read by Jonathan Davis. 12 cass. (Running Time: 18 hrs.). 2000. 39.95 Blckstn Audio.
In March 1847, the U.S. Navy delivers eight thousand soldiers on the beaches of Vera Cruz. They are led by the army's commanding general, Winfield Scott, a heroic veteran of the war. He leads his troops against the Mexican dictator & it becomes clear the final conflict will occur at the gates & fortified walls of the ancient capital, Mexico City. Cut off from communications & their only supply line, the Americans learn about their enemy, themselves & the horror of war.

Gone for Soldiers: A Novel of the Mexican War. unabr. ed. Jeff Shaara. Read by Jonathan Davis. 12 cass. (Running Time: 18 hrs.). 2000. 96.00 (978-0-7366-5454-8(2), 5325) Books on Tape.
A tale of the men who helped define the United States. Thirteen years before the Civil War, many who would become leaders on both sides in that war invaded Mexico to chasten Mexican General Santa Ana. Although it secured the Souhwest for a nation fulfilling its "manifest destiny," the Mexican-American War has since faded into oblivion. While most of the future Civil War generals make an appearance, Shaara focuses on the veteran Major-General Winfield Scott and his observant protege, Robert E. Lee.

Gone from Danger. Perf. by Joan Baez. 1 cass., 1 CD. 8.78 (ANGEL 59357); audio compact disk 12.78 CD Jewel box. (ANGEL 59357) NewSound.

Gone Missing. unabr. ed. Jean Ure. Read by Kate Byers. 3 CDs. (Running Time: 3 hrs. 25 mins.). (YA). (gr. 5-8). 2008. audio compact disk 29.95 (978-1-4056-5745-7(6), Chivers Child Audio) AudioGO.

Gone the Dreams & Dancing. unabr. ed. Douglas C. Jones. Narrated by George Guidall. 9 cass. (Running Time: 12 hrs. 30 mins.). 1997. 78.00 (978-0-7887-1308-8(6), 95150E7) Recorded Bks.
Set in 1875, it follows the long friendship between a young Comanche chief & a seasoned Army wagoner who becomes his spokesman & comrade.

***Gone 'til November.** unabr. ed. Wallace Stroby. Narrated by Karen White. (Running Time: 7 hrs. 0 mins. 0 sec.). 2010. audio compact disk 69.99 (978-1-4001-4562-1(7)) Pub: Tantor Media. Dist(s): IngramPubServ

***Gone 'til November: A Novel.** unabr. ed. Wallace Stroby. Narrated by Karen White. (Running Time: 7 hrs. 0 mins.). 2010. 34.99 (978-1-4001-9562-6(4)); 14.99 (978-1-4001-8562-7(9)) Tantor Media.

***Gone 'til November: A Novel.** unabr. ed. Wallace Stroby. Narrated by Karen White. (Running Time: 7 hrs. 0 mins. 0 sec.). (ENG.). 2010. 24.99 (978-1-4001-6562-9(8)); audio compact disk 34.99 (978-1-4001-1562-4(0)) Pub: Tantor Media. Dist(s): IngramPubServ

Gone to Earth, Mary Webb. Read by Flo Gibson. 6 cass. (Running Time: 8 hrs.). (YA). (gr. 8 up). 1997. 41.95 (5020) Audio Bk Con.
Hazel Woodus is a creature of the wilds. A gentle minister & a demanding country squire vie for her love. There is humor, tragedy & memorable descriptions of Wales.

Gone to Earth. unabr. ed. Mary Webb. Narrated by Flo Gibson. (Running Time: 7 hrs. 42 mins.). 1999. 24.95 (978-1-55685-502-3(8)) Audio Bk Con.

Gone to Texas: The Vengeance of Josey Wales. unabr. ed. Forrest Carter. Narrated by Ed Sala. 4 cass. (Running Time: 5 hrs. 45 mins.). 2000. 35.00 (978-0-7887-2486-2(X), 95561E7) Recorded Bks.
One day, Josie's world was shattered when his cabin & family were reduced to charred skeletons. Now a loner following his own outlaw code, Josie is headed for a new life.

Gone Tomorrow. abr. ed. Lee Child. Read by Dick Hill. 5 CDs. (Running Time: 6 hrs. 30 mins.). (Jack Reacher Ser.). (ENG.). 2009. audio compact disk 29.95 (978-0-7393-4071-4(9), Random AudioBks) Pub: Random Audio Pubg. Dist(s): Random

***Gone Tomorrow.** abr. ed. Lee Child. Read by Dick Hill. (ENG.). 2010. audio compact disk 14.99 (978-0-307-75092-1(2), Random AudioBks) Pub: Random Audio Pubg. Dist(s): Random

Gone Tomorrow. unabr. ed. Lee Child. (Jack Reacher Ser.). 2009. audio compact disk 44.95 (978-0-7393-6591-5(6), Random AudioBks) Pub: Random Audio Pubg. Dist(s): Random

***Gone Tomorrow.** unabr. ed. Lee Child. Read by Dick Hill. 12 CDs. (Running Time: 14 hrs.). 2009. audio compact disk 100.00 (978-1-4159-6288-6(X), BksonTape) Pub: Random Audio Pubg. Dist(s): Random

Gone Wild, unabr. ed. James W. Hall. Narrated by George Guidall. 10 cass. (Running Time: 14 hrs. 30 mins.). (Thorn Ser.). 1995. 85.00 (978-0-7887-0264-8(5), 94473E7) Recorded Bks.
Allison Farleigh watches helplessly as her oldest daughter is brutally gunned down by poachers in Borneo - an incident that catastrophically changes her life.

Gone with the Wind. unabr. ed. Margaret Mitchell. Narrated by Linda Stephens. 36 cass. (Running Time: 50 hrs. 30 mins.). 2001. 199.00 (978-0-7887-4976-6(5), 96052E7) Recorded Bks.
The spectacular production of the Civil War & the tempestuous love between Rhett Butler & Scarlett O'Hara.

Gone with the Wind, Pts. 1 & 2. unabr. ed. Margaret Mitchell. Read by Liza Ross. 40 CDs. (Running Time: 46 hrs.). 2001. audio compact disk (978-0-7531-0726-3(0)) ISIS Audio GBR.
World's biggest best-seller after the Bible, portrays the soul of a people divided, living through the events of a catalystic world is the loves and lives of unforgettable characters.

Gone with the Wind, Set. unabr. ed. Margaret Mitchell. 28 cass. (Running Time: 50 hrs.). (YA). (gr. 9-12). 2004. 79.99 (978-0-7887-8957-1(0), 00414) Recorded Bks.

Gone with the Wind: The Author's Letters. Read by Richard Harwell. 1 cass. (Running Time: 60 min.). 10.95 (OP-76-11-24, HarperThor) HarpC GBR.

Goneboy: A Walkabout. collector's ed. Gregory Gibson. Read by Edward Lewis. 8 cass. (Running Time: 12 hrs.). 1999. 64.00 (978-0-7366-4749-6(X), 5087) Books on Tape.
Gregory Gibson's eighteen year old son was dead, shot in the doorway of his college library by a fellow student gone berserk. College officials, would later learn, he had received an anonymous warning about the murderer. Gibson came to the realization that he had to do something before he destroyed himself. He resolved to discover & document exactly who was to blame for his sons death & why. He decided to go on a walkabout. His wayward mission begins with a visit to the man who sold the gun to the killer & ends, like a hardboiled mystery, in a place no one could have predicted.

Goneboy: A Walkabout. unabr. ed. Gregory Gibson. Read by Edward Lewis. 8 cass. (Running Time: 12 hrs.). 1999. 64.00 (978-0-7366-4702-1(3), 5087) Books on Tape.

Gong Meditation 2: A Shower of Sound. Perf. by Hans De Back. 1 cass. (Running Time: 1 hr.). 10.00 (978-1-57863-055-4(X), Red) Red Wheel Weiser.
Traditional Asian gongs sounded in a very fine, subtle interplay. A dramatic yet meditative performance, also for therapeutic practice.

Gono & the Magic Hat. (J). (ps-4). 1985. bk. (978-0-318-59510-8(9)) Listen USA.

Gono & the Magic Hat. Joseph Currier. 1 read-along cass. (Running Time: 14 min.). (WellinWorld Ser.). (J). (ps-4). 1985. bk. 8.95 incl. bk. (978-0-88684-179-9(8), TC:114591) Listen USA.
A Wellin story about making decisions. From a children series developed to promote better health habits & more cooperative personal relationships.

Gonzo Marketing. abr. ed. Christopher Locke. 2004. 10.95 (978-0-7435-4790-1(X)) Pub: S&S Audio. Dist(s): S and S Inc

Goober Peas. (Song Box Ser.). (gr. 1-2). bk. 8.50 (978-0-7802-0942-8(7)) Wright Group.

Goober Peas: 1 Big Book, 6 Each of 1 Student Book, & 1 Cassette. (Song Box Ser.). (gr. 1-2). 68.95 (978-0-7802-0943-5(5)) Wright Group.

Good. Frank Cappelli. 1 cass. (J). (ps up). 8.98 (978-0-929304-03-8(9)) Peanut Heaven.
Music for children designed not only to entertain, but also to reinforce basic educational concepts & a sense of self-esteem.

Good Afternoon, Ladies & Gentlemen! Intermission Scripts from the Met's Broadcasts. Boris Goldovsky. 1 cass. (Running Time: 90 min.). 1984. 7.95 (978-0-253-32587-7(0)) Ind U Pr.
Boris Goldovsky, intermission commentator on the Metropolitan Opera broadcasts, has collected 26 of his radio scripts into a book with accompanying audiocassette.

Good & Beautiful God. unabr. ed. James Bry Smith. (Running Time: 6 hrs. 12 mins. 0 sec.). (ENG.). 2009. audio compact disk 24.98 (978-1-59644-797-4(4), Hovel Audio) christianaud.

***Good & Beautiful God: Falling in Love with the God Jesus Knows.** unabr. ed. James Bryan Smith. Narrated by Arthur Morey. (ENG.). 2009. 14.98 (978-1-59644-798-1(2), Hovel Audio) christianaud.

***Good & Beautiful Life: Putting on the Character of Christ.** unabr. ed. James Bryan. Narrated by Arthur Morey. (ENG.). 2010. 14.98 (978-1-59644-256-6(5), Hovel Audio) christianaud.

***Good & Beautiful Life: Putting on the Character of Christ.** unabr. ed. James Bryan Smith & James Bryan. Narrated by Arthur Morey. (Running Time: 8 hrs. 0 mins. 0 sec.). (ENG.). 2010. audio compact disk 24.98 (978-1-59644-255-9(7), Hovel Audio) christianaud.

Good & Dead. unabr. collector's ed. Jane Langton. Read by Mary Peiffer. 8 cass. (Running Time: 8 hrs.). 1992. 48.00 (978-0-7366-2223-3(3), 3013) Books on Tape.
Too many parishioners of New England church are dying. The flock, so devout on Sundays, breaks most commandments the other six. Homer Kelly must untangle murder from seemingly natural death.

Good & Evil: The Problem of Shadow. Read by Murray Stein. 2 cass. (Running Time: 2 hrs.). (Psychological Approach to the Bible Ser.: Pt. I, No. 4). 1988. 14.00 (978-0-7822-0287-8(X), 359-4) C G Jung IL.

Good Angels. Ben Young. 1997. 4.95 (978-0-7417-6025-8(8)) Win Walk.

Good Apprentice. unabr. abr. ed. Iris Murdoch. Read by Miriam Margolyes. 14 cass. (Running Time: 6 hrs.). 2004. 47.95 (978-1-931056-90-8(0), N Millennium Audio) New Millenn Enter.
A beautifully orchestrated tale about the difficulty of being good. Edward Baltram is overwhelmed by guilt. His nasty little prank has gone horribly wrong: he has fed his closest friend a sandwich laced with a hallucinogenic drug and the young man has fallen out of a window to his death. Stuart Cuno, Edward's stepbrother, has renounced both sex and a promising academic career to live a monklike life helping others. As stuart seeks salvation, Edward searches for forgiveness and redemption through a reunion with his famous father, Jesse Bultram. it is in Jesse's unusual household that the complex affairs of Edward's extended family begin to unfold.

Good as Gold. unabr. ed. Joseph Heller. Read by Dan Lazar. 9 cass. (Running Time: 13 hrs. 30 mins.). 72.00 (978-0-7366-0529-8(0), 1503) Books on Tape.
Meet Bruce Gold, 48 & ready for a change. He settles on government service. There is a hitch, however: to land the job, Gold must bring to the marriage couch Andrea Conover, the darling daughter of an influential Washington anti-Semite, whose chief delight is baiting Bruce. And Andrea will not marry Bruce until he has the government job.

Good Association. 1 cass. (Running Time: 1 hr.). 12.99 (713) Yoga Res Foun.

Good Athlete: II Timothy 2:5. Ed Young. (J). 1978. 4.95 (978-0-7417-1022-2(6), A0022) Win Walk.

Good Behavior. unabr. collector's ed. Donald E. Westlake. Read by Michael Kramer. 6 cass. (Running Time: 9 hrs.). (Dortmunder Ser.). 1997. 48.00 (978-0-7366-3673-5(0), 4350) Books on Tape.
John Dortmunder's one of the slyest burglars going, but by God, he has bad luck! While fleeing the police during his latest caper, he falls through the roof of the Silent Sisterhood of St. Filumena & tumbles into the lap of trouble.

Good Benito. unabr. ed. Alan P. Lightman. Read by Alexander Adams. 4 cass. (Running Time: 4 hrs.). 1995. 24.00 (978-0-7366-2980-5(7), 3671) Books on Tape.
Volatile nature of human relationships forces scientist to reconcile his ordered world with his emotions. Deeply moving, wryly funny.

Good, Better, Blessed: Living with Purpose, Power & Passion. unabr. ed. Joel Osteen. Read by Joel Osteen. 5 CDs. (Running Time: 5 hrs. 0 mins. 0 sec.). (ENG.). 2008. audio compact disk 29.99 (978-0-7435-8168-4(7)) Pub: S&S Audio. Dist(s): S and S Inc

Good Boats. unabr. collector's ed. Roger C. Taylor. Read by Bob Erickson. 7 cass. (Running Time: 7 hrs.). 1985. 42.00 (978-0-7366-0524-3(X), 1498) Books on Tape.
Taylor shares his favorite designs with fellow boat lovers. We learn how to interpret boat plans & we also pick up some basic seamanship.

Good Book: Reading the Bible with Mind & Heart. Peter J. Gomes. 2004. 10.95 (978-0-7435-4791-8(8)) Pub: S&S Audio. Dist(s): S and S Inc

Good Book Method. abr. ed. Jeanie Eller. Read by Jeanie Eller. 6 cass. (Running Time: 9 hrs. 35 mins.). 1990. (978-1-928606-30-7(X)) Action Readg.
Christian learn to read program.

***Good Boss, Bad Boss: How to Be the Best... & Learn from the Worst.** unabr. ed. Robert I. Sutton. Read by Robert I. Sutton. Read by Bob Walter. (Running Time: 6 hrs. 30 mins.). (ENG.). 2010. 16.98 (978-1-60024-782-8(2)); audio compact disk 24.98 (978-1-60024-781-1(4)) Pub: Hachet Audio. Dist(s): HachBkGrp

Good Brothers Looking for Good Sisters. Jawanza Kunjufu. 1 cass. (Running Time: 60 mins.). 1999. 5.95 (AT18) African Am Imag.

Good Business: Leadership, Flow & the Making of Meaning. abr. ed. Mihaly Csikszentmihalyi. 2004. 15.95 (978-0-7435-4792-5(6)) Pub: S&S Audio. Dist(s): S and S Inc

Good-bye see Sir John Betjeman Reading His Poetry

Good-Bye & Amen. unabr. ed. Beth Gutcheon. Narrated by Paul Boehmer. (Running Time: 6 hrs. 30 mins. 0 sec.). (ENG.). 2008. audio compact disk 19.99 (978-1-4001-5981-9(4)); audio compact disk 59.99 (978-1-4001-3981-1(3)) Pub: Tantor Media. Dist(s): IngramPubServ

Good-Bye & Amen. unabr. ed. Beth Gutcheon. Read by Joyce Bean. Narrated by Paul Boehmer. (Running Time: 6 hrs. 30 mins. 0 sec.). (ENG.). 2008. audio compact disk 29.99 (978-1-4001-0981-4(7)) Pub: Tantor Media. Dist(s): IngramPubServ

Good Bye Mr. Chips. James Hilton. Read by Santiago Munévar. (Running Time: 3 hrs.). 2002. 16.95 (978-1-60083-216-1(4), Audiofy Corp) Iofy Corp.

Good-bye My Fancy see Twentieth-Century Poetry in English, No. 17, Walt Whitman Speaks for Himself

Good Children: A Novel of Suspense. unabr. ed. Kate Wilhelm. Read by Carrington MacDuffie. (Running Time: 8.5 hrs. 0 mins.). (ENG.). 2009. 29.95 (978-1-4332-3057-8(7)); 54.95 (978-1-4332-3053-0(4)); audio compact disk 76.00 (978-1-4332-3054-7(2)) Blckstn Audio.

Good Citizens Audio CD. Adapted by Benchmark Education Company Staff. Based on a work by Vickey Herold. (Early Explorers Set C Ser.). (J). (gr. 2). 2008. audio compact disk 10.00 (978-1-60437-550-3(7)) Benchmark Educ.

Good Citizens Can Help Audio CD. Adapted by Benchmark Education Company Staff. Based on a work by Cynthia Swain. (Early Explorers Set C Ser.). (J). (gr. k). 2008. audio compact disk 10.00 (978-1-60437-508-4(6)) Benchmark Educ.

Good Conscience: Heb. 13:17-25. Ed Young. 1992. 4.95 (978-0-7417-1945-4(2), 945) Win Walk.

Good Daughters. unabr. ed. Mary Hocking. Read by Hugh Ross. 8 cass. (Running Time: 12 hrs.). (Isis Ser.). (J). 2004. 69.95 (978-1-85089-733-0(6), 90043) Pub: ISIS Lrg Prnt GBR. Dist(s): Ulverscroft US

***Good Daughters: A Novel.** unabr. ed. Joyce Maynard. Read by Joyce Maynard. (ENG.). 2010. (978-0-06-206212-3(3), Harper Audio); (978-0-06-200695-0(9), Harper Audio) HarperCollins Pubs.

Good Decisions. Betty L. Randolph. Read by Betty L. Randolph. Read by Leonard Baron. Ed. by Success Education Institute International Staff. 1 cass. (Educational Ser.). 1989. bk. 14.98 Ocean Format. (978-1-55909-258-6(0), 460P); bk. Music Format. (460PM) Randolph Tapes.
Features 60,000 messages with the left-right brain.

Good Detective. unabr. ed. H. R. F. Keating. Read by Frederick Davidson. 4 cass. (Running Time: 5 hrs. 30 mins.). 1995. 32.95 (978-0-7861-0823-7(1), 1646) Blckstn Audio.
A call out of the blue is about to ruin Assistant Chief Constable Ned French's career, perhaps even his life, because a case from way back has returned to haunt him.

Good Detective. unabr. ed. H. R. F. Keating. Read by Frederick Davidson. (Running Time: 5 hrs. 30 mins.). 2010. 29.95 (978-1-4417-1881-5(8)); audio compact disk 55.00 (978-1-4417-1878-5(8)) Blckstn Audio.

Good Dog. unabr. ed. 4 cass. (Running Time: 4 hrs. 45 min.). (J). 2004. 35.00 (978-1-4025-2204-8(5)) Recorded Bks.

Good Dog: The Story of Orson Who Changed My Life. Jon Katz. Read by Tom Stechschulte. (Running Time: 23400 sec.). 2006. audio compact disk 29.99 (978-1-4281-1340-4(1)) Recorded Bks.

Good Dog. Stay. unabr. ed. Anna Quindlen. Read by Anna Quindlen. (Running Time: 0 hr. 45 mins. 0 sec.). (ENG.). 2007. audio compact disk 15.00 (978-0-7435-7199-9(1)) Pub: S&S Audio. Dist(s): S and S Inc

Good Earth. Pearl S. Buck. Read by Laura García. (Running Time: 3 hrs.). 2002. 16.95 (978-1-60083-272-7(5), Audiofy Corp) Iofy Corp.

Good Earth. Pearl S. Buck. Read by George Guidall. 7 Cass. (Running Time: 12.5 Hrs.). 29.95 (978-1-4025-2808-8(6)) Recorded Bks.

Good Earth. Pearl S. Buck. 2004. audio compact disk 39.95 (978-1-4193-1960-0(4)) Recorded Bks.

Good Earth. collector's ed. Pearl S. Buck. Read by Roses Prichard. 8 cass. (Running Time: 12 hrs.). 1998. 64.00 (978-0-7366-4256-9(0), 4755) Books on Tape.
This great classic tells the story of peasant Wang Lung of the family he founded, of its rise to dynasty, of the gods he implored, of the earth that sustained him & of the land he made to prosper against the ravages of nature & the attacks of man.

Good Earth. unabr. ed. Pearl S. Buck. Read by Anthony Heald. 8 cass. (Running Time: 37800 sec.). (J). 2007. 19.95 (978-1-4332-0407-4(X)); audio compact disk 19.95 (978-1-4332-0408-1(8)) Blckstn Audio.

Good Earth. unabr. ed. Pearl S. Buck. Read by Anthony Heald. 1 MP3-CD. (Running Time: 10 hrs. 30 mins.). (J). 2007. 29.95 (978-1-4332-0409-8(6)); 65.95 (978-1-4332-0405-0(3)) Blckstn Audio.

Good Earth. unabr. ed. Pearl S. Buck. Read by Anthony Heald. 9 CDs. (Running Time: 10 hrs. 30 mins.). 2007. audio compact disk 81.00 (978-1-4332-0406-7(1)) Blckstn Audio.

Good Earth. unabr. ed. Pearl S. Buck. Read by Kate Reading. 8 cass. (Running Time: 12 hrs.). 2001. 64.00 (978-0-7366-8490-3(5)); audio compact disk 80.00 (978-0-7366-8514-6(6)) Books on Tape.
Wang Lung, a poor Chinese peasant, realizes the value of the land, acquires it, and after much deprivation becomes rich.

Good Earth, unabr. ed. Pearl S. Buck. Narrated by George Guidall. 9 cass. (Running Time: 12 hrs. 15 mins.). 1992. 78.00 (978-1-55690-671-8(4), 92318E7) Recorded Bks.
Nobel Prize-winning author tells the life story of Wang Lung, a poor farmer living in pre-revolutionary China who clings to the land as vast change sweeps his country.

Good Eating Habits. (Running Time: 45 min.). (Health Ser.). 9.98 (978-1-55909-138-1(X), 113) Randolph Tapes.
Instills good eating, healthy habits & patterns for fitness for life!.

Good Enough to Dream. unabr. collector's ed. Roger Kahn. Read by Michael Russotto. 9 cass. (Running Time: 13 hrs. 30 min.). 1990. 72.00 (978-0-7366-1765-9(5), 2604) Books on Tape.
What is Roger Kahn, best-selling author of The Boys of Summer, doing owning a near-bankrupt minor league baseball team? What is this bunch of major league rejects doing playing their hearts out for an organization that pays peanuts & rations practice baseballs? They - & you - are finding out if the dreams that baseball is made of can come true in real life. This funny, poignant story of one special season will make you hesitate before you ever call anything "bush league" again.

Good Faith. Jane Smiley. 13 CDs. (Running Time: 16 hrs.). 2004. audio compact disk 49.99 (978-1-4025-3635-9(6), 00752) Recorded Bks.

Good Faith. unabr. ed. Jane Smiley. 11 cass. (Running Time: 16 hrs.). 2003. 99.00 (978-1-4025-4360-9(3)) Recorded Bks.
New Jersey realtor Joe Stratford's life is just starting to come together. After a difficult divorce, he is eager to start over again. It's 1982, and times are changing. The realty world that was once so familiar to the honest Joe has become more competitive. Marcus Burns, a New Yorker, has come to town looking for a luxurious home and new business prospects. He has befriended Joe, and offers him a plan to get rich quick. Convincingly, Marcus offers Joe a vision of extravagant homes, country clubs, and shops spreading throughout the countryside.

Good Faith. unabr. ed. Jane Smiley. Read by Richard Poe. 9 cass. (Running Time: 16 hrs.). 2004. 34.99 (978-1-4025-3634-2(8), 02634) Recorded Bks.
A masterly novel about some very American seductions: money, sex, and real estate.

Good Fall. unabr. ed. Ha Jin. (Running Time: 8 hrs. 30 mins.). 2009. 29.95 (978-1-4417-1146-5(5)); audio compact disk 29.95 (978-1-4417-1145-8(7)) Blckstn Audio.

Good Fall: Stories. unabr. ed. Ha Jin. (Running Time: 8 hrs. 30 mins.). 2009. 54.95 (978-1-4417-1142-7(2)); audio compact disk 76.00 (978-1-4417-1143-4(0)) Blckstn Audio.

Good Fight. abr. ed. Jerry Ahern. Read by Alan Zimmerman. 3 vols. (Running Time: 4 hrs. 30 mins.). (Defender Ser.: No. 10). 2003. 22.00 (978-1-58807-030-2(1)) Am Pubng Inc.

***Good Fight.** abr. ed. Peter Beinart. Read by David Slavin. (ENG.). 2006. (978-0-06-120573-6(7), Harper Audio); (978-0-06-120574-3(5), Harper Audio) HarperCollins Pubs.

Good Fight. unabr. ed. Jerry Ahern. Read by Alan Zimmerman. 2 vols. No. 10. 2003. (978-1-58807-537-6(0)) Am Pubng Inc.

Good Fight. unabr. ed. Jerry Ahern. Read by Alan Zimmerman. 3 vols. No. 10. 2004. audio compact disk (978-1-58807-703-5(9)) Am Pubng Inc.

Good Fight. unabr. ed. Jerry Ahern. Read by Alan Zimmerman. 4 vols. No. 10. 2004. audio compact disk 28.00 (978-1-58807-272-6(X)) Am Pubng Inc.

Good Fight of Faith. Kenneth Copeland. 6 cass. 1982. bk. 30.00 Set incl. study guide. (978-0-938458-40-1(X)) K Copeland Pubns.
Learning how to fight the good fight of faith.

Good Fight of Faith. Creflo A. Dollar. 2008. audio compact disk 14.00 (978-1-59944-753-7(3)) Creflo Dollar.

Good Food. Velda L. Largen & Deborah L. Bence. (gr. 9-12). 2004. tchr. ed. 200.00 (978-1-59070-113-5(5)); audio compact disk 192.00 (978-1-59070-115-7(1)) Goodheart.

Good Food ABC-Read-Along with Mimi: A Fun Nutritional Headstart Pack. Mimi Morganstern. Illus. by Barbara Bergier. Narrated by Boshie Skolnik. (J). (ps-3). 2000. per. 8.99 (978-0-9700522-2-3(7)) M Morganstern.

Good Food from Sweden. Inga Norberg. (Hippocrene International Cookbook Ser.). (ENG.). 1996. audio compact disk 10.95 (978-0-7818-0486-8(8)) Hippocrene Bks.

Good Foundation. (Paws & Tales Ser.: No. 1). 1999. 3.99 (978-1-57972-380-4(2)) Insight Living.
A children's radio drama modeling Christian valuesWithout following Paw Paw Chuck?s plan, C.J. and Staci build a tree house that is a disaster waiting to happen.

Good Foundation. (Paws & Tales Ser.: No. 1). (J). 2001. audio compact disk 5.99 (978-1-57972-382-8(9)) Insight Living.

Good Friday Murder. abr. ed. Lee Harris. Read by Judith R. Seto. Music by Anne Rebold. 3 cass. (Running Time: 4 hrs. 30 mins.). (Christine Bennett Mystery Ser.). 1997. 19.95 (978-0-9658148-0-5(7), SA111) Pub: Scheherazade Audio. Dist(s): Penton Overseas
The mother of "idiot savant" twins was brutally murdered in her Brooklyn apartment on Good Friday. If the twins didn't do it, who did? Ex-nun Christine Bennett finds out forty years later & finds unexpected romance along the way.

Good Friends. Rory. Perf. by Al Jarreau et al. 1 cass. (J). 1998. 14.99 (978-1-892377-09-8(8)); 9.99 CD. Roar Music Inc.
Collection of friendship songs for kids who loves singing & performing.

Good Friends. unabr. ed. Read by Peter Himmelman. Perf. by Peter Himmelman. 1 cass. (Running Time: 28 min.). Dramatization. (J). 1986. 8.95 (978-1-58452-005-4(1), 4345); 8.95 Spanish version. (978-1-58452-014-6(0), 5345) Spinoza Co.

***Good Fuck Spoiled.** unabr. ed. Laura Lippman. Read by Linda Emond & Francois Battiste. (ENG.). 2008. (978-0-06-176302-1(0), Harper Audio); (978-0-06-176301-4(2), Harper Audio) HarperCollins Pubs.

Good German. abr. ed. Joseph Kanon. 2004. 15.95 (978-0-7435-1867-3(5), Audioworks) Pub: S&S Audio. Dist(s): S and S Inc

Good German: A Novel. unabr. ed. Joseph Kanon. Read by Michael Kramer. 14 cass. (Running Time: 21 hrs.). 2001. 112.00 (978-0-7366-8318-0(6)); 136.00 (978-0-7366-8459-0(X)) Books on Tape.
Jake Geismar is in postwar Berlin to find his mistress, but finds an American soldier's corpse that sends him into international intrigue.

***Good Girls Don't Have to Dress Bad: A Style Guide for Every Woman.** Zondervan. (Running Time: 4 hrs. 36 mins. 48 sec.). (ENG.). 2010. 14.99 (978-0-310-41273-1(0)) Zondervan.

Good Girls, Good Food, Good Fun: The Story of USO Hostesses During World War II. Meghan K. Winchell. (Gender & American Culture Ser.). (ENG., 2008. 15.00 (978-0-8078-8730-1(7)); audio compact disk 15.00 (978-0-8078-8732-5(3)) U of NC Pr.

Good Good Sheriff. Joe Vernetti. Narrated by Dave Giorgio & Julie Gorham. 5 CDs. (Running Time: 5 hrs., 52 min., 37 secs.). 2006. audio compact disk 21.95 (978-1-60031-010-2(9)) Spoken Books.

Good Grammar Matters, Pt. I. unabr. ed. Steven Redden. 4 cass. (Running Time: 4 hrs.). 1992. pap. bk. 39.50 (978-0-88432-527-7(X), S04050) J Norton Pubs.
A convenient reference for anyone wishing to improve his-her grammar; provides the basics of English grammatical structures through an effective & easy-to-follow sequence of exercises exclusively designed to teach through repetition & memorization. Each lesson begins with a simple, non-technical explanation & examples of wrong usage, followed by a variety of listening & speaking exercises using the correct forms.

Good Grammar Matters, Pt. II. unabr. ed. Steven Redden. 4 cass. 1992. pap. bk. 39.50 (978-0-88432-528-4(8), S04060) J Norton Pubs.

Good Grammar Matters! Part 1 CDs & Booklet. Steven Redden. 4 CDs. (Running Time: 4 hrs. 15 min.). 2005. audio compact disk 39.50 (978-1-57970-127-7(2), S04050D, Audio-For) J Norton Pubs.

Good Grammar Matters! Part 2 CDs & Booklet. Steven Redden. 4 CDs. (Running Time: 4 hrs.). 2005. audio compact disk 39.50 (978-1-57970-128-4(0), S04060D, Audio-For) J Norton Pubs.

Good Grief. abr. ed. Lolly Winston. 4 Cass. (Running Time: 6 Hours). 2004. 23.98 (978-1-58621-693-1(7)) Hachet Audio.

Good Grief. abr. ed. Lolly Winston. Read by Amanda Foreman. (ENG.). 2005. 9.99 (978-1-59483-173-7(4)) Pub: Hachet Audio. Dist(s): HachBkGrp

Good Grief: A Novel. abr. ed. Lolly Winston. Read by Amanda Foreman. (Running Time: 6 hrs.). (ENG.). 2009. 35.98 (978-1-60788-032-5(6)) Pub: Hachet Audio. Dist(s): HachBkGrp

***Good Grief: Turning the Showers of Disappointment & Pain into Sunshine.** unabr. ed. Granger Westberg. (Running Time: 2 hrs. 0 mins. 0 sec.). (ENG.). 2010. audio compact disk 9.98 (978-1-61045-057-7(4)) christianaud.

Good Griselle. unabr. ed. Jane Yolen. Narrated by John McDonough. 1 cass. (Running Time: 30 mins.). (gr. k up). 1997. 10.00 (978-0-7887-1281-4(0), 95168E7) Recorded Bks.
In the Paris of long ago beautiful Griselle has lived alone since her soldier husband disappeared in action. She fills her life with making lace & caring for the woodland animals & birds that come to her yard. She has won the love & respect of the stone angels on the cathedral wall, & the rancor of the gargoyles who propose a wager. The gargoyles bet the angels that they can cause Griselle to act with cruelty.

Good Griselle. unabr. ed. Jane Yolen. Read by John McDonough. 1 cass. (Running Time: 30 min.). (J). (gr. 1). 1997. bk. 31.70 (40520); Rental 6.50 Recorded Bks.
About good & evil, beautiful Griselle has lived alone since her soldier husband disappeared in action. She fills her life with making lace & caring for the woodland animals & birds that come to her yard. She has won the love & respect of the stone angels on the cathedral wall, & the rancor of the gargoyles who propose a wager. The gargoyles bet the angels that they can cause Griselle to act with cruelty.

Good Ground. Composed by Robertson Jalonda. Contrib. by Richard Cheri. 2007. audio compact disk 17.00 (978-1-58459-361-4(X)) Wrld Lib Pubns.

Good Ground for the Word. Gloria Copeland. 3 cass. 1992. 15.00 Set. (978-0-88114-866-4(0)) K Copeland Pubns.
Biblical teaching on hearing from God.

Good Guy. unabr. ed. Dean Koontz. 9 cass. (Running Time: 13 hrs. 30 mins.). 2007. 110.00 (978-1-4159-3874-4(1)); audio compact disk 110.00 (978-1-4159-3635-1(8)) Books on Tape.

Good Guy. unabr. ed. Dean Koontz. Read by Richard Ferrone. 8 CDs. (Running Time: 32400 sec.). (ENG.). 2007. audio compact disk 44.95 (978-0-7393-3293-1(7), Random AudioBks) Pub: Random Audio Pubg. Dist(s): Random

Good Guys. abr. ed. Joe Pistone et al. Read by Joe Pistone & Bill Bonanno. (ENG.). 2005. 14.98 (978-1-59483-134-8(3)) Pub: Hachet Audio. Dist(s): HachBkGrp

Good Guys. abr. ed. Joe Pistone et al. Read by Joe Pistone & Bill Bonanno. (Running Time: 6 hrs.). (ENG.). 2009. 49.98 (978-1-60024-935-8(3)) Pub: Hachet Audio. Dist(s): HachBkGrp

Good Hair. Benilde Little. Narrated by Kim Staunton. 5 cass. (Running Time: 6 hrs. 15 mins.). 1996. 48.00 (978-0-7887-4833-2(5), F0001E7) Recorded Bks.
When a working class girl from Newark & an Ivy League surgeon from Boston fall in love, class differences threaten to destroy their romance. Benilde Little's novel is humorous, sexy & touching.

Good Harbor. abr. ed. Anita Diamant. 2005. 23.95 (978-0-7435-5374-2(8)) Pub: S&S Audio. Dist(s): S and S Inc

Good Harbor. unabr. ed. Anita Diamant. Read by Linda Emond. 6 vols. (Running Time: 9 hrs.). 2002. bk. 54.95 (978-0-7927-2534-3(4), CSL 423, Chivers Sound Lib); audio compact disk 79.95 (978-0-7927-9867-5(8), SLD 118, Chivers Sound Lib) AudioGO.
When kathleen Levine is diagnosed with breast cancer, her life is thrown into turmoil. Frightened and burdened by secrets, she meets Joyce Tabachnik, a freelance writer with literary aspirations, and a once-in-a-lifetime friendship is born. Joyce has just bought a small house in Glouster, Massachusetts, where she hopes to write as well as vacation with her family. And like Kathleen, Joyce is at a fragile place in her life.

Good Health. 1 cass. (Running Time: 1 hr. 30 mins.). (SmartReader Ser.). (J). 1999. pap. bk. & tchr. ed. 19.95 (978-0-7887-0125-2(8), 79313T3) Recorded Bks.
To be healthy, you need to know about diet, exercise & other factors that determine your total well-being. Here is a simple guide to staying healthy & fit.

Good Health. Barry Tesar. 1 cass. (Running Time: 1 hr.). (Subliminal Inspiration Ser.). 1992. (978-1-56470-022-3(4)) Success Cass.
Subliminal program.

Good Health: Body, Mind & Spirit. Created by Anne H. Spencer-Beacham. 1. 2003. audio compact disk (978-1-932163-44-5(1)) Infinity Inst.

Good Health Now (Mind, Body & Spirit) Norman J. Caldwell. Read by Norman J. Caldwell. Ed. by Achieve Now Institute Staff. 1 cass. (Running Time: 20 min.). (Health-Imaging Ser.). 1988. 9.97 (978-1-56273-076-5(2)) My Mothers Pub.
Preprogramming for good health.

Good Heart. 2 CDs. 2006. audio compact disk 17.00 (978-1-933207-16-2(7)) Ransomed Heart.

Good Hearts. Reynolds Price. (Running Time: 30 min.). 8.00 (NL 47) Am Audio Prose.
Price, who is now paraplegic due to cancer surgery, also talks about the effect his illness has had on his work.

Good Husband Material. Trisha Ashley. Read by Tanya Myers. 10 cass. (Storysound Ser.). (J). 2003. 84.95 (978-1-85903-540-5(X)) Pub: Mgna Lrg Print GBR. Dist(s): Ulverscroft US

Good Husband of Zebra Drive. Alexander McCall Smith. (No. 1 Ladies' Detective Agency Ser.: No. 8). 2007. 24.99 (978-1-4281-2510-0(8)) Recorded Bks.

Good Husband of Zebra Drive. unabr. ed. Alexander McCall Smith. 7 CDs. (Running Time: 30600 sec.). (No. 1 Ladies' Detective Agency Ser.: No. 8). 2007. audio compact disk 29.99 (978-1-4281-2548-3(5)) Recorded Bks.

Good in a Room: How to Sell Yourself (and Your Ideas) & Win over Any Audience. Stephanie Palmer. Read by Judith Brackley. (Playaway Adult Nonfiction Ser.). 2008. 54.99 (978-1-60640-557-4(8)) Find a World.

Good in a Room: How to Sell Yourself (and Your Ideas) & Win over Any Audience. unabr. ed. Stephanie Palmer. Narrated by Judith Brackley. (Running Time: 7 hrs. 0 mins. 0 sec.). (ENG.). 2008. 19.99 (978-1-4001-5672-6(6)); audio compact disk 29.99 (978-1-4001-0672-1(9)) Pub: Tantor Media. Dist(s): IngramPubServ

Good in a Room: How to Sell Yourself (And Your Ideas) & Win over Any Audience. unabr. ed. Stephanie Palmer. Narrated by Judith Brackley. (Running Time: 7 hrs. 0 mins. 0 sec.). (ENG.). 2008. audio compact disk 59.99 (978-1-4001-3672-8(5)) Pub: Tantor Media. Dist(s): IngramPubServ

Good in Bed. abr. ed. Jennifer Weiner. Read by Paula Cale. 5 CDs. (Running Time: 50 hrs. 0 mins. 0 sec.). (Cannie Shapiro Ser.: Vol. 1). 2005. audio compact disk 14.95 (978-0-7435-4499-3(4)) Pub: S&S Audio. Dist(s): S and S Inc

Good in Bed. unabr. ed. Jennifer Weiner. Read by Laura Hicks. 10 vols. (Running Time: 15 hrs.). (Cannie Shapiro Ser.: Bk. 1). 2001. bk. 84.95

(978-0-7927-2497-1(6), CSL 386, Chivers Sound Lib); audio compact disk 110.95 (978-0-7927-9923-8(2), SLD 074, Chivers Sound Lib) AudioGO.
Cannie Shapiro never wanted to be famous. The smart, sharp, plus-sized pop culture reporter was perfectly content writing about other people's lives on the pages of the Philadelphia Examiner. But the day she opened up a national woman's magazine to find out that her ex-boyfriend had been chronicling their ex-sex life is the day her life changed forever.

Good Karma Divorce: Avoid Litigation, Turn Negative Emotions into Positive Actions, & Get on with the Rest of Your Life. unabr. abr. ed. Michele F. Lowrance. Read by Michele F. Lowrance. (ENG.). 2010. 25.00 (978-0-307-70421-4(1), Random AudioBks) Pub: Random Audio Pubg. Dist(s): Random

Good Kid, Bad Adult. Contrib. by John Heffron. (Running Time: 43 mins.). (YA). (gr. 11). 2005. audio compact disk 16.98 (978-1-929243-69-3(3)) Uproar Ent.

Good Life: Following God for Successful Living. Narrated by Max E. McLean. 2002. audio compact disk Rental 9.95 (978-1-931047-26-5(X)) Fellow Perform Arts.

Good Life: Health, Wealth & Happiness. Dick Sutphen. 1 cass. (Running Time: 1 hr.). (RX17 Ser.). 1986. 14.98 (978-0-87554-295-9(6), RX104) Valley Sun.
You now focus the power of your subconscious mind upon attaining health, wealth & happiness. What you believe, your mind can help you achieve. You have a divine right to health, wealth & happiness. You are now open & receptive to the good life. You are deserving of the best life has to offer. Happiness & success are self-bestowed.

Good life a newspapering & other Adventures. Ben Bradlee. 2004. 15.95 (978-0-7435-4793-2(4)) Pub: S&S Audio. Dist(s): S and S Inc

Good Life Wasted. Dave Ames. 2007. audio compact disk 28.00 (978-1-933309-52-1(0)) Pub: A Media Intl. Dist(s): Natl Bk Netwk

Good Life... with Fred Pryor. PUEI. 2007. audio compact disk 49.95 (978-1-934147-14-6(1), Fred Pryor) P Univ E Inc.

Good Listener. Betty L. Randolph. (Running Time: 45 min.). (Educational Ser.). 1989. 9.98 (978-1-55909-122-0(3), 98S) Randolph Tapes.
Discusses how to listen, be attentive & really hear what is being said.

Good Little Christmas Tree. unabr. ed. Ursula Moray Williams. Read by Bernard Cribbins. 1 cass. (Running Time: 1 hr.). 2001. 9.95 (CTC870, Chivers Child Audio) AudioGO.
The Christmas tree of a poor peasant family leaves their cottage on Christmas Eve & goes into the forest in search of pretty things with which to decorate himself.

Good Little Christmas Tree. unabr. ed. Ursula Moray Williams. Read by Bernard Cribbins. 1 CD. (Running Time: 40 mins.). 2002. audio compact disk (978-1-85549-824-2(3)) Cover To Cover GBR.
A timeless story that captures the spirit of Christmas, with six traditional carols.

Good Little Girl. Lawrence David. Read by Christina Moore. 1 cass. (Running Time: 15 mins.). (YA). 1998. pap. bk. 25.24 (978-0-7887-2991-1(8), 40873) Recorded Bks.
Miranda's busy parents have trouble making time for her. She's patient until the day her alter ego, Lucretia, takes over. Lucretia knows how to get what she wants, but she isn't very nice. Now Miranda is afraid she'll never regain control of herself.

Good Little Girl. Lawrence David. Read by Christina Moore. 1 cass. (Running Time: 15 mins.). (YA). 1999. pap. bk. & wbk. ed. 100.70 (978-0-7887-3021-4(5), 46838) Recorded Bks.

Good Little Girl. unabr. ed. David Lawrence. Narrated by Christina Moore. 1 cass. (Running Time: 15 mins.). (gr. k up). 1999. 10.00 (978-0-7887-2961-4(6), 95735E7) Recorded Bks.

Good Luck Duck. unabr. ed. Meindert DeJong. Read by Jim Weiss. 1 CD. (Running Time: 1 hr. 12 mins.). (J). (ps-3). 2007. audio compact disk 14.95 (978-1-882513-89-5(4)) Greathall Prods.

Good Luck Pony. Elizabeth Koda-Callan. (J). 1993. 8.95 (978-1-55994-893-7(0), HarperChildAud) HarperCollins Pubs.

Good Luck, Ronald Morgan! Patricia Reilly Giff. Read by Jeff Woodman. 1 cass. (Running Time: 15 mins.). (YA). 1999. stu. ed. 90.70 (978-0-7887-3867-8(4), 47032) Recorded Bks.
Ronald isn't having any fun with his best friend away at the lake. Even his new dog refuses to learn tricks. When someone moves in next door, Ronald hopes his luck will change. But out steps a girl with a cat!.

Good Luck, Ronald Morgan! unabr. ed. Patricia Reilly Giff. Narrated by Jeff Woodman. 1 cass. (Running Time: 15 mins.). (YA). 2000. pap. bk. 24.24 (978-0-7887-3796-1(1), 41040X4) Recorded Bks.

Good Luck, Ronald Morgan! unabr. ed. Patricia Reilly Giff. Narrated by Jeff Woodman. 1 cass. (Running Time: 15 mins.). (gr. k up). 2000. 10.00 (978-0-7887-3812-8(7), 96057E7) Recorded Bks.

Good Man in Africa. unabr. ed. William Boyd. Read by Ian Whitcomb. 9 cass. (Running Time: 9 hrs.). 1997. 72.00 (978-0-7366-3638-4(2), 4299) Books on Tape.
Worldly success doesn't burden Morgan Leafy, a representative of Her Majesty in tropical Kinjanja in this wickedly funny tale. Falling back on his deep-laid reserves of misanthropy & guile, Morgan has to fight off the sea of humiliation, betrayal & juju that threatens to wash over him.

***Good Man Is Hard to Find & Other Stories.** unabr. ed. Flannery O'Connor. (Running Time: 6 hrs. 30 mins.). 2010. 29.95 (978-1-4417-6913-8(7)); 44.95 (978-1-4417-6910-7(2)); audio compact disk 24.95 (978-1-4417-6912-1(9)); audio compact disk 69.00 (978-1-4417-6911-4(0)) Blckstn Audio.

***Good Man Jesus & the Scoundrel Christ.** unabr. ed. Philip Pullman. Read by Philip Pullman. 1 MP3-CD. (Running Time: 3 hrs.). 2010. 19.99 (978-1-4418-5797-2(4), 9781441857972, Brilliance MP3); 19.99 (978-1-4418-5799-6(0), 9781441857996, BAD); 39.97 (978-1-4418-5798-9(2), 9781441857989, Brinc Audio MP3 Lib); 39.97 (978-1-4418-5800-9(8), 9781441858009, BADLE); audio compact disk 19.99 (978-1-4418-5795-8(8), 9781441857958, Bril Audio CD Unabri); audio compact disk 59.97 (978-1-4418-5796-5(6), 9781441857965, BriAudCD Unabrid) Brilliance Audio.

Good Man of Nanking. unabr. ed. John Rabe. Read by Anna Fields. 6 cass. (Running Time: 9 hrs.). 2001. 29.95 (978-0-7861-1915-8(2)) Pub: Blckstn Audio. Dist(s): Penton Overseas
A unique and gripping document: the recently discovered diaries of a German businessman, John Rabe, who saved so many lives in the infamous siege of Nanking in 1937, that he is now honored as the Oskar Schindler of China.

Good Man of Nanking: The Diaries of John Rabe. unabr. ed. John Rabe. Read by Anna Fields. 6 cass. (Running Time: 8 hrs. 30 mins.). 2000. 44.95 (978-0-7861-1779-6(6), 2578) Blckstn Audio.
A unique document: the recently discovered diaries of a German businessman, John Rabe, who saved so many lives in the infamous siege of Nanking in 1937 that he is honored as the Oskar Schindler of China. As the Japanese army closed in on the city & all foreigners were ordered to evacuate, Rabe felt it would shame him before his Chinese workers & dishonor the Fatherland if he abandoned them.

Good Man of Nanking: The Diaries of John Rabe. unabr. ed. John Rabe. Read by Anna Fields. 8 CDs. (Running Time: 8 hrs. 30 mins.). 2000. audio compact disk 64.00 (978-0-7861-9874-0(5), 2578) Blckstn Audio.

Good Manager. Betty L. Randolph. Read by Betty L. Randolph. Read by Leonard Baron. Ed. by Success Education Institute International Staff. 1 cass. (Success Ser.). 1989. 9.98 (978-1-55909-133-6(9), 109S); 9.98 (978-1-55909-134-3(7), 109X) Randolph Tapes.
Includes Male-Female voice tracks with the right-left brain.

Good Marriage: How & Why Love Lasts. abr. ed. Judith S. Wallerstein & Sandra Blakeslee. 4 cass. 1999. 21.95 Set. (70338) Courage-to-Change.
When so many marriages fail miserably why do others succeed? Based on a study of 50 happily married couples.

Good Marriage Set: How & Why Love Lasts. Judith S. Wallerstein & Sandra Blakeslee. Read by Anne Mattingly. 4 cass. (Running Time: 6 hrs.). 1995. 21.95 (978-1-55935-182-9(9), 693460) Soundelux.

Good Masters! Sweet Ladies! Voices from a Medieval Village. unabr. ed. Laura Amy Schlitz. Narrated by Christina Moore. 2 CDs. (Running Time: 1 hrs. 30 mins.). (J). (gr. 4-8). 2008. audio compact disk 30.75 (978-1-4361-1963-4(4)); 30.75 (978-1-4361-1958-0(8)) Recorded Bks.
Laura Amy Schlitz wrote the Newbery Medal winner Good Masters! Sweet Ladies! for the students at the school where she is a librarian. The 22 monologues introduce readers to everyone in a medieval village, from the town half-wit, to Nelly the Sniggler, to the Lord's daughter.

Good Medicine. Mark Cosgrove. 1997. pap. bk. 17.95 (978-0-7866-3188-9(0), 96782BCD) Mel Bay.

Good Medicine: How to Turn Pain into Compassion with Tonglen Meditation. unabr. ed. Pema Chödrön. 2 CDs. (Running Time: 2 hrs. 30 min.). 2001. audio compact disk 24.95 (978-1-56455-846-6(0), AE00504) Sounds True.
A simple & elegant meditation system "for ordinary people like ourselves." Through tonglen, we can use the difficulties in life as a way to befriend ourselves, accept the past we have rejected & widen our circle of compassion. These traditional breathing meditations cut through obstacles "on the spot".

Good Memory. Betty L. Randolph. 1 stereo cass. (Running Time: 45 min.). (Self-Hypnosis Ser.). 9.98 (978-1-55909-146-6(0), 806) Randolph Tapes.
Promotes use of your subconscious. A sleep program that increases your mind power.

Good Memory. Betty L. Randolph. Read by Betty L. Randolph. Read by Leonard Baron. Ed. by Success Education Institute International. 1 cass. (Running Time: 60 min.). (Educational Ser.). 1989. bk. 10.98 90 min. extended length stereo music. (978-1-55909-182-4(7), 24B); 9.98 (978-1-55909-007-0(3), 24) Randolph Tapes.
Remember facts, names, places, etc. without effort! Subliminal messages are heard 3-5 minutes before becoming ocean sounds or music.

Good Monsters. Contrib. by Jars of Clay & Terry Hemmings. 2006. audio compact disk 17.98 (978-5-558-20311-0(0)) Essential Recs.

Good Morning Exercises for Kids. 1 CD. (J). (ps-3). 2001. pap. bk. 14.95 (KIM 9098CD) Kimbo Educ.

Good Morning Exercises for Kids. Georgiana Stewart. 1 LP. (J). (ps-3). 2001. pap. bk. 11.95 (KIM 9098) Kimbo Educ.

Good Morning Exercises for Kids. Georgiana Stewart. 1 cass. . (J). 2001. pap. bk. 11.95 (978-0-937124-22-2(2), KIM 9098C) Kimbo Educ.
How do you start the day a great way?...With easy, fun movement exercises & all-time favorite songs. Classics such as Oh, What a Beautiful Morning & Carolina in the Morning set the stage for clapping, skipping, stretching, sit-ups & more. Includes guide with lyrics nd instructions. (Fitness & Dancing, Exercises).

Good Morning, Good Night. 1 cass. (Musical Poems for Families Ser.: Vol. I). (J). (ps up). 9.98 (232) MFLP CA.
Elegant musical interpretations of poems by William Wordsworth, Rudyard Kipling, Rachel Field, Robert Louis Stevenson, Emily Bronte, Margaret Wise Brown, David Spangler & others.

Good Morning, Gorillas. Mary Pope Osborne. (Running Time: 40 mins.). (Magic Tree House Ser.: No. 26). (J). (gr. k-3). 2003. pap. bk. 17.00 (978-0-8072-1174-8(5), Listening Lib) Pub: Random Audio Pubg. Dist(s): Random

Good Morning, Granny Rose! unabr. ed. Warren Ludwig. 1 cass. (Running Time: 7 min.). (J). (gr. k-4). 1992. bk. 26.90 (978-0-8045-6668-1(2), 6668) Spoken Arts.
An Arkansas folktale with Granny Rose & her old dog, Henry.

Good Morning, Irene. unabr. ed. Carole Nelson Douglas. Narrated by Virginia Leishman & Patrick Tull. 9 cass. (Running Time: 12 hrs. 30 mins.). 1999. 80.00 (978-0-7887-2487-9(8), 95562E7) Recorded Bks.
The lovely & capable Irene Addler returns to action in France, where a corpse with a strangely familiar tattoo sets her detective's mind in motion. You will find yourself rubbing shoulders with the Crown Prince of Monaco, the divine Sarah Burnhardt & of course, Sherlock Holmes himself.

Good Morning, Killer. unabr. ed. April Smith. 8 cass. (Running Time: 12 hrs.). 2003. 72.00 (978-0-7366-9151-2(0)) Books on Tape.

***Good Morning Nantwich: Adventures in Breakfast Radio.** abr. ed. Phill Jupitus. Read by Phill Jupitus. (Running Time: 6 hrs. 40 mins.). (ENG.). 2010. audio compact disk 23.95 (978-0-00-735755-0(9)) Pub: HarpC GBR. Dist(s): IPG Chicago

Good-Morrow see Palgrave's Golden Treasury of English Poetry

Good-Morrow see Love Poems of John Donne

Good-Morrow see Treasury of John Donne

Good Mother. unabr. ed. Sue Miller. Read by Donada Peters. 9 cass. (Running Time: 13 hrs. 30 min.). 1987. 72.00 (978-0-7366-1154-1(1), 2078) Books on Tape.
Anna Dunlap is being torn in two...by love for her daughter, Molly & by passion for her lover, a painter with liberal ideas about personal freedom. It is a classic problem, hers to solve...which, remarkably, she does.

Good Mother. unabr. ed. Sue Miller. Narrated by Barbara McCulloh. 9 cass. (Running Time: 12 hrs. 45 mins.). 1988. 78.00 (978-1-55690-199-7(2), 88160E7) Recorded Bks.
Anna Dunlap's ex-husband accuses her lover of molesting Molly, Anna's child. The allegation leads to a bitter legal conflict.

Good Mother - Stratford Festival. Kathy M. Dixon. 2 CDs. (Running Time: 3 hrs.). 2005. audio compact disk 15.95 (978-0-660-18817-1(1)) Pub: Canadian Broadcasting CAN. Dist(s): Georgetown Term

Good News. Music by James V. Marchionda. 2004. audio compact disk 17.00 (978-1-58459-211-2(7)) Wrld Lib Pubns.
More than a dozen songs specifically for children and youth, but with appeal to choirs and assemblies of all ages! These are tried-and-true songs that have been incorporated into Fr. Marchionda's missions and retreats throughout the country. The scripturally sound texts and lyrical, singable melodies speak across the generations. Perfect for combined children's and adult choirs and 2-part choirs.

Good News about Injustice Audio Book: A Witness of Courage in a Hurting World. 10th rev. ed. Gary A. Haugen. (ENG.). audio compact disk 16.00 (978-0-8308-5570-4(X)) InterVarsity.

Good News about Injustice Audio Book: A Witness of Courage in a Hurting World. 10th rev. ed. Gary A. Haugen. (ENG.). 2009. audio compact disk 20.00 (978-0-8308-3711-3(6)) InterVarsity.

Good News about Sex & Marriage. Marcellino D'Ambrosio. 2005. audio compact disk 34.95 (978-1-932927-30-6(1)) Ascensn Pr.

Good News about Sex & Marriage, Set. 5 CDs. 2005. audio compact disk 29.95 (978-1-932645-73-6(X)) Ascensn Pr.

Good News about Sex & Marriage: Answers to Your Honest Questions about Catholic Teaching. Christopher West. 2005. 25.00 (978-1-932927-29-0(8)) Ascensn Pr.

Good News about Sex & Marriage: Answers to Your Honest Questions about Catholic Teaching. Christopher West. Read by Paul Smith. 5 cass. (Running Time: 7 hrs.). 2005. 40.95 (978-0-86716-703-0(3)) St Anthony Mess Pr.
BEST-SELLER NOW AVAILABLE IN AUDIO! The author, a diocesan director of marriage and family life, answers the questions about human sexuality and marriage that he always encounters in the numerous adult audiences he addresses. He provides thoughtful responses that present Catholic Church teaching in a fresh, thoroughly appealing, and convincing manner. A Servant Book.

Good News According to Mark. Richard Rohr. Read by Richard Rohr. 10 cass. (Running Time: 10 hrs.). 74.95 incl. study guide & vinyl album. (AA1907) Credence Commun.
Brings to light the central themes of the gospel; relates them to spiritual needs & for desire to grow in discipleship.

Good News, Bad News: New Stories for Listening & Discussion. Roger Barnard. 1997. 24.75 (978-0-19-435058-7(4)) OUP.

Good News, Bad News: New Stories for Listening & Discussion. Roger Barnard. 1998. audio compact disk 24.75 (978-0-19-435059-4(2)) OUP.

Good News Daily Leader's. Northwestern Publishing House Staff. (Vacation Bible Study Ser.). 2001. audio compact disk (978-0-8100-1324-7(X)) Northwest Pub.

Good News for Bad Days: Living a Soulful Life. unabr. ed. Paul Keenan. Narrated by John McDonough. 5 cass. (Running Time: 6 hrs. 15 mins.). 1998. 45.00 (978-0-7887-2488-6(6), 95563 E7) Recorded Bks.
Father Keenan has helped scores of troubled people with his radio programs, "Religion on the Line" & "As You Think." Discover the adventure & creativity involved in living a soulful life.

Good News for the Middle Aged: Psalms 91:6. Ed Young. 1979. 4.95 (978-0-7417-1096-3(X), A0096) Win Walk.

Good News from John: Based on the Gospel of John. Cindy Holtrop & Shirley Cooman. (Running Time: 1 hr.). (Noel Ser.). 15.95 (978-1-56212-265-2(7), 416102) FaithAliveChr.

***Good News in the Badlands: Americana Gospel Folk Music.** Composed by Bob Ayanian. (ENG.). 2009. audio compact disk 16.95 (978-0-9824881-4-0(9)) Lighthouse Trails OR.

Good News of Jesus Christ. abr. ed. Read by Marvin Miller. 6 cass. 35.70 (C-709) Audio Bk.
From the King James Bible, the complete four gospels of the New Testament.

Good News of the Kingdom, Album 1. Derek Prince. 4 cass. 19.95 (I-GNK1) Derek Prince.

Good News of the Kingdom, Album 2. Derek Prince. 3 cass. 14.95 (I-GNK2) Derek Prince.

Good News of the Risen Lord. Eugene LaVerdiere. Read by Eugene LaVerdiere. 2 cass. (Running Time: 1 hr. 59 min.). 16.95 set. (TAH156) Alba Hse Comns.

Good News of 1938: Celebration of MGM's Rosalie. Hosted by James Stewart. 1 cass. (Running Time: 1 hr.). 2001. 6.98 (2218) Radio Spirits.

Good News of 1939: Wallace Berry. Perf. by Robert Young & Wallace Berry. 1 cass. (Running Time: 1 hr.). 2001. 6.98 (2100) Radio Spirits.

***Good News We Almost Forgot: Rediscovering the Gospel in a 16th Century Catechism.** unabr. ed. Kevin DeYoung. Narrated by Adam Verner. (ENG.). 2010. 14.98 (978-1-59644-390-7(1), Hovel Audio); audio compact disk 24.98 (978-1-59644-389-1(8), Hovel Audio) christianaud.

Good Night. Short Stories. Jim Weiss. As told by Jim Weiss. 1 cass. (Running Time: 1 hr.). Dramatization. (Storyteller's Version Ser.). (J). (ps up). 1989. 10.95 (978-1-882513-01-7(0), 1124-01) Greathall Prods.
A bedtime tape with six vignettes that take the listener into scenes which bring about feelings of safety and love. A minute of gentle music follows each vignette.

Good Night: Off to Sleep. Read by Jim Weiss. 1 cass.1 CD. (Running Time: 1 hr.). (J). (GHP1) NewSound.

Good Night: Restful Sleep. Roxanne E. Daleo. 1 cass. (J). 1999. 12.95 Hlth Jrnys.

Good Night: Sleep Well. unabr. ed. Roxanne E. Daleo. Read by Roxanne E. Daleo. 1 cass. (Running Time: 31 min.). (MindWorks for Children Ser.: Vol. 1). (J). (ps-6). 1988. 12.95 (978-1-889447-11-7(0)) Mindwrks Chldrn.
Designed to give children the tools they need to relax body & mind. Regular use of these tapes will help children develop self-confidence & a healthy mental attitude, improve concentration & problem-solving abilities, & stimulate creativity.

Good Night Baby: A Collection of Lullabies. Rachel Coleman. (J). 2006. audio compact disk 9.99 (978-1-933543-35-2(3)) Tw Li Ha Pr LLC.

Good Night Evening Star. Perf. by Sequoyah. 1 CD. 1999. audio compact disk 16.98 (978-1-57908-479-0(6), 5330) Platinm Enter.

Good Night for Ghosts. unabr. ed. Mary Pope Osborne. Read by Mary Pope Osborne. (Magic Tree House Ser.: No. 42). (J). (gr. 1). 2009. audio compact disk 14.95 (978-0-7393-7294-4(7), Listening Lib) Pub: Random Audio Pubg. Dist(s): Random

Good Night, Good Knight. Shelley Moore Thomas. Narrated by L. J. Ganser. (Running Time: 15 mins.). 2000. 10.00 (978-1-4025-4187-2(2)) Recorded Bks.

Good Night Gorilla. 2004. 8.95 (978-1-55592-424-9(7)); audio compact disk 12.95 (978-1-55592-897-1(8)) Weston Woods.

Good Night Gorilla. (J). 2004. pap. bk. 18.95 (978-1-55592-419-5(0)); pap. bk. 18.95 (978-1-55592-422-5(0)); pap. bk. 38.75 (978-1-55592-421-8(2)); pap. bk. 38.75 (978-1-55592-423-2(9)); pap. bk. 32.75 (978-1-55592-426-3(3)); pap. bk. 32.75 (978-0-7882-0247-6(2)); pap. bk. 14.95 (978-1-55592-425-6(5)) Weston Woods.

Good Night, Mr. Holmes. unabr. ed. Carole Nelson Douglas. Narrated by Virginia Leishman. 9 cass. (Running Time: 13 hrs. 15 mins.). 1998. 78.00 (978-0-7887-2489-3(4), 95564E7) Recorded Bks.
Behold the incomparable Irene Adler - rising opera star & amateur sleuth extraordinaire. In defiance of the stuffy restrictions of victorian society, this

American woman joyfully flaunts her many talents & even outsmarts Sherlock Holmes.

Good Night My Angel. Kathleen Gibson. 1 cass. (Running Time: 35 min.). (J). (ps-2). 1995. 10.00 (978-1-888862-04-1(1), RR1120) Rompin Records.
Songs for quiet times, specifically designed to help children relax & be tranquil.

Good-Night Owl. 2004. cass. & flmstrp 30.00 (978-0-89719-514-0(0)) Weston Woods.

Good-Night Owl. (J). 2004. bk. 24.95 (978-1-56008-206-4(2)) Weston Woods.

Good-Night Owl! 2004. 8.95 (978-0-89719-914-8(6)) Weston Woods.

Good Night Warrior: 84 Favorite Bedtime Bible Stories Read by Sheila Walsh. unabr. ed. Sheila Walsh. (Gigi, God's Little Princess Ser.). (J). 2009. audio compact disk 19.99 (978-1-4003-1449-2(6)) Nelson.

Good Night Wish. Perf. by Shambhavi Christian. 1 cass. (Running Time: 1 hr. 8 mins.). (J). 2001. 10.95 (105320, Siddha Yoga Pubs); audio compact disk 15.95 (106320, Siddha Yoga Pubs) SYDA Found.
These lullabies for children of all ages are soothing traveling companions on the road to sweet dreams. The images and ideas for many of these songs came from conversations that singer/songwriter Shambhavi Christian had with Gurumayi Chidvilasananda. This happy collaboration carries the Guru's message of love, protection, and guidance to children everywhere.

Good Night's Sleep. Rick Brown. Read by Rick Brown. Ed. by John Quatro. 1 cass. (Running Time: 30 min.). (Subliminal - Easy Listening Ser.). 1993. 10.95 (978-1-57100-012-5(7), E131); 10.95 (978-1-57100-036-1(4), J131); 10.95 (978-1-57100-060-6(7), N131); 10.95 (978-1-57100-084-2(4), S131); 10.95 (978-1-57100-108-5(5), W131); 10.95 (978-1-57100-132-0(8), H131) Sublime Sftware.
Transitions from hypnosis to sleep.

Good Night's Sleep. Michael P. Kelly. 1 cass. 1992. 14.95 (978-1-883700-05-8(1)) ThoughtForms.
Self help.

Good Ol' Boys. 1 cass. (Running Time: 30 min.). 8.00 (C0640B090, HarperThor); 8.00 (ME-82-10-01, HarperThor) HarpC GBR.

Good Old Boys. abr. ed. Elmer Kelton. Read by Bernard Bridges. Ed. by Steve Holland. 4 cass. (Running Time: 6 hrs.). (Texas Tradition Ser.: No. 1). 1995. 25.00 (978-1-883268-06-0(0), 694032) Spellbinders.
Relates, with humor, great insight, & integrity the feelings of cowboy Hewey Calloway struggling to find a place for himself in a new era in the West.

Good Old Boys & the Women Who Love Them. Barbara McBride-Smith. (Running Time: 51 mins.). 2005. audio compact disk 14.95 (978-0-87483-763-6(4)) Pub: August Hse. Dist(s): Natl Bk Netwk

Good Old Crunchy Stories. As told by Nancy K. Duncan. (Running Time: 1 hour 21 mins). 2002. audio compact disk 15.00 (978-0-9719007-0-7(1)) STORY PERFORM.
I call these "crunchy" stories because they are like my favorite kind of cookie. When you get to the end - there's a "crunch." A surprise waiting to happen. Ideal for grades 5 - 12, this tape includes these stories: Tushi (a Duncan family story about an alive wedding present), How People Were Made (a Miwok creation story from California), My Dad (told to me by an Iowa 4th grader), The Big White House (a funny ghost story given to me by Jackie Torrence), and The Pocket People (which you need to see to believe.).

Good Old Days: They Were Terrible. unabr. ed. Heywood Hale Broun. Perf. by Otto Bettman & Viola S. Thomas. 1 cass. (Running Time: 56 min.). 12.95 (40095) J Norton Pubs.
Archivist Dr. Bettman interviewed by Broun, culls a horrifying pictorial survey of the good old days. He describes life in America at the turn of the century, with guest Viola Scott Thomas, Curator of the Museum of Immigration.

Good Old-Fashioned Christmas see Best of Benchley

Good Omens: The Nice & Accurate Prophecies of Agnes Nutter, Witch. unabr. ed. Neil Gaiman & Terry Pratchett. Read by Martin Jarvis. 10 CDs. (Running Time: 12 hrs. 30 mins.). 2009. audio compact disk 39.99 (978-0-06-173581-3(7), Harper Audio) HarperCollins Pubs.

***Good Omens: The Nice & Accurate Prophecies of Agnes Nutter, Witch.** unabr. ed. Neil Gaiman & Terry Pratchett. Read by Martin Jarvis. (ENG.). 2009. (978-0-06-196707-8(6), Harper Audio); (978-0-06-196708-5(4), Harper Audio) HarperCollins Pubs.

Good People. unabr. ed. Marcus Sakey. Read by Joyce Bean & Dan John Miller. (Running Time: 8 hrs.). 2008. 39.25 (978-1-4233-6693-5(X), 9781423366935, BADLE); 39.25 (978-1-4233-6691-1(3), 9781423366911, Brlnc Audio MP3 Lib); audio compact disk 87.25 (978-1-4233-6689-8(1), 9781423366898, BriAudCD Unabrid) Brilliance Audio.

Good People. unabr. ed. Marcus Sakey et al. (Running Time: 8 hrs.). 2008. 24.95 (978-1-4233-6692-8(1), 9781423366928, BAD); 24.95 (978-1-4233-6690-4(5), 9781423366904, Brilliance MP3); audio compact disk 32.95 (978-1-4233-6688-1(3), 9781423366881, Bril Audio CD Unabri) Brilliance Audio.

Good Peoples. Narrated by Peter Francis James. 8 CDs. (Running Time: 9 hrs. 45 mins.). audio compact disk 78.00 (978-0-7887-8966-3(X)) Recorded Bks.

Good Peoples. Marcus Major. Narrated by Peter Francis James. 7 cass. (Running Time: 9 hrs. 45 mins.). 2000. 64.00 (978-0-7887-4942-1(0), F0007E7) Recorded Bks.
Myles Moore, 28, has almost convinced himself that single life in Philadelphia is just fine but when he meets Marisa Marrero, all thoughts of solitude fly away. Now he must put his male ego aside & learn to understand this person he has come to love.

Good Pick: Early Explorers Early Set A Audio CD. Benchmark Education Staff. (J). 2006. audio compact disk 10.00 (978-1-4108-7622-5(5)) Benchmark Educ.

Good Poems: Selected & Introduced by Garrison Keillor. abr. ed. Garrison Keillor. Read by Garrison Keillor. 4 CDs. (Running Time: 4 hrs. 30 mins.). (ENG.). 2002. audio compact disk 26.95 (978-1-56511-694-8(1), 1565116941) Pub: HighBridge. Dist(s): Workman Pub

Good Practice Audio CD Set: Communication Skills in English for the Medical Practitioner. Marie McCullagh & Rosalind Wright. (Running Time: 1 hr. 40 mins.). (ENG.). 2008. audio compact disk 42.00 (978-0-521-75592-4(1)) Cambridge U Pr.

Good Practice Details. GLC. 1997. audio compact disk (978-0-7506-2657-6(7), Arch Sci Pr) Sci Tech Bks.

Good Provider. unabr. ed. Jessica Stirling. Read by Kara Wilson. 10 cass. (Running Time: 10 hrs.). (Nicholson Quartet Ser.). 1993. bk. 84.95 (978-0-7451-6314-7(9), CAB 483) AudioGO.

***Good Psychologist: A Novel.** unabr. ed. Noam Shpancer. Narrated by William Dufris. (Running Time: 7 hrs. 0 mins.). 2010. 14.99 (978-1-4001-8927-4(6)); 19.99 (978-1-4001-6927-6(5)); audio compact disk 29.99 (978-1-4001-1927-1(8)) Pub: Tantor Media. Dist(s): IngramPubServ

***Good Psychologist (Library Edition) A Novel.** unabr. ed. Noam Shpancer. Narrated by William Dufris. (Running Time: 7 hrs. 30 mins. 0 sec.). (ENG.). 2010. audio compact disk 71.99 (978-1-4001-4927-8(4)) Pub: Tantor Media. Dist(s): IngramPubServ

Good Rat: A True Story. unabr. ed. Jimmy Breslin. Narrated by Richard M. Davidson et al. 6 CDs. (Running Time: 7 hrs.). (ENG.). 2008. audio compact disk 29.95 (978-1-60283-376-0(1)) Pub: AudioGO. Dist(s): Perseus Dist

Good Rat: A True Story. unabr. ed. Jimmy Breslin. Read by Richard M. Davidson. (YA). 2008. 59.99 (978-1-60514-959-2(4)) Find a World.

Good Samaritan, Set. unabr. ed. Nicola Thorne. Read by Joanna David. 8 cass. (Running Time: 12 hrs.). 1999. 69.95 (978-0-7540-0357-1(4), CAB1780) AudioGO.
Lois enjoys a privileged lifestyle: happily married, she's a pillar of the community. Wendy, her urban sister, seems equally fortunate: for there is a man she may marry & a whirl of parties to attend. What neither of them expects is Oliver, a proud, enigmatic beggar, befriended by Lois. But what does Oliver think of them? And what dark secrets from his past is he keeping?.

Good Samaritan Strikes Again. unabr. ed. Patrick F. McManus. Narrated by Norman Dietz. 4 cass. (Running Time: 5 hrs. 15 mins.). 1992. 37.00 (978-0-7887-3774-9(0), 95991E7) Recorded Bks.
Gently pokes fun at the oddities of sacred institutions like friendship, marriage & even hunting & fishing.

Good Samaritan Strikes Again. unabr. ed. Patrick F. McManus. Narrated by Norman Dietz. 5 CDs. (Running Time: 5 hrs. 15 mins.). 2000. audio compact disk 48.00 (978-0-7887-4656-7(1), C1192E7) Recorded Bks.

Good Scent from a Strange Mountain: Stories. Robert Olen Butler. Read by Robert Olen Butler. 2 cass. (Running Time: 3 hrs.). (American Audio Prose Library Reading). 1994. 13.95 set. (978-1-55644-398-5(6), 14011); 25.00 incl. interview. (978-1-55644-400-5(1), 14013); 13.95 interview, 1 cass., 58 min. (978-1-55644-399-2(4), 14012) Am Audio Prose.
The author's training as an actor is evident in this polished reading performance from his 1993 Pulitzer Prize winning collection. The stories he has chosen to read range in mood from the slyly comic to the openly spiritual. In the interview, listeners curious about how & why fiction is produced will be fascinated.

Good Shepherd. Edward Hays. 1 cass. (Running Time: 60 min.). 9.95 (For Peace Pubng) Ave Maria Pr.
In an age when many claim to speak in the name of the Shepherd, these two conferences will help you bring into focus the true voice of the Good Shepherd.

Good Shepherd. collector's ed. C. S. Forester. Read by Richard Green. 7 cass. (Running Time: 10 hrs. 30 mins.). 1981. 56.00 (978-0-7366-0364-5(6), 1348) Books on Tape.
A convoy is ploughing through icy, submarine-infested North Atlantic seas during the most critical day of WWII. In charge is Commander George Krause, an untested veteran of the U. S. navy.

***Good Soldier.** unabr. ed. Ford Madox Ford. Narrated by Gildart Jackson. (Running Time: 8 hrs. 30 mins.). 2010. 15.99 (978-1-4001-8947-2(0)); 19.99 (978-1-4001-6947-4(X)); audio compact disk 66.99 (978-1-4001-4947-6(9)); audio compact disk 27.99 (978-1-4001-1947-9(2)) Pub: Tantor Media. Dist(s): IngramPubServ

Good Soldier: A Tale of Passion. unabr. ed. Ford Madox Ford. Read by Frank Muller. 4 Cass. (Running Time: 7 Hrs.). 19.95 (978-1-4025-4528-3(2)) Recorded Bks.

Good Soldier: A Tale of Passion. unabr. ed. Ford Madox Ford. Narrated by Frank Muller. 5 cass. (Running Time: 7 hrs.). 1986. 44.00 (978-1-55690-200-0(X), 86410E7) Recorded Bks.
On the face of it Captain Edward Ashburnham's life was unimpeachable. But behind the mask where passion seethes, the captain's "good" life was rotting away.

***Good Soldiers.** unabr. ed. David Finkel. Read by Mark Boyett. (Running Time: 11 hrs.). 2010. 24.99 (978-1-4418-5145-1(3), 9781441851451, Brilliance MP3); 39.97 (978-1-4418-5146-8(1), 9781441851468, Brlnc Audio MP3 Lib); 39.97 (978-1-4418-5147-5(X), 9781441851475, BADLE); audio compact disk 29.99 (978-1-4418-5143-7(7), 9781441851437, Bril Audio CD Unabri); audio compact disk 92.97 (978-1-4418-5144-4(5), 9781441851444, BriAudCD Unabrid) Brilliance Audio.

***Good Son.** unabr. ed. Michael Gruber. (Running Time: 13 hrs. 30 mins.). 2010. 29.95 (978-1-4417-3730-4(8)); 79.95 (978-1-4417-3726-7(X)); audio compact disk 29.95 (978-1-4417-3729-8(4)); audio compact disk 109.00 (978-1-4417-3727-4(8)) Blckstn Audio.

Good Sons. unabr. ed. K. C. Constantine. Read by Lloyd James. 7 cass. (Running Time: 10 hrs. 30 min.). (Mario Balzic Ser.). 1998. 56.00 (978-0-7366-4015-2(0), 4513) Books on Tape.
Mario Balzic is in retirement, & Det. Rugs Carlucci takes on a brutal rape & a Pittsburgh crime family.

Good Sports. abr. ed. Rick Wolf. Read by Chris Smith. 2 cass. (Running Time: 3 hrs.). Dramatization. bk. 16.95 set. (978-1-56703-031-0(9)) High-Top Sports.

Good Student. Rick Brown. Read by Rick Brown. Ed. by John Quatro. 1 cass. (Running Time: 30 min.). (Subliminal - Easy Listening Ser.). 1993. 10.95 (978-1-57100-006-4(2), E117); 10.95 (978-1-57100-030-9(5), J117); 10.95 (978-1-57100-054-5(2), N117); 10.95 (978-1-57100-078-1(X), S117); 10.95 (978-1-57100-102-3(6), W117); 10.95 (978-1-57100-126-9(3), H117) Sublime Sftware.
Praises & encourages, enhances learning.

Good Study Habits. 1 cass. (Running Time: 1 hr.). 1992. 9.98 (978-1-56470-018-6(6)) Success Cass.
Subliminal program.

Good Study Habits. Barrie Konicov. 1 cass. (YA). 11.98 (978-0-87082-299-5(3), 053) Potentials.
Now is the time to bring out the hidden talents in your child. More concerned parents purchase this tape for their children than any other tape we offer. Studying can be fun, learning can be enjoyable.

Good Study Habits. Barrie Konicov. 1 CD. (J). 2003. audio compact disk 16.98 (978-0-87082-963-5(7)) Potentials.
More concerned parents purchase this program for their children than any other program we offer. The results are amazing! Studying can be fun; learning can be enjoyable. Now is the time to bring out the hidden potential in your child.You will find the self-hypnosis on track 1 and the subliminal on track 2. The easy-listening music of the subliminal, together with the self-hypnosis, is the original format which most people love and with which they are most familiar.

Good Stuff. Perf. by Eric Bibb. 1 cass.; 1 CD. 1998. 10.98 (978-1-56628-157-7(1), 75265); audio compact disk 15.98 CD. (978-1-56628-156-0(3), 75265D) MFLP CA.

Good Stuff. Perf. by Eric Bibb. 1 cass., 1 CD. 7.98 (EB 75265); audio compact disk 12.78 CD Jewel box. (EB 75265) NewSound.

Good Stuff Inside. Larry Chesley. 1 cass. 7.98 (978-1-55503-736-9(4), 069407); 7.95 (978-1-57734-228-1(3), 06005756) Covenant Comms.
Finding the best in ourselves & others.

Good Terrorist. unabr. ed. Doris Lessing. Read by Nadia May. 10 cass. (Running Time: 14 hrs. 30 mins.). 1999. 69.95 (978-0-7861-1530-3(0), 2380) Blckstn Audio.
Timely portrait of the kind of personalities - who they are, how they function, what makes them tick - that can be drawn to this dangerous & frightening way of life.

Good Terrorist. unabr. ed. Doris Lessing. Read by Nadia May. (Running Time: 50400 sec.). 2008. audio compact disk & audio compact disk 29.95 (978-1-4332-3427-9(0)); audio compact disk & audio compact disk 99.00 (978-1-4332-3426-2(2)) Blckstn Audio.

Good That Lives after Them. Bob Wilson. Ed. by John Kings. 1 cass. 1982. bk. 10.00 (978-0-9608192-1-8(5)) B Wilson.

Good, the Bad, & the Undead. unabr. ed. Kim Harrison. Read by Marguerite Gavin. (Hollows Ser.: Bk. 2). (YA). 2008. 64.99 (978-1-60514-640-9(4)) Find a World.

Good, the Bad, & the Undead. unabr. ed. Kim Harrison. Read by Marguerite Gavin. (Running Time: 14 hrs. 30 mins. 0 sec.). (Hollows Ser.: Bk. 2). (ENG.). 2007. audio compact disk 39.99 (978-1-4001-0472-7(6)); audio compact disk 29.99 (978-1-4001-5472-2(3)); audio compact disk 79.99 (978-1-4001-3472-4(2)) Pub: Tantor Media. Dist(s): IngramPubServ

Good, the Bad & the Very Slimy. unabr. ed. R. L. Stine. (Rotten School Ser.: No. 3). (J). 2005. audio compact disk 17.95 (978-0-06-082073-2(X)) HarperCollins Pubs.

Good, the Bad, the Ugly: Luke 10:25-37. Ed Young. 1993. 4.95 (978-0-7417-1952-2(5), 952) Win Walk.

Good Thief. unabr. ed. Hannah Tinti. Read by William Dufris. (Running Time: 11 hrs.). 2009. 24.99 (978-1-4233-8532-5(2), 9781423385325, Brilliance MP3); 24.99 (978-1-4233-8534-9(9), 9781423385349, BAD); 39.97 (978-1-4233-8533-2(0), 9781423385332, Brlnc Audio MP3 Lib); 39.97 (978-1-4233-8535-6(7), 9781423385356, BADLE); audio compact disk 34.99 (978-1-4233-8530-1(6), 9781423385301, Bril Audio CD Unabri); audio compact disk 92.97 (978-1-4233-8531-8(4), 9781423385318, BriAudCD Unabrid) Brilliance Audio.

Good Things Do, Too, Come in Brown Packaging, Vol. 1. Poems. David Jedidah. Read by Rael Jedidiah. Ed. by Rael Jedidish. Illus. by Rael Jedidish. 1 cass. 1998. spiral bd. (978-1-892981-00-4(9), BKOIGT) Divinity Seven.

Good Times. unabr. collector's ed. Russell Baker. Read by Michael Prichard. 8 cass. (Running Time: 12 hrs.). 1990. 64.00 (978-0-7366-1735-2(3), 2574) Books on Tape.
In this sequel to Growing Up, the autobiography of his boyhood, Russell Baker relates the striving of his early career & contrasts it to the country's sunny years under Truman, Eisenhower & Kennedy. Baker rose steadily, from newsboy to college paper, from police reporter to rewrite man, from White House correspondent to Washington columnist. In contrast, these stages read like a successful resume, but it is Baker's recall of detail that makes the story live. Nothing was easy, success never is. Behind every triumph lies a pitfall, behind every joy a hard lesson. Baker tells it all, from the mean streets of Baltimore to a seat at the coronation of Queen Elizabeth II, & from watching Ike fish to sharing LBJ's calculated secrets.

Good Times & Bedtimes. Read by Si Kahn. 1 cass. (Running Time: 35 min.). (Family Ser.). (J). (gr. 1-7). 1993. 9.98 (8027); audio compact disk 14.98 (8027) Rounder Records.
Adults & children alike will love Si Kahn's zany & touching look at the most universal family ritual: bedtime.

Good to Be Free. Contrib. by Karen Peck & New River & Phil Johnson. Prod. by Phil Johnson & Michael Sykes. 2005. audio compact disk 15.98 (978-5-559-13573-1(9)) Sprg Hill Music Group.

***Good to Great.** unabr. ed. Jim Collins. Read by Jim Collins. (ENG.). 2008. (978-0-06-179126-0(1), Harper Audio) HarperCollins Pubs.

***Good to Great.** unabr. ed. Jim Collins. Read by Jim Collins. (ENG.). 2010. (978-0-06-204587-4(3), Harper Audio) HarperCollins Pubs.

Good to Great: Why Some Companies Make the Leap... And Others Don't. Jim Collins. Narrated by Rick Rohan. 5 cass. (Running Time: 7 hrs. 30 mins.). 54.00 (978-1-4025-0255-2(9)); audio compact disk 72.00 (978-1-4025-2077-8(8)) Recorded Bks.

Good to Great: Why Some Companies Make the Leap... And Others Don't. abr. ed. Jim Collins. 4 cass. (Running Time: 6 hrs.). 2001. 26.95 (978-0-694-52607-9(X)) HarperCollins Pubs.

Good to Great: Why Some Companies Make the Leap... And Others Don't. abr. ed. Jim Collins. Read by Jim Collins. 5 CDs. (Running Time: 6 hrs.). 2001. audio compact disk 29.99 (978-0-694-52608-6(8)) HarperCollins Pubs.

Good to Great: Why Some Companies Make the Leap... & Other's Don't. unabr. ed. Jim Collins. Read by Jim Collins. 2005. audio compact disk 39.95 (978-0-06-079441-5(0)) HarperCollins Pubs.

Good to Great & the Social Sectors: A Monograph to Accompany Good to Great. unabr. abr. ed. Jim Collins. Read by Jim Collins. (Running Time: 5400 sec.). 2006. audio compact disk 17.00 (978-0-06-134102-1(9), Harper Audio) HarperCollins Pubs.

Good to Great series, Pt. 1. 2005. audio compact disk 24.95 (978-1-59834-105-8(7)) Walk Thru the Bible.

Good Versus Evil. (Running Time: 20 hrs.). 2004. 59.98 (978-1-57019-713-0(X)) Radio Spirits.

***Good Walk Spoiled.** J. M. Gregson. 2010. 71.95 (978-1-4079-0929-5(0)); audio compact disk 79.95 (978-1-4079-0930-1(4)) Pub: Soundings Ltd GBR. Dist(s): Ulverscroft US

Good Walk Spoiled: Days & Nights on the PGA Tour. John Feinstein. Read by Michael Kramer. 2000. 104.00 (978-0-7366-4841-7(0)); audio compact disk 120.00 (978-0-7366-7501-7(9)) Books on Tape.

Good Walk Spoiled: Days & Nights on the PGA Tour. abr. ed. John Feinstein. (Running Time: 2 hrs. 30 mins.). (ENG.). 2006. 14.98 (978-1-59483-657-2(4)) Pub: Hachet Audio. Dist(s): HachBkGrp

Good Walk Spoiled: Days & Nights on the PGA Tour. unabr. ed. John Feinstein. Read by Michael Kramer. 13 cass. (Running Time: 90 mins. per cass.). 2000. 78.00 (5191) Books on Tape.
A behind-the-scenes study of men's professional golfers. It follows a turbulent year on the PGA tour, sharing portraits of superstars & rising players, the pressures of a high-profile sport & dramatic tournament moments.

Good War Pt. I: An Oral History of World War II. unabr. collector's ed. Studs Terkel. Read by Christopher Hurt. 8 cass. (Running Time: 12 hrs.). 1988. 64.00 (978-0-7366-1268-5(8), 2179-A) Books on Tape.
An oral history of World War II. Personal accounts by ordinary Americans at home & abroad.

Good War Pt. II: An Oral History of World War II. collector's ed. Studs Terkel. Read by Christopher Hurt. 8 cass. (Running Time: 12 hrs.). 1988. 64.00 (978-0-7366-1269-2(6), 2179-B) Books on Tape.

Good Wife: A Novel. unabr. ed. Stewart O'Nan. Read by Laural Merlington. (Running Time: 9 hrs.). 2005. 39.25 (978-1-59710-329-9(2), 9781597103299, BADLE); 24.95 (978-1-59710-328-2(4), 9781597103282,

BAD); 39.25 (978-1-59335-988-1(8), 9781593359881, Brlnc Audio MP3 Lib); 24.95 (978-1-59335-987-4(X), 9781593359874, Brilliance MP3); 74.25 (978-1-59600-290-6(5), 9781596002906, BriAudUnabridg); 29.95 (978-1-59600-289-0(1), 9781596002890, BAU); audio compact disk 82.25 (978-1-59600-292-0(1), 9781596002920, BriAudCD Unabrid) Brilliance Audio.
Please enter a Synopsis.

Good Wife: A Novel. unabr. rev. ed. Stewart O'Nan. Read by Laural Merlington. (Running Time: 9 hrs.). 2005. audio compact disk 29.95 (978-1-59600-291-3(3), 9781596002913) Brilliance Audio.

Good Will, Good Health. unabr. ed. Perf. by Eknath Easwaran. 1 cass. (Running Time: 1 hr.). 1989. 7.95 (978-1-58638-548-4(8)) Nilgiri Pr.

Good Wives. unabr. ed. Louisa May Alcott. 7 cass. (Running Time: 10 hrs.). 1997. 49.95 (978-0-7861-1051-3(1), 1823) Blckstn Audio.
Takes up three years after the close of "Little Women." The March girls & their friend Laurie are young adults with only their futures to find. Along the way they all face painful trials from Meg's difficult lessons in housekeeping to Laurie's heartbreak in a love tragedy - each of the girls finds happiness, although not always in the way they expect.

Good Wives. unabr. ed. Louisa May Alcott. Read by C. M. Hebert. (Running Time: 34200 sec.). 2007. audio compact disk 29.95 (978-0-7861-6154-6(X)) Blckstn Audio.

Good Wives. unabr. ed. Louisa May Alcott & C. M. Hebert. (Running Time: 34200 sec.). 2007. audio compact disk 72.00 (978-0-7861-6153-9(1)) Blckstn Audio.

Good Woman. Danielle Steel. Read by Jay O. Sanders. (Playaway Adult Fiction Ser.). (ENG.). 2009. 104.99 (978-1-60812-693-4(5)) Find a World.

Good Woman. abr. ed. Danielle Steel. Read by Jay O. Sanders. 5 CDs. (Running Time: 6 hrs.). 2008. audio compact disk 19.99 (978-1-4233-2046-3(8), 9781423320463, BACD) Brilliance Audio.

Good Woman. abr. ed. Danielle Steel. Read by Jay O. Sanders. (Running Time: 6 hrs.). 2009. audio compact disk 14.99 (978-1-4233-2047-0(6), 9781423320470, BCD Value Price) Brilliance Audio.

Good Woman. unabr. ed. Danielle Steel. Read by Jay O. Sanders. 1 MP3-CD. (Running Time: 10 hrs.). 2008. 24.95 (978-1-4233-2042-5(5), 9781423320425, Brilliance MP3); 39.25 (978-1-4233-2045-6(X), 9781423320456, BADLE); 39.25 (978-1-4233-2043-2(3), 9781423320432, Brlnc Audio MP3 Lib) Brilliance Audio.

Good Woman. unabr. ed. Danielle Steel. Read by JAY O. SANDERS. (Running Time: 10 hrs.). 2008. 24.95 (978-1-4233-2044-9(1), 9781423320449, BAD) Brilliance Audio.

Good Woman. unabr. ed. Danielle Steel. Read by Jay O. Sanders. 8 CDs. (Running Time: 10 hrs.). 2008. audio compact disk 38.99 (978-1-4233-2040-1(9), 9781423320401, Bril Audio CD Unabri); audio compact disk 102.25 (978-1-4233-2041-8(7), 9781423320418, BriAudCD Unabrid) Brilliance Audio.

***Good Yarn.** abr. ed. Debbie Macomber. Read by Linda Emond. (ENG.). 2005. (978-0-06-079701-0(0), Harper Audio); (978-0-06-084585-8(6), Harper Audio) HarperCollins Pubs.

Good Yarn. abr. ed. Debbie Macomber. Read by Linda Emond. (Blossom Street Ser.: No. 2). 2005. audio compact disk 29.95 (978-0-06-058200-5(6)) HarperCollins Pubs.

Good Year. abr. ed. Peter Mayle. Read by Ben Chaplin. (Running Time: 18000 sec.). (ENG.). 2006. audio compact disk 27.95 (978-0-7393-3991-6(5), Random AudioBks) Pub: Random Audio Pubg. Dist(s): Random

Good Years, 1900-1914. unabr. ed. Walter Lord. Read by Noah Waterman. 9 cass. (Running Time: 13 hrs.). 1996. 62.95 (978-0-7861-1000-1(7), 1777) Blckstn Audio.
This is about the years from the turn of the century to the First World War, when for a span of time that was never going to end Americans enjoyed the best of all possible worlds. Walter Lord brings to life the big moments of this era. You will fight the Boxer Rebellion with an American missionary of amazing military talent. You will see McKinely shot & be convinced that everything will be all right; watch Theodore Roosevelt go trust-busting; visit that stifling armory the night men went wild for Woodrow Wilson. You will tour the world with the Great White Fleet; battle of the flames of San Francisco that day when Caruso, William James, John Barrymore, & Jack London were among the present; & race with Peary to the Pole.

***Goodby, World, Goodby.** Contrib. by Mosie Lister & Camp Kirkland. (ENG.). 2008. audio compact disk 24.99 (978-5-557-43536-9(0)) Lillenas.

Goodbye Baby Blue. Frank Ryan. Read by Michael Tudor Barnes. 10 cass. (Running Time: 15 hrs.). 2001. 84.95 (978-1-86042-687-2(5), 26875) Pub: Soundings Ltd GBR. Dist(s): Ulverscroft US

Goodbye, Columbus: And Five Short Stories. unabr. ed. Philip Roth. Perf. by John Rubinstein et al. 6 cass. (Running Time: 8 hrs.). 2001. 32.00 (978-1-59040-050-0(X), Phoenix Audio) Pub: Amer Intl Pub. Dist(s): PerseuPGW
Neil Klugman (he of poor Newark) and pretty, spirited Brenda Patimkin (she of suburban Short Hills) meet one summer and dive into an affair that is as much about social class and suspicion as it is about love. Goodbye Columbus is accompanied by five short stories that range in tone from inconoclastic to the astonishingly tender and illuminate the subterranean conflicts between parents and children and friends and neighbors in the American Jewish Diaspora.

Goodbye Curate. Fred Secombe. Read by Fred Secombe. 5 cass. 1999. 39.95 (65468) Pub: Soundings Ltd GBR. Dist(s): Ulverscroft US

Goodbye, Darkness. unabr. ed. Read by Christopher Hurt. 11 cass. (Running Time: 1 hr. 30 min. per cass.). 1979. Rental 11.95 Set. (1682) Books on Tape.
This exercise in autobiographical exorcism transports us to those times when the cause was clear, the case convincing, the fighting bitter & implacable.

Goodbye, Darkness: A Memoir of the Pacific War. William Manchester. Read by Barrett Whitener. (Running Time: 54000 sec.). 2007. 79.95 (978-0-7861-6923-8(0)); audio compact disk 99.00 (978-0-7861-6922-1(2)) Blckstn Audio.

Goodbye, Darkness: A Memoir of the Pacific War. unabr. ed. William Manchester. Read by Barrett Whitener. (Running Time: 54000 sec.). 2007. 29.95 (978-0-7861-4860-8(8)); audio compact disk 29.95 (978-0-7861-6046-4(2)); audio compact disk 29.95 (978-0-7861-7152-1(9)) Blckstn Audio.

Goodbye, Darkness: A Memoir of the Pacific War. unabr. ed. William Manchester. Read by Barrett Whitener. (YA). 2007. 84.99 (978-1-60252-903-8(5)) Find a World.

Goodbye, Darkness: A Memoir of the Pacific War. unabr. collector's ed. William Manchester. Read by Christopher Hurt. 11 cass. (Running Time: 16 hrs. 30 mins.). 1984. 88.00 (978-0-7366-0725-4(0), 1682) Books on Tape.
This exercise in autobiographical exorcism transports us to those times when the cause was clear, the case convincing, the fighting bitter & implacable.

Goodbye for Now. Perf. by Kathy Troccoli. 1 cass. 1999. 8.98 (978-0-7601-2726-1(3)) Brentwood Music.

Goodbye, Good Men. Michael Rose. 9 CDs. (Running Time: 9 hrs.). 2002. audio compact disk 44.95 (978-1-57058-467-1(2)) St Joseph Communs.
These days Catholics and non-Catholics alike are asking, "How did the American Catholic priesthood go from an image of wise, strong men like Spencer Tracy in Boys Town and Bing Crosby in Going My Way, to an image of "pedophile priests"?" In the best-selling book Goodbye, Good Men, Catholic author and investigative reporter Michael S. Rose provides the shocking answer - an answer that you won"t hear from the mainstream news media! Now, by special arrangement with the publisher, St. Joseph Communications has produced an exclusive audio version of Goodbye, Good Men read by popular Catholic apologist and radio personality Tim Staples. A one-time seminarian that experienced first-hand many of the types of incidents recounted in this eye-opening book, Staples brings a real passion to the narration that greatly enhances the presentation of this challenging material.

Goodbye, Mr. Chips see Lincoln: The Prairie Years

Goodbye, Mr. Chips. James Hilton. Read by Martin Jarvis. (CSA Word Classics (Playaway) Ser.). (ENG.). 2009. 59.99 (978-1-60775-707-8(9)) Find a World.

Goodbye, Mr. Chips. unabr. ed. James Hilton. Read by Martin Jarvis. (Classics Collection). 2001. 7.95 (978-1-57815-237-7(2), Media Bks Audio) Media Bks NJ.

Goodbye, Mr Chips. unabr. ed. James Hilton. Read by Martin Jarvis. (Running Time: 2 hrs. 0 mins. 0 sec.). (ENG.). 2008. audio compact disk 19.95 (978-1-934997-14-7(5)) Pub: CSAWord. Dist(s): PerseuPGW

***Goodbye Quilt.** abr. ed. Susan Wiggs. (Running Time: 6 hrs.). 2011. 9.99 (978-1-4558-0490-0(8), 9781455804900, BAD); audio compact disk 24.99 (978-1-4233-5210-5(6), 9781423352105, BACD) Brilliance Audio.

***Goodbye Quilt.** unabr. ed. Susan Wiggs. (Running Time: 12 hrs.). 2011. 39.97 (978-1-4233-5207-5(6), 9781423352075, Brlnc Audio MP3 Lib); 39.97 (978-1-4233-5209-9(2), 9781423352099, BADLE); 24.99 (978-1-4233-5206-8(8), 9781423352068, Brilliance MP3); 24.99 (978-1-4233-5208-2(4), 9781423352082, BAD); audio compact disk 92.97 (978-1-4233-5205-1(X), 9781423352051, BriAudCD Unabrid); audio compact disk 34.99 (978-1-4233-5204-4(1), 9781423352044, Bril Audio CD Unabri) Brilliance Audio.

Goodbye, Saigon. 1 cass. (Running Time: 1 hr.). 10.95 (H0200B090, HarperThor) HarpC GBR.

Goodbye Soldier. unabr. ed. Spike Milligan. Read by Spike Milligan. 6 cass. (Running Time: 8 hrs. 15 min.). (Spike Milligan's War Biography Ser.: Vol. 6). 1997. 54.95 (978-1-85695-912-4(0), 950108) Pub: ISIS Audio GBR. Dist(s): Ulverscroft US
Lance Bombadier Milligan, is a member of the Combined Services Entertainment, in charge of entertaining the troops. They make their way across Europe via romantic Rome & venereal Venice, to Vienna where Spike continues to demoralize the troops from the stage despite frenzied protests from Eisenhower, Churchill & Stalin.

***Goodbye Summer.** abr. ed. Patricia Gaffney. Read by Jan Maxwell. (ENG.). 2005. (978-0-06-083508-8(7), Harper Audio); (978-0-06-083507-1(9), Harper Audio) HarperCollins Pubs.

Goodbye Summer. unabr. abr. ed. Patricia Gaffney. Read by Jan Maxwell. 4 CDs. (Running Time: 6 hrs.). 2004. audio compact disk 29.95 (978-0-06-054850-6(9)) HarperCollins Pubs.

***Goodbye, Sweet Prince.** unabr. ed. Catherine Marshall. Adapted by C. Archer. Narrated by Jaimee Draper. (Catherine Marshall's Christy Ser.). (ENG.). 2010. 7.00 (978-1-60814-710-6(X), SpringWater) Oasis Audio.

Goodbye to a River. unabr. collector's ed. John Graves. Read by Wolfram Kandinsky. 7 cass. (Running Time: 10 hrs. 30 mins.). 1987. 56.00 (978-0-7366-1132-9(0), 2055) Books on Tape.
October is the best month on the Brazos...especially the part near Fort Worth, where John Graves grew up. As a boy he hunted, fished & camped by the river. In 1957 he learned the river would be dammed, drowning much he remembered. So he took a belated canoe trip on it, alone, to bid it farewell-this is the story of that trip.

Goodbye to All That. abr. ed. Robert Graves. Read by Martin Jarvis. 4 CDs. (Running Time: 5 hrs.). (ENG.). 2009. audio compact disk 26.95 (978-1-934997-31-4(5)) Pub: CSAWord. Dist(s): PerseuPGW

Goodbye to All That: An Autobiography. Robert Graves. 2007. audio compact disk 15.99 (978-1-906147-03-7(5)) CSA Telltapes GBR.

Goodbye to All That: An Autobiography. unabr. ed. Robert Graves. Read by Sean Barrett. 10 cass. (Running Time: 12 hrs.). 1995. 84.95 (978-1-85089-750-7(6), 90051) Pub: ISIS Audio GBR. Dist(s): Ulverscroft US
One of the great autobiographies of the 20th century, Robert Graves wrote "Goodbye to All That" when about to leave England after much personal turmoil. In it, the intractable experience of the First World War is digested by Graves' poetic imagination into literature. At the same time, it is one of the most candid self portraits ever drawn, while containing vivid sketches of his close friends.

Goodbye to All That: An Autobiography. unabr. collector's ed. Robert Graves. Read by Richard Green. 8 cass. (Running Time: 12 hrs.). 1985. 64.00 (978-0-7366-0467-3(7), 1439) Books on Tape.
Autobiographical statement about World War I & the disillusionment that set in afterward.

Goodbye to Berlin. Christopher Isherwood. Read by Michael York. 6 cass. 54.95 (978-0-7927-3377-5(0), CSL 717); audio compact disk 74.95 (978-0-7927-3378-2(9), SLD 717) AudioGO.

***Goodbye to Goldie.** Fran Manushkin. Illus. by Tammie Lyon. (Katie Woo Ser.). (ENG.). 2010. audio compact disk 8.95 (978-1-4048-6242-5(0)) CapstoneDig.

Goodbye to Shy: For the Bashful in All of Us. abr. ed. Leil Lowndes. Read by Leil Lowndes. (Running Time: 14400 sec.). 2006. audio compact disk 23.95 (978-1-59316-083-8(6)) Listen & Live.

Goodey's Last Stand. unabr. ed. Charles Alverson. Narrated by Frank Muller. 4 cass. (Running Time: 6 hrs.). 1981. 35.00 (978-1-55690-201-7(8), 81050E7) Recorded Bks.
Joe Goodey is a cop's cop in the City by the Bay until he accidentally guns down a relative of the mayor. After becoming a private eye, his first customer happens to be the mayor. There's a lot of funny stuff going on out there in the San Francisco night, but Goodey's not going to find much to laugh at until he grabs himself a killer.

Goodfinding: Optimizing Your Aptitude for Health & Happiness. William G. DeFoore. (ENG.). 2005. audio compact disk 29.99 (978-0-9785244-2-5(X)) Halcyon Life.

Goodknyght! Steve Barlow & Steve Skidmore. Read by Graham Seed. 6 CDs. (Running Time: 24240 sec.). (Tales of the Dark Forest Ser.). (J). 2005. audio compact disk 59.95 (978-0-7540-6695-8(9)) AudioGo GBR.

Goodmans: Live in Texas. Contrib. by Happy Goodman Family. (Gospel Legacy Video Ser.). 2007. 19.98 (978-5-557-63536-3(X)) Pt of Grace Ent.

Goodness & Mercy: A Selection of Inspirational Poems. Poems. Elfrida Arrindell. Read by Elfrida Arrindell. 1 cass. (Running Time: 45 min.). 12.00 (978-0-9664317-1-1(5)) E R Arrindell NLD.

***Goodness of God: Assurance of Purpose in the Midst of Suffering.** unabr. ed. Randy Alcorn. Narrated by Randy Alcorn. (Running Time: 3 hrs. 36 mins. 26 sec.). (ENG.). 2010. 12.59 (978-1-60814-724-3(X)); audio compact disk 17.99 (978-1-59859-774-5(4)) Oasis Audio.

Goodness of God: Logos Sept. 28, 1997. Ben Young. 1997. 4.95 (978-0-7417-6049-4(5), B0049) Win Walk.

Goodness of the Devil. unabr. ed. Claudio Naranjo. 1 cass. 1969. 11.00 (04201) Big Sur Tapes.

Goodnews. Davis Ken. 2004. DVD & audio compact disk 21.99 (978-1-894300-74-2(2)) Crown Video Dupl CAN.

Goodnight. Perf. by Bronn Journey Staff. 1 cass., 1 CD. (J). 7.98 (PHIL 14); audio compact disk 12.78 CD Jewel box. (PHIL 14) NewSound.
Includes: "Close Your Eyes," "Greensleeves," "When You Wish Upon a Star" & more.

Goodnight Everyone. Lone Morton & Mary Risk. Tr. by Marie-Therese Bougard. Photos by Jakki Wood. 1 cass. (Running Time: 20 min.). (I Can Read Bks.).Tr. of Bonne Nuit a Tous. (ENG & FRE.). (J). (ps up). 1998. bk. 9.95 (978-0-7641-7188-8(7)) Barron.
Repeats every word of the bilingual text in both languages so that children can hear exactly how the words sound.

Goodnight Moon see Buenas Noches, Luna

Goodnight Moon. 9.95 (978-1-59112-150-3(7)) Live Oak Media.

Goodnight Moon. 2004. 8.95 (978-1-56008-387-0(5)); 8.95 (978-0-7882-0306-0(1)); cass. & flmstrp 30.00 (978-1-56008-677-2(7)) Weston Woods.

Goodnight Moon. (J). 2004. bk. 24.95 (978-0-89719-774-8(7)); pap. bk. 32.75 (978-1-55592-233-7(3)); pap. bk. 32.75 (978-1-55592-234-4(1)) Weston Woods.

Goodnight Moon. Margaret Wise Brown. 1 cass. (Running Time: 35 min.). (J). 2001. pap. bk. 15.95 (VX-60C) Kimbo Educ.
A classic tale of the little rabbit who bids goodnight to every familiar object in his room. Includes book.

Goodnight Moon. Margaret Wise Brown. Illus. by Clement Hurd. 14 vols. (Running Time: 4 mins.). 1984. pap. bk. 35.95 (978-1-59519-259-2(X)); 9.95 (978-1-59112-145-9(0)); audio compact disk 12.95 (978-1-59519-256-1(5)) Live Oak Media.

Goodnight Moon. Margaret Wise Brown. Illus. by Clement Hurd. 11 vols. (Running Time: 4 mins.). (J). 1984. pap. bk. 18.95 (978-1-59519-257-8(3)) Pub: Live Oak Media. Dist(s): AudioGO

Goodnight Moon. Margaret Wise Brown. (J). 1994. bk. 29.95 (978-0-317-07120-7(3)) Live Oak Media.
The tale of the little rabbit who bids goodnight to every familiar object in his room.

Goodnight Moon. Margaret Wise Brown. Illus. by Clement Hurd. 1 cass., 5 bks. (Running Time: 30 min.). (J). pap. bk. 32.75 Weston Woods.
All the while, the big warm room grows gradually darker until, in the near obscurity, sleep arrives. This perennial favorite of young children conveys the descending colors of bedtime peace & calm, while the gentle narration & piano lullaby illuminate the quite poetry of the text.

Goodnight Moon. Margaret Wise Brown. Illus. by Clement Hurd. 1 cass. (Running Time: 30 min.). (J). (ps-3). bk. 24.95 Weston Woods.

Goodnight Moon. Margaret Wise Brown. Illus. by Clement Hurd. 1 cass. (Running Time: 3 min.). (J). (ps-3). 2004. pap. bk. 8.95 (978-0-89719-976-6(6), RAC298) Weston Woods.

Goodnight Moon. Margaret Wise Brown. Illus. by Clement Hurd. 1 cass. (J). (ps-3). 2004. pap. bk. 14.95 (978-0-89719-775-5(5), PRA298) Weston Woods.

Goodnight Moon. abr. ed. Margaret Wise Brown. Read by Si Kahn et al. Illus. by Clement Hurd. 1 cass. (J). (ps up). 1989. 8.95 (978-0-89845-988-3(5)) HarperCollins Pubs.

Goodnight Moon. abr. ed. Margaret Wise Brown. Illus. by Clement Hurd. (Share a Story Ser.). (J). (ps-1). 2007. 9.99 (978-0-06-114270-3(0), HarperFestival) HarperCollins Pubs.

Goodnight Moon. unabr. ed. Margaret Wise Brown. Read by Linda Terheyden. Illus. by Clement Hurd. 11 vols. (Running Time: 4 mins.). (J). (gr. k-3). 1984. bk. 25.95 (978-0-941078-30-6(2)); pap. bk. 16.95 (978-0-941078-28-3(0)); pap. bk. 33.95 Reading Chest. (978-0-941078-29-0(9)) Live Oak Media.
The tale of the little rabbit who bids goodnight to every familiar object in his room.

Goodnight Moon. unabr. ed. Margaret Wise Brown & Clement Hurd. 1 cass. (J). 2000. pap. bk. 7.98 (T170SP, Listening Lib) Random Audio Pubg.
Still a favorite of many sleepy children, this is a perfect addition to a bedtime tradition that started so long ago.

Goodnight Moon. unabr. abr. ed. Margaret Wise Brown & Si Kahn. Illus. by Clement Hurd. (Share a Story Ser.). (J). (ps up). 1998. 9.99 (978-0-694-70094-3(0)) HarperCollins Pubs.

Goodnight Nobody. abr. ed. Jennifer Weiner. Read by Emily Skinner. CDs 5. (Running Time: 5 hrs. 30 mins. 0 sec.). (ENG.). 2008. audio compact disk 14.99 (978-0-7435-6958-3(X)) Pub: S&S Audio. Dist(s): S and S Inc

Goodnight Sleep Tight. Brian Alman. 1992. audio compact disk 22.50 (978-0-87630-669-7(5)) Taylor and Fran.

Goodnight, Sleep Tight. Marylee Sunsen & Nancy Stewart. 1 cass. (Running Time: 37 min.). (J). 1987. 9.95 (978-1-885430-02-1(7), FS1001); audio compact disk 15.95 CD. (978-1-885430-10-6(8), FS1010) Frnds St Music.
Traditional & original lullabies.

Goodnight Sweet Prince. David Dickinson. 9 cass. (Soundings Ser.). (J). 2005. 76.95 (978-1-84283-826-6(1)) Pub: ISIS Lrg Prnt GBR. Dist(s): Ulverscroft US

Goodnight, Sweet Prince, Set. unabr. ed. Emma Blair. Read by Kara Wilson. 10 cass. 2000. 84.95 (978-0-7540-0406-6(6), CAB 1829) Pub: Chivers Audio Bks GBR. Dist(s): AudioGO
Nancy Thompson is poor & uneducated. She does heavy duty agricultural work for Bill McCabe. By contrast, Rose Drummond is beautiful & spoiled. When Rose suffers a miscarriage, Nancy becomes her personal maid & is able to bid farewell to her previous life.

Goodnight Trail. abr. ed. Ralph Compton. Read by Jim Gough. 4 cass. (Running Time: 6 hrs.). (Trail Drive Ser.: Vol. 1). 1997. Rental 24.95 (978-1-890990-00-8(0)) Otis Audio.
Texas history buffs will relish this hard-hitting tale about maverick longhorn cattle, Texas rangers, the battles between the Comanches & the white man & the fierce struggle to tame the harsh land.

Goodwill Tour: From Moreland to Moscow: Lewis Grizzard Live. unabr. ed. Lewis Grizzard. Read by Lewis Grizzard. 1 cass. 1987. 9.98 (978-0-945258-01-8(1), STC-007); audio compact disk 9.98 CD. (978-0-945258-05-6(4), STCD-007) Sthrn Tracks.
Southern humor.

Goof-Proof Grammar. Margaret Bynum. 2 CDs. (Smart Audio Ser.). 2004. audio compact disk 19.99 (978-1-58926-066-5(X)) Oasis Audio.
This is a no-nonsense grammar guide that gives you just the skills you need. Now you can learn to recognize and wipe out embarrassing errors - quickly and easily - while you drive, exercise or relax. It goes straight to the grammar trouble spots and answers the nagging questions that plague you when-ever you write.

Goof-Proof Grammar. unabr. ed. Debra Giffen & Margaret M. Bynum. Read by Margaret M. Bynum & Mel Alpern. 2 cass. (Running Time: 50 min.). (Smart Tapes Ser.). 1994. pap. bk. 19.99 Set. (978-1-55678-054-7(0), 3230) Oasis Audio.
A quick, easy way to clear up the top 10 trouble spots whenever you speak or write. You'll learn to find your errors & fix them in less than an evening.

Goofy Greats. (Silly-Wacky-Goofy-Flaky Ser.). (J). 1997. 7.00 (978-1-57375-064-6(6)) Audioscope.

Goofy Jokes & Really Great Riddles, Vol. 1. unabr. ed. Charline Spektor. Perf. by Jessica Ambrose et al. 1 cass. (Running Time: 1 hrs.). (J). 1998. 12.95 (978-1-885608-28-4(4)) Airplay.
A collection of jokes & riddles for young listeners from a group of kids who really know. Includes magic motion music.

Goofy Jokes & Really Great Riddles with Poster. abr. ed. Perf. by Joke Ensemble Staff & Magic Motion Music. 1 cass. (Running Time: 1 hr.). (J). 2000. 7.95 (978-1-885608-33-8(0)) Airplay.
A collection of the very best jokes for young listeners & is great for long rides, short days, hard nights & all the moments in between. Over 100 jokes, riddles & tongue twisters that will entertain the kids.

Goofy Movie. 1 cass. (J). 7.99 Norelco.; audio compact disk 13.99 CD. (978-1-55723-623-4(2)); audio compact disk 13.99 (978-1-55723-624-1(0)) W Disney Records.

Goofy Movie. 1 cass. (J). (ps-3). 1995. 7.99 (978-1-55723-621-0(6)) W Disney Records.

Google Speaks: Secrets of the World's Greatest Billionaire Entrepreneurs, Sergey Brin & Larry Page. unabr. ed. Janet Lowe. Read by Sean Pratt. (Running Time: 7 hrs.). (ENG.). 2009. 24.98 (978-1-59659-402-9(0), GildAudio) Pub: Gildan Media. Dist(s): HachBkGrp

Google Story. abr. ed. David A. Vise & Mark Malseed. Read by Adam Grupper. (Running Time: 21600 sec.). (ENG.). 2005. audio compact disk 29.95 (978-0-7393-2161-4(7)) Pub: Random Audio Pubg. Dist(s): Random

Google Story. unabr. ed. David A. Vise & Mark Malseed. Read by Stephen Hoye. 10 CDs. (Running Time: 10 hrs.). 2005. audio compact disk 76.50 (978-1-4159-2494-5(5)); 72.00 (978-1-4159-2493-8(7)) Books on Tape.
THE GOOGLE STORY is the definitive account of the populist media company powered by the world's most advanced technology that in a few short years has revolutionized access to information about everything for everybody everywhere. In 1998, Moscow-born Sergey Brin and Midwest-born Larry Page dropped out of graduate school at Stanford University to, in their own words, "change the world" through a search engine that would organize every bit of information on the Web for free. While the company has done exactly that in more than one hundred languages, Google's quest continues as it seeks to add millions of library books, television broadcasts, and more to its searchable database. Readers will learn about the amazing business acumen and computer wizardry that started the company on its astonishing course; the secret network of computers delivering lightning-fast search results; the unorthodox approach that has enabled it to challenge Microsoft's dominance and shake up Wall Street. Even as it rides high, Google wrestles with difficult choices that will enable it to continue expanding while sustaining the guiding vision of its founders' mantra: DO NO EVIL.

Googled: The End of the World as We Know It. unabr. ed. Ken Auletta. (Running Time: 16 hrs.). 2009. 44.97 (978-1-4418-2102-7(3), 9781441821027, BADLE) Brilliance Audio.

Googled: The End of the World as We Know It. unabr. ed. Ken Auletta. Read by Jim Bond. (Running Time: 14 hrs.). 2009. 39.97 (978-1-4418-2100-3(7), 9781441821003, Brlnc Audio MP3 Lib); 24.99 (978-1-4418-2099-0(X), 9781441820990, Brilliance MP3); 24.99 (978-1-4418-2101-0(5), 9781441821010, BAD); audio compact disk 97.97 (978-1-4418-2098-3(1), 9781441820983, BriAudCD Unabrid); audio compact disk 29.99 (978-1-4418-2097-6(3), 9781441820976, Bril Audio CD Unabri) Brilliance Audio.

***Goon Show: Enter Bluebottle.** Created by Spike Milligan. Narrated by Harry Secombe & Peter Sellers. 2 CDs. (Running Time: 2 hrs. 0 mins. 0 sec.). (ENG.). 2010. audio compact disk 24.95 (978-0-563-38859-3(5)) Pub: AudioGO. Dist(s): Perseus Dist

Goon Show: Moriarty, Where Are You? unabr. ed. Read by Spike Milligan. Narrated by Full Cast Production Staff. (Running Time: 2 hrs. 0 mins. 0 sec.). (ENG.). 2010. audio compact disk 24.95 (978-1-60283-837-6(2)) Pub: AudioGO. Dist(s): Perseus Dist

***Goon Show Compendium, Volume Five.** Narrated by Spike Milligan et al. (Running Time: 8 hrs. 0 mins. 0 sec.). (ENG.). 2010. audio compact disk 79.95 (978-1-4084-2728-6(1)) Pub: AudioGO. Dist(s): Perseus Dist

***Goon Show: Series Four, Part One: The Golden Age of BBC Radio Comedy.** Narrated by Spike Milligan et al. (Running Time: 2 hrs. 0 mins. 0 sec.). (ENG.). 2011. audio compact disk 24.95 (978-1-4084-6771-8(2)) Pub: AudioGO. Dist(s): Perseus Dist

Goon Show Specials, Vol. 16. BBC Radio Collection Staff. 2 cass. 1999. 16.85 Set. (978-0-563-55823-1(7)) BBC WrldWd GBR.

***Gooney Bird Collection.** unabr. ed. Lois Lowry. Read by Lee Adams. 6 CDs. (Running Time: 7 hrs. 1 min.). (Gooney Bird Ser.). (J). (gr. 1-3). 2009. audio compact disk 45.00 (978-0-7393-7280-7(7), Listening Lib) Pub: Random Audio Pubg. Dist(s): Random

Gooney Bird Collection: Gooney Bird Greene; Gooney Bird & the Room Mother; Gooney the Fabulous; Gooney Bird Is So Absurd. unabr. ed. Lois Lowry. Read by Lee Adams. (Gooney Bird Ser.: Nos. 1-4). (ENG.). (J). (ps). 2009. audio compact disk 34.00 (978-0-7393-7278-4(5), Listening Lib) Pub: Random Audio Pubg. Dist(s): Random

Goons at Christmas. Spike Milligan et al. 2 cass. 1998. 15.00 Set. (978-0-563-55719-7(2)) BBC WrldWd GBR.

Goops & How to Be Them: A Manual of Manners for Polite Children. Barbara Ross. Ed. by Pam Atherton. (J). (gr. 1-6). 1999. 6.95 (978-0-9712368-1-3(X)) Goops Unltd.
100 year old Book of Children's Manners each manner taught in rhyme. Written in 1900 by Gelett Burgess reintroduced by Barbara Ross 1998.

Goose. 2004. bk. 24.95 (978-1-55592-078-4(0)); pap. bk. 18.95 (978-1-55592-140-8(X)); pap. bk. 38.75 (978-1-55592-631-1(2)); pap. bk. 32.75 (978-1-55592-235-1(X)); pap. bk. 14.95 (978-1-55592-079-1(9)); audio compact disk 12.95 (978-1-55592-939-8(7)) Weston Woods.

Goose. Molly Garrett Bang. Narrated by Laura Dern. 1 cass. (Running Time: 6 min.). (J). (gr. k-2). 2004. 8.95 (978-1-55592-974-9(5)) Weston Woods.
A baby goose, adopted at birth by a family of woodchucks feels like an outcast until she discovers that she can fly.

Goose Chase Set: Capturing the Energy of Change in Logistics. Jim Tompkins. 2 cass. 1998. 19.95 (978-0-9658659-3-7(2)) Tompkins Pr. Management.

Goose Girl. Shannon Hale. Read by Cynthia Bishop. (Running Time: 10 hrs.). (Books of Bayern Ser.: Bk. 1). 2005. 38.95 (978-1-60083-553-7(8)) Iofy Corp.

Goose Girl. unabr. ed. Shannon Hale. Read by Full Cast Production Staff. (Books of Bayern Ser.: Bk. 1). (J). 2006. 54.99 (978-1-59895-457-9(1)) Find a World.

Goosebumps Horrorland. unabr. ed. R. L. Stine. Read by Alissa Hunnicutt & Jeff Woodman. (J). 2008. 54.99 (978-1-60514-559-4(9)) Find a World.

***Gopher I Couldn't Defuse.** Gary Schwind. 2009. audio compact disk 6.95 (978-0-578-03128-6(0)) Groovy Ruta.

Gopher in the Garden see Rolling Harvey down the Hill

Gopher Vanishes: Ralphie the Gopher. Rich Stim & Andrea Ross. (J). (gr. k-6). 2008. audio compact disk 12.95 (978-1-933781-14-3(9)) TallTales Aud.

GoPortuguese: Speak & Read the Pimsleur Way. Pimsleur Staff. (Running Time: 7 hrs. 30 mins. 0 sec.). (Go Ser.). (ENG.). 2009. audio compact disk 29.99 (978-0-7435-9659-6(5)) Pub: S&S Audio. Dist(s): S and S Inc

Gorbachev Era. unabr. collector's ed. Read by Michael Prichard. Ed. by Alexander Dallin & Condoleezza Rice. 8 cass. (Running Time: 8 hrs.). 1986. 48.00 (978-0-7366-0600-4(9), 1567) Books on Tape.
Who runs the Soviet Union & how? What will change under Gorbachev? What is life in the USSR like today? Answers to these & other questions are given in this program by top Soviet experts from Standford University, the University of California, the University of Toronto & the Sorbonne.

Gordon: A Fable. Julian Padowicz. Read by Julian Padowicz. 2 cass. (Running Time: 2 hrs.). 1998. 14.95 Set. (978-1-881288-20-6(X), BFI AudioBooks) BusnFilm Intl.
A satire about a divorced advertising writer who commutes to Madison Avenue from trendy Westport, Conn., & is knee deep in self-inflicted trouble when something bizarre happens.

Gordon Banks: Goalie. Read by Gordon Banks. 1 cass. 9.95 (7146) Lets Talk Assocs.
Gordon Banks talks about the people & events which influenced his career & his own approach to his speciality.

Gordon Bok: A Rouge's Gallery of Songs for Twelve-String. 1 cass. 9.98 (C-94) Folk-Legacy.
Bok continues to amaze us all.

Gordon Bok: A Tune for November. 1 cass. 9.98 (C-40) Folk-Legacy.
Gordon's first Folk-Legacy recording. Some fine sea songs.

Gordon Bok: Another Land Made of Water. Poems. 1 cass., 1 CD. 9.98 (C-72); audio compact disk 14.98 CD. (CD-72) Folk-Legacy.
Mysterious, poetic narration with music.

Gordon Bok: Bay of Fundy. 1 cass. 9.98 (C-54) Folk-Legacy.
Another strong recording by an important artist.

Gordon Bok: Clear Away in the Morning. 1 cass. 9.98 (C-1001) Folk-Legacy.
A compilation of sea songs from his earlier records.

Gordon Bok: Cold as a Dog & the Wind Northeast. Contrib. by Ruth Moore. 1 cass. 9.98 (C502) Folk-Legacy.
Reciting Maine ballads.

Gordon Bok: Ensemble. 1 cass., 1 CD. 9.98 (C-112); audio compact disk 14.98 CD. (CD-112) Folk-Legacy.
A wide-ranging program by Gordon with a full chorus of friends.

Gordon Bok: Jeremy Brown & Jeannie Teal. 1 cass. 9.98 (C-84) Folk-Legacy.
A delightful Christmas story, plus fine songs.

Gordon Bok: Peter Kagan & the Wind. 1 cass. 9.98 (C-44) Folk-Legacy.
One of Gordon's finest recordings, mostly sea songs.

Gordon Bok: Return to the Land. 1 cass., 1 CD. 9.98 (C-118); audio compact disk 14.98 CD. (CD-118) Folk-Legacy.
One of Gordon's stongest performances, nicely varied.

Gordon Bok: Schooners. 1 cass., 1 CD. 9.98 (C-504); audio compact disk 14.98 CD. (CD-504) Folk-Legacy.
Celebrating the great coastal schooners in song, with friends.

Gordon Bok: Seal Djiril's Hymn. Contrib. by Ann M. Muir. 1 cass. 9.98 (C-48) Folk-Legacy.
Beautiful songs & "tellings.".

Gordon Bok & Cindy Kallet: Neighbors. 1 cass., 1 CD. 9.98 (C-5040); audio compact disk 14.98 CD. (CD-5040) Folk-Legacy.
Two superb artists combine exceptional talents.

Gordon Bok & Friends Vol. 1: The February Tapes. 1 cass. 9.98 (C-500) Folk-Legacy.
Fighting winter doldrums with song.

Gordon Bok & Friends Vol. 2: The February Tapes. 1 cass. 9.98 (C-501) Folk-Legacy.
Continuing the battle, & winning.

Gordon Hill: The Referee's Side. Read by Gordon Hill. 1 cass. 9.95 (978-0-89811-094-4(7), 7145) Lets Talk Assocs.
Gordon Hill talks about the people & events which influenced his career & his own approach to his speciality.

Gordon MacQuarrie Trilogy. abr. ed. Gordon MacQuarrie. Read by Karl Schmidt. Ed. by Zack Taylor. 6 cass. (Running Time: 7 hrs. 30 min.). 1994. 45.00 set. (978-1-57223-017-0(7), 177) Willow Creek Pr.
Entertaining stories from the pages of the Gordon MacQuarrie trilogy. Classic hunting & fishing yarns from a master storyteller. Winner of the 1995 Ben Franklin award - Best Audio.

Gordon Smith's Introduction to the Spirit World. Gordon Smith. 2006. bk. (978-1-4019-1169-0(2), 417) Hay Hse GBR.

Gordon Weaver. unabr. ed. Gordon Weaver. Read by Gordon Weaver. 1 cass. (Running Time: 29 min.). 1989. 10.00 New Letters.
Weaver reads from a short story, "The Cold", & is interviewed.

Gore Vidal: When National Security Rules. Gore Vidal. 1 cass. (Running Time: 60 min.). 10.95 (K0360B090, HarperThor) HarpC GBR.

Gorgon Slayer. unabr. ed. Gary Paulsen. Narrated by Jeff Woodman. 1 cass. (Running Time: 1 hr.). (Gary Paulsen's World of Adventure Ser.: Bk. 7). (gr. 4 up). 10.00 (978-0-7887-1108-4(3), 95101E7) Recorded Bks.
During his summer vacation, 11-year-old Warren Trumbull is working for Prince Charming's Damsel in Distress Rescue Agency. Young & inexperienced, he always gets the last & worst assignments. But in a world of dragons, warlocks & cyclopes, even the smallest job is plenty dangerous. Now he's on his way to fight a Gorgon. He'll need all his strength & a secret weapon, to conquer this nasty monster. Available to libraries only.

Gorgon's Head see Favorite Children's Stories: A Collection

Gorgon's Head. Nathaniel Hawthorne. (J). 1978. (G-3) Jimcin Record.

Gorilla City. unabr. ed. Charlie Small. Read by Andrew Dennis. 2 CDs. (Running Time: 1 hr. 50 mins.). (Amazing Adventures of Charlie Small Ser.: Bk. 1). (J). (gr. 3-6). 2007. audio compact disk 30.00 (978-0-7393-6308-9(5), Listening Lib) Pub: Random Audio Pubg. Dist(s): Random
No one knows the full story of Charlie Small. At least, not yet. His battered journal was found washed up on a remote, windswept shore. And at first we thought it an elaborate hoax. Surely no 8-year-old could have had so many wild adventures, witnessed so many extraordinary things, lived such an incredible life - and still only be eight. And yet . . . there was something so vivid in the telling that we were persuaded to send the journal and some of its boggling content for analysis. And only one conclusion could be drawn. Everything in the journal of Charlie Small is true! In his first adventure, Gorilla City, Charlie wrestles a deadly river croc, rides a steam-powered rhino, and becomes tribal chief in a city of gorillas.

Gorilla My Dreams. E. J. Gold. 2 cass. (Running Time: 2 hrs. 30 min.). 18.98 set. (TP038) Union Label.
A lighthearted television interview on the subject of transformation, presented on audiocassette.

Gorky Park. unabr. ed. Martin Cruz Smith. Narrated by Henry Strozier. 10 cass. (Running Time: 15 hrs.). (Arkady Renko Ser.: No. 1). 1983. 85.00 (978-1-55690-202-4(6), 83055E7) Recorded Bks.
Moscow investigator Arkady Renko is called in when three frozen bodies turn up in Gorky Park, the city's pleasure garden. But he hits a sharp & complicated turn with the arrival of the KGB's Pribluda. Suddenly, his access to a routine investigation is blocked. Why?.

Gorky Park. unabr. collector's ed. Martin Cruz Smith. Read by Wolfram Kandinsky. 10 cass. (Running Time: 15 hrs.). (Arkady Renko Ser.: No. 1). 1983. 80.00 (978-0-7366-0735-3(8), 1692) Books on Tape.
Three mutilated bodies are dicovered in Moscow's Gorky Park, frozen solid in deep snow. When Chief Homicide Investigator Arkady Renko of the local police finds a surly KGB officer at the site, he suspects that these are no ordinary murders. And as he presses forward with his investigations & finds his every move monitored by the KGB, he finds out he was right!.

Gorman & Kane: Powder River. 1 cass. 9.98 (C-76) Folk-Legacy.
Western songs & tunes authentically performed.

Gormans: Portrait of the Navaho Artists. Interview. Interview with R. C. Gorman & Carl Gorman. 1 cass. (Running Time: 30 min.). 9.95 (G0550B090, HarperThor) HarpC GBR.

Gormenghast. Mervyn Peake. Read by Robert Whitfield. 13 cass. (Running Time: 19 hrs.). (Gormenghast Trilogy: Bk. 2). 2000. 85.95 (978-0-7861-1875-5(X), 2674); audio compact disk 128.00 (978-0-7861-9800-9(1), 2674) Blckstn Audio.
A doomed lord, an emergent hero, & an array of bizarre creatures haunt the world of Gormenghast.

Gormenghast. Mervyn Peake. 2009. audio compact disk 130.95 (978-0-7531-4138-0(8)) Pub: Isis Pubng Ltd GBR. Dist(s): Ulverscroft US

Gormenghast. unabr. ed. Mervyn Peake. Read by Edmund Dehn. 16 cass. (Running Time: 24 hrs.). (Gormenghast Trilogy: Bk. 2). (J). 2004. 104.95 (978-1-85695-977-3(5), 951105) Pub: ISIS Lrg Prnt GBR. Dist(s): Ulverscroft US

GoRussian: Speak & Read the Pimsleur Way. Pimsleur Staff. (Running Time: 7 hrs. 30 mins. 0 sec.). (Go Ser.). (ENG.). 2009. audio compact disk 29.99 (978-0-7435-9658-9(7)) Pub: S&S Audio. Dist(s): S and S Inc

Goshawk Squadron. unabr. ed. Derek Robinson. Read by Terry Wale. 8 cass. (Soundings Ser.). 2006. 69.95 (978-1-84559-357-5(X)) Pub: ISIS Lrg Prnt GBR. Dist(s): Ulverscroft US

***Gospel.** Sydney Bauer. Read by Bill Ten Eyck. (Running Time: 17 hrs. 58 mins.). 2010. 119.99 (978-1-74214-628-7(7), 9781742146287) Pub: Bolinda Pubng AUS. Dist(s): Bolinda Pub Inc

Gospel. unabr. ed. Sydney Bauer. Read by Bill Ten Eyck. (Running Time: 17 hrs. 58 mins.). 2009. audio compact disk 123.95 (978-1-74214-492-4(6), 9781742142494) Pub: Bolinda Pubng AUS. Dist(s): Bolinda Pub Inc

Gospel: A Synopsis of Romans: the Power of God. 4. 2004. audio compact disk 28.00 (978-1-59548-005-7(6)) A Wommack.

Gospel: The Power of God. Andrew Wommack. 4 cass. (Running Time: 5 hrs. 16 min.). 19.00 Set. (978-1-881541-15-8(0), 1014) A Wommack.
This tape series reveals the great theme of Romans which is the power of the gospels. The book of Romans is Paul's great masterpiece on the doctrine of grace. Nowhere else in scripture is the mystery of God's grace revealed more thoroughly or more simply.

***Gospel According to Coco Chanel: Life Lessons from the World's Most Elegant Woman.** unabr. ed. Karen Karbo. Read by Bernadette Dunne. (Running Time: 7 hrs. 30 mins.). 2010. 29.95 (978-1-4417-6962-6(5)); 54.95 (978-1-4417-6959-6(5)); audio compact disk 69.00 (978-1-4417-6960-2(9)) Blckstn Audio.

Gospel According to Dawn: A Woman's Work of Spiritual Imagination. Dawn Annette Mills. 3 cass. (Running Time: 3 hrs.). 2002. 29.95 (978-0-9714807-2-8(9), 001CAS, Lvng Trad) Living Tradtn Audio.

Gospel According to Dawn: A Woman's Work of Spiritual Imagination. Dawn Annette Mills. Read by Sister Dawn Annette Milss. 3 CDs. (Running Time: 3 hrs.). 2002. audio compact disk 39.95 (978-0-9714807-1-1(0), 001CD, Lvng Trad) Living Tradtn Audio.

Gospel According to Jesus. John MacArthur, Jr. 6 cass. 19.95 (20170, HarperThor) HarpC GBR.

***Gospel According to Jesus: A Faith that Restores All Things.** unabr. ed. Chris Seay. 2010. audio compact disk 24.99 (978-0-8499-4936-4(X)) Nelson.

Gospel According to Jesus: A New Translation & Guide to His Essential Teachings for Believers & Unbelievers. abr. ed. Read by Stephen Mitchell. Tr. by Stephen Mitchell. 2 cass. (Running Time: 3 hrs.). 1995. 16.95 (978-0-944993-75-0(3)) Audio Lit.
A provocative and moving image of Jesus as a real person and as a great spiritual teacher.

Gospel According to Jesus: What Is Authentic Faith? rev. ed. John F. MacArthur. (Running Time: 12 hrs. 29 mins. 0 sec.). (ENG.). 2009. 19.99 (978-0-310-77242-2(7)) Zondervan.

Gospel According to John: A Biblical Interpretation. Concept by Ermance Rejebian. (ENG.). 2007. 5.99 (978-1-60339-145-0(2)); audio compact disk 5.99 (978-1-60339-146-7(0)) Listenr Digest.

Gospel According to Larry. Janet Tashjian. Read by Jesse Eisenberg. 4 cass. (Running Time: 6 hrs.). (J). (gr. 7 up). 2004. 32.00 (978-0-8072-2305-5(0), Listening Lib); audio compact disk 45.00 (978-1-4000-8618-4(3), Listening Lib) Random Audio Pubg.

Gospel According to Lost - CD. unabr. ed. Chris Seay. 2009. audio compact disk 16.99 (978-0-8499-4598-4(4)) Nelson.

Gospel According to Matthew So. 2004. audio compact disk 14.95 (978-1-889710-10-5(5)) Visual Entnmnt.

Gospel According to Oprah. unabr. ed. Marcia Z. Nelson. 4 CDs. (Running Time: 4 hrs. 15 mins. 0 sec.). (ENG.). 2005. audio compact disk 21.98 (978-1-59644-284-9(0), Hovel Audio) christianaud.
In this book, religion reporter Marcia Nelson explores the spiritual dimensions that are prevalent in all aspects of the Oprah Winfrey media

empire, pointing out that there are several major Christian themes that weave through these aspects of her life and work.

***Gospel According to Oprah.** unabr. ed. Marcia Z. Nelson. Narrated by Marguerite Gavin. (ENG.). 2005. 12.98 (978-1-59644-285-6(9), Hovel Audio) christianaud.

Gospel According to St. John. Read by George Vafiadis. (Playaway Adult Nonfiction Ser.). 2008. 39.99 (978-1-60640-824-7(0)) Find a World.

Gospel According to St. John. Narrated by George Vafiadis. (Running Time: 7320 sec.). (Unabridged Classics in MP3 Ser.). (ENG.). 2008. audio compact disk 24.00 (978-1-58472-649-4(0), In Aud) Sound Room.

Gospel According to St. Mark. 1 cass. 1995. 14.95 (978-1-57050-027-5(4)) Multilingua.

***Gospel According to the Simpsons: The Spiritual Life of the World's Most Animated Family.** unabr. ed. Mark Pinsky. Narrated by Lloyd James. (ENG.). 2005. 14.98 (978-1-59644-209-2(3), Hovel Audio) christianaud.

Gospel According to the Simpsons: The Spiritual Life of the World's Most Animated Family. unabr. ed. Mark I. Pinsky. Narrated by Lloyd James. 1 MP3CD. (Running Time: 7 hrs. 45 mins. 0 sec.). (ENG.). 2005. lp 19.98 (978-1-59644-207-8(7), Hovel Audio); audio compact disk 24.98 (978-1-59644-208-5(5), Hovel Audio) christianaud.

***Gospel According to Tolkien: Visions of the Kingdom in Middle Earth.** unabr. ed. Ralph Wood. Narrated by Nadia May. (ENG.). 2005. 14.98 (978-1-59644-213-9(1), Hovel Audio) christianaud.

Gospel According to Tolkien: Visions of the Kingdom in Middle-Earth. unabr. ed. Ralph C. Wood. Narrated by Nadia May. 1 MP3CD. (Running Time: 7 hrs. 0 mins. 0 sec.). (ENG.). 2005. lp 19.98 (978-1-59644-211-5(5), Hovel Audio); audio compact disk 24.98 (978-1-59644-212-2(3), Hovel Audio) christianaud.

Gospel Birds & Other Stories of Lake Wobegon. Garrison Keillor. 2 cass., 3 CDs. 14.38 Set, blisterpack. (PHC 21152); audio compact disk 23.98 CD Set, Jewel box. (PHC 25701) NewSound.

Gospel Birds & Other Stories of Lake Wobegon. abr. unabr. ed. Garrison Keillor. 3 CDs. (Running Time: 3 hrs.). (ENG.). 1993. audio compact disk 29.95 (978-1-56511-010-6(2), 1565110102) Pub: HighBridge. Dist(s): Workman Pub

Gospel Celebration. Mauldin et al. 2001. 75.00 (978-0-633-01217-5(3)); 11.98 (978-0-633-01215-1(7)); audio compact disk 85.00 (978-0-633-01218-2(1)); audio compact disk 16.98 (978-0-633-01216-8(5)) LifeWay Christian.

Gospel Christmas. Sonya Tinsley. (BookNotes Ser.). 1998. bk. 13.99 (978-0-88088-407-5(X)) Peter Pauper.

Gospel Classics. Contrib. by Mark Hayes. (Sacred Performer Collections Ser.). (ENG.). 2003. audio compact disk 9.95 (978-0-7390-3106-3(6)) Alfred Pub.

Gospel Code: Novel Claims about Jesus, Mary Magdalene, & Da Vinci. unabr. ed. Ben Witherington, III. Narrated by Grover Gardner. 1 MP3 D. (Running Time: 6 hrs. 0 mins. 0 sec.). (ENG.). 2005. lp 19.98 (978-1-59644-147-7(X), Hovel Audio); audio compact disk 23.98 (978-1-59644-148-4(8), Hovel Audio) christianaud.
Dan Brown's International best-seller The DaVinci Code has raised many questions in the minds of readers. The DaVinci Code, in blurring the lines between fact and fiction, popularizes the speculations and contentions of numerous more serious books that are also attracting wide attention. How should we respond to such claims that we now have documents that reveal secrets about Jesus, secrets long suppressed by the church and other religious institutions? Do these new documents successfully debunk traditional views about Jesus and early Christianity? Ben Witherington confronts these claims with the sure-footedness of a New Testament scholar, yet in the plain language than any interested reader can follow. He takes us back to the early centuries after Jesus' death and tells us what we really can know about Jesus, Mary Magdalene, the canonical Gospels and their Gnostic rivals.

***Gospel Code: Novel Claims about Jesus, Mary Magdalene, & Da Vinci.** unabr. ed. Ben Witherington III. Narrated by Grover Gardner. (ENG.). 2005. 14.98 (978-1-59644-149-1(6), Hovel Audio) christianaud.

Gospel Collection. Contrib. by Oak Ridge Boys. 2008. audio compact disk 13.99 (978-5-557-43696-0(0)) Sprg Hill Music Group.

Gospel Dobro. Ken Eidson & Tom Swatzell. 1994. pap. bk. 18.95 (978-0-7866-1241-3(X), 95257P) Mel Bay.

Gospel Duck, Vol. 1. Len Mink. 1 cass. (Running Time: 60 min.). (J). 2001. 9.99 (978-0-88114-727-8(3), PM076) Mink Ministries.

Gospel Duck Goes to Camp. Contrib. by Len Mink. 1 cass. (Running Time: 60 min.). (J). (ps-3). 2000. 9.99 (978-0-88114-785-8(0), PM479) Mink Ministries.

Gospel Duck Goes to School. Len Mink. 1 cass. (Running Time: 60 min.). (J). 2001. 9.99 (978-0-9620866-1-8(4), PM477) Mink Ministries.

Gospel Duck Goes to the Zoo. Len Mink. 1 cass. (Running Time: 60 min.). (J). 2001. 9.99 (978-0-9620866-4-9(9), PM478) Mink Ministries.

Gospel Duets with Treasured Friends. Contrib. by Brenda Lee & Terry Hemmings. 2007. audio compact disk 13.99 (978-5-557-92866-3(9)) Pt of Grace Ent.

Gospel Food for Hungry Christians: Images & Reflections from the Gospel. Comment by John Shea. 6 cass. (Running Time: 1 hr. 30 mins.). (Gospel Food Ser.). 2004. 29.95 (978-0-87946-250-5(7), 333) ACTA Pubns.
Enjoy this enlightening and entertaining discussion of the Gospel of Luke, lead by the renowned theologian and storyteller John Shea. With his classic wit and insightful observations, Shea leads listeners through all the major stories and parables contained in the Gospel of Luke, offering new and informative interpretations of this sacred text.

Gospel Food for Hungry Christians: Images & Reflections from the Gospel. Narrated by John Shea. 6 cass. (Running Time: 6 hrs.). 2004. 29.95 (978-0-87946-276-5(0), 335) ACTA Pubns.
Enjoy this enlightening and entertaining discussion of the Gospel of John, lead by the renowned theologian and storyteller John Shea. With his classic wit and insightful observations, Shea leads listeners through all the major stories and parables contained in the Gospel of John, offering new and informative interpretations of this sacred text. This set of audio tapes was recorded live, re-mastered in a sound studio, and divided into discrete segments on six audio cassette tapes.

Gospel Food for Hungry Christians: Mark - Images & Reflections from the Gospel. John Shea. Read by John Shea. 6. (Running Time: 1 hr. 30 mins.). (Gospel Food Ser.). 2004. 29.95 (978-0-87946-238-3(8), 332) ACTA Pubns.

Gospel Food for Hungry Christians: Matthew - Images & Reflections from the Gospel. John Shea. Read by John Shea. 6 cass. (Running Time: 1 hr. 30 mins.). (Gospel Food Ser.). 2004. 29.95 (978-0-87946-228-4(0), 331) ACTA Pubns.
A fresh look at the gospel of Matthew. Join noted theologian John Shea as he journeys through the gospel. Learn from his marvelous scriptural and theological insights. His captivating stories and examples drawn from everyday life bring new meaning to the gospel.

Gospel Food for Hungry Christians: John: Images & Reflections from the Gospel. (Running Time: 22500 sec.). (Gospel Food Ser.). 2008. audio compact disk 29.95 (978-0-87946-352-6(X)) ACTA Pubns.

Gospel Food for Hungry Christians: Luke: Images & Reflections from the Gospel. (Running Time: 23460 sec.). (Gospel Food Ser.). 2008. audio compact disk 29.95 (978-0-87946-351-9(1)) ACTA Pubns.

Gospel Food for Hungry Christians: Mark: Images & Reflections from the Gospel. (Running Time: 14820 sec.). (Gospel Food Ser.). 2008. audio compact disk 29.95 (978-0-87946-350-2(3)) ACTA Pubns.

Gospel Food for Hungry Christians: Matthew: Images & Reflections from the Gospel. (Running Time: 22680 sec.). (Gospel Food Ser.). 2008. audio compact disk 29.95 (978-0-87946-349-6(X)) ACTA Pubns.

Gospel Fun Songs for Kids. Arranged by Joseph Linn. 1 cass. (Running Time: 1 hr.). (J). 1996. 12.99 (TA-9205C); 15.99 (TA-9205S) Lillenas.
Do kids love gospel music? They will with this collection! These 17 great gospel songs are colorful, lively & fun, fun, fun! They offer Bible stories & biblical truth in a form that kids will thoroughly enjoy. Arranged in unison with optional harmony parts. The format is clear, flexible & very practical anytime children sing. perfect for Sunday School, children's choir, VBS Christian school or at home.

Gospel Fun Songs for Kids. Arranged by Joseph Linn. 1 CD. (Running Time: 1 hr.). (YA). 1996. audio compact disk 19.99 (DC-9205S) Lillenas.

Gospel Fun Songs for Kids. Arranged by Jospeh Linn. 10 cass. (Running Time: 10 hrs.). (J). 1996. bk. 54.99 (TA-9205PK) Lillenas.

Gospel Gangstaz: Do or Die. 1 cass. 1999. 10.98 (KMGC9532); audio compact disk 16.98 (KMGD9532) Provident Mus Dist.

Gospel Gangstaz Gang Affiliated. 1 cass. 1999. 10.98 (KMGC9460); audio compact disk 16.98 (KMGD9460) Provident Mus Dist.

Gospel Greats: My Prayer. Perf. by Commissioned et al. 2002. audio compact disk Verity Records.

Gospel Greats: Songs of Triumph, Vol. 10. Perf. by Yolanda Adams et al. 2003. audio compact disk Verity Records.

Gospel Greats Vol. 8: The Diary of a Worshiper. audio compact disk 9.98 Provident Music.

Gospel Greats Live, Vol. 2. 1 CD. 2000. audio compact disk 9.99 (978-0-7601-3408-5(1), SO33210, Verity) Pub: Brentwood Music. Dist(s): Provident Mus Dist
Includes: "Mighty God," "Unconditional," "Thank You," "Jesus Saves" & more.

Gospel in Slow Motion. Ronald Knox. 10 cass. 39.95 (929) Ignatius Pr.
A series of sermons delivered on the Gospels by the great English preacher.

Gospel Kids Presents Action Praise. Perf. by Gospel Kids. 1 cass. 10.98 (978-1-57908-218-5(1)); audio compact disk 15.98 CD. (978-1-57908-217-8(3)) Platinm Enter.

Gospel Kids Presents Christian Soldiers. Perf. by Gospel Kids. 1 cass. 10.98 (978-1-57908-224-6(6)); audio compact disk 15.98 CD. (978-1-57908-223-9(8)) Platinm Enter.

Gospel Kids Presents Easter Praise. 1 cass. 10.98 (978-1-57908-289-5(0), 1376); audio compact disk 15.98 CD. (978-1-57908-288-8(2), 1376) Platinm Enter.

Gospel Latino. (SPA.). 2008. audio compact disk 14.99 (978-987-01-0047-8(3)) Pub: Peniel ARG. Dist(s): Zondervan

Gospel Library. Steven Sanders. 6 cass. (Running Time: 6 hrs. 10 min.). (BibleQuizmania Ser.). 49.95 Set, vinyl album. (978-0-929536-18-7(5)) Emb Cassettes.
Includes: Teachings of the Master; The Easter Story; & The Promise Child.

Gospel Light: Jesus Stories for Spiritual Consciousness. John Shea. 1 cass. 1999. 16.95 (978-0-8245-3015-0(2), Crossroad Classic) Pub: Crossroad NY. Dist(s): IPG Chicago

Gospel Light Set: Jesus Stories for Spiritual Consciousness. abr. ed. John Shea. Read by John Shea. 2 cass. (Running Time: 3 hrs.). 1998. 16.95 (978-0-87946-190-4(X), 351) ACTA Pubns.
Retelling & analysis of key stories from the gospels.

Gospel Music of Johnny Cash. Contrib. by Johnny Cash. 2008. audio compact disk 19.99 (978-5-557-48891-4(X)) Gaither Music Co.

Gospel Never Changes. Contrib. by Martha Bolton & Marty Parks. (ENG.). 1996. 12.00 (978-0-00-520101-5(2)) Lillenas.

***Gospel Never Changes: A Musical Drama for the Senior Choir.** Contrib. by Martha Bolton & Marty Parks. (ENG.). 1996. audio compact disk 90.00 (978-0-00-520103-9(9)) Lillenas.

Gospel of Grace: Logos May 24,1998. Ben Young. 1998. 4.95 (978-0-7417-6083-8(5), B0083) Win Walk.

Gospel of Healing. Elbert Willis. 1 cass. (Review of Divine Healing Ser.). 4.00 Fill the Gap.

Gospel of Jesus. abr. unabr. ed. Read by Garrison Keillor. Ed. by Daniel L. Johnson. (Running Time: 8 hrs.). (ENG.). 2006. audio compact disk 39.95 (978-1-59887-016-9(5), 1598870165) Pub: Penguin-HghBrdg. Dist(s): Penguin Grp USA

Gospel of Jesus the Messiah: The Synoptic View. Read by Ronald Bickram. 4 CDs. 2002. audio compact disk (978-0-9715877-3-1(6)) R Bickram.
This work is a dramatic reading of the book, "The Gospel of Jesus the Messiah. In addition to vocal enhancement, environmental sounds and music are interspersed throughout the set.

Gospel of John. Raymond E. Brown. (Running Time: 8 hrs. 40 min.). 2004. 59.00 (978-1-904756-01-9(8)) STL Dist NA.

Gospel of John. Richard Rohr. 10 cass. (Running Time: 8 hrs. 41 min.). 69.95 Set. (AA2337) Credence Commun.
Rohr explains what the text meant when written & how it applies to American culture today.

Gospel of John: A verse-by-verse Commentary. Chuck Smith. (ENG.). 2003. 25.99 (978-1-932941-44-9(4)) Word For Today.

Gospel of Judas. unabr. ed. Simon Mawer. Read by Graeme Malcolm. (ENG.). 2005. 14.98 (978-1-59483-418-9(0)) Pub: Hachet Audio. Dist(s): HachBkGrp

Gospel of Life: Text & Commentary. Read by George Rutler. 5 cass. 24.95 set. (5512-C) Ignatius Pr.
The official text of Pope John Paul II's powerful encyclical Evangelium Vitae: The Gospel of Life. This tape series that emphasizes the sanctity of all human life is especially essential in today's age, an age in what our Holy Father calls, "The Culture of Death" that we live in.

Gospel of Luke. Richard Rohr. 10 cass. (Running Time: 8 hrs. 44 min.). 69.95 Set, incl. study guide. (AA2299) Credence Commun.
Rohr gives explanations of what the text meant when written & how it applies to American culture today.

***Gospel of Mark.** Based on a work by Charles B. Sprawls. (ENG.). 2010. audio compact disk 19.99 (978-1-59950-715-6(3)) GraphicAudio.

Gospel of Matthew. Richard Rohr. Read by Richard Rohr. 10 cass. (Running Time: 9 hrs. 30 min.). 1991. 41.95 Set. (978-7-900781-45-1(5), AA2521) Credence Commun.
Rohr's Commentary on the Gospel of Matthew.

Gospel of Matthew, Set. Stephen Doyle. 5 cass. (Running Time: 7 hrs. 14 min.). 1998. 42.95 INCL. SCRIPT. (TAH402) Alba Hse Comns.
Explores the depth of the gospel, covering the formation, sources & development including The Sermon on the Mount, The Beatitudes, etc.

Gospel of Matthew: An Audio Course. Senior Rev. Donald. 2007. audio compact disk 69.95 (978-0-9795255-2-0(7)) Now You Know.

Gospel of Our Lord Jesus Christ. Read by Douglas Wilson. 1996. 14.00 (978-1-59128-290-7(X)); 18.00 (978-1-59128-292-1(6)) Canon Pr ID.

***Gospel of Ruth: Loving God Enough to Break the Rules.** unabr. ed. Carolyn Custis James. (Running Time: 7 hrs. 38 mins. 0 sec.). (ENG.). 2009. 16.99 (978-0-310-77170-8(6)) Zondervan.

Gospel of St. John. Scott Hahn. 15 cass. 1995. 64.95 Set. (148-C) Ignatius Pr.
This study course on the Gospel of John consists of actual lectures that Scott gave in his classes at the University of Steubenville. Now you, too, can listen in while one of the best Catholic apologists in the country makes the Gospel of John come alive. Scott shows just how "Catholic" the Fourth Gospel really is.

Gospel of the Second Coming Set: The Long-Awaited Sequel! Timothy Freke & Peter Gandy. Read by Ax Norman. Told to Timothy Freke. 4 CDs. 2007. audio compact disk 23.95 (978-1-4019-1840-8(9)) Hay House.

Gospel of Thomas, Set. Stephan Hoeller. 3 cass. 1999. 26.00 (40035) Big Sur Tapes.
1982 Los Angeles.

Gospel of Thomas: The Hidden Sayings of Jesus. unabr. ed. Read by Jacob Needleman. Interview with Jacob Needleman. Tr. by Marvin Meyer. Interview with Michael Toms. 1 cass. (Running Time: 1 hr. 30 min.). 1997. 11.95 (978-1-57453-157-2(3)) Audio Lit.
Discovered in 1945, this text reveals a Jesus who takes his place alongside the masters of all the great wisdom teachings of the world.

Gospel Outtakes (The Good Cuts) 1 cass. 10.98 (978-1-57908-285-7(8), 1356); audio compact disk 15.98 CD. (978-1-57908-284-0(X), 1356) Platinm Enter.

Gospel para bebes Volumen 1. (SPA.). 2008. audio compact disk 14.99 (978-987-01-0042-3(2)) Pub: Peniel ARG. Dist(s): Zondervan

Gospel Pedal Steel Guitar. Dewitt Scott. 1997. pap. bk. 19.95 (978-0-7866-2931-2(2), 96709BCD) Mel Bay.

Gospel Sing-Along. Anna Laura Page et al. (ENG.). 2001. audio compact disk 35.00 (978-0-7390-1689-3(X), 19972); audio compact disk 12.95 (978-0-7390-1690-9(3)) Alfred Pub.

Gospel Songs Cassette Promo Pak. Greg Skipper & Stan Pethel. 1994. 8.00 (978-0-7673-0159-6(5)) LifeWay Christian.

Gospel Songs Choir Cassette. Greg Skipper. 1994. 11.98 (978-0-7673-0656-0(2)) LifeWay Christian.

Gospel Songs Stereo/Split Acc Cassette. Greg Skipper & Stan Pethel. 1994. 40.00 (978-0-7673-0690-4(2)) LifeWay Christian.

Gospel Spirituality, Set. John Shea. 6 cass. 1994. 29.95 (978-0-87946-097-6(0), 325) ACTA Pubns.
Master storyteller & theologian John Shea leads listeners through an "audio retreat" on the spirituality of Jesus found in the Gospels.

Gospel Truth. Contrib. by Tom Fettke. Prod. by Tom Fettke. (ENG.). 1993. audio compact disk 90.00 (978-0-00-501802-6(1)) Lillenas.

Gospel Truth about Mary. 2006. audio compact disk 39.95 (978-1-888992-77-9(8)) Catholic Answers.

Gospel Violin. 2001. audio compact disk 15.98 (978-0-7866-5765-0(0)) Mel Bay.

Gospel Violin. Bill Guest. 1990. bk. 16.95 (978-0-7866-1027-3(1), 94427P) Mel Bay.

Gospel Violin. Bill Guest. 1990. 9.98 (978-0-87166-995-7(1), 94427C) Mel Bay.

Gospel's Best: Choirs. Contrib. by Various Artists et al. 2008. audio compact disk 9.99 (978-5-557-43695-3(2)) Pt of Grace Ent.

Gospel's Best: Men. Contrib. by Various Artists et al. 2008. audio compact disk 9.99 (978-5-557-43694-6(4)) Pt of Grace Ent.

Gospel's Best: Women. Contrib. by Various Artists et al. 2008. audio compact disk 9.99 (978-5-557-43693-9(6)) Pt of Grace Ent.

Gospels Bible. Ty Fischer & Emily Fischer. Perf. by Steve Scheffler. 1998. 6.95 (978-1-930710-88-7(7)) Veritas Pr PA.

Gospels Come to Life. Michael W. Smith. 2004. 29.95 (978-0-9725538-1-0(9)) Gospels Come To Life.

Gospels from the New Revised Standard Version of the Bible Audiobook. Read by Stephen Schnetzer. 5 cass. 2005. 14.95 (978-1-56585-990-6(1)); audio compact disk 19.95 (978-1-59803-006-8(X)) Teaching Co.

Gospels of Saints Matthew, Mark, Luke & John: King James Version, unabr. ed. Narrated by James Hamilton. 8 cass. (Running Time: 9 hrs. 30 mins.). 1980. 70.00 (978-1-55690-373-1(1), 80100E7) Recorded Bks.

Gospels of the New Testament. unabr. ed. Read by George Vafiadis. 10 cds. (Running Time: 8 hrs 42 mins). 2002. audio compact disk 49.95 (978-1-58472-368-4(8), 029, In Aud) Pub: Sound Room. Dist(s): Baker Taylor
King James Version of Matthew, Mark, Luke and John.

Gospel's Top 20 Songs of the Century: Volume 2. Contrib. by Ken Harding. 2005. audio compact disk 18.98 (978-5-558-78717-7(1)) Pt of Grace Ent.

Gospodin Iz San-Francisco. Ivan A. Bunin. 1 cass. (Running Time: 1 hr.).Tr. of Gentleman from San-Francisco. (RUS.). 1996. pap. bk. 24.50 (978-1-58085-578-5(4)) Interlingua VA.
Includes dual language Russian-English text, advanced level. The combination of written text & clarity & pace of diction will open the door for intermediate & advanced students to genuine comprehension & the use of literary texts for advancement in rapid understanding of written & oral language materials. The audio text plus written text concept makes foreign languages accessible to a much wider range of students than books alone.

Gossamer. unabr. ed. Lois Lowry. Read by Anne Twomey. 2 cass. (Running Time: 2 hrs. 49 mins.). (J). (gr. 4-7). 2006. 24.00 (978-0-7393-3569-7(3), Listening Lib); audio compact disk 30.00 (978-0-7393-3560-4(X), Listening Lib) Pub: Random Audio Pubg. Dist(s): Random

Gossamer. unabr. ed. Lois Lowry. Read by Anne Twomey. 3 CDs. (Running Time: 9780 sec.). (ENG.). (J). (gr. 5-9). 2006. audio compact disk 27.00 (978-0-7393-3526-0(X), Listening Lib) Pub: Random Audio Pubg. Dist(s): Random

Gossip see Little Women: With Good Wives

Gossip Girl. abr. ed. Cecily von Ziegesar. Read by Christina Ricci. (Gossip Girl Ser.: No. 1). (ENG.). (gr. 10 up). 2005. 14.98 (978-1-59483-233-8(1)) Pub: Hachet Audio. Dist(s): HachBkGrp

Gossip Girl. abr. ed. Cecily von Ziegesar. Read by Christina Ricci. (Running Time: 2 hrs.). (ENG.). 2009. 24.98 (978-1-60024-987-7(6)) Pub: Hachet Audio. Dist(s): HachBkGrp

***Got a Problem?** FESS PARKER & Cerebellum Academic Team Staff. (Running Time: 11 mins.). (Lesson Booster Ser.). 2008. cd-rom 79.95 (978-1-59443-691-8(6)) Cerebellum.

Got off Your Knees: Audio Book on CD. unabr. ed. Sheila Walsh. 2010. audio compact disk 24.99 (978-1-4003-1625-0(1)) Nelson.

Got Teens? As told by Scarlett Bishop. 3 cass. (Running Time: 1 hr. 30 min.). 2000. 15.00 (978-0-9628301-8-1(6)) M Bishop Minis.

***Got the Life.** abr. ed. Fieldy. Read by William Dufris. (ENG.). 2009. (978-0-06-180532-5(7), Harper Audio) HarperCollins Pubs.

***Got the Life: My Journey of Addiction, Faith, Recovery, & Korn.** unabr. ed. Fieldy. Read by William Dufris. (ENG.). 2009. (978-0-06-171947-9(1)) HarperCollins Pubs.

Got the Look. James Grippando. Read by Nick Sullivan. 2006. audio compact disk 29.95 (978-0-7927-3962-3(0), CMP 898) AudioGO.

Got the Look. James Grippando. Read by Nick Sullivan. 8 cass. (Running Time: 45480 sec.). (Sound Library). 2006. 69.95 (978-0-7927-3892-3(6), CSL 898); audio compact disk 94.95 (978-0-7927-3893-0(4), SLD 898) AudioGO.

Got the Look. abr. ed. James Grippando. Read by Jonathan Davis. (Running Time: 21600 sec.). (Jack Swyteck Ser.). 2006. audio compact disk 29.95 (978-0-06-085283-2(6)) HarperCollins Pubs.

***Got the Look.** abr. ed. James Grippando. Read by Jonathan Davis. (ENG.). 2006. (978-0-06-087833-7(9), Harper Audio); (978-0-06-087834-4(7), Harper Audio) HarperCollins Pubs.

Got to be Real. 11 cass. (Running Time: 14 hrs. 30 mins.). 94.00 (978-0-7887-9360-8(8)); audio compact disk 116.00 (978-1-4025-3483-6(3)) Recorded Bks.

Got to Make It! 2nd collector's ed. Jack E. Eadon. Lyrics by Jack E. Eadon. Music by Tom Sievers et al. 1 CD enclosed. (Running Time: 2 hr., 23 min., 21 secs.). 2004. per. 16.95 (978-0-9753300-6-7(3), 0063) Pub: Eloquence Pr. Dist(s): Baker Taylor

Got Your Number. Stephanie Bond. Narrated by C. J. Critt. 9 cass. (Running Time: 12 hrs.). 82.00 (978-1-4025-1740-2(8)) Recorded Bks.

Gotas de Lluvia. 2nd rev. ed. Carlos Gonzalez. 1 CD. (Running Time: .52 mins.).Tr. of Rain Drops. (SPA.). 2004. audio compact disk 15.00 (978-1-56491-100-1(4)) Imagine Pubs.

Gotha Speaks to Earth. George King. 2009. audio compact disk (978-0-937249-55-0(6)) Aetherius Soc.

Gotham Tragic. unabr. collector's ed. Kurt Wenzel. Narrated by Henry Strozier. 9 cass. (Running Time: 12 hrs.). 2004. 42.95 (978-1-4025-7519-8(X), RH016) Recorded Bks.
The holy book for the world's 1.3 billion Muslims is, of course, the Holy Qur'an (or Koran). This is the book that needed to be consulted in order to complete the research for Gotham Tragic . This novel is about a successful, debauched writer who marries a Muslim lady and converts to Islam, leaving his vices behind him and shocking the world.

Gotta Dance. 1 LP. (J). 2001. pap. bk. 11.95 (KIM 9143) Kimbo Educ.
Dance to the beat of Boot Scootin' Boogie, Charlie Brown, We Are Family, Let's Twist Again, Iko Iko, It's a Beautiful Life, Teach Me How to Shimmy, Hound Dog & more! Motivate your kids with foot-stomping, hand-clapping, high-energy Gotta Dance music! Guide with lyrics & instructions for Boot Scootin' Boogie included.

Gotta Dance! 1 cass. (Running Time: 40 min.). (J). (gr. k-5). 1996. pap. bk. 10.95 (KIM 9143C); pap. bk. 14.95 (KIM 9143CD) Kimbo Educ.
Dance to the beat of Boot Scootin? Boogie, Charlie Brown, We Are Family, Let?s Twist Again, Iko Iko, It?s a Beautiful Life, Teach Me How to Shimmy, Hound Dog & more! Motivate your kids with foot-stomping, hand-clapping, high-energy Gotta Dance music! Guide with lyrics & instructions for Boot Scootin' Boogie included. (Fitness and Dancing).

Gotta Have Gospel! The World's Top Gospel Artists & Songs. Contrib. by Various Artists & Michael Coleman. 2008. audio compact disk 18.98 (978-5-557-39779-7(5)) Integrity Music.

Gotta Have Gospel! The World's Top Gospel Artists & Songs 5. (Gotta Have Gospel! Ser.). 2007. audio compact disk 18.98 (978-5-557-59909-2(6)) GospoCen.

Gotta Have Gospel! Worship: The World's Top Worship Artists & Songs. 2007. audio compact disk 16.98 (978-5-557-70344-4(6)) Integrity G.

Gotta Have Musica Cristiana! 2. Contrib. by Don Moen & Mike Herron. 2007. audio compact disk 15.98 (978-5-557-70340-6(3)) Pt of Grace Ent.

Gotta Hop! David S. Jack. 1 cass. (J). 8.78 (KE 2003) NewSound.

Gotta Hop! Perf. by David S. Jack. Music by David S. Jack. Contrib. by Susan J. Cooper. 1 cass. (Running Time: 30 min.). (J). (ps-3). 1990. 9.95 (978-0-942181-08-1(5), TD 2003) Ta-Dum Prodns.
More high-energy fun, with lots of humor & lots of participation. This Parents' Choice Award winning cassette contains such favorites as the title song "Gotta Hop," that super-popular, pre-historic rock hit "The Dinosaur Dip" & the unforgettable "Miranda the Panda".

Gotta Keep on Tryin' Virginia DeBerry & Donna Grant. Read by Virginia DeBerry & Donna Grant. (Playaway Adult Fiction Ser.). 2008. 69.99 (978-1-60640-592-5(6)) Find a World.

Gotta Keep on Tryin' unabr. ed. 9 cass. (Running Time: 36000 sec.). 2008. 92.25 (978-1-4233-4975-4(X), 9781423349754, BrilAudUnabridg); audio compact disk 97.25 (978-1-4233-4977-8(6), 9781423349778, BriAudCD Unabrid) Brilliance Audio.

Gotta Keep on Tryin' unabr. ed. Virginia DeBerry & Donna Grant. Read by Virginia DeBerry & Donna Grant. 1 MP3-CD. (Running Time: 36000 sec.). 2008. audio compact disk 39.25 (978-1-4233-4979-2(2), 9781423349792, Brlnc Audio MP3 Lib); audio compact disk 24.95 (978-1-4233-4978-5(4), 9781423349785, Brilliance MP3); audio compact disk 36.95 (978-1-4233-4976-1(8), 9781423349761, Bril Audio CD Unabri) Brilliance Audio.

Gotta Keep on Tryin' A Novel. abr. ed. Virginia DeBerry & Donna Grant. Read by Virginia DeBerry and Donna Grant. (Running Time: 6 hrs.). 2008. audio compact disk 14.99 (978-1-4233-4983-9(0), 9781423349839, BCD Value Price) Brilliance Audio.

Gotta Keep on Tryin' A Novel. unabr. ed. Virginia DeBerry & Donna Grant. (Running Time: 10 hrs.). 2008. 39.25 (978-1-4233-4981-5(4), 9781423349815, BADLE); 24.95 (978-1-4233-4980-8(6), 9781423349808, BAD) Brilliance Audio.

Gouda. Jay O'Callahan. Perf. by Jay O'Callahan. 2 CDs. (Running Time: 116 mins 46 sec). Dramatization. (J). 2006. audio compact disk 22.95 (978-1-877954-53-5(5)) Pub: Artana Prodns. Dist(s): Rounder Kids Mus Dist
Ted touched a button and a false wall opened. The back of the UPS truck was a dressing room, and there was the secret of the Gouda!.

Gouda, Set. unabr. ed. Jay O'Callahan. 2 cass. (Running Time: 2 hrs.). 1989. 18.00 (978-1-877954-37-5(3), A15C) Artana Prodns.
Teddy, Laura & Meave are on a wild chase to discover "The Gouda's" amazing secret. High technology, a UPS truck & New Orleans jazz.

Gould's book of Fish. Richard Flanagan. Read by Humphrey Bower. (Running Time: 11 hrs.). 2009. 84.99 (978-1-74214-225-8(7), 9781742142258) Pub: Bolinda Pubng AUS. Dist(s): Bolinda Pub Inc

Gould's Book of Fish. unabr. ed. Richard Flanagan. Read by Humphrey Bower. 9 CDs. (Running Time: 11 hrs.). 2004. audio compact disk 93.95 (978-1-74093-374-2(5)); 64.00 (978-1-74093-288-2(9)) Pub: Bolinda Pubng AUS. Dist(s): Bolinda Pub Inc
Published in hardcover to outstanding acclaim on both sides of the Atlantic, and winner of the prestigious Commonwealth Writers Prize, Gould's Book of Fish is a marvelously imagined epic of nineteenth-century Australia - a world of convicts and colonists, thieves and catamites, whose bloody history is recorded in a very unusual taxonomy of fish. Widely hailed as a masterpiece and a work of genius, it stands out as one of the best novels of recent years.

Gould's book of Fish. unabr. ed. Richard Flanagan. Read by Humphrey Bower. (Running Time: 11 hrs.). 2008. 43.95 (978-1-74214-031-5(9), 9781742140315) Pub: Bolinda Pubng AUS. Dist(s): Bolinda Pub Inc

Gourmandise see Gourmet Rhapsody

Gourmet Rhapsody. unabr. ed. Muriel Barbery. Tr. by Alison Anderson.Tr. of Gourmandise. (ENG.). 2009. audio compact disk 24.95 (978-1-61573-032-2(X), 161573032X) Pub: HighBridge. Dist(s): Workman Pub

***Governator: From Muscle Beach to His Quest for the White House, the Improbable Rise of Arnold Schwarzenegger.** unabr. ed. Ian Halperin. (ENG.). 2010. (978-0-06-206303-8(0), Harper Audio); (978-0-06-200710-0(6), Harper Audio) HarperCollins Pubs.

Government Accounting & Auditing Update 1994-95. William A. Broadus, Jr. 2 cass. 1994. 129.00 incl. wkbk. (736453VC) Am Inst CPA.
This annual course clarifies the most significant recent accounting & auditing pronouncements for state & local government entities. Course material is drawn from standards & other pronouncements issued by the GASB, AICPA, OMB, PCIE, & GAO during the past year. The course will also alert you to important pending or emerging pronouncements on government accounting & auditing.

Government Accounting & Auditing Update 1994-95. William A. Broadus, Jr. 2 cass. (Running Time: 10 hrs.). 1995. bk. 129.00 set. (736455EZ) Am Inst CPA.

Government & Citizenship Audio CD Theme Set: Set of 6 Set A. Adapted by Benchmark Education Staff. (English Explorers Ser.). (J). (gr. 3-6). 2007. audio compact disk 60.00 (978-1-4108-9840-1(7)) Benchmark Educ.

Government & Industry Pt. 2: Track Two. 2 cass. 1990. 17.00 set.; 25.50 set. Recorded Res.
Topics covered include national policy, Darpa & NASA, & semiconductors & consumer electronics.

Government & the Individual. unabr. ed. Nathaniel Branden. 1 cass. (Running Time: 56 min.). 12.95 (573) J Norton Pubs.
The principles of a proper political system - Individual rights - Freedom vs. compulsion.

Government Auditing Standards: 1994 Yellow Book. Lucinda V. Upton & Betty A. King. 3 cass. 1994. bk. 199.00 set. (CPE2506) Bisk Educ.
Gain a complete understanding & working knowledge of the 1994 Government Auditing Standards revisions.

Government Giveaways for Entrepreneur. Matthew Lesko. 1 cass. (Running Time: 2 hrs.). 1992. 19.95 (978-1-878346-11-7(3)) Info USA.

Government in America. 4th ed. George C. Edwards. (C). 1999. (978-0-321-04396-2(0)) Addson-Wesley Educ.

Government in Our Society, The Role Of. unabr. ed. Milton Friedman & Joseph Clark. 1 cass. (Running Time: 58 min.). 12.95 (152) J Norton Pubs.

Government in the Future. Speeches. Noam Chomsky. 1 CD. (Running Time: 57 mins.). 2006. audio compact disk 12.95 (978-1-57970-406-3(9), C27002D, Audio-For) J Norton Pubs.
Discussion of the problems of advanced industrial society and possibilities for overcoming these problems within the framework of libertarian socialism (anarchism).

Government in the Future. unabr. ed. Noam Chomsky. 1 cass. (Running Time: 57 min.). 12.95 (27002) J Norton Pubs.
Discussion of the problems of advanced industrial society & possibilities for overcoming these problems within the framework of libertarian socialism (anarchism).

Government on File. rev. ed. (gr. 6-12). 2004. audio compact disk 149.95 (978-0-8160-5815-0(6)) Facts On File.

Government Sanction of the Oil Cartel. unabr. ed. D. T. Armentano. 1 cass. (Running Time: 53 min.). 12.95 (224) J Norton Pubs.

Governmental Authorities of Russia, Federal to Regional. 6th rev. ed. BIA. (J). 2006. audio compact disk 289.00 (978-1-4187-5226-2(6)) Bus Info Agency.

Governmental Authorities of Russia, Federal to Regional. 6th rev. ed. BIA. (J). 2006. audio compact disk 249.00 (978-1-4187-5225-5(8)) Bus Info Agency.

Governmental Immunity. 1 cass. 1989. bk. 45.00 (AC-530) PA Bar Inst.

Gower Street. unabr. ed. Claire Rayner. Read by Doreen Mantle. 10 cass. (Running Time: 13 hrs. 15 min.). (Performers Ser.: Vol. 1). (J). 2001. 84.95 (978-1-85903-454-5(3)) Pub: Mgna Lrg Print GBR. Dist(s): Ulverscroft US

Gower Street. unabr. ed. Claire Rayner. Read by Doreen Mantle. 12 CDs. (Performers Ser.: Vol. 1). (J). 2002. audio compact disk 99.95 (978-1-85903-557-3(4)) Pub: Mgna Lrg Print GBR. Dist(s): Ulverscroft US

Grab a Partner. Sally K. Albrecht et al. (ENG.). 2001. audio compact disk 39.95 (978-0-7390-1839-2(6)) Alfred Pub.

Grab Another Partner! Sally K. Albrecht. Composed by Jay Althouse. (ENG.). 2003. audio compact disk 29.95 (978-0-7390-3040-0(X)) Alfred Pub.

Grabbing the Family Jewels. unabr. ed. Gaby Hauptmann. Read by Veronika Hyks. 7 cass. (Running Time: 10 hrs. 48 mins.). (Isis Cassettes Ser.). (J). 2004. 61.95 (978-0-7531-1840-5(8)) Pub: ISIS Lrg Prnt GBR. Dist(s): Ulverscroft US

Grace. (Soundtraks Ser.). 2007. audio compact disk 8.99 (978-5-557-56226-3(5)) Christian Wrld.

Grace. Contrib. by Jim Brickman & David Grow. Prod. by David Grow. 2005. audio compact disk 17.98 (978-5-559-05263-2(9)) BMG Records GBR.

***Grace.** Morris Gleitzman. Read by Mary-Anne Fahey. (Running Time: 3 hrs. 38 mins.). (J). 2010. 54.99 (978-1-74214-602-7(3), 9781742146027) Pub: Bolinda Pubng AUS. Dist(s): Bolinda Pub Inc

Grace. Derek Prince. 3 cass. 17.85 Set. (075-076-077) Derek Prince.
The message of the miracle of Christ's birth is summed up in one beautiful word of measureless meaning: grace.

Grace. Jane Roberts Wood. Narrated by Kate Forbes. 7 cass. (Running Time: 9 hrs. 15 mins.). 65.00 (978-1-4025-0598-0(1)); audio compact disk 78.00 (978-1-4025-3491-1(4)) Recorded Bks.

Grace. unabr. ed. Richard Paul Evans. Read by John Dossett. (Running Time: 5 hrs. 0 mins. 0 sec.). (ENG.). 2008. audio compact disk 29.99 (978-0-7435-7483-9(4)) Pub: S&S Audio. Dist(s): S and S Inc

Grace. unabr. ed. Morris Gleitzman. Read by Morris Gleitzman. Read by Mary-Anne Fahey. (Running Time: 3 hrs. 38 mins.). (J). 2009. audio compact disk 54.95 (978-1-74214-527-3(2), 9781742145273) Pub: Bolinda Pubng AUS. Dist(s): Bolinda Pub Inc

***Grace.** unabr. ed. Shelley Shepard Gray. (Running Time: 10 hrs.). (Sisters of the Heart Ser.: Bk. 4). 2010. 29.95 (978-1-4417-7109-4(3)); 59.95 (978-1-4417-7106-3(9)); audio compact disk 90.00 (978-1-4417-7107-0(7)) Blckstn Audio.

Grace. unabr. ed. James Joyce. Read by Richard Setlok. 2 cass. (Running Time: 2 hrs. 10 min.). 1993. lib. bdg. 18.95 Set. (978-1-883049-20-1(2)) Sound Room.
A collection of stories from "Dubliners." "Grace," "Arby," "After the Race," "Clay," "A Little Cloud," & "Counterparts." "Audio Best of the Year" - Publishers Weekly.

Grace. unabr. ed. Short Stories. James Joyce. Read by Richard Setlok. 2 cass. (Running Time: 2 hrs. 14 min.). (Commuter's Library). 1993. bk. 16.95 (978-1-883049-01-0(6), Commuters Library) Sound Room.
A collection of stories from "Dubliners." "Grace," a moving story of alcoholism & friendship, & "Araby," a famous story of first love. Also included are the stories: "After the Race," "Clay," "A Little Cloud," & "Counterparts".

Grace: Come Boldly to the Throne. Kenneth Copeland. 6 cass. 1990. 30.00 Set. (978-0-88114-914-2(4)) K Copeland Pubns.
Biblical teaching on prayer.

Grace - Actual & Sanctifying. 1 cass. (Running Time: 60 min.). (Mother Angelica Live Ser.). 10.00 (978-1-55794-057-5(6), T8) Eternal Wrd TV.

Grace Alone. Created by Maranatha! Music. (Praise Ser.). 1998. audio compact disk 13.99 (978-7-01-255826-2(1)) Maranatha Music.

Grace & Favour. abr. ed. Caroline Upcher. Read by Leslie Ash. 2 cass. 1998. 16.85 Set. (978-0-00-105545-2(3)) Ulvrscrft Audio.

Grace & Mercy. Bobby Hilton. 4 cass. 2002. 65.00 (978-1-930766-12-9(2)) Pub: Bishop Bobby. Dist(s): STL Dist NA

Grace & Mercy, Set. Bobby Hilton. 4 cass. (Running Time: 6 hrs.). 2002. 22.00 (978-1-930766-11-2(4)) Pub: Bishop Bobby. Dist(s): STL Dist NA
Religious ministry program.

Grace & the Heart of Being. Christopher Love. Read by Christopher Love. 1 cass. (Running Time: 90 min.). 1997. 10.95 (978-1-891820-00-7(1)) World Sangha Pubg.
Self-hypnosis meditation for healing, self-improvement & realizing our full & powerful potential as spiritual beings.

Grace & Truth Paradox: Responding with Christlike Balance. unabr. ed. Randy C. Alcorn. Narrated by Randy C. Alcorn. (ENG.). 2007. 9.09 (978-1-60814-231-6(0)); audio compact disk 12.99 (978-1-59859-272-6(6)) Oasis Audio.

Grace Awakening. 2 cass. (Running Time: 2 hrs.). 2004. 48.00 (978-1-57972-578-5(3)); audio compact disk 48.00 (978-1-57972-579-2(1)) Insight Living.

Grace Awakening. abr. ed. Charles R. Swindoll. Read by Richard Fredricks. (Running Time: 4 hrs.). 2006. 39.25 (978-1-4233-0332-9(6), 9781423303329, BADLE); 39.25 (978-1-4233-0330-5(X), 9781423303305, Brlnc Audio MP3 Lib); audio compact disk 24.95 (978-1-4233-0329-9(6), 9781423303299, Brilliance MP3) Brilliance Audio.
Maybe you've known about grace for years. You grew up with it. You heard about it from the pulpits, in Bible classes, from radio and TV preachers. But maybe there's more to grace than they told you. Yes, it's God's "unmerited favor to lost sinners," but did anyone tell you how grace can change you? How it can revolutionize the way you live? Grace can give you freedom. Freedom to be creative, spontaneous. Freedom to think outside the box. Grace can make you want to know God, to be close to Him. Grace can cure your fears, improve your outlook, help you look at life through the lens of joy rather than the fog of pessimism. Grace can strengthen your relationships, giving you freedom to be yourself - and freedom to let others be themselves - without feeling a need to judge, control, or manipulate one another. And yes, grace is God's incredible gift to each of us that shows His love daily in overflowing measures, giving us reason for hope and joy. For the growing number of people who feel that there should be something more to their walk with God than the sometimes grim face of religion, The Grace Awakening offers a glorious alternative: the truth that sets us free.

Grace Awakening. abr. ed. Charles R. Swindoll. Read by Richard Fredricks. (Running Time: 4 hrs.). 2006. 24.95 (978-1-4233-0331-2(8), 9781423303312, BAD) Brilliance Audio.

Grace Awakening Devotional: A Thirty Day Walk in the Freedom of Grace, Charles R. Swindoll. 8 cass. (Running Time: 15 hrs.). 1996. 39.95 (978-1-57972-025-4(0)) Insight Living.
Bible study on living a life of grace.

Grace Awakening Devotional: A Thirty Day Walk in the Freedom of Grace. abr. ed. Charles R. Swindoll. Read by Richard Fredricks. 3 cass. (Running Time: 4 hrs.). 2003. 44.25 (978-1-59355-285-5(8), 1593552858); 19.95 (978-1-59355-284-8(X), 159355284X); audio compact disk 21.95 (978-1-59355-286-2(6), 1593552866); audio compact disk 62.25 (978-1-59355-287-9(4), 1593552874) Brilliance Audio.
Maybe you've known about grace for years. You grew up with it. You heard about it from the pulpits, in Bible classes, from radio and TV preachers. But maybe there's more to grace than they told you. Yes, it's God's "unmerited favor to lost sinners," but did anyone tell you how grace can change you? How it can revolutionize the way you live? Grace can give you freedom. Freedom to be creative, spontaneous. Freedom to think outside the box. Grace can make you want to know God, to be close to Him. Grace can cure your fears, improve your outlook, help you look at life through the lens of joy rather than the fog of pessimism. Grace can strengthen your relationships, giving you freedom to be yourself - and freedom to let others be themselves - without feeling a need to judge, control, or manipulate one another. And yes, grace is God's incredible gift to each of us that shows His love daily in overflowing measures, giving us reason for hope and joy. For the growing number of people who feel that there should be something more to their walk with God than the sometimes grim face of religion, The Grace Awakening offers a glorious alternative: the truth that sets us free.

Grace Cavalieri. unabr. ed. Read by Grace Cavalieri. 1 cass. (Running Time: 29 min.). 1985. 10.00 New Letters.
Grace Cavalieri's reading includes selections from "Body Fluids" & "Creature Comforts".

Grace Compilation. abr. ed. Francine Rivers. Narrated by Anita Lustrea. 10 CDs. (Running Time: 12 hrs. 0 mins. 0 sec.). (Lineage of Grace Ser.: Bks. 1-5). (ENG.). 2004. audio compact disk 34.99 (978-1-58926-645-2(5)) Oasis Audio.

Grace (Eventually) Thoughts on Faith. unabr. ed. Anne Lamott. Read by Anne Lamott. (Running Time: 6 hrs.). (ENG.). (gr. 8). 2007. audio compact disk 34.95 (978-0-14-314208-9(9), PengAudBks) Penguin Grp USA.

Grace for the Journey: Logos June 14, 1998. Ben Young. 1998. Rental 4.95 (978-0-7417-6086-9(X), B0086) Win Walk.

Grace Happens: Stories of Everyday Encounters with Grace. abr. ed. Bob Libby. Read by Raymond H. McPhee. 2 cass. (Running Time: 3 hrs. 45 min.). 1995. 17.95 set. (978-0-9646530-0-9(1)) Luna Media.
Transforming accounts of grace & forgiveness offer mind-healing, soul-soothing & heart-opening insights by author Bob Libby.

Grace in the Wilderness: After the Liberation, 1945-1948. unabr. ed. Aranka Siegal. Narrated by Christina Moore. 5 pieces. (Running Time: 7 hrs.). (gr. 6 up). 1998. 44.00 (978-0-7887-2217-2(4), 95516E7) Recorded Bks.
What was it like to be a teenage survivor in the first years after the Holocaust? In this sequel to "Upon the Head of the Goat," the Hungarian girl, Piri, shares her experiences.

Grace in the Wilderness: After the Liberation, 1945-1948, Class Set. unabr. ed. Aranka Siegal. Read by Christina Moore. 5 cass., 10 bks. (Running Time: 7 hrs.). (YA). 1998. bk. 124.70 (978-0-7887-2539-5(4), 46709) Recorded Bks.
What was it like to be a teenage survivor in the first years after the Holocaust? The Hungarian girl, Piri, shares her experiences.

Grace in the Wilderness: After the Liberation, 1945-1948, Homework Set. unabr. ed. Aranka Siegal. Read by Christina Moore. 5 cass. (Running Time: 7 hrs.). (YA). (gr. 7). 1998. bk. 58.24 (978-0-7887-2234-9(4), 40718) Recorded Bks.

Grace Like Rain. Contrib. by Todd Agnew. (Ultimate Tracks (Word Tracks) Ser.). 2006. audio compact disk 8.99 (978-5-558-14522-9(6), Word Music) Word Enter.

***Grace Notes: Daily Readings with Philip Yancey.** Philip Yancey. (Running Time: 17 hrs. 13 mins. 0 sec.). (ENG.). 2009. 19.99 (978-0-310-77326-9(1)) Zondervan.

Grace of Awakening. Swami Amar Jyoti. 1 cass. 1982. 9.95 (M-35) Truth Consciousness.
In melting of ego, invoking His Grace, the shoreless Ocean of consciousness floods in.

Grace of Faith. Reuven Doron. 1 cass. (Running Time: 90 mins.). (Ways of God Ser.: Vol. 8). 2000. 5.00 (RD04-008) Morning NC.
Through the teaching in this eight-part series, Reuven does an excellent job of explaining God's ways versus man's ways.

Grace of Giving. Gloria Copeland. 1 cass. 1989. 5.00 (978-0-88114-823-7(7)); 20.00 Set. (978-1-57562-003-9(0)) K Copeland Pubns.
Biblical teaching on giving.

Grace of Giving. Elbert Willis. 1 cass. (Learning Lordship Ser.). 4.00 Fill the Gap.

Grace of Giving Series, Set. Elbert Willis. 4 cass. 13.00 Fill the Gap.

Grace of God. Read by Wayne Monbleau. 6 cass. (Running Time: 8 hrs.). 1982. 45.00 Set. (978-0-944648-19-3(3), 300) Loving Grace Pubns.
Religious.

***Grace of God.** unabr. ed. Andy Stanley. 2010. audio compact disk 24.99 (978-1-4003-1676-2(6)) Nelson.

Grace of Grit. Elbert Willis. 1 cass. (Spirit of a Finisher Ser.). 4.00 Fill the Gap.

Grace of Grit: Faithfulness. Elbert Willis. 1 cass. (Faithfulness Through Love Ser.). 4.00 Fill the Gap.

***Grace of Silence: A Memoir.** unabr. ed. Michele Norris. Read by Michele Norris. (Running Time: 6 hrs.). (ENG.). 2010. audio compact disk 32.00 (978-0-307-74891-1(X), Random AudioBks) Pub: Random Audio Pubg. Dist(s): Random

Grace of Sri Krishna. Swami Amar Jyoti. 2 cass. 1989. 12.95 (K-110) Truth Consciousness.
Wondrous examples from the life of Sri Krishna, of the benevolence, mercy, & grace of God.

Grace of the Guru. Swami Amar Jyoti. 1 cass. 1975. 9.95 (E-21) Truth Consciousness.
Nothing greater than the Sad-Guru. The Guru's real work. Why we need a Guru.

Grace of Yeilding. Derek Prince. 1 cass. (I-4040) Derek Prince.

Grace Paley. Interview. Interview with Grace Paley & Kay Bonetti. 1 cass. 1986. 13.95 (978-1-55644-166-0(5), 6102) Am Audio Prose.
An interview in which Paley's fervor for effecting social change is discussed.

Grace Paley. unabr. ed. Ed. by Jim McKinley. Prod. by Rebekah Presson. 1 cass. (Running Time: 29 min.). (New Letters on the Air Ser.). 1994. 10.00 (010394) New Letters.
The writer many consider to be the best short story writer in America has recently published her "New & Collected Poems." Now 71, Paley reads poems about aging & about political activism, she calls herself a "combative pacifist & cooperative anarchist, & says she means her writing to be always clear & comprehensible.

Grace Paley. unabr. ed. Grace Paley. Read by Grace Paley. Interview with Robert Stewart. Prod. by Rebekah Presson. 1 cass. (Running Time: 29 min.). 1991. 10.00 (010491) New Letters.
One of the finest short fiction writers of our time talks about the influence of her heritage & her location on her writing. Paley also reads a light story titled "Loving," & a darker one, "Living".

Grace Schulman. unabr. ed. Read by Grace Schulman. 1 cass. (Running Time: 29 min.). 1985. 10.00 New Letters.
New York poet Grace Schulman reads from "Burn Down The Icons" & "Hemispheres".

Grace Tape. unabr. ed. David E. Roy. Read by David E. Roy. 1 cass. (Running Time: 1 hr. 27 min.). 1993. 10.95 (978-0-9641965-0-6(6)) Ctr Healing Jrny.
Contains a new look at grace & eight guided imagery exercises designed to help listeners learn to bring their spiritual depth to growth & healing. The exercises held with self-esteem, problem solving, empowerment & healing shame wounds.

Grace That Teaches: Logos July 5, 1998. Ben Young. 1998. 4.95 (978-0-7417-6089-0(4), B0089) Win Walk.

Grace, the Life of the Believer. Chuck Smith. (ENG.). 2001. audio compact disk 22.99 (978-1-932941-13-5(4)) Word For Today.

Grace Through Self-Control. unabr. ed. Myrtle Smyth. 1 cass. (Running Time: 1 hrs. 3 min.). (Myrtle Smyth Audiotapes Ser.: Vol. 23). 1999. 8.95 (978-1-893107-25-0(6), M23) Healing Unltd.

Grace to Hugh. 1 cass. (Running Time: 30 min.). (Paws & Tales Ser.: Vol. 2). 2001. 3.99 (978-1-57972-381-1(0)) Insight Living.
After a suspicious fire is put out at the Collins Mansion, C.J. discovers a clue that tells him who started the fire.

Grace to Hugh. (Paws & Tales Ser.: Vol. 2). (J). 2001. audio compact disk 5.99 (978-1-57972-383-5(7)) Insight Living.

Grace Trilogy Bk. 1: Love. abr. ed. Margaret Perron et al. 2 cass. (Running Time: 3 hrs.). 1998. 17.95 (978-1-57453-272-2(3)) Audio Lit.
The friendship of three women & what they learned about life & spirituality during the course of one extraordinary year. The birth & subsequent death of a daughter launches these women on a remarkable odyssey of personal growth & spiritual discovery.

Grace under Fire: Letters of Faith in Times of War. unabr. ed. Andrew Carroll. Read by Patrick G. Lawlor. (Running Time: 4 hrs. 30 mins. 0 sec.). (ENG.). 2007. audio compact disk 24.99 (978-1-4001-0373-7(8)) Pub: Tantor Media. Dist(s): IngramPubServ

Grace under Fire: Letters of Faith in Times of War. unabr. ed. Read by Patrick G. Lawlor. Ed. by Andrew Carroll. (Running Time: 4 hrs. 30 mins. 0 sec.). (ENG.). 2007. audio compact disk 19.99 (978-1-4001-5373-2(5)); audio compact disk 49.99 (978-1-4001-3373-4(4)) Pub: Tantor Media. Dist(s): IngramPubServ

Grace Walk Conference. Based on a book by Steve McVey. 8 cass. (Running Time: 8 Hours). 1996. 40.00 (978-0-9664736-3-6(9)); audio compact disk 40.00 (978-0-9664736-4-3(7)) Grace Walk.
Conference regarding the Christian's Identity in Christ.

Grace Yoga: Beside Still Waters. Arlene Bjork. 2005. audio compact disk 14.95 (978-1-59975-210-5(7)) Indep Pub IL.

Graceful Passages: A Companion for Living & Dying. 2 CDs. (Running Time: 3 hrs.). 2003. pap. bk. 24.95 (95007) Parallax Pr.
Offers compassion, comfort, and emotional healing for those facing life-threatening illness, grieving the loss of a loved one, or simply overcome by life's burdens.

Graceful Waiting: Bringing Eternal Truths into A Temporal World. Mac Hammond. 2008. audio compact disk 6.00 (978-1-57399-378-4(6)) Mac Hammond.

Graceful Waiting: Pulling God's Promises from Heaven to Earth. Mac Hammond. 2009. audio compact disk 30.00 (978-1-57399-387-6(5)) Mac Hammond.

Graceland. Perf. by Ladysmith Black Mambazo et al. 1 cass. (Running Time: 80 min.). (J). (ps up). 9.98 (2145); audio compact disk 17.98 CD. (D2145) MFLP CA.
This remarkable concert video showcases unforgettable rousing performances. Uplifting & instills a vision of world unity.

Graceland. unabr. ed. Chris Abani. Read by Chris Abani. 8 cass. (Running Time: 12 hrs. 30 min.). 2005. 89.75 (978-1-4193-0229-9(9)) Recorded Bks.

Graceland. unabr. collector's ed. Chris Abani. Narrated by Chris Abani. 11 CDs. (Running Time: 12 hrs. 30 min.). 2005. audio compact disk 39.95 (978-1-4193-0302-9(3)) Recorded Bks.
The Elvis Oke of Chris Abani's novel is a child left to fend for himself in the urban jungle of Lagos , Nigeria . He has a talent for Elvis impersonations (hence the name) and wants to make it big so he can escape his violent and tumultuous life. In a place where angels fear to tread and only fools rush in, Elvis searches for redemption and a small piece of graceland.

GraceLife Audio Album. Read by Lee Lefebre. 8 cass. (GraceLife Conference Ser.). 1993. 39.99 Set. (978-1-57838-121-0(5)) CrossLife Express.
Christian living.

Graceling. unabr. ed. Kristin Cashore. Read by David Baker. 11 CDs. (Running Time: 12 hrs. 30 mins.). (YA). (gr. 7 up). 2009. audio compact disk 65.00 (978-1-934180-70-9(X)) Full Cast Audio.

Gracestoration. Dottie Bingham. Read by Dottie Bingham. 1 cass. (Running Time: 1 hr. 50 min.). (ICEL Three Ser.). 1996. 6.00 (978-1-57838-055-8(3)) CrossLife Express.

Gracey. unabr. ed. James Moloney. Read by Kate Hosking & Peter Hardy. 5 cass. (Running Time: 6 hrs. 15 mins.). (YA). 2000. 40.00 (978-1-74030-107-7(2), 500326) Pub: Bolinda Pubng AUS. Dist(s): Bolinda Pub Inc

Gracey. unabr. ed. James Moloney. 5 CDs. (Running Time: 6 hrs. 15 mins.). (YA). 2002. audio compact disk 63.95 (978-1-74030-604-1(X)) Pub: Bolinda Pubng AUS. Dist(s): Bolinda Pub Inc

Gracias. unabr. ed. Semilla de Mostaza. 1 CD. (Running Time: 1 hr. 30 mins.). 2002. audio compact disk 9.99 (978-0-8297-3722-6(7)) Zondervan.

Gracias. unabr. ed. De Mostaza Semilla & Zondervan Publishing Staff. (SPA.). 2002. 9.99 (978-0-8297-3724-0(3)) Pub: Vida Pubs. Dist(s): Zondervan

Gracias Unplugged: Logos November 23, 1997. Ben Young. 1997. 4.95 (978-0-7417-6057-9(6), B0057) Win Walk.

Gracie for President. 6 cass. 24.98 Set. Moonbeam Pubns.

Gracie's Girl. unabr. ed. Ellen Wittlinger. Narrated by Stina Nielsen. 4 pieces. (Running Time: 5 hrs.). (gr. 3 up). 2002. 37.00 (978-1-4025-1468-5(9)) Recorded Bks.
Bess Cunningham has never been popular, and she plans to do something about it. She's got a fresh style with plenty of unique clothes, and she's the new stage manager for the musical at her middle school. She couldn't care less about the volunteer work her parents do at a soup kitchen until she meets Grace Jarvis Battle. The kind, elderly woman reminds Bess of her grandmothers except for one significant difference - Grace lives on the street and finds food in dumpsters. Because of Grace, Bess begins to think about her priorities and realizes there are more important things in life than trying to win friends with a few wild outfits.

Gracious Imperatives. bk. 13.00 (978-0-687-76223-1(5)) Abingdon.

Gracious Plenty: A Novel. unabr. ed. Sheri Reynolds. Read by Bernadette Dunne. 4 cass. (Running Time: 6 hrs.). 1998. 32.00 (978-0-7366-4143-2(2), 4647) Books on Tape.
Badly burned when she was just four, Finch grows into a courageous & feisty loner. As she tends to the flowers in the local cemetery, she discovers she can hear the voices of those who have gone before. With the help of her spectral friends, Finch learns to embrace the living in this novel of dreams & regrets.

Graciousness of Jesus: The Glory of the Senses. Jonathan Murro. 1 cass. 7.95 (978-0-917189-13-5(2)) A R Colton Fnd.

Grade School Musical. Robin Sammons Berry. Read by Twin Sisters Productions. (Twin Sisters Productions: Growing Minds with Music (Playaway) Ser.). (J). 2008. 44.99 (978-1-60252-967-0(1)) Find a World.

Graded Repertoire for Guitar, Volume 1. Stanley Yates. 2003. audio compact disk 9.98 (978-0-7866-6224-1(7)) Mel Bay.

GradeKeeper. (Timesaving Software Tools for Teachers Ser.). 2004. audio compact disk 19.99 (978-1-57690-706-1(6)) TCR Inc.

Gradual Psalms with Alleluia Verses & Tracts: Year A, B, & C for the Revised Common Lectionary. Bruce E. Ford. 2007. audio compact disk 85.00 (978-0-89869-557-1(0)) Church Pub Inc.

Graduate. unabr. ed. Charles Webb. Read by Scott Brick. (Running Time: 8.5 hrs. NaN mins.). 2008. 29.95 (978-1-4332-5546-5(4)); audio compact disk 19.95 (978-1-4332-5545-8(6)); audio compact disk 54.95 (978-1-4332-5543-4(X)); audio compact disk 70.00 (978-1-4332-5544-1(8)) Blckstn Audio.

Graduate. unabr. ed. Charles Webb. Read by William Hope. 4 cass. (Running Time: 6 hrs.). 2002. 39.95 (978-0-7540-0861-3(4), CAB 2283) Pub: Chivers Pr GBR. Dist(s): AudioGO

Graduate Education Services in Malaysia: A Strategic Reference 2006. Compiled by Icon Group International, Inc. Staff. 2007. ring bd. 195.00 (978-0-497-82344-3(6)) Icon Grp.

Graduate Education Symposium: Implications of Continuing Fragmentation in Surgery. 2 cass. (General Sessions Ser.: C85-SP1). 15.00 (8543) Am Coll Surgeons.

***Graduated Soloing Book/CD Set: The Mimi Fox Guitar Method.** Mimi Fox. (ENG.). 2010. lib. bdg. 19.99 (978-0-7866-8138-9(1)) Mel Bay.

Graduation Day: Luke 23:46. Ed Young. 1999. 4.95 (978-0-7417-2212-6(7), 1212) Win Walk.

Graduation of Jake Moon. unabr. ed. Barbara Park. Read by Fred Savage. 2 vols. (Running Time: 2 hrs. 20 mins.). (J). (gr. 4-7). 2004. pap. bk. 29.00 (978-0-8072-8722-4(9), Listening Lib); 23.00 (978-0-8072-8721-7(0), Listening Lib) Random Audio Pubg.

Graf Spee: The Life & Death of a Raider. unabr. ed. Dudley Pope. Read by Bill Kelsey. 7 cass. (Running Time: 10 hrs. 30 min.). 1995. 56.00 (978-0-7366-3099-3(6), 3775) Books on Tape.
It was the pride of the German navy - & the subject of a sea hunt virtually without parallel in maritime history. But what happened to the Graf Spee on December 17, 1939 remains a puzzle. As three hopelessly outgunned British cruisers faced her off the coast of Uruguay, why did the captain scuttle his ship?.

Graffiti for the Johns of Heaven. James Broughton. 1 cass. 1986. 9.95 SPD-Small Pr Dist.

Graffiti on the Fence. unabr. ed. Elaine Forrestal. Read by Peter Hardy. 2 cass. (Running Time: 2 hrs. 30 mins.). 2002. (978-1-74030-349-1(0)) Bolinda Pubng AUS.

Grail. unabr. ed. Stephen R. Lawhead. Narrated by Robert Whitfield. 10 CDs. (Running Time: 12 hrs.). 2001. audio compact disk 80.00 (978-0-7861-9596-1(7), ZP2889); audio compact disk 19.95 (978-0-7861-9374-5(3), PZM2889) Blckstn Audio.
Drought, plague, and war have left the Isle of the Mighty battered and its heart, the beloved Arthur, grievously injured, until a secret relic is brought before the dying King; it is a Holy Grail that heals his wounds and restores his vigor. But soon evil enters the royal court in the guise of a beautiful maiden: a soulless, malevolent force capable of seducing the King's loyal champion, confounding the sage whom some call Merlin, and carrying the sacred Grail, and Arthur's adored Queen, off into the dark unknown. Now Arthur faces the greatest challenge of his sovereignty: a quest of recovery that must lead the noble liege through realms of magic and the undead, on a trail that winds inexorably toward a grim confrontation with his most foul nemesis and his destiny.

Grail. unabr. ed. Stephen R. Lawhead. Narrated by Robert Whitfield. 9 cass. (Running Time: 12 hrs.). 2002. 62.95 (978-0-7861-2138-0(6), P2888) Blckstn Audio.

Grail Murders: Being the Third Journal of Sir Roger Shallot Concerning Certain Wicked Conspiracies & Horrible Murders Perpetrated in the Reign of King Henry the Eighth. unabr. ed. Michael Clynes, pseud. 7 cass. 1998. 76.95 Set. (978-1-85903-158-2(7)) Pub: Magna Story GBR. Dist(s): Ulverscroft US

Grail Tree. unabr. ed. Jonathan Gash. Narrated by Christopher Kay. 6 cass. (Running Time: 8 hrs.). (Lovejoy Mystery Ser.). 1999. 53.00 (978-1-84197-028-8(X), H1027E7) Recorded Bks.
The Holy Grail has surfaced once again n the antiques world. Lovejoy is not unduly amazed - it's hardly the first time such a claim has been made. Even the fact that the owner is an ex-clergyman is nothing to write home about. Or it wasn't until someone somewhere takes him seriously. The cup itself is unsurprisingly stolen, but worst of all, the owner is found dead in rather gruesome circumstances.

Grail Tree. unabr. ed. Jonathan Gash. Narrated by Christopher Kay. 7 CDs. (Running Time: 8 hrs.). (Lovejoy Mystery Ser.). 2001. audio compact disk 67.00 (978-1-84197-098-1(0), C1142E7) Recorded Bks.
The Holy Grail has surfaced once again in the antiques world. Lovejoy is not unduly amazed until the cup is stolen, & the owner is found dead in rather gruesome circumstances.

Grain of Truth. unabr. ed. Nina Bawden. Read by Phyllida Law. 6 cass. (Running Time: 9 hrs.). 2000. 54.95 (978-0-7540-0446-2(5), CAB 1869) AudioGO.
A gentle old man falls down the stairs & dies. Did he fall or was he pushed? His delicate, day-dreaming daughter-in-law, Emma, insists she is guilty. But to her husband, Henry, & her friend, Holly, this is unthinkable. Guilt is simply Emma's obsession. Emma, Holly & Henry tell the story in turn, yet each of their accounts is full of deception.

Grainger & Friends. 2004. audio compact disk 14.95 (978-0-8258-5352-4(4)) Fischer Inc NY.

***Grainne.** Duirling. (ENG.). 11.95 (978-0-8023-7042-6(X)) Pub: Clo Iar-Chonnachta IRL. Dist(s): Dufour

Gramatica Ritmica. Diego Marulanda. Ed. by Ramiro Puerta & Agustina Tocalli - Beller. Prod. by Sara Jordan. Composed by Sara Jordan. Illus. by Glen Wyand. 1 cass. (Running Time: 50 min. 46 secs.). (SPA.). (J). 1995. pap. bk. 14.95 (978-1-895523-66-9(4), JMP S09K) Jordan Music.
Ten upbeat Spanish grammar songs that teach basic grammar rules: nouns, pronouns, adjectives, and the conjugation of verbs in present and past tenses. Exciting exercises and crossword puzzles are included in the lyrics book.

Gramatica Ritmica. abr. ed. Diego Marulanda. Prod. by Sara Jordan. Composed by Sara Jordan. 1 CD. (Running Time: 30 min.). (Songs that Teach Spanish Ser.). (SPA.). (J). (gr. 4-7). 1995. audio compact disk 13.95 (978-1-894262-15-6(8), JMP S09CD) Pub: S Jordan Publ. Dist(s): CrabtreePubCo

Gramatica Viva: Interactive Spanish Grammar. Mediatheque Publisher Services. 2003. audio compact disk 22.60 (978-0-13-111796-9(3)) Pearson Educ CAN CAN.

Gramela Pamela Explains What's a YEBEN! ??? unabr. ed. Pamela Walter. Read by Pamela Walter. Adapted by Seth D. Walter. 1 cass. (Running Time: 25 min.). (J). (gr. k-3). 1999. bk. 7.95 (978-1-929110-27-8(8), 0-92791-1) Colter Enterp.
Introduces the YEBEN!s in this delightful trip to The Heartland - the secret place inside us that no one else can see.

Gramercy Park. Paula Cohen. Narrated by Alyssa Bresnahan. 11 cass. (Running Time: 15 hrs. 30 mins.). 99.00 (978-1-4025-3336-5(5)) Recorded Bks.

***Grammaire en Dialogues: Niveau Intermediaire.** Claire Miquel. (FRE.). 2001. pap. bk. 39.95 (978-2-09-035216-0(7)) Cle Intl FRA.

Grammar. 1 CD. (Running Time: 1 hr.). (J). 2001. pap. bk. 13.95 (RL 929CD) Kimbo Educ.
Grammar made fun! 11 songs & "follow along" book teach the tools for great writing. Nouns, pronouns & verbs! Includes book.

Grammar, Vol. 1. unabr. ed. Brad Caudle & Richard Caudle. Perf. by T. J. Rockenstein et al. 1 cass. (Running Time: 37 min.). (Rock 'N Learn Ser.). (J). (gr. 1-5). 1994. pap. bk. 12.99 (978-1-878489-29-6(1), RL929) Rock N Learn.
"Top 40" type songs with educational lyrics teach the basics of grammar. Covers nouns, proper nouns, pronouns, verbs & linking verbs & verb tense. Includes illustrated book.

Grammar & Usage Seminar, Set. Fred Pryor Seminars Staff. 6 cass. 59.95 (10500AX) Nightingale-Conant.
End the frustration & embarrassment that poor grammar skills & usage cause. In this fastpaced live seminar, you'll learn simple, easy-to-apply guidelines that answer virtually all your questions about grammar, punctuation, capitalization & spelling - without having to memorize countless complicated rules & definitions. Includes workbook.

Grammar & Usage Seminar: End Embarassing, Mistake-Ridden Communications in Your Organization Forever. 6 cass. 59.95 Set incl. wkbk. (10501AS) Pryor Resources.
Cut grammar & usage confusion down to size with easy-to-understand tips & guidelines that work on the job. Master simple rules & how-tos that are always appropriate & correct for even the most difficult times.

Grammar Bible: Answers to the Top 500 Questions That Commonly Bewilder Us! abr. ed. Michael Strumpf & Ariel Douglas. Read by Michael Strumpf. 2 cass. (Running Time: 2 hrs.). 1996. 15.00 Set. (978-0-679-44914-0(0), Random AudioBks) Random Audio Pubg.
With "The Grammar Bible" as your guide, you'll find practical, pointed, lucid examples of everyday grammar quandaries that occur in both speaking & writing. Here is everything you need to know about common & proper nouns, verb tenses & moods, punctuation & capitalization, objects & subjects, phrases & clauses - plus, how to decide between the politically correct & the merely correct; what to do if textbook, dictionary, & style sheet all disagree; & much, much more.

Grammar Connections Bk. 1: An Advanced Course for Reference & Practice. Lynda Berish & Sandra Thibaudeau. 2 cass. (Running Time: 3 hrs.). 2002. (978-0-13-332362-7(5)) Longman.

Grammar Connections Bk. 2: An Advanced Course for Reference & Practice. Lynda Berish & Sandra Thibaudeau. 2002. 21.85 (978-0-13-333296-4(9)) Longman.

***Grammar Dimensions, Bk. 4.** 3rd ed. Frodesen. (ENG.). (C). 2000. 37.95 (978-0-8384-0287-0(9)) Pub: Heinle. Dist(s): CENGAGE Learn

Grammar Dimensions: Platinum Edition. 2000. audio compact disk (978-0-8384-1267-1(X)) Heinle.

Grammar for Business Professionals. PUEI. 2005. 69.95 (978-1-933328-09-6(6), CareerTrack) P Univ E Inc.

Grammar for Business Professionals. unabr. ed. Read by Pat Cramer. 6 cass. 69.50 set. (S03000) J Norton Pubs.
Writing expert Pat Cramer demystifies the often puzzling world of grammar, word usage, sentence structure & punctuation. You'll be able to add impact to the ideas you express.

Grammar for Business Professionals: Never Again Be Embarrassed - Or Unsure - About Your Writing Skills. Patricia Cramer. 6 cass. (Running Time: 5 hrs. 49 min.). 79.95 Set. (V10014) CareerTrack Pubns.
In this program, communication expert Pat Cramer demystifies the often puzzling world of grammar, word usage, sentence structure & punctuation. And she does it with wit & style. You're guaranteed to learn a lot - & have a great time in the process! Pat will give you a renewed sense of confidence in your ability to present a polished, professional image in all your business communication.

Grammar for Success. unabr. ed. Richard Lederer & Richard Dowis. Read by Richard Lederer. 8 cass. (Running Time: 8 hrs.). 2000. (978-1-931187-17-6(7), GS) Word Success.

Grammar Girl's: Quick & Dirty Tips for Better Writing. unabr. ed. Mignon Fogarty. (Running Time: 6 hrs. 0 mins. 0 sec.). (ENG.). 2008. audio compact disk 29.95 (978-1-4272-0434-9(9)) Pub: Macmill Audio. Dist(s): Macmillan

Grammar Grooves. abr. ed. Jennifer Moore. Lyrics by Jennifer Moore. Prod. by Sara Jordan. Composed by Sara Jordan. 1 CD. (Running Time: 30 min.). (Songs that Teach Language Arts Ser.). (ENG.). (J). (gr. 4-7). 1994. audio compact disk 13.95 (978-1-894262-17-0(4), JMP 109CD) Pub: S Jordan Publ. Dist(s): CrabtreePubCo

Grammar Grooves: Primary. Jennifer Moore. Lyrics by Jennifer Moore. Ed. by Debby Seed & Pat Findlay. Prod. by Sara Jordan. Composed by Sara Jordan. Illus. by Glen Wyand. Engineer Mark Shannon. 1 cass. (Running Time: 47 min. 6 secs.). (J). (gr. 3-5). 1994. pap. bk. 14.95 (978-1-895523-54-6(0), JMP109K) Jordan Music.
Tap your toes to the Grammar Grooves! These 10 songs teach basic grammar rules (nouns and pronouns, adjectives, verbs, tenses, adverbs, and punctuation). Entertaining activities and crossword puzzles are included in the lyrics book to help reinforce learning even further. A bonus complement of music accompaniment tracks comes in handy karaoke performances and music night productions!.

Grammar in Action 3. Barbara Foley & Elizabeth R. Neblett. Ed. by Elizabeth Foley. Bk. 3. (ENG., (C). 1998. suppl. ed. 41.95 (978-0-8384-6730-5(X)) Pub: Heinle. Dist(s): CENGAGE Learn

***Grammar in Context, Bk. 1.** 4th ed. ELBAUM. (C). 2005. 59.95 (978-1-4130-0740-4(6)); audio compact disk 59.95 (978-1-4130-0739-8(2)) Pub: Heinle. Dist(s): CENGAGE Learn

***Grammar in Context Basic.** 4th ed. Sandra N. Elbaum. (ENG.). (C). 2006. 60.95 (978-1-4130-0826-5(7)) Pub: Heinle. Dist(s): CENGAGE Learn

***Grammar Minutes, Gr. 4 Ebook: 100 Minutes to Better Basic Skills.** Carmen S. Jones. (J). 2009. 14.99 (978-1-60689-946-5(5)) Creat Teach Pr.

***Grammar Minutes, Gr. 5 Ebook: 100 Minutes to Better Basic Skills.** Kathleen Hex. (J). 2009. 14.99 (978-1-60689-947-2(3)) Creat Teach Pr.

***Grammar Minutes, Gr. 6 Ebook: 100 Minutes to Better Basic Skills.** Colleen Dobelmann. (J). 2009. 14.99 (978-1-60689-948-9(1)) Creat Teach Pr.

Grammar Plus Set: A Basic Skills Course. 2nd ed. Judy DeFilippo et al. 2 cass. 1994. 41.91 (978-0-201-53498-6(3)) AddisonWesley.
English as a second language.

Grammar Rock. 1 cass., 1 CD. (Schoolhouse Rock Ser.). (J). 7.18 Blisterpack. (KID 72611); audio compact disk 11.98 CD Jewel box. (KID 72612) NewSound.

Grammar Rock. Rhino Records Staff. 1 cass., 1 CD. (Schoolhouses Rock Ser.). 1998. 11.89 CD. (978-1-56826-772-2(X)) Rhino Enter.

Grammar Rock. Rhino Records Staff. 1 cass., 1 CD. (Schoolhouses Rock Ser.). (J). 1998. 7.89 (978-1-56826-771-5(1), 72612) Rhino Enter.
Includes "Lolly, Lolly, Lolly, Get Your Adverbs Her" and "Conjunction Junction".

Grammar Rules! Easy Guidelines for Mistake-Free Written & Verbal Communication. abr. ed. Patricia Cramer. 2 cass. (Running Time: 3 hrs.). 2000. 17.95 (978-1-55977-963-0(2)) CareerTrack Pubns.

Grammar Sense. Contrib. by Susan Kesner Bland. (Grammar Sense Ser.). 2004. audio compact disk & audio compact disk 39.95 (978-0-19-437815-4(2)) OUP.

Grammar Sense, Level 2. Cheryl Pavlik. Contrib. by Susan Kesner Bland. (Grammar Sense Ser.). 2004. audio compact disk 39.95 (978-0-19-437814-7(4)) OUP.

Grammar Sense, No. 1. Cheryl Pavlik. Contrib. by Susan Kesner Bland. (Grammar Sense Ser.). 2004. audio compact disk 39.95 (978-0-19-437813-0(6)) OUP.

Grammar Snobs Are Great Big Meanies: A Guide to Language for Fun & Spite. June Casagrande. Read by Shelly Frasier. (Playaway Adult Nonfiction Ser.). (ENG.). 2009. 50.00 (978-1-60775-628-6(5)) Find a World.

Grammar Snobs Are Great Big Meanies: A Guide to Language for Fun & Spite. unabr. ed. June Casagrande. Read by Shelly Fraser. (Running Time: 5 hrs. 30 mins. 0 sec.). (ENG.). 2006. audio compact disk 24.99 (978-1-4001-0218-1(9)) Pub: Tantor Media. Dist(s): IngramPubServ

Grammar Snobs Are Great Big Meanies: A Guide to Language for Fun & Spite. unabr. ed. June Casagrande. Read by Shelly Frasier. (Running Time: 5 hrs. 30 mins. 0 sec.). (ENG.). 2006. audio compact disk 19.99 (978-1-4001-5218-6(6)); audio compact disk 49.99 (978-1-4001-3218-8(5)) Pub: Tantor Media. Dist(s): IngramPubServ

Grammar Songs. 1 CD. (Running Time: 1 hr.). (YA). (gr. 2 up). 2001. pap. bk. & tchr. ed. 22.95 (1CD) Audio Memory.
Sixteen lively songs cover parts of speech, plurals, capitals, Greek and Latin roots, tenses, irregular verbs, apostrophes, commas, quotation marks and more.

Grammar Songs. 2004. audio compact disk 22.95 (978-1-883028-10-7(8)) Audio Memory.

Grammar Songs. 1 cass. (Running Time: 1 hr.). (J). (gr. k-7). 2001. wbk. ed. 10.95 (THR 101C) Kimbo Educ.
You remember "I before E" & "30 Days Hath September..." 12 rap, country & rock songs teach grammar & punctuation skills through music. Songs include Commas, Vowels, Quotation Marks, Syllables, Verbs, Plurals, Periods, Capital Letters & more. Reproducible workbook & lyrics included.

Grammar Songs. Audio. 1 cass. (Running Time: 1 hr.). 1996. pap. bk. & tchr. ed. 19.95 (978-1-883028-05-3(1), 1) Audio Memory.
Covers parts of speech, plurals, punctuation rules, Greek & Latin roots, capitalization, tenses, irregular verbs, apostrophes, commas, quotation marks, etc.

Grammar Tools. Glazier. 1 CD. (Running Time: 1 hr.). 2002. audio compact disk 13.95 (978-0-8384-6772-5(5)) Heinle.

Grammarchants. Carolyn Graham. Ed. by Marilyn Rosenthal. Contrib. by Joseph Mennonna. (Jazz Chants Ser.). 1993. 24.50 (978-0-19-434641-2(2)) OUP.

Grammarchants: More Jazz Chants CD. Carolyn Graham. 2003. audio compact disk & audio compact disk 24.50 (978-0-19-438604-3(X)) OUP.

Grammardog Guide to A Connecticut Yankee. unabr. ed. Mary Jane McKinney. (ENG.). 2005. cd-rom & audio compact disk 14.95 (978-1-60857-108-6(4)) Grammardog.

Grammardog Guide to A Midsummer Night's Dream. unabr. ed. Mary Jane McKinney. (ENG.). 2005. cd-rom & audio compact disk 14.95 (978-1-60857-156-7(4)) Grammardog.

Grammardog Guide to A Tale of Two Cities. unabr. ed. Mary Jane McKinney. (ENG.). 2003. cd-rom & audio compact disk 14.95 (978-1-60857-145-1(9)) Grammardog.

Grammardog Guide to Alice's Adventures in Wonderland. unabr. ed. Mary Jane McKinney. (ENG.). 2006. cd-rom & audio compact disk 14.95 (978-1-60857-126-0(2)) Grammardog.

Grammardog Guide to Anthem. unabr. ed. Mary Jane McKinney. (ENG.). 2004. cd-rom & audio compact disk 14.95 (978-1-60857-101-7(7)) Grammardog.

Grammardog Guide to As You Like It. unabr. ed. Mary Jane McKinney. (ENG.). 2005. cd-rom & audio compact disk 14.95 (978-1-60857-149-9(1)) Grammardog.

Grammardog Guide to Bartleby the Scrivener. unabr. ed. Mary Jane McKinney. (ENG.). 2003. cd-rom & audio compact disk 14.95 (978-1-60857-103-1(3)) Grammardog.

Grammardog Guide to Benito Cereno. unabr. ed. Mary Jane McKinney. (ENG.). 2003. cd-rom & audio compact disk 14.95 (978-1-60857-104-8(1)) Grammardog.

Grammardog Guide to Billy Budd. unabr. ed. Mary Jane McKinney. (ENG.). 2003. cd-rom & audio compact disk 14.95 (978-1-60857-105-5(X)) Grammardog.

Grammardog Guide to Chopin Short Stories. unabr. ed. Mary Jane McKinney. (ENG.). 2006. cd-rom & audio compact disk 14.95 (978-1-60857-107-9(6)) Grammardog.

Grammardog Guide to Civil Disobedience. unabr. ed. Mary Jane McKinney. (ENG.). 2007. cd-rom & audio compact disk 14.95 (978-1-60857-100-0(9)) Grammardog.

Grammardog Guide to Conrad Short Stories. unabr. ed. Mary Jane McKinney. (ENG.). 2005. cd-rom & audio compact disk 14.95 (978-1-60857-128-4(9)) Grammardog.

Grammardog Guide to Crane Short Stories. unabr. ed. Mary Jane McKinney. (ENG.). 2005. cd-rom & audio compact disk 14.95 (978-1-60857-109-3(2)) Grammardog.

Grammardog Guide to Daisy Miller. unabr. ed. Mary Jane McKinney. (ENG.). 2008. cd-rom & audio compact disk 14.95 (978-1-60857-090-4(8)) Grammardog.

Grammardog Guide to David Copperfield. unabr. ed. Mary Jane McKinney. (ENG.). 2006. cd-rom & audio compact disk 14.95 (978-1-60857-129-1(7)) Grammardog.

Grammardog Guide to Dr. Jekyll & Mr. Hyde. unabr. ed. Mary Jane McKinney. (ENG.). 2005. cd-rom & audio compact disk 14.95 (978-1-60857-130-7(0)) Grammardog.

Grammardog Guide to Emma. unabr. ed. Mary Jane McKinney. (ENG.). 2007. cd-rom & audio compact disk 14.95 (978-1-60857-175-8(0)) Grammardog.

Grammardog Guide to Ethan Frome. unabr. ed. Mary Jane McKinney. (ENG.). 2008. cd-rom & audio compact disk 14.95 (978-1-60857-179-6(3)) Grammardog.

Grammardog Guide to Evangeline. unabr. ed. Mary Jane McKinney. (ENG.). 2008. cd-rom & audio compact disk 14.95 (978-1-60857-098-0(3)) Grammardog.

Grammardog Guide to Frankenstein. unabr. ed. Mary Jane McKinney. (ENG.). 2003. cd-rom & audio compact disk 14.95 (978-1-60857-131-4(9)) Grammardog.

Grammardog Guide to Great Expectations. unabr. ed. Mary Jane McKinney. (ENG.). 2003. cd-rom & audio compact disk 14.95 (978-1-60857-132-1(7)) Grammardog.

Grammardog Guide to Gulliver's Travels. unabr. ed. Mary Jane McKinney. (ENG.). 2007. cd-rom & audio compact disk 14.95 (978-1-60857-171-0(8)) Grammardog.

Grammardog Guide to Hamlet. unabr. ed. Mary Jane McKinney. (ENG.). 2005. cd-rom & audio compact disk 14.95 (978-1-60857-151-2(3)) Grammardog.

Grammardog Guide to Hard Times. unabr. ed. Mary Jane McKinney. (ENG.). 2006. cd-rom & audio compact disk 14.95 (978-1-60857-133-8(5)) Grammardog.

Grammardog Guide to Hawthorne Short Stories. unabr. ed. Mary Jane McKinney. (ENG.). 2005. cd-rom & audio compact disk 14.95 (978-1-60857-110-9(6)) Grammardog.

Grammardog Guide to Heart of Darkness. unabr. ed. Mary Jane McKinney. (ENG.). 2003. cd-rom & audio compact disk 14.95 (978-1-60857-134-5(3)) Grammardog.

Grammardog Guide to Henry IV, Part I. unabr. ed. Mary Jane McKinney. (ENG.). 2007. cd-rom & audio compact disk 14.95 (978-1-60857-169-7(6)) Grammardog.

Grammardog Guide to Henry V. unabr. ed. Mary Jane McKinney. (ENG.). 2006. cd-rom & audio compact disk 14.95 (978-1-60857-164-2(5)) Grammardog.

Grammardog Guide to Hound of the Baskervilles. unabr. ed. Mary Jane McKinney. (ENG.). 2004. cd-rom & audio compact disk 14.95 (978-1-60857-135-2(1)) Grammardog.

Grammardog Guide to Huckleberry Finn. unabr. ed. Mary Jane McKinney. (ENG.). 2003. cd-rom & audio compact disk 14.95 (978-1-60857-111-6(4)) Grammardog.

Grammardog Guide to Jane Eyre. unabr. ed. Mary Jane McKinney. (ENG.). 2003. cd-rom & audio compact disk 14.95 (978-1-60857-136-9(X)) Grammardog.

Grammardog Guide to Jude the Obscure. unabr. ed. Mary Jane McKinney. (ENG.). 2008. cd-rom & audio compact disk 14.95 (978-1-60857-093-5(2)) Grammardog.

Grammardog Guide to Julius Caesar. unabr. ed. Mary Jane McKinney. (ENG.). 2005. cd-rom & audio compact disk 14.95 (978-1-60857-152-9(1)) Grammardog.

Grammardog Guide to Kidnapped. unabr. ed. Mary Jane McKinney. (ENG.). 2007. cd-rom & audio compact disk 14.95 (978-1-60857-170-3(X)) Grammardog.

Grammardog Guide to King Lear. unabr. ed. Mary Jane McKinney. (ENG.). 2005. cd-rom & audio compact disk 14.95 (978-1-60857-153-6(X)) Grammardog.

Grammardog Guide to Legend of Sleepy Hollow. unabr. ed. Mary Jane McKinney. (ENG.). 2006. cd-rom & audio compact disk 14.95 (978-1-60857-113-0(0)) Grammardog.

Grammardog Guide to Life on the Mississippi. unabr. ed. Mary Jane McKinney. (ENG.). 2006. cd-rom & audio compact disk 14.95 (978-1-60857-114-7(9)) Grammardog.

Grammardog Guide to Little Women. unabr. ed. Mary Jane McKinney. (ENG.). 2007. cd-rom & audio compact disk 14.95 (978-1-60857-176-5(9)) Grammardog.

Grammardog Guide to London Short Stories. unabr. ed. Mary Jane McKinney. (ENG.). 2006. cd-rom & audio compact disk 14.95 (978-1-60857-115-4(7)) Grammardog.

Grammardog Guide to Lord Jim. unabr. ed. Mary Jane McKinney. (ENG.). 2006. cd-rom & audio compact disk 14.95 (978-1-60857-137-6(8)) Grammardog.

Grammardog Guide to Lord of the Flies. unabr. ed. Mary Jane McKinney. (ENG.). 2003. cd-rom & audio compact disk 14.95 (978-1-60857-138-3(6)) Grammardog.

Grammardog Guide to Macbeth. unabr. ed. Mary Jane McKinney. (ENG.). 2005. cd-rom & audio compact disk 14.95 (978-1-60857-154-3(8)) Grammardog.

Grammardog Guide to Middlemarch. unabr. ed. Mary Jane McKinney. (ENG.). 2007. cd-rom & audio compact disk 14.95 (978-1-60857-166-6(1)) Grammardog.

Grammardog Guide to Moby Dick. unabr. ed. Mary Jane McKinney. (ENG.). 2003. cd-rom & audio compact disk 14.95 (978-1-60857-116-1(5)) Grammardog.

Grammardog Guide to Much Ado about Nothing. unabr. ed. Mary Jane McKinney. (ENG.). 2006. cd-rom & audio compact disk 14.95 (978-1-60857-157-4(2)) Grammardog.

Grammardog Guide to Narrative of the Life of Frederick Douglass. unabr. ed. Mary Jane McKinney. (ENG.). 2007. cd-rom & audio compact disk 14.95 (978-1-60857-165-9(3)) Grammardog.

Grammardog Guide to Nature. unabr. ed. Mary Jane McKinney. (ENG.). 2007. cd-rom & audio compact disk 14.95 (978-1-60857-173-4(4)) Grammardog.

Grammardog Guide to O. Henry Short Stories. unabr. ed. Mary Jane McKinney. (ENG.). 2005. cd-rom & audio compact disk 14.95 (978-1-60857-117-8(3)) Grammardog.

Grammardog Guide to Oliver Twist. unabr. ed. Mary Jane McKinney. (ENG.). 2006. cd-rom & audio compact disk 14.95 (978-1-60857-140-6(8)) Grammardog.

Grammardog Guide to Othello. unabr. ed. Mary Jane McKinney. (ENG.). 2005. cd-rom & audio compact disk 14.95 (978-1-60857-158-1(0)) Grammardog.

Grammardog Guide to Outcasts of Poker Flat. unabr. ed. Mary Jane McKinney. (ENG.). 2008. cd-rom & audio compact disk 14.95 (978-1-60857-097-3(5)) Grammardog.

Grammardog Guide to Poe Short Stories. unabr. ed. Mary Jane McKinney. (ENG.). 2005. cd-rom & audio compact disk 14.95 (978-1-60857-118-5(1)) Grammardog.

Grammardog Guide to Pride & Prejudice. unabr. ed. Mary Jane McKinney. (ENG.). 2004. cd-rom & audio compact disk 14.95 (978-1-60857-141-3(6)) Grammardog.

Grammardog Guide to Richard III. unabr. ed. Mary Jane McKinney. (ENG.). 2006. cd-rom & audio compact disk 14.95 (978-1-60857-159-8(9)) Grammardog.

Grammardog Guide to Rikki Tikki Tavi. unabr. ed. Mary Jane McKinney. (ENG.). 2007. cd-rom & audio compact disk 14.95 (978-1-60857-167-3(X)) Grammardog.

Grammardog Guide to Rip Van Winkle. unabr. ed. Mary Jane McKinney. (ENG.). 2007. cd-rom & audio compact disk 14.95 (978-1-60857-168-0(8)) Grammardog.

Grammardog Guide to Romeo & Juliet. unabr. ed. Mary Jane McKinney. (ENG.). 2005. cd-rom & audio compact disk 14.95 (978-1-60857-160-4(2)) Grammardog.

Grammardog Guide to Self-Reliance. unabr. ed. Mary Jane McKinney. (ENG.). 2007. cd-rom & audio compact disk 14.95 (978-1-60857-172-7(6)) Grammardog.

Grammardog Guide to Sense & Sensibility. unabr. ed. Mary Jane McKinney. (ENG.). 2007. cd-rom & audio compact disk 14.95 (978-1-60857-142-0(4)) Grammardog.

Grammardog Guide to Sherlock Holmes Stories. unabr. ed. Mary Jane McKinney. (ENG.). 2005. cd-rom & audio compact disk 14.95 (978-1-60857-143-7(2)) Grammardog.

Grammardog Guide to Tess of the D'Urbervilles. unabr. ed. Mary Jane McKinney. (ENG.). 2004. cd-rom & audio compact disk 14.95 (978-1-60857-146-8(7)) Grammardog.

Grammardog Guide to the Awakening. unabr. ed. Mary Jane McKinney. (ENG.). 2003. audio compact disk 14.95 (978-1-60857-102-4(5)) Grammardog.

Grammardog Guide to the Call of the Wild. unabr. ed. Mary Jane McKinney. (ENG.). 2004. cd-rom & audio compact disk 14.95 (978-1-60857-106-2(8)) Grammardog.

Grammardog Guide to the Comedy of Errors. unabr. ed. Mary Jane McKinney. (ENG.). 2006. cd-rom & audio compact disk 14.95 (978-1-60857-150-5(5)) Grammardog.

Grammardog Guide to the House of the Seven Gables. unabr. ed. Mary Jane McKinney. (ENG.). 2008. cd-rom & audio compact disk 14.95 (978-1-60857-094-2(0)) Grammardog.

Grammardog Guide to the Importance of Being Earnest. unabr. ed. Mary Jane McKinney. (ENG.). 2008. cd-rom & audio compact disk 14.95 (978-1-60857-096-6(7)) Grammardog.

Grammardog Guide to the Innocents Abroad. unabr. ed. Mary Jane McKinney. (ENG.). 2006. cd-rom & audio compact disk 14.95 (978-1-60857-112-3(2)) Grammardog.

Grammardog Guide to the Mayor of Casterbridge. unabr. ed. Mary Jane McKinney. (ENG.). 2005. cd-rom & audio compact disk 14.95 (978-1-60857-139-0(4)) Grammardog.

Grammardog Guide to the Merchant of Venice. unabr. ed. Mary Jane McKinney. (ENG.). 2005. cd-rom & audio compact disk 14.95 (978-1-60857-155-0(6)) Grammardog.

Grammardog Guide to the Picture of Dorian Gray. unabr. ed. Mary Jane McKinney. (ENG.). 2006. cd-rom & audio compact disk 14.95 (978-1-60857-099-7(1)) Grammardog.

Grammardog Guide to the Prince & the Pauper. unabr. ed. Mary Jane McKinney. (ENG.). 2005. cd-rom & audio compact disk 14.95 (978-1-60857-119-2(X)) Grammardog.

Grammardog Guide to the Red Badge of Courage. unabr. ed. Mary Jane McKinney. (ENG.). 2003. cd-rom & audio compact disk 14.95 (978-1-60857-120-8(3)) Grammardog.

Grammardog Guide to the Rime of the Ancient Mariner. unabr. ed. Mary Jane McKinney. (ENG.). 2008. cd-rom & audio compact disk 14.95 (978-1-60857-177-2(7)) Grammardog.

Grammardog Guide to the Rocking-Horse Winner. unabr. ed. Mary Jane McKinney. (ENG.). 2008. cd-rom & audio compact disk 14.95 (978-1-60857-092-8(4)) Grammardog.

Grammardog Guide to the Scarlet Letter. unabr. ed. Mary Jane McKinney. (ENG.). 2003. cd-rom & audio compact disk 14.95 (978-1-60857-121-5(1)) Grammardog.

Grammardog Guide to the Secret Garden. unabr. ed. Mary Jane McKinney. (ENG.). 2007. cd-rom & audio compact disk 14.95 (978-1-60857-178-9(5)) Grammardog.

Grammardog Guide to the Song of Myself. unabr. ed. Mary Jane McKinney. (ENG.). 2008. cd-rom & audio compact disk 14.95 (978-1-60857-091-1(6)) Grammardog.

Grammardog Guide to the Taming of the Shrew. unabr. ed. Mary Jane McKinney. (ENG.). 2006. cd-rom & audio compact disk 14.95 (978-1-60857-161-1(0)) Grammardog.

Grammardog Guide to the Tempest. unabr. ed. Mary Jane McKinney. (ENG.). 2005. cd-rom & audio compact disk 14.95 (978-1-60857-162-8(9)) Grammardog.

Grammardog Guide to Tom Sawyer. unabr. ed. Mary Jane McKinney. (ENG.). 2004. cd-rom & audio compact disk 14.95 (978-1-60857-122-2(X)) Grammardog.

Grammardog Guide to Treasure Island. unabr. ed. Mary Jane McKinney. (ENG.). 2004. cd-rom & audio compact disk 14.95 (978-1-60857-147-5(5)) Grammardog.

Grammardog Guide to Twain Short Stories. unabr. ed. Mary Jane McKinney. (ENG.). 2005. cd-rom & audio compact disk 14.95 (978-1-60857-123-9(8)) Grammardog.

Grammardog Guide to Twelfth Night. unabr. ed. Mary Jane McKinney. (ENG.). 2006. cd-rom & audio compact disk 14.95 (978-1-60857-163-5(7)) Grammardog.

Grammardog Guide to Uncle Tom's Cabin. unabr. ed. Mary Jane McKinney. (ENG.). 2006. cd-rom & audio compact disk 14.95 (978-1-60857-124-6(6)) Grammardog.

Grammardog Guide to up from Slavery. unabr. ed. Mary Jane McKinney. (ENG.). 2007. cd-rom & audio compact disk 14.95 (978-1-60857-095-9(9)) Grammardog.

Grammardog Guide to Walden. unabr. ed. Mary Jane McKinney. (ENG.). 2007. cd-rom & audio compact disk 14.95 (978-1-60857-174-1(2)) Grammardog.

Grammardog Guide to White Fang. unabr. ed. Mary Jane McKinney. (ENG.). 2004. cd-rom & audio compact disk 14.95 (978-1-60857-125-3(4)) Grammardog.

Grammardog Guide to Wuthering Heights. unabr. ed. Mary Jane McKinney. (ENG.). 2003. cd-rom & audio compact disk 14.95 (978-1-60857-148-2(3)) Grammardog.

***Grammarifics: Teaches the Parts of Speech.** (ENG., (J). 2006. audio compact disk 189.00 (978-1-55576-390-9(1)) EDCON Pubng.

Grammie Stories Vol. 1: True Stories about People Living in the Real World. unabr. ed. Margot S. Biestman. Illus. by Margot S. Biestman. Ed. by Alice Boatwright. Music by Jeff Wessman. Contrib. by Lou Judson. 1 cass. (Running Time: 1 hr.). Dramatization. (ENG.). (J). (gr. k-6). 1993. pap. bk. 7.95 (978-0-936865-09-6(1)) Pergot Pr.
Side A: Margot invents a plan to keep herself out of trouble - instead of pestering adults to gain attention. Side B - Margot discovers that her cruelty leads to being bullied. By trying to be "cool" (or someone she isn't), she has failed herself.

Grammie Stories Vol. 2: Grammie at School. unabr. ed. Margot S. Biestman. Contrib. by Alice Boatwright et al. 2 cass. Dramatization. (J). (gr. k-6). 1993. 23.00 Set.; 12.00 ea. Pergot Pr.
Tape 1: Grammie & Miss Kennedy's School, Grammie & Ruthwood - Until Something Awful Happened. Tape 2: Grammie & the Fire, Grammie, Shyness, & I'll-Do-It-When-(& If)-I'm Ready.

Grammie Stories - When Grammie Was Little. unabr. ed. Alice Boatwright & Margot S. Biestman. Music by Jeff Wessman. Contrib. by Lou Judson. 2 cass. (Running Time: 1 hr. per cass.). Dramatization. (J). (gr. k-6). 1992. 15.00 Set. (978-0-936865-08-9(3)) Pergot Pr.
An author/teacher offers insights into family & school behavior through real life stories for children from 3-93. Each story has an important message of caring & respect for feelings & experiences we have all shared. Develops self-esteem, promotes mutual sharing of values between generations, & stimulates problem-solving.

Grammie Stories - When Grammie Was Little Vol. 2: Grammie & the Rosebud Fairy; Grammie & Good Times with Her Mother. unabr. ed. Margot S. Biestman. Illus. by Margot S. Biestman. Ed. by Alice Boatwright. Music by Jeff Wessman. Contrib. by Lou Judson. 1 cass. (Running Time: 1 hr.). Dramatization. (J). (gr. k-6). 1992. pap. bk. 7.95 (978-0-936865-10-2(5)) Pergot Pr.
Side A: Margot relishes her adventures with an imaginary friend, who keeps her from feeling lonely. Side B: Margot finds joy when her mother spends special time alone with her, sharing simple pleasures.

***Grammr in Cntxt Bk 2 4e-Aud CD.** 4th ed. Sandra N. Elbaum. (C). 2005. audio compact disk 90.95 (978-1-4130-0745-9(7)) Pub: Heinle. Dist(s): CENGAGE Learn

***Grammr in Cntxt Bk 3 4e-Aud CD.** 4th ed. Sandra N. Elbaum. (C). 2005. audio compact disk 115.95 (978-1-4130-0749-7(X)) Pub: Heinle. Dist(s): CENGAGE Learn

***Grammr in Cntxt Bk 3 4e-Tape.** 4th ed. ELBAUM. (C). 2005. 115.95 (978-1-4130-0820-3(8)) Pub: Heinle. Dist(s): CENGAGE Learn

Gran Gatsby. abr. ed. F. Scott Fitzgerald. Read by Hernando Iván Cano. 3 CDs.Tr. of Great Gatsby. (SPA.). 2003. audio compact disk 17.00 (978-958-43-0197-0(7)) YoYoMusic.

Grand Adventure. Chuck Missler. 2 cass. (Running Time: 2.5 hours +). (Briefing Packages by Chuck Missler). 1992. vinyl bd. 14.95 Incl. notes . (978-1-880532-73-7(5)) Koinonia Hse.
Come on the journey of discovery between the miracle of our origin and the mystery of our destiny. Why should we take the Bible seriously? And what does it mean to take it seriously?All creation seems to proclaim the existence of a creator.From the fine-tuned environment in which we live to recent discoveries in biochemistry, scientists all around the world are frantically searching for new answers where the traditional theories have failed.Missler's unique perspective will bring new and provocative insights that will inspire a breath-taking excitement for the adventure of our destiny.

Grand Adventure. Chuck Missler. 2 CD's. (Running Time: 120 mins.). (Briefing Packages by Chuck Missler). 1995. audio compact disk 19.95 (978-1-57821-306-1(1)) Koinonia Hse.

Grand Army of the Republic: Civil War Veterans, Department of Massachusetts, 1866-1947. Compiled by A. Dean Sargent. 2002. audio compact disk 25.00 (978-0-7884-2130-3(1)) Heritage Bk.

Grand Benediction: Jude 22-25. Ed Young. 1989. 4.95 (978-0-7417-1745-0(X), 745) Win Walk.

Grand Canyon. Donald Davis. (Running Time: 49 mins.). 2005. audio compact disk 14.95 (978-0-87483-739-1(1)) Pub: August Hse. Dist(s): Natl Bk Netwk

Grand Canyon. unabr. ed. Gary McCarthy. Read by Gene Engene. 12 cass. (Running Time: 17 hrs.). 1996. 64.95 (978-1-55686-706-4(9)) Books in Motion.
Here is the bold adventure story of William Dunn, an educated & achieved mountain man, whose life becomes forever entertwined with the wild, unforgettable Grand Canyon.

Grand Canyon: Gem of the Southwest. unabr. ed. Drew Cozby. Read by Drew Cozby. 1 cass. (Running Time: 1 hr. 08 min.). (Audio Tour Ser.). 1999. bk. (978-1-928677-00-0(2)) Yaki Point Prods.
General information about the canyon & surrounding area: history, geology, ecology, weather, etc.

Grand Canyon East Tour. 2004. audio compact disk (978-0-9755800-1-1(9)) Waypoint Tours.

Grand Canyon Village & West Tour. 2004. audio compact disk (978-0-9755800-0-4(0)) Waypoint Tours.

Grand Canyon's East Rim Drive: Walkabout Audio Tours. Patrick T. Houlihan & Betsy Houlihan. 1 cass. (Running Time: 1 hr.). 2000. 9.00 (978-1-931544-17-7(4)) Walkabout Audio.
A description of the views from the overlooks on the East Rim Drive (Desert View Drive). Also a discussion of geology, prehistory, measuring the Grand Canyon by reaches & river miles & many of the historic people who played a part in the history of the Grand Canyon, from Spanish Explorers to contemporaries.

Grand Canyon's East Rim Drive - Eastbound: Desert View Drive - Walkabout Audio Tours. Patrick T. Houlihan & Betsy Houlihan. 1 CD. (Running Time: 1 hr). 2000. audio compact disk 16.00 (978-1-931544-19-1(0)) Walkabout Audio.

Grand Canyon's East Rim Drive - Westbound: Desert View Drive - Walkabout Audio Tours. Patrick T. Houlihan & Betsy Houlihan. 1 CD. (Running Time: 1 hr). 2000. audio compact disk 16.00 (978-1-931544-18-4(2)) Walkabout Audio.

Grand Canyon's Historic Village: Walkabout Audio Tours. Patrick T. Houlihan & Betsy Houlihan. 1 cass. (Running Time: 1 hr). 2000. 9.00 (978-1-931544-14-6(X)); audio compact disk 16.00 (978-1-931544-13-9(1)) Walkabout Audio.
A walking tour of historic Grand Canyon Village. Also a discussion of buildings, architecture, historic characters of the village & the art that remains in the buildings of the village.

Grand Canyon's West Rim Drive: Walkabout Audio Tours. Patrick T. Houlihan & Betsy Houlihan. 1 cass. (Running Time: 1 hr). 2000. 9.00 (978-1-931544-16-0(6)); audio compact disk 16.00 (978-1-931544-15-3(8)) Walkabout Audio.
A description from the overlooks on the West Rim Drive on the South Rim of the Grand Canyon. Also a discussion of the geology, history of mining at the canyon, the story of Bright Angel Trail & the history of the Houasupai Indians who live within the canyon.

Grand Central Station & The Great Gildersleeve: "Miracle for Christmas" & "Why the Chimes Rang" unabr. ed. 1 cass. (Running Time: 60 min.). Dramatization. 7.95 Norelco box. (DD-5560) Natl Recrd Co.
Miracle for Christmas: From New York...Pillsbury's best enriched flour brings you...Grand Central Station! A traditional Christmas play about the mysterious appearance of Dr. Mason, thought to be killed in an accident, & Mac, an ambulance driver, who learns the true meaning of Christmas. You could shed a tear or two in this drama you will long remember. Gaylan Drake is the announcer. Why the Chimes Rang starring Harold Peary: With LeRoy, Marjorie, Birdie, the Judge, & Peavy. Gildy wants to impress his girlfriend with an expensive Christmas gift. He calls on her at the Children's Hospital & reads a story to the children. He learns an "impressive" story himself. Poignant presentation! Sponsored by Kraft Foods & broadcast December 14, 1949.

Grand Design. abr. unabr. ed. Stephen W. Hawking & Leonard Mlodinow. Read by Steve West. (ENG.). 2010. audio compact disk 30.00 (978-0-7393-4426-2(9), Random AudioBks) Pub: Random Audio Pubg. Dist(s): Random

Grand Entertainment: Colonial Williamsburg Celebrates Christmas. 1 CD. (Running Time: 1 hr.). 2003. audio compact disk 17.95 (978-1-931592-00-0(4)) Colonial Williamsburg.
Since the first organized Christmas celebration drew visitors to Colonial Williamsburg in 1936, nothing quite matches the beauty, imagination, excitement, pageantry, sights, smells, sounds, and grandeur of the Christmas season in Colonial Williamsburg. "A Grand Entertainment" brings the magic sounds of Christmas in Colonial Williamsburg to life. From the refined notes of classic pieces played on period instruments to the rich voices raised in songs remembered from Christmases long ago, and the frivolity of a tavern balladeer, listeners are carried away to a season of Grand Entertainment in Colonial Williamsburg. This recording includes performances by The Governor's Musick, The Fifes and Drums of Colonial Williamsburg, The Choir of the College of William & Mary, The William & Mary Botetourt Chamber Singers, Lee Welch, The Colonial Williamsburg Carolers and Rex Ellis.

Grand Expectations Pt. 1: The United States, 1945-1974. collector's ed. James T. Patterson. Read by Bill Kelsey. 13 cass. (Running Time: 19 hrs. 30 min.). 1997. 104.00 (978-0-7366-3728-2(1)) Books on Tape.
A dramatic & brilliant account of the period from the end of World War II in 1945 to the resignation of Richard Nixon in 1974. In the late-forties, America enjoyed the greatest prosperity that the world had ever known. From this boom came a national euphoria that led to an unprecedented faith in government & the American Dream, a feeling that no expectation was too grand. But this optimistic spirit would be shaken by the events of the 60s & early 70s, the assassinations of the Kennedys & Martin Luther King, the debacle in Vietnam & the scandal of Watergate.

Grand Expectations Pt. 2: The United States, 1945-1974. collector's ed. James T. Patterson. Read by Bill Kelsey. 12 cass. (Running Time: 18 hrs.). 1997. 96.00 (978-0-7366-3729-9(X)) Books on Tape.

***Grand Finale.** unabr. ed. Janet Evanovich. Read by C. J. Critt. (ENG.). 2009. (978-0-06-125743-8(5), Harper Audio); (978-0-06-125742-1(7), Harper Audio) HarperCollins Pubs.

Grand Finale. unabr. ed. Janet Evanovich. 2009. audio compact disk 14.99 (978-0-06-073698-9(4), Harper Audio) HarperCollins Pubs.

Grand Finale: Encourage Yourself. Contrib. by Donald Lawrence and the Tri-City Singers. 2007. 14.99 (978-5-557-56873-9(5)) Pt of Grace Ent.

Grand Finale: Encourage Yourself. Contrib. by Donald Lawrence. 2007. 14.99 (978-5-557-51654-9(9)) Pt of Grace Ent.

Grand Hotel see Theatre Highlights

Grand Hymns of the Faith. Contrib. by Kenon D. Renfrow. (Sacred Performer Collections Ser.). (ENG.). 2003. audio compact disk 9.95 (978-0-7390-3064-6(7)) Alfred Pub.

Grand Junction: Barriers to Quality (Follow-Up to General Session) unabr. ed. Innovation Groups Staff. 1 cass. (Running Time: 1 hrs. 30 min.). (Transforming Local Government Ser.: Vol. 14). 1999. 10.00 (978-1-882403-70-7(3), IG9914) Alliance Innov.

Grand Jury, Pt. 1. unabr. ed. Philip Friedman. Read by Jonathan Reese. 10 cass. (Running Time: 15 hrs.). 1996. 80.00 (978-0-7366-3535-6(1), 4180-A) Books on Tape.
Susan Linwood & David Clark are strangers when they're sworn in as members of the Grand Jury, the only secret proceedings in American jurisprudence.

Grand Jury, Pt. 2. Philip Friedman. Read by Jonathan Reese. 8 cass. (Running Time: 12 hrs.). 1996. 64.00 (4180-B) Books on Tape.
Two members of a Grand Jury launch a dangerous investigation when the facts of a case don't add up. Gritty and complex.

Grand Jury Practice. 1986. bk. 55.00; 35.00 PA Bar Inst.

Grand Meaulnes. Alain-Fournier. Read by Michael Maloney. 6 vols. (Running Time: 9 hrs.). 2003. 54.95 (978-0-7540-0956-6(4)) Pub: Chivers Audio Bks GBR. Dist(s): AudioGO

Grand Meaulnes. Alain-Fournier. pap. bk. 21.95 (978-88-7754-838-2(X)) Pub: Cideb ITA. Dist(s): Distribks Inc

Grand Old Duke of York. unabr. ed. Maureen Roffey & Bernard Lodge. Read by Brownie Macintosh & Julie Thompson. 1 cass. (Running Time: 6 min.). (J). (gr. k-4). 1994. pap. bk. 17.90 (978-0-8045-6766-4(2), 6766) Spoken Arts.
Singalong.

Grand Passion. Jayne Ann Krentz. Narrated by Richard Ferrone. 9 cass. (Running Time: 11 hrs. 45 mins.). 71.00 (978-1-4025-2526-1(5)); audio compact disk 111.00 (978-1-4025-3074-6(9)) Recorded Bks.

Grand Passion. Jayne Ann Krentz. 2004. 10.95 (978-0-7435-4794-9(2)) Pub: S&S Audio. Dist(s): S and S Inc

Grand Passion. Perf. by John Tesh. 1 cass., 1 CD. 8.78 (GTS 9804); audio compact disk 13.58 CD Jewel box. (GTS 9804) NewSound.

Grand Passion. unabr. ed. Jayne Ann Krentz. Read by Mary Peiffer. 8 cass. (Running Time: 12 hrs.). 1994. 64.00 (978-0-7366-3447-2(9), 4091) Books on Tape.
Cleo Robbins sees the man of her dreams, but they don't click. His help when danger strikes puts them on the same track.

***Grand Pursuit.** unabr. ed. Sylvia Nasar. (Running Time: 17 hrs. 0 mins. 0 sec.). (ENG.). 2011. audio compact disk 49.99 (978-1-4423-4014-5(2)) Pub: S&S Audio. Dist(s): S and S Inc

Grand Slam. unabr. ed. Susan Moody. Read by Julia Franklin. 8 cass. (Running Time: 10 hrs. 35 min.). 1998. 83.95 Set. (978-1-85903-229-9(X)) Pub: Magna Story GBR. Dist(s): Ulverscroft US
Who killed Lady Portia Wickham? Although the two women have never met, Cassie Swann feels an instant rapport with the sensual Portia after briefly seeing her portrait during an evening of bridge-playing at Halkam Court. But why was Portia Wickham walking up her own drive in the rain, after midnight? How did the murderer know she would be there? It is the arrest of Lady Wickham's young butler, Jamie, which forces Cassie to seek out the real killer - plunging herself into extreme danger.

Grand Slam: Bobby Jones, America & the Story of Golf. Mark Frost. Read by Grover Gardner. 14 cass. (Running Time: 19 hrs.). 2004. 99.95 (978-0-7861-2925-6(5), 3403) Blckstn Audio.

Grand Slam: Bobby Jones, America, & the Story of Golf. unabr. ed. Mark Frost. Read by Grover Gardner. 16 CDs. (Running Time: 19 hrs.). 2000. audio compact disk 120.00 (978-0-7861-8191-9(5), 3403) Blckstn Audio.

Grand Slam into Murder: A Kate Morlan Mystery. Christine Davis. Read by Christine Davis. 2 cass. (Running Time: 2 hrs.). 1987. 9.95 (978-0-938451-03-7(0)) Selena Pr.
A lakeshore country house... a weekend bridge party... & murder.

Grand Sophy. unabr. ed. Georgette Heyer. Read by John Westbrook. 10 cass. (Running Time: 12 hrs.). (Isis Ser.). (J). 2001. 84.95 (978-1-85089-736-1(0), 90045) Pub: ISIS Lrg Prnt GBR. Dist(s): Ulverscroft US

Grand Staff-Capers: A Musical Voyage Through the Lines & Spaces. Composed by Cynthia Pace. 2008. pap. bk. 10.95 (978-1-4234-4224-0(5), 1423442245) H Leonard.

Grand Sweep: 365 Days from Genesis Through Revelation - A Bible Study for Individuals & Groups. J. Ellsworth Kalas. Orig. Title: Three Hundred Sixty Five Days from Genesis Through Revelation. 1997. stu. ed. 100.00 (978-0-687-01861-1(7)) Abingdon.

Grand Teton National Park: Circle Tour. 1 cass. (Running Time: 90 min.). (Guided Auto Tape Tour). 12.95 (P2); Comp Comms Inc.

Grand Tu Seras Grand. Matt Maxwell. 1 cass. 12.95 (978-0-8442-1434-4(5), Natl Textbk Co) M-H Contemporary.
Features upbeat songs to help young students expands their knowledge of French.

Grand Weaver: How God Shapes Us Through the Events of Our Lives. unabr. ed. Ravi Zacharias. Read by Ravi Zacharias. (Running Time: 6 hrs. 0 mins. 0 sec.). (ENG.). 2007. audio compact disk 24.99 (978-0-310-26953-3(9)) Zondervan.

Grand Weaver: Why Are You the Way You Are? unabr. ed. Ravi Zacharias. (Running Time: 6 hrs. 0 mins. 0 sec.). (ENG.). 2007. 12.99 (978-0-310-26954-0(7)) Zondervan.

***Grandaunt Tiger (Chinese/English)** (CHI & ENG.). audio compact disk 9.95 (978-957-747-255-7(9)) Pub: Grimm Pr TWN. Dist(s): Chinasprout

***¿Grande o pequeño? Audio CD.** Francisco Blane. Adapted by Benchmark Education Company, LLC. (My First Reader's Theater Ser.). (SPA.). (J). 2009. audio compact disk 10.00 (978-1-935470-63-2(9)) Benchmark Educ.

Grandees, unabr. collector's ed. Stephen Birmingham. Read by Jonathan Reese. 9 cass. (Running Time: 13 hrs. 30 min.). 1993. 72.00 (978-0-7366-2334-6(5), 3113) Books on Tape.
The Jewish Sephardim made their mark in the United States in trade & banking, & closed ranks to form a durable aristocracy.

Grandes Esperanzas. abr. ed. Charles Dickens. Read by Daniel Quintero. 3 CDs.Tr. of Great Expectations. (SPA.). 2003. audio compact disk 17.00 (978-958-8218-25-0(X)) YoYoMusic.

Grandes Historias de Antiquo Testamento: Great Stories of Great Lives from the Old Testament. Charles R. Swindoll. (SPA.). 2007. audio compact disk 30.00 (978-1-57972-784-0(9)) Insight Living.

Grandes Son Tu Maravillas. unabr. ed. Witt & Murrell. (SPA.). 1999. 7.99 (978-0-8297-2505-6(9)) Pub: Vida Pubs. Dist(s): Zondervan

Grandfather. Tom Brown, Jr.. Narrated by Tom Brown, Jr. Music by Karl Direske. (ENG.). 2007. 24.95i (978-1-60326-003-9(X)); audio compact disk 44.95i (978-1-60326-002-2(1)) Tracker Pubng.

Grandfather's Clock see Favorite American Poems

Grandfather's Greatest Hits. Perf. by David Holt et al. 1 cass. (Running Time: 32 min.). 1992. 9.98 (978-0-942303-26-1(1), HW1251) Pub: High Windy Audio. Dist(s): August Hse
In the right hands, old songs like "John Henry," "Dixie," & "Wreck of the Old 97" sound as fresh & dynamic today as they did on the original 78s. Holt has provided extensive liner notes revealing new information about the histories of the 14 songs provided here. Grammy nominee.

Grandfather's Greatest Hits. Perf. by David Holt et al. 1 cass. (Running Time: 32 min.). 1992. audio compact disk 15.98 (978-0-942303-27-8(X)) Pub: High Windy Audio. Dist(s): August Hse

Grandfather's Journey. Allen Say. Narrated by B. D. Wong. (J). (gr. k-5). 2009. bk. 29.95 (978-0-545-10696-2(6)); pap. bk. 18.95 (978-0-545-12708-0(4)); audio compact disk 12.95 (978-0-545-10694-8(X)) Weston Woods.

Grandma Jasmine: The Gifts of Musical Stories. unabr. ed. Silvia Silk. Read by Silvia Silk. 1 cass. (Running Time: 0 hr. 44 min.). Orig. Title: My Friendly Snowman. (J). (ps-3). 1993. 10.99 (978-0-938861-05-8(0), 10007) Jasmine Texts.
Five stories that include a song with each story. Also music for social development skills.

Grandma Loves You. Ed. by Publications International Staff. (J). 2007. audio compact disk 3.98 (978-1-4127-3906-1(3)) Pubns Intl Ltd.

Grandma Moses - The Art World's Senior Citizen. Weiss Kelly. 1 cass. 8.95 (193) Am Fed Astrologers.
An AFA Convention workshop tape.

Grandma Slid down the Mountain. Perf. by Cathy Fink. 1 cass. (Running Time: 38 min.). (Family Ser.). (J). 1984. 9.98 (8010); audio compact disk 14.98 (8010) Rounder Records.
Cathy Fink's first not-for-kids only album became an industry standard & continues to please kids & adults alike & was applauded in many "BEST" lists.

Grandmas & Mothers-in-Law: On to the Next Thing. Nancy Wilson. (ENG.). 2008. audio compact disk 20.00 (978-1-59128-227-3(6)) Canon Pr ID.

Grandma's Boy. unabr. ed. Donald Davis. 1 cass. (Running Time: 58 mins.). (American Storytelling Ser.). (gr. 3 up). 1999. 12.00 (978-0-87483-582-3(8)) Pub: August Hse. Dist(s): Natl Bk Netwk
Grandma's house was a magical place. The author paints the picture & we follow with images stored from personal experience.

Grandma's Lap Stories. Donald Davis. (Running Time: 57 mins.). 1997. audio compact disk 14.95 (978-0-87483-752-0(9)) Pub: August Hse. Dist(s): Natl Bk Netwk

Grandma's Lap Stories. Read by Donald Davis. 1 cass. (Running Time: 53 min.). (ps-2). 1997. 12.00 (978-0-87483-431-4(7)) Pub: August Hse. Dist(s): Natl Bk Netwk
Stories for young children retold from the Appalachian oral tradition.

Grandma's Patchquilt Quilt: A Children's Sampler. Prod. by Phil Rosenthal. 1 cass. (Running Time: 30 min.). (J). (ps-4). 1987. 9.98 (978-1-879305-02-1(X)) Am Melody.
A delightful musical patchwork of children's songs performed by some of America's finest folk artists. Parents' Choice Award recording.

Grandma's Patchwork Quilt. 1 CD. (Running Time: 34 min.). 2003. audio compact disk 9.98 (978-1-879305-34-2(8)) Am Melody.

Grandmother in Heaven see Philip Levine

Grandmother Moon: Hindu & Indian. Elizabeth Gauerke. 1 cass. 7.95 (399) Am Fed Astrologers.
Moon eclipses & nodes to predict.

Grandmother of Time: A Woman's Book of Celebrations, Spells & Sacred Objects for Every Month of the Year. Zsuzsanna E. Budapest. Read by Zsuzsanna E. Budapest. 1 cass. (Running Time: 60 min.). 1990. 9.95 HarperCollins Pubs.

***Grandmothers: Heart to Heart Encouragement.** unabr. ed. Rebecca Barlow Jordan. (Running Time: 3 hrs. 28 mins. 0 sec.). (Day-Votionsâ,¢ Ser.). (ENG.). 2010. 13.99 (978-0-310-39566-9(6)) Zondervan.

Grandmothers' Stories: Wise Woman Tales from Many Cultures. Burleigh Muten. Narrated by Olympia Dukakis. 2 CDs. (Running Time: 1 hr. 29 mins. 41 sec.). (J). (gr. 1-4). 2001. audio compact disk 19.99 (978-1-84148-419-8(9)) BarefootBksMA.
Stories from all over the world which portray strong female figures who are resourceful and shrewd, but also full of warmth and kindness.

Grandpa, Grandpa. Joy Cowley. 1 read-along cass. (J). 1986. 5.95 incl. bk. (978-0-86867-045-4(6)) Wright Group.
Rhyme & repetition emphasized. About a child who wants to go fishing with Grandpa. This story also teaches one, two, three.

Grandpa Grumpy Pants Audio Book. Cullen Porter. (ENG.). (J). 2008. audio compact disk 12.95 (978-1-932278-51-4(6)) Pub: Mayhaven Pub. Dist(s): Baker Taylor

Grandpa Sings-Alone Favorite Tales. Duncan Sings-Alone. 1 cass. (Running Time: 54 mins.). (J). 2000. 11.95 (978-1-929590-03-2(2)) Two Canoes.
Traditional native American tales & legends told by master storyteller & cherokee elder, Duncan Sings-Alone.

Grandpa Sings-Alone's Favorite Tales. Duncan Sings-Alone. 1 CD. (Running Time: 54 mins.). (J). 2000. 16.95 (978-1-929590-02-5(4)) Two Canoes.
Traditional Native American tales & legends told by master storyteller & Cherokee elder, Duncan Sings-Alone.

Grandparent-Grandchild Relationship. Lois Khan. Read by Lois Khan. 1 cass. (Running Time: 90 min.). 1988. 10.95 (978-0-7822-0431-5(7), 309-6) C G Jung IL.

Grandparenting in a Changing World. Eda J. LeShan. Narrated by Barbara Caruso. 6 CDs. (Running Time: 6 hrs. 30 mins.). 2000. audio compact disk 58.00 (978-0-7887-4773-1(8), C1264E7) Recorded Bks.
Guides today's baffled grandparents through the challenges they face with their grandchildren. Explores the special demands of teenage grandchildren, visitation rights, resolving conflicts & more.

Grandparenting in a Changing World, unabr. ed. Eda J. LeShan. Narrated by Barbara Caruso. 5 cass. (Running Time: 6 hrs. 30 mins.). 2000. 44.00 (978-0-7887-4062-6(8), 96162E7) Recorded Bks.

Grandparents Are Special. Text by Allyson Rothburd. 1 cass. (gr. 3-8). 2001. 6.00 (978-0-86647-142-8(1)) Pro Lingua.

Grandparents Are Special. Allyson Rothburd. 1 CD. (gr. 3-8). 2005. pap. bk. & tchr. ed. 24.00 (978-0-86647-220-3(7)) Pro Lingua.

Grandparents Are Special. Allyson Rothburd. 1 CD. (gr. 3-8). 2005. pap. bk. & stu. ed. 19.00 (978-0-86647-221-0(5)); audio compact disk 15.00 (978-0-86647-219-7(3)) Pro Lingua.

Grandparents from "Life Studies" see Twentieth-Century Poetry in English, No. 32-33, Recordings of Poets Reading Their Own Poetry

Grandpa's Hat. unabr. ed. Ben B. Boothe. Read by Ben B. Boothe. Ed. by Paulette Boothe. 1 cass. (Running Time: 1 hr.). (J). (gr. 6 up). 1991. 8.95 (978-1-878162-01-4(2)) Unicorn Pr USA.
Unique stories from heartland America. Witty, humorous, & heartwarming stories conveying traditional values from the history of America...inspirational...motivational.

Grandpa's Secret. Barbara Davoll & Dennis Hockerman. 1 cass. (Christopher Churchmouse Ser.). (J). (ps-2). 1993. 11.99 (3-0002) David C Cook.

Grandpa's Storybook Collection/Audio CD: And the Winner Is. As told by Jamie Moore. Illus. by Adam Murray. (ENG.). (J). 2008. audio compact disk 9.99 (978-1-935282-00-6(X)) Pot Heights.

Grands Moments de l'Athenee. Louis Jouvet. 1 CD. (FRE.). 1995. 29.95 (1364-AD) Olivia & Hill.
Louis Jouvet dies in 1951 in his dressingroom at the Theatre de l'Athenee in Paris. A devilish look, a great stature, a voice that could be recognized instantly. This prize-winning record enables us to hear Jouvet in his most famous roles.

Granite & Cypress see Poetry of Robinson Jeffers

Granny. Brendan O'Carroll. Read by Donada Peters. 2000. 32.00 (978-0-7366-5518-7(2)) Books on Tape.

Granny. unabr. ed. Brendan O'Carroll. Read by Donada Peters. 4 cass. (Running Time: 6 hrs.). 2000. 24.95 (978-0-7366-5716-7(9)) Books on Tape.
The final installment of the Agnes Browne saga follows the Dublin widow & her brood all the way to Agnes' happy end.

Granny & the Desperadoes. unabr. ed. Peggy Parish. Narrated by C. J. Critt. 1 cass. (Running Time: 15 mins.). (gr. k up). 1998. 10.00 (978-0-7887-2623-1(4), 95627E7) Recorded Bks.
Granny Guntry's apple pie is stolen & she finds the culprits eating the pie in the woods. Although they are infamous desperadoes, Granny has no fear & puts them to work doing chores.

Granny Awards: SoundTrax. Janet Gardner. (ENG.). 1997. audio compact disk 59.95 (978-0-7390-2738-7(7)) Alfred Pub.

Granny Dan. Danielle Steel. Read by Patrice Donnell & Lewis Arlt. 4 cass. (Running Time: 6 hrs.). 1999. 24.95 (4986) Books on Tape.
A simple box, filled with mementos from a grandmother, offers the greatest legacy of all: an unexpected gift of a life transformed.

Granny Dan. unabr. ed. Danielle Steel. Read by Patrice Donnell & Lewis Arlt. 4 cass. (Running Time: 6 hrs.). 1999. 29.95 (978-0-7366-4579-9(9), 4986) Books on Tape.
She was the cherished grandmother who sang songs in Russian, loved to roller-skate, and spoke little of her past. But when granny Dan died, all that remained was a box wrapped in brown paper, tied with string. Inside, an old pair of satin toe shoes, a gold locker, and a stack of letters tied with ribbon. it was her legacy, her secret past, waiting to be discovered by the granddaughter who loved her but never really knew her. it was a story waiting to be told.

Granny Dan. unabr. ed. Danielle Steel. Read by Patrice Donnell & Lewis Arlt. 8 cass., 5 CDs. (Running Time: 12 hrs.). 1999. (Random AudioBks) Random Audio Pubg.
A simple box filled with mementos from a grandmother offers the greatest legacy of all: an unexpected gift of a life transformed, a long-forgotten history of youth & beauty, love & dreams.

Granny Dan, Set. unabr. ed. Danielle Steel. 4 cass. 1999. 25.00 (FS9-43432) Highsmith.

Granny Groggin. Jill Eggleton. (Sails Literacy Ser.). (gr. 3 up). 10.00 (978-0-7578-6992-1(0)) Rigby Educ.

Granny Nothing. Catherine MacPhail. Read by Sophie Aldred. 3 CDs. (J). (ps-3). 2005. DVD, audio compact disk, audio compact disk 29.95 (978-0-7540-6676-7(2), Chivers Child Audio) AudioGO.

Granny Nothing & the Shrunken Head. Catherine MacPhail. 3 CDs. 2005. audio compact disk 29.95 (978-0-7540-6711-5(4), Chivers Child Audio) AudioGO.

Granny Project. unabr. ed. Anne Fine. Read by Christian Rodska. 3 CDs. (Running Time: 3 hrs. 45 mins.). (J). (gr. 4-6). 2007. audio compact disk 29.95 (978-1-4056-5734-1(0), Chivers Child Audio) AudioGO.

***Granny Torrelli Makes Soup.** unabr. ed. Sharon Creech. Read by Donna Murphy. (ENG.). 2005. (978-0-06-085017-3(5)); (978-0-06-085016-6(7)) HarperCollins Pubs.

Granny Torrelli Makes Soup. unabr. ed. Sharon Creech. Read by Donna Murphy. (J). 2008. 34.99 (978-1-60514-641-6(2)) Find a World.

Granny Torrelli Makes Soup. unabr. ed. Sharon Creech. Read by Donna Murphy. (Running Time: 9000 sec.). (J). (gr. 4-7). 2005. audio compact disk 17.95 (978-0-06-112212-5(2), HarperChildAud) HarperCollins Pubs.

Granny Was a Buffer Girl. Berlie Doherty. (J). 1988. 27.95 (978-0-8161-7771-4(6), Macmillan Ref) Gale.

Grannyman. Judy Schachner. Read by John McDonough. 1 cass. (Running Time: 15 mins.). (YA). 1999. stu. ed. 178.20 (978-0-7887-3669-8(8), 46972) Recorded Bks.
Ever since Simon was a kitten, he has helped out around the house, playing with the babies. But now he is old. He feels tired & useless. Can his family help him find a reason to go on?.

Grannyman. unabr. ed. Judy Schachner. Narrated by John McDonough. 1 cass. (Running Time: 15 mins.). (gr. k up). 2000. 10.00 (978-0-7887-3508-0(X), 95902E7) Recorded Bks.

Grannyman. unabr. ed. Judy Schachner. Read by John McDonough. 1 cass. (Running Time: 15 mins.). (YA). 2000. pap. bk. 32.99 (978-0-7887-3640-7(X), 41005X4) Recorded Bks.

Granny's Wonderful Chair. unabr. ed. Frances Browne. Narrated by Flo Gibson. 3 cass. (Running Time: 3 hrs. 18 min.). (J). (gr. 1-6). 2003. 24.95 (978-1-55685-674-7(1),) Audio Bk Con.
Fairy-story book including: "The Christmas Cuckoo", "The Lords of the White & Grey Castles", "The Greedy Shepherd", "The Story of Fairyfoot", "The Story of Childe Charity", "Sour & Civil", "The Story of Merrymind" "Prince Wisewit's Return".

Grant. Max Byrd. Narrated by George Guidall. 12 CDs. (Running Time: 13 hrs. 30 mins.). audio compact disk 118.00 (978-0-7887-9885-6(5)) Recorded Bks.

Grant. abr. unabr. ed. John Mosier. 6 cass. (Running Time: 380 hrs. NaN mins.). 2006. 25.95 (978-0-7861-4489-1(0)); audio compact disk 29.95 (978-0-7861-7670-0(9)) Blckstn Audio.

Grant. unabr. ed. Max Byrd. Narrated by George Guidall. 10 cass. (Running Time: 13 hrs. 30 mins.). 2001. 92.00 (978-0-7887-5322-0(3), 96569E7) Recorded Bks.
A novel that sheds light on the final, embattled years of Ulysses S. Grant's life. After failing to secure a third presidential nomination, Grant goes bankrupt at the same time he learns he has throat cancer.

Grant. unabr. ed. Mosier John. Read by Brian Emerson. 2006. audio compact disk 45.00 (978-0-7861-6741-8(6)) Blckstn Audio.

Grant. unabr. ed. John Mosier. Frwd. by Wesley K. Clark. (Running Time: 23400 sec.). (Great Generals Ser.). 2006. 44.95 (978-0-7861-4666-6(4)) Blckstn Audio.

Grant. unabr. ed. John Mosier. Read by Brian Emerson. Frwd. by Wesley K. Clark. 8 CDs. (Running Time: 23400 sec.). (Great Generals Ser.). 2006. audio compact disk 25.95 (978-0-7861-7242-9(8)) Blckstn Audio.

Grant Pt. 1: A Biography. unabr. ed. William S. McFeely. Read by Jeff Riggenbach. 11 cass. (Running Time: 32 hrs.). 1995. 76.95 (978-0-7861-0890-9(8), 1678A,B) Blckstn Audio.
Having once said "a military life had no charms to me," U. S. Grant entered West Point "to get through the course, secure a detail for a few years as assistant professor of mathematics at the Academy & afterwards obtain a permanent position as professor at some respectable college. But the course his life took was quite different. Little did he ever dream that he would serve with distinction in the Mexican War, lead the Union to victory in the Civil War, struggle through eight years as President of the United States & wage bitter personal battles against alcoholism, insolvency & cancer.

Grant Pt. 1: A Biography. unabr. collector's ed. William S. McFeely. Read by Dick Estell. 12 cass. (Running Time: 18 hrs.). 1989. 96.00 (978-0-7366-1593-8(8), 2456A) Books on Tape.
Ulysses Grant showed little aptitude for the common careers open to young men, so he went off to West Point. He showed no great scholastic aptitude, fared better during the Mexican War, but when that contest was over he returned home. It was all downhill - from farmer to collector of rents to shop clerk. To such a man the Civil War spelled opportunity. Grant reached out & took it. His early war years, in the Mississippi theatre, were brilliant. His ruthless pursuit of victory brought him to Lincoln's notice. Grant never looked back. In war he was strong & decisive, but these virtues did not last. His years as president were a disgrace & only when he again found himself in battle, his last with cancer, did he summon his heroic energies.

Grant Pt. 2: A Biography. unabr. ed. William S. McFeely. Read by Jeff Riggenbach. 8 cass. (Running Time: 32 hrs.). 1995. 56.95 (978-0-7861-0891-6(6), 1678A,B) Blckstn Audio.

Grant Pt. 2: A Biography. unabr. collector's ed. William S. McFeely. Read by Dick Estell. 9 cass. (Running Time: 13 hrs. 30 min.). 1989. 72.00 (978-0-7366-1594-5(6), 2456B) Books on Tape.

Grant & Sherman: The Friendship That Won the Civil War. abr. ed. Charles Bracelen Flood. Read by Charles Bracelen Flood. 5 CDs. (Running Time: 6 hrs.). 2005. audio compact disk 29.95 (978-0-06-085741-7(2)) HarperCollins Pubs.

***Grant & Sherman: The Friendship That Won the Civil War.** abr. ed. Charles Bracelen Flood. Read by Charles Bracelen Flood. (ENG.). 2007. (978-0-06-089377-4(X), Harper Audio); (978-0-06-089378-1(8), Harper Audio) HarperCollins Pubs.

Grant & Sherman: The Friendship That Won the Civil War. unabr. ed. Charles Bracelen Flood. 2005. audio compact disk 49.95 (978-0-06-085740-0(4)) HarperCollins Pubs.

Grant Comes East. abr. rev. ed. Newt Gingrich & William R. Forstchen. Read by Boyd Gaines. 5 CDs. (Running Time: 6 hrs. 0 mins. 0 sec.). (ENG.). 2004. audio compact disk 29.95 (978-1-59397-440-4(X)) Pub: Macmill Audio. Dist(s): Macmillan

Grant Money 2010: How to Find the Right Backers. Mervin L. Evans. 3 Audio CD. (Running Time: 3 Hours). 2009. cass. & DVD 79.99 (978-0-914391-06-7(2)) Comm People Pr.

Grant Rogers: Catskill Mountain Songmaker. 1 cass. 9.98 (C-27) Folk-Legacy.
Continuing an old tradition in the Catskills.

Grant Scandals. (Presidency Ser.). 10.00 Esstee Audios.
Presents Grant as both a war hero & president.

Grant Writing. 2nd abr. ed. Bev Browning. Read by Brett Barry. (Running Time: 12600 sec.). (For Dummies Ser.). 2007. audio compact disk 14.95 (978-0-06-117590-9(0)) HarperCollins Pubs.

Grant Writing: A Basic Guide. Karen Jean Matsko Hood. 2006. 29.95 (978-1-59434-237-0(7)); audio compact disk 24.95 (978-1-59434-236-3(9)) Whspmg Pine.

***Grant Writing for Dummies 2nd Ed.** abr. ed. Beverly Browning. Read by Brett Barry. (ENG.). 2006. (978-0-06-128726-8(1), Harper Audio); (978-0-06-128725-1(3), Harper Audio) HarperCollins Pubs.

Grantraeet see Fir Tree

Grants & Contract Cash: Writing Proposals That Get the Funding You Need. Chuck Schuler. 1 cass. (Running Time: 90 mins.). 1994. 79.00 (978-1-884667-05-3(8)) Prime Concepts Grp.
Business training.

Grant's Indian. Narrated by Peter Johnson. (ENG.). 2009. 15.00 (978-0-9819842-2-3(3)) PeteJohnson.

Granville Affaire. Una-Mary Parker. Read by Sheila Mitchell. 7 cass. (Running Time: 9 hrs. 30 mins.). (Isis Cassettes Ser.). 2006. 61.95 (978-0-7531-3625-6(2)) Pub: ISIS Lrg Prnt GBR. Dist(s): Ulverscroft US

Granville Affaire. Una-Mary Parker. (Isis (CDs) Ser.). 2007. audio compact disk 84.95 (978-0-7531-2689-9(3)) Pub: ISIS Lrg Prnt GBR. Dist(s): Ulverscroft US

Granville Legacy. Una-Mary Parker. (Isis Cassettes Ser.). 2007. 61.95 (978-0-7531-3715-4(1)) Pub: ISIS Lrg Prnt GBR. Dist(s): Ulverscroft US

Granville Sisters. unabr. ed. Una-Mary Parker. Read by Sheila Mitchell. 7 cass. (Running Time: 8 hrs. 55 mins.). (Isis Cassettes Ser.). 2006. 61.95 (978-0-7531-3545-7(0)) Pub: ISIS Lrg Prnt GBR. Dist(s): Ulverscroft US

Grapefruit Delights Journal: A Daily Journal. Karen Jean Matsko Hood. 2005. audio compact disk 13.95 (978-1-59649-968-3(0)) Whsprng Pine.

Grapefruit Delights Menu Cookbook: A Collection of Grapefruit-themed Menus. Karen Jean Matsko Hood. 2005. audio compact disk 13.95 (978-1-59649-964-5(8)) Whsprng Pine.

Grapefruit Juice Diet. D. E. Treynor. 1 cass. (Running Time: 1 hr. 05 min.). 12.50 Alpha Tape.
Excellent way to lose weight & retain your strength.

Grapes Making see Twentieth-Century Poetry in English, No. 12, Recordings of Poets Reading Their Own Poetry

Grapes of Wrath. Frank Galati. 1994. 5.99 (978-1-55994-924-8(4)) HarperCollins Pubs.

Grapes of Wrath. Frank Galati. Narrated by Dylan Baker. 18 CDs. (Running Time: 21 hrs.). audio compact disk 169.00 (978-1-4025-3087-6(0)) Recorded Bks.

Grapes of Wrath. unabr. ed. Frank Galati. Read by Emily Bergl & Shirley Knight. (YA). 2008. 34.99 (978-1-60514-886-1(5)) Find a World.

Grapes of Wrath. unabr. ed. Frank Galati. Narrated by Dylan Baker. 15 cass. (Running Time: 21 hrs.). 1999. 120.00 (978-0-7887-2914-0(4), 95707E7) Recorded Bks.
Tragic portrait of a migrant family traveling from the dust bowl to California. Created from camp records & Steinbeck's own experience working in a migrant camp.

Graph It! Sundance/Newbridge, LLC Staff. (Early Math Ser.). (gr. k-1). 2000. 12.00 (978-1-58273-870-3(X)) Sund Newbrdge.

Graphic Arts. unabr. ed. Incl. Graphic Arts: Al: Art Director - Publishing; Graphic Arts: David: Director - Graphic Arts Studio; Graphic Arts: Stan: Partner - Graphics Design Firm; (Selections from the Career Strategy Cassette Library). 11.95 per cass. J Norton Pubs.
In-depth interviews of young men & women with 5 - 10 years job experience. Guides to career planning for college students making intelligent decisions about their future careers.

Graphic Arts: Al: Art Director - Publishing see Graphic Arts

Graphic Arts: David: Director - Graphic Arts Studio see Graphic Arts

Graphic Arts: Stan: Partner - Graphics Design Firm see Graphic Arts

Graphic Design. Sherry Stinson et al. 2009. 49.95 (978-0-7637-7634-3(3)) Jones Bartlett.

***Graphic Flash Collection (Playaway)** (Playaway Ser.). (ENG.). audio compact disk 29.20 (978-1-4342-2999-1(8)) CapstoneDig.

Graphic Organizers CD: Building Comprehension Skills. Joan Westley. (J). 2005. audio compact disk 19.95 (978-1-60184-112-4(4)) Primry Concpts.

***Graphic Revolve Classics 1 (Playaway)** (Playaway Ser.). (ENG.). audio compact disk 29.20 (978-1-4342-3000-3(7)) CapstoneDig.

***Graphic Revolve Mythology 1 (Playaway)** (Playaway Ser.). (ENG.). audio compact disk 29.20 (978-1-4342-3001-0(5)) CapstoneDig.

***Graphic Science Collection II: A Journey Through the Digestive System with Max Axiom/the Powerful World of Energy with Max Axiom.** Created by Playaway. (Playaway Children Ser.). (ENG.). (J). 2009. 39.99 (978-1-61587-675-4(8)) Find a World.

***Graphic Science Collection III: The Solid Truth about States of Matter with Max Axiom/Understandin Viruses with Max Axiom.** Created by Playaway. (Playaway Children Ser.). (ENG.). (J). 2009. 39.99 (978-1-61545-859-2(X)) Find a World.

***Graphic Sparks (Audio CD - Complete Set Spring 2008)** (Graphic Sparks Ser.). (ENG.). 2008. audio compact disk 175.80 (978-1-4342-0651-0(3)) CapstoneDig.

***Graphic Sparks (Audio CD - Fall 2007)** (Graphic Sparks Ser.). (ENG.). 2007. audio compact disk 87.90 (978-1-4342-0342-7(5)) CapstoneDig.

***Graphic Sparks (Audio CD - Spring 2008)** (Graphic Sparks Ser.). (ENG.). 2008. audio compact disk 87.90 (978-1-4342-0649-7(1)) CapstoneDig.

***Graphic Spin Fairy Tales (Playaway)** (Playaway Ser.). (ENG.). audio compact disk 43.80 (978-1-4342-3004-1(X)) CapstoneDig.

GraphicAudio. 2007. audio compact disk (978-1-59950-207-6(0)); audio compact disk (978-1-59950-216-8(X)); audio compact disk 19.99 (978-1-59950-217-5(8)); audio compact disk 19.99 (978-1-59950-218-2(6)); audio compact disk 19.99 (978-1-59950-219-9(4)) GraphicAudio.

GraphicAudio. 2007. audio compact disk 19.99 (978-1-59950-206-9(2)); audio compact disk 19.99 (978-1-59950-208-3(9)); audio compact disk 19.99 (978-1-59950-209-0(7)); audio compact disk 19.99 (978-1-59950-210-6(0)) GraphicAudio.

GraphicAudio. Created by GraphicAudio. 2007. audio compact disk 19.99 (978-1-59950-228-1(3)) GraphicAudio.

Grasping Life with Both Hands (Even with Gloves on): Approaches to the Christian-Zen Meeting see Grasping Life with Both Hands (Even with Gloves on): The Meeting Between Zen and Christianity

Grasping Life with Both Hands (Even with Gloves on): Christian Mind, Empty Mind see Grasping Life with Both Hands (Even with Gloves on): The Meeting Between Zen and Christianity

Grasping Life with Both Hands (Even with Gloves on): Everyday Emptiness see Grasping Life with Both Hands (Even with Gloves on): The Meeting Between Zen and Christianity

Grasping Life with Both Hands (Even with Gloves on): Freedom - How Tasty! see Grasping Life with Both Hands (Even with Gloves on): The Meeting Between Zen and Christianity

Grasping Life with Both Hands (Even with Gloves on): Nonattachment & Social Concern see Grasping Life with Both Hands (Even with Gloves on): The Meeting Between Zen and Christianity

Grasping Life with Both Hands (Even with Gloves on): Sin, Ignorance & the Art of Emptiness see Grasping Life with Both Hands (Even with Gloves on): The Meeting Between Zen and Christianity

Grasping Life with Both Hands (Even with Gloves on) The Meeting Between Zen & Christianity. Silvio Fittipaldi. 9 cass. Incl. Grasping Life with Both Hands (Even with Gloves on) Approaches to the Christian-Zen Meeting. 1980.; Grasping Life with Both Hands (Even with Gloves on) Christian Mind, Empty Mind. 1980.; Grasping Life with Both Hands (Even with Gloves on) Everyday Emptiness. 1980.; Grasping Life with Both Hands (Even with Gloves on) Freedom - How Tasty! 1980.; Grasping Life with Both Hands (Even with Gloves on) Nonattachment & Social Concern. 1980.; Grasping Life with Both Hands (Even with Gloves on) Sin, Ignorance & the Art of Emptiness. 1980.; Grasping Life with Both Hands (Even with Gloves on) The Story of the Christian-Zen Meeting. 1980.; Grasping Life with Both Hands (Even with Gloves on) Word & Silence. 1980.; Grasping Life with Both Hands (Even with Gloves on) Zen Mind, Empty Mind. 1980.; 1980. 28.00 Set.; 4.50 ea. Pendle Hill.

Grasping Life with Both Hands (Even with Gloves on): The Story of the Christian-Zen Meeting see Grasping Life with Both Hands (Even with Gloves on): The Meeting Between Zen and Christianity

Grasping Life with Both Hands (Even with Gloves on): Word & Silence see Grasping Life with Both Hands (Even with Gloves on): The Meeting Between Zen and Christianity

Grasping Life with Both Hands (Even with Gloves on): Zen Mind, Empty Mind see Grasping Life with Both Hands (Even with Gloves on): The Meeting Between Zen and Christianity

Grasping the Ways of the Lord. Adrian Van Kaam & Susan Muto. 4 cass. (Running Time: 5 hrs. 50 min.). 1995. 34.95 Set. (TAH337) Alba Hse Comns.
Fr. Van Kaam & Dr. Muto guide us through an awakening of the spirit in this four part audio-cassette program, & answer some of the questions that may be foremost in our minds as we strive to uncover God's will in our lives.

Grass Crown. Colleen McCullough. (Masters of Rome Ser.: No. 2). 2004. 14.95 (978-0-7435-4795-6(0)) Pub: S&S Audio. Dist(s): S and S Inc

Grass Crown. unabr. ed. Colleen McCullough. Read by Donada Peters. 12 cass. (Running Time: 18 hrs.). (Masters of Rome Ser.: No. 2). 1992. 96.00 (978-0-7366-2103-8(2), 2908A); 104.00 (2908B) Books on Tape.
The second installment of the author's acclaimed series on ancient Rome. An astonishing work, fiction at its best.

Grass-Cutting Sword. Catherynne M. Valente. 2006. audio compact disk 19.95 (978-0-8095-6229-9(4)) Diamond Book Dists.

Grass-Cutting Sword. Catherynne M. Valente. 2006. audio compact disk 29.95 (978-0-8095-6230-5(8)) Diamond Book Dists.

Grass Dancer. unabr. ed. Susan Power. Read by Susan Power. (Running Time: 9 hrs.). 2009. 24.99 (978-1-4233-9380-1(5), 9781423393801, Brilliance MP3); 39.97 (978-1-4233-9381-8(3), 9781423393818, Brlnc Audio MP3 Lib); 24.99 (978-1-4233-9382-5(1), 9781423393825, BAD); 39.97 (978-1-4233-9383-2(X), 9781423393832, BADLE) Brilliance Audio.

Grass for His Pillow: The Way Through the Snow. unabr. ed. Lian Hearn. Read by Aiko Nakasone & Kevin Grey. 8 CDs. (Running Time: 9 hrs. 30 mins.). Bk. 2. (ENG.). 2003. audio compact disk 34.95 (978-1-56511-799-0(9), 1565117999) Pub: HighBridge. Dist(s): Workman Pub

Grass Is Always Greener. Jeffrey Archer. Narrated by Andrew Sachs. 2000. pap. bk. 16.95 (978-0-00-105653-4(0)) Pub: HarpC GBR. Dist(s): Trafalgar

Grass Is always Greener over the Septic Tank. Erma Bombeck. Narrated by Barbara Rosenblat. 4 CDs. (Running Time: 4 hrs. 15 mins.). audio compact disk 39.00 (978-0-7887-8968-7(6)) Recorded Bks.

Grass Is Always Greener over the Septic Tank. unabr. ed. Erma Bombeck. Narrated by Barbara Rosenblat. 3 cass. (Running Time: 4 hrs. 15 mins.). 2001. 32.00 (978-0-7887-4985-8(4), 96188E7) Recorded Bks.
Join the station wagon train to the suburbs. In new lands like the Suburbian Gems sub-division, settlers from the city brave dangers like endless cul-de-sacs, overly helpful insurance salesmen & epic battles at school board meetings.

Grass Kingdom. unabr. ed. Jory Sherman. Read by Maynard Villers. 12 cass. (Running Time: 16 hrs. 30 min.). 1996. 64.95 (978-1-55686-650-0(X)) Books in Motion.
A Lone Star dynasty, bound by blood, the Baron kingdom is one of the largest ranches in Texas. But now their rule is threatened by oil drilling, drought, marauders & uncontrolled ambition.

Grass Roots. unabr. ed. Stuart Woods. Read by Barrett Whitener. 8 cass. (Running Time: 12 hrs.). (Will Lee Ser.: No. 4). 2002. 32.95 (978-1-58788-150-3(0), 1587881500, BAU) Brilliance Audio.
Will Lee has returned to his roots to kick off his campaign for the Senate. A prominent lawyer, he has come back to his hometown of Delano, Georgia, to plan his strategies...and to argue an explosively controversial case that could seriously damage his political career. For Delano is a town with a dark secret - a smoldering hotbed of racial hatred and moral outrage, held in the thrall of a sinister white-supremacist group called The Elect... a breeding ground for violent, evil forces that will stop at nothing to keep the candidate out of office. At first, Will Lee was running for the Senate. But now he is running for his life.

Grass Roots. unabr. ed. Stuart Woods. Read by Barrett Whitener. (Running Time: 12 hrs.). (Will Lee Ser.: No. 4). 2005. 39.25 (978-1-59600-707-9(9), 9781596007079, BADLE); 24.95 (978-1-59600-706-2(0), 9781596007062, BAD); audio compact disk 24.95 (978-1-59600-704-8(4), 9781596007048, Brilliance MP3); audio compact disk 39.25 (978-1-59600-705-5(2), 9781596007055, Brlnc Audio MP3 Lib) Brilliance Audio.

Grass Roots. unabr. ed. Stuart Woods. Read by Barrett Whitener. (Running Time: 43200 sec.). (Will Lee Ser.: No. 4). 2007. audio compact disk 102.25 (978-1-4233-3370-8(5), 9781423333708, BriAudCD Unabrid); audio compact disk 38.95 (978-1-4233-3369-2(1), 9781423333692, Bril Audio CD Unabri) Brilliance Audio.

Grass Roots Research Project. ACT Staff. 1 cass. (Workshop Ser.). 8.95 (008) Am Fed Astrologers.

Grass Widow & Her Cow. unabr. ed. Barbara Paynter. Read by Anita Wright. 3 cass. (Running Time: 4 hr. 30 min.). (Reminiscence Ser.). 1998. 34.95 (978-0-7531-0346-3(X), 980317) Pub: ISIS Audio GBR. Dist(s): Ulverscroft US
An account of country life during wartime Britain. The true story, based on the letters written to her husband stationed in the Middle East, of a young woman who knew nothing about farms or animals, but who determinedly "did her bit" for the war effort by turning her well-ordered home into a farm.

Grass Widow's Tale. unabr. ed. Ellis Peters, pseud. Read by Diana Bishop. 6 CDs. (Running Time: 7 hrs.). (Inspector George Felse Mystery Ser.: Vol. 7). 1999. audio compact disk 64.95 (978-0-7531-0707-2(4), 107074) Pub: ISIS Audio GBR. Dist(s): Ulverscroft US

Grass Widow's Tale. unabr. ed. Ellis Peters, pseud. Read by Diana Bishop. 6 cass. (Running Time: 7 hrs.). (Inspector George Felse Mystery Ser.: Vol. 7). (J). 1995. 54.95 (978-1-85695-989-6(9), 950709) Pub: ISIS Lrg Prnt GBR. Dist(s): Ulverscroft US
"Listen to who's talking. I'm not the one who goes hobnobbing with gunmen & such." Such is Bunty Felse's light-hearted reply to her husband's parting words of caution, when George is called away to London on urgent police business. To shake off the black mood, she goes out to the local pub - where a chance meeting with a distraught stranger proves that her farewell words to George were horribly mistaken. Caught up in a terrifying situation, Bunty struggles desperately to hold on to her life.

Grasshopper see Richard Wilbur Readings

Grasshopper. Barbara Vine, pseud. Read by Emilia Fox. 12 cass. (Running Time: 17 hrs. 30 min.). 2001. 45.95 (978-0-7540-0601-5(8)) AudioGO.
A group of twenty something slackers spend their nights walking the roofs of Maida Vale. On one of these walks they see a couple through an open window, a sighting with profound consequences that reverberate through all their lives.

Grasshopper. collector's unabr. ed. Barbara Vine, pseud. Read by Bernadette Dunne. 12 cass. (Running Time: 18 hrs.). 2000. 96.00 (978-0-7366-5656-6(1)) Books on Tape.
A psychological thriller & coming-of-age novel about a young woman with a love of dangerous heights.

Grasshopper. unabr. ed. Barbara Vine, pseud. Read by Bernadette Dunne. 9 cass. (Running Time: 12 hrs.). 2000. 34.95 (978-0-7366-4954-4(9)) Books on Tape.

Grasshopper. unabr. ed. Barbara Vine, pseud. Narrated by Jill Tanner. 15 cass. (Running Time: 21 hrs. 15 mins.). 2000. 122.00 (978-0-7887-4857-8(2), 96355E7) Recorded Bks.
Young Clodagh Brown loves to climb, especially the giant electrical pylons that form a neat row outside her parents? home. When this obsession breeds tragedy, her shamed family sends her to London for college. As a respite from insufferable classes, she begins climbing atop the local houses with her unique band of friends. But it is a practice that lands the group in a kidnapping scandal & leads to a terrifying climax on the rooftops.

Grasshopper on the Road. abr. ed. Arnold Lobel. Illus. by Arnold Lobel. 1 cass. (I Can Read Bks.). (J). (gr. k-3). 1991. 8.99 (978-1-55994-436-6(6), TBC 4366) HarperCollins Pubs.

***Grasshopper on the Road.** unabr. ed. Arnold Lobel. Read by Mark Linn-baker. (ENG.). 2009. (978-0-06-196709-2(2)); (978-0-06-190159-1(8)) HarperCollins Pubs.

Grasshopper Trap. unabr. ed. Patrick F. McManus. Narrated by Norman Dietz. 6 CDs. (Running Time: 6 hrs. 30 mins.). 2001. audio compact disk 58.00 (978-0-7887-7172-9(8), C1425) Recorded Bks.
The author maintains just the right balance between baffled innocence & conspiratorial confidence. Since 1979, this humorist has been delighting readers with hilarious stories recounting his childhood in rural Idaho & relating his misadventures in the great outdoors. Whether you're a sportsman or a couch potato, he will have you laughing out loud at his escapades. In this collection of 30 tall tales, the author introduces you to the perils of Trailer Trials & Mean Tents. This story unveils an ingenious invention for catching fish bait in motion.

Grasshopper Trap. unabr. ed. Patrick F. McManus. Narrated by Norman Dietz. 5 cass. (Running Time: 6 hrs. 30 mins.). 2000. 45.00 (978-0-7887-4885-1(8), 96037E7) Recorded Bks.
A collection of tall tales from the great outdoors. Includes: "Trailer Trails," "Mean Tents." "The Grasshopper Trap" & "Hunting Camp Etiquette".

Grassroots Action by Alaska's Conservationists. Hosted by Nancy Pearlman. 1 cass. (Running Time: 30 min.). 10.00 (710) Educ Comm CA.

***Gratitud.** (SPA.). 2009. audio compact disk 11.99 (978-0-8297-6158-0(6)) Pub: CanZion. Dist(s): Zondervan

Gratitude see Classical Russian Poetry

Gratitude. Executive Producer Donna Auguste. (YA). 2004. audio compact disk (978-0-9762377-4-7(1)) Leave a Little Room Found.

Gratitude. unabr. ed. Angeles Arrien. (Running Time: 3:02:03). 2009. audio compact disk 24.95 (978-1-59179-686-2(5)) Sounds True.

Gratitude: Reflections on What We Owe to Our Country. unabr. ed. William F. Buckley, Jr. Read by Robin Lawson. 3 cass. (Running Time: 16200 sec.). 1991. 23.95 (978-0-7861-0217-4(9), 1191) Blckstn Audio.
What do we owe to our country? Service, answers William F. Buckley. Voluntary national service. A surprising (to those who do not know him well) call to service by the nation's patriarchal conservative thinker & writer. Offers a plan for universal voluntary national service for men & women eighteen years & older.

Gratitude: Reflections on What We Owe to Our Country. unabr. collector's ed. William F. Buckley, Jr. Read by Jonathan Reese. 5 cass. (Running Time: 5 hrs.). 1992. 30.00 (978-0-7366-2324-7(8), 3104) Books on Tape.
The author's ideas on reviving American youths' interest in government.

Gratitude: The Theory of Relativity. Mary Ellen Edmunds. 2006. audio compact disk 12.95 (978-1-59038-674-3(4)) Deseret Bk.

Gratitude Effect. unabr. ed. John F. DeMartini. Read by Erik Synnestvedt. (Running Time: 6 hrs.). (ENG.). 2008. 24.98 (978-1-59659-301-5(6), GildAudio) Pub: Gildan Media. Dist(s): HachBkGrp

***GrATTITUDE: Practicing Contagious Optimism for Positive Change.** Zondervan Publishing Staff & Ace Collins. (Running Time: 4 hrs. 5 mins. 7 sec.). (ENG.). 2010. 14.99 (978-0-310-41232-8(3)) Zondervan.

***Grave.** 2010. audio compact disk (978-1-59171-204-6(1)) Falcon Picture.

Grave. James Heneghan. Narrated by Gerard Doyle. 5 pieces. (Running Time: 6 hrs. 30 mins.). (gr. 6 up). 2003. 46.00 (978-1-4025-1717-4(3)) Recorded Bks.
13-year-old Tom Mullen has spent his entire life in foster homes. One night, while visiting a recently discovered mass grave at the local cemetery, he falls through a hole in time and finds himself in 1847 Ireland. Taken in by the first caring family he has ever known, Tom must find a way to help them survive the famine and disease that grips their country.

Grave Concerns. unabr. ed. Rebecca Tope. Read by Christopher Kay. 10 cass. (Running Time: 10 hrs.). 2001. 84.95 (978-1-86042-996-5(3)) Pub: Soundings Ltd GBR. Dist(s): Ulverscroft US
Drew Slocome is determined to revolutionize the whole death industry with his peaceful Repose Cemetery, by offering inexpensive, ecologically sound burials - a popular choice. But the body of an elderly women is discovered just before Drew opens for business. The police are unconcerned, suspecting it is the body of a vagrant. Genevieve Slater wants to hire Drew, to prove that the body is that of her missing mother. Drew realizes helping her might land him in trouble with the law, but for a man looking to escape money worries, Genevieve's offer proves impossible to resist.

Grave Consequences. unabr. ed. Allan Zullo. Read by John Ratzenberger. 2008. 1.37 (978-1-4233-8065-8(7), 9781423380658, BAD) Brilliance Audio.

Grave Endings. unabr. ed. Rochelle Krich. Read by Deanna Hurst. (Running Time: 10 hrs.). (Molly Blume Ser.). 2004. 39.25 (978-1-59710-332-9(2), 1597103322, BADLE); 24.95 (978-1-59710-333-6(0), 1597103330, BAD) Brilliance Audio.

Grave Endings: A Novel of Suspense. abr. ed. Rochelle Majer Krich. Read by Deanna Hurst. 5 CDs. (Running Time: 6 hrs.). (Molly Blume Ser.: No. 3). 2004. audio compact disk 74.25 (978-1-59355-945-8(3), 1593559453, BACDLib Ed) Brilliance Audio.
Only weeks before her wedding to Rabbi Zack Abrams, true crime writer Molly Blume receives news she thought she'd never hear. . . After almost six years, the LAPD has finally identified the man who brutally murdered Molly's best friend, Aggie Lasher, leaving her body in a Dumpster. His name is Randy Creeley, a handyman who, since his teenage years, has supported his drug habit with petty thievery. The only link between Creeley is a gold locket, its face embossed with the image of Rachel's Tomb in Bethlehem; on the back is the inscription "To Aggie. Best friends." The other "best friend" is Molly, who goes from her bridal shower to the police department, where she confirms to detectives that she gave Aggie the locket to celebrate Aggie's then-new position as a social worker at Rachel's Tent, a private social services agency for women - and named after the ancestral Rachel, who is a symbol of compassion. Coiled inside the locket is a thin red thread, part of a longer thread Molly had wound around the tomb seven times when she had visited the historic site - a thread that, according to Jewish mysticism, protects its wearers, just as Rachel protects her "children." But closure eludes Molly: Randy Creeley has been found dead of an overdose - and the police, burdened with a backlog of unsolved murders, are grateful to consider the cold case closed. Still, the case gnaws at Molly. She wants the real killer to pay for Aggie's murder. And when she learns that Creeley's death was neither accidental nor suicide - in fact that someone had killed

the handyman in order to prevent him from talking to the police - Molly investigates further. . .and her search for the truth places her in increasing jeopardy.

Grave Endings: A Novel of Suspense. unabr. ed. Rochelle Majer Krich. Read by Deanna Hurst. 1 MP3-CD. (Running Time: 10 hrs.). (Molly Blume Ser.: No. 3). 2004. 24.95 (978-1-59335-726-9(5), 1593357265, Brilliance MP3); 39.25 (978-1-59335-860-0(1), 1593358601, Brinc Audio MP3 Lib); 32.95 (978-1-59355-472-9(9), 1593554729, BAU); 82.25 (978-1-59355-473-6(7), 1593554737, BrilAudUnabridg) Brilliance Audio.

Stabbings, even fatal ones, are not uncommon in Los Angeles. But the stabbing death of Aggie Lasher - a vibrant young woman dedicated to helping others and, it seemed, deeply loved by everyone who knew her - was especially tragic. For almost six years crime writer Molly Blume has been obsessed by the mystery of her best friend's murder: If she had been with Aggie, would the killer have chosen another victim? Will the killer ever be caught? When Molly's LAPD pal Detective Andy Connors shows her a locket found on the body of a dead man, suddenly the case seems solved. Molly had given that locket to Aggie. Still coiled inside it is the red-thread good-luck charm that Molly had brought back years ago from Rachel's Tomb in Bethlehem, a thread with the reputed mystical power to protect its wearer. The presumed murderer - a good-looking aspiring actor named Randy Creeley - was found dead of an overdose in his shabby Hollywood apartment. But Molly is plagued by unanswered questions. And though she should be focused on her wedding, only weeks away, she is driven to find out more - about Creeley; about his nervous sister, Trina; about his missing girlfriend, Doreen. About Aggie, who, it turns out, didn't tell her best friend everything. The more Molly discovers, the more she wonders: Was Aggie's life snuffed out so an addict could shoot up? Or has Creeley been framed? What if Aggie was deliberately murdered by someone else, someone who is ready to kill again to ensure that his motives stay buried with Aggie and Randy Creeley? Molly's search for the truth sends her scurrying for answers in an L.A. tourists seldom see. But closure is elusive, and seeking it can exact a stiff price - sometimes even a life. Rochelle Krich's third Molly Blume mystery is irresistible: an inexorably compelling chiller.

Grave Goods. Ariana Franklin, pseud. (Running Time: 11 hrs.). (ENG.). (gr. 12 up). 2009. audio compact disk 39.95 (978-0-14-314412-0(X), PengAudBks) Penguin Grp USA.

***Grave Goods.** unabr. ed. Ariana Franklin, pseud. Read by Kate Reading. 9 CDs. (Running Time: 10 hrs. 45 mins.). 2009. audio compact disk 110.00 (978-1-4159-6266-4(9), BksonTape) Pub: Random Audio Pubg. Dist(s): Random

Grave Maurice. Martha Grimes. Read by Donada Peters. (Richard Jury Novel Ser.). 2002. 90.00 (978-0-7366-8681-5(9)); audio compact disk 117.00 (978-0-7366-8769-0(6)) Books on Tape.

Grave Mistake. Ron Ellis. 7 cass. (Running Time: 9 hrs. 15 mins.). (Story Sound Ser.). (J). 2005. 61.95 (978-1-85903-823-9(9)) Pub: Mgna Lrg Print GBR. Dist(s): Ulverscroft US

Grave Peril. Jim Butcher. 10 CDs. (Running Time: 11 hrs). (Dresden Files Ser.: Bk. 3). 2004. audio compact disk 49.95 (978-0-9657255-5-2(3), Buzzy Audio) Buzzy Multimed.

Grave Peril. Jim Butcher. 1 CD MP-3. (Running Time: 10 hrs). (Dresden Files Ser.: Bk. 3). 2005. 34.95 (978-0-9657255-9-0(6)) Buzzy Multimed.

Grave Robber. (Start-to-Finish Books). (J). (gr. 2-3). (978-1-893376-06-9(0), F01K2) D Johnston Inc.

Grave Robber. (Start-to-Finish Books). (J). (gr. 2-3). 2002. 100.00 (978-1-58702-979-0(0)) D Johnston Inc.

***Grave Secret.** unabr. ed. Charlaine Harris. Narrated by Alyssa Bresnahan. 1 Playaway. (Running Time: 10 hrs.). 2009. 59.75 (978-1-4407-2810-5(0)); 67.75 (978-1-4407-2807-5(0)) Recorded Bks.

***Grave Secret.** unabr. ed. Charlaine Harris. Read by Alyssa Bresnahan. 9 CDs. (Running Time: 10 hrs.). (Harper Connelly Ser.: Bk. 4). 2009. audio compact disk 92.75 (978-1-4407-2808-2(9)) Recorded Bks.

***Grave Secret.** unabr. collector's ed. Charlaine Harris. Narrated by Alyssa Bresnahan. 9 CDs. (Running Time: 10 hrs.). 2009. audio compact disk 51.95 (978-1-4407-2809-9(7)) Recorded Bks.

Grave Secrets. abr. ed. Kathy Reichs. Read by Katherine Borowitz. 4 CDs. (Running Time: 50 hrs. 0 mins. 0 sec.). No. 5. (ENG.). 2002. audio compact disk 30.00 (978-0-7435-2502-2(7), Audioworks) Pub: S&S Audio. Dist(s): S and S Inc

Grave Secrets. abr. ed. Kathy Reichs. Read by Katherine Borowitz. (Temperance Brennan Ser.: No. 5). 2004. 15.95 (978-0-7435-4796-3(9)) Pub: S&S Audio. Dist(s): S and S Inc

Grave Secrets. unabr. ed. Kathy Reichs. Read by Katherine Borowitz. 1 CD. (Running Time: 10 hrs.). (Temperance Brennan Ser.: No. 5). 2002. audio compact disk 29.95 (978-0-7927-2664-7(2), CMP 481, Chivers Sound Lib) AudioGO.

Summer, 1982, Soldiers enter a Guatermalan village and massacre its women and children. Today, families refer to their lost members as "the disappeared." Enter Temperance Brennan, about to confront the most heartbreaking case of her career. Out of shallow graves fading clues emerge. Something savage happened two decades ago. It is happening again? Four girls are missing and a human rights investigator is murdered. Will Tempe be the next victim.

Grave Secrets. unabr. ed. Kathy Reichs. Read by Katherine Borowitz. (Temperance Brennan Ser.: No. 5). 2004. 21.95 (978-0-7435-5084-0(6)) Pub: S&S Audio. Dist(s): S and S Inc

Grave Secrets, Set. unabr. ed. Peter N. Walker. 6 cass. 1998. 69.95 (978-1-85903-024-0(6)) Pub: Magna Story GBR. Dist(s): Ulverscroft US

Grave Talent. unabr. ed. Laurie R. King. Narrated by Alyssa Bresnahan. 10 cass. (Running Time: 14 hrs. 15 mins.). (Kate Martinelli Mystery Ser.: No. 1). 1996. 85.00 (978-0-7887-0395-9(1), 94587E7) Recorded Bks.

When detective Martinelli hunts for a sadist who is strangling six-year-old girls, she thinks she may be falling into a trap.

Gravedigger's Daughter. unabr. ed. Joyce Carol Oates. Read by Bernadette Dunne. 17 CDs. (Running Time: 21 hrs.). 2007. audio compact disk 129.00 (978-1-4159-4424-0(5), BksonTape) Pub: Random Audio Pubg. Dist(s): Random

In 1936 the Schwarts, an immigrant family desperate to escape Nazi Germany, settle in a small town in upstate New York, where the father, a former high school teacher, is demeaned by the only job he can get: gravedigger and cemetery caretaker. After local prejudice and the family's own emotional frailty result in unspeakable tragedy, the gravedigger's daughter, Rebecca, begins her astonishing pilgrimage into America, an odyssey of erotic risk and imaginative daring, ingenious self-invention, and, in the end, a bittersweet - but very "American" - triumph. "You are born here, they will not hurt you" - so the gravedigger has predicted for his daughter, which will turn out to be true.

Graven Images. unabr. ed. Paul Fleischman. Read by Paul Michael et al. 2 cass. (Running Time: 2 hrs. 6 mins.). (J). (gr. 4-7). 2006. 23.00 (978-0-307-24328-7(1), Listening Lib); audio compact disk 24.00 (978-0-307-28573-7(1), Listening Lib) Pub: Random Audio Pubg. Dist(s): Random

Graven Images Still in Vogue: Exodus 20:4-6. Ed Young. 1985. 4.95 (978-0-7417-1429-9(9), 429) Win Walk.

***Graveyard Book.** unabr. ed. Neil Gaiman. Read by Neil Gaiman. (ENG.). 2008. (978-0-06-170739-1(2)); (978-0-06-170741-4(4)) HarperCollins Pubs.

Graveyard Book. unabr. ed. Neil Gaiman. Read by Neil Gaiman. (J). (gr. 4-7). 2008. audio compact disk 29.95 (978-0-06-155189-5(9), HarperChildAud) HarperCollins Pubs.

Graveyard Book. unabr. ed. Neil Gaiman. (Running Time: 7 hrs. 45 mins.). (YA). (gr. 5-8). 2008. 56.75 (978-1-4361-9878-3(X)); 56.75 (978-1-4361-5879-4(6)); audio compact disk 76.75 (978-1-4361-5884-8(2)) Recorded Bks.

Graveyard Book. unabr. collector's ed. Neil Gaiman. 7 CDs. (Running Time: 7 hrs. 45 mins.). (YA). (gr. 5-8). 2008. audio compact disk 29.95 (978-1-4361-5888-6(5)) Recorded Bks.

Graveyard Mystery. Jerry Stemach. (Nick Ford Mysteries Ser.). 1999. audio compact disk 18.95 (978-1-4105-0128-8(0)) D Johnston Inc.

Graveyard Mystery, Vol. 1. Jerry Stemach. Ed. by Gail Portnuff Venable & Dorothy Tyack. Illus. by Phillip Dizick. Narrated by Ed Smaron. Contrib. by Ted S. Hasselbring. (Start-to-Finish Bks.). (J). (gr. 2-3). 2001. 35.00 (978-1-58702-723-9(2)) D Johnston Inc.

Graveyard Mystery, Vol. 1. unabr. ed. Jerry Stemach. Ed. by Jerry Stemach. Ed. by Gail Portnuff Venable & Dorothy Tyack. Illus. by Phillip Dizick. Narrated by Ed Smaron. Contrib. by Ted S. Hasselbring. 1 cass. (Running Time: 1 hr.). (Start-to-Finish Books). (J). (gr. 2-3). 2001. 7.00 (978-1-58702-707-9(0), F01) D Johnston Inc.

In this story, a cancer research center in St. Louis has asked Nick Ford to find seeds from native grasses in Missouri. His search takes Nick and the kids to a pioneer cemetery where Ken and Jeff learn that someone is digging up old graves. The tombstone of every disturbed grave marks the death of a man in 1862. Kris and Mandy drive to Hannibal, Missouri to research the events of 18621. They learn about Mark Twain and about the Civil War.

Graveyard of Ghost Tales. unabr. ed. Read by Vincent Price. 1 cass. Incl. Bond of Reunion. (J). (CP 1429); Ghostly Hand of Spital House. (J). (CP 1429); Hand of Glory. (J). (CP 1429); Harp Notes in the Mist. (J). (CP 1429); Lavender Evening Dress. (J). (CP 1429); Leg of Gold. (J). (CP 1429); Magic Candle to Find Treasure. (J). (CP 1429); Protection Against the Hand of Glory. (J). (CP 1429); Tale of the White Dove. (J). (CP 1429); (J). 1984. 9.95 (978-1-55994-066-5(2), CP 1429) HarperCollins Pubs.

Graveyard Position. Robert Barnard & Robert Barnard. 7 CDs. (Running Time: 8 hrs.). (Soundings (CDs) Ser.). (J). 2005. audio compact disk 71.95 (978-1-84559-140-3(2)) Pub: ISIS Lrg Prnt GBR. Dist(s): Ulverscroft US

Graveyard Position. unabr. ed. Robert Barnard & Robert Barnard. 6 cass. (Running Time: 8 hrs.). (Soundings Ser.). (J). 2005. 54.95 (978-1-84559-097-0(X)) Pub: ISIS Lrg Prnt GBR. Dist(s): Ulverscroft US

Graveyard Shift. abr. unabr. ed. Jack Higgins. Perf. by Patrick Macnee. 4 cass. (Running Time: 6 hrs.). 2004. 25.00 (978-1-59007-160-1(3)) Pub: New Millenn Enter. Dist(s): PerseuPGW

All the creeps and thugs are out during the graveyard shift. It takes a special person to handle people and their weapons at that hour of the morning. This story brings suspense and police action to the fore. Not an hour you want to be out.

***Graveyard Shift.** unabr. ed. Jack Higgins. (Running Time: 5 hrs.). (Nick Miller Ser.). 2010. 24.99 (978-1-4418-4461-3(9), 9781441844613, Brilliance MP3); 24.99 (978-1-4418-4463-7(5), 9781441844637, BAD); 39.97 (978-1-4418-4462-0(7), 9781441844620, Brinc Audio MP3 Lib); 39.97 (978-1-4418-4464-4(3), 9781441844644, BADLE) Brilliance Audio.

***Graveyard Shift.** unabr. ed. Jack Higgins. Read by Michael Page. (Running Time: 5 hrs.). (Nick Miller Ser.). 2010. audio compact disk 29.99 (978-1-4418-4459-0(7), 9781441844590, Bril Audio CD Unabri); audio compact disk 87.97 (978-1-4418-4460-6(0), 9781441844606, BriAudCD Unabrid) Brilliance Audio.

Graveyard Shift. unabr. ed. Jack Higgins. Perf. by Patrick Macnee. 5 CDs. (Running Time: 6 hrs.). 2004. audio compact disk 29.95 (978-1-59007-161-8(1)) Pub: New Millenn Enter. Dist(s): PerseuPGW

Graveyard Tales. 1 cass. (Running Time: 45 min.). (J). 11.95 (978-1-879991-02-6(0), 107C) Natl Storytlng Network.

One of the highlights of the National Storytelling Festival each year is the Saturday night ghost-story telling near the historic Old Jonesborough Cemetery. This is a time for shadows, chills, the ghost tales that put us in touch with our fears. Includes spine-tingling stories from ghost-story tellers Gayle Ross, The Folktellers, Kathryn Windham, Mary Carter Smith, Laura Simms, & Jackie Torrence.

Graveyard Tales. Short Stories. Perf. by Gayle Ross et al. 1 CD. (Running Time: 46 mins.). 2002. audio compact disk 12.95 (978-1-879991-29-3(2), Natl Storytell) Natl Storytlng Network.

The night is chill - let us gather 'round the campfire. Come a little closer, and you'll hear deliciously frightful tales of the supernatural. Graveyard Tales presents six ghost stories that stretch the scope of reality in disturbing, yet exciting ways - giving us safe passage to the dark side and back again. This special collection, recorded live at the National Storytelling Festival, celebrates this country's favorite stories - from Jack tales and ghost stories to legends, folk and fairy tales, and personal remembrances. Here, for your enjoyment, is the best in American storytelling.

Gravitational Marketing: The Science of Attracting Customers. unabr. ed. Jimmy Vee et al. Read by Travis Miller. (Running Time: 6 hrs.). (ENG.). 2009. 24.98 (978-1-59659-408-1(X), GildAudio) Pub: Gildan Media. Dist(s): HachBkGrp

Gravitational Pull & Inertia. Swami Amar Jyoti. 1 cass. 1977. 9.95 (O-5) Truth Consciousness.

All forces are one force, Shakti. Will, key to understanding all phenomena. The gunas, or qualities of mind. Elimination of ego.

Gravity. Sundance/Newbridge, LLC Staff. (Early Science Ser.). (gr. k-3). 2007. audio compact disk 12.00 (978-1-4007-6471-6(8)); audio compact disk 12.00 (978-1-4007-6472-3(6)); audio compact disk 12.00 (978-1-4007-6470-9(X)) Sund Newbrdge.

Gravity. unabr. ed. Tess Gerritsen. Read by William Dufris. 10 vols. (Running Time: 15 hrs.). 2000. bk. 84.95 (978-0-7927-2388-2(0), CSL 277, Chivers Sound Lib) AudioGO.

Emma Watson, a brilliant research physician, has been training for the mission of a lifetime: to study living beings in space. Emma's estranged husband, Jack McCallum shared her dreams of space travel, but a medical condition has grounded & embittered him. He must watch from the sidelines as his wife prepares for her first mission. Once aboard the International Space Station, things start go terribly wrong. In space, the cells rapidly multiply & begin to infect the crew - with agonizing & deadly results.

Gravity. unabr. ed. Tess Gerritsen. Read by William Dufris. 10 CDs. (Running Time: 15 hrs.). 2001. audio compact disk 94.95 (978-0-7927-9934-4(8), SLD 085, Chivers Sound Lib) AudioGO.

Emma Watson has been training for the mission of a lifetime: to study living beings in space. Her estranged husband, Jack, has a medical condition that forces him to watch from the sidelines as things start to go terribly wrong.

Gravity & Grace: Insights into Christian Ministry. Richard Rohr. 1 cass. (Running Time: 1 hr.). 2001. 8.95 (A6451) St Anthony Mess Pr.

Ministers are the gloves that God wears to touch us. He invites us to touch others on the edge of our society, according to our unique life and gifts.

Gray Fox: Robert E. Lee & the Civil War. unabr. ed. Burke Davis. Read by Christopher Hurt. 9 cass. (Running Time: 13 hrs.). 1990. 62.95 (978-0-7861-0167-2(9), 1149) Blckstn Audio.

Robert E. Lee, a Christian & a gentleman, was the mot remarkable man to emerge from the Civil War & is one of the greatest tragic figures of American history. Reserved & unflappable, savvy & fearless, shrewd & tenacious, fatherly & kind, these are but a few of the words commonly used to describe this noble hero.

***Gray Fox: Robert E. Lee & the Civil War.** unabr. ed. Burke Davis. Read by Christopher Hurt. (Running Time: 13 hrs.). 2010. 29.95 (978-1-4417-4652-8(8)); audio compact disk 109.00 (978-1-4417-4649-8(8)) Blckstn Audio.

Gray Fox: Robert E. Lee & the Civil War. unabr. collector's ed. Burke Davis. Read by Dick Estell. 10 cass. (Running Time: 15 hrs.). 1988. 80.00 (978-0-7366-1399-6(4), 2288) Books on Tape.

Of the many remarkable figures in the Civil War, none can approach Robert E. Lee.

Gray Squirrel at Pacific Avenue. Geri Harrington. Narrated by Alexi Komisar. Illus. by Michele Chopin Roosevelt. 1 cass. (Smithsonian's Backyard Ser.). (J). (ps-2). 1995. 5.00 (978-1-56899-120-7(7), C5006) Soundprints.

There's no place like home, but not for Gray Squirrel! His yard behind the pink house on Pacific Avenue is full of danger! An orange cat & a brown dog chase him back & forth across the fence. The toils & troubles of Gray Squirrel abound.

Gray Wolf & Other Stories. unabr. ed. George MacDonald. Read by Thomas Whitworth. 4 cass. (Running Time: 6 hrs.). (J). 2006. 32.95 (978-0-7861-0163-4(6), 1146) Blckstn Audio.

A Collection of seven fairy tales & stories certain to delight both young & old.

Grayheart. Tara K. Harper. Read by Karen White. 2002. 88.00 (978-0-7366-8488-0(3)) Books on Tape.

Grays. abr. ed. Whitley Strieber. 2006. 14.95 (978-1-59397-936-2(3)) Pub: Macmill Audio. Dist(s): Macmillan

Grays. unabr. ed. Whitley Strieber. Narrated by Stephen Lang. 10 CDs. 2006. audio compact disk 94.95 (978-0-7927-4035-3(1), SLD 946) AudioGO.

Grays. unabr. ed. Whitley Strieber. Narrated by Stephen Lang. 2 CDs. (Running Time: 40620 sec.). 2006. audio compact disk 59.95 (978-0-7927-4557-0(4), CMP 946) AudioGO.

Grays. unabr. ed. Whitley Strieber & Whitley Strieber. Narrated by Stephen Lang. (Running Time: 11 hrs. 0 mins. 0 sec.). (ENG.). 2006. audio compact disk 44.95 (978-1-59397-934-8(7)) Pub: Macmill Audio. Dist(s): Macmillan

Grayson. unabr. ed. Lynne Cox. Read by Lynne Cox. (YA). 2007. 34.99 (978-1-59895-927-7(1)) Find a World.

Grayson. unabr. ed. Lynne Cox. Read by Lynne Cox. (Running Time: 9900 sec.). (ENG.). 2006. audio compact disk 24.95 (978-1-59887-055-8(6), 1598870556) Pub: HighBridge. Dist(s): Workman Pub

GRE Vocabulary Builder. 2nd unabr. rev. ed. Ewald Neumann. Read by James Davis & Heidi Davis-Spargo. 3 cass. (Running Time: 4 hrs. 30 min.). (Vocabulary Builder Ser.). (C). 1994. pap. bk. 24.95 Set. (978-0-9625001-1-4(9)) Spargo Comns.

A study aid for the verbal portion of the GRE Exam including: a 64 page book, 3 - 90 minute cassettes & 200 Flash Cards.

Grease: Piano Play-along Volume 53. Created by Hal Leonard Corporation Staff. 2008. pap. bk. 14.95 (978-1-4234-4681-1(X), 142344681X) H Leonard.

Greasing the Piñata. unabr. ed. Tim Maleeny. Read by Amando Duran. (Running Time: 8 hrs. NaN mins.). (Cape Weathers Investigation Ser.). 2008. 29.95 (978-1-4332-5216-7(3)); audio compact disk 70.00 (978-1-4332-5215-0(5)); audio compact disk 54.95 (978-1-4332-5214-3(7)) Blckstn Audio.

Great Adventure. Steven Curtis Chapman. 1 CD. (Running Time: 1 hr.). 2001. bk. 10.97 (978-0-8499-9506-4(X)) Nelson.

Great Adventure: A Journey Through the Bible. Jeff Cavins. 2005. audio compact disk 39.95 (978-1-932645-82-8(9)) Ascensn Pr.

Great Adventure Bible Timeline Seminar. 2003. audio compact disk 13.95 (978-1-932645-21-7(7)) Ascensn Pr.

Great Adventure Bible Timeline Seminar AC. 2003. 13.95 (978-1-932645-19-4(5)) Ascensn Pr.

Great Adventure Starter Pack AC. 2003. 11.95 (978-1-932645-24-8(1)) Ascensn Pr.

Great Adventures of Sherlock Holmes. Prod. by Saddleback Educational Publishing. (Saddleback's Illustrated Classics Ser.). (YA). 2005. audio compact disk 24.95 (978-1-56254-901-5(4)) Saddleback Edu.

Great American Banjo Collection. 1 cass., 1 CD. 11.18 Double. (CMH 1785); audio compact disk 15.98 CD Jewel box, double. (CMH 1785) NewSound.

Great American Bestsellers: The Books That Shaped America. Instructed by Peter Conn. (ENG.). 2009. 129.95 (978-1-59803-533-9(9)); audio compact disk 179.95 (978-1-59803-534-6(7)) Teaching Co.

Great American Classics. unabr. ed. Short Stories. 10 cds. (YA). 2002. audio compact disk 49.95 (978-1-58472-366-0(1), In Aud) Pub: Sound Room. Dist(s): Baker Taylor

Includes The Legend of Sleepy Hollow, The Red Badge of Courage, The Notorious Jumping Frog of Calaveras County, The Gift of the Magi, Miss Tempy's Watchers, Desiree's Baby, The Call of the Wild, and Bernice Bobs Her Hair.

Great American Essays. 7 cass. (Running Time: 7 hrs.). 1989. 49.00 (C-134); 39.00 incl. album. Jimcin Record.

Words of great Americans.

Great American Essays. unabr. collector's ed. Read by Walter Covell et al. 7 cass. (Running Time: 7 hrs.). (Jimcin Recording Ser.). 1986. 42.00 (978-0-7366-3902-6(0), 9134) Books on Tape.

Includes: Ralph Waldo Emerson's "Self-Reliance;" Henry David Thoreau's "Walking" & "Civil Disobedience;" Mark Twain's "Hunting the Deceitful Turkey" & "Reply to a Begging Letter;" & Thomas Paine's "The American Crisis".

Great American Essays: A Collection. unabr. ed. Read by Walter Covell et al. 7 cass. (Running Time: 1 hr. ea.). Incl. Abraham Lincoln. James Russell Lowell. 1985. (C-134); American Crisis. Thomas Paine. 1985. (C-134); Art of Publicity. P. T. Barnum. 1985. (C-134); Civil Disobedience. Henry David Thoreau. 1985. (C-134); Hunting the Deceitful Turkey. Mark Twain. 1985. (C-134); Life of Fear. John Burrough. 1985. (C-134); Other People's Dogs.

Eugene Field. 1985. (C-134); Reply to a Begging Letter. Benjamin Franklin. 1985. (C-134); Self-Reliance. Ralph Waldo Emerson. 1985. (C-134); Short Month. Bradford Torry. 1985. (C-134); Union & Its New Constitution. Alexander Hamilton. 1985. (C-134); Walking. Henry David Thoreau. 1985. (C-134); 1985. 49.00 (C-134); 12.50 rental. Jimcin Record.

Great American Humor: 16 Complete Stories. unabr. ed. Short Stories. John Irving et al. Read by John Irving et al. 4 cass. (Running Time: 4 hrs. 30 min.). 2004. 22.95 (978-1-57270-041-3(6), M41041u) Pub: Audio Partners. Dist(s): PerseuPGW
Includes "Pension Grillparzer" & "Casey at the Bat".

Great American Humorists Set: George Burns One Hundred Years One Hundred Stories; Love, Groucho. abr. ed. George Burns & Groucho Marx. Read by John Byner & Frank Ferrante. Perf. by John Byner & Frank Ferrante. 2 cass. (Running Time: 2 hr.). 1999. 14.95 CLAMSHELL. (978-1-929243-04-4(9), UPR1004-4) Uproar Ent.

Great American Humorists Set: George Burns: 100 Years, 100 Stories & Groucho Marx: Love, Groucho. George Burns & Groucho Marx. Read by John Byner & Frank Ferrante. Perf. by John Byner & Frank Ferrante. Intro. by Dick Cavett. 2 CDs. (Running Time: 2 hrs.). (Spoken Word Humor Ser.). 1999. audio compact disk 19.95 (978-1-929243-03-7(0), UPR1004-2) Uproar Ent.
"100 Years, 100 Stories" includes a tribute by Milton Berle & excerpts from "The Burns & Allen Radio Show." "Love, Groucho" includes the letters Groucho wrote to his daughter Miriam. Both recordings provide real insight into two of America's favorite humorists.

Great American Mousical. unabr. ed. Julie Andrews. (J). 2007. 17.99 (978-0-06-125449-9(5), HarperChildAud) HarperCollins Pubs.

Great American Music: Broadway Musicals. Instructed by Bill Messenger. 8 cass. (Running Time: 12 hrs.). 54.95 (978-1-59803-199-7(6)) Teaching Co.

Great American Music: Broadway Musicals. Instructed by Bill Messenger. 16 CDs. (Running Time: 12 hrs.). 2006. audio compact disk 69.95 (978-1-59803-201-7(1)) Teaching Co.

Great American Novel. Interview. Interview with Francine Gray & Larry McMurtry. 1 cass. (Running Time: 1 hr.). 10.95 (F0290B090, HarperThor) HarpC GBR.

Great American Novel. unabr. ed. Philip Roth. Read by James Daniels. (Running Time: 15 hrs.). 2010. audio compact disk 29.99 (978-1-4418-0563-8(X), 9781441805638) Brilliance Audio.

***Great American Novel.** unabr. ed. Philip Roth. Read by James Daniels. (Running Time: 15 hrs.). 2010. 24.99 (978-1-4418-0565-2(6), 9781441805652, Brilliance MP3); 39.97 (978-1-4418-0566-9(4), 9781441805669, Brinc Audio MP3 Lib); 24.99 (978-1-4418-0567-6(2), 9781441805676, BAD); 39.97 (978-1-4418-0568-3(0), 9781441805683, BADLE); audio compact disk 92.97 (978-1-4418-0564-5(8), 9781441805645, BriAudCD Unabrid) Brilliance Audio.

Great American Poetry: Three Centuries of Classics. unabr. ed. Poems. Anthology Staff. Read by Julie Harris et al. 2 cass. (Running Time: 1 hr. 45 mins.). (Great American Ser.). 2004. 16.95 (978-0-945353-77-5(4), D20377u) Pub: Audio Partners. Dist(s): PerseuPGW
33 classic poems by 14 of America's most influential poets.

Great American Sermons. unabr. ed. Speeches. Jonathan Edwards et al. Narrated by Don Randall et al. 3 CDs. (Running Time: 3 hrs. 9 mins.). (ENG.). 2006. audio compact disk 25.95 (978-0-9790364-0-8(2)) A Audiobooks.
Essential listening for understanding the development of religious thought in America?or for just hearing a rousing good sermon! Dynamic performances bring these classic pieces of Americana to life!Included in this audiobook:"A Sermon In Praise of Swearing"; "Sinners in the Hands of an Angry God" by Jonathan Edwards; "A Sermon of War" by Theodore Parker; "Uses and Abuses of the Bible" by Lucretia Mott; "On Being Born Again" by Dwight Moody; and "The Dogma of Hell" by Octavius Frothingham.

Great American Short Stories. 2 cass. 15.95 set. (8145Q) Filmic Archives.
Includes Poe's "The Tell Tale Heart"; Stockton's "The Lady or The Tiger"; Twain's "The Celebrated Jumping Frog of Calaveras County"; O. Henry's "The Gift of the Magi"; Harte's "Outcasts of Poker Flat" & Bierce's "An Occurrence at Owl Creek Bridge".

Great American Short Stories. unabr. ed. 6 cass. (Running Time: 9 hrs.). (J). (gr. 1-8). 1999. 40.00 (LL 0028, Chivers Child Audio) AudioGO.

Great American Short Stories. unabr. ed. Read by George Backman et al. 6 cass. (Running Time: 6 hrs. 28 min.). Incl. Episode of War. Stephen Crane. 1979. (CXL521CX); Furnished Room. 1979. (CXL521CX); Gift of the Magi. O. Henry. 1979. (CXL521CX); Haircut. Ring Lardner. 1979. (CXL521CX); Interview with a Lemming. James Thurber. 1979. (CXL521CX); Lady or the Tiger. Frank Richard Stockton. 1979. (CXL521CX); Notorious Jumping Frog of Calaveras County. Mark Twain. 1979. (CXL521CX); Occurrence at Owl Creek Bridge. Ambrose Bierce. 1979. (CXL521CX); Outcasts of Poker Flat. Bret Harte. 1979. (CXL521CX); Return of a Private. Hamlin Garland. 1979. (CXL521CX); Rip Van Winkle. Washington Irving. Read by George Baekman. (J). 1979. (CXL521CX); Tell-Tale Heart. Edgar Allan Poe. 1979. (CXL521CX); To Build a Fire & Other Stories. Jack London. 1979. (CXL521CX); Treasurer's Report: And Other Aspects of Community Singing. Robert Benchley. 1979. (CXL521CX); Unlighted Lamps. Michael Anderson, Jr. 1979. (CXL521CX); What Stumped the Bluejays? 1979. (CXL521CX); Young Goodman Brown. Nathaniel Hawthorne. 1979. (CXL521CX); (Cassette Library). 1979. 44.98 (978-0-8072-2991-0(1), CXL521CX, Listening Lib); (Listening Lib) Random Audio Pubg.
Various readers give a panoramic overview of the short story in America. Seventeen miniature masterpieces - flashes of insight, truth & beauty.

Great American Short Stories, Set. unabr. ed. Edgar Allan Poe et al. Read by Edward Blake et al. 2 cass. 1999. 15.95 trade pkg. (978-0-8072-3518-8(0), BTCB109CXR, Listening Lib) Random Audio Pubg.
Also includes readings by Richard Pyatt. Includes "The Tell-Tale Heart," "The Lady or the Tiger?," "The Celebrated Jumping Frog of Calaveras County," "The Gift of the Magi," "The Outcasts of Poker Flat" & "An Occurrence at Owl Creek Bridge".

Great American Short Stories, Vol. I. unabr. ed. 7 cass. (Running Time: 1 hr. 30 min. per cass.). Incl. Ambitious Guest. Nathaniel Hawthorne. 1981. (C-54); Baker's Bluejay Yarn. Mark Twain. 1981. (C-54); Bartleby, the Scrivener. Herman Melville. 1981. (C-54); Blue Hotel. Stephen Crane. 1981. (C-54); Law of Life. Jack London. 1981. (C-54); Man & the Snake. Ambrose Bierce. 1981. (C-54); Minister's Black Veil. Nathaniel Hawthorne. 1981. (C-54); MS Found in a Bottle. Edgar Allan Poe. 1981. (C-54); Occurrence at Owl Creek Bridge. Ambrose Bierce. 1981. (C-54); Open Boat. Stephen Crane. 1981. (C-54); Outcasts of Poker Flat. Bret Harte. 1981. (C-54); Paul's Case. Willa Cather. 1981. (C-54); Princess & the Puma. O. Henry. 1981. (C-54); Tennessee's Partner. Bret Harte. 1981. (C-54); Under the Lion's Paw. Hamlin Garland. 1981. (C-54); 1,000,000 Pound Bank-Note & Other New Stories. Mark Twain. 1981. (C-54); 1981. 49.00 (C-54) Jimcin Record.

Great American Short Stories, Vol. 1. unabr. ed. Silhouette Staff. 7 cass. (Running Time: 10 hrs.). 1981. 49.95 (978-0-7861-0513-7(5), 2013) Blckstn Audio.
This is a delightful collection of short stories by several of America's greatest writers.

Great American Short Stories, Vol. 1. unabr. collector's ed. 7 cass. (Running Time: 10 hrs. 30 min.). 1982. 56.00 (978-0-7366-3856-2(3), 9054) Books on Tape.
Includes: "Bartleby the Scrivener" by Herman Melville; "The Blue Hotel" & "The Open Boat" by Stephen Crane; "The Minister's Black Veil" & "The Ambitious Guest" by Nathaniel Hawthorne; "The One Million Pound Bank Note" & "Baker's Bluejay Yarn" by Mark Twain; "The Princess & the Puma" by O. Henry; "Under the Lion's Paw" by Hamlin Garland; "The Law of Life" by Jack London; "An Occurrence at Owl Creek Bridge" & "The Man & the Snake" by Ambrose Bierce; "Paul's Case" by Willa Cather; "MS Found in a Bottle" by Edgar Allan Poe; "The Outcast of Poker Flat" & "Tennessee's Partner" by Bret Harte.

Great American Short Stories, Vol. 2. unabr. ed. 7 cass. (Running Time: 10 hrs.). 1984. 49.95 (978-0-7861-0600-4(X), 2089) Blckstn Audio.
This is a delightful collection of short stories by several of America's greatest writers.

Great American Short Stories, Vol. 2. unabr. collector's ed. 7 cass. (Running Time: 10 hrs. 30 min.). 1983. 56.00 (978-0-7366-3884-5(9), 9111) Books on Tape.
Includes: "Marjorie Daw" by Thomas Bailey Aldrich; "The McWilliams & the Burglar Alarm" & "The McWilliams & the Lightning" by Mark Twain; "The Phonograph & the Graft" & "The Lotus & the Bottle" by O. Henry; "The Wild Horse of Tartary" by Clara Morris; "The Legend of the Rose of the Alhambra" & "The Phantom Island" by Washington Irving; "The Great Stone Face" & "My Kinsman, Major Molineau" by Nathaniel Hawthorne; "Chickamauga" & "The Coup de Grace" by Ambrose Bierce; "The Premature Burial" & "The Oblong Box" by Edgar Allan Poe; "A Mystery of Heroism" by Stephen Crane; "The Descent of Man" by Edith Wharton; "The Boy Who Drew Cats" by Lafcadio Hearn; & "The Altar of the Dead" by Henry James.

Great American Short Stories, Vol. 3. unabr. ed. Silhouette Staff. 7 cass. (Running Time: 10 hrs.). 1984. 49.95 (978-0-7861-0601-1(8), 2090) Blckstn Audio.
This is a delightful collection of short stories by several of America's greatest writers.

Great American Short Stories, Vol. 3. unabr. collector's ed. 7 cass. (Running Time: 10 hrs. 30 min.). 1983. 56.00 (978-0-7366-3886-9(5), 9114) Books on Tape.
Contains "The Bride Comes to Yellow Sky" by Stephen Crane; "Mrs. Higginbotham's Catastrophe" & "The Birthmark" by Nathaniel Hawthorne; "Editha" by William Dean Howells; "The Courting of Sister Wisby" by Sarah Orne Jewett; "The Damned Thing" & "Beyond the Wall" by Ambrose Bierce; "The Gold Bug" by Edgar Allan Poe; "Jimmy Rose" & "The Fiddler" by Herman Melville; "The Stout Gentleman" by Washington Irving; "Even Unto Death" by Jack London; "Louisa" by Mary E. Wilkins Freeman; "Mliss" by Bret Harte; "The Bar Sinister" by Richard Harding Davis; "The Ghostly Kiss" by Lafcadio Hearn; & "The Californian's Tale" by Mark Twain.

Great American Short Stories Vol. II: A Collection. unabr. ed. 7 cass. (Running Time: 10 hrs. 30 min.). Incl. Altar of the Dead. Henry James. 1984. (C-111); Boy Who Drew Cats. Lafcadio Hearn. 1984. (C-111); Chickamauga. Ambrose Bierce. 1984. (C-111); Coup de Grace. Ambrose Bierce. 1984. (C-111); Descent of Man. Edith Wharton. 1984. (C-111); Great Stone Face. Nathaniel Hawthorne. 1984. (C-111); Legend of the Rose of the Alhambra. Washington Irving. 1984. (C-111); Lotus & the Bottle. O. Henry. 1984. (C-111); Majorie Daw. Thomas Bailey Aldrich. 1984. (C-111); McWilliams & the Burglar Alarm. Mark Twain. 1984. (C-111); Mrs. McWilliams & the Lighting. Mark Twain. 1984. (C-111); My Kinsman, Major Molineux. Nathaniel Hawthorne. 1984. (C-111); Mystery of Heroism. Stephen Crane. 1984. (C-111); Oblong Box. Edgar Allan Poe. 1984. (C-111); Phantom Island. Washington Irving. 1984. (C-111); Phonograph & the Graft. O. Henry. 1984. (C-111); Premature Burial. Edgar Allan Poe. 1984. (C-111); Wild Horse of Tartary. Clara Morris. 1984. (C-111); 1984. 44.00 (C-111) Jimcin Record.

Great American Short Stories Vol. III: A Collection. unabr. ed. 7 cass. (Running Time: 1 hr. 30 min. per cass.). Incl. Bar Sinister. Richard Harding Davis. 1984. (C-114); Beyond the Wall. Ambrose Bierce. 1984. (C-114); Birthmark. Nathaniel Hawthorne. 1984. (C-114); Bride Comes to Yellow Sky. Stephen Crane. 1984. (C-114); Californian's Tale. Mark Twain. 1984. (C-114); Courting of Sister Wisby. Sarah Orne Jewett. 1984. (C-114); Damned Thing. Ambrose Bierce. 1984. (C-114); Editha. William Dean Howells. 1984. (C-114); Even unto Death. Jack London. 1984. (C-114); Fiddler. Herman Melville. 1984. (C-114); Ghostly Kiss. Lafcadio Hearn. 1984. (C-114); Gold Bug. Edgar Allan Poe. 1984. (C-114); Jimmy Rose. Herman Melville. 1984. (C-114); Louisa. Mary E. Wilkins Freeman. 1984. (C-114); M'Liss. Bret Harte. 1984. (C-114); Mr. Higginbotham's Catastrophe. Nathaniel Hawthorne. 1984. (C-114); Stout Gentleman. Washington Irving. 1984. (C-114); 1984. 44.00 (C-114) Jimcin Record.
Seventeen famous stories.

Great American Songwriters for Solo Singers: 12 Contemporary Settings of Favorites from the Great American Songbook for Solo Voice & Piano (High Voice) Alfred Publishing Staff. (For Solo Singers Ser.). (ENG.). 2009. audio compact disk 13.95 (978-0-7390-6056-8(2)) Alfred Pub.

Great American Songwriters for Solo Singers: 12 Contemporary Settings of Favorites from the Great American Songbook for Solo Voice & Piano (Low Voice) Alfred Publishing Staff. (For Solo Singers Ser.). (ENG.). 2009. audio compact disk 13.95 (978-0-7390-6059-9(7)) Alfred Pub.

Great American Speeches: Abraham Lincoln see Great American Speeches: 1950-1963

Great American Speeches: Acceptance of Nomination & Eulogy for John Kennedy see Great American Speeches: 1950-1963

Great American Speeches: Address before Congress see Great American Speeches: 1950-1963

Great American Speeches: Farewell to His Troops see Great American Speeches, Set, 1775-1896

Great American Speeches: First Inaugual Address see Great American Speeches, Set, 1775-1896

Great American Speeches: First Inaugural Address see Great American Speeches, Set, 1775-1896

Great American Speeches: First Inaugural Address & Declaration of War see Great American Speeches: 1931-1947

Great American Speeches: Fourteen Points see Great American Speeches: 1898-1918

Great American Speeches: Liberty or Death see Great American Speeches, Set, 1775-1896

Great American Speeches: Loyal Opposition see Great American Speeches: 1931-1947

Great American Speeches: Morgenthau's Plan see Great American Speeches: 1931-1947

Great American Speeches: Naboth's Vineyard see Great American Speeches: 1898-1918

Great American Speeches: Nobel Prize Speech see Great American Speeches: 1950-1963

Great American Speeches: On His Ninetieth Birthday see Great American Speeches: 1931-1947

Great American Speeches: On Secession see Great American Speeches, Set, 1775-1896

Great American Speeches: On the Admission of Louisiana see Great American Speeches, Set, 1775-1896

Great American Speeches: On the War of 1812 see Great American Speeches, Set, 1775-1896

Great American Speeches: Opening Statement of the Fourth Kennedy-Nixon Address see Great American Speeches: 1950-1963

Great American Speeches: Opening Statement of the Fourth Kennedy-Nixon Debate & Inaugural Address see Great American Speeches: 1950-1963

Great American Speeches: Order of the Day see Great American Speeches: 1931-1947

Great American Speeches: Soldier's Pay see Great American Speeches: 1898-1918

Great American Speeches: The Crime Against Kansas see Great American Speeches, Set, 1775-1896

Great American Speeches: The Cross of Gold Speech see Great American Speeches, Set, 1775-1896

Great American Speeches: The House Divided Speech, the Cooper Union Speech & the Gettysburg Address see Great American Speeches, Set, 1775-1896

Great American Speeches: The Man with the Muck Rake see Great American Speeches: 1898-1918

Great American Speeches: The March of the Flag see Great American Speeches: 1898-1918

Great American Speeches: The Marshall Plan see Great American Speeches: 1931-1947

Great American Speeches: The Truman Doctrine see Great American Speeches: 1931-1947

Great American Speeches: To the Jury: Self-Defense see Great American Speeches: 1898-1918

Great American Speeches: War Comes to Europe see Great American Speeches: 1931-1947

Great American Speeches: 1898-1918. abr. ed. Read by Ed Begley et al. 2 cass. Incl. Great American Speeches: Fourteen Points. Woodrow Wilson. (SWC 2031); Great American Speeches: Naboth's Vineyard. William Jennings Bryan. (SWC 2031); Great American Speeches: Soldier's Pay. Robert M. LaFollette. (SWC 2031); Great American Speeches: The Man with the Muck Rake. Theodore Roosevelt. (SWC 2031); Great American Speeches: The March of the Flag. Albert Jeremiah Beveridge. (SWC 2031); Great American Speeches: To the Jury: Self-Defense. Clarence S. Darrow. (SWC 2031); Public Education. Mark Twain. (SWC 2031); 1984. 19.95 (978-0-694-50389-6(4), SWC 2031) HarperCollins Pubs.

Great American Speeches: 1931-1947. abr. ed. Ed. by John Graham. 2 cass. Incl. Great American Speeches: First Inaugural Address & Declaration of War. Franklin D. Roosevelt. Read by Franklin D. Roosevelt. (SWC 2033); Great American Speeches: Loyal Opposition. Wendell Willkie. Read by Wendell Willkie. (SWC 2033); Great American Speeches: Morgenthau's Plan. Will Rogers. Read by Will Rogers. (SWC 2033); Great American Speeches: On His Ninetieth Birthday. Oliver Wendell Holmes. Read by Oliver Wendell Holmes. (SWC 2033); Great American Speeches: Order of the Day. Dwight D. Eisenhower. Read by Dwight D. Eisenhower. (SWC 2033); Great American Speeches: The Marshall Plan. George C. Marshall. Read by George C. Marshall. (SWC 2033); Great American Speeches: The Truman Doctrine. Harry S. Truman. Read by Harry S. Truman. (SWC 2033); Great American Speeches: War Comes to Europe. Herbert Hoover. Read by Herbert Hoover. (SWC 2033); 1984. 19.95 (978-0-694-50391-9(6), SWC 2033) HarperCollins Pubs.

Great American Speeches: 1950-1963. abr. ed. Ed. by John Graham. 2 cass. Incl. Great American Speeches: Abraham Lincoln. Carl Sandburg. Read by Carl Sandburg. (SWC 2035); Great American Speeches: Acceptance of Nomination & Eulogy for John Kennedy. Adlai Stevenson. Read by Adlai Stevenson. (SWC 2035); Great American Speeches: Address before Congress. Douglas MacArthur. Read by Douglas MacArthur. (SWC 2035); Great American Speeches: Nobel Prize Speech. William Faulkner. Read by William Faulkner. (SWC 2035); Great American Speeches: Opening Statement of the Fourth Kennedy-Nixon Address. Richard M. Nixon. Read by Richard M. Nixon. (SWC 2035); Great American Speeches: Opening Statement of the Fourth Kennedy-Nixon Debate & Inaugural Address. John F. Kennedy. Read by John F. Kennedy. (SWC 2035); 1984. 19.95 (978-0-694-50392-6(4), SWC 2035) HarperCollins Pubs.

Great American Speeches Set: 1775-1896. abr. ed. Read by Melvyn Douglas et al. 2 cass. Incl. Great American Speeches: Farewell to His Troops. Robert E. Lee. (SWC 2016); Great American Speeches: First Inaugual Address. Thomas Jefferson. (SWC 2016); Great American Speeches: First Inaugural Address. George Washington. (SWC 2016); Great American Speeches: Liberty or Death. Patrick Henry. (SWC 2016); Great American Speeches: On Secession. Robert Toombs. (SWC 2016); Great American Speeches: On the Admission of Louisiana. Josiah Quincy. (SWC 2016); Great American Speeches: On the War of 1812. Henry Clay. (SWC 2016); Great American Speeches: The Crime Against Kansas. Charles Sumner. (SWC 2016); Great American Speeches: The Cross of Gold Speech. William Jennings Bryan. (SWC 2016); Great American Speeches: The House Divided Speech, the Cooper Union Speech & the Gettysburg Address. Abraham Lincoln. (SWC 2016); 1984. 19.95 (978-0-694-50377-3(0), SWC 2016) HarperCollins Pubs.

Great American Speeches Set: 1931-1947. unabr. ed. Ed. by John Graham. 2 cass. (Running Time: 1 hr. 45 mins.). 17.95 (H113) Blckstn Audio.
In their own voices, great statesmen of this century deliver some of the most important speeches of their time, including F.D.R.'s Declaration of War, & George C. Marshall reading "The Marshall Plan." Also included are Oliver Wendell Holmes, Jr. "On His Ninetieth Birthday"; Herbert Hoover: "War Comes to Europe" & Dwight D. Eisenhower: "Order of the Day.".

Great American Speeches Set: 1950-1963. Ed. by John Graham. 2 cass. (Running Time: 60 mins. per cass.). 17.95 (H114) Blckstn Audio.
Carl Sandburg speaks about Abraham Lincoln & John F. Kennedy delivers his "First Inaugural Address." Also included are Douglas MacArthur's "Address Before Congress"; Adlai Stevenson's "Acceptance of Nomination" & "Eulogy for John F. Kennedy"; & Richard Nixon's "Opening Statement from the Fourth Kennedy-Nixon Debate.".

Great American Stories: 10 Classics. unabr. ed. Ambrose Bierce et al. Ed. by Mark Twain. Narrated by Patrick Fraley. 5 CDs. (Running Time: 5 hrs. 30

mins.). (ENG.). 2003. audio compact disk 29.95 (978-1-57270-303-2(2)) Pub: AudioGO. Dist(s): Perseus Dist

Great American Stories: 10 Classics. unabr. ed. Short Stories. Mark Twain et al. Read by Patrick Fraley et al. 4 cass. (Running Time: 5 hrs. 30 min.). (Great American Ser.). 2004. 19.95 (978-0-945353-96-6(0), F40396u) Pub: Audio Partners. Dist(s): PerseuPGW
Stories included are: Mark Twain's "The One-Million Pound Bank Note," "The Celebrated Jumping Frog of Calaveras County," "A Visit to Niagara" & "A Mysterious Visit"; Stephen Crane's "The Blue Hotel" & "The Bride Comes to Yellow Sky"; Ambrose Bierce's "The Eyes of the Panther" & "An Occurrence at Owl Creek Bridge"; & Jack London's "The Love of Life" & "To Build a Fire".

Great American Suspense: 5 Classics. unabr. ed. Short Stories. Edgar Allan Poe et al. Read by Geraint Wyn Davies. 2 cass. (Running Time: 3 hrs.). (Great American Ser.). 2000. 17.95 (978-1-57270-136-6(6), N21136u) Pub: Audio Partners. Dist(s): PerseuPGW
Anthology Masterpiece including works by: Edgar Allan Poe, Nathaniel Hawthorne, Ambrose Bierce, F. Marion Crawford & Robert W. Chambers.

Great American Women's Fiction. unabr. ed. Willa Cather et al. Read by Chris McGlasson. (Running Time: 16500 sec.). (Audio Editions Ser.). (ENG.). 2006. audio compact disk 25.95 (978-1-57270-546-3(9)) Pub: AudioGO. Dist(s): Perseus Dist

Great American Women's Fiction: Ten Classics. unabr. ed. Short Stories. Willa Cather et al. Read by Chris McGlasson et al. 4 cass. (Running Time: 5 hrs. 30 mins.). (Great American Ser.). 2004. 19.95 (978-1-57270-006-2(8), F40006u) Pub: Audio Partners. Dist(s): PerseuPGW
Stories included are: Willa Cather's "On the Divide" & "The Garden Lodge"; Kate Chopin's "A Point at Issue," "The Story of an Hour," "Desiree's Baby," & "A Pair of Silk Stockings"; Charlotte Perkins Gilman's "The Yellow Wallpaper" & "Three Thanksgivings"; & Edith Wharton's "The Pelican" & "The Fullness of Life".

Great American Writers: 21 Stories. unabr. ed. Short Stories. Ann Beattie et al. Read by Edward Asner et al. 6 cass. (Running Time: 7 hrs. 20 mins.). (Great American Ser.). 2004. 24.95 (978-1-57270-021-5(1), M61021u) Pub: Audio Partners. Dist(s): PerseuPGW
Stories from 19 of this century's most renowned authors.

Great Americans in History: A Collection of Biographies. Eric Braun. Read by Full Cast Production Staff. (Playaway Children Ser.). (ENG.). (J). 2009. 35.00 (978-1-60775-607-1(2)) Find a World.

Great Ancient Civilizations of Asia Minor, Pts. I-II. Instructed by Kenneth Harl. 12 CDs. (Running Time: 12 hrs.). 2001. bk. 69.95 (978-1-56585-337-9(7), 363) Teaching Co.

Great Ancient Civilizations of Asia Minor, Vol. 2. Instructed by Kenneth Harl. 6 cass. (Running Time: 6 hrs.). 2001. 129.95 (978-1-56585-089-7(0)); audio compact disk 179.95 (978-1-56585-338-6(5)) Teaching Co.

Great Ancient Civilizations of Asia Minor: Parts I-II. Instructed by Kenneth Harl. 12 cass. (Running Time: 12 hrs.). 54.95 (978-1-56585-088-0(2), 363) Teaching Co.

Great Ancient Goddess. Marija Gimbutas. 2 cass. 18.00 set. (A0261-89) Sound Photosyn.
Gimbutas is the archeologist from whom Riane Eisler gathered much of her "Chalice & the Blade" material. Elegant & reliable.

Great & Abominable Church in Prophecy. unabr. ed. Duane S. Crowther. Read by Duane S. Crowther. 1 cass. (Running Time: 90 min.). 1988. 13.98 (978-0-88290-332-3(2), 1825) Horizon Utah.
This tape talks of Nephi's prophecy of the great & most abominable church which is among the Gentile people. Carefully documented from the scriptures, this tape tells of the wickedness this church will exercise.

Great & Terrible Beauty. Libba Bray. Read by Josephine Bailey. 8 cass. (Running Time: 11 hrs.). (Gemma Doyle Trilogy: Bk. 1). (J). (gr. 8 up). 2004. 50.00 (978-0-8072-2067-2(1), Listening Lib); audio compact disk 60.00 (978-1-4000-8621-4(3), Listening Lib) Random Audio Pubg.

Great & Terrible Beauty. unabr. ed. Libba Bray. Read by Josephine Bailey. (Running Time: 40740 sec.). (Gemma Doyle Trilogy: Bk. 1). (ENG.). (J). (gr. 9-12). 2007. audio compact disk 44.00 (978-0-8072-2376-5(X), Listening Lib) Pub: Random Audio Pubg. Dist(s): Random

Great Anglo-Boer War, Pt. 1. unabr. ed. Byron Farwell. Read by Bill Kelsey. 8 cass. (Running Time: 12 hrs.). 1994. 64.00 (978-0-7366-2868-6(1), 3574-A) Books on Tape.
The Boer War (1899-1902) pitted a sturdy pioneer people against the might of the British Empire at its zenith.

Great Anglo-Boer War, Pt. 2. unabr. ed. Byron Farwell. Read by Bill Kelsey. 8 cass. (Running Time: 12 hrs.). 1994. 64.00 (978-0-7366-2869-3(X), 3574-B) Books on Tape.

Great Architect: Tests & Examinations; Initiation. Jonathan Murro & Ann Ree Colton. 1 cass. 7.95 A R Colton Fnd.

Great Are You Lord. Created by Maranatha! Music. (Praise Ser.). 1999. audio compact disk 9.99 (978-7-01-610884-5(8)) Maranatha Music.

Great Aussie Bites. unabr. ed. Margaret Clark. Read by Stig Wemyss. 2 CDs. (Running Time: 2 hrs. 5 mins.). (Aussie Bites Ser.). (J). 2002. audio compact disk 43.95 (978-1-74030-598-3(1)) Pub: Bolinda Pubng AUS. Dist(s): Bolinda Pub Inc

Great Aussie Bites, Vol. 2. unabr. ed. Sherryl Clark. 2 CDs. (Running Time: 2 hrs. 10 mins.). (Great Aussie Bites Ser.: Vol. 2). (J). 2002. audio compact disk 43.95 (978-1-74030-599-0(X)) Pub: Bolinda Pubng AUS. Dist(s): Bolinda Pub Inc

Great Aussie Bites, Vol. 3. unabr. ed. Max Dann. 2 CDs. (Running Time: 2 hrs. 5 mins.). (Great Aussie Bites Ser.: Vol. 3). (J). 2002. audio compact disk 43.95 (978-1-74030-605-8(8)) Pub: Bolinda Pubng AUS. Dist(s): Bolinda Pub Inc

Great Authors - Mark Twain Collected Stories. unabr. ed. Mark Twain. Read by Thomas Becker. (YA). 2007. 39.99 (978-1-59895-982-6(4)) Find a World.

Great Authors: Arthur Conan Doyle: Sherlock Holmes Mysteries: Arthur Conan Doyle: Sherlock Holmes Mysteries. Arthur Conan Doyle. Read by Ralph Cosham. (Running Time: 4 hrs. 30 mins.). 2003. 22.95 (978-1-59912-067-6(4), Audiofy Corp) Iofy Corp.

Great Authors: Edgar Allan Poe: Collected Stories & Poems: Edgar Allan Poe: Collected Stories & Poems. Edgar Allan Poe. Read by Ralph Cosham. (Running Time: 4 hrs.). 2003. 22.95 (978-1-59912-068-3(2), Audiofy Corp) Iofy Corp.

Great Authors: Edith Wharton: Edith Wharton. Edith Wharton. Read by Ralph Cosham. (Running Time: 5 hrs.). 2003. 22.95 (978-1-59912-069-0(0), Audiofy Corp) Iofy Corp.

Great Authors: H. G. Wells: Collected Sci Fi: H. G. Wells: Collected Sci Fi. H. G. Wells. Read by Ralph Cosham. (Running Time: 4 hrs.). 2003. 22.95 (978-1-59912-070-6(4), Audiofy Corp) Iofy Corp.

Great Authors: Joseph Conrad- Heart of Darkness: Joseph Conrad- Heart of Darkness. Joseph Conrad. Read by Ralph Cosham. (Running Time: 4 hrs.). 2003. 20.95 (978-1-59912-072-0(0), Audiofy Corp) Iofy Corp.

Great Authors: Mark Twain- Collected Stories: Mark Twain- Collected Stories. Mark Twain. Read by Thomas Becker. (Running Time: 4 hrs. 30 mins.). 2003. 22.95 (978-1-59912-073-7(9), Audiofy Corp) Iofy Corp.

Great Authors of the Western Literary Tradition, I-VII. 2nd ed. Instructed by James Heffernan et al. 42 CDs. (Running Time: 42 hrs.). 2004. bk. 199.95 (978-1-56585-976-0(6), 2100) Teaching Co.

Great Authors of the Western Literary Tradition, Pts. I-VII, Vol. 1. Instructed by Arnold Weinstein et al. 40 cass. (Running Time: 60 hrs.). 1993. 399.95 (978-1-56585-014-9(9)) Teaching Co.

Great Authors of the Western Literary Tradition Vol. 2: The Literature of Ancient Greece & Rome. Instructed by S. Georgia Nugent & Michael Sugrue. 5 cass. (Running Time: 7 hrs. 30 mins.). 1993. 399.95 (978-1-56585-015-6(7)) Teaching Co.

Great Authors of the Western Literary Tradition Vol. 3: Medieval Literature & the Birth of English. Instructed by John Fleming. 6 cass. (Running Time: 9 hrs.). 1993. 399.95 (978-1-56585-016-3(5)) Teaching Co.

Great Authors of the Western Literary Tradition Vol. 4: The Literature of the Renaissance. Instructed by Arnold Weinstein et al. 6 cass. (Running Time: 9 hrs.). 1993. 399.95 (978-1-56585-017-0(3)) Teaching Co.

Great Authors of the Western Literary Tradition Vol. 5: Neo-Classical & Romantic Literature. Instructed by Arnold Weinstein et al. 6 cass. (Running Time: 9 hrs.). 1993. 399.95 (978-1-56585-018-7(1)) Teaching Co.

Great Authors of the Western Literary Tradition Vol. 6: The 19th Century: Realism & Naturalism. Instructed by Arnold Weinstein et al. 6 cass. (Running Time: 9 hrs.). 1993. 399.95 (978-1-56585-019-4(X)) Teaching Co.

Great Authors of the Western Literary Tradition Vol. 7: The 20th Century: Modernism & Existentialism. Instructed by Arnold Weinstein et al. 6 cass. (Running Time: 9 hrs.). 1993. 399.95 (978-1-56585-020-0(3)) Teaching Co.

Great Authors of the Western Literary Tradition, 2nd Edition, I-VII. 2nd ed. Instructed by James Heffernan et al. 42 cass. (Running Time: 42 hrs.). 2004. bk. 149.95 (978-1-56585-974-6(X), 2100) Teaching Co.

Great Awakening: Rev. 7:1-17. Ed Young. 1986. 4.95 (978-0-7417-1563-0(5), 563) Win Walk.

Great Awakening: Seven Ways to Change the World. unabr. ed. Jim Wallis. Read by Jim Wallis. Frwd. by Jimmy Carter. 11 CDs. (Running Time: 14 hrs.). 2008. audio compact disk 44.95 (978-0-06-136709-0(5), Harper Audio) HarperCollins Pubs.

Great Baltimore Fire! Pete Petersen. Music by Charlie Poole. Narrated by Ross Ballard. (ENG.). 2004. audio compact disk 28.95 (978-0-9717801-4-9(5)) Mtn Whispers Pubng.

Great Battles of the Ancient World, Vol. I-II. Instructed by Garrett Fagan. 12 cass. (Running Time: 12 hrs.). 2005. 54.95 (978-1-59803-047-1(7), 3757); audio compact disk 69.95 (978-1-59803-049-5(3), 3757) Teaching Co.

Great Big Enormous Turnip, the; Three Poor Tailors. 2004. 8.95 (978-1-56008-912-4(1)); cass. & flmstrp 30.00 (978-1-56008-678-9(5)) Weston Woods.

Great Big Especially Beautiful Easter Egg. James Stevenson. (J). 1980. 49.21 (978-0-676-31107-5(5)) SRA McGraw.

Great Big Mysteries. abr. ed. Richard Scarry. Perf. by Carol Channing. 1 cass. Incl. Great Big Mysteries: Great Big Mystery Book. (J). (CP 1730); Great Big Mysteries: Please & Thank You Book. (J). (CP 1730); Great Big Mysteries: The Great Steamboat Mystery. (J). (CP 1730); (J). 1984. 8.98 (978-0-89845-137-5(X), CP 1730) HarperCollins Pubs.

Great Big Mysteries: Great Big Mystery Book see Great Big Mysteries

Great Big Mysteries: Please & Thank You Book see Great Big Mysteries

Great Big Mysteries: The Great Steamboat Mystery see Great Big Mysteries

Great Big Praise for a Great Big God Bk. 1: 118 Fun, Exciting, Singable Songs for Younger Children. 1 cass. (Running Time: 1 hr.). (YA). 2001. 24.99 (TA-9304S) Lillenas.

Great Big Praise for a Great Big God Bk. 2: 98 Fun, Exciting, Singable Songs for Older Kids. 1 cass. (Running Time: 1 hr.). (YA). 2001. 24.99 (TA-9305S) Lillenas.

Great Big Schoolhouse. (J). (CP 1588) HarperCollins Pubs.

Great Big World. Lyrics by Joe McDermott. 1 CD. (Running Time: 30 min.). (J). (ps-3). 2000. audio compact disk 14.95 (MA264-CD) Big Kids Prods.
Ten original songs cover getting close to the alligators, going to the beach and taking a backyard trip to Hawaii.

Great Black Speeches. 1 cass. (Running Time: 60 mins.). (J). (gr. 4 up). 1999. 13.00 (CDSWC-2070) African Am Imag.

Great Black Speeches. abr. ed. Perf. by Claudia McNeil & Norman Matlock. Ed. by John Graham. 1 cass. Incl. Great Black Speeches: An Appeal to the British People. Frederick Douglass. (SWC 2070); Great Black Speeches: Atlanta Exposition Address. Booker T. Washington. (SWC 2070); Great Black Speeches: O Ye Sons of Africa. Frances Maria Stewart. (SWC 2070); Great Black Speeches: Rather Die Freemen Than Live to Be Slaves. Henry Highland Garnet. (SWC 2070); 1991. 13.00 (978-1-55994-381-9(5), SWC 2070, Harper Audio) HarperCollins Pubs.

Great Black Speeches: An Appeal to the British People see Great Black Speeches

Great Black Speeches: Atlanta Exposition Address see Great Black Speeches

Great Black Speeches: O Ye Sons of Africa see Great Black Speeches

Great Black Speeches: Rather Die Freemen Than Live to Be Slaves see Great Black Speeches

Great Books. Prod. by Michael Enright. Hosted by Michael Enright & B. Meyer. Hosted by B. Meyer. 3 CDs. (Running Time: 3 hrs.). 2005. audio compact disk 24.95 (978-0-660-19216-1(0)) Pub: Canadian Broadcasting CAN. Dist(s): Georgetown Term

Great Books, Vol. 2. Prod. by Michael Enright. Hosted by Michael Enright & B. Meyer. Hosted by B. Meyer. 3 CDs. (Running Time: 3 hrs.). 2005. audio compact disk 24.95 (978-0-660-19217-8(9)) Pub: Canadian Broadcasting CAN. Dist(s): Georgetown Term

Great Books, Vol. 3. Prod. by Michael Enright. Hosted by Michael Enright & B. Meyer. Hosted by B. Meyer. 3 CDs. (Running Time: 3 hrs.). 2005. audio compact disk 24.95 (978-0-660-19218-5(7)) Pub: Canadian Broadcasting CAN. Dist(s): Georgetown Term

Great Books: My Adventures with Homer, Rousseau, Woolf & Other Indestructible Writers of the Western World, abr. ed. David Denby. Read by Edward Asner. 4 cass. (Running Time: 6 hrs.). 1997. 25.95 (978-1-57453-179-4(4)) Audio Lit.
Denby returns to his alma mater to re-experience the freshman humanities courses. What relevance do the thinkers of the past have to our current life? The answer surprised Denby and will enlighten his audience.

Great Books (This Morning) abr. ed. Bruce Meyer & Michael Enright. 2 CDs. (Running Time: 2 hrs.). 2004. audio compact disk 19.95 (978-0-660-19298-7(5)) Pub: Can Mus Civil CAN. Dist(s): U of Wash Pr

Great Books (This Morning), Vol. 3. abr. ed. Bruce Meyer & Michael Enright. 2 CDs. (Running Time: 2 hrs.). 2004. audio compact disk 19.95 (978-0-660-19305-2(1)) Pub: Can Mus Civil CAN. Dist(s): U of Wash Pr

Great Brain. unabr. ed. John D. Fitzgerald. 1 read-along cass. (Running Time: 1 hr. 18 min.). (Children's Cliffhangers Ser.). (J). (gr. 4-6). 1986. 15.98 incl. bk. & guide. (978-0-8072-1142-7(7), SWR53SP, Listening Lib) Random Audio Pubg.
The story of life in turn-of-the century Utah, where mean schoolmasters get their come-uppance & even Skeleton Cabe is no match for the awesome powers of Tom's great brain.

Great Brain. unabr. ed. John D. Fitzgerald. 3 cass. (Running Time: 5 hrs.). (YA). (gr. 3 up). 2002. pap. bk. 35.00 (978-0-8072-0859-5(0), LYA 376 SP, Listening Lib) Random Audio Pubg.
Ten year old Tom D. Fitzgerald is known to everyone as The Great Brain. J.D., The Great Brain's sometimes confounded but always admiring younger brother, tells his story. Such people as Mr. Standish, the mean schoolmaster regret the day they came up against The great Brain. But others, like the Jensen kids lost in Skeleton Cave, Basil, the Greek kid, or Andy, who has lost his leg and his friends, know that Tom's great brain never fails to find a way home.

Great Brain. unabr. ed. John D. Fitzgerald. 3 cass. (Running Time: 4 hrs. 39 mins.). (Great Brain Ser.). (J). (gr. 3-7). 2004. 30.00 (978-0-8072-0735-2(7), Listening Lib) Random Audio Pubg.

Great Bridge: The Epic Story of the Building of the Brooklyn Bridge. David McCullough. Read by Grover Gardner. 1990. audio compact disk 136.00 (978-0-7366-6050-1(X)) Books on Tape.

Great Bridge: The Epic Story of the Building of the Brooklyn Bridge. abr. ed. David McCullough. Read by Edward Herrmann. 2004. 21.95 (978-0-7435-3989-0(3)) Pub: S&S Audio. Dist(s): S and S Inc

Great Bridge: The Epic Story of the Building of the Brooklyn Bridge. abr. ed. David McCullough. Read by Edward Herrmann. 7 CDs. (Running Time: 110 hrs. 0 mins. 0 sec.). (ENG.). 2004. audio compact disk 39.95 (978-0-7435-3723-0(8), Audioworks) Pub: S&S Audio. Dist(s): S and S Inc

Great Bridge: The Epic Story of the Building of the Brooklyn Bridge. unabr. ed. David McCullough. Read by Grover Gardner. 14 cass. (Running Time: 21 hrs.). 1990. 112.00 (978-0-7366-1766-6(3), 2605) Books on Tape.
In the years around 1870, the idea of building a great bridge to span the East River seemed ludicrous. Critics said that it couldn't be done. But there is more to this story than the history of an engineering miracle. It is the narrative of a remarkable decade, and a poignant memoir of those who had a hand in constructing this great bridge.

Great Bridge: The Epic Story of the Building of the Brooklyn Bridge. unabr. ed. David McCullough. Read by Nelson Runger. 19 cass. (Running Time: 27 hrs. 30 mins.). 2006. 109.75 (978-1-4193-6308-5(5)) Recorded Bks.
In the years around 1870, the concept of building a great bridge to span the East River between the great cities of Manhattan and Brooklyn required a vision and determination comparable to that which went into the building of the pyramids. Throughout the 14 years of its construction, the odds against the successful completion of the bridge seemed staggering. But this is not merely the saga of an engineering miracle: it is a sweeping narrative of the social climate of the time and of the heroes and rascals who had a hand in either constructing or obstructing the great enterprise.

Great Bridge: The Epic Story of the Building of the Brooklyn Bridge. unabr. collector's ed. David McCullough. Read by Grover Gardner. 17 CDs. (Running Time: 25 hrs. 30 mins.). 2001. audio compact disk 136.00 Books on Tape.
In the years around 1870, the idea of building a great bridge to span the East River between New York & Brooklyn required vision & determination comparable to that needed to build the Pyramids. Once begun, its completion was never more than an even bet. Construction dragged on for 14 years. Safety was appalling. Political fortunes waxed & waned, as did public emotion over the project. But this is not merely history of an engineering miracle, it is the narrative of a remarkable decade, of the time & of its heroes & rascals, & a poignant memoir of those who had a hand in constructing or obstructing this great enterprise.

Great Britain: Edinburgh - Your Personal Guide (Six Walking Tours) 2 cass. (Running Time: 2 hrs.). 19.95 (CC427) Comp Comms Inc.
Discover Sir Walter Scott Monument, St. Andrews Square, Calton Hill & Grassmarket.

Great Britain: London - A Traveler's Companion (Overview) 1 cass. (Running Time: 60 min.). 11.95 (CC426) Comp Comms Inc.
Highlights four different areas of London, explaining what to see along with the history of each area.

Great Britain: London - Your Personal Guide (Four Walking Tours) (Running Time: 2 hrs.). 19.95 (CC424) Comp Comms Inc.
The tour start & ends at Trafalgar Square with stops along historic Whitehall, Downing Street, a visit to the Houses of Parliament, Westminister Abbey & Buckingham Palace.

Great British Speeches: A Solemn Hour see Great British Speeches, Vol. 4, 1867-1940

Great British Speeches: Before the Battle of Hastings see Great British Speeches: 1597-1625

Great British Speeches: Campaign Speech see Great British Speeches, Vol. 4, 1867-1940

Great British Speeches: Declining the Poll see Great British Speeches: 1628-1780

Great British Speeches: Easter see Great British Speeches: 1597-1625

Great British Speeches: Election Speech see Great British Speeches: 1783-1812

Great British Speeches: Farewell Message see Great British Speeches, Vol. 4, 1867-1940

Great British Speeches: Let Us Go to the King & the Peasant's Rising see Great British Speeches: 1597-1625

Great British Speeches: On Augustine's Mission to England see Great British Speeches: 1597-1625

Great British Speeches: On Meaning see Great British Speeches: 1597-1625

Great British Speeches: On Secret Influence see Great British Speeches: 1783-1812

Great British Speeches: On the Love of Our Country see Great British Speeches: 1783-1812

Great British Speeches: On the Nativity of the Apostles Peter & Paul see Great British Speeches: 1597-1625

Great British Speeches: On the Petition of Right see Great British Speeches: 1628-1780

Great British Speeches: Restoring Peace with America see Great British Speeches: 1628-1780

Great British Speeches: Speech at Limehouse see Great British Speeches, Vol. 4, 1867-1940

Great British Speeches: Speech at the Stake see Great British Speeches: 1597-1625

Great British Speeches: Speech on the Scaffold see Great British Speeches: 1597-1625

Great British Speeches: The Deliverance of Europe see Great British Speeches: 1783-1812

Great British Speeches: The Flight of the Sparrow see Great British Speeches: 1597-1625

Great British Speeches: The Reform Bill see Great British Speeches, Vol. 4, 1867-1940

Great British Speeches: The Use of Money see Great British Speeches: 1628-1780

Great British Speeches: 1597-1625. abr. ed. Read by Brian Bedford et al. Ed. by John Graham. 2 cass. Incl. Great British Speeches: Before the Battle of Hastings. William the Conqueror. (SWC 2061); Great British Speeches: Easter. John Donne. (SWC 2061); Great British Speeches: Let Us Go to the King & the Peasant's Rising. John Ball. (SWC 2061); Great British Speeches: On Augustine's Mission to England. Ethelbert. (SWC 2061); Great British Speeches: On Meaning. John Wyclif. (SWC 2061); Great British Speeches: On the Nativity of the Apostles Peter & Paul. Bede. (SWC 2061); Great British Speeches: Speech at the Stake. Thomas Cranmer. (SWC 2061); Great British Speeches: Speech on the Scaffold. Walter Raleigh. (SWC 2061); Great British Speeches: The Flight of the Sparrow. Edwin of Deira's Alderman. (SWC 2061); 1984. 19.95 (978-0-694-50416-9(5), SWC 2061) HarperCollins Pubs.

Great British Speeches: 1628-1780. abr. ed. Read by Brian Bedford et al. Ed. by John Graham. 2 cass. Incl. Great British Speeches: Declining the Poll. Edmund Burke. (SWC 2062); Great British Speeches: On the Petition of Right. John Eliot. (SWC 2062); Great British Speeches: Restoring Peace with America. William Pitt. (SWC 2062); Great British Speeches: The Use of Money. John Wesley. (SWC 2062); 1984. 19.95 (978-0-694-50417-6(3), SWC 2062) HarperCollins Pubs.

Great British Speeches: 1783-1812. abr. ed. Read by Brian Bedford & Patrick MaGee. Ed. by John Graham. 2 cass. Incl. Great British Speeches: Election Speech. Henry Brougham. (SWC 2063); Great British Speeches: On Secret Influence. Charles James Fox. (SWC 2063); Great British Speeches: On the Love of Our Country. Richard Price. (SWC 2063); Great British Speeches: The Deliverance of Europe. William Pitt. (SWC 2063); 1984. 19.95 (978-0-694-50418-3(1), SWC 2063) HarperCollins Pubs.

Great British Speeches Vol. 4: 1867-1940. abr. ed. Read by Brian Bedford et al. Ed. by John Graham. 2 cass. Incl. Great British Speeches: A Solemn Hour. Winston L. S. Churchill. Perf. by Winston L. S. Churchill. (SWC 2065); Great British Speeches: Campaign Speech. William E. Gladstone. (SWC 2065); Great British Speeches: Farewell Message. Edward VIII. Perf. by Edward VIII. (SWC 2065); Great British Speeches: Speech at Limehouse. David Lloyd George. (SWC 2065); Great British Speeches: The Reform Bill. Benjamin Disreali. (SWC 2065); 1972. 22.00 (978-0-694-50420-6(3), SWC 2065) HarperCollins Pubs.

Great Canadian War Stories. Read by John Born. Ed. by Muriel Whitaker. 4 cass. (ENG., 2002. 39.95 (978-0-88864-388-9(8)) U Alberta Pr CAN.
Shows how the experience of Canada at war captured the imagination of fiction writers across the country. Chronicles the scope of Canadian war efforts in the first half of the twentieth century.

Great Capitalists: What They Have Done. Interview with Leonard Peikoff & Richard Salsman. 1 cass. (Philosophy: Who Needs It? Ser.). 1998. 12.95 (LPXXC75) Second Renaissance.

Great Captains Unveiled. unabr. collector's ed. Basil H. Liddell-Hart. Read by Stuart Courtney. 8 cass. (Running Time: 12 hrs.). 1985. 64.00 (978-0-7366-0477-2(4), 1452) Books on Tape.
Analyzes the careers of six of the greatest military leaders in history. These include Genghis Khan, founder of the Mongol Empire & Subutai, his chief general; Marshall Saxe, 18th century French military prophet; Gustavus Adolphus, founder of modern war; Wallenstein, the German enigma & German Wolfe, whom Hart terms "grandsire of the United States".

Great Catch. 1 cass. (J). (978-0-944391-75-4(3)) DonWise Prodns.
Narrates biblical story designed especially for children.

Great Catherine: The Life of Catherine the Great, Empress of Russia. unabr. ed. Carolly Erickson. Narrated by Davina Porter. 11 cass. (Running Time: 15 hrs. 15 mins.). 1995. 91.00 (978-0-7887-0102-3(9), 94383E7) Recorded Bks.
A biography of the Russian queen, who ascended to the throne in 1762.

Great Central Railway see Sir John Betjeman Reading His Poetry

Great Chase. unabr. ed. Harvey Rosenfeld. Read by Barrett Whitener. 9 cass. (Running Time: 13 hrs.). 2002. 62.95 (978-0-7861-2181-6(5), 2932) Blckstn Audio.
On October 3, 1951, Bobby Thomson's "shot heard around the world" ended one of the most dramatic pennant races ever. Interviews, contemporary newspaper articles, and memoirs of participants are used to describe the intense rivalry and provide a day-by-day look at the Giants' pennant run, including a fascinating examination of the strategy of the final game.

Great Chase, Set. Charles Davis. 2 cass. 11.98 (978-1-55503-815-1(8), 07001223) Covenant Comms.
A fast-paced novel of adventure & romance.

***Great Chase: The Dodgers-Giants Pennant Race Of 1951.** unabr. ed. Harvey Rosenfeld. Read by Barrett Whitener. (Running Time: 13 hrs. NaN mins.). (ENG.). 2011. 29.95 (978-1-4417-8361-5(X)); audio compact disk 105.00 (978-1-4417-8359-2(8)) Blckstn Audio.

Great Cheese Conspiracy. unabr. ed. Jean Van Leeuwen. Read by Full Cast Production Staff. (J). 2007. 34.99 (978-1-60252-484-2(X)) Find a World.

Great Chicago Fire. unabr. ed. Read by Ernie Winstanley. 1 cass. (Running Time: 1 hr.). 1993. 7.95 (978-1-882071-13-5(1), 015) B-B Audio.
From the nearly forgotten files of a great Chicago newspaper, this on-the-scene account brings to life the all-encompassing fire of 1871. Covered by a reporter on the street, it describes in graphic detail the destruction, fear and heroism coupled with h.

Great Christmas Comedy: Selected Sketches. 1 cass. (Running Time: 60 min.). Incl. Bob Hope & Frank Sinatra. Perf. by Bob Hope & Frank Sinatra. (CC-5550); Jack Benny & Fred Allen. Perf. by Jack Benny & Fred Allen. (CC-5550); Night Before Christmas. Perf. by Charlie McCarthy. (CC-5550); Santa Claus Sits Down. Perf. by Fred Allen & Harry Von Zell. (CC-5550); 7.95 (CC-5550) Natl Recrd Co.
In the first sketch, starring Charlie McCarthy & Edgar Bergen, Charlie must recite The Night Before Christmas before he gets his Christmas present from Bergen; Charlie really butchers the poem. In the second sketch, starring Bob Hope & Frank Sinatra, Hope thinks he is receiving an expensive gift from Sinatra & worries about what to get him in return. In the third sketch, starring Jack Benny & Fred Allen, they shop for Christmas gifts for each other in the best bargain basement available. They wind up buying one another the same 59 cent gift. In the fourth sketch, starring Fred Allen, St. Nick refuses to make his trip this year & gives some funny "historical" reasons why.

Great Christmas Kidnapping Caper. unabr. ed. Jean Van Leeuwen. Read by Daniel Bostick & Full Cast Production Staff. (J). 2007. 39.99 (978-1-60252-904-5(3)) Find a World.

***Great Classic Family Favorites: Unabridged Stories.** Ed. by Audiobooks America BBC. (Running Time: 6 hrs. 0 mins. 0 sec.). (ENG.). 2011. audio compact disk 24.95 (978-1-60283-937-3(9)) Pub: AudioGO. Dist(s): Perseus Dist

Great Classic Hauntings: 6 Unabridged Stories. unabr. ed. Short Stories. Ambrose Bierce et al. Read by Geraint Wyn Davies. 2 cass. (Running Time: 2 hrs. 30 mins.). 2000. 17.95 (978-1-57270-147-2(1), N21147u) Pub: Audio Partners. Dist(s): PerseuPGW
A brilliant collection including works by Ambrose Bierce, Robert Louis Stevenson, Washington Irving, J. Sheridan Le Fanu, Edgar Allan Poe & Saki.

Great Classic Horror: Five Unabridged Classic Tales of Dark, Eerie Power. unabr. ed. Geraint Wyn Davies. 3 CDs. 2009. audio compact disk 19.95 (978-1-60283-641-9(8)) AudioGO.

Great Classic Love Stories. unabr. ed. William Shakespeare et al. 7 CDs. (Running Time: 8 hrs. 30 mins. 0 sec.). (ENG.). 2010. audio compact disk 24.95 (978-1-60283-871-0(2)) Pub: AudioGO. Dist(s): Perseus Dist

***Great Classic Mysteries: Unabridged Stories.** Ed. by Audiobooks America BBC. (Running Time: 6 hrs. 0 mins. 0 sec.). (ENG.). 2010. audio compact disk 24.95 (978-1-60283-935-9(2)) Pub: AudioGO. Dist(s): Perseus Dist

Great Classic Science. unabr. ed. H. G. Wells et al. 7 CDs. (Running Time: 8 hrs. 30 mins. 0 sec.). (ENG.). 2010. audio compact disk 24.95 (978-1-60283-874-1(7)) Pub: AudioGO. Dist(s): Perseus Dist

Great Classic Stories: 22 Unabridged Classics. unabr. ed. Derek Jacobi et al. Read by Kerry Shale et al. (ENG.). 2006. audio compact disk 29.95 (978-1-57270-561-6(2)) Pub: AudioGO. Dist(s): Perseus Dist

Great Classic Stories No. 2. unabr. ed. Jerome K. Jerome. Read by Martin Jarvis & Hugh Laurie. (Running Time: 7 hrs. 30 mins. 0 sec.). (Great Classic Stories Ser.). (ENG.). 2008. audio compact disk 31.95 (978-1-934997-06-2(4)) Pub: CSAWord. Dist(s): PerseuPGW

***Great Classic Stories II.** (Running Time: 7 hrs. 30 mins. 0 sec.). (ENG.). 2010. audio compact disk 29.95 (978-1-60998-012-2(3)) Pub: AudioGO. Dist(s): Perseus Dist

Great Classic Stories 3: 20 Unabridged Classics. unabr. ed. Read by Patrick Malahide & Richard Pasco. Narrated by Stephen Fry et al. (Running Time: 7 hrs. 30 mins. 0 sec.). (Great Classic Stories Ser.). 2009. audio compact disk 31.95 (978-1-934997-25-3(0)) Pub: CSAWord. Dist(s): PerseuPGW

Great Classical Composers. unabr. ed. David Allen et al. Read by Richard Mayes et al. 8 cass. (Running Time: 12 hrs.). 2001. 34.95 (978-1-57270-238-7(9), E81238a, Audio Editions) Pub: Audio Partners. Dist(s): PerseuPGW
Provides an individual biography of each composer along with dramatization & interwoven interludes that are examples of the music created by that musician. The narrations include the fascinating details of the ups & downs of each life, including the struggles each faced & the public response to his musical creations.

Great Claus & Little Claus. Hans Christian Andersen. 1 cass. (J). 10.95 (978-0-8045-0873-5(9), SAC 873) Spoken Arts.

Great Co-Mission. John MacArthur, Jr. 2 cass. 7.95 (22-19, HarperThor) HarpC GBR.

Great Collection of the Lives of the Saints: September. 12 cass. (Running Time: 14 hrs.). 2003. 65.00 (978-0-9674413-0-6(7)) St Vladimirs.

Great Commandment: Matthew 22:27-40. Ed Young. 1985. 4.95 (978-0-7417-1439-8(6), 439) Win Walk.

Great Commission. Speeches. Joel Osteen. 1 Cass. (Running Time: 30 Mins.). (J). 2000. 6.00 (978-1-59349-049-2(6), JA0049) J Osteen.

Great Commission. abr. ed. Reinhard Bonnke. 2001. audio compact disk 7.00 (978-1-933106-50-2(6)) E-R-Productions.

Great Commission: Acts 1:18. Ed Young. 1983. 4.95 (978-0-7417-1274-5(1), 274) Win Walk.

Great Communication = Great Production Quick Study. 1995. 31.95 (978-0-87814-473-0(0)) PennWell Corp.

Great Compassion Repentance. audio compact disk 15.00 (978-0-88139-713-0(X)) Buddhist Text.

Great Composers, 1 cass. 1999. (NBFLS7); audio compact disk (NCHCZ7) Time-Life.
Begin with Beethoven: Symphony No. 6 "Pastoral," Symphony No. 5 Berlin Philharmonic Orchestra, Herbert von Karajan, conductor Piano Concerto No. 5 "Emperor" Wilhelm Kempff, piano, Berlin Philharmonic Orchestra, Ferdinand Leitner, conductor, Piano sonata No.14 "Moonlight.".

Great Concertos. audio compact disk 24.98 CD. (978-1-57908-201-7(7), 1216) Platinm Enter.

Great Contemporaries. unabr. collector's ed. Winston L. S. Churchill. Read by David Case. 8 cass. (Running Time: 12 hrs.). 1990. 64.00 (978-0-7366-2238-7(1), 3028) Books on Tape.
Great Contemporaries is a collection of essays about 21 men whom Winston S. Churchill felt contributed to the course of the world in which he lived. The central theme is a group of British statesmen who shone in the late 1800s & early in this century - Balfour, Chamberlain, Rosebery, Morley, Asquith & Curzon. Others whose acquaintance we make through Churchill's eyes include George Bernard Shaw, Hindenburg, Lawrence of Arabia, Marshall Foch, Leon Trotsky, Philip Snowden, Clemenceau & King George V.

Great Controversy. Ellen G. White. 25 CDs. (Running Time:). audio compact disk (978-1-883012-08-3(2)) Remnant Pubns.

Great Conversations: Talking to Writers: The Sunday Edition. abr. ed. Told to Michael Enright. 2 CDs. (Running Time: 7200 sec.). (Great Conversations Ser.). 2005. audio compact disk 19.95 (978-0-660-19385-4(X)) Canadian Broadcasting CAN.

Great Conversations with Michael Enright: Volume 2, Vol. 2. abr. ed. Interview. 2 CDs. (Running Time: 7200 sec.). (Ideas Ser.). 2006. audio compact disk 19.95 (978-0-660-19548-3(8), CBC Audio) Canadian Broadcasting CAN.

Great Country Duets. (Running Time: 29 mins.). 2006. audio compact disk 5.95 (978-1-59987-523-1(3)) Braun Media.

Great Coverup: Ecc. 1:1-2. Ed Young. 1993. 4.95 (978-0-7417-1975-1(4), 975) Win Walk.

Great Crash 1929. unabr. ed. John Kenneth Galbraith. Read by John MacDonald. 7 cass. (Running Time: 7 hrs.). 1987. 40.00 (978-0-7366-1109-1(6), 2035) Books on Tape.
Economic & social account of events leading up to the 1929 stock market crash, making comparisons with the mood of the 1980's.

Great Crash 1929. unabr. ed. John Kenneth Galbraith. Narrated by Nelson Runger. 5 cass. (Running Time: 6 hrs. 30 mins.). 1987. 44.00 (978-1-55690-203-1(4), 89350E7) Recorded Bks.
An account of the great financial crash of 1929. With grace & wit, America's foremost economist examines the boom & bust that led to the sock market crash of 1929.

Great Crooners. Delilah Jones. (CD Ser.). 2001. bk. 16.98 (978-1-56799-301-1(X), Friedman-Fairfax) M Friedman Pub Grp Inc.

***Great Day! A Choral Celebration for Christmas.** Contrib. by Mosie Lister. (ENG.). 1994. audio compact disk 90.00 (978-0-00-503932-8(0)) Lillenas.

Great Day of the Lord. 2003. audio compact disk 8.00 (978-0-9747608-0-3(3)) D Waltz.

***Great Death.** unabr. ed. John Smelcer. Narrated by Lorna Raver. 3 CDs. (Running Time: 3 hrs. 42 mins.). (YA). (gr. 6-9). 2009. audio compact disk 30.00 (978-0-7393-7177-0(0), Listening Lib) Pub: Random Audio Pubg. Dist(s): Random

Great Debate: Advocates & Opponents of the American Constitution. Instructed by Thomas L. Pangle. 2007. 89.95 (978-1-59803-364-9(6)); audio compact disk 39.95 (978-1-59803-365-6(4)) Teaching Co.

Great Debate: Does God Exist? Greg Bahnsen & Gordon Stein. (ENG.). 1985. 12.00 (978-0-9678317-7-0(6)) Covenant Media.

Great Deception. Joe Schimmel. 1 cass. 3.00 (JS1) Evang Outreach.

***Great Deception.** Carl Sommer. (Quest for Success Ser.). (ENG.). (YA). 2009. bk. 19.95 (978-1-57537-329-4(7)); pap. bk. 11.95 (978-1-57537-378-2(5)) Advance Pub.

***Great Deception / el Gran Engaño.** ed. Carl Sommer. (Quest for Success Bilingual Ser.). (ENG & SPA.). (YA). 2009. bk. 21.95 (978-1-57537-428-4(5)) Advance Pub.

Great Deliverance. unabr. ed. Elizabeth George. Read by Donada Peters. 8 cass. (Running Time: 12 hrs.). (Inspector Lynley Ser.). 1994. 64.00 (978-0-7366-2624-8(7), 3364) Books on Tape.
Roberta Teys sits by her father's headless corpse, an axe in her lap. "I did it," she says, "& I'm not sorry." Inspector Thomas Lynley & Detective Sergeant Barbara Havers, both of Scotland Yard, discover a labyrinth of crimes that reverberate through the surrounding countryside...& their own lives as well.

Great Deliverance-mp3: Justification. 9. 2005. 28.00 (978-1-59128-557-1(7)) Canon Pr ID.

Great Deliverance-tape: Justification. 9 cass. 2005. 35.00 (978-1-59128-559-5(3)) Canon Pr ID.

***Great Deluge.** abr. ed. Douglas Brinkley. Read by Kyf Brewer. (ENG.). 2006. (978-0-06-120934-5(1), Harper Audio); (978-0-06-120932-1(5), Harper Audio) HarperCollins Pubs.

Great Deluge: Hurricane Katrina, New Orleans, & the Mississippi Gulf Coast. abr. ed. Douglas Brinkley. Read by Kyf Brewer. (Running Time: 21600 sec.). 2006. audio compact disk 29.95 (978-0-06-112894-3(5)) HarperCollins Pubs.

Great Democracies: A History of the English-Speaking Peoples, Volume 4, Vol. 4. unabr. ed. Winston S. Churchill. 11 CDs. (Running Time: 42720 sec.). 2006. audio compact disk 99.95 (978-0-7927-4493-1(4), SLD 1023) AudioGO.

Great Depression. 10.00 (HD412) Esstee Audios.

Great Depression. 1 cass. (Running Time: 1 hr.). 10.95 (G0450B090, HarperThor) HarpC GBR.

Great Depression Ahead: How to Prosper in the Crash Following the Greatest Boom in History. abr. ed. Harry S. Dent, Jr.. Read by Harry S. Dent, Jr. (Running Time: 6 hrs. 0 mins. 0 sec.). (ENG.). 2009. audio compact disk 29.99 (978-0-7435-8075-5(3)) Pub: S&S Audio. Dist(s): S and S Inc

Great Detective Stories. Arthur Conan Doyle et al. Read by David Case. (Running Time: 2 hrs.). 2002. 17.95 (978-1-59912-075-1(5), Audiofy Corp) Iofy Corp.

Great Detective Stories. unabr. ed. Short Stories. Edgar Allan Poe et al. Read by David Case. 2 cds. (Running Time: 2 hrs 14 mins). (YA). 2002. audio compact disk 18.95 (978-1-58472-254-0(1), 058, In Aud) Pub: Sound Room. Dist(s): Baker Taylor
Contains The Purloined Letter, The Biter Bit and The Man In The Passage.

Great Detective Stories: The Purloined Letter, the Crooked Man, the Man in the Passage. Edgar Allan Poe et al. Read by David Case. (Playaway Adult Fiction Ser.). 2008. 39.99 (978-1-60640-825-4(9)) Find a World.

Great Detective Stories: The Purloined Letter, the Crooked Man, the Man in the Passage. Edgar Allan Poe et al. Narrated by David Case. (Running Time: 8040 sec.). (Unabridged Classics in MP3 Ser.). (ENG.). 2008. audio compact disk 24.00 (978-1-58472-662-3(8), In Aud) Sound Room.

Great Detectives, Vol. 1, Set. 6 cass. (Running Time: 6 hrs.). vinyl bd. 24.95 (978-1-57816-026-6(X), GD1011) Audio File.
Includes: "Bulldog Drummond" (1940s); "Ellery Queen" (3-27-43); "The Fat Man" (10-3-47); "Nick Carter, Master Detective" (8-15-48); "The Man Called X" (9-30-44); "Philip Marlowe" (1-8-49); "Richard Diamond, Private Detective" (2-9-51); "Sam Spade" (8-8-48); "The Shadow" (1-19-41); "Sherlock Holmes" (1933); "The Thin Man" (10-10-43); "Yours Truly, Johnny Dollar" (4-4-50).

Great Detectives, Vol. 2, Set. 6 cass. (Running Time: 6 hrs.). 24.95 bookshelf album. (978-1-57816-027-3(8), GD2021) Audio File.
Includes: "Barry Craig, Confidential Investigator" (12-5-51); "Boston Blackie" (1-23-45); "Bulldog Drummond" (1-17-47); "Casey, Crime Photographer" (3-20-47); "The Fat Man" (1-17-51); "Jeff Regan, Investigator" (8-14-48); "Mr. & Mrs. North" (9-19-54); "Mr. Keen, Tracer of Lost Persons" (10-6-49); "Richard Diamond, Private Detective" (1-12-51); "Sam Spade, Detective" (4-10-49); "The Shadow" (9-14-47); "Sherlock Holmes" (2-22-48).

Great Dinosaur Mystery: A Musical Fossil Fantasy. Perf. by DinoRock Performers Staff. (J). 9.98; audio compact disk 14.98 Rounder Records.
Kids can solve "The Great Dinosaur Mystery". It's a mystery & Detective Joe Kafootsi is on the case, plunging into the Mesozoic Era with singing paleontologist Dr. Vander PlasterCaster. How can the fossils at the museum's dinosaur exhibit be coming to life? Cryptic messages from ancient creatures are the only clues. What are the dinosaurs trying to tell us? It all adds up to another fossil fantasy from DinoRock.

Great Dinosaur Mystery Solved! abr. ed. Ken Ham. (Ken Ham's Creation Audio Ser.). 2005. audio compact disk 15.99 (978-0-89051-447-4(X)) Master Bks.
Internationally known author and speaker Ken Ham brings a ?new way of thinking? to the table for Christians, emphasizing that dinosaurs are no mystery when studied in the light of Scripture. Junior high to adult level.

Great Discoveries, Personal Audio Guide, Florence Italy's, Basilica di San Lorenzo, Basilica of St. Lawrence: Formated for CD Players. Scripts. William Browne. Narrated by Christopher Kent. 2 CDs. (Running Time: 1 hr.

24 mins.). 2005. audio compact disk Rental 21.95 (978-1-59971-123-2(0)) AardGP.
One hour and twenty-four minutes of playtime provide today's independent traveler with an unparalleled audio tour of the Basilica di San Lorenzo, the Medici Chapels and Michelangelo's New Sacristy and Laurentian Library. One of Florence's most precious treasures and the city's oldest church, the Basilica is a Renaissance masterpiece designed by great Florentine maestro Fillipo Brunelleschi. Generations of Medici's, Florence's wealthiest and most powerful family, put some of the world's greatest artists to work here, men like Michelangelo, Donatello and Fillipo Lippi. It is also important for its historical connection to the Medici's. This was their family church and generations of the great and not so great Medici are buried here. Professional narrators delight, inform and amuse as they guide the listener and discuss San Lorenzo's remarkable history and the lives and deaths of the Medici Dukes, Florence's ruling family for over three-hundred years. The absolute jewel of the Medici Chapels is Michelangelo's New Sacristy, the heart of the museum and a fatal attraction for the thousands of people who visit each year. Michelangelo spent over fourteen years of his life designing and building the New Sacristy, which contains some of his most important works and the tomb of the greatest of the Medici, Lorenzo the Magnificent. Visitors will view the Laurentian Library, built by Michelangelo to house the Medici's century's old collection of 15,000 precious books, papyri and manuscripts, some collected by the original Medici godfather, Cosimo the Elder. Many of these historic and irreplaceable documents are on display today. Michelangelo designed everything in this reading room including the stalls. This 37 track audio tour is in standard CD format, on 2 CD's, ready for play on any CD player. Not for use on MP3 players.

Great Discoveries, Personal Audio Guide, Florence Italy's, Basilica di San Lorenzo, Basilica of St. Lawrence: MP3 Format. Scripts. William Browne. Narrated by Christopher Kent. 1 CD. (Running Time: 1 hr. 24 mins.). 2005. Rental 19.95 (978-1-59971-115-7(X)) AardGP.

Great Discoveries, Personal Audio Guide, Florence Italy's, Galleria dell' Accademia, Academy Gallery: Home to Michelangelo's David. MP3 Format. Scripts. William Browne. Narrated by Christopher Kent. 1. (Running Time: 1 hr 12 min). Dramatization. (YA). 2005. 19.95 (978-1-59971-102-7(8)) AardGP.
One hour and twelve minutes of playtime provides today's independent traveler with an unparalleled audio tour of the Florentine home to Michelangelo's magnificent statue, David. Professional narrators delight, inform and amuse the listener as they explain the Accademia's great history and discuss the wonderful art contained therein. This 14 track audio tour is in MP3 format, on 1 CD, ready for copying to any MP3 device library. Not for use on a regular CD player.

Great Discoveries, Personal Audio Guide, Florence Italy's, Palazzo Vecchio, Old Palace MP3 Format: MP3 Format. William Browne. Narrated by Christopher Kent. 1 CD. (Running Time: 1 hr. 43 mins.). 2005. Rental 19.95 (978-1-59971-103-4(6)) AardGP.

Great Discoveries, Personal Audio Guide, Florence Italy's, Pitti Palace, Palazzo Pitti: MP3 Format. Scripts. 1. (Running Time: 3 hrs. 40 mins.). 2005. Rental 19.95 (978-1-59971-101-0(X)) AardGP.
Three hours and forty minutes of playtime provide today?s independent traveler with an unparalleled audio tour of Italy?s grandest Renaissance palace. Now one of the world?s great museums, the Pitti Palace was, from the 16th century on, home to the ruling families of Florence, Tuscany and Italy. The Medici?s, the Lorraine?s, the Bourbon's, the Bonaparte?s and the Savoy?s resided here. Professional narrators delight, inform and amuse as they present the palaces history, its great works of art, and the lives of the people, while guiding the listener through the Palatine Galleries and Royal Apartments. Its countless rambling rooms house several museums, the most important of which is the Palatine Gallery, whose beautiful salons are filled from floor to ceiling with paintings from the Medici private collection. It was in these rooms that the Medici accumulated the collections of great and not so great works of art that create the unique character of the Palatine Galleries. It is one of the largest and most important collections in the world containing works by Michelangelo, Raphael, Titian, Botticelli, Lippi, Tintoretto, Peter Paul Rubins, and others. This 42 track audio tour of the Palatine Galleries and the Royal Apartments is in MP3 format, on one CD, ready for copying to any MP3 device library. Not for use on a regular CD player.

Great Discoveries, Personal Audio Guide, Florence Italy's, Santa Croce Basilica, Basilica of the Holy Cross: Formated for CD Players. Scripts. William Browne. Narrated by Christopher Kent. 2 CDs. (Running Time: 1 hr. 49 mins.). 2005. audio compact disk 21.95 (978-1-59971-129-4(X)) AardGP.
One hour and forty-nine minutes of playtime provide today's independent traveler with an unparalleled audio tour of Santa Croce, perhaps the most beautiful Gothic church in all of Italy. The basilica's spectacular interior is most famous for its art and its tombs. As a burial place, the church, known as the "Westminster Abbey" of Florence, contains more skeletons of Renaissance celebrities than any other church in Italy. Here you will find the monumental tombs and mortal remains of Michelangelo, Galileo, Machiavelli, Gioacchino Rossini, and Ugo Foscolo. Although exiled from Florence and buried in Ravenna, Dante, the great poet and father of the Italian language, is honored with a cenotaph. The tombs are grand with some realistic carvings of the great and the good in final repose. Professional narrators delight, inform and amuse as they guide the listener along, while discussing Santa Croce's remarkable history, its spectacular medieval and Renaissance art, and the lives of its famous residents in final repose. This 37 track audio tour is in standard CD format, on 2 CD's, ready for play on any CD player. Not for use on MP3 players.

Great Discoveries, Personal Audio Guide, Florence Italy's, Santa Croce Basilica, Basilica of the Holy Cross: MP3 Format. Scripts. William Browne. Narrated by Christopher Kent. 1 CD. (Running Time: 1 hr. 49 mnis.). 2005. 19.95 (978-1-59971-114-0(1)) AardGP.

Great Discoveries, Personal Audio Guide, Florence Italy's, Santa Maria Novella Basilica: Formated for CD Players. Scripts. William Browne. Narrated by Christopher Kent. 2 CDs. (Running Time: 1 hr. 43 mins.). 2005. audio compact disk 21.95 (978-1-59971-126-3(5)) AardGP.
One hour and forty-tree minutes of playtime provide today's independent traveler with an unparalleled audio tour of Santa Maria Novella, the mother church of Florence's Dominican Order and one of the most picturesque churches in all of Florence. The Dominicans, or the Domini Canes (the Hounds of God), mission was to hunt down heresy and punish the heretics. Its members are referred to as black friars, the mendicant friars who revolutionized religious life in Europe during the high Middle Ages. Here visitors will see Brunelleschi's pulpit, chiefly famous as the spot from which the Dominican monks first denounced Galileo as a heretic for espousing the Copernican theory of the universe. Professional narrators delight, inform and amuse as they guide the listener and discuss the many treasures that fill the churches interior, not the least of which is a groundbreaking painting by Masaccio, a crucifix by Giotto and no fewer than three major fresco cycles. This 15 track audio tour is in standard CD format, on 2 CD's, ready for play on any CD player. Not for use on MP3 players.

Great Discoveries, Personal Audio Guide, Florence Italy's, Santa Maria Novella Basilica: MP3 Format. Scripts. William Browne. Narrated by Christopher Kent. 1 CD. (Running Time: 1 hr. 43 mins.). 2005. 19.95 (978-1-59971-112-6(5)) AardGP.
One hour and forty-tree minutes of playtime provide today?s independent traveler with an unparalleled audio tour of Santa Maria Novella, the mother church of Florence?s Dominican Order and one of the most picturesque churches in all of Florence. The Dominicans, or the Domini Canes (the Hounds of God), mission was to hunt down heresy and punish the heretics. Its members are referred to as black friars, the mendicant friars who revolutionized religious life in Europe during the high Middle Ages. Here visitors will see Brunelleschi?s pulpit, chiefly famous as the spot from which the Dominican monks first denounced Galileo as a heretic for espousing the Copernican theory of the universe. Professional narrators delight, inform and amuse as they guide the listener and discuss the many treasures that fill the churches interior, not the least of which is a groundbreaking painting by Masaccio, a crucifix by Giotto and no fewer than three major fresco cycles. This 15 track audio tour of Santa Maria Novella is in MP3 format, on one CD, and ready for copying to any MP3 device library. Not for use on a regular CD player.

Great Discoveries, Personal Audio Guide, Florence Italy's, Uffizi Gallery, Galleria degli Uffizi: Formated for CD Players. Scripts. Jessica Krzywicki. Narrated by Christopher Kent. 4 CDs. (Running Time: 4 hrs. 28 mins.). 2005. audio compact disk 26.95 (978-1-59971-127-0(3)) AardGP.
Four hours and twenty-eight minutes of playtime provide today's independent traveler with an unparalleled audio tour of the Uffizi Gallery, known simply as the Uffizi, one of the world's greatest art galleries and home to a collection of medieval, Renaissance and other paintings by some of the most hallowed names in Italian and European art. The exhibition area is composed of over 45 rooms that contain about 1,700 paintings, 300 sculptures, 46 tapestries, and 14 pieces of furniture and ceramics. Here you will find paintings by the early masters like Cimabue and Giotto and magnificent Renaissance works by Veneziano, Uccello, Leonardo, Michelangelo, Raphael, Lippi, Botticelli, Giorgione, Titian, Tintoretto, and many others. Two of the world's most famous paintings, Botticelli's "Birth of Venus" and "La Primavera" are displayed here. Professional narrators delight, inform and amuse as they guide the listener through the many rooms containing historically important works of early 13th through the late 18th century artists. The most important pieces, by the most prominent European artist of their time, have been carefully selected for discussion. This 35 track audio tour is in standard CD format, on 4 CD's, ready for play on any CD player. Not for use on MP3 players.

Great Discoveries Personal Audio Guide Florence's Baptistery of St. John, Battistero di San Giovanni: MP3 Format. Scripts. William Browne. Narrated by Christopher Kent. 1 CD. (Running Time: 36 min). 2005. 19.95 (978-1-59971-106-5(0)) AardGP.
Thirty-six minutes of playtime provide today's independent traveler with an unparalleled audio tour of Florence Italy's Baptistery of St. John, (Battistero di San Giovanni). Professional narrators delight, inform and amuse the listener as they explain the Baptistery's history (from Roman antiquity), her artwork and Ghiberti's magnificent "Gates of Paradise". This 4 track audio tour is in MP3 format, on one CD, ready for copying to any MP3 device library. Not for use on a regular CD player.

Great Discoveries, Personal Audio Guide, to Florence Italy's Piazza Della Signoria, Signoria Square: MP3 Format. Scripts. William Browne. Narrated by Christopher Kent. 1CD. (Running Time: 1 hr. 19 mins.). 2005. Rental 19.95 (978-1-59971-105-8(2)) AardGP.
One hour and nineteen minutes of playtime provide today's independent traveler with an unparalleled audio tour of the Piazza della Signoria, the centuries old heart of Florentine political life. Professional narrators delight, inform and amuse the listener as they explain the piazza's great history and discuss the wonderful works of art contained in this one-of-a-kind outdoor museum. This 14 track audio tour is in MP3 format, on one CD, ready for copying to any MP3 device library. Not for use on a regular CD player.

Great Discoveries, Personal Audio Guide, to Florence's Duomo, Cathedral of Santa Maria del Fiore: MP3 Format. Scripts. William Browne. Narrated by Christopher Kent. 1. (Running Time: 2 hrs 3 mins). Dramatization. 2005. 19.95 (978-1-59971-100-3(1)) AardGP.
Two hour and three minutes of playtime provide today's independent traveler with an unparalleled audio tour of Florence Italy's greatest cathedral, the Cathedral of Santa Maria del Fiore, better known as the Duomo. Professional narrators delight, inform and amuse the listener as they explain the Duomo's great history, including descriptions Brunelleschi's great Dome and Giotto's magnificent Campanile (Bell Tower). This 20 track audio tour is in MP3 format, on 1 CD, ready for copying to any MP3 device library. Not for use on a regular CD player.

Great Discoveries ¿Personal Audio Guide to Venice Italy¿s, Ca' Rezzonico (Rezzonico Palace) MP3 Format. Scripts. Stephen Soncini. Narrated by Christopher Kent. 1 CD. (Running Time: 2 hrs. 10 mins.). 2005. Rental 19.95 (978-1-59971-113-3(3)) AardGP.
Two hours and ten minutes of playtime provide today's independent traveler with an unparalleled audio tour of this majestic but imposing 17th century marble palace that today is a gallery dedicated to 18th century Venetian art. Ca' Rezzonico stands on the right bank of the Grand Canal at its junction with the rio di San Barnaba. It is one of the few palaces in Venice Italy permitting public insight into what lies behind the ornamental, but often secretive, facades of the many exquisite buildings that line the Grand Canal. Ca' Rezzonico was acquired by the City Council of Venice to display its vast collections of 18th century Venetian art. It is one of the finest museums in Venice, largely because of its unique character, where objects designed for great palazzo's are displayed in a palace, thus the contents and the building harmonize in a way not possible in a purposely built museum. Today the palazzo is furnished with contents more magnificent than at any time in its history. This 23 track audio tour is in MP3 format, on one CD, ready for copying to any MP3 device library. Not for use on a regular CD player.

Great Discoveries, Personal Audio Guide, Venice Italy's, Accademia Galleries: MP3 Format. Scripts. Jennifer Dennis. Narrated by Christopher Kent. 1. (Running Time: 2 hrs. 10 mins.). 2005. 19.95 (978-1-59971-124-9(9)) AardGP.
Two hours and ten minutes of playtime provide today's independent traveler with an unparalleled audio tour of the Accademia Galleries of Venice, home to an unparalleled collection of paintings from the Venetian masters of the 13th through the 18th centuries. Five hundred years of Venetian art are displayed in the Galleries, which for consistency, clarity of display and quality cannot be equaled anywhere in the world. Professional narrators delight, inform and amuse as they guide the listener along while discussing the lives and the art of the great Venetian medieval and Renaissance painters. The works of Vittore Carpaccio, Giovanni Bellini, Gentile Bellini, Andrea Mantegna, Giorgione, Lorenzo Lotto, Tiziano Vecellio (Titian), Jacopo Tintoretto, Paolo Veronese, Gian Battista Tiepolo, Canaletto, Francesco Guardi, Giambattista Piazzetta, Pietro Longhi and others are displayed here. This 21 track audio tour is in MP3 format, on one CD, ready for copying to any MP3 device library. Not for use on a regular CD player.

Great Discoveries, Personal Audio Guide, Venice Italy's, Ca' D'Oro: MP3 Format. Scripts. Jessica Krzywicki. 1 CD. (Running Time: 1 hr. 34 mins.). 2005. 19.95 (978-1-59971-131-7(1)) AardGP.
One hour and thirty-four minutes of playtime provide today's independent traveler with an unparalleled audio tour of one of the most charming buildings in all of Venice. The ca' d'Oro is one of the older palaces, or palazzi, lining the Grand Canal, its harmony of design and color continue to fascinate and charm Venetians and visitors alike. The palace has always been known as Ca' d'Oro (Golden House) due to the long lost gilded decorations which once adorned its facade. In 1922, the palaces last owner, Baron Giorgio Franchetti, bequeathed both the palace and his private collection of artworks to the state. Extensive renovations were preformed to return it to its former glory and the colors of this beautiful mansion's exterior once again reflect in Venice's Grand Canal. The Ca d'Oro, which is also known as the Giorgio Franchetti Gallery, is now open to the public and it houses a collection of important Venetian paintings and other artworks. This 14 track audio tour is in MP3 format, on one CD, ready for copying to any MP3 device library. Not for use on a regular CD player.

Great Discoveries, Personal Audio Guide, Venice Italy's, Piazza San Marco: MP3 Format. Scripts. James Sweeney. Narrated by Christopher Kent. 1 CD. (Running Time: 1 hr. 1 minute). 2005. 19.95 (978-1-59971-121-8(4)) AardGP.
One hour and one minute of playtime provide today's independent traveler with an unparalleled audio tour of this majestic square, which, according to most Venetians, is the only place in the city "worthy of having the sky for its roof." Piazza San Marco is a majestic trapezoid shaped space whose sheer scale alone defies one's senses. It is as overwhelming as it is exhilarating; overwhelming for its size and the hordes of tourists it holds, and exhilarating because, as squares go, this one is nearly perfect in its shape and architectural details. Professional narrators delight, inform and amuse as they guide the listener along while discussing the symmetry of the piazza and its history. The majesty of its bordering buildings, the beautiful St. Mark's Basilica, the imposing Doge's Palace and the Bell Tower (Campanile) can leave even the most callused traveler dumbstruck. On a sunny day the sun reflects off the Basilica's mosaics, creating a golden glow which reinforces the myths and stories surrounding the history of this magnificent edifice. Napoleon once described Piazza San Marco as the "finest drawing room in Europe." This 14 track audio tour is in MP3 format, on one CD, ready for copying to any MP3 device library. Not for use on a regular CD player.

Great Discoveries, Personal Audio Guide, Venice Italy's, Santa Maria della Salute: MP3 Format. Scripts. Stephen Soncini. Narrated by Christopher Kent. 1 CD. (Running Time: 1 hr. 28 mins.). 2005. 19.95 (978-1-59971-128-7(1)) AardGP.
One hour and twenty-eight minutes of playtime provide today's independent traveler with an unparalleled audio tour of this, the most brilliant architectural jewel in the Venetian crown, a soaring baroque structure unlike any other. La Salute lifts its gleaming drum of white istrian stone high above the city's tiled rooftops as its silhouette dominates the southern terminus of the Grand Canal. The church sits at the entrance to Venice Italy like some great lady, on the threshold of her salon, with her domes and scrolls, her scalloped buttresses and statues forming a pompous crown, her wide steps placed on the ground like the train of a great robe. Throughout history, great plagues, wars, and disease have stimulated great art and architecture. La Salute is a case in point. In 1630, a plague had struck Venice taking some 45,000 people, over a quarter of its citizens, to early graves. In the midst of this horror, the Venetian Senate made a pact with God, "Stop the plague and we will build a church to honor the Virgin Mary." The pact worked, the plague came to a sudden end, most likely due to cooler weather, and the Senate set about honoring their promise to God by building the Basilica di Santa Maria della Salute or the Basilica of St. Mary of Good Health. Professional narrators delight, inform and amuse as they guide the listener through this magnificent cathedral as they discuss her remarkable history and remarkable art. La Salute contains masterpieces and great works aplenty including two of Titian's greatest paintings, "the Pentecost" and "St. Mark Enthroned with Other Saints." The large Sacristy contains an additional wealth of unforgettable Titian paintings as well as the work of other artists. Outstanding among these is one of Tintoretto's most famous paintings, the "Wedding at Cana." This 17 track audio tour is in MP3 format, on one CD, ready for copying to any MP3 device library. Not for use on a regular CD player.

Great Discoveries, Personal Audio Guide, Venice Italy's, Santa Maria Gloriosa dei Frari Basilica: MP3 Format. Scripts. James Sweeney. Narrated by Christopher Kent. 1 CD. (Running Time: 2 hrs. 17 mins.). 2005. 19.95 (978-1-59971-130-0(3)) AardGP.
Two hours and seventeen minutes of playtime provide today's independent traveler with an unparalleled audio tour of this truly unique monument. Santa Maria Gloriosa dei Frari Basilica (the Frari) is the mother church for Venice's Franciscan Order and one of the most beautiful Gothic churches in Italy. Built in the shape of a Latin cross, it is a classic example of a Gothic style which can only be described as Franciscan because it avoids ostentatious spires, pinnacles and flying buttresses. The harmony and beauty of the lines, spaces, vaults, ribbing and crosses render this building a true masterpiece of Venetian art and history. Professional narrators delight, inform and amuse as they guide the listener along while describing the churches remarkable history and its magnificent art. Its spectacular interior is most famous for its art and the monumental tombs of rich and famous Venetians it contains. The grandeur of its architecture, the harmony of its lines, the magnificent monuments along the walls, the gradual rise of the double order of steps, the stained-glass windows shining above and casting their soft glow below, seem to move ones eye towards a single point, "the Assumption" by Titian, the most precious of all of the Basilica's masterpieces. Everything focuses from above, drawing one's eye toward the brilliant light, which holds the visitor in a sense of inexpressible spiritual wonder. The totality of the setting adds to the power and splendor that have made Titian's masterpiece famous throughout the centuries. The artist knew exactly how to use the whole of the architecture to perfectly frame his painting, which the great sculptor Canova described as the most beautiful picture in the world. Tiziano Vecellio, known throughout the world as simply Titian, is buried here in the Frari, in a rather simple tomb designed by Canova, which stands along the right aisle of the church. The Frari contains many other masterpieces by some of the greatest Renaissance artist, in fact too many to mention in this writing. This 29 track audio tour is in MP3 format, on one CD, ready for copying to any MP3 device library. Not for use on a regular CD player.

Great Discoveries' Personal Audio Guide, Venice Italy's, Scuola Grande di San Rocco, Grand Scuola of St. Roch: Formatted for CD Players. Scripts. Jennifer Dennis. Narrated by Christopher Kent. 2 CDs. (Running Time: 1 hr. 27 mins.). 2005. audio compact disk 21.95 (978-1-59971-140-9(0)) AardGP.
One hour and twenty-seven minutes of playtime provide today's independent traveler with an unparalleled audio tour of the Scuola Grande di San Rocco, a striking 16th century Renaissance building that exhibits traces of successive enhancements up through the Baroque period. It is one of the most important treasure chests of Venetian paintings and a shrine to followers of Jacopo Tintoretto. This rather small building containing only three rooms is an absolute must see when visiting Venice. Professional narrators delight, inform and amuse as they guide the listener through this dazzling monument to the work of Jacopo Tintoretto. The Scuola holds the largest collection of his work anywhere. The series of the more than 50 dark and dramatic works took the artist more than 20 years to complete, making this the richest of the many confraternity guilds or scuola that once flourished in Venice. The walls of the rooms and the ceilings of the upper floor are completely covered with canvasses by Tintoretto. They represent one of the most important picture cycles of art history. The most renowned of these is Tintoretto's stunning "Crucifixion", which is hanging in the Albergo Room. The paintings on the ceilings are so alluring that the museum provides mirrors to use for standing and looking at each piece. There are also some interesting easel works by Titian, Tiepolo, and Giorgione. On the staircase are canvasses by Pietro Negri and Antonio Zanchi. This 14 track audio tour is in standard CD format, on 2 CD's, ready for play on any CD player. Not for use on MP3 players.

Great Discoveries, Personal Audio Guide, Venice Italy's, Scuola Grande di San Rocco, Grand Scuola of St. Roch: MP3 Format. Scripts. Jennifer Dennis. Narrated by Christopher Kent. 1 CD. (Running Time: 1 hr. 27 mins.). 2005. 19.95 (978-1-59971-132-4(X)) AardGP.

Great Discoveries ¿Personal Audio Guide#8255; Venice Italy¿s, Santa Maria Gloriosa dei Frari Basilica: Formatted for CD Players. Scripts. James Sweeney. Narrated by Christopher Kent. 2 CDs. (Running Time: 2 hrs. 17 mins.). 2005. audio compact disk Rental 19.95 (978-1-59971-135-5(4)) AardGP.
Two hours and seventeen minutes of playtime provide today's independent traveler with an unparalleled audio tour of this truly unique monument. Santa Maria Gloriosa dei Frari Basilica (the Frari) is the mother church for Venice's Franciscan Order and one of the most beautiful Gothic churches in Italy. Built in the shape of a Latin cross, it is a classic example of a Gothic style which can only be described as Franciscan because it avoids ostentatious spires, pinnacles and flying buttresses. The harmony and beauty of the lines, spaces, vaults, ribbing and crosses render this building a true masterpiece of Venetian art and history. Professional narrators delight, inform and amuse as they guide the listener along while describing the churches remarkable history and its magnificent art. Its spectacular interior is most famous for its art and the monumental tombs of rich and famous Venetians it contains. The grandeur of its architecture, the harmony of its lines, the magnificent monuments along the walls, the gradual rise of the double order of steps, the stained-glass windows shining above and casting their soft glow below, seem to move ones eye towards a single point, "the Assumption‿ by Titian, the most precious of all of the Basilica's masterpieces. Everything focuses from above, drawing one's eye toward the brilliant light, which holds the visitor in a sense of inexpressible spiritual wonder. The totality of the setting adds to the power and splendor that have made Titian's masterpiece famous throughout the centuries. The artist knew exactly how to use the whole of the architecture to perfectly frame his painting, which the great sculptor Canova described as the most beautiful picture in the world. Tiziano Vecellio, known throughout the world as simply Titian, is buried here in the Frari, in a rather simple tomb designed by Canova, which stands along the right aisle of the church. The Frari contains many other masterpieces by some of the greatest Renaissance artist, in fact too many to mention in this writing. This 29 track audio tour is in standard CD format, on 2 CD's, ready for play on any CD player. Not for use on MP3 players.

Great Divide. unabr. ed. T. Davis Bunn. Read by Buck Schirner. (Running Time: 13 hrs.). 2005. 39.25 (978-1-59600-566-2(1), 9781596005662, BADLE); 24.95 (978-1-59600-565-5(3), 9781596005655, BAD); 39.25 (978-1-59600-564-8(5), 9781596005648, Brlnc Audio MP3 Lib); 24.95 (978-1-59600-563-1(7), 9781596005631, Brilliance MP3) Brilliance Audio.
When attorney Marcus Glenwood resigns from his prestigious corporate law firm to retreat to the small town of Rocky Mount, North Carolina, and rebuild his life after a devastating personal tragedy, he has no idea that the biggest, most emotionally trying case of his entire career is about to fall into his backyard. It is a fragile and spiritually wounded Glenwood who first meets his distraught clients, Alma and Austin Hall. Their daughter, Gloria, has disappeared in China while investigating the slavelike labor practices of a factory owned by the international giant New Horizons, the world's largest manufacturer of sports shoes and athletic gear. Moved and persuaded by Alma's pleading, Marcus agrees to take their case. But he cannot know how quickly his investigation will begin to untangle a web of greed and deceit stretching from Washington D.C., across international borders - or how desperately his former law colleagues will try to prevent him from uncovering the truth.

***Great Divide.** unabr. ed. T. Davis Bunn. Read by Buck Schirner. (Running Time: 14 hrs.). 2010. audio compact disk 89.97 (978-1-4418-4056-1(7), 9781441840561, BriAudCD Unabrid); audio compact disk 29.99 (978-1-4418-4055-4(9), 9781441840554, Bril Audio CD Unabri) Brilliance Audio.

Great Divorce. unabr. ed. C. S. Lewis. Read by Robert Whitfield. 2003. audio compact disk 22.00 (978-0-06-057295-2(7)) HarperCollins Pubs.

Great East Mojave. Hosted by Nancy Pearlman. 1 cass. (Running Time: 29 min.). 10.00 (412) Educ Comm CA.

Great Eating Contest. unabr. ed. Shea. 1 cass. (Running Time: 20 min.). (Fun to Read Ser.). (J). (gr. 3-6). 1983. bk. 16.99 (978-0-934898-40-9(5)); pap. bk. 9.95 (978-0-934898-28-7(6)) Jan Prods.
The kids of Pepper Street choose Jody to represent them in a pizza eating contest, only to find out that she hates pizza. The humorous way in which they solve their problem will delight readers.

Great Economic Thinkers. Narrated by Louis Rukeyser. (Audio Classics Ser.). 1988. (978-0-938935-30-8(5), 10200) Knowledge Prod.
From classical economics to monetarism & supply-side ideas, these presentations express the views of history's most important economists. Particular emphasis is placed on explaining each thinker's attitude toward capitalism. Includes The Classical Economists; Karl Marx: Das Kapital; Early Austrian Economics; Alfred Marshall & Neoclassicism; Welfare Capitalism Begins; Walras: Markets in Equilibrium; Institutionalism; Schumpteter & Dynamic Economic Change; The Chicago School; The Free Market Process; The Keynesian Revolution; The Keynesian Heritage; Monetarism & Supply Side Economics.

Great Economic Thinkers Boxed Set. unabr. ed. Robert Hebert et al. Read by Louis Rukeyser. (Running Time: 126000 sec.). (Audio Classics Ser.). 2008. audio compact disk 99.95 (978-0-7861-5892-8(1)) Blckstn Audio.

Great Electric Blanket Caper. Read by Donald James. 1 cass. (Running Time: 60 min.). (J). 1990. 11.95 Sheba Bks Intl.
Tells of the exploits of Sheba the cat.

Great Elephant Chase. unabr. ed. Gillian Cross. Read by Jenny Agutter. 6 cass. (Running Time: 6 hrs.). (J). 1997. 49.95 (LL 3367, Chivers Child Audio) AudioGO.

***Great Emergence: How Christianity Is Changing & Why.** unabr. ed. Phyllis Tickle. Narrated by Pam Ward. (ENG.). 2008. 12.98 (978-1-59644-576-5(9), Hovel Audio) christianaud.

Great Emergence: How Christianity Is Changing & Why. unabr. ed. Phyllis Tickle. Narrated by Pam Ward. (Running Time: 5 hrs. 0 mins. 0 sec.). (ENG.). 2008. audio compact disk 21.98 (978-1-59644-575-8(0), Hovel Audio) christianaud.

Great English Literature of the 17th Century: Diary of Samuel Pepys see Great English Literature of the 17th Century: Pilgrim's Progress

Great English Literature of the 17th Century: Pilgrim's Progress. abr. ed. John Bunyan et al. Read by Robert Speaight et al. 6 cass. (Running Time: 4 hrs. 41 min.). Incl. Great English Literature of the 17th Century: Diary of Samuel Pepys. Samuel Pepys. Read by John Franklyn. 1986. (PCC 12); Great English Literature of the 17th Century: Treasury of John Dryden. John Dryden. Read by Robert Speaight. 1986. (PCC 12); Treasury of John Donne. John Donne. Read by Robert Speaight. 1986. (PCC 12); Great English Literature of the 17th Century: Pilgrim's Progress. John Milton. Read by Robert Speaight & Robert Eddison. 1986. (PCC 12); Great English Literature of the 17th Century: Pilgrim's Progress. John Bunyan. Read by Christopher Casson. 1986. (PCC 12); 1986. 55.00 set. (978-0-8045-0012-8(6), PCC 12) Spoken Arts.
Includes Pilgrim's Progress, Pepys' Diary, & poetry by Donne,Dryden, & Milton.

Great English Literature of the 17th Century: Treasury of John Dryden see Great English Literature of the 17th Century: Pilgrim's Progress

Great English Literature of the 18th Century. abr. ed. Alexander Pope et al. Read by Pamela Mant et al. 6 cass. (Running Time: 4 hrs. 55 min.). Incl. Alexander Pope: The Rape of the Lock. Alexander Pope. Read by Robert Speaight & Maxine Audley. 1986. (PCC 13); Gulliver's Travels. Jonathan Swift. Read by Denis Johnson. 1986. (PCC 13); Robinson Crusoe: The Complete Story of Robinson Crusoe. 1 cass. (Running Time: 1 hr.). Daniel Defoe. Read by John Franklyn & Pamela Mant. 1986. (PCC 13); Treasury of Goldsmith, Gray & Collins. Oliver Goldsmith. Read by Christopher Casson. 1986. (PCC 13); Treasury of Pope. Alexander Pope. 1986. (PCC 13); Treasury of William Blake. William Blake. Read by Wendy Hiller et al. 1986. (PCC 13); 1986. 55.00 (978-0-8045-0013-5(4), PCC 13) Spoken Arts.

Great Escape. Paul Brickhill. Read by Robert Whitfield. (Running Time: 27000 sec.). 2003. audio compact disk 24.95 (978-0-7861-9611-1(4), 1952) Blckstn Audio.

Great Escape. Paul Brickhill. Read by Robert Whitfield. 2008. audio compact disk 19.95 (978-1-4332-4961-7(8)) Blckstn Audio.

Great Escape. Jack Van Impe. 1991. 7.00 (978-0-934803-22-9(6)) J Van Impe.
Sermon cassette asserting that Christians depart earth before the Tribulation Hour.

Great Escape. unabr. ed. Paul Brickhill. Read by Robert Whitfield. 6 cass. (Running Time: 8 hrs. 30 mins.). 2003. 44.95 (978-0-7861-1169-5(0), 1952) Blckstn Audio.
With only their bare hands & the crudest of homemade tools, they sank shafts, built underground railroads, forged passports, drew maps, faked weapons & tailored German uniforms & civilian clothes.

Great Escape. unabr. ed. Paul Brickhill. Read by Robert Whitfield. 7 CDs. (Running Time: 8 hrs. 30 mins.). 2000. audio compact disk 56.00 (978-0-7861-9880-1(X), 1952) Blckstn Audio.
With only their bare hands & the crudest of homemade tools, they sank shafts, built underground railroads, forged passports, drew maps, faked weapons & tailored German uniforms & civilian clothes. They developed a fantastic security system to protect themselves from the German "ferrets" who prowled the compounds with nerve-racking tenacity & suspicion.

Great Escape. unabr. ed. Paul Brickhill. Read by Robert Whitfield. 1 CD. (Running Time: 7 hrs. 30 mins.). 2001. audio compact disk 19.95 (zm1952) Blckstn Audio.

Great Escape: Nine Jews Who Fled Hitler & Changed the World. unabr. ed. Kati Marton. Read by Anna Fields. (Running Time: 9 hrs. 30 mins. 0 sec.). (ENG.). 2006. audio compact disk 34.99 (978-1-4001-0309-6(6)); audio compact disk 69.99 (978-1-4001-3309-3(2)); audio compact disk 24.99 (978-1-4001-5309-1(3)) Pub: Tantor Media. Dist(s): IngramPubServ

Great Expectations see Works of Charles Dickens

Great Expectations see Grandes Esperanzas

Great Expectations. Charles Dickens. Contrib. by Geraldine McEwan & Douglas Hodge. 5 CDs. (Running Time: 5 hrs. 35 mins.). 2006. audio compact disk 59.95 (978-0-7927-3990-6(6), BBCD 141) AudioGO.

Great Expectations. Charles Dickens. Read by Anais 9000. 2008. 33.95 (978-1-60112-175-2(X)) Babblebooks.

Great Expectations. Charles Dickens. Read by Martin Jarvis. 13 cass. (Running Time: 17 hrs. 30 min.). 77.95 (CC/010) C to C Cassettes.
Pip receives from an anonymous benefactor the chance of rising above his home at the village forage. His expectations of wealth are unfulfilled & he returns to the Essex marshes penniless & dispirited to be reunited with his good friend Joe Gargery & finally Estella.

Great Expectations. Charles Dickens. Read by Martin Jarvis. 12 cass. (Running Time: 17 hrs. 30 min.). 1998. 44.95 Set. (13109FA) Filmic Archives.
Tale of Pip, an orphan, who has the chance to rise above his small-village life on the Essex marsh when an anonymous benefactor leaves him a sum of money. Depicts the development of moral character through Pip's searches & struggles at the same time he teaches lessons about class, trust, humility, & gratitude.

Great Expectations. Charles Dickens. Read by Anton Lesser. (Complete Classics (Playaway) Ser.). (ENG.). 2009. 114.99 (978-1-60775-752-8(4)) Find a World.

Great Expectations. Charles Dickens. Read by Anton Lesser. (Running Time: 5 hrs. 15 mins.). (C). 2000. 28.95 (978-1-60083-746-3(8)) Iofy Corp.

Great Expectations. Charles Dickens. Read by Daniel Quintero. (Running Time: 3 hrs.). 2003. 16.95 (978-1-60083-288-8(1), Audiofy Corp) Iofy Corp.

Great Expectations. Charles Dickens. Read by Ray Verna. 12 cass. (Running Time: 18 hrs.). 1993. 69.80 Set. (978-1-56544-003-6(X), 350017); Rental 11.30 30 day rental Set. (350017) Literate Ear.
Little Pip, an orphan raised by a resentful older sister, seems an unlikely possessor of great expectations. Unknown to Pip, his life is shaped by a small generous act of childhood. In striving to better himself socially, Pip's expectations lead him to betray his friends & protectors.

Great Expectations. Charles Dickens. Read by Anton Lesser. 4 CDs. (Running Time: 5 hrs. 15 mins.). (Works of Charles Dickens). (J). (gr. 9-12). 1996. audio compact disk 28.98 (978-962-634-082-0(7), NA408212) Naxos.
Story of a struggling orphan who finds his expectations of wealth unfulfilled after he becomes the benefactor of an anonymous donor.

Great Expectations. Charles Dickens. Read by Anton Lesser. 4 cass. (Running Time: 5 hrs. 15 mins.). (Works of Charles Dickens). 1996. 22.98 (978-962-634-582-5(9), NA408214, Naxos AudioBooks) Naxos.

Great Expectations. Charles Dickens. 1 cass. (Running Time: 1 hr.). (Radiobook Ser.). 1987. 4.98 (978-0-929541-44-0(8)) Radiola Co.

Great Expectations. Charles Dickens. Read by Frank Muller. 14 CDs. (Running Time: 16 Hrs.). 2005. audio compact disk 34.95 (978-1-4193-2368-3(7)) Recorded Bks.

Great Expectations. Charles Dickens. Narrated by Flo Gibson. 2007. audio compact disk 42.95 (978-1-55685-943-4(0)) Audio Bk Con.

Great Expectations. abr. ed. Charles Dickens. (Classics Collection). 2001. 7.95 (978-1-57815-244-5(5), Media Bks Audio) Media Bks NJ.

Great Expectations. abr. ed. Charles Dickens. Perf. by Paul Scofield. 2 cass. (Running Time: 3 hrs.). 2004. 18.00 (978-1-931056-58-8(7), N Millennium Audio) New Millenn Enter.
Pip Learn, a young man without expectations, the opportunity to shun kind friends & to feel the pleasure of being a benefactor & learn humility & repentance.

Great Expectations. abr. ed. Charles Dickens. Read by Paul Scofield. 3 CDs. (Running Time: 3 hrs.). 2004. audio compact disk 24.95 (978-1-59007-573-9(0)) Pub: New Millenn Enter. Dist(s): PerseuPGW

Great Expectations. abr. ed. Charles Dickens. Read by Hugh Laurie. (Running Time: 3 hrs.). (ENG.). (gr. 12 up). 2005. audio compact disk 14.95 (978-0-14-305816-8(9), PengAudBks) Penguin Grp USA.

Great Expectations, unabr. ed. Charles Dickens. Narrated by Flo Gibson. 11 cass. (Running Time: 16 hrs. 30 mins.). (gr. 10 up). 2000. 34.95 (978-1-55685-623-5(7)) Audio Bk Con.
A frightening encounter with an escaped convict on the moors in Kent, a mysterious call to Miss Havisham's strange house, his love for the beautiful cold Estalla & his ups & downs with Joe Gargery all lead to Pip's expectations & his struggle to redeem himself morally.

***Great Expectations.** unabr. ed. Charles Dickens. Read by Charlton Griffin. (Running Time: 20:29). 2008. 61.60 Audio Conn.

Great Expectations. unabr. ed. Charles Dickens. Read by Martin Jarvis. 10 cass. (Running Time: 17 hrs. 30 mins.). (gr. 9-12). 2004. 44.95 (978-1-57270-063-5(7), F91063u) Pub: Audio Partners. Dist(s): PerseuPGW
Someone has left the orphan, Pip, a sum of money, but who is this benefactor? Dickens depicts the development of moral character & explores the significance of class.

Great Expectations. unabr. ed. Charles Dickens. Narrated by Martin Jarvis. (Running Time: 63000 sec.). (Cover to Cover Classics Ser.). (ENG.). 2006. audio compact disk 42.95 (978-1-57270-567-8(1)) Pub: AudioGO. Dist(s): Perseus Dist

Great Expectations. unabr. ed. Charles Dickens. Read by Frederick Davidson. 13 cass. (Running Time: 19 hrs.). 1994. 85.95 (978-0-7861-0493-2(7), 1444) Blckstn Audio.
Standing as one of the most revered works in all of English literature, "Great Expectations" traces the development of Philip Pirrip, called Pip, from a boy of shallow aspirations to a man of depth & character. Reared by his sister & her husband, Pip is also influenced by the eccentric Miss Havisham, who was jilted on her wedding night & who has brought up her adopted niece Estella to hate men. As a young man, Pip is informed that an unknown benefactor has provided money for his education & expects to make him his heir. Forsaking his humbler friends - particularly the faithful Joe - he sets off to London with the firm intention of becoming a gentleman & realizing his "great expectations".

Great Expectations. unabr. ed. Charles Dickens. Read by Frederick Davidson. 2 pieces. (Running Time: 19 mins.). 2007. 39.95 (978-0-7861-8960-1(6), 1444) Blckstn Audio.

Great Expectations. unabr. ed. Charles Dickens. Read by Gene Engene. 16 cass. (Running Time: 21 hrs. 30 min.). Dramatization. 1990. 69.95 (978-1-55686-330-1(6), 330) Books in Motion.
While visiting his parents gravesite, Pip, a young orphan living with his sister, encounters a convict on the run. In spite of his fear of the man, Pip befriends the convict & gives aid, an act that spells considerable consequence for Pip later in life.

Great Expectations. unabr. ed. Charles Dickens. 13 cass. (Running Time: 19 hrs. 30 mins.). 2002. 104.00 (978-0-7366-8641-9(5)) Books on Tape.
Follows the orphan Pip, who is left a mysterious fortune and comes of age as he deals with the ambiguous consequences of his inheritance. From the novel's opening, when Pip encounters the convict Magwitch amid the swirling fog on the marshes, we strive with Pip to unravel the mystery he is drawn into and urge him to save himself from the fate of the beautiful Estella, raised to have no heart. Dickens is all heart; we laugh while we learn.

Great Expectations. unabr. ed. Charles Dickens. 16 CDs. (Running Time: 19 hrs. 30 mins.). 2002. audio compact disk 42.50 (978-0-7366-8642-6(8)) Pub: Books on Tape. Dist(s): NetLibrary CO

Great Expectations. unabr. ed. Charles Dickens. Read by Michael Page. 14 cass. (Running Time: 20 hrs.). 2002. 34.95 (978-1-59086-153-0(1), 1590861531, BAU) Brilliance Audio.

Great Expectations. unabr. ed. Charles Dickens. Read by Michael Page. (Running Time: 20 hrs.). 2004. 44.25 (978-1-59335-391-9(X), 159335391X, Brlnc Audio MP3 Lib) Brilliance Audio.
Great Expectations chronicles the progress of Pip from childhood through adulthood. As he moves from the marshes of Kent to London society, he encounters a variety of extraordinary characters: from Magwitch, the escaped convict, to Miss Havisham and her ward, the arrogant and beautiful Estella. In this fascinating story, Dickens shows the dangers of being driven by a desire for wealth and social status. Pip must establish a sense of self against the plans which others seem to have for him - and somehow discover a firm set of values and priorities.

Great Expectations. unabr. ed. Charles Dickens. Read by Michael Page. (Running Time: 20 hrs.). 2004. 44.25 (978-1-59710-335-0(7), 1597103357, BADLE); 29.95 (978-1-59710-334-3(9), 1597103349, BAD) Brilliance Audio.

Great Expectations. unabr. ed. Charles Dickens. Read by Michael Page. (Running Time: 20 hrs.). 2005. audio compact disk 112.25 (978-1-59737-132-2(7), 9781597371322, BriAudCD Unabrid); audio compact disk 44.95 (978-1-59737-131-5(9), 9781597371315, Bril Audio CD Unabri) Brilliance Audio.

Great Expectations. unabr. ed. Charles Dickens. Read by Martin Jarvis. (YA). 2008. 104.99 (978-1-60514-642-3(0)) Find a World.

Great Expectations. unabr. ed. Charles Dickens. Read by Anton Lesser. 15. (Running Time: 68959 sec.). (Complete Classics Ser.). 2007. audio compact disk 89.98 (978-962-634-462-0(8), Naxos AudioBooks) Naxos.

Great Expectations, unabr. ed. Charles Dickens. Narrated by Frank Muller. 11 cass. (Running Time: 16 hrs.). 1987. 91.00 (978-1-55690-204-8(2), 87850E7) Recorded Bks.
Young Pip is endowed by a secret benefactor & sets about discovering his or her identity. Dickens supplied two endings to his great novel, both are recorded leaving the listener to judge.

Great Expectations. unabr. ed. Charles Dickens. Read by Michael Page. 2 MP3-CDs. (Running Time: 20 hrs.). 2004. 29.95 (978-1-59335-159-5(3), 1593351593) Soulmate Audio Bks.
Great Expectations chronicles the progress of Pip from childhood through adulthood. As he moves from the marshes of Kent to London society, he encounters a variety of extraordinary characters: from Magwitch, the escaped convict, to Miss Havisham and her ward, the arrogant and beautiful Estella. In this fascinating story, Dickens shows the dangers of being driven by a desire for wealth and social status. Pip must establish a sense of self against the plans which others seem to have for him - and somehow discover a firm set of values and priorities.

Great Expectations. unabr. ed. Charles Dickens. Narrated by Simon Vance. (Running Time: 18 hrs. 0 mins. 0 sec.). (Tantor Unabridged Classics Ser.). (ENG.). 2008. 34.99 (978-1-4001-5632-0(7)); audio compact disk 44.99 (978-1-4001-0632-5(X)); audio compact disk 89.99 (978-1-4001-3632-2(6)) Pub: Tantor Media. Dist(s): IngramPubServ

Great Expectations. unabr. ed. Charles Dickens & Frederick Davidson. (Running Time: 68400 sec.). 2007. audio compact disk 120.00 (978-0-7861-6024-2(1)) Blckstn Audio.

Great Expectations. unabr. collector's ed. Charles Dickens. Read by Vanessa Benjamin. 12 cass. (Running Time: 18 hrs.). (J). 1977. 96.00 (978-0-7366-4198-2(X), 4696) Books on Tape.
Pip, an orphan, helps an escaped prisoner & from these beginnings moves upward in life's great struggle.

Great Expectations, Set. unabr. ed. Charles Dickens. Read by Frederick Davidson. 13 cass. 1999. 85.95 (FS9-34210) Highsmith.

Great Expectations: An A+ Audio Study Guide. unabr. ed. Charles Dickens. (Running Time: 30 mins.). (ENG.). 2006. 5.98 (978-1-59483-708-1(2)) Pub: Hachet Audio. Dist(s): HachBkGrp

Great Expectations: Preparing for Childbirth. 1 cassette. (Running Time: 60:24 mins.). 1983. 12.95 (978-1-55841-030-5(9)) Emmett E Miller.
Techniques adapted from childbirth education, meditation and hypnotherapeutic sources. Tested in Dr. Miller's medical practice, these techniques help you experience a smoother pregnancy and easier delivery. For use by both mother and father.

Great Expectations: The Joy of Pregnancy & Birthing. 1 CD. 1983. audio compact disk 16.95 (978-1-55841-118-0(6)) Emmett E Miller.

***Great Expectations: Value-Priced Edition.** Charles Dickens. Narrated by Full Cast. (Running Time: 5 hrs. 35 mins. 0 sec.). (ENG.). 2010. audio compact disk 14.95 (978-1-60283-984-7(0)) Pub: AudioGO. Dist(s): Perseus Dist

Great Expectations & Hard Times. abr. ed. Charles Dickens. 2001. 12.99 (978-1-57815-258-2(5)) Media Bks NJ.

Great Explanations. Nora Randall. 1990. 12.00 (978-0-88961-155-9(6)) Pub: Can Scholars Pr CAN. Dist(s): IngramPubServ

Great Explorers: The European Discovery of America. unabr. ed. Samuel Eliot Morison. Read by Frederick Davidson. (Running Time: 25 hrs. 30 mins.). 2009. 44.95 (978-1-4332-9543-0(1)); audio compact disk 140.00 (978-1-4332-9542-3(3)) Blckstn Audio.

Great Explorers Pt. 1: The European Discovery of America. unabr. ed. Samuel Eliot Morison. Read by Frederick Davidson. 12 cass. (Running Time: 27 hrs. 30 mins.). 1995. 83.95 (978-0-7861-0802-2(9), 1626A,B) Blckstn Audio.
A master seaman himself, Morison personally retraced the voyages of the early explorers, charting his travels in maps & photographs, then compared these to the maps & travelogues of the early sailors. The result, the magnificent, two-volume "The European Discovery of America". "The Great Explorers" abridges this work, bringing together the chapters on the Cabots, Verrazzano, Cartier, Gilbert, Frobisher, Davis, Columbus, Magellan, & Drake, as well as a detailed description of the English, French, & Spanish ways of seafaring.

Great Explorers Pt. 1: The European Discovery of America. unabr. ed. Samuel Eliot Morison. Read by Wolfram Kandinsky. 9 cass. (Running Time: 13 hrs. 30 mins.). 1988. 72.00 (2195-A) Books on Tape.
Historical account of the European explorers & the attitude of mind which led to their discovery of America.

Great Explorers Pt. 2: The European Discovery of America. unabr. ed. Samuel Eliot Morison. Read by Frederick Davidson. 7 cass. (Running Time: 27 hrs. 30 mins.). 1995. 49.95 (978-0-7861-0803-9(7), 1626A,B) Blckstn Audio.
Bringing together the chapters on the Cabots, Verrazzanok Cartier, Gilbert, Frobisher, Davis, Columbus & Magellan as well as a detailed description of the English, French & Spanish ways of seafaring.

Great Explorers Pt. 2: The European Discovery of America. unabr. ed. Samuel Eliot Morison. Read by Wolfram Kandinsky. 10 cass. (Running Time: 15 hrs.). 1988. 80.00 (2195-B) Books on Tape.
Historical account of the European explorers & the attitude of mind which led to their discovery of America.

Great Explorers Pts. 1-2: The European Discovery of America. unabr. ed. Samuel Eliot Morison. Read by Wolfram Kandinsky. 19 cass. (Running Time: 28 hrs. 30 mins.). 1988. 115.00 (978-0-7366-1287-6(4), 2195-A/B) Books on Tape.
Historical account of the European explorers & the attitude of mind which led to their discovery of America. Part 1 of 2.

Great Explorers of the World. David Angus. Read by Kerry Shale et al. (Running Time: 2 hrs. 30 mins.). 2005. 20.95 (978-1-60083-747-0(6)) Iofy Corp.

Great Explorers of the World. David Angus. Read by Kerry Shale et al. 2 CDs. (Running Time: 2 hrs. 30 min.). 2003. audio compact disk 17.98 (978-962-634-291-6(9)) Naxos.
Here are the stories of nine great adventures and the lives of the men who took part in them.

Great Explorers of the World. David Angus. Read by Kerry Shale et al. 2 cass. (Running Time: 2 hrs. 30 min.). 2003. 13.98 (978-962-634-791-1(0), NA229112) Naxos.

Great Explorers of the World: Marco Polo; Ibn Battuta; Christopher Columbus; Bartolomeu Diaz Vasco da Gama; Ferdinand Magellan; Captain Cook Lewis & Clark; Livingstone & Stanley; the Apollo Mission. unabr. ed. David Angus. Read by Sam Dastor et al. (J). 2006. 39.99 (978-1-59895-344-2(3)) Find a World.

Great Failure: A Bartender, a Monk, & My Unlikely Path to Truth. Natalie Goldberg. 6 CDs. 2004. audio compact disk 29.95 (978-1-59179-073-0(5), AW00873D) Sounds True.

Great Figures of the New Testament, Pts. I-II. Instructed by Amy J. Levine. 12 cass. (Running Time: 12 hrs.). 2002. bk. 54.95 (978-1-56585-541-0(8), 6206); bk. 69.95 (978-1-56585-543-4(4), 6206) Teaching Co.

Great Figures of the Old Testament, Pts. I-II. Instructed by Amy J. Levine. 12 cass. (Running Time: 12 hrs.). 2002. bk. 54.95 (978-1-56585-544-1(2), 6203); bk. 69.95 (978-1-56585-546-5(9), 6203) Teaching Co.

Great Fire. Shirley Hazzard. Narrated by Virginia Leishman. 10 CDs. (Running Time: 11 hrs. 15 mins.). 2004. audio compact disk 29.99 (978-1-4025-8112-0(2), 01602) Recorded Bks.

Great Fire. Jim Murphy. (YA). 2003. audio compact disk 26.95 (978-1-883332-92-1(3)) Audio Bkshelf.

Great Fire. Jim Murphy. Read by Taylor Mali. 2 cass. (Running Time: 3 hrs.). (YA). 2003. 19.95 (978-1-883332-86-0(9)) Audio Bkshelf.

Great Fire. unabr. ed. Shirley Hazzard. 10 CDs. (Running Time: 11 hrs. 25 min.). 2004. audio compact disk 79.75 (978-1-4025-8127-4(0)) Recorded Bks.

Great Fire. unabr. ed. Jim Murphy. Read by Taylor Mali. (J). 2008. 34.99 (978-1-60514-807-6(5)) Find a World.

Great Fire, unabr. ed. Jim Murphy. Narrated by John McDonough. 3 pieces. (Running Time: 3 hrs.). (gr. 7 up). 1998. 27.00 (978-0-7887-2077-2(5), 95430E7) Recorded Bks.
In 1871 a small fire breaks out in the O'Leary's bar, but when the flames are finally extinguished a week later, more than half the city of Chicago lies in ruins & nearly 100,000 people are homeless.

Great Fire of London see Diary of Samuel Pepys

***Great Fire of Rome: The Fall of the Emperor Nero & His City.** unabr. ed. Stephen Dando Collins. (Running Time: 9 hrs. 30 mins.). 2010. audio compact disk 29.95 (978-1-4417-5648-0(5)) Blckstn Audio.

***Great Fire of Rome: The Fall of the Emperor Nero & His City.** unabr. ed. Stephen Dando-Collins. (Running Time: 9 hrs. 30 mins.). 2010. 29.95 (978-1-4417-5649-7(3)); 59.95 (978-1-4417-5645-9(0)); audio compact disk 90.00 (978-1-4417-5646-6(9)) Blckstn Audio.

Great Flood. 2004. 8.95 (978-0-7882-0302-2(9)) Weston Woods.

Great French & Russian Short Stories, Vol. 1. collector's ed. 7 cass. (Running Time: 10 hrs. 30 min.). 1982. 56.00 (978-0-7366-3857-9(1), 9055) Books on Tape.
A wide selection of literary masterworks from the 19th century.

Great French & Russian Short Stories, Vol. 1. unabr. ed. Read by Walter Zimmerman et al. 7 cass. (Running Time: 20 hrs.). (Great French & Russian Stories Ser.: Vol. 1). 1982. 49.95 (978-0-7861-0545-8(3), 2040A,B) Blckstn Audio.
This collection of 19th-century masterworks provides rich insights into human nature & social conditions in Russia & France during this turbulent era.

Great French & Russian Short Stories, Vol. 2. Leo Tolstoy et al. Read by Walter Zimmerman. 8 cass. (Running Time: 12 hrs.). 1989. 49.00 incl. album. (C-119) Jimcin Record.
Tolstoy, Poushkin, Flaubert & others.

Great French & Russian Short Stories, Vol. 2. collector's ed. 8 cass. (Running Time: 12 hrs.). 1983. 64.00 (978-0-7366-3890-6(3), 9119) Books on Tape.
Offers 18 works by important 19th century French & Russian writers.

Great French & Russian Short Stories, Vol. 2. unabr. ed. Read by Walter Zimmerman. 8 cass. (Running Time: 20 hrs.). (Great French & Russian Stories Ser.: Vol. 2). 1982. 56.95 (978-0-7861-0546-5(1), 2040A,B) Blckstn Audio.
This collection of 19th-century masterworks provides rich insights into human nature & social conditions in Russia & France during this turbulent era.

Great French & Russian Stories, Vol. 2. unabr. ed. Read by Walter Zimmerman. 8 cass. (Running Time: 1 hrs. 30 min. per cass.). 1983. 50.00 (9119) Books on Tape.
A wide selection of literary masterworks from the 19th century.

Great French & Russian Stories Vol. 1: A Collection. unabr. ed. Read by Cindy Hardin et al. 7 cass. (Running Time: 1 hr. 30 min. per cass.). Incl. Christ in Flanders. Honoré de Balzac. 1981. (C-55); False Jewels. Guy de Maupassant. 1981. (C-55); Honest Thief & Other Stories. Fyodor Dostoyevsky. 1981. (C-55); In the Moonlight. Guy de Maupassant. 1981. (C-55); Kiss. Anton Chekhov. 1981. (C-55); Long Exile. Leo Tolstoy. 1981. (C-55); Lottery Ticket. Anton Chekhov. 1981. (C-55); Love. Guy de Maupassant. 1981. (C-55); Love's Awakening. Guy de Maupassant. 1981. (C-55); Mysterious Mansion. Honoré de Balzac. 1981. (C-55); Necklace. Guy de Maupassant. 1981. (C-55); Overcoat. Nikolai Gogol. 1981. (C-55); Piece of String. Guy de Maupassant. 1981. (C-55); Regret. Guy de Maupassant. 1981. (C-55); Shot. Alexander Pushkin. 1981. (C-55); Useless Beauty. Guy de Maupassant. 1981. (C-55); Wedding. Fyodor Dostoyevsky. 1981. (C-55); Zodiminsky's Duel. Alexandre Dumas. 1981. (C-55); 1981. 49.00 (C-55) Jimcin Record.

Great from God's Perspective. Dan Corner. 1 cass. 3.00 (37) Evang Outreach.

Great Fuzz Frenzy. unabr. ed. Janet Stevens & Susan Stevens Crummel. 1 CD. (Running Time: 14 mins.). (J). (gr. k-3). 2006. bk. 29.95 (978-0-8045-4154-1(X), SACD4155); bk. 27.99 (978-0-8045-6940-8(1), SAC6941) Spoken Arts.
It's big, round, and really fuzzy. But, what is it? Whatever it is, there's no end of trouble when this big, round, fuzzy thing tumbles into the prairie-dog town. Who would have guessed that its arrival would cause a great fuzz frenzy? And, what will happen when all the fuzz is gone?.

Great Gamble: The Soviet War in Afghanistan. unabr. ed. Gregory Feifer. (Running Time: 10 hrs. 0 mins. 0 sec.). (ENG.). 2009. audio compact disk 69.99 (978-1-4001-4057-2(9)); audio compact disk 24.99 (978-1-4001-6057-0(X)); audio compact disk 34.99 (978-1-4001-1057-5(2)) Pub: Tantor Media. Dist(s): IngramPubServ

Great Game. unabr. ed. Perf. by Eknath Easwaran. 1 cass. (Running Time: 1 hr.). 1992. 7.95 (978-1-58638-549-1(6)) Nilgiri Pr.

Great Game: The Struggle for Empire in Central Asia. unabr. collector's ed. Peter Hopkirk. Read by David Case. 14 cass. (Running Time: 21 hrs.). 1993. 112.00 (978-0-7366-2525-8(9), 3278) Books on Tape.
Struggle between Czarist Russia & Victorian England over India was the first "Cold War".

Great Gatsby see Gran Gatsby

Great Gatsby. F. Scott Fitzgerald. Narrated by David Fendig. (ENG.). 2007. audio compact disk 24.95 (978-1-55685-905-2(8)) Audio Bk Con.

Great Gatsby. F. Scott Fitzgerald. Read by Tim Robbins. 1975. 14.95 (978-0-06-074339-0(5)); audio compact disk 14.95 (978-0-06-074338-3(7)) HarperCollins Pubs.

Great Gatsby. F. Scott Fitzgerald. Read by William Hope. (Running Time: 2 hrs. 30 mins.). 1999. 22.95 (978-1-60083-748-7(4)) Iofy Corp.

Great Gatsby. F. Scott Fitzgerald. Read by Hernando Iván Cano. (Running Time: 3 hrs.). 2003. 16.95 (978-1-60083-283-3(0), Audiofy Corp) Iofy Corp.

Great Gatsby. F. Scott Fitzgerald. Narrated by Christopher Reeve. (Running Time: 2 hrs. 30 mins.). 2006. 14.95 (978-1-59912-983-9(3)) Iofy Corp.

Great Gatsby. F. Scott Fitzgerald. 2005. audio compact disk 5.25 (978-1-4193-2927-2(8)) Recorded Bks.

Great Gatsby. unabr. ed. F. Scott Fitzgerald. Narrated by David Fendig. 4 cass. (Running Time: 6 hrs. 20 mins.). 2001. 19.95 (978-1-55685-657-0(1)) Audio Bk Con.
This great American novel describes the lavish lifestyle, along with the cruelty & ugliness of Long Island society during the Jazz Age, told through the eyes of Nick Carraway. The book follows events surrounding the enigmatic & super rich Jay Gatsby.

Great Gatsby. unabr. ed. F. Scott Fitzgerald. Read by Alexander Scourby. 3 cass. (Running Time: 4 hrs. 30 mins.). 2004. 19.95 (978-0-945353-41-6(3), M30341u) Pub: Audio Partners. Dist(s): PerseuPGW
Nick Carraway, fascinated by the enigmatic Gatsby, becomes his confidante & accomplice in his plan to recapture the heart of Daisy Buchanan.

Great Gatsby. unabr. ed. F. Scott Fitzgerald. Read by Alexander Scourby. 4 CDs. (Running Time: 4 hrs. 30 mins.). 2002. audio compact disk 27.95 (978-1-57270-256-1(7)) Pub: Audio Partners. Dist(s): PerseuPGW

Great Gatsby. unabr. ed. F. Scott Fitzgerald. Narrated by Alexander Scourby. (ENG.). 2008. audio compact disk 19.95 (978-1-60283-412-5(1)) Pub: AudioGO. Dist(s): Perseus Dist

Great Gatsby. unabr. ed. F. Scott Fitzgerald. Read by Anthony Heald. (Running Time: 18000 sec.). 2007. 34.95 (978-1-4332-1045-7(2)); audio compact disk 19.95 (978-1-4332-1047-1(9)); audio compact disk 36.00 (978-1-4332-1046-4(0)) Blckstn Audio.

Great Gatsby. unabr. ed. F. Scott Fitzgerald. Read by Alexander Scourby. 3 cass. (Running Time: 4 hrs. 30 min.). 29.95 set. (8007Q) Filmic Archives.
Use this unabridged audio version as an aid to students with reading problems, or as reinforcement for the whole class. However you use this classic, you will find Scourby's reading magnificent, & will agree that Gatsby is fundamental for a complete audio collection.

Great Gatsby. unabr. ed. F. Scott Fitzgerald. Read by Alexander Scourby. (YA). 2008. 44.99 (978-1-60252-755-3(5)) Find a World.

Great Gatsby. unabr. ed. F. Scott Fitzgerald. Read by Tim Robbins. 5 cass. (Running Time: 7 hrs.). (gr. 9-12). 2002. 27.95 (978-0-06-009890-2(2)); audio compact disk 19.99 (978-0-06-009891-9(0)) HarperCollins Pubs.

Great Gatsby, unabr. ed. F. Scott Fitzgerald. Narrated by Frank Muller. 3 cass. (Running Time: 4 hrs. 30 mins.). 1984. 26.00 (978-1-55690-205-5(0), 84072E7) Recorded Bks.
The life of Jay Gatsby appears charmed to outsiders. It is a life that is rotten at heart.

Great Gatsby. unabr. ed. F. Scott Fitzgerald. Narrated by Robertson Dean & Dawkins Dean. 4 CDs. (Running Time: 5 hrs. 0 mins. 0 sec.). 2009. audio compact disk 19.99 (978-1-4001-1424-5(1)); audio compact disk 39.99 (978-1-4001-4424-2(8)) Pub: Tantor Media. Dist(s): IngramPubServ

***Great Gatsby.** unabr. ed. F. Scott Fitzgerald. Read by Tim Robbins. (ENG.). 2004. (978-0-06-082458-7(1), Harper Audio); (978-0-06-082459-4(X), Harper Audio) HarperCollins Pubs.

Great Gatsby: An A+ Audio Study Guide. unabr. ed. F. Scott Fitzgerald & Lawrence Pressman. Read by Lawrence Pressman. (Running Time: 1 hr.). (ENG.). 2006. 5.98 (978-1-59483-555-1(1)) Pub: Hachet Audio. Dist(s): HachBkGrp

Great Gatsby: An A+ Audio Study Guide. unabr. ed. F. Scott Fitzgerald & Lawrence Pressman. Read by Lawrence Pressman. (Running Time: 1 hr.). (ENG.). 2009. 14.98 (978-1-60788-166-7(7)) Pub: Hachet Audio. Dist(s): HachBkGrp

Great Gatsby & Other Stories. unabr. ed. F. Scott Fitzgerald. Read by Alexander Scourby. 6 cass. (Running Time: 6 hrs. 37 min.). Incl. Babylon Revisited. F. Scott Fitzgerald. 1977. (CXL507CX); Bridal Party. 1977. (CXL507CX); Lost Decade. 1977. (CXL507CX); Three Hours Between Planes. 1977. (CXL507CX); 1977. 44.98 (978-0-8072-2935-4(0), CXL507CX, Listening Lib) Random Audio Pubg.
This collection includes "The Great Gatsby" along with four of his short stories. In these works, Fitzgerald's freshness of vision, keen observations & his unique position as both representative & critic of the jazz age combine to capture these tumultuous times.

Great Gatsby & Other Stories, Set. unabr. ed. F. Scott Fitzgerald. Read by Alexander Scourby. 6 cass. (Running Time: 6 hrs. 36 mins.). 44.95 (L153) Blckstn Audio.
Includes "The Bridal Party," "Three Hours Between Planes," "Babylon Revisited" & "The Lost Decade.".

Great Gatsby & Other Stories, Set. unabr. ed. F. Scott Fitzgerald. Read by Alexander Scourby. 6 cass. 1999. 44.95 (FS9-50922) Highsmith.

Great Gatsby CD Low Price. F. Scott Fitzgerald. Read by Robbins Tim. 1975. audio compact disk 19.95 (978-0-06-115355-6(9)) HarperCollins Pubs.

Great Gatsby, with EBook. unabr. ed. F. Scott Fitzgerald. Narrated by Robertson Dean & Dawkins Dean. (Running Time: 5 hrs. 0 mins. 0 sec.). (ENG.). 2009. 19.99 (978-1-4001-6424-0(9)) Pub: Tantor Media. Dist(s): IngramPubServ

***Great Gatsby, with EBook.** unabr. ed. F. Scott Fitzgerald. Narrated by Robertson Dean. (Running Time: 5 hrs. 0 mins.). 2009. 13.99 (978-1-4001-8424-8(X)) Tantor Media.

Great Ghost Stories - Volume 1, Set. unabr. ed. J. Sheridan Le Fanu et al. Narrated by Grover Gardner et al. 3 cass. (Running Time: 4 hrs. 30 min.). Incl. Golden Arm. Mark Twain.; Lady's Maid's Bell. Edith Wharton.; Madame Crowl's Ghost & Ghost Stories of the Tiled House. J. Sheridan Le Fanu.; Markheim. Robert Louis Stevenson.; Upper Berth. F. Marion Crawford.; What Was It? Fitz James O'Brien.; 1984. (978-1-55685-006-6(9)) Audio Bk Con.
These eerie tales & authors were mentioned by Edith Wharton as having influenced her in the writing of her own ghost stories. Wharton's choices have a lingering, mystifying & frightening quality.

Great Ghost Stories, Volume I. Narrated by Flo Gibson et al. (ENG.). 2007. audio compact disk 19.95 (978-1-55685-918-2(X)) Audio Bk Con.

Great Ghost Stories, Volume II, Vol. II, Set. unabr. ed. Narrated by Grover Gardner et al. 3 cass. (Running Time: 4 hrs. 30 min.). Incl. Canterville Ghost. Oscar Wilde. (J).; Doll's Ghost. F. Marion Crawford.; Old Nurse's Story. Elizabeth Gaskell.; Thrawn Janet. Robert Louis Stevenson.; Watcher. J. Sheridan Le Fanu.; 1999. 16.95 (978-1-55685-007-3(7)) Audio Bk Con.
More chilling tales including, "The Doll's Ghost", Thrawn Janet", "The Watcher", "The Old Nurse's Story" & "Canterville Ghost".

Great Ghost Stories, Volume 3, Vol. 3. unabr. ed. Henry James et al. Read by Flo Gibson. 6 cass. (Running Time: 8 hrs. 30 mins.). (gr. 6-12). 1997. 24.95 (978-1-55685-447-7(1), 447-1) Audio Bk Con.
More chilling tales, including, "The Romance of Certain Clothes", "The Judge's House", "John Granger" & "The Shadow".

Great Gift see Zawadi Kuu

Great Gildersleeve. Perf. by Harold Peary. 1 cass. (Running Time: 60 min.). 7.95 (CC-3693) Natl Recrd Co.
Throckmorton P. Gildersleeve, the water commissioner, gets LeRoy interested in school activities; Gildy then decides to get the Jolly Boys to start a band. In "Our Miss Brooks," Miss Brooks' landlady, Mrs. Davis, has been dating Henry Pringel, the butcher & is thinking of marrying him after knowing him only a few weeks; then Miss Brooks learns that the butcher is a con-man & has been in jail.

Great Gildersleeve. Perf. by Harold Peary. 1 cass. (Running Time: 60 min.). 1944. 7.95 (CC-6060) Natl Recrd Co.
In the first episode, water commissioner Throckmorton P. Gildersleeve opposes incumbent Mayor Twilliger in the upcoming election for Mayor. Gildy also tries to get his future mother-in-law out of town. In the second episode Gildy is a juror in Judge Hooker's court hearing a bank robbery case. He unknowingly is given a $1,000 bribe to free the bank robber.

Great Gildersleeve. Contrib. by Harold Peary. (Running Time: 10800 sec.). 2004. 9.98 (978-1-57019-556-3(0)) Radio Spirits.

Great Gildersleeve. Perf. by Harold Peary. 1 cass. (Running Time: 60 min.). (Old Time Radio Classic Singles Ser.). 4.95 (978-1-57816-104-1(5), GG110) Audio File.
Includes: 1) Gildy runs for Mayor. 6/18/44. 2) plus Screen Guild Players (1940s) "Gildersleeve's Bad Day" radio version of the film. Lady Esther Products.

Great Gildersleeve. Contrib. by Harold Peary. (Running Time: 10800 sec.). 2004. 9.98 (978-1-57019-555-6(2)) Radio Spirits.

Great Gildersleeve. unabr. ed. 1 cass. (Running Time: 57 min.). 12.95 (#494) J Norton Pubs.
Side One has Gildersleeve & his neighbor Bullard competing for the affections of the same girl. On Side Two, Hal Perry (the original Gildersleeve) talks about the programs & introduces two excerpts from past episodes.

Great Gildersleeve, Set. Perf. by Willard Waterman. 2 cass. (Running Time: 2 hrs.). vinyl bd. 10.95 (978-1-57816-054-9(5), GG2401) Audio File.
Includes: "October 4, 1950" Gildy has been appointed chairman of the Summerfield Community Chest fund drive & nephew Leroy is going to be the quarterback in the benefit football game. "October 11, 1950" If Summerfield gets a new mayor, will Gildersleeve lose his job as water commissioner? "October 18, 1950" Mr. Gildersleeve decides to buy himself a new suit...& then tries to fashion a new image to go with it. "October 25, 1950" Gildersleeve is hopeful that he will be named to the "Sons of Summerfield" Lodge.

Great Gildersleeve, Vol. 1. collector's ed. Perf. by Harold Peary. 6 cass. (Running Time: 9 hrs.). 1998. bk. 34.98 (4008) Radio Spirits.
The Great Gildersleeve was radio's first great spinoff series, featuring the character of Fibber McGee's nemesis, Throckmorton P. Gildersleeve. Continuing the role he perfected on Fibber McGee and Molly, Harold Peary, as Gildersleeve, rode the train out of Wistful Vista and into the town of Summerfield, where he assumed custody of his orphaned niece and nephew and was appointed water commissioner. Includes Moving to Summerfield, Bad Case of the Sneezes, Mail Order Rabbits, House Hunting and 14 more.

Great Gildersleeve, Vol. 2. (Running Time: 2 hrs.). 2004. audio compact disk 12.95 (978-1-57816-172-0(X)) Audio File.

Great Gildersleeve, Vol. 3. collector's ed. Perf. by Walter Tetley et al. 6 cass. (Running Time: 9 hrs.). 2001. bk. 34.98 (4198) Radio Spirits.
Eighteen classic comedies including "Preparing for Grass Lake," "The New Teacher," "Leroy Is Expelled," "Leila Returns," "Talents in the Family," "Uninvited," "Leroy's Debt," "Leila's Friend," "Peavey's Wife Is Ill," "Leroy Is a Problem," "The Homemaking Class" and more.

Great Gildersleeve, Vol.2. (Running Time: 2 hrs.). 2004. 10.95 (978-1-57816-168-3(1)) Audio File.

Great Gildersleeve: Baby Needs a Name & Welfare Worries. 1 cass. (Running Time: 1 hr.). 2001. 6.98 (2331) Radio Spirits.

Great Gildersleeve: Be Kind to Birdie & Leroy's Magical Date. 1 cass. (Running Time: 1 hr.). 2001. 6.98 (2329) Radio Spirits.

Great Gildersleeve: Bronco vs. Marshall & Christmas Competition. 1 cass. (Running Time: 1 hr.). 2001. 6.98 (1979) Radio Spirits.

Great Gildersleeve: Christmas Eve & New Year's Eve. 1 cass. (Running Time: 1 hr.). 2001. 6.98 (2101) Radio Spirits.

Great Gildersleeve: Christmas Show & Lost Presents. 1 cass. (Running Time: 1 hr.). 2001. 6.98 (2437) Radio Spirits.

Great Gildersleeve: Crush on French Teacher & Baseball Diamond. 1 cass. (Running Time: 1 hr.). 2001. 6.98 (1745) Radio Spirits.

Great Gildersleeve: Dueling over Adeline & No Women Allowed. 1 cass. (Running Time: 1 hr.). 2001. 6.98 (2330) Radio Spirits.

Great Gildersleeve: Election Mischief & Mayor for a Day. 1 cass. (Running Time: 1 hr.). 2001. 6.98 (2327) Radio Spirits.

Great Gildersleeve: Engagement Notices & The French D. P. 1 cass. (Running Time: 1 hr.). 2001. 6.98 (2037) Radio Spirits.

Great Gildersleeve: Gilder-Mom! & A Job for Bronco. 1 cass. (Running Time: 1 hr.). 2001. 6.98 (1959) Radio Spirits.

Great Gildersleeve: Gildersleeve vs. Golf & Problems with Leroy's Teacher. 1 cass. (Running Time: 1 hr.). 2001. 6.98 (2601) Radio Spirits.

Great Gildersleeve: Gildy Finds Himself Engaged to Two Women & Water Shortage in Town. 1 cass. (Running Time: 1 hr.). 2001. 6.98 (2139) Radio Spirits.

Great Gildersleeve: Gildy Forgets Court Date & Pervus Tries to Sell Gildy. 1 cass. (Running Time: 1 hr.). 2001. 6.98 (1871) Radio Spirits.

Great Gildersleeve: Gildy Gets Leroy a Dog for Christmas & Gildy Falls in Love. 1 cass. (Running Time: 1 hr.). 2001. 6.98 (1743) Radio Spirits.

Great Gildersleeve: Gildy Goes Christmas Shopping & The Mayor Criticizes Gildersleeve. 1 cass. (Running Time: 1 hr.). 2001. 6.98 (2219) Radio Spirits.

Great Gildersleeve: Gildy Plays Hooky & Is Adeline Having an Affair? 1 cass. (Running Time: 1 hr.). 2001. 6.98 (1850) Radio Spirits.

Great Gildersleeve: Gildy Ponders Life & The End-of-the-Month Water Bills! 1 cass. (Running Time: 1 hr.). 2001. 6.98 (1560) Radio Spirits.

Great Gildersleeve: Gildy Teaches Leroy Money Management & Bessie's Love Problems. 1 cass. (Running Time: 1 hr.). 2001. 6.98 (1742) Radio Spirits.

Great Gildersleeve: Gildy Waits for Important Call & Gildy May Get His Job Back. 1 cass. (Running Time: 1 hr.). 2001. 6.98 (1741) Radio Spirits.

Great Gildersleeve: Gildy's Girlfriend & Young Doctor? & Trouble with Young Doctor. 1 cass. (Running Time: 1 hr.). 2001. 6.98 (1749) Radio Spirits.

Great Gildersleeve: Gildy's Jealousy Gets the Best of Him & Has Gildy Proposed to Miss DelRay? 1 cass. (Running Time: 1 hr.). 2001. 6.98 (2416) Radio Spirits.

Great Gildersleeve: Hurrying Hattie Home & Adoption Dilemma. 1 cass. (Running Time: 1 hr.). 2001. 6.98 (2332) Radio Spirits.

Great Gildersleeve: In Love with a Voice & Double Date with Marjorie. 1 cass. (Running Time: 1 hr.). 2001. 6.98 (1891) Radio Spirits.

Great Gildersleeve: Leila Spoils Gildersleeve's Dinner & Gildersleeve Faces Re-Election. 1 cass. (Running Time: 1 hr.). 2001. 6.98 (2240) Radio Spirits.

Great Gildersleeve: Leila's New Beau & Leroy Goes to a Party. 1 cass. (Running Time: 1 hr.). 2001. 6.98 (2458) Radio Spirits.

Great Gildersleeve: Leroy Gets the Flu & The Hobby. 1 cass. (Running Time: 1 hr.). 2001. 6.98 (2179) Radio Spirits.

Great Gildersleeve: Leroy Has a Toothache & New Blood in the Water Department. 1 cass. (Running Time: 1 hr.). 2001. 6.98 (1748) Radio Spirits.

Great Gildersleeve: Leroy Has the Left-Out Blues & Peavey is M. I. A. 1 cass. (Running Time: 1 hr.). 2001. 6.98 (1504) Radio Spirits.

Great Gildersleeve: Love, Life & Leila Ransom. Perf. by Harold Peary. 8 CDs. (Running Time: 8 hrs). Dramatization. 2005. audio compact disk 25.95 (978-0-9770819-0-5(7)) Choice Vent.
Join Throckmorton P. Gildersleeve as he raises his orphaned niece and nephew in the small town of Summerfield in this critically acclaimed radio comedy spun off from the popular Fibber McGee & Molly radio series. Set against the backdrop of American life early in World War II, listen and laugh as Gildersleeve becomes the Water Commissioner and romances the widow Leila Ransom while trying to cope with local politics, wartime rationing, woman in the workplace, and the mysteries of love with ensuing hilarity.Harold Peary stars as Gildersleeve and is joined by an outstanding group of supporting players including Walter Tetley as Leroy, Lurene Tuttle as Marjorie, Lillian Randolph as Birdie, Shirley Mitchell as Leila Ransom, Earle Ross as Judge Hooker, Richard LeGrand as Mr. Peavy, and Arthur Q. Bryan as Floyd the Barber. This 8 CD digitally remastered audio collection features 16 episodes as broadcast during the classic 1942-43 second season of this series that aired for more than 15 years during the Golden Age of Radio. Also included is a Program Booklet with photographs and essays by noted radio historian Anthony Tollin.

Great Gildersleeve: Love, Life & Leila Ransom. Perf. by Harold Peary. (ENG.). 2008. audio compact disk 31.95 (978-1-57019-856-4(X)) Radio Spirits.

Great Gildersleeve: Mousetrap Invention & Election Woes for Gildersleeve. 1 cass. (Running Time: 1 hr.). 2001. 6.98 (2281) Radio Spirits.

Great Gildersleeve: Radio episode/hal perry Discussion. (ENG.). 2008. audio compact disk 12.95 (978-1-57970-513-8(8), Audio-For) J Norton Pubs.

Great Gildersleeve: Test Drive & Mayor Catches Gildersleeve Relaxing at the Office. 1 cass. (Running Time: 1 hr.). 2001. 6.98 (1747) Radio Spirits.

Great Gildersleeve: The Diplomat & Need for a New Car. 1 cass. (Running Time: 1 hr.). 2001. 6.98 (2118) Radio Spirits.

Great Gildersleeve: The Engagement Ring & New Year's Party. 1 cass. (Running Time: 1 hr.). 2001. 6.98 (1930) Radio Spirits.

Great Gildersleeve: The Haunted House & Detective Gildersleeve. 1 cass. (Running Time: 1 hr.). 2001. 6.98 (2578) Radio Spirits.

Great Gildersleeve: The Jolly Boys Band & The New Neighbors. 1 cass. (Running Time: 1 hr.). 2001. 6.98 (1904) Radio Spirits.

Great Gildersleeve: The New Flame & The Inherited Baby. 1 cass. (Running Time: 1 hr.). 2001. 6.98 (2079) Radio Spirits.

Great Gildersleeve: The Strange Visitor & Gildy Needs a Babysitter. 1 cass. (Running Time: 1 hr.). 2001. 6.98 (2014) Radio Spirits.

Great Gildersleeve: The Whole Town Is Talking & JoAnne Meets Leila. 1 cass. (Running Time: 1 hr.). 2001. 6.98 (2476) Radio Spirits.

Great Gildersleeve: Who Is Gildy's Secretary? And Gildy to Speak on the Radio. 1 cass. (Running Time: 1 hr.). 2001. 6.98 (1744) Radio Spirits.

Great Gildersleeve: Wounded Vanity & Sweet Adeline. 1 cass. (Running Time: 1 hr.). 2001. 6.98 (2328) Radio Spirits.

Great Gildersleeve: 2-Month Anniversary & Gildy Takes Leroy Fishing. 1 cass. (Running Time: 1 hr.). 2001. 6.98 (1746) Radio Spirits.

Great Gildersleeve No. 2: Harold Peary's Last Show & Willard Waterman's First Show. unabr. ed. 1 cass. (Running Time: 60 min.). Dramatization. 1950. 7.95 Norelco box. (CC-9803) Natl Recrd Co.
Harold Peary's last show: Throckmorton P. Gildersleeve prepares to take his little family for a vacation on a houseboat. The show has an unusual twist ending. With Walter Tetley as LeRoy & Richard Crenna as Bronco. Kraft Foods. Willard Waterman's first show: When Gildersleeve returns from a vacation, he learns that Marjorie's husband, Bronco, has a black eye. When he finds out the reason, he also learns a happy secret. Of course, everyone knows the secret already. Kraft Foods.

Great Gildersleeve Vol. 2: The Lost Episodes from 1951! Perf. by Willard Waterman. 1 cass. (Running Time: 60 min.). 4.95 (978-1-57816-105-8(3), GG223) Audio File.
Includes: 1) Harold Peary's last show as Gildersleeve (6/14/50). 2) Willard Waterman's first show as Gildersleeve (9/6/50).

Great Gildersleeve Vol. 2: The Lost Episodes from 1951!, collector's ed. Perf. by Willard Waterman et al. 6 cass. (Running Time: 9 hrs..). 1998. bk. 34.98 (4388) Radio Spirits.
The Great Gildersleeve was radio's first great spinoff series, featuring the character of Fibber McGee's nemesis, Throckmorton P. Gildersleeve. Continuing the role he perfected on Fibber McGee and Molly, Harold Peary, as Gildersleeve, rode the train out of Wistful Vista and into the town of Summerfield, where he assumed custody of his orphaned niece and nephew and was appointed water commissioner. Includes Naming the Twins, Bronco Runs the House, Babysitting Twins, Leroy's Driving Lesson, Bronco's Mother Overstays Visit, Falling for Rumson's Sister and 12 more.

***Great Gildersleeve, Volume 1.** RadioArchives.com. (Running Time: 600). (ENG.). 2003. audio compact disk 29.98 (978-1-61081-006-7(6)) Radio Arch.

Great Gildesleeve: The Haunted House & Detective Gildersleeve. 1 cass. (Running Time: 1 hr.). 2001. 6.98 (2578) Radio Spirits.

Great Gilly Hopkins. Katherine Paterson. (J). 1979. bk. 21.33 (978-0-394-78371-0(9)) Random.

***Great Gilly Hopkins.** unabr. ed. Katherine Paterson. Read by Alyssa Bresnahan. (ENG.). 2009. (978-0-06-190271-0(3)); (978-0-06-184550-5(7)) HarperCollins Pubs.

Great Gilly Hopkins, unabr. ed. Katherine Paterson. Narrated by Alyssa Bresnahan. 4 pieces. (Running Time: 4 hrs. 45 mins.). (gr. 4 up). 1997. 35.00 (978-0-7887-0740-7(X), 94917E7) Recorded Bks.
In three years, 11-year-old Gilly Hopkins has been in three foster homes & has perfected the art of driving people crazy, especially those responsible for her. Now she's headed for home number four.

Great Gilly Hopkins. unabr. ed. Katherine Paterson. Narrated by Alyssa Bresnahan. 4 CDs. (Running Time: 4 hrs. 45 mins.). (gr. 4 up). 2000. audio compact disk 39.00 (978-0-7887-4737-3(1), C1220E7) Recorded Bks.

Great Go-Cart Race. (Paws & Tales Ser.: Vol. 14). (J). 2001. 3.99 (978-1-57972-412-2(4)); audio compact disk 5.99 (978-1-57972-413-9(2)) Insight Living.

Great God: In the Fathers Presence. Perf. by Campus Crusade Singers. Contrib. by Randy Ray. Arranged by Ric Flauding. 1 cass. . (Running Time: 1 hr.). 1999. 10.98 (978-1-57919-131-3(2)) Randolf Prod.
Praise & worship.

Great God: In the Fathers Presence. Perf. by Campus Crusade Singers. Prod. by Randy Ray. 1 cass., 1 CD. (Running Time: 1 hr.). 1999. audio compact disk 14.98 CD. (978-1-57919-132-0(0)) Randolf Prod.
Praise & worship.

Great God Who Saves. Contrib. by Laura Story. 2008. audio compact disk 11.99 (978-5-557-48003-1(X)) INO Rec.

Great Golf. Shelley L. Stockwell & John Goode. Read by John Goode & Shelley Lessin Stockwell. 1991. 14.95 (978-0-912559-20-9(9)) Creativity Unltd Pr.
Improve your game, free your mind, build confidence, play focused & relaxed while having fun. Hypnosis on one side, motivational music & pep talk on the other.

Great Gondolfo see Adventures of Sherlock Holmes

Great Good Place & in the Cage, unabr. ed. Henry James. Narrated by Flo Gibson. 3 cass. (Running Time: 4 hrs.). (gr. 10 up). 2000. 16.95 (978-1-55685-630-3(X)) Audio Bk Con.
In "The Great Good Place" Dane searches for peace & a respite from the demands of success. The fascinating searching novella "In the Cage" tells of a young girl in a Mayfair post office becoming aware of the great social world & of a certain gentleman's affairs through the telegrams they send.

Great Good Thing. unabr. ed. Roderick Townley. Read by Blair Brown. 2 vols. (Running Time: 3 hrs. 4 mins.). (Middle Grade Cassette Librariestm Ser.). (J). (gr. 4-6). 2004. pap. bk. 29.00 (978-0-8072-1001-7(3), S YA 302 SP, Listening Lib); 23.00 (978-0-8072-0497-9(8), Listening Lib) Random Audio Pubg.
Sylvie is a 12-year-old princess & has been for the more than 80 years the book she lives in was first printed. But Sylvie has a restless urge to explore & go beyond the margins of her book. Sylvie breaks the rule of all storybook characters when she looks at her reader & gets to know the shy young Claire. When Claire falls asleep with the book open, Sylvie then enters her dreams.

***Great Grammar & Painless Proofreading.** PUEI. 2009. audio compact disk 199.00 (978-1-935041-70-2(3), CareerTrack) P Univ E Inc.

Great-Grandma Heroine! Barbara Sobel. 1 cass. (Running Time: 10 min.). (J). 1986. 16.59 incl. hardcover. Jan Prods.

Great Green Squishy Mean Concert. unabr. ed. Monty Harper. 1 CD. (Running Time: 52 mins.). (J). 2005. audio compact disk 15.00 (978-0-9701081-6-6(8)) Monty Harper.
Monty Harper is a gifted songwriter who truly appeals to his targeted age group. The children sang along and requested the CD again, a true testament to his talent. His lyrics are kid-friendly and his music is catchy and tuneful.

Great Grizzly Wilderness: A Story of a Pacific Rain Forest. Audrey Fraggalosch. 1 cass. (Running Time: 35 min.). (J). (gr. k-4). 2001. pap. bk. 19.95 (SP 7015C) Kimbo Educ.
A mother grizzly bear & her cubs awaken from their winter hibernation to explore the rainforest & search for food. Includes readalong book.

Great Grizzly Wilderness: A Story of the Pacific Rain Forest. Audrey Fraggalosch. Read by Randye Kaye. 1 cass. (Running Time: 14 min.). (Habitat Ser.). (J). (ps-3). 2000. 19.95 (978-1-56899-840-4(6)) Soundprints.

Great Guitar Picking Tunes. William Bay. 2000. pap. bk. 9.95 (978-0-7866-5317-1(5), 98054BCD) Mel Bay.

Great Gypsy. Kimberly Willis Holt. Read by Emily Janice Card. (Piper Reed Ser.: No. 2). (J). 2009. 35.00 (978-1-60775-600-2(5)) Find a World.

Great Gypsy. unabr. ed. Kimberly Willis Holt. Read by Emily Janice Card. (Piper Reed Ser.: No. 2). (J). (gr. 3). 2008. audio compact disk 19.95 (978-0-7393-6185-6(6), Listening Lib) Pub: Random Audio Pubg. Dist(s): Random

Great Harry: The Extravagant Life of Henry VIII. unabr. ed. Carolly Erickson. Narrated by Nelson Runger. 15 cass. (Running Time: 19 hrs.). 1988. 120.00 (978-1-55690-206-2(9), 88430E7) Recorded Bks.
The life & times of Henry VIII of England.

Great Historical Shakespeare Recordings. Perf. by Charles Laughton et al. Featuring Henry Irving et al. 2 CDs. (Running Time: 2 hrs. 30 mins.). (Classic Drama Ser.). 2000. audio compact disk 17.98 (978-962-634-200-8(5), NA220012, Naxos AudioBooks) Naxos.
A unique and unusual compilation of some of the greatest recordings from the beginning of the recording era. Includes a wide range of works.

Great Historical Shakespeare Recordings. Read by Historical Recordings. (Running Time: 2 hrs.). 2004. 20.95 (978-1-60083-749-4(2)) Iofy Corp.

Great Historical Shakespeare Recordings. abr. ed. Perf. by Charles Laughton et al. Featuring Henry Irving et al. 2 cass. (Running Time: 2 hrs. 30 mins.). (Classic Drama Ser.). 2000. 13.98 (978-962-634-700-3(7), NA220014, Naxos AudioBooks) Naxos.

Great Hits for Harmonica. Phil Duncan. 1996. pap. bk. 18.95 (978-0-7866-1318-2(1), 95405P) Mel Bay.

Great Home Business. unabr. ed. Gary Null. 1 cass. (Running Time: 58 min.). 12.95 (945) J Norton Pubs.
The author takes you step-by-step through all the basics: how to select a profitable business, advertising & promotion, tax advantages, legal matters, bookkeeping, pricing. Actual case histories of home entrepreneurs will show you how others did it & give you ideas for your own successful home business.

***Great House.** Nicole Krauss. 2010. audio compact disk 39.99 (978-1-4498-5487-4(7)) Recorded Bks.

Great House of God. abr. ed. Max Lucado. Narrated by Alan Scott. (ENG.). 2003. 10.49 (978-1-60814-232-3(9)) Oasis Audio.

Great House of God. unabr. abr. ed. Max Lucado. Narrated by Alan Scott. 3 CDs. (Running Time: 3 hrs.). (ENG.). 2003. audio compact disk 14.99 (978-1-58926-245-4(X), T10M-003D) Oasis Audio.

***Great Hunger.** Dan Cushman. 2009. (978-1-60136-473-9(3)) Audio Holding.

Great Hunger. Dan Cushman. (Running Time: 0 hr. 24 mins.). 2000. 10.95 (978-1-60083-520-9(1)) Iofy Corp.

Great Hunger, unabr. ed. Cecil Woodham-Smith. Read by Frederick Davidson. 13 cass. (Running Time: 19 hrs.). 1999. 85.95 (978-0-7861-1495-5(9), 2346) Blckstn Audio.
The Potato famine of the 1840's killed one million Irish peasants and sent hundreds of thousands to the new world.

***Great Hunger: Ireland 1845-1849.** unabr. ed. Cecil Woodham-Smith. Read by Frederick Davidson. (Running Time: 18 hrs. 30 mins.). 2010. 44.95 (978-1-4417-6742-4(8)); audio compact disk 123.00 (978-1-4417-6740-0(1)) Blckstn Audio.

Great Hunt. abr. ed. Robert Jordan. Read by Mark Rolston. 2 cass. (Running Time: 3 hrs.). (Wheel of Time Ser.: Bk. 2). 2000. 7.95 (978-1-57815-133-2(3), 1092, Media Bks Audio) Media Bks NJ.
Legend fades to myth & even myth is long forgotten when the Age that gave it birth returns again. So many tales about each of the Hunters & so many Hunters to tell of.

Great Hunt. abr. ed. Scripts. Robert Jordan. Perf. by Mark Rolston. 2 cass. (Running Time: 3 hrs.). (Wheel of Time Ser.: Bk. 2). 2003. 16.95 (978-1-59007-363-6(0), N Millennium Audio); audio compact disk 20.95 (978-1-59007-364-3(9), N Millennium Audio) Pub: New Millenn Enter. Dist(s): PerseuPGW

Great Hunt. abr. ed. Robert Jordan. Read by Mark Rolston. 2 cass. (Running Time: 3 hrs.). (Wheel of Time Ser.: Bk. 2). 1994. 16.95 Set. (978-1-879371-53-8(7), 40210) Pub Mills.
Rand al'Thor, the farmboy who is thought to be the Dragon Reborn, refuses to accept his fate as the leader long prophesied who will save the world, but in the saving, destroy it.

Great Hunt. unabr. ed. Robert Jordan. (Wheel of Time Ser.: Bk. 2). 2008. (978-1-55927-955-0(9)); (978-1-55927-956-7(7)) Macmill Audio.

Great Hunt. unabr. rev. ed. Robert Jordan. Read by Kate Reading & Michael Kramer. 22 CDs. (Running Time: 27 hrs. 0 mins. 0 sec.). (Wheel of Time Ser.: Bk. 2). (ENG.). 2004. audio compact disk 59.95 (978-1-59397-433-6(7)) Pub: Macmill Audio. Dist(s): Macmillan

Great Hunt, Pt. 1. unabr. ed. Robert Jordan. Read by Kate Reading & Michael Kramer. 10 cass. (Running Time: 15 hrs.). (Wheel of Time Ser.: Bk. 2). 1997. 80.00 (978-0-7366-3563-9(7), 4208-A) Books on Tape.
Young Rand learns that he's The Dragon reborn when he unwittingly uses his powers to subdue the Dark One's warriors.

Great Hunt, Pt. 2. Robert Jordan. Read by Kate Reading & Michael Kramer. 8 cass. (Running Time: 12 hrs.). (Wheel of Time Ser.: Bk. 2). 1997. 64.00 (4208-B) Books on Tape.

Great Hurricane: 1938. Cherie Burns. Read by Anna Fields. (Running Time: 7 mins.). 2005. 44.95 (978-0-7861-3750-3(9)) Blckstn Audio.

Great Hurricane: 1938. unabr. ed. Cherie Burns. 5 cass. (Running Time: 21600 sec.). 2005. 27.95 (978-0-7861-3545-5(X), E3515); audio compact disk 29.95 (978-0-7861-7779-0(9), ZE3515); audio compact disk 29.95 (978-0-7861-8002-8(1), ZM3515) Blckstn Audio.

Great Hurricane: 1938. Cherie Burns. Read by Anna Fields. (Running Time: 21600 sec.). 2005. audio compact disk 55.00 (978-0-7861-7646-5(6)) Blckstn Audio.

Great Hymns: F Horn/Eb Horn - Grade 3-4. James Curnow. 2002. pap. bk. 12.95 (978-90-431-1035-8(3), 9043110353) H Leonard.

Great Hymns of the Church: The Choirs of the Cathedral of St Philip, Atlanta, Georgia. Cd & Robert L. Simpson. audio compact disk 18.00 (978-0-89869-286-0(5)) Church Pub Inc.

Great Hymnwriters (Portraits in Song) Medium High Voice. Composed by Jay Althouse & Patti Drennan. (ENG.). 2006. audio compact disk 12.95 (978-0-7390-4313-4(7)) Alfred Pub.

Great Hymnwriters (Portraits in Song) Medium Low Voice. Composed by Jay Althouse & Patti Drennan. (ENG.). 2006. audio compact disk 12.95 (978-0-7390-4314-1(5)) Alfred Pub.

Great Idea Is Worth a 1,000 Words: Winning Keys to Educational Wellness. abr. ed. Perf. by Angela Brown et al. 1 cass. (Running Time: 30 mins.). (Words of Wellness Ser.: Vol. 2). 2000. 12.95 (978-0-9673451-7-8(0), LLP302) Life Long Pubg.
Easy tips that will generate new ideas, how to capitalize on non-traditional thinking, how to use your creativity to promote yourself & your career.

Great Ideas. Earl Nightingale. Read by Earl Nightingale. 6 cass. 45.00 Set. (316A) Nightingale-Conant.

Great Ideas. Herb True. 6 cass. 49.95; 10.00 ea. Team Intl Inc.
Laugh along with Herb's "live" audience as you listen to pick-me-up messages about laughter, love & managing for the best of life.

Great Ideas: Listening & Speaking Activities for Students of American English. Leo Jones & Victoria F. Kimbrough. 1 cass. (Running Time: hrs. mins.). (ENG., 1987. 24.00 (978-0-521-32052-8(6)) Cambridge U Pr.

Great Ideas: Listening & Speaking Activities for Students of American English. Leo Jones & Victoria F. Kimbrough. 1 cass. 19.95 Midwest European Pubns.
Activities designed for intermediate & advanced students.

Great Ideas Audio Sampler: Listening & Speaking Activities for Students of American English. Leo Jones & Victoria F. Kimbrough. 1 cass. (Running Time: 1 hr.). pap. bk. Cambridge U Pr.
A unique collection of absorbing and enjoyable activities designed to improve the listening and speaking abilities of intermediate to high-intermediate students. Students are encouraged to exchange their ideas and opinions about a wide range of topics, including entertainment, current events, employment, strange phenomena, the future, and advertising. Photographs, advertisements, maps and drawings, cartoons, and excerpts from magazines and newspapers help stimulate this exchange. Specially designed communication activities motivate students to share information by providing each student with some information that the other does not have. Accompanying cassette consists of both scripted and authentic recordings of people speaking naturally, with the normal pauses, hesitations, and interruptions that occur in everyday spoken language.

***Great Ideas: A Retrospective, Vol. 1: Episodes 1-26.** unabr. ed. Mortimer J. Adler. Read by Mortimer J. Adler. (Running Time: 13 hrs.). 2010. 29.95 (978-1-4417-0477-1(9)); audio compact disk 109.00 (978-1-4417-0474-0(4)) Blckstn Audio.

***Great Ideas: A Retrospective, Vol. 2: Episodes 27-52.** unabr. ed. Mortimer J. Adler. Read by Mortimer J. Adler. (Running Time: 13 hrs.). 2010. 29.95 (978-1-4417-4547-7(5)); audio compact disk 109.00 (978-1-4417-4544-6(0)) Blckstn Audio.

Great Ideas of Classical Physics. Instructed by Steven J. Pollock. 12 CDs. (Running Time: 12 hrs.). 2006. 69.95 (978-1-59803-253-6(4)); 129.95 (978-1-59803-252-9(6)) Teaching Co.

Great Ideas of Philosophy. unabr. ed. Daniel N. Robinson. 5 cass. (Running Time: 25 hrs.). 1999. 299.95 (490) Teaching Co.
Covers more than 2,000 years of philosophical thought. After identifying & explaining the recurring questions humans have pondered, Professor Robinson demonstrates their connections to one another across centuries of debates. Course 490, 5 parts, 50 lectures.

Great Ideas of Philosophy, I-V. 2nd ed. Instructed by Daniel Robinson. 30 cass. (Running Time: 30 hrs.). 2004. bk. 119.95 (978-1-56585-979-1(0), 4200); bk. 169.95 (978-1-56585-981-4(2), 4200) Teaching Co.

Great Ideas of Philosophy, Vol. 2. Instructed by Daniel Robinson. 5 cass. (Running Time: 5 hrs.). 1997. 299.95 (978-1-56585-140-5(4)) Teaching Co.

Great Ideas of Philosophy, Vol. 3. Instructed by Daniel Robinson. 5 cass. (Running Time: 5 hrs.). 1997. 299.95 (978-1-56585-141-2(2)) Teaching Co.

Great Ideas of Philosophy, Vol. 4. Instructed by Daniel Robinson. 5 cass. (Running Time: 5 hrs.). 1997. 299.95 (978-1-56585-142-9(0)) Teaching Co.

Great Ideas of Philosophy, Vol. 5. Instructed by Daniel Robinson. 5 cass. (Running Time: 5 hrs.). 1997. 299.95 (978-1-56585-143-6(9)) Teaching Co.

Great Ideas of Philosophy, Vols. I-V. Instructed by Daniel Robinson. 25 cass. (Running Time: 25 hrs.). 1997. 299.95 (978-1-56585-139-9(0)); audio compact disk 449.95 (978-1-56585-356-0(3)) Teaching Co.

Great Ideas of Psychology, Pts. I-IV. Instructed by Daniel Robinson. 24 cass. (Running Time: 24 hrs.). 1997. 249.95 (978-1-56585-185-6(4)); audio compact disk 129.95 (978-1-56585-368-3(7)) Teaching Co.

Great Ideas of Psychology, Vol. 2. Instructed by Daniel Robinson. 6 cass. (Running Time: 6 hrs.). 1997. 249.95 (978-1-56585-186-3(2)) Teaching Co.

Great Ideas of Psychology, Vol. 3. Instructed by Daniel Robinson. 6 cass. (Running Time: 6 hrs.). 1997. 249.95 (978-1-56585-187-0(0)) Teaching Co.

Great Ideas of Psychology, Vol. 4. Instructed by Daniel Robinson. 6 cass. (Running Time: 6 hrs.). 1997. 249.95 (978-1-56585-188-7(9)) Teaching Co.

Great Ideas (Seventy-Five Ideas in Seventy-Five Minutes) 1 cass. (America's Supermarket Showcase '96 Ser.). 1996. 11.00 (NGA96-033) Sound Images.

Great Improvisation: Franklin, France, & the Birth of America. abr. ed. Stacy Schiff. Read by Jason Culp. 8 CDs. (Running Time: 10 hrs.). (ENG.). 2005. audio compact disk 37.95 (978-0-7393-2038-9(6)) Pub: Random Audio Pubg. Dist(s): Random

Great Improvisation: Franklin, France, & the Birth of America. unabr. ed. Stacy Schiff. Read by Susan Denaker. 14 CDs. (Running Time: 22 hrs.). 2005. audio compact disk 112.00 (978-1-4159-1983-5(6)); 96.00 (978-1-4159-1979-8(8)) Books on Tape.
An unexamined story of the Revolution complete with international intrigue and Benjamin Franklin's adventures in Paris.

Great Influenza: The Epic Story of the Deadliest Plague in History. unabr. ed. John M. Barry. Read by Scott Brick. 16 CDs. (Running Time: 20 hrs.). (ENG.). (gr. 12 up). 2006. audio compact disk 39.95 (978-0-14-305882-3(7), PengAudBks) Penguin Grp USA.

Great Inventors & Their Inventions. Donald B. Lemke et al. (Playaway Children Ser.). (ENG.). (J). (gr. k). 2009. 39.99 (978-1-60775-753-5(2)) Find a World.

Great Inventors & Their Inventions: Gutenberg - Bell - Marconi - the Wright Brothers. David Angus. Read by Benjamin Soames. (Playaway Children Ser.). (ENG.). (J). (gr. k). 2009. 39.99 (978-1-60812-512-8(2)) Find a World.

Great Inventors & Their Inventions: Gutenberg, Bell, Marconi, the Wright Brothers. David Angus. Read by Benjamin Soames. (Running Time: 9192 sec.). (Junior Classics Ser.). (J). (gr. 3-7). 2006. audio compact disk 17.98 (978-962-634-419-4(9), Naxos AudioBooks) Naxos.

Great Is the Lord: Sax & Guitar. 1 cass., 1 CD. (Instrumental Praise Ser.). 1999. 7.99 (978-0-7601-2669-1(0), 83061-0502-483061-0502-2) Provident Music.
Favorite praise choruses & cherished hymns performed by solo instruments & full orchestra. Includes: "At the Cross," "Blessed Assurance," "Change My Heart, O God," "Great Is the Lord," "He Who Began a Good Work in You," "His Name is Wonderful," "How I Love Jesus," "I Sing Praises to Your Name," "I Will Enter His Gates," "Jesus Is All the World to Me," "O How I Love Jesus," "Shine, Jesus, Shine" (Lord, the Light of Your Love), " Something Beautiful," "Sweet, Sweet Spirit," "Trust & Obey" & "When I Look into Your Holiness".

Great Is the Lord: Sax & Guitar. Perf. by Brentwood Music Staff. 1 cass., 1 CD. (Instrumental Praise Ser.). 1999. audio compact disk 10.99 (978-0-7601-2670-7(4), 83061-0502-2) Pub: Brentwood Music. Dist(s): Provident Mus Dist

Great Is Thy Faithfulness. Perf. by Robert Kochis & Robin Kochis. 1 cass. (Running Time: 44 mins.). 1999. 10.95 (T8570); audio compact disk 15.95 (K1140) Liguori Pubns.
Songs include: "Great Is Thy Faithfulness," "Blest Art They," "Not Too Far from Here," "Taste & See" & many more.

Great Is Thy Faithfulness. Ovid Young. 1998. 11.98 (978-0-7673-9949-4(8)); audio compact disk 16.98 (978-0-7673-9937-1(4)) LifeWay Christian.

Great Joy. Kate DiCamillo. Narrated by Jane Curtin. 1 CD. (Running Time: 9 mins.). (J). (gr. k-3). 2008. audio compact disk 12.95 (978-0-545-10683-2(4)) Weston Woods.

Great Joy. Kate DiCamillo. Narrated by Jane Curtin. Illus. by Bagram Ibatoulline. 1 CD. (Running Time: 9 mins.). (J). (gr. k-3). 2008. bk. 29.95 (978-0-545-10687-0(7)) Weston Woods.

Great Keinplatz Experiment: And Other Tales of Twilight & the Unseen. unabr. ed. Arthur Conan Doyle. 1 cass. (Running Time: 74 min.). Dramatization. 1981. 7.95 (S-9) Jimcin Record.
Sherlock Holmes' creator turns to the supernatural in these stories.

Great Kid's Shows. 1 cass. (Running Time: 60 min.). Incl. Jack Armstrong. (J). (GE-3924); Little Orphan Annie. (J). (GE-3924); Superman. (J). (GE-3924); Tom Mix. (J). (GE-3924); (J). 7.95 (GE-3924) Natl Recrd Co.
"Little Orphan Annie" adventure finds Annie & Joe Corntassle opposing Singapore Kirby; Superman episode is "The Strange Land of Aleria"; Tom Mix provides action, mystery, & a mile-a-minute thrills in an episode from the adventure known as "Secret Mission"; Jack Armstrong, the All-American Boy waving the flag for Hudson High, is featured in "The Luminous Dragon's Eye Ring".

Great Leaders Collection. David A. Adler. Illus. by Alexander Wallner & Robertand the Johnand theCasilla. 55 vols. (Running Time: 45 mins.). 1990. pap. bk. 85.95 (978-1-59112-845-8(5)) Live Oak Media.

Great Leaders of Our Time: Speeches That Made History. 16 cass. 49.97 Set. Moonbeam Pubns.
Americans have found both their presidents & life in the White House sources of never-ending interest. The president finds himself at the center of all sorts of events, including wars & political struggles. This collections of speeches help us to understand our presidents as men, statesmen & as the dominant symbols of their period. Speeches from Truman, Eisenhower, Roosevelt & Kennedy are included & replicas of each president's campaign buttons & a beautiful parchment scroll of each president's inaugural speech.

Great Light of God. Paramhansa Yogananda. 11.50 (978-0-87612-432-1(5)) Self Realization.

Great Light of God. Paramhansa Yogananda. 1 cass. 1993. 11.50 (2016) Self Realization.
Paramahansa Yogananda speaks of that immense light of God, & of the indescribable joy experienced by one who perceives that Unseen Reality. He explains why the spiritual science of Kriya Yoga gives the greatest proof of God's existence & how, through its practice, you realize that you are not a man or a woman, but a part of the eternal consciousness, the infinite blessedness of Spirit.

Great Light of God. Paramhansa Yogananda. (Running Time: 1 hr. 2 mins.). (Collector's (Self-Realization Fellowship) Ser.). 2006. audio compact disk 14.00 (978-0-87612-443-7(0)) Self Realization.

Great Light of the World: The Best of Bebo Norman. Contrib. by Bebo Norman. 2007. audio compact disk 13.99 (978-5-557-60942-5(3)) Essential Recs.

Great Lion of God. collector's ed. Taylor Caldwell. Narrated by John McDonough. 24 cass. (Running Time: 34 hrs. 30 mins.). 2002. 84.95 (978-1-4025-1165-3(5), K0022) Recorded Bks.
A sweeping novel of the life and times of Paul of Tarsus. A man with uniquely human qualities, Paul faced a world much like that of today, yet two millennia in the past. An extremely intelligent and passionate man, he spread Judeo-Christianity throughout the world. From his work arose the foundation for the morals and philosophy of contemporary Western thought.

Great Lion of God. unabr. ed. Taylor Caldwell. Narrated by John McDonough. 24 cass. (Running Time: 34 hrs. 30 mins.). 2002. 177.00 (978-0-7887-5092-2(5)) Recorded Bks.

Great Little Book of Affirmations: Incredibly Simple Questions - Amazingly Powerful Results! rev. unabr. ed. Noah St. John. Frwd. by Joe Vitale, Jr. (Running Time: 2 hrs.). (ENG.). 2008. audio compact disk 19.98 (978-1-59659-134-9(X), GildAudio) Pub: Gildan Media. Dist(s): HachBkGrp

Great Lives: A Man of Grit & Grace. unabr. ed. Charles R. Swindoll. Narrated by Raymond Todd. (Running Time: 10 hrs. 0 mins. 0 sec.). (ENG.). 2009. audio compact disk 28.98 (978-1-59644-690-8(0), christianSeed) christianaud.

Great Lives: A Man of Heroic Endurance. unabr. ed. Charles R. Swindoll. Read by Raymond Todd. (Running Time: 13 hrs. 42 mins. 0 sec.). (ENG.). 2009. audio compact disk 28.98 (978-1-59644-692-2(7), christianSeed) christianaud.

Great Lives: A Man of Heroism & Humility. unabr. ed. Charles R. Swindoll. Read by Raymond Todd. (Running Time: 6 hrs. 0 mins. 0 sec.). (ENG.). 2009. audio compact disk 24.98 (978-1-59644-688-5(9), christianSeed) christianaud.

Great Lives: A Man of Integrity & Forgiveness. unabr. ed. Charles Swindoll. Narrated by Michael Kramer. (Running Time: 9 hrs. 0 mins. 0 sec.). (ENG.). 2008. audio compact disk 24.98 (978-1-59644-641-0(2), christianSeed) christianaud.

Great Lives: A Man of Passion & Destiny. unabr. ed. Charles Swindoll. Narrated by Michael Kramer. (Running Time: 12 hrs. 0 mins. 0 sec.). (ENG.). 2008. audio compact disk 28.98 (978-1-59644-645-8(5), christianSeed) christianaud.

Great Lives: A Man of Selfless Dedication. unabr. ed. Charles Swindoll. Narrated by Raymond Todd. (Running Time: 12 hrs. 48 mins. 0 sec.). (ENG.). 2008. audio compact disk 28.98 (978-1-59644-643-4(9), christianSeed) christianaud.

Great Lives: A Woman of Strength & Dignity. unabr. ed. Charles Swindoll. Narrated by Kate Reading. (Running Time: 7 hrs. 42 mins. 0 sec.). (ENG.). 2008. audio compact disk 24.98 (978-1-59644-639-7(0), christianSeed) christianaud.

Great Lives: The Greatest Life of All. unabr. ed. Charles Swindoll. Narrated by Kate Reading. (Running Time: 11 hrs. 12 mins. 0 sec.). (ENG.). 2008. audio compact disk 28.98 (978-1-59644-647-2(1), christianSeed) christianaud.

***Great Lives: David: A Man of Passion & Destiny.** unabr. ed. Charles Swindoll. Narrated by Michael Kramer. (ENG.). 2008. 16.98 (978-1-59644-646-5(3), christianSeed) christianaud.

***Great Lives: Elijah.** unabr. ed. Charles Swindoll. Narrated by Raymond Todd. (ENG.). 2009. 14.98 (978-1-59644-689-2(7), christianSeed) christianaud.

***Great Lives: Esther: A Woman of Strength & Dignity.** unabr. ed. Charles Swindoll. Narrated by Pam Ward. (ENG.). 2008. 14.98 (978-1-59644-640-3(4), christianSeed) christianaud.

***Great Lives: Job.** unabr. ed. Charles Swindoll. Narrated by Michael Kramer. (ENG.). 2009. 16.98 (978-1-59644-693-9(5), christianSeed) christianaud.

***Great Lives: Joseph: A Man of Integrity & Forgiveness.** unabr. ed. Charles Swindoll. Narrated by Michael Kramer. (ENG.). 2008. 14.98 (978-1-59644-642-7(0), christianSeed) christianaud.

***Great Lives: Moses: A Man of Selfless Dedication.** unabr. ed. Charles Swindoll. Narrated by Raymond Todd. (ENG.). 2008. 16.98 (978-1-59644-644-1(7), christianSeed) christianaud.

***Great Lives: Paul.** unabr. ed. Charles Swindoll. Narrated by Raymond Todd. (ENG.). 2009. 16.98 (978-1-59644-691-5(9), christianSeed) christianaud.

Great Lobster Chase. unabr. collector's ed. Mike Brown. Read by Richard Wulf. 7 cass. (Running Time: 10 hrs. 30 mins.). 1987. 56.00 (978-0-7366-1205-0(X), 2123) Books on Tape.
Stories from the lives of the Maine coast lobster fishermen.

Great Love Poems. Weller. 1 cass. (Running Time: 1 hr. 04 min.). 1996. pap. bk. 5.95 Boxed set. (29307-6) Dover.

Great Lover. Jill Dawson. 2009. 76.95 (978-0-7531-4199-1(X)); audio compact disk 99.95 (978-0-7531-4200-4(7)) Pub: Isis Pubng Ltd GBR. Dist(s): Ulverscroft US

Great March on Washington. 1 cass. (Running Time: 60 mins.). 1999. 12.95 (WC-909) African Am Imag.

Great Masters: Robert & Clara Schumann - Their Lives & Music. Instructed by Robert Greenberg. 4 cass. (Running Time: 6 hrs.). 2002. bk. 29.95 (978-1-56585-526-7(4), 759) Teaching Co.

Great Masters: Shostakovich - His Life & Music. Instructed by Robert Greenberg. 8 CDs. (Running Time: 6 hrs.). 2002. bk. 39.95 (978-1-56585-530-4(2), 760) Teaching Co.

Great Masters: Shostakovich - His Life & Music. Instructed by Robert Greenberg. 4 cass. (Running Time: 6 hrs.). 2002. bk. 29.95 (978-1-56585-529-8(9), 760) Teaching Co.

Great Masters: Beethoven: His Life & Music. Instructed by Robert Greenberg. 8 CDs. (Running Time: 6 hrs.). 2001. bk. 39.95 (978-1-56585-380-5(6), 755); 29.95 (978-1-56585-222-8(2), 755) Teaching Co.

Great Masters: Brahms: His Life & Music. Instructed by Robert Greenberg. 8 CDs. (Running Time: 6 hrs.). 2002. bk. 39.95 (978-1-56585-382-9(2), 757) Teaching Co.

Great Masters: Brahms: His Life & Music. Instructed by Robert Greenberg. 4 cass. (Running Time: 6 hrs.). 2002. bk. 29.95 (978-1-56585-224-2(9), 757) Teaching Co.

Great Masters: Haydn: His Life & Music. Instructed by Robert Greenberg. 4 pieces. (Running Time: 6 hrs.). (C). 2000. bk. 29.95 (978-1-56585-218-1(4), 751); bk. 39.95 (978-1-56585-376-8(8), 751) Teaching Co.

Great Masters: Liszt: His Life & Music. Instructed by Robert Greenberg. 8 CDs. (Running Time: 6 hrs.). 2002. bk. 39.95 (978-1-56585-383-6(0), 758) Teaching Co.

Great Masters: Liszt: His Life & Music. Instructed by Robert Greenberg. 4 cass. (Running Time: 6 hrs.). 2002. bk. 29.95 (978-1-56585-225-9(7), 758) Teaching Co.

Great Masters: Mahler: His Life & Music. Instructed by Robert Greenberg. 4 cass. (Running Time: 6 hrs.). 2001. 29.95 (978-1-56585-223-5(0), 756); audio compact disk 39.95 (978-1-56585-381-2(4), 756) Teaching Co.

Great Masters: Mozart: His Life & Music. Instructed by Robert Greenberg. 8 CDs. (Running Time: 6 hrs.). 2000. bk. 39.95 (978-1-56585-377-5(6), 752); 29.95 (978-1-56585-219-8(2), 752) Teaching Co.

Great Masters: Robert & Clara Schumann: Their Lives & Music. Instructed by Robert Greenberg. 8 CDs. (Running Time: 6 hrs.). 2002. bk. 39.95 (978-1-56585-527-4(2), 759) Teaching Co.

Great Masters: Stravinsky: His Life & Music. Instructed by Robert Greenberg. 4 cass. (Running Time: 6 hrs.). 2000. 29.95 (978-1-56585-221-1(4), 754); audio compact disk 39.95 (978-1-56585-379-9(2), 754) Teaching Co.

Great Masters: Tchaikovsky: His Life & Music. Instructed by Robert Greenberg. 4 pieces. (Running Time: 6 hrs.). (C). 2000. bk. 29.95 (978-1-56585-220-4(6), 753); bk. 39.95 (978-1-56585-378-2(4), 753) Teaching Co.

Great McGoniggle's Gray Ghost. unabr. ed. Scott Corbett. 1 read-along cass. (Running Time: 39 min.). (Follow the Reader Ser.). (J). (gr. 2-3). 1981. 15.98 incl. bk. & guide. (978-0-8072-0006-3(9), FTR 54 SP, Listening Lib) Random Audio Pubg.
With a valuable gift certificate at stake, the great McGoniggle urges his friend, Ken, to acts of bravery & imagination. The plan requires nerves of steel & hearts of gold.

Great Meadow. unabr. ed. Dirk Bogarde. Read by Dirk Bogarde. 4 cass. (Running Time: 4 hrs.). 1993. 39.95 set. (978-0-7451-4176-3(5), CAB 859) AudioGO.
From 1927 to 1934, Dirk Bogarde lived in a remote cottage in Sussex Downs with his sister & their Nanny. Seen through the eyes of an innocent, shrewd young boy, Great Meadow recaptures an idyllic childhood, a time of love & gentleness, while the world beyond prepared for war.

Great Melbourne Cup Mystery. unabr. ed. Arthur W. Upfield. Read by Stig Wemyss. 4 cass. (Running Time: 6 hrs.). 1998. (978-1-86340-727-4(8), 570826) Bolinda Pubng AUS.
Melbourne during the Depression. Someone has struck at the heart of Australia's soul: they have killed the horse that would have won the Melbourge Cup. For what motive? Only Tom Pink, the rider of the murdered horse can find out.

great Melbourne Cup Mystery. unabr. ed. Arthur W. Upfield. Read by Stig Wemyss. (Running Time: 5 hrs. 30 mins.). (Inspector Napoleon Bonaparte Mysteries). 2009. audio compact disk 57.95 (978-1-74214-110-7(2), 9781742141107) Pub: Bolinda Pubng AUS. Dist(s): Bolinda Pub Inc

Great Memory. Dick Sutphen. 1 cass. (Running Time: 1 hr.). (RX17 Ser.). 1986. 14.98 (978-0-87554-322-2(7), RX131) Valley Sun.
You have a great memory. Your memory gets better every day. Your memory is improving. You retain everything you desire to remember. You have the power & ability to remember everything you desire to remember. You have memory power. You have the power & ability to create your own reality. "Memory file" are your key words for contioned response.

Great Memory. unabr. ed. Robert L. Montgomery. Read by Robert L. Montgomery. 2 cass. (Running Time: 2 hrs. 35 min.). (Smart Tapes Ser.). (gr. 10-12). 1994. pap. bk. 19.99 (978-1-55678-051-6(6), 3220) Oasis Audio.
Breakthrough techniques for remembering everything you read, hear & study. Have instant recall of names, phone numbers, appointments & test material. The fun, interactive approach makes learning easy.

Great Memory: Remember Everything You Hear, Read, & Study. unabr. ed. Robert Montgomery. Narrated by Robert Montgomery. 2 CDs. (Running Time: 3 hrs.). (Smart Audio Ser.). (ENG.). 2002. audio compact disk 19.99 (978-1-58926-024-5(4), Oasis Kids) Oasis Audio.
The breakthrough techniques in this program are the result of intensive research into the best way to train the human mind. In just minutes a day, remember every name you hear; instantly recall facts and numbers; keep track of appointments in your head, and more. It's fun and effective. Get ready to listen, laugh and expand your mind. Includes a pocket guidebook.

Great Memory: Remember Everything You Hear, Read, & Study. unabr. ed. Robert Montgomery. Narrated by Robert Montgomery. (Smart Tapes Ser.). (ENG.). 2007. 13.99 (978-1-60814-081-7(4)) Oasis Audio.

Great Memory: Remember Everything You Hear, Read, Study. unabr. ed. Robert L. Montgomery & Robert Montgomery. Read by Michael Coon. Narrated by Robert Montgomery. (Running Time: 9000 sec.). (ENG.). 2007. audio compact disk 12.99 (978-1-59859-188-0(6)) Oasis Audio.

Great Minds: G. W. F. Hegel & Karl Marx. Instructed by Michael Sugrue & Darren M. Staloff. 2 cass., 4 lectures. (Running Time: 3 hrs.). (SuperStar Teachers Ser.). 19.95 Set. (978-1-56585-147-4(1)) Teaching Co.
The beginning lectures focus on Hegel & the Phenomenology of Geist & his Philosophy of history, continuing with Marx & the problem of alienation & ideology & historical materialism.

Great Minds of Medicine. 1999. 25.00 (978-0-671-04722-1(1), Audioworks) S&S Audio.

Great Minds of Medicine: With Health Magazine. Unapix Entertainment Staff. 2004. 15.95 (978-0-7435-4797-0(7)) Pub: S&S Audio. Dist(s): S and S Inc

Great Minds of Science: With Discover Magazine. Unapix Entertainment Staff. 2004. 15.95 (978-0-7435-4798-7(5)) Pub: S&S Audio. Dist(s): S and S Inc

Great Minds of the Western Intellectual Tradition. 2nd ed. Darren Staloff & Michael Sugrue. 6 pts., 70 lectures. 249.91 Set. Teaching Co.
Tour of the greatest philosophical minds of the Western tradition. It is panoramic, extremely well taught, & swiftly becomes an irresistible immersion in the progress of the mind to understand itself & its place in the rest of being.

Great Minds of the Western Intellectual Tradition, Pts. I-VII. 3rd rev. ed. Instructed by Darren Staloff et al. 42 CDs. (Running Time: 42 hrs.). 2000. bk. 179.95 (978-1-56585-354-6(7), 470); 134.95 (978-1-56585-126-9(9), 470) Teaching Co.

Great Minds of the Western Intellectual Tradition Vol. 2: The Christian Age. Instructed by Philip Cary & Jeremy Adams. 6 cass. (Running Time: 6 hrs.). 2000. 399.95 (978-1-56585-127-6(7)) Teaching Co.

Great Minds of the Western Intellectual Tradition Vol. 3: From the Renaissance to the Age of Reason. 3rd rev. ed. Instructed by Darren Staloff et al. 6 cass. (Running Time: 6 hrs.). 2000. 399.95 (978-1-56585-128-3(5)) Teaching Co.

Great Minds of the Western Intellectual Tradition Vol. 4: The Age of Ideology. 3rd rev. ed. Instructed by Darren Staloff et al. 6 cass. (Running Time: 6 hrs.). 2000. 399.95 (978-1-56585-130-6(7)) Teaching Co.

Great Minds of the Western Intellectual Tradition Vol. 4: The Enlightenment & Its Critics. Instructed by Alan Kors et al. 6 cass. (Running Time: 6 hrs.). 2000. 399.95 (978-1-56585-129-0(3)) Teaching Co.

Great Minds of the Western Intellectual Tradition Vol. 6: Modernism & the Age of Analysis. 3rd rev. ed. Instructed by Darren Staloff et al. 6 cass. (Running Time: 6 hrs.). 2000. 399.95 (978-1-56585-131-3(5)) Teaching Co.

Great Minds of the Western Intellectual Tradition Vol. 7: The Crisis of Modernity. 3rd rev. ed. Instructed by Darren Staloff et al. 6 cass. (Running Time: 6 hrs.). 2000. 399.95 (978-1-56585-132-0(3)) Teaching Co.

Great Misunderstanding. Featuring Dave Ramsey. 2002. audio compact disk (978-0-9720044-8-0(3)) Lampo Inc.

Great Modern Stories. unabr. ed. Narrated by Martin Jarvis & Harriet Walter. 4 CDs. (Running Time: 5 hrs.). (ENG.). 2009. audio compact disk 26.95 (978-1-934997-36-9(6)) Pub: CSAWord. Dist(s): PerseuPGW

Great Moments of the 20th Century. 3 CDs. (Running Time: 4 hrs. 30mins.). 2001. bk. 59.98 (R2 75868) Rhino Enter.

Great Money Binge: Spending Our Way to Socialism. unabr. ed. George Melloan. Narrated by Johnny Heller. (Running Time: 10 hrs. 0 mins. 0 sec.). (ENG.). 2009. 24.99 (978-1-4001-6467-7(2)); audio compact disk 69.99 (978-1-4001-4467-9(1)); audio compact disk 34.99 (978-1-4001-1467-2(5)) Pub: Tantor Media. Dist(s): IngramPubServ

***Great Money Binge: Spending Our Way to Socialism.** unabr. ed. George Melloan. Narrated by Johnny Heller. (Running Time: 10 hrs. 0 mins.). 2009. 16.99 (978-1-4001-8467-5(3)) Tantor Media.

Great Morning (This Morning), Vol. 2. abr. ed. Bruce Meyer & Michael Enright. 2 CDs. (Running Time: 2 hrs.). 2004. audio compact disk 19.95 (978-0-660-19304-5(3)) Pub: Can Mus Civil CAN. Dist(s): U of Wash Pr

Great Mulation of 1842. Mae R. Wilson-Ludlam. 1 cass. 8.95 (855) Am Fed Astrologers.

Great Music of Christmas: St John's Cathedral, Denver, Colorado. Donald Pearson. (ENG.). audio compact disk 18.00 (978-0-89869-169-6(9)) Church Pub Inc.

Great Music of Holy Week & Easter: Choirs of St Mark's Cathedral, Seattle, Washington. J. Melvin Butler. (ENG.). audio compact disk 18.00 (978-0-89869-282-2(2)) Church Pub Inc.

Great Mutiny: India 1857. collector's unabr. ed. Christopher Hibbert. Read by David Case. 12 cass. (Running Time: 18 hrs.). 2000. 96.00 (978-0-7366-5925-3(0)) Books on Tape.
The 1857 mutiny in India that besieged the British touched off that country's fight for independence.

Great Mysteries: Experiencing Catholic Faith from the Inside Out. Andrew M. Greeley. Read by Paul Smith. Frwd. by Robert Barron. 4 cass. (Running Time: 6 hrs.). 2005. 33.95 (978-0-86716-701-6(7)) St Anthony Mess Pr.
?In Greeley?s vision, God is an agent of life and life to the full?Greeley interprets Christianity as the proclamation of light in the midst of darkness, final victory after many losses, life trumping death. What he sees in all Christian doctrine?is God?s exuberant, childlike, irrepressible ?Yes.???from the foreword by Rev. Robert Barron.

Great Mystery AudioBook: Fourteen Wedding Sermons. Peter J. Leithart. Read by Aaron Wells. (ENG.). 2007. audio compact disk 20.00 (978-1-59128-299-0(3)) Canon Pr ID.

Great Mystery Series: Ellery Queen's Mystery Magazine, abr. ed. Haskell Barken et al. Read by Roddy McDowall et al. 4 cass. (Running Time: 6 hrs.). (Great Mysteries - Louis L'Amour Ser.). 2000. 12.99 (978-1-57815-155-4(4), 4404, Media Bks Audio) Media Bks NJ.

Great Mystery Series: Top Female Sleuths by Eight of the Best Women Mystery Writers, abr. ed. Sara Paretsky & Nancy Pickard. Read by Lorri Holt & Gina Leishman. 4 cass. (Running Time: 5 hrs.). (Great Mysteries - Louis L'Amour Ser.). 1991. 12.99 (978-1-57815-154-7(6), 4403, Media Bks Audio) Media Bks NJ.

Great Mystery Series: Women Titles, abr. ed. Agatha Christie & Dorothy L. Sayers. Read by Juliet Mills. 4 cass. (Running Time: 5 hrs.). (Great Mysteries - Louis L'Amour Ser.). 2000. 12.99 (978-1-57815-153-0(8), 4402, Media Bks Audio) Media Bks NJ.

Great Narrative Poems of the Romantic Age. Poems. Read by John Moffatt et al. 2 cass. (Running Time: 2 hrs. 16 mins.). 1996. 13.98 (978-962-634-592-4(6), NA209214, Naxos AudioBooks) Naxos.
Anthology including the works of the masters of the Romantic Age, such as Samuel Taylor Coleridge, George Crabbe, John Keats, William Morris, Alfred Lord Tennyson and William Wordsworth.

Great Narrative Poems of the Romantic Age. Read by Sarah Woodward. (Running Time: 2 hrs. 15 mins.). 2000. 20.95 (978-1-60083-750-0(6)) Iofy Corp.

***Great Negotiations: Agreements That Changed the Modern World.** unabr. ed. Fredrik Stanton. (Running Time: 10 hrs.). 2011. 29.95 (978-1-4417-7242-8(1)); 65.95 (978-1-4417-7239-8(1)); audio compact disk 90.00 (978-1-4417-7240-4(5)) Blckstn Audio.

Great Nemo see Osbert Sitwell Reading His Poetry

Great New Stories. 2004. 22.50 (978-0-01-208140-2(X)) Your Story.

Great New Stories, Vol. 2. 2004. 22.50 (978-0-01-208141-9(8)); audio compact disk 22.50 (978-0-01-210511-5(2)) Your Story.

Great Night of Shiva. unabr. ed. Swami Amar Jyoti. 1 cass. (Running Time: 1 hr.). 2000. 9.95 (978-0-933572-58-4(1), K-171) Truth Consciousness.
Mahadeva, the Great Lord, the Auspicious in the form of the Transformer, through destruction he makes transformation and renewal possible.

Great Omission: Reclaiming Jesus Essential Teachings on Discipleship. unabr. ed. Dallas Willard. (Running Time: 7 hrs. 42 mins. 0 sec.). (ENG.). 2007. audio compact disk 26.98 (978-1-59644-494-2(0), Hovel Audio) christianaud.

***Great Omission: Reclaiming Jesus's Essential Teachings on Discipleship.** unabr. ed. Dallas Willard. Narrated by Grover Gardner. (ENG.). 2007. 16.98 (978-1-59644-495-9(9), Hovel Audio) christianaud.

Great One, Set. abr. ed. William A. Henry, III. Read by Frank Ferrante. 2 cass. (Running Time: 3 hrs.). 1993. 16.95 (978-1-879371-14-9(6)) Pub Mills.
Two-time Pulitzer Prize winning critic William A. Henry, III delivers the definitive biography of the legendary Jackie Gleason.

Great Orchestral Melodies. 2 CDs. (Running Time: 3 hrs.). audio compact disk 24.98 (978-1-57908-200-0(9), 1215) Platinm Enter.

Great Paintings Renaissance to Impressionism: The Frick Collection. Robb Lazarus et al. 1994. audio compact disk 79.95 (978-1-886664-02-9(1)); audio compact disk 79.95 (978-1-886664-03-6(X)) Digital Collect.

Great Paintings Renaissance to Impressionism: The Frick Collection: Jewel Case. Robb Lazarus et al. 1994. audio compact disk 49.95 (978-1-886664-33-3(1)); audio compact disk 49.95 (978-1-886664-34-0(X)) Digital Collect.

***Great Penguin Rescue: 40,000 Penguins, a Devastating Oil Spill, & the Inspiring Story of the World's Largest Animal Rescue.** unabr. ed. Dyan deNapoli. (Running Time: 9 hrs. 0 mins.). 2010. 15.99 (978-1-4001-8963-2(2)) Tantor Media.

***Great Penguin Rescue: 40,000 Penguins, a Devastating Oil Spill, & the Inspiring Story of the World's Largest Animal Rescue.** unabr. ed. Dyan deNapoli. Narrated by Coleen Marlo. (Running Time: 9 hrs. 0 mins. 0 sec.). 2010. 24.99 (978-1-4001-6963-4(1)); audio compact disk 83.99 (978-1-4001-4963-6(0)); audio compact disk 34.99 (978-1-4001-1963-9(4)) Pub: Tantor Media. Dist(s): IngramPubServ

***Great Penguin Rescue (Library Edition) 40,000 Penguins, a Devastating Oil Spill, & the Inspiring Story of the World's Largest Animal Rescue.** unabr. ed. Dyan deNapoli. (Running Time: 9 hrs. 0 mins.). 2010. 34.99 (978-1-4001-9963-1(8)) Tantor Media.

Great Perfection Preliminaries, Set. Tr. by Lisa Leghorn. Contrib. by Chagdud Tulku. 3 cass. (Running Time: 4 hrs.). 1997. 18.00 (978-1-881847-28-1(4)) Padma Pub CA.
While teaching the Dudjom Tersar Ngondro, Tulku explains the importance of this practice in establishing the foundations for & enhancing one's receptivity to the Great Perfection teachings.

Great Pharaohs of Ancient Egypt. Instructed by Bob Brier. 6 cass. (Running Time: 6 hrs.). bk. 29.95 (978-1-56585-964-7(2), 3588); bk. 39.95 (978-1-56585-966-1(9), 3588) Teaching Co.

Great Philosophical Debates: Free Will & Determinism. Instructed by Shaun Nichols. 2008. 129.95 (978-1-59803-460-8(X)); audio compact disk 69.95 (978-1-59803-461-5(8)) Teaching Co.

Great Physician's Rx for Women's Health. unabr. ed. Jordan S. Rubin & Nicki Rubin. Read by Rebecca Gallagher. Told to Wilson Panchetta. (Running Time: 6 hrs. 45 mins. 20 sec.). 2007. audio compact disk 25.99 (978-1-59859-218-4(1)) Oasis Audio.

Great Physician's Rx for Women's Health. unabr. ed. Jordan S. Rubin et al. (ENG.). 2007. 18.19 (978-1-60814-233-0(7)) Oasis Audio.

Great Pierpont Morgan. unabr. ed. Frederick L. Allen. Read by Nick Bernard. 7 cass. (Running Time: 10 hrs.). 1996. 49.95 (978-0-7861-0439-0(2), 1391) Blckstn Audio.
That John Pierpont Morgan built his family fortune into a colossal financial & industrial empire is beyond doubt. His ascent to power & use (or abuse) of it, however, has been for many years a subject of outspoken controversy. In 1901, Morgan formed the U.S. Steel Corp., which became the first billion dollar corporation in the world, & through his firm came enormous funds from abroad to develop American resources. But he was widely criticized for backing the sale of obsolete carbines to the Union army during the Civil War; for his gold speculations during the same period; & for the harsh terms of his loan of gold to the Federal Government during the 1895 crisis. At the same time, he was an ardent sportsman, a renowned art collector & a generous philanthropist.

Great Pierpont Morgan. unabr. ed. Frederick L. Allen. Read by Walter Zimmerman. 7 cass. (Running Time: 10 hrs. 30 mins.). 1988. 56.00 (978-0-7366-1420-7(6), 2306) Books on Tape.
Examines personal life of Morgan, as well as his complex financial activity. Here is Morgan buying out Andrew Camegie & forming one of the biggest corporations yet known; here is Morgan trying unsuccessfully to dominate the vestry of his church & here is Morgan testifying before the Pujo Committee that character was the primary basis for credit.

Great Plan of Happiness. Jack Christianson. 2004. 9.95 (978-1-57734-695-1(5)) Covenant Comms.

Great Poetry: Poetry Is Life & Vice Versa. 2 CDs. (Running Time: 7200 sec.). (This Morning Ser.). 2006. audio compact disk 19.95 (978-0-660-19610-7(7), CBC Audio) Canadian Broadcasting CAN.

Great Poets: John Keats. John Keats. Read by Samuel West et al. 1. (Running Time: 4088 sec.). (Great Poets Ser.). 2007. audio compact disk 14.98 (978-962-634-489-7(X), Naxos AudioBooks) Naxos.

Great Poets: Oliver Wendell Holmes. unabr. ed. Oliver Wendell Holmes. (Running Time: 1 hr. 15 mins.). 2009. audio compact disk 14.98 (978-962-634-954-0(9), Naxos AudioBooks) Naxos.

Great Poets: Robert Burns. unabr. ed. Robert Burns. (Running Time: 1 hr. 15 mins.). 2009. audio compact disk 14.98 (978-962-634-938-0(7), Naxos AudioBooks) Naxos.

Great Poets: William Mcgonagall. unabr. ed. William Topaz McGonagall. (Running Time: 1 hr.). 2009. audio compact disk 14.98 (978-962-634-893-2(3), Naxos AudioBooks) Naxos.

Great Poets - Emily Dickinson. unabr. ed. Emily Dickinson. Read by Teresa Gallagher. (YA). 2008. 34.99 (978-1-60514-704-8(4)) Find a World.

Great Poets: Emily Dickinson. abr. ed. Emily Dickinson. Read by Teresa Gallagher. (Running Time: 4606 sec.). (Great Poets Ser.). 2008. audio compact disk 14.98 (978-962-634-856-7(9), Naxos AudioBooks) Naxos.

Great Poets: Gerard Manley Hopkins. Gerard Manley Hopkins. Read by Jeremy Northam. (Great Poets (Playaway) Ser.). 2008. 34.99 (978-1-60640-532-1(2)) Find a World.

Great Poets: John Milton. abr. ed. John Milton. Read by Samantha Bond & Derek Jacobi. (Running Time: 4761 sec.). (Great Poets Ser.). 2008. audio compact disk 14.98 (978-962-634-855-0(0), Naxos AudioBooks) Naxos.

Great Poets of the Romantic Age. Read by Michael Sheen. (Running Time: 2 hrs. 30 mins.). 1998. 20.95 (978-1-60083-751-7(4)) Iofy Corp.

Great Poets of the Romantic Age. unabr. ed. Poems. Read by Michael Sheen. 2 CDs. (Running Time: 2 hrs. 38 mins.). 1994. audio compact disk 17.98 (978-962-634-021-9(5), NA202112, Naxos AudioBooks) Naxos.
Contains the works of the greatest Romantic poets including William Blake, William Wordsworth, Percy Bysshe Shelley, Samuel Taylor Coleridge, John Keats, Lord Byron and John Clare.

Great Poets of the Romantic Age. unabr. ed. Poems. Read by Michael Sheen. 2 cass. (Running Time: 2 hrs. 38 mins.). 1994. 22.98 (978-962-634-521-4(7), NA202114, Naxos AudioBooks) Naxos.

Great Poets of the Romantic Age. unabr. ed. William Wordsworth et al. Read by Robert Speaight et al. 6 cass. (Running Time: 4 hrs. 30 min.). 1986. 55.00 (978-0-8045-0014-2(2), PCC 14) Spoken Arts.
Includes: Treasury of William Wordsworth, Rime of the Ancient Mariner, George Gordon Lord Byron, Treasury of Percy Shelley, Treasury of John Keats & Letters of the Romantic Poets.

Great Poets Percy Bysshe Shelley. abr. ed. Percy Bysshe Shelley. Read by Bertie Carvel. (Running Time: 4698 sec.). (Great Poets Ser.). 2008. audio compact disk 14.98 (978-962-634-861-1(5), Naxos AudioBooks) Naxos.

Great Poets: Rudyard Kipling. Rudyard Kipling. Read by Robert Glenister et al. 1. (Running Time: 4348 sec.). 2007. audio compact disk 14.98 (978-962-634-474-3(1), Naxos AudioBooks) Naxos.

Great Poets: W. B. Yeats. W. B. Yeats. Read by Jim Norton et al. 1. (Running Time: 3869 sec.). (Great Poets Ser.). 2007. audio compact disk 14.98 (978-962-634-490-3(3), Naxos AudioBooks) Naxos.

Great Poets: William Blake. William Blake. Read by Stephen Critchlow et al. 1. (Running Time: 3764 sec.). 2007. audio compact disk 14.98 (978-962-634-472-9(5), Naxos AudioBooks) Naxos.

Great Poets William Wordsworth. abr. ed. William Wordsworth. Read by Oliver Ford Davies & Jasper Britton. (Running Time: 4690 sec.). (Great Poets Ser.). 2008. audio compact disk 14.98 (978-962-634-860-4(7), Naxos AudioBooks) Naxos.

Great Polarities. Manly P. Hall. 5 cass. (Running Time: 150 min.). 1999. 40.00 set incl. album. (978-0-89314-129-5(1), S800172) Philos Res.

Great Prayers of the Bible. unabr. ed. Warren W. Wiersbe. Read by Warren W. Wiersbe. 3 cass. (Running Time: 3 hrs.). 1989. 14.95 (978-0-8474-2363-7(8)) Back to Bible.
Examines the prayer life of some Bible characters, with encouragement to become a person of prayer.

Great Presidents, Vol. 2. Instructed by Allan Lichtman. 6 cass. (Running Time: 6 hrs.). 2000. 249.95 (978-1-56585-232-7(X)) Teaching Co.

Great Presidents, Vol. 3. Instructed by Allan Lichtman. 6 cass. (Running Time: 6 hrs.). 2000. 249.95 (978-1-56585-233-4(8)) Teaching Co.

Great Presidents, Vol. 4. Instructed by Allan Lichtman. 6 cass. (Running Time: 6 hrs.). 2000. 249.95 (978-1-56585-234-1(6)) Teaching Co.

Great Presidents, Vols. I-IV. Instructed by Allan Lichtman. 24 CDs. (Running Time: 24 hrs.). 2000. bk. 129.95 (978-1-56585-387-4(3), 8100); 99.95 (978-1-56585-231-0(1), 8100) Teaching Co.

Great Principles of Science: Course 1100. Instructed by Robert M. Hazen. 30 cass. (Running Time: 30 hrs.). 2000. 299.95 Teaching Co.
Five parts, 60 lectures to provide you with a clear & bracing overview of the scientific world - from the laws of motion first formulated 300 years ago by Sir Isaac Newton, to the latest marvels of contemporary research.

Great Profundo & Other Stories. unabr. ed. Bernard M. Laverty & Bernard Maclaverty. Read by Denys Hawthorne. 5 cass. (Running Time: 5 hrs. 17 min.). 1995. 49.95 (978-1-85089-738-5(7), 90046) Pub: ISIS Audio GBR. Dist(s): Ulverscroft US
Ranging from the deserted windswept coast of a troubled Ireland to the sun-drenched landscapes of Portugal, Bernard Mac Laverty's stories portray the insecurity & flickering hope of the afflicted & estranged with deep compassion & gentle irony.

Great Prophet Melchizedek. Speeches. As told by Glenn Kimball. 1 CD. (Running Time: 01:19:36). 2005. audio compact disk 15.00 (978-1-59772-043-4(7), Your Own Wrld Bks) Your Own Wrld.
THE GREAT PROPHET MELCHIZEDEK: From a lecture at the Sheraton Wild Horse Pass July 2003 by Glenn Kimball1- It contains a playbill with the whole list of the names for the various brothers and sisters of Jesus. This has never been done before. You will be amazed at the various names and how they are connected to each other.2- It contains the history of Melchizedek from a variety of ancient manuscript sources. Melchizedek is the only name of an ancient order associated with Jesus himself. This work tracks the disappearance and reappearance of Melchizedek. God promised him that he would not die. He became a member of those who were granted the gift to remain on the earth and intervene in the lives of men until the return of the messiah. I quote some recent stories illustrating possible sightings of these men. Most of you have known someone who appeared suddenly, performed some sort of rescue and then disappeared as suddenly as he came.3- Lastly, I connect Melchizedek with a probable sighting at the time of King Arthur. The evidence is amazing. England is filled with the traditions and teachings of Melchizedek. It is my contention that at least one of the most famous sightings of Melchizedek comes in the personage of someone you will instantly recognize from British history. Certainly, the Magi who came to the birth of Jesus were from the fraternal orders in Great Britain. The Latin for Druid is the word Magi. These men filled the world for thousands of years as wise men, kings, priests, astrologers, mentors and the mysterious ?undead? who came from time to time to perform quiet rescues.

Great Psychedelic Armadillo Picnic: A Walk in Austin. unabr. ed. Kinky Friedman. Read by Stephen Hoye. 3 CDs. (Running Time: 3 hrs.). 2004. audio compact disk 45.00 (978-1-4159-1326-0(9)); 36.00 (978-1-4159-1325-3(0)) Books on Tape.
This travelog introduces the history of Texas as well as points out the restaurants, activities, and everything else that might interest visitors to Austin. But what sets it apart is Friedman's ability to entertain listeners. His recommendations come from personal experience, and he usually adds an offbeat anecdote to spice up his choices. Not exactly a typical Texan, novelist Friedman founded the band Kinky Friedman and the Texas Jewboys and brags about always wearing his brontosaurus-foreskin boots. Knowledgeable about music, especially country and rock, he provides historical tidbits about Texans Janis Joplin, Willie Nelson, and Stevie Ray Vaughn, among others. The book's craziness does not detract, though, from the helpful information included.

Great Pursuit. unabr. ed. Tom Sharpe. Read by Donald Monat. 7 cass. (Running Time: 10 hrs. 30 min.). 1988. 56.00 (978-0-7366-1304-0(8), 2211) Books on Tape.
Comic novel satirizing the world of publishing.

Great Putting - Right Now! Mental Keys to Confident Putting. abr. ed. Patrick J. Cohn & Robert K. Winters. Read by Patrick J. Cohn & Robert K. Winters. 1 cass. (Running Time: 74 mins.). 1998. 12.00 (978-1-885999-09-2(7)) Peak Perform.
Two leading golf & sport psychologists colaborate to record the most practical instructional program in the golf market. Will improve attitude, confidence & focus in putting.

Great Pyramid Robbery. unabr. collector's ed. John Minahan. Read by Grover Gardner. 7 cass. (Running Time: 10 hrs. 30 min.). 1990. 56.00 (978-0-7366-1767-3(1), 2606) Books on Tape.
Rawlings is trying to crack the spectacular $8 million heist of a New York armored car company. When his cover is blown, he gets orders to track suspects in drag. One flees to Egypt, with Rawlings in hot pursuit. The chase leads Rawlings to the Great Pyramid of Cheops. He finds a secret chamber replete with its treasures, even the mummy of Cheops himself!.

Great Pyramids. Erik Johansen. Narrated by Larry A. McKeever. (Ancient Egyptian Mystery Ser.). (J). 2004. 10.95 (978-1-58659-122-9(3)); audio compact disk 14.95 (978-1-58659-356-8(0)) Artesian.

Great Question on Prayer Thematic. 1999. pap. bk. 35.00 (978-0-933173-84-2(9)) Chging Church Forum.

Great Radio Detectives. 4 cass. (Four DET-1). 1988. 14.95 (978-0-929541-49-5(9)) Radiola Co.
Eight Old-Time Radio Detective Shows.

Great Radio Detectives. (Running Time: 4 hrs.). 2002. 29.95 (978-1-57019-510-5(2)) Radio Spirits.

Great Radio Detectives. Radio Yesteryear Staff. 4 cass. 1996. 16.95 Set. (978-0-929541-57-0(X)) Radiola Co.

Great Radio Voices: Selected Broadcasts. unabr. ed. 1 cass. (Running Time: 60 min.). Dramatization. 7.95 Norelco box. (DD-5336) Natl Recrd Co.
Walter Winchell: "Good evening, Mr. & Mrs. North & South America & all the ships & clippers at sea. Let's go to press!" The 5/18/41 edition of the Jurgen's Journal (with lotions of love). Louella Parsons: "Hello, to all of you from Hollywood!" In this 11/9/47 program her guest is Joan Crawford. Woodbury Soap ("for the skin you love to touch"). Bill Stern: October 20, 1950, the 12th anniversary of the Colgate Sports Newsreel. An all-star cast of famous voices from prior years - Joe Lewis, Babe Ruth, Eleanor Roosevelt, Jo DiMaggio, Eddie Cantor, Jim Stewart, etc. Gabriel Heatter: "There's good news tonight!" August 13, 1945, news of Japan's offer to surrender, possible civil strife & the tone of expectancy in the U.S. as we await the end of World War II.

Great Raid. movie tie-in unabr. ed. William B. Breuer. Read by Patrick G. Lawlor. 8 CDs. (Running Time: 32400 sec.). 2005. audio compact disk 29.95 (978-0-7861-7730-1(6), ZE3525) Blckstn Audio.

Great Raid: Rescuing the Doomed Ghost of Bataan & Corregidor. movie tie-in unabr. ed. William B. Breuer. Read by Patrick G. Lawlor. 1 MP3-CD. (Running Time: 32400 sec.). 2005. audio compact disk 29.95 (978-0-7861-7961-9(9), ZM3525); 29.95 (978-0-7861-3657-5(X), E3525) Blckstn Audio.
Before General Douglas MacArthur could fulfill his stirring promise of "I shall return" and re-take the Philippines from Japanese control, a remarkable rescue mission would have to take place. Captured American soldiers had been held at the notorious Cabanatuan prison camp for more than 33 months. Emaciated and ill from brutal mistreatment, a mere 511 POWs remained from the 25,000-strong fighting force that MacArthur had been ordered to abandon on February 23, 1942. On the morning of January 28, 1945, a small band of Army Rangers set out on an audacious and daring rescue effort: to penetrate 30 miles into Japanese controlled territory, storm the camp, and escape with the POWs, carrying them if necessary.

Great Raid: Rescuing the Doomed Ghosts of Bataan & Corregidor. William B. Breuer & Patrick G. Lawlor. (Running Time: 32400 sec.). 2005. audio compact disk 72.00 (978-0-7861-7593-2(1)) Blckstn Audio.

Great Raid: The Most Daring Rescue Mission of Our Time Is a Story That Has Never Been Told. William B. Breuer. Read by Patrick G. Lawlor. (Running Time: 32400 sec.). 2005. 59.95 (978-0-7861-3768-8(1)) Blckstn Audio.

Great Railway Bazaar: By Train Through Asia. unabr. ed. Paul Theroux. Read by Michael Prichard. 10 cass. (Running Time: 15 hrs.). 1984. 64.00 (978-0-7366-0924-1(5), 1867) Books on Tape.
This records a solitary traveler's reflections as he traverses two continents - through the deserts of Iran, the war zone of Vietnam, the snowfields of Japan & Siberia - on the trains with the wonderful names.

Great Railway Bazaar: By Train Through Asia, unabr. ed. Paul Theroux. Narrated by Frank Muller. 8 cass. (Running Time: 11 hrs. 30 mins.). 1983. 70.00 (978-1-55690-207-9(7), 83078E7) Recorded Bks.
Theroux boarded a train at London's Victoria Station & followed the rails as far as he could to India & beyond.

***Great Reflation: How Investors Can Profit from the New World of Money.** unabr. ed. Anthony J. Boeckh. Read by Don Hagen. (Running Time: 10 hrs.). (ENG.). 2010. 29.98 (978-1-59659-665-8(1), GildAudio) Pub: Gildan Media. Dist(s): HachBkGrp

Great Republic: A History of America. abr. ed. Read by Winston L. S. Churchill. Ed. by Winston L. S. Churchill. 4 cass., 5 CDs. (Running Time: 6 hrs.). 1999. audio compact disk 29.95 (978-0-375-40818-2(5), Random AudioBks) Random Audio Pubg.
The legacy of a man of superhuman energy, great intellectual powers, & the utmost simplicity of soul. It is an enthralling love song to America by one of the great men of our century.

***Great Reset.** unabr. ed. Richard Florida. Read by Eric Conger. (ENG.). 2010. (978-0-06-199299-5(2), Harper Audio) HarperCollins Pubs.

***Great Reset: How New Ways of Living & Working Drive Post-Crash Prosperity.** unabr. ed. Richard Florida. Read by Eric Conger. (ENG.). 2010. (978-0-06-198862-2(6), Harper Audio) HarperCollins Pubs.

Great River Road. Contrib. by Jason Upton. Prod. by Michael Tyrrell & Michael Demus. 2005. audio compact disk 16.98 (978-5-559-10059-3(5)) Gotee Records.

Great River, Wide Land. unabr. collector's ed. Armstrong Sperry. Read by Paul Shay. 7 cass. (Running Time: 7 hrs.). (J). 1987. 42.00 (978-0-7366-1236-4(X), 2154) Books on Tape.
The story of the Rio Grand River & how it influenced the settlement of the west.

Great Rope Swing Misadventure. Short Stories. Bil Lepp. (Running Time: 55 mins.). 2006. audio compact disk 12.95 (978-1-891852-52-7(3)) Pub: Quarrier Pr. Dist(s): WV Book Co

Great Rose see Twentieth-Century Poetry in English, No. 1, Recordings of Poets Reading Their Own Poetry

Great Royal Race. Short Stories. Carl Sommer. Narrated by Carl Sommer. 1 cass. Dramatization. (Another Sommer-Time Story Ser.). (J). (gr. 1-4). 2003. bk. 16.95 (978-1-57537-557-1(5)) Advance Pub.

Great Royal Race. Carl Sommer. Narrated by Carl Sommer. 1 cass. Dramatization. (Another Sommer-Time Story Ser.). (J). (gr. k-4). 2003. lib. bdg. 23.95 (978-1-57537-758-2(6)) Advance Pub.

***Great Royal Race / la Gran Carrera Real.** ed. Carl Sommer. Illus. by Dick Westbrook. (Another Sommer-Time Story Bilingual Ser.). (ENG & SPA.). (J). 2009. bk. 26.95 (978-1-57537-177-1(4)) Advance Pub.

Great Salesperson: The Ultimate Guide to Influencing Others. Scripts. Alan J. Parisse. 6 CDs. (Running Time: 520 mins.). 2005. audio compact disk 79.95 (978-0-9726981-1-5(6)) Flagstaff Pubng.
This 6-CD set audio program discusses the 7 rules of selling from establishing credibility to taking risks and going beyond the norm. It then tests the rules against the finest salespeople, medical doctors, to provide significant insights into what does and does not work in the business of selling, leading and communicating.

Great Santini. abr. ed. Pat Conroy. Read by Dick Hill. (Running Time: 9 hrs.). 2010. audio compact disk 26.99 (978-1-4418-1485-2(X), 9781441814852, BACD) Brilliance Audio.

Great Santini. abr. ed. Pat Conroy. Read by Dick Hill. (Running Time: 9 hrs.). 2010. audio compact disk 14.99 (978-1-4418-1486-9(8), 9781441814869, BCD Value Price) Brilliance Audio.

Great Santini. unabr. ed. Pat Conroy. Read by Jonathan Marosz. 11 cass. (Running Time: 11 hrs.). 1995. 44.00 (978-0-7366-2978-2(5), 3669) Books on Tape.
A stern but lovable Marine rules home with iron fist. But wife & son don't always agree. Raucous & endearing.

Great Santini. unabr. ed. Pat Conroy. Read by Dick Hill. (Running Time: 19 hrs.). 2010. 29.99 (978-1-4418-1483-8(3), 9781441814838, BAD); 44.97 (978-1-4418-1482-1(5), 9781441814821, Brlnc Audio MP3 Lib); 44.97 (978-1-4418-1484-5(1), 9781441814845, BADLE); 29.99 (978-1-4418-1481-4(7), 9781441814814, Brilliance MP3) Brilliance Audio.

Great Santini. unabr. ed. Pat Conroy. Read by Frank Muller & Dick Hill. (Running Time: 20 hrs.). 2010. audio compact disk 39.99 (978-1-4418-1479-1(5), 9781441814791, Bril Audio CD Unabri) Brilliance Audio.

Great Santini. unabr. ed. Pat Conroy. Read by Dick Hill. (Running Time: 20 hrs.). 2010. audio compact disk 107.97 (978-1-4418-1480-7(9), 9781441814807, BriAudCD Unabrid) Brilliance Audio.

Great Santini, Set. unabr. ed. Pat Conroy. Read by David Hilder. 12 cass. 1999. 83.95 (FS9-51140) Highsmith.

***Great Scenes from Great Plays.** RadioArchives.com. (Running Time: 600). (ENG.). 2009. audio compact disk 29.98 (978-1-61081-087-6(2)) Radio Arch.

Great Scientific Ideas That Changed the World. Instructed by Steven L. Goldman. 18 cass. (Running Time: 18 hrs.). 79.95 (978-1-59803-302-1(6)) Teaching Co.

Great Scientific Ideas That Changed the World. Instructed by Steven L. Goldman. 18 CDs. (Running Time: 18 hrs.). 2007. audio compact disk 99.95 (978-1-59803-303-8(4)) Teaching Co.

Great Scientists & Their Discoveries. David Angus. Read by Bnjamin Soames & Clare Corbett. (Running Time: 22229 sec.). (Junior Classics Ser.). (J). (gr. 4-7). 2007. audio compact disk 17.98 (978-962-634-440-8(7), Naxos AudioBooks) Naxos.

Great Scientists & Their Discoveries. unabr. ed. David Angus. Read by Benjamin Soames. (J). 2007. 39.99 (978-1-60252-559-7(5)) Find a World.

Great Sea Adventures. abr. ed. Daniel Defoe et al. Perf. by Robert Carlile. 6 cass. (Running Time: 4 hrs. 41 min.). Dramatization. 1987. 55.00 (978-0-8045-0031-9(2), PCC 31) Spoken Arts.
Condensed versions of "Robinson Crusoe," "Captains Courageous," "Treasure Island," "Kidnapped," "The Sea Wolf" & "Moby Dick".

Great Secret. unabr. ed. L. Ron Hubbard. Read by Bruce Boxleitner. 2 CDs. (Running Time: 2 hrs.). (Stories from the Golden Age Ser.). 2008. audio compact disk 9.95 (978-1-59212-249-3(3)) Gala Pr LLC.

Great Self Within: Anthropos & Pleroma in Gnostic Myth & Psychological Reality. Robert Moore. Read by Robert Moore. 1 cass. (Running Time: 80 min.). 1993. 10.95 (978-0-7822-0428-5(7), 511) C G Jung IL.
Robert Moore addresses the psychological deep structures underlying Gnostic myths of the Anthropos (the supreme divinity) & the Pleroma. Parallels with Jung's understanding of the collective unconscious & the archetypal Self will be examined & discussed in terms of their clinical & spiritual significance.

Great Self Within: Men & the Quest for Significance. Robert Moore. Read by Robert Moore. Read by Michael Meade. Perf. by Michael Meade. Ed. by William Booth. . (Running Time:). 1991. cass. & video 18.95 set. (978-0-915408-43-6(0), C108) Ally Pr.
Michael Meade tells the Russian fairy tale, "The Firebird & Princess Vasilisa." Then Jungian psychologist Robert Moore talks on the archetype of the king & the human desire to be more than ordinary.

Great Shame: And the Triumph of the Irish in the English-Speaking World. unabr. ed. Thomas Keneally. Narrated by John McDonough. 24 cass. (Running Time: 36 hrs.). 2000. 176.00 (978-0-7887-4371-9(6), 96316E7) Recorded Bks.
The struggle of the Irish to survive during the nineteenth century. Amidst famine, massive emigration to America & deportation to Australia, the Irish persevered. The message is ultimately one of hope.

Great Short Stories from Around the World. unabr. ed. 10 cass. (Running Time: 14 hrs. 30 mins.). 1990. 69.95 set. (978-0-7861-0613-4(1), 2103) Blckstn Audio.
This collection provides a wide selection of literary masterworks by authors of numerous nationalities.

Great Short Stories from Around the World. unabr. collector's ed. 10 cass. (Running Time: 15 hrs.). 1991. 80.00 (978-0-7366-3960-6(8), 9212) Books on Tape.
A wide collection of short stories from France, Germany, England, Japan, Sweden, Italy, Russia, & many other countries.

Great Shower Singer & Sailing with John & Kitty. Howard W. Gabriel, III. (J). (gr. k-8). 1987. 2.95 (978-0-936997-04-9(4), T87-02) M & H Enter.
In the First Story Three Children Figure Out How to Get a Super Voice Out of the Shower & into Stardom, but End up into More Hot Water. In the Second Story a Man Plans to Become a Real Tough Sailor by Sailing from Alaska to Hawaii All by Himself - Well Not Exactly!.

Great Siege. unabr. collector's ed. Ernle Bradford. Read by Walter Zimmerman. 6 cass. (Running Time: 6 hrs.). 1987. 36.00 (978-0-7366-0932-6(6), 1876) Books on Tape.
Modern day Malta is still the main British naval base in the Mediterranean & a NATO headquarters, but its role as a fortress is centuries old. Bradford researches the study of the great siege of 1565 & the important role Malta was destined to fulfill.

***Great Slave.** Zane Grey. 2009. (978-1-60136-474-6(1)) Audio Holding.

Great Slave. Zane Grey. (Running Time: 0 hr. 42 mins.). 1998. 10.95 (978-1-60083-458-5(2)) Iofy Corp.

Great Sled Race Vol. 2: Denny & I. abr. ed. Short Stories. Mike Anderson. 1 CD. (Running Time: 73 mins.). (J). 2000. audio compact disk 15.00 (978-1-929050-10-9(0), MW10400) MW Prods.
Six stories about two boys growing up in a midwestern town during the 1960's.

Great Smoky Mountains National Park. 2 cass. (Running Time: 1 hr. 30 min.). 12.95 Gattinburg to Cherokee. (CCI-327); 11.95 Cherokee to Gattinburg. (CCI-327A) Comp Comms Inc.
The Great Smoky Mountains wrap around 800 square miles of Appalachian splendor. Sixteen of its peaks rise more than 6,000 feet into the sky. The highway follows a trail originally used by Indians & climbs a respectable distance of 4,743 feet into the air.

Great Smoky Mountains National Park: Gatlinburg to Cherokee. 1 cass. (Running Time: 90 min.). (Guided Auto Tape Tour). 12.95 (P1) Comp Comms Inc.

Great Soap Operas: Selected Episodes. 1 cass. (Running Time: 60 min.). Incl. Backstage Wife. (GE-3630); Goldbergs. (GE-3630); Just Plain Bill. (GE-3630); Ma Perkins. (GE-3630); 7.95 (GE-3630) Natl Recrd Co.
"Ma Perkins," America's mother of the air, tries to get to the bottom of family problems. "Backstage Wife" is the story of a little Iowa girl who fell in love with & married a Broadway matinee idol. "Just Plain Bill" is the story of Bill Davidson, barber of Hartville, who, in this episode, attends the reading of a girl's last will & is disturbed at the thought that one of the beneficiaries may be her murderer. "The Goldbergs" is the warm hearted story of Molly Goldberg & her family & friends.

Great Songs of Power & Praise. Contrib. by Don Marsh. 1996. 90.00 (978-0-00-513371-2(8), 75608553); 11.98 (978-0-00-513373-6(4), 75608552); audio compact disk 16.98 (978-0-00-513374-3(2), 75608550) Pub: Brentwood Music. Dist(s): H Leonard

Great Souls: Six Who Changed the Century. unabr. ed. David Aikman. Read by David Aikman. 13 cass. (Running Time: 19 hrs.). 2000. 85.95 (978-0-7861-1902-8(0), 2695); audio compact disk 128.00 (978-0-7861-9792-7(7), 2695) Blckstn Audio.
The "Great Souls" chronicled by Aikman, a former senior correspondent for Time Magazine, are Billy Graham, Mother Teresa, Aleksandr Solzhenitsyn, Pope John Paul II, Elie Wiesel & Nelson Mandela.

Great Souls & Great Works; God As Omnipresence. Ann Ree Colton & Jonathan Murro. 1 cass. 7.95 A R Colton Fnd.

Great Speeches Vol. 1: Ronald Reagan. Ed. by Pent. 1 cass. 1995. audio compact disk 10.98 (978-1-885959-19-5(2), JRCS 7046, Speechworks) Jerden Recs.
Highlights of major speeches given by President Ronald Reagan, from his address before the Republican convention when he accepted the nomination in 1980, the "Evil Empire" speech, to farewell address in 1988.

Great Speeches & Soliloquies. William Shakespeare. (Running Time: 2 hrs. 30 mins.). 1998. 20.95 (978-1-60083-752-4(2)) Iofy Corp.

Great Speeches & Soliloquies. abr. ed. Speeches. William Shakespeare. Read by Simon Russell Beale et al. 2 cass. (Running Time: 2 hrs. 38 mins.).

Dramatization. (Classic Literature with Classical Music Ser.). 1994. 34.98 (978-962-634-515-3(2), NA201514, Naxos AudioBooks) Naxos.
Selection of key speeches from "Hamlet," "Romeo and Juliet," "The Tempest," and others remind the listener of Shakespeare's extraordinary gift for penetrating human nature.

Great Speeches & Soliloquies. abr. ed. Speeches. William Shakespeare. Read by Simon Russell Beale et al. 2 CDs. (Running Time: 2 hrs. 38 mins.). Dramatization. (Classic Literature with Classical Music Ser.). 1994. audio compact disk 17.98 (978-962-634-015-8(0), NA201512, Naxos AudioBooks) Naxos.
Selection of key speeches from "Hamlet," "Romeo and Juliet," "The Tempest," and others remind the listener of Shakespeare's extraordinary gift for penetrating human nature.

Great Speeches in History. Read by Norman Rodway et al. (Playaway Young Adult Ser.). (ENG.). (YA). 2009. 39.99 (978-1-60812-513-5(0)) Find a World.

Great Speeches in History. Speeches. Read by Norman Rodway et al. 2 CDs. (Running Time: 2 hrs. 38 mins.). 1996. audio compact disk 17.98 (978-962-634-083-7(5), NA208312, Naxos AudioBooks) Naxos.
From Socrates to Lincoln - some of history's most significant figures with their most important speeches.

Great Speeches of the 20th Century. Rhino Records Staff. 4 CDs. (Running Time: 6 hrs.). 1993. bk. 39.98 (978-0-930589-05-9(X), R2 70567); bk. 29.98 (R4 70567) Rhino Enter.

Great Speeches of the 20th Century Vol. 1: Presidential Addresses. 1 CD. (Running Time: 1 hr. 30 mins.). 2001. audio compact disk 9.98 (R2 71812) Rhino Enter.

Great Speeches of the 20th Century Vol. 2: The New Frontier. 1 CD. (Running Time: 1 hr. 30 mins.). 2001. audio compact disk 9.98 (R2 71813) Rhino Enter.

Great Speeches of the 20th Century Vol. 3: Dreams & Realities. 1 CD. (Running Time: 1 hr. 30 mins.). 2001. audio compact disk 9.98 (R2 71814) Rhino Enter.

Great Spirit. rev. ed. Sydney Banks. Read by Sydney Banks. (J). (gr. 4). 2001. (978-1-55105-370-7(5)); audio compact disk 14.95 (978-1-55105-368-4(3)) Lone Pine.

Great Spirituals (Portraits in Song) An Anthology or Program for Solo Voice & Piano for Concert & Worship (High Voice) Composed by Tom Fettke & Mark Hayes. (Portraits in Song Ser.). (ENG.). 2007. audio compact disk 12.95 (978-0-7390-4837-5(6)) Alfred Pub.

Great Spirituals (Portraits in Song) An Anthology or Program for Solo Voice & Piano for Concert & Worship (Low Voice) Composed by Tom Fettke & Mark Hayes. (Portraits in Song Ser.). (ENG.). 2007. audio compact disk 12.95 (978-0-7390-4840-5(6)) Alfred Pub.

Great Steinplatz Experiment see Tales of the Supernatural

Great Stone Face see Great American Short Stories, Vol. II, A Collection

Great Stone Face see Ten All Time Favorite Stories

Great Stone Face see Childhood Legends

Great Stone Face. Nathaniel Hawthorne. (J). (823) Audio Bk.

Great Stone Face. Nathaniel Hawthorne. 10.00 (LSS1114) Esstee Audios.

Great Stone Face. Nathaniel Hawthorne. (SWC 1197) HarperCollins Pubs.

Great Stone Face. unabr. ed. Nathaniel Hawthorne. Read by Walter Covell. 1 cass. (Running Time: 76 min.). Dramatization. 1983. 7.95 (S-49) Jimcin Record.
Considered the best of all Hawthorne's short stories. The search for a noble & honest man.

Great Stone Face. unabr. ed. Nathaniel Hawthorne. Read by Robert S. Breen. (Running Time: 50 min.). 10.95 (978-0-8045-0940-4(9), 7028) Spoken Arts.

Great Stone Face & Other Stories. unabr. ed. Short Stories. Nathaniel Hawthorne. Narrated by Nelson Runger. 2 cass. (Running Time: 2 hrs.). 1986. 18.00 (978-1-55690-208-6(5), 86120E7) Recorded Bks.
Tales of the White Mountains, including "The Ambitious Guest," "The Great Carbuncle" "Sketches from Memory" & the title story.

Great Stories, Vol. 3. 2006. 24.50 (978-1-60079-049-2(6)) YourStory.

Great Stories Vol. 1: Dramatized Audio Stories. 6 cass. 2006. 22.50 (978-1-60079-011-9(9)); 22.50 (978-1-60079-034-8(8)) YourStory.

Great Stories Vol. 2: Dramatized Audio Stories. 6 cass. 2006. 22.50 (978-1-60079-012-6(7)); 22.50 (978-1-60079-035-5(6)) YourStory.

Great Stories Vol. 3: Dramatized Audio Stories. 6 cass. 2006. 22.50 (978-1-60079-013-3(5)); 22.50 (978-1-60079-036-2(4)) YourStory.

Great Stories Vol. 4: 6 Cassette Dramatized Audio Stories. 2006. 22.50 (978-1-60079-014-0(3)) YourStory.

Great Stories Vol. 4: 6 CD Dramatized Audio Stories. 2006. 22.50 (978-1-60079-037-9(2)) YourStory.

Great Stories Vol. 5: 6 Cassette Dramatized Audio Stories. 2006. 22.50 (978-1-60079-015-7(1)) YourStory.

Great Stories Vol. 5: 6 CD Dramatized Audio Stories. 2006. 22.50 (978-1-60079-038-6(0)) YourStory.

Great Stories Vol. 6: 6 Cassette Dramatized Audio Stories. 2006. 22.50 (978-1-60079-016-4(X)) YourStory.

Great Stories Vol. 7: 6 Cassette Dramatized Audio Stories. 2006. 22.50 (978-1-60079-017-1(8)) YourStory.

Great Stories Vol. 7: 6 CD Dramatized Audio Stories. 2006. 22.50 (978-1-60079-040-9(2)) YourStory.

Great Stories Volume 6 Vol. 6: 6 CD Dramatized Audio Stories. 2006. 22.50 (978-1-60079-039-3(9)) YourStory.

Great Switcheroo. abr. ed. Roald Dahl. Perf. by Patricia Neal. 1 cass. 1984. 12.95 (978-0-694-50295-0(2), SWC 1545) HarperCollins Pubs.

Great Tales of Mystery. 7 cass. (Running Time: 10 hrs. 30 min.). 49.00 incl. albums. (C-166) Jimcin Record.
Stories by Baroness Orczy, G. K. Chesterton & others.

Great Tales of Mystery. unabr. collector's ed. 7 cass. (Running Time: 10 hrs. 30 min.). 1987. 56.00 (978-0-7366-3930-9(6), 9168) Books on Tape.
This collection of nine short stories incl.: "The Mystery of Marie Roget" by Edgar Allan Poe, "The Queer Feet" by G. K. Chesterton, "The Invisible Man" by G. K. Chesterton, "The Mysterious Death on the Undergroun Railway" by Baroness Orczy, & others.

Great Taos Bank Robbery. unabr. ed. Tony Hillerman. Read by Jonathan Marosz. 5 cass. (Running Time: 5 hrs.). 1994. 30.00 (978-0-7366-2819-8(3), 3530) Books on Tape.
A collection of essays about life in New Mexico, by the prize-winning mystery writer & former professor of journalism.

Great Taos Bank Robbery. unabr. abr. ed. Tony Hillerman. Read by Tony Hillerman. 1 CD. (Running Time: 1 hr. 30 min.). 2005. audio compact disk 14.95 (978-0-06-081512-7(4)) HarperCollins Pubs.

Great Teacher: Failure: Exodus 2:11-3:1. Ed Young. 1984. 4.95 (978-0-7417-1417-6(5), 417) Win Walk.

Great Teacher on Something's Happening! J. Krishnamurti. 2 cass. 18.00 set. (A0170-0) Sound Photosyn.
Considered by many an avatar, glimpse this extraordinary life.

Great Tennessee Monkey Trial. Peter Goodchild. Contrib. by Sharon Gless. (Running Time: 6720 sec.). 2006. audio compact disk 25.95 (978-1-58081-352-5(6)) Pub: L A Theatre. Dist(s): NetLibrary CO

Great Tennessee Monkey Trial. unabr. ed. Peter Goodchild. Read by Edward Asner. (YA). 2008. 34.99 (978-1-60514-887-8(3)) Find a World.

Great Tennessee Monkey Trial. unabr. ed. Peter Goodchild & Edward Asner. Perf. by Tyne Daly et al. 2 cass. (Running Time: 2 hrs. 2 mins.). 2001. 22.95 (978-1-58081-057-9(8), RDP11) L A Theatre.
The Scopes Trial, over the right to teach the theory of evolution in the public schools, revealed the importance of intellectual freedom, as codified by the Founding fathers in the Bill of Rights. The trial, in a small-town Tennessee courtroom in 1925, set the stage for the ongoing national debate over freedom of inquiry & the separation of Church & State in a democratic society.

Great Terror: A Reassessment. unabr. ed. Robert Conquest. Read by Frederick Davidson. (Running Time: 31 hrs. 0 mins.). 2008. 44.95 (978-1-4332-5802-2(1)); audio compact disk 160.00 (978-1-4332-5799-5(8)) Blckstn Audio.

Great Terror Pt. 1: A Reassessment. unabr. ed. Robert Conquest. Read by Frederick Davidson. 12 cass. (Running Time: 23 hrs. 30 mins.). 1992. 83.95 (978-0-7861-0372-0(8), 1328A,B) Blckstn Audio.
The definitive work on Stalin's purges, "The Great Terror" was universally acclaimed when it first appeared in 1968. Edmund Wilson hailed it as "the only scrupulous, non-partisan, & adequate book on the subject." And Harrison Salisbury called it "brilliant...not only an odyssey of madness, tragedy & sadism, but a work of scholarship & literary craftsmanship." And in recent years it has received equally high praise in Russia, where it is now considered the authoritative work on the period, & has been serialized in Neva, one of their leading periodicals.

Great Terror Pt. 2: A Reassessment. unabr. ed. Robert Conquest. Read by Frederick Davidson. 11 cass. (Running Time: 23 hrs. 30 mins.). 1992. 76.95 (978-0-7861-0373-7(6), 1328A,B) Blckstn Audio.

Great Things see Poetry of Thomas Hardy

Great Things. Contrib. by Ken Reynolds. 2008. audio compact disk 13.99 (978-5-557-51936-6(X)) Integrity Music.

Great Time Coming: The Life of Jackie Robinson from Baseball to Birmingham. unabr. ed. David Falkner. Narrated by Richard M. Davidson. 11 cass. (Running Time: 15 hrs.). 2000. 91.00 (978-0-7887-0482-6(6), 94675E7) Recorded Bks.
Portrays the rise to stardom of Jackie Robinson, the first African-American to play on a major-leauge baseball team.

Great Train Robbery. Michael Crichton. Narrated by Simon Prebble. 8 CDs. (Running Time: 8 hrs. 45 mins.). 2000. audio compact disk 78.00 (978-0-7887-4745-8(2), C1231E7) Recorded Bks.
Edward Pierce charms the most prominent of the well-to-do as he cunningly orchestrates a masterpiece of crime - the most daring train robbery of the century. Who would suspect that a gentleman of breeding could mastermind the daring theft of a fortune in gold? Who could predict the consequences of making the extraordinary robbery aboard the pride of England's industrial era, the mighty steam locomotive? Fact, as lively as legend & studded with all suspense & style of a modern fiction master.

Great Train Robbery. unabr. ed. Michael Crichton. Narrated by Simon Prebble. 6 cass. (Running Time: 8 hrs. 45 mins.). 1975. 56.00 (978-0-7887-4038-1(5), 95911E7) Recorded Bks.
In this classic caper novel made into a popular motion picture, best-selling author Michael Crichton introduces you to the ingenious thief, a handsome gentleman of good breeding, who orchestrated the most shocking crime of the century.

Great Transformation. Read by M. Basilea Schlink. 1 cass. (Running Time: 30 min.). 1985. (0272) Evang Sisterhood Mary.
Discusses how our cross can become golden & a commission for Jesus followers as seen in the light of Scripture.

Great Transformation: The Beginning of Our Religious Traditions. abr. ed. Karen Armstrong. Read by Karen Armstrong. 10 Cds. (Running Time: 43200 sec.). (ENG.). 2006. audio compact disk 44.95 (978-0-7393-2532-2(9), Random AudioBks) Pub: Random Audio Pubg. Dist(s): Random

Great Tree of Avalon: A Child of the Dark Prophecy. unabr. ed. 8 cass. (Running Time: 14 hrs.). 2004. 50.00 (978-1-4000-9100-3(4), Listening Lib) Random Audio Pubg.

Great Truths from the Mahabharata. Swami Amar Jyoti. 1 dolby cass. 1983. 9.95 (K-57) Truth Consciousness.
Illustrations from the great epic "Mahabharata" showing the need to search beyond superficial solutions to find the fundamental cause, deepest truth & real solution.

Great Turkey Walk. Kathleen Karr. Read by Tom Stechschulte. 4 cass. (Running Time: 5 hrs.). (YA). 1999. stu. ed. 204.30 (978-0-7887-3632-2(9), 46973) Recorded Bks.
Even though brawny Simon Green has just completed third grade for the fourth time, he is nobody's fool. He plans to make himself rich by driving a flock of turkeys from his home in eastern Missouri to the 1860 boomtown of Denver. Includes study guide.

Great Turkey Walk. unabr. ed. Kathleen Karr. Narrated by Tom Stechschulte. 4 pieces. (Running Time: 5 hrs.). (gr. 5 up). 1999. 36.00 (978-0-7887-3522-6(5), 95861E7) Recorded Bks.

Great Turkey Walk. unabr. ed. Kathleen Karr. Narrated by Tom Stechschulte. 4 cass. (Running Time: 5 hrs.). (YA). (gr. 5 up). 2000. pap. bk. 59.00 (978-0-7887-3631-5(0), 41006X4) Recorded Bks.

Great UFO Frame-up. Randy Horton. Narrated by Larry A. McKeever. (Adventure Ser.). (J). 2000. audio compact disk 14.95 (978-1-58659-281-3(5)) Artesian.

Great UFO Frame-Up. unabr. ed. Randy Horton. Narrated by Larry A. McKeever. 1 cass. (Running Time: 40 min.). (Take Ten Ser.). (J). (gr. 3-12). 2000. 10.95 (978-1-58659-017-8(0), 54107) Artesian.

Great Unraveling: Losing Our Way in the New Century. unabr. abr. ed. Paul Krugman. Read by Paul Krugman. 4 CDs. (Running Time: 6 hrs.). 2003. audio compact disk 29.95 (978-0-06-058178-7(6)) HarperCollins Pubs.

Great Upheaval: America & the Birth of the Modern World, 1788-1800. abr. ed. Jay Winik. Read by Sam Tsoutsouvas. (Running Time: 45000 sec.). 2007. audio compact disk 34.95 (978-0-06-136706-9(0), Harper Audio) HarperCollins Pubs.

Great Voices Collection, Set. unabr. ed. Anais Nin et al. Read by Anais Nin et al. 4 cass. (Running Time: 4 hrs.). 1996. bk. 39.00 (978-1-55994-975-0(9), BGS 001, Harper Audio) HarperCollins Pubs.
Selections include: Anais Nin reading portions of her diary, Ernest Hemingway reading "In Harry's Bar in Venice" & "The Fifth Column", James Joyce reading from "Ulysses" & "Finnegan's Wake" & E. E. cummings reading from "Xaipe".

***Great Wall Chinese Textbook CD-ROM Book 1.** (CHI.). 2006. audio compact disk 14.95 (978-7-900689-24-5(9)) Pub: Beijing Lang CHN. Dist(s): China Bks

Great War: The Opening Shots - August 1914 - May 1915. Max Arthur. 2 cass. (Running Time: 3 hrs. 0 mins. 0 sec.). (Forgotten Voices Ser.). (ENG., 2003. 17.50 (978-1-85686-667-5(X), Audiobks) Pub: Random GBR. Dist(s): IPG Chicago

Great War & Modern Memory. unabr. ed. Interview with Paul Fussell. 1 cass. (Running Time: 56 min.). 12.95 (40216) J Norton Pubs.
With Heywood Hale Broun, author Fussell creates a vision of World War I in terms of a highly educated young British officer, the scion of well-regulated society, hurled into the indescribable horrors of trench warfare.

Great War & Modern Memory. unabr. collector's ed. Paul Fussell. Read by Christopher Hurt. 11 cass. (Running Time: 16 hrs. 30 min.). 1985. 88.00 (978-0-7366-0709-4(9), 1672) Books on Tape.
This is an absorbing exploration of the ongoing consequences of World War I. Fussell writes of the blood & muck in the trenches & of the literary means by which that experience was assimilated, remembered & mythologized.

Great War in Africa. unabr. ed. Byron Farwell. Read by Bill Kelsey. 8 cass. (Running Time: 12 hrs.). 1994. 64.00 (978-0-7366-2625-5(5), 3365) Books on Tape.
Remote from the main events of WW I, campaigns in Africa looked like a sideshow. But fascinating sideshows they were, fought with spears & airplanes, knobkerries & armored cars, pangas, machine guns & bare hands. A colorful, anecdotal narrative, including the true story behind the African Queen, this history brings to life a cast of splendid & memorable eccentrics.

Great Weep see Piece of String

Great Weight, Great Shape - Hypnosis. Created by Laura Rubinstein. 1 CD. (Running Time: 50 mins). (LBR Relaxation Ser.: No. 4). 1999. audio compact disk (978-0-9749845-3-7(1)) L Rubinstein.
Hypnosis CD. Track 1 is to be used as a power nap which will wake you up at the end. Track 2 is to be used to fall asleep to.

Great White Brotherhood - the Spiritual Hierarchy of Earth. George King. 2007. audio compact disk (978-0-937249-38-3(6)) Aetherius Soc.

Great White Man-Eating Shark. 2004. bk. 24.95 (978-0-89719-878-3(6)); 8.95 (978-1-56008-913-1(X)); cass. & flmstrp 30.00 (978-0-89719-633-8(3)) Weston Woods.

Great White Man Eating Shark. (J). 2004. pap. bk. 14.95 (978-0-7882-0690-0(7)) Weston Woods.

Great White Man-Eating Shark. 2004. 8.95 (978-1-56008-140-1(6)) Weston Woods.

Great White Man-Eating Shark: A Cautionary Tale. Margaret Mahy. 1 cass. (Running Time: 10 min.). (J). (ps-4). 8.95 (RAC348) Weston Woods.
Caramel Cove becomes deserted when Norvin, a boy who resembles a shark, pretends to be one.

Great White Shark. 1 cass. (Running Time: 35 min.). (J). 2001. 19.95 (SP 4006C) Kimbo Educ.

Great White Shark: Ruler of the Sea. Kathleen Weidner Zoehfeld. Illus. by Steven James Petruccio. Narrated by Peter Thomas. 1 cass. (Smithsonian Oceanic Collection). (J). (ps-2). 1995. 5.00 (978-1-56899-127-6(4), C4006) Soundprints.
Try as she might, White Shark cannot hunt like the older great whites & her attempts leave her hungry & hopeless. The fast-paced excitement of this story will leave all children rooting for White Shark to reign someday as ruler of the sea!.

Great White Throne: Rev. 20:11-15. Ed Young. 1987. 4.95 (978-0-7417-1583-8(X), 583) Win Walk.

Great White Whale. Contrib. by Secret & Whisper. Prod. by Travis Saunders & Danny R. McBride. 2008. audio compact disk 13.99 (978-5-557-50310-5(2)) Tooth & Nail.

Great Will Serve. Elbert Willis. 1 cass. (Resurrection Living Ser.). 4.00 Fill the Gap.

Great Women Composers. Gail Smith. 2002. per. 24.95 (978-0-7866-6585-3(8), 96008BCD) Mel Bay.

Great Women Composers Cd. Gail Smith. 1997. audio compact disk 15.98 (978-0-7866-2533-8(3)) Mel Bay.

Great Women Practitioners. Tr. by Lisa Leghorn. Contrib. by Chagdud Tulku. 2 cass. (Running Time: 3 hrs.). 1996. 14.00 () Padma Pub CA.
Recounts the life histories of several such women in the Tibetan tradition: Machig Labdron, Yeshe Tsogyal, Mandarava & his mother, Delog Dawa Drolma.

Great Women Rulers in World History. Cerebellum Academic Team Staff. Executive Producer Ronald M. Miller. (Running Time: 1 hr.). (Just the Facts Ser.). (gr. 7 up). 2010. 29.95 (978-1-59163-600-7(0)) Cerebellum.

Great Women Writers Read Their Work. abr. ed. Anais Nin et al. Read by Anais Nin et al. 6 cass. (Running Time: 4 hrs. 58 min.). 55.00 (978-0-8045-0044-9(4), PCC 44) Spoken Arts.
Selections from Nin's "Diary," Smith's "Strange Fruit" & "Our Faces, Our Words," & Skinner's drama, "The Loves of Charles II." Also 26 poems & short stories by Dorothy Parker.

Great Wonder: The Building of the Great Pyramid. Annabelle Howard. Illus. by Stephen Wells. 1 cass. Dramatization. (Smithsonian Odyssey Ser.). (ENG.). (J). (gr. 2-5). 1996. 7.95 (978-1-56899-358-4(7), C6002) Soundprints.
It is a really hot day in Washington, DC. Kevin & his friends look for relief in the Early Civilizations exhibit of the Smithsonian Institution's National Museum of Natural History. They sit down in a small dark theater, where it is cool & quiet, to watch a film about the building of the Great Pyramid in Egypt. Kevin is fascinated by this amazing engineering event & wants to share his excitement with his friend Emma. But, when he nudges her, he hits his elbow against a hard stone surface. It's not long before he realizes he is in King Khufu's burial chamber inside the Great Pyramid almost 4,000 years ago.

***Great Work Great Career.** unabr. ed. Stephen R. Covey & Jennifer Colosimo. (Running Time: 2 hrs. 30 mins. 0 sec.). (ENG.). 2010. audio compact disk 19.99 (978-1-936111-14-4(X)) Pub: Franklin Covey. Dist(s): S and S Inc

Great World & Timothy Colt. unabr. ed. Louis Auchincloss. Read by Brian Emerson. 7 cass. (Running Time: 10 hrs.). 1997. 49.95 Set. (978-0-7861-1199-2(2), 1964) Blckstn Audio.
The story of a large Manhattan law firm - the kind of latter-day Olympus so rich & influential, so full of good grey heads, that it appears more a seat of government than a place of business.

***Great World & Timothy Colt.** unabr. ed. Louis Auchincloss. Read by Brian Emerson. (Running Time: 9 hrs. 30 mins.). 2010. 29.95 (978-1-4417-1351-3(4)); audio compact disk 90.00 (978-1-4417-1348-3(4)) Blckstn Audio.

Great World Religions. 2nd ed. 2003. 169.95 (978-1-59803-532-2(0)) Teaching Co.

Great World Religions, Pts. I-V. Instructed by Robert Oden et al. 25 cass. (Running Time: 37 hrs. 30 mins.). 1994. 299.95 (978-1-56585-160-3(9)) Teaching Co.

Great World Religions: Beliefs, Practices & Histories. unabr. ed. Robert A. Oden, Jr. et al. Read by Robert A. Oden, Jr. et al. Ed. by Teaching Company Staff. 2 cass. (Running Time: 3 hrs.). 1995. 19.95 set. (978-1-56585-116-0(1)) Teaching Co.
A look at the "New Religious Right," "Religious Fundamentalism," the Islamic Society, Judaism & Gandhi: "All Religions are True".

Great World Religions: Buddhism. 2nd ed. Instructed by Malcolm David Eckel. 6 cass. (Running Time: 6 hrs.). 2003. bk. 29.95 (978-1-56585-781-0(X), 6105); bk. 39.95 (978-1-56585-783-4(6), 6105) Teaching Co.

Great World Religions: Christianity. 2nd ed. Instructed by Luke Timothy Johnson. 6 cass. (Running Time: 6 hrs.). 2003. bk. 29.95 (978-1-56585-785-8(2), 6101); bk. 39.95 (978-1-56585-787-2(9), 6101) Teaching Co.

Great World Religions: Hinduism. 2nd ed. Instructed by Mark Muesse. 6 cass. (Running Time: 6 hrs.). 2003. bk. 29.95 (978-1-56585-789-6(5), 6104); bk. 39.95 (978-1-56585-791-9(7), 6104) Teaching Co.

Great World Religions: Islam. 2nd ed. Instructed by John Esposito. 6 CDs. (Running Time: 6 hrs.). 2003. bk. 39.95 (978-1-56585-648-6(1), 6102); bk. 29.95 (978-1-56585-646-2(5), 6102) Teaching Co.

Great World Religions: Judaism. 2nd ed. Instructed by Isaiah Gafni. 6 cass. (Running Time: 6 hrs.). 2003. bk. 29.95 (978-1-56585-793-3(3), 6103); bk. 39.95 (978-1-56585-795-7(X), 6103) Teaching Co.

Great World Religions Vol. 2: God & His Prophet: The Religion of Islam: Beliefs, Practices, & Histories. Instructed by John Swanson. 5 cass. (Running Time: 7 hrs. 30 mins.). 1994. 299.95 (978-1-56585-161-0(7)) Teaching Co.

Great World Religions Vol. 3: God & God's People: The Religion of Judaism: Beliefs, Practices, & Histories. Instructed by William Scott Green. 5 cass. (Running Time: 7 hrs. 30 mins.). 1994. 299.95 (978-1-56585-162-7(5)) Teaching Co.

Great World Religions Vol. 4: Confucius, the Tao, the Ancestors & the Buddha: The Religions of China: Beliefs, Practices, & Histories. Instructed by Robert Henricks. 5 cass. (Running Time: 7 hrs. 30 mins.). 1994. 299.95 (978-1-56585-163-4(3)) Teaching Co.

Great World Religions Vol. 5: Hindu, Buddhist, Muslim, Sikh: The Religions of India: Beliefs, Practices, & Histories. Instructed by Diana Eck. 5 cass. (Running Time: 7 hrs. 30 mins.). 1994. 299.95 (978-1-56585-164-1(1)) Teaching Co.

Great Worship Songs for Kids: 10 Sing-A-Long Favorites!! Created by Brentwood-Benson Music Publishing. (J). (gr. 4-7). 2008. 12.99 (978-5-557-45438-4(1), Brentwood-Benson Music); audio compact disk 7.99 (978-5-557-45439-1(X), Brentwood-Benson Music) Brentwood Music.

Great Worship Songs for Kids, Volume 2: 10 Sing-A-Long Favorites!! Created by Brentwood-Benson Music Publishing. (Great Worship Songs Ser.). (J). (ps-3). 2008. 12.99 (978-5-557-42743-2(0), Brentwood-Benson Music); audio compact disk 7.99 (978-5-557-42744-9(9), Brentwood-Benson Music) Brentwood Music.

Great Writers: Their Lives & Works. 6 hrs. (Running Time: 9 hrs.). 1996. 39.95 (978-1-56585-021-7(1)) Teaching Co.

Greater Damnation. Joe Schimmel. 1 cass. 3.00 (JS2) Evang Outreach.

Greater Energy at Your Finger Tips. Michael R. Gach. (Running Time: 30 min.). (Greater Energy Ser.). 1987. 9.95 (978-0-945093-00-8(4)) Enhanced Aud Systs.
Explains how acupressure relieves tension & energizes the body.

Greater Energy for Women Only. Michael R. Gach. 1 cass. (Running Time: 40 min.). (Greater Energy Ser.). 1988. 9.95 (978-0-945093-02-2(0)) Enhanced Aud Systs.

Greater Self Confidence. Michael P. Kelly. 1 cass. 1992. 14.95 (978-1-883700-15-7(9)) ThoughtForms.
Self help.

Greater Than Every Suffering. Read by M. Basilea Schlink. 1 cass. (Running Time: 30 min.). 1985. (0228) Evang Sisterhood Mary.
God offers us hidden strength; The biblical solution to this problem.

Greater Than Napoleon. unabr. collector's ed. Basil H. Liddell-Hart. Read by John MacDonald. 7 cass. (Running Time: 7 hrs.). 1986. 42.00 (978-0-7366-0572-4(X), 1544) Books on Tape.
This is the story of Publius Cornelius Scipio Africanus-the romance of his personality, his political importance as the founder of Rome's world dominion & his military work which has great value.

Greater Than Yourself: The Ultimate Lesson of True Leadership. unabr. ed. Steve Farber. Read by Steve Farber. (Running Time: 4 hrs.). (ENG.). 2009. 24.98 (978-1-59659-389-3(X), GildAudio); audio compact disk 29.98 (978-1-59659-286-5(9)) Pub: Gildan Media. Dist(s): HachBkGrp

Greatest. Joanie Greggains. 1 cass. (Running Time: 60 min.). 1989. 9.95 Peter Pan.

Greatest Aces. unabr. collector's ed. Edward H. Sims. Read by Justin Hecht. 7 cass. (Running Time: 10 hrs. 30 min.). 1983. 56.00 (978-0-7366-0528-1(2), 1502) Books on Tape.
Account of the greatest aerial missions as recalled by the top World War II aces of the R.A.F., U.S.A.A.F. & the Luftwaffe.

***Greatest Americans Series: Speeches from George Washington, Abraham Lincoln & Thomas Jefferson with Washington's Farewell Address.** unabr. ed. George Washington. Narrated by Robin Field. (Running Time: 4 hrs. 42 mins. 0 sec.). (ENG.). 2010. audio compact disk 18.98 (978-1-59644-966-4(7), MissionAud) christianaud.

Greatest Battle: Stalin, Hitler, & the Desperate Struggle for Moscow That Changed the Course of World War II. unabr. ed. Andrew Nagorski. Read by Michael Prichard. (YA). 2008. 64.99 (978-1-60514-581-5(5)) Find a World.

Greatest Battle: Stalin, Hitler, & the Desperate Struggle for Moscow That Changed the Course of World War II. unabr. ed. Andrew Nagorski. Narrated by Michael Prichard. (Running Time: 14 hrs. 0 mins. 0 sec.). (ENG.). 2007. audio compact disk 39.99 (978-1-4001-0507-6(2)); audio compact disk 29.99 (978-1-4001-5507-1(X)) Pub: Tantor Media. Dist(s): IngramPubServ

Greatest Battle: Stalin, Hitler, & the Desperate Struggle for Moscow That Changed the Course of World War II. unabr. ed. Andrew Nagorski. Read by Michael Prichard. (Running Time: 14 hrs. 0 mins. 0 sec.). (ENG.). 2007. audio compact disk 79.99 (978-1-4001-3507-3(9)) Pub: Tantor Media. Dist(s): IngramPubServ

Greatest Bible Stories Ever Told!, Vol. 1. Darian Sewell. (J). 2005. audio compact disk 20.00 (978-0-9802006-0-7(1)) DARIAN Enter.

Greatest Bible Stories Ever Told!, Vol. 2. Executive Producer Darian Sewell. (J). 2007. audio compact disk 10.00 (978-0-9802006-1-4(X)) DARIAN Enter.

Greatest Blessing. Neville Goddard. 1 cass. (Running Time: 62 min.). 1965. 8.00 (107) J & L Pubns.
Neville taught Imagination Creates Reality. He was a powerfully influential teacher of God as Consciousness.

***Greatest Book on Coaching for Small Business.** Terry Ostrowiak. 2010. 8.99 (978-0-9827081-1-8(4)) AuthorsDig.

Greatest Cat Stories of the 20th Century. unabr. ed. Lilian Jackson Braun & Sharyn McCrumb. Read by Susan Anspach. 4 cass. (Running Time: 6 hrs.). 2001. 25.00 (978-1-59040-094-4(1), Phoenix Audio) Pub: Amer Intl Pub. Dist(s): PerseuPGW

***Greatest Coach Ever: Timeless Wisdom & Insights from John Wooden.** unabr. ed. Fellowship of Christian Athletes. (Running Time: 5 hrs. 12 mins. 0 sec.). (ENG.). 2010. audio compact disk 21.98 (978-1-61045-002-7(7)) christianaud.

Greatest Course That Never Was. unabr. ed. J. Michael Veron. Read by Buck Schimer. (Running Time: 9 hrs.). 2005. 39.25 (978-1-59600-803-8(2), 9781596008038, BADLE); 24.95 (978-1-59600-802-1(4), 9781596008021, BAD); audio compact disk 24.95 (978-1-59600-800-7(8), 9781596008007, Brilliance MP3); audio compact disk 39.25 (978-1-59600-801-4(6), 9781596008014, Brlnc Audio MP3 Lib) Brilliance Audio.
Charley Hunter broke the biggest story in golf history. The young law student unearthed the life and career of the greatest player who never lived, and then spent years successfully attempting to bring Beau Stedman's story to light. His actions did not go unnoticed. Now, it is time for Charley to put the whole experience behind him . . . pass the bar, learn the ropes at the new firm, and settle into a promising legal career. But he's been receiving these intriguing notes attached to clipped obituaries that have caught hold of his curiosity. Charley knows that he has to focus on his future, but the old man has promised so much. The old man is Moonlight McIntyre, an eccentric old caddie from Augusta National, and his promise is one that he can't possibly keep. Charley has heard that the old man is crazy. . .delusional, but Moonlight claims he can reward the young lawyer's faith by disclosing unrivaled stories that he would be the first to hear. And, in the process, they would unearth the Atlantis of the golden age of golf. "Secrets," Moonlight said, "were easier to keep back then." How can Charley believe the eccentric old man with a story that no one else is able to vouch for, when he's got briefs piling up on his desk that demand his attention? He can't just pick up and trek across the country in search of what might be one of the biggest stories in sports history. There may not be a career waiting for him when he gets back. But there is something about Moonlight that he can't resist . .

Greatest Course There Never Was. abr. ed. Michael Veron. Read by Buck Schimer. 5 cass. (Running Time: 6 hrs.). 2001. audio compact disk 69.25 (978-1-58788-395-8(3), 1587883953) Brilliance Audio.

Greatest Course There Never Was. unabr. ed. Michael Veron. Read by Buck Schimer. 7 cass. (Running Time: 9 hrs.). 2001. 32.95 (978-1-58788-105-3(5), 1587881055, BAU); 78.25 (978-1-58788-106-0(3), 1587881063) Brilliance Audio.

Greatest Crimes of the Century, Vol. I. abr. ed. 2 cass. 10.95 (978-0-89926-211-6(2)) Audio Bk.
Reenactments of six of the most heinous crimes of the last 100 years, including: The Lindbergh Kidnapping; Bluebeard-the French Mass Murder; The Al Capone Story; The Scandal of Harry Thaw; Stanford White, & Evelyn Nesbit; Mata Hari; & The Great Train Robbery.

Greatest Detectives. 8 cass. (Running Time: 12 hrs.). 2003. 39.98 (978-1-57019-538-9(2), 4333); audio compact disk 39.98 (978-1-57019-537-2(4), 4334) Radio Spirits.
During the Golden Age of Radio, millions of listeners tuned in to the adventures of their favorite sleuths. Return to the scene of the crime with 10 of radio's most popular gumshoes.

Greatest Energizer Tunes Ever! Eric Jensen. 2005. 18.95 (978-1-4129-4229-4(2)) Pub: Corwin Pr. Dist(s): SAGE

Greatest Ever Bank Robbery: The Collapse of the Savings & Loan Industry. unabr. ed. Martin Mayer. Read by Grover Gardner. 9 cass. (Running Time: 13 hrs. 30 min.). 1991. 72.00 (978-0-7366-2053-6(2), 2864) Books on Tape.
In the early 1980s soaring interest rates threatened savings & loan associations, many of them small local businesses, because the old mortgages they held paid them less than what they had to pay depositors. The solution - deregulation. Deregulation attracted a new breed of entrepreneur - men who bought their way into S&Ls, men who regarded deposit insurance as a guarantee of solvency, men who looked at reward rather than risk. After all, it was other people's money.

Greatest Evil. unabr. collector's ed. William X. Kienzle. Read by Edward Holland. 7 cass. (Running Time: 10 hrs. 30 min.). (Father Koesler Mystery Ser.: No. 20). 1998. 56.00 (978-0-7366-4529-4(2), 4720) Books on Tape.
In his twentieth investigative outing, the redoubtable Father Koesler prepares to welcome Father Zacheay Tully into his parish.

Greatest Faith: Win in Every Situation You Encounter. Speeches. Creflo A. Dollar. 7 cass. (Running Time: 6 hrs.). 2005. Rental 29.00 (978-1-59089-903-8(2)); audio compact disk 40.00 (978-1-59089-904-5(0)) Creflo Dollar.

Greatest Feeling in the World: Matthew 6:12. Ed Young. (J). 1979. 4.95 (978-0-7417-1083-3(8), A0083) Win Walk.

Greatest Folksingers of the Sixties. Perf. by New Lost City Ramblers et al. 1 cass. (Running Time: 60 min.). (Vanguard Folk Ser.). (J). 10.98 (2253); audio compact disk 16.98 (D2253) MFLP CA.

Greatest Generation. abr. ed. Tom Brokaw. Read by Tom Brokaw. 4 CDs. (Running Time: 4 hrs.). (Tom Brokaw Ser.). (ENG.). 1998. audio compact disk 30.00 (978-0-375-40566-2(6)) Pub: Random Audio Pubg. Dist(s): Random

Greatest Generation, unabr. ed. Tom Brokaw. Narrated by Nelson Runger. 9 cass. (Running Time: 12 hrs. 45 mins.). 1999. 87.00 (978-0-7887-3133-4(5), 95825E7) Recorded Bks.
Tom Brokaw went to Normandy for the 40th anniversary of D-Day & was convinced that those who served during World War II are "the greatest generation any society has ever produced." This is a collection of over 50 veterans of that war sharing their experiences & life stories.

Greatest Gift. unabr. ed. Keith A. Butler, II. 1 cass. (Running Time: 1 hr. 30 mins.). 2001. 5.00 (A181) Word Faith Pubng.

Greatest Gift: The Courageous Life & Martyrdom of Sister Dorothy Stang. unabr. ed. Binka Le Breton. Read by Binka Le Breton. Read by Elizabeth Bowyer. (Running Time: 21600 sec.). 2008. audio compact disk 29.95 (978-0-86716-877-8(3)) St Anthony Mess Pr.

Greatest Gift (It's a Wonderful Life) Philip V. Stern. Read by Andy Williams. 1 cass. (Running Time: 30 min.). 1996. 10.98 (978-1-57511-017-2(2)) Pub Mills.
The original classic short story which inspired the film "It's a Wonderful Life." This story was originally intended by its author as a personal Christmas gift for his loved ones & close friends.

Greatest Gifts Our Children Give to Us, Vol. 1. Steven W. Vannoy. Ed. by Allison St. Claire. 1 cass. 1997. (978-0-9637226-3-8(8)) Vannoy Grp.
Inspiring life stories & insightful lessons gleaned from the hearts of America's children. A rare collection of real-life tales that are rich with diversity & cross-generational ties.

Greatest Golf Stories Ever Told: Gallery Shy & Dormie One, Vol. 1. abr. ed. William C. Gault & Holworthy Hall. Read by Douglas Rowe. 1 cass. (Running Time: 1 hr. 40 min.). 1996. pap. bk. 12.95 (978-1-56703-046-4(7)) High-Top Sports.
"Gallery Shy" & "Dormie One" two of golf's greatest short stories as told by the game's greatest new storyteller, Douglas Rowe, will run the gamut of your emotions. From the exhilaration of a straight & powerful drive to the depression of a maddening rub of the green, we follow brilliant golfers through a National Open (Gallery Shy) & a National Amateur (Dormie One).

Greatest Hits. Contrib. by Keith Green et al. Prod. by Bill Hearn. 2008. 13.99 (978-5-557-47790-1(X)) Pt of Grace Ent.

Greatest Hits. Perf. by Kenny G. 1 cass., 1 CD. 8.78 (ACB 18991); audio compact disk 14.38 CD. (ACB 18991) NewSound.

Greatest Hits. Gary Rosen & Bill Shontz. Perf. by Gary Rosen & Bill Shontz. 1 cass. (Rosenshontz Ser.). (J). (ps-6). 8.98 (978-1-56896-079-1(4)); 8.98 (978-1-56896-080-7(8)); audio compact disk 15.98 CD. (978-1-56896-081-4(6)); audio compact disk 15.98 (978-1-56896-082-1(4)) Lightyear Entrtnmnt.

Greatest Hits: Act I. Poems. 1 CD. Dramatization. (YA). 1990. audio compact disk (978-1-883731-10-6(0)) Poetry Alive.

Greatest Hits: Act I. abr. ed. Poems. Read by Poetry Alive! Staff. 1 cass. (Running Time: 45 min.). Dramatization. (Something Is Going to Happen Ser.). 1990. 9.95 (978-1-883731-07-6(0)) Poetry Alive.
Collection of poems, remastered with enhanced sound effects, performed as theater. Includes, among others, the written work of Tennyson, Poe, Giovanni, Dickinson & Dunbar.

Greatest Hits: Act II. (YA). 1990. audio compact disk (978-1-883731-11-3(9)) Poetry Alive.

Greatest Hits: Act II. Poems. Read by Poetry Alive! Staff. 1 cass. (Running Time: 42 min.). Dramatization. (Something Is Going to Happen Ser.). 1990. 9.95 (978-1-883731-06-9(2)) Poetry Alive.
A collection of poems, remastered with enhanced sound effects, performed as theater. Includes, among others, the written work of Brooks, Browning, Dunbar, Dickinson, Whitman, & Shakespeare.

Greatest Hits for Charity. Perf. by Raffi & Ziggy Marley. 1 cass. (Running Time: 1 hr.). 2001. 8.99 Rounder Records.
An all-star roster of children's performers join forces on Bright Spaces to benefit the program for homeless children, which provides safe, educational & stimulating play areas for children in homeless shelters.

Greatest Hits for Charity. Perf. by Raffi & Ziggy Marley. 1 CD. (Running Time: 1 hr.). (J). 2001. audio compact disk 12.99 Rounder Records.

***Greatest Hits of the National Lampoon.** Contrib. by John Belushi et al. (ENG.). 2004. audio compact disk (978-1-929243-64-8(2)) Uproar Ent.

Greatest Job You Never Thought Of: How Anyone Can Find Career Satisfaction & Financial Independence in Sales. Frank Felker. 2004. audio compact disk 14.95 (978-0-9759400-2-0(3)) Powerhse VA.
Like millions of other executives, middle managers, factory, telecom and technical workers whose jobs have been down-sized, right-sized, sent offshore or just plain evaporated in recent years, Frank Felker found himself without a job but with plenty of bills to pay and a family to feed. Out of desperation he took a job he never wanted - salesman - in an industry he knew nothing about. The results, in short, were amazing. His path to success and how anyone can follow it are what The Greatest Job You Never Thought Of is all about.

Greatest Knight. unabr. ed. Elizabeth Chadwick. Read by Christopher Scott. 14 cass. (Soundings Ser.). 2006. 99.95 (978-1-84559-427-5(4)) Pub: ISIS Lrg Prnt GBR. Dist(s): Ulverscroft US

Greatest Knight. unabr. ed. Elizabeth Chadwick. Read by Christopher Scott. 16 CDs. (Running Time: 66600 sec.). (Soundings (CDs) Ser.). 2006. audio compact disk 109.95 (978-1-84559-459-6(2)) Pub: ISIS Lrg Prnt GBR. Dist(s): Ulverscroft US

Greatest Life of All: Jesus. Charles R. Swindoll. (ENG.). 2007. audio compact disk 58.00 (978-1-57972-804-5(9)) Insight Living.

Greatest Love. (Dovetales Ser.: Tape 15). pap. bk. 6.95 (978-0-944391-50-1(8)); 4.95 (978-0-944391-30-3(3)) DonWise Prodns.

Greatest Love Story Ever Told. Jack Van Impe. 1977. 7.00 (978-0-934803-24-3(2)) J Van Impe.
Combines Old Testament prophetical statements concerning the Saviour's death with fulfilled New Testament passages.

Greatest Man in Cedar Hole. Stephanie Doyon. Narrated by Jeff Woodman. (Running Time: 51900 sec.). 2005. audio compact disk 39.99 (978-1-4193-4384-1(X)) Recorded Bks.

Greatest Man in the World see World of James Thurber

Greatest Management Principle in the World. Michael LeBoeuf. Read by Michael LeBoeuf. 6 cass. 45.00 Set. (149A) Nightingale-Conant.
How to manage others, yourself & your boss.

Greatest Minds & Ideas of All Time. unabr. ed. Will Durant. Read by John Little. 2 cass. (Running Time: 3 hrs.). 2003. 18.95 (978-1-57270-347-6(4)) Pub: Audio Partners. Dist(s): PerseuPGW
This is a collection of essays in which Durant presents the most remarkable events, people, and ideas the world has known. It is the 'best of' world history, the high-points of humanity.

Greatest Minds & Ideas of All Time. unabr. ed. Will Durant. Narrated by John Little. 3 CDs. (Running Time: 3 hrs.). (ENG.). 2003. audio compact disk 24.95 (978-1-57270-348-3(2)) Pub: AudioGO. Dist(s): Perseus Dist

Greatest Miracle in the World. Og Mandino. (Running Time: 2 hrs.). 2007. audio compact disk 17.95 (978-0-88391-123-5(X)) F Fell Pubs Inc.

Greatest Miracle in the World. abr. ed. Og Mandino. 2 cass. (Running Time: 2 hrs.). 1996. audio compact disk 17.95 (978-0-8119-0840-5(2)) F Fell Pubs Inc.
Offers priceless wisdom to those searching for a higher meaning & purpose in life. Mandino also offers a special timeless message entitled "The God Memorandum." Here is a spell-binding narrative revealing exciting new secrets for your personal happiness & success. Learn why you have lost your self-esteem & what you can do to regain it. Discover the ragpicker who rescues humans after they quit on themselves & you will learn the four simple rules that can help you perform a miracle in your life.

Greatest Miracle of All. Hugh Howard & Margaret Howard. 1 cass. 8.95 (978-1-55503-556-3(6), 311154) Covenant Comms.

Greatest Mysteries. 2001. audio compact disk 69.98 (978-1-57019-430-6(0)) Radio Spirits.

Greatest Mystery in the World, unabr. ed. Og Mandino. Narrated by Nelson Runger. 3 cass. (Running Time: 4 hrs. 30 mins.). 1998. 26.00 (978-0-7887-1880-9(0), 95302E7) Recorded Bks.
Discover new ways to enrich each new day, with the practical step-by-step approach found in this "guide to a better life.".

Greatest News in History: 1 Corinthians 15:13-17. Ed Young. 1997. 4.95 (978-0-7417-2133-4(3), 1133) Win Walk.

Greatest of All Gifts. abr. ed. Robert Bowman. 2 CDs. (Running Time: 2 hrs. 25 min.). (YA). (gr. 7 up). 2001. audio compact disk 15.00 (978-0-9713530-0-8(X), GOAG) Smart Smarter.
Follows the life of Mayela Celayan and her struggle against oppression and discrimination.

Greatest of Friends, unabr. collector's ed. Keith Alldritt. Read by David Case. 5 cass. (Running Time: 7 hrs. 30 min.). 1996. 40.00 (978-0-7366-3516-5(5), 4153) Books on Tape.
At Franklin Roosevelt's memorial service, Winston Churchill wept openly. He had lost a colleague, confidant & above all, a friend.

Greatest of These Is Love. unabr. ed. Myrtle Smith. Prod. by David Keyston. 1 cass. (Running Time: 55 min.). (Myrtle Smyth Audiotapes Ser.). 1998. , CD. (978-1-893107-09-0(4), M9, Cross & Crown) Healing Unltd.

Greatest of These Is Love: Bible Passages Proclaiming God's Love for Us, & Our Love for God & Each Other. abr. ed. 2006. 5.95 (978-0-7435-5575-3(9), Sound Ideas) Pub: S&S Audio. Dist(s): S and S Inc

Greatest of These Is Love: Bible Passages Proclaiming God's Love for Us, & Our Love for God & Each Other. abr. ed. Created by Simon and Schuster Audio Staff. (Running Time: 1 hr. 0 mins. 0 sec.). (ENG.). 2006. audio compact disk 7.95 (978-0-7435-5449-7(3), Sound Ideas) Pub: S&S Audio. Dist(s): S and S Inc

***Greatest Person to Ever Live.** Read by Jane Robelot. Prod. by Elmer L. Towns. (Running Time: 11460 sec.). (ENG.). 2009. audio compact disk 13.95 (978-0-578-02151-5(X)) Sapphire Dig.

Greatest Player Who Never Lived. unabr. ed. Michael Veron. Read by Buck Schirner. (Running Time: 6 hrs.). 2005. 39.25 (978-1-59600-799-4(0), 9781596007994, BADLE); 24.95 (978-1-59600-798-7(2), 9781596007987, BAD); audio compact disk 24.95 (978-1-59600-796-3(6), 9781596007963, Brilliance MP3); audio compact disk 39.25 (978-1-59600-797-0(4), 9781596007970, Brlnc Audio MP3 Lib) Brilliance Audio.
Unwritten in the annals of the sporting world is the story of a man with unlimited potential who was denied his rightful place in the lore of golf... It is a story that might never have been told had Charley Hunter not accepted a summer internship at Butler & Yates, a prestigious Atlanta law firm. Bobby Jones, the legendary amateur golfer, had once been a partner at the firm and his old legal files had been severely neglected over the years. The task of cataloging those files soon presents Charley with the remnants of a man's life, as he pieces together a tale that spans decades. Who is this mysterious golfer with a golden swing, whose life and career Jones followed with such interest? An accused felon fleeing from the law? Or a man falsely accused, whose only crime was being in the wrong place at the wrong time? And why would one of the greatest athletes of all time risk his spotless reputation to help a man he met only once? Charley quickly learns that there is a compelling tale buried within the files of Bobby Jones. Charley uncovers stories of unfulfilled promise, fleeting justice, near captures, and unyielding friendship - and to what end? Charley hopes to find the truth. But what he ultimately finds will change his life and understanding of life forever.

Greatest Player Who Never Lived: A Golf Story. unabr. ed. Michael Veron. Read by Buck Schirner. 5 CDs. (Running Time: 6 hrs.). 2000. audio compact disk 57.25 (978-1-58788-183-1(7), 1587881837, Unabridge Lib Edns) Brilliance Audio.

Greatest Power. unabr. ed. Wendelin Van Draanen. Read by Marc Cashman. (Gecko & Sticky Ser.: Bk. 1). (ENG.). (J). (gr. 3). 2009. audio compact disk 25.00 (978-0-7393-7922-6(4), Listening Lib) Pub: Random Audio Pubg. Dist(s): Random

Greatest Power Source. Kenneth E. Hagin. (How to Be an Overcomer Ser.). bk. 17.00 Faith Lib Pubns.

Greatest Praise Songs of the Church Instrumental. Created by Maranatha! Music. Contrib. by Thomas Vegh & Randy Alward. 2005. audio compact disk 9.99 (978-5-559-08347-6(X)) Maranatha Music.

Greatest Problem in Marriage: Isiah 53:6. Ed Young. (J). 1981. 4.95 (978-0-7417-1161-8(3), A0161) Win Walk.

Greatest Questions Ever Asked. Dan Corner. 1 cass. 3.00 (38) Evang Outreach.

Greatest Salesman in the World see Vendedor Mas Grande del Mundo

Greatest Salesman in the World. Og Mandino. (Running Time: 9000 sec.).Tr. of Vendedor Mas Grande del Mundo. 2007. audio compact disk 14.95 (978-0-88391-157-0(4)) F Fell Pubs Inc.

Greatest Salesman in the World. Og Mandino. 1 cass.Tr. of Vendedor Mas Grande del Mundo. 10.00 (SP100000) SMI Intl.
Hear the amazing story of the ancient scrolls, passed from hand to hand for thousands of years, that contain secrets used by merchants & traders to acquire wealth. The wisdom of the scrolls can influence your life & bring you the fortune of prosperity & riches.

Greatest Salesman in the World. abr. ed. Og Mandino. 2 cass. (Running Time: 2 hrs.).Tr. of Vendedor Mas Grande del Mundo. 1996. 17.95 (978-0-8119-0839-9(9)) F Fell Pubs Inc.
Recounts the legend of Hafid, a camel boy who lived a thousand years ago & came into the possession of ten ancient scrolls which contain the wisdom necessary for the boy to achieve all his ambitions.

Greatest Salesman in the World. unabr. ed. Og Mandino.Tr. of Vendedor Mas Grande del Mundo. 2007. 17.95 (978-0-88391-078-8(0)) F Fell Pubs Inc.

Greatest Salesman Part II: The End of the Story see Vendedor Mas Grande del Mundo: El Final de la Historia

Greatest Science. Swami Amar Jyoti. 1 cass. 1982. 9.95 (O-23) Truth Consciousness.
The Yogic science of force & energy, creation & evolution, relativity & reality. Relationship of the soul & Pure Consciousness. On transmigration, liberation & Enlightement.

Greatest Secret of All: Moving Beyond Abundance to a Life of True Fulfillment. Marc Allen. (ENG.). 2008. audio compact disk 17.95 (978-1-57731-640-4(1)) Pub: New Wrld Lib. Dist(s): PerseuPGW

Greatest Show off Earth. unabr. ed. Margaret Mahy. Read by Richard Mitchley. 3 cass. (Running Time: 3 hrs.). (J). 1997. 30.00 (LL 0052, Chivers Child Audio) AudioGO.

Greatest Show off Earth, Set. unabr. ed. Margaret Mahy. Read by Richard Mitchley. 3 cass. (Running Time: 2 hrs. 58 min.). (J). (gr. 4-6). 1995. 23.98 (978-0-8072-7518-4(2), YA870CX, Listening Lib) Random Audio Pubg.
All fun is forbidden on gloomy Space Station Vulnik so Delphinium blasts off into hyperspace & smack into the middle of the missing Wonder Show - the Greatest Show off Earth. In the space adventure of a lifetime, Delphinium & her two passengers find themselves in a thrilling escapade beyond their wildest dreams.

Greatest Show off Earth, Set. unabr. ed. Read by Richard Mitchley. Ed. by Margaret Mahy. 3 cass. (Running Time: 2 hrs. 58 min.). (J). (gr. 4-6). 1995. 28.98 (978-0-8072-7519-1(0), YA870SP, Listening Lib) Random Audio Pubg.

Greatest Show on Earth: The Evidence for Evolution. unabr. ed. Richard Dawkins. Read by Richard Dawkins. Read by Lalla Ward. 14 CDs. (Running Time: 16 hrs. 30 mins. 0 sec.). (ENG.). 2009. audio compact disk 39.99 (978-0-7435-7927-8(5)) Pub: S&S Audio. Dist(s): S and S Inc

Greatest Shows of the 20th Century. Selected by Walter Cronkite. 10 vols. (Running Time: 10 hrs.). (10-Hour Collections). bk. 39.98 (978-1-57019-616-4(8), OTR47102) Pub: Radio Spirits. Dist(s): AudioGO

Greatest Shows Selected by Walter Cronkite. Radio Spirits Staff. Read by Walter Cronkite. 2005. audio compact disk 39.98 (978-1-57019-623-2(0)) Radio Spirits.

Greatest Speeches of All Time. Ed. by Pent. 1 cass. 1997. audio compact disk 10.95 (978-1-885959-48-5(6), JRAB9400) Jerden Recs.
Highlights of famous speeches given by the great orators of the 20th century.

Greatest Speeches of All Time: Volumes 1 And 2. unabr. ed. Read by Original Recorded Speeches. (YA). 2006. 39.99 (978-1-59895-337-4(0)) Find a World.

Greatest Speeches of All-Time, Volume III. Created by Speechworks. (Running Time: 2580 sec.). 2007. audio compact disk 15.95 (978-1-885959-72-0(9), Speechworks) Jerden Recs.

Greatest Sports Shows. 2004. 29.95 (978-1-57019-727-7(X)) Radio Spirits.

Greatest Stars of Bluegrass Music for Fiddle. Martin Norgaard. 2002. bk. 27.95 (978-0-7866-6613-3(7), 97050BCD) Mel Bay.

Greatest Stories Ever. unabr. ed. Short Stories. Read by George Vafiadis. 10 cds. 2002. audio compact disk 49.95 (978-1-58472-367-7(X), In Aud) Pub: Sound Room. Dist(s): Baker Taylor
King James Version. Includes the Creation, Adam and Eve, Cain and Abel, Noah's Ark, the testing of Abraham, Joseph sold into slavery in Egypt, Moses birth and life in Egypt, the deliverance of Israel, the Ten Commandments, Samson and Delilah, David and Goliath, the wisdom of Solomon, the birth of Christ, the Last Supper, Crucifixion and Death, the Resurrection, Miracles and Parables, and many others.

Greatest Stories of All Time. unabr. ed. King James Version. Read by George Vafiadis. (YA). 2006. 49.99 (978-1-59895-168-4(8)) Find a World.

Greatest Stories of All Time: Best-Loved Bible Stories. Narrated by George Vafiadis. (J). 2005. audio compact disk 39.95 (978-1-58472-692-0(X), In Aud) Sound Room.

Greatest Stories of All Time: 177 Famous Stories from the Bible. Created by InAudio. (Running Time: 42600 sec.). (J). 2003. audio compact disk 14.95 (978-1-58472-516-9(8), In Aud) Sound Room.

Greatest Story Ever Told. Jeff Cavins. audio compact disk (978-1-932927-45-0(X)) Ascensn Pr.

Greatest Story Ever Told: And Her Name Was Mary & Blessed among Women. Perf. by Warren Parker. 1 cass. (Running Time: 1 hr.). 2001. 6.98 (2220) Radio Spirits.

Greatest Story Ever Told: Luke 15:11-32. (J). 1982. 4.95 (978-0-7417-1223-3(7), 223) Win Walk.

***Greatest Story Ever Told: The Timeless Bestselling Life of Jesus Christ.** abr. ed. Fulton Oursler. Read by Edward Herrmann. (Running Time: 6 hrs. 0 mins. 0 sec.). (ENG.). 2010. audio compact disk 21.98 (978-1-61045-101-7(5), christaudio) christianaud.

Greatest Story Never Told. Ron Watson. 1 cass. 8.95 (360) Am Fed Astrologers.
Unlock Bible prophesy for spiritual growth.

Greatest Success in the World see Exito Mas Grande del Mundo

Greatest Thing in the World. Contrib. by Peter B. Allen. (Running Time: 30 min.). 2004. audio compact disk 15.95 (978-5-559-57278-9(0)) Pub: Pt of Grace Ent. Dist(s): STL Dist NA

Greatest Thing in the World. unabr. ed. Henry Drummond. (ENG.). 2005. 1.98 (978-1-59659-054-0(8), GildAudio) Pub: Gildan Media. Dist(s): HachBkGrp

Greatest Thing in the World. unabr. ed. Henry Drummond. 1 CD. (Running Time: 1 hr. 0 mins. 0 sec.). (ENG.). 2004. audio compact disk 12.98 (978-1-59644-025-8(2), Hovel Audio) christianaud.
Drummond's memorable homily on love-the supreme good- retains all its original freshness and vitality in this oral rendition. Widely quoted and read, his message on love from First Corinthians sold over 12 million copies. Involving God's two greatest commands to love Him and love one another, this message is just as needed today as it was back then.

***Greatest Thing in the World.** unabr. ed. Henry Drummond. Narrated by Paul Eggington. (Running Time: 1 hr. 0 mins. 0 sec.). (ENG.). 2004. 8.98 (978-1-59644-024-1(4), Hovel Audio) christianaud.

Greatest Thing in the World: Walking in Love. Henry Drummond. Read by Charlie Tremendous Jones. (Laws of Leadership Ser.). (ENG.). 2007. audio compact disk 19.95 (978-1-933715-52-0(9)) Executive Bks.

Greatest Thing since Sliced Bread. unabr. ed. Don Robertson. Narrated by Tony Barbour. 6 cass. (Running Time: 8 hrs.). 1980. 51.00 (978-1-55690-209-3(3), 80180E7) Recorded Bks.
Ten year old Morris Bird III sets out across Cleveland in 1944 & becomes an unwitting hero.

Greatest Threat: Iraq, Weapons of Mass Destruction, & the Crisis of Global Security. unabr. ed. Richard Butler. Read by Robert Whitfield. 9 CDs. (Running Time: 11 hrs. 30 mins.). 2003. audio compact disk 72.00 (978-0-7861-9284-7(4), 3085); 56.95 (978-0-7861-2419-0(9), 3085) Blckstn Audio.
Tells the inside story of the UN's failed attempt to stop Saddam and explains the terrible cost of that failure.

Greatest Trade Ever: The Behind-the-Scenes Story of How John Paulson Defied Wall Street & Made Financial History. unabr. ed. Gregory Zuckerman. Read by Marc Cashman. (ENG.). 2009. audio compact disk 40.00 (978-0-307-71331-5(8), Random AudioBks) Pub: Random Audio Pubg. Dist(s): Random

Greatest Weapon of Life: Prayer. Voice by Eddie Long. 2008. audio compact disk 20.00 (978-1-58602-360-7(8)) Pub: E L Long. Dist(s): Anchor Distributors

Greatest Western Stories of the 20th Century. unabr. ed. Louis L'Amour. Read by Burt Reynolds. 4 cass. (Running Time: 6 hrs.). 2001. 25.00 (978-1-59040-083-6(6)) Pub: Amer Intl Pub. Dist(s): PerseuPGW

Greatly Needed: Empathy: Ezekiel 3:15. Ben Young. (YA). 2000. 4.95 (978-0-7417-6222-1(6), B0222) Win Walk.

***Greatness: The 16 Characteristics of True Champions.** unabr. ed. Don Yaeger. (Running Time: 7 hrs. 30 mins.). (ENG.). 2011. 19.98 (978-1-60941-228-9(1)); audio compact disk & audio compact disk 24.98 (978-1-60941-227-2(3)) Pub: Hachet Audio. Dist(s): HachBkGrp

Greatness in You. unabr. ed. Read by Bob Richards. 1 cass. (Running Time: 30 min.). 15.00 B R Motivational.
A recorded live speech by Bob Richards, concentrated on the individual & his or her capacity to achieve greatness, & the opportunities in our great American Society.

Greatness of Christ-mp3. Read by Douglas Wilson. 1991. 12.00 (978-1-59128-224-2(1)) Canon Pr ID.

Greatness of Christ-tape. Read by Douglas Wilson. 6 cass. 1991. 15.00 (978-1-59128-226-6(8)) Canon Pr ID.

Greatness of Faith. Hyrum Smith. 1 cass. 3.95 (978-1-57734-403-2(0), 34441441) Covenant Comms.

Greatness of Faith & The Marvelous Gift. Don J. Black. 1 cass. 5.98 (978-1-55503-044-5(0), 060013) Covenant Comms.
Two talks on The Savior.

Greatness of Gone with the Wind, Featuring Elliot Engel. 2000. bk. 15.00 (978-1-890123-20-8(X)) Media Cnslts.

Greatness of Humility. unabr. ed. Swami Amar Jyoti. 1 cass. (Running Time: 1 hr. 30 min.). (Satsangs of Swami Amar Jyoti Ser.). 1998. 9.95 (978-0-933572-29-4(8), K162) Truth Consciousness.
Humility opens us to connection with the Lord. What makes one genuinely humble? Taking responsibility for our virtues & vices.

Greatness of Sri Rama. Swami Amar Jyoti. 1 cass. 1991. 9.95 (K-134) Truth Consciousness.
Under all tribulations, Rama perfectly lived Dharma. Violence & nonviolence in Nature & human affairs.

Greatness of Veritatis Splendor. Fr. Hardon. 9 cass. 36.00 Set. (94F) IRL Chicago.

Greatness of Women. Don J. Black. 1 cass. 7.98 (978-1-55503-811-3(5), 06005055) Covenant Comms.
A lively & loving tribute to the women in our lives.

Greatness to Spare: The Heroic Sacrifices of the Men Who Signed the Declaration of Independence, abr. ed. T. R. Fehrenbach. Read by Timothy P. Miller. 2 cass. (Running Time: 3 hrs.). 1998. 17.95 (978-0-9655275-2-1(2)) Vis Aud Pub Inc.
On July 4, 1776, John Hancock was the first to sign the Declaration of Independence. Over the following four years, fifty-five other men signed, branding themselves "leaders of the revolution" against the crown of England. In signing, they put their futures on the line for this new concept in which they believed liberty. Here are the stories of forty-two of these men, patriots who made heroic personal sacrifices. During seven years of war these men were constantly hunted & their families persecuted.

Grecian Urn. (Paws & Tales Ser.: Vol. 26). (J). 2002. 3.99 (978-1-57972-434-4(5)) Insight Living.

Greeblies: Five Tall Stories about Gross Little Bugs. unabr. ed. Robert Greenberg. Read by Stig Wemyss. (Running Time: 6900 sec.). (J). 2007. audio compact disk 43.95 (978-1-74093-982-9(4), 9781740939829) Pub: Bolinda Pubng AUS. Dist(s): Bolinda Pub Inc

Greece. Contrib. by Time-Life Audiobooks Staff. (Lost Civilizations Ser.). 1999. (978-1-57042-730-5(5)) Hachet Audio.

Greece: Athens - Your Personal Guide. (Running Time: 60 min.). 1990. 12.95 (CC504) Comp Comms Inc.
Takes you to the Acropolis crowned by the Parthenon by way of the Parliament building, National Gardens, & visits to Hadrian's Arch & the Temple of Olympian Zeus. You will also visit the Agora, the principal market & meeting place of Ancient Athens. You'll pass some fine Orthodox churches on your way to Monastiraki Square before you visit Kerameikos, Athens' oldest cemetery.

Greece & Rome: An Integrated History of the Ancient Mediterranean. Instructed by Robert Garland. 2008. 199.95 (978-1-59803-416-5(2)); audio compact disk 99.95 (978-1-59803-417-2(0)) Teaching Co.

Greece Long Ago. Compiled by Benchmark Education Staff. 2005. audio compact disk 10.00 (978-1-4108-5504-6(X)) Benchmark Educ.

Greed & Glory on Wall Street: The Fall of the House of Lehman. Ken Auletta. Read by Jim Micheals. 7 cass. (Running Time: 1 hr. 30 min. per cass.). 1991. 70.00 incl. outline. (978-0-942563-16-0(6)); Rental 15.00 incl. outline. (978-0-942563-17-7(4)) CareerTapes.
This is the more than just the story of the fall of investment banking house, Lehman Brothers. It is a spellbinding look into human nature. It is a story of jealousy, greed, ego & error; a tale of primal combat between two men from irrevocably different & hostile worlds.

Greed, Bribes & Scandals: The Ancient Olympics. unabr. ed. David Gilman Romano. Read by Suzanne Bona & Thane Maynard. 1 cass. (Running Time: 60 min.). (IMS Audio Ser.). (C). 1999. 9.95 (978-0-9675626-0-5(0)) Inst Medit.
Learn about the rituals and rules of the ancient Olympics as well as the various events and customs. Bribery, cheating & scandal were as much a part of the ancient Olympics as they are today.

Greed, Bribes & Scandals: The Ancient Olympics. unabr. ed. David Gilmon Romano. Read by Suzanne Bona & Thane Maynard. 1 CD. (Running Time: 1 hr.). (IMS Audio Ser.). (YA). (gr. 13 up). 1999. audio compact disk 9.95 (978-0-9675626-1-2(9)) Inst Medit.
We learn about the rituals & rules of the ancient olympics as well as the various events & customs. Bribery, cheating & scandal were as much a part of the ancient olympics as they are today.

Greedy Gray Octopus: Audiocassette. (gr. k-3). 10.00 (978-0-7635-6368-4(4)) Rigby Educ.

Greedy Old Fat Man. unabr. ed. Paul Galdone. 1 cass. (Running Time: 7 min.). (J). (gr. k-4). 1987. bk. 24.90 (978-0-8045-6556-1(2), 6556) Spoken Arts.

Greek. Created by Berlitz. (Berlitzin 60 Minutes Ser.). (GRE & ENG., 2008. audio compact disk 9.95 (978-981-268-389-2(5)) Pub: Berlitz Pubng. Dist(s): Langenscheidt

Greek. Athena Economides & Collins Educational Staff. Ed. by Rosi McNab. (Running Time: 3 hrs. 0 mins. 0 sec.). (Collins Easy Learning Audio Course Ser.). (ENG.). 2009. audio compact disk 19.95 (978-0-00-731365-5(9)) Pub: HarpC GBR. Dist(s): IPG Chicago

Greek. Penton Overseas, Inc. Staff. 2 cass. (Running Time: 80 min.). (Language - Thirty Library). bk. 16.95 set in vinyl album. Moonbeam Pubns.
Using the proven method based on the famous U.S. Military accelerated language learning program, Language/30 courses stress conversationally useful words & phrases.

Greek. unabr. ed. Ed. by Charles Berlitz. 2 cass. (Running Time: 1 hr. 30 mins.). (Language/30 Brief Course Ser.). pap. bk. 21.95 (AF1024) J Norton Pubs.
Quick, highly condensed introduction to the words & phrases you'll need to communicate effectively in the country you're visiting. Cassettes & phrase guide book are in a vinyl album.

Greek: Language/30. rev. ed. Educational Services Corporation Staff. Intro. by Charles Berlitz. 2 cass. (GRE.). 1994. pap. bk. 21.95 (978-0-910542-74-6(0)) Educ Svcs DC.
Greek self-teaching language course.

Greek Adventure: Lord Byron & Other Eccentrics in the War of Greek Independence. unabr. ed. David Howarth. Narrated by Tom West. 6 cass. (Running Time: 9 hrs.). 1982. 51.00 (978-1-55690-210-9(7), 82018E7) Recorded Bks.
A detailed account of the 1821 War of Independence fought by the Greeks against their Turkish overlords.

Greek & Persian Wars. Instructed by John R. Hale. 2008. 129.95 (978-1-59803-428-8(6)); audio compact disk 69.95 (978-1-59803-429-5(4)) Teaching Co.

Greek & Roman Deities As Personifications of Divine Principles. Instructed by Manly P. Hall. 5 cass. 8.50 ea. o.p. Pt. 1: Divine Dynasty - Uranus, Cronus, & Zeus. (800160-A) Philos Res.

Greek & Roman Deities As Personifications of Divine Principles. Instructed by Manly P. Hall. 5 cass. (Running Time: 150 min.). 1999. 40.00 Set. incl. album. (978-0-89314-130-1(5), S800160) Philos Res.

Greek & Roman Myths. unabr. ed. Thomas Bulfinch. 1 cass. (Running Time: 1 hr.). 1996. 16.95 (978-1-885608-06-2(3)) Airplay.
The director of the Metropolitan Museum reads Classic Greek & Roman myths.

Greek Basic Course: Level Three. S. Oblensky & P. Sapountzis. 6 cass. (Multilingual Books Intensive Cassette Foreign Language Ser.). (GRE.). (C). 1999. spiral bd. 120.00 (978-1-58214-024-7(3)) Language Assocs.

Greek Basic Course (FSI), Vol. 1. 13 CDs. (Running Time: 11 hrs. 30 min.). (Foreign Service Institute Basic Course Ser.). (GRE.). 2005. audio compact disk 225.00 (978-1-57970-187-1(6), AFR301D) J Norton Pubs.

Greek Classics. Minds Eye Staff. 4 cass. Dramatization. 1995. 16.95 Set. (978-1-55935-187-4(X)) Soundelux.
Includes "Oedipus the King" & "The Odyssey".

Greek Classics: The Odyssey & Oedipus, the King. 4 cass. (Running Time: 4 hrs.). 2001. 29.95 (SNDX009) Lodestone Catalog.

Greek Folk Dancing w/Music CD. Vicki Corona. (Celebrate the Cultures Ser.: 1-23A). 1980. pap. bk. 24.95 (978-1-58513-116-7(4)) Dance Fantasy.

Greek for Speakers of English: Level 1. unabr. ed. 10 cass. (Running Time: 10 hrs.). (Pimsleur Tapes Ser.). (GRE.). 1963. 230.00 set. (18800, Pimsleur) S&S Audio.
A twenty-lesson-unit program based upon the Pimsleur Spoken Language Programmed Instructional Method, providing basic beginning language training to the ACTFL Novice Level.

Greek I: Learn to Speak & Understand Greek with Pimsleur Language Programs. 2nd rev. ed. Pimsleur Staff. 16 CDs. (Running Time: 160 hrs. 0 mins. 0 sec.). (Comprehensive Ser.). (ENG.). 2002. audio compact disk 345.00 (978-0-7435-0889-6(0), Pimsleur) Pub: S&S Audio. Dist(s): S and S Inc
Program provides a method of self-practice with an expert teacher and native speakers in lessons specially designed to work with the way the mind naturally acquires language information.

Greek Interpreter see Memoirs of Sherlock Holmes

Greek Interpreter. 1981. (S-40) Jimcin Record.

Greek Legacy: Classical Origins of the Modern World. Instructed by Daniel Robinson. 6 cass. (Running Time: 6 hrs.). 29.95 (978-1-56585-123-8(4)) Teaching Co.

Greek Legacy: Classical Origins of the Modern World. Instructed by Daniel N. Robinson. 6 CDs. (Running Time: 6 hrs.). audio compact disk 39.95 (978-1-59803-209-3(7)) Teaching Co.

Greek Lives. Plutarch. Read by Nicholas Farrell. (Running Time: 5 hrs.). 2005. 28.95 (978-1-60083-754-8(9)) Iofy Corp.

Greek Lives: Lycurgus; Themistocles; Pericles; Alexander; Demosthenes & Others. Plutarch. Read by Nicholas Farrell. (C). 2003. pap. bk. 41.98 (978-962-634-289-3(7), Naxos AudioBooks) Naxos.

Greek (Modern) II Vol. 2: Learn to Speak & Understand Greek with Pimsleur Language Programs. unabr. ed. Pimsleur Staff & Pimsleur. (Running Time: 16 hrs. 0 mins. 0 sec.). (Comprehensive Ser.). (ENG.). 2008. audio compact disk 345.00 (978-0-7435-5253-0(9), Pimsleur) Pub: S&S Audio. Dist(s): S and S Inc

Greek, Modern Poetry: Reader 1. unabr. ed. 3 cass. (Running Time: 2 hrs.). 1994. bk. 34.95 (978-0-88432-526-0(1), SGFR180) J Norton Pubs.

Greek Myths. Read by Jim Weiss. 1 cass. (J). (gr. k-6). 1999. 9.95 (1124-02); audio compact disk 14.95 (1124002) Greathall Prods.

Greek Myths. Short Stories. As told by Jim Weiss. 1 cass. (Running Time: 1 hr.). Dramatization. (Storyteller's Version Ser.). (J). (gr. k up). 1989. 10.95 (978-1-882513-02-4(9), 1124-02) Greathall Prods.
A 1990 Booklist Editor's Choice, this tape makes Hercules, King Midas and Perseus and Medusa understandable to children with strong emphasis on character over violence.

Greek Myths. Read by Jim Weiss. 1 cass., 1 CD. (Running Time: 1 hr.). (J). (GHP2) NewSound.

Greek Myths. unabr. ed. Read by Andrew Sachs. Retold by Geraldine McCaughrean. 2 CDs. (Running Time: 3 hrs.). (J). 2002. audio compact disk 21.95 (978-0-7540-6517-3(0), CHCD 017, Chivers Child Audio) AudioGO.

Greek Myths, Vol. 1. unabr. collector's ed. Robert Graves. Read by David Case. 12 cass. (Running Time: 18 hrs.). 1992. 96.00 (978-0-7366-2112-0(1), 2916) Books on Tape.
Stories of the most important gods & heroes of Ancient Greece.

Greek Myths, Vol. 2. unabr. collector's ed. Robert Graves. Read by David Case. 12 cass. (Running Time: 18 hrs.). 1992. 96.00 (978-0-7366-2277-6(2), 3065) Books on Tape.
Retelling of Greek legends of gods & heroes.

Greek Myths I: Zeus & the Mighty Gods of Olympus. Ed. by Jerry Stemach et al. As told by Noe Venable. Narrated by Noe Venable. Illus. by Michael Letwenko et al. Contrib. by Ted S. Hasselbring. (Start-to-Finish Books). (J). (gr. 2-3). 2001. 35.00 (978-1-58702-864-9(6)) D Johnston Inc.

Greek Myths I: Zeus & the Mighty Gods of Olympus. Noe Venable. (Myths & Legends Ser.). 2001. audio compact disk 18.95 (978-1-4105-0183-7(3)) D Johnston Inc.

Greek Myths II: Heroes, Lovers, & Mortal Man. Ed. by Jerry Stemach et al. As told by Noe Venable. Narrated by Noe Venable. Illus. by Michael Letwenko & Edward Letwenko. Contrib. by Ted S. Hasselbring. (Start-to-Finish Books). (J). (gr. 2-3). 2001. 35.00 (978-1-58702-867-0(0)) D Johnston Inc.

Greek Myths II: Heroes, Lovers, & Mortal Man. Noe Venable. (Myths & Legends Ser.). 2001. audio compact disk 18.95 (978-1-4105-0184-4(1)) D Johnston Inc.

Greek Myths II: Heroes, Lovers, & Mortal Man. unabr. ed. Ed. by Jerry Stemach et al. As told by Noe Venable. Narrated by Noe Venable. Illus. by Michael Letwenko & Edward Letwenko. Contrib. by Ted S. Hasselbring. 1 cass. (Running Time: 1 hr.). (Start-to-Finish Books). (J). (gr. 2-3). 2001. 7.00 (978-1-58702-695-9(3), H03) D Johnston Inc.
Recounts some of the most vivid tales in all of mythology. Whereas Greek Myths I contained tales of the major Greed gods, this book focuses on minor gods and human offspring of the gods. Don't be fooled by the word, "minor" however. The tales in this book are actually some of the most famous of Greek myths. From Pandoras box, to the creation of mankind, and from Orpheus and Furidice to the labors of Hercules, the tales contained in this book.

Greek Myths 1: Zeus & the Mighty Gods of Olympus. unabr. ed. Ed. by Jerry Stemach et al. As told by Noe Venable. Narrated by Noe Venable. Illus. by Michael Letwenko et al. Contrib. by Ted S. Hasselbring. 1 cass. (Running Time: 1 hr.). (Start-to-Finish Books). (J). (gr. 2-3). 2001. 7.00 (978-1-58702-694-2(5), H02) D Johnston Inc.
Greek Myths I focuses on the major Greek gods and goddesses who Greeks lived on Olympus and ruled over heaven and Earth. Packed with comedy and adventure, Greek Myths I is sure to bring to life for your students. YOur students will see how the Greeks used myths to explain the world around them. They will also get a sense of what the gods meant to the people who worshipped them.

Greek New Testament. Narrated by Panos Zachariou. 13 cass. (Running Time: 19 hrs. 30 min.). (GRE.). 2000. 39.99 (978-7-902030-37-3(6)) Chrstn Dup Intl.

Greek Phrase Book Pack. rev. ed. Collins Publishers Staff. (ENG & GRE.). 2003. pap. bk. 13.99 (978-0-00-765098-9(1)) Pub: HarpC GBR. Dist(s): Trafalgar

Greek Poetry, A Recital of Ancient. unabr. ed. Stephen G. Daitz. 4 cass. Incl. Greek Poetry, A Recital of Ancient: Selections from Homer's "Illiad" (S23600); Greek Poetry, A Recital of Ancient: Selections from Homer's "Odyssey" (S23600); Greek Poetry, A Recital of Ancient: Selections from the Lyric Poets. (S23600); Selections from Tragedy & Comedy. (S23600); 59.50 incl. bklet. Set. (S23600); 15.00 J Norton Pubs.
An unusual presentation of Greek poetry in the restored historical pronunciation, in the original rhythms, & with the musical pitch accents.

Greek Poetry, A Recital of Ancient: Selections from Homer's "Illiad" see Greek Poetry, A Recital of Ancient

Greek Poetry, A Recital of Ancient: Selections from Homer's "Odyssey" see Greek Poetry, A Recital of Ancient

Greek Poetry, A Recital of Ancient: Selections from the Lyric Poets see Greek Poetry, A Recital of Ancient

Greek Thought. Sophia Schreiber. Narrated by Larry A. McKeever. (Ancient Greek Mystery Ser.). (J). 2007. 10.95 (978-1-58659-133-5(9)); audio compact disk 14.95 (978-1-58659-367-4(6)) Artesian.

Greek Tragedy. Instructed by Elizabeth Vandiver. 6 cass. (Running Time: 6 hrs.). 2000. 129.95 (978-1-56585-026-2(2)) Teaching Co.

Greek Tragedy, Pts. I-II. Instructed by Elizabeth Vandiver. 12 CDs. (Running Time: 12 hrs.). 2000. audio compact disk 69.95 (978-1-56585-284-6(2), 217) Teaching Co.

Greek Tragedy, Pts. I-II, Vol. 1. Instructed by Elizabeth Vandiver. 12 cass. (Running Time: 12 hrs.). 54.95 (978-1-56585-025-5(4), 217) Teaching Co.

Greek Tragedy, Vol. 2. Instructed by Elizabeth Vandiver. 6 CDs. (Running Time: 6 hrs.). 2000. audio compact disk 179.95 (978-1-56585-285-3(0)) Teaching Co.

Greek Treasure: A Biographical Novel of Henry & Sophia Schliemann. unabr. ed. Irving Stone. Read by Penelope Dellaporta. 15 cass. (Running Time: 22 hrs. 30 mins.). 1979. 120.00 (978-0-7366-0154-2(6), 1154) Books on Tape.
Heinrich Schliemann was the discoverer of Troy. This story is of that early archaeological adventurer. Schliemann went to Asia Minor not only for artifacts but also to find a woman. At age 47 he met 17-year-old Sophia Engastromeno, he took her as his companion for the rest of his life.

***Greek Vol 2 Cds & Text.** Foreign Service Institute. (ENG & GRE.). 2005. pap. bk. 255.00 (978-1-57970-302-8(X), Audio-For) J Norton Pubs.

Greek Vol 2 Earworms. (EARWORMS Ser.). 2009. audio compact disk 24.95 (978-0-8416-1070-5(3)) Pub: Berlitz Pubng. Dist(s): Langenscheidt

Greek vs. Hebraic Thinking. Stephen Mansfield. 1 cass. (Running Time: 90 mins.). (Studies in Church History Ser.: Vol. 3). 2000. 5.00 (SM02-003) Morning NC.
An in-depth look at different philosophies that have influenced church history, this series provides excellent keys for understanding how to effectively confront the important issues of our times.

Greek Way. unabr. ed. Edith Hamilton. Read by Nadia May. 6 cass. (Running Time: 8 hrs. 30 mins.). 1994. 44.95 (978-0-7861-0678-3(6), 1466) Blckstn Audio.
"What the Greeks discovered, how they brought a new world to birth out of the dark confusions of an old world that had crumbled away, is full of meaning for us today who have seen an old world swept away." Based on a thorough study of Greek life & civilization, of Greek literature, philosophy, & art, "The Greek Way" interprets their meaning & brings a realization of the refuge & strength the past can be to us in the troubled present. Miss Hamilton's book must take its place with the few interpretative volumes which are permanently rooted & profoundly alive in our literature.

Greek Wedding. unabr. ed. Jane Aiken Hodge. Read by Norma West. 10 cass. (Running Time: 10 hrs.). 1999. 84.95 (978-0-7540-0339-7(6), CAB1762) Pub: Chivers Audio Bks GBR. Dist(s): AudioGO
Brett Renshaw's relationship with Phyllida Vannick was a stormy one. Yet, bankrupt as he was, how could he refuse to let her charter his yacht? Romance & adventure abound as a young girl is embroiled in the turbulent Greek War of Independence.

Greek with Ease see Nuovo Greco Senza Sforzo

Green. Ed. by Robert A. Monroe. 1 cass. (Running Time: 30 min.). (Meta Music Ser.). 1989. 12.95 (978-1-56102-211-3(X)) Inter Indus.
Enjoy a musical voyage with Hemi-Sync. A good tape for meditation or simply relaxing into conscious dreams.

Green, abr. ed. Troon McAllister, pseud. Read by Chris McDonald. 4 cass. (Running Time: 6 hrs.). 2001. 24.95 (978-1-57511-062-2(8)) Pub Mills.
When Eddie Caminetti, an unknown golfing hustler, is recruited to represent his country in the Ryder Cup - golf's prestigious biennial contest which pits the best U.S. players against their European peers - a comical clash erupts as the gruff con-artist competes for the coveted cup & a big payoff from the big shots. The huckster goes head-to-head with the sacrosanct rules of the green & its stuffy golf elite.

Green: The Beginning & the End. unabr. ed. Ted Dekker. Narrated by Tim Gregory. (Running Time: 15 hrs. 0 mins. 0 sec.). (Books of History Chronicles: Bk. 0). (ENG.). 2009. 25.89 (978-1-60814-518-8(2)); audio compact disk 36.99 (978-1-59859-579-6(2)) Oasis Audio.

Green Acres: Joshua 158:16-19. Ed Young. 1991. 4.95 (978-0-7417-1849-5(9), 849) Win Walk.

Green Algae & Bubble Gum Wars. unabr. ed. Annie Bryant. (Beacon Street Girls Ser.: No. 13). (ENG.). (J). (gr. 4). 2008. audio compact disk 19.95 (978-0-7393-7323-1(4), Listening Lib) Pub: Random Audio Pubg. Dist(s): Random

Green & Pleasant Land. unabr. ed. Teresa Crane. Narrated by Briony Sykes. 12 cass. (Running Time: 16 hrs. 30 mins.). 1999. 101.00 (978-1-84197-017-2(4), H1017E7) Recorded Bks.
England in the 1920's & the aftermath of The Great War brings the dawning of new hopes. In this time of turbulent change & political unrest, the lives of three women become inextricably intertwined. From frivolous twenties London & the elegant country house parties, to the lush & tropical hills of madeira, this is a story told with warmth & humour. A magnificent saga of three women & their search for happiness in a world of changing values & new freedoms.

Green & Pleasant Land. unabr. ed. Teresa Crane. Narrated by Briony Sykes. 15 CDs. (Running Time: 16 hrs. 30 mins.). 1999. audio compact disk 127.00 (978-1-84197-095-0(6), C1127E7) Recorded Bks.
England in the 1920s & the aftermath of The Great War bring the dawning of new hopes. In this time of turbulent change & political unrest, the lives of three women become inextricably intertwined.

Green & Pleasant Land, Set. unabr. ed. Teresa Crane. Narrated by Briony Sykes. 12 cass. 1999. 101.00 (H1017K4, Clipper Audio) Recorded Bks.

Green Bananas. (gr. k-3). 10.00 (978-0-7635-6369-1(2)) Rigby Educ.

Green Bay Tree. unabr. ed. Louis Bromfield. Read by Flo Gibson. 7 cass. (Running Time: 10 hrs.). (gr. 8 up). 1999. 25.95 (978-1-55685-591-7(5)) Audio Bk Con.
Follow beautiful Lily Shane's life & loves. As a grandchild of pioneers see her develop into a woman of the world.

Green Behind the Ears. unabr. ed. Faith Addis. Narrated by Briony Sykes. 6 cass. (Running Time: 7 hrs. 30 mins.). 1999. 53.00 (978-1-84197-016-5(6), H1016) Recorded Bks.
Faith & Brian & their ups & downs as they welcome their young guests to their farmhouse set amidst the beautiful Devon Countryside. When Brian & Faith Addis do their sums at the end of their first year providing country holidays for children, they find they are running at a small but steady loss. Whilst Brian is already into a new project, raising pansies for seed, Faith is not yet ready to give up. A choice has to be made however & the Addis's opt for the pansies. Arming themselves with such skills as hedge-laying & clamping, it's time to give peace & horticulture a chance.

Green Bottle: One Cop's War Against the Mob. unabr. ed. Stuart M. Kaminsky. Read by Nick Sullivan. 8 vols. (Running Time: 9 hr. 30 min.). (Rockford Files Ser.). 1999. bk. 69.95 (978-0-7927-2300-4(7), CSL 189, Chivers Sound Lib) AudioGO.
Jim Rockford is expecting a quiet day of lazing around the beach & evading the bill collectors. Lucky for him, he's just found a missing green bottle for a rich & very grateful client. That takes care of last month's bills. But it's not long before Rockford is mixed up in a case of stolen property with thugs who would like to rearrange his anatomy. And it all leads back to the case of the green bottle, which wasn't quite as simple as it looked.

Green Bottle: One Cop's War Against the Mob. unabr. ed. Stuart M. Kaminsky. Read by Nick Sullivan. 8 cass. (Running Time: 12 hrs.). (Rockford Files Ser.). 2000. 59.95 (CSL 189) Pub: Chivers Audio Bks GBR. Dist(s): AudioGO
Jim Rockford is spending a quiet day of lazing around the beach and evading the bill collectors. Lucky for him, he's just found a missing green bottle for a rich and very grateful client. That takes care of last month's bills. But it's not long before Rockford is mixed up in a case of stolen property with thugs who would like to rearrange his anatomy. And it all leads back to the case of the green bottle, which wasn't quite as simple as it looked.

***Green Brain.** unabr. ed. Frank Herbert. Narrated by Scott Brick. (Running Time: 7 hrs. 0 mins. 0 sec.). (ENG.). 2010. 19.99 (978-1-4001-6488-2(5)); 14.99 (978-1-4001-8488-0(6)); audio compact disk 29.99 (978-1-4001-1488-7(8)) Pub: Tantor Media. Dist(s): IngramPubServ

***Green Brain (Library Edition)** unabr. ed. Frank Herbert. Narrated by Scott Brick. (Running Time: 7 hrs. 0 mins. 0 sec.). (ENG.). 2010. audio compact disk 59.99 (978-1-4001-4488-4(4)) Pub: Tantor Media. Dist(s): IngramPubServ

Green Building Materials in Italy: A Strategic Reference 2006. Compiled by Icon Group International, Inc. Staff. 2007. ring bd. 195.00 (978-0-497-36039-9(X)) Icon Grp.

***Green Business Practices for Dummies.** abr. ed. Lisa Swallow. (ENG.). 2009. (978-0-06-176483-7(3), Harper Audio); (978-0-06-176482-0(5), Harper Audio) HarperCollins Pubs.

***Green Cleaning for Dummies.** abr. ed. Elizabeth Goldsmith & Betsy Sheldon. (ENG.). 2008. (978-0-06-176492-9(2), Harper Audio); (978-0-06-176493-6(0), Harper Audio) HarperCollins Pubs.

Green Darkness, Pt. 1. unabr. ed. Anya Seton. Read by Penelope Dellaporta. 9 cass. (Running Time: 13 hrs. 30 min.). Incl. Pt. 2. Green Darkness. 8 cass. (Running Time: 12 hrs.). Anya Seton. Read by Penelope Dellaporta. 1979. 64.00 (1184-B); 1979. 72.00 (978-0-7366-0182-5(1), 1184-A) Books on Tape.
This story of troubled love takes place simultaneously during 2 periods of time: today & 400 years ago. We meet Richard & Celia Marsdon, an attractive young couple, whose family traces its lineage back to medieval England. Richard's growing depression creates a crisis in Celia, & she falls desperately ill. Lying unconscious & near death, Celia's spirit journeys backward to a time four centuries earlier when another Celia loved Marsdon.

Green Day: The Unauthorized Biography of Green Day. Ben Graham. 1 CD. (Running Time: 1 hr.). (Maximum Ser.). (ENG.). 2001. audio compact disk 14.95 (978-1-84240-127-9(0)) Pub: Chrome Dreams GBR. Dist(s): IPG Chicago

Green Door see Favorite Stories by O. Henry

Green Eagle Score. collector's ed. Richard Stark, pseud. Read by Michael Kramer. 4 cass. (Running Time: 6 hrs.). 2000. 32.00 (978-0-7366-5586-6(7)) Books on Tape.
Parker has never said no to a challenge as long as it paid off in big bills. So when an ex-con spotted a real honey of a heist, Parker wasn't worried that the money was in a safe. That the safe was in a busy office. Or that the office was smack in the middle of an Air Force base guarded by M.P.s holding very nasty guns. Parker had the brains to plan the caper & the guts to pull it off. But he didn't have the heart to kill a nervous dame. And nothing could throw a curve into this score like a fidgety female or a screwball so unexpected it could take Parker right out of the game.

***Green Eagle Score.** unabr. ed. Richard Stark, pseud. Narrated by Stephen R. Thorne. 4 CDs. (Running Time: 4 hrs. 39 mns.). 2010. audio compact disk 59.95 (978-0-7927-7142-5(7)) AudioGO.

***Green Eagle Score: A Parker Novel.** Richard Stark. Narrated by Stephen Thorne. (Running Time: 4 hrs. 39 mins. 0 sec.). (ENG.). 2011. audio compact disk 19.95 (978-1-60998-137-2(5)) Pub: AudioGO. Dist(s): Perseus Dist

Green Eggs & Ham. Dr. Seuss. (J). 1960. 17.68 (978-0-394-12953-2(9)) SRA McGraw.

Green Eggs & Ham & Other Servings of Dr. Seuss. unabr. ed. Dr. Seuss. (Running Time: 2 hrs. 15 mins.). (ENG.). (J). (ps). 2003. audio compact disk 19.99 (978-0-8072-1992-8(4), Listening Lib) Pub: Random Audio Pubg. Dist(s): Random

Green Eggs & Ham & Other Servings of Dr. Seuss. unabr. collector's ed. Dr. Seuss. 2 cass. (Running Time: 55 mins.). (J). (ps-3). 2005. 23.00 (978-0-307-24671-4(X), BksonTape); audio compact disk 20.40 (978-0-307-24672-1(8), BksonTape) Pub: Random Audio Pubg. Dist(s): NetLibrary CO
9 complete stories at a great price! Featuring: Green Eggs and Ham read by Jason Alexander; One Fish Two Fish Red Fish Blue Fish read by David Hyde Pierce; Oh, the Thinks You Can Think! read by Michael McKean; I'm Not Going to Get Up Today read by Jason Alexander; Oh Say Can You

Say? read by Michael McKean; Fox in Socks read by David Hype Pierce;I Can Read with My Eyes Shut read by Michael McKean;Hop on Pop read by David Hype Pierce; Dr. Seuss's ABC read by Jason Alexander.

***Green-Eyed Demon.** unabr. ed. Jaye Wells. Narrated by Not Yet Named. (Running Time: 10 hrs. 0 mins.). (Sabina Kane Ser.). 2011. 24.99 (978-1-4001-6904-7(6)); 16.99 (978-1-4001-8904-5(7)); 34.99 (978-1-4001-1904-2(9)) Tantor Media.

***Green-Eyed Demon (Library Edition)** unabr. ed. Jaye Wells. Narrated by Not Yet Named. (Running Time: 10 hrs. 0 mins.). (Sabina Kane Ser.). 2011. 83.99 (978-1-4001-4904-9(5)); 34.99 (978-1-4001-9904-4(2)) Tantor Media.

***Green for Life: Audio Book.** Boutenko. (ENG.). 2010. 24.95 (978-0-9704819-0-0(X)) Raw Family.

Green Gardens of God: Memories of Extraordinary American Places. Allen L. Scarbrough. Narrated by Tom Power. (ENG.). 2007. audio compact disk 15.95 (978-1-60031-023-2(0)) Spoken Books.

Green Glass Sea. unabr. ed. Ellen Klages. Narrated by Julie Dretzin. 7 cass. (Running Time: 7 hrs. 30 mins.). (J). (gr. 4 up). 2007. 67.75 (978-1-4281-4634-1(2)); audio compact disk 97.75 (978-1-4281-4639-6(3)) Recorded Bks.

Green Grass Grew All Around. Transcribed by Dix Bruce. 1998. pap. bk. 22.95 (978-0-7866-4383-7(8), 96706CDP) Mel Bay.

Green Grass Grew All Around: Family Folk Songs. Perf. by Phil Rosenthal. 1 cass. (Running Time: 40 min.). (J). (ps-5). 1995. 9.98 (978-1-879305-18-2(6), AM-C-116); audio compact disk 14.98 (978-1-879305-19-9(4), AM-CD-5116) Am Melody.
A lively collection of new & old folk songs performed by acclaimed singer-musician Phil Rosenthal & his talented family. The spirited performances invite singing along.

Green Grass, Running Water. abr. ed. Thomas King. Narrated by Thomas King. Prod. by CBC Radio Staff. 4 cass. (Running Time: 5 hrs.). (Between the Covers Collection). (ENG.). 1998. 24.95 (978-0-86492-244-1(2)) Goose Ln Eds CAN.
When four ancient Natives escape from a mental hospital & set out to fix the world, they get no further than Blossom, Alberta.

Green Grow the Victims. Jeanne M. Dams. 5 cass. (Running Time: 7 hrs. 30 min.). (Hilda Johansson Mystery Ser.: Bk. 3). 2002. 40.00 (978-0-7366-8629-7(0)) Books on Tape.
Turn-of-the-century housekeeper/detective Hilda Johansson must solve both a disappearance and a murder.

Green Grow the Victims. Jeanne M. Dams. (Hilda Johansson Mystery Ser.: Bk. 3). 2002. audio compact disk 48.00 (978-0-7366-8735-5(1)) Books on Tape.

Green Hell: How Environmentalists Plan to Control Your Life & What You Can Do to Stop Them. unabr. ed. Steven Milloy. (Running Time: 8 hrs. 0 mins.). 2009. audio compact disk 24.95 (978-1-4332-7585-2(6)) Blckstn Audio.

Green Hell: How Environmentalists Plan to Control Your Life & What You Can Do to Stop Them. unabr. ed. Steven Milloy. (Running Time: 8 hrs. 0 mins.). (ENG.). 2009. 29.95 (978-1-4332-7586-9(4)); 54.95 (978-1-4332-7582-1(1)); audio compact disk 70.00 (978-1-4332-7583-8(X)) Blckstn Audio.

Green Helmet. unabr. ed. Jon Cleary. 4 cass. (Sound Ser.). 2004. 44.95 (978-1-85496-043-6(1)) Pub: UlverLrgPrint GBR. Dist(s): Ulverscroft US

Green Helmet, unabr. ed. Jon Cleary. Read by Gordon Griffin. 4 cass. (Running Time: 6 hrs.). 1999. 44.95 (60431) Pub: Soundings Ltd GBR. Dist(s): Ulverscroft US

Green Hills of Africa. unabr. ed. Ernest Hemingway. Read by Alexander Adams. 6 cass. (Running Time: 9 hrs.). 2001. 29.95 (978-0-7366-5675-7(8)) Books on Tape.
The story of two months Hemingway spent on safari in East Africa.

Green Hills of Africa. unabr. ed. Ernest Hemingway. Read by Josh Lucas. 2006. 17.95 (978-0-7435-6356-7(5), Audioworks); audio compact disk 29.95 (978-0-7435-6444-1(8)) Pub: S&S Audio. Dist(s): S and S Inc

Green Hills of Africa. unabr. collector's ed. Ernest Hemingway. Read by Wolfram Kandinsky. 6 cass. (Running Time: 9 hrs.). 1989. 48.00 (978-0-7366-1661-4(6), 2511) Books on Tape.
In the winter of 1933 Ernest Hemingway & his wife Pauline set out on a two-month safari in the big-game country of East Africa, camping out on the great Serengeti Plain at the foot of Mount Kilimanjaro. "I had quite a trip," he told his friend Philip Percival, & he later used these experiences to create Green Hills of Africa. Rich in description & refreshingly alive to the character of the country, it is one of Hemingway's most revealing aesthetic statements. His writing, as Carl Van Doren remarked, "sings like poetry without ever ceasing to be prose, easy, intricate & magical".

Green Hills of Earth see SF Soundbook

Green Hills of Earth. unabr. ed. Robert A. Heinlein. Read by Tom Weiner. (Running Time: 9 hrs. NaN mins.). 2009. 29.95 (978-0-7861-7415-7(3)); audio compact disk 59.95 (978-0-7861-4651-2(6)); audio compact disk 80.00 (978-0-7861-6783-8(1)) Blckstn Audio.

Green Hills of Earth. unabr. ed. Robert A. Heinlein. 1 cass. (Running Time: 57 min.). Dramatization. 12.95 (#491) J Norton Pubs.
This is a radio dramatization of Robert Heinlein's story. An engineer, blinded in an accident, turns to singing & composing, & soon becomes a sort of outer-space hero.

Green Hills of Earth. unabr. collector's ed. Robert A. Heinlein. Read by Paul Shay. 8 cass. (Running Time: 8 hrs.). 1988. 48.00 (978-0-7366-1289-0(0), 2196) Books on Tape.
Science fiction short stories; includes "Deliah & the Space-Rigger", "The Black Pits of Luna", "We Also Walk Dogs", & many others.

Green hills of Earth: Robert heinlein's Story. (ENG.). 2008. audio compact disk 12.95 (978-1-57970-517-6(0), Audio-For) J Norton Pubs.

Green Hornet. 1 CD. (Running Time: 1 hr.). Dramatization. (Old-Time Radio Blockbusters Ser.). 2002. audio compact disk 4.98 (978-1-57019-394-1(0), OTR7705) Pub: Radio Spirits. Dist(s): AudioGO
Incl.: "Paid in Full," and "Escape for Revenge.".

Green Hornet. Created by Radio Spirits. (Running Time: 10800 sec.). 2004. 9.98 (978-1-57019-638-6(9)) Radio Spirits.

Green Hornet. unabr. ed. 1 cass. (Running Time: 50 min.). Incl. Green Hornet: Clenched Fist. (#750); Green Hornet: Ghost Who Talked Too Much. (#750); 12.95 (#750) J Norton Pubs.
Two episodes from the popular radio suspense series. He hunts the biggest of all game-racketeers, saboteurs & public enemies who try to destroy America. They feel the weight of the law by the sting of the Green Hornet.

Green Hornet. 1998th ed. 6 cass. (Running Time: 6 hrs.). 1998. bk. 24.98 (4345) Radio Spirits.

Green Hornet, Vol. 1. collector's ed. 6 cass. (Running Time: 9 hrs.). 1998. bk. 34.98 (4391) Radio Spirits.
The Green Hornet was really Britt Reid, daring young publisher of the Daily Sentinel, who, along with his faithful valet Kato, matched wits with the underworld. 18 thrill-packed adventures that ran between the 1930s and 1945.

Green Hornet, Vol. 2. collector's ed. Created by George W. Trendle. 6 cass. (Running Time: 9 hrs.). 2000. bk. 34.98 (4547) Radio Spirits.
Britt Reid, grandnephew of the Lone Ranger and publisher of the Daily Sentinel newspaper is the infamous Green Hornet. "The Green Hornet" buzzed into homes across the country promoting law and order, while staying just one step ahead of the law himself. Enjoy 18 crime-busting adventures.

Green Hornet: Clenched Fist see Green Hornet

Green Hornet: Ghost Who Talked Too Much see Green Hornet

Green Hornet: Paid in Full & Escape for Revenge. 1 CD. (Running Time: 1 hr.). (Old-Time Radio Blockbusters Ser.). 2001. audio compact disk 4.98 (7705) Radio Spirits.

Green Hornet: Political Racket & Parking Lot Racket. 1 cass. (Running Time: 1 hr.). 2001. 6.98 (2477) Radio Spirits.

Green Hornet: Put it on Ice & A Pair of Nylons. 1 cass. (Running Time: 1 hr.). 2001. 6.98 (2282) Radio Spirits.

Green Hornet: Road to Ruin & A Matter of Evidence. 1 cass. (Running Time: 1 hr.). 2001. 6.98 (2015) Radio Spirits.

Green Hornet: Spies & Rackets. Perf. by Various. (ENG.). 2009. audio compact disk 39.98 (978-1-57019-889-2(6)) Radio Spirits.

***Green Hornet: The Biggest Game.** Perf. by Al Hodge & Raymond Toyo. 2010. audio compact disk 39.98 (978-1-57019-918-9(3)) Radio Spirits.

Green Hornet: The Letter & Youth Takes the Headlines. 1 cass. (Running Time: 1 hr.). 2001. 6.98 (2417) Radio Spirits.

Green Hornet: The Quiz Program Clue & Giuseppi's Secret. 1 cass. (Running Time: 1 hr.). 2001. 6.98 (2536) Radio Spirits.

Green Hornet: The Wrapped Book & The Prodigal Brother. 1 cass. (Running Time: 1 hr.). 2001. 6.98 (2518) Radio Spirits.

Green Hour. Frederic Tuten. Narrated by Celeste Lawson. (Running Time: 7 hrs.). 2003. 27.95 (978-1-59912-669-2(9)) Iofy Corp.

Green Hour. unabr. ed. Frederic Tuten. Read by Celeste Lawson. 6 CDs. (Running Time: 7 hrs.). 2003. audio compact disk 48.00 (978-0-7861-9133-8(3), 3098); 39.95 (978-0-7861-2463-3(6), 3098) Blckstn Audio.
Tells the story of Dominique, an art historian who cannot choose between two men who embody the critical schism in her life: unquenchable idealism and material happiness.

Green House: Healing Beyond Medicine Series. Joseph Michael Levry. (ENG.). 2001. 19.00 (978-1-885562-10-4(1)) Root Light.

Green Jasper. K. M. Grant. 8 cass. (YA). 2006. 59.75 (978-1-4193-9465-2(7)); audio compact disk 74.75 (978-1-4193-9470-6(3)) Recorded Bks.

Green Knight. unabr. ed. Iris Murdoch. Read by Eva Haddon. 16 cass. (Running Time: 21 hrs.). 1996. 104.95 (978-1-85695-469-3(2), 950912) Pub: ISIS Audio GBR. Dist(s): Ulverscroft US
When defending himself with his umbrella against a nocturnal assailant, Professor Lucas Graffe unintentionally kills him.

Green Latern - Hero's Quest: Justice League of America. Dennis O'Neil. 2009. audio compact disk 19.99 (978-1-59950-540-4(1)) GraphicAudio.

Green Leaf in Drought Time: James 1:1-8, 619. Ed Young. 1987. 4.95 (978-0-7417-1619-4(4), 619) Win Walk.

***Green Like God: Unlocking the Divine Plan for Our Planet.** unabr. ed. Jonathan Merritt. Narrated by Jonathan Merritt. (Running Time: 5 hrs. 13 mins. 17 sec.). (ENG.). 2010. 17.49 (978-1-60814-668-0(5)); audio compact disk 24.99 (978-1-59859-717-2(5)) Oasis Audio.

Green Living. abr. ed. Liz Barclay et al. Read by Michael Grosvenor & Brett Barry. 3 CDs. (Running Time: 3 hrs.). 2008. audio compact disk 14.95 (978-0-06-167283-5(1), Harper Audio) HarperCollins Pubs.

***Green Living for Dummies.** abr. ed. Liz Barclay. Read by Brett Barry & Michael Grosvenor. (ENG.). 2008. (978-0-06-170732-2(5)); (978-0-06-170734-6(1)) HarperCollins Pubs.

Green Living for Dummies. abr. ed. Yvonne Jeffery et al. Read by Brett Barry. (Playaway Adult Nonfiction Ser.). (ENG.). 2009. 59.99 (978-1-60812-582-1(3)) Find a World.

***Green Mama: The Guilt-Free Guide to Helping You & Your Kids Save the Planet.** Tracey Bianchi. (Running Time: 5 hrs. 29 mins. 53 sec.). (ENG.). 2010. 13.99 (978-0-310-39573-7(9)) Zondervan.

Green Man. 2004. pap. bk. 14.95 (978-1-56008-207-1(0)); 8.95 (978-0-89719-905-6(7)); cass. & flmstrp 30.00 (978-0-89719-505-8(1)) Weston Woods.

Green Man. Kingsley Amis. Read by Steven Pacey. 6 cass. (Running Time: 9 hrs.). 2002. 54.95 (978-0-7540-0689-3(1), CAB 2111) AudioGO.

Green Man. Kate Sedley. 2009. 69.95 (978-1-4079-0650-8(X)); audio compact disk 84.95 (978-1-4079-0651-5(8)) Pub: Soundings Ltd GBR. Dist(s): Ulverscroft US

Green Man, unabr. collector's ed. Kingsley Amis. Read by Richard Green. 7 cass. (Running Time: 7 hrs.). 1981. 42.00 (978-0-7366-0233-4(X), 1229) Books on Tape.
This ghost story takes place in an English medieval coaching inn that has been converted into a Class-A restaurant called "The Green Man".

Green Mansions. W. H. Hudson. Read by Patrick Treadway. 8 cass. (Running Time: 9 hrs.). 1989. 49.95 (978-1-55686-293-9(8), 293) Books in Motion.
The Indians of the South American jungle want Mr. Abel to kill the beautiful girl in the forest named Rima. She possessed the ability to sooth the most venomous & irritable snakes by her mere presence. The Indians thought that she was evil, Mr. Abel wasn't so sure.

Green Mansions. abr. ed. W. H. Hudson. Read by Brian Parry & Jill Daly. Ed. by Beth Baxter. 2 cass. (Running Time: 3 hrs.). 1993. 12.95 (978-1-882071-06-7(9), 008) B-B Audio.
An astonishing journey into the green dark of the South American rain forests, where our adventurer falls in love with Rima, a girl of a magnificent race. Join our hero on this trip as his love leads him to discover the greatest joy as well as the darkes.

Green Mansions. unabr. ed. W. H. Hudson. Read by Walter Zimmerman & Jim Killavey. 6 cass. (Running Time: 9 hrs.). Dramatization. 1982. 29.00 incl. album. (C-69) Jimcin Record.
Exotic love story of mysterious Rima.

Green Mansions. unabr. ed. W.H. Hudson. Read by Flo Gibson. 6 cass. (Running Time: 8 hrs. 10 min.). 1998. 24.95 (978-1-55685-557-3(5)) Audio Bk Con.
A haunting tale of a Venezuelan's love for Rima, the bird girl & descendant of a mysterious race, who lives in the heart of the jungle.

Green Mansions. unabr. collector's ed. W. H. Hudson. Read by Jim Roberts. 6 cass. (Running Time: 9 hrs.). 1982. 48.00 (978-0-7366-3862-3(8), 9069) Books on Tape.
Based on an Indian legend, "Green Mansions" is a memorable romance of the jungle.

Green Mars. unabr. ed. Kim Stanley Robinson. Narrated by Richard Ferrone. 20 cass. (Running Time: 27 hrs. 45 mins.). 2001. 167.00 (978-0-7887-4983-4(8), 96114E7) Recorded Bks.
The decisions & actions of a fascinating diverse group of colonists will ultimately determine whether Mars will simply be a sanctuary for scientists, a source of raw materials for Earth or something else.

Green Meadow Stream. Bernie Krause. 1 cass. (Running Time: 60 min.). (Wild Sanctuary Ser.). 1994. audio compact disk 15.95 CD. (2320, Creativ Pub) Quayside.
Sierra Nevada mountains streams flow gently, wildflowers sway in the breeze, & songbirds sing the praises of a glorious summer day.

Green Meadow Stream. Bernie Krause. 1 cass. (Running Time: 60 min.). (Wild Sanctuary Ser.). 1994. 9.95 (2319, NrthWrd Bks) TandN Child.

Green Metropolis: What the City Can Teach the Country about True Sustainability. unabr. ed. David Owen. Narrated by Patrick G. Lawlor. 1 MP3-CD. (Running Time: 10 hrs. 0 mins. 0 sec.). (ENG.). 2009. 24.99 (978-1-4001-6371-7(4)); audio compact disk 34.99 (978-1-4001-1371-2(7)); audio compact disk 69.99 (978-1-4001-4371-9(3)) Pub: Tantor Media. Dist(s): IngramPubServ

***Green Metropolis: What the City Can Teach the Country about True Sustainability.** unabr. ed. David Owen. Narrated by Patrick G. Lawlor. (Running Time: 10 hrs. 0 mins.). 2009. 16.99 (978-1-4001-8371-5(5)) Tantor Media.

Green Mile. abr. ed. Stephen King & Frank Muller. 2006. 29.95 (978-0-7435-6334-5(4), Audioworks) Pub: S&S Audio. Dist(s): S and S Inc

Green Mile. unabr. ed. Stephen King. Read by Frank Muller. 12 CDs. (Running Time: 18 hrs.). 2001. audio compact disk 49.95 Books on Tape.
Welcome to Cold Mountain Penitentiary, home to the Depression-worn men of E Block. Convicted killers all, each awaits his turn to walk the Green Mile, keeping a date with "Old Sparky," Cold Mountain's electric chair. Prison guard Paul Edgecombe has seen his share of oddities in his years working the Mile. But he's never seen anyone like John Coffey, a man with the body of a giant and the mind of a child, condemned for a crime terrifying in its violence and shocking in its depravity. In this place of ultimate retribution, Edgecombe is about to discover the terrible, wondrous truth about Coffey, a truth that will challenge his most cherished beliefs...and yours.

Green Mile. unabr. abr. ed. Stephen King. Read by Frank Muller. 12 CDs. (Running Time: 140 hrs. 0 mins. 0 sec.). (ENG.). 1999. audio compact disk 49.95 (978-0-671-04725-2(6), Audioworks) Pub: S&S Audio. Dist(s): S and S Inc
Here this history-making serial novel - from cliffhanger to cliffhanger - in its entirety. When it first appeared, one volume per month, Stephen King's The Green Mile was an unprecedented publishing triumph: all six volumes ended up on the New York Times bestseller list - simultaneously - and delighted millions of fans the world over. Welcome to Cold Mountain Penitentiary, home to the Depression-worn men of E Block. Convicted killers all, each awaits his turn to walk the Green Mile, keeping a date with "Old Sparky," Cold Mountain's electric chair. Prison guard Paul Edgecombe has seen his share of oddities in his years working the Mile. But he's never seen anyone like John Coffey, a man with the body of a giant and the mind of a child, condemned for a crime terrifying in its violence and shocking in its depravity. In this place of ultimate retribution, Edgecombe is about to discover the terrible, wondrous truth about Coffey, a truth that will challenge his most cherished beliefs...and yours.

***Green Mill Murder.** unabr. ed. Kerry Greenwood. Read by Stephanie Daniel. (Running Time: 6 hrs. 23 mins.). (Phryne Fisher Mystery: Ser.). 2010. audio compact disk 77.95 (978-1-74214-681-2(3), 9781742146812) Pub: Bolinda Pubng AUS. Dist(s): Bolinda Pub Inc

Green Money: A Starletta Duvall Mystery. Judith Smith-Levin. Narrated by Andrea Johnson. 7 cass. (Running Time: 9 hrs.). 62.00 (978-1-4025-0980-3(4)) Recorded Bks.

Green Monster. unabr. ed. Rick Shefchik. (Running Time: 6.5 hrs. NaN mins.). 2008. 29.95 (978-1-4332-5231-0(7)); 44.95 (978-1-4332-5229-7(5)); audio compact disk 60.00 (978-1-4332-5230-3(9)) Blckstn Audio.

Green Pastures: Scripture Songs. TRILOGY Scripture Songs. (ENG.). 2007. audio compact disk 15.95 (978-0-9817124-8-2(7)) Trilogy Script.

Green Politics. Fritjof Capra. 5 cass. 45.00 (OC23W) Sound Horizons AV.

Green Recovery: Get Lean, Get Smart, & Emerge from the Downturn on Top. unabr. ed. Andrew S. Winston. Read by Andrew S. Winston. (Running Time: 3 hrs. 30 mins.). (ENG.). 2009. 17.98 (978-1-59659-438-8(1), GildAudio) Pub: Gildan Media. Dist(s): HachBkGrp

Green Recovery: Get Lean, Get Smart, & Emerge from the Downturn on Top. unabr. ed. Andrew S. Winston. Read by Andrew S. Winston. (Running Time: 3 hrs. 30 mins.). (ENG.). 2009. audio compact disk 19.98 (978-1-59659-398-5(9), GildAudio) Pub: Gildan Media. Dist(s): HachBkGrp

Green Revolution. Judy Leonard. 1 cass. (Running Time: 39 min.). (Nature's Lullabyes Ser.). (J). 1994. 9.95 (2752, NrthWrd Bks) TandN Child.
This up-beat tape entices kids to care about the Earth with songs about ecology, nature, & recycling. Song lyrics are enclosed so children can sing along with the instrumental versions of the songs on Side Two. Activity book included.

***Green Ring Conspiracy.** AIO Team. (Adventures in Odyssey Ser.). (ENG.). (J). 2011. audio compact disk 24.99 (978-1-58997-652-8(5)) Tyndale Hse.

Green Ripper. unabr. ed. John D. MacDonald. Read by Michael Prichard. 7 cass. (Running Time: 10 hrs.). (Travis McGee Ser.: Vol. 18). 2001. 29.95 (978-0-7366-6785-2(7)) Books on Tape.
When McGee's true love is murdered, it comes close to finishing him.

Green Ripper. unabr. collector's ed. John D. MacDonald. Read by Michael Prichard. 7 cass. (Running Time: 7 hrs.). (Travis McGee Ser.: Vol. 18). 1980. 42.00 (978-0-7366-0474-1(X), 1449) Books on Tape.
In this Travis McGee adventure our hero falls deeply in love with Gretel, his live-aboard boatmate. But this woman who means everything to him is horribly & impersonally murdered. Desperate & half-demented, McGee sets out to find the killers.

Green River Rising. abr. ed. Tim Willocks. Read by Dick Hill. 2 cass. (Running Time: 3 hrs.). 2000. 7.95 (978-1-57815-034-2(5), 1051, Media Bks Audio) Media Bks NJ.
The thrilling, dark, violent & sexy story of one man's moral choices in an amoral maelstrom of prison rioting.

Green River, Running Red: The Real Story of the Green River Killer - America's Deadliest Serial Murderer. abr. ed. Ann Rule. Read by Michele Pawk. 2004. 15.95 (978-0-7435-4899-1(X)) Pub: S&S Audio. Dist(s): S and S Inc

Green River, Running Red: The Real Story of the Green River Killer - America's Deadliest Serial Murderer. abr. ed. Ann Rule. Read by Michele Pawk. (Running Time: 6 hrs. 0 mins. 0 sec.). (ENG.). 2007. audio compact disk 14.95 (978-0-7435-6107-5(4)) Pub: S&S Audio. Dist(s): S and S Inc

Green River, Running Red: The Real Story of the Green River Killer - America's Deadliest Serial Murderer. unabr. ed. Ann Rule. Narrated by Barbara Caruso. 14 cass. (Running Time: 20 hrs.). 2005. 109.75 (978-1-4193-0911-3(0), 97886) Recorded Bks.

Green River Trail, abr. ed. Ralph Compton. Read by Jim Gough. 4 cass. (Running Time: 6 hrs.). (Trail Drive Ser.: Vol. 13). 2000. 24.95 (978-1-890990-27-5(2), 99027) Otis Audio.
The year was 1853. For a handful of cowboys turned California gold rushers, it was time to go home. Then Lonnie Kilgore & his fellow Texans met Western legend & former mountain man Jim Bridger, who told them of a lush range waiting to be claimed in Northern Utah. Now, the Texans have purchased land on the Green River & come to San Antonio to gather up some longhorns. But with Indian trouble, law trouble, & woman trouble along for the ride, the cowboys are finding out the truth about this paradise: to live on land you bought & paid for, you have to be willing to die.

Green Smoke. Rosemary Manning. (J). 1992. 24.95 (978-0-8161-9242-7(1), Macmillan Ref) Gale.

Green Stick. unabr. ed. Malcolm Muggeridge. Read by Frederick Davidson. 10 cass. (Running Time: 14 hrs. 30 mins.). (Chronicles of Wasted Time Ser.: 1). 1989. 69.95 (978-0-7861-0042-2(7), 1041) Blckstn Audio.
The son of a pioneer socialist, as a youth the author embraced utopian socialism & Soviet communism. Later, serving as the Manchester Guardian's man in Moscow, his leftest verve vanished. When his editor refused to print his expose of the Russian famine in which millions were to perish, he left Russia. His descriptions are vibrant & his criticism of modern phenomena is severe.

Green Stick, Chronicle 1. unabr. ed. Malcolm Muggeridge. Read by Frederick Davidson. 10 cass. (Running Time: 1 hr. 30 min. per cass.). 69.95 Set. (1041) Blckstn Audio.
Through scores of intellectual, social, political, & religious endeavors, Muggeridge's life touched the heart of 20th century history. Chronicles the time he wasted in the leftist intellectual pursuits of his youth.

Green Tea see Classic Ghost Stories, Vol. 1, A Collection

Green Tea. 1980. (C-30) Jimcin Record.

Green Tea. unabr. ed. J. Sheridan Le Fanu. Read by Walter Covell. 1 cass. (Running Time: 82 min.). Dramatization. 1982. 7.95 (S-20) Jimcin Record.
Chilling tale Of Strange & awful visions.

Green Tea & Squire Toby's Will. unabr. ed. J. Sheridan Le Fanu. Read by Flo Gibson. 2 cass. (Running Time: 2 hrs. 34 mins.). 2001. vinyl bd. 14.95 (978-1-55685-664-8(4)) Audio Bk Con.
First story is of an English cleric's bout with a malignant spectral presence. The second is a chilling tale of sibling rivalry over a disputed inheritance. Both are full of suspense & terror.

Green Team. Richard Marcinko. (Rogue Warrior Ser.). 2004. 10.95 (978-0-7435-4587-7(7)) Pub: S&S Audio. Dist(s): S and S Inc

Green Team. Richard Marcinko & John Weisman. Read by Richard Marcinko. 2 cass. (Running Time: 3 hrs.). 1998. 9.98 Set. (978-0-671-58141-1(4), 391487, Audioworks) Pub: S&S Audio. Dist(s): Lndmrk Audiobks
Espionage & intrigue.

Green Thumb. unabr. ed. Rob Thomas. Narrated by Johnny Heller. 4 cass. (Running Time: 5 hrs. 30 mins.). (gr. 7 up). 1999. 36.00 (978-0-7887-3524-0(1), 95879E7) Recorded Bks.

Green Thumb. unabr. ed. Rob Thomas. Narrated by Johnny Heller. 4 cass. (Running Time: 5 hrs. 30 mins.). (YA). 2000. pap. bk. 59.00 (978-0-7887-3641-4(8), 41007); 204.30 (978-0-7887-3671-1(X), 46974) Recorded Bks.
Grady Jacobs is a 13-year-old geek. He's also a brilliant botanist. So when he's invited to join an experimental reforestation project deep in the Amazon, he jumps at the chance to do some real research. There are deadly side effects to the project, though & Grady soon finds himself running for his life.

Green to Gold: How Smart Companies Use Environmental Strategy to Innovate, Create Value, & Build Competitive Advantage. unabr. ed. Daniel C. Esty & Andrew S. Winston. Read by Fred Stella. (Running Time: 11 hrs.). 2009. 39.97 (978-1-4233-7090-1(2), 9781423370901, BADLE); 39.97 (978-1-4233-7088-8(0), 9781423370888, Brinc Audio MP3 Lib); 24.99 (978-1-4233-7089-5(9), 9781423370895, BAD); 24.99 (978-1-4233-7087-1(2), 9781423370871, Brilliance MP3); audio compact disk 97.97 (978-1-4233-7086-4(4), 9781423370864, BriAudCD Unabrid); audio compact disk 29.99 (978-1-4233-7085-7(6), 9781423370857, Bril Audio CD Unabri) Brilliance Audio.

Green Trap. unabr. ed. Ben Bova. Read by Stefan Rudnicki & Kathe Mazure. (Running Time: 36000 sec.). 2007. 59.95 (978-1-4332-0616-0(1)); audio compact disk 29.95 (978-1-4332-0618-4(8)); audio compact disk 72.00 (978-1-4332-0617-7(X)) Blckstn Audio.

Green Woods: Upon a Celtic Path. Perf. by Paul Machlis. 1 cass., 1 CD. 7.98 (RM 8163); audio compact disk 14.38 CD Jewel box. (RM 8163) NewSound.

Greenaway see Sir John Betjeman Reading His Poetry

Greener Shore: A Novel of the Druids of Hibernia. unabr. ed. Morgan Llywelyn. Narrated by Simon Vance. 9 CDs. (Running Time: 12 hrs. 30 mins. 0 sec.). (ENG.). 2006. audio compact disk 69.99 (978-1-4001-3253-9(3)); audio compact disk 24.99 (978-1-4001-5253-7(4)); audio compact disk 34.99 (978-1-4001-0253-2(7)) Pub: Tantor Media. Dist(s): IngramPubServ
The sequel to Morgan Llywelyn's glorious Celtic fantasy, Druids, The Greener Shore is a beautifully told adventure story. After Julius Caesar triumphs over Gaul, the druid Ainvar and his three wives sail west to the brilliant green island of Hibernia. Here, Ainvar and his clan try to reestablish themselves. Ainvar's "senior" wife, Briga, provides constant wisdom and support for him. Strong, sensible, and with druidic powers of her own, Briga overcomes all obstacles. Readers who appreciate strong female characters will love this woman of the druids.

Greenlings, Set. unabr. ed. Redland Rose. Read by Elihu Blotnick. 3 cass. (Running Time: 4 hrs. 30 min.). 1999. 21.00 (978-0-915090-87-7(2), Calif St) Firefall.
A satire/celebration of the running scene at the Marina Green, San Francisco: lust propels a drifting sailor into the mysteries of motion, after he is overwhelmed by the beauty of a red-headed runner at rest.

Greenmantle. unabr. ed. John Buchan. Read by Robert Whitfield. 7 cass. (Running Time: 10 hrs.). 1996. 49.95 (978-0-7861-1015-5(5), 1793) Blckstn Audio.
Richard Hannay, South African mining engineer & war hero whom we met in "The Thirty-Nine Steps," travels across war torn Europe in search of a German plot & an Islamic Messiah. He is joined by three others: John S. Blenkiron, an American who is determined to battle the Kaiser; Peter Pienaar, an old Boer Scout; & the colorful Sandy Arbuthnot, who is modeled on Lawrence of Arabia. Disguised, they travel through Germany to Constantinople & the Russian border to confront their enemies: the hideous Stumm & the evil beauty Hilda von Einem. Their success or failure could change the outcome of the First World War.

Greensleeves. 1 cd. audio compact disk 10.98 (978-1-57908-396-0(X), 1669) Platinm Enter.

Greenway. unabr. ed. Jane Adams. 5 cass. 1998. 63.95 Set. (978-1-85903-119-3(6)) Pub: Magna Story GBR. Dist(s): Ulverscroft US

Greenwichtown: A Novel. Joyce Palmer. Narrated by Robin Miles. 7 cass. (Running Time: 9 hrs. 45 mins.). 62.00 (978-1-4025-1591-0(X)) Recorded Bks.

Greenwitch. unabr. ed. Susan Cooper. Read by Alex Jennings. 3 vols. (Running Time: 4 hrs. 24 mins.). (Dark Is Rising Sequence Ser.). (J). (gr. 4-7). 2004. 36.00 (978-0-8072-0664-5(4), Listening Lib) Random Audio Pubg.

***Greetings from Afghanistan, Send More Ammo: Dispatches from Taliban Country.** unabr. ed. Benjamin Tupper. Narrated by Johnny Heller. (Running Time: 5 hrs. 0 mins. 0 sec.). (ENG.). 2010. 19.99 (978-1-4001-6775-3(2)); 13.99 (978-1-4001-8775-1(3)); audio compact disk 59.99 (978-1-4001-4775-5(1)); audio compact disk 24.99 (978-1-4001-1775-8(5)) Pub: Tantor Media. Dist(s): IngramPubServ

Greg & Steve Readers Varity Pack. Ed. by Creative Teacing Press. (Sing & Read with Greg & Steve Ser.). (J). (ps-3). 2006. pap. bk. 56.87 (978-1-59198-421-4(1)) Creat Teach Pr.

Greg Iles: Mortal Fear, Spandau Phoenix, the Footprints of God. abr. ed. Greg Iles. (Running Time: 18 hrs.). 2008. audio compact disk 34.95 (978-1-4233-5240-2(8), 9781423352402) Brilliance Audio.

Greg Iles: The Quiet Game, Turning Angel, & Blood Memory. abr. ed. Greg Iles. Narrated by Dick Hill & Joyce Bean. (Running Time: 18 hrs.). 2006. audio compact disk 34.95 (978-1-4233-1680-0(0), 9781423316800, BACD) Brilliance Audio.
The Quiet Game: Penn Cage is no stranger to death. As a Houston prosecutor he sent sixteen men to death row, and watched seven of them die. But now, in the aftermath of his wife's death, the grief-stricken father packs up his four-year-old daughter, Annie, and returns to his hometown in search of healing. But peace is not what he finds there. After twenty years away, Penn is stunned to find his own family trapped in a web on intrigue and danger. Turning Angel: Turning Angel marks the long-awaited return of Penn Cage, the lawyer hero of The Quiet Game, and introduces Drew Elliott, the highly respected doctor who saved Penn's life in a hiking accident when they were boys. Drew and Penn sit on the school board of their alma mater, St. Stephen's Prep. When the nude body of a young female student is found, the entire community is shocked - but no one more than Penn, who discovers that his best friend was entangled in a passionate relationship with the girl and may be accused of her murder. Blood Memory: Catherine "Cat" Ferry is a forensic odontologist, a specialist in bite marks and the clues they provide. In a desperate effort to regain control over a life spiraling out of control, Cat retreats to her hometown of Natchez, Mississippi. But her family's secluded antebellum estate provides no sanctuary. Driven by fragments of her past, Cat attempts a forensic reconstruction of a decades-old crime.

Greg Iles CD Collection 3: Dead Sleep, Sleep No More, True Evil. abr. ed. Greg Iles. (Running Time: 18 hrs.). 2008. audio compact disk 36.95 (978-1-4233-5247-1(5), 9781423352471, BACD) Brilliance Audio.

Greg Iles CD Collection 4: Black Cross, 24 Hours, Third Degree. abr. ed. Greg Iles. (Running Time: 18 hrs.). 2009. audio compact disk 34.99 (978-1-4233-7967-6(5), 9781423379676, BACD) Brilliance Audio.

Gregg Braden Audio Collection: Awakening the Power of Spiritual Technology. Gregg Braden. 7 CDs. (Running Time: 30600 sec.). 2004. audio compact disk 39.95 (978-1-59179-251-2(7), W899D) Sounds True.

Gregg Shorthand: G-21 Series & G-23 Series. 22 cass. 1987. 270.00 set incl. student guide. Reinforcement Lrn.

Gregor & the Code of Claw. unabr. ed. Suzanne Collins. Read by Paul Boehmer. 7 CDs. (Running Time: 9 hrs.). (Underland Chronicles: Bk. 5). (J). (gr. 4-7). 2008. audio compact disk 55.00 (978-0-7393-6488-8(X), Listening Lib) Pub: Random Audio Pubg. Dist(s): Random
Everyone has been trying to keep Gregor from seeing the final prophecy, The Prophecy of Time. It says something awful: It calls for the warrior's death. The warrior being Gregor, of course. Now, an army of rats is quickly approaching and Gregor's mom and little sister, Boots, are still in Regalia. The entire existence of the Underland is in Gregor's hands and time is running out. There is a code that must be cracked, a new princess to contend with Gregor's burgeoning dark side, and a war designed to end all wars.In this suspenseful final installment in the acclaimed Underland Chronicles, Suzanne Collins unfolds the fate of the Underland and the great warrior, Gregor the Overlander, in a manner that can only be described as masterful.

Gregor & the Code of Claw. unabr. ed. Suzanne Collins. Read by Suzanne Collins. Read by Paul Boehmer. (Underland Chronicles: Bk. 5). (ENG.). (J). (gr. 4). 2008. audio compact disk 37.00 (978-0-7393-6486-4(3), Listening Lib) Pub: Random Audio Pubg. Dist(s): Random

Gregor & the Curse of the Warmbloods. unabr. ed. Suzanne Collins. Read by Paul Boehmer. 5 cass. (Running Time: 7 hrs. 48 mins.). (Underland Chronicles: Bk. 3). (J). (gr. 4-7). 2005. 40.00 (978-0-307-28088-6(8), Listening Lib); audio compact disk 46.75 (978-0-307-28378-8(X), Listening Lib) Pub: Random Audio Pubg. Dist(s): NetLibrary CO

Gregor & the Curse of the Warmbloods. unabr. ed. Suzanne Collins. Read by Paul Boehmer. 7 CDs. (Running Time: 28080 sec.). (Underland Chronicles: Bk. 3). (ENG.). (J). (gr. 5). 2005. audio compact disk 45.00 (978-0-307-28267-5(8), Listening Lib) Pub: Random Audio Pubg. Dist(s): Random

Gregor & the Marks of Secret. unabr. ed. Suzanne Collins. Read by Mark Bramhall & Paul Boehmer. (Underland Chronicles: Bk. 4). (ENG.). (J). (gr. 4). 2008. audio compact disk 39.00 (978-0-7393-6482-6(0), Listening Lib) Pub: Random Audio Pubg. Dist(s): Random

Gregor & the Prophecy of Bane. unabr. ed. Suzanne Collins. 4 cass. (Running Time: 6 hrs. 34 mins.). (Underland Chronicles: Bk. 2). (J). (gr. 4-8). 2005. 35.00 (978-0-307-20730-2(7), Listening Lib) Random Audio Pubg.
In this accessible, almost-cinematic fantasy, Gregor and his two-year-old sister fall into an amazing underground world. Taken in by people who have lived beneath the earth for centuries, the 11-year-old learns about the giant-sized talking creatures that also reside there, including bats, cockroaches, and vicious rats. Gregor just wants to get home, but a prophecy hints that he may be the "overlander" destined to save the humans from the warlike rodents. He is reluctant until he learns that his father, who disappeared from their New York City home a few years before, is a prisoner of the rats. Gregor is not an eager hero, but with common sense, quick thinking, and determination he grows into the role. His sister, who provides some comic relief, also plays a key part because of her ability to befriend creatures, especially the giant cockroaches. Plot threads unwind smoothly, and the pace of the book is just right. Exciting scenes and cliff-hanger chapters are balanced by decisions and interactions that drive the action. Gregor is not the most compelling figure at first, but as the story progresses he becomes more interesting, maturing through the challenges he faces. Supporting characters are generally engaging, particularly the enigmatic warrior rat that claims to support the protagonist's mission.

Gregor & the Prophecy of Bane. unabr. ed. Suzanne Collins. Read by Paul Boehmer. 5 CDs. (Running Time: 6 hrs. 34 mins.). (Underland Chronicles: Bk. 2). (J). (gr. 4-7). 2005. audio compact disk 42.50 (978-0-307-24611-0(6), BksonTape); audio compact disk 42.50 (978-0-307-28337-5(2), Listening Lib) Pub: Random Audio Pubg. Dist(s): NetLibrary CO
A prophecy foretells that Gregor has a role to play in the Underland's uncertain future.

Gregor & the Prophecy of Bane. unabr. ed. Suzanne Collins. Read by Paul Boehmer. (Running Time: 23640 sec.). (Underland Chronicles: Bk. 2). (ENG.). (J). (gr. 5-7). 2005. audio compact disk 39.00 (978-0-307-28268-2(6), Listening Lib) Pub: Random Audio Pubg. Dist(s): Random

Gregor the Overlander. unabr. ed. Suzanne Collins. Read by Paul Boehmer. (Running Time: 23640 sec.). (Underland Chronicles: Bk. 1). (ENG.). (J). (gr. 5-7). 2005. audio compact disk 39.00 (978-0-307-28269-9(4), Listening Lib) Pub: Random Audio Pubg. Dist(s): Random

Gregorg Bateson e l'Ecologia Della Mante. Ed. by Cristiana Grocometti. Narrated by Maurizio Falyhera. (Visions of the World Ser.). (ITA.). 1999. bk. 19.95 (978-1-58214-129-9(0)) Language Assocs.

Gregorg Bateson e l'Ecologia Della Mente. Ed. by Cristiana Grocometti. Narrated by Maurizio Falyhera. (Visions of the World Ser.). (ITA.). 1999. bk. 29.95 (978-1-58214-130-5(4)) Language Assocs.

Gregorian Anthology. Monks of Solesmes Staff. 1 CD. 1998. audio compact disk 16.95 (978-1-55725-201-2(7), 930-063) Paraclete MA.

Gregorian Chant Intonations & the Role of Rhetoric: With Accompanying CD. Columba Kelly. (Studies in Gregorian Chant: Vol. 1). 2003. bk. 119.95 (978-0-7734-6872-6(2)) E Mellen.

Gregorian Chant Rediscovered. Monks of Solesmes Staff. 1 CD. 1995. audio compact disk 16.95 (978-1-55725-136-7(3), 930-069) Paraclete MA.

Gregorian Chants. Bernada Ri. 3 cass. (Running Time: 2 hrs. 30 min.). 1992. 23.95 set. (TAH262) Alba Hse Comns.
4 Sundays of advent & Christmas Mass.

Gregorian Christmas: Puer Natus Est. Perf. by Religious Monks. 1987. audio compact disk 15.95 (179) GIA Pubns.

Gregorian Melodies, Popular Chants, Vol. 1. Perf. by Monks of Solesmes Staff. 2001. audio compact disk 16.95 (978-1-55725-293-7(9)) Paraclete MA.

Gregorian Melodies Popular Chants, Vol. 2. Solesmes. Directed By Dom Richard Gagne. audio compact disk 16.95 (978-1-55725-338-5(2)) Paraclete MA.

Gregorian Requiem: Chants of the Requiem Mass. Gloriae Dei Cantores Schola. Prod. by Elizabeth C. Patterson. 2008. audio compact disk 16.95 (978-1-55725-519-8(9)) Paraclete MA.

Gregorian Requiem: Chants of the Requiem Mass. Contrib. by Gloriae Dei Schola. 1 CD. 1996. audio compact disk 16.95 (978-1-55725-166-4(5), GDCD021) Paraclete MA.
Exquisite Chant repertoire from the Gloriae Dei Cantores Schola that tells of the birth of the soul into the kingdom of heaven. This Schola has been lauded by the New York Times for its "expert renditions of Gregorian chant".

Gregorian Sampler. Monks of Solesmes Staff. 1 CD. 1988. audio compact disk 16.95 (978-1-55725-117-6(7), 930-062) Paraclete MA.

Gregory Orr. unabr. ed. Read by Gregory Orr. 1 cass. (Running Time: 29 min.). 1985. 10.00 New Letters.
Gregory Orr includes readings from "Burning the Empty Nests" & "The Red House".

Gregory's Shadow. Don Freeman. Illus. by Don Freeman. 11 vols. (Running Time: 12 mins.). 2003. bk. 28.95 (978-1-59112-537-2(5)); pap. bk. 39.95 (978-1-59112-536-5(7)) Live Oak Media.

Gregory's Shadow. Don Freeman. Illus. by Don Freeman. 11 vols. (Running Time: 12 mins.). (Readalongs for Beginning Readers Ser.). (J). 2003. bk. 25.95 (978-1-59112-238-8(4)); pap. bk. 37.95 (978-1-59112-239-5(2)); audio compact disk 12.95 (978-1-59112-487-0(5)) Live Oak Media.

Gregory's Shadow. Don Freeman. Read by Jim Weiss. 11 vols. (Running Time: 12 mins.). (Readalongs for Beginning Readers Ser.). (J). 2005. pap. bk. 16.95 (978-1-59112-237-1(6)) Pub: Live Oak Media. Dist(s): AudioGO

Greig Cephalopolysyndactyly Syndrome - A Bibliography & Dictionary for Physicians, Patients, & Genome Researchers. Compiled by Icon Group International, Inc. Staff. 2007. ring bd. 28.95 (978-0-497-11226-4(4)) Icon Grp.

Grendel. unabr. ed. John Gardner. Read by Wolfram Kandinsky. 5 cass. (Running Time: 5 hrs.). 30.00 (978-0-7366-0796-4(X), 1747) Books on Tape.
It is comic, grotesque, at times sad & peopled with fantastic characters: a wise but formidable dragon; a royal bully, old King Hrothgar, whose marauding is over & a stranger literally from another world, Beowulf, defender of mandkind, half dragon, half computer, with empty eyes. In the story of Beowulf, Grendel, devourer of men, signifies the dread that lies beyond human knowledge. But the truth is even darker. Grendel haunts the warrior feast-hall because he is in love with an ideal vision of man & God, a vision betrayed when humanity fails his test.

Grendel. unabr. ed. John Gardner. Narrated by George Guidall. 4 cass. (Running Time: 5 hrs. 30 mins.). (gr. 9). 1997. 35.00 (978-0-7887-1103-9(2), 95096E7) Recorded Bks.
Retelling of Beowulf, the earliest epic in British literature. Focusing on the monster who fights Beowulf, the tale shows young adults the other side of the heroic coin.

Gretel Ehrlich. unabr. ed. Gretel Ehrlich. 1 cass. (Running Time: 29 min.). (New Letters on the Air Ser.). 1992. 10.00 (111591) New Letters.
The author of "Islands, the Universe, Home," writes essays about the natural world found in & about her Wyoming home.

***Grey Ghost.** Adapted by Siren Audio Studios. Prod. by Siren Audio Studios. Based on a novel by Dale N. Smith. (ENG.). 2010. audio compact disk (978-0-9844180-3-9(2)) Siiren Audio.

Grey Is the Color of Hope. unabr. ed. Irina Ratushinskaya. Read by Gretel Davis. 12 cass. (Running Time: 16 hrs.). 2001. 94.95 (978-1-85089-791-0(3), 90011) Pub: ISIS Audio GBR. Dist(s): Ulverscroft US
When she was just twenty-eight years old, Irina Ratushinskaya was imprisoned because of the poetry she had written. This is the gripping account of her years spent in a Soviet labor camp & of the women who survived the brutal conditions of such a place.

Grey Islands. John Steffler. Narrated by John Steffler. Narrated by Frank Holden. (Running Time: 9000 sec.). 2006. audio compact disk 24.95 (978-0-9737586-0-3(0)) Rattling Bks CAN.

Grey King. Susan Cooper. Read by Richard Mitchley & Alex Jennings. 5 CDs. (Running Time: 5 hrs. 41 mins.). (Dark Is Rising Sequence Ser.). (J). (gr. 4-7). 2004. audio compact disk 40.00 (978-0-8072-1785-6(9), Listening Lib) Random Audio Pubg.

Grey King. unabr. ed. Susan Cooper. Read by Richard Mitchley. 4 vols. (Running Time: 5 hrs. 41 mins.). (Dark Is Rising Sequence Ser.). (J). (gr. 4-7). 2004. 38.00 (978-0-8072-8878-8(0), Listening Lib); 32.00 (978-0-8072-8877-1(2), Listening Lib) Random Audio Pubg.
Will is the last-born of the Old Ones, immortals dedicated to saving the world from the forces of evil. Now it is Will's task to wake with the golden harp the

six who must be roused from their long slumber in the Welsh hills to prepare for the last battle between the Dark & the Light.

Grey Mask. Patricia Wentworth. 2008. 61.95 (978-0-7531-3806-9(9)); audio compact disk 79.95 (978-0-7531-2787-2(3)) Pub: ISIS Audio GBR. Dist(s): Ulverscroft US

Grey Seas Under. unabr. ed. Farley Mowat. Read by Grover Gardner. 8 cass. (Running Time: 12 hrs.). 1994. 64.00 (978-0-7366-2846-4(0), 3554) Books on Tape.
Passionate tale of the courage of men & of a small, ocean-going salvage tug.

Grey Squirrel at Pacific Ave. 1 cass. (Running Time: 35 min.). (J). (gr. k-4). 2001. pap. bk. 19.95 (SP 5006C) Kimbo Educ.
The antics & troubles of Grey Squirrel.

Greyfriars Bobby. unabr. ed. Eleanor Atkinson. Read by Peter Joyce. 5 cass. 1997. 49.95 (978-1-86015-445-4(X)) Pub: UlverLrgPrint GBR. Dist(s): Ulverscroft US
One dog's loyalty changes the lives of those around him &, ultimately, the conditions of the poor living in Edinburgh.

Greygallows. unabr. ed. Barbara Michaels, pseud. Read by Jacqueline King. 8 cass. (Running Time: 9 hrs. 48 mins.). 2000. 34.95 (978-1-57270-141-0(2), N81141u) Pub: Audio Partners. Dist(s): PerseuPGW
Ignoring the mysterious past of Baron Clare, Lucy Cartwright accepts his marriage proposal and follows him innocently to his estate. She has no idea that he is leading her into a world of betrayal & danger.

Greyling. unabr. ed. Jane Yolen. 1 cass. (Running Time: 14 min.). (J). (ps-5). 1993. bk. 25.90 (978-0-8045-6678-0(X), 6678) Spoken Arts.

Greywolf's Hoss. Jane Coleman. (Running Time: 0 hr. 30 mins.). 1998. 10.95 (978-1-60083-464-6(7)) Iofy Corp.

***Greywolf's Hoss.** Jane Candia Coleman. 2009. (978-1-60136-439-5(3)) Audio Holding.

Grian an Fhomhair: Sean-Nos Songs from Connemara. Contrib. by Aine Bean Mhaitiu. (ENG.). 2001. 14.95 (978-0-8023-7145-4(0)); audio compact disk 21.95 (978-0-8023-8145-3(6)) Pub: Clo Iar-Chonnachta IRL. Dist(s): Dufour

Grid. Philip Kerr. 1999. (978-1-57042-779-4(8)) Hachet Audio.

Grid. unabr. ed. Philip Kerr. Read by Geoffrey Howard. 9 cass. (Running Time: 13 hrs. 30 min.). 1996. 72.00 (978-0-7366-3468-7(1), 4112) Books on Tape.
The sparkling new Yu Corp. building in downtown L.A. is a monument to human genius. It talks to you; it forecasts the weather. It reads your body temperature & knows if you use drugs. It darkens windows to reduce mid-day glare & tends to the tree in its atrium. Truly a culmination of art & function. Just one problem: it's also a serial killer.

Grief: Program from the Award Winning Public Radio Series. Hosted by Fred Goodwin. Comment by John Hockenberry. Contrib. by Ken Doka et al. 1 cass. (Running Time: 1 hr.). (Infinite Mind Ser.). 1998. audio compact disk 21.95 (978-1-888064-27-8(7), LCM 37) Lichtenstein Creat.
Grief is a natural dimension of human life. As poet (and undertaker) Thomas Lynch puts it, "Grief is a sign of our humanity. It's the tax we pay on our attachments." Although grief that evolves into clinical depression may demand medical treatment, too often American culture unnecessarily pathologizes grief, or tries to fit the most individual of processes into simplistic "stage" models. This week we speak with leading experts on grief, visit the Day of the Dead celebration in Oaxaca, Mexico, and hear from teenagers in East Harlem who have experienced the death of family and friends. With commentary by John Hockenberry.

Grief: Reality & Recovery. 2007. audio compact disk 17.99 (978-1-934570-08-1(7)) Lanphier Pr.

Grief - A Stepping Stone to Peace: How to Help a Family in Crisis. Illus. by Angela Brown & Mary Louise Selph. Prod. by Les Lingle. 1 cass. (Running Time: 30 mins.). (Words of Wellness - Your Show for Simple Solutions Ser.: Vol. 320). 2000. 12.95 (978-1-930995-13-0(X), LLP320) Life Long Pubg.
Ever lost a child? Know someone who has? Kids aren't supposed to die before their parents. Tips include coping strategies & how to move form grief to grace.

Grief & the Holidays. Doug Manning. 1 cass. 1986. 9.95 (978-1-892785-17-6(X)) In-Sight Bks Inc.
The Holidays are always difficult for people in grief. Day gives warm wisdom & practical advice to get people through these holiday depressions.

Grief-Bereavement Becomes Alcoholism in Many Combat Veterans. 1 cass. (Care Cassettes Ser.: Vol. 19, No. 8). 1992. 10.80 Assn Prof Chaplains.

***Grief Encounters.** Stuart Pawson & Jonathan Keeble. 2010. 71.95 (978-1-84652-770-8(8)); audio compact disk 79.95 (978-1-84652-771-5(6)) Pub: Magna Story GBR. Dist(s): Ulverscroft US

Grief Observed. (Running Time: 7200 sec.). 2005. 22.95 (978-0-7861-3780-0(0)); audio compact disk 24.00 (978-0-7861-7586-4(9)); audio compact disk 29.95 (978-0-7861-7861-2(2)) Blckstn Audio.

Grief Recovery, Set. John W. James & Russell Friedman. 3 cass. (Running Time: 4 hrs. 45 mins.). 2004. instr.'s hndbk. ed. 19.99 (978-1-4025-1158-5(2), 01204) Recorded Bks.

Grief Recovery Handbook: The Action Program for Moving Beyond Death, Divorce, & Other Losses. unabr. ed. John W. James & Russell Friedman. Narrated by Brian Keeler. 4 cass. (Running Time: 4 hrs. 45 mins.). 2002. 44.00 (978-0-7887-5347-3(9), 96570) Recorded Bks.
A tool for understanding and completing the grieving process.

Grief, Trauma, & Loss. 2004. audio compact disk 13.95 (978-1-930429-70-3(3)) Love Logic.

Grief, Trauma & Loss: Helping Children Cope. unabr. ed. Foster W. Cline. 1 CD. (Running Time: 1 hr. 30 mins.). 1999. audio compact disk 12.95 (978-0-944634-57-8(5), 0194486) Pub: Love Logic. Dist(s): Penton Overseas
Help is here for parents and educators to guide children in coping with life stresses: grief, loss and trauma. Cline discusses many topics such as explaining death and funerals, senseless violence and talking with teens when a friend commits suicide.

Grievance: A Rugs Carlucci Novel. unabr. ed. K. C. Constantine. Read by Norman Dietz. 8 vols. (Running Time: 12 hrs.). 2000. bk. 69.95 (978-0-7927-2407-0(0), CSL 296, Chivers Sound Lib) AudioGO.
If Lyons accomplished his business objectives, he has since paid the ultimate price. For he has just been found in the trunk of his Jaguar, bent over a bag of golf clubs & sporting a small-caliber bullet wound at the base of his skull.

Grieving: The Pain & the Promise. Deanna Edwards. 2 cass. 2004. 11.95 (978-1-57734-852-8(4)) Covenant Comms.

Grieving Children. Interview with Mother Angelica et al. 1 cass. (Running Time: 60 min.). (Mother Angelica Live Ser.). 1987. 10.00 (978-1-55794-101-5(7), T52) Eternal Wrd TV.

Grieving Our Losses & Living with Hope, Vol. 3. Perf. by Dudley Riggle. (Running Time: 1 hr. 15 min.). (Issues In Living & Dying Ser.). 1996. 19.95 (978-1-886909-06-9(7), A222) Dynam Comm.

***Grieving the Loss of a Loved One: A Devotional Companion.** Kathe Wunnenberg. (Running Time: 4 hrs. 55 mins. 0 sec.). (ENG.). 2009. 14.99 (978-0-310-30450-0(4)) Zondervan.

Grieving the Loss of Your Pet see Healing from the Loss of a Pet

Grievous Sin. unabr. ed. Faye Kellerman. Read by Bernadette Dunne. 9 cass. (Running Time: 13 hrs. 30 min.). (Peter Decker & Rina Lazarus Novel Ser.). 1996. 72.00 (978-0-7366-3321-5(9), 3973) Books on Tape.
The day following a childbirth should be a peaceful, happy time for both mother & father. But Rina, who's just delivered a baby, & Peter Decker, her husband, are a bundle of nerves. The hospital's budget woes & staff cuts have compromised security in the nursery, which scares especially Peter, an edgy L.A. cop.

***Griff Carver, Hallway Patrol.** unabr. ed. Jim Krieg. (ENG.). (J). 2011. audio compact disk 28.00 (978-0-307-91537-5(9), Listening Lib) Pub: Random Audio Pubg. Dist(s): Random

Griffe. Lise Pascal. pap. bk. 21.95 (978-88-7754-629-6(8)) Pub: Cideb ITA. Dist(s): Distribks Inc

Griffin & Sabine: An Extraordinary Correspondence. Nick Bantock. 1 cass. (Running Time: 90 min.). Dramatization. 1991. 10.95 (978-1-879371-42-2(1), 30000) Pub Mills.
This is a story that is partly a romance, partly a mystery & completely a work of art. The reader has the delightful forbidden sensation of reading someone else's mail. The complete correspondence tells an extraordinary story in an extraordinary way.

Griffin & Sabine Trilogy. unabr. ed. Nick Bantock. Read by Maxwell Caulfield et al. 3 cass. (Running Time: 2 hrs.). 1994. 24.95 Set. (978-1-879371-58-3(8), 70000) Pub Mills.
It started with a mysterious & seemingly innocent postcard, but from that point nothing was to remain the same in the life of Griffin Moss, a quiet artist living in London. Over the course of this best-selling trilogy, Griffin's world is turned upside down by Sabine, a strangely exotic woman living on a tropical island thousands of miles away. Beginning in "Griffin & Sabine", the relationship between the title characters unfolds in a series of postcards & letter. "Sabine's Notebook", the second book, follows Griffin on a journey while he struggles to maintain his precarious link to reality, & to Sabine. Finally, The "Golden Mean" builds toward a powerful conclusion that will satisfy the millions of readers & listeners entranced by the imaginative & enigmatic union of Griffin & Sabine.

Griffin & the Minor Canon. unabr. ed. Frank Richard Stockton. Read by Jack Benson. (Running Time: 82 min.). Dramatization. 7.95 (N-43) Jimcin Record.
Mythical monster comes to life & is befriended by a country cleric.

Grifter's Game. unabr. ed. Lawrence Block. Read by Alan Sklar. 4 cass. (Running Time: 5 Hrs). 2005. 39.95 (978-0-7927-3668-4(0), CSL 814); audio compact disk 59.95 (978-0-7927-3669-1(9), SLD 814) AudioGO.

Grifter's Game. unabr. ed. Lawrence Block. Narrated by Alan Sklar. (Running Time: 19140 sec.). (Hard Case Crime Ser.). (ENG.). 2008. audio compact disk 19.95 (978-1-60283-452-1(0)) Pub: AudioGO. Dist(s): Perseus Dist

Grilling Season. unabr. ed. Diane Mott Davidson. Narrated by Barbara Rosenblat. 8 cass. (Running Time: 11 hrs. 30 mins.). (Goldy Schulz Culinary Mysteries Ser.: No. 7). 1998. 75.00 (978-0-7887-1871-7(1), 95293E7) Recorded Bks.
A bizarre twist of a woman seeking her ex-husband, comes across his dead girlfriend instead & decides to solve the case. Faced with all the strange happenings in her life, she is marvelled at the kindness & attentiveness showed to her by her new husband.

Grillo en Times Square, Set. unabr. ed. George Selden. Narrated by Graciela Lecube. 3 cass. (Running Time: 4 hrs.). (SPA.). (J). (gr. 4). 1999. 27.00 (978-1-55690-877-4(6), 93319) Recorded Bks.
Whimsical story of the friendship between a cat, a mouse & a cricket in the heart of New York City.

Grim Grotto. Illus. by Lemony Snicket, pseud. Narrated by Tim Curry. 6 CDs. (Running Time: 6 hrs. 15 mins.). (Series of Unfortunate Events Ser.: Bk. 11). (J). (gr. 5 up). 2004. audio compact disk 52.75 (978-1-4193-1781-1(4)) Recorded Bks.

Grim Grotto. Illus. by Lemony Snicket, pseud. Narrated by Tim Curry. 5 cass. (Running Time: 6 hrs. 15 mins.). (Series of Unfortunate Events Ser.: Bk. 11). (YA). (gr. 6 up). 2004. 47.75 (978-1-4193-0565-8(4)) Recorded Bks.

Grim Grotto. unabr. abr. ed. Read by Tim Curry. Illus. by Lemony Snicket. 4 cass. (Running Time: 5 hrs. 30 mins.). (Series of Unfortunate Events Ser.: Bk. 11). (J). (gr. 3-6). 2004. 20.00 (978-0-06-057946-3(3), HarperChildAud) HarperCollins Pubs.

Grim Grotto. unabr. abr. ed. Lemony Snicket, pseud. Read by Tim Curry. (Series of Unfortunate Events Ser.: Bk. 11). (J). (gr. 3-6). 2004. audio compact disk 25.99 (978-0-06-057947-0(1), HarperChildAud) HarperCollins Pubs.

Grim Pickings. unabr. ed. Jennifer Rowe. Read by Lise Rodgers. 10 cass. (Running Time: 15 hrs.). 1998. (978-1-86340-605-5(0), 551105) Bolinda Pubng AUS.
An engrossing murder mystery.

Grim Reaper. Bernard Knight. Narrated by Paul Matthews. 9 cass. (Running Time: 12 hrs.). (Crowner John Mystery Ser.). 82.00 (978-1-84197-420-0(X)) Recorded Bks.

***Grim Reaper's Dance.** unabr. ed. Judy Clemens. (Running Time: 8 hrs. 30 mins.). 2010. 29.95 (978-1-4417-4984-0(5)); 54.95 (978-1-4417-4980-2(2)); audio compact disk 76.00 (978-1-4417-4981-9(0)) Blckstn Audio.

***Grim Smile of the Five Towns.** Arnold Bennett. Read by Anais 9000. 2009. 27.95 (978-1-60112-236-0(5)) Babblebooks.

Grim Tuesday. Garth Nix. Read by Allan Corduner. 4 cass. (Running Time: 7 hrs.). (Keys to the Kingdom Ser.: No. 2). (J). (gr. 4-7). 2004. 35.00 (978-0-8072-1728-3(X), Listening Lib) Random Audio Pubg.

Grimm Fairy Tales: Hansel & Gretel, Snow White, Frog Prince. Short Stories. 1 CD. (Running Time: 60 mins.). Dramatization. (J). 2005. 12.00 (978-0-9773525-0-0(1)) Hollywood Cliche.
Hollywood ClichE presents a delightful new reading of classic traditional fairy tales. Endorsed by teachers and parents alike. We know you will enjoy these famous folk tales passed down from elders to youngsters the world over and have entertained many generations of children.ReaderMichael McFall is a Graduate of the American Conservatory Theatre and Co-star in Academy Award Best Picture Forrest Gump. Among his other Film and TV credits include Made in America and Tales of the City and roles on Emmy winning shows such as ER, NYPD Blue, Fraiser and Star Trek: Voyager.

Grimm Tales. Nox Arcana. Narrated by Joseph Vargo. Music by Joseph Vargo & William Piotrowski. (ENG.). 2008. audio compact disk 13.99 (978-0-9788857-5-5(9)) Monolith.

***Grimm's Animal Stories & Fairy Tales.** Jacob W. Grimm & Wilhelm K. Grimm. Narrated by Flo Gibson. (ENG.). (J). 2010. audio compact disk 16.95 (978-1-60646-143-3(5)) Audio Bk Con.

Grimm's Animal Stories & Fairy Tales. unabr. ed. Jacob W. Grimm & Wilhelm K. Grimm. Narrated by Flo Gibson. (Running Time: 2 hrs. 45 mins.). (J). (gr. k-2). 1992. 14.95 (978-1-55685-225-1(8)) Audio Bk Con.

Grimm's Animal Stories & Fairy Tales, Set. unabr. ed. Jacob W. Grimm & Wilhelm K. Grimm. Read by Flo Gibson. 2 cass. (Running Time: 3 hrs.). (J). (gr. 1 up). 1992. 20.95 Audio Bk Con.
The Grimm Brothers best stories are included in this collection. Among them are such old favorites as: "The White Snake," "The Table, the Ass, & the Stick," "How Mrs. Fox Married Again," "Old Sultan," "The Six Swans," "The Golden Swan," "The Queen Bee," "The Frog Prince," "Snow White & Rose Red," "The Three Feathers," "The Elves," "The Angel Mothers," & "Little Snow White.".

Grimm's Fairy Tales. 4 cass. (Running Time: 4 hrs.). 2001. 29.95 (SNDX003) Lodestone Catalog.
Featuring "Snow White & the Seven Dwarfs", "Hansel & Gretel", "Rumpelstiltskin," & the Fisherman & His Wife.

Grimms' Fairy Tales. Short Stories. Jacob W. Grimm & Wilhelm K. Grimm. Read by Laura Paton. 2 CDs. (Running Time: 2 hrs. 20 mins.). (J). (gr. k-2). 1994. audio compact disk 17.98 (978-962-634-005-9(3), NA200512) Naxos.
Collection of 13 tales including "Snow White," "Hansel and Gretel," "Rumplestiltsken," and "Cinderella".

Grimms' Fairy Tales. Short Stories. Jacob W. Grimm & Wilhelm K. Grimm. Read by Laura Paton. 2 cass. (Running Time: 2 hrs. 20 mins.). (Junior Classics Ser.). (J). (ps-3). 1994. 13.98 (978-962-634-505-4(5), NA200514, Naxos AudioBooks) Naxos.
Collection of 13 tales including "Snow White," "Hansel and Gretel," Rumplestiltsken" and "Cinderella.".

***Grimm's Fairy Tales.** unabr. ed. Brothers Grimm. Narrated by Robin Field. (ENG.). 2010. 14.98 (978-1-59644-972-5(1), MissionAud); audio compact disk 24.98 (978-1-59644-971-8(3), MissionAud) christianaud.

Grimms' Fairy Tales. unabr. ed. Jacob W. Grimm & Wilhelm K. Grimm. 5 cass. Incl. Hansel & Gretel. (J). (D-311); Rumpelstiltskin. (J). (D-311); (J). 29.75 (D-311) Audio Bk.
Eleven tales by the Grimm Brothers.

Grimm's Fairy Tales, Vol. 2. unabr. ed. Jacob W. Grimm et al. 3 CDs. audio compact disk 17.98 (978-962-634-303-6(6), NA330412) Naxos.

Grimpow: The Invisible Road. unabr. ed. Rafael Abalos. Read by Richard McGonagle. 11 CDs. (Running Time: 13 hrs. 20 mins.). (J). (gr. 4-7). 2007. audio compact disk 75.00 (978-0-7393-6124-5(4), Listening Lib) Pub: Random Audio Pubg. Dist(s): Random
Grimpow has no idea who the dead man is, but hidden in his leather bag is a treasure that will change the boy's life forever. Daggers encrusted with rubies and emeralds, silver coins, jewels, and a letter with a golden seal depicting a snake swallowing its own tail. And clutched in the man's firm grip - a stone. A stone that will shape Grimpow's destiny. For when he holds it in his hand, strange things begin to happen. Visions of places he's never been fill his mind, and he finds that he can read the odd language in the letter, a message meant for someone else entirely. So begins Grimpow's journey with the stone: a centuries-long search that has driven sane men crazy, turned peaceful men to violence, and made knights into cowards. Only the one who is chosen can unlock the stone's secrets. No man has ever succeeded. But no boy has ever tried.

Grimpow: The Invisible Road. unabr. ed. Rafael Abalos. Read by Richard McGonagle. 11 CDs. (Running Time: 48000 sec.). (ENG.). (J). (gr. 5 up). 2007. audio compact disk 50.00 (978-0-7393-5963-1(0), Listening Lib) Pub: Random Audio Pubg. Dist(s): Random

Gringo Amigo. unabr. ed. Gary McCarthy. Read by Gene Engene. 6 cass. (Running Time: 6 hrs. 42 min.). 2001. 39.95 (978-1-55686-815-3(4)) Books in Motion.
The California Gold Country of 1849 is the setting for this historical novel revealing the true story behind the infamous Mexican Vaquero Joaquin Murieta. Irish immigrant miner Michael Callahan becomes the "Gringo Amigo" after defending Mexican miners from white claim jumpers.

Grip of the Shadow Plague. Brandon Mull. (Fablehaven Ser.: Bk. 3). audio compact disk 39.95 (978-1-59038-899-0(2), Shadow Mount) Deseret Bk.

Gris & That: The Words of Ed Grisamore. Read by Ed Grisamore. 2006. audio compact disk 12.00 (978-0-9785562-0-4(8)) Socio Pub.

Grit Laskin: A Few Simple Words. 1 cass. 9.98 (C-5511); 14.98 (CD-557) Folk-Legacy.
From bright humor to dark concern from this Canadian.

Gritanilla. Miguel de Cervantes Saavedra. (SPA.). pap. bk. 20.95 (978-88-7754-897-9(5)) Pub: Cideb ITA. Dist(s): Distribks Inc

Grito de Independencia. unabr. ed. Abuelo Historias Del. (SPA.). 2007. audio compact disk 13.00 (978-958-8318-01-7(7)) Pub: Yoyo Music COL. Dist(s): YoYoMusic

Grits Vol. 1: What Makes Us Southerners. Kathryn Tucker Windham. 1 CD. (Running Time: 1 hr.). (American Storytelling Ser.). 2001. audio compact disk 16.95 (978-0-87483-627-1(1)) Pub: August Hse. Dist(s): Natl Bk Netwk

Grits Vol. 1: What Makes Us Southerners. Kathryn Tucker Windham. 1 cass. (Running Time: 1 hr.). (American Storytelling Ser.). 2001. 12.00 (978-0-87483-626-4(3)) Pub: August Hse. Dist(s): Natl Bk Netwk
Included in Grits are ten stories full of humor and wit, including "Piano Lessons," "The Green Rubber Bathing Suit," "Iced Tea," and "Listen to the Morning".

Grits: the Greatest H9ts. Contrib. by Grits. 2007. audio compact disk 19.99 (978-5-557-62811-2(8)) Gotee Records.

Grizzly & the Gadgets & Further Fables for Our Time. abr. ed. James Thurber. Read by Peter Ustinov. 1 cass. 1984. 12.95 (978-0-694-50251-6(0), SWC 1412) HarperCollins Pubs.

Grizzly Bear. unabr. collector's ed. Thomas McNamee. Read by Richard Wulf. 9 cass. (Running Time: 13 hrs. 30 min.). 1987. 72.00 (978-0-7366-1188-6(6), 2108) Books on Tape.
Man & bear are omnivorous, predatory, intelligent...each at the top of his respective food chain. Each has little to fear from any creature...except ourselves & the other.

Grizzly King. unabr. ed. James Oliver Curwood. Read by Jack Sondericker. 4 cass. (Running Time: 4 hrs. 30 min.). Dramatization. (J). 1991. 26.95 (978-1-55686-372-1(1), 372) Books in Motion.
The book from which came almost line for line the script for the hit motion picture "The Bear.".

Grizzly Pass. unabr. ed. Will C. Knott. Read by Maynard Villers. 4 cass. (Running Time: 4 hrs. 18 min.). (Golden Hawk Ser.: Bk. 3). 1995. 26.95 (978-1-55686-640-1(2)) Books in Motion.
Golden Hawk was faced with a cruel choice; he must save a wagon train led by a preacher he hated, from Indians led by a warrior chief he respected.

***Grmmr in Cntxt Bk 2 4e-Tape.** 4th ed. ELBAUM. (C). 2005. 90.95 (978-1-4130-0746-6(5)) Pub: Heinle. Dist(s): CENGAGE Learn

Gro Harlem Brundtland: Saving Earth from Decline. (Running Time: 65 min.). 1989. 13.95 (K0710B090, HarperThor) HarpC GBR.

Grommet Saves the World & Boots & All. unabr. ed. Sherryl Clark & James Moloney. Read by Francis Greenslade. 2 cass. (Running Time: 2 hrs. 50 mins.). (Aussie Chomps: Ser.). (J). 2003. 24.00 (978-1-74030-980-6(4)) Pub: Bolinda Pubng AUS. Dist(s): Bolinda Pub Inc

Groosham Grange. Anthony Horowitz. Read by Nickolas Grace. 3 CDs. (Groosham Grange Ser.: Bk. 1). (J). 2004. audio compact disk 29.95 (978-0-7540-6642-2(8), Chivers Child Audio) AudioGO.

***Groove Alchemy.** Stanton Moore. (ENG.). 2010. pap. bk. 44.99 (978-1-4234-9627-4(2), 1423496272) Pub: Hudson Music. Dist(s): H Leonard

Groove Book, Vol. 1. John Mackay. Read by John Mackay. Ed. by Byron Duckwall. 1 cass. 1992. pap. bk. 12.50 (978-1-883617-04-2(9)) Evergreen Music.
Music book & cassette. 25 piano grooves in the pop, rock, jazz & other various styles for the contemporary professional or amateur musician. The book contains a piano score & the tape plays all 25 examples.

Groove Book: A Study in Musical Styles for Bass. Marc Ensign. 1999. pap. bk. 14.95 (978-0-7866-3261-9(5)) Mel Bay.

***Groovin' & Other Uplifting Piano Pieces: The Debra Wanless Intermediate Piano Library.** Created by Hal Leonard Corp. Debra Wanless. (ENG.). 2010. pap. bk. 12.99 (978-1-4234-9749-3(X), 142349749X) H Leonard.

Gros-Calin, Set. Romain Gary. 4 cass. (FRE.). 1995. 36.95 (1678-LV) Olivia & Hill.
The intriguing story of an "object," called Gros-Calin & its possessor. Follow the streets of Paris as this story reveals the identity of Gros-Calin.

Gross: The Hits, the Flops: The Summer That Ate Hollywood. unabr. ed. Peter Bart. Read by Jonathan Tindle. 7 cass. (Running Time: 11 hrs. 30 mins.). 2000. 49.95 (978-0-7861-1710-9(9), 2506) Blckstn Audio.
Refers to the movie box office income & comments on the movie business.

Gross Songs Kids Love to Sing. Prod. by Twin Sisters Productions Staff. 1 CD. (Running Time: 30:00). (J). 2005. audio compact disk 4.99 (978-1-57583-805-2(2)) Twin Sisters.
OOOO! Yuck! Kids are sure to sing along and laugh together with this all-new collection of gross songs! Even adults will wrinkle their noses and smile at the thought of "Greasy Grimy Gopher Guts!" Over 30 minutes of musicadd up to hours of fun at home, school, and camp. BONUS! Includes 50 fun things to do with kids!.

Grotesque Imagination of Charles Dickens: A Light & Enlightening Lecture, Featuring Elliot Engel. 2000. bk. 15.00 (978-1-890123-37-6(4)) Media Cnslts.

Groucho Marx. Perf. by Groucho Marx. 1 cass. (Running Time: 60 min.). 1956. 7.95 (CC-8830) Natl Recrd Co.
Groucho at his best with contestants on his quiz program & W. C. Fields in eight of his funniest comedy skits.

Groucho Marx: Is the World Funny? see Buckley's Firing Line

Groucho Marx - W. C. Fields. Perf. by Charlie McCarthy & Don Ameche. 1 cass. (Running Time: 60 min.). (Old Time Radio Classic Singles Ser.). 4.95 (978-1-57816-106-5(1), GW126) Audio File.
Includes: 1) "You Bet Your Life" Quiz show with Groucho, guests & the "Secret Word" (1956). 2) W. C. Fields Best Comedy Routines. Eight selected skits.

Grouch's Christmas. 1 cass. (J). 1995. bk. 6.98 (Sony Wonder) Sony Music Ent.
The re-release of the holiday book & tape package includes a full color, 24-page story book with accompanying audio cassette. Everyone on Sesame Street is looking forward to Christmas - except for Oscar the Grouch! Can sardine cookies with chocolate icing & a Christmas tree with old tin cans & orange peels help change Oscar's mind about the holiday season?.

Ground Beneath Her Feet: A Novel. unabr. ed. Salman Rushdie. Narrated by Steven Crossley. 20 cass. (Running Time: 27 hrs. 15 mins.). 1999. 163.00 (978-0-7887-4350-4(3), 95939E7) Recorded Bks.
Imaginative maze of ancient mythology & pop culture.

Ground Beneath Her Feet: A Novel. unabr. ed. Salman Rushdie & Pat Milton. Read by Steven Crossley. Narrated by Richard Poe. 13 cass. (Running Time: 19 hrs.). 1999. 104.00 (978-0-7887-3747-3(3), 95939E5) Recorded Bks.
Modern retelling of the myth of Orpheus. An imaginative maze of ancient mythology & pop culture.

Ground Money. abr. ed. Rex Burns. Read by Charlton Griffin. 2 vols. No. 6. 2003. (978-1-58807-670-0(9)) Am Pubng Inc.

Ground of Infinity: A Series of Satsangs in Boulder, CO. Featuring Adyashanti. (ENG.). 2009. audio compact disk 65.00 (978-1-933986-56-2(5)) Open Gate Pub.

Ground Truth: The Untold Story of America under Attack on 9/11. unabr. ed. John Farmer. Narrated by Patrick G. Lawlor. 1 MP3-CD. (Running Time: 12 hrs. 0 mins. 0 sec.). (ENG.). 2009. audio compact disk 24.99 (978-1-4001-6359-5(5)); audio compact disk 75.99 (978-1-4001-4359-7(4)); audio compact disk 37.99 (978-1-4001-1359-0(8)) Pub: Tantor Media. Dist(s): IngramPubServ

Ground Zero & the Human Soul: The Search for the New Ordinary Life. Interview. Lynn Jericho & Bethene LeMahieu. 6 cass. (Running Time: 6 hrs.). 2003. wbk. ed. 49.95 (978-0-9723312-0-3(4)) Foursquare Conversions.
These are unsettling times! Fear and caution have replaced security and optimism in less than two years. Uncertainty and trauma are everywhere. What you are feeling is real. Until now no one has envisioned the individual within our new environment. Who am I? What do I want? How can I create my future? What does it mean to be human? Has my soul changed during the last two years and how do I find out? We rarely ask ourselves these questions. Today, these questions resonate loudly and carry a personal moral imperative. Our institutions ? national, religious, academic ? cannot dictate or define our individual response. We can seek our own answers in our inner life ... searching for our personal harmony, our personal truth, our personal goodness, our confrontation with evil in our own ?New Ordinary Life.? 9/11 made us realize that we all have a life decision to make. One choice takes us back to our lives on ?September 10th,? a life that seemed safe and secure but wasn?t. (Many have already made this choice.) Another choice is to live on ?September 11th? ? a life of fear, betrayal, shock, anger and disbelief with no future path. We see this, today, among many of us. There is a third option ? to evolve into ?September 12th??New Ordinary Life,? following a modern and thoughtful path to a healing, freeing, tolerant and empowering existence. In their new audio book, GROUND ZERO And The HUMAN SOUL: THE SEARCH FOR THE NEW ORDINARY LIFE, Lynn Jericho and Bethene LeMahieu, Ed.D. provide insights, inspirations and practical empowering exercises to help us to focus on ?9/12?, that ?New Ordinary Life.? They help us to explore a future where we are responsible for our own humanity. They talk together about the need to develop an understanding and a tolerance/acceptance of others, to move beyond terrorism, trauma and tragedy and to confront and acknowledge evil. Their conversations are lively, incisive, inspired, uniquely creative and truly practical.GROUND ZERO And The HUMAN SOUL is a series of six discussions between Lynn and Bethene designed to help us examine our lives and the complexities of our human soul in today?s world. We know we have changed, but how? September 11, 2001, and the times since, weren?t just ordinary days. Our decisions about our ?New Ordinary Life? can impact not just our world but the world as a whole. For a harmonious future life, it is crucial that we each explore this new reality.

Groundbreaking Service: 11 Kings 12:1-16. Ed Young. 1984. 4.95 (978-0-7417-1382-7(9), 382) Win Walk.

Grounded for Life? Michael Weir Allred. 2004. 9.95 (978-1-57734-692-0(0)); audio compact disk 10.95 (978-1-57734-693-7(9)) Covenant Comms.

Groundhog see Richard Eberhart Reading His Poetry

Groundhog see Caedmon Treasury of Modern Poets Reading Their Own Poetry

Groundhog see Twentieth-Century Poetry in English, No. 1, Recordings of Poets Reading Their Own Poetry

Grounding Meditation. Created by Ken Mellor. 1 MP3 File. (Running Time: 60 mins). 2002. 22.95 (978-0-9775658-9-4(0)) AwakenNet AUS.

Grounds for Suspicion Readalong. Michael Coleman. 1 cass. (Running Time: 1 hr.). (Ten-Minute Mysteries Ser.). (YA). (gr. 6-12). 1994. pap. bk. 12.95 (978-0-7854-1051-5(1), 40759) Am Guidance.

Groundswell: Winning in a World Transformed by Social Technologies. unabr. ed. Charlene Li & Josh Bernoff. Read by Josh Bernoff. (Running Time: 8 hrs. 30 mins.). (ENG.). 2008. 24.98 (978-1-59659-231-5(1), GildAudio) Pub: Gildan Media. Dist(s): HachBkGrp

Groundswell: Winning in a World Transformed by Social Technologies. unabr. ed. Charlene Li & Josh Bernoff. Read by Josh Bernoff. 6 CDs. (Running Time: 8 hrs. 30 mins.). (ENG.). 2008. audio compact disk 29.98 (978-1-59659-212-4(5), GildAudio) Pub: Gildan Media. Dist(s): HachBkGrp

Group A Strep - Current & Evolving Problems. Contrib. by Michael A. Gerber et al. 1 cass. (American Academy of Pediatrics UPDATE: Vol. 16, No. 1). 1998. 20.00 Am Acad Pediat.

Group & Club Tours: Your Guide to Ideas & Possibilities. 1 cass. (Running Time: 23 min.). 32.95 (CFSS/CS27) Ctr Self Suff.

Group B Strep in Pregnancy. Contrib. by Sebastian Faro et al. 1 cass. (American College of Obstetrics & Gynecologists UPDATE: Vol. 22, No. 5). 1998. 20.00 Am Coll Obstetric.

Group Genius: The Creative Power of Collaboration. unabr. ed. Keith Sawyer. Read by Jonathan Marosz. (Running Time: 8 hrs.). (ENG.). 2008. 24.98 (978-1-59659-186-8(2), GildAudio) Pub: Gildan Media. Dist(s): HachBkGrp

Group Piano, Bk. 2. Gayle Kowalchyk et al. 1 CD. (Alfred's Basic Piano Library). (ENG.). 1997. audio compact disk 14.95 (978-0-7390-0222-3(8), 18087) Alfred Pub.

Group Piano Course, Bk. 3. Gayle Kowalchyk et al. 3/2 CDs. (Alfred's Basic Piano Library). (ENG.). 1998. audio compact disk 14.95 (978-0-7390-0223-0(6), 18090) Alfred Pub.

Group Piano Solos for Adult. E. L. Lancaster & Kenon D. Renfrow. 1 CD. (Running Time: 1 hr. 30 mins.). 1997. audio compact disk 7.95 (978-0-7390-1508-7(7), 14567) Alfred Pub.

Group Treatment for Asperger Syndrome: A Social Skills Curriculum. Lynn Adams. 2005. pap. bk. 24.95 (978-1-59756-022-1(7)) Plural Pub Inc.

Groups. 1 cass. (First Steps in Science Ser.). (J). 12.00 (6351-0, Natl Textbk Co) M-H Contemporary.
Helps children discover the process of scientific investigation. Part of the First Steps in Science Program.

Groups: Program from the Award Winning Public Radio Series. Interview. Hosted by Fred Goodwin. Comment by John Hockenberry. 1 CD. (Running Time: 1 hr.). 1999. audio compact disk 21.95 (978-1-932479-51-5(1), LCM 88) Lichtenstein Creat.
Do groups really have their own personality and behavior? Are there really such things as "mass hysteria" and "mass hallucination?" The latest research on why people in groups behave the way they do, and how some are turning these theories to their advantage. With commentary by John Hockenberry.

Group's Christmas Caroling Kit. Group Publishing Staff. 1 cass. 1992. pap. bk. 16.99 (978-1-55945-151-2(3)) Group Pub.

Grouse in the Heather: An Chearc Fhraoigh. Contrib. by P. J. and Marcus Hernon. (ENG.). 1999. audio compact disk 21.95 (978-0-8023-8100-2(6)) Pub: Clo Iar-Chonnachta IRL. Dist(s): Dufour

Grover & the Package. 1 cass. (Sesame Street Ser.). (J). 1995. bk. 6.98 (Sony Wonder) Sony Music Ent.
While Grover is taking a walk one day, a delivery man accidentally drops a package near him. Can the little blue monster catch up to the delivery man in time to return the package?.

Grover Thompson: Young People Out of Control. Prod. by Grover Thompson. 2007. audio compact disk 12.00 (978-1-4276-2102-3(0)) AardGP.

Grover's Orange Book. Jane Zion Brauer. 1991. act. bk. ed. 24.50 (978-0-19-434418-0(5)) OUP.

Grover's Overtures. 1 cass. (Running Time: 11 min.). (Golden's Sesame Street Ser.). (J). 1994. bk. 6.99 (14427, Gold Bks) RH Chldrns.
Grover is on his way to play his toy cannon at the end of the 1812 Overture. As he runs through the Monsterpolitan Opera House he hears lots of different overtures but he cannot find the 1812 Overture! Will he get there in time to play his cannon.

Grow Big Songs, Vol. 1. Woody Guthrie & Arlo Guthrie. 1 cass. (Running Time: 25 min.). (J). 1992. 8.98 (4-45021) Warner Bros.
10 songs with lyrics.

Grow Big Songs, Vol. 2. Woody Guthrie & Arlo Guthrie. Read by Guthrie Family. 1 cass. (J). 1992. 8.98 (978-1-880528-03-7(7), 4-45022) Warner Bros.

Grow, Grow, Grow: God Made Me to Grow Up! Perf. by Karyn Henley. 1. (Running Time: approx. 30 minutes). (J). 2004. audio compact disk 8.99 (978-0-9743197-2-8(4), PLCD5) Child Sens Comm.

Grow Old Along with Me the Best Is Yet to Be. unabr. ed. Poems. Read by Edward Asner et al. Ed. by Sandra Haldeman Martz. 2 cass. (Running Time: 3 hrs.). 1996. 17.95 (978-1-57453-054-4(2)) Audio Lit.
Asks: How do we look at each other as we grow older? Our children grow up, our lovers age & our lives take on different dimensions. The poems & prose in this collection revel in the joys of being older, not necessarily wiser & continually involved with the process of living.

Grow Up: Luke 7:31-35, Matthew 7:24-27. Ed Young. 1993. 4.95 (978-0-7417-1971-3(1), 971) Win Walk.

Grow Wings & Fly: Keys to Motivational Skills. abr. ed. Andrea Nierenberg. 1 cass. (Running Time: 40 mins.). (Nierenberg Success Program). 1998. 12.99 (978-0-9725972-1-0(2)) Nierenberg Group.
Learn how you can have more joy and personal growth while "flying over" disappointments in life. The author teaches you how to "take off", achieve your goals, discover hidden potential, and control difficulty.

Grow Younger, Live Longer: Ten Steps to Reverse Aging. abr. ed. Deepak Chopra & David Simon. Read by Deepak Chopra. 5 CDs. (Running Time: 5 hrs.). (Deepak Chopra Ser.). (ENG.). 2001. audio compact disk 24.95 (978-0-375-41976-8(4), Random AudioBks) Pub: Random Audio Pubg. Dist(s): Random

Grow Your Money: 101 Easy Tips to Plan, Save, & Invest. Jonathan D. Pond. Read by Dick Hill. (Playaway Adult Nonfiction Ser.). (ENG.). 2009. 65.00 (978-1-60775-623-1(4)) Find a World.

Grow Your Money: 101 Easy Tips to Plan, Save, & Invest. unabr. ed. Jonathan D. Pond. Narrated by Dick Hill. 9 CDs. (Running Time: 11 hrs. 0 mins. 0 sec.). (ENG.). 2007. audio compact disk 34.99 (978-1-4001-0585-4(4)); audio compact disk 69.99 (978-1-4001-3585-1(0)) Pub: Tantor Media. Dist(s): IngramPubServ

Grow Your Money: 101 Easy Tips to Plan, Save, & Invest. unabr. ed. Jonathan D. Pond. Read by Dick Hill. 1 MP3-CD. (Running Time: 11 hrs. 0 mins. 0 sec.). (ENG.). 2007. audio compact disk 24.99 (978-1-4001-5585-9(1)) Pub: Tantor Media. Dist(s): IngramPubServ

Grow Your Own Money Tree! David P. Schloss. Read by David P. Schloss. 1 CD. (Running Time: 43 mins.). (ENG.). 2007. audio compact disk 10.95 (978-0-9629230-6-7(0)) D P Schloss.

Grow Your Own Money Tree! unabr. ed. David P. Schloss. Read by David P. Schloss. 1 cass. (Running Time: 42 min.). (ENG.). 1997. 9.95 (978-0-9629230-2-9(8)) D P Schloss.
This 45 - minute financial audio cassette shares with the listener powerful strategies for financial success!A few of the topics are: Why people fail financially and how you can avoid their mistakes! The variables for financial success! How to win the most important card game of your life! An explanation of mutual funds and their charges! An explanation of compound interest and tax-deferred growth! A better way to invest in mutual funds! How to be victorious in the money game and win your retirement and much more! Endorsed by: Jason Fohr, Regional Vice President, IDEX mutual funds.

Growing a Business. Paul Hawken. 2004. 7.95 (978-0-7435-4799-4(3)) Pub: S&S Audio. Dist(s): S and S Inc

Growing & Managing a Business. unabr. ed. Kathleen R. Allen. Narrated by Eric Conger. 2 CDs. (Running Time: 2 hrs. 30 mins.). (New York Times Pocket MBA Ser.). 2003. audio compact disk 19.95 (978-1-885408-99-0(4)) Listen & Live.

Growing & Managing a Business: 25 Keys to Building Your Company. Kathleen R. Allen. Read by Eric Conger. 2 cass. (Running Time: 2 hrs.). (New York Times Pocket MBA Ser.). 2000. pap. bk. 27.95 Listen & Live.
Learn the 25 keys in managing the growth of a business, including identifying your competitive advantage, implementing a total quality strategy & creating a visionary corporate culture.

Growing & Managing a Business: 25 Keys to Building Your Company. unabr. ed. Kathleen R. Allen. Read by Eric Conger. 2 cass. (Running Time: 2 hrs. 30 mins.). (New York Times Pocket MBA Ser.). 2000. 16.95 (978-1-885408-40-2(4), LL033) Listen & Live.

Growing Deep in the Christian Life. 2005. audio compact disk 62.00 (978-1-57972-685-0(2)); audio compact disk 62.00 (978-1-57972-686-7(0)) Insight Living.

Growing Deeper CD Series. 2004. audio compact disk 27.00 (978-1-59834-054-9(9)) Walk Thru the Bible.

Growing Faith: Being Good Stewards. 2003. (978-1-932614-03-9(6)); audio compact disk (978-1-932614-02-2(8)) Bookworks.

Growing Faith: Confidently Facing Fear. 2003. (978-1-932614-07-7(9)); audio compact disk (978-1-932614-06-0(0)) Bookworks.

Growing Faith: Faith That Works. 2003. (978-0-9710612-3-1(8)); audio compact disk (978-0-9710612-2-4(X)) Bookworks.

Growing Faith: Faithful Relationships. 2003. (978-1-932614-05-3(2)); audio compact disk (978-1-932614-04-6(4)) Bookworks.

Growing Faith: God Every Day. 2003. (978-1-932614-13-8(3)); audio compact disk (978-1-932614-12-1(5)) Bookworks.

Growing Faith: God's Helping Hand. 2003. (978-1-932614-01-5(X)); audio compact disk (978-1-932614-00-8(1)) Bookworks.

Growing Faith: Joyful Living. 2003. (978-0-9710612-5-5(4)); audio compact disk (978-0-9710612-4-8(6)) Bookworks.

Growing Faith: Lift up Your Heart. 2003. (978-0-9710612-1-7(1)); audio compact disk (978-0-9710612-0-0(3)) Bookworks.

Growing Faith: Raising Kids in God's Grace. 2003. (978-0-9710612-7-9(0)); audio compact disk (978-0-9710612-6-2(2)) Bookworks.

Growing Faith: The Power of Prayer. 2003. (978-1-932614-09-1(5)); audio compact disk (978-1-932614-08-4(7)) Bookworks.

Growing Faith: With God There's Hope. 2003. (978-0-9710612-9-3(7)); audio compact disk (978-0-9710612-8-6(9)) Bookworks.

Growing Faith: You Are Not Alone. 2003. (978-1-932614-11-4(7)); audio compact disk (978-1-932614-10-7(9)) Bookworks.

Growing Godward. Swami Amar Jyoti. 1 cass. 1980. 9.95 (P-30) Truth Consciousness.
Preparing the ground to see Him. Conscious effort makes the breakthrough. Doing everything for God for even 30 days will change our lives.

Growing Hand. unabr. ed. 1 cass. (Running Time: 20 min.). Dramatization. (Magic Looking Glass Ser.). (J). (gr. 2-6). 1989. 9.95 (978-0-7810-0017-8(3), NIM-CW-126-3-91) NIMCO.
A story of Irish descent.

Growing Healthy Cell Gro Audio. House to House Staff. 2004. 35.00 (978-1-886973-50-3(4)) Hse2HsePubns.

Growing in Awareness of Christ Today, Set. Benedict J. Groeschel. 2 cass. (Running Time: 1 hrs. 58 min.). 1999. 19.95 (TAH420) Alba Hse Comns.
To assist us in regaining a real sense of mystery in the presence of Christ, Fr. Groeschel leads this revealing & intuitive exploration back into the effective sense of that presence.

Growing in English Language Skills. Mary Finocchiaro & Violet Lavanda. (J). (gr. 9-12). 1987. 32.00 (978-0-13-366022-7(2), 58444) Prentice ESL.

Growing in Faith. Rick Joyner. 6 cass. (Running Time: 9 hrs.). 2000. 30.00 (RJ15-000) Morning NC.
With fresh & practical messages centering on faith, this tape series will enable you to better understand essential principles of the Christian walk.

Growing in Faith. Rick Joyner. 1 cass. (Running Time: 90 min.). (Growing in Faith Ser.: Vol. 2). 2000. 5.00 (RJ14-002) Morning NC.

Growing in God's Word. Prod. by Twin Sisters Productions Staff. 1 CD. (Running Time: 30 min). (J). 2005. audio compact disk 6.99 (978-1-57583-813-7(3)) Twin Sisters.
Begin building a solid foundation for Christian growth with new, original Scripture memory songs! Impress God's Word upon tender hearts and minds with contemporary, easy-to-sing, uplifting, and worshipful original music. Kids and families will sing and learn what God says about love, trust, grace, strength, worship, and more. Sung by kids for kids, these Scripture memory songs are ideal for use at home, church, and school! BONUS! The ENHANCED CD includes 63 pages of sheet music that can be printed from your own computer!.

Growing in Grace: Daniel: Dan. 1:8. Ed Young. 1988. Rental 4.95 (978-0-7417-1674-3(7), 674) Win Walk.

Growing in Grace: Peter: Gal. 2:11-14. Ed Young. 1988. 4.95 (978-0-7417-1675-0(5), 675) Win Walk.

***Growing in Intimacy with God.** Mason Betha.Tr. of 2009. (ENG.). 2008. audio compact disk 24.99 (978-1-60989-002-5(7)) Born To Succee.

Growing in Marriage. Mark Crow. 5 cass. (Running Time: 5 hrs.). 2001. (978-1-931537-04-9(6)) Vision Comm Creat.

Growing in the Christian Life. Ord L. Morrow. Read by Ord L. Morrow. 1 cass. (Running Time: 1 hr. 30 min.). 1988. 4.95 (978-0-8474-2319-4(0)) Back to Bible.
Features messages that focus on what happens when Christ lives out his life in us & gives tips for growing in faith.

Growing in the Spirit. Contrib. by Gospel Light Publications Staff. 3 cass. 1997. 17.99 Set. (978-7-5116-0035-6(2)) Gospel Lght.
Spirituality.

Growing into Holiness. Swami Amar Jyoti. 1 cass. 1975. 9.95 (M-54) Truth Consciousness.
Transcending dogmas & conjectures, aspiring to Perfection. Fulfilling God's conditions.

Growing into Sattwa. Swami Amar Jyoti. 1 cass. 1976. 9.95 (M-58) Truth Consciousness.
The three gunas & spiritual seeking. Advice to seekers on transcending into sattwa.

Growing into Sonship. Speeches. Creflo A. Dollar. 3 cass. (Running Time: 4 hrs.). 2002. 15.00 (978-1-59089-462-0(6)); audio compact disk 21.00 (978-1-59089-463-7(4)) Creflo Dollar.

Growing Old & How to Cope with It. unabr. ed. Alfons Deeken. Read by Al Covaia. 3 cass. 14.95 set. (938) Ignatius Pr.
"A splendid, cheering book!" Filled with practical aids & examples from literature & philosophy. It will appeal to young & old alike.

Growing Old with Grace. unabr. ed. Leopold Bellak & Robert Neil Butler. 1 cass. (Running Time: 56 min.). 12.95 (978-0-88432-221-4(1), C40205) J Norton Pubs.
Bellak & Butler discuss with Heywood Hale Broun how to grow old & face it with equanimity. They describe some of the services available & some of the techniques of postponing the inevitable as long as possible.

Growing Old with Wisdom & Grace: When I Am an Old Woman I Shall Wear Purple, If I Had My Life to Live over I Would Pick More Daisies, Grow Old Along with Me the Best Is Yet to Be, unabr. ed. Sandra Haldeman-Martz. Contrib. by Cch Pounder & Ellen Burstyn. 6 cass. (Running Time: 9 hrs.). (Papier-Mache Press Anthologies Ser.). 1998. bk. 49.95 (978-1-57453-229-6(4)) Audio Lit.

Growing Pains of Adrian Mole. unabr. ed. Sue Townsend. Read by Nicholas Barnes. 6 cass. (Running Time: 6 hrs.). (Adrian Mole Ser.: Vol. 3). (J). 1995. 54.95 Set. (978-0-7451-4379-8(2), CAB 1063) AudioGO.
Adrian is fifteen & still wobbling through the welter of parents, Pandora, & his American pen pal, on a course of intellectual obscurity. But changes are afoot with the awful threat of a new sibling. Meanwhile, his voice just can't be trusted to stay at the same pitch for a single sentence!.

Growing Pumpkins. Sundance/Newbridge, LLC Staff. (Early Science Ser.). (gr. k-3). 2007. audio compact disk 12.00 (978-1-4007-6182-1(4)); audio compact disk 12.00 (978-1-4007-6181-4(6)); audio compact disk 12.00 (978-1-4007-6183-8(2)) Sund Newbrdge.

Growing Rock: A Native American Tale. Sandra Robbins. 1 cass. (Running Time: 32 min.). (See-More Ser.). (J). (ps). 1993. 5.50 (978-1-882601-17-2(3)) See-Mores Wrkshop.
Created for children based on Shadow Box Theatre's Production. Side 1 - word for word rendition of companion book with musical accompaniment. Side 2 - guided activity (movement, acting, singing) rendition of story with musical.

Growing Rock: A Native American Tale. Sandra Robbins. Music by Jeff Olmsted. 1 cd. (Running Time: 32). (See-More's Stories Ser.). (J). 1993. pap. bk. 16.95 (978-1-882601-39-4(4)) See-Mores Wrkshop.

Growing Rock: A Native American Tale. Sandra Robbins. Illus. by Iku Oseki. (See-More's Stories Ser.). (J). (ps-4). 1993. pap. bk. 11.95 (978-1-882601-15-8(7)) See-Mores Wrkshop.

Growing Strong in the Seasons of Life. Charles R. Swindoll. (Running Time: 60 min.). 1994. 12.99 (978-0-310-41368-4(0)) Zondervan.
A one-year devotional build around the seasons of life.

Growing Strong in the Seasons of Life. abr. ed. Charles R. Swindoll. (Running Time: 1 hr. 0 mins. 0 sec.). (ENG.). 2003. 10.99 (978-0-310-26051-6(5)) Zondervan.

***Growing the Church in the Power of the Holy Spirit: Seven Principles of Dynamic Cooperation.** Zondervan. (Running Time: 10 hrs. 35 mins. 0 sec.). (ENG.). 2009. 16.99 (978-0-310-78243-8(0)) Zondervan.

Growing Through Personal Crisis. Harmon Hartzell & June Avis. 1 cass. (Running Time: 60 min.). 1989. 9.95 HarperCollins Pubs.

Growing Up. unabr. ed. Wanda E. Brunstetter. Read by Ellen Grafton. (Running Time: 4 hrs.). (Rachel Yoder Ser.). 2009. 39.97 (978-1-4418-0691-8(1), 9781441806918, Brlnc Audio MP3 Lib); 14.99 (978-1-4418-0690-1(3), 9781441806901, Brilliance MP3); 14.99 (978-1-4418-0692-5(X), 9781441806925, BAD); 39.97 (978-1-4418-0693-2(8), 9781441806932, BADLE); audio compact disk 14.99 (978-1-4418-0688-8(1), 9781441806888, Bril Audio CD Unabri); audio compact disk 44.97 (978-1-4418-0689-5(X), 9781441806895, BriAudCD Unabrid) Brilliance Audio.

Growing Up. unabr. collector's ed. Russell Baker. Read by Michael Prichard. 7 cass. (Running Time: 10 hrs. 30 mins.). 1983. 56.00 (978-0-7366-0910-4(5), 1853) Books on Tape.
Traces the youth of Russell Baker, the 1979 Pulitzer Prize winning columnist of the New York Times.

Growing up Bin Laden: Osama's Wife & Son Take Us Inside Their Secret World. unabr. ed. Jean Sasson et al. Narrated by Mel Foster et al. (Running Time: 14 hrs. 0 mins. 0 sec.). 2009. audio compact disk 79.99 (978-1-4001-4407-5(8)) Pub: Tantor Media. Dist(s): IngramPubServ

Growing up bin Laden: Osama's Wife & Son Take Us Inside Their Secret World. unabr. ed. Jean Sasson et al. Narrated by Mel Foster et al. (Running Time: 14 hrs. 0 mins. 0 sec.). (ENG.). 2009. 29.99 (978-1-4001-6407-3(9)); audio compact disk 39.99 (978-1-4001-1407-8(1)) Pub: Tantor Media. Dist(s): IngramPubServ

***Growing up bin Laden: Osama's Wife & Son Take Us Inside Their Secret World.** unabr. ed. Jean Sasson et al. Narrated by Lorna Raver et al. (Running Time: 14 hrs. 0 mins.). 2009. 19.99 (978-1-4001-8407-1(X)) Tantor Media.

Growing up Brady: I Was a Teenage Greg. Barry Williams & Chris Kreski. Read by Barry Williams. 2 cass. (Running Time: 3 hrs.). 1992. 15.95 Set. (978-1-879371-35-4(9), 20260) Pub Mills.
This audio reveals explicit & surprising facts from behind the scenes of the national phenomenon known as "The Brady Bunch." The audio includes recollections from the show's cast members, written in an amiable style & discloses all about the show's cast & crew, the producers, & the scripts.

Growing up Christian-mp3. Read by Douglas Wilson. 1995. 9.50 (978-1-59128-269-3(1)) Canon Pr ID.

Growing up Christian-tape. Read by Douglas Wilson. 4 cass. 1995. 12.00 (978-1-59128-271-6(3)) Canon Pr ID.

Growing up Cuban in Decatur, Georgia. Carmen Agra Deedy. 1 cass. (Running Time: 60 mins.). (ps-3). 1995. 10.95 (978-1-56145-060-2(X)) Peachtree Pubs.

Growing up Cuban in Decatur, Georgia. Carmen Agra Deedy. (Running Time: 1 hr.). (gr. 8 up). 2004. audio compact disk 14.95 (978-1-56145-318-4(8)) Peachtree Pubs.

Growing up in America: Many Families, Many Cultures. Joe Giordano. Narrated by George Guidall. 6 cass. (Running Time: 6 hrs.). (Growing Up in America Ser.: Vol. 1). 1997. 49.95 Set. (978-1-891207-00-6(8)) Ethnic Prods.
A narrated series of 12 half-hour audio tapes. How ethnic, racial & religious traditions continue to exert powerful influences in American family life & personal identity.

Growing up in God's Family. unabr. ed. Charles R. Swindoll. 8 cass. (Running Time: 7 hrs.). 1998. 39.95 (978-1-57972-286-9(5)) Insight Living.

Growing up in Mississippi. Bertha M. Davis. Narrated by Ericka Dill. (ENG.). 2007. audio compact disk 21.95 (978-1-60031-018-8(4)) Spoken Books.

Growing up in the Gorbals. unabr. ed. Ralph Glasser. Read by Joe Dunlop. 8 cass. (Running Time: 11 hrs. 30 min.). (Isis Ser.). (J). 2001. 69.95 (978-1-85089-762-0(X), 8907X) Pub: ISIS Lrg Prnt GBR. Dist(s): Ulverscroft US

Growing up Is No Fun: the Standards '95-'05. Contrib. by Huntingtons & B. Ebel. 2005. audio compact disk 13.98 (978-5-558-97848-3(1)) Tooth & Nail.

Growing up Jamaican. Yvette Gladstone. Prod. by Ayodele Arowosegbe. (YA). 2007. audio compact disk 15.00 (978-1-4276-2823-7(8)) AardGP.

Growing up King: An Intimate Memoir. abr. ed. Dexter Scott King. (ENG.). 2005. 14.98 (978-1-59483-350-2(8)) Pub: Hachet Audio. Dist(s): HachBkGrp

Growing up Lutheran: What Does This Mean? abr. ed. Suzann Johnson Nelson & Janet Letnes Martin. (Running Time: 3 hrs.). (ENG.). 2005. audio compact disk 19.95 (978-1-56511-998-7(3), 1565119983) Pub: HighBridge. Dist(s): Workman Pub

Growing up, Not Old. 1 cass. 1995. 14.95 (978-1-882389-21-6(2)) Wilarvi Communs.
Some new skills & specifics on improving the emotional quality of life to keep oneself growing.

***Growing up Republican.** abr. ed. Patricia Beard. Read by Patricia Beard. (ENG.). 2007. (978-0-06-147286-2(7), Harper Audio); (978-0-06-147287-9(5), Harper Audio) HarperCollins Pubs.

Growing up Republican Set: Conversations with Christine Todd Whitman. Patricia Beard. 2 cass. 1996. 18.00 (978-0-694-51695-7(3), 651724) HarperCollins Pubs.
Drawing on extensive & exclusive interviews with Whitman & capturing her voice & ideas succinctly on audio, this in-depth biography chronicles the Republican Party's most dynamic & visible woman. The governor's cooperation gave Beard access to her family & friends for a personal angle on what makes her tick.

Growing up Responsible, Pts. 1 & 2. Bruce A. Baldwin. Read by Bruce A. Baldwin. 2 cass. (Running Time: 80 min. per cass.). 1986. 14.95 set. (978-0-933583-02-3(8), PDC#871-872) Direction Dynamics.
Book on Tape: Chapters from "Beyond the Cornucopia Kids." Part 1: Defines how discipline & success are intimately related & the seven necessary discipline products that parents must help create. Part 2: focuses on common parental problems with discipline procedures, including "soft spots," & the seven emotionally destructive parental response styles.

Growing up Rich: A Novel. unabr. ed. Anne Bernays. Read by Nancy Dannevik. 8 cass. (Running Time: 12 hrs.). 1979. 64.00 (978-0-7366-0164-1(3), 1166) Books on Tape.
The story concerns a young princess of upper class New York Jewish society who at a twist of fate is removed from her family to an adopted one, from privilege not so much to poverty as to ordinariness & from Manhattan to Brooklyn.

Growing up Spiritually. Kenneth Copeland. 4 cass. 1989. 20.00 Set. (978-0-88114-911-1(X)) K Copeland Pubns.
Biblical teaching on spiritual maturity.

Growing up Spiritually. David T. Demola. 8 cass. 32.00 (S-1050) Faith Fellow Min.

Growing up Spiritually. Taffi L. Dollar. 20.00 (978-1-59089-027-1(2)) Pub: Creflo Dollar. Dist(s): STL Dist NA

Growing up, Spiritually. Kenneth E. Hagin. 4 cass. 16.00 (48H) Faith Lib Pubns.

Growing up Spiritually. Gary V. Whetstone. Adapted by Faye Whetstone. (Theology Ser.: Vol. TH 202). 1997. 120.00 (978-1-58866-114-2(8)) Gary Whet Pub.

Growing up with Astrology & Astrologers. Bernice P. Grebner & Welsch. 1 cass. 8.95 (668) Am Fed Astrologers.
An AFA Convention workshop tape.

Growing up with Character. Howard W. Gabriel, III. (Character Building Stories for Children Ser.: Vol. 1). (J). (gr. k-8). 1987. 5.95 (978-0-936997-03-2(6), T87-01) M & H Enter.
Six Exciting, Fun Packed, Character Building Adventure Stories for Children & the Entire Family, about Love, Courage, Curiosity, Patience, Integrity & Service to Others.

Growing up with Ella Jenkins: Rhythms, Songs & Rhymes. Perf. by Ella Jenkins. 1 cass. (Running Time: 35 min.). (J). (ps). 1990. (0-9307-45032-4-9) Smithsonian Folkways.
Nursery school children join Ella in a 20-song collection including "Little Orphan Annie," "I'm Changing" & "Hickory Dickory Dock".

Growing up with Hockey Night in Canada. Contrib. by Mark Lee. 1 CD. (Running Time: 1 hr.). 2005. audio compact disk 12.95 (978-0-660-19000-6(1)) Pub: Canadian Broadcasting CAN. Dist(s): Georgetown Term

Growing up with "Shoeless Joe" The Greatest Natural Player in Baseball History. 3rd ed. E. Joe Thompson, Sr. & Jack L. Thompson, Sr. Ed. by Mary Jane McCloskey. 1 cass. 1997. 19.95 (978-0-9662531-2-2(4), 003) JTI Pub.
Tragic life story of major league baseball player banished from the game for life, after being implicated in the 1919 World Series Black Sox Scandal, who claimed his innocence on his death-bed in 1951.

***Growing up with Tamales/Los Tamales de Ana: Los tamales de Ana.** Gwendolyn Zepeda. Read by Gabriela Cavallero. (ENG & SPA., (J). (ps-3). 2009. bk. 23.95 (978-0-9815686-9-0(6)) Lorito Bks.

Growing up with the Classics. Read by Carol Quiroga. Perf. by Julia M. Lakhani. 1 cass., 1 CD. (Running Time: 45 min.). (Children's Treasury of Piano Music Classics & Favorite Poems Ser.). (J). (ps-2). 1990. (978-1-893305-00-7(7), CP102) Classic Prods Inc.
Selections by 23 different authors & composers from around the world over the past 200 years.

***Growing up with the Classics (CD) Clas[illegible]s for Children by the Masters.** Perf. by Julia Muench. (Running Time [illegible] (ENG.). (J). 1998. audio compact disk 19.95 (978-1-893305-01[illegible] Classic Prods Inc.

Growing Vegetable Soup. Lois Ehlert. (Metro Reading Ser.). (J). (gr. k). 2000. 8.46 (978-1-58120-980-8(0)) Metro Teaching.

***Growing with Purpose: Connecting with God Every Day.** unabr. ed. Jon Walker. (Running Time: 8 hrs. 18 mins. 0 sec.). (ENG.). 2009. 18.99 (978-0-310-77343-6(1)) Zondervan.

Growing Your Company Without Debt: How Today's Small Business Can Get Cash by Tomorrow. unabr. ed. Jeff Callender. Read by Jeff Callender. 1 cass. (Running Time: 15 min.). 1996. 2.95 (978-1-889095-02-8(8)) Dash Point Pubng.
Description of how factoring (purchase/sale of accounts receivable) can benefit small to medium-sized businesses.

Growler Radio Vol. 1: I Am Not a Pig! Bob Sakayama. Perf. by Zebe et al. 1 CD. (Running Time: 30 min.). (J). (gr. k-6). 1994. audio compact disk 13.00 (978-1-893185-96-8(6), GR1/CD, Growler Tapes) TNG Earth.
Kids encounter the swine laurel.

Growler Radio Vol. 1: I Am Not a Pig! Bob Sakayama. Perf. by Lynne Raymond et al. 1 cass. (Running Time: 30 min.). (J). (gr. k-6). 1994. 7.00 (978-1-893185-04-3(4), GR1, Growler Tapes) TNG Earth.

Growler Radio Vol. 2: The Sky Rider Problem. Bob Sakayama. Perf. by Zebe et al. 1 CD. (Running Time: 30 min.). (J). (gr. k-6). 1994. audio compact disk 13.00 (978-1-893185-95-1(8), GR2/CD, Growler Tapes) TNG Earth.
Something's wrong with the sky rider passenger kits.

Growler Radio Vol. 2: The Sky Rider Problem. Bob Sakayama. Perf. by Lynne Raymond et al. 1 cass. (Running Time: 30 min.). (J). (gr. k-6). 1994. 7.00 (978-1-893185-05-0(2), GR2, Growler Tapes) TNG Earth.
Somethings wrong with the sky raiders passenger kites.

Growler Radio Vol. 3: Way Out. Bob Sakayama. Perf. by Zebe et al. 1 CD. (Running Time: 30 min.). (J). (gr. k-6). 1994. audio compact disk 13.00 (978-1-893185-94-4(X), GR3/CD, Growler Tapes) TNG Earth.
Starting out in the back seat of a car, the kids end up falling through a way out.

Growler Radio Vol. 3: Way Out. Bob Sakayama. Perf. by Lynne Raymond et al. 1 cass. (Running Time: 30 min.). (J). (gr. k-6). 1994. 7.00 (978-1-893185-06-7(0), GR3, Growler Tapes) TNG Earth.
Starting out in the back seat of a car - the kids end up falling thru a way out.

Growler Radio Vol. 4: Imposimazoo. Bob Sakayama. Perf. by Zebe et al. 1 CD. (Running Time: 30 min.). (J). (gr. k-6). 1994. audio compact disk 13.00 (978-1-893185-93-7(1), GR4/CD, Growler Tapes) TNG Earth.
An ancient, mythological creature was discovered sealed in a tomb.

Growler Radio Vol. 4: Imposimazoo. Bob Sakayama. Perf. by Lynne Raymond et al. 1 cass. (Running Time: 30 min.). (J). (gr. k-6). 1994. 7.00 (978-1-893185-07-4(9), GR4, Growler Tapes) TNG Earth.

Growler Radio Vol. 5: Book of Lies. Bob Sakayama. Perf. by Zebe et al. 1 CD. (Running Time: 30 min.). (J). (gr. k-6). 1994. audio compact disk 13.00 (978-1-893185-92-0(3), GR5/CD, Growler Tapes) TNG Earth.
A package containing 2 books gets mistakenly delivered.

Growler Radio Vol. 5: Book of Lies. Bob Sakayama. Perf. by Lynne Raymond et al. 1 cass. (Running Time: 30 min.). (J). (gr. k-6). 1994. 7.00 (978-1-893185-08-1(7), GR5, Growler Tapes) TNG Earth.

Growler Radio Vol. 6: Dry Water. Sakayama Bob. Perf. by Lynne Raymond et al. 1 cass. (Running Time: 30 min.). Dramatization. (J). (gr. k-6). 1995. 7.00 (978-1-893185-09-8(5), GR6, Growler Tapes) TNG Earth.
The wetness has been removed from water.

Growler Radio Vol. 6: Dry Water. Bob Sakayama. Perf. by Zebe et al. 1 CD. (Running Time: 30 min.). (J). (gr. k-6). 1994. audio compact disk 13.00 (978-1-893185-91-3(5), GR6/CD, Growler Tapes) TNG Earth.

Growler Radio Vol. 7: Summer Radio. Bob Sakayama. Perf. by Lynne Raymond et al. 1 cass. (Running Time: 30 min.). (J). (gr. k-6). 1995. 7.00 (978-1-893185-10-4(9), GR7, Growler Tapes) TNG Earth.
Weird snow buries Growlerville.

Growler Radio Vol. 7: Summer Snow. Bob Sakayama. Perf. by Zebe et al. 1 CD. (Running Time: 30 min.). (J). (gr. k-6). 1994. audio compact disk 13.00 (978-1-893185-90-6(7), GR7/CD, Growler Tapes) TNG Earth.

Growler Radio Vol. 8: Invisibility Crisis. Bob Sakayama. Perf. by Zebe et al. 1 CD. (Running Time: 30 min.). Dramatization. (J). 1994. audio compact disk 13.00 (978-1-893185-89-0(3), GR8/CD, Growler Tapes) TNG Earth.
An ancestral enchantment gets out of control.

Growler Radio Vol. 8: Invisibility Crisis. Bob Sakayama. Perf. by Lynne Raymond et al. 1 cass. (Running Time: 30 min.). (J). (gr. k-6). 1995. 7.00 (978-1-893185-11-1(7), GR8, Growler Tapes) TNG Earth.

Growler Radio Vol. 9: Time Stop. Bob Sakayama. Perf. by Lynne Raymond et al. 1 cass. (Running Time: 30 min.). (J). (gr. k-6). 1995. 7.00 (978-1-893185-12-8(5), GR9, Growler Tapes) TNG Earth.
Free magic samples over the phone result in difficulties.

Growler Radio Vol. 9: Time Stop. Bob Sakayama. Perf. by Zebe et al. 1 CD. (Running Time: 30 min.). (J). (gr. k-6). 1995. audio compact disk 13.00 (978-1-893185-88-3(5), GR9/CD, Growler Tapes) TNG Earth.

Growler Radio Vol. 10: Mad Rainbow. Bob Sakayama. Perf. by Zebe et al. 1 CD. (Running Time: 30 min.). (J). (gr. k-6). 1995. audio compact disk 13.00 (978-1-893185-87-6(7), GR10/CD, Growler Tapes) TNG Earth.
Kids get hit by the seed packets of the mad rainbow tree.

Growler Radio Vol. 10: Mad Rainbow. Bob Sakayama. Perf. by Lynne Raymond et al. 1 cass. (Running Time: 30 min.). (J). (gr. k-6). 1995. 7.00 (978-1-893185-13-5(3), Growler Tapes) TNG Earth.
The kids get hit by seed packets of the mad rainbow tree.

Growler Radio Vol. 11: Time in 2 Bottles. Bob Sakayama. Perf. by Zebe et al. 1 CD. (Running Time: 30 min.). (J). (gr. k-6). 1995. audio compact disk 13.00 (978-1-893185-86-9(9), GR11/CD, Growler Tapes) TNG Earth.
Kids discover problems with time travel.

Growler Radio Vol. 11: Time in 2 Bottles. Bob Sakayama. Perf. by Lynne Raymond et al. 1 cass. (Running Time: 30 min.). (J). (gr. k-6). 1995. 7.00 (978-1-893185-14-2(1), GR11, Growler Tapes) TNG Earth.

Growler Radio Vol. 12: Wave of the Future. Bob Sakayama. Perf. by Zebe et al. 1 CD. (Running Time: 30 min.). (J). (gr. k-6). 1995. audio compact disk 13.00 (978-1-893185-85-2(0), GR12/CD, Growler Tapes) TNG Earth.
The kids see themselves as teenagers.

Growler Radio Vol. 12: Wave of the Future. Bob Sakayama. Perf. by Lynne Raymond et al. 1 cass. (Running Time: 30 min.). (J). (gr. k-6). 1995. 7.00 (978-1-893185-15-9(X), GR12, Growler Tapes) TNG Earth.

Growler Radio Vol. 13: Voice Throw. Bob Sakayama. Perf. by Zebe et al. 1 CD. (Running Time: 30 min.). (J). (gr. k-6). 1995. audio compact disk 13.00 (978-1-893185-84-5(2), GR13/CD, Growler Tapes) TNG Earth.
The kids run into problems backstage.

Growler Radio Vol. 13: Voice Throw. Bob Sakayama. Perf. by Lynne Raymond et al. 1 cass. (Running Time: 30 min.). (J). (gr. k-6). 1995. 7.00 (978-1-893185-16-6(8), GR13, Growler Tapes) TNG Earth.

Growler Radio Vol. 14: Nothing for Christmas. Bob Sakayama. Perf. by Zebe et al. 1 CD. (Running Time: 30 min.). (J). (gr. k-6). 1995. audio compact disk 13.00 (978-1-893185-83-8(4), GR14/CD, Growler Tapes) TNG Earth.
Why do the little Huhu all want nothing?.

Growler Radio Vol. 14: Nothing for Christmas. Bob Sakayama. Perf. by Lynne Raymond et al. 1 cass. (Running Time: 30 min.). (J). (gr. k-6). 1995. 7.00 (978-1-893185-17-3(6), GR14, Growler Tapes) TNG Earth.
Why do the little Hu Hu all want nothing.

Growler Radio Vol. 15: Recipe for Disaster. Bob Sakayama. Perf. by Zebe et al. 1 CD. (Running Time: 30 min.). (J). (gr. k-6). 1997. audio compact disk 13.00 (Growler Tapes) TNG Earth.
Kids discover a robotic device named "Sweetie Pie.".

Growler Radio Vol. 15: Recipe for Disaster. Bob Sakayama. Perf. by Lynne Raymond et al. 1 cass. (Running Time: 30 min.). (J). (gr. k-6). 1998. 7.00 (978-1-893185-18-0(4), GR15, Growler Tapes) TNG Earth.
The kids discover a robotic device named "Sweetie Pie.".

Growler Radio Vol. 16: Seeds of Doubt. Bob Sakayama. Perf. by Zebe et al. 1 CD. (Running Time: 30 min.). (J). (gr. k-6). 1997. audio compact disk 13.00 (978-1-893185-81-4(8), GR16/CD, Growler Tapes) TNG Earth.
Kids encounter upsy crystals & the doubt bush.

Growler Radio Vol. 17: Edible Incredible. Bob Sakayama. Perf. by Zebe et al. 1 CD. (Running Time: 30 min.). (J). (gr. k-6). 1997. audio compact disk 13.00 (978-1-893185-80-7(X), GR17/CD, Growler Tapes) TNG Earth.
Everything becomes edible.

Growler Radio Vol. 17: Edible Incredible. Bob Sakayama. Perf. by Lynne Raymond et al. 1 cass. (Running Time: 30 min.). (J). (gr. k-6). 1998. 7.00 (978-1-893185-20-3(6), GR17, Growler Tapes) TNG Earth.

Growler Radio Vol. 18: The Ring of Truth. Bob Sakayama. Perf. by Zebe et al. 1 CD. (Running Time: 30 min.). (J). (gr. k-6). 1998. audio compact disk 13.00 (978-1-893185-79-1(6), GR18/CD, Growler Tapes) TNG Earth.
The kids find the ring of truth & an encrusted clay called scratch.

Growler Radio Vol. 18: The Ring of Truth. Bob Sakayama. Perf. by Lynne Raymond et al. 1 cass. (Running Time: 30 min.). (J). (gr. k-6). 1998. 7.00 (978-1-893185-21-0(4), GR18, Growler Tapes) TNG Earth.

Growler Radio Vol. 19: Stuck on a Sneeze. Bob Sakayama. Perf. by Zebe et al. 1 CD. (Running Time: 30 min.). (J). (gr. k-6). 1998. audio compact disk 13.00 (978-1-893185-78-4(8), GR19/CD, Growler Tapes) TNG Earth.
The kids learn about the sneeze trees.

Growler Radio Vol. 19: Stuck on a Sneeze. Bob Sakayama. Perf. by Lynne Raymond et al. 1 cass. Dramatization. (J). (gr. k-6). 1998. 6.00 (978-1-893185-22-7(2), GR19, Growler Tapes) TNG Earth.

Growler Radio Vol. 20: Toxic Obnoxic. Bob Sakayama. Perf. by Zebe et al. 1 CD. (Running Time: 30 min.). (J). (gr. k-6). 1998. audio compact disk 13.00 (978-1-893185-77-7(X), GR20/CD, Growler Tapes) TNG Earth.
Dr. Growler's Growlershine poses a danger in Growlerville.

Growler Radio Vol. 20: Toxic Obnoxic. Bob Sakayama. Perf. by Lynne Raymond et al. 1 cass. (Running Time: 30 min.). (Growler Radio Ser.). (J). (gr. k-6). 1998. 7.00 (978-1-893185-23-4(0), Growler Tapes) TNG Earth.
Dr. Growler's Growlershine poses a danger to Growlerville.

Growler Radio Vol. 21: Bottomless Bag. Bob Sakayama. Perf. by Lynne Raymond et al. 1 cass. (Running Time: 30 min.). (J). (gr. k-6). 1999. 7.00 (978-1-893185-24-1(9)) TNG Earth.
The kids discover a bag that's bigger on the inside then the outside in this science fiction adventure.

Growler Radio Vol. 21: Bottomless Bag. Bob Sakayama. Perf. by Zebe et al. 1 CD. (Running Time: 30 min.). (J). (gr. k-6). 1999. audio compact disk 13.00 (978-1-893185-76-0(1), GR21/CD, Growler Tapes) TNG Earth.
The kids discover a bag that's bigger on the inside than on the outside.

Growler Radio Vol. 22: The Noise Thief. Bob Sakayama. Perf. by Lynne Raymond et al. 1 cass. (Running Time: 30 min.). (J). (gr. k-6). 1999. 7.00 (978-1-893185-25-8(7)) TNG Earth.
The noise thief escapes from the forbidden zone in this science fiction adventure.

Growler Radio Vol. 22: The Noise Thief. Bob Sakayama. Perf. by Zebe et al. 1 CD. (Running Time: 30 min.). (J). (gr. k-6). 1999. audio compact disk 13.00 (978-1-893185-75-3(3), GR22/CD, Growler Tapes) TNG Earth.
The Noise Thief escapes from the forbidden zone.

Growler Radio Vol. 23: Glitch. Bob Sakayama. Perf. by Zebe et al. 1 cass. (Running Time: 30 min.). (J). (gr. k-6). 1999. 7.00 (978-1-893185-26-5(5), GR23, Growler Tapes); audio compact disk 13.00 (978-1-893185-70-8(2), GR23/CD, Growler Tapes) TNG Earth.
A dormant encrusted jewel threatens chaos upon activation.

Growler Radio Vol. 25: Camouflage. Bob Sakayama. 1 cass. (Running Time: 30 min.). (J). (gr. k-6). 2000. 7.00 (978-1-893185-28-9(1)) TNG Earth.
Mother Huhu had a slight accident during the taping of her show. But not to worry. Everything that escaped has been recaptures and is being held in small glass containment traps spread out on the lawn, waiting to be put back into the vault by the baby Huhu. What else could possibly go wrong?.

Growler Radio Vol. 26: Timefish. Bob Sakayama. 1 cass. (Running Time: 30 min.). (J). (gr. k-6). 2001. 7.00 (978-1-893185-29-6(X)); audio compact disk 13.00 (978-1-893185-67-8(2)) TNG Earth.
The Timefish evolved the ability to create an opening in time called a temporal vortex, through which they can travel to other time zones in search of better survival conditions. But is this temporal vortex a dangerous place for the Baby Huhu? And what is Professor Growler doing with all those fake crickets.

Growler Radio Vol. 27: All Things Being Equal. Bob Sakayama. 1 CD. (Running Time: 30 min.). (J). (gr. k-6). 2001. audio compact disk 13.00 (978-1-893185-66-1(4)); 7.00 (978-1-893185-30-2(3)) TNG Earth.
During a renovation of Oldold's historic residence, a sealed basement room was discovered and opened. During the next rainstorm, weird purple flies started popping up everywhere. Then citizens started having trouble making up their minds. To top it off, there's an anti-magic candidate running in the election.

Growler Tapes. 4 cass. (Running Time: 2 hrs.). (J). 2001. 24.95 (EAMU001) Lodestone Catalog.

Growler Tapes Classic Series, Vols. 1-4, Set. Bob Sakayama. Perf. by Sky Burdahl et al. 2 CDs. (Running Time: 1 hr. 35 min.). (J). (ps-5). 1986. audio compact disk 46.00 (978-1-893185-97-5(4), GTI-4/2CD, Growler Tapes) TNG Earth.
Stories include "Cutting the Cord," "A Sign from the Sky," "Square Bubbles" & "1/4 Past 20.".

Growler Tapes Classics Vol. 1: Cutting the Cord. Bob Sakayama. Perf. by Sky Burdahl et al. 1 CD. (Running Time: 19 min.). Dramatization. (J). (ps-5). 1983. audio compact disk 13.00 (978-1-893185-74-6(5), GTI/CD, Growler Tapes) TNG Earth.
In the dark the kids lose a key they need to get home. They find a strange recycling plant & the Growlers who do the sorting.

Growler Tapes Classics Vol. 2: A Sign from the Sky. Bob Sakayama. Perf. by Sky Burdahl et al. 1 CD. (Running Time: 25 min.). Dramatization. (J). (ps-5). 1984. audio compact disk 13.00 (978-1-893185-73-9(7), GTII/CD, Growler Tapes) TNG Earth.
The kids weren't the only ones to see where the shooting star landed.

Growler Tapes Classics Vol. 3: Square Bubbles. Bob Sakayama. Perf. by Sky Burdahl et al. 1 CD. (Running Time: 27 min.). Dramatization. (J). (ps-5). 1985. audio compact disk 13.00 (978-1-893185-72-2(9), GTIII/CD, Growler Tapes) TNG Earth.
The kids try to find the source of the square bubbles.

Growler Tapes Classics Vol. 4: Quarter Past Twenty. Bob Sakayama. Perf. by Sky Burdahl et al. 1 CD. (Running Time: 25 min.). Dramatization. (J). (ps-5). 1986. audio compact disk 13.00 (978-1-893185-71-5(0), GT IV/CD, Growler Tapes) TNG Earth.
The kids win a contest on late night Huhu radio.

Growler Tapes I: Cutting the Cord. Bob Sakayama. Perf. by Lynne Raymond et al. 1 cass. (Running Time: 19 min.). (Growler Tapes Ser.). (J). (ps-5). 1993. 7.00 (978-1-893185-00-5(1), GT1, Growler Tapes) TNG Earth.
In the dark the kids drop & lose a key - they need to get home. They find a strange recycling plant, & the Growlers who do the sorting at the plant.

Growler Tapes II: A Sign from the Sky. Bob Sakayama. Perf. by Lynne Raymond et al. 1 cass. (Running Time: 24 min.). (Growler Tapes Ser.). (J). (ps-5). 1993. 7.00 (978-1-893185-01-2(X), GT2, Growler Tapes) TNG Earth.
The kids weren't the only ones to see where that shooting star landed.

Growler Tapes III: Square Bubbles. Bob Sakayama. Perf. by Lynne Raymond et al. 1 cass. (Running Time: 19 min.). (Growler Tapes Ser.). (J). (ps-5). 1993. 7.00 (978-1-893185-02-9(8), GT3, Growler Tapes) TNG Earth.
The kids try to find the source of the square bubbles.

Growler Tapes IV: Quarter Past Twenty. Bob Sakayama. Perf. by Lynne Raymond et al. 1 cass. (Running Time: 24 min.). (Growler Tapes Ser.). (J). (ps-5). 1993. 7.00 (978-1-893185-03-6(6), GT4, Growler Tapes) TNG Earth.
The kids win a contest on late night Hu Hu Radio.

Growler Tapes 16: Seeds of Doubt. Bob Sakayama. Perf. by Lynne Raymond et al. 1 cass. (Running Time: 30 min.). (J). (gr. k-6). 1998. 7.00 (978-1-893185-19-7(2), GR16, Growler Tapes) TNG Earth.
The kids encounter upsy crystals & the doubt bush.

Grown a Foot or Two. Scott Simmons. 1 cass. 1998. 9.95 (978-1-57008-568-0(4), Bkcraft Inc) Deseret Bk.

Grown Man Now. Jane B. Schulz. Read by Jane B. Schulz. Prod. by Daniel T. de Wit. Des. by Mary S. de Wit. (ENG.). (YA). 2008. 24.95 (978-1-935095-06-4(4)) intwowit.

Grown-up Christmas List. Contrib. by Amy Grant. (Ultimate Tracks (Word Tracks) Ser.). 2006. audio compact disk 8.98 (978-5-558-27164-5(7), Word Music) Word Enter.

Grown up Christmas List. Contrib. by Amy Grant. (Mastertrax Ser.). 2007. audio compact disk 9.98 (978-5-557-55749-8(0)) Pt of Grace Ent.

Grown-up's Halloween: Fantasies & Fables for the Philosophically Fiendish. unabr. ed. (Running Time: 23400 sec.). 2006. 44.95 (978-0-7861-4873-8(X)); audio compact disk 29.95 (978-0-7861-7123-1(5)) Blckstn Audio.

Grown-up's Halloween: Fantasies & Fables for the Philosophically Fiendish. unabr. ed. Yuri Rasovsky. Read by Full Cast Production Staff. (Running Time: 23400 sec.). 2006. audio compact disk 45.00 (978-0-7861-6037-2(3)) Blckstn Audio.

Grownups Are Strange. Bill Harley. (J). 2004. audio compact disk 15.00 (978-1-878126-39-9(3)) Round Riv Prodns.
An upbeat title song & stories about camping out & third grade teachers. Grownups Are Strange; Grandma vs. the Headless Man; Happy Birthday Mrs. Nottingham!!!/Birthday Waltz.

Grownups Are Strange. unabr. ed. Bill Harley. Read by Bill Harley. 1 cass. (Running Time: 50 min.). (J). (gr. 4-8). 1990. 10.00 (978-1-878126-03-0(2), RRR106) Round Riv Prodns.

Growth from Gratitude: The Best of Lynn Jones. 2010. audio compact disk (978-0-9769068-6-5(4)) Mid A Bks & Tapes.

Growth in Discipleship: A Retreat for Religious. Eugene Trainer. 8 cass. 57.95 incl. shelf-case. (TAH001) Alba Hse Comns.
Prayer, personality, spirituality, stages of growth, discernment, models of Church & religion & total response to the Gospel.

Growth Is Messy/Preparation for Relationships. Marianne Williamson. Read by Marianne Williamson. 1 cass. (Running Time: 90 mins.). (Lectures on a Course in Miracles). 1999. 10.00 (978-1-56170-227-5(7), M730) Hay House.

Growth of America 1878-1928. unabr. ed. Clarence B. Carson. (Running Time: 45000 sec.). (Basic History of the United States Ser.). 2007. audio compact disk 90.00 (978-0-7861-6016-7(0)); audio compact disk 29.95 (978-0-7861-6017-4(9)) Blckstn Audio.

Growth of an Expanding Mission see Cremcimiento de una Mision que se Expande

Growth of an Expanding Mission: A Study of Acts 10:1-10:18. unabr. ed. Charles R. Swindoll. 10 cass. (Running Time: 8 hrs. 15 mins.). 1998. 48.95 (978-1-57972-254-8(7)) Insight Living.

Growth or No Growth - The Battle Lines Are Drawn. Hosted by Nancy Pearlman. 1 cass. (Running Time: 29 min.). 10.00 (313) Educ Comm CA.

Growth Series, Set. Elbert Willis. 4 cass. 13.00 Fill the Gap.

Grudge Can Be Art (an Essay from Things I've Learned from Women Who've Dumped Me) abr. ed. Andy Selsberg. Read by Andy Selsberg. Ed. by Ben Karlin. (Running Time: 15 mins.). (ENG.). 2008. 1.98 (978-1-60024-338-7(X)) Pub: Hachet Audio. Dist(s): HachBkGrp

Gruesome Twosome. unabr. ed. Keith Brumpton. Read by Toby Longworth. 6 CDs. (Running Time: 6 hrs. 30 mins.). (J). (gr. 5-7). 2006. audio compact disk 59.95 (978-1-4056-5534-7(8), Chivers Child Audio) AudioGO.

Grumpuss: The Original Otherworld Audio Theater Production, Set. unabr. ed. Travis E. Pike. Read by Travis E. Pike. 2 cass. (Running Time: 1 hr. 24 min.). Dramatization. (YA). (gr. 7-12). 1998. 16.95 (978-1-892900-02-9(5), 98-3107) Otherworld Ent.
A fantasy-adventure tale of an enormous pre-historic cat & the courageous knight sent to vanquish or tame it. Told entirely in rhyme, features original music & sound effects.

Grumpy Bear. (Sails Literacy Ser.). (gr. k up). 10.00 (978-0-7578-5419-4(2)) Rigby Educ.

Grumpy Pumpkins. unabr. ed. Judy Delton. Narrated by Christina Moore. 1 cass. (Running Time: 1 hr.). (Pee Wee Scouts Ser.: No. 5). (J). (gr. 2-5). 1997. 10.00 (978-0-7887-0752-0(3), 94929E7) Recorded Bks.
Six-year-old Molly Duff is so excited, she can hardly sit still - the Pee Wee Scouts are planning a Halloween party.

Grumpy Pumpkins. unabr. ed. Judy Delton. Read by Christina Moore. 1 cass. (Running Time: 1 hr.). (Pee Wee Scouts Ser.: No. 5). (J). (gr. 2-5). 1997. pap. bk. 22.24 (978-0-7887-1828-1(2), 40608); Rental 6.50; 70.70 (978-0-7887-2385-8(5), 46656) Recorded Bks.
Six-year-old Molly Duff is so excited, she can hardly sit still - the Pee Wee Scouts are planning a Halloween party.

Grumpy Shepherd. Contrib. by Joe Cox & Nylea L. Butler-Moore. (gr. 2-6). bk. 40.00 (978-0-687-05037-6(5)) Abingdon.

Grumpy Shepherd: Listening Tape - Music & Speaking Parts. Joe Cox. (gr. 2-6). 1998. 12.00 (978-0-687-06653-7(0)) Abingdon.

Grundo Beach Party. Will Ryan. Ed. by Mary Becker. Illus. by David High et al. (J). (ps). 1986. bk. (978-0-318-60971-3(1)) Alchemy Comms.

Grunge Rock Sessions for Guitar. Ed. by Ed Lazano. Contrib. by Randy Young & Peter Marunzak. 1 CD. (Running Time: 1 hr.). 1998. pap. bk. 12.95 (978-0-8256-1627-3(1), AM945175) Music Sales.

Grupos. 1 cass. (Primeros Pasos en Ciencia Ser.). (SPA.). (J). 12.00 (7451-0, Natl Textbk Co) M-H Contemporary.
Helps children discover the process of scientific investigation. Part of the First Steps in Science Program.

Guadalcanal. Richard B. Frank. Read by Grover Gardner. 9 cass. (Running Time: 13 hrs. 30 min.). 1991. 72.00 (2824-B) Books on Tape.

Guadalcanal. unabr. ed. Richard B. Frank. Read by Grover Gardner. 9 cass. (Running Time: 13 hrs. 30 min.). 1991. 72.00 (978-0-7366-2007-9(9), 2824-A) Books on Tape.
Eight months to the day after Pearl Harbor, the First U.S. Marine Division landed on the remote Pacific island of Guadalcanal. They seized the airfield early on, but then ran into a kind of resistance they came to know well in the months ahead. Japanese soldiers never surrendered, no matter the odds, & when the island was finally secured (six months later) it had cost us 7000 lives. Guadalcanal, 10 years in the writing, is the definitive story of this critical campaign.

Guadalupe River Valley Travel Guide: Driving Trip in the Texas Hill Country by way of Rte. 27 & Center Point River Road. 2nd enl. exp. ed. 2007. pap. bk. 20.00 (978-0-9676931-5-6(2)) Skyline Ranch.

Guan Yin Bodhisattva Is Our Brother. Contrib. by Hua. (978-0-88139-600-3(1)) Buddhist Text.

Guaranteed for Eternity. 2 cass. 7.95 (22-10, HarperThor) HarpC GBR.

Guaranteed Fresh. Perf. by Suzanne Westenhoefer. 1 CD. (Running Time: 1 hr.). 2003. audio compact disk 16.95 (978-1-929243-47-1(2)) Uproar Ent.
Uproariously funny comedy from the #1 performing "not-angry" lesbian comedian.

Guaranteed Return. Bill Winston. 4 cass. (Running Time: 3hr.38min.). (C). 2004. 20.00 (978-1-931289-18-4(2)) Pub: B Winston Min. Dist(s): Anchor Distributors

Guard Us Sleeping: Compline: Psalms, Prayers & Hymns for the Night. Perf. by Society of Saint John the Evangelist. 1 CD. (Running Time: 1 hr. 12 mins.). 2004. audio compact disk 14.95 (978-1-56101-255-8(6)) Pub: Cowley Pubns. Dist(s): Rowman

Guard Your Heart. Music by Judy Rogers. 1 cass. (Running Time: 1 hr.). (J). (gr. k-8). 2002. 8.50 Christian Liberty.
Latest recordings teaches children to gain a heart of wisdom and how to guard it.

***Guardian.** John Saul. 2010. audio compact disk 29.99 (978-1-4418-4127-8(X)) Brilliance Audio.

Guardian. abr. ed. Nicholas Sparks. Read by Anne Twomey. (ENG.). 2005. 14.98 (978-1-59483-321-2(4)) Pub: Hachet Audio. Dist(s): HachBkGrp

Guardian. abr. ed. Nicholas Sparks. Read by Anne Twomey. (Running Time: 6 hrs.). (ENG.). 2009. 49.98 (978-1-60788-033-2(4)) Pub: Hachet Audio. Dist(s): HachBkGrp

Guardian. unabr. ed. Dee Henderson. Narrated by Tom Stechschulte. 8 cass. (Running Time: 10 hrs. 30 mins.). (O'Malley Ser.: Vol. 2). 2001. 79.75 (978-1-4025-9478-6(X), K1108MC) Recorded Bks.

Guardian. unabr. ed. John Saul. Read by David Regal. (Running Time: 12 hrs.). 2008. 39.25 (978-1-4233-5258-7(0), 9781423352587, BADLE); 24.95 (978-1-4233-5257-0(2), 9781423352570, BAD); audio compact disk 39.25 (978-1-4233-5256-3(4), 9781423352563, Brinc Audio MP3 Lib); audio compact disk 24.95 (978-1-4233-5255-6(6), 9781423352556, Brilliance MP3) Brilliance Audio.

Guardian. unabr. ed. Nicholas Sparks. Read by Isabelle Keating. (ENG.). 2005. 14.98 (978-1-59483-280-2(3)) Pub: Hachet Audio. Dist(s): HachBkGrp

Guardian Angel. unabr. ed. Sara Paretsky. Read by Donada Peters. 9 cass. (Running Time: 13 hrs. 30 min.). (V. I. Warshawski Novel Ser.). 1992. 72.00 (978-0-7366-2203-5(9), 2998) Books on Tape.
Elderly woman falls prey to unscrupulous neighbors who think she's an easy mark. They didn't think they'd have to contend with V.I. Warshawski.

Guardian Angel. unabr. ed. Sara Paretsky. Narrated by Barbara Rosenblat. 10 cass. (Running Time: 14 hrs.). (V. I. Warshawski Novel Ser.). 1992. 85.00 (978-1-55690-669-5(2), 92233E7) Recorded Bks.
Private eye V. I. Warshawski investigates political corruption in Chicago.

Guardian Angel Guidance (Hypnosis), Vol. 17. Jayne Helle. 1 cass. (Running Time: 28 min.). 1997. 15.00 (978-1-891826-16-0(6)) Introspect.
Everyone has a guardian angel just waiting to be recognized. Discover yours, & receive clearer guidance.

Guardian Angels in the Chart. Mary E. Korpan-Roy. Read by Mary E. Korpan-Roy. 1 cass. (Running Time: 90 min.). 1994. 8.95 (1153) Am Fed Astrologers.
Protective influences in the horoscope.

***Guardian of Lies.** unabr. ed. Steve Martini. Read by George Guidall. (ENG.). 2009. (978-0-06-190229-1(2), Harper Audio); (978-0-06-190230-7(6), Harper Audio) HarperCollins Pubs.

***Guardian of Lies.** unabr. ed. Steve Martini. Read by George Guidall. (Paul Madriani Ser.: Bk. 10). 2010. audio compact disk 19.99 (978-0-06-201089-6(1), Harper Audio) HarperCollins Pubs.

Guardian of the Dead. Roy Lewis & Martyn Waites. 2009. 54.95 (978-1-84652-410-4(3)); audio compact disk 64.95 (978-1-84652-411-0(3)) Pub: Magna Story GBR. Dist(s): Ulverscroft US

***Guardian of the Horizon.** abr. ed. Elizabeth Peters. Read by Barbara Rosenblat. (ENG.). 2004. (978-0-06-077915-3(2), Harper Audio); (978-0-06-081383-3(0), Harper Audio) HarperCollins Pubs.

Guardian of the Horizon. abr. ed. Elizabeth Peters, pseud. Read by Barbara Rosenblat. (Amelia Peabody Ser.: No. 16). 2004. audio compact disk 29.95 (978-0-06-058684-3(2)) HarperCollins Pubs.

***Guardian of the Horizon.** unabr. ed. Elizabeth Peters. Read by Barbara Rosenblat. (ENG.). 2004. (978-0-06-078288-7(9), Harper Audio) HarperCollins Pubs.

***Guardian of the Horizon.** unabr. ed. Elizabeth Peters. Read by Barbara Rosenblat. (ENG.). 2004. (978-0-06-081502-8(7), Harper Audio) HarperCollins Pubs.

Guardian of the Horizon. unabr. ed. Elizabeth Peters, pseud. Read by Barbara Rosenblat. 9 cass. (Running Time: 15 hrs.). (Amelia Peabody Ser.: No. 16). 2004. 34.95 (978-0-06-059006-2(8)) HarperCollins Pubs.

Guardian of the Horizon. unabr. ed. Elizabeth Peters, pseud. Narrated by Barbara Rosenblat. 10 cass. (Running Time: 14 hrs. 45 min.). (Amelia Peabody Ser.: No. 16). 2004. 99.75 (978-1-4025-7478-8(9), 97641) Recorded Bks.

Guardian of the Horizon. unabr. collector's ed. Elizabeth Peters, pseud. Narrated by Barbara Rosenblat. (Amelia Peabody Ser.: No. 16). 2004. audio compact disk 44.95 (978-1-4025-7744-4(3), CC040); 39.95 (978-1-4025-7479-5(7)) Recorded Bks.
Victorian Egyptologist Amelia Peabody Emerson and her growing family are in top-notch form. With antiquities to uncover, and nefarious villains to confront, there is never a dull moment.

Guardian of the Light & the Way of the Lonely Ones. Instructed by Manly P. Hall. 8.95 (978-0-89314-131-8(3), C800106) Philos Res.

Guardian of the Pool: A Story from Nelson Mandela's Favorite African Folktales. Read by Gillian Anderson. Compiled by Nelson Mandela. (Running Time: 6 mins.). (ENG.). 2009. 1.99 (978-1-60024-835-1(7)) Pub: Hachet Audio. Dist(s): HachBkGrp

Guardians see Poetry of Geoffrey

Guardianships & Advance Directives. 2 cass. (Running Time: 2 hrs.). 1999. 25.00 Set; incl. outline. (ACX993) Am Law Inst.
Live recording from the Elder Law Update teleseminar series.

Guarding Your Heart. Jack Deere. 1 cass. (Running Time: 90 mins.). (Proverbs Ser.: Vol. 4). 2000. 5.00 (JD08-004) Morning NC.
Practical wisdom for everyday living is brought to life in Jack's thorough exposition of this important book of the Bible.

Guarding Your Thoughts. Speeches. Joel Osteen. 1 Cass. (Running Time: 30 Mins.). (J). 2000. 6.00 (978-1-59349-058-4(5), JA0058) J Osteen.

Guards. Ken Bruen. 2009. 44.95 (978-0-7531-4477-0(8)); audio compact disk 59.95 (978-0-7531-4478-7(6)) Pub: Isis Pubng Ltd GBR. Dist(s): Ulverscroft US

Guards! Guards! unabr. ed. Terry Pratchett. Read by Nigel Planer. 9 CDs. (Running Time: 9 hrs. 45 mins.). (Discworld Ser.). (J). 2000. audio compact disk 89.95 (978-0-7531-0697-6(3), 106973) Pub: ISIS Lrg Prnt GBR. Dist(s): Ulverscroft US

Guards! Guards! unabr. ed. Terry Pratchett. Read by Nigel Planer. 8 cass. (Running Time: 9 hrs. 45 min.). (Discworld Ser.). (J). 2001. 69.95 (978-0-7531-0016-5(9), 951202) Pub: ISIS Lrg Prnt GBR. Dist(s): Ulverscroft US
The dragons lie...not dead, not asleep, but...dormant. And although the space they occupy isn't like the normal space, nevertheless, they are packed in tightly. And presumably, somewhere there's a key.

Guardship. unabr. ed. James Nelson. Read by Peter Wickham. 14 CDs. (Running Time: 15 hrs.). (Sound Ser.). (J). 2002. audio compact disk 104.95 (978-1-84283-409-1(6)) Pub: ISIS Lrg Prnt GBR. Dist(s): Ulverscroft US
With the bounty from his years as a pirate - a life he intends to renounce and keep forever secret - Thomas Marlowe purchases a fine Virginia plantation from a beautiful yound widow, Elizabeth Tinling. Soon afterwards, while defending her honour, he kills the favourite son of one of the colony's most powerful families in a duel. But in a clever piece of manoeuvring he manages to win command of The Plymouth Prize, the colony's decrepit guardship, and is charged with leading the King's sailors in bloody pitched battle against against the cut-throats who infest the waters off Virginia's shores. A threat from his illicit past appears, however, as an old pirate enemy plots to seize the colony's wealth, forcing Marlowe to choose between losing all - or facing the one man he fears.

Guardship. unabr. ed. James Nelson. Read by Peter Wickham. 12 cass. (Running Time: 15 hrs.). (Sound Ser.). 2002. 94.95 (978-1-84283-162-5(3)) Pub: UlverLrgPrint GBR. Dist(s): Ulverscroft US

Guatemala: A Culture of Fear. 1 cass. (Running Time: 30 min.). (Horizon Ser.). 9.95 (HO-87-03-25, HarperThor) HarpC GBR.

Gucci Mamas. unabr. ed. Cate Kendall. Read by Danielle Carter. (Running Time: 9 hrs. 5 mins.). 2008. audio compact disk 87.95 (978-1-74093-991-1(3), 9781740939911) Pub: Bolinda Pubng AUS. Dist(s): Bolinda Pub Inc

Guerilla Copywriting. David Garfinkel & Jay Conrad Levinson. 2 CDs. 2006. audio compact disk 59.95 (978-1-933596-20-4(1)) Pub: Morgan James Pubng. Dist(s): IngramPubServ

Guerilla P. R. Wired. unabr. ed. Michael K. Levine. Read by Lloyd James. 9 CDs. (Running Time: 11 hrs. 30 mins.). 2002. audio compact disk 72.00 (978-0-7861-9425-4(1), 3009) Blckstn Audio.
Shows you how to get noticed now and help you craft a message that is both powerful and profitable in today's fast moving, wired world.

Guerilla Season. unabr. ed. Paul Thomas. Read by David Tredinnick. 5 cass. (Running Time: 11 hrs. 25 mins.). 2001. (978-1-74030-112-1(9), 500426) Bolinda Pubng AUS.

Guerilla Selling LIVE. PUEI. 2006. audio compact disk 89.95 (978-1-933328-71-3(1), CareerTrack) P Univ E Inc.

Guermantes Way. Marcel Proust. Read by Neville Jason. Tr. by C. K. Scott Moncrieff from FRE. Adapted by Neville Jason. 3 cass. (Running Time: 3 hr. 30 mins.). (Remembrance of Things Past Ser.: Vol. V). 1997. 17.98 (978-962-634-616-7(7), NA311614, Naxos AudioBooks) Naxos.
Describes the struggles for political, social and sexual supremacy played out beneath a veneer of elegant manners.

Guermantes Way. abr. ed. Marcel Proust. Read by Neville Jason. Tr. by C. K. Scott Moncrieff from FRE. Adapted by Neville Jason. 3 CDs. (Running Time: 3 hrs. 30 mins.). (Remembrance of Things Past Ser.: Vol. V). 1997. audio compact disk 22.98 (978-962-634-116-2(5), NA311612, Naxos AudioBooks) Naxos.

Guermantes Way, Pt. 2. Marcel Proust. Read by Neville Jason. Tr. by C. K. Scott Moncrieff from FRE. Adapted by Neville Jason. 3 cass. (Running Time: 3 hrs. 30 mins.). (Remembrance of Things Past Ser.: Vol. VI). 1998. 17.98 (978-962-634-641-9(8), NA314114, Naxos AudioBooks) Naxos.
Continues the story of Marcel's entry into Parisian aristocratic society.

Guermantes Way, Vol. 2. abr. ed. Marcel Proust. Read by Neville Jason. Tr. by C. K. Scott Moncrieff from FRE. Adapted by Neville Jason. 3 CDs. (Running Time: 3 hrs. 30 mins.). (Remembrance of Things Past Ser.: Vol. VI). 1997. audio compact disk 22.98 (978-962-634-141-4(6), NA314112, Naxos AudioBooks) Naxos.

Guernica. unabr. ed. Dave Boling. Narrated by Paul Boehmer. (Running Time: 13 hrs. 0 mins. 0 sec.). (ENG.). 2008. audio compact disk 24.99 (978-1-4001-5873-7(7)); audio compact disk 75.99 (978-1-4001-3873-9(6)) Pub: Tantor Media. Dist(s): IngramPubServ

Guernica. unabr. ed. Dave Boling. Read by Lloyd James. (Running Time: 13 hrs. 0 mins. 0 sec.). (ENG.). 2008. audio compact disk 37.99 (978-1-4001-0873-2(X)) Pub: Tantor Media. Dist(s): IngramPubServ

Guernsey Literary & Potato Peel Pie Society. unabr. ed. Mary Ann Shaffer & Annie Barrows. 7 CDs. (Running Time: 8 hrs.). 2008. audio compact disk 80.00 (978-1-4159-5440-9(2), BksonTape) Pub: Random Audio Pubg. Dist(s): Random
I wonder how the book got to Guernsey? Perhaps there is some sort of secret homing instinct in books that brings them to their perfect readers. January 1946: London is emerging from the shadow of the Second World War, and writer Juliet Ashton is looking for her next book subject. Who could imagine that she would find it in a letter from a man she's never met, a native of the island of Guernsey, who has come across her name written inside a book by Charles Lamb. As Juliet and her new correspondent exchange letters, Juliet is drawn into the world of this man and his friends - and what a wonderfully eccentric world it is. The Guernsey Literary and Potato Peel Pie Society - born as a spur-of-the-moment alibi when its members were discovered breaking curfew by the Germans occupying their island - boasts a charming, funny, deeply human cast of characters, from pig farmers to phrenologists, literature lovers all. Juliet begins a remarkable correspondence with the society's members, learning about their island, their taste in books, and the impact the recent German occupation has had on their lives. Captivated by their stories, she sets sail for Guernsey, and what she finds will change her forever.

Guernsey Literary & Potato Peel Pie Society. unabr. ed. Mary Ann Shaffer & Annie Barrows. (Running Time: 8 hrs.). (ENG.). 2008. 17.50 (978-0-7393-6844-2(3), Listening Lib) Pub: Random Audio Pubg. Dist(s): Random

Guernsey Literary & Potato Peel Pie Society. unabr. ed. Mary Ann Shaffer & Annie Barrows. Read by Paul Boehmer & Juliet Mills. 7 CDs. (Running Time: 8 hrs.). (ENG.). 2008. audio compact disk 34.95 (978-0-7393-6843-5(5), Random AudioBks) Pub: Random Audio Pubg. Dist(s): Random

Guerra y la Paz. abr. ed. Leo Tolstoy. 2. (Running Time: 7200 sec.). (SPA.). 2007. audio compact disk 16.95 (978-1-933499-12-3(5)) Fonolibro Inc.

Guerre d'Algerie, Set. 7 cass. (Running Time: 10 hrs.). (FRE.). 1991. 59.95 (1243-RF) Olivia & Hill.
A series broadcast on France-Culture. The participants & witnesses to the Algerian War finally speak about their experiences, many for the first time. Based on texts, audio archives & interviews.

Guerre des Boutons, Set. abr. ed. Louis Pergaud. Read by Sophie Arthuys. 3 cass. (FRE.). (J). 1995. bk. 39.95 (1GA071) Olivia & Hill.
Children of two neighboring towns wage a bitter war which consists of pulling off the buttons of their opponents, forcing the loser to return home with his pants around his ankles.

Guerre d'Indochine, Set. 5 cass. (FRE.). 1991. 46.95 (1459-RF) Olivia & Hill.
Thirty-five years after the eight-year war which pit France against Vietnam, Laos & Cambodia (1945-54), the main protagonists speak out. A fascinating document on a forgotten war.

Guerrilla Dating Tactics: Gen. 24:1-14. Ed Young. 1993. 4.95 (978-0-7417-1958-4(4), 958) Win Walk.

***Guerrilla Lovers: Changing the World with Revolutionary Compassion.** unabr. ed. Vince Antonucci. Narrated by Adam Verner. (ENG.). 2010. 14.98 (978-1-59644-873-5(3)); audio compact disk 24.98 (978-1-59644-872-8(5)) christianaud.

Guerrilla Marketing, unabr. exp. rev. ed. Jay Conrad Levinson. Read by David Hilder. 9 cass. (Running Time: 13 hrs.). 1995. 62.95 (978-0-7861-0771-1(5), 1620) Blckstn Audio.
Included in this completely revised & expanded edition are Levinson's wisdom on: (1) the fastest-growing markets in the nineties with tips on how to reach & keep them; (2) strategies for marketing during a recession; (3) the most up-to-date information on what consumers in the nineties care most about; (4) new programs for targeted prospects; (5) how to use the technological explosion for bigger profits; & (6) management lessons for the twenty-first centur.

Guerrilla Marketing: Put Your Advertising on Steroids! abr. ed. 2006. audio compact disk 39.95 (978-1-933596-15-0(5)) Pub: Morgan James Pubng. Dist(s): IngramPubServ
"This is Barely Legal...But You Can Still Get Away With It"A Review of Guerrilla Marketing: Put Your Advertisingon Steroidsby Mark Joyner, International Best Selling Author of The Confidential Internet Intelligence ManuscriptI guess it's human nature to be tempted bythings that are forbidden - or barely legal, for that matter.There's something wickedly delicious about"getting away with something" that makes us feel like the "catthat swallowed the canary."Face it. We all want an unfair advantage if the prize is appetizingenough. Olympic athletes took steroids before the anabolic drug was banned - for the prize of a gold medal. What would you do for the prize of having an Internet business that is insanelyprofitable? I doubt that you'd do anything illegal... but if it werelegal, you'd do almost anything, wouldn't you? What the heck am I talking about, you ask? Here it is: Just when Ithought I'd read every valuable book on marketing, Jay Conrad Levinson revivesmy amazement yet again.Given the fact that Jay has always been famous (and notorious) for his unconventionaland revolutionary ideas, I shouldn't be surprised that he has pioneeredyet another blockbuster concept: steroidal marketing.In his new book, Guerrilla Marketing: Put Your Advertising on Steroids, Jay tookthe proven concepts of the world's most successful companies, and synthesizedthem into a new type of marketing that any Internet business canuse to make mega-profits. Among other things, he shows you how to make your Internet business insanelyprofitable on a tiny marketing budget - and use stealth tacticsto snatch business away from your competitors. Those 2 things alone arewell worth the cover price. Somewhere along the way, I must have gotten pretty smug about Internetmarketing because it took someone like Jay to give me a jolt in the headwith his new arsenal of innovative strategies. He reveals thingsthat most so-called marketing "gurus" don't even know - but if they did, it would boost even their business by at least 30% to40%. What can you expect from the man who made "guerrilla marketing" a householdword, and masterminded 3 out of the 10 most successful advertisingcampaigns of the 20th century (including the Marlboro Man, GreenGiant, and Fly the Friendly Skies)? Guerrilla Marketing: Put Your Advertising on Steroids is definitely a treasure, and I recommend that you check out howJay invented this amazing method of marketing. "Ask almost any successful entrepreneur what the best book is for building a small business, and one of Levinson's titles will surely come up." - Entrepreneur Business Success Guide Buy Now to check out insidersecrets that even marketing heavyweights don't know.

Guerrilla Marketing Attack: New Strategies, Tactics & Weapons for Winning Big Profits from Your Small Business. unabr. ed. Jay Conrad Levinson. Read by Jeff Riggenbach. 5 cass. (Running Time: 7 hrs.). 1996. 39.95 (978-0-7861-0934-0(3), 1683) Blckstn Audio.
Provides solid, practical, cost-effective advice on how to take advantage of the most recent advances in marketing. These advances could save your company & give you an all-important competitive edge.

Guerrilla Marketing During Tough Times: Is Your Business Slowing Down? Jay Conrad Levinson. Read by Jay Conrad Levinson. 2005. audio compact disk 39.95 (978-1-933596-12-9(0)) Pub: Morgan James Pubng. Dist(s): IngramPubServ
Is Your Business Slowing Down? Find Out Why Here!Guerrilla Marketing guru Jay Conrad Levinson shows you exactly why your business is slowing down in tough economic times and exactly what you can do about it.

Guerrilla Marketing for the Home-based Business, Set. unabr. ed. Jay Conrad Levinson & Seth Godin. Read by Barrett Whitener. 4 cass. (Running Time: 5 hrs. 30 mins.). 1997. 32.95 (978-0-7861-1095-7(3), 1861) Blckstn Audio.
Home-based businesses are not just small versions of big marketing conglomerates. They are faced with totally different issues, problems & opportunities requiring specific skills & tactics. Discover the secrets of the most successful home-based entrepreneurs, quit wasting time & money on strategies that will not & can not work & exploit eleven proven methods.

Guerrilla Marketing for the New Millennium: Lessons from the Father of Guerrilla Mktg. Jay Conrad Levinson. Read by Jay Conrad Levinson. 2005. audio compact disk 39.95 (978-1-933596-09-9(0)) Pub: Morgan James Pubng. Dist(s): IngramPubServ
READ by Jay Conrad LevinsonHistory is full of stories where tiny, unadvanced armies have handily defeated better equipped and much larger armies. The history of these battles is the history of guerrilla warfare. There are similar stories in business. One example is that of the "Marlboro Man". Before the Marlboro Man, the Marlboro brand of cigarettes was ranked 31st - almost rock bottom. After the introduction of the Marlboro Man, and the guerrilla branding campaign to promote it, Marlboro became the #1 brand in a multi-billion dollar industry. It may shock you how many of the "big business" names (that are now household words) started out as struggling small businesses. The history of the ascent of these icons is the history of guerrilla marketing. Until 1984, the principles of guerrilla marketing were known only by a select few people in the world. They jealously kept this information quiet with almost fanatical secrecy. And who can blame them? If you had some special knowledge that allowed you to rise to the top of your field, would you want this information to be made public? Of course not! The balance of power was dramatically upset by a maverick marketing genius named Jay Conrad Levinson - a man who is arguably the most respected marketer in the world. He is the man who coined the term "guerrilla marketing" and introduced these secrets to the average Joe. His concepts are so successful that he has sold over 14 million books on the subject (in 41 languages), his books are required reading in the most respected MBA programs in the world, and he is now the most widely read and respected author of business books in the world. And Jay did all this "from scratch". That is, the success of the "Guerrilla Marketing" brand is a testament to the very principles Jay himself teaches. It just so happens that he is also one of the creators of the Marlboro Man. (Think what you will about tobacco, but you can not deny the power of the marketing behind Marlboro - arguably the most successful marketing campaign in history, and the most widely recognized brand in the world.)So, what then, is Guerrilla Marketing all about? Let"s take a segment from Jay"s new book "Guerrilla Marketing for the New Millennium" to learn:"Marketing is absolutely every bit of contact any part of your business has with any segment of the public. Guerrillas view marketing as a circle that begins with your ideas for generating revenue and continues on with the goal of amassing a large number of repeat and referral customers. "The three key words in that paragraph are every, repeat, and referral. If your marketing is not a circle, it"s a straight line that leads directly into Chapters 7, 11, or 13 in the bankruptcy courts. How is Guerrilla Marketing different from traditional marketing?"Guerrilla marketing means marketing that is unconventional, non-traditional, not by-the-book, and extremely flexible. Eighteen factors make it different from old-fashioned marketing:" Jay then goes on to list 18 things that separate guerrillas from "mere mortals."(See below for info on this new book - it"s recognized as his most powerful work yet.)So, how then, does this information apply to those of us marketing on the Internet? Far more than you think! The Internet is not just a new guerrilla battlefield - it"s the ultimate guerrilla battlefield. There have been more small business mega-success stories in the last 5 years than in the combined history of business. And there are clearly two factors that have influenced this more than anything: 1. The Internet 2. Guerrilla Marketing Ever wonder why big businesses are totally blowing it online? Because they are not guerrilla thinkers! These big bloated bureaucracies are sluggish and set in their ways. This means that someone like you can step in and out-maneuver them. (More and more big businesses are turning to small business entrepreneurs to teach them how to market online - the tables have turned!)So, start thinking like a guerrilla right now. You have the advantage - all you have to do is take it.Here"s the definitive place to get started - where you will find an easy to follow step by step plan for launching a "guerrilla attack".

***Guerrilla Marketing Goes Green: Winning Strategies to Improve Your Profits & Your Planet.** unabr. ed. Jay Conrad Levinson & Shel Horowitz. Read by Erik Synnestvedt. (Running Time: 7 hrs. 30 mins.). (ENG.). 2010. 29.98 (978-1-59659-653-5(8), GildAudio) Pub: Gildan Media. Dist(s): HachBkGrp

Guerrilla Marketing Mastery for Franchisees. Jay Conrad Levinson & Todd Woods. 2006. audio compact disk 97.00 (978-1-60037-133-2(7)) Pub: Morgan James Pubng. Dist(s): IngramPubServ

Guerrilla Marketing on the Go! Become a World Class Guerrilla Marketer While Driving Your Car, Walking, Jogging, or Listening to Your Portable MP3 Player. Mitch Meyerson & Jay Conrad Levinson. 2006. audio compact disk 19.95 (978-1-60037-147-9(7)) Pub: Morgan James Pubng. Dist(s): IngramPubServ

Guerrilla Marketing Weapons: One Hundred Affordable Marketing Methods for Maximizing Profits from Your Small Business. unabr. ed. Jay Conrad Levinson. Read by Barrett Whitener. 5 cass. (Running Time: 7 hrs.). 1996. 39.95 (978-0-7861-1017-9(1), 1795) Blckstn Audio.
These 100 targeted weapons add potency to a marketing attack & substantially increase profits. Most important, they work for all types of small & medium businesses, even for nonprofit organizations. All the weapons are inexpensive to implement & fully half of them are absolutely cost-free, a bonanza that liberates cash flow. And there are 14 powerhouse weapons that help start-up businesses & five substantial lifts to an already running operation.

Guerrilla Marketing Weapons: 100 Affordable Marketing Methods for Maximizing Profits from Your Small Business. unabr. ed. Jay Conrad Levinson. Read by Barrett Whitener. (Running Time: 23400 sec.). 2007. audio compact disk 55.00 (978-0-7861-5810-2(7)); audio compact disk 29.95 (978-0-7861-5811-9(5)) Blckstn Audio.

Guerrilla Marketing 101 Bootlegged! Lessons from the Father of Guerrilla Marketing. Speeches. Jay Conrad Levinson. 6 CDs. (Running Time: 18000 sec.). 2005. audio compact disk 59.95 (978-1-933596-30-3(9)) Pub: Morgan James Pubng. Dist(s): IngramPubServ
*This 6-volume CD set contains over 5 hours of business-building secrets personally presented by Jay Conrad Levinson, Father of the Worldwide Guerrilla Marketing Revolution.The topics you will learn include:*20 differences between traditional and Guerrilla Marketing*100 Guerrilla Marketing weapons*How Memes can increase your profits*12 personality traits of successful Guerrillas*How to launch a Guerrilla Marketing Attack - and WIN!*16 monumental secrets of Guerrilla Marketing*And much, much more!If you're serious about learning the secrets that can propel you to business success, you need to listen to these audios!.*

Guerrilla Negotiating. Jay Levinson. Narrated by Edward Lewis. (Running Time: 8 hrs. 30 mins.). 1999. 27.95 (978-1-59912-498-8(X)) Iofy Corp.

An Asterisk (*) at the beginning of an entry indicates that the title is appearing for the first time.

Guerrilla Negotiating. unabr. ed. Jay Conrad Levinson. Read by Edward Lewis. 7 cass. (Running Time: 8 hrs. 30 mins.). 2000. 44.95 (978-0-7861-1767-3(2), 2570); audio compact disk 56.00 (978-0-7861-9883-2(4), 2570) Blckstn Audio.
Learn how to negotiate by using unconventional weapons & tactics to get what you want.

Guerrilla Negotiating. unabr. ed. Jay Conrad Levinson et al. Read by Edward Lewis. 1 CD. (Running Time: 12 hrs.). 2001. audio compact disk 19.95 (zm2570) Blckstn Audio.

Guerrilla P. R. unabr. ed. Michael K. Levine. Read by Christopher Hurt. 6 cass. (Running Time: 8 hrs. 30 mins.). 1993. 44.95 (978-0-7861-0467-3(8), 1419) Blckstn Audio.
In clear & concise language, Michael Levine, one of the top public relations counselors in the country, reveals the same procedures he uses every day to get press on major stars - & how those strategies can be utilized on little or no budget. Using case histories & tips from his own experiences, & providing important weapons in any P.R. arsenal - including the Ten Commandments of Guerrilla P.R. & a start-up list of important contacts - Levine shows you how to think like a publicist & map out a strategy for success. This book, written by the head of a major public relations firm, is for people who need to engage the media & want quick & ingenious methods to bridge the gap between their message & the public.

Guerrilla P. R. How You Can Wage an Effective Publicity Campaign... Without Going Broke. Michael K. Levine. Frwd. by Melvin Belli. 2005. audio compact disk 63.00 (978-0-7861-7849-0(3)) Blckstn Audio.

Guerrilla P. R. Wired. Michael K. Levine. Narrated by Lloyd James. (Running Time: 11 hrs. 30 mins.). 2002. 34.95 (978-1-59912-499-5(8)) Iofy Corp.

Guerrilla P. R. Wired. unabr. ed. Michael K. Levine. Read by Lloyd James. 8 cass. (Running Time: 11 hrs. 30 mins.). 2002. 56.95 (978-0-7861-2351-3(6), 3009) Blckstn Audio.
Shows you how to get noticed now and help you craft a message that is both powerful and profitable in today's fast moving, wired world.

Guerrilla P. R. 2. 0: Wage an Effective Publicity Campaign without Going Broke. unabr. ed. Michael Levine. (Running Time: 12 hrs. 0 mins.). (ENG.). 2009. 29.95 (978-1-4332-9568-3(7)); 72.95 (978-1-4332-9564-5(4)); audio compact disk 105.00 (978-1-4332-9565-2(2)) Blckstn Audio.

Guerrilla Selling: Unconventional Weapons & Tactics for Increasing Your Sales. unabr. ed. Bill Gallagher et al. Read by David Hilder. 6 cass. (Running Time: 8 hrs. 30 mins.). 1995. 44.95 (978-0-7861-0665-3(4), 1567) Blckstn Audio.
Practical tips & ideas that anyone can apply immediately to increase their corporate sales & personal income. Every salesperson in today's competitive market should read this book.

Guerrilla Selling Live: Unconventional Weapons & Tactics for Increasing Your Sales. Orvel R. Wilson. 6 cass. (Running Time: 6 hrs.). 1996. 59.95 Set, incl. wkbk. (13650PAY) Nightingale-Conant.
This program shows you how to use speed & mobility as well as energy & imagination to generate greater income & excel in every aspect of your sales career.

Guerrilla Teleselling: New Unconventional Weapons & Tactics to Sell When You Can't Be There in Person. unabr. ed. Jay Conrad Levinson et al. Read by Edward Lewis. 6 cass. (Running Time: 8 hrs. 30 mins.). 2000. 44.95 (978-0-7861-1734-5(6), 2539) Blckstn Audio.
Applies guerrilla sales & marketing tactics to the unique, high-pressure environment of electronic communications, this groundbreaking resource is packed with valuable tips, expert advice & insider secrets on finding, closing & increasing sales by phone & fax as well as via e-mail & the Internet.

***Guerrilla Teleselling: New Unconventional Weapons & Tactics to Sell When You Can't Be There in Person.** unabr. ed. Jay Conrad Levinson et al. Read by Edward Lewis. (Running Time: 8 hrs.). 2010. 29.95 (978-1-4417-1374-2(3)); audio compact disk 76.00 (978-1-4417-1372-8(7)) Blckstn Audio.

Guerrilla Trading Tactics with Oliver Velez: Tools for Today's Active & Short-Term Investors. Speeches. Oliver Velez. (Running Time: 180 Mins.). (Trade Secrets Audio Ser.). 2002. 19.95 (978-1-59280-006-3(8)) Marketplace Bks.
Reap large market gains - consistently - when you master the unique market style of Oliver Velez, called "Guerrilla Trading". Practiced by the world's most successful short-term traders, this "hit and run" market move gets you in and out of trades quickly - at the right times - with profits in tow. Available at www.traderslibrary.com/tradesecrets ttp://www.traderslibrary.com/tradesecrets. Even veteran market professionals admit that today's investment arena is more confusing than ever before. Market trends, if they develop at all, tend to be short-lived, and fundamental valuations are frequently invalid. So what can you do to succeed in such a chaotic financial environment? Adopt a "guerrilla" style of trading. Forget long-term thinking. Abandon buy-and-hold strategies. Instead, hit the market with quick, profit-grabbing attacks. Relying on time-tested technical trading patterns for entry and exit cues, Oliver Velez shows how to raid the markets for consistent short-term profits using "guerrilla" tactics that boast historic success rates of 80% or more - and now he shares these winning market moves with you.

Guess Who Got the Last Hotdog? unabr. ed. Short Stories. Steven D. Bunnell & Jack Sondericker. 2 cass. (Running Time: 2 hrs. 30 min.). Dramatization. 1992. 16.95 (978-1-55686-438-4(8), 438) Books in Motion.
Here is an array of humorous & emotionally sincere short stories about family life that will leave listeners uplifted & pleased they took the time to enjoy the experience.

Guest List. unabr. ed. Fern Michaels. Read by Jen Taylor. 8 vols. (Running Time: 10 hrs. 30 min.). 2001. bk. 69.95 (978-0-7927-2400-1(3), CSL 289, Chivers Sound Lib) AudioGO.
Abby has been reunited with her sister, Mallory, ater a tragic accident separated them. But while the two sisters make up for lost time, danger hides in the shadows. Abby & Mallory have planned a sumptuous party unaware that their gathering will include an uninvited guest who will do anything to keep the past hidden.

Guest of Honor. Short Stories. Robert Reed. Narrated by Amy Bruce. 1 CD. (Running Time: 80 mins.). (Great Science Fiction Stories Ser.). 2004. audio compact disk Rental 10.99 (978-1-884612-39-8(3)) AudioText.

Guest of Honor. unabr. ed. Robert Reed. Read by Amy Bruce. Ed. by Allan Kaster. 1 cass. (Running Time: 1 hr. 23 min.). (Great Science Fiction Stories Ser.). 1996. 10.99 (978-1-884612-08-4(3)) AudioText.

Guests at His Table. 1 cass. (Running Time: 30 min.). 1985. (0252) Evang Sisterhood Mary.
Questions & answers about the sacrament of Holy Communion; Christians, such as God needs today.

Guests of My Life. Elizabeth Watson. 5 cass. Incl. Guests of My Life: Alan Paton - For You Departed. 1978.; Guests of My Life: Emily Dickinson - Burglar! Banker-Father! 1978.; Guests of My Life: Katherine Mansfield - All Is Well! 1978.; Guests of My Life: Rabindranath Tagore - Let It Be Not Death, But Completeness. 1978.; Guests of My Life: Rainer Maria Rilke - Over the Nowhere Arches the Everywhere. 1978.; 1978. 17.50 Set.; 4.50 ea. Pendle Hill.

Guests of My Life: Alan Paton - For You Departed see Guests of My Life

Guests of My Life: Emily Dickinson - Burglar! Banker-Father! see Guests of My Life

Guests of My Life: Katherine Mansfield - All Is Well! see Guests of My Life

Guests of My Life: Rabindranath Tagore - Let It Be Not Death, But Completeness see Guests of My Life

Guests of My Life: Rainer Maria Rilke - Over the Nowhere Arches the Everywhere see Guests of My Life

Guests of the Ayatollah. abr. ed. Mark Bowden. Read by Mark Bowden. 2006. 23.95 (978-0-7435-6512-7(6), Audioworks) Pub: S&S Audio. Dist(s): S and S Inc

Guia de Las Chicas Buenas para Hacerlo Como Las Chicas Malas: Una Guia Indispensable para el Placer y la Seduccion. abr. ed. Barbara Keesling. 4 CDs. (Running Time: 18000 sec.). (SPA.). 2006. audio compact disk 24.95 (978-1-933499-37-6(0)) Fonolibro Inc.

Guia para el Exito en la Cuidadania. Haiyun Weimholt. (SPA & ENG.). 2005. audio compact disk 25.00 (978-0-9761856-2-8(8)) Knowledgelenders.

Guidance: The Dance That Leads Us Home. unabr. ed. Carol Howe. 3 cass. (Running Time: 4 hrs.). 1995. 24.95 Set. (978-1-889642-06-2(1)) C Howe.
Do you wish to understand the true meaning of "guidance?" There is no authority "out there" who knows how to offer peace, security, & abundance. However, our inner intuition does! This workshop, which engages the senses, the intellect & the heart: Clarifies the source of trustworthy, loving guidance, always available to everyone. Shows how releasing fear automatically accesses intuition. Reveals the rewards of following our in-born wisdom & the guaranteed frustration when we do not.

Guidance for Personal Transformation. Swami Amar Jyoti. 1 cass. 1980. 9.95 (N-10) Truth Consciousness.
The science of virtues & vices; understanding & overcoming arrogance, indecisiveness, fear & negativity. Guru helps us always.

Guidance in Prayer from Three Women Mystics: Julian of Norwich, Teresa of Avila, Theresa of Lisieux. Margaret Dorgan. Read by Margaret Dorgan. 7 cass. (Running Time: 7 hrs.). 59.95 incl. bibliography & vinyl album. Credence Commun.
Combines two major developments in the church - rising feminine awareness & renewed interest in mysticism.

Guidance of the Divine Mother. Swami Amar Jyoti. 1 cass. 1982. 9.95 (K-48) Truth Consciousness.
Divine Mother, the Law of Perfection, the manifestation of the Lord. When we let go, She takes care of everything.

Guide Me to Eternity. Christine Monson. 11.95 (978-1-56236-710-7(2)) Pub: Aspen Bks. Dist(s): Origin Bk Sales

Guide to Accountant's Liability in Audit & SEC Practice. Ralph S. Janvey. 3 cass. bk. 159.00 set. (CPE4390) Bisk Educ.
Get information to help you avoid liability in the audit & securities area, plus learn the rules & regulations that affect accounting practice, financial reporting, & the misuse of information & disclosure requirements.

Guide to Achieving the Edge. Daniel Singer. 3 cass. (Running Time: 40 min.). 1991. pap. bk. 29.95 set. (978-1-880802-00-7(7)) Edgetrng.
"Psychology" mental conditioning for tennis & sport.

Guide to Debt Restructuring. Christopher B. Andersen & Vincent J. Intrieri. 3 cass. bk. 159.00 set, incl. textbk. & quizzer. (CPE4110) Bisk Educ.
Learn the warning signs of a company in trouble, out-of-court alternatives to Chapter 11, the pros & cons of Chapter 11 filing, pre-bankruptcy planning, & how to handle the transition from workout to turnaround.

Guide to Good Food: Chapter Review Games CD Individual License (Windows) Velda L. Largen & Deborah L. Bence. (gr. 9-12). 2004. audio compact disk 64.00 (978-1-59070-114-0(3)) Goodheart.

Guide to Good Food: Teacher's Resource. Velda L. Largen & Deborah L. Bence. 2002. audio compact disk 195.80 (978-1-56637-771-3(4)) Goodheart.

Guide to Growth: Your Career, Relationships with Others, Spirituality, Your Relationship with Yourself. Patricia Clason. Read by Patricia Clason. 8 cass. (Running Time: 8 hrs.). 82.95 set. ArGee Prods.

Guide to Helping Elderly Relatives Near & Far. Pamela A. Erickson & Gordon Wolfe. 2 cass. (Running Time: 1 hrs. 32 min.). 1997. 24.95 Set. (978-0-9633185-8-9(6)) Eldercare Pr.
Guides seniors & adult children through the maze of problems & possibilities families with aging relatives may face.

Guide to Intermediate Meditation. unabr. ed. Swami Rama. 1 cass. (Running Time: 28 mins.). 1990. 7.95 (978-0-89389-162-6(2), CS208MO) Himalayan Inst.
Clear & practical instructions provide continued guidance in the journey to deepened meditation.

Guide to Learning Haitian Creole. Fequiere Vilsaint & Maude Heurtelou. (ENG & CRP.). 2004. lib. bdg. 39.50 (978-1-58432-195-8(4)) Educa Vision.

Guide to Limited Liability Companies. William L. Raby. 6 cass. bk. 159.00 set. (CPE0590) Bisk Educ.
Learn how to set up a limited liability company, the tax consequences of converting from various business forms to an LLC, & potential problems to avoid.

Guide to Night Sounds. Lang Elliott. 1 cass. (Running Time: 65 min.). 1994. audio compact disk 16.95 CD. (2655, Creativ Pub) Quayside.
Fascinating sounds of the night with this unique audio guide that features 60 night-active mammals, birds, reptiles, & insects in North America. Includes 40-page booklet.

Guide to Night Sounds. Lang Elliott. 1 cass. (Running Time: 65 min.). 1994. 12.95 (2654, NrthWrd Bks) TandN Child.

Guide to Non-Jazz Improvisation: Banjo Edition. Dan Fox & Dick Weissman. (ENG.). 2009. lib. bdg. 24.99 (978-0-7866-7593-7(4)) Mel Bay.

Guide to Non-Jazz Improvisation: Flute Edition. Dan Fox & Dick Weissman. (ENG.). 2009. lib. bdg. 24.99 (978-0-7866-7477-0(6)) Mel Bay.

Guide to Non-Jazz Improvisation: Guitar Edition. Dan Fox & Dick Weissman. (ENG.). 2009. lib. bdg. 24.99 (978-0-7866-0751-8(3)) Mel Bay.

Guide to Non-Jazz Improvisation: Piano Edition. Dick Weissman & Dan Fox. (ENG.). 2009. lib. bdg. 24.99 (978-0-7866-7552-4(7)) Mel Bay.

Guide to Pass PSI Real Estate Exam, Version. 3. 0. 3rd ed. 2004. audio compact disk 48.99 (978-0-7931-8805-5(9), Dearbrn Real Est Ed) Kaplan Pubng.

Guide to Personal Peace: The Control of Stress, Worry, Depression & Anxiety. H. J. Roberts. Read by H. J. Roberts. 3 cass. (Running Time: 2 hrs. 30 min.). 1994. bk. 24.95 Set. (978-0-9633260-4-1(X)) Sunshine Sentinel.
A treasure of information about stress, worry, depression & anxiety - & practical advice concerning their control - based on the experience of "The Best Doctor in the U.S." These insights minimize medicalese & psychiatric jargon.

Guide to Recognizing Your Saints: A Memoir. unabr. ed. Dito Montiel. Read by Jason Collins. 6 CDs. (Running Time: 18000 sec.). 2006. 19.95 (978-0-7861-4642-0(7), E3850); audio compact disk 19.95 (978-0-7861-6793-7(9), ZE3850); audio compact disk 29.95 (978-0-7861-7424-9(2), ZM3850) Blckstn Audio.

Guide to Recognizing Your Saints: A Memoir. unabr. ed. Dito Montiel. Read by Jason Collins. (Running Time: 18000 sec.). 2006. 54.95 (978-0-7861-4703-8(2)); audio compact disk 63.00 (978-0-7861-6590-2(1)) Blckstn Audio.

Guide to Relaxation. Dick Lutz. Read by Dick Lutz. 6 cass. (Running Time: 2 hrs. 10 min.). 1987. 29.95 (978-0-931625-17-6(3)) DIMI Pr.
Enables one to try six different types of relaxation narrations.

Guide to Serenity. abr. ed. Robert A. Monroe. Read by Robert A. Monroe. (Mind Food Ser.). 1983. 14.95 (978-1-56102-407-0(4)) Inter Indus.
Progressive relaxation into refreshing sleep.

Guide to Successful Dating. Nancy Van Pelt. 3 CDs. (Running Time: 3 hrs). 2006. audio compact disk 24399.00 (978-0-8127-0402-0(9)) Review & Herald.

Guide to Successful Marriage. Nancy Van Pelt. 2006. audio compact disk 24.99 (978-0-8127-0403-7(7)) Review & Herald.

Guide to Successful Naturalization. Helen Weimholt. 2004. audio compact disk 19.99 (978-0-9761856-0-4(1)) Knowledgelenders.

Guide to the Bodhisattva's Way of Life: A Buddhist Poem for Today. unabr. ed. Shantideva. Read by Rupert Brookes. Tr. by Geshe Kelsang Gyatso & Neil Elliot. Narrated by Michael Sington. 4 CDs. (Running Time: 4 hrs. 30 mins. 0 sec.). (ENG., 2005. audio compact disk 24.95 (978-0-9548790-1-3(5)) Pub: Tharpa Pubns GBR. Dist(s): IPG Chicago

Guide to the Fiduciary Duties of Directors of Charitable Corporations. 1 cass. (Running Time: 50 min.). 1993. 95.00 Incl. study guide. (Y607) Am Law Inst.
Examines the fiduciary duties of care, loyalty, & obedience & looks at ways counsel can help directors carry out responsibilities.

Guide to the Project Management Body of Knowledge. 4th ed. Created by Project Management Institute. (ENG.). 2008. audio compact disk 65.95 (978-1-933890-74-6(6)) Proj Mgmt Inst.

Guide to Therapy for Irritable Bowel Syndrome. Leonard Weinstock & Thomas Lipsitz. Read by Leonard Weinstock & Thomas Lipsitz. 2 CDs. (Running Time: 1 hr. 32 mins.). 2000. audio compact disk 19.95 (978-0-9707125-0-9(2)) Specialists Gastro.
Easy & effective stress reducing strategies to manage the symptoms of irritable bowel syndrome. Education, stress modification & relaxation therapy for IBS.

Guide to Uniform Capitalization & Inventory Tax Accounting. 3 cass. bk. 159.00 set. (CPE4340) Bisk Educ.
Get step-by-step analysis of tax accounting for inventories & long-term contracts concentrating on developments in the law since 1986.

Guide to Wine. Julian Curry. Read by Julian Curry. (Running Time: 5 hrs.). 2005. 28.95 (978-1-60083-756-2(5)) Iofy Corp.

Guide to Wine. Julian Curry. 4 CDs. (Running Time: 5 hrs. 15 min.). 2003. audio compact disk 28.98 (978-962-634-290-9(0), NA429012, Naxos AudioBooks) Naxos.
The whole subject is introduced and explained - how wine is made, the different grapes, the different blends, vintages, wine-growing areas and types. In an entertaining and informal style, he also teaches how to taste wine, how to choose it, to keep it. Other topics such as food and wine, fortified wines, champagnes and the New World experience are also covered.

Guide to Wine. unabr. ed. Julian Curry. Read by Julian Curry. (YA). 2007. 44.99 (978-1-60252-713-3(X)) Find a World.

Guidebook to Re-Evaluation Counseling. Harvey Jackins. 1 cass. 10.00 (978-1-885357-97-7(4)) Rational Isl.

***Guided Energy-Based Practices: Tools for Self-Care.** Kelly Gordon. (ENG.). 2010. audio compact disk 9.99 (978-1-4507-2828-7(6)) Indep Pub IL.

Guided Imagery. Bernie S. Siegel. 1 cass. 10.00 (OC113M) Sound Horizons AV.

Guided Imagery - Loss Bereavement & New Hope. Carole Riley. 2 cass. (Running Time: 3 hrs.). 1991. 18.95 set. (TAH239) Alba Hse Comns.
A cassette program for those who are coming to grips with their own loss or grieving as well as their caregivers. Also for group study & sharing, self help & discussion.

Guided Imagery & Other Approaches to Healing. Rubin Battino. 2 cass. (Running Time: 3 hrs.). 2000. reel tape 19.95 (978-1-899836-59-8(4)) Crown Hse GBR.

Guided Imagery Astral Voyage. Bruce Goldberg. (ENG.). 2005. audio compact disk 17.00 (978-1-57968-069-5(0)) Pub: B Goldberg. Dist(s): Baker Taylor

Guided Imagery Astral Voyage. Scripts. Bruce Goldberg. Read by Bruce Goldberg. 1 cass. (Running Time: 25 mins.). (ENG.). 2007. 13.00 (978-1-885577-87-0(7)) Pub: B Goldberg. Dist(s): Baker Taylor
Takes you on a guided tour out-of-the-body to explore other dimensions. You are safely instructed to return to your physical body following this trip.

Guided Instruction for Coping with Anxiety & Stress. unabr. ed. James D. Cowart. Read by Leo A. Kominek. 2 cass. (Running Time: 2 hrs.). 1996. Set, manual. (978-1-892776-00-6(6)); J&L Mental Health.
Includes Tape 1, Side A: "Introduction & Graduated Exposure," Side B: "Learning to Relax;" Tape 2, Side A: "Learning to Identify Realistic & Unrealistic Thoughts," & Side B: "Learning to Counter Unrealistic Thoughts".

Guided Listening: A Textbook for Music. Eleanor Hammer & Malcolm Cole. 1 cass. (C). 1991. (978-0-697-11005-3(2)); (978-0-697-17038-5(1)) Brown & Benchmark.

Guided Meditation. Glenn Harrold. 1 cass. (Running Time: 1 hr. 30 mins.). 2002. 11.95 (978-1-901923-10-0(X)); audio compact disk 17.95 (978-1-901923-30-8(4)) Pub: Divinit Pubing GBR. Dist(s): Bookworld

Guided Meditation. Narrated by Sivananda Radha. 1 CD. (Running Time: 40 mins.). 2002. audio compact disk 15.95 (978-0-931454-97-4(2)) Pub: Timeless Bks. Dist(s): Baker Taylor
Two separate meditations. One is on the Light and the other is a mental journey to the ice cave of Lord Siva.

Guided Meditation: Create your inner Sanctuary. unabr. ed. Kelly Howell. 1 CD. (Running Time: 60 min.). 1997. audio compact disk 14.95 (978-1-881451-93-8(3)) Brain Sync.
Offers a unique combination of sound frequencies & verbal techniques that produce a state of expanded body-mind awareness ideal for meditation. While guided on a transformative journey, an inner calm & a profound connection to self is established. In this state one feels nourished, creativity comes alive, & a surge in personal power is experienced. The ability to love & receive love is enhanced & it is possible to direct the will to achieve new goals. This meditation creates the ability to expand beyond the boundaries of the body & access enlightened states of being.

Guided Meditation: Revitalize Mind, Body & Spirit. unabr. ed. Read by Kelly Howell. 1 cass. (Running Time: 60 min.). 1992. 11.95 (978-1-881451-14-3(3)) Brain Sync.

Guided Meditation: Six Essential Practices to Cultivate Love, Awareness, & Wisdom. unabr. ed. Jack Kornfield. 2 CDs. (Running Time: 7200 sec.). 2007. audio compact disk 19.95 (978-1-59179-625-1(3), AW01191D) Sounds True.

Guided Meditation & Relaxation. Todd Norian. Perf. by Todd Norian. 1 cass. (Running Time: 1 hr. 6 min.). 1998. 10.98 (978-1-929553-02-0(1), 6101) T Norian.

Four guided meditations on breath awareness, slow motion movement, & loving kindness. Also included is a relaxation exercise.

Guided Meditation for Beginners. unabr. ed. Rama. Read by Rama. 1 cass. (Running Time: 24 mins.). 1990. 7.95 (978-0-89389-160-2(6), CS207MO) Himalayan Inst.

Purposes & benefits of meditation are explained, & a practical method of meditation is given.

Guided Meditation for Children: Help Anxious Children Calm down, Manage Feelings & Sleep Better. Diane L. Tusek. Read by Diane L. Tusek. (ENG.). (J). 2009. 39.99 (978-1-61574-703-0(6)) Find a World.

Guided Meditation for Discovering You: Living Life with Confidence, Direction & Peace. Diane L. Tusek. Read by Diane L. Tusek. (ENG.). 2009. 39.99 (978-1-61574-704-7(4)) Find a World.

Guided Meditation for Healing Trauma (PTSD) Belleruth Naparstek. Perf. by Belleruth Naparstek. Music by Steven Mark Kohn. Engineer Bruce Gigax. 1 CD. (Running Time: 1 hr.). (Health Journeys Ser.). 1999. audio compact disk 17.98 (978-1-881405-23-8(0), 50) Hlth Jrnys.

Designed by Psychotherapist Belleruth Naparstek to reduce isolation, terror, shame and despair; restore a sense of inner goodness, hope, growth, purpose and meaning; replenish self-esteem and a sense of spiritual connection and protection - not by reliving the trauma, but by metaphorically shifting it, incrementally over time, with repeated listening. With affirmations.

Guided Meditation for Pregnancy, Labor & Delivery: Relax, Relieve Anxiety, & Sleep Better During Pregnancy. Diane L. Tusek. Read by Diane L. Tusek. (ENG.). 2009. 39.99 (978-1-61574-706-1(0)) Find a World.

Guided Meditation for Procedures or Surgery: Relax, Relieve Anxiety, Sleep Better, Heal Faster. Diane L. Tusek. Read by Diane L. Tusek. (ENG.). 2009. 39.99 (978-1-61587-738-6(X)) Find a World.

Guided Meditation for Relaxation & Deep Sleep: Feeling Calm as Your Mind Is Gently Quieting Down. Diane L. Tusek. Read by Diane L. Tusek. (ENG.). 2009. 39.99 (978-1-61574-707-8(9)) Find a World.

Guided Meditation for Stress & Anxiety. Diane L. Tusek. Read by Diane L. Tusek. (ENG.). 2009. 39.99 (978-1-61574-708-5(7)) Find a World.

Guided Meditation Series by Vicky Thurlow: Guided Meditations. Concept by Vicky Thurlow. Voice by Vicky Thurlow. (ENG.). 2008. audio compact disk 134.55 (978-0-9817095-0-5(8)) DVT Invest.

***Guided Meditation to Help with Caregiver Stress.** Belleruth Naparstek. Read by Belleruth Naparstek. (Playaway Adult Nonfiction Ser.). (ENG.). 2010. 39.99 (978-1-61587-382-1(1)) Find a World.

Guided Meditation to Help You with Rheumatoid Arthritis or Lupus. Belleruth Naparstek. Composed by Steven Mark Kohn. 1 cass. (Running Time: 50 mins.). (Health Journeys Ser.). 1992. 12.98 (978-1-881405-25-2(7)) Hlth Jrnys.

Designed to help reduce inflammation, soreness, excess fluid; replace eroded bone & joint tissue; help calm overactive, misguided immune cells; reduce pain & fatigue.

Guided Meditation to Help You with Rheumatoid Arthritis or Lupus. Belleruth Naparstek. Perf. by Belleruth Naparstek. Music by Steven Mark Kohn. 1 CD. (Running Time: 50 minutes). (Health Journeys Ser.: 2137). 1992. audio compact disk 17.98 (978-1-881405-69-6(9)) Hlth Jrnys.

Designed by Psychotherapist Belleruth Naparstek to help reduce inflammation, soreness, excess fluid; replace eroded bone and joint tissue; help calm overactive, misguided immune cells, encourage gentleness toward the self; reduce pain and fatigue; and encourage feelings of relaxation, safety, love and peace. With affirmations.

Guided Meditation to Support the Evolution of Your Soul. Jane E. Hart. (ENG.). 2007. audio compact disk 10.00 (978-0-9753047-3-0(9)) J E Hart.

Guided Meditations. Earnie Larsen. 1 cass. (Running Time: 90 min.). 1986. 10.95 (978-1-56047-001-4(1), A102) E Larsen Enterprises.

Starts with instructions on how to prepare one's self to meditate, the follows with six separate guided mediations.

Guided Meditations. Jan Tober. Read by Jan Tober. Read by Mark Geisler. Ed. by Lee Carroll. 1 cass. (Running Time: 1 hrs.). (Kryon Seminar Ser.). 1997. 10.00 Set. (978-1-888053-05-0(4)) Kryon Writings.

Two half-hour meditations accompanied by harp.

Guided Meditations: For Calmness, Awareness, & Love. Dharmachari Bodhipaksa. 1 CD. (Running Time: 73 mins, 50 secs). 2002. audio compact disk 14.45 (978-0-9724414-0-7(9)) Wildmind.

Three down-to-earth guided meditations from the Buddhist tradition, including the Mindfulness of Breathing practice, the Development of Lovingkindness (Metta Bhavana), and Walking Meditation.

Guided Meditations for Adults: Salvation, Joy, Faith, Healing. abr. ed. Jane E. Ayer. 1 cass. (Running Time: 90 mins.). (Quiet Place Apart Ser.). 1996. 8.95 (978-0-88489-394-3(4)); audio compact disk 14.95 (978-0-88489-424-7(X)) St Marys.

Using meditations in daily life, in retreats, in planning, in meetings & in liturgies is the perfect way for one to introduce some quiet time for personal thought. A leader's guide that includes directions for preparing the meditations, the meditations scripts & suggestions for follow-up is also available.

Guided Meditations for Advent, Christmas, New Year & Epiphany. abr. ed. Jane E. Ayer. 1 CD. (Running Time: 90 mins.). (Quiet Place Apart Ser.). 1997. audio compact disk 14.95 (978-0-88489-519-0(X)) St Marys.

Meditations on the themes of birthing, naming, offering & journeying. Can be used by youth ministers, catechists, teachers & pastors. A leader's guide that includes directions for preparing the meditations, the meditations scripts & suggestions for follow-up is also available.

Guided Meditations for Advent, Christmas, New Year & Epiphany. abr. ed. Jane E. Ayer. 1 cass. (Running Time: 90 mins.). (Quiet Place Apart Ser.). (J). 1997. 9.95 (978-0-88489-518-3(1)) St Marys.

Guided Meditations for Junior High: Good Judgment, Gifts, Obedience, Inner Blindness. abr. ed. Jane E. Ayer. 1 CD. (Running Time: 90 mins.). (Quiet Place Apart Ser.). (YA). (gr. 9-10). 1997. audio compact disk 14.95 (978-0-88489-502-2(5)) St Marys.

Meditations that can be used by youth ministers, catechists, teachers & liturgists. A leader's guide that includes directions for preparing the meditations, the meditations scripts & suggestions for follow-up is also available.

Guided Meditations for Junior High: Good Judgment, Gifts, Obedience, Inner Blindness. abr. ed. Jane E. Ayer. 1 cass. (Running Time: 90 mins.). (Quiet Place Apart Ser.). (YA). (gr. 9-10). 2003. 8.95 (978-0-88489-501-5(7)) St Marys.

Guided Meditations for Lent, Holy Week, Easter & Pentecost. abr. ed. Jane E. Ayer. 1 cass . (Running Time: 90 mins.). (Quiet Place Apart Ser.). 1997. 9.95 (978-0-88489-521-3(1)); audio compact disk 14.95 (978-0-88489-522-0(X)) St Marys.

Meditations on the themes of desert surrender, promise keeping, why are you crying? & on fire. These meditations can be used by youth ministers, catechists, speakers & teachers. A leader's guide that includes directions for preparing the meditations, the meditations scripts & suggestions for follow-up is available.

Guided Meditations for Love & Wisdom. unabr. ed. Sharon Salzberg. (Running Time: 2:09:00). 2009. audio compact disk 19.95 (978-1-59179-707-4(1)) Sounds True.

Guided Meditations for Ordinary Time: Courage, Loss, Gratitude & Needs. abr. ed. Jane E. Ayer. 1 cass. (Running Time: 90 mins.). (Quiet Place Apart Ser.). 1998. 9.95 (978-0-88489-587-9(4)); audio compact disk 14.95 (978-0-88489-588-6(2)) St Marys.

These meditations can be used by youth ministers, catechists, speakers & teachers. A leader's guide that includes directions for preparing the meditations, the meditations scripts & suggestions for follow-up is available.

***Guided Meditations for Self-Healing.** Jack Kornfield. (Running Time: 2:00:00). 2010. audio compact disk 19.95 (978-1-60407-202-0(4)) Sounds True.

Guided Meditations for Stress Reduction: Body Scanning & Mindfulness of Breathing Practices. Bodhipaksa. 1 CDs. (Running Time: 56 mins.). 2004. audio compact disk 14.95 (978-0-9724414-2-1(5)) Wildmind.

Mindfulness has been shown in clinical trials to be an effective way of reducing stress. It is a form of focused awareness that helps to prevent the runaway thinking that gives rise to physical and emotional hyper-arousal.The two meditations on this CD help us to develop this transformative quality of mindfulness, by means of which we practice acceptance of our present-moment experience in a non-judgmental way.Although the meditations on this CD are Buddhist in origin, they can be practiced by people who follow any spiritual tradition or none at all.

Guided Meditations for the Soul Vol. 1: Letting Go, Letting God; A Journey Home. unabr. ed. Linda Cox. 1 cass. (Running Time: 60 min.). 1996. 11.00 (978-1-890272-01-2(9)) Purple Pr.

Experience the freedom that is yours when you surrender what no longer serves you to God. Re-awaken your Heart/Self by remembering your Divinity on a journey back to God.

Guided Meditations for the Soul Vol. 2: Letting Go, Letting God; Inner Child - Self Healing. unabr. ed. Linda Cox. 1 cass. (Running Time: 60 min.). 1996. 11.00 (978-1-890272-02-9(7)) Purple Pr.

Experience the freedom that is yours when you surrender what no longer serves you to God. Creating a safe place where you can connect with & nurture your inner child/self.

Guided Meditations for the Soul Vol. 3: Angel Empowerment; Healing Doors. unabr. ed. Linda Cox. 1 cass. (Running Time: 60 min.). 1996. 11.00 (978-1-890272-03-6(5)) Purple Pr.

Allow the angelic realm to assist you in reclaiming your power through love. Allow yourself the healing you deserve, as you move through the dooways of higher consciousness.

Guided Meditations for the Soul Vol. 4: Magical Child, Loves Your Inner Child; Forgiveness: Self-Others. unabr. ed. Linda Cox. 1 cass. (Running Time: 60 min.). 1996. 11.00 (978-1-890272-04-3(3)) Purple Pr.

Let your magical child unfold your memories of unconditional Love/God. Allow your soul the freedom forgiveness offers, when you have the willingness to forgive.

Guided Meditations for the Soul Vol. 5: Relaxation-Transformation; Smoking Cessation. unabr. ed. Linda Cox. 1 cass. (Running Time: 60 min.). 1996. 11.00 (978-1-890272-05-0(1)) Purple Pr.

Create positive changes to transform & empower you in all areas of your life. Making a decision to be free, by surrendering your addiction to a Higher Power.

Guided Meditations for Youth on Personal Themes. unabr. ed. Jane Aresenault & Jean Cedor. Ed. by Robert P. Stamschror. 1 cass. (Running Time: 90 min.). (Quiet Place Apart Ser.). (YA). (gr. 9-12). 2003. 7.95 (978-0-88489-354-7(5)) St Marys.

The audiocassette contains high-quality recordings of the meditation scripts against a background of original music.

Guided Meditations for Youth on Personal Themes. unabr. ed. Jane Aresenault & Jean Cedor. Ed. by Robert P. Stamschror. 1 cass. (Running Time: 90 min.). (Quiet Place Apart Ser.). (YA). (gr. 9-12). 2003. pap. bk. 9.95 (978-0-88489-347-9(2)) St Marys.

Guided Meditations for Youth on Sacramental Life. unabr. ed. Jane Arsenault & Jean Cedor. Ed. by Robert P. Stamschror. Illus. by Elaine Kohner. 1 cass. (Running Time: 90 min.). (Quiet Place Apart Ser.). (YA). (gr. 9-12). 2003. pap. bk. 9.95 (978-0-88489-308-0(1)) St Marys.

The audiocassette contains the meditation scripts with original background music. These meditations can be used with young people in a variety of settings.

Guided Meditations for Youth on Sacramental Life. unabr. ed. Jane Arsenault & Jean Cedor. 1 cass. (Running Time: 90 min.). (Quiet Place Apart Ser.). (YA). (gr. 9-12). 2003. 7.95 (978-0-88489-309-7(X)) St Marys.

Guided Meditations Help for Infertility. Belleruth Naparstek. Perf. by Belleruth Naparstek. Music by Steven Mark Kohn. 2 CDs. (Running Time: 75 min.). (Health Journeys Ser.: 2125). 2001. audio compact disk 19.98 (978-1-881405-65-8(6)) Hlth Jrnys.

A double audio set. Four different guided imagery exercises for the full range of relevant issues, from conception to resolution. Designed by Psychotherapist Belleruth Naparstek to relax mind and body, reinforce self-esteem and promote feelings of protection and support, while 1) envisioning successful fertilization - inside or outside the body; 2) repeating calming affirmations; 3) gaining respit from daunting procedures and help with general coping; and 4) helping with grief, resolution and reclaiming one's life.

Guided Meditations II. Byron Katie International. (ENG.). 2007. audio compact disk 16.50 (978-1-890246-84-6(0)) B Katie Int Inc.

Guided Meditations on Covenant: Consecrated, Intimacy, a New Covenant, Fidelity. Jane E. Ayer. (Quiet Place Apart Ser.). 2003. 11.95 (978-0-88489-704-0(4)); audio compact disk 17.95 (978-0-88489-705-7(2)) St Marys.

Guided Meditations on Discipleship: Readiness, Faithfulness, Conviction & Transformation. Jane E. Ayer. (Running Time: 090 min.). (Quiet Place Apart Ser.). 2003. audio compact disk 17.95 (978-0-88489-655-5(2)) St Marys.

Guided Meditations on Discipleship: Readiness, Faithfulness, Conviction, Transformation. Scripts. Jane E. Ayer. Read by Jane E. Ayer. 1 cass. (Running Time: 90 mins.). (Quiet Place Apart Ser.). 2003. 11.95 (978-0-88489-654-8(4)) St Marys.

Reading of the meditation script is accompanied by specially composed background music.

Guided Meditations on God's Justice & Compassion: Accountability, Judgment, Acknowledgment, Selfishness. Jane E. Ayer. Read by Jane E. Ayer. 1 CD. (Running Time: 90 mins.). (Quiet Place Apart Ser.). 2003. audio compact disk 17.95 (978-0-88489-652-4(8)) St Marys.

Meditations are accompanied by specially composed background music. Appropriate for use by youth ministers.

Guided Meditations on God's Justice & Compassion: Accountability, Judgment, Acknowledgment, Selfishness. Jane E. Ayer. Read by Jane E. Ayer. 1 cass. (Running Time: 90 mins.). (Quiet Place Apart Ser.). (C). 2003. 11.95 (978-0-88489-651-7(X)) St Marys.

The reading of the meditation script is accompanied by specially composed background music.

Guided Meditations on God's Reign: Benevolence, Kingdom Now, Sharing, New Jerusalem. Narrated by Jane E. Ayer. (Quiet Place Apart Ser.). 2003. 11.95 (978-0-88489-706-4(0)); audio compact disk 17.95 (978-0-88489-707-1(9)) St Marys.

Guided Meditations on Images of God: Mother, Potter, Compassion, Love. Jane E. Ayer. (Running Time: 090 min.). (Quiet Place Apart Ser.). 2003. 11.95 (978-0-88489-610-4(2)); audio compact disk 17.95 (978-0-88489-611-1(0)) St Marys.

Guided Meditations on the Chakras & the Love Principles. Arleen Lorrance & Diane K. Pike. 1 cass. (Running Time: 2 hrs.). 9.95 Teleos Inst.

Guided relaxation exercises & practice in directing energy through the energy centers.

Guided Meditations on the Lamrim: The Gradual Path to Enlightenment. Thubten Chodron. 14 CDs. (Running Time: 48 hrs.). 2000. audio compact disk 99.95 (978-0-9707641-0-2(3)) Dharma Friendship.

Guided meditations in the Buddhist tradition of Lamrim.

Guided Meditations on the Paschal Mystery: Consequences, Idolatry, Revelation, Reconciliation. Jane E. Ayer. (Running Time: 090 min.). (Quiet Place Apart Ser.). 2003. 11.95 (978-0-88489-613-5(7)) St Marys.

Guided Meditations on the Paschal Mystery: Consequences, Idolatry, Revelation, Reconciliation. Jane E. Ayer. (Running Time: 090 min.). (Quiet Place Apart Ser.). 2003. audio compact disk 17.95 (978-0-88489-614-2(5)) St Marys.

Guided Meditations with Katie. 2004. audio compact disk 15.00 (978-1-890246-94-5(8)) B Katie Int Inc.

Guided Meditations with Relaxation Music. June McIntyre. Read by June McIntyre. 1 cass. (Running Time: 45 min.). 1994. 11.98 (978-1-889045-00-9(4)) J McIntyre.

Spoken meditations with positive affirmations leading the listener into a positive state. Each meditation has soothing digital music with sounds of the entire orchestra in the background, followed by instrumental music.

Guided Meditations with Relaxation Music. June McIntyre. Read by June McIntyre. Illus. by Coe Savage. Photos by Joseph Boyles. 1 cass. (Running Time: 45 min.). (J). (ps up). 1996. pap. bk. 14.98 CD. (978-1-889045-05-4(5)) J McIntyre.

Guided Mindfulness Meditation. Jon Kabat-Zinn. 4 CDs. (Running Time: 9900 sec.). 2005. audio compact disk 29.95 (978-1-59179-359-5(9), W966D) Sounds True.

Guided Option Meditation Program. Created by Barry Neil Kaufman. 3 CDs. (Running Time: 78 mins., 74 mins., 69 mins.). 2005. audio compact disk 65.00 (978-1-887254-19-9(6)) Epic Century.

Each meditation focuses on a theme in a most relaxing and restful atmosphere. The journey within is further enhanced by interweaving the strong, yet gentle voice of Barry Neil Kaufman with soft musical themes of Daniel Kobialka's Timeless Motion and Going Home.These soothing meditations invite you to take a journey into yourself, to become an active participant in the visualization (at times, applying content from your own life), and create continuous opportunities to nurture the most relaxed, easy, centered and loving part of yourself. Therefore, as you change and grow, the meditations change and grow.Always a part of The Option Process teaching programs, they are now available in these captivating recorded versions aimed at helping each person explore their inner space , and maximize a series of intentions.

Guided Reading: Strategies That Work (Grades 1-3) Perf. by Nancy Nos. 6 cass., handbk. (Running Time: 4 hrs. 12 mins.). 2000. 85.00 (978-1-886397-32-3(5)) Bureau of Educ.

Live educator's workshop includes a comprehensive resource handbook.

Guided Reflections in Demello Spirituality. James R. Dolan. 2 cass. (Running Time: 2 hrs. 45 min.). 1995. 17.95 Set. (TAH352) Alba Hse Comns.

Wonderfully reflective material for those busy times when we need a spiritual uplift but can't seem to find the time for a traditional retreat. Whether you are familiar with the Demello style or not, this audio cassette series will prove to be refreshing & comforting experience.

Guided Relaxation. Richard Latham. (ENG.). 2008. audio compact disk 17.95 (978-0-9550584-7-9(3)) Pub: Meditainment Ltd GBR. Dist(s): H B Fenn Co

Guided Relaxation: Let Go of Stress & Pressure. unabr. ed. Kelly Howell. 1 cass. (Running Time: 60 min.). 1994. 11.95 (978-1-881451-24-2(0)) Brain Sync.

Guided into a calm state of inner peace, the mind, body & spirit are refreshed & revitalized. The listener is verbally led through a systematic release of all physical tension & mental stress. Alpha frequencies assist in this release & help increase visual imagery & creativity. The "triple induction method" is used to further enhance the receptivity of the mind to numerous positive suggestions. "Guided Relaxation" opens the mind & nurtures the body, where the exploration of unlimited possibilities can begin.

Guided Relaxation: Let Go of Stress & Pressure. unabr. ed. Kelly Howell. 1 CD. (Running Time: 60 min.). 2005. audio compact disk 14.95 (978-1-881451-47-1(X)) Brain Sync.

Guided Relaxation & Breathing. unabr. ed. Rolf Sovik. Read by Rolf Sovik. 1 cass. (Running Time: 22 mins.). 1998. 6.95 (978-0-89389-161-9(4)) Himalayan Inst.

Clear, systematic relaxation & diaphragmatic breathing instruction.

Guided Relaxation for an Inward Journey. Scripts. 1 CD. (Running Time: 46.22 minutes). 2001. audio compact disk 16.95 (978-0-9707146-1-9(0)) St John Deane.

Guided relaxation w/music for deep relaxation.

Guided Relaxation for Body Mind Soul. Govinda. Read by Karen Petrella. Ed. by Dietmar R. Rittner. 1 cass. (Running Time: 1 hr.). (ViViD-Process Ser.). 1993. 12.95 (978-1-884027-01-7(6)) Magic Sunrise.

A guided relaxation with wonderful background-music to let go of tension & stress. Includes color healing.

Guided Traveler Experience: A Personal Journey into the Seven Decisions. (ENG.). 2008. 225.00 (978-0-9629620-9-7(0)) Lightning Crown Pub.

Guided Yoga. 1 CD. (Running Time: 1 hr.). 2001. audio compact disk 39.95 (978-0-9706865-0-3(1)) All Day Pr.

Guided Yoga Relaxations. Rolf Sovik. (Running Time: 1 hr. 1 min. 15 sec.). 2004. audio compact disk 18.95 (978-0-89389-226-5(2), CD238MO) Himalayan Inst.

Guidelines for Singleness & Marriage. 6 cass. 19.95 (20136, HarperThor) HarpC GBR.

Guidelines Nineteen Eighty-Five. 1 cass. 10.00 (978-1-885357-98-4(2)) Rational Isl.
Guidelines for the re-evaluation counseling communities.

Guidelines Nineteen Eighty-Six. 2 cass. 10.00 (978-1-885357-99-1(0)) Rational Isl.

Guidelines to a Healing. Elbert Willis. 1 cass. (Learning Divine Healing Ser.). 4.00 Fill the Gap.

Guidelines to Starting & Maintaing a Church Dance Ministry. Denita Hedgeman. 2007. audio compact disk 19.99 (978-1-60247-668-4(3)) Tate Pubng.

Guideposts Inspiration. unabr. ed. (Running Time: 3 hrs. 46 mins. 39 sec.). (Best of Guideposts Ser.). (ENG.). 2009. 10.49 (978-1-60814-588-1(3)); audio compact disk 14.99 (978-1-59859-636-6(5)) Oasis Audio.

Guideposts Junction: Volume 1: Angels, Angels/All for One/Run This Race. Contrib. by Jodi Benson & Wally T Turtle. (Running Time: 1 hr. 30 mins.). (Guideposts Junction DVD Ser.). (J). (ps-3). 2007. 9.99 (978-5-557-62801-3(0)) Pt of Grace Ent.

Guideposts Junction: Volume 2: It's the Little Things/Yes! I Can Do It/Just a Prayer Away. Contrib. by Jodi Benson & Wally T Turtle. (Running Time: 1 hr. 30 mins.). (Guideposts Junction DVD Ser.). (J). (ps-3). 2007. 9.99 (978-5-557-62800-6(2)) Pt of Grace Ent.

Guide's Greatest Prayer Stories. Short Stories. Read by Jay Kiernan & Kim Snyder. Ed. by Helen Lee. (Running Time: 80 minutes). (J). 2004. audio compact disk 10.99 (978-0-8280-1862-3(6), 79-976) Review & Herald.
Here are 12 exciting stories that will boost your confidence in God's willingness to answer prayer. Read by Jay Kiernan and Kim Snyder; complete with sound effects.

Guiding Grandparents in the Stepfamily. Elizabeth A. Einstein. Read by Elizabeth A. Einstein. 1 cass. (Stepfamily Living Ser.: No. 5). 1997. 9.95 (978-1-884944-11-6(6)) E Einstein.
Explores ways for grandparents to understand the complex stepfamily & offers suggestions for making a positive difference.

Guiding Principles for the Biblical Counselor: A Tool for Effective Counseling & Discipleship. 14 cass. 2001. (978-1-931787-01-7(8)) Fundament Christ End.

Guiding Your Child Through Peer Pressure. abr. ed. Dennis Rainey & Ashley Rainey. 3 cass. (Running Time: 3 hrs.). 1993. 14.95 Set. (978-1-57229-034-1(X)) FamilyLife.

Guilding a Faith Worth Dying For: Creed. Ben Young. (Faith Worth Dying for Ser.). 2000. 4.95 (978-0-7417-6214-6(5), B0214) Win Walk.

Guilt. Anne Schraff. Narrated by Larry A. McKeever. (Standing Tall 3 Mystery Ser.). (J). 2003. 10.95 (978-1-58659-108-3(8)); audio compact disk 14.95 (978-1-58659-347-6(1)) Artesian.

Guilt. unabr. ed. John Lescroart. Read by David Colacci. (Running Time: 17 hrs.). 2009. 24.99 (978-1-4233-8689-6(2), 9781423386896, Brilliance MP3); 44.97 (978-1-4233-8690-2(6), 9781423386902, Brlnc Audio MP3 Lib); 44.97 (978-1-4233-8692-6(2), 9781423386926, BADLE); 29.99 (978-1-4233-8691-9(4), 9781423386919, BAD); audio compact disk 97.97 (978-1-4233-8688-9(4), 9781423386889, BriAudCD Unabrid); audio compact disk 38.99 (978-1-4233-8687-2(6), 9781423386872, Bril Audio CD Unabri) Brilliance Audio.

Guilt: Ease & Peace. Steven Gurgevich. (ENG.). 2005. audio compact disk 19.95 (978-1-932170-32-0(4), HWH) Tranceformation.

Guilt: The Noble Emotion. 2nd ed. Lois F. Timmins. 1 cass. (Running Time: 55 min.). 1986. 12.95 (978-0-931814-11-2(1)) Comn Studies.
Guilt helps in achieving the highest qualities of human potential: generosity, self-sacrifice, unselfishness, honesty, & duty. Insight into guilt helps in sorting values & standards, & inspires improvement in actions.

Guilt & Shame: A Fertile Garden. Earl Hackett. (Running Time: 90 min.). 1986. 10.80 (0203) Assn Prof Chaplains.

***Guilt by Association.** unabr. ed. Marcia Clark. (Running Time: 11 hrs.). (ENG.). 2011. 24.98 (978-1-60941-979-0(0)); audio compact disk & audio compact disk 29.98 (978-1-60941-978-3(2)) Pub: Hachet Audio. Dist(s): HachBkGrp

Guilt Free. (Running Time: 45 min.). (Educational Ser.). 9.98 (978-1-55909-120-6(7), 97) Randolph Tapes.

Guilt Free: Ocean. Eldon Taylor. Read by Eldon Taylor. Ed. by Leslie Brice. 1 cass. (Running Time: 1 hr.). 1992. 16.95 (978-1-56705-315-9(7)) Gateways Inst.
Self improvement.

Guilt Free: Soundtrack: Musical Themes. Eldon Taylor. 1 cass. (Running Time: 62 min.). 16.95 (978-0-940699-53-3(2), 5321C) Progress Aware Res.
Musical soundtrack with underlying subliminal affirmations.

Guilt Free: Soundtrack: Synthesized Moments. Eldon Taylor. 1 cass. (Running Time: 62 min.). 16.95 (978-0-940699-80-9(X), 5321D) Progress Aware Res.

Guilt Free: Soundtrack: Tropical Lagoon. Eldon Taylor. 1 cass. (Running Time: 62 min.). 16.95 incl. script. (978-0-940699-81-6(8), 5321A) Progress Aware Res.
Environmental soundtrack with underlying subliminal affirmations.

Guilt-Free Motherhood, Set, Pt. 1. Joni Hilton. 2 cass. (Running Time: 3 hrs.). (Raincoast Journeys Ser.). 1996. 9.98 Set, Digital. (978-1-55503-914-1(6), 07001312) Covenant Comms.
How to raise great kids & have fun doing it.

Guilt-Free Motherhood, Set, Pt. 2. Joni Hilton. 2 cass. 9.98 (978-1-55503-967-7(7), 07001347) Covenant Comms.

Guilt-Free Play - Quality Work: Stop Wasting Your Time. Neil A. Fiore. 1 CD. (Running Time: 58 mins.). 2004. audio compact disk 19.95 (978-0-9760524-1-8(5)) Self Leadshp.

Guilt Free Play, Quality Work. unabr. ed. Neil Fiore. (ENG.). 2007. 14.98 (978-1-59659-110-3(2), GildAudio) Pub: Gildan Media. Dist(s): HachBkGrp

Guilt: My Feeling-Response to Acts of Wrongdoing: Shame: My Fear of Failure, Inadequacy & Abandonment. Earl Hackett. 1986. 10.80 (0203) Assn Prof Chaplains.

Guilt Relief - Peace of Mind. Norman J. Caldwell. Read by Norman J. Caldwell. Ed. by Achieve Now Institute Staff. 1 cass. (Running Time: 20 min.). (Better Health Ser.). 1988. 9.97 (978-1-56273-054-3(1)) My Mothers Pub.
Set yourself free - harmony now in your daily life. Feel wonderful inside & out - you're worth it!.

Guilt Relief - Peace of Mind: Set Yourself Free-Harmony comes Through Release & the Ability to Let Go. 1. 1988. 14.95 (978-1-56273-008-6(8)) My Mothers Pub.

Guilt, Shame, Rejection. Derek Prince. 1 cass. 5.95 (4346) Derek Prince.
Nearly all of us experience these three negative emotions at one time or another, but the death of Jesus on the cross offers us full deliverance & victory.

Guilt, the Real & the False. Dan Corner. 1 cass. 3.00 (39) Evang Outreach.

Guilty. abr. ed. Karen Robards. Read by Joyce Bean. (Running Time: 6 hrs.). 2009. audio compact disk 14.99 (978-1-4233-2840-7(X), 9781423328407, BCD Value Price) Brilliance Audio.

Guilty. unabr. ed. Karen Robards. Read by Joyce Bean. (Running Time: 11 hrs.). 2008. 24.95 (978-1-4233-2837-7(X), 9781423328377, BAD); 39.25 (978-1-4233-2838-4(8), 9781423328384, BADLE); audio compact disk 38.95 (978-1-4233-2833-9(7), 9781423328339, Bril Audio CD Unabri); audio compact disk 24.95 (978-1-4233-2835-3(3), 9781423328353, Brilliance MP3); audio compact disk 102.25 (978-1-4233-2834-6(5), 9781423328346, BriAudCD Unabrid); audio compact disk 39.25 (978-1-4233-2836-0(1), 9781423328360, Brlnc Audio MP3 Lib) Brilliance Audio.

Guilty: Liberal Victims & Their Assault on America. abr. ed. Ann Coulter. Read by Ann Coulter. (ENG.). 2009. audio compact disk 29.95 (978-0-7393-6960-9(1), Random AudioBks) Pub: Random Audio Pubg. Dist(s): Random

Guilty: Liberal Victims & Their Assault on America. unabr. ed. Ann Coulter. Narrated by Margy Moore. 9 CDs. (Running Time: 10 hrs. 30 mins.). 2009. audio compact disk 90.00 (978-1-4159-5840-7(8), BksonTape) Pub: Random Audio Pubg. Dist(s): Random

Guilty: Thirty Years of Randy Newman, Set. 4 cass. 1998. 59.98 (978-1-56826-986-3(2)) Rhino Enter.

Guilty Always Run. Perf. by Tyrone Power. 1 cass. (Running Time: 60 min.). 1954. 7.95 (MM-5135) Natl Recrd Co.
In "The Guilty Always Run", a man finds everything has turned against him, his wife distrusts him, his best friend turns against him & a bartender blackmails him all because of a girl he did not even want to see. In "Just a Nickle", an attorney leaves home without his wallet, or any identification. If he had a nickle, just "chicken feed" he would not go to jail, not get beat-up & not get involved in murder.

Guilty as Sin. abr. ed. Tami Hoag. Read by Joyce Bean. 4 cass. (Running Time: 6 hrs.). 2002. 62.25 (978-1-58788-641-6(3), 1587886413, Lib Edit) Brilliance Audio.
A cold-blooded kidnapper has been playing a twisted game with a terrified Minnesota town. Now a respected member of the community stands accused of a chilling act of evil. But when a second boy disappears, a frightened public demands to know: Have the police caught the wrong man? Is the nightmare continuing . . . Or just beginning? Prosecutor Ellen North believes she's building a case against a guilty man - and that he has an accomplice in the shadows. As she prepares for the trial of her career, Ellen suddenly finds herself swept into a cruel contest of twisted wits, a dark game of life and death . . . With an evil mind as guilty as sin. "Accomplished and scary." - Cosmopolitan "Guilty as Sin is a page-turner." - Chicago Tribune.

Guilty as Sin. abr. ed. Tami Hoag. Read by Joyce Bean. (Running Time: 6 hrs.). 2006. 39.25 (978-1-4233-0084-7(X), 9781423300847, BADLE); 24.95 (978-1-4233-0083-0(1), 9781423300830, BAD); 24.95 (978-1-4233-0081-6(5), 9781423300816, Brilliance MP3); audio compact disk 39.25 (978-1-4233-0082-3(3), 9781423300823, Brlnc Audio MP3 Lib); audio compact disk 16.99 (978-1-4233-1930-6(3), 9781423319306, BCD Value Price) Brilliance Audio.

Guilty as Sin. abr. ed. Tami Hoag. Read by Adrienne Barbeau. 4 cass. 1996. 23.00 Set. (978-1-56876-057-5(4)) Soundlines Ent.

Guilty Conscience. Michael Underwood. Read by Patricia Gallimore. 6 cass. (Running Time: 9 hrs.). 1999. 54.95 (67851) Pub: Soundings Ltd GBR. Dist(s): Ulverscroft US

Guilty Conscience. unabr. ed. Michael Underwood. Read by Patricia Gallimore. 6 cass. (Sound Ser.). 2004. 54.95 (978-1-85496-785-5(1)) Pub: UlverLrgPrint GBR. Dist(s): Ulverscroft US

Guilty Party. unabr. ed. Marie Joseph. Read by Karen Cass. 4 cass. (Running Time: 6 hrs.). 2000. 44.95 (978-1-86042-328-4(0), 23280) Pub: Soundings Ltd GBR. Dist(s): Ulverscroft US
Emma Danton, marrying almost straight from school, goes to live in Lancashire with Mervyn, her husband, in his strange, possessive sister's house. Emma meets Andrew Farlane, an ex-actor, with whom she falls unwillingly & blindly in love.

Guilty Pleasures. abr. ed. Laurell K. Hamilton. Read by Kimberly Alexis. (Running Time: 7 hrs.). (Anita Blake, Vampire Hunter Ser.: No. 1). (ENG.). (gr. 12 up). 2009. audio compact disk 29.95 (978-0-14-314510-3(X), PengAudBks) Penguin Grp USA.

Guilty Pleasures. abr. ed. Lawrence Sanders. 2004. 10.95 (978-0-7435-4800-7(0)) Pub: S&S Audio. Dist(s): S and S Inc

Guilty Pleasures. abr. ed. Lawrence Sanders & Lawrence Sanders. Read by Boyd Gaines. 2 cass. (Running Time: 3 hrs. 0 mins. 0 sec.). (ENG., 1998. 18.00 (978-0-671-57691-2(7), Audioworks) Pub: S&S Audio. Dist(s): S and S Inc

Guilty Pleasures. unabr. ed. Patricia Briggs & Laurell K. Hamilton. Read by Kimberly Alexis. (Running Time: 10 hrs.). (Anita Blake, Vampire Hunter Ser.: No. 1). (ENG.). (gr. 12 up). 2009. audio compact disk 34.95 (978-0-14-314401-4(4), PengAudBks) Penguin Grp USA.

Guilty River. unabr. ed. Wilkie Collins. Narrated by Flo Gibson. 3 cass. (Running Time: 4 hrs. 22 mins.). 2003. 16.95 (978-1-55685-660-0(1)) Audio Bk Con.
A haunting tale as two men vie for the same lovely lass.

Guilty Thing Surprised. unabr. ed. Ruth Rendell. Read by Christopher Ravenscroft. 6 cass. (Running Time: 9 hrs.). (Inspector Wexford Mystery Ser.: Bk. 5). 2000. 49.95 (978-0-7451-4399-6(7), CAB 1083) Pub: Chivers Audio Bks GBR. Dist(s): AudioGO
The Nightingales were a very happy couple. If a husband and wife never discuss anything but weather and sleep, are waited on hand and foot, and childless, then what is there to argue about? Someone had reason to argue with Elizabeth. Someone was alone with her that September night and had killed her. Inspector Wexford soon discovered that beneath the placid surface of the Nightingales' lives, were secrets no one had ever suspected.

Guimont Psalms from the Lectionary for Mass. Michel Guimont. 1 cass. 1999. 10.95 (CS-445); 10.95 (CS-445); audio compact disk 15.95 (CD-445) GIA Pubns.

Guineaman. unabr. ed. Richard Woodman. Read by Joe Dunlop. 8 cass. (Running Time: 10 hrs. 30 min.). (William Kite Trilogy: Bk. 1). (J). 2003. 69.95 (978-1-84283-332-2(4)); audio compact disk 84.95 (978-1-84283-690-3(0)) Pub: ISIS Lrg Prnt GBR. Dist(s): Ulverscroft US

Guinness Irish Black Whistle. Created by Walton Manufacturing Ltd. 1999. pap. bk. 23.95 (978-0-7866-5309-6(4)) Waltons Manu IRL.

Guitar. Perf. by Louie Shelton. 1 CD. (Running Time: 50 Min.). 1996. audio compact disk 15.98 (978-1-56896-141-5(3), 54171-2) Lightyear Entrtnmnt.
Louie Shelton has been viewed as a supreme session guitarist. This album showcases the skill, versatility & passion of an acclaimed guitarist, producer & composer.

Guitar. Tim Brookes. Narrated by Tim Brookes. (Running Time: 11 hrs. 30 mins.). 2005. 34.95 (978-1-59912-500-8(5)) Iofy Corp.

Guitar: An American Life. Tim Brookes. Read by Tim Brookes. (Running Time: 13 hrs. 18 mins.). 2005. 29.95 (978-0-7861-8071-4(4)); reel tape 79.95 (978-0-7861-3492-2(5)) Blckstn Audio.

Guitar: An American Life. Tim Brookes. Read by Tim Brookes. (Running Time: 41400 sec.). 2005. audio compact disk 99.00 (978-0-7861-7888-9(4)) Blckstn Audio.

Guitar Axis Masterclass Octaves. audio compact disk 12.95 (978-1-932016-00-0(7), GA001CD) Guitar Ax.

Guitar Axis Masterclass Target Tones. audio compact disk 12.95 (978-0-7579-9429-6(6), GA003CD, Warner Bro) Alfred Pub.

Guitar Axis Masterclass Turnarounds. audio compact disk 12.95 (978-0-7579-9428-9(8), GA002CD, Warner Bro) Alfred Pub.

***Guitar Basics.** Created by Alfred Publishing. (Play (Alfred) Ser.). (ENG.). 2010. (978-0-7390-6566-2(1)) Alfred Pub.

***Guitar Boy.** M. J. Auch. Read by David Baker. (ENG.). (YA). 2010. audio compact disk 45.00 (978-1-936223-38-1(4)) Full Cast Audio.

Guitar Chop Shop. M. Smith. (ENG.). 2001. audio compact disk 10.95 (978-1-929395-33-0(7)) Pub: Workshop Arts. Dist(s): Alfred Pub

Guitar Chords. Armstrong & George Taylor. 1 CD. 2004. audio compact disk 12.95 (978-0-7119-8771-5(8), AM969661) Music Sales.

Guitar Class Method, Vol. 1. William Bay. 1972. spiral bd. 17.95 (978-0-7866-0912-3(5), 93300P) Mel Bay.

Guitar Class Method, Vol. 1. William Bay. 1976. 9.98 (978-0-87166-531-7(X), 93300C) Mel Bay.

Guitar Class Method, Volume 1, Vol. 1. Created by Mel Bay Publications Inc. 1996. audio compact disk 9.98 (978-0-7866-2350-1(0), 93300CD) Mel Bay.

Guitar Collection of Antonio Curio. Antonio Curio. 1999. pap. bk. 19.95 (978-0-7866-3192-6(9), 96800BCD) Mel Bay.

Guitar for the Absolute Beginner, Bk. 1. Workshop Arts Staff. (ENG.). 1997. audio compact disk 10.00 (978-0-7390-1077-8(8), 14977) Alfred Pub.

Guitar for the Absolute Beginner, Bk. 2. Workshop Arts Staff. (ENG.). 1997. audio compact disk 9.95 (978-0-7390-1080-8(8), 14980) Alfred Pub.

Guitar Highway Rose. unabr. ed. Brigid Lowry. Read by Kate Hosking. 4 cass. (Running Time: 5 hrs.). 2002. (978-1-876584-16-0(5), 590688) Bolinda Pubng AUS.
Rosie is restless. She wants a nose-ring, & more. She wants to do something, be someone, be someone else. Asher is the new boy in her class. He has dreadlocks, a guitar & a bad case of the gypsy blues. And he just wants to get away. Sometimes we know we shouldn't & that's exactly why we do.

Guitar Highway Rose. unabr. ed. Brigid Lowry. Read by Kate Hosking. 4 CDs. (Running Time: 4 hrs. 45 mins.). (YA). (gr. 7-10). 2006. audio compact disk 63.95 (978-1-74093-890-7(9)) Pub: Bolinda Pubng AUS. Dist(s): Bolinda Pub Inc

Guitar Landscape. Stefan Grossman. 1992. 10.98 (978-1-56222-348-9(8), 94513C) Shanachie Recs.

Guitar Lullaby. Ricardo Cobo. 1 cass. (Running Time: 1 hr.). 9.95 (978-1-55961-622-5(9)) Relaxtn Co.

Guitar Made Easy. Karen Hogg. (ENG.). 2001. audio compact disk 10.00 (978-1-929395-25-5(6)) Pub: Workshop Arts. Dist(s): Alfred Pub

Guitar Method, Bk. 1. Gary Turner. (Progressive Ser.). 2004. pap. bk. 19.95 (978-1-86469-068-2(6), 256-073) Kolala Music SGP.

Guitar Method Bk. 1: Supplementary Songbook. Brett Duncan. (Progressive Ser.). 1997. pap. bk. (978-1-875726-07-3(1)) Kolala Music SGP.

Guitar Method Bar Chords. Gary Turner. (Progressive Ser.). 2004. pap. bk. 19.95 (978-1-86469-067-5(4), 256-075) Kolala Music SGP.

Guitar Method Book. Gary Turner. (Progressive Ser.). (SPA.). 2004. pap. bk. 14.95 (978-1-875726-99-8(3), 256-072) Kolala Music SGP.

Guitar Method Chords. Gary Turner. (Progressive Ser.). 2004. pap. bk. 19.95 (978-1-86469-066-8(6), 256-076) Kolala Music SGP.

Guitar Method Fingerpricking. Gary Turner. (Progressive Ser.). 2004. pap. bk. 19.95 (978-1-86469-071-2(2), 256-077) Kolala Music SGP.

Guitar Method for Young Beginners Supplementary Songbook A. Andrew Scott. (J). 1997. pap. bk. (978-0-947183-82-0(5)) Kolala Music SGP.

Guitar Method Lead. Gary Turner. (Progressive Ser.). 2004. pap. bk. 19.95 (978-1-86469-070-5(4), 256-078) Kolala Music SGP.

Guitar Method Rhythm. Gary Turner. (Progressive Ser.). 2004. pap. bk. 19.95 (978-1-86469-069-9(0), 256-079) Kolala Music SGP.

Guitar Method Theory. Peter Gelling. (Progressive Ser.). 2004. pap. bk. 19.95 (978-1-86469-075-0(5), 256-080) Kolala Music SGP.

Guitar Method 1. Gary Turner. (Progressive Ser.). 2004. pap. bk. & suppl. ed. 19.95 (978-1-86469-133-7(6), 256-071) Kolala Music SGP.

Guitar Music of Cuba. Elias Barreiro. 1996. bk. 24.95 (978-0-7866-2303-7(9), MB96178BCD) Mel Bay.

Guitar of Big Bill Broonzy. Woody Mann. (Stefan Grossman's Guitar Workshop Ser.). 1999. pap. bk. 24.95 (978-0-7866-5025-5(7)) Mel Bay.

Guitar of Blind Blake. Woody Mann. (Stefan Grossman's Guitar Workshop Ser.). 1999. audio compact disk 24.95 (978-0-7866-4997-6(6)) Mel Bay.

Guitar of Lonnie Johnson. Woody Mann. (Stefan Grossman's Guitar Workshop Ser.). 1999. pap. bk. 24.95 (978-0-7866-4998-3(4)) Mel Bay.

Guitar of Peter Finger - Advanced Fingerstyle Composition: Intermediate Level. Peter Finger. 1998. pap. bk. 22.95 (978-0-7866-2592-5(9), 96993BCD) Mel Bay.

Guitar of Tim Sparks - Fingerstyle Excursions. Tim Sparks. 1998. pap. bk. 22.95 (978-0-7866-4105-5(3), 96992BCD) Mel Bay.

Guitar One Presents Lesson Lab: The Best of 1995-2000. Cherry Lane Music Staff. (Instrument Instruction). 2002. bk. 19.95 (978-1-57560-415-2(9), HL02500330) Pub: Cherry Lane. Dist(s): H Leonard

Guitar Rock: 1974-1975. 1 cass. (Running Time: 1 hr. 30 min.). 1999. 9.99 (GRCM63); audio compact disk 9.99 (GSCM11) Time-Life.

Guitar School, Bk. 2. Jerry Snyder. 1 CD. (ENG.). 1999. audio compact disk 9.00 (978-0-7390-0816-4(1), 18498) Alfred Pub.

Guitar Serenity. (Running Time: 60 mins.). 2002. audio compact disk 15.99 (978-1-904972-65-5(9)) Global Jrny GBR GBR.

Guitar Shop - Getting Your Sound: Handy Guide. Tobias Hurwitz. (ENG.). 1999. audio compact disk 10.00 (978-0-7390-2559-8(7)) Alfred Pub.

Guitar Shop - Tricks & Special Effects: Handy Guide. Ethan Fiks. (ENG.). 1999. audio compact disk 10.00 (978-0-7390-2560-4(0)) Alfred Pub.

Guitar Solos. William Foden. Perf. by Ron Purcell & Gregory Newton. 2001. bk. 14.95 (978-0-7866-3408-8(1)) Mel Bay.

Guitar Today, No. 1. Perf. by Jerry Snyder. 1987. 8.95 (978-0-7390-1806-4(X), 340) Alfred Pub.

Guitar Today, No. 1. Perf. by Jerry Snyder. 1987. pap. bk. 17.45 (978-0-7390-1805-7(1), 344) Alfred Pub.

Guitar Today, No. 1. Perf. by Jerry Snyder. 1 CD. (ENG.). 1995. audio compact disk 10.95 (978-0-7390-0811-9(0)) Alfred Pub.

Guitar Today: A Beginning Acoustic & Electric Guitar Method. Jerry Snyder. 1 CD. (ENG.). 1996. audio compact disk 10.95 (978-0-7390-0707-5(6), 14152) Alfred Pub.

Guitar Toons No. 1: Music Book. D. R. Auten. Ed. by Jim Kirlin. Interview with Jim Kirlin. Illus. by Bruce Kunkel. Interview with Bruce Kunkel. 1 cass., 1 CD. 1999. bk. CD. (978-0-9669881-0-9(8)) D R Auten.
Arrangements of songs played solo on acousting guitar. Songs contain sounds of animals.

Guitar Warm-Up Studies & Solos. William Bay. 2000. pap. bk. 5.95 (978-0-7866-5085-9(0), 98592BCD) Mel Bay.

Guitare Basse. (FRE.). 1997. bk. 21.95 (978-0-7692-1319-4(7), Warner Bro) Alfred Pub.

Guitarist's Link to Sight Reading. Jerry E. Jennings. 2004. bk. 19.95 (978-0-9700038-0-5(3), JJ10000) Pub: J Jennings Pubng. Dist(s): Music Sales

Guitarra de Amor. Perf. by Anthony Arizaga. 1 cass., 1 CD. (SPA.). 7.98 (DUR 7); audio compact disk 12.78 CD Jewel box. (DUR 7) NewSound.

Guitarra del Sol. Perf. by Anthony Arizaga. 1 cass., 1 CD. (SPA.). 7.98 (DUR 5); audio compact disk 12.78 CD Jewel box. (DUR 5) NewSound.

Guitarra Ritmos Basicos. 1 CD. (SPA.). 2003. pap. bk. 14.95 (978-1-928827-65-8(9)) Mayas Music.
The CD contains examples and rhythms taught in the book.

Guitarra Suave. Perf. by Anthony Arizaga. 1 cass. 9.98; audio compact disk 15.98 Lifedance.
Guitars, piano, winds, accordion, vocals, sitar, bass & percussion. Sweet & sensual favorites, in an evocative Caribbean style. Includes "Black Orpheus," "Do It Again," "How Insensitive," "Is It a Crime," "Let's Stay Together," "Mas Que Nada," "The Shadow of Your Smile," "Smooth Operator," "This Masquerade" & "Wicked Game." Demo CD or cassette available.

Guitars for Christmas: 20 Christmas Carols for One or Two Guitars. Created by Hal Leonard Corporation Staff. Barrie Carson Turner. 2007. pap. bk. 17.95 (978-1-902455-75-4(4), 1902455754) Pub: Schott Music Corp. Dist(s): H Leonard

Guitarscapes: Intermediate Level. Vincent Sadovsky. 1998. pap. bk. 19.95 (978-0-7866-3051-6(5), 96571BCD) Mel Bay.

Guitropolis. Ron Manus. (ENG.). 1997. audio compact disk 24.95 (978-0-88284-775-7(9)) Alfred Pub.

Guitropolis: Lab Set, CD-ROM Set. Alfred Publishing Staff. (ENG.). 1900. audio compact disk (978-0-7390-2555-0(4)) Alfred Pub.

Gujarat, Vol. 1. 1 cass. 1993. (F93031) Multi-Cultural Bks.

Gujarat, Vol. 2. 1 cass. 1993. (F93032) Multi-Cultural Bks.

Gulag Archipelago Vol. 1, Pt. 1: The Prison Industry & Perpetual Motion. unabr. ed. Aleksandr Solzhenitsyn. Read by Frederick Davidson. 10 cass. (Running Time: 27 hrs. 30 mins.). 1989. 59.95 (978-0-7861-0333-1(7), 1291A,B); 62.95 (978-0-7861-0332-4(9), 1291A,B) Blckstn Audio.
Examines in its totality the Soviet apparatus of repression from its inception following the October Revolution of 1917. This volume involves us in the innocent victim's arrest, preliminary detention, & the stages by which he is transferred across the breadth of the Soviet Union to his ultimate destination: the hard-labor camp.

Gulag Archipelago Vol. 2, Pt. 1: The Destructive Labor Camps & the Soul & Barbed Wire. unabr. ed. Aleksandr Solzhenitsyn. Read by Frederick Davidson. 8 cass. (Running Time: 27 hrs. 30 mins.). 1989. 56.95 (978-0-7861-0334-8(5), 1292A,B); 76.95 (978-0-7861-0335-5(3), 1292A,B) Blckstn Audio.
The first four-fifths of this volume cover the fate of prisoners in what the author calls the "Destructive-Labor Camps," felling timber, building canals & railroads, mining gold, without equipment or adequate food or clothing, & subject always to the caprices of the camp authorities. Most tragic of all is the life of the women prisoners ... & of the luckless children they bear.

Gulag Archipelago Vol. 3: Katorga, Exile, Stalin Is No More. unabr. ed. Aleksandr Solzhenitsyn. Read by Frederick Davidson. 15 cass. (Running Time: 22 hrs.). 1989. 95.95 (978-0-7861-0336-2(1), 1293) Blckstn Audio.
In this final volume of both a literary masterpiece & living memorial to the untold millions of Soviet martyrs, Solzhenitsyn's epic narrative moves to its astounding climax. We now see that this great cathedral of a book not only commemorates those massed victims but celebrates the unquenched spirit of resistance which flickered & then burst into flame even in Stalin's "special camps." This volume contains the final three parts: Katorga, Exile & Stalin Is No More.

Guleesh see Irish Fairy Tales

Gulf Conspiracy. unabr. ed. Ken McClure. Read by John Keogh. (Running Time: 30600 sec.). 2006. audio compact disk 87.95 (978-1-74093-737-5(6)) Pub: Bolinda Pubng AUS. Dist(s): Bolinda Pub Inc

Gulf Crisis. Daniel Ellsberg et al. 2 cass. 18.00 set. (A0767-90) Sound Photosyn.
Apt commentary by astute observers on the threat of war.

Gulf Screen Guild Theatre: History Is Made at Night & Waterloo Bridge. 1 cass. (Running Time: 1 hr.). 2001. 6.98 (1659) Radio Spirits.

Gulf Stream: Tiny Plankton, Giant Bluefin, & the Amazing Story of the Powerful River in the Atlantic. Stan Ulanski. (ENG., 2008. 14.00 (978-0-8078-8714-1(5)); audio compact disk 14.00 (978-0-8078-8716-5(1)) U of NC Pr.

Gulf War Anthology of Poetry. Poems. William J. Simmons, Sr.. Read by William J. Simmons, Sr. Interview with LaTashe Jackson. 1 cass. (Running Time: 60 min.). 1996. 10.00 (978-0-9656133-3-0(X)) Simmons Ent & Servs.
Accounts of the Gulf War before, during & after.

Gulf War; Black: Two Short Plays. unabr. ed. Joyce Carol Oates. 1994. 19.95 (978-1-58081-152-1(3)) L A Theatre.

Gulistan, Vol. 1. Music by Farida Khanum. 1 cass. 1991. (B91033); audio compact disk (CD B91033) Multi-Cultural Bks.
Ghazals.

Gulistan, Vol. 2. Music by Farida Khanum. 1 cass. 1991. (B91034); audio compact disk (CD B91034) Multi-Cultural Bks.

Gulistan, Vol. 3. Music by Iqbal Bano. 1 cass. 1991. (B91035); audio compact disk (CD B91035) Multi-Cultural Bks.

Gulistan, Vol. 4. Music by Iqbal Bano. 1 cass. 1991. (B91036); audio compact disk (CD B91036) Multi-Cultural Bks.
Thumri & Dadra.

Gulistan, Vol. 5. Music by Reshma. 1 cass. 1991. (B91037); audio compact disk (CD B91037) Multi-Cultural Bks.
Folk & Sufi songs.

Gulistan, Vol. 6. Music by Reshma. 1 cass. 1991. (B91038); audio compact disk (CD B91038) Multi-Cultural Bks.
Folk & Sofi songs.

Gulistan, Vol. 7. Music by Tahira Syed. 1 cass. 1991. (B91039); audio compact disk (CD B91039) Multi-Cultural Bks.
Ghazals.

Gulistan, Vol. 8. Music by Tahira Syed. 1 cass. 1991. (B91040); audio compact disk (CD B91040) Multi-Cultural Bks.
Geet & Folk songs.

Gullah - Carry Me Home. Marlena Smalls. Perf. by Hallelujah Singers Staff. 1 cass., 1 CD. (Running Time: 53 min.). 1999. 11.95 (978-1-889974-14-9(5)) Ziplow Prodns.
More songs from the Gullah culture of the South Carolina Sea Islands.

Gullah - Carry Me Home. unabr. ed. Marlena Smalls. Perf. by Hallelujah Singers. 1 cass. (Running Time: 90 mins.). 1999. 14.95 (978-1-889974-13-2(7)) Ziplow Prodns.

Gullah - Heritage Not Hate: One Woman's Journey. unabr. ed. Marlena Smalls. Read by Marlena Smalls. 1 cass. (Running Time: 1 hr. 30 mins.). 2000. 16.95 Ziplow Prodns.
One woman's discovery of her Gullah roots.

Gullah - Songs of Hope, Faith & Freedom. unabr. ed. Marlena Smalls. Perf. by Hallelujah Singers Staff. 1 cass. (Running Time: 50 min.). 1997. 11.95 (978-1-889974-05-7(6)) Ziplow Prodns.
Songs & stories of the Gullah culture of the South Carolina Sea Islands.

Gullah - Songs of Hope, Faith & Freedom. unabr. ed. Perf. by Marlena Smalls & Hallelujah Singers Staff. 1 CD. (Running Time: 50 min.). 1997. audio compact disk 16.95 (978-1-889974-03-3(X)) Pub: Ziplow Prodns. Dist(s): Bookworld

Gullah Gullah Island: Jump up & Sing Binyah's Favorite Songs. Rhino Records Staff. 1 CD. (Running Time: 1 hr. 30 mins.). (J). (gr. 4-7). 1998. audio compact disk 11.98 (978-1-56826-924-5(2), R2 75313); 7.98 (978-1-56826-923-8(4), R4 75312) Rhino Enter.
Get preschoolers jumping and singing along with Binyah's favorite songs from the popular Nick Jr. TV series. Includes complete lyrics.

Gullah Night Before Christmas. Virginia M. Geraty. 1 cass. (Running Time: 20 hrs. NaN mins.). (Night Before Christmas Ser.). (ENG.). (J). (ps-3). 1998. 9.95 (978-1-56554-396-6(3)) Pelican.

Gullah Night Before Christmas. Virginia Mixson Geraty. 1 cass. (J). 1998. 9.95 Pelican.

Gullible's Travels. Steve Allen. Read by Steve Allen. Read by Jayne Meadows. 1 cass. (Running Time: 1 hr.). (ENG.). (gr. 3-10). 1995. 22.98 (978-1-57392-029-2(0)) Prometheus Bks.
Steve Allen introduces young people to the brain and its proper use. Critical thinking has never been so much fun!.

Gullible's Travels: Commentary on Jonathan Swift's Political Satire. Instructed by Manly P. Hall. 8.95 (978-0-89314-132-5(1), C830828) Philos Res.

Gullible's Travels: The Adventures of a Bad Taste Tourist. Cash Peters. Read by Cash Peters. (Running Time: 28800 sec.). 2007. 54.95 (978-1-4332-0070-0(8)); audio compact disk 63.00 (978-1-4332-0071-7(6)); audio compact disk 29.95 (978-1-4332-0072-4(4)) Blckstn Audio.

Gulliver's Travels see Great English Literature of the 18th Century

Gulliver's Travels. Jonathan Swift. Narrated by David Thorn. Music by David Thorn. Engineer Bobbie Frohman. Des. by B. J. Bedford. 9 Cds. (Running Time: 10 Hrs.). (J). 2004. audio compact disk (978-0-9793777-5-4(7)) Alcazar AudioWorks.

Gulliver's Travels. Jonathan Swift. Narrated by Paul Albertson. (ENG.). 2008. 12.95 (978-0-9801087-4-3(8)) Alpha DVD.

Gulliver's Travels. Jonathan Swift. Read by Hal Girard. (J). (D-303) Audio Bk.

Gulliver's Travels. Jonathan Swift. Read by Pamela Garelick. (Running Time: 43200 sec.). (J). 2007. 72.95 (978-0-7861-4970-4(1)) Blckstn Audio.

Gulliver's Travels. Jonathan Swift. Read by Martin Shaw. 2 cass. (Running Time: 3 hrs.). (YA). (gr. 7 up). 1999. 16.99 (978-0-00-105241-3(1)) Pub: HarpC GBR. Dist(s): Trafalgar

Gulliver's Travels. Jonathan Swift. Read by Neville Jason. (Running Time: 4 hrs.). 2000. 24.95 (978-1-60083-757-9(3)) Iofy Corp.

Gulliver's Travels. Jonathan Swift. Narrated by Walter Covell. (Running Time: 11 hrs.). 2006. 30.95 (978-1-59912-140-6(9)) Iofy Corp.

Gulliver's Travels. Jonathan Swift. Read by Walter Covell. 8 cass. (Running Time: 12 hrs.). 1989. 48.00 incl. album. (C-154) Jimcin Record.
Famous mythical journeys.

Gulliver's Travels. Jonathan Swift. (J). 1985. 4.95 (978-0-87188-164-9(0)) McGraw.

Gulliver's Travels. Jonathan Swift. 1 cass. 3.98 Clamshell. (978-1-55886-108-4(4), BB/PT 435) Smarty Pants.

Gulliver's Travels. Jonathan Swift. Read by David Case. (Running Time: 39600 sec.). (Unabridged Classics in Audio Ser.). (ENG.). 2006. audio compact disk 69.99 (978-1-4001-3272-0(X)) Pub: Tantor Media. Dist(s): IngramPubServ

Gulliver's Travels. abr. ed. Jonathan Swift. Narrated by Hal Gerard. 2 cass. (Running Time: 50 min.). 12.95 (978-0-89926-130-0(2), 818) Audio Bk.

Gulliver's Travels. abr. ed. Jonathan Swift. Read by Neville Jason. 3 CDs. (Running Time: 4 hrs.). (J). (gr. 6-12). 1996. audio compact disk 22.98 (978-962-634-077-6(0), NA307712) Naxos.
The images of Gulliver among the miniature Lilliputians & the giants of Brobdingnag, the crazy scientists & the rational horses create a series of novel delights & challenging insights.

Gulliver's Travels. abr. ed. Jonathan Swift. Read by Neville Jason. 3 cass. (Running Time: 4 hrs.). (J). 1996. 17.98 (978-962-634-577-1(2), NA307714, Naxos AudioBooks) Naxos.

Gulliver's Travels. abr. ed. Jonathan Swift. Perf. by Joel Grey. 4 cass. (Running Time: 6 hrs.). 2004. 25.00 (978-1-59007-115-1(8)) Pub: New Millenn Enter. Dist(s): PerseuPGW
The voyages of an eighteenth-century Englishman carry him to such strange places as Lilliput, where people are six inches tall, and Brobdingnag, a land peopled by giants.

Gulliver's Travels. abr. ed. Jonathan Swift. Read by Denis Johnston. 1 cass. (Running Time: 43 min.). 10.95 (978-0-8045-0856-8(9), SAC 856) Spoken Arts.
Chapters I, III & V from Voyage to Lilliput.

Gulliver's Travels. abr. ed. Jonathan Swift. Read by Robert Hardy. 2 cass. (Running Time: 3 hrs.). (Hodder Headline Ser.). 2001. Trafalgar.

***Gulliver's Travels.** abr. ed. Jonathan Swift. Compiled by James Baldwin. Narrated by Simon Vance. (ENG.). 2010. 10.98 (978-1-59644-974-9(8), MissionAud); audio compact disk 12.98 (978-1-59644-973-2(X), MissionAud) christianaud.

Gulliver's Travels. unabr. ed. Jonathan Swift. Read by Pamela Garelick. (Running Time: 43200 sec.). (J). 2007. audio compact disk 90.00 (978-0-7861-5826-3(3)) Blckstn Audio.

Gulliver's Travels. unabr. ed. Jonathan Swift. Read by Pamela Garelick. (Running Time: 12 hrs.). 2010. audio compact disk 29.95 (978-0-7861-6967-2(2)) Blckstn Audio.

Gulliver's Travels. unabr. ed. Jonathan Swift. Read by David Case. 8 cass. (Running Time: 12 hrs.). 2001. 29.95 (978-0-7366-6816-3(0)) Books on Tape.
One of the great works of satire pertinent to the events of the 18th-century & of continuing significance for today's readers.

Gulliver's Travels. unabr. ed. Jonathan Swift. Read by David Case. (J). 2006. 49.99 (978-1-59895-685-6(X)) Find a World.

Gulliver's Travels, unabr. ed. Jonathan Swift. Narrated by Norman Dietz. 8 cass. (Running Time: 10 hrs. 45 mins.). 1999. 70.00 (978-1-55690-211-6(5), 88888E7) Recorded Bks.
Here is the perfect opportunity to rediscover the world of Lemuel Gulliver, a world of little people & great contradictions, of fantastically sighted quadrupeds & unrelentingly myopic bipeds.

***Gulliver's Travels.** unabr. ed. Jonathan Swift. Read by Jasper Britton. 9 CDs. (Running Time: 10 hrs. 57 mins.). 2010. audio compact disk 59.98 (978-1-84379-419-6(5), Naxos AudioBooks) Naxos.

Gulliver's Travels. unabr. collector's ed. Jonathan Swift. Read by David Case. 8 cass. (Running Time: 12 hrs.). (Jimcin Recording Ser.). (J). 1994. 64.00 (978-0-7366-2727-6(8), 9174) Books on Tape.
Gulliver undertakes four voyages, all of which end in disaster. They take him to Lilliput where he is a giant amongst tiny people. He goes next to Brobdingnag, a land of giants where he is a tiny person. His next voyage to Laputa is largely an allegory of English political life under the Whigs.

Gulliver's Travels, Pack. Jonathan Swift & Gill Harvey. Read by Jonathan Kydd. Illus. by Peter Dennis. (Young Reading CD Packs Ser.). (J). (gr. k-3). 2006. pap. bk. 9.99 (978-0-7945-1206-4(2), UsborneU) EDC Pubng.

Gulliver's Travels, Set. Jonathan Swift. Read by Robert L. Halvorson. 8 cass. (Running Time: 720 min.). 56.95 (14) Halvorson Assocs.

Gulliver's Travels, Set. unabr. ed. Jonathan Swift. Read by Grover Gardner. 6 cass. (Running Time: 9 hrs.). 1994. 24.95 (978-1-55685-343-2(2)) Audio Bk Con.
A biting & ribald satire of manners & mores disguised as a fantastic journey to incredible lands. Gulliver's wits & endurance are taxed by the fabulous inhabitants of Lilliput, Brobdingnag, Laputa & other amazing places.

Gulliver's Travels: A Voyage to Lilliput. abr. ed. Jonathan Swift. Perf. by Anthony Quayle. 2 cass. 1984. 19.95 (978-0-694-50408-4(4), SWC 2053) HarperCollins Pubs.

Gulliver's Travels: An A+ Audio Study Guide. unabr. ed. Jayne Lewis & Jonathan Swift. (Running Time: 30 mins.). (ENG.). 2006. 5.98 (978-1-59483-709-8(0)) Pub: Hachet Audio. Dist(s): HachBkGrp

Gulliver's Travels: And Alexander Pope's Verses on Gulliver's Travels. Jonathan Swift. Narrated by Flo Gibson. (ENG.). 2008. audio compact disk 29.95 (978-1-60646-062-7(5)) Audio Bk Con.

Gulliver's Travels: And Alexander Pope's Verses on Gulliver's Travels. adpt. ed. Jonathan Swift. (Bring the Classics to Life: Level 4 Ser.). (ENG.). 2008. audio compact disk 12.95 (978-1-55576-572-9(6)) EDCON Pubng.

***Gulliver's Travels: And Alexander Pope's Verses on Gulliver's Travels.** unabr. ed. Jonathan Swift. Read by Pam Garelick. (Running Time: 12 hrs.). 2010. audio compact disk 29.95 (978-1-4417-6411-9(9)) Blckstn Audio.

***Gulliver's Travels: Bring the Classics to Life.** adpt. ed. Jonathan Swift. (Bring the Classics to Life Ser.). 2008. pap. bk. 21.95 (978-1-55576-613-9(7)) EDCON Pubng.

Gulliver's Travels: The Houyhnhnms. abr. ed. Jonathan Swift. Read by Michael Redgrave. 1 cass. (J). 1984. 12.95 (978-0-694-50076-5(3), SWC 1099) HarperCollins Pubs.

Gulliver's Travels, with EBook. unabr. ed. Jonathan Swift. Narrated by David Case. (Running Time: 11 hrs. 0 mins. 0 sec.). (ENG.). 2009. audio compact disk 32.99 (978-1-4001-0902-9(7)); audio compact disk 22.99 (978-1-4001-5902-4(4)) Pub: Tantor Media. Dist(s): IngramPubServ

Gulliver's Travels, with eBook. unabr. ed. Jonathan Swift. Narrated by David Case. (Running Time: 11 hrs. 0 mins. 0 sec.). (ENG.). 2009. audio compact disk 65.99 (978-1-4001-3902-6(3)) Pub: Tantor Media. Dist(s): IngramPubServ

Gully see Russell Banks

***Gum, Geckos, & God: A Familyâ€(tm)s Adventure in Space, Time, & Faith.** James S. Spiegel. (Running Time: 5 hrs. 51 mins. 0 sec.). (ENG.). 2009. 12.99 (978-0-310-77235-4(4)) Zondervan.

GUMP & CO. Winston Groom. 2004. 10.95 (978-0-7435-4801-4(9)) Pub: S&S Audio. Dist(s): S and S Inc

Gun. unabr. collector's ed. C. S. Forester. Read by Richard Brown. 7 cass. (Running Time: 7 hrs.). 1992. 42.00 (978-0-7366-2176-2(8), 2973) Books on Tape.
Napoleon's troops in Spain try to prop up his brother King Joseph. Spaniards hate a master & rebel. A remarkable cannon transforms the rebels into a besieging army.

***Gun: The AK-47 & the Evolution of War.** unabr. ed. C. J. Chivers. (Running Time: 18 hrs. 30 mins.). 2010. 22.99 (978-1-4001-8914-4(4)); audio compact disk 49.99 (978-1-4001-1914-1(6)) Pub: Tantor Media. Dist(s): IngramPubServ

***Gun: The AK-47 & the Evolution of War.** unabr. ed. C. J. Chivers. Narrated by Michael Prichard. (Running Time: 18 hrs 30 mins. 0 sec.). 2010. 34.99 (978-1-4001-6914-6(3)) Pub: Tantor Media. Dist(s): IngramPubServ

Gun Gentlemen. collector's unabr. ed. Max Brand. Read by Jonathan Marosz. 6 cass. (Running Time: 6 hrs.). 1995. 36.00 (978-0-7366-3011-5(2), 3697) Books on Tape.
When gunslingers Lucky Bill & Matt Morgan end up in the same small town, trouble's not far behind. A pretty lass named Molly Aiken may be the winner's prize. Someone's going to end up dead.

Gun Ketch. unabr. ed. Dewey Lambdin. 9 cass. (Running Time: 13 hrs. 30 mins.). (Alan Lewrie Naval Adventures Ser.). 2002. 72.00 (978-0-7366-8701-0(7)) Books on Tape.
A fighter, rogue, and ladies man, Alan Lewrie has done the unthinkable and gotten himself hitched - to a woman and a ship! The woman Caroline Chiswick. The ship is the gun ketch ALACRITY, bound for the Bahamas and a bloody game of cat and mouse with the pirates who ply the lunatic winds there. But while war comes naturally to the young husband, politics doesn't. Sure that a powerful Bahamian merchant is behind a scourge of piracy, Lewrie runs afoul of the Royal Governor, who holds the most precious hostage of all. From the windswept Carolinas to the exotic East Indies, Alan Lewrie fights and frolics with all the wild abandon of the high seas themselves. He's a true swashbuckling naval hero in the age of great sailing ships.

***Gun (Library Edition) The AK-47 & the Evolution of War.** unabr. ed. C. J. Chivers. (Running Time: 18 hrs. 30 mins.). 2010. 49.99 (978-1-4001-9914-3(X)) Tantor Media.

***Gun (Library Edition) The AK-47 & the Evolution of War.** unabr. ed. C. J. Chivers. Narrated by Michael Prichard. (Running Time: 18 hrs. 30 mins. 0 sec.). 2010. audio compact disk 119.99 (978-1-4001-4914-8(2)) Pub: Tantor Media. Dist(s): IngramPubServ

Gun Man. unabr. ed. Loren D. Estleman. Narrated by Mark Hammer. 6 cass. (Running Time: 8 hrs.). 1992. 51.00 (978-1-55690-675-6(7), 92231E7) Recorded Bks.
Eugene Morner killed his first man at age twelve & gave life to a legend; soon he found he could hire out his swift, unerring gun to the highest bidders on both sides of the law.

Gun Play at Convict Lake. Narrated by Ed Delaney. (ENG., 2009. 14.95 (978-0-9706798-1-9(5)) Talahi Media.

Gun, with Occasional Music. unabr. ed. Jonathan Lethem. Read by Nick Sullivan. (YA). 2008. 64.99 (978-1-60514-643-0(9)) Find a World.

Gundam Throne Ein Hg Model Kit. Diamond Staff. 2008. 21.99 (978-1-60584-035-2(1)) Diamond Book Dists.

Gunfighters of the Old West, Set. Dave Southworth. Read by Dave Southworth. 4 cass. (Running Time: 8 hrs.). 1998. 24.95 (978-1-890778-03-3(6)) Wld Horse Pub.

Gung Ho! Turn on the People in Any Organization. abr. ed. Ken Blanchard & Sheldon Bowles. Read by Agnes Herrmann. 2 CDs. (Running Time: 1 hr. 30 mins.). (ENG.). 2002. audio compact disk 18.00 (978-0-553-71294-0(2)) Pub: Random Audio Pubg. Dist(s): Random

Gunga Din see Classics of English Poetry for the Elementary Curriculum

Gunga Din see Famous Story Poems

Gunman's Gold. unabr. ed. E. R. Slade. Read by Gene Engene. 4 cass. (Running Time: 5 hrs. 36 min.). 1994. 26.95 (978-1-55686-504-6(X)) Books in Motion.
Lee Calloway was gold hunting in New Mexico, but his avocation was cut short when he was mistaken for a bandit & jailed. To clear his name, he broke jail & went after the real bandit.

Gunman's Justice, unabr. collector's ed. P. A. Bechko. Read by Christopher Lane. 5 cass. (Running Time: 5 hrs.). 1994. 30.00 (978-0-7366-2870-9(3), 3575) Books on Tape.
When Thorne Stevens gives up gunslinging & hell-raising, he does it in the middle of a range war. Bad time to be a pacifist.

Gunman's Rhapsody. Robert B. Parker. Narrated by Ed Begley. 4 cass. (Running Time: 5 hrs. 30 mins.). 38.00 (978-1-4025-0788-5(7)) Recorded Bks.

Gunman's Rhapsody. collector's ed. Robert B. Parker. Read by Ed Begley, Jr. 4 cass. (Running Time: 5 hrs. 30 mins.). 2002. 29.95 (978-1-4025-0789-2(5), 96917) Recorded Bks.
Details the time Wyatt Earp and his brothers spend in Tombstone, culminating in the shootout at the O.K. Corral.

Gunman's Rhapsody. unabr. ed. Robert B. Parker. Read by Ed Begley, Jr. 5 CDs. (Running Time: 6 hrs.). 2004. audio compact disk 34.95 (978-1-59007-082-6(8)) Pub: New Millenn Enter. Dist(s): PerseuPGW
The longstanding rivalry between the Earps and the cowboys may stem from cultural difference (the Clantons were ranchers who held Confederate sympathies during the Civil War; the Earps were townsfolk who had Union loyalties), and it may be exacerbated by alcohol, machismo, and fiery accusations from both sides. But the spark that leads to the final conflagration is simpler: Wyatt falls in love with Josie Marcus, Sheriff Johnny Behan's beautiful, self-assured companion.

Gunman's Rhapsody. unabr. ed. Robert B. Parker. Read by Ed Begley, Jr. 4 cass. (Running Time: 6 hrs.). 2004. 25.00 (978-1-59007-081-9(X)) New Millenn Enter.

Gunmetal Justice. abr. ed. Matthew S. Hart. Read by Charlton Griffin. 2 vols. 2003. (978-1-58807-738-7(1)) Am Pubng Inc.

Gunmetal Justice. abr. ed. Matthew S. Hart. Read by Charlton Griffin. 2 vols. (Cody's Law Ser.: No. 1). 2003. 18.00 (978-1-58807-243-6(6)) Am Pubng Inc.

Gunner Kelly. unabr. ed. Anthony Price. Read by John Livesey. 6 cass. (Running Time: 9 hrs.). (Isis Ser.). (J). 1999. 54.95 (978-0-7531-0498-9(9), 990113) Pub: ISIS Lrg Prnt GBR. Dist(s): Ulverscroft US
Colonel Butler & Dr. Audley, two of the most brilliant & formidable men in British Intelligence are at odds. Each is concealing his activities from the other & each is keeping a jump or two ahead of the CIA, the KGB, the IRA & other old rivals & enemies. Why has Dr. Audley turned up at the remote West Country village of Duntisbury Royal, as guest of the young lady of the manor, the grand-daughter of the General Maxwell who was killed recently by a car bomb? Colonel Butler sends in a man from German Intelligence posing as an archeologist. And is launched into a story which goes back to the war years.

Gunner Myrdal. Interview with Gunner Myrdal. 1 cass. (Running Time: 30 min.). Incl. Werner Von Braun. Ed. by Wernher Von Braun. 1969. (L057); 1969. 8.95 (L057) TFR.
The late Swedish sociologist looks back at his landmark book on racism, "An American Dilemma" & compares it with his work on Vietnam, "Asian Drama." Also includes an interview with Werner von Braun, recorded in 1969.

Gunny. abr. ed. Johnny Quarles. Read by Jef Fontana. 4 cass. (Running Time: 6 hrs.). Dramatization. 1998. 24.95 (978-1-890990-12-1(4)) Otis Audio.
Clayton Crist was a skinny kid from Tennessee when he first donned Confederate gray. By the time the war ended, he was a lightening-fast gunny, playing his trade from San Antonio to Dodge City. Now the hour of the gun is past. The years have blurred his vision, love has torn an aching hole in his heart & the face of every man he laid low is etched eternally on his conscience. The aging gunslinger is a marked man - pursued by name-hungry young guns. But there's one last ride Clayton Crist is determined to make - the one that will lead him home.

Gunpowder Plot: Terror & Faith in 1605. unabr. ed. Antonia Fraser. 12 cass. (Running Time: 16 hrs. 30 min.). 2003. 102.00 (978-1-84197-738-6(1)) Recorded Bks.

Gunrunners on the Missouri. unabr. ed. M. Lehman. Read by Sean Morgan. 4 cass. (Running Time: 5 hrs.). Dramatization. 1991. 26.95 (978-1-55686-376-9(4), 376) Books in Motion.
A small band of trappers buy a sternwheeler to get back upriver. They find themselves caught up in a river war against sinister factions determined to control river shipping.

***Guns.** Doris Baizley. Contrib. by Edward Asner et al. (Running Time: 3660 sec.). (L. A. Theatre Works Audio Theatre Collections). (ENG.). 2010. audio compact disk 18.95 (978-1-58081-701-1(7)) L A Theatre.

Guns. unabr. ed. Ed McBain, pseud. Read by Michael Prichard. 7 cass. (Running Time: 7 hrs.). (87th Precinct Ser.). 1987. 42.00 (978-0-7366-1169-5(X), 2092) Books on Tape.
Colley Donato, twenty-nine, has just been promoted. He used to be small-time. Now he's killed a cop & all hell is about to break loose.

Gun's for a Peacemaker. Luke Short. (Running Time: 0 hr. 54 mins.). 1999. 10.95 (978-1-60083-511-7(2)) Iofy Corp.

***Guns for a Peacemaker.** Luke Short. 2009. (978-1-60136-440-1(7)) Audio Holding.

***Guns, Germs & Steel.** unabr. ed. Jared M. Diamond. Read by Doug Ordunio. (Running Time: 16 hrs. 30 mins.). (ENG.). 2011. audio compact disk 25.00 (978-0-307-93242-6(7), Random AudioBks) Pub: Random Audio Pubg. Dist(s): Random

Guns, Germs & Steel: The Fates of Human Societies. abr. ed. Jared M. Diamond. Read by Grover Gardner. (YA). 2006. 44.99 (978-1-59895-532-3(2)) Find a World.

Guns, Germs & Steel: The Fates of Human Societies. abr. ed. Read by Grover Gardner. Jared Diamond. 5 CDs. (Running Time: 6 hrs.). (ENG.). 2001. audio compact disk 29.95 (978-1-56511-514-9(7), 1565115147) Pub: HighBridge. Dist(s): Workman Pub

Guns, Germs, & Steel: The Fates of Human Societies. collector's unabr. ed. Jared M. Diamond. Read by Doug Ordunio. 11 cass. (Running Time: 16 hrs. 30 min.). 1999. 88.00 (978-0-7366-4629-1(9), 5014) Books on Tape.
Dismantles racially based theories of human history & chronicles the way the modern world came to be.

Guns, Germs, & Steel: The Fates of Human Societies. unabr. ed. Jared M. Diamond. Read by Doug Ordunio. 11 cass. (Running Time: 16 hrs. 30 min.). 1999. 88.00 (978-0-7366-5666-5(9), 5014) Books on Tape.
Why did Eurasians conquer, displace, or decimate Native Americans, Australians and Africans, instead of the reverse? In this groundbreaking book, evolutionary biologist Jared Diamond stunningly dismantles racially based theories of human history by revealing the environmental factors actually responsible for shaping the modern world. Societies that had a head start in food production advanced beyond the hunter-gatherer stage, and then developed writing, technology and government, and organized religion - as well as nasty germs and potent weapons of war.

Guns of Arrest. unabr. ed. Philip McCutchan. Read by Christopher Scott. 7 cass. (Running Time: 10 hrs.). 2000. 61.95 (978-1-86042-524-0(0), 25240) Pub: Soundings Ltd GBR. Dist(s): Ulverscroft US
Lieutenant St. Vincent Halfhyde, RN, appointed to the battleship Prince Consort, is ordered to proceed to South Africa upon a special mission to apprehend a highly placed Admiralty civilian who has fled the country with secret blueprints of the forthcoming naval construction program.

Guns of August. unabr. ed. Barbara W. Tuchman. Read by Jack Hrkach. 13 cass. (Running Time: 19 hrs. 30 min.). 1983. 104.00 (978-0-7366-0779-7(X), 1733) Books on Tape.
The first 30 days of battle in the summer of 1914 - a month which determined the course of World War I & ultimately the political shape of our present world. Beginning with the funeral of Edward VII, the author traces each step that lead to the inevitable clash.

Guns of August. unabr. ed. Barbara W. Tuchman. Narrated by Ian Stuart. 12 cass. (Running Time: 17 hrs. 30 mins.). 1986. 97.00 (978-1-55690-212-3(3), 86170E7) Recorded Bks.
A detailed account of Europe's descent into world war in 1914.

Guns of August. unabr. ed. Barbara W. Tuchman & Nadia May. (Running Time: 19 hrs. NaN mins.). 2008. 44.95 (978-0-7861-7319-8(X)); 99.95 (978-0-7861-4779-3(2)); audio compact disk 120.00 (978-0-7861-6295-6(3)) Blckstn Audio.

Guns of Avalon. Roger Zelazny. Read by Roger Zelazny. 2 vols. (Chronicles of Amber: Bk. 2). 2002. (978-1-58807-506-2(0)) Am Pubng Inc.

Guns of Avalon. Roger Zelazny. Read by Roger Zelazny. 2 vols. (Chronicles of Amber: Bk. 2). 2003. audio compact disk 25.00 (978-1-58807-254-2(1)); audio compact disk (978-1-58807-685-4(7)) Am Pubng Inc.

Guns of Avalon. abr. ed. Roger Zelazny. Read by Roger Zelazny. 2 vols. (Running Time: 3 hrs.). (Chronicles of Amber: Bk. 2). 2002. 18.00 (978-1-58807-127-9(8)) Am Pubng Inc.
Across the worlds of Shadow, Corwin, Prince of blood royal, heir to the throne of Amber, gathers his forces for an assault that will yeild up to him the crown that is rightfully his. But, a growing darkness of his own doing threatens Corwin's plans, an evil that stretches to the heart of the perfect kingdom itself where the demonic forces of Chaos mass to annihilate Amber and all who would rule there.

Guns of Dorking Hollow. unabr. collector's ed. Max Brand. Read by Jonathan Marosz. 7 cass. (Running Time: 7 hrs.). 1994. 42.00 (978-0-7366-2864-8(9), 3570) Books on Tape.
An encounter with a wily colonel sends Donnegan, a young gunfighter, on a life-or-death mission.

Guns of Heaven. unabr. ed. Pete Hamill. Narrated by Christian Conn. 5 CDs. 2006. audio compact disk 59.95 (978-0-7927-4484-9(5), SLD 1014) AudioGO.

Guns of Mark Jardine. (Western Audiobooks Ser.). audio compact disk 9.95 (978-1-59212-224-0(8)) Gala Pr LLC.

Guns of Mark Jardine. L. Ron Hubbard. Read by Geoffrey Lewis. 1 cass. 1995. 8.99 (978-0-88404-939-5(6)) Bridge Pubns Inc.
Mark Jardine, 30 years old, clean cut & a crack shot, is drawn to lawless Arizona to avenge the death & torture of his best friend. But Jardine doesn't count on coming between beautiful landowner Barbara Alan & someone who wants her ranch - someone who will kill for it.

Guns of Mark Jardine. L. Ron Hubbard. Read by Geoffrey Lewis. 2002. 9.95 (978-1-59212-015-4(6)) Gala Pr LLC.

Guns of Mark Jardine. abr. ed. L. Ron Hubbard. Read by Geoffrey Lewis. 1 cass. (Running Time: 1 hr.). 1993. 9.95 (978-0-88404-828-2(4)) Bridge Pubns Inc.

Guns of Navarone. Alistair MacLean. Contrib. by Toby Stephens et al. 2 CDs. (Running Time: 2 hrs. 5 mins.). 2006. audio compact disk 64.95 (978-0-7927-4342-2(3), BBCD 170) AudioGO.

Guns of Navarone. unabr. ed. Alistair MacLean. Read by Steven Pacey. 8 cass. (Running Time: 12 hrs.). 2000. 59.95 (978-0-7451-4126-8(9), CAB 809) Pub: Chivers Audio Bks GBR. Dist(s): AudioGO
Twelve hundred British soldiers isolated on the small island of Kheros wait to die as the savage guns of Navarone blast them. Courageously, Captain Keith Mallory assumes the task of silencing the guns of Navarone forever.

Guns of the Timberlands. unabr. ed. Louis L'Amour. Read by Jason Culp. (ENG.). 2010. 20.00 (978-0-307-73734-2(9), Random AudioBks) Pub: Random Audio Pubg. Dist(s): Random

***Gunsights.** unabr. ed. Elmore Leonard. Read by Josh Clark. (ENG.). 2010. (978-0-06-199371-8(9), Harper Audio); (978-0-06-199753-2(6), Harper Audio) HarperCollins Pubs.

Gunslinger. Stephen King. 4 cass. (Running Time: 6 hrs.). (Dark Tower Ser.). 1989. Penguin Grp USA.

Gunslinger. unabr. ed. Stephen King. 3 cass. Library cd. (Running Time: 7 hrs. 30 min.). (Dark Tower Ser.: Bk. 1). 2003. 58.00 (978-1-4025-5859-7(7), 97135) Recorded Bks.

Gunslinger. unabr. ed. Stephen King. Narrated by George Guidall. 6 CDs Library ed. (Running Time: 7 hrs. 30 min.). (Dark Tower Ser.: Bk. 1). 2003. audio compact disk 58.00 (978-1-4025-5944-0(5), C2306) Recorded Bks.

Gunslinger. unabr. collector's ed. Stephen King. Narrated by George Guidall. 6 cass. (Running Time: 7 hrs. 30 min.). (Dark Tower Ser.: Bk. 1). 2003. 34.95 (978-1-4025-5860-3(0), RG118) Recorded Bks.
Follows the journeys of the heroic Roland of Gilead. Roland is the last gunslinger - replete with dusty Old West garb and a duo of six-shooters - and he is searching for the elusive man in black. A solitary traveler, Roland treks endlessly through desperate surroundings, passing derelict outposts, participating in violent showdowns. He finally arrives at a way station in the middle of the desert where he meets a young boy named Jake. Together they will battle unspeakable enemies before facing a dreadful decision.

Gunsmith. unabr. ed. C. K. Crigger. Read by Stephanie Brush. 8 cass. (Running Time: 10 hrs. 48 min.). (Time Travel Gunsmith Ser.). 2001. 49.95 (978-1-55686-921-1(5)) Books in Motion.
Boothenay Irons is a modern day gunsmith with the power of time travel when handling an antique weapon. Through use of an 1811 Blunderbus, Boothenay and client travel to England.

Gunsmoke. 3 cass. (Running Time: 3 hrs.). (3-Hour Collectors' Editions Ser.). 2002. 9.98 (978-1-57019-580-8(3), 27834) Radio Spirits.

Gunsmoke. Read by William Conrad et al.. (Running Time:). 2006. cd-rom 39.98 (978-1-57019-779-6(4)) Radio Spirits.

Gunsmoke. Radio Spirits Staff. Read by William Conrad. 3 CDs. (Running Time: 3 hrs.). (3-Hour Collectors' Editions Ser.). 2005. audio compact disk 9.98 (978-1-57019-581-5(1), 27832) Radio Spirits.

Gunsmoke, Set. Perf. by William Conrad. 2 cass. (Running Time: 2 hrs.). vinyl bd. 10.95 (978-1-57816-055-6(3), GS2401) Audio File.
Includes: "The Kentucky Tolmans" (8-9-52) A mountain girl asks Marshall Dillon to arrest her father. "The Lost Rifle" (7-29-56) The townspeople blame Matt for not arresting a man suspected of murder because the man is a friend of his. "Sweet & Sour" (8-5-56) Matt & Chester come to the aid of a damsel apparently in distress, only to discover that she enjoys having men fight over her. "Braggart's Boy" (12-9-56) Marshall Dillon & his deputy meet the mild-mannered son of a Dodge City braggart.

Gunsmoke, Vol. 2. collector's ed. Perf. by William Conrad et al. 6 cass. (Running Time: 9 hrs.). 2000. bk. 34.98 (4176) Radio Spirits.
Dodge City Marshal Matt Dillon, "the first man they look for and the last they want to meet," in 18 western adventures include Sunny Afternoon, Land Deal, Scared Kid, Twelfth Night, Pucket's New year, Doc's Revenge, How to Cure a Friend, Romeo, Bureaucrat, Kitty's Outlaw, Who Lives by the Sword, The Hunter, Bringing Down Father, Man Who Would Be Marshal and 4 more.

Gunsmoke: A House Ain't a Home & The Piano. Perf. by William Conrad. 1 cass. (Running Time: 1 hr.). 2001. 6.98 (1892) Radio Spirits.

Gunsmoke: Annie Oakley & No Sale. Perf. by William Conrad. 1 cass. (Running Time: 1 hr.). 2001. 6.98 (1660) Radio Spirits.

Gunsmoke: Belle's Back see Gunsmoke: Three Western Classics

Gunsmoke: Ben Slade's Saloon & Carmen. Perf. by William Conrad. 1 cass. (Running Time: 1 hr.). 2001. 6.98 (1960) Radio Spirits.

Gunsmoke: Chester's Hanging & Poor Pearl. Perf. by William Conrad. 1 cass. (Running Time: 1 hr.). 2001. 6.98 (2119) Radio Spirits.

Gunsmoke: Executioner, Indian Crazy & Doc's Reward. Perf. by William Conrad. 1 cass. (Running Time: 1 hr.). 2001. 6.98 (2016) Radio Spirits.

Gunsmoke: Gunshot Wound see Gunsmoke: Three Western Classics

Gunsmoke: Hinka-Do & The Mortgage. Perf. by William Conrad. 1 cass. (Running Time: 1 hr.). 2001. 6.98 (2241) Radio Spirits.

Gunsmoke: Indian Scout & Doc Quits. Perf. by William Conrad. 1 cass. (Running Time: 1 hr.). 2001. 6.98 (2537) Radio Spirits.

Gunsmoke: Laurie Suitor & Unwanted Deputy. Perf. by William Conrad. 1 cass. (Running Time: 1 hr.). 2001. 6.98 (2159) Radio Spirits.

Gunsmoke: No Sale see Gunsmoke: Three Western Classics

Gunsmoke: Sweet & Sour & Snake Bite. Perf. by William Conrad. 1 cass. (Running Time: 1 hr.). 2001. 6.98 (1851) Radio Spirits.

Gunsmoke: Tail to the Wind, Speak Me Fair & Braggarts' Boy. Perf. by William Conrad. 1 cass. (Running Time: 1 hr.). 2001. 6.98 (1980) Radio Spirits.

Gunsmoke: Tara & Fingered. Perf. by William Conrad. 1 cass. (Running Time: 1 hr.). 2001. 6.98 (2419) Radio Spirits.

Gunsmoke: The Bottle Man, Robin Hood & Chester's Murder. Perf. by William Conrad. 1 cass. (Running Time: 1 hr.). 2001. 6.98 (2038) Radio Spirits.

Gunsmoke: The Kentucky Tolmans & The Lynching. Perf. by William Conrad. 1 cass. (Running Time: 1 hr.). 2001. 6.98 (2180) Radio Spirits.

Gunsmoke: The Old Lady & Cavalcade. Perf. by William Conrad. 1 cass. (Running Time: 1 hr.). 2001. 6.98 (2283) Radio Spirits.

Gunsmoke: The Preacher, Dutch George & Cows & Cribs. Perf. by William Conrad. 1 cass. (Running Time: 1 hr.). 2001. 6.98 (1546) Radio Spirits.

Gunsmoke: The Queue & Kitty's Kidnap. Perf. by William Conrad. 1 cass. (Running Time: 1 hr.). 2001. 6.98 (2418) Radio Spirits.

Gunsmoke: The Round-Up & Meshoogah. Perf. by William Conrad. 1 cass. (Running Time: 1 hr.). 2001. 6.98 (2198) Radio Spirits.

Gunsmoke: The Stallion & Little Bird. Perf. by William Conrad. 1 cass. (Running Time: 1 hr.). 2001. 6.98 (1872) Radio Spirits.

Gunsmoke: Thick 'n' Thin & Box of Rocks. Perf. by William Conrad. 1 cass. (Running Time: 1 hr.). 2001. 6.98 (2602) Radio Spirits.

Gunsmoke: Three Western Classics. Perf. by William Conrad. 1 cass. (Running Time: 60 min.). Incl. Gunsmoke: Belle's Back. (WW-5930); Gunsmoke: Gunshot Wound. (WW-5930); Gunsmoke: No Sale. (WW-5930); 7.95 (WW-5930) Natl Recrd Co.
In the first episode, Kitty & her partner are offered a large sum of money by two men that want to buy the saloon & Kitty & Marshall Dillon suspect it may be a crooked deal. In "Belle's Back", Marshall's old flame returns to Dodge City with a very unlikely story as to why she has been gone for three years. The last episode is about a man who learns that he will soon die of a bullet wound he received & seeks revenge against two brothers who caused it.

Gunsmoke: Three Westerns. Perf. by William Conrad. 1 cass. (Running Time: 60 min.). (Old Time Radio Classic Singles Ser.). 1997. 4.95 (978-1-57816-107-2(X), GS128) Audio File.
Includes: 1) "No Sale" (8/26/56). 2) "Belle's Back" (9/9/56). 3) "Gunshot Wound" (10/14/56).

Gunsmoke: Wind & Flashback. Perf. by William Conrad. 1 cass. (Running Time: 1 hr.). 2001. 6.98 (2140) Radio Spirits.

Gurbani. 1 CD. (Running Time: 1 hr.). 1994. audio compact disk (CD D94005) Multi-Cultural Bks.

Gurbani, Vol. 1. Perf. by Bhai Gurmej Singh Ragi Staff. 1 cass. 1994. (D94005) Multi-Cultural Bks.

Gurbani, Vol. 2. Music by Bhai Hari Singh Ragi Staff. 1 cass. 1994. (D94006) Multi-Cultural Bks.

Gurbani, Vol. 3. Music by Bhai Nirmal Singh Ragi Staff. 1 cass. 1994. (D94007) Multi-Cultural Bks.

Gurbani, Vol. 4. Music by Bhai Ravinder Singh Ragi Staff. 1 cass. 1994. (D94008) Multi-Cultural Bks.

Gurdjieff & C. G. Jung. unabr. ed. Stephan Hoeller. 1 cass. (Running Time: 1 hr. 30 min.). 1981. 11.00 (40002) Big Sur Tapes.
Compares The Fourth Way of the Asian teach Gurdjieff & the Western Analytical Psychology of Jung.

Gurdjieff & the Mysteries of Time. unabr. ed. Stephan Hoeller. 1 cass. (Running Time: 1 hr. 30 min.). 1981. 11.00 (40003) Big Sur Tapes.
Elaborates on Gurdjieff's method for breaking through the mundane experience of time which is either cyclical or linear & can be psychologically unsatisfactory.

Gurdjieff Versus Ouspensky: The Dervish & the Intellectual. unabr. ed. Stephan Hoeller. 1 cass. (Running Time: 1 hr. 30 min.). 1981. 11.00 (40008) Big Sur Tapes.
Compares Gurdjieff, the pragmatic practicing magus, the technician of transformation, with Ouspensky, the ponderous disciplined, serious-minded intellectual.

Gurkhas. unabr. ed. Byron Farwell. Read by Bill Kelsey. 6 cass. (Running Time: 9 hrs.). 1994. 48.00 (978-0-7366-2626-2(3), 3366) Books on Tape.
India gave Britain many treasures, but none more valuable than its Gurkhas. Recruited from fierce hill tribes, these warriors bore British arms for more than a century. They asked no quarter & gave none.

Gurney's Release. unabr. ed. Sam Llewellyn. Read by Simon J. Williamson. 10 cass. (Running Time: 13 hrs. 15 min.). 1998. 57.95 Set. (978-1-85903-182-7(X)) Pub: Magna Story GBR. Dist(s): Ulverscroft US
George le Fanu Gurney, formerly of His Majesty's Navy, & now, in 1828, a prosperous Norfolk ship-builder, sets off with his wife to inspect her inheritance, a plantation in Jamaica. Along with the crew of his twelve gun schooner, 'Vandal', they sail into danger. For Gurney, the danger lies in the slave markets of the Bight of Benin, where human life is cheap & quickly sold. For his wife, it lies in the hatred of powerful Jamaicans who know she holds the key to their ruin.

Gurps Character Assistant. Gurps Staff. 2005. audio compact disk 19.95 (978-1-55634-740-5(5)) Pub: Sovrgn Pr. Dist(s): PSI Ga

Gurren Lagann Part 1 SE w/ CD (sub-only) (YA). 2008. DVD 39.98 (978-1-60496-011-2(6)) Bandai Ent.

Guru. Yogi Hari. 1 cass. (Running Time: 1 hr.). (Adoration Ser.). 9.95 (ADG) Nada Prodns.
Nada Mala for Master Sivananda. A garland of music offered at the lotue feet of the Master to celebrate his centenary, including Mantras, Bhajans & Chants that glorify all Gurus: Guru Mantras; Jai Guru Dev (chant); Dheeray Dheeray Ja; Ganga Kinaray; Paravata Pehai Sohana & Ananda Kutir Kay.

Guru: Messenger of Truth. Mrinalini Mata. 1984. 8.50 (2402) Self Realization.
The author, who trained under Paramahansa Yogananda, reveals the stages of spiritual evolution, qualities of a true guru (omniscience, wisdom, compassion, omnipotence & humility) & qualities of a true disciple (loyalty, faith, devotion & obedience).

Guru As Prophet. abr. ed. Ruchira Avatar Adi Da Samraj. 1 cass. 1997. 11.95 (978-1-57097-044-3(0), AT-UP) Dawn Horse Pr.
Avatar Adi Da speaks on the Emis' role as prophet in the world which is to create "an aggravation, a criticism, an undermining of the usual life".

Guru-Disciple. 2 cass. (Running Time: 2 hrs.). (Essence of Yoga Ser.). 14.95 (ST-29) Crystal Clarity.
Includes: Discipleship as a process of becoming more open; Yogananda's approach to discipleship; challenging the guru as a means of stengthening your faith; why true discipleship makes you a disciple of life; why vibrations & consciousness are more important than knowledge.

Guru-Disciple Relationship. Swami Amar Jyoti. 1 cass. 1989. 9.95 (E-33) Truth Consciousness.
In-depth view of the most personal, yet most universal & highest relationship. Oneness with the Master begins at initiation.

Guru, Faith & Satsang. ed. Da Avabhasa. 1 cass. (Method of the Siddhas Ser.). 1996. 11.95 (AT-UP) Dawn Horse Pr.

Guru Purnima Nineteen Eighty-One. Swami Amar Jyoti. 2 cass. 1981. 12.95 (E-20) Truth Consciousness.
Guru's perfection. Formal & informal initiation. When longing is born, He finds a way to meet us.

Guru Sharanam: Devotional Chants from India. Sri Ramesh Prem. 1 cass. 1993. 8.00 (2904) Self Realization.
Performed & recorded in India by disciples of Paramahansa Yogananda in honor of the centennial anniversary of his birth. Music & lyrics by Sri Ramesh Prem.

Guru Within. Swami Amar Jyoti. 1 dolby cass. 1985. 9.95 (E-30) Truth Consciousness.
Master is an embodiment of conscience, Viveka, the Royal Preceptor. On mind, intellect & ego. Bringing conscience to life.

Guru's Story see Childlike Simplicity

Gus the Rattler. Jerry Cardinal. (YA). 2000. audio compact disk 10.00 (978-1-4276-1118-5(1)) AardGP.

***Gust Front.** unabr. ed. John Ringo. Read by Marc Vietor. (Running Time: 26 hrs.). (Legacy of Aldenata Ser.). 2010. 44.97 (978-1-4418-6617-2(5), 9781441866172, Brilnc Audio MP3 Lib); 29.99 (978-1-4418-6616-5(7), 9781441866165, Brilliance MP3); 44.97 (978-1-4418-6618-9(3), 9781441866189, BADLE); audio compact disk 39.99 (978-1-4418-6614-1(0), 9781441866141); audio compact disk 99.97 (978-1-4418-6615-8(9), 9781441866158, BriAudCD Unabrid) Brilliance Audio.

Gustav Mahler Adagietto. fac. ed. Gustav Mahler. (Faber Edition Ser.). (ENG.). 1998. audio compact disk 125.50 (978-0-571-51322-2(0)) Pub: Faber Mus Ltd GBR. Dist(s): Alfred Pub

Gustavo Cisneros: Un Empresario Global. abr. ed. Pablo Bachelet. Prologue by Carlos Fuentes. 5 CDs. (Running Time: 16800 sec.). (SPA.). 2005. audio compact disk 29.95 (978-0-9728598-6-8(1)) Fonolibro Inc.
Gustavo Cisneros, uno de los grandes empresarios globales, forma parte de una dinastia iniciada por su padre, Diego Cisneros, en la que la segunda generacion no solo mantiene sino que supera los logros de la primera. El autor relata de forma amena, y no especializada, el entramado de un negocio con muchas cabezas que, conforme se va haciendo mas grande, se hace mucho mas complejo. Uno siente que esta en el consejo de administracion de la organizacion, volando con Cisneros a Miami, Nueva York o Madrid, e incluso vive en carne propia y en tiempo real el vertigo de negociaciones complejas y, sobre todo, arriesgadas. Gustavo Cisneros es presentado en toda su complejidad, con sus triunfos y sus fracasos. En este sentido, las experiencias de Galerias Preciados, o, mucho despues, el intento de crear una unica plataforma de satelite para America Latina con Murdoch, Ascarraga y Marinho son tan fascinantes como los exitos de CADA, Venevision, Univision, o la operacion ultrasecreta para convertir la Organizacion Cisneros en el franquiciador de Coca-Cola en Venezuela. Gustavo Cisneros, "el adelantado", como lo define Carlos Fuentes en su prologo, es una historia de riesgos premiados. Tambien, de errores admitidos. Es una historia de oportunos cambios de velocidad. Del negocio del consumo perecedero, Cisneros pasa al negocio de las comunicaciones. De la generacion de flujo de caja, a la generacion de valor. Y siempre antes del siguiente paso, la consolidacion interna. La saga empresarial de Cisneros posee, como toda vida, luces y sombras, derrotas y victorias como las detalladamente descritas en este audio libro.

Gut Feelings: The Intelligence of the Unconscious. Gerd Gigerenzer. Read by Dick Hill. (Playaway Adult Nonfiction Ser.). 2008. 59.99 (978-1-60640-981-7(6)) Find a World.

Gut Feelings: The Intelligence of the Unconscious. unabr. ed. Gerd Gigerenzer. Narrated by Dick Hill. (Running Time: 7 hrs. 30 mins. 0 sec.). (ENG.). 2007. audio compact disk 29.99 (978-1-4001-0505-2(6)) Pub: Tantor Media. Dist(s): IngramPubServ

Gut Feelings: The Intelligence of the Unconscious. unabr. ed. Gerd Gigerenzer. Read by Dick Hill. (Running Time: 7 hrs. 30 mins. 0 sec.). (ENG.). 2007. audio compact disk 59.99 (978-1-4001-3505-9(2)); audio compact disk 19.99 (978-1-4001-5505-7(3)) Pub: Tantor Media. Dist(s): IngramPubServ

***Guts.** unabr. ed. Gary Paulsen. (Running Time: 3 hrs.). 2011. 39.97 (978-1-4558-0474-0(6), 9781455804740, Brlnc Audio MP3 Lib); 39.97 (978-1-4558-0476-4(2), 9781455804764, BADLE); 12.99 (978-1-4558-0473-3(8), 9781455804733, Brilliance MP3); 12.99 (978-1-4558-0475-7(4), 9781455804757, BAD); audio compact disk 39.97 (978-1-4558-0472-6(X), 9781455804726, BriAudCD Unabrid); audio compact disk 12.99 (978-1-4558-0471-9(1), 9781455804719, Bril Audio CD Unabri) Brilliance Audio.

Gutter & the Grave. Ed McBain, pseud. Read by Richard Ferrone. 3 cass. (Running Time: 17880 sec.). 2006. 29.95 (978-0-7927-3870-1(5), CSL 893) AudioGO.

Gutter & the Grave. unabr. ed. Ed McBain, pseud. Read by Richard Ferrone. 4 CDs. (Running Time: 17880 sec.). (Hard Case Crime Ser.). 2006. audio compact disk 49.95 (978-0-7927-3871-8(3), SLD 893) AudioGO.

Guy de Maupassant Stories, Set. unabr. ed. Guy de Maupassant. Read by Flo Gibson. 3 cass. (Running Time: 4 hrs. 30 min.). 1993. 16.95 (978-1-55685-293-0(2)) Audio Bk Con.
Included in the nineteen stories in this collection are: "In Various Roles," "A Useful House," "Two Little Soldiers," "Ghosts," "The New Sensation," "The Thief," "On Perfumes," "In His Sweetheart's Livery," "The Confession," "Lost," "A Country Excursion," "The Relics," "Margot's Tapers," "The Accent," "Profitable Business," & "The Log".

Guy Lee's How to Make a Living Teaching Guitar (and other musical instruments) Guy Buckman Lee. 2005. audio compact disk 24.95 (978-0-9747795-2-2(0)) Guytar Pub.

Guy Noir: Radio Private Eye. abr. unabr. ed. Garrison Keillor & Walter Bobbie. (Running Time: 1 hr. 20 mins.). (ENG.). 2002. audio compact disk 14.95 (978-1-56511-749-5(2), 1565117492) Pub: HighBridge. Dist(s): Workman Pub

Guy Not Taken. unabr. ed. Jennifer Weiner. Read by Mary Catherine Garrison & Jordan Bridges. 2006. 17.95 (978-0-7435-6119-8(8)) Pub: S&S Audio. Dist(s): S and S Inc

Guy Not Taken. unabr. ed. Jennifer Weiner. Read by Mary Catherine Garrison & Jordan Bridges. (Running Time: 7 hrs. 0 mins. 0 sec.). (ENG.). 2009. audio compact disk 14.99 (978-0-7435-8043-4(5)) Pub: S&S Audio. Dist(s): S and S Inc

Guying the Guides see Best of Mark Twain

Guys are Waffles, Girls are Spaghetti. unabr. ed. Bill Farrel et al. Narrated by Bill Farrel & Pam Farrel. (Running Time: 4 hrs. 41 mins. 40 sec.). (ENG.). 2009. 16.09 (978-1-60814-582-9(4)); audio compact disk 22.99 (978-1-59859-628-1(4)) Oasis Audio.

***Guys Read: Funny Business.** unabr. ed. Jon Scieszka et al. Illus. by Mac Barnett. (ENG.). 2010. (978-0-06-200766-7(1)); (978-0-06-206256-7(5)) HarperCollins Pubs.

Guzin Najim's the Promise. unabr. ed. Sandra Lee. Read by Lise Rodgers. 7 cass. (Running Time: 10 hrs.). 2004. 56.00 (978-1-74093-357-5(5)); audio compact disk 87.95 (978-1-74093-508-1(X)) Pub: Bolinda Pubng AUS. Dist(s): Bolinda Pub Inc

Gwalior Gharana. Music by Ulhas Kashalkar. 1 cass. 1997. (A97024) Multi-Cultural Bks.

Gwalior Gharana. Music by Laxman Rao Pandit. 1 cass. 1997. (A97021) Multi-Cultural Bks.

Gwalior Gharana. Music by Malini Rajurkar. 1 cass. 1997. (A97022) Multi-Cultural Bks.

Gwalior Gharana. Music by Veena Sahasrabuddhe. 1 cass. 1997. (A97023) Multi-Cultural Bks.

Gwendolyn Brooks I. unabr. ed. Gwendolyn Brooks. Read by Gwendolyn Brooks. Prod. by Rebekah Presson. 1 cass. (Running Time: 29 min.). 1988. 10.00 (110488) New Letters.
Brooks won the 1950 Pulitzer Prize in poetry for "Annie Allen". On this program, she reads poetry & talks about the widely anthologized poem "We Real Cool".

Gwendolyn Brooks II. unabr. ed. Gwendolyn Brooks. Read by Gwendolyn Brooks. 1 cass. (Running Time: 29 min.). 1989. 10.00 New Letters.
Brooks reads poetry & is interviewed.

Gwendolyn Brooks Reading Her Poetry. Gwendolyn Brooks. Read by Gwendolyn Brooks. 1 cass. (Running Time: 60 mins.). (YA). (gr. 4 up). 1999. 11.95 (CAE1) African Am Imag.

Gwenhwyfar: The White Spirit. unabr. ed. Mercedes Lackey. Narrated by Anne Flosnik. (Running Time: 15 hrs. 0 mins. 0 sec.). 2009. 29.99 (978-1-4001-6381-6(1)); audio compact disk 39.99 (978-1-4001-1381-1(4)); audio compact disk 79.99 (978-1-4001-4381-8(0)) Pub: Tantor Media. Dist(s): IngramPubServ

***Gwenhwyfar: The White Spirit.** unabr. ed. Mercedes Lackey. Narrated by Anne Flosnik. (Running Time: 15 hrs. 0 mins.). 2009. 20.99 (978-1-4001-8381-4(2)) Tantor Media.

Gwilan's Harp & Intracom. Ursula K. Le Guin. 1 cass. (Running Time: 1 hr.). 1984. 12.00 (978-0-694-50298-1(7), SWC 1556) HarperCollins Pubs.

***Gym Teacher from the Black Lagoon.** Mike Thaler. Narrated by Joey Stack. 1 CD. (Running Time: 9 mins.). (J). (ps-3). 2009. audio compact disk 12.95 (978-0-545-19682-6(5)) Weston Woods.

***Gym Teacher from the Black Lagoon.** Mike Thaler. Narrated by Joey Stack. Illus. by Jared Lee. 1 CD. (Running Time: 9 mins.). (J). (ps-3). 2009. pap. bk. 18.95 (978-0-545-19706-9(6)) Weston Woods.

Gynecologic Laser: Status, 1986. Moderated by Francis J. Major. 2 cass. (Gynecology & Obstetrics Ser.: GO-7). 1986. 19.00 (8646) Am Coll Surgeons.

Gynecology & Obstetrics: Urologic Aspects of Gynecological Practice & Surgery. Moderated by Jack R. Robertson. (Postgraduate Courses Ser.). 1986. 57.00 (8616(C86-PG6)) Am Coll Surgeons.
improves the quality of female patient urogynecologic care through a cooperative effort of both the urologic & gynecologic specialities.

***Gypsy-Bachelor of Manchester: The Life of Mrs. Gaskell's Demon.** Felicia Bonaparte. (Victorian Literature & Culture Ser.). (ENG.). 27.50 (978-0-8139-2930-9(X)) U Pr of Va.

Gypsy Guitar 1: The Secrets. Denis Roux & Samy Daussat. audio compact disk 19.95 (978-0-7579-2762-1(9), ML96655, Warner Bro) Alfred Pub.

Gypsy in Amber, unabr. ed. Martin Cruz Smith. Narrated by Walt MacPherson. 4 cass. (Running Time: 5 hrs. 30 mins.). (Roman Grey - Sergeant Isidore Mystery Ser.: Vol. 1). 1983. 35.00 (978-1-55690-213-0(1), 83050E7) Recorded Bks.
When you are a gypsy who was raised by non-gypsies, you have an identity problem. When you are a gypsy, an antique dealer & you've been entrusted with a very old highboy in which a dead body is discovered, you have a major problem.

Gypsy Lord. abr. ed. Kat Martin. Read by Victoria Pryne. 1 cass. (Running Time: 90 min.). 1995. 5.99 (978-1-57096-011-6(9), RAZ 912) Romance Alive Audio.
When Lady Catherine Barrington is bartered to save her from a Romany whipping, she has no idea that her deliverer is Dominic Edgemont, heir to the Marquis of Gravenwold. When Catherine & her Gypsy Lord meet again in the glittering social whirl of London, she must decide between vengeance or love.

Gypsy Moon: Exotic Spanish Guitar Set to Tribal Dance Rhythms. Contrib. by Deva Priyo. (Running Time: 2880 sec.). 2007. audio compact disk 17.98 (978-1-59179-575-9(3)) Sounds True.

Gypsy Morph. unabr. ed. Terry Brooks. (Running Time: 15 hrs.). (Genesis of Shannara Ser.: Bk. 3). 2008. 39.25 (978-1-4233-2279-5(7), 9781423322795, BADLE) Brilliance Audio.

Gypsy Morph. unabr. ed. Terry Brooks. Read by Phil Gigante. 1 MP3-CD. (Running Time: 15 hrs.). (Genesis of Shannara Ser.: Bk. 3). 2008. 24.95 (978-1-4233-2276-4(2), 9781423322764, Brilliance MP3); 39.25 (978-1-4233-2277-1(0), 9781423322771, Brlnc Audio MP3 Lib); 24.95 (978-1-4233-2278-8(9), 9781423322788, BAD); audio compact disk 33.99 (978-1-4233-2274-0(6), 9781423322740, Bril Audio CD Unabri); audio compact disk 107.25 (978-1-4233-2275-7(4), 9781423322757, BriAudCD Unabrid) Brilliance Audio.

Gypsy Rizka. Lloyd Alexander. Read by Ron Keith. 4 cass. (Running Time: 5 hrs. 45 mins.). (YA). 1999. 213.20 (978-0-7887-3953-8(0), 47053) Recorded Bks.
Rizka, the young gypsy girl who lives in Greater Dunitsa, walks around in her ragbag clothes, playing tricks on deserving rogues. The town leaders are convinced she is bad for business. If only they could find a way to run her out of town!.

Gypsy Rizka. unabr. ed. Lloyd Alexander. Narrated by Ron Keith. 4 cass. (Running Time: 5 hrs. 45 mins.). (J). 2000. pap. bk. 58.99 (978-0-7887-3954-5(9), 41059X4) Recorded Bks.

Gypsy Rizka. unabr. ed. Lloyd Alexander. Narrated by Ron Keith. 4 pieces. (Running Time: 5 hrs. 45 mins.). (gr. 5 up). 2000. 35.00 (978-0-7887-3893-7(3), 95860E7) Recorded Bks.

Gypsy Soul, Heart of Passion. Perf. by Aurora Juliana Ariel & Bruce BecVar. Prod. by Aurora Juliana Ariel. Composed by Bruce BecVar. (ENG.). 2009. 16.95 (978-0-9816501-4-2(7)) Aeos Inc.

Gypsy Sun, Gypsy Moon. Perf. by Sunyata. 1 cass., 1 CD. 7.98 (SOP 7171); audio compact disk 11.98 CD Jewel box. (SOP 7171) NewSound.

***Gypsy Swing & Hot Club Rhythm for Guitar.** Dix Bruce. (ENG., 2007. pap. bk. 15.95 (978-0-7866-7772-6(4)) Mel Bay.

***Gypsy Swing & Hot Club Rhythm II for Guitar.** Dix Bruce. 2009. pap. bk. 16.95 (978-0-7866-8019-1(9)) Mel Bay.

***Gypsy Swing & Hot Club Rhythm II for Mandolin.** Dix Bruce. 2009. pap. bk. 16.95 (978-0-7866-8020-7(2)) Mel Bay.

Gypsy Violin. Mary Ann Harbar. 1997. spiral bd. 15.00 (978-0-7866-1651-0(2), 95538CDP) Mel Bay.

***Gypsy Wind.** unabr. ed. Lisa Jackson. Read by Teri Clark Linden. (Running Time: 7 hrs.). 2010. 19.99 (978-1-4418-8427-5(0), 9781441884275, Brilliance MP3); 39.97 (978-1-4418-8428-2(9), 9781441884282, Brlnc Audio MP3 Lib); 39.97 (978-1-4418-8429-9(7), 9781441884299, BADLE); audio compact disk 19.99 (978-1-4418-8425-1(4), 9781441884251, Bril Audio CD Unabri); audio compact disk 79.97 (978-1-4418-8426-8(2), 9781441884268, BriAudCD Unabrid) Brilliance Audio.

H

H. G. Wells: The Science Fiction of H. G. Wells. unabr. ed. Short Stories. H. G. Wells. Read by Ralph Cosham. 6 cass. (Running Time: 9 hrs.). (Great Authors Ser.). 1999. 34.95 (978-1-883049-71-3(7), Commuters Library) Sound Room.
As a young man, shortly after the turn of the century, Wells wrote science fiction ("The Time Machine") that still reigns as some of the best. Also includes: "The Country of the Blind," "The Truth about Pyecraft," "The Door in the Wall.

H. G. Wells Science Fiction Stories. H. g. Wells. Narrated by Flo Gibson. 2009. audio compact disk 16.95 (978-1-60646-097-9(8)) Audio Bk Con.

H. G. Wells Science Fiction Stories. unabr. ed. H. G. Wells. Read by Flo Gibson. 2 cass. (Running Time: 2 hrs. 30 min.). (YA). (gr. 8 up). 1998. 14.95 (978-1-55685-576-4(1)) Audio Bk Con.
Includes "The Star," "The Remarkable Case of Davidson's Eyes," "The Country of the Blind," & "Under the Knife".

H. G. Wells War of the Worlds Dramatized Audio Book: 2 Hour Drama Old Time Radio Style Recorded in the U. K. Based on a book by H. G. Wells. Adapted by Sidney Williams. 2 CDs. (Running Time: 2 hrs). Dramatization. (YA). 2005. audio compact disk 34.95 (978-1-59971-032-7(3)) AardGP.
Sidney Williams Adaptaion of H.G. Well The War of The Worlds This is the first Dramatized Audio do the novel in the period in which it was intended. A clever adaptation by Sidney Williams. Also Recorded in the UK The acting is Great Starring Martyn Tott, Nell Brooker, Simon Watts, John Tott,Patricia Tott. Music and special effects are all new creations of talented Jim Stewart. All this effectively evokes a period feel. A faithful adaptation of the Wells novel, but small enough changes to make it very interesting. Produced By Troy Thayne for MindsEyeTheater.com This First Installment is free for the blind and disabled. Visit http://www.fearyoucanhear.com also for more information.

H. I. S. Songs for Children. unabr. ed. Ralph McCoy et al. Read by Steve H. Herrera. 1 cass. (Running Time: 60 min.). (J). 1994. 7.95 (978-1-885819-07-9(2)) His Songs.
Scripture songs for children.

H Is for Homicide. unabr. collector's ed. Sue Grafton. Read by Mary Peiffer. 6 cass. (Running Time: 9 hrs.). (Kinsey Millhone Mystery Ser.). 1994. 48.00 (978-0-7366-2728-3(6), 3458) Books on Tape.
Claims adjuster Parnell Perkins's death looked strangely suspicious to Kinsey Millhone, especially when she found hints of a massive insurance

scam. Kinsey goes undercover in LA's gang hideouts, realizing she may have to cross bad man Raymond Maldonado.

H L Hunley. Tom Chaffin. 2008. audio compact disk 29.95 (978-1-4332-4876-4(X)) Blckstn Audio.

H. L. Hunley: The Secret Hope of the Confederacy. unabr. ed. Tom Chaffin. (Running Time: 8.5 hrs. NaN mins.). 2008. 29.95 (978-1-4332-4877-1(8)); 54.95 (978-1-4332-4874-0(3)); audio compact disk 70.00 (978-1-4332-4875-7(1)) Blckstn Audio.

H. L. Mencken Baby Book. unabr. collector's ed. H. L. Mencken. Read by Grover Gardner. Comment by Howard Markel & Frank A. Oski. 6 cass. (Running Time: 9 hrs.). 1991. 48.00 (978-0-7366-2054-3(0), 2865) Books on Tape.
Mencken's baby care articles appeared in The Delineator magazine in 1907, then as a book under the omniscient marquee "What You Ought to Know about Your Baby." "Questions for Mothers" after each chapter contains the original answers, followed by more modern ones.

H. M. S. Pinafore see Gilbert & Sullivan: The D'Oyly Carte Opera Company

H. M. S. Richards Reads the Bible Vols. 1-4: Hear the Word of the Lord. Read by H. M. S. Richards. 60 cass. 194.95 Set. (978-0-922615-00-1(4)) Hampton Hill.
Contains the King James Version of the Holy Bible.

H. M. S. Richards Reads the Bible: Hear the Word of the Lord Vol. 1: The Old Testament (Gen. 1.1 - Sam. 24.11) Read by H. M. S. Richards. 15 cass. 1987. 49.95 (978-0-922615-01-8(2)) Hampton Hill.

H. M. S. Richards Reads the Bible: Hear the Word of the Lord Vol. 2: The Old Testament (1 Sam. 24.12 - Psalms 107.22) Read by H. M. S. Richards. 15 cass. 1988. 49.95 (978-0-922615-02-5(0)) Hampton Hill.

H. M. S. Richards Reads the Bible: Hear the Word of the Lord Vol. 3: The Old Testament (Psalms 107.23 - Malachi 4) Read by H. M. S. Richards. 15 cass. (Running Time: 22 hrs.). 1988. 49.95 (978-0-922615-03-2(9)) Hampton Hill.

H. M. S. Richards Reads the Bible: Hear the Word of the Lord Vol. 4: The New Testament (Matthew 1 - Revelation 22) Read by H. M. S. Richards. 15 cass. 1988. 49.95 (978-0-922615-04-9(7)) Hampton Hill.

H. M. S. Surprise. Patrick O'Brian. Narrated by Simon Vance. (Running Time: 13 hrs.). 2004. 41.95 (978-1-59912-501-5(3)) Iofy Corp.

H. M S Surprise. Patrick O'Brian. Narrated by Patrick Tull. 14 CDs. (Running Time: 16 hrs.). (Aubrey-Maturin Ser.). 2000. audio compact disk 134.00 (978-0-7887-4904-9(8), C1279E7) Recorded Bks.
When Jack Aubrey's prize money fails to come through, he is thrown into a debtors' prison, threatening his chances to marry the lovely Sophia Williams. Jack escapes on the HMS Surprise, bound for the East Indies. Available to libraries only.

H. M. S. Surprise. unabr. ed. Patrick O'Brian. Read by Simon Vance. 9 pieces. (Running Time: 13 hrs.). 2004. reel tape 39.95 (978-0-7861-2765-8(1)); audio compact disk 49.95 (978-0-7861-8597-9(X)) Blckstn Audio.
Third in the series of Aubrey-Maturin adventures, this book is set among the strange sights and smells of the Indian subcontinent and in the distant waters ploughed by the ships of the East India Company. Aubrey is on the defensive, pitting wits and seamanship against an enemy enjoying overwhelming local superiority. But somewhere in the Indian Ocean lies the prize that could make him rich beyond his wildest dreams: the ships sent by Napoleon to attack the China Fleet.

H. M. S. Surprise. unabr. ed. Patrick O'Brian. Narrated by Patrick Tull. 11 cass. (Running Time: 16 hrs.). (Aubrey-Maturin Ser.). 91.00 (978-1-55690-710-4(9), 92410E7) Recorded Bks.
When Jack Aubrey's prize money fails to come through, he is thrown into a debtors' prison, threatening his chances to marry the lovely Sophia Williams. Jack escapes on the HMS Surprise, bound for the East Indies. Available to libraries only.

H. M. S Surprise. unabr. ed. Patrick O'Brian. Read by Simon Vance. (YA). 2007. 69.99 (978-1-59895-854-6(2)) Find a World.

H. M. S. Surprise. unabr. ed. Patrick O'Brian & Patrick Tull. 14 CDs. (Running Time: 16 hrs.). audio compact disk 49.95 (978-1-4025-2828-6(0)) Recorded Bks.

H. M. S. Surprise, Vol. 3. unabr. ed. Patrick O'Brian. Read by Simon Vance. 10 CDs. (Running Time: 13 hrs.). 2000. audio compact disk 30.00 (978-0-7861-8633-4(X), 3289) Blckstn Audio.

H. M. S. Surprise, Vol. 3. unabr. ed. Patrick O'Brian. Read by Simon Vance. 9 cass. (Running Time: 13 hrs.). 2004. 62.95 (978-0-7861-2756-6(2), 3289) Blckstn Audio.

H. O. M. E. on la Grange. Robert A. Wilson. 1 cass. 9.00 (A0406-89) Sound Photosyn.
Tim Leary does an intro & RAW is off & running in the political & space age arenas.

H. R. H. abr. ed. Danielle Steel. Read by Jay O. Sanders. (Running Time: 21600 sec.). (ENG.). 2007. audio compact disk 14.99 (978-0-7393-5811-5(1), Random AudioBks) Pub: Random Audio Pubg. Dist(s): Random

H. R. H. unabr. ed. Danielle Steel. Read by Jay O'Sanders. 7 cass. (Running Time: 10 hrs. 30 mins.). 2006. 63.00 (978-1-4159-3270-4(0)); audio compact disk 76.50 (978-1-4159-3271-1(9)) Pub: Books on Tape. Dist(s): NetLibrary CO

H. Ross Perot: How to Be the Best. (Running Time: 60 min.). 1989. 11.95 (K0450B090, HarperThor) HarpC GBR.

Ha-Ha. abr. ed. Dave King. Read by Terry Kinney. (ENG.). 2005. 14.98 (978-1-59483-192-8(0)) Pub: Hachet Audio. Dist(s): HachBkGrp

Ha-Ha: A Novel. abr. ed. Dave King. Read by Terry Kinney. (Running Time: 6 hrs.). (ENG.). 2009. 44.98 (978-1-60024-939-6(6)) Pub: Hachet Audio. Dist(s): HachBkGrp

Ha-Ha: A Novel. unabr. ed. Dave King. Narrated by Richard Poe. 10 cass. (Running Time: 12 hrs. 30 mins.). 2005. 94.75 (978-1-4193-2070-5(X)) Recorded Bks.
Wounded in Vietnam, Howard Kapostash is unable to speak, read or write, although his intelligence is normal. Now middle-aged, he lives a lonely existence. But then his former high school sweetheart entrusts her nine-year-old son to Howard when she enters drug rehab. Suddenly a father figure, Howard begins to open up, and the emotional wounds of his past start to heal.

Ha' Penny see Tales from a Troubled Land

Habia una Vez. Dorothy S. Bishop. 1 cass. (Running Time: 60 min.). (Read Along & Learn Ser.). (J). 1989. 15.00 (978-0-8442-7331-0(7), Natl Textbk Co) M-H Contemporary.
Three well-known stories retold in Spanish: "Los tres osos," "El muchacho y el burro" & "La gallinata".

Habibi. Naomi Shihab Nye. Read by Christina Moore. 4 cass. (Running Time: 6 hrs.). (YA). 1999. stu. ed. 106.70 (978-0-7887-3672-8(8), 46975) Recorded Bks.
Fourteen-year-old Liyana Abboud loves St. Louis, Missouri. But her father is moving the family to his embattled homeland, Jerusalem. Suddenly Liyana finds herself in a threatening world. Helps young adults view those who are different from a whole new perspective.

Habibi. unabr. ed. Naomi Shihab Nye. Narrated by Christina Moore. 4 cass. (Running Time: 6 hrs.). (YA). 2000. pap. bk. 49.24 (978-0-7887-3642-1(6), 41008X4) Recorded Bks.

Habibi, unabr. ed. Naomi Shihab Nye. Narrated by Christina Moore. 4 pieces. (Running Time: 6 hrs.). (gr. 5 up). 2000. 36.00 (978-0-7887-3532-5(2), 95880E7) Recorded Bks.

Habit: Program from the Award Winning Public Radio Series. Interview. Hosted by Fred Goodwin. Comment by John Hockenberry. 1 CD. (Running Time: 1 hr.). 2001. audio compact disk 21.95 (978-1-932479-52-2(X), LCM 169) Lichtenstein Creat.
Why do we do the things we do - over and over and over again? In this show, we explore habit. Guests include Dr. Ann Graybiel, a professor of neuroanatomy in the Department of Brain and Cognitive Sciences at MIT; Dr. Kurt Fischer, the director of the Mind, Brain & Education program at the Harvard University Graduate School of Education; Dr. Bruce Masek, the clinical director of Child Psychology at Massachusetts General Hospital and an associate professor at Harvard Medical School; and stand-up comic Sean Conroy. Commentary by John Hockenberry.

Habit of Rivers: Reflections on Trout Streams & Fly Fishing. abr. ed. Ted Leeson. Narrated by Lloyd James. (Running Time: 16200 sec.). (Field & Stream Ser.). 2007. audio compact disk 28.00 (978-1-933309-32-3(6)) Pub: A Media Intl. Dist(s): Natl Bk Netwk

Habit 1- Be Proactive: The Habit of Choice. unabr. ed. Stephen R. Covey. Read by Stephen R. Covey. 2006. 9.95 (978-1-933976-17-4(9)) Pub: Franklin Covey. Dist(s): S and S Inc

Habit 2 -Begin with the End in Mind: The Habit of Vision. unabr. ed. Stephen R. Covey. Read by Stephen R. Covey. 2006. 9.95 (978-1-933976-18-1(7)) Pub: Franklin Covey. Dist(s): S and S Inc

Habit 3- Put First Things First: The Habit of Integrity & Execution. unabr. ed. Stephen R. Covey. Read by Stephen R. Covey. 2006. 9.95 (978-1-933976-19-8(5)) Pub: Franklin Covey. Dist(s): S and S Inc

Habit 4 -Think Win-Win: The Habit of Mutual Benefit. unabr. ed. Stephen R. Covey. Read by Stephen R. Covey. 2006. 9.95 (978-1-933976-20-4(9)) Pub: Franklin Covey. Dist(s): S and S Inc

Habit 5 Seek First to Understand then to be Understood: The Habit of Mutual Understanding. unabr. ed. Stephen R. Covey. Read by Stephen R. Covey. 2006. 9.95 (978-1-933976-21-1(7)) Pub: Franklin Covey. Dist(s): S and S Inc

Habit 6 Synergize: The Habit of Creative Cooperation. unabr. ed. Stephen R. Covey. Read by Stephen R. Covey. 2006. 9.95 (978-1-933976-22-8(5)) Pub: Franklin Covey. Dist(s): S and S Inc

Habit 7 Sharpen the Saw: The Habit of Renewal. unabr. ed. Stephen R. Covey. Read by Stephen R. Covey. 2006. 9.95 (978-1-933976-23-5(3)) Pub: Franklin Covey. Dist(s): S and S Inc

Habitantes Del Silencio. VV Staff. (SPA.). 2005. audio compact disk 15.95 (978-84-204-9420-3(8)) Pub: Alfaguara Ediciones ESP. Dist(s): Santillana

Habitation of Dragons, Set. unabr. ed. J. Keith Miller. Read by J. Keith Miller. 3 cass. (Running Time: 4 hrs. 30 mins.). 1997. audio compact disk 21.95 (978-0-9655275-0-7(6)) Vis Aud Pub Inc.
Forty-two separate personal experiences of the author in which he discovered how applying Christian principles can heal personal relationships.

***Habitation of the Blessed, Bk. 1.** unabr. ed. Catherynne Valente. Read by Ralph Lister. (Running Time: 10 hrs.). (Prester John Trilogy). 2010. 24.99 (978-1-4418-7026-1(1), 9781441870261, BAD) Brilliance Audio.

***Habitation of the Blessed: A Dirge for Prester John Volume One.** unabr. ed. Catherynne M. Valente. Read by Ralph Lister. (Running Time: 10 hrs.). (Prester John Ser.). 2010. 24.99 (978-1-4418-7024-7(5), 9781441870247, Brilliance MP3); 39.97 (978-1-4418-7025-4(3), 9781441870254, Brlnc Audio MP3 Lib); 39.97 (978-1-4418-7027-8(X), 9781441870278, BADLE); audio compact disk 99.97 (978-1-4418-7023-0(7), 9781441870230, BriAudCD Unabrid) Brilliance Audio.

***Habitation of the Blessed Vol. 1: A Dirge for Prester John.** unabr. ed. Catherynne Valente. Read by Ralph Lister. (Running Time: 11 hrs.). (Prester John Trilogy). 2010. audio compact disk 32.99 (978-1-4418-7022-3(9), 9781441870223, Bril Audio CD Unabri) Brilliance Audio.

Habitats Around the World Audio CD. Adapted by Benchmark Education Company Staff. Based on a work by Margaret McNamara. (Content Connections Ser.). (J). (gr. k-2). 2008. audio compact disk 10.00 (978-1-60634-892-5(2)) Benchmark Educ.

Habitats Audio CD Theme Set: Set of 6 Set A. Adapted by Benchmark Education Staff. (English Explorers Ser.). (J). (gr. 3-6). 2007. audio compact disk 60.00 (978-1-4108-9835-7(0)) Benchmark Educ.

***HáBitats Por Todo el Mundo Audio Cd.** Debra Castor. Adapted by Benchmark Education Company, LLC. (Content Connections Ser.). (SPA.). (J). 2009. audio compact disk 10.00 (978-1-935472-57-5(7)) Benchmark Educ.

***Habitos Diarios para Vencer en la Vida.** Tr. of Daily Habits for Overcoming in Life. (SPA.). 2006. audio compact disk 18.00 (978-0-944129-29-6(3)) High Praise.

Habits: Developing Habits That Will Change Your Life. abr. ed. Doug Fields. (Super-Ser.). 2006. audio compact disk 60.00 (978-5-558-25705-2(9)) Group Pub.

Habits of Highly Effective People. Stephen R. Covey. 6 cass. bk. 129.00 set. (CPE4320) Bisk Educ.
Highly effective individuals share seven fundamental traits - learn how to develop these habits in yourself, plus discover how to free yourself from the weaknesses of others & take responsibility for your own life, & how to maximize your efforts to achieve your goals.

Habits of Nature. Rupert Sheldrake. 2 cass. 18.00 (OC121) Sound Horizons AV.

Habits That Block Love: 1 John 5:-2:21. Ben Young. 1996. 4.95 (978-0-7417-6009-8(6), B0009) Win Walk.

Habits to Highly Effective Friendships. Tim Burt & Renee Burt. 4. (Running Time: 4 hrs.). 2001. 20.00 (978-1-57399-111-7(2)) Mac Hammond.
Godly relationships are vital to our Christian lives. You can't become the person God meant you to be without them. In this in-depth teaching on relationships, Tim and Renee Burt explain that you must first know God's true purpose for friendships before they can be effective avenues of blessing. Whether you need understaning on how to become a friend or how to be a better friend, this tape series is for you.

Habla Ingles con Confianzail. Carlos A. Sanchez. 2 cass. (Running Time: 3 hrs.). (SPA & ENG.). 2002. 15.95 (978-1-891368-25-7(7), C101C) Casa Ed KARISA.
A self development program that provides ideas and exercises so the listener can overcome the fear of speaking English.

Hablame! Cassette Program. C. Dixon Anderson & R. Alan Meredith. 10 cass. Harcourt Coll Pubs.

Hablan los Ninos, Level 1. Dade County Public Schools. 7 cass. (Spanish for Young Americans Ser.). (J). 175.00 (978-0-8442-7085-2(7), Natl Textbk Co) M-H Contemporary.
First-level program with 70 lessons develops a 400-word vocabulary, beginning with the words of immediate use & interest to children.

Hablan Mas los Ninos, Level 2. Dade County Public Schools. 6 cass. (Spanish for Young Americans Ser.). (J). 150.00 (978-0-8442-7135-4(7), Natl Textbk Co) M-H Contemporary.
Expands & builds vocabulary & structures. 50 lessons.

Hablando de Negocios. Marisa de Prada & M. Bovet. 1 cass. (Running Time: 1 hr.). (SPA.). 2000. 29.95 (978-84-7711-156-6(1), EDI1561) Pub: Edelsa ESP. Dist(s): Continental Bk
Designed for the students with a basic knowledge of Spanish who need to focus on business situations. The lessons are thematically classified to facilitate location of vocabulary necessary for each event.

Hablando Ingles Americano: English Explained in Spanish. Mark Frobose. (SPA.). 1993. 49.00 (978-1-893564-08-4(8)) Macmill Audio.

Hablar el Idioma de Su Cliente: Audio CD/Cassette, Vol. 1. Bess I. Kennedy. Perf. by Juan Escobar et al. 1 cass. (Hablar el Idioma de Su Cliente). (SPA & ENG.). (C). 1997. audio compact disk 19.95 (978-0-9660225-3-7(X), PCHC-1) Manzana.
Eight situational dialogues in Spanish & 3 listening comprehension exercises.

Hablar el Idioma de Su Cliente, A Spanish Course for Patient Registration, Student Edition: Speaking your Client's Language. Bess Ives Kennedy. (Hablar el Idioma de Su Cliente).Tr. of Speaking Your Client's Language. (SPA & ENG.). 2006. stu. ed. & spiral bd. 25.20 (978-0-9660225-8-2(0), PRSE-0966022580) Manzana.

Hablemos Espanol! 6th ed. Teresa Méndez-Faith & Mary McVey Gill. (SPA.). 1998. lab manual ed. 47.95 (978-0-03-025461-1(2)); lab manual ed. (978-0-03-025512-0(0)) Harcourt Coll Pubs.

Hablemos Espanol! Instructor's Kit. 6th ed. Teresa Méndez-Faith & Mary McVey Gill. (SPA.). 1998. bk. & tchr. ed. (978-0-03-025511-3(2)) Harcourt Coll Pubs.

Hacia las Cumbres. Mariano de Blas.Tr. of To the Mountain Top. (SPA.). 2008. audio compact disk 24.95 (978-1-935405-04-7(7)) Hombre Nuevo.

Hacia las Estrellas. abr. ed. L. Ron Hubbard. Read by Daniel Quintero. 3 CDs.Tr. of To the Stars. (SPA.). 2005. audio compact disk 17.00 (978-958-8218-51-9(9)) YoYoMusic.

Hacia un Cambio de Actitud Mental. unabr. ed. Hugo Tapias. Read by Fernando Gutierrez.Tr. of Towards a Change of Attitude. (SPA.). 2001. audio compact disk 13.00 (978-958-43-0144-4(6)) YoYoMusic.

.hack OST. (YA). 2003. audio compact disk 14.98 (978-1-59409-052-3(1)) Bandai Ent.

Hacker Cracker: A Journey from the Mean Streets of Brooklyn to the Frontiers of Cyberspace. abr. ed. David Chanoff. 1 cass. (Running Time: 1 hr. 30 mins.). 2002. 25.95 (978-0-06-009053-1(7)) HarperCollins Pubs.

***Hacking Work: Breaking Stupid Rules for Smart Results.** unabr. ed. Bill Jensen & Josh Klein. Read by Walter Dixon. (Running Time: 6 hrs. 30 mins.). (ENG.). 2010. 27.98 (978-1-59659-678-8(3), GildAudio) Pub: Gildan Media. Dist(s): HachBkGrp

***Hacking Work: Breaking Stupid Rules for Smart Results.** unabr. ed. Bill Jensen & Josh Klein. Read by Walter Dixon. (Running Time: 6 hrs.). (ENG.). 2010. audio compact disk 29.98 (978-1-59659-533-0(7), GildAudio) Pub: Gildan Media. Dist(s): HachBkGrp

. hack//legend of the twighlight Soundtrack. (YA). 2003. audio compact disk (978-1-59409-335-7(0)) Bandai Ent.

Hack//Roots OST I. Prod. by Bandai Entertainment. (YA). 2007. 14.98 (978-1-59409-835-2(2)) Bandai Ent.

Hack//Roots OST II. Prod. by Bandai Entertainment. (YA). 2007. 14.98 (978-1-59409-836-9(0)) Bandai Ent.

Hadassah: One Night with the King. Tommy Tenney & Mark Andrew Olsen. (Running Time: 3 hrs.). 2005. audio compact disk 19.99 (978-0-7642-0047-2(X)) Pub: Bethany Hse. Dist(s): Baker Pub Grp

Hades Factor. Robert Ludlum & Gayle Lynds. Read by Michael Prichard. (Covert-One Ser.). 2001. audio compact disk 104.00 (978-0-7366-7143-9(9)) Books on Tape.

Hades Factor. abr. ed. Robert Ludlum & Gayle Lynds. Read by Joseph Campanella. 5 CDs. (Running Time: 6 hrs. 0 mins. 0 sec.). (Covert-One Ser.). (ENG.). 2006. audio compact disk 14.95 (978-1-59397-943-0(6)) Pub: Macmill Audio. Dist(s): Macmillan

Hades Factor. unabr. ed. Robert Ludlum & Gayle Lynds. Read by Michael Prichard. 13 CDs. (Running Time: 19 hrs. 30 mins.). (Covert-One Ser.). 2001. audio compact disk 104.00 Books on Tape.
Lt. Col. Jonathan Smith is determined to uncover the cause of a doomsday virus that threatens millions.

Hades Factor. unabr. ed. Robert Ludlum & Gayle Lynds. Read by Michael Prichard. 11 cass. (Covert-One Ser.). 2001. 88.00 (978-0-7366-7038-8(6)) Books on Tape.

Hades Factor. unabr. ed. Robert Ludlum & Gayle Lynds. Narrated by George Guidall. 10 cass. (Running Time: 13 hrs. 30 mins.). (Covert-One Ser.). 2000. 88.00 (978-0-7887-7152-1(3), 96710K8) Recorded Bks.
Sets one brave man on a race against the clock to prevent world wide plague. When a mysterious disease strikes a researcher at NIH, her fiancee, Lt. Col. Jonathan Smith, vows to find what forces are responsible for her death. But as the disease spreads, every month becomes crucial.

Hades Factor. unabr. ed. Robert Ludlum & Gayle Lynds. Narrated by George Guidall. 12 CDs. (Running Time: 13 hrs. 30 mins.). (Covert-One Ser.). 2001. audio compact disk 116.00 (978-1-4025-0917-9(0), C1580) Recorded Bks.
The Hades Factor sets one brave man on a race against the clock to prevent worldwide plague. In three widely spaced locations, three apparently unrelated people die a horrible death. Ravaged by high fever, they succumb to a virus that dissolves their lungs. Local authorities are helpless. After this mysterious disease strikes a researcher at NIH, her fiancee, Lt. Col. Jonathan Smith, vows to find what forces are responsible for her death. Every hour is crucial. From Washington, D.C. to Baghdad, the breathless pace of The Hades Factor never lets up.

Hadrian Memorandum. abr. ed. Allan Folsom. Read by Holter Graham & Scott Sowers. 6 CDs. (Running Time: 7 hrs. 0 mins. 0 sec.). (ENG.). 2009. audio compact disk 29.99 (978-1-4272-0771-5(2)) Pub: Macmill Audio. Dist(s): Macmillan

Hadrian's Walls. Robert Draper. Narrated by Peter Bradbury. 10 cass. (Running Time: 14 hrs. 15 mins.). 88.00 (978-1-4025-1596-5(0)) Recorded Bks.

Hafiz: The Scent of Light. Hafiz. 2002. audio compact disk 15.95 (978-1-56455-958-6(0)) Sounds True.

Hag see Spirits & Spooks for Halloween

Hagakure: the Book of the Samurai: The Book of the Samurai. Yamamoto. Read by Pedro Montoya. (Running Time: 3 hrs.). 2001. 16.95 (978-1-60083-265-9(2), Audiofy Corp) Iofy Corp.

Hagalo! Haga Dieta Set: Moderacion No Privacion. Michelle Present. Read by Maria Cea. 2 CDs. (Running Time: 140 min.). (SPA.). 1999. audio compact disk 25.00 (978-0-9659120-5-1(1)) Michelle Present.

Hagase Ciudadano. Jaime A. Lopez. (SPA & ENG., 2000. pap. bk. 14.95 (978-0-9676584-0-7(3), PHC8403) HCCo.

Haggard. unabr. ed. Christopher Nicole. Read by Clifford Norgate. 12 cass. (Running Time: 18 hrs.). (Isis Ser.). (J). 1999. 94.95 (978-0-7531-0489-7(X), 981110) Pub: ISIS Lrg Prnt GBR. Dist(s): Ulverscroft US
The first part of the Haggard family saga takes us from the West Indies & the end of the American War of Independence to the England of the Napoleonic Wars. Traces the fortunes of Haggard & the women he loved & abused; above all, as he relates the tragedy of a nabob at the dawn of a more humanitarian age who found the tide of history too strong for him.

Haggard's Inheritance. unabr. ed. Christopher Nicole. Read by Clifford Norgate. 12 cass. (Running Time: 20 hrs. 30 mins.). (Isis Ser.). (J). 1999. 94.95 (978-0-7531-0490-3(3), 990111) Pub: ISIS Lrg Prnt GBR. Dist(s): Ulverscroft US
Following the sudden suicide of his father, Roger Haggard has assumed the position of head of the family & become one of the richest & most powerful men in England. Meanwhile, Roger daringly proposes to & is accepted by the beautiful Meg, a mere tinker's daughter but she cruelly jilts him. Broken-hearted, he heaves the family estate in the hands of his half-sister Alice & with Lord Byron's help, makes a glittering debut into London's foremost political & social circles but a corrupt few are determined to bring about the downfall of Roger Haggard.

Hai, Ima! 3: Audio CD Program. Elise Wackett & Misho Okutsu. (JPN.). audio compact disk 159.95 (978-0-8219-2627-7(6)) EMC-Paradigm.

Haida & Paul Horn: The Adventures of a Killer Whale & a Jazz Musician. l.t. ed. Shirley E. Forbing. Illus. by Jan Beaton & Sherry Beaton. Music by Paul Horn. Narrated by Norman Eisley. 1 CD. (Running Time: 1 hr.). (YA). 2001. per. 21.95 (978-0-9708743-0-6(8)) Wild Animal.

Haiku: A Novel. unabr. ed. Andrew Vachss. Read by Christopher Lane. (Running Time: 6 hrs.). 2009. 24.99 (978-1-4418-0807-3(8), 9781441808073, Brilliance MP3); 24.99 (978-1-4418-0809-7(4), 9781441808097, BAD); 39.97 (978-1-4418-0808-0(6), 9781441808080, Brlnc Audio MP3 Lib); 39.97 (978-1-4418-0843-1(4), 9781441808431, BADLE); audio compact disk 29.99 (978-1-4418-0805-9(1), 9781441808059, Bril Audio CD Unabri); audio compact disk 79.97 (978-1-4418-0806-6(X), 9781441808066, BriAudCD Unabrid) Brilliance Audio.

Haiku Poems: A Collection of Haiku Poetry. 2006. 29.95 (978-1-59649-040-6(3)); audio compact disk 24.95 (978-1-59649-747-4(5)) Whspmg Pine.

Hail, Hail, the Gang's All Here! unabr. ed. Ed McBain, pseud. Read by Jonathan Marosz. 6 cass. (Running Time: 6 hrs.). (87th Precinct Ser.: Bk. 25). 1997. 36.00 (978-0-7366-3752-7(4), 4427) Books on Tape.
A nude dancer turns up in an alley with a knife in her chest.

Hail, Holy Queen. Scripts. Scott Hahn. Read by Matt Arnold. 3 CDs. (Running Time: 3 hrs.). 2001. audio compact disk 23.95 (978-1-57058-421-3(4), 5611-cd) St Joseph Communs.
Reading or listening to Hail Holy Queen, you'll gain a profound understanding of the nature of God's covenant family. In His family nothing is missing. Everything Jesus has He shares with us; His divine life; His Father and His mother as well. With great conviction, Scott explores how the many Old Testament types, our deepest human needs, and even creation itself all tell us that a family without a mother is incomplete. You'll discover that the apostles, who gathered with Mary in Jerusalem at Pentecost, and the early Christians, who painted her image in the catacombs and dedicated their churches to her, knew and taught this since the earliest times.Building on these scriptural and historical foundations, Dr. Hahn presents a new look at Marian doctrines: her Immaculate Conception, Perpetual Virginity, Assumption and Coronation. Hail Holy Queen-The Mother of God in the Word of God guides modern-day readers through passages filled with great mystery. Rediscover the ancient art and science of reading the scriptures to gain a more profound understanding of their truthfulness and relevance to faith and the practice of Catholicism in the contemporary world.

Hail, Holy Queen: The Mother of God in the Word of God. Scott Hahn. Narrated by Gus Lloyd. 3 cass. (Running Time: 3 hrs. 30 mins.). 29.00 (978-1-4025-1749-5(1)) Recorded Bks.

Hail Mary, Holy Hour of Reparation. Interview with Mother Angelica et al. 1 cass. (Running Time: 60 min.). 1987. 10.00 (978-1-55794-087-2(8), T38) Eternal Wrd TV.

Hail the Conquering Hero, Pt. 1. unabr. ed. Frank Yerby. Read by Dan Lazar. 8 cass. (Running Time: 12 hrs.). 1982. 64.00 (978-0-7366-0433-8(2), 1405-A) Books on Tape.
In the imaginary Caribbean Republic of Costa Verde, Frank Yerby sets in motion the unrestrained powers of bribery, blackmail, murder & torture. Against these he balances the strength of an untested United States Ambassador, James Randolph Rush. Rush makes discoveries that impinge on international politics: among other items, trading oil for nuclear weapons & trafficking in illegal drugs.

Hail the Conquering Hero, Pt. 2. Frank Yerby. Read by Dan Lazar. 8 cass. (Running Time: 12 hrs.). 1982. 64.00 (1405-B) Books on Tape.

Hail to the Chief. unabr. ed. Ed McBain, pseud. Read by Jonathan Marosz. 5 cass. (Running Time: 5 hrs.). (87th Precinct Ser.: Bk. 28). 1995. 30.00 (978-0-7366-3199-0(2), 3863) Books on Tape.
Street cops become hardened to the horrific crimes they see. But these murders are bad, really bad: six naked bodies in a ditch, all of them young, two of them female, one of them an infant. A phone tip leads two detectives to a private street war, where even veteran cops can get caught in a crossfire of unthinkable violence & revenge.

Hail to the Dragon Slayer. Arthur A. Lemann. 1 cass. 1998. 14.95 (978-1-891643-06-4(1)) Pontalba Pr.

Hail to Thee, Chicago: City Anthem. Estella A. Johnson-Hunt & John E. King. Perf. by Jeff Felton. 1 cass. 1994. 5.00 (978-1-884991-08-0(4)); audio compact disk 10.00 CD. (978-1-884991-09-7(2)) Estarion LPI.

Hailey's War. abr. ed. Jodi Compton. (Running Time: 5 hrs.). 2008. audio compact disk 14.99 (978-1-59600-883-0(0), 9781596008830, BCD Value Price) Brilliance Audio.
Please enter a Synopsis.

Hailey's War. unabr. ed. Jodi Compton. (Running Time: 9 hrs.). 2010. 24.99 (978-1-59710-838-6(3), 9781597108386, BAD) Brilliance Audio.

Hailey's War. unabr. ed. Jodi Compton. Read by Angela Dawe. (Running Time: 8 hrs.). 2010. 24.99 (978-1-59335-702-3(8), 9781593357023, Brilliance MP3); 39.97 (978-1-59710-839-3(1), 9781597108393, BADLE); 39.97 (978-1-59335-836-5(9), 9781593358365, Brlnc Audio MP3 Lib); audio compact disk 92.97 (978-1-4233-0172-1(2), 9781423301721, BriAudCD Unabrid); audio compact disk 34.99 (978-1-4233-0170-7(6), 9781423301707, Bril Audio CD Unabri) Brilliance Audio.

Haircut see Great American Short Stories

Haircut see Fourteen American Masterpieces

Haircutting. Milady Publishing Company Staff. 1 cass. (Standard Ser.: Chapter 7). 1995. 11.95 (978-1-56253-279-6(0), Milady) Pub: Delmar. Dist(s): CENGAGE Learn

Hairy Bear. J. Melser. 1 read-along cass. (J). 1986. 5.95 incl. bk. (978-0-86867-043-0(X)) Wright Group.
Did you ever hear a noise in the middle of the night? The Daddy Bear did but he was too lazy to go downstairs to see what was there.

Hairy Man. unabr. ed. David Holt. Read by David Holt. 1 cass. (Running Time: 44 min.). (YA). (ps up). 1981. 9.98 (978-0-942303-00-1(8)) Pub: High Windy Audio. Dist(s): August Hse
Traditional & contemporary folktales with outstanding music. ALA Notable.

Hairyman & Other Wild Tales. Read by David Holt. 1 cass. (Running Time: 44 min.). (J). 8.95 (WW722C) Weston Woods.

Haitian: Learn to Speak & Understand Haitian Creole with Pimsleur Language Programs. Pimsleur Staff & Pimsleur. (Running Time: 50 hrs. 0 mins. 0 sec.). (Compact Ser.). (ENG.). 2004. audio compact disk 115.00 (978-0-7435-3849-7(8), Pimsleur) Pub: S&S Audio. Dist(s): S and S Inc

Haitian Creole: Short Course, Set. 1995th ed. Paul Pimsleur. 5 cass. (Pimsleur Language Learning Ser.). 1995. pap. bk. & stu. ed. 149.95 (0671-57929-0) SyberVision.

Haitian Creole, Basic: Learn to Speak & Understand Haitian Creole with Pimsleur Language Programs. Pimsleur. (Running Time: 5 hrs. 0 mins. 0 sec.). (Basic Ser.). (ENG.). 2010. audio compact disk 24.95 (978-0-7435-7240-8(8), Pimsleur) Pub: S&S Audio. Dist(s): S and S Inc

Haitian Creole Basic Course CDs & Text. Albert Valdman. 16 CDs. (Running Time: 15 hrs. 30 mins.). (CRP.). 2005. audio compact disk 245.00 (978-1-57970-110-9(8), AFCR10D) J Norton Pubs.

Haitian Creole, Compact: Learn to Speak & Understand Haitian Creole with Pimsleur Language Programs. unabr. ed. Pimsleur Staff & Pimsleur. 5 CDs. (Running Time: 50 hrs. 0 mins. 0 sec.). (Compact Ser.). (CRP & ENG.). 2005. audio compact disk 49.95 (978-0-7435-5057-4(9), Pimsleur) Pub: S&S Audio. Dist(s): S and S Inc

Haitian Creole, Comprehensive: Learn to Speak & Understand Haitian Creole with Pimsleur Language Programs. Pimsleur. (Running Time: 16 hrs. 0 mins. 0 sec.). (Comprehensive Ser.). (ENG.). 2010. audio compact disk 345.00 (978-0-7435-7239-2(4), Pimsleur) Pub: S&S Audio. Dist(s): S and S Inc

Haitian Creole, Conversational: Learn to Speak & Understand Haitian Creole with Pimsleur Language Programs. Pimsleur. (Running Time: 8 hrs. 0 mins. 0 sec.). (Conversational Ser.). (ENG.). 2010. audio compact disk 49.95 (978-0-7435-7241-5(6), Pimsleur) Pub: S&S Audio. Dist(s): S and S Inc

Haitian Creole for Speakers of English, Compact. unabr. ed. 5 cass. (Running Time: 5 hrs.). (Pimsleur Tapes Ser.). 1995. 129.00 set. (18490, Pimsleur) S&S Audio.
A ten-lesson-unit program based upon the Pimsleur Spoken Language Programmed Instructional Method, providing basic beginning language training to the ACTFL Novice Level.

Haitian Creole Newspaper Reader. Kate Howe. 1990. 13.00 (978-1-881265-16-0(1)) Dunwoody Pr.

Haitian Creole Newspaper Reader, Set. Kate Howe & Lyonel Desmarattes. 2 cass. (Running Time: 60 min. per cass.). (CRP.). 1990. 13.00 (3080) Dunwoody Pr.
Forty-two selections provide an introduction to the language, culture & politics for a linguistically sophisticated beginner.

Haitian Health Resources (HHR) Laurent Pierre-Philippe. 1997. audio compact disk (978-1-58432-014-2(1)) Educa Vision.

Haj, Pt. 1. unabr. ed. Leon Uris. Read by Michael Prichard. 7 cass. (Running Time: 10 hrs. 30 min.). 1985. 56.00 (978-0-7366-0657-8(2), 1619-A) Books on Tape.
Until the Jews came, the village of Tabah was little changed from one Arab generation to another. Tabah was ruled by Haj Ibrahim, a man who had mastered the complex ways of his people. He was the Haj, a leader to be feared & respected; a man at once compassionate & merciless, loving & cruel, visionary & blind. Forced to leave Tabah during the struggle for Palestine, his family fled to a refugee camp near Jericho. But the Haj cannot play a defeatist role, & his fight against the refugee system is a struggle at once lonely, gallant & doomed.

Hajimete-no Tin Whistle. Excerpts. Bill Ochs. Perf. by Bill Ochs. Tr. by Kaori Ono & Hidekazu Sakamoto from ENG. Voice by Kaori Ono. 1 CD. (Running Time: 48 minutes). (JPN., (J). 2006. audio compact disk 12.95 (978-0-9727516-2-9(9)) Pub: Pnnywhstlrs Pr. Dist(s): Bk Clearing Hse
CD includes spoken instruction in Japanese, plus 31 tunes and musical exercises. Most tracks include guitar accompaniment. CD includes two bonus tracks, the music for which can be found at www.pennywhistle.com.

Hajimete-no Tin Whistle Learn-to-Play Tin Whistle Set: Includes Clarke Meg D Whistle in Clamshell Pack: Book, Whistle & Compact Disc. Excerpts. Bill Ochs. Perf. by Bill Ochs. Tr. by Kaori Ono & Hidekazu Sakamoto from JPN. Narrated by Kaori Ono. 1 CD. (Running Time: 48 minutes). (J). 2006. audio compact disk 15.95 (978-0-9727516-4-3(5)) Pub: Pnnywhstlrs Pr. Dist(s): Bk Clearing Hse
CD includes spoken instruction in Japanese, plus all tunes and musical exercises. Most tracks include guitar accompaniment. CD also includes two bonus tracks, the music for which can be found at www.pennywhistle.com. There are 31 tunes in all.

Hal Leonard Guitar Method, Vol. 2. 2nd ed. Will Schmid & Greg Koch. (Hal Leonard Guitar Method Ser.). 2000. pap. bk. 9.99 (978-0-634-01313-3(0), 0634013130) H Leonard.

Hal Leonard Guitar Method, Vol. 3. 2nd ed. Will Schmid & Greg Koch. (Hal Leonard Guitar Method Ser.). 2000. pap. bk. 9.95 (978-0-634-01416-1(1), 0634014161) H Leonard.

Hal Leonard Tenor Saxophone Method: Jazz Saxophone: Tenor. Dennis Taylor. 2008. pap. bk. 14.99 (978-1-4234-2634-9(7), 1423426347) H Leonard.

Halbach on Principles & Techniques of Estate Planning. Read by Edward C. Halbach. (Running Time: 6 hrs.). 1992. 115.00 Incl. tape materials. (ES-55268) Cont Ed Bar-CA.
Prof. Edward C. Halbach, nationally recognized authority, teaches the "advanced basics" of estate planning. He begins with an overview of estate & generation-skipping taxes & selected aspects of income tax legislation, & then focuses on living trust, the fundamentals of testamentary planning, & the basics of intervivos planning (including types of ownership & gifts).

Halcyon Days. unabr. ed. Steven Dietz. Perf. by Anne Archer et al. 1 cass. (Running Time: 1 hr. 35 min.). 1996. 19.95 (978-1-58081-005-0(5)) L A Theatre.
Senator Eddy Bowman cannot see the point of invading a miniscule Caribbean island to rescue a bunch of overly tanned medical students. But as the 1983 U. S. invasion of Grenada gets underway, the Senator finds himself at odds.

Haldeman Diaries Set: Inside the Nixon White House. abr. ed. H. R. Haldeman. Read by Robert Foxworth. 4 cass. (Running Time: 6 hrs.). 1994. 24.95 (978-1-879371-86-6(3)) Pub Mills.
An unvarnished view, from the ultimate insider - Chief of Staff H.R. Haldeman - of the inner-workings of the Nixon White House. A riveting portrait of that period's more celebrated events.

Half a Heart. Rosellen Brown. Read by Jayne Atkinson & Lisa Gay Hamilton. 2004. 15.95 (978-0-7435-4802-1(7)) Pub: S&S Audio. Dist(s): S and S Inc

Half a Heart. unabr. ed. Rosellen Brown. Read by Carrington MacDuffie. 12 vols. (Running Time: 18 Hrs.). 2000. bk. 96.95 (978-0-7927-2414-8(3), CSL 303, Chivers Sound Lib) AudioGO.
Miriam Veneer, a former civil rights activist, finds her comfortable white upper-middle-class life shattered with the appearance, after almost eighteen years, of her biracial daughter Veronica.

Half a Life. unabr. ed. V. S. Naipaul. 2001. 40.00 (978-0-7366-8435-4(2)) Books on Tape.
A scrupulously honest and hauntingly sad look at what it's like to be poor and fatherless in America, it shows how a girl without means or promise and with only a loving mother, chutzpah, a bit of fraud, and a lot of luck turned herself into somebody." Begins with the Ciments' immigration from Montreal's middle-class Jewish suburbs to the fringe desert communities of Los Angeles, a landscape and culture so alien that their father loses the last vestiges of his sanity.

Half-a-Moon Inn. unabr. ed. Paul Fleischman. Narrated by Steven Crossley. 2 pieces. (Running Time: 1 hr. 45 mins.). (gr. 6 up). 1998. 19.00 (978-0-7887-2066-6(X), 95419E7) Recorded Bks.
Twelve-year-old Aaron is mute. He lives with his mother & depends on her completely. When a sudden blizzard strands his mother in town, Aaron sets out in the snow to look for his mother & embarks on a perilous adventure.

Half & Half. Kenneth H. Kim. Narrated by Larry A. McKeever. (Sport Ser.). (J). 2000. 10.95 (978-1-58659-037-6(5)); audio compact disk 14.95 (978-1-58659-291-2(2)) Artesian.

Half Baked Living: Hos. 6:1-7. Ed Young. 1988. 4.95 (978-0-7417-1657-6(7), 657) Win Walk.

Half-Breed. unabr. ed. Loren Robinson. Read by Ron Varela. 6 cass. (Running Time: 6 hrs. 30 min.). (American Blend Ser.: Bk. 4). 2001. 39.95 (978-1-55686-843-6(X)) Books in Motion.
Lynn Genet grew up in Oklahoma Territory despising his Indian blood. Losing his family and job to liquor, Genet is lost in a world where he has no place.

***Half Broke Horses.** unabr. ed. Jeannette Walls. Read by Jeannette Walls. 1 Playaway. (Running Time: 8 hrs.). 2009. 59.75 (978-1-4407-5812-6(3)); 67.75 (978-1-4407-5809-6(3)); audio compact disk 92.75 (978-1-4407-5810-2(7)) Recorded Bks.

Half Broke Horses. unabr. ed. Jeannette Walls. Read by Jeannette Walls. 8 CDs. (Running Time: 9 hrs. 0 mins. 0 sec.). (ENG., 2009. audio compact disk 39.99 (978-0-7435-9722-7(2)) Pub: S&S Audio. Dist(s): S and S Inc

***Half Broke Horses.** unabr. collector's ed. Jeannette Walls. Read by Jeannette Walls. 8 CDs. (Running Time: 8 hrs.). 2009. audio compact disk 44.95 (978-1-4407-5811-9(5)) Recorded Bks.

Half Broken Things. unabr. ed. Morag Joss. Read by Anita Wright & Stephen Perring. 9 cass. (Running Time: 10 hrs. 8 mins.). (Isis Cassettes Ser.). (J). 2004. 76.95 (978-0-7531-1803-0(3)) Pub: ISIS Lrg Prnt GBR. Dist(s): Ulverscroft US

Half Broken Things. unabr. ed. Morag Joss. 9 CDs. (Running Time: 10 hrs. 8 mins.). (Isis (CDs) Ser.). (J). 2004. audio compact disk 84.95 (978-0-7531-2353-9(3)) Pub: ISIS Lrg Prnt GBR. Dist(s): Ulverscroft US

***Half Brother.** unabr. ed. Kenneth Oppel. Read by Daniel diTomasso. (Running Time: 10 hrs.). 2010. 39.97 (978-1-4418-7154-1(3), 9781441871541, BADLE); 24.99 (978-1-4418-7153-4(5), 9781441871534, BAD) Brilliance Audio.

***Half Brother.** unabr. ed. Kenneth Oppel. Read by Daniel diTomasso. 1 MP3-CD. (Running Time: 9 hrs.). (YA). 2010. 24.99 (978-1-4418-7151-0(9), 9781441871510, Brilliance MP3); 39.97 (978-1-4418-7152-7(7), 9781441871527, Brlnc Audio MP3 Lib); audio compact disk 29.99 (978-1-4418-7149-7(7), 9781441871497, Bril Audio CD Unabri); audio compact disk 87.97 (978-1-4418-7150-3(0), 9781441871503, BriAudCD Unabrid) Brilliance Audio.

Half-Chick. unabr. ed. 1 cass. (Running Time: 20 min.). Dramatization. (Magic Looking Glass Ser.). (J). (gr. 2-6). 1989. 9.95 (978-0-7810-0047-5(5), NIM-CW-130-5-C) NIMCO.
A Spanish folk tale.

***Half Empty.** unabr. ed. David Rakoff. Read by David Rakoff. (Running Time: 7 hrs.). (ENG.). 2010. audio compact disk 30.00 (978-0-307-73884-4(1), Random AudioBks) Pub: Random Audio Pubg. Dist(s): Random

Half-Hearted, Set. unabr. ed. John Buchan. Read by Flo Gibson. 6 cass. (Running Time: 8 hrs. 30 min.). 1997. 24.95 (978-1-55685-493-4(5), 493-5) Audio Bk Con.
The moors of Scotland form a lovely backdrop for the romance of our "half-hearted" hero whose truly heroic nature comes to fruition on the battlefields of the Far East.

Half Hidden. unabr. ed. Emma Blair. Read by Leonie Mellinger. 10 cass. (Running Time: 10 hrs.). 1997. 84.95 Set. (978-0-7451-6737-4(3), CAB 1353) AudioGO.
It's 1940, & Holly learns that her fiance, Martin, has been killed in Dunkirk. Working as a nurse in Nazi-occupied Jersey, she struggles to cope with Martin's death. But then she meets Peter, a German doctor, & their friendship turns to love. But will her loyalty to Martin's memory & the threat of war destroy their newfound love?.

Half Light. unabr. ed. Frances Fyfield. Read by Di Langford. 10 CDs. (Running Time: 15 hrs.). 2001. audio compact disk 89.95 (978-0-7531-1056-0(3), 110563) Pub: ISIS Audio GBR. Dist(s): Ulverscroft US

Half Light. unabr. ed. Frances Hegarty. Read by Di Langford. 8 cass. (Running Time: 9 hrs. 45 min.). (Isis Ser.). (J). 1997. 69.95 (978-0-7531-0180-3(7), 970707) Pub: ISIS Lrg Prnt GBR. Dist(s): Ulverscroft US
Elizabeth Young is a picture restorer with modest needs - complete privacy & the beauty of the painting she painstakingly brings back to life. But as she works alone in her basement flat, she becomes haunted by the echo of mysterious footsteps & a silent figure in the shadows. When a wealthy recluse invites her to restore his remarkable collection at his luxurious residence, it sees to be the refuge she seeks. Too late, she realizes her error, as privacy becomes her nemesis.

Half Magic. unabr. ed. Edward Eager. 2 cass. (Running Time: 3 hrs.). (J). (gr. 1-8). 1999. 23.00 (LL 0142, Chivers Child Audio) AudioGO.

Half Magic. unabr. ed. Edward Eager. Read by Words Take Wing Repertory Company Staff. 2 cass. (Running Time: 3 hrs. 30 mins.). (Words Take Wingtm Ser.). (J). (gr. 3-7). 1998. 23.00 (978-0-8072-8065-2(8), YA992CX, Listening Lib) Random Audio Pubg.
Jane finds a magic charm which grants half of any wish. Her brother Mark & her sisters, Katherine & Martha, take turns double wishes, leading to strange happenings.

Half Magic. unabr. ed. Edward Eager. Read by Words Take Wing Repertory Company Staff. 2 vols. (Running Time: 3 hrs. 30 mins.). (Words Take Wingtm Ser.). (J). (gr. 3-7). 1999. pap. bk. 29.00 (978-0-8072-8066-9(6), YA992SP, Listening Lib) Random Audio Pubg.

Half Magic. unabr. ed. Edward Eager & Full Cast Production Staff. (ENG.). (J). (gr. 3). 2008. audio compact disk 27.00 (978-0-7393-6517-5(7), Listening Lib) Pub: Random Audio Pubg. Dist(s): Random

Half-Moon & Empty Stars. Gerry Spence. Read by Jonathan Marosz. 2001. audio compact disk 104.00 (978-0-7366-8544-3(8)) Books on Tape.

Half-Moon & Empty Stars. unabr. ed. Gerry Spence. Read by Jonathan Marosz. 11 cass. (Running Time: 16 hrs. 30 mins.). 2001. 88.00 (978-0-7366-7637-3(6)) Books on Tape.
Relates the gripping stories of two women - Charlie Redtail's mother and his woman, Willow - who struggle, each in her own way, to save Charlie from the gas chamber. It is the story of brothers, half-blooded Arapahoe twins: Charlie, who goes the way of the Native American, and Billy, who becomes a wealthy Wall Street banker, resulting in a conflict of cultures that explodes in murder. Charlie is dragged to trial in a small, prejudiced backwater Wyoming town, a trial that erupts into an astonishing courtroom drama that only Spence, the famous lawyer, can tell.

Half-Moon Investigations. unabr. ed. Eoin Colfer. Read by Sean Patrick Reilly. 5 cass. (Running Time: 7 hrs. 17 mins.). (J). (gr. 4-7). 2006. 40.00 (978-0-7393-3570-3(7), Listening Lib) Pub: Random Audio Pubg. Dist(s): Random
Fletcher Moon has never been like other kids. For one thing, he has had to suffer the humiliating nickname "Half Moon" because of his short stature. But the real reason Fletcher is different is that ever since he was a baby he's had a nose for sniffing out mysteries. And let's just say, it's not a skill that has been appreciated by many people, including his own family. That doesn't bother Fletcher, though. After graduating at the top of his Internet class, he is officially certified as the youngest detective in the world. He even has a silver-plated detective's badge to prove it. Everything is going along fine until two things happen: a classmate hires him to solve a crime, and his prized badge is stolen. All signs point to the town's most notorious crime family, the Sharkeys. As Fletcher follows the clues, evidence of a conspiracy begins to emerge. But before he can crack the case, Fletcher finds himself framed for a serious crime. To clear his name he will have to pair up with the unlikeliest of allies and go on the run from the authorities. Fletcher has twelve hours to find the guilty party - or he is the guilty party.

Half-Moon Investigations. unabr. ed. Eoin Colfer. Read by Sean Patrick Reilly. 6 CDs. (Running Time: 7 hrs. 17 mins.). (J). (gr. 4-7). 2007. audio compact disk 42.50 (978-0-7393-3561-1(8), Listening Lib) Pub: Random Audio Pubg. Dist(s): NetLibrary CO

Half-Moon Investigations. unabr. ed. Eoin Colfer. Read by Sean Patrick Reilly. 6 CDs. (Running Time: 26220 sec.). (ENG.). (J). (gr. 5). 2006. audio compact disk 34.00 (978-0-7393-3528-4(6), Listening Lib) Pub: Random Audio Pubg. Dist(s): Random

Half Moon Street. unabr. ed. Paul Theroux. Narrated by Davina Porter. 4 cass. (Running Time: 6 hrs.). 35.00 (978-1-55690-214-7(X), 87210E7) Recorded Bks.
At the Hemisphere Institute she was called Mopsy. At the Jasmine Escort Agency & to most of the men they sent her to, she was Dr. Lauren Slaughter. She found the work similar in many respects & when people (day or night) asked her what she did the rest of the time she said simply: "Research." Available to libraries only.

***Half the Blood of Brooklyn: A Novel.** unabr. ed. Charlie Huston. Read by Scott Brick. (Running Time: 7 hrs. 30 mins.). 2010. 29.95 (978-1-4417-5323-6(0)); 54.95 (978-1-4417-5319-9(2)); audio compact disk 69.00 (978-1-4417-5320-5(6)) Blckstn Audio.

***Half the Church: Recapturing God's Global Vision for Women.** unabr. ed. Carolyn Custis James. (ENG.). 2011. 18.99 (978-0-310-55586-5(8)) Zondervan.

Half the Sky: Turning Oppression into Opportunity for Women Worldwide. unabr. ed. Nicholas D. Kristof & Sheryl WuDunn. Narrated by Cassandra Campbell. 8 CDs. (Running Time: 10 hrs.). 2009. audio compact disk 34.95 (978-1-59887-928-5(6), 1598879286) Pub: HighBridge. Dist(s): Workman Pub

Halfhyde & the Admiral. Philip McCutchan. Read by Christopher Scott. 6 cass. (Running Time: 7 hrs. 30 mins.). (Halfhyde Adventures Ser.: No. 15). (J). 2004. 54.95 (978-1-84283-336-0(7)) Pub: ISIS Lrg Prnt GBR. Dist(s): Ulverscroft US

Halfhyde & the Chain Gangs. unabr. ed. Philip McCutchan. Read by David Tarkenter. 6 cass. (Running Time: 7 hrs.). (Halfhyde Adventures Ser.: No. 12). 2002. 54.95 (978-1-84283-146-5(1)) Pub: UlverLrgPrint GBR. Dist(s): Ulverscroft US
Murder and chicanery involving a consignment of gold bullion stalk St Vincent Halfhyde as he takes the square-rigged ship Glen Hallandale on government service from Devonport dockyard to Cape Town. His "cargo" consists of a large draft of convicts from Dartmoor Prison, volunteers for the fight against the Boers in South Africa - volunteers who travel in chain gangs and under strong escort or armed warders in Halfhyde's hastily converted holds.

Halfhyde & the Flag Captain. unabr. ed. Philip McCutchan. Read by Christopher Scott. 6 cass. (Running Time: 6 hrs.). (Halfhyde Adventures Ser.: No. 7). 2001. 54.95 (978-1-86042-835-7(5)) Pub: Soundings Ltd GBR. Dist(s): Ulverscroft US
The safety of the British Ambassador to Uruguay is jeopardized by a revolutionary coup. With the attention being focussed on their ambassador rather than on their traitor, von Merkatz steams confidently up the River Plate and with lavish promises immediately makes allies of the new Uruguayan regime. The British are ill-prepared to contest von Merkatz's certain triumph.

Halfhyde for the Queen. Philip McCutchan. Read by Christopher Scott. 6 cass. (Running Time: 9 hrs.). (Halfhyde Adventures Ser.: No. 5). 2001. 54.95 (978-1-86042-771-8(5), 27715) Pub: Soundings Ltd GBR. Dist(s): Ulverscroft US
Halfhyde's desperate attempt to save his sovereign's life takes him from the seedy, treacherous backstreets of Torremolinos to the more familiar, yet equally dangerous, Scottish Highlands.

Halfhyde Goes to War. unabr. ed. Philip McCutchan. Read by Christopher Scott. 6 cass. (Running Time: 9 hrs.). (Halfhyde Adventures Ser.: No. 13). (J). 2003. 54.95 (978-1-84283-226-4(3)) Pub: ISIS Lrg Prnt GBR. Dist(s): Ulverscroft US

Halfhyde Line. Philip McCutchan. 6 cass. (Halfhyde Adventures Ser.: No. 11). 2003. 54.95 (978-1-84283-099-4(6)) Pub: UlverLrgPrint GBR. Dist(s): Ulverscroft US

Halfhyde on the Amazon. unabr. ed. Philip McCutchan. Read by David Tarkenter. 6 cass. (Running Time: 7 hrs.). (Halfhyde Adventures Ser.: No. 14). (J). 2003. 54.95 (978-1-84283-279-0(4)); audio compact disk 64.95 (978-1-84283-688-0(9)) Pub: ISIS Lrg Prnt GBR. Dist(s): Ulverscroft US
A horribly mutilated corpse is found aboard the "Taronga Park", and when Detective Inspector Todhunter is embarked to sail with the ship, Halfhyde is unclear whether the policeman's investigations are confined to the murder.

Halfhyde on the Yangtze. unabr. ed. Philip McCutchan. Read by Christopher Scott. 6 cass. (Running Time: 6 hrs. 30 mins.). (Halfhyde Adventures Ser.: No. 8). 2002. 54.95 (978-1-86042-885-2(1)) Pub: UlverLrgPrint GBR. Dist(s): Ulverscroft US
Far up the Yangtze, the European residents in Chungking are threatened with rebellion and massacre by the Chinese. Tactful intervention in rescuing the terrified civilians is essential. No sooner has the naval party landed at Chungking than the unfortunate Captain Watkiss is captured, leaving Lieutenant Halfhyde with a dilemma: should he effect the safe removal of the stranded Europeans, or pursue Watkiss' Chinese captors.

Halfhyde on Zanatu. unabr. ed. Philip McCutchan. Read by Graham Roberts. 4 cass. (Running Time: 6 hrs.). (Halfhyde Adventures Ser.: No. 9). (J). 2002. 44.95 (978-1-86042-974-3(2)) Pub: ISIS Lrg Prnt GBR. Dist(s): Ulverscroft US

Halfhyde Ordered South. Philip McCutchan. Read by Christopher Scott. 7 cass. (Running Time: 8 hrs. 30 min.). (Halfhyde Adventures Ser.: No. 6). 2001. 61.95 (978-1-86042-683-4(2)) Pub: UlverLrgPrint GBR. Dist(s): Ulverscroft US
Ordered to take part in a diplomatic mission to Chile, Lieutenant St. Vincent Halfhyde of the Royal Navy once again finds himself under the thumb of his old compatriot the incoherent and blustering Captain Watkiss. They are to deliver an obsolete battleship to the Chilean government.. But soon they learn the real purpose of the mission, and it is not long before the pair are caught up in political double-dealing, escaped prisoners and treason.

Halfhyde to the Narrows. unabr. ed. Philip McCutchan. 6 cass. (Running Time: 9 hrs.). (Halfhyde Adventures Ser.: No. 4). 2001. 54.95 (978-1-86042-636-0(0), 26360) Pub: Soundings Ltd GBR. Dist(s): Ulverscroft US

Halftime. unabr. ed. Read by Bob Buford. (Running Time: 5 hrs. 0 mins. 0 sec.). (ENG.). 2008. audio compact disk 29.99 (978-0-310-28958-6(0)) Zondervan.

***Halftime: Moving from Success to Significance.** unabr. ed. Bob Buford. (Running Time: 6 hrs. 17 mins. 0 sec.). 2008. 19.99 (978-0-310-28959-3(9)) Zondervan.

Halftime & Game Plan: Changing Your Game Plan from Success to Significance/Winning Strategies for the 2nd Half of Your Life. abr. ed. Bob Buford. (Running Time: 2 hrs. 50 mins. 0 sec.). (ENG.). 2003. 10.99 (978-0-310-26052-3(3)) Zondervan.

Halfway Home. Mary Sheldon. Narrated by Barbara Rosenblat. 7 cass. (Running Time: 9 hrs. 30 mins.). 69.00 (978-1-4025-0609-3(0)) Recorded Bks.

Halfway Home. unabr. ed. Mary Sheldon. Narrated by Barbara Rosenblat. 7 cass. (Running Time: 9 hrs. 30 mins.). 2002. 37.95 (978-1-4025-0610-9(4), RF586) Recorded Bks.
Arriving home from school one day, eight-year-old Alexis is devastated when she learns of her mother's abandonment. Now 40, Alexis is drawn back into her tragic past through the eyes of a troubled teen. The emotional reading by Barbara Rosenblat lends heartbreaking awareness to every single sentiment.

***Halfway to the Grave: A Night Huntress Novel.** unabr. ed. Jeaniene Frost. (Running Time: 13 hrs. 0 mins.). (Book One of the Night Huntress Ser.). 2010. 72.95 (978-1-4417-3181-4(4)); audio compact disk 105.00 (978-1-4417-3182-1(2)) Blckstn Audio.

***Halfway to the Grave: A Night Huntress Novel.** unabr. ed. Jeaniene Frost. (Running Time: 13 hrs.). (Book One of the Night Huntress Ser.). 2010. 29.95 (978-1-4417-3185-2(7)) Blckstn Audio.

***Halfway to the Grave: A Night Huntress Novel.** unabr. ed. Jeaniene Frost. Read by Tavia Gilbert. (Running Time: 13 hrs.). (Night Huntress Ser.). 2010. audio compact disk 24.95 (978-1-4417-3184-5(9)) Blckstn Audio.

Halim el-Dabh Live at Starwood. Perf. by Halim El-Dabh & Seeds of Time. 1. 2002. audio compact disk 12.95 (978-1-59157-027-1(1)) Assn for Cons.
A live performance of sacred music from Africa by Professor Halim El-Dabh and the percussion ensemble Seeds of Time at the 2002 Starwood Festival.

Hall Bedroom see Classic Ghost Stories, Vol. 2, A Collection

Hall Bedroom. unabr. ed. Mary E. Wilkins Freeman. Read by Cindy Hardin. 1 cass. (Running Time: 58 min.). Dramatization. 1982. 8.95 (S-45) Jimcin Record.
Chilling stories of the supernatural.

Hall Bedroom & The Shadows on the Wall. Mary E. Wilkins Freeman. 1 cass. 1989. 8.95 (S-45) Jimcin Record.
Chilling stories of the supernatural.

Hall Johnson Collection: For Voice & Piano. 2 CDs. 2004. audio compact disk 34.95 (978-0-8258-4964-0(0)) Fischer Inc NY.

Hall Monitor, Vol. 3. Annie Auerbach. Read by Denis Lawrence. (Running Time: 26 mins.). (J). (gr. 2-5). 2004. pap. bk. 17.00 (978-0-8072-1988-1(6), Listening Lib) Random Audio Pubg.

Hall of Faith: 12 Stories of the Bible's Greates Heroes. Marshall Younger et al. Created by Focus on the Family Staff. (Running Time: 4 hrs. 0 mins.). (Adventures in Odyssey Audio Ser.). (ENG.). (J). 2008. audio compact disk 24.99 (978-1-58997-489-0(1)) Pub: Focus Family. Dist(s): Tyndale Hse

Hall of Fame. Capital Radio. (Running Time: 1 hr.). 2005. 16.95 (978-1-59912-938-9(8)) Iofy Corp.

Hall of Fame. Perf. by Andrae Crouch. 1 cass. 10.98 (978-1-57908-456-1(7)); audio compact disk 16.98 (978-1-57908-455-4(9)) Platinm Enter.

Hall of Fame Legends. 2006. audio compact disk 5.95 (978-1-59987-528-6(4)) Braun Media.

Hall of Fantasy: The Hand of Botar & The Castle of Levoca. Perf. by Richard Thorne. 1 cass. (Running Time: 1 hr.). 2001. 6.98 (1750) Radio Spirits.

Hall of Fantasy: The Man in Black & The Crawling Things. Perf. by Richard Thorne. 1 cass. (Running Time: 1 hr.). 2001. 6.98 (1505) Radio Spirits.

***Halla la longitud Audio CD.** April Barth. Adapted by Benchmark Education Co., LLC. (Content Connections Ser.). (SPA.). (J). 2010. audio compact disk 10.00 (978-1-61672-200-5(2)) Benchmark Educ.

***¿Halla las figuras sólidas? Audio CD.** April Barth. Adapted by Benchmark Education Co., LLC. (Content Connections Ser.). (SPA.). (J). 2010. audio compact disk 10.00 (978-1-61672-199-2(5)) Benchmark Educ.

***Halle, Hodie!** Composed by Douglas E. Wagner. (Running Time: 2 mins.). (ENG.). 2010. audio compact disk 26.99 (978-1-4234-8702-9(8), 1423487028) Pub: Shawnee Pr. Dist(s): H Leonard

Hallelu et Adonai. Contrib. by Ted Pearce & Be'er Sheva. 2008. audio compact disk 16.98 (978-5-557-47912-7(0)) Pt of Grace Ent.

Hallelujah. 1 cass., 1 CD. 10.98 (978-1-57908-359-5(5), 5310); audio compact disk 15.98 CD. (978-1-57908-358-8(7)) Platinm Enter.

***Hallelujah.** Composed by Leonard Cohen. (ENG.). 2010. pap. bk. 6.99 (978-1-4234-9321-1(4), 1423493214) H Leonard.

Hallelujah. Contrib. by Bethany Dillon. (Mastertrax Ser.). 2006. audio compact disk 9.98 (978-5-558-01832-5(1)) Pt of Grace Ent.

Hallelujah! Rev. 19:1-10. Ed Young. 1987. 4.95 (978-0-7417-1580-7(5), 580) Win Walk.

Hallelujah! The Welcome Table: A Lifetime of Memories with Recipes. unabr. ed. Maya Angelou. 3 CDs. (Running Time: 2 hrs.). 2004. audio compact disk 25.50 (978-1-4159-0330-8(1)) Pub: Books on Tape. Dist(s): NetLibrary CO

Hallelujah! The Welcome Table: A Lifetime of Memories with Recipes. unabr. ed. Maya Angelou. 2 cass. (Running Time: 2 hrs.). 2004. 24.00 (978-1-4159-0329-2(8), BksonTape) Random Audio Pubg.
Angelou shares memories pithy and poignant - and the recipes that helped to make them both indelible and irreplaceable. Angelou tells us about the time she was expelled from school for being afraid to speak - and her mother baked a delicious maple cake to brighten her spirits. She gives us her recipe for short ribs along with a story about a job she had as a cook at a Creole restaurant (never mind that she didn't know how to cook and had no idea what Creole food might entail). There was the time in London when she attended a wretched dinner party full of wretched people; but all wasn't lost - she did experience her initial taste of a savory onion tart. She recounts her very first night in her new home in Sonoma, California, when she invited M. F. K. Fisher over for cassoulet, and the evening Deca Mitford roasted a chicken when she was beyond tipsy - and created Chicken Drunkard Style. And then there was the hearty brunch Angelou made for a homesick Southerner, a meal that earned her both a job offer and a prophetic compliment: "If you can write half as good as you can cook, you are going to be famous." Maya Angelou is renowned in her wide and generous circle of friends as a marvelous chef. Her kitchen is a social center. From fried meat pies, chicken livers, and beef Wellington to caramel cake, bread pudding, and chocolate éclairs, the one hundred-plus recipes included here are all tried and true, and come from Angelou's heart and her home.

Hallelujah Chorus. Mormon Tabernacle Choir. 1 cass. 2.37 (3111415); audio compact disk 8.98 (3333124) Covenant Comms.

Hallelujah! Christ Jesus Is Born. 1 cass. (Max Lucado's God Came Near Ser.). 1998. 8.98 Mastertrax. (978-1-58229-056-0(3)) Brentwood Music.

Hallelujah! Christ Jesus Is Born. Perf. by Max Lucado. 1 cass. 1999. 8.99 (Howard Bks) S and S.
A song of praise & words of inspiration for the Christmas season.

Hallelujah! Great Choruses from Handel's Messiah. Perf. by His Majestie's Clerkes. 1 cass., 1 CD. 1998. 9.98; audio compact disk 16.98 CD. Lifedance.

Hallelujah Handel. Susan Hammond. 1 cass. 1995. 10.98; 18.98 Consort Bk Sales.

Hallelujah Hop. Contrib. by Dale Mathews. Created by Brentwood Kids Company. Prod. by David Huff. 1 CD. 1999. audio compact disk 12.98 (978-1-55897-781-5(3)) Provident Music.

Hallelujah Jesus. Contrib. by Monk & Neagle. (Mastertrax Ser.). 2007. audio compact disk 9.98 (978-5-557-71915-5(6)) Pt of Grace Ent.

Hallelujah, Jesus Is Born! Contrib. by Bradley Knight & Geron Davis. 2008. audio compact disk 7.00 (978-5-557-40857-8(6), Brentwood-Benson Music) Brentwood Music.

Hallelujah, Jesus Is Born! Contrib. by Bradley Knight. Created by Bradley Knight & Geron Davis. Created by Geron Davis. 2008. audio compact disk 16.98 (978-5-557-40889-9(4), Brentwood-Benson Music) Brentwood Music.

Hallelujah, Jesus Is Born! Alto. Contrib. by Johnathan Crumpton et al. Prod. by Bradley Knight & Geron Davis. 2008. audio compact disk 5.00 (978-5-557-40862-2(2), Brentwood-Benson Music) Brentwood Music.

Hallelujah, Jesus Is Born: Bass. Contrib. by Bradley Knight & Geron Davis. 2008. audio compact disk 5.00 (978-5-557-40860-8(6), Brentwood-Benson Music) Brentwood Music.

Hallelujah, Jesus Is Born! Bass Guitar (Full Mix-Right, Bass Guitar-Left) Contrib. by Johnathan Crumpton et al. Prod. by Bradley Knight & Geron Davis. 2008. audio compact disk 7.00 (978-5-557-40858-5(4), Brentwood-Benson Music) Brentwood Music.

Hallelujah, Jesus Is Born: Satb. Contrib. by Bradley Knight. Created by Bradley Knight & Geron Davis. Created by Geron Davis. 2008. audio compact disk 90.00 (978-5-557-40888-2(6), Brentwood-Benson Music) Brentwood Music.

Hallelujah, Jesus Is Born! Soprano. Contrib. by Johnathan Crumpton. Prod. by Geron Davis & Bradley Knight. 2008. audio compact disk 5.00 (978-5-557-40865-3(7), Brentwood-Benson Music) Brentwood Music.

Hallelujah, Jesus Is Born! Tenor. Contrib. by Bradley Knight & Geron Davis. 2008. audio compact disk 5.00 (978-5-557-40861-5(4), Brentwood-Benson Music) Brentwood Music.

Hallelujah, What a Savior! 25 Hymn Stories Celebrating Christ Our Redeemer. Kenneth W. Osbeck. 1 CD. (Running Time: 1 hr. 30 mins.). 2002. audio compact disk 11.99 (978-0-8254-3436-5(X)) Kregel.
The real-life stories behind twenty-five favorite songs of the death and resurrection of Christ. Includes rendition of each song in the book.

Halley's Comet: Once in a Lifetime. unabr. ed. William Gutsch, Jr. Read by Leonard Nimoy. 1 cass. 1986. 7.95 (S 1788) HarperCollins Pubs.

Hallmark Playhouse: Cimarron & Goodbye Mr. Chips. Perf. by Richard Thorne & Ronald Colman. 1 cass. (Running Time: 1 hr.). 2001. 6.98 (1661) Radio Spirits.

Hallowed Hunt. Lois McMaster Bujold. Read by Marguerite Gavin. (Running Time: 59400 sec.). 2007. 89.95 (978-1-4332-0103-5(8)); audio compact disk 108.00 (978-1-4332-0104-2(6)); audio compact disk 29.95 (978-1-4332-0105-9(4)) Blckstn Audio.

Hallowed Journey. 15 CDs. 2004. bk. 49.95 (978-1-57734-841-2(9)) Covenant Comms.

Hallowed Journey Set: Dramatized Book of Mormon. 15 CDs. audio compact disk 59.95 (978-1-57734-059-1(0), 0400483) Covenant Comms.

Hallowed Journey Set: Dramatized Book of Mormon. 13 cass. 2004. 49.95 (978-1-55503-214-2(1), 040029) Covenant Comms.
Make learning the Book of Mormon fun!.

Hallowed Murder. unabr. ed. Ellen Hart. Read by Carol Jordan Stewart. 6 cass. (Running Time: 8 hrs.). (Jane Lawless Mystery Ser.). 1995. 39.95 Set. (978-1-888348-00-2(3), HCB101) Hall Closet.
Starring lesbian sleuth Jane Lawless & her outrageous sidekick Cordelia Thorn. Jane searches for clues to a murder & risks her own life to ensnare a cunning killer.

Halloween. Gail Gibbons. Illus. by Gail Gibbons. Read by Larry Robinson. 14 vols. (Running Time: 7 mins.). 1985. pap. bk. & tchr. ed. 37.95 Reading Chest. (978-0-941078-86-3(8)) Live Oak Media.

Halloween. unabr. ed. Gail Gibbons. Illus. by Gail Gibbons. Read by Larry Robinson. 1 cass. (Running Time: 6 mins.). (J). (gr. k-3). 1985. bk. 24.95

(978-0-941078-87-0(6)); pap. bk. 15.95 (978-0-941078-85-6(X)) Live Oak Media.
Describes the history, traditions, & customs of the holiday.

Halloween. unabr. ed. Gail Gibbons. 1 cass. (Running Time: 6 min.). (J). (gr. k-3). 1985. pap. bk. 33.95 incl. 4 pap. bks. & guide. Live Oak Media.

Halloween: Invitation to the Occult? Chuck Missler. 2 CD's. (Running Time: 112 min). (Briefing Packages by Chuck Missler). 2003. audio compact disk 19.95 (978-1-57821-231-6(6)) Koinonia Hse.
The celebration of the pagan festival of Halloween is now a $2.4 billion merchandiser's market. Fifty percent of Americans will decorate for Halloween (compared to over 80% for Christmas). It is now the third most popular party activity, after the Superbowl and New Year's Eve. This is always a difficult time for Christians, especially those with children. It is also a dangerous time for some, since many of the seemingly "harmless" involvements associated with Halloween can also be "entries" for the occult, and can prove very tragic for the unwary.

Halloween Classics. unabr. ed. Radio Spirits Publishing Staff & Bram Stoker. 2006. audio compact disk 9.98 (978-1-57019-782-6(2)) Radio Spirits.

Halloween Dream. unabr. ed. Phyllis Dolgin. 1 cass. (Running Time: 7 min.). (Holidays Are Fun Ser.). (J). (ps-2). 1985. 16.99 incl. hardcover. (978-0-87386-010-9(1)) Jan Prods.
Bruno is invited to his first costume party & he has to decide what character he wants to be.

Halloween Fun. 1 cass. (Running Time: 1 hr.). (J). 2001. pap. bk. 10.95 (KIM 9113C); pap. bk. 11.95 (KIM 9113); pap. bk. 14.95 (KIM 9113CD) Kimbo Educ.

Halloween Havoc. Audio Scope Staff. 1 cass. (J). 1996. 5.00 (978-1-57375-375-3(0), 667308); audio compact disk 5.00 CD. (978-1-57375-488-0(9), 667295) Audioscope.

Halloween Horror: And Other Cases. unabr. ed. Seymour Simon. Narrated by Johnny Heller. 1 cass. (Running Time: 1 hr.). (Einstein Anderson, Science Detective Ser.). (gr. 3 up). 2001. 10.00 (978-0-7887-4657-4(X), 96291E7) Recorded Bks.
Adam "Einstein" Anderson uses science to solve all sorts of problems & mysteries, usually while telling bad jokes & puns.

Halloween Horror & Other Stories. unabr. ed. Seymour Simon. Narrated by Johnny Heller. 1 cass. (Running Time: 1 hr.). (J). 2001. pap. bk. & stu. ed. 23.24 Recorded Bks.

Halloween Howls. (Running Time: 42 min.). 7.99; audio compact disk 11.99 CD. MFLP CA.
Festive halloween music for dancing, decorating, or dressing up.

Halloween in the United States. unabr. ed. Maria Latona. Ed. by Marybeth Hageman. 3 cass. (English for You! Ser.). 1998. 39.95 Set, incl. tchr's. guide, student texts, worksheets. (48000) Recorded Bks.
ESL students will understand & enjoy celebrations along with their native speaker friends. Student texts contain key vocabulary & a wide range of exercises including: conversation practice, comprehension, discussion, writing, grammar, & critical thinking.

Halloween Misfits. Audrey Smith. 1 CD. (Running Time: 12:24 min.). (J). 2004. pap. bk. 14.95 (978-0-9722673-4-2(4)) Audrey Prods.

Halloween Night. unabr. ed. 1 CD. (Running Time: 60 mins.). 2001. audio compact disk 5.99 (978-1-896617-08-4(5), SMA005) Stuffed Moose CAN.
Including Gruesome Graveyard, Creepy Castle, Dr. Death's Laboratory, and Scream on. Seven background tracks.

***Hallowe'En Party: A BBC Full-Cast Radio Drama.** Agatha Christie. Narrated by John Moffatt & Full Cast Production Staff. (Running Time: 1 hr. 30 mins. 0 sec.). (ENG.). 2010. audio compact disk 24.95 (978-1-84607-041-9(4)) Pub: AudioGO. Dist(s): Perseus Dist

Hallowe'En Party: A BBC Full-Cast Radio Drama. unabr. ed. Agatha Christie. Read by John Moffatt. 6 cass. (Running Time: 7 hrs. 2 mins.). 2003. 29.95 (978-1-57270-330-8(X)) Pub: Audio Partners. Dist(s): PerseuPGW

Hallowe'En Party: A BBC Full-Cast Radio Drama. unabr. ed. Agatha Christie. Narrated by John Moffatt. (Running Time: 25320 sec.). (Hercule Poirot Mystery Ser.). (ENG.). 2006. audio compact disk 29.95 (978-1-57270-535-7(3)) Pub: AudioGO. Dist(s): Perseus Dist

Hallowe'En Party: A BBC Full-Cast Radio Drama. unabr. ed. Agatha Christie. Read by John Moffatt. 6 CDs. (Hercule Poirot Mystery Ser.). 2000. audio compact disk 64.95 (978-0-7540-5335-4(0), CCD 026) Pub: Chivers Audio Bks GBR. Dist(s): AudioGO
At a Hallowe'en party, 13-year-old Joyce boasts that she has witnessed a murder. When no-one believes her, she storms off. Within hours, her body is found, drowned in an apple-bobbing tub. Hercule Poirot must now establish whether he is looking for a murderer or a double-murderer.

Hallowe'En Party: A BBC Full-Cast Radio Drama, Set. unabr. ed. Agatha Christie. Read by John Moffatt. 6 cass. (Running Time: 9 hrs). 1999. 54.95 (978-0-7540-0377-9(9), CAB1800) AudioGO.
At a Hallowe'en party, Joyce, a hostile 13 year-old, boasts that she has witnessed a murder. When no-one believes her, she storms off. Within hours, her body is found, still in the house, drowned in an apple-bobbing tub. Hercule Poirot is called to the scene, but first he must establish whether he is looking for a murderer or a double-murderer.

Halloween Party *C-1566841283. Tape. 1 cass. (Running Time: 60 min.). (J). 7.95 (978-0-9652802-5-9(X)) Timeless Prods.
Halloween stories, sound effects, music.

Halloween Sampler, No. 2. 2004. 99.00 (978-1-58997-038-0(1)) Nelson.

Halloween Spooky Sounds. rev. ed. John Sereda. 2003. audio compact disk (978-1-894877-49-7(7)) Ghost Hse Bks CAN.

Halloween Spooky Sounds CD, Vol. 1. rev. ed. John Sereda. (Running Time: 48 mins.). 2003. audio compact disk (978-1-894877-51-0(9)) Ghost Hse Bks CAN.

Halloween Stories from Mosses from an Old Manse & Other Tales, Set. unabr. ed. Nathaniel Hawthorne. Read by Michael Russotto & Flo Gibson. 2 cass. (Running Time: 3 hrs.). (gr. 5 up). 1992. 14.95 (978-1-55685-243-5(6)) Audio Bk Con.
"Young Goodman Brown, "Feathertop: A Moralized Legend," "An Old Woman's Tale," "Graves & Goblins," "The Appeal of Alice Doane," & "The Ghost of Dr. Harris" are full of tricks & treats.

Halloween Tree. unabr. ed. Ray Bradbury. 1 MP3-CD. (Running Time: 2 hrs.). 2008. 19.95 (978-1-4332-3217-6(0)) Blckstn Audio.

Halloween Tree. unabr. ed. Ray Bradbury. Read by Jerry Robbins & Colonial Radio Players. 2 CDs. (Running Time: 2 hrs.). 2008. audio compact disk 14.95 (978-1-4332-3216-9(2)) Blckstn Audio.

Halloween Tree. unabr. ed. Ray Bradbury & A. Full Cast. (Running Time: 2 hrs. NaN mins.). 2008. 22.95 (978-1-4332-3213-8(8)); audio compact disk 27.00 (978-1-4332-3214-5(6)) Blckstn Audio.

***Halls of Ivy.** Perf. by Ronald Colman & Benita Hume. 2010. audio compact disk 18.95 (978-1-57019-920-2(5)) Radio Spirits.

Halls of Ivy. collector's ed. Perf. by Ronald Colman et al. 1 DVD. (Running Time: 3 hrs.). (TV from Yesteryear Ser.). 2001. bk. 9.98 (7807) Radio Spirits.
Contains three classic television shows and three complete old time radio shows. Includes Boston Blackie and Dragnet.

Halls of Ivy, Set. unabr. ed. 2 cass. (Running Time: 2 hrs.). 10.95 (978-1-57816-002-0(2), HI2401) Audio File.
Four shows, including the first & the last of the radio broadcast.

Halls of Ivy: A Son's True Intellect & A Slight Misunderstanding. Perf. by Ronald Colman & Benita Colman. 1 cass. (Running Time: 1 hr.). 2001. 6.98 Radio Spirits.

Halls of Ivy: College Bound. Perf. by Ronald Colman. 6 cass. (Running Time: 6 hrs.). 1999. 19.98 (AB239) Radio Spirits.

Halls of Ivy: Female Department Head & Dinner a Week Early. Perf. by Ronald Colman & Benita Colman. 1 cass. (Running Time: 1 hr.). 2001. 6.98 (1506) Radio Spirits.

Halls of Ivy: Music Student to Drop Out of College & New Psychology Professor. Perf. by Ronald Colman & Benita Colman. 1 cass. (Running Time: 1 hr.). 2001. 6.98 (2120) Radio Spirits.

Halls of Justice. Lee Gruenfeld. Read by Barry Williams. 4 cass. (Running Time: 6 hrs.). 1996. 24.95 Set. (978-1-57511-021-9(0)) Pub Mills.
Two sisters are brutally attacked leaving them badly traumatized. Their case falls into the hands of Deputy DA Sal Milano, a man of strong moral conviction & a brilliant legal strategist. But when departmental politics & legal maneuverings lead to a legal misstep in the trial of the perpetrator the sisters concoct a remarkable scheme to exact revenge on their attacker. Their shocking plan sets of a chain of events which will leave no one involved with the case unscathed.

Halls of Justice. unabr. ed. Lee Gruenfeld. Read by Barrett Whitener. 12 cass. (Running Time: 18 hrs.). 1996. 83.95 (978-0-7861-0997-5(1), 1774) Blckstn Audio.
Santa Monica Deputy District Attorny Sal Milano finds himself prosecuting what seems to be the most explosive & high-profile case of his career. A small-time thug with ties to the mob is charged with raping twin sisters, one of them the stunning Diane Pierman, a celebrated attorney & Sal's longtime court rival. When the case is suddenly thrown out on a technicality, Sal finds his hopes of rising to political office seemingly ruined. But he hasn't counted on the determination of the Pierman sisters. A few days after the trial, one of them hunts down their assailant & kills him. Neither one will talk, & both are charged with murder one. Now Sal has the case of a lifetime, the headlines & attention he needs for his own ambitions. But everything depends on prosecuting & convicting two beautiful women, who, in the eyes of the public, have righted a grievous wrong.

Halls of Justice. unabr. ed. Lee Gruenfeld. Read by Barrett Whitener. (Running Time: 17 hrs. 0 mins.). 2010. 44.95 (978-1-4417-0727-7(1)); audio compact disk 123.00 (978-1-4417-0724-6(7)) Blckstn Audio.

Hallucinogens & Contemporary North American Shamanic Practices. Ralph Metzner. 1 cass. 9.00 (A0212-87) Sound Photosyn.
ICSS '87 with Tom Pinkson.

***Halo.** unabr. ed. Alexandra Adornetto. (Running Time: 13 hrs.). (YA). 2010. 24.99 (978-1-4418-7525-9(5), 9781441875259, BAD); 39.97 (978-1-4418-7526-6(3), 9781441875266, BADLE) Brilliance Audio.

***Halo.** unabr. ed. Alexandra Adornetto. Read by Alexandra Adornetto. 1 MP3-CD. (Running Time: 15 hrs.). (YA). 2010. 24.99 (978-1-4418-7523-5(9), 9781441875235, Brilliance MP3); 39.97 (978-1-4418-7524-2(7), 9781441875242, Brinc Audio MP3 Lib); audio compact disk 24.99 (978-1-4418-7521-1(2), 9781441875211, Bril Audio CD Unabri); audio compact disk 69.97 (978-1-4418-7522-8(0), 9781441875228, BriAudCD Unabrid) Brilliance Audio.

Halo, Set. unabr. ed. Eric Nylund & William C. Dietz. Narrated by Todd McLaren. (Running Time: 34 hrs. 0 mins. 0 sec.). (ENG.). 2008. audio compact disk 29.95 (978-1-4001-2031-4(4)) Pub: Tantor Media. Dist(s): IngramPubServ

Halo on the Sword. Mary Purcell. 7 cass. 28.95 (719) Ignatius Pr.
Portrayal of the life of St. Joan of Arc.

Halos. unabr. ed. Kristen Heitzmann. Narrated by Katherine Kellgren. 8 cass. (Running Time: 11:50 hrs.). 2005. 79.75 (978-1-4025-9080-1(6)) Recorded Bks.

Halsey's Typhoon: The True Story of a Fighting Admiral, an Epic Storm, & an Untold Rescue. unabr. ed. Bob Drury & Tom Clavin. Read by Eric Conger. (YA). 2007. 59.99 (978-1-59895-797-6(X)) Find a World.

Halsey's Typhoon: The True Story of a Fighting Admiral, an Epic Storm, & an Untold Rescue. unabr. ed. Bob Drury & Tom Clavin. Read by Eric Conger. (ENG.). 2007. audio compact disk 36.95 (978-1-59887-086-2(6), 1598870866) Pub: HighBridge. Dist(s): Workman Pub

Halting Bedtime Hassles: Teleseminar Package. Perf. by Jody Johnston Pawel. (ENG.). 2008. 19.95 (978-1-929643-00-4(4)) Ambris Publ.

***Halt's Peril.** John Flanagan. (Running Time: 9 hrs.). (Ranger's Apprentice Ser.: Bk. 9). (ENG.). (J). 2010. audio compact disk 39.95 (978-0-14-242851-1(5), PengAudBks) Penguin Grp USA.

Hamaca de la Vaca. Alma Flor Ada. (Cuentos Para Todo el Ano Ser.). (SPA., (J). (gr. k-3). 4.95 (978-1-58105-248-0(0)) Santillana.

Hamatreya see Poetry of Ralph Waldo Emerson

Hamburger, Fries, Pie, & a Drink. Victor Harris. 1 cass. 7.98 (978-1-55503-785-7(2), 06005004) Covenant Comms.
Daring to do the right thing.

Hamburger, Fries, Pie & a Drink. Victor Harris. 1 cass. 3.95 (978-1-57734-382-0(4), 34441212) Covenant Comms.

Hamdden. 2005. audio compact disk (978-1-85644-883-3(5)) UWACES GBR.

Hamdulillah Vol. II: Fes Festival of World Sacred Music. Perf. by Francoise Atlan. 2 CDs. (Running Time: 2 hrs. 24 min.). 1999. audio compact disk 21.98 (978-1-56455-648-6(4), MM00108D) Sounds True.
Includes: Christian-Muslim canticles from medieval Spain; the Sufi music of Azerbaijan, Iran & Turkey; Arab-Andalusian vocal & instrumental performances; classical Indian dhrupad chant the multi-cultural music of Baghdad; Sephardic songs by Parisian diva Francoise Atlan; Muslim-Jewish synagogue music; "Moroccan roll" & much more.

Hamel the Camel - A Different Mammal. Read by Robert Perinchief. Music by Dan Sullivan. (J). bk. 16.95 (978-1-880396-45-2(9), JP9645-9) Jalmar Pr.

Hamiltons of Ballydown. Anne Doughty. (Soundings (CDs) Ser.). 2006. audio compact disk 99.95 (978-1-84559-441-1(X)) Pub: ISIS Lrg Prnt GBR. Dist(s): Ulverscroft US

Hamiltons of Ballydown. unabr. ed. Anne Doughty. Read by Caroline Lennon. 10 cass. (Soundings Ser.). 2006. 84.95 (978-1-84559-425-1(8)) Pub: ISIS Lrg Prnt GBR. Dist(s): Ulverscroft US

Hamlet see Hearing Great Poetry: From Chaucer to Milton

Hamlet. (DD-7080) Natl Recrd Co.

Hamlet. (Audio BookNotes Guide). 2002. audio compact disk 9.95 (978-1-929011-03-2(2)) Scholarly Audio.

Hamlet. William Shakespeare. Narrated by John Gielgud. (Running Time: 2 hrs.). (C). 2006. 14.95 (978-1-60083-044-0(7)) Iofy Corp.

Hamlet. William Shakespeare. Perf. by Anton Lesser et al. 4 cass. (Running Time: 3 hrs. 20 mins.). Dramatization. (Plays of William Shakespeare Ser.). 1997. 22.98 (978-962-634-624-2(8), NA412414, Naxos AudioBooks) Naxos.
The first in Shakespeare's great series of tragedies. This version uses the text of the New Cambridge Shakespeare, used by the Royal Shakespeare Company and educational institutions across the world.

Hamlet. William Shakespeare. Perf. by Anton Lesser et al. 4 CDs. (Running Time: 3 hrs. 20 mins.). Dramatization. (Plays of William Shakespeare Ser.). 1997. audio compact disk 28.98 (978-962-634-124-7(6), NA412412, Naxos AudioBooks) Naxos.

Hamlet. William Shakespeare. Contrib. by John Gielgud et al. 2008. 39.99 (978-1-60514-644-7(7)) Find a World.

Hamlet. abr. ed. William Shakespeare. 3 CDs. (Running Time: 3 hrs.). 2005. audio compact disk 19.95 (978-0-660-18964-2(X)) Pub: Canadian Broadcasting CAN. Dist(s): Georgetown Term

Hamlet. abr. ed. William Shakespeare. (R[illegible]g Time: 30 mins.). (ENG.). 2006. 5.98 (978-1-59483-854-5(2)) Pu[illegible]het Audio. Dist(s): HachBkGrp

Hamlet. abr. ed. William Shakespeare. 1 c[illegible] (Monarch Notes Ser.). 1985. 7.95 (978-0-671-54409-6(8)) S&S Audio.
Intended as a supplement to classroom study, offering plot summary, interpretive theme, information on literary theme & style. The flashcards outline the author's life.

Hamlet. abr. ed. William Shakespeare. Perf. by Dublin Gate Theatre Staff. 1 cass. (Running Time: 51 min.). Dramatization. 10.95 (978-0-8045-0781-3(3), SAC 781) Spoken Arts.
Using key scenes & bridges, a complete telling of Hamlet.

Hamlet. abr. ed. William Shakespeare. Read by Full Ensemble Cast. (YA). 2006. 34.99 (978-1-59895-508-8(X)) Find a World.

***Hamlet.** abr. ed. William Shakespeare. (ENG.). 2003. (978-0-06-074327-7(1), Caedmon); (978-0-06-079953-3(6), Caedmon) HarperCollins Pubs.

Hamlet, unabr. ed. William Faulkner. Narrated by Mark Hammer. 12 cass. (Running Time: 16 hrs. 30 mins.). 2001. 97.00 (978-1-55690-916-0(0), 93412E7) Recorded Bks.
Published in 1940, the first book in a trilogy that includes "The Town" & "The Mansion". Through the eyes of Ratliff, the novel's hero & teller of tall tales, witness the terrifying rise to prominence of the Snopeses, white trash who insinuate their way into the tiny hamlet of Frenchman's Bend like steady drips of poison.

Hamlet. unabr. ed. William Shakespeare. Read by Arkangel Cast. Narrated by Simon Russell Beale et al. (Arkangel Shakespeare Ser.). (ENG.). 2005. audio compact disk 24.95 (978-1-932219-08-1(0)) Pub: AudioGO. Dist(s): Perseus Dist

Hamlet. unabr. ed. William Shakespeare. Perf. by Paul Scofield & Diana Wynyard. 3 cass. (Running Time: 3 hrs 29 min.). Dramatization. 20.00 (H102) Blckstn Audio.
Hamlet, Prince of Denmark, is told that his father was murdered by his Uncle, who then married Hamlet's mother, the queen. Once he determines the truth, the prince sets out to seek revenge - with tragic consequences.

Hamlet. unabr. ed. William Shakespeare. Read by Audio Partners Staff. 2 cass. (Running Time: 3 hrs. 25 mins.). (Arkangel Shakespeare Ser.). 2004. 17.95 (978-1-932219-48-7(X), Atlntc Mnthly) Pub: Grove-Atltc. Dist(s): PerseuPGW

Hamlet. unabr. ed. William Shakespeare. Perf. by Paul Scofield & Diana Wynyard. 4 cass. Dramatization. 1984. 35.92 (978-0-89845-132-0(9), CP 232) HarperCollins Pubs.
Cast includes: Wilfrid Lawson, Zena Walker, Roland Culver, Charles Heslop, Edward De Souza, Donald Houston, Richard Dare, Eric Jones, Peter Bayliss, John Warner, Christopher Guinee, Robert Eddison, Aubrey Woods, Esmond Knight, Barry Ingham, Charles Gray.

Hamlet. unabr. ed. William Shakespeare. 3 cass. 1999. 20.00 (FS9-50929) Highsmith.

Hamlet. unabr. ed. William Shakespeare. Perf. by Ronald Pickup et al. 4 cass. 22.95 (SCN 085) J Norton Pubs.
A man caught up in a web of his own making & condemned to an ever-increasing course of violence.

Hamlet, unabr. ed. William Shakespeare. Narrated by Frank Muller. 3 cass. (Running Time: 4 hrs.). 1999. 28.00 (978-1-55690-215-4(8), 90011E7) Recorded Bks.
A single-voice performance of the complete text with glossary & introduction.

Hamlet. unabr. ed. William Shakespeare. 2 cass. (Running Time: 2 hrs.). Dramatization. 2000. pap. bk. 40.20 (40113E5); 28.00 (21510E5) Recorded Bks.

Hamlet: John Gielgud's Classic 1948 Recording. William Shakespeare. Read by John Gielgud. (Running Time: 12369 sec.). 2006. audio compact disk 22.98 (978-962-634-417-0(2), Naxos AudioBooks) Naxos.

Hamlet: Prince of Denmark. unabr. ed. William Shakespeare. Read by Grover Gardner. 3 cass. (Running Time: 4 hrs. 30 min.). 1991. 16.95 (978-1-55685-229-9(0)) Audio Bk Con.
Hamlet, Prince of Denmark, encounters his father's ghost. When he learns that his uncle, now king & married to his mother, was responsible for his royal father's death, he sets out to avenge the murder.

Hamlet: The Storm Within. Music by Lee Kweller. Text by Joshua Brown & John Esposito. 1 cass. (Running Time: 9 min.). (Educational Song Ser.: Vol. 3). (YA). (gr. 7-12). 1998. stu. ed. 19.98 (978-1-57649-003-7(3), 76003) Arkadia Ent.
Based on Shakespeare's classic play about youth, madness, genius, love & more, depending on whom you ask. Hamlet is widely recognized as one of the greatest works of literature ever produced in the English language.

Hamlet - Prince of Denmark. unabr. ed. William Shakespeare. Read by Anton Lesser & Full Cast Production Staff. (YA). 2008. 54.99 (978-1-60514-582-2(3)) Find a World.

Hamlet on the Stage. unabr. ed. Thomas M. Parrott. 1 cass. (Running Time: 21 min.). (Shakespeare's Critics Ser.). 1953. 12.95 (23101) J Norton Pubs.
Astute first-hand observations on the performance of famous actors from Edwin Booth to Maurice Evans who have portrayed the character Hamlet.

Hamlet One Voice. abr. ed. Perf. by David Ian Davies. 1 cass. (Running Time: 40 min.). Dramatization. 2000. (978-0-9708022-0-0(X)) One Voice.

Hamlet, Prince of Denmark. William Shakespeare. Retold by John Bergez. (Classic Literature Ser.). 2003. pap. bk. 69.00 (978-1-4105-0004-5(7)); audio compact disk 18.95 (978-1-4105-0195-0(7)) D Johnston Inc.

Hamlet Prince of Denmark. William Shakespeare. (Running Time: 3 hrs. 15 mins.). 2001. 28.95 (978-1-60083-758-6(1)) Iofy Corp.

Hamlet, Prince of Denmark. unabr. ed. William Shakespeare. Ed. by Naxos Audiobooks Staff. 2 cass. (Running Time: 3 hrs. 23 mins.). (New Cambridge Shakespeare Audio Ser.). (ENG.). 1997. 29.99 (978-0-521-62561-6(0)) Cambridge U Pr.

Hamlet, Prince of Denmark, Set. William Shakespeare. Contrib. by Naxos Audiobooks Staff. (Running Time: 3 hrs. 22 mins. 42 sec.). (New Cambridge Shakespeare Audio Ser.). (ENG.). 1997. audio compact disk 38.99 (978-0-521-62560-9(2)) Cambridge U Pr.

Hamlet Read Along. Prod. by Saddleback Educational Publishing. (Saddleback's Illustrated Classics Ser.). (YA). 2006. 24.95 (978-1-56254-905-3(7)) Saddleback Edu.

Hamlet Rethought. unabr. ed. Salvador De Madariaga. 1 cass. (Running Time: 26 min.). 1968. 12.95 J Norton Pubs.
A re-examination of Hamlet, which rejects certain common views on both Hamlet & Ophelia - particularly the views that Hamlet could not make up his mind.

Hamlet's Dresser. unabr. ed. Bob Smith. Read by Bob Smith. 1 CD. (Running Time: 10 hrs.). 2003. audio compact disk 24.95 (978-0-7861-9067-6(1), 3043); 49.95 (978-0-7861-2341-4(9), 3043) Blckstn Audio.
Bob Smith grew up in a town named for Shakespeare's birthplace, Stratford, Connecticut. His troubled childhood was spent in a struggle to help his devastated parents care for his severely retarded sister. But at age ten, Smith stumbled onto a line from The Merchant of Venice: "In sooth I know not why I am so sad." In the language of Shakespeare, he had found a window through which to view the world. When he was a teenager, the American Shakespeare Festival moved into Stratford, and Smith became Hamlet's dresser. As he watched the plays from backstage, his life's passion took shape. Here is the tender and lyrical prose, Smith tells the story of a life shaped by poetry.

Hamlet's Dresser. unabr. ed. Bob Smith. Read by Bob Smith. 8 CDs. (Running Time: 41400 sec.). 2003. audio compact disk 64.00 (978-0-7861-9343-1(3), 3043) Blckstn Audio.

Hamlet's Dresser. unabr. ed. Bob Smith. Read by Bob Smith. 8 CDs. 2004. audio compact disk 39.95 (978-0-7861-9096-6(5)); reel tape 35.95 (978-0-7861-2400-8(8)) Blckstn Audio.
When he was a teenager, the American Shakespeare Festival moved into Stratford, and Smith became Hamlet's dresser. As he watched the plays from backstage, his life's passion took shape. Here, in tender and lyrical prose, Smith tells the story of a life shaped by.

Hamlet's Trap. Janice Greene. (Running Time: 4235 sec.). (Pageturners Ser.). (J). 2004. 10.95 (978-1-56254-712-7(7), SP7127) Saddleback Edu.

Hammer of Eden. Ken Follett. 2 cass. (Running Time: 3 hrs.). 1998. 15.00 Set. (978-0-333-74610-3(4)) Ulvrscrft Audio.
The governor of California has received a terrorist threat. If this demand is not met, the group threatens to trigger an earthquake in exactly four weeks time.

Hammer of Eden. abr. ed. Ken Follett. Read by Anthony Heald. 3 cass. (Running Time: 3 hrs.). 1999. 24.00 (FS9-43295) Highsmith.

Hammer of Eden. unabr. ed. Ken Follett. Read by Alexander Adams. 9 cass. (Running Time: 13 hrs. 30 mins.). 1998. 72.00 (4727); 72.00 (978-0-7366-4534-8(9), 4727) Books on Tape.
The broadcast, by a controversial talk-radio host, of a terrorist threat to create a man-made earthquake in California is seen as folly by mot people. But no so by Judy Maddox, a young FBI agent with an agenda. Nursing the terrifying suspicion that the threat may be all too real, Judy, against orders, begins to investigate. She quickly discovers that indeed it is possible to trigger an earthquake deliberately. When a tremor in a remote desert region shows signs of being machine generated. Judy's suspicions are confirmed. Racing the clock, Judy must track down the elusive Stop Now group before they can carry out their promise to level San Francisco.

Hammer of Eden. unabr. ed. Ken Follett. Read by Alexander Adams. 11 CDs. (Running Time: 13 hrs. 12 mins.). 2000. audio compact disk 88.00 (978-0-7366-5145-5(4)) Books on Tape.
A young FBI agent races against the clock to stop a terrorist group from triggering a man-made earthquake in San Francisco.

Hammer of Eden. unabr. ed. Ken Follett. Read by Alexander Adams. 8 cass. (Running Time: 8 hrs.). 1999. 39.95 (FS9-40133) Highsmith.

Hammer of God. unabr. ed. Arthur C. Clarke. Narrated by George Guidall. 5 CDs. (Running Time: 5 hrs. 30 mins.). 2000. audio compact disk 49.75 (978-0-7887-3394-9(X), C10000E7) Recorded Bks.
The asteroid is named Kali, for the Hindu goddess of death & destruction & she is locked on a course to the sun - her only impediment the small green planet directly in her path, the planet Earth. For Captain Robert Singh, of the Goliath, Kali is a career-making challenge. He is tasked with altering the huge asteroid's course enough to minimize or eliminate the damage to his home planet. But someone wants his mission to fail - someone wants Kali to complete her ordained mission of destruction.

Hammer of God. unabr. ed. Arthur C. Clarke. Narrated by George Guidall. 4 cass. (Running Time: 5 hrs. 30 mins.). 1994. 3.00 (978-1-55690-962-7(4), 94105E7) Recorded Bks.

Hammer of God. unabr. ed. Karen Miller. Narrated by Josephine Bailey. (Running Time: 22 hrs. 0 mins. 0 sec.). (Godspeaker Ser.). (ENG.). 2010. 39.99 (978-1-4001-6318-2(8)); audio compact disk 54.99 (978-1-4001-1318-7(0)); audio compact disk 109.99 (978-1-4001-4318-4(7)) Pub: Tantor Media. Dist(s): IngramPubServ

***Hammer of God.** unabr. ed. Karen Miller. Narrated by Josephine Bailey. (Running Time: 22 hrs. 0 mins.). (Godspeaker Ser.). 2010. 24.99 (978-1-4001-8318-0(9)) Tantor Media.

Hammered Dulcimer Classics. Carole Koenig. 1994. 10.98 (978-1-56222-987-0(7), 95107C) Mel Bay.

Hammered Fiddle Tunes. Rick Thum. 2002. bk. 22.95 (978-0-7866-6621-8(8), 97206BCD) Mel Bay.

Hammerhead. Ken McCoy & Ken Mccoy. 2008. 69.95 (978-1-84652-227-7(7)); audio compact disk 79.95 (978-1-84652-228-4(5)) Pub: Magna Story GBR. Dist(s): Ulverscroft US

Hammett & Goodbye Pops. Joe Gores. Read by Joe Gores. 1 cass. (Running Time: 36 min.). 1985. 13.95 (978-1-55644-144-8(4), 5111) Am Audio Prose.
Gores reads excerpts from "Hammet" & short story "Goodbye Pops".

Hammy's House of Horror, Set. unabr. ed. Kaye Umansky. Read by Sandi Toksvig. 3 cass. (J). (gr. 1-8). 1999. 24.95 (CCA 3552, Chivers Child Audio) AudioGO.

Hampstead: London's Over-the-Hill Suburb. Gerald J. Morse. 1 cass. (Walking Tours on Cassette Ser.). 1987. 9.95 (978-0-939969-07-4(6), LE 11) Talk-a-Walk.
A walk through Hampstead, London. Detailed street map included.

Hamster Revolution: How to Manage Your E-Mail Before It Manages You. unabr. ed. Mike Song et al. Read by Oliver Wyman. (Running Time: 2 hrs. 30 mins. 0 sec.). (ENG.). 2007. audio compact disk 19.95 (978-1-4272-0080-8(7)) Pub: Macmill Audio. Dist(s): Macmillan

Hamster Revolution for Meetings: How to Meet Less & Get More Done. unabr. ed. Mike Song et al. Read by Erik Synnestvedt. (Running Time: 3 hrs.). (ENG.). 2009. 14.98 (978-1-59659-435-7(7), GildAudio) Pub: Gildan Media. Dist(s): HachBkGrp

Hamster/Hamper & Guinea-Pig in the Garage. Lucy Daniels. 2 cass. (Running Time: 2 hrs.). (J). 1998. (978-1-84032-032-9(X), HoddrStoughton) Hodder General GBR.
Two Animal Ark adventures, "Hamster in a Hamper," & "Guinea-pig in the Garage".

Hana & the Dragon & other tales from Japan Vol. 2: Musical Adventures with Elizabeth Falconer. Perf. by Elizabeth Falconer. 1 CD. (Running Time: 57:08). (J). 2000. audio compact disk 15.00 (978-0-9770499-3-6(0)) Koto World.
Five Japanese folktales of friendship and sharing, with koto musical accompaniment. Recipient of a Parents' Choice Silver Honor and a Storytelling World Honors Award.

Hana's Suitcase. Fumiko Ishioka & George Brady. 2005. audio compact disk 15.95 (978-0-660-19270-3(5)) Canadian Broadcasting CAN.

Hana's Suitcase: A True Story. unabr. ed. Karen Levine. Read by Stephanie Wolfe. 1 MP3-CD. (Running Time: 2 hrs.). 2009. 39.97 (978-1-4233-8233-1(1), 9781423382331, Brlnc Audio MP3 Lib); 19.99 (978-1-4233-8232-4(3), 9781423382324, Brilliance MP3); 39.97 (978-1-4233-8235-5(8), 9781423382355, BADLE); 19.99 (978-1-4233-8234-8(X), 9781423382348, BAD); audio compact disk 19.99 (978-1-4233-8230-0(7), 9781423382300, Bril Audio CD Unabri) Brilliance Audio.

Hana's Suitcase: A True Story. unabr. ed. Karen Levine. Read by Stephanie Wolfe. 2 CDs. (Running Time: 2 hrs.). (YA). (gr. 5-8). 2009. audio compact disk 42.97 (978-1-4233-8231-7(5), 9781423382317, BriAudCD Unabrid) Brilliance Audio.

Hancock's Half Hour. Tony Hancock. 2 cass. Dramatization. (BBC Humor Ser.). 1991. 14.95 set. Minds Eye.
Dramatizations produced by the BBC.

Hancock's Half Hour, Vol. 10. Ray Galton & Alan Simpson. 2 cass. (Running Time: 2 hrs.). 1998. 15.00 Set. (978-0-563-55729-6(X)) BBC WrldWd GBR.
Britian's episodes of the Hancock's Half Hour.

Hancock's Half Hour: The Very Best Episodes. unabr. ed. Created by Ray Galton & Alan Simpson. (Running Time: 2 hrs. 0 mins. 0 sec.). (ENG.). 2010. audio compact disk 24.95 (978-1-60283-841-3(0)) Pub: AudioGO. Dist(s): Perseus Dist

***Hancock's Half Hour: The Very Best Episodes, Vol. 2.** Ray Galton. (Running Time: 2 hrs. 0 mins. 0 sec.). (ENG., 2010. audio compact disk 24.95 (978-0-563-50408-5(0)) Pub: AudioGO. Dist(s): Perseus Dist

Hand. D. Hastings-Nield. (Anatomy Project). 1997. audio compact disk 189.95 (978-1-85070-835-3(5), Parthenon Pbng) Pub: CRC Pr. Dist(s): Taylor and Fran

Hand Drumming Essentials. C. A. Grosso. (ENG.). 2003. audio compact disk 10.00 (978-0-7390-3283-1(6)) Alfred Pub.

Hand Drums for Beginners. John Marshall. (ENG.). 2000. audio compact disk 10.00 (978-0-7390-0325-1(9)) Alfred Pub.

Hand, Handwriting & the Child with Nonverbal Learning Disorder. Peg Bledsoe. 1 cass. (Running Time: 88 min.). 1997. bk. 15.00 (978-1-58111-009-8(X)) Contemporary Medical.
Components of movement needed for writing of child with NLD. Factors & strategies to help develop hand function.

Hand, Handwriting, & the Child with Nonverbal Learning Disorders. Contrib. by Peg Bledsoe. 1 cass. (Running Time: 1 hrs. 30 min.). 20.00 (19-003A) J W Wood.
An occupational therapist discusses components of movement needed for writing, development of the arm & its relationship to NLD dysfunction, factors in the environment & strategies to help develop hand function, suggestions for home activities.

Hand I Fan With. unabr. ed. Tina McElroy Ansa. Read by Tonya Jordan. 12 cass. (Running Time: 18 hrs.). 1997. 96.00 (978-0-7366-3660-5(9), 4334) Books on Tape.
Ansa returns us to the small town of Mulberry, Georgia, with its eccentric & nosy folk. Affirms life as it laughs at it.

Hand in Hand. 1 cass.; 1 CD. 1998. 9.98 (978-1-56628-059-4(1), 42569); audio compact disk 15.98 CD. (978-1-56628-058-7(3)) MFLP CA.

Hand in Hand. Lori Wilke. 1 cass. 1993. 9.95 (978-1-56043-380-4(9)); audio compact disk 14.99 CD. (978-1-56043-381-1(7)) Destiny Image Pubs.

Hand in Hand. Perf. by Lori Wilke. 1 cass., 1 CD. (Running Time: 44 min.). 1992. 9.98 (978-1-891916-07-6(6)); 9.98 (978-1-891916-27-4(0)); audio compact disk 14.98 CD. (978-1-891916-08-3(4)) Spirit To Spirit.
Ministry to the Believer.

Hand in Hand: Helping Children Celebrate Diversity. Colleen Aalsburg Wiessner et al. (Diversity Ser.). (gr. 3-6). 1997. tchr. ed. 35.75 (978-1-56212-260-7(6), 116000) FaithAliveChr.

Hand in the Glove. unabr. ed. Rex Stout. Read by Judith West. 5 cass. (Running Time: 7 hrs.). (Stout, Rex Ser.). 2003. 27.95 (978-1-57270-349-0(0)) Pub: Audio Partners. Dist(s): PerseuPGW
"Dol" Bonner is a beautiful young New Yorker who runs a licensed detective agency. The year is 1937 and she and her friends are smart, savvy, and full of fast, no-nonsense talk.

Hand in the Glove. unabr. ed. Rex Stout. Narrated by Judith West. 6 CDs. (Running Time: 7 hrs.). (Stout, Rex Ser.). (ENG.). 2003. audio compact disk 29.95 (978-1-57270-350-6(4)) Pub: AudioGO. Dist(s): Perseus Dist

Hand Me Another Brick. Charles R. Swindoll. 2006. audio compact disk 50.00 (978-1-57972-743-7(3)) Insight Living.

Hand Me Another Brick. unabr. ed. Charles R. Swindoll. 8 cass. (Running Time: 6 hrs. 30 mins.). 1998. 39.95 (978-1-57972-303-3(9)) Insight Living.

Hand of Evil. abr. ed. J. A. Jance. Read by Karen Ziemba. (Running Time: 6 hrs. 0 mins. 0 sec.). No. 3. (ENG.). 2009. audio compact disk 14.99 (978-0-7435-9755-5(9)) Pub: S&S Audio. Dist(s): S and S Inc

Hand of Evil. unabr. ed. J. A. Jance. Read by Karen Ziemba. 9 cass. (Running Time: 10 hrs. 30 mins.). (Ali Reynolds Ser.: No. 3). 2007. 72.75 (978-1-4281-6908-1(3)); audio compact disk 102.75 (978-1-4281-6910-4(5)) Recorded Bks.

Hand of Evil. unabr. ed. J. A. Jance. Read by Karen Ziemba. (Running Time: 10 hrs. 30 mins. 0 sec.). No. 3. (ENG.). 2007. audio compact disk 39.95 (978-0-7435-6840-1(0)) Pub: S&S Audio. Dist(s): S and S Inc

Hand of Fate. Michael Underwood. Read by Tim Hardy. 5 cass. (Running Time: 7 hrs. 30 min.). 1999. 49.95 (66073) Pub: Soundings Ltd GBR. Dist(s): Ulverscroft US

Hand of Fate. unabr. ed. Lis Wiehl & April Henry. Narrated by Pam Turlow. (Running Time: 8 hrs. 0 mins. 12 sec.). (Triple Threat Ser.). (ENG.). 2010. 20.99 (978-1-60814-643-7(X)); audio compact disk 29.99 (978-1-59859-700-4(0)) Oasis Audio.

Hand of Fu-Manchu. Read by John Bolen. Ed. by Sax Rohmer. (Running Time: 7 hrs.). (Fu-Manchu Ser.: Vol. 3). 2002. 27.95 (978-1-60083-621-3(6), Audiofy Corp) Iofy Corp.

Hand of Fu-Manchu. unabr. ed. Read by Gary Martin. Ed. by Sax Rohmer. 6 cass. (Running Time: 8 hrs. 30 mins.). (Fu-Manchu Ser.: Vol. 3). 1994. 44.95 (978-0-7861-0794-0(4), 2132) Blckstn Audio.
Concealed from civilization high in the mountains of Tibet, the immaculate Empress of Si Fan was kept. Her handmaidens were blind; no one could look upon her ageless beauty. Her servants were mute, rendering them incapable of revealing the awesome ceremonies they witnessed. And her sire was the all-powerful threat to six continents, the master of evil - Dr. Fu Manchu.

Hand of Fu-Manchu. unabr. ed. Sax Rohmer, pseud. Read by John Bolen. (Fu-Manchu Ser.: Vol. 3). (ENG.). 2002. audio compact disk 72.00 (978-1-4001-3052-8(2)) Pub: Tantor Media. Dist(s): IngramPubServ

Hand of Fu-Manchu. unabr. ed. Ed. by Sax Rohmer, pseud. (Running Time: 6 hrs. 53 mins.). (Fu-Manchu Ser.: No. 3). (ENG.). 2002. audio compact disk 20.00 (978-1-4001-5052-6(3)) Pub: Tantor Media. Dist(s): IngramPubServ
Unabridged Audiobook. 1 MP3 CD - 6 hours, 53 minutes. Narrated by John Bolen.Sir Gregory Hale returns to London from Mongolia with a mysterious Tulun-Nur chest that holds the ?key to India?, a vital secret of the Fu Manchu's notorious Si-Fan organization. Unfortunately Hale is murdered before he is able to disclose the secret to Nayland Smith. The Burmese police commissioner and Dr. Petrie launch a mission to affront the brilliant but deadly master criminal before he succeeds in his malignant and fantastic plot to take over the world.In pursuit of the Devil Doctor, Smith and Petrie must escape numerous assassination attempts and battle an insect army. They are faced with multiple mysteries including: the Zagazig Code, the Shrine of Seven Lamps, and the Chapel of Satan. The future of the free world depends on the success of Smith and Petrie defeating the villainous Hand of Fu Manchu.This is the third novel of the Fu Manchu series.This audiobook is on one CD, encoded in MP3 format and will only play on computers and CD players that have the ability to play this unique format.

Hand of Fu-Manchu. unabr. ed. Ed. by Sax Rohmer, pseud. 6 CDs. (Running Time: 6 hrs. 53 min.s). (Fu-Manchu Ser.: Vol. 3). (ENG.). 2002. audio compact disk 36.00 (978-1-4001-0052-1(6)) Pub: Tantor Media. Dist(s): IngramPubServ
Unabridged Audiobook. 6 CDs - 6 hours, 53 minutes. Narrated by John Bolen.Sir Gregory Hale returns to London from Mongolia with a mysterious Tulun-Nur chest that holds the ?key to India?, a vital secret of the Fu Manchu's notorious Si-Fan organization. Unfortunately Hale is murdered before he is able to disclose the secret to Nayland Smith. The Burmese police commissioner and Dr. Petrie launch a mission to affront the brilliant but deadly master criminal before he succeeds in his malignant and fantastic plot to take over the world.In pursuit of the Devil Doctor, Smith and Petrie must escape numerous assassination attempts and battle an insect army. They are faced with multiple mysteries including: the Zagazig Code, the Shrine of Seven Lamps, and the Chapel of Satan. The future of the free world depends on the success of Smith and Petrie defeating the villainous Hand of Fu Manchu.This is the third novel of the Fu Manchu series.

Hand of Fu-Manchu, Set. unabr. ed. Read by Gary Martin. Ed. by Sax Rohmer. 6 cass. (Running Time: 9 hrs.). (Fu-Manchu Ser.: Vol. 3). 1994. 29.00 in vinyl album. (C-252) Jimcin Record.
Nayland Smith & his friend Dr. Petrie are again on the trail of the sinister Dr. Fu Manchu.

Hand of Fu-Manchu, with EBook. unabr. ed. Sax Rohmer, pseud. Narrated by John Bolen. (Running Time: 7 hrs. 0 mins. 0 sec.). (Fu-Manchu Ser.). (ENG.). 2009. audio compact disk 27.99 (978-1-4001-1113-8(7)); audio compact disk 19.99 (978-1-4001-6113-3(4)) Pub: Tantor Media. Dist(s): IngramPubServ

Hand of Fu-Manchu, with eBook. unabr. ed. Sax Rohmer, pseud. Narrated by John Bolen. (Running Time: 7 hrs. 0 mins. 0 sec.). (Fu-Manchu Ser.). (ENG.). 2009. audio compact disk 55.99 (978-1-4001-4113-5(3)) Pub: Tantor Media. Dist(s): IngramPubServ

Hand of Glory see Graveyard of Ghost Tales

Hand of Glory. unabr. ed. Sophie Masson. Read by Richard Aspel. 6 cass. (Running Time: 8 hrs.). (YA). 2004. 48.00 (978-1-74093-250-9(1)); audio compact disk 83.95 (978-1-74093-518-0(7)) Pub: Bolinda Pubng AUS. Dist(s): Bolinda Pub Inc

Hand of God. Swami Amar Jyoti. 1 cass. 1982. 9.95 (R-42) Truth Consciousness.
The known & the unknown, no gap in creation. God's hand never leaves us. Perfect relationship between Creator & creation.

Hand of God: Releasing God's Unlimited Power. Speeches. Creflo A. Dollar. 3 cass. (Running Time: 3 hrs.). 2006. 15.00 (978-1-59944-036-1(9)); audio compact disk 21.00 (978-1-59944-037-8(7)) Creflo Dollar.

Hand of Oberon. Roger Zelazny. Read by Roger Zelazny. 2 vols. (Chronicles of Amber: Bk. 4). 2002. (978-1-58807-514-7(1)) Am Pubng Inc.

Hand of Oberon. Roger Zelazny. Read by Roger Zelazny. 2 vols. (Chronicles of Amber: Bk. 4). 2003. audio compact disk 25.00 (978-1-58807-256-6(8)); audio compact disk (978-1-58807-687-8(3)) Am Pubng Inc.

Hand of Oberon. abr. ed. Roger Zelazny. Read by Roger Zelazny. 2 vols. (Running Time: 3 hrs.). (Chronicles of Amber: Bk. 4). 2002. 18.00 (978-1-58807-129-3(4)) Am Pubng Inc.
Across the mysterious Black Road, demons swarm into Shadow. The ancient, secret source of the royal family's power is revealed, and an unholy pact between a prince of the realm and the forces of Chaos threaten all the known worlds with absolute obliteration. The hour of battle is at hand. Now Corwin and the remaining princes of Amber must call upon all their superhuman powers to defeat their brother-turned-traitor before he can walk the magical Pattern that created Amber and remake the universe in his own image.

Hand of Poetry: Five Mystic Poets of Persia. abr. ed. Created by Omega Publications. 4 CDs. (Running Time: 14400 sec.). 1993. audio compact disk 49.95 CD Set. (978-0-930872-62-5(2)) Omega Pubns NY.

Hand of Providence. abr. ed. Ron Carter. Read by Ron Carter. 1 cass. (Running Time: 1 hr.). (Prelude to Glory Ser.: Vol. 4). 2003. 7.99 (978-1-57345-883-2(X)) Deseret Bk.
British General John Burgoyne sets out from Canada with a massive army. Losing the help of his Indian allies and slowed by the nearly impassable terrain, the flamboyant Burgoyne finds himself locked in the battle of his life at a place called Saratoga. There, under the heroic leadership of General Benedict Arnold, the rustic American force claims an unlikely victory, and a turning point is reached in the American Revolution.

Hand of Providence. unabr. ed. Mary Beth Brown. 5 cass. (Running Time: 6 hrs.). 2004. 27.99 (978-1-58926-741-1(9), 6741); audio compact disk 29.99 (978-1-58926-742-8(7), 6742) Oasis Audio.
The Strong and Quiet Faith of Ronald Reagan is an uplifting biography that emphasizes the powerful impact his faith had on his ideas, motives, and actions. According to recent opinion polls, Ronald Reagan is the most popular of modern presidents, and yet to most biographers the man is still an enigma. This is because, as Brown explains, no one has ever focused on this great man¿s faith. This book explores the life and personality of Ronald Reagan by focusing on his deep-felt Christian beliefs and showing how faith guided him along his distinguished career and led him to his unprecedented success.

Hand of Providence. unabr. ed. Mary Beth Brown. Narrated by Chris Fabry. (ENG.). 2004. 20.99 (978-1-60814-002-2(4)) Oasis Audio.

Hand of Providence: The Strong & Quiet Faith of Ronald Reagan. unabr. ed. Mary Beth Brown. Read by Chris Fabry. Prod. by Oasis Audio Staff. 6

CDs. (Running Time: 7 hrs.). 2006. audio compact disk 48.00 (978-0-7861-8433-0(7), 3346) Blckstn Audio.

Hand Papermaking & Healing. Harriet Hope. 1 cass. 9.00 (A0265-89) Sound Photosyn.
This Catholic nun makes paper in a very Zen, meditative way. Very beautiful & inspiring.

***Hand That First Held Mine.** unabr. ed. Maggie O'Farrell. (Running Time: 13 hrs. 30 mins.). 2010. 79.95 (978-1-4417-2942-2(9)); audio compact disk 109.00 (978-1-4417-2943-9(7)) Blckstn Audio.

Hand that First Held Mine. unabr. ed. Maggie O'Farrell. (Running Time: 13 hrs. 30 mins.). 2010. 29.95 (978-1-4417-2946-0(1)); audio compact disk 32.95 (978-1-4417-2945-3(3)) Blckstn Audio.

Hand That Signed the Paper see Dylan Thomas Reading His Poetry

Hand to Hand Combat with Satan. Don J. Black. 1 cass. 2004. 9.95 (978-1-55503-071-1(8), 0600784) Covenant Comms.
Recognizing the devil's influence & how to resist it.

Handbags & Gladrags. Sally Worboyes. 2009. 69.95 (978-1-4079-0460-3(4)); audio compact disk 79.95 (978-1-4079-0461-0(2)) Pub: Soundings Ltd GBR. Dist(s): Ulverscroft US

***Handbook for Boys.** abr. ed. Walter Dean Myers. Read by Peter Francis James. (ENG.). 2005. (978-0-06-083921-5(X)); (978-0-06-083920-8(1)) HarperCollins Pubs.

Handbook for Boys. unabr. ed. Walter Dean Myers. Read by James Peter Francis. (YA). 2008. 54.99 (978-1-60514-583-9(1)) Find a World.

Handbook for Citizenship. Margaret Seely. (C). 1990. 26.40 (978-0-13-372814-9(5)) Longman.

Handbook for Citizenship. 2nd ed. Margaret Seely. 1989. bk. 12.95 (978-0-88084-324-9(1)) Alemany Pr.

Handbook for Itinerant & Resource Teachers of Blind & Visually Impaired Students. 1 cass. (Running Time: 1 hr.). 2003. 30.00 Natl Fed Blind.
A complete guide for anyone interested in working with the blind student. It discusses topics ranging from travel training, to teaching Braille, understanding medical assessments, and much more.

***Handbook for Lightning Strike Survivors: A Novel.** unabr. ed. Michele Young-Stone. Narrated by Coleen Marlo. (Running Time: 11 hrs. 0 mins.). 2010. 17.99 (978-1-4001-8729-4(X)); 24.99 (978-1-4001-6729-6(9)); audio compact disk 34.99 (978-1-4001-1729-1(1)); audio compact disk 83.99 (978-1-4001-4729-8(8)) Pub: Tantor Media. Dist(s): IngramPubServ

Handbook for the Heart: Original Writings on Love. abr. ed. Read by Michael Tucker & Jill Eikenberry. Ed. by Richard Carlson & Benjamin Shield. Frwd. by John Gray. 2 cass. 2001. 7.95 (978-1-57815-202-5(X), Media Bks Audio) Media Bks NJ.

Handbook for the Soul. abr. ed. Read by Blair Brown & James Coburn. Ed. by Richard Carlson & Benjamin Shield. Frwd. by Marianne Williamson. 2 cass. 2001. 7.95 (978-1-57815-201-8(1), Media Bks Audio) Media Bks NJ.

Handbook of Ecological Modelling & Informatics. Ed. by S. E. Jorgensen et al. 2009. bk. 360.00 (978-1-84564-207-5(4)) Pub: WIT Pr GBR. Dist(s): Computational Mech MA

Handbook of Parenting V5 Practical Issues in Pa: Being & Becoming a Parent. 2nd rev. ed. Bornstein. 2003. audio compact disk 180.00 (978-0-8058-4842-7(8)) Pub: L Erlbaum Assocs. Dist(s): Taylor and Fran

Handbook of Pronunciation of English Words. J. Sethi & D. V. Jindal. 2 cass. (Running Time: 3 hrs.). 2002. bk. 15.00 (978-81-203-0670-7(8)) Prentice Hall India IND.

Handbook of Win-Win Policy Analysis: A CD-Rom Production. Ed. by Stuart S. Nagel. 69.00 (978-1-59033-417-1(5)) Nova Sci Pubs.

Handbook to Prayer. unabr. ed. Kenneth Boa. Read by Duncan Michael MacGregor. 12 cass. (Running Time: 18 hrs.). 1993. 39.00 set. (978-1-884330-01-8(0)) Trnty House.
Audio version of the book Handbook to Prayer. This is a devotional prayer guide.

Handbook to Renewal: Renewing Your Mind with Affirmations from Scripture. unabr. ed. Kenneth Boa. Read by Duncan Michael MacGregor. 12 cass. (Running Time: 18 hrs.). 1996. 39.95 Set. (978-1-884330-04-9(5)) Trnty House.
Daily prayer guide.

Handbuch zum Ablesen Stromzählers. Tr. by Tara Schneider from ENG. Virgil Johnson. (GER.). 2006. audio compact disk 118.08 (978-0-9755301-3-9(5)) V Johnson Tech.

Handedness: Program from the Award Winning Public Radio Series. Interview. Hosted by Fred Goodwin. Comment by John Hockenberry. 1CD. (Running Time: 1 hr). (Infinite Mind Ser.). 2002. audio compact disk 21.95 (978-1-888064-91-9(9), LCM 204) Lichtenstein Creat.
What do Leonardo da Vinci, Albert Einstein, Oprah Winfrey, and The Infinite Mind's host, Dr. Fred Goodwin, have in common? They're all left-handed. In this all-new program, we'll explore what handedness had to do with the development of language; the connection between left handedness and dyslexia, alcoholism, and shorter life expectancies; and why lefties may have a creative edge.Plus, verbal wizard Richard Lederer on southpaws, righteousness, and the radical turkey (it had two left wings); and commentary by John Hockenberry.

Handel: Messiah. 2 cass. 17.98 (1500139) Covenant Comms.
Complete Messiah with the Philadelphia Philharmonic Symphony Orchestra.

Handel: The Greatest Hits. 1 cass,. audio compact disk 10.98 CD. (978-1-57908-158-4(4), 3604) Platinm Enter.

Handel Three Sonatas for Flute & Piano: Telemann Three Duet Sonatas for Two Flutes. Richard Wyton. 2 vols. 1997. pap. bk. 29.98 (978-1-59615-319-6(9), 586-070) Pub: Music Minus. Dist(s): Bookworld

Handel's Last Chance. Composed by George Frideric Handel. (Composer's Specials Ser.). 1998. audio compact disk 12.95 (978-0-634-00886-3(2), 0634008862) H Leonard.

Handel's Last Chance - ShowTrax. 1 CD. (Running Time: 1 hr.). 2000. audio compact disk 12.95 (00841336) H Leonard.

Handel's Messiah. 2 cass. 17.98 (1500139) Covenant Comms.

Handel's Messiah. 1 cass., 1 CD. audio compact disk 10.98 CD. (978-1-57908-386-1(2), 1550) Platinm Enter.

Handel's Messiah. Contrib. by London Philharmonic Orchestra & Royal Philharmonic Orchestra. 2007. audio compact disk 12.98 (978-5-557-71868-4(0)) Madacy Ent Grp CAN.

Handel's Messiah. Perf. by London Symphony Orchestra. 1993. 4.99 (978-1-930800-05-2(3), Prop Voice); audio compact disk 5.99 (978-1-930800-04-5(5), Prop Voice) Iliad TN.

***Handel's Messiah: Comfort for God's People.** Calvin R. Stapert. (Running Time: 5 hrs. 30 mins. 0 sec.). (ENG.). 2010. audio compact disk 21.98 (978-1-61045-044-7(2)) christianaud.

Handful of Dust. unabr. collector's ed. Evelyn Waugh. Read by David Case. 8 cass. (Running Time: 8 hrs.). 1991. 48.00 (978-0-7366-2055-0(9), 2866) Books on Tape.
Satirizes that stratum of English life where all the characters have money, but lack practically every other credential. Murderously urbane, it depicts the breakup of a marriage in the London gentry, where the errant wife suffers from terminal boredom & becomes enamored of a social parasite & professional lunch-goer.

Handful of Purpose. 2001. 6.00 (978-1-58602-046-0(3)) E L Long.

Handful of Silver. Meg Hutchinson. Read by Julia Sands. 10 cass. (Running Time: 13 hr. 15 min.). 1999. 98.95 (978-1-85903-195-7(1)) Ulvrscrft Audio.
Wheelchair-bound Ester Kerral is horrified when her father forces her into an arranged marriage, in order to save his ailing business. Esther must struggle as best she can to survive a loveless marriage & build a business in a man's world.

Handle. collector's ed. Richard Stark, pseud. Read by Michael Kramer. 4 cass. (Running Time: 6 hrs.). 2000. 32.00 (978-0-7366-5639-9(1)) Books on Tape.
The Baron ran a gambling island right off the Texas coast in the Gulf's blue waters. To Parker, it was just a floating crap game with class. To the Big Boys, it was competition they couldn't stomach. They wanted a specialist to rob the Baron blind, pluck him like a chicken, & burn this paradise island into the sea. That's why they sent for Parker. His price was 200 grand in cash & Crystal - a beautiful little blond. So the pot was sweet, but the heist soon had so many twists it smelled like a brand-new lemon - & Parker knew the line between success & failure on this score would be exactly the length of the barrel of a .38.

Handle with Care. unabr. ed. Jodi Picoult. 1 Playaway. (Running Time: 18 hrs. 30 mins.). 2009. 61.75 (978-1-4361-9829-5(1)); 113.75 (978-1-4361-9826-4(7)) Recorded Bks.

Handle with Care. unabr. ed. Jodi Picoult. Read by Celeste Ciulla et al. 15 CDs. (Running Time: 18 hrs. 30 mins.). 2009. audio compact disk 123.75 (978-1-4361-9827-1(5)) Recorded Bks.

Handle with Care. unabr. ed. Jodi Picoult. Read by Celesete Cuilla et al. 15 CDs. (Running Time: 18 hrs. 30 mins.). 2009. audio compact disk 44.99 (978-1-4361-9840-0(2)) Recorded Bks.

Handling a Chapter Eleven Reorganization. Read by John Ryan et al. (Running Time: 5 hrs. 45 min.). 1992. 115.00 Incl. 446p. tape materials. (BU-55261) Cont Ed Bar-CA.

Handling a Fall. Elbert Willis. 1 cass. (Developing Stability Ser.). 4.00 Fill the Gap.

Handling a Narcotics Case. 4 cass. (Running Time: 5 hrs. 30 min.). 85.00 (T7-9313) PLI.
This December 1990 program discusses pre-trial & trial practice techniques of narcotics cases.

Handling Attorney Malpractice Cases. Read by William Elfving & William McLean. (Running Time: 2 hrs. 45 min.). 1991. 89.00 Incl. Ethics: 1 hr., & 115p. tape materials. (TO-55212) Cont Ed Bar-CA.
Covers all the factors that must be considered in handling a legal malpractice case, including the initial screening & evaluation; details of trial preparation & strategy; & presentation of the case in the courtroom.

Handling Business Valuations for Audits & Tax Disputes. 1 cass. (Running Time: 55 min.). (Business Valuation Discount Planning & Tax Dispute Techniques Ser.). 1995. 75.00 Incl. study guide. (M233) Am Law Inst.
This fundamental program examines the special valuation issues that surround taxpayers & their lawyers, business appraisers, the Internal Revenue Service, & the Tax Court during tax controversies. Discussion topics include the taxpayer's burden of proof: rules of confidentiality & privilege, protection of communications, & the appraisal report & other sources as evidence; audits & administrative appeals: the IRS's view & review of valuation issues, administrative appeals & the IRS Appeals Office, & protection of the appraiser's credibility; & valuation disputes & the Tax Court: battle of the appraisers, review appraisers & rebuttal appraisers, & preparing appraisers & providing legal context. The Tax Court process, including procedures, appraiser testimony, & dispute resolution alternatives is discussed as well.

Handling Civil Appeals. Read by Carl Anderson et al. (Running Time: 2 hrs. 30 min.). 1992. 89.00 Incl. 117p. tape materials. (CP-55203) Cont Ed Bar-CA.
Eminent appellate court judge & leading appellate lawyers teach the essentials of combining winning style & strategy. Covers deciding whether to appeal; protecting client rights during appeal; perfecting the appeal & preparing the record; motions; preparing a cogent brief; & presenting your case effectively in oral arguments.

Handling Conflict Between People: National Association of Evangelicals, 47th Annual Convention, Columbus, Ohio, March 7-9, 1989. Marilyn Moravec. 1 cass. (Workshops Ser.: No. 25-Wednesd). 1989. 4.25 ea. 1-8 tapes.; 4.00 ea. 9 tapes or more. Nat Assn Evan.

Handling Corporate Employment Law Problems. 8 cass. (Running Time: 11 hrs.). bk. 75.00 incl. 459-page course handbook. (T6-9143) PLI.

Handling Customer Complaints, Closing Techniques, Overcoming Objections, Laliaphobia, Preliminary Rapport, Negotiations. Persuasive Communications Staff. 6 cass. (Running Time: 45 min. per cass.). 1981. 125.00 incl. vinyl binder & wkbks. Persuasive Comns.
Live classroom situations that deal with actual problems that are encountered every day in business. Benefits new & experienced salespeople, sales managers, marketing personnel, dealers, distributors.

Handling Depression: Guidelines for a Happy Creative Life. Carole Riley. 3 cass. (Running Time: 3 hrs.). 1990. 25.95 set. (TAH228) Alba Hse Comns.
A clear succinct presentation that helps us define depression, name its conscious & unconscious causes & the physical, emotional & spiritual effects & gives suggestions for remedies, what we can do humanly, psychologically, & spiritually to assess ourself & take creative beneficial action to becoming well.

Handling Difficult People: With Practical Techniques for Improving Customer Care & Patient Care, for All Levels Such As Office Manager, Doctor, Nurse, Practice Administrator, Dentist, & Executives, Who Want to Implement Total Quality Management in Their Organization, & for All Types of Businesses. Daniel Farb. 2004. audio compact disk 49.95 (978-1-932634-53-2(3)) Pub: UnivofHealth. Dist(s): AtlasBooks

Handling Disappointment. Konicov. 1 cass. 11.98 (978-0-87082-328-2(0), 054) Potentials.
Shows how to clear away the debris, enabling you to deal with disappointment & begin to enjoy a more positive outlook.

Handling Essay Questions on the New Jersey State Bar Examination. Contrib. by Howard H. Kestin. (Running Time: 12 hrs.). 1984. 75.00 incl. program handbook. NJ Inst CLE.
Shows the listener how to relate facts to principles of law, organize the orderly flow of answers, use effective writing techniques, employ available time advantageously.

Handling Excuses: Knowing the Best Things to Do & Say. Jane K. Cleland. 1 cass. (Running Time: 60 min.). (Improving Accounts Receivable Collections: Tape 5). 1991. 39.50 (978-1-877680-11-3(7)) Tiger Pr.
Tape 5 covers over a dozen debtor excuses, discusses what each reveals about the situation & tells accounts receivable collectors exactly what to do & say no matter what excuse is offered.

Handling Fear. Marianne Williamson. 4 cass. (Running Time: 4 hrs.). 1998. 25.00 (978-1-56170-583-2(7), M864) Hay House.
Lectures on handling fear & bringing success to your life.

Handling Fear: Talks on Spirituality & Modern Life. Marianne Williamson. 4 CDs. 2004. audio compact disk 23.95 (978-1-4019-0411-1(4)) Hay House.

Handling Fear/Giving Yourself Credit. Marianne Williamson. Read by Marianne Williamson. 1 cass. (Running Time: 90 mins.). (Lectures on a Course in Miracles). 1999. 10.00 (978-1-56170-228-2(5), M731) Hay House.

Handling Job-Related Stress. 1 cass. (Professional Issues Ser.). 1985. 8.95 (1565G) Hazelden.

Handling Land Use & Environmental Problems of Real Estate. unabr. ed. Contrib. by Nicholas A. Robinson. 8 cass. (Running Time: 11 hrs. 30 min.). 1989. 50.00 course handbk. (T7-9203) PLI.
This recording of PLI's March 1989 program analyzes the impact of substantive & procedural land use & environmental regulations on real estate transactions & identifies effective techniques for the real estate, environmental & governmental attorney. Among the topics discussed are: environmental impact statutes, scoping & mitigation measures for environmental assessments, the environmental audit, developers' responsibility for environmental infrastructure, wetland regulation, clean-up of hazardous contaminants & critical habitat laws.

Handling Mind Storms. Elbert Willis. 1 cass. (Increasing Spiritual Assurance Ser.). 4.00 Fill the Gap.

Handling Mortgage Foreclosures in New Jersey. Contrib. by Michael S. Ackerman et al. (Running Time: 4 hrs.). 1983. 70.00 NJ Inst CLE.
You will be guided through handling Chapter 13 & Chapter 7 bankruptcy situations, the new foreclosure rule that sets up the office of foreclosures, recent cases involving foreclosures & bankruptcy, HUD & VA foreclosure procedures.

Handling Patient Telephone Calls Effectively. pap. bk. 52.95 (978-0-89970-252-0(X), OP378185) AMA.
Real-life vignettes of typical calls that come into the medical office, learn how to deal with all types of situations in a professional manner.

Handling Social Security Disability Claims. 1988. bk. 110.00; 60.00 PA Bar Inst.

Handling Social Security Disability Claims. Contrib. by Louis D. Balk et al. (Running Time: 4 hrs.). 1983. 70.00 incl. program handbook. NJ Inst CLE.
Teaches you how to prepare & present social security disability claims effectively & profitably, offering guidance through the entire procedure from the client interview to the appeal process.

Handling Teenage Rebellion: Eph. 2:1-3, 11 Tim. 3:1-7, 731. Ed Young. 1989. 4.95 (978-0-7417-1731-3(X), 731) Win Walk.

Handling the Purchase & Sale of an Ongoing Business. Contrib. by Ronald J. Cappucio & Michael A. Kulzer. (Running Time: 4 hrs.). 1984. 65.00 incl. program handbook. NJ Inst CLE.
Discusses the following topics: basic methods for buying & selling a corporate business, factors to be considered in selecting a taxable method, deciding the form of the acquiring entity, tax accounting considerations.

Handling Waiting Periods. Elbert Willis. 1 cass. (Faith School Ser.: Vol. 1). 4.00 Fill the Gap.

Handmaid of the Lord. unabr. ed. Adrienne Von Speyr. Read by Cynthia Splatt. 6 cass. 24.95 set. (944) Ignatius Pr.
Von Speyr's first book after her conversion shows how Mary's assent to God's will is what defines & sanctifies every aspect of her life.

Handmaiden, Vol. 2. Daughters of St Paul. 1991. audio compact disk 14.95 (978-0-8198-3342-6(8), 332-110) Pauline Bks.

Handmaiden: Songs of Mary. Daughters of St Paul. audio compact disk 14.95 (978-0-8198-3334-1(7), 332-109) Pauline Bks.

Handmaid's Tale. Margaret Atwood. Read by Margaret Atwood. 1 cass. (Running Time: 30 min.). 8.95 (AMF-17) Am Audio Prose.
Readings from "A Handmaid's Tale" & discussion of the novel with the author.

Handmaid's Tale. Margaret Atwood & Michael O'Brien. 2 CDs. (Running Time: 2 hrs.). (ENG.). 2004. audio compact disk 19.95 (978-0-86492-341-7(4)) Pub: BTC Audiobks CAN. Dist(s): U Toronto Pr

Handmaid's Tale. unabr. ed. Margaret Atwood. 3 CDs. (Running Time: 3 hrs.). 2004. audio compact disk 39.95 (978-0-563-52463-2(4)) AudioGO.
The handmaid of the title is Offred, one of the few fertile women in a totalitarian theocratic state. Offred serves the Commander and his wife Serena Joy. Every month she must have impersonal sex with the Commander until she becomes pregnant.

Handmaid's Tale. unabr. ed. Margaret Atwood. Read by Joanna David. 8 cass. (Running Time: 12 hrs.). 2001. 59.95 (978-0-7451-6808-1(6), CAB 518) Pub: Chivers Audio Bks GBR. Dist(s): AudioGO
In the repressive and insular Republic of Gilead, Offred is allowed one function: to breed. If she deviates, she will be hanged at the wall or sent to die slowly of radiation sickness. But old feelings and memories from the days before the Republic still stir inside her. And the repressive state cannot obliterate desire - neither Offred's nor that of the two men on whom her future hangs.

Handmaid's Tale. unabr. ed. Margaret Atwood. Narrated by Betty Harris. 8 cass. (Running Time: 11 hrs.). 1988. 70.00 (978-1-55690-216-1(6), 88060E7) Recorded Bks.
Sometime in the near future the role of Offred, a young woman, is reduced to that of handmaid to an aging Commander of the Faithful.

***Hands, Grooves, & Fills: Book & DVD Pack.** Pat Petrillo. (ENG.). 2007. pap. bk. 39.95 (978-1-4234-2632-5(0), 1423426320) Pub: Hudson Music. Dist(s): H Leonard

Hands of God. Paul Ferrini. 2003. audio compact disk 16.95 (978-1-879159-57-0(0)) Heartways Pr.

Hands of the Strangler. unabr. ed. J. R. Roberts, pseud. Narrated by Randall James Stanton. 2 cass. (Running Time: 3 hrs.). (Gunsmith Ser.: No. 97). 1996. 12.95 Set. (978-1-882071-40-1(9)) B-B Audio.
Clint Adams cant resist getting tangled in other folks troubles-especially when those folks are pretty females. When the Gunsmith heads for London, hes looking for peace and quiet. Instead he finds that hes up to his neck in murder.

Hands-Off Manager: How to Mentor People & Allow Them to Be Successful. unabr. ed. Steve Chandler & Duane Black. Narrated by Nick Landrum. 5 CDs. (ENG.). 2008. audio compact disk 24.95 (978-1-60283-476-7(8)) Pub: AudioGO. Dist(s): Perseus Dist

Hands-On Bible Curriculum: Grades 1 & 2 - Fall 2001. 1 CD. (Running Time: 30 mins.). (J). 2001. audio compact disk 14.99 Group Pub.
Contains music, skits and drama.

Hands-On Bible Curriculum: Grades 1 & 2 - Spring 2001. 1 CD. (Running Time: 30 mins.). (J). 2001. audio compact disk 14.99 Group Pub.

Hands-On Bible Curriculum: Grades 1 & 2 - Summer 2001. 1 CD. (Running Time: 30 mins.). (J). 2001. audio compact disk 14.99 Group Pub.

Hands-On Bible Curriculum: Grades 3 & 4 - Fall 2001. 1 CD. (Running Time: 30 mins.). (J). 2001. audio compact disk 14.99 Group Pub.

Hands-On Bible Curriculum: Grades 3 & 4 - Spring 2001. 1 CD. (Running Time: 30 mins.). (J). 2001. audio compact disk 14.99 Group Pub.

Hands-On Bible Curriculum: Grades 3 & 4 - Summer 2001. 1 CD. (Running Time: 30 mins.). (J). 2001. audio compact disk 14.99 Group Pub.

Hands-On Bible Curriculum: Grades 5 & 6 - Fall 2001. 1 CD. (Running Time: 30 mins.). (J). 2001. audio compact disk 14.99 Group Pub.

Hands-On Bible Curriculum: Grades 5 & 6 - Spring 2001. 1 CD. (Running Time: 30 mins.). (J). 2001. audio compact disk 14.99 Group Pub.

Hands-On Bible Curriculum: Grades 5 & 6 - Summer 2001. 1 CD. (Running Time: 30 mins.). (J). 2001. audio compact disk 14.99 Group Pub.

Hands-On Bible Curriculum: Pre-K & K Ages 5 & 6. 1 CD. (Running Time: 30 mins.). (J). 2001. audio compact disk 14.99 Group Pub.

Hands-On Bible Curriculum: Pre-K & K Ages 5 & 6 - Fall 2001. 1 CD. (Running Time: 30 mins.). (J). 2001. audio compact disk 14.99 Group Pub.

Hands-On Bible Curriculum: Pre-K & K Ages 5 & 6 - Spring 2001. 1 CD. (Running Time: 30 mins.). (J). 2001. audio compact disk 14.99 Group Pub.

Hands-On Bible Curriculum: Preschool Ages 3 & 4 - Fall 2001. 1 CD. (Running Time: 30 mins.). (J). 2001. audio compact disk 14.99 Group Pub.

Hands-On Bible Curriculum: Preschool Ages 3 & 4 - Spring 2001. 1 CD. (Running Time: 30 mins.). (J). 2001. audio compact disk 14.99 Group Pub.

Hands-On Bible Curriculum: Preschool Ages 3 & 4 - Summer 2001. 1 CD. (Running Time: 30 mins.). (J). 2001. audio compact disk 14.99 Group Pub.

Hands-On Bible Curriculum: Toddlers & 2s - Fall 2001. 1 CD. (Running Time: 30 mins.). (J). 2001. audio compact disk 14.99 Group Pub.

Hands-On Bible Curriculum: Toddlers & 2s - Summer 2001. 1 CD. (Running Time: 30 mins.). (J). 2001. audio compact disk 14.99 Group Pub.

Hands-On Bible Curriculum: Toddlers & 2s , Spring 2001. 1 CD. (Running Time: 30 mins.). (J). 2001. audio compact disk 14.99 Group Pub.
Contains music, skits and drama.

Hands on Leadership: Nehm 2:12-20. Ed Young. 1990. 4.95 (978-0-7417-1805-1(7), 805) Win Walk.

Handshake in Space: The Apollo-Soyuz Test Project. Sheri Tan. Illus. by Higgins Bond. Dramatization. (Smithsonian Odyssey Ser.). (J). (gr. 1-6). 1998. 7.95 (978-1-56899-542-7(3), C6010) Soundprints.

Handshake in Space: The Apollo-Soyuz Test Project. Sheri Tan. Illus. by Higgins Bond. (J). (gr. 1-6). 2009. pap. bk. 9.95 (978-1-59249-203-9(7)) Soundprints.

Handsome Brown & the Aggravating Goats. Short Stories. Erskine Caldwell. Read by Erskine Caldwell. 1 cass. (Running Time: 55 min.). 13.95 (978-1-55644-068-7(5), 3041) Am Audio Prose.

Handwriting Reveals Personality. Kathy G. Stevens. 1 cass. (Running Time: 49 min.). (Handwriting Analysis - Personality Analysis Ser.). 1986. 8.95 Listen USA.

Handyman. Carolyn See. Read by Jonathan Marosz. 5 cass. (Running Time: 7 hrs. 30 min.). 1999. 24.95 (978-0-7366-4689-5(2)) Books on Tape.
This breathtaking visual novel explores the surprises of destiny & the origins of fame.

Handyman. collector's ed. Carolyn See. Read by Jonathan Marosz. 5 cass. (Running Time: 7 hrs. 30 min.). 1999. 40.00 (978-0-7366-4612-3(4), 4998) Books on Tape.

Handyman, unabr. ed. Carolyn See. Read by Gil Bellows. 4 cass. (Running Time: 6 hrs.). 1999. 24.95 (978-1-57511-059-2(8)) Pub Mills.
A young artist becomes disillusioned with his career & decides to become a handyman. In the process he discovers that he has the ability to repair more than just broken down appliances.

Hang in There & Surviving Earthly Battles. David Litchford. 1 cass. 1996. 9.98 (978-1-57734-084-3(1), 06005446) Covenant Comms.
A strategy for surviving earthly battles.

Hang On: 1 Peter 1:3-13. Ed Young. 1982. 4.95 (978-0-7417-1266-0(0), 266) Win Walk.

Hang on Tightly: Let Go Lightly. unabr. ed. Ram Dass. 1 cass. (Running Time: 1 hr. 25 min.). 1980. 11.00 (00606) Big Sur Tapes.
Speaking through personal anecdotes, Ram Dass addresses the question: What does it mean to honor your incarnation properly? He believes that once you have a spiritual perspective, everything in your life becomes part of the process of spiritual unfolding.

Hang on to Our Identity. Arynne Simon. 1 cass. 1995. 14.95 (978-1-882389-17-9(4)) Wilarvi Communs.
Hang on to one's own identity in marriage, in family & in work; a program for polishing skills in interpersonal relations.

***Hang-Tree Rebellion.** Peter Dawson. 2009. (978-1-60136-409-8(1)) Audio Holding.

Hang-Tree Rebellion. Peter Dawson. (Running Time: 1 hr. 30 mins.). 2000. 10.95 (978-1-60083-529-2(5)) Iofy Corp.

Hanged Man's House, Set. unabr. ed. E. X. Ferrars. Read by Clive Mantle. 6 cass. (Running Time: 6 hrs.). 1999. 54.95 (978-0-7540-0396-0(5), CAB1819) AudioGO.

Hanged Man's Song. unabr. ed. John Sandford, pseud. 6 cass. (Running Time: 9 hrs.). 2003. 62.00 (978-1-4025-6117-7(2)) Recorded Bks.

Hanging Curve. Troy Soos. Narrated by Johnny Heller. 8 CDs. (Running Time: 9 hrs.). (Mickey Rawlings Baseball Ser.: Vol. 6). 2000. audio compact disk 78.00 (978-0-7887-4767-0(3), C1260E7) Recorded Bks.
Critically-acclaimed novelist & baseball historian Troy Soos evokes the spirit of 1920s America in this compelling mystery. St. Louis Browns infielder Mickey Rawlings plays in a semi-pro game against the East St. Louis Cubs, a well-known black team. But the real battle begins after the winning black pitcher is found hanging from the backstop.

Hanging Curve, unabr. ed. Troy Soos. Narrated by Johnny Heller. 8 cass. (Running Time: 9 hrs.). (Mickey Rawlings Baseball Ser.: Vol. 6). 1999. 60.00 (978-0-7887-4057-2(1), 96129E7) Recorded Bks.

Hanging Fire. unabr. ed. Jessica Mann. Read by Anne Scott-Pendlebury. 6 cass. (Running Time: 8 hrs.). 1999. 54.95 (978-0-7531-0373-9(7), 980411) Pub: ISIS Audio GBR. Dist(s): Ulverscroft US
Tess Redpath has been working for The Argus nearly all her working life. Within minutes of meeting the paper's new proprietor, she finds herself without a job. Life without deadlines feels empty & miserable & gets worse when Tess's married lover, a high ranking officer, decides it's all over. Trying to drag herself back from despair, she decides to work freelance on the stories she has already started. Her flat is ransacked & set on fire & she begins to realize that she has stumbled on something really big.

Hanging Garden. unabr. ed. Ian Rankin. Read by Stuart Langton. 8 cass. (Running Time: 12 hrs.). 1999. 64.00 (4877) Books on Tape.
Detective Inspector Rebus is caught in the middle of two investigations, one involving a suspected Nazi war criminal, the other a dispute between two rival gangs. And when his daughter is nearly killed, Rebus knows there's nothing he won't do to punish the men responsible - even if it means making a deal with the devil himself.

Hanging in the Hotel. Simon Brett. Read by Geoffrey Howard. (Running Time: 8 mins. 30 sec.). 2005. 54.95 (978-0-7861-3695-7(2)); audio compact disk 63.00 (978-0-7861-7682-3(2)) Blckstn Audio.

Hanging in the Hotel. unabr. ed. Simon Brett. Read by Geoffrey Howard. (Running Time: 8 mins. 30 sec.). 2005. 29.95 (978-0-7861-7920-6(1)) Blckstn Audio.

Hanging in the Hotel. unabr. ed. Simon Brett. 8 cass. (Running Time: 8 hrs. 30 mins.). (Isis Cassettes Ser.). (J). 2004. 69.95 (978-0-7531-1989-1(7)); audio compact disk 79.95 (978-0-7531-2351-5(7)) Pub: ISIS Lrg Prnt GBR. Dist(s): Ulverscroft US

Hanging Matter. unabr. ed. Margaret Duffy. Read by Marie McCarthy. 8 cass. (Running Time: 10 hrs.). (Sound Ser.). (J). 2003. 69.95 (978-1-84283-460-2(6)) Pub: ISIS Lrg Prnt GBR. Dist(s): Ulverscroft US

Hanging Time. Leslie Glass. Read by Jane E. Lawder. 4 cass. (Running Time: 360 min.). No. 2. 2000. 25.00 (978-1-58807-059-3(X)) Am Pubng Inc.

Hanging Time. abr. ed. Leslie Glass. Read by M. J. Wilde. 4 vols. No. 2. 2003. (978-1-58807-577-2(X)) Am Pubng Inc.

Hanging Up. Delia Ephron. Narrated by C. J. Critt. 9 CDs. (Running Time: 10 hrs.). audio compact disk 89.00 (978-0-7887-4747-2(9)) Recorded Bks.

Hanging Up. Delia Ephron. Narrated by C. J. Critt. 9 CDs. (Running Time: 10 hrs.). 2000. audio compact disk 89.00 (C1233E7) Recorded Bks.
Eve Mozell has a wonderful husband & a creative job. She also has a temperamental teenage son, a domineering sister & a demented old father. As she deals with daily crises, her life is filled with phone calls. These conversations are marvelous reflection of modern life.

Hanging Up. unabr. ed. Delia Ephron. Narrated by C. J. Critt. 7 cass. (Running Time: 10 hrs.). 1995. 60.00 (978-0-7887-4082-4(2), 96169E5) Recorded Bks.

***Hanging Valley.** unabr. ed. Peter Robinson. Narrated by James Langton. (Running Time: 8 hrs. 30 mins. 0 sec.). (Inspector Banks Mystery Ser.). 2010. 24.99 (978-1-4001-6270-3(X)); 16.99 (978-1-4001-8270-1(0)); audio compact disk 34.99 (978-1-4001-1270-8(2)); audio compact disk 83.99 (978-1-4001-4270-5(9)) Pub: Tantor Media. Dist(s): IngramPubServ

Hangjab Brothers in the Case of the Creatures from Calumet City. Created by Danny D'Agostino. 4 CDs. (Running Time: 4 hrs 42 mins). Dramatization. (YA). (gr. 5-9). 2002. audio compact disk 25.00 (978-0-935367-09-6(8)) Hillary Pr.
"Creatures From Calumet City" is a 4.7 hour comedy, sci-fi thriller, the first audio-movie-book produced in the US, featuring full dramatic acting, complete sound effects, and a digital electronic music score. The recording is sold as a 4 CD set,supplied in a jewel case, shrink wrapped. The sound effects and score and the acting bring the story alive, and allow the listener to "see" the entire action in one's mind's eye. The sound effects and score use state-of-the-art digital technology, including digital synthesizers and computer software. STORY CONTENT: Stan and Leroy Hangjab, two street-wise detectives from the Southside of Chicago, and the precocious 13 year old Richard T. McCormick, the 4th, rescue the city from the clutches of the evil genius Dr. Stein and his mutant, insect humanoids. Hear Mayor Daley erupt, "I want this situation turned 360 degrees around!" and the Chinese politicians, "Nobody in this room know nothing! Get better advice from dog!" The story has many other colorful comedy characters such as General George C. Patent (comedy spelling). "Creatures" is supported by an exciting web site, featuring audio samples.

***Hangman.** unabr. ed. Faye Kellerman. Read by Mitchell Greenberg. (ENG.). 2010. (978-0-06-204125-8(8), Harper Audio) HarperCollins Pubs.

***Hangman: A Decker/Lazarus Novel.** unabr. ed. Faye Kellerman. Read by Mitchell Greenberg. (ENG.). 2010. (978-0-06-200900-5(1), Harper Audio) HarperCollins Pubs.

Hangman's Beautiful Daughter. unabr. ed. Sharyn McCrumb. Narrated by Sally Darling. 7 cass. (Running Time: 10 hrs. 30 mins.). (Ballad Ser.: No. 2). 1993. 60.00 (978-1-55690-786-9(9), 93104E7) Recorded Bks.
A young preacher's wife, new to her husband's Appalachian parish, begins to understand her new neighbors when she helps the sheriff cope with the aftermath of a violent crime.

Hangman's Creek. unabr. ed. Matt Braun. Read by Gene Engene. 4 cass. (Running Time: 5 hrs. 30 min.). (Luke Starbuck Ser.: Bk. 1). 2001. 26.95 (978-1-58116-062-8(3)) Books in Motion.
Luke Starbuck got to be foreman of the largest spread in the Panhandle by knowing horseflesh and fistfights better than all other men. And when horse thieves decimate area ranches, Starbuck is called on to stop the lawlessness.

Hangman's Holiday & Other Stories. unabr. ed. Dorothy L. Sayers. Read by Ian Carmichael. 12 cass. (Running Time: 18 hrs.). (Lord Peter Wimsey Mystery Ser.: Bk. 9). 2000. 49.95 (978-0-7451-6661-2(X), CAB 1277) Pub: Chivers Audio Bks GBR. Dist(s): AudioGO
The incredible Mr. Egg is introduced, a salesman extraordinaire, whose powers of deduction are just as keen as Lord Peter Wimsey's.

Hank & Chloe. unabr. ed. Jo-Ann Mapson. Read by Kate Forbes. 8 vols. (Running Time: 12 hrs.). 2000. bk. 69.95 (978-0-7927-2229-8(9), CSL 118, Chivers Sound Lib) AudioGO.
33-year-old Chloe Morgan is a part-time waitress and horse trainer living in Southern California. Though surrounded by a troupe of colorful friends, the only creatures Chloe allows herself to love are Hannah, her German shepard, and Absalom, her horse. But a quirk in the weather and a sudden funeral service cause her to encounter Henry Oliver, a local college professor. The two are drawn to one another despite very different backgrounds.

Hank Ferguson: Behind These Walls. 1 cass. 9.98 (C-13) Folk-Legacy.
Country songs by a former inmate from Tennessee.

Hank of Hair: An Exquisite Danse Macabre. unabr. ed. Charlotte Jay. Read by Richard Aspel. 3 cass. (Running Time: 4 hrs. 30 min.). 1999. (978-1-876584-31-3(9), 590892) Bolinda Pubng AUS.
'For I prefer beauty always a little soured. When it comes to me as a spoonful of syrup, I spit it out' Gilbert Hand hasn't been the same since his wife died. He's moved to a dull but respectable hotel where silence seems to brood in the hall & stairway. In a secret drawer he discovers a long, thick hank of human hair & his world narrows down to two people-himself & the murderer.

Hank the Cowdog & Monkey Business. John R. Erickson. 2 cass. (Running Time: 2 hrs.). (Hank the Cowdog Ser.: No. 14). (J). (gr. 2-5). 1990. 16.95 set. (978-0-87719-182-7(4)) Lone Star Bks.

Hank the Cowdog & Monkey Business. unabr. ed. John R. Erickson. Read by John R. Erickson. 2 cass. (Running Time: 3 hrs.). (Hank the Cowdog Ser.: No. 14). (J). 2002. 17.99 (978-1-59188-314-2(8)) Maverick Bks.
A convoy of circus trucks is passing through the ranch. The last truck in the column hits a bump and a large red box falls off and comes to rest in the horse pasture. Hank and Drover investigate the box and discover that it contains a circus monkey. Pete advises Hank not to open it, but Hank's curiosity gets the best of him.

Hank the Cowdog & Monkey Business. unabr. ed. John R. Erickson. Read by John R. Erickson. 3 CDs. (Running Time: Approx. 3 hours). (Hank the Cowdog Ser.: No. 14). (J). 2002. audio compact disk 19.99 (978-1-59188-614-3(7)) Maverick Bks.

Hank the Cowdog & Monkey Business. unabr. ed. John R. Erickson. Read by John R. Erickson. 2 cass. (Hank the Cowdog Ser.: No. 14). (J). (gr. 2-5). 1998. 17.00 (21656) Recorded Bks.

Hank the Cowdog's Greatest Hits. John R. Erickson. Illus. by Gerald L. Holmes. (Hank the Cowdog Ser.). (J). (gr. 2-5). 1985. (978-0-318-61642-1(4)) Maverick Bks.

Hank Williams Story. John Garton. 4 CDs. (Running Time: 4 hrs.). (ENG., 2001. audio compact disk 24.95 (978-1-84240-009-8(6)) Pub: Chrome Dreams GBR. Dist(s): IPG Chicago
Charts the life and work of this renowned country musician and songwriting genius. With his troubled marriages and continual problems with drink and drugs, Hank Williams' life story makes fascinating, yet tragic listening.

Hanna & the Silver Unicorn. Jerry Cardinal. (YA). 2006. audio compact disk 10.00 (978-1-4276-1117-8(3)) AardGP.

Hannah-Barbera: Cartoon Sound FX. (J). 2002. audio compact disk 16.98 (978-1-56826-479-0(8), 71828) Rhino Enter.
Almost 100 cartoon sound effects for computers, home videos, parties and more, plus special-occasion greetings and answering machine messages by your favorite characters.

Hannah Coulter. unabr. ed. Wendell Berry. Read by Susan Denaker. 7 CDs. (Running Time: 8 hrs. 6 mins. 0 sec.). (ENG.). 2008. audio compact disk 23.98 (978-1-59644-533-8(5)) christianaud.

***Hannah Coulter: A Novel.** unabr. ed. Wendell Berry. Narrated by Susan Denaker. (Yasmin Peace Ser.). (ENG.). 2008. 14.98 (978-1-59644-534-5(3), christaudio) christianaud.

***Hannah's Dream.** unabr. ed. Diane Hammond. Read by Laura Flanagan. (ENG.). 2008. (978-0-06-177887-2(7), Harper Audio) HarperCollins Pubs.

***Hannah's List.** abr. ed. Debbie Macomber. Read by Tanya Eby & Fred Stella. 5 CDs. (Running Time: 6 hrs.). (Blossom Street Ser.: No. 6). 2010. audio compact disk 24.99 (978-1-4233-4785-9(4), 9781423347859, BACD) Brilliance Audio.

***Hannah's List.** abr. ed. Debbie Macomber. Read by Fred Stella. (Running Time: 6 hrs.). (Blossom Street Ser.). 2010. 9.99 (978-1-4418-9358-1(X), 9781441893581, BAD) Brilliance Audio.

***Hannah's List.** unabr. ed. Debbie Macomber. Read by Fred Stella. (Running Time: 10 hrs.). (Blossom Street Ser.: No. 6). 2010. 39.97 (978-1-4233-4784-2(6), 9781423347842, BADLE) Brilliance Audio.

***Hannah's List.** unabr. ed. Debbie Macomber. Read by Fred Stella. (Running Time: 10 hrs.). (Blossom Street Ser.: No. 6). 2010. 24.99 (978-1-4233-4783-5(8), 9781423347835, BAD); 39.97 (978-1-4233-4782-8(X), 9781423347828, Brlnc Audio MP3 Lib); 24.99 (978-1-4233-4781-1(1), 9781423347811, Brilliance MP3) Brilliance Audio.

***Hannah's List.** unabr. ed. Debbie Macomber. Read by Tanya Eby & Fred Stella. 9 CDs. (Running Time: 10 hrs.). (Blossom Street Ser.: No. 6). 2010. audio compact disk 87.97 (978-1-4233-4780-4(3), 9781423347804, BriAudCD Unabrid); audio compact disk 34.99 (978-1-4233-4779-8(X), 9781423347798, Bril Audio CD Unabri) Brilliance Audio.

Hannah's Miracle Child: How a Woman of Remarkable Faith Received Remarkable Results. Marty Copeland. (ENG.). 2006. audio compact disk 5.00 (978-1-57562-908-7(9)) K Copeland Pubns.

Hannah's Quest. rev. ed. Gina Beth Clark. 1 CD. (Running Time: 1 hr. 30 mins.). 2002. audio compact disk 19.95 (978-0-9712681-5-9(0), 043-010) G B C Audio Bk.

Hannah's Quest. rev. ed. Gina Beth Clark. 1 cass. (Running Time: 1 hr. 30 mins.). 2002. 19.95 (978-0-9717408-0-8(1)) G B C Audio Bk.

Hannah's Wreath. Kaye Jacobs Volk. 1 cass. 5.95 (978-1-57734-340-0(9), 07001924) Covenant Comms.

Hannibal, abr. ed. Thomas Harris. Read by Thomas Harris. 4 cass. (Running Time: 6 hrs.). 1999. 27.95 (FS9-51022) Highsmith.

Hannibal. abr. ed. Thomas Harris. Read by Thomas Harris. 5 CDs. (Running Time: 21600 sec.). (ENG.). 2006. audio compact disk 14.99 (978-0-7393-4343-2(2), Random AudioBks) Pub: Random Audio Pubg. Dist(s): Random

Hannibal. unabr. ed. Ernle Bradford. Narrated by Peter Jones. 7 cass. (Running Time: 9 hrs. 45 mins.). 1993. 60.00 (978-1-55690-810-1(5), 93119E7) Recorded Bks.
Biography of the brilliant, one-eyed Cartheginian general who swore eternal enmity to Rome at the age of nine; as commander of a vast polyglot army, he crossed the Alps bringing war to Italy, where he successfully campaigned for 15 years.

Hannibal. unabr. ed. Thomas Harris. Read by Daniel Gerroll. 8 cass. (Running Time: 12 hrs.). 1999. 32.00 (4975); 44.95 (978-0-7366-4568-3(3), 4975) Books on Tape.
Seven years have passed since Dr. Hannibal Lecter escaped from custody, seven years since FBI Special Agent Clarice Starling interviewed him in a maximum security hospital for the criminally insane. Starling has never forgotten her encounters with Lecter and the metallic rasp of his seldom-used voice still sounds in her dreams. Mason Verger remembers Dr. Lecter too, and is obsessed with revenge. He was Dr. Lecter's sixth victim and he has survived to rule his own butcher's empire. From his respirator, Berger monitors every twitch in his world-wide web. Soon he sees that to draw the doctor, he must have the most exquisite and innocent-appearing bait; he must have what Dr. Lecter likes best.

Hannibal, unabr. ed. Thomas Harris. Read by Daniel Gerroll. 8 cass. (Running Time: 13 hrs.). 1999. 39.95 (FS9-51203) Highsmith.

Hannibal, unabr. ed. Ross Leckie. Narrated by Paul Matthews. 8 cass. (Running Time: 11 hrs. 30 mins.). 2000. 73.00 (978-1-84197-084-4(0), H1092E7) Recorded Bks.
Hannibal, the most infamous, the most brilliant & most feared of Carthage's generals, was hated by the Romans for centuries after he died. Now Hannibal tells his own story, a story of love, strife, adventure & ultimately of war. Of all Rome's opponents, Hannibal came closest to annihilating her. Victory after victory followed him through Italy & he managed to maintain a mercenary army in Italy for almost 20 years.

Hannibal. unabr. ed. Ross Leckie. Narrated by Paul Matthews. 10 CDs. (Running Time: 11 hrs. 30 mins.). 2000. audio compact disk 101.00 (978-1-84197-166-7(9), C1284E7) Recorded Bks.

Hannibal. unabr. collector's ed. Ernle Bradford. Read by Walter Zimmerman. 6 cass. (Running Time: 9 hrs.). 1985. 36.00 (978-0-7366-0777-3(3), 1731) Books on Tape.
Examines the campaign during the Second Punic War when Hannibal set out to invade Italy with a small force of select troops, crossed the Alps with a full baggage train intending to take Rome. For sixteen years the campaign continued & Bradford examines the tactics of the major battles & traces the reasons, including political naivete, why Hannibal failed to conquer the Romans.

Hannibal Rising. unabr. ed. Thomas Harris. Read by Thomas Harris. (YA). 2007. 54.99 (978-0-7393-7487-0(7)) Find a World.

Hans Brinker or the Silver Skates. abr. ed. Mary Mapes Dodge. (Running Time: 50 min.). Dramatization. 10.95 (978-0-8045-1112-4(8), SAC 1112) Spoken Arts.

Hans Brinker or the Silver Skates, unabr. ed. Mary Mapes Dodge. Narrated by John McDonough. 8 pieces. (Running Time: 10 hrs. 15 mins.). (gr. 4 up). 1996. 67.00 (978-0-7887-0639-4(X), 94818E7) Recorded Bks.
Provides a fascinating look at daily life in Holland & has inspired generations of American children to appreciate the people & culture of this industrious country. The heartwarming story that made this Dutch boy a symbol for goodness & devotion.

Hans Brinker, or the Silver Skates. unabr. ed. Mary Mapes Dodge. Read by Christine Marshall. (Running Time: 32400 sec.). (J). 2006. 59.95 (978-0-7861-4356-6(8)); audio compact disk 72.00 (978-0-7861-7495-9(1)); audio compact disk 29.95 (978-0-7861-7810-0(8)) Blckstn Audio.

Hans Brinker or the Silver Skates, Set. Mary Mapes Dodge. Read by Flo Gibson. 6 cass. (Running Time: 9 hrs.). (J). 1990. 24.95 (978-1-55685-166-7(9)) Audio Bk Con.
A touching tour of Holland with the poor but valiant Brinker family & a young boy's skating excursion, full of Dutch history & art lore, culminating in the exciting race for the silver skates.

Hans Brinker or the Silver Skates, Set. Mary Mapes Dodge. Read by John McDonough. 8 cass. (Running Time: 10 hr. 15 min.). (J). (gr. 4). 1996. pap. bk. 77.75 (978-0-7887-1551-8(8), 40114) Recorded Bks.
This is the heartwarming story that provides a fascinating look at daily life in Holland.

Hans Bronson's Gold Medal Mission. Kathie Hill. 1994. 11.98 (978-0-7673-0806-9(9)); audio compact disk 85.00 (978-0-7673-0808-3(5)) LifeWay Christian.

Hans Bronsons Gold Medal Mission. Kathie Hill. 1995. 75.00 (978-0-7673-0807-6(7)) LifeWay Christian.

Hans Christian Andersen: His Poems & the Story of His Life. unabr. ed. Poems. Hans Christian Andersen. Read by Siobhan McKenna. 1 cass. 1984. 12.95 (978-0-694-50232-5(4), SWC 1366) HarperCollins Pubs.

Hans Christian Andersen: Holiday Fairy Tales. Based on a story by Hans Christian Andersen. (ENG.). 2007. 5.00 (978-1-60339-095-8(2)); audio compact disk 5.00 (978-1-60339-096-5(0)) Listenr Digest.

Hans Christian Andersen: Tales of Love & Wonder. Perf. by Mary-Ellen Bradley. 1 cass. (J). 1996. 10.00 (978-1-889777-00-9(5)) M-E Bradley Talecrftr.
Consists of storyteller's favorite tales from Hans Christian Andersen. Includes: "The Steadfast Tin Soldier," "The Nightingale," "The Princess & the Pea," "The Emperor's New Clothes".

Hans Christian Andersen & Tubby the Tuba. Read by Danny Kaye. 1 cass. (J). (gr. 3 up). 7.98 (237) MFLP CA.
Danny Kaye breathes his magic into the cobbler-turned-storyteller who journeys to the big city in search of his dreams. Includes: "The Ugly Duckling," "Tumbelina," "Inchworm" & others. Also includes Danny's rendition of the orchestral story of Tubby the Tuba who dreams of giving up his boring oom-pahs to play a real tune.

Hans Christian Andersen Classic Stories. Contrib. by Shirley Keller. As told by Diane Wolkstein. (Running Time: 3258 sec.). (J). (ps-3). 2005. audio compact disk 14.95 (978-0-87483-767-4(7)) Pub: August Hse. Dist(s): Natl Bk Netwk

Hans Christian Andersen in Central Park. Perf. by Diane Wolkstein. Music by Shirley Keller. Contrib. by Rachel Zucker. (Running Time: 53 min.). (J). (gr. k-6). 1977. 10.00 (978-1-879846-04-3(7)) Cloudstone NY.
Diane Wolkstein tells six Andersen favorites in her clear lively delivery. Highlighted by Shirley Keller on guitar, kazoo, & kalimba. Danish melody on recorder. Last song sung by Rachel Zucker, Diane Wolkstein's six year old daughter.

Hans Christian Andersen in Central Park. Read by Diane Wolkstein. 1 cass. (Running Time: 53 min.). (J). (ps-12). 1981. 8.95 (978-0-89719-933-9(2), WW713C) Weston Woods.
The author has been telling the stories of Hans Christian Andersen in New York City's Central Park since 1967. Collection includes "the Ugly Duckling," "the Emperor's New Clothes," & many more Andersen favorites.

Hans Christian Andersen Stories for Children: Grown-Ups May Listen If They Wish. unabr. ed. Hans Christian Andersen. Read by Aurora Wetzel. Tr. by L. W. Kingsland. 1 cass. (Running Time: 90 min.). (J). (ps up). 1997. 9.95 (978-1-887393-13-3(7), 036) Aurora Audio.
Includes: Side A: The Wild Swans; The High Jumpers. Side B: The Flying Trunk; Little Claus & Big Claus.

Hans Christian Andersen Stories for Grown-Ups: Children May Listen If They Wish. unabr. ed. Hans Christian Andersen. Read by Aurora Wetzel. Tr. by L. W. Kingsland. 1 cass. (Running Time: 75 min.). (J). (ps up). 1997. 9.95 (978-1-887393-11-9(0), 032) Aurora Audio.
Includes Side A: Story of a Mother; Five from a Peapod; She Was Good for Nothing. Side B: Everything in its Right Place; Gardener & the Family; Absolutely True.

Hans Christian Andersen Story, Set. abr. ed. Hans Christian Andersen et al. Read by Laurine Richards. 1 cass. (Running Time: 60 min.). (J). (gr. k-4). 1989. 9.95 Incl. picture cards. (978-0-938451-06-8(5)) Selena Pr.

Hans Christian Andersen's Best Known Stories. abr. ed. Hans Christian Andersen. 2 cass. (Running Time: 1 hr. 38 min.). Incl. Constant Tin Soldier. (J). (838); Little Match Girl. Based on a story by Hans Christian Andersen. (J). (838); Thumbelina. Illus. by Hans Christian Andersen. (J). (838); Tinder-Box. Based on a story by Hans Christian Andersen. (J). (838); Ugly Duckling. Robert Van Nutt. Illus. by Robert Van Nutt. (J). (838); (J). 12.95 (978-0-89926-150-8(7), 838) Audio Bk.

Hans de Back in Concert. Perf. by Hans De Back. 1 cass. (Running Time: 1 hr.). 10.00 (978-1-57863-057-8(6), Red); audio compact disk 16.95 (978-1-57863-056-1(8), Red) Red Wheel Weiser.
This widely-acclaimed Dutch sound therapist is rapidly becoming one of Europe's most gifted artists. Performing on Nepalese, Tibetan & Bhutan bells & bowls, 10 tone Chink drum & a Japanese 16-string koto, de Back keeps his audience spellbound. All pieces are interwoven with nature's sounds.

Hans Juergensen & John Ciardi: World War II. unabr. ed. Poems. Hans Juergensen. Read by Hans Juergensen. Read by John Ciardi. 1 cass. (Running Time: 29 min.). 1986. 10.00 New Letters.
These two authors & veterans share poems & tales about their World War II experiences.

Hansel & Gretel see Grimms' Fairy Tales

Hansel & Gretel see Uses of Enchantment: The Meaning and Importance of Fairy Tales

Hansel & Gretel see Hansel et Gretel

Hansel & Gretel. (J). 2005. pap. bk. 18.95 (978-0-439-80423-3(X)); pap. bk. 14.95 (978-0-439-80422-6(1)) Weston Woods.
The classic story of a woodcutter's two lost children, who find a house in the forest made of sweets and candy that belongs to a hungry witch. James Marshall's zany illustrations provide a fresh interpretation to this childhood favorite.

Hansel & Gretel. Read by Famous Theater Company Staff. 1 cass. (J). (ps-2). 2.98 (978-1-55886-032-2(0)) Smarty Pants.
A children's fairy tale about a brother & sister, an evil witch & a gingerbread house.

Hansel & Gretel. Naomi Fox. Illus. by Neal Fox. Narrated by Robert Guillaume. 1 cass. (Running Time: 15 min.). Dramatization. (Confetti Company Proudly Presents Ser.). (J). (ps-1). 1992. bk. 9.95 (978-1-882179-12-1(9)) Confetti Ent.
The Confetti Company, a cast of children, reenact the classic fairy tale with a modern upbeat tempo.

Hansel & Gretel. Read by Hollywood Studio Orchestra Staff. 1 cass. (J). (ps-2). 3.98 incl. poster. (978-1-55886-040-7(1)) Smarty Pants.

Hansel & Gretel. Adapted by Claudie Stanke. Illus. by Andre Pijet. 1 cass. (Running Time: 15 mins.). (Classic Stories Ser.). (J). (ps-2). audio compact disk 9.95 (978-2-921997-81-2(9)) Coffragants CAN.
You have to beware of strangers when you are alone. Their kindness may be a disguise. But sometimes you can outsmart bad people.

***Hansel & Gretel.** Weston Woods Staff. (J). audio compact disk 12.95 (978-0-439-80416-5(7)) Weston Woods.

Hansel & Gretel & Other Children's Favorites. (J). 2005. audio compact disk (978-1-933796-32-1(4)) PC Treasures.

Hansel & Gretel Classic Read along Audio Book. Prod. by PC Treasures Staff. (J). 2007. (978-1-60072-056-7(0)) PC Treasures.

Hansel et Gretel. Tr. of Hansel & Gretel. (FRE.). pap. bk. 12.95 (978-2-89558-055-3(3)) Pub: Coffragants CAN. Dist(s): Penton Overseas

Hansel et Gretel. Joujou Turenne. 1 cass., bklet. (Running Time: 50 mins.). (Best-Sellers Ser.).Tr. of Hansel & Gretel. (FRE., (J). (gr. k-3). audio compact disk 9.95 (978-2-921997-79-9(7)) Pub: Coffragants CAN. Dist(s): Penton Overseas

Hanukkah Lights: Stories from the Festival of Lights. unabr. ed. Chaim Potok et al. Read by Theodore Bikel et al. 2 cass. (Running Time: 2 hrs.). 2001. 18.00 (978-1-57453-459-7(9)) Audio Lit.
An inspiring, thought-provoking and often humorous anthology of Hanukkah stories.

Hanyu for Beginning Students. Peter Chang & Alyce Mackerras. 1 cass. 1993. 49.99 (978-0-88727-212-7(6)) Cheng Tsui.

Hanyu for Intermediate Students Stage 1. Peter Chang & Alyce Mackerras. 1 cass. 1993. 54.99 (978-0-88727-214-1(2)) Cheng Tsui.

Hanyu for Intermediate Students Stage 2, Vol. 2. Peter Chang & Alyce Mackerras. 1 cass. 1993. 47.99 (978-0-88727-240-0(1)) Cheng Tsui.

Hanyu for Intermediate Students Stage 3. Peter Chang et al. 1 CD. (Running Time: 1 hr. 30 mins.). (Hanyu Ser.). (CHI & ENG.). (YA). (gr. 10-12). 1999. audio compact disk 100.00 (978-0-88727-338-4(6)) Cheng Tsui.

Hanyu for Senior Students 4. Peter Chang et al. 1 CD. (Running Time: 1 hr. 30 mins.). (Hanyu Ser.). 2005. audio compact disk 100.00 (978-0-88727-296-7(7)) Cheng Tsui.

Hanyu Pinyin Workbook: Practice Using Hanyu Pinyin - - the standard romanization of Mandarin Chinese. Scripts. Jia-Fang Eubanks. Ed. by Curtis Eubanks. 1 CD. (Running Time: 66 mins). (CHI & ENG., (J). 2006. per. & wbk. ed. 15.95 (978-0-9778334-0-5(2)) Ahong Pub LLC.
The author reads the workbook text on the included audio CD.

Hap Palmer's Holiday Magic. Hap Palmer. 1 cass., 1 CD. (J). bk. 11.95 (EA649C); audio compact disk 14.95 CD. (EA649CD) Kimbo Educ.
New & traditional holiday songs selected to be enjoyed by all faiths.

Haphazard House. unabr. ed. Mary Wesley. Read by Jane Asher. 5 cass. (Running Time: 5 hrs. 5 min.). 1993. 49.95 (978-1-85089-655-5(0), 91072) Pub: ISIS Audio GBR. Dist(s): Ulverscroft US
When a painter sells every picture at his first one-man exhibition, he & his daughter, Lisa, back a winning horse with the proceeds making it possible to buy a romantic house on the Devon/Cornwall border.

HAPM Component Life Manual. Hapm Publications Ltd. Staff & Construction Audit Ltd. Staff. 2000. cd-rom 441.00 (978-0-419-24910-8(9), Spon) Pub: Routledge. Dist(s): Taylor and Fran

Hapm Life Manual Bk & CD. HAPM LTD. 1960. 450.00 (978-0-419-25990-9(2)) Taylor and Fran.

Happenin' Holidays. Mark Bradford. 1 CD. (Running Time: 1 hr.). Dramatization. 1998. pap. bk. 15.00 (978-1-58302-126-2(4), DHH-11) One Way St.
Collection of ten religious musical performance pieces created for use with puppetry.

Happenin' Holidays Through the Year. 2000. audio compact disk 15.00 (978-1-58302-158-3(2)) One Way St.
This Christian music has a great variety of upbeat, fun songs as well as strong message songs, to take you through a year of holidays.

Happenin' Hymns, Vol. 1. Mark Bradford. 1 CD. (Running Time: 1 hr.). Dramatization. 1997. pap. bk. 15.00 (978-1-58302-122-4(1), DHH-01) One Way St.
Collection of ten religious musical performance pieces, created for use with puppetry.

Happenin' Hymns, Vol. 2. Mark Bradford. 1 CD. (Running Time: 1 hr.). Dramatization. 1998. pap. bk. 15.00 (978-1-58302-124-8(8), DHH-02) One Way St.

Happens All the Time. Pamela Golden. 1 cass. 1993. (MPC7001) Miramar Images.

***Happens Every Day.** unabr. ed. Isabel Gillies. 1 Playaway. (Running Time: 6 hrs. 30 mins.). 2009. 59.75 (978-1-4407-2826-6(7)); 51.75 (978-1-4407-2823-5(2)) Recorded Bks.

***Happens Every Day.** unabr. ed. Isabel Gillies. Read by Isabel Gillies. 6 CDs. (Running Time: 6 hrs. 30 mins.). 2009. audio compact disk 72.75 (978-1-4407-2824-2(0)) Recorded Bks.

***Happens Every Day.** unabr. collector's ed. Isabel Gillies. 6 CDs. (Running Time: 6 hrs. 30 mins.). 2009. audio compact disk 29.99 (978-1-4407-2825-9(9)) Recorded Bks.

***Happenstance Found.** unabr. ed. P. W. Catanese. Narrated by Richard Poe. 1 Playaway. (Running Time: 8 hrs. 15 mins.). (Books of Umber Ser.: Bk. 1). (YA). (gr. 5-8). 2009. 59.75 (978-1-4407-2130-4(0)); 61.75 (978-1-4407-2121-2(1)); audio compact disk 87.75 (978-1-4407-2125-0(4)) Recorded Bks.

***Happenstance Found.** unabr. collector's ed. P. W. Catanese. Narrated by Richard Poe. 7 CDs. (Running Time: 8 hrs. 15 mins.). (Books of Umber Ser.: Bk.1). (YA). (gr. 5-8). 2009. audio compact disk 44.95 (978-1-4407-2552-4(7)) Recorded Bks.

Happiest Toddler on the Block: The New Way to Stop the Daily Battle of Wills & Raise a Secure & Well-Behaved One- to Four-Year-Old. Harvey Karp. Narrated by Johnny Heller. 8 CDs. (Running Time: 9 hrs. 30 mins.). 2004. audio compact disk 22.99 (978-1-4025-9431-1(3), 01822) Recorded Bks.

Happily Ever After. Pleasant Rowland. 5 cass. Dramatization. (J). (ps-1). 1990. 80.00 set. (978-0-201-28613-7(0)) AddisonWesley.
Readings of the ten folktales in the Happily Ever After Program, with simple aural & visual activities.

Happily Ever After & Feed My Sheep. Ed Pinegar. 1 cass. 1997. 9.98 (978-1-57734-110-9(4), 06005535) Covenant Comms.
Find out what everyone wants in a mate.

Happily-Ever-After Love Stories, More or Less. Read by Carol Birch. 1 cass. (Running Time: 47 min.). (J). 2004. 8.95 (978-0-89719-977-3(4), WW724C) Weston Woods.

Happily Married see Matrimonios Felices: Para mantener el amor Encendido

Happiness. (BI13A) Master Mind.

Happiness. Jack Boland. 1 cass. 8.95 (978-0-88684-089-1(9)) Listen USA.
Learn how to recognize happiness & how to be happy.

Happiness. Windham Hill Staff. 1 cass. 1998. 15.00 (978-1-56170-553-5(5)) Hay House.

Happiness: A Guide to Developing Life's Most Important Skill. Matthieu Ricard. 2 CDs. (Running Time: 7200 sec.). 2007. audio compact disk 19.95 (978-1-59179-555-1(9), AW01118D) Sounds True.

Happiness: Program from the Award Winning Public Radio Series. Hosted by Fred Goodwin. Comment by John Hockenberry. Contrib. by David Myers et al. 1 cass. (Running Time: 1 hr.). (Infinite Mind Ser.). 1998. audio compact disk 21.95 (978-1-888064-42-1(0), LCM 13) Lichtenstein Creat.
Happiness is an elusive state of mind. Often, the harder one looks, the harder it is to find. Yet, it may be as natural as breathing, and simply paying attention to our daily lifestyle choices may make us feel better. Dr. Goodwin explores several perspectives on the matter.

Happiness: The Novel Formerly Known as Generica. 2nd abr. ed. Will Ferguson. Narrated by Ron Halder. 3 cass. (Running Time: 4 hrs.). (ENG.). 2003. 19.95 (978-0-86492-367-7(8)) Pub: BTC Audiobks CAN. Dist(s): U Toronto Pr
In this hilarious send-up of America's self-improvement industry, an underpaid New York editor stakes his flagging career on the rambling magnum opus of a self-help guru only to realize that he's created a monster. Formerly known as Generica, Will Ferguson's satiric first novel won the Leacock Medal for Humour.

***Happiness Advantage: The Seven Principles of Positive Psychology That Fuel Success & Performance at Work.** unabr. ed. Shawn Achor. Read by Shawn Achor. (ENG.). 2010. audio compact disk 35.00 (978-0-307-74934-5(7), Random AudioBks) Pub: Random Audio Pubg. Dist(s): Random

Happiness & Inner Contentment: Cultivate & Experience Unconditional Happiness & Inner Contentment. Mark Bancroft. Read by Mark Bancroft. 1 cass., bklet. (Running Time: 1 hr.). (General Self-Development/Improvement Ser.). 1999. 12.95 (978-1-58522-017-5(5), 914, EnSpire Aud) EnSpire Pr.
Two complete sessions plus printed instruction manual/guidebook. With Healing music soundtrack.

Happiness & Inner Contentment: Cultivate & Experience Unconditional Happiness & Inner Contentment. Mark Bancroft. Read by Mark Bancroft. 1 CD, bklet. (Running Time: 1 hr.). (General Self-Development/Improvement Ser.). 2006. audio compact disk 20.00 (978-1-58522-065-6(5)) EnSpire Pr.
Two complete sessions plus printed instructionmanual/guidebook. With healing music soundtrack.

Happiness & Joy: Enjoy Every Day of your Life! Created by Christine Sherborne. (ENG.). 2007. audio compact disk 19.95 (978-0-9582712-1-9(6)) Pub: Colourstory AUS. Dist(s): APG

Happiness Cake. Linda Arnold. 1 cass. (Running Time: 45 min.). (J). (ps-3). 1988. 9.98 Incl. lyrics. (978-1-889212-01-2(6), CAAR2) Ariel Recs.
Original children's songs composed & performed by Linda Arnold.

Happiness Cake. Perf. by Linda Arnold. 1 cass. (J). (ps-7). 9.98 (234) MFLP CA.
Linda's heartwarming tunes & fresh, effervescent voice connect us with the innocence of childhood & its simple joys. Songs include: "Dinosaur Knocking at My Door," "Rockin' at the Zoo," "Our Family," & many more.

Happiness Cake. Perf. by Linda Arnold. 1 cass. (J). 10.98 (978-1-57471-449-4(X), YM122-CN); audio compact disk 13.98 (978-1-57471-453-1(8), YM123-CD) Youngheart Mus.
Songs include: "Barnyard Talk"; "Our Family"; "Rockin' at the Zoo"; "Abazaba Scooby Dooby"; "Pirate Song"; "Dr. DoReMi"; "There's a Lot of Magic in Tears"; "Mama Don't Allow"; "Be a Friend"; "L.O.V.E."; "Happiness Cake" & more.

***Happiness for Dummies.** abr. ed. W. Doyle Gentry. (ENG.). 2008. (978-0-06-176494-3(9), Harper Audio); (978-0-06-176495-0(7), Harper Audio) HarperCollins Pubs.

Happiness Hypothesis: Finding Modern Truth in Ancient Wisdom - Why the Meaningful Life Is Closer Than You Think. unabr. ed. Jonathan Haidt. Read by George K. Wilson. (Running Time: 11 hrs.). (ENG.). 2007. audio compact disk 39.98 (978-1-59659-097-7(1), GildAudio) Pub: Gildan Media. Dist(s): HachBkGrp

Happiness Is: Matthew 5:1-9. Ed Young. (J). 1978. 4.95 (978-0-7417-1030-7(7), A0030) Win Walk.

Happiness Is... Simple Steps to a Life of Joy. unabr. ed. A. R. Bernard. Read by Richard Allen. 3 CDs. (Running Time: 4 hrs. 0 mins. 0 sec.). (ENG.). 2007. audio compact disk 24.99 (978-1-4001-0556-4(0)); audio compact disk 49.99 (978-1-4001-3556-1(7)); audio compact disk 19.99 (978-1-4001-5556-9(8)) Pub: Tantor Media. Dist(s): IngramPubServ

Happiness Is a Choice. Frank Minirth & Paul Meier. Read by Frank Minirth & Paul Meier. 1 cass. (Running Time: 85 min.). (Minirth & Meier Home Counseling Audio Library). 1994. 9.95 (978-1-56707-037-8(X)) Dallas Christ Recs.
The symptoms causes & cures of depression.

Happiness Is a Choice. abr. ed. Barry Neil Kaufman. Read by Susan Clark. 2 cass. (Running Time: 3 hrs.). 1998. 17.95 (978-1-57453-259-3(6)) Audio Lit.
Reveals that people who are most successful at finding happiness, despite their widely varying life circumstances and backgrounds, share certain traits, beliefs and attitudes. Stories of people from all over the world illustrate the healing power of love and the limitless potential of the human spirit.

Happiness Is a Choice Set: New Life Clinic. Frank Minirth et al. 2 cass. (Running Time: 3 hrs.). (Minirth Meier New Life Clinic Ser.). 1995. 12.95 (978-1-886463-05-9(0)) Oasis Audio.
Depression is always curable. Clinical depression has many symptoms. Headaches, fatigue, anxiety, hopelessness & more. Helps the listener identify the emotional & spiritual causes & the steps to conquering the problem.

Happiness Is a Decision/Softening. Marianne Williamson. Read by Marianne Williamson. 1 cass. (Running Time: 90 mins.). (Lectures on a Course in Miracles). 1999. 10.00 (978-1-56170-229-9(3), M732) Hay House.

Happiness Is a Serious Problem. Dennis Prager. Read by Jonathan Marosz. 1999. 32.00 (978-0-7366-4467-9(9)) Books on Tape.

Happiness Is a Serious Problem: A Human Nature Repair Manual. unabr. ed. Dennis Prager. Read by Jeff Riggenbach. 4 cass. (Running Time: 5 hrs. 30 mins.). 1999. 32.95 (978-0-7861-1513-6(0), 2363) Blckstn Audio.
Prager, a lecturer & theologian, points out several aspects of what happiness is. He points out one must distinguish happiness from fun, avoid envy, not think of oneself as a victim, believe life has a purpose or meaning & develop a philosophy of life.

Happiness Is a Serious Problem: A Human Nature Repair Manual. unabr. ed. Dennis Prager. Read by Jonathan Marosz. 4 cass. (Running Time: 6 hrs.). 1999. 32.00 (4911) Books on Tape.
The author, a talk-radio host, asserts that we're actually obligated to be happy, because it makes us better people. Achieving that happiness won't be easy, though: to the author, it requires a continuing process of counting your blessings & giving up any expectations that life is supposed to be wonderful.

Happiness Is an Inside Job: Practicing for a Joyful Life. unabr. ed. Sylvia Boorstein. Read by Pam Ward. (Running Time: 14400 sec.). 2007. 19.95 (978-1-4332-0829-4(6)); 44.95 (978-1-4332-0832-4(6)); audio compact disk 29.95 (978-1-4332-0831-7(8)); audio compact disk & audio compact disk 45.00 (978-1-4332-0833-1(4)) Blckstn Audio.

Happiness Is an Inside Job: Practicing for a Joyful Life. unabr. ed. Sylvia Boorstein. Read by Pam Ward. (Running Time: 14400 sec.). 2008. audio compact disk 19.95 (978-1-4332-0830-0(X)) Blckstn Audio.

***Happiness Is Here - Simple Strategies for Staying Happy.** Read by Kellie Poulsen-Grill. Created by Kellie Poulsen-Grill. (ENG.). 2009. audio compact disk 30.00 (978-0-9843566-0-7(6)) Whirlwind OR.

Happiness Is... Humility: Matthew 5:3. Ed Young. (J). 1979. 4.95 (978-0-7417-1032-1(3), A0032) Win Walk.

Happiness Is... Meekness: Matthew 5:5. Ed Young. 1979. 4.95 (978-0-7417-1036-9(6), A0036) Win Walk.

Happiness Is... Mercy: Matthew 5:7. Ed Young. (J). 1979. 4.95 (978-0-7417-1039-0(0)) Win Walk.

Happiness Is... Mourning: Matthew 5:4. Ed Young. 1979. 4.95 (978-0-7417-1034-5(X), A0034) Win Walk.

Happiness Is... Persecution: Matthew 5:10-12. Ed Young. (J). 1979. 4.95 (978-0-7417-1044-4(7), A0042) Win Walk.

Happiness Is... Purity: Matthew 5:8. Ed Young. (J). 1979. 4.95 (978-0-7417-1040-6(4)) Win Walk.

Happiness Is... Reconciliation: Matthew 5:9. Ed Young. (J). 1979. 4.95 (978-0-7417-1041-3(2)) Win Walk.

Happiness Is Righteousness: Matthew 5:6. Ed Young. (J). 1979. 4.95 (978-0-7417-1037-6(4)) Win Walk.

Happiness Is Your Destiny. Stuart Wilde. Read by Stuart Wilde. 2 cass. (Running Time: 3 hrs.). 1996. 16.95 (978-1-56170-285-5(4), 297) Hay House.
You have a divine right to be happy!.

Happiness Lives Within You. unabr. ed. Trenna Daniells. Read by Trenna Daniells. 1 cass. (Running Time: 30 min.). (One to Grow on Ser.). (J). (gr. k-6). 1982. 9.95 (978-0-918519-09-2(8), SR68523) Trenna Prods.
An age old concept is explored as a young girl's search for happiness takes her around the world & into adulthood. In frustration she almost gives up & then finds her answer in a reflecting pool. True happiness in not found in things, money or other people but rather comes from within ourselves.

Happiness Lives Within You -the Girl Who Looked for Happiness. Trenna Daniells. Narrated by Trenna Daniells. (ENG.). (J). 2009. (978-0-918519-53-5(5)) Trenna Prods.

Happiness Makes up in Height see Robert Frost Reads

Happiness Now. Robert Holden. (Running Time: 2 hrs.). 16.95 (978-1-84032-164-7(4), HoddrStoughton) Pub: Hodder General GBR. Dist(s): Trafalgar

Happiness Now! Timeless Wisdom for Feeling Good Fast. Robert Holden. Read by Robert Holden. 2007. audio compact disk 39.95 (978-1-4019-2061-6(6)) Hay House.

***Happiness Project.** unabr. ed. Gretchen Rubin. Read by Gretchen Rubin. (ENG.). 2009. (978-0-06-200228-0(7), Harper Audio) HarperCollins Pubs.

***Happiness Project: Or, Why I Spent a Year Trying to Sing in the Morning, Clean My Closets, Fight Right, Read Aristotle, & Generally Have More Fun.** unabr. ed. Gretchen Rubin. Read by Gretchen Rubin. (ENG.). 2009. (978-0-06-199692-4(0), Harper Audio) HarperCollins Pubs.

Happiness Sold Separately. abr. ed. Lolly Winston. Read by Melinda Wade. (Running Time: 6 hrs.). (ENG.). 2006. 14.98 (978-1-59483-526-1(8)) Pub: Hachet Audio. Dist(s): HachBkGrp

Happiness Sold Separately. abr. ed. Lolly Winston. Read by Melinda Wade. (Running Time: 6 hrs.). (Replay Edition Ser.). (ENG.). 2007. audio compact disk 14.98 (978-1-59483-956-6(5)) Pub: Hachet Audio. Dist(s): HachBkGrp

Happiness Sold Separately. abr. ed. Lolly Winston. Read by Melinda Wade. (Running Time: 6 hrs.). (ENG.). 2009. 39.98 (978-1-60788-266-4(3)) Pub: Hachet Audio. Dist(s): HachBkGrp

Happiness, the Way of Life. Ormond McGill. 2000. (978-1-933332-14-7(X)) Hypnotherapy Train.

Happy: Simple Steps to Get the Most Out of Life. unabr. ed. Ian K. Smith. Read by Ian K. Smith. (Running Time: 5 hrs. 0 mins. 0 sec.). (ENG.). 2010. audio compact disk 24.99 (978-1-4272-0864-4(6)) Pub: Macmill Audio. Dist(s): Macmillan

Happy Anniversary: As it Happens. 2 CDs. (Running Time: 90 mins.). 2005. audio compact disk 19.95 (978-0-660-19223-9(3)) Pub: Canadian Broadcasting CAN. Dist(s): Georgetown Term

***Happy at Last: The Thinking Person's Guide to Finding Joy.** unabr. ed. Richard O'Connor. Read by Rick Adamson. 8 CDs. (Running Time: 10 hrs.). 2008. audio compact disk 79.95 (978-0-7927-5662-0(2)) AudioGO.

Happy at Last: The Thinking Person's Guide to Finding Joy. unabr. ed. Richard O'Connor. Read by Rick Adamson. 4 CDs. (Running Time: 5 hrs. 0 mins. 0 sec.). (ENG.). 2008. audio compact disk 24.95 (978-1-4272-0532-2(9)) Pub: Macmill Audio. Dist(s): Macmillan

Happy B-I-R-T-H-D-A-Y: Sing, Color'n Say. Phillip Siadi & Lenore Paxton. Read by Phillip Siadi & Lenore Paxton. 1 cass. (Running Time: 46 min.). (World of Language Activity Pack Ser.). (J). (ps-3). 1995. 5.95 (978-1-880449-28-8(5)) Wrldkids Pr.
Song, music, learning to say "Happy Birthday" in 10 languages, language lesson, narrative regarding birthday folklore, facts, celebrations in many countries. Companion coloring book included.

Happy B-I-R-T-H-D-A-Y: Sing, Color'n Say. 2nd ed. Lenore Paxton & Phillip Siadi. Read by Lenore Paxton & Phillip Siadi. 1 cass. (Running Time: 46 min.). (World of Language Activity Pack Ser.). (J). (ps-3). 1994. pap. bk. 7.95 (978-1-880449-09-7(9)) Wrldkids Pr.

Happy Birthday see Feliz Cumpleanos

Happy Birthday see Bon Anniversaire

Happy Birthday. abr. ed. Danielle Steel. (Running Time: 6 hrs.). 2011. audio compact disk 14.99 (978-1-4233-2097-5(2), 9781423320975, BCD Value Price); audio compact disk 26.99 (978-1-4233-2096-8(4), 9781423320968, BACD) Brilliance Audio.

Happy Birthday. abr. ed. Danielle Steel. (Running Time: 6 hrs.). 2013. audio compact disk 19.99 (978-1-4233-8878-4(X), 9781423388784, BACD) Brilliance Audio.

Happy Birthday. unabr. ed. Danielle Steel. (Running Time: 12 hrs.). 2011. 24.99 (978-1-4233-2092-0(1), 9781423320920, Brilliance MP3); 39.97 (978-1-4233-2093-7(X), 9781423320937, Brlnc Audio MP3 Lib); 39.97 (978-1-4233-2095-1(6), 9781423320951, BADLE); 24.99 (978-1-4233-2094-4(8), 9781423320944, BAD); audio compact disk 38.99 (978-1-4233-2090-6(5), 9781423320906, Bril Audio CD Unabri); audio compact disk 92.97 (978-1-4233-2091-3(3), 9781423320913, BriAudCD Unabrid) Brilliance Audio.

Happy Birthday. unabr. ed. Danielle Steel. (Running Time: 10 hrs.). 2013. 39.97 (978-1-4233-8875-3(5), 9781423388753, Brlnc Audio MP3 Lib); 39.97 (978-1-4233-8877-7(1), 9781423388777, BADLE); 24.99 (978-1-4233-8874-6(7), 9781423388746, Brilliance MP3); 24.99 (978-1-4233-8876-0(3), 9781423388760, BAD); audio compact disk 102.97 (978-1-4233-8873-9(9), 9781423388739, BriAudCD Unabrid); audio compact disk 38.99 (978-1-4233-8872-2(0), 9781423388722, Bril Audio CD Unabri) Brilliance Audio.

Happy Birthday: Personalized Happy Birthday Tape. Michael Rosenbaum. Perf. by Cindy Rosenbaum & Sheri. 1 cass. (Running Time: 18 min.). (J). (ps-5). 1995. 6.95 Happy Kids Prods.
5 personalized, original "Happy Birthday" songs that sings your child's name over 35 times. Songs include "Make a Wish", "The Great Birthday Surprise" & 3 others. Over 230 names available.

Happy Birthday, Danny & the Dinosaur! abr. ed. Syd Hoff. Illus. by Syd Hoff. (I Can Read Bks.). (J). (ps-3). 2007. 9.99 (978-0-06-133539-6(8), HarperFestival) HarperCollins Pubs.

Happy Birthday, Danny & the Dinosaur! Book & Tape. abr. ed. Syd Hoff. Illus. by Syd Hoff. 1 cass. (Running Time: 030 min.). (I Can Read Bks.). (J). (ps-2). 1999. 8.99 (978-0-694-70102-5(5), HarperFestival) HarperCollins Pubs.

Happy Birthday, Gus!/Feliz Cumpleanos, Gus! Jacklyn Williams. (Read-It! Readers: Gus the Hedgehog Orange Level Ser.). (J). (gr. k-4). 2008. audio compact disk 9.27 (978-1-4048-4458-2(9)) CapstoneDig.

Happy Birthday, Moon. 2004. 8.95 (978-0-89719-918-6(9)); cass. & flmstrp 30.00 (978-0-89719-518-8(3)) Weston Woods.

Happy Birthday, Moon. (J). 2004. bk. 24.95 (978-1-56008-031-2(0)) Weston Woods.

Happy Birthday Moon. 2004. pap. bk. 32.75 (978-1-55592-236-8(8)); 8.95 (978-0-7882-0304-6(5)); audio compact disk 12.95 (978-1-55592-873-5(0)) Weston Woods.

Happy Birthday Moon. (J). 2004. pap. bk. 18.95 (978-1-55592-805-6(6)); pap. bk. 18.95 (978-1-55592-773-8(4)); pap. bk. 38.75 (978-1-55592-822-3(6)); pap. bk. 38.75 (978-1-55592-788-2(2)); pap. bk. 32.75 (978-1-55592-237-5(6)); pap. bk. 14.95 (978-1-55592-657-1(6)) Weston Woods.

Happy Birthday, Moon. Frank Asch. 1 cass., 5 bks. (Running Time: 6 min.). (J). pap. bk. 32.75 Weston Woods.
Bear must travel across the river, through a forest & up a mountain to give his friend, the moon, a birthday present.

Happy Birthday, Moon. Frank Asch. 1 cass. (Running Time: 6 min.). (J). (ps-4). bk. 24.95 Weston Woods.

Happy Birthday, Moon. Frank Asch. 1 cass. (Running Time: 6 min.). (J). (ps-4). 1990. 8.95 (978-1-56008-107-4(4), RAC281) Weston Woods.

Happy Birthday, Moon. Frank Asch. 1 cass. (Running Time: 6 min.). (J). (ps-4). 1990. pap. bk. 14.95 (978-1-56008-032-9(9), PRA281) Weston Woods.

Happy Birthday, Moon; Rose for Pinkerton, A; Doctor de Soto; Leo the Late Bloomer. 2004. cass. & flmstrp (978-0-89719-754-0(2)) Weston Woods.

Happy Birthday, Mrs. Piggle-Wiggle. unabr. ed. Betty MacDonald & Anne Macdonald Canham. Read by Karen White. 3 CDs. (Running Time: 3 hrs. 38 mins.). (J). (ps-3). 2007. audio compact disk 24.00 (978-0-7393-6152-8(X), Listening Lib) Pub: Random Audio Pubg. Dist(s): Random

Happy Birthday Plus Jokes & Riddles. 1 cass. 1994. 5.98 (978-5-553-53180-5(2)) Peter Pan.

Happy Birthday, Sam. Pat Hutchins. Illus. by Pat Hutchins. Read by Linda Terheyden. 11 vols. (Running Time: 5 mins.). (J). (gr. k-3). 2005. pap. bk. 16.95 (978-0-87499-287-8(7)) AudioGO.
Even though he's a year older, Sam still can't reach doorknobs, light switches, or sink faucets. However, a thoughtful birthday gift of a chair from his grandfather sets things right.

Happy Birthday, Sam. Pat Hutchins. 1 cass. (Running Time: 35 min.). (J). (ps-3). 2001. pap. bk. 15.95 (VX-97C) Kimbo Educ.
Sam still can't reach doorknobs, light switches or faucets. His grandfather helps him out. Includes read along book.

Happy Birthday, Sam. Pat Hutchins. Illus. by Pat Hutchins. 14 vols. (Running Time: 5 mins.). 1994. pap. bk. 35.95 (978-1-59519-041-3(4)); 9.95 (978-1-59112-046-9(2)); audio compact disk 12.95 (978-1-59519-039-0(2)) Live Oak Media.

Happy Birthday, Sam. Pat Hutchins. Illus. by Pat Hutchins. 11 vols. (Running Time: 5 mins.). (J). 1994. pap. bk. 18.95 (978-1-59519-040-6(6)) Pub: Live Oak Media. Dist(s): AudioGO

Happy Birthday, Sam. unabr. ed. Pat Hutchins. Illus. by Pat Hutchins. Read by Linda Terheyden. 14 vols. (Running Time: 5 mins.). (J). 1994. pap. bk. & tchr. ed. 33.95 Reading Chest. (978-0-87499-289-2(3)) Live Oak Media.
Even though he's a year older, Sam still can't reach door-knobs, light switches, or sink faucets. However, a thoughtful birthday gift of a chair from his grandfather sets things right.

Happy Birthday to You! see Dr. Seuss Audio Collection

Happy Child for Happy Dreams. Read by Mary Richards. 1 cass. (Running Time: 45 min.). (J). 2007. audio compact disk 19.95 (978-1-56136-169-4(0)) Master Your Mind.

Happy Children. Barry Tesar. 1 cass. (Running Time: 1 hr.). (Subliminal Inspiration Ser.). 9.98 (978-1-56470-016-2(X)) Success Cass.
Subliminal program.

Happy Christmas. (Happy Christmas Ser.). 2005. audio compact disk 13.98 (978-5-558-77739-0(7)) Tooth & Nail.

Happy Couples School! Get Love's Gifts by Mastering Love's Challenges, Set. David Grudermeyer & Rebecca Grudermeyer. 2 cass. 18.95 (T-63) Willingness Wrks.

Happy Day. 2004. bk. 24.95 (978-0-7882-0550-7(1)); pap. bk. 14.95 (978-0-7882-0615-3(X)) Weston Woods.

Happy Day, the; Where Does the Butterfly Go When It Rains? 2004. 8.95 (978-1-56008-914-8(8)); cass. & flmstrp 30.00 (978-1-56008-679-6(3)) Weston Woods.

Happy Days. unabr. ed. Laurent Graff. (Running Time: 6 hrs. NaN mins.). 2009. 19.95 (978-1-4332-1589-6(6)); audio compact disk 28.00 (978-1-4332-1586-5(1)); audio compact disk 22.95 (978-1-4332-1585-8(3)) Blckstn Audio.

Happy Days. unabr. collector's ed. H. L. Mencken. Read by Daniel Grace. 8 cass. (Running Time: 8 hrs.). (H. L. Mencken Author Collection: Pt. 1). 1975. 48.00 (978-0-913369-92-0(6), 1002) Books on Tape.
Growing up in Baltimore a century ago.

Happy Days & Holidays. Perf. by Kayleen Anderson & Gary Romer. 1 cass. 1998. 8.00 (978-1-890672-15-7(7)) Phil Don.
Various songs of holidays.

Happy Dream. Kenneth Wapnick. 1 CD. (Running Time: 2 hrs. 20 mins. 11 secs.). 2007. 11.00 (978-1-59142-303-4(1), 3m137); audio compact disk 14.00 (978-1-59142-302-7(3), CD137) Foun Miracles.

Happy Easter. 2004. 8.95 (978-0-7882-0058-8(5)); cass. & flmstrp 30.00 (978-0-89719-596-6(5)) Weston Woods.

Happy Easter. Kurt Wiese. 1 cass., 5 bks. (Running Time: 4 min.). (J). pap. bk. 32.75 Weston Woods.
Mama Rabbit sends her children out to collect eggs to paint before Easter.

Happy Easter. Kurt Wiese. 1 cass. (Running Time: 4 min.). (J). (ps-4). 1989. pap. bk. 14.95 (978-1-56008-014-5(0), PRA336); 8.95 (978-0-89719-996-4(0), RAC336) Weston Woods.

Happy Easter, Gus! Created by Picture Window Books. (Running Time: 537 sec.). (Read-It! Readers: Gus the Hedgehog Orange Level Ser.). (ENG.). (J). (ps-4). 2008. audio compact disk 9.27 (978-1-4048-4534-3(8)) CapstoneDig.

Happy Endings. Trisha Ashley. 2009. 54.95 (978-0-7531-3396-5(2)); audio compact disk 71.95 (978-0-7531-3397-2(0)) Pub: Isis Pubng Ltd GBR. Dist(s): Ulverscroft US

Happy Ever After. abr. ed. Nora Roberts. Read by Angela Dawe. 5 CDs. (Running Time: 5 hrs.). (Bride Quartet Ser.). 2010. audio compact disk 14.99 (978-1-4233-6902-8(5), 9781423369028, BACD) Brilliance Audio.

***Happy Ever After.** abr. ed. Nora Roberts. Read by Angela Dawe. (Running Time: 6 hrs.). (Bride Quartet Ser.: Bk. 4). 2010. 14.99 (978-1-4418-9237-9(0), 9781441892379, BAD) Brilliance Audio.

Happy Ever After. abr. ed. Nora Roberts. (Running Time: 6 hrs.). (Bride Quartet Ser.). 2011. audio compact disk 9.99 (978-1-4233-6903-5(3), 9781423369035, BCD Value Price) Brilliance Audio.

Happy Ever After. unabr. ed. Nora Roberts. (Running Time: 10 hrs.). (Bride Quartet Ser.). 2010. 39.97 (978-1-4233-6901-1(7), 9781423369011, BADLE); 24.99 (978-1-4233-6900-4(9), 9781423369004, BAD) Brilliance Audio.

Happy Ever After. unabr. ed. Nora Roberts. Read by Angela Dawe. 1 MP3-CD. (Running Time: 9 hrs.). (Bride Quartet Ser.). 2010. 39.97 (978-1-4233-6899-1(1), 9781423368991, Brlnc Audio MP3 Lib); 24.99 (978-1-4233-6898-4(3), 9781423368984, Brilliance MP3); audio compact disk 92.97 (978-1-4233-6897-7(5), 9781423368977, BriAudCD Unabrid); audio compact disk 34.99 (978-1-4233-6896-0(7), 9781423368960, Bril Audio CD Unabri) Brilliance Audio.

Happy Failure see Melville: Six Short Novels

Happy Family; Old House; Drop of Water. unabr. ed. Hans Christian Andersen. Narrated by Aurora Wetzel. 1 cass. (J). (ps up). 1995. 9.95 (978-1-887393-08-9(0)) Aurora Audio.
Less familiar stories of HCA.

Happy Feet. Perf. by Fred Penner. 1 cass. (J). (ps-5). 1992. 10.98 (978-0-945267-50-8(9), YM083-CN); audio compact disk 13.98 (978-0-945267-51-5(7), YM083-CD) Youngheart Mus.
Songs include: "Happy Feet"; "You Can Count on Me"; "At the Codfish Ball"; "How Would You Feel If You Were a Wheel"; "Allergies"; "Red Red Robin"; "I Have a Heart"; "A Shine on Your Shoes"; "Oo Babba Loo"; "What You Need" & more.

Happy Feet & Silly Beat. Read by Joanie Bartels. 2 cass. (Running Time: 66 min.). (Magic Series Gift Collection). (J). pap. bk. set incl. 2 lyric bks. (978-1-881225-11-9(9)) Discov Music.
Two full length audio cassettes, plus two full color lyric books with words to dancin' & sillytime songs.

Happy for No Good Reason. Swami Shankarananda. 1 CD. (Running Time: 72 mins.). 2005. pap. bk. 24.95 (978-0-915801-10-7(8)) Rudra Pr.

Happy for No Reason: 7 Steps to Being Happy from the Inside Out. abr. ed. Marci Shimoff. Read by Marci Shimoff. Jack L. Canfield. Told to Carol Kline. (Running Time: 5 hrs. 0 mins. 0 sec.). (ENG.). 2008. audio compact disk 29.95 (978-0-7435-6843-2(5)) Pub: S&S Audio. Dist(s): S and S Inc

Happy Golden Years. 1 cass. 10.00 (978-1-58506-020-7(8), 47) New Life Inst OR.
Helps you enjoy the wonderful experiences & opportunities of your older years.

Happy Halloween, Gus!/Feliz Halloween, Gus! Jacklyn Williams. (Read-It! Readers: Gus the Hedgehog Orange Level Ser.). (J). (gr. k-4). 2008. audio compact disk 9.27 (978-1-4048-4462-9(7)) CapstoneDig.

Happy Hanukah: A Compact Disk to Celebrate the Festival of Dedication. Judith S. Rubenstein. 1 cass. (Running Time: 0.30). 2003. audio compact disk 15.99 Granite Hills Pr.

Happy Hanukah CD: Companion Recording of Happy Hanukah A Music Book to Celebrate the Festival of Dedication. Voice by Judith Rubenstein. 1 CD. (Running Time: 30 min.). 2002. audio compact disk 15.95 (978-1-929468-10-2(5)) Granite Hills Pr.
Hanukah songs parallel the music book: "Happy Hanukah: A Music Book to Celebrate the Festival of Dedication" sold separately ISBN 1929468067 $15.95. The songs you want to sing they way you want to sing them.

Happy, Happy Kwanzaa: Kwanzaa for the World. 1 cass. (Running Time: 13 mins.). (J). (gr. k-6). 1999. 6.95 (978-0-9673762-0-2(3)) BrassHeart.
A joyful ode to the African American celebration of thanksgiving & community. Side 1 has an original song that introduces the seven principles of Kwanzaa . An original story, "A Family Kwanzee," is on side 2.

Happy, Happy Kwanzaa: Kwanzaa for the World. Bunny Hull. Composed by Bunny Hull. Illus. by Synthia Saint-James. 1 CD. (Running Time: 20 mins.). (J). (gr. k-5). 2003. pap. bk. 16.95 (978-0-9721478-1-1(0), KCC/HHKCD810, Kids Creative Classics) BrassHeart.
Kwanzaa offers principles of life that can benefit us all, no matter what race, religion or culture. This package, used in schools, by teachers and families nationwide is one that provides a platform that shares these principles in a way that are simple and understandable by children. ?Happy Happy Kwanzaa?...the Kwanzaa song of choice in most elementary schools everywhere.

Happy, Happy Kwanzaa! Kwanzaa for the World with Book & Crayons. Synthia Saint James & Bunny Hull. Illus. by Synthia Saint James. 1 cass. (Running Time: 12 mins.). 2000. bk. 10.95 (978-0-9673762-2-6(X)) BrassHeart.
Includes original song along with story and sing-a-long coloring book.

***Happy Heart.** unabr. ed. Wanda E. Brunstetter. Read by Ellen Grafton. (Running Time: 3 hrs.). (Rachel Yoder - Always Trouble Somewhere Ser.). 2010. 14.99 (978-1-4418-1184-4(2), 9781441811844, Brilliance MP3); 39.97 (978-1-4418-1185-1(0), 9781441811851, Brlnc Audio MP3 Lib); 14.99 (978-1-4418-1186-8(9), 9781441811868, BAD); audio compact disk 44.97 (978-1-4418-1183-7(4), 9781441811837, BriAudCD Unabrid) Brilliance Audio.

***Happy Heart.** unabr. ed. Wanda E. Brunstetter & #5 Rachel Yoderndash;always Trouble. Read by Ellen Grafton. (Running Time: 3 hrs.). (Rachel Yoder - Always Trouble Somewhere Ser.). 2010. audio compact disk 14.99 (978-1-4418-1182-0(6), 9781441811820) Brilliance Audio.

Happy Holiday. abr. ed. Nina Mattikow. Perf. by Purple Balloon Players. 3 cass. (Running Time: 3 hrs.). Dramatization. (Triple Packs Ser.). (J). 1992. 11.95 Set. (978-1-55569-534-7(5), 23004) Great Am Audio.
The perfect way to celebrate the spirit of Christmas is with our happy little package filled with classic stories & songs.

Happy Holiday, Love Barney. 1 cass. (Running Time: 1 hr.). (J). 9.98 Long Cass. Blister. (978-1-57132-180-0(2), 9566) Lyrick Studios.

Happy Holiday, Love Barney. (J). 1997. 9.98 CD. Lyrick Studios.
The purple dinosaur croons traditional Christmas songs as well as some new holiday tunes.

Happy Holidays from Meeka & Her Cool Cousins. Perf. by Meeka. Contrib. by Art Halperin. 1 cass. (J). 10.98 (978-1-57471-443-2(0), YM114-CN); audio compact disk 13.98 (978-1-57471-446-3(5), YM114-CD) Youngheart Mus.
Songs include: "What Child Is This?"; "Xmas & Chanukah"; "Snow"; "Postcard to Grandma"; "Christmas in the Caribbean"; "What Was That?"; "Tick Tock"; "Christmas Again"; "O Christmas Tree"; "Don't Cut My Tree"; "Why Only on Christmas?" & more.

Happy Hour. Perf. by Salt of the Earth. 1 cass. 10.98 (978-1-57908-255-0(6), 1328); audio compact disk 15.98 CD. (978-1-57908-254-3(8), 1328) Platinm Enter.

Happy Hour Deck & Disc. 2002. pap. bk. 14.95 (978-1-931918-00-8(7)) Compass Labs.

Happy International Birthdays. Vicki Corona. 1 cass. (Running Time: 15 mins.). 1993. 14.95 (978-1-58513-078-8(8)) Dance Fantasy.

Happy Isles of Oceania Pt. I: Paddling the Pacific. unabr. collector's ed. Paul Theroux. Read by Michael Prichard. 8 cass. (Running Time: 12 hrs.). 1993. 64.00 (978-0-7366-2526-5(7), 3279-A) Books on Tape.
Theroux's true tale of paddling the Pacific in a kayak. He expected paradise - & found it.

Happy Isles of Oceania Pt. II: Paddling the Pacific. unabr. collector's ed. Paul Theroux. Read by Michael Prichard. 9 cass. (Running Time: 13 hrs. 30 mins.). 1993. 72.00 (978-0-7366-2527-2(5), 3279-B) Books on Tape.

Happy Lion. 2004. pap. bk. 14.95 (978-1-56008-086-2(8)); 8.95 (978-1-56008-141-8(4)) Weston Woods.

Happy Lion. Louise Fatio. 1 cass. (Running Time: 8 min.). (J). (ps-4). pap. bk. 12.95 (PRA363); 8.95 (RAC363) Weston Woods.
A lion in a Paris zoo tries to return his friends' visits by venturing into town to see them.

Happy Man see Donald Hall

Happy Marriage: A Novel. unabr. ed. Rafael Yglesias. Read by Grover Gardner. (Running Time: 13 hrs. 0 mins.). 2010. 79.95 (978-1-4417-2538-7(5)); audio compact disk 109.00 (978-1-4417-2539-4(3)) Blckstn Audio.

Happy Marriage: A Novel. unabr. ed. Rafael Yglesias. Read by Grover Gardner. (Running Time: 11 hrs. 30 mins.). 2010. 29.95 (978-1-4417-2542-4(3)) Blckstn Audio.

***Happy Marriage: A Novel.** unabr. ed. Rafael Yglesias. Read by Grover Gardner. (Running Time: 11 hrs. 30 mins.). 2010. audio compact disk 29.95 (978-1-4417-2541-7(5)) Blckstn Audio.

Happy Owls. 2004. 8.95 (978-1-56008-915-5(6)); 8.95 (978-0-7882-0273-5(1)); cass. & flmstrp 30.00 (978-1-56008-680-2(7)) Weston Woods.

Happy Place see Madeline & Other Bemelmans

Happy Prince see Favorite Children's Stories: A Collection

Happy Prince - The Canterville Ghost - Lord Arthur Saville's Crime see Principe Feliz - El Fantasma de Canterville - El Crimen de Lord Arturo Saville

Happy Prince - the Canterville Ghost - Lord Arthur Saville's Crime. Oscar Wilde. Read by Carlos Zambrano. (Running Time: 3 hrs.). 2002. 16.95 (978-1-60083-235-2(0), Audiofy Corp) Iofy Corp.

Happy Prince & Other Stories. Oscar Wilde. Read by Anton Lesser. (Running Time: 2 hrs. 30 mins.). 2002. 20.95 (978-1-60083-759-3(X)) Iofy Corp.

Happy Prince & Other Stories. Short Stories. Oscar Wilde. Read by Anton Lesser. 2 cass. (Running Time: 2 hrs. 32 mins.). (J). 1998. 13.98 (978-962-634-639-6(6), NA213914, Naxos AudioBooks) Naxos.
Includes the Happy Prince, The Remarkable Rocket, The Nightingale and the Rose, The Selfish Giant, The Young King, The Devoted Friend and The Star Child.

Happy Prince & Other Stories. unabr. ed. Oscar Wilde. Read by Johanna Ward. 4 cass. (Running Time: 5 hrs. 30 mins.). 1995. 32.95 (978-0-7861-0672-1(7), 1574) Blckstn Audio.
The Happy Prince lived in the Palace of Sans Souci, where sorrow was not allowed to enter, & only pleasure was experienced. Then, a gilded statue set on top of a high column allowed him to see all the wretchedness of the poor, the sick & the lonely who inhabited his great city. What develops is a story of sacrifice & redemption that is a parable for our time. This program includes nine of Oscar Wilde's magical & haunting fairy tales.

Happy Prince & Other Stories. unabr. ed. Oscar Wilde. Read by Walter Zimmerman. (Running Time: 82 min.). Dramatization. Incl. Remarkable Rocket. 1980. (N-44); Selfish Giant. (J). (gr. k-6). 1980. (N-44); 1980. 7.95 (N-44) Jimcin Record.
Heartwarming stories of charity, pride & love.

Happy Prince & Other Tales. unabr. ed. Short Stories. Oscar Wilde. Read by Anton Lesser. 2 CDs. (Running Time: 2 hrs. 32 mins.). (Junior Classics Ser.). (J). (ps-3). 1998. audio compact disk 17.98 (978-962-634-139-1(4), NA213912, Naxos AudioBooks) Naxos.
Includes: "The Happy Prince," "The Remarkable Rocket," "The Nightingale and the Rose," "The Selfish Giant," "The Young King," "The Devoted Friend " and "The Star Child.".

Happy Prince & Other Tales by Oscar Wilde. Oscar Wilde. (Running Time: 1 hr. 3 mins. 0 sec.). (PlainTales Classics Ser.). (ENG.). (J). (gr. 2-4). 2009. audio compact disk 12.95 (978-0-9819032-3-1(1)) Pub: PlainTales. Dist(s): IPG Chicago

***Happy Princess.** unabr. ed. Stephanie Perry Moore. Narrated by Debora Raell. (Running Time: 2 hrs. 30 mins. 0 sec.). (Carmen Browne Ser.). (ENG.). 2010. audio compact disk 12.98 (978-1-61045-086-7(8), christaudio) christianaud.

Happy Prisoner. unabr. ed. Monica Dickens. Read by Sheila Mitchell. 10 cass. (Running Time: 13 hrs. 12 min.). 2001. 84.95 (978-1-85695-425-9(0), 92081) Pub: ISIS Audio GBR. Dist(s): Ulverscroft US
Oliver has been confined to bed following the amputation of one leg & the effect of shrapnel scraping his heart. As he lies in bed, Oliver observes how his family are responding to the changing world as the war ends.

***Happy Reading, Happy Learning with Dr. Jean & Dr. Holly: Literacy Music Collection.** Created by Rourke Classroom. (ENG.). (J). 2010. audio compact disk (978-1-61590-439-6(5)) Rourke FL.

***Happy Reading, Happy Learning with Dr. Jean & Dr. Holly: Math Music Collection.** Created by Rourke Classroom. (ENG.). (J). 2010. audio compact disk (978-1-61590-440-2(9)) Rourke FL.

***Happy Reading, Happy Learning with Dr. Jean & Dr. Holly: Science Music Collection.** Created by Rourke Classroom. (ENG.). (J). 2010. audio compact disk (978-1-61590-441-9(7)) Rourke FL.

Happy Stories & Silly Songs: Stories & Songs That Encourage Children to Listen & Join In, Vol. 1. unabr. ed. Charlotte Rivera. Read by Charlotte Rivera. Perf. by Dennis O'Hanlon. 1 cass. (Running Time: 30 min.). (J). (ps-1). 1999. 10.00 (978-0-9671654-0-0(7)) Charlotte Rivera.
Incl. three stories & nine songs, both tradition & original.

Happy Thanksgiving, Gus!/Feliz Dia de Gracia, Gus! Jacklyn Williams. Illus. by Doug Cushman. (Running Time: 993 sec.). (Read-It! Readers: Gus the Hedgehog Orange Level Ser.). (J). (gr. k-4). 2008. audio compact disk 9.27 (978-1-4048-4460-5(0)) CapstoneDig.

Happy Thoughts with Sandy D. Dandelion & Friends. Holly Scarabosio. 1 CD. (Running Time: 5 mins.). (J). 2002. pap. bk. 13.95 (978-0-9721445-0-6(1)) Dande Prodns.

Happy Time Sing Along. 1 cass. (Running Time: 1 hr.). (J). 2001. pap. bk. 10.95 (KIM 1225C) Kimbo Educ.
Big band versions of Oh Susanna, Camptown Races, Home on the Range, Clementine, Yellow Bird & more. Includes guide.

Happy to Be Here. Perf. by Parachute Express Staff. 1 cass., 1 CD. (J). 7.98 (TLR 1011); audio compact disk 11.18 CD Jewel box. (TLR 1011) NewSound.

Happy Trails: More Western Themes. Perf. by Erich Kunzel & Cincinnati Pops Orchestra. 1 cass., 1 CD. 7.98 (TA 30191); audio compact disk 12.78 CD Jewel box. (TA 80191) NewSound.

***Happy Traum Bluegrass Pack: Includes Bluegrass Guitar book/CD & Easy Bluegrass & Country Guitar DVD.** Happy Traum. (ENG.). 2010. pap. bk. 39.95 (978-1-4234-9689-2(2), 1423496892) Pub: Homespun Video. Dist(s): H Leonard

Happy Tunes & More! Totally Terrific Tunes for Singing & Dancing. Pamela Ott. 1 cass. (Running Time: 1 hr. 30 mins.). 14.95 (978-1-886655-00-3(6), 85076) Corwin Pr.

Happy Tunes & More! Totally Terrific Tunes for Singing & Dancing. Pamela Ott. 1 CD. (Teaching Tunes Ser.). 2000. audio compact disk 14.95 (978-0-8039-6872-1(8), 85075) Corwin Pr.

Happy Valentine's Day, Gus!/Feliz Dia de la Amistad, Gus! Jacklyn Williams. Illus. by Doug Cushman. (Read-It! Readers: Orange Level Ser.). (SPA.). (J). (gr. k-4). 2008. audio compact disk 9.27 (978-1-4048-4456-8(2)) CapstoneDig.

Happy Wife Happy Life. Allen Jeff. 2004. DVD & audio compact disk 22.99 (978-1-894300-91-9(2)) Crown Video Dupl CAN.

Happy Woman Blues. Perf. by Lucinda Williams. Anno. by John Morthland. 1 cass. (Running Time: 35 min.). 1990. (0-9307-400030-9307-40003-2-8); audio compact disk (0-9307-40003-2-8) Smithsonian Folkways.
Songs include "Lafayette," "I Lost It" & "Happy Woman Blues".

Happy Women: Best of Women's Short Stories Volume 3. unabr. ed. Louisa May Alcott et al. Read by Juliet Stevenson & Harriet Walter. (Running Time: 5 hrs. 10 mins. 10 sec.). (Best of Women's Short Stories Ser.). (ENG.). 2009. audio compact disk 26.95 (978-1-934997-39-0(0)) Pub: CSAWord. Dist(s): PerseuPGW

***Happy Yoga 1.** abr. ed. Steve Ross. (ENG.). 2006. (978-0-06-135548-6(8), Harper Audio) HarperCollins Pubs.

***Happy Yoga 2.** abr. ed. Steve Ross. (ENG.). 2006. (978-0-06-135549-3(6), Harper Audio) HarperCollins Pubs.

***Harbor Lights.** unabr. ed. Sherryl Woods. Read by Christina Traister. (Running Time: 11 hrs.). (Chesapeake Shores Ser.). 2010. 19.99 (978-1-4418-5001-0(5), 9781441850010, Brilliance MP3); 39.97 (978-1-4418-5002-7(3), 9781441850027, Brlnc Audio MP3 Lib); 19.99 (978-1-4418-5003-4(1), 9781441850034, BAD); 39.97 (978-1-4418-5004-1(X), 9781441850041, BADLE); audio compact disk 19.99 (978-1-4418-4999-1(8), 9781441849991, Bril Audio CD Unabri); audio compact disk 79.97 (978-1-4418-5000-3(7), 9781441850003, BriAudCD Unabrid) Brilliance Audio.

Harbor of Hope Film Score. Prod. by Joshua Stone. 1 cass. 9.95 Aquarius Prods.
Contains music specially composed for the Harbor of Hope video, as well as other very relaxing, healing music. A great tape to use during a meditation.

Harbour Hill. unabr. ed. Judith Saxton. Read by Anne Dover. 8 cass. (Running Time: 10 hrs. 30 min.). (Sound Ser.). (J). 2003. 69.95 (978-1-84283-470-1(3)) Pub: ISIS Lrg Prnt GBR. Dist(s): Ulverscroft US

Harc: Inside Chants. Contrib. by Ruth Cunningham & Ana Hernandez. 1. 2005. audio compact disk 18.00 (978-0-89869-504-5(X)) Church Pub Inc.

Harcourt Ciencias Set: Text on Tape. Harcourt School Publishers Staff. (Harcourt Ciencias Ser.). (SPA.). (gr. 3 up). 2003. 133.50 (978-0-15-316901-4(X)) Harcourt Schl Pubs.

Harcourt Ciencias Set: Text on Tape. Harcourt School Publishers Staff. (Harcourt Ciencias Ser.). (SPA.). (gr. 4 up). 2003. 163.20 (978-0-15-316908-3(7)) Harcourt Schl Pubs.

Harcourt Ciencias Set: Text on Tape. Harcourt School Publishers Staff. (Harcourt Ciencias Ser.). (SPA.). (gr. 5 up). 2003. 207.70 (978-0-15-316917-5(6)) Harcourt Schl Pubs.

Harcourt Math: Bear in a Square: Big Book Cassette. 2nd ed. Harcourt School Publishers Staff. (J). 2002. 14.00 (978-0-15-321880-4(0)) Harcourt Schl Pubs.

Harcourt Math: Five Little Ducks: Big Book Cassette. 2nd ed. Harcourt School Publishers Staff. (J). 2002. 14.00 (978-0-15-321878-1(9)) Harcourt Schl Pubs.

Harcourt Science Set: Text on Tape. Harcourt School Publishers Staff. (J). (gr. 6). 1999. 109.20 (978-0-15-315439-3(X)) Harcourt Schl Pubs.

Hard-Boiled Detectives. Radio Spirits Staff. Read by Jack Webb. 10 CDs. (Running Time: 10 hrs.). 2007. 39.98 (978-1-57019-788-8(1), OTR 43732) Pub: Radio Spirits. Dist(s): AudioGO

***Hard-Boiled Wonderland & the End of the World.** unabr. ed. Haruki Murakami. Read by Adam Sims & Ian Porter. 11 CDs. (Running Time: 14 hrs.). 2010. audio compact disk 62.98 (978-962-634-338-8(9), Naxos AudioBooks) Naxos.

Hard Call: Great Decisions & the Extraordinary People Who Made Them. abr. ed. John McCain & Mark Salter. Read by John McCain & Daniel Hugh Kelly. (YA). 2007. 54.99 (978-1-60252-642-6(7)) Find a World.

Hard Call: Great Decisions & the Extraordinary People Who Made Them. unabr. abr. ed. John McCain & Mark Salter. Read by John McCain & Daniel Hugh Kelly. (Running Time: 8 hrs.). (ENG.). 2007. 14.98 (978-1-59483-944-3(1)) Pub: Hachet Audio. Dist(s): HachBkGrp

Hard Candy. unabr. ed. Andrew Vachss. Read by Phil Gigante. (Running Time: 7 hrs.). (Burke Ser.). 2010. audio compact disk 29.99 (978-1-4418-2115-7(5), 9781441821157, Bril Audio CD Unabri) Brilliance Audio.

***Hard Candy.** unabr. ed. Andrew Vachss. Read by Phil Gigante. (Running Time: 7 hrs.). (Burke Ser.). 2010. 24.99 (978-1-4418-2117-1(1), 9781441821171, Brilliance MP3); 24.99 (978-1-4418-2119-5(8), 9781441821195, BAD); 39.97 (978-1-4418-2118-8(X), 9781441821188, Brlnc Audio MP3 Lib); 39.97 (978-1-4418-2120-1(1), 9781441821201, BADLE); audio compact disk 79.97 (978-1-4418-2116-4(3), 9781441821164, BriAudCD Unabrid) Brilliance Audio.

Hard Currency. unabr. ed. Stuart M. Kaminsky. Narrated by Mark Hammer. 7 cass. (Running Time: 9 hrs. 45 mins.). (Inspector Porfiry Rostnikov Mystery Ser.: No. 9). 1995. 60.00 (978-0-7887-0412-3(5), 94604E7) Recorded Bks.
Leaving Russia on a routine investigation, Rostnikov flies to sunny Cuba. The assignment turns ominous, however, when the KGB wants an innocent man convicted of murder. With tropical intrigue, a pretty assistant & a few double agents, Rostnikov is trapped once again between his conscience & his country.

Hard Detective. unabr. ed. H. R. F. Keating. Read by Sheila Mitchell. 6 cass. (Running Time: 9 hrs.). 2000. 54.95 (978-0-7540-0555-1(0), CAB 1978) Pub: Chivers Audio Bks GBR. Dist(s): AudioGO
Detective Chief Inspector Harriet Martins has earned the nickname the "hard detective", but she's had to be unyielding to make it in a man's world.

Hard Eight. Janet Evanovich. Narrated by C. J. Critt. 7 cass. (Running Time: 10 hrs.). (Stephanie Plum Ser.: No. 8). 69.00 (978-1-4025-2385-4(8)) Recorded Bks.

Hard Eight. abr. ed. Janet Evanovich. Read by Lorelei King. 3 CDs. (Running Time: 3 hrs. 0 mins. 0 sec.). (Stephanie Plum Ser.: No. 8). (ENG.). 2005. audio compact disk 19.95 (978-1-59397-747-4(6)) Pub: Macmill Audio. Dist(s): Macmillan

Hard Eight. unabr. ed. Janet Evanovich. Narrated by C. J. Critt. 7 cass. (Running Time: 10 hrs.). (Stephanie Plum Ser.: No. 8). 2002. 37.95 (978-1-4025-2386-1(6), RG083) Recorded Bks.
Stephanie is hired to find a missing child. But things aren't always what they seem and Stephanie must determine if she's working for the right side of the law. Plus, there's the Morelli question: can a Jersey girl keep her head on straight when more than just bullets are aimed for her heart? And with the Plum and Morelli relationship looking rocky, is it time for Ranger to move in for the kill? Janet Evanovich's latest thriller proves that Hard Eight will never be enough.

Hard Eight. unabr. ed. Janet Evanovich. Narrated by C. J. Critt. 9 CDs. (Running Time: 10 hrs.). (Stephanie Plum Ser.: No. 8). 2002. audio compact disk 89.00 (978-1-4025-2965-8(1), C1854) Recorded Bks.

Hard Eight. unabr. rev. ed. Janet Evanovich. Read by Lorelei King. 9 CDs. (Running Time: 9 hrs. 0 mins. 0 sec.). (Stephanie Plum Ser.: No. 8). (ENG., 2002. audio compact disk 34.95 (978-1-55927-724-2(6)) Pub: Macmill Audio. Dist(s): Macmillan

Hard Evidence. John Lescroart. Read by David Colacci. (Dismas Hardy Ser.: No. 3). 2009. 90.00 (978-1-60775-522-7(X)) Find a World.

Hard Evidence. abr. ed. John Lescroart. Read by David Colacci. (Running Time: 6 hrs.). (Dismas Hardy Ser.: No. 3). 2008. audio compact disk 14.99 (978-1-4233-2309-9(2), 9781423323099, BCD Value Price) Brilliance Audio.

Hard Evidence. unabr. ed. John Lescroart. Read by David Colacci. (Running Time: 17 hrs.). (Dismas Hardy Ser.: No. 3). 2007. 39.25 (978-1-4233-2307-5(6), 9781423323075, BADLE); 24.95 (978-1-4233-2306-8(8), 9781423323068, BAD); 102.25 (978-1-4233-2301-3(7), 9781423323013, BrilAudUnabridg); audio compact disk 24.95 (978-1-4233-2304-4(1), 9781423323044, Brilliance MP3); audio compact disk 38.95 (978-1-4233-2302-0(5), 9781423323020, Bril Audio CD Unabri); audio compact disk 122.25 (978-1-4233-2303-7(3), 9781423323037, BriAudCD Unabrid); audio compact disk 39.25 (978-1-4233-2305-1(X), 9781423323051, Brlnc Audio MP3 Lib) Brilliance Audio.

Hard Fall. unabr. ed. Ridley Pearson. Read by Michael Russotto. 10 cass. (Running Time: 15 hrs.). 1993. 80.00 (978-0-7366-2528-9(3), 3280) Books on Tape.
When a flight training specialist is killed, it puts a FBI agent back on the trail of an elusive terrorist.

Hard Frost. unabr. ed. R. D. Wingfield. Read by Robin Browne. 12 cass. (Running Time: 14 hrs. 30 min.). (Jack Frost Ser.: Bk. 4). 2001. 94.95 (978-0-7531-0099-8(1), 970613) Pub: ISIS Audio GBR. Dist(s): Ulverscroft US
The body of an eight-year-old boy has been found, bound, gagged & stripped naked. Detective Inspector Jack Frost, who should have been on holiday, has had this case dumped on him, as no other officers were available. Then another boy is reported missing. The ransom demand: $25,000 or the boy dies like the first!.

Hard Frost. unabr. ed. R. D. Wingfield. Read by Robin Browne. 13 CDs. (Running Time: 19 hrs. 30 min.). (Jack Frost Ser.: Bk. 4). 2001. audio compact disk 99.95 (978-0-7531-1252-6(3), 1252-3) Pub: ISIS Audio GBR. Dist(s): ISIS Pub

***Hard Girls.** abr. ed. Martina Cole. Read by Nicola Duffett. (Running Time: 6 hrs. 8 mins.). (ENG.). 2009. audio compact disk 24.95 (978-1-4055-0728-8(4)) Pub: Little BrownUK GBR. Dist(s): IPG Chicago

Hard Landing. unabr. ed. Stephen Leather. 13 CDs. (Running Time: 15 hrs. 17 mins.). (Isis (CDs) Ser.). (J). 2004. audio compact disk 99.95 (978-0-7531-2315-7(0)) Pub: ISIS Lrg Prnt GBR. Dist(s): Ulverscroft US

Hard Landing. unabr. ed. Stephen Leather. Read by Martyn Read. 12 cass. (Running Time: 48000 sec.). (Isis Cassettes Ser.). 2004. 94.95 (978-0-7531-1974-7(9)) Pub: ISIS Lrg Prnt GBR. Dist(s): Ulverscroft US

Hard Light. Michael Crummey. Read by Ron Hynes. (Running Time: 4800 sec.). 2003. audio compact disk 19.95 (978-0-9734223-3-7(5)) Rattling Bks CAN.

Hard Look at Comparisons. unabr. ed. Bernice P. Grebner. Read by Bernice P. Grebner. (Running Time: 90 min.). 1988. 8.95 (729) Am Fed Astrologers.
Describes the impact of hard aspects in Comparison Charts.

Hard Love. unabr. ed. Ellen Wittlinger. Read by Mark Webber. 3 cass. (Running Time: 4 hrs. 58 mins.). (J). (gr. 7 up). 2004. 30.00

(978-0-8072-8866-5(7), Listening Lib); pap. bk. 38.00 (978-0-8072-0865-6(5), LYA 283 SP, Listening Lib) Random Audio Pubg.
When John first meets Marisol, their friendship is based on a shared interest in homemade zines, dysfunctional families and dreams of escape. Unfortunately, John mistakes their growing intimacy for love, and a disastrous date to his junior prom leaves that friendship in ruins. As John attempts to fix things, he realizes just how hard love can be.

Hard Metal. 1 CD. 2003. audio compact disk (978-1-932616-02-6(0)) Feng Shui Para.
If You are the Element HARD METAL...In Feng Shui you are the personal Trigram CHIEN (pronounced "chi'n") and you represent the oldest male - or the EmperorWhen in balance, you are organized, focused, analytical, insightful and wise. You are a brilliant trail blazer, extremely creative and original in your thoughts and ideas and you are a powerful leader, too.When you are not in balance, you can be defensive, withdrawn, picky, arrogant, self absorbed, emotionally unavailable, isolated, detached and sorrowful.The above is just a brief excerpt from the HARD METAL audio program. Discover the hidden mysteries of your life, recorded in China's ancient art, history and science. Learn about your lucky number and season, along with the kind of homes and offices that support you, and the types of locations that can deplete your business, health and finances. You will learn specific power directions to help you negotiate a sale, communicate with your friends and family, increase your wealth, improve your health, along with optimum directions to capitalize on to enhance love and good fortune in your life. This and more is available, today, on Suzee's audio program... HARD METAL.

Hard Optimism Audio: How to Succeed in a World Where Positive Wins. Price Pritchett. Narrated by Eric Conger. (ENG.). 2007. 9.95 (978-0-944002-44-5(7)) Pritchett.

Hard Prayer (audio CD) Galway Kinnell. (ENG.). 2007. audio compact disk 12.95 (978-1-57970-459-9(X), Audio-For) J Norton Pubs.

Hard Rain. abr. ed. David A. Rollins. (Running Time: 6 hrs.). 2009. audio compact disk 26.95 (978-1-4233-3268-8(7), 9781423332688, BACD) Brilliance Audio.

Hard Rain. unabr. ed. Barry Eisler. Read by Dick Hill. 7 cass. (Running Time: 10 hrs.). (John Rain Ser.: Bk. 2). 2003. 32.95 (978-1-59086-954-3(0), 1590869540, BAU); 82.25 (978-1-59086-955-0(9), 1590869559, Unabridge Lib Edns) Brilliance Audio.
John Rain - half-Japanese, half-American, raised in both countries but at home in neither - is trying to leave his life as a freelance assassin. After killing a CIA officer who hunted him halfway around the globe, Rain goes underground, hoping to find the peace that has eluded him. But then Tatsu, his old nemesis from the Japanese FBI, comes to him with one last job: to find and eliminate a killer at large, a creature with neither compassion nor compunction, whose activities could tip the balance of power in Japan's corrupt politics and who seems to have designs on Rain's few friends. To protect them, Rain will have to pursue his most dangerous quarry yet through the crosshairs of the CIA and the Japanese mafia, where the differences between friend and foe and truth and deceit are as murky as the rain-slicked streets of Tokyo.

Hard Rain. unabr. ed. Barry Eisler. Read by Dick Hill. (Running Time: 36000 sec.). (John Rain Ser.: Bk. 2). 2004. audio compact disk 39.25 (978-1-59335-637-8(4), 1593356374, Brinc Audio MP3 Lib) Brilliance Audio.

Hard Rain. unabr. ed. Barry Eisler. Read by Dick Hill. (Running Time: 10 hrs.). (John Rain Ser.). 2004. 24.95 (978-1-59710-338-1(1), 1597103381, BAD) Brilliance Audio.

Hard Rain. unabr. ed. Barry Eisler. Read by Dick Hill. (Running Time: 10 hrs.). (John Rain Ser.: Bk. 2). 2004. 39.25 (978-1-59710-339-8(X), 159710339X, BADLE) Brilliance Audio.

Hard Rain. unabr. ed. Barry Eisler. Read by Dick Hill. (Running Time: 10 hrs.). (John Rain Ser.: Bk. 2). 2004. 24.95 (978-1-59335-213-4(1), 1593352131) Soulmate Audio Bks.

***Hard Rain.** unabr. ed. Barry Eisler. Read by Dick Hill. (Running Time: 10 hrs.). 2010. audio compact disk 29.99 (978-1-4418-4107-0(5), 9781441841070, Bril Audio CD Unabri); audio compact disk 89.97 (978-1-4418-4108-7(3), 9781441841087, BriAudCD Unabrid) Brilliance Audio.

Hard Rain. unabr. ed. David Rollins. Read by Mel Foster. (Running Time: 14 hrs.). (Vin Cooper Ser.). 2010. 24.99 (978-1-4233-3266-4(0), 9781423332664, BAD); 39.97 (978-1-4233-3265-7(2), 9781423332657, Brinc Audio MP3 Lib); 39.97 (978-1-4233-3267-1(9), 9781423332671, BADLE); audio compact disk 97.97 (978-1-4233-3263-3(6), 9781423332633, BriAudCD Unabrid) Brilliance Audio.

Hard Rain. unabr. ed. David A. Rollins. Read by Mel Foster. (Running Time: 14 hrs.). (Vin Cooper Ser.). 2010. 24.99 (978-1-4233-3264-0(4), 9781423332640, Brilliance MP3); audio compact disk 36.99 (978-1-4233-3262-6(8), 9781423332626, Bril Audio CD Unabri) Brilliance Audio.

Hard Revolution. abr. ed. George P. Pelecanos. Read by Lance Reddick. (ENG.). 2005. 14.98 (978-1-59483-234-5(X)) Pub: Hachet Audio. Dist(s): HachBkGrp

Hard Revolution: A Novel. George P. Pelecanos. Read by Charles Canada. 7 vols. 2004. bk. 59.95 (978-0-7927-3184-9(0), CSL 640, Chivers Sound Lib); bk. 79.95 (978-0-7927-3185-6(9), SLD 640, Chivers Sound Lib); bk. 29.95 (978-0-7927-3186-3(7), CMP 640, Chivers Sound Lib) AudioGO.

Hard Revolution: A Novel. abr. ed. George P. Pelecanos. Read by Lance Reddick. (Running Time: 6 hrs.). (ENG.). 2009. 49.98 (978-1-60024-577-0(3)) Pub: Hachet Audio. Dist(s): HachBkGrp

Hard Row. unabr. ed. Margaret Maron. Read by C. J. Critt. 8 cass. (Running Time: 9 hrs.). (Deborah Knott Mystery Ser.: No. 13). 2007. 67.75 (978-1-4281-5599-2(6)); audio compact disk 92.75 (978-1-4281-5601-2(1)) Recorded Bks.

Hard Scrabble. unabr. collector's ed. John Graves. Read by Wolfram Kandinsky. 8 cass. (Running Time: 12 hrs.). 1993. 64.00 (978-0-7366-2473-2(2), 3236) Books on Tape.
John Graves wrests a home & a living for his family out of 400 acres of rough Texas hill country.

Hard Stop. unabr. ed. Chris Knopf. (Running Time: 10 hrs. 0 mins.). (ENG.). 2009. 29.95 (978-1-4332-5881-7(1)); audio compact disk 24.95 (978-1-4332-5880-0(3)) Blckstn Audio.

Hard Stop: A Sam Acquillo Hamptons Mystery. unabr. ed. Chris Knopf. (Running Time: 10 hrs. 0 mins.). (ENG.). 2009. 59.95 (978-1-4332-5877-0(3)); audio compact disk 80.00 (978-1-4332-5878-7(1)) Blckstn Audio.

Hard Tack & Coffee. unabr. ed. John D. Billings. Read by David Hilder. 7 cass. (Running Time: 10 hrs.). 2000. 49.95 (978-0-7861-1856-4(3), 2655) Blckstn Audio.
Provides a fascinating first-person look at everyday life for the footsoldier in the U.S. Army of one hundred years ago.The author served in the Army of the Potomac.

Hard Tack & Coffee: Life in the Army of the Potomac. unabr. ed. John D. Billings. Read by Jim Roberts. 9 cass. (Running Time: 13 hrs. 30 min.). 1993. 54.00 set in vinyl album. (C-240) Jimcin Record.
This first person account of the life of a Union soldier during the Civil War was first published in 1888 & became an immediate best seller.

***Hard Tack & Coffee: Or the Unwritten Story of Army Life.** unabr. ed. John D. Billings. Read by Edward Lewis. (Running Time: 10 hrs.). 2010. 29.95 (978-1-4417-4180-6(1)); audio compact disk 90.00 (978-1-4417-4177-6(1)) Blckstn Audio.

Hard Target, Set. abr. ed. Robert Tine. Read by Arnold Vosloo. 2 cass. (Running Time: 3 hrs.). 1993. 16.95 (978-1-56876-015-5(9)) Soundlines Ent.
An ungodly crime in the French Quarter of New Orleans brings Natasha Binder to enlist the help of Chance Boudreaux to help find her missing father. They stumble onto a group of insidious sportsmen who use humans as targets. Now they have vowed to hunt Chance to his death, but he is downright impossible to kill.

Hard Texas Winter. unabr. ed. Preston Lewis. Read by Rusty Nelson. 4 cass. (Running Time: 5 hrs. 18 min.). 1998. 26.95 (978-1-55686-820-7(0)) Books in Motion.
Crippled & embittered by the war, Morgan Garrett left his native Alabama to seek a new life in the West.

Hard Time. abr. ed. Sara Paretsky. Contrib. by Jean Smart. 2008. 59.99 (978-1-60640-664-9(7)) Find a World.

Hard Time. unabr. ed. Sara Paretsky. Read by Jean Smart. 8 cass. (Running Time: 12 hrs.). (V. I. Warshawski Novel Ser.). 2001. 40.00 (978-1-59040-005-0(4), Phoenix Audio) Pub: Amer Intl Pub. Dist(s): PerseuPGW
On her way home from a party, V. I. stops to help a woman lying in the street. Her Good Samaritan act sends her straight into a case that exposes dark hidden truths behind the razzle-dazzle of the entertainment industry.

Hard Time, Set. abr. ed. Sara Paretsky. Read by Jean Smart. 4 cass. (V. I. Warshawski Novel Ser.). 1999. 25.00 (FS9-51084) Highsmith.

Hard Times. Charles Dickens. Contrib. by John Woodvine et al. 4 CDs. (Running Time: 4 hrs.). 2006. audio compact disk 49.95 (978-0-7927-4329-3(6), BBCD 156) AudioGO.

Hard Times. Charles Dickens. 4 cass. (Running Time: 4 hrs.). 1998. 24.35 Set. (978-0-563-55755-5(9)) BBC WrldWd GBR.
A novel of unresolvable tensions & contradictions & wonderfully entertaining.

Hard Times. Charles Dickens. Read by Fredrick Davidson. 9 CDs. (Running Time: 11 hrs. 30 mins.). 2004. audio compact disk 81.00 (978-0-7861-8145-2(1), 1448) Blckstn Audio.

Hard Times. Charles Dickens. Read by Stephen Thorne. 9 cass. (Running Time: 10 hrs. 30 min.). 59.95 (CC/019) C to C Cassettes.
A portrait of life in a Lancashire mill town in the 1840's.

Hard Times. Charles Dickens. Read by Harriet Walter. 2 cass. (Running Time: 3 hrs.). 1996. 12.00 Set. (978-1-878427-53-3(9), XC449) Cimino Pub Grp.
Set in the North of England during the 19th Century. Thomas Gradgrind's advice to his two children, Louisa & young Tom, on how to become "models" in society is set against a background of wealth & poverty, where the rich marry for money & the poor cannot afford to divorce, where greed leads to gambling & crime, where the rich rule & the poor suffer. "Hard Times" is full of drama, love, comedy, pathos & finally a slender thread of hope.

Hard Times. Charles Dickens. Read by Anton Lesser. (Running Time: 4 hrs.). 2001. 24.95 (978-1-60083-760-9(3)) Iofy Corp.

Hard Times. Based on a book by Charles Dickens. Abr. by Deems Weldon. 2007. 5.00 (978-1-60339-113-9(4)); audio compact disk 5.00 (978-1-60339-114-6(2)) Listenr Digest.

Hard Times. Charles Dickens. Read by Anton Lesser. 3 cass. (Running Time: 4 hrs.). (Works of Charles Dickens). 1997. 17.98 (978-962-634-610-5(8), NA311014, Naxos AudioBooks) Naxos.
In this openly political novel, discover the terrible human consequences of a ruthless materialistic philosophy in the lives of the Gradgrind family, brought up to believe that only "Facts! Facts! Facts!" have any meaning.

Hard Times. Charles Dickens. Read by Paul Scofield. 2 cass. (Running Time: 3 hrs.). 2001. (N Millennium Audio) New Millenn Enter.

***Hard Times.** Charles Dickens. Narrated by Flo Gibson. (ENG.). 2010. audio compact disk 31.95 (978-1-60646-174-7(5)) Audio Bk Con.

Hard Times. abr. ed. Charles Dickens. 2001. 7.95 (978-1-57815-238-4(0), Media Bks Audio) Media Bks NJ.

Hard Times. abr. ed. Charles Dickens. Read by Anton Lesser. 3 CDs. (Running Time: 4 hrs.). (Works of Charles Dickens). 1997. audio compact disk 22.98 (978-962-634-110-0(6), NA311012, Naxos AudioBooks) Naxos.
In this openly political novel, discover the terrible human consequences of ruthless materialistic philosophy in the lives of the Gradgrind family, brought up to believe that only "Facts! Facts! Facts!" have any meaning.

Hard Times. abr. ed. Charles Dickens. Perf. by Paul Scofield. 2 cass. (Running Time: 3 hrs.). (Ultimate Classics Ser.). 2004. 18.00 (978-1-931056-64-9(1), N Millennium Audio) New Millenn Enter.
In the squalor of a textile town, successful businessman and arch-pragmatist Thomas Gradgrind, proclaiming that he is a self-made, teaches his children to suppress their imaginations and embrace hard facts. He arranges the marriage of his daughter Louisa to Josiah Bounderby, an unattractive, boastful manufacturer who is thirty years older than she. Gradgrind believes that eh has succeeded as a father when his son Thomas goes to work in Bounderby's bank. When Tom steals from his employer and Louisa flees the horrors of her marriage, Gradgrind must acknowledge the error of his lifelong devotion to facts and utility.

Hard Times. abr. ed. Charles Dickens. Read by Paul Scofield. 3 CDs. (Running Time: 3 hrs.). 2004. audio compact disk 24.95 (978-1-59007-574-6(9)) Pub: New Millenn Enter. Dist(s): PerseuPGW

Hard Times. unabr. ed. Charles Dickens. 8 cass. (Running Time: 11 hrs.). 2003. 34.95 (978-1-57270-336-0(9)) Pub: Audio Partners. Dist(s): PerseuPGW
Dickens' powerful and withering portrait of Coketown, a Lancashire mill town, in the 1840s. The novel is particularly harsh in indicting England's educational system, represented by Thomas Gradgrind, who runs a school in which he focuses on driving wonder, fancy, and imagination from children's minds to be replaced only by facts. Gradgrind finally sees the error of his ways and abandons Utilitarianism and resolves to learn the "philosophy" of the circus.

Hard Times. unabr. ed. Charles Dickens. Read by Frederick Davidson. 8 cass. (Running Time: 11 hrs. 30 mins.). 1994. 56.95 (978-0-7861-0497-0(X), 1448) Blckstn Audio.
Thomas Gradgrind is a practical man who believes in facts & statistics & has brought up his two children Louisa & Tom accordingly, thoroughly suppressing the imaginative sides of their nature. They are raised in ignorance of love & affection, & the consequences are devastating. No other work of Dickens presents so harsh an indictment against the attitude of life he associated with Utilitarianism. With savage bitterness he exposes the devilish institutions that exploited the vulnerable labor class.

Hard Times. unabr. ed. Charles Dickens. Read by Frederick Davidson. (Running Time: 41400 sec.). 2007. 19.95 (978-0-7861-4827-1(6)); audio compact disk 19.95 (978-0-7861-6148-5(5)); audio compact disk 29.95 (978-0-7861-7164-4(2)) Blckstn Audio.

Hard Times. unabr. ed. Charles Dickens. Read by Martin Jarvis. 8 cass. (Running Time: 12 hrs.). 2000. 59.95 (978-0-7540-0084-6(2), CAB 1507) Pub: Chivers Audio Bks GBR. Dist(s): AudioGO
A powerful and withering portrait of a Lancashire mill town in the 1840's.

Hard Times. unabr. ed. Charles Dickens. Read by Martin Jarvis. 8 CDs. (Running Time: 12 hrs.). 2001. audio compact disk 79.95 (978-0-7540-5423-8(3), CCD 114) Pub: Chivers Audio Bks GBR. Dist(s): AudioGO
Portrait of a Lancashire mill town in the 1840's. In the persons of Gangrind and Bouderby he stigmatized the prevalent philosophy of Utilitarianism which allowed human beings to be enslaved to machines and reduced to numbers.

Hard Times. unabr. ed. Charles Dickens. Read by Martin Jarvis. (YA). 2007. 69.99 (978-1-60252-836-9(5)) Find a World.

Hard Times. unabr. ed. Charles Dickens. Read by Denise Bryer & Martin Jarvis. Adapted by Ian Cotterell. 4 cass. 22.95 (SCN 200) J Norton Pubs.
Dickens' attack on utilitarianism & the industrial process that together seemed to be turning the working class into mere cogs, with no regard for the individual.

Hard Times, unabr. ed. Charles Dickens. Narrated by Patrick Tull. 9 cass. (Running Time: 13 hrs.). 78.00 (978-1-55690-712-8(5), 92427E7) Recorded Bks.
Dickens classic presents a relentless indictment against the callous greed of Victorian industrial society & its misapplied utilitarian philosophy. Available to libraries only.

Hard Times. unabr. ed. Charles Dickens. Narrated by Simon Prebble. (Running Time: 10 hrs. 30 mins. 0 sec.). (Tantor Unabridged Classics Ser.). (ENG.). 2009. audio compact disk 32.99 (978-1-4001-1036-0(X)); audio compact disk 65.99 (978-1-4001-4036-7(6)); audio compact disk 22.99 (978-1-4001-6036-5(7)) Pub: Tantor Media. Dist(s): IngramPubServ

Hard Times. unabr. ed. Charles Dickens. Read by Peter Joyce. 6 cass. (Running Time: 8 hrs. 30 min.). 1998. 54.95 (978-1-86015-454-6(9)) Pub: UlverLrgPrint GBR. Dist(s): Ulverscroft US
Mr. Gradind is a practical man, but his emphasis on facts & figures alone supresses his children's natural sense of wonder.

Hard Times. unabr. collector's ed. Charles Dickens. Read by Jill Masters. 9 cass. (Running Time: 13 hrs. 30 min.). 1983. 72.00 (978-0-7366-3980-4(2), 9528) Books on Tape.
An indictment of the insensitivity & greed rampant in Victorian industrial society. In the squalor of a textile town, arch pragmatist Thomas Gradgrind teaches utility. Facts & conformity rule. So when Louisa, his daughter, marries banker Josiah Bounderby, the alliance seems predestined. But appearances deceive & Louisa rebels against husband & father. Gradgrind realizes the error of his ways.

Hard Times, Set. Charles Dickens. Read by Flo Gibson. 7 cass. (Running Time: 10 hrs.). 1995. 25.95 (978-1-55685-374-6(2)) Audio Bk Con.
Self-made cotton mill owner & braggart Josiah Bounderby marries Thomas Gradgrind Esquire's daughter. He accuses a dismissed laborer of stealing from his bank, but the culprit turns out to be his brother-in-law. This novel was dramatized as "The Sons of Toil" or "Under the Earth".

***Hard Times: Unabridged Value-Priced Edition.** Charles Dickens. Narrated by Martin Jarvis. (Running Time: 11 hrs. 0 mins. 0 sec.). (ENG.). 2010. audio compact disk 14.95 (978-1-60283-985-4(9)) Pub: AudioGO. Dist(s): Perseus Dist

Hard to Receive. John Arnott. 1 cass. 1996. 7.00 (978-0-7684-0003-8(1)) Destiny Image Pubs.

Hard Truth. abr. ed. Nevada Barr. Read by Joyce Bean. 4 cass. (Running Time: 6 hrs.). (Anna Pigeon Ser.: No. 13). 2005. 62.25 (978-1-59086-664-1(9), 9781590866641, BAudLibEd); audio compact disk 74.25 (978-1-59086-666-5(5), 9781590866665, BACDLib Ed) Brilliance Audio.
Please enter a Synopsis.

Hard Truth. abr. ed. Nevada Barr. Read by Joyce Bean. (Running Time: 21600 sec.). (Anna Pigeon Ser.: No. 13). 2006. audio compact disk 16.99 (978-1-59600-439-9(8), 9781596004399, BCD Value Price) Brilliance Audio.
Just three days after her wedding to Sheriff Paul Davidson, Anna Pigeon moves from Mississippi to Colorado to assume her new post as district ranger at Rocky Mountain National Park, where three girls have disappeared during a religious retreat. Two of the children reappear a month later, clad only in filthy underwear and claiming to remember nothing of the intervening weeks. The girls are frightened and traumatized, but they forge a bond with the pair of campers who discover them - a wheelchair-bound paraplegic and her elderly aunt. With the reappearance of the children comes an odd and unsettling presence in the park, a sense of disembodied evil and unspeakable terrors: small animals are mercilessly slaughtered, and a sinister force seems to still control the girls. As Anna investigates, she finds herself caught up in the machinations of a paranoid religious sect bent on protecting their secrets and keeping the girls sequestered from law enforcement and psychiatric help. Following the trail of the many suspects, especially that of the cult's intense youth-group leader, Anna comes to find the force against which the children's minds have been broken. This evil has the eyes of a visionary and the soul of the devil. Anna will discover the truth - even if it kills her.

Hard Truth. abr. ed. Nevada Barr. Read by Joyce Bean. (Running Time: 6 hrs.). (Anna Pigeon Ser.). 2006. 24.95 (978-1-4233-0087-8(4), 9781423300878, BAD) Brilliance Audio.

Hard Truth. abr. ed. Nevada Barr. Read by Joyce Bean. (Running Time: 6 hrs.). (Anna Pigeon Ser.: No. 13). 2006. 39.25 (978-1-4233-0088-5(2), 9781423300885, BADLE); audio compact disk 39.25 (978-1-4233-0086-1(6), 9781423300861, Brinc Audio MP3 Lib); audio compact disk 24.95 (978-1-4233-0085-4(8), 9781423300854, Brilliance MP3) Brilliance Audio.

Hard Truth. abr. unabr. ed. Mariah Stewart. Read by Anna Fields. 7 pieces. (Running Time: 27000 sec.). 2006. 29.95 (978-0-7861-4480-8(7)); audio compact disk 29.95 (978-0-7861-7249-8(5)) Blckstn Audio.

Hard Truth. unabr. ed. Nevada Barr. Read by Barbara Rosenblat. 8 cass. (Running Time: 11 hrs. 45 mins.). (Anna Pigeon Ser.: No. 13). 2005. 79.75 (978-1-4193-3886-1(2), 98025); audio compact disk 119.75 (978-1-4193-3888-5(9), C3286) Recorded Bks.
Just married Anna is bound for Rocky Mountain National Park and a new post as Park Ranger. But no sooner does she arrive that she finds herself involved in the vanishing case of three young girls. When two of the girls suddenly reappear claiming to know nothing of the whereabouts of the third, Anna begins to suspect an evil presence lurking within the tranquil mountain sanctuary.

Hard Truth. unabr. ed. Nevada Barr. (Anna Pigeon Ser.: No. 13). 2005. 34.99 (978-1-4193-2674-5(0)); audio compact disk 34.99 (978-1-4193-2675-2(9)) Recorded Bks.

Hard Truth. unabr. ed. Nevada Barr. Read by Anna Fields. (Running Time: 27000 sec.). (Anna Pigeon Ser.: No. 13). 2006. audio compact disk 55.00 (978-0-7861-6744-9(0)) Blckstn Audio.

Hard Truth. unabr. ed. Mariah Stewart. Read by Anna Fields. (Running Time: 27000 sec.). 2006. 54.95 (978-0-7861-4643-7(5)) Blckstn Audio.

***Hard Truth-ABR.** Nevada Barr & #13 Anna Pigeon Series. 2010. audio compact disk 9.99 (978-1-4418-5649-4(8)) Brilliance Audio.

Hard Way. Lee Child. Read by Dick Hill. (Jack Reacher Ser.). 2009. 74.99 (978-1-60775-882-2(2)) Find a World.

Hard Way. abr. ed. Lee Child. Read by Dick Hill. (Running Time: 6 hrs.). (Jack Reacher Ser.). 2007. audio compact disk 14.99 (978-1-4233-0639-9(2), 9781423306399, BCD Value Price) Brilliance Audio.

Hard Way. unabr. ed. Lee Child. Read by Dick Hill. (Running Time: 12 hrs.). (Jack Reacher Ser.). 2006. 39.25 (978-1-59710-887-4(1), 9781597108874, BADLE); 24.95 (978-1-59710-886-7(3), 9781597108867, BAD); 82.25 (978-1-59600-326-2(X), 9781596003262, BrilAudUnabridg); 32.95 (978-1-59600-325-5(1), 9781596003255); audio compact disk 102.25 (978-1-59600-329-3(4), 9781596003293, BriAudCD Unabrid); audio compact disk 36.95 (978-1-59600-328-6(6), 9781596003286); audio compact disk 24.95 (978-1-59600-330-9(8), 9781596003309, Brilliance MP3); audio compact disk 39.25 (978-1-59600-331-6(6), 9781596003316, Brlnc Audio MP3 Lib) Brilliance Audio.
Please enter a Synopsis.

Hard Wood. 1 CD. 2003. audio compact disk (978-1-932616-03-3(9)) Feng Shui Para.
If You are the Element HARD WOOD...In Feng Shui you are the personal Trigram CHEN (pronounced "chen") and you represent the oldest son. When in balance, you are patient, a clear thinker, open minded, capable of leadership, intelligent, able to thrive under pressure and a good organizer. You can grow any business, are open to change, the arts, and new ideas. When you are not in balance, you can be demanding, fault finding, arrogant, judgmental, impatient, addicted to doing, or depressed. You stuff your emotions then erupt with anger. The above is just a brief excerpt from the HARD WOOD audio program.

Hard Work: My Life on & off the Court. unabr. ed. Roy Williams. Frwd. by Tim Crothers & John Grisham. 2009. audio compact disk 29.95 (978-1-61573-020-9(6), 1615730206) Pub: HighBridge. Dist(s): Workman Pub

Hardball. abr. ed. Sara Paretsky. Read by Susan Ericksen. (Running Time: 6 hrs.). (V. I. Warshawski Ser.). 2009. audio compact disk 26.99 (978-1-4233-1997-9(4), 9781423319979, BACD) Brilliance Audio.

Hardball. abr. ed. Sara Paretsky. Read by Susan Ericksen. (Running Time: 6 hrs.). (V. I. Warshawski Ser.). 2010. audio compact disk 14.99 (978-1-4233-1998-6(2), 9781423319986, BCD Value Price) Brilliance Audio.

Hardball. unabr. ed. Sara Paretsky. Read by Susan Ericksen. (Running Time: 14 hrs.). (V. I. Warshawski Ser.). 2009. 24.99 (978-1-4233-1993-1(1), 9781423319931, Brilliance MP3); 39.97 (978-1-4233-1994-8(X), 9781423319948, Brlnc Audio MP3 Lib); 39.97 (978-1-4233-1996-2(6), 9781423319962, BADLE); 24.99 (978-1-4233-1995-5(8), 9781423319955, BAD); audio compact disk 36.99 (978-1-4233-1991-7(5), 9781423319917, Bril Audio CD Unabri); audio compact disk 99.97 (978-1-4233-1992-4(3), 9781423319924, BriAudCD Unabrid) Brilliance Audio.

Hardcase. unabr. ed. Bill Pronzini. Read by John Michalski. 6 CDs. (Running Time: 7 hrs. 15 mins.). (Nameless Detective Mystery Ser.). 2007. audio compact disk 64.95 (978-0-7927-4794-9(1)) AudioGO.

Hardcastle. John Yount. Read by John Yount. Interview with Kay Bonetti. 1 cass. 1986. 13.95 (978-1-55644-169-1(X), 6121) Am Audio Prose.
The chapter on coon hunting from this novel in which Bill Music & Regus Patoff Bone take a young coon hound & a pint of high proof moonshine into the woods & discuss their jobs; Music is uncomfortable about his new job as a company goon at the local mine, & Bone is cynical about his job as a mine guard.

Hardening into Print see Richard Eberhart Reading His Poetry

Hardening of the Arteries: Hebrews 3:7-19. Ed Young. 1991. 4.95 (978-0-7417-1883-9(9), 883) Win Walk.

***Harder than I Thought: Adventures of a 21st Century CEO.** unabr. ed. Robert D. Austin et al. Read by Authors. (Running Time: 8 hrs.). (ENG.). 2011. 34.00 (978-1-59659-648-1(1), GildAudio); audio compact disk 39.98 (978-1-59659-636-8(8), GildAudio) Pub: Gildan Media. Dist(s): HachBkGrp

Harder They Come. Michael Thelwell. Read by Michael Thelwell. 1 cass. (Running Time: 45 min.). 1981. 13.95 (978-1-55644-025-0(1), 1141) Am Audio Prose.
Beautiful reading makes the Jamaican patois come to life for Western ears.

Hardest Part of Love. unabr. ed. Catherine Ryan Hyde. Read by Anthony Heald. (Running Time: 32400 sec.). 2008. 59.95 (978-1-4332-1316-8(8)); audio compact disk 29.95 (978-1-4332-1318-2(4)); audio compact disk & audio compact disk 70.00 (978-1-4332-1317-5(6)) Blckstn Audio.

Hardest Word: Daniel 3:18. Ed Young. (J). 1980. 4.95 (978-0-7417-1115-1(X), A0115) Win Walk.

Harding & the Scandals. 10.00 (HT401) Esstee Audios.

Harding Scandals. (Presidency Ser.). 10.00 Esstee Audios.
Presents a tale of naivete in power.

Hardly Knew Her. unabr. ed. Laura Lippman. Read by Linda Emond & Francois Battiste. 8 CDs. (Running Time: 9 hrs. 30 mins.). 2008. audio compact disk 39.95 (978-0-06-166159-4(7), Harper Audio) HarperCollins Pubs.

***Hardly Knew Her.** unabr. ed. Laura Lippman. Read by Linda Emond & Francois Battiste. 2008. (978-0-06-176305-2(5), Harper Audio); (978-0-06-176303-8(9), Harper Audio); (978-0-06-171009-4(1)); (978-0-06-171019-3(9)) HarperCollins Pubs.

***Hardness Factor.** abr. ed. Steven Lamm. Read by Steven Lamm. (ENG.). 2005. (978-0-06-083939-0(2), Harper Audio); (978-0-06-083940-6(6), Harper Audio) HarperCollins Pubs.

Hardness Factor: How to Achieve Your Best Health & Sexual Fitness at Any Age. unabr. abr. ed. Steven Lamm & Secor Couzens. Read by Steven Lamm. (Running Time: 012600 sec.). 2005. audio compact disk 22.95 (978-0-06-076009-0(5)) HarperCollins Pubs.

Hardness of Heart. 3 Tapes. 2004. 15.00 (978-1-59548-012-5(9)); audio compact disk 21.00 (978-1-59548-013-2(7)) A Wommack.

Hardness of Heart. Created by AWMI. (ENG.). 2006. audio compact disk 25.00 (978-1-59548-079-8(X)) A Wommack.

Hardness of Heart. Created by Awmi. (ENG.). 2006. 25.00 (978-1-59548-078-1(1)) A Wommack.

Hardship of Accounting see Robert Frost in Recital

Hardware. unabr. ed. Linda Barnes. Narrated by C. J. Critt. 8 cass. (Running Time: 10 hrs. 45 mins.). (Carlotta Carlyle Mystery Ser.). 2000. 70.00 (978-0-7887-0262-4(9), 94471E7) Recorded Bks.

Hardware - Software Wrap-Up. 2 cass. 1990. 16.00 set. Recorded Res.

Hardy & Manchild. unabr. ed. Benjamin DeMott. 1 cass. (Running Time: 50 min.). 1968. 12.95 (23069) J Norton Pubs.
Five of Hardy's poems are presented as illustrating the simultaneity of contradictory feelings experienced by the poet.

Hardy Boys #1: the Tower Treasure. unabr. ed. Franklin W. Dixon. Read by Bill Irwin. (ENG.). (J). (gr. 4). 2008. audio compact disk 19.99 (978-0-7393-6681-3(5), Listening Lib) Pub: Random Audio Pubg. Dist(s): Random

Hardy Breed. unabr. ed. Giles Lutz. Narrated by Frank Muller. 4 cass. (Running Time: 5 hrs. 30 mins.). 1979. 35.00 (978-1-55690-217-8(4), 79070E7) Recorded Bks.
Texas in 1825 & a tough pioneer, new in town, proves he's tough in the face of opposition & jeers from local "guns".

Hardy Family. Perf. by Mickey Rooney. 1 cass. (Running Time: 60 min.). Incl. Hardy Family: Junior Executive. (CC-5030); Hardy Family: The Night Watchman. (CC-5030); 7.95 (CC-5030) Natl Recrd Co.
In "Junior Executive", Andy telephones a large company for a job & the company gives him a title instead of a large salary; thinking he is an executive, he makes office changes. that get him in trouble. In "The Night Watchman", Andy announces that he has just got a job as a private eye, which is actually a job as a night watchman.

Hardy Family: Andy Takes up Knitting & Andy Bets on Horses. Perf. by Mickey Rooney. 1 cass. (Running Time: 1 hr.). 2001. 6.98 (1751) Radio Spirits.

Hardy Family: Junior Executive see Hardy Family

Hardy Family: The Night Watchman see Hardy Family

Hare & Other Stories. Catherine Fisher. 1 cass. (J). 1996. 19.95 (978-0-8464-4838-9(6)) Beekman Bks.

Hare & the Tortoise. 2004. bk. 24.95 (978-0-7882-0553-8(6)); pap. bk. 14.95 (978-0-7882-0618-4(4)) Weston Woods.

Hare & the Tree Spirit: A Story from Nelson Mandela's Favorite African Folktales. Read by Sophie Okonedo. Compiled by Nelson Mandela. (Running Time: 5 mins.). (ENG.). 2009. 1.99 (978-1-60024-860-3(8)) Pub: Hachet Audio. Dist(s): HachBkGrp

Hare Hare Yukai. Perf. by Aya Hirano. (YA). 2007. 9.98 (978-1-59409-839-0(5)) Bandai Ent.

Hare Hare Yukai 45 RPM Record. Perf. by Aya Hirano. (YA). 2007. 12.00 (978-1-59409-855-0(7)) Bandai Ent.

Hare Krishna Mahamantra. 1 cass.; 1 CD. 4.95 (CD-12); audio compact disk 14.95 CD. Bhaktivedanta.

Hare Krisma Classics & Originals. 1 cass.; 1 CD. 4.95 (CD-2); audio compact disk 14.95 CD. Bhaktivedanta.

Hare-Raising Tale. unabr. ed. Elizabeth Levy. Read by William Dufris & Christine Marshall. Illus. by Mordicai Gerstein. 1 CD. (Running Time: 3420 sec.). (First Chapter Bks.). (YA). (gr. 7-11). 2006. audio compact disk 15.95 (978-1-59519-703-0(6)); 12.95 (978-1-59519-702-3(8)) Live Oak Media.
With the markings of a map of the world on his fur, Jill thinks her new dog Fletcher is an excellent candidate for show and tell. But when the class rabbit mysteriously disappears, Fletcher isn't such a hit anymore; in fact, he's the prime suspect!.

Hare's Big Tug-of-War/How the Sky Got Its Stars. Created by Steck-Vaughn Staff. (Running Time: 586 sec.). (Primary Take-Me-Home Books Level A Ser.). 1998. 9.80 (978-0-8172-8665-1(9)) SteckVau.

Hari Om: A Mantra for Meditation. Voice by Sivananda Radha. 1 CD. (Running Time: 59 mins.). 1997. audio compact disk 15.95 (978-0-931454-87-5(5)) Pub: Timeless Bks. Dist(s): Baker Taylor
Swami Radha chants a traditional ancient mantra effective in keeping the mind centered while working or for meditation.

Hari Om: For Meditation. Sivananda Radha. (Running Time: 60 min.). 1994. 9.95 (978-0-931454-35-6(2)) Timeless Bks.
Swami Radha chants traditional ancient Mantra. Effective in keeping the mind centered while working, or for meditation.

Harinama Cintamani. Srila B. Thakura. 4 cass. 18.00 Set, incl. 1 vinyl album. Bhaktivedanta.
Conversation between Lord Caitanya Mahaprabhu & Srila Haridasa Thakura on the subject of chanting the Holy Name to achieve ecstatic love of God. Draw grace from the guru & Lord for faster growth & improve mental concentration on the Name to foster taste, attachment, & absorption in it. See the Lord, his qualities, & pastimes within the Name.

Hariprasad Chaurasia (Flute), Vol. 1. Music by Hariprasad Chaurasia. 1 cass. (Music Today Presents Ser.). 1992. (A92024) Multi-Cultural Bks.

Hariprasad Chaurasia (Flute), Vol. 2. Music by Hariprasad Chaurasia. 1 cass. (Music Today Presents Ser.). 1992. (A92025) Multi-Cultural Bks.

Hark! abr. ed. Ed McBain, pseud. Read by Ron McLarty. (87th Precinct Ser.: Bk. 54). 2004. 15.95 (978-0-7435-3993-7(1)) Pub: S&S Audio. Dist(s): S and S Inc

Hark! unabr. ed. Ed McBain, pseud. Narrated by Michael Arkin. 8 cass. (Running Time: 11 hrs. 15 mins.). (87th Precinct Ser.: Bk. 54). 2004. 69.75 (978-1-4193-0460-6(7), 97841MC) Recorded Bks.

Hark! the Herald Angels Sing. Virginia Reynolds. 2005. bk. 15.00 (978-0-7567-8640-3(1)) DIANE Pub.

Harlan Coben CD Collection: Promise Me, the Woods. abr. ed. Harlan Coben. (Running Time: 12 hrs.). 2009. audio compact disk 29.99 (978-1-4418-0153-1(7), 9781441801531, BACD) Brilliance Audio.

***Harlan Coben CD Collection 2: Hold Tight, Long Lost.** abr. ed. Harlan Coben. (Running Time: 11 hrs.). 2010. audio compact disk 19.99 (978-1-4418-6991-3(3), 9781441869913, BACD) Brilliance Audio.

Harlem. Walter Dean Myers. Read by Ruby Dee & Ossie Davis. 1 cass. (Running Time: 10 min.). 1997. bk. 27.90 (978-0-8045-6852-4(9), 6852) Spoken Arts.

Harlem Globetrotters: Clown Princes of Basketball. (High Five Reading - Purple Ser.). (ENG.). (gr. 4-5). 2007. audio compact disk 5.95 (978-1-4296-1426-9(9)) CapstoneDig.

Harlem Globetrotters: Clown Princes of Basketball. Robbie Butler. (High Five Reading Ser.). (ENG.). (gr. 4 up). 2001. audio compact disk 5.95 (978-0-7368-9506-4(X)) CapstoneDig.

Harlem Renaissance Remembered: Duke Ellington, Langston Hughes, Countee Cullen & the Sound of the Harlem Renaissance. unabr. ed. Jonathan Gross. Read by Mack Jay Jordan. 1 CD. (Running Time: 1 hr.). 2010. audio compact disk 14.99 (978-1-4418-0883-7(3), 9781441808837, Bril Audio CD Unabri) Brilliance Audio.

***Harlem Renaissance Remembered: Duke Ellington, Langston Hughes, Countee Cullen & the Sound of the Harlem Renaissance.** unabr. ed. Jonathan Gross. Read by Jay Jordan. 1 MP3-CD. (Running Time: 1 hr.). 2010. 14.99 (978-1-4418-1136-3(2), 9781441811363, Brilliance MP3) Brilliance Audio.

***Harlem Renaissance Remembered: Duke Ellington, Langston Hughes, Countee Cullen & the Sound of the Harlem Renaissance.** unabr. ed. Jonathan Gross & Jay Jordan. 1 MP3-CD. (Running Time: 1 hr.). 2010. 39.97 (978-1-4418-1137-0(0), 9781441811370, Brlnc Audio MP3 Lib) Brilliance Audio.

***Harlem Renaissance Remembered: Duke Ellington, Langston Hughes, Countee Cullen & the Sound of the Harlem Renaissance.** unabr. ed. Jay Jordan. Read by Jonathan Gross. (Running Time: 1 hr.). 2010. 39.97 (978-1-4418-1139-4(7), 9781441811394, BADLE); 14.99 (978-1-4418-1138-7(9), 9781441811387, BAD); audio compact disk 39.97 (978-1-4418-0884-4(1), 9781441808844, BriAudCD Unabrid) Brilliance Audio.

Harlequin. Laurell K. Hamilton. Read by Cynthia Holloway. (Anita Blake, Vampire Hunter Ser.: No. 15). 2009. 89.99 (978-1-60775-701-6(X)) Find a World.

Harlequin. abr. ed. Laurell K. Hamilton. Read by Cynthia Holloway. (Running Time: 7 hrs.). (Anita Blake, Vampire Hunter Ser.: No. 15). 2008. audio compact disk 19.99 (978-1-59600-049-0(X), 9781596000490, Bri Audio Pbk Audbks) Brilliance Audio.

Harlequin. unabr. ed. Laurell K. Hamilton. Read by Cynthia Holloway. (Running Time: 16 hrs.). (Anita Blake, Vampire Hunter Ser.: No. 15). 2007. 44.25 (978-1-59737-892-5(5), 9781597378925, BADLE); 29.95 (978-1-59737-891-8(7), 9781597378912, BAD); 102.25 (978-1-59600-045-2(7), 9781596000452); audio compact disk 46.95 (978-1-59600-046-9(5), 9781596000469); audio compact disk 122.25 (978-1-59600-048-3(1), 9781596000483, BACDLib Ed); audio compact disk 29.95 (978-1-59737-889-5(5), 9781597378895, Brilliance MP3); audio compact disk 44.25 (978-1-59737-890-1(9), 9781597378901, Brlnc Audio MP3 Lib) Brilliance Audio.

Harlequin Ichthyosis - A Bibliography & Dictionary for Physicians, Patients, & Genome Researchers. Compiled by Icon Group International, Inc. Staff. 2007. ring bd. 28.95 (978-0-497-11227-1(2)) Icon Grp.

Harlequin Tea Set & Other Stories. unabr. ed. Agatha Christie. Read by Alexandra Thomas. 4 cass. 1998. 21.95 Set. (978-1-55935-260-4(4)) Soundelux.
Includes "The Mystery of the Spanish Chest," & "The Edge" along with seven other stories about the darker side of human nature.

Harley Elliott. unabr. ed. Read by Harley Elliott. 1 cass. (Running Time: 29 min.). 1985. 10.00 New Letters.
Harley Elliot's books include "Animals That Stand in Dreams" & "The Secret Lover Poems".

Harley, Like a Person. unabr. ed. Cat Bauer. Narrated by Carine Montbertrand. 7 pieces. (Running Time: 9 hrs.). (gr. 10 up). 2002. 61.00 (978-0-7887-9402-5(7)) Recorded Bks.
Harley Columba may still be in high school, but she's growing up fast. With trouble at home and a stunted social life, she feels more like a survivor than a student. The only thing that keeps her sane is drawing and painting. The man who calls himself her father is a drunken jerk. He and Harley don't look alike, and her mother refuses to talk about the past. To make sense of her life, Harley decides she must find out the truth about her father: his identity and his connection to her artistic talent. It is a search that will take her from her tiny home town to the streets of New York City. Harley, like a person is a brutally honest portrait of a troubled teenage girl. As Harley grows more rebellious, her story is not sweetened with artificial hope.

Harlot by the Side of the Road. unabr. ed. Jonathan Kirsch. Read by Geoffrey Howard. 9 cass. (Running Time: 13 hrs. 30 mins.). 1999. 72.00 (5031) Books on Tape.
The Old Testament is filled with some of the most startling & explicit stories in all of Western literature.

Harm Done. Ruth Rendell. Read by Donada Peters. (Inspector Wexford Mystery Ser.: Bk. 18). 1999. audio compact disk 96.00 (978-0-7366-6297-0(9)) Books on Tape.

Harm Done. Ruth Rendell. Narrated by Davina Porter. 13 CDs. (Running Time: 15 hrs.). (Inspector Wexford Mystery Ser.: Bk. 18). audio compact disk 124.00 (978-0-7887-4740-3(1)) Recorded Bks.

Harm Done. collector's ed. Ruth Rendell. Read by Donada Peters. 10 cass. (Running Time: 15 hrs.). (Inspector Wexford Mystery Ser.: Bk. 18). 1999. 80.00 (978-0-7366-4794-6(5), 5142) Books on Tape.
A three-year-old child returns, unable to explain where she'd been or why she'd been away for three days. Shortly after, a convicted pedophile is released into the community. Then the child of a wealthy executive disappears & not long after, a suspect in the kidnapping is found stabbed to death. Chief Inspector Wexford looks for connections & finds himself focusing on domestic violence.

Harm Done. unabr. ed. Ruth Rendell. Read by Donada Peters. 12 CDs. (Running Time: 18 hrs.). (Inspector Wexford Mystery Ser.: Bk. 18). 2001. audio compact disk 96.00 Books on Tape.

Harm Done. unabr. ed. Ruth Rendell. Read by Donada Peters. 10 cass. (Running Time: 15 hrs.). (Inspector Wexford Mystery Ser.: Bk. 18). 2000. 34.95 (978-0-7366-4699-4(X)) Books on Tape.

Harm Done, unabr. ed. Ruth Rendell. Narrated by Davina Porter. 11 cass. (Running Time: 15 hrs.). (Inspector Wexford Mystery Ser.: Bk. 18). 1999. 91.00 (978-0-7887-4033-6(4), 96151E7) Recorded Bks.
Chief Inspector Wexford tackles a volatile issue that is dividing the residents of Kingsmarkham - the various guises of domestic abuse.

Harmful Intent. unabr. ed. Robin Cook. Read by Donada Peters. 9 cass. (Running Time: 13 hr. 30 min.). 1992. 72.00 (978-0-7366-2225-7(X), 3015) Books on Tape.
Charged with malpractice, anesthesiologist Jeffrey Rhodes seeks to clear his name by following a fugitive trail into the heart of a medical nightmare.

Harmless. unabr. ed. Dana Reinhardt. 5 CDs. (Running Time: 5 hrs. 57 mins.). (YA). (gr. 7 up). 2006. audio compact disk 36.00 (978-0-7393-4853-6(1)) Books on Tape.

Harmless. unabr. ed. Dana Reinhardt. Read by Lynde Houck et al. (Running Time: 21420 sec.). (ENG.). (J). (gr. 7 up). 2007. audio compact disk 35.00 (978-0-7393-3865-0(X), Listening Lib) Pub: Random Audio Pubg. Dist(s): Random

Harmless Ones; The Television Consciousness. Jonathan Murro. 1 cass. 1990. 7.95 A R Colton Fnd.

Harmonic Meditations: Music from the Heart of the Cosmos. David Hykes. 1 CD. (Running Time: 4260 sec.). 2005. audio compact disk 16.98 (978-1-59179-253-6(3), M901D) Sounds True.

Harmonic Overtones: Magical Vibrations in Voice & Music. Text by Dick de Ruiter. Music by Vincent Vrolijk. 2 vols. (Running Time: 50 mins.). 2005. bk. 23.50 (978-90-74597-58-6(0)) Pub: Binkey Kok NLD. Dist(s): Red Wheel Weiser

Harmonic Resonance. Jim Oliver. 1 cass. (Running Time: 1 hr.). 9.95 (978-1-55961-335-4(1)) Relaxtn Co.

Harmonic Throat Singing. Perf. by Tuvan Throat Singers. 1 cass. 9.00 (A0414-85) Sound Photosyn.
Courtesy of Ralph Leighton & Richard Feynman.

Harmonic Wealth: The Secret of Attracting the Life You Want. James Arthur Ray. 2009. 14.98 (978-0-7662-4230-2(7)) Gaiam Intl.

Harmonic Wealth: The Secret of Attracting the Life You Want. unabr. abr. ed. James Arthur Ray. Read by James Arthur Ray. 2008. audio compact disk 29.95 (978-1-4013-8891-1(4), Hyperion Audio) Pub: Hyperion. Dist(s): HarperCollins Pubs

Harmonica Americana Complete Beginners Kit. Jon Gindick. Illus. by Art Ellis. 2 cass. 1996. pap. bk. 29.95 (978-0-930948-08-5(4)) Cross Harp.

Harmonica Chuck: Take It Like You Find It, Leave It Like It Is. Prod. by Patrick Joseph O'Connor. Interview with Patrick Joseph O'Connor. Comment by Charlie Phillips. Music by Charlie Phillips. 2006. audio compact disk 10.00 (978-1-929731-04-6(3)) Rowfant.

Harmonica for Kids. Bobby Joe Holman. 2004. audio compact disk 9.95 (978-0-8256-1699-0(9)) Music Sales.

Harmonica Humdrums see Carl Sandburg's Poems for Children

Harmonica Jam Trax. Ralph Agresta. 1997. audio compact disk 12.95 (978-0-8256-1641-9(7), AM945318) Pub: Music Sales. Dist(s): H Leonard

Harmonica Positions. 1 cass. 9.95 Musical I Pr.

Harmonious Relationships. Eldon Taylor. 2 cass. (Running Time: 62 min. per cass.). (Omniphonics Ser.). 29.95 incl. script Set. (978-1-55978-818-2(6), 4019) Progress Aware Res.

3-D soundtrack with underlying subliminal affirmations, night & day versions.

Harmonising. Ed. by Peter Samuels. (Running Time: 60 mins.). 2002. audio compact disk 15.99 (978-1-904451-29-7(2)) Global Jrny GBR GBR.

Harmonizing Religion & Science. Steve Kellmeyer. 2005. audio compact disk 11.95 (978-0-9767368-5-1(3)) Bridegroom.

Harmonizing Your Chakras. Elena Bussolino. Illus. by Albert Bussolino. Music by Rizwan Ahmad. Engineer Khalid Muhammad. Orig. Title: Original. 2000. 12.95 (978-0-9706743-0-2(9)) Bagatto.

Harmonizing Your Chakras. Elena Bussolino & Anna Florentis. Orig. Title: Original. (ENG.). 2000. 7.99 (978-0-9720314-0-0(5)) Bagatto.

Harmonizing Your Craniosacral System: 17 Exercises for Relaxation & Self-Treatment. abr. ed. Daniel Agustoni. (Running Time: 4171 sec.). (ENG.). 2008. audio compact disk 17.95 (978-1-84409-126-3(0)) Pub: Findhorn Pr GBR. Dist(s): IPG Chicago

Harmony. S. Eckels. 1 cass. (Running Time: 60 min.). 11.95 (978-0-938586-87-6(4), H) Whole Person.

Intricately woven to support your relaxation or meditation rituals. Classical guitarist Steven Zdenek Eckels draws on Gregorian chant, Native American melodies, the rhythms of Lake Superior, & the spirit of the North Woods for inspiration to compose his musical prayers for healing. Summer or winter, he prepares his creative spirit by hiking along the rocky wind-swept shore, then returns to his cozy studio to compose in front of the picture window or fireplace, accompanied by the aromas of cedar, sage, pine, or angelica. Music composed in this peaceful environment is certain to bring you peace of mind.

***Harmony: A New Way of Looking at Our World.** unabr. ed. Charles Hrh The Prince Of Wales. (ENG.). 2010. (978-0-06-200700-1(9), Harper Audio); (978-0-06-206804-0(0), Harper Audio) HarperCollins Pubs.

Harmony Harris Cuts Loose. Jenny Oldfield. 3 CDs. (Running Time: 10380 sec.). (J). 2005. audio compact disk 29.95 (978-0-7540-6740-5(8)) AudioGo GBR.

Harmony of the Cosmos. Swami Amar Jyoti. 1 cass. 1982. 9.95 (K-46) Truth Consciousness.

Discovering the inherent harmony. Whirlpools in the cosmic ocean. How Lord Shiva brought celestial Ganga to earth.

Harmony Ranch. Perf. by Riders in the Sky. 1 cass. (J). (ps-5). 9.98 (2153); audio compact disk 15.98 (D2153) MFLP CA.

A superb collection of children's songs presented with tight harmonies & expert musicianship. Songs include: "How Does He Hodle?," "Great Grand-Dad" & "The Cowboy's ABC.".

Harm's Way. Catherine Aird. Read by Bruce Montague. 6 vols. (Running Time: 9 hrs.). 2003. 54.95 (978-0-7540-8347-4(0)) Pub: Chivers Audio Bks GBR. Dist(s): AudioGO

Harm's Way. abr. ed. Stephen White. Read by Dick Hill. (Running Time: 6 hrs.). (Dr. Alan Gregory Ser.). 2005. audio compact disk 16.99 (978-1-59600-421-4(5), 9781596004214, BCD Value Price) Brilliance Audio.

When Dr. Alan Gregory's good friend Peter Arvin is found bloody and dying on the stage of a Colorado theatre, suspicion soars that he has become the second victim of a killer whose first prey was discovered amid the elaborate scenery of the road company's production of the Broadway show Miss Saigon. Alan is immediately asked to respond to two pleas for help: one from the police, who would like a psychological profile of the murderer, and one from Peter's widow, who is desperate to know the meaning of her dead husband's secrets. As Alan struggles to cope with the complexities of his new marriage and the shattering personal consequences of his friend's murder, provocative clues lead him down a trail that winds from the Front Range of the Rockies to the casinos of the Colorado high country and finally to the grandeur outside Jackson Hole, Wyoming. His journey takes him deep into Peter's past and inevitably toward the discovery of harrowing truths about the human heart - about the struggle for survival and the quest for forgiveness - that seem always just out of his reach, obscured by the smoke of a long-forgotten fire.

Harm's Way. abr. ed. Stephen White. Read by Dick Hill. (Running Time: 6 hrs.). (Dr. Alan Gregory Ser.). 2006. 24.95 (978-1-4233-0091-5(2), 9781423300915, BAD); audio compact disk 24.95 (978-1-4233-0089-2(0), 9781423300892, Brilliance MP3) Brilliance Audio.

Harm's Way. unabr. ed. J. L. Fikes & E. B. Boatner. Read by Rusty Nelson. 6 cass. (Running Time: 7 hrs. 24 min.). 2001. 39.95 (978-1-55686-779-8(4)) Books in Motion.

An assassin is killing Harmony Falls residents and Sheriff Harvey Blunt suspects a backwoodsman named Macklin. But Macklin and weapons expert Oley Fermo know Macklin is not the killer.

Harm's Way. unabr. collector's ed. Stephen White. Read by Michael Kramer. 7 cass. (Running Time: 10 hrs. 30 min.). (Dr. Alan Gregory Ser.). 1997. 56.00 (978-0-913369-39-5(X), 4215) Books on Tape.

When Alan Gregory, a psychiatrist, finds his friend dead in a Colorado community theater, it looks like the victim knew - even trusted - his killer.

Harnessing Desires. unabr. ed. Perf. by Eknath Easwaran. 1 cass. (Running Time: 1 hr.). 1990. 7.95 (978-1-58638-550-7(X)) Nilgiri Pr.

Harnessing Peacocks. unabr. ed. Mary Wesley. Read by Carole Boyd. 7 cass. (Running Time: 10 hrs. 30 min.). (Isis Ser.). (J). 1994. 61.95 (978-1-85089-660-9(7), 91041) Pub: ISIS Lrg Prnt GBR. Dist(s): Ulverscroft US

Harnessing Personal Power: How to Recognize & Manage Your Impact, Set. David Grudermeyer & Rebecca Grudermeyer. 2 cass. 18.95 (T-24) Willingness Wrks.

Harnessing Your Emotions. 3 CDs. 2004. audio compact disk 21.00 (978-1-59548-014-9(5)) A Wommack.

Harnessing Your Emotions. Created by Awmi. 4 cass. (ENG.). 2004. 25.00 (978-1-59548-020-0(X)) A Wommack.

Harnessing Your Emotions. Andrew Wommack. 3 cass. (Running Time: 4 hrs. 40 min.). 14.00 Set. (978-1-881541-02-8(9), 1005) A Wommack.

This three-tape series ministers on how to find our identity with Christ. Bible-based teaching revealing God's best for you. This is life-changing & one of the major keys to a victorious life in Christ.

Harold & the Purple Crayon. (HEB.). 2004. 8.95 (978-0-7882-0267-4(7)); cass. & flmstrp 30.00 (978-0-89719-551-5(5)) Weston Woods.

Harold & the Purple Crayon. (J). 2004. bk. 24.95 (978-1-56008-236-1(4)); pap. bk. 14.95 (978-0-7882-0602-3(8)) Weston Woods.

Harold & the Purple Crayon. Crockett Johnson. 1 cass. (Running Time: 8 min.). (J). (ps-3). pap. bk. 12.95 Weston Woods.

This is the ingeniously imaginative story of a small boy who, with his magic crayon, draws himself in & out of a series of adventures.

Harold B Lee: A Dramatized History. Brian Kelly & Petrea Kelly. 2004. 5.98 (978-1-57734-973-0(3)); audio compact disk 5.98 (978-1-57734-974-7(1)) Covenant Comms.

Harold B Lee: Remembering the Miracles. L. Brent Goates. 4 CDs. 2004. audio compact disk 21.95 (978-1-57734-971-6(7)) Covenant Comms.

Harold Robbins. Interview with Harold Robbins. 1 cass. (Running Time: 25 min.). 1977. 11.95 (L065) TFR.

Robbins tells why he believes himself to be the greatest writer in the world & he also explains why it's impossible for any other writer to manufacture a "Robbins".

Harold Soloman: Tennis in Perspective. Read by Harold Soloman. 1 cass. 9.95 (978-0-89811-120-0(X), 7177) Lets Talk Assocs.

Harold Soloman talks about the people & events which influenced his career, & his own approach to his specialty.

Harold Taylor: Academic Freedom see Buckley's Firing Line

Harold Witt. unabr. ed. Read by Harold Witt. 1 cass. (Running Time: 29 min.). Incl. Winesburg by the Sea; 1987. 10.00 New Letters.

California author of some ten books reads from his works.

Harold y el Lapiz Color Morado. Crockett Johnson. (J). 2004. 8.95 (978-1-56008-917-9(2)) Weston Woods.

Harold's Fairy Tale. 2004. 8.95 (978-1-56008-918-6(0)); cass. & flmstrp 30.00 (978-0-89719-532-4(9)) Weston Woods.

Harold's Fairy Tale. (J). 2004. pap. bk. 14.95 (978-0-7882-0686-3(9)) Weston Woods.

Harp Guitar Artistry. Contrib. by Stephen Bennett. (Running Time: 45 mins.). 2005. 24.95 (978-5-558-09186-1(X)) Mel Bay.

Harp Notes in the Mist see Graveyard of Ghost Tales

Harp School, Vol. 1. Shinichi Suzuki. (Suzuki Method Core Materials Ser.). (ENG.). 1999. audio compact disk 15.95 (978-0-87487-287-3(1), Warner Bro) Alfred Pub.

Harp School, Vol. 2. Shinichi Suzuki. (Suzuki Method Core Materials Ser.). (ENG.). 1999. audio compact disk 15.95 (978-0-87487-288-0(X), Warner Bro) Alfred Pub.

Harp That Once. (23300-A) J Norton Pubs.

Harp, the Stones, & the North Wind. Lynn Taylor. 1 cass. 9.00 (A0203-87) Sound Photosyn.

From ICSS '87 with Bill Lyon on tape.

Harper & Moon. unabr. ed. Ramon Royal Ross. Narrated by Ramon Royal Ross. 5 cass. (Running Time: 6 hrs.). (gr. 7 up). 2002. 45.00 (978-0-7887-9660-9(7)) Recorded Bks.

Still haunted by early memories of growing up in an abusive family, 17-year-old Moon can't separate himself from his past. Twelve-year-old Harper comes from a world full of love and support. Despite their differences, they become the best of friends. Just prior to World War II, they spend the summer in the wilds of Washington State, with reclusive storekeeper and mountaineer, Olinger. But when winter comes, a blustery snowstorm hits, and Moon is missing. Risking his own life, Harper searches frantically for his friend. But what he finds is Olinger, dead, in a snowbank - and Moon is standing over him! Their friendship is put to the ultimate test as Harper struggles with what he believes to be the truth and the serious evidence stacking up against Moon.

Harriet & the Promised Land. unabr. ed. Jacob Lawrence. Narrated by Ruby Dee. Music by Wayne Abravanel. 1 cass. (Running Time: 8 min.). (J). 1997. pap. bk. 16.95 (978-0-8045-6848-7(0), 6848) Spoken Arts.

Covers the life of a poet from birth through what might have been her death - via her arrival by chariot in the promised land.

Harriet & the Roller Coaster. unabr. ed. Nancy Carlson. Illus. by Nancy Carlson. Read by Peter Fernandez. 11 vols. (Running Time: 6 mins.). (J). (gr. k-3). bk. 24.95 (978-0-941078-56-6(6)); pap. bk. 15.95 (978-0-941078-54-2(X)); pap. bk. & tchr. ed. 31.95 Reading Chest. (978-0-941078-55-9(8)) Live Oak Media.

Harriet's friend, George, dares Harriet to ride the rollercoaster, which he assures her will scare her to death. Harriet shows George that one person's idea of terror can be another's delight.

Harriet & Walt. unabr. ed. Nancy Carlson. Illus. by Nancy Carlson. Read by Peter Fernandez. 11 vols. (Running Time: 7 mins.). (J). (gr. k-3). bk. 24.95 (978-0-941078-59-7(0)); pap. bk. 15.95 (978-0-941078-57-3(4)); pap. bk. & tchr. ed. 31.95 Reading Chest. (978-0-941078-58-0(2)) Live Oak Media.

Harriet harbors "unsisterly" thoughts toward little brother Walt. When her friend George puts those thoughts into words Harriet takes Walt's side & learns that responsibility can be fun.

Harriet Lerner on Intimacy. Harriet Lerner. 2 CDs. (Running Time: 1 hr 30 mins). 2006. audio compact disk 19.95 (978-1-59179-486-8(2), AW00266D) Sounds True.

A heart-to-heart session that confronts cherished myths about relationships and offers practical ideas for overcoming the obstacles to authentic, enduring intimacy.

Harriet Said. Beryl Bainbridge. 5 cass. (Soundings Ser.). (J). 2005. 49.95 (978-1-84283-989-8(6)); audio compact disk 59.95 (978-1-84559-001-7(5)) Pub: ISIS Lrg Prnt GBR. Dist(s): Ulverscroft US

Harriet Spies Again. Helen Ericson. Read by Anne Bobby. 3 vols. (Running Time: 4 hrs. 33 mins.). (J). (gr. 3-7). 2004. pap. bk. 36.00 (978-0-8072-2091-7(4), Listening Lib); 30.00 (978-0-8072-1642-2(9), Listening Lib); audio compact disk 35.00 (978-0-8072-2015-3(9), Listening Lib) Random Audio Pubg.

Harriet the Spy. Louise Fitzhugh. Read by Anne Bobby. 4 cass. (Running Time: 7 hrs.). (J). 2000. 30.00 (978-0-7366-9094-2(8)) Books on Tape.

Harriet M. Welsch, determined to be a famous author, writes down everything she sees in her secret notebook. But her life is turned upside down when her classmates find her spy notebook & read it aloud.

Harriet the Spy. Louise Fitzhugh. Read by Anne Bobby. 6 CDs. (Running Time: 6 hrs. 56 mins.). (J). (gr. 3-7). 2004. audio compact disk 42.50 (978-0-8072-1780-1(8), Listening Lib) Pub: Random Audio Pubg. Dist(s): NetLibrary CO

Harriet the Spy. unabr. ed. Louise Fitzhugh. Read by Anne Bobby. 4 cass. (Running Time: 6 hrs.). (J). (gr. 1-8). 1999. 32.00 (LL 0133, Chivers Child Audio) AudioGO.

Harriet the Spy. unabr. ed. Louise Fitzhugh. Read by Anne Bobby. 4 cass. (YA). 1999. 29.98 (FS9-43439) Highsmith.

Harriet the Spy. unabr. ed. Louise Fitzhugh. Read by Anne Bobby. 4 vols. (Running Time: 6 hrs. 56 mins.). (J). (gr. 3-7). 1999. pap. bk. 38.00 (978-0-8072-8069-0(0), YA993SP, Listening Lib); 32.00 (978-0-8072-8068-3(2), YA993CX, Listening Lib) Random Audio Pubg.

Harriet M. Welsch is determined to grow up to be a famous author. She keeps a secret notebook & writes down everything she sees each day.

Harriet the Spy. unabr. ed. Louise Fitzhugh. Read by Anne Bobby. (Running Time: 24960 sec.). (ENG.). (J). (gr. 3-7). 2007. audio compact disk 28.00 (978-0-7393-3899-5(4), Listening Lib) Pub: Random Audio Pubg. Dist(s): Random

Harriet Tubman. 10.00 Esstee Audios.

Harriet Tubman. unabr. ed. Robert Hogrogian. 1 cass. (Running Time: 15 min.). (People to Remember Ser.: Set I). (J). (gr. 4-7). 1979. bk. 16.99 (978-0-934898-47-8(2)); pap. bk. 9.95 (978-0-934898-06-5(5)) Jan Prods.

The captivating story of the woman who risked her life to help other find freedom.

Harriet Tubman: Conductor on the Underground Railroad. Ann Petry. Read by Peter Francis James. 5 cass. (Running Time: 6 hrs. 30 mins.). (YA). 1999. pap. bk. 59.20 (978-0-7887-3011-5(8), 40893); 116.30 (978-0-7887-3041-2(X), 46858) Recorded Bks.

Born a plantation slave in 1820, Harriet Tubman dreamed of freedom. Risking life & limb, she escaped to become a conductor on the Underground Railroad. A symbol of strength & hope, this legendary "Moses" led scores of her people to freedom.

Harriet Tubman: Conductor on the Underground Railroad, unabr. ed. Ann Petry. Narrated by Peter Francis James. 5 pieces. (Running Time: 6 hrs. 30 mins.). (gr. 6 up). 1999. 46.00 (978-0-7887-2981-2(0), 95753E7) Recorded Bks.

Harriet Tubman: The Moses of Her People. Alan Venable. (Step into History Ser.). 2000. audio compact disk 18.95 (978-1-4105-0139-4(6)) D Johnston Inc.

Harriet Tubman: The Moses of Her People. Alan Venable. Ed. by Jerry Stemach. Illus. by Jack Nichols. 2000. audio compact disk 200.00 (978-1-58702-452-8(7)) D Johnston Inc.

Harriet Tubman- The Moses of Her People. Alan Venable. Ed. by Jerry Stemach et al. Illus. by Jack Nichols. Narrated by Denise Jordan Walker. Contrib. by Ted S. Hasselbring. (Start-to-Finish Books: Vol. 1). (J). (gr. 2-3). 2000. 35.00 (978-1-58702-453-5(5)) D Johnston Inc.

Harriet's Halloween Candy. unabr. ed. Nancy Carlson. Illus. by Nancy Carlson. Read by Peter Fernandez. 14 vols. (Running Time: 6 mins.). (J). pap. bk. & tchr. ed. 31.95 Reading Chest. (978-0-941078-52-8(3)) Live Oak Media.

Harriet is afraid that her huge hoard of Halloween candy will be stolen. She finally takes the ultimate step & consumes all of it at once, she is then taught a lesson by her stomach.

Harriet's Halloween Candy. unabr. ed. Nancy Carlson. Illus. by Nancy Carlson. Read by Peter Fernandez. 11 vols. (Running Time: 6 mins.). (J). (gr. k-3). bk. 24.95 (978-0-941078-53-5(1)); pap. bk. 15.95 (978-0-941078-51-1(5)) Live Oak Media.

Harriet's Recital. unabr. ed. Nancy Carlson. Illus. by Nancy Carlson. Read by Peter Fernandez. 11 vols. (Running Time: 5 mins.). (J). (gr. k-3). 1985. bk. 24.95 (978-0-941078-69-6(8)); pap. bk. 15.95 (978-0-941078-67-2(1)); pap. bk. 31.95 Reading Chest. (978-0-941078-68-9(X)) Live Oak Media.

Harriet's scheduled debut as a ballerina in her dancing class recital brings on an attack of anxiety but Harriet proves herself a true trouper by dancing her way out of her stagefright.

Harris & Me: A Summer Remembered. unabr. ed. Gary Paulsen. Read by Steven Boyer. 4 cass. (Running Time: 3 hrs. 45 mins.). (YA). (gr. 5-8). 2007. 41.75 (978-1-4281-3707-3(6)) Recorded Bks.

Harrod's Landing. unabr. ed. Tom E. Neet. Read by Lynda Evans. 6 cass. (Running Time: 7 hrs. 48 min.). (Mel Tippett Detective Ser.: Bk. 4). 1996. 39.95 (978-1-55686-664-7(X)) Books in Motion.

Mel Tippett has herself as a client when she is accused of murder & is forced to prove her innocence.

Harrogate Secret. unabr. ed. Catherine Cookson. Read by Susan Jameson. 10 cass. (Running Time: 10 hrs.). 1993. 84.95 (978-0-7451-5862-4(5), CAB 415) AudioGO.

Harry: The Work with Byron Katie: the Ressurection of a Dead Man. 2000. audio compact disk 24.00 (978-1-890246-26-6(3)) B Katie Int Inc.

Harry, a History: The True Story of a Boy Wizard, His Fans, & Life Inside the Harry Potter Phenomenon. unabr. ed. Melissa Anelli. Narrated by Renée Raudman. 1 MP3-CD. (Running Time: 11 hrs. 0 mins. 0 sec.). (ENG.). 2009. 24.99 (978-1-4001-6162-1(2)); audio compact disk 69.99 (978-1-4001-4162-3(1)) Pub: Tantor Media. Dist(s): IngramPubServ

Harry, a History: The True Story of a Boy Wizard, His Fans, & Life Inside the Harry Potter Phenomenon. unabr. ed. Melissa Anelli. Read by Renée Raudman. Narrated by Renée Raudman. 9 CDs. (Running Time: 11 hrs. 0 mins. 0 sec.). (ENG.). 2009. audio compact disk 34.99 (978-1-4001-1162-6(5)) Pub: Tantor Media. Dist(s): IngramPubServ

Harry & Chicken; Harry the Explorer. unabr. ed. Dyan Sheldon. Read by Charlotte Coleman. 2 cass. (Running Time: 3 hrs.). (J). (gr. 1-8). 1999. 18.95 (CCA 3484, Chivers Child Audio) AudioGO.

Harry & the Lady Next Door. abr. ed. Gene Zion. Illus. by Margaret Bloy Graham. (I Can Read Bks.). (J). (ps-3). 2008. 9.99 (978-0-06-133609-6(2), HarperFestival) HarperCollins Pubs.

Harry & the Lady Next Door Book. abr. ed. Gene Zion. Read by Becca Lish. Illus. by Margaret Bloy Graham. Contrib. by Becca Lish. 1 Cassette. (Running Time: 35 min.). (I Can Read Bks.). (J). (ps-3). 1996. pap. bk. 8.99 (978-0-694-70035-6(5)) HarperCollins Pubs.

***Harry Bosch Box Set.** unabr. ed. Michael Connelly. Read by Len Cariou. (Running Time: 27 hrs. 30 mins.). (ENG.). 2010. 32.98 (978-1-60788-726-3(6)); audio compact disk 49.98 (978-1-60788-725-6(8)) Pub: Hachet Audio. Dist(s): HachBkGrp

Harry Byrd of Virginia. Ronald Heinemann. 2006. 35.00 (978-0-8139-2381-9(6)) U Pr of Va.

Harry Caray: Voice of the Fans. Janell Hughes. (ENG.). 2006. audio compact disk 16.00 (978-0-9818365-1-5(8)) Baseball Voice.

Harry Cox: English Love Songs. 1 cass. 9.98 (C-20) Folk-Legacy.

Unaccompanied songs from a very important traditional singer.

Harry Crews. Interview. Interview with Harry Crews & Kay Bonetti. 1 cass. (Running Time: 1 hr.). 13.95 (978-1-55644-043-4(X), 2052) Am Audio Prose.

Crews speaks of his family's nomadic lifestyle, the uniqueness of the South, & his uneasiness in being classified as a peculiarly Southern writer. Interview provides significant insight into his other works.

Harry Freedman. Harry Freedman. 2004. audio compact disk 15.95 (978-0-662-33323-4(3)) Pub: Canadian Broadcasting CAN. Dist(s): Georgetown Term

Harry Golden: States' Rights see Buckley's Firing Line

Harry Heathcote of Gangoil. Anthony Trollope. 1 CD. (Running Time: 3.8 hours). 2007. 27.95 (978-1-60112-008-3(7)) Babblebooks.

Harry Heathcote of Gangoil: A Tale of Australian Bush Life. unabr. ed. Anthony Trollope. Read by Peter Joyce. 3 cass. 1997. 34.95 (978-1-86015-450-8(6)) Pub: UlverLrgPrint GBR. Dist(s): Ulverscroft US
An honest man finds himself at odds with his neighbors in the untamed wilderness of colonial Australia.

Harry Kalas: Voice of the Phillies. Janell Hughes. (ENG.). 2007. audio compact disk 16.00 (978-0-9818365-4-6(2)) Baseball Voice.

Harry Mark Petrakis. unabr. ed. Harry Mark Petrakis. Read by Harry Mark Petrakis. 1 cass. (Running Time: 29 min.). 1986. 10.00 New Letters.
Harry Mark Petrakis, a Greek storyteller from Chicago, reads a story called "Pa & the Sad Turkeys" from "The Petrakis Reader".

Harry Potter, Nos. 1-7. unabr. ed. J. K. Rowling. Read by Jim Dale. (ENG.). (J). 2007. audio compact disk, audio compact disk, audio compact disk 454.75 (978-0-7393-5224-3(5), Listening Lib) Pub: Random Audio Pubg. Dist(s): Random

Harry Potter & the Chamber of Secrets. collector's ed. J. K. Rowling. Read by Jim Dale. 6 cass. (Running Time: 9 hrs.). (Harry Potter Ser.: Year 2). (YA). (gr. 3 up). 1999. 38.00 (978-0-7366-9130-7(8)) Books on Tape.
Harry Potter is in trouble. His attempts to hop the train back to the Hogwarts School of Witchcraft & Wizardry to begin his second year fail. Then his only other transportation option, a magical flying car, crashes into a Whomping Willow. When he finally gets to school, strange things are happening & he hears an eerie voice talking about escaping & killing. A rumor starts that Harry is the long dreaded heir of one of the school's founders, who purportedly created a Chamber of Secrets which houses a monster that can only be released by the heir. Mystery & ghosts swirl among all the more typical student concerns, eccentric faculty & just plain fanciful fun & horror of traditional British school.

Harry Potter & the Chamber of Secrets. unabr. ed. J. K. Rowling. Read by Jim Dale. 8 CDs. (Running Time: 9 hrs. 25 mins.). (Harry Potter Ser.: Year 2). (YA). (gr. 3 up). 2000. audio compact disk 60.00 (978-0-7366-5091-5(1)) Books on Tape.
In Harry's second year at Hogwarts, new torments & horrors arise. Someone or something is turning Hogwarts students to stone. Could it be Percy Weasley, who's been acting so strange? Could it possibly be Hagrid, the Gamekeeper, whose mysterious past is finally told? Or could it be the one everyone at Hogwarts most suspects... Harry Potter himself!.

Harry Potter & the Chamber of Secrets. unabr. ed. J. K. Rowling. Read by Stephen Fry. 6 cass. (Running Time: 9 hrs. 40 mins.). (Harry Potter Ser.: Year 2). 2002. (978-1-85549-987-4(8)) Cover To Cover GBR.
Harry, determined to discover Hogwarts' Chamber of Secrets, realizes he can speak Parselmouth - which turns out to be very useful indeed.

Harry Potter & the Chamber of Secrets. unabr. ed. J. K. Rowling. Read by Jim Dale. 8 CDs. (Running Time: 9 hrs. 36 mins.). (Harry Potter Ser.: Year 2). (ENG.). (J). (gr. 3-8). 1999. audio compact disk 49.95 (978-0-8072-8194-9(8), Listening Lib) Pub: Random Audio Pubg. Dist(s): Random

Harry Potter & the Chamber of Secrets. unabr. ed. J. K. Rowling. Read by Jim Dale. 6 vols. (Running Time: 9 hrs. 18 mins.). (Harry Potter Ser.: Year 2). (J). (gr. 3 up). 2004. pap. bk. 46.00 (978-0-8072-8207-6(3), S YA 137 SP, Listening Lib); audio compact disk 55.00 (978-0-8072-8601-2(X), S YA 137 CD, Listening Lib); 40.00 (978-0-8072-8206-9(5), LL0160, Listening Lib) Random Audio Pubg.
In Harry's second year at Hogwarts, new torments & horrors arise. Someone or something is turning Hogwarts students to stone. Could it be Percy Weasley, who's been acting so strange? Could it possibly be Hagrid, the Gamekeeper, whose mysterious past is finally told? Or could it be the one everyone at Hogwarts most suspects... Harry Potter himself!.

Harry Potter & the Deathly Hallows. unabr. ed. J. K. Rowling. Read by Jim Dale. 12 cass. (Running Time: 21 hrs. 39 mins.). (Harry Potter Ser.: Year 7). (J). (gr. 4-7). 2007. 90.00 (978-0-7393-6040-8(X), Listening Lib); audio compact disk 79.95 (978-0-7393-6038-5(8), Listening Lib); audio compact disk 90.00 (978-0-7393-6041-5(8), Listening Lib) Pub: Random Audio Pubg. Dist(s): Random

Harry Potter & the Goblet of Fire. collector's ed. J. K. Rowling. Read by Jim Dale. 12 cass. (Running Time: 18 hrs.). (Harry Potter Ser.: Year 4). (YA). (gr. 3 up). 2000. 39.95 (978-0-7366-5519-4(0)) Books on Tape.
Harry returns for his fourth year at Hogwarts, facing dangers & delights as he pitches headfirst into near adulthood.

Harry Potter & the Goblet of Fire. collector's unabr. ed. J. K. Rowling. Read by Jim Dale. 9 cass. (Running Time: 9 hrs.). (Harry Potter Ser.: Year 4). (YA). (gr. 3 up). 2000. 36.00 (978-0-7366-5847-8(5)); audio compact disk 33.95 (978-0-7366-5848-5(3)) Books on Tape.

Harry Potter & the Goblet of Fire. unabr. ed. J. K. Rowling. Read by Jim Dale. 12 cass. (Running Time: 18 hrs.). (Harry Potter Ser.: Year 4). (YA). (gr. 3 up). 2000. 60.00 (L193) Blckstn Audio.
Fourth in the seven-part tale of Harry Potter's training as a wizard & his coming of age. Harry wants to get away from the pernicious Dursleys & go to the International Quidditch Cup with Hermione, Ron, & the Weasleys. He wants to be a normal, fourteen-year -old wizard, but unfortunately for Harry, he's not normal - not even by wizarding standards.

Harry Potter & the Goblet of Fire. unabr. ed. J. K. Rowling. Read by Stephen Fry. 14 cass. (Running Time: 20 hrs. 55 mins). (Harry Potter Ser.: Year 4). 2002. (978-1-85549-989-8(4)) Cover To Cover GBR.
It is Harry's fourth year at Hogwarts and there are spells to be learnt and potions to be brewed. Harry is expecting these: however, other quite unexpected events are already on the march.

Harry Potter & the Goblet of Fire. unabr. ed. J. K. Rowling. Read by Jim Dale. 17 CDs. (Running Time: 21 hrs.). (Harry Potter Ser.: Year 4). (ENG.). (J). (gr. 3-8). 2000. audio compact disk 69.95 (978-0-8072-8259-5(6), Listening Lib) Pub: Random Audio Pubg. Dist(s): Random

Harry Potter & the Goblet of Fire. unabr. ed. J. K. Rowling. Read by Jim Dale. 12 cass. (Running Time: 20 hrs. 37 mins.). (Harry Potter Ser.: Year 4). (J). (gr. 3 up). 2004. 55.00 (978-0-8072-8793-4(8), LL0190, Listening Lib); audio compact disk 100.00 (978-0-8072-8603-6(6), S YA 270 CD, Listening Lib) Random Audio Pubg.
"The pivotal fourth novel in the seven-part tale of Harry Potter's training as a wizard is now available on audio! Harry wants to go to the International Quidditch Cup with Hermione, Ron, and the Weasleys. He wants to find out about the mysterious event that's supposed to take place at Hogwarts this year. He wants to be a normal, fourteen-year-old wizard. Unfortunately for Harry Potter, he's not normal-even by wizarding standards. And in his case, different can be deadly.".

Harry Potter & the Goblet of Fire. unabr. ed. J. K. Rowling & Jim Dale. 12 vols. (Running Time: 20 hrs. 37 mins.). (Harry Potter Ser.: Year 4). (J). 2004. pap. bk. 65.00 (978-0-8072-1196-0(6), S YA 270 SP, Listening Lib) Random Audio Pubg.

Harry Potter & the Half-Blood Prince. unabr. ed. J. K. Rowling. Read by Jim Dale. 17 CDs. (Running Time: 19 hrs.). (Harry Potter Ser.: Year 6). (ENG.). (J). (gr. 4-8). 2005. audio compact disk 75.00 (978-0-307-28365-8(8), Listening Lib) Pub: Random Audio Pubg. Dist(s): Random

Harry Potter & the Half-Blood Prince. unabr. collector's ed. J. K. Rowling. Read by Jim Dale. 12 cass. (Running Time: 18 hrs. 34 mins.). (Harry Potter Ser.: Year 6). (J). (gr. 4-8). 2005. 60.00 (978-0-307-28366-5(6), BksonTape) Random Audio Pubg.

Harry Potter & the Half-Blood Prince. unabr. collector's ed. J. K. Rowling. Read by Jim Dale. 17 CDs. (Running Time: 18 hrs. 34 mins.). (Harry Potter Ser.: Year 6). (J). (gr. 4-8). 2005. audio compact disk 90.00 (978-0-307-28367-2(4), BksonTape) Random Audio Pubg.

Harry Potter & the Order of the Phoenix. unabr. ed. J. K. Rowling. Read by Jim Dale. 23 CDs. (Running Time: 27 hrs.). (Harry Potter Ser.: Year 5). (ENG.). (J). (gr. 3-8). 2003. audio compact disk 75.00 (978-0-8072-2029-0(9), Listening Lib) Pub: Random Audio Pubg. Dist(s): Random

Harry Potter & the Order of the Phoenix. unabr. ed. J. K. Rowling. Read by Jim Dale. 23 CDs. (Running Time: 26 hrs. 30 mins.). (Harry Potter Ser.: Year 5). (J). 2004. audio compact disk 90.00 (978-0-8072-2031-3(0), Listening Lib); 60.00 (978-0-8072-2030-6(2), Listening Lib) Random Audio Pubg.
Dumbledore lowered his hands and surveyed Harry through his half-moon glasses. 'It is time,' he said 'for me to tell you what I should have told you five years ago, Harry. Please sit down. I am going to tell you everything.'.

Harry Potter & the Philosopher's Stone. unabr. ed. J. K. Rowling. Read by Stephen Fry. 6 cass. (Running Time: 8 hrs. 25 mins.). (Harry Potter Ser.: Year 1). 2002. (978-1-85549-394-0(2)); audio compact disk (978-1-85549-652-1(6)) Cover To Cover GBR.
Harry Potter thought he was just ordinary - until his eleventh birthday that is. Then he discovered he was to be one of our finest wizards . .

Harry Potter & the Prisoner of Azkaban. unabr. ed. J. K. Rowling. Read by Jim Dale. 7 cass. (Running Time: 10 hrs. 30 min.). (Harry Potter Ser.: Year 3). (YA). (gr. 3 up). 2000. 38.00 (L150) Blckstn Audio.
For twelve long years the dreaded fortress of Azkaban held an infamous prisoner named Sirius Black. Convicted of killing thirteen people with a single curse, he was said to be the heir apparent to the Dark Lord, Voldemort. Now he has escaped leaving only two clues as to where he might be headed: Harry Potter's defeat of You-Know-Who was Black's downfall as well. And the Azkaban guards heard Black muttering in his sleep, "He's at Hogwarts... he's at Hogwarts." Harry Potter isn't safe, not even within the walls of his magical school, surrounded by his friends. Because on top of it all there may well be a traitor in their midst.

Harry Potter & the Prisoner of Azkaban. unabr. ed. J. K. Rowling. Read by Jim Dale. 10 CDs. (Running Time: 11 hrs. 48 mins.). (Harry Potter Ser.: Year 3). (YA). (gr. 3 up). 2000. audio compact disk 49.46 (978-0-7366-5096-0(2)) Books on Tape.

Harry Potter & the Prisoner of Azkaban. unabr. ed. J. K. Rowling. Read by Jim Dale. 10 CDs. (Running Time: 12 hrs.). (Harry Potter Ser.: Year 3). (ENG.). (J). (gr. 3-8). 2000. audio compact disk 54.95 (978-0-8072-8232-8(4), Listening Lib) Pub: Random Audio Pubg. Dist(s): Random

Harry Potter & the Prisoner of Azkaban. unabr. ed. J. K. Rowling. Read by Jim Dale. 7 vols. (Running Time: 11 hrs. 41 mins.). (Harry Potter Ser.: Year 3). (J). 2004. pap. bk. 52.00 (978-0-8072-8316-5(9), LYA 160 SP, Listening Lib) Random Audio Pubg.
Harry's ready to start his third year at Hogwarts and this adventure promises to be better than his last. Hermione and Ron are back as well. An escaped prisoner from the famous wizard prison, Azkaban, is rumored to be after Harry and everyone wants to keep an eye on him. His name is Sirius Black, a follower of Lord Voldemort. And he will stop at nothing to find Harry Potter, eve if it means laying siege to the very walls of Hogwarts.

Harry Potter & the Prisoner of Azkaban. unabr. ed. J. K. Rowling. Read by Jim Dale. 7 cass. (Running Time: 11 hrs. 41 mins.). (Harry Potter Ser.: Year 3). (J). (gr. 3 up). 2004. 46.00 (978-0-8072-8315-8(0), LL0164, Listening Lib); audio compact disk 65.00 (978-0-8072-8602-9(8), Listening Lib) Random Audio Pubg.

Harry Potter & the Sorcerer's Stone see Harry Potter y la Piedra Filosofal

Harry Potter & the Sorcerer's Stone. collector's unabr. ed. J. K. Rowling. Read by Jim Dale. 6 cass. (Running Time: 9 hrs.). (Harry Potter Ser.: Year 1). (YA). (gr. 3 up). 1999. 33.95 (978-0-7366-9000-3(X), 4195) Books on Tape.
Harry Potter's terrible life with his wretched aunt & uncle changes forever with the arrival of a mysterious letter that carries with it an invitation to an astonishing place, an infamous school for wizards. He begins to discover some clues about his illustrious birthright.

Harry Potter & the Sorcerer's Stone. unabr. ed. J. K. Rowling. Read by Jim Dale. 6 cass. (Harry Potter Ser.: Year 1). (YA). (gr. 3 up). 1999. 37.98 (LL 0146, Chivers Child Audio) AudioGO.
Harry Potter has no ideas how famous he is. That's because he's being raised by his miserable muggle aunt & uncle who are terrified Harry will learn that he's a wizard, just as his parents were. Everything changes when Harry is summoned to attend an infamous school for wizards & he begins to discover some clues about his illustrious birthright.

Harry Potter & the Sorcerer's Stone. unabr. ed. J. K. Rowling. Read by Jim Dale. 6 cass. (Running Time: 9 hrs.). (Harry Potter Ser.: Year 1). (YA). (gr. 3 up). 2000. 38.00 (L282) Blckstn Audio.
Harry Potter has no idea how famous he is. That's because he's being raised by his miserable aunt & uncle who are terrified Harry will learn that he's really a wizard, just as his parents were. But everything changes when Harry is summoned to attend an infamous school for wizards & he begins to discover some clues about his illustrious birthright. From the surprising way he is greeted by a loveable giant, to the unique curriculum & colorful faculty at this unusual school, Harry finds himself drawn deep inside a mystical world he never knew existed, & closer to his own noble destiny.

Harry Potter & the Sorcerer's Stone. unabr. ed. J. K. Rowling. Read by Jim Dale. 7 CDs. (Running Time: 8 hrs. 12 mins.). (Harry Potter Ser.: Year 1). (YA). (gr. 3 up). 2000. audio compact disk 49.95 (978-0-7366-5092-2(X)) Books on Tape.
Harry Potter's terrible life with his wretched aunt & uncle changes forever with the arrival of a mysterious letter that carries with it an invitation to an astonishing place, an infamous school for wizards. He begins to discover some clues about his illustrious birthright.

Harry Potter & the Sorcerer's Stone. unabr. ed. J. K. Rowling. Read by Stephen Fry. 6 cass. (Harry Potter Ser.: Year 1). (YA). (gr. 3 up). 1999. 37.98 (FS9-50964) Highsmith.
Harry Potter has no ideas how famous he is. That's because he's being raised by his miserable muggle aunt & uncle who are terrified Harry will learn that he's a wizard, just as his parents were. Everything changes when Harry is summoned to attend an infamous school for wizards & he begins to discover some clues about his illustrious birthright.

Harry Potter & the Sorcerer's Stone. unabr. ed. J. K. Rowling. 7 cass. (Running Time: 12 hrs.). (Harry Potter Ser.: Year 1). (YA). (gr. 3 up). pap. bk. 62.00 (978-0-8072-1547-0(3), Listening Lib) Random Audio Pubg.

Harry Potter & the Sorcerer's Stone. unabr. ed. J. K. Rowling. Read by Jim Dale. 7 CDs. (Running Time: 8 hrs. 17 mins.). (Harry Potter Ser.: Year 1). (ENG.). (J). (gr. 3-8). 1999. audio compact disk 49.95 (978-0-8072-8195-6(6), Listening Lib) Pub: Random Audio Pubg. Dist(s): Random

Harry Potter & the Sorcerer's Stone. unabr. ed. J. K. Rowling. Read by Jim Dale. 6 cass. (Running Time: 8 hrs. 17 mins.). (Harry Potter Ser.: Year 1). (J). (gr. 3 up). 2004. 40.00 (978-0-8072-8118-5(2), LL0146, Listening Lib); audio compact disk 50.00 (978-0-8072-8600-5(1), S YA 108 CD, Listening Lib); pap. bk. 46.00 (978-0-8072-8119-2(0), S YA 108 SP, Listening Lib) Random Audio Pubg.
Harry Potter's terrible life with his wretched aunt & uncle changes forever with the arrival of a mysterious letter that carries with it an invitation to an astonishing place, an infamous school for wizards. He begins to discover some clues about his illustrious birthright.

Harry Potter y la Piedra Filosofal. J. K. Rowling. Read by Christopher E. Smith. 8 cd. (Running Time: 8 hrs. 20 mins.). (Harry Potter Ser.: Year 1).Tr. of Harry Potter & the Sorcerer's Stone. (SPA.). 2004. bk. 49.95 (978-84-7888-856-6(X)) Emece ESP.

Harry Roskolenko. unabr. ed. Harry Roskolenko. Read by Harry Roskolenko. 1 cass. (Running Time: 29 min.). 1986. 10.00 New Letters.
World traveler Roskolenko reads from his works & is remembered in an interview with a long-time friend & traveling companion.

Harry S. Truman. Read by Jack Perkins. 1 cass. (Running Time: 45 min.). 1997. 9.95 A & E Home.

Harry S. Truman. Soundworks. 1 cass. 1995. audio compact disk 10.98 (978-1-885959-17-1(6), JRCS 7038) Jerden Recs.
Highlights of major speeches given by President Harry S. Truman, from 1948 to 1953.

Harry S. Truman. unabr. ed. Robert H. Ferrell. Narrated by Nelson Runger. 16 cass. (Running Time: 23 hrs. 15 mins.). 1996. 128.00 (978-0-7887-0398-0(6), 94590E7) Recorded Bks.
Ferrell documents Truman's ambition & powerful commitment to service, along with his shrewdness & exceptional ability to judge people.

Harry S. Truman: A Journey to Independence - An Intimate Audio Portrait. Perf. by Harry S. Truman. Narrated by Lauren Bacall et al. 4 cass. (Running Time: 60 min. per cass.). 1998. 12.98 Boxed set. (4350) Radio Spirits.
Reveals the president of common sense, personal responsibility, & integrity.

Harry S. Truman: A Journey to Independence - An Intimate Audio Portrait, Set. unabr. ed. Read by Lauren Bacall et al. Intro. by Bill Clinton. 4 cass. (Running Time: 4 hrs.). 1995. 21.95 (978-1-55935-179-9(9), 492935) Soundelux.
In the first 120 days of Truman's presidency, the war in Europe was won, the atomic age began & the United Nations was born.

Harry S. Truman: A Life. unabr. ed. Robert H. Ferrell. Read by Jeff Riggenbach. 15 cass. (Running Time: 23 hrs. 30 mins.). 1997. 95.95 (978-0-7861-1094-0(5), 1860) Blckstn Audio.
Few U.S. presidents have captured the imagination of the American people as has Harry S. Truman, "the man from Missouri." In this major biography, Robert H. Ferrell, widely regarded as an authority on the thirty-third president, challenges the popular characterization of Truman as a man who rarely sought the offices he received, revealing instead a man who - with modesty, commitment to service, & basic honesty - moved with method & system toward the presidency.

Harry S. Truman: The Honest President. unabr. ed. Merle Miller. 1 cass. (Running Time: 56 min.). 12.95 (40050) J Norton Pubs.
In an interview with Heywood Hale Broun, Miller gives an account of a candid, brilliant & honest man who he believes was never fully appreciated as President but to whom history will be more than kind.

Harry S. Truman: The 33rd President, 1945-1953. unabr. ed. Robert Dallek. Read by William Dufris. Ed. by Arthur M. Schlesinger, Jr. & Sean Wilentz. 5 CDs. (Running Time: 6 hrs. 0 mins. 0 sec.). (ENG.). 2008. audio compact disk 29.95 (978-1-4272-0543-8(4)) Pub: Macmill Audio. Dist(s): Macmillan

Harry the Dirty Dog. 2004. bk. 24.95 (978-0-7882-0692-4(3)); pap. bk. 18.95 (978-1-55592-427-0(1)); pap. bk. 32.75 (978-1-55592-238-2(4)); pap. bk. 32.75 (978-1-55592-239-9(2)); pap. bk. 32.75 (978-1-55592-429-4(8)); pap. bk. 14.95 (978-1-55592-658-8(4)); audio compact disk 12.95 (978-1-55592-913-8(3)) Weston Woods.

Harry the Dirty Dog. (J). 2004. pap. bk. 38.75 (978-1-55592-430-0(1)) Weston Woods.

Harry the Dirty Dog. Gene Zion. Illus. by Margaret Bloy Graham. 1 cass., 5 bks. (Running Time: 30 min.). (J). pap. bk. 32.75 Weston Woods.

Harry the Dirty Dog. Gene Zion. Illus. by Margaret Bloy Graham. 1 cass. (Running Time: 30 min.). (J). (ps-2). bk. 24.95; pap. bk. 12.95 Weston Woods.
Harry, the little white dog with black spots, runs away before bath time & plays outside, until he changes into a black dog with white spots. Back home again, he must use all his wits & tricks to convince his family who he really is.

Harry the Dirty Dog. unabr. ed. Prod. by Paul Gagne. Narrated by Bruce Johnson. Music by Ernest V. Troost. 1 cass. (Running Time: 7 min.). (J). 1997. 8.95 (978-1-56008-813-4(3), RAC359) Weston Woods.
Harry, the little white dog with black spots, runs away before bathtime & plays outside until he changes into a black dog with white spots.

Harry the Dirty Dog. unabr. ed. Gene Zion. 1 CD. (Running Time: 9 mins.). (SPA.). (J). (ps-2). 2006. pap. bk. 18.95 (978-0-439-90593-0(1)) Weston Woods.

Harry the Dirty Dog & Other Animal Stories: Harry the Dirty Dog, Officer Buckle & Gloria, I, CROCODILE, Flossie & the Fox, Norman the Doorman. unabr. ed. Gene Zion et al. Read by Patricia C. McKissack et al. (J). 2007. 44.99 (978-1-60252-684-6(2)) Find a World.

Harry the Poisonous Centipede: A Story to Make You Squirm. unabr. ed. Lynne Reid Banks. Read by Lynne Reid Banks. 2 cass. (Running Time: 1 hr. 31 mins.). (J). (gr. 1-3). 1998. pap. bk. 23.00 (978-0-8072-7997-7(8), YA962SP, Listening Lib); 23.00 (978-0-8072-7996-0(X), LL0127, Listening Lib) Random Audio Pubg.
Harry must never visit Hoo-Mins! But he & his friend George venture into the UP-Pipe World - the land of the Hoo-Mins.

Harry the Poisonous Centipede: A Story to Make You Squirm, Set. unabr. ed. Lynne Reid Banks. Read by Lynne Reid Banks. 2 cass. (J). (gr. 1-8). 1999. 16.98 (LL 0127, Chivers Child Audio) AudioGO.

Harry the Sixty Lb. Guard Cat. unabr. ed. Roger W. Bretemitz. 1 cass. (Running Time: 20 min.). (J). (gr. k-5). 1997. 8.95 (978-1-893417-01-4(8), 001) Vector Studios.
A Canadian Lynx guards million dollar boat, scares off burglar & gets reward from police & Marina Society.

Harry Truman: A New View. Prod. by A&E Television Network Staff. 1 cass. 1997. 9.95 (978-0-7670-0001-7(3)) A & E Home.
Historical - U.S.

Harry Tuft: Across the Blue Mountain. 1 cass. 9.98 (C-63) Folk-Legacy.
A varied collection, some old, some new, well sung.

Harry's Picture. unabr. ed. Susan Kempler. 1 cass. (Running Time: 7 min.). (Read It Alone Ser.). (J). (ps-3). 1985. 16.99 incl. hardcover. (978-0-87386-006-2(3)) Jan Prods.
Harry loves to take pictures with his old camera. He encounters more than he bargained for when he goes to photograph a traffic jam; for there holding up all the traffic is a mother cat & her kittens.

***Harry's Pony.** unabr. ed. Barbara Ann Porte. (ENG.). 2008. (978-0-06-169466-0(5)); (978-0-06-171338-5(4)) HarperCollins Pubs.

Harsh Cry of the Heron: The Last Tale of the Otori. unabr. ed. Lian Hearn. Read by Julia Fletcher & Henri Lubatti. 16. (Running Time: 72000 sec.). Bk. 4. (ENG.). 2006. audio compact disk 46.95 (978-1-59887-067-1(X), 159887067X) Pub: HighBridge. Dist(s): Workman Pub

Harstairs House. unabr. ed. Amanda Grange. 6 cass. (Soundings Ser.). (J). 2005. 54.95 (978-1-84559-117-5(8)) Pub: ISIS Lrg Prnt GBR. Dist(s): Ulverscroft US

Hart Crane. unabr. ed. Nathan Asch. 1 cass. (Running Time: 15 min.). 1959. 12.95 (23049) J Norton Pubs.
Having lived with him at one time, Asch recalls Crane's idiosyncracies, his alcoholism & homosexuality, during an agonizing period for the great poet.

Hart Crane, On. unabr. ed. Robert Park. 1 cass. (Running Time: 57 min.). 1963. 12.95 (23197) J Norton Pubs.
Park discusses Hart Crane's split personality & unhappy life & relates them to the dichotomies in his poetry. He reads & interprets passages from "Crane's Voyages" & "the Bridge".

Hart's Hope. Orson Scott Card. Read by Stefan Rudnicki. (Running Time: 11 mins.). 2005. 65.95 (978-0-7861-3676-6(6)); audio compact disk 81.00 (978-0-7861-7690-8(3)) Blckstn Audio.

Hart's Hope. unabr. ed. Orson Scott Card. Read by Stefan Rudnicki. (Running Time: 11 mins.). 2005. 29.95 (978-0-7861-7952-7(X)) Blckstn Audio.

Hart's War. unabr. ed. John Katzenbach. Narrated by Frank Muller. 14 cass. (Running Time: 19 hrs. 45 mins.). 1999. 112.00 (978-0-7887-3748-0(1), 95949E7) Recorded Bks.
The horrors of a German POW camp & the suspense of a legal battle collide in this World War II thriller. Someone has killed a popular southern prisoner in Stalag Luft 13. All the evidence points to a Black lieutenant who was target of his racial slurs. Now it's up to navigator Tommy Hart to be the lieutenant's legal defense. As Hart prepares for the trial, however, he begins to think that they are being set up.

Haruhi Character CD. Perf. by Aya Hirano. (YA). 2007. 9.98 (978-1-59409-841-3(7)) Bandai Ent.

Haruhi no Tsumeawase. Perf. by Aya Hirano. (YA). 2007. 9.98 (978-1-59409-842-0(5)) Bandai Ent.

Harvard Medical School Guide to Lowering Your Cholesterol. abr. ed. Mason W. Freeman. Narrated by Alan Sklar. (Running Time: 10800 sec.). 2005. audio compact disk 22.95 (978-1-933310-01-5(4)) STI Certified.

Harvard Medical School Guide to Overcoming Thyroid Problems. Jeffrey R. Garber. 2007. audio compact disk 22.95 (978-1-933310-17-6(0)) STI Certified.

Harvard Medical School Guide to Taking Control of Asthma: A Comprehensive Prevention & Treatment Plan for You & Your Family. abr. ed. Christopher H. Fanta et al. Read by Barrett Whitener. Told to Nancy Waring. (Running Time: 10800 sec.). 2006. audio compact disk 22.95 (978-1-933310-03-9(0)) STI Certified.

Harvard Yard in April: April in Harvard Yard see Twentieth-Century Poetry in English, No. 26, Recordings of Poets Reading Their Own Poetry

Harvest. T. D. Jakes. (ENG.). 2008. 19.99 (978-1-4245-0825-9(8)) Tre Med Inc.

Harvest. abr. ed. Rick Joyner. 2004. 19.99 (978-0-7684-0212-4(3)) Destiny Image Pubs.

Harvest. unabr. ed. Tess Gerritsen. Narrated by George Guidall. 11 CDs. (Running Time: 12 hrs. 30 mins.). 1999. audio compact disk 96.00 (978-0-7887-3716-9(3), C1073E7) Recorded Bks.
A second-year medical resident notices that the paperwork for a donor heart is missing & she begins to uncover horrifying clues to where the mysterious organ was harvested.

Harvest. unabr. ed. Tess Gerritsen. Narrated by George Guidall. 9 cass. (Running Time: 12 hrs. 30 mins.). 1997. 80.00 (978-0-7887-0790-2(6), 94940E7) Recorded Bks.
Second-year medical resident notices that the paperwork for a donor heart is missing & she begins to uncover horrifying clues to where the mysterious organ was harvested.

Harvest. unabr. ed. Tess Gerritsen. Narrated by George Guidall. 9 cass. (Running Time: 12 hrs. 30 mins.). 2002. 42.95 (978-0-7887-8251-0(7), RD732) Recorded Bks.
A second-year resident selected for Boston's Bayside Hospital's elite cardiac transplant team, Dr. Abby DiMatteo is just beginning to learn the nightmares involved in finding a donor heart for a transplant victim. But when a wealthy private patient checks into the hospital, and a donor heart appears without the proper paperwork, Abby uncovers some horrifying clues to where the mysterious organ was harvested. Brilliantly conceived and flawlessly executed, Harvest spins the listener into an explosive world of medical miracles, lethal greed and unforgiveable conspiracy.

***Harvest.** unabr. ed. Belva Plain. Read by Joyce Bean. (Running Time: 12 hrs.). 2010. 24.99 (978-1-4418-4145-2(8), 9781441841452, Brilliance MP3); 39.97 (978-1-4418-4146-9(6), 9781441841469, Brinc Audio MP3 Lib); 24.99 (978-1-4418-4147-6(4), 9781441841476, BAD); 39.97 (978-1-4418-4148-3(2), 9781441841483, BADLE) Brilliance Audio.

Harvest Audio BK. T. D. Jakes. 2008. audio compact disk 24.99 (978-0-7684-2666-3(9)) Destiny Image Pubs.

Harvest Blessing, Vol. I: Looking. 4 cass. (Running Time: 45 min. per cass.). 29.50 (9200) Franciscan Comns.
Includes Looking Back, Looking at Know, Looking Alone, & Looking Beyond.

Harvest Celebration. Marina Bokelman. Read by Marina Bokelman. 1 cass. (Running Time: 1 hr.). (Seasonal Medicine Wheel Ser.). 1991. 9.95 (978-1-886139-03-9(2), SMW-3) Sacred Paw.
Attunement with seasonal energy, Fall healing issues, transformational process work.

Harvest for Hope: A Guide to Mindful Eating. abr. ed. Jane Goodall et al. Read by Tippi Hedren. (ENG.). 2005. 14.98 (978-1-59483-267-3(6)) Pub: Hachet Audio. Dist(s): HachBkGrp

Harvest for Hope: A Guide to Mindful Eating. abr. ed. Jane Goodall et al. Read by Tippi Hedren. (Running Time: 6 hrs.). (ENG.). 2009. 49.98 (978-1-60788-082-0(2)) Pub: Hachet Audio. Dist(s): HachBkGrp

***Harvest Hunting.** unabr. ed. Yasmine Galenorn. (Running Time: 11 hrs. 0 mins.). (Sisters of the Moon Ser.). 2010. 34.99 (978-1-4001-9765-1(1)); 24.99 (978-1-4001-6765-4(5)); 17.99 (978-1-4001-8765-2(6)); audio compact disk 83.99 (978-1-4001-4765-6(4)); audio compact disk 34.99 (978-1-4001-1765-9(8)) Pub: Tantor Media. Dist(s): IngramPubServ

Harvest Hymn see Sir John Betjeman Reading His Poetry

Harvest of Justice. 7684th ed. 1989. audio compact disk 16.00 (978-1-58459-071-2(8)) Wrld Lib Pubns.

Harvest of Sunflowers. unabr. ed. Ruth Silvestre. Read by Ruth Silvestre. 6 cass. (Running Time: 7 hrs. 48 mins.). (Isis Cassettes Ser.). (J). 2006. 54.95 (978-0-7531-3436-8(5)) Pub: ISIS Lrg Prnt GBR. Dist(s): Ulverscroft US

Harvest of the Earth: Rev. 14:6-20, 573. Ed Young. 1987. 4.95 (978-0-7417-1573-9(2), 573) Win Walk.

Harvest of the Earth: Rev. 14:6-20, 574. Ed Young. 1987. Rental 4.95 (978-0-7417-1574-6(0), 574) Win Walk.

Harvest on the Don. unabr. collector's ed. Mikhail Sholokhov. Read by Wolfram Kandinsky. 11 cass. (Running Time: 16 hrs. 30 min.). 1986. 88.00 (978-0-7366-0839-8(7), 1790) Books on Tape.
Sholokhov continues the dramatic story of the impact of revolution on the people of his native Russia. We see the same Don village, Gremyachy Log, to which has come Davidov, representative of the Party's drive to revolutionize village agriculture. The peasants see a vision of a better life in the plans of this man. Yet to-the-death opposition lurks just beneath the surface.

Harvest Song: Music from Around the World Inspired by Working the Land. 1 CD. (Running Time: 1 hr.). 1995. pap. bk. 19.95 (978-1-55961-297-5(5)); pap. bk. 16.95 (978-1-55961-298-2(3)) Relaxtn Co.

Harvest Your Dreams. Gary V. Whetstone. 6 cass. (Running Time: 9 hrs.). (Empowerment Ser.). 1998. pap. bk. 50.00 (978-1-58866-186-9(5), VE027A) Gary Whet Pub.
Dare to dream boldly, but don't limit yourself to earthly manifestations. God also has purposed eternal dreams for you to fulfill ! Through this series, learn how to sow.

Harvester. unabr. ed. Gene Stratton-Porter. Read by Mary Starkey. 12 cass. (Running Time: 13 hrs.). 1989. 64.95 (978-1-55686-295-3(4), 112674) Books in Motion.
David Langston is the collector & seller of medicinal herbs taken from the forest near his home. David is a fine upstanding young man in search of the woman of his dreams; she came to him in a vision. He knows she is attainable & he must find her.

Harvesting Church Seminar. Frank Damazio. 6 cass. (Running Time: 9 hrs.). 2000. 39.99 (978-1-886849-37-2(4)) CityChristian.

Harvesting God's Promises. Gary V. Whetstone. 4 cass. (Running Time: 6 hrs.). (Empowerment Ser.). 1998. bk. 35.00 (978-1-58866-187-6(3), VE028A) Gary Whet Pub.
Have you heard God's promises for you personally? Many christians have not. Or do you have a promise from God but don't know what to do with it?.

Harvesting the Heart. unabr. ed. Jodi Picoult. Contrib. by Cassandra Campbell. (Running Time: 18 hrs.). (ENG.). (gr. 12 up). 2008. audio compact disk 39.95 (978-0-14-314332-1(8)) Penguin Grp USA.

Harvey Penick, Set. gif. ed. Harvey Penick & Bud Shrake. 1 cass. (Running Time: 180 min.). 1993. 24.00 (978-0-671-99329-0(1), Audioworks) S&S Audio.

Harvey Penick's Little Red Book. abr. ed. Harvey Penick. Read by Jack Whitaker. 2004. 7.95 (978-0-7435-4803-8(5)) Pub: S&S Audio. Dist(s): S and S Inc

Harvey's Life - Now What? Audio Book. Brian H. Porter. (ENG.). 2009. 14.98 (978-1-932278-65-1(6)) Pub: Mayhaven Pub. Dist(s): Baker Taylor

***Has Christianity Failed You?** unabr. ed. Ravi Zacharias. (Running Time: 8 hrs. 10 mins. 35 sec.). (ENG.). 2010. 31.99 (978-0-310-26956-4(3)) Zondervan.

Has Christianity Failed You? unabr. ed. Ravi Zacharias. (Running Time: 8 hrs. 10 mins. 35 sec.). (ENG.). 2010. 18.99 (978-0-310-26957-1(1)) Zondervan.

Has the Contraceptive Mentality Affected Religious Life?; Growth in Holiness; Antidote to the Contraceptive Mentality; Arch. Cacciavillan. Fr. Mankowski & Fr. Henchey. 1 cass. (National Meeting of the Institute, 1993 Ser.). 4.00 (93N1) IRL Chicago.

Hasenwinkel Road Travel Guide: Drive the Texas Hill Country by way of Hasenwinkel Road. 2nd enl. exp. ed. 2007. pap. bk. 20.00 (978-0-9676931-7-0(9)) Skyline Ranch.

Hashish Eater: Edited, with notes, &C. , by Donald Sidney-Fryer. Clark Ashton Smith. Anno. by Donald Sidney-Fryer. 2008. pap. bk. 15.00 (978-0-9793806-8-6(5)) Hippocampus Pr.

Hasidic & Sufi Teaching Stories. unabr. ed. James Fadiman. 1 cass. (Running Time: 59 min.). 1980. 11.00 (03202) Big Sur Tapes.

Hasidic Archetypes. unabr. ed. Zalman Schachter-Shalomi. Read by Zalman Schachter-Shalomi. 5 cass. (Running Time: 6 hrs. 39 min.). 1994. 46.00 Set. (31002) Big Sur Tapes.
The stories, rituals & symbols of Hasidic tradition provide a rich resource for living soulfully. Rabbi Schachter skillfully weaves these elements together, creating a framework for experience & understanding that can help enrich life in the world.

Hastened to the Grave. unabr. ed. Jack Olsen. Read by Susie Breck. (Running Time: 12 hrs.). 2009. 39.97 (978-1-4233-8623-0(X), 9781423386230, Brinc Audio MP3 Lib); 39.97 (978-1-4233-8625-4(6), 9781423386254, BADLE); 24.99 (978-1-4233-8622-3(1), 9781423386223, Brilliance MP3); 24.99 (978-1-4233-8624-7(8), 9781423386247, BAD) Brilliance Audio.

Hasty Death. unabr. ed. Marion Chesney. Narrated by Davina Porter. 6 CDs. (Running Time: 23700 sec.). (Edwardian Murder Mysteries Ser.). 2006. audio compact disk 64.95 (978-0-7927-4476-4(4), SLD 1006) AudioGO.

Hat. 2004. 8.95 (978-0-89719-906-3(5)); cass. & flmstrp 30.00 (978-0-89719-506-5(X)) Weston Woods.

Hat. unabr. ed. Jan Brett. 1 cass. (Running Time: 15 min.). (J). 2001. bk. 27.95 (978-0-8045-6855-5(3), 6855) Spoken Arts.
When Lisa's woolen stocking flies off the clothesline, Hedgie finds it and pokes his nose in. He tries to pull it out, but the stocking gets stuck on his prickles - and the fun begins.

Hat Full of Rabbits-4. Thomas Henry Kelly. 2006. audio compact disk 35.00 (978-1-56142-207-4(X)) T Kelly Inc.

Hat Full of Sky. abr. ed. Terry Pratchett. 4 cass. (Running Time: 6 hrs). (Discworld Ser.). 2004. 34.95 (978-0-06-059772-6(0)) HarperCollins Pubs.

Hat Full of Sky. unabr. ed. Terry Pratchett. Read by Stephen Briggs. 7 CDs. (Running Time: 10 hrs. 30 mins.). (Discworld Ser.). (J). (gr. 6-10). 2004. audio compact disk 34.95 (978-0-06-074768-8(4), HarperChildAud) HarperCollins Pubs.

***Hat Full of Sky.** unabr. ed. Terry Pratchett. Read by Stephen Briggs. (ENG.). 2004. (978-0-06-082465-5(4), Harper Audio); (978-0-06-082466-2(2), Harper Audio) HarperCollins Pubs.

Hat, the; Tilly's House; Pig Pig Grows up; Bear Hunt. 2004. (978-0-89719-850-9(6)); cass. & flmstrp (978-0-89719-706-9(2)) Weston Woods.

Hatbox Baby. unabr. ed. Carrie Brown. Read by Grover Gardner. 8 vols. (Running Time: 11 hrs.). 2001. bk. 69.95 (978-0-7927-2430-8(5), CSL 319, Chivers Sound Lib) AudioGO.
On a summer morning in 1933, a baby is delivered in a hatbox to the Century of Progress Exposition in Chicago. Born three months early, this tiny baby is brought by his desperate young father to the fair's famous baby doctor, Leo Hoffman, to be saved.

Hatchet. Gary Paulsen. Read by Peter Coyote. 3 cass. (Running Time: 4 hrs. 35 mins.). (J). 2000. 24.00 (978-0-7366-9051-5(4)) Books on Tape.
Haunted by his parents divorce & the secret that caused it, young Brian Robeson, the sole survivor of a plane crash in the Canadian wilderness, must draw on untested skills & strength to survive.

Hatchet. Gary Paulsen. 4 cass. (Running Time: 222 min.). (J). (gr. 4-6). 2001. audio compact disk 33.00 (978-0-8072-0506-8(0), Listening Lib) Random Audio Pubg.

Hatchet. Gary Paulsen. (J). 1989. 21.33 (978-0-07-540595-5(4)) SRA McGraw.

Hatchet. abr. ed. Gary Paulsen. 3 cass. (Running Time: 3 hrs. 30 mins.). (J). 1992. 14.39 (978-0-553-70027-5(8), 391964, Random AudioBks) Random Audio Pubg.
On his way to visit his recently divorced father in the Canadian mountains, thirteen-year-old Brian Robeson is the only survivor when the single-engine plane crashes. His body battered, his clothes in shreds, Brian must now stay alive in the boundless Canadian wilderness. More than a survival story, Hathcet is a tale of tough decisions. When all is stripped down to the barest essentials, Brian discovers some stark and simple truths: Self-pity doesn't work. Despair doesn't work. And if Brian is to survive physically as well as mentally, he must discover courage.

Hatchet. unabr. ed. Gary Paulsen. Read by Peter Coyote. 4 CDs. (Running Time: 3 hrs. 42 mins.). (ENG.). (J). (gr. 5). 2004. audio compact disk 19.99 (978-0-8072-0477-1(3), Listening Lib) Pub: Random Audio Pubg. Dist(s): Random

Hatchet. unabr. ed. Gary Paulson. 3 CDs. (Running Time: 3 hrs. 42 mins.). (J). (gr. 5-9). 2004. audio compact disk 25.50 (978-0-8072-1155-7(9), Listening Lib) Pub: Random Audio Pubg. Dist(s): NetLibrary CO
Heart-stopping story of a boy who, following a plane crash in the Canadian wilderness, must learn to survive with only a hatchet and his own wits.

Hatchet. unabr. ed. Gary Paulson. Read by Peter Coyote. 3 vols. (Running Time: 3 hrs. 42 mins.). (J). (gr. 5-9). 2004. pap. bk. 36.00 (978-0-8072-8319-6(3), YA161SP, Listening Lib); 30.00 (978-0-8072-8318-9(5), LL0174, Listening Lib) Random Audio Pubg.
Haunted by his parents' divorce & the secret that caused it, young Brian Roberson, the sole survivor of a plane crash in the Canadian wilderness, must draw on untested skills & strength to survive.

Hatchling. unabr. ed. Kathryn Lasky. (Running Time: 5.5 hrs. NaN mins.). (Guardians of Ga'Hoole Ser.: Bk. 7). 2009. audio compact disk 34.95 (978-1-4332-2621-2(9)); audio compact disk 50.00 (978-1-4332-2622-9(7)) Blckstn Audio.

Hatchling. unabr. ed. Kathryn Lasky. Read by Pamela Garelick. (Running Time: 5 hrs. 30 mins.). (Guardians of Ga'Hoole Ser.: Bk. 7). 2010. 29.95 (978-1-4332-2625-0(1)) Blckstn Audio.

***Hatchling.** unabr. ed. Kathryn Lasky. Read by Pamela Garelick. (Running Time: 5 hrs. 30 mins.). (Guardians of Ga'Hoole Ser.: Bk. 7). 2010. audio compact disk 24.95 (978-1-4332-2624-3(3)) Blckstn Audio.

Hate Crimes. Hosted by Leonard Peikoff. 1 cass. (Philosophy: Who Needs It? Ser.). 1998. 12.95 (LPXXC58) Second Renaissance.

Hate Mail from Cheerleaders: And Other Adventures from the Life of Reilly. unabr. ed. Rick Reilly. Read by Lloyd James. (YA). 2008. 59.99 (978-1-60514-584-6(X)) Find a World.

Hate Mail from Cheerleaders: And Other Adventures from the Life of Reilly. unabr. ed. Rick Reilly. Read by Lloyd James. (Running Time: 10 hrs. 0 mins. 0 sec.). (ENG.). 2007. audio compact disk 69.99 (978-1-4001-3555-4(9)) Pub: Tantor Media. Dist(s): IngramPubServ

Hate Mail from Cheerleaders: And Other Adventures from the Life of Reilly. unabr. ed. Rick Reilly. Read by Lloyd James. Intro. by Lance Armstrong. (Running Time: 10 hrs. 0 mins. 0 sec.). (ENG.). 2007. audio compact disk 34.99 (978-1-4001-0555-7(2)); audio compact disk 24.99 (978-1-4001-5555-2(X)) Pub: Tantor Media. Dist(s): IngramPubServ

***Hate That Cat.** unabr. ed. Sharon Creech. Read by Scott Wolf. (ENG.). 2008. (978-0-06-170611-0(6)); (978-0-06-170612-7(4)) HarperCollins Pubs.

Hate That Cat. unabr. ed. Sharon Creech. Read by Scott Wolf. (J). (gr. 4-7). 2008. audio compact disk 14.95 (978-0-06-165822-8(7), HarperChildAud) HarperCollins Pubs.

Hate That Cat. unabr. ed. Sharon Creech. Read by Scott Wolf. 1 CD. (Running Time: 1 hr. 3 mins.). (J). (gr. 4-7). 2008. audio compact disk 20.00 (978-0-7393-7679-9(9), Listening Lib) Pub: Random Audio Pubg. Dist(s): Random

Hater. unabr. ed. David Moody. Read by Gerard Doyle. (Running Time: 9.5 hrs. 0 mins.). (ENG.). 2009. 29.95 (978-1-4332-9289-7(0)); 59.95 (978-1-4332-9285-9(8)); audio compact disk 90.00 (978-1-4332-9286-6(6)) Blckstn Audio.

Haters. abr. ed. Alisa Valdes-Rodriguez. Read by Flora Diaz. (Running Time: 6 hrs.). (ENG.). 2006. 9.98 (978-1-59483-801-9(1)) Pub: Hachet Audio. Dist(s): HachBkGrp

Haters. abr. ed. Alisa Valdes-Rodriguez. Read by Flora Diaz. (Running Time: 6 hrs.). (ENG.). 2009. 19.98 (978-1-60788-268-8(X)) Pub: Hachet Audio. Dist(s): HachBkGrp

Haters. unabr. ed. Alisa Valdes-Rodriguez. Read by Johanna Parker. 8 cass. (Running Time: 9 hrs. 50 mins.). (YA). (gr. 8 up). 2006. 59.75 (978-1-4281-2198-0(6)); audio compact disk 87.75 (978-1-4281-2203-1(6)) Recorded Bks.

Hateship, Friendship, Courtship, Loveship, Marriage: Stories. unabr. ed. Alice Munro. Read by Kymberly Dakin. 6 cass. (Running Time: 10 hrs.). 2002. 29.95 (978-1-57270-291-2(5)) Pub: Audio Partners. Dist(s): PerseuPGW
Collection of characters a subtly revealed and personal stories unfold. The fate of a housekeeper is unintentionally reversed by a teenage girl's practical joke. A college student vising her aunt stumbles on a long-hidden secret and its meaning in her life. And an inveterate philanderer finds the tables turned when he puts his wife into an old-age home.

Hateship, Friendship, Courtship, Loveship, Marriage: Stories. unabr. ed. Alice Munro. Read by Kymberly Dakin. 6 vols. (Running Time: 7 hrs. 30 mins.). 2002. bk. 54.95 (978-0-7927-2526-8(3), CSL 415, Chivers Sound Lib) AudioGO.
Here's another collection of short but sure-to-please stories. This is the tenth collection of stories from Canada's matchless chronicle of women's external fates, inner lives, and painful journeys toward and away from self-understanding. These particular nine tales are set mostly in native

Ontario or in Western Canada and they're sure to leave listeners mesmerized once again.

Hateship, Friendship, Courtship, Loveship, Marriage: Stories. unabr. ed. Alice Munro. Narrated by Kymberly Dakin. 8 CDs. (Running Time: 10 hrs.). (Audio Editions Ser.). (ENG.). 2002. audio compact disk 39.95 (978-1-57270-292-9(3)) Pub: AudioGO. Dist(s): Perseus Dist
Collection of characters a subtly revealed and personal stories unfold. The fate of a housekeeper is unintentionally reversed by a teenage girl's practical joke. A college student vising her aunt stumbles on a long-hidden secret and its meaning in her life. And an inveterate philanderer finds the tables turned when he puts his wife into an old-age home.

Hatfield-McCoy Feud: They Were Reckless Mountain Boys. unabr. ed. Jimmy Gray & Jan Gray. Ed. by Joe Loesch. 1 cass. (Running Time: 60 min.). (Americana Ser.). 1995. 9.95 (978-1-887262-04-0(0), AudioMagazine) Natl Tape & Disc.
An original documentary describing the famed Hatfield-McCoy feud in Kentucky & West Virginia. With a host narrator, character voices, background music & sound effects.

Hatfield-McCoy Feud: They Were Reckless Mountain Boys. unabr. ed. Jimmy Gray & Jan Gray. Narrated by Bennie Shipley. Prod. by Joe Loesch. 1 cass. (Running Time: 1 hr.). (Wild West Ser.). 1999. 12.95 (978-1-887729-63-5(1)) Toy Box Prods.
For years, rifle shots echoes through the mountains of Kentucky & West Virginia. Dark secrets were hidden far back in the hollows & no stranger dared go there. The law stayed away & justice was found in the barrel of a gun.

Hatha Yoga Devanand: Ejercicio de Ralajcion-Primer Nivel. Luis F. Rivera. Perf. by Alfredo J. Santi. 1 cass. (Running Time: 21 min.). 1998. bk. 10.00 (978-1-893261-05-1(0)) USA Dev Yoga.

Hatha Yoga Exercises. 1 cass. (Running Time: 1 hr.). 12.99 (602) Yoga Res Foun.

Hating Whitey: And Other Progressive Causes. David Horowitz. Read by Jeff Riggenbach. 7 cass. (Running Time: 10 hrs.). 2001. 49.95 (978-0-7861-1979-0(9), 2749) Blckstn Audio.
Ideological hatred of whites is now a growth industry, boosted by "civil rights" activists & liberal academics. These once-youthful radicals, now entrenched in positions of power & influence, peddle a warmed-over version of the Marxist creed that supported the Communist empire & excuses intolerance to the point of thuggery.

***Hating Whitey & Other Progressive Causes.** unabr. ed. David Horowitz. Read by Jeff Riggenbach. (Running Time: 9 hrs. 30 mins.). 2010. 29.95 (978-1-4417-6716-5(9)); audio compact disk 90.00 (978-1-4417-6714-1(2)) Blckstn Audio.

Hatred's Kingdom. Dore Gold. Read by Nadia May. 8 CDs. (Running Time: 10 hrs.). 2003. audio compact disk 64.00 (978-0-7861-9189-5(9), 3130) Blckstn Audio.

Hatred's Kingdom. unabr. ed. Dore Gold. Read by Nadia May. 1 MP3. (Running Time: 10 hrs.). 2003. audio compact disk 24.95 (978-0-7861-8924-3(X), 3130); 49.95 (978-0-7861-2477-0(6), 3130) Blckstn Audio.
Provides the startling evidence of how Saudi Arabia not only is linked to terror, but in fact has spawned the current wave of global terrorism.

Hatred's Kingdom. unabr. ed. Dore Gold. Read by Nadia May. 7 pieces. 2004. reel tape 35.95 (978-0-7861-2484-8(9)); audio compact disk 39.95 (978-0-7861-9196-3(1)) Blckstn Audio.

Hats, Hats, Hats/Thanksgiving Day. Steck-Vaughn Staff. (J). 2002. (978-0-7398-5904-9(8)) SteckVau.

Hats Off! A Tribute to Merle Haggard. 1 cass., 1 CD. 7.98 (CMH 8024); audio compact disk 11.18 CD Jewel box. (CMH 8024) NewSound.

Hats off to Connecticut! unabr. ed. Perf. by Melissa Jones School, Fourth Grade Students. Prod. by Phil Rosenthal. 1 cass. (Running Time: 30 min.). (J). (gr. k-5). 1992. 6.50 (978-1-879305-14-4(3), AMC113) Am Melody.
The story of Connecticut, including its history, as well as songs, facts & anecdotes about the state, performed by the Fourth Grade Students of Melissa Jones School of Guilford, CT. Musical accompaniment on banjo, mandolin, guitar & piano by Phil Rosenthal & Gale Mack.

Hattie Big Sky. unabr. ed. Kirby Larson. Read by Kirsten Potter. 7 CDs. (Running Time: 8 hrs. 30 mins.). (J). (gr. 4-7). 2007. audio compact disk 60.00 (978-0-7393-5132-1(X), Listening Lib) Pub: Random Audio Pubg. Dist(s): Random

Hattie Big Sky. unabr. ed. Kirby Larson. Read by Kirsten Potter. (Running Time: 30660 sec.). (ENG.). (J). (gr. 5-12). 2007. audio compact disk 37.00 (978-0-7393-5051-5(X), Listening Lib) Pub: Random Audio Pubg. Dist(s): Random

Hattie's Mill. unabr. ed. Marcia Willett. Read by June Barrie. 8 cass. (Running Time: 8 hrs.). 1997. 69.95 (978-0-7540-0060-0(5), CAB 1483) AudioGO.
Hattie Weatherall's heart leapt when she first saw Abbot's Mill. With her dog & assortment of wild fowl for company, she sets about renovating the mill. As Hattie settles in, she befriends two young boatmen: Toby, who is recovering from a broken marriage, & Joss, whose problems are not so easily solved. But when Joss turns to Hattie for support, the motherly love that blossoms enables them both to heal old wounds.

Haughty Snail-King see Gathering of Great Poetry for Children

Haunted. unabr. ed. Kelley Armstrong. Read by Laural Merlington. Narrated by Laural Merlington. (Running Time: 13 hrs. 30 mins. 0 sec.). (Women of the Otherworld Ser.: Bk. 5). (ENG.). 2008. audio compact disk 29.99 (978-1-4001-5740-2(4)); audio compact disk 79.99 (978-1-4001-3740-4(3)); audio compact disk 39.99 (978-1-4001-0740-7(7)) Pub: Tantor Media. Dist(s): IngramPubServ

***Haunted.** unabr. ed. Jessica Verday. (Running Time: 9 hrs. 30 mins.). (Hollow Trilogy). 2010. 29.95 (978-1-4417-5955-9(7)); 59.95 (978-1-4417-5951-1(4)); audio compact disk 90.00 (978-1-4417-5952-8(2)) Blckstn Audio.

***Haunted.** unabr. ed. Jessica Verday. (Running Time: 9 hrs. 15 mins.). (Hollow Trilogy). 2010. audio compact disk 29.95 (978-1-4417-5954-2(9)) Blckstn Audio.

Haunted & the Haunters. unabr. ed. Edward Bulwer-Lytton. Read by Jim Killavey. 1 cass. (Running Time: 90 min.). Dramatization. 1982. 7.95 (S-25) Jimcin Record.
A story of strange visions & manifestations.

Haunted Asheville. 2001. 14.95 (978-0-9649370-5-5(0)) Shadowbox.

Haunted Beach House. Susannah Brin. Narrated by Larry A. McKeever. (Chillers Ser.). (J). 2001. audio compact disk 14.95 (978-1-58659-297-4(1)) Artesian.

Haunted Beach House. unabr. ed. Susannah Brin. Narrated by Larry A. McKeever. 1 cass. (Running Time: 40 min.). (Take Ten Ser.). (J). (gr. 3-12). 2001. 10.95 (978-1-58659-058-1(8), 54128) Artesian.

Haunted Bookshop, Set. Christopher Morley. Read by Flo Gibson. 4 cass. (Running Time: 6 hrs.). (J). 1996. 19.95 (978-1-55685-424-8(2)) Audio Bk Con.
Parnassus, the bookshop on wheels, has found a home in Brooklyn where Helen & Roger Mifflin, Bock the dog (short for Boccaccio), the lovely apprentice Titania, & Aubrey Gilbert, an advertising agent, match wits with literary spirits & evil plotters for Germany's revenge.

Haunted Castle on Hallows Eve. unabr. ed. Mary Pope Osborne. Read by Mary Pope Osborne. (Running Time: 1 hr. 16 mins.). (Magic Tree House Ser.: No. 30). (ENG.). (J). 2004. audio compact disk 12.00 (978-1-4000-9105-8(5), ImaginStudio) Pub: Random Audio Pubg. Dist(s): Random

Haunted Dog House. Sandi Johnson. Perf. by Van Buchanan. 1 cass. (Spooky Ser.). (J). 2000. 8.99 (978-1-929063-51-2(2), 150) Moons & Stars.
Story with theme song & spooky tunes.

Haunted Dog House. Sandi Johnson. Perf. by Van Buchanan. 1 CD. (Spooky Ser.). (J). (ps-6). 2000. audio compact disk 12.99 (978-1-929063-52-9(0), 151) Moons & Stars.

Haunted Fort Niagara. R. G. Hilson. Narrated by Paul Strickwerda. 2007. audio compact disk 9.95 (978-1-60031-021-8(4)) Spoken Books.

Haunted Forts & Battlefields of Niagra. Robert Hilson. Narrated by Frank Traynor. 1 CD. (Running Time: 35 mins., 14 secs.). 2006. audio compact disk 9.95 (978-1-60031-009-6(5)) Spoken Books.

Haunted Ground. unabr. ed. Erin Hart. 10 CDs. (Running Time: 12 hrs.). 2003. audio compact disk 81.60 (978-0-7366-9325-7(4)) Pub: Books on Tape. Dist(s): NetLibrary CO

Haunted Hawaii, Vol. 2. As told by Jeff Gere. (Running Time: 66 mins). 2005. audio compact disk 16.95 (978-0-9762190-1-9(8)) J Gere.

Haunted Hearts: Tales of Love & Tragedy. Sherry Norfolk. 1 cass. (Running Time: 1 hr.). 1998. 12.00 (978-0-87483-537-3(2)) Pub: August Hse. Dist(s): Natl Bk Netwk
Six tales woven together by traditional & original hammer dulcimer music, to lead one on a voyage of discovery, pursuing the elusive but priceless treasure of perfect love.

Haunted Hotel. unabr. ed. Wilkie Collins. Read by Walter Covell. 4 cass. (Running Time: 6 hrs.). (J). 1984. 28.00 incl. album. (C-131) Jimcin Record.

Haunted Hotel. unabr. collector's ed. Wilkie Collins. Read by Walter Covell. 7 cass. (Running Time: 7 hrs.). (J). 1984. 42.00 (978-0-7366-3899-9(7), 9131) Books on Tape.
As was the practice with Victorian novelists, Collins wrote his fair share of ghost stories. This novel was the first in which the supernatural is of central interest.

Haunted Hotel, Set. Wilkie Collins. Read by Flo Gibson. 4 cass. (Running Time: 6 hrs.). (J). 1990. 19.95 (978-1-55685-174-2(X)) Audio Bk Con.
Set in England & Venice, this tale of horror follows the doomed enchantress, Countess Narona, through a series of grotesque conspiracies.

Haunted Hound. Anne Schraff. Narrated by Larry A. McKeever. (Standing Tall 1 Mystery Ser.). (J). 2000. audio compact disk 14.95 (978-1-58659-267-7(X)) Artesian.

Haunted Hound. unabr. ed. Anne Schraff. Narrated by Larry A. McKeever. 1 cass. (Running Time: 40 min.). (Standing Tall 1 Mystery Ser.). (J). 2000. 10.95 (978-1-58659-095-6(2), 54135) Artesian.

Haunted House see Classic Ghost Stories, Vol. 2, A Collection

Haunted House. unabr. ed. Mary Hooper. Read by Tom Lawrence. 2 CDs. (Running Time: 1 hr. 42 mins.). (J). (gr. 3-6). 2007. audio compact disk 21.95 (978-1-4056-5663-4(8), ChiversChildren) AudioGO GBR.

Haunted House at Latchford. unabr. ed. J. H. Riddell. Read by Walter Covell. 4 cass. (Running Time: 6 hrs.). 1984. 28.00 (C-108) Jimcin Record.
Victorian tale of the supernatural.

Haunted in Death. J. D. Robb, pseud. Read by Susan Ericksen. (In Death Ser.). 2009. 44.99 (978-1-60775-669-9(2)) Find a World.

Haunted in Death. unabr. ed. J. D. Robb, pseud. Read by Susan Ericksen. (Running Time: 3 hrs.). (In Death Ser.). 2006. 39.25 (978-1-4233-2541-3(9), 9781423325413, BADLE); 24.95 (978-1-4233-2540-6(0), 9781423325406, BAD); 39.25 (978-1-4233-2539-0(7), 9781423325390, Brlnc Audio MP3 Lib); audio compact disk 62.25 (978-1-4233-2537-6(0), 9781423325376, BriAudCD Unabrid); audio compact disk 19.95 (978-1-4233-2536-9(2), 9781423325369, Bril Audio CD Unabri); audio compact disk 24.95 (978-1-4233-2538-3(9), 9781423325383, Brilliance MP3) Brilliance Audio.
Please enter a Synopsis.

Haunted in Death. unabr. ed. J. D. Robb, pseud. Read by Susan Ericksen. (Running Time: 10800 sec.). (In Death Ser.). 2007. 44.25 (978-1-4233-3718-8(2), 9781423337188, BrilAudUnabridg) Brilliance Audio.

Haunted Kids: True Ghost Stories. unabr. ed. Allan Zullo. Read by John Ratzenberger. 1 MP3-CD. (Running Time: 2 hrs.). (Haunted Kids Ser.). 2008. 31.97 (978-1-4233-6915-8(7), 9781423369158, Brlnc Audio MP3 Lib); 31.97 (978-1-4233-6917-2(3), 9781423369172, BADLE); 14.95 (978-1-4233-6916-5(5), 9781423369165, BAD); 14.95 (978-1-4233-6914-1(9), 9781423369141, Brilliance MP3); audio compact disk 37.97 (978-1-4233-6913-4(0), 9781423369134, BriAudCD Unabrid); audio compact disk 19.95 (978-1-4233-6912-7(2), 9781423369127, Bril Audio CD Unabri) Brilliance Audio.

Haunted Mask II. R. L. Stine. (Goosebumps Ser.: No. 36). (J). (gr. 3-7). 1996. 7.98 (978-0-7634-0083-5(1)) W Disney Records.

Haunted Monastery. unabr. ed. Robert H. Van Gulik. Narrated by Frank Muller. 3 cass. (Running Time: 4 hrs. 15 mins.). (Judge Dee Mysteries Ser.). 1986. 26.00 (978-1-55690-218-5(2), 86530E7) Recorded Bks.
Judge Dee takes refuge from a storm in a Taoist monastery & discovers three unsolved crimes.

Haunted Palace see Fall of the House of Usher & Other Works

Haunted Waters. unabr. ed. Chris Fabry & Jerry B. Jenkins. Contrib. by Samantha Beach & Blain Hogan. (Running Time: 10800 sec.). (Red Rock Mystery Ser.: No. 1). (J). (gr. 3-7). 2005. 11.99 (978-1-58926-856-2(3), 6856) Pub: Oasis Audio. Dist(s): TNT Media Grp

Haunted Waters. unabr. ed. Jerry B. Jenkins. Read by Chris Fabry. (Red Rock Mystery Ser.). (J). 2007. 34.99 (978-1-60252-699-0(0)) Find a World.

Haunted Waters: A Dramatic Audio Experience. unabr. ed. Jerry B. Jenkins & Chris Fabry. (Red Rock Mysteries Ser.). (ENG.). 2005. 10.49 (978-1-60814-355-9(4)) Oasis Audio.

Haunted Youth Center. unabr. ed. George Khoury. 1 cass. (Running Time: 20 min.). (J). (gr. 4-8). 1983. bk. 16.99 (978-0-934898-50-8(2)); pap. bk. 9.95 (978-0-934898-18-8(9)) Jan Prods.
Strange & eerie happenings occur at a town youth center.

Haunter of the Dark. unabr. ed. H. P. Lovecraft. Read by Erik Bauersfeld. 1 cass. (Running Time: 1 hr.). (C). 1995. 7.95 (978-0-940884-77-9(1)) Necronomicon.

Haunting Hour: Destination Unknown & The Two Mr. Brandts. 1 cass. (Running Time: 1 hr.). 2001. 6.98 (1752) Radio Spirits.

***Haunting in Plymouth.** Paula Chretien. (YA). 2009. 12.00 (978-1-4276-4710-8(0)) AardGP.

Haunting of Charles Dickens. unabr. ed. Lewis Buzbee. Read by Ralph Lister. (Running Time: 10 hrs.). (YA). 2010. 39.97 (978-1-4233-6952-3(1), 9781423369523, Brlnc Audio MP3 Lib); 39.97 (978-1-4233-6954-7(8), 9781423369547, BADLE); 24.99 (978-1-4233-6953-0(X), 9781423369530, BAD); 24.99 (978-1-4233-6951-6(3), 9781423369516, Brilliance MP3); audio compact disk 79.97 (978-1-4233-6950-9(5), 9781423369509, BriAudCD Unabrid); audio compact disk 29.99 (978-1-4233-6949-3(1), 9781423369493, Bril Audio CD Unabri) Brilliance Audio.

Haunting of Hill House. unabr. ed. Shirley Jackson. Read by David Warner. 4 cass. (Running Time: 6 hrs.). 2001. 25.00 (978-1-59040-104-0(2), Phoenix Audio) Pub: Amer Intl Pub. Dist(s): PerseuPGW

***Haunting of Hill House.** unabr. ed. Shirley Jackson. (Running Time: 7 hrs. NaN mins.). (ENG.). 2010. 29.95 (978-1-4417-8083-6(1)); audio compact disk 24.95 (978-1-4417-8082-9(3)) Blckstn Audio.

***Haunting of Hill House.** unabr. ed. Shirley Jackson. Read by To be Announced. (Running Time: 7 hrs. NaN mins.). (ENG.). 2010. 44.95 (978-1-4417-8080-5(7)); audio compact disk 69.00 (978-1-4417-8081-2(5)) Blckstn Audio.

Haunting of Hillside School. unabr. ed. Kristiana Gregory. (Running Time: 1 hr. 15 mins. 0 sec.). (Cabin Creek Mysteries Ser.). (ENG.). (J). 2008. 10.49 (978-1-60814-106-7(3), SpringWater) Oasis Audio.

Haunting of Hillside School. unabr. ed. Kristiana Gregory. 2 CDs. (Running Time: 1 hr. 18 mins. 3 sec.). (Cabin Creek Mysteries Ser.: Bk. 4). (ENG.). (J). (gr. 3-5). 2008. audio compact disk 14.99 (978-1-59859-411-9(7)) Oasis Audio.

Haunting of Hiram. unabr. ed. Eva Ibbotson. Read by Prunella Scales. 4 cass. (Running Time: 4 hrs.). (J). 1997. 32.95 (CCA 3369, Chivers Child Audio) AudioGO.

Haunting of Josie. unabr. ed. Kay Hooper. Read by Traci Svendsgaard. (Running Time: 6.5 hrs. 0 mins.). 2008. 29.95 (978-1-4332-2905-3(6)); 44.95 (978-1-4332-2901-5(3)); audio compact disk 40.00 (978-1-4332-2902-2(1)) Blckstn Audio.

Haunting of Lamb House, unabr. ed. Joan Aiken. Read by John Rye. 6 cass. (Running Time: 6 hrs. 45 min.). (Isis Ser.). (J). 1993. 54.95 (978-1-85695-659-8(8), 931107) Pub: ISIS Lrg Prnt GBR. Dist(s): Ulverscroft US

Haunting of Lamb House. unabr. ed. Joan Aiken. Read by John Franklyn-Robbins et al. 5 cass. (Running Time: 7 hrs. 15 mins.). 1993. 44.00 (978-1-55690-862-0(8), 93304E7) Recorded Bks.
Three stories of literary hauntings at an old English country house, once home to writers Henry James & E.F. Benson.

Haunting Rachel. unabr. ed. Kay Hooper. Read by Kate Fleming. 6 vols. (Running Time: 9 hrs.). 2001. bk. 54.95 (978-0-7927-2502-2(6), CSL 391, Chivers Sound Lib) AudioGO.
Ten years ago, Rachel Grants fiance, Thomas, disappeared. His body was never found. Now there's a stranger in town, a man who could be Thomas's twin. He's been watching Rachel for days. He has the locket she gave Thomas before he vanished. And he says he owed her father three million dollars. But there's no record of the loan, nor a shred of proof that this man is who he claims to be. And he's always nearby as accidents begin to threaten Rachel's life.

Haunting Rose. deluxe unabr. ed. Mickee Madden & Glennora Jean. 8 cass. (Running Time: 14 hrs). 2001. lib. bdg. 50.00 (978-0-932079-04-6(0), 79040) TimeFare AudioBks.

Haunting Tales: Live from Culbertson Mansion. Short Stories. Retold by Mary Hamilton. 1 CD. (Running Time: 70 minutes). (YA). 2001. audio compact disk 15.00 (978-1-885556-06-6(3)) Hidden Sprng.
Haunting Tales that could have been told during, or are set in, Victorian times. Titles include: "Sam'l" "The Beaded Bag" "Tailypo" "Sop Doll" "Promises to Keep" "The Men in the Open Grave" (all recorded live), plus "The Woman in Brown" "Mr. Fox" (studio recordings).

Haunting World War I Poets: A Literary Lecture, Featuring Eleanor Poe Barlow & Elliot Engel. 2001. bk. 15.00 (978-1-890123-42-0(0)) Media Cnslts.

Haus An Den Klippen. Medaglia & Seiffarth. audio compact disk 12.95 (978-0-8219-3798-3(7)) EMC-Paradigm.

Hausa. unabr. ed. Foreign Service Institute Staff. 15 cass. (Running Time: 15 hrs. 30 mins.). (YA). (gr. 10-12). 1976. pap. bk. 295.00 (978-0-88432-109-5(6), AFHA01) J Norton Pubs.
The major language of the northern region of Nigeria, is also used widely in commerce & trade in West Africa. Teaches the basic phonology & language structure & provides a basic vocabulary.

Hausa Newspaper Reader, Set. Philip J. Jaggar. 2 cass. (Running Time: 2 hrs. per cass.). (HAU.). 1996. 24.00 (3125) Dunwoody Pr.
Aimed at intermediate to advanced learners. Forty-four selections cover a variety of topics & are extracted from "Gaskiya Ta Fi Kwabo," "Nasiha," "Al-Mizan," "Magori," & the magazines "Rana" & "Lokaci.".

Hauser Kaspar. Archim Seiffarth. pap. bk. 20.95 (978-88-7754-991-4(2)) Pub: Cideb ITA. Dist(s): Distribks Inc

Hausmann, or Distinction. Paul LaFarge & Erik Bauersfeld. 9 cass. (Running Time: 13 hrs.). 2002. 62.95 (978-0-7861-2591-3(8), 3192) Blckstn Audio.

Haussmann, or the Distinction. Paul LaFarge. Read by Erik Bauersfeld. (Running Time: 11 hrs. 30 mins.). 2003. 36.95 (978-1-59912-502-2(1)) Iofy Corp.

Haussmann, or the Distinction. unabr. ed. Paul LaFarge. Read by Erik Bauersfeld. 10 CDs. (Running Time: 13 hrs.). 2006. audio compact disk 80.00 (978-0-7861-8948-9(7), 3192) Blckstn Audio.

Hauts de Hurle-Vent, Set. Emily Brontë. Read by Christine Deis. 3 cass.Tr. of Wuthering Heights. (FRE.). 1992. 31.95 (1529-VSL) Olivia & Hill.
The passionate love story of the ill-fated lovers, Cathy & Heathcliff.

Havana. Paul Monette. Read by Gregory Harrison. 2 cass. (Running Time: 3 hrs.). 1990. 15.95 set. (978-0-9627187-5-5(0), 40010) Pub Mills.
From the Christmas 1990 blockbuster Universal motion picture, a Sidney Pollack (Out of Africa) film starring Robert Redford, Lena Olin, Raul Julia. On the eve of the Cuban revolution, Jack Weil, mercenary, ladies' man & a well-known gambler, falls in love with Roberta Duran, the wife of a leading Castro revolutionary sought by the secret police.

Havana. abr. ed. Stephen Hunter. Read by William Dufris. (Running Time: 6 hrs.). (Earl Swagger Ser.). 2005. audio compact disk 16.99 (978-1-59600-402-3(9), 9781596004023, BCD Value Price) Brilliance Audio.

Havana. unabr. ed. Stephen Hunter. Read by William Dufris. (Running Time: 13 hrs.). (Earl Swagger Ser.). 2003. 32.95 (978-1-59355-168-1(1), 1593551681, BAU) Brilliance Audio.

Havana. unabr. ed. Stephen Hunter. Read by William Dufris. (Running Time: 13 hrs.). (Earl Swagger Ser.). 2004. 39.25 (978-1-59335-515-9(7), 1593355157, Brlnc Audio MP3 Lib) Brilliance Audio.
High summer in Cuba, 1953, and Havana gleams with possibility. Flush with booming casinos, sex and drugs, Havana is a lucrative paradise for everyone from the Mafia, Domino Sugar, and United Fruit to pimps, porn-makers, and anyone looking to grab a piece of the action - including the Cuban government, which naturally honors the interests of its old ally, Uncle Sam. Of course, where there's paradise, trouble can't be far behind.

Trouble, in this case, makes its entrance in the terrifically charismatic and silver-tongued form of a young revolutionary named Fidel Castro. The Caribbean is fast becoming a strategic Cold War hub, and Soviet intelligence has taken Castro under its wing. The CIA's response is to send the one man capable of eliminating Castro: the legendary gunfighter and ex-Marine hero Earl Swagger, who proved his lethal talent in the national bestsellers Hot Springs and Pale Horse Coming. In Cuba, Earl finds himself up to his neck in treacherous ambiguity where the old rules about honor and duty don't apply, and where Earl's target seems to have more guts and good luck than anyone else in Cuba.

Havana. unabr. ed. Stephen Hunter. Read by William Dufris. (Running Time: 13 hrs.). (Earl Swagger Ser.). 2004. 39.25 (978-1-59710-340-4(3), 1597103403, BADLE); 24.95 (978-1-59710-341-1(1), 1597103411, BAD) Brilliance Audio.

Havana. unabr. ed. Stephen Hunter. Read by William Dufris. (Running Time: 46800 sec.). (Earl Swagger Ser.). 2007. audio compact disk 102.25 (978-1-4233-3374-6(8), 9781423333746, BriAudCD Unabrid); audio compact disk 38.95 (978-1-4233-3373-9(X), 9781423333739, Bril Audio CD Unabri) Brilliance Audio.

Havana. unabr. ed. Stephen Hunter. Read by William Dufris. (Running Time: 13 hrs.). (Earl Swagger Ser.). 2004. 24.95 (978-1-59335-247-9(6), 1593352476) Soulmate Audio Bks.

***Havana: The 47th Samurai.** abr. ed. Stephen Hunter. (Running Time: 12 hrs.). 2010. audio compact disk 19.99 (978-1-4418-5036-2(8), 9781441850362) Brilliance Audio.

***Havana-ABR.** Stephen Hunter & #7 Earl Swagger. 2010. audio compact disk 9.99 (978-1-4418-5650-0(1)) Brilliance Audio.

Havana Bay. Martin Cruz Smith. Read by Edward Lewis. 8 cass. (Running Time: 12 hrs.). (Arkady Renko Ser.: No. 4). 1999. 64.00 (978-0-7366-4580-5(2), 4987) Books on Tape.

Havana Bay. abr. ed. Martin Cruz Smith. Read by Stephen Lang. 4 cass. (Arkady Renko Ser.: No. 4). 1999. 25.95 (FS9-50901) Highsmith.

Havana Bay. unabr. ed. Martin Cruz Smith. Narrated by Frank Muller. 8 cass. (Running Time: 11 hrs. 45 mins.). (Arkady Renko Ser.: No. 4). 1999. 70.00 (978-0-7887-3476-2(8), 95891E7) Recorded Bks.
Russian detective, Arkady Renko, explores the dark side of Cuba while investigating the fatal accident of a Soviet comrade. Smith paints a stunning backdrop of dazzling excesses & stark deprivation.

Havana Bay. unabr. ed. Martin Cruz Smith. Narrated by Frank Muller. 10 CDs. (Running Time: 11 hrs. 45 mins.). (Arkady Renko Ser.: No. 4). 2000. audio compact disk 70.00 (978-0-7887-3969-9(7), C1088E7) Recorded Bks.

Havana Bay. unabr. collector's ed. Martin Cruz Smith. Read by Edward Lewis. 10 CDs. (Running Time: 11 hrs. 48 mins.). (Arkady Renko Ser.: No. 4). 2000. audio compact disk 80.00 (978-0-7366-5186-8(1)) Books on Tape.
The body of a Russian embassy official is found floating in Havana Bay & Arkady Renko, the memorable detective from Gorky Park, is sent to identify it. Renko, however, refuses to positively identify the body. The Russian is soon followed in death by a Cuban boxer & a prostitute. Although none of these cases are supposed to be investigated, Renko cannot be stopped. He speaks no Spanish, knows nothing about Cuba & as a Russian in post Cold War Cuba, is a pariah. However there is something about havana, the rhythms of waves against the sea wall, the insinuation of music in the air & finally, Ofelia herself, a Cuban detective.

Havana Dreams. Wendy Gimbel. Read by Anna Fields. 5 cass. (Running Time: 7 hrs. 30 min.). 1999. 27.95 (978-0-7861-1705-5(2)) Blckstn Audio.
The story of four generations of Cuban women, through whose lives the author illuminates a vivid picture of Cuba in our century.

Havana Dreams. unabr. ed. Wendy Gimbel. Read by Anna Fields. 6 CDs. (Running Time: 7 hrs.). 2003. audio compact disk 48.00 (978-0-7861-9877-1(X), 2415) Blckstn Audio.

Havana Dreams: A Story of Cuba. unabr. ed. Wendy Gimbel. Read by Anna Fields. 5 cass. (Running Time: 7 hrs.). 1999. 39.95 (978-0-7861-1586-0(6), 2415) Blckstn Audio.
Story of four generations of Cuban women, through whose lives the author illuminates a vivid picture - both personal and historical - of Cuba in our century.

Havana Dreams: A Story of Cuba. unabr. ed. Wendy Gimbel. Read by Anna Fields. 6 CDs. (Running Time: 7 hrs. 30 mins.). 2000. audio compact disk 48.00 (z2415) Blckstn Audio.

Havana Heat. Darryl Brock. Narrated by Tom Parker. (Running Time: 10 hrs.). 2002. 30.95 (978-1-59912-503-9(X)) Iofy Corp.

Havana Heat. unabr. ed. Darryl Brock. Read by Tom Parker. 7 cass. (Running Time: 10 hrs.). 2002. 49.95 (978-0-7861-2192-2(0), 2939); audio compact disk 64.00 (978-0-7861-9532-9(0), 2939) Blckstn Audio.
Transports readers to 1911 America, where real-life pitcher Luther "Dummy" Taylor is trying to work his arm back into fighting shape. Though deaf, Taylor helped lead John McGraw's New York Giants to the pennant, winning 115 games between 1900 and 1908. But an injury relegates him to the minors, and he dreams of one last shot at the big barnstorming trip to Cuba. In Cuba, Taylor faces off against the tough Havana teams...and meets a deaf Cuban boy with a spectacular pitching arm. In young Luis, Taylor sees his chance for redemption-and a way to win them both Giants uniforms. But baseball's changing politics and the growing unrest in Cuba threaten his plans and force him to confront the choices that have brought him to this crossroads in his life.

Havana Nocturne: How the Mob Owned Cuba... And Then Lost It to the Revolution. T. J. English. Read by Mel Foster. (Playaway Adult Nonfiction Ser.). (ENG.). 2009. 69.99 (978-1-60775-785-6(0)) Find a World.

Havana Nocturne: How the Mob Owned Cuba... And Then Lost It to the Revolution. unabr. ed. T. J. English. Narrated by Mel Foster. 11 CDs. (Running Time: 13 hrs. 0 mins. 0 sec.). (ENG.). 2008. audio compact disk 75.99 (978-1-4001-3769-5(1)) Pub: Tantor Media. Dist(s): IngramPubServ

Havana Nocturne: How the Mob Owned Cuba... And Then Lost It to the Revolution. unabr. ed. T. J. English. Read by Mel Foster. Narrated by Mel Foster. 2 MP3-CDs. (Running Time: 13 hrs. 0 mins. 0 sec.). (ENG.). 2008. 24.99 (978-1-4001-5769-3(2)); audio compact disk 37.99 (978-1-4001-0769-8(5)) Pub: Tantor Media. Dist(s): IngramPubServ

Havana Twist. Lia Matera. Narrated by Anna Fields. (Running Time: 7 hrs. 30 mins.). 2000. 27.95 (978-1-59912-504-6(8)) Iofy Corp.

Havana Twist. Lia Matera. Read by Susan Anspach. 2 cass. (Running Time: 3 hrs.). 2001. 18.00 (978-1-59040-159-0(X), Phoenix Audio) Pub: Amer Intl Pub. Dist(s): PerseuPGW

Havana Twist. Lia Matera. Read by Anna Fields. 7 CDs. (Running Time: 7 hrs.). (Willa Jansson Mystery Ser.). 2000. audio compact disk 56.00 (978-0-7861-9884-9(2), 2565) Blckstn Audio.
When attorney Willa Jansson's mother doesn't return with the rest of her peacenik tour group from Cuba, she fears the feds might consider the trip "trading with the enemy." Willa risks her career & passport following her mother's trail from Havana to Mexico City, from California back to Havana...all the while keeping barely one step ahead of two angry governments & at least one ruthless killer.

Havana Twist. unabr. ed. Lia Matera. Read by Anna Fields. 5 cass. (Running Time: 7 hrs.). (Willa Jansson Mystery Ser.). 2000. 39.95 (978-0-7861-1762-8(1), 2565) Blckstn Audio.

Havana Twist. unabr. ed. Lia Matera. Read by Anna Fields. 1 CD. (Running Time: 8 hrs.). (Willa Jansson Mystery Ser.). 2001. audio compact disk 19.95 (zm2565) Blckstn Audio.
Willa risks her career & passport by rushing to Cuba to retrace her mother's steps. But she finds that nothing there is quite as it seems. Following clues to neighborhoods tourists never see, through secret tunnels beneath the street, Willa is manipulated, misled & nearly arrested.

Have a Backyard Picnic: The Bugville Critters. unabr. ed. Robert Stanek, pseud. Narrated by Ginny Westcott. (Running Time: 18 mins.). (ENG.). (J). 2008. 4.95 (978-1-57545-327-9(4), RP Audio Pubng) Pub: Reagent Press. Dist(s): OverDrive Inc

Have a Bad Day: The Bugville Critters. unabr. ed. Robert Stanek, pseud. Narrated by Ginny Westcott. (Running Time: 21 mins.). (ENG.). (J). 2008. 5.95 (978-1-57545-328-6(2), RP Audio Pubng) Pub: Reagent Press. Dist(s): OverDrive Inc

Have a Ball. Perf. by Jill Gallina & Michael Gallina. 1 cass. (Running Time: 1 hr.). (J). 2001. pap. bk. 10.95 (KIM 0835C) Kimbo Educ.
Original games & songs by Jill & Michael Gallina set the tone for exciting ball playing activities. Ideal for use with any type of ball yet well suited for use with foam balls. Develop ball handling skills, motor coordination & more. Good for limited spaces. Youngsters will love Hot Potato, Roly Poly, Loop Ball & others. Includes guide.

Have a Good Day. 2000. vinyl bd. 10.00 (978-1-58602-005-7(6)) E L Long.

Have a Little Faith: A True Story. unabr. ed. Mitch Albom. Read by Mitch Albom. 4 CDs. (Running Time: 5 hrs.). 2009. audio compact disk 29.99 (978-1-4013-9419-6(1), Hyperion Audio) Pub: Hyperion. Dist(s): HarperCollins Pubs

***Have a Little Faith: A True Story.** unabr. ed. Mitch Albom. Read by Mitch Albom. 4 CDs. 2009. audio compact disk 40.00 (978-0-307-70403-0(3), BksonTape) Pub: Random Audio Pubg. Dist(s): Random

Have a New Husband by Friday: How to Change His Attitude, Behavior & Communication in 5 Days. Kevin Leman. 2009. audio compact disk 24.99 (978-0-8007-4453-3(5)) Pub: Revell. Dist(s): Baker Pub Grp

Have a New Kid by Friday: How to Change Your Child's Attitude, Behavior & Character in 5 Days. Kevin Leman. 2008. audio compact disk 22.99 (978-1-59859-343-3(9)) Oasis Audio.

Have a New Kid by Friday: How to Change Your Child's Attitude, Behavior & Character in 5 Days. Kevin Leman. (Running Time: 4 hrs. 56 mins.). 2008. audio compact disk 24.99 (978-0-8007-4438-0(1)) Pub: Revell. Dist(s): Baker Pub Grp

***Have a New You by Friday: How to Accept Yourself, Boost Your Confidence & Change Your Life in 5 Days.** unabr. ed. Kevin Leman. Narrated by Wayne Shepherd. (Running Time: 6 hrs. 16 mins. 3 sec.). (ENG.). 2010. 18.19 (978-1-60814-726-7(6)); audio compact disk 25.99 (978-1-59859-778-3(7)) Oasis Audio.

Have a Nice Decade: The Seventies' Pop Culture Box, Set. 7 cass. 1998. bk. 99.98 (978-1-56826-925-2(0)) Rhino Enter.

Have a Sleepover: The Bugville Critters. unabr. ed. Robert Stanek, pseud. Narrated by Victoria Charters. (Running Time: 12 mins.). (ENG.). (J). 2008. 4.95 (978-1-57545-330-9(4), RP Audio Pubng) Pub: Reagent Press. Dist(s): OverDrive Inc

Have a Surprise Party: The Bugville Critters. unabr. ed. Robert Stanek, pseud. Narrated by Ginny Westcott. (Running Time: 20 mins.). (ENG.). (J). 2008. 5.95 (978-1-57545-331-6(2), RP Audio Pubng) Pub: Reagent Press. Dist(s): OverDrive Inc

Have Gun, Will Travel, Vol. 1. collector's ed. Perf. by John Dehner. 6 cass. (Running Time: 9 hrs.). 1998. bk. 34.98 (4394) Radio Spirits.
Paladin, a western soldier of fortune, could be hired to do the dirty work others wouldn't... for a hefty price. 18 episodes of this western series.

Have Gun, Will Travel, Vol. 2. collector's ed. Perf. by John Dehner. 6 cass. (Running Time: 9 hrs.). 2000. bk. 34.98 (4549) Radio Spirits.
Paladin wore black, wined and dined beautiful women and announced his services with a simple card which read: Have Gun, Will travel and the symbol of a white chess knight, a Paladin.

Have Gun, Will Travel: About Face & Return Engagement. Perf. by John Dehner. 1 cass. (Running Time: 1 hr.). 2001. 6.98 (2419) Radio Spirits.

Have Gun, Will Travel: Bad Bert & The Boss. Perf. by John Dehner. 1 cass. (Running Time: 1 hr.). 2001. bk. 6.98 (1893) Radio Spirits.

Have Gun, Will Travel: Birds of a Feather & Homecoming. Perf. by John Dehner. 1 cass. (Running Time: 1 hr.). 2001. 6.98 (2459) Radio Spirits.

Have Gun, Will Travel: Ceasar's Wife & Bring Him Back Alive. Perf. by John Dehner. 1 cass. (Running Time: 1 hr.). 2001. 6.98 (1667) Radio Spirits.

Have Gun, Will Travel: Comanche & That Was No Lady. Perf. by John Dehner. 1 cass. (Running Time: 1 hr.). 2001. 6.98 (2538) Radio Spirits.

Have Gun, Will Travel: Dad-Blamed Luck & Five Days to Yuma. Perf. by John Dehner. 1 cass. (Running Time: 1 hr.). 2001. 6.98 (1507) Radio Spirits.

Have Gun, Will Travel: Death of a Young Gunfighter & Five Books of Owen Deaver. Perf. by John Dehner. 1 cass. (Running Time: 1 hr.). 2001. 6.98 (1664) Radio Spirits.

Have Gun, Will Travel: Delta Queen & Little Guns. Perf. by John Dehner. 1 cass. (Running Time: 1 hr.). 2001. 6.98 (1671) Radio Spirits.

Have Gun, Will Travel: Dusty & Lucky Penny. Perf. by John Dehner. 1 cass. (Running Time: 1 hr.). 2001. 6.98 (1676) Radio Spirits.

Have Gun, Will Travel: Eat Crow & For the Birds. Perf. by John Dehner. 1 cass. (Running Time: 1 hr.). 2001. 6.98 (1674) Radio Spirits.

Have Gun, Will Travel: Helen of Adajinian & The Lady. Perf. by John Dehner. 1 cass. (Running Time: 1 hr.). 2001. 6.98 (2080) Radio Spirits.

Have Gun, Will Travel: Hey Boy's Revenge & Monster of Moonridge. Perf. by John Dehner. 1 cass. (Running Time: 1 hr.). 2001. 6.98 (1663) Radio Spirits.

Have Gun, Will Travel: Nellie Watson's Boy & Deadline. Perf. by John Dehner. 1 cass. (Running Time: 1 hr.). 2001. 6.98 (1675) Radio Spirits.

Have Gun, Will Travel: No Visitors & Contessa Marie Desmoulins. Perf. by John Dehner. 1 cass. (Running Time: 1 hr.). 2001. 6.98 (2242) Radio Spirits.

Have Gun, Will Travel: Search for Wylie Dawson & Apache Concerto. Perf. by John Dehner. 1 cass. (Running Time: 1 hr.). 2001. 6.98 (1669) Radio Spirits.

Have Gun, Will Travel: Somebody Out There Hates Me & Dollhouse. Perf. by John Dehner. 1 cass. (Running Time: 1 hr.). 2001. 6.98 (1831) Radio Spirits.

Have Gun, Will Travel: Stopover in Tombstone & Brothers Lost. Perf. by John Dehner. 1 cass. (Running Time: 1 hr.). 2001. 6.98 (2260) Radio Spirits.

Have Gun, Will Travel: The Colonel & the Lady & Gunshy. Perf. by John Dehner. 1 cass. (Running Time: 1 hr.). 2001. 6.98 (1665) Radio Spirits.

Have Gun, Will Travel: The Gunsmith & Pat Murphy. Perf. by John Dehner. 1 cass. (Running Time: 1 hr.). 2001. 6.98 (1666) Radio Spirits.

Have Gun, Will Travel: The Lonely One & French Leave. Perf. by John Dehner. 1 cass. (Running Time: 1 hr.). 2001. 6.98 (2478) Radio Spirits.

Have Gun, Will Travel: The Map, Martha Nell & From Here to Boston. Perf. by John Dehner. 1 cass. (Running Time: 1 hr.). 2001. 6.98 (1981) Radio Spirits.

Have Gun, Will Travel: The Outlaw & The Hanging Corpse. Perf. by John Dehner. 1 cass. (Running Time: 1 hr.). 2001. 6.98 (2284) Radio Spirits.

Have Gun, Will Travel: The Warrant & My Son Must Die. Perf. by John Dehner. 1 cass. (Running Time: 1 hr.). 2001. 6.98 (1673) Radio Spirits.

Have Gun, Will Travel: Too Too Solid Town & Doctor from Vienna. Perf. by John Dehner. 1 cass. (Running Time: 1 hr.). 2001. 6.98 (1670) Radio Spirits.

Have Gun, Will Travel: Viva & Extended Viva. Perf. by John Dehner. 1 cass. (Running Time: 1 hr.). 2001. 6.98 (1672) Radio Spirits.

Have Gun, Will Travel: Winchester Quarantine & The Return of Doctor Thackeray. Perf. by John Dehner. 1 cass. (Running Time: 1 hr.). 2001. 6.98 (1662) Radio Spirits.

Have Gun, Will Travle: Irish Luck & Dressed to Kill. Perf. by John Dehner. 1 cass. (Running Time: 1 hr.). 2001. 6.98 (1668) Radio Spirits.

Have It All. Eldon Taylor. Read by Eldon Taylor. Ed. by Leslie Brice. 6 cass. (Running Time: 6 hrs.). 1992. 69.95 set. (978-1-56705-369-2(6)) Gateways Inst.
Self improvement.

Have It All. Eldon Taylor. Read by Eldon Taylor. Interview with XProgress Aware Staff. Music by Steven Halpern. Interview with XProgress Aware. 1 cass. (Running Time: 62 min.). (EchoTech Ser.). 16.95 incl. script. (978-1-55978-344-6(3), 9908) Progress Aware Res.
Gentle coaching & soundtrack with underlying subliminal affirmations with tones & frequencies to alter brain wave activity.

Have It All: Classic. Eldon Taylor. Read by Eldon Taylor. Ed. by Leslie Brice. 1 cass. (Running Time: 1 hr.). 1992. 16.95 (978-1-56705-218-3(5)) Gateways Inst.
Self improvement.

Have It All: Easy. Eldon Taylor. Read by Eldon Taylor. Ed. by Leslie Brice. 1 cass. (Running Time: 1 hr.). 1992. 16.95 (978-1-56705-219-0(3)) Gateways Inst.

Have It All: Echotech. Eldon Taylor. Read by Eldon Taylor. Ed. by Leslie Brice. 1 cass. (Running Time: 1 hr.). 1992. 19.95 (978-1-56705-002-8(6)) Gateways Inst.

Have It All: Ocean. Eldon Taylor. Read by Eldon Taylor. Ed. by Leslie Brice. 1 cass. (Running Time: 1 hr.). 1992. 16.95 (978-1-56705-220-6(7)) Gateways Inst.

Have It All: Soundtrack: Leisure Listening. Eldon Taylor. 1 cass. (Running Time: 62 min.). 1998. 16.95 (978-0-940699-28-1(1), 5318B) Progress Aware Res.
Musical soundtrack with underlying subliminal affirmations.

Have It All: Soundtrack: Musical Themes. Eldon Taylor. 1 cass. (Running Time: 62 min.). 1998. 16.95 incl. script. (978-0-940699-29-8(X), 5318C) Progress Aware Res.

Have It All: Soundtrack: Synthesized Moments. Eldon Taylor. 1 cass. (Running Time: 62 min.). 1998. 16.95 (978-0-940699-82-3(6), 5318D) Progress Aware Res.

Have It All: Soundtrack: Tropical Lagoon. Eldon Taylor. 1 cass. (Running Time: 62 min.). 1998. 16.95 incl. script. (978-0-940699-83-0(4), 5318A) Progress Aware Res.
Environmental soundtrack with underlying subliminal affirmations.

Have Mercy on Me, O God: The Great Canon of St. Andrew of Crete. abr. ed. J. Michael Thompson. 1 cass. (Running Time: 1 hr. 5 mins.). 2005. 14.95 (978-0-8146-7936-4(6)); audio compact disk 16.95 (978-0-8146-7937-1(4)) Liturgical Pr.

Have Polls Closed? How Journalists Influenced the '88 Campaign. Moderated by Sanford Ungar. 1 cass. (Running Time: 1 hr.). 10.95 (G0380B090, HarperThor) HarpC GBR.

Have Space Suit, Will Travel. Robert A. Heinlein. Read by Will Mcauliffe. (Running Time: 8 hrs.). 2003. 34.95 (978-1-60083-419-6(1)) Iofy Corp.

Have Space Suit, Will Travel. unabr. ed. Robert A. Heinlein. Read by Full Cast Production Staff. (J). 2007. 49.99 (978-1-60252-560-3(9)) Find a World.

Have Spacesuit Will Travel. Robert A. Heinlein. 8 CDs. (Running Time: 8 hours). (J). 2003. 33.00 (978-1-932076-40-0(9)) Full Cast Audio.
One of the greatest young adult science fiction novels ever writter, a galaxy spanning adventure that manages to be profound, hilarious, and deeply moving. One minute Kip Russell is walking around his own backyard, testing out an old space suit and dreaming about going to the moon-the next he is the captive of a space pirate and on his way to the very place he had been dreaming of. At first, the events are so unreal he thinks he might be having a nightmare . . . but when he discovers other prisoners aboard the spaceship he knows the ordeal is all too real. Kip and his fellow abductees, the daughter of a world-renowned scientist and a beautiful creature from an alien planet, have been skyjacked by a monstrous extraterrestrial who is flying them to the moon-on a journey toward a fate worse than death. . .

Have the States Become Irrelevant? unabr. ed. Meldrin Thomson et al. 1 cass. (Running Time: 1 hr. 29 min.). 12.95 (330) J Norton Pubs.

Have the Time of Your Life in Retirement: The help-yourself guide for a fun, fulfilling Retirement. Dave Brazier. 2007. audio compact disk 14.99 (978-1-60462-089-4(7)) Tate Pubng.

Have Trouble at School: The Bugville Critters. unabr. ed. Robert Stanek, pseud. Narrated by Ginny Westcott. (Running Time: 17 mins.). (ENG.). (J). 2008. 4.95 (978-1-57545-332-3(0), RP Audio Pubng) Pub: Reagent Press. Dist(s): OverDrive Inc

Have We Met Before? Emma B. Donath. 1 cass. 8.95 (401) Am Fed Astrologers.
Open workshop using her book.

Have You Ever Seen a Chimpanzee. Silvia Silk. (J). (gr. 4 up). 1984. (978-0-938861-09-6(3)) Jasmine Texts.

Have You Found Him? Neville Goddard. 1 cass. (Running Time: 62 min.). 1965. 8.00 (83) J & L Pubns.
Neville taught Imagination Creates Reality. He was a powerfully influential teacher of God as Consciousness.

Have You Seen My Country Lately? America's Wake-Up Call. unabr. ed. Jerry Doyle. Read by Jerry Doyle. (Running Time: 9 hrs. 0 mins. 0 sec.). (ENG.). 2009. audio compact disk 29.99 (978-1-4423-0068-2(X)) Pub: S&S Audio. Dist(s): S and S Inc

Have You Seen My Daddy? Short Stories. Eddy G. Mora. Created by Eddy G. Mora. Narrated by Lawlor Ron. 1 CD. (Running Time: 19.4). Dramatization. (Toby & Tig Ser.: Vol. 1). (J). (ps-5). 2002. audio compact disk 9.99 (978-0-9671753-2-4(1)) Mora Art Studio.
This audio CD brings to life the book 'Have you seen my daddy?' The audio fx and music create a background for the vivid narration and characters that interact throughout the story. Children will want to listen and add to their imagination.

Have You Seen My Daddy? deluxe l.t. ed. Eddy G. Mora. Ed. by April Martin. 1. (Running Time: 19.4 mins.). Dramatization. (Toby & Tig Ser.: Vol. 1). (J). (ps-5). 1999. per. 7.99 (978-0-9671753-0-0(5)) Mora Art Studio.

Have You Suffered Enough? Be Free of the Hidden Core Issues That Destroy Love & Sabotage Your Life. Bill Ferguson. Read by Bill Ferguson. 2001. 18.00 (978-1-878410-32-0(6)); audio compact disk 18.00 (978-1-878410-33-7(4)) Return Heart.

Have Your Cake & Eat it Too: How to Build a Profitable Business, Turn it over to Your Employees, & Walk away with a Mountain of Cash. Glenn Ribble. Read by Glenn Ribble. 1 CD. (Running Time: 55min 06sec). 2005. pap. bk. 12.95 (978-1-932226-40-9(0)) Pub: Wizard Acdmy. Dist(s): Baker Taylor

When you arrive at the office before dawn and all is dark around remember it is about to be morning and all with it the promise of a new day. Promise only to the extent of your desire to see what others cannot, to do what other will not, and so to realize what others say is folly. It is time to be about the work. Enjoy the day of work.In all do well among men and they will do well to you and yours.Trust. Believe. Become.Includes:55min 06sec Audio CD39 page booklet.

Have Yourself a Looney Tunes Christmas. 1 cass. (Running Time: 1 hr.). (J). 2002. 10.98 (978-1-56826-468-4(2), 71767); audio compact disk 16.98 (978-1-56826-467-7(4), 71767) Rhino Enter.

Have Yourself a Looney Tunes Christmas. 1 cass. (Running Time: 30 min.). 1998. (978-1-58138-017-0(8), R475499); (978-1-58138-018-7(6), R275499) Sellthrough Ent.

The Bugs Bunny & friends cartoon characters sing Christmas music.

Haveli. unabr. ed. Suzanne Fisher Staples. Narrated by Christina Moore. 6 pieces. (Running Time: 8 hrs. 15 mins.). (gr. 8 up). 2001. 51.00 (978-0-7887-0373-7(0), 94564E7) Recorded Bks.

The adventures of a free-spirited Pakistani girl trapped in an arranged marriage continue, in this sequel to "Shabanu." Portrays vividly the grace, beauty & occasional harshness of Pakistan's culture & customs.

Haven. unabr. ed. John R. Maxim. Read by Dick Hill. (Running Time: 13 hrs.). 2008. 24.95 (978-1-4233-5439-0(7), 9781423354390, Brilliance MP3); 24.95 (978-1-4233-5441-3(9), 9781423354413, BAD); 39.25 (978-1-4233-5440-6(0), 9781423354406, Brlnc Audio MP3 Lib); 39.25 (978-1-4233-5442-0(7), 9781423354420, BADLE) Brilliance Audio.

Having. Paul R. Scheele. 1 cass. (Running Time: 40 min.). (Personal Celebration Ser.). 1992. 9.95 (978-0-925480-77-4(0)) Learn Strategies.

Helps you have whatever brings you richness.

Having a Baby. Barrie Konicov. 1 cass. 11.98 (978-0-87082-329-9(9), 055) Potentials.

Many couples are now choosing home delivery rather than the sterile atmosphere of a hospital. Designed to condition mother, making the delivery as pleasant as possible.

Having a Baby: The Owner's Manual to a Happy & Healthy Pregnancy. abr. ed. Michael F. Roizen & Mehmet C. Oz. Read by Michael F. Roizen & Mehmet C. Oz. (Running Time: 6 hrs. 0 mins. 0 sec.). (ENG.). 2009. audio compact disk 29.99 (978-0-7435-7397-9(8)) Pub: S&S Audio. Dist(s): S and S Inc

Having a Godly Self-Image. Speeches. Joel Osteen. 1 Cass. (Running Time: 30 Mins.). (J). 2000. 6.00 (978-1-59349-050-8(X), JA0049) J Osteen.

Having a Good Cry. 1 cass. (Running Time: 1 hr.). 10.95 (I0040B090, HarperThor) HarpC GBR.

Having a Good Cry: Effeminate Feelings & Pop-Culture Forms. Robyn R. Warhol. (Theory & Interpretation of Narrative Ser.). 2003. audio compact disk 9.95 (978-0-8142-9011-8(6)) Pub: Ohio St U Pr. Dist(s): Chicago Distribution Ctr

Having a Healthy Self-Image. Speeches. Joel Osteen. 1 Cass. (Running Time: 30 Mins.). 2002. 6.00 (978-1-59349-160-4(3), JA0160) J Osteen.

Having a Mary Heart in a Martha World. unabr. ed. Joanna Weaver. 2004. 27.99 (978-1-58926-834-0(2), 6834) Pub: Oasis Audio. Dist(s): TNT Media Grp

Having a Mary Heart in a Martha World. unabr. ed. Joanna Weaver. Narrated by Jill Gajkowski. (Running Time: 7 hrs. 0 mins. 38 sec.). (ENG.). 2005. audio compact disk 29.99 (978-1-58926-835-7(0), 6835) Oasis Audio.

Having A Mary Heart in A Martha World. unabr. ed. Joanna Weaver. Narrated by Jill Gajkowski. (Running Time: 7 hrs. 0 mins. 38 sec.). (ENG.). 2005. 20.99 (978-1-60814-003-9(2)) Oasis Audio.

Having a Mary Spirit: Allowing God to Change Us from the Inside Out. unabr. ed. Joanna Weaver. Narrated by Joanna Weaver. (Running Time: 7 hrs. 9 mins. 0 sec.). (ENG.). 2006. 16.09 (978-1-60814-004-6(0)); audio compact disk 22.99 (978-1-59859-158-3(4)) Oasis Audio.

Having A Mary Spirit: An Oasis Audio Production. unabr. ed. Joanna Weaver. Read by Joanna Weaver. (Running Time: 25200 sec.). 2006. audio compact disk 55.00 (978-0-7861-5948-2(0)) Blckstn Audio.

Having a Relaxed & Easy Going Attitude. Speeches. Joel Osteen. 1 Cass. (Running Time: 30 mins.). 2002. Rental 6.00 (978-1-59349-149-9(2), JA0149) J Osteen.

Having an Effortless & Joyless Job. 1 cass. (Running Time: 60 min.). 1998. 10.00 (978-1-930455-16-0(X)) E P Inc Pubng Co.

Learn to enjoy the job you have now.

Having Archaic & Eating It Too. Terence McKenna. 2 cass. 18.00 set. (A0461-89) Sound Photosyn.

The Second Annual State of the Stone Address, a doozey in Carson City.

Having Beautiful Relationships. Terry Cole-Whittaker. Read by Terry Cole-Whittaker. 1 cass. (Running Time: 1 hr.). 1991. 10.00 (978-1-56170-035-6(5), 259) Hay House.

Terry helps you to define your vision of a beautiful relationship & what you can do to manifest it. She ends with two powerful meditations.

Having It All. unabr. ed. Jennifer James. Read by Jennifer James. 1 cass. (Running Time: 1 hr. 4 min.). 1986. 9.95 (978-0-915423-17-0(0)) Jennifer J.

Discusses what it means to have it all. Focuses on what gives our lives passion, joy, & bliss, & how to tap the sources.

Having It All: Achieving Your Life's Goals & Dreams. abr. unabr. ed. John Assaraf. Read by John Assaraf. (Running Time: 3 hrs. 0 mins. 0 sec.). (ENG., 2007. audio compact disk 19.95 (978-0-7435-7116-6(9)) Pub: S&S Audio. Dist(s): S and S Inc

Having Our Say: The Delany Sisters' First 100 Years, unabr. ed. A. Elizabeth Delany. Read by Iona Morris. Illus. by Sarah L. Delany. 6 cass. (Running Time: 9 hrs.). 1995. 48.00 (692820) Books on Tape.

Sadie Delany, 104 & her sister Betty, 102, draw from a century of African American experience in these inspiring & entertaining memoirs.

Having Our Say: The Delany Sisters' First 100 Years. unabr. ed. A. Elizabeth Delany & Amy Hill Hearth. Read by Iona Morris. Illus. by Sarah L. Delany. 6 cass. (Running Time: 9 hrs.). 1995. 48.00 (3635) Books on Tape.

From a century of African American experience & in the punchy memoirs from Sadie Delany, 104 & her sister Betty, 102.

Having Something to Say When You Have to Say Something. abr. ed. Randy Horn. Read by Randy Horn. 2 cass. (Running Time: 2 hrs. 17 min.). 1998. 19.95 Set; incl. wkbk. (978-1-57294-105-2(7), 11-0225) SkillPath Pubns.

Easily & powerfully teaches the organizing principles of successful presentations, delivering the ground rules & strategies that banish missteps & stage fright forever.

Having the New Horizon in View. Ren Changhui. 4 pieces. 2003. 29.95 (978-7-88703-131-0(1), HANETA) China Bks.

Havoc. abr. ed. Jack Du Brul. Read by J. Charles. (Running Time: 21600 sec.). (Philip Mercer Ser.). 2007. audio compact disk 14.99 (978-1-59737-353-1(2), 9781597373531, BCD Value Price) Brilliance Audio.

Jack Du Brul's Havoc links an ancient weapon in the hands of modern terrorists, an agenda of greed couched in faith, a fabled tomb thought lost forever, and ultimately the enduring power of myth.

Havoc. unabr. ed. Jack Du Brul. Read by J. Charles. (Running Time: 43200 sec.). (Philip Mercer Ser.). 2006. audio compact disk 107.25 (978-1-59600-019-3(8), 9781596000193, BACDLib Ed) Brilliance Audio.

Havoc. unabr. ed. Jack Du Brul. Read by J. Charles. (Running Time: 12 hrs.). (Philip Mercer Ser.). 2006. 39.25 (978-1-59710-343-5(8), 9781597103435, BADLE); 24.95 (978-1-59710-342-8(X), 9781597103428, BAD); 87.25 (978-1-59600-017-9(1), 9781596000179, BrilAudUnabridg); audio compact disk 24.95 (978-1-59335-783-2(4), 9781593357832, Brilliance MP3); audio compact disk 39.25 (978-1-59335-917-1(9), 9781593359171, Brlnc Audio MP3 Lib); audio compact disk 38.95 (978-1-4233-0613-9(9), 9781423306139, Bril Audio CD Unabri) Brilliance Audio.

Havoc, in Its Third Year. unabr. ed. Ronan Bennett. Read by Nick Rawlinson. 8 CDs. (Running Time: 9 hrs. 17 mins.). (Isis (CDs) Ser.). (J). 2006. audio compact disk 79.95 (978-0-7531-2498-7(X)) Pub: ISIS Lrg Prnt GBR. Dist(s): Ulverscroft US

Havoc, in Its Third Year. unabr. ed. Ronan Bennett. 7 cass. (Running Time: 9 hrs. 35 mins.). (Isis Cassettes Ser.). (J). 2006. 61.95 (978-0-7531-2183-2(2)) Pub: ISIS Lrg Prnt GBR. Dist(s): Ulverscroft US

Hawaii. James A. Michener. Read by Larry McKeever. 1991. 96.00 (978-0-7366-2057-4(5)); 96.00 (978-0-7366-2058-1(3)) Books on Tape.

Hawaii. National Textbook Company Staff. 1 cass. (Discover America Ser.). 15.00 (978-0-8442-7496-6(8), Natl Textbk Co) M-H Contemporary.

Offers a fascinating introduction to key locations in the country. Especially designed for intermediate ESL students, combines language learning with American culture study.

Hawaii, Pt. 1. unabr. ed. James A. Michener. Read by Larry McKeever. 12 cass. (Running Time: 18 hrs.). 1991. 96.00 (978-0-7366-2056-7(7), 2867A) Books on Tape.

The masterful tale begins with the geologic origin of Hawaii & then describes the peopling of the islands by Polynesians, Americans, & Asians.

Hawaii, Pt. 2. James A. Michener. Read by Larry McKeever. 12 cass. (Running Time: 18 hrs.). 1991. 96.00 (2867-B) Books on Tape.

Hawaii, Pt. 3. James A. Michener. Read by Larry McKeever. 12 cass. (Running Time: 18 hrs.). 1991. 96.00 (2867-C) Books on Tape.

Hawaii: Circle Island Tour & Polynesian Cultural Center. (Running Time: 2 hrs.). 12.95 (CC241) Comp Comms Inc.

You'll drive along the windward coast, soon you're at the Polynesian Cultual, next you visit Waimea Fall park.

Hawaii: Kauai - The Garden Island. 1 cass. (Running Time: 90 min.). 12.95 (CC244) Comp Comms Inc.

Begin in Lihue town, move on to Wailua River & then visit the Kilauea lighthouse.

Hawaii: Maui - The Valley Island. 1 cass. (Running Time: 60 min.). 12.95 (CC243) Comp Comms Inc.

Begin in Kahului & Wailuku, soon you're entering the lush Iao Valley, Lahaina & more.

Hawaii: Oahu - Diamond Head & Eastern Coast. (Running Time: 75 min.). 12.95 (CC240) Comp Comms Inc.

Your Hawaiian guide will point out all of the sights & tell you all about Hawaii's past and present.

Hawaii: Oahu - Pearl Harbour & Historic Honolulu. (Running Time: 75 min.). 12.95 (CC242) Comp Comms Inc.

Visit historic Pearl Harbor, the Bishop Museum, the Foster Botanical Gardens, Punchbowl National Museum & much more.

Hawaii & Pacific Islands Seafood: An Informative & Interactive Recipe Book & Guide for the Professional or Weekend Chef. Ocean Resource Center Staff. 1999. cd-rom 4.95 (978-0-8248-2198-2(X)) UH Pr.

Hawaii Kidz Sing-a-Long. (J). audio compact disk 9.15 (978-0-931548-76-5(4), 09502-000) Island Heritage.

Hawaii Lectures - 2 CD Set. rev. ed. Sydney Banks. 2003. audio compact disk (978-1-55105-424-7(8)) Lone Pine Publ CAN.

Hawaii Loa - Aloha Is Love. 2003. audio compact disk 20.00 (978-0-89610-908-7(9)) Island Heritage.

Hawaii Loa - Hawaiian Memories. 2000. audio compact disk 16.99 (978-0-89610-946-9(1)) Island Heritage.

Hawaii Loa - Hawaiian Memories Aloha Shirt. 2000. audio compact disk 18.99 (978-0-89610-947-6(X)) Island Heritage.

Hawaiian - English Mini-Book Set with Audio. Claudia Schwalm. (HAW., 2000. pap. bk. 21.95 (978-1-57371-034-3(2)) Cultural Cnnect.

Hawaiian Astrology. Roberleigh Deal. 1 cass. 8.95 (080) Am Fed Astrologers.

Sign rulership and descriptions, symbology.

Hawaiian Drum Dance Chants: Sounds of Power in Time. Anno. by Elizabeth Tatar. 1 cass. 1989. (0-9307-400150-9307-40015-2-3); audio compact disk v. (0-9307-40015-2-3) Smithsonian Folkways.

Recordings made between 1923 & 1989, featuring solo chants or chanting accompanied by dancers, drum & percussion.

Hawaiian Language: Its Spelling & Pronunciation: Ka 'Olelo Hawai'i: Ka Pela me ka Ho'opuka 'ana. Kalena Silva & Kauanoe Kamana. 2000. pap. bk. & wbk. ed. 15.95 (978-0-9665331-7-0(8)); pap. bk. & wbk. ed. 15.95 (978-0-9665331-6-3(X)) Hale Kuamoo.

Hawaiian Luau Celebrations. 1 cass. 1996. 14.95 (978-1-58513-067-2(2), 1HE) Dance Fantasy.

Hawaiian Luau Cooking. Bess Press. 2004. audio compact disk 4.95 (978-1-57306-204-6(9)) Bess Pr.

Hawaiian Sentence Book. Robert L. Snakenberg. 1 cass. 1987. pap. bk. 19.95 Bess Pr.

Hawaiian Values Series. Susan Entz & Sheri Galarza. Illus. by Bruce Hale. 1999. bk. 29.95 (978-1-57306-095-0(X)) Bess Pr.

Hawaiian Word Book. Frwd. by Robert L. Shakenberg. 1 cass. 1987. pap. bk. 19.95; 7.95 Bess Pr.

Hawai'iloa. Lilinoe Andrews. Illus. by Lilinoe Andrews. (HAW.). (J). (gr. 1-3). 1994. pap. bk. 6.95 (978-1-890270-18-6(0)) Aha Punana Leo.

Hawaii's Sacred Lands. Hosted by Nancy Pearlman. 1 cass. (Running Time: 30 min.). 10.00 (1108) Educ Comm CA.

***Hawk & Fisher (Book 1) Hawk & Fisher.** Simon R. Green. 2010. audio compact disk 19.99 (978-1-59950-684-5(X)) GraphicAudio.

***Hawk & Fisher (Book 2) Winner Takes All.** Simon R. Green. 2010. audio compact disk 19.99 (978-1-59950-692-0(0)) GraphicAudio.

***Hawk & Fisher (Book 3) The God Killer.** Simon R. Green. 2010. audio compact disk 19.99 (978-1-59950-698-2(X)) GraphicAudio.

***Hawk & Fisher (Book 4) Wolf in the Fold.** Simon R. Green. 2010. audio compact disk 19.99 (978-1-59950-708-8(0)) GraphicAudio.

Hawk & the Dove: Paul Nitze, George Kennan, & the History of the Cold War. unabr. ed. Nicholas Thompson. Narrated by Michael Prichard. (Running Time: 15 hrs. 30 mins. 0 sec.). (ENG.). 2009. audio compact disk 39.99 (978-1-4001-1353-8(9)); audio compact disk 79.99 (978-1-4001-4353-5(5)); audio compact disk 29.99 (978-1-4001-6353-3(6)) Pub: Tantor Media. Dist(s): IngramPubServ

Hawk & the Heather. abr. ed. Robin Lee Hatcher. Read by Noel Taylor. 1 cass. (Running Time: 90 min.). 1995. 5.99 (978-1-57096-013-0(5), RAZ 914) Romance Alive Audio.

Beautiful & proud, Heather FitzHugh has hated the Dukes of Hawksbury & Tanner Montgomery since childhood. Will her plans for revenge be able to withstand his passionate nature & the heady sensuality of his caresses? Or will she succumb to love?.

Hawk, I'm Your Brother. 1 cass. (SPA.). (J). (gr. k-6). 1989. 5.95 (978-0-929937-07-6(4)) SW Series.

A young boy takes a young red-tailed hawk from its nest because he wants to learn to fly. He learns that he can't keep the bird.

Hawk, I'm Your Brother. Byrd Baylor. 1 cass. (J). (gr. k-6). 1988. 5.95 (978-0-929937-01-4(5)) SW Series.

A young boy takes a young red-tailed hawk from its nest because he wants to learn to fly. He learns that he can't keep the bird.

Hawk Nelson Is My Friend. Contrib. by Hawk Nelson. 2008. audio compact disk 13.99 (978-5-557-47151-0(0)) BEC Recordings.

Hawk Nelson Is My Friend. Contrib. by Hawk Nelson. Prod. by David Bendeth. 2008. audio compact disk 18.99 (978-5-557-47786-4(1)) BEC Recordings.

Hawk O'Toole's Hostage. unabr. ed. Sandra Brown. Narrated by Richard Ferrone. 4 cass. (Running Time: 5 hrs. 30 mins.). 1997. 36.00 (978-0-7887-0925-8(9), 95065L8) Recorded Bks.

When Miranda Price falls prey to a seductive captor & is held hostage on a modern Indian reservation, she is caught between her heart & her pride.

Hawk Roosting see Poetry & Voice of Ted Hughes

Hawkes Harbor. unabr. ed. S. E. Hinton. Read by Dick Hill. (Running Time: 6 hrs.). 2004. 39.25 (978-1-59710-345-9(4), 1597103454, BADLE); 24.95 (978-1-59710-344-2(6), 1597103446, BAD); 39.25 (978-1-59335-937-9(3), 1593359373, Brlnc Audio MP3 Lib); 24.95 (978-1-59335-921-8(7), 1593359217, Brilliance MP3); 29.95 (978-1-59600-123-7(2), 1596001232); audio compact disk 29.95 (978-1-59600-125-1(9), 1596001259); audio compact disk 82.25 (978-1-59600-126-8(7), 1596001267, BriAudCD Unabrid) Brilliance Audio.

Dr. Phillip McDevitt, director of Terrace View Asylum, is intrigued by his newest patient, a troubled young man recently transferred from the state hospital for the criminally insane. Jamie Sommers suffers from depression, partial amnesia, and an unaccountable fear of the dark. Dr. McDevitt is determined to help Jamie conquer his demons, but the more he probes the young man's fractured memories, the stranger his case becomes.... An orphan and a bastard, Jamie grew up tough enough to handle almost anything. Taking to the sea, he found danger and adventure in exotic ports all over the world. He's survived foreign prisons, smugglers, pirates, gunrunners, and even a shark attack. But what he discovered in the quiet seaside town of Hawkes Harbor, Delaware, was enough to drive him almost insane - and change his life forever. Hawkes Harbor is a compelling and unpredictable new novel by one of America's most honored storytellers.

Hawkrise. unabr. ed. Aileen Armitage. Read by Marilyn Finlay. 6 cass. (Running Time: 6 hrs. 30 min.). 1998. 54.95 (978-1-85695-261-3(4), 961009) Pub: ISIS Audio GBR. Dist(s): Ulverscroft US

Charismatic Vincent Gregg, the valley's first socialist MP, loses his seat because of his philandering ways. He enlists as a private in the Great War, but once again finds himself torn between greed & socialist principles. The war is a testing time for the young men of Hawksmoor too. Robert Hardcastle, has had to face the horror of Flanders. Conscientious objector Hal Pearson has had to endure the scorn of the entire community, while his brother Eddie, too young to fight, follows his father to the mill & tastes the bittersweet pangs of first love.

Hawks of Kamalon: An Interplanetary Adventure. unabr. ed. Michael Reisig. Read by Cameron Beierle. 12 cass. (Running Time: 12 hrs. 18 min.). 2001. 64.95 (978-1-55686-972-3(X)) Books in Motion.

A small squadron of British and American aircraft depart at dawn on a long-range strike into the heart of Germany. But as they cross the English Channel, the squadron vanishes... drawn thousands of light years across the galaxy by Kamalon's "Sensitive Mother." Ten men and their aircraft are greeted by a roaring crowd near a field before the provincial capitol in Kamalon, on the continent of Azra; a land in desperate need of champions.

Hawksmoor. unabr. ed. Peter Ackroyd. Read by Derek Jacobi. 8 cass. (Running Time: 12 hrs.). 1999. 69.95 (978-0-7540-0348-9(5), CAB1771) AudioGO.

Eighteenth century London is a city where squalor & superstition vie with elegance & enlightenment as the brilliant architect Nicholas Dwyer is commissioned to build several new churches. Two hundred & fifty years later, the legacy of the past lives on, as CID Detective Nicholas Hawksmoor investigates a series of macabre murders on the sites of certain eighteenth century churches.

Hawksmoor. unabr. ed. Peter Ackroyd. Read by Derek Jacobi. 10 CDs. (Running Time: 15 hrs.). 2002. audio compact disk 94.95 (978-0-7540-5509-9(4), CCD200) Pub: Chivers Pr GBR. Dist(s): AudioGO

Hawksmoor. unabr. ed. Aileen Armitage. Read by Marilyn Finlay. 12 cass. (Running Time: 15 hrs. 15 min.). (Isis Ser.). (J). 1995. 94.95 (978-1-85695-236-1(3), 951108) Pub: ISIS Lrg Prnt GBR. Dist(s): Ulverscroft US

Hawksong. Amelia Atwater-Rhodes. Narrated by Alyssa Bresnahan. 5 cass. (Running Time: 6 hrs. 45 mins.). (Kiesha'ra Ser.: Bk. 1). (YA). 2003. 48.75 (978-1-4193-1621-0(4)) Recorded Bks.

Hawthorn Farm. unabr. ed. Fred Archer. Read by Daniel Philpott. 6 cass. (Running Time: 9 hrs.). 2001. 54.95 (000915) Pub: ISIS Audio GBR. Dist(s): Ulverscroft US

Hawthorne. unabr. ed. Henry James. Narrated by Flo Gibson. 3 cass. (Running Time: 4 hrs. 30 mins.). (gr. 10 up). 2000. 16.95 (978-1-55685-652-5(0)) Audio Bk Con.

James' admiration for one of America's greatest authors contagious. His life, novels & short stories are touched upon with reverence.

Hawthorne & the Real: Bicentennial Essays. Millicent Bell. 2005. audio compact disk 9.95 (978-0-8142-9060-6(4)) Pub: Ohio St U Pr. Dist(s): Chicago Distribution Ctr

Hawthorne Heritage. unabr. ed. Teresa Crane. Read by Rowena Cooper. 14 cass. (Running Time: 14 hrs.). 2001. 110.95 (978-0-7540-0634-3(4), CAB2056) Pub: Chivers Audio Bks GBR. Dist(s): AudioGO
Jessica Hawthorne's parents acquired their fortune in the newly outlawed slave trade. Jessica grows up at Melbury New Hall in Suffolk, & surrounded by grandeur & respect money can buy, but without the furnishings of affection. She turns to her best friend & as events in her family take a tragic turn, it is Robert who will help Jessica change the course of her life.

Hawthorns Bloom in May. Anne Doughty. 2007. 69.95 (978-1-84559-807-5(5)); audio compact disk 84.95 (978-1-84559-808-2(3)) Pub: Soundings Ltd GBR. Dist(s): Ulverscroft US

Hay Fever. Noel Coward. 1 cass. (Running Time: 1 hr.). (Radiobook Ser.). 1987. 4.98 (978-0-929541-45-7(6)) Radiola Co.

Hay Fever. unabr. ed. Noel Coward. Perf. by Eric Stoltz et al. 1 cass. (Running Time: 1 hr. 35 mins.). 2001. 25.95 (978-1-58081-155-2(8), TPT135) Pub: L A Theatre. Dist(s): NetLibrary CO
A country house weekend goes haywire when the guests & their hosts play a game of romantic musical chairs.

Hay Fever, Set unabr. ed. Noel Coward. Narrated by Flo Gibson. 2 cass. (Running Time: 2 hr. 21 min.). Dramatization. (gr. 10 up). 1999. pap. bk. 14.95 (978-1-55685-618-1(0)) Audio Bk Con.
An irresistible comedy when a group of bohemian protagonist wreak emotional havoc on their houseguests.

Hayden Carruth. Hayden Carruth. (Listener's Guide Ser.). (ENG.). 2000. audio compact disk 12.00 (978-1-55659-998-9(6)) Pub: Copper Canyon. Dist(s): Consort Bk Sales

Haydn Concerto in D Major, HobXVIII/11. Composed by Joseph Haydn. 2006. pap. bk. 34.98 (978-1-59615-019-5(X), 159615019X) Pub: Music Minus. Dist(s): H Leonard

Hayduke Lives! A Novel, unabr. collector's ed. Edward Abbey. Read by Paul Shay. 10 cass. (Running Time: 15 hrs.). 1990. 80.00 (978-0-7366-1824-3(4), 2660) Books on Tape.
Presumed dead by those who stalked him, whereabouts unknown to those who knew him, Hayduke lives & he does it with the same fiery vengeance & inspired scheming that made him the hero of eco-warriors everywhere.When he appears this time, it's to take on Goliath, the worlds' largest mobile earth-moving machine, now munching its way through the desert in search of toothsome minerals.

Hayek. unabr. ed. Eamonn Butler. Read by Jeff Riggenbach. 4 cass. (Running Time: 5 hrs. 30 mins.). 1993. 32.95 (978-0-7861-0485-7(6), 1437) Blckstn Audio.
Here is a readable presentation of the essential thought of F. A. Hayek: Nobel prizewinner in 1974 & author of the bestselling "The Road to Serfdom." Hayek's influence in helping a generation to understand the nature of society & the errors of collectivism goes far beyond that of any other writer of his period. Having been decades ahead of his time when he began to write, Hayek is proving to be one of the most seminal thinkers of our age.

Hayek: His Contribution to the Political & Economic Thought of Our Time. unabr. ed. Eamonn Butler. Read by Jeff Riggenbach. (Running Time: 4 hrs. 30 mins.). 2010. 19.95 (978-1-4417-1761-0(7)); audio compact disk 49.00 (978-1-4417-1758-0(7)) Blckstn Audio.

Hayek's Theory of the Business Cycle. unabr. ed. Murray Newton Rothbard. 1 cass. (Running Time: 52 min.). 12.95 (291) J Norton Pubs.
Rothbard comments on the 1974 Nobel Prize to Friedrich von Hayek & lucidly explains Hayek's theory of the business cycle as it relates to money supply.

Hayley Mills Let's Get Together. Prod. by Walt Disney Records Staff. 1 cass. (Archive Collections). (J). 1998. 22.50 (978-0-7634-0398-0(9)) W Disney Records.

Haymarket Riot. 10.00 Esstee Audios.
The famous confrontation between anarchism & the authorities in Chicago.

Haymeadow. Gary Paulsen. Read by Richard Thomas. 3 cass. (Running Time: 4 hrs. 40 mins.). (J). 2000. 24.00 (978-0-7366-9056-0(5)) Books on Tape.
Tale of courage, survival & coming-of-age as young John Barron struggles against the elements to win his father's love.

Haymeadow. unabr. ed. Gary Paulsen. Read by Richard Thomas. 3 vols. (Running Time: 4 hrs. 40 mins.). (J). (gr. 5-9). 2004. pap. bk. 36.00 (978-0-8072-0452-8(8), Listening Lib) Random Audio Pubg.

Haymeadow. unabr. ed. Gary Paulsen. Read by Richard Thomas. 3 cass. (Running Time: 4 hrs. 40 mins.). (J). (gr. 5-9). 2004. 30.00 (978-0-8072-0451-1(X), Listening Lib) Random Audio Pubg.

Haymeadow. unabr. ed. Gary Paulsen. Read by Peter Coyote & Richard Thomas. (ENG.). (J). (gr. 4). 2009. audio compact disk 25.00 (978-0-307-58294-2(9), Listening Lib) Pub: Random Audio Pubg. Dist(s): Random

Hayseed. unabr. ed. Frank Roderus. Read by Jack Sondericker. 4 cass. (Running Time: 5 hrs. 36 min.). 2001. 26.95 (978-1-55686-997-6(5)) Books in Motion.
Young Arnie Rasmussen leaves his parents' Wyoming ranch to find the beautiful Katherine Mulraney, who has disappeared from the ranching community under strange circumstances.

Hayward Sanitarium. Text by Last Minute Productions Staff. Directed By Last Minute Productions Staff. 5 CDs. (Running Time: 5 hrs.). Dramatization. 2005. audio compact disk 39.95 (978-1-59938-061-2(7)) Lode Cat.

Hayward Sanitarium, Bk. 1, Episodes 1-8. Mathew Baucco & David A. Johnson. Perf. by Mike Kelleher et al. Prod. by Tony G. Brewer. 5 cass. (Running Time: 5 hrs.). 1996. 44.95 (978-0-9642427-9-1(6), LMPD125) Lodestone Catalog.
Something is wrong at Hayward Sanitarium. Horribly wrong. Dr. Richard Atwater is trying to find out what it is. Unwittingly, he starts down a long, dark path - from which he may be unable to escape. With its own particular method of making your hair stand on end, each half-hour episode of Hayward Sanitarium tells its own story, but also contributes to the larger, developing mystery. Hayward Sanitarium specializes in treating casualties of occult research, a fact that should clue you in to the nature of this cleverly plotted & intensely intellectual series.

Hayward Sanitarium Episodes 9-10: The Arrest; Breakout. Matthew Baucco & David A. Johnson. Perf. by Mike Kelleher et al. Prod. by Richard Fish. 1 cass. 12.95 (978-1-57677-067-2(2), LMPD005) Lodestone Catalog.

Hazard. Jo Beverley. Narrated by Anne Flosnik. 10 cass. (Running Time: 13 hrs. 30 mins.). 2002. 88.00 (978-1-4025-4203-9(8)) Recorded Bks.

Hazard of New Fortunes. William Dean Howells. Narrated by Flo Gibson. 12 cass. (Running Time: 16 hrs 40 mins.). 2005. 39.95 (978-1-55685-854-3(X)) Audio Bk Con.

Hazard of New Fortunes. William Dean Howells. Read by Anais 9000. 2008. 33.95 (978-1-60112-208-7(X)) Babblebooks.

Hazardous Aquatic Life. unabr. ed. Kenneth Kizer. Read by Ken Hull & Jim Meuninck. Ed. by Jim Meuninck et al. 3 cass. (Running Time: 85 min.). Dramatization. 1988. 10.95 (978-0-939865-05-5(X)) Meunincks Media.
Describes First-aid & avoidance tips for scuba divers.

***Hazardous Materials: Awareness & Operations.** rev. ed. International Association of Fire Chiefs Staff & National Fire Protection Association Staff. 2010. 295.95 (978-0-7637-7702-9(1)) Jones Bartlett.

Hazardous Materials: Awareness & Operations DVD Series. International Association of Fire Chiefs Staff & National Fire Protection Association. 2006. 1500.95 (978-0-7637-4205-8(8)) Jones Bartlett.

Hazardous to Your Health: Toxics, Torts & Environmental Bureaucracy. unabr. ed. Read by Newt Gingrich et al. 8 cass. (Running Time: 11 hrs.). (National Conference Program Ser.). 1993. bk. 82.95 set. (978-0-945999-34-8(8)); bk. 110.95 (978-0-945999-35-5(6)) Independent Inst.
Despite the hazards from chemical substances, consumer products & manufacturing processes, pork-barrel politics have created disinfectives for private & public parties to take precautions against toxic hazards plus overwhelming political incentives to pursue even greater harm. The conference, part of The Institute's greater project Toxic Liability, addresses these issues to foster an in-depth understanding of the causes & remedies of the hazardous substance problem.

Hazardous Waste - Transport & Treatment. Hosted by Nancy Pearlman. 1 cass. (Running Time: 29 min.). 10.00 (210) Educ Comm CA.

Hazardous Waste & Cleanup Liability. Phillip D. Reed & Michael Rodburg. (Running Time: 11 hrs.). 1992. pap. bk. 295.00 incl. course book. NY Law Pub.
Topics include RCRA, CERCLA & state statutes; hazardous waste management; regulatory issues; criminal & civil liability; environmental audits & compliance programs.

Hazardous Waste & Real Property Transactions. Read by John Adams et al. (Running Time: 3 hrs. 15 min.). 1990. 80.00 Incl. 549p. tape materials. (RE-54135) Cont Ed Bar-CA.

Hazardous Waste Law & Practice under RCRA. Richard G. Stoll et al. 2 cass. (Running Time: 2 hrs. 23 min.). (Environmental Law Ser.). 1995. 89.00 Set, incl. study materials, 154p. (M235) Am Law Inst.
Helps practitioners make more sense out of the RCRA regulatory scheme. Explains the basic structure of the regulations, key RCRA programs, recent developments, & anticipated changes. Includes: origins, framework, & scope; definitions of solid waste & hazardous waste; framework & standards for generators & transporters; standards (& permits) for treatment, storage, & disposal facilities; the land ban; enforcement.

Hazardous Waste Litigation: Advanced Tactics & Practice. unabr. ed. Contrib. by Randy M. Mott. 8 cass. (Running Time: 11 hrs. 30 min.). 1989. 50.00 course handbk. (T7-9207) PLI.
This recording of PLI's June 1989 seminar is designed for the experienced practitioner in law firms, corporations & the government. Strong emphasis is placed on a structured review of key practice issues & topics, e.g., expansion of the liability net: are there liability defenses left, allocation of liability, the Superfund process: representing clients in the administrative void, technical help: the use of experts, selection of the remedy: CERCLA & RCRA issues, public participation: citizen involvement, anxiety & litigation, settling claims, cost recovery under SARA: public & private actions. This program assumes a knowledge of the basic concepts of hazardous waste litigation.

Hazardous Waste Treatment Equipment in India: A Strategic Reference 2006. Compiled by Icon Group International, Inc. Staff. 2007. ring bd. 195.00 (978-0-497-36012-2(8)) Icon Grp.

Hazardous Waste Treatment Equipment in Singapore: A Strategic Reference 2006. Compiled by Icon Group International, Inc. Staff. 2007. ring bd. 195.00 (978-0-497-82413-6(2)) Icon Grp.

Hazardous Wastes, Superfund, & Toxic Substances. 11 cass. (Running Time: 15 hrs.). 1996. 197.50 Set; incl. study guide. (MB25) Am Law Inst.
Advanced course intended for lawyers & environmental managers who need to keep their skills & knowledge updated in the area of hazardous substances regulation & cleanup.

Hazards of Geriatric Pharmacology. Speeches. (Running Time: 55 mins). 2004. audio compact disk 29.95 (978-0-9762468-0-0(5)) LifeCare Med.
Audio and PowerPoint presentation of lecture on Hazards of Geriatric Pharmacology. Presentation is oriented toward emergency medical services and health care professionals to enhance the delivery of quality care to the older patient.

Haze. unabr. ed. L. E. Modesitt, Jr. Narrated by William Dufris. (Running Time: 10 hrs. 30 mins. 0 sec.). (ENG.). 2009. audio compact disk 69.99 (978-1-4001-4291-0(1)); audio compact disk 34.99 (978-1-4001-1291-3(5)); audio compact disk 24.99 (978-1-4001-6291-8(2)) Pub: Tantor Media. Dist(s): IngramPubServ

Hazelden Lectures, Album 1. 6 cass. (Running Time: 60 min. per cass.). Incl. Hazelden Lectures: AA & the Self; Help Group Movement. Daniel J. Anderson. 1986. (1521); Hazelden Lectures: Anxiety; Conflicts. Daniel J. Anderson. 1986. (1521); Hazelden Lectures: Constitutional Factors in Chemical Dependency; The Pleasure Factor in Addiction. Richard O. Heilman. 1986. (1521); Hazelden Lectures: Historical & Cultural Attitudes. Daniel J. Anderson. 1986. (1521); Hazelden Lectures: Nature of Drug Dependency; Addiction to the Addicted. Richard O. Heilman. 1986. (1521); Hazelden Lectures: Psychoactive Drugs. Dee Smith. 1986. (1521); 1986. 39.95 Set. (1521); 7.95 each. Hazelden.
Explores the complexity of chemical dependency by examining ways in which culture, personality & physiology interact.

Hazelden Lectures, Album 2. 6 cass. (Running Time: 60 min. per cass.). Incl. Hazelden Lectures: Chemical Dependency in the Family. Harold A. Swift. 1986.; Hazelden Lectures: Death of a Salesman; King Baby. Edward D. Juergen & Robert E. Brissett. 1986.; Hazelden Lectures: Diagnosis of Drug Dependency; The Real Drug Problem. Richard O. Heilman. 1986.; Hazelden Lectures: It Never Was There Before; Ya, But! Edward D. Juergens. 1986.; Hazelden Lectures: The Dependent Woman; The Liberated Woman. Patricia C. McGuire. 1986.; Hazelden Lectures: What to Do about Charles. Charles W. Crewe. 1986.; 1986. 7.95; 39.95 Set. (1589) Hazelden.
Recovery from chemical dependency involves learning all you can about your disease, your family, your job, & most of all, about yourself. This lecture series combines information with personal experiences.

Hazelden Lectures, Album 3. 6 cass. (Running Time: 60 min. per cass.). Incl. Hazelden Lectures: Coping With Unmanageability. Jack Hafner. 1986.; Hazelden Lectures: Negative Beliefs; Loss of Control. Rock Stack. 1986.; Hazelden Lectures: Powerlessness & Unmanageability; Higher Power, Managing, Manipulating & Intellectualizing. John P. Burns. 1986.; Hazelden Lectures: Recovering Self; Esteem-Change (Not Chance) Richard O. Heilman. 1986.; Hazelden Lectures: Spiritual Awakening; Group Dynamics. Damian McGuits. 1986.; Hazelden Lectures: Women, Alcoholic & Enablers; Gratitude & Sobriety. Bonnie-Jean Kimball & Genny Carlin. 1986.; 1986. 7.95 ea.; 39.95 Set. (1588) Hazelden.
Examines AA concepts one needs to understand while working on personal change & growth.

Hazelden Lectures, Album 4. 6 cass. (Running Time: 60 min. per cass.). Incl. Hazelden Lectures: Step Eleven & Step Twelve. Paul Hilton & Charles Minshek. 1986.; Hazelden Lectures: Step Five, Steps Six & Seven. Gordon Grimm & Paul Hilton. 1986.; Hazelden Lectures: Step One & Step Two. Fred Holmquist & Damian McElrath. 1986.; Hazelden Lectures: Step Three & Step Four. Edward D. Juergens & Damian McElrath. 1986.; Hazelden Lectures: Steps Eight & Nine, Step Ten. Patricia McGuire & John P. Burns. 1986.; Hazelden Lectures: What to Expect from AA. Charles Crewe. 1986.; 1986. 7.95 each.; 39.95 Set. (1587) Hazelden.
Covers each of the Twelve Steps of the AA Program.

Hazelden Lectures, Album 5. 6 cass. (Running Time: 60 min. per cass.). Incl. Hazelden Lectures: Step Eight, Step Nine. 1986.; Hazelden Lectures: Step Five, Steps Six & Seven. 1986.; Hazelden Lectures: Step One, Step Two. 1986.; Hazelden Lectures: Step Ten, Step Eleven. 1986.; Hazelden Lectures: Step Three, Step Four. 1986.; Hazelden Lectures: Step Twelve; Double Winners. 1986.; 1986. 7.95 each.; 39.95 Set. (1508) Hazelden.
The speakers blend personal experiences with individual interpretations of each Step.

Hazelden Lectures, Album 6. 6 cass. (Running Time: 60 min. per cass.). Incl. Hazelden Lectures: Bond of Friendship; Caring, Sharing, Sparing. 1986.; Hazelden Lectures: Getting Better: Coping with Stress; The Twelve Steps: A Prescription for Recovery. 1986.; Hazelden Lectures: Growing Up; When Your Wife Is an Alcoholic. 1986.; Hazelden Lectures: Humility; Anonymity. 1986.; Hazelden Lectures: Loving Yourself; Family Forgiveness. 1986.; Hazelden Lectures: Sexuality; Symptoms of Co-Dependency. 1986.; 1986. 7.95; 39.95 Set. (1518) Hazelden.
Explores families, relationships, Friendship & personal growth.

Hazelden Lectures, Album 8. 6 cass. (Running Time: 60 min. per cass.). Incl. Hazelden Lectures: Are We Really Letting Go? Is My Well Running Dry? 1986.; Hazelden Lectures: Dry Drunk Revisited; Shame: A Spiritual Block to Serenity. 1986.; Hazelden Lectures: Living vs Existing; Hope. 1986.; Hazelden Lectures: Maturity; 24 Hours. 1986.; Hazelden Lectures: Our Big Ego; Anger Is a Motivator. 1986.; Hazelden Lectures: Sense & Nonsense-Well; Adjusted. 1986.; 1986. 7.95 ea.; 39.95 Set. (1538) Hazelden.
Explores sober living, hope, acceptance, & serenity as well as complacency, egotism & the dry drunk syndrome.

Hazelden Lectures, Album 9. 6 cass. (Running Time: 60 min. per cass.). Incl. Hazelden Lectures: Detaching With Love; Why Didn't We Do This Before? 1986.; Hazelden Lectures: Essentials of Recovery; Recovery. 1986.; Hazelden Lectures: Intimacy; Personal Relationships. 1986.; Hazelden Lectures: My Payoffs for Feeling Inadequate; Great Expectations. 1986.; Hazelden Lectures: Three Decisions; The Challenge of Love. 1986.; Hazelden Lectures: Using Time; Guilt. 1986.; 1986. 7.95 ea.; 39.95 Set. (1529) Hazelden.
Typical problems experienced by people in treatment, & by AA & Al-Anon members, are described in this lecture series.

Hazelden Lectures, Album 9. Damian McElrath. 6 cass. (Running Time: 60 min. per cass.). Incl. Hazelden Lectures: Detaching With Love; Why Didn't We Do This Before? 1986.; Hazelden Lectures: Essentials of Recovery; Recovery. 1986.; Hazelden Lectures: Intimacy; Personal Relationships. 1986.; Hazelden Lectures: My Payoffs for Feeling Inadequate; Great Expectations. 1986.; Hazelden Lectures: Three Decisions; The Challenge of Love. 1986.; Hazelden Lectures: Using Time; Guilt. 1986.; 1986. 7.95 ea. Hazelden.

Hazelden Lectures, Album 10. 6 cass. (Running Time: 60 min. per cass.). Incl. Hazelden Lectures: Confidentiality & the Law. David Evan. 1986.; Hazelden Lectures: Confrontation in Group Counseling. Genny Carlin. 1986.; Hazelden Lectures: Ethics in Counseling. LeClair Bissell. 1986.; Hazelden Lectures: Handling Job-Related Stress. Bruce Fischer. 1986.; Hazelden Lectures: Patient Assessment & Referral. Tim Plant. 1986.; Hazelden Lectures: Professionalism in Counseling. David Oughton. 1986.; 1986. 7.95; 39.95 Set. (1568) Hazelden.
Provides information for chemical dependency, family, & EAP counselors, doctors, therapists, & other professional who provide services to dependent people.

Hazelden Lectures, Album 11. 4 cass. (Running Time: 60 min. per cass.). Incl. Hazelden Lectures: A Look at Relapse; Another Look at Step One. Charles W. Crewe & James G. Jensen. 1986.; Hazelden Lectures: Alcoholism: A Merry-go-Round Named Denial - Free to Care. Joseph L. Kellermann & Terence Williams. 1986.; Hazelden Lectures: The Last Major Talk of Dr. Bob. 1986.; Hazelden Lectures: Treatment & AA - Humility. 1986.; 1986. 7.95 ea.; 29.95 Set. (5750) Hazelden.
Discusses Several important topics for recovering people & AA members. Includes best-selling author Joseph Kellerman talking about the roles one adopts on the "Merry-go-round Named Denial.".

Hazelden Lectures, Album 12. 6 cass. (Running Time: 60 min. per cass.). Incl. Hazelden Lectures: Prayer & Meditation; Adventures in Meditation. Pat Kearns & Joe Klaas. 1986.; Hazelden Lectures: Renewal; Imaging. Ed Juergens & Elene Loescher. 1986.; Hazelden Lectures: Rules for Relationships; Sexuality & Spirituality. Marilyn Mason. 1986.; Hazelden Lectures: Spiritual Awakening; Building Self-Esteem. Jerry Dollard & Karen Casey. 1986.; Hazelden Lectures: Telling Your Story; Intimacy. Rock Stack & Pat. 1986.; Hazelden Lectures: Transitions; Problems in Recovery. Mary Farr & Jim Emmert. 1986.; 1986. 7.95 each.; 39.95 Set. (5600) Hazelden.
Takes a positive, hopeful approach to some of the problems one may encounter on the recovery road & presents the spiritual tools that can be employed to bring growth & renewal.

Hazelden Lectures: A Look at Relapse; Another Look at Step One see Hazelden Lectures

Hazelden Lectures: AA & the Self; Help Group Movement see Hazelden Lectures

Hazelden Lectures: Alcoholism: A Merry-go-Round Named Denial - Free to Care see Hazelden Lectures

Hazelden Lectures: Anxiety; Conflicts see Hazelden Lectures

Hazelden Lectures: Are We Really Letting Go? Is My Well Running Dry? see Hazelden Lectures

Hazelden Lectures: Bond of Friendship; Caring, Sharing, Sparing see Hazelden Lectures

Hazelden Lectures: Chemical Dependency in the Family see Hazelden Lectures

Hazelden Lectures: Confidentiality & the Law see Hazelden Lectures

Hazelden Lectures: Confrontation in Group Counseling see Hazelden Lectures

Hazelden Lectures: Constitutional Factors in Chemical Dependency; The Pleasure Factor in Addiction see Hazelden Lectures

Hazelden Lectures: Coping With Unmanageability see Hazelden Lectures

Hazelden Lectures: Death of a Salesman; King Baby see Hazelden Lectures

Hazelden Lectures: Detaching With Love; Why Didn't We Do This Before? see Hazelden Lectures

Hazelden Lectures: Diagnosis of Drug Dependency; The Real Drug Problem see Hazelden Lectures

Hazelden Lectures: Dry Drunk Revisited; Shame: A Spiritual Block to Serenity see Hazelden Lectures

Hazelden Lectures: Essentials of Recovery; Recovery see Hazelden Lectures

Hazelden Lectures: Ethics in Counseling see Hazelden Lectures

Hazelden Lectures: Getting Better: Coping with Stress; The Twelve Steps: A Prescription for Recovery see Hazelden Lectures

Hazelden Lectures: Growing Up; When Your Wife Is an Alcoholic see Hazelden Lectures

Hazelden Lectures: Handling Job-Related Stress see Hazelden Lectures

Hazelden Lectures: Historical & Cultural Attitudes see Hazelden Lectures

Hazelden Lectures: Humility; Anonymity see Hazelden Lectures

Hazelden Lectures: Intimacy; Personal Relationships see Hazelden Lectures

Hazelden Lectures: It Never Was There Before; Ya, But! see Hazelden Lectures

Hazelden Lectures: Living vs Existing; Hope see Hazelden Lectures

Hazelden Lectures: Loving Yourself; Family Forgiveness see Hazelden Lectures

Hazelden Lectures: Maturity; 24 Hours see Hazelden Lectures

Hazelden Lectures: My Payoffs for Feeling Inadequate; Great Expectations see Hazelden Lectures

Hazelden Lectures: Nature of Drug Dependency; Addiction to the Addicted see Hazelden Lectures

Hazelden Lectures: Negative Beliefs; Loss of Control see Hazelden Lectures

Hazelden Lectures: Our Big Ego; Anger Is a Motivator see Hazelden Lectures

Hazelden Lectures: Patient Assessment & Referral see Hazelden Lectures

Hazelden Lectures: Powerlessness & Unmanageability; Higher Power, Managing, Manipulating & Intellectualizing see Hazelden Lectures

Hazelden Lectures: Prayer & Meditation; Adventures in Meditation see Hazelden Lectures

Hazelden Lectures: Professionalism in Counseling see Hazelden Lectures

Hazelden Lectures: Psychoactive Drugs see Hazelden Lectures

Hazelden Lectures: Recovering Self; Esteem-Change (Not Chance) see Hazelden Lectures

Hazelden Lectures: Renewal; Imaging see Hazelden Lectures

Hazelden Lectures: Rules for Relationships; Sexuality & Spirituality see Hazelden Lectures

Hazelden Lectures: Sense & Nonsense-Well; Adjusted see Hazelden Lectures

Hazelden Lectures: Sexuality; Symptoms of Co-Dependency see Hazelden Lectures

Hazelden Lectures: Spiritual Awakening; Building Self-Esteem see Hazelden Lectures

Hazelden Lectures: Spiritual Awakening; Group Dynamics see Hazelden Lectures

Hazelden Lectures: Step Eight, Step Nine see Hazelden Lectures

Hazelden Lectures: Step Eleven & Step Twelve see Hazelden Lectures

Hazelden Lectures: Step Five, Steps Six & Seven see Hazelden Lectures

Hazelden Lectures: Step One & Step Two see Hazelden Lectures

Hazelden Lectures: Step One, Step Two see Hazelden Lectures

Hazelden Lectures: Step Ten, Step Eleven see Hazelden Lectures

Hazelden Lectures: Step Three & Step Four see Hazelden Lectures

Hazelden Lectures: Step Three, Step Four see Hazelden Lectures

Hazelden Lectures: Step Twelve; Double Winners see Hazelden Lectures

Hazelden Lectures: Steps Eight & Nine, Step Ten see Hazelden Lectures

Hazelden Lectures: Telling Your Story; Intimacy see Hazelden Lectures

Hazelden Lectures: The Dependent Woman; The Liberated Woman see Hazelden Lectures

Hazelden Lectures: The Last Major Talk of Dr. Bob see Hazelden Lectures

Hazelden Lectures: Three Decisions; The Challenge of Love see Hazelden Lectures

Hazelden Lectures: Transitions; Problems in Recovery see Hazelden Lectures

Hazelden Lectures: Treatment & AA - Humility see Hazelden Lectures

Hazelden Lectures: Using Time; Guilt see Hazelden Lectures

Hazelden Lectures: What to Do about Charles see Hazelden Lectures

Hazelden Lectures: What to Expect from AA see Hazelden Lectures

Hazelden Lectures: Women, Alcoholic & Enablers; Gratitude & Sobriety see Hazelden Lectures

HazMat Awarement. Delmar Learning Staff & NATMI Staff. 2009. audio compact disk 19.95 (978-1-4354-9746-7(5)) Pub: Delmar. Dist(s): CENGAGE Learn

HCD Agents & Managers Directory, Vol. 20. Hollywood Creative Directory Staff. (Agents & Managers Directory Ser.: Vol. 20). 2000. pap. bk. 54.95 (978-1-928936-08-4(3)) Hollywood Creat Dir.

HCD International Film Buyers. 2001. pap. bk. 59.95 (978-1-928936-13-8(X)) Hollywood Creat Dir.

HCD Producers Directory, Vol. 40. 40th ed. pap. bk. 59.95 (978-1-928936-07-7(5)) Hollywood Creat Dir.

HCSB Experiencing the Word New Testament. unabr. ed. Michael Stanton. Read by David Payne. Prod. by David Payne. 16 CDs. (Holman CSB Audio Ser.). (ENG., 2002. audio compact disk 49.99 (978-1-58640-015-6(0)) BH Pubng Grp.

HCSB Share Jesus Without Fear New Testament. William Fay. 3.99 (978-0-8054-2298-6(6)) BH Pubng Grp.

HDTV Equipment in Detail: Workshop Two. 2 cass. 1990. 17.00 set. Recorded Res.

He Bear, She Bear see Berenstain Bears' Christmas

He Came to His Own. Read by Basilea Schlink. 1 cass. (Running Time: 30 min.). 1985. (0273) Evang Sisterhood Mary.

A new perspective that adds a deeper dimension to our Christmas; The Name of Jesus - the help we need in every situation.

He Came to Us. Contrib. by Don Marsh. 1993. 11.98 (978-1-55897-429-6(6), 75602270) Pub: Brentwood Music. Dist(s): H Leonard

He Cannot Read Minds. Elbert Willis. 1 cass. (Understanding Satan's Strate Ser.). 4.00 Fill the Gap.

He Comes in Glory - The Second Coming of Jesus Christ. unabr. ed. Duane S. Crowther. Read by Duane S. Crowther. 1 cass. (Running Time: 90 min.). 1984. 13.98 (978-0-88290-396-5(9), 1812) Horizon Utah.

Features a treatment of the second coming. Many major events which must precede the second coming are discussed.

***He Comes Next.** abr. ed. Ian Kerner. Read by Ian Kerner. (ENG.). 2006. (978-0-06-085300-6(X), Harper Audio); (978-0-06-085299-3(2), Harper Audio) HarperCollins Pubs.

He Did Deliver Me from Bondage. Scripts. Colleen C. Harrison. 8 CDs. 2003. audio compact disk 35.95 (978-1-930738-15-7(3)) Windhaven Pub.

The full audio text for the book He Did Deliver Me from Bondage by Colleen C. Harrison. Narrated by Colleen C. Harrison and Philip A. Harrison.

He Doomsayer, Vol. I. unabr. ed. Jerry Ahern. Read by Charlie O'Dowd. 2 cass. (Running Time: 3 hrs.). (Survivalist Ser.: No. 4). 2003. 18.00 (978-1-58807-306-8(8)) Am Pubng Inc.

He Gave Gifts. unabr. ed. Charles R. Swindoll. 5 cass. (Running Time: 5 hrs.). 1998. 25.95 (978-1-57972-247-0(4)) Insight Living.

He Hawaii Au. Punana Leo Curriculum Development Committee Staff. Illus. by George Keonaona Lorch. 1 cass. (HAW.). (J). 1989. pap. bk. 5.95 (978-1-890270-12-4(1)) Aha Punana Leo.

He Is. Contrib. by Aaron Jeoffrey. (Praise Hymn Soundtracks Ser.). 2006. audio compact disk 8.98 (978-5-558-35314-3(7)) Pt of Grace Ent.

He Is Able. Created by Maranatha! Music. (Praise Ser.). 1999. audio compact disk 9.99 (978-7-01-611184-5(9)) Maranatha Music.

He Is Born. 2004. 7.99 (978-0-8474-2579-2(7)); audio compact disk 9.99 (978-0-8474-1912-8(6)) Back to Bible.

He Is Exalted: Live Worship. Contrib. by Twila Paris. Prod. by David Hamilton. Contrib. by Don Moen & Chris Thomason. 2005. audio compact disk 13.99 (978-5-558-84226-5(1)) Integrity Music.

He Is Exalted: Trumpet & Cello. 1 cass. (Instrumental Praise Ser.). 1999. 7.99 (978-0-7601-2671-4(2), 83061-0503-483061-0503-2); audio compact disk 10.99 (978-0-7601-2672-1(0), 83061-0503-2) Provident Music.

Favorite praise choruses & cherished hymns performed by solo instruments & full orchestra. Includes: "Blessed Be the Name of the Lord," "Fairest Lord Jesus," "For the Beauty of the Earth," "Give Thanks," "Great Is Thy Faithfulness," "He is Exalted," "Holy Ground," "I Stand in Awe," "In Moments Like These," "It Is Well with My Soul," "Jesus Paid It All," "Just As I Am," "My Jesus, I Love Thee," "My Savior's Love," & "There Is a Redeemer".

He Is Exalted with We Bow Down. Contrib. by Jarrod Brandt. 2007. audio compact disk 24.99 (978-5-557-54317-0(1)) Allegis.

He Is Lord. Perf. by Crystal Gayle. 2006. audio compact disk 12.95 (978-1-59987-412-8(1)) Braun Media.

He Is My Defense. Perf. by Marty Goetz. 1 CD. 2000. audio compact disk 13.99 (978-0-7601-3462-7(6), SO36143) Pub: Brentwood Music. Dist(s): Provident Mus Dist

A timeless collection of Messianic Worship offered as a sacrifice of praise to the Holy One of Israel. Contains 14 Scripture based songs including "H Iis My Defense," "Lamb of God," "Hineni" & more.

***He Is Not Silent: Preaching in a Postmodern World.** unabr. ed. Albert Mohler. Narrated by Raymond Todd. (ENG.). 2008. 14.98 (978-1-59644-603-8(X), Hovel Audio) christianaud.

He Is Not Silent: Preaching in a Postmodern World. unabr. ed. Albert Mohler. Narrated by Albert Mohler. (Running Time: 5 hrs. 0 mins. 0 sec.). (ENG.). 2008. audio compact disk 24.98 (978-1-59644-602-1(1), Hovel Audio) christianaud.

He Is Risen. Lloyd Larson. 1 CD. (Running Time: 1 hr.). (ENG.). 2001. audio compact disk 29.95 (978-0-7390-1979-5(1), 20009) Alfred Pub.

He Is Risen: The True Meaning of Easter. (Bible Stories for Kids Ser.). 2000. 7.98 (978-1-887729-78-9(X)) Toy Box Prods.

He Is Risen: The True Meaning of Easter. Joe Loesch. Ed. by Cheryl J. Hutchinson. Illus. by Brian T. Cox. (Bible Stories for Kids Ser.). (J). (ps-3). 2000. pap. bk. 14.95 (978-1-887729-74-1(7)) Toy Box Prods.

He Is Risen: The True Meaning of Easter. Joe Loesch. Ed. by Cheryl J. Hutchinson. Illus. by Brian T. Cox. (Bible Stories for Kids Ser.). (J). (ps-3). 2000. pap. bk. 16.95 (978-1-887729-75-8(5)) Toy Box Prods.

He Is the One. Evelyn Murray. Read by Evelyn Murray. 6 cass. (Running Time: 6 hrs.). 1998. 24.00 Set. (978-1-893072-03-9(7)) Evelyn Murray.

John awoke out of a coma in the hospital telling of his dream over & over. He was miraculously healed & released, went searching for this man in his dreams & was a successful.

He Is the Prince of Peace. 1985. (0231) Evang Sisterhood Mary.

***He Is There & He Is Not Silent.** unabr. ed. Francis Schaeffer. (ENG.). 2011. 10.98 (978-1-59644-173-6(9), Hovel Audio) christianaud.

He Is There & He Is Not Silent. 30th unabr. ed. Francis Schaeffer. Frwd. by Chuck Colson. 4 CDs. (Running Time: 3 hrs. 45 mins. 0 sec.). (ENG.). 2006. audio compact disk 21.98 (978-1-59644-270-2(0), Hovel Audio) christianaud.

In He is There and He is not Silent, Francis Schaeffer - philosopher, popular speaker, and founder of L'Abri Fellowship in the Swiss Alps - addresses some of the most perplexing questions to believers and unbelievers alike:Does God Exist?Does it make Sense to believe in God?Can we ever Know God?During his life, Francis Schaeffer welcomed questioners and doubters from all walks of life to L'Abri Fellowship. For Schaeffer, Christianity expressed the ultimate truth. That is why he never shunned doubts and questions by honest seekers. He knew the truths in the Bible would always prove themselves when they were thoroughly investigated by an open mind and heart.From the intriguing late night discussions at L'Abri came a series of compelling books that every Christian should own, especially this classic, He is There and He is not Silent.

***He is there & He Is Not Silent: Does it Make Sense to Believe in God?** unabr. ed. Francis A. Schaeffer. Narrated by Kate Reading. (ENG.). 2006. 12.98 (978-1-59644-271-9(9), Hovel Audio) christianaud.

He Kills Coppers. unabr. ed. Jake Arnott. 9 cass. (Isis Ser.). (J). 2002. 76.95 (978-0-7531-1380-6(5)) Pub: ISIS Lrg Prnt GBR. Dist(s): Ulverscroft US

He Knew He Was Right. Anthony Trollope. Narrated by Flo Gibson. 23 Cass. (Running Time: 33 Hrs. 32 Mins.). 2005. 63.95 (978-1-55685-853-6(1)) Audio Bk Con.

He Knows My Heart: Vicki Yoh'e. Perf. by Vicki Yoh'e. 1 cass., 1 CD. 1997. 10.98 (978-0-7601-1939-6(2)); audio compact disk 16.98 CD. (978-0-7601-1940-2(6)) Provident Mus Dist.

Featuring songs of honest, integrity, faith & commitment.

He Knows Too Much: Level 6. Alan Maley. Contrib. by Philip Prowse. (Running Time: 3 hrs. 18 mins.). (Cambridge English Readers Ser.). (ENG., 1999. 17.00 (978-0-521-65606-1(0)) Cambridge U Pr.

He Lahui Kanaka 'Oiwi Anei Ko Hawai'i Nei? William H. Wilson. Illus. by Brook Parker. 1 cass. (HAW.). (J). (gr. 4). 1999. pap. bk. 5.95 (978-1-58191-054-1(1)) Aha Punana Leo.

He Leadeth Me. Walter Ciszek. 8 cass. 32.95 (907) Ignatius Pr.

Personal account of a priest's 23 years in Siberian labor camps.

He Leadeth Me. Perf. by Cissy Houston. 1 cass. 10.98 (978-1-57908-234-5(3), 1312); audio compact disk 15.98 CD. (978-1-57908-233-8(5)) Platinm Enter.

He Leka Na Kahilina. Hokulani Cleeland. Illus. by Brook Parker. 1 cass. (HAW.). (J). (gr. 1-3). 1999. pap. bk. 5.95 (978-1-58191-051-3(7)) Aha Punana Leo.

He Lives. Contrib. by Lari Goss. 2007. audio compact disk 24.98 (978-5-557-53095-8(9), Word Music) Word Enter.

He Lives, Set. Perf. by Gospel Miracles. 1 cass., 1 CD. (Running Time: 52 mins.). 1999. 10.98 (978-1-57908-506-3(7), 1030); audio compact disk 16.98 (978-1-57908-505-6(9), 1030) Platinm Enter.

He Lives! Luke 24:1-12. Ed Young. 1999. 4.95 (978-0-7417-2213-3(5), 1213) Win Walk.

He Lives (Easter) John 19:32-20:9. Ed Young. 1988. 4.95 (978-0-7417-1655-2(0), 655) Win Walk.

He Loved Me Enough to Be Late. T. D. Jakes. 1 cass. 2001. 6.00 (978-1-57855-256-6(7)) T D Jakes.

He Loved Me with a Cross. Contrib. by Lari Goss. 1995. 11.98 (978-0-00-512560-1(X), 75608356) Pub: Brentwood Music. Dist(s): H Leonard

He Loves Me! Learning to Live in the Father's Affection. unabr. ed. Wayne Jacobsen. Narrated by Wayne Jacobsen. (Running Time: 5 hrs. 13 mins. 57 sec.). (ENG.). 2008. 16.09 (978-1-60814-008-4(3)); audio compact disk 22.99 (978-1-59859-522-2(9)) Oasis Audio.

He Lumi Hou Ko Ka Hale. Hokulani Cleeland. Illus. by Brook Parker. 1 cass. (HAW.). (J). (gr. 1-2). 1999. pap. bk. 5.95 (978-1-58191-052-0(5)) Aha Punana Leo.

He Mala'ai Ka'u. Aha Punana Leo Curriculum Development Committee. Illus. by Nelson Makua. 1 cass. (HAW.). (J). 1989. pap. bk. 5.95 (978-1-890270-15-5(6)) Aha Punana Leo.

He Mau Hana Ka'u E Hana Ai. Hau'oli Motta & William H. Wilson. Illus. by Brook Parker. 1 cass. (HAW.). (J). 1999. pap. bk. 6.95 (978-1-58191-079-7(7)) Aha Punana Leo.

He Mau Mikilima Hau No Ioane. Margaret Beaver. Tr. by Hiapo K. Perreira from ACE. Illus. by Cara Brunk. (HAW.). (J). (gr. 1-2). 1996. pap. bk. 3.95 (978-1-890270-28-5(8)) Aha Punana Leo.

He-Motions: Even Strong Men Struggle. abr. ed. T. D. Jakes. Read by Richard Allen. 3 cass. (Running Time: 4 hrs.). 2004. 19.95 (978-1-59600-118-3(6), 1596001186); 49.25 (978-1-59600-119-0(4), 1596001194, BAudLibEd); audio compact disk 69.25 (978-1-59600-121-3(6), 1596001216, BACDLib Ed) Brilliance Audio.

Do you find it difficult to express how you feel and what you need in your personal relationships? Do you have trouble communicating and developing relationships with other men? Does the weight of responsibility drag you down? Do you wonder why it seems difficult to get the support and encouragement you need from your wife? Do you often feel that there is a stronger, more effective leader inside you waiting to be developed? Do you wonder what God's plan is for you? As a man, you may often feel the pressure of fulfilling many roles in life: husband, father, son, businessman, member of the church community. Now T. D. Jakes comes to your aid with a guidebook to help you understand your own needs for emotional and spiritual support. He offers practical, sound answers to assist you in expressing your needs and having them met in healthy and wholesome ways by those you love. This is a candid, no-holds-barred look at sexuality, spirituality, and the seldom mentioned but extremely important emotions that shape success in every area of a man's life. Using examples from his own life, as well as from the lives of the thousands of men he has counseled, Jakes gives detailed advice on how to move from struggle to success, from victim to victory. And ladies, He-Motions is also for you. Inspirational and refreshingly honest, this is the ultimate source for women seeking to comprehend and care for the men in their lives. It helps you decode men's often baffling behavior and provides eye-opening insights for greater intimacy and healing in your relationships. He-Motions brings clarity and hope to men and helps them strengthen their relationships with themselves, with the women in their lives, and with their Lord. It gives women the solutions they seek as they relate to the men they love. It is a book that will bring you closer together and closer to God.

He-Motions: Even Strong Men Struggle. abr. ed. T. D. Jakes. Read by Richard Allen. (Running Time: 4 hrs.). 2006. 39.25 (978-1-4233-0296-4(6), 9781423302964, BADLE); 9.99 (978-1-4233-0295-7(8), 9781423302957, BAD); 39.25 (978-1-4233-0294-0(X), 9781423302940, Brinc Audio MP3 Lib) Brilliance Audio.

***He-Motions: Even Strong Men Struggle.** abr. ed. T. D. Jakes. Read by Richard Allen. (Running Time: 4 hrs.). 2010. audio compact disk 14.99 (978-1-4418-7816-8(5), 9781441878168, BCD Value Price) Brilliance Audio.

He-Motions: Even Strong Men Struggle. abr. ed. T. D. Jakes. Read by Richard Allen. (Running Time: 4 hrs.). 2006. audio compact disk 9.99 (978-1-4233-0293-3(1), 9781423302933, Brilliance MP3) Brilliance Audio.

He Pepe Wale No Au. Laiana Wong. Illus. by Maile Andrade. 1 cass. (HAW.). (J). 1999. pap. bk. 5.95 (978-1-58191-071-1(1)) Aha Punana Leo.

He Reigns. Contrib. by Newsboys. (Worship Tracks (Word Tracks) Ser.). 2006. audio compact disk 8.98 (978-5-558-26903-1(0), Word Music) Word Enter.

He Reigns: The Worship Collection. Contrib. by Newsboys. 2005. audio compact disk 16.98 (978-5-558-78006-2(1)) Pt of Grace Ent.

He Said She Said. 1 CD. (Running Time: 1 hr. 30 mins.). 2005. audio compact disk 12.95 (978-0-660-18648-1(9)) Pub: Canadian Broadcasting CAN. Dist(s): Georgetown Term

A hilarious collection of sketch comedy from some of the most entertaining comedians on the scene today. It's full of sharp insight and truth all wrapped up and twisted with paradox and contradiction.

He Said, She Said. Deborah Tannen. (Portable Professor Ser.). 2004. audio compact disk 39.95 (978-0-7607-5006-3(8)) Barnes & Noble Inc.

***He Saw, He Left, He Conquered.** Featuring Ravi Zacharias. 1986. audio compact disk 9.00 (978-1-61256-015-1(6)) Ravi Zach.

He Sees You When You're Sleeping. unabr. ed. Mary Higgins Clark & Carol Higgins Clark. 4 vols. (Running Time: 6 hrs.). 2001. bk. 39.95 (978-0-7927-2536-7(0), CSL 425, Chivers Sound Lib) AudioGO.

A perfect story for the holidays, a delightful and warmhearted tale of perseverance, redemption and love.

He Sees You When You're Sleeping. unabr. ed. Mary Higgins Clark & Carol Higgins Clark. Read by Carol Higgins Clark. 4 CDs. (Running Time: 6 hrs.). 2002. audio compact disk 49.95 (978-0-7927-2742-2(8), SLD 425, Chivers Sound Lib) AudioGO.

For 46 years Sterling Brooks has waited to be deemed fit for entrance into heaven. Now he must prove his worthiness by helping someone else. In Rockefeller Center, he meets a heartbroken seven-year-old named Marissa who has been separated from her father and grandmother, now in the Witness Protection Program. Two mobsters, the Badgett brothers, have put a price on their heads. Can Sterling save the day and earn his entrance into heaven?.

He Sees You When You're Sleeping. unabr. ed. Mary Higgins Clark & Carol Higgins Clark. 5 cass. (Running Time: 50 hrs. 0 mins. 0 sec.). (ENG.). 2001.

audio compact disk 30.00 (978-0-7435-2333-2(4), Audioworks) Pub: S&S Audio. Dist(s): S and S Inc

Meet Sterling Brooks. His was not an exemplary life; his misdeeds were few. His were sins of omission, not of commission. A few days before Christmas, Sterling watches those around him gain passage through the celestial gates. The Hevenly Council poses a test - Sterling will be sent back to earth and given an opportunity to prove his worthiness by helping someone else. And so, Sterling Brooks finds himself in Manhattan, at the skating rink in Rockefeller Center. Among the skaters is a sad-faced young girl named Marissa whose family has been forced into the Federal Witness Protection Program because the mobster Blogett brothers have put a price on their heads. Using his ability to go back and forth in time, Sterling masterminds a plan to eliminate the Blogett brothers and reunite Marissa with her loved ones. Filed with suspense and humor, He Sees You When You're Sleeping is a perfect story for the holidays, a delightful and warmhearted tale of perserverance, redemption, and love.

He Sees You When You're Sleeping. unabr. ed. Mary Higgins Clark & Carol Higgins Clark. 2004. 15.95 (978-0-7435-4521-1(4)) Pub: S&S Audio. Dist(s): S and S Inc

He Sent Love. 2006. audio compact disk 14.00 (978-0-9786707-5-7(2)) Concord I Minis.

He Shall Arise. Tom Fettke. 1998. 8.00 (978-0-7673-9975-3(7)); 75.00 (978-0-7673-9959-3(5)); 11.98 (978-0-7673-9941-8(2)); audio compact disk 12.00 (978-0-7673-9967-8(6)); audio compact disk 85.00 (978-0-7673-9933-3(1)); audio compact disk 16.98 (978-0-7673-9932-6(3)) LifeWay Christian.

He Shall Thunder in the Sky. unabr. ed. Elizabeth Peters, pseud. Narrated by Barbara Rosenblat. 12 cass. (Running Time: 17 hrs. 15 mins.). (Amelia Peabody Ser.: Vol. 12). 2000. 103.00 (978-0-7887-4850-9(5), 96110E7) Recorded Bks.

In 1914 the tides of war rise, Egypt is threatened by attacks. Espionage abounds, pulling in several members of the Peabody Emerson household even as they embark on a new archaeological season. Amidst a growing tangle of disguises & deception, Emerson's nemesis, the Master Criminal, appears. As increasing perils threaten the Peabody Emerson's, their expedition & Egypt, help arrives from a most unlikely source.

He Shall Thunder in the Sky. unabr. ed. Elizabeth Peters, pseud. Narrated by Barbara Rosenblat. 15 CDs. (Running Time: 17 hrs. 15 mins.). (Amelia Peabody Ser.). 2001. audio compact disk 119.00 (978-0-7887-6176-8(5), C1400) Recorded Bks.

He Still Heals Series. unabr. ed. Steve Thompson. 7 cass. (Running Time: 10 hrs. 30 mins.). 2000. 35.00 (SAO1-000) Morning NC.

Learn about the healing power of God that is available to believers today.

He Still Leads. Contrib. by Christopher Phillips et al. 2008. audio compact disk 7.00 (978-5-557-48392-6(6), Brentwood-Benson Music); audio compact disk 7.00 (978-5-557-48391-9(8), Brentwood-Benson Music); audio compact disk 7.00 (978-5-557-48390-2(X), Brentwood-Benson Music) Brentwood Music.

He Still Leads: Alto. Contrib. by Christopher Phillips et al. 2008. audio compact disk 5.00 (978-5-557-48396-4(9), Brentwood-Benson Music); audio compact disk 5.00 (978-5-557-48386-5(1), Brentwood-Benson Music) Brentwood Music.

He Still Leads: Bass. Contrib. by Christopher Phillips et al. 2008. audio compact disk 5.00 (978-5-557-48394-0(2), Brentwood-Benson Music); audio compact disk 5.00 (978-5-557-48384-1(5), Brentwood-Benson Music) Brentwood Music.

He Still Leads: Drums. Contrib. by Christopher Phillips et al. 2008. audio compact disk 7.00 (978-5-557-48393-3(4), Brentwood-Benson Music) Brentwood Music.

He Still Leads: Satb. Contrib. by Christopher Phillips et al. 2008. audio compact disk 10.00 (978-5-557-48398-8(5), Brentwood-Benson Music) Brentwood Music.

He Still Leads: Soprano. Contrib. by Christopher Phillips et al. 2008. audio compact disk 5.00 (978-5-557-48397-1(7), Brentwood-Benson Music); audio compact disk 5.00 (978-5-557-48387-2(X), Brentwood-Benson Music) Brentwood Music.

He Still Leads: Tenor. Contrib. by Christopher Phillips et al. 2008. audio compact disk 5.00 (978-5-557-48395-7(0), Brentwood-Benson Music); audio compact disk 5.00 (978-5-557-48385-8(3), Brentwood-Benson Music) Brentwood Music.

He Still Moves Stones: Everyone Needs a Miracle. abr. ed. Max Lucado. Narrated by Max Lucado. (ENG.). 2003. 10.49 (978-1-60814-009-1(1)) Oasis Audio.

He Still Moves Stones: Everyone Needs a Miracle. unabr. abr. ed. Max Lucado. Narrated by Max Lucado. 2 CDs. (Running Time: 2 hrs. 18 mins. 0 sec.). (ENG.). 2003. audio compact disk 14.99 (978-1-58926-243-0(3), T10M-001D); 11.99 (978-1-58926-242-3(5), T10M-0010) Oasis Audio.

Though suffering comes from many different directions and causes, our suffering is real, and we often have no place to turn, thinking we are alone in our pain. Yet, in these situations, God is waiting, ready to step in and lift the burden.

He Touched Me. 2005. audio compact disk 9.99 (978-5-559-07889-2(1)) Pt of Grace Ent.

He Touched Me: Best of Bill Gaither. Perf. by Bill Gaither Trio, The. 2002. audio compact disk Provident Mus Dist.

He Was Placed in the Tomb. Monks of Solesmes Staff. 1 CD. 1997. audio compact disk 16.95 (978-1-55725-193-0(2), 930-070) Paraclete MA.

He Was Singin' This Song: A Collection of Traditional Songs of the American Cowboy, with Music & Stories. abr. ed. Jim B. Tinsley. Read by Jim B. Tinsley. Contrib. by Michael M. Murphey. 2 cass. (Running Time: 3 hrs.). 1998. 18.95 Set. (978-1-57453-263-0(4)) Audio Lit.

Traces the history of the cowboy from colonial America to the selling of the West in songs & stories.

He Who Fears the Wolf. unabr. ed. Karin Fossum. 5 cass. (Running Time: 29340 sec.). (Inspector Sejer Mystery Ser.). 2005. 49.95 (978-0-7927-3697-4(4), CSL 825); audio compact disk 74.95 (978-0-7927-3698-1(2), SLD 825) AudioGO.

He Will Help You: Conquering Vices with the Virtue of Christ, Talk on CD. Read by Curtis Castillow. 2006. audio compact disk 13.95 (978-1-59038-731-3(7)) Desert Bks.

He Will Not Leave Us. 1 cass. (Running Time: 30 min.). 1985. (0258) Evang Sisterhood Mary.

Includes: Not Alone in Suffering; Following in His Footsteps; I Am Not Alone: There Is Power in Hope.

Head & Heart: American Christianities. unabr. ed. Garry Wills. Read by Mel Foster. (YA). 2008. 84.99 (978-1-60514-888-5(1)) Find a World.

Head & Heart: American Christianities. unabr. ed. Garry Wills. Read by Mel Foster. 16 CDs. (Running Time: 20 hrs. 0 mins. 0 sec.). (ENG.). 2007. audio compact disk 49.99 (978-1-4001-0578-6(1)); audio compact disk 34.99 (978-1-4001-5578-1(9)); audio compact disk 99.99 (978-1-4001-3578-3(8)) Pub: Tantor Media. Dist(s): IngramPubServ

Head & Heart to Resume Success; Head & Heart to Interview Success. Deborah P. Bloch. Read by Deborah P. Bloch. 2 cass. (Running Time: 3 hrs.). 1995. 24.95 Boxed Set. (978-0-9645872-0-5(3)) D P Bloch.

Resume writing & job interviews. On each cassette, one side is an ordered, linear approach & the other utilizes visualizations, affirmations & meditations.

Head Case. unabr. ed. Liza Cody. Read by Lindsay Sandison. 6 cass. (Running Time: 7 hrs.). (Isis Ser.). (J). 1994. 54.95 (978-1-85695-745-8(4), 940201) Pub: ISIS Lrg Prnt GBR. Dist(s): Ulverscroft US

Head for Business. Jon Naunton. 2003. 17.50 (978-0-19-457353-5(2)) OUP.

Head for Business: Intermediate Class. Jon Naunton. 2 CDs. (Running Time: 2 hrs.). 2003. cd-rom, audio compact disk, audio compact disk 35.95 (978-0-19-457367-2(2)) OUP.

Head for Business Upper-Intermediate: Class Audio. Jon Naunton. 2 CDs. (Running Time: 2 hrs.). 2003. cd-rom, audio compact disk, audio compact disk 35.95 (978-0-19-457368-9(0)) OUP.

Head for Business Upper-Intermediate: Class Cassettes. Jon Naunton. 2 cass. (Running Time: 3 hrs.). 2003. 31.95 (978-0-19-457345-0(1)) OUP.

Head Games: A Body of Evidence Thriller. unabr. ed. Christopher Golden. Narrated by Julie Dretzin. 5 pieces. (Running Time: 6 hrs. 15 mins.). (gr. 9 up). 2002. 45.00 (978-1-4025-2226-0(6)) Recorded Bks.

Head Games: 5 Cassettes (unabridged) unabr. ed. Nick Earls. 5 cass. (Running Time: 6 hrs. 40 mins.). 2004. 40.00 (978-1-74030-698-0(8)) Pub: Bolinda Pubng AUS. Dist(s): Lndmrk Audiobks

Head Injury: Context for Ministry. 1 cass. (Care Cassettes Ser.: Vol. 15, No. 2). 1988. 10.80 Assn Prof Chaplains.

Head-Long. Michael Frayn. Read by Frederick Davidson. 10 CDs. (Running Time: 11 hrs. 30 mins.). 2000. audio compact disk 80.00 (978-0-7861-9839-9(7), 2631) Blckstn Audio.

The boorish landowner, Martin Clay & his scrupulous art historian wife find themselves enlisted to assess the value of three dusty paintings. So begins a wild trail of lies & concealments, soaring hopes & sudden panics as Martin embarks on an obsessive quest to prove his hunch, win over his wife & resolve one of the great mysteries of European art.

Head-Long. unabr. ed. Michael Frayn. Read by Frederick Davidson. 8 cass. (Running Time: 11 hrs. 30 mins.). 2000. 56.95 (978-0-7861-1832-8(6), 2631) Blckstn Audio.

Martin Clay, a philosopher & his scrupulous art historian wife find themselves enlisted to assess the value of three dusty paintings. So begins a wild trail of lies & concealments, soaring hopes & sudden panics as Martin embarks on an obsessive quest to prove his hunch, win over his wife & resolve one of the great mysteries of European art.

Head of the Dragon. Lani Despres. 1 cass. 8.95 (649) Am Fed Astrologers.

An AFA Convention workshop tape.

Head over Heels. unabr. ed. Susan Anderson. Read by Anna Fields. 7 cass. (Running Time: 10 hrs. 30 mins.). 2001. 56.00 (978-0-7366-8496-5(4)) Books on Tape.

Veronica Davis swore she'd never voluntarily step foot in the family honky-tonk again. But now circumstances have brought her back, and it's even worse than she remembers, thanks to Cooper Blackstock, a bossy bartender with an agenda all his own. With his strange, manly charm, Cooper has gotten Veronica to start serving drinks at the bar again, working a rough, inebriated crowd that thinks that her shapely body is public property. Veronica feels obliged to help lift the bar back into solvency, because it will be the sole financial help available for her near-orphaned niece. The question is: when will Cooper Blackstock stop being the irritatingly cock-sure man that he is, and when will Veronica find herself, against all her best instincts, falling in love with him.

Head over Heels. unabr. ed. Sam Bailey & Jenny Bailey. Read by William McInnes. (Running Time: 6 hrs. 50 mins.). 2009. audio compact disk 77.95 (978-1-74214-471-9(3), 9781742144719) Pub: Bolinda Pubng AUS. Dist(s): Bolinda Pub Inc

Head over Heels. unabr. ed. Jill Mansell. Read by Patricia Gallimore. 13 CDs. (Running Time: 15 hrs. 52 mins.). (Isis (CDs) Ser.). (J). 2006. audio compact disk 99.95 (978-0-7531-2497-0(1)) Pub: ISIS Lrg Prnt GBR. Dist(s): Ulverscroft US

Head over Heels. unabr. ed. Jill Mansell. Read by Polly March. 11 cass. (Running Time: 14 hrs. 15 mins.). (Isis Cassettes Ser.). (J). 2006. 89.95 (978-0-7531-3479-5(9)) Pub: ISIS Lrg Prnt GBR. Dist(s): Ulverscroft US

Head over Heels in the Dales. Gervase Phinn. 8 cass. (Running Time: 12 hrs.). 2002. 69.95 (978-0-7540-0887-3(8), CAB 2309) Pub: Chivers Audio Bks GBR. Dist(s): AudioGO

Head over Heels in the Dales. Gervase Phinn. Read by Gervase Phinn. 2 cass. (Running Time: 3 hrs.). (ENG., 2002. (978-0-14-180363-0(0), PengAudBks) Penguin Grp USA.

When an angelic-faced girl of six asks him how to spell "sex" Gervase finds himself faced with one of those familiar situations, floored by a child's innocent remark. And news of an early retirement makes him seriously consider applying for the senior post, but his fiancee Christine makes it clear she wants to see her future husband other than at weekends. While in the office, the aptly named Mrs. Savage continues her magisterial rule with her incomprehensible memos.

Head Shot. unabr. ed. Quintin Jardine. Read by James Bryce. 10 cass. (Running Time: 11.5 hrs.). (Isis Ser.). (J). 2002. 84.95 (978-0-7531-1359-2(7)) Pub: ISIS Lrg Prnt GBR. Dist(s): Ulverscroft US

Head Shot. unabr. ed. Quintin Jardine. Read by James Bryce. 10 CDs. (Running Time: 12 hrs. 4 min.). (Isis Ser.). (J). 2003. audio compact disk 89.95 (978-0-7531-2227-3(8)) Pub: ISIS Lrg Prnt GBR. Dist(s): Ulverscroft US

Head Trip: Adventures on the Wheel of Consciousness. unabr. ed. Jeff Warren. Read by Raymond Todd. (Running Time: 41400 sec.). 2007. 32.95 (978-1-4332-0675-7(7)); 85.95 (978-1-4332-0673-3(0)); audio compact disk 32.95 (978-1-4332-0676-4(5)); audio compact disk 29.95 (978-1-4332-0677-1(3)); audio compact disk & audio compact disk 99.00 (978-1-4332-0674-0(9)) Blckstn Audio.

Head Wounds: A Sam Acquillo Hamptons Mystery. unabr. ed. Chris Knopf & Richard Ferrone. (Running Time: 10 hrs. NaN mins.). 2008. 29.95 (978-1-4332-2865-0(3)); 65.95 (978-1-4332-2861-2(0)); audio compact disk 80.00 (978-1-4332-2862-9(9)) Blckstn Audio.

Headache Relief. 1 cassette. (Running Time: 63 minutes, 40 seconds). 1985. 12.95 (978-1-55841-012-1(0)) Emmett E Miller.

Powerful mind-body approaches for most headaches. Four separate experiences to relieve and trace the cause of your pain, plus brief morning and evening meditations to keep you comfortable.

Headache Relief. 1 CD. 1986. audio compact disk 16.95 (978-1-55841-106-7(2)) Emmett E Miller.

Powerful mind-body approaches for most headaches. Four separate experiences to relive and trace the cause of your pain, plus brief morning and evening meditations to keep you comfortable.

Headache Relief. Steven Gurgevich. (ENG.). 2002. audio compact disk 19.95 (978-1-932170-21-4(9), HWH) Tranceformation.

Headache Relief. Martin Rossman. 1 CD. (Running Time: 1 hr. 15 mins.). (Guided Self-Healing Ser.). 2006. audio compact disk 15.95 (978-1-59179-189-8(8), W824D) Sounds True.

Headache Relief. Eldon Taylor. 1 cass. (Running Time: 62 min.). (Inner Talk Ser.). 16.95 (978-1-55978-305-7(2), 5367A) Progress Aware Res.

Soundtrack - Tropical Lagoon with underlying subliminal affirmations.

Headache Relief: Babbling Brook. Eldon Taylor. 1 cass. 16.95 (978-1-55978-490-0(3), 5367F) Progress Aware Res.

Headache Relief: Harmonies. Eldon Taylor. Read by Eldon Taylor. Ed. by Leslie Brice. 1 cass. (Running Time: 1 hr.). 1992. 16.95 (978-1-56705-146-9(4)) Gateways Inst.

Self improvement.

Headache Relief: Music Theme. Eldon Taylor. 1 cass. 16.95 (978-1-55978-146-6(7), 5367C) Progress Aware Res.

Headache Relief: Ocean. Eldon Taylor. Read by Eldon Taylor. Ed. by Leslie Brice. 1 cass. (Running Time: 1 hr.). 1992. 16.95 (978-1-56705-147-6(2)) Gateways Inst.

Headache Relief: Stream. Eldon Taylor. Read by Eldon Taylor. Ed. by Leslie Brice. 1 cass. (Running Time: 1 hr.). 1992. 16.95 (978-1-56705-148-3(0)) Gateways Inst.

Headache Relief (Clear Mind) Norman J. Caldwell. Read by Norman J. Caldwell. Ed. by Achieve Now Institute Staff. 1 cass. (Running Time: 20 min.). (Health-Imaging Ser.). 1988. 9.97 (978-1-56273-078-9(9)) My Mothers Pub.

Relax your mind & head with ease.

Headaches. 1 cass. (Running Time: 1 hr.). 2001. 9.95 (CA609) Pub: VisnQst Vid Aud. Dist(s): TMW Media

Headaches. unabr. ed. Don Colbert. Read by Greg Wheatley. 1 cass. (Running Time: 1 hr.). (Bible Cure for...Ser.). 2003. 7.99; audio compact disk 9.99 Oasis Audio.

Headaches. unabr. ed. Read by Robert S. Friedman & Kelly Howell. 1 cass. (Running Time: 60 min.). (Sound Techniques for Healing Ser.). 1993. 11.95 (978-1-881451-18-1(6)) Brain Sync.

A healthy blood flow to the brain is established as tension in the head, neck & shoulders disappears. Head pain is dramatically relieved & comfort restored.

Headaches, Heartaches & People-Aches: The Cross & Holiness. Edmund McCaffrey. 1 cass. 4.00 (95C2) IRL Chicago.

Headed for the Future - ShowTrax. Perf. by America Sings. Arranged by Mac Huff. 1 CD. (Running Time: 5 mins.). (Pop Choral Ser.). 2000. audio compact disk 19.95 (08201131) H Leonard.

Greet the millennium with this updated treatment of a classic Neil Diamond hit! Performed in the 1999 Macy's Thanksgiving Parade, it's a great choice for pop/show groups.

Headhunters. Jules Bass. Narrated by Barbara Rosenblat. 8 cass. (Running Time: 10 hrs. 30 mins.). 74.00 (978-0-7887-9581-7(3)); audio compact disk 89.00 (978-1-4025-1554-5(5)) Recorded Bks.

Headin' Home. Marty Hamby. 1997. 8.00 (978-0-7673-3034-3(X)); 75.00 (978-0-7673-3032-9(3)); 11.98 (978-0-7673-3031-2(5)); audio compact disk 85.00 (978-0-7673-3033-6(1)) LifeWay Christian.

Headless Bicycle Rider, unabr. ed. Tom B. Stone. Narrated by Jeff Woodman. 2 cass. (Running Time: 2 hrs. 30 mins.). (Graveyard School Ser.: No. 3). (gr. 3-7). 2001. 19.00 (978-0-7887-0707-0(8), 94882E7) Recorded Bks.

An adventure of spooky danger & grisly humor centers around a school so weird that its students are dying to go to class.

Headless Cupid, unabr. ed. Zilpha Keatley Snyder. Narrated by Johnny Heller. 4 pieces. (Running Time: 5 hrs. 30 mins.). (gr. 6 up). 1996. 35.00 (978-0-7887-0692-9(6), 94866E7) Recorded Bks.

When David's new stepsister arrives, she introduces David to a strange world of witchcraft & the occult. At first, spells & potions are fun, but when rocks start flying around the house David begins to fear the strange forces at work.

Headless Cupid, Set. Zilpha Keatley Snyder. Read by Johnny Heller. 4 cass. (Running Time: 5 hr. 30 min.). (J). (gr. 6). 1996. pap. bk. 47.75 (978-0-7887-1546-4(1), 40344) Recorded Bks.

Headless Horseman see Legend of Sleepy Hollow

Headless Trainman. unabr. ed. Allan Zullo. Read by John Ratzenberger. 2008. 1.37 (978-1-4233-8067-2(3), 9781423380672, BAD) Brilliance Audio.

Headlines & Footnotes: A Collection of Topical Songs. Pete Seeger & Mark Greenberg. 1 cass. (Running Time: 74 min.). (YA). 1999. 14.00 Smithsonian Folkways.

Includes song notes, photos & lyrics.

Headlong. unabr. ed. Michael Frayn. Read by Robert Powell. 10 cass. (Running Time: 15 hrs.). 2001. 84.95 (978-0-7540-0567-4(4), CAB1990) Pub: Chivers Audio Bks GBR. Dist(s): AudioGO

Martin Clay, a young would-be art historian, believes he has found one of the world's long lost great treasures. His find could make his professional reputation & a lot of money. The treasure he has found is in someone else's possession & to get his hands on it he needs to set up a classic sting.

Headlong. unabr. ed. Michael Frayn. Narrated by Steven Crossley. 9 cass. (Running Time: 12 hrs. 45 mins.). 2001. 81.00 (978-0-7887-5467-8(X), 96602x7) Recorded Bks.

When philosopher Martin Clay & his art historian wife assess a neglected painting owned by a loutish man, Martin believes the painting is a valuable masterwork. He's willing to stake everything on his hunch & he hopes to finagle the painting away from its owner in the process.

Headmaster. unabr. ed. R. F. Delderfield. Read by Christian Rodska. 12 cass. (Running Time: 18 hrs.). (To Serve Them All My Days Ser.: Bk. 2). 2000. 79.95 (CAB 713) Pub: Chivers Audio Bks GBR. Dist(s): AudioGO

Having survived the horrors of World War I, David Powlett-Jones makes the adjustment to a changing society and emerges as a schoolmaster of rare talent. But will his experiences serve him well when he must confront the deaths of the many pupils he had nurtured in school during World War II?.

Heads or Tails: Stories from the Sixth Grade, unabr. ed. Jack Gantos. Narrated by Greg Longenhagen. 4 pieces. (Running Time: 4 hrs. 30 mins.). (gr. 6 up). 1997. 35.00 (978-0-7887-1105-3(9), 95098E7) Recorded Bks.

Story of a quirky sixth-grader & the dazzlingly wacky world he lives in. How can you grow up right when a neighbor feeds spoiled pork chops to an alligator in the canal behind your family's run-down rental home? You have a pest for a little brother & an older sister who mocks your belief in UFOs?.

Heads or Tails: Stories from the Sixth Grade. unabr. ed. Jack Gantos. Read by Greg Longenhagen. 4 cass. (Running Time: 4 hrs. 05 min.). (J). (gr. 2). 1997. Rental 11.50 Recorded Bks.

Heads-up Baseball: Playing the Game One Pitch at a Time. abr. ed. Ken Ravizza & Tom Hanson. Frwd. by Hank Aaron. (Running Time: 16200 sec.). (J). (ps-7). 2005. audio compact disk 28.00 (978-1-932378-89-4(8)) Pub: A Media Intl. Dist(s): Natl Bk Netwk

Headship of Jesus. Derek Prince. 2 cass. 1990. 5.95 ea. Derek Prince.

God made Jesus head over all things! How does this affect our personal lives, our families, our churches - & the church?.

Headshot! Carol Eason. Read by Carol Eason. 3 CDs. (Running Time: 3 hrs.). (Mercenary Ser.: No. 12). 2005. audio compact disk (978-1-58807-969-5(4)); audio compact disk 25.00 (978-1-58807-336-5(X)) Am Pubng Inc.
Hank Frost, the wise-cracking, one-eyed mercenary captain, is hired by the hot-tempered daughter of the assassinated patriarch of Miami's anti-Castro underground. His mission: Cut the three-way connection between Havana, Colombia's M-19 terrorists, and Florida drug smugglers. But Frost discovers that more than drugs are being smuggled - arms and explosives are being traded to the M-19 for military protection and to pro-Castro terrorists in Miami. As Frost fights Castro's death squads, M-19 guerillas, and murderous professional hitmen, it's hard to figure out if the fiery beauty who hired him wants him as a lover - or as a target.

Headshot. Axel Kilgore. Read by Carol Eason. Abr. by Odin Westgaard. 2 vols. No. 12. 2004. (978-1-58807-659-5(8)) Am Pubng Inc.

Headshot! abr. ed. Axel Kilgore. Read by Charlton Griffin. Abr. by Odin Westgaard. 2 vols. No. 12. 2004. 18.00 (978-1-58807-168-2(5)) Am Pubng Inc.

Headstart for the Philippines: Learn Tagalog or Philipino Quickly. Dofensc Language Institute Staff. 14 cass. (Intensive Cassette Ser.). (TAG.). (C). 1998. spiral bd. 225.00 (978-1-58214-008-7(1)) Language Assocs.

Headwaters of the Mississippi River. Hosted by Nancy Pearlman. 1 cass. (Running Time: 30 min.). 10.00 (913) Educ Comm CA.

Headwind. unabr. ed. John J. Nance. Read by John J. Nance. 8 cass. (Running Time: 12 hrs.). 2001. 87.25 (978-1-58788-821-2(1), 1587888211, Unabridge Lib Edns); 34.95 (978-1-58788-820-5(3), 1587888203, BAU) Brilliance Audio.
In Athens, a Boeing 737 noses into the gate, and its crew is suddenly confronted by Greek officials waiting to arrest one of its passengers, a beloved ex-President of the United States, John Harris. Captain Craig Dayton, believing Harris' life is in danger, stages a daring escape by backing the jet away from the gate without clearance and taking off down a vacant runway. The dilemma for Captain Dayton and his precious cargo is that Peru has signed an Interpol warrant for President Harris' arrest, using the same treaty employed to extradite former Chilean dictator Augusto Pinochet. The Peruvian government alleges that Harris is personally responsible for a supposed CIA-led strike against a biological weapons factory during his term of office. But the nightmare for Harris - and the U.S. State Department - is this: There is no place to hide, because almost every nation in the world has signed the treaty and every one of them must honor the warrant and give Peru what it wants - a president to humiliate on the international stage. Captain Dayton flies Harris and his crew on an against-the-clock mission around the world to find a safe haven, while Harris' rumpled and out-gunned lawyer wrestles an international team of legal sharks snapping at their biggest prize yet.

Headwind. unabr. ed. John J. Nance. Read by John J. Nance. (Running Time: 12 hrs.). 2004. 39.25 (978-1-59335-362-9(6), 1593353626, Brinc Audio MP3 Lib) Brilliance Audio.

Headwind. unabr. ed. John J. Nance. Read by John J. Nance. (Running Time: 12 hrs.). 2004. 39.25 (978-1-59710-347-3(0), 1597103470, BADLE) Brilliance Audio.

Headwind. unabr. ed. John J. Nance. Read by John J. Nance. (Running Time: 12 hrs.). 2004. 24.95 (978-1-59335-034-5(1), 1593350341) Soulmate Audio Bks.

Headwind. unabr. ed. John J. Nance. Read by John J. Nance. (Running Time: 12 hrs.). 2004. 24.95 (978-1-59710-346-6(2), 1597103462, BAD) Brilliance Audio.

Heal the Hurt That Runs Your Life: Discover & Heal the Inner Issues That Destroy Love & Sabotage Life. Bill Ferguson. Read by Bill Ferguson. 2 cass. (Running Time: 108 min.). 1996. 16.00 (978-1-878410-22-1(9)) Return Heart.
Find and heal the inner issues that run your life, These Issues: failure, worthless, not good enough, etc., are only thoughts, but they sabotage every aspect of life.

Heal the Hurt That Sabotages Your Life: Be Free of the Inner Issues That Destroy Love & Create Suffering. Bill Ferguson. 2 Cds. (Running Time: 2 hrs. 18 mins.). 2004. audio compact disk 21.95 (978-1-878410-37-5(7)) Return Heart.

Heal Thyself. White Eagle. Read by Ylana Hayward. (Running Time: 2 hrs. 4 mins.). audio compact disk 15.95 (978-0-85487-148-3(9)) Pub: White Eagle GBR. Dist(s): DeVorss

Heal Thyself: Using Your Inner Power to Heal. Richard Jafolla & Mary-Alice Jafolla. Read by Richard Jafolla & Mary-Alice Jafolla. (Health & Healing Ser.). 1986. 12.95 (290) Stppng Stones.
Motivational tapes that work on the subconscious mind (subliminal) & conscious mind to bring about self-improvement.

Heal Us Lord: Songs of Mercy. Perf. by Still Waters. 1 cass. (Running Time: 46 min.). 1993. 12.00 (978-1-884479-01-4(4)); audio compact disk 16.00 CD. (978-1-884479-09-0(X)) Spirit Song.
Meditative religious songs sung by Still Waters family music ministry.

Heal Us Today: Stories of Jesus the Healer. Bert Polman. (Running Time: 25 mins.). (Scripture Alive Ser.). 2000. 15.95 (978-1-56212-431-1(5), 415111) FaithAliveChr.

Heal Your Body. Glenn Harrold. 1 cass. (Running Time: 1 hr. 30 mins.). 2002. 11.95 (978-1-901923-09-4(6)) Pub: Divinit Pubing GBR. Dist(s): Bookworld

Heal Your Body. Glenn Harrold. 2 CDs. (Running Time: 3 hrs.). 2003. audio compact disk 17.95 (978-1-901923-29-2(0)) Pub: Divinit Pubing GBR. Dist(s): Bookworld

Heal Your Body. unabr. ed. Dick Sutphen. Read by Dick Sutphen. 1 cass. (Running Time: 1 hr.). (Spirit Guide Meditations). 1999. 14.98 (978-0-87554-631-5(5), SG104) Valley Sun.
Connect with the spirit guide to focus combined energies. Fill every cell & every atom with the universal light of life energy.

Heal Your Hang-Ups: Depression, Alcohol & Drug Addiction. (ENG.). 2008. audio compact disk 10.00 (978-0-9815046-0-5(4)) Pub: BBCSPub. Dist(s): Baker Taylor

Heal Your Heart: Coping with the Loss of a Pet. (ENG.). 2009. audio compact disk 18.00 (978-0-615-29858-0(3)) HPL.

Heal Your Life see Cure Su Vida

Heal Your Life: Consciousness & Energy Medicine. Caroline Myss & Ron Roth. 2000. 55.00 (978-1-893869-65-3(2)) Celbrtng Life.

Heal Your Life & Honor Your Soul's Intention: A Seven-Fold Path of Love to Living with an Awakened Spirit, Set. unabr. ed. Meredith Young Sowers. 8 cass. (Running Time: 8 hrs.). 1998. pap. bk. 75.00 (978-1-883478-10-0(3)) Stillpoint.
A guide to connecting with God as the energy of divine love. Work with a gifted "intuitive" healer & spiritual teacher to explore the real issues behind your illness & your inability to create positive outcomes.

Heal Yourself of Anything Example Glaucoma. Nancy Lynne Harris. 2006. audio compact disk 10.95 (978-0-9636781-5-7(9)) BBCSPub.

Heal Yourself with Medical Hypnosis: The Most Immediate Way to Use Your Mind-Body Connection. Andrew Weil & Steven Gurgevich. 2 CDs. (Running Time: 8100 sec.). 2005. audio compact disk 19.95 (978-1-59179-356-4(4), W963D) Sounds True.

Heal Yourself with Sound & Music. Don Campbell. 6 CDs. (Running Time: 22500 sec.). 2006. audio compact disk 39.95 (978-1-59179-496-7(X), AW00477D) Sounds True.

Healed by the Word of God, Confessions. Robb Thompson. audio compact disk 10.00 (978-1-889723-47-1(9)) Pub: Family Harvest. Dist(s): Harrison Hse

Healed in Your Love. Daughters of St Paul. 2003. audio compact disk 16.95 (978-0-8198-3383-9(5), 332-120) Pauline Bks.

Healed of Multiple Sclerosis. Mother Angelica & Father Michael. 1 cass. (Running Time: 60 min.). (Mother Angelica Live Ser.). 1988. 10.00 (978-1-55794-108-4(4), T59) Eternal Wrd TV.
The author tells about struggling with the revages of multiple sclerosis.

Healed Without Scars. David Evans. 2004. audio compact disk 7.99 (978-2-901008-39-2(9)) Pub: Whitaker Hse. Dist(s): Anchor Distributors

Healer. Contrib. by Lari Goss. 1997. 24.95 (978-0-7601-1810-8(8), 75600296) Pub: Brentwood Music. Dist(s): H Leonard

Healer. unabr. ed. Terry Teykl. 6 cass. 1996. 25.00 Set. (978-1-57892-030-3(2)) Prayer Pt Pr.
Sermon/teaching the Healer.

Healer Within. Eldon Taylor. 2 cass. (Running Time: 62 min. per cass.). (Omniphonics Ser.). 29.95 incl. script Set. (978-1-55978-810-6(0), 4011) Progress Aware Res.
3-D soundtrack with underlying subliminal affirmations, night & day versions.

Healers, Helpers, Wizards & Guides: A Healing Journey. Bertie Ryan Synowiec. 3 cass. (Running Time: 4 hrs. 30 min.). 2000. 24.95 Boxed set. (978-1-885335-17-3(2)) Positive Support.

Healing. Kenneth Copeland. 8 cass. 1982. bk. 40.00 Set incl. study guide. (978-0-938458-37-1(X)) K Copeland Pubns.
The biblical principles of healing.

Healing. Mary Flora. 2003. audio compact disk 12.00 (978-1-886983-16-8(X)) CDM Pubns.

Healing. Gayl Jones. Read by Rebecca Nicholas. 7 cass. (Running Time: 10 hrs. 30 min.). 1999. 39.95 (978-0-7366-4588-1(8)) Books on Tape.
Harlan Jane Eagleton is a faith healer, traveling by bus to small towns, converting skeptics, restoring minds & bodies, but before that she was a minor rock star's manager & before that a beautician. She's had a fling with her rock star's ex-husband & an Afro-German horse dealer. Along the way she's somehow lost her own husband, a medical anthropologist now traveling with a medicine woman in Africa. Harlan tells her story from the end backwards, drawing us constantly deeper into her world & the mystery at the heart of her tale, the story of her first healing.

Healing. Betty L. Randolph. 1 stereo cass. (Running Time: 45 min.). (Self-Hypnosis Ser.). 9.98 (978-1-55909-147-3(9), 807) Randolph Tapes.
Healing Relaxation. Music background & spoken word.

Healing. Uma Silbey. Read by Uma Silbey. 1 cass. (Running Time: 45 min.). 10.00 UMA.
Guided spoken meditation with sound background.

Healing. Vincent M. Walsh. 1 cass. 1986. 4.00 Key of David.

Healing. collector's ed. Gayl Jones. Read by Rebecca Nicholas. 7 cass. (Running Time: 10 hrs. 30 min.). 1999. 56.00 (978-0-7366-4565-2(9)) Books on Tape.
Harlan Jane Eagleton is a faith healer, traveling by bus to small towns, converting skeptics, restoring minds & bodies, but before that she was a minor rock star's manager & before that a beautician. She's had a fling with her rock star's ex-husband & an Afro-German horse dealer. Along the way she's somehow lost her own husband, a medical anthropologist now traveling with a medicine woman in Africa. Harlan tells her story from the end backwards, drawing us constantly deeper into her world & the mystery at the heart of her tale, the story of her first healing.

Healing, Vol. 1. unabr. ed. Chris Yaw. Perf. by Scott Hiltzik. 1 cass. (Running Time: 1 hr.). (Living Words Ser.). 1998. 9.98 (978-1-893613-00-3(3)); audio compact disk 11.98 CD. (978-1-893613-04-1(6)) Living Wds.
Bible verses arranged by topic & read with music in the background.

Healing: Awakening the Healer Within - Releasing the Blocks. Diana Keck. Read by Diana Keck. 9.95 (978-0-929653-05-1(X), TAPE 301) Mntn Spirit Tapes.

Healing: Forever Settled Series. Kenneth W. Hagin, Jr. 3 cass. 1995. 12.00 Set. (34J) Faith Lib Pubns.

Healing: Hearing the Melody. Kenneth Wapnick. 4 cassettes. 2003. audio compact disk 26.00 (978-1-59142-109-2(8), CD88) Foun Miracles.
Using the example and symbolism of music-Beethoven, Schubert, and Wagner-the workshop develops the theme of listening to others, hearing the inner melody or song (melos) that sings both of Heaven and our need to return. Listening with Jesus prevents judgment, and allows our healing heart to touch another's pain with "the gentle hands of forgiveness." Thus are we healed together and as one, learning that the melody of love is our Self.

Healing: Hearing the Melody. Kenneth Wapnick. 1 CD. 2006. 21.00 (978-1-59142-273-0(6), 3m88) Foun Miracles.

Healing: Is It God's Will? Kenneth Copeland. 1 cass. (Healing Ser.: No. 1). 1982. 5.00 (978-0-938458-91-3(4)) K Copeland Pubns.
Indepth biblical study on healing.

Healing: Key to Spiritual Balance. Mary Ellen Flora. (Running Time: 60 min.). 1992. 9.95 (978-0-9631993-3-1(1)) CDM Pubns.
Side 1 teaches self-healing techniques such as grounding, centering, amusement, and present time. Side 2 provides a clear and powerful self-healing session using spiritual techniques from side 1 and more.

Healing: Meditation Scriptures on the Biblical Promises for Healing. Excerpts. Compiled by Steven B. Stevens. Voice by Steven B. Stevens. Engineer Thomas A. Webb. Executive Producer Thomas A. Webb. 1 CD. (Running Time: 41 mins). (Promises for Life Ser.). 2005. audio compact disk 14.95 (978-0-9726363-2-2(3), CD-101, Promises for Life) Brite Bks.
Selected meditation scriptures focused on Bible Promises for Healing.Un-unabridged, non-commentary, non-denominational audio reading of like topic bible promises from multiple translations all on the subject of Healing.

Healing: Music, Meditation & Prayer. Marianne Williamson. 1 cass. (Running Time: 45 min.). 1997. 10.95 (978-1-56170-434-7(2), M819) Hay House.
Will bring a soothing, peaceful space into your life, helping to heal your body, mind, & soul.

Healing: Music, Meditation & Prayer. Marianne Williamson. 1 CD. (Running Time: 1 hr.). 1998. audio compact disk 12.95 (978-1-56170-533-7(0), M832) Hay House.

Healing: Radiation Therapy-Energy for Healing - Healing Through Chemotherapy. Diana Keck. 1 cass. 9.95 (978-0-929653-06-8(8), TAPE 302) Mntn Spirit Tapes.

Healing: The Decision to Join. unabr. ed. Carol Howe. 3 cass. (Running Time: 4 hrs. 30 min.). 1995. 23.95 Set. (978-1-889642-10-9(X)) C Howe.
For all those who suffer from physical illness, emotional pain, or deprivation in any area of life, this workshop presents the revolutionary "one size fits all" solution & provides: Insights into the true origin of all sickness or deprivation & the part we play in its occurrence. Specific instructions for resolving the conflict in our minds, leading inevitably to healing & wholeness. Clarification of the important difference between rescuing & being truly helpful.

Healing: The Healing Light - Directing Healing to Others. Diana Keck. Read by Diana Keck. 1 cass. 9.95 (978-0-929653-04-4(1), TAPE 300) Mntn Spirit Tapes.

Healing: The Message & Method of Jesus. Derek Prince. 1 cass. (I-4132) Derek Prince.

Healing - Secrets, Vol. 1. adpt. ed. Read by Adrian Plass et al. Adapted by Paul McCusker. Prod. by Dave Arnold. (Running Time: 240 hrs. 0 mins.). (Radio Theatre Ser.). (ENG.). (J). (gr. 3). 2007. audio compact disk 14.97 (978-1-58997-504-0(9), Tyndale Ent) Tyndale Hse.

Healing a Heartbreak. Richard Jafolla & Mary-Alice Jafolla. Read by Richard Jafolla & Mary-Alice Jafolla. (Overcoming Ser.). 1986. 12.95 (190) Stppng Stones.
Works on the subconscious mind (subliminal) & conscious mind to bring about self-improvement.

Healing Across Time & Space: Guided Journeys to Your Past, Future, & Parallel Lives. Cyndi Dale. 2008. audio compact disk 19.95 (978-1-59179-667-1(9)) Sounds True.

Healing Affirmations & Harp: Relax into Healing Series (Spoken Audio CD & Booklet) Nancy Hopps. (Relax Into Healing Ser.). 2007. pap. bk. 19.95 (978-0-9785985-5-6(5), Relas into Healing) Pub: Syner Systs. Dist(s): Baker Taylor

Healing & Counseling with Animals. rev. ed. Penelope Smith. 2 cass. (Running Time: 2 hrs.). (Interspecies Telepathic Connection Tape Ser.: No. 4). 1994. 19.95 set. (978-0-936552-16-3(6)) AnimaMundi.
Learn straightforward methods to help animals through emotional trauma, fear, injury, illness, & death (not a substitute for veterinary assistance but ways to promote healing). Bodywork & counselling in-person & at a distance. Contacting animals who have died. Spirit transfer. Entities. Insights into Penelope's seasoned approach to counselling with animals.

Healing & Freeing the Inner Child. Martha B. Beveridge. 1 cass. (Running Time: 60 min.). 1994. 9.95 (978-1-889237-29-9(9)) Options Now.
Learn how the child you were impacts your life today. This cassette is important for parents & vital for understanding your intimate relationships.

Healing & Health: How Spiritual Gifts Operate. Derek Prince. 1 cass. (B-2002) Derek Prince.

Healing & Love. Kenneth Copeland. 2006. audio compact disk 30.00 (978-1-57562-866-0(X)) K Copeland Pubns.

Healing & Love. Kenneth Copeland. 4 cass. 1982. 30.00 Set incl. study guide. (978-0-938458-63-0(9)) K Copeland Pubns.
Healing & love.

Healing & Non-Ordinary Consciousness. Stanislov Grof. 4 cass. 1993. 36.00 set. (OC336-71) Sound Horizons AV.

Healing & Personal Health: Natural Killer Cells. Patricia O'Malley. Perf. by Barry Weiss. 1 cass. (Running Time: 50 min.). 1998. 11.95 (978-1-892450-19-7(4), 115) Pub: Promo Music. Dist(s): Penton Overseas
Experience the birth of new & healthy cells & take control of your own health & healing, once again.

Healing & Physical Illness Inspired by Shamanic Traditions. Lewis Mehl. 1 cass. 9.00 (A0215-87) Sound Photosyn.
From ICSS '87 with Ruth Inge Heinze & Stanley Krippner on this tape.

Healing & Preventing Autism. unabr. ed. Jenny McCarthy & Jerry Kartzinel. (Running Time: 5 hrs. 0 mins.). (ENG.). 2009. 19.95 (978-1-4332-7092-5(7)); audio compact disk 19.95 (978-1-4332-7091-8(9)) Blckstn Audio.

Healing & Preventing Autism. unabr. ed. Jenny McCarthy & Jerry Kartzinel. Read by Tavia Gilbert. (Running Time: 5 hrs. 0 mins.). (ENG.). 2009. 34.95 (978-1-4332-7088-8(9)); audio compact disk 40.00 (978-1-4332-7089-5(7)) Blckstn Audio.

Healing & Releasing Meditations. unabr. ed. Carolyn Ann O'Riley. 1 cass. (Running Time: 30 mins.). 2000. audio compact disk 12.50 (978-1-891870-11-8(4)) Archangels Pen.
Archangel Michael inspired meditation tape. Side A: "A Meditation to Heal or Release a Relationship"; Side B: "A Meditation to Sever the Cords That Keep You Stuck.".

Healing & Releasing the Emotional Pain. Eldon Taylor. 1 cass. (Running Time: 62 min.). (Inner Talk Ser.). 16.95 incl. script. (978-1-55978-527-3(6), 53812F) Progress Aware Res.
Soundtrack - Brook with underlying subliminal affirmations.

Healing & Releasing the Emotional Pain: Classics. Eldon Taylor. 1 cass. 16.95 (978-1-55978-636-2(1), 53812L) Progress Aware Res.

Healing & Salvation. Robert Reeves. 1986. 10.80 (0101) Assn Prof Chaplains.

Healing & Spirituality: The Sacred Quest for Transformation of Body & Soul. Joan Z. Borysenko. 2 CDs. 2005. audio compact disk 18.95 (978-1-4019-0430-2(0)) Hay House.

Healing & Spirituality: The Sacred Quest for Transformation of Body & Soul, Set. Joan Borysenko. Read by Joan Borysenko. 2 cass. (Running Time: 2 hrs.). 2000. 18.95 (978-1-56170-770-6(8), 4069) Hay House.
How to heal spiritually by delving into body/mind issues.

Healing & the Atonement. Mike Craig. 1 cass. (Running Time: 90 mins.). (He Still Heals Ser.: Vol. 4). 2000. 5.00 (SAO1-004) Morning NC.
Learn about the healing power of God that is available to believers today.

Healing & Transformation - The Buddhist Approach. Sogyal Rinpoche. 1 cass. 9.00 (A0109-84) Sound Photosyn.
A wonderful laugh along talk.

Healing & Wellness: Your 10-Day Spiritual Action Plan. Kenneth Copeland & Gloria Copeland. (ENG.). 2009. pap. bk. 20.00 (978-1-57562-962-9(3)) K Copeland Pubns.

Healing Angels. Steven Gurgevich. (ENG.). 2005. audio compact disk 19.95 (978-1-932170-37-5(5), HWH) Tranceformation.

Healing Anger & Depression: Removing Barriers to Health & Happiness. William G. DeFoore. (ENG.). 2004. audio compact disk 29.99 (978-0-9785244-3-2(8)) Halcyon Life.

Healing Anointing Series. Kenneth E. Hagin. 8 cass. 32.00 (32H) Faith Lib Pubns.

Healing Anxiety & Depression: The Revolutionary Brain Based Program That Allows You to See. unabr. abr. ed. Daniel G. Amen et al. Read by Alan Sklar. 4 CDs. (Running Time: 7 hrs. 30 mins.). (ENG.). 2003. audio compact disk 29.95 (978-1-56511-801-0(4), 1565118014) Pub: HighBridge. Dist(s): Workman Pub

Healing Art of Conscious Breathing. John C. Meneghini. 1 CD. (Running Time: 73 mins). (ENM.). 2002. audio compact disk 19.99 (978-0-9721765-0-7(0)) Sadhana Concepts Inc.

Healing Arts Collection. Kathleen Milner. Perf. by Kathleen Milner. 5 cass. 1995. bk. 165.00 (978-1-886903-99-9(9)) K Milner.
Titles include: Journey to Sacred Mountain - Side 2, Ancient Symbology; Candle Meditation - Side 2, Crystal Cave; When the Angels Came - Side 2, music only "Passageways" by Richard Bennette; Atlantian Heart Chakra - Side 2, music only "Atlantis" by Paul Lincoln; Past Life Regression - Side 2, "Healing with Colors.".

Healing Back Pain: The Mind-Body Connection. abr. rev. ed. John E. Sarno. Read by John E. Sarno. 3 CDs. (Running Time: 3 hrs. 0 mins. 0 sec.). (ENG.). 2004. audio compact disk 19.95 (978-1-55927-995-6(8)) Pub: Macmill Audio. Dist(s): Macmillan

Healing Belongs to Us. Kenneth E. Hagin. 4 cass. 16.00 (58H) Faith Lib Pubns.

Healing Breath. Neil Douglas-Klotz. 6 CDs. 2004. audio compact disk 69.95 (978-1-59179-075-4(1), AF00706D) Sounds True.
Perhaps the most recognized passage from the Sermon on the Mount, the Beatitudes (or "Blessed are ..." sayings) are among Jesus' most beloved-and most misunderstood-teachings. On The Healing Breath, acclaimed teacher and author Neil Douglas-Klotz leads listeners through the Beatitudes as spoken in Jesus' native Aramaic to show how this seemingly simple set of statements reveals a profound source of divine connection. With 12 in-depth sessions including 24 "body prayers"-authentic meditations of the ancient Middle East that use body awareness, breath, sound, and gentle movement-Douglas-Klotz helps listeners open fully to the transformative power of The Healing Breath.

Healing Breezes: Acts 3 1-26. Ed Young. 1997. 4.95 (978-0-7417-2152-5(X), A1152) Win Walk.

Healing Chakra: Light to Awaken My Soul. Ilchi Lee. 2005. pap. bk. 20.00 (978-1-932843-10-1(8)) Healing Society.

Healing Circle. Laura Day. 2000. audio compact disk 14.95 (978-0-9679579-0-6(7)) Laura Day Inc.

Healing Classics. Kenneth E. Hagin. 6 cass. 24.00 set. (57H) Faith Lib Pubns.

Healing Codependency with Gospel Principles. John C. Turpin. 1 cass. 2004. 3.95 (978-1-57734-405-6(7), 34441476) Covenant Comms.

Healing Connection: The Story of a Physician's Search for the Link beetween Faith & Health. Harold G. Koenig & Gregg Lewis. 6 CDs. (Running Time: 375 min). 2005. audio compact disk 14.95 (978-1-932031-85-0(5)) Pub: Templeton Pr. Dist(s): Chicago Distribution Ctr

Healing Crystal Secrets. Brett Bravo. 1 cass. 8.95 (638) Am Fed Astrologers.
An AFA Convention workshop tape.

Healing Depression the Natural Way. Elizabeth Joyce. 1 cass. (Running Time: 1 hr.). 1992. 12.00 (978-1-57124-009-5(8)) Creat Seminars.
Overview of techniques to deal with depression.

Healing Dream: The Ascleplad Experience. Eldon Taylor. 1 cass. (Running Time: 62 min.). (Inner Talk Ser.). 16.95 incl. script. (978-1-55978-022-3(3), 5422C) Progress Aware Res.
Soundtrack - Musical Themes with underlying subliminal affirmations & audible meditation.

Healing Drones. Kay Gardner. 1 cass. (Running Time: 1 hr.). 1996. 9.95 (978-1-55961-355-2(6)); audio compact disk 14.95 (978-1-55961-354-5(8)) Relaxtn Co.

Healing Drum: African Ceremonial & Ritual Music. Yaya Diallo. 2003. audio compact disk 14.95 (978-0-89281-505-0(1), Inner Trad) Inner Tradit.

Healing Drum Kit: Drumming for Personal Wellness & Creative Expression. Christine Stevens. 2 CDs. (Running Time: 2 hrs. 30 mins.). 2005. 59.95 (978-1-59179-278-9(9), T930D) Sounds True.

***Healing Drums: A Medical Intuitive's Guide to Shamanic Journey.** (ENG.). 2010. audio compact disk 14.99 (978-0-9845677-0-6(4)) Queens Crt Pr.

Healing Encounters. Ron Roth. 6 cass. (Running Time: 4 hrs. 30 min.). 1993. 49.95 Set. (978-1-893869-10-3(5)) Celbrtng Life.
Takes the listener through the Sacred Scriptures & shares with us the role Jesus played in helping people who needed healing & how Jesus deals with people.

Healing Energy - Sleep. Read by Mary Richards. 12.95 (501) Master Your Mind.
Focuses on ways to relax into sleep with the soothing sound of the surf, letting the suggestions lull you into a feeling of well being.

Healing Faith. Kenneth E. Hagin. 1 cass. 4.95 (SH27) Faith Lib Pubns.

Healing, Faith, & You: An Investigation of the Power of God to Heal. 6. (Running Time: 6 hrs.). 2002. 30.00 (978-1-57399-120-9(1)) Mac Hammond.
Healing is one of God's most basic provisions in Scripture. Yet, it seems to be one of those things that we have the most difficulty receiving from the Lord. It's for that reason that Mac Hammond began teaching the basic principles of healing.

Healing Fear. 2nd ed. Created by Catherine Sweet. 1CD. 2003. audio compact disk 14.95 (978-0-9744587-0-0(8)) Sweet Sp.

Healing Feelings... from Your Heart. Karol K. Truman. 2008. audio compact disk 39.95 (978-0-911207-08-8(2)) Olympus Distributing Corp.

Healing Fire: Healing Beyond Medicine Series. Joseph Michael Levry. (ENG.). 2000. 19.00 (978-1-885562-08-1(X)) Root Light.

Healing Fire of Christ. Paul Glynn. 7 CDs. (Running Time: 7 hrs.). 2003. audio compact disk 38.95 (978-1-57058-550-0(4)) St Joseph Communs.
What are miracles? Why do miracles still Happen? The subject of miraculous activity is one that has compelled believers for millennia. This book describes and recounts some of the most fascinating stories that have taken place not on the dusty pages of some centuries-old manuscript, but here and now in our own modern world.Fr. Paul Glynn, a Marist priest, takes the reader on a trip around the world to the sites of miraculous happenings, including healings, apparitions and conversions, including Lourdes, Knock and Fatima.

Healing Flame of St Germain: Healing Cellular Memory in the Body. Heraty Eugenie. (ENG.). 2007. 16.98 (978-1-934332-03-0(8), Heal Voice) Inter Med Pub.

Healing for Healers: How to Give Without Giving It All Away. abr. ed. Karla McLaren. Read by Karla McLaren. 1 cass. (Running Time: 1 hr. 30 min.). 1999. 11.00 (978-0-9656583-3-1(3)) Laughing Tree Pr.
Explains energy exchange between healers & their clients, & provides a complete healing process for the maintenance of the aura, chakras, & energy body of healers.

***Healing for the Angry Heart.** Lisa Bevere. 2010. audio compact disk 29.99 (978-1-933185-56-9(2)) Messengr Intl.

Healing for the Angry Heart CD Series. 2007. audio compact disk 34.99 (978-1-933185-22-4(8)) Messengr Intl.

Healing for the Angry Heart CD Series. Lisa Bevere. 2008. 34.99 (978-1-933185-38-5(4)) Messengr Intl.

***Healing for the Angry Heart Life Message Series.** Bevere Lisa. 2010. audio compact disk 0.00 (978-1-933185-66-8(X)) Messengr Intl.

Healing Force: Using Your Mind to Help Heal. Dick Sutphen. 1 cass. (Running Time: 1 hr.). (RX17 Ser.). 1986. 14.98 (978-0-87554-308-6(1), RX117) Valley Sun.
You have the power & ability to accelerate your healing. Your body is now filled wih positive healing energy. You consciously & subconsciously choose perfect health. You are healing, you are healed. You now focus the unlimited power of your mind upon healing your body. You think positively about your health & visualize yourself as healed.

Healing from Cancer: Positive Imagery for People with Cancer. 1 CD. 1989. audio compact disk 16.95 (978-1-55841-117-3(8)) Emmett E Miller.
Healing imagery helps you grow stronger while you empower your army of white cells ridding your body of unwelcome guests. Designed to help strengthen your immune and healing responses.

Healing from Loss: An Audio CD & Journal for Getting in Touch with Your Soul. Scripts. Read by Susan Beverly. Music by Vinnie Hazeltine. Directed By Suzanna Mallow. 1 CD. (Running Time: 1 hr). 2005. audio compact disk 18.00 (978-0-9763972-1-2(8)) S Pub Co.
Tracki one of the audio CD contains a guided imagery script and the haunting music of Vinnie Hazeltine. Track two contains only Vinnie's soothing instrumental music.

Healing from Rejection. Benny Hinn. 5 cass. 1993. 30.00 (978-1-881256-15-1(4)) Wrld Outreach Church.

Healing from the Core: A Journey Home to Ourselves. unabr. ed. Suzanne Scurlock-Durana. 3 cass. (Running Time: 2 hrs. 13 min.). 1996. 29.00 Set. (978-1-893226-01-2(8)); 75.00 Set. (978-1-893226-00-5(X)) Heal from Core.
Self-healing, relaxation, energizing explorations: covers basic overview, eating, movement, breathing, nature elements, helping others & grounding.

Healing from the Core: Basic Relaxation & Energizing Exercises. Voice by Suzanne Scurlock-Durana. 2000. 10.00 (978-1-893226-05-0(0)); audio compact disk 18.00 (978-1-893226-02-9(6)) Heal from Core.

Healing from the Core: Mini Series: the complete guide to learning how to feel fully alive: grounded, energized, relaxed, with healthy Boundaries. Voice by Suzanne Scurlock-Durana. 2003. audio compact disk 39.00 (978-1-893226-04-3(2)) Heal from Core.

Healing from the Core: Release & Renewal. Voice by Suzanne Scurlock-Durana. 2004. audio compact disk 35.00 (978-1-893226-08-1(5)) Heal from Core.

Healing from the Core: The complete guide to learning how to feel fully alive: grounded, energized, relaxed with healthy Boundaries. Voice by Suzanne Scurlock-Durana. 2003. audio compact disk 99.00 (978-1-893226-03-6(4)) Heal from Core.

Healing from the Core: The Five Principles of Living Joyfully. Voice by Suzanne Scurlock-Durana. 2003. 10.00 (978-1-893226-07-4(7)); audio compact disk 18.00 (978-1-893226-06-7(9)) Heal from Core.

Healing from the Inside Out. Interview with Bernie S. Siegel & Michael Toms. 2 cass. (Running Time: 1 hr. 30 min.). (New Dimensions Ser.). 1997. 16.95 (978-1-56170-447-7(4), 992) Hay House.
Expands on his unconventional opinions that, Health is a state of mind. It has nothing to do with your body, & you're not sick when you're laughing or loving...choose joy for your life.

Healing from the Loss of a Pet. Peggy Haymes & Susan Lautemann. Orig. Title: Grieving the Loss of Your Pet. 2006. audio compact disk 19.95 (978-0-9741775-2-6(0)) W Summit.

Healing Garden. Patricia O'Malley. Perf. by Barry Weiss. 1 cass. (Running Time: 50 min.). 1998. 11.95 (978-1-892450-25-8(9), 123) Pub: Promo Music. Dist(s): Penton Overseas
Learn how to call on beautiful angels to assist you to heal & to allow the healing to move through you, around you & in you.

Healing Grief: Reclaiming Life after Any Loss. unabr. ed. James Van Praagh. Narrated by Jonathan Marosz. 5 cass. (Running Time: 9 hrs. 30 min.). 2000. 40.00 (978-0-7366-5003-8(2)) Books on Tape.
An inspiring new perspective on grief from a world-renowned medium who has become an expert at helping people cope with unresolved sorrow.

Healing Grief: Reclaiming Life after Any Loss. unabr. collector's ed. James Van Praagh. Read by Jonathan Marosz. 5 cass. (Running Time: 7 hrs. 30 mins.). 2001. 20.00; audio compact disk 24.00 Books on Tape.

Healing Grief: The Etheric Bridge. unabr. ed. Kim Falcone & Steven Falcone. Read by Steven Falcone. 1 cass. (Running Time: 58 min.). 1994. 10.95 (978-1-887799-05-8(2), 1-822-884) Creat Aware.
This program uses imagery as a medium for symbolic communication & helps to bring feelings of grief & anger to closure.

Healing Habits of the Mind: Healing Your Relationship with Food. Created by Kathryn A. Kelley. 1. 2004. audio compact disk 30.00 (978-0-9763665-0-8(9)) K Institute of Integr.
A powerful guided mediation and bi-lateral music therapy through deep relaxation and information processing to relieve unwanted or unhealthy habits related to food. This technique allows the individual to replace unhealthy habits with life-giving behaviors natually, while resting!.

Healing Habits of the Mind: Learning to Appreciate Your Own Gifts & Talents: Enhancing Your Self-Esteem. Created by Kathryn A. Kelley. 1. 2004. audio compact disk Rental 30.00 (978-0-9763665-1-5(7)) K Institute of Integr.
A Powerful guided mediation and bi-laterial music therapy through deep relaxation and information processing to relieve feelings of lack of self-worth and change unwanted behaviors that surround these feelings, allowing the individual to begin life-giving behaviors naturally.

Healing Habits of the Mind: Living a LIfe of freedom & Purpose: Overcoming Anxiety. 2004. audio compact disk Rental 30.00 (978-0-9763665-2-2(5)) K Institute of Integr.

Healing Happens. William Wait. 1 cass. 7.98 (978-1-55503-414-6(4), 06004601) Covenant Comms.
Deals with our need for spiritual & emotional healing.

***Healing Happens: Relaxation Hypnosis with Paul Dale Anderson.** Paul Dale Anderson. Perf. by Paul Dale Anderson. (ENG.). 2010. audio compact disk 21.00 (978-0-937491-12-6(8)) TwoAM Pubns.

Healing Harmonies. Jim Oliver. 1 CD. (Running Time: 1 hr.). audio compact disk 14.95 (978-1-55961-301-9(7)) Relaxtn Co.

Healing Harmonies: Music Composed to Balance & Soothe. Jim Oliver. 2 cass. (Running Time: 2 hrs.). 1992. 16.95 (978-1-55961-166-4(9)) Relaxtn Co.

Healing Heart. Ragini E. Michaels. Read by Ragini E. Michaels. Music by Divyam Ambodha. 1 cass. (Running Time: 30 min.). (Remembrance Ser.). 1988. 14.95 (978-0-9628686-6-5(3), FTAT-104) Facticity Tr.
Works to heal wounds of the heart & evoke the heart's capacity to forgive, to accept & to allow the love to flow. Soothing combination of feminine voice & original music.

Healing Heart, abr. ed. Norman Cousins. Read by William Conrad. 2 cass. (Running Time: 3 hrs.). 2000. 7.95 (978-1-57815-136-3(8), 1095, Media Bks Audio) Media Bks NJ.
A dramatic account of the trauma highlights & the importance of the patient's role in combating serious illness. The author addresses the problem of panic & helplessness produced by any serious illness.

Healing Heart. unabr. collector's ed. Norman Cousins. Read by Ken Ohst. 4 cass. (Running Time: 4 hrs.). 1985. 24.00 (978-0-7366-0648-6(3), 1609) Books on Tape.
Cousins deals with the most common cause of death in the U. S. More people die from heart attacks & heart disease than any other malady. This highlights the importance of the patient's role in combating serious illness. It is also the story of a team effort, a partnership between the patient & his physician.

Healing Heart: Comfort. Roxanne E. Daleo. 1 cass. (J). 1999. 12.95 Hlth Jrnys.

Healing Heart: Comfort. unabr. ed. Roxanne E. Daleo. Read by Roxanne E. Daleo. 1 cass. (Running Time: 32 min.). (MindWorks for Children Ser.: Vol. 3). 1988. 12.95 (978-1-889447-13-1(7)) Mindwrks Chldrn.
Designed to give children the tools they need to relax body & mind. Regular use of these tapes will help children develop self-confidence & a healthy mental attitude, improve concentration & problem-solving abilities, & stimulate creativity.

***Healing Hearts: A Memoir of a Female Heart Surgeon.** unabr. ed. Kathy Magliato. Narrated by Renée Raudman. (Running Time: 8 hrs. 30 mins. 0 sec.). (ENG.). 2010. 19.99 (978-1-4001-6673-2(X)); 29.99 (978-1-4001-9673-9(6)); 14.99 (978-1-4001-8673-0(0)); audio compact disk 29.99 (978-1-4001-1673-7(2)); audio compact disk 59.99 (978-1-4001-4673-4(9)) Pub: Tantor Media. Dist(s): IngramPubServ

Healing Humor: Live Happy - Be Healthy. Based on a work by Becky Cortino. (ENG.). 2009. 15.00 (978-0-9799093-4-4(1)) Heart Clown.

Healing Imagery: Mind-Body Connection. Carla Czybora. Music by Jim Adams. 1 cass. 10.00 New Bgnnngs.
Features self hypnosis, guided imagery, metaphysically presenting the mind-body connection for the listeners personal use toward healing visualization.

Healing Imagery for People Facing Cancer. Patricia Palmer. 1998. 39.95 (978-0-9650240-5-1(9)) TouchStar.

Healing Imagery for People Facing Surgery Set: Two Guided Imagery. unabr. ed. Patricia Palmer. 2 cass. (Running Time: 42 min.). 1999. 18.95 (978-0-9650240-7-5(5), TSA-100) TouchStar.
An aid in mobilizing one's inner healing resources to feel calmer before surgery, decrease the need for pain medications & accelerate the recovery process.

Healing Images: Affirmations for Envisioning Yourself As an Attractive, Whole & Unique Individual. Bernie S. Siegel. Read by Bernie S. Siegel. Music by Jerry Florence. 1 cass. (Running Time: 60 min.). (Prescriptions for Living Ser.). (ENG.). 1990. 10.95 (978-0-937611-77-7(8), 708) Hay House.
Dr. Siegel helps us release all resistance to the healing process & embrace our inner strength & love.

Healing Images for Children: Relax & Imagine. Nancy Klein. Narrated by Roger Klein. (ENG.). (J). (ps-9). 1999. audio compact disk 15.95 (978-0-9636027-3-2(X)) Pub: Inner Coach. Dist(s): IPG Chicago
Healing images for children: Relax and imagine CD is a guide for parents and professionals to assist them in teaching children relaxation and guided imagery. A stand alone or in combination with the book.

***Healing in Golden Atlantis.** Diana Cooper. Andrew Brel. (Running Time: 0 hr. 56 mins. 12 sec.). (Information & Meditation Ser.). (ENG.). 2010. audio compact disk 14.95 (978-1-84409-522-3(3)) Pub: Findhorn Pr GBR. Dist(s): IPG Chicago

Healing in the Word. Kenneth W. Hagin, Jr. 4 cass. 16.00 (11J) Faith Lib Pubns.

Healing Initiations in the Shamanic Mysteries. Nicki Scully. 2 cass. 18.00 set. (A0693-90) Sound Photosyn.
The healing underworld is evoked, with a discussion of the rule of shamanic allies (totemic animals & deities) & the creative inner forces they symbolize.

Healing Instruction. C. S. Lovett. Read by C. S. Lovett. 1 cass. (Running Time: 50 min.). 6.95 (539) Prsnl Christianity.
Gives you private instruction for making the healing laws work in your own body.

Healing into Wholeness: An Expanded Model of the Self for Today's Addiction Treatment. unabr. ed. Jacquelyn Small. 1 cass. (Running Time: 1 hr. 30 min.). (C). 1994. 11.00 (978-0-939344-12-3(2)) Eupsychian.
A view of addiction treatment emphasizing a shift away from pathologizing clients to more holistic, positive approaches.

Healing Is for Today. Gary V. Whetstone. 9 cass. (Running Time: 13 hrs. 30 mins.). (Practical Ministry Ser.: PM101). 1996. pap. bk. 170.00 (978-1-58866-020-6(6)) Gary Whet Pub.
Jesus gave the Great Commission: Preach, Teach & Heal! One-third of the believer's responsibility is to heal the sick. Become equipped in the healing ministry of Jesus Christ.

Healing Is the Children's Bread. Kenneth W. Hagin, Jr. 1 cass. (Running Time: 1 hr.). 2002. 5.95 (SH30) Faith Lib Pubns.

***Healing ISIS: Meditations for Relaxation Clearing & Re-Intergration.** Natalie Kimbrough. (ENG.). 2010. audio compact disk 12.00 (978-1-4507-2804-1(9)) Indep Pub IL.

Healing Journey. 1 CD. 1980. audio compact disk 16.95 (978-1-55841-109-8(7)) Emmett E Miller.
Effective for any illness or imbalance, physical, mental or emotional. Features the music of Raphael, with Dr. Miller's voice at its beguiling best. Relax deeply in a safe place, contact and gently awaken your inner healer, and guide the healing energy to the part of you that thirsts for it.

Healing Journey. Narrated by Emmett Miller. Music by Raphael. 1 cassette. (Running Time: 55:05 mins). 1980. 12.95 (978-1-55841-016-9(3)) Emmett E Miller.

Healing Journey. Emmett E. Miller. Read by Emmett E. Miller. Music by Raphael. 1 cass. (Running Time: 1 hr.). 1996. 10.95 (978-1-56170-366-1(4), 391) Hay House.
Words & music to facilitate the healing process.

Healing Journey. unabr. ed. Marci Archambeault. Read by Marci Archambeault. 1 cass. (Running Time: 1 hr.). 1994. pap. bk. 14.95 (978-1-888861-00-6(2)) Quest MA.
Meditation will help you to discover what is holding you back in life. It will help you to overcome fear & addictions. The "Healing Journey" will empower you to become the person you were meant to be.

Healing Journey, Vol. 1. Carl Hammerschlag. 2 cass. 1991. 20.00 Set. (978-1-889166-24-7(3)) Turtle Isl Pr.
The greatest power we have is the power to choose. Here is a message about how to confront the fears that entrap us & choose paths which can liberate us. How can we balance the need for predict-ability with the passion

for change? Here's how to conquer inertia & make the leap of faith that sustains us in health.

Healing Journey: An Invitation to Wholeness. Nicholas Harnan. 6 cass. (Running Time: 5 hrs. 26 min.). 39.95 incl. shelf-case. (THOA033) Alba Hse Comns.
Includes: "Journey to the Heart", "The Kingdom of Heaven Is Within You", "Become As A Little Child", "Healing Our Hurting Child", "Coming Home to Ourself", "The Holy Trinity Within You".

Healing Journey - the Voice of the Angels. 2005. audio compact disk 12.99 (978-0-9776140-3-5(4)) Journeymakers.

Healing Lifetimes: Then & Now. unabr. ed. Galexis. 2 cass. (Running Time: 3 hrs.). 1997. 19.95 Set. (978-1-56089-056-0(8), G137) Visionary FL.
How to release limiting influences from other lifetimes so as to free up this current lifetime emotionally & spiritually. Includes questions & answers & meditation.

Healing Light Meditation. Laura Kern. Read by Laura Kern. 1 cass. (Running Time: 1 hr.). 1995. 10.00 (978-1-887541-01-5(2)) L Kern.
Spoken audio cassette with background music for relaxation & meditation. Subject: allowing body, mind, & spirit to be cleansed by a healing light.

Healing Liturgies. 1 cass. (Care Cassettes Ser.: Vol. 17, No. 1). 1990. 10.80 Assn Prof Chaplains.

Healing, Living, & Being. Mitchell May. 6 cass. 1998. 45.00 Set. (430) Hay House.
Guides you in a rich, inspiring, & transformational journey of healing - while learning very practical ways to facilitate personal & spiritual growth. Also experience one of his powerful group healing sessions.

Healing, Living, & Being. Mitchell M. May. 2 cass. (Running Time: 2 hrs.). 1998. 16.95 (978-1-56170-486-6(5), 429) Hay House.

Healing Love Through the Tao: Cultivating Female & Male Sexual Energy. Mantak Chia. Illus. by Juan Li. Pref. by Felix Morrow. 1988. 9.95 Heal Tao Bks.

Healing Mantras. Shri Anandi Ma & Shri Dileepji Pathak. 1 CD. (Running Time: 1 hr. 15 min.). 2000. stu. ed. 16.98 (978-1-56455-748-3(0), AW00455D) Sounds True.
Shri Anandi Ma, respected master of the Kundalini Maha Yoga lineage, chants three mantras specifically said to reestablish balance on the level of the prana. These chants can, according to the traditional understanding, impart a powerful healing impulse to the entire human system ? body, mind, and spirit.

Healing Meditation. Michael P. Bovines. Read by Michael P. Bovines. Ed. by Christian Flint. 1 cass. (Running Time: 40 min.). (Healing Ser.). 1993. pap. bk. 9.98 (978-1-885768-02-5(8), M303) Circle of Light.
The Healing Meditation is designed to assist you in connecting with God's healing light. The guided imagery & relaxing music creates within you a new state of being that allows for optimum healing energy to flow through you.

Healing Meditation: Guided Meditation. Concept by Vicky Thurlow. Voice by Vicky Thurlow. (ENG.). 2008. audio compact disk 14.95 (978-0-9817055-9-0(6)) DVT Invest.

Healing Meditation: Nourish Mind Body & Spirit. Kelly Howell. 2000. audio compact disk 14.95 (978-1-881451-67-9(4)) Brain Sync.

Healing Meditation: Nourish Mind Body & Spirit. unabr. ed. Kelly Howell. 1 cass. (Running Time: 60 mins.). 1994. 11.95 (978-1-881451-25-9(9)) Brain Sync.
The listener is gently guided on a path that travels to a safe, secure, & serene place to heal. On the path one encounters elements that ground, center, & nurture a sense of connectedness & well-being. The melodic music combined with delta frequencies gradually decreases the activity of the brain & it becomes able to process the numerous healing suggestions being offered. Scientists have found that the delta frequencies trigger deep restorative sleep & healing. "Healing Meditation" creates the opportunity for the body to strengthen its immune system & regenerate on a cellular level.

Healing Meditations. unabr. ed. Connirae Andreas. 2 cass. (Running Time: 2 hrs. 20 mins.). 1998. 19.95 (978-0-9705492-5-9(3)) N L P Comp.
Nourish your spirit & your being with these five life affirming meditations.

Healing Meditations: Enhance Your Immune System & Find the Key to Good Health. Bernie S. Siegel & Bernie Siegel. 2 CDs. 2003. audio compact disk 18.95 (978-1-4019-0142-4(5), 1425) Hay House.

Healing Meditations & Affirmations. Ron Roth. 3 cass. (Running Time: 2 hrs. 15 min.). 1989. 24.95 Set. (978-1-893869-11-0(3)) Celbrtng Life.

Healing Migraines: Guided Spiritual Meditations. unabr. ed. John D. Lentz. 1 CD. (Running Time: 42 min.). 2005. audio compact disk 14.95 (978-0-9740978-2-4(9)) Pub: Healing Words. Dist(s): STL Dist NA

Healing Mind: Medical Hypnosis for Mind-Body Healing. Scripts. Steven Gurgevich. Prod. by Steven Gurgevich. 1 CD. (Running Time: 42 mins). (ENG.). 2003. audio compact disk 19.95 (978-1-932170-03-0(0), HWH) Tranceformation.

Healing Mind & Body. Eknath Easwaran. Read by Eknath Easwaran. 1 cass. (Running Time: 1 hr.). 1988. 7.95 (978-1-58638-551-4(8)) Nilgiri Pr.

Healing Mind System: Tap into Your Highest Potential for Health & Well Being. abr. ed. Jeffrey Thompson. (Running Time: 1:00:00). 2005. audio compact disk 19.98 (978-1-55961-771-0(3)) Sounds True.

Healing Miracles. William McGarey. 1 cass. (Running Time: 60 min.). 1989. 9.95 HarperCollins Pubs.

***Healing Miracles of Archangel Raphael.** Doreen Virtue. 2011. audio compact disk 19.95 (978-1-4019-3140-7(5)) Hay House.

Healing Music. Perf. by Jim Oliver et al. 4 cass., 4 CDs. 1999. pap. bk. 29.95 Set. (45350); audio compact disk 34.95 CD. (45351) Courage-to-Change.
Use music to promote wholeness & enhance well-being.

Healing Music: Four Pioneers Explore the Healing Power of Music. Jim Oliver. 4 CDs. (Running Time: 4 hrs.). 1994. bk. 29.95 (978-1-55961-296-8(7)); audio compact disk 34.95 (978-1-55961-295-1(9)) Relaxtn Co.

Healing Music Story Sampler. 1 cass. 7.95 (978-1-55961-483-2(8)) Relaxtn Co.

Healing of Anger; The Healing of Sadism. Jonathan Murro. 7.95 A R Colton Fnd.

Healing of Cancer: Journeys of Self-Discovery. Voice by Diana Hunt. Orig. Title: The Healing of Cancer: Journeys of Self-Discovery. 2003. cass. & cd-rom 16.95 (978-0-9755286-0-0(2)) D Hunt LLC.

Healing of Cancer: Journeys of Self-Discovery see Healing of Cancer: Journeys of Self-Discovery

Healing of Damaged Emotions: Matt. 8:17 John 5:1-9. Ed Young. (J). 1980. 4.95 (978-0-7417-1112-0(5), A0112) Win Walk.

Healing of Harms. Contrib. by Fireflight. Prod. by Skidd Mills. Contrib. by Will McGinniss & Mark Stuart. 2006. audio compact disk 11.99 (978-5-558-32770-0(7)) Flicker.

Healing of Ignorance; Science & Religion. Ann Ree Colton & Jonathan Murro. 1 cass. 7.95 A R Colton Fnd.

Healing of the Mind: God's Kitchen. Ann Ree Colton & Jonathan Murro. 1 cass. 7.95 A R Colton Fnd.
Discusses the goal of God-Realization.

Healing of the Mind: James 5::13-16. Ed Young. (J). 1980. 4.95 (978-0-7417-1119-9(2), A0119) Win Walk.

Healing of Time: A Millennium Retreat. Richard Rohr. 4 cass. (Running Time: 4 hrs.). 2001. 39.95 (A3277) St Anthony Mess Pr.
About letting go, healing, looking forward and moving on.

Healing on All Levels. Swami Amar Jyoti. 1 cass. 1980. 9.95 (K-38) Truth Consciousness.
The secret of healing as a natural process, physical, astral & spirtual. Being truthful to our understanding at each level.

Healing Our Brokenness. George Maloney. 3 cass. (Running Time: 4 hrs. 20 min.). 1995. 27.95 Set. (TAH350) Alba Hse Comns.
In this penetrating reflection, Fr. Maloney leads us through the experiences of brokenness in all area of life - in our daily existence, in the church, & in our world. He guides us to an understanding of the effects our brokenness have on us & the community of humankind.

Healing Our Concepts. unabr. ed. Carol Howe. 6 cass. (Running Time: 9 hrs.). 1993. 49.95 Set. (978-1-889642-15-4(0)) C Howe.
Identify the blocks to the experience of joy & creativity. Understand the power & process of releasing & forgiving. Welcome the opportunities for growth & service through relationships. Explore issues of commitment, development of intuition, & decision-making. Begin to change the perception of your world in order to be truly free.

Healing Our Planet. Emmett Miller. (ENG.). 2007. audio compact disk 16.95 (978-1-55841-139-5(9)) Emmett E Miller.

Healing Our Psychic Wounds/Faith in God Only. Marianne Williamson. Read by Marianne Williamson. 1 cass. (Running Time: 90 mins.). (Lectures on a Course in Miracles). 1999. 10.00 (978-1-56170-403-3(2), M811) Hay House.

Healing Ourselves, Healing Our Planet. Vivienne Verdon-Roe. 1 cass. 9.00 (A0703-90) Sound Photosyn.
This dynamic woman takes an honest look at the world today.

Healing Ourselves, Healing Our World. John Robbins. 1 cass. (Running Time: 90 min.). 1989. 11.00 (04801) Big Sur Tapes.

Healing Pain & Grief. Elena Bussolino & Anna Florentis. (ENG.). 2000. 7.99 (978-0-9720314-1-7(3)) Bagatto.

Healing Pain & Grief: Releasing & Unloading Unnecessary Baggage, Allowing Room for Healing to Take Place. 2001. audio compact disk 17.95 (978-0-9706743-7-1(6)) Bagatto.

Healing Pain & Grief: Releasing & Unloading Unnecessary Baggage, Allowing Room for Healing to Take Place. Elena Bussolino. Illus. by Albert Bussolino. Music by Rizwan Ahmad. Engineer Khalid Muhammad. Orig. Title: Original. 2001. 12.95 (978-0-9706743-5-7(X)) Bagatto.

Healing Partnerships: Affirmations to Create Mutual Respect & Trust Between You & Your Doctor. Bernie S. Siegel. Read by Bernie S. Siegel. Music by Jerry Florence. 1 cass. (Running Time: 60 mins.). (Prescriptions for Living Ser.). (ENG.). 1990. 10.00 (978-0-937611-76-0(X), 707) Hay House.
Dr. Siegel encourages a harmonious relationship between us & the people in our health-care team.

Healing Passages. 4 cass. (Running Time: 4 hrs.). 1997. 29.95 (978-1-55961-444-3(7)) Relaxtn Co.

Healing Passages: Four Pioneers Explore the Healing Power of Music. Laraaji et al. 4 CDs. (Running Time: 4 hrs.). 1997. bk. 34.95 (978-1-55961-442-9(0)) Relaxtn Co.

Healing Path: How the Hurts in Your Past Can Lead You to a More Abundant Life. abr. ed. Dan B. Allender. 2 cass. (Running Time: 3 hrs.). (ENG.). 1999. 14.95 (978-1-57856-155-1(8), WaterB Pr) Pub: Doubday Relig. Dist(s): Random
Takes us beyond self-discovery to God-discovery, giving the tools to excavate the riches that hid beneath the surface of our pain.

Healing, Power, & the Miraculous. Rick Joyner. 2006. audio compact disk 34.99 (978-1-59933-006-8(7)) Pub: Morning NC. Dist(s): Destiny Image Pubs

Healing, Power, & the Miraculous. Rick Joyner. (Running Time: 4 hrs. 35 mins.). 2007. 34.99 (978-1-4245-0688-0(3)) Tre Med Inc.

Healing Power of Animal Communication. rev. unabr. ed. Penelope Smith. 1 cass. (Running Time: 46 min.). 1994. 6.95 (978-0-936552-17-0(4)) AnimaMundi.
How you can help heal animals through direct communication with them & how animals can assist you in your journey of self-discovery. Understanding exactly what our animal companions think & feel enhances all healing approaches & results in a reverence for all life.

Healing Power of Garlic. Morton Walker. 1 cass. (Running Time: 25 min.). 1999. 10.00 (AC28) Am Media.
A review of garlic's properties: an antibiotic against colds & infections; anti-inflammatory against arthritis; an immune stimulant against cancer; etc.

Healing Power of Gratitude - Thanksgiving 2001. Myrtle Smyth. Prod. by David Keyston. 1 cass. (Running Time: 60 min.). (Myrtle Smyth Audiotape Ser.). 2001. 8.95 (978-1-893107-47-2(7)) Pub: Healing Unltd. Dist(s): Bookmark CA

***Healing Power of Kindness: Releasing Judgment, Vol. 1.** Kenneth Wapnick. 2009. 10.00 (978-1-59142-459-8(3)) Foun Miracles.

Healing Power of Love & Intimacy. Read by Dean Ornish. 2 cass. (Running Time: 2 hrs. 10 min.). (Love & Survival Ser.). 1999. 17.95 Set. (83-0055) Explorations.
Teaches how survival depends on these feelings. Dr. Ornish reviews the scientific studies from his own research & the studies of others supporting the powerful role they play in health & illness.

Healing Power of Meditation; Abiding Joy. Ann Ree Colton. 1 cass. 7.95 A R Colton Fnd.

Healing Power of Nature: Thoughts from Thoreau's Walden. Instructed by Manly P. Hall. 8.95 (978-0-89314-133-2(X), C590308) Philos Res.

Healing Power of Prayer: The Surprising Connection between Prayer & Your Health. abr. ed. Chester L. Tolson & Harold Koenig. Read by J. Charles. (Running Time: 3 hrs.). 2006. 24.95 (978-1-4233-0351-0(2), 9781423303510, BAD) Brilliance Audio.

Healing Power of Prayer: The Surprising Connection Between Prayer & Your Health. abr. ed. Chester L. Tolson & Harold G. Koenig. Read by J. Charles. 2 cass. (Running Time: 3 hrs.). 2003. 17.95 (978-1-59355-248-0(3), 1593552483); audio compact disk 19.95 (978-1-59355-250-3(5), 1593552505); 44.25 (978-1-59355-249-7(1), 1593552491); audio compact disk 62.25 (978-1-59355-251-0(3), 1593552513) Brilliance Audio.
It's not just hype or hope or a spiritual cliche. It's a scientific fact: Prayer heals. Recent medical and psychological studies claim that prayer can relieve stress, improve attitudes, and mend bodies. Prayer generates peace, power, and health - a triple preventative that guards against anxiety and disease. It's a simple act that heals. According to Chester Tolson and Harold Koenig, prayer helps people function at their best when life serves them the worst. Even on good days, it enhances the mind-body-soul connection. In The Healing Power of Prayer, these authors explain the nature of prayer, what happens when we pray, the restorative benefits of prayer, how to organize prayer, and much more. Their facts and insights will encourage believers to increase, the fainthearted to revive, and skeptics to begin a life of prayer.

Healing Power of Prayer: The Surprising Connection Between Prayer & Your Health. abr. ed. Chester L. Tolson & Harold G. Koenig. Read by J. Charles. (Running Time: 10800 sec.). 2006. audio compact disk 24.95 (978-1-4233-0349-7(0), 9781423303497, Brilliance MP3) Brilliance Audio.

Healing Power of Prayer: The Surprising Connection between Prayer & Your Health. abr. ed. Chester L. Tolson & Harold G. Koenig. Read by J. Charles. (Running Time: 3 hrs.). 2006. 39.25 (978-1-4233-0352-7(0), 9781423303527, BADLE); 39.25 (978-1-4233-0350-3(4), 9781423303503, Brlnc Audio MP3 Lib) Brilliance Audio.

Healing Power of Psalms. unabr. ed. Samuel Chiel & Henry Dreher. Read by Grover Gardner. 3 cass. (Running Time: 4 hrs. 30 mins.). 2001. 28.00 (978-0-7366-6045-7(3)) Books on Tape.
The most beloved collection of prayers for Jews & Christians. The Psalms' ageless beauty & themes of compassion & mercy can have a dramatic healing effect on the mind, spirit & sometimes even the body.

Healing Power of the Family: An Illustrated Overview of Life with the Distubed Foster or Adoptive Child. Narrated by Richard Delaney. Prod. by Northwest Media. 2006. cass. & cd-rom 21.95 (978-1-933848-09-9(X)) NW Media.
A non-technical approach to understanding and treating disturbed foster and adoptive children.

Healing Power of the Family: An Illustrated Overview of Life with the Disturbed Foster or Adopted Child. unabr. ed. Richard J. Delaney. 2 cass. (Running Time: 1 hr. 29 min.). 1998. 21.95 (978-1-892194-02-2(3)) Wood N Barnes.
A tribute to foster & adoptive parents & to their potent influence upon the disturbed children who have joined their families.

Healing Powers of Tone & Chant. Don Campbell & Tim Wilson. Read by Don Campbell. 2 cass. (Running Time: 2 hrs.). 1994. 10.95 (978-0-8356-1906-6(0), Quest) Pub: Theos Pub Hse. Dist(s): Natl Bk Netwk

Healing Prayer: Generate Healing for Yourself or Someone You Know. Mark Bancroft. Read by Mark Bancroft. 1 cass., bklet. (Running Time: 1 hr.). (Alternative Health & Healing Ser.). 1999. 12.95 (978-1-58522-036-6(1), 203) EnSpire Pr.
Two complete sessions plus printed instructionmanual/guidebook. With healing music soundtrack.

Healing Prayer: Generate Healing for Yourself or Someone You Know. Mark Bancroft. Read by Mark Bancroft. 1 CD, bklet. (Running Time: 1 hr.). (Alternative Health & Healing Ser.). 2006. audio compact disk 20.00 (978-1-58522-040-3(X)) EnSpire Pr.

Healing Prayers. Ron Roth. 1 cass. (Running Time: 1 hr.). 1998. 10.95 (978-1-56170-504-7(7), 369); audio compact disk 10.95 (978-1-56170-531-3(4), 445) Hay House.

Healing Presence of Christ. Edd Anthony. Read by Edd Anthony. 2007. audio compact disk 16.95 (978-1-881586-24-1(3)) Canticle Cass.

Healing, Psychosomatic Medicine, & the Judaeo-Christian Tradition, Set. Jeffrey B. Satinover. Read by Jeffrey Burke Satinover. 2 cass. (Running Time: 2 hrs. 20 min.). 1994. 18.95 (978-0-7822-0462-9(7), 539) C G Jung IL.

Healing Relationships: Your Relationship to Life & Creation. Bernie S. Siegel. 1 cass. (Running Time: 1 hr.). 1999. 10.95 (978-1-56170-650-1(7), 483) Hay House.
A lecture on how to heal all relationships.

Healing Relationships: Your Relationship to Life & Creation. Bernie S. Siegel. One CD. 2007. audio compact disk 10.95 (978-1-4019-0673-3(7)) Hay House.

Healing, Remission & Miracle Cures. Brendan O'Regan. 2 cass. 18.00 (OC138) Sound Horizons AV.

Healing Rosary of Our Mother of Perpetual Help. Read by George Keavney. 2 cass. (Running Time: 95 mins.). 1999. 10.95 (T8692); audio compact disk 14.95 (K5200) Liguori Pubns.
Covers the Joyful Mysteries, the Living Mysteries, the Sorrowful Mysteries & the Glorious Mysteries.

Healing Sands. unabr. ed. Nancy Rue & Stephen Arterburn. Narrated by Pam Turlow. (Running Time: 13 hrs. 16 mins. 14 sec.). (Sullivan Crisp Ser.). (ENG.). 2009. 27.99 (978-1-60814-594-2(8)); audio compact disk 39.99 (978-1-59859-642-7(X)) Oasis Audio.

Healing Scarcity, Embracing Abundance. Galexis. 2 cass. (Running Time: 3 hrs.). 1994. 17.95 Set. (978-1-56089-032-4(0)) Visionary FL.
Here, in exquisite detail, are healing approaches to issues around time, money, & love. No meditation.

Healing School. Gloria Copeland. 6 cass. 1983. 30.00 Set, incl. study guide. (978-1-57562-130-2(4)) K Copeland Pubns.
Biblical teaching on healing.

Healing School. Gloria Copeland. 2006. audio compact disk 30.00 (978-1-57562-825-7(2)) K Copeland Pubns.

Healing Scriptures. Kenneth Copeland. 1 cass. (Running Time: 1 hr.). 1981. 5.00 (978-0-88114-738-4(9)) K Copeland Pubns.

Healing Scriptures. David T. Demola. 1 cass. (Running Time: 1 hr.). 4.00 (1-084) Faith Fellow Min.

Healing Scriptures. Kenneth E. Hagin. (Running Time: 4363 sec.). (Faith Library). 2006. audio compact disk 10.00 (978-1-00-000174-7(1)) Harrison Hse.

Healing Scriptures & Prayers: Old Testament Scriptures. Jeff Doles. Read by Jeff Doles. 1. (Running Time: 61 minutes). 2003. audio compact disk 14.99 (978-0-9744748-2-3(7)) Walking Barefoot.
Sit back and relax as the Scriptures from the Old Testament wash over you and stir up your faith to receive God's healing promises. The prayers on this CD will help you exercise your faith as you present God's Word before Him with joy and expectation. The gentle acoustic background music will refresh you as you meditate on the healing Word of God. 1/ The Healing Scriptures 2/ The LORD Who Heals 3/ Healing Scriptures from the Psalms 4/ Healing Scriptures from the Book of Proverbs 5/ Healing Scriptures from the ProphetsGreat for home use, in the car, in healing rooms and ministries, or wherever you want to create an atmosphere that is conducive for faith and healing.

Healing Scriptures & Prayers No. 2: New Testament Scriptures. Jeff Doles. Read by Jeff Doles. (Running Time: 66:43). 2004. audio compact disk 11.99 (978-0-9744748-3-0(5)) Walking Barefoot.
Sit back and relax as the Scriptures from the New Testament wash over you and stir up your faith to receive God's healing promises. The prayers on this CD will help you exercise your faith as you present God's Word before Him with joy and expectation. The gentle acoustic background music will refresh

you as you meditate on the healing Word of God.Over 60 minutes of soaking prayer from the New Testament Scriptures to help you receive your healing from God.(This recording is adapted from the book, Healing Scriptures and Prayers, by Jeff Doles)Tracks:1/ Praying With Expectation Authority for Healing Prayer2/ Asking in Jesus' Name Exercising Faith3/ The Faithful, Faith-filled Work of Jesus The Goodness of God Toward Us4/ Faith Redeemed from the Curse5/ The Holy Spirit Dwelling Within Us6/ Spiritual Warfare and Healing Prayer7/ The Prayer of Faith Confidence in God8/ Spirit, Soul and BodyBONUS TRACKS (based on Deuteronomy 28):9/ Choosing Life10/ A New and Better Covenant11/ Close.

Healing Scriptures & Prayers No. 3: The Healing Names of God. Jeff Doles. Narrated by Jeff Doles. (Running Time: 70 mins.). 2005. audio compact disk 14.99 (978-0-9744748-4-7(3)) Walking Barefoot.
Sit back and relax as these Scriptures on the healing names of God wash over you and stir up your faith to receive God's healing promises. The prayers on this CD will help you exercise your faith as you present God's Word before Him with joy and expectation. The gentle acoustic background music will refresh you as you meditate on the healing Word of God. 1/ The Healing Names of God 2/ The LORD Will Provide 3/ The LORD Who Heals You 4/ The LORD My Banner 5/ The LORD Who Sanctifies You 6/ The LORD Is Peace 7/ The LORD of Hosts 8/ The LORD My Shepherd 9/ The LORD Our Righteousness10/ The LORD is There11/ Almighty God12/ Everlasting God13/ God Most High14/ The Living God15/ God Who ForgivesGreat for home use, in the car, in healing rooms and ministries, or wherever you want to create an atmosphere that is conducive for faith and healing.

Healing Scriptures & Prayers No. 4: The Healing Ministry of Jesus. Jeff Doles. (Running Time: 71 mins). 2006. audio compact disk 14.99 (978-0-9744748-5-4(1)) Walking Barefoot.

Healing Scriptures with Instrumental Music: Spiritual Workout for Everyday Living. C. W. Productions Staff. 1 cass. 1997. 4.00 (978-0-9640854-2-8(9)) M J Beth.
Meditation tape.

Healing Series. 5 cass. 20.00 (S-1000) Faith Fellow Min.

Healing Series. Mike Craig. 6 cass., 6 videos. 30.00 Set. (MSMA-014) Morning NC.
Dr. Mike Craig, who is currently practicing medicine in Charlotte, offers his professional perspective in a refreshing manner.

Healing Sleep: Sound Sleep & Deep Sleep: for Nights When Thoughts Keep Churning. Kelly Howell. 2 CDs. (Running Time: 7200 sec.). 2006. audio compact disk 24.95 (978-1-881451-64-8(X)) Brain Sync.
Slip on your headphones and close your eyes. Within minutes you'll feel like you're floating and then start to slowly swirl and drift. Soothing Delta waves, associated with deep restorative sleep woven into dreamy music, making it easy for you to get the rest you need. As your brain is massaged, pestering concerns are gently washed away, your mind is eased into the deepest levels of sleep.

Healing Sounds. unabr. ed. Janet Bray. 1 cass. 1988. 9.00 (978-1-56964-763-9(1), A0374-88) Sound Photosyn.
1988 ICSS, with Kevin Setchko. Flute & Tibetan Bells bathe the listener in the land of All-Is-Well.

Healing Sounds of the Didgeridoo: An Invitation to a Personal Spiritual Journey. Dick de Ruiter & Vincent Vrolijk. (Running Time: 47 mins.). 2002. bk. 19.95 (978-90-74597-48-7(3)) Pub: Binkey Kok NLD. Dist(s): Red Wheel Weiser

Healing Spirit of Ra Ma Da Sa. Joseph Michael Levry. (Healing Beyond Medicine Ser.). 2006. 19.00 (978-1-885562-07-4(1)) Root Light.

Healing Starts from the Heart. David Steindl-Rast. 2 cass. (Running Time: 1 hr. 56 min.). 1984. 18.00 (05102) Big Sur Tapes.
Seeks beneath the doctrine & dogma in all religion for the meanings.

Healing Stones. unabr. ed. Nancy Rue & Stephen Arterburn. Narrated by Pam Turlow. (Running Time: 12 hrs. 54 mins. 28 sec.). (Sullivan Crisp Ser.). (ENG.). 2009. 24.49 (978-1-60814-544-7(1)); audio compact disk 34.99 (978-1-59859-535-2(0)) Oasis Audio.

Healing Stories, Vol. 1. Carl Hammerschlag. 2 cass. (Running Time: 1 hr. 20 min.). 1997. 29.95 Set. (978-1-889166-09-4(X)) Turtle Isl Pr.
Tales about old certainties & new possibilities.

Healing Stories Tape 1: Stories of Preconception. Carl A. Hammerschlag. Read by Carl A. Hammerschlag. Read by Lisa Cohen. 1 cass. (Running Time: 43 min.). 1997. 29.95 (978-1-889166-10-0(3)) Turtle Isl Pr.

Healing Stories Tape 2: Stories of Liberation. Carl A. Hammerschlag. Read by Carl A. Hammerschlag. Read by Lisa Cohen. 1 cass. (Running Time: 40 min.). 1997. 29.95 (978-1-889166-11-7(1)) Turtle Isl Pr.

Healing Stream. Susan A. Rothmann et al. Read by Susan A. Rothmann. Music by S. W. Mexcur. 1 cass. (Running Time: 1 hr.). (Fertile Imagination Ser.). 1998. 15.95 (978-0-9660540-6-4(7), F3004) Fertil Solns.
Guided imagery & music designed for people with loss or grief especially related to fertility who want to move forward with their lives. Designed to promote healing & wellness, & to help people cope with grief, depression & anxiety.

Healing Support for Your Surgery, Set. Marilyn Winfield. Read by Marilyn Winfield. 4 cass. (Running Time: 1 hr. 52 mins.). 2000. 49.95 (978-0-9679210-0-6(7)) Pathwy Heal.
Guided visualization techniques to help a patient with their surgery.

Healing Support for Your Surgery No. 1: Releasing Your Fears. Marilyn Winfield. Read by Marilyn Winfield. 1 cass. (Running Time: 21 mins.). 2000. (978-0-9679210-1-3(5)) Pathwy Heal.
Guided visualization techniques to help patients release their fears.

Healing Support for Your Surgery No. 2: Pre-Surgery. Marilyn Winfield. Read by Marilyn Winfield. 1 cass. (Running Time: 29 mins.). 2000. (978-0-9679210-2-0(3)) Pathwy Heal.
Guided visualizations for the patient before surgery.

Healing Support for Your Surgery No. 3: During Surgery. Marilyn Winfield. Read by Marilyn Winfield. 1 cass. (Running Time: 29 mins.). 2000. (978-0-9679210-3-7(1)) Pathwy Heal.
Guided visualization techniques to be used during surgery.

Healing Support for Your Surgery No. 4: Post Surgery. Marilyn Winfield. Read by Marilyn Winfield. 1 cass. (Running Time: 29 mins.). 2000. (978-0-9679210-4-4(X)) Pathwy Heal.
Guided visualization techniques to be used after surgery.

Healing the Adult Survivor of Child Abuse. 1998. 24.95 (978-1-58557-009-6(5)) Dynamic Growth.

Healing the Bitter Pool. Derek Prince. 1 cass. (B-2022) Derek Prince.

Healing the Body Through Faith Imaging. John Mergenhagen. 5 cass. (Running Time: 4 hrs. 7 min.). 1994. 40.95 Set. (TAH303) Alba Hse Comns.
This comprehensive presentation on healing is the result of over 20 years of study & personal experience in the healing ministries. These practical lessons on healing will certainly help you understand as well as apply faith-imaging in your own life & others in need of healing.

Healing the Body with the Mind & Heart: A Journey into Health. abr. ed. Angela P. Trafford. 1 cass. (Running Time: 25 min.). 1992. 10.00 INCL. SCRIPT. (978-0-9674748-9-2(2)) APT-Self Heal.
Recommended for anyone interested in spiritual & self-improvement of the body.

Healing the Child Within. Charles L. Whitfield. 1 cass. (Running Time: 60 min.). 1988. 9.95 (978-0-932194-93-0(1)) Health Comm.

Healing the Coyote in Me: The Navajo Coyoteway Blessing Ceremony. John C. Cook & Owen D. Owens. (ENG.). 2008. audio compact disk (978-0-9762377-2-3(5)) Leave a Little Room Found.

Healing the Dream of Sickness. Kenneth Wapnick. 4 CDs. 2005. audio compact disk 23.00 (978-1-59142-220-4(5), CD75) Foun Miracles.

Healing the Dream of Sickness. Kenneth Wapnick. 2009. 18.00 (978-1-59142-386-7(4)) Foun Miracles.

Healing the Emotional Body: Ending Pain, Embracing Joy. Galexis. 2 cass. (Running Time: 3 hrs.). 1995. 17.95 Set. (978-1-56089-033-1(9)) Visionary FL.
Learn to feel your power, passion, & love, as the Emotional Body is a vital connection home. Includes meditation on Side 4.

Healing the Emotions, Set. Tr. by Tsering Everest. Contrib. by Chagdud Tulku. 2 cass. (Running Time: 1 hr. 30 min.). (Archival Ser.). 18.00 () Padma Pub CA.
Tulku discusses how our emotional suffering can be reduced & ultimately eliminated, by the power of faith & compassion.

Healing the Father Wound. John Bradshaw. (Running Time: 14400 sec.). 2008. audio compact disk 100.00 (978-1-57388-124-1(4)) J B Media.

Healing the Feminine Betrayal of the Feminine. Judith Barr. 1 cass. (Spoken Word on Behalf of the Feminine Ser.). 1994. 12.32 (978-1-886264-03-8(1)) Mysteries of Life.
Women's spirituality - psychology.

Healing the Grief: ... Of the Loss of a Love One. unabr. ed. Read by John E. Welshons. Interview with Mark Victor Hansen. 2 cass. (Running Time: 2 hrs. 20 min.). 1995. 18.95 Set. (978-1-928732-02-0(X)) Open Heart NJ.
Questions & answers on dealing with grief after the death/loss of a loved one.

Healing the Heart: Opening to Love & Joy. Heraty Eugenie. (ENG.). 2007. 16.98 (978-1-934332-02-3(X), Heal Voice) Inter Med Pub.

Healing the Heart Series. John Gray. 12 cass. (Running Time: 12 hrs.). 1996. 79.95 (978-1-886095-18-2(3)) Genesis Media Grp.

Healing the Holidays Set: It's Never Too Late to Have a Happy Holiday. David Grudermeyer & Rebecca Grudermeyer. 2 cass. 18.95 incl. handouts. (T-43) Willingness Wrks.

Healing the Hurt Behind Addictions. unabr. ed. Carol Howe. 3 cass. (Running Time: 4 hrs. 30 min.). 1996. 23.95 Set. (978-1-889642-09-3(6)) C Howe.
All of us are concerned with addictive or compulsive behavior, in ourselves or others. This profound, yet simple, message integrates the absolutely essential element of true spirituality into the recovery process. See how healing must occur & addictions fade automatically as hidden guilt is acknowledged & released. Understand that everyone needs to recover from the false belief in unworthiness that has driven our lives. Choose to become aware of the peace that dwells within, offering safety, serenity, & comfort.

Healing the Inner Child. Brett Bravo. 1 cass. (Running Time: 60 min.). 1992. 8.95 (1010) Am Fed Astrologers.

Healing the Inner Masculine. unabr. ed. Marion Woodman. 4 cass. (Running Time: 5 hrs. 44 min.). 1990. 36.00 Set. (11801) Big Sur Tapes.
Healing the masculine is not a project limited by gender; Woodman is concerned with ways in which we all embody both masculine & feminine archetypes, & therefore examines both in depth, paying special attention to how they shape each other & contribute to the development of a whole psyche.

Healing the Masculine. Read by Robert Moore. 1 cass. (Running Time: 90 min.). 1987. 10.95 (978-0-7822-0175-8(X), 231) C G Jung IL.
What are the keys to understanding how archetypal psychology relates to men in our culture today? Healing the Masculine gives you a firm foundation in the principles of Jungian psychology, including detailed overviews of four primary masculine archetypes: The King, The Warrior, The Magus (or Magician), & The Lover.

Healing the Pain: Emotional Recovery for Adult Children of Alcoholics. unabr. ed. Lynne Logan. Read by Lynne Logan. 1 cass. (Running Time: 1 hrs.). 1995. 11.00 (978-1-890907-05-1(7), 0006) Heaven Only.
Characteristics of alcoholism, problems with relationships, treatment, how to heal from past traumas & forgiveness.

Healing the Past. John Gray. 2 cass. (Running Time: 2 hrs.). 1996. 17.95 (978-1-886095-17-5(5)) Genesis Media Grp.

Healing the Past. Eldon Taylor. 1 cass. (Running Time: 62 min.). (Inner Talk Ser.). 16.95 incl. script. (978-1-55978-616-4(7), 53869F) Progress Aware Res.
Soundtrack - Brook with underlying subliminal affirmations.

Healing the Planet. 1 cassette. 1980. 12.95 (978-1-55841-101-2(1)) Emmett E Miller.

Healing the Shadow - Our Wounded & Disowned Self. Jacquelyn Small. 1 cass. (Running Time: 60 min.). (Awakening in Time Ser.: Vol. 2). 1991. 10.00 (978-0-939344-05-5(X)) Eupsychian.
This tape series offers transformational education, guidance & practical exercises for awakening the listener to deeper levels of knowledge & healing of one's Self. Jacquelyn describes the shadow then, through guided imagery, leads the listener on a healing journey of introduction & acceptance of this often unconscious & misunderstood aspect of their being.

Healing the Shame That Binds You. John Bradshaw. Read by John Bradshaw. 2 cass. (Running Time: 2 hrs. 12 min.). 1989. Rental 13.95 (978-1-55874-043-3(0)) Health Comm.
In an emotionally revealing way Bradshaw shows us how toxic shame is the core problem in our compulsions, co-dependencies, addictions & the drive to superachieve. This important book breaks new ground in the core issues of societal & personal breakdown.

Healing the Shame That Binds You. John Bradshaw. (Running Time: 14400 sec.). 2008. audio compact disk 100.00 (978-1-57388-151-7(1)) J B Media.

Healing the Soul see Sanando las Heridas del Alma

***Healing the Wound.** John Eldredge. (ENG.). 2011. audio compact disk 14.99 (978-1-933207-45-2(0)) Ransomed Heart.

Healing the Wounded. Interview with Mother Angelica. Contrib. by Briege McKenna. 1 cass. (Running Time: 60 min.). (Mother Angelica Live Ser.). 10.00 (978-1-55794-060-5(6), T11) Eternal Wrd TV.

Healing the Wounded Child. Paul Ferrini. Read by Paul Ferrini. Perf. by Michael Gray. 1 cass. (Running Time: 1 hr.). 1991. 10.00 (978-1-879159-11-2(2)) Heartways Pr.
A potent healing tape that accesses old feelings of pain, fragmentation, self-judgment & separation & brings them into the light of conscious awareness & acceptance.

Healing the Wounded Heart. 1 cass. (Running Time: 90 mins.). 2000. 7.95 (978-1-886463-89-9(1)) Oasis Audio.

Healing the Wounded Spirit: Getting Past the Pain. Mike Atkins. 1. 2005. audio compact disk 8.00 (978-0-9759218-6-9(X)) M Atkins Min.

Healing the Wounded Woman. Read by Linda Leonard. 1 cass. (Running Time: 90 min.). 1980. 10.95 (978-0-7822-0145-1(8), 078) C G Jung IL.

Healing Thoughts. Created by Patricia Anne Slabaugh. 2006. audio compact disk 17.99 (978-0-615-19568-1(7)) Pat A Sla.

Healing Through Centers. Mae R. Wilson-Ludlam. 1 cass. 8.95 (839) Am Fed Astrologers.

Healing Through Centers Using Rays & Astrology. Mae R. Wilson-Ludlam. 1 cass. (Running Time: 90 min.). 1986. 8.95 (601) Am Fed Astrologers.

Healing Through Communication: How We Create Words; How Others Manipulate Us with Words & Symbols. Instructed by Manly P. Hall. 8.95 (978-0-89314-134-9(8), C820321) Philos Res.

Healing Through Forgiveness. John Mergenhagen. 2 cass. (Running Time: 1 hr. 38 min.). 1990. 16.95 set. (TAH229) Alba Hse Comns.
Describes the process of total forgiveness & explains what total forgiveness is not. The presentation is meant to teach a process & also provide an experience of forgiving others completely, fully & totally.

Healing Through the Centers. Mae R. Wilson-Ludlam. 1 cass. 8.95 (444) Am Fed Astrologers.
Initiate self-healing.

Healing Through the Character of God. Read by Wayne Monbleau. 2 cass. (Running Time: 2 hrs.). 1994. 10.00 Set. (978-0-944648-35-3(5), LGT-1230) Loving Grace Pubns.
Religious.

Healing Through the Mind see Curacion por el Pensamiento

Healing Through the Rosary. Scripts. Eugene Koshenina. Narrated by Robert DeGrandis. Music by Cecilia Kittley. 2 CDs. (Running Time: 1 hr. 30 mins.). 2000. 9.95 (978-0-9722438-1-0(X)) Eugene Chu.
Stories, Songs, and Prayers.

Healing Through the Rosary. Scripts. Eugene Koshenina. Narrated by Robert DeGrandis. Music by Cecilia Kittley. Prod. by Eugene Chu Koshenina Staff. 2 CDs. (Running Time: 2 hours 26 mins.). 2000. audio compact disk Rental 19.95 (978-0-9722438-0-3(1)) Eugene Chu.
Stories, Songs, and MeditationsMore Musice with Ave Maria.

Healing Tools. Read by Joseph Le Page. Music by Jack Lee. 3 CDs. (Running Time: 3 hrs). 2003. audio compact disk 22.00 (978-0-9744303-2-4(3)) Integrative Yoga.

Healing Touch Journeys: Healing Meditations, Chants & Exercises. Photos by Ron Lavin. 1 CD. (Running Time: 1 hr. 6 mins.). 2003. audio compact disk 15.00 (978-1-929537-08-2(5)) P Price.

Healing Touch Journeys: Healing Meditations, Chants & Exercises, Vol. 1. Ron Lavin. Photos by Ron Lavin. 1 CD. (Running Time: 1 hr. 5 mins.). (One Light Healing Touch Journeys Ser.). 2002. audio compact disk 15.00 (978-1-929537-07-5(7)) P Price.

Healing Trauma. Peter A. Levine. 6 CDs. (Running Time: 6 hrs 45 mins). 2005. audio compact disk 69.95 (978-1-59179-329-8(7), AF00941D) Sounds True.
Are you experiencing physical or emotional symptoms that no one is able to explain? If so, you may be suffering a traumatic reaction to a past event, teaches Dr. Peter A. Levine. On Healing Trauma, this respected therapist and teacher brings you face to face with an effective new treatment - not a "talking" cure, but a deep physiological process for releasing your past traumas. Medical researchers have known for decades that survivors of accidents, disasters, and childhood trauma often endure lifelong symptoms ranging from anxiety and depression to unexplained physical pain. As a young stress researcher at UC-Berkeley, Dr. Levine made a remarkable discovery: that all animals, including humans, are born with a natural ability to rebound from these distressing situations. On Healing Trauma, you will learn Dr. Levine's four-phase method of somatic healing. You will learn how and where you are storing unresolved distress, how to become more aware of your body's physiological responses to danger, and specific methods to free yourself from trauma. Now you can learn to address unexplained symptoms at their source - your body - and return to the natural state you were meant to live in, with Healing Trauma.

Healing Trauma: Guided Imagery for Post Traumatic Stress (PTSD) Belleruth Naparstek. Read by Steven Mark Kohn. Composed by Steven Mark Kohn. Engineer Bruce Gigax. 1 cass. (Running Time: 1 hr.). (Health Journeys Ser.). 1999. 12.95 (978-1-881405-24-5(9), 51) Hlth Jrnys.
Designed to renew a positive connection with the body & the emotions; reduce isolation, terror, shame & despair; restore a sense of inner goodness.

Healing Triad: Master Vibrant Health in a Polluted World. 2 cass. 19.95 Set. (978-0-929167-13-8(9)) Apple-a-Day.
Discussion in detoxification & rejuvenation for the whole body via the digestion, colon, & liver.

Healing Trust. 2004. audio compact disk 20.95 (978-1-930429-66-6(5)) Love Logic.

Healing Trust: Rebuilding the Broken Bond for the Child with Reactive Attachment Disorder. unabr. ed. Nancy Thomas. Interview with Bert Gurule. 2 cass. (Running Time: 3 hrs.). 1998. 18.95 (978-0-944634-55-4(9)) Pub: Love Logic. Dist(s): Penton Overseas
Focuses on reestablishing trust & connection between unbonded children & the adults significant in their lives.

Healing Vibrations. Scripts. Martin Brofman. 1 CD. (Running Time: 61 mins.). (ENG.). 2004. audio compact disk 17.99 (978-1-84409-024-2(8)) Pub: Findhorn Pr GBR. Dist(s): IPG Chicago
These meditations were conceived by Martin Brofman, healer, author, and teacher, to help you get in contact with the nature of your energies, and gently work with them inorder to return yourself to a sense of well-being, balance and inner peace.

Healing Visions. Angelo Rue & Mannion Rue. 3 cass. (Running Time: 3 hrs.). 1987. 39.95 Set. (978-1-55612-047-3(8), LL7047, SheWard) Rowman.
Helps for those counseling women who have had an abortion or those affected by this event.

Healing Visions. Andrew Schwartz & Nancy L. Tubesing. 1 cass. (Running Time: 47 min.). 1995. 11.95 (978-1-57025-067-5(7)) Whole Person.
Guided imagery provides a powerful source for renewal & healing. Six images that will restore balance & well-being.

Healing Waters. Perf. by Michelle Tumes. 1 cass. 1999. (751-321-3658) Brentwood Music.

Healing Waters. unabr. ed. Nancy Rue & Stephen Arterburn. Narrated by Pam Turlow. (Running Time: 12 hrs. 0 mins. 0 sec.). (Sullivan Crisp Ser.). (ENG.). 2009. 25.89 (978-1-60814-550-8(6)); audio compact disk 36.99 (978-1-59859-606-9(3)) Oasis Audio.

Healing Wings of Music, Set. Michael Ballam. 2 cass. 14.98 (119114) Covenant Comms.
Talk plus music-music as a tool to heal body & spirit.

Healing with Color: A Meditation to Awaken Your Power Within. D., Carolyn Porter. Contrib. by Jonn Serrie. (Running Time: 3526 sec.). 2006. audio compact disk 15.00 (978-0-9711150-6-4(0)) Empow IL.

Healing with Herbs. Dulal C. Koley. 1 cass. 8.95 (521) Am Fed Astrologers.

Healing with Hypnosis. Mel Bucholtz. 8 cass. 72.00 (OC106) Sound Horizons AV.

Healing with Spirit. Caroline Myss. Interview with Michael Toms. 1 cass. (Running Time: 45 min.). (New Dimensions Ser.). 1997. reel tape 10.95 (978-1-56170-380-7(X), 810) Hay House.

Healing with Spirit. Caroline Myss & Michael Toms. 1 CD. (Running Time: 90 min.). 2005. audio compact disk 10.95 (978-1-4019-0448-7(3)) Hay House.

Healing with the Angels. Doreen Virtue. 1 CD. 2004. audio compact disk 10.95 (978-1-4019-0422-7(X)) Hay House.

Healing with the Angels: How the Angels Can Assist You in Every Area of Your Life. Doreen Virtue. 1 cass. (Running Time: 1 hrs.). 1998. 10.95 (978-1-56170-624-2(8), 462) Hay House.
How angels can assist you in healing your life.

Healing with the Energy of Angels. 3 cass. (Running Time: 5 hrs.). 1999. 29.95 Edin Bks.
Join Stevan Thayer on a guided healing journey into the realm of angels. Learn to harness the power of prayer & direct spiritual forgiveness to bring your life's vision into the world.

Healing with the Lord's Prayer. abr. ed. Marsha Jean Burack. 2 CDs. (Running Time: 2 Hours). 2002. audio compact disk 29.95 (978-1-880441-18-3(7)) Reiki Heal.

Healing with the Lord's Prayer & Reiki. abr. ed. Marsha Jean Burack. 2 CDs. (Running Time: 60 Mins.). 2002. audio compact disk 29.95 (978-1-880441-01-5(2)) Reiki Heal.

Healing with the power of your Mind: Healing with meditation & creative Visualisation. Elena Bussolino. 2001. 12.95 (978-0-9720314-6-2(4)) Bagatto.

Healing with the Power of Your Mind: Healing with Meditation & Creative Visualization. Elena Bussolino. Illus. by Albert Bussolino. Music by Rizwan Ahmad. Engineer Khalid Muhammad. 2000. 12.95 (978-0-9706743-1-9(7)) Bagatto.

Healing with Vitamins. Lynne Palmer. Read by Lynne Palmer. 1 cass. (Running Time: 90 min.). 1994. 8.95 (1122) Am Fed Astrologers.

Healing Within Hypnosis with Tina Taylor. Nick Kemp & Tina Taylor. (Running Time: 57 mins.). audio compact disk 24.95 (978-0-9545993-2-4(2)) Pub: Human Alchemy GBR. Dist(s): Crown Hse

Healing Word. Cathy Duplantis. (ENG.). 2005. 12.00 (978-0-9743829-7-5(3)) J Duplantis.

***Healing Words to Change Your Life.** Suzette Caldwell. 2010. audio compact disk 11.00 (978-0-9828041-0-0(5)) Prayer Institute.

Healing Wounded Emotions. Martin H. Padovani. Read by Martin H. Padovani. Read by Andrea Star. Frwd. by John Powell. 3 cass. (Running Time: 3 hrs. 15 min.). (YA). (gr. 9 up). 1987. pap. bk. 7.95 (978-0-89622-333-2(7)) Twenty-Third.
A self-help guide to healing emotions.

Healing Wounded Emotions. Martin H. Padovani. Read by Martin H. Padovani. Read by Andrea Star. 3 cass. (Running Time: 3 hrs. 15 min.). (YA). (gr. 9 up). 1988. 24.95 (978-0-89622-375-2(2)) Twenty-Third.

Healing Wounded Relationships. Ginger Chalford. 1 cass. (Running Time: 90 min.). 1988. 8.95 (640) Am Fed Astrologers.

Healing Your Aloneness: The Inner Bonding Workshop. Margaret Paul. Instructed by Margaret Paul. 6 Cass. (Running Time: 8 hrs). 2002. 200.00 (978-0-912389-11-0(7)) Evolving Pubns.
The full 12 hour weekend Inner Bonding Workshop, with lectures, demonstrations, questions and discussions with audience, exercises and visualizations. Includes workbook and Introductory Video.

Healing Your Appetite, Healing Your Life: A Spiritual Approach to Life & Weight Management. abr. ed. Doreen Virtue. 1 CD. 2005. audio compact disk 10.95 (978-1-4019-0656-6(7)) Hay House.

Healing Your Aura & Chakras: Accessing Your Energetic Wisdom. abr. ed. Karla McLaren. Read by Karla McLaren. 1 cass. (Running Time: 1 hr. 30 min.). 1999. 11.00 (978-0-9656583-2-4(5)) Laughing Tree Pr.
A body-based centering process that makes aura & chakra healing simple & natural.

Healing Your Back. Scripts. 1 cassette. (Running Time: 1 hr. 18 min, 52 sec). 1986. 12.95 (978-1-55841-005-3(8)); audio compact disk 16.95 (978-1-55841-104-3(6)) Emmett E Miller.
Most back pain is cuased or exacerbated by stress. Four experiences to relieve stress and pain, discover and disconnect your triggers, start and end each day in the right frame of mind and body. Change the behaviors that lead to re-injury.

Healing Your Body, Mind & Soul. Sylvia Browne. 2 cass. 16.95 Set. (463) Hay House.
Explains how to reprogram your cell memory & eliminate your physical, emotional, & spiritual challenges.

Healing Your First Three Chakras. 1 CD. (Running Time: 1 hr. 19 mins.). 2004. audio compact disk 18.95 (978-0-9741450-1-3(7)) Queens Crt Pr.
Christel Nani, RN, is one of the rare Medical Intuitives who also has a substantial background in Western Medicine. A gifted healer and savant clairvoyant, she worked for sixteen years as an ER and trauma nurse, often knowing a person's diagnosis before the tests came back. Nani is a leader in her field, widely referred to by colleagues and clients alike as "the real thing."Her extensive knowledge of the chakra system - the spiritual energy centers of the body - enables her to pinpoint the causes of emotional, physical, and spiritual distress. The chakras make up the mind-body connection and reveal much about your life. They are highly sensitive barometers of health that become ill before your body does. In this live presentation, Christel explains the ways in which your thinking and fears affect your vital first three chakras and how to heal them.

Healing Your Heart with Archangel Chamuel. Elisabeth Constantine. (Running Time: 55 mins.). (Light Meditations Series I Ser.). (ENG.). 2004. audio compact disk 17.99 (978-1-84409-041-9(8)) Pub: Findhorn Pr GBR. Dist(s): IPG Chicago

Healing Your Inner Child. Read by Mary Richards. (Short Strengthening Ser.). 6.00 (086) Master Your Mind.

Healing Your Marriage with Love & Affection. Creflo A. Dollar. 15.00 (978-1-59089-033-2(7)) Pub: Creflo Dollar. Dist(s): STL Dist NA

Healing Your Mind, Healing Your Heart. Christopher Jackson. 1999. 10.95 (978-0-87159-801-1(9)) Unity Schl Christ.

Healing Your Past Lives. Roger Woolger. (Running Time: 1 hr. 15 mins.). 2006. bk. 19.95 (978-1-59179-183-6(9), K818D) Sounds True.

Healing Your Wounded Ego (Principle #10: Manage Your Own Morale) Ephesians 4:26-27. Ed Young. 1997. 4.95 (978-0-7417-2131-0(7), 1131) Win Walk.

Healing Yourself & Your Relationships by Pulling Out of the Collective Unconscious. Phyllis Light. 2 cass. (Running Time: 1 hr. 32 min.). (C). 1996. 19.95 (978-0-9648935-2-8(5)) Lght Unltd.
Seminar that presents how the collective unconscious contributes to many of the realtionship challenges people face. Empowers listeners to create more joyful, lasting relationships.

Healing Yourself with Light: Your Temple of Angelic Healing. 2nd ed. 1997. 59.95 (978-1-893027-00-8(7)) Path of Light.

Healing Yourself with Light Vol. 2: Your System & Cells. 2nd ed. 1997. 59.95 (978-1-893027-01-5(5)) Path of Light.

Healing Yourself with Your Mind - Blood Pressure. Robert E. Griswold. Read by Robert E. Griswold. 1 cass. (Super Strength Ser.). 1994. 10.95 (978-1-55848-314-9(4)) EffectiveMN.
Two complete non-subliminal programs with ideas, information & techniques to help tap the natural healing power of the mind & spirit.

Healing Yourself with Your Own Voice. unabr. abr. ed. Don Campbell. 1 CD. (Running Time: 3600 sec.). 2006. audio compact disk 14.95 (978-1-59179-437-0(4), AW00105D) Sounds True.

Health: Spanish Section Summaries. B. E. Pruitt et al. audio compact disk 89.97 (978-0-13-251078-3(2)) PH School.

Health & Altered State of Consciousness. Andrew Weil. 1 cass. (Running Time: 1 hr.). 1976. 11.00 (02604) Big Sur Tapes.
Since mind & body are thoroughly intertwined, all illness has a psychosomatic component. The part of the mind which most directly affects our health is the unconscious, transmitting its reactions - via the autonomic nervous system. This channel, generally closed to the conscious, rational mind, is open when one is high on drugs or in an altered state induced by hypnosis or biofeedback. Whether or not a cure works depends more on the patient's faith in the cure than on the scientific principle involved. One of the chief values of altered states is that people can learn that it is possible for them to have a healthier & happier existence, & once having had this reinforcement, they can continue to work toward these goals in "ordinary" consciousness.

Health & Fitness As It Pertains to Life & Godliness. Marty Copeland. 4 cass. (Running Time: 6 hrs.). 2001. 20.00 (978-1-57562-312-2(9), TKC312-9) K Copeland Pubns.

Health & Healing. Dick Sutphen. 1 cass. (Running Time: 1 hr.). (Only Subliminals Ser.). 1990. 12.98 (978-0-87554-447-2(9), T207) Valley Sun.
One hour of soothing, digitally mastered stereo music with positive subliminal suggestions phrased for maximum acceptance by your subconscious mind.

Health & Healing. Eldon Taylor. Read by Eldon Taylor. Interview with XProgress Aware Staff. 1 cass. (Running Time: 62 min.). 16.95 incl. script. (978-1-55978-288-3(9), 020102) Progress Aware Res.
Verbal coaching soundtrack with underlying subliminal affirmations & sound matrix frequencies for brain entrainment.

Health & Healing: Guided Meditation for Health & Healing. Voice by Susan/Sisler Boyes. 2007. audio compact disk 9.50 (978-1-4276-1420-9(2)) AardGP.

Health & Integrated Consciousness. unabr. ed. Andrew Weil. 6 cass. (Running Time: 5 hrs. 51 min.). 1976. 56.00 Set. (02605) Big Sur Tapes.
Explains his vast experience with other cultures & the history of medical practices all over the world, since developed in such works as his bestseller, "Spontaneous Healing". Here he presents his findings in a lively informal setting that conveys a depth & breadth unparalled in the field.

Health & Physical Diseases. Swami Jyotirmayananda. Read by Swami Jyotirmayananda. 1 cass. (Running Time: 45 min.). 10.00 (824) Yoga Res Foun.

Health & Physical Fitness. Shad Helmstetter. 1 cass. (Self-Talk Cassettes Ser.). 10.95 (978-0-937065-21-1(8)) Grindle Pr.

Health & Safety. (J). 1970. 11.95; audio compact disk 14.95 CD. Ed Activities.

Health & Sickness Audio Tape: Basic information regarding health & sickness in Haitian Creole. Maude Heurtelou. (CRP.). (YA). 2006. 12.00 (978-1-58432-342-6(6)) Educa Vision.

Health & the Zodiac: Introduction to Astro-Psychology. Instructed by Manly P. Hall. 8.95 (978-0-89314-135-6(6), C610514) Philos Res.

Health & Vitality. Read by Mary Richards. (Subliminal Impact Ser.). 12.95 (603) Master Your Mind.
Explains how to achieve a healthful balance of work & play, relaxation & exercise.

Health & Well Being. Christopher Love. Read by Christopher Love. 1 cass. (Running Time: 30 min.). 1997. 10.95 (978-1-891820-16-8(8)) World Sangha Pubg.
Self-hypnosis meditation for healing, self-improvement & realizing our full & powerful potential as spiritual beings.

Health & Wellbeing: Energize & Harmonize your Body. Created by Christine Sherborne. (ENG.). 2007. audio compact disk 19.95 (978-0-9582712-3-3(2)) Pub: Colourstory AUS. Dist(s): APG

Health & Wellness. 1 cassette. 1980. 12.95 (978-1-55841-018-3(X)) Emmett E Miller.
Four imagery experiences for developing wisdom and balance at each of the four levels - mind, body, emotion and spirit. Part 4 includes drum rhythums and movement to help you open to the life force within.

Health & Wellness. 1 CD. 1980. audio compact disk 16.95 (978-1-55841-110-4(0)) Emmett E Miller.
Four imagery experiences for developing widom and balance at each of the four levels - mind, body, emotion and spirit. Part 4 includes drum rhythums to help you open to the life force within.

Health & Wellness. Eldon Taylor. Read by Eldon Taylor. Ed. by Leslie Brice. 8 cass. (Running Time: 8 hrs.). 1992. 89.95 set. (978-1-56705-260-2(6)) Gateways Inst.
Self improvement.

Health & Wellness. Eldon Taylor. 8 cass. 119.95 Set. (978-1-55978-394-1(X), A103) Progress Aware Res.

Health & Wholeness: Creative Visualizations for Creating a New Reality. Created by Stanley Haluska. 1 CD. (Running Time: 70 mins). 2004. audio compact disk 15.00 (978-0-9668872-4-2(7), AP109) Awakening Pubns Inc.

Health & Wholeness: Creative Visualizations into Self Empowerment & Spiritual Identity. (ENG.). 2009. 15.95 (978-0-9758866-4-9(9)) Awakening Pubns Inc.

Health, Astrology & Spirituality. Miss Dee. 1 cass. 8.95 (270) Am Fed Astrologers.
What are people learning through body ailments.

Health Care & Social Justice. William F. Maestri. 1 cass. (Running Time: 40 min.). 1986. 7.95 (TAH166) Alba Hse Comns.
Principles for a vision of health care.

Health-Care CareerVision: View What You'd Do. JIST Publishing Editors. 2007. pap. bk. 22.95 (978-1-59357-463-5(0), JIST Works) JIST Pubng.

Health Care Decisions at the End of Life: An Evangelical Perspective: Proceedings of the 45th Annual Convention of Evangelicals Buffalo, New York. Read by Roger C. Sider. 1 cass. (Running Time: 60 min.). 1987. 4.00 (338) Nat Assn Evan.

Health Care Law & Litigation. 12 cass. (Running Time: 17 hrs.). 1999. 395.00 Incl. study guide. (AE34) Am Law Inst.

Health Care Law & Litigation: Thursday-Friday, October 29-30, 1998, Washington, D. C. (Loews L'Enfant Plaza Hotel) unabr. ed. Manuel Del Valle. 8 cass. (Running Time: 12 hrs.). 1998. 345.00 Incl. course materials. (MC04) Am Law Inst.
Provides practitioners with critical background information & recent developments in major legal areas affecting the health care industry.

Health Care Litigation Seminar: Top Partners on Negotiations, Settlements & Winning Legal Strategies for Success. Ed. by ReedLogic Staff. 2006. pap. bk. 499.95 (978-1-59701-087-0(1)) Aspatore Bks.

Health Care Reform Now! A Prescription for Change. unabr. ed. George Halvorson. Read by John J. Nance. 1 MP3-CD. (Running Time: 10 hrs.). 2008. 24.95 (978-1-4233-6967-7(X), 9781423369677, Brilliance MP3); 39.25 (978-1-4233-6970-7(X), 9781423369707, BADLE); 24.95 (978-1-4233-6969-1(6), 9781423369691, BAD); audio compact disk 102.25 (978-1-4233-6966-0(1), 9781423369660, BriAudCD Unabrid); audio compact disk 36.95 (978-1-4233-6965-3(3), 9781423369653, Bril Audio CD Unabri) Brilliance Audio.

Health Care Reform Now! A Prescription for Change. unabr. ed. George Halvorson. Read by John J. Nance. 1 MP3-CD. (Running Time: 10 hrs.). 2008. 39.25 (978-1-4233-6968-4(8), 9781423369684, Brinc Audio MP3 Lib) Brilliance Audio.

Health, Healing & Spiritual Energy. 2002. audio compact disk 14.95 (978-0-9728185-1-3(0)) InGenius Inc.

Health Healing & Spiritual Energy. abr. ed. Speeches. Edward Strachar. 1 cass. (Running Time: 60 mins.). 2002. 14.95 (978-0-9719358-9-1(0)) InGenius Inc.

Health, Healing & Spiritual Energy: Lessons, Stories & Examples from a Spiritual Healer. Short Stories. Greg Joseph. 6 cass. (Running Time: 6 hrs.). 2002. 59.95 (978-0-9719358-0-8(7)) InGenius Inc.

Health, Healing & Spiritual Energy II: Applying the Lessons & Strengthening the Connection. Short Stories. Greg Joseph. 8 cass., 1 video. (Running Time: 8 hrs.). 2002. 149.95 (978-0-9719358-1-5(5)) InGenius Inc.
A video / audio program with inspirational stories, meditation techniques and lessons to allow you to achieve health.

Health in the Buddhist Tradition, Pt. 1. Osel Tendzin. 8 cass. 1981. 81.00 Vajradhatu.
Illness of body, speech & mind is caused by unnecessary complications such as overthinking, overacting & overtalking. The discipline of simplicity leads to healthiness.

Health in the Buddhist Tradition, Pt. 1. Read by Osel Tendzin. 8 cass. 1981. 81.00 (A068) Vajradhatu.
Six talks. Illness of body, speech & mind is caused by unnecessary complications: overthinking, overacting & overtalking. The discipline of simplicity leads to healthiness.

Health in the Buddhist Tradition, Pt. 2. Osel Tendzin. 6 cass. 1982. 65.50 Vajradhatu.
A continuation of themes presented in the first Health in the Buddhist Tradition course.

Health in the Buddhist Tradition, Pt. 2. Read by Osel Tendzin. 6 cass. 1982. 65.50 (A069) Vajradhatu.
Five talks. This is a continuation of the themes presented in the first Health in the Buddhist Tradition course.

Health in the Light of Yoga, No. 1. Swami Jyotirmayananda. 1 cass. (Running Time: 1 hr.). 1990. 12.99 Yoga Res Foun.

Health in the Light Yoga. (117) Yoga Res Foun.

Health Insurance Services in Ukraine: A Strategic Reference 2006. Compiled by Icon Group International, Inc. Staff. 2007. ring bd. 195.00 (978-0-497-82447-1(7)) Icon Grp.

Health Journey Meditation. Belleruth Naparstek. 2001. (978-1-58621-153-0(6)) Hachet Audio.

Health Journey Meditations. Belleruth Naparstek. 2001. (978-1-58621-151-6(X)); (978-1-58621-152-3(8)); (978-1-58621-159-2(5)) Hachet Audio.

Health Journeys. Belleruth Naparstek. 2001. (978-1-58621-143-1(9)); (978-1-58621-144-8(7)); (978-1-58621-149-3(8)); (978-1-58621-158-5(7)); (978-1-58621-165-3(X)) Hachet Audio.

Health Journeys. abr. ed. Belleruth Naparstek. 2 cass. (Running Time: 3 hrs.). 2001. (978-1-58621-161-5(7)) Hachet Audio.

Health Journeys: For Anyone Concerned with General Wellness. Belleruth Naparstek. Composed by Steven Mark Kohn. 1 cass. (Running Time: 32 min.). (Health Journeys Ser.). 1993. 12.95 (978-1-881405-01-6(X), 6) Hlth Jrnys.
Designed to uplift & relax; help the body eliminate unhealthy cells & tissue; invoke a sense of connection with the universe to strengthen body, mind & spirit.

Health Journeys: For People Experiencing Stress. Belleruth Naparstek. 1 cass. (Running Time: 90 min.). 1999. 17.00 (22226) Courage-to-Change.
Meditations to alleviate general anxiety, promote feelings of safety & a more compassionate perspective on yourself, walking meditation to both calm & energize & affirmations that combat negative thinking.

Health Journeys: For People Experiencing Stress. Belleruth Naparstek. Composed by Steven Mark Kohn. 1 cass. (Running Time: 1 hr. 10 mins.). 1995. 14.98 Hlth Jrnys.
Exercise alleniates anxiety, promotes a powerful sense of peace, love & protection, includes a soothing, walking meditation & positive affirmations.

Health Journeys: For People Experiencing Stress. Belleruth Naparstek. Composed by Steven Mark Kohn. 1 cass. (Running Time: 1 hr. 10 min.). (Health Journeys Ser.). 2000. 14.95 (978-1-881405-03-0(6), 15) Hlth Jrnys.
The first exercise alleviates anxiety; the second promotes a powerful sense of peace, love & protection; the third guides a soothing, walking meditation; the fourth is positive affirmations.

Health Journeys: For People with Depression. Belleruth Naparstek. Composed by Steven Mark Kohn. 1 cass. (Running Time: 36 min.). (Health Journeys Ser.). 1993. 12.95 (978-1-881405-00-9(1), 4) Hlth Jrnys.
Designed to reduce hopelessness & self-hatred; mobilize energy; reduce fatigue; inspire feelings of love, hope & gratitude; connect with inner strength; reduce anxiety.

Health Journeys: Power over Smoking. Belleruth Naparstek. Read by Belleruth Naparstek. 1 cass. (Running Time: 1 hr.). 1997. 12.00 Hachet Audio.

Health Journeys: Power over Smoking. Belleruth Naparstek. 2001. (978-1-58621-160-8(9)) Hachet Audio.

Health Journeys for Anyone Concerned with General Wellness. Belleruth Naparstek. 2001. (978-1-58621-147-9(1)); (978-1-58621-148-6(X)) Hachet Audio.

Health Journeys for People Coping with Headaches. Belleruth Naparstek. 2 cass. (Running Time: 3 hrs.). 2001. (978-1-58621-150-9(1)) Hachet Audio.

Health Journeys for People Experiencing Stress. abr. ed. Belleruth Naparstek. 2 cass. (Running Time: 2 hrs.). 2001. (978-1-58621-162-2(5)) Hachet Audio.
These inspiring and beautifully crafted Health Journeys programs offer guided imagery at its finest. The author's soothing voice and Steve Kahn's inspiring music combine perfectly to increase physical and emotional healing Guided imagery is the gently technique of directing the imagination to help the mind and body relax, heal, and perform better.

Health Journeys for People Managing Pain. Belleruth Naparstek. 2001. (978-1-58621-156-1(0)) Hachet Audio.

Health Journeys for People Recovering from Stroke. Belleruth Naparstek. 2001. (978-1-58621-163-9(3)) Hachet Audio.

Health Journeys for People with Asthma. Belleruth Naparstek. 2001. (978-1-58621-141-7(2)) Hachet Audio.

Health Journeys for People with Cancer. Belleruth Naparstek. 2001. (978-1-58621-142-4(0)) Hachet Audio.

Health Journeys for People with Depression. Belleruth Naparstek. 2001. (978-1-58621-145-5(5)) Hachet Audio.

Health Journeys for People with Diabetes. Belleruth Naparstek. 1 cass. (Running Time: 90 min.). 2001. (978-1-58621-146-2(3)) Hachet Audio.

Health Journeys for People with Multiple Sclerosis. Belleruth Naparstek. 2001. (978-1-58621-155-4(2)) Hachet Audio.

Health Journeys Meditation to Help You Recover from Alcohol & Other Drugs. Belleruth Naparstek. 2001. (978-1-58621-140-0(4)) Hachet Audio.

Health Law & the Elderly. Read by Stephen A. Feldman. 1 cass. 1989. 20.00 (AL-72) PA Bar Inst.

Health Law Primer: Patient Care-Regulation of Facilities-HMOs & PPOs-Medical Staff Issues-Joint Ventures. 1987. bk. 95.00; 45.00 PA Bar Inst.

Health Literacy in Patient Care: Helping Your Patients Understand. Susan Labuda Schrop. LuAnne Stockton et al. 2005. cd-rom & audio compact disk 50.00 (978-0-9817031-0-7(0)) NE Ohio Univs.

Health, Nutrition & Growth: Basic concepts to know about health, nutrition & Growth. Maude Heurtelou. (ENG.). (YA). 2006. 12.00 (978-1-58432-341-9(8)) Educa Vision.

Health on File. 2nd ed. Victoria Chapman and Associates Staff. (gr. 6-12). 2002. audio compact disk 149.95 (978-0-8160-4681-2(6)) Facts On File.

Health Plans, HIPAA, & COBRA Update: Current ERISA, Tax, & Other Issues for Attorneys, Administrators, Insurers, & Consultants. 3 cass. (Running Time: 3 hrs. 30 min.). 1999. 165.00 Set; incl. 220p. study guide. (D285) Am Law Inst.

Health Policy & the Church's Ministry. Lowell Mays. 1986. 10.80 (0208) Assn Prof Chaplains.

Health Talk: Audio CD Program Sampler. Holt, Rinehart and Winston Staff. 1997. audio compact disk 20.33 (978-0-03-052954-2(9)) Holt McDoug.

Health Talk Program. Holt, Rinehart and Winston Staff. (SPA & ENG.). 1998. 128.33 (978-0-03-051907-9(1)) Holt McDoug.

Health: Total Wellness: Building the Mind & Body You Want. abr. ed. Health Magazine. (Running Time: 1 hr.). (ENG.). 2006. 9.99 (978-1-59483-747-0(3)) Pub: Hachet Audio. Dist(s): HachBkGrp

Health, Wealth & Happiness. Dick Sutphen. 1 cass. (Running Time: 1 hr.). (Only Subliminals Ser.). 1990. 12.98 (978-0-87554-452-6(5), T212) Valley Sun.
One hour of soothing, digitally mastered stereo music with positive subliminal suggestions phrased for maximum acceptance by your subconscious mind.

Healthcare Fraud & Abuse Introduction: Healthcare Billing Compliance Training & Planning for Small Practices to Hospitals & Health Systems, for Doctors, Nurses, Dentists, Therapists, Podiatrists, Osteopaths, Physicians Assistants, Practice Administrators, Compliance Officers, & All Allied Health Professionals. Daniel Farb. 2004. audio compact disk 49.95 (978-1-932634-54-9(1)) Pub: UnivofHealth. Dist(s): AtlasBooks

Healthcare Fraud & Abuse Introduction 10 Users. Daniel Farb. 2005. audio compact disk 149.95 (978-1-59491-167-5(3)) Pub: UnivofHealth. Dist(s): AtlasBooks

Healthcare Fraud & Abuse Introduction 100 Users. Daniel Farb. 2005. audio compact disk 899.95 (978-1-59491-223-8(8)) Pub: UnivofHealth. Dist(s): AtlasBooks

Healthcare Fraud & Abuse Introduction 25 Users. Daniel Farb. 2005. audio compact disk 299.95 (978-1-59491-221-4(1)) Pub: UnivofHealth. Dist(s): AtlasBooks

Healthcare Fraud & Abuse Introduction 5 Users: Healthcare Billing Compliance Training & Planning for Small Practices to Hospitals & Health Systems, for Doctors, Nurses, Dentists, Therapists, Podiatrists, Osteopaths, Physicians Assistants, Practice Administrators, Compliance Officers, & All Allied Health Professionals. Daniel Farb. 2005. audio compact disk 99.95 (978-1-59491-132-3(0)) Pub: UnivofHealth. Dist(s): AtlasBooks

Healthcare Fraud & Abuse Introduction 50 Users. Daniel Farb. 2005. audio compact disk 499.95 (978-1-59491-222-1(X)) Pub: UnivofHealth. Dist(s): AtlasBooks

Healthcare Information Systems: How to Re-Engineer Installed Systems, Vol. 2. A. Laurence Jr Smith. 2007. per. 56.00 (978-0-9797236-1-2(2)) A L Smith.

Healthful Sleep. Belleruth Naparstek. Composed by Steven Mark Kohn. 1 cass. (Running Time: 1 hr.). 2000. 12.98 (978-1-881405-11-5(7)) Hlth Jrnys.
Designed to promote peaceful sleep; create relaxed feelings of safety & calm; release muscular tension in the body; clear the mind of worry & obsessive thinking.

Healthier Alternatives. May Jideofo. 2007. audio compact disk 17.99 (978-1-60247-641-7(1)) Tate Pubng.

Healthier Mouth. 1 cass. (Health Ser.). 12.98 (108) Randolph Tapes.
Feel confident at the dentist's. Encourages better care of one's mouth.

Healthier You! 1 cass. (Health Ser.). 12.98 (82) Randolph Tapes.
Use your mind to help your body. Keeps body balanced & in harmony. Boosts your resistance! Your healing brain!.

Healthiest Man in the World. abr. ed. A. J. Jacobs. Read by A. J. Jacobs. (Running Time: 6 hrs. 0 mins. 0 sec.). (ENG.). 2012. audio compact disk 29.99 (978-0-7435-9876-7(8)) Pub: S&S Audio. Dist(s): S and S Inc

HealthStyle & Stress Success Gift Box. Krs Edstrom. 3 cass. (Running Time: 2 hrs.). 1996. bk. 32.00 (978-1-886198-50-0(0)) Soft Stone Pub.

Healthtalk. 94th ed. Holt, Rinehart and Winston Staff. (SPA & ENG.). 1994. 118.80 (978-0-03-097768-8(1)) Holt McDoug.
Health Talk Audiocassettes paraphrase 16 of Holt Health's most important chapters in both English and Spanish. This audio program is especially useful with auditory learners, students with limited reading proficiency, or Spanish-speaking students.

Healthtalk: Sampler. 94th ed. Holt, Rinehart and Winston Staff. (SPA & ENG.). 1994. 10.00 (978-0-03-098640-6(0)) Holt McDoug.

HealthWalking. 2 cass. 39.95 (2018) SyberVision.
Includes video & training guide.

Healthy Aging: A Lifelong Guide to Your Physical & Spiritual Well-Being. abr. ed. Andrew Weil. Read by Andrew Weil. 4 CDs. (Running Time: 18000 sec.). (ENG.). 2005. audio compact disk 27.50 (978-0-7393-1409-8(2), Random AudioBks) Pub: Random Audio Pubg. Dist(s): Random

Healthy & Thin Forever: Making Changes for a Healthier Lifestyle. Dora C. Fowler. 3 cass. (Running Time: 2 hrs. 15 min.). 1993. bk. 39.95 Set, incl. 48p. bk. (978-1-57323-006-3(5)) Natl Inst Child Mgmt.
Weight loss & eating habits.

Healthy Anger & Your Health: Using Healthy Emotions to Heal Your Body. William G. DeFoore. 2006. audio compact disk 29.99 (978-0-9785244-9-4(7)) Halcyon Life.

Healthy At 100. unabr. ed. John Robbins. Read by Raymond Todd. 9 cass. (Running Time: 27000 sec.). 2006. 29.95 (978-0-7861-4605-5(2)) Blckstn Audio.

Healthy At 100: The Scientifically Proven Secrets of the World's Healthiest & Longest-Lived People. unabr. ed. John Robbins. (Running Time: 10 mins.). (J). 2006. 59.95 (978-0-7861-4770-0(9)) Blckstn Audio.

Healthy At 100: The Scientifically Proven Secrets of the World's Healthiest & Longest-Lived Peoples. unabr. ed. John Robbins. Read by Raymond Todd. 11 CDs. (Running Time: 27000 sec.). 2006. audio compact disk 29.95 (978-0-7861-6894-1(3)); audio compact disk 72.00 (978-0-7861-6376-2(3)) Blckstn Audio.

Healthy Attitudes about Wealth. Jack Deere. 1 cass. (Running Time: 90 min.). (Proverbs Ser.: Vol. 5). 2000. 5.00 (JD08-005) Morning NC.
Practical wisdom for everyday living is brought to life in Jack's thorough exposition of this important book of the Bible.

Healthy Back: Relief from Neck, Shoulder, & Back Pain; Based on the Work of Dr. Moshe Feldenkrais. Scripts. Jack Heggie. 1 CD. (Running Time: 71 Mins.). 2005. audio compact disk 16.95 (978-1-884605-22-2(2)) Genesis II.
Feldenkrais Method?! equipment required. These four specially developed exercises gently guide you through the basic movements of the spine?increasing your range of motion and flexibility, while releasing tension, stress, and pain. Use A Healthy Back? for less than 20 minutes a day and:?Relieve stress and strain?Reduce or eliminate pain in your neck, shoulders, and back?Ease back stress from exercise, yard work, gardening, lifting, cleaning and other activities?Increase flexibility without straining?Improve your range of motion?Improve your posture?look and feel better?Relax more fully, sleep more soundlyWho will benefit from A Healthy Back???Anyone who experiences tension, stress or pain in their neck, shoulders or back.?Desk-Bound People?Professionals, Managers, Sales People, Accountants, ComputerOperators, Word Processors, etc.?People Who Are Active?Gardeners, Athletes, Carpenters, Construction Workers, Delivery People, Drivers, People Who Travel, etc.

Healthy Balancing. 1 cass. (Running Time: 40 min.). (Guided Meditation Ser.: No. 2). 11.95 (978-1-57025-001-9(4), HBT) Whole Person.
Side A: Inner Harmony. Feeling pulled in too many directions? Listen as the narrator leads the way to an energy-restoring, relaxing balance. Side B: Regaining Equilibrium. When your life is out of focus, take time to rebalance yourself. View metaphors for rebalancing on a mental movie screen. Helps to put priorities back in order.

Healthy Beginnings. Lorraine Bayes & Dennis Westphall. Perf. by Tickle Tune Typhoon Staff. 1 CD. (Running Time: 52 min.). (J). (gr. k-6). 1993. audio compact disk 14.98 (978-0-945337-11-9(6), TTTCD007) Tickle Tune Typhoon.
Collection of songs promoting healthy attitudes & habits through music. Lyrics cover physical, mental & emotional aspects of health, encouraging children to take care of themselves on the outside as well as in the inside.

Healthy Beginnings. Perf. by Tickle Tune Typhoon Staff. 1 cass. (J). 9.98 (978-1-56628-019-8(2), MFLP2502) MFLP CA.
Healthy Beginnings for newborn infants.

***Healthy Body: CD add-on Set.** Perf. by Millmark Education Staff. (ConceptLinks Ser.). 2009. audio compact disk 50.00 (978-1-61618-346-2(2)) Millmark Educ.

***Healthy Body Audio CD.** Perf. by Millmark Education Staff. (ConceptLinks Ser.). 2008. audio compact disk 28.00 (978-1-4334-0250-0(5)) Millmark Educ.

***Healthy Body SB1 Audio CD Body Systems.** Perf. by Millmark Education Staff. (Content Literacy Libraries Ser.). 2008. audio compact disk (978-1-4334-0448-1(6)) Millmark Educ.

***Healthy Body SB2 Audio CD Energy to Live.** Perf. by Millmark Education Staff. (Content Literacy Libraries Ser.). 2008. audio compact disk (978-1-4334-0449-8(4)) Millmark Educ.

***Healthy Body SB3 Audio CD Fighting Disease.** Perf. by Millmark Education Staff. (Content Literacy Libraries Ser.). 2008. audio compact disk (978-1-4334-0450-4(8)) Millmark Educ.

***Healthy Body SB4 Audio CD Making Good Decisions.** Perf. by Millmark Education Staff. (Content Literacy Libraries Ser.). 2008. audio compact disk (978-1-4334-0451-1(6)) Millmark Educ.

Healthy Child for Happy Dreams. Read by Mary Richards. 1 cass. (Running Time: 45 min.). (J). 2007. audio compact disk 19.95 (978-1-56136-170-0(4)) Master Your Mind.

Healthy Choices. Read by Nancy L. Tubesing. Music by Steven Zdenek Eckels. 1 cass. (Running Time: 34 min.). 1995. 11.95 (978-1-57025-092-7(8)) Whole Person.
Using the power of your mind, promote wellness in all areas of your life, including: lifestyle, eating, exercise, stress, relationships & change, with vivid sensory images.

Healthy Dose of Motivation: Includes 'The Aladdin Factor' & 'Dare to Win' abr. rev. ed. Mark Victor Hansen & Jack L. Canfield. 6 CDs. (Running Time: 6 hrs. 0 mins. 0 sec.). (ENG.). 2004. audio compact disk 29.95 (978-1-59397-517-3(1)) Pub: Macmill Audio. Dist(s): Macmillan

Healthy Earth: Early Explorers Fluent Set B Audio CD. Sandra Sarsha. Adapted by Benchmark Education Staff. (J). 2007. audio compact disk 10.00 (978-1-4108-8246-2(2)) Benchmark Educ.

Healthy Eating Freeway Guide. Contrib. by Penny Steward. (Playaway Adult Nonfiction Ser.). (ENG.). 2009. 34.99 (978-1-60812-574-6(2)) Find a World.

Healthy Family Is: The Basics. Walter Kempler. 3 cass. 1986. 44.95 Kempler Inst.
Provides a fundamental prespective for working with any family in trouble; practical tools to impact stuck family processes; live examples of these tools in action. Topics include: "The Psychology of Man Reconsidered," "All the Diagnosis You'll Ever Need" & "A New Approach to an Old Matter" with two interviews by Dr. Walter Kempler.

Healthy Food, Healthy Hearts, Healthy Arteries. Michael Klaper. 1 cass. (Running Time: 30 min.). (Help Yourself to Health Ser.). 7.00 (978-0-929274-02-7(4)) Gentle World.
One of a series of tapes discussing the relationship between a diet free of animal products & improving one's health or a particular disease.

Healthy Grieving. Thomas Junior Strawser. 1 CD. (Running Time: 1 hr.,10 mins.). 2002. audio compact disk (978-0-9755695-3-5(8)) My Lvng Solutions.
1 CD teaching application of these principles when a loved one is lost due to death, separation isolation, or divorce. It offers spiritual engineering techniques to provide the foundation and develop the skills of healthy grieving. These non-religious, comforting practices combine with practical tools that have helped thousands through painful and trying experiences.

Healthy Habits. (J). (ps-3). 2001. pap. bk. 14.95 (RT 116C); pap. bk. 16.95 (RT 116CD) Kimbo Educ.
Nutrition, the food groups, dental hygiene, fire safety & more. Motivating songs & lyric book chock-full of activities.

Healthy Habits for Early Learners. Sara Jordan & Renie Marshall. Lyrics by Sara Jordan. Illus. by Glen Wyand & Katherien Chorney. Prod. by Mark Shannon. Engineer Mark Shannon. 1 cass. (Running Time: 49 mins. 20 secs.). (J). (gr. k-4). 1997. pap. bk. 14.95 (978-1-895523-86-7(9), JMP116K) Jordan Music.
Award winning songs about nutrition, the food pyramid, dental hygiene, personal and fire safety and much more. The lyrics book also includes activities.

Healthy Habits for Early Learners. abr. ed. Sara Jordan. Prod. by Sara Jordan. (Running Time: 53 mins.). (Songs that Teach Early Learning Ser.). (ENG.). (J). (gr. 4-7). 1997. audio compact disk 13.95 (978-1-894262-28-6(X)) Pub: S Jordan Publ. Dist(s): CrabtreePubCo

Healthy Happy Songs. Ed. by Publications International Staff. (J). 2007. audio compact disk 3.98 (978-1-4127-3796-8(6)) Pubns Intl Ltd.

Healthy Heart Walking: Walking Workouts for a Lifetime of Fitness. unabr. ed. American Heart Association Staff. Read by Rita Moreno. 1 CD. (Running Time: 10 hrs. 0 mins. 0 sec.). (ENG.). 2004. audio compact disk 14.00 (978-0-7435-3949-4(4), Sound Ideas) Pub: S&S Audio. Dist(s): S and S Inc
Walk your Way to Health and Well-Being.

Healthy Love vs. Neurotic Love. unabr. ed. Nathaniel Branden. 1 cass. (Running Time: 1 hr. 9 min.). 12.95 (603) J Norton Pubs.
The psychological preconditions of being able to love; distinguishing healthy love from neurotic love.

Healthy Nails. Rick Brown. Read by Rick Brown. Ed. by John Quatro. 1 cass. (Running Time: 30 min.). (Subliminal - Easy Listening Ser.). 1993. 10.95 (978-1-57100-003-3(8), E106); 10.95 (978-1-57100-027-9(5), J106); 10.95 (978-1-57100-051-4(8), N106); 10.95 (978-1-57100-075-0(5), S106); 10.95 (978-1-57100-099-6(2), W106); 10.95 (978-1-57100-123-8(9), H106) Sublime Sftware.
Stop biting & have healthy nails.

Healthy, Pain Free, Drug Free, Childbirth. unabr. ed. Missy Frantz & Curt Frantz. Read by Missy Frantz & Curt Frantz. 2 cass. (Running Time: 1 hr. 50 min.). 1993. 14.00 set. (978-0-9644405-0-0(4)) Alt Health Choices.
Details health risks of pain killer used during labor, describes 13 attitudes & actions one can take to facilitate having drug free-pain free childbirth.

Healthy People 2010. U. S. Department of Health and Human Services Staff. (C). 2000. audio compact disk 42.95 (978-0-7637-1701-8(0), 1701-0) Jones Bartlett.

Healthy Pregnancy & Successful Labor. 1999. Hlth Jrnys.

Healthy Sexual Response-Ability. Martha B. Beveridge. 1 cass. (Running Time: 90 min.). 1994. 9.95 (978-1-889237-31-2(0)) Options Now.
If you struggle with sexual wounds & want to heal this vital creative part of you, this cassette will give you guidance & hope.

Healthy Sleep: Fall Asleep Easily, Sleep More Deeply, Sleep Through the Night, Wake up Refreshed. unabr. ed. Andrew Weil & Rubin Naiman. 2 CDs. (Running Time: 2 hrs. 15 mins.). 2007. audio compact disk 19.95 (978-1-59179-583-4(4), AW01152D) Sounds True.

Healthy Teeth & Gums. Barrie Konicov. 1 cass. 11.98 (978-0-87082-330-5(2), 056) Potentials.
Learn how to direct your body's energy to heal your gums & teeth & have a healthy mouth.

Healthy Teeth & Gums. Eldon Taylor. 1 cass. (Running Time: 62 min.). (Inner Talk Ser.). 16.95 incl. script. (978-1-55978-131-2(9), 5379C) Progress Aware Res.
Soundtrack - Musical Themes with underlying subliminal affirmations.

Healthy Teeth & Gums: Babbling Brook. Eldon Taylor. 1 cass. (Running Time: 60 min.). 1999. 16.95 (978-1-55978-541-9(1), 5379F) Progress Aware Res.

Healthy Teeth & Gums: Stream. Eldon Taylor. Read by Eldon Taylor. Ed. by Leslie Brice. 1 cass. (Running Time: 1 hr.). 1992. 16.95 (978-1-56705-317-3(3)) Gateways Inst.
Self improvement.

Healthy Water for a Longer Life: A Summary. Martin Fox. 1 cass. (Running Time: 45 min.). 1986. 8.00 (978-0-9617432-2-2(0)) Health Water Res.
Harmful & beneficial substances in our drinking water.

Healthy, Wealthy, & Wise. Patricia J. Crane & Rick Nichols. Read by Patricia J. Crane & Rick Nichols. 2 cass. (Running Time: 2 hrs. 15 min.). 1999. 16.95 Set. (978-1-893705-08-1(0)) Hlth Horiz.
Workshop recorded live, outlining principles for living in connection with Divine Wisdom, & creating health & wealth.

Healthy Weight Loss. Created by Sharon Penchina. Narrated by Sharon Penchina. Prod. by Imagine. Created by Stuart Hoffman. 1. (Running Time: 21:52). 2003. audio compact disk 14.95 (978-0-9740684-1-1(1)) Two Imagine.
Create a powerful mindset for success! Lose weight and fell good about yourself. Successful change depends upon the mind's acceptance of constructive suggestions. This CD features narrative that makes it easy and comfortable for the subconscious mind to accept positive suggestions to promote positive change.After being safely guided into a deep state of mental and physical relaxation, you will hear suggestions designed to release self-destructive behavior, increase confidence and self-esteem, and promote eating healthy foods in the correct portions to ensure your ideal body weight. Motivates you to exercise more and remain a healthy eater forever!.

Hear & Gone in 60 Seconds! 1 CD. (Running Time: 29 min.). (J). (ps-3). 2003. audio compact disk 14.98 (978-1-57940-092-7(2)) Pub: Rounder Records. Dist(s): Rounder Kids Mus Dist

Hear Me. unabr. ed. Philip Levine. Read by Philip Levine. 1 cass. (Running Time: 1 hr. 2 min.). (Watershed Tapes of Contemporary Poetry). 1977. 12.95 (23630) J Norton Pubs.
Selected poems.

Hear Me, America! And Other Verse & Prose. Jack B. Carmichael. 1999. lib. bdg. 21.95 (978-0-9626948-5-1(1)) Dynamics MI.

Hear Me Now: Tragedy in Cambodia. unabr. ed. Sophal L. Stagg et al. Read by Susan O'Malley. 4 cass. (Running Time: 5 hrs. 30 mins.). 1997. 32.95 (978-0-7861-1246-3(8), 2154) Blckstn Audio.
Story portrays a young girl & her family in their unyielding attempts to endure against an avalanche of suffering & pain, all the while clinging to life & dreaming of peace.

Hear Me Now: Tragedy in Cambodia. unabr. ed. Sophal L. Stagg et al. Read by Susan O'Malley. 4 cass. (Running Time: 6 hrs.). 1999. 24.95 (978-0-7861-1548-8(3)) Blckstn Audio.
Deeply moving & personal story portrays a young Cambodian girl & her family trying to survive the suffering & pain of the violent upheavals of the '70s. Clinging to hope amidst the horrors of starvation, separation from her family, torture & execution, the author conveys her spirit of optimism for a brighter future.

Hear My Worship. Jaime Jamgochian. (Praise Hymn Soundtracks Ser.). 2006. audio compact disk 8.98 (978-5-558-16195-3(7)) Pt of Grace Ent.

Hear No Evil. James Grippando. Read by Nick Sullivan. 9 vols. 2004. bk. 44.95 (978-0-7927-3272-3(3), SLD 675, Chivers Sound Lib); bk. 54.95 (978-0-7927-3273-0(1), CMP 675, Chivers Sound Lib) AudioGO.

***Hear No Evil.** abr. ed. James Grippando. Read by Campbell Scott. (ENG.). 2004. (978-0-06-081782-4(8), Harper Audio); (978-0-06-081783-1(6), Harper Audio) HarperCollins Pubs.

Hear That Lonesome Whistle Blow: Railroads in the West. unabr. ed. Dee Brown. Narrated by George Guidall. 8 cass. (Running Time: 11 hrs.). 1991. 70.00 (978-1-55690-219-2(0), 91205E7) Recorded Bks.
When train service began in 1869, America's Great Transcontinental Railroad was a symbol of the pioneer's Manifest Destiny. By the late 1800s, the romantic ideal had become a lost cause of epic proportions, a corrupt enterprise built upon a bedrock of paltry ethics & unbridled greed. He takes us on a journey through a frontier long since vanished into popular myth.

Hear the Angels Singing Anthem. Tim Van Brummelen. 2000. 5.00 (978-0-687-33810-8(7)) Abingdon.

Hear Them Ring! The Bells of Christmas. Gloriae Dei Cantores. 1 CD. 1995. audio compact disk 16.95 (978-1-55725-140-4(1), 930-091) Paraclete MA.

Hear Them Ring: the Bells of Christmas see Bells of Christmas

Hear Ye Israel, Set, Vol. I. Michael Ballam. 2 cass. (Running Time: 3 hrs.). 14.98 (978-1-57734-011-9(6), 1100769) Covenant Comms.
A musical journey through ancient & modern Israel.

Hear Ye Israel, Set, Vol. 2. Michael Ballam. 2 cass. 14.98 (978-1-57734-012-6(4), 1100777) Covenant Comms.

Heard! Baker Publishing Group Staff. Created by Green Key Books Staff. 14 CDs. (God's Word New Testament Ser.). 2004. audio compact disk 39.99 (978-1-932587-55-5(1)) Baker Pub Grp.

Hearing. abr. ed. John Lescroart. Read by Robert Lawrence. (Running Time: 6 hrs.). (Dismas Hardy Ser.: No. 7). 2008. audio compact disk 14.99 (978-1-4233-5157-3(6), 9781423351573, BCD Value Price) Brilliance Audio.

Hearing. abr. ed. James Mills. 2 cass. (Running Time: 3 hrs.). 1998. 17.98 Set. (978-1-57042-597-4(3)) Hachet Audio.

Hearing. unabr. ed. John Lescroart. Read by Robert Lawrence. 10 cass. (Running Time: 15 hrs.). (Dismas Hardy Ser.: No. 7). 2001. 107.25 (978-1-58788-176-3(4), 1587881764); 34.95 (978-1-58788-175-6(6), 1587881756, BAU) Brilliance Audio.
The call comes at midnight. It looks like a tragic and petty murder - a rising star in San Francisco's legal firmament found shot in a dark alley. But for homicide lieutenant Abe Glitsky, the crime cuts horribly close to home - unknown to anyone, the victim was his daughter. Seething, Glitsky leans hard on his only suspect - a homeless heroin addict found lingering over his daughter's body, with her jewelry in his pocket and a smoking gun in his hand. The city's embattled, ambitious D.A. Sharron Pratt sees an opportunity to revive her troubled administration by publicly declaring war on the killer and vowing to deliver a death penalty, putting the case on the fast track to certain conviction. Unable to watch a man die for Pratt's political gain, Dismas Hardy warily takes on the defense. But as Hardy's crusade to secure his client a fair hearing ensues, a lethal web of political corruption, legal conspiracy, and cold-blooded murder begins to unravel. In a case that will send shock waves through San Francisco and echo in the private lives of its most prominent citizens, the hearing is just the beginning.

Hearing. unabr. ed. John Lescroart. Read by Robert Lawrence. (Running Time: 15 hrs.). (Dismas Hardy Ser.: No. 7). 2004. 39.25 (978-1-59335-457-2(6), 1593354576, Brlnc Audio MP3 Lib) Brilliance Audio.

Hearing. unabr. ed. John Lescroart. Read by Robert Lawrence. (Running Time: 15 hrs.). (Dismas Hardy Ser.: No. 7). 2004. 39.25 (978-1-59710-349-7(7), 1597103497, BADLE); 24.95 (978-1-59710-348-0(9), 1597103489, BAD) Brilliance Audio.

Hearing. unabr. ed. John Lescroart. Read by Robert Lawrence. (Running Time: 54000 sec.). (Dismas Hardy Ser.: No. 7). 2007. audio compact disk 117.25 (978-1-4233-3408-6(6), 9781423334088, BriAudCD Unabrid); audio compact disk 38.95 (978-1-4233-3407-1(8), 9781423334071, Bril Audio CD Unabri) Brilliance Audio.

Hearing. unabr. ed. John Lescroart. Read by Robert Lawrence. (Running Time: 15 hrs.). (Dismas Hardy Ser.: No. 7). 2004. 24.95 (978-1-59335-088-8(0), 1593350880) Soulmate Audio Bks.

Hearing. unabr. ed. James Mills. Narrated by Richard Ferrone. 7 cass. (Running Time: 10 hrs.). 1999. 66.00 (978-0-7887-2920-1(9), 95676E7) Recorded Bks.
Draws you into a world of political intrigue where a scrap of information can soil the cleanest reputation. Judge Gus Parham has been nominated for the U.S. Supreme Court. His record is exemplary; his appointment seems certain. How, then, did someone discover a chapter from his past that he thought was dead & buried?.

Hearing: Program from the Award Winning Public Radio Series. Interview. Hosted by Fred Goodwin. 1 CD. (Running Time: 1 hr). (Infinite Mind Ser.). 2003. audio compact disk 21.95 (978-1-932479-06-5(6), LCM 257) Lichtenstein Creat.
In this hour, we explore the sense of hearing. Guests include Dr. Brenda Ryals, a professor and hearing researcher at James Madison University; Dr. Albert Bregman, a professor of psychology and hearing researcher at McGill University in Montreal, Canada; Dr. Sarah Woolley, a postdoctoral fellow in Behavioral Neurobiology at The University of California at Berkeley; Dr. Natan Bauman, the founder and director of The Hearing, Balance and Speech Center in Connecticut; Ms. Kathy Peck, the founder of the grassroots organization H.E.A.R - Hearing Education and Awareness for Rockers; Dr. David Silbersweig, a neurologist and psychiatrist who directs the neuropsychiatry program at Cornell University; and Mr. Randy Thom, a re-recording mixer and sound designer for Skywalker Sound, a division of Lucas Digital.

Hearing Chords & Differences in Chord Types. Duane Shinn. 1 cass. 19.95 (ET-2) Duane Shinn.
Explains how to distinguish between the basic kinds of triads.

Hearing Eye. 6 cass. 55.00 (978-0-614-25226-2(1)) Pub: UWA Pub AUS. Dist(s): Intl Spec Bk

***Hearing from God.** Katie Souza. (ENG.). 2011. audio compact disk 10.00 (978-0-7684-0264-3(6)) Pub: Expected End. Dist(s): Destiny Image Pubs

Hearing from God Each Morning: 365 Daily Devotions. unabr. ed. Joyce Meyer. Narrated by Laural Merlington. (Running Time: 12 hrs. 5 mins. 51 sec.). (ENG.). 2010. 11.19 (978-1-60814-647-5(2)) Oasis Audio.

Hearing from the Councils of Heaven. Phillip Halverson. 1 cass. (Running Time: 1 hr). 2005. 5.00 (978-1-57399-241-1(0)) Mac Hammond.
The Holy Spirit wants to help you and reveal Himself to you in prayer. Find out how you can hear from the councils of heaven and pray the hidden wisdom of God.

***Hearing God.** unabr. ed. Peter Lord. (ENG.). 2010. 17.99 (978-0-9830140-4-1(3)) Sozo Media.

Hearing God: Developing a Conversational Relationship with God. unabr. ed. Dallas Willard. 8 CDs. (Running Time: 8 hrs. 30 mins. 0 sec.). (ENG.). 2005. audio compact disk 26.98 (978-1-59644-055-5(4), Hovel Audio) christianaud.
Being close to God means communicating with Him-telling Him what is on our hearts in prayer and hearing and understanding what he is saying to us. It is this second half of our conversation with God that is so important but that also can be so difficult. How do we hear his voice? How can we be sure that what we think we hear is not our own subconscious? What role does the Bible play? What if what God says to us is not clear?The key, says best-selling author Dallas Willard, is to focus not so much on individual actions and decisions as on building our personal relationship with our creator. In this updated classic, originally published as In Search of Guidance, the author provides a rich, spiritual insight into how we can hear Goda??s voice clearly and develop an intimate partnership with Him in the work of His kingdom.

***Hearing God: Developing a Conversational Relationship with God.** unabr. ed. Dallas Willard. Narrated by Grover Gardner. (ENG.). 2005. 14.98 (978-1-59644-053-1(8), Hovel Audio) christianaud.

Hearing God: Developing a Conversational Relationship with God. unabr. ed. Dallas Willard. Narrated by Grover Gardner. 1 MP3 CD. (Running Time: 8 hrs. 30 mins. 0 sec.). (ENG.). 2005. lp 19.98 (978-1-59644-054-8(6), Hovel Audio) christianaud.

Hearing God - An Introduction. Rick Joyner. 1 cass. (Running Time: 90 mins.). (Hearing God Ser.: Vol. 1). 2000. 5.00 (RJ10-001) Morning NC.
"Principles of Spiritual Warfare" & "Putting on the Full Armor of God." These tapes highlight practical truths that lead to certain victory in spirtual warfare.

Hearing God Series. Rick Joyner. 6 cass. (Running Time: 9 hrs.). 2000. 30.00 (RJ10-000) Morning NC.
The Lord said that His sheep know His voice. This set of tapes contains essential teaching for every believer to recognize when God is speaking.

Hearing God's Voice. Derek Prince. 2 cass. 11.90 Set. (057-058) Derek Prince.
Throughout all dispensations, to hear God's voice has always been the basic, unvarying requirement for all ongoing relationships with God.

Hearing God's Voice. abr. ed. Henry and Richard Blackaby. Read by Mel Foster. (Running Time: 3 hrs.). 2007. 24.95 (978-1-4233-0399-2(7), 9781423303992, BAD) Brilliance Audio.

Hearing God's Voice. abr. ed. Henry Blackaby & Richard King. Read by Mel Foster. (Running Time: 3 hrs.). 2007. 39.25 (978-1-4233-0398-5(9), 9781423303985, Brlnc Audio MP3 Lib); 39.25 (978-1-4233-0400-5(4), 9781423304005, BADLE); audio compact disk 24.95 (978-1-4233-0397-8(0), 9781423303978, Brilliance MP3) Brilliance Audio.

Hearing God's Voice. abr. ed. Henry T. Blackaby & Richard King. Read by Mel Foster. 3 CDs, Library ed. (Running Time: 3 hrs.). 2002. audio compact disk 62.25 (978-1-59086-690-0(8), 1590866908, CD Lib Edit); 17.95 (978-1-59086-687-0(8), 1590866878, Nova Audio Bks); 44.25 (978-1-59086-688-7(6), 1590866886, CD Lib Edit); audio compact disk 24.95 (978-1-59086-689-4(4), 1590866894, CD Unabridged) Brilliance Audio.
Based on classic Experiencing God principles, Hearing God's Voice is for those who are ready to listen. Beloved author Henry Blackaby and his son Richard help those who are listening to discern the voice of God, to identify ways He speaks, and to respond to revelations of His will. God speaks to individuals in ways that are personal and unique to each person. God will never say anything that contravenes what He has said in the Bible. After you learn to listen to God, hearing from God will be as natural as communicating with a close friend.

Hearing God's Voice, Vol. 4. Paul L. Cox. Hosted by Paul L. Cox. Featuring Scott Abke & JoAnn Seel. 4 cass. (Running Time: 223). 2000. 22.00 (978-0-9702183-8-4(9)) Aslans Pl.

Hearing God's Voice Series. Jack Deere. 6 cass. (Running Time: 9 hrs.). 2000. 30.00 (JD04-000) Morning NC.
These messages are an outstanding collection that lay a solid & practical foundation for discerning God's voice.

Hearing Great Poetry: From Chaucer to Milton. abr. ed. Poems. Read by Mark Van Doren. Perf. by Hurd Hatfield et al. 1 cass. Incl. Collar. George Herbert. (SWC 1021); Death Be Not Proud & The Bait. John Donne. (SWC 1021); Fresh Spring. Edmund Spenser. (SWC 1021); Hamlet. William Shakespeare. (SWC 1021); Lycidas. John Milton. (SWC 1021); Midsummer Night's Dream: Act III, Scene 1. William Shakespeare. (SWC 1021); Patient Grissell: The Basket-Maker's Song. Thomas Dekker. (SWC 1021); Prologue to the Legend of Good Women. Geoffrey Chaucer. (SWC 1021); Sonnet XXX. William Shakespeare. (SWC 1021); Tragical History of Doctor Faustus. Christopher Marlowe. (SWC 1021); Volpone: Act III, Scene 6. Ben Jonson. (SWC 1021); 1984. 12.95 (978-0-694-50017-8(8), SWC 1021) HarperCollins Pubs.

Hearing Restored. Barrie Konicov. 1 cass. 11.98 (978-0-87082-331-2(0), 057) Potentials.
Through suggestion & self-hypnosis the author, Barrie Konicov, reveals how complete or partial hearing may be restored. Listen...to your heart.

Hearing the Gentle Brother: White Eagle Readings. Read by Ylana Hayward. audio compact disk 17.95 (978-0-85487-143-8(8)) Pub: White Eagle GBR. Dist(s): DeVorss

Hearing the Voice of God. Read by Wayne Monbleau. 4 cass. 1994. 20.00 Set. (978-0-944648-37-7(1), LGT-1237) Loving Grace Pubns.

Hearing the Voice of God. Featuring Bill Winston. 4. (ENG.). 2001. audio compact disk 32.00 (978-1-59544-070-9(4)) Pub: B Winston Min. Dist(s): Anchor Distributors
You can avoid the pitfalls of life by listening to the voice of God. In this powerful series by Pastor Winston, you will learnto train your spirit-the real you-to hear God's voice. You will learn that righteousness is a key factor in hearing God's voice.And, once He speaks to you, you will never be the same again.Walk in the wisdom of God by hearing the Voice of God.

Hearing the Voice of God. Featuring Bill Winston. 4. 2004. audio compact disk Rental 32.00 (978-1-59544-030-3(5)) B Winston Min.

Hearing the Voice of God. Bill Winston. 4 cass. (Running Time: 2hr.29min.). (C). 2003. 20.00 (978-1-931289-38-2(7)) Pub: B Winston Min. Dist(s): Anchor Distributors

Hearing the Voice of God. unabr. ed. Read by Gayle D. Erwin. 1 cass. (Running Time: 1 hr.). 1992. 4.95 (978-1-56599-516-1(3), C-16) Yahshua Pub.
Hebrews 1: 1-3, John 10: 1-30.

Hearing the Wisdom of Jesus. Richard Rohr. 1 cass. (Running Time: 1 hr.). 2001. 8.95 (A6721) St Anthony Mess Pr.
Ongoing reform, renewal and regeneration of the Church requires an ever closer, clearer discovery of the intention, the teaching and the mind of Jesus as presented in Scripture.

Hear's a Journey Driving Tour Through Provence in France: From Avignon East to l'Isle Sur la Sorgue, Fontaine de Vaucluse, Abbey Notre-Dame of Senanque, Gordes & Roussillon. Interview. Narrated by Francis Dumaurier & Ann Williams. 1 cass. (Running Time: 90 min.). 2003. 15.95 (978-0-9726774-2-4(9)) Hear's A Journey.
Hear's A Journey Driving Tour Through Provence is a daylong driving excursion through the enchanting countryside of the Vaucluse, east of Avignon. Designed for use in a car's tape player, the expert commentary is relayed by Frenchman , Francis Dumaurier and American , Ann Williams. They convey an array of information about the towns and sites one will stop to visit as well as insights about the region. Directions are also provided en route.The audio cassette tour is supplemented by an Informational Booklet that includes a driving map with directions, individual town maps that note parking, major sites, market days, festivals and other useful advice.

Hear's a Journey Driving Tour Through Tuscany in Italy: From Siena Northwest to the Hilltop Towns of Monteriggioni, San Gimignano & Volterra. Interview. Narrated by Fausto Lombard & Ann Williams. 1 cass. (Running Time: 90 minutes). 2003. 15.95 (978-0-9726774-0-0(2)) Hear's A Journey.
Hear's a Journey Driving Tour Through Tuscany is a daylong driving excursion through the majestic countryside northwest of Siena. Developed for use in a car's tape player, the expert commentary is relayed by Italian, Fausto Lombard and American, Ann Williams. They discuss an array of topics about the town and sites one will stop to visit as well as insights about the region. Directions are also provided en route.The audio cassette tour is supplemented by an Informational Booklet that includes a driving map and directions, individual town maps that note parking, major sites, market dats, festivals and other useful information.

Hear's a Journey Driving Tour Through T[illegible]cany in Italy: From Siena South to the Abbey Monte Oliveto M[illegible]re & the Hilltop Towns of Pienza & Montepulciano. Interview. N[illegible]ed by Fausto Lombard & Ann Williams. 1 cass. (Running Time: 90 minu[illegible]). 2003. 15.95 (978-0-9726774-1-7(0)) Hear's A Journey.
Hear's A Journey Driving Tour Through Tuscany is a daylong driving excursion through the striking and entrancing countryside south of Siena. Designed for use in a car's tape player, the expert commentary is relayed by Italian, Fausto Lombard and American, Ann Williams. They discuss an array of topics about the towns and sites one will stop and visit as well as insights about the area. Directions are also provided en route.The audio cassette tour is likewise supplemented by an Informational Booklet that includes driving map and directions, individual town maps that note parking, major sites, market days, festivals and other useful information.

Hearsay. Irving Younger. Read by Irving Younger. 3 cass. (Running Time: 3 hrs.). 1985. pap. bk. 70.00 Set. (978-0-943380-38-4(3)) PEG MN.
Recognizing hearsay.

Hearsay. Perf. by Irving Younger. Created by Irving Younger. 2 CDs. (Running Time: 3 hours). 2004. pap. bk. 199.00 (978-1-932831-03-0(7)) PEG MN.

Hearsay & the Right to Confrontation, Pt. 1. 1 cass. (Running Time: 53 min.). (Basic Concepts in the Law of Evidence Ser.). 1975. 15.00 (EYX12) Natl Inst Trial Ad.

Hearsay & the Right to Confrontation, Pt. 2. 1 cass. (Running Time: 54 min.). (Basic Concepts in the Law of Evidence Ser.). 1975. 15.00 (EYX13) Natl Inst Trial Ad.

Hearsay I. 1 cass. (Running Time: 30 min.). (Basic Concepts in the Law of Evidence Ser.). 1975. 15.00 (EYX07) Natl Inst Trial Ad.

Hearsay II. 1 cass. (Running Time: 52 min.). (Basic Concepts in the Law of Evidence Ser.). 1975. 15.00 (EYX08) Natl Inst Trial Ad.

Hearsay III. 1 cass. (Running Time: 58 min.). (Basic Concepts in the Law of Evidence Ser.). 1975. 15.00 (EYX09) Natl Inst Trial Ad.

Hearsay IV. 1 cass. (Running Time: 48 min.). (Basic Concepts in the Law of Evidence Ser.). 1975. 15.00 (EYX10) Natl Inst Trial Ad.

Hearsay Rule & Its Exceptions. David F. Binder. 1 cass. (Running Time: 1 hr.). 1985. 15.00 PA Bar Inst.

Hearsay Update. 1 cass. (Running Time: 49 min.). (Basic Concepts in the Law of Evidence Ser.). 1975. 15.00 (EYX15) Natl Inst Trial Ad.

Hearse Case Scenario. unabr. ed. Tim Cockey. Read by Bruce Reizen. 8 cass. (Running Time: 11 hrs.). (Hearse Ser.). 2002. 32.95 (978-1-58788-794-9(0), 1587887940, BAU); 78.25 (978-1-58788-795-6(9), 1587887959, Unabridge Lib Edns) Brilliance Audio.
Nightclub owner Shrimp Martin has been shot, and Hitchcock Sewell already knows who-done-it. It's his friend, Lucy Taylor, who went directly to Hitch's funeral home and placed the smoking gun on his desk. As it happens, Shrimp survives the gunshot wound, but he doesn't survive the knife that is plunged into his heart as he lies in his hospital bed. The police would like to question Lucy Taylor. But she has slipped away from Hitch's custody, hooked up with Hitch's ex-wife Julia, and the two have disappeared. Matters get more complicated when Shrimp's younger brother, also a friend of Lucy's, turns up dead. Is Lucy on a rampage? Is Julia somehow involved? As Hitch begins to nose about, he is joined by a private eye named Pete, who is in the full bloom of a mid-life crisis. A felonious painter, a Miles Davis wannabe, an Ida Lupino look-alike, the Great White Hope of Baltimore professional basketball, and one very angry dance instructor are just some of the characters Hitch and Pete encounter in this tale of greed, obsession, and misplaced loyalties.

Hearse Case Scenario. unabr. ed. Tim Cockey. Read by Bruce Reizen. (Running Time: 11 hrs.). (Hearse Ser.). 2004. 39.25 (978-1-59335-361-2(8), 1593353618, Brlnc Audio MP3 Lib) Brilliance Audio.

Hearse Case Scenario. unabr. ed. Tim Cockey. Read by Bruce Reizen. (Running Time: 11 hrs.). (Hearse Ser.). 2004. 39.25 (978-1-59710-350-3(0), 1597103500, BADLE); 24.95 (978-1-59710-351-0(9), 1597103519, BAD) Brilliance Audio.

Hearse Case Scenario. unabr. ed. Tim Cockey. Read by Bruce Reizen. (Running Time: 11 hrs.). (Hearse Ser.). 2004. 24.95 (978-1-59335-033-8(3), 1593350333) Soulmate Audio Bks.

Hearst Legacy. Frank Browning. 1 cass. (Running Time: 30 min.). 9.95 (H0270B090, HarperThor) HarpC GBR.

Hearsts: Father & Son. unabr. ed. William R. Hearst, Jr. & Jack Casserly. Read by Jeff Riggenbach. 9 cass. (Running Time: 13 hrs. 30 min.). 1994. 62.95 (1390) Blckstn Audio.
The founder of the largest U.S. Pewar media empire, William Randolf Hearst, Sr., changed the face of American jounalism forever. He was larger than life, an ambitious congressman, then a reclusive yet active

businessman in the famous castle ensconced above the Pacific at San Simeon.

Hearsts: Father & Son. unabr. ed. William Randolph Hearst, Jr. & Jack Casserly. Read by Jeff Riggenbach. 9 cass. (Running Time: 13 hrs.). 2006. 62.95 (978-0-7861-0438-3(4), 1390) Blckstn Audio.

Heart: Repairs & Maintenance. abr. ed. Robert A. Monroe. Read by Robert A. Monroe. (Running Time: 30 min.). (Human Plus Ser.). 1989. 14.95 (978-1-56102-013-3(3)) Inter Indus.
Establish improvement in heart function.

Heart Advice from the Lama, Set. Tr. by Lisa Leghorn. Contrib. by Chagdud Tulku. 4 cass. (Running Time: 6 hrs.). 1998. 24.00 (978-1-881847-27-4(6)) Padma Pub CA.
Intimate advice from Tulku, at the heart of which is his own guru yoga, illuminated by the stories he tells about his lamas & the impact their advice has had on him.

Heart Aflame. Daya Mata. 1984. 6.50 (2106) Self Realization.
Presents simple down-to-earth ways of creating an intimate, personal relationship with God. Topics include: Keys to deeper levels of meditation; The simplicity of divine love; How to cultivate a loving companionship with God; The most satisfying relationship; Expansion of consciousness; The purpose of Yoga; What is emotional maturity?; How to live peacefully with others.

Heart Alighed - Psalms of David, Vol. 2. Charles R. Swindoll. 1 cass. 1998. 11.98 (978-5-559-01217-9(3)) Word Enter.

Heart Aligned: Songs of Praise from the Psalms of David. abr. ed. Charles R. Swindoll. 2 CDs. 1998. audio compact disk 16.99 (978-5-559-01215-5(7)) Pt of Grace Ent.

Heart Alive with Love. Thomas Merton. 1 cass. 8.95 (AA2373) Credence Commun.

Heart & Guts of Prosperity. Speeches. Creflo A. Dollar. 5 CDs. (Running Time: 6 hrs.). 2004. audio compact disk 34.00 (978-1-59089-859-8(1)) Creflo Dollar.

Heart & Passion. Read by Osel Tendzin. 1 cass. 1975. 10.00 (A097) Vajradhatu.
One talk. The human realm is characterized by passion. Feeling one's heart produces the ambition to utilize this life for the benefit of others.

Heart & Soul. Betty Stevenson. 1 cass. 9.95 (978-1-57734-286-1(0), 06005837) Covenant Comms.
An incredible story of inspiration & hope.

Heart & Soul. Perf. by Kathy Troccoli. 1 cass. 1984. Brentwood Music.
The follow-up to a best selling debut release, features the classics, Holy, Holy & I Belong to You.

Heart & Soul. Winans, The. 1 cass., 1 CD. 10.98 (45888-4); audio compact disk 15.98 CD. (45888-2) Warner Christian.

Heart & Soul. abr. ed. Maeve Binchy. Read by Sile Bermingham. (ENG.). 2009. audio compact disk 29.95 (978-0-7393-7723-9(X), Random AudioBks) Pub: Random Audio Pubg. Dist(s): Random

***Heart & Soul.** abr. ed. Maeve Binchy. Read by Sile Bermingham. (ENG.). 2011. audio compact disk 14.99 (978-0-307-91421-7(6), Random AudioBks) Pub: Random Audio Pubg. Dist(s): Random

Heart & Soul Gospel Music Workout Compilation. 1 cass. 10.98 (978-1-57908-448-6(6)); audio compact disk 16.98 (978-1-57908-447-9(8)) Platinm Enter.

Heart & Soul of Freedom: Liberation from Limitation. Guy Finley. (ENG.). 2002. 24.95 (978-1-929320-39-4(6)) Life of Learn.

Heart & Soul of Freedom: Liberation from Limitation. Guy Finley. 7 cass. (Running Time: 10 hrs. 30 mins.). 2002. audio compact disk 39.95 (978-1-929320-12-7(4)) Life of Learn.

Heart & Soul of Ireland Version B: Dublin to Shannon. Ronald Hutton. Read by Ronald Hutton. Ed. by Craig Mayes. 3 cass. (Running Time: 3 hrs. 4 min.). (Personal Courier Ser.). 1990. 26.95 (978-1-878877-02-4(X), 02-X) Educ Excursions.
British historian Dr. Ronald Hutton enchants the listener with the legends of Finn MacCumail & the Fianna, St. Brendan, St. Bridget of the Curragh, & many more...as he relives the history of Ireland from the Tain Bo Culaigne to the Easter Rising of 1916. Structured along a popular southern route across the Emerald Isle.

Heart & Soul of Ireland, Version A: Shannon to Dublin. unabr. ed. Ronald Hutton. Read by Ronald Hutton. Ed. by Craig Mayes. 3 cass. (Running Time: 3 hrs. 4 min.). (Personal Courier Ser.). 1990. 26.95 Set. (978-1-878877-01-7(1)) Educ Excursions.
An excursion through the ancient legends, folk tales, & history of the Emerald Isle. For travelling convenience, the tape is laid out along a route from Shannon to Dublin as Ronald Hutton delights listeners with tales of Finn MacCumail & the Fianna, ancient Gaelic literature, & tragic tales from history.

Heart & Sout of Freedom: Liberation from Limitation. Guy Finley. 2002. 24.95 (978-1-929320-11-0(6)) Life of Learn.
Timeless answers that point the way to a life without limits. Provides tools for finding inner freedom. Soul-stirring, empowering and inspiring.

Heart Aroused: Poetry & the Preservation of the Soul in Corporate America. Read by David Whyte. 3 CDs. (Running Time: 180 mins). 2005. audio compact disk 33.00 (978-1-932887-11-2(3)) Pub: Many Rivers Pr. Dist(s): Partners-West

Heart Asks Pleasure First see Poems & Letters of Emily Dickinson

Heart at Work: Stories & Strategies for Building Self-Esteem & Reawakening the Soul at Work. abr. ed. Jack L. Canfield. Read by Jack L. Canfield. 4 cass. (Running Time: 6 hrs.). 2004. 25.00 (978-1-59007-116-8(6)) Pub: New Millenn Enter. Dist(s): PerseuPGW
Emphasizing thanking people for a job well done, these vignettes intend to encourage people to inject kindness into corporate America. Despite the enjoyable subject matter, these lessons could be learned in less than four tapes, relieving listeners of repetition of content and some of the tedious narrative.

Heart Attacks: Prevent & Survive. l.t. ed. Tom Smith & Patrick O'brian. 1995. 18.95 (978-1-85695-000-8(X)) Pub: ISIS Lrg Prnt GBR. Dist(s): Transaction Pubs

Heart Broken Open. unabr. ed. 1 cass. (Running Time: 1 hr. 13 min.). 2001. 12.00 (978-1-887984-09-6(7)); audio compact disk 15.00 (978-1-887984-08-9(9)) The Gangaji Fnd.
Reflections on the life and teachings of Jesus.

Heart Chakra Meditations. Layne Redmond. 2 CDs. (Running Time: 7200 sec.). 2005. audio compact disk 19.95 (978-1-59179-350-2(5), W951D) Sounds True.
The transcendental, humming pulse of consciousness can be heard in the center of the fourth chakra: the human body's heart center. As this chakra is balanced and energized, faith, devotion, and harmony in our relationships unfold. Here, world renowned drummer and author Layne Redmond offers Chakra Meditations: Opening the Heart-two CDs specially recorded to purify the heart chakra, and fine-tune our receptivity for love at the core of our entire being. On CD One, Layne offers listeners a complete series of pranayama exercises, guided meditations, and a unique shavasana (relaxation) practice to balance and tone the heart chakra. On CD Two, she presents a masterful chanting practice that blends Christian, Jewish, Islamic, Hindu and Buddhist traditions, and is the perfect accompaniment to meditation, massage, yoga, or trance work. Also included is a 20-minute recording of the human heartbeat- a powerful healing sound that opens our hearts, and connects us to all of life.

Heart Condition. 2001. audio compact disk 15.00 (978-1-58302-179-8(5)) One Way St.
Six songs cover the theme of the heart. This collection helps the listener understand that Dr. Jesus is the cure for all our heart aches.

Heart Connections. 1992. 59.95 (978-1-893027-26-8(0)) Path of Light.

Heart Cry: Tale of Discovery. abr. ed. 2006. audio compact disk 14.99 (978-0-7684-2423-2(2)) Destiny Image Pubs.

Heart Disease. unabr. ed. Don Colbert. Read by Greg Wheatley. 1 cass. (Running Time: 1 hr.). (Bible Cure for...Ser.). 2003. 7.99; audio compact disk 9.99 Oasis Audio.

Heart Disease: Ancient Truths, Natural Remedies & the Latest Findings for Your Health Today. unabr. ed. Don Colbert. Narrated by Greg Wheatley. 1 CD. (Running Time: 1 hr. 30 mins.). (Bible Cure Ser.). (ENG.). 2003. audio compact disk 9.99 (978-1-58926-191-4(7), S56L-022D) Oasis Audio.

Heart Disease: Prevention. Contrib. by Arthur Levy. 2006. DVD 69.95 Apogee Communications.

Heart Disease: The Heart of the Matter. Interview. Jill Eisen. 3 CDs. (Running Time: 3 hrs). 2006. audio compact disk 24.95 (978-0-660-19619-0(0), CBC Audio) Canadian Broadcasting CAN.

Heart Disease & Cancer. unabr. ed. Don Colbert. Narrated by Steve Hiller. 4 CDs. (Running Time: 3 hrs.). (Bible Cure Ser.). (ENG.). 2004. audio compact disk 18.99 (978-1-58926-605-6(6)) Oasis Audio.
Are you suffering from heart disease? In this concise, easy-to-read booklet you?ll discover a wealth of information to help you reverse and overcome heart disease! Learn biblical secrets on health and the latest medical research that can set you free from heart disease. You?ll discover findings that your doctor may never have told you. Ways you can reverse clogged arteries: Key foods to avoid-and vital foods to eat-for heart health and healing; Amazing antioxidants-your powerful weapons against heart disease; Discover how to prevent or lower high blood pressure.

Heart Disease & Woman: Awareness & Treatment. Contrib. by Arthur Levy. 2006. DVD 69.95 Apogee Communications.

Heart Earth: A Memoir. abr. ed. Ivan Doig. Read by Ivan Doig. 2 cass. (Running Time: 3 hrs.). 1993. 16.95 (978-0-939643-48-6(0)) Audio Pr.

Heart Earth: A Memoir. abr. ed. Ivan Doig. Read by Ivan Doig. 2 cass. (Running Time: 3 hrs.). Dramatization. 1993. 16.95 Set. (3560, NrthWrd Bks) TandN Child.
Doig was inspired to write "Heart Earth" when he found old letters his mother wrote to her brother, a sailor, during the year prior to her death in 1945.

Heart Earth: A Memoir. unabr. collector's ed. Ivan Doig. Read by Grover Gardner. 4 cass. (Running Time: 4 hrs.). 1994. 24.00 (978-0-7366-2871-6(1), 492818) Books on Tape.
Against the backdrop of WWII, the Doigs migrate from boomtime Arizona to the high country of their Montana origins. It's a drama that builds as only real life can. Doig re-creates the nomadic existence of his family as he works to make it secure.

Heart for God. 4.95 (C9) Carothers.

***Heart for God.** Ave Murray. Narrated by Ave Murray. Ed. by Lael Westmoreland. Music by Lael Westmoreland. Des. by Rhema Release Media. (ENG.). (J). 2010. audio compact disk 20.00 (978-0-9823078-2-3(9)) Barrier Breaker.

Heart for Israel Worship. 2002. audio compact disk Provident Mus Dist.

Heart Full of Diamonds. unabr. ed. Anne Jenner. 2002. 18.00 (978-1-930923-03-4(1)) MediaBay Audio.
Marilee is on the run from her abusive husband, Tony, who she has vowed to kill her. Marilee gets away from Chicago and starts a new life next to neighbors Richard and his son Derreck in Salt Lake City. But just as she settles into her new life, Tony's thugs appear, but this time Marilee has nowhere to hide. Is there a way out? Or will Marilee have to involve Richard, whom she's begun to fall in love with.

Heart Full of Lies: A True Story of Desire & Death. abr. ed. Ann Rule. Read by Blair Brown & Blair Brown. (Running Time: 6 hrs. 0 mins. 0 sec.). (ENG.). 2006. audio compact disk 14.95 (978-0-7435-5520-3(1), S&S Encore) Pub: S&S Audio. Dist(s): S and S Inc

Heart Full of Turquoise. abr. ed. Joe Hayes. 1 cass. (Running Time: 1 hr. 10 min.). (J). (gr. 1-8). 1988. 10.95 (978-0-939729-10-4(5)) Trails West Pub.
Features eight Pueblo Indian tales.

Heart Has Its Reasons, Set. Kerry Blair. 2 cass. 1999. 13.95 (978-1-57734-480-3(4), 07002114) Covenant Comms.
Would you give up Mr. Perfect for Mr. Right?.

Heart Hermeneutics. Rick Joyner. 1 cass. (Running Time: 90 mins.). (Foundation Ser.: Vol.1). 2000. 5.00 (RJ04-001) Morning NC.
Firmly establishing basic Christian principles, these messages also illuminate some of the primary enemies of truth, such as legalism & the control spirit.

Heart (Improving Your Cardiovascular System) Norman J. Caldwell. Read by Norman J. Caldwell. Ed. by Achieve Now Institute Staff. 1 cass. (Running Time: 20 min.). (Health-Imaging Ser.). 1988. 9.97 (978-1-56273-077-2(0)) My Mothers Pub.
We share ways to build, strengthen & love your heart muscle.

Heart in Ice. unabr. ed. Iris Gower. 6 cass. (Isis Ser.). (J). 2002. 54.95 (978-0-7531-1284-7(1)) Pub: ISIS Lrg Prnt GBR. Dist(s): Ulverscroft US

Heart in Motion: Digitally Remastered. Contrib. by Amy Grant. 2007. audio compact disk 13.99 (978-5-557-62603-3(4)) Pt of Grace Ent.

Heart Is a Chocking Hazard (an Essay from Things I've Learned from Women Who've Dumped Me) abr. ed. Stephen Colbert. Read by Stephen Colbert. Ed. by Ben Karlin. (Running Time: 15 mins.). (ENG.). 2008. 1.98 (978-1-60024-333-2(9)) Pub: Hachet Audio. Dist(s): HachBkGrp

Heart Is a Lonely Hunter. unabr. ed. Carson Mc Cullers. Read by Cherry Jones. 9 CDs. (Running Time: 13 hrs. 30 mins.). 2004. audio compact disk 39.95 (978-0-06-076486-9(4)) HarperCollins Pubs.

***Heart Is A Lonely Hunter.** unabr. ed. Carson Mc Cullers. Read by Cherry Jones. (ENG.). 2004. (978-0-06-081385-7(7), Harper Audio); (978-0-06-078262-7(5), Harper Audio) HarperCollins Pubs.

Heart Like His. Virginia H. Pearce. 2006. audio compact disk 14.95 (978-1-59038-696-5(5)) Desert Bks.

Heart Like His: Intimate Reflections on the Life of David. abr. ed. Beth Moore. Narrated by Beth Moore. (ENG.). 2005. 13.99 (978-1-60814-082-4(2)); audio compact disk 19.99 (978-1-59859-104-0(5)) Oasis Audio.

Heart Matters: Loving God the Way He Loves You. abr. ed. Juanita Bynum. Narrated by Kiersten Kingsley. (ENG.). 2007. 6.99 (978-1-60814-010-7(5)); audio compact disk 9.99 (978-1-59859-305-1(6)) Oasis Audio.

Heart, Mediastinum & Great Vessels. D. Hastings-Nield. (Anatomy Project). 1997. audio compact disk 189.95 (978-1-85070-801-8(0), Parthenon Pbng) Pub: CRC Pr. Dist(s): Taylor and Fran

***Heart Mender: A Story of Second Chances.** unabr. ed. Andy Andrews. 2010. audio compact disk 24.99 (978-0-7852-3151-6(X)) Nelson.

Heart, Mind & Soul on Him. Swami Amar Jyoti. 1 cass. 1982. 9.95 (M-34) Truth Consciousness.
Transcending all rungs of the evolutionary ladder; coming home.

Heart of a Champion. unabr. ed. Carl Deuker. Narrated by Greg Longenhagen. 5 pieces. (Running Time: 6 hrs.). (gr. 8 up). 1997. 44.00 (978-0-7887-0791-9(4), 94941E7) Recorded Bks.
Seth, whose father died when he was young, meets Jimmy & his father at the baseball field. Jimmy lives & breathes baseball & an easy friendship develops as both boys play baseball together. Seth soon realizes that he will never be the super ballplayer that Jimmy is, but he practices, dreaming that he will make the varsity team like Jimmy.

Heart of a Champion: Expanding Your Heart for God & Others. Doug Fields. (Super-Ser.). 2007. audio compact disk 40.00 (978-5-557-78140-4(4)) Group Pub.

Heart of a Child. Betsy Rose. 1 cass. (Running Time: 32 min.). 2003. 11.00 (PC49A); audio compact disk 15.00 (PC49CD) Parallax Pr.

Heart of a Doctor. Sara Blaine. Read by Judith Franklyn. 4 cass. (Running Time: 6 hrs.). 1999. 44.95 (66588) Pub: Soundings Ltd GBR. Dist(s): Ulverscroft US

Heart of a Doctor. Sara Blaine. 4 cass. (Sound Ser.). 2004. 44.95 (978-1-85496-658-2(8)) Pub: UlverLrgPrint GBR. Dist(s): Ulverscroft US

Heart of a Dog. Robert Astle. 2002. (978-0-921833-84-0(9)) Sig2nature Eds CAN.

Heart of a Friendship: Friends Again? Narrated by H. J. Arrington. (Running Time: 30 hrs. NaN mins.). (ENG.). (J). 2002. 9.95 (978-1-56554-888-6(4)) Pelican.

Heart of a Love Song. Perf. by William Becton. 1 cass. 10.98 (978-1-57908-232-1(7), 1318); audio compact disk 15.98 CD. (978-1-57908-231-4(9)) Platinm Enter.

***Heart of a Man.** John Eldredge. (ENG.). 2011. audio compact disk 22.99 (978-1-933207-41-4(8)) Ransomed Heart.

Heart of a Man. unabr. collector's ed. Georges Simenon. Read by Michael Prichard. 6 cass. (Running Time: 6 hrs.). 1982. 36.00 (978-0-7366-0532-8(0), 1506) Books on Tape.
The story of a successful French actor who must change his wild-ways because of a deteriorating physical condition.

Heart of a Mentor. Don Nori. 4 cass. 25.00 Set. (978-1-56043-391-0(4)) Destiny Image Pubs.

Heart of a Mother: Mothering from Birth to Adolescence. Featuring The Ransomed Heart Women's Team. 2008. audio compact disk 21.00 (978-1-933207-25-4(6)) Ransomed Heart.

Heart of a Mother Music CD. Perf. by Laurie Z et al. Prod. by World Sound Productions. (ENG.). 2008. audio compact disk 12.95 (978-1-880878-17-0(8)) Sparkle Present.

Heart of a Perfect Man. unabr. ed. Lynne Logan. Read by Lynne Logan. 1 cass. (Running Time: 1 hrs.). 1995. 11.00 (978-1-890907-01-3(4), 0002) Heaven Only.
Biblical principals of a godly man.

Heart of a Shepherd. unabr. ed. Rosanne Parry. Read by Kirby Heyborne. 3 CDs. (Running Time: 3 hrs. 42 mins.). (J). (gr. 4-7). 2009. audio compact disk 30.00 (978-0-7393-8016-1(8), Listening Lib) Pub: Random Audio Pubg. Dist(s): Random

Heart of a Warrior. abr. ed. Johanna Lindsey. Read by Laural Merlington. (Running Time: 6 hrs.). (Ly-san-ter Ser.). 2009. audio compact disk 14.99 (978-1-4233-6641-6(7), 9781423366416) Brilliance Audio.

Heart of a Warrior. unabr. ed. Johanna Lindsey. Read by Laural Merlington. (Running Time: 10 hrs.). (Ly-san-ter Ser.). 2009. 24.99 (978-1-4233-6637-9(9), 9781423366379, Brilliance MP3); 24.99 (978-1-4233-6639-3(5), 9781423366393, BAD); 39.97 (978-1-4233-6638-6(7), 9781423366386, Brinc Audio MP3 Lib); 39.97 (978-1-4233-6640-9(9), 9781423366409, BADLE); audio compact disk 29.99 (978-1-4233-6635-5(2), 9781423366355, Bril Audio CD Unabri); audio compact disk 97.97 (978-1-4233-6636-2(0), 9781423366362, BriAudCD Unabrid) Brilliance Audio.

Heart of Adoption. Perf. by Steve Sweat / Young. Lyrics by Tera Sweat. Arranged by Amy B. Lacey. Music by John Carter & Jay Richards. 2005. audio compact disk 15.95 (978-1-59971-309-0(8)) AardGP.

Heart of America. Mike Trout. 1 cass. 1998. 16.99 (978-0-310-22363-4(6)) Zondervan.

Heart of America. abr. ed. Mike Trout. (Running Time: 2 hrs. 30 mins. 0 sec.). (ENG.). 2003. 9.99 (978-0-310-26053-0(1)) Zondervan.

Heart of Autumn see Robert Penn Warren Reads Selected Poems

Heart of Awareness. Sister Ishpriya. Read by Sister Ishpriya. 6 cass. (Running Time: 5 hrs. 10 min.). 1992. 49.95 Set. (978-7-900781-10-9(2), AA2506) Credence Commun.
Sr. Ishpriya focuses on the disciplines of awareness.

Heart of Bamboo: Poetry & Music in the Zen Tradition. Sam Hamill. (Listener's Guide to Poetry Ser.: Vol. 2). (ENG.). 1999. audio compact disk 12.00 (978-1-55659-999-6(4)) Pub: Copper Canyon. Dist(s): Consort Bk Sales

Heart of Change: Real-Life Stories of How People Change Their Organizations. unabr. ed. John P. Kotter & Dan S. Cohen. Read by Oliver Wyman. 5 CDs. (Running Time: 5 hrs. 30 mins. 0 sec.). (ENG.). 2008. audio compact disk 29.95 (978-1-4272-0234-5(6)) Pub: Macmill Audio. Dist(s): Macmillan

Heart of Danger. unabr. ed. Gerald Seymour. Read by Nigel Graham. 12 cass. (Running Time: 14 hrs. 50 min.). (Isis Ser.). (J). 1995. 94.95 (978-1-85695-888-2(4), 950904) Pub: ISIS Lrg Prnt GBR. Dist(s): Ulverscroft US

Heart of Danger. unabr. ed. Gerald Seymour. Read by Nigel Graham. 15 CDs. (Running Time: 22 hrs. 30 min.). (Isis Ser.). (J). 2002. audio compact disk 104.95 (978-0-7531-1250-2(7), 1250-7) Pub: ISIS Lrg Prnt GBR. Dist(s): Ulverscroft US
In the wrecked Groat village of Rosenovici, a mass grave is uncovered & the mutilated body of a young Englishwoman, Dorrie Mowat, is exhumed. Her mother, who loathed Dorrie in life, becomes obsessed to discover the truth of her daughter's death. But with civil war tearing apart the former Yugoslavia, none of the authorities there or in England are interested in a "minor" war crime. Dorrie's mother hires Bill Penn, private investigator, M15 reject. For Penn this should be a chance to pick up a good fee for a trip to safe Zagreb & the writing of a useless report. But Penn begins to learn of the last hours of Dorrie's life & the image of the young woman draws him

inexorably towards the killing grounds behind the lines, to find the truth of her death & perhaps the truth about himself.

Heart of Darkness. 1984. (1098) Books on Tape.

Heart of Darkness. 1979. (C-5) Jimcin Record.

Heart of Darkness. Joseph Conrad. Narrated by Flo Gibson. (ENG.). 2008. audio compact disk 19.95 (978-1-55685-986-1(4)) Audio Bk Con.

Heart of Darkness. Joseph Conrad. Read by Michael Thompson. (Running Time: 4 hrs. 30 min.). 21.95 (HarperThor) HarpC GBR.

Heart of Darkness. Joseph Conrad. Read by Ralph Cosham. (Running Time: 3 hrs. 45 mins.). 2002. 20.95 (978-1-59912-077-5(1), Audiofy Corp) Iofy Corp.

Heart of Darkness. Joseph Conrad. Read by Scott Brick. (Running Time: 4 hrs. 45 mins.). 2002. 25.95 (978-1-60083-630-5(5), Audiofy Corp) Iofy Corp.

Heart of Darkness. Joseph Conrad. Read by Ray Verna. 3 cass. (Running Time: 4 hrs.). 1993. 32.00 Set. (978-1-56544-021-0(8), 350010); Rental 6.80 30 day rental Set. (350010) Literate Ear.
This volume is said to be a slightly fictionalized record of Conrad's nightmare experience in the Congo, where his health was seriously imperiled & his view of human nature permanently darkened.

Heart of Darkness. Joseph Conrad. Narrated by Ralph Cosham. (Running Time: 13500 sec.). (Unabridged Classics in MP3 Ser.). (ENG.). 2008. audio compact disk 14.95 (978-1-58472-518-3(4), In Aud); audio compact disk 24.00 (978-1-58472-519-0(2), In Aud) Sound Room.

Heart of Darkness. Joseph Conrad. Narrated by Scott Brick. (ENG.). 2005. audio compact disk 58.00 (978-1-4001-3061-0(1)) Pub: Tantor Media. Dist(s): IngramPubServ

***Heart of Darkness.** Joseph Conrad. Read by David Case. (Running Time: 14400 sec.). (ENG.). 2007. audio compact disk 19.95 (978-1-4332-0383-1(9)) Blckstn Audio.

Heart of Darkness. abr. ed. Joseph Conrad. Read by Joss Ackland. 2 cass. (Running Time: 3 hrs). (YA). (gr. 9-12). 1999. 16.99 (978-0-00-105049-5(4)) Pub: HarpC GBR. Dist(s): Trafalgar

Heart of Darkness. abr. ed. Joseph Conrad. Perf. by Christopher Cazenove. 4 cass. (Running Time: 6 hrs.). 2004. 25.00 (978-1-59007-117-5(4)) Pub: New Millenn Enter. Dist(s): PerseuPGW
the novel tells the story of Marlow, a seaman who undertakes his own journey into the African jungle to find the tormented white trader Kurtz.

Heart of Darkness. abr. ed. Joseph Conrad. (Classic Stage Ser.). 2004. audio compact disk 14.99 (978-1-894003-31-5(4)) Pub: Scenario Prods CAN. Dist(s): Baker Taylor

Heart of Darkness. unabr. ed. Joseph Conrad. Read by Dan O'Herlihy. 4 cass. 23.80 (E-413) Audio Bk.

Heart of Darkness. unabr. ed. Joseph Conrad. Read by Frederick Davidson. 3 cass. (Running Time: 4 hrs. 30 min.). (J). (gr. 9-12). 1994. 23.95 (978-0-7861-0442-0(2), 1394) Blckstn Audio.
Marlow, the story's narrator, tells his friends of an experience in the British Congo where he once ran a river steamer for a trading company. He tells of the ivory traders' cruel exploitation of the natives there. Chief among these is a greedy & treacherous European named Kurtz, a man who has used savagery to obtain semi-divine power over the natives. While Marlow tries to get Kurtz back down the river, Kurtz tries to justify his actions & motions, asserting that he has seen into the very heart of things.

Heart of Darkness. unabr. ed. Joseph Conrad. Read by Frederick Davidson. (Running Time: 4 hrs.). 1998. audio compact disk 36.00 (978-1-4332-0380-0(4)) Blckstn Audio.

Heart of Darkness. unabr. ed. Joseph Conrad. Read by David Case. 4 CDs. (Running Time: 14400 sec.). 2007. audio compact disk 19.95 (978-1-4332-0382-4(0)) Blckstn Audio.

Heart of Darkness. unabr. ed. Joseph Conrad. Read by David Case. (Running Time: 14400 sec.). 2007. audio compact disk 29.95 (978-0-7861-5867-6(0)); audio compact disk 36.00 (978-0-7861-5866-9(2)) Blckstn Audio.

Heart of Darkness. unabr. ed. Joseph Conrad. Read by Jack Sondericker. 4 cass. (Running Time: 4 hrs. 30 min.). 1987. 26.95 (978-1-55686-232-8(6)) Books in Motion.
Based on Conrad's personal experience in Central Africa and parallels many of the events that occurred while he worked his way up the Congo River.

Heart of Darkness. unabr. ed. Joseph Conrad. 4 cass. (Running Time: 6 hrs.). 2001. 24.95 (978-0-7366-6820-0(9)) Books on Tape.
Conrad's classic river journey in the African jungle.

Heart of Darkness. unabr. ed. Joseph Conrad. Read by Alistair Maydon. 8 cass. (Running Time: 11 hrs.). (Isis Ser.). 1993. 69.95 set. (978-1-85089-731-6(X), 89084) Eye Ear.
These three Joseph Conrad stories describe the three stages of manhood. "Youth" explores a young boy's reactions to his first sea-voyage. "Heart of Darkness" is set in the west African jungle & concerns the search of a long-lost explorer. "The End of the Tether" introduces us to an old sea-captain discovering the corruptions of his crew.

Heart of Darkness. unabr. ed. Joseph Conrad. Read by Ralph Cosham. (YA). 2007. 39.99 (978-1-59895-855-3(0)) Find a World.

Heart of Darkness. unabr. ed. Joseph Conrad. Read by Alistair Maydon. 8 cass. (Running Time: 12 hrs.). 2001. 69.95 (89084) Pub: ISIS Audio GBR. Dist(s): Ulverscroft US

Heart of Darkness, unabr. ed. Joseph Conrad. Narrated by Michael Thompson. 3 cass. (Running Time: 4 hrs. 30 mins.). 1989. 26.00 (978-1-55690-220-8(4), 89470E7) Recorded Bks.
Marlow, Conrad's famous maritime wanderer & narrator, spins a story with a mysterious thread: how he shipped on a steamer bound for Africa, how he landed on the banks of "the big river" & how he first heard the name Kurtz, the enigmatic figure at the heart of darkness.

Heart of Darkness. unabr. ed. Joseph Conrad. Read by Ralph Cosham. 4 cds. (Running Time: 3 hrs 44 mins). 2002. pap. bk. (978-1-58472-258-8(4), In Aud) Sound Room.
Adventure in the Belgian Congo.

Heart of Darkness. unabr. ed. Joseph Conrad. Read by Ralph Cosham. 4 cds. (Running Time: 3 hrs 44 mins). 2002. audio compact disk 26.95 (978-1-58472-256-4(8), 017, In Aud) Pub: Sound Room. Dist(s): Baker Taylor

Heart of Darkness. unabr. ed. Joseph Conrad. Narrated by Scott Brick. (Running Time: 4 hrs. 30 mins. 0 sec.). (ENG.). 2008. 19.99 (978-1-4001-5846-1(X)); audio compact disk 19.99 (978-1-4001-0846-6(2)); audio compact disk 39.99 (978-1-4001-3846-3(9)) Pub: Tantor Media. Dist(s): IngramPubServ

Heart of Darkness, Set. unabr. ed. Joseph Conrad. Read by Frederick Davidson. 3 cass. 1999. 23.95 (FS9-51135) Highsmith.

Heart of Darkness, Set. unabr. ed. Joseph Conrad. Read by Ralph Cosham. 2 cass. (Running Time: 3 hrs.). 24.95 (978-1-883049-78-2(4), Commuters Library) Sound Room.
An intriguing tale of adventure in the Belgian Congo by one of the great prose stylists of the last century.

Heart of Darkness: An A+ Audio Study Guide. unabr. ed. John Jones. (Running Time: 1 hr.). (ENG.). 2006. 5.98 (978-1-59483-710-4(4)) Pub: Hachet Audio. Dist(s): HachBkGrp

Heart of Darkness & Other Stories, Set. unabr. ed. Joseph Conrad. Read by Norman Barrs. 6 cass. (Running Time: 8 hrs. 20 min.). Incl. Lagoon. (CXL 525CX); Lord Jim. Joseph Conrad. (CXL 525CX); Secret Sharer. (CXL 525CX); Typhoon. (CXL 525CX); Youth. (CXL 525CX); 1985. 44.98 (978-0-8072-3012-1(X), CXL 525CX, Listening Lib) Random Audio Pubg.
Conrad's best works are represented in this collection, which features his novel, "Heart of Darkness", the allegorical tale of a man's journey up a river in search of a madman. This was the basis for the movie "Apocalyse Now". Master of the psychological tale, Conrad created an important literary heritage for the 20th century fiction writer.

Heart of Darkness, The Nigger of the Narcissus. Joseph Conrad. Read by Wolfram Kandinsky. 7 cass. (Running Time: 10 hrs.30 mins.). 1978. 56.00 (978-0-7366-0090-3(6)) Books on Tape.
Narcissus is an adventure at sea, Darkness is a journey into Africa.

Heart of Darkness; Typhoon. Joseph Conrad. Read by Michael M. Thompson & George Guidall. 5 Cass. (Running Time: 7.5 Hrs.). 19.95 (978-1-4025-1148-6(5)) Recorded Bks.

Heart of Darkne16. unabr. ed. Joseph Conrad. Narrated by Flo Gibson. 3 cass. (Running Time: 4 hrs. 30 mins.). 2003. 16.95 (978-1-55685-707-2(1)) Audio Bk Con.
Set in the Belgian Congo jungle Marlow searches for the powerful ivory trader Kurtz in an atmosphere of evil.

Heart of David. unabr. ed. Rick Joyner. 3 cass. (Running Time: 4 hrs. 30 mins.). 2000. 15.00 (RJ13-000) Morning NC.
"Restoring the Tabernacle of David," "Restoration is Hard Work" & "the Kingdom is Here - Dwell in it." These tapes not only address the need for a foundation of truth; they impart the essential devotion of having a love for the truth.

Heart of Enlightenment. Jangon Kongtrul. Read by Jangon Kongtrul. 3 cass. 1984. 34.00 (A173) Vajradhatu.

Heart of Fire. unabr. ed. Linda Howard. Read by Tanya Eby Sirois & Tanya Eby. 1 MP3-CD. (Running Time: 11 hrs.). 2009. 39.97 (978-1-4233-6312-5(4), 9781423363125, Brlnc Audio MP3 Lib) Brilliance Audio.

Heart of Fire. unabr. ed. Linda Howard. Read by Tanya Eby. 1 MP3-CD. (Running Time: 11 hrs.). 2009. 24.99 (978-1-4233-6311-8(6), 9781423363118, Brilliance MP3); 24.99 (978-1-4233-6313-2(2), 9781423363132, BAD) Brilliance Audio.

Heart of Fire. unabr. ed. Linda Howard. Read by Tanya Eby Sirois & Tanya Eby. 10 CDs. (Running Time: 11 hrs.). 2009. audio compact disk 92.97 (978-1-4233-6310-1(8), 9781423363101, BriAudCD Unabrid) Brilliance Audio.

Heart of Fire. unabr. ed. Linda Howard. Read by Tanya Eby. 10 CDs. (Running Time: 11 hrs.). 2009. audio compact disk 29.99 (978-1-4233-6309-5(4), 9781423363095, Bril Audio CD Unabri) Brilliance Audio.

Heart of Fire. unabr. ed. Linda Howard. Read by Tanya Eby. (Running Time: 11 hrs.). 2009. 39.97 (978-1-4418-5027-0(9), 9781441850270, BADLE) Brilliance Audio.

Heart of Flesh: A Feminist Spirituality for Women & Men. unabr. ed. Joan Chittister. Read by Joan Chittister. 1997. 7.00 (978-1-890890-35-3(9)) Benetvision.

Heart of Forgiveness. Tara Singh. 1 cass. (Running Time: 1 hr. 30 min.). (Exploring a Course in Miracles Ser.). 1986. 9.95 (978-1-55531-023-3(0), #A007) Life Action Pr.
A session on Relationship & the part forgiveness plays. Forgiveness is a basic principle in a Course In Miracles.

Heart of God Revealed: Luke 2:11. Ed Young. 1982. 4.95 (978-0-7417-1270-7(9), 270) Win Walk.

***Heart of Ice.** unabr. ed. Lis Wiehl & April Henry. (Faith & Consequences Ser.). 2011. audio compact disk 24.99 (978-1-4003-1681-6(2)) Nelson.

Heart of India. unabr. ed. Mark Tully. Read by Mark Tully. 8 cass. (Running Time: 8 hrs.). 1997. 69.95 Set. (978-0-7451-6759-6(4), CAB 1375) AudioGO.
With many experiences in India, Mark Tully has collated a series of stories which describe the unique atmosphere of the country. This anthology includes stories about the impact of traditional village life in India: A barren wife visits a holy man; a son plots revenge against his father's murderer, & a woman is persuaded by her friends to spurn an arranged marriage. Based on fact, these fictional stories capture the essence of all things Indian.

Heart of Jabez CD Pack. 2002. audio compact disk (978-1-931713-31-3(6)) Word For Today.

Heart of Justice. unabr. ed. William J. Coughlin. Read by Dick Hill. (Running Time: 11 hrs.). 2009. 39.97 (978-1-4233-8627-8(2), 9781423386278, Brlnc Audio MP3 Lib); 39.97 (978-1-4233-8629-2(9), 9781423386292, BADLE); 24.99 (978-1-4233-8626-1(4), 9781423386261, Brilliance MP3); 24.99 (978-1-4233-8628-5(0), 9781423386285, BAD) Brilliance Audio.

***Heart of Lies: A Novel.** Zondervan. (Irish Angel Ser.). (ENG.). 2011. 14.99 (978-0-310-41302-8(8)) Zondervan.

Heart of Me. Perf. by Kathy Troccoli. 2002. audio compact disk Reunion Recs.

***Heart of Memory: A Novel.** Zondervan. (ENG.). 2011. 12.99 (978-0-310-41343-1(5)) Zondervan.

Heart of Midlothian see Cambridge Treasury of English Prose: Austen to Bronte

Heart of Perfect Wisdom. Perf. by Robert Gass & On Wings of Song. 1 cass. (Running Time: 1 hr.). 9.98 (SA234) White Dove NM.
The latest in the chant series, based on the Heart Sutra, chanted by Buddhists around the world. Side One, Gate Gate, uses male voices, Celtic harp & Tibetan bells. Side Two features Tibetan & Mongolian overtone chanting with Tibetan bells & Nepalese bamboo flutes.

Heart of Praise. 2005. audio compact disk (978-0-9772969-3-4(8)) PFC Inc.

Heart of Princess Osra. unabr. ed. Anthony Hope-Hawkins. Read by Patrick Treadway. 6 cass. (Running Time: 6 hrs.). Dramatization. 1991. 39.95 (978-1-55686-384-4(5), 384) Books in Motion.
Beautiful Princess Osra attracts & breaks the hearts of many suitors, but she finds herself caught in webs of romance, mystery, intrigue & royal adventure.

Heart of Religious Vocation, Set. Joan Chittister. 2 cass. (Running Time: 2 hrs.). 1995. 17.95 Credence Commun.
When religious leaders in charge of vocations for the congregations met, they invited Joan Chittister to give them direction & inspriation. She did. In two firey talks on the heart of religious vocation, Chittister packed an uncommon amount of scripture, social analysis, religious history & personal feminine spirituality. Required viewing for all religious, salutary viewing for anybody in ministry, religious or not.

***Heart of Remarriage.** unabr. ed. Greg Smalley. Narrated by Maurice England. (ENG.). 2010. 14.98 (978-1-59644-994-7(2), christianSeed); audio compact disk 24.98 (978-1-59644-993-0(4), christianSeed) christianaud.

Heart of Rock 'N' Roll: 1958. 1 cass. 1999. 9.99 (MYN7J4); audio compact disk 9.99 (M94MN0) Time-Life.

Heart of Rock 'N' Roll: 1959. 1 cass. 1999. 9.99 (TTBVA0); audio compact disk 9.99 (TUBVEO) Time-Life.

***Heart of Stone: A Novel.** unabr. ed. Jill Marie Landis. (Running Time: 9 hrs. 36 mins. 0 sec.). (Irish Angel Ser.). (ENG.). 2010. 15.99 (978-0-310-39575-1(5)) Zondervan.

***Heart of the Artist: A Character-Building Guide for You & Your Ministry Team.** Rory Noland. (Running Time: 11 hrs. 46 mins. 0 sec.). (ENG.). 2008. 16.99 (978-0-310-30451-7(2)) Zondervan.

Heart of the Beloved. Read by Wayne Monbleau. 2 cass. 1995. 10.00 Set. (978-0-944648-36-0(3), LGT-1241) Loving Grace Pubns.
Religious.

Heart of the Celts. 1 cass. 9.98; audio compact disk 15.98 Lifedance.
Gaelic vocals, winds, guitar, electronic instruments, fiddle & more accompany native Irishwomen singing haunting love songs of the Celts with sweet poetry. A few contemporary pieces as well as traditionals. Demo CD or cassette available.

***Heart of the City: Nine Stories of Love & Serendipity on the Streets of New York.** unabr. ed. Ariel Sabar. (Running Time: 9 hrs.). 2011. 29.95 (978-1-4417-6836-0(X)); 59.95 (978-1-4417-6833-9(5)); audio compact disk 29.95 (978-1-4417-6835-3(1)); audio compact disk 76.00 (978-1-4417-6834-6(3)) Blckstn Audio.

Heart of the Dreaming. Di Morrissey. Read by Natalie Bate. 12 cass. (Running Time: 18 hrs.). 2000. (978-1-876584-70-2(X), 591108) Bolinda Pubng AUS.
At twenty-one Queenie Hanlon has the world at her feet. At twenty-two her life lies in ruins. A series of disasters has robbed her of everything she has ever loved. Everything except Tingulla, her ancestral home & her spirit's dreaming place. Now she is about to lose that, too.

***Heart of the Dreaming.** Di Morrissey. Read by Natalie Bate. (Running Time: 16 hrs. 15 mins.). 2010. 109.99 (978-1-74214-625-6(2), 9781742146256) Pub: Bolinda Pubng AUS. Dist(s): Bolinda Pub Inc

***Heart of the Dreaming.** unabr. ed. Di Morrissey. Read by Natalie Bate. 13 CDs. (Running Time: 16 hrs. 15 mins.). 2009. audio compact disk 34.95 (978-1-74233-283-3(8)) Pub: Bolinda Pubng AUS. Dist(s): Bolinda Pub Inc

Heart of the Dreaming. unabr. ed. Di Morrissey. Read by Natalie Bate. (Running Time: 16 hrs. 15 mins.). 2009. audio compact disk 113.95 (978-1-74214-445-0(4), 9781742144450) Pub: Bolinda Pubng AUS. Dist(s): Bolinda Pub Inc

Heart of the Family. unabr. collector's ed. Elizabeth Goudge. Read by Wanda McCaddon. 10 cass. (Running Time: 15 hrs.). 1983. 80.00 (978-0-7366-0485-7(5), 1460) Books on Tape.
Courage & integrity are lyrically interwoven in this story of a brotherhood of spirit as well as of blood. It takes the intrusion of a stranger, an Austrian victimized by war & ravaged by guilt & hatred, to provide a spirited catalyst to help the troubled family find its own peace.

Heart of the Five Love Languages. unabr. ed. Gary Chapman. Narrated by Chris Fabry. (ENG.). 2008. 6.99 (978-1-60814-011-4(3)); audio compact disk 9.99 (978-1-59859-392-1(7)) Oasis Audio.

Heart of the Gospel. 2002. audio compact disk (978-1-931713-29-0(4)) Word For Today.

Heart of the Gospel. 2001. (978-1-931713-03-0(0)) Word For Today.

***Heart of the Matter.** abr. ed. Emily Giffin. Read by Cynthia Nixon. 4 CDs. (Running Time: 5 hrs. 30 mins. 0 sec.). 2010. audio compact disk 24.99 (978-1-4272-0959-7(6)) Pub: Macmill Audio. Dist(s): Macmillan

***Heart of the Matter.** unabr. ed. Emily Giffin. Narrated by Cynthia Nixon. 1 Playaway. (Running Time: 10 hrs. 30 mins.). 2010. 94.95 (978-0-7927-7205-7(9)); audio compact disk 89.95 (978-0-7927-7148-7(6)) AudioGO.

***Heart of the Matter.** unabr. ed. Emily Giffin. Read by Cynthia Nixon. 8 CDs. (Running Time: 10 hrs. 30 mins. 0 sec.). 2010. audio compact disk 39.99 (978-1-4272-0961-0(8)) Pub: Macmill Audio. Dist(s): Macmillan

Heart of the Matter. unabr. ed. Graham Greene. Read by Michael Kitchen. 8 cass. (Running Time: 12 hrs.). 2000. 69.95 (978-0-7540-0438-7(4), CAB 1861) AudioGO.
Scobie is an officer in a war-torn West African state. When he is passed over for a promotion, he borrows money to send his wife away on holiday. In her absence, he falls in love with Helen, a young widow & his life is transformed. With an inability to distinguish between love, pity & responsibility, Scobie moves towards his final damnation.

Heart of the Matter, unabr. ed. Graham Greene. Read by Joseph Porter. 8 cass. (Running Time: 11 hrs. 30 mins.). 1994. 56.95 (978-0-7861-0479-6(1), 1431) Blckstn Audio.
The first half of this novel ranks with Greene's best writing. Scobie, a British policeman on the west coast of Africa during World War II, is the quintessential Greene protagonist. After 15 years of foreign service, he has the respect of local swindlers for not succumbing to their bribes; his longstanding servant is devoted to him; he knows how to handle both his superiors & his subordinates; but in matters of love & faith his life is destined to unravel. After he borrows from the wrong man to placate his discontented wife, a love affair lays him open to blackmail & disrupts the psychic balance of his religion, which is precisely where the novel goes wrong.

***Heart of the Matter.** unabr. ed. Graham Greene. Read by Joseph Porter. (Running Time: 11 hrs. 30 mins.). 2010. audio compact disk 100.00 (978-1-4417-0481-8(7)) Blckstn Audio.

***Heart of the Matter.** unabr. ed. Graham Greene. Read by Joseph Porter. (Running Time: 10 hrs. 5 mins.). 2011. 29.95 (978-1-4417-0484-9(1)); audio compact disk 29.95 (978-1-4417-0483-2(3)) Blckstn Audio.

Heart of the Mountain Man. abr. ed. William W. Johnstone. Read by Jim Gough. 4 cass. (Running Time: 6 hrs.). (Mountain Man Ser.: No. 25). 2002. 24.95 (978-1-890990-88-6(4), 99088) Otis Audio.
Western with sound effects.

Heart of the Movies. Music by Sally Harmon. 1 cass.; 1 CD. 1998. 9.98; audio compact disk 15.98 CD. Lifedance.
Sophisticated album of songs from "Titanic," "Toy Story" & "Batman Forever".

***Heart of the Night.** abr. ed. Barbara Delinsky. Read by Sandra Burr. (Running Time: 6 hrs.). 2010. audio compact disk 9.99 (978-1-4418-6697-4(3), 9781441866974, BCD Value Price) Brilliance Audio.

Heart of the Night. unabr. ed. Barbara Delinsky. Read by Sandra Burr. 10 cass. (Running Time: 13 hrs.). 2003. 97.25 (978-1-58788-825-0(4), 1587888254); 34.95 (978-1-58788-824-3(6), 1587888246) Brilliance Audio.
Dear Reader, When I think of Heart of the Night, I think of one of the characters in the book, late-night disc jockey Jared Snow. So do many of my readers, if the mail they send me is any indication. It's his voice - always his voice - there on the radio, as soothing as a massage and twice as sexy. For me, Jared Snow is also a concept, the idea that a single voice on the radio is heard by many different people, with a different effect on each. I wrote Heart of the Night in 1988. I was still writing category romances at the time, but this book is different. In the solving of the kidnapping of a society wife, it has a strong element of mystery. In the relationship between twins

Savannah and Susan, it explores the issue of sibling rivalry. And yes, it has a love story, but one that is deeper, stronger, and hotter than I had been allowed by the constraints of the genre. How does Jared Snow fit in? As Savannah and Susan look for the missing woman, the trail they follow leads to one desperate voice, that of an anonymous caller who pours out her heart to a certain radio personality. My writing style has changed since I wrote this book, but the heart and soul of my characters have not. The emotional intensity here is the very same that marks my current work. Please enjoy Heart of the Night as much as I did then -and do now. Warmly, Barbara Delinsky.

Heart of the Night. unabr. ed. Barbara Delinsky. Read by Sandra Burr. (Running Time: 13 hrs.). 2004. 39.25 (978-1-59335-459-6(2), 1593354592, Brlnc Audio MP3 Lib) Brilliance Audio.

Heart of the Night. unabr. ed. Barbara Delinsky. Read by Sandra Burr. (Running Time: 13 hrs.). 2004. 39.25 (978-1-59710-355-8(1), 1597103551, BADLE); 24.95 (978-1-59710-354-1(3), 1597103543, BAD) Brilliance Audio.

***Heart of the Night.** unabr. ed. Barbara Delinsky. Read by Sandra Burr. (Running Time: 15 hrs.). 2010. audio compact disk 89.97 (978-1-4418-4062-2(1), 9781441840622, BriAudCD Unabrid); audio compact disk 29.99 (978-1-4418-4061-5(3), 9781441840615, Bril Audio CD Unabri) Brilliance Audio.

Heart of the Night. unabr. ed. Barbara Delinsky. Read by Sandra Burr. (Running Time: 13 hrs.). 2004. 24.95 (978-1-59335-089-5(9), 1593350899) Soulmate Audio Bks.

Heart of the Piano Concerto. Created by Hal Leonard Corporation Staff. 2006. pap. bk. 34.98 (978-1-59615-020-1(3), 1596150203) Pub: Music Minus. Dist(s): H Leonard

Heart of the Psalms. unabr. ed. Read by Wayne Monbleau. Perf. by Dick Tilton. 1 cass. (Running Time: 45 min.). 1993. 10.00 (978-0-944648-11-7(8)) Loving Grace Pubns.

The reading of the Psalms over a beautiful, sensitive & meditative score.

Heart of the Sea. Nora Roberts. Read by Patricia Daniels. (Irish Trilogy: Vol. 3). 2009. 69.99 (978-1-60775-876-1(8)) Find a World.

***Heart of the Sea.** abr. ed. Nora Roberts. Read by Patricia Daniels. (Running Time: 6 hrs.). (Irish Trilogy: Vol. 3). 2010. audio compact disk 9.99 (978-1-4418-5094-2(5), 9781441850942, BCD Value Price) Brilliance Audio.

Heart of the Sea. unabr. ed. Nora Roberts. Read by Patricia Daniels. (Running Time: 10 hrs.). (Irish Trilogy: Vol. 3). 2005. 49.97 (978-1-59600-969-1(1), 9781596009691, BADLE); 24.95 (978-1-59600-968-4(3), 9781596009684, BAD); audio compact disk 39.25 (978-1-59600-967-7(5), 9781596009677, Brlnc Audio MP3 Lib); audio compact disk 24.95 (978-1-59600-966-0(7), 9781596009660, Brilliance MP3); audio compact disk 97.25 (978-1-59600-965-3(9), 9781596009653, BriAudCD Unabrid); audio compact disk 36.95 (978-1-59600-964-6(0), 9781596009646, Bril Audio CD Unabri) Brilliance Audio.

Darcy Gallagher has always believed in the pull of fate, the magic of legend . . . and the importance of money. She longs to find a rich man who will sweep her away - into a world filled with glamour and adventure, and the exotic life that is her destiny. A wealthy businessman with Irish blood, Trevor Magee has come to Ardmore to build a theater - and uncover secrets hidden in his family's past. He thought he had given up on love long ago, but Darcy Gallagher tempts him like no women ever has. She's gorgeous, intelligent, and she knows what she wants - and he's more than willing to give it to her. But as their mutual attraction flares into passion, they look into their hearts - and find out what happens when you truly believe. .

Heart of the Soul. abr. ed. Gary Zukav & Linda Francis. Based on a work by Linda Francis. 6 CDs. (Running Time: 70 hrs. 0 mins. 0 sec.). (ENG.). 2001. audio compact disk 32.00 (978-0-7435-0905-3(6), Sound Ideas) Pub: S&S Audio. Dist(s): S and S Inc

Heart of the Sunset. unabr. ed. Rex Ellingwood Beach. Read by Gene Engene. 8 cass. (Running Time: 11 hrs. 30 min.). Dramatization. 1991. 49.95 (978-1-55686-366-0(7), 366) Books in Motion.

A Texas romance set against the backdrop of the failed Mexican revolution of the early 1900's.

Heart of the World. 1 cass. (Running Time: 58 min.). 2003. 9.95 (978-1-58467-016-2(9)) Gentle Wind.

Heart of the World. Hans Urs Von Balthasar. 7 cass. 28.95 (910) Ignatius Pr.

Lyrical meditation on Our Lord's love for the Church.

Heart of Troy. Ed Lange. 2 CDs. (Running Time: 2 hours). Dramatization. 2004. audio compact disk 16.95 (978-1-892613-13-4(1), FamClassAudBks) NYS Theatre Inst.

An historical drama centering on the indomitable, true-life characters of Betsey Howard Hart and her husband, Richard P. Hart, "The Heart of Troy" journeys through time and explores the life of this remarkable couple during years of momentous change in the 1800s. At a time when steamboats changed a river, the Erie Canal changed a state, and railroads changed a world, Troy and Albany locked horns in bitter rivalry, with Erastus Corning, Emma Willard, and others figuring prominently by their contributions and accomplishments.

Heart of Understanding: Commentaries on the Prajnaparamita Heart Sutra. Thich Nhat Hanh. 2 CDs. (Running Time: 120 min.). (ENG.). 2002. audio compact disk 19.00 (978-1-888375-27-5(2), 75272) Pub: Parallax Pr. Dist(s): PerseuPGW

MERGE WITH LOOKING DEEPLY - 464 "Form is emptiness, emptiness is form, form does not differ from emptiness, emptiness does not differ from form." Recorded at the Green Gulch Zen Center, Muir Beach, California, on April 19, 1987, Thich Nhat Hanh discusses.

Heart of Valor. unabr. ed. Tanya Huff. Narrated by Marguerite Gavin. (Running Time: 12 hrs. 0 mins. 0 sec.). (Confederation Ser.). (ENG.). 2009. audio compact disk 29.99 (978-1-4001-5989-5(X)); audio compact disk 79.99 (978-1-4001-3989-7(9)) Pub: Tantor Media. Dist(s): IngramPubServ

Heart of Valor. unabr. ed. Tanya Huff. Narrated by Marguerite Gavin. (Running Time: 12 hrs. 0 mins. 0 sec.). (Confederation Ser.). (ENG.). 2009. audio compact disk 39.99 (978-1-4001-0989-0(2)) Pub: Tantor Media. Dist(s): IngramPubServ

***Heart of Valor.** unabr. ed. L. J. Smith. Read by Khristine Hvam. (Running Time: 7 hrs.). 2010. 39.97 (978-1-4418-7212-8(4), 9781441872128, BADLE) Brilliance Audio.

***Heart of Valor.** unabr. ed. L. J. Smith. Read by Trish Telep Editors & Khristine Hvam. (Running Time: 7 hrs.). 2010. audio compact disk 19.99 (978-1-4418-7208-1(6), 9781441872081, Bril Audio CD Unabri) Brilliance Audio.

***Heart of Valor.** unabr. ed. Trish Telep Editors & L. J. Smith. Read by Khristine Hvam. (Running Time: 7 hrs.). 2010. 39.97 (978-1-4418-7211-1(6), 9781441872111, Brlnc Audio MP3 Lib); 19.99 (978-1-4418-7210-4(8), 9781441872104, Brilliance MP3); audio compact disk 59.97 (978-1-4418-7209-8(4), 9781441872098, BriAudCD Unabrid) Brilliance Audio.

Heart of War. abr. ed. Lucian K. Truscott, IV. Read by David Dukes. 4 cass. (Running Time: 6 hrs.). 2001. 25.00 (978-1-59040-179-8(4), Phoenix Audio) Pub: Amer Intl Pub. Dist(s): PerseuPGW

Heart of War, Pt. 1. unabr. collector's ed. John Masters. Read by Walter Zimmerman. 9 cass. (Running Time: 13 hrs. 30 min.). (Loss of Eden Ser.). 1986. 72.00 (978-0-7366-0757-5(9), 1715A) Books on Tape.

The middle years of WWII were desperate for the English. Britain never broke, but some British bent - an adjutant sleeps with his commander's wife, a pilot weeps for his fallen foes, a woman donates herself along with the coffee & biscuits she distributes at the canteen - this is their story.

Heart of War, Pt. 2. collector's ed. John Masters. Read by Walter Zimmerman. 10 cass. (Running Time: 15 hrs.). (Loss of Eden Ser.). 1986. 80.00 (978-0-7366-0758-2(7), 1715-B) Books on Tape.

Heart of Wisdom: An Explanation of the Heart Sutra. Geshe Kelsang Gyatso. Narrated by Michael Sington. 6 CDs. (Running Time: 6 hrs. 0 mins. 0 sec.). (ENG.). 2003. audio compact disk 29.95 (978-0-948006-84-5(6)) Pub: Tharpa Pubns GBR. Dist(s): IPG Chicago

Heart of Yoga. Shiva Rea. 4 CDs. (Running Time: 4 hrs. 30 mins.). 2002. audio compact disk 39.95 (978-1-59179-025-9(5), AW00660D) Sounds True.

Vinyasa or "flow" yoga is traditional yoga, energized with movement and the breath. At studios and workshops across the country, flow yoga is in high demand, and growing more popular every day. Now, this offers two of the most popular flow yoga classes, bringing these exhilarating alternative to yoga students everywhere. Yoga Chant and Yoga Trance Dance.

Heart Only Knows. Kerry Blair. 5 cass. 2004. 21.95 (978-1-57734-862-7(1)) Covenant Comms.

Heart Palpitations: Possible Causes, Testing, & Therapies. unabr. ed. Gary S. Ross. Interview with Kathleen S. Ross. 1 cass. (Running Time: 44 min.). (Natural Treatment Ser.). 1994. 15.00 (978-1-891875-01-4(9)) Creat Hlth Wrks.

Explains possible root causes of heart palpitations (cardiac arrythmias). Includes helpful testing & effective natural treatments.

***Heart Revolution: Experience the Power of a Turned Heart.** unabr. ed. Sergio de La Mora. (Running Time: 6 hrs. 0 mins. 0 sec.). (ENG.). 2011. audio compact disk 21.98 (978-1-61045-024-9(8)) christianaud.

Heart-Shaped Box. unabr. ed. Joe Hill. Read by Stephen Lang. 9 CDs. (Running Time: 39600 sec.). 2007. audio compact disk 39.95 (978-0-06-123587-0(3)) HarperCollins Pubs.

***Heart-Shaped Box.** unabr. ed. Joe Hill. Read by Stephen Lang. (ENG.). 2007. (978-0-06-126240-1(4), Harper Audio); (978-0-06-126239-5(0), Harper Audio) HarperCollins Pubs.

Heart Song. unabr. ed. V. C. Andrews. Read by Laurel Lefkow. 10 CDs. (Running Time: 37200 sec.). (Isis Ser.). 2003. audio compact disk 89.95 (978-0-7531-1108-6(X)) Pub: ISIS Lrg Prnt GBR. Dist(s): Ulverscroft US

Heart Songs. Joseph Linn. 1991. bk. 75.00 (978-0-685-68448-1(2), MU-9137C) Lillenas.

Heart Songs: 20 Arrangements for Ladies' Choir or Ensemble. Contrib. by Joseph Linn. 1991. 12.99 (978-0-00-530559-1(4)) Lillenas.

Heart Sounds. unabr. ed. Instructed by Jill S. Flateland. 6 cass. (Running Time: 9 hrs.). 1990. 79.00 cass. & soft-bound bk. (HT32) Ctr Hlth Educ.

Hear actual heart sounds! Learn how to interpret heart sounds the easy way with this complete set of tapes that allow you to hear actual abnormal & extra heart sounds. These include S3 & S4, mitral stenosis, & aortic valve lesions. Differentiate between systolic & diastolic murmurs & learn to recognize the 6 most common congenital heart defects.

Heart Sounds: What They Teach Us. unabr. ed. Antonio C. De Leon, Jr. 12 cass. (Running Time: 20 hrs.). 1973. bk. 275.00 Humetrics Corp.

Heart Spirit: Inspiration. Roger Williams & Will Masters. Read by Roger Williams & Vicki Williams. 1 cass. (Running Time: 47 min.). 1997. 10.00 (978-1-888112-09-4(6)) Global Dharma Ctr.

An inspirational combination of ambient & tech0-pop music.

Heart Stream-Music. 2007. audio compact disk 16.95 (978-1-56136-421-3(5)) Master Your Mind.

Heart Takes Wing. Kathy Kituai. Music by Nitya Parker. 2008. pap. bk. 14.95 (978-1-921479-12-0(4), InterPressAUS) Pub: Interactive Pubns AUS. Dist(s): CD Baby

Heart That Makes a Home Audio Album. Instructed by Bruce Wilkinson. 1999. 19.95 (978-1-885447-53-1(1)) Walk Thru the Bible.

It's what every wife longs for. To draw closer. Become more intimate. And enjoy a richer, more rewarding marriage with her husband. Fortunately, that's exactly what God wants for you. And He has a plan to help you get there. In six remarkable 26-minute sessions, you'll discover precisely what the role of the wife was designed to be. Not according to our culture. Not according to psychologists. But according to the unchanging truth of God's Word.

Heart Zones: Music to Boost Vitality. Doc Childre. 2000. 9.95 (978-1-879052-48-2(2)); audio compact disk 15.95 (978-1-879052-47-5(4)) HeartMath.

HeartAid Project. Photos by Eric Chapelle. 1 CD. (Running Time: 1 hr. 11 mins.). 2002. audio compact disk (978-1-891319-72-3(8)) Spring Hill CO.

Heartbeat. unabr. ed. 1 cass. (Running Time: 1 hrs. 30 min.). 2004. 10.75 (978-1-4025-8482-4(2)) Recorded Bks.

Heartbeat. unabr. ed. Sharon Creech. Read by Mandy Siegfried. (J). 2004. audio compact disk 17.95 (978-0-06-074485-4(5), HarperChildAud) HarperCollins Pubs.

***Heartbeat.** unabr. ed. Sharon Creech. (ENG.). 2005. (978-0-06-085015-9(9)); (978-0-06-085014-2(0)) HarperCollins Pubs.

Heartbeat: Voices of First Nations Women. Prod. by Rayna Green & Howard Bass. 1 cass. 1995. (0-9307-404150-9307-40415-2-9); audio compact disk (0-9307-40415-2-9) Smithsonian Folkways.

Ceremonial & social songs traditionally sung by women & material that combines traditional & contemporary themes & musical forms.

***Heartbeat Away.** unabr. ed. Michael Palmer. Read by Robert Petkoff. (Running Time: 11 hrs. 30 mins. 0 sec.). (ENG.). 2011. audio compact disk 39.99 (978-1-4272-0993-1(6)) Pub: Macmill Audio. Dist(s): Macmillan

Heartbeat Away. unabr. collector's ed. Barbara Rogan. Read by Rebecca Nicholas. 7 cass. (Running Time: 10 hrs. 30 min.). 2000. 56.00 (978-0-7366-4982-7(4)) Books on Tape.

A housekeeper, a ghost & an emergency room doctor find that there is life after death in the hospitals & jazz clubs of New York.

Heartbeat Hypno: Movement & Exercise. Jay Irvin. (ENG.). 2008. audio compact disk 25.00 (978-0-9768912-6-0(3)) eMotion Inc.

Heartbeat Musical Therapy Series. 3 cass. (Running Time: 4 hrs. 30 mins.). 1998. 12.95 ea.; audio compact disk 15.95 CD. Audio Therapy.

Various artists perform lullabies & nursery rhymes mixed with the sound of an actual heartbeat.

Heartbeat Two: More Voices of First Nations Women. Music by Sharon Burch et al. 1 cass. 1995. (093074041543093074041529 (RH)); audio compact disk (093074041529 (RH)) Smithsonian Folkways.

American Indian women from the U.S. & Canada perform contemporary & traditional songs & music: Kiowa, Lakota, Maliseet, Navajo, Paiute, Ojibwe/Cree, Pomo, Salish, & Yupi'k.

Heartbeats. Mary M. Slappey. Read by Mary M. Slappey. (Running Time: 30 min). 1986. 10.00 Interspace Bks.

Heartbreak Hotel. unabr. ed. Anne Rivers Siddons. Narrated by Alyssa Bresnahan. 8 cass. (Running Time: 10 hrs. 45 mins.). 1999. 70.00 (978-0-7887-0295-2(5), 94488E7) Recorded Bks.

A young women coming-of-age in the south of the 1950s, amid the racial revolution & the strife of a humid Alabama summer.

Heartbreak House. George Bernard Shaw. Narrated by Flo Gibson. (ENG.). 2007. audio compact disk 19.95 (978-1-55685-937-3(6)) Audio Bk Con.

Heartbreak House, Set. George Bernard Shaw. Read by Flo Gibson. 3 cass. (Running Time: 4 hrs.30 mins.). (gr. 9 up). 1997. 16.95 (978-1-55685-459-0(5), 495-5) Audio Bk Con.

In this allegorical play the eccentric Captain Shotover's home hosts a cast who each represent some evil in the modern world due to apathy, confusion, or lack of purpose. The first bombs of the war kill the greedy capitalist Boss Mangan & in the end there is a note of optimism.

Heartbreaker. Karen Robards. Read by Lisa Jandovitz. 9 CDs. 2004. audio compact disk 44.95 (978-0-7927-3287-7(1), SLD 274, Chivers Sound Lib) AudioGO.

Heartbreaker. abr. ed. Robert Ferrigno. Read by John Glover. 3 cass. 1999. 24.00 (FS9-43425) Highsmith.

Heartbreaker. unabr. ed. Julie Garwood. Read by Laura Hicks. 10 vols. (Running Time: 15 hrs.). 2001. bk. 84.95 (978-0-7927-2394-3(5), CSL 283, Chivers Sound Lib) AudioGO.

In the still shadows of the confessional, the penitent kneels & makes a bone-chilling disclosure: that he describes his murderous past & how he stalked his victim, worked his way into her life & then took that life in a violent rage & his plans to kill again.

Heartbreaker. unabr. ed. Julie Garwood. Read by Laura Hicks. 12 CDs. (Running Time: 18 hrs.). 2001. audio compact disk 110.95 (978-0-7927-9930-6(5), SLD 081, Chivers Sound Lib) AudioGO.

In the still shadows of the confessional, the penitent kneels and makes a bone-chilling disclosure: Bless me father, for I will sin... Slowly, tauntingly, the man describes his murderous past - how he stalked his victim, worked his way into her life, and then took that life in a violent rage and his plans to kill again. I'm a heartbreaker. And I do so love a challenge.

Heartbreaker. unabr. ed. Karen Robards. Read by Lisa Jandovitz. 8 vols. (Running Time: 12 hrs.). 2000. bk. 69.95 (978-0-7927-2252-6(3), CSL 141, Chivers Sound Lib) AudioGO.

Nothing in anchorwoman Lynn Nelson's high-profile TV career prepares her for an adventurous vacation in Utah's mountain wilderness. Lynn, a divorced mother, and her daughter Rory set out with their guide, handsome Jess Feldman. But in a terrifying moment, Lynn and Rory fall off a cliff! Now Jess must risk his life to save them.

Heartbreakers. unabr. ed. Pamela Wells. Narrated by Stina Nielsen. 7 CDs. (Running Time: 9 hrs.). (YA). (gr. 9 up). 2008. audio compact disk 97.75 (978-1-4281-8329-2(9)); 67.75 (978-1-4281-8324-7(8)) Recorded Bks.

This irresistible debut novel from author Pamela Wells touches on a subject all teenagers can relate to - broken hearts. When Sydney, Raven, and Kelly all get dumped on the same night, Alexia - who's never had a serious boyfriend - is happy to have her three BFFs back. To avoid future disasters the girls make a list of 20 rules, including "never ask or beg The Ex to date you again." But staying single is sometimes harder than splitting up in the first place. Soon all four girls, especially Alexia, are doing a little heartbreaking themselves.

***Heartbreaking Work of Staggering Genius.** unabr. ed. Dave Eggers. Narrated by Dion Graham. 1 Playaway. (Running Time: 13 hrs. 30 mins.). 2010. 64.75 (978-1-4407-6419-6(0)); 98.75 (978-0-7887-9470-4(1)) Recorded Bks.

***Heartbreaking Work of Staggering Genius.** unabr. ed. Dave Eggers. Narrated by Dion Graham. 12 CDs. (Running Time: 13 hrs. 30 mins.). 2010. audio compact disk 39.99 (978-1-4407-6417-2(4)) Recorded Bks.

***Heartbreaking Work of Staggering Genius.** unabr. collector's ed. Dave Eggers. Narrated by Dion Graham. 12 CDs. (Running Time: 13 hrs. 30 mins.). 2010. audio compact disk 56.95 (978-1-4407-6418-9(2)) Recorded Bks.

Heartfire. unabr. ed. Orson Scott Card. Read by Full Cast Production Staff. (Running Time: 43200 sec.). (Tales of Alvin Maker Ser.). 2007. 72.95 (978-1-4332-0772-3(9)) Blckstn Audio.

Heartfire. unabr. ed. Orson Scott Card. Read by Emily Janice Card et al. (Running Time: 43200 sec.). (Tales of Alvin Maker Ser.). 2007. audio compact disk 29.95 (978-1-4332-0774-7(5)); audio compact disk 90.00 (978-1-4332-0773-0(7)) Blckstn Audio.

***Heartfulness- Transformation in Christ.** Thomas Keating. (ENG.). 2009. audio compact disk 50.00i (978-0-9841302-0-7(9)) Contemp Outreach.

Heartland. unabr. ed. Davis Bunn. Narrated by Tim Lundeen. (ENG.). 2007. 17.49 (978-1-60814-012-1(1)) Oasis Audio.

Heartland. unabr. ed. Davis Bunn. Narrated by Tim Lundeen. (Running Time: 39600 sec.). (ENG.). 2007. audio compact disk 24.99 (978-1-59859-223-8(8)) Oasis Audio.

Heartland. unabr. ed. Perf. by Nancy Rockland-Miller. 1 cass. (Running Time: 40 min.). (J). (gr. k-5). 1996. 9.98 (978-0-9649933-3-4(3)) Mud Pie Prods.

Original children's songs about families, self-esteem, adventures.

Heartless. abr. ed. Diana Palmer. Read by Phil Gigante. 4 CDs. (Running Time: 5 hrs.). 2009. audio compact disk 19.99 (978-1-4233-8262-1(5), 9781423382621, BACD) Brilliance Audio.

Heartless. abr. ed. Diana Palmer. Read by Phil Gigante. (Running Time: 5 hrs.). 2010. audio compact disk 14.99 (978-1-4233-8263-8(3), 9781423382638, BCD Value Price) Brilliance Audio.

***Heartless.** unabr. ed. Gail Carriger. (Running Time: 11 hrs.). (Parasol Protectorate Ser.). (ENG.). 2011. 26.98 (978-1-60941-366-8(0)) Pub: Hachet Audio. Dist(s): HachBkGrp

Heartless. unabr. ed. Diana Palmer. Read by Phil Gigante. 1 MP3-CD. (Running Time: 9 hrs.). 2009. 24.99 (978-1-4233-8258-4(7), 9781423382584, Brilliance MP3); 39.97 (978-1-4233-8259-1(5), 9781423382591, Brlnc Audio MP3 Lib); 39.97 (978-1-4233-8261-4(7), 9781423382614, BADLE); 24.99 (978-1-4233-8260-7(9), 9781423382607, BAD); audio compact disk 34.99 (978-1-4233-8256-0(0), 9781423382560, Bril Audio CD Unabri); audio compact disk 87.97 (978-1-4233-8257-7(9), 9781423382577, BriAudCD Unabrid) Brilliance Audio.

Heartlink with Your Angel. 1 cass. (Running Time: 60 mins.). 1999. 12.00 Edin Bks.

Using a technique given during meditation, Stevan will teach you how to use angelic energy for healing & become part of a worldwide, spititual evolution.

Heartmates: A Guide for the Spouse & Family of the Heart Patient. rev. unabr. ed. Rhoda F. Levin. 1998. 24.95 (978-0-9637795-4-0(0)) MinervaPress.

Hearts. Hilma Wolitzer. Read by Hilma Wolitzer. 1 cass. (Running Time: 37 min.). 1983. 13.95 (978-1-55644-087-8(1), 3141) Am Audio Prose.

Readings by the Brooklyn-born author of "In the Flesh" & "Endings".

Hearts & Hands. Perf. by Tickle Tune Typhoon Staff. 1 cass. (J). 8.98 (2235) MFLP CA.
Joining hearts together, reaching out with helping hands, believing in ourselves & growing strong within the human family are the powerful themes in this album.

Hearts & Hands. Tickle Tune Typhoon Staff. 1 cass. (Running Time: 44 min.). (J). (gr. k-5). 1991. 9.98 (978-0-945337-09-6(4), TTT006) Tickle Tune Typhoon.
This recording combines musical styles ranging from latin grooves to boogie woogie. Song titles include Brains, Grammer Rapper, Dolphin Dance, I Believe In Me.

Heart's Delight. abr. ed. Marilyn Robbins. 1 cass. (Running Time: 90 min.). (Listen to Love Ser.). 3.98 (906R) Audio Bk.

Heart's Desire. Laura Pedersen. Narrated by Katie Hale. 2008. audio compact disk 35.95 (978-1-60031-046-1(X)) Spoken Books.

Heart's Desire. unabr. ed. Michael Taylor. Read by Maggie Mash. 12 cass. (Running Time: 16 hrs.). (Story Sound Ser.). (J). 2004. 94.95 (978-1-85903-641-9(4)) Pub: Mgna Lrg Print GBR. Dist(s): Ulverscroft US

Hearts Do Not Break. Ivy Preston. Read by Anne Cater. 5 cass. (Running Time: 7 hrs. 30 mins.). (Sound Ser.). 2004. 49.95 (978-1-85496-559-2(X), 6559x) Pub: UlverLrgPrint GBR. Dist(s): Ulverscroft US

Hearts Do Not Break, Set. Ivy Preston. Read by Anne Cater. 5 cass. 1999. 49.95 (6559X) Pub: Soundings Ltd GBR. Dist(s): ISIS Pub

Hearts, Hands & Hides. 1 cass. . 9.98; audio compact disk 15.98 Lifedance.
Native American flute, drums, electronic instruments & vocals. Although this was meant to showcase the use of drums in many Native American songs, the rhythm actually enhances the movement for these full-bodied ensemble. Demo casette or CD available.

Hearts in Atlantis. Stephen King. Narrated by Stephen King. Narrated by William Hurt. 16 cass. (Running Time: 20 hrs. 15 mins.). 2001. 132.00 (978-0-7887-5992-5(2)) Recorded Bks.
These five novellas, all rooted in the 19602, tackle everything from the fears and dangers of a precarious childhood to the horrors of the Vietnam War.

Hearts in Atlantis. Stephen King. 20 CDs. (Running Time: 210 hrs. 0 mins. 0 sec.). (ENG.). 2001. audio compact disk 49.95 (978-0-7435-0987-9(0), Audioworks) Pub: S&S Audio. Dist(s): S and S Inc

Hearts in Atlantis. Stephen King. 2006. 29.95 (978-0-7435-6335-2(2), Audioworks) Pub: S&S Audio. Dist(s): S and S Inc

Hearts in Atlantis. unabr. ed. Stephen King. Narrated by Stephen King. Narrated by William Hurt. 20 CDs. (Running Time: 20 hrs. 15 mins.). 2001. audio compact disk 140.00 (978-0-7887-6167-6(6)) Recorded Bks.
With these five novellas, rooted in the 1960s, Stephen King tackles the horrors of the Vietnam war & the fears & dangers of a precarious childhood. In the title story, a group of college students discover sex, rock-and-roll & the art of protest. When obsessed with a card game, they risk flunking out & getting drafted. Low Men in Yellow Coats features 11-year-old Bobby, whose problems escalate from being neglected by a bitter mother to being stalked by other predators. His story continues until 1999, when, as a middle-aged man, he returns to his hometown to find the final secret that awaits him. Hearts in Atlantis is a tribute to all those people whose living rooms were flooded with TV broadcasts of the Vietnam war. It's a cultural education for those who are too young to remember.

Hearts in Hiding. Betsy Brannon Green. 6 cass. 2004. 24.95 (978-1-57734-824-5(9)) Covenant Comms.

Heart's Needle see Twentieth-Century Poetry in English, No. 27, Recordings of Poets Reading Their Own Poetry

Hearts of Horses. unabr. ed. Molly Gloss. (Running Time: 9 hrs. 30 mins. 0 sec.). (ENG.). 2009. audio compact disk 34.99 (978-1-4001-1196-1(X)) Pub: Tantor Media. Dist(s): IngramPubServ

Hearts of Horses. unabr. ed. Molly Gloss. Narrated by Renée Raudman. (Running Time: 9 hrs. 30 mins. 0 sec.). 2009. audio compact disk 24.99 (978-1-4001-6196-6(7)); audio compact disk 69.99 (978-1-4001-4196-8(6)) Pub: Tantor Media. Dist(s): IngramPubServ

Hearts of Space. (Running Time: 1 hr. 17 min.). (Universe Collection: No. 4). (11203-4); audio compact disk (11203-2) NewSound.

Hearts on Pilgrimage. Compiled by Sara Singleton. 4 cass. (Running Time: 5 hrs.). 2003. 29.99 (978-1-58926-138-9(0)) Oasis Audio.
A daily devotional experience filled with music, Prayer and Scripture. Provides 15 minutes of devotional worship for each workday of the month.

Hearts on Pilgrimage. Compiled by Sara Singleton. 4 CDs. (Running Time: 5 hrs.). 2004. audio compact disk 29.99 (978-1-58926-049-8(X)) Oasis Audio.
Hearts on Pilgrimage provides fifteen minutes of devotional worship for each workday of the month.

Heart's Wisdom: Four Meditations for Cultivating Love, Compassion, Joy, & Equanimity. Bodhipaksa. Narrated by Bodhipaksa. (ENG.). 2007. audio compact disk 21.95 (978-0-9724414-4-5(1)) Pub: Wildmind. Dist(s): New Leaf Dist

Heart.Seeds: Affirmations for Awakening Our Creative Spirit. 2nd rev. ed. John-Robert Coleman. Narrated by Gemma Roskum. Contrib. by Erik Robinson. 1. (Running Time: 30 min.). 1997. 10.00 (978-0-9718638-1-1(4)) Heart Seeds.

Heartsick. unabr. ed. Chelsea Cain. Read by Carolyn McCormick. 9 CDs. (Running Time: 10 hrs.). (Gretchen Lowell Ser.: No. 1). 2007. audio compact disk 39.95 (978-0-7927-5022-2(5)) AudioGO.

Heartsick. unabr. ed. Chelsea Cain. Read by Carolyn McCormick. 9 CDs. (Running Time: 11 hrs. 0 mins. 0 sec.). No. 1. (ENG.). 2007. audio compact disk 39.95 (978-1-4272-0195-9(1)) Pub: Macmill Audio. Dist(s): Macmillan

Heartsongs. Leon Thurman & Anna P. Langness. Intro. by Thomas R. Verny. 1986. pap. bk. (978-0-318-60184-7(2)) Music Study.

Heartsongs Collection: Heartsongs & Journey Through Heartsongs. unabr. ed. Mattie J. T. Stepanek. Read by Mattie J. T. Stepanek. 1 cass. (Running Time: 1 hr. 30 mins.). 2002. 12.98 (978-0-7868-6953-4(4)) Pub: Hyperion. Dist(s): HarperCollins Pubs

Heartsongs Collection: The Poetry of Mattie J. T. Stepanek. unabr. ed. Mattie J. T. Stepanek. Narrated by Mattie J. T. Stepanek. (Running Time: 4 hrs. 9 mins. 9 sec.). (ENG.). 2009. audio compact disk 22.99 (978-1-59859-682-3(9)) Oasis Audio.

Heartsteps. Julia Cameron. 2001. (978-0-333-78256-9(9)) Macmillan UK GBR.

***Heartstone.** unabr. ed. Phillip Margolin. (Running Time: 11 hrs.). 2010. 14.99 (978-1-61106-108-6(3), 9781611061086, BAD); 39.97 (978-1-61106-109-3(1), 9781611061093, BADLE) Brilliance Audio.

***Heartstone.** unabr. ed. Phillip Margolin. Read by Mel Foster. (Running Time: 12 hrs.). 2010. 14.99 (978-1-61106-106-2(7), 9781611061062, Brilliance MP3); 39.97 (978-1-61106-107-9(5), 9781611061079, Brlnc Audio MP3 Lib); audio compact disk 19.99 (978-1-61106-104-8(0), 9781611061048, Bril Audio CD Unabri); audio compact disk 69.97 (978-1-61106-105-5(9), 9781611061055, BriAudCD Unabrid) Brilliance Audio.

Heartstone. unabr. ed. Read by Michael Russotto. Ed. by Phillip Margolin. 8 cass. (Running Time: 12 hrs.). 1996. 64.00 (978-0-7366-3214-0(X), 3877) Books on Tape.
Richie Walters, all-American boy. Elaine Murray, cheerleader. They made the perfect couple. And that evening at Lookout Point - Richie fumbling at the buttons of her blouse, Elaine thrilled & afraid - they were about to take the big step. But they never would. Death came to Richie, suddenly & savagely. And Elaine would die too. But not that night, or the next. She would live just long enough to know how lucky Richie had been.

Heartstones. unabr. ed. Ruth Rendell. Read by Geraldine Somerville. 2 cass. (Running Time: 2 hrs.). (Mini-CAB Audio Bks.). 1994. 24.95 Set. (978-0-7451-4279-1(6), CAB 962) AudioGO.
Luke is the widowed father of two girls, Elvira & Spinny, who are both very watchful, as Luke plans to remarry. He has chosen Mary Leonard as his bride, which now poses a threat to the girls. Then Mary falls to her death, & it was definitely not an accident.

Heartstones. unabr. ed. Ruth Rendell. 2000. 18.00 (89720K8) Recorded Bks.

Heartstones. unabr. ed. Ruth Rendell. Narrated by Alexandra O'Karma. 2 cass. (Running Time: 2 hrs. 15 mins.). 1989. 18.00 (978-1-55690-221-5(2), 89720E7) Recorded Bks.
Elvira's obsession with her father & jealousy of her sister lead to tragedy. Shows how even the most unsuspicious people are capable of the worst kind of horrors.

Heartstopper. Joy Fielding. Read by Judith West. (Playaway Adult Fiction Ser.). (ENG.). 2009. 80.00 (978-1-60775-534-0(3)) Find a World.

Heartstopper. abr. ed. Joy Fielding. Read by Judith West. (Running Time: 21600 sec.). 2008. audio compact disk 14.99 (978-1-4233-2550-5(8), 9781423325505, BCD Value Price) Brilliance Audio.

Heartstopper. unabr. ed. Joy Fielding. (Running Time: 13 hrs.). 2007. 39.25 (978-1-4233-2546-8(X), 9781423325468, Brlnc Audio MP3 Lib); 24.95 (978-1-4233-2545-1(1), 9781423325451, Brilliance MP3); 92.25 (978-1-4233-2542-0(7), 9781423325420, BrilAudUnabridg); audio compact disk 107.25 (978-1-4233-2544-4(3), 9781423325444, BriAudCD Unabrid); audio compact disk 36.95 (978-1-4233-2543-7(5), 9781423325437, Bril Audio CD Unabri) Brilliance Audio.

Heartstopper. unabr. ed. Joy Fielding. Read by Judith West. (Running Time: 13 hrs.). 2007. 39.25 (978-1-4233-2548-2(6), 9781423325482, BADLE); 24.95 (978-1-4233-2547-5(8), 9781423325475, BAD) Brilliance Audio.

Heartwood. abr. ed. James Lee Burke. Read by Will Patton. (Billy Bob Holland Ser.). 2004. 15.95 (978-0-7435-4819-9(1)) Pub: S&S Audio. Dist(s): S and S Inc

Heartwood. unabr. ed. James Lee Burke. Read by Alan Sklar. 12 CDs. (Running Time: 18 hrs.). (Billy Bob Holland Ser.). 2001. audio compact disk 110.95 (978-0-7927-9993-1(3), SLD 044, Chivers Sound Lib) AudioGO.

Heartwood, Set. abr. ed. James Lee Burke. Read by Will Patton. 4 cass. 1999. 25.00 (FS9-50997) Highsmith.

***Heartwood: A Novel.** unabr. ed. Belva Plain. (ENG.). 2011. audio compact disk 40.00 (978-0-307-87617-1(9), Random AudioBks) Pub: Random Audio Pubg. Dist(s): Random

***Heat.** abr. ed. Stuart Woods. Read by Tony Roberts. (ENG.). 2005. (978-0-06-084200-0(8), Harper Audio); (978-0-06-084201-7(6), Harper Audio) HarperCollins Pubs.

Heat. unabr. ed. Campbell Armstrong. Read by Ric Jerrom. 10 cass. (Running Time: 15 hrs.). 2001. 69.95 (978-0-7540-0096-9(6), CAB 1519) Pub: Chivers Audio Bks GBR. Dist(s): AudioGO
Frank Pagan, Special Branch's counter-terrorist agent, is being observed. His apartment is broken into and a photo of his dead wife is stolen. But Pagan's thoughts are turned to a mortally alluring woman: Carlotta, a ruthless terrorist who Pagan must bring to justice. Indifferent to the destruction she leaves behind, Carlotta crosses the line that separates duty from obsession.

Heat. unabr. ed. Mike Lupica. Read by Paolo Andino. 5 CDs. (Running Time: 6 hrs. 14 mins.). (YA). (gr. 5-8). 2006. audio compact disk 38.25 (978-0-307-28598-0(7)) Pub: Books on Tape. Dist(s): NetLibrary CO

Heat. unabr. ed. Mike Lupica. Read by Paolo Andino. 4 cass. (Running Time: 6 hrs. 14 mins.). (YA). (gr. 5-8). 2006. 35.00 (978-0-307-28597-3(9), Listening Lib) Pub: Random Audio Pubg. Dist(s): Random

Heat. unabr. ed. Mike Lupica. Read by Paolo Andino. 5 CDs. (Running Time: 22440 sec.). (ENG.). (J). (gr. 7). 2006. audio compact disk 30.00 (978-0-307-28441-9(7), Listening Lib) Pub: Random Audio Pubg. Dist(s): Random

Heat. unabr. ed. Ed McBain, pseud. Read by Jonathan Marosz. 7 cass. (Running Time: 7 hrs.). (87th Precinct Ser.: Bk. 35). 1998. 42.00 (978-0-7366-4110-4(6), 4615) Books on Tape.
Too many unanswered questions emerge after an artist's suicide. Detective Steve Carella wants answers.

Heat, unabr. ed. Stuart Woods. Narrated by Richard Ferrone. 7 cass. (Running Time: 10 hrs. 30 mins.). 1994. 60.00 (978-0-7887-0064-4(2), 94320E7) Recorded Bks.
The Justice Department wants to bring back Jesse Warden, an ex-DEA agent serving time for a crime he didn't commit, to take on a lethal assignment that no one else wants. To earn his freedom, the battered ex-cop must destroy the Aryan Universe, a deadly, reclusive cult living deep in the Idaho mountains. But are his greatest enemies the cultists, or the heads of the federal agency that sent him?.

Heat: An Amateur's Adventures as Kitchen Slave, Line Cook, Pasta-Maker, & Apprentice to a Dante-Quoting Butcher in Tuscany. abr. ed. Bill Buford. Read by Bill Buford. 5 CDs. (Running Time: 21600 sec.). (ENG.). 2006. audio compact disk 29.95 (978-0-7393-1545-3(5)) Pub: Random Audio Pubg. Dist(s): Random

Heat: Today's Hottest Christian Rock. 2007. audio compact disk 19.98 (978-5-557-57587-4(1)) INO Rec.

***Heat Islands.** unabr. ed. Randy Wayne White. Narrated by Dick Hill. (Running Time: 10 hrs. 30 mins. 0 sec.). (Doc Ford Ser.). (ENG.). 2010. 24.99 (978-1-4001-6669-5(1)); 16.99 (978-1-4001-8669-3(2)); audio compact disk 69.99 (978-1-4001-4669-7(0)); audio compact disk 34.99 (978-1-4001-1669-0(4)) Pub: Tantor Media. Dist(s): IngramPubServ

***Heat Lighting.** John Sandford. Read by Richard Ferrone. (Running Time: 6 hrs.). (ENG.). 2011. audio compact disk 14.95 (978-0-14-242909-9(0), PengAudBks) Penguin Grp USA.

Heat Lightning. abr. ed. John Sandford, pseud. Read by Eric Conger. (Running Time: 10 hrs.). No. 2. (ENG.). (gr. 12 up). 2008. audio compact disk 29.95 (978-0-14-314363-5(8), PengAudBks) Penguin Grp USA.

Heat Lightning. unabr. ed. John Sandford, pseud. Read by Eric Conger. 9 CDs. (Running Time: 10 hrs.). No. 2. (ENG.). (gr. 12 up). 2008. audio compact disk 39.95 (978-0-14-314362-8(X), PengAudBks) Penguin Grp USA.

Heat Wave. unabr. ed. Richard Castle. Narrated by Johnny Heller. 1 MP3-CD. (Running Time: 6 hrs. 30 mins. 0 sec.). 2009. 19.99 (978-1-4001-6425-7(7)); audio compact disk 59.99 (978-1-4001-4425-9(6)); audio compact disk 29.99 (978-1-4001-1425-2(X)) Pub: Tantor Media. Dist(s): IngramPubServ

***Heat Wave.** unabr. ed. Richard Castle. Narrated by Johnny Heller. (Running Time: 6 hrs. 30 mins.). 2009. 14.99 (978-1-4001-8425-5(8)) Tantor Media.

Heat Wave. unabr. ed. Penelope Lively. Narrated by Davina Porter. 6 cass. (Running Time: 8 hrs.). 1997. 51.00 (978-0-7887-0853-4(8), 94999E7) Recorded Bks.
A poignant tale of a mother's obsessive love & disillusionment repeated in her daughter's own marriage.

Heathen Days. unabr. collector's ed. H. L. Mencken. Read by Daniel Grace. 8 cass. (Running Time: 8 hrs.). 1976. 48.00 (978-0-7366-0032-3(9), 1044) Books on Tape.
"Heathen Days" covers the years from 1890 to 1936 & puts the lash to many politicos of that era.

Heather! An Unabashed, Unauthorized Celebration of All Things Locklear. abr. ed. Jodie Gould. Read by Jodie Gould. 2 cass. (Running Time: 3 hrs.). 1996. 16.95 Set. (978-1-882071-64-7(6)) B-B Audio.
Heather is hot. After single handedly rescuing Melrose Place from the ratings doldrums with her portrayal of that hilariously over-the-top bitch Amanda Woodward, Heather Locklear has emerged as one of the leading stars of the nineties.With insights a.

Heather Hill. unabr. collector's ed. Elleston Trevor. Read by Gary Martin. 5 cass. (Running Time: 7 hrs. 30 min.). (Woodlander Ser.). (J). 1992. 40.00 (978-0-7366-2091-8(5), 2897) Books on Tape.
Adventures of inhabitants of Deep Wood continue.

Heather Hills of Stonewycke. unabr. ed. Michael R. Phillips & Judith Pella. Narrated by Davina Porter. 7 cass. (Running Time: 10 hrs. 15 mins.). (Stonewycke Trilogy: Bk. 1). 2001. 64.00 (978-0-7887-5146-2(8), K0034E7) Recorded Bks.
In 19th-century Scotland, Maggie Duncan is torn between her obligations as dutiful daughter & her hatred of her father's cruel pursuit of money & power.

Heather McHugh. unabr. ed. Read by Heather McHugh. 1 cass. (Running Time: 29 min.). 1985. 10.00 New Letters.
Heather McHugh is author of "Dangers" & "A World of Difference".

Heather Miller: Once upon a Time. Perf. by Heather Miller. 1 cass. 1999. 10.98 (KMGC8669); audio compact disk 16.98 (KMGD8669) Provident Mus Dist.

Heating for Robin Hood. Seth Feldman. 1 CD. (Running Time: 1 hr. 30 mins.). 2005. audio compact disk 12.95 (978-0-660-18914-7(3)) Pub: Canadian Broadcasting CAN. Dist(s): Georgetown Term

Heaven see Philip Levine

Heaven. Creflo A. Dollar & Taffi L. Dollar. 10.00 (978-1-59089-113-1(9)) Pub: Creflo Dollar. Dist(s): STL Dist NA

Heaven. Angela Johnson. Narrated by Andrea Johnson. 3 CDs. (Running Time: 2 hrs. 45 mins.). (gr. 7 up). audio compact disk 29.00 (978-1-4025-1969-7(9)) Recorded Bks.

Heaven. John MacArthur, Jr. 8 cass. (John MacArthur's Bible Studies). 24.75 (HarperThor) HarpC GBR.

Heaven. Joni Eareckson Tada. Read by Joni Eareckson Tada. 2 cass. (Running Time: 60 min. per cass.). 1995. 16.99 (978-0-310-20003-1(2)) Zondervan.

Heaven. abr. ed. Randy C. Alcorn. 10 cass. 2004. 29.99 (978-0-8423-7946-5(0), Tyndale Audio) Tyndale Hse.

Heaven. abr. ed. Randy C. Alcorn. 9 CDs. (Running Time: 11 hrs.). (ENG.). 2004. audio compact disk 32.99 (978-0-8423-7968-7(1)) Tyndale Hse.

Heaven. unabr. ed. Angela Johnson. Narrated by Andrea Johnson. 2 pieces. (Running Time: 2 hrs. 45 mins.). (gr. 7 up). 2001. 26.00 (978-0-7887-4563-8(8), 96334E7) Recorded Bks.
Heaven is the name for the small town where Marley lives. She thought so until the mysterious letter arrived.

Heaven. unabr. ed. Angela Johnson. Narrated by Andrea Johnson. 2 cass. (Running Time: 2 hrs. 45 mins.). (YA). 2001. pap. bk. & stu. ed. 40.24 Recorded Bks.

Heaven. unabr. ed. Read by Lorelei King. Ed. by V. C. Andrews. 10 cass. (Running Time: 13 hrs. 40 min.). (Isis Ser.). (J). 1995. 84.95 (978-1-85695-865-3(5), 940904) Pub: ISIS Lrg Prnt GBR. Dist(s): Ulverscroft US

Heaven. unabr. ed. Read by Donada Peters. Ed. by V. C. Andrews. 10 cass. (Running Time: 15 hrs.). (Casteel Ser.). 1990. 80.00 (978-0-7366-1736-9(1), 2576) Books on Tape.
Mountain folks say the prettiest flower grows closest to the dung heap. If Heaven Casteel was the prettiest, smartest girl in the hills & she was - then her family was the meanest & most lowdown. Despite a father who rode her & a mother who worked her like a mule, Heaven clung to hope for herself & for her brother, Tom.

Heaven, Pts. 1-7. 7 cass. (Running Time: 60 min.). (Mother Angelica Live Ser.). 10.00 (978-1-55794-080-3(0), T31) Eternal Wrd TV.

Heaven: Biblical Answers to Common Questions. unabr. ed. Randy C. Alcorn. Narrated by Randy C. Alcorn. (Running Time: 0 hr. 59 mins. 5 sec.). (ENG.). 2008. 6.99 (978-1-60814-015-2(6)); audio compact disk 9.99 (978-1-59859-447-8(8)) Oasis Audio.

Heaven: My Father's House. abr. ed. Anne Graham Lotz. 1 CD. (Running Time: 1 hr. 30 mins.). 2001. audio compact disk 18.99 (978-0-8499-6348-3(6)) Nelson.

Heaven: Obstacles & Opportunities. 2006. audio compact disk 27.95 (978-1-888992-76-2(X)) Catholic Answers.

Heaven: Our Enduring Fascination with the Afterlife. unabr. ed. Lisa Miller. Read by Linda Emond. 8 CDs. (Running Time: 9 hrs. 30 mins. 0 sec.). 2010. audio compact disk 39.99 (978-0-7435-3283-9(X)) S and S Inc.

Heaven: Out of Body Adventure. Jack Van Impe. 1 cass. (Running Time: 90 min.). 1992. J Van Impe.
Religious commentary.

Heaven: Songs for the Soul-Winning Church. Contrib. by Wayne Haun et al. 2007. audio compact disk 90.00 (978-5-557-54406-1(2)) Lillenas.

Heaven: The Heart's Deepest Longing. unabr. ed. Peter Kreeft. Read by Mark Taheny. 6 cass. 24.95 set. (126) Ignatius Pr.
Fascinating & upbeat exploration of the hunger for heaven that no modern promises or answers can satisfy: a thorough & joyous venture into the psychological, philisophical & religious dimensions of this search for total joy & the ultimate reality that grounds it.

Heaven: Your Real Home. abr. ed. Joni Eareckson Tada. (Running Time: 2 hrs. 0 mins. 0 sec.). (ENG.). 2003. 10.99 (978-0-310-26054-7(X)) Zondervan.

Heaven Pt. 1: Logos August 30. 1998. Ben Young. 1998. 4.95 (978-0-7417-6096-8(7), B0096) Win Walk.

Heaven Pt. 1: Secrets. Mother Angelica. 1 cass. (Running Time: 60 min.). (Mother Angelica Live Ser.). 10.00 (978-1-55794-073-5(8), T24) Eternal Wrd TV.

Heaven Pt. 2: Joys. Mother Angelica. 1 cass. (Running Time: 60 min.). (Mother Angelica Live Ser.). 10.00 (978-1-55794-074-2(6), T25) Eternal Wrd TV.

Heaven Pt. 2: Logos September 6, 1998. Ben Young. 1998. 4.95 (978-0-7417-6097-5(5), B0097) Win Walk.

Heaven Pt. 3: Work. Mother Angelica. 1 cass. (Running Time: 60 min.). (Mother Angelica Live Ser.). 10.00 (978-1-55794-075-9(4), T26) Eternal Wrd TV.

Heaven Pt. 4: Companionship in Heaven. Mother Angelica. 1 cass. (Running Time: 60 min.). (Mother Angelica Live Ser.). 10.00 (978-1-55794-076-6(2), T27) Eternal Wrd TV.

Heaven Pt. 5: Music & Beauty in Heaven. Mother Angelica. 1 cass. (Running Time: 60 min.). (Mother Angelica Live Ser.). 10.00 (978-1-55794-077-3(0), T28) Eternal Wrd TV.

Heaven Pt. 6: Knowledge. Mother Angelica. 1 cass. (Running Time: 60 min.). (Mother Angelica Live Ser.). 10.00 (T29) Eternal Wrd TV.

Heaven Pt. 7: Body & Soul. 1 cass. (Running Time: 60 min.). (Mother Angelica Live Ser.). 10.00 (978-1-55794-079-7(7), T30) Eternal Wrd TV.

Heaven & Earth. abr. ed. Nora Roberts. Read by Sandra Burr. 4 CDs. (Running Time: 4 hrs.). (Three Sisters Island Trilogy: Vol. 2). 2004. audio compact disk 14.99 (978-1-59355-322-7(6), 1593553226, BCD Value Price) Brilliance Audio.
Ripley Todd just wants to live a quiet, peaceful kind of life. Her job as a sheriff's deputy keeps her busy and happy, and she has no trouble finding men when she wants them - which, lately, isn't all that often. She's perfectly content, except for one thing: she has special powers that both frighten and confuse her-and though she tries hard to hide them, she can't get them under control... Distraction soon arrives in the handsome form of MacAllister Booke - a researcher who's come to investigate the rumors of witchcraft that haunt Three Sisters Island. Right from the start, he knows there's something extraordinary about Ripley Todd. It's not just her blazing green eyes and her sultry smile. There's something else. Something he can detect, but she'll never admit. Fascinated by her struggle with her amazing abilities, he becomes determined to help her accept who she is - and find the courage to open her heart. But before Ripley and Mac can dream of what lies in the future, they must confront the pain of the past. For Three Sisters shelters centuries of secrets-and a legacy of danger that plagues them still.... "A storytelling wizard." -Publishers Weekly.

Heaven & Earth. unabr. ed. Nora Roberts. Read by Sandra Burr. (Running Time: 9 hrs.). (Three Sisters Island Trilogy: Vol. 2). 2001. 69.25 (978-1-58788-225-8(6), 1587882256, Unabridge Lib Edns) Brilliance Audio.

Heaven & Earth. unabr. ed. Nora Roberts. Read by Sandra Burr. (Running Time: 32400 sec.). (Three Sisters Island Trilogy: Vol. 2). 2004. audio compact disk 39.25 (978-1-59335-360-5(X), 159335360X, Brlnc Audio MP3 Lib) Brilliance Audio.

Heaven & Earth. unabr. ed. Nora Roberts. Read by Sandra Burr. (Running Time: 9 hrs.). (Three Sisters Island Trilogy: Vol. 2). 2004. 39.25 (978-1-59710-357-2(8), 1597103578, BADLE); 24.95 (978-1-59710-356-5(X), 159710356X, BAD) Brilliance Audio.

Heaven & Earth. unabr. ed. Nora Roberts. Read by Sandra Burr. (Running Time: 32400 sec.). (Three Sisters Island Trilogy: Vol. 2). 2007. audio compact disk 92.25 (978-1-4233-3418-7(3), 9781423334187, BriAudCD Unabrid); audio compact disk 34.95 (978-1-4233-3417-0(5), 9781423334170, Bril Audio CD Unabri) Brilliance Audio.

Heaven & Earth. unabr. ed. Nora Roberts. Read by Sandra Burr. (Running Time: 9 hrs.). (Three Sisters Island Trilogy: Vol. 2). 2004. 24.95 (978-1-59335-032-1(5), 1593350325) Soulmate Audio Bks.

Heaven & Earth: Making the Psychic Connection. unabr. ed. James Van Praagh. Read by Barrett Whitener. 6 vols. (Running Time: 9 hrs.). 2002. bk. 54.95 (978-0-7927-2722-4(3), CSL 508, Chivers Sound Lib); audio compact disk 64.95 (978-0-7927-2750-7(9), SLD 508, Chivers Sound Lib) AudioGO.
For the last several years he has worked with tens of thousands of people, refining techniques that we can use on our own. Combining his own inspiring experiences with testimony from others who have been touched by their spirit family and guides.

***Heaven & Earth-ABR.** Nora Roberts & #2 Three Sisters Island Trilogy. 2010. audio compact disk 9.99 (978-1-4418-5663-0(3)) Brilliance Audio.

Heaven & Hell. abr. ed. John Jakes. Read by George Grizzard. 2 cass. (Running Time: 6 hrs.). 2001. 18.00 (978-1-59040-085-2(2), Phoenix Audio) Pub: Amer Intl Pub. Dist(s): PerseuPGW

Heaven & Hell, Pt. 1. unabr. collector's ed. John Jakes. Read by Michael Kramer. 11 cass. (Running Time: 16 hrs. 30 min.). (North & South Trilogy: Vol. 3). 1994. 88.00 (978-0-7366-2820-4(7), 3531-A) Books on Tape.
The Civil War may be over, but in this conclusion to the North & South Trilogy, the battles of the heart have just begun.

Heaven & Hell, Pt. 2. collector's ed. John Jakes. Read by Michael Kramer. 10 cass. (Running Time: 15 hrs.). 1994. 80.00 (978-0-7366-2821-1(5), 3531-B) Books on Tape.

Heaven & Hell: What Happens When You Die? Chuck Missler. 2 CDs. (Running Time: 112 mins.). 2003. audio compact disk 19.95 (978-1-57821-234-7(0)) Koinonia Hse.
What Happens When You Die?We don't like to think about death. It's not a pleasant subject, and we avoid even discussing it seriously or giving it any diligent study. Yet our appointment with death is the most certain event in our future. We all know of personal examples when death has come suddenly to people, without warning, without preparations; car accidents, stray bullets, unforeseen strokes. When it comes our time, what do we expect death to be like? How will we enter eternity?Each Audio Briefing Pack contains two high-quality cassette tapes, with extensive supporting study notes, all packaged in a sturdy clear-plastic case.

Heaven below, the Heaven above. abr. ed. Emily Dickinson. Read by Lyn Dalebout. 1 cass. (Running Time: 1 hr.). Dramatization. (Poetry of Nature Ser.). 1994. 10.95 (978-0-939643-61-5(8), 3598, NrthWrd Bks) TandN Child.
Dickinson's unique form of poetry is full of her private certainty and hypersensitive wonder of the world. A selection of poems that highlight her perceptive vision concerning the magic and meaning to be found in the pleasures of heaven and earth.

***Heaven Calling: Hearing Your Father's Voice Every Day of the Year.** Zondervan. (Running Time: 7 hrs. 55 mins. 30 sec.). (ENG.). 2010. 14.99 (978-0-310-42703-2(7)) Zondervan.

***Heaven Came Down: Higher Praise Christmas.** Perf. by Ocean's Edge Music. Prod. by Clay Hecocks. (ENG.). 2010. audio compact disk 9.99 (978-1-932283-16-7(1)) Calvry Chap Ch.

Heaven Eyes. unabr. ed. David Almond. Read by Amanda Plummer. 3 cass. (Running Time: 5 hrs. 7 mins.). (J). (gr. 5-9). 2004. 30.00 (978-0-8072-8879-5(9), Listening Lib) Random Audio Pubg.
Erin Law & her friends are Damaged Children, the label given to them by Maureen, the woman who runs the orphanage that they live in, because they have no parents to take care of them. Sometimes there is nothing left but to run away, to run for freedom. That is what Erin & two friends do, run away one night downriver on a raft. What they find on their journey is stranger than you can imagine, maybe & you might not think it's true. But Erin will tell you it is all true & the proof is a girl named Heaven Eyes, who sees through all the darkness in the world to the joy that lies beneath.

Heaven for Kids. unabr. ed. Randy C. Alcorn. Narrated by Randy C. Alcorn. (ENG.). (J). 2006. 10.49 (978-1-60814-014-5(8)) Oasis Audio.

Heaven for Kids. unabr. ed. Randy C. Alcorn. Narrated by Randy C. Alcorn. (Running Time: 3 hrs. 50 mins. 25 sec.). (ENG.). (J). (gr. 3-7). 2006. audio compact disk 14.99 (978-1-59859-166-8(5)) Oasis Audio.

Heaven Is a Decision We Make/Judge Not. Marianne Williamson. Read by Marianne Williamson. 1 cass. (Running Time: 90 mins.). (Lectures on a Course in Miracles). (ENG.). 1999. 10.00 (978-1-56170-754-6(6), M878) Hay House.

***Heaven Is for Real: A Little Boy's Astounding Story of His Trip to Heaven & Back.** unabr. ed. Todd Burpo. Contrib. by Lynn Vincent. Narrated by Dean Gallagher. (Running Time: 4 hrs. 15 mins. 2 sec.). (ENG.). 2010. 13.99 (978-1-60814-791-5(6)); audio compact disk 19.99 (978-1-59859-919-0(4)) Oasis Audio.

***Heaven Is High: A Barbara Holloway Novel.** unabr. ed. Kate Wilhelm. (Running Time: 9.5 hrs. NaN mins.). (Barbara Holloway Mysteries Ser.). (ENG.). 2011. 29.95 (978-1-4417-7900-7(0)); audio compact disk 29.95 (978-1-4417-7899-4(3)) Blckstn Audio.

***Heaven Is High: A Barbara Holloway Novel.** unabr. ed. Kate Wilhelm. Read by To be Announced. (Running Time: 9.5 hrs. NaN mins.). (Barbara Holloway Mysteries Ser.). (ENG.). 2011. 59.95 (978-1-4417-7897-0(7)); audio compact disk 90.00 (978-1-4417-7898-7(5)) Blckstn Audio.

Heaven Is Real: Lessons on Earthly Joy - From the Man Who Spent 90 Minutes in Heaven. Don Piper & Cecil Murphey. Read by Don Piper. (Running Time: 7 hrs.). (ENG.). (gr. 8). 2007. audio compact disk 29.95 (978-0-14-314270-6(4), PengAudBks) Penguin Grp USA.

Heaven on Earth. Marilyn Pappano. Narrated by Cristine McMurdo-Wallis. 9 cass. (Running Time: 12 hrs. 30 mins.). 82.00 (978-1-4025-2144-7(8)) Recorded Bks.

Heaven on Earth. Featuring Bill Winston. 3. 2004. 15.00 (978-1-59544-038-9(0)); audio compact disk 24.00 (978-1-59544-039-6(9)) Pub: B Winston Min. Dist(s): Anchor Distributors

Heaven on Earth: 15-Minute Miracles to Change the World. Danny Seo. 2004. 10.95 (978-0-7435-4820-5(5)) Pub: S&S Audio. Dist(s): S and S Inc

Heaven on Earth Marriage. C. S. Lovett. Read by C. S. Lovett. 1 cass. (Running Time: 24 min.). 5.95 (504) Prsnl Christianity.
Offers counsel for recovering the thrill of marriage once things have become stale.

Heaven; Scripture & the Church. Joseph F. Girzone. Read by Joseph F. Girzone. 1 cass. (Running Time: 90 min.). 1992. 7.95 (978-0-911519-14-3(9)) Richelieu Court.
Girzone's public talk on these topics.

Heaven Sent - audio Book. Alison Longstaff. Perf. by Jason Carter. 12 CDs. (Running Time: 14 hrs). (Cliffside Chapel Ser.: 1 - Audio). 2004. audio compact disk 48.00 (978-0-9687329-1-5(7)) Longstaff Pub.
Unabridged performance of edgy, romantic adventure, delightfully read by Shakespearean actor, Jason Carter.

Heaven Series. Ed Young. 4. 2000. 24.95 (978-0-7417-0032-2(8)) Win Walk.

Heaven Symbolic Almighty Beam. Serafin Lanot. 1 cass. 8.95 (755) Am Fed Astrologers.

Heaven, Texas. unabr. collector's ed. Susan Elizabeth Phillips. Read by Anna Fields. 8 cass. (Running Time: 12 hrs.). (Chicago Stars Bks.: No. 2). 1996. 64.00 (978-0-7366-3322-2(7), 3974) Books on Tape.
It seems like an easy assignment for an assertive but sweet woman like Gracie Snow: track down her friend, Bobby Denton, a famous ex-jock, & bring him to Heaven (Texas, that is) to shoot a movie. How could he refuse a glamorous offer like that?.

Heaven to Earth. Tom Fettke. 2007. audio compact disk 24.99 (978-5-557-69947-1(3)) Lillenas.

***Heaven Trilogy: Heaven's Wager, When Heaven Weeps, & Thunder of Heaven.** unabr. ed. Ted Dekker. Narrated by Tim Gregory. (Running Time: 44 hrs. 15 mins. 0 sec.). (Heaven Trilogy). (ENG.). 2010. audio compact disk 89.99 (978-1-59859-881-0(3)) Oasis Audio.

Heavenly. Stacie Ruth & Carrie Beth. 2009. audio compact disk 17.95 (978-1-60615-007-8(3)) Pub: WinePress Pub. Dist(s): Spring Arbor Dist

Heavenly Hoedown. 2001. audio compact disk 15.00 (978-1-58302-199-6(X)) One Way St.
This is a great collection of ten toe-tapping tunes with a country flavor. All the songs convey a biblical truth.

***Heavenly Man: The Remarkable True Story of Chinese Christian Brother Yun.** unabr. ed. Brother Yun & Paul Hattaway. Narrated by Cristofer Jean. (ENG.). 2008. 14.98 (978-1-59644-651-9(X), Hovel Audio) christianaud.

Heavenly Man: The Remarkable True Story of Chinese Christian Brother Yun. unabr. ed. Brother Yun & Paul Hattaway. Narrated by Cristofer Jean et al. (Running Time: 10 hrs. 0 mins. 0 sec.). (ENG.). 2008. lp 19.98 (978-1-59644-650-2(1), Hovel Audio); audio compact disk 24.98 (978-1-59644-649-6(8), Hovel Audio) christianaud.

Heavenly Peace. (ENG.). 2008. 15.98 (978-0-9789562-0-2(6)) TimeArt.

Heavenly Perspective. Rick Joyner. 1 cass. (Running Time: 90 mins.). (Call To Leadership Ser.). 2000. 5.00 (RJ01-003) Morning NC.
Rick addresses the qualities required of spiritual leaders in these times.

Heavenly Pleasures. Kerry Greenwood. Read by Louise Siversen. (Running Time: 8 hrs. 25 mins.). (Corinna Chapman Mystery: Ser.). 2009. 74.99 (978-1-74214-240-1(0), 9781742142401) Pub: Bolinda Pubng AUS. Dist(s): Bolinda Pub Inc

Heavenly Pleasures. unabr. ed. Kerry Greenwood. Read by Louise Siversen. (Running Time: 30300 sec.). (Corinna Chapman Mystery: Ser.). 2008. audio compact disk 83.95 (978-1-921334-98-6(3), 9781921334986) Pub: Bolinda Pubng AUS. Dist(s): Bolinda Pub Inc

Heavenly Relationships: Guided Meditations to Enhance Your Relationships. Alma Daniel. Music by Gerald Jay Markoe. 1 cass. (Running Time: 60 min.). 10.95 (LA114); audio compact disk 15.95 (LA114D) Lghtwrks Aud & Vid.
Including selections like "Heavenly Relationship with Your Beloved", "Sharing & Space" & "Commitment", this series of 6 meditations focus us on balancing our relationships with others & with ourself.

Heavenly Skies & Lullabies: Illustrated Songbook & CD. Kathy Reilly Fallon & Frank Pellegrino. Illus. by Becky Kelly. (J). (ps-3). 2006. bk. 29.95 (978-1-933626-06-2(2), Llumina Pr) Media Creations Inc.

Heaven's Command: An Imperial Progress. unabr. collector's ed. Jan Morris. Read by David Case. 15 cass. (Running Time: 22 hrs. 30 min.). (Pax Britannica Trilogy: Vol. 1). 1996. 120.00 (978-0-7366-3416-8(9), 4062) Books on Tape.
Begins in 1837, when Queen Victoria takes the throne.

***Heaven's Fury.** Stephen Frey. (Running Time: 10 hrs. 0 mins. 0 sec.). (ENG.). 2010. audio compact disk 29.95 (978-0-61998-059-7(X)) Pub: AudioGO. Dist(s): Perseus Dist

Heaven's Hero. Contrib. by Marty Hamby & Steve Mauldin. (ENG.). 2005. audio compact disk 59.99 (978-5-558-57735-8(5), Brentwood-Benson Music) Brentwood Music.

Heaven's Keep. William Kent Krueger. Read by Buck Schirner. (Playaway Adult Fiction Ser.). (ENG.). 2009. 64.99 (978-1-4418-0994-0(5)) Find a World.

Heaven's Keep. unabr. ed. William Kent Krueger. Read by Buck Schirner. (Running Time: 10 hrs.). (Cork O'Connor Ser.). 2009. 24.99 (978-1-4233-4186-4(4), 9781423341864, Brilliance MP3); 39.97 (978-1-4233-4187-1(2), 9781423341871, Brlnc Audio MP3 Lib); 39.97 (978-1-4233-4189-5(9), 9781423341895, BADLE); 24.99 (978-1-4233-4188-8(0), 9781423341888, BAD); audio compact disk 89.97 (978-1-4233-4185-7(6), 9781423341857, BriAudCD Unabrid); audio compact disk 34.99 (978-1-4233-4184-0(8), 9781423341840, Bril Audio CD Unabri) Brilliance Audio.

Heaven's Net Is Wide. unabr. ed. Lian Hearn. Read by Julia Fletcher & J. Paul Boehmer. (ENG.). 2007. audio compact disk 44.95 (978-1-59887-101-2(3), 1598871013) Pub: HighBridge. Dist(s): Workman Pub

Heaven's Price. abr. ed. Sandra Brown. Read by Robin Mattson. 3 CDs. (Running Time: 10800 sec.). (ENG.). 2006. audio compact disk 14.99 (978-0-7393-2494-3(2), Random AudioBks) Pub: Random Audio Pubg. Dist(s): Random

Heaven's Price, unabr. ed. Sandra Brown. Narrated by Peter Francis James. 5 cass. (Running Time: 6 hrs. 30 mins.). 1997. 44.00 (978-0-7887-0859-6(7), 95008E7) Recorded Bks.
Knee injuries force a Broadway dancer to move to a small town to recuperate. But her attractive landlord diverts her attention & brings new feelings to life in her heart.

Heaven's Prisoners. James Lee Burke. (Dave Robicheaux Ser.). 2004. 10.95 (978-0-7435-4821-2(3)) Pub: S&S Audio. Dist(s): S and S Inc

Heaven's Prisoners. unabr. ed. James Lee Burke. Narrated by Mark Hammer. 8 cass. (Running Time: 11 hrs.). (Dave Robicheaux Ser.). 1996. 79.75 (978-0-7887-0623-3(3), 94797E7) Recorded Bks.
When a plane crash brings a young girl into Dave Robicheaux life, she also brings murder, deception & the world of home-grown crime with her.

***Heaven's Spite.** unabr. ed. Lilith Saintcrow. Read by Joyce Bean. (Running Time: 8 hrs.). (Jill Kismet Ser.). 2010. 39.97 (978-1-4418-8686-6(9), 9781441886866, Brlnc Audio MP3 Lib); 24.99 (978-1-4418-8685-9(0), 9781441886859, Brilliance MP3); 24.99 (978-1-4418-8687-3(7), 9781441886873, BAD); 39.97 (978-1-4418-8688-0(5), 9781441886880, BADLE) Brilliance Audio.

***Heaven's Spite.** unabr. ed. Lilith Saintcrow. Read by Angela Dawe & Joyce Bean. (Running Time: 8 hrs.). (Jill Kismet Ser.). 2010. audio compact disk 79.97 (978-1-4418-8684-2(2), 9781441886842, BriAudCD Unabrid); audio compact disk 29.99 (978-1-4418-8683-5(4), 9781441886835, Bril Audio CD Unabri) Brilliance Audio.

Heaven's Touch: Healing Beyond Medicine Series. Joseph Michael Levry. 2001. 19.00 (978-1-885562-13-5(6)) Root Light.

***Heaven's Wager.** unabr. ed. Ted Dekker. Narrated by Tim Gregory. (Running Time: 16 hrs. 11 mins. 42 sec.). (Martyr's Song Ser.: Vol. 1). (ENG.). 2010. 24.49 (978-1-60814-777-9(0)); audio compact disk 34.99 (978-1-59859-808-7(2)) Oasis Audio.

Heavier Than Heaven: A Biography of Kurt Cobain. abr. unabr. ed. Charles R. Cross. Read by Lloyd James. 9 cass. (Running Time: 54000 sec.). 2006. 25.95 (978-0-7861-4542-3(0)); audio compact disk 25.95 (978-0-7861-7136-1(7)) Blckstn Audio.

Heavier Than Heaven: A Biography of Kurt Cobain. unabr. ed. Charles R. Cross. Read by Lloyd James. (Running Time: 54000 sec.). 2006. 72.95 (978-0-7861-4708-3(3)); audio compact disk 29.95 (978-0-7861-7600-7(8)); audio compact disk 99.00 (978-0-7861-6585-8(5)) Blckstn Audio.

Heavy Construction Equipment in France: A Strategic Reference 2007. Compiled by Icon Group International, Inc. Staff. 2007. ring bd. 195.00 (978-0-497-35950-8(2)) Icon Grp.

Heavy Construction Equipment in Nigeria: A Strategic Reference 2006. Compiled by Icon Group International, Inc. Staff. 2007. ring bd. 195.00 (978-0-497-82373-3(X)) Icon Grp.

Heavy Metal Drumming. Jim Latta. (Progressive Ser.). 1997. pap. bk. 19.95 (978-0-947183-75-2(2), 256-086) Kolala Music SGP.

Heavy Weather. abr. ed. P. G. Wodehouse. Read by Martin Jarvis. 4 CDs. (Running Time: 5 hrs. 0 mins. 0 sec.). (Blandings Castle Saga Ser.). (ENG.). 2009. audio compact disk 26.95 (978-1-934997-23-9(4)) Pub: CSAWord. Dist(s): PerseuPGW

Heavy Weather. unabr. ed. P. G. Wodehouse. Read by Frederick Davidson. 6 cass. (Running Time: 8 hrs. 30 mins.). 1991. 44.95 (978-0-7861-0252-5(7), 1220) Blckstn Audio.
Gloom lay like a mantle over the Mammoth Publishing Company, heaviest in the office of the proprietor, Lord Tilbury. On his desk lay a letter, brief but blasting: "Dear Sir: Enclosed find cheque for the advance you paid me on those Reminiscences of mine. I have been thinking it over & have decided not to publish them after all. Yours truly, G. Threepwood." Not conceding defeat, Lord Tilbury set about retrieving his fortunes, leading himself into situations most distressing for a newly made peer, little knowing that he was toying with the happiness of Sue Brown & Ronnie Fish, never guessing that his final obstacle would be the rotund form of the Empress of Blandings, Lord Emsworth's prize pig.

Heavyweight Championship: James 2:14:26, 624. Ed Young. 1987. 4.95 (978-0-7417-1624-8(0), 624) Win Walk.

Heber J Grant: A Dramatized History. Petrea Kelly. 2004. 9.95 (978-1-59156-377-8(1)); audio compact disk 11.95 (978-1-59156-378-5(X)) Covenant Comms.

Heber J Grant: Exemplar to the Saints. Matthew Haslam. 4 cass. 2004. 16.95 (978-1-59156-380-8(1)); audio compact disk 17.95 (978-1-59156-381-5(X)) Covenant Comms.

Hebreu sans Peine, Vol. 1. 1 cass. (Running Time: 1 hr., 30 min.). (FRE & HEB.). 2000. bk. 75.00 (978-2-7005-1321-9(5)) Pub: Assimil FRA. Dist(s): Distribks Inc

Hebreu sans Peine, Vol. 2. 1 cass. (Running Time: 1 hr., 30 min.). (FRE & HEB.). 2000. bk. 75.00 (978-2-7005-1322-6(3)) Pub: Assimil FRA. Dist(s): Distribks Inc

Hebrew. Penton Overseas, Inc. Staff. 4 cass. (Running Time: 2 hrs. 30 mins.). (HEB.). 1996. 49.95 (978-1-57451-002-7(9), HE57) CLL Cupertino.
Provides practice in 90% of our most commonly used words. All directions and practice sentences are spoken in one of 27 languages as well as English. The content is the same in all languages.

Hebrew. Penton Overseas, Inc. Staff. 4 cass. (Running Time: 2 hrs. 30 mins.). (HEB.). 1996. 49.95 (978-1-57451-001-0(0), HE35) CLL Cupertino.

Hebrew. Penton Overseas, Inc. Staff. 2 cass. (Running Time: 80 min.). (Language - Thirty Library). bk. 16.95 set in vinyl album. Moonbeam Pubns.
Using the proven method based on the famous U.S. Military accelerated language learning program, Language/30 courses stress conversationally useful words & phrases.

Hebrew. Paul Pimsleur. 16 cass. (Pimsleur Language Learning Ser.). 1982. pap. bk. & stu. ed. 345.00 (0671-57932-0) SyberVision.

Hebrew. unabr. ed. Ed. by Charles Berlitz. 2 cass. (Running Time: 1 hr. 30 mins.). (Language/30 Brief Course Ser.). pap. bk. 21.95 (AF1025) J Norton Pubs.
Quick, highly condensed introduction to the words & phrases you'll need to communicate effectively in the country you're visiting. Cassettes & phrase guide book are in a vinyl album.

Hebrew. 2nd ed. Pimsleur Staff. 4 CDs. (Running Time: 400 hrs. 0 mins. NaN sec.). (Basic Ser.). (HEB & ENG.). 2001. audio compact disk 19.95 (978-0-671-79085-1(4), Pimsleur) Pub: S&S Audio. Dist(s): S and S Inc

Hebrew: Language/30. rev. ed. Educational Services Corporation Staff. Intro. by Charles Berlitz. 2 cass. (HEB.). 1995. pap. bk. 21.95 (978-0-910542-80-7(5)) Educ Svcs DC.
Hebrew self-teaching language course.

Hebrew: Learn to Speak & Understand Hebrew with Pimsleur Language Programs. 2nd unabr. ed. Pimsleur. Created by Pimsleur. 8 CDs. (Running Time: 80 hrs. 0 mins. 0 sec.). (Instant Conversation Ser.). (HEB & ENG.). 2005. audio compact disk 49.95 (978-0-7435-5119-9(2), Pimsleur) Pub: S&S Audio. Dist(s): S and S Inc

Hebrew Audio Vocabulary Builder. unabr. ed. 1 cass. 12.95 (SHE010) J Norton Pubs.
101 words & phrases for the traveler.

Hebrew Basic Course. unabr. ed. Foreign Service Institute Staff. 24 cass. (Running Time: 35 hrs.). (HEB.). (J). (gr. 10-12). 1971. pap. bk. 285.00 (978-0-88432-040-1(5), AFH345) J Norton Pubs.
Designed to teach you to speak & read modern Hebrew, the ordinary, informal speech of educated native Israelis. It is not intended as a text for the study of the Old Testament or other Hebrew literature. Emphasis is on unaccented, conversational spoken Hebrew, although reading & writing skills are acquired as study progresses. The text includes a 15-page glossary & a section on the Hebrew alphabet.

Hebrew Basic Course (FSI) 25 CDs. (Running Time: 24 hrs.). (HEB.). 2005. audio compact disk 285.00 (978-1-57970-129-1(9), AFH345D) J Norton Pubs.

Hebrew Bible. Lawrence H. Schiffman. 2008. audio compact disk 29.99 (978-1-4361-7434-3(1)) Recorded Bks.

Hebrew Bible - New Testament (Spoken Word) Read by Shmoo-eloff Abraham. 16 cass. 1994. 39.97 (978-1-58968-065-4(0), 9501A) Chrstn Dup Intl.

Hebrew for Speakers of English, One. unabr. ed. 16 cass. (Running Time: 12 hrs. 30 min.). (Pimsleur Tapes Ser.). 1982. 345.00 set. (18526, Pimsleur) S&S Audio.
Spoken foreign-language proficiency training. Twenty-five, half-hour, intensive, spoken-language lesson units to be completed at the rate of one lesson per day for 30 days. By achieving eighty-percent correct answers to the questions in each unit, the Pimsleur Spoken Language Programmed Instructional Method will enable the learner to achieve the ACTFL Intermediate-Low Spoken Proficiency Level.

Hebrew I: Learn to Speak & Understand Hebrew with Pimsleur Language Programs. 2nd ed. Pimsleur Staff & Pimsleur. 16 CDs. (Running Time: 160 hrs. 0 mins. 0 sec.). (Comprehensive Ser.). (ENG.). 2001. audio compact disk 345.00 (978-0-7435-0041-8(5), Pimsleur) Pub: S&S Audio. Dist(s): S and S Inc

Hebrew III: Learn to Speak & Understand Hebrew with Pimsleur Language Programs. 3rd unabr. ed. Pimsleur. (Running Time: 16 hrs. 0 mins. 0 sec.). (Comprehensive Ser.). (ENG.). 2009. audio compact disk 345.00 (978-0-7435-5255-4(5), Pimsleur) Pub: S&S Audio. Dist(s): S and S Inc

Hebrew in a Minute. 1 cass. (Language in a Minute Cassette Ser.). 5.95 (978-1-878427-00-7(8), XC1027) Cimino Pub Grp.
Feel at home in any foreign country with these 101 esssential words & phrases. Hear each word introduced in English, hear them pronounced by a Voice of America instructor. Practice at your own pace, you can check yourself with the wallet sized dictionary included.

Hebrew in 60 Minutes. (In 60 MINUTES Ser.). 2009. audio compact disk 9.95 (978-981-268-610-7(X)) Pub: Berlitz Pubng. Dist(s): Langenscheidt

Hebrew New Testament. Contrib. by Christian Duplications International Staff. 16 cass. (HEB.). 1994. 39.98 Set. (978-7-902030-50-2(3)) Chrstn Dup Intl.
Bible.

Hebrew/Greek Tutor Bundle. Findex. 2004. audio compact disk 69.95 (978-1-57264-294-2(7)) Parsons Tech.

Hebrews. (LifeLight Bible Studies: Course 12). 13.95 (20-2303) Concordia.

Hebrews. Michael Pearl. 12 CDs. 2005. audio compact disk (978-1-892112-67-5(1)) No Greater Joy.

Hebrews. Michael Pearl. (ENG.). 2006. (978-1-934794-27-2(9)) No Greater Joy.

Hebrews Commentary. Chuck Missler. 1 CD-ROM. (Running Time: 20 hrs.). 2000. cd-rom 39.95 (978-1-57821-129-6(8)) Koinonia Hse.
The Epistle to the Hebrews is one of the two greatest theological treatises of the New Testament. This letter is, in a real way, the "Leviticus" of the New Testament, detailing how the Lord Jesus Christ is both the fulfillment and the successor to all that had gone on before.

Hebrews Commentary. Chuck Missler. 16 CD's. (Running Time: 16 hours aprox). (Chuck Missler Commentaries). 2008. audio compact disk 69.95 (978-1-57821-409-9(2)) Koinonia Hse.

Hebrews Highlights: Cd Album. Created by Awmi. (ENG.). 2009. audio compact disk 35.00 (978-1-59548-175-7(3)) A Wommack.

Heckler. unabr. ed. Ed McBain, pseud. Read by Jonathan Marosz. 6 cass. (Running Time: 6 hrs.). (87th Precinct Ser.: Bk. 12). 1996. 36.00 (978-0-7366-3254-6(9), 3911) Books on Tape.
Few things are as frustrating as anonymous phone calls. You want to strangle the caller, but you can't grab a voice. So when citizens in the 87th precinct get death threats over the phone, they vent their anger on the local boys in blue.

***Hector & the Search for Happiness.** unabr. ed. François Lelord. Tr. by Lorenza Garcia. (ENG.). 2010. audio compact disk 26.95 (978-1-61573-107-7(5), 1615731075) Pub: HighBridge. Dist(s): Workman Pub

Hedda Gabbler. Henrik Ibsen. 2 CDs. (Running Time: 7200 sec.). 2005. audio compact disk 19.95 (978-0-660-19468-4(6)) Canadian Broadcasting CAN.

Hedda Gabler. Henrik Ibsen. (Running Time: 2 hrs. 30 mins.). 2006. 20.95 (978-1-60083-761-6(1)) Iofy Corp.

Hedda Gabler. Henrik Ibsen. Narrated by Flo Gibson. (ENG.). 2007. audio compact disk 16.95 (978-1-55685-912-0(0)) Audio Bk Con.

Hedda Gabler. Perf. by Juliet Stevenson et al. Ed. by Henrik Ibsen. 2 cass. (Running Time: 2 hrs. 25 mins.). 2002. 13.98 (978-962-634-765-2(1), NA226514, Naxos AudioBooks) Naxos.
Hedda Gabler, a General's daughter marries dull George Tesman and foresees a life of middleclass tedium ahead when they return from a honeymoon they could not afford, to a house they cannot afford. Increasingly, she is drawn into the clutches of her admirer, Judge Brack, who seeks to establish a menage a trois. Then a former flame arrives in the brilliant Eilert Lovborg to rival her husband for an academic post. After a drunken orgy, the manuscript of his treatise falls into her hands and she destroys it. Discovery traps her, her romantic ideas are shattered, and there seems only one way out of the net, the pistols of her father, the General.

Hedda Gabler. unabr. ed. Perf. by Juliet Stevenson et al. Ed. by Henrik Ibsen. 2 CDs. (Running Time: 2 hrs. 30 mins.). 2002. audio compact disk 17.98 (978-962-634-265-7(X)) Naxos.

Hedda Gabler, Set. unabr. ed. Henrik Ibsen. Read by Flo Gibson. 2 cass. (Running Time: 3 hrs.). (gr. 8 up). 1991. 14.95 (978-1-55685-221-3(5)) Audio Bk Con.
Hedda, bored by her husband & jealous of her former lover Lovborg's success, lures Eilert Lovborg back to dissipation & secretly burns his manuscript. She gives him a pistol & urges him to "die beautifully." His death in a brawl threatens her with exposure.

Hedgie's Surprise. Jan Brett. Narrated by Randye Kaye. 1 cass. (Running Time: 1 hr.). (J). (gr. k-3). 2001. bk. (978-0-8045-6883-8(9), 6883) Spoken Arts.
Every morning Tomten steals an egg from Henny's nest, and then runs away to cook it and gobble it down for breakfast.

Hedingham Harvest. unabr. ed. Geoffrey Robinson. Read by Christopher Kay. 7 cass. (Running Time: 8 hrs.). (Sound Ser.). 2002. 61.95 (978-1-86042-671-1(9)) Pub: UlverLrgPrint GBR. Dist(s): Ulverscroft US
true story of village life inVictorian rural England. Active though he was with a succession of servant girls and neighbours' wives, my grandfather did not neglect almost nightly his reluctant wife.

Hedy West: Old Times & Hard Times. 1 cass. 9.98 (C-32) Folk-Legacy.
Songs & ballads from a long family traditionalist.

Heel, Toe, Away We Go. 1 cass. (Running Time: 35 min.). (J). (gr. k-3). 2001. pap. bk. 10.95 (KIM 7050C) Kimbo Educ.
Improve coordination skills through familiar folk dances in an easy style. Sailor's Hompipe, Glow Worm, Little Brown Jug & more. Includes guide.

Heel, Toe, Away We Go. Georgiana Stewart. 1 cass. (Running Time: 35 min.).Tr. of Talon y Dedo, Vamanos Todos. (SPA & ENG.). (J). (ps-3). 2001. pap. bk. 10.95 (KMS 7050C); pap. bk. 11.95 (KMS 7050) Kimbo Educ.
Improve coordination through familiar folk dances in an easy style. Side A - English translation. Side B - Spanish narration. Manual in English with narration script in Spanish.

Hegel in 90 Minutes. unabr. ed. Paul Strathern. Read by Robert Whitfield. (Running Time: 5400 sec.). (Philosophers in 90 Minutes Ser.). 2006. 14.95 (978-0-7861-3681-0(2)); audio compact disk 16.00 (978-0-7861-5945-1(6)) Blckstn Audio.

Hegemony or Survival: America's Quest for Full Spectrum Dominance. unabr. rev. ed. Noam Chomsky. Read by Brian Jones. 6 CDs. (Running Time: 7 hrs. 0 mins. 0 sec.). (American Empire Project Ser.). (ENG., 2003. audio compact disk 34.95 (978-1-55927-941-3(9), 890606) Pub: Macmill Audio. Dist(s): Macmillan

Heidegger & a Hippo Walk Through Those Pearly Gates: Using Philosophy (And Jokes!) to Explain Life, Death, the Afterlife, & Everything in Between. unabr. ed. Thomas Cathcart & Daniel Klein. Read by Thomas Cathcart. 4 CDs. (Running Time: 5 hrs.). (ENG.). (gr. 12 up). 2009. audio compact disk 29.95 (978-0-14-314498-4(7), PengAudBks) Penguin Grp USA.

Heidegger & a Hippo Walk through Those Pearly Gates: Using Philosophy (and Jokes!) to Explore Life, Death, the Afterlife, & Everything in Between. unabr. ed. Thomas Cathcart & Daniel Klein. (Running Time: 1 hr. 0 mins.). (ENG.). 2009. 29.95 (978-1-4417-0012-4(9)); 59.95 (978-1-4417-0008-7(0)); audio compact disk 76.00 (978-1-4417-0009-4(9)) Blckstn Audio.

Heidegger in 90 Minutes. Paul Strathern. Read by Robert Whitfield. (Running Time: 5400 sec.). (Philosophers in 90 Minutes Ser.). 2006. audio compact disk 16.00 (978-0-7861-5943-7(X)) Blckstn Audio.

Heidegger in 90 Minutes. unabr. ed. Paul Strathern. Read by Robert Whitfield. (Running Time: 5400 sec.). (Philosophers in 90 Minutes Ser.). 2006. 14.95 (978-0-7861-3683-4(9)) Blckstn Audio.

Heidelberg Castle/David David. Cynthia Todd & Debbie Ziemann. Illus. by Circe Woessner. (Sing Me a Song Ser.). (J). (ps-3). 1999. bk. 15.95 (978-1-879056-00-8(3)) Alpenhorn Pr.

Heidi. Johanna Spyri. 1 CD. (J). 1999. audio compact disk 49.95 Audio Bk Con.
Heidi, an orphan, goes to live with her old grandfather & his goats in the Swiss Alps, where she meets Peter, the goat boy, his blind grandmother & the villagers of Dorfli. She is taken away to Frankfurt to be a companion to the invalid Clara who later finds health & strength when they return to the mountain Heidi has learned love.

***Heidi.** Johanna Spyri. Narrated by Flo Gibson. (ENG.). (J). 2010. audio compact disk 29.95 (978-1-60646-172-3(9)) Audio Bk Con.

Heidi. Johanna Spyri. 2 CDs. (Running Time: 1 hr. 50 mins.). 2006. audio compact disk 29.95 (978-0-7927-3991-3(4), BBCD 142) AudioGO.

Heidi. Johanna Spyri. Read by Teresa Gallagher. (Running Time: 2 hrs. 30 mins.). 2001. 20.95 (978-1-60083-762-3(X)) Iofy Corp.

Heidi. Johanna Spyri. Read by Teresa Gallagher. 2 cass. (Running Time: 2 hrs. 30 min.). 2003. 13.98 (978-962-634-785-0(6), Naxos AudioBooks); audio compact disk 17.98 (978-962-634-285-5(4), Naxos AudioBooks) Naxos.
Initially, life in the Swiss Alps proves to be rather difficult for Heidi, but eventually she wins the heart of her grandfather and befriends Peter, a young goatherd.

Heidi. abr. ed. Johanna Spyri. Read by Claire Bloom. 1 cass. (Running Time: 60 min.). (J). (gr. k-6). 10.98 (308) MFLP CA.
Heartwarming story of the little girl who brings so much joy to all she meets. Her love for life in the Swiss Alps with her grandfather, her friendship with the invalid girl she helps to heal, & her gift of caring make this book unforgettable.

Heidi. abr. ed. Johanna Spyri. 1 cass. (Running Time: 50 min.). Dramatization. (J). 10.95 (978-0-8045-1109-4(8), SAC 1109) Spoken Arts.

Heidi. abr. adpt. ed. Johanna Spyri. (Bring the Classics to Life: Level 1 Ser.). (ENG.). (gr. 4-7). 2008. audio compact disk 12.95 (978-1-55576-418-0(5)) EDCON Pubng.

Heidi. unabr. ed. Ed. by Johanna Spyri. Narrated by Flo Gibson. 6 cass. (Running Time: 9 hrs.). (J). 1984. 24.95 (978-1-55685-055-4(7)) Audio Bk Con.
Heidi, an orphan, goes to live with her old grandfather & his goats in the Swiss Alps, where she meets Peter, the goat boy, his blind grandmother & the villagers of Dorfli. She is taken away to Frankfurt to be a companion to the invalid Clara who later finds health & strength when they return to the mountain Heidi has learned love.

Heidi, unabr. ed. Johanna Spyri. Read by Johanna Ward. 5 cass. (Running Time: 7 hrs.). 1994. 39.95 (978-0-7861-0644-8(1), 1460) Blckstn Audio.
High in the Swiss Alps, Heidi, a five year old orphan, comes to live with her grandfather. His neighbors say he is a fierce old hermit, of whom they are all afraid. Heidi, however, proves to be a remarkable, unaffected child, who quickly charms her grandfather. However, her Aunt Dete doesn't understand, & it is a sad day when she takes Heidi to live in a strange city with a strange family who want a companion for their young invalid daughter Klara. Heidi does her best to be a friend to Klara, but her longing for home becomes too much to bear.

Heidi. unabr. ed. Johanna Spyri. Read by Johanna Ward. 7 CDs. (Running Time: 7 hrs.). 2000. audio compact disk 56.00 (978-0-7861-9827-6(3), 1460) Blckstn Audio.
Heidi, a five-year-old orphan, comes to live with her mean old grandfather. She soon proves to be a unaffected child & quickly charms her grandfather.

Heidi. unabr. ed. Johanna Spyri. Read by Marilyn Langbehn. 8 cass. (Running Time: 7 hrs. 45 min.). 1989. 49.95 (978-1-55686-297-7(0), 297) Books in Motion.
An effervescent little orphaned girl goes to the Alps to live with her grandfather.

Heidi. unabr. ed. Johanna Spyri. Read by Marnie MacAdam. (Running Time: 8 hrs.). 2006. 39.25 (978-1-4233-1111-9(6), 9781423311119, BADLE); 24.95 (978-1-4233-1110-2(8), 9781423311102, BAD) Brilliance Audio.

Heidi. unabr. ed. Johanna Spyri. Read by Marnie MacAdam. (Running Time: 28800 sec.). (Classic Collection (Brilliance Audio) Ser.). (J). (gr. 4-7). 2006. audio compact disk 87.25 (978-1-4233-1107-2(8), 9781423311072, BriAudCD Unabrid); audio compact disk 39.25 (978-1-4233-1109-6(4), 9781423311096, Brinc Audio MP3 Lib); audio compact disk 32.95 (978-1-4233-1106-5(X), 9781423311065, Bril Audio CD Unabri); audio compact disk 24.95 (978-1-4233-1108-9(6), 9781423311089, Brilliance MP3) Brilliance Audio.
In this treasured story, the orphan child, Heidi, is sent to live with her embittered Grandfather high in the Swiss Alps. Heidi's innocent joy of life and genuine concern and love for all living things become the old man's salvation. From the goatherder Peter and his family to the sickly girl Clara and her desperate father, Heidi's special charm enriches everyone she meets. Unselfish to the core, Heidi's goodness overcomes all obstacles - even those seemingly insurmountable. Remembered and loves as a child's story, Heidi remains a testimony of redemption and salvation for all ages. Uplifting and enjoyable, Heidi makes superior family listening.

Heidi. unabr. ed. Johanna Spyri. Read by Frances Cassidy. (J). 2006. 39.99 (978-1-59895-683-2(3)) Find a World.

Heidi. unabr. ed. Johanna Spyri. Narrated by John McDonough. 8 cass. (Running Time: 10 hrs. 45 min.). (J). (gr. 2). 1997. 16.50 Recorded Bks.
Heidi, a small orphaned girl, is sent to live with her reclusive grandfather high in the Swiss Alps where she spends glorious days playing on the hills with the goat boy, Peter. And when Heidi is sent to a cold city to care for an invalid, she works a miracle there that reflects her love of the wild freedom of her beloved mountains.

Heidi, unabr. ed. Johanna Spyri. Narrated by John McDonough. 8 cass. (Running Time: 10 hrs. 45 mins.). (gr. 6 up). 1997. 69.00 (978-0-7887-0677-6(2), 94710E7) Recorded Bks.

Heidi. unabr. ed. Johanna Spyri. Narrated by Frances Cassidy. (Running Time: 6 hrs. 0 mins. 0 sec.). (ENG.). (J). (gr. 4-7). 2008. 19.99 (978-1-4001-5883-6(4)); audio compact disk 45.99 (978-1-4001-3883-8(3)) Pub: Tantor Media. Dist(s): IngramPubServ

Heidi. unabr. ed. Johanna Spyri. Read by Frances Cassidy. (Running Time: 6 hrs. 0 mins. 0 sec.). (ENG.). (J). (gr. 4-7). 2008. audio compact disk 22.99 (978-1-4001-0883-1(7)) Pub: Tantor Media. Dist(s): IngramPubServ

Heidi. unabr. collector's ed. Johanna Spyri. Read by Frances Cassidy. 6 cass. (Running Time: 6 hrs.). (J). (gr. 4-7). 1994. 36.00 (978-0-7366-2872-3(X), 3577) Books on Tape.
Heidi shares her grandfather's frugal life in the Swiss Alps. One of the best-loved stories in children's literature.

Heidi: A BBC Radio Full-Cast Dramatization. Johanna Spyri. (Running Time: 2 hrs. 0 mins. 0 sec.). (ENG.). 2009. audio compact disk 24.95 (978-1-60283-755-3(4)) Pub: AudioGO. Dist(s): Perseus Dist

Heidi Chronicles. Wendy Wasserstein. Contrib. by Kaitlin Hopkins et al. (Playaway Adult Fiction Ser.). 2008. 39.99 (978-1-60640-944-2(1)) Find a World.

Heidi Chronicles. unabr. ed. Wendy Wasserstein. Read by Martha Plimpton et al. 2 CDs. (Running Time: 7200 sec.). (L. A. Theatre Works). 2003. audio compact disk 25.95 (978-1-58081-268-9(6), CDTPT183) Pub: L A Theatre. Dist(s): NetLibrary CO
The tale of a baby-boomer?s long, hard road from ?60s confusion to ?90s self-made woman. . . or so she hopes.

Heidi Joyce's Comedy Stand up Against Domestic Violence, Vol. 1. Perf. by Heidi Joyce et al. 2000. 14.95 (978-1-929243-06-8(5)) Uproar Ent.

Heidi Joyce's Comedy Stand up Against Domestic Violence, Vol. 1. Perf. by Heidi Joyce et al. (Heidi Joyce's Comedy Stand Up Against Domestic Violence: Vol. I). 2000. audio compact disk 19.95 (978-1-929243-05-1(7)) Uproar Ent.

Heidi Joyce's Comedy Stand up Against Domestic Violence, Vol. 2. unabr. ed. Perf. by Heidi Joyce et al. (Heidi Joyce's Comedy Stand Up Against Domestic Violence: Vol. II). 2001. audio compact disk 19.95 (978-1-929243-32-7(4)) Uproar Ent.

Heidi Muller: Between the Water & the Wind. 1 cass. 9.98 (C-562) Folk-Legacy.
The first recording of a glorious singer.

Heidi Muller: Cassiopeia. 1 cass., 1 CD. 9.98 (C-560); audio compact disk 14.98 CD. (CD-560) Folk-Legacy.
A lovely collection of songs by a great singer from Seattle.

Heidi Muller: Giving Back. 1 cass., 1 CD. 9.98 (C-563); audio compact disk 14.98 CD. (CD-563) Folk-Legacy.
Heidi's lastest recording, with many of her fine new songs.

Heidi Muller: Matters of the Heart. 1 cass., 1 CD. 9.98 (C-561); audio compact disk 14.98 CD. (CD-561) Folk-Legacy.
More songs offered by one of the finest voices going.

Heifer Project's Gifts of Animals & Raffi Sings "Evergreen, Everblue" Hosted by Nancy Pearlman. 1 cass. (Running Time: 28 min.). 10.00 (1205) Educ Comm CA.

Heigh Ho Banjo: Bluegrass Salutes Favorite Disney Songs. 1 cass., 1 CD. 7.98 (CMH 8019); audio compact disk 11.18 CD Jewel box. (CMH 8019) NewSound.

Heigh Ho Banjo: Bluegrass Salutes Favorite Disney Songs. 1 cass., 1 CD. (J). 7.98 (CMH 8019); audio compact disk 11.18 CD Jewel box. (CMH 8019) NewSound.

Heights. unabr. ed. Peter Hedges. (Running Time: 8 hrs.). (ENG.). (gr. 12 up). 2010. audio compact disk 29.95 (978-0-14-314531-8(2), PengAudBks) Penguin Grp USA.

Heights of Zervos. unabr. ed. Colin Forbes. Read by Sean Barrett. 8 cass. (Running Time: 10 hrs.). 2001. 69.95 (978-1-85089-611-1(9), 91011) Pub: ISIS Audio GBR. Dist(s): Ulverscroft US
It is April 1941...The monastery on the Zervos mountain dominates the only escape route for the small British expeditionary force. The German army is

invading Greece. Ian Macomber, Grapos, Lieutenant Prentice & Sergeant Ford, are the only four men who stand in the way of the Nazis.

Heinemann Australian Student Dictionary Edictionary. 2001. audio compact disk 26.95 (978-0-86462-732-2(7), Heinemann Pear) Pearson EdAUS AUS.

Heinemann eEnglish Links Four. Marguerite O'Hara & Michael Pryor. (J). 2000. audio compact disk 39.60 (978-0-86462-609-7(6), Heinemann Pear) Pearson EdAUS AUS.

Heinemann eEnglish Links One. Sara Wawer & Michael Pryor. (J). 2000. audio compact disk 39.60 (978-0-86462-606-6(1), Heinemann Pear); audio compact disk 39.60 (978-0-86462-778-0(5), Heinemann Pear) Pearson EdAUS AUS.

Heinemann eEnglish Links Three. Marguerite O'Hara & Michael Pryor. (J). 2000. audio compact disk 39.60 (978-0-86462-608-0(8), Heinemann Pear) Pearson EdAUS AUS.

Heinemann eEnglish Links Two. Sara Wawer & Michael Pryor. (J). 2000. audio compact disk 39.60 (978-0-86462-607-3(X), Heinemann Pear) Pearson EdAUS AUS.

Heinemann English Language: VCE Units 3 And 4. Louise Taunt & Debbie De Laps. (YA). 2001. stu. ed. 40.70 (978-0-86462-722-3(X), Heinemann Pear) Pearson EdAUS AUS.

Heinemann English Zone. Andrea Hayes et al. (J). 2002. tchr. ed. 113.30 (978-1-74081-102-6(X), Heinemann Pear) Pearson EdAUS AUS.

Heinemann English Zone 2, Vol. 2. Andrea Hayes. (J). 2003. tchr. ed. 113.30 (978-1-74081-106-4(2), Heinemann Pear) Pearson EdAUS AUS.

Heinemann Foundation English. Tony Glasson & McGee. (J). 2001. tchr. ed. 96.80 (978-0-86462-721-6(1), Heinemann Pear); stu. ed. 41.80 (978-0-86462-719-3(X), Heinemann Pear) Pearson EdAUS AUS.

***Heinle Picture Dictionary.** Jann Huizenga & Heinle. (ENG.). (C). 2004. 169.95 (978-0-8384-4406-1(7)) Pub: Heinle. Dist(s): CENGAGE Learn

Heinrich Boll: Das Brot der Fruhen Jahre. 1 cass. (Running Time: 1 hr.). (German Literary Criticism Ser.). (GER.). 2001. 12.95 (G07554) J Norton Pubs.
Recorded at the University of Exeter in England.

Heir. abr. ed. Barbara Taylor Bradford. Narrated by John Lee. (Running Time: 6 hrs. 0 mins. 0 sec.). Bk. 2. (ENG.). 2007. audio compact disk 29.95 (978-1-4272-0244-4(3)) Pub: Macmill Audio. Dist(s): Macmillan

***Heir.** abr. ed. Barbara Taylor Bradford. (Running Time: 6 hrs. 0 mins. 0 sec.). 2011. audio compact disk 14.99 (978-1-4272-1190-3(6)) Pub: Macmill Audio. Dist(s): Macmillan

Heir. abr. ed. Johanna Lindsey. Read by Laural Merlington. (Running Time: 3 hrs.). (Reid Family Ser.). 2009. audio compact disk 14.99 (978-1-4233-6633-1(6), 9781423366331) Brilliance Audio.

Heir. unabr. ed. Barbara Taylor Bradford. Narrated by John Lee. 13 CDs. (Running Time: 16 hrs. 20 mins.). (Ravenscar Ser.: Bk. 2). 2007. audio compact disk 112.95 (978-0-7927-5047-5(0)) AudioGO.

Heir. unabr. ed. Barbara Taylor Bradford. Read by John Lee. (Running Time: 17 hrs. 0 mins. 0 sec.). Bk. 2. (ENG.). 2007. audio compact disk 39.95 (978-1-4272-0243-7(5)) Pub: Macmill Audio. Dist(s): Macmillan

Heir. unabr. ed. Catherine Coulter. Read by Steven Crossley. 10 cass. (Running Time: 13 hrs. 30 mins.). 1997. 85.00 (978-0-7887-0655-4(1), 94832E7) Recorded Bks.
This richly layered tale set in early 19th century England has been rewritten for the 90s audience. When a couple is forced to marry to gain inheritance, their marriage of convenience exposes intrigue & a family secret that threatens to destroy them.

Heir. unabr. ed. Johanna Lindsey. Read by Laural Merlington. (Running Time: 9 hrs.). (Reid Family Ser.). 2009. 24.99 (978-1-4233-6629-4(8), 9781423366294, Brilliance MP3); 24.99 (978-1-4233-6631-7(X), 9781423366317, BAD); 39.97 (978-1-4233-6630-0(1), 9781423366300, Brlnc Audio MP3 Lib); 39.97 (978-1-4233-6632-4(8), 9781423366324, BADLE); audio compact disk 29.99 (978-1-4233-6627-0(1), 9781423366270, Bril Audio CD Unabri); audio compact disk 92.97 (978-1-4233-6628-7(X), 9781423366287, BriAudCD Unabrid) Brilliance Audio.

Heir Apparent. unabr. ed. Vivian Vande Velde. Narrated by Carine Montbertrand. 8 cass. (Running Time: 10 hrs.). (YA). 2005. 64.75 (978-1-4193-2654-7(6), 97958) Recorded Bks.
Vivian Vande Velde is an Edgar Award-winning author of fiction for young adults. Heir Apparent, a Junior Library Guild Selection and winner of the Anne Spencer Lindbergh Prize for Best Children's Fantasy Novel, has been called "consistently entertaining" by Publishers Weekly. This clever and imaginative fantasy, featuring a marvelous reading from narrator Carine Montbertrand, will lure curious listeners into the virtual reality world of a medieval-styled arcade game that might just be deadly.

Heir Hunter. unabr. ed. Chris Larsgaard. Narrated by Pete Bradbury. 10 cass. (Running Time: 14 hrs.). 2000. 91.00 (978-0-7887-4881-3(5), 96232E7) Recorded Bks.
A dazzling page-turner peppered with murder, robbery & conspiracy. Nick Merchant is an heir hunter. His globetrotting, life-threatening task is to find an heir for the mysterious Gerald Jacobs & collect a chunk of the 22 million bucks Jacobs left behind.

Heir of Redclyffe. Charlotte M. Yonge. Read by Anais 9000. 2008. 33.95 (978-1-60112-113-4(X)) Babblebooks.

Heir of the Whole World. unabr. ed. Gilbert Highet. Read by Gilbert Highet. 1 cass. (Running Time: 30 min.). 9.95 (23300-A) J Norton Pubs.

Heir to the Dragon. abr. ed. Robert N. Charrette. 2 cass. (Running Time: 3 hrs.). (Battletech). 2002. 9.95 (978-1-931953-29-0(5)) Listen & Live.

Heir to the Empire. unabr. ed. Timothy Zahn. Read by Larry McKeever. 11 cass. (Running Time: 16 hrs. 30 min.). (Star Wars: Vol. 1). (J). 1995. 88.00 Set. (3753) Books on Tape.
The Rebel Alliance has taken care of business, but the last Imperial warlord plots to shatter the New Republic's peace. Dramatic & breathtaking.

Heiress. Janet Dailey. Read by Shelley Thompson. 16 cass. (Running Time: 18 hrs. 49 min.). 2001. 41.95 (978-0-7540-0593-3(3)) AudioGO.
Two women meet each other for the first time across their father's grave. They are bound together by a fateful secret, they are sisters but only one is legitimate & only one can claim the legacy that truly marks her as the Heiress.

Heiress. unabr. ed. Janet Dailey. Read by Kate Harper. 16 vols. (Running Time: 24 hrs.). 2001. bk. 124.95 (978-0-7927-2448-3(8), CSL 337, Chivers Sound Lib) AudioGO.
Two women, who could almost be twins. Abbie Lawson is gently bred & raised in luxury, Rachel Farr is the love child of Dean Lawson & a fiery artist. Rachel's life has been modest & lonely. Their father's death will set off a fierce competition, of each sister trying to prove which one of them their father loved best by fighting to inherit his legacy.

Heiress. unabr. ed. Ruth Goetz & Augustus Goetz. Perf. by Amy Irving et al. 2 CDs. (Running Time: 2 hrs. 5 mins.). 2002. audio compact disk 25.95 (978-1-58081-231-3(7), CDWTA6) Pub: L A Theatre. Dist(s): NetLibrary CO
Set in New York City in 1850, centers on painfully shy Catherine and her austere father. When Catherine falls in love with a handsome suitor, her father threatens to disinherit her, convinced that the young man could only be interested in Catherine's fortune.

Heiress Bride. abr. ed. Catherine Coulter. Read by Anne Flosnik. 5. (Running Time: 21600 sec.). (Bride Ser.). 2007. audio compact disk 14.99 (978-1-59737-808-6(9), 9781597378086, BCD Value Price) Brilliance Audio.

Heiress Bride. abr. ed. Catherine Coulter. Read by Emma Samms. 2 cass. (Running Time: 3 hrs.). (Bride Trilogy: Bk. 3). 1992. 15.95 Set. (978-1-879371-23-1(5), 40100) Pub Mills.
The year is 1807 & the mysterious intrigue of the Sherbrookes continues. At the ripe age of 19 years & on her second society debut in London, "The Heiress Bride," Joan "Sinjun" Sherbrooke meets, falls madly in love with & marries a Scottish nobleman in search of a royal heiress for his bride.

Heiress Bride. unabr. ed. Catherine Coulter. Read by Anne Flosnik. (Running Time: 12 hrs.). (Bride Ser.). 2006. 39.25 (978-1-59737-806-2(2), 9781597378062, BADLE); 24.95 (978-1-59737-805-5(4), 9781597378055, BAD); 87.25 (978-1-59737-800-0(3), 9781597378000, BrilAudUnabridg); audio compact disk 39.25 (978-1-59737-804-8(6), 9781597378048, Brlnc Audio MP3 Lib); audio compact disk 102.25 (978-1-59737-802-4(X), 9781597378024, BriAudCD Unabrid); audio compact disk 36.95 (978-1-59737-801-7(1), 9781597378017, Bril Audio CD Unabri); audio compact disk 24.95 (978-1-59737-803-1(8), 9781597378031, Brilliance MP3) Brilliance Audio.
Dear Reader, Welcome to the exciting conclusion of the English Regency Bride Trilogy, The Heiress Bride. You met Sinjun Sherbrooke in The Sherbrooke Bride and in The Hellion Bride, a delightful, quite endearing fifteen-year-old who, I hope, charmed your socks off. Now she's nineteen, blessed with Sherbrooke blue eyes, wit to burn, and a wonderful sense of humor. She is also bored with the London Season until she spies Colin Kinross, the Scottish earl of Ashburnham, across the dance floor at a London ball. When she overhears Colin complain that he must find a wealthy bride quickly in order to survive, Sinjun promptly introduces herself as the answer to his prayers. Despite all odds, Sinjun manages an elopement to Scotland to begin her life in a drafty old castle that holds more revelations and surprises than Sinjun could ever imagine. You'll also meet another ghost, Pearlin' Jane, who teams up with the Virgin Bride. Do enjoy Sinjun. She's one hell of a bride. Please write to me at P.O. Box 17, Mill Valley, CA 94942 or email me at ReadMoi@aol.com and let me know which of the three Bride novels you like best. Catherine Coulter.

Heirloom. Perf. by Steve Hall & Mary B. Carlson. 1 cass., 1 CD. 7.98 (BANK 15); audio compact disk 12.78 CD Jewel box. (BANK 15) NewSound.

Heirlooms. Contrib. by Amy Grant. (Mastertrax Ser.). 2007. audio compact disk 9.98 (978-5-557-55751-1(2)) Pt of Grace Ent.

Heirlooms. Contrib. by Amy Grant. 2006. audio compact disk 8.98 (978-5-558-27161-4(2), Word Music) Word Enter.

Heirs & Graces. unabr. ed. Gerald Hammond & Cathleen McCarron. Contrib. by Cathleen McCarron. 6 vols. (Story Sound CD Ser.). (J). 2006. audio compact disk 64.95 (978-1-85903-949-6(9)) Pub: Mgna Lrg Print GBR. Dist(s): Ulverscroft US

Heirs & Graces, Vol. 5. unabr. ed. Gerald Hammond. Contrib. by Cathleen McCarron. (Story Sound Ser.). (J). 2006. 49.95 (978-1-85903-899-4(9)) Pub: Mgna Lrg Print GBR. Dist(s): Ulverscroft US

Heirs Together: Solving the Mystery of a Satisfying Marriage. 8 cass. (Running Time: 7 hrs. 30 min.). 2000. 40.00 (978-1-57399-119-3(8)) Mac Hammond.
This series shines the light of God's Word on the husband-wife relationship with remarkable frankness, insight, and humor. Learn the four attitude adjustments you must make to have a happy marriage, your spouse's "top five" needs, and much more.

***Heist Society.** Ally Carter. Contrib. by Angela Dawe. (Playaway Children Ser.). (J). 2010. 54.99 (978-1-4418-4853-6(3)) Find a World.

Heist Society. unabr. ed. Ally Carter. Read by Renée Raudman & Angela Dawe. (Running Time: 7 hrs.). 2010. 24.99 (978-1-4418-2675-6(0), 9781441826756, Brilliance MP3); 24.99 (978-1-4418-2677-0(7), 9781441826770, BAD); 39.97 (978-1-4418-2676-3(9), 9781441826763, Brlnc Audio MP3 Lib); 39.97 (978-1-4418-2678-7(5), 9781441826787, BADLE); audio compact disk 24.99 (978-1-4418-2673-2(4), 9781441826732, Bril Audio CD Unabri); audio compact disk 71.97 (978-1-4418-2674-9(2), 9781441826749, BriAudCD Unabrid) Brilliance Audio.

Hele 'O Kawika Laua 'O Kamuela I Ka Pule. Hokulani Cleeland. Illus. by Brook Parker. 1 cass. (HAW.). (J). (gr. k-1). 1999. pap. bk. 5.95 (978-1-58191-055-1(X)) Aha Punana Leo.

Helen see George Seferis

Helen Barolini. Interview. Interview with Helen Barolini & Kay Bonetti. 1 cass. (Running Time: 55 min.). 1983. 13.95 (978-1-55644-065-6(0), 3022) Am Audio Prose.
Interview concerns issues surrounding the concepts of ethnic literature & its place in the larger American tradition, her feminism, & problems peculiar to her particular choice of subject matter.

Helen Baylor: The Definitive Gospel Collection. Contrib. by Helen Baylor. (Definitive Gospel Collection). 2008. audio compact disk 7.99 (978-5-557-49743-5(9), Word Records) Word Enter.

Helen Baylor Live... The Testimony Continues. Perf. by Helen Baylor. 1 cass., 1 CD. (Running Time: 90 min.). 1999. video & audio compact disk 19.98 (978-0-7601-2631-8(3)) Buena Vista Home Video.
Recorded live in Denver, Colorado before a full capacity crowd at Heritage Christian Center says all that need be said.

Helen Baylor Live... The Testimony Continues. Perf. by Helen Baylor. 1 CD. 1999. audio compact disk 16.98 (978-0-7601-2630-1(5)) Provident Music.

Helen Baylor Live...The Testimony Continues. Perf. by Helen Baylor. 1 cass. 1999. 10.98 (978-0-7601-2629-5(1)) Provident Music.

Helen Bonchek Schneyer: Somber, Sacred & Silly. 1 cass., 1 CD. 9.98 (C-553); audio compact disk 14.98 CD. (CD-553) Folk-Legacy.
Wide ranging program, powerfully sung.

Helen, Ethel & the Crazy Quilt Audio Book: Based on the 1890 Letters Between Helen Keller & Ethel Orr. Nancy Orr Johnson Jensen. (ENG.). (J). 2007. 9.95 (978-1-932278-24-8(9)) Pub: Mayhaven Pub. Dist(s): Baker Taylor

Helen Hath No Fury. unabr. ed. Gillian Roberts. Narrated by Christina Moore. 6 cass. (Running Time: 7 hrs. 45 mins.). (Amanda Pepper Mystery Ser.). 2002. 57.00 (978-1-4025-1705-1(X)) Recorded Bks.
Amanda Pepper is not the usual gumshoe; she teaches English in one of Philadelphia's most exclusive schools. In a world of old families and solid wealth, Amanda's cases test her wit, wisdom, and social graces. During a lively discussion of The Awakening at Amanda's book club meeting, a member, Helen Coulter, vigorously denounces the main character's suicide as cowardly. When Helen tragically falls from the roof of her house the very next day, Amanda finds it very strange that the death is ruled a suicide. Immediately, she smells foul play. As she begins an investigation, Amanda will follow an increasingly dangerous path - one leading toward a cold-blooded killer ready to strike again.

Helen Hayes: My Life in Three Acts. unabr. ed. Helen Hayes & Katherine Hatch. Read by James MacArthur. 6 cass. (Running Time: 8 hrs. 30 mins.). 1998. 44.95 (978-0-7861-1296-8(4), 2200) Blckstn Audio.
Helen Hayes speaks with wit, wisdom & candor on topics both public & private. She treats us to anecdotes about Ethel Barrymore, John Ford, Al Capone. At the same time she reflects more seriously on the painful parts of her life.

Helen Keller. Cerebellum Academic Team. (Running Time: 30 mins.). (Just the Facts Ser.). 2010. 24.95 (978-1-59163-387-7(7)) Cerebellum.

Helen Keller. Dorothy Herrmann. Read by Mary Peiffer. 1998. 80.00 (978-0-7366-4233-0(1)) Books on Tape.

Helen Keller. unabr. ed. Dorothy Herrmann. Read by Mary Peiffer. 10 cass. (Running Time: 15 hrs.). 1998. 80.00 (4739) Books on Tape.
Portrays Helen Keller's childhood & her relationship with her teacher Annie Sullivan.

Helen Keller. unabr. ed. Robert Hogrogian. 1 cass. (Running Time: 20 min.). (People to Remember Ser.: Set II). (J). (gr. 4-7). 1979. bk. 16.99 (978-0-934898-57-7(X)); pap. bk. 9.95 (978-0-934898-15-7(4)) Jan Prods.
An inspirational story of a woman's courage & determination.

Helen Keller: Courageous Advocate. Scott R. Welvaert. Illus. by Cynthia Martin & Keith Tucker. (Graphic Biographies Ser.). (ENG.). (gr. 3-4). 2007. audio compact disk 6.95 (978-1-4296-1470-2(6)) CapstoneDig.

Helen Keller: Facing Her Challenges - Challenging the World. Janet Benge. Illus. by Kennon James. 1 cass. Dramatization. (Another Great Achiever Ser.). (J). 2003. lib. bdg. 23.95 (978-1-57537-793-3(4)); 16.95 (978-1-57537-593-9(1)) Advance Pub.

Helen Keller: From Tragedy to Triumph. unabr. ed. Katherine E. Wilkie. Read by Marguerite Gavin. 3 cass. (Running Time: 4 hrs.). (Childhood of Famous Americans Ser.). (gr. 1-3). 2001. pap. bk. 35.95 (978-0-7861-2066-6(5), K2827) Blckstn Audio.
Listen & enjoy the story of the childhood of Helen Keller, a courageous little girl who overcame severe physical limitations & turned tragedy into triumph with the loving help of a determined teacher.

Helen Keller (INK Audiocassette) Courageous Advocate. (Graphic Library Biographies I Ser.). (ENG.). 2006. audio compact disk 5.95 (978-0-7368-7452-6(6)) CapstoneDig.

Helen Kemp: A Portrait (DVD) Helen Kemp. 2007. 49.95 (978-1-929187-22-5(X)) Choristers.

Helen Lawrenson. Interview with Helen Lawrenson. 1 cass. (Running Time: 25 min.). 1980. 11.95 (L042) TFR.
The author of "Latins are Lousy Lovers" tells about her bawdy life & rates her lovers which includes presidential adviser Bernard Baruch, Harlem gangster Bumpy Johnson & Robbin Stephen Wise.

Helen Schneyer: Ballads, Broadsides & Hymns. 1 cass. 9.98 (C-50) Folk-Legacy.
Powerful performance by a great singer.

Helen Schneyer: On the Hallelujah Line. 1 cass. 9.98 (C-85) Folk-Legacy.
Gospel song collection of traditional hammered dulcimer artist ever.

Helen Schucman, A Gift of God. Kenneth Wapnick. 2 CDs. 2005. audio compact disk 14.00 (978-1-59142-181-8(0), CD108) Foun Miracles.

Helena. Perf. by Robert Kochis & Robin Kochis. 1 cass. (Running Time: 45 mins.). 1999. 10.95 (T8699); audio compact disk 15.95 (K5140) Liguori Pubns.
Songs include: "I Surrender All," "Be with Me Lord," "I Cannot Tell All," "Fairest Lord Jesus" & more.

Helicopter Man. Elizabeth Fensham. Read by Stig Wemyss. (Running Time: 3 hrs. 35 mins.). (J). 2009. 54.99 (978-1-74214-374-3(1), 9781742143743) Pub: Bolinda Pubng AUS. Dist(s): Bolinda Pub Inc

Helicopter Man. unabr. ed. Elizabeth Fensham. Read by Stig Wemyss. (Running Time: 3 hrs. 35 mins.). (J). 2007. audio compact disk 54.95 (978-1-74093-926-3(3), 9781740939263) Pub: Bolinda Pubng AUS. Dist(s): Bolinda Pub Inc

Helicopters, Drill Sergeants & Consultants: Parenting Styles & the Messages They Send. Jim Fay. Read by Jim Fay. Ed. by Bert Gurule Mizke. 1 cass. (Running Time: 90 mins.). 1994. 12.95 (978-0-944634-04-2(4)) Pub: Love Logic. Dist(s): Penton Overseas
Parenting expert & humorous story teller, Jim Fay, helps parents identify their parenting style, then shares practical, stress-free techniques to help parents enjoy parenting to the fullest.

Helicopters, Drill Sergeants & Consultants: Parenting Styles & the Messages They Send. unabr. ed. Jim Fay & Bert Gurule Mizke. Perf. by Jim Fay & Bert Gurule Mizke. 1 CD. (Running Time: 1 hr. 20 mins.). 2000. audio compact disk 13.95 (978-1-930429-08-6(8)) Pub: Love Logic. Dist(s): Penton Overseas
Parenting expert helps you identify your parenting style & the powerful message this style sends to the children.

Helicopters in India: A Strategic Reference 2007. Compiled by Icon Group International, Inc. Staff. 2007. ring bd. 195.00 (978-0-497-36013-9(6)) Icon Grp.

Helicopters in Japan: A Strategic Reference 2006. Compiled by Icon Group International, Inc. Staff. 2007. ring bd. 195.00 (978-0-497-82327-6(6)) Icon Grp.

Helicopters in United Kingdom: A Strategic Reference 2006. Compiled by Icon Group International, Inc. Staff. 2007. ring bd. 195.00 (978-0-497-82453-2(1)) Icon Grp.

Heliocentric, Pt. 1. T. Patrick Davis. 1 cass. 8.95 (508) Am Fed Astrologers.
Basics - includes rectification techniques.

Heliocentric, Pt. 2. T. Patrick Davis. 1 cass. 8.95 (509) Am Fed Astrologers.
Geo & helio differ - notes on Chiron.

Heliocentric Astrology: A Spiritual Map. Stephanie Clement. 1 cass. (Running Time: 90 min.). 1990. 8.95 (753) Am Fed Astrologers.

Hell Pt. 1: Logos August 9,1998. Ben Young. 1998. 4.95 (978-0-7417-6093-7(2), B0093) Win Walk.

Hell Pt. 2: Logos August 16, 1998. Ben Young. 1998. 4.95 (978-0-7417-6095-1(9), B0095) Win Walk.

Hell along the Chugwater. unabr. ed. John D. Heisner. Read by Maynard Villers. 4 cass. (Running Time: 5 hrs. 30 min.). (Chinook Ser.: Bk. 2). 1995. 26.95 (978-1-55686-623-4(2)) Books in Motion.
Jackson Kane is Chinook, a peaceable man until aroused. Large ranchers attempting to destory small ranchers receive Chinook's wrath.

Hell & Its Torments. Robert Bellarmine. Narrated by Charles A. Coulombe. 1 cass. (Running Time: 90 mins.). 2000. 7.00 (20135) Cath Treas.
Originally delivered in Latin as one of five sermons on the "Four Last Things" (Death, Judgement, Hell & Heaven) to a congregation largely consisting of faculty & students at the University of London in Belgium. A novel &

vigorous consideration of the reality of Hell & its punishments, one that will certainly inspire people to do whatever is necessary not to go there.

Hell Creek Cabin. unabr. collector's ed. Frank Roderus. Read by Allen Cornell. 7 cass. (Running Time: 7 hrs.). 1995. 42.00 (978-0-7366-2989-8(0), 3678) Books on Tape.
A winter storm brings two strangers to an isolated Wyoming cabin. Their ominous behavior could spell danger for their hosts.

Hell Gate. unabr. ed. Linda Fairstein. Read by Barbara Rosenblat. 10 CDs. (Running Time: 11 hrs.). (ENG.). (gr. 12 up). 2010. audio compact disk 39.95 (978-0-14-314532-5(0), PengAudBks) Penguin Grp USA.

***Hell Gate.** unabr. ed. Linda Fairstein. Narrated by Barbara Rosenblat. 1 Playaway. (Running Time: 11 hrs. 15 mins.). 2010. 64.75 (978-1-4407-7180-4(4)); 92.75 (978-1-4407-7177-4(4)); audio compact disk 123.75 (978-1-4407-7178-1(2)) Recorded Bks.

***Hell Gate.** unabr. collector's ed. Linda Fairstein. Narrated by Barbara Rosenblat. 10 CDs. (Running Time: 11 hrs. 15 mins.). 2010. audio compact disk 39.95 (978-1-4407-7179-8(0)) Recorded Bks.

He'll Give His Angels Charge over Thee: 91st Psalm. (Myrtle Smyth Audiotape Ser.). 2001. 8.95 (978-1-893107-46-5(9)) Pub: Healing Unltd. Dist(s): Bookmark CA

Hell High Water. unabr. ed. Peter Heller. Read by Patrick G. Lawlor. 9 CDs. (Running Time: 9 hrs. 30 mins. 0 sec.). (ENG.). 2004. audio compact disk 34.99 (978-1-4001-0141-2(7)) Pub: Tantor Media. Dist(s): IngramPubServ

Hell House. unabr. ed. Richard Matheson. Read by Ray Porter. (Running Time: 9 hrs. 0 mins.). (ENG.). 2009. 29.95 (978-1-4332-5175-7(2)); 59.95 (978-1-4332-5172-6(8)); audio compact disk 90.00 (978-1-4332-5173-3(6)) Blckstn Audio.

Hell Is Always Today. unabr. ed. Jack Higgins. Perf. by Patrick Macnee. 4 cass. (Running Time: 6 hrs.). 2004. 25.00 (978-1-59007-193-9(X)) New Millenn Enter.
A heart-stopping, gripping tale set in the dark, violent storm of World War II. In 1943, a British intelligence operative, two American Rangers, an extraordinary woman, and an American Mafia overlord parachute into Nazi-occupied Sicily to convince the Sicilian Mafian king to back invading American forces.

***Hell Is Always Today.** unabr. ed. Jack Higgins. Read by Michael Page. (Running Time: 5 hrs.). (Nick Miller Ser.). 2010. 24.99 (978-1-4418-4469-9(4), 9781441844699, Brilliance MP3); 39.97 (978-1-4418-4470-5(8), 9781441844705, Brlnc Audio MP3 Lib); 39.97 (978-1-4418-4472-9(4), 9781441844729, BADLE); 24.99 (978-1-4418-4471-2(6), 9781441844712, BAD); audio compact disk 29.99 (978-1-4418-4467-5(8), 9781441844675, Bril Audio CD Unabri); audio compact disk 87.97 (978-1-4418-4468-2(6), 9781441844682, BriAudCD Unabrid) Brilliance Audio.

Hell Is Too Crowded. unabr. collector's ed. Jack Higgins. Read by Larry McKeever. 4 cass. (Running Time: 4 hrs.). 1985. 24.00 (978-0-7366-0502-1(9), 1476) Books on Tape.
The face swimming at him out of the fog. The strange woman appearing suddenly with invitation to her flat for a drink. That was the last thing Matt Brady remembered. When he woke, police were all around & the body of the girl was lying near him. He was charged with murder & sent to prison, but few prisons can hold Brady. He had to find out the truth behind this crazy nightmare.

Hell No We Won't Go: Vietnam at Home. Peter Knutson. Music by David Hahn. 2 cass. (Running Time: 74 min.). 1993. pap. bk. 9.95 set incl. 49p. bklet. (978-0-9640663-1-1(9)) Loki Pr.
A spoken-word memoir of resistance to the Vietnam War, with musical accompaniment.

Hell on the Draw. 25.00 (978-1-59040-247-4(2)) Pub: Amer Intl Pub. Dist(s): PerseuPGW

Hell Only Breaks Loose Once see Middle-Aged Man on the Flying Trapeze

Hell or High Water: Surviving Tibet's Tsangpo River. unabr. ed. Peter Heller. Read by Patrick G. Lawlor. (Running Time: 9 hrs. 30 mins. 0 sec.). (ENG.). 2004. audio compact disk 69.99 (978-1-4001-3141-9(3)); audio compact disk 19.99 (978-1-4001-5141-7(4)) Pub: Tantor Media. Dist(s): IngramPubServ

Hell, Purgatory, Paradise: Dante's "Divine Comedy", Course 253. Instructed by William R. Cook & Ronald B. Herzman. 4 cass. (Running Time: 6 hrs.). 19.95 (253) Teaching Co.
Eight lectures give a fascinating look at the turbulent & energetic world of Dante's Florence, a world which has surprising parallels with our own time, including everything from runaway inflation to the breakdown of family values.

***Hell to Pay: Operation Downfall & the Invasion of Japan, 1945-47.** unabr. ed. D. M. Giangreco. Narrated by Danny Campbell. (Running Time: 15 hrs. 0 mins.). 2010. 20.99 (978-1-4001-8908-3(X)); 29.99 (978-1-4001-6908-5(9)); audio compact disk 39.99 (978-1-4001-1908-0(1)) Pub: Tantor Media. Dist(s): IngramPubServ

***Hell to Pay (Library Edition) Operation Downfall & the Invasion of Japan, 1945-47.** unabr. ed. D. M. Giangreco. Narrated by Danny Campbell. (Running Time: 15 hrs. 0 mins.). 2010. 39.99 (978-1-4001-9908-2(5)); audio compact disk 95.99 (978-1-4001-4908-7(8)) Pub: Tantor Media. Dist(s): IngramPubServ

Hell Town, abr. ed. Dalton Walker. Read by Dick Wilkinson. 2 cass. (Running Time: 3 hrs.). (Shiloh Ser.: Bk. 5). 1999. Rental 16.95 (978-1-890990-31-2(0)) Otis Audio.
Frank Hoven holds a small border town in a rage of terror, governing a labor camp where no one finds mercy. Every lawman wants him stopped, but only Shiloh has the guts as he infiltrates the camp's inner circle to battle Hoven.

Hell Without Hell. Jack Van Impe. 1977. 7.00 (978-0-934803-30-4(7)) J Van Impe.
Sermon cassette in which the author asserts that Hell is not the grave as the cultists claim.

Hella Nation: Looking for Happy Meals in Kandahar, Rocking the Side Pipe, Wingnut's War Against the GAP, & Other Adventures with the Totally Lost Tribes of America. unabr. ed. Evan Wright. Read by Paul Boehmer & Paul Boehmer. (Running Time: 14 hrs. 30 mins. 0 sec.). (ENG.). 2009. audio compact disk 24.99 (978-1-4001-6230-7(0)); audio compact disk 69.99 (978-1-4001-4230-9(X)) Pub: Tantor Media. Dist(s): IngramPubServ

Hella Nation: Looking for Happy Meals in Kandahar, Rocking the Side Pipe, Wingnut's War Against the GAP, & Other Adventures with the Totally Lost Tribes of America. unabr. ed. Evan Wright. Read by Paul Boehmer. Narrated by Paul Boehmer. (Running Time: 14 hrs. 30 mins. 0 sec.). (ENG.). 2009. audio compact disk 34.99 (978-1-4001-1230-2(3)) Pub: Tantor Media. Dist(s): IngramPubServ

***Hellcats: The Epic Story of World War II's Most Daring Submarine Raid.** unabr. ed. Peter Sasgen. Narrated by Grover Gardner. (Running Time: 9 hrs. 35 mins. 31 sec.). (ENG.). 2010. 20.99 (978-1-60814-785-4(1), SpringWater); audio compact disk 29.99 (978-1-59859-790-5(6), SpringWater) Oasis Audio.

Hellfire. Cameron Forbes. Read by Peter Byrne. (Running Time: 18 hrs. 15 mins.). 2009. 114.99 (978-1-74214-175-6(7), 9781742141756) Pub: Bolinda Pubng AUS. Dist(s): Bolinda Pub Inc

Hellfire. unabr. ed. Cameron Forbes. Read by Peter Byrne. (Running Time: 18 hrs. 15 mins.). 2008. audio compact disk 123.95 (978-1-921415-52-4(5), 9781921415524) Pub: Bolinda Pubng AUS. Dist(s): Bolinda Pub Inc

Hellfire. unabr. ed. Cameron Forbes. Read by Peter Byrne. (Running Time: 18 hrs. 15 mins.). 2009. 54.95 (978-1-74214-043-8(2), 9781742140438) Pub: Bolinda Pubng AUS. Dist(s): Bolinda Pub Inc

Hellfire. unabr. ed. Diana Gabaldon. Narrated by Jeff Woodman. 1 cass. (Running Time: 75 mins.). 2003. 13.00 (978-1-4025-5789-7(2)) Recorded Bks.
Story of intrigue and mystery set in an indelibly drawn world of 18th-century London. Here is the prequel to a captivating new trilogy featuring Lord John Grey, one of the most fascinating and engaging characters to emerge from Diana Gabaldon?s best-selling series.

Hellfire. unabr. collector's ed. Diana Gabaldon. Narrated by Jeff Woodman. 2003. audio compact disk 13.00 (978-1-4025-5981-5(X)) Recorded Bks.

Hellfire Club. abr. ed. Peter Straub. 2004. 15.95 (978-0-7435-4822-9(1)) Pub: S&S Audio. Dist(s): S and S Inc

***Hellhole.** unabr. ed. Brian Herbert & Kevin J. Anderson. Read by Scott Brick. (Running Time: 15 hrs. 0 mins. 0 sec.). (Hell Hole Trilogy). (ENG.). 2011. audio compact disk 49.99 (978-1-4272-1142-2(6)) Pub: Macmill Audio. Dist(s): Macmillan

***Hellhound of Wall Street: How Ferdinand Pecora's Investigation of the Great Crash Forever Changed American Finance.** unabr. ed. Michael Perino. (Running Time: 12 hrs. 30 mins.). 2010. 18.99 (978-1-4001-8856-7(3)); 24.99 (978-1-4001-6856-9(2)); 34.99 (978-1-4001-9856-6(9)); audio compact disk 83.99 (978-1-4001-4856-1(1)); audio compact disk 34.99 (978-1-4001-1856-4(5)) Pub: Tantor Media. Dist(s): IngramPubServ

Hellhound on His Trail: The Stalking of Martin Luther King, Jr. & the International Hunt for His Assassin. unabr. ed. Hampton Sides. Read by Hampton Sides. 12 CDs. (Running Time: 15 hrs.). 2010. 45.00 (978-0-7393-5892-4(8), Random AudioBks) Pub: Random Audio Pubg. Dist(s): Random

***Hellion & the Highlander.** unabr. ed. Lynsay Sands. Read by Marianna Palk. (ENG.). 2010. (978-0-06-204134-0(7), Harper Audio); (978-0-06-199436-4(7), Harper Audio) HarperCollins Pubs.

Hellion Bride. abr. ed. Catherine Coulter. Read by Anne Flosnik. (Running Time: 21600 sec.). (Bride Ser.). 2006. audio compact disk 16.99 (978-1-59737-798-0(8), 9781597377980, BCD Value Price) Brilliance Audio.

Hellion Bride. abr. ed. Catherine Coulter. Read by Juliet Mills. 2 cass. (Running Time: 3 hrs.). (Bride Trilogy: Bk. 2). 1992. 15.95 Set. (978-1-879371-22-4(7), 40090) Pub Mills.
The royal Sherbrooke saga continues in this mystery adventure of 19th century Jamaica on the Sherbrooke Plantation where the young Ryder Sherbrooke meets his bride to be & the tribulations of their relationship bring them back to their England homeland.

Hellion Bride. unabr. ed. Catherine Coulter. Read by Anne Flosnik. (Running Time: 11 hrs.). (Bride Ser.). 2005. 39.25 (978-1-59737-796-6(1), 9781597377966, BADLE); 24.95 (978-1-59737-795-9(3), 9781597377959, BAD); 32.95 (978-1-59737-789-8(9), 9781597377898, BAU); 87.25 (978-1-59737-790-4(2), 9781597377904, BrilAudUnabridg); audio compact disk 36.95 (978-1-59737-791-1(0), 9781597377911, Bril Audio CD Unabri); audio compact disk 24.95 (978-1-59737-793-5(7), 9781597377935, Brilliance MP3); audio compact disk 102.25 (978-1-59737-792-8(9), 9781597377928, BriAudCD Unabrid); audio compact disk 39.25 (978-1-59737-794-2(5), 9781597377942, Brinc Audio MP3 Lib) Brilliance Audio.
Dear Reader, Ryder Sherbrooke is a fun-loving rake with a secret. When he travels to Jamaica to solve the mystery of the supernatural goings-on at the Sherbrooke sugar plantation, he finds another mystery as well - a sophisticated nineteen-year-old girl, Sophia Stanton-Greville, who wants to bed him. And not, he believes, because she is simply enthralled with his handsome self or his boundless charm. Sophia has successfully controlled every man in her orbit until she meets Ryder Sherbrooke, a man she knows immediately is different from the others, a man she sees as one of hell's own sons. Ryder, confident as only a successful rake can be when it comes to knowing women, sets out to teach her who is in charge. It's said she already has three lovers. Is she indeed the outrageous tease she appears? A seductress? Or is she an innocent with an ugly and terrifying secret? As to Ryder's secret, you will see. You will also meet Douglas and Alexandra Sherbrooke from The Sherbrooke Bride; Sinjun Sherbrooke; and the Virgin Bride. The Heiress Bride will feature Sinjun Sherbrooke and Colin Kinross, an impoverished Scottish earl, who does his best to sink the unsinkable Sinjun. Please write me at P.O. Box 17, Mill Valley, CA 94942, e-mail me at ReadMoi@aol.com, and visit my website at www.catherinecoulter.com. Catherine Coulter.

***Hellion in Her Bed.** unabr. ed. Sabrina Jeffries. (Running Time: 11 hrs.). (Hellions of Halstead Hall Ser.). 2010. 19.99 (978-1-4418-3663-2(2), 9781441836632, BAD); 39.97 (978-1-4418-3664-9(0), 9781441836649, BADLE) Brilliance Audio.

***Hellion in Her Bed.** unabr. ed. Sabrina Jeffries. Read by Antony Ferguson. (Running Time: 10 hrs.). (Hellions of Halstead Hall Ser.). 2010. 19.99 (978-1-4418-3661-8(6), 9781441836618, Brilliance MP3); 39.97 (978-1-4418-3662-5(4), 9781441836625, Brlnc Audio MP3 Lib) Brilliance Audio.

***Hellion in Her Bed.** unabr. ed. Sabrina Jeffries. Read by Ralph Lister & Antony Ferguson. (Running Time: 10 hrs.). (Hellions of Halstead Hall Ser.). 2010. audio compact disk 19.99 (978-1-4418-3659-5(4), 9781441836595, Bril Audio CD Unabri); audio compact disk 79.97 (978-1-4418-3660-1(8), 9781441836601, BriAudCD Unabrid) Brilliance Audio.

Hello. Emmet L. Robinson. Read by Emmet L. Robinson. 1 cass. (Running Time: 51 min.). 1991. 14.95 King Street.
How to get paid for answering your business telephone.

Hello after Goodbye. Contrib. by Johnathan Crumpton & Richard Kingsmore. Prod. by Ed Kee. (ENG.). 2008. audio compact disk 24.99 (978-5-557-48383-4(7), Brentwood-Benson Music) Brentwood Music.

Hello Bunny Alice. unabr. ed. Laura Wilson. Read by Anna Bentinck. 7 cass. (Running Time: 10 hrs. 4 mins.). (Isis Cassettes Ser.). (J). 2004. 61.95 (978-0-7531-1791-0(6)); audio compact disk 84.95 (978-0-7531-1852-8(1)) Pub: ISIS Lrg Prnt GBR. Dist(s): Ulverscroft US

Hello, Claudia! unabr. ed. Barbara Brooks Wallace. Narrated by Christina Moore. 3 cass. (Running Time: 3 hrs. 45 mins.). (gr. 3 up). 2002. 28.00 (978-1-4025-2227-7(4)) Recorded Bks.
Claudia and Janice are best friends and have been in the same class at school. When Janice moves away, Claudia must start fourth grade without her and look for ways they can still stay close.

Hello, Darkness. abr. ed. Sandra Brown. Read by Victor Slezak. 2007. 17.95 (978-0-7435-6100-6(7)); audio compact disk 14.95 (978-0-7435-6539-4(8)) Pub: S&S Audio. Dist(s): S and S Inc

Hello English, Bk. 1. 2 cass. (Running Time: 30 min.). 29.95 (Natl Textbk Co) M-H Contemporary.
Designed to speed the development of English language skills youngs students need for academic success & personal confidence.

Hello English, Bk. 2. 2 cass. (Running Time: 30 min.). 29.95 (Natl Textbk Co) M-H Contemporary.
Designed to speed the development of English Language skills younger students need for academic success & personal confidence.

Hello English, Bk. 3. 2 cass. (Running Time: 30 min.). 29.95 (Natl Textbk Co) M-H Contemporary.

Hello English, Bk. 4. 2 cass. (Running Time: 30 min.). 1994. 29.95 (978-0-8442-0417-8(X), Natl Textbk Co) M-H Contemporary.

Hello English, Bk. 5. 2 cass. (Running Time: 30 min.). 29.95 (978-0-8442-0420-8(X), Natl Textbk Co) M-H Contemporary.

Hello English, Bk. 6. 2 cass. 29.95 (Natl Textbk Co) M-H Contemporary.

Hello Everybody. Rachel Buchman. (J). 1986. audio compact disk 14.95 (978-0-939065-61-5(4)) Gentle Wind.

Hello Everybody. Rachel Buchman. 1 cass. (J). (GW1038) NewSound.
Songs, fingerplays & lullabies for toddlers.

Hello Everybody, I'm George Kell! Narrated by George Kell. 1998. 19.95 (978-1-57167-239-1(7)) Pub: Sports Pub. Dist(s): IngramPubServ
Pertains to Tiger Baseball Player Hall of Famer.

Hello Everybody, I'm George Kell! Read by George Kell. 1998. 19.95 Sports Pub.

Hello Everybody! Playsongs & Rhymes from a Toddler's World. Rachel Buchman. 1 cass. (J). (ps-1). 1986. 9.95 (978-0-939065-34-9(7)) Gentle Wind.
Features playsongs, rhymes & lullabyes such as "Pussy Willow Riddle," "A Tickling Rhyme" & "Little Red Wagon".

Hello, Good Friend. Contrib. by Rocket Summer. Prod. by Tim O'Heir & Bryce Avary. 2005. audio compact disk 13.99 (978-5-558-93304-8(6)) Pt of Grace Ent.

Hello, Goodbye, I Love You: The Story of Aloha A Guide Dog for the Blind. Frwd. by Michael Hingson. (ENG.). (J). 2004. audio compact disk Rental 16.95 (978-0-9685097-4-6(6)) Pinata Pubng.

***Hello, Hello: Echo Songs & Activities for Young Singers.** Composed by John Jacobson. (ENG.). 2007. pap. bk. 29.95 (978-1-4234-2604-2(5), 1423426045) H Leonard.

Hello, I'm Sir Frettirick! Let's Say Hello to Our New Friends! Lou Stratten. Ed. by Judy Bennett. Illus. by Sal Denaro. Des. by MMR Design Solutions. (J). (ps-2). 2006. pap. bk. 6.95 (978-0-9747173-1-9(2)) L Stratten.

Hello in Japanese, Vol. 1. Keiko Inoue. 3 cass. (YA). (gr. 9-12). 1990. 39.50 set. (978-0-89346-352-6(3)) Heian Intl.
Audiotape accompaniment to the textbook-workbook set Hello in Japanese; for use in high school classrooms.

Hello in Japanese, Vol. 2. Keiko Inoue. 3 cass. (JPN.). (YA). (gr. 9-12). 1991. 39.50 set. (978-0-89346-351-9(5)) Heian Intl.

Hello Kitty Bakes a Cake. John Whitman. 1 cass. (J). 1995. 7.99 (978-1-57375-152-0(9)) Audioscope.

Hello Lord. Music by Michael John Poirier. 1986. 11.00 (978-1-58459-114-6(5), 002670); audio compact disk 16.00 (978-1-58459-115-3(3), 002677) Wrld Lib Pubns.

Hello Lord D. Contrib. by Michael John Poirier. 2007. audio compact disk 17.00 (978-1-58459-215-0(X)) Wrld Lib Pubns.

Hello Mars! (J). 2005. cass. & cd-rom 24.95 (978-0-9771381-6-6(X)) Geoffrey Williams.

Hello, Mrs. Piggle Wiggle. Betty Bard MacDonald. Read by John McDonough. 3 cass. (Running Time: 3 hrs. 15 mins.). (YA). 2000. pap. bk. 40.20 (978-0-7887-4171-5(3), 41089); 97.30 (978-0-7887-4172-2(1), 47082) Recorded Bks.
Parents turn to Mrs. Piggle-Wiggle when their precious sons & daughters come down with annoying habits. She always supplies the perfect fun-filled treatment for even the most stubborn cases.

Hello, Mrs. Piggle Wiggle. unabr. ed. Betty Bard MacDonald. 2 cass. (Running Time: 3 hrs. 4 mins.). (J). (gr. 2-5). 2004. 23.00 (978-0-8072-1182-3(6), S YA 1018 CX, Listening Lib) Random Audio Pubg.

Hello, Mrs. Piggle Wiggle. unabr. ed. Betty Bard MacDonald. Narrated by John McDonough. 3 pieces. (Running Time: 3 hrs. 15 mins.). (gr. 1 up). 2000. 27.00 (978-0-7887-4000-8(8), 96096E7) Recorded Bks.

Hello, Mrs Piggle Wiggle. unabr. ed. Betty Bard MacDonald. 2 vols. (Running Time: 3 hrs. 4 mins.). (J). (gr. 2-5). 2004. pap. bk. 29.00 (978-0-8072-1184-7(2), S YA 1018 SP, Listening Lib) Random Audio Pubg.

Hello Rhythm. Perf. by Jackie Silberg. 1 cass. (J). 1988. 10.95 (978-0-939514-24-3(9)) Miss Jackie.
Features Miss Jackie with songs, rhymes, & rhythm games & activities.

Hello Sadness see Bonjour Tristesse

Hello, This Is God Calling! Proceedings of the 45th Annual Convention National Association of Evangelicals Buffalo, New York. Read by Pamela Heim. 1 cass. (Running Time: 60 min.). 1987. 4.00 (321) Nat Assn Evan.

Hello World! Perf. by Red Grammer. 1 cass. (J). (ps-6). 1995. 10.00 (978-1-886146-11-2(X)); audio compact disk 15.00 CD. (978-1-886146-12-9(8)) Red Note Recs.

Hello World It's Me. unabr. ed. Thurley Fowler. (Aussie Bites Ser.). (J). 2002. audio compact disk 39.95 (978-1-74030-844-1(1)) Pub: Bolinda Pubng AUS. Dist(s): Bolinda Pub Inc

***Hell's Bay.** unabr. ed. James W. Hall. Narrated by Ed Sala. (Running Time: 11 hrs. 30 mins.). (Thorn Mysteries Ser.). 2010. 17.99 (978-1-4001-8558-0(0)) Tantor Media.

***Hell's Bay.** unabr. ed. James W. Hall. Narrated by Ed Sala. (Running Time: 11 hrs. 30 mins. 0 sec.). (Thorn Mysteries Ser.). (ENG.). 2010. 24.99 (978-1-4001-6558-2(X)); audio compact disk 34.99 (978-1-4001-1558-7(2)); audio compact disk 69.99 (978-1-4001-4558-4(9)) Pub: Tantor Media. Dist(s): IngramPubServ

Hell's Children. unabr. ed. Will C. Knott. Read by Maynard Villers. 4 cass. (Running Time: 4 hrs. 48 min.). (Golden Hawk Ser.: Bk. 4). 1996. 26.95 (978-1-55686-685-2(2)) Books in Motion.
Hawk is enlisted to help guide a wagon train through Indian country where a murderous horde of Bannock Indians were waiting in ambush.

***Hell's Corner.** David Baldacci. Read by Ron McLarty & Orlagh Cassidy. (Running Time: 7 hrs.). (ENG.). 2011. audio compact disk & audio compact disk 14.98 (978-1-60941-385-9(7)) Pub: Hachet Audio. Dist(s): HachBkGrp

***Hell's Corner.** abr. ed. David Baldacci. Read by Orlagh Cassidy & Ron McLarty. (Running Time: 7 hrs.). (ENG.). 2010. 19.98 (978-1-60788-656-3(1)); audio compact disk 29.98 (978-1-60788-655-6(3)) Pub: Hachet Audio. Dist(s): HachBkGrp

***Hell's Corner.** unabr. ed. David Baldacci. Read by Orlagh Cassidy & Ron McLarty. (Running Time: 14 hrs.). (ENG.). 2010. 26.98 (978-1-60788-658-7(8)); audio compact disk 39.98 (978-1-60788-657-0(X)) Pub: Hachet Audio. Dist(s): HachBkGrp

***Hell's Gate.** unabr. ed. Stephen Frey. Read by Erik Steele. 1 Playaway. (Running Time: 11 hrs. 37 mins.). 2009. 94.95 (978-0-7927-6529-5(X)); 59.95 (978-0-7927-6528-8(1)); audio compact disk 94.95 (978-0-7927-6055-9(7)) AudioGO.

Hell's Gate: Terror at Bobby Mackey's Music World. Read by John Boles. 2 cass. 1993. 14.95 set. (978-0-9630499-6-4(8)); 5.95 electronic bk., 3.5" DOS diskette. (978-0-9630499-7-1(6)) B J Fitz.

Bobby Mackey, a well-known country music singer, buys a night club to renovate & showcase his music. His family & workers are terrorized by demonic spirits who don't want them there.

Hell's Gate: Terror at Bobby Mackey's Music World. Douglas Hensley. Read by John Boles. 2 cass. (Running Time: 3 hrs.). 1993. pap. bk. 11.95 (978-0-9630499-8-8(4)) B J Fitz.

Hell's High-Graders. Cliff Farrell. (Running Time: 0 hr. 54 mins.). 2000. 10.95 (978-1-60083-544-5(9)) Iofy Corp.

***Hell's High-Graders!** Cliff Farrell. 2009. (978-1-60136-441-8(5)) Audio Holding.

Hellstrom's Hive. unabr. ed. Frank Herbert. Read by Scott Brick. 10 CDs. (Running Time: 12 hrs. 30 mins. 0 sec.). (ENG.). 2008. audio compact disk 34.99 (978-1-4001-0564-9(1)); audio compact disk 24.99 (978-1-4001-5564-4(9)); audio compact disk 69.99 (978-1-4001-3564-6(8)) Pub: Tantor Media. Dist(s): IngramPubServ

Hellstrom's Hive. unabr. ed. Frank Herbert. Read by Scott Brick. (YA). 2008. 59.99 (978-1-60514-867-0(9)) Find a World.

Helmet: Ephesians 6:17, 648. Ed Young. 1988. 4.95 (978-0-7417-1648-4(8), 648) Win Walk.

Helmet for My Pillow. unabr. ed. Robert Leckie. Narrated by Tom West. 6 cass. (Running Time: 9 hrs. 30 mins.). 1982. 51.00 (978-1-55690-222-2(0), 82032E7) Recorded Bks.

A first-hand account of war in the Pacific seen from the front lines.

Helmet for My Pillow. unabr. ed. Robert Leckie. Narrated by Tom West. 6 cass. (Running Time: 9 hrs. 30 mins.). 2002. 34.95 (978-0-7887-6447-9(0), RC996) Recorded Bks.

This is one of the most outstanding personal accounts ever written by an American soldier who fought in World War II. Marine Corps infantryman Robert Leckie paints a grueling, bluntly honest vision of war in all its mud, sweat, and blood: the exhilaration of boot camp; the aftershock of furious combat in the Pacific rainforests; and the intense mental suffering that comes with overexposure to night attacks, sleeplessness, and pure terror.

***Helmet for My Pillow: From Parris Island to the Pacific.** unabr. ed. Robert Leckie. Narrated by John Allen Nelson. (Running Time: 10 hrs. 0 mins.). 2010. 34.99 (978-1-4001-9050-8(9)); 24.99 (978-1-4001-6050-1(2)); 16.99 (978-1-4001-8050-9(3)); audio compact disk 69.99 (978-1-4001-4050-3(1)); audio compact disk 34.99 (978-1-4001-1050-6(5)) Pub: Tantor Media. Dist(s): IngramPubServ

Helmet of Horror: The Myth of Theseus & the Minotaur. unabr. ed. Victor Pelevin. (Running Time: 3 hrs.). (Myths Ser.). 2006. 39.25 (978-1-4233-1159-1(0), 9781423311591, BADLE); 24.95 (978-1-4233-1158-4(2), 9781423311584, BAD); 49.25 (978-1-4233-1153-9(1), 9781423311539, BrilAudUnabridg); 19.95 (978-1-4233-1152-2(3), 9781423311522); audio compact disk 62.25 (978-1-4233-1155-3(8), 9781423311553, BriAudCD Unabrid); audio compact disk 39.25 (978-1-4233-1157-7(4), 9781423311577, Brinc Audio MP3 Lib); audio compact disk 24.95 (978-1-4233-1156-0(6), 9781423311560, Brilliance MP3) Brilliance Audio.

The Helmet of Horror is a cyber age retelling of the Myth of Theseus and the Minotaur by one of Russia's most lauded and respected writers. They have never met, they have been assigned strange pseudonyms, they inhabit identical rooms which open out onto very different landscapes, and they have entered into a dialogue from which they cannot escape - a discourse defined and destroyed by the Helmet of Horror. Its wearer is the dominant force they call Asterisk, a force for good and ill in which the Minotaur is forever present and Theseus is the great unknown. Victor Pelevin has created a mesmerizing world where the surreal and the hyperreal collide. The Helmet of Horror is structured according to the internet exchanges of the 21st century, yet instilled with the figures and narratives of classical mythology. It is a labyrinthine examination of epistemological uncertainty that radically reinvents the myth of Theseus and the Minotaur for an age where information is abundant but knowledge is ultimately unattainable. "According to one definition, a myth is a traditional story, usually explaining some natural or social phenomenon. According to another, it is a widely held but false belief or idea. This duality of meaning is revealing. It shows that we naturally considered stories and explanations that come from the past untrue - or at least treat them with suspicion. This attitude, apart from creating new jobs in the field of intellectual journalism, gives some additional meaning to our life. The past is a quagmire of mistakes; we are here to find the truth." From Victor Pelevin's introduction to The Helmet of Horror.

Helmet of Horror: The Myth of Theseus & the Minotaur. unabr. ed. Victor Pelevin. Read by Dick Hill et al. (Running Time: 10800 sec.). (Myths Ser.). 2006. audio compact disk 19.95 (978-1-4233-1154-6(X), 9781423311546) Brilliance Audio.

Helmut Backhaus: Die Nacht Hat Kein Gesicht. unabr. ed. 1 cass. (Running Time: 1 hr.). (GER.). 18.95 (CGE320) J Norton Pubs.

***Help.** L. Ron Hubbard. 2010. audio compact disk 15.00 (978-1-4031-6833-7(4)); audio compact disk 15.00 (978-1-4031-6847-4(4)); audio compact disk 15.00 (978-1-4031-6840-5(7)); audio compact disk 15.00 (978-1-4031-6846-7(6)); audio compact disk 15.00 (978-1-4031-6837-5(7)); audio compact disk 15.00 (978-1-4031-6836-8(9)); audio compact disk 15.00 (978-1-4031-6845-0(8)); audio compact disk 15.00 (978-1-4031-6839-9(3)); audio compact disk 15.00 (978-1-4031-6831-3(8)); audio compact disk 15.00 (978-1-4031-6832-0(6)); audio compact disk 15.00 (978-1-4031-6843-6(1)); audio compact disk 15.00 (978-1-4031-6841-2(5)); audio compact disk 15.00 (978-1-4031-6835-1(0)); audio compact disk 15.00 (978-1-4031-6844-3(X)); audio compact disk 15.00 (978-1-4031-6842-9(3)); audio compact disk 15.00 (978-1-4031-6834-4(2)); audio compact disk 15.00 (978-1-4031-6838-2(5)) Bridge Pubns Inc.

Help. unabr. ed. Kathryn Stockett. Read by Jenna Lamia et al. 15 CDs. (Running Time: 18 hrs.). (gr. 12 up). 2009. audio compact disk 39.95 (978-0-14-314418-2(9), PengAudBks) Penguin Grp USA.

Help. unabr. ed. Kathryn Stockett. Read by Octavia Spencer et al. 15 CDs. (Running Time: 18 hrs.). 2009. audio compact disk 120.00 (978-1-4159-6125-4(5), BksonTape) Pub: Random Audio Pubg. Dist(s): Random

Help! Level 1. Philip Prowse. Contrib. by Philip Prowse. (Running Time: hrs. mins.). (Cambridge English Readers Ser.). (ENG., 1999. 9.45 (978-0-521-65614-6(1)) Cambridge U Pr.

Help for Abuse Victims: 2007 CCEF Annual Conference. Featuring Sarah Lipp. (ENG.). 2007. audio compact disk 11.99 (978-1-934885-06-2(1)) New Growth Pr.

Help for Couples: A Guide for Adults from Dysfunctional Families. Daniel M. Ryan & Susan Hagberg. 1989. 9.95 R & H Cassettes.

Problems in relationships encountered by adults who grew up in dysfunctional families & suggestions for how to deal with the problems.

Help for Stutterers. unabr. ed. Read by C. Woodruff Starkweather. 1 cass. 1999. 12.95 (978-0-88432-222-1(X), AF1520) J Norton Pubs.

Advises on the best way of finding a clinician, the types of therapy available, & the cost, length of time needed, & likely success of each kind of treatment.

Help for Your Journey CD. Nancy Leigh DeMoss. (ENG.). 2007. audio compact disk 12.00 (978-0-940110-90-8(3)) Life Action Publishing.

***Help, I Can't Stop Laughing! A Nonstop Collection of Life's Funniest Stories.** Adapted by Ann Spangler. Told to Shari MacDonald. (Running Time: 4 hrs. 26 mins. 0 sec.). (ENG.). 2009. 14.99 (978-0-310-30453-1(9)) Zondervan.

Help! I Have a Teenager, Vol. 1. 2 cass. 1995. 14.95 Set, incl. 4p. pamphlet. Wrldview Pub Inc.

Ten parenting sessions on how to get out of power struggles, & turn over responsibility.

Help! I'm a Classroom Gambler. Pete Johnson. Narrated by Paul Chequer. (Running Time: 13680 sec.). (J). (gr. 5-8). 2007. audio compact disk 29.95 (978-1-4056-5585-9(2)) AudioGo GBR.

Help, I'm a Substitute Music Teacher: A Collection of Games & Activities. 1987. bk. 14.95 (978-0-7935-2888-2(7)) H Leonard.

Help! I'm Stuck with These People for the Rest of Eternity. Susan Gaddis. 2003. 50.00i (978-1-932505-09-2(1)) Et Fnd Cu.

Help in Avoiding the Mistakes of Youth: Ecc. 11:7-12:1. Ed Young. 1994. 4.95 (978-0-7417-2009-2(4), 1009) Win Walk.

Help Me I've Fallen & I Can't Get up Audio BK. T. D. Jakes. 2008. audio compact disk 24.99 (978-0-7684-2672-4(3)) Destiny Image Pubs.

Help Me Remember: Bible Stories for Children. Elaine Blanchard. 2005. pap. bk. 24.00 (978-0-8298-1600-6(3)) Pilgrim OH.

Help Me with My Teenager: A step-by-step Guide for Parents that Works. Christina Botto. Read by Sandra Johnson. (ENG.). 2007. audio compact disk 24.95 (978-0-9786553-6-5(2)) Dreamervision Pub.

Help Me with My Teenager: A Step by Step Guide for Parents That Works. Christina Botto. (ENG.). 2008. 19.95 (978-1-934965-12-2(X)) Pub: Dreamervision Pub. Dist(s): Dreamervision Dist

Help! We Have Strange Powers! R. L. Stine. (Goosebumps HorrorLand Ser.: No. 10). (ENG.). (J). (gr. 4-7). 2009. audio compact disk 29.95 (978-0-545-13876-5(0)); audio compact disk 9.95 (978-0-545-13853-6(1)) Scholastic Inc.

Help with the Stress of Herpes. Michael P. Kelly. 1 cass. 1992. 14.95 (978-1-883700-03-4(5)) ThoughtForms.

Self help.

Help Your Student: Succeed in High School & College. Instructed by Tim McGee. 2 cass., 4 lectures. (Running Time: 3 hrs.). (SuperStar Teachers Ser.). 1999. 19.95 Set. (978-1-56585-148-1(X)) Teaching Co.

"Lecture One: Motivation & Teamwork," outlines the ground rules for academic success. In "Lecture Two: The Keys to Academic Success," parents of high school students are shown important ways to improve their child's school success & the chief role they play in it. The focus is on the art of studying with an emphasis on synthesis & learning. In "Lecture Three: Planning, Financing & Admission," McGee addresses the issues of college admission such as school selection, financial aid, college admissions, & athletic scholarships. In the "Final Lecture: The First Day, the First Month & the First Year," the focus is on helping the parent support the college-bound student.

Help Yourself! Safety & Self-Esteem Songs for Young Children. Cathy Fink & Marcy Marxer. 1 cass. (Running Time: 40 min.). (J). (ps-4). 1998. 9.98 (978-1-57940-023-1(X), 8021); audio compact disk 14.98 (978-1-57940-022-4(1)) Rounder Records.

Using humor & bouncy melodies, this audio educates children about nutrition, self-reliance, stranger danger, & other important topics in this wonderful collection of songs.

Help Yourself Audiotherapy Series. 6 cass. 2001. 69.95 (978-1-889577-12-8(X)) Media Psy Assocs.

This self-help audiotape program covers six topics: making crucial choices and major life changes; how to develop self-confidence and a positive self-image; how to manage stress; overcoming anxiety, depression, and anger.

Help Yourself Heal Vol.1: Hope for Cancer Patients & Their Families. Bill L. Little. Interview with Candice Coleman & Gay Carlstom. 4 cass. (Steps One to Three Ser.). 1997. Set. (978-0-9663283-0-1(2)) Cancer Support.

Explains the proven 8-step cancer fighting techniques based on seven years of clinical research & 20 years experience. The set includes the 8-step program, pain management, positive input for patients & family, relaxation & help for chemotherapy.

Help Yourself Heal - Menopause. unabr. ed. Linda Mackenzie. Read by Linda Mackenzie. 1 cass. (Running Time: 1 hr.). 1999. 9.95 (978-0-9656432-7-6(1)) Creat Hlth & Spirit.

Natural remedies & visualizations.

Help Yourself in Reading Quran. Faisal Abdur-Razak. 2 cass. (Running Time: 2 hrs.). 2000. pap. bk. 12.00 (978-1-894264-01-3(0)) Al-Attique Pubs CAN.

Help Yourself to Health. Michael Klaper. 10 cass. (978-0-929274-16-4(4)) Gentle World.

Helper. Francis Frangipane. 1 cass. (Running Time: 90 mins.). (Abide in Him Ser.: Vol. 3). 2000. 5.00 (FF08-003) Morning NC.

A subject Francis teaches on with great gifting, this series deals with the advantages of walking in the "abiding principle".

***Helper.** unabr. ed. Catherine Marshall. Narrated by Renee Ertl. (Running Time: 5 hrs. 15 mins. 50 sec.). (ENG.). 2010. 18.19 (978-1-60814-695-6(2)); audio compact disk 25.99 (978-1-59859-747-9(7)) Oasis Audio.

Helper: The Power of the Enneagram Individual Type Audio Recording. Scripts. Based on a work by Enneagram Institute Staff. 1 CD. (Running Time: 60 mins.). 2004. audio compact disk 10.00 (978-0-9755222-1-9(3)) Enneagr.

Type Two Individual Type Audio Recording (ITAR) in CD format from the audio tapeset The Power of the Enneagram. Includes a 25 minute introduction to the system as a whole, as well as a 35 minute exposition on Type Two. An excellent way for therapists or business consultants to introduce the Enneagram to clients, or to work with the Enneagram in ongoing situations.

Helping Animals: Early Explorers Emergent Set B Audio CD. Katherine Scraper. Adapted by Benchmark Education Staff. (J). 2007. audio compact disk 10.00 (978-1-4108-8202-8(0)) Benchmark Educ.

Helping Children & Adolescents Cope with Divorce: A Guide for Counselors, Teachers, & Parents. Michael S. Prokop. (Running Time: 54 min.). (J). 9.95 (978-0-933879-32-4(6)) Alegra Hse Pubs.

Helping Children Grieve, Vol. 1. Doug Manning. 1 cass. (Running Time: 20 min.). 1991. 9.95 (978-1-892785-18-3(8)) In-Sight Bks Inc.

Provides guidance & assurances for parents as they help children deal with grief in a healthy manner.

Helping Children Understand & Express Their Feelings. Stephanie Marston. Read by Stephanie Marston. 1 cass. (Running Time: 45 min.). (Magic of Encouragement Audio Ser.). 1991. 10.95 (978-1-56170-015-8(0), 244) Hay House.

Accepting your children's feelings is essential to raising children with high self-esteem. In this tape, you will learn the negative impact of denial & the five keys for acknowledging your children's feelings.

Helping Clients to Structure Commercial Acquisitions. Mark Morris. 2006. audio compact disk 199.95 (978-1-59701-095-5(2)) Aspatore Bks.

Helping Families Face a Tragic Death. Vern Albrecht. 1986. 10.80 (0106A) Assn Prof Chaplains.

Helping Fido Welcome Your Baby. Suzanne Hetts & Daniel Q. Estep. (ENG.). 2007. audio compact disk 29.95 (978-0-9749542-8-8(4)) Island Dg Pr.

Helping Friends: Early Explorers Emergent Set B Audio CD. Katherine Scraper. Adapted by Benchmark Education Staff. (J). 2007. audio compact disk 10.00 (978-1-4108-8201-1(2)) Benchmark Educ.

Helping Hercules. unabr. ed. Francesca Simon. Read by Sophie Aldred. 2 CDs. (Running Time: 3 hrs.). (J). 2002. audio compact disk 21.95 (978-0-7540-6546-3(4), CHCD 046) AudioGO.

Susan is whisked back in time to ancient Greece, and finds that helping Hercules clean out the Augean stables is much, much worse than tidying her room. One hair-raising experience follows another as she goes down to the Underworld with Orpheus, just misses being turned into stone by Medusa, and rides on the winged horse, Pegasus.

Helping Kids Build a Healthy Self-Esteem. unabr. ed. Ray Levy & Joe Cates. 1 cass. (Running Time: 1 hr. 30 mins.). 2002. bk. 12.95 (978-0-9701173-4-2(5)) Cates Levy.

An aid for parents and/or teachers of children/youth 18 years and younger to help in building healthy self-esteem.

Helping the Confused Resident. unabr. ed. Charlotte Eliopoulos. Read by Charlotte Eliopoulos. 1 cass. (Running Time: 20 min.). 1991. 15.00 (978-1-882515-14-1(5)) Hlth Educ Netwk.

Describes nursing measures to improve the function & quality of life for confused nursing home residents.

Helping the Helpers. D. Copeland et al. 1986. 10.80 (0810) Assn Prof Chaplains.

Helping Young People Meet the Challenges They Face. unabr. ed. Myrtle Smith. Prod. by David Keyston. 1 cass. (Running Time: 1 hr. 10 min.). (Myrtle Smyth Audiotapes Ser.). 1998. , CD. (978-1-893107-12-0(4), M12, Cross & Crown) Healing Unltd.

Helping Your At-Risk Students Be More Successful Readers, Set. Mary Howard. Read by Mary Howard. 6 cass. (Running Time: 3 hr. 58 min.). (J). (gr. 1-3). 1997. 75.00 Incl. resource hdbk. (978-1-886397-12-5(0)) Bureau of Educ.

Live audio seminar.

Helping Your Child Manage Stress, Pressure & Anxiety. Bettie B. Youngs. 6 cass. 29.95 (5013) SyberVision.

Schoolwork, making friends, loneliness, divorce: your child suffers from stress, fear & anxiety just as you do. And how you respond now will strongly influence your child's ability to handle the pressures of adulthood.

Helping Your Children with Their Anger. William G. DeFoore. (ENG.). 2004. audio compact disk 29.99 (978-0-9814740-1-4(2)) Halcyon Life.

Helping Your Struggling Students Be More Successful Readers & Writers, Set. Mitzi Merrill. 6 cass. (Running Time: 4 hr. 34 min.). (J). (gr. 6-12). 1998. 75.00 Incl. handbk. (978-1-886397-18-7(X)) Bureau of Educ.

Helps for the Scrupulous. abr. ed. Russell M. Abata. Read by Thomas Santa. Ed. by Kenneth Daust. 2 cass. (Running Time: 2 hrs. 20 min.). 1995. 14.95 (978-0-89243-895-2(9), T8710) Liguori Pubns.

A starting point for overcoming fears & returning to a normal life.

Helter Skelter. abr. ed. Vincent Bugliosi. 4 cass. (Running Time: 6 hrs.). 2001. 25.00 (978-1-59040-165-1(4), Phoenix Audio) Pub: Amer Intl Pub. Dist(s): PerseuPGW

Helter Skelter. abr. ed. Vincent Bugliosi. Read by Robert Foxworth. 4 cass. (Running Time: 6 hrs.). 2004. 25.00 (978-1-59007-179-3(4)) Pub: New Millenn Enter. Dist(s): PerseuPGW

Is Everage just an average Australian housewife who stumbled into megastardom? Did she really strike a sympathetic chord with audiences at her one-woman shows just by talking about long-suffering husband Norm, three unusual kids, and one eccentric mother? Don't you believe it! Everage is every bit the clever creation of performer/impersonator Barry Humphries - from her trademark harlequin glasses to her astounding adventures which mock suburban life and then some. Popular abroad, she should take America by storm. This is "Dame Edna's" riotous story. Although the finer satiric jabs at things peculiarly Australian may slip by, the humor is quite universal - but with a decidedly offbeat twist that may not be for everyone.

Hematuria & Proteinuria - Office Problems. Contrib. by F. Bruder Stapleton et al. 1 cass. (American Academy of Pediatrics UPDATE: Vol. 16, No. 7). 1998. 20.00 Am Acad Pediat.

Heme Aqui Senor. unabr. ed. Jocelyn Arias. (SPA.). 2001. 9.99 (978-0-8297-3584-0(4)) Pub: Vida Pubs. Dist(s): Zondervan

Hemingses of Monticello: An American Family. unabr. ed. Annette Gordon-Reed. Read by Karen White. 3 MP3-CDs. (Running Time: 31 hrs. 30 mins. 0 sec.). (ENG.). 2008. 44.99 (978-1-4001-5975-8(X)); audio compact disk 119.99 (978-1-4001-3975-0(9)); audio compact disk 59.99 (978-1-4001-0975-3(2)) Pub: Tantor Media. Dist(s): IngramPubServ

Hemingway Short Stories. unabr. ed. Ernest Hemingway. Read by Alexander Scourby. 2 cass. (Running Time: 1 hr. 25 min.). Incl. Short Happy Life of Francis Macomber. 1984. (CB100CX); Snows of Kilimanjaro. 1984. (CB100CX); (Cassette Bookshelf Ser.). 1984. 15.98 Set, Library ed. (978-0-8072-3400-6(1), CB100CX, Listening Lib) Random Audio Pubg.

Features two of Hemingway's best loved, flowing chronicles of human nature.

Hemingway Short Stories: My Old Man, up in Michigan, Out of Season. (ENG.). 2007. (978-1-60339-063-7(4)); cd-rom & audio compact disk (978-1-60339-064-4(2)) Listenr Digest.

Hemingway Women: Those Who Love Him - The Wives & Others. unabr. collector's ed. Bernice Kert. Read by Kimberly Schraf. 14 cass. (Running Time: 21 hrs.). 1999. 112.00 (978-0-7366-4666-6(3), 5048) Books on Tape.

The movements of the women that were Hemingway heroines & their real-life.

Hemingway's France. unabr. ed. Winston S. Conrad. Narrated by Tom Parker. 2 CDs. (Running Time: 2 hrs. 30 mins.). 2002. audio compact disk 16.00 (978-0-7861-9575-6(4), 2914) Blckstn Audio.
Ernest Hemingway's literary ambitions took root in France in the 1920s among some of the most extravagantly creative artists of the twentieth century. Pablo Picasso, Georges Braque, James Joyce, T.S. Eliot, Gertrude Stein, F. Scott Fitzgerald, Ezra Pound, Cole Porter, Sergey Diaghilev, and others were drawn to the left bank of the Seine in Paris after World War I. Hemingway joined them and, with the publication of his book The Sun Also Rises, which epitomized Paris during the jazz era, became one of the most powerful forces in the vortex of talent and experimentation.

Hemingway's France. unabr. ed. Winston S. Conrad. Narrated by Tom Parker. 2 cass. (Running Time: 2 hrs. 30 mins.). 2002. 17.95 (978-0-7861-2164-9(5), 2914) Blckstn Audio.

Hemingway's "The Old Man & the Sea" unabr. ed. Charles K. Hofling. 1 cass. (Running Time: 44 min.). 1968. 12.95 (23053) J Norton Pubs.
Examination of Hemingway's techniques of plotting from the viewpoint of depth psychology.

Hemispheres - Book 1 (High Beginning) - Audio CDs (2) Scott Cameron et al. (Hemispheres Ser.). (C). 2007. audio compact disk 38.44 (978-0-07-319929-0(X), 007319929X, ESL/ELT) Pub: McGrw-H Hghr Educ. Dist(s): McGraw

Hemispheres - Book 2 (Low Intermediate) - Audio CDs (2) Scott Cameron et al. (Hemispheres Ser.). (C). 2007. audio compact disk 38.44 (978-0-07-321302-6(0), 0073213020, ESL/ELT) Pub: McGrw-H Hghr Educ. Dist(s): McGraw

Hemispheres - Book 3 (Intermediate) - Audio CDs (2) Scott Cameron et al. (Hemispheres Ser.). (C). 2007. audio compact disk 38.44 (978-0-07-321306-4(3), 0073213063, ESL/ELT) Pub: McGrw-H Hghr Educ. Dist(s): McGraw

Hemispheres - Book 4 (High Intermediate) - Audio CDs (2) Susan Iannuzzi & Diana Renn. (Hemispheres Ser.). (C). 2007. audio compact disk 38.44 (978-0-07-321310-1(1), 0073213101, ESL/ELT) Pub: McGrw-H Hghr Educ. Dist(s): McGraw

Hemlock Bay. unabr. ed. Catherine Coulter. Read by Sandra Burr. 8 CDs. (Running Time: 9 hrs.). (FBI Thriller Ser.: No. 3). 2001. audio compact disk 96.25 (978-1-58788-526-6(3), 1587885263, CD Unabrid Lib Ed) Brilliance Audio.
FBI Agent Dillon Savich is on a challenging case involving the kidnapping of two teenage boys when trouble boils up in his personal life. His younger sister Lily has crashed her Explorer into a redwood in California's Hemlock Bay. Is it another suicide attempt, the second since the loss of her young daughter some seven months before? Savich and Sherlock discover that four of Lily's paintings, left to her by their very famous grandmother, artist Sarah Elliot, now worth millions, are at the heart of an intricate conspiracy. Lily and art broker Simon Russo are thrust into ever-widening circles of danger that radiate from a notorious collector's locked room. Dillon and his sister Lily both have to face their worst fears to survive.

Hemlock Bay. unabr. ed. Catherine Coulter. Read by Sandra Burr. 6 cass. (Running Time: 9 hrs.). (FBI Thriller Ser.: No. 6). 2001. 29.95 (978-1-58788-498-6(4), 1587884984, BAU); 69.25 (978-1-58788-499-3(2), 1587884992, CD Unabrid Lib Ed); audio compact disk 37.95 (978-1-58788-525-9(5), 1587885255, CD Unabridged) Brilliance Audio.

Hemlock Bay. unabr. ed. Catherine Coulter. Read by Sandra Burr. (Running Time: 9 hrs.). (FBI Thriller Ser.: No. 6). 2004. 24.95 (978-1-59335-290-5(5), 1593352905, Brilliance MP3); 39.25 (978-1-59335-546-3(7), 1593355467, Brlnc Audio MP3 Lib) Brilliance Audio.

Hemlock Bay. unabr. ed. Catherine Coulter. Read by Sandra Burr. (Running Time: 9 hrs.). (FBI Thriller Ser.: No. 6). 2004. 39.25 (978-1-59710-360-2(8), 1597103608, BADLE); 24.95 (978-1-59710-361-9(6), 1597103616, BAD) Brilliance Audio.

Hemochromatosis - A Bibliography & Dictionary for Physicians, Patients, & Genome Researchers. Compiled by Icon Group International, Inc. Staff. 2007. ring bd. 28.95 (978-0-497-11228-8(0)) Icon Grp.

Hemodynamic Monitoring. unabr. ed. Instructed by April Kimball. 5 cass. (Running Time: 7 hrs.). 1990. 79.00 cass. & soft-bound bk. (HT11) Ctr Hlth Educ.
Treat your cardiac patients with supreme skill & confidence. Actual case studies guide you through critical hemodynamic parameters & help you determine accurate therapy. In this unique course the information is presented clearly & in detail.

Hemophilia - A Bibliography & Dictionary for Physicians, Patients, & Genome Researchers. Compiled by Icon Group International, Inc. Staff. 2007. ring bd. 28.95 (978-0-497-11229-5(9)) Icon Grp.

Hemp - A Renewable Resource. Hosted by Nancy Pearlman. 1 cass. (Running Time: 29 min.). 10.00 (1033) Educ Comm CA.

Hen Flower see Poetry & Voice of Galway Kinnell

Hen Who Wouldn't Give up & the Otter Who Wanted to Know. Jill Tomlinson. Read by Maureen Lipman. (Running Time: 7920 sec.). (J). (ps-3). 2001. audio compact disk 21.95 (978-0-7540-6738-2(6)) AudioGo GBR.

Henceforth, From the Mind see Twentieth-Century Poetry in English, No. 2, Recordings of Poets Reading Their Own Poetry

Henderson the Rain King. unabr. ed. Saul Bellow. Read by Joe Barrett. (Running Time: 13 hrs.). (Audible Modern Classic Ser.). 2009. 39.97 (978-1-4233-9352-8(X), 9781423393528, Brlnc Audio MP3 Lib); 24.99 (978-1-4233-9351-1(1), 9781423393511, Brilliance MP3); 39.97 (978-1-4233-9353-5(8), 9781423393535, BADLE); audio compact disk 29.99 (978-1-4233-9349-8(X), 9781423393498, Bril Audio CD Unabri); audio compact disk 99.97 (978-1-4233-9350-4(3), 9781423393504, BriAudCD Unabrid) Brilliance Audio.

Henk Badings: Trios-Cosmos. Vartan Manoogian. 2008. audio compact disk 15.00 (978-1-931569-17-0(7)) Pub: U of Wis Pr. Dist(s): Chicago Distribution Ctr

Henny Penny see Three Little Pigs & Other Fairy Tales

Henny Penny. 1 cass. (Running Time: 35 min.). (J). (gr. k-4). 1992. bk. 16.95 (SAC-6C) Kimbo Educ.
A famous tale that begins when the gullible Henny Penny is hit on the head with an acorn & believes the sky is falling. Includes read along book & guide.

Henny-Penny. Illus. by Jane Wattenberg. Retold by Jane Wattenberg. 1 cass. (Running Time: 8 min.). (J). (gr. k-3). 2001. bk. 26.90 (978-0-8045-6877-7(4)) Spoken Arts.
Come flock along as Henny-Penny and her barnyard pals take a side-splitting trip around the world in search of... King Kong? King Tut? Or is it Elvis? Along the way the gang breezes by many international landmarks such as the Egyptian pyramids and the Leaning Tower of Pisa. But when they meet up with that mean ball of fur Foxy-Loxy, their plans suddenly go a-fowl!.

Henny-Penny. l.t. ed. Short Stories. Illus. by Graham Percy. 1 cass. (Running Time: 10 mins.). Dramatization. (J). (ps-3). 2001. bk. 8.99 (978-84-86154-39-4(1)) Pub: Peralt Mont ESP. Dist(s): imaJen

Henny Penny. unabr. ed. Paul Galdone. 1 cass. (Running Time: 8 min.). (J). (gr. k-4). 1987. pap. bk. 17.90 (978-0-8045-6520-2(1), 6520) Spoken Arts.
"The sky is falling!" says Henny Penny. "I must go and tell the king!".

Henrietta Who? unabr. ed. Catherine Aird. Read by Robin Bailey. 6 cass. (Running Time: 9 hrs.). (Inspector C. D. Sloan Mystery Ser.). 2001. 49.95 (978-0-7451-5707-8(6), CAB 517) Pub: Chivers Audio Bks GBR. Dist(s): AudioGO
Henrietta Jenkins lived with her widowed mother while she went to college. But her life soon changed dramatically: just before her 21st birthday, her mother's body was found on a quiet country road, apparently the victim of a hit-and-run. It's not long before the case turns into a murder hunt, and the postmortem of Grace Jenkins reveals that she never had any children. In which case, who was Henrietta?.

Henry & Beezus. Beverly Cleary. (Henry Huggins Ser.). (J). (gr. 1-4). 1981. 16.00 (978-0-394-66100-1(1)) SRA McGraw.

Henry & Beezus. unabr. ed. Beverly Cleary. Read by William Roberts. 2 cass. (Running Time: 3 hrs.). (Henry Huggins Ser.). (J). (gr. 1-4). 1999. 17.95 (L191) Blckstn Audio.
The gang on Klickitat Street is at it again! And Henry Huggins & his dog Ribsy find themselves in the middle of all the zaniness. Henry is determined to buy a new red bike to replace his old scooter. But, even with the help of Beezus & Robert, he just keeps coming up short - until an unexpected bit of luck comes his way.

***Henry & Beezus.** unabr. ed. Beverly Cleary. Read by Stockard Channing & William Roberts. (J). 2010. audio compact disk 14.99 (978-0-06-177406-5(5), HarperChildAud) HarperCollins Pubs.

***Henry & Beezus.** unabr. ed. Beverly Cleary. Read by William Roberts. (ENG.). 2010. (978-0-06-206218-5(2)); (978-0-06-176819-4(7)) HarperCollins Pubs.

Henry & Beezus. unabr. ed. Beverly Cleary. Read by William Roberts. 2 vols. (Running Time: 2 hrs. 31 mins.). (Henry Huggins Ser.). (J). (gr. 3-7). 1997. pap. bk. 29.00 (978-0-8072-7607-5(3), YA897SP, Listening Lib); 23.00 (978-0-8072-7606-8(5), YA897CX, Listening Lib) Random Audio Pubg.
Henry Huggins is determined to buy a shiny new red bike to show up Scooter. Beezus helps Henry reach his goals & turn his humiliating situation into a business success.

Henry & Mudge. unabr. ed. Cynthia Rylant. Narrated by George Guidall. 1 cass. (Running Time: 15 mins.). (Henry & Mudge Ser.). (gr. 1 up). 1997. 10.00 (978-0-7887-0902-9(X), 95040E7) Recorded Bks.
Teaches lessons about friendship & security as it follows the adventures of a small boy & his best friend, an enormous Great Dane.

Henry & Mudge & Annie's Good Move. Cynthia Rylant. 14 vols. (Running Time: 9 mins.). (Henry & Mudge Ser.). (J). (ps-3). 2002. pap. bk. & tchr.'s planning gde. ed. 29.95 (978-0-87499-966-2(9)) Live Oak Media.
Henry is a big help to his cousin Annie when he realizes she has the moving day jitters.

Henry & Mudge & Annie's Good Move. Cynthia Rylant. Illus. by Suçie Stevenson. 14 vols. (Running Time: 9 mins.). (Henry & Mudge Ser.). 2002. pap. bk. 31.95 (978-1-59112-647-8(9)); 9.95 (978-0-87499-963-1(4)); audio compact disk 12.95 (978-1-59112-645-4(2)) Live Oak Media.

Henry & Mudge & Annie's Good Move. Cynthia Rylant. Narrated by George Guidall. (Running Time: 15 mins.). (Henry & Mudge Ser.). (gr. 1 up). 10.00 (978-1-4025-0750-2(X)) Recorded Bks.

Henry & Mudge & Annie's Good Move. abr. ed. Cynthia Rylant. Illus. by Suçie Stevenson. 11 vols. (Running Time: 9 mins.). (Henry & Mudge Ser.). (J). (ps-3). 2002. bk. 25.95 (978-0-87499-965-5(0)); pap. bk. 16.95 (978-0-87499-964-8(2)) Pub: Live Oak Media. Dist(s): AudioGO

Henry & Mudge & the Bedtime Thumps. unabr. ed. Cynthia Rylant. Narrated by George Guidall. 1 cass. (Running Time: 15 mins.). (Henry & Mudge Ser.). (gr. 1 up). 1997. 10.00 (978-0-7887-1113-8(X), 95107E7) Recorded Bks.
Henry & his pet, Mudge, are going to visit Grandma & they worry about how she will react to a large, slobbering dog rambling around her small house.

Henry & Mudge & the Best Day of All. unabr. ed. Cynthia Rylant. Narrated by George Guidall. 1 cass. (Running Time: 15 mins.). (Henry & Mudge Ser.). (gr. 1 up). 10.00 (978-0-7887-1787-1(1), 95258E7) Recorded Bks.
Follows the adventures of a small boy & his best friend, an enormous Great Dane. Available to libraries only.

Henry & Mudge & the Best Day of All. unabr. ed. Cynthia Rylant. Read by George Guidall. 1 cass. (Running Time: 15 min.). (Henry & Mudge Ser.). (J). (gr. k-3). 1997. bk. 22.24 (978-0-7887-1820-5(7), 40600) Recorded Bks.
Follows the adventures of a small boy & his best friend - an enormous Great Dane.

Henry & Mudge & the Careful Cousin. Cynthia Rylant. Read by John Beach. Illus. by Suçie Stevenson. 1 cass. (Henry & Mudge Ser.). (J). (gr. k-3). 2000. pap. bk. 19.97 (978-0-7366-9183-3(9)) Books on Tape.
When proper Cousin Annie comes to visit, Henry isn't sure how she'll react to big, drooly Mudge & is pleasantly surprised to discover that she & Mudge share a talent for Frisbee.

Henry & Mudge & the Careful Cousin. Cynthia Rylant. 1 cass. (Running Time: 35 min.). (Henry & Mudge Ser.). (J). (gr. k-3). 2001. pap. bk. 15.95 (VX-94C) Kimbo Educ.
When proper cousin Annie comes to visit, Henry isn't too sure how she will react to big, drooly Mudge. But, he is pleasantly surprised!.

Henry & Mudge & the Careful Cousin. Cynthia Rylant. Illus. by Suçie Stevenson. 14 vols. (Running Time: 12 mins.). (Henry & Mudge Ser.). 1999. pap. bk. 31.95 (978-1-59112-570-9(7)); 9.95 (978-0-87499-531-2(0)) Live Oak Media.

Henry & Mudge & the Careful Cousin. Cynthia Rylant. Illus. by Suçie Stevenson. (Running Time: 12 mins.). (Henry & Mudge Ser.). (J). (gr. k-3). 1999. 12.95 (978-1-59112-369-9(0)) Live Oak Media.

Henry & Mudge & the Careful Cousin. Cynthia Rylant. Illus. by Suçie Stevenson. 1 cass. (Running Time: 30 mins.). (Henry & Mudge Ser.). (J). (gr. k-3). 2000. pap. bk. 15.98 (T 6564 SP, Listening Lib) Random Audio Pubg.

Henry & Mudge & the Careful Cousin. unabr. ed. Cynthia Rylant. Read by John Beach. Illus. by Suçie Stevenson. 14 vols. (Running Time: 12 mins.). (Henry & Mudge Ser.). (J). 1999. pap. bk. 29.95 Reading Chest. (978-0-87499-530-5(2)) Live Oak Media.
When proper Cousin Annie comes to visit, Henry isn't too sure how she'll react to big, drooly Mudge.

Henry & Mudge & the Careful Cousin. unabr. ed. Cynthia Rylant. Read by John Beach. Illus. by Suçie Stevenson. 11 vols. (Running Time: 12 mins.). (Henry & Mudge Ser.). (J). (gr. k-3). 1999. bk. 25.95 (978-0-87499-529-9(9)); pap. bk. 16.95 (978-0-87499-528-2(0)) Pub: Live Oak Media. Dist(s): AudioGO
When proper Cousin Annie comes to visit, Henry isn't too sure how she'll react to big, drooly Mudge & their rough & tumble ways.

Henry & Mudge & the Forever Sea. Cynthia Rylant. Read by John Beach. Illus. by Suçie Stevenson. 1 cass. (Henry & Mudge Ser.). (J). (gr. k-3). 2000. pap. bk. 19.97 (978-0-7366-9187-1(1)) Books on Tape.
Henry, his father & his big red dog Mudge spend a day at the beach while on summer vacation. Leisurely activities such as splashing waves, eating hot dogs & cherry sno-cones & chasing an errant crab provide a days adventures.

Henry & Mudge & the Forever Sea. Cynthia Rylant. 1 cass. (Running Time: 35 min.). (Henry & Mudge Ser.). (J). (gr. k-3). 2001. pap. bk. 15.95 (VX-605C) Kimbo Educ.
Henry, his father & his big red dog Mudge spend a day at the beach while on summer vacation. Includes book to read along with.

Henry & Mudge & the Forever Sea. Cynthia Rylant. Illus. by Suçie Stevenson. (Henry & Mudge Ser.). 9.95 (978-1-59112-170-1(1)) Live Oak Media.

Henry & Mudge & the Forever Sea. Cynthia Rylant. Illus. by Suçie Stevenson. 11 vols. (Running Time: 8 mins.). (Henry & Mudge Ser.). 2000. bk. 28.95 (978-1-59112-575-4(8)); pap. bk. 31.95 (978-1-59112-574-7(X)); 9.95 (978-0-87499-604-3(X)) Live Oak Media.

Henry & Mudge & the Forever Sea. Cynthia Rylant. Illus. by Suçie Stevenson. (Running Time: 8 mins.). (Henry & Mudge Ser.). (J). (gr. k-3). 2000. 12.95 (978-1-59112-373-6(9)) Live Oak Media.

Henry & Mudge & the Forever Sea. unabr. ed. Cynthia Rylant. Read by John Beach. Illus. by Suçie Stevenson. 11 vols. (Running Time: 8 mins.). (Henry & Mudge Ser.). (J). (gr. k-3). 2000. bk. 25.95 (978-0-87499-606-7(6)); pap. bk. 16.95 (978-0-87499-605-0(8)); pap. bk. & tchr. ed. 29.95 Reading Chest. (978-0-87499-607-4(4)) Live Oak Media.
Rylant & Stevenson once again demonstrate that simple pleasures can be adventurous. Henry, his father & his red dog Mudge spend a day at the beach while on summer vacation. Leisurely activities such as splashing waves, eating hot dogs & cherry sno-cones & chasing an errant crab provide a day's adventures.

Henry & Mudge & the Happy Cat. unabr. ed. Cynthia Rylant. Narrated by George Guidall. 1 cass. (Running Time: 15 mins.). (Henry & Mudge Ser.). (gr. 1 up). 1997. 10.00 (978-0-7887-1340-8(X), 95189E7) Recorded Bks.
One night, Henry & his parents find a stray cat on their doorstep. It's not a pretty cat, but it is very friendly. Once it meets Mudge, it is also a very happy cat. What will happen, now, if someone claims Mudge's scruffy new friend?.

Henry & Mudge & the Long Weekend. Cynthia Rylant. 1 cass. (Running Time: 35 min.). (Henry & Mudge Ser.). (J). (gr. k-3). 2001. pap. bk. 15.95 (VX-601C) Kimbo Educ.
"No snow" no sun, no fun, Bo-o-ring!" Until Henry's mother suggests a creative solution that engages everyone's interest.

Henry & Mudge & the Long Weekend. Cynthia Rylant. Illus. by Suçie Stevenson. (Henry & Mudge Ser.). 9.95 (978-1-59112-296-8(1)) Live Oak Media.

Henry & Mudge & the Long Weekend. Cynthia Rylant. Illus. by Suçie Stevenson. 11 vols. (Running Time: 11 mins.). (Henry & Mudge Ser.). 2000. bk. 28.95 (978-1-59112-577-8(4)); pap. bk. 31.95 (978-1-59112-576-1(6)) Live Oak Media.

Henry & Mudge & the Long Weekend. Cynthia Rylant. Illus. by Suçie Stevenson. (Running Time: 11 mins.). (Henry & Mudge Ser.). (J). (gr. k-3). 2000. 12.95 (978-1-59112-375-0(5)) Live Oak Media.

Henry & Mudge & the Long Weekend. unabr. ed. Cynthia Rylant. Read by John Beach. Illus. by Suçie Stevenson. 14 vols. (Running Time: 11 mins.). (Henry & Mudge Ser.). (J). 2000. pap. bk. 29.95 Reading Chest. (978-0-87499-603-6(1)) Live Oak Media.
No snow, no sun, no fun, Bo-o-ring! That's Henry's vision of a long winter weekend, until his mother suggests transforming appliance cartons into a castle, a creative solution that engages everyone's interest & provides a starring role for Mudge's canine capers.

Henry & Mudge & the Long Weekend. unabr. ed. Cynthia Rylant. Read by John Beach. Illus. by Suçie Stevenson. 11 vols. (Running Time: 11 mins.). (Henry & Mudge Ser.). (J). (gr. k-3). 2000. bk. 25.95 (978-0-87499-602-9(3)); pap. bk. 16.95 (978-0-87499-601-2(5)) Pub: Live Oak Media. Dist(s): AudioGO

Henry & Mudge & the Sneaky Crackers. Cynthia Rylant. 14 vols. (Running Time: 9 mins.). (Henry & Mudge Ser.). (J). 2002. pap. bk. & tchr.'s planning gde. ed. 29.95 (978-0-87499-958-7(8)) Live Oak Media.
Henry and his dog Mudge become spies.

Henry & Mudge & the Sneaky Crackers. Cynthia Rylant. Illus. by Suçie Stevenson. 11 vols. (Running Time: 9 mins.). (Henry & Mudge Ser.). 2002. bk. 28.95 (978-1-59112-639-3(8)); pap. bk. 31.95 (978-1-59112-640-9(1)); 9.95 (978-0-87499-955-6(3)); audio compact disk 12.95 (978-1-59112-637-9(1)) Live Oak Media.

Henry & Mudge & the Sneaky Crackers. Cynthia Rylant. Narrated by George Guidall. (Running Time: 15 mins.). (Henry & Mudge Ser.). (gr. 1 up). 10.00 (978-0-7887-9368-4(3)) Recorded Bks.

Henry & Mudge & the Sneaky Crackers. abr. ed. Cynthia Rylant. 11 vols. (Running Time: 9 mins.). (Henry & Mudge Ser.). (J). 2002. pap. bk. 16.95 (978-0-87499-956-3(1)) Pub: Live Oak Media. Dist(s): AudioGO

Henry & Mudge & the Sneaky Crackers. abr. ed. Cynthia Rylant. Illus. by Suçie Stevenson. 11 vols. (Running Time: 9 mins.). (Henry & Mudge Ser.). (J). 2002. bk. 25.95 (978-0-87499-957-0(X)) Live Oak Media.

Henry & Mudge & the Snowman Plan. Cynthia Rylant. 14 vols. (Running Time: 10 mins.). (Henry & Mudge Ser.). (J). 2002. pap. bk. & tchr.'s planning gde. ed. 29.95 (978-0-87499-970-9(7)) Live Oak Media.
Henry's father helps him participate in a snowman-building contest.

Henry & Mudge & the Snowman Plan. Cynthia Rylant. Illus. by Suçie Stevenson. 14 vols. (Running Time: 10 mins.). (Henry & Mudge Ser.). 2002. pap. bk. 31.95 (978-1-59112-652-2(5)); 9.95 (978-0-87499-967-9(7)) Live Oak Media.

Henry & Mudge & the Snowman Plan. Cynthia Rylant. Illus. by Suçie Stevenson. (Running Time: 10 mins.). (Henry & Mudge Ser.). (J). (gr. k-3). 2002. 12.95 (978-1-59112-649-2(5)) Live Oak Media.

Henry & Mudge & the Snowman Plan. abr. ed. Cynthia Rylant. 11 vols. (Running Time: 10 mins.). (Henry & Mudge Ser.). (J). 2002. bk. 25.95 (978-0-87499-969-3(3)); pap. bk. 16.95 (978-0-87499-968-6(5)) Pub: Live Oak Media. Dist(s): AudioGO

Henry & Mudge & the Snowman Plan. unabr. ed. Cynthia Rylant. Narrated by George Guidall. 1 cass. (Running Time: 15 mins.). (Henry & Mudge Ser.). (gr. 1 up). 1999. 10.00 (978-1-4025-0706-9(2), 96928) Recorded Bks.
In January, there's a lot of snow on the ground. One day when Henry and his big dog Mudge go outside to play, they see a sign in a store window. It says: SNOWMAN CONTEST, SATURDAY AT THE PARK. Henry runs home to tell his dad. On Saturday, the park is filled with people building all kinds of fancy snowmen. There are many dogs there, too. While Mudge makes friends, Henry and his dad get to work. They will need to make a very unusual snowman to win this contest!.

Henry & Mudge & the Starry Night. Cynthia Rylant. Illus. by Suçie Stevenson. 14 vols. (Running Time: 9 mins.). (Henry & Mudge Ser.). 2002. pap. bk.

31.95 (978-1-59112-644-7(4)); 9.95 (978-0-87499-959-4(6)); audio compact disk 12.95 (978-1-59112-641-6(X)) Live Oak Media.

Henry & Mudge & the Starry Night. abr. ed. Cynthia Rylant. 11 vols. (Running Time: 9 mins.). (Henry & Mudge Ser.). (J). 2002. bk. 25.95 (978-0-87499-961-7(8)); pap. bk. & tchr.'s planning gde. ed. 29.95 (978-0-87499-962-4(6)) Live Oak Media.
Mudge and Henry and his parents are off on a camping trip.

Henry & Mudge & the Starry Night. abr. ed. Cynthia Rylant. Narrated by George Guidall. 1 cass. (Running Time: 15 mins.). (Henry & Mudge Ser.). (gr. 1 up). 2002. 10.00 (978-0-7887-9978-5(9)) Recorded Bks.
Henry, his parents, and his dog Mudge are going camping at Bear Lake. They will cook on a campfire, sleep in a tent, but will they see a bear.

Henry & Mudge & the Wild Wind. unabr. ed. Cynthia Rylant. Narrated by George Guidall. 1 cass. (Running Time: 15 mins.). (Henry & Mudge Ser.). (gr. 1 up). 1998. 10.00 (978-0-7887-2214-1(X), 95513E7) Recorded Bks.
Henry's dog Mudge is unhappy when a thunderstorm begins & wants to go inside & hide. How can Henry help him weather the storm?.

Henry & Mudge Get the Cold Shivers. Cynthia Rylant. Read by John Beach. Illus. by Suçie Stevenson. 1 cass. (Henry & Mudge Ser.). (J). (gr. k-3). 2000. pap. bk. 19.97 (978-0-7366-9186-4(3)) Books on Tape.
When Mudge gets sick & has to go to the vet, he & Henry share some scary moments, but Henry once again shows his devotion to his canine friend as he pampers him through his cold.

Henry & Mudge Get the Cold Shivers. Cynthia Rylant. 1 cass. (Running Time: 35 min.). (Henry & Mudge Ser.). (J). (gr. k-3). 2001. pap. bk. 15.95 (VX-93C) Kimbo Educ.
When Mudge gets sick & has to go to the vet, both he & Henry share some scary moments. Readalong.

Henry & Mudge Get the Cold Shivers. Cynthia Rylant. Illus. by Suçie Stevenson. 14 vols. (Running Time: 9 mins.). (Henry & Mudge Ser.). 1999. pap. bk. 31.95 (978-1-59112-572-3(3)) Live Oak Media.

Henry & Mudge Get the Cold Shivers. Cynthia Rylant. Illus. by Suçie Stevenson. (Running Time: 9 mins.). (Henry & Mudge Ser.). (J). (gr. k-3). 1999. 9.95 (978-0-87499-527-5(2)); 12.95 (978-1-59112-371-2(2)) Live Oak Media.

Henry & Mudge Get the Cold Shivers. unabr. ed. Cynthia Rylant. Read by John Beach. Illus. by Suçie Stevenson. 14 vols. (Running Time: 9 mins.). (Henry & Mudge Ser.). (J). 1999. pap. bk. 29.95 Reading Chest. (978-0-87499-526-8(4)) Live Oak Media.
When Mudge gets sick & has to go to the vet, both he & Henry share some scary moments.

Henry & Mudge Get the Cold Shivers. unabr. ed. Cynthia Rylant. Read by John Beech. Illus. by Suçie Stevenson. 11 vols. (Running Time: 9 mins.). (Henry & Mudge Ser.). (J). (gr. k-3). 1999. bk. 25.95 (978-0-87499-525-1(6)) Live Oak Media.

Henry & Mudge Get the Cold Shivers. unabr. ed. Cynthia Rylant. Read by John Beach. Illus. by Suçie Stevenson. 11 vols. (Running Time: 9 mins.). (Henry & Mudge Ser.). (J). (gr. k-3). 1999. pap. bk. 16.95 (978-0-87499-524-4(8)) Pub: Live Oak Media. Dist(s): AudioGO

Henry & Mudge Get the Cold Shivers. unabr. ed. Cynthia Rylant. Illus. by Suçie Stevenson. 1 cass. (Running Time: 30 mins.). (Henry & Mudge Ser.). (J). (gr. k-3). 2000. pap. bk. 15.98 (T 6565 SP, Listening Lib) Random Audio Pubg.

Henry & Mudge in Puddle Trouble. Cynthia Rylant. Read by Suzanne Toren. Illus. by Suçie Stevenson. 1 cass. (Henry & Mudge Ser.). (J). (gr. k-3). 2000. pap. bk. 19.97 (978-0-7366-9192-5(8)) Books on Tape.
Henry & Mudge celebrate spring by finding a March flower good enough to eat, an April puddle big enough for a surprise splasher & a May litter of kittens that Mudge watches over.

Henry & Mudge in Puddle Trouble. Cynthia Rylant. 1 cass. (Running Time: 35 min.). (Henry & Mudge Ser.). (J). (gr. k-3). 2001. pap. bk. 15.95 (VX-441C) Kimbo Educ.
Henry & his lovable dog, Mudge, are perfect friends for new readers.

Henry & Mudge in Puddle Trouble. Cynthia Rylant. Illus. by Suçie Stevenson. (Henry & Mudge Ser.). 9.95 (978-1-59112-151-0(5)) Live Oak Media.

Henry & Mudge in Puddle Trouble. Cynthia Rylant. Illus. by Suçie Stevenson. 14 vols. (Running Time: 15 mins.). (Henry & Mudge Ser.). 1998. pap. bk. 31.95 (978-1-59112-580-8(4)); 9.95 (978-0-87499-444-5(6)); audio compact disk 12.95 (978-1-59112-379-8(8)) Live Oak Media.

Henry & Mudge in Puddle Trouble. Cynthia Rylant. Illus. by Suçie Stevenson. 11 vols. (Running Time: 15 mins.). (Henry & Mudge Ser.). (J). 2005. pap. bk. 18.95 (978-1-59112-380-4(1)) Pub: Live Oak Media. Dist(s): AudioGO

Henry & Mudge in Puddle Trouble. unabr. ed. Cynthia Rylant. Read by Suzanne Toren. Illus. by Suçie Stevenson. 14 vols. (Running Time: 15 mins.). (Henry & Mudge Ser.). 1998. pap. bk. 29.95 Reading Chest. (978-0-87499-443-8(8)) Live Oak Media.
Henry & his lovable dog Mudge celebrate spring by finding a March flower good enough to eat, an April puddle big enough for a surprise splasher & a May litter of kittens that Mudge watches over.

Henry & Mudge in Puddle Trouble. unabr. ed. Cynthia Rylant. Read by Suzanne Toren. Illus. by Suçie Stevenson. 11 vols. (Running Time: 15 mins.). (Henry & Mudge Ser.). (J). (gr. k-3). 1998. bk. 25.95 (978-0-87499-442-1(X)); pap. bk. 16.95 (978-0-87499-441-4(1)) Pub: Live Oak Media. Dist(s): AudioGO

Henry & Mudge in the Family Trees. Cynthia Rylant. Narrated by George Guidall. (Running Time: 15 mins.). (Henry & Mudge Ser.). (gr. 1 up). 10.00 (978-0-7887-9976-1(2)) Recorded Bks.

Henry & Mudge in the Green Time. Cynthia Rylant. Read by Suzanne Toren. Illus. by Suçie Stevenson. 1 cass. (Henry & Mudge Ser.). (J). (gr. k-3). 2000. pap. bk. 19.97 (978-0-7366-9191-8(X)) Books on Tape.
Captures the essence of childhood during the summer with three adventures. Welcome chapter in the life of a boy & his dog.

Henry & Mudge in the Green Time. Cynthia Rylant. Illus. by Suçie Stevenson. 11 vols. (Running Time: 10 mins.). (Henry & Mudge Ser.). 1999. bk. 28.95 (978-1-59112-579-2(0)); pap. bk. 31.95 (978-1-59112-578-5(2)); 9.95 (978-0-87499-420-9(9)); audio compact disk 12.95 (978-1-59112-377-4(1)) Live Oak Media.

Henry & Mudge in the Green Time. Cynthia Rylant. Illus. by Suçie Stevenson. 11 vols. (Running Time: 10 mins.). (Henry & Mudge Ser.). (J). 2005. pap. bk. 18.95 (978-1-59112-378-1(X)) Pub: Live Oak Media. Dist(s): AudioGO

Henry & Mudge in the Green Time. Cynthia Rylant. (Henry & Mudge Ser.). (J). (gr. k-3). 1988. bk. 30.66 (978-0-676-87199-9(2)) SRA McGraw.

Henry & Mudge in the Green Time. unabr. ed. Cynthia Rylant. 1 cass. (Running Time: 35 min.). (Henry & Mudge Ser.). (J). (gr. k-3). 2001. pap. bk. 15.95 (VX-421C) Kimbo Educ.
A welcome chapter in the life of a boy & his dog. The essence of childhood during the summer is captured with three adventures.

Henry & Mudge in the Green Time. unabr. ed. Cynthia Rylant. Read by Suzanne Toren. Illus. by Suçie Stevenson. 11 vols. (Running Time: 10 mins.). (Henry & Mudge Ser.). (J). (gr. k-3). 1999. bk. 25.95 (978-0-87499-422-3(5)); pap. bk. 16.95 (978-0-87499-421-6(7)); pap. bk. & tchr. ed. 29.95 Reading Chest. (978-0-87499-423-0(3)) Live Oak Media.
Henry & his big dog Mudge share their prime time together in three adventures.

Henry & Mudge in the Green Time. unabr. ed. Cynthia Rylant. Illus. by Suçie Stevenson. 1 cass. (Running Time: 30 mins.). (Henry & Mudge Ser.). (J). (gr. k-3). 2000. pap. bk. 15.98 (T 6566 SP, Listening Lib) Random Audio Pubg.

Henry & Mudge in the Sparkle Days. Cynthia Rylant. Read by Suzanne Toren. Illus. by Suçie Stevenson. 1 cass. (Henry & Mudge Ser.). (J). (gr. k-3). 2000. pap. bk. 19.97 (978-0-7366-9185-7(5)) Books on Tape.
Henry & Mudge enjoy the delights of winter in these three stories.

Henry & Mudge in the Sparkle Days. Cynthia Rylant. 1 cass. (Running Time: 35 min.). (Henry & Mudge Ser.). (J). (gr. k-3). 2001. pap. bk. 15.95 (VX-499C) Kimbo Educ.

Henry & Mudge in the Sparkle Days. Cynthia Rylant. Illus. by Suçie Stevenson. 14 vols. (Running Time: 11 mins.). (Henry & Mudge Ser.). 1999. pap. bk. 31.95 (978-1-59112-582-2(0)); 9.95 (978-0-87499-498-8(5)) Live Oak Media.

Henry & Mudge in the Sparkle Days. Cynthia Rylant. Illus. by Suçie Stevenson. (Running Time: 11 mins.). (Henry & Mudge Ser.). (J). (gr. k-3). 1999. 12.95 (978-1-59112-381-1(X)) Live Oak Media.

Henry & Mudge in the Sparkle Days. Cynthia Rylant. Illus. by Suçie Stevenson. 11 vols. (Running Time: 11 mins.). (Henry & Mudge Ser.). (J). 2005. pap. bk. 18.95 (978-1-59112-382-8(8)) Pub: Live Oak Media. Dist(s): AudioGO

Henry & Mudge in the Sparkle Days. unabr. ed. Cynthia Rylant. Read by Suzanne Toren. Illus. by Suçie Stevenson. 14 vols. (Running Time: 11 mins.). (Henry & Mudge Ser.). (J). 1999. pap. bk. 29.95 Reading Chest. (978-0-87499-501-5(9)) Live Oak Media.

Henry & Mudge in the Sparkle Days. unabr. ed. Cynthia Rylant. Read by Suzanne Toren. Illus. by Suçie Stevenson. 11 vols. (Running Time: 11 mins.). (Henry & Mudge Ser.). (J). (gr. k-3). 1999. bk. 25.95 (978-0-87499-500-8(0)); pap. bk. 16.95 (978-0-87499-499-5(3)) Pub: Live Oak Media. Dist(s): AudioGO

Henry & Mudge in the Sparkle Days. unabr. ed. Cynthia Rylant. Illus. by Suçie Stevenson. 1 cass. (Running Time: 30 mins.). (Henry & Mudge Ser.). (J). (gr. k-3). 2000. pap. bk. 15.98 (T 6567 SP, Listening Lib) Random Audio Pubg.

Henry & Mudge Take the Big Test. unabr. ed. Cynthia Rylant. Narrated by George Guidall. 1 cass. (Running Time: 15 mins.). (Henry & Mudge Ser.). (gr. 1 up). 1997. 10.00 (978-0-7887-0744-5(2), 94921E7) Recorded Bks.
Perfect for beginning readers. Full of the sunny adventures of a young boy & his enormous but good-natured dog.

Henry & Mudge under the Yellow Moon. Cynthia Rylant. Read by Suzanne Toren. Illus. by Suçie Stevenson. 1 cass. (Henry & Mudge Ser.). (J). (gr. k-3). 2000. pap. bk. 19.97 (978-0-7366-9184-0(7)) Books on Tape.
The three short chapters of this beginning reader focus on autumn activities.

Henry & Mudge under the Yellow Moon. Cynthia Rylant. 1 cass. (Running Time: 35 min.). (Henry & Mudge Ser.). (J). (gr. k-3). 2001. pap. bk. 15.95 Kimbo Educ.
3 easy-to-read stories that celebrate fall.

Henry & Mudge under the Yellow Moon. Cynthia Rylant. Illus. by Suçie Stevenson. 11 vols. (Running Time: 11 mins.). (Henry & Mudge Ser.). 1998. bk. 28.95 (978-1-59112-585-3(5)); pap. bk. 31.95 (978-1-59112-584-6(7)); audio compact disk 12.95 (978-1-59112-383-5(6)) Live Oak Media.

Henry & Mudge under the Yellow Moon. Cynthia Rylant. Read by Suzanne Toren. Illus. by Suçie Stevenson. 14 vols. (Running Time: 11 mins.). (Henry & Mudge Ser.). (J). (gr. k-3). 1998. pap. bk. & tchr. ed. 29.95 Reading Chest. (978-0-87499-447-6(0)) Live Oak Media.
Three easy-to-read stories that celebrate the fall & speak directly to the concerns of children.

Henry & Mudge under the Yellow Moon. Cynthia Rylant. Illus. by Suçie Stevenson. 11 vols. (Running Time: 11 mins.). (Henry & Mudge Ser.). (J). 2005. pap. bk. 18.95 (978-1-59112-384-2(4)) Pub: Live Oak Media. Dist(s): AudioGO

Henry & Mudge under the Yellow Moon. unabr. ed. Cynthia Rylant. Read by Suzanne Toren. Illus. by Suçie Stevenson. 11 vols. (Running Time: 11 mins.). (Henry & Mudge Ser.). (J). (gr. k-3). 1998. bk. 25.95 (978-0-87499-446-9(2)); pap. bk. 16.95 (978-0-87499-445-2(4)) Pub: Live Oak Media. Dist(s): AudioGO

Henry & Mudge under the Yellow Moon. unabr. ed. Cynthia Rylant. Illus. by Suçie Stevenson. 1 cass. (Running Time: 30 mins.). (Henry & Mudge Ser.). (J). (gr. k-3). 1999. pap. bk. 15.98 (T 6426 SP, Listening Lib) Random Audio Pubg.

***Henry & Ribsy.** unabr. ed. Beverly Cleary. Read by Neil Patrick Harris. (ENG.). 2009. (978-0-06-180562-2(9)); (978-0-06-176246-8(6)) HarperCollins Pubs.

Henry & Ribsy, unabr. ed. Beverly Cleary. Narrated by Jeff Woodman. 2 pieces. (Running Time: 2 hrs.). (Henry Huggins Ser.). (gr. 3 up). 19.00 (978-0-7887-0534-2(2), 94729E7) Recorded Bks.
If Henry can keep his dog, Ribsy, out of trouble for a month, Mr. Huggins promises to take them both fishing. It sounds easy, but then again, nothing is ever easy for Henry & Ribsy! Available to libraries only.

Henry & the Clubhouse. unabr. ed. Beverly Cleary. Read by Neil Patrick Harris. (Running Time: 12600 sec.). (Henry Huggins Ser.). (J). 2006. audio compact disk 22.00 (978-0-06-089836-6(4)) HarperCollins Pubs.

***Henry & the Clubhouse.** unabr. ed. Beverly Cleary. Read by Neil Patrick Harris. (ENG.). 2006. (978-0-06-122908-4(3)); (978-0-06-122907-7(5)) HarperCollins Pubs.

Henry & the Clubhouse. unabr. ed. Beverly Cleary. Narrated by Jeff Woodman. 2 pieces. (Running Time: 2 hrs. 45 mins.). (Henry Huggins Ser.). (gr. 3 up). 19.00 (978-0-7887-0603-5(9), 94782E7) Recorded Bks.
Third-grader Henry Huggins is about to fulfill a young boy's dream: he & his friends are about to build a "boys only" clubhouse. Available to libraries only.

Henry & the Paper Route. Beverly Cleary. Read by Jeff Woodman. 2 cass. (Running Time: 3 hrs.). (Henry Huggins Ser.). (J). (gr. 1-4). 1999. wbk. ed. 91.70 (47033) Recorded Bks.
Henry Huggins is tired of sitting around peeling the covering off a golfball. He wants to do something important. He wants a paper route like Scooter.

***Henry & the Paper Route.** abr. ed. Beverly Cleary. Read by Neil Patrick Harris. (ENG.). 2006. (978-0-06-122898-8(2)); (978-0-06-122899-5(0)) HarperCollins Pubs.

Henry & the Paper Route. unabr. ed. Beverly Cleary. Read by Neil Patrick Harris. 3 cds. (Running Time: 12600 sec.). (Henry Huggins Ser.). (J). (gr. 4-7). 2006. audio compact disk 22.00 (978-0-06-089831-1(3), HarperChildAud) HarperCollins Pubs.

Henry & the Paper Route. unabr. ed. Beverly Cleary. Narrated by Jeff Woodman. 2 cass. (Running Time: 3 hrs.). (Henry Huggins Ser.). (J). (gr. 1-4). 2000. pap. bk. 34.24 (978-0-7887-3797-8(X), 41041X4) Recorded Bks.

Henry & the Paper Route, unabr. ed. Beverly Cleary. Narrated by Jeff Woodman. 2 pieces. (Running Time: 3 hrs.). (Henry Huggins Ser.). (gr. 3 up). 2000. 21.00 (978-0-7887-3821-0(6), 96014E7) Recorded Bks.

Henry Builds a Cabin. 2004. bk. 24.95 (978-1-55592-176-7(0)); audio compact disk 12.95 (978-1-55592-890-2(0)); 8.95 (978-1-55592-834-6(X)) Weston Woods.
Johnson tells the story of a frugal bear named Henry who sets about building a small cabin in the woods and ends up with a much bigger home than he and his friends ever imagined. Narrated by James Naughton with music by Jon Carroll.

Henry David Thoreau: Activist. unabr. ed. Joseph Schiffman. 1 cass. (Running Time: 25 min.). (Six American Authors Ser.). 1968. 12.95 (23043) J Norton Pubs.
Discussion of Thoreau's style of expression & relevance to our time.

Henry el Explorador. Tr. of Henry the Explorer. (SPA.). 2004. 8.95 (978-0-7882-0298-8(7)) Weston Woods.

Henry Esmond, Set. William Makepeace Thackeray. Read by Flo Gibson. 12 cass. (Running Time: 17 hrs. 30 min.). 1996. 39.95 (978-1-55685-409-5(9)) Audio Bk Con.
An historical novel peopled with such characters as Addison, Steele, Congreve & James Edward, the old Pretender to the throne of England. Henry Esmond, heir to the Castlewood estate, keeps this a secret to enhance the lives of his beloved cousins.

Henry Ford. unabr. ed. 1 cass. (Running Time: 1 hr. 14 min.). (History Maker Ser.). 12.95 (41016) J Norton Pubs.
Through Ford, & his development of the Model T car, autos were produced quickly & cheaply. The tale of a man with limited education who became a commercial genius & changed the world's lifestyle.

Henry Ford. unabr. ed. Hazel B. Aird. Read by Lloyd James. 3 cass. (Running Time: 4 hrs.). (Childhood of Famous Americans Ser.). (gr. 1-3). 2001. 35.95 (978-0-7861-2060-4(6), K2821) Blckstn Audio.

Henry Hikes to Fitchburg. 2004. bk. 24.95 (978-1-55592-080-7(2)); audio compact disk 12.95 (978-1-55592-953-4(2)) Weston Woods.

Henry Hikes to Fitchburg. Donald B. Johnson. 1 cass. (Running Time: 5 min.). (J). (gr. k-4). 2004. 8.95 (978-1-55592-975-6(3)) Weston Woods.
Two friends agree to meet 30 miles away in Fitchburg. Henry elects to take a very long nature walk, while his friend chooses to work to earn his train fare.

Henry Holzer: The Walter Polovchak Case & Constitutional Law. (Running Time: 60 min.). (Long Beach City College). 1983. 9.00 (F150) Freeland Pr.
A discussion of the efect of freedom on a young Russian defector & the legal processes which were hindering his bid for freedom (by the Consitutional attorney who undertook his defense.).

Henry Hudson: English Explorer of the Northwest Passage. unabr. ed. Josepha Sherman. Read by Eileen Stevens. 1 MP3-CD. (Running Time: 2 hrs.). (Library of Explorers & Exploration Ser.). 2009. 39.97 (978-1-4233-9388-7(0), 9781423393887, Brinc Audio MP3 Lib); 19.99 (978-1-4233-9387-0(2), 9781423393870, Brilliance MP3); 39.97 (978-1-4233-9389-4(9), 9781423393894, BADLE); audio compact disk 19.99 (978-1-4233-9385-6(6), 9781423393856, Bril Audio CD Unabri) Brilliance Audio.

Henry Hudson: English Explorer of the Northwest Passage. unabr. ed. Josepha Sherman. Read by Eileen Stevens. 2 CDs. (Running Time: 2 hrs.). (Library of Explorers & Exploration Ser.). (J). (gr. 4-7). 2009. audio compact disk 39.97 (978-1-4233-9386-3(4), 9781423393863, BriAudCD Unabrd) Brilliance Audio.

Henry Huggins. Beverly Cleary. Read by Neil Patrick Harris. (Running Time: 2 hrs. 30 mins.). (J). 2001. 18.00 (PH294) Blckstn Audio.
Nothing ever happens to Henry Huggins. Nothing, that is, until a stray dog named Ribsy comes into his life. Pretty soon, Henry and Ribsy are wreaking havoc on the city bus, getting a ride in a police car with sirens wailing, and winning a prize at the dog show.

***Henry Huggins.** unabr. ed. Beverly Cleary. Read by Neil Patrick Harris. (ENG.). 2004. (978-0-06-079043-1(1)); (978-0-06-081434-2(9)) HarperCollins Pubs.

Henry Huggins, unabr. ed. Beverly Cleary. Narrated by Barbara Caruso. 2 pieces. (Running Time: 3 hrs.). (Henry Huggins Ser.). (gr. 3 up). 1994. 19.00 (978-0-7887-0020-0(0), 94219E7) Recorded Bks.
Henry Huggins is in the third grade. He lives with his Mom & Dad in a square white house on Klickitat Street. Except for having his tonsils out when he was six & breaking his arm when he was seven, nothing exciting ever happens to Henry. But that is before he meets Ribsy, a hungry black & tan mongrel with a nasty case of fleas.

Henry Huggins. unabr. ed. Beverly Cleary. Narrated by Barbara Caruso. 3 CDs. (Running Time: 3 hrs.). (Henry Huggins Ser.). (gr. 3 up). 2000. audio compact disk 27.00 (978-0-7887-4218-7(3), C1157E7) Recorded Bks.

Henry Huggins. unabr. anniv. ed. Beverly Cleary. Read by Neil Patrick Harris. 3 CDs. (Running Time: 2 hrs. 30 mins.). (Henry Huggins Ser.). (J). (gr. 3-5). 2001. 20.00 (978-0-694-52525-6(1)) HarperCollins Pubs.

Henry IV Pt. 2: Texts & Contexts. abr. ed. William Shakespeare. Perf. by Swan Theatre Players. 1 cass. (Running Time: 53 min.). Dramatization. 10.95 (978-0-8045-0816-2(X), SAC 7116) Spoken Arts.
The complete play in key scenes & arts, with narrative bridges.

Henry IV Pt.1: Texts & Contexts. abr. ed. William Shakespeare. Perf. by Swan Theatre Players. 1 cass. (Running Time: 52 min.). Dramatization. 10.95 (978-0-8045-0815-5(1), SAC 7115) Spoken Arts.
The complete play using key scenes, acts & bridges.

Henry IV Vol. 2: Texts & Contexts. unabr. ed. William Shakespeare. Read by Audio Partners Staff. 2 cass. (Running Time: 3 hrs. 3 mins.). (Arkangel Shakespeare Ser.). 2004. 17.95 (978-1-932219-50-0(1), Atlntc Mnthly) Pub: Grove-Atltic. Dist(s): PerseuPGW
King Henry's health is failing, and England is still in turmoil. Prince Hal has proved his courage, but the conniving Falstaff and his ribald companions lurk in the wings, waiting for Hal to ascend the throne. Performed by Julian Glover, Jamie Glover, Richard Griffiths, and the Arkangel cast.

Henry Iv, Part. unabr. ed. William Shakespeare. Read by Arkangel Cast Staff. Narrated by Jamie Glover et al. (Arkangel Shakespeare Ser.). (ENG.). 2005. audio compact disk 24.95 (978-1-932219-09-8(9)) Pub: AudioGO. Dist(s): Perseus Dist

Henry Iv, Part. unabr. ed. William Shakespeare. Read by Arkangel Cast Staff. Narrated by Jamie Glover et al. (Arkangel Shakespeare Ser.). (ENG.). 2005. audio compact disk 24.95 (978-1-932219-10-4(2)) Pub: AudioGO. Dist(s): Perseus Dist
In the early 15th century, civil war is rife in England. King Henry's health is failing - and Falstaff and his ribald companions waste the nights in revelry, anticipating the moment when Prince Hal will ascend the throne. The king fears his son's hedonistic nature will lead the kingdom to ruin. But when news arrives that the king has passed, the prince surprises his friends. This wonderful production is performed by Julian Glover, Jamie Glover, Richard Griffiths, and the Arkangel cast.

Henry IV, Part 1. unabr. ed. William Shakespeare. Narrated by Flo Gibson. (Running Time: 3 hrs. 3 mins.). 2004. 14.95 (978-1-55685-766-9(7)) Audio Bk Con.

Henry IV, Part 2, Vol. 2. unabr. ed. William Shakespeare. Narrated by Flo Gibson. (Running Time: 3 hrs. 18 mins.). 2005. 16.95 (978-1-55685-767-6(5)) Audio Bk Con.

***Henry James Short Stories.** Henry James. Narrated by Flo Gibson. 2009. audio compact disk 29.95 (978-1-60646-095-5(1)) Audio Bk Con.

Henry James Short Stories, Set. unabr. ed. Short Stories. Henry James. Read by Flo Gibson. 6 cass. (Running Time: 8 hrs. 30 min.). 1993. 24.95 (978-1-55685-302-9(5)) Audio Bk Con.
"The Beast of the Jungle" (considered to be one of Henry James' best), "The Altar of the Dead," "The Birthplace," "The Liar," & "The Middle Years" comprise this deeply sensitive & provocative collection.

Henry Kaufmann, Wall Street Guru. (Running Time: 60 min.). 1989. 11.95 (K0490B090, HarperThor) HarpC GBR.

Henry Mencken Conversing. abr. ed. H. L. Mencken. 1 cass. 1984. 12.95 (978-0-694-50064-2(X), SWC 1082) HarperCollins Pubs.
A conversation with Donald Howe Kirkley, Sr. of the "Baltimore Sun".

Henry Miller. Featuring Henry Miller. 1 cass. (FRE.). 1996. 21.95 (1809-LQP) Olivia & Hill.
Unique document. Unedited recording of a rare interview, in French, granted by Miller during his last visit to Paris in September 1969.

Henry Miller: An Interview. 1 cass. (Running Time: 60 min.). 10.95 (OP-77-12-20, HarperThor) HarpC GBR.

Henry Miller's People. abr. ed. Read by Mitchell Ryan. 2 cass. (Running Time: 3 hrs.). 1995. 15.95 (978-0-944993-55-2(9)) Audio Lit.
Focuses on Henry Miller's insights into the human character. The pieces range from the delightfully raucous to the metaphysically illuminating, including portraits of the famous Walt Whitman, Blase Cendrars & the less-than-famous Max, Mademoiselle Claude - people in Miller's life.

Henry Pruden: The Conceptual Framework for Technical Market Analysis. Read by Henry Pruden. 1 cass. 30.00 Dow Jones Telerate.
A conceptual framework must bring all of the elements of technical market analysis together into an integrated whole, combining the four key ingredients of technical market analysis; price, volume, time & sentiment. Coordinating these various elements is frequently among the most critical problems the technical trader will face. This session will present a conceptual framework which allows the technical trader to see how the various elements of price, volume, time & sentiment fit together into a meaningful, mutually reinforcing whole.

Henry Reed, Inc. abr. ed. Keith Robertson. 1 cass. (Running Time: 52 mins.). Dramatization. (J). (gr. 4-7). pap. bk. 15.95 (978-0-670-36801-3(6)); 9.95 (978-0-670-36799-3(0)) Live Oak Media.
Young Henry Reed records the efforts of a summer vacation spent in learning the lessons of free enterprise.

Henry Reed, Inc., Set. abr. ed. Keith Robertson. Illus. by Robert McCloskey. 11 vols. (Running Time: 52 mins.). Dramatization. (J). (gr. 4-7). bk. 24.95 Incl. cloth bk. (978-0-670-36800-6(8)) Live Oak Media.

***Henry Shortbull Swallows the Sun.** Jill Kalz. Illus. by Sahin Erkocak. Contrib. by Miles Tagmeyer. (Pfeffernut County Ser.). (ENG.). 2008. audio compact disk 11.93 (978-1-4048-5386-7(3)) CapstoneDig.

Henry Taylor. unabr. ed. Henry Taylor. Read by Henry Taylor. 1 cass. (Running Time: 29 min.). 1989. 10.00 New Letters.
Taylor reads his poetry & is interviewed.

Henry the Explorer see Henry el Explorador

Henry the Explorer. 2004. 8.95 (978-1-56008-919-3(9)); cass. & flmstrp 30.00 (978-0-89719-533-1(7)) Weston Woods.

***Henry the Fourth.** abr. ed. William Shakespeare. Read by Harry Andrews & Pamela Brown. (ENG.). 2005. (978-0-06-112606-2(3), Caedmon); (978-0-06-089640-9(X), Caedmon) HarperCollins Pubs.

***Henry the Fourth, Part 2.** abr. ed. William Shakespeare. (ENG.). 2006. (978-0-06-112643-7(8), Caedmon) HarperCollins Pubs.

Henry the Little Cactus. unabr. ed. Roger W. Bretemitz. 1 cass. (Running Time: 20 min.). Dramatization. (J). (gr. k-5). 1997. 8.95 (978-1-893417-02-1(6), 002) Vector Studios.
A little cactus finds a home in the city with a little kitten, & a dog named Peppy. They feed & give it love. Music & sound effects in background.

Henry V. Claire McEachern. Narrated by Flo Gibson. 2008. audio compact disk 19.95 (978-1-55685-998-4(8)) Audio Bk Con.

***Henry V.** abr. ed. Claire McEachern. (ENG.). 2006. (978-0-06-112641-3(1), Caedmon); (978-0-06-112642-0(X), Caedmon) HarperCollins Pubs.

Henry V. unabr. ed. Claire McEachern. Narrated by Flo Gibson. (Running Time: 3 hrs. 16 mins.). 2004. 16.95 (978-1-55685-763-8(2)) Audio Bk Con.

Henry V. unabr. ed. Claire McEachern. Read by Full Ensemble Cast. (YA). 2006. 34.99 (978-1-59895-626-9(4)) Find a World.

Henry V. unabr. collector's ed. Desmond Seward. Read by Bob Hanrott. 7 cass. (Running Time: 10 hrs. 30 min.). 1999. 56.00 (978-0-7366-4452-5(0), 4897) Books on Tape.
The author reexamines the life of Henry V - the ruthless military genius whose armies swept across Normandy in the early fifteenth century, reviving the long-dormant Hundred Years War. Henry emerges as an intolerant bigot, who zealously persecuted & burned English heretics; a brilliant political tactician; & a strict & often sadistic administrator of occupied France who kept the populace in line through the systematic use of terror & artificially induced famine. Henry's disastrous policies of conquest overseas ended by bankrupting the monarchy & plunging the country into the bloody Wars of the Roses.

Henry Vi. unabr. ed. William Shakespeare. Read by David Tennant & Amanda Root. (Running Time: 9540 sec.). (Arkangel Shakespeare Ser.). (ENG.). 2005. audio compact disk 24.95 (978-1-932219-12-8(9)) Pub: AudioGO. Dist(s): Perseus Dist

Henry Vi, Part 1. unabr. ed. William Shakespeare. Read by Audio Partners Staff. 2 cass. (Running Time: 2 hrs. 39 mins.). (Arkangel Shakespeare Ser.). 2004. 17.95 (978-1-932219-52-4(8), Atlntc Mnthly) Pub: Grove-Atltic. Dist(s): PerseuPGW
Henry V is dead, and his infant son Henry VI occupies the throne. While the French, led by Joan of Arc, threaten to win back territories lost to Henry V, a power struggle develops between the young king's guardians, leading to the Wars of the Roses. Performed by David Tennant, Amanda Root, and the Arkangel cast.

Henry Vi, Vol. 2, Part 2. unabr. ed. William Shakespeare. Read by Audio Partners Staff. 2 cass. (Running Time: 3 hrs. 1 min.). (Arkangel Shakespeare Ser.). 2004. 17.95 (978-1-932219-53-1(6), Atlntc Mnthly) Pub: Grove-Atltic. Dist(s): PerseuPGW
The young king's new queen is beautiful - and ruthless. Supported by the powerful Duke of Suffolk, Margaret plots the overthrow of her enemies, including the ambitious Duke of York. The common people revolt, and England erupts in civil war. Performed by David Tennant, Kelly Hunter, and the Arkangel cast.

Henry Vi, Vol. 3, Part 3. unabr. ed. William Shakespeare. Read by Audio Partners Staff. 2 cass. (Running Time: 2 hrs. 55 mins.). (Arkangel Shakespeare Ser.). 2004. 17.95 (978-1-932219-54-8(4), Atlntc Mnthly) Pub: Grove-Atltic. Dist(s): PerseuPGW

Henry VI, Part Three, Pt. 3. unabr. ed. William Shakespeare. Read by David Tennant et al. (Running Time: 10500 sec.). (Arkangel Shakespeare Ser.). (ENG.). 2005. audio compact disk 24.95 (978-1-932219-14-2(5)) Pub: AudioGO. Dist(s): Perseus Dist

Henry VI, Part Two. unabr. ed. William Shakespeare. Read by Norman Rodway et al. Narrated by David Tennant et al. (Running Time: 10860 sec.). (Arkangel Shakespeare Ser.). (ENG.). 2005. audio compact disk 24.95 (978-1-932219-13-5(7)) Pub: AudioGO. Dist(s): Perseus Dist

Henry VIII. unabr. ed. William Shakespeare. Read by Paul Jesson et al. Narrated by Arkangel Cast Staff. (Running Time: 10140 sec.). (Arkangel Shakespeare Ser.). (ENG.). 2005. audio compact disk 24.95 (978-1-932219-15-9(3)) Pub: AudioGO. Dist(s): Perseus Dist
Smitten with Anne Boleyn, Henry resolves to divorce his wife, even if it means breaking with Rome. The great king and his powerful advisors - Wolsey, Cramner, Cromwell - are vividly portrayed against the backdrop of one of England's most dramatic episodes. Performed by Paul Jesson, Jane Lapotaire, and the Arkangel cast.

Henry VIII. unabr. ed. William Shakespeare. Read by Audio Partners Staff. 2 cass. (Running Time: 2 hrs. 49 mins.). (Arkangel Shakespeare Ser.). 2004. 17.95 (978-1-932219-55-5(2), Atlntc Mnthly) Pub: Grove-Atltic. Dist(s): PerseuPGW

Henry VIII. unabr. ed. William Shakespeare. 2 cass. (Running Time: 3 hrs.). (Arkangel Complete Shakespeare Ser.). 2001. 17.95 (PengAudBks) Penguin Grp USA.

Henry VIII, Set. unabr. ed. William Shakespeare. Read by Grover Gardner. 2 cass. (Running Time: 3 hrs.). 1992. 14.95 (978-1-55685-242-8(8)) Audio Bk Con.
Henry VIII foils a plot by the scheming Cardinal Wolsey, rejects his twenty-year marriage to the tragic Katharine of Aragon, & falls in love with Anne Boleyn.

Henry VIII: The Politics of Tyranny. unabr. ed. Jasper Ridley. Read by Richard Brown. 15 cass. (Running Time: 22 hrs. 30 min.). 1994. 120.00 (978-0-7366-2680-4(8), 3416) Books on Tape.
Colorful picture of life & times of this formidable English ruler.

Henry's Freedom Box: A True Story from the Underground Railroad. Ellen Levine. Illus. by Kadir Nelson. Narrated by Jerry Dixon. Music by David Mansfield. 1 CD. (Running Time: 10 mins.). (J). (gr. 2-5). 2009. bk. 29.95 (978-0-545-13455-2(2)); audio compact disk 12.95 (978-0-545-13445-3(5)) Weston Woods.

Hen's Teeth & Horse's Toes: Further Reflections in Natural History. unabr. collector's ed. Stephen Jay Gould. Read by Larry McKeever. 10 cass. (Running Time: 15 hrs.). 1986. 80.00 (978-0-7366-0661-5(0), 1623) Books on Tape.
What color is a zebra? Did an asteroid bring mass extinction to the earth sixty-five million years ago? Why do animals walk, fly, swim & slither but never roll? Behind each question & each answer lie concepts central to science & in particular to an understanding of evolution, the centerpiece of biology.

Hepatitis: Liver Healing. Steven Gurgevich. (ENG.). 2002. audio compact disk 19.95 (978-1-932170-13-9(8), HWH) Tranceformation.

Hepatitis-C Set: All Natural Holistic Protocol. Judith Knilans. Read by Sherril Wolff. Interview with Sherril Wolff & Terry Beardsley. 2 cass. 1999. bk. 35.00 (978-0-9673817-0-1(3)) Hepatitis.
To date Hepatitis C has no known cure, however, a natural protocol explained b this recording has had very excellent results.

Hephaistos Problem: An Exploration of the Wounded Creative Instincts. Murray Stein. Read by Murray Stein. 3 cass. (Running Time: 3 hrs. 50 min.). 1993. 24.95 set. (978-0-7822-0438-4(4), 519) C G Jung IL.
The Greek god Hephaistos, blacksmith & artist, & patron of artisans & crafts people, provides a compelling insight into the problem of wounded creativity. Himself lame & imperfect, yet ingenious & resourceful, Hephaistos symbolizes the painful outcome of the clash between matriarchal & patriarchal values. This seminar, consisting of three presentations followed by discussion, explores the Hephaistos myth & its affect on contemporary men & women with a focus on therapeutic strategies for the healing & enhancement of creative potential.

Her Deadly Mischief: A Baroque Mystery. unabr. ed. Beverle Graves Myers. (Running Time: 8 hrs. 0 mins.). (ENG.). 2009. 29.95 (978-1-4332-9462-4(1)); 54.95 (978-1-4332-9458-7(3)); audio compact disk 76.00 (978-1-4332-9459-4(1)) Blckstn Audio.

Her Father's House. unabr. ed. Belva Plain. 10 cass. (Running Time: 15 hrs.). 2002. 81.00 (978-0-7366-8673-0(8)); audio compact disk 96.00 (978-0-7366-8674-7(6)) Books on Tape.
Donald Wolfe, a young lawyer, arrives in New York City. Idealistic and ambitious, he marries Lillian out of infatuation and little else. Their marriage is shaky, but they have a child, Tina, and for her, Donald would give up everything. When his flawed marriage begins to fail, he must consider a step that would force him into flight and a life of hiding. Tina develops into an exceptional young woman, who at university falls in love with the lawyer Gilbert. Together, they go to New York, where she learns the truth about her family's past - a truth that must change her regard for the father who has protected and cherished her.

Her Father's House. unabr. ed. Emma Sinclair. Read by Nicolette McKenzie. 18 cass. (Running Time: 22 hrs. 30 min.). (Sound Ser.). (J). 2003. 109.95 (978-1-84283-416-9(9)) Pub: ISIS Lrg Prnt GBR. Dist(s): Ulverscroft US

Her Father's Sins. unabr. ed. Josephine Cox. Read by Maggie Ollerenshaw. 8 cass. (Running Time: 8 hrs.). 1997. 69.95 Set. (978-0-7451-6773-2(X), CAB 1389) AudioGO.

***Her Fearful Symmetry.** unabr. ed. Audrey Niffenegger. Narrated by Bianca Amato. 1 Playaway. (Running Time: 13 hrs. 45 mins.). 2009. 64.75 (978-1-4407-5836-2(0)); 92.75 (978-1-4407-5833-1(6)); audio compact disk 123.75 (978-1-4407-5834-8(4)) Recorded Bks.

Her Fearful Symmetry. unabr. ed. Audrey Niffenegger. Read by Bianca Amato. 12 CDs. (Running Time: 14 hrs. 0 mins. 0 sec.). 2009. audio compact disk 39.99 (978-0-7435-9930-6(6)) Pub: S&S Audio. Dist(s): S and S Inc

***Her Fearful Symmetry.** unabr. collector's ed. Audrey Niffenegger. Narrated by Bianca Amato. 12 CDs. (Running Time: 13 hrs. 45 mins.). 2009. audio compact disk 39.99 (978-1-4407-5835-5(2)) Recorded Bks.

Her First American see Lore Segal

Her First Ball see Garden Party

Her Husband. Diane Middlebrook. Read by Bernadette Dunne. (Running Time: 11 hrs.). 2003. 34.95 (978-1-59912-505-3(6)) Iofy Corp.

Her Husband: Hughes & Plath - A Marriage. unabr. ed. Diane Middlebrook. Read by Bernadette Dunne. 1 MP3. (Running Time: 11 hrs. 30 mins.). 2004. audio compact disk 24.95 (978-0-7861-8723-2(9), 3215); 56.95 (978-0-7861-2651-4(5), 3215) Blckstn Audio.
Presents a portrait of Hughes as a man, as a poet, and as a husband haunted¿and nourished¿his entire life by the aftermath of his first marriage. How marriages fail and how men fail in marriages is one of the book¿s central themes.

Her Husband: Hughes & Plath: Portrait of a Marriage. unabr. ed. Diane Middlebrook. Read by Bernadette Dunne. 9 CDs. (Running Time: 12 hrs.). 2004. audio compact disk 72.00 (978-0-7861-8888-8(X)) Blckstn Audio.

Her Husband Ted Hughes & Sylvia Plath: A Marriage. unabr. ed. Diane Middlebrook. Read by Bernadette Dunne. 8 pieces. 2004. reel tape 39.95 (978-0-7861-2654-5(X)); audio compact disk 44.95 (978-0-7861-8882-6(0)) Blckstn Audio.

Her Little Majesty: The Life of Queen Victoria. unabr. ed. Carolly Erickson. Narrated by Nelson Runger. 9 cass. (Running Time: 12 hrs. 30 mins.). 1997. 78.00 (978-0-7887-1229-6(2), 95142E7) Recorded Bks.
At a time when women were believed to be inferior, Victoria rose from her emotionally deprived childhood to become the beloved leader of a vast empire.

Her Majesty's Yankee. unabr. ed. Tom Nichols. Read by Rusty Nelson. 8 cass. (Running Time: 9 hrs. 24 min.). (John Whyte Ser.: Bk. 1). 2001. 49.95 (978-1-55686-877-1(4)) Books in Motion.
Britain's John Whyte leaves military service in India and emigrates to America. A meeting with President Lincoln propels Whyte into Union military service in the Civil War.

Her Man of Affairs. unabr. ed. Elizabeth Mansfield. Read by Flo Gibson. 5 cass. (Running Time: 7 hrs.). 1999. 20.95 (978-1-55685-610-5(5)) Audio Bk Con.
A regency love story. The beautiful, willful & extravagant Lady Theodora Fairchild was on the brink of financial ruin until David Mackenzie took over her business affairs. He despaired over a passion that society would never approve of.

Her Mother Before Her: Stories of Mothers & Grandmothers. Jocelyn Riley. 1 cass. (Running Time: 22 min.). (YA). 1992. 8.00 (978-1-877933-22-6(8)) Her Own Words.
Documentary.

***Her Mother's Keeper.** unabr. ed. Nora Roberts. Read by Therese Plummer. (Running Time: 5 hrs.). 2010. 24.99 (978-1-4418-5412-4(6), 9781441854124, Brilliance MP3); 39.97 (978-1-4418-5413-1(4), 9781441854131, Brinc Audio MP3 Lib); 39.97 (978-1-4418-5414-8(2), 9781441854148, BADLE); audio compact disk 24.99 (978-1-4418-5410-0(X), 9781441854100, Bril Audio CD Unabri); audio compact disk 79.97 (978-1-4418-5411-7(8), 9781441854117, BriAudCD Unabrid) Brilliance Audio.

Her Name Is Barbra. abr. ed. Randall Riese. Read by Isabel Liss. Ed. by Jocelyn Kaye. 2 cass. (Running Time: 3 hrs.). 1997. 16.95 (978-1-882071-48-7(4)) B-B Audio.
The name alone summons flashes of br[illegible] talent and temperament, explosive outbursts of demonstrative p[illegible] & an untamed ego. But who is the real Barbra Streisand; the Jewish g[illegible] from Flatbush, who grew up to become the biggest multi-media star of [illegible]

Her Own Place. unabr. ed. Dori Sanders. Narrated by Kim Staunton. 5 cass. (Running Time: 6 hrs. 45 mins.). 1998. 44.00 (978-0-7887-0404-8(4), 94837E7) Recorded Bks.
Abandoned by her husband to raise five children & run a farm alone, Mae Lee Barnes transforms her life to meet the vagaries of fortune & the changing times.

Her Own Rules. unabr. ed. Barbara Taylor Bradford. Read by Kate Reading. 6 cass. (Running Time: 9 hrs.). 1996. 48.00 (978-0-7366-3469-4(X), 4113) Books on Tape.
Meredith Stratton, at 44 the owner of six elegant, international inns, should be happy. But she comes down with a strange, debilitating illness that baffles her doctors. Desperate for relief, she sees a psychiatrist & through therapy discovers the truth behind her past.

Her Own Rules. unabr. abr. ed. Barbara Taylor Bradford. Read by Redgrave Lynn. 2 CDs. (Running Time: 3 hrs.). 2005. audio compact disk 14.95 (978-0-06-076363-3(9)) HarperCollins Pubs.

Her Own Words: Pioneer Women's Diaries. Jocelyn Riley. 1 cass. (Running Time: 15 min.). (YA). 1986. 8.00 (978-1-877933-32-5(5)) Her Own Words.
Documentary.

Her Secret Guardian. Linda Needham. Narrated by Anne Flosnik. 8 cass. (Running Time: 11 hrs. 15 mins.). 74.00 (978-0-7887-5980-2(9)); audio compact disk 97.00 (978-1-4025-1549-1(9)) Recorded Bks.

Her Secret Guardian. unabr. ed. Linda Needham. 2001. 71.00 (L1005L8) Recorded Bks.

Her Story & the Amber Gods. unabr. ed. Harriet P. Spofford. Read by Flo Gibson. 2 cass. (Running Time: 3 hrs.). 1992. 14.95 (978-1-55685-238-1(X)) Audio Bk Con.
The strangely powerful "Her Story" & the complex symbolic romance "The Amber Gods" form a lyric & haunting pair.

Her Time Has Come: Mary Magdalene in the 21st Century. Deborah Rose. 2005. 15.00 (978-0-9761311-4-4(5)) Illuminated Sea.

Her Victory, Pt. 1. unabr. collector's ed. Alan Sillitoe. Read by Penelope Dellaporta. 7 cass. (Running Time: 10 hrs. 30 min.). 1985. 56.00 (978-0-7366-0817-6(6), 1767-A) Books on Tape.

Her Victory, Pt. 2. collector's ed. Alan Sillitoe. Read by Penelope Dellaporta. 7 cass. (Running Time: 10 hrs. 30 min.). 1985. 56.00 (978-0-7366-0818-3(4), 1767-B) Books on Tape.
A remarkable woman as ally & lover.

Her Way. abr. ed. Catherine Cookson. 2 cass. (Running Time: 3 hrs.). 1996. 16.95 (978-0-552-14560-2(2), Corgi RHG) Pub: Transworld GBR. Dist(s): Trafalgar

Her Way: The Hopes & Ambitions of Hillary Rodham Clinton. unabr. abr. ed. Jeff Gerth & Don Van Natta, Jr. Read by Erik Singer. (Running Time: 6 hrs.). (ENG.). 2007. 14.98 (978-1-59483-938-2(7)) Pub: Hachet Audio. Dist(s): HachBkGrp

Her Way - the Hopes & Ambitions of Hilary Rodham Clinton. abr. ed. Jeff Gerth & Don Van Natta. Read by Erik Singer. (YA). 2007. 54.99 (978-1-60252-905-2(1)) Find a World.

Hera. Read by Lois Khan. 1 cass. (Running Time: 2 hrs.). (Facing the Gods Ser.: No. 2). 1987. 12.95 (978-0-7822-0116-1(4), 286) C G Jung IL.

Heraldic Message. 1 cass. 8.98 (KGOC24) Ken Mills Found.
Kenneth G. Mills conducts The Star-Scape Singers - traditional & new Christmas carols - total of 11.

Herb - Herbal Remedies: Bilingual: English & German. Thomas Brendler et al. 2001. audio compact disk 84.00 (978-3-88763-092-8(0)) Pub: Medpharm Sci Pubs DEU. Dist(s): Balogh
The Herb-CD is used as the basis of the Amercan "PDR - Physicians Desk Reference for Herbal Medicines". In addition the CD contains the complete

Commission E Monographs - new translated. Herb-CD now features over 900 plants, for which the following can be accessed.

Herb of Grace see Pilgrim's Inn

Herbal Harmonies: Gingko Biloba. 1 CD. (Running Time: 1 hr.). 2001. audio compact disk 16.00 (93-0191) Relaxtn Co.
Unwind and recharge with the unique music collection. Based on proven principles of psychoacoustic and created by the Harmonix Ensemble, a group of therapists, researchers and musicians, this set explores the mood-altering effects similar to an herbal supplement.

Herbal Harmonies: Ginseng. 1 CD. (Running Time: 1 hr.). 2001. audio compact disk 16.00 (93-0195) Relaxtn Co.

Herbal Harmonies: Kava Kava. 1 CD. (Running Time: 1 hr.). 2001. audio compact disk 16.00 (93-0190) Relaxtn Co.

Herbal Harmonies: Musical Nutrition for Your Soul. 3 CDs. (Running Time: 3 hrs.). 2000. audio compact disk 30.00 (978-1-55961-627-0(X), 93-0187) Relaxtn Co.

Herbal Medicine: Expanded Commission e Monographs. Ed. by Mark Blumenthal. (ENG.). 2000. audio compact disk 59.95 (978-0-9670772-3-9(0)) Thieme Med Pubs.

Herbal Verbal. Alfreda C. Doyle. 1 cass. (Running Time: 45 min.). (YA). (gr. 9-12). 1989. 12.95 (37 SOR 21CT) Sell Out Recordings.
Features a poetry reading on herbal cures, uses and folklore. Geraniums, roses, mint, aloe vera, castor oil, and others are presented.

Herbal Verbal Immune System Poetry. unabr. ed. Poems. Poet's Workshop Staff. Read by Poet's Workshop Staff. 1 cass. (Running Time: 30 min.). 9.95 (37SOR HV006) Sell Out Recordings.
A poetry narrative on herbs, etc. that help the immune system.

Herbal Verbal Rhymes. unabr. ed. Alfreda C. Doyle. Read by Alfreda C. Doyle. 1 cass. (Running Time: 30 min.). (Alfreda's Radio Ser.: Vol. 2). (J). (gr. 5-9). 1998. 25.95 (978-1-56820-306-5(3)) Story Time.
Stories that educate, entertain, inform & rhyme.

Herbert Hoover. (Presidency Ser.). 10.00 Esstee Audios.
Describes man who served his nation & who gave his name to a depression.

Herbert Hoover & Other Great Conservatives. 2008. audio compact disk 12.95 (978-1-57970-526-8(X), Audio-For) J Norton Pubs.

Herbert Hoover & Other Great Conservatives (1959-1964) unabr. ed. Read by Herbert Hoover. 1 cass. (Running Time: 28 min). 12.95 (#135) J Norton Pubs.
In part one President Hoover appeared on the Manion Forum, during which he discussed the importance of maintaining U. S. vigilance against communism. The second part recaps statements made by famous conservatives on another Manion broadcast.

Herbert Scott. unabr. ed. Read by Herbert Scott. 1 cass. (Running Time: 29 min.). 1985. 10.00 New Letters.
Herbert Scott reads from his books "Disguises & Groceries".

***Herbert's Wormhole.** unabr. ed. Peter Nelson. Read by Jonathan Davis. (ENG.). 2009. (978-0-06-177628-1(9), KTegenBooks); (978-0-06-190176-8(8), KTegenBooks) HarperCollins Pubs.

Herbie Hancock, Vol. 20. Contrib. by Herbie Hancock. 2003. pap. bk. 14.95 (978-0-634-06140-0(2), 00843013) H Leonard.

Herbie Jones. unabr. ed. Suzy Kline. Read by Jim Fyfe. 1 cass. (Running Time: 60 mins.). (Follow the Reader Ser.). (J). (gr. 3-4). 1988. pap. bk. 17.00 (978-0-8072-0150-3(2), FTR128SP, Listening Lib) Random Audio Pubg.
Herbie's promoted from the lowest reading group...& brokenhearted to leave his best friend behind.

Herbs & Herbal Remedies, Vol. 3, Set. Jonathan Parker. Read by Jonathan Parker. 2 CDs. (Running Time: 2 hrs.). (Natural Health Ser.: Vol. 5). 1999. audio compact disk (978-1-58400-054-9(6)) QuantumQuests Intl.

Herbs & Herbal Remedies, Vol. 6. Jonathan Parker. 2 cass. (Running Time: 2 hrs.). 1998. 17.00 Set. (978-1-58400-004-4(X)) QuantumQuests Intl.

Herbs & Immunity Audio Seminar. unabr. ed. Michael Weiner. 2 cass. (Running Time: 1 hr. 30 min.). 1990. 12.50 set. (978-0-912845-05-0(8)) Quantum Bks.
A complete reference to the 15 most important & commonly available immune-enhancing herbs, & a primer on the immune system. An insert lists all scientific references.

Herbs, Nutrition & Healing: Live Nutritional Seminar. unabr. ed. Humbart Smokey Santillo. Read by Humbart Smokey Santillo. 4 cass. (Running Time: 5 hrs. 30 min.). 1984. cass. & audio compact disk 40.00 set. (978-0-934252-22-5(X)) Hohm Pr.
Contains the basics of herbology & extends into a comprehensive coverage of therapies used in clinics throughout the world. It correlates historical herbology with the most recent in American & Chinese herbal philosophies. Concentrated, easy to understand information which can be of assistance to anyone who has the interest.

Hercule Poirot's Christmas: A Holiday Mystery. Agatha Christie. 2 CDs. (Running Time: 1 hr. 20 mins. 0 sec.). Orig. Title: A Holiday for Murder. (ENG., 2001. audio compact disk 24.95 (978-0-563-53511-9(3)) Pub: AudioGO. Dist(s): Perseus Dist

Hercule Poirot's Greatest Cases. unabr. ed. 28 CDs. audio compact disk 249.95 (978-0-7927-4347-7(4), BBCD172) AudioGO.

Hercule Poirot's Greatest Cases, Set. unabr. ed. Agatha Christie. (Hercule Poirot Ser.). (ENG.). 2007. audio compact disk 150.00 (978-1-60283-316-6(8)) Pub: AudioGO. Dist(s): Perseus Dist

Hercules. 1 cass. (Play Packs Ser.). (J). bk. 14.99 (978-0-7634-0261-7(3)); 13.99 Norelco. (978-0-7634-0232-7(X)); audio compact disk 22.99 CD. (978-0-7634-0234-1(6)); audio compact disk 22.99 (978-0-7634-0235-8(4)) W Disney Records.

Hercules. 1 cass. (Sing-Along Ser.). (J). 1997. bk. 11.99 (978-0-7634-0201-3(X)) W Disney Records.

Hercules. 2004. 8.95 (978-1-56008-920-9(2)); 8.95 (978-0-7882-0251-3(0)); cass. & flmstrp 30.00 (978-1-56008-681-9(5)) Weston Woods.

Hercules. Adapted by Ann Braybrooks. Illus. by Disney Staff. Narrated by Danny DeVito. 1 cass. (Read-Along Ser.). (J). 1997. bk. 7.99 (978-0-7634-0202-0(8)) W Disney Records.

Hercules. Alan Menken. Contrib. by David Zippel & Michael Bolton. 1 cass. (J). 1997. 13.99 (978-0-7634-0233-4(8)) W Disney Records.

Hercules. unabr. ed. Read by Cynthia Bishop. Retold by Geraldine McCaughrean. 4 CDs. (Running Time: 4 hrs. 15 mins.). (YA). (gr. 5-8). 2009. audio compact disk 38.00 (978-1-934180-25-9(4)) Full Cast Audio.

Hercules, Vol. 3. abr. ed. Bernard Evslin. Read by Kevin Sorbo & Michael Hurst. 1 cass. (Running Time: 60 min.). (Enchanted Tales Ser.). (J). 1997. 16.95 (978-1-888453-06-5(0), BMP Audio) BMP Music.
Stories included: The Twins; The Serpents; Chiron; The Vision; The Taskmaster; The Nemean Lion; & The Hydra.

Hercules; Make Way for Ducklings, Mike Mulligan & His Steam Shovel; Millions of Cats. 2004. (978-0-89719-800-4(X)); cass. & flmstrp (978-0-89719-709-0(7)) Weston Woods.

Here & Here see Shamanic Drumming

Here & Now. Perf. by Lori Wilke. 1 cass. (Running Time: 4 min.). 1992. 9.98 Sound track. (978-1-891916-28-1(9)) Spirit To Spirit.

Here & Now. unabr. ed. Kimberla Lawson Roby. Narrated by Donna Bailey. 8 cass. (Running Time: 10 hrs. 45 mins.). 2001. 68.00 (978-0-7887-5118-9(2), F0021E7) Recorded Bks.
A powerful story of two women learning to accept their losses.

Here & Now: Living in the Spirit. Henri J. M. Nouwen. Read by Murray Bodo. 3 CDs. (Running Time: 3 hrs. 30 mins.). 2005. audio compact disk 24.95 (978-0-86716-733-7(5)) St Anthony Mess Pr.
Henri Nouwen notes, ?It is hard to live in the present. The past and the future keep harassing us.? He reminds us that Jesus came to wipe away the burden of the past as well as any worries of the future. With Nouwen as our exceptional guide, we realize that the Spirit of God is ever with us, gracing us in the many places of our everyday lives. We notice small miracles that reflect the divine mystery permeating our world.This audiobook describes the hardships and harmony of prayer, forgiveness and gratitude, competition and compassion, and the ongoing process of conversion through our loving?or perhaps, not so loving?encounters with friends and family. Nouwen says his insights are an expression of his own spiritual journey and a way of sharing about God?s love in his life.

Here & Now: Living in the Spirit. unabr. ed. Henri J. M. Nouwen. Read by Murray Bodo. 2 cass. (Running Time: 3 hrs.). 2000. 14.95 (978-0-86716-435-0(2), A4352) St Anthony Mess Pr.
The spiritual life is not a life then & there, but a life here & now. It is a life in which the spirit of God is revealed in the ordinary encounters of everyday.

Here at the New Yorker. unabr. ed. Brendan Gill. Read by Wolfram Kandinsky. 10 cass. (Running Time: 15 hrs.). 1984. 80.00 (978-0-7366-0116-0(3), 1123) Books on Tape.
For more than 50 years "The New Yorker" has boldly recorded the contemporary scene in succinct prose veined with urbane wit. Celebrates 2 anniversaries: The fiftieth of the magazine & the fourtieth of the author's employment there & offers a view of the literary nottables of the last half-century.

Here Burns My Candle. unabr. ed. Liz Curtis Higgs. Read by Liz Curtis Higgs. (ENG.). 2010. audio compact disk 35.00 (978-0-307-71484-8(5), Random AudioBks) Pub: Random Audio Pubg. Dist(s): Random

Here Come the Blobbies. Jorge Tello. Illus. by Jorge Tello. 1 CD. (J). 2004. pap. bk. 15.89 (978-1-932179-32-3(1)) Pers Pubng.

Here Comes Jesus. unabr. ed. Peter Enns. Read by Peter Enns. Ed. by Lock Wolverton. 4 cass. (Running Time: 22 min.). (Stories to Remember Ser.). (J). (gr. 1-4). 1987. 5.98 (978-0-943593-39-5(5)) Kids Intl Inc.
Contains six scripturally accurate Bible stories about the last days of Jesus Christ.

Here Comes the Bride! 1 CD. (Running Time: 90 mins.). 1999. audio compact disk 7.95 (978-0-9650258-3-6(7), Persnickety Pr) Pub: DBP & Assocs. Dist(s): Penton Overseas
The perfect shower gift for the jittery bride-to-be! Humorous songs about "getting hitched" that will have her rolling down the aisle with laughter. Also includes intimate mood music for the wedding night.

Here Comes the Cat! 2004. bk. 24.95 (978-1-56008-013-8(2)); pap. bk. 14.95 (978-0-7882-0658-0(3)); pap. bk. 32.75 (978-1-55592-240-5(6)); 8.95 (978-0-7882-0077-9(1)) Weston Woods.

Here Comes the Cat. 2004. cass. & flmstrp 30.00 (978-0-89719-601-7(5)) Weston Woods.

Here Comes the Cat! Vladimir Vagin. Illus. by Frank Asch. 1 cass., 5 bks. (Running Time: 7 min.). (J). pap. bk. 32.75 Weston Woods.
A cat descends upon a peaceful mouse settlement. Historic collaboration between American author-illustrator & a Soviet artist.

Here Comes the Cat! Vladimir Vagin. Illus. by Frank Asch. 1 cass. (Running Time: 7 min.). (J). (ps-4). 1989. pap. bk. 12.95 (PRA341) Weston Woods.

Here Comes the Cat! Vladimir Vagin & Frank Asch. Read by Vladimir Vagin & Frank Asch. 1 cass. (Running Time: 7 min.). (J). (ps-4). 1989. 8.95 (978-0-89719-995-7(2), RAC341) Weston Woods.

Here Comes the New Year! Lois Brownsey et al. (ENG.). 1999. audio compact disk 24.95 (978-0-7390-0951-2(6)) Alfred Pub.

***Here Comes the Strikeout.** unabr. ed. Leonard Kessler.Tr. of Aqui viene el que se Poncha!. (ENG.). 2007. (978-0-06-143478-5(7)) HarperCollins Pubs.

Here Comes the Strikeout! Book & Tape. abr. ed. Leonard Kessler. Illus. by Leonard Kessler. 1 cass. (I Can Read Bks.). (J). (gr. k-3). 1990. 8.99 (978-1-55994-231-7(2), TBC 2312) HarperCollins Pubs.

Here Comes Tod! unabr. ed. Philippa Pearce. Read by Bernard Cribbins. 1 cass. (Running Time: 1 hrs., 30 min.). (J). (gr. 1-8). 1999. 9.95 (CTC 781, Chivers Child Audio) AudioGO.

Here I Am. Lori Wilke. 1 cass. 1993. 9.95 (978-1-56043-382-8(5)); audio compact disk 14.99 CD. (978-1-56043-383-5(3)) Destiny Image Pubs.

Here I Am. Perf. by Lori Wilke. 1 cass., 1 CD. (Running Time: 47 min.). 1988. 9.98 Set. (978-1-891916-05-2(X)); 9.98 (978-1-891916-12-0(2)); audio compact disk 14.98 CD. (978-1-891916-06-9(8)) Spirit To Spirit.
Ministry to the Lord.

Here I Am: Travis Meadows Recording. (Book of Life Ser.). 2001. audio compact disk (978-1-890525-59-0(6)) Bk of Hope.

Here I Am to Worship. Contrib. by Michael W. Smith. (Praise Hymn Soundtracks Ser.). 2002. audio compact disk 8.98 (978-5-552-46219-3(X)) Pt of Grace Ent.

Here I Stand: Elders' Wisdom, Children's Songs. 1 CD. (Running Time: 1 hr. 10 min.). (J). (gr. 3 up). 1996. audio compact disk 13.00 Smithsonian Folkways.
Songs create a blueprint for oral history & multi-generational projects.

Here If You Need Me: A True Story. abr. unabr. ed. Kate Braestrup. (Running Time: 5 hrs. 30 mins.). (ENG.). 2007. 14.98 (978-1-59483-930-6(1)) Pub: Hachet Audio. Dist(s): HachBkGrp

Here in Me. Arrow Records. 2008. audio compact disk 13.99 (978-1-59944-731-5(2)) Creflo Dollar.

Here Is Love. Contrib. by Ed Hogan. 2007. audio compact disk 24.99 (978-5-557-54320-0(1)) Lillenas.

Here Is Thumbkin! More Action Songs for Every Month. 1 CD. (Running Time: 1 hr.). (J). 2001. pap. bk. 14.95 (KIM 9157CD); pap. bk. 10.95 (KIM 9157C) Kimbo Educ.
Here are rhymes & rhythms for learning & action. Each rhyme is sung once followed by an instrumental with finger plays or simple activities & then sung again to reinforce language. "Three Little Kittens", "Mary Had a Little Lamb", "Old King Cole", "Dance Thumbkin Dance", "Three Wishes", "30 Days Has September," "ABC Song" & more! Includes guide with lyrics & activities.

***Here Is Where: Discovering America's Great Forgotten History.** unabr. ed. Andrew Carroll. Read by Andrew Carroll. (Running Time: 8 hrs.). (ENG.). 2011. audio compact disk 35.00 (978-0-307-75070-9(1), Random AudioBks) Pub: Random Audio Pubg. Dist(s): Random

Here Lies: An Autobiography. unabr. ed. Eric Ambler. Read by Richard Brown. 8 cass. (Running Time: 12 hrs.). 1989. 64.00 (978-0-7366-1494-8(X), 2370) Books on Tape.
Ambler peels back the layers of experience that have affected his life with the familiar skill he uses to unfold the plot of one of his novels.

Here Lies a Lady see Twentieth-Century Poetry in English, No. 5, Recordings of Poets Reading Their Own Poetry

Here Lies the Librarian. unabr. ed. Richard Peck. Read by Lara Everly. 3 CDs. (Running Time: 3 hrs. 41 mins.). (J). (gr. 4-7). 2006. audio compact disk 30.00 (978-0-307-28596-6(0), Listening Lib); 30.00 (978-0-307-28595-9(2), Listening Lib) Pub: Random Audio Pubg. Dist(s): Random
Peewee idolizes Jake, a big brother whose dream of auto mechanic glory are fueled by the hard road coming to link their Indiana town and futures with the twentieth century. And motoring down the road comes Irene Ridpath, a young librarian with plans to astonish them all and turn Peewee's life upside down. This novel, with its quirky characters, folksy setting, classic cars, and hilariously larger-than-life moments, is vintage Richard Peck - an offbeat, deliciously wicked comedy that is also unexpectedly moving.

Here on Earth. abr. ed. Alice Hoffman. Read by Susan Ericksen & Sandra Burr. (Running Time: 6 hrs.). 2009. audio compact disk 14.99 (978-1-4418-0740-3(3), 9781441807403, BCD Value Price) Brilliance Audio.

Here on Earth, unabr. ed. Alice Hoffman. Read by Susan Ericksen. 8 cass. (Running Time: 10 hrs.). 1997. 73.25 (978-1-56100-830-8(3), 1561008303, Unabridge Lib Edns) Brilliance Audio.
March Murray, along with her fifteen-year-old daughter, Gwen, returns to the small Massachusetts town where she grew up to attend the funeral of Judith Dale, the beloved housekeeper who raised her. After nearly twenty years of living in California, March is thrust into the world of her past. She finds that Mrs. Dale knew more of life than March could have ever suspected; that her brother Alan, whose tragic history has left him grief-stricken, has turned to alcohol as his only solace; and that Hollis, the boy she once loved, is the man she can't seem to stay away from. "Here on Earth" is the dramatic and lyrical account of the joys of love, as well as the destruction that love can release. Erotic, disturbing, and compelling, this is without a doubt Alice Hoffman's most unforgettable novel.

Here on Earth. unabr. ed. Alice Hoffman. Read by Susan Ericksen. (Running Time: 9 hrs.). 2009. 19.99 (978-1-4418-0736-6(5), 9781441807366, Brilliance MP3); 39.97 (978-1-4418-0737-3(3), 9781441807373, Brlnc Audio MP3 Lib); 24.99 (978-1-4418-0738-0(1), 9781441807380, BAD); 39.97 (978-1-4418-0739-7(X), 9781441807397, BADLE) Brilliance Audio.

***Here on Earth.** unabr. ed. Alice Hoffman. Read by Susan Ericksen. (Running Time: 9 hrs.). 2010. audio compact disk 19.99 (978-1-4558-0095-7(3), 9781455800957, Bril Audio CD Unabri); audio compact disk 69.97 (978-1-4558-0096-4(1), 9781455800964, BriAudCD Unabrid) Brilliance Audio.

Here, There Be Dragons. unabr. ed. James A. Owen. Read by James Langton. (Running Time: 8 hrs. 30 mins. 0 sec.). (ENG.). (YA). 2008. audio compact disk 34.95 (978-0-7435-6910-1(5)) Pub: S&S Audio. Dist(s): S and S Inc

Here Today. Ann M. Martin. Read by Judy Kaye. 4 cass. (J). 2004. 32.00 (978-1-4000-9045-7(8), Listening Lib); audio compact disk (978-1-4000-9487-5(9), Listening Lib) Random Audio Pubg.

Here Today... Gone to Tomorrow: Asimov's All Time Favorite Travel Stories. unabr. ed. C. M. Kornbluth & Bob Shaw. Ed. by Isaac Asimov & Martin Greenberg. 4 pieces. (Running Time: 6 hrs.). (Science Fiction Library). 1997. 21.95 (978-1-55656-258-7(6)) Pub: Dercum Audio. Dist(s): APG

Here We All Are. Ram Dass. 3 CDs. (ENG., 2005. audio compact disk 19.95 (978-1-4019-1044-0(0)) Hay House.
nbsp;nbsp;nbsp;nbsp;Telling his story in “three chapters,” Ram Dass explains how he moved from the structured academic world to wide-open experiences with psychedelics (and Timothy Leary). This thirst for knowledge led him to India, where he encountered a man who taught him to “just be here now.” nbsp;nbsp;nbsp;nbsp;Ram Dass shares with us how we can all attain a state of well-being. The result is that we’ll become more centered, and we’ll learn to see the God in each other, which ultimately leads to an overwhelming sense of oneness with, and love for, our fellow humans. nbsp;nbsp;nbsp;nbsp;As Ram Dass says, “We’re all the same . . . and here we all are.” Includes the bonus CD, Be Here Now, which features music from.

Here We All Are. unabr. ed. Tomie dePaola. 1 cass. (Running Time: 40 mins.). (Fairmount Avenue Ser.: Vol. 2). (J). (gr. 2-5). 2004. pap. bk. 17.00 (978-0-8072-0655-3(5), LDTR 246 SP, Listening Lib) Random Audio Pubg.
In this delightful sequel, the author illustrates and shares engaging childhood memories about siblings, school, and life as a 5-year-old.

Here We Go. 2004. DVD & audio compact disk 14.99 (978-1-894300-88-9(2)) Crown Video Dupl CAN.

Here We Go Again: Genisis 20:1-18. Ed Young. 1994. 4.95 (978-0-7417-2036-8(1), 1036) Win Walk.

Here We Go Again: My Life in Television. Betty White. 2004. 10.95 (978-0-7435-4823-6(X)) Pub: S&S Audio. Dist(s): S and S Inc

***Here We Go Again: My Life in Television.** abr. ed. Betty White. Read by Betty White. (Running Time: 30 hrs. 0 mins. 0 sec.). (ENG.). 2010. audio compact disk 14.99 (978-1-4423-3969-9(1)) Pub: S&S Audio. Dist(s): S and S Inc

Here We Go Loopty Loo. 1 cass. (Running Time: 37 min.). (J). 1998. 10.95 (KUB8000C); audio compact disk 14.95 (KUB8000CD) Kimbo Educ.
12 old-time favorites updated with a new beat. Rock & roll & rhythm & blues! Circle games, finger plays, echo songs & dances include Bear Hunt, Chuckle Bug, Head, Shoulders, Knees & more.

Here with Us. Contrib. by Joy Williams. (Mastertrax Ser.). 2005. audio compact disk 9.98 (978-5-558-80579-6(X)) Essential Recs.

Hereaftersthis see Three Little Pigs & Other Fairy Tales

Hereditary Hemorrhagic Telangiectasia - A Bibliography & Dictionary for Physicians, Patients, & Genome Researchers. Compiled by Icon Group International, Inc. Staff. 2007. ring bd. 28.95 (978-0-497-11230-1(2)) Icon Grp.

Hereditary Neuropathy with Liability to Pressure Palsies - A Bibliography & Dictionary for Physicians, Patients, & Genome Researchers. Compiled by Icon Group International, Inc. Staff. 2007. ring bd. 28.95 (978-0-497-11231-8(0)) Icon Grp.

Hereditary Nonpolyposis Colorectal Cancer - A Bibliography & Dictionary for Physicians, Patients, & Genome Researchers. Compiled by Icon Group International, Inc. Staff. 2007. ring bd. 28.95 (978-0-497-11232-5(9)) Icon Grp.

Heredity. Compiled by Benchmark Education Staff. 2005. audio compact disk 10.00 (978-1-4108-5479-7(5)) Benchmark Educ.

Here's How to Do Therapy: Hands-on Core Skills in Speech- Language Pathology. Debra M. Dwight. 2005. pap. bk. 79.95 (978-1-59756-002-3(2)) Plural Pub Inc.

Here's the Bright Side: Of Failure, Fear, Cancer, Divorce, & Other Bum Raps. unabr. ed. Betty Rollin. Read by Pam Ward. (Running Time: 9000 sec.). 2007. 22.95 (978-0-7861-6873-6(0)); 14.95 (978-0-7861-4921-6(3)); audio compact disk 19.95 (978-0-7861-7051-7(4)); audio compact disk 27.00 (978-0-7861-6872-9(2)); audio compact disk 14.95 (978-0-7861-5925-3(1)) Blckstn Audio.

Here's the Deal: Don't Touch Me. unabr. ed. Howie Mandel & Josh Young. Read by Howie Mandel. (ENG.). 2009. audio compact disk 30.00 (978-0-307-70448-1(3), Random AudioBks) Pub: Random Audio Pubg. Dist(s): Random

***Here's the Story.** abr. ed. Maureen Mccormick. Read by Maureen Mccormick. (ENG.). 2008. (978-0-06-171342-2(2)); (978-0-06-171343-9(0)) HarperCollins Pubs.

Here's the Story: Surviving Marcia Brady & Finding My True Voice. abr. ed. Maureen McCormick. Read by Maureen McCormick. 5 CDs. (Running Time: 6 hrs.). 2008. audio compact disk 29.95 (978-0-06-168657-3(3), Harper Audio) HarperCollins Pubs.

Heresy. abr. ed. S. J. Parris. Read by John Lee. (ENG.). 2010. audio compact disk 30.00 (978-0-307-71429-9(2), Random AudioBks) Pub: Random Audio Pubg. Dist(s): Random

Heretic. Bernard Cornwell. Read by Tim Pigott-Smith. (Grail Quest Ser.: No. 3). 1975. 9.99 (978-0-06-074336-9(0)) HarperCollins Pubs.

***Heretic.** abr. ed. Bernard Cornwell. Read by Tim Pigott-Smith. (ENG.). 2005. (978-0-06-078450-8(4), Harper Audio); (978-0-06-083886-7(8), Harper Audio) HarperCollins Pubs.

Heretic. unabr. abr. ed. Bernard Cornwell. Read by Tim Pigott-Smith. 6 cass. (Running Time: 8 hrs. 30 min.). (Grail Quest Ser.: No. 3). 2003. 25.95 (978-0-06-056613-5(2)) HarperCollins Pubs.

Heretic & the Historian: The Dead Sea Scrolls: Who Wrote Them? - Josephus Flavius: Hero or Traitor? unabr. ed. Shmuel Irons. Read by Shmuel Irons. 2 cass. (Running Time: 3 hrs.). 19.95 Set. (978-1-889648-15-6(9)) Jwish Her Fdtn.

A clear view of ancient history based on the Bible & Talmud & other ancient primary sources. A new way of looking at the past.

Heretic As Religious Genius: A Psychoanalytic Understanding of Submission & Dissent. Read by David Dalrymple. 1 cass. (Running Time: 90 min.). 1991. 10.95 (978-0-7822-0052-2(4), 446) C G Jung IL.

***Heretics.** G. K. Chesterton. (ENG.). 2009. audio compact disk 19.95 (978-1-936231-03-4(4)) Cath Audio.

Heretics. collector's ed. G. K. Chesterton. Read by Bill Kelsey. 8 cass. (Running Time: 8 hrs.). 1996. 48.00 (978-0-7366-3391-8(X), 4040) Books on Tape.

A collection of 20 free-ranging essays. Chesterton attacks Nietzsche, George Bernard Shaw, H. G. Wells, hypocrisy, faddism, & muddy thinking. He takes to task the English gutter press of the early 20th century & chides Rudyard Kipling for not having spent enough of his life in England. With equal vigor, he defends the institutions he holds dear: the family, his country & his church.

Heretic's Apprentice. unabr. ed. Ellis Peters, pseud. Read by Stephen Thorne. 8 cass. (Running Time: 12 hrs.). (Chronicles of Brother Cadfael Ser.: Vol. 16). 2000. 59.95 (978-0-7451-4397-2(0), CAB 1081) Pub: Chivers Audio Bks GBR. Dist(s): AudioGO

In the summer of 1143, William of Lythwood returns to Shrewsbury from pilgrimage, in a coffin. His young attendant, Elave, searches for a burial place for his heretic master. But Elave has heretic views of his own, and having drunkenly expressed them, he faces capital charges! The woman that Elave adores, becomes a reluctant prosecution witness, and before long, a violent death takes place. brother Cadfael's task is therefore two-fold: to rebut the heresy charges and solve the murder.

Heretic's Apprentice. unabr. ed. Ellis Peters, pseud. Narrated by Patrick Tull. 6 cass. (Running Time: 9 hrs.). (Chronicles of Brother Cadfael Ser.: Vol. 16). 1997. 51.00 (978-0-7887-1074-2(5), 95087E7) Recorded Bks.

It is the summer of 1143, & Brother Cadfael wants nothing more than to tend his roses. But a coffin, a heresy & a murder will drag him away from his beloved garden.

Heretic's Daughter. unabr. ed. Kathleen Kent. Read by Mare Winningham. (Running Time: 10 hrs.). (ENG.). 2008. 19.98 (978-1-60024-451-3(3)) Pub: Hachet Audio. Dist(s): HachBkGrp

Heretic's Daughter. unabr. ed. Kathleen Kent. Read by Mare Winningham. (Running Time: 10 hrs. 30 mins.). (ENG.). 2009. audio compact disk 19.98 (978-1-60024-823-8(3)) Pub: Hachet Audio. Dist(s): HachBkGrp

Heretics of Dune. collector's ed. Frank Herbert. Read by John Edwardson. 14 cass. (Running Time: 21 hrs.). (Dune Chronicles). 2000. 112.00 (978-0-7366-5453-1(4)) Books on Tape.

On Arrakis, now called Rakis, known to legend as Dune, ten times ten centuries have passed. The planet is becoming desert again. The Lost Ones are returning home from the far reaches of space. The great sandworms are dying & the Bene Gesserit & the Bene Tleilax struggle to direct the future of Dune. The children of Dune's children awaken as from a dream, wielding the new power of a heresy called love.

Heretics of Dune. unabr. ed. Frank Herbert & Frank Herbert. 17 CDs. (Running Time: 18 hrs. 30 mins. 0 sec.). (ENG.). 2008. audio compact disk 59.95 (978-1-4272-0316-8(4)) Pub: Macmill Audio. Dist(s): Macmillan

Herge. Interview with Jacques Chancel. 1 cass. (Radioscopie Ser.). 1992. 16.95 (1537-RF) Olivia & Hill.

Creator of famous comic strip "Tintin."

Heriberto. 2003. audio compact disk 3.60 (978-0-8297-4143-8(7)) Zondervan.

Heriberto. unabr. ed. 2003. 2.00 (978-0-8297-4145-2(3)) Zondervan.

Heritage see Poetry of Countee Cullen

Heritage. Keith Halligan. (Running Time: 1 hr.). 2002. audio compact disk 15.99 (978-1-904972-50-1(0)) Global Jrny GBR GBR.

Heritage, No. 1. 1 cass. 10.00 (978-1-893165-42-7(6)) Rational Isl.

Shared experiences of Native Americans, about being Native American & about Native Americans using re-evaluation counseling.

Heritage, No. 2. 4 cass. 10.00 ea. (978-1-893165-43-4(4)) Rational Isl.

Shared experiences of Native Americans about being Native American & about Native Americans using re-evaluation counseling.

Heritage, Pt. 1. unabr. collector's ed. Peter Driscoll. Read by Rupert Keenlyside. 7 cass. (Running Time: 10 hrs. 30 min.). 1985. 56.00 (978-0-7366-0740-7(4), 1697A) Books on Tape.

The Lombard family - tightly-knit, wealthy, conservative - finds its loyalties split when massacre, terrorism & torture cripple their beloved Algeria.

Heritage, Pt. 2. unabr. collector's ed. Peter Driscoll. Read by Rupert Keenlyside. 8 cass. (Running Time: 12 hrs.). 1985. 64.00 (978-0-7366-0741-4(2), 1697B) Books on Tape.

Heritage Vol. 2: Les Maitres du Pain. l.t. ed. Bernard Lenteric. (French Ser.). 1995. bk. 30.99 (978-2-84011-112-2(8)) Pub: UlverLrgPrint GBR. Dist(s): Ulverscroft US

Heritage & How to Advance Liberty. unabr. ed. Ralph Bradford & Leonard E. Read. 1 cass. (Running Time: 1 hr. 24 min.). 12.95 (107) J Norton Pubs.

Heritage Books Archives: Births & Deaths Abstracted from the Camp Point Journal, Camp Point, Adams County, Illinois, 1873-1903. Joseph J. Beals & Sandy. 2002. audio compact disk 33.00 (978-0-7884-2205-8(7)) Heritage Bk.

Heritage Not Hate: Discovering Gullah & Finding Myself. Marlena Smalls. 1 cass. (Running Time: 90 min.). Date not set. 14.95 (978-1-889974-16-3(1)) Pub: Ziplow Prodns. Dist(s): Bookworld

Heritage Not Hate: Discovering Gullah & Finding Myself. Marlena Smalls. Read by Marlena Smalls. 1 cass. (Running Time: 90 mins.). 2000. 14.95 Ziplow Prodns.

Heritage of Hymns. Robert C. Bowden. 1 cass. 7.98 (100080); audio compact disk 14.95 (2800659) Covenant Comms.

Spiritual favorites.

Heritage of Our Country, Vol. 6. 2004. 45.00 (978-0-01-208134-1(5)) Your Story.

Heritage of Our Country Activity Book. 2006. 24.50 (978-1-60079-047-8(X)) YourStory.

Heritage of Our Country Album 6: 12 Cassette Dramatized Audio Stories. 2006. 45.00 (978-1-60079-005-8(4)) YourStory.

Heritage of Our Country Album 6: 12 CD Dramatized Audio Stories. 2006. 45.00 (978-1-60079-028-7(3)) YourStory.

Heritage of the Desert. unabr. ed. Zane Grey. Read by Robert Morris. 6 cass. (Running Time: 8 hrs. 30 mins.). 1995. 44.95 (978-0-7861-0886-2(X), 1520) Blckstn Audio.

Jack Hare, a tough young cowboy, owed his life to August Naab, the stern but kind old settler who rescued him from sure death & offered him refuge. But Hare soon learned that Naab's Utah ranch was little more than an island paradise surrounded by a sea of danger.

Heritage of the Desert. unabr. ed. Zane Grey. Read by Gene Engene. 6 cass. (Running Time: 8 hrs. 30 min.). 39.95 (978-1-55686-120-8(6), 120) Books in Motion.

A story beautifully told in the magnificent Zane Grey fashion. Moving & exciting with new perils in every chapter. The action is intermingled with tender love between Jack Hare & the beautiful half-breed maiden Mescal.

Heritage of the Desert, Set. unabr. ed. Zane Grey. Read by Robert Morris. 6 cass. 1999. 44.95 (FS9-34231) Highsmith.

Heritage of World Civilizations: Teaching & Learning Classroom Edition. 2nd ed. Craig. trans. & audio compact disk 99.97 (978-0-13-191770-5(6)) PH School.

Heritage of World Civilizations, Teaching & Learning Classroom Edition: Instructor's Manual with Tests. 2nd ed. Craig. bk. & tchr. ed. 18.97 (978-0-13-191378-3(6)) PH School.

Heritage of World Civilizations, Teaching & Learning Classroom Edition: School Binding. 2nd ed. Craig. bk. & stu. ed. 62.47 (978-0-13-192867-1(8)) PH School.

Heritage of World Civilizations, Teaching & Learning Classroom Edition: TestGen. 2nd ed. Craig. bk. 49.97 (978-0-13-191379-0(4)) PH School.

Heritage of World Civilizations, Teaching & Learning Classroom Edition 2: History Notes. 2nd ed. Craig. bk. 9.97 (978-0-13-191574-9(6)) PH School.

Heritage Studies Listening Cassette A. 7.50 (978-1-57924-762-1(8)) BJUPr.

Heritage Studies Listening Cassette B (grades 4-6) 7.50 (978-1-59166-101-6(3)) BJUPr.

Heritage, Vintage & Retro Collection. Prod. by Primedia Staff. 2004. audio compact disk 36.95 (978-1-929180-58-5(6)) Creating Keepsakes.

Heritieres-Aurelie. l.t. ed. Jacques Duquesne. (French Ser.). 2001. bk. 30.99 (978-2-84011-412-3(7)) Pub: UlverLrgPrint GBR. Dist(s): Ulverscroft US

Herland. Charlotte Perkins Gilman. Read by Anais 9000. 2008. 27.95 (978-1-60112-019-9(2)) Babblebooks.

Herman Melville. collector's ed. Elizabeth Hardwick. Read by Karen White. 3 cass. (Running Time: 4 hrs. 30 min.). 2000. 28.00 (978-0-7366-5441-8(0)) Books on Tape.

Now, a century after his death, a popular surge of interest in Melville calls for Hardwick's rich analysis of the whole of Melville's works, uneven as it is & the challenging shape of his life, a story of the creative history of an extraordinary American genius.

Herman Melville. unabr. ed. Elizabeth Hardwick. Read by Karen White. 3 cass. (Running Time: 4 hrs.). 2000. 17.95 (978-0-7366-5689-4(8)) Books on Tape.

Herman Melville: Collected Stories. Herman Melville. Narrated by Walter Covell. (Running Time: 5 hrs. 30 mins.). (C). 1979. 33.95 (978-1-59912-858-0(6)) Iofy Corp.

Herman Melville: Moby-Dick. unabr. ed. Herman Melville. Adapted by Henry Reed. 2 cass. 15.95 (SCN 094) J Norton Pubs.

Captures the atmosphere of Melville's novel, concentrating on the obsessive hunt for the White whale & the final cataclysmic encounter between Captain Ahab & Moby Dick.

Herman Melville: The World a Ship. unabr. ed. Joseph Schiffman. 1 cass. (Running Time: 24 min.). (Six American Authors Ser.). 1969. 12.95 (23035) J Norton Pubs.

The life, thought, art & relevance of Melville.

Herman Wouk. Interview with Herman Wouk. 1 cass. (Running Time: 35 min.). 1972. 13.95 (L082) TFR.

Wouk talks about "The Winds of War," his account of World War II, which mixes grandscale reality & individual-sized fiction. He also talks about his strenuous research on the real-life characters who walk through the pages of the book.

Hermanita; El Diente Molesto, Set. (Coleccion Chiquilines - Imagen y Sonido). (SPA.). (J). bk. 15.95 (978-950-11-0627-5(6), SGM276) Pub: Sigmar ARG. Dist(s): Continental Bk

Hermann Goerring Talks. 10.00 (HE826) Esstee Audios.

In interviews with a psychologist during the trials at Nuremberg, Goerring gives personal views of the entire Holocaust.

Hermann Sons Road Travel Guide: Driving Trip in the Texas Hill Country y way of Hermann Sons Road. 2007. pap. bk. 20.00 (978-0-9676931-6-3(0)) Skyline Ranch.

Hermes. Read by Murray Stein. 1 cass. (Running Time: 2 hrs.). (Facing the Gods Ser.: No. 3). 1987. 12.95 (978-0-7822-0278-6(0), 287) C G Jung IL.

Hermes & the Creation of Space. Murray Stein. 1 cass. (Running Time: 1 hr. 22 min.). 1995. 10.95 (978-0-7822-0487-2(2), 563) C G Jung IL.

This lecture explores the archetypal pattern of boundary & container as illustrated by the myth of Hermes.

Hermes in the New World. Peter L. Wilson. 2 cass. 1992. 18.00 set. (OC298-66) Sound Horizons AV.

Hermetic Astrology & Healing. Elayne J. Manago. 1 cass. 8.95 (558) Am Fed Astrologers.

Sign function reveals blocks & healing.

Hermetic Wisdom. Eternal Quest Staff. 1 cass. (Running Time: 1 hr.). 1989. 8.95 (978-0-8356-1912-7(5)) Theos Pub Hse.

Sealed or hermetic wisdom, rhythm in life, trusting the hologram, subliminal consciousness.

Hermit & the Wild Woman, the Other Two & More, unabr. ed. Edith Wharton. Read by Flo Gibson. 4 cass. (Running Time: 5 hrs.). 1995. 19.95 (978-1-55685-385-2(8)) Audio Bk Con.

"The Hermit & the Wild Woman," a strange mystical tale set in Medieval Italy, "The Last Asset," on divorce & manipulation; "The Other Two," a brilliant study of a mannered quadrangle & considered by many to be Wharton's best, "The Pretext," on love unrequited & "The Best Man,".

Hermit of Cape Rosier see Twentieth-Century Poetry in English, No. 28, Recordings of Poets Reading Their Own Poetry

Hermit of Eyton Forest. Ellis Peters, pseud. Narrated by Roe Kendall. (Running Time: 8 hrs. 30 mins.). 2000. 27.95 (978-1-59912-670-8(2)) Iofy Corp.

Hermit of Eyton Forest. unabr. ed. Ellis Peters. Read by Roe Kendall. 6 cass. (Running Time: 8 hrs. 30 mins.). (Chronicles of Brother Cadfael Ser.: Vol. 14). 2001. 44.95 (978-0-7861-1964-6(0), 2735); audio compact disk 56.00 (978-0-7861-9760-6(9), 2735) Blckstn Audio.

The year is 1142 & all England is in the iron grip of civil war. Within the sheltered cloisters of the Benedictine Abbey of St. Peter & St. Paul, a chain of events begin with the sad demise of Richard Ludel, Lord of Eaton, whose 10-year-old son & heir, also named Richard, is a pupil at the Abbey. The boy refuses to surrender his new powers to his formidable grandmother Dionysis. The hermit Cuthred's arrival heralds a series of mishaps for the monks. When Richard disappears & a corpse is found in Eyton Forest, Brother Cadfael is forced to leave the tranquility of his herb garden & devote his knowledge of human nature to tracking down a ruthless murderer.

Hermit of Eyton Forest. unabr. ed. Ellis Peters, pseud. Narrated by Patrick Tull. 6 cass. (Running Time: 8 hrs. 15 mins.). (Chronicles of Brother Cadfael Ser.: Vol. 14). 51.00 (978-0-7887-0308-9(0), 94501E7) Recorded Bks.

Shortly after he inherits the powerful position of Lord Eaton, 10-year-old Richard Ludel disappears from Shrewsbury Abbey, where he had been a student. Did he run away or was he kidnapped? Cadfael suspects the hermit of Eyton Forest, a mysterious man rumored to have holy powers, knows the answer. Available to libraries only.

Hermit of Peking: The Hidden Life of Sir Edmund Backhouse. unabr. collector's ed. Hugh R. Trevor-Roper. Read by Bill Kelsey. 10 cass. (Running Time: 15 hrs.). 1997. 80.00 (978-0-913369-51-7(9), 4261) Books on Tape.

Carefully backtracking to original sources, Trevor-Roper unearthed the bizarre truth: that this Hermit of Peking had swindled millions in fraudulent arms deals & in other highly imaginative & sophisticated frauds.

Hermit Thrush Sings. Susan Butler. Read by Kate Forbes. 5 cass. (Running Time: 6 hrs. 45 mins.). (YA). 1999. stu. ed. 223.80 (978-0-7887-3869-2(0), 47034) Recorded Bks.

Before the great Disaster, the people of Maynor (once the state of Maine) were free to travel & there were no mutant birmbas to fear. Because the young orphan Leora has a webbed hand, she is a mutant outcast in her own village. When she accidentally learns that the feared birmbas are friendly, she ventures into the forbidden Outside.

Hermit Thrush Sings. unabr. ed. Susan Butler. Narrated by Kate Forbes. 5 cass. (Running Time: 6 hrs. 45 mins.). (YA). 2000. pap. bk. 69.95 (978-0-7887-3798-5(8), 41042X4) Recorded Bks.

Hermit Thrush Sings, unabr. ed. Susan Butler. Narrated by Kate Forbes. 5 pieces. (Running Time: 6 hrs. 45 mins.). (gr. 7 up). 2000. 46.00 (978-0-7887-3826-5(7), 96045E7) Recorded Bks.

Hermit's Cave, Vol. 1. collector's ed. Perf. by Mel Johnson. 6 cass. (Running Time: 9 hrs.). 1998. bk. 34.98 (4105) Radio Spirits.

Eighteen horrific episodes from 1940 to 1943 with the old Hermit who stands at the mouth of his cave, warning the weak of heart not to listen. Digitally restored and remastered.

Hermit's Cave, Vol. 2. collector's ed. Perf. by Mel Johnson. 9 CDs. (Running Time: 9 hrs.). 1998. bk. 39.98 (4106) Radio Spirits.

Hermit's Cave: Hanson's Ghost. 1945. (MM-5795) Natl Recrd Co.

Hermit's Peak. Michael McGarrity. (Kevin Kerney Ser.: Bk. 4). 2004. 14.95 (978-0-7435-4824-3(8)) Pub: S&S Audio. Dist(s): S and S Inc

***Hero.** Mike Lupica. (Running Time: 5 hrs.). (ENG.). (J). 2010. audio compact disk 29.95 (978-0-14-242819-1(1), PengAudBks) Penguin Grp USA.

Hero. unabr. collector's ed. W. Somerset Maugham. Read by Jill Masters. 6 cass. (Running Time: 9 hrs.). 1985. 48.00 (978-0-7366-0789-6(7), 1741) Books on Tape.

Five years can change a man & when they have been spent in the bush fighting Boers, the changes are profound. When Jamie Parson comes home with captain's pips & a Victoria cross, he is no longer the boy he was. But not to his parents & sweetheart, Mary - they expect him to fit in. Happiness remains a shadow & Jamie finds the moral struggle as relentless as the military.

Hero: Becoming the Man She Desires. Fred Stoeker & Jasen Stoeker. Contrib. by Mike Yorkey. (ENG.). 2009. audio compact disk 26.99 (978-1-934384-31-2(3)) Pub: Treasure Pub. Dist(s): STL Dist NA

***Hero: The Life & Legend of Lawrence of Arabia.** abr. ed. Michael Korda. (ENG.). 2010. (978-0-06-203453-7(3), Harper Audio); (978-0-06-206809-5(1), Harper Audio) HarperCollins Pubs.

Hero, Adventurer, King & Priest: Becoming a Man of God. Kenneth Copeland & Edwin L. Cole. 5 cass. 1997. 25.00 Set. (978-1-57562-209-5(2), 04-2700) K Copeland Pubns.

God designed manhood to be an adventure. And He gave man a desire for responsibility & challenge. But today's men are finding their roles in life increasingly difficult & confusing.

Hero & Heroine: The Mythic Dimension in Times of Transition & Growth. Read by Jean Shinoda Bolen. 4 cass. (Running Time: 6 hrs.). 1989. 31.95 Set. (978-0-7822-0024-9(5), 361) C G Jung IL.

Hero & the Crown. Robin McKinley. (J). 1986. bk. 34.66 (978-0-676-31297-3(7)) RandomHse Pub.

Hero & the Crown, unabr. ed. Robin McKinley. Read by Rosalyn Alexander. 8 cass. (Running Time: 10 hrs. 45 min.). (YA). (gr. 8). 1992. 69.00 (978-1-55690-590-2(4), 92126) Recorded Bks.

Aerin-sol sets out in quest of the Crown of Damar.

***Hero at Large.** unabr. ed. Janet Evanovich. Read by C. J. Critt. (ENG.). 2010. (978-0-06-201603-4(2), Harper Audio); (978-0-06-201463-4(3), Harper Audio) HarperCollins Pubs.

***Hero at Large.** unabr. ed. Janet Evanovich. Read by C. J. Critt. 2010. audio compact disk 14.99 (978-0-06-201460-3(9), Harper Audio) HarperCollins Pubs.

***Hero Found: The Greatest POW Escape of the Vietnam War.** unabr. ed. Bruce B. Henderson. (Running Time: 10 hrs. 0 mins.). 2010. 16.99 (978-1-4001-8702-7(8)) Tantor Media.

***Hero Found: The Greatest POW Escape of the Vietnam War.** unabr. ed. Bruce B. Henderson. Narrated by Todd McLaren. (Running Time: 11 hrs. 0 mins. 0 sec.). (ENG.). 2010. 24.99 (978-1-4001-6702-9(7)); audio compact disk 69.99 (978-1-4001-4702-1(6)); audio compact disk 34.99 (978-1-4001-1702-4(X)) Pub: Tantor Media. Dist(s): IngramPubServ

Hero Game. unabr. ed. Pete Johnson. Read by Stuart McLoughlin. 4 CDs. (Running Time: 4 hrs. 16 mins.). (YA). (gr. 5-8). 2006. audio compact disk 29.95 (978-1-4056-5523-1(2), Chivers Child Audio) AudioGO.

Hero in Every Heart: Messages to Motivate & Inspire the Best in You. H. Jackson Brown, Jr. 1 cass. 1996. 12.99 Nelson.

Hero in the Shadows: Waylander the Slayer Stalks an Ancient Evil. David Gemmell. Narrated by Christopher Kay. 14 CDs. (Running Time: 16 hrs.). audio compact disk 134.00 (978-0-7887-9865-8(0)) Recorded Bks.

Hero Journey. Gwynne Spencer. Created by Gwynne Spencer. Interview with Laura Lee. Prod. by Paul Robear. Contrib. by Scott Sanders. 3 cass. (Running Time: 3 hrs.). 2001. 24.95 (978-1-889071-23-7(4), 6225) Radio Bookstore.

THE HERO JOURNEY - Everybody walking the planet has a story to share, and everybody's story matters. You are the hero of your own life story. Long ago, Joseph Campbell observed in THE HERO WITH A THOUSAND FACES that all over the world, through all the myths and legends, through all the stories of every culture, there is one identical monomyth. The names and faces and places of the story change, but the structure is the same. He called it The Hero Journey and mapped it out in its infinite variations using thousands of examples from his vast knowledge of story and myth. In this three tape set, you'll learn not just the secret formula of the hero journey, but how it manifests itself in daily life, in the waking world and the dream world. Included is an entertaining and wide-ranging conversation with Laura Lee that takes listeners on a journey through movies, novels, real world events and back to their own life stories again and again. Once you see the Hero Journeyevident in your own life, nothing is by accident any longer, says Gwynne Spencer to Laura Lee. It is all part of the map, the interlocking plan that guides our lives, our destiny, our mutual purpose on this planet and perhaps beyond. Whether you're a writer or storyteller looking for plots, a businessman charting the course of a new enterprise, or a regular ordinary mortal looking for answers to life's questions, you'll enjoy this three-hour romp through mythic structure and archetypal encounter.

Hero of Cape Lonely Light. Geoffrey T. Williams. Narrated by Dennis F. Regan. Composed by Stephen J. O'Connor. (J). 2005. audio compact disk 15.99 (978-1-59971-166-9(4)) AardGP.

A cat and a lonely lighthouse keeper save a storm-tossed ship from sinking and a young sailor from drowning.

Hero of the Pacific: The Life of Marine Legend John Basilone. unabr. ed. James Brady. Narrated by Grover Gardner. (Running Time: 7 hrs. 41 mins. 0 sec.). (ENG.). 2010. 20.99 (978-1-60814-537-9(9), SpringWater); audio compact disk 29.99 (978-1-59859-597-0(0), SpringWater) Oasis Audio.

Hero Tales: How Common Lives Reveal the Uncommon Genius of America. Theodore Roosevelt & Henry Cabot Lodge. Read by Patrick Cullen. (Running Time: 5 hrs. 30 mins.). (YA). 2003. 24.95 (978-1-59912-506-0(4)) Iofy Corp.

Hero Tales: How Common Lives Reveal the Uncommon Genius of America. unabr. ed. Theodore Roosevelt & Henry Cabot Lodge. Read by Lloyd James. 4 cass. (Running Time: 7 hrs.). 2001. 32.95 (978-0-7861-2473-2(3), 3102) Blckstn Audio.

Hero Tales: How Common Lives Reveal the Uncommon Genius of America. unabr. ed. Theodore Roosevelt & Henry Cabot Lodge. Read by Lloyd James. 5 CDs. (Running Time: 7 hrs.). 2003. audio compact disk 40.00 (978-0-7861-8797-3(2), 3102) Blckstn Audio.

Hero Tales: How Common Lives Reveal the Uncommon Genius of America. unabr. ed. Theodore Roosevelt & Henry Cabot Lodge. Read by Lloyd James. (YA). 2008. 49.99 (978-1-60514-725-3(7)) Find a World.

Hero Tales: How Common Lives Reveal the Uncommon Genius of America. unabr. ed. Theodore Roosevelt & Henry Cabot Lodge. Narrated by Maurice England. (Running Time: 6 hrs. 25 mins. 42 sec.). (ENG.). 2009. 18.89 (978-1-60814-532-4(8), SpringWater); audio compact disk 26.99 (978-1-59859-592-5(X), SpringWater) Oasis Audio.

Hero, the Wild Man, & the Goddess: The Story of Gilgemesh, Enkido, & Ishtar. Ralph Metzner. 1 cass. 10.50 (A0326-88) Sound Photosyn.

From Shamanism Before & Beyond History, at Ojai.

***Hero Type.** collector's unabr. ed. Barry Lyga. Narrated by Jonathan Todd Ross. 8 CDs. (Running Time: 9 hrs. 15 mins.). (YA). (gr. 8 up). 2009. audio compact disk 41.95 (978-1-4361-6283-8(1)) Recorded Bks.

***Hero Type.** unabr. ed. Barry Lyga. Narrated by Jonathan Todd Ross. 1 Playaway. (Running Time: 9 hrs. 15 mins.). (YA). (gr. 8 up). 2009. 56.75 (978-1-4407-0393-5(0)); 61.75 (978-1-4361-6274-6(2)); audio compact disk 87.75 (978-1-4361-6279-1(3)) Recorded Bks.

Herodotus Pt. 1: The Histories. unabr. ed. Herodotus. Read by Bill Kelsey. 10 cass. (Running Time: 10 hrs.). 2001. 80.00 (978-0-7366-8377-7(1)) Books on Tape.

A chronicle of the ancient Persians, Egyptians, and Greeks, leavened with many entertaining and socially observant digressions.

Herodotus Pt. 2: The Histories. unabr. ed. Herodotus. Read by Bill Kelsey. 10 cass. (Running Time: 10 hrs.). 2001. 80.00 (978-0-7366-8378-4(X)) Books on Tape.

Herodotus Pts. I-II: The Father of History. Instructed by Elizabeth Vandiver. 12 CDs. (Running Time: 12 hrs.). 2002. bk. 69.95 (978-1-56585-289-1(3), 2353) Teaching Co.

Herodotus Pts. I-II, Vol. 1: The Father of History. Instructed by Elizabeth Vandiver. 12 cass. (Running Time: 12 hrs.). bk. 54.95 (978-1-56585-034-7(3), 2353) Teaching Co.

Herodotus Vol. 2: The Father of History. Instructed by Elizabeth Vandiver. 6 cass. (Running Time: 6 hrs.). 2002. 129.95 (978-1-56585-035-4(1)); audio compact disk 179.95 (978-1-56585-290-7(7)) Teaching Co.

Heroes. Perf. by Hilton Ruiz. 1 cass., 1 CD. 7.98 (TA 33338); audio compact disk 12.78 CD Jewel box. (TA 83338) NewSound.

Heroes. unabr. ed. Dante Gebel. (Running Time: 18000 sec.). (SPA.). (gr. 8). 2006. audio compact disk 19.99 (978-0-8297-4756-0(7)) Pub: Vida Pubs. Dist(s): Zondervan

Heroes: From Alexander the Great & Julius Caesar to Churchill & de Gaulle. Paul Johnson. Read by James Adams. (Playaway Adult Nonfiction Ser.). 2008. 64.99 (978-1-60640-760-8(0)) Find a World.

Heroes: From Alexander the Great & Julius Caesar to Churchill & de Gaulle. unabr. ed. Paul Johnson. Read by James Adams. (Running Time: 39600 sec.). 2007. 19.95 (978-1-4332-0659-7(5)); 54.95 (978-1-4332-0657-3(9)); audio compact disk 19.95 (978-1-4332-0660-3(9)); audio compact disk 29.95 (978-1-4332-0661-0(7)); audio compact disk & audio compact disk 63.00 (978-1-4332-0658-0(7)) Blckstn Audio.

Heroes Set: Or, Greek Fairy Tales for My Children. Charles Kingsley. Read by Flo Gibson. 4 cass. (Running Time: 6 hrs.). (J). (gr. 4-5). 1987. 19.95 (978-1-55685-091-2(3)) Audio Bk Con.

These myths include tales of Perseus, Theseus, the Twelve Labors of Heracles, Jason's Quest for the Golden Fleece & the Argonauts.

Heroes Vol. 3: And Other Secrets, Surprises & Sensational Stories. AIO Team Staff. Created by Focus on the Family Staff. 4 CDs. (Running Time: 3 hrs. 20 mins.). (Adventures in Odyssey Ser.: Vol. 3). (ENG.). (J). 2005. audio compact disk 24.99 (978-1-58997-072-4(1)) Pub: Focus Family. Dist(s): Tyndale Hse

Heroes among Us: Firsthand Accounts of Combat from America's Most Decorated Warriors in Iraq & Afghanistan. Read by Lloyd James. Ed. by Chuck Larson. Afterword by John McCain. Frwd. by Tommy Franks. (Playaway Adult Nonfiction Ser.). 2008. 64.99 (978-1-60640-857-5(7)) Find a World.

Heroes among Us: Firsthand Accounts of Combat from America's Most Decorated Warriors in Iraq & Afghanistan. unabr. ed. Read by Robertson Dean & Lloyd James. Ed. by Chuck Larson. Frwd. by Tommy Franks. Afterword by John S. McCain. (Running Time: 9 hrs. 30 mins. 0 sec.). (ENG.). 2008. audio compact disk 24.99 (978-1-4001-5652-8(1)); audio compact disk 34.99 (978-1-4001-0652-3(4)) Pub: Tantor Media. Dist(s): IngramPubServ

Heroes among Us: Firsthand Accounts of Combat from America's Most Decorated Warriors in Iraq & Afghanistan. unabr. ed. Chuck Larson. Read by Robertson Dean. Narrated by Lloyd James. (Running Time: 9 hrs. 30 mins. 0 sec.). (ENG.). 2008. audio compact disk 69.99 (978-1-4001-3652-0(0)) Pub: Tantor Media. Dist(s): IngramPubServ

Heroes among Us: Ordinary People, Extraordinary Choices. unabr. ed. John Quinones. Narrated by Arthur Morey. 1 MP3-CD. (Running Time: 6 hrs. 30 mins. 0 sec.). (ENG.). 2009. audio compact disk 19.99 (978-1-4001-6056-3(1)); audio compact disk 59.99 (978-1-4001-4056-5(0)); audio compact disk 29.99 (978-1-4001-1056-8(4)) Pub: Tantor Media. Dist(s): IngramPubServ

Heroes & Hell'yuns: Tales of the New River Gorge. Melody Bragg. Music by Mike Morningstar. (ENG.). 1997. 12.95 (978-0-9795156-2-0(9)) Mtn Whispers Pubng.

Heroes & Hell'yuns: Tales of the New River Gorge, 2. Short Stories. 1 CD. (Running Time: 74 mins.). Dramatization. (ENG.). (YA). 2005. audio compact disk 14.95 (978-0-9795156-0-6(2)) Mtn Whispers Pubng.

Heroes & Hell'yuns: Tales of the New River Gorge (Vol. 2) Melody Bragg. Music by Mike Morningstar. Narrated by Ross Ballard. (ENG.). 2005. audio compact disk 12.95 (978-0-9717801-0-1(2)) Mtn Whispers Pubng.

Heroes & Heroines. (Running Time: 1 hr.). 2002. 16.95 (978-1-60083-764-7(6)) Iofy Corp.

Heroes & Heroines from Classic Tales. abr. ed. Excerpts. Intro. by Benjamin Soames. 1 CD. (Running Time: 1 hr. 8 mins.). (J). 1998. audio compact disk 14.98 (978-962-634-155-1(6), NA115512, Naxos AudioBooks) Naxos.

An introduction to favorite classics. Includes excerpts from "Pinocchio," "Peter Pan," "King Arthur," "Tales from the Norse Legends." "Anne of Green Gables," "The Railway Children," "Kidnapped" and others.

Heroes & Heroines from Classic Tales. abr. ed. Excerpts. Intro. by Benjamin Soames. 1 cass. (Running Time: 1 hr. 8 mins.). (J). 1999. 9.98 (978-962-634-655-6(8), NA115514, Naxos AudioBooks) Naxos.

An introduction to favorite classics. Includes excerpts from Pinocchio, Peter Pan, King Arthur, Tales from the Norse Legends, Anne of Green Gables, The Railway Children, Kidnapped and others.

Heroes & Heroines in Music: Cassette. Wendy-Ann Ensor. 1982. 18.00 (978-0-19-321107-0(6)) OUP.

Heroes & Martyrs: Emma Goldman, Sacco & Vanzetti, & the Revolutionary Struggle. Howard Zinn. (AK Press Audio Ser.). (ENG.). 2000. audio compact disk 20.00 (978-1-902593-26-5(X)) Pub: AK Pr GBR. Dist(s): Consort Bk Sales

Heroes & Outlaws of the Bible. Narrated by Don Reid. 3 cass. 2003. 13.99 (978-0-89221-531-7(3), 303-037) Pub: New Leaf. Dist(s): Spring Arbor Dist

Down home reflections of History's most colorful men and women as told by Don Reid of the Statler Brothers.

Heroes at Home: Help & Hope for America's Military Families. abr. ed. Ellie Kay. Read by Ellie Kay. 3 CDs. (Running Time: 3 hrs.). 2004. audio compact disk 62.25 (978-1-59355-605-1(5), 1593556055); 17.95 (978-1-59355-602-0(0), 1593556020); 44.25 (978-1-59355-603-7(9), 1593556039); audio compact disk 19.95 (978-1-59355-604-4(7), 1593556047) Brilliance Audio.

Filled with actual stories of life in the military, this encouraging book provides helpful guidance to families on active duty and insight to their extended families, friends, and churches. From her perspective as the wife of an air force pilot and mom with five school-age kids, the author includes practical ideas on how to cope with frequent moves, pre-deployment readiness, and how to stay in touch when families are separated.

Heroes at Home: Help & Hope for America's Military Families. abr. ed. Ellie Kay. Read by Ellie Kay. (Running Time: 3 hrs.). 2006. 39.25 (978-1-4233-0324-4(5), 9781423303244, BADLE); 24.95 (978-1-4233-0323-7(7), 9781423303237, BAD); 39.25 (978-1-4233-0322-0(9), 9781423303220, Brlnc Audio MP3 Lib); 24.95 (978-1-4233-0321-3(0), 9781423303213, Brilliance MP3) Brilliance Audio.

Heroes for Young Readers Activity Guide Audio CDs for Books 1-4. Renee Meloche. (Running Time: 1 hr. 5 min.). 2007. audio compact disk 14.99 (978-1-57658-396-8(1)) YWAM Pub.

Heroes for Young Readers Activity Guide Audio CDs for Books 13-16. Renee Taft Meloche. (ENG.). 2005. audio compact disk 14.99 (978-1-57658-399-9(6)) YWAM Pub.

Heroes for Young Readers Activity Guide Auido CDs for Books 5-8. Renee Taft Meloche. (ENG.). 2005. audio compact disk 14.99 (978-1-57658-397-5(X)) YWAM Pub.

Heroes for Young Readers Activity Guide Auido CDs for Books 9-12. Renee Taft Meloche. (ENG.). 2005. audio compact disk 14.99 (978-1-57658-398-2(8)) YWAM Pub.

Heroes for Young Readers Activity Guide Package Books 1-4: Includes: Activity Guide, Audio CD, & Books 1-4. Renee Meloch. Illus. by Bryan Pollard. 1CD. (Heroes for Young Readers Ser.). (ENG.). 2005. bk. 55.94 (978-1-57658-375-3(9)) YWAM Pub.

Heroes for Young Readers Activity Guide Package Books 13-16: Includes: Activity Guide, Audio CD, & Books 13-16. Renee Taft Meloche. Illus. by Bryan Pollard. (ENG.). 2006. bk. 55.94 (978-1-57658-378-4(3)) YWAM Pub.

Heroes for Young Readers Activity Guide Package Books 5-8: Includes: Activity Guide, Audio CD, & Books 5-8. Renee Taft Meloche. Illus. by Bryan Pollard. 1CD. (Heroes for Young Readers Ser.). (ENG.). 2005. bk. 57.94 (978-1-57658-376-0(7)) YWAM Pub.

Heroes for Young Readers Activity Guide Package Books 9-12: Includes: Activity Guide, Audio CD, & Books 9-12. Renee Taft Meloche. Illus. by Bryan Pollard. 1 CD. (Heroes for Young Readers Ser.). (ENG.). 2005. bk. 55.94 (978-1-57658-377-7(5)) YWAM Pub.

Heroes, Gods & Monsters of the Greek Myths. Bernard Evslin. Read by Richard Kiley & Julie Harris. 6 cass. (Running Time: 5 hrs. 2 min.). 1988. 55.00 (978-0-8045-0007-4(X), PCC 7) Spoken Arts.

Heroes, Gods & Monsters of the Greek Myths, Pt. 1. unabr. ed. Bernard Evslin. Read by Julie Harris & Richard Kiley. (Running Time: 55 min.). 10.95 (SAC 989) Spoken Arts.

Includes stories of Zeus, Hera, Hades, Demeter, Birth of the Twins, Athene, Poseidon, Hephaestus & Hermes.

Heroes, Gods & Monsters of the Greek Myths, Pt. 2. unabr. ed. Bernard Evslin. Read by Julie Harris & Richard Kiley. 10.95 (SAC 1000) Spoken Arts.

Includes Artemis, Apollo, Sons of Apollo, Aphrodite & Phaethon.

Heroes, Gods & Monsters of the Greek Myths, Vol. 3. unabr. ed. Bernard Evslin. Read by Julie Harris & Richard Kiley. 1 read-along cass. (Running Time: 58 min.). 10.95 (SAC 1001) Spoken Arts.

Includes stories of Persus, Narcissus & Echo.

Heroes, Gods & Monsters of the Greek Myths, Vol. 4. Bernard Evslin. Perf. by Julie Harris & Richard Kiley. 1 read-along cass. (Running Time: 56 min.). 1986. 10.95 (SAC 1002) Spoken Arts.

Stories of Theseus & Pandora.

Heroes, Gods & Monsters of the Greek Myths, Vol. 5. Bernard Evslin. Perf. by Julie Harris & Richard Kiley. 1 read-along cass. (Running Time: 57 min.). 1986. 10.95 (SAC 1003) Spoken Arts.

Stories of Arion, Orpheus & Atalanta.

Heroes, Gods & Monsters of the Greek Myths, Vol. 6. Bernard Evslin. Perf. by Julie Harris & Richard Kiley. 1 read-along cass. (Running Time: 48 min.). 1986. 10.95 (SAC 1004) Spoken Arts.

Stories of Prometheus, Daedalus & the love story of Eros & Psyche.

Heroes in Mythology. unabr. ed. Read by Jim Weiss. 2001. audio compact disk 13.46 Books on Tape.

Featuring Odin and the Norse men: Prometheus, Bringer of Fire; Thesus and the Minotaur. Three of the world's greatest adventures, each featuring a quest for Wisdom. From Norse mythology, the central story of Odin, King of the Norse Gods, who seeks wisdom before facing a fierce foe. Then meet the ancient Greek gods and titans in the famed tale of Prometheus which has inspired some of the world's greatest masterpieces. Finally, follow daring Theseus, bold hero and wise man, as he enters the maze-like Labyrinth to face the monstrous half-man, half-bull, the mighty Minotaur.

Heroes in Mythology. unabr. ed. Read by Jim Weiss. 1 cass. (Running Time: 60 mins.). (J). 2001. 9.86 Books on Tape.

Heroes in Mythology: Theseus, Prometheus & Odin. Short Stories. As told by Jim Weiss. 1 cass. (Running Time: 1 hr.). Dramatization. (Storyteller's Version Ser.). (J). (gr. 2 up). 2000. 9.95 (978-1-882513-24-6(X), 1124-24) Greathall Prods.

Three of the world's greatest adventures, each featuring a quest for wisdom. Includes: "Theseus and the Minotaur," "Prometheus, Bearer of Fire" and "Odin and the Norse Men".

Heroes in Mythologym: Theseus, Prometheus & Odin. As told by Jim Weiss. 1 CD. (Running Time: 1 hr.). Dramatization. (Storyteller's Version Ser.). (J). (gr. 2-6). 2000. audio compact disk 13.95 (978-1-882513-49-9(5), 1124-024) Greathall Prods.

Heroes of American History. unabr. ed. 2 cass. (Running Time: 3 hrs.). (Full - Cast Productions Ser.). (J). 2002. 19.95 (978-1-931953-09-2(0)) Listen & Live.

Original production presents the exciting biographies of three of America's greatest men: George Washington, military general and first President of our great land; Daniel Boone, courageous pioneer and explorer; and Benjamin Franklin, inventor and beloved statesman.

Heroes of History. unabr. ed. Will Durant. Read by Grover Gardner. (YA). 2008. 74.99 (978-1-60514-585-3(8)) Find a World.

Heroes of History. unabr. collector's ed. Winston L. S. Churchill. Read by David Case. 6 cass. (Running Time: 6 hrs.). 1990. 36.00 (978-0-7366-1825-0(2), 2661) Books on Tape.

A collection of short biographical sketches taken from Churchill's four-volume work "The History of the English-Speaking Peoples".

***Heroes of History: A Brief History of Civilization from Ancient Times to the Dawn of the Modern Age.** Will Durant. Narrated by Grover Gardner. (Running Time: 12 hrs. 35 mins. 0 sec.). (ENG.). 2011. audio compact disk 29.95 (978-1-60998-201-0(0)) Pub: AudioGO. Dist(s): Perseus Dist

Heroes of History: A Brief History of Civilization from Ancient Times to the Dawn of the Modern Age. unabr. ed. Will Durant. Read by Grover Gardner. 10 cass. (Running Time: 15 hrs.). 2003. 34.95 (978-1-57270-343-8(1)) Pub: Audio Partners. Dist(s): PerseuPGW

Heroes of History: A Brief History of Civilization from Ancient Times to the Dawn of the Modern Age. unabr. ed. Will Durant. Narrated by Grover Gardner. 12 CDs. (Running Time: 15 hrs.). (Audio Editions Ser.). (ENG.). 2003. audio compact disk 39.95 (978-1-57270-344-5(X)) Pub: AudioGO. Dist(s): Perseus Dist

Heroes of History for Young Readers Activity Guide Package Books 1-4: Includes: Activity Guide, Audio CD, & Books 1-4. Renee Taft Meloche. Illus. by Bryan Pollard. (ENG.). 2007. bk. 55.94 (978-1-932096-49-1(3)) Pub: Emerald WA. Dist(s): YWAM Pub

Heroes of the Faith: The Lives of Four Christians Whose Examples Offer Hope. unabr. ed. Diana Waring. Read by Diana Waring. 1 cass. (Running Time: 1 hr. 30 mins.). 1999. 8.95 (978-1-930514-11-9(5)) Diana Waring.

Heroes of the Greek Myths. Bernard Evslin. Perf. by Richard Kiley & Frances Sternhagen. 10.95 (978-0-8045-1133-9(0), SAC 1133) Spoken Arts.

Heroes of the Valley. unabr. ed. Jonathan Stroud. Read by David Thorn. 11 CDs. (Running Time: 13 hrs. 28 mins.). (YA). (gr. 5 up). 2009. audio compact disk 65.00 (978-0-7393-8222-6(5), Listening Lib) Pub: Random Audio Pubg. Dist(s): Random

Heroes of the Valley. unabr. ed. Jonathan Stroud. (ENG.). (J). (gr. 5). 2009. audio compact disk 50.00 (978-0-7393-8220-2(9), Listening Lib) Pub: Random Audio Pubg. Dist(s): Random

Heroic Australian women in War. unabr. ed. Susanna De Vries. Read by Beverley Dunn. (Running Time: 12 hrs. 10 mins.). 2009. audio compact disk 98.95 (978-1-921415-33-3(9), 9781921415333) Pub: Bolinda Pubng AUS. Dist(s): Bolinda Pub Inc

Heroic Bible Stories: Jonah & the Whale/Joseph & His Brothers. unabr. ed. Listening Library Staff & Rabbit Ears Books Staff. Read by Jason Robards & Reuben Blades. (Running Time: 2760 sec.). (Rabbit Ears Ser.). (ENG.). (J). (gr. 1). 2007. audio compact disk 11.95 (978-0-7393-3874-2(9), Listening Lib) Pub: Random Audio Pubg. Dist(s): Random

Heroic Business Dynasties. Edwin A. Locke. 4 cass. (Running Time: 4 hrs. 30 min.). 49.95 Set. (EL54D) Second Renaissance.

The pivotal, creative role of business leaders by presenting the remarkable histories of three companies: Ford Motor Co., IBM & Dupont.

***Heroic Conservatism.** unabr. ed. Michael J. Gerson. Read by Alan Nebelthau. (ENG.). 2007. (978-0-06-155441-4(3)); (978-0-06-155448-3(0)) HarperCollins Pubs.

Heroic Life of Al Capsella. unabr. ed. Judith Clarke. Read by Stig Wemyss. 4 cass. (Running Time: 4 hrs. 30 mins.). (YA). 2000. 32.00 (978-1-74030-090-2(4), 500121) Pub: Bolinda Pubng AUS. Dist(s): Bolinda Pub Inc

Heroic Life of Al Capsella. unabr. ed. Judith Clarke. Read by Stig Wemyss. 4 CDs. (Running Time: 4 hrs. 30 mins.). (YA). (gr. 5-8). 2007. audio compact disk 57.95 (978-1-74093-462-6(8)) Pub: Bolinda Pubng AUS. Dist(s): Bolinda Pub Inc

Heroic Symphony. Anna Harwell Celenza. Illus. by JoAnn E. Kitchel. (J). 2004. bk. 21.95 (978-1-57091-509-3(1)) Charlesbridge.

Heroine see Winter's Tales

Heroines. Eileen Favorite. 2008. audio compact disk 29.99 (978-1-4281-8530-2(5)) Recorded Bks.

***Heroine's Bookshelf: Life Lessons, from Jane Austen to Laura Ingalls Wilder.** unabr. ed. Erin Blakemore. Read by Tavia Gilbert. (Running Time: 8 hrs. 30 mins.). 2010. 19.95 (978-1-4417-6197-2(7)); audio compact disk 19.95 (978-1-4417-6196-5(9)) Blckstn Audio.

***Heroine's Bookshelf (Library Edition) Life Lessons, from Jane Austen to Laura Ingalls Wilder.** unabr. ed. Erin Blakemore. Read by Tavia Gilbert. (Running Time: 8 hrs. 30 mins.). 2010. 24.95 (978-1-4417-6194-1(2)); audio compact disk 30.00 (978-1-4417-6195-8(0)) Blckstn Audio.

Heroism in Modern American Literature. 4 cass. (Running Time: 6 hrs.). 1997. 49.95 Set. (978-1-56114-389-4(8), MB45D) Second Renaissance.
The concept of American heroism as portrayed in "Shane", "A Separate Peace" & "One Flew Over the Cuckoo's Nest".

Heroism of the Fathers Is the Legacy of the Sons. Douglas W. Phillips et al. 2 CDs. (Running Time: 1 hr. 30 mins.). 2002. audio compact disk 15.00 (978-0-9724173-3-4(8)) Pub: Vsn Forum. Dist(s): STL Dist NA

Heron see Gathering of Great Poetry for Children

Heros & Anti-Heroes. 10.00 (HT405) Esstee Audios.

Hero's Journey. Gary McAuley. 1 cass. (Running Time: 1 hr. 30 min.). 2001. 13.95 (978-0-9701926-1-5(4), SW401C) Sunwest.

Hero's Self-Understanding in Othello, Lear & Macbeth. unabr. ed. Robert Heilman. 1 cass. (Running Time: 33 min.). 1965. 12.95 (23091) J Norton Pubs.
An analysis of Shakespeare's exploration of man's mingled openness & his resistance to self-knowledge.

Hero's Way: Business Leaders, Politicians, & Other Notables Explore the Nature of Heroism. abr. ed. Robert L. Dilenschneider. 2004. 24.95 (978-1-59007-608-8(7)); audio compact disk 34.95 (978-1-59007-609-5(5)) Pub: New Millenn Enter. Dist(s): PerseuPGW

Hero's Welcome: Easter Service. Ed Young. 1991. 4.95 (978-0-7417-1856-3(1), 856) Win Walk.

Hero's 2 Journeys. Speeches. Michael Hauge & Christopher Vogler. Instructed by Michael Hauge & Christopher Vogler. 3 CDs. (Running Time: 3 hrs. 15 mins.). 2003. audio compact disk 29.95 (978-1-880717-47-9(6), 829-035) Writers AudioShop.
Make your story the best it can be - on 2 levels. Hear each superstar teacher present his unique approach to . . . 1) The OUTER JOURNEY, the essential structural principles driving every successful plot, and 2) The INNER JOURNEY, the deeper storyline that makes a story truly great. Full of specific examples. Suitable for all writers, actors, filmmakers, studio executives, game designers and developers, storytellers and anyone with a passion for movies and stories.

Herotica: A Collection of Women's Erotic Fiction. Ed. by Susie Bright. 2 cass. (Running Time: 3 hrs.). 1995. 16.95 Set. (978-1-886238-02-2(2), 8022) Passion Press.
Susie Bright's ground-breaking anthology of new women's erotic fiction explores what is sexually exciting to a variety of different modern women characters in the ten short stories. Witty, thoughtful, & incisive, Herotica delivers a banquet of non-stop sensual delights.

Herotica Vol. 3: A New Collection of Erotic Writing by Women. Ed. by Susie Bright. 2 cass. (Running Time: 3 hrs.). 2001. 16.95 (978-1-886238-18-3(9)); audio compact disk 24.95 (978-1-886238-17-6(0)) Passion Press.

Herotica Vol. 4: A New Collection of Erotic Writing by Women. Ed. by Marcy Sheiner. 2 CDs. (Running Time: 3 hrs.). 2001. audio compact disk 24.95 (978-1-886238-21-3(9)) Passion Press.

Herotica Vol. 4: A New Collection of Erotic Writing by Women. Ed. by Marcy Sheiner. 2 cass. (Running Time: 3 hrs.). 1999. 16.95 (978-1-886238-22-0(7)) Passion Press.

Herotica Vol. 5: A New Collection of Erotic Writing by Women. Ed. by Marcy Sheiner. 2 cass. (Running Time: 3 hrs.). 2001. 16.95 (978-1-886238-33-6(2)); audio compact disk 24.95 (978-1-886238-32-9(4)) Passion Press.

Herotica 6. Ed. by Marcy Sheiner. 2 cass. (Running Time: 3 hrs.). 2003. 16.95 (978-1-886238-38-1(3)); audio compact disk 24.95 (978-1-886238-37-4(5)) Passion Press.

Herotics Two. abr. ed. Ed. by Susie Bright & Joani Blank. 2 cass. (Running Time: 3 hrs.). 1996. 16.95 Set. (978-1-886238-05-3(7)) Passion Press.
Take a trip around the world with this amazing collection of woman-authored erotic short stories. From Rubenesque, a fantasy encounter in a staid San Francisco restaurant filled with strangers...to the sexy lover's surprise on a sultry tropical beach in Boca Chica, this successor to the original volume in the Herotic series provides the listener with a continuous erotic joy ride.

Herring-Gull see Twentieth-Century Poetry in English, No. 25, Recordings of Poets Reading Their Own Poetry

Herring Shed. Jay O'Callahan. Perf. by Jay O'Callahan. 1 cass. (Running Time: 52 min.). (YA). (gr. 9 up). 1983. bk. 10.00 (978-1-877954-01-6(2)) Artana Prodns.
World War II comes home to a Nova Scotia fishing village. A touching story told through the eyes of a 14 year-old girl.

Herself. Hortense Calisher. Read by Hortense Calisher. 1 cass. (Running Time: 52 min.). 13.95 (978-1-55644-095-3(2), 4031) Am Audio Prose.
Calisher performs "Herself" & excerpts from "Mysteries of Motion".

Hertford O'Donnell's Warning see Classic Ghost Stories, Vol. 2, A Collection

Herzlich Willkommen Neu: Deutsch in Restaurant und Tourismus. Ulrike Cohen. 2 cass. (Running Time: 1 hr. 20 mins.). (GER.). 2005. 19.95 (978-3-468-49546-5(3)) Langenscheidt.

Herzlich Willkommen Neu Set: Deutsch in Restaurant und Tourismus. Ulrike Cohen. 2 cass. (Running Time: 1 hr. 35 mins.). (GER.). 2005. 26.50 (978-3-468-49545-8(5)) Langenscheidt.

Herzog. unabr. ed. Saul Bellow. Read by Wolfram Kandinsky. 13 cass. (Running Time: 19 hrs.). 1994. 85.95 (978-0-7861-0343-0(4), 1300) Blckstn Audio.
Moses Herzog, great sufferer, joker & moaner, cuckold, charmer, & man of our time. Seeing himself as a survivor of his private disasters, but also those of the age, Herzog cannot keep from asking what he calls the "piercing" questions. The answers he finds will matter not only to him but to listeners of Saul Bellow's magnificent novel.

Herzog. unabr. ed. Saul Bellow. Read by Wolfram Kandinsky. (Running Time: 64800 sec.). 2006. audio compact disk 120.00 (978-0-7861-6290-1(2)); audio compact disk 44.95 (978-0-7861-7304-4(1)) Blckstn Audio.

Herzog. unabr. ed. Saul Bellow. (Running Time: 18 hrs.). 2009. audio compact disk 34.95 (978-1-4417-1189-2(9)) Blckstn Audio.

Herzog. unabr. ed. Saul Bellow. Read by Malcolm Hillgartner. (Running Time: 18 hrs. 0 mins.). 2009. 29.95 (978-1-4417-1190-8(2)); 95.95 (978-1-4417-1186-1(4)); audio compact disk 123.00 (978-1-4417-1187-8(2)) Blckstn Audio.

Herzog, Set. unabr. ed. Saul Bellow. Read by Wolfram Kandinsky. 13 cass. 1999. 85.95 (FS9-51101) Highsmith.

He's Able. Perf. by Dreyfus and The Wings of Faith. Prod. by Dottie Peoples. 1 cass. 1997. audio compact disk 15.98 CD. (D2205) Diamante Music Grp.

***He's Alive.** 2010. audio compact disk (978-1-59171-254-1(8)) Falcon Picture.

He's Alive. Contrib. by Russell Mauldin. 2007. audio compact disk 24.98 (978-5-557-53094-1(0), Word Music) Word Enter.

He's Been Faithful. Contrib. by Vicki Yohe. Prod. by Sanchez Harley & Geron Davis. Contrib. by Demetrus Stewart & Michelle S. Duffie. 2005. audio compact disk 17.99 (978-5-558-87058-9(3)) Pt of Grace Ent.

He's Been Faithful. abr. unabr. ed. Carol Cymbala & Spangler. 2001. 17.99 (978-0-310-23668-9(1)) Zondervan.

He's Been Faithful: Trusting God to Do What Only He Can Do. abr. ed. Carol Cymbala. (Running Time: 2 hrs. 0 mins. 0 sec.). (ENG.). 2004. 17.99 (978-0-310-26055-4(8)) Zondervan.

He's Dreaming Now. Neville Goddard. 1 cass. (Running Time: 62 min.). 1970. 8.00 (81) J & L Pubns.
Neville taught Imagination Creates Reality. He was a powerfully influential teacher of God as Consciousness.

He's Got It All in Control. 2005. 7.99 (978-5-558-93894-4(3)) Christian Wrld.

He's Got to Go. unabr. ed. Sheila O'Flanagan. Read by Caroline Lennon. 12 cass. (Running Time: 18 hrs.). 2003. 96.95 (978-0-7540-0976-4(9), CAB 2398) AudioGO.

He's Just Not That into You: The No-Excuses Truth to Understanding Guys. unabr. ed. Greg Behrendt & Liz Tuccillo. 2004. 11.95 (978-0-7435-4508-2(7)) Pub: S&S Audio. Dist(s): S and S Inc

He's Just Not That into You: The No-Excuses Truth to Understanding Guys. unabr. movie tie-in ed. Greg Behrendt & Liz Tuccillo. Read by Greg Behrendt & Liz Tuccillo. 3 CDs. (Running Time: 3 hrs. 30 mins. 0 sec.). (ENG.). 2009. audio compact disk 14.99 (978-0-7435-7817-2(1)) Pub: S&S Audio. Dist(s): S and S Inc

He's Still the King of Kings: A Musical Worshiping the Chris of Christmas. Contrib. by Mosie Lister. (ENG.). 1998. audio compact disk 16.99 (978-5-559-27369-3(4)) Lillenas.

He's Still the Lamb. Contrib. by Russell Mauldin. 1994. 11.98 (978-0-7601-0243-5(0), 75602047); 85.00 (978-0-7601-0244-2(9), 75606280); 4.00 (978-0-7601-0245-9(7), 75602048); 4.00 (978-0-7601-0246-6(5), 75602049) Pub: Brentwood Music. Dist(s): H Leonard

Hesped - Rabbi Yaakov Weinberg, ZT"L; Shailos U'Teshuvos. Sheftel Neuberger et al. 1 cass. (Running Time: 90 mins.). 1999. 8.00 (T60TB) Torah Umesorah.

Hesse Between Music. abr. ed. Hermann Hesse & Ralph Manheim. Perf. by Fred Haines. Tr. by Del Caro et al. 1 cass. 1984. 12.95 (978-0-694-50284-4(7), SWC 1516) HarperCollins Pubs.
German conductor & music producer, Joachim-Emst Berendt, set a narration of Hesse's work to music. The performance is by Fred Haines & The Group Between.

Hester Roon. Norah Lofts. 2008. 89.95 (978-1-4079-0051-3(X)); audio compact disk 99.95 (978-1-4079-0052-0(8)) Pub: Soundings Ltd GBR. Dist(s): Ulverscroft US

Het Management Support Plan: De volgende generatie Bedrijfsvoering. Jacob Korthuis.Tr. of Management Support Plan: the next generation business Management. (DUT.). 2008. audio compact disk 31.27 (978-0-9786598-7-5(2)) BCE Inst Inc.

Hetty Hackett's Farm. (Sails Literacy Ser.). (gr. k up). 10.00 (978-0-7578-2649-8(0)) Rigby Educ.

***Hewey Calloway 1: The Smiling Country.** Elizabeth Kelton. 2010. audio compact disk 19.99 (978-1-59950-709-5(9)) GraphicAudio.

***Hewey Calloway 2: The Good Old Boys.** Elmer Kelton. 2011. audio compact disk 19.99 (978-1-59950-731-6(5)) GraphicAudio.

***Hewey Calloway 3: Six Bits A Day.** Elmer Kelton. 2011. audio compact disk 19.99 (978-1-59950-742-2(0)) GraphicAudio.

Hey, Al. Arthur Yorinks. (J). 1987. 18.66 (978-0-676-87122-7(4)) SRA McGraw.

Hey, Al. Arthur Yorinks. Illus. by Richard Egielski. 1 cass. (Running Time: 8 min.). (J). (gr. k-3). 2001. pap. bk. 15.90 (978-0-8045-6872-2(3)) Spoken Arts.
Al, a janitor, and his faithful dog, Eddie, live in a single room on the West Side. They eat together, they work together, they do everything together. So what's the problem? You name it. Their tiny home is crowded and cramped; their life is an endless struggle. Al and Eddie are totally miserable until a large and mysterious bird offesr them a change of fortune.

Hey, Andrew! Teach Me Some Greek! - Pronunciation Cassette Tape for Level 3, Level 4: A Biblical Greek Pronunciation Tape. Read by Karen Mohs & Amy Mohs. Perf. by Amy Mohs et al. Text by Karen Mohs. 1 cass. (Running Time: 33.5 mins). (J). 1999. suppl. ed. 8.00 (978-1-931842-40-2(X), GR-TP-34) Greek n Stuff.
This pronunciation cassette tape is designed to be used with the Hey, Andrew! Teach Me Some Greek! Level 3 and Level 4 workbooks. It features the Greek Alphabet Song and pronunciations of the letters, words, and paradigms taught in the third and fourth levels.

Hey, Andrew! Teach Me Some Greek! - Pronunciation Cassette Tape for Level 5, Level 6: A Biblical Greek Pronunciation Tape. Read by Karen Mohs & Amy Mohs. Perf. by Amy Mohs et al. Text by Karen Mohs. 1 cass. (Running Time: 77.5 mins.). (J). 1999. suppl. ed. 8.00 (978-1-931842-41-9(8), GR-TP-56) Greek n Stuff.
This pronunciation cassette tape is designed to be used with the Hey, Andrew! Teach Me Some Greek! Level 5 and Level 6 workbooks. It features the Greek Alphabet Song and pronunciations of the letters, words, and paradigms taught in the fifth and sixth levels.

Hey, Andrew! Teach Me Some Greek! - Pronunciation Cassette Tape for the Reader, Level 1, Level 2: A Biblical Greek Pronunciation Tape. Read by Karen Mohs & Amy Mohs. Perf. by Amy Mohs et al. Text by Karen Mohs. 1 cass. (Running Time: 25 mins). (J). 1999. suppl. ed. 8.00 (978-1-931842-39-6(6), GR-TP-R12) Greek n Stuff.
This pronunciation cassette tape is designed to be used with the Hey, Andrew! Teach Me Some Greek! Reader and the Level 1 and Level 2 workbooks. It features the Greek Alphabet Song, a reading of the Reader, and pronunciations of the letters and words taught in the first two levels.

Hey, Andrew! Teach Me Some Greek! - Pronunciation CD for Level 3, Level 4: A Biblical Greek Pronunciation CD. Read by Karen Mohs & Amy Mohs. Perf. by Amy Mohs et al. Text by Karen Mohs. 1 CD. (Running Time: 13 mins.). (J). 1999. suppl. ed. 10.00 (978-1-931842-37-2(X), GR-CD-34) Greek n Stuff.
This pronunciation CD is designed to be used with the Hey, Andrew! Teach Me Some Greek! Level 3 and Level 4 workbooks. It features the Greek Alphabet Song and pronunciations of the letters, words, and paradigms taught in the third and fourth levels.

Hey, Andrew! Teach Me Some Greek! - Pronunciation CD for Level 5, Level 6: A Biblical Greek Pronunciation CD. Read by Karen Mohs & Amy Mohs. Perf. by Amy Mohs et al. Text by Karen Mohs. 1 CD. (Running Time: 32 mins). (J). 1999. suppl. ed. 10.00 (978-1-931842-38-9(8), GR-CD-56) Greek n Stuff.
This pronunciation CD is designed to be used with the Hey, Andrew! Teach Me Some Greek! Level 5 and Level 6 workbooks. It features the Greek Alphabet Song and pronunciations of the letters, words, and paradigms taught in the fifth and sixth levels.

Hey, Andrew! Teach Me Some Greek! - Pronunciation CD for the Reader, Level 1, Level 2: A Biblical Greek Pronunciation CD. Read by Karen Mohs & Amy Mohs. Perf. by Amy Mohs et al. Text by Karen Mohs. 1 CD. (Running Time: 15 mins). (J). 1999. suppl. ed. 10.00 (978-1-931842-36-5(1), GR-CD-R12) Greek n Stuff.
This pronunciation CD is designed to be used with the Hey, Andrew! Teach Me Some Greek! Reader and the Level 1 and Level 2 workbooks. It features the Greek Alphabet Song, a reading of the Reader, and pronunciations of the letters and words taught in the first two levels.

Hey Diddle Diddle; Baby Bunting; Milkmaid. 2004. 8.95 (978-1-56008-838-7(9)); cass. & flmstrp 30.00 (978-0-89719-649-9(X)) Weston Woods.

Hey Diddle Diddle; Baby Bunting; Milkmaid, the; House That Jack Built, the; Old Mother Hubbard & Her Dog; Old Woman & Her Pig. 2004. (978-0-89719-809-7(3)); cass. & flmstrp (978-0-89719-718-2(6)) Weston Woods.

Hey Frank ... pass the Beans! Jack McCall. (ENG.). 2007. audio compact disk (978-0-9767676-2-6(7)) Bradford F.

Hey, Good Looking. abr. ed. Fern Michaels. Read by Laural Merlington. 2006. 14.95 (978-0-7435-5419-0(1), Audioworks) Pub: S&S Audio. Dist(s): S and S Inc

Hey, Good Looking. abr. ed. Fern Michaels. Read by Laural Merlington. (Running Time: 50 hrs. 0 mins. 0 sec.). (ENG.). 2008. audio compact disk 14.99 (978-0-7435-7238-5(6)) Pub: S&S Audio. Dist(s): S and S Inc

Hey, It's Franklin! 1 CD. (Running Time: 36 mins.). (J). (ps-2). 2000. audio compact disk 13.98 (978-0-7379-0161-0(6), R2 79974) Rhino Enter.
Traditional & original songs from the Franklin series.

Hey, It's Franklin! unabr. ed. 1 cass. (Running Time: 36 mins.). (J). (ps-2). 2000. 9.98 (978-0-7379-0160-3(8), R4 79973) Rhino Enter.

Hey, Kids! (10-lesson edition All-English version) Book 1 Student's Book (with CD) English Language Teaching. 2003. spiral bd. (978-0-7428-1051-8(8)) CCLS Pubg Hse.

Hey, Kids! (10-lesson edition All-English version) Book 2 Student's Book (with CD) English Language Teaching. 2003. spiral bd. (978-0-7428-1052-5(6)) CCLS Pubg Hse.

Hey, Kids! (10-lesson edition All-English version) Book 3 Student's Book (with CD) English Language Teaching. 2003. spiral bd. (978-0-7428-1053-2(4)) CCLS Pubg Hse.

Hey, Kids! (10-lesson edition All-English version) Book 4 Student's Book (with CD) English Language Teaching. 2003. spiral bd. (978-0-7428-1054-9(2)) CCLS Pubg Hse.

Hey, Kids! (10-lesson edition) Book 1 CD: English Language Teaching. 2003. audio compact disk (978-0-7428-0904-8(8)) CCLS Pubg Hse.

Hey, Kids! (10-lesson edition) Book 1 Student's Book (with CD) English Language Teaching. 2003. spiral bd. (978-0-7428-0913-0(7)) CCLS Pubg Hse.

Hey, Kids! (10-lesson edition) Book 2 CD: English Language Teaching. 2003. audio compact disk (978-0-7428-0905-5(6)) CCLS Pubg Hse.

Hey, Kids! (10-lesson edition) Book 2 Student's Book (with CD) English Language Teaching. 2003. spiral bd. (978-0-7428-0914-7(5)) CCLS Pubg Hse.

Hey, Kids! (10-lesson edition) Book 3 CD: English Language Teaching. 2003. audio compact disk (978-0-7428-0906-2(4)) CCLS Pubg Hse.

Hey, Kids! (10-lesson edition) Book 3 Student's Book (with CD) English Language Teaching. 2003. spiral bd. (978-0-7428-0915-4(3)) CCLS Pubg Hse.

Hey, Kids! (10-lesson edition) Book 4 CD: English Language Teaching. 2003. audio compact disk (978-0-7428-0907-9(2)) CCLS Pubg Hse.

Hey, Kids! (10-lesson edition) Book 4 Student's Book (with CD) English Language Teaching. 2003. spiral bd. (978-0-7428-0916-1(1)) CCLS Pubg Hse.

Hey, Kids! (8-lesson edition) Book 1 CD: English Language Teaching. 2003. audio compact disk (978-0-7428-0899-7(8)) CCLS Pubg Hse.

Hey, Kids! (8-lesson edition) Book 1 Student's Book (with CD) English Language Teaching. 2003. spiral bd. (978-0-7428-0908-6(0)) CCLS Pubg Hse.

Hey, Kids! (8-lesson edition) Book 2 CD: English Language Teaching. 2003. audio compact disk (978-0-7428-0900-0(5)) CCLS Pubg Hse.

Hey, Kids! (8-lesson edition) Book 2 Student's Book (with CD) English Language Teaching. 2003. spiral bd. (978-0-7428-0909-3(9)) CCLS Pubg Hse.

Hey, Kids! (8-lesson edition) Book 3 CD: English Language Teaching. 2003. audio compact disk (978-0-7428-0901-7(3)) CCLS Pubg Hse.

Hey, Kids! (8-lesson edition) Book 3 Student's Book (with CD) English Language Teaching. 2003. spiral bd. (978-0-7428-0910-9(2)) CCLS Pubg Hse.

Hey, Kids! (8-lesson edition) Book 4 CD: English Language Teaching. 2003. audio compact disk (978-0-7428-0902-4(1)) CCLS Pubg Hse.

Hey, Kids! (8-lesson edition) Book 4 Student's Book (with CD) English Language Teaching. 2003. spiral bd. (978-0-7428-0911-6(0)) CCLS Pubg Hse.

Hey, Look Me Over. 1997. audio compact disk 12.95 (978-0-7692-1624-9(2), Warner Bro) Alfred Pub.

Hey, Ludwig! Perf. by Ric Louchard. 1 cass., 1 CD. (Running Time: 51 min.). (J). 1993. 9.98 (978-1-56628-015-0(X), 42537); audio compact disk 15.98 CD. (978-1-56628-014-3(1), 42537D) MFLP CA.
Classical piano solos for playful times - energetic & warmhearted pieces where the composers let their own joy & playfulness stand out front.

Hey, New Kid! Betsy Duffey. Read by Johnny Heller. 1 cass. (Running Time: 1 hr. 15 mins.). (YA). 2000. pap. bk. 22.24 (978-0-7887-4173-9(X), 41093); 70.70 (978-0-7887-4174-6(8), 47086) Recorded Bks.
Cody's father is a secret agent for the F.B.I. & his mother is an American Gladiator. Cody himself is a plant expert, skates like a pro & has a pet emu. Well... not really. He's the new kid in third grade & he wants people to like him.

Hey, New Kid! unabr. ed. Betsy Duffey. Narrated by Johnny Heller. 1 cass. (Running Time: 1 hr. 15 mins.). (gr. 2 up). 2000. 10.00 (978-0-7887-4004-6(0), 96027E7) Recorded Bks.

Hey, Picasso. 1 CD. (Running Time: 40 mins.). 2004. audio compact disk 14.98 (978-1-57940-103-0(1)) Rounder Records.

Hezekiah Walker Live in London. Perf. by Love Fellowship Crusade Choir. 1997. 10.98; audio compact disk 15.98 CD. Brentwood Music.
Contemporary Gospel. Includes "If You Need a Friend," "To Be Like Jesus," "I Am Waiting," "Jesus Is My Help," & more.

HF Radio Systems & Circuits. 2nd rev. ed. Ed. by William E. Sabin & Edgar O. Schoenike. 1998. bk. 89.00 (978-1-884932-04-5(5), NoblePubng) SciTech Pub.

Hi, Cat! Ezra Jack Keats. 1 readalong cass. (Running Time: 5 min.). (J). 1990. pap. bk. 15.95 Live Oak Media.
Archie's temporary adoption of a cat while on his way to meet his pals proves to be the undoing of the show he plans to put on as the cat turns in its own spontaneous performance.

Hi, Cat! Ezra Jack Keats. 11 vols. (Running Time: 5 mins.). (J). (gr. k-3). 1990. pap. bk. 9.95 (978-0-87499-179-6(X)) Live Oak Media.

Hi, Cat! Ezra Jack Keats. Illus. by Ezra Jack Keats. (Running Time: 5 mins.). 1998. 9.95 (978-1-59112-059-9(4)) Live Oak Media.

Hi, Cat! unabr. ed. Ezra Jack Keats. Illus. by Ezra Jack Keats. Read by Jerry Terheyden. 11 vols. (Running Time: 5 mins.). (J). (gr. k-3). 1998. bk. 25.95 (978-0-87499-180-2(3)) Live Oak Media.
Befriending a stray cat proves to be the undoing of the impromptu street show Archie attempts to put on with his friend Peter.

Hi, Cat!, Set. Ezra Jack Keats. 11 vols. (Running Time: 5 mins.). (J). (gr. k-3). 1990. bk. & stu. ed. 33.95 incl. four books & guide to reading & language arts skills activities. (978-0-87499-181-9(1)) Live Oak Media.
Archie's temporary adoption of a cat while on his way to meet his pals proves to be the undoing of the show he plans to put on as the cat turns in its own spontaneous performance.

Hi Dad... Bye, Dad. Ed Young. 1990. 4.95 (978-0-7417-1806-8(5), 806) Win Walk.

Hi, Fly Guy. Tedd Arnold. (Fly Guy Ser.). (ENG.). (J). (ps-3). 2008. audio compact disk 18.95 (978-0-545-09139-8(X)) Scholastic Inc.

Hi Ho Librario! Songs, Chants, & Stories to Keep Kids Humming. Judy Freeman. 1 cass. (Running Time: 45 min.). (J). (gr. k-6). 1997. pap. bk. 34.95 (978-1-890604-02-8(X)) RockHill Comns.
Teaches children to love books & reading & to appreciate & use the library properly. Accompanying book links the pieces on the cassette to children's literature & gives tips for use in the classroom.

Hi, Kids! Audio CD: ELT - English Language Teaching. Waldyr Lima. 2003. audio compact disk (978-0-7428-0903-1(X)) CCLS Pubg Hse.

Hi Lo to Hollywood. unabr. ed. Max Evans. 4 cass. (Running Time: 6 hrs.). 2001. 25.00 (978-1-59040-100-2(X), Phoenix Audio) Pub: Amer Intl Pub. Dist(s): PerseuPGW

Hi-Tech Shaman at the Spiritual Olympics. E. J. Gold. 1 cass. (Running Time: 1 hr.). 15.00 (MT025) Union Label.
70s radio satire pieces including Enterview, panel with Reschad Feild & others, from Pacifica.

Hi Tops: the Musical. Prod. by Ernie Rettino & Debby Kerner Rettino. (Running Time: 1 hr. 28 mins.). (YA). (gr. 7-12). 2008. 9.99 (978-5-557-41362-6(6)) Maranatha Music.

Hiawatha. 2004. pap. bk. 32.75 (978-1-55592-241-2(4)); pap. bk. 14.95 (978-0-7882-0666-5(4)); 8.95 (978-0-7882-0060-1(7)); cass. & flmstrp 30.00 (978-0-89719-598-0(1)) Weston Woods.

Hiawatha. Henry Wadsworth Longfellow. Illus. by Susan Jeffers. 1 cass., 5 bks. (Running Time: 8 min.). (J). pap. bk. 32.75 Weston Woods.
The beautiful tradition of The American Indian is captured in the story of Hiawatha's boyhood.

Hiawatha. Henry Wadsworth Longfellow. 1 cass. (Running Time: 8 min.). (J). (gr. k-6). 1989. 8.95 (978-0-89719-997-1(9), RAC338) Weston Woods.

Hiawatha. Henry Wadsworth Longfellow. Illus. by Susan Jeffers. 1 cass. (Running Time: 8 min.). (J). (gr. k-6). 1989. bk. 24.95 (978-1-56008-015-2(9), HRA338); pap. bk. 12.95 (PRA338) Weston Woods.

Hiawatha. unabr. ed. Henry Wadsworth Longfellow. 3 CDs. audio compact disk 22.98 (978-962-634-340-1(0), NA334012) Naxos.

Hiccup: How to Train Your Dragon. unabr. ed. Cressida Cowell. Narrated by Gerard Doyle. 4 cass. (Running Time: 4 hrs. 30 mins.). (J). 2005. 37.75 (978-1-4193-2947-0(2), 97970) Recorded Bks.
Author Cressida Cowell has written several warmly received books for children. Booklist calls How to Train Your Dragon a "wildly enjoyable comic fantasy." Hiccup Horrendous Haddock III may be the son of the brave leader of the mighty Viking tribe the Hairy Hooligans, but he certainly doesn't feel very heroic. When Hiccup and the other boys his age are challenged to pick baby dragons from the dragon nursery, Hiccup actually manages to catch a small one. But now how will he train his stubborn new pet?.

Hickle the Pickle. Josephine A. Smith. Read by Josephine A. Smith. 1 cass. (Running Time: 24 min.). (J). (gr. 1-3). 1992. pap. bk. 5.00 (978-1-881958-08-6(6)) Hickle Pickle.
Read out loud story, Hickle the Pickle, the cover will also have the title in braille for the blind.

Hickory B Hopp Cassette. Stephen Cosgrove. 2004. 5.00 (978-1-58804-393-1(2)) PCI Educ.

Hickory Dickory Dock. Agatha Christie. Read by Hugh Fraser. (Running Time: 21840 sec.). (Hercule Poirot Mystery Ser.). 2006. 27.95 (978-1-57270-565-4(5)) Pub: Audio Partners. Dist(s): PerseuPGW

Hickory Dickory Dock. unabr. ed. Agatha Christie. Narrated by Hugh Fraser. 5 CDs. (Running Time: 21840 sec.). (Hercule Poirot Mystery Ser.). (ENG.). 2006. audio compact disk 27.95 (978-1-57270-564-7(7)) Pub: AudioGO. Dist(s): Perseus Dist

Hickory Dickory Dock; or, Go, Mouse, Go! Audio CD. Adapted by Benchmark Education Company Staff. Based on a work by Jeffrey B. Fuerst. (Reader's Theater Nursery Rhymes & Songs Ser.). (J). (gr. k-1). 2008. audio compact disk 10.00 (978-1-60437-984-6(7)) Benchmark Educ.

Hickory, Dickory, Dock/Jack & Jill. Created by Steck-Vaughn Staff. (Running Time: 302 sec.). (Primary Take-Me-Home Books Level K Ser.). 1998. 9.80 (978-0-8172-8653-8(5)) SteckVau.

Hidden. unabr. ed. Steven Savile. Narrated by Naoko Mori. (Running Time: 2 hrs. 30 mins. 0 sec.). (ENG.). 2010. audio compact disk 24.95 (978-1-60283-827-7(5)) Pub: AudioGO. Dist(s): Perseus Dist

***Hidden: Sisters of the Heart series, Book 1.** unabr. ed. Shelley Shepard Gray. Read by Kirsten Potter. (Running Time: 8 hrs.). (Sisters of the Heart Ser.: Bk. 1). 2010. 29.95 (978-1-4417-7088-2(7)); 34.95 (978-1-4417-7085-1(2)); audio compact disk 55.00 (978-1-4417-7086-8(0)) Blckstn Audio.

Hidden Agenda. Norman Dodd. Read by Norman Dodd. 1 cass. 1998. (978-0-912986-26-5(3)) Am Media.

Hidden Agendas. Tom Clancy. Read by Steve Pieczenik. 4 cass. (Running Time: 4 hrs.). (Tom Clancy's Net Force Ser.). (YA). 1998. (978-1-84032-156-2(3), HoddrStoughton) Hodder General GBR.
A team of highly trained operatives whose homeground is the Virtual Reality world of the Net.

Hidden Agendas. Tom Clancy. Read by Kerry Shale. (Running Time: 3 hrs.). (Tom Clancy's Net Force Ser.). (YA). (gr. 5-8). 1999. (978-1-84032-161-6(X), HoddrStoughton) Hodder General GBR.
It is 2010 & the Internet has become the world's central nervous system. If terrorists are going to subvert the New World order, this is where they will strike. A new organization is therefore needed, to deter them.

Hidden Agendas, Set. abr. ed. Tom Clancy. Read by Kerry Shale. 4 cass. (Tom Clancy's Net Force Ser.). (YA). 1999. 24.00 (FS9-51093) Highsmith.

Hidden Answers Revealed Through Prayer of Tongues. Creflo A. Dollar. 30.00 (978-1-59089-037-0(X)) Pub: Creflo Dollar. Dist(s): STL Dist NA

Hidden Aspects in the Horoscopes. William Henry. 1 cass. 8.95 (152) Am Fed Astrologers.
New techniques to analyze natal, progressed and directed chart.

Hidden Aspects of Today's Inflation. unabr. ed. Ludwig M. Lachman. 1 cass. (Running Time: 34 min.). (Symposium on the Geographical Aspects of Inflation Ser.: No. 1). 12.95 (461) J Norton Pubs.

Hidden Assassins. Robert Wilson. Read by Sean Barrett. 14 cass. (Running Time: 65400 sec.). (Isis Cassettes Ser.). 2007. 99.95 (978-0-7531-3650-8(3)); audio compact disk 109.95 (978-0-7531-2616-5(8)) Pub: ISIS Lrg Prnt GBR. Dist(s): Ulverscroft US

Hidden Beauty. unabr. ed. Tessa Barclay. Read by Anne Dover. 18 cass. (Running Time: 24 hrs.). 1999. 109.95 (978-1-86042-562-2(3), 25623) Pub: Soundings Ltd GBR. Dist(s): Ulverscroft US
Corie Duggan is the mainstay of a stage-struck family, but she turns her back on the theatre to become a famous photographer. Her sister Beryl becomes "Lynette Lee," one of the first TV sweethearts, but at great cost in health & emotional well-being. Misled by passion Corie makes a mistake when she allows herself to be involved with Sasha Lenoir, her sister's ambitious & selfish agent. Lynette has innocently given her heart to Sasha so Corie must end their affair. She goes abroad, meeting Drew Richter, an American public relations consultant. Lynette becomes seriously ill but begs Corie to help keep it secret so that her career won't be ended.

Hidden Church of the Holy Grail. Instructed by Manly P. Hall. 8.95 (978-0-89314-136-3(4), C711219) Philos Res.

Hidden Cost of Mental Illness: Program from the award winning public radio Series. Interview. Hosted by Fred Goodwin. Comment by John Hockenberry. 1 CD. (Running Time: 1hr). (Infinite Mind Ser.). 2002. audio compact disk 21.95 (978-1-888064-80-3(3), LCM 218) Lichtenstein Creat.
What are the hidden costs of mental illnesses? In recent weeks, the White House and Capitol Hill have weighed the potential benefits and costs of requiring health insurers to provide treatment for psychiatric disorders. This week on "The Infinite Mind" we turn to the cost of NOT treating them. Dr. Peter Kramer guest hosts this program for the vacationing Dr. Fred Goodwin. Guests include Ronald Kessler, a sociologist at the Harvard Medical School Department of Health Care Policy; Paul Greenberg, an economist at the Analysis Group in Cambridge, Massachusetts; and Dr. Greg Simon of Seattle's pioneering Group Health Cooperative. And sharing a front-line view of the frequent intersections between untreated psychiatric illnesses and hospital emergency rooms are Dr. Herbert Pardes, president and chief executive officer of the New York Presbyterian Hospital; and Dr. David Goldschmitt, who runs the emergency room at New York University Downtown Hospital. Commentary by John Hockenberry.

Hidden Degrees. Rose Cosentino. 1 cass. (Running Time: 90 min.). 1990. 8.95 (868) Am Fed Astrologers.

Hidden Depths. unabr. ed. Joyce Holms. Read by James Bryce. 7 cass. (Running Time: 32400 sec.). (Soundings Ser.). 2006. 61.95 (978-1-84559-181-6(X)) Pub: ISIS Lrg Prnt GBR. Dist(s): Ulverscroft US

Hidden Diary of Marie Antoinette. Carolly Erickson. Read by Carrington MacDuffie. 7 cass. 59.95 (978-0-7927-3772-8(5), CSL 852); audio compact disk 89.95 (978-0-7927-3773-5(3), SLD 852); audio compact disk 29.95 (978-0-7927-3841-1(1), CMP 852) AudioGO.

Hidden Diary of Marie Antoinette. abr. ed. Carolly Erickson. Read by Maggi-Meg Reed. 2005. 14.95 (978-1-59397-830-3(8)) Pub: Macmill Audio. Dist(s): Macmillan

Hidden Empire. Kevin J. Anderson. Narrated by George Guidall. 14 cass. (Running Time: 20 hrs. 15 mins.). (Saga of Seven Suns Ser.: Bk. 1). 126.00 (978-1-4025-2404-2(8)) Recorded Bks.

Hidden Empire. unabr. ed. Kevin J. Anderson. Narrated by George Guidall. 14 cass. (Running Time: 20 hrs. 15 mins.). (Saga of Seven Suns Ser.: Bk. 1). 2002. 57.95 (978-1-4025-2405-9(6), RG093) Recorded Bks.
Hidden Empire is the fist volume in The Saga of the Seven Suns, modeled after the Star Wars and X-Files universes. Anderson has become the foremost science fiction writer of the century, bringing to life vivid characters and worlds that delight his fans across the galaxy. The Klikiss, a now extinct alien civilization, left behind vast technological information that has been discovered by two xenoarchaeologists. One discovery, a device that converts gas planets into life-giving suns is quickly put to the test with unimaginable results. Arising out of the test is a new alien species that threatens every human. Mankind is left with the dim reality-either fight the new alien life form or face humiliation, death and extinction. This riveting adventure swings you from one wonderous realm to another as the Hidden Empire is sought after and exposed.

Hidden Empire. unabr. ed. Orson Scott Card. Read by Orson Scott Card. Read by Rusty Humphries & Stefan Rudnicki. (Running Time: 9 hrs. 0 mins. 0 sec.). No. 2. 2009. audio compact disk 39.99 (978-1-4272-0777-7(1)) Pub: Macmill Audio. Dist(s): Macmillan

***Hidden Empire.** unabr. ed. Orson Scott Card. Read by Orson Scott Card. Read by Stefan Rudnicki & Rusty Humphries. 8 CDs. (Running Time: 9 hrs.). 2009. 89.95 (978-0-7927-6622-3(9)) AudioGO.

Hidden Flame. abr. ed. Janette Oke & Davis Bunn. Narrated by Aimee Lilly. (Running Time: 7 hrs. 0 mins. 57 sec.). (Acts of Faith Ser.). (ENG.). 2009. 18.19 (978-1-60814-593-5(X)); audio compact disk 25.99 (978-1-59859-641-0(1)) Oasis Audio.

Hidden Gospel. Neil Douglas-Klotz. 3 CDs. (Running Time: 2 hrs 45 mins). 2005. audio compact disk 24.95 (978-1-59179-371-7(8), AW00429D) Sounds True.
If we could travel back to the world of ancient Palestine and hear Jesus teach in his native tongue, what would we learn? On The Hidden Gospel, listeners join Neil Douglas-Klotz, the brilliant translator and bestselling author of Prayers of the Cosmos (over 100,000 sold), as he delves into early New Testament scriptures written in Aramaic - the original language of Jesus and his followers. Overlooked for centuries by all but a small minority of the world's Christians, these sacred texts reveal a very different Christ, long shrouded by the veils of language and time. Now, through years of passionate scholarship, Neil Douglas-Klotz revives the teachings of Jesus as we have never heard them before - and shows us meditations to interpret and reflect on these words just as the early Christians did. What we will discover hidden within these scriptures may surprise many - a visionary Christ who transcends the narrow constructs of good and evil to offer us a grand cosmology based on the earthy wisdom of a desert people.

Hidden Grail: Sir Percival & the Fisher King. abr. ed. Read by Odds Bodkin Storytelling Library Staff. 2 CDs. (Running Time: 1 hr. 30 mins.). Dramatization. (Odds Bodkin Musical Story Collection). (J). (gr. 2 up). 2003. bk. 24.95 (978-1-882412-25-9(7)) Pub: Rivertree. Dist(s): Penton Overseas
This classic Arthurian legend of knights in armor contains character voices & music on 12 string guitar & grand Celtic harp.

Hidden Grail: Sir Percival & the Fisher King. abr. ed. Read by Odds Bodkin Storytelling Library Staff. 2 cass. (Running Time: 1 hrs. 30 mins.). Dramatization. (Odds Bodkin Musical Story Collection). (gr. 2 up). 2003. bk. 18.95 (978-1-882412-26-6(5)) Pub: Rivertree. Dist(s): Penton Overseas

Hidden Heresy. Jim Craddock. Read by Jim Craddock. 1 cass. (Running Time: 43 min.). (ICEL Three Ser.). 1996. 6.00 (978-1-57838-051-0(0)) CrossLife Express.
Biblical doctrine.

Hidden Hindrances. Elbert Willis. 1 cass. (Prosperity Insights Ser.). 4.00 Fill the Gap.

Hidden History. unabr. ed. Melody Carlson. Narrated by Sherri Berger. (Running Time: 6 hrs. 30 mins. 12 sec.). (Grace Chapel Inn Ser.). (ENG.). 2009. 18.19 (978-1-60814-475-4(5)); audio compact disk 25.99 (978-1-59859-557-4(1)) Oasis Audio.

Hidden in God. Lori Wilke. 1 cass. 1992. 7.00 (978-1-56043-902-8(5)) Destiny Image Pubs.

Hidden in His Hands. 1985. (0203) Evang Sisterhood Mary.

Hidden in Plain View. abr. ed. Blair S. Walker. Read by Eric Jerome Dickey. 4 cass. 2001. 12.99 (978-1-57815-207-0(0), Media Bks Audio) Media Bks NJ.

Hidden in Plain View. abr. ed. Blair S. Walker. Read by Eric Jerome Dickey. 4 cass. (Running Time: 6 hrs.). 1999. 24.95 (978-1-57511-061-5(X)) Pub Mills.
Reporter Darryl Billups puts himself in harm's way while investigating a string of racially motivated murders.

Hidden Kitchens: Stories & More from NPR's the Kitchen Sisters with Jay Allison. abr. ed. Davia Nelson & Nikki Silva. Told to Jay Allison. Afterword by Alice Waters. 5 CDs. (Running Time: 3 hrs. 0 mins. 0 sec.). (ENG.). 2005. audio compact disk 19.95 (978-1-59397-833-4(2)) Pub: Macmill Audio. Dist(s): Macmillan

Hidden Life. unabr. ed. Adele Geras. Narrated by Maggie Mash. (Running Time: 16 hrs. 15 mins.). 2009. 61.75 (978-1-4407-0993-7(9), Clipper Audio); audio compact disk 123.75 (978-1-4361-9231-6(5), Clipper Audio) Recorded Bks.

Hidden Life. unabr. collector's ed. Adele Geras. Narrated by Maggie Mash. 14 CDs. (Running Time: 16 hrs. 15 mins.). 2009. audio compact disk 69.95 (978-1-4361-9232-3(3), Clipper Audio) Recorded Bks.

Hidden Life of Dogs. abr. ed. Elizabeth Marshall Thomas. 2006. 14.98 (978-1-59483-762-3(7)) Pub: Hachet Audio. Dist(s): HachBkGrp

Hidden Life of Dogs, unabr. ed. Elizabeth Marshall Thomas. Narrated by Barbara Caruso. 3 cass. (Running Time: 3 hrs. 45 mins.). 1994. 26.00 (978-0-7887-0028-6(6), 94227E7) Recorded Bks.
Thomas' best-selling study, spanning 30 years & including chapters on dingoes & wolves, provides a picture of dog life that goes way beyond the tail-wagging canine most of us think of.

Hidden Magic. Vivian Vande Velde. 2 cass. (J). 13.58 Set, blisterpack. (BYA 957) NewSound.
Jennifer is a princess who had the misfortune of falling in love with Prince Alexander who is both very handsome - & very conceited.

Hidden Magic. unabr. ed. Vivian Vande Velde. Read by Full Cast Production Staff. 2 cass. (J). (gr. 1-8). 1999. 23.00 (LL 0116, Chivers Child Audio) AudioGO.

Hidden Magic. unabr. ed. Vivian Vande Velde. Perf. by Words Take Wing Repertory Company Staff. 2 cass. (Running Time: 2 hrs. 27 min.). (J). (gr. 5 up). 1998. pap. bk. 21.98 (978-0-8072-7972-4(2), YA957SP, Listening Lib); 16.98 (978-0-8072-7971-7(4), 396012, Listening Lib) Random Audio Pubg.
Jennifer & Alexander enter the enchanted forest & must contend with a witch, a giant, a dragon & an evil enchantress. Norman, a sorcerer helps them, & they discover they need all the help they can get before this adventure is over.

Hidden Magic, Set. unabr. ed. Vivian Vande Velde. 2 cass. (YA). 1999. 16.98 (FS9-34628) Highsmith.

Hidden Man. Michael Underwood. Read by Judith Franklyn. 5 cass. (Running Time: 7 hrs. 30 min.). 1999. 49.95 (65476) Pub: Soundings Ltd GBR. Dist(s): Ulverscroft US

Hidden Man. unabr. ed. David Ellis. Read by Luke Daniels. (Running Time: 11 hrs.). 2009. 24.99 (978-1-4233-7927-0(6), 9781423379270, Brilliance MP3); 24.99 (978-1-4233-7929-4(2), 9781423379294, BAD); 39.97 (978-1-4233-7928-7(4), 9781423379287, Brinc Audio MP3 Lib); 39.97 (978-1-4233-7930-0(6), 9781423379300, BADLE); audio compact disk 79.97 (978-1-4233-7926-3(8), 9781423379263, BriAudCD Unabrid); audio compact disk 29.99 (978-1-4233-7925-6(X), 9781423379256, Bril Audio CD Unabri) Brilliance Audio.

Hidden Man. unabr. ed. Michael Underwood. Read by Judith Franklyn. 5 cass. (Sound Ser.). 2004. 49.95 (978-1-85496-547-9(6)) Pub: UlverLrgPrint GBR. Dist(s): Ulverscroft US

Hidden Man: An Unveiling of the Subconscious Mind. E. W. Kenyon. Read by Stephen Sobozenski. 6 Cass. (Running Time: 420 Min.). 2001. 28.00 (978-1-57770-028-9(7)) Kenyons Gospel.
A study of the Recreated Human Spirit.

Hidden Masks of Anger. unabr. ed. Lynne Logan. Read by Lynne Logan. 1 cass. (Running Time: 1 hrs.). 1995. 11.00 (978-1-890907-03-7(0), 0004) Heaven Only.
Anger & how it affects our lives, relationships, physical & well-being. How to resolve anger & achieve forgiveness.

Hidden Messages. Maxine Taylor. 1 cass. 8.95 (338) Am Fed Astrologers.
Discover programming messages given by parents.

Hidden Messages of the Decanates. Glenda Tomosovich. 1 cass. 8.95 (348) Am Fed Astrologers.
Understanding through planet & cusp decans.

Hidden Paycheck: Employer Sales Presentation. abr. ed. Robert A. Robinson. Read by H. Paul Springer & J. P. Daiu. Ed. by John Campbell. 1 cass. (Running Time: 28 min.). (ECA Benefit Communications Ser.). 1991. pap. bk. 10.95 (978-1-884780-08-0(3)) Phoenix Pubng.
Instructional audio cassette of insurance sales presentation for selling payroll deduction plans of insurance.

Hidden Personalities of the Chart. Ginger Chalford. 1 cass. (Running Time: 90 min.). 1984. 8.95 (047) Am Fed Astrologers.

Hidden Places. Lynn Austin. Narrated by Ruth Ann Phimister. 11 cass. (Running Time: 15 hrs.). 2002. 94.00 (978-1-4025-4415-6(4)) Recorded Bks.

Hidden Poetry of the Jewish Prayerbook: The What, How & Why of Jewish Liturgy. Speeches. Reuven Kimelman. Voice by Reuven Kimelman. Concept by Sergiu Simmel. Prod. by Sergiu Simmel. Des. by Joanne Franklin. Engineer David Sparr. 10 CDs. (Running Time: 10.5 hrs). (ENG & HEB., 2005. bk. 225.00 (978-0-9769330-0-7(4)) O Learn Co.

Hidden Poetry of the Jewish Prayerbook: The What, How & Why of Jewish Liturgy. Reuven Kimelman. Ed. by Sergiu Simmel. Engineer David Sparr. (ENG, HEB & ARC.). 2006. bk. 100.00 (978-0-9769330-1-4(2)) O Learn Co.

Hidden Power. Judith Cutler. Narrated by Patricia Gallimore. 7 cass. (Running Time: 10 hrs. 15 mins.). 2002. 67.00 (978-1-84197-424-8(2)) Recorded Bks.

Hidden Power. James K. Van Fleet. 1 cass. 10.00 (SP100072) SMI Intl.
How to tap the unlimited, infinite, & inexhaustible power of your subconscious mind to reach your desired goals. Learn the techniques to gain greater wealth, enjoy better health, improve personal relationships & achieve spiritual goals.

Hidden Power. Ben Young. 2000. 4.95 (978-0-7417-6162-0(9), B0162) Win Walk.

Hidden Power: Presidential Marriages That Shaped Our Recent History. abr. ed. Kati Marton. Read by Jane Alexander. 3 cass. (Running Time: 5 hrs.). 2001. 25.00 (Random AudioBks) Random Audio Pubg.

Hidden Power of Humility CD Series. 2007. audio compact disk 19.99 (978-1-933185-15-6(5)) Messengr Intl.

Hidden Powers. Colin Wilson. 2 cass. 18.00 (OC93) Sound Horizons AV.

Hidden Prey. abr. ed. John Sandford, pseud. 5 CDs. (Running Time: 6 hrs.). (ENG.). (gr. 8). 2005. audio compact disk 12.95 (978-0-14-305775-8(8), PengAudBks) Penguin Grp USA.

Hidden Prey. unabr. ed. John Sandford, pseud. Read by Richard Ferrone. 11 CDs. (Running Time: 12 hrs. 25 mins.). (Prey Ser.). 2004. audio compact disk 109.75 (978-1-4025-8825-9(9)); 89.75 (978-1-4025-8823-5(2)) Recorded Bks.
Now a statewide troubleshooter, Detective Lucas Davenport is plunged into a murder investigation that involves a Russian corpse, 50-year-old bullets, and some high-level government connections.

Hidden Prince. Retold by Jeffrey E. Burkart. (J). 2003. bk. 9.99 (978-0-570-07174-7(7)) Concordia.

Hidden Profits in Mobile Home Investing: How a Real Estate Investor Stumbled on to the Lucrative World of Mobile Home Investing! Speeches. Jerry Hoganson. (Running Time: 46 mins). 2006. audio compact disk 13.95 (978-1-933723-04-4(1)) Ascend Beyond Pubng.

***Hidden Reality: Parallel Universes & the Deep Laws of the Cosmos.** abr. unabr. ed. Brian Greene. (ENG.). 2011. audio compact disk 45.00 (978-0-7393-8352-0(3), Random AudioBks) Pub: Random Audio Pubg. Dist(s): Random

Hidden Riches. abr. ed. Nora Roberts. Read by Sandra Burr. 3 CDs. (Running Time: 3 hrs.). 2004. audio compact disk 14.99 (978-1-59600-105-3(4), 1596001054) Brilliance Audio.
When Dora Conroy, a Philadelphia antiques dealer, purchases a curious selection of auction items - objects she judges to be humorous novelties, she unknowingly becomes the deadly focus of an international smuggler. When robberies and death surround her merchandise, Dora seeks help from her intriguing upstairs tenant, former cop Jed Skimmerhorn. They discover a shadowy path leading across the continent to the smuggler, a man who will stop at nothing to recover his hidden riches. Like the treasures he craves, Dora and Jed find they are susceptible to his crushing grasp.

Hidden Riches. abr. ed. Nora Roberts. Read by Sandra Burr. 2 cass. (Running Time: 3 hrs.). 2000. 7.95 (978-1-57815-011-3(6), 1004, Media Bks Audio) Media Bks NJ.
An antique dealer becomes the deadly focus of an international smuggler in a jewel of romantic suspense where precious treasures are masked in tawdry disguises & the price tags are written in blood.

Hidden Riches. unabr. ed. Nora Roberts. Read by Sandra Burr. (Running Time: 14 hrs.). 2004. 24.95 (978-1-59335-800-6(8), 1593358008, Brilliance MP3); 39.25 (978-1-59335-934-8(9), 1593359349, Brlnc Audio MP3 Lib); 29.95 (978-1-59600-104-6(6), 1596001046) Brilliance Audio.
When Dora Conroy, a Philadelphia antiques dealer, purchases a curious selection of auction items - objects she judges to be humorous novelties, she unknowingly becomes the deadly focus of an international smuggler. When robberies and death surround her merchandise, Dora seeks help from her intriguing upstairs tenant, former cop Jed Skimmerhorn. They discover a shadowy path leading across the continent to the smuggler, a man who will stop at nothing to recover his hidden riches. Like the treasures he craves, Dora and Jed find they are susceptible to his crushing grasp.

Hidden Riches. unabr. ed. Nora Roberts. Read by Sandra Burr. (Running Time: 14 hrs.). 2004. 39.25 (978-1-59710-362-6(4), 1597103624, BADLE); 24.95 (978-1-59710-363-3(2), 1597103632, BAD) Brilliance Audio.

Hidden Riches. unabr. ed. Nora Roberts. Read by Sandra Burr. (Running Time: 50400 sec.). 2008. audio compact disk 112.25 (978-1-4233-5602-8(0), 9781423356028, BriAudCD Unabrid); audio compact disk 38.95 (978-1-4233-5601-1(2), 9781423356011, Bril Audio CD Unabri) Brilliance Audio.

Hidden River. unabr. ed. Adrian McKinty. 9 cass. (Running Time: 12 hrs. 30 mins.). 2005. 72.95 (978-0-7861-2847-1(X), 3377); audio compact disk 90.00 (978-0-7861-8330-2(6), 3377) Blckstn Audio.

Hidden River. unabr. ed. Adrian McKinty. Read by Gerard Doyle. 20 cass. (Running Time: 10 hrs.). 2005. reel tape 29.95 (978-0-7861-2885-3(2), E3377); audio compact disk 29.95 (978-0-7861-8363-0(2), 3377); audio compact disk 29.95 (978-0-7861-8291-6(1), ZE3377) Blckstn Audio.

Hidden Staircase. abr. ed. Carolyn Keene. Read by Laura Linney. 2 cass. (Running Time: 3 hrs. 12 mins.). (Nancy Drew Mystery Stories: Vol. 2). (J). (gr. 4-7). 2004. 23.00 (978-0-8072-0758-1(6), Listening Lib) Random Audio Pubg.
Nancy Drew is out to solve the mysterious happenings at an old stone mansion.

Hidden Staircase. unabr. ed. Carolyn Keene. Read by Laura Linney. (Running Time: 11520 sec.). (Nancy Drew Ser.). (ENG.). (J). (gr. 3-7). 2007. audio compact disk 14.95 (978-0-7393-5058-4(7), Listening Lib) Pub: Random Audio Pubg. Dist(s): Random

Hidden Talents. unabr. collector's ed. Jayne Ann Krentz. Read by Mary Peiffer. 8 cass. (Running Time: 12 hrs.). 1996. 64.00 (978-0-7366-3448-9(7), 4092) Books on Tape.
When Serenity's accountant saves her business - & her life - she sees him in a whole new light.

Hidden Treasure. Stephen Bly. Narrated by L. J. Ganser. 7 CDs. (Running Time: 7 hrs. 30 mins.). 2000. audio compact disk 69.00 (978-1-4025-3811-7(1)) Recorded Bks.

Hidden Treasure. Hull Bunny. Read by Elayne J. Taylor. Illus. by Kye Fleming. 1 CD. (Running Time: 23 mins.). (Young Masters Ser.). (J). (ps). 2007. bk. 13.95 (978-0-9721478-8-0(8)) BrassHeart.

Hidden Treasure. Mark Hanby. 2 cass. 1995. 14.00 Set. (978-1-56043-887-8(8)) Destiny Image Pubs.

Hidden Treasure 2: The Skinners of Goldfield. Stephen Bly. Narrated by L. J. Ganser. 6 cass. (Running Time: 7 hrs. 30 mins.). 54.00 (978-1-4025-1770-9(X)) Recorded Bks.

Hidden Treasures. Dave Arnold et al. Prod. by Focus on the Family Staff. 4 CDs. (Running Time: 6 hrs.). (Adventures in Odyssey Ser.: Vol. 32). (ENG.). (J). 2004. audio compact disk 24.99 (978-1-56179-748-6(0)) Pub: Focus Family. Dist(s): Tyndale Hse

Hidden Treasures. Gloria Copeland. 2006. audio compact disk (978-1-57562-835-6(X)) K Copeland Pubns.

Hidden Treasures. abr. ed. Leigh Keno et al. (ENG.). 2005. 14.98 (978-1-59483-448-6(2)) Pub: Hachet Audio. Dist(s): HachBkGrp

Hidden Treasures: Heaven's Astonishing Help with Your Money Matters. Leslie Householder. Read by Leslie Householder. (ENG.). 2007. audio compact disk 29.95 (978-0-9765310-5-0(4)) Thoughts A.

Hidden Treasures: Short Stories by Relatively Obscure Authors. Short Stories. Ed. by Gary Gabriel. 1 cass. (Running Time: 60 min.). (Audio-Drama Ser.: Vol. 6). 14.95 Lend-A-Hand Soc.

***Hidden Truth.** unabr. ed. Dawn Cook. Read by Marguerite Gavin. (Running Time: 12 hrs. 15 mins.). 2010. 29.95 (978-1-4417-5403-5(2)); audio compact disk 29.95 (978-1-4417-5402-8(4)) Blckstn Audio.

Hidden Victory: A Historical Novel of Jesus. unabr. ed. Herbert F. Smith. Narrated by Richard Ferrone. 17 CDs. (Running Time: 19 hrs. 45 min.). 2003. audio compact disk 160.00 (978-1-4025-6936-4(X)) Recorded Bks.
Hidden Victory can be approached as revelation, as history, and as adventure. Solidly rooted in the four gospels, it also draws on contemporary theological studies of Christ. Historically based details of Biblical culture mix with fictional conversations and minor characters to create a full panorama of the world Jesus inhabited. Saint John described Jesus as a rich mine of treasures. This novel does indeed dig deep into the character of Christ. From the opening chapter, as Jesus contemplates death, to the final powerful image, Hidden Victory puts the listener by Jesus' side as he fulfills his Father's will on earth.

Hidden Victory: A Novel of Jesus. Herbert F. Smith. Narrated by Richard Ferrone. 14 cass. (Running Time: 19 hrs. 45 mins.). 114.00 (978-1-4025-2182-9(0)) Recorded Bks.

Hidden Ways to Wealth. Lynn M. Scheurell. Created by Fracka Future. (ENG.). 2009. audio compact disk (978-0-9801550-6-8(1)) Mizrahi Press.

***Hidden Wholeness: The Journey Toward an Undivided Life.** Parker J. Palmer. Read by Stefan Rudnicki. (Playaway Adult Nonfiction Ser.). (ENG.). 2010. 59.99 (978-1-4417-0238-8(5)) Find a World.

Hidden Wholeness: The Journey toward an Undivided Life. unabr. ed. Parker J. Palmer. (Running Time: 9 hrs. 0 mins.). (ENG.). 2009. 59.95 (978-1-4417-0231-9(8)); audio compact disk 90.00 (978-1-4417-0232-6(6)) Blckstn Audio.

Hidden Wholeness: The Journey toward an Undivided Life. unabr. ed. Parker J. Palmer. (Running Time: 9 hrs. 30 mins.). 2010. 29.95 (978-1-4417-0235-7(0)) Blckstn Audio.

Hidden Wholeness: The Journey toward an Undivided Life. unabr. ed. Parker J. Palmer. Read by Stefan Rudnicki. (Running Time: 9 hrs. 30 mins.). 2010. audio compact disk 34.95 (978-1-4417-0234-0(2)) Blckstn Audio.

Hidden Wisdom: Corinthians 1. Ben Young. 2000. 4.95 (978-0-7417-6163-7(7), B0163) Win Walk.

Hidden Wisdom: The Ancient Meaning of the Dead Sea Scrolls. Kenneth Hanson. 4 CDs. (Running Time: 14280 sec.). (Explorer Ser.). 2003. audio compact disk 19.95 (978-0-9707422-5-4(8)) Reel Prodns.
It was one of the greatest discoveries in history. In 1947 a Bedouin shepherd boy uncovered an entire library of ancient scrolls that had remained hidden in a desert cave near the dead sea for nearly 2000 years.The story of the Dead Sea Scrolls is a tale of discovery, adventure, intrigue and faith.But what truths do they contain? What do they mean for us today?.

Hidden Wounds: Matt. 26:20-25; 47-50. Ed Young. 1987. 4.95 (978-0-7417-1590-6(2), 590) Win Walk.

Hidden Years. Neil Boyd. Read by Andrea Star et al. 3 cass. (Running Time: 3 hrs. 10 min.). Dramatization. (YA). (gr. 9 up). 1987. 24.95 (978-0-89622-343-1(4)) Twenty-Third.
A fictional dramatic telling of the life of Jesus before his ministry.

Hide. Contrib. by Joy Williams. (Mastertrax Ser.). 2005. audio compact disk 9.98 (978-5-558-93071-9(3)) Pt of Grace Ent.

Hide. abr. ed. Lisa Gardner. Read by Maggie-Meg Reed. (Running Time: 18000 sec.). (ENG.). 2008. audio compact disk 14.99 (978-0-7393-5823-8(5)) Pub: Random Audio Pubg. Dist(s): Random

Hide. unabr. ed. Lisa Gardner. 7 cass. (Running Time: 10 hrs.). 2007. 70.00 (978-1-4159-3703-7(6)); audio compact disk 90.00 (978-1-4159-3550-7(5)) Books on Tape.

Hide. unabr. ed. Lisa Gardner. Read by Maggie-Meg Reed. 9 CDs. (Running Time: 11 hrs.). (ENG.). 2007. audio compact disk 39.95 (978-0-7393-2154-6(4)) Pub: Random Audio Pubg. Dist(s): Random

Hide & Die. unabr. ed. Stella Whitelaw. Read by Julia Franklin. 7 cass. 2007. 61.95 (978-1-84559-288-2(3)) Pub: ISIS Audio GBR. Dist(s): Ulverscroft US

Hide & Seek. 1999. (978-1-57042-736-7(4)) Hachet Audio.

Hide & Seek. Swami Amar Jyoti. 1 cass. 1979. 9.95 (R-20) Truth Consciousness.
Our game of hiding under the blanket. Light is everywhere, all is Brahma. On awakening & unfoldment. It is not beyond but within us.

***Hide & Seek.** Jack Ketchum. Read by Wayne June. 1 MP3-CD. (Running Time: 6 mins.). 2009. 19.95 (978-1-897331-09-5(6), AudioRealms) Dorch Pub Co.

Hide & Seek. Fern Michaels. Read by Laural Merlington. (Sisterhood Ser.: No. 10). 2008. 69.99 (978-1-60640-593-2(4)) Find a World.

Hide & Seek. abr. ed. Fern Michaels. Read by Laural Merlington. (Running Time: 3 hrs.). (Sisterhood Ser.: No. 10). 2008. audio compact disk 14.99 (978-1-4233-4484-1(7), 9781423344841, BCD Value Price) Brilliance Audio.

Hide & Seek. unabr. ed. Wilkie Collins. Read by Flo Gibson. 10 cass. (Running Time: 14 hrs. 30 min.). (YA). (gr. 10 up). 1998. 44.95 (978-1-55685-578-8(8)) Audio Bk Con.
The mystery of the beautiful deaf-mute Mary Grice's (or Madonna's) origins unravel with pathos & humor & with a series of unforgettable characters.

Hide & Seek. unabr. ed. Jack Ketchum. Read by Wayne June. 5 CDs. (Running Time: 6 mins.). 2009. audio compact disk 29.95 (978-1-897304-40-2(4)) Dorch Pub Co.

Hide & Seek. unabr. ed. Fern Michaels. (Running Time: 7 hrs.). (Sisterhood Ser.: No. 8). 2007. 39.25 (978-1-4233-4480-3(4), 9781423344803, Brlnc Audio MP3 Lib); 24.95 (978-1-4233-4479-7(0), 9781423344797, Brilliance MP3); 39.25 (978-1-4233-4482-7(0), 9781423344827, BADLE); 24.95 (978-1-4233-4481-0(2), 9781423344810, BAD) Brilliance Audio.

Hide & Seek. unabr. ed. Fern Michaels. Read by Laural Merlington. (Running Time: 25200 sec.). (Sisterhood Ser.: No. 8). 2007. 74.25 (978-1-4233-4476-6(6), 9781423344766, BrilAudUnabridg); audio compact disk 82.25 (978-1-4233-4478-0(2), 9781423344780, BriAudCD Unabrid); audio compact disk 29.95 (978-1-4233-4477-3(4), 9781423344773, Bril Audio CD Unabri) Brilliance Audio.

Hide & Seek. unabr. ed. James Patterson. Read by Kimberly Schraf. 6 cass. (Running Time: 9 hrs.). 1996. 48.00 (978-0-7366-3379-6(0), 4029) Books on Tape.
How could she do it? That's what fans of Maggie Bradford, legendary vocalist, ask themselves. How could she murder her husband, a popular figure in his own right & father of her two children.

Hide & Seek. unabr. ed. James Patterson. Narrated by C. J. Critt & George Guidall. 6 cass. (Running Time: 9 hrs.). 1996. 51.00 (978-0-7887-0518-2(0), 94713E7) Recorded Bks.
In the celebrity trial of the century, world famous music star Maggie Bradford is charged with murder - again.

Hide & Seek. unabr. collector's ed. Sherryl Woods. Read by Frances Cassidy. 6 cass. (Running Time: 6 hrs.). 1994. 36.00 (978-0-7366-2778-8(2), 3497) Books on Tape.
Looking for a link between a psychopath & his victim, a young woman finds that her own lover might hold the key to solving the case.

Hide & Seek Fog. 2004. 8.95 (978-1-56008-921-6(0)); cass. & flmstrp 30.00 (978-1-56008-682-6(3)) Weston Woods.

Hide & Seek Fog; Kiss for Little Bear, A; Little House, the; Whose Mouse Are You? 2004. (978-0-89719-830-1(1)); cass. & flmstrp (978-0-89719-738-0(0)) Weston Woods.

Hide & Seek Game. Swami Amar Jyoti. 1 cass. 1976. 9.95 (J-6) Truth Consciousness.
What are we seeking & why are we hiding? Everyone is drunk with something, not wanting to end the play.

Hide & Seek/All Kinds of Fish. Created by Steck-Vaughn Staff. (Running Time: 322 sec.). (Primary Take-Me-Home Books Level K Ser.). 1998. 9.80 (978-0-8172-8656-9(X)) SteckVau.

Hide This Cd Counter Display Prepack. (HIDE THIS CD Ser.). 2007. audio compact disk 99.50 (978-0-8416-2712-3(6)) Pub: Berlitz Pubng. Dist(s): Langenscheidt

Hide This French CD. Created by Berlitz Publishing. (Running Time: 3600 sec.). (Berlitz Hide This CD Ser.). (FRE & ENG., 2006. audio compact disk 9.95 (978-981-246-969-4(9)) Pub: APA Pubns Serv SGP. Dist(s): IngramPubServ

Hide This Spanish CD, Pack. Created by Berlitz Publishing. (Running Time: 3600 sec.). (Berlitz Hide This CD Ser.). (SPA & ENG.). 2006. audio compact disk 9.95 (978-981-246-968-7(0)) Pub: APA Pubns Serv SGP. Dist(s): IngramPubServ

Hide Yourself Away. unabr. ed. Mary Jane Clark. Read by Melissa delany Del Valle. 6 cass. (KEY News Ser.: Bk. 7). 2005. bk. 59.95 (978-0-7927-3284-6(7), CSL 680); bk. 89.95 (978-0-7927-3285-3(5), SLD 680); audio compact disk 29.95 (978-0-7927-3286-0(3), CMP 680) AudioGO.

Hideaway. unabr. ed. Dean Koontz. Read by Michael Hanson & Carol Cowan. (Running Time: 15 hrs.). 2005. 39.25 (978-1-59710-365-7(9), 9781597103657, BADLE) Brilliance Audio.

Hideaway. unabr. ed. Dean Koontz. Read by Michael Hanson and Carol Cowan. (Running Time: 15 hrs.). 2005. 24.95 (978-1-59710-364-0(0), 9781597103640, BAD) Brilliance Audio.

Hideaway. unabr. ed. Dean Koontz. Read by Carol Cowan & Michael Hanson. (Running Time: 54000 sec.). 2005. 29.95 (978-1-59355-332-6(3), 9781593553326, BAU); 92.25 (978-1-59355-333-3(1), 9781593553333, BrilAudUnabridg); audio compact disk 40.95 (978-1-59355-334-0(X), 9781593553340, Bril Audio CD Unabri); audio compact disk 112.25 (978-1-59355-335-7(8), 9781593553357, BriAudCD Unabrid); audio compact disk 24.95 (978-1-59335-712-2(5), 9781593357122, Brilliance MP3); audio compact disk 39.25 (978-1-59335-846-4(6), 9781593358464, Brlnc Audio MP3 Lib) Brilliance Audio.
The New York Times #1 bestseller by the author of Dragon's Tears. Pronounced clinically dead after his car plunges into an icy river, Hatch Harrison is miraculously revived by a special team of doctors. Now Hatch approaches each day with a new appreciation . . . until he starts to see terrifying images of madness and murder. For he brought something back from his visit with death - and its murderous rampage has just begun.

Hideaway. unabr. ed. Dean Koontz. Read by Michael Hanson & Carol Cowan. 9 cass. (Running Time: 14 hrs.). 1992. 54.00 (978-0-9624010-2-2(1), 112708) Readers Chair.
Although accident victim Hatch Harrison dies en route to the hospital, a brilliant physician miraculously resuscitates him. Given this second chance, Hatch & his wife, Lindsey, approach each day with a new appreciation for the beauty of life, until a series of mysterious & frightening events bring them face-to-face with the unknown. Includes an Exclusive Conversation with Dean Koontz.

Hide'n Find. W. Mark Wattenford. 2007. audio compact disk 14.99 (978-1-60247-210-5(6)) Tate Pubng.

Hideous Error of Women Priests. Perf. by John Vennari. 1 cass. (Running Time: 90 mins.). 7.00 (20207) Cath Treas.
Demonstrates the true agenda behind the woman priest movement, its program for the establishment of a goddess religion & its connection to New Age occultism. It shows that these feminists "are not angry at a male priesthood, they're actually angry at male-divinity. Their goal is a complete destruction of Catholicism in order to replace it with a feminist, witchcraft religion. Female Eucharistic ministers, lady lectors & alter girls are only stepping stones to this occultic agenda.".

Hideous Kinky. Esther Freud. Read by Esther Freud. 2 cass. 1998. 16.85 Set. (978-1-901768-20-6(1)) Pub: CSA Telltapes GBR. Dist(s): Ulverscroft US

Hideous Kinky. abr. ed. Esther Freud. Read by Esther Freud. 2 cass. (Running Time: 3 hrs.). 1999. 17.95 (978-1-57270-099-4(8), M21099) Pub: Audio Partners. Dist(s): PerseuPGW
An English mother, intent on exploring the hippy/spiritual life of Morocco, takes her two young daughters with her on a lighthearted adventure with overtones of pathos & risk. In the voice of the 5-year old daughter who narrates the story, Freud perfectly captures the yearning for a normal life.

Hideout. Eve Bunting. Read by Johnny Heller. 3 cass. (Running Time: 3 hrs.). (YA). 1999. 107.80 (978-0-7887-3240-9(4), 46897) Recorded Bks.
Twelve-year-old Andy Dubin has left his home to get away from his new stepfather. When he finds a key to a seldom-used penthouse in a luxurious hotel, he thinks he has discovered the perfect hideout. But suddenly he is plunged into the most terrifying experience of his life. A tale of a young man learning to adjust to some of life's difficult changes.

Hideout. unabr. ed. Eve Bunting. Narrated by Johnny Heller. 3 pieces. (Running Time: 3 hrs.). (gr. 5 up). 1999. 27.00 (978-0-7887-3242-3(0), 95847E7) Recorded Bks.

Hideout. unabr. ed. Eve Bunting. Narrated by Johnny Heller. 3 cass. (Running Time: 3 hrs.). (YA). 2000. pap. bk. 41.25 (978-0-7887-3213-3(7), 95847X4) Recorded Bks.

Hiding from Love: How to Change the Withdrawal Patterns That Isolate & Imprison You. John Townsend. (ENG.). 2008. 14.99 (978-0-310-30454-8(7)) Zondervan.

Hiding God's Law in Our Hearts. (Power Tool Box Ser.: Vol. 1). (J). (gr. 1-6). 1998. ring bd. 164.99 (978-1-57405-043-1(5)) CharismaLife Pub.

Hiding God's Law in Our Hearts, Qtr. 1. Contrib. by Charisma Life Publishers Staff. 1 CD. (Power Tool Box Ser.). (J). (gr. 1-7). 1998. audio compact disk 15.99 (978-1-57405-429-3(5)) CharismaLife Pub.

Hiding in the Twelfth House. Beverly J. Farrell. 1 cass. (Running Time: 90 min.). 1988. 8.95 (612) Am Fed Astrologers.

Hiding my Candy. Chablis. 2004. 7.95 (978-0-7435-4825-0(6)) Pub: S&S Audio. Dist(s): S and S Inc

Hiding Place. Contrib. by Don Moen. (Chill Cafe Ser.). 2007. audio compact disk 13.99 (978-5-557-57586-7(3)) Integrity Music.

Hiding Place. John Sherrill & Elizabeth Sherrill. 2006. audio compact disk (978-0-7861-8988-5(6)) Blckstn Audio.

Hiding Place. John Sherrill et al. Read by Nadia May. Perf. by Julie Harris. 2003. audio compact disk 24.95 (978-0-7861-9423-0(5)) Blckstn Audio.

Hiding Place. abr. ed. Read by Carole Boyd. Perf. by Julie Harris. 4 cass. (Running Time: 6 hrs. 30 min.). (Life of Glory Ser.). 2003. 25.99; audio compact disk 25.99 Oasis Audio.

Hiding Place. adpt. ed. Corrie Ten Boom. Adapted by Dave Arnold & Philip Glassborow. (Running Time: 240 hrs. 0 mins.). (Radio Theatre Ser.). (ENG.). (J). (gr. 3). 2007. audio compact disk 14.97 (978-1-58997-513-2(8), Tyndale Ent) Tyndale Hse.

Hiding Place. unabr. ed. Corrie Ten Boom. Narrated by Bernadette Dunne. (Running Time: 9 hrs. 30 mins. 0 sec.). (ENG.). 2009. audio compact disk 24.98 (978-1-59644-682-3(X), Hovel Audio) christianaud.

Hiding Place. unabr. ed. Corrie Ten Boom et al. Read by Nadia May. (Running Time: 8.5 hrs. 0 mins.). 2009. audio compact disk 19.95 (978-1-4332-6046-9(8)) Blckstn Audio.

Hiding Place. unabr. ed. John Sherrill et al. Read by Nadia May. Perf. by Julie Harris. 6 cass. (Running Time: 9 hrs.). 2003. 44.95 (978-0-7861-0647-9(6), 1461) Blckstn Audio.
Corrie ten Boom was an old-maid watchmaker living contentedly with her spinster sister & their elderly father in the tiny house over their shop in Holland. With the Nazi invasion & occupation of Holland, she & her family became leaders in the Dutch Underground, hiding Jewish people in their home & aiding their escape from the Nazis. For their efforts, all but Corrie found death in a concentration camp.

Hiding Place. unabr. ed. John Sherrill et al. Read by Tom Parker. Perf. by Julie Harris. 8 CDs. (Running Time: 10 hrs.). 2000. audio compact disk 64.00 (978-0-7861-9923-5(7), z1461) Blckstn Audio.

***Hiding Place.** unabr. ed. Corrie ten Boom. Narrated by Bernadette Dunne. (ENG.). 2009. 14.98 (978-1-59644-683-0(8), Hovel Audio) christianaud.

Hiding Place. unabr. ed. Collin Wilcox. Read by Larry McKeever. 8 cass. (Running Time: 8 hrs.). (Frank Hastings Ser.). 1996. 48.00 (978-0-7366-3404-5(5), 4050) Books on Tape.
How well do parents know their children? Mrs. Towers thought her daughter June was a good girl. Why, then, did the pretty teen turn up dead atop a rubbish heap in San Francisco's Golden Gate Park?.

Hierarchy-Nature Healing; The Healing of Guilt. Ann Ree Colton & Jonathan Murro. 1 cass. 7.95 A R Colton Fnd.

Higglety Pigglety Pop!: Or There Must Be More to Life see Maurice Sendak

Higglety Pigglety Pop! Or There Must Be More to Life. 1 cass. (J). (ps-1). 2002. 10.95 (978-0-8126-0055-1(X)) Pub: Cricket Bks. Dist(s): PerseuPGW

High: Stories of Survival from Everest & K2. unabr. ed. Read by Eric Conger et al. Ed. by Clint Willis. Contrib. by Matt Dickinson et al. 4 cass. (Running Time: 6 hrs.). 2000. pap. bk. 38.95 (LC028) Listen & Live.
A unique perspective on climbing these two peaks, from early exploration disasters, to the modern tragedies. Reminds us why they Everest & K2 are among the world's most dangerous places, yet why the best climbers can't stay away from them.

High: Stories of Survival from Everest & K2. unabr. ed. Short Stories. Read by Eric Conger et al. Ed. by Clint Willis. Contrib. by David Roberts et al. 4 cass. (Running Time: 6 hrs.). (Mountains Ser.). 2000. 24.95 (978-1-885408-35-8(8), LL028) Listen & Live.

High Altar. unabr. ed. Howard H. Hilton. Read by Kevin Foley. 8 cass. (Running Time: 9 hrs. 24 min.). (Howard H. Hilton International Mystery Ser.). 1996. 49.95 (978-1-55686-654-8(2)) Books in Motion.
An aristocratic Spaniard is obsessed with stealing an ornately-carved altar, crafted from over a ton of silver, from an obscure cathedral in the upper reaches of the Peruvian Andes.

High Blood Pressure. Read by Robert S. Friedman & Kelly Howell. 1 cass. (Running Time: 60 min.). (Sound Techniques for Healing Ser.). 1993. 11.95 (978-1-881451-21-1(6)) Brain Sync.
A remarkable, totally calm state is induced in which fears & anxieties just seem to vanish. In this deep realm of relaxation, blood pressure naturally lowers.

High Blood Pressure: Ancient Truths, Natural Remedies & the Latest Findings for Your Health Today. unabr. ed. Don Colbert. Read by Tim Lundeen.Tr. of Cura biblica para la presion alta, La. 7.99 (978-1-58926-803-6(2)) Oasis Audio.

High Blood Pressure: Ancient Truths, Natural Remedies & the Latest Findings for Your Health Today. unabr. ed. Don Colbert. Narrated by Tim Lundeen. (Bible Cure Ser.).Tr. of Cura biblica para la presion alta, La. (ENG.). 2004. audio compact disk 9.99 (978-1-58926-804-3(0)) Oasis Audio.

High Call & Personal Cost of the Gospel. 2005. (978-1-59024-195-0(9)); audio compact disk (978-1-59024-194-3(0)) B Hinn Min.

High Calling: The Courageous Life & Faith of Space Shuttle Columbia Commander Rick Husband. abr. ed. Evelyn Husband & Donna VanLiere. Read by Evelyn Husband. 5 CDs. (Running Time: 6 hrs.). 2004. audio compact disk 27.99 (978-1-58926-613-1(7)); 24.99 (978-1-58926-611-7(0)) Oasis Audio.
Rick Husband wanted to be an astronaut since his fourth birthday. His determination to pursue his dreams proved successful when he entered the NASA space shuttle program. Husband's years at NASA served not only to increase his integrity and character, but also to increase his faith in a Creator that could not be denied in the vastness of space. His story is not only inspirational, but exhilarating and invigorating as he served a faithful God. Evelyn Husband is the widow of Rick Husband, commander of the ill-fated Columbia Space Shuttle Mission that tragically ended on February 1, 2003. Evelyn is the mother of two children.

High Chimes. Read by Steve Scherf. 4 cass. 1998. 25.95 Set. (890067) Penton Overseas.
Modern-day Robin Hood, Newfoundland's Captain Peter Kerrivan is dogged by his own Sheriff of Nottingham who is prepared to bend every rule in the book to put Kerrivan behind bars. Before the action is over, a Canadian Cabinet minister is sweating to cover crimes that go straight to the top, & two honest cops must put things right.

High Cholesterol: Ancient Truths, Natural Remedies & the Latest Findings for Your Health Today. unabr. ed. Don Colbert. Narrated by Greg Wheatley. (Running Time: 1 hr. 30 mins.). (Bible Cure Ser.). (ENG.). 2004. audio compact disk 9.99 (978-1-58926-683-4(8)) Oasis Audio.

High Conquest: The Story of Mountaineering. unabr. collector's ed. James R. Ullman. Read by Larry McKeever. 8 cass. (Running Time: 12 hrs.). 1990. 64.00 (978-0-7366-1719-2(1), 2560) Books on Tape.
Beginning with the days when man looked upon mountains as the home of angry gods, James Ramsey Ullman leads swiftly through the stirring pageant of mountaineering history; the pioneering ascents in the Alps & the disastrous conquest of the Matterhorn; the journeys of exploration in the Rockies & Andes, Africa & Alaska; & finally the Himalayan expeditions. A climber of considerable experience, Ullmann also discusses the mountaineering craft & describes the most attractive mountain regions in the United States.

High Cost of Free Love: James 14, Matthew 7:14-15. Ed Young. 1995. 4.95 (978-0-7417-2057-3(4), 1057) Win Walk.

High Cost of Holy Living: 1 Peter 1:13-25. Ed Young. 1982. 4.95 (978-0-7417-1268-4(7), 268) Win Walk.

High Cost of Loving. Ben Young. 1996. 4.95 (978-0-7417-6014-2(2), B0013) Win Walk.

High Cost of Low Living: Romans 1:24-32. Ed Young. 1996. 4.95 (978-0-7417-2106-8(6), 1106) Win Walk.

High Country. Nevada Barr. 2009. audio compact disk 9.99 (978-1-4418-2651-0(3)) Brilliance Audio.

High Country. Nevada Barr. Narrated by Barbara Rosenblat. 6 cass. (Running Time: 9 hrs. 30 mins.). (Anna Pigeon Ser.: No. 12). 2004. 29.99 (978-1-4025-6983-8(1), 03864) Recorded Bks.

High Country. abr. ed. Nevada Barr. Read by Joyce Bean. 4 cass. (Running Time: 6 hrs.). (Anna Pigeon Ser.: No. 12). 2004. 62.25 (978-1-59086-659-7(2), 1590866592, BAudLibEd); audio compact disk 74.25 (978-1-59086-661-0(4), 1590866614, BACDLib Ed) Brilliance Audio.
It's fall in the Sierra Mountains, and Anna Pigeon is slinging hash in Yosemite National Park's historic Ahwahnee Hotel. Four young people, all seasonal park employees, have disappeared, and two weeks of work by crack search-and-rescue teams have failed to turn up a single clue; investigators are unsure as to whether the four went AWOL for reasons of their own - or died in the park. Needing an out-of-park ranger to work undercover, Anna is detailed to dining-room duty; but after a week of waiting tables, she knows the missing employees are only the first indications of a sickness threatening the park. Her twenty-something roommates give up their party-girl ways and panic; her new restaurant colleagues regard her with suspicion and fear. But when Anna's life is threatened and her temporary supervisor turns a deaf ear, she follows the scent of evil, taking a solo hike up a snowy trial to the high country, seeking answers. What waits for her is a nightmare of death and greed - and perhaps her final adventure. "Barr's trademark pleasures [are] evocative natural descriptions, mounting suspense, and Anna Pigeon's never-say-die spirit." - Kirkus Reviews.

High Country. abr. ed. Nevada Barr. Read by Joyce Bean. (Running Time: 6 hrs.). (Anna Pigeon Ser.: No. 12). 2005. audio compact disk 16.99 (978-1-59600-393-4(6), 9781596003934, BCD Value Price) Brilliance Audio.

High Country. abr. ed. Nevada Barr. Read by Joyce Bean. (Running Time: 6 hrs.). (Anna Pigeon Ser.). 2006. 24.95 (978-1-4233-0095-3(5), 9781423300953, BAD) Brilliance Audio.

High Country. abr. ed. Nevada Barr. Read by Joyce Bean. (Running Time: 6 hrs.). (Anna Pigeon Ser.: No. 12). 2006. 39.25 (978-1-4233-0096-0(3), 9781423300960, BADLE); 24.95 (978-1-4233-0093-9(9), 9781423300939, Brilliance MP3); audio compact disk 39.25 (978-1-4233-0094-6(7), 9781423300946, Brlnc Audio MP3 Lib) Brilliance Audio.
It's fall in the Sierra Mountains, and Anna Pigeon is slinging hash in Yosemite National Park's historic Ahwahnee Hotel. Four young people, all seasonal park employees, have disappeared, and two weeks of work by crack search-and-rescue teams have failed to turn up a single clue; investigators are unsure as to whether the four went AWOL for reasons of their own - or died in the park. Needing an out-of-park ranger to work undercover, Anna is detailed to dining-room duty; but after a week of waiting tables, she knows the missing employees are only the first indications of a sickness threatening the park. Her twenty-something roommates give up their party-girl ways and panic; her new restaurant colleagues regard her with suspicion and fear. But when Anna's life is threatened and her temporary supervisor turns a deaf ear, she follows the scent of evil, taking a solo hike up a snowy trial to the high country, seeking answers. What waits for her is a nightmare of death and greed - and perhaps her final adventure. "Barr's trademark pleasures [are] evocative natural descriptions, mounting suspense, and Anna Pigeon's never-say-die spirit." - Kirkus Reviews.

High Country. unabr. ed. Nevada Barr. Narrated by Barbara Rosenblat. 8 CDs. (Running Time: 9 hrs. 30 mins.). (Anna Pigeon Ser.: No. 12). 2004. audio compact disk 34.99 (978-1-4025-7366-8(9), 01462) Recorded Bks.
With each breathtaking, New York Times best-selling entry in her acclaimed Anna Pigeon mystery series, author Nevada Barr earns more and more fans. Loaded with intrigue and adventure, High Country showcases Barr at the top of her game. Anna is lodged in Yosemite National Park's historic Ahwahnee Hotel when four employees disappear. Elite rescue teams are unable to discover any clues, so it falls to Anna to work undercover and determine whether the group vanished willingly-or suffered an unthinkable fate somewhere in the park. Quickly, the intrepid ranger learns the disappearances indicate a far more sinister problem. And when Anna herself is threatened, her supervisor is hardly concerned. Seeking to root out the evil, Anna hikes a snowy trail to the high country, only to discover a disturbing reality that may end her adventures once and for all.

High Country Fall. unabr. ed. Margaret Maron. Read by C. J. Critt. 8 CDs. (Running Time: 9 hrs.). (Deborah Knott Mystery Ser.: No. 10). 2005. audio compact disk 89.75 (978-1-4193-1661-6(3), C3018) Recorded Bks.
Judge Knott is finally ready to marry her long-time friend Deputy Sheriff Dwight Bryant and settle down - or is she? She jumps at a chance to fill in for a judge in the high country of North Carolina. But ugly murder haunts the beauty of the Smoky Mountains.

High Crimes. Perf. by Steve Scherf & Maggie Scherf. Music by Michael Creber. 4 cass. (Running Time: 6 hrs.). 25.99 Set. (978-1-894144-00-1(7)) Am Listeners.
High seas smuggling to the tune of $300 million.

***High Crimes.** abr. ed. Joseph Finder. (Running Time: 6 hrs. 0 mins. 0 sec.). (ENG.). 2010. audio compact disk 14.99 (978-1-4272-1160-6(4)) Pub: Macmill Audio. Dist(s): Macmillan

High Crimes. abr. movie tie-in ed. Joseph Finder. Narrated by J. Charles. 3 CDs. (Running Time: 3 hrs.). 2001. audio compact disk 24.95 (978-1-58788-924-0(2)); audio compact disk 53.25 (978-1-58788-925-7(0), Lib Edit) Brilliance Audio.
Claire Heller Chapman has the perfect life. She's a Harvard Law professor, a criminal defense attorney, happily married to Tom & has a six-year-old daughter she adores. Then Tom is arrested by a team of government agents & accused of a 13-year-old wartime atrocity. Claire soon discovers that her husband is not who he says he is, that once he had a different name, even a different face. Now Claire must defend Tom in a top-secret military court-martial. As her career & even her life, are put in jeopardy, she must try to believe in her husband's innocence - even when everything indicates that he is a killer.

High Crimes: The Fate of Everest in an Age of Greed. unabr. ed. Michael Kodas. Read by Holter Graham. (Running Time: 21600 sec.). 2008. audio compact disk 29.95 (978-1-4013-8893-5(0), Hyperion Audio) Pub: Hyperion. Dist(s): HarperCollins Pubs

High Dark. unabr. ed. Ann Darr. Read by Ann Darr. 1 cass. (Running Time: 1 hr.). (Watershed Tapes of Contemporary Poetry Ser.). 12.95 (23616) J Norton Pubs.

***High Deryni.** unabr. ed. Katherine Kurtz. Read by Jeff Woodman. (Running Time: 13 hrs.). (Chronicles of the Deryni Ser.). 2010. 39.97 (978-1-4418-1599-6(6), 9781441815996, Brlnc Audio MP3 Lib); 39.97 (978-1-4418-1600-9(3), 9781441816009, BADLE); 24.99 (978-1-4418-1598-9(8), 9781441815989, Brilliance MP3); audio compact disk 87.97 (978-1-4418-1597-2(X), 9781441815972, BriAudCD Unabrid); audio compact disk 29.99 (978-1-4418-1596-5(1), 9781441815965, Bril Audio CD Unabri) Brilliance Audio.

High Efficiency Meetings. Learn Inc. Staff. pap. bk. 49.95 (978-1-55678-010-3(9), 3007, Lrn Inc) Oasis Audio.
Presents methods for improving business conferences.

High Efficiency Meetings. unabr. ed. 3 cass. 49.95 set, incl. guide bk. & forms. (S02050) J Norton Pubs.
A fast-paced program that teaches a method of planning & follow-up that will result in a much better use of everyone's time in meetings. You'll also learn a system that will help you maintain control while allowing an open exchange of ideas.

High efficiency selling: how superior sales people get that Way: How Superior Salespeople Get That Way. abr. ed. Stephan Schiffman. 2004. 10.95 (978-0-7435-4826-7(4)) Pub: S&S Audio. Dist(s): S and S Inc

High Energy. Richard Jafolla & Mary-Alice Jafolla. Read by Richard Jafolla & Mary-Alice Jafolla. (Health & Healing Ser.). 1986. 12.95 (370) Stppng Stones.
Motivational tapes that work on the subconscious mind (subliminal) & conscious mind to bring about self-improvement.

High Energy. Eldon Taylor. 1 cass. (Running Time: 62 min.). (Inner Talk Ser.). 16.95 (978-1-55978-304-0(4), 5365A) Progress Aware Res.
Soundtrack - Tropical Lagoon with underlying subliminal affirmations.

High Energy: Babbling Brook. Eldon Taylor. 1 cass. 16.95 (978-1-55978-488-7(1), 5365F) Progress Aware Res.

High Energy: Easy. Eldon Taylor. Read by Eldon Taylor. Ed. by Leslie Brice. 1 cass. (Running Time: 1 hr.). 1992. 16.95 (978-1-56705-140-7(5)) Gateways Inst.
Self improvement.

High Energy: Music Theme. Eldon Taylor. 1 cass. 16.95 (978-1-55978-144-2(0), 5365C) Progress Aware Res.

High Energy: Ocean. Eldon Taylor. Read by Eldon Taylor. Ed. by Leslie Brice. 1 cass. (Running Time: 1 hr.). 1992. 16.95 (978-1-56705-141-4(3)) Gateways Inst.

High Energy: Rhythm. Eldon Taylor. Read by Eldon Taylor. Ed. by Leslie Brice. 1 cass. (Running Time: 1 hr.). 1992. 16.95 (978-1-56705-142-1(1)) Gateways Inst.

High Energy: Stream. Eldon Taylor. Read by Eldon Taylor. Ed. by Leslie Brice. 1 cass. (Running Time: 1 hr.). 1992. 16.95 (978-1-56705-318-0(1)) Gateways Inst.

High Energy Living. abr. ed. Sudhir Jonathan Foust. 1 cass. (Running Time: 1 hr. 30 min.). 2004. 11.95 (978-0-7435-3943-2(5)) Pub: S&S Audio. Dist(s): S and S Inc

High Exposure: An Enduring Passion for Everest & Other Unforgiving Places. abr. ed. David F. Breashears. Read by David F. Breashears. Read by Michael Gross. 4 cass. (Running Time: 6 hrs.). 2001. 25.00 (978-1-59040-025-8(9), Phoenix Audio) Pub: Amer Intl Pub. Dist(s): PerseuPGW
Hear what it's like to confront death on the world's most notorious and dangerous mountain. This is the story of famed IMAX cinematographer, adventurer and mountaineer David F. Breashears, whose terrifying experiences on Mount Everest in 1996 became the defining moment in his life.

High Fidelity. collector's ed. Nick Hornby. Read by David Case. 6 cass. (Running Time: 9 hrs.). 2000. 48.00 (978-0-7366-5522-4(0)) Books on Tape.
Rob is a pop music junkie who runs his own semi-failing record store. His girlfriend, Laura, has just left him & he's both miserable & relieved. After all, he could have spent his life with someone who has a bad record collection. Rob seeks refuge in the company of Barry & Dick, the offbeat clerks at his store who endlessly review their top five films, top five Elvis Costello songs & top five episodes of Cheers. Rob tries dating a singer called Marie. Maybe its just that he's always wanted to sleep with someone who has a record contract but then he sees Laura again & Rob begins to think that a life as a episode of Thirtysomething might not be so bad.

***High Financier: The Lives & Time of Siegmund Warburg.** unabr. ed. Niall Ferguson. (Running Time: 12 hrs. 0 mins.). 2010. 17.99 (978-1-4001-8498-9(3)); 34.99 (978-1-4001-9498-8(9)) Tantor Media.

***High Financier: The Lives & Time of Siegmund Warburg.** unabr. ed. Niall Ferguson. Narrated by James Langton. 2 MP-3 CDs. (Running Time: 17 hrs. 30 mins. 0 sec.). 2010. 29.99 (978-1-4001-6498-1(2)); audio compact disk 95.99 (978-1-4001-4498-3(1)); audio compact disk 39.99 (978-1-4001-1498-6(5)) Pub: Tantor Media. Dist(s): IngramPubServ

High Five. abr. ed. Janet Evanovich. Read by Debi Mazar. 3 CDs. (Running Time: 3 hrs. 0 mins. 0 sec.). (Stephanie Plum Ser.: No. 5). (ENG.). 2005. audio compact disk 19.95 (978-1-55927-964-2(8)) Pub: Macmill Audio. Dist(s): Macmillan

High Five. abr. ed. Janet Evanovich. (Stephanie Plum Ser.: No. 5). 2001. (978-0-333-76587-6(7)) Macmillan UK GBR.

High Five. abr. ed. Janet Evanovich. (Stephanie Plum Ser.: No. 5). 2001. 7.95 (978-1-57815-264-3(X)) Media Bks NJ.

High Five. abr. ed. Janet Evanovich. (Stephanie Plum Ser.: No. 5). 2002. audio compact disk 11.99 (978-1-57815-545-3(2)) Media Bks NJ.

High Five. unabr. ed. Janet Evanovich. 7 cass. (Running Time: 10 hrs.). (Stephanie Plum Ser.: No. 5). 1999. 58.00 (978-0-7887-3664-3(7)) Recorded Bks.
Bounty hunter Stephanie Plumb has just nabbed a "little person" who is on the wanted list when she receives a frantic call from her mother about her missing uncle Fred. It seems Fred had a dispute with the garbage company just before he disappeared. When Stephanie finds pictures of a garbage bag full of body parts, it's clear this is something more than an old man wandering off.

High Five. unabr. ed. Janet Evanovich. Narrated by C. J. Critt. 8 CDs. (Running Time: 9 hrs. 30 mins.). (Stephanie Plum Ser.: No. 5). 2000. audio compact disk 75.00 (978-0-7887-4200-2(0), C1129E7) Recorded Bks.
Join America's favorite bounty hunter as she scrambles to make an honest living, keep her family happy & find true love. Stephanie juggles high-powered scams, lusts & fun.

High Five. unabr. ed. Janet Evanovich. Narrated by C. J. Critt. 7 cass. (Running Time: 9 hrs. 30 mins.). (Stephanie Plum Ser.: No. 5). 1999. 60.00 (978-0-7887-3464-9(4), 95857E7) Recorded Bks.

High Five! The Magic of Working Together. unabr. abr. ed. Ken Blanchard et al. Read by Sheldon Bowles. 5 CDs. (Running Time: 240 min.). 2001. 24.00 (978-0-694-52486-0(7)) HarperCollins Pubs.

High Five: The Secrets of Sharp, Savvy Winning Teams. abr. ed. Ken Blanchard & Sheldon M. Bowles. Read by Sheldon M. Bowles. 3 cass. (Running Time: 4 hrs.). 2000. 22.00; audio compact disk 24.00 HarperCollins Pubs.

***High Five Reading Audio CDs, Blue Level.** (High Five Reading - Blue Ser.). (ENG.). 2007. audio compact disk 59.50 (978-1-4296-1530-3(3)) CapstoneDig.

***High Five Reading Audio CDs, Green Level.** (High Five Reading - Green Ser.). (ENG.). 2007. audio compact disk 59.50 (978-1-4296-1532-7(X)) CapstoneDig.

***High Five Reading Audio CDs I.** (High Five Reading Level I Ser.). (ENG.). 2007. audio compact disk 158.60 (978-1-4296-1483-2(8)) CapstoneDig.

***High Five Reading Audio CDs Level II.** (High Five Reading Level II Ser.). (ENG.). 2007. audio compact disk 158.60 (978-1-4296-1484-9(6)) CapstoneDig.

***High Five Reading Audio CDs, Purple Level.** (High Five Reading - Purple Ser.). (ENG.). 2007. audio compact disk 59.50 (978-1-4296-1533-4(8)) CapstoneDig.

***High Five Reading Audio CDs, Red Level.** (High Five Reading - Red Ser.). (ENG.). 2007. audio compact disk 59.50 (978-1-4296-1531-0(1)) CapstoneDig.

***High Five Reading Audio CDs, Red Level I.** (High Five Reading - Red Ser.). (ENG.). 2007. audio compact disk 39.65 (978-1-4296-1477-1(3)) CapstoneDig.

***High Five Reading Audiocassettes, Blue Level I.** (High Five Reading - Blue Ser.). 2005. audio compact disk 33.95 (978-0-7368-5909-7(8)) CapstoneDig.

***High Five Reading Audiocassettes, Blue Level II.** (High Five Reading - Blue Ser.). 2005. audio compact disk 33.01 (978-0-7368-5913-4(6)) CapstoneDig.

***High Five Reading Audiocassettes I.** (High Five Reading Level I Ser.). 2005. audio compact disk 77.35 (978-0-7368-5902-8(0)) CapstoneDig.

***High Five Reading Audiocassettes II.** (High Five Reading Level II Ser.). (ENG.). 2005. audio compact disk 107.10 (978-0-7368-5906-6(3)) CapstoneDig.

***High Five Reading CDs, Blue Set I.** (High Five Reading - Blue Ser.). (ENG.). 2007. audio compact disk 29.75 (978-1-4296-1475-7(7)) CapstoneDig.

***High Five Reading CDs, Blue Set II.** (High Five Reading - Blue Ser.). (ENG.). 2007. audio compact disk 39.65 (978-1-4296-1476-4(5)) CapstoneDig.

***High Five Reading CDs, Green Set I.** (High Five Reading - Green Ser.). (ENG.). 2007. audio compact disk 39.65 (978-1-4296-1479-5(X)) CapstoneDig.

***High Five Reading CDs, Green Set II.** (High Five Reading - Green Ser.). (ENG.). 2007. audio compact disk 39.65 (978-1-4296-1480-1(3)) CapstoneDig.

***High Five Reading CDs, Purple Set I.** (High Five Reading - Purple Ser.). (ENG.). 2007. audio compact disk 39.65 (978-1-4296-1481-8(1)) CapstoneDig.

***High Five Reading CDs, Purple Set II.** (High Five Reading - Purple Ser.). (ENG.). 2007. audio compact disk 39.65 (978-1-4296-1482-5(X)) CapstoneDig.

***High Five Reading CDs, Red Set II.** (High Five Reading - Red Ser.). (ENG.). 2007. audio compact disk 39.65 (978-1-4296-1478-8(1)) CapstoneDig.

High Five USA Reading Audiocassettes, Green Level II. 5 cass. (High Five Reading - Green Ser.). (ENG.). (gr. 4 up). 2003. audio compact disk 17.85 (978-0-7368-2862-8(1)) CapstoneDig.

High Five USA Reading Audiocassettes I. 15 cass. (High Five Reading Level I Ser.). (ENG.). (gr. 4 up). 2002. audio compact disk 47.60 (978-0-7368-9582-8(5)) CapstoneDig.

High Five USA Reading Audiocassettes II. 15 cass. (High Five Reading Level II Ser.). (ENG.). (gr. 4 up). 2004. audio compact disk 77.35 (978-0-7368-3862-7(7)) CapstoneDig.

High Five USA Reading Audiocassettes, Purple Level I. 5 cass. (High Five Reading - Purple Ser.). (ENG.). (gr. 4 up). 2002. audio compact disk 33.01 (978-0-7368-9211-7(7)) CapstoneDig.

High Five USA Reading Audiocassettes, Purple Level II. 5 cass. (High Five Reading - Purple Ser.). (ENG.). (gr. 4 up). 2004. audio compact disk 33.01 (978-0-7368-3865-8(1)) CapstoneDig.

High Five USA Reading Audiocassettes, Red Level I. 5 cass. (High Five Reading - Red Ser.). (ENG.). (gr. 4 up). 2002. audio compact disk 11.90 (978-0-7368-9566-8(3)) CapstoneDig.

High Five USA Reading Audiocassettes, Red Level II. 5 cass. (High Five Reading - Red Ser.). (ENG.). (gr. 4 up). 2003. audio compact disk 33.01 (978-0-7368-2857-4(5)) CapstoneDig.

High Five USA Reading, Green Level I. 5 vols. (gr. 4 up). bk. 250.95 (978-0-7368-9570-5(1), High Five) Red Brick Lrning.

High Five USA Reading, Green Level II. 5 vols. (gr. 4 up). bk. 250.95 (978-0-7368-2860-4(5), High Five) Red Brick Lrning.

High Five USA Reading, Purple Level I. 5 vols. (gr. 4 up). bk. 250.95 (978-0-7368-9516-3(7), High Five) Red Brick Lrning.

High Five USA Reading, Purple Level II. 5 vols. (gr. 4 up). bk. 250.95 (978-0-7368-3863-4(5), High Five) Red Brick Lrning.

High Five USA Reading, Red Level I. 5 vols. (gr. 4 up). bk. 250.95 (978-0-7368-9544-6(2), High Five) Red Brick Lrning.

High Five USA Reading, Red Level II. 5 vols. (gr. 4 up). bk. 250.95 (978-0-7368-2855-0(9), High Five) Red Brick Lrning.

High Flight. abr. ed. David Hagberg. Read by Bruce Watson. 4 vols. (Kirk McGarvey Ser.). 2003. (978-1-58807-679-3(2)) Am Pubng Inc.

High Focus: Activate Lucid Thinking. Kelly Howell. 1 CD. (Running Time: 60 mins.). 2004. audio compact disk 14.95 (978-1-881451-97-6(6)) Brain Sync.
Perhaps your energy is dragging, but you need to be in top form for a meeting or exam or presentation. Maybe concentrating on a single task has never been one of your strong points. Now you can easily reach high-performance brain states, ideal for increasing cognition and focusing on any task that requires your full attention.Simply slip on your headphones, and listen to High Focus. Within minutes your brain waves will become energized and organized. Suddenly, the high Beta waves kick your brain into high gear and your mind focuses in like a laser beam. You'll feel alert and energized as your ability to think, concentrate ans store information is dramatically improved.

High Focus: Activate Lucid Thinking. unabr. ed. Kelly Howell. 1 cass. (Running Time: 60 min.). 1991. 11.95 (978-1-881451-01-3(1)) Brain Sync.
Ideal for energy boosts or when laser-sharp concentration is needed, also combines high beta frequencies that research has shown is associated with cognition & alertness.

High Frequency German Course. Mark Frobose. 6 CDs. 2004. audio compact disk 49.00 (978-1-893564-07-7(X)) Macmill Audio.

High Gravel Blind. Paul Dunn. Read by Damien Atkins. 1 CD. (Running Time: 1 hr.). 2005. audio compact disk 15.95 (978-0-660-19268-0(3)) Canadian Broadcasting CAN.

High Hand. unabr. ed. Gary Phillips. Narrated by Patricia R. Floyd. 6 cass. (Running Time: 8 hrs. 15 mins.). 2004. 56.00 (978-1-4025-3597-0(X)) Recorded Bks.

High Hostage. Anne Worboys. Read by Sharon Mayer. 4 cass. (Running Time: 6 hrs.). 1999. 44.95 (67355) Pub: Soundings Ltd GBR. Dist(s): Ulverscroft US

High-Impact Business Writing: How to Write Clear & Concise Memos, Proposals, Letters & Reports. Instructed by Ronnie Moore. 4 cass. (Running Time: 4 hrs. 8 min.). 59.95 Set, incl. wkbk., 44p. (Q10180) CareerTrack Pubns.
Program highlights: Simple ways to organize your content so your writing has better "flow"; 5 guidelines for crisp, concise writing; How to "unsmother" your verbs & set them free to work harder; Using the active voice: how to add impact & urgency to your writing; Proven strategies for writing to sell.

High-Impact Business Writing: How to Write Faster, More Easily & with Far Greater Impact. abr. ed. Ronnie Moore. 2 cass. 2000. 17.95 (978-1-55977-912-8(8)) CareerTrack Pubns.

High Impact Communication. Bert Decker. 6 cass. (Running Time: 6 hrs.). 1992. 59.95 set. (271A) Nightingale-Conant.

High Impact Facilitation. Terry R. Bacon et al. 4 cass. (Running Time: 4 hrs.). 1997. Set. (978-1-57740-027-1(5), ILW017) Lore Intl Inst.
Provides an understanding of group dynamics & behaviors & specific techniques & processes that lead you closer to the goal of becoming a facilitative leader.

High Impact Leader: Authentic, Resilient Leadership That Gets Results. Bruce J. Avolio & Fred Luthans. Read by Chris Ryan. (Running Time: 16200 sec.). 2007. audio compact disk 28.00 (978-1-933309-14-9(8)) Pub: A Media Intl. Dist(s): Natl Bk Netwk

High-Impact Leadership. Mark Sanborn. 4 cass. (Running Time: 3 hrs. 49 min.). 59.95 Set. (Q10096) CareerTrack Pubns.
This program is an affordable, convenient way for you to get high-quality leadership training - so you can take your people boldly into the future.

High-Impact Leadership: How to Be More Than a Manager. Mark Sanborn. 4 cass. 1995. 19.95 (978-1-55977-068-2(6)) CareerTrack Pubns.

High Impact Learning Systems. Robert O. Brinkerhoff. 1 cass. (Running Time: 40 min.). 1997. (978-1-57740-058-5(5)) Lore Intl Inst.

High Impact Options Trading. 1. (Running Time: 90 mins.). (Trade Secrets Audio Ser.). 2002. 19.95 (978-1-931611-67-1(X)) Marketplace Bks.
When it comes to powerhouse options strategies, Price Headley of BigTrends.com is an industry leader, and his new workshop provides a hands-on overview of the top options strategies. Traders will learn to: 1) Target the best stocks and leverage them with options, 2) Spot trends before the crowd does, 3) Use a powerful indicator - Acceleration Bands - to find upcoming buying surges and pinpoint trend changes. And discover the awesome power of market timing indicators like the put/call ratio. Great for improving marketing timing & general trading skills.

High Interest Rates: Neh. 5;1-13. Ed Young. 1990. 4.95 (978-0-7417-1810-5(3), 810) Win Walk.

High Jinx. unabr. ed. William F. Buckley, Jr. Read by Christopher Hurt. 5 cass. (Running Time: 7 hrs.). (Blackford Oakes Mystery Ser.). 1990. 39.95 (978-0-7861-0106-1(7), 1099) Blckstn Audio.
The year is 1954, Stalin has died in Moscow & a deadly earnest power play nears its conclusion. Meanwhile, British & American commandos, their mission to liberate a Soviet satellite country, have met a disastrous end. Jinxed. The communications system between English & American intelligence has been penetrated. Jinxed. There is a spook in their midst. High Jinx. And higher still when the risk becomes one Blacky alone must take.

High Jinx. unabr. collector's ed. William F. Buckley, Jr. Read by Michael Prichard. 6 cass. (Running Time: 9 hrs.). (Blackford Oakes Mystery Ser.). 1995. 48.00 (978-0-7366-2913-3(0), 3610) Books on Tape.
In 1954, the KGB plots to topple the Kremlin while Blackford Oakes tracks a traitor from Stockholm to Buckingham Palace.

High John the Conqueror. unabr. ed. John W. Wilson. Narrated by Peter Jay Fernandez. 5 cass. (Running Time: 6 hrs. 45 mins.). (Tcu Press Texas Tradition Ser.). 1998. 49.75 (978-1-4193-1213-7(8), S1071MC); audio compact disk 69.75 (978-1-4193-1215-1(4), CS021MC) Recorded Bks.

High King. unabr. ed. Lloyd Alexander. Read by James Langton. (Running Time: 26640 sec.). (Chronicles of Prydain Ser.). (ENG.). (J). (gr. 5-7). 2008. audio compact disk 34.00 (978-0-7393-6357-7(3), Listening Lib) Pub: Random Audio Pubg. Dist(s): Random

***High King of Montival.** unabr. ed. S. M. Stirling. Narrated by Todd McLaren. (Running Time: 17 hrs. 0 mins. 0 sec.). (Change Ser.: BBk. 4). 2010. audio compact disk 95.99 (978-1-4001-3684-1(9)) Pub: Tantor Media. Dist(s): IngramPubServ

***High King of Montival.** unabr. ed. S. M. Stirling. Narrated by Todd McLaren. (Running Time: 16 hrs. 30 mins.). (Change Ser.: Bk. 4). 2010. 39.99 (978-1-4001-2684-2(3)); 21.99 (978-1-4001-7684-7(0)); 29.99 (978-1-4001-5684-9(X)); audio compact disk 39.99 (978-1-4001-0684-4(2)) Pub: Tantor Media. Dist(s): IngramPubServ

High Life, Low Life, Level 4. Alan R. Battersby. Contrib. by Philip Prowse. (Running Time: 2 hrs. 26 mins.). (Cambridge English Readers Ser.). (ENG.). 2001. 15.75 (978-0-521-78816-8(1)) Cambridge U Pr.

High Lonesome. unabr. ed. Louis L'Amour. Read by David Strathairn. 5 CDs. (Running Time: 3 hrs. 40 mins.). (Louis L'Amour Ser.). (ENG.). 2005. audio compact disk 21.00 (978-0-7393-2017-4(3)) Pub: Random Audio Pubg. Dist(s): Random
Many a hardcase had died trying to tale the bank and settle an old score at the same time. But he never counted on meeting a beautiful woman and her trail-savvy but reckless father, headed a straight for Apache country. Now Considine and his gang can either ride like hell for the border just ahead of an angry posse, or join the old man and his daughter in a desperate last stand against blood-hungry warriors. The choice is simple: risk the hangman's noose or an Apache bullet. From the Paperback edition.

high Lord. unabr. ed. Trudi Canavan. Read by Richard Aspel. (Running Time: 21 hrs. 35 mins.). (Black Magician Trilogy). 2009. 54.95 (978-1-74214-080-3(7), 9781742140803) Pub: Bolinda Pubng AUS. Dist(s): Bolinda Pub Inc

High Middle Ages, Pts. I-II. Instructed by Philip Daileader. 12 CDs. (Running Time: 12 hrs.). 2001. bk. 69.95 (978-1-56585-392-8(X), 869); 54.95 (978-1-56585-260-0(5), 869) Teaching Co.

High Middle Ages, Vol. 2. Instructed by Philip Daileader. 6 cass. (Running Time: 6 hrs.). 2001. 129.95 (978-1-56585-261-7(3)) Teaching Co.

High Midnight. unabr. ed. Stuart M. Kaminsky. Read by Christopher Lane. 4 cass. (Running Time: 5 hrs. 30 mins.). (Toby Peters Mystery Ser.: No. 6). 1995. 32.95 (978-0-7861-0765-0(0), 1614) Blckstn Audio.
Someone wants Gary Cooper to make a movie he isn't interested in making, & whoever it is wants him badly enough to get nasty about it. Cooper takes to the hills, accompanied by a writer named Ernest Hemingway, chased by men with blood in their eyes & murder in their hearts. The problem is that Cooper can't shoot straight & Hemingway can't operate without native bearers & an elephant gun. Toby Peters can't shoot either, but he doesn't need help...much. Just give him a bowl of cereal & time to decide his next move & Toby will get everything straightened out. Now, if he can only keep Lombardi the gangster from making good on his threat to turn him into kosher hot dogs.

High Missouri. unabr. ed. Winfred Blevins. Read by Michael Taylor. 12 cass. (Running Time: 15 hrs. 48 min.). 2001. 64.95 (978-1-58116-068-0(2)) Books in Motion.
Would-be poet Dylan Campbell signs up with Nor West Co. to bring God to the Indians - and to break with his father in Montreal. Making his way across the vast Saskatchewan toward the legendary Missouri, Dylan must contend with acts of violence and evil, to struggle for his life.

High Mountain Meditation. Read by Mary Richards. 12.95 (502) Master Your Mind.
Creates one's own mountaintop setting where one can go & meet a higher self or to experience a feeling of inner peace.

High Noon. 1 cass. (Running Time: 30 min.). (Paws & Tales Ser.: Vol. 4). 2001. 3.99 (978-1-57972-355-2(1)) Insight Living.
Hugh McClaw, the town bully has warned the ?Club? his cousin Joey is coming to town for a visit and they have plans to make trouble for them and even take over their fort.

High Noon. (Paws & Tales Ser.: Vol. 4). (J). 2001. audio compact disk 5.99 (978-1-57972-385-9(3)) Insight Living.

High Noon. Nora Roberts. Read by Susan Ericksen. (Playaway Adult Fiction Ser.). 2008. 89.99 (978-1-60640-594-9(2)) Find a World.

High Noon. abr. ed. Nora Roberts. Read by Susan Ericksen. (Running Time: 6 hrs.). 2008. audio compact disk 14.99 (978-1-4233-3736-2(0), 9781423337362, BCD Value Price) Brilliance Audio.

High Noon. unabr. ed. Nora Roberts. Read by Susan Ericksen. 1 MP3-CD. (Running Time: 16 hrs.). 2007. 24.95 (978-1-4233-3731-7(X), 9781423337317, Brilliance MP3); 39.25 (978-1-4233-3734-8(4), 9781423337348, BADLE); 24.95 (978-1-4233-3733-1(6), 9781423337331, BAD); 102.25 (978-1-4233-3728-7(X), 9781423337287, BrilAudUnabridg); audio compact disk 39.25 (978-1-4233-3732-4(8), 9781423337324, Brinc Audio MP3 Lib); audio compact disk 122.25 (978-1-4233-3730-0(1), 9781423337300, BriAudCD Unabrid); audio compact disk 39.95 (978-1-4233-3729-4(8), 9781423337294, Bril Audio CD Unabri) Brilliance Audio.

High Noon. unabr. ed. Karen Southwick. Read by Sneha Mathan. 7 cass. (Running Time: 10 hrs.). 2000. 49.95 (978-0-7861-1872-4(5), 2671) Blckstn Audio.
In 1982, a little upstart named Sun was making waves in the high-tech industry with its groundbreaking workstation technology, even as early competitors dismissed the company as not worth losing sleep over. Since then, Sun Microsystems has become a formidable presence in the industry, making its own rules & taking no prisoners & is currently poised to reach the highest point of its ascendancy, the challenge of Microsoft's dominance over the future of computing.

***High Noon: The Inside Story of Scott Mcnealy & the Rise of Sun Microsystems.** unabr. ed. Karen Southwick. Read by Sneha Mathan. (Running Time: 10 hrs. NaN mins.). (ENG.). 2011. 29.95 (978-1-4417-8489-6(6)); audio compact disk 90.00 (978-1-4417-8487-2(X)) Blckstn Audio.

High on Arrival. abr. ed. Mackenzie Phillips. Read by Mackenzie Phillips. (Running Time: 6 hrs. 0 mins. 0 sec.). 2009. audio compact disk 29.99 (978-1-4423-0366-9(2)) Pub: S&S Audio. Dist(s): S and S Inc

High Performance. Read by Mary Richards. 12.95 (401); 12.95 (600) Master Your Mind.
Discusses how to focus your creative gift & skill to perform.

High Performance Living: A Seminar for Total Mind-Body Wellness. Ken Dychtwald. Read by Ken Dychtwald. 6 cass. 34.95 Set. (175A) Nightingale-Conant.

High-Performance Mentoring Facilitator's Guide: A Multimedia Program for Training Mentor Teachers. James B. Rowley & Patricia Hart. 1999. 34.95 (978-0-7619-7526-7(8), 85342) Pub: Corwin Pr. Dist(s): SAGE

High-Performance Mind: Brainwave Development Exercises. Anna Wise. 4 CDs. (Running Time: 6 hrs.). 1998. audio compact disk 29.95 (978-1-55961-467-2(6)) Relaxtn Co.

High-Performance Mind; Brainwave Development Exercises. Anna Wise. 4 cass. 1998. 26.95 (978-1-55961-468-9(4)) Relaxtn Co.

High-Performance Mind; Brainwave Development Exercises, Set. Anna Wise. 4 cass. 1998. 29.95 Relaxtn Co.

High Performance Radio. Blake Brooker. 2005. audio compact disk 15.95 (978-0-660-19296-3(9)) Canadian Broadcasting CAN.

High Performance Super Learning Meditation CD-ROM. 1 CDS. 2007. audio compact disk 29.00 (978-1-921183-09-6(8)) One-on-One AUS.

High-Performance Teamwork. Doug Jones. 6 cass. 59.95 Set. (10550AX) Nightingale-Conant.
Business experts from Peter Drucker to Alvin Toffler are calling the shift from bureaucratic management to teamwork the Second Industrial Revolution. Now, Doug Jones shows you how to use this concept to build your business...improve your performance...& develop the successful team mentality. He reveals how to design, build, train, cultivate, motivate & reward a high-performance team step-by-step. Learn to translate your team's common purpose into attainable goals...use the latest tools to improve internal communications...even develop the sense of connectedness that makes work more enjoyable.

High Places: Psalm 18. Ed Young. 1989. 4.95 (978-0-7417-1766-5(2), 766) Win Walk.

High Places: Spontaneous Instrumental Worship. Contrib. by Rick Joyner. Prod. by Leonard Jones. (ENG.). 2008. audio compact disk 16.99 (978-7-5124-0108-2(6)) EagleStar.

High Plains Tango. Robert James Waller. 2005. audio compact disk 53.55 (978-1-4159-2137-1(7)) Pub: Books on Tape. Dist(s): NetLibrary CO

High Plains Tango. unabr. ed. Robert James Waller. 6 cassettes. (Running Time: 9 hrs.). 2005. 54.00 (978-1-4159-2020-6(6)) Books on Tape.

High Point. (High Point Ser.). (gr. 6-12). bk. & tchr. ed. 91.16 (978-0-7362-0934-2(4)); bk., tchr. ed., tchr.'s training gde. ed. 91.16 (978-0-7362-0966-3(2)) Hampton-Brown.

High Point. (High Point Ser.). (gr. 6-12). 2000. bk., tchr. ed., tchr.'s training gde. ed. 91.16 (978-0-7362-0902-1(6)) Hampton-Brown.

High Point, Pack. (gr. 6-12). reel tape 136.10 (978-0-7362-1534-3(4)); audio compact disk 65.00 (978-0-7362-1248-9(5)) Hampton-Brown.

High Point: The Basics Bookshelf. 3 vols. (gr. 6-12). bk. 487.59 (978-0-7362-1279-3(5)); bk. 531.44 (978-0-7362-1280-9(9)) Hampton-Brown.

High Point Level: With Selection Tapes. (High Point Ser.). (gr. 4-12). reel tape 547.00 (978-0-7362-1260-1(4)) Hampton-Brown.

High Points & Lows: Life, Faith & Figuring It All Out. unabr. ed. Austin Carty. Narrated by Austin Carty. (Running Time: 4 hrs. 45 mins. 0 sec.). (ENG.). 2010. 13.99 (978-1-60814-622-2(7)); audio compact disk 19.99 (978-1-59859-676-2(4)) Oasis Audio.

High Price of Being Nice. Louise Jenkins. 1 cass. 8.95 (173) Am Fed Astrologers.
Relationship needs vs. selfishness.

High Priest of Harmful Matter. Jello Biafra. 2 cass. (Running Time: 2 hrs.). (AK Press Audio Ser.). 2001. 11.98 (978-1-902593-14-2(6), AK Pr San Fran) AK Pr Dist.
Tales from the trial, censorship, Tipper Gore & more.

High Priest of Harmful Matter. Jello Biafra. 2 CDs. (AK Press Audio Ser.). (ENG.). 1999. audio compact disk 16.98 (978-1-902593-13-5(8)) Pub: AK Pr GBR. Dist(s): Consort Bk Sales

***High Priests & Priestesses of Golden Atlantis.** Diana Cooper. Andrew Brel. (Running Time: 0 hr. 54 mins. 24 sec.). (Information & Meditation Ser.). (ENG.). 2010. audio compact disk 14.95 (978-1-84409-520-9(7)) Pub: Findhorn Pr GBR. Dist(s): IPG Chicago

High Probability Chart Reading. Frwd. by John A. Murphy. (Trade Secrets Audio Ser.). 2000. 19.95 (978-1-883272-69-2(6)) Marketplace Bks.

High Probability Selling. Jacques Werth & Nicholas E. Ruben. 4 CDs. 2003. audio compact disk 39.85 (978-0-9631550-6-1(7)) Abba Pub PA.

High Probability Selling. Jacques Werth & Nicholas E. Ruben. 2003. (978-0-9631550-5-4(9)) Abba Pub PA.

High Profile. unabr. ed. Robert B. Parker. Read by Scott Sowers. 5 CDs. (Running Time: 21600 sec.). (Jesse Stone Ser.: No. 6). (ENG.). 2007. audio compact disk 29.95 (978-0-7393-1868-3(3)) Pub: Random Audio Pubg. Dist(s): Random

High Rhulain. Brian Jacques. Narrated by Brian Jacques. (Running Time: 41400 sec.). (Redwall Ser.). (J). (gr. 3-7). 2005. audio compact disk 29.99 (978-1-4193-4320-9(3)) Recorded Bks.

High Rise Glorious Skittle Skat Roarious Sky Pie Angel Food Cake. unabr. ed. Nancy Willard. Narrated by Christina Moore. 1 cass. (Running Time: 30 mins.). (gr. 3 up). 1997. 10.00 (978-0-7887-0604-2(7), 94783E7) Recorded Bks.
Birthday presents for mothers are always hard to find. So when a young girl's mother asks for a High Rise Glorious Skittle Skat Roarious Sky Pie Angel Food Cake for her birthday, the girl knows the recipe will require some detective work. Delectable tale of food, magic & love as heavenly as the gorgeous birthday cake.

High Rise Private Eyes Case of the Desperate Duck. Cynthia Rylant. Illus. by Suçie Stevenson. Narrated by William Dufris. (J). (gr. k-3). 2007. 12.95 (978-1-4301-0063-8(X)) Live Oak Media.

High-Rise Private Eyes Series. Cynthia Rylant. Illus. by G. Brian Karas. 44 vols. (Running Time: 65 mins.). 2003. pap. bk. 61.95 (978-1-59112-430-6(1)); pap. bk. 68.95 (978-1-59112-858-8(7)) Live Oak Media.

High Rising. unabr. ed. Angela Thirkell. Read by Jilly Bond. 6 cass. (Running Time: 7 hrs. 12 min.). (Isis Ser.). (J). 2003. 54.95 (978-0-7531-1666-1(9)); audio compact disk 64.95 (978-0-7531-2235-8(9)) Pub: ISIS Lrg Prnt GBR. Dist(s): Ulverscroft US

High Risk OB. Instructed by Cynthia F. Krening. 3 cass. (Running Time: 7 hrs.). 1990. 79.00 cass. & soft-bound bk. (HT37) Ctr Hlth Educ.
Prompt assessment & treatment are imperative in high risk obstetric patients if the life of mother & child are to be saved. Learn critical features of nursing care for women with HELLP syndrome, pre-term labor, PROM & multiple gestation.

High Road North Road Trip. 1000th ed. Scripts. Narrated by Michael Hice et al. 2 cass. (Running Time: 2 hours). 2004. audio compact disk 19.50 (978-0-9759930-2-6(X)) Galloping Glries.
The High Road from Santa Fe to Taos through the foothills of the Sangre de Cristo Mountains is one of the richest local byways in terms of history, culture and landscape.This CD road trip will guide you through the geology and history of the area, weaving the story of Indian Peblos and Spanish settlers, their conflicts and triumphs. As you meander through mountain villages, your guides unveil the culture and traditions of New Mexico. Music by local musicians highlights the trip.

High Road to China. unabr. ed. Jon Cleary. Read by Gordon Griffin. 9 cass. (Running Time: 13 hrs. 30 mins.). 1999. 69.95 (20354) Pub: Soundings Ltd GBR. Dist(s): Ulverscroft US

High School Heart Stoppers: A Mighty Change Within. Victor Harris. 1 cass. 7.98 (978-1-55503-935-6(9), 06005268) Covenant Comms.
High school challenges & conversion.

High School Musical. Created by Walt Disney Records Staff. (J). (gr. 4-7). 2006. audio compact disk 13.99 (978-5-558-57366-4(X)) W Disney Records.

High School Resources. Created by Standard Publishing. (Encounter Curriculum Ser.). 2006. 13.99 (978-0-7847-5875-5(1)) Standard Pub.

***High School Sweethearts.** Prod. by Siren Audio Studios. Adapted by L. N. Nolan. Based on a novel by L. N. Nolan. (ENG.). 2010. audio compact disk 25.99 (978-0-9844180-5-3(9)) Siiren Audio.

High School Teacher's Convenience Kit. Created by Standard Publishing. (Encounter Curriculum Ser.). 2006. 24.99 (978-0-7847-5877-9(8)) Standard Pub.

High Season: English for the Hotel & Tourist Industry. Keith Harding. 1995. 17.50 (978-0-19-451309-8(2)) OUP.

High Self Esteem: Babbling Brook. Eldon Taylor. 1 cass. 16.95 (978-1-55978-455-9(5), 5305F) Progress Aware Res.

High Self-Esteem: Classic. Eldon Taylor. Read by Eldon Taylor. Ed. by Leslie Brice. 1 cass. (Running Time: 1 hr.). 1992. 16.95 (978-1-56705-052-3(2)) Gateways Inst.
Self improvement.

High Self-Esteem: Easy. Eldon Taylor. Read by Eldon Taylor. Ed. by Leslie Brice. 1 cass. (Running Time: 1 hr.). 1992. 16.95 (978-1-56705-053-0(0)) Gateways Inst.

High Self-Esteem: Harmonies. Eldon Taylor. Read by Eldon Taylor. Ed. by Leslie Brice. 1 cass. (Running Time: 1 hr.). 1992. 16.95 (978-1-56705-054-7(9)) Gateways Inst.

High Self-Esteem: Ocean. Eldon Taylor. Read by Eldon Taylor. Ed. by Leslie Brice. 1 cass. (Running Time: 1 hr.). 1992. 16.95 (978-1-56705-055-4(7)) Gateways Inst.

High Self Esteem: Soundtrack: Leisure Listening. Eldon Taylor. 1 cass. (Running Time: 62 min.). 16.95 (978-0-940699-10-6(9), 5305B) Progress Aware Res.
Musical soundtrack with underlying subliminal affirmations.

High Self Esteem: Soundtrack: Musical Themes. Eldon Taylor. 1 cass. (Running Time: 62 min.). 16.95 incl. script. (978-0-940699-11-3(7), 5305C) Progress Aware Res.

High Self Esteem: Soundtrack: Synthesized Moments. Eldon Taylor. 1 cass. (Running Time: 62 min.). 16.95 (978-0-940699-74-8(5), 5305D) Progress Aware Res.

High Self Esteem: Soundtrack: Tropical Lagoon. Eldon Taylor. 1 cass. (Running Time: 62 min.). 16.95 (978-0-940699-75-5(3), 5305A) Progress Aware Res.
Environmental soundtrack with underlying subliminal affirmations.

High Self-Esteem: Stream. Eldon Taylor. Read by Eldon Taylor. Ed. by Leslie Brice. 1 cass. (Running Time: 1 hr.). 1992. 16.95 (978-1-56705-056-1(5)) Gateways Inst.
Self improvement.

High Self-Esteem: Whisper. Eldon Taylor. Read by Eldon Taylor. Ed. by Leslie Brice. 1 cass. (Running Time: 1 hr.). 1992. 16.95 (978-1-56705-199-5(5)) Gateways Inst.

High Self-Esteem & Self-Image for Busy People. Bob Griswold. Read by Deirdre M. Griswold. 2000. 11.98 (978-1-55848-213-5(X)) EffectiveMN.

***High Self-Esteem & Unshakable Confidence: The Science of Feeling Great!** unabr. ed. Made for Success. Read by Larry Iverson & Zig Ziglar. (Running Time: 7 hrs.). (Made for Success Ser.). 2010. audio compact disk 34.95 (978-1-4417-6798-1(3)) Blckstn Audio.

***High Self-Esteem & Unshakable Confidence (Library Edition) The Science of Feeling Great!** unabr. ed. Made for Success. Read by Larry Iverson & Zig Ziglar. (Running Time: 7 hrs.). (Made for Success Ser.). 2010. audio compact disk 105.00 (978-1-4417-6797-4(5)) Blckstn Audio.

High Self Esteem, Success & Prosperity. Christopher Love. Read by Christopher Love. 1 cass. (Running Time: 30 min.). 1997. 10.95 (978-1-891820-20-5(6)) World Sangha Pubg.
Self-hypnosis meditation for healing, self-improvement & realizing our full & powerful potential as spiritual beings.

High Sierra. Perf. by Humphrey Bogart & Ida Lupino. 1943. (DM-5110) Natl Recrd Co.

High Society. unabr. ed. Ben Elton. Read by Greg Wagland. 12 CDs. (Running Time: 11 hrs. 57 min.). (Isis Ser.). (J). 2003. audio compact disk 99.95 (978-0-7531-1836-8(X)); 84.95 (978-0-7531-1812-2(2)) Pub: ISIS Lrg Prnt GBR. Dist(s): Ulverscroft US
The war on drugs has been lost. The simple fact is that the whole world is rapidly becoming one vast criminal network. From pop stars and royal princes to crack whores and street kids, from the Groucho Club toilets to the poppy fields of Afghanistan, we are all partners in crime. Here is a story about Britain today, a criminal nation in which everybody is either breaking the law or knows people who do.

High Society: The Life of Grace Kelly. unabr. ed. Donald Spoto. Narrated by George K. Wilson. (Running Time: 10 hrs. 0 mins.). 2009. 16.99 (978-1-4001-8511-5(4)) Tantor Media.

High Society: The Life of Grace Kelly. unabr. ed. Donald Spoto. Narrated by George K. Wilson. 1 MP3-CD. (Running Time: 10 hrs. 0 mins. 0 sec.). 2010. 24.99 (978-1-4001-6511-7(3)); audio compact disk 34.99 (978-1-4001-1511-2(6)); audio compact disk 69.99 (978-1-4001-4511-9(2)) Pub: Tantor Media. Dist(s): IngramPubServ

High Speed Success: Good, Better, Best. Tommy Newberry. Read by Tommy Newberry. 1 cass. (Running Time: 91 min.). 1994. 15.00 (978-1-886669-01-7(5)) One Percent Club.
Demonstrates how the principles of personal development help successful individuals cope with & manage change in all six areas of life.

High Stakes. unabr. ed. Dick Francis. Read by Geoffrey Howard. 4 cass. (Running Time: 5 hrs. 30 mins.). 2003. 32.95 (978-0-7861-0906-7(8), 1715) Blckstn Audio.
Steven Scott is relatively new to horses. A successful, wealthy inventor, he takes up horse racing as a hobby - a hobby that soon brings him winner after winner under the inspired guidance of his trainer, Jody Leeds. But just when Steven is winning at both women & horses, he discovers deceit in his own stables. Termination of the troublemaker marks Steven for his own termination & much sooner than he can imagine.

High Stakes. unabr. ed. Dick Francis. Read by Geoffrey Howard. 5 CDs. (Running Time: 5 hrs. 30 mins.). 2000. audio compact disk 40.00 (978-0-7861-9918-1(0), 1715) Blckstn Audio.

High Stakes. unabr. ed. Dick Francis. Read by Tony Britton. 6 cass. (Running Time: 9 hrs.). 2000. 49.95 (978-0-7451-4047-6(5), CAB 744) Pub: Chivers Audio Bks GBR. Dist(s): AudioGO
When your horse has just sprinted past the winning post, racing seems a very cozy and civilized hobby. But the pleasure of a day at Sandown Race Park is spoiled for Steven Scott when he fires the trainer of his horses. Although Jody Leeds seems to be a bright young workaholic, Scott suspects he is a crook. And it isn't long before Scott finds out that the worst is yet to come.

High Stakes: Big Time Sports & Downtown Redevelopment. Timothy J. Curry et al. (Urban Life & Urban Landscape Ser.). 2004. audio compact disk 9.95 (978-0-8142-9029-3(9)) Pub: Ohio St U Pr. Dist(s): Chicago Distribution Ctr

High Stand, unabr. ed. Hammond Innes. Narrated by Eric Conger. 8 cass. (Running Time: 12 hrs.). 1989. 70.00 (978-1-55690-223-9(9), 88994E7) Recorded Bks.
The disappearance of Tom Halliday leads Philip Redfern, his attorney, to the Pacific Northwest to investigate the estate. The trail leads from Halliday's gold mine in the Yukon to a modern ghost town & secrets even more dangerous Halliday curse.

High Tech-High Touch. abr. ed. John Naisbitt et al. Read by Michael McConnohie. 1 cass. (Running Time: 180 min.). 1999. 17.95 (978-1-55935-327-4(9)) Soundelux.
Examination of the ubiquitous fusion of technology, spirituality & new-millenium culture.

High Tide. Jude Deveraux. Read by Jenna Stern. 2004. 15.95 (978-0-7435-4182-4(0)) Pub: S&S Audio. Dist(s): S and S Inc

High Tide, Set. abr. ed. Jude Deveraux. Read by Kim Cattrall. 4 cass. 1999. 24.00 (FS9-51088) Highsmith.

High Tide in Hawaii. Mary Pope Osborne. (Running Time: 40 mins.). (Magic Tree House Ser.: No. 28). (J). (gr. k-3). 2003. pap. bk. 17.00 (978-0-8072-1176-2(1), Listening Lib) Pub: Random Audio Pubg. Dist(s): Random

***High Tide in Tucson.** abr. ed. Barbara Kingsolver. Read by Barbara Kingsolver. (ENG.). 2005. (978-0-06-089450-4(4), Harper Audio); (978-0-06-089451-1(2), Harper Audio) HarperCollins Pubs.

High Tide in Tucson: Essays from Now or Never, unabr. ed. Barbara Kingsolver. Narrated by Suzanne Toren. 7 cass. (Running Time: 9 hrs. 15 mins.). 1998. 60.00 (978-0-7887-2605-7(6), 95445E7) Recorded Bks.
Kingsolver gently directs listeners' attention to an elusive place where ecology meets poetry in 25 illuminating essays.

High Tide in Tucson Set: Essays from Now or Never. abr. ed. Barbara Kingsolver. Read by Barbara Kingsolver. 2 cass. (Running Time: 3 hrs.). 1995. 18.00 (978-0-694-51577-6(9), 393199) HarperCollins Pubs.

High Time to Kill. Raymond Benson. Read by Robert Whitfield. 1 CD. (Running Time: 30600 sec.). (James Bond Ser.). 2003. audio compact disk 24.95 (978-0-7861-9063-8(9), 3049) Blckstn Audio.

High Time to Kill. unabr. ed. Raymond Benson. Read by Robert Whitfield. 7 CDs. (Running Time: 10 hrs.). 2003. audio compact disk 56.00 (978-0-7861-9337-0(9), 3049); 49.95 (978-0-7861-2347-6(8), 3049) Blckstn Audio.
From England to Belgium to the icy heights of the legendary mountain Kangchenjunga, Bond must pit his strength and guile against the most resourceful criminal minds he has ever encountered.

High Touch with High Tech: Spiritual Assessment on the Computer. 1 cass. (Care Cassettes Ser.: Vol. 22, No. 4). 1995. 10.80 Assn Prof Chaplains.

High Trust Selling: Make More Money in Less Time with Less Stress. abr. ed. Todd Duncan. Read by Todd Duncan. 4 cass. (Running Time: 4 hrs.). (Smart Audio Ser.). 2004. 25.99 (978-1-58926-339-0(1)) Oasis Audio.

High Trust Selling: Make More Money in Less Time with Less Stress. abr. unabr. ed. Todd Duncan. Narrated by Todd Duncan. 4 CDs. (Running Time: 5 hrs.). (Smart Audio Ser.). (ENG.). 2004. audio compact disk 25.99 (978-1-58926-340-6(5)) Oasis Audio.
A Wall Street Journal best-seller! There is a major difference between being a sales person in business and being in business as a salesperson. Being successful in sales has a lot to do with what's on the inside of a person, and the person's ability to establish and foster loyal relationships.

High Trust Selling: Make More Money in Less Time with Less Stress. unabr. ed. Todd Duncan. Narrated by Todd Duncan. (ENG.). 2004. 18.19 (978-1-60814-234-7(5)) Oasis Audio.

High-Ways: TITLE was changed to High-Ways - see new ISBN Number. (ENG.). 2008. audio compact disk 15.00 (978-0-9654372-4-0(8)) Insight Inc.

High, Wide & Lonesome: Growing up on the Colorado Frontier. unabr. ed. Hal Borland. Narrated by Robert Gorman. 6 cass. (Running Time: 9 hrs.). 1988. 51.00 (978-1-55690-224-6(7), 88890E7) Recorded Bks.
The author recounts his youth on the high plains of Colorado in the first years of the 20th Century in 1910.

High Window. abr. ed. Raymond Chandler. Read by Elliott Gould. 3 CDs. (Running Time: 3 hrs.). 2004. audio compact disk 25.00 (978-1-59007-102-1(6)) Pub: New Millenn Enter. Dist(s): PerseuPGW
A wealthy Pasadena widow with a mean streak, a missing daughter-in-law with a past, and a gold coin worth a small fortune-the elements don't quite add up until Marlowe discovers evidence of murder, rape, blackmail, and the worst kind of human exploitation.

High Window. abr. unabr. ed. Raymond Chandler. Read by Elliott Gould. 2 cass. (Running Time: 3 hrs.). 2004. 18.00 (978-1-59007-101-4(8)) Pub: New Millenn Enter. Dist(s): PerseuPGW

High-Wire Henry. Mary Calhoun. Read by Christina Moore. 1 cass. (Running Time: 15 mins.). (YA). 2000. pap. bk. 33.00 (978-0-7887-4175-3(6), 41090); 178.30 (978-0-7887-4176-0(4), 47083) Recorded Bks.
Henry the cat is green with envy ever since a new puppy joined the family. Has everyone forgotten how special Henry is? But when the silly puppy chases a squirrel out onto a narrow roof ledge, it is Henry to the rescue! Now he must put his jealousy aside to attempt a dangerous high-wire act.

High-Wire Henry. unabr. ed. Mary Calhoun. Narrated by Christina Moore. 1 cass. (Running Time: 15 mins.). (gr. 1 up). 2000. 10.00 (978-0-7887-4001-5(6), 96049E7) Recorded Bks.

High Wizardry. Diane Duane. Read by Christina Moore. 5 cass. (Running Time: 8 hrs.). (YA). (gr. 5 up). 2000. pap. bk. 58.25 (978-0-7887-3799-2(6), 41043); 124.80 (978-0-7887-3870-8(4), 47035) Recorded Bks.
Twice, young wizards Nita & Kit have successfully thwarted a dark power called The Lone One. But when Nita's 10-year-old sister finds Nita's manual of spells, she becomes a powerful wizard herself. Now she is headed toward her own confrontation with The Lone One. Includes an exclusive interview with the author.

High Wizardry. unabr. ed. Diane Duane. Narrated by Christina Moore. 6 pieces. (Running Time: 8 hrs.). (gr. 5 up). 2000. 44.00 (978-0-7887-3831-9(3), 96043E7) Recorded Bks.

Higher. Neal Bascomb. 7 cass. (Running Time: 11 hrs. 15 mins.). 2004. 29.99 (978-1-4025-5601-2(2), 03234) Recorded Bks.

Higher Abdication. (ENG.). 2007. (978-1-60339-045-3(6)); cd-rom & audio compact disk (978-1-60339-046-0(4)) Listenr Digest.

Higher Authority. abr. ed. Stephen White. Read by Dick Hill. 5 CDs. (Running Time: 21600 sec.). (Dr. Alan Gregory Ser.). 2005. audio compact disk 16.99 (978-1-59600-407-8(X), 9781596004078, BCD Value Price) Brilliance Audio.
The sudden death of Utah's Senator Orrin Hatch propels his successor, Lester Horner, first into Hatch's Senate seat and then on to become the first Mormon associate justice of the U.S. Supreme Court. Carried along with Horner is Blythe Oaks, an ambitious and intelligent woman who is also Horner's favorite law clerk and fellow Mormon. But Blythe's reputation - and, by extension, Lester Horner's - is threatened when a female former employee accuses her of sexual harassment and career sabotage. In Higher Authority White shifts his focus from Dr. Alan Gregory, the hero of Privileged Information and the national bestseller Private Practices, to Alan's fiancée, Lauren Crowder. The pool-shooting deputy D.A.'s life is already complicated enough as she picks her way through her relationship with Alan at the same time she is fighting her quiet and dignified battle with multiple sclerosis. But since Blythe's accuser happens to be Lauren's kid sister, aspiring stand-up comic Teresa Crowder, Lauren plunges into the case. And she gets immediate help from an old law school buddy, Robin Torr, whose practice is in Salt Lake City. When, suddenly, Blythe Oaks is savagely murdered in Washington D.C., the lengths to which someone will go to protect secrets that might prove embarrassing to higher authorities in the church are starkly revealed. And as Crowder and Torr probe more and more deeply into these secrets, with timely help from Alan Gregory and his old friend Detective Sam Purdy of the Boulder, Colorado police, White's tough but determined women find the body count growing and themselves placed in jeopardy by a remorseless killer.

Higher Authority. abr. ed. Stephen White. Read by Dick Hill. (Running Time: 6 hrs.). (Dr. Alan Gregory Ser.). 2006. 24.95 (978-1-4233-0099-1(8), 9781423300991, BAD); audio compact disk 24.95 (978-1-4233-0097-7(1), 9781423300977, Brilliance MP3) Brilliance Audio.

Higher Authority. unabr. collector's ed. Stephen White. Read by Kimberly Schraf. 10 cass. (Running Time: 15 hrs.). (Dr. Alan Gregory Ser.). 1995. 80.00 (978-0-7366-3042-9(2), 3724) Books on Tape.
Lauren Crowder, deputy D.A. in Salt Lake City, already has enough on her plate. But when her kid sister accuses a prominent judge's law clerk of sexual harrassment, she lends a hand. When someone kills the clerk, Crowder & her team guess the motive: cover for the Mormon Church. The further they dig, the more bodies they find & the closer they come to closing in on a remorseless killer.

Higher Calling. Rick Joyner. 1 cass. (Running Time: 90 mins.). (Growing in Faith Ser.: Vol. 5). 2000. 5.00 (RJ14-005) Morning NC.
With fresh & practical messages centering on faith, this tape series will enable you to better understand essential principles of the Christian walk.

Higher Communication. Swami Amar Jyoti. 1 cass. 1989. 9.95 (R-95) Truth Consciousness.
God & Master always communicate with us; we receive to the extent we are conscious. The hierarchy of communication.

Higher Consciousness, Tape 1. Pat Carroll. Read by Pat Carroll. Ed. by Tony Carroll. 1 cass. (Running Time: 30 min.). 10.00 Inner-Mind Concepts.
Presents metaphysical exercises into one's consciousness.

Higher Consciousness, Tape 2. Pat Carroll. Read by Pat Carroll. Ed. by Tony Carroll. 1 cass. (Running Time: 30 min.). 10.00 Inner-Mind Concepts.
Explains how to open the mind to the universe & react to the deepest part of one's subconciousness.

Higher Dedication. Swami Amar Jyoti. 1 cass. 1995. 9.95 (M-96) Truth Consciousness.
A higher perspective for proceeding on the path. Letting go of the past; avoiding fear & negativity. Healing ourselves & our world.

Higher Education & Post-Graduate Executive Programs in France: A Strategic Reference 2006. Compiled by Icon Group International, Inc. Staff. 2007. ring bd. 195.00 (978-0-497-35951-5(0)) Icon Grp.

Higher Education in a Learning Society: Meeting New Demands for Education & Training. Jerold W. Apps. (Higher Education Ser.). 1988. bk. 38.45 (978-1-55542-115-1(6), Jossey-Bass) Wiley US.

Higher Ethics. Swami Amar Jyoti. 1 cass. 1977. 9.95 (K-14) Truth Consciousness.
Preparation for true seeking. What higher ethics are, why they are necessay. Fulfilling the terms & conditions for peace.

Higher Ground. Music by Steven Halpern. 1 cass. 9.95 (LA129); audio compact disk 14.95 (A129D) Lghtwrks Aud & Vid.
This recording offers a deeper experience than mere relaxation. "Higher Ground" provides a sonic matrix that entrains your brain into the alpha & theta brainwave states associated with relaxation & meditation.

Higher Message of Jesus. unabr. ed. Swami Amar Jyoti. 1 cass. (Satsangs of Swami Amar Jyoti Ser.). (C). 1996. 9.95 (K-160) Truth Consciousness.
The message & mission of Jesus were uncompromisingly spiritual. Assuming responsibility, not taking advantage of Holy Ones. The spirit of Christmas.

Higher Mission. Swami Amar Jyoti. 1 cass. 1976. 9.95 (O-2) Truth Consciousness.
Did we come on earth to care for the body & control the mind? Raja Yoga & natural Law. Distinguishing between control & release.

Higher Power of Lucky. unabr. ed. Susan Patron. Read by Cassandra Campbell. 3 CDs. (Running Time: 3 hrs. 38 mins.). (J). (gr. 4-7). 2007. audio compact disk 30.00 (978-0-7393-4851-2(5), Listening Lib) Pub: Random Audio Pubg. Dist(s): Random
Lucky, age ten, can't wait another day. The meanness gland in her heart and the crevices full of questions in her brain make running away from Hard Pan, California (population 43), the rock-bottom only choice she has. It's all Brigitte's fault- -for wanting to go back to France. Guardians are supposed to stay put and look after girls in their care! Instead Lucky is sure that she'll be abandoned to some orphanage in Los Angeles where her beloved dog, HMS Beagle, won't be allowed. She'll have to lose her friends Miles, who lives on cookies, and Lincoln, future U.S. president (maybe) and member of the International Guild of Knot Tyers. Just as bad, she'll have to give up eavesdropping on twelve-step anonymous programs where the interesting talk is all about Higher Powers. Lucky needs her own - and quick. But she hadn't planned on a dust storm. Or needing to lug the world's heaviest survival-kit backpack into the desert.

Higher Power of Lucky. unabr. ed. Susan Patron. Read by Cassandra Campbell. 3 CDs. (Running Time: 13080 sec.). (ENG.). (J). (gr. 3-7). 2007. audio compact disk 27.00 (978-0-7393-3879-7(X), Listening Lib) Pub: Random Audio Pubg. Dist(s): Random

Higher Power Tools. Bob Meehan. Perf. by Bob Meehan. (ENG.). 2008. 14.95 (978-0-9702327-6-2(4)) Meek Pubng.

Higher Praise - Devotions. Prod. by Clay Hecocks. Engineer Michael Grosso. 2001. audio compact disk 11.99 (978-1-932283-11-2(0)) Pub: Calvry Chap Ch. Dist(s): STL Dist NA

Higher Praise - You Are There. Prod. by Clay Hecocks. Engineer Michael Grosso. 2003. audio compact disk 11.99 (978-1-932283-10-5(2)) Pub: Calvry Chap Ch. Dist(s): STL Dist NA

Higher Self see Ser Superior

Higher Self: Aligning to Your Higher Self. Instructed by Stuart Wilde. 1 cass. (Self-Help Tape Ser.). 9.95 (978-0-930603-24-3(9)) White Dove NM.
The Higher Self is a collective body of energy - it is the inner you. Within it is all the knowledge that you will ever need & through it you can experience a limitless understanding of the physical plane as well as the "unseen dimensions" that lie close at hand.

Higher Self: The Magic of Inner & Other Fulfillment. Deepak Chopra. 6 cass. (Running Time: 6 hrs.). 1992. 59.95 (978-1-55525-070-6(X), 255A) Nightingale-Conant.
On this fascinating odyssey, Dr. Chopra will reveal how to eliminate fear & other obstacles to spirituality & liberate your emotional body & live in a state of total freedom & more. Open a window into eternity & a doorway to the infinite with the higher self. And discover boundless fulfillment in life. Includes chart.

Higher Self: The Magic of Inner & Other Fulfillment. abr. ed. Deepak Chopra. 2 CDs. (Running Time: 20 hrs. 0 mins. 0 sec.). (ENG., 2001. audio compact disk 20.00 (978-0-7435-0921-3(8), Nightgale) Pub: S&S Audio. Dist(s): S and S Inc
In this revolutionary program Dr. Chopra combines modern science and ancient spirituality to show how to reach the higher self and its empowering source of intelligence.

Higher Self: The Magic of Inner & Other Fulfillment. unabr. ed. Deepak Chopra. 2 cass. 13.95 set. (87028) Books on Tape.
Why are you here? What do you really need? How can you get it? Inside you there's a "you" who really knows the answers to these questions - a "higher self" that resides in each of us that is naturally boundless, totally intelligent & completely free.

Higher Self Communication. 2003. audio compact disk 17.98 (978-1-933441-05-4(4)) Quantum Heal.

Higher-Self Exploration. Dick Sutphen. 1 cass. (Running Time: 1 hr.). (RX17 Ser.). 14.98 (978-0-87554-410-6(X), RX205) Valley Sun.

Higher Self Guidance, Vol. 4, set. Jonathan Parker. Read by Jonathan Parker. 2 CDs. (Running Time: 2 hrs.). (Guided Meditation Ser.: Vol. 6). 1999. audio compact disk (978-1-58400-059-4(7)) QuantumQuests Intl.

Higher Self Meditation. Read by Mary Richards. (Stress Reduction Ser.). 9.95 (092) Master Your Mind.

Higher Self Meditation. Read by Mary Richards. 1 cass. (Running Time: 45 min.). (Energy Break Ser.). 2007. audio compact disk 19.95 (978-1-56136-154-0(2)) Master Your Mind.

Higher-Self Transition. 1 cass. (Tara Sutphen Sleep Programming Tapes Ser.). 11.98 (978-0-87554-554-7(8), 2103) Valley Sun.

Higher Speed General Recording: 225 Series. National Shorthand Reporters Association. 3 cass. 9.00 (225-4). (CT-15); 9.00 (225-5). (CT-16); 9.00 (225-6). (CT-17) Natl Ct Report.
Testimony shorthand dictation at 225 wpm, jury charge dictation at 200 wpm, & literary dictation at 180 wpm. 225-4 consists of past Certificate of Proficiency examinations.

Higher Speed General Recording: 230 Series. National Shorthand Reporters Association. 9.00 (230-4). (CT-18); 9.00 (230-4). (CT-19) Natl Ct Report.
Testimony at 230 wpm, jury charge dictation at 210 wpm & literary dictation at 180 wpm.

Higher Speed General Recording: 240 Series. National Shorthand Reporters Association. 1 cass. 9.00 (240-4). (CT-20); 9.00 (240-5). (CT-21) Natl Ct Report.
Dictation testimony at 240 wpm, jury charge dictation at 220 wpm., & literary dictation 190 wpm.

Higher Speed General Recording: 250 Series. National Shorthand Reporters Association. 3 cass. 9.00 (250-3). (CT-22); 9.00 (250-4). (CT-23); 9.00 (250-5). (CT-24) Natl Ct Report.
Shorthand dictation testimony at 250 wpm, jury charge dictation at 230 wpm, & literary dictation at 195 wpm.

Higher Speed General Recording: 260 Series. National Shorthand Reporters Association. 5 cass. 9.00 (260-4). (CT-25); 9.00 (260-5). (CT-26); 9.00 (260-6). (CT-27); 9.00 (260-7). (CT-28); 9.00 (260-8). (CT-29) Natl Ct Report.
Shorthand dictation testimony at 260 wpm, jury charge dictation at 250 wpm, & literary dictation at 200 wpm. Recordings 260-4 & 260-6 consist entirely of former Certificate of Merit examinations.

Highest Chosen Ideal. Swami Amar Jyoti. 1 cass. 1982. 9.95 (M-23) Truth Consciousness.
Aspiration & longing for the Light, the ultimate essence of the universe. Real meaning of renunciation.

Highest Civilization. Swami Amar Jyoti. 1 cass. 1982. 9.95 (A-19) Truth Consciousness.
Outer modes may change, but not the Truth. Making civilization flourish. What is required of us?.

***Highest Duty.** unabr. ed. Chesley B. Sullenberger. Read by Chesley B. Sullenberger. Read by Michael Mcconnohie. (ENG.). 2009. (978-0-06-196711-5(4), Harper Audio); (978-0-06-196710-8(6), Harper Audio) HarperCollins Pubs.

Highest Duty: My Search for What Really Matters. unabr. ed. Chesley B. Sullenberger. Read by Chesley B. Sullenberger. Read by Michael McConnohie. 8 CDs. (Running Time: 9 hrs. 30 mins.). 2009. audio compact disk 39.99 (978-0-06-195325-5(3), Harper Audio) HarperCollins Pubs.

Highest Formula. Swami Amar Jyoti. 1 cass. 1980. 9.95 (P-32) Truth Consciousness.
Using the seasoned formulas. Readiness for absolute knowledge. The foremost duty of a seeker. Taking benefit of dreams.

Highest Glory. John Devries. 2001. 75.00 (978-0-633-01446-9(X)); 11.98 (978-0-633-01444-5(3)); audio compact disk 85.00 (978-0-633-01447-6(8)) LifeWay Christian.

Highest Glory. John DeVries. 2001. audio compact disk 16.98 (978-0-633-01445-2(1)) LifeWay Christian.

Highest Goal: The Secret That Sustains You in Every Moment. unabr. ed. Michael Ray. Read by Jonathan Marosz. (Running Time: 5 hrs. 30 mins.). (ENG.). 2008. 24.98 (978-1-59659-245-2(1), GildAudio) Pub: Gildan Media. Dist(s): HachBkGrp

Highest Hit. unabr. ed. Nancy Willard. Narrated by Christina Moore. 2 pieces. (Running Time: 2 hrs. 45 mins.). (gr. 4 up). 1997. 19.00 (978-0-7887-1109-1(1), 95102E7) Recorded Bks.
All ages will enjoy spirited Kate & benefit from the sage advice of Kate's best friend, 75-year-old Mr. Goldberg: we strengthen out integrity every time we choose the high road in any difficult situation.

Highest Praise. Contrib. by Nicole Binion. 2004. audio compact disk 15.99 (978-0-7684-0200-1(X)) Destiny Image Pubs.

Highest Relationship. Swami Amar Jyoti. 1 cass. 1980. 9.95 (E-17) Truth Consciousness.
Most sacred relationship is between Guru & disciple. How the master helps us. Harmonizing all relationships.

Highest Tide. unabr. ed. Jim Lynch. Read by Fisher Stevens. 6 CDs. (Running Time: 7 hrs. 30 mins. 0 sec.). (ENG.). 2005. audio compact disk 29.95 (978-1-59397-827-3(8)) Pub: Macmill Audio. Dist(s): Macmillan

Highest Tide: A Novel. Jim Lynch. 6 CDs. 2005. audio compact disk 64.95 (978-0-7927-3753-7(9), SLD 843, Chivers Sound Lib) AudioGO.

Highest Tide: A Novel. Jim Lynch. Read by Fisher Stevens. 2005. 17.95 (978-1-59397-828-0(6)) Pub: Macmill Audio. Dist(s): Macmillan

Highgate Rise. unabr. ed. Anne Perry. Read by Kenneth Shanley. 10 cass. (Running Time: 13 hrs. 15 min.). (Thomas Pitt Ser.). 1999. 98.95 (978-1-85903-219-0(2)) Pub: Magna Story GBR. Dist(s): Ulverscroft US
A fire in the peaceful suburb of Highgate was set by an arsonist. The wife of a prominent doctor died in it. Police inspector Pitts & his wife become enmeshed in the sinister web.

Highgate Rise. unabr. ed. Anne Perry. Read by Davina Porter. 10 cass. (Running Time: 13 hrs.). (Thomas Pitt Ser.). 2006. 89.75 (978-1-4193-4456-5(0), 96095); audio compact disk 119.75 (978-1-4193-4564-7(8), C3351) Recorded Bks.

Highland Fling. unabr. ed. Nancy Mitford. Read by Carol Marsh. 6 cass. (Running Time: 6 hrs. 14 min.). 2001. 54.95 (978-1-85089-867-2(7), 92075) Pub: ISIS Audio GBR. Dist(s): Ulverscroft US
This book conveys the essence of life as the 'Bright Young People' lived it during the 1920s & 1930s. We observe Lady Brenda Chadlington 'blowing smoke through her nostrils like a horse in cold weather,' we encounter a splendid Scots ballad, & hear about a curious & very intoxicating drink made of cabbage & oatmeal.

Highland King Vol. 2: The Scottish Lute. Ronn McFarlane. 2003. pap. bk. 35.00 (978-0-7866-7251-6(X)) Mel Bay.

Highland Laddie Gone. unabr. ed. Sharyn McCrumb. 4 cass. (Running Time: 6 hrs.). 2002. (978-1-74030-755-0(0)) Bolinda Pubng AUS.

Highland Laddie Gone. unabr. ed. Sharyn McCrumb. Narrated by Davina Porter. 5 cass. (Running Time: 6 hrs. 15 mins.). (Elizabeth MacPherson Ser.: No. 3). 1992. 44.00 (978-1-55690-678-7(1), 92220E7) Recorded Bks.
The Glencoe Scottish games, a summer festival where several hundred kilt-clad Americans celebrate their Scottish roots, is off to a bad start when Colin Campbell, a troublemaker from the Campbell clan, is found dead in his cottage with a "skian dubh" in his chest.

Highland Lady. Colleen Faulkner. Narrated by Jill Tanner. 8 cass. (Running Time: 11 hrs. 15 mins.). 82.00 (978-1-4025-3247-4(4)) Recorded Bks.

Highland Lord. Colleen Faulkner. Narrated by Jill Tanner. 8 cass. (Running Time: 10 hrs. 45 mins.). 72.00 (978-1-4025-3443-0(4)) Recorded Bks.

Highland Memories. Keith Halligan. (Running Time: 1 hr.). 2002. audio compact disk 15.99 (978-1-904972-17-4(9)) Global Jrny GBR GBR.

Highland Ring. Ed. by Robert A. Monroe. 1 cass. (Running Time: 30 min.). (Meta Music Ser.). 1986. 12.95 (978-1-56102-212-0(8)) Inter Indus.
An uplifting & awakening Scottish theme which can awaken feelings of ecstasy & joy.

***Highland Scandal.** unabr. ed. Julia London. (Running Time: 11 hrs.). (Scandalous Ser.). 2011. 39.97 (978-1-4418-5165-9(8), 9781441851659, BADLE); 24.99 (978-1-4418-5164-2(X), 9781441851642, BAD) Brilliance Audio.

***Highland Scandal.** unabr. ed. Julia London. (Running Time: 11 hrs.). (Scandalous Ser.). 2011. 24.99 (978-1-4418-5162-8(3), 9781441851628, Brilliance MP3); audio compact disk 19.99 (978-1-4418-5160-4(7), 9781441851604, Bril Audio CD Unabri) Brilliance Audio.

***Highland Scandal.** unabr. ed. Julia London. Read by Anne Flosnik. (Running Time: 11 hrs.). (Scandalous Ser.). 2011. 39.97 (978-1-4418-5163-5(1), 9781441851635, Brlnc Audio MP3 Lib); audio compact disk 69.97 (978-1-4418-5161-1(5), 9781441851611, BriAudCD Unabrid) Brilliance Audio.

Highlander: Love & Hate. Colin Harvey. 2009. audio compact disk 15.95 (978-1-84435-359-0(1)) Pub: Big Finish GBR. Dist(s): Natl Bk Netwk

Highlander: Secret of the Sword. Jonathan Clements. 2009. audio compact disk 15.95 (978-1-84435-360-6(5)) Pub: Big Finish GBR. Dist(s): Natl Bk Netwk

Highlander: the Lesson. Trevor Baxendale. 2009. audio compact disk 15.95 (978-1-84435-358-3(3)) Pub: Big Finish GBR. Dist(s): Natl Bk Netwk

Highlanders. Doctor Who. 2 CDs. 2001. cd-rom 13.99 (978-0-563-47755-6(5)) London Brdge.

Highlander's Touch. unabr. ed. Karen Marie Moning. (Running Time: 11 hrs.). (Highlander Ser.). 2007. 39.25 (978-1-4233-4145-1(7), 9781423341451, BADLE); 24.95 (978-1-4233-4144-4(9), 9781423341444, BAD) Brilliance Audio.

Highlander's Touch. unabr. ed. Karen Marie Moning. Read by Phil Gigante. 10 cass. (Running Time: 39600 sec.). (Highlander Ser.). 2007. 92.25 (978-1-4233-4139-0(2), 9781423341390, BrilAudUnabridg); audio compact disk 97.25 (978-1-4233-4141-3(4), 9781423341413, BriAudCD Unabrid); audio compact disk 39.25 (978-1-4233-4143-7(0), 9781423341437, Brlnc Audio MP3 Lib); audio compact disk 24.95 (978-1-4233-4142-0(2), 9781423341420, Brilliance MP3); audio compact disk 29.95 (978-1-4233-4140-6(6), 9781423341406, Bril Audio CD Unabri) Brilliance Audio.

Highlighting Galatians, I. Dan Corner. 1 cass. 3.00 (101) Evang Outreach.

Highlighting Stepfamily Living. Nancee N. Kempler. 4 cass. (Running Time: 6 hrs.). Incl. Highlighting Stepfamily Living: Blending Families. 1 cass. 8.50; Highlighting Stepfamily Living: Realistic Expectations. 1 cass. 8.50; Highlighting Stepfamily Living: Stepfamily Parenting. 1 cass. 8.50; Highlighting Stepfamily Living: Your way, My way, Our way. 1 cass. 8.50; 1988. 31.50 set. Kempler Inst.
Discusses how one can improve chances for success in a new family.

Highlighting Stepfamily Living: Blending Families see Highlighting Stepfamily Living

Highlighting Stepfamily Living: Realistic Expectations see Highlighting Stepfamily Living

Highlighting Stepfamily Living: Stepfamily Parenting see Highlighting Stepfamily Living

Highlighting Stepfamily Living: Your way, My way, Our way see Highlighting Stepfamily Living

Highlights from Carnegie Hall Concert. Perf. by Liza Minnelli. 1 cass., 1 CD. 7.98 (TA 35505); audio compact disk 12.78 CD Jewel box. (TA 85505) NewSound.

Highlights from True Hallucinations. Terence McKenna. Read by Terence McKenna. 1 cass. 9.00 (A0423-84) Sound Photosyn.
An audio adventure - treat your ears to selected scenes from the Sound Photosynthesis musical & sound effected production of Terence performing his novel.

Highlights in Space 2008. United Nations Office for Outer Space Affairs Staff et al. 2009. audio compact disk 35.00 (978-92-1-101190-6(6)) Untd Nat Pubns.

***Highlights in Space 2009.** United Nations Staff. 2010. audio compact disk 15.00 (978-92-1-101216-3(3)) Untd Nat Pubns.

Highlights of Clutterology(R) Eliminate the Clutter in Your Life & Get Organized. Created by Nancy Miller. Based on a book by Nancy Miller. (ENG.). 2007. audio compact disk 12.95 (978-1-891440-44-1(6)) CPM Systems.

Highlights of Glory-'Ninety-Three Camp & Believers' Conv. Kenneth. 1 cass. 1994. (978-0-88114-953-1(5)) K Copeland Pubns.
Biblical teaching on the Glory of God.

Highlights of the Franchise Law. Read by Michael A. Doctrow. 1 cass. 1990. 20.00 (AL-79) PA Bar Inst.

Highlights of Western Civilization Pts. I-VI: A Great Courses Anthology. Instructed by Bob Brier et al. 32 cass. (Running Time: 32 hrs.). 2003. 349.95 (978-1-56585-650-9(3)) Teaching Co.

Highlights of Western Civilization Pts. I-VI: A Great Courses Anthology. Instructed by Bob Brier et al. Intro. by Jeremy McInerney. Instructed by Phillip Cary et al. 32 CDs. (Running Time: 32 hrs.). 2003. audio compact disk 499.95 (978-1-56585-652-3(X)) Teaching Co.

Highly Confident: The Crime & Punishment of Michael Milken. unabr. collector's ed. Jesse Kornbluth. Read by Jonathan Reese. 11 cass. (Running Time: 16 hrs. 30 min.). 1993. 88.00 (978-0-7366-2431-2(7), 3195) Books on Tape.
"The clearest picture of Michael Milken to date." (The Wall Street Journal).

Highly Effective Living: The 7 Habits in Your Life. Ed. by Simon and Schuster Staff. 1 cass. (Running Time: 90 mins.). 1999. 12.00 (978-0-671-58262-3(3), Sound Ideas) S&S Audio.
Self-help, Personal growth.

Highly Recommended: English for the Hotel & Catering Industry. 3rd rev. ed. Trish Stott & Rod Revell. 2005. 21.95 (978-0-19-457467-9(9)) OUP.

Highly Recommended: English for the Hotel & Catering Industry Class. 3rd rev. ed. Stott. 2005. audio compact disk 21.95 (978-0-19-457466-2(0)) OUP.

Highness in Hiding. unabr. l.t. ed. Nigel Tranter. Read by Colin Bower. 9 cass. (Running Time: 13 hrs. 30 min.). (Story Sound Ser.). (J). 1996. 79.95 (978-1-85903-094-3(7), 30947) Pub: Mgna Lrg Print GBR. Dist(s): Ulverscroft US
The quashing of the Jacobite Rising of 1745 saw an end to the ambitions of the exiled royal house of Stuart to regain the throne. But the English government, army & navy strove unsuccessfully to apprehend the young Prince Charles Edward.

***Highway Cats.** unabr. ed. Janet Taylor Lisle. Narrated by James Jenner. 1 Playaway. (Running Time: 2 hrs. 30 mins.). (J). (gr. 4-7). 2009. 54.75 (978-1-4407-2041-3(X)); 30.75 (978-1-4407-2032-1(0)); audio compact disk 30.75 (978-1-4407-2036-9(3)) Recorded Bks.

***Highway Cats.** unabr. collector's ed. Janet Taylor Lisle. Narrated by James Jenner. 2 CDs. (Running Time: 2 hrs. 30 mins.). (J). (gr. 4-7). 2009. audio compact disk 28.95 (978-1-4407-2557-9(8)) Recorded Bks.

Highway Home Through Texas. Keith Miller. 1 cass. 1993. pap. bk. 12.95 (978-1-55725-064-3(2)) Paraclete MA.

Highway of Prayer: Preparing the Way for a National Move of God. Lynne Hammond. 3 CDs. 2005. audio compact disk 15.00 (978-1-57399-284-8(4)) Mac Hammond.
God can reach any nation, if someone will build Him a highway. You can do it! You can help revolutionize the spiritual landscape of your nation. Pray... and prepare the way for a national move of God.

Highway to a Rodeo. abr. ed. 1 cass. 1997. 17.00 (978-1-883268-42-8(7)) Spellbinders.

Highway to Black Rose. unabr. ed. B. J. Conners. Read by Jane Rice. Ed. by Richard Haywood. 2 cass. 1996. 17.00 Set. (978-1-883268-40-4(0)) Spellbinders.
Loretta Starke, lady trucker, has a gig hauling equipment for a rock band on a cross country tour. Lead singer, Rita Thorne, is as wild off stage as on. Rita "The Black Rose" is found dead in Loretta's sleeper. Can Loretta prove her innocence?.

Highway to Evil. unabr. ed. B. J. Conners. Read by Jane Rice. Ed. by Richard Haywood. 2 cass. (Running Time: 3 hrs.). 1996. 17.00 Set. (978-1-883268-38-1(9)) Spellbinders.
The secrets of the Mercedes family draw Loretta Starke, "The Concrete Angel", into a web of evil & mystery. She soon finds herself on someone's "A" list as both suspect & victim of murder.

Highway to Fear. unabr. ed. B. J. Conners. Read by Jane Rice. Ed. by Richard Haywood. 2 cass. (Running Time: 3 hrs.). (Concrete Angel Trucking Adventure Ser.). 1995. 17.00 Set. (978-1-883268-23-7(0)) Spellbinders.
The story of a lady truck driver who rescues a young boy from an abusive home.

Highway to Holiness: The Three-Part Process of Sanctification in Your Body, Your Mind, & Your Spirit. 4 cass. (Running Time: 4 hrs.). (Passing the Test Ser.: 6). 2002. 20.00 (978-1-57399-155-1(4)) Mac Hammond.
If there was a road that led you far from sorrow and took you toward everlasting joy, would you travel that route even if there was a price to pay? At times, the price of the journey seems too high, but as Mac Hammond reveals in this installment of the Passing the Test series, the rewards greatly outweigh the sacrifice.

Highway to Lust. unabr. ed. B. J. Conners. Read by Jane Rice. 2 cass. (Running Time: 3 hrs.). 17.00 Set. (978-1-883268-34-3(6)) Spellbinders.
Loretta Starke is called in to solve a mystery...illegal immigrants are being smuggled into San Diego for slave labor. She discovers there is a link between the smugglers & a mysterious "baby farm" operated in the basement of a Beverly Hills hospital. Handsome & wimpy, Dr. Jonathan Powers, finds himself involved in Loretta's plan to bust the gang.

Highway to Murder, Set. B. J. Conners. 2 cass. 1995. 17.00 (978-1-883268-29-9(X)) Spellbinders.

Highway to Survival. unabr. ed. B. J. Conners. Read by Jane Rice. Ed. by Richard Haywood. 2 cass. (Running Time: 3 hrs.). 1996. 17.00 Set. (978-1-883268-43-5(5)) Spellbinders.
Loretta Starke becomes an heiress & gets caught up in the search for lost Spanish treasure. But first, she must deal with the guardian of this treasure, the Apache Thunder God & para-military bad guys in a mountain mini-war.

Highway to Terror. abr. ed. 1 cass. 1997. 17.00 (978-1-883268-51-0(6)) Spellbinders.

Highwayman see Classics of English Poetry for the Elementary Curriculum

Highwayman see Famous Story Poems

Highwayman. Helen Cannam. Read by Sally Hague. 5 cass. (Storysound Ser.). (J). 2000. 49.95 (978-1-85903-308-1(3)) Pub: Mgna Lrg Print GBR. Dist(s): Ulverscroft US

Highwaymen: Riding for the Band. Louis L'Amour. Read by Willie Nelson et al. 1 cass. 1995. 11.95 (978-1-55935-173-7(X)); audio compact disk 14.95 (978-1-55935-160-7(8)) Soundelux.

Hija de la Fortuna see Daughter of Fortune

Hiki I Na 'Elala Ke Kokua la 'Oe. Lilinoe Andrews. Illus. by Brook Parker. 1 cass. (HAW.). (J). (gr. k-2). 1999. pap. bk. 5.95 (978-1-58191-056-8(8)) Aha Punana Leo.

Hilarious Generosity see Generosidad Hilarante

Hilarious Generosity, Charles R. Swindoll. 2 cass. (Running Time: 4 hrs.). 1996. 11.95 (978-1-57972-023-0(4)) Insight Living.

Hilarious Generosity. Charles R. Swindoll. (ENG.). 2007. audio compact disk 24.00 (978-1-57972-763-5(8)) Insight Living.

Hilarious Homeschool Workshop. unabr. ed. Diana Waring. Read by Diana Waring. 1 cass. (Running Time: 1 hr. 30 mins.). 1997. 8.95 (978-1-930514-04-1(2)) Diana Waring.

Hilarith: The Best of Lesbian Humor. Perf. by Kate Clinton et al. 4 cass. (Running Time: 4 hrs.). (Spoken Word Humor Ser.). 1999. 29.95 Set, clamshell. (978-1-929243-01-3(4), UPR1002) Uproar Ent.
Featuring the top four performing Lesbian comediennes. Kate Clinton, Suzanne Westenhoefer, Marga Gomez, & Karen Williams.

Hilary Caine Mysteries. M. J. Elliott. (ENG.). 2008. audio compact disk 9.95 (978-1-60245-162-9(1)) GDL Multimedia.

Hilary Masters. unabr. ed. Read by Hilary Masters. 1 cass. (Running Time: 29 min.). 1985. 10.00 New Letters.
Author Hilary Masters, son of Edgar Lee Masters, reads from his Autobiographical work, "Last Stands," Notes from Memory.

Hilda Morley. unabr. ed. Read by Hilda Morley. 1 cass. (Running Time: 29 min.). 1985. 10.00 New Letters.
New York author of "A Blessing Outside Us" reads about the lives of women in history & the present.

Hildegarde, Eckhart, Etc. Matthew Fox. 2 cass. 18.00 (OC89L) Sound Horizons AV.

Hill Bachelors. unabr. ed. William Trevor. Read by Sean Barrett. 6 cass. (Running Time: 6 hrs. 20 mins.). 2001. (978-0-7531-1157-4(8)) ISIS Audio GBR.

Hill of Devi. unabr. collector's ed. E. M. Forster. Read by David Case. 6 cass. (Running Time: 6 hrs.). 1995. 36.00 (978-0-7366-3016-0(3), 3700) Books on Tape.
E.M. Forster's year as a Maharajah's private secretary helped him understand India's cultural paradoxes. Background for "A Passage to India".

Hill of Fire. Thomas P. Lewis. 1 cass. (Running Time: 30 min.). (I Can Read Bks.). (J). (gr. 2-4). 1987. bk. 5.98 (JC-168) HarperCollins Pubs.
Includes uninterrupted narration & appropriate background music.

Hill of Fire. unabr. abr. ed. Thomas P. Lewis. Illus. by Joan Sandin. 1 cass. (I Can Read Bks.). (J). (gr. k-3). 1990. 8.99 (978-1-55994-232-4(0), TBC 2320) HarperCollins Pubs.

Hill Towns. abr. ed. Anne Rivers Siddons. 2 cass. (Running Time: 3 hrs.). 1993. 16.00 set. (978-1-55994-718-3(7)) HarperCollins Pubs.

***Hill Towns.** abr. ed. Anne Rivers Siddons. Read by Marcia Gay Harden. (ENG.). 2005. (978-0-06-087923-5(8), Harper Audio); (978-0-06-087922-8(X), Harper Audio) HarperCollins Pubs.

Hill Towns. unabr. ed. Anne Rivers Siddons. Read by Kate Reading. 10 cass. (Running Time: 15 hrs.). 1994. 80.00 (978-0-7366-2574-6(7), 3323) Books on Tape.
Something so terrible happened to Catherine Gaillard as a child that for 30 years she can't leave Tennessee. But when she does, it's to Italy. Italy transforms Cat, but the transformation threatens her husband. Then a painter joins Cat's group in the hill towns of Tuscany. He understands her.

Hill Worth Dying For: Daniel 3:1-18. Ed Young. 1995. 4.95 (978-0-7417-2069-6(8), 1069) Win Walk.

***Hilliker Curse: My Pursuit of Women.** unabr. ed. James Ellroy. Read by James Ellroy. 2010. audio compact disk 35.00 (978-0-307-87585-3(7), Random AudioBks) Pub: Random Audio Pubg. Dist(s): Random

Hillinger's California. unabr. ed. Charles Hillinger. Read by Jeff Riggenbach. 8 CDs. (Running Time: 10 hrs.). 2003. audio compact disk 64.00 (978-0-7861-9139-0(2), 3151); 49.95 (978-0-7861-2518-0(7), 3151) Blckstn Audio.
The California revealed here is not the stereotypical land of movie stars, sensational trials, or tourist snapshots but instead a remarkable patchwork of out-of-the-way places and everyday people.

Hillinger's Secured Transactions Audio CD Set. Ingrid Hillinger. audio compact disk 74.00 (978-0-314-17079-8(0)) West.

Hills Beyond. unabr. collector's ed. Thomas Wolfe. Read by John Edwardson. 10 cass. (Running Time: 15 hrs.). 1997. 80.00 (978-0-7366-3639-1(0), 4300) Books on Tape.
Wolfe stands among our nation's greatest writers, a figure whose stylish prose was admired by William Faulkner & honored by Jack Kerouac. The collection includes "The Lost Boy".

Hills Is Lonely. unabr. ed. Lillian Beckwith. Read by Hannah Gordon. 8 cass. (Running Time: 8 hrs.). 1994. 69.95 Set. (978-0-7451-4366-8(0), CAB 1049) AudioGO.
When Lillian Beckwith advertised for a quiet place in the country, she received the following unorthodox description of life in isolated Hebridean: "Surely it's that quiet when even the sheeps is lonely & as the sea it's as near as I use it myself everyday for the refusals..." Intrigued by her would-be landlady's letter, Lillian journeys to Hebridean.

Hillsong Kids: MPEG Video Library, Volume 1. Created by Hillsong Kids. (J). (gr. 4-7). 2008. 79.95 (978-5-557-57361-0(5)) Hillsong Pubng AUS.

Hillsong United: All of the Above. Contrib. by Hillsong United. 2007. audio compact disk 19.95 (978-5-557-81256-6(3)) Integrity Music.

Hilma Wolitzer. Interview. Interview with Hilma Wolitzer & Kay Bonetti. 1 cass. (Running Time: 1 hr.). 1983. 13.95 (978-1-55644-088-5(X), 3142) Am Audio Prose.
Wolitzer's insights on "the inner life" as the source of her fiction, & her debts to & qualms about some aspects of the women's movement as it relates to women writers.

Him Her Him Again the End of Him. unabr. ed. Patricia Marx. Read by Hillary Huber. (Running Time: 27000 sec.). 2007. 29.95 (978-0-7861-4793-9(8)); 59.95 (978-0-7861-4796-0(2)); audio compact disk 29.95 (978-0-7861-6246-8(5)); audio compact disk 29.95 (978-0-7861-7204-7(5)) Blckstn Audio.

Him Her Him Again the End of Him. unabr. ed. Patricia Marx. Read by Carrington MacDuffie. (Running Time: 10 mins.). (YA). 2007. audio compact disk 72.00 (978-0-7861-6241-3(4)) Blckstn Audio.

Himachal Pradesh, Vol. 1. Music by Folk Artistes Ensemble. 1 cass. 1993. (F93003) Multi-Cultural Bks.

Himachal Pradesh, Vol. 2. Music by Folk Artistes Ensemble. 1 cass. 1993. (F93004) Multi-Cultural Bks.

Himalaya. Michael Palin. Read by Michael Palin. 8 cass. 2005. 69.95 (978-0-7927-3756-8(3), CSL 844, Chivers Sound Lib); audio compact disk 89.95 (978-0-7927-3757-5(1), SLD 844, Chivers Sound Lib) AudioGO.

Himalaya. unabr. ed. Michael Palin. Narrated by Michael Palin. (Running Time: 6 hrs. 0 mins. 0 sec.). (ENG.). 2010. audio compact disk 49.95 (978-1-60283-834-5(8)) Pub: AudioGO. Dist(s): Perseus Dist

Himalayan Nights. Agni Howard. 2003. audio compact disk 15.95 (978-1-56589-752-6(8)) Pub: Crystal Clarity. Dist(s): Natl Bk Netwk

Himalayan Sunrise. Donald Walters. 2002. audio compact disk 15.95 (978-1-56589-772-4(2)) Pub: Crystal Clarity. Dist(s): Natl Bk Netwk

Himalayan Touch. Donald Walters. 2003. audio compact disk 15.95 (978-1-56589-773-1(0)) Pub: Crystal Clarity. Dist(s): Natl Bk Netwk

***Himnos Clasicos: Coleccion Instrumental, Volume 3.** Created by Patmos Music. (ENG.). 2000. audio compact disk 9.99 (978-1-58802-209-7(9)) Ed Patmos.

Himnos para Ninos. 2003. 1.30 (978-0-8297-3745-5(6)); audio compact disk 1,50 (978-0-8297-3743-1(X)) Zondervan.

Himnos Para Ninos. Serie Vida para Niños 1. CD. (Running Time: 30 min.). (SPA.). 2003. audio compact disk 4.99 (978-0-8297-3742-4(1)) Pub: Vida Pubs. Dist(s): Zondervan

Himnos para Ninos. unabr. ed. Serie Ninos. (SPA.). 2003. 3.99 (978-0-8297-3744-8(8)) Pub: Vida Pubs. Dist(s): Zondervan

Himpressions: The Blackwoman's Guide to Pampering the Blackman. Valerie Shaw. Read by Valerie Shaw. 1 cass. 1996. 12.00 (978-0-694-51693-3(7), 628162) HarperCollins Pubs.
Shaw is an "African-American Helen Gurley Brown," delivering no-nonsense advice straight from the hip, encouraging women to recognize their power & influence to effect positive change. This audio is offered in a fresh girlfriend-to-girlfriend style, dispensing warm, wise & witty advice.

Himself Took the Leper. Lynne Hammond. 2009. audio compact disk 6.00 (978-1-57399-419-4(7)) Mac Hammond.

Hind & the Panther see Treasury of John Dryden

Hindenburg Murders. abr. ed. Max Allan Collins. Read by Charlie O'Dowd. 4 vols. 2000. (978-1-58807-606-9(7)) Am Pubng Inc.

Hindenburg Murders. abr. ed. Max Allan Collins. Read by Charlie O'Dowd. 4 cass. (Running Time: 360 min.). 2000. 25.00 (978-1-58807-041-8(7)) Am Pubng Inc.
The date is May 3, 1937. The legendary Hindenburg has just left Frankfurt on its final, fateful voyage across the Atlantic. And passenger Leslie Charteris has a terrible sense of foreboding.

Hindenburg Murders. unabr. ed. Max Allan Collins. Narrated by Jeff Woodman. 7 CDs. (Running Time: 7 hrs.). 2001. audio compact disk 58.00 (978-1-4025-1010-6(1), C1589) Recorded Bks.
Leslie Charteris, legendary creator of the Saint mystery series, is a passenger on what is to be the last fatal flight of the Hindenburg. Uneasy to find the dirigible under Nazi control, Charteris becomes even more apprehensive with the disappearance of a Gestapo agent. Asked to investigate, he begins digging into the background of his fellow passengers, unearthing uncomfortable secrets along the way. Ultimately, he will be the only person with the truth behind the devastating fire.

Hindenburg Murders. unabr. ed. Max Allan Collins. Narrated by Jeff Woodman. 6 cass. (Running Time: 7 hrs.). 2001. 57.00 (978-0-7887-5451-7(3), 96371x7) Recorded Bks.
Charteris, a famous mystery writer, is a passenger on the last fatal flight of the Hindenburg. Uneasy to find the dirigible under Nazi control, Charteris' apprehension increases with the disappearance of a Gestapo agent. Asked to investigate, he becomes the only person with the truth behind the devastating fire. Includes an exclusive interview with the author.

Hindi. 2 cass. (Running Time: 80 min.). (Language - Thirty Library). bk. 16.95 set in vinyl album. Moonbeam Pubns.
Using the proven method based on the famous U.S. Military accelerated language learning program, Language/30 courses stress conversationally useful words & phrases.

Hindi. 24 cass. 167.75 Set. U MI Lang Res.

Hindi. R. Snelland & Simon Weightman. 1 cass. (Running Time: 60 min.). (Language Complete Course Packs Ser.). 1993. 17.95 (Passport Bks) McGraw-Hill Trade.

Hindi. unabr. ed. Ed. by Charles Berlitz. 2 cass. (Running Time: 1 hr. 30 mins.). (Language/30 Brief Course Ser.). pap. bk. 21.95 (AF1045) J Norton Pubs.
Quick, highly condensed introduction to the words & phrases you'll need to communicate effectively in the country you're visiting. Cassettes & phrase guide book are in a vinyl album.

Hindi: A Complete Course for Beginners. unabr. ed. Living Language Staff. 6 CDs. (Running Time: 6 hrs. 42 mins.). (World Languages Ser.). 2008. audio compact disk 72.00 (978-1-4000-2441-4(2), LivingLang) Pub: Random Info Grp. Dist(s): Random
Comprehensive self-study courses that meet the growing demands for new language offerings. Covering everything from grammar and vocabulary to cultural and practical information through the proven learning techniques from Living Language, the World Language Series will be a must-have. Includes 250+ page coursebook and a dictionary.

Hindi: Language/30. rev. ed. Educational Services Corporation Staff. Intro. by Charles Berlitz. 2 cass. (HIN.). 1995. pap. bk. 21.95 (978-0-910542-79-1(1)) Educ Svcs DC.
Hindi self-teaching language course.

Hindi: Learn to Speak & Understand Hindi with Pimsleur Language Programs. Pimsleur Staff. (Running Time: 5 hrs. 0 mins. 0 sec.). (Quick & Simple Ser.). (ENG.). 2006. audio compact disk 24.95 (978-0-7435-5256-1(3), Pimsleur) Pub: S&S Audio. Dist(s): S and S Inc

Hindi: Learn to Speak & Understand Hindi with Pimsleur Language Programs. abr. ed. Pimsleur Staff. (Running Time: 8 hrs. 0 mins. 0 sec.). (Conversational Ser.). (ENG.). 2006. audio compact disk 49.95 (978-0-7435-5257-8(1), Pimsleur) Pub: S&S Audio. Dist(s): S and S Inc

Hindi: Learn to Speak & Understand Hindi with Pimsleur Language Programs. unabr. ed. Pimsleur. Created by Pimsleur. (Running Time: 16 hrs. 0 mins. 0 sec.). (Comprehensive Ser.). (ENG.). 2006. audio compact disk 345.00 (978-0-7435-5258-5(X), Pimsleur) Pub: S&S Audio. Dist(s): S and S Inc

Hindi Bible - New Testament (Spoken Word) New - Hindi Transalation, Major Language of India. Read by Steven Paul. 16 cass. 1994. 39.97 (978-1-58968-062-3(6), 9201A) Chrstn Dup Intl.

Hindi Chants & Temple Music. unabr. ed. 1 cass. 1994. 12.95 (978-0-88432-386-0(2), C11128) J Norton Pubs.

Hindi New Testament: Old Version. 2002. 35.00 (978-1-57449-167-8(9), 107711) Pub: Hosanna NM. Dist(s): Am Bible

Hindi Newspaper Reader. (ENG & HIN.). 1990. 24.00 (978-0-931745-63-8(2)) Dunwoody Pr.

Hindi Newspaper Reader, Set. James W. Stone & Roshna M. Kapadia. 3 cass. (Running Time: 1 hr. 30 min. per cass.). (HIN.). 1990. 24.00 (3044) Dunwoody Pr.
Fifty-one selections provide the intermediate student with practice in reading journalistic Hindi. Intended for the learner who has the basic reading competence usually obtained in a year of classwork.

Hindi sans Peine. 1 cass. (Running Time: 1 hr., 30 min.). (FRE & HIN.). 2000. bk. 75.00 (978-2-7005-1335-6(5)) Pub: Assimil FRA. Dist(s): Distribks Inc

Hindrance to Hearing God's Voice. Rick Joyner. 1 cass. (Running Time: 90 mins.). (Hearing God Ser.: Vol. 5). 2000. 5.00 (RJ10-005) Morning NC.
"Principles of Spiritual Warfare" & "Putting on the Full Armor of God." These tapes highlight practical truths that lead to certain victory in spirtual warfare.

Hindrances to Healing. Matthew W. Peterson. 1 cass. (Running Time: 90 mins.). (He Still Heals Ser.: Vol. 2). 2000. 5.00 (SA01-002) Morning NC.
Learn about the healing power of God that is available to believers today.

Hindrances to Hearing God. Jack Deere. 1 cass. (Running Time: 90 mins.). (Hearing God's Voice Ser.: Vol. 6). 2000. 5.00 (JD04-006) Morning NC.
These messages are an outstanding collection that lay a solid & practical foundation for discerning God's voice.

Hindrances to Moving in the Prophetic. Rick Joyner. 1 cass. (Running Time: 90 mins.). (Prophetic Ministry & Gifts Ser.: Col. 3). 2000. 5.00 (RJ06-003) Morning NC.
These messages contain advanced teaching on the prophetic ministry, including discussion of strongholds & hindrances.

Hindrances to Spiritual Gifts. Jack Deere. 1 cass. (Running Time: 90 mins.). (Receiving Spiritual Gifts Ser.: Vol. 2). 2000. 5.00 (JD03-002) Morning NC.
This is a powerful debunking of aguments against the use of spiritual gifts & reveals major hindrances to believers walking in the power of God.

Hinds' Feet on High Places. Hannah Humard. 1 cass. (Running Time: 0 hr. 96 min.). (Christian Audio Classics Ser.). 1996. 4.97 (978-1-55748-715-5(4)) Barbour Pub.

Hinds' Feet on High Places. abr. ed. Hannah Hurnard. Read by Flo Schmidt. 2 pieces. 11.99 (978-1-58926-674-2(9)) Oasis Audio.

Hinds' Feet on High Places. abr. ed. Hannah Hurnard. Narrated by Flo Schmidt. (ENG.). 2004. 10.49 (978-1-60814-235-4(3)); audio compact disk 14.99 (978-1-58926-625-4(0)) Oasis Audio.

Hinds' Feet on High Places. unabr. ed. Hannah Hurnard. Read by Nadia May. (Running Time: 6 hrs. 30 mins.). 2010. 29.95 (978-0-7861-7269-6(X)); audio compact disk 69.00 (978-1-4417-2614-8(4)) Blckstn Audio.

Hind's Feet on High Places: An Allegory Dramatizing the Journey Each of Us Must Take Before We Can Live in "High Places" unabr. ed. Hannah Hurnard. Read by Nadia May. 5 cass. (Running Time: 7 hrs.). 2003. 39.95 (978-0-7861-0902-9(5), 1710) Blckstn Audio.
Follow Much-Afraid on her spiritual journey through difficult places with her two companions, Sorrow & Suffering. Learn how Much-Afraid overcomes her tormenting fears as she passes through many dangers & mounts at last to the High Places. There she gains a new name & returns to her valley of service, transformed by her union with the loving Shepherd.

Hind's Feet on High Places: An Allegory Dramatizing the Journey Each of Us Must Take Before We Can Live in "High Places" unabr. ed. Hannah Hurnard. Read by Nadia May. 5 cass. (Running Time: 7 hrs. 30 mins.). 1999. 27.95 (978-0-7861-1547-1(5)) Blckstn Audio.

Hindsight. unabr. ed. Peter Dickinson. Read by Joe Dunlop. 6 cass. (Running Time: 7 hrs. 30 min.). 2001. 54.95 (978-1-85089-776-7(X), 89073) Pub: ISIS Audio GBR. Dist(s): Ulverscroft US
During the war, schoolboy Paul Rogers encounters 'Mad Molly' Benison, a notorious beauty of the Twenties. At her Sunday teas in the conservatory he observed the events leading up to a night of tragedy.

Hindu & Christian Experience of God. unabr. ed. Bede Griffiths. 2 cass. (Running Time: 1 hr. 57 min.). 1983. 18.00 Set. (03303) Big Sur Tapes.
What happens when we get beyond the ego, beyond the sense experience? What is the ultimate reality & how do we experience that? Fr. Bede discusses these & other questions from both Hindu & Christian perspectives.

Hindu Astrology: Ashtaka Varga 1 & 2. R. G. Krishnan. 1 cass. 8.95 (624) Am Fed Astrologers.
An AFA Convention workshop tape.

Hindu Astrology: Ashtaka Varga 3. R. G. Krishnan. 1 cass. 8.95 (625) Am Fed Astrologers.

Hindu Vedic Astrology. Anders Johansson. 1 cass. 8.95 (175) Am Fed Astrologers.
Presentation of Maha Dasa Shadvarga for predictions and interpreting.

Hinduism. Arwind Vasavada. 2 cass. (Running Time: 3 hrs. 15 min.). (Common Territory, Different Maps: the Archetypal Underpinnings of Religious Practice Ser.). 1994. 21.95 set. (978-0-7822-0476-6(7), 552) C G Jung IL.

Hinduism. unabr. ed. Gregory Kozlowski. Read by Ben Kingsley. Ed. by Walter Harrelson & Mike Hassell. 2 cass. (Running Time: 3 hrs.). Dramatization. (Religion, Scriptures & Spirituality Ser.). 1994. 17.95 (978-1-56823-012-2(5), 10455) Pub: Knowledge Prod. Dist(s): APG
Hinduism began in India about 1800 B.C.E.; several other religions & philosophies are its offspring, including Buddhism & the Jain tradition (both 6th century B.C.E.) & the Sikh tradition (15th century C.E.). These three traditions flourish today primarily in India; Buddhism has flourished in southeast Asia. Vedanta, another offspring, is worldwide, as are Yoga, transcendental meditation, & other spiritual & meditative exercises related to Hinduism.

Hinduism. unabr. ed. Gregory C. Kozlowski. Read by Ben Kingsley. (Running Time: 10800 sec.). (Religion, Scriptures, & Spirituality Ser.). 2006. audio compact disk 25.95 (978-0-7861-6481-3(6)) Pub: Blckstn Audio. Dist(s): NetLibrary CO

Hints on Child Training. unabr. ed. H. Clay Trumbull. Read by Harold N. Cropp. 4 cass. (Running Time: 5 hrs. 30 mins.). 1995. 32.95 (978-0-7861-0883-1(5), 1552) Blckstn Audio.
Fortified with common sense & Biblical wisdom, Trumbull's straightforward guide has established its place as a classic work in the field of child rearing. Written over 100 years ago, it is completely free of modernist influence. Will give you a whole new perspective on your joy as a parent & a lot more hope!.

Hip Chick's Guide to Macrobiotics: A Philosophy for Achieving a Radiant Mind & Fabulous Body. unabr. ed. Jessica Porter. Narrated by Jessica Porter. Narrated by William Dufris & Dan Bernard. (Running Time: 7 hrs. 30 mins. 0 sec.). (ENG.). 2009. 19.99 (978-1-4001-6529-2(6)); 14.99 (978-1-4001-8529-0(7)); audio compact disk 49.99 (978-1-4001-4529-4(5)); audio compact disk 24.99 (978-1-4001-1529-7(9)) Pub: Tantor Media. Dist(s): IngramPubServ

Hip Grooves for Hand Drums: How to Play Funk, Rock & World-Beat Patterns on Any Drum. Alan Dworsky & Betsy Sansby. (J). 2001. bk. 24.95 (978-0-9638801-5-4(2)) Pub: Dancing Hands. Dist(s): SCB Distributors

Hip Hop & His Famous Face. Gary Oliver et al. 1 cass. (Wonder Woods Ser.). (J). (ps-3). 1995. 11.99 (3-1234) David C Cook.

Hip-Hop Approach to SAT-Level Vocabulary Building. unabr. ed. Flocabulary. Read by Flocabulary. (YA). 2008. 34.99 (978-1-60252-961-8(2)) Find a World.

Hip Hop High School. Alan Lawrence Sitomer. Read by Sisi Aisha Johnson. 7. (Running Time: 7 hrs. 50 mins.). 2007. 49.75 (978-1-4281-0483-9(6)) Recorded Bks.

Hip Hop High School. Alan Lawrence Sitomer & Sisi Aisha Johnson. 7. (Running Time: 7 hrs. 50 mins.). 2007. audio compact disk 77.75 (978-1-4281-0488-4(7)) Recorded Bks.

Hip Hop Hymns for Kids. 1 cass. (J). (C5584N) Brentwood Music.
Mixed with a '90s hip-hop beat, this recording introduces the next generation to the timeless teaching of the great hymns. Features: Amazing Grace, Joyful, Joyful, Jesus Loves Me, All Hail the Power & more.

Hip-Hop Improvisation: One Beat, One Chord at a Time. Walter Beasley. DVD & audio compact disk 29.95 (978-0-7579-2377-7(1), 908072, Warner Bro) Alfred Pub.

Hip-Hop Kid Pop. unabr. ed. Lisa M. Nelson & Ophir Shur. Perf. by Bright Ideas Staff. 1 cass. (Running Time: 40 min.). (J). (ps-4). 1994. 9.98 (978-1-883212-03-2(0), BID008); audio compact disk 11.98 CD. Brght Ideas CA.
13 original songs that promote self-esteem.

Hip-Hop U. S. History. unabr. ed. Flocabulary. Read by Flocabulary. 2008. 34.99 (978-1-60252-968-7(X)) Find a World.

Hip-Hop vs. MAAT: A Psycho/Social Analysis of Values. Jawanza Kunjufu. 1 cass. (Running Time: 60 mins.). 1999. 5.95 (AT11) African Am Imag.
What are values? Where do we learn them? How do our values affect our decisions regarding abortion or adoption, marriage or "shacking," gun control & other controversial issues.

Hip Hope Hits 2008: The Hottest Positive Hip Hop of the Year. Contrib. by Toby McKeehan & Joey Elwood. 2007. audio compact disk 13.99 (978-5-557-62810-5(X)) Gotee Records.

Hip Hope 2006. Contrib. by Toby McKeehan & Joey Elwood. 2005. 17.98 (978-5-558-92014-7(9)) Gotee Records.

Hip Stories for Hip Kids Vol. 1: Rat Fink's Hip Stories. Ed 'Big Daddy' Roth & Art Greenhaw. (Running Time: 1 hr. 04 min.). (Rat Fink Ser.). (YA). 1995. 12.00 (978-1-888092-09-7(2), AD1002) Lght Crust Dghboys.
Legendary hot rod artist & car designer Ed Roth teams with Texas musician, Light Crust Doughboy band member Art Greenhaw for songs & stories featuring Rat Fink & friends.

HIPAA Focused Training 1 Five Users: HIPAA Regulations, HIPAA Training, HIPAA Compliance, & HIPAA Security for the Administrator of a HIPAA Program, for Beginners to Advanced, from Small Practice to Large Hospital or Health System Including Chief Privacy Officers, Nurses, Doctors, Dentists, Risk Managers, Compliance Officers, & Practice Administrators. Daniel Farb. 2005. audio compact disk 99.95 (978-1-59491-133-0(9)) Pub: UnivofHealth. Dist(s): AtlasBooks

HIPAA Focused Training 1 Overview: HIPAA Regulations, HIPAA Training, HIPAA Compliance, & HIPAA Security for the Administrator of a HIPAA Program, for Beginners to Advanced, from Small Practice to Large Hospital or Health System Including Chief Privacy Officers, Nurses, Doctors, Dentists, Risk Managers, Compliance Officers, & Practice Administrators. Daniel Farb. 2004. audio compact disk 49.95 (978-1-932634-34-1(7)) Pub: UnivofHealth. Dist(s): AtlasBooks

HIPAA Focused Training 1 Ten Users. Daniel Farb. 2005. audio compact disk 149.95 (978-1-59491-168-2(1)) Pub: UnivofHealth. Dist(s): AtlasBooks

HIPAA Focused Training 2 Business Associates & Covered Entities: HIPAA Regulations, HIPAA Training, HIPAA Compliance, & HIPAA Security for the Administrator of a HIPAA Program, for Beginners to Advanced, from Small Practice to Large Hospital or Health System Including Chief Privacy Officers, Nurses, Doctors, Dentists, Risk Managers, Compliance Officers, & Practice Administrators. Daniel Farb. 2004. audio compact disk 49.95 (978-1-932634-35-8(5)) Pub: UnivofHealth. Dist(s): AtlasBooks

HIPAA Focused Training 2 Five Users: HIPAA Regulations, HIPAA Training, HIPAA Compliance, & HIPAA Security for the Administrator of a HIPAA Program, for Beginners to Advanced, from Small Practice to Large Hospital or Health System Including Chief Privacy Officers, Nurses, Doctors, Dentists, Risk Managers, Compliance Officers, & Practice Administrators. Daniel Farb. 2005. audio compact disk 99.95 (978-1-59491-134-7(7)) Pub: UnivofHealth. Dist(s): AtlasBooks

HIPAA Focused Training 2 Ten Users. Daniel Farb. 2005. audio compact disk 149.95 (978-1-59491-169-9(X)) Pub: UnivofHealth. Dist(s): AtlasBooks

HIPAA Focused Training 3A Five Users: HIPAA Regulations, HIPAA Training, HIPAA Compliance, & HIPAA Security for the Administrator of a HIPAA Program, for Beginners to Advanced, from Small Practice to Large Hospital or Health System Including Chief Privacy Officers, Nurses, Doctors, Dentists, Risk Managers, Compliance Officers, & Practice Administrators. Daniel Farb. 2005. audio compact disk 99.95 (978-1-59491-135-4(5)) Pub: UnivofHealth. Dist(s): AtlasBooks

HIPAA Focused Training 3A Privacy Uses & Disclosures: HIPAA Regulations, HIPAA Training, HIPAA Compliance, & HIPAA Security for the Administrator of a HIPAA Program, for Beginners to Advanced, from Small Practice to Large Hospital or Health System Including Chief Privacy Officers, Nurses, Doctors, Dentists, Risk Managers, Compliance Officers, & Practice Administrators. Daniel Farb. 2004. audio compact disk 49.95 (978-1-932634-36-5(3)) Pub: UnivofHealth. Dist(s): AtlasBooks

HIPAA Focused Training 3A Ten Users. Daniel Farb. 2005. audio compact disk 149.95 (978-1-59491-170-5(3)) Pub: UnivofHealth. Dist(s): AtlasBooks

HIPAA Focused Training 3B Five Users: HIPAA Regulations, HIPAA Training, HIPAA Compliance, & HIPAA Security for the Administrator of a HIPAA Program, for Beginners to Advanced, from Small Practice to Large Hospital or Health System Including Chief Privacy Officers, Nurses, Doctors, Dentists, Risk Managers, Compliance Officers, & Practice Administrators. Daniel Farb. 2005. audio compact disk 69.95 (978-1-59491-136-1(3)) Pub: UnivofHealth. Dist(s): AtlasBooks

Hipaa Focused Training 3b Psychotherapy & Country Doctors. Daniel Farb. 2004. audio compact disk 29.95 (978-1-932634-37-2(1)) Pub: UnivofHealth. Dist(s): AtlasBooks

HIPAA Focused Training 3b Ten Users: Psychotherapy & Country Doctors, 10 Users. Daniel Farb. 2005. audio compact disk 104.95 (978-1-59491-171-2(1)) Pub: UnivofHealth. Dist(s): AtlasBooks

HIPAA Focused Training 3C Five Users: HIPAA Regulations, HIPAA Training, HIPAA Compliance, & HIPAA Security for the Administrator of a HIPAA Program, for Beginners to Advanced, from Small Practice to Large Hospital or Health System Including Chief Privacy Officers, Nurses, Doctors, Dentists, Risk Managers, Compliance Officers, & Practice Administrators. Daniel Farb. 2005. audio compact disk 99.95 (978-1-59491-137-8(1)) Pub: UnivofHealth. Dist(s): AtlasBooks

HIPAA Focused Training 3C Marketing: HIPAA Regulations, HIPAA Training, HIPAA Compliance, & HIPAA Security for the Administrator of a HIPAA Program, for Beginners to Advanced, from Small Practice to Large Hospital or Health System Including Chief Privacy Officers, Nurses, Doctors, Dentists, Risk Managers, Compliance Officers, & Practice Administrators. Daniel Farb. 2004. audio compact disk 49.95 (978-1-932634-38-9(X)) Pub: UnivofHealth. Dist(s): AtlasBooks

HIPAA Focused Training 3C Ten Users. Daniel Farb. 2005. audio compact disk 149.95 (978-1-59491-172-9(X)) Pub: UnivofHealth. Dist(s): AtlasBooks

HIPAA Focused Training 3d: Notice of Privacy Practices, 10 Users. Daniel Farb. 2005. audio compact disk 149.95 (978-1-59491-173-6(8)) Pub: UnivofHealth. Dist(s): AtlasBooks

HIPAA Focused Training 3D Five Users: HIPAA Regulations, HIPAA Training, HIPAA Compliance, & HIPAA Security for the Administrator of a HIPAA Program, for Beginners to Advanced, from Small Practice to Large Hospital or Health System Including Chief Privacy Officers, Nurses, Doctors, Dentists, Risk Managers, Compliance Officers, & Practice Administrators. Daniel Farb. 2005. audio compact disk 99.95 (978-1-59491-138-5(X)) Pub: UnivofHealth. Dist(s): AtlasBooks

HIPAA Focused Training 3D Notice of Privacy Practices: HIPAA Regulations, HIPAA Training, HIPAA Compliance, & HIPAA Security for the Administrator of a HIPAA Program, for Beginners to Advanced, from Small Practice to Large Hospital or Health System Including Chief Privacy Officers, Nurses, Doctors, Dentists, Risk Managers, Compliance Officers, & Practice Administrators. Daniel Farb. 2004. audio compact disk 49.95 (978-1-932634-39-6(8)) Pub: UnivofHealth. Dist(s): AtlasBooks

HIPAA Focused Training 4a: Data & Security Security, 100 Users. Daniel Farb. 2005. audio compact disk 899.95 (978-1-59491-208-5(4)) Pub: UnivofHealth. Dist(s): AtlasBooks

HIPAA Focused Training 4A Data & Computer Security: HIPAA Regulations, HIPAA Training, HIPAA Compliance, & HIPAA Security for the Administrator of a HIPAA Program, for Beginners to Advanced, from Small Practice to Large Hospital or Health System Including Chief Privacy Officers, Nurses, Doctors, Dentists, Risk Managers, Compliance Officers, & Practice Administrators. Daniel Farb. 2004. audio compact disk 49.95 (978-1-932634-40-2(1)) Pub: UnivofHealth. Dist(s): AtlasBooks

HIPAA Focused Training 4A Five Users: HIPAA Regulations, HIPAA Training, HIPAA Compliance, & HIPAA Security for the Administrator of a HIPAA Program, for Beginners to Advanced, from Small Practice to Large Hospital or Health System Including Chief Privacy Officers, Nurses, Doctors, Dentists, Risk Managers, Compliance Officers, & Practice Administrators. Daniel Farb. 2005. audio compact disk 99.95 (978-1-59491-139-2(8)) Pub: UnivofHealth. Dist(s): AtlasBooks

HIPAA Focused Training 4A Ten Users. Daniel Farb. 2005. audio compact disk 149.95 (978-1-59491-174-3(6)) Pub: UnivofHealth. Dist(s): AtlasBooks

HIPAA Focused Training 4A 25 Users. Daniel Farb. 2005. audio compact disk 299.95 (978-1-59491-206-1(8)) Pub: UnivofHealth. Dist(s): AtlasBooks

HIPAA Focused Training 4A 50 Users. Daniel Farb. 2005. audio compact disk 499.95 (978-1-59491-207-8(6)) Pub: UnivofHealth. Dist(s): AtlasBooks

HIPAA Privacy Certificate Program: HIPAA Regulations, HIPAA Training, HIPAA Compliance, & HIPAA Security for the Administrator of a HIPAA Program, for Beginners to Advanced, from Small Practice to Large Hospital or Health System Including Chief Privacy Officers, Nurses, Doctors, Dentists, Risk Managers, Compliance Officers, & Practice Administrators. Daniel Farb. 2004. audio compact disk 299.95 (978-0-9743674-5-3(1)) Pub: UnivofHealth. Dist(s): AtlasBooks

HIPAA Privacy Compliance Planning: HIPAA Regulations, HIPAA Training, HIPAA Compliance, & HIPAA Security for the Administrator of a HIPAA Program, for Beginners to Advanced, from Small Practice to Large Hospital or Health System Including Chief Privacy Officers, Nurses, Doctors, Dentists, Risk Managers, Compliance Officers, & Practice Administrators. Daniel Farb. 2004. audio compact disk 49.95 (978-1-932634-41-9(X)) Pub: UnivofHealth. Dist(s): AtlasBooks

HIPAA Regulatory Documents: The Documents of HIPAA as a Convenient Reference in a Searchable CD-ROM for Healthcare Corporations, Hospitals, Doctors, Nurses, Dentists, & Allied Health Professionals. Daniel Farb. 2004. audio compact disk 29.95 (978-1-59491-097-5(9)) Pub: UnivofHealth. Dist(s): AtlasBooks

HIPAA 3B Psychotherapy & Country Doctors: HIPAA Regulations, HIPAA Training, HIPAA Compliance, & HIPAA Security for the Administrator of a HIPAA Program, for Beginners to Advanced, from Small Practice to Large Hospital or Health System Including Chief Privacy Officers, Nurses, Doctors, Dentists, Risk Managers, Compliance Officers, & Practice Administrators, Embedded in a Fictional Hospital Story. Daniel Farb. 2003. audio compact disk 29.95 (978-1-932634-31-0(2)) Pub: UnivofHealth. Dist(s): Atlas Bks USA

Hiperactividad y Deficiencia de Atencion en la Ninez. unabr. ed. John F. Taylor. Read by Timothy Taylor. 1 cass. (Running Time: 38 min.). (Answers to ADD Ser.). (SPA.). 1994. 9.95 (978-1-883963-16-3(8)) ADD Plus.
Toddlers & young children with ADD/ADHD, diagnosis of ADD/ADHD, genetic factors, early signs in infancy, personality features, a successful screening checklist.

Hippo & Friends. Claire Selby. (Running Time: 1 hr. 10 mins.). 2006. audio compact disk 23.10 (978-0-521-68018-9(2)) Cambridge U Pr.

Hippo & Friends: Starter. Claire Selby. Told to Lesley McKnight. (Running Time: 1 hr. 10 mins.). (J). (ps-3). 2006. audio compact disk 23.10 (978-0-521-68006-6(9)) Cambridge U Pr.

Hippo & Friends 1. Claire Selby. Told to Lesley McKnight. (Running Time: 1 hr. 10 mins.). (J). (ps-3). 2006. audio compact disk 23.10 (978-0-521-68012-7(3)) Cambridge U Pr.

Hippopotamus. unabr. ed. Stephen Fry. [illegible]ed by Stephen Fry. 7 cass. (Running Time: 9 hrs.). 2000. 63.00 (97[illegible]84197-129-2(4), H1127E7) Recorded Bks.
Often shocking, Ted Wallace, theatre critic & failed poet, has opinions on everything. Often rather crude, rather long opinions, they are fueled by vast amounts of whiskey. Just as life?s at its lowest ebb, Ted meets Jane Swann, whose godfather he was until her mother fired him. She has a financially interesting proposal for Ted, & since he?s just been sacked for pointing out a new play?s deficiencies from the theatre stalls, he?s got nothing better to do. As it involves a few drinks with his old friend Lord Logan at Swafford Hall, the witnessing of alleged miracles & other fantastic phenomena, Ted agrees to her plan.

Hippopotamus. unabr. ed. Stephen Fry. Narrated by Stephen Fry. 8 CDs. (Running Time: 9 hrs.). 2000. audio compact disk 82.00 (978-1-84197-169-8(3), C1287E7) Recorded Bks.

Hippopotamus Pool. unabr. ed. Elizabeth Peters, pseud. Narrated by Barbara Rosenblat. 10 cass. (Running Time: 14 hrs. 30 mins.). (Amelia Peabody Ser.: No. 8). 2000. 85.00 (978-0-7887-0607-3(1), 94617E7) Recorded Bks.
The spunky Victorian Egyptologist Amelia Peabody Emerson has returned to the exotic Nile valley. Parasol aloft and hot on the trail of an unexplored tomb, she must outwit a shadowy evildoer, a questionable antiquities dealer, and her loquacious son, Ramses.

Hire a Hangman. unabr. ed. Collin Wilcox. Read by Larry McKeever. 6 cass. (Running Time: 9 hrs.). (Frank Hastings Ser.). 1991. 48.00 (978-0-7366-2059-8(1), 2868) Books on Tape.
Brice Hanchett was almost legend...& believed it. Chief of surgery at a San Francisco hospital & head of its transplant team, he let power get to him. He played God. Now Hanchett is history, shot down in cold blood. The cops find lots of suspects. All had motives, but there has to be a clue to the killer. It's up to Frank Hastings of homicide to find it.

Hire & Keep the Best People: 21 Practical & Proven Techniques You Can Use Immediately! unabr. ed. Brian Tracy. (Running Time: 1 hr.). (ENG.). 2008. 9.98 (978-1-59659-221-6(4), GildAudio) Pub: Gildan Media. Dist(s): HachBkGrp

Hire Principle. (Paws & Tales Ser.: No. 32). 2002. 3.99 (978-1-57972-482-5(5)); audio compact disk 5.99 (978-1-57972-483-2(3)) Insight Living.

Hire the One with the Turban: Cultural Diversity in the 1990's. unabr. ed. Jennifer James. Read by Jennifer James. 2 cass. (Running Time: 2 hrs.). 14.95 set. Jennifer J.

Hired Lad. Ian Campbell Thomson. Read by Christopher Scott. 4 cass. (Soundings Ser.). (J). 2005. 44.95 (978-1-84283-625-5(0)) Pub: ISIS Lrg Prnt GBR. Dist(s): Ulverscroft US

***Hired Man.** Jan Irving. (ENG.). 2010. 14.99 (978-1-61581-993-5(2)) Dreamspinner.

Hiring Fair, Set unabr. ed. Jessica Stirling. Read by Vivien Heilbron. 12 cass. (Stalker Trilogy: Vol. 2). 1999. 96.95 (CAB 1515) AudioGO.

Hiring the Best. Contrib. by Ann M. McGill. 1 cass. (Running Time: 25 mins.). pap. bk. 99.95 (1037AV); pap. bk. 99.95 (1037AV) J Wilson & Assocs.

Hiring the Best People, Set. Steve Penny. Read by Steve Penny. 2 cass. (Running Time: 2 hrs.). 1993. pap. bk. 60.00 Hiring the Best.
How to get the maximum information during your hiring interviews in the minimum amount of time. Includes over 200 questions that probe ability, motivation & manageability along with how to evaluate what you hear.

Hiroshima. John Hersey. Read by George Guidall. 3 Cass. (Running Time: 6 Hrs.). 19.95 (978-1-4025-6290-7(X)) Recorded Bks.

Hiroshima. John Hersey. Narrated by Jack Foreman & George Guidall. 4 cass. (Running Time: 6 hrs.). 2001. 37.00 (978-0-7887-4639-0(1), 96373E7) Recorded Bks.
Returns to Hiroshima to find the survivors - & to tell their fates.

Hiroshima. John Hersey. Read by Edward Asner. Narrated by Emily Woo Zeller. (Running Time: 17400 sec.). (ENG.). 2007. audio compact disk 25.95 (978-1-57270-840-2(9)) Pub: AudioGO. Dist(s): Perseus Dist

Hiroshima. John Hersey. Narrated by George Guidall. (Running Time: 21600 sec.). 2005. audio compact disk 19.99 (978-1-4193-6496-9(0)) Recorded Bks.

Hiroshima. unabr. ed. John Hersey. Read by Edward Asner. 4 cass. (Running Time: 5 hrs. 15 mins.). 2004. 21.95 (978-1-57270-003-1(3), E40003u) Pub: Audio Partners. Dist(s): PerseuPGW
A dramatic, journalistic account of the effect of the U.S. bombing on Hiroshima, Japan, on August 6, 1945. Includes a chapter written 40 years after the original book, entitled "Aftermath," describing what became of each of the six featured people.

Hiroshima. unabr. ed. John Hersey. Read by Jack Foreman. 2 cass. (Running Time: 3 hrs.). 1982. 18.00 (978-1-55690-225-3(5), 82016) Recorded Bks.
Accounts of survivors of the U. S. atomic attack on the Japanese city of Hiroshima on August 6, 1945, the day the city was destroyed by the first atomic bomb. Told through the memories of six survivors.

Hiroshima. unabr. ed. John Hersey. Read by Edward Asner. (YA). 2007. 74.99 (978-1-60252-837-6(3)) Find a World.

Hiroshima. unabr. ed. Laurence Yep. Narrated by Nelson Runger. 1 cass. (Running Time: 45 mins.). (gr. 4 up). 1997. 10.00 (978-0-7887-1111-4(3), 95104E7) Recorded Bks.
Weaves a counterpoint of information about the atomic bomb & a moving story of a young girl who lives through the fateful day it was dropped on her city. Introduction to a controversial piece of history that still inflames debates today.

Hiroshima. unabr. ed. Laurence Yep. Read by Nelson Runger. 1 cass. (Running Time: 45 min.). (J). (gr. 2). 1997. pap. bk. 21.24 (978-0-7887-1269-2(1), 40515); Rental 6.50 Recorded Bks.

Hiroshima. unabr. collector's ed. John Hersey. Read by Dan Lazar. 4 cass. (Running Time: 4 hrs.). 1981. 24.00 (978-0-7366-0319-5(0), 1307) Books on Tape.
The story of six human beings who lived through the greatest single man-made disaster in history. John Hersey tells what these 6 - a clerk, a widowed seamstress, a physician, a Methodist minister, a young surgeon & a German Catholic Priest - were doing at 8:15 on August 6, 1945, when Hiroshima was destroyed by the first atom bomb ever dropped on a city.

Hiroshima & the Aftermath. John Hersey. Read by John Hersey. 1 cass. (Running Time: 55 min.). 1988. 13.95 (978-1-55644-292-6(0), 8051) Am Audio Prose.
Dignified reading performance of the first chapter of this classic account of six survivors of Hiroshima, & a selection from "The Aftermath," Hersey's 1986 revisiting of those remaining.

Hiroshima Survivors. 1 cass. (Running Time: 30 min.). 9.95 (H0260B090, HarperThor) HarpC GBR.

His Arms Around You. Becky McLean Simmons. 1 cass. 9.95 (3111334); audio compact disk 14.95 (333387) Covenant Comms.
A contemporary album reflecting on Christ.

***His Brain, Her Brain: How Divinely Designed Differences Can Strengthen Your Marriage.** unabr. ed. Walt and Barb Larimore. (Running Time: 6 hrs. 1 mins. 0 sec.). (ENG.). 2009. 14.99 (978-0-310-77139-5(0)) Zondervan.

His Bright Light: The Story of Nick Traina, Set. unabr. ed. Danielle Steel. Read by Traci Godfrey. 6 cass. 1999. 27.50 (FS9-43265) Highsmith.

His Brother's Debt. unabr. ed. Louis L'Amour. Read by Stan Winiarski & John Malloy. 1 cass. (Running Time: 1 hr. 20 min.). 1993. 7.95 (978-1-882071-27-2(1), 029) B-B Audio.
His Brothers DebtRock Cassidy is a tall, strongly built man. Men had often said they would hate to face him in a shootout! But he has a secret; Rock Cassidy is yellow! Will he let his secret keep him on the run for life or will he face his accuser.

His Brother's Debt; Big Medicine; Turkey Feather Riders. abr. ed. Louis L'Amour. 2 cass. (Running Time: 3 hrs.). (Louis L'Amour Collector Ser.). 2000. 7.95 (978-1-57815-101-1(5), 1072, Media Bks Audio) Media Bks NJ.
The brave men & women who settled the American frontier.

***His Christmas Pleasure.** unabr. ed. Cathy Maxwell. (ENG.). 2010. (978-0-06-200896-1(X), Harper Audio) HarperCollins Pubs.

His Divine Character. Elbert Willis. 1 cass. (Understanding the Holy Spirit Ser.). 4.00 Fill the Gap.

His Excellency: George Washington. unabr. ed. Joseph J. Ellis. Narrated by Nelson Runger. 10 cass. (Running Time: 14 hrs. 45 mins.). 2004. 89.75 (978-1-4193-0725-6(8), 97058MC) Recorded Bks.

His Excellency: George Washington. unabr. ed. Joseph J. Ellis. 8 cass. (Running Time: 14 hrs.). 2004. 34.99 (978-1-4025-9301-7(5), 04104) Recorded Bks.
Washington has always been a larger-than-life and enigmatic figure. On the day he was given command of the continental army, he recorded only the temperature and where he ate dinner in his journal. But recently, his papers were catalogued at the University of Virginia. Ellis had primary access to the 90-volume papers, allowing him to paint a thorough and fascinating portrait. From the French and Indian War to Mount Vernon, from the American Revolution to the presidency, Ellis delivers the definitive biography of the greatest American icon.

His Excellency: George Washington. unabr. ed. Joseph J. Ellis. Read by Nelson Runger. 13 CDs. (Running Time: 14 hrs.). 2004. audio compact disk 34.99 (978-1-4025-4476-7(6), 01702) Recorded Bks.

His Father's Son: The Life of Randolph Churchill. collector's ed. Winston S. Churchill. Read by David Case. 14 cass. (Running Time: 21 hrs.). 1999. 112.00 (978-0-7366-4728-1(7), 5066) Books on Tape.
Son of Winston Churchill, Randolph established himself as one of the most respected political journalists of his generation, the first to warn the world, in 1932, that Hitler's rise to power could mean war with England.

His Fleece Was White As Snow! (YA). 2003. audio compact disk 15.00 (978-1-58302-242-9(2)) One Way St.
This children's Easter musical is a sequel to the Christmas musical, "Mary Had a Little Lamb." It's about fifty minutes long with all animal characters: four lambs, two donkeys, a hen and a rooster. This tells the Biblical Easter story from the point of view of animals who were present. Written by Dan Barker.

His Fleece Was White As Snow: Accomp. CD - Mono Track (Instruments Only) (YA). 2003. audio compact disk 60.00 (978-1-58302-245-0(7)) One Way St.

His Fleece Was White As Snow: Accomp. CD - Split Track. (YA). 2003. audio compact disk 60.00 (978-1-58302-244-3(9)) One Way St.

His Glory Gang: Inside Out & Upside down: Ambassadors of Jesus Christ: Teaching Tracts & Ministry Aids. abr. ed. Sharon I. Hopf. (ENG.). 2009. audio compact disk 9.99 (978-1-60799-923-2(4)) Tate Pubng.

His Honor. 2004. audio compact disk 14.95 (978-0-8258-5351-7(6)) Fischer Inc NY.

His Illegal Self. unabr. ed. Peter Carey. Read by Stefan Rudnicki. (Running Time: 28800 sec.). 2008. 29.95 (978-1-4332-0920-8(9)); 54.95 (978-1-4332-0918-5(7)); audio compact disk 29.95 (978-1-4332-0921-5(7)); audio compact disk & audio compact disk 29.95 (978-1-4332-0922-2(5)); audio compact disk & audio compact disk 63.00 (978-1-4332-0919-2(5)) Blckstn Audio.

His Illegal Self. unabr. ed. Peter Carey. Read by Stefan Rudnicki. (YA). 2008. 59.99 (978-1-60514-779-6(6)) Find a World.

His Image in My Countenance. Tomas Kofod & Ane Marie Kofod. (Running Time: 4080 sec.). 2008. audio compact disk 12.99 (978-1-59955-149-4(7)) CFI Dist.

His Last Bow. Arthur Conan Doyle. Read by Tom Whitworth. (Playaway Young Adult Ser.). (ENG.). 2009. 60.00 (978-1-60775-632-3(3)) Find a World.

His Last Bow. Arthur Conan Doyle. Narrated by Frederick Davidson. (Running Time: 7 hrs.). (YA). 1999. 27.95 (978-1-59912-507-7(2)) Iofy Corp.

His Last Bow. Arthur Conan Doyle. Narrated by Walter Covell. (Running Time: 6 hrs. 30 mins.). 2006. 30.95 (978-1-59912-139-0(5)) Iofy Corp.

His Last Bow. Arthur Conan Doyle. Read by Tom Whitworth. (Running Time: 27000 sec.). (ENG.). 2005. audio compact disk 19.99 (978-1-4001-5169-1(4)); audio compact disk 59.99 (978-1-4001-3169-3(3)); audio compact disk 29.99 (978-1-4001-0169-6(7)) Pub: Tantor Media. Dist(s): IngramPubServ

His Last Bow. unabr. ed. Arthur Conan Doyle. Narrated by Ian Whitcomb. (Running Time: 8 hrs. 0 mins. 0 sec.). (ENG.). 2009. audio compact disk 55.99 (978-1-4001-4132-6(X)) Pub: Tantor Media. Dist(s): IngramPubServ

***His Last Bow.** unabr. ed. Arthur Conan Doyle. Narrated by Simon Prebble. (Running Time: 7 hrs. 0 mins. 0 sec.). (ENG.). 2010. 19.99 (978-1-4001-6520-9(2)); 14.99 (978-1-4001-8520-7(3)); audio compact disk 27.99 (978-1-4001-1520-4(5)); audio compact disk 55.99 (978-1-4001-4520-1(1)) Pub: Tantor Media. Dist(s): IngramPubServ

His Last Bow: Some Reminiscences of Sherlock Holmes. unabr. ed. Short Stories. Arthur Conan Doyle. Read by Frederick Davidson. 6 CDs. (Running Time: 7 hrs.). 2000. audio compact disk 48.00 (978-0-7861-9939-6(3), 2471) Blckstn Audio.
This collection of eight world-famous cases from Doctor Watson's portfolio illustrate the singular mental faculties of Sherlock Holmes. In the course of these investigations, Holmes himself is struck down by a virulent Eastern disease & we are reintroduced to his remarkable brother Mycroft - "all other men are specialists, but his specialism is omniscience.".

His Last Bow: Some Reminiscences of Sherlock Holmes. unabr. ed. Arthur Conan Doyle. Read by Walter Covell. 6 cass. (Running Time: 9 hrs.). 1994. 29.00 set in vinyl cassette album. (C-256) Jimcin Record.
More classic Holmes.

His Last Bow: Some Reminiscences of Sherlock Holmes. unabr. collector's ed. Arthur Conan Doyle. Read by Thomas Whitworth. 8 cass. (Running Time: 8 hrs.). 1993. 48.00 (978-0-7366-2335-3(3), 3114) Books on Tape.
A collection of Sherlock Holmes' mysteries including "The Adventure of Wisteria Lodge" plus seven other stories.

His Last Bow, with EBook. unabr. ed. Arthur Conan Doyle. Narrated by Ian Whitcomb. (Running Time: 8 hrs. 0 mins. 0 sec.). (ENG.). 2009. 19.99 (978-1-4001-6132-4(0)); audio compact disk 27.99 (978-1-4001-1132-9(3)) Pub: Tantor Media. Dist(s): IngramPubServ

***His Last Bow, with EBook.** unabr. ed. Arthur Conan Doyle. Narrated by Ian Whitcomb. (Running Time: 8 hrs. 0 mins.). 2009. 15.99 (978-1-4001-8132-2(1)) Tantor Media.

***His Last Bow, with eBook.** unabr. ed. Arthur Conan Doyle. Narrated by Ian Whitcomb. (Running Time: 8 hrs. 0 mins.). 2009. 27.99 (978-1-4001-9132-1(7)) Tantor Media.

His Legs Ran About see Poetry & Voice of Ted Hughes

His Love Is Calling Us. 1985. (0220) Evang Sisterhood Mary.

His Love Surrounds Me. Stephanie Kemp. 1 cass. 7.98 (1000772) Covenant Comms.
Favorite primary songs & hymns by a bright & beautiful new artist.

His Majesty's Dragon. abr. ed. Naomi Novik. Read by David Thorn. (Running Time: 21600 sec.). (Temeraire Ser.). (ENG.). 2007. audio compact disk 29.95 (978-0-7393-5413-1(2), Random AudioBks) Pub: Random Audio Pubg. Dist(s): Random

His Name. Neville Goddard. 1 cass. (Running Time: 62 min.). 1963. 8.00 (36) J & L Pubns.
Neville taught Imagination Creates Reality. He was a powerfully influential teacher of God as Consciousness.

His Name Is Mudd. 1 cass. (Running Time: 59 min. per cass.). 1978. 10.00 (HS330) Esstee Audios.
The ordeal of Dr. Samuel Mudd, a Confederate sympathizer arrested & charged with conspiracy in President Lincoln's assassination.

His Name Is Wonderful see Su Nombre es Admirable

His Name Is Wonderful. Charles R. Swindoll. 6 cass. (Running Time: 9 hrs.). 1998. 30.95 (978-1-57972-074-2(9)) Insight Living.
Bible study exploring the many names & titles of Christ, their meanings, symbolism & historical perspective.

His Name Shall Be Called Wonderful. Kenneth E. Hagin. 1 cass. 4.95 (SH21) Faith Lib Pubns.

His Name Was David: Sing, Color'n Say. Phillip Siadi & Lenore Paxton. Read by Phillip Siadi & Lenore Paxton. 1 cass. (Running Time: 45 min.). (World of Language Bible Story Ser.). (J). (ps-3). 1993. 5.95 (978-1-880449-32-5(3)) Wrldkids Pr.
Song, coloring book present story of David & Goliath with musical effects, dramatic narrative expands on song with indepth "facts" about story. Children learn to say a phrase in 10 different languages.

His Name Was David: Sing, Color'n Say. 2nd ed. Lenore Paxton & Phillip Siadi. Read by Lenore Paxton & Phillip Siadi. 1 cass. (Running Time: 45 min.). (World of Language Bible Story Ser.). (J). (ps up). 1994. pap. bk. 7.95 (978-1-880449-12-7(9)) Wrldkids Pr.

His Needs, Her Needs: Building an Affair-Proof Marriage. Willard F. Harley, Jr. Read by Wayne Shepherd. 5 CDs. (Running Time: 6 hrs.). (gr. 13 up). 2002. audio compact disk 29.99 (978-0-8007-4423-6(3)) Pub: Revell. Dist(s): Baker Pub Grp

***His Other Wife: A Novel.** unabr. ed. Deborah Bedford. (Running Time: 7.5 hrs. NaN mins.). (ENG.). 2011. 29.95 (978-1-4417-7672-3(9)); 44.95 (978-1-4417-7669-3(9)); audio compact disk 24.95 (978-1-4417-7671-6(0)); audio compact disk 69.00 (978-1-4417-7670-9(2)) Blckstn Audio.

His Personal Prisoner. Les Savage. (Running Time: 0 hr. 30 mins.). 2000. 10.95 (978-1-60083-551-3(1)) Iofy Corp.

***His Personal Prisoner.** Les Savage, Jr. 2009. (978-1-60136-442-5(3)) Audio Holding.

His Purpose of Descent. Elbert Willis. 1 cass. (Understanding the Holy Spirit Ser.). 4.00 Fill the Gap.

His Relation to Jesus. Elbert Willis. 1 cass. (Understanding the Holy Spirit Ser.). 4.00 Fill the Gap.

His Strength Is Perfect. Contrib. by Steven Curtis Chapman. (Mastertrax Ser.). 2006. audio compact disk 9.98 (978-5-558-01825-7(9)) Pt of Grace Ent.

His Voice for Your Need. Mark Crow. 5 cass. (Running Time: 7 hrs. 30 mins.). 2002. (978-1-931537-35-3(6)) Vision Comm Creat.

His Way: The Unauthorized Biography of Frank Sinatra. unabr. ed. Kitty Kelley. Read by Anna Fields. 15 cass. (Running Time: 22 hrs. 30 mins.). 2000. 120.00 (978-0-7366-4821-9(6), 5165) Books on Tape.
The unglossed biography of Frank Sinatra, the multi-talented legendary singer who topped the entertainment industry for more than fifty years. Sinatra worshipers will recoil from the book's concentration on claimed faults. Some observers do praise his good qualities though.

Hispanic-American Experience on File. (gr. 6-12). 2002. audio compact disk 149.95 (978-0-8160-4222-7(5)) Facts On File.

Hispanic Children's Folklore with Jose-Luis Orozco see Lirica Infantil con Jose-Luis Orozco

Hispanic Children's Folklore with Jose-Luis Orozco 4: Animales y Movimiento. Contrib. by Jose-Luis Orozco. (SPA.). (J). (gr. k-2). 12.00 (978-1-57417-020-7(1), AC5052); audio compact disk 16.00 (978-1-57417-004-7(X), AC1658) Pub: Arcoiris Recs. Dist(s): Lectorum Pubns

Hispanic Children's Folklore with Jose-Luis Orozco 5: Letras, Colores y Numeros. Contrib. by Jose-Luis Orozco. (SPA.). (J). (gr. k-2). 12.00 (978-1-57417-016-0(3), AC5053); audio compact disk 16.00 (978-1-57417-005-4(8), AC1662) Pub: Arcoiris Recs. Dist(s): Lectorum Pubns

Hispanic Heritage. 1 cass. (Running Time: 1 hr.). 10.95 (H0080B090, HarperThor) HarpC GBR.

Hiss, Don't Bite. Vayu Naidu. 1 cass. (Running Time: 022 min.). (Under the Banyan Ser.). (YA). (gr. 2 up). 1998. bk. 11.99 (978-81-86838-31-0(7)) APG.
Fairy tales & folklore.

Hissy Fit. Mary Kay Andrews. Read by Moira Driscoll. 9 cass. 79.95 (978-0-7927-3339-3(8), CSL 701); audio compact disk 110.95 (978-0-7927-3340-9(1), SLD 701) AudioGO.

***Hissy Fit.** abr. ed. Mary Kay Andrews. Read by Isabel Keating. (ENG.). 2004. (978-0-06-082426-6(3), Harper Audio); (978-0-06-082427-3(1), Harper Audio) HarperCollins Pubs.

Hissy Fit. abr. ed. Mary Kay Andrews. Read by Isabel Keating. 2005. audio compact disk 14.95 (978-0-06-087470-4(8)) HarperCollins Pubs.

Histoire Contemporaine see Treasury of French Prose

Histoire de la Bibliotheque Nationale. Emmanuel L. Ladurie. 1 cass. (Running Time: 60 mins.). (College de France Lectures). (FRE.). 1996. 21.95 (1859-LQP) Olivia & Hill.

Histoire de l'Occident Mediterraneen au Moyen Age. Pierre Toubert. 1 cass. (Running Time: 60 mins.). (College de France Lectures). (FRE.). 1996. 21.95 (1848-LQP) Olivia & Hill.

Histoire des Mentalites Religieuses dans l'Occident Moderne. Jean Delumeau. 1 cass. (Running Time: 60 mins.). (College de France Lectures). (FRE.). 1996. 21.95 (1853-LQP) Olivia & Hill.

Histoire d'O, Set. Pauline Reage. Read by C. Deis & G. Bejean. 4 cass.Tr. of Story of O. (FRE.). 1991. 34.95 (1480-VSL) Olivia & Hill.
This erotic novel describing the complete degradation of a young woman into a sex object was a literary event when it was first published under a pseudonym in the early 1950s.

Histoires Celebres. Ntc. 1 cass. 2001. 15.00 (978-0-8442-1402-3(7)) Glencoe.
Features four French stories, customized for ease of reading by intermediate students.

Histoires Comme Ca. Rudyard Kipling. Read by Michael Lonsdale. 1 cass.Tr. of Just So Stories. (FRE.). 1992. 16.95 (1575-RF) Olivia & Hill.
Kipling's famous stories on French National Radio (with musical interludes).

Histoires D'Animaux. Henri Bosco. Read by D. Cagnard. 1 cass. (FRE.). 1995. 18.95 (1732-DI) Olivia & Hill.
The professor wrote these tales for his students, in which animals speak, participate in intricate plots & unexpected twists.

Histoires de Rencontres. l.t. ed. Maeve Binchy. (French Ser.). 2001. bk. 30.99 (978-2-84011-430-7(5)) Pub: UlverLrgPrint GBR. Dist(s): Ulverscroft US

Histology: A Colour Atlas. Santelli. 2004. audio compact disk 20.00 (978-81-8061-378-4(X)) Jaypee Brothers IND.

Historia de Abraham. (Heroes de la Fe Ser.). 2000. (978-1-57697-781-1(1)) Untd Bible Amrcas Svce.

Historia de Abraham y Elias. (SPA.). (J). 2004. audio compact disk (978-1-933218-01-4(0)) Untd Bible Amrcas Svce.

Historia de Abu-Dir, el Tintorero y Abu-Sir, el Barbero - Cuento de las Mil y una Noches. unabr. ed. Read by Laura Garcia.Tr. of Arabian Nights Tale. (SPA.). 2002. audio compact disk 13.00 (978-958-43-0142-0(X)) YoYoMusic.

Historia de Dos Ciudades. abr. ed. Charles Dickens. Read by Guillermo Piedrahita. 3 CDs.Tr. of Tale of Two Cities. (SPA.). 2001. audio compact disk 17.00 (978-958-9494-58-5(7)) YoYoMusic.

Historia Del Patito Ping. Tr. of Story about Ping. (SPA.). 2004. 8.95 (978-0-7882-0257-5(X)) Weston Woods.

Historia Escondida de Juan Luis Guerra. Dario Tejada. 7 cass. (Running Time: 10 hrs.). (SPA.). 2004. 37.95 (978-1-4025-7674-4(9)) Recorded Bks.

Historia Sagrada Bible. Narrated by Rocha. (SPA.). 2007. audio compact disk 79.99 (978-1-930034-35-8(0)) Casscomm.

Historia Viva. abr. ed. Hillary Rodham Clinton. Read by Anna Silvetti. 7. (Running Time: 28800 sec.). (SPA.). 2007. audio compact disk 24.95 (978-1-933499-15-4(X)) Fonolibro Inc.

Historian. abr. ed. Elizabeth Kostova. Read by Joanne Whalley et al. (ENG.). 2005. 14.98 (978-1-59483-240-6(4)) Pub: Hachet Audio. Dist(s): HachBkGrp

Historian. abr. ed. Elizabeth Kostova. Read by Joanne Whalley et al. (Running Time: 12 hrs.). (ENG.). 2008. audio compact disk 14.98 (978-1-60024-278-6(2)) Pub: Hachet Audio. Dist(s): HachBkGrp

Historian. abr. ed. Elizabeth Kostova. Read by Joanne Whalley et al. (Running Time: 12 hrs.). (ENG.). 2009. 59.98 (978-1-60788-050-9(4)) Pub: Hachet Audio. Dist(s): HachBkGrp

Historian. abr. ed. Elizabeth Kostova. Read by Joanne Whalley et al. 10 CDs. (Running Time: 12 hrs.). (ENG.). 2009. audio compact disk 19.98 (978-1-60024-861-0(6)) Pub: Hachet Audio. Dist(s): HachBkGrp

Historian. unabr. ed. Elizabeth Kostova. 17 CDs. 2005. audio compact disk 126.65 (978-1-4159-2901-8(7)); 129.00 (978-1-4159-2900-1(9)) Books on Tape.
Based on the legend of Vlad the Impaler, this is the story of a young girl who discovers an ancient and disturbing book in her father's library, one which will lead to terrible loss and tragedy, as well as uncovering Dracula's resting place.

Historians I Have Known. unabr. ed. A. L. Rowse. Read by David Case. 6 cass. (Running Time: 9 hrs.). 1996. 31.20 (978-0-7366-3607-0(2), 4262) Books on Tape.
In the course of his distinguished career, A. L. Rowse has known most of the leading historians of our time in the U. S. & Britain.

Historias Biblicas. Logan Marshall. Narrated by Adolpho Stambulsky. Prod. by Ralph LaBarge. (J). 2006. 12.95 (978-0-9798626-9-4(8)) Alpha DVD.

Historias de amor en la Biblia. P. Juan Rivas. (SPA.). (YA). 2004. audio compact disk 18.95 (978-1-935405-81-8(0)) Hombre Nuevo.

Historias para Conversar: Nivel Basico. José Siles Artés. 1 cass. (Running Time: 1 hr. 30 mins.). (SPA & ENG., audio compact disk (978-84-7143-640-5(X)) Sociedad General ESP.

Historias para Conversar: Nivel Medio. José Siles Artés. 1 cass. (Running Time: 1 hr. 30 mins.). (SPA & ENG., (978-84-7143-641-2(8)) Sociedad General ESP.

Historias para Conversar: Nivel Superior. José Siles Artés. 1 cass. (Running Time: 1 hr. 30 mins.). (SPA & ENG., (978-84-7143-642-9(6)) Sociedad General ESP.

Historias para Conversar: Nivel Umbral. José Siles Artés. 1 cass. (Running Time: 1 hr. 30 mins.). (SPA & ENG., (978-84-7143-639-9(6)) Sociedad General ESP.

Historic Film of Glenn Canyon Before & after the Dam. Hosted by Nancy Pearlman. 1 cass. (Running Time: 28 min.). 10.00 (1214) Educ Comm CA.

Historic London. unabr. ed. Ronald Hutton. Read by Ronald Hutton. Ed. by Craig Mayes. 3 cass. (Running Time: 3 hrs.). (Personal Courier Ser.). 1992. 24.95 set. (978-1-878877-09-3(7), 09-7) Educ Excursions.
Experience the history of this venerable city from the Roman walls of Londinium to the medieval Isle of Thorney & Westminster Abbey to the 19th-century Houses of Parliament. Hear tales of England's kings & queens, heroes & heroines, whose lives thread a colorful tapestry throughout London as you explore the city. Winner: Best Audiotape - 1993 Benjamin Franklin Awards.

Historic Ocala. David Cook. 2007. audio compact disk 34.95 (978-1-893619-78-4(8)) Pub: Hist Pub Network. Dist(s): Partners Bk Dist

Historic Pre & Amillennialism: Logos 03/14/99. Ben Young. 1999. 4.95 (978-0-7417-6123-1(8), B0123) Win Walk.

Historic Preservation Law: An Introduction & Recent Developments. American Bar Association, Real Property, Probate and Trust Law Section Staff. 1 cass. (Running Time: 1 hr. 10 min.). 1983. pap. bk. 25.00 (PC:543-0049-01) Amer Bar Assn.
Surveys current state of the law.

Historic Presidential Speeches (1908-1993) Compiled by Library of Congress Staff. 6 CDs. (Running Time: 9 hrs.). 2001. bk. 79.98 (R2 71970) Rhino Enter.

Historic Problem: The Jews vs. the Arabs: Hebrews 6:11-12. Ed Young. (J). 1980. 4.95 (978-0-7417-1147-2(8), A0147) Win Walk.

Historical & Cultural Attitudes. 1 cass. (Introduction to Chemical Dependency Ser.). 1974. 8.95 (1480G) Hazelden.

Historical Apologetics: Augustine; Anselm. John Robbins. 1 cass. (Introduction to Apologetics Ser.: No. 2). 5.00 Trinity Found.

Historical Apologetics: Joseph Butler & William Paley; Friedrich Schleiermacher & Soren Kierkegaard. John Robbins. 1 cass. (Introduction to Apologetics Ser.: No. 4). 5.00 Trinity Found.

Historical Apologetics: Thomas Aquinas; John Calvin & Martin Luther. John Robbins. 1 cass. (Introduction to Apologetics Ser.: No. 3). 5.00 Trinity Found.

Historical Books on Cassette, Pt. 1. Read by Robert Baram. 12 cass. (Running Time: 75 min. per cass.). 32.95 (978-0-8198-3337-2(1)) Pauline Bks.
Listening to the Bible Series.

Historical Books on Cassette, Pt. 2. Read by Robert Baram. 12 cass. (Running Time: 85 min. per cass.). 32.95 (978-0-8198-3338-9(X)) Pauline Bks.

Historical Development of American Education see Educational Thought of the Founding Fathers

Historical Evolution of Romantic Love. unabr. ed. Nathaniel Branden. 1 cass. (Running Time: 1 hr. 24 min.). 12.95 (601) J Norton Pubs.
Love in primitive societies; the Greek & Roman view; the Christian attack on sexuality; individualism, capitalism & the birth of romantic love.

Historical Fiction Series. Margaret K. Wetterer. 33 vols. (Running Time: 48 mins.). (J). (gr. 1-6). 2000. pap. bk. 45.95 (978-0-87499-580-0(9)) Live Oak Media.
Includes: "Kate Shelley & the Midnight Express," "Keep the Lights Burning, Abbie" & "The Snow Walker.".

Historical Fiction Series. Margaret K. Wetterer et al. Illus. by Mary O. Young et al. 33 vols. (Running Time: 48 mins.). 2000. pap. bk. 51.95 (978-1-59112-859-5(5)) Live Oak Media.

Historical Foundations of Christianity. Rick Joyner. 1 cass. (Running Time: 90 mins.). (Church History & the Coming Move of God Ser.: Vol. 2). 2000. 5.00 (RJ11-002) Morning NC.
Church history is brought to life with practical applications & insights into how the enemy uses the same strategy against every new move of God.

Historical Heroes - Winston Churchill, Robert E. Lee, Sir Walter Raleigh Vol. 2: Three Literary Lectures. Featuring Elliot Engel. 3 cass. (Running Time: 3 hrs.). 1998. bk. 30.00 (978-1-890123-15-4(3), GS2) Media Cnslts.

***Historical Icons: Coretta Scott King.** Cerebellum Academic Team. (Running Time: 30 mins.). (Just the Facts Ser.). 2010. 24.95 (978-1-59163-537-6(3)) Cerebellum.

***Historical Icons: Famous African Americans.** Cerebellum Academic Team. (Running Time: 30 mins.). (Just the Facts Ser.). 2010. 24.95 (978-1-59163-262-7(5)) Cerebellum.

***Historical Icons: Famous Explorers.** Cerebellum Academic Team. (Running Time: 30 mins.). (Just the Facts Ser.). 2010. 24.95 (978-1-59163-307-5(9)) Cerebellum.

***Historical Icons: Famous Irish-Americans.** Cerebellum Academic Team. (Running Time: 30 mins.). (Just the Facts Ser.). 2010. 24.95 (978-1-59163-265-8(X)) Cerebellum.

***Historical Icons: Gandhi.** Cerebellum Academic Team. (Running Time: 30 mins.). (Just the Facts Ser.). 2010. 24.95 (978-1-59163-308-2(7)) Cerebellum.

***Historical Icons: Great Women in American History.** Cerebellum Academic Team. (Running Time: 30 mins.). (Just the Facts Ser.). 2010. 24.95 (978-1-59163-267-2(6)) Cerebellum.

***Historical Icons: Leonardo Da Vince.** Cerebellum Academic Team. (Running Time: 30 mins.). (Just the Facts Ser.). 2010. 24.95 (978-1-59163-316-7(8)) Cerebellum.

***Historical Icons: Mandela - Man of Vision.** Cerebellum Academic Team. (Running Time: 1 hr.). (Just the Facts Ser.). 2010. 29.95 (978-1-59163-309-9(5)) Cerebellum.

***Historical Icons: Martin Luther King.** Cerebellum Academic Team. (Running Time: 30 mins.). (Just the Facts Ser.). 2010. 24.95 (978-1-59163-264-1(1)) Cerebellum.

***Historical Icons: Michelangelo.** Cerebellum Academic Team. (Running Time: 30 mins.). (Just the Facts Ser.). 2010. 24.95 (978-1-59163-313-6(3)) Cerebellum.

***Historical Icons: Napolean.** Cerebellum Academic Team. (Running Time: 30 mins.). (Just the Facts Ser.). 2010. 24.95 (978-1-59163-311-2(7)) Cerebellum.

***Historical Icons: Picasso.** Cerebellum Academic Team. (Running Time: 30 mins.). (Just the Facts Ser.). 2010. 24.95 (978-1-59163-312-9(5)) Cerebellum.

***Historical Icons: Raphael.** Cerebellum Academic Team. (Running Time: 30 mins.). (Just the Facts Ser.). 2010. 24.95 (978-1-59163-315-0(X)) Cerebellum.

***Historical Icons: Vincent Van Gogh.** Cerebellum Academic Team. (Running Time: 30 mins.). (Just the Facts Ser.). 2010. 24.95 (978-1-59163-314-3(1)) Cerebellum.

***Historical Icons: Winston Churchill.** Cerebellum Academic Team. (Running Time: 30 mins.). (Just the Facts Ser.). 2010. 24.95 (978-1-59163-310-5(9)) Cerebellum.

Historical Inventions on File. Diagram Group. (YA). (gr. 6-12). 2002. audio compact disk 149.95 (978-0-8160-4442-9(2)) Facts On File.

Historical Jesus, Pts. I-II. Instructed by Bart D. Ehrman. 12 CDs. (Running Time: 12 hrs.). 2000. bk. 69.95 (978-1-56585-363-8(6), 643); 54.95 (978-1-56585-175-7(7), 643) Teaching Co.

Historical Jesus, Vol. 2. Instructed by Bart D. Ehrman. 6 cass. (Running Time: 6 hrs.). 2000. 129.95 (978-1-56585-176-4(5)) Teaching Co.

Historical Part of Bible: Sin, Sanctification, New Birth. Finis J. Dake, Sr. (J). (gr. k up). 5.95 (978-1-55829-032-7(X)) Dake Publishing.
Bible study.

Historical Science Experiments on File. Diagram Group. (YA). (gr. 6-12). 2002. audio compact disk 149.95 (978-0-8160-4443-6(0)) Facts On File.

Historical Sketch of the Cherokee. Read by Willena Robinson. Des. by Willena Robinson. 2005. 29.95 (978-1-882182-14-5(6)) Cherokee Lang & Cult.

Historical Survey. unabr. ed. Narrated by Wu-Chi Liu. 1 cass. (Running Time: 27 mins.). 1969. 14.95 (23146) J Norton Pubs.
Discusses the value of Chinese literature produced in the Han, Tang, Sung & subsequent dynasties.

Historical Timeline Figures. 2004. audio compact disk 25.00 (978-1-931397-11-7(2)) Geography Mat.

Historical Tour of Ancient Israel. 10.00 (RME103) Esstee Audios.

Histories. unabr. ed. Herodotus. Read by Bernard Mayes. (YA). 2008. 144.99 (978-1-60514-726-0(5)) Find a World.

Histories. unabr. ed. Herodotus. Read by Bernard Mayes. Tr. by George Rawlinson. 12 cass. (Running Time: 41 hrs. 30 mins.). 2001. 83.95 (978-0-7861-1591-4(2), 2420A,B) Blckstn Audio.

Histories. unabr. ed. Tacitus. Read by James Adams. (Running Time: 36000 sec.). (Classic Collection (Blackstone Audio) Ser.). 2008. 19.95 (978-1-4332-1256-7(0)); audio compact disk 19.95 (978-1-4332-1257-4(9)) Blckstn Audio.

Histories. unabr. ed. Tacitus & Tacitus. Read by James Adams. (Running Time: 36000 sec.). 2008. 65.95 (978-1-4332-3459-0(9)) Blckstn Audio.

Histories, Pt. 1. unabr. ed. Herodotus. Read by Bernard Mayes. 12 cass. (Running Time: 18 hrs.). 1999. 83.95 (2420A) Blckstn Audio.
Herodotus is not only the father of the art & the science of historical writing but also one of the Western tradition's most compelling storytellers. He infused his magnificent history with a continuous awareness of the mythic & the wonderful, & virtually defined the rational, humane spirit that is the enduring legacy of Greek civilization.

Histories, Pt. II. Herodotus. Read by Bernard Mayes. 9 cass. (Running Time: 41 hrs. 30 mins.). 1999. 62.95 (978-0-7861-1598-3(X), 2420A,B) Blckstn Audio.
Herodotus is not only the father of the art and the science of historical writing but also one of the Western traditions most compelling storytellers. In tales such as that of Gyges, who murders Candaules, the king of Lydia, & usurps his throne & his marriage bed, thereby bringing on, generations later, war with the Persians, Herodotus laid bare the intricate human entanglements at the core of great historical events.

Histories & Stories from the Older Testament. Douglas Wilson et al. (ENG.). 2007. audio compact disk 35.00 (978-1-59128-492-5(9)) Canon Pr ID.

Histories of Tacitus. unabr. ed. Cornelius Tacitus. Read by Frederick Davidson. 7 cass. (Running Time: 10 hrs.). 2001. 49.95 (978-0-7861-2004-8(5), 2774) Blckstn Audio.
In taking up history, Tacitus joined the line of succession of those who described & interpreted their own period & he covered the story from the political situation that followed Nero's death to the close of the Flavian dynasty.

History. Contrib. by Matthew West. Prod. by Kenny Greenberg & Jason Houser. 2005. audio compact disk 13.99 (978-5-558-98205-3(5)) Sigma F RUS.

History, Bks. 8 & 9, set. unabr. ed. Herodotus. Read by Robert L. Halvorson. 4 cass. (Running Time: 360 min.). 28.95 (72) Halvorson Assocs.

History & Functions of the House of Representatives. Cerebellum Academic Team. (Running Time: 30 mins.). (Just the Facts Ser.). 2001. 24.95 (978-1-59163-290-0(0)) Cerebellum.

History & Functions of the Presidency. Cerebellum Academic Team. (Running Time: 30 mins.). (Just the Facts Ser.). 2001. 24.95 (978-1-59163-286-3(2)) Cerebellum.

History & Functions of the Secretary of State. Cerebellum Academic Team. (Running Time: 30 mins.). (Just the Facts Ser.). 2003. 24.95 (978-1-59163-287-0(0)) Cerebellum.

History & Functions of the Supreme Court. Cerebellum Academic Team. (Running Time: 30 mins.). (Just the Facts Ser.). 2001. 24.95 (978-1-59163-280-1(3)) Cerebellum.

History & Functions of the United Nations. Cerebellum Academic Team. (Running Time: 30 mins.). (Just the Facts Ser.). 2001. 24.95 (978-1-59163-288-7(9)) Cerebellum.

History & Functions of the Vice Presidency. Cerebellum Academic Team. (Running Time: 30 mins.). (Just the Facts Ser.). 2003. 24.95 (978-1-59163-292-4(7)) Cerebellum.

History & Use of the I Ching. unabr. ed. John Blofeld. 1 cass. (Running Time: 1 hr. 22 min.). 1978. 11.00 (02901) Big Sur Tapes.
A concise history of the I Ching & its uses, including consideration of whether the I Ching was intended as a book of wisdom for us to study or as a book of divination for us to use.

History, Baseball, & the Art of the Narrative. Doris Kearns Goodwin. 1 cass. (Running Time: 58 mins.). 2001. 12.95 Smithson Assocs.

History Boys. abr. ed. Alan Bennett. Contrib. by Clive Merrison & Richard Griffiths. (Running Time: 9000 sec.). (ENG.). 2007. audio compact disk 19.95 (978-1-60283-025-7(8)) Pub: AudioGO. Dist(s): Perseus Dist

History Boys. unabr. ed. Alan Bennett. Richard Griffiths & Clive Merrison. 2 CDs. (Running Time: 2 hrs. 30 mins.). 2007. audio compact disk 29.95 (978-0-7927-4987-5(1)) AudioGO.

History Channel Presents Events That Shaped Our Lives from CBS News: With Historical Broadcasts from Walter Cronkite & Dan Rather. Created by Radio Spirits. 2004. audio compact disk 9.98 (978-1-57019-736-9(9)) Radio Spirits.

History Ends in Green. Read by Terence McKenna. 6 cass. (Running Time: 7 hrs. 30 min.). 1992. bk. 39.95 set. (978-1-56176-907-0(X)) Mystic Fire.
McKenna examines the nature of language & the techniques of ecstasy that have developed in non-Western societies to navigate to & from invisible worlds.

History in the Making: The Easiest Way to Preserve Your Family History. Louise Bobrow. 2 cass. (Running Time: 3 hrs.). 2000. pap. bk. 24.95 (978-0-9665319-6-1(5)) Gmlf Bk Grp.

History Lights the Way. Ed. by Ames Sweet & Ann Warner. 1 cass. (Running Time: 1 hr. 30 min.). Dramatization. 1994. 6.50 (978-0-933685-25-3(4), TP-18) A A Grapevine.
Articles about AA history.

History Man, Set. unabr. ed. Malcolm Bradbury. Read by Paul Shelley. 8 cass. 2000. 69.95 (978-0-7540-0407-3(4), CAB 1830) AudioGO.
Howard Kirk is the trendiest of radical tutors at a fashionable university. Timid vice-chancellors pale before his threats of disruption. Reactionary colleagues are crushed beneath his merciless Marxist logic. Women are drawn by his progressive promiscuity. A self-appointed revolutionary hero, Howard always comes out on top.

History of a Young Man with Spectacles. Arthur Machen. 1981. (S-4) Jimcin Record.

***History of Air Warfare.** unabr. ed. John Andreas Olsen. Read by Steve Van Doren. (Running Time: 17 hrs. NaN mins.). (ENG.). 2010. 44.95 (978-1-4417-7658-7(3)); 89.95 (978-1-4417-7655-6(9)); audio compact disk 34.95 (978-1-4417-7657-0(5)); audio compact disk 123.00 (978-1-4417-7656-3(7)) Blckstn Audio.

History of American Literature, Pt. 1. audio compact disk 80.97 (978-0-13-435354-8(4)) P-H.

History of American Literature, Pt. I & II. audio compact disk 145.97 (978-0-13-435352-4(8)) P-H.

History of American Literature, Pt. II. audio compact disk 80.97 (978-0-13-435353-1(6)) P-H.

History of Ancient Egypt, Pts. I-IV. Instructed by Robert Brier. 24 CDs. (Running Time: 24 hrs.). 1999. bk. 129.95 (978-1-56585-333-1(4), 350); 99.95 (978-1-56585-084-2(X), 350) Teaching Co.

History of Ancient Egypt, Vol. 2. Instructed by Robert Brier. 6 cass. (Running Time: 6 hrs.). 1999. 249.95 (978-1-56585-085-9(8)); audio compact disk 359.95 (978-1-56585-334-8(2)) Teaching Co.

History of Ancient Egypt, Vol. 3. Instructed by Robert Brier. 6 cass. (Running Time: 6 hrs.). 1999. 249.95 (978-1-56585-086-6(6)); audio compact disk 359.95 (978-1-56585-335-5(0)) Teaching Co.

History of Ancient Egypt, Vol. 4. Instructed by Robert Brier. 6 cass. (Running Time: 6 hrs.). 1999. 249.95 (978-1-56585-087-3(4)); audio compact disk 359.95 (978-1-56585-336-2(9)) Teaching Co.

History of Ancient Rome, Pts. I-IV. Instructed by Garrett Fagan. 24 CDs. (Running Time: 24 hrs.). 1999. bk. 129.95 (978-1-56585-327-0(X), 340); 99.95 (978-1-56585-078-1(5), 340) Teaching Co.

History of Ancient Rome, Vol. 2. Intro. by Garrett Fagan. 6 cass. (Running Time: 6 hrs.). 1999. 249.95 (978-1-56585-079-8(3)) Teaching Co.

History of Ancient Rome, Vol. 2. Instructed by Garrett Fagan. 6 CDs. (Running Time: 6 hrs.). 1999. audio compact disk 359.95 (978-1-56585-328-7(8)) Teaching Co.

History of Ancient Rome, Vol. 3. Instructed by Garrett Fagan. 6 cass. (Running Time: 6 hrs.). 1999. 249.95 (978-1-56585-080-4(7)); audio compact disk 359.95 (978-1-56585-329-4(6)) Teaching Co.

History of Ancient Rome, Vol. 4. Instructed by Garrett Fagan. 6 cass. (Running Time: 6 hrs.). 1999. 249.95 (978-1-56585-081-1(5)); audio compact disk 359.95 (978-1-56585-330-0(X)) Teaching Co.

History of Ancient Sparta: Valor, Virtue, & Devotion in the Greek Golden Age. unabr. ed. Timothy B. Shutt. 7 CDs. 2009. audio compact disk 98.75 (978-1-4361-7817-4(7)) Recorded Bks.

History of Britain Vol. I: At the Edge of the World? 3000 BC-AD 1603. Simon Schama. Read by Stephen Thorne. (Chivers Audio Bks.). 2003. audio compact disk 115.95 (978-0-7540-8780-9(8)) Pub: Chivers Audio Bks GBR. Dist(s): AudioGO

History of Britain Vol. I: At the Edge of the World? 3000 BC-AD 1603. Simon Schama. Read by Stephen Thorne. 2003. 110.95 (978-0-7540-8387-0(X)) Pub: Chivers Audio Bks GBR. Dist(s): AudioGO

History of Britain Vol. III: The Fate of Empire, 1776-2000. Simon Schama. Read by Stephen Thorne. 13 cass. 99.95 (978-0-7927-3379-9(7), CSL 718); audio compact disk 124.95 (978-0-7927-3380-5(0), SLD 718); audio compact disk 49.95 (978-0-7927-3381-2(9), CMP 718) AudioGO.

History of British Military Bands Vol. 1: Cavalry & Corps. Gordon Turner & Alwyn Turner. 1 CD. (C). 1997. bk. 240.00 (978-1-873376-01-0(4)) Pub: Spellmount Pubs GBR. Dist(s): St Mut

History of British Military Bands Vol. III: Infantry & Irish. Gordon Turner & Alwyn Turner. 1 CD. (Running Time: 1 hr.). 1999. bk. 280.00 (978-1-873376-28-7(6)) Pub: Spellmount Pubs GBR. Dist(s): St Mut

History of Calvinism in America-mp3. 1998. 15.00 (978-1-59128-314-0(0)) Canon Pr ID.

History of Calvinism in America-tape. 8 cass. 1998. 28.00 (978-1-59128-316-4(7)) Canon Pr ID.

History of Christian Theology. Instructed by Phillip Cary. 2008. 199.95 (978-1-59803-485-1(5)); audio compact disk 99.95 (978-1-59803-486-8(3)) Teaching Co.

***History of Christianity.** unabr. ed. Paul Johnson. Read by Nadia May. (Running Time: 14 hrs. 30 mins.). 2010. 44.95 (978-1-4417-4671-9(4)); audio compact disk 160.00 (978-1-4417-4668-9(4)) Blckstn Audio.

History of Christianity, Pt. 1. unabr. collector's ed. Paul Johnson. Read by Richard Brown. 12 cass. (Running Time: 18 hrs.). 1992. 96.00 (978-0-7366-2279-0(9), 3067-A) Books on Tape.
It is almost 200 years since the birth of Jesus Christ...during these two millennia Christianity has proved more influential in shaping human destiny

than any other institutional philosophy, but there are now signs that its period of predominance is drawing to a close, thereby inviting a retrospect & a balance sheet.

History of Christianity, Pt. 2. unabr. collector's ed. Paul Johnson. Read by Richard Brown. 11 cass. (Running Time: 16 hrs. 30 min.). 1992. 88.00 (978-0-7366-2280-6(2), 3067-B) Books on Tape.

History of Christianity: Part 1 Of 2, Vol. 1. unabr. ed. Paul Johnson. Read by Nadia May. 10 cass. (Running Time: 29 hrs.). 1989. 69.95 (978-0-7861-0066-8(4), 1063A,B) Blckstn Audio.
Paul Johnson provides the listener with a panoramic overview of the events which have shaped our twentieth century Western lifestyle.

History of Christianity: Part 2 Of 2, Vol. 2. unabr. ed. Paul Johnson. Read by Nadia May. 10 cass. (Running Time: 29 hrs.). 1989. 69.95 set. (978-0-7861-0067-5(2), 1063A,B) Blckstn Audio.

History of Christianity in the Reformation Era, Pts. I-III. Instructed by Brad Gregory. 18 pieces. (Running Time: 18 hrs.). (C). bk. 79.95 (978-1-56585-192-4(7), 690) Teaching Co.

History of Christianity in the Reformation Era, Pts. I-III. Instructed by Brad Gregory. 18 CDs. (Running Time: 18 hrs.). (C). 2001. bk. 99.95 (978-1-56585-370-6(9), 690) Teaching Co.

History of Christianity in the Reformation Era, Vol. 2. Instructed by Brad Gregory. 6 cass. (Running Time: 6 hrs.). 2001. 199.95 (978-1-56585-193-1(5)) Teaching Co.

History of Christianity in the Reformation Era, Vol. 3. Instructed by Brad Gregory. 6 cass. (Running Time: 6 hrs.). 2001. 199.95 (978-1-56585-194-8(3)) Teaching Co.

History of Classical Music. Richard Fawkes. Read by Robert Powell. (Running Time: 5 hrs. 15 mins.). (C). 2001. 28.95 (978-1-60083-766-1(2)) Iofy Corp.

History of Classical Music. Richard Fawkes. Read by Robert Powell. 4 cass. (Running Time: 5 hrs. 15 mins.). 1997. 22.98 (978-962-634-640-2(X), NA414014, Naxos AudioBooks); audio compact disk 28.98 (978-962-634-140-7(8), NA414012, Naxos AudioBooks) Naxos.
Music of the western classical tradition spans some 14 centuries, from the emergence of Gregorian chant to the sounds of the present day. 150 musical excerpts illustrate the narrative.

History of Classical Music. unabr. ed. Richard Fawkes. Read by Robert Powell. (YA). 2007. 39.99 (978-1-60252-561-0(7)) Find a World.

History of Classical Music, Set. Richard Fawkes. (Running Time: 5 hrs. 21 mins.). (ENG.). (gr. 9-11). 1998. 28.99 (978-0-521-63741-1(4)) Cambridge U Pr.

History of Classical Music/The History of Opera. Richard Fawkes. Read by Robert Powell. 8 cass. (Running Time: 12 hrs.). 2003. bk. (978-962-634-757-7(0), Naxos AudioBooks) Naxos.

***History of Clearing.** L. Ron Hubbard. (ITA.). 2010. audio compact disk 15.00 (978-1-4031-6822-1(9)); audio compact disk 15.00 (978-1-4031-6828-3(8)); audio compact disk 15.00 (978-1-4031-6814-6(8)); audio compact disk 15.00 (978-1-4031-6817-7(2)); audio compact disk 15.00 (978-1-4031-6819-1(9)); audio compact disk 15.00 (978-1-4031-6830-6(X)); audio compact disk 15.00 (978-1-4031-6815-3(6)); audio compact disk 15.00 (978-1-4031-6821-4(0)); audio compact disk 15.00 (978-1-4031-6824-5(5)); audio compact disk 15.00 (978-1-4031-6818-4(0)); audio compact disk 15.00 (978-1-4031-6825-2(3)); audio compact disk 15.00 (978-1-4031-6826-9(1)); audio compact disk 15.00 (978-1-4031-6829-0(6)); audio compact disk 15.00 (978-1-4031-6823-8(7)); audio compact disk 15.00 (978-1-4031-6816-0(4)); audio compact disk 15.00 (978-1-4031-6820-7(2)); audio compact disk 15.00 (978-1-4031-6827-6(X)) Bridge Pubns Inc.

History of Danish Dreams. abr. ed. Peter Hoeg. Read by Maxwell Caulfied. 4 cass. (Running Time: 6 hrs.). 1995. 24.95 Set. (978-1-57511-006-6(7), 70020) Pub Mills.
Through a series of vividly imagined & wildly colorful characters, Hoeg gives us a very different account of the twentieth century, which in Denmark encompasses the transition from a medieval society to a modern welfare state with its accompanying cultural revolutions. The cast includes a count who builds a wall around his estate & stops all of his clocks to prevent the passage of time; an old lady who presides over a powerful newspaper dynasty & predicts the future accurately in print without ever learning to read & write; & Adonis Jensen, who causes his vagabound parents great sorrow through his inability to steal.

History of Economics. John Robbins. 1 cass. (Introduction to Economics Ser.: No. 2). 5.00 Trinity Found.

History of England from the Tudors to the Stuarts, Pts. I-IV. Instructed by Robert Bucholz. 24 cass. (Running Time: 24 hrs.). 2003. bk. 99.95 (978-1-56585-654-7(6), 8470); bk. 129.95 (978-1-56585-656-1(2), 8470) Teaching Co.

History of English Literature. Perry Keenlyside. Read by Derek Jacobi. (Running Time: 5 hrs.). (C). 2005. 28.95 (978-1-60083-767-8(0)) Iofy Corp.

History of English Literature. Perry Keenlyside. Read by Derek Jacobi. 4 cass. (Running Time: 5 hrs. 15 min.). 2001. 22.98 (978-962-634-721-8(X), NA422114, Naxos AudioBooks); audio compact disk 28.98 (978-962-634-221-3(8), NA422112, Naxos AudioBooks) Naxos.
Tells the remarkable story of the world's richest literary resource. The story-telling, the poetry, the growth of the novel & the great histories & essays which have informed the language & the imagination wherever English is spoken.

History of Ethics, Set. unabr. ed. Henry Sidgwick. Read by Robert L. Halvorson. 8 cass. (Running Time: 720 min.). 56.95 (76) Halvorson Assocs.

History of Europe, 1 of 2. unabr. ed. J. M. Roberts. Read by Frederick Davidson. 14 cass. (Running Time: 41 hrs.). 2003. 89.95 (978-0-7861-2387-2(7), 3064A,B) Blckstn Audio.
Traces the development of the European identity over the course of thousands of years, ranging across empires and religions, economics, science, and the arts. Antiquity, the age of Christendom, the Middle Ages, early modern history, and the old European order are all surveyed in turn, with particular emphasis given to the turbulent twentieth century.

History of Europe, 2 of 2. unabr. ed. J. M. Roberts. Read by Frederick Davidson. 14 cass. (Running Time: 41 hrs.). 2003. 89.95 (978-0-7861-2399-5(0), 3064A,B) Blckstn Audio.

History of Europe- Part A. unabr. ed. J. M. Roberts. Read by Frederick Davidson. (Running Time: 19 hrs. 50 mins.). 2008. audio compact disk 120.00 (978-1-4332-5037-8(3)) Blckstn Audio.

History of Europe- Part B. unabr. ed. J. M. Roberts. Read by Frederick Davidson. (Running Time: 18 hrs. 0 mins.). 2008. audio compact disk 120.00 (978-1-4332-5038-5(1)) Blckstn Audio.

History of Freedom, Vol. 2. Instructed by J. Rufus Fears. 6 cass. (Running Time: 6 hrs.). 2001. 199.95 (978-1-56585-134-4(X)) Teaching Co.

History of Freedom, Vol. 3. Instructed by J. Rufus Fears. 6 cass. (Running Time: 6 hrs.). 2001. 199.95 (978-1-56585-135-1(8)) Teaching Co.

History of Freedom, Vols. I-III. Instructed by J. Rufus Fears. 18 cass. (Running Time: 18 hrs.). 79.95 (978-1-56585-133-7(1), 480) Teaching Co.

History of Freedom, Vols. I-III. Instructed by J. Rufus Fears. 18 CDs. (Running Time: 18 hrs.). 2001. bk. 99.95 (978-1-56585-355-3(5), 480) Teaching Co.

History of God. Karen Armstrong. 1975. audio compact disk 9.99 (978-0-06-074335-2(2)) HarperCollins Pubs.

History of God: The 4,000-Year Quest of Judaism, Christianity & Islam. abr. ed. Karen Armstrong. Read by Karen Armstrong. 2004. audio compact disk 29.95 (978-0-06-059185-4(4)) HarperCollins Pubs.

History of Greece. unabr. ed. Cyril E. Robinson. 12 cass. (Running Time: 17 hrs. 19 min.). 2000. 88.00 (978-1-929718-07-8(1), 90014) Audio Conn.
The thrilling story of the rise to power & influence of the greatest civilization the world has ever known.

History of Hand Knitting. Richard Rutt. (ENG.). 2007. audio compact disk 29.95 (978-0-9796073-4-9(5)) Knitting Out.

History of Hand Knitting. abr. ed. Richard Rutt. Read by Melissa Hughes. (YA). 2008. 54.99 (978-1-60514-980-6(2)) Find a World.

History of Hands. David Citino. 2006. audio compact disk 9.95 (978-0-8142-9121-4(X)) Pub: Ohio St U Pr. Dist(s): Chicago Distribution Ctr

History of Hapkido. 1986. 12.95 (TC-16) ITA Inst.
Follow the development of Hapkido from its humble beginning to the formation of the International Hapkido Federation.

History of Henry Esmond. William Makepeace Thackeray. Read by Anais 9000. 2008. 33.95 (978-1-60112-080-9(X)) Babblebooks.

History of Henry Esmond. unabr. ed. William Makepeace Thackeray. Read by Gordon Griffin. 16 cass. (Running Time: 20 hrs. 28 min.). (Isis Ser.). (J). 2003. 104.95 (978-0-7531-1825-2(4)) Pub: ISIS Lrg Prnt GBR. Dist(s): Ulverscroft US
Follows the troubled progress of Henry Esmond Esq., a gentleman and officer in Marlborough's army.

History of Henry Esmond. unabr. ed. William Makepeace Thackeray. Read by Gordon Griffin. 18 CDs. (Running Time: 20 hrs. 28 mins.). (Isis (CDs) Ser.). (J). 2005. audio compact disk 116.95 (978-0-7531-2465-9(3)) Pub: ISIS Lrg Prnt GBR. Dist(s): Ulverscroft US

History of Hip-Hop: The Roots of Rap. Thomas Hatch. (High Five Reading Ser.). (ENG., (gr. 4-5). 2005. audio compact disk 5.95 (978-0-7368-5760-4(5)) CapstoneDig.

History of Hip-Hop: The Roots of Rap. Thomas Hatch. (High Five Reading - Blue Ser.). (ENG.). (gr. 1-2). 2007. audio compact disk 5.95 (978-1-4296-1429-0(3)) CapstoneDig.

History of Hitler's Empire. 2nd rev. ed. Instructed by Thomas Childers. 6 CDs. (Running Time: 6 hrs.). bk. 39.95 (978-1-56585-385-0(7), 805); 29.95 (978-1-56585-229-7(X), 805) Teaching Co.

History of Hitler's Empire, Course 805. Instructed by Thomas Childers. 4 cass. (Running Time: 6 hrs.). 19.95 (805) Teaching Co.
An intense realism underlies this look at 1930's Germany, which leaves the often chilling impression that Hitler's political ambition reached its climax only through many accidents of chance & circumstance. Exhibits techniques used by the Nazis that we now take for granted: polling, direct mailings, exit interviews. Eight lectures.

History of Indian Policy: Syllabus. Judith Bachman. (J). 1978. 146.10 (978-0-89420-149-3(2)) Natl Book.

History of Ireland: An Introduction. Ed. by Ciaran Brady. Prod. by Stephen F. Browne. 7 CDs. (Running Time: 7 hrs.). 2002. audio compact disk 59.99 (978-1-872310-00-8(1)) Irish Audio Lib.
The combined work of 14 of Ireland's historians, seven hours in duration, covers from 6,000 BC to the present day.

History of Joseph Smith by His Mother. Lucy Mack Smith. 5 cass. 2004. 19.95 (978-1-57734-721-7(8)); audio compact disk 24.95 (978-1-57734-751-4(X)) Covenant Comms.

History of Latin America. unabr. ed. George Pendle. Read by Fred Williams. 7 cass. (Running Time: 10 hrs.). 1995. 49.95 (978-0-7861-0892-3(4), 1669) Blckstn Audio.
An authoritative & concise introduction to an area of such great economic potential is certainly needed. This history has been written by a specialist who was closely connected with Latin America for over forty years. His text emphasizes how many races & classes have contributed to the civilization of this great landmass, with its vast mountain ranges, rivers, prairies, forests & deserts: Indians, European conquistadores, priests, planters, African slaves, caudillos, liberal intellectuals & commercial pioneers.

History of Literature, Set. abr. ed. Thomas Carlyle. Read by Robert L. Halvorson. 5 cass. (Running Time: 450 min.). 35.95 (86) Halvorson Assocs.

History of Love. Nicole Krauss. 2005. audio compact disk 34.99 (978-1-4193-3342-2(9)) Recorded Bks.

History of Luck. unabr. ed. Jandy Nelson. (Running Time: 7 hrs.). 2010. audio compact disk 24.99 (978-1-4418-2019-8(1), 9781441820198, Bril Audio CD Unabri) Brilliance Audio.

History of Marion County, Ohio, Containing a History of the County: Its Townships, Towns, Churches, Schools, Etc.; General & Local Statistics, Military Record, Portraits of Early Settlers & Prominent Men. Conaway Leggett and Co. Staff. 2002. audio compact disk 25.00 (978-0-7884-2154-9(9)) Heritage Bk.

History of Music in Western Civilization: Fascinating Discussions by 15 Prominent Music Authorities, with Musical Examples. unabr. abr. ed. Highbridge Staff. Told to Christopher Hogwood & Wilfrid Mellers. 12 CDs. (Running Time: 10 hrs. 30 mins.). (ENG.). 1996. audio compact disk 99.95 (978-1-56511-185-1(0), 1565111850) Pub: HighBridge. Dist(s): Workman Pub

History of Music of the Western World CD Set. Contrib. by Anthony Rooley et al. 12 CDs. (Running Time: 11 hrs. 40 mins.). 2006. audio compact disk 69.50 (978-1-57970-373-8(9), SCD100, Audio-For) J Norton Pubs.
For anyone who likes music and would like to know more about it. Stimulating discussions by 15 prominent authorities are illustrated with hundreds of musical examples.

History of Music of the Western World (1100 to 1980) unabr. ed. 12 cass. 1996. 79.00 set. (11100) Books on Tape.
An Audio-Forum presentation. Journey through nine centuries of music, from Gregorian chants & medieval love songs to Baroque, ballet & jazz. Outstanding music appreciation course.

History of Neuroscience in Autobiography. Sidney Brenner & Gerald Fischbach. Ed. by Larry Squire. (ENG.). 2006. audio compact disk 20.95 (978-0-12-373641-3(2), Acad Press) Sci Tech Bks.

History of Now: A Novel. unabr. ed. Klein, Daniel Klein. Read by Carrington MacDuffie. (Running Time: 1 hr. 0 mins.). (ENG.). 2009. 29.95 (978-1-4332-9893-6(7)); 65.95 (978-1-4332-9889-9(9)); audio compact disk 100.00 (978-1-4332-9890-5(2)) Blckstn Audio.

History of Opera. Richard Fawkes. (Running Time: 5 hrs. 18 mins.). (ENG.). 2000. audio compact disk 34.99 (978-0-521-78752-9(1)) Cambridge U Pr.

History of Opera. Richard Fawkes. Read by Robert Powell. (Running Time: 5 hrs. 15 mins.). (C). 2003. 28.95 (978-1-60083-768-5(9)) Iofy Corp.

History of Opera. Richard Fawkes. Read by Robert Powell. 4 cass. (Running Time: 5 hrs. 15 mins.). 1999. 22.98 (978-962-634-676-1(0), NA417614, Naxos AudioBooks); audio compact disk 28.98 (978-962-634-176-6(9), NA417612, Naxos AudioBooks) Naxos.
Since its origins in the 16th century, opera has been an extravagant and costly affair, arousing great passions. More than 115 musical examples trace the history of opera and operetta up to the present day.

History of Our World. Heidi Hayes Jacobs & Michal L. LeVasseur. Contrib. by Dorling Kindersley Publishing Staff et al. stu. ed. 151.97 (978-0-13-130787-2(8)) PH School.

History of Our World: Guided Reading. Heidi Hayes Jacobs & Michal L. LeVasseur. Contrib. by Dorling Kindersley Publishing Staff et al. (ENG & SPA.). cass. & audio compact disk 54.47 (978-0-13-130783-4(5)) PH School.

History of Philosophy. unabr. ed. Frank Barr. 2 cass. 1983. 18.00 set. (978-1-56964-754-7(2), A0004-83) Sound Photosyn.
Brilliant Barr, gives a wonderful densely packed talk. To get the most from this one, note taking & multiple listenings are necessary.

History of Psychology: A Cultural Perspective. Cherie Goodenow O'Boyle. 2006. audio compact disk (978-0-8058-5786-3(9)) L Erlbaum Assocs.

History of Rasselas, Prince of Abissinia. unabr. ed. Samuel Johnson. Read by Walter Zimmerman. 4 cass. (Running Time: 6 hrs.). 1982. 32.95 (978-0-7861-0522-9(4), 2021) Blckstn Audio.
This is a didactic romance which Dr. Johnson published in 1759. Rasselas, a son of the Emperor of Abyssinia, weary of the joys of the "happy valley," escapes to Egypt. Here he studies the various conditions of men's lives, concluding that happiness eludes philosophers, hermits & the wealthy. The plot is charmed with its wise & humane melancholy.

History of Rasselas, Prince of Abissinia. unabr. ed. Samuel Johnson. Read by Walter Zimmerman. 4 cass. (Running Time: 5 hrs.). 1984. 29.00 incl. album. (C-101) Jimcin Record.
"The History of Rasselas" deals with the flight into Egypt of a young prince who tires of a life of ease & complacency & seeks to plumb the eternal verities.

History of Religious Life up to Vatican II. Fr. Hardon. 16 cass. 64.00 Set. (94A) IRL Chicago.

***History of Research & Investigation.** L. Ron Hubbard. (SWE.). 2010. audio compact disk 15.00 (978-1-4031-7137-5(8)); audio compact disk 15.00 (978-1-4031-7136-8(X)); audio compact disk 15.00 (978-1-4031-7131-3(9)); audio compact disk 15.00 (978-1-4031-7134-4(3)); audio compact disk 15.00 (978-1-4031-7135-1(1)); audio compact disk 15.00 (978-1-4031-7126-9(2)); audio compact disk 15.00 (978-1-4031-7122-1(X)); audio compact disk 15.00 (978-1-4031-7130-6(0)); audio compact disk 15.00 (978-1-4031-7133-7(5)); audio compact disk 15.00 (978-1-4031-7128-3(9)); audio compact disk 15.00 (978-1-4031-7123-8(8)); audio compact disk 15.00 (978-1-4031-7138-2(6)); audio compact disk 15.00 (978-1-4031-7124-5(6)); audio compact disk 15.00 (978-1-4031-7125-2(4)); audio compact disk 15.00 (978-1-4031-7129-0(7)); audio compact disk 15.00 (978-1-4031-7127-6(0)); audio compact disk 15.00 (978-1-4031-7132-0(7)) Bridge Pubns Inc.

History of Russia Pts. I-III: From Peter the Great to Gorbachev. Instructed by Mark Steinberg. 18 CDs. (Running Time: 18 hrs.). 2003. bk. 99.95 (978-1-56585-633-2(3), 8380) Teaching Co.

History of Russia Pts. I-III: From Peter the Great to Gorbachev, Instructed by Mark Steinberg. 18 cass. (Running Time: 18 hrs.). 2003. bk. 79.95 (978-1-56585-631-8(7), 8380) Teaching Co.

***History of Science.** unabr. ed. Peter Whitfield. Read by Peter Whitfield. 4 CDs. (Running Time: 5 hrs. 8 mins.). 2010. audio compact disk 28.98 (978-962-634-993-9(X)) Naxos.

History of Science: Antiquity to 1700, Pts. I-III. Instructed by Lawrence Principe. 18 cass. (Running Time: 18 hrs.). 2002. bk. 79.95 (978-1-56585-558-8(2), 1200); bk. 99.95 (978-1-56585-560-1(4), 1200) Teaching Co.

History of Science: 1700-1900, Parts I-III. Instructed by Frederick Gregory. 18 cass. (Running Time: 18 hrs.). 2003. bk. 79.95 (978-1-56585-835-0(2), 1210); bk. 99.95 (978-1-56585-837-4(9), 1210) Teaching Co.

History of Taekwon-Do. James S. Benko. 1986. 12.95 (TC-1) ITA Inst.
Follow the development of Taekwon-Do from the formation of the Hwa Rang warriors of Silla, to the establishment of the major Taekwon-Do organizations of today.

History of the American People. unabr. ed. Paul Johnson. Read by Nadia May. (Running Time: 48 hrs. 50 mins.). (ENG.). 2009. audio compact disk 169.00 (978-1-4332-9750-2(7)) Blckstn Audio.

History of the American People. unabr. ed. Paul Johnson. Read by Nadia May. (Running Time: 48 hrs.). (ENG.). 2010. 59.95 (978-0-7861-8952-6(5)) Blckstn Audio.

***History of the American People.** unabr. ed. Paul Johnson. Read by Nadia May. (Running Time: 48 hrs.). 2010. audio compact disk 59.95 (978-1-4417-4752-5(4)) Blckstn Audio.

History of the American People, Pt. 1. unabr. ed. Paul Johnson. Read by Nadia May. 15 cass. (Running Time: 51 hrs.). 2003. 95.95 (978-0-7861-1333-0(2), 2228A,B,C) Blckstn Audio.
A portrait of people from their fragile origins through their struggles for independence & nationhood, their efforts & sacrifices to deal with the "organic sin" of slavery & the preservation of the Union to their explosive growth & emergence as a world power & its sole superpower. Emphasizes the role of religion in American history & how early America was linked to England's history & culture.

History of the American People, Pt. 1. unabr. ed. Paul Johnson. Read by Bill Kelsey. 10 cass. (Running Time: 15 hrs.). 1998. 80.00 (4756-A) Books on Tape.
Paul Johnson's narrative is a provocative reinterpretation of American history, from the first settlements to the Clinton administration.

History of the American People, Pt. 2. unabr. ed. Paul Johnson. Read by Nadia May. 11 cass. (Running Time: 51 hrs.). 2003. 76.95 (978-0-7861-1341-5(3), 2228A,B,C) Blckstn Audio.

History of the American People, Pt. 2. unabr. ed. Paul Johnson. Read by Bill Kelsey. 12 cass. (Running Time: 18 hrs.). 1998. 96.00 (4756-B) Books on Tape.
Grasps what makes America unique: a blend of moral fervor & an optimistic, pioneering spirit.

History of the American People, Pt. 3. unabr. ed. Paul Johnson. Read by Nadia May. 9 cass. (Running Time: 51 hrs.). 2003. 49.95 (978-0-7861-1342-2(1), 2228A,B,C) Blckstn Audio.

History of the American People, Pt. 3. unabr. ed. Paul Johnson. Read by Bill Kelsey. 12 cass. (Running Time: 18 hrs.). 1998. 96.00 (4756-C) Books on Tape.

History of the American Revolution. Scripts. Narrated by Adolph Connard, III. 1 CD. (Running Time: 30 mins.). (J). (gr. 5 up). 1999. pap. bk. 18.95 My Fathers Busn.
Introduces the battles, campaigns, people & places of the American Revolution, supported by instrumental & four-part choral background music. Selections including "Lexington," "Battle of Bunker Hill" & "The Swamp Fox" emphasize battle locales, military heroes & other topics. A print insert includes the narrative script & song lyrics.

History of the Arab Peoples. unabr. ed. Albert H. Hourani. Read by Nadia May. 15 cass. (Running Time: 22 hrs.). 1995. 95.95 (978-0-7861-0859-6(2), 1657) Blckstn Audio.
A panoramic view encompassing twelve centuries of Arab history & culture. Looks at all sides of this rich & venerable civilization: the beauty of the Alhambra & the great mosques, the importance attached to education, the achievements of Arab science - but also internal conflicts, wide-spread poverty, the role of women & the contemporary Palestinian question.

History of the Bible: The Making of the New Testament Canon. Instructed by Bart D. Ehrman. 6 cass. (Running Time: 6 hrs.). 2005. 89.95 (978-1-59803-072-3(8)); audio compact disk 39.95 (978-1-59803-074-7(4)) Teaching Co.

History of the Church to 1500. Fr. Hardon. 9 cass. 36.00 Set. (94E) IRL Chicago.

History of the Conquest of Mexico. W. H. Prescott. Read by Kerry Shale. (Running Time: 5 hrs.). 2005. 28.95 (978-1-60083-769-2(7)) Iofy Corp.

History of the Conquest of Mexico. unabr. ed. William H. Prescott. Read by Kerry Shale. 4 CDs. (Running Time: 5 hrs.). 2003. audio compact disk 28.98 (978-962-634-282-4(X), Naxos AudioBooks) Naxos.

History of the Donner Party: A Tragedy of the Sierra. C. F. McGlashan. Read by Anais 9000. 1 CD. (Running Time: 7.2 hours). 2006. 16.95 (978-1-60112-003-8(6)) Babblebooks.

History of the English Language, Course 800. Instructed by Seth Lerer. 18 cass. (Running Time: 18 hrs.). 2000. 199.95 (800) Teaching Co.
A thorough understanding of our common language - from its origins as a Teutonic dialect through the literary & cultural achievements of its 1500-year span to the state of American speech today. Three parts, 36 lectures present English as an organic phenomenon, constantly changing according to time, place & the innovations of human genius.

History of the English Language, Vols. I-III. Instructed by Seth Lerer. 18 CDs. (Running Time: 18 hrs.). 1998. bk. 99.95 (978-1-56585-384-3(9), 800); 79.95 (978-1-56585-226-6(5), 800) Teaching Co.

History of the English Language Vol. 2: Making Modern English. Instructed by Seth Lerer. 6 cass. (Running Time: 6 hrs.). 1998. 199.95 (978-1-56585-227-3(3)) Teaching Co.

History of the English Language Vol. 3: English in America & Beyond. Instructed by Seth Lerer. 6 cass. (Running Time: 6 hrs.). 1998. 199.95 (978-1-56585-228-0(1)) Teaching Co.

History of the English Language, 2nd Edition. Instructed by Seth Lerer. (ENG.). 2008. 199.95 (978-1-59803-400-4(6)); audio compact disk 99.95 (978-1-59803-401-1(4)) Teaching Co.

History of the English People. unabr. ed. Paul Johnson. Read by Nadia May. 14 cass. (Running Time: 20 hrs. 30 mins.). 1989. 89.95 (978-0-7861-0096-5(6), 1089) Blckstn Audio.
This is a provocative & panoramic survey of 2,000 years of English history. Johnson tells the story of how a small nation, living in a geographical backwater, developed unique economic & political institutions, expanded its territory & saddled upon it the frame of a modern industrial society.

***History of the English People.** unabr. ed. Paul Johnson. Read by Nadia May. (Running Time: 20 hrs. 30 mins.). 2010. 44.95 (978-1-4417-4665-8(X)); audio compact disk 123.00 (978-1-4417-4662-7(5)) Blckstn Audio.

History of the English Speaking Peoples Vol. 1: The Birth of Britain. Winston L. S. Churchill. Read by Richard Matthews. 2002. 88.00 (978-0-7366-8811-6(0)) Books on Tape.

History of the English Speaking Peoples Vol. 1: The Birth of Britain. unabr. collector's ed. Winston L. S. Churchill. Read by Richard Green. 12 cass. (Running Time: 18 hrs.). 1988. 96.00 (978-0-7366-1421-4(4), 2307) Books on Tape.
Churchill imagines England's beginnings, moves through Roman, Arthur, Magna Carta & ends with the founding of the Tudor dynasty.

History of the English Speaking Peoples Vol. 2: The New World. unabr. collector's ed. Winston L. S. Churchill. Read by Richard Green. 10 cass. (Running Time: 15 hrs.). 1990. 80.00 (978-0-7366-1688-1(8), 2534) Books on Tape.
In 1939, just before the outbreak of war, Winston Churchill completed the original draft of his great history. First projected as two volumes, it doubled in size as Churchill got into it & was finally published as four. The second volume, The New World, presents a galaxy of great personages & stirring events: Henry VIII, Mary Queen of Scots, Queen Elizabeth I & the defeat of the Spanish Armada, the sailing of the Mayflower & settling of America, Cromwell & the Great Revolution. The book ends with the corrupt but colorful reign of the "Merry Monarch," Charles II.

History of the English Speaking Peoples Vol. 3: The Age of Revolution. unabr. collector's ed. Winston L. S. Churchill. Read by David Case. 9 cass. (Running Time: 13 hrs. 30 min.). 1991. 72.00 (978-0-7366-1921-9(6), 2745) Books on Tape.
In 1939, just before the outbreak of World War II, Winston Churchill completed the original draft of his history. Volume III, THE AGE OF REVOLUTION, covers the years between 1688 & 1815.

History of the English Speaking Peoples Vol. 4: The Great Democracies. unabr. collector's ed. Winston L. S. Churchill. Read by David Case. 9 cass. (Running Time: 13 hrs. 30 min.). 1991. 72.00 (978-0-7366-1982-0(8), 2799) Books on Tape.
Churchill examines events from 1815 to the turn of the century with emphasis on British-American relations.

History of the Jews. unabr. ed. Paul Johnson. Read by Nadia May. (Running Time: 104400 sec.). 2007. audio compact disk 160.00 (978-0-7861-6050-1(0)); audio compact disk 44.95 (978-0-7861-6051-8(9)) Blckstn Audio.

History of the Jews, Pt. 1. unabr. ed. Paul Johnson. Read by Nadia May. 12 cass. (Running Time: 32 hrs.). 1989. 83.95 (978-0-7861-0023-1(0), 1023A,B) Blckstn Audio.
A provocative survey capturing 4,000 years of the extraordinary history of the Jews - as a people, a culture & a nation. This historical magnum opus covers far more than the basics of Jewish history. It shows the impact of Jewish character on the world: their genius, imagination & most of all, their ability to persevere despite severe persecutions.

History of the Jews, Pt. 1. unabr. ed. Paul Johnson. Read by Richard Brown. 12 cass. (Running Time: 18 hrs.). 1990. 96.00 (978-0-7366-2503-6(8), 3261-A) Books on Tape.
A national best seller, this brilliant book surveys the impact of Jewish genius & imagination on the world during the past 4000 years. The Jews played a major role in the creation of the modern world & its component parts: first the great religious themes...monetheism, the concept of personal worth & the development of Christianity...also in the evolution of capitalism & the revolutionary developments of 19th & 20th century Western culture.

History of the Jews, Pt. 2. unabr. ed. Paul Johnson. Read by Nadia May. 10 cass. (Running Time: 32 hrs.). 1989. 69.95 (978-0-7861-0024-8(9), 1023A,B) Blckstn Audio.
A provocative survey capturing 4,000 years of the extraordinary history of the Jews - as a people, a culture & a nation. This historical magnum opus covers far more than the basics of Jewish history. It shows the impact of Jewish character on the world: their genius, imagination & most of all, their ability to persevere despite severe persecutions.

***History of the Medieval World: From the Conversion of Constantine to the First Crusade.** unabr. ed. Susan Wise Bauer. Narrated by John Lee. (Running Time: 24 hrs. 0 mins.). 2010. 54.99 (978-1-4001-9493-3(8)); 26.99 (978-1-4001-8493-4(2)) Tantor Media.

***History of the Medieval World: From the Conversion of Constantine to the First Crusade.** unabr. ed. Susan Wise Bauer. Narrated by John Lee. (Running Time: 22 hrs. 30 mins. 0 sec.). (ENG.). 2010. 39.99 (978-1-4001-6493-6(1)); audio compact disk 109.99 (978-1-4001-4493-8(0)); audio compact disk 54.99 (978-1-4001-1493-1(4)) Pub: Tantor Media. Dist(s): IngramPubServ

History of the Middle East. unabr. ed. Peter Mansfield. Read by Richard Brown. 12 cass. (Running Time: 17 hrs. 30 mins.). 2003. 83.95 set. (978-0-7861-0280-8(2), 1246) Blckstn Audio.
In this masterly work of synthesis, Peter Mansfield, drawing on his experience as a journalist & historian, explores two centuries of history in the Middle East. He forms a picture of the historical, political, & social history of the meeting point of Occident & Orient, from Bonaparte's marauding invasion of Egypt to the start of the Gulf War.

History of the Middle East. unabr. ed. Peter Mansfield. Read by Richard Brown. 12 pieces. 2004. reel tape 44.95 (978-0-7861-2224-0(2)) Blckstn Audio.

History of the Middle East. unabr. ed. Peter Mansfield. Read by Richard Brown. (Running Time: 61200 sec.). 2007. audio compact disk 120.00 (978-0-7861-5795-2(X)) Blckstn Audio.

History of the Middle East. unabr. ed. Peter Mansfield. Read by Richard Brown. 14 CDs. (Running Time: 61200 sec.). 2006. audio compact disk 34.95 (978-0-7861-7389-1(0)) Blckstn Audio.

History of the Middle East. unabr. ed. Peter Mansfield & Richard Brown. (Running Time: 61200 sec.). 2007. audio compact disk 44.95 (978-0-7861-6966-5(4)) Blckstn Audio.

History of the Modern Libertarian Movement. unabr. ed. Ralph Raico. 1 cass. (Running Time: 42 min.). 12.95 (734) J Norton Pubs.
Raico discusses the libertarian movement's place in history, & offers a scathing analysis of Jimmy Carter, Gerald Ford, Lester Maddox, & the Republican & Democratic Parties.

History of the Musical. Richard Fawkes. Read by Kim Criswell. 4 cass. (Running Time: 5 hrs. 15 min.). 2001. 22.98 (978-962-634-727-0(9), NA422714, Naxos AudioBooks); audio compact disk 28.98 (978-962-634-227-5(7), NA422712, Naxos AudioBooks) Naxos.
Entertaining undertaking traces the musical from its origins in classical music through to its flowering in America.

History of the Olympics. unabr. ed. John Goodbody. Read by Barry Davies. (YA). 2008. 54.99 (978-1-60514-990-5(X)) Find a World.

History of the Olympics. unabr. ed. John Goodbody. Read by David Davies. (Running Time: 22811 sec.). 2008. audio compact disk 28.98 (978-962-634-870-3(4), Naxos AudioBooks) Naxos.

History of the Peloponnesian War. unabr. ed. Thucydides. Read by Pat Bottino. Tr. by Richard Crawley. 16 cass. (Running Time: 23 hrs. 30 mins.). 1996. 99.95 (978-0-7861-0978-4(5), 1755) Blckstn Audio.
The Peloponnesian War broke out in 431 BC & continued intermittently for twenty-seven years. It pitted an all-powerful land force (Sparta & its allies), against a supremely powerful naval force (Athens). Thucydides actually participated in this conflict, a war which he realized would have a greater influence on the history of Greece than any other war.

History of the Peloponnesian War. unabr. ed. Thucydides. Read by Pat Bottino. (Running Time: 79200 sec.). 2007. audio compact disk 130.00 (978-0-7861-5909-3(X)); audio compact disk 44.95 (978-0-7861-5910-9(3)) Blckstn Audio.

History of the Rebellion & Civil Wars in England see Cambridge Treasy Burton

History of the Sacraments. Joseph Martos. 7 cass. (Running Time: 6 hrs. 52 min.). 1986. 53.95 incl. shelf-case. (TAH158) Alba Hse Comns.
Utilizes insights of contemporary theology to reveal the sacred mystery, the uplifting poetry, the healing power, & the meaning of the sacraments.

History of the Second World War, Pt. 1. unabr. collector's ed. Basil H. Liddell-Hart. Read by Bernard Mayes. 12 cass. (Running Time: 18 hrs.). 1980. 96.00 (978-0-7366-0145-0(7), 1147-A) Books on Tape.
Basil H. Liddell Hart, English military strategist & historian, served as a captain during World War I & later developed a theory of mobile warfare employing tanks & infantry. His theories were adopted by the Germans, who called them "Blitzkrieg".

History of the Second World War, Pt. 2. unabr. collector's ed. Basil H. Liddell-Hart. Read by Bernard Mayes. 12 cass. (Running Time: 18 hrs.). 1980. 96.00 (978-0-7366-0146-7(5), 1147-B) Books on Tape.

History of the Supreme Court, Pts. I-III. Instructed by Peter Irons. 18 cass. (Running Time: 18 hrs.). 2003. bk. 79.95 (978-1-56585-750-6(X), 8570); bk. 99.95 (978-1-56585-751-3(8), 8570) Teaching Co.

History of the Twentieth Century: The Concise Edition of the Acclaimed World History. unabr. ed. Martin Gilbert. Read by John Curless. 22 cass. (Running Time: 30 hrs.). 2006. 109.75 (978-1-4025-2268-0(1), 97105) Recorded Bks.

History of the Twentieth Century Vol. 1, Pt. 1: 1900-1933. unabr. collector's ed. Martin Gilbert. Read by David Case. 14 cass. (Running Time: 21 hrs.). 1999. 112.00 (978-0-7366-4322-1(2), 4821-A) Books on Tape.
A complete history of the century covers the period 1900 through 1933, from the embarrassment of the Boer War to the looming horror of the Second World War, predetermined by the rise to power of Hitler. In between lie 37 chapters - one for each year & three for the intricacies of the First World War - that recount in great detail the political, social, economic, moral, technological, & military advancements & retreats of the first third of this century.

History of the Twentieth Century Vol. 1, Pt. 2: 1900-1933. unabr. collector's ed. Martin Gilbert. Read by David Case. 13 cass. (Running Time: 19 hrs. 30 min.). 1999. 104.00 (978-0-7366-4323-8(0), 4821-B) Books on Tape.
A complete history, from the embarrassment of the Boer War to the looming horror of the Second World War, predetermined by the rise to power of Hitler. In between lie 37 chapters - one for each year & three for the intricacies of the First World War - that recount in great detail the political, social, economic, moral, technological, & military advancements & retreats of the first third of this century.

History of the Twentieth Century Vol. 2: 1933-1951. collector's ed. Martin Gilbert. Read by David Case. 9 cass. (Running Time: 13 hrs. 30 min.). 2000. 72.00 (978-0-7366-5038-0(5)); 120.00 (978-0-7366-5039-7(3)); 56.00 (978-0-7366-5040-3(7)) Books on Tape.
Gilbert charts the approach of the Second World War, a war in which more than forty-six million people were killed & which caused revolutionary upheavals in the world's social & political order. He takes the story to the end of 1951, with the United States & the Soviet Union grappling to establish the primacy of their respective systems & when, amid the continuing conflict in Korea, the specter of nuclear war threatened to become a terrible reality.

History of the U. S. Economy in the 20th Century. Instructed by Timothy Taylor. 5 cass. (Running Time: 7 hrs. 30 mins.). 1996. 39.95 (978-1-56585-153-5(6)) Teaching Co.

History of the United States. Instructed by Darren Staloff et al. 7 cass. (Running Time: 52 hrs., 30 min.). 199.95 incl. course guide. (830) Teaching Co.
Experience the history of the nation as an ongoing evolution of intellectual & social forces, within which even the facts known for years bristle with fresh, provocative meaning. Learn not only what happened, but why - & what all of it may mean for the country's future. Course 830 incls. 7 parts with 70 lectures.

History of the United States, Parts I-VII. 2nd ed. Instructed by Patrick Allitt et al. 42 cass. (Running Time: 42 hrs.). 2003. bk. 149.95 (978-1-56585-760-5(7), 8500); bk. 199.95 (978-1-56585-761-2(5), 8500) Teaching Co.

History of the United States: Greatest Americans of the Early Republic 40 Stories of Inspiration & Success. Ed. by Ross M. Armetta. Narrated by Ross M. Armetta. 6 Cds. (Running Time: 7 Hours 30mins. Aprox.). 2005. audio compact disk 35.95 (978-1-59733-500-3(2), Antecdent Wisdom) InfoFount.
6 CDs of Wisdom, Joy, and Honor Energizing, informative, and entertaining for the whole family.INSPIRATIONAL ROCKET FUEL - FIRE UP YOUR IMAGINATION, DREAMS, AND CHARACTHER.The Greatest Americans series of audiobooks is a must have for anyone seeking to improve themselves. This series provides lucid examples of individuals who determined to improve themselves, their lot, and humanity whatever the effort, risks, and hardships they had to endure. It is also quite invigorating and enriching to the spirit as it gives you a dramatic appreciation of the power of good in humanity in overcoming bad, the efforts of our Founding Fathers, and our gift of this blessed land. The Greatest Americans audiobook set consists of 6 CDs (40 Biographies approx. 7.5 hours total playing time) with the following contents The Founding Fathers (3 CDs) Great Early Presidents Great Inventors Giants of the Military and Freedom Literary Giants These biographies bring the subject?s life in focus to make them known to the reader on a human level, rather than give the general history of their time. We have striven to give to the careful listener an idea of the spirit of those who engaged in work so remarkable. We believe the listener will appreciate more highly the success of the great founders and leaders of many fields of the early republic, from knowing more intimately the details of their lives, struggles, and of their education. THE history of humanity is made up of the biographies' of people. We appreciate and understand our heritage most thoroughly, in those periods where we know of the personal lives of many of the actors. Detailed list of contents of Greatest Americans: stories of inspiration and success. The Founding Fathers 3 (disks) 1 George Washington /Alexander Hamilton and John Paul Jones 2 John Adams / Benjamin Franklin 3 Thomas Jefferson / John Jay and Frances E. Willard with 3a Great Inventors of the Early Republic Thomas Edison Samuel Morse Robert Fulton Eli Whitney Elias Howe Cyrus H. McCormick Chauncey Jerome Oliver Evans Jacob Perkins Eli Terry 4 Great Early Presidents 1 (disk) John Quincy Adams / Andrew Jackson and The Story of American Women and their education. 5 Giants of the Military and Freedom 1 (disk) Oliver H. Perry David G. Farragut Robert. E. Lee Stonewall Jackson George G. Meade Frederick Douglas 6 Literary Giants of the Early Republic 1 (disk) Introduction to Early American Literature Henry Longfellow Washington Irving William Cullen Bryant James Fennimore Cooper Ralph Waldo Emerson Edgar Allan Poe Nathaniel Hawthorne Henry D. Thoreau James Russell Lowell Walt Whitman Louisa Alcott Russell Conwell Harriet Beecher Stowe Benjamin Franklin?s 13 virtues.

History of the United States: Parts I-VII. Instructed by Darren Staloff et al. 35 cass. (Running Time: 52 hrs. 30 mins.). 1996. 399.95 (978-1-56585-245-7(1)) Teaching Co.

History of the United States Vol. 2: Maturation & Independence. Instructed by Darren Staloff. 5 cass. (Running Time: 7 hrs. 30 mins.). 1996. 399.95 (978-1-56585-246-4(X)) Teaching Co.

History of the United States Vol. 3: The Making of a Nation. Instructed by Louis P. Masur. 5 cass. (Running Time: 7 hrs. 30 mins.). 1996. 399.95 (978-1-56585-247-1(8)) Teaching Co.

History of the United States Vol. 4: The Crisis of Nationhood. Instructed by Louis P. Masur. 5 cass. (Running Time: 7 hrs. 30 mins.). 1996. 399.95 (978-1-56585-248-8(6)) Teaching Co.

History of the United States Vol. 5: The Making of Modern America. Instructed by James Shenton. 5 cass. (Running Time: 7 hrs. 30 mins.). 1996. 399.95 (978-1-56585-249-5(4)) Teaching Co.

History of the United States Vol. 6: Liberalism & the Cold War. Instructed by James Shenton. 5 cass. (Running Time: 7 hrs. 30 mins.). 1996. 399.95 (978-1-56585-250-1(8)) Teaching Co.

History of the United States Vol. 7: Consensus & Conflict. Instructed by James Shenton & Darren Staloff. 5 cass. (Running Time: 7 hrs. 30 mins.). 1996. 399.95 (978-1-56585-253-2(2)) Teaching Co.

History of the World. Julian Barnes. 9. (Running Time: 39240 sec.). 2007. audio compact disk 67.98 (978-962-634-475-0(X), Naxos AudioBooks) Naxos.

History of the World. unabr. ed. Julian Barnes. Read by Tony Robinson. 8 cass. (Running Time: 12 hrs.). 2001. 69.95 (90052) Pub: ISIS Audio GBR. Dist(s): Ulverscroft US

History of the World. unabr. ed. Julian Barnes. Read by Tony Robinson. 8 cass. (Running Time: 10 hrs. 25 min.). (Isis Ser.). 1994. 69.95 Set. (978-1-85089-730-9(1), 90052) Eye Ear.
With imaginative craft, & using a whole flotilla of historic & symbolic ships, this wittily individual book surveys human existence buoyantly, but never lets you forget the dark depths beneath.

History of the World. unabr. ed. J. M. Roberts. Read by Frederick Davidson. 16 cass. (Running Time: 55 hrs.). 2001. 99.95 (978-0-7861-2547-0(0), 3179A,B,C) Blckstn Audio.

History of the World. unabr. ed. J. M. Roberts. Read by Frederick Davidson. 13 cass. (Running Time: 55 hrs.). 2003. 85.95 (978-0-7861-2594-4(2), 3179A,B,C); 69.95 (978-0-7861-2595-1(0), 3179A,B,C) Blckstn Audio.

History of the World, Pt 1. unabr. ed. J. M. Roberts. Read by Frederick Davidson. 16 cass. (Running Time: 1 hr. 30 min. per cass.). 1997. 99.95 Set. (978-0-7861-1188-6(7), 1945-A) Blckstn Audio.

An Asterisk (*) at the beginning of an entry indicates that the title is appearing for the first time.

History of the World, Pt. 2. unabr. ed. J. M. Roberts. Read by Frederick Davidson. 13 cass. (Running Time: 1 hr. 30 min. per cass.). 1997. 85.95 Set. (978-0-7861-1189-3(5), 1945-B) Blckstn Audio.

History of the World, Pt. 3. unabr. ed. J. M. Roberts. Read by Frederick Davidson. 8 cass. (Running Time: 1 hr. 30 min. per cass.). 1997. 56.95 Set. (978-0-7861-1190-9(9), 1945-C) Blckstn Audio.

History of the World Cup. Brian Glanville. Read by Bob Wilson. 4 cass. (Running Time: 4 hrs. 35 mins.). 2002. 17.98 (978-962-634-767-6(8), Naxos AudioBooks); audio compact disk 19.98 (978-962-634-267-1(6), Naxos AudioBooks) Naxos.
Released especially to coincide with the start of the 2002 tournament in South Korea and Japan, this recording gives a commanding account of the history of the tournament, starting with the story of how the World Cup came into being.

History of the World Cup, 1930-2002. unabr. abr. ed. Brian Glanville. Read by Bob Wilson. 4 CDs. (Running Time: 16974 sec.). 2006. audio compact disk 28.98 (978-962-634-404-0(0), Naxos AudioBooks) Naxos.

History of the Young Man. Robert Louis Stevenson. 1 cass. 1989. 7.95 (S-69) Jimcin Record.
A Robert Louis Stevenson mystery.

History of the Young Man with Spectacles see Tales of Terror & the Supernatural: A Collection

History of the Young Man with the Cream Tarts. unabr. ed. Robert Louis Stevenson. Read by Jim Killavey. 1 cass. (Running Time: 80 min.). Dramatization. 1986. 7.95 (S-69) Jimcin Record.

History of Theatre. David Timson. Read by Derek Jacobi. (Running Time: 5 hrs.). (C). 2004. 28.95 (978-1-60083-772-2(7)) Iofy Corp.

History of Theatre. David Timson. Read by Derek Jacobi. 4 cass. (Running Time: 5 hrs.). (YA). (gr. 10 up). 2000. 22.98 (978-962-634-699-0(X), NA419914, Naxos AudioBooks); audio compact disk 28.98 (978-962-634-199-5(8), NA419912, Naxos AudioBooks) Naxos.
This bold undertaking covers western theater from ancient Greece to the present day.

History of Tom Jones, a Foundling. Henry Fielding. Read by Maurice West. (Running Time: 3 hrs.). 2001. 37.95 (978-1-60083-773-9(5)) Iofy Corp.

History of Tom Jones, a Foundling. unabr. ed. Henry Fielding. Read by Ken Danziger. (Running Time: 36 hrs. 0 mins.). 2010. 59.95 (978-1-4417-2772-5(8)); 99.95 (978-1-4417-2768-8(X)); audio compact disk 160.00 (978-1-4417-2769-5(8)) Blckstn Audio.

History of Warfare. unabr. ed. John Keegan. Read by Frederick Davidson. 14 cass. (Running Time: 20 hrs. 30 mins.). 2003. 89.95 (978-0-7861-0690-5(5), 1475) Blckstn Audio.
Starting with the premise that all civilizations owe their origins to warmaking, Keegan probes the meanings, motivations & methods underlying war in different societies over the course of more than two thousand years. Following the progress of human aggression in its full historical sweep - from the strangely ritualistic combat of Stone Age peoples to the warfare of mass destruction in the present age - his illuminating & lively narrative gives us all the world's great warrior cultures, including the Zulus, the samurai & the horse peoples of the steppe, as well as the famed warmakers of the West.

History of Warfare. unabr. ed. John Keegan. Narrated by Ian Stuart. 12 cass. (Running Time: 18 hrs. 15 mins.). 1994. 97.00 (978-0-7887-0025-5(1), 94224E7) Recorded Bks.
Eminent military historian John Keegan recounts the evolution of warfare from the stone age to the nuclear age.

History of Warfare. unabr. collector's ed. John Keegan. Read by David Case. 14 cass. (Running Time: 21 hrs.). 1994. 112.00 (978-0-7366-2777-1(4), 3496) Books on Tape.
Sweeping view of the place of warfare in human culture & a brilliant exposition of the human impulse toward violence.

History of Wells & Kennebunk from the Earliest Settlement to the Year 1820, at Which Time Kennebunk Was Set off & Incorporated, with Biographical Sketches. Edward E. Bourne. 2002. audio compact disk 24.00 (978-0-7884-2166-2(2)) Heritage Bk.

History of Western Music. 4th ed. Claude V. Palisca. (C). 2001. 47.00 (978-0-393-97733-2(1)) Norton.

History of Western Music & the Norton Anthology of Western Music Vol. 1: Recordings. 4th ed. Donald Jay Grout & Claude Palisca. 6 CDs. (C). 2001. 85.20 (978-0-393-10366-3(8)) Norton.

History of Western Music & the Norton Anthology of Western Music Vol. II: Recordings. 4th ed. Donald Jay Grout. Ed. by Claude Palisca. 6 CDs. (C). 2001. (978-0-393-10367-0(6)) Norton.

History of Western Society. 7th ed. (gr. 6-12). 2003. audio compact disk (978-0-618-17061-6(8), 3-35959) CENGAGE Learn.

History of World Literature. Instructed by Grant L. Voth. 2007. 249.95 (978-1-59803-358-8(1)); audio compact disk 129.95 (978-1-59803-359-5(X)) Teaching Co.

History Shorts: The Craft of the Historian. unabr. ed. 3 cass. (Running Time: 4 hrs. 15 mins.). 1990. 26.00 (978-1-55690-229-1(8), 90055E7) Recorded Bks.
Selected articles from A Sense of History, a collection of the best of The American Heritage Magazine.

History Shorts: The Robber Barons. unabr. ed. 3 cass. (Running Time: 3 hrs. 45 mins.). 1990. 26.00 (978-1-55690-226-0(3), 90056E7) Recorded Bks.

History Shorts: Two World Wars & in Between. unabr. ed. 3 cass. (Running Time: 4 hrs. 30 mins.). 1990. 26.00 (978-1-55690-227-7(1), 90057E7) Recorded Bks.

History Shorts Vol. 1: 1660-1814. unabr. ed. 3 cass. (Running Time: 4 hrs.). 1989. 26.00 (978-1-55690-230-7(1), 89495E7) Recorded Bks.
History stories combining the informative & the entertaining bring the past alive for a general audience.

History Shorts Vol. 2: 1831-1845. unabr. ed. 3 cass. (Running Time: 4 hrs.). 1989. 26.00 (978-1-55690-231-4(X), 89496E7) Recorded Bks.
History stories, combining the informative & the entertaining, bring the past alive for a general audience.

History Shorts Vol. 3: 1841-1964. unabr. ed. 9 cass. (Running Time: 12 hrs. 45 mins.). 1989. 78.00 (978-1-55690-228-4(X), 89498E7) Recorded Bks.
History stories combining the informative & the entertaining bring the past alive for a general audience.

History Shorts Vol. 4: 1846-1861. unabr. ed. 3 cass. (Running Time: 4 hrs. 30 mins.). 1989. 26.00 (978-1-55690-232-1(8), 89497E7) Recorded Bks.

History Songs. 1 cass. (Running Time: 42 min.). bk. & tchr. ed. 12.95 (978-1-883028-07-7(8), 5) Audio Memory.
Eleven songs teach over one hundred dates & events of American History from 1492 to the 1990s - a musical timeline with dramatic sound effects. Features children & adult singers with lively, memorable melodies & full orchestration.

History Songs. 1 CD. (Running Time: 1 hr.). 2001. pap. bk., tchr. ed., wbk. ed. 15.95 (5CD) Audio Memory.
Eleven songs create a musical time line, teaching over 100 dates and events in American history from 1492 to 1991.

History Songs. 2004. audio compact disk 15.95 (978-1-883028-09-1(4)) Audio Memory.

History via the Scenic Route: Getting off the Textbook Interstate, Set. unabr. ed. Diana Waring. Read by Diana Waring. 4 cass. (Running Time: 4 hrs.). 1995. 20.95 (978-1-930514-01-0(8)) Diana Waring.

Historyscope Book of the BAttle Reports of the American Civil War: A chronological review of the major campaigns & battles by theater of War. Ed. by Donagh Bracken. (ENG.). 2007. audio compact disk 19.99 (978-1-933909-04-2(8)) Hist Pub.

***Hit.** Tara Moss. Read by Tara Moss. (Running Time: 11 hrs. 55 mins.). 2009. 74.99 (978-1-74214-271-5(0), 9781742142715) Pub: Bolinda Pubng AUS. Dist(s): Bolinda Pub Inc

Hit. unabr. ed. Tara Moss. Read by Tara Moss. (Running Time: 11 hrs. 55 mins.). 2006. audio compact disk 98.95 (978-1-74093-855-6(0)) Pub: Bolinda Pubng AUS. Dist(s): Bolinda Pub Inc

***Hit.** unabr. ed. Tara Moss. Read by Tara Moss. (Running Time: 11 hrs. 55 mins.). 2010. 43.95 (978-1-74214-581-5(7), 9781742145815) Pub: Bolinda Pubng AUS. Dist(s): Bolinda Pub Inc

Hit & Hope. unabr. ed. David Owen. Read by Barrett Whitener. 4 CDs. (Running Time: 4 hrs.). 2003. audio compact disk 32.00 (978-0-7861-9187-1(2), 3140); 32.95 (978-0-7861-2506-7(3), 3140) Blckstn Audio.
Takes a delightfully irreverent look at the game of golf and all the absurd behavior it inspires.

Hit & Hope. unabr. ed. David Owen. Read by Barrett Whitener. 3 pieces. 2004. reel tape 24.95 (978-0-7861-2568-5(3)) Blckstn Audio.

***Hit & Run.** Susan Dunlap. 2009. (978-1-60136-543-9(8)) Audio Holding.

Hit & Run. Cath Staincliffe. (Soundings (CDs) Ser.). 2006. audio compact disk 64.95 (978-1-84559-446-6(0)) Pub: ISIS Lrg Prnt GBR. Dist(s): Ulverscroft US

***Hit & Run.** unabr. ed. Lawrence Block. Read by Richard Poe. (ENG.). 2008. (978-0-06-174602-4(9)); (978-0-06-174799-1(8)) HarperCollins Pubs.

Hit & Run. unabr. ed. Lawrence Block. Narrated by Richard Poe. (Running Time: 8 hrs. 30 mins.). 2008. 56.75 (978-1-4361-6500-6(8)); audio compact disk 92.75 (978-1-4361-0728-0(8)) Recorded Bks.
Named Grand Master of the Mystery Writers of America and a four-time winner of the Edgar and Shamus Awards, Lawrence Block enjoys a well-deserved reputation as one of the premier mystery writers of all time. The fourth novel in Block's John Keller series finds hit-man Keller immersed in his real passion: stamp collecting. But for a man like Keller, danger is always close at hand.

Hit & Run. unabr. ed. Cath Staincliffe. Read by Julia Franklin. 6 cass. (Soundings Ser.). 2006. 54.95 (978-1-84559-389-6(8)) Pub: ISIS Lrg Prnt GBR. Dist(s): Ulverscroft US

Hit & Run: How Jon Peters & Peter Guber Took Sony for a Ride in Hollywood. unabr. ed. Nancy Griffin & Kim Masters. Read by Kate Reading. 13 cass. (Running Time: 19 hrs. 30 min.). 1996. 104.00 Set. (978-0-913369-28-9(4), 4181) Books on Tape.
Jon Peters, a semi-literate, seventh-grade drop out & Peter Guber, his well-educated but uncentered soul mate, formed a partnership based on a near pathological hunger for money. Incredibly, Sony chose them to run one of Hollywood's great studios. It had all the ingredients for an outrageous tale, which indeed it became.

Hit & run how jon peters & peter guber took sony for a ride in hollywood: How Jon Peters & Peter Guber Took Sony for a Ride in Hollywood. Nancy Griffin. Read by John Slattery. 2004. 13.95 (978-0-7435-4832-8(9)) Pub: S&S Audio. Dist(s): S and S Inc

Hit-Away Kid. unabr. ed. Matt Christopher. Narrated by Norman Dietz. 1 cass. (Running Time: 1 hr.). (gr. 1 up). 10.00 (978-0-7887-0380-5(3), 94571E7) Recorded Bks.
Barry McGee likes being the star of his neighborhood baseball team. In fact, he likes it so much that he's willing to cheat once in a while to help his game. But when a pitcher from a rival team discovers that the Hit-Away Kid isn't nearly as good as everyone thinks, Barry must decide which is more important: winning or playing fair. Available to libraries only.

***Hit Hard.** unabr. ed. Joey Kramer. Read by Holter Graham. (ENG.). 2009. (978-0-06-190231-4(4), Harper Audio); (978-0-06-190232-1(2), Harper Audio) HarperCollins Pubs.

Hit Hard: A Story of Hitting Rock Bottom at the Top. unabr. ed. Joey Kramer. Read by Holter Graham. 2009. audio compact disk 34.99 (978-0-06-171467-2(4), Harper Audio) HarperCollins Pubs.

***Hit List.** abr. ed. Lawrence Block. Read by Lawrence Block. (ENG.). 2004. (978-0-06-078318-1(4), Harper Audio) HarperCollins Pubs.

***Hit List.** abr. ed. Lawrence Block. Read by Lawrence Block. (ENG.). 2004. (978-0-06-081433-5(0), Harper Audio) HarperCollins Pubs.

Hit List. unabr. ed. Chris Ryan. Narrated by Gordon Griffin. 11 CDs. (Running Time: 13 hrs.). 2001. audio compact disk 99.00 (978-1-84197-163-6(4), C1414) Recorded Bks.
Chris Ryan was a member of the SAS for 10 years. Awarded the Military Medal for an amazing escape from Iraq during the Gulf War, he now selects & trains potential recruits, as well as being the author of five bestselling books. Neil Slater left the SAS at the end of his tether. However, as he tries to make a new life for himself in the normal world, he discovers that some habits are hard to break. When his reactions to an attempted kidnapping cause him to lose his job, he is soon to realize that you can take the man out of the system, but you can't take the system out of the man - particularly not when the system has other ideas.

***Hit List Unabridged CDs.** Laurell K. Hamilton. (Running Time: 19 hrs.). (ENG.). 2011. audio compact disk 39.95 (978-0-14-314563-9(0), PengAudBks) Penguin Grp USA.

Hit Parade. unabr. ed. Lawrence Block. 1 MP3 CD. (Running Time: 28200 sec.). 2006. audio compact disk 29.95 (978-0-7927-4244-9(3), Chivers Sound Lib) AudioGO.

Hit Parade. unabr. ed. Lawrence Block. Read by Lawrence Block. 6 cass. (Running Time: 28200 sec.). 2006. 54.95 (978-0-7927-4243-2(5), Chivers Sound Lib); audio compact disk 74.95 (978-0-7927-4050-6(5), Chivers Sound Lib) AudioGO.

Hit Parade. unabr. ed. Lawrence Block. Read by Lawrence Block. 7 CDs. (Running Time: 28800 sec.). (John Keller Mystery Ser.). 2006. audio compact disk 39.95 (978-0-06-089792-5(9), Harper Audio) HarperCollins Pubs.

***Hit Parade.** unabr. ed. Lawrence Block. Read by Lawrence Block. (ENG.). 2006. (978-0-06-113478-4(3), Harper Audio); (978-0-06-113477-7(5), Harper Audio) HarperCollins Pubs.

Hit the Ground Running: A Manual for New Leaders. unabr. ed. Jason Jennings. Read by Jason Jennings. (Running Time: 7 hrs.). (ENG.). 2009. 24.98 (978-1-59659-375-6(X), GildAudio) Pub: Gildan Media. Dist(s): HachBkGrp

Hit the Ground Running: A Manual for New Leaders. unabr. ed. Jason Jennings. Read by Jason Jennings. (Running Time: 7 hrs.). (ENG.). 2009. audio compact disk 29.98 (978-1-59659-287-2(7)) Pub: Gildan Media. Dist(s): HachBkGrp

Hit the Ground Running: A Woman's Guide to Success for the First 100 Days on the Job. abr. ed. Liz Cornish. Read by Beth Richmond. (Running Time: 16200 sec.). 2008. audio compact disk 28.00 (978-1-933309-39-2(3)) Pub: A Media Intl. Dist(s): Natl Bk Netwk

Hit the Road Austin. 2nd ed. Created by Margaret Harrist. 1 CD. (Running Time: 86 minutes). 2002. audio compact disk 18.95 (978-0-9740225-0-5(0)) Hit the Road.
A driving audio tour of Austin, Texas with tour guides Wally Pryor and Mary Gordon Spence.

Hit Time: A Georgia Barnett Mystery. Ardella Garland. Narrated by Starla Benford. 6 CDs. (Running Time: 6 hrs. 30 mins.). 2002. audio compact disk 58.00 (978-1-4025-3822-3(7)) Recorded Bks.

Hit Time: A Georgia Barnett Mystery. Yolanda Joe. Narrated by Starla Benford. 5 cass. (Running Time: 6 hrs. 30 mins.). 39.00 (978-1-4025-1255-1(4)) Recorded Bks.

***Hitch-Hiker.** 2010. audio compact disk (978-1-59171-205-3(X)) Falcon Picture.

***Hitch-22: A Memoir.** Christopher Hitchens. Read by Author. (Running Time: 17 hrs.). (ENG.). 2011. audio compact disk & audio compact disk 19.98 (978-1-60941-281-4(8)) Pub: Hachet Audio. Dist(s): HachBkGrp

Hitch-22: A Memoir. unabr. ed. Christopher Hitchens. (Running Time: 17 hrs.). (ENG.). 2010. 24.98 (978-1-60788-233-6(7)) Pub: Hachet Audio. Dist(s): HachBkGrp

Hitch-22: A Memoir. unabr. ed. Christopher Hitchens. Read by Christopher Hitchens. 15 CDs. (Running Time: 17 hrs.). (ENG., 2010. audio compact disk 34.98 (978-1-60788-232-9(9)) Pub: Hachet Audio. Dist(s): HachBkGrp

Hitchcock Astrologically Unveiled. Roger Mock. 1 cass. 8.95 (564) Am Fed Astrologers.
Chart of the master of mystery.

Hitched. abr. ed. Carol Higgins Clark. Read by Carol Higgins Clark. (Regan Reilly Mystery Ser.: No. 9). 2006. 17.95 (978-0-7435-5420-6(5), Audioworks) Pub: S&S Audio. Dist(s): S and S Inc

Hitched. abr. ed. Carol Higgins Clark. Read by Carol Higgins Clark. (Running Time: 4 hrs. 30 mins. 0 sec.). No. 9. (ENG.). 2008. audio compact disk 14.99 (978-0-7435-7237-8(8)) Pub: S&S Audio. Dist(s): S and S Inc

Hitchhike Poker & The Barking Death. Perf. by Gregory Peck & William Powell. 1 cass. (Running Time: 60 min.). Dramatization. (Suspense Ser.). 6.00 Once Upon Rad.
Radio broadcasts - mystery & suspense.

Hitchhiker. Perf. by Orson Welles. 1 cass. 10.00 (MC1015) Esstee Audios.
Radio drama.

Hitchhiker's Guide to the Galaxy: Douglas Adams Live in Concert. unabr. ed. Douglas Adams. Read by Douglas Adams. (YA). 2008. 34.99 (978-1-60514-838-0(5)) Find a World.

Hitchhiker's Guide to the Galaxy: Quandary Phase. unabr. ed. Douglas Adams. 2 CDs. (Running Time: 8580 sec.). (ENG.). 2005. audio compact disk 24.95 (978-1-57270-488-6(8)) Pub: AudioGO. Dist(s): Perseus Dist

Hitchhiker's Guide to the Galaxy: Quintessential Phase. Douglas Adams. (Hitchhiker's Guide to the Galaxy: Ser.). (ENG.). 2007. audio compact disk 19.95 (978-1-60283-306-7(0)) Pub: AudioGO. Dist(s): Perseus Dist

Hitchhiker's Guide to the Galaxy: Quintessential Phase. unabr. ed. Douglas Adams. Contrib. by Simon Jones & Geoffrey McGivern. 2 CDs. (Running Time: 2 hrs. 10 mins.). 2006. audio compact disk 29.95 (978-0-7927-3858-9(6), BBCD130) AudioGO.

Hitchhiker's Guide to the Galaxy: Secondary Phase. Douglas Adams. (BBC Radio Ser.). (ENG.). 2009. audio compact disk 24.95 (978-1-60283-545-0(4)) Pub: AudioGO. Dist(s): Perseus Dist

Hitchhiker's Guide to the Galaxy: Secondary Phase. unabr. ed. Douglas Adams. 3 CDs. 2008. audio compact disk 39.95 (978-0-7927-5626-2(6)) AudioGO.

Hitchhiker's Guide to the Galaxy: The Complete Radio Series. unabr. ed. Douglas Adams. 14 CDs. (ENG.). 2008. audio compact disk 99.95 (978-1-60283-479-8(2)) Pub: AudioGO. Dist(s): Perseus Dist

Hitchhiker's Guide to the Galaxy: The Tertiary Phase. unabr. ed. Douglas Adams. Contrib. by Simon Jones et al. 3 CDs. (Running Time: 3 hrs. 10 mins.). 2005. audio compact disk 39.95 (978-0-7927-3591-5(9), BBCD106) AudioGO.

Hitchhiker's Guide to the Galaxy: The Tertiary Phase. unabr. ed. Douglas Adams. Read by Simon Jones & Geoffrey McGivern. 3 CDs. (Running Time: 3 Hrs. 10 Mins.). (ENG.). 2005. audio compact disk 29.95 (978-1-57270-469-5(1)) Pub: AudioGO. Dist(s): Perseus Dist
The brand new third installment of Douglas Adams's classic time travel tale, The Hitchhiker's Guide to the Galaxy Tertiary Phase, is now available on audio. The long-awaited CD-which revives the BBC's popular radio series with this new six-part dramatization of Adams's book Life, the Universe and Everything-features 25 minutes of exclusive and previously unheard footage and features the author himself playing the role of Agrajag. The plot picks up where the second radio series left off: Arthur Dent and Ford Prefect escape from prehistoric Earth on a time-traveling sofa while a pack of homicidal robots blow up Lords Cricket Ground. Armed only with a rabbit bone, a worn dressing gown, and a spaceship that looks remarkably like an Italian bistro, Arthur embarks on an intergalactic journey to save the universe.Several members of the original BBC Radio 4 cast reunited for this special audio production, including Simon Jones as Arthur Dent, Geoffrey McGivern as Ford Prefect, Susan Sheridan as Trillian, Mark Wing-Davey as Zaphod Beeblebrox, and Stephen Moore as Marvin the Paranoid Android. Richard Griffiths, Chris Langham, Joanna Lumley, and cricket commentators Fred Trueman and Henry Blofeld also star in this brilliant satire replete with incisive comedic wit.

Hitchhiker's Guide to the Galaxy Quandary Phase. unabr. ed. Douglas Adams. Contrib. by Simon Jones et al. 2 CDs. (Running Time: 2 hrs. 25 mins.). 2005. audio compact disk 29.95 (978-0-7927-3737-7(7), BBCD129) AudioGO.

Hitchhiker's Guide to the Universe, Vol. 5. unabr. ed. Douglas Adams. Read by Douglas Adams. 3 CDs. (Running Time: 6 hrs.). 2004. audio compact disk 39.95 (978-1-59007-257-8(X)) Pub: New Millenn Enter. Dist(s): PerseuPGW

Hite Report: A Nationwide Study of Female Sexuality. unabr. ed. Shere Hite. Read by Roses Prichard. 12 cass. (Running Time: 18 hrs.). 1981. 96.00 (1316) Books on Tape.
Shere Hite distributed questionnaires consisting of some 60 questions to 3000 women across the country, from every age & economic group & from all walks of life. Her questionnaire sought to reveal the complex nature of female sexuality. "The Hite Report" presents what the women who answered said, in their own words & in their own way.

Hitler, Pt. 1 unabr. ed. Joachim C. Fest. Read by Frederick Davidson. 15 cass. (Running Time: 44 hrs.). 1991. 95.95 (978-0-7861-0260-0(8), 1228A, B) Blckstn Audio.
This work has become the leading nonfiction best seller in Germany since its publication & is now widely read in seventeen translations. Joachim Fest shows Hitler as the receptacle of the dreads & resentments of a shaken social order, gifted with an uncanny instinct for all that was hollow behind the appearance of power, at home & abroad. Though a warped human being, he was neither clown nor puppet, as many liked to think; Hitler appears here as an enormously astute politician, impressing & hypnotizing Germans & foreigners alike with the scope of his projects & the theatricality of their presentation. In the last analysis, however, Fest uncovers in Hitler a constantly destructive personality who aimed at & achieved destruction on an unprecedented scale, not least because an insecure world gave him his opportunities.

Hitler, Pt. 2. unabr. ed. Joachim C. Fest. Read by Frederick Davidson. 15 cass. (Running Time: 44 hrs.). 1991. 95.95 (978-0-7861-0261-7(6), 1228A, B) Blckstn Audio.
Fest shows Hitler as the receptacle of the dreads & resentment of a shaken social order, gifted with an uncanny instinct for all that was hollow behind the appearance of power, at home & abroad. Though a warped human being, he was neither clown not puppet, as many liked to think; Hitler appears here as an enormously astute politician, impressing & hypnotizing Germans & foreigner s alike with the scope of his projects & the theartricality of their presentation.

Hitler & Stalin: Parallel Lives. unabr. ed. Alan Bullock. Read by John MacDonald. 12 cass. (Running Time: 18 hrs.). 1994. 96.00 (978-0-7366-2729-0(4), 3459-A); 96.00 (3459-B); 104.00 (3459-C) Books on Tape.
This full-scale dual biography examines Hitler & Stalin not in the traditional context of their conflicts with the Western Alliance but from a freshly revealing perspective: against the background of Berlin-Moscow relations.

Hitler & the Holocaust. Robert S. Wistrich. Narrated by George Guidall. 7 cass. (Running Time: 9 hrs. 15 mins.). 65.00 (978-1-4025-1364-0(X)) Recorded Bks.

Hitler Book: The Secret Dossier Prepared for Stalin from the Interrogations of Hitler's Personal Aides. unabr. ed. Henrik Eberle & Matthias Uhl. Narrated by Michael Prichard. (Running Time: 15 hrs. 30 mins. 0 sec.). (ENG.). 2006. audio compact disk 39.99 (978-1-4001-0203-7(0)); audio compact disk 79.99 (978-1-4001-3203-4(7)) Pub: Tantor Media. Dist(s): IngramPubServ

Hitler Book: The Secret Dossier Prepared for Stalin from the Interrogations of Hitler's Personal Aides. unabr. ed. Henrik Eberle & Matthias Uhl. Narrated by Michael Prichard. (Running Time: 15 hrs. 30 mins. 0 sec.). (ENG.). 2006. audio compact disk 29.99 (978-1-4001-5203-2(8)) Pub: Tantor Media. Dist(s): IngramPubServ

***Hitler in the Crosshairs: A GI's Story of Courage & Faith.** unabr. ed. John Woodbridge & Maurice Possley. (ENG.). 2010. audio compact disk 41.99 (978-0-310-57864-2(7)) Zondervan.

Hitler of History. unabr. ed. John Lukacs. Read by Edward Lewis. 6 cass. (Running Time: 9 hrs.). 1998. 48.00 (978-0-7366-4212-5(9), 4710) Books on Tape.

Hitler Youth. unabr. ed. Susan Campbell Bartoletti. Read by Kathrin Kana. 4 CDs. (Running Time: 15840 sec.). (ENG.). (J). (gr. 5-12). 2006. audio compact disk 30.00 (978-0-7393-3662-5(2), Listening Lib) Pub: Random Audio Pubg. Dist(s): Random

Hitler Youth: Growing up in Hitler's Shadow. unabr. ed. Susan Campbell Bartoletti. 2006. (978-0-7393-3678-6(9), Listening Lib); audio compact disk 32.30 (978-0-7393-3677-9(0), Listening Lib) Pub: Random Audio Pubg. Dist(s): NetLibrary CO

Hitler's Angels. unabr. ed. Kris Rusch. Read by Susan O'Malley. 5 cass. (Running Time: 7 hrs.). 1998. 39.95 (978-0-7861-1371-2(5), 2278) Blckstn Audio.
A gripping crime novel set in Germany on the eve of Adolf Hitler's ascension, based on the true-life affair Hitler had with his niece, Geli Raubal. A fascinating exploration of the might-have-beens of this dark & fateful time.

Hitler's Holy Relics: A True Story of Nazi Plunder & the Race to Recover the Crown Jewels of the Holy Roman Empire. unabr. ed. Sidney Kirkpatrick. Read by Charles Stransky. 9 CDs. (Running Time: 10 hrs. 45 mins.). 2010. audio compact disk 34.95 (978-1-61573-043-8(5), 1615730435) Pub: HighBridge. Dist(s): Workman Pub

Hitler's Inferno. unabr. ed. 1 cass. (Running Time: 1 hr. 48 min.). 12.95 (#486) J Norton Pubs.
Narrated sketch of Hitler's rise to power & his attempts at world conquest. It includes recording clips from Hitler's speeches. Another portion of the recording offers a collection of songs then popular in Germany.

Hitler's Inferno: A recorded time Capsule. 2008. audio compact disk 12.95 (978-1-57970-522-0(7), Audio-For) J Norton Pubs.

Hitler's Niece: A Novel. Ron Hansen. Narrated by Paul Hecht. 9 CDs. (Running Time: 10 hrs. 30 mins.). 2000. audio compact disk 89.00 (978-0-7887-4756-4(8), C1244E7) Recorded Bks.
Passionate & eventful, this fictional biography is as compelling as a psychological thriller. As Hitler stands poised to unleash his reign of horror, his 23-year-old niece is found dead. He's calling it suicide, but the disturbing secrets she's taking to her grave would destroy the rising fuhrer's messianic image.

Hitler's Niece: A Novel. unabr. ed. Ron Hansen. Narrated by Paul Hecht. 8 cass. (Running Time: 10 hrs. 30 mins.). 1999. 70.00 (978-0-7887-4043-5(1), 96120E7) Recorded Bks.

Hitler's Pope: The Secret History of Pius XII. unabr. ed. John Cornwell. Read by David Case. 12 cass. (Running Time: 18 hrs.). 2000. 34.95 (978-0-7366-4770-0(8)) Books on Tape.
This highly controversial book alleges that Pius XII, Pope during WW II, was a willing dupe for the Nazis.

Hitler's Pope: The Secret History of Pius XII. unabr. collector's ed. John Cornwell. Read by David Case. 12 cass. (Running Time: 18 hrs.). 1999. 96.00 (978-0-7366-4818-9(6), 5149) Books on Tape.
Pope Pius XII indifference to the plight of the European Jews, as his public silence allowed the Nazis to destroy & massacre millions of Jews before & during World War II.

Hitler's Scientists: Science, War, & the Devil's Pact. abr. ed. John Cornwell. 5 CDs. (Running Time: 6 hrs.). 2003. audio compact disk 29.95 (978-1-59316-018-0(6), 750455) Listen & Live.
A gripping, in-depth account of Germany's horrific abuse of science and its consequences- then and now. By the first decade of the twentieth century, Germany was the Mecca of science and technology in the world. However, by the beginning of the First World War, Germany began to display some of the features that would blight the conduct of ideal science through the rest of the century.

Hitler's War. unabr. ed. Harry Turtledove. Narrated by John Allen Nelson. 2 MP3-CDs. (Running Time: 17 hrs. 0 mins. 0 sec.). (War That Came Early Ser.). (ENG.). 2009. 34.99 (978-1-4001-6388-5(9)); audio compact disk 99.99 (978-1-4001-4388-7(8)); audio compact disk 49.99 (978-1-4001-1388-0(1)) Pub: Tantor Media. Dist(s): IngramPubServ

***Hitler's War.** unabr. ed. Harry Turtledove. Narrated by John Allen Nelson. (Running Time: 17 hrs. 0 mins.). (War That Came Early Ser.). 2009. 21.99 (978-1-4001-8388-3(X)); 49.99 (978-1-4001-9388-2(5)) Tantor Media.

***Hitman: The Untold Story of Johnny Martorano, Whitey Bulger's Enforcer & the Most Feared Gangster in the Underworld.** unabr. ed. Howie Carr. Read by To be announced. (Running Time: 16 hrs. NaN mins.). (ENG.). 2011. 29.95 (978-1-4417-7602-0(8)) Blckstn Audio.

***Hitman: The Untold Story of Johnny Martorano, Whitey Bulger's Enforcer & the Most Feared Gangster in the Underworld.** unabr. ed. Howie Carr. Read by To Be Announced. (Running Time: 16 hrs. NaN mins.). (ENG.). 2011. 85.95 (978-1-4417-7599-3(4)) Blckstn Audio.

***Hitman: The Untold Story of Johnny Martorano, Whitey Bulger's Enforcer & the Most Feared Gangster in the Underworld.** unabr. ed. Howie Carr. Read by To be announced. (Running Time: 16 hrs. NaN mins.). 2011. audio compact disk 34.95 (978-1-4417-7601-3(X)) Blckstn Audio.

***Hitman: The Untold Story of Johnny Martorano, Whitey Bulger's Enforcer & the Most Feared Gangster in the Underworld.** unabr. ed. Howie Carr. Read by To be Announced. (Running Time: 16 hrs. NaN mins.). (ENG.). 2011. audio compact disk 118.00 (978-1-4417-7600-6(1)) Blckstn Audio.

Hits on the Web: Writers Harbrace Handbook. Robert Keith Miller. audio compact disk 33.95 (978-0-8384-8083-0(7)) Heinle.

Hits on the Web - Avenidas. Marinelli & Oramas. (C). bk. & stu. ed. 88.95 (978-0-8384-7499-0(3)) Heinle.

Hits on the Web - Ciao. 4th ed. Federici. (C). bk. & stu. ed. 148.95 (978-0-8384-7921-6(9)); bk. & stu. ed. 166.95 (978-0-8384-7922-3(7)) Heinle.

Hits on the Web - Motifs. 2nd ed. Jansma. (C). bk. 111.95 (978-0-8384-8081-6(0)); bk. 154.95 (978-0-8384-8190-5(6)) Heinle.

Hits on the Web - Puentes. 3rd ed. Marinelli & Oramas. (C). bk. & stu. ed. 81.95 (978-0-8384-7500-3(0)) Heinle.

Hits on the Web - Saludos. Ozete. (C). bk. 84.95 (978-0-8384-8391-6(7)) Heinle.

Hits on the Web - Tu Diras. 2nd ed. John R. Gutiérrez-Candelaria. (C). bk. 88.95 (978-0-8384-8402-9(6)) Heinle.

Hits on the Web Sundance. 2nd ed. Mark Connelly. audio compact disk 51.95 (978-0-8384-8346-6(1)) Heinle.

Hitting Secrets of the Pros: Big League Sluggers Reveal the Tricks of Their Trade. abr. ed. Wayne Stewart. Read by Michael Kramer. (Running Time: 16200 sec.). 2006. audio compact disk 28.00 (978-1-933309-10-1(5)) Pub: A Media Intl. Dist(s): Natl Bk Netwk

Hitting the Ideal Wall. Hosted by Andrew C. Jacobs. 2009. audio compact disk 9.95 (978-0-9823699-5-1(6)) Ideal Jacobs.

***Hittite.** unabr. ed. Ben Bova. Read by Stefan Rudnicki. (Running Time: 11 hrs. 0 mins.). 2010. 29.95 (978-1-4417-2816-6(3)); 65.95 (978-1-4417-2812-8(0)); audio compact disk 100.00 (978-1-4417-2813-5(9)) Blckstn Audio.

HIV-AIDS: Peer Puppet Program. 6 cass. (Running Time: 9 hrs). (J). (gr. k-6). 1996. 185.00 Set, incl. prevention manual. (252300-SG) Sunburst Comm.
An effective approach to teaching students about critical health issues, based on the premise that kids listen to kids.

HIV & Sexuality Issues. Directed By Gerald T. Rogers. Contrib. by Dennis C. Daley. (Living Sober 2 Ser.: Segment L). 1996. pap. bk. 89.00 NTSC. (978-1-56215-069-3(3), Jossey-Bass) Wiley US.

HIV/AIDS & the Mind: Program from the Award Winning Public Radio Series. Interview. Hosted by Fred Goodwin. 1 CD. (Running Time: 1hr.). (Infinite Mind Ser.). 2001. audio compact disk 21.95 (978-1-888064-70-4(6), LCM 190) Lichtenstein Creat.
It's been twenty years since the Federal Centers for Disease Control and Prevention (CDC) reported the first cases of the illness that is now known as AIDS. Its been years since we've understood how HIV - the virus that causes AIDS - spreads. So why are there 40,000 new cases of HIV every year in the United States alone? This show features a discussion about the psychology of HIV transmission and prevention.

HLA Blood Test for Paternity: Turek v. Hardy. 1 cass. (Running Time: 1 hr.). 1983. 15.00 PA Bar Inst.

Hmmm? Tackling Some of Life's Most Difficult Questions. Kurt Johnston. (Super-Ser.). 2007. audio compact disk 30.00 (978-5-557-78143-5(9)) Group Pub.

Hmong: Laotian Refugees in U. S. 1 cass. (Running Time: 30 min.). 8.00 (HO-85-09-25, HarperThor) HarpC GBR.

Hmong Teaching Set. unabr. ed. University of Iowa, CEEDE Staff. 5 cass. (Tales of Marvel & Wonder Ser.). 1988. 99.00 Set, incl. tchr's. guide, activity masters, ESL grammar activity masters & the ESL grammar activity masters tchr's. guide. (978-0-7836-1091-7(2), 9991) Triumph Learn.
Twenty-three Indochinese fables.

HMOs: A Primer on the Law of Health Maintenance Organizations. 1986. bk. 90.00; 50.00 PA Bar Inst.

HMS Beagle: The Story of Darwin's Ship. unabr. collector's ed. Keith S. Thomson. Read by Stuart Langton. 7 cass. (Running Time: 10 hrs. 30 min.). 1996. 56.00 (978-0-7366-3494-6(0), 4134) Books on Tape.
We know a great deal about Darwin's voyage on the HMS Beagle & what it meant to science, but we know almost nothing of the ship & its crew. Thomson, an evolutionary biologist & maritime historian, tells the Beagle's story, from humble origins to great renown.

HMS Marlborough Will Enter Harbour see Monsarrat at Sea

HMS Ulysses. unabr. ed. Alistair MacLean. Read by Peter Joyce. 10 cass. (Running Time: 15 hrs.). 1995. 84.95 (978-1-85496-341-3(4), 63414) Pub: Soundings Ltd GBR. Dist(s): Ulverscroft US

***HMS Unseen.** abr. ed. Patrick Robinson. (ENG.). 2004. (978-0-06-081846-3(8), Harper Audio); (978-0-06-081847-0(6), Harper Audio) HarperCollins Pubs.

H.M.S. Unseen. abr. ed. Patrick Robinson. 2 cass. (Running Time: 3 hrs.). 1999. 16.85 Set. (978-1-85686-721-4(8)) Ulvrscrft Audio.

H.M.S. Unseen, unabr. ed. Patrick Robinson. Narrated by George Guidall. 11 cass. (Running Time: 16 hrs.). 1999. 96.00 (978-0-7887-3463-2(6), 95874E7) Recorded Bks.
Robinson blows listeners out of the water with his adrenaline-charged technothrillers. Here, he portrays the world in crisis as a dangerous terrorist pits nation against nation to promote his own chilling agenda. Includes an exclusive interview with the author.

H.M.S. Unseen. unabr. ed. Patrick Robinson. Narrated by George Guidall. 14 CDs. (Running Time: 16 hrs.). 2001. audio compact disk 134.00 (978-0-7887-7186-6(8), C1436) Recorded Bks.
An explosive H.M.S. Unseen portrays the world in crisis as a dangerous terrorist pits nation against nation to promote his own chilling agenda. While on a training mission, the British submarine H.M.S. Unseen mysteriously disappears. A year later three planes are shot from the sky, one of them carrying the Vice President of the United States. As wily U.S. Security Advisor Arnold Morgan scrambles to prevent international turmoil, he suspects the lost sub has been modified to carry anti-aircraft weapons. Morgan knows only one person who could mastermind this scheme - an Iraqi terrorist believed to be dead. Acclaimed on both sides of the Atlantic, Patrick Robinson blows readers out of the water with his adrenaline-charged tales.

Ho for a Hat! see Twentieth-Century Poetry in English, No. 31, Recordings of Poets Reading Their Own Poetry: William Jay Smith Reading His Poems for Children

Ho Lee Chow! Chinese for Kids. Carole Marsh. (Of All the Gaul Ser.). (J). (gr. k-6). 1994. 19.95 (978-0-7933-7360-4(3)) Gallopade Intl.

Hoarding & Clutter: Program from the Award Winning Public Radio Series. Interview. Hosted by Fred Goodwin. 1 CD. (Running Time: 1 hr.). (Infinite Mind Ser.). 2002. audio compact disk 21.95 (978-1-888064-69-8(2), LCM 229) Lichtenstein Creat.
When does enough become too much? And why is it so hard for compulsive savers to know the difference? This show looks at hoarding, which involves the accumulation and inability to throw away unneeded possessions, to the point that a home may become so filled with stuff that furniture and rooms can no longer be used for their intended purposes. Guests include Dr. Randy Frost, a pioneer researcher in the study of clinical hoarding and Dr. Sanjaya Saxena, a neurobiologist who is pinpointing where in the brain the problem seems to originate. Author Denise Linn, addresses non-clinical forms of hoarding with tips on how to recognize - and get rid of - clutter.

Hoax. abr. ed. Robert K. Tanenbaum. Read by Lee Sellars. 2004. 15.95 (978-0-7435-3992-0(3)) Pub: S&S Audio. Dist(s): S and S Inc

Hoax. abr. movie tie-in unabr. ed. Clifford Irving. Read by Joe Barrett. 8 cass. (Running Time: 52200 sec.). 2006. 25.95 (978-0-7861-4546-1(3)); audio compact disk 25.95 (978-0-7861-7132-3(4)) Blckstn Audio.

Hoax. unabr. ed. Clifford Irving. Read by Joe Barrett. (Running Time: 52200 sec.). 2006. 65.95 (978-0-7861-4702-1(4)); audio compact disk 81.00 (978-0-7861-6591-9(X)) Blckstn Audio.

Hoax. unabr. ed. Clifford Irving. Read by Joe Barrett. (YA). 2006. 69.99 (978-1-59895-566-8(7)) Find a World.

Hoax. unabr. movie tie-in ed. Clifford Irving. Read by Joe Barrett. (Running Time: 52200 sec.). 2006. audio compact disk 29.95 (978-0-7861-7571-0(0)) Blckstn Audio.

Hoax of Scientific Creationism. John Robbins. 1 cass. (Christianity & Science Ser.: No. 1). 5.00 Trinity Found.

Hobart. unabr. ed. Anita Briggs. Read by Full Cast Production Staff. (J). 2007. 34.99 (978-1-60252-504-7(8)) Find a World.

Hobart. unabr. ed. Robert A. Heinlein. 1 cassette. (Running Time: 30 minutes). (J). 2003. 12.00 (978-1-932076-31-8(X)) Full Cast Audio.

Hobart Smith of Saltville, VA. 1 cass. 9.98 (C-17) Folk-Legacy.
Traditional songs, ballads & banjo tunes by a true master.

Hobbit. J. R. R. Tolkien. 5 CDs. (Running Time: 4 hrs.). 2001. audio compact disk 39.95 (BMDD009) Lodestone Catalog.
Follow Bibo Baggins from his nice dry hobbit hole, past Mirkwood & down into the gullet of the dragon Smaug's stolen mountain fortress.

Hobbit. J. R. R. Tolkien. 6 cass. (Running Time: 4 hrs.). (J). (gr. k up). 29.98 Incl. wooden box. (318) MFLP CA.
Children & adults alike love this adventure story of Bilbo Baggins, the hobbit, hired by the dwarfs to regain their mountain kingdom from a terrible dragon.

Hobbit. J. R. R. Tolkien. 5 CDs. audio compact disk 39.95 (BMDD009, Random AudioBks) Random Audio Pubg.
Tolkien's middle earth, this BBC production features an original score written for Renaissance-era instruments, ensemble acting, innovative sound techniques designed to present a hobbit's-eye view of Bilbo's adventures.

Hobbit. J. R. R. Tolkien. 5 CDs. (Running Time: 3 hrs. 35 min.). (YA). 2001. audio compact disk 45.00 (978-0-8072-0526-6(5), Listening Lib) Random Audio Pubg.

Hobbit. J. R. R. Tolkien. Narrated by Rob Inglis. 10 CDs. (Running Time: 11 hrs. 15 mins.). 2000. audio compact disk 87.00 (978-0-7887-3727-5(9), C1084E7) Recorded Bks.
Recounts the travels & mishaps of Bilbo Baggins, a home-loving Hobbit who accompanies 13 dwarves & the wizard Gandalf in search of the lost treasure of the dwarves, reputed to be located in the den of a fire-breathing dragon named Smaug.

Hobbit. abr. ed. J. R. R. Tolkien. 5 CDs. (Running Time: 7 hrs. 30 mins.). 2001. audio compact disk 45.00 Books on Tape.

Hobbit. abr. ed. J. R. R. Tolkien. 4 cass. 1995. 29.95 (8245Q) Filmic Archives.
Bilbo Baggins enjoys a quiet & contented life, with no desire to travel far from the comforts of home. Then one day the wizard Gandalf & a band of dwarves arrive unexpectedly & enlist his services as a burglar. "The Hobbit" became an instant success when it was first published & now, more than fifty years later this epic tale of elves, dwarves, trolls, goblins, myth, magic, & adventure, with its reluctant hero Bilbo Baggins, has lost none of its appeal.

Hobbit. abr. ed. J. R. R. Tolkien. 4 CDs. (Running Time: 4 hrs. 30 mins.). (ENG.). 2001. audio compact disk 29.95 (978-1-56511-552-1(X), 156511552X) Pub: HighBridge. Dist(s): Workman Pub

Hobbit. abr. ed. J. R. R. Tolkien. Contrib. by Ensemble Cast Staff. 2009. audio compact disk 19.95 (978-1-59887-898-1(0), 1598878980) Pub: HighBridge. Dist(s): Workman Pub

Hobbit. abr. ed. J. R. R. Tolkien. 6 CDs. (Running Time: 5 hrs.). Dramatization. (J). 1994. audio compact disk 29.95 Wood-branded gift box. (978-1-55935-119-5(5)) Soundelux.
Open the enchanted door to "Middle Earth". Here is the first part of the great epic - the story of a middle-aged Hobbit who joins a band of dwarfs seeking to reclaim their treasure from the dreadful dragon Smaug.

Hobbit. unabr. ed. J. R. R. Tolkien. Full Cast Production Staff. Narrated by Michael Kilgariff. 4 CDs. (ENG.). 2008. audio compact disk 29.95 (978-1-60283-454-5(7)) Pub: AudioGO. Dist(s): Perseus Dist

Hobbit. unabr. ed. J. R. R. Tolkien. 4 cass. (Running Time: 4 hrs.). (J). 2000. 30.00 (978-0-7366-9181-9(2)) Books on Tape.
Hobbit's eye view of Bilbo's adventures.

Hobbit. unabr. ed. J. R. R. Tolkien. 4 cass. (Running Time: 3 hrs. 35 min.). (Middle Earth Chronicles: Vol. 2). (J). 2000. 32.00 (978-0-8072-8340-0(1), LL0186, Listening Lib) Random Audio Pubg.
Bilbo Baggins, the hobbit, is a peaceful sort of cozy hole in the Shire, a place where adventures are uncommon and rather unwanted. So when the wizard Gandalf whisks him away on a treasure hunting expedition with a troop of rowdy dwarves, he's not entirely thrilled.

Hobbit. unabr. ed. J. R. R. Tolkien. Narrated by Rob Inglis. 8 cass. (Running Time: 11 hrs. 15 mins.). (gr. 6). 1991. 70.00 (978-1-55690-233-8(6), 91121E7) Recorded Bks.
The prelude to the epic "The Lord of the Rings," this tale of dragons & elves, hobbits & kings, is truly one of the most enchanting adventure stories of all time.

Hobbit. unabr. ed. J. R. R. Tolkien. Narrated by Rob Inglis. 1 CD. 1999. audio compact disk 87.00 (C1084) Recorded Bks.

Hobbit. unabr. ed. J. R. R. Tolkien. Read by Rob Inglis. 10 CDs. (Running Time: 11 hrs.). 2004. audio compact disk 39.99 (978-0-7887-8982-3(1), 00222) Recorded Bks.
Like every other hobbit, Bilbo Baggins likes nothing better than a quiet evening in his snug hole in the ground, dining on a sumptuous dinner in front of a fire. But when a wandering wizard captivates him with tales of the unknown, Bilbo becomes restless. Soon he joins the wizard?s band of homeless dwarves in search of giant spiders, savage wolves, and other dangers. Bilbo quickly tires of the quest for adventure and longs for the security of his familiar home. But before he can return to his life of comfort, he must face the greatest threat of all - a treasure-troving dragon named Smaug.

Hobbit. unabr. ed. J. R. R. Tolkien. Read by Rob Inglis. 7 cass. (Running Time: 11 hrs.). (gr. 6-8). 2004. 29.99 (978-0-7887-8956-4(2), 00404) Recorded Bks.

Hobbit: Radio Dramatization. J. R. R. Tolkien. 4 CDs. (Running Time: 6 hrs.). (Lord of the Rings Ser.). (J). 2002. audio compact disk 49.95 (978-0-563-53047-3(2)) AudioGO.

Hobbit & The Fellowship of the Ring. abr. ed. J. R. R. Tolkien. Read by J. R. R. Tolkien. 1 cass. (Running Time: 49 min.). (J). 1996. 12.00 (978-1-55994-631-5(8), DCN 1477) HarperCollins Pubs.
In this rare recording, J. R. R. Tolkien leads you in prose, poems & song into the fantastic world of the greatest fantasy series ever written, "The Lord of the Rings." Includes one of Tolkien's unpublished poems.

Hobbit & The Fellowship of the Ring. unabr. ed. J. R. R. Tolkien. Read by J. R. R. Tolkien. 1 cass. (Running Time: 49 mins.). 12.00 (H132) Blckstn Audio.
Tolkien leads you in prose, poems & song into the fantastic world of the greatest fantasy series ever written.

Hobbit Soundtrack-on Cd. Prod. by Myattic Studio. (YA). 2000. audio compact disk 89.95 (978-0-7365-3274-7(9)) Films Media Grp.

***Hobby Farming for Dummies.** abr. ed. Theresa Husarik. (ENG.). 2008. (978-0-06-176484-4(1), Harper Audio); (978-0-06-176485-1(X), Harper Audio) HarperCollins Pubs.

Hobgoblin Proxy. unabr. ed. J. T. Petty. Read by L. J. Ganser. 3 cass. (Running Time: 2 hrs. 45 mins.). (Clemency Pogue Ser.). (J). 2006. 24.75 (978-1-4193-4366-7(1), 98054) Recorded Bks.
In this fresh and funny second book of acclaimed author JT Petty's series, it's up to Clemency Pogue to save the land of Make-Believe and all its creatures. For Kennethurchin to complete the change from human to hobgoblin, his proxy made of clay and named Inky must completely dissolve. If not, the land of Make-Believe will disappear forever. But Inky won't dissolve anytime soon since he rarely bathes.

Hobson's Choice. Harold Brighouse. 2 cass. & 2 CDs. (Running Time: 6 hrs.). 2003. audio compact disk 17.99 (978-1-58926-173-0(9), C05M-0050) Oasis Audio.

Hobson's Choice. adpt. ed. Harold Brighouse. 2 CDs. (Running Time: 2 hrs. 30 mins.). (ENG.). 2003. audio compact disk 17.99 (978-1-58926-325-3(1)) Oasis Audio.

Hoc Va Vui: Vietnamese Language, Stages A, B and 2. National Vietnamese Curriculum Project Staff. 1 cass. (Running Time: 50 mins.). (VIE.). EducServs AUS.

Hockey - Improve & Win. Norman J. Caldwell. Read by Norman J. Caldwell. Ed. by Achieve Now Institute Staff. 1 cass. (Running Time: 20 min.). (Sports Achievement Ser.). 1988. 9.97 (978-1-56273-088-8(6)) My Mothers Pub.
Increase your power & accuracy, more energy & confidence.

Hockey Mystery. Gertrude Chandler Warner. (Running Time: 5400 sec.). (Boxcar Children Ser.: No. 80). (J). 2005. audio compact disk 14.95 (978-0-7861-7489-8(7)) Blckstn Audio.

Hockey Mystery. unabr. ed. Gertrude Chandler Warner. Read by Aimee Lilly. 2 cass. (Running Time: 1 hr. 50 min.). (Boxcar Children Ser.: No. 80). (J). 2003. 12.99 (978-1-58926-121-1(6), A65L-0120, Oasis Kids) Oasis Audio.
Henry, Jessie, Violet and Bennie have become friends with Kevin Reynolds, their favorite hockey star. He wants to build an ice rink in Greenfield, but now, equipment is missing, and someone is trying to ruin plans for the rink. They must help their new friend solve this mystery!.

Hockey Mystery. unabr. ed. Gertrude Chandler Warner. Narrated by Aimee Lilly. (Boxcar Children Ser.). (ENG.). (J). 2003. 10.49 (978-1-60814-088-6(1)) Oasis Audio.

Hockey Mystery. unabr. ed. Gertrude Chandler Warner. Narrated by Aimee Lilly. 2 CDs. (Running Time: 1 hr. 50 min.). (Boxcar Children Ser.: No. 80). (ENG.). (J). 2003. audio compact disk 14.99 (978-1-58926-127-3(5), A65L-012D, Oasis Kids) Oasis Audio.

Hockey sur Glace. unabr. ed. Short Stories. Peter LaSalle. Narrated by Johnny Heller. 3 cass. (Running Time: 3 hrs. 45 mins.). 1997. 26.00 (978-0-7887-1309-5(4), 95151E7) Recorded Bks.
Nostalgic collection of literary stories of hockey & growing up in the Northeast will inspire you to acquire a new appreciation for the fastest game on two feet.

Hockey Sweater & Other Stories. Roch Carrier & Alexander Hausvater. Tr. by Sheila Fischman from ENG. 1 cass. (Running Time: 1 hr. 30 mins.). Dramatization. Orig. Title: Le Chandail de Hockey. (FRE & ENG.). 2001. 14.95 (978-0-86492-332-5(5)); audio compact disk 16.95 (978-0-86492-333-2(3)) Pub: BTC Audiobks CAN. Dist(s): U Toronto Pr

Hocus Pocus. unabr. ed. Kurt Vonnegut. Read by George Ralph. (Running Time: 7 hrs.). 2007. 39.25 (978-1-4233-3048-6(X), 9781423330486, BADLE); 24.95 (978-1-4233-3047-9(1), 9781423330479, BAD); audio compact disk 39.25 (978-1-4233-3046-2(3), 9781423330462, Brlnc Audio MP3 Lib); audio compact disk 24.95 (978-1-4233-3045-5(5), 9781423330455, Brilliance MP3) Brilliance Audio.

Hocus Pocus. unabr. ed. Kurt Vonnegut. Read by George Ralph. (Running Time: 7 hrs.). 2010. audio compact disk 29.99 (978-1-4418-3570-3(9), 9781441835703, Bril Audio CD Unabri); audio compact disk 89.97 (978-1-4418-3571-0(7), 9781441835710, BriAudCD Unabrid) Brilliance Audio.

Hocus Pocus. unabr. ed. Kurt Vonnegut. Narrated by Norman Dietz. 7 cass. (Running Time: 9 hrs. 45 mins.). 1991. 60.00 (978-1-55690-234-5(4), 91210E7) Recorded Bks.
A wry parable of a college professor turned tutor that roams the world we live in.

***Hocus-Pocus & Frisby.** 2010. audio compact disk (978-1-59171-189-6(4)) Falcon Picture.

***Hocus Pocus & the giant fairy, Gog.** unabr. ed. Laura Milligan. Read by Mary-Anne Fahey. (Running Time: 2 hrs. 36 mins.). (J). 2010. audio compact disk 43.95 (978-1-74214-731-4(3), 9781742147314) Pub: Bolinda Pubng AUS. Dist(s): Bolinda Pub Inc

***Hocus Pocus Versus the Stinky Pong.** unabr. ed. Laura Milligan. Read by Mary-Anne Fahey. (Running Time: 2 hrs. 45 mins.). (J). 2010. audio compact disk 54.95 (978-1-74214-670-6(8), 9781742146706) Pub: Bolinda Pubng AUS. Dist(s): Bolinda Pub Inc

Hodder History the Roman Empire Brita. 2006. audio compact disk 449.00 (978-0-340-91686-5(9), HodderMurray) Pub: Hodder Edu GBR. Dist(s): Trans-Atl Phila

Hoeren - Brummen - Sprechen: Angewandte Phonetik im Unterricht Deutsch als Fremdsprache: Handbuch. I. Cauneau. (GER.). (C). 1992. 38.00 (978-3-12-675353-1(1)) Pub: Klett Ernst Verlag DEU. Dist(s): Intl Bk Import

Hogan. unabr. ed. Curt Sampson. Read by Tom Parker. 5 cass. (Running Time: 7 hrs.). 2004. 39.95 (978-0-7861-1358-3(8), 2267) Blckstn Audio.

Hogan. unabr. ed. Curt Sampson. (Running Time: 25200 sec.). 2007. audio compact disk 29.95 (978-0-7861-5958-1(8)); audio compact disk 55.00 (978-0-7861-5957-4(X)) Blckstn Audio.

Hogarth: A Life & a World. unabr. ed. Jenny Uglow. 10 cass. (Running Time: 15 hrs.). 2001. 80.00 (978-0-7366-6719-7(9)); 72.00 (978-0-7366-6720-3(2)) Books on Tape.

Hogfather. unabr. ed. Terry Pratchett. Read by Nigel Planer. 8 cass. (Running Time: 8 hrs.). (Discworld Ser.). (J). 1999. 69.95 (978-0-7531-0520-7(9), 991202) Pub: ISIS Lrg Prnt GBR. Dist(s): Ulverscroft US
It's the night before Hogwatch & it's too quiet. There's snow, there are robins, there are trees covered with decorations, but there's a notable lack of the fat man who delivers toys. He's gone. Susan the governess has to find him before morning, otherwise the sun won't rise. Unfortunately her only helpers are a raven with an eyeball fixation, the Death of Rats & oh, a god of hangovers. Worse still, someone is coming down the chimney. This time he's carrying a sack instead of scythe, but there's still something regrettably familiar ."You'd better watch out.".

Hogfather. unabr. ed. Terry Pratchett. Read by Nigel Planer. 10 CDs. (Running Time: 11 hrs.). (Discworld Ser.). (J). 2001. audio compact disk 89.95 (978-0-7531-0759-1(7), 107597) Pub: ISIS Lrg Prnt GBR. Dist(s): Ulverscroft US

Hok Lee & the Dwarfs see Favorite Children's Stories: A Collection

Hoko River Archaeological Site Complex: The Rockshelter (45CA21), 1,000-100 B. P. Dale R. Croes. Contrib. by Barbara Stucki & Rebecca Wigen. 2005. audio compact disk 18.00 (978-0-9768928-0-9(4)) Pub: D Croes. Dist(s): Wash St U Pr

Hokus Pokus. abr. ed. Fern Michaels. Read by Laural Merlington. (Running Time: 3 hrs.). (Sisterhood Ser.: No. 9). 2009. audio compact disk 14.99 (978-1-4233-4493-3(6), 9781423344933, BCD Value Price) Brilliance Audio.

Hokus Pokus. unabr. ed. Fern Michaels. Read by Laural Merlington. (Running Time: 7 hrs.). (Sisterhood Ser.: No. 9). 2008. 24.95 (978-1-4233-4490-2(1), 9781423344902, BAD); 39.25 (978-1-4233-4491-9(X), 9781423344919, BADLE); audio compact disk 24.95 (978-1-4233-4488-9(X), 9781423344889, Brilliance MP3); audio compact disk 29.95 (978-1-4233-4486-5(3), 9781423344865, Bril Audio CD Unabri); audio compact disk 82.25 (978-1-4233-4487-2(1), 9781423344872, BriAudCD Unabrid); audio compact disk 39.25 (978-1-4233-4489-6(8), 9781423344896, Brlnc Audio MP3 Lib) Brilliance Audio.

Holcroft Covenant. unabr. collector's ed. Robert Ludlum. Read by Michael Prichard. 13 cass. (Running Time: 19 hrs. 30 min.). 1983. 104.00 (978-0-7366-0808-4(7), 1758) Books on Tape.
Noel Holcroft, a young American architect, flies to Geneva where he sees an astonishing document. Drawn up more than 30 years ago by 3 ostensibly repentant Nazis, it is the key to a $780 million fund sequestered by the trio to aid survivors of the holocaust. All that is required is Holcroft's signature.

Hold Back Time. unabr. ed. Allene Frances. Read by Stephanie Brush. 8 cass. (Running Time: 10 hrs. 42 min.). 2001. 49.95 (978-1-58116-041-3(0)) Books in Motion.
Movie, stars, including the late Mona Sterling, have sought the "fountain of youth," in an effort to continue their careers. And now, cosmetic marketing manager Joy Mitchell may have stumbled upon her company's secret formula, a formula that just might have killed Sterling.

Hold Fast. Contrib. by MercyMe. (Soundtraks Ser.). 2006. audio compact disk 8.99 (978-5-558-04456-0(X)) Christian Wrld.

Hold God Trustworthy. Neville Goddard. 1 cass. (Running Time: 62 min.). 1964. 8.00 (71) J & L Pubns.
Neville taught Imagination Creates Reality. He was a powerfully influential teacher of God as Consciousness.

Hold Me Close, Let Me Go: A Mother, a Daughter & an Adolescence Survived. abr. ed. Adair Lara. 4 cass. (Running Time: 360 mins.). 2001. 24.95 (978-1-57511-090-5(3)) Pub Mills.
When Adair Lara's daughter Morgan turns 13, she changes from a sweet, loving child into an angry, secretive teenager spinning out of control. Thus begins a five-year trip into chaos as Morgan spirals into a world of drinking, drugs, and crime. Lara's story will evoke shocks of recognition in parents while offering hope for beating seemingly insurmountable odds.

Hold Me, Lord: Songs for Prayer. Composed by Matthew Baute. 2008. audio compact disk 17.00 (978-1-58459-370-6(9)) Wrld Lib Pubns.

Hold Me Tight: Seven Conversations for a Lifetime of Love. unabr. ed. Sue Johnson. Read by Sandra Burr. (Running Time: 9 hrs.). 2008. 39.25 (978-1-4233-6370-5(1), 9781423363705, BADLE); 24.95 (978-1-4233-6369-9(8), 9781423363699, BAD); audio compact disk 24.95 (978-1-4233-6367-5(1), 9781423363675, Brilliance MP3); audio compact disk 29.95 (978-1-4233-6365-1(5), 9781423363651, Bril Audio CD Unabri); audio compact disk 39.25 (978-1-4233-6368-2(X), 9781423363682, Brlnc Audio MP3 Lib); audio compact disk 92.25 (978-1-4233-6366-8(3), 9781423363668, BriAudCD Unabrid) Brilliance Audio.

Hold Me While I Cry. Contrib. by Karen Peck & New River. (Spring Hill Studio Tracks Plus Ser.). 2005. audio compact disk 9.98 (978-5-559-13563-2(1)) Sprg Hill Music Group.

Hold My Hand - Or Else! unabr. ed. Margaret Clark. Read by Kate Hosking. 3 cass. (Running Time: 3 hrs. 30 mins.). (YA). 2000. 28.00 (978-1-74030-204-3(4), 500743) Pub: Bolinda Pubng AUS. Dist(s): Bolinda Pub Inc

Hold my hand - or Else. unabr. ed. Judith Clarke. Read by Kate Hosking. (Running Time: 3 hrs. 30 mins.). (YA). 2004. audio compact disk 28.00 (978-1-74093-405-3(9)) Pub: Bolinda Pubng AUS. Dist(s): Bolinda Pub Inc

Hold My Name. Carolyn Coleman. 1 cass. (Running Time: 30 mins.). 2002. bk. 12.99 (978-0-9726960-1-2(6)) Carol Coleman.

Hold On. Perf. by Gary Chapman. 1 cass. 1999. 8.98 (978-0-7601-3157-2(0)) Provident Music.

Hold On. Contrib. by Daniel Doss. (Mastertrax Ser.). 2008. audio compact disk 9.98 (978-5-557-46037-8(3)) Pt of Grace Ent.

Hold on, the Light Will Come: And Other Lessons My Songs Have Taught Me. Michael McLean. 2003. bk. 21.95 (978-1-59038-088-8(6), Shadow Mount) Pub: Deseret Bk. Dist(s): Bookworld

Hold on to Hope. Jack R. Christianson. 1 cass. 1996. 9.95 (978-1-57008-232-0(4), Bkcraft Inc) Deseret Bk.

Hold on to Me. unabr. ed. Read by Peter Himmelman. Perf. by Peter Himmelman. 1 cass. (Running Time: 30 min.). Dramatization. (J). 1989. 8.95 (978-1-58452-007-8(8), 4370); 8.95 Spanish version. (978-1-58452-016-0(7), 5370) Spinoza Co.

Hold on to Your Peace. Short Stories. Joel Osteen. 1 Cass. (Running Time: 30 Mins.). 2002. 6.00 (978-1-59349-158-1(1), JA0158) J Osteen.

Hold Still. unabr. ed. Nina LaCour. (Running Time: 8 hrs.). (ENG.). (gr. 7 up). 2009. audio compact disk 29.95 (978-0-14-314504-2(5), PengAudBks) Penguin Grp USA.

Hold the Anchovies. (Paws & Tales Ser.: Vol. 16). (J). 2001. 3.99 (978-1-57972-416-0(7)); audio compact disk 5.99 (978-1-57972-417-7(5)) Insight Living.

Hold the Dream. unabr. ed. Barbara Taylor Bradford. Read by Lindsay Sandison. 22 cass. (Running Time: 27 hrs. 30 min.). (Emma Harte Ser.: No. 2). (J). 2004. 117.25 (978-1-85695-995-7(3), 950903) Pub: ISIS Lrg Prnt GBR. Dist(s): Ulverscroft US
Now eighty years old, Emma Harte is ready to hand over the reins of the vast business empire she created. To her favorite grandchild, Paul McGill Failey, Emma bequeaths her mighty retailing empire with these heartfelt words: "I charge you to hold my dream". A towering international success, this is the powerfully moving tale of one woman's determination to 'hold the dream' which was entrusted to her, & in so doing find the happiness & passion which is her legacy.

Hold Tight. Harlan Coben. Read by Scott Brick. (Playaway Adult Fiction Ser.). (ENG.). 2009. 75.00 (978-1-60775-535-7(1)) Find a World.

Hold Tight. abr. ed. Harlan Coben. Read by Scott Brick. (Running Time: 6 hrs.). 2009. audio compact disk 14.99 (978-1-4233-2755-4(1), 9781423327554, BCD Value Price) Brilliance Audio.

Hold Tight. unabr. ed. Harlan Coben. Read by Scott Brick. (Running Time: 12 hrs.). 2008. 24.95 (978-1-4233-2752-3(7), 9781423327523, BAD); 39.25 (978-1-4233-2753-0(5), 9781423327530, BADLE); audio compact disk 38.95 (978-1-4233-2748-6(9), 9781423327486, Bril Audio CD Unabri); audio compact disk 24.95 (978-1-4233-2750-9(0), 9781423327509, Brilliance MP3); audio compact disk 102.25 (978-1-4233-2749-3(7), 9781423327493, BriAudCD Unabrid); audio compact disk 39.25 (978-1-4233-2751-6(9), 9781423327516, Brlnc Audio MP3 Lib) Brilliance Audio.

Hold Tight the Thread. Jane Kirkpatrick & Barbara Rosenblat. 8 CDs. 2004. audio compact disk 34.99 (978-1-58926-659-9(5)) Oasis Audio.

Hold Your Horses: Genesis 17:1-27. Ed Young. 1994. 4.95 (978-0-7417-2031-3(0), 1031) Win Walk.

Holdin' On. Perf. by Blind Boys of Alabama Staff. 1 cass. 10.98 (978-1-57908-236-9(X), 1311); audio compact disk 15.98 CD. (978-1-57908-235-2(1)) Platinm Enter.

Holding Back: Restraint, Rarely & Safely. rev. ed. Bernard Allen. Illus. by Barbara Maines. 1998. 74.95 (978-1-873942-91-8(5)) Pub: P Chapman GBR. Dist(s): SAGE

Holding Hands at 35,000 Feet. Perf. by Denison Marrs. 1 CD. 1999. audio compact disk 16.98 (978-1-57908-480-6(X)) Platinm Enter.

Holding Hands with You: Exploring the First Fifty Lessons of the Course. Tara Singh. 25 cass. 1992. 175.00 set. (1A900) Life Action Pr.
Tara Singh's best sharings on the first 50 lessons of the workbook in A Course in Miracles. Introduces the listener to key steps that will enable him/her to make his own discoveries about the lessons.

Holding Heaven. unabr. ed. Jerry B. Jenkins. Narrated by Jerry B. Jenkins. (ENG.). 2005. 8.39 (978-1-60814-236-1(1)); audio compact disk 11.99 (978-1-59859-078-4(2)) Oasis Audio.

Holding On see Philip Levine

Holding on to Hope. Nancy Guthrie. 2004. audio compact disk 14.99 (978-1-58926-048-1(1)) Oasis Audio.

Holding on to Hope: A Pathway Through Suffering to the Heart of God. abr. ed. Nancy Guthrie. Read by Nancy Guthrie. 1 cass. (Running Time: 1 hr.). 2002. 11.99 (978-1-58926-047-4(3), T09B-0320) Oasis Audio.

Holding on to Your Dreams. Speeches. Joel Osteen. 8 audio cass. (J). 2001. 32.00 (978-1-931877-05-3(X)) J Osteen.

Holding on to Your Dreams. Speeches. Joel Osteen. 4 CDs. (J). 2002. audio compact disk 32.00 (978-1-931877-22-0(X), JCS001) J Osteen.

Holding One Another: Being Separate Together. Andre Papineau. 1 cass. (Running Time: 1 hr.). 2001. 8.95 (A6591) St Anthony Mess Pr.
In the process of maturing, each person has two yearnings: one is to be separate and distinct; the other is to be part of a whole. Papineau shows how to balance these essential human needs.

Holding Possibility As Probability/Heaven on Earth. Marianne Williamson. Read by Marianne Williamson. 1 cass. (Running Time: 90 mins.). (Lectures on a Course in Miracles). 1999. 10.00 (978-1-56170-230-5(7), M733) Hay House.

Holding the Dream. abr. ed. Nora Roberts. Read by Sandra Burr. (Running Time: 3 hrs.). (Dream Trilogy: Bk. 2). 2009. audio compact disk 14.99 (978-1-4233-7905-8(5), 9781423379058, BCD Value Price) Brilliance Audio.

Holding the Dream. unabr. ed. Nora Roberts. Read by Sandra Burr. (Running Time: 12 hrs.). (Dream Trilogy: Bk. 2). 2008. 39.25 (978-1-4233-7889-1(X), 9781423378891, BADLE); 39.25 (978-1-4233-7887-7(3), 9781423378877, Brlnc Audio MP3 Lib); 24.95 (978-1-4233-7888-4(1), 9781423378884, BAD); 24.95 (978-1-4233-7886-0(5), 9781423378860, Brilliance MP3); audio compact disk 102.25 (978-1-4233-7885-3(7), 9781423378853, BriAudCD Unabrid); audio compact disk 34.95 (978-1-4233-7884-6(9), 9781423378846, Bril Audio CD Unabri) Brilliance Audio.

Holding the Line: Women in the Great Arizona Mine Strike of 1983. unabr. ed. Barbara Kingsolver. Narrated by Suzanne Toren. 7 cass. (Running Time: 10 hrs.). 1996. 62.00 (978-0-7887-3951-4(4), 96081E7) Recorded Bks.
When Barbara Kingsolver began covering the 1983 mine strike in Clifton, Arizona, she expected to find it run by men. Instead she discovered scores of women holding the picket lines, being beaten, arrested & tear-gassed.

Holding the Zero. unabr. ed. Gerald Seymour. Read by Sean Barrett. 10 cass. (Running Time: 15 hrs.). (Isis Ser.). (J). 2001. 84.95 (978-0-7531-0862-8(3), 000403); audio compact disk 104.95 (978-0-7531-0890-1(9), 108909) Pub: ISIS Lrg Prnt GBR. Dist(s): Ulverscroft US
Gus Peake should have stayed at home, but an old family debt draws him to the remote wastes of Northern Iraq & to a forgotten war between Kurdish guerrillas & Saddam Hussein's military strength.

Hole in My Life. Jack Gantos. 3 cass. (Running Time: 4 hrs. 20 mins.). (YA). (gr. 7 up). 2003. 30.00 (978-0-8072-1645-3(3), Listening Lib) Pub: Random Audio Pubg. Dist(s): Random

Hole in My Stocking. Rhonda Johnson. 1 disc. (J). 2005. audio compact disk 9.95 (978-0-9763635-5-2(0)) Beyond the Stars.

Hole in One. Catherine Aird. Read by Bruce Montague. 4 cass. 39.95 (978-0-7927-3776-6(8), CSL 854); audio compact disk 59.95 (978-0-7927-3777-3(6), SLD 854) AudioGO.

***Hole in Our Gospel: What Does God Expect of Us? The Answer That Changed My Life & Might Just Change the World.** unabr. ed. Richard Stearns. Read by Tommy Creswell. (Running Time: 10 hrs. 30 mins. 0 sec.). (ENG.). 2009. audio compact disk 24.98 (978-1-59644-027-2(9)) christianaud.

Hole in Texas: A Novel. unabr. ed. Herman Wouk. Read by Jonathan Davis. (ENG.). 2005. 14.98 (978-1-59483-322-9(2)) Pub: Hachet Audio. Dist(s): HachBkGrp

Hole in the Dike. 2004. bk. 24.95 (978-0-7882-0569-9(2)); 8.95 (978-1-56008-922-3(9)); cass. & flmstrp 30.00 (978-0-89719-626-0(0)) Weston Woods.

Hole in the Sky. Phyllis U. Hiller. 1 cass. 1979. pap. bk. 10.95 (978-1-884877-06-3(0)) Creat Mats Lib.

Hole in the Top of the World. unabr. ed. Fay Weldon. Perf. by Barbara Bain et al. 1 cass. (Running Time: 1 hr. 28 min.). 1995. 19.95 (978-1-58081-086-9(1)) L A Theatre.
Walter Matthau plays a renowned & much married scientist, presently working in Antarctica with his latest mistress. Complicatiions arise when one of his former wives comes knocking on his igloo door. Witty, provocative, & very funny!.

Hole in the Wall. unabr. ed. Arthur Morrison. 5 cass. 1996. 49.95 (978-1-86015-431-7(X)) Pub: UlverLrgPrint GBR. Dist(s): Ulverscroft US
Young Stephen Kemp is taken to live with his grandfather after the death of his mother. Nat Kemp is determined to keep his grandson away from the seamier side of the Docklands but Stephen has a natural inquistiveness that will not be quelled.

Hole Is to Dig. 2004. cass. & flmstrp 30.00 (978-1-56008-683-3(1)) Weston Woods.

Hole Is to Dig. (J). 2004. bk. 24.95 (978-0-7882-0551-4(X)); pap. bk. 14.95 (978-0-7882-0616-0(8)); 8.95 (978-1-56008-923-0(7)) Weston Woods.

Hole Is to Dig. Ruth Krauss. Illus. by Maurice Sendak. 14 vols. (Running Time: 8 mins.). 1990. pap. bk. 39.95 (978-1-59519-044-4(9)); 9.95 (978-1-59112-060-5(8)); audio compact disk 12.95 (978-1-59519-042-0(2)) Live Oak Media.

Hole Is to Dig. Ruth Krauss. Read by Linda Terheyden. Illus. by Maurice Sendak. Interview with Maurice Sendak. 14 vols. (Running Time: 8 mins.). 1990. pap. bk. & tchr. ed. 37.95 Reading Chest. (978-0-87499-175-8(7)) Live Oak Media.

Hole Is to Dig. Ruth Krauss. Read by Linda Terheyden. Illus. by Maurice Sendak. Interview with Maurice Sendak. 11 vols. (Running Time: 8 mins.). (J). (gr. k-3). 1990. pap. bk. 25.95 (978-0-87499-174-1(9)); pap. bk. 16.95 (978-0-87499-173-4(0)) Live Oak Media.

Holes. Louis Sachar. Read by Kerry Beyer. 3 cass. (Running Time: 4 hrs. 30 mins.). (J). 2000. 24.00 (978-0-7366-9104-8(9)) Books on Tape.
With his luck, Stanley Yelnats isn't surprised when a miscarriage of justice sends him to a harsh juvenile detention center. While the warden claims that hard labor digging holes builds character, it becomes clear that she is using Stanley to hunt for a fortune, buried by a Wild West outlaw.

Holes. unabr. ed. Louis Sachar. Read by Kerry Beyer. 3 cass. (J). (gr. 1-8). 1999. 23.98 (LL 0143, Chivers Child Audio) AudioGO.

Holes. unabr. ed. Louis Sachar. Read by Kerry Beyer. 3 cass. (YA). 1999. 23.98 (FS9-43384) Highsmith.

Holes. unabr. ed. Louis Sachar. Read by Kerry Beyer. 3 vols. (Running Time: 4 hrs. 30 mins.). (J). (gr. 5-9). 2004. pap. bk. 36.00 (978-0-8072-8072-0(0), Listening Lib); audio compact disk 32.30 (978-0-8072-8611-1(7), S YA 994 CD, Listening Lib) Pub: Random Audio Pubg. Dist(s): NetLibrary CO

Holes. unabr. ed. Louis Sachar. Read by Kerry Beyer. (Running Time: 16620 sec.). (ENG.). (J). (gr. 4-7). 2006. audio compact disk 19.95 (978-0-7393-3176-7(0), Listening Lib) Pub: Random Audio Pubg. Dist(s): Random

Holes. unabr. ed. Louis Sachar. Narrated by Kerry Beyer. 3 cass. (Running Time: 3 hrs.). (J). pap. bk. 29.00 (LL1034AC) Weston Woods.

Holford Will Case see Martin Hewitt, Investigator

Holford Will Case. unabr. ed. Arthur Morrison. Read by Walter Covell. 1 cass. (Running Time: 52 min.). Dramatization. 1981. 7.95 (S-14) Jimcin Record.
Which is the real will? Detective Martin Hewitt, Sherlock Holmes greatest rival, tries to find out.

Holiday Action Songs. 2 cass. (J). 16.95 set. (KIM 3080C) Kimbo Educ.

Holiday Caroling. 1 cass. 1998. 31.98 (978-1-56826-872-9(6)) Rhino Enter.

Holiday Celebration. Perf. by Peter, Paul and Mary. 1 cass. (J). 9.98 (457); audio compact disk 17.98 (D457) MFLP CA.
The three original folk bards performing Christmas songs & carols live, with full orchestra & choir. Songs include: "The Cherry Tree Carol," "A Soalin," "Children Go Where I Send Thee," "Light One Candle" & many more.

Holiday Cheer. Paul R. Scheele. Read by Paul R. Scheele. 1 cass. (Running Time: 16 min.). (Paraliminal Tapes Ser.). 1989. 14.95 (978-0-925480-10-1(X)) Learn Strategies.
Brings joy, love & peace into listeners' life during holidays.

Holiday Classics. 1 CD. (Running Time: 30 min.). (J). 2001. audio compact disk 12.98 (978-1-892309-41-9(6)) Pub: Baby Einstn. Dist(s): Penton Overseas

Holiday Classics. 1 cass., 1 CD. 15.98 (978-1-57908-379-3(X), 1543) Platinm Enter.

Holiday Classics. unabr. ed. Radio Spirits Publishing Staff. 2006. audio compact disk 39.98 (978-1-57019-786-4(5)) Radio Spirits.

Holiday Collection. abr. ed. Read by Julie Harris. Ed. by HarperCollins Publishers Ltd. Staff. 1 CD. (Running Time: 1 hr. 30 mins.). 2002. audio compact disk 6.99 (978-0-06-051999-5(1)) HarperCollins Pubs.

Holiday Concert. 1997. audio compact disk 12.95 (978-0-7692-1650-8(1), Warner Bro) Alfred Pub.

Holiday for Murder see Hercule Poirot's Christmas: A Holiday Mystery

Holiday Fun: Activity Fun Pack. Sally A. Bonkrude. Ed. by Steve Bondrude & Karla Lange. Illus. by Terri Bahn. 1 cass. Dramatization. (J). (ps-3). 1988. bk. 21.95 (978-0-924829-05-5(2)); 6.95 (978-0-924829-13-0(3)) Musical Imag.
Songs about holidays such as Halloween, Thanksgiving, Christmas, Easter, Valentine's Day & St. Patrick's Day.

Holiday Guitar. Cathy Ellis. Perf. by René González & Donn Legge. Illus. by Patricia Moya. Interview with Patricia Moya. 1 cass. (Complete Guide for the Guitar Ser.: Vol. 2). (YA). (gr. 6-12). 1997. bk. & wbk. ed. 25.95 (978-1-879542-26-6(9), EFM HG2) Ellis Family Mus.
Supplement to the series features 18 graded (easy to advanced) performance pieces for guitar ensemble &/or classroom for Christmas & Hannukah, plus traditional holiday pieces.

Holiday Help for Foster Children: A Basic Guide to Help Foster Children During the Holidays. Karen Jean Matsko Hood. 2006. 29.95 (978-1-59434-319-3(5)) Whsprng Pine.

Holiday Hits for Solo Singers: Contemporary Arrangements of 11 Popular Holiday Songs. Andy Beck. (For Solo Singers Ser.). (ENG.). 2009. audio compact disk 15.95 (978-0-7390-5866-4(5)) Alfred Pub.

Holiday Humor: 8 Holiday Laughs. Created by Radio Spirits. (Running Time: 10800 sec.). 2004. audio compact disk 9.98 (978-1-57019-773-4(3)) Radio Spirits.

Holiday in Death. abr. ed. J. D. Robb, pseud. Read by Susan Ericksen. 4 cass. (Running Time: 6 hrs.). (In Death Ser.:). 2001. 44.25 (978-1-58788-440-5(2), 1587884402, Lib Edit) Brilliance Audio.
#7 in the Bestselling Series When Computer Technology Brings Lovers Together, Dating Can Be a Deadly Game. . . No one likes to be alone during the holidays. For New York's most posh dating service, Personally Yours, it is the season to bring lonely hearts together. But Lt. Eve Dallas, on the trail of a ritualistic serial killer, has made a disturbing discovery: all of the victims have been traced to Personally Yours. Eve soon enters an elite world of people searching for their one true love - and one killer searching for his next victim. From Nora Roberts writing as J.D. Robb.

Holiday in Death. abr. ed. J. D. Robb, pseud. Read by Susan Ericksen. (Running Time: 21600 sec.). (In Death Ser.). 2007. audio compact disk 14.99 (978-1-4233-1417-2(4), 9781423314172, BCD Value Price) Brilliance Audio.

Holiday in Death. unabr. ed. J. D. Robb, pseud. Read by Susan Ericksen. (Running Time: 9 hrs.). (In Death Ser.). 2006. 39.25 (978-1-4233-0104-2(8), 9781423301042, BADLE); 24.95 (978-1-4233-0103-5(X), 9781423301035, BAD); audio compact disk 39.25 (978-1-4233-0102-8(1), 9781423301028, Brlnc Audio MP3 Lib); audio compact disk 92.25 (978-1-4233-1415-8(8), 9781423314158, BriAudCD Unabrid); audio compact disk 36.95 (978-1-4233-1414-1(X), 9781423314141, Bril Audio CD Unabri) Brilliance Audio.

Holiday in Death. unabr. ed. J. D. Robb, pseud. Read by Susan Ericksen. 1. (Running Time: 32400 sec.). (In Death Ser.). 2006. audio compact disk 24.95 (978-1-4233-0101-1(3), 9781423301011, Brilliance MP3) Brilliance Audio.

Holiday in Death. unabr. ed. J. D. Robb, pseud. Read by Susan Ericksen. (Running Time: 32400 sec.). (In Death Ser.). 2007. 82.25 (978-1-4233-3719-5(0), 9781423337195, BrilAudUnabridg) Brilliance Audio.

Holiday in Israel. Fred Berk & Lucy Venable. (C). 1977. pap. bk. 15.00 (978-0-685-08560-8(0)) Dance Notation.

Holiday Inn. 1947. (DD-5085) Natl Recrd Co.

Holiday Jazz Chants. Carolyn Graham. (Jazz Chants Ser.). 1999. 24.50 (978-0-19-434928-4(4)) OUP.

Holiday Jazz Chants. Carolyn Graham. (Jazz Chants Ser.). 1999. audio compact disk 24.50 (978-0-19-435249-9(8)) OUP.

Holiday Magic. 1 cass. (Running Time: 1 hr.). (J). 2001. pap. bk. 11.95 (EA 649C); audio compact disk 14.95 (EA 649CD) Kimbo Educ.
Original & traditional songs with vocals by Hap, Baby's Carol, Merry Hula, The Angel Band, Merry Christmas Santa, Rudolph, Feliz Navidad, Chanukkah & more. Includes guide.

Holiday Magic. Perf. by Hap Palmer. 1 cass. (Running Time: 1 hr.). (J). 2001. 9.95 (HP 108); audio compact disk 14.95 (HP 108 CD) Hap-Pal Music.
Easy to learn activity songs for pre-school & primary grade learners which tap children's natural desire to move, sing & make-believe. The whole child is engaged in developing movement skills, enriching language, experiencing basic math & science concepts & stimulating imaginative powers. Each song is repeated in an instrumental version. Complete guide with lyrics & activities included.

Holiday Memory see Dylan Thomas Reading

***Holiday Messages 2009.** Charles R. Swindoll. 2009. audio compact disk 24.00 (978-1-57972-867-0(7)) Insight Living.

Holiday Piggyback Songs: New Songs Sung to Childhood Favorites. 1 cass. (Running Time: 1 hr.). (J). 2001. pap. bk. 10.95 (KIM 9151C); pap. bk. 14.95 (KIM 9151CD) Kimbo Educ.
Original songs about the holidays have been created & set to famous tunes such as Bingo, Twinkle Twinkle & The Farmer in the Dell. These easy-to-sing songs are a springboard for natural learning. Includes Easter, Thanksgiving, Hanukkah, Christmas, Kwanzaa, Chinese New Year, Martin Luther King Day, Cinco de Mayo, Passover, Independence Day, Columbus Day, Halloween, Lincoln's Birthday & more. Includes song guide.

Holiday Song Search. Sally K. Albrecht et al. 1 CD. (Running Time: 1 hr. 30 mins.). (ENG.). 2001. audio compact disk 14.95 (978-0-7390-1491-2(9), 20090) Alfred Pub.

Holiday Song Search: Soundtrax. Sally K. Albrecht et al. 1 CD. (Running Time: 1 hr. 30 mins.). (ENG.). 2001. audio compact disk 59.95 (978-0-7390-1490-5(0), 20089) Alfred Pub.

Holiday Songs & Rhythms. Perf. by Hap Palmer. 1 LP. (J). pupil's gde. ed. 11.95 (EA 538); 11.95 (EA 538C) Kimbo Educ.
We Wish You a Merry Christmas - Hanukkah - Things I'm Thankful For - Easter Time Is Here Again & more.

Holiday Songs for All Occasions. Perf. by Jill Gallina. 1 cass . (Running Time: 1 hr.). (J). 2001. pap. bk. 10.95 (KIM 0805C); pap. bk. 11.95 (KIM 0805); pap. bk. 14.95 (KIM 0805CD) Kimbo Educ.
Holidays are more fun with these original tunes by Jill Gallina. Dances, games & more included with songs for Christmas, Hanukkah, Columbus Day, Flag Day, Easter, Halloween, Martin Luther King & St. Patrick's Day, plus Happy Birthday. Includes guide.

Holiday Stories: Audio Book: Christmas Bazaar, Daniel Is coming home, & the Nativity, Vol. 1.1. ed. Rochelle O'Neal Thorpe. Composed by Rochelle O'Neal Thorpe. Based on a book by Wiggles Press. (ENG.). (YA). 2009. pap. bk. 9.95 (978-0-9823906-3-4(7)) Wiggles Pr.

Holiday Times. Ella Jenkins. 1 CD. (Running Time: 1 hr.). (J). 2001. audio compact disk 15.00 (FC 45041CD) Kimbo Educ.

Holiday Times. Perf. by Ella Jenkins. 1 cass. (Running Time: 33 min.). (J). (gr. k-5). 1996. (0-9307-450410-9307-45041-2-3); audio compact disk (0-9307-45041-2-3) Smithsonian Folkways.
Twenty-six songs, poems & stories related to winter holidays. Jenkins & friends sing & play ukulele, harmonica, guitar, pipe organ, flute & percussion.

Holiday to Remember (Medley) A Multi-Traditional Choral Celebration - ShowTrax. Arranged by Mac Huff & John Jacobson. 1 CD. (Running Time: 30 mins.). 2000. audio compact disk 59.95 (08742313) H Leonard.
This sparkling choral show is a snap to put together. With 8 flexible sections, it's wonderfully adaptable for everything from holiday concerts to caroling to singing for the local Rotary Club. Includes: "Happy Holidays"; "A Holiday to Remember"; "Once Upon a Wintertime"; "Let It Snow! Let it Snow! Let It Snow"; "A Marshmallow World"; "Frosty, the Snow Man"; "White Christmas"; "Happy Kwanzaa"; "We Wish You a Merry Christmas"; "Feliz Navidad"; "Happy Hannukkah, My Friend"; "Rockin Around the Christmas Tree"; "Rudolph, the Red-Nosed Reindeer"; "Santa Bring Back My Baby to Me"; "I Saw Mommy Kissing Santa Claus"; "Christmas Chopsticks"; "Jingle Bells"; "Jingle Bell Rock"; "Away in a Manger" & "Do You Hear What I Hear?".

Holiday with Violence. unabr. ed. Ellis Peters, pseud. Read by Eva Haddon. 7 cass. (Running Time: 10 hrs. 30 min.). 1994. 61.95 (978-1-85695-714-4(4), 940410) Pub: ISIS Audio GBR. Dist(s): Ulverscroft US
It should have been a wonderful holiday for the four young people traveling to Venice, so it was a shock to find, on arriving in Turin, that their elderly traveling companion has been the victim of robbery with violence. They continue on their way only to find that trouble is following them. They have inadvertently walked off with crucial evidence of a more serious crime & someone desperately wants to retrieve it.

Holiday with Violence. unabr. ed. Ellis Peters, pseud. Read by Eva Haddon. 10 CDs. (Running Time: 10 hrs. 30 mins.). (Isis Ser.). (J). 2000. audio compact disk 89.95 (978-0-7531-0698-3(1), 106981) Pub: ISIS Lrg Prnt GBR. Dist(s): Ulverscroft US

Holidays. 10.00 (RJ124) Esstee Audios.

Holidays: Menu Cookbook, Music by the San Francisco String Quartet. Sharon O'Connor. (Sharon O'Connor's Menus & Music Ser.). 1989. bk. 24.95 (978-1-883914-05-9(1)) Menus & Music.

Holidays & Special Times. 1998. 14.99 (978-1-60689-177-3(4)) Pub: Youngheart Mus. Dist(s): Creat Teach Pr

Holidays & Special Times. Contrib. by Flo Gibson. 1 CD. (J). audio compact disk 14.95 (YM9CD) Kimbo Educ.

Holidays & Special Times. Contrib. by Flo Gibson. 1 cass . (Running Time: 1 hr.). (J). 2001. pap. bk. 10.95 (YM9C); pap. bk. 14.95 (YM9) Kimbo Educ.
Greg & Steve highlight many favorite holidays with Peter Cottontail, Jingle Bell Rock, Halloween on Parade, Happy Thanksgiving to All, Love Is..., Songs for Birthdays & more. Includes guide.

Holidays & Special Times. Perf. by Greg Scelsa. Music by Steve Millang. 1 cass. (J). 1990. 10.98 (YM009-CN); lp 12.98 (YM009-R); audio compact disk 13.98 CD. (YM009-CD) Youngheart Mus.
Songs include: "If You Feel Like Rockin'"; "Halloween on Parade"; "The Party Line"; "Jingle Bell Rock"; "Music Makes the World Go 'Round"; "Somebody's Birthday"; "This Land Is Your Land"; "Peter Cottontail"; "Love Is..."; "A Man Named King"; "Happy Thanksgiving to All" & "Goodbye & Farewell.".

Holidays on Ice. David Sedaris. 2002. 17.00 (978-1-57042-744-2(5)) Hachet Audio.
Sedaris skewers the absurd conventions and contrivances of the holiday season, to hilarious effect. Special guest Ann Magnuson performs "Merry Christmas to our Friends and Family," and Amy Sedaris also peppers the stories with comical characters.

Holidays on Ice. abr. ed. David Sedaris. Read by David Sedaris. Read by Amy Sedaris & Ann Magnuson. 3 CDs. (Running Time: 3 hrs.). (ENG.). 2001. audio compact disk 24.98 (978-1-58621-222-3(2)) Pub: Hachet Audio. Dist(s): HachBkGrp

Holidays on Ice. abr. ed. David Sedaris. (Running Time: 2 hrs.). (ENG.). 2006. 14.98 (978-1-59483-733-3(3)) Pub: Hachet Audio. Dist(s): HachBkGrp

Holidays on Ice. unabr. ed. David Sedaris. Read by David Sedaris. Read by Ann Magnuson & Amy Sedaris. (Running Time: 4 hrs.). (ENG.). 2008. 19.98 (978-1-60024-488-9(2)); audio compact disk 26.98 (978-1-60024-487-2(4)) Pub: Hachet Audio. Dist(s): HachBkGrp

Holidays on Ice. unabr. ed. David Sedaris. Read by David Sedaris. Read by Ann Magnuson & Amy Sedaris. (Running Time: 4 hrs.). (ENG.). 2009. 29.98 (978-1-60024-942-6(6)) Pub: Hachet Audio. Dist(s): HachBkGrp

Holier-Than-Thou People: Luke 18:9-14. Ed Young. 1993. 4.95 (978-0-7417-1961-4(4), 961) Win Walk.

Holiness. unabr. ed. Henry Blackaby. Read by Mel Foster. (Running Time: 2 hrs.). 2006. 39.25 (978-1-4233-0336-7(9), 9781423303367, BADLE); 24.95 (978-1-4233-0335-0(0), 9781423303350, BAD); 39.25 (978-1-4233-0334-3(2), 9781423303343, Brlnc Audio MP3 Lib) Brilliance Audio.
"If there is anything that characterizes God's people in America today, it is the loss of the fear of God," states Henry Blackaby. When you do not fear God, he contends, you will not fear sin. The troubling result of this issue is that many Christians fail to recognize that they have sinned against God. The lack of holiness within the Church has reached epidemic levels. "True revival can only come," notes Blackaby, "when the people of God return to a healthy, holy fear of Him." God, in His holiness, is grieved by our lack of it. In his worthy book, Blackaby urges believers to look inward, to see sin from God's perspective, and to live the standard that He has set up in Scripture. He writes, "The salvation of the nation has little do with Washington or Hollywood - it has to do with the people of God!".

Holiness. unabr. ed. Henry T. Blackaby. Read by Mel Foster. (Running Time: 2 hrs.). 2003. 17.95 (978-1-59355-289-3(0), 1593552890); 44.25 (978-1-59355-290-9(4), 1593552904, BAudLibEd); audio compact disk 19.95 (978-1-59355-291-6(2), 1593552912, BACD); audio compact disk 62.25 (978-1-59355-292-3(0), 1593552920, BACDLib Ed) Brilliance Audio.

Holiness: God's Plan for Fullness of Life. unabr. ed. Henry T. Blackaby. Read by Mel Foster. (Running Time: 7200 sec.). 2006. audio compact disk 24.95 (978-1-4233-0333-6(4), 9781423303336, Brilliance MP3) Brilliance Audio.

Holiness: Life in His Presence. Speeches. Creflo A. Dollar. 4 cass. (Running Time: 5 hrs.). 2003. 20.00 (978-1-59089-790-4(0)); audio compact disk 28.00 (978-1-59089-791-1(9)) Creflo Dollar.

***Holiness: Day by Day: Transformational Thoughts for Your Spiritual Journey.** unabr. ed. Jerry Bridges. Narrated by Arthur Morey. (ENG.). 2009. 16.98 (978-1-59644-840-7(7), Hovel Audio); audio compact disk 26.98 (978-1-59644-839-1(3), Hovel Audio) christianaud.

Holiness of God. unabr. ed. Read by Grover Gardner. 6 CDs. (Running Time: 6 hrs. 30 mins. 0 sec.). (ENG.). 2006. audio compact disk 24.98 (978-1-59644-413-3(4), Hovel Audio) christianaud.

***Holiness of God.** unabr. ed. R. C. Sproul. Narrated by Grover Gardner. (ENG.). 2006. 14.98 (978-1-59644-414-0(2), Hovel Audio) christianaud.

Holiness of God: Logos Sept. 14, 1997. Ben Young. 1997. 4.95 (978-0-7417-6047-0(9), B0047) Win Walk.

Holiness on God: Isaiah 6:3. Ed Young. 1990. 4.95 (978-0-7417-1830-3(8), 830) Win Walk.

Holiness the Jesus Way. Derek Prince. 1 cass. 1988. 5.95 (I-4246) Derek Prince.
The New Testament way to holiness in Jesus: not effort, but Union; not struggling, but yielding; not works, but faith.

Holiness Truth & the Presence of God. J. C. Ryle. 1 cass. 1991. 15.00 (978-951-24-0035-5(9)) Mrngstar Pubns.
Inspirational.

Holiness vs. Legalism. Jack Deere. 1 cass. (Running Time: 90 mins.). (Intimacy with God & the End-Time Church Ser.: Vol. 5). 2000. 5.00 (JD09-005) Morning NC.
Oneness with the Father is essential for every believer in these last days & the teaching in this six-tape series will impart a heartfelt hunger for intimate fellowship with Him.

Holistic Accent. 1 cass. (Care Cassettes Ser.: Vol. 1, No. 6). 1974. 10.80 Assn Prof Chaplains.

Holistic Approach & Its Shadow: The Healing of Psychophysiological Disorders. August Cwik. Read by August Cwik. 2 cass. (Running Time: 2 hrs. 15 min.). 1991. 18.95 set. (978-0-7822-0349-3(3), 471) C G Jung IL.
This workshop focuses on several paths to the psychological "healing" of disorders of the body as imaged in two fairy tales, " The Story of Hoc Lee & the Dwarfs" & "Godfather Death".

Holistic Approach to Cancer. Ralph Alan Dale. Read by Ralph Alan Dale. 1 cass. (Running Time: 45 min.). 1977. 9.00 (7) Dialectic Pubng.
The main ways to treat & to prevent cancer.

Holistic Approach to Cancer Treatment. unabr. ed. David Simon & Deepak Chopra. Read by David Simon & Deepak Chopra. 1 cass. (Running Time: 1 hr.). 2000. 10.95 Hay House.

Holistic Astrology: Esoteric Approach. Joan Kellogg. 1 cass. 8.95 (190) Am Fed Astrologers.
Understanding crisis points as spiritual opportunities.

Holistic Astrology at Work. Patricia Hardin. 1 cass. 1992. 8.95 (1040) Am Fed Astrologers.

Holistic Counseling. Patricia Hardin. 1 cass. 8.95 (616) Am Fed Astrologers.
An AFA Convention workshop tape.

Holistic Health Care & the Church. 1 cass. (Care Cassettes Ser.: Vol. 11, No. 1). 1984. 10.80 Assn Prof Chaplains.

Holistic Health Habits for Menopausal Women. unabr. ed. Mercedes Leidlich. Read by Mercedes Leidlich. 1 cass. (Running Time: 1 hr.). 1992. 10.95 in Norelco box. (978-1-882174-11-9(9), MLL-012) UFD Pub.
This tape explains in detail preventive measures that can be taken by a menopausal woman to stave off the two most serious complications of post-menopause - heart disease & osteoporosis. Topics covered are symptoms of menopause & post-menopause & preventive health measures including diet, exercise, & psychological well-being.

Holistic Hypnoanalysis. 1995. (978-1-932163-29-2(8)) Infinity Inst.

Holistic Hypnoanalysis Course. 10 CDs. 2003. audio compact disk (978-1-932163-45-2(X)) Infinity Inst.

Holistic Pathways to Health. Ralph Alan Dale. Read by Ralph Alan Dale. 1 cass. (Running Time: 90 min.). 1977. 9.00 (3) Dialectic Pubng.
The main ways to prevent illness.

Holistic Vision of Life & Health. Yeshi Donden. 7 cass. 63.00 (OC11W) Sound Horizons AV.

Holla: the Best of Trin-I-Tee 5:7. Contrib. by Trin-I-Tee 5 7. Prod. by Percy Bady et al. 2007. audio compact disk 11.99 (978-5-557-66405-9(X)) GospoCen.

Holland Suggestions: A Novel. John Dunning. Narrated by Jack Garrett. 7 CDs. (Running Time: 8 hrs. 15 mins.). audio compact disk 69.00 (978-1-4025-2081-5(6)) Recorded Bks.

Holland Suggestions: A Novel. unabr. ed. John Dunning. Narrated by Jack Garrett. 6 cass. (Running Time: 8 hrs. 15 mins.). 2001. 58.00 (978-0-7887-5450-0(5)) Recorded Bks.
When contractor Jim Ryan receives an anonymous package, in it he finds a photograph of a mountain cave that may hold the key to a missing chapter in his life.

Holler if You hear Me: Searching for Tupac Shakur. Michael Eric Dyson. Narrated by J. D. Jackson. 5 cass. (Running Time: 7 hrs. 30 mins.). 45.00 (978-1-4025-1237-7(6)) Recorded Bks.

Hollow. Nora Roberts. Read by Marie Caliendo. (Sign of Seven Trilogy: Bk. 2). 2009. 99.99 (978-1-60812-690-3(0)) Find a World.

Hollow. abr. ed. Nora Roberts. Read by Marie Caliendo. (Running Time: 6 hrs.). (Sign of Seven Trilogy: Bk. 2). 2008. audio compact disk 14.99 (978-1-4233-3782-9(4), 9781423337829, BCD Value Price) Brilliance Audio.

Hollow. unabr. ed. Agatha Christie. Read by Hugh Fraser. 5 cass. (Running Time: 7 hrs. 12 mins.). 2004. 27.95 (978-1-57270-405-3(5)) Pub: Audio Partners. Dist(s): PerseuPGW
Hercule Poirot arrives at The Hollow for a weekend luncheon just in time to see Gerda Christow standing, revolver in hand, over the body of her husband. It seems obvious that she has killed her wayward spouse, but Poirot doesn't believe things are that simple. What does Christow's death have to do with his current and former lovers, both of whom are nearby? What secrets are the weekend guests hiding in this case of love, deceit, mystery, and death?.

Hollow. unabr. ed. Agatha Christie. Narrated by Hugh Fraser. 6 CDs. (Running Time: 9 hrs.). (Mystery Masters Ser.). (ENG.). 2004. audio compact disk 29.95 (978-1-57270-406-0(3)) Pub: AudioGO. Dist(s): Perseus Dist

Hollow. unabr. ed. Agatha Christie. 1 cass. (Running Time: 90 min.). 2002. (978-0-00-713968-2(3)) Zondervan.

Hollow. unabr. ed. Nora Roberts. Read by Marie Caliendo. (Running Time: 11 hrs.). (Sign of Seven Trilogy: Bk. 2). 2008. 39.25 (978-1-4233-3780-5(8), 9781423337805, BADLE); 24.95 (978-1-4233-3779-9(4), 9781423337799, BAD); audio compact disk 39.25 (978-1-4233-3778-2(6), 9781423337782, Brlnc Audio MP3 Lib); audio compact disk 97.25 (978-1-4233-3776-8(X), 9781423337768, BriAudCD Unabrid); audio compact disk 24.95 (978-1-4233-3777-5(8), 9781423337775, Brilliance MP3); audio compact disk 36.95 (978-1-4233-3775-1(1), 9781423337751, Bril Audio CD Unabri) Brilliance Audio.

***Hollow.** unabr. ed. Jessica Verday. (Running Time: 17 hrs. 30 mins.). (Hollow Trilogy). 2010. 29.95 (978-1-4417-5199-7(8)); 72.95 (978-1-4417-5195-9(5)); audio compact disk 34.95 (978-1-4417-5198-0(X)); audio compact disk 105.00 (978-1-4417-5196-6(3)) Blckstn Audio.

Hollow Core. Lesley Horton & Maggie Mash. 2008. 76.95 (978-1-84652-211-6(0)); audio compact disk 99.95 (978-1-84652-212-3(9)) Pub: Magna Story GBR. Dist(s): Ulverscroft US

Hollow Hills. unabr. ed. Mary Stewart. Read by Stephen Thorne. 12 cass. (Running Time: 18 hrs.). (Merlin Ser.: Bk. 2). 2000. 79.95 (978-0-7451-4052-0(1), CAB 749) Pub: Chivers Audio Bks GBR. Dist(s): AudioGO
Tells the entrancing story of King Arthur's boyhood. From his birth to the accession of the throne, Merlin's guardianship of the young Arthur is brilliantly portrayed, as are the strife and violence of the turbulent times in which Arthur comes into maturity.

Hollow Kingdom. unabr. ed. 6 cass. (Running Time: 8 hrs. 30 min.). (J). 2003. 58.00 (978-1-4025-6941-8(6)) Recorded Bks.
In 19th-century England, Kate and her sister Emily return to the family estate after their father dies. There, under the guardianship of a distant uncle, they live in a small lodge with two great-aunts. One evening while out late and unable to find their way home, they encounter a nest of goblins. Clare Dunkle unites the human realm and the underworld of the goblin in a fascinating and exciting tale.

Hollow Men. unabr. ed. Charles J. Sykes. Read by Michael Wells. 8 cass. (Running Time: 11 hrs. 30 mins.). 1991. 56.95 (978-0-7861-0248-8(9), 1217) Blckstn Audio.
Documents the politicization & intellectual impoverishment of American higher education.

Hollow Night. Cynthia Harrod-Eagles. Read by Terry Wale. 4 cass. (Running Time: 5 hrs.). (Soundings Ser.). (J). 2004. 44.95 (978-1-84283-660-6(9)) Pub: ISIS Lrg Prnt GBR. Dist(s): Ulverscroft US

Hollowpoint. unabr. ed. Rob Reuland. Read by David Colacci. 5 cass. (Running Time: 7 hrs.). 2001. 27.95 (978-1-58788-466-5(6), 1587884666, BAU); 61.25 (978-1-58788-467-2(4), 1587884674, Unabridge Lib Edns) Brilliance Audio.
There was a time when Assistant District Attorney Andrew Giobberti pursued his job with vigor and a certain glee. He sent hundreds of perps upstate and commanded the respect of the tough Brooklyn cops whose investigations he steered. Now he mostly thinks about his next drink and the girl he can persuade to share it with him. A hand has reached into his chest and removed something that made the whole machine run. She was five years old, and her name was Opal. Over the course of one impossibly hot August, Gio's life comes apart. It's been a year since his daughter died, but the loss carves away at him still. A case much like others crosses his desk: young girl, dead from a gunshot wound, crackhead mother, very guilty looking boyfriend. Something in this ordinary if tawdry case uncovers a vast well of grief and rage in him, and it's unclear who will be the target of his urge to avenge a pointless death. His steely associate, Stacey - with whom he shares his bed but nothing more - watches with alarm as he lurches toward an act that could prove to be destruction or redemption. He's badly in need of one of them.

Hollowpoint. unabr. ed. Rob Reuland. Read by David Colacci. (Running Time: 7 hrs.). 2004. 39.25 (978-1-59335-356-8(1), 1593353561, Brlnc Audio MP3 Lib) Brilliance Audio.

Hollowpoint. unabr. ed. Rob Reuland. Read by David Colacci. (Running Time: 7 hrs.). 2004. 39.25 (978-1-59710-369-5(1), 1597103691, BADLE); 24.95 (978-1-59710-368-8(3), 1597103683, BAD) Brilliance Audio.

Hollowpoint. unabr. ed. Rob Reuland. Read by David Colacci. (Running Time: 7 hrs.). 2004. 24.95 (978-1-59335-028-4(7), 1593350287) Soulmate Audio Bks.

Holly. unabr. ed. Jude Deveraux. Read by Jennifer Wiltsie. 2004. 15.95 (978-0-7435-4833-5(7)) Pub: S&S Audio. Dist(s): S and S Inc

Holly. unabr. ed. Jude Deveraux. Read by Jennifer Wiltsie. (Running Time: 6 hrs. 0 mins. 0 sec.). (ENG.). 2006. audio compact disk 14.95 (978-0-7435-5522-7(8), S&S Encore) Pub: S&S Audio. Dist(s): S and S Inc

Holly Days Songs of Praise. Arranged by Kathie Hill. 1996. 8.00 (978-0-7673-3134-0(6)) LifeWay Christian.

Holly Days Songs of Praise. Kathie Hill. 1996. 75.00 (978-0-7673-3132-6(X)); 11.98 (978-0-7673-3131-9(1)); audio compact disk 85.00 (978-0-7673-3133-3(8)) LifeWay Christian.

Holly Daze. Mary Miche. 1 cass. (J). (ps-6). 1988. 11.50 (978-1-883505-05-9(4)) Song Trek Music.
Selection of 20 songs for Thanksgiving, Halloween, Chanukah, Christmas, New Years & Martin Luther King's birthday for children.

Holly Tree. (9501) Books on Tape.

Hollyhocks & Purple Clover. JoAnne Lower. Read by JoAnne Lower. Perf. by Martha Towey. 1 cass. (Running Time: 1 hr.). 1995. (978-1-888940-01-5(8)) J Lower Ent.
Personal stories of a young girl growing up on an Iowa farm.

Hollywood: A Novel of America in the 1920's. unabr. ed. Gore Vidal. Read by Grover Gardner. 13 cass. (Running Time: 16 hrs. 30 min.). (American Chronicles Ser.). 1993. 104.00 (978-0-7366-2529-6(1), 3281) Books on Tape.
As WW I approaches, the fledgling California movie industry draws Caroline Sanford in front of the cameras.

Hollywood & the Black Actor. unabr. ed. Interview with Heywood Hale Broun et al. 1 cass. (Heywood Hale Broun Ser.). 12.95 (40016) J Norton Pubs.
Talk with Don Bogle & Rosalind Cash: An Interpretive History of Blacks in American Films.

Hollywood & TV Classics. 1 cass. (Running Time: 60 min.). (At the Sound of the Beep Ser.). 1989. 6.95 (978-1-55569-337-4(7), 6160) Great Am Audio.
Features pre-recorded answering machine messages from Phantom of the Opera to Scarlett and Rhett.

Hollywood Audio Tour by Scott's L. A. Narrated by Scott Carter. Des. by Paul Whitney. (ENG.). 2007. audio compact disk 17.95 (978-0-9788500-1-2(7)) Scotts LA.

Hollywood Babes. unabr. ed. Prod. by Listening Library Staff. 3 cass. (Running Time: 4 hrs. 56 mins.). 2005. 30.00 (978-1-4000-9938-2(2), Listening Lib) Pub: Random Audio Pubg. Dist(s): Random

Hollywood Buzz. unabr. ed. Margit Liesche. (Running Time: 9 hrs. NaN mins.). 2009. 29.95 (978-1-4332-6548-8(6)); audio compact disk 80.00 (978-1-4332-6545-7(1)); audio compact disk 59.95 (978-1-4332-6544-0(3)) Blckstn Audio.

Hollywood Crows. unabr. ed. Joseph Wambaugh. Read by Christian Rummel. (Running Time: 11 hrs. 30 mins.). (ENG.). 2008. 19.98 (978-1-60024-154-3(9)) Pub: Hachet Audio. Dist(s): HachBkGrp

Hollywood Crows: A Novel. unabr. ed. Joseph Wambaugh. Read by Christian Rummel. (Running Time: 11 hrs. 30 mins.). (ENG.). 2009. audio compact disk 19.98 (978-1-60024-851-1(9)) Pub: Hachet Audio. Dist(s): HachBkGrp

Hollywood Distributor's Directory, Vol. 11. Hollywood Creative Directory Staff. 2000. pap. bk. (978-1-928936-02-2(4)) Hollywood Creat Dir.

Hollywood Divorces. abr. ed. Jackie Collins. 2004. 15.95 (978-0-7435-4834-2(5)) Pub: S&S Audio. Dist(s): S and S Inc

***Hollywood Hills: A Novel.** Joseph Wambaugh. Read by Christian Rummel. (Running Time: 11 hrs.). (ENG.). 2011. audio compact disk & audio compact disk 19.98 (978-1-60941-287-6(7)) Pub: Hachet Audio. Dist(s): HachBkGrp

***Hollywood Hills: A Novel.** unabr. ed. Joseph Wambaugh. Read by Christian Rummel. (Running Time: 11 hrs.). (ENG.). 2010. 26.98 (978-1-60788-975-5(7)); audio compact disk 34.98 (978-1-60788-974-8(9)) Pub: Hachet Audio. Dist(s): HachBkGrp

Hollywood Hulk Hogan: The Story of Terry Bollea. abr. ed. Hulk Hogan. Read by Hulk Hogan. 2006. 10.95 (978-0-7435-6218-8(6)) Pub: S&S Audio. Dist(s): S and S Inc

Hollywood in the Thirties. unabr. ed. Interview with Heywood Hale Broun & Joan Blondell. 1 cass. (Heywood Hale Broun Ser.). 12.95 (40002) J Norton Pubs.
Broun talks with the author of "Center Door Fancy".

Hollywood Kids. Jackie Collins. 2004. 13.95 (978-0-7435-4835-9(3)) Pub: S&S Audio. Dist(s): S and S Inc

Hollywood Kremlin. Short Stories. Bruce Sterling. Narrated by Gordon H. Williams. 1 CD. (Running Time: 80 mins.). (Great Science Fiction Stories Ser.). 2004. audio compact disk 10.99 (978-1-884612-40-4(7)) AudioText.

Hollywood Kremlin. unabr. ed. Bruce Sterling. Read by Gordon H. Williams. Ed. by Allan Kaster. 1 cass. (Running Time: 1 hr. 22 min.). (Great Science Fiction Stories Ser.). 1996. 10.99 (978-1-884612-11-4(3)) AudioText.
In this witty story, a smuggling operation in the Soviet province of Azerbaijan struggles to maintain itself amidst political turmoil. This is the first Leggy Starlitz story.

Hollywood Moon: A Novel. unabr. ed. Joseph Wambaugh. Read by Christian Rummel. (Running Time: 11 hrs. 30 mins.). (ENG.). 2009. 19.98 (978-1-60024-775-0(X)) Pub: Hachet Audio. Dist(s): HachBkGrp

***Hollywood Moon: A Novel.** unabr. ed. Joseph Wambaugh. Read by Christian Rummel. (Running Time: 12 hrs.). (ENG.). 2010. audio compact disk 19.98 (978-1-60788-640-2(5)) Pub: Hachet Audio. Dist(s): HachBkGrp

Hollywood Musicals. Friedman-Fairfax and Sony Music Staff. 1 CD. (CD Ser.). 1993. pap. bk. 15.98 (978-1-56799-039-3(8), Friedman-Fairfax) M Friedman Pub Grp Inc.

Hollywood Nocturnes. unabr. collector's ed. James Ellroy. Read by Michael Prichard. 8 cass. (Running Time: 8 hrs.). 1996. 64.00 (978-0-7366-3255-3(7), 3912) Books on Tape.
James Ellroy's bizarre tales hook us because of their unusual mix of brutality, noir realism & humor. "Hollywood Nocturnes" is quintessential Ellroy: bluesy, black & sizzling suspense.

Hollywood Station. unabr. ed. Joseph Wambaugh. Narrated by Adam Grupper. 10 CDs. (Running Time: 42720 sec.). 2006. audio compact disk 94.95 (978-0-7927-4521-1(3), SLD 1051); audio compact disk 59.95 (978-0-7927-4569-3(8), CMP 1051) AudioGO.

Hollywood Station. unabr. ed. Joseph Wambaugh. Read by Adam Grupper. (YA). 2007. 69.99 (978-1-59895-459-3(8)) Find a World.

Hollywood Station. unabr. ed. Joseph Wambaugh. Read by Adam Grupper. (Running Time: 11 hrs.). (ENG.). 2006. 14.98 (978-1-59483-803-3(8)) Pub: Hachet Audio. Dist(s): HachBkGrp

Hollywood Station. unabr. ed. Joseph Wambaugh. Read by Adam Grupper. (Running Time: 11 hrs.). (ENG.). 2008. audio compact disk 14.98 (978-1-60024-243-4(X)) Pub: Hachet Audio. Dist(s): HachBkGrp

Hollywood Station. unabr. ed. Joseph Wambaugh. Read by Adam Grupper. (Running Time: 11 hrs.). (ENG.). 2009. 19.98 (978-1-60788-287-9(6)) Pub: Hachet Audio. Dist(s): HachBkGrp

Hollywood Studios: House Style in the Golden Age of the Movies. unabr. ed. Ethan Mordden. Read by Barrett Whitener. 9 cass. (Running Time: 13 hrs.). 1997. bk. 62.95 (978-0-7861-1217-3(4), 1996) Blckstn Audio.
Hollywood in the years between 1929 &1948 was a town of moviemaking empires. The great studios were estates of talent. It was the Golden Age of the Movies & each studio made its contribution. But how did the studios, "growing up" in the same time & place, develop so differently? What combinations of talents & temperaments gave them their signature styles?.

***Hollywood Studios: House Style in the Golden Age of the Movies.** unabr. ed. Ethan Mordden. Read by Barrett Whitener. (Running Time: 12 hrs. 30 mins.). 2010. 29.95 (978-1-4417-0741-3(7)); audio compact disk 105.00 (978-1-4417-0738-3(7)) Blckstn Audio.

Hollywood the Hard Way: A Cowboy's Journey. unabr. ed. Patti Dickinson. Read by Rusty Nelson. 6 cass. (Running Time: 8 hrs.). 2001. 39.95 (978-1-55686-986-0(X)) Books in Motion.
After discharge from the Navy at the end of World War II, 20-year-old Jerry Van Meter accepts the challenge from the wager of his pioneer grandfather and movie cowboy Jimmy Wakely that no one could travel by horseback to California in 50 days. The result is a true life adventure of the actual trip taken on an Osage pony in 1945.

Hollywood Tough. unabr. ed. Stephen J. Cannell. Read by Paul Michael. 6 cass. (Running Time: 10 hrs.). (Shane Scully Ser.: No. 3). 2003. 54.95 (978-0-7927-2830-6(0), Chivers Sound Lib) AudioGO.

Hollywood Tough. unabr. rev. ed. Stephen J. Cannell. 8 CDs. (Running Time: 10 hrs.). (Shane Scully Ser.: No. 3). (ENG.). 2003. audio compact disk 42.00 (978-1-55927-823-2(4)) Pub: Macmill Audio. Dist(s): Macmillan

Hollywood vs. America: Popular Culture & the War Against Traditional Values. unabr. ed. Michael Medved. Read by David Hilder. 10 cass. (Running Time: 14 hrs. 30 mins.). 1995. 69.95 (978-0-7861-0715-5(4), 1593) Blckstn Audio.
One of the nation's best known film critics examines how Hollywood has broken faith with its public, creating movies, television & popular music that exacerbate every serious social problem we face, from teenage pregnancies to violence in the streets. In hard-hitting chapters on "The Attack on Religion," "The Addiction to Violence," "Promoting Promiscuity," "The Infatuation with Foul Language" & other subjects, Medved outlines the underlying themes that turn up again & again in our popular culture.

Hollywood Wives - the New Generation. abr. ed. Jackie Collins. 2004. 15.95 (978-0-7435-4836-6(1)) Pub: S&S Audio. Dist(s): S and S Inc

Hollywood's Greatest Hits, Vol. 1. Perf. by Erich Kunzel & Cincinnati Pops Orchestra. 1 cass., 1 CD. 7.98 (TA 30168); audio compact disk 12.78 Jewel box. (TA 80168) NewSound.

Hollywood's Greatest Hits, Vol. 2. Perf. by Erich Kunzel & Cincinnati Pops Orchestra. 1 cass., 1 CD. 7.98 (TA 30319); audio compact disk 12.78 CD Jewel box. (TA 80319) NewSound.

Hollywood's Magical Island-Catalina. Prod. by Greg Reitman. 1 cass, 1 cd. (Running Time: 1 hr). 2005. audio compact disk 24.95 (978-0-9769566-2-4(4)) BLUE WTR.
HOLLYWOOD?S MAGICAL ISLAND-CATALINATHROUGH THE REMARKABLE EYE of first time film director, Greg Reitman, we get a first hand glimpse of The Magic Isle. While exploring historical, social, and environmental changes, the film captures the mystical splendors, natural beauty and romance of Santa Catalina Island. Using a mix of rare 16mm, archival film and old black and white stills, inter-cut with interviews of islanders, historians and celebrities; the viewer is taken on a journey during America?s golden era. It begins with the acquisition of the Santa Catalina Island Company in 1919 led by William Wrigley, Jr. He set a course for Catalina?s future in the world of art, sports, music and entertainment that was unmatched in US history even through present day. The film documents architectural achievements, many are first of a kind buildings and innovations that transformed Catalina from a simple island into a modern day state-of-the-art playground. The film highlights many of the individuals including stars of the Big Band Era, Marilyn Monroe, and the island?s role as Hollywood?s secret playground for the stars. The island even played a role in helping to elect a President. We witness the island?s tragedy and heartache ? deftly captured in the film with heartfelt interviews and a score that tugs at the emotions. Utilizing interviews with Jean-Michel Cousteau, heirs of the Wrigley family, residents and visitors of the island; we learn of William Wrigley, Jr?s dream of preserving the island?s natural beauty as well as providing a magical place for all to enjoy. The film concludes with Art Good Jazz Trax, Fender?s Catalina Island Blues Festival, and a visual kaleidoscope of modern day Catalina Island as an ecological paradise highlighting the revival of the island as a place of leisure and entertainment.

Holman Christian Standard Bible. David Payne. 48 cass. 2004. 99.97 (978-1-55819-946-0(2)) BH Pubng Grp.

Holman Christian Standard Bible. Read by David Payne. 2005. 24.99 (978-1-59859-002-9(2)); audio compact disk 45.99 (978-1-59859-001-2(4)) Oasis Audio.

Holmes on the Range. unabr. ed. Steve Hockensmith. Read by William Dufris. 8 CDs. (Running Time: 9 hrs. 30 mins. 0 sec.). (Holmes on the Range Ser.). (ENG.). 2006. audio compact disk 34.99 (978-1-4001-0225-9(1)); audio compact disk 69.99 (978-1-4001-3225-6(8)); audio compact disk 24.99 (978-1-4001-5225-4(9)) Pub: Tantor Media. Dist(s): IngramPubServ

Holmward Bound: An Evening with Bill Holm. Speeches. Read by Bill Holm. Music by Bill Holm. Prod. by Scott Beyers. 1 CD. (Running Time: 73 mins.). (Evening With Ser.: Vol. 1). 2001. audio compact disk 14.95 (978-0-9665212-2-1(6)) EssayAudio.

Holmward Bound: An Evening with Bill Holm. Speeches. Bill Holm. Read by Bill Holm. Prologue by Scott Beyers. 1 cass. (Running Time: 75 mins.). 2001. 11.95 (978-0-9665212-5-2(0), 5) EssayAudio.
*An evening captured live with author Bill Holm. Take Bill Holm's booming voice, wit, poetry and piano-playing home with you or along with you in the car. Come along and spend and evening traveling with Bill as he visits his favorite places, both real and imagined, with wonderful stories and live readings from his latest book "Eccentric Islands: Travels Real and Imaginary".Excerpt from track list:2. Your Mail Gets More Interesting3. Hallelujah at the Sioux Falls Airport4. We Travel To See Something Inside Us5. Madagascar, Politics, and A Good-Smelling God6. The President of Rocks, January 19977. Lutheran Singing in Madagascar8. Islands9. My Best Icelandic Teachers10 Icelandic Recycling on a Summer Night..... 13 A Nation of Tightwads * Spouting the Foam of Poetry * Ragtime Piano Medley.*

Holocarboxylase Synthetase Deficiency - A Bibliography & Dictionary for Physicians, Patients, & Genome Researchers. Compiled by Icon Group International, Inc. Staff. 2007. ring bd. 28.95 (978-0-497-11233-2(7)) Icon Grp.

Holocaust & Genocide. 2004. audio compact disk 525.00 (978-0-340-81418-5(7), HodderMurray) Pub: Hodder Edu GBR. Dist(s): Trans-Atl Phila

Holocaust Memorial Speech. Shirley Rose. 1 cass. 1993. 5.00 (978-0-9636347-2-6(0)) Rose Pub CA.
Speech on Holocaust delivered April 18, 1993.

Holonomic Brain Theory. Karl Pribram. 2 cass. 18.00 set. (A0277-88) Sound Photosyn.
The definitive word from the originator of the concept.

Holonomic Consciousness Paradigm. unabr. ed. Stanislav Grof & Christina Grof. 2 cass. (Running Time: 2 hrs. 49 min.). 1982. 18.00 (00804) Big Sur Tapes.

Holt Biology: Visualizing Life. Holt, Rinehart and Winston Staff. (ENG & SPA.). 1994. 115.80 (978-0-03-076419-6(X)) Holt McDoug.

Holt Chemistry, Set. 4th ed. Myers. 2004. audio compact disk 598.33 (978-0-03-038073-0(1)) Holt McDoug.

Holt Chemistry: Guided Reading Program. 4th ed. Holt, Rinehart and Winston Staff. 2003. audio compact disk 113.33 (978-0-03-068528-6(1)) Holt McDoug.

Holt Chemistry: Guided Reading Program. 4th ed. Holt, Rinehart and Winston Staff. (SPA.). 2004. audio compact disk 228.80 (978-0-03-068368-8(8)) Holt McDoug.

Holt Ciencias y Technologia: Earth: Guided Reading Program. Holt, Rinehart and Winston Staff. (SPA.). 2001. audio compact disk 247.13 (978-0-03-065349-0(5)) Holt McDoug.

Holt Ciencias y Technologia: Guided Reading Program: Texas Edition - Grade 6. 2nd ed. Holt, Rinehart and Winston Staff. 2001. audio compact disk 238.00 (978-0-03-065488-6(2)) Holt McDoug.

Holt Ciencias y Technologia: Guided Reading Program: Texas Edition - Grade 7. 2nd ed. Holt, Rinehart and Winston Staff. 2001. audio compact disk 238.00 (978-0-03-065489-3(0)) Holt McDoug.

Holt Ciencias y Technologia: Guided Reading Program: Texas Edition - Grade 8. 2nd ed. Holt, Rinehart and Winston Staff. 2001. audio compact disk 238.00 (978-0-03-065491-6(2)) Holt McDoug.

Holt Ciencias y Technologia: Life: Guided Reading Program. Holt, Rinehart and Winston Staff. (SPA.). 2001. audio compact disk 247.13 (978-0-03-065348-3(7)) Holt McDoug.

Holt Ciencias y Technologia: Physics: Guided Reading Program. Holt, Rinehart and Winston Staff. (SPA.). 2001. audio compact disk 247.13 (978-0-03-065351-3(7)) Holt McDoug.

Holt French 1: Bien Dit! Created by Rheinhart And Winston Holt. 2008. audio compact disk 67.95 (978-0-03-079714-9(4)) Holt McDoug.

Holt Literature & Language Arts: Interactive Reading Tutor: California Edition. 3rd ed. Holt, Rinehart and Winston Staff. 2002. audio compact disk 54.13 (978-0-03-067654-3(1)); audio compact disk 54.13 (978-0-03-067656-7(8)); audio compact disk 54.13 (978-0-03-067657-4(6)) Holt McDoug.

Holt Literature & Language Arts, Grade 10: Audio Library - California Edition. 3rd ed. Holt, Rinehart and Winston Staff. 2002. audio compact disk 137.33 (978-0-03-066167-9(6)) Holt McDoug.

Holt Literature & Language Arts, Grade 10: Interactive Reading Tutor: California Edition. 3rd ed. Holt, Rinehart and Winston Staff. 2002. audio compact disk 54.13 (978-0-03-067659-8(2)) Holt McDoug.

Holt Literature & Language Arts, Grade 10: Selections Library. 3rd ed. Holt, Rinehart and Winston Staff. (SPA.). 2002. audio compact disk 137.33 (978-0-03-067726-7(2)) Holt McDoug.

Holt Literature & Language Arts, Grade 11: Audio Library - California Edition. 3rd ed. Holt, Rinehart and Winston Staff. 2002. audio compact disk 137.33 (978-0-03-066168-6(4)) Holt McDoug.

Holt Literature & Language Arts, Grade 11: Interactive Reading Tutor: California Edition. 3rd ed. Holt, Rinehart and Winston Staff. 2002. audio compact disk 54.13 (978-0-03-067661-1(4)) Holt McDoug.

Holt Literature & Language Arts, Grade 11: Selections Library. 3rd ed. Holt, Rinehart and Winston Staff. (SPA.). 2002. audio compact disk 137.33 (978-0-03-067727-4(0)) Holt McDoug.

Holt Literature & Language Arts, Grade 12: Audio Library - California Edition. 3rd ed. Holt, Rinehart and Winston Staff. 2002. audio compact disk 137.33 (978-0-03-066169-3(2)) Holt McDoug.

Holt Literature & Language Arts, Grade 12: Selections Library. 3rd ed. Holt, Rinehart and Winston Staff. (SPA.). 2002. audio compact disk 137.33 (978-0-03-067728-1(9)) Holt McDoug.

Holt Literature & Language Arts, Grade 6: Audio Library - California Edition. 3rd ed. Holt, Rinehart and Winston Staff. 2002. audio compact disk 137.33 (978-0-03-066162-4(5)) Holt McDoug.

Holt Literature & Language Arts, Grade 6: Selections Library. 3rd ed. Holt, Rinehart and Winston Staff. (SPA.). 2002. audio compact disk 137.33 (978-0-03-067721-2(1)) Holt McDoug.

Holt Literature & Language Arts, Grade 7: Audio Library - California Edition. 3rd ed. Holt, Rheinhart and Winston Staff. 2002. audio compact disk 137.33 (978-0-03-066163-1(3)) Holt McDoug.

Holt Literature & Language Arts, Grade 7: Selections Library. 3rd ed. Holt, Rinehart and Winston Staff. (SPA.). 2002. audio compact disk 136.99 (978-0-03-067722-9(X)) Holt McDoug.

Holt Literature & Language Arts, Grade 8: Audio Library - California Edition. 3rd ed. Holt, Rinehart and Winston Staff. 2002. audio compact disk 137.33 (978-0-03-066164-8(1)) Holt McDoug.

Holt Literature & Language Arts, Grade 8: Selections Library. 3rd ed. Holt, Rinehart and Winston Staff. (SPA.). 2002. audio compact disk 137.33 (978-0-03-067723-6(8)) Holt McDoug.

Holt Literature & Language Arts, Grade 9: Audio Library - California Edition. 3rd ed. Holt, Rinehart and Winston Staff. 2002. audio compact disk 137.33 (978-0-03-066166-2(8)) Holt McDoug.

Holt Literature & Language Arts, Grade 9: Interactive Reading Tutor: California Edition. 3rd ed. Holt, Rinehart and Winston Staff. 2002. audio compact disk 54.13 (978-0-03-067658-1(4)) Holt McDoug.

Holt Literature & Language Arts, Grade 9: Selections Library. 3rd ed. Holt, Rinehart and Winston Staff. (SPA.). 2002. audio compact disk 137.33 (978-0-03-067724-3(6)) Holt McDoug.

Holt Literature & Language Arts 2: Audio CD Library: Summaries in Spanish - California Edition. 3rd ed. Holt, Rinehart and Winston Staff. 2002. audio compact disk 30.40 (978-0-03-067974-2(5)); audio compact disk 30.40 (978-0-03-067976-6(1)); audio compact disk 30.40 (978-0-03-067977-3(X)); audio compact disk 30.40 (978-0-03-067978-0(8)); audio compact disk 30.40 (978-0-03-067979-7(6)); audio compact disk 30.40 (978-0-03-067981-0(8)); audio compact disk 30.40 (978-0-03-067982-7(6)) Holt McDoug.

Holt Literature & Languge Arts, Grade 12: Interactive Reading Tutor: California Edition. 3rd ed. Holt, Rinehart and Winston Staff. 2002. audio compact disk 54.13 (978-0-03-067662-8(2)) Holt McDoug.

Holt-Oram Syndrome - A Bibliography & Dictionary for Physicians, Patients, & Genome Researchers. Compiled by Icon Group International, Inc. Staff. 2007. ring bd. 28.95 (978-0-497-11234-9(5)) Icon Grp.

Holt Science & Technology, Set. Holt, Rinehart and Winston Staff. 2004. audio compact disk 598.33 (978-0-03-038079-2(0)); audio compact disk 598.33 (978-0-03-038081-5(2)); audio compact disk 598.33 (978-0-03-038082-2(0)) Holt McDoug.

Holt Science & Technology, Set. 4th ed. Holt, Rinehart and Winston Staff. 2004. audio compact disk 598.33 (978-0-03-038069-3(3)); audio compact disk 598.33 (978-0-03-038071-6(5)); audio compact disk 598.33 (978-0-03-038072-3(3)) Holt McDoug.

Holt Science & Technology: Earth: Guide to Reading. Holt, Rinehart and Winston Staff. 2000. audio compact disk 244.86 (978-0-03-054396-8(7)) Holt McDoug.

Holt Science & Technology: Earth: Guided Reading Program. Holt, Rinehart and Winston Staff. 2001. audio compact disk 244.86 (978-0-03-065346-9(0)) Holt McDoug.

Holt Science & Technology: Earth: Guided Reading Program - California Edition. Holt, Rinehart and Winston Staff. 2000. audio compact disk 152.93 (978-0-03-055677-5(0)) Holt McDoug.

Holt Science & Technology: Guided Reading Audio CD Program. 5th ed. Holt, Rinehart and Winston Staff. 2004. audio compact disk 244.86 (978-0-03-030011-0(8)); audio compact disk 244.86 (978-0-03-030016-5(9)); audio compact disk 244.86 (978-0-03-030036-3(3)) Holt McDoug.

Holt Science & Technology: Guided Reading Audio CD Program. 5th ed. Holt, Rinehart and Winston Staff. (SPA.). 2004. audio compact disk 41.76 (978-0-03-030611-2(6)); audio compact disk 41.76 (978-0-03-030612-9(4)); audio compact disk 41.76 (978-0-03-030613-6(2)); audio compact disk 41.76 (978-0-03-030614-3(0)); audio compact disk 41.76 (978-0-03-030616-7(7)); audio compact disk 41.76 (978-0-03-030617-4(5)); audio compact disk 41.76 (978-0-03-030618-1(3)); audio compact disk 41.76 (978-0-03-030619-8(1)); audio compact disk 41.76 (978-0-03-030621-1(3)); audio compact disk 41.76 (978-0-03-030622-8(1)); audio compact disk 41.76 (978-0-03-030623-5(X)); audio compact disk 41.76 (978-0-03-030624-2(8)); audio compact disk 41.76 (978-0-03-030626-6(4)); audio compact disk 41.76 (978-0-03-030627-3(2)); audio compact disk 41.76 (978-0-03-030628-0(0)); audio compact disk 252.06 (978-0-03-030091-2(6)); audio compact disk 252.06 (978-0-03-030096-7(7)); audio compact disk 252.06 (978-0-03-030101-8(7)) Holt McDoug.

Holt Science & Technology: Guided Reading Audio CD Program - Short Course. 5th ed. Holt, Rinehart and Winston Staff. 2004. audio compact disk 44.33 (978-0-03-030536-8(5)); audio compact disk 44.33 (978-0-03-030537-5(3)); audio compact disk 44.33 (978-0-03-030541-2(1)); audio compact disk 44.33 (978-0-03-030546-7(2)); audio compact disk 44.33 (978-0-03-030551-1(9)); audio compact disk 44.33 (978-0-03-030561-0(6)); audio compact disk 44.33 (978-0-03-030564-1(0)); audio compact disk 44.33 (978-0-03-030566-5(7)); audio compact disk 44.33 (978-0-03-030567-2(5)); audio compact disk 44.33 (978-0-03-030571-9(3)) Holt McDoug.

Holt Science & Technology: Guided Reading Audio CD Program - Short Version. 5th ed. Holt, Rinehart and Winston Staff. 2004. audio compact disk 41.76 (978-0-03-030532-0(2)) Holt McDoug.

Holt Science & Technology: Guided Reading Audio CD Program - Short Version. 5th ed. Holt, Rinehart and Winston Staff. 2004. audio compact disk 41.76 (978-0-03-030534-4(9)); audio compact disk 41.76 (978-0-03-030576-4(4)) Holt McDoug.

Holt Science & Technology: Guided Reading Audio Program. 4th ed. Holt, Rinehart and Winston Staff. 2004. audio compact disk 228.80 (978-0-03-037104-2(X)); audio compact disk 228.80 (978-0-03-037106-6(6)); audio compact disk 228.80 (978-0-03-037107-3(4)) Holt McDoug.

Holt Science & Technology: Guided Reading Program. Holt, Rinehart and Winston Staff. (SPA.). 2001. audio compact disk 336.00 (978-0-03-054438-5(6)) Holt McDoug.

Holt Science & Technology: Guided Reading Program: California Edition. Holt, Rinehart and Winston Staff. (SPA.). 2000. audio compact disk 366.93 (978-0-03-055637-1(6)) Holt McDoug.

Holt Science & Technology: Guided Reading Program: Texas Edition - Grade 6. Holt, Rinehart and Winston Staff. 2001. audio compact disk 238.00 (978-0-03-064509-9(3)) Holt McDoug.

Holt Science & Technology: Guided Reading Program: Texas Edition - Grade 7. Holt, Rinehart and Winston Staff. 2001. audio compact disk 238.00 (978-0-03-064511-2(5)) Holt McDoug.

Holt Science & Technology: Guided Reading Program: Texas Edition - Grade 8. Holt, Rinehart and Winston Staff. 2001. audio compact disk 238.00 (978-0-03-064512-9(3)) Holt McDoug.

Holt Science & Technology: Guided Reading Short Version. 5th ed. Holt, Rinehart and Winston Staff. 2004. audio compact disk 41.76 (978-0-03-030533-7(0)) Holt McDoug.

Holt Science & Technology: Guided Reading Short Version. 5th ed. Holt, Rinehart and Winston Staff. 2004. audio compact disk 41.76 (978-0-03-030556-6(X)) Holt McDoug.

Holt Science & Technology: Life: Guide to Reading. Holt, Rinehart and Winston Staff. 2000. audio compact disk 244.86 (978-0-03-054377-7(0)) Holt McDoug.

Holt Science & Technology: Life: Guided Reading Program. Holt, Rinehart and Winston Staff. 2000. audio compact disk 244.86 (978-0-03-065344-5(4)) Holt McDoug.

Holt Science & Technology: Life: Guided Reading Program - California Edition. Holt, Rinehart and Winston Staff. 2000. audio compact disk 152.93 (978-0-03-055654-8(6)) Holt McDoug.

Holt Science & Technology: Physics: Guide to Reading. Holt, Rinehart and Winston Staff. 2000. audio compact disk 244.86 (978-0-03-054406-4(8)) Holt McDoug.

Holt Science & Technology: Physics: Guided Reading Program. Holt, Rinehart and Winston Staff. 2001. audio compact disk 244.86 (978-0-03-065347-6(9)) Holt McDoug.

Holt Science & Technology: Physics: Guided Reading Program - California Edition. Holt, Rinehart and Winston Staff. 2000. audio compact disk 152.93 (978-0-03-055712-5(7)) Holt McDoug.

Holt Science & Technology Course A-E: Guided Reading Program. 2nd ed. Holt, Rinehart and Winston Staff. 2001. audio compact disk 217.20 (978-0-03-064928-8(5)) Holt McDoug.

Holt Science & Technology Course F-J: Guided Reading Program. 2nd ed. Holt, Rinehart and Winston Staff. 2001. audio compact disk 217.20 (978-0-03-064943-1(9)) Holt McDoug.

Holt Science & Technology Course K-O: Guided Reading Program. 2nd ed. Holt, Rinehart and Winston Staff. 2001. audio compact disk 217.20 (978-0-03-064958-5(7)) Holt McDoug.

Holt Science & Technology Module I: Guided Reading Program. 2nd ed. Holt, Rinehart and Winston Staff. 2001. audio compact disk 43.46 (978-0-03-066196-9(X)) Holt McDoug.

Holt Science & Technology Module L: Guided Reading Program. 2nd ed. Holt, Rinehart and Winston Staff. 2001. audio compact disk 43.46 (978-0-03-066199-0(4)) Holt McDoug.

Holt Science & Technology Module D: Guided Reading Program. 2nd ed. Holt, Rinehart and Winston Staff. 2001. audio compact disk 43.46 (978-0-03-066189-1(7)) Holt McDoug.

Holt Science & Technology Module M: Guided Reading Program. 2nd ed. Holt, Rinehart and Winston Staff. 2001. audio compact disk 43.46 (978-0-03-066201-0(X)) Holt McDoug.

Holt Science & Technology Module A: Guided Reading Program. 2nd ed. Holt, Rinehart and Winston Staff. 2001. audio compact disk 43.46 (978-0-03-066186-0(2)) Holt McDoug.

Holt Science & Technology Module B: Guided Reading Program. 2nd ed. Holt, Rinehart and Winston Staff. 2001. audio compact disk 43.46 (978-0-03-066187-7(0)) Holt McDoug.

Holt Science & Technology Module E: Guided Reading Program. 2nd ed. Holt, Rinehart and Winston Staff. 2001. audio compact disk 43.46 (978-0-03-066191-4(9)) Holt McDoug.

Holt Science & Technology Module F: Guided Reading Program. 2nd ed. Holt, Rinehart and Winston Staff. 2001. audio compact disk 43.46 (978-0-03-066192-1(7)) Holt McDoug.

Holt Science & Technology Module G: Guided Reading Program. 2nd ed. Holt, Rinehart and Winston Staff. 2001. audio compact disk 43.46 (978-0-03-066193-8(5)) Holt McDoug.

Holt Science & Technology Module H: Guided Reading Program. 2nd ed. Holt, Rinehart and Winston Staff. 2001. audio compact disk 43.46 (978-0-03-066194-5(3)) Holt McDoug.

Holt Science & Technology Module J: Guided Reading Program. 2nd ed. Holt, Rinehart and Winston Staff. 2001. audio compact disk 43.46 (978-0-03-066197-6(8)) Holt McDoug.

Holt Science & Technology Module K: Guided Reading Program. 2nd ed. Holt, Rinehart and Winston Staff. 2001. audio compact disk 43.46 (978-0-03-066198-3(6)) Holt McDoug.

Holt Science & Technology Module N: Guided Reading Program. 2nd ed. Holt, Rinehart and Winston Staff. 2001. audio compact disk 43.46 (978-0-03-066202-7(8)) Holt McDoug.

Holt Science & Technology Module O: Guided Reading Program. 2nd ed. Holt, Rinehart and Winston Staff. 2001. audio compact disk 43.46 (978-0-03-066203-4(6)) Holt McDoug.

Holt Science & Technology Pt. I: Spanish Guided Reading. 3rd ed. Holt, Rinehart and Winston Staff. (SPA.). 2002. audio compact disk 43.46 (978-0-03-069566-7(X)) Holt McDoug.

Holt Science & Technology Pt. L: Spanish Guided Reading. 3rd ed. Holt, Rinehart and Winston Staff. (SPA.). 2002. audio compact disk 43.46 (978-0-03-069591-9(0)) Holt McDoug.

Holt Science & Technology Pt. C: Spanish Guided Reading. 3rd ed. Holt, Rinehart and Winston Staff. (SPA.). 2002. audio compact disk 43.46 (978-0-03-069518-6(X)) Holt McDoug.

Holt Science & Technology Pt. D: Spanish Guided Reading. 3rd ed. Holt, Rinehart and Winston Staff. (SPA.). 2002. audio compact disk 43.46 (978-0-03-069519-3(8)) Holt McDoug.

Holt Science & Technology Pt. M: Spanish Guided Reading. 3rd ed. Holt, Rinehart and Winston Staff. (SPA.). 2002. audio compact disk 43.46 (978-0-03-069592-6(9)) Holt McDoug.

Holt Science & Technology Pt. A: Spanish Guided Reading. 3rd ed. Holt, Rinehart and Winston Staff. (SPA.). 2002. audio compact disk 43.46 (978-0-03-069516-2(3)) Holt McDoug.

Holt Science & Technology Pt. B: Spanish Guided Reading. 3rd ed. Holt, Rinehart and Winston Staff. (SPA.). 2002. audio compact disk 43.46 (978-0-03-069517-9(1)) Holt McDoug.

Holt Science & Technology Pt. E: Spanish Guided Reading. 3rd ed. Holt, Rinehart and Winston Staff. (SPA.). 2002. audio compact disk 43.46 (978-0-03-069521-6(X)) Holt McDoug.

Holt Science & Technology Pt. F: Spanish Guided Reading. 3rd ed. Holt, Rinehart and Winston Staff. (SPA.). 2002. audio compact disk 43.46 (978-0-03-069522-3(8)) Holt McDoug.

Holt Science & Technology Pt. G: Spanish Guided Reading. 3rd ed. Holt, Rinehart and Winston Staff. (SPA.). 2002. audio compact disk 43.46 (978-0-03-069523-0(6)) Holt McDoug.

Holt Science & Technology Pt. H: Spanish Guided Reading. 3rd ed. Holt, Rinehart and Winston Staff. (SPA.). 2002. audio compact disk 43.46 (978-0-03-069564-3(3)) Holt McDoug.

Holt Science & Technology Pt. J: Spanish Guided Reading. 3rd ed. Holt, Rinehart and Winston Staff. (SPA.). 2002. audio compact disk 43.46 (978-0-03-069567-4(8)) Holt McDoug.

Holt Science & Technology Pt. K: Spanish Guided Reading. 3rd ed. Holt, Rinehart and Winston Staff. (SPA.). 2002. audio compact disk 43.46 (978-0-03-069568-1(6)) Holt McDoug.

Holt Science & Technology Pt. N: Spanish Guided Reading. 3rd ed. Holt, Rinehart and Winston Staff. 2002. audio compact disk 43.46 (978-0-03-069593-3(7)) Holt McDoug.

Holt Science & Technology Pt. O: Spanish Guided Reading. 3rd ed. Holt, Rinehart and Winston Staff. (SPA.). 2002. audio compact disk 43.46 (978-0-03-069594-0(5)) Holt McDoug.

Holt Science & Technology, Tennessee Edition: Guided Reading Audio CD Program. 3rd ed. Holt, Rinehart and Winston Staff. 2003. audio compact disk 228.80 (978-0-03-069104-1(4)); audio compact disk 228.80 (978-0-03-069128-7(1)); audio compact disk 228.80 (978-0-03-069157-7(5)) Holt McDoug.

Holt Student One Stop: Elements of Language, Introductory Course. Created by Holt Rinehart & Winston. (ENG.). 2008. audio compact disk 65.95 (978-0-03-094754-4(5)) Holt McDoug.

Holt Student One Stop: Modern Chemistry. Created by Holt Rinehart & Winston. 2009. audio compact disk 80.95 (978-0-03-036791-5(3)) Holt McDoug.

Holy Ambition CD Series. 2005. audio compact disk 34.95 (978-1-59834-002-0(6)) Walk Thru the Bible.

***Holy Available: Surrendering to the Transforming Presence of God Every Day of Your Life.** unabr. ed. Zondervan. (Running Time: 7 hrs. 51 mins. 10 sec.). (ENG.). 2010. 18.99 (978-0-310-87452-2(1)) Zondervan.

Holy Bible. 2003. audio compact disk 49.95 (978-1-58134-421-9(X)) CrosswayIL.

Holy Bible. Alexander Scourby. 12 cass. 2004. 21.99 (978-0-88368-829-8(8)) Whitaker Hse.

Holy Bible. unabr. ed. Crossway Books Staff. Narrated by Marquis Laughlin. 20 CDs. (Running Time: 21 hrs. 19 mins. 4 sec.). (Proven Wisdom Ser.). (ENG.). 2003. audio compact disk 39.99 (978-1-58926-362-8(6)) Oasis Audio.

Holy Bible. unabr. rev. ed. Narrated by Marquis Laughlin. (ENG.). 2005. 19.99 (978-1-60814-318-4(X)) Oasis Audio.

Holy Bible: King James Version - Deluxe. Read by Alexander Scourby. 48 cass. 79.99 (978-0-529-10266-9(8), WBC-153) Nelson.

Holy Bible: King James Version - Dramatized. 48 cass. 99.99 (978-0-529-07294-8(7), WBC-25) Nelson.

Holy Bible: King James Version - Dramatized. Narrated by Alexander Scourby. 48 cass. 99.99 (978-0-529-10267-6(6), WBC-154) Nelson.

Holy Bible: King James Version - Dramatized New Testament. 12 cass. 24.99 (978-0-529-07529-1(6)) Nelson.

Holy Bible: King James Version - New Testament. Narrated by Alexander Scourby. 12 cass. 1996. 24.99 (978-0-529-10453-3(9)) Nelson.

Holy Bible: New International Version - Dramatized. 48 cass. 109.99 (978-0-529-07293-1(9), WBC-9) Nelson.

Holy Bible: New International Version - Dramatized. Read by Stephen Johnston. 48 cass. 1996. 69.99 (978-0-529-10241-6(2), WBC-41) Nelson.

Holy Bible: New International Version - Dramatized New Testament. 12 cass. 24.99 (978-0-529-07528-4(8), WBC-40) Nelson.

Holy Bible: New Testament. 2003. 39.95 (978-1-58134-422-6(8)) CrosswayIL.

Holy Bible: New Testament. unabr. ed. Perf. by Alexander Scourby. 12 cass. (Running Time: 18 hrs.). 1991. 19.95 Incl. black nylon case with handle. (978-1-56563-142-7(0)) Hendrickson MA.
The world's best-loved translation of the Bible is brought to life in this powerful, word-for-word narration by renowned British dramatist Alexander Scourby. A convenient way to hear God's word at any time of the day. The nylon carrying case helps keep the cassettes protected and organized at home or on the go. And the limited lifetime warranty ensures years of listening pleasure.

Holy Bible: The New Testament. unabr. ed. Narrated by Peter Francis James et al. 22 CDs. (Running Time: 23 hrs.). 2004. audio compact disk 49.99 (978-1-4025-6979-1(3), 01342) Recorded Bks.
At long last, an unabridged contemporary version of The New Testament, approved by the American Bible Society, is available. This is the most authentic and accessible translation of the Bible available on audio. The end product of an impressive undertaking by the American Bible Society, this exquisite version features contemporary language that aids comprehension while enhancing the enjoyment of this all-time classic text. Included in this spectacular production are the Gospels of Matthew, Mark, Luke and John, the Acts, the Letters of Paul, General Letters, and the book of Revelation. Compelling performances by several of the world's finest narrators help make this luminous rendition of The Holy Bible an utter treasure.

Holy Bible: The New Testament. unabr. collector's ed. 18 cass. (Running Time: 23 hrs.). 2004. 59.99 (978-1-4025-9172-3(1), RH193) Recorded Bks.

Holy Bible, King James Version, Complete New Testament. Read by Alexander Scourby. (Running Time: 18 hrs.). 2005. 29.95 (978-1-933092-95-9(5), Audiofy Corp) Iofy Corp.

Holy Bible, King James Version, Complete Old Testament. Read by Alexander Scourby. (Running Time: 55 hrs.). 2005. 51.95 (978-1-933092-94-2(7), Audiofy Corp) Iofy Corp.

Holy Bible (KJV) Created by AWMI. (ENG.). 2005. 20.00 (978-1-59548-058-3(7)) A Wommack.

Holy Bible, KJV, Complete Old & New Testament. Read by Alexander Scourby. (Running Time: 74 hrs.). 2005. 74.95 (978-1-933092-96-6(3), Audiofy Corp) Iofy Corp.

Holy Bible on Cassette: The Complete New Testament King James Version. Read by Stephen Johnston. 11 cass. (Running Time: 16 hrs. 30 min.). 1997. 19.95 Set. (978-0-9659197-0-8(6)) Stephen Co.
Word for word reading of King James Version of the Bible (New Testament) with musical background.

Holy Bible on MP3. 2003. audio compact disk (978-1-883012-07-6(4)) Remnant Pubns.

Holy Bible on Tape. unabr. ed. Read by Alexander Scourby. 48 cass. 129.95 Set. (978-1-879010-05-5(4)) Vision Mktg.

Holy Body. 2003. audio compact disk (978-0-9748215-3-5(5)) Sensuous Myst.

Holy Books Rap 'N' Poster. 1 cass. pap. bk. 14.99 (978-1-55945-693-7(0)) Group Pub.

Holy Books Rap 'N' Poster. Interview with James Ward. 1 cass. 14.99 Incl. poster. Group Pub.

Holy Chariot. David A. Cooper. 6 cass. (Running Time: 9 hrs.). 1999. 59.95 Set. (83-0057) Explorations.
Rabbi Cooper teaches how to use the principles of the Holy Chariot, the precursor of Kabbalistic Study, in daily actions & thoughts. Twelve lessons to reach the realm where all of creation interlocks & unfolds in the present moment.

Holy Christ Is Born in Me Today. Kenneth Wapnick. 1 CD. (Running Time: 2 hrs. 41 mins. 45 secs.). 2007. 13.00 (978-1-59142-317-1(1), 3m47); audio compact disk 16.00 (978-1-59142-316-4(3), CD47) Foun Miracles.

Holy City. Meg Henderson. Narrated by Eileen McCallum. 8 cass. (Running Time: 11 hrs.). 72.00 (978-1-84197-275-6(4)) Recorded Bks.

***holy City.** unabr. ed. Patrick McCabe. Read by Humphrey Bower. (Running Time: 6 hrs.). 2010. audio compact disk 63.95 (978-1-74214-657-7(0), 9781742146577) Pub: Bolinda Pubng AUS. Dist(s): Bolinda Pub Inc

Holy Communion Preparation Prayers, Pt. 2. Perf. by Jane M. deVyver. 1 cass. (Running Time: 1 hrs.). (Treasury of Orthodox Christian Prayers Ser.: Vol. 1). 1993. 6.95 (978-1-881211-13-6(4)) Firebird Videos.
Side 1: Canon of Repentance & Canon of Preparation for Holy Communion. Side 2: Prayers in Preparation for Holy Communion & Thanksgiving After Communion.

Holy Cow. Sarah Macdonald. Read by Kate Hosking. (Running Time: 10 hrs. 30 mins.). 2009. 84.99 (978-1-74214-260-9(5), 9781742142609) Pub: Bolinda Pubng AUS. Dist(s): Bolinda Pub Inc

Holy Cow: An Indian Adventure. unabr. ed. Sarah Macdonald. Read by Kate Hosking. 7 cass. (Running Time: 10 hrs. 30 mins.). 2004. 56.00 (978-1-74093-160-1(2)); audio compact disk 87.95 (978-1-74093-506-7(3)) Pub: Bolinda Pubng AUS. Dist(s): Bolinda Pub Inc

Holy Culture. Contrib. by Cross Movement. 2004. 12.99 (978-5-559-97325-8(4)) BEC Recordings.

Holy Dating: Passion for Holiness Series. Ed Young. 2000. 4.95 (978-0-7417-6211-5(0), B0211) Win Walk.

Holy Diner: A Complete Introduction to Judaism, Set. 18 cass. (Running Time: 1 hr. per cass.). 95.00 (978-0-9676554-0-6(4)) A HaTorah.
Topics include: Judaism & Feminism; Creation; Origin of Man; After Life; Shabbos; Life Is for Pleasure; Prayer; Independence; Who is God?; Sex; The Exodus; Israel; Ahavas Israel; Suffering; Oral Law; Intellect in Judaism; God's Love & Patience; Misconceptions about Judaism.

***Holy Discontent.** unabr. ed. Bill Hybels. (Running Time: 3 hrs. 24 mins. 0 sec.). (ENG.). 2007. 12.99 (978-0-310-27736-1(1)) Zondervan.

Holy Discontent: Fueling the Fire That Ignites Personal Vision. unabr. ed. Bill Hybels. Read by Larry Black. (Running Time: 3 hrs. 24 mins. 0 sec.). (ENG.). 2007. audio compact disk 19.99 (978-0-310-27735-4(3)) Zondervan.

Holy Disorders. Edmund Crispin. 2008. 61.95 (978-0-7531-3055-1(6)); audio compact disk 79.95 (978-0-7531-3056-8(4)) Pub: ISIS Audio GBR. Dist(s): Ulverscroft US

Holy Eucharist. Perf. by John F. O'Connor. 1 cass. (Running Time: 47 min.). 7.00 (20068) Cath Treas.
Every Catholic should know & believe the dogma of the "Real Presence," the test of faith first presented by Christ to his apostles & followers.

Holy Eucharist, Foundation of Christian Family & Religious Family. Fr. Hardon. 1 cass. (National Meeting of the Institute, 1993 Ser.). 4.00 (93N4) IRL Chicago.

Holy Family: The Gleaming Brain. Ann Ree Colton & Jonathan Murro. 1 cass. 7.95 A R Colton Fnd.

Holy Father: Pope Benedict XVI: Pontiff for a New Era. unabr. ed. Greg Tobin. Read by John McDonough. 4 cass. (Running Time: 5 hrs. 15 mins.). 2006. 39.75 (978-1-4193-8288-8(8), 98310) Recorded Bks.
In Holy Father, celebrated papal commentator Greg Tobin surveys the extraordinary legacy of John Paul II and examines the new head of the Church, Pope Benedict XVI. Who is the German-born Joseph Ratzinger? Tobin sheds light on every chapter of the new Pope's life, from his childhood to his seminary education and through the career that led to the papacy. Tobin also provides an insider's look at the conclave that captivated the entire world while electing Ratzinger as the new Pope. And finally, Tobin discusses the significant issues facing today's Church and predicts how Benedict XVI is likely to react.

Holy Fire: Kissing the Dust from Jesus Feet. Ann Ree Colton & Jonathan Murro. 1 cass. 7.95 A R Colton Fnd.

***Holy Fools.** unabr. ed. Joanne Harris. Read by Suzanne Bertish. (ENG.). 2004. (978-0-06-081492-2(6), Harper Audio); (978-0-06-078453-9(9), Harper Audio) HarperCollins Pubs.

Holy Gampopa. Vajracarya. 1 cass. 1970. 10.00 Vajradhatu.
Discusses the relationship of Milarepa's realization to work with his disciples, & the story of Gampopa's development.

Holy Gampora. Read by Chogyam Trungpa. 1 cass. 1970. 10.00 (A042) Vajradhatu.
One talk. The relationship of Milarepa's realization to work with his disciples, & the story of Gampopa's development.

Holy Garment. 2003. 10.00 (978-1-58602-159-7(1)); audio compact disk 20.00 (978-1-58602-160-3(5)) E L Long.

Holy God. Contrib. by Brian Doerksen. Prod. by Philip Janz. 2007. audio compact disk 29.98 (978-5-557-93548-7(7)) Integrity Music.

Holy God, Holy People: Take Time to Be Holy, the World Rushes On. Hugh D. Morgan. 2007. pap. bk. 14.99 (978-1-85049-222-1(0)) Bryntirion Pr GBR.

Holy Grail - Excerpts. unabr. ed. Excerpts. Thomas Malory. Narrated by John Franklyn-Robbins. 3 cass. (Running Time: 4 hrs. 30 mins.). 1999. 26.00 (978-1-55690-722-7(2), 92408E7) Recorded Bks.
Selections from Mallory's great epic Le Morte d'Arthur, recounting some of the legends of the Knights of the Round Table & their search for the Holy Grail.

Holy Ground. Contrib. by Various Artists. (Songs 4 Worship Ser.). 2008. audio compact disk 19.98 (978-5-557-43332-7(5)) Integrity Music.

Holy Ground. Created by Word Music. (Worship Tracks (Word Tracks) Ser.). 2006. audio compact disk 8.98 (978-5-558-26900-0(6), Word Music) Word Enter.

***Holy Ground: Walking with Jesus as a Former Catholic.** unabr. ed. Chris A. Castaldo. (Running Time: 6 hrs. 38 mins. 0 sec.). (ENG.). 2009. 12.99 (978-0-310-77344-3(X)) Zondervan.

Holy Hip Hop: Taking the Gospel to the Street. Contrib. by Christopher Martin. 2004. audio compact disk 9.98 (978-5-559-61747-3(4)) Pt of Grace Ent.

Holy Holy Holy. Perf. by Tom Wurth. 2006. audio compact disk 9.95 (978-1-59987-424-1(5)) Braun Media.

Holy Hour. Music by Michael John Poirier. 1998. 11.00 (978-1-58459-107-8(2)) Wrld Lib Pubns.

Holy Hour. Perf. by Michael John Poirier. 1998. audio compact disk 16.00 (978-1-58459-091-0(2)) Wrld Lib Pubns.

Holy Hunger. Perf. by Jeannie Tenney. 1 cass. (Running Time: 90 mins.). 1999. 10.99 (978-0-7684-0196-7(8)); audio compact disk 15.99 (978-0-7684-0195-0(X)) Destiny Image Pubs.

Holy Is the Lamb. Perf. by Oleta Adams. 1 cass. 1999. 7.98 (978-0-7601-2755-1(7)) Brentwood Music.

Holy Land, Then & Now. Gary V. Whetstone. Adapted by June Austin. (Theology Ser.: Vol. TH 206). 1996. 80.00 (978-1-58866-134-0(2)) Gary Whet Pub.

Holy Love & the Body/Finding Your Truth. Marianne Williamson. Read by Marianne Williamson. 1 cass. (Running Time: 90 mins.). (Lectures on a Course in Miracles). 1999. 10.00 (978-1-56170-231-2(5), M734) Hay House.

Holy Man. unabr. ed. Susan Trott & Ben Mikaelsen. Narrated by Lynne Thigpen & Ed Sala. 3 cass. (Running Time: 3 hrs. 15 mins.). (gr. 4 up). 1996. 26.00 (978-0-7887-0560-1(1), 94739E7) Recorded Bks.
On a distant mountain top lives an aging wise man named Joe. Each chapter tells the story of one person in the long line of pilgrims waiting to see him.

Holy Man's Journey. unabr. ed. Susan Trott. Narrated by Lynne Thigpen. 3 cass. (Running Time: 3 hrs. 45 mins.). 1999. 26.00 (978-0-7887-1305-7(1), 95143E7) Recorded Bks.
Rejoin Joe, the Holy Man, on the enlightened path where you left him. Knowing that Anna will succeed him, he embarks on an important journey that may be his last.

Holy Moses. Box Toy Box Productions Staff. 2000. (978-1-887729-83-3(6)) Toy Box Prods.

Holy Night. 2004. 8.95 (978-1-56008-924-7(5)); cass. & flmstrp 30.00 (978-1-56008-684-0(X)) Weston Woods.

Holy of Holies Tape Pack. 2002. (978-1-931713-37-5(5)) Word For Today.

Holy One. Contrib. by Rush of Fools. (Mastertrax Ser.). 2008. audio compact disk 9.98 (978-5-557-36652-6(0)) Pt of Grace Ent.

Holy One. Sharon E. Swanepoel. 2008. audio compact disk 14.99 (978-0-9772647-3-5(4)) GGMI.

Holy One: A Cross Between. 1 cass. 1999. 7.98 (978-0-7601-2939-5(8)) Provident Music.

Holy Power: Some Ways to Use It. Richard Rohr. Read by Richard Rohr. 1 cass. (Running Time: 59 min.). 1992. 9.95 (978-7-900783-69-1(5), AA2560) Credence Commun.
How Holy Power is used in a healthy way.

Holy Quran. Read by Mustafa Ozcan Gunesdogdu. 1 CD. (Running Time: 1 hr.). 1995. audio compact disk 9.95 (978-1-931445-00-9(1)) A S R Media.
Starts with adhan recitation & also a few short suras from Holy Qur'an.

Holy Quran, Pt. 30. Muhammed S. Haque. (Running Time: 90 min.). 1997. pap. bk. 7.75; 3.00 (978-0-933057-06-7(7)) Namuk Intl Inc.
Includes each Surah & page number.

Holy Quran Pt. 3: Juz'u 'Amma. 5th rev. ed. Tr. by Al-Hajj Muhammad Shamsul Haque. 1 cass. (Running Time: 90 min.). (ARA & ENG., 1985. per. 4.75 (978-0-933057-02-9(4)) Namuk Intl Inc.
With modern English translations, word meanings & salat (prayer) guidance. Arabic recited by famous Qaaris.

Holy Quran Pts. 1-3, Set: "Surah Al-Baqarah" with Word Meaning & Tajwid Rules & Examples. Al-Hajj M. Haque. Tr. by Al-Hajj M. Haque from ARA. Tr. by Al-Hajj Muhammad Shamsul Haque from ARA. Anno. by Al-Hajj Muhammad Shamsul Haque. 2 cass. (Running Time: 3 hr.). 1993. pap. bk. 6.00 (978-0-933057-33-3(4)) Namuk Intl Inc.
Includes Appendices: A: Al-Muqatta'at - The Luminous Abbreviated Letters of the Qur'aan; B: Word Meanings with their component parts; & C: Tajweed Rules in Summary with Examples. Recitations by famous Qaari.

Holy Quran with Modern English Translations & Anno Haque. Muhammad S. Haque. 1 cass. (J). 1998. bk. 25.00 (978-0-933057-05-0(9), WOQHO002T) Namuk Intl Inc.

Holy Relationship. Charles Muir & Caroline Muir. Read by Charles Muir & Caroline Muir. 1 cass. (Running Time: 1 hr. 40 min.). (Tantra: The Art of Conscious Loving Ser.). 1989. 15.00 (978-1-882570-01-0(4)) Hl Goddess.
Charles & Caroline Muir reveal the secrets of this age-old science which will enable your sexual sharing to heal, energize, awaken consciousness & unfold the depths of Love & Joy. In this double length cassette you will learn the exciting concepts of Tantra that keep a couple in harmony, forming a team that serves, empowers, uplifts & heals. A wealth of information, humorously presented. Keep your relationship growing & flourishing throughout the years.

Holy Road. Michael Blake. 7 cass. (Running Time: 12 hrs.). 2004. 29.99 (978-0-7887-8960-1(0), 00444) Recorded Bks.

Holy Road. unabr. ed. Michael Blake. Narrated by Bruce Boxleitner. 10 CDs. (Running Time: 12 hrs.). 2002. audio compact disk 111.00 (978-1-4025-2928-3(7)) Recorded Bks.
Eleven years have passed since former Lt. John Dunbar became the Comanche warrior Dances With Wolves. Now married to Stands With A Fist, he and his three children live peacefully in the village of Ten Bears. But when a group of white rangers attacks, Stands With A Fist and her infant daughter are carried off. Along with Kicking Bird and Wind In His Hair, Dances With Wolves decides to fight back. He knows that he alone can move among the white people to rescue his wife and child.

Holy Road: A Novel. abr. ed. Michael Blake. Read by Bruce Boxleitner. 6 cass. (Running Time: 9 hrs.). 2004. 29.95 (978-1-59007-066-6(6)); audio compact disk 39.95 (978-1-59007-067-3(4)) Pub: New Millenn Enter. Dist(s): PerseuPGW

Holy Road: A Novel. unabr. ed. Michael Blake. Read by Bruce Boxleitner. 8 cass. (Running Time: 12 hrs.). 2001. 74.00 (978-0-7887-9435-3(3), 96775) Recorded Bks.
Eleven years have passed since former Lt. John Dunbar became a Comanche warrior. Now married to Stands With a Fist, he and his three children live peacefully in the village of Ten Bears. But when a group of white rangers attacks the village, unspeakable violence erupts.

Holy Rosary. 1 cass. (Running Time: 60 min.). 1988. 10.00 (978-1-55794-102-2(5), T53) Eternal Wrd TV.

Holy Rule. Thomas Merton. 1 cass. (Running Time: 60 min.). (Humility Ser.). 4.50 (AA2105) Credence Commun.
Discussions on the beginning of humility & growth of that trait.

***Holy Rule of St. Benedict.** unabr. ed. Saint Benedict of Nursia. Narrated by John Polhamus. (ENG.). 2005. 10.98 (978-1-59644-063-0(5), Hovel Audio) christianaud.

Holy Rule of St. Benedict. unabr. ed. Saint Benedict of Nursia. 3 CDs. (Running Time: 4 hrs. 0 mins. 0 sec.). (Mystics Ser.). (ENG.). 2005. audio compact disk 18.98 (978-1-59644-064-7(3), Hovel Audio) christianaud.

Holy Russia. unabr. collector's ed. Fitzroy Maclean. Read by Wolfram Kandinsky. 12 cass. (Running Time: 18 hrs.). 1991. 96.00 (978-0-7366-1950-9(X), 2771) Books on Tape.
This remarkable story of Russia, based on the author's 40 years of travel & study in Central Asia & the Caucasus, makes the country come alive. Blood-stained & tumultuous, Russia has come down through the ages to emerge in the 20th century as a giant in chains.

Holy Sacrifice of the Mass, Set. Perf. by William Biersach & Charles A. Coulombe. 9 pts. on 16 cass. (Running Time: 17 hrs.). 59.00 (20149) Cath Treas.
The Tridentine Mass is examined, explored, & explained in the light of the Traditions of the Church & compared with the Novus Ordo with respect to dogmatic clarity & devotional flavor. Learn the meaning & origin of the priest's vestments, altar accouterments, various liturgical prayers, & the rubrics. Learn, too, how the Truths of the Faith have been expressed in other Rites of the Catholic Church.

Holy Sanctuary, Bible. adpt. ed. Created by Tyndale House Publishers Staff. (ENG.). 2006. audio compact disk 19.97 (978-1-4143-1033-6(1)) Tyndale Hse.

Holy Sanctuary Bible. adpt. ed. Created by Tyndale House Publishers Staff. Dramatization. (ENG.). 2006. audio compact disk 99.97 (978-1-4143-0741-1(1)) Tyndale Hse.

Holy Sanctuary Bible-NLT. unabr. ed. Created by Tyndale House Publishers Staff. (ENG.). 2006. audio compact disk 49.97 (978-1-4143-0743-5(8)) Tyndale Hse.

Holy Sanctuary New Testament. Created by Tyndale House Publishers Staff. (ENG.). 2006. audio compact disk 19.97 (978-1-4143-0744-2(6)) Tyndale Hse.

Holy Sanctuary New Testament-NLT. adpt. ed. Created by Tyndale House Publishers Staff. (ENG.). 2006. audio compact disk 39.97 (978-1-4143-0742-8(X)) Tyndale Hse.

Holy Secret. Read by James Ferrell. 2008. audio compact disk 24.95 (978-1-59038-739-9(2)) Deseret Bk.

Holy Singleness: Passion for Holiness Series. Ben Young. 2000. 4.95 (978-0-7417-6210-8(2), B0210) Win Walk.

Holy Smoke. unabr. ed. Anna Campion & Jane Campion. Read by Nicki Paull. 6 CDs. (Running Time: 6 hrs. 30 mins.). 2003. audio compact disk 77.95 (978-1-74093-085-7(1)) Pub: Bolinda Pubng AUS. Dist(s): Bolinda Pub Inc

Holy Smoke: 5 Cassettes (unabridged) unabr. ed. Anna Campion & Jane Campion. Read by Nicki Paull. 5 cass. (Running Time: 6 hrs. 30 mins.). 2001. 40.00 (978-1-74030-477-1(2)) Pub: Bolinda Pubng AUS. Dist(s): Bolinda Pub Inc

Holy Soul Jelly Roll: Poems & Songs, 1949-1993. Allen Ginsberg. Read by Allen Ginsberg. 4 CDs. (Running Time: 6 hr.). 2001. bk. 49.98 (R2 71693) Rhino Enter.

Holy Spirit. 2003. 10.00 (978-1-881541-84-4(3)) A Wommack.

Holy Spirit. 2. 2004. audio compact disk Rental 14.00 (978-1-881541-96-7(7)) A Wommack.

Holy Spirit. Kenneth Copeland. 6 cass. 1983. bk. 30.00 Set incl. study guide. (978-0-938458-23-4(X)) K Copeland Pubns.
Understanding the Holy Spirit.

Holy Spirit. Mark Crow. 6 cass. (Running Time: 6 hrs.). 2001. (978-1-931537-07-0(0)) Vision Comm Creat.

Holy Spirit. Kenneth E. Hagin. 6 cass. 24.00 (18H) Faith Lib Pubns.

Holy Spirit. Chester P. Michael. 1985. 24.00 (978-0-940136-20-5(1)) Open Door Inc.

Holy Spirit. Gary V. Whetstone. 9 cass. (Running Time: 13 hrs. 30 mins.). (Theology Ser.: TH104). 1996. 170.00 (978-1-58866-094-7(X), BT 104 A00) Gary Whet Pub.
Develop a deeper, personal, intimate fellowship with the Holy Spirit. This course will explore in detail His personality, attributes & spiritual gifts.

Holy Spirit. Featuring Bill Winston. 4 CDs. 2005. audio compact disk 32.00 (978-1-59544-131-7(X)) Pub: B Winston Min. Dist(s): Anchor Distributors

Holy Spirit: A Safe Guide, Vol. 2. Creflo A. Dollar. 5 cass. (Running Time: 5 hrs.). 2005. Rental 25.00 (978-1-59089-936-6(9)); audio compact disk 34.00 (978-1-59089-938-0(5)) Creflo Dollar.

Holy Spirit: Activating God's Power in Your Life. unabr. ed. Billy Graham. Narrated by Jack Garrett. 8 cass. (Running Time: 10 hrs. 45 mins.). 1988. 71.00 (978-0-7887-5480-7(7), K0064L8) Recorded Bks.
An inspiring & thought-provoking work based on the author's personal quest to understand the most mysterious aspect of Trinity. Using Biblical passages to illustrate his points, he helps the reader to understand the power of the Holy Spirit & His relevance in everyday life.

Holy Spirit: Before & after Pentecost. Derek Prince. 1 cass. (B-3014) Derek Prince.

Holy Spirit: From Genesis to Pentecost. Speeches. Andrew Fleming. 4 CDs. (Running Time: 4 hours). 2005. audio compact disk 20.00 (978-0-9767583-9-6(3)) Illumination MA.

Holy Spirit: Logos November 30, 1997. Ben Young. 1997. 4.95 (978-0-7417-6058-6(4), B0058) Win Walk.

Holy Spirit: The Boundless Energy of G. Ron Roth. 2 CDs. (Running Time: 2 hrs.). (ENG.). 2005. audio compact disk 18.95 (978-1-4019-0660-3(5)) Hay House.

Holy Spirit: The Boundless Energy of God. Ron Roth. 4 cass. (Running Time: 3 hrs.). 1995. 34.95 Set. (978-1-893869-09-7(1)) Celbrtng Life.

Holy Spirit: The Boundless Energy of God. Ron Roth. 2 cass. (Running Time: 2 hrs.). 1998. 16.95 (978-1-56170-544-3(6), 450) Hay House.

Holy Spirit & His Gifts. Bill Williams. 4 cass. 2005. 20.00 (978-1-59544-130-0(1)) Pub: B Winston Min. Dist(s): Anchor Distributors

Holy Spirit & the Anointing. Creflo A. Dollar. 3 cass. (Running Time: 4 hrs. 30 mins.). 2000. 15.00 (978-1-931172-44-8(7), TS239, Kidz Faith) Pub: Creflo Dollar. Dist(s): STL Dist NA

Holy Spirit As Guide. Derek Prince. 1 cass. (Running Time: 1 hr.). 1991. 5.95 (I-4330) Derek Prince.
Have you tried to become righteous by following rules? Have you failed? Only the guidance of the Holy Spirit can bring righteousness.

Holy Spirit audio Book. Reinhard Bonnke. 2009. audio compact disk 7.00 (978-1-933106-74-8(3)) E-R-Productions.

***Holy Spirit Baptism.** abr. ed. Reinhard Bonnke. (ENG.). 2010. audio compact disk (978-1-936081-01-1(6)) Casscomm.

Holy Spirit CD Series. 2004. audio compact disk 22.00 (978-1-59834-007-5(7)) Walk Thru the Bible.

Holy Spirit Come. Perf. by Lori Wilke. 1 cass. (Running Time: 5 min.). 1988. 9.98 Sound track. (978-1-891916-18-2(1)) Spirit To Spirit.

Holy Spirit Hovers over the Universe. unabr. ed. George Maloney. 4 cass. (Running Time: 4 hrs. 59 min.). 1993. 33.95 Set. (TAH292) Alba Hse Comns.
An enjoyable seven talk series on the Holy Spirit. You will also be armed with a biblical understanding of Holy Spirit & practical guides to enable you to open yourself to the Holy Spirit & to experience the Spirit in a way you never thought possible.

Holy Spirit in Action. Homer Rhea. 1 cass. 1998. bk. 34.99 (978-5-559-09310-9(6)) Pathway Pr.

Holy Spirit in Luke. Eugene LaVerdiere. 4 cass. (Running Time: 4 hrs.). 2001. 32.95 (A7020) St Anthony Mess Pr.
Explains Luke from both symbolic and cultural perspectives.

Holy Spirit in You. Derek Prince. 2 cass. 11.90 Set. (060-061) Derek Prince.
To enjoy the wealth of the kingdom, we must recognize the Holy Spirit as its sole administrator.

Holy Spirit in You, Set. Mac Hammond. 8 cass. (Running Time: 8 hrs.). 1995. Mac Hammond.
The awesome, living spirit of God dwelling inside you. It's a staggering concept. Let this series give you biblical answers to your questions about the "baptism" of the Holy Spirit.

Holy Spirit Inside. Tim Enloe. (ENG.). 2008. audio compact disk 17.99 (978-0-9794331-1-5(8)) E M Pubns.

Holy Spirit Is a Person. Gordon Clark. 1 cass. (Lectures on the Holy Spirit: No. 1). 5.00 Trinity Found.

Holy Spirit Is a Person. Derek Prince. 1 cass. (I-3016) Derek Prince.

Holy Spirit, Rain down with the Comforter Has Come. Contrib. by Marty Parks. 2007. audio compact disk 24.99 (978-5-557-54328-6(7)) Allegis.

Holy Spirit Speaks Vol. 3: Are You Listening ? Speeches. Creflo A. Dollar. 7 CDs. (Running Time: 6 hrs.). 2005. audio compact disk 34.00 (978-1-59089-951-9(2)) Creflo Dollar.

Holy Spirit Speaks Vol. 3: Are You Listening? Speeches. Creflo A. Dollar. 7 cass. (Running Time: 6 hrs.). 2005. Rental 25.00 (978-1-59089-950-2(4)) Creflo Dollar.

Holy Spirit, Use Me. Alexa S. Lambert. 1 cass. (Running Time: 30 min.). (J). (gr. 7 up). 8.99 (978-0-9639375-1-3(0)) ASL Music.
Contemporary Christian cassette with 10 original songs.

Holy Terror in the Hebrides. unabr. collector's ed. Jeanne M. Dams. Read by Kate Reading. 5 cass. (Running Time: 7 hrs. 30 min.). (Dorothy Martin Mystery Ser.: Bk. 3). 1999. 40.00 (978-0-7366-4296-5(X), 4789) Books on Tape.
The promise of fine food lures Dorothy Martin to the cottage of her friends Tom & Lynn on the island of Iona in the Hebrides. But when Tom is stricken with chest pains & remains in London, Dorothy's traveling companions turn out to be an ecumenical group from the States that are anything but ecumenical. And when one of the group dies in an "accidental" fall, it is up to Dorothy to find the killer.

Holy Thief. unabr. ed. Ellis Peters, pseud. Read by Stephen Thorne. 8 cass. (Running Time: 12 hrs.). (Chronicles of Brother Cadfael Ser.: Vol. 19). 2000. 59.95 (978-0-7451-6594-3(X), CAB 1210) Pub: Chivers Audio Bks GBR. Dist(s): AudioGO
In this 19th chronicle of Brother Cadfael, the death of the Earl of Essex, known thief and marauder, returns the Benedictine Abbey back to the good brothers. Brother Cadfael never expects the theft of Saint Winifred's holy bones, and even a murder, as the result of the disinternment. Indeed, a killer nearly gets away, but carnal and spiritual intrigue unfold to answer Brother Cadfael's prayers.

***Holy Thief.** unabr. ed. William Ryan. Read by Simon Vance. (Running Time: 10 hrs. 0 mins. 0 sec.). (ENG., 2010. audio compact disk 39.99 (978-1-4272-1039-5(X)) Pub: Macmill Audio. Dist(s): Macmillan

Holy Treasure! David Williams. Read by Sion Probert. 6 vols. (Running Time: 9 hrs.). 2003. 54.95 (978-0-7540-8313-9(6)) Pub: Chivers Audio Bks GBR. Dist(s): AudioGO

Holy Trinity. Father Kricek. 7 cass. 28.00 Set. (92H) IRL Chicago.

Holy Trinity & the Cross, Set. Benedict J. Groeschel. 2 cass. (Running Time: 2 hrs. 18 min.). 1999. 19.95 (TAH412) Alba Hse Comns.
In the call to prayer, Fr. Groeschel continues his Good Friday addresses by presenting this year a new theme for reflection & preparation: The Holy Trinity.

Holy War. Rose-Mae Carvin. (Running Time: 065 min.). (YA). (gr. 8 up). 2000. 9.95 (978-0-89084-913-2(7), 050500) BJUPr.

Holy War. unabr. ed. John Bunyan. Narrated by George E. Sarris. 6 cass. (Running Time: 6 hrs. 30 mins.). 2003. 30.00 (978-0-9665233-4-8(2)); audio compact disk 50.00 (978-0-9665233-5-5(0)) STL Dist NA.
A parable which tells the story of the fall & redemption of mankind as only he could. El Shaddai once rules over the great city Mansoul, but was betrayed through Ear Gate & Eye Gate into the hands of Diabolus.

Holy War, Inc: Inside the Secret World of Osama Bin Laden. abr. ed. Peter Bergen. 2004. 15.95 (978-0-7435-4837-3(X)) Pub: S&S Audio. Dist(s): S and S Inc

Holy War, Inc. Inside the Secret World of Osama Bin Laden. abr. ed. Peter L. Bergen. 1 CD. audio compact disk 30.00 S&S Audio.

***Holy Water: A Novel.** unabr. ed. James P. Othmer. (Running Time: 10 hrs. 30 mins.). 2010. 16.99 (978-1-4001-8671-6(4)) Tantor Media.

***Holy Water: A Novel.** unabr. ed. James P. Othmer. Narrated by William Dufris. (Running Time: 9 hrs. 30 mins. 0 sec.). (ENG.). 2010. 24.99 (978-1-4001-6671-8(3)); audio compact disk 34.99 (978-1-4001-1671-3(6)); audio compact disk 69.99 (978-1-4001-4671-0(2)) Pub: Tantor Media. Dist(s): IngramPubServ

***Holy Wild: Trusting in the Character of God.** unabr. ed. Mark Buchanan. Narrated by Lloyd James. (ENG.). 2006. 16.98 (978-1-59644-378-5(2), Hovel Audio) christianaud.

Holy Wild: Trusting in the Character of God. unabr. ed. Mark Buchanan. Narrated by Lloyd James. 8 CDs. (Running Time: 6 hrs. 30 mins. 0 sec.). (ENG.). 2006. audio compact disk 28.98 (978-1-59644-377-8(4), Hovel Audio) christianaud.

Holy Women & Mystics. Richard Woods. 1 cass. (Running Time: 1 hr.). 2001. 17.95 (A6850) St Anthony Mess Pr.
Presents an overview of holy women in Church history with an eye on their meaning for women today.

Holy Work: Passion for Holiness Series. Ben Young. 2000. 4.95 (978-0-7417-6209-2(9), B0209) Win Walk.

Homage. unabr. ed. Julian Rathbone. Read by Russell Bentley. 8 cass. (Running Time: 11 hrs. 55 mins.). (Isis Ser.). (J). 2002. 69.95 (978-0-7531-1379-0(1)) Pub: ISIS Lrg Prnt GBR. Dist(s): Ulverscroft US
British private eye, Chris Shovelin, answers a call for help from the other side of the world. Arriving in San Diego he discovers Jefferson, the friend in need, lying on the floor of his apartment with a hole in his head. Shovelin's instinct is to run, but China Heart, chic and mega-rich, wants him to take over where Jefferson failed and find Jerry Lennox, her missing brother. Catastrophic air crashes, extortion, drugs and murder, all play their part in bringing about a tumultuous climax.

Homage. unabr. ed. Julian Rathbone. Read by Russell Bentley. 8 CDs. (Running Time: 8 hrs.). (Isis Ser.). (J). 2002. audio compact disk 79.95 (978-0-7531-1574-9(3)) Pub: ISIS Lrg Prnt GBR. Dist(s): Ulverscroft US
Reformed alcoholic, ageing hippy, victim of a dysfunctional marriage, British private eye Chris Shovelin answers a call for help from the other side of the world. Arriving in San Diego he discovers Jefferson, the friend in need, lying on the floor of his apartment with a hole in his head. Shovelin's instinct is to run, but China Heart, chic and mega-rich, wants him to take over where Jefferson failed and find Jerry Lennox, his missing brother.

Homage to Catalonia. unabr. ed. George Orwell. Read by Frederick Davidson. 6 cass. (Running Time: 8 hrs. 30 mins.). (gr. 9-12). 1992. 44.95 (978-0-7861-0298-3(5), 1262) Blckstn Audio.
In 1936, George Orwell went to Spain to report on the Civil War & instead joined the P.O.U.M. militia to fight against the Fascists. In this now justly famous account of his experience, he describes both the bleak & the comic aspects of trench warfare on the Aragon front, the Barcelona uprising in May, 1937, his nearly fatal wounding just two weeks later, & his escape from Barcelona into France after the P.O.U.M. was suppressed. As important as the story of the war itself is Orwell's uncompromising effort to sort out the partisan politics that plagued the Republican cause.

Homage to Catalonia. unabr. collector's ed. George Orwell. Read by Richard Green. 8 cass. (Running Time: 8 hrs.). 1978. 48.00 (978-0-7366-0097-2(3), 1105) Books on Tape.
In 1936, Eric Blair, a novelist, critic & political satirist known by the pseudonym George Orwell, went to Spain to write about the Spanish Civil War. This book is his eyewitness account of that conflict. Nothing written since is as moving & alive with the terrors & triumphs of the time past.

Homage to Catalonia: Fighting the Spanish Civil War. unabr. ed. George Orwell. Narrated by Patrick Tull. 6 cass. (Running Time: 8 hrs.). 1989. 51.00 (978-1-55690-235-2(2), 89398E7) Recorded Bks.
Fighting the Spanish Civil War - youth against Fascism in 1936. Histories can explain causes & effects but usually fail to convey to later generations the spirit that moved men & women to act.

Homage to the Sun. Kyriacos Markides. 3 cass. 27.00 (OC111) Sound Horizons AV.

Homage to Theodore Roethke. unabr. ed. Stanley Kunitz. Read by Stanley Kunitz. 1 cass. (Running Time: 35 min.). (YM-YWHA Poetry Center Ser.). 1966. 12.95 (23264) J Norton Pubs.

Hombre de la Mascara de Hierro: La Ultima Aventura de los Tres Mosqueteros. abr. ed. Alejandro Dumas. Contrib. by Eduardo Serrano. (Running Time: 7200 sec.). (SPA.). 2007. audio compact disk 16.95 (978-1-933499-43-7(5)) Fonolibro Inc.

hombre de pan de jengibre Audio CD. Benchmark Education Company. Based on a work by Brenda Parkes. (Shared Reading Classics Ser.). (J). (gr. k-2). 2009. audio compact disk 10.00 (978-1-60634-979-3(1)) Benchmark Educ.

Hombre de Pasion y Destino. 2003. audio compact disk 62.50 (978-1-57972-519-8(8)) Insight Living.

Hombre Invisible. abr. ed. H. G. Wells. Read by Guillermo Piedrahita. 3 CDs.Tr. of Invisible Man. (SPA.). 2002. audio compact disk 17.00 (978-958-9494-75-2(7)) YoYoMusic.

Hombre Maleducado. Idries Shah. Tr. by Rita Wirkala. Illus. by Rose Mary Santiago. (J). (ps-3). 2006. pap. bk. 18.95 (978-1-933779-07-2(1), Hoopoe Books) ISHK.

Hombre Que Era Nadie. unabr. ed. Edgar Wallace. Read by Hernando Iván Cano. 3 CDs. (SPA.). 2002. audio compact disk 17.00 (978-958-8161-51-8(7)) YoYoMusic.

Hombre Que No Lavabo Los Platos. Tr. of Man Who Didn't Wash His Dishes, the. (SPA.). 2004. 8.95 (978-0-7882-0289-6(8)) Weston Woods.

Hombre Que Rie. abr. ed. Victor Hugo. Read by Laura García. 3 CDs. (SPA.). 2002. audio compact disk 17.00 (978-958-8161-44-0(4)) YoYoMusic.

***Hombre Que Vendio Su Sombra.** abr. ed. Adalberto Von Chamiso. Read by Adriana Sema. (SPA.). 2008. audio compact disk 17.00 (978-958-8318-48-6(3)) Pub: Yoyo Music COL. Dist(s): YoYoMusic

Hombre y el Zorro. Idries Shah. Tr. by Rita Wirkala. Illus. by Sally Mallam. (J). (ps). 2006. pap. bk. 28.95 (978-1-933779-03-4(9), Hoopoe Books) ISHK.

Hombre y la Mujer, Como Entenderse Mejor Hacia Una Vida Sexual Sana see How Men & Women Can Better Understand Each Other: How to Have a Healthy Sexual Life

Hombrecito de Mazapan. l.t. ed. Short Stories. Illus. by Graham Percy. 1 cass. (Running Time: 10 mins.). Dramatization.Tr. of Gingerbread Man. (SPA.). (J). (ps-3). 2001. bk. 9.95 (978-84-86154-09-7(X)) Peralt Mont ESP.

Hombrecito de Pan de Jengibre. Created by Rigby Staff. 1992. 10.40 (978-0-435-05340-6(X), Rigby PEA) Pearson EdAUS AUS.

Hombres de Valor Adorando. 2002. audio compact disk One Voice.

Hombres Son de Marte, las Mujeres Son de Venus. John Gray. Narrated by Francisco Rivela. 8 cass. (Running Time: 10 hrs. 30 mins.).Tr. of Men Are from Mars, Women Are from Venus. 74.00 (978-1-4025-0379-5(2)) Recorded Bks.

Hombres Valientes see Hombres Victoriosos

Hombres Victoriosos. Voice by Carlos Arzola. Prod. by Chris Richards. Orig. Title: Hombres Valientes. (SPA.). 1999. 7.99 (978-1-885630-52-0(2)); audio compact disk 12.99 (978-1-885630-53-7(0)) Jayah Producc.

Home see Favorite American Poems

Home. unabr. ed. Richard McKenzie. Read by Barrett Whitener. 7 cass. (Running Time: 7 hrs.). 1997. 42.00 (4301) Books on Tape.
A look at America's overburdened foster-parenting system has sparked a debate on the care of abused & orphaned children: should they be raised in foster homes or in private orphanages.

Home. unabr. ed. Marilynne Robinson. Narrated by Maggi-Meg Reed. 10 CDs. (Running Time: 12 hrs. 30 mins.). 2008. audio compact disk 94.95 (978-0-7927-5634-7), Chivers Sound Lib) AudioGO.

Home. unabr. ed. Marilynne Robinson. Read by Maggi-Meg Reed. 10 CDs. (Running Time: 12 hrs. 30 mins. 0 sec.). (ENG.). 2008. audio compact disk 44.95 (978-1-4272-0510-0(8)) Pub: Macmill Audio. Dist(s): Macmillan

Home. unabr. ed. Witold Rybczynski. Read by Nadia May. 6 cass. (Running Time: 8 hrs. 30 mins.). 1992. 44.95 (978-0-7861-0315-7(9), 1276) Blckstn Audio.
T.S. Eliot once wrote, "home is where one starts from." In this illuminating book, Rybczynski's program is to explain how very long it took us to arrive at this starting point. He walks us through five centuries of homes both great & small, from the smoke-filled manor halls of the Middle Ages to the Ralph Lauren-designed environments of today, on a house tour like no other, one that delightfully explicates the very idea of "home." Along the way, he skillfully weaves into his work the enlightening confluences of social & economic conditions & national character.

Home: A Memoir of My Early Years. unabr. ed. Julie Andrews. Read by Julie Andrews. 11 CDs. (Running Time: 13 hrs.). 2008. audio compact disk 44.95 (978-1-4013-8894-2(9), Hyperion Audio) Pub: Hyperion. Dist(s): HarperCollins Pubs

Home: Memoir of Growing up in an Orphanage. unabr. ed. Richard McKenzie. Read by Barrett Whitener. 7 cass. (Running Time: 7 hrs.). 1996. 27.30 Set. (4301) Books on Tape.
America's overburdened foster-parenting system has sparked a debate on the care of abused & orphaned children: should they be raised in foster homes or in private orphanages.

Home: The Architecture of Our Lives. John Edwards. 2006. audio compact disk 29.95 (978-0-06-114263-5(8)) HarperCollins Pubs.

Home Again. Annie Smith. Narrated by Christina Moore. 7 cass. (Running Time: 10 hrs.). 64.00 (978-1-4025-3433-1(7)) Recorded Bks.

***Home Again.** unabr. ed. Kristin Hannah. (Running Time: 13 hrs.). 2010. 24.99 (978-1-4418-4434-7(1), 9781441844347, BAD); 39.97 (978-1-4418-4439-2(2), 9781441844392, BADLE) Brilliance Audio.

***Home Again.** unabr. ed. Kristin Hannah. Read by Tanya Eby. (Running Time: 13 hrs.). 2010. 39.97 (978-1-4418-4432-3(5), 9781441844323, Brinc Audio MP3 Lib); 24.99 (978-1-4418-4430-9(9), 9781441844309, Brilliance MP3); audio compact disk 89.97 (978-1-4418-4428-6(7), 9781441844286, BriAudCD Unabrid); audio compact disk 29.99 (978-1-4418-4423-1(6), 9781441844231, Bril Audio CD Unabri) Brilliance Audio.

Home Alone Companion Tape for Cats. abr. ed. Nina Mattikow. 1 cass. (Running Time: 60 min.). Dramatization. (Pet Cassettes Ser.). 1992. 9.95 (978-1-55569-552-1(3), 41006) Great Am Audio.
Studies have shown that cats respond positively to certain sounds of music & nature. We have captured these sounds on tape to provide companionship while you're away. You can leave home & know that your feline friend is not alone.

Home Alone Companion Tape for Dogs. abr. ed. Nina Mattikow. 1 cass. (Running Time: 60 min.). Dramatization. (Pet Cassettes Ser.). 1992. 9.95 (978-1-55569-549-1(3), 41003) Great Am Audio.
Comforting, stimulating sounds of music & nature will make it easier on both of you when you're not home. Keep your dog occupied, content & free from loneliness with sounds that will soothe.

Home & Away. abr. ed. Kevin Kling. 1 cass. (Running Time: 1 hr. 12 min.). 2001. 11.95 (978-1-57453-142-8(5)) Audio Lit.

***Home at Last: Stories for chidlren about Homelessness.** Ralph da Costa Nunez. (ENG.). (J). 2010. 5.00 (978-0-9825533-1-2(5)) Homes Homeless.

Home at the End of the World. abr. rev. ed. Michael Cunningham & Blair Brown. Read by Colin Farrell & Dallas Roberts. 6 CDs. (Running Time: 7 hrs. 30 mins. 0 sec.). (ENG.). 2004. audio compact disk 24.95 (978-1-59397-541-8(4)) Pub: Macmill Audio. Dist(s): Macmillan

Home at the End of the World. unabr. ed. Michael Cunningham. Contrib. by Original Motion Picture Cast. 9 cass. 2005. bk. 79.99 (978-0-7927-3258-7(8), CSL 670); bk. 99.99 (978-0-7927-3259-4(6), SLD 670) AudioGO.

Home at the End of the World. unabr. rev. ed. Michael Cunningham & Blair Brown. Read by Colin Farrell et al. 11 CDs. (Running Time: 12 hrs. 0 mins. 0 sec.). (ENG.). 2004. audio compact disk 44.95 (978-1-55927-990-1(7)) Pub: Macmill Audio. Dist(s): Macmillan

Home Before Dark. unabr. ed. Susan Wiggs. Read by Tanya Eby. 7 cass. (Running Time: 10 hrs.). 2003. 34.95 (978-1-59086-694-8(0), 1590866940); 82.25 (978-1-59086-712-9(2), 1590867122, CD Unabrid Lib Ed) Brilliance Audio.
In her career as a photojournalist, free-spirited Jessie Ryder has seen the world through her camera lens. But she's never traveled far enough to escape a painful moment that has haunted her for the past sixteen years: the day she gave her baby daughter away. Now, facing a life-altering crisis, she's decided to fix the broken pieces of her heart and seek out Lila, even if it means she has to upset the world of Lila's adoptive mother...her very own sister, Luz. Like a Technicolor tornado bursting into Luz's picture-perfect life, Jessie returns to her Texas hometown with a shattering request. She wants to tell Lila the truth. As Luz and her husband struggle with what Jessie's return may mean to rebellious Lila, their seemingly solid marriage falters. Old secrets are exposed. Then, just as Jessie comes to terms with the past, life's bittersweet irony plays its hand. She meets Dustin Matlock, a young father who has survived a devastating loss. And Jessie begins to see the hopeful possibilities that lie buried in the most wrenching tragedies. Though she aches to reach out to those she loves, Jessie stands at the crossroads. She is leaving behind the only life she knows and blindly leaping into the unknown. Now the choice she makes will affect the life of her daughter and challenge the meaning of sisterhood. As Jessie and Luz examine the true meaning of love, loyalty and family, they are drawn into an emotional tug-of-war filled with moments of unexpected humor, surprising sweetness and unbearable sadness. But as the pain, regrets and mistakes of the past slowly rise to the surface, a new picture emerges - a picture filled with hope, promise and the redeeming power of the human heart.

Home Before Dark. unabr. ed. Susan Wiggs. Read by Tanya Eby. (Running Time: 10 hrs.). 2004. 39.25 (978-1-59335-376-6(6), 1593353766, Brlnc Audio MP3 Lib) Brilliance Audio.

Home Before Dark. unabr. ed. Susan Wiggs. Read by Tanya Eby. (Running Time: 10 hrs.). 2004. 39.25 (978-1-59710-371-8(3), 1597103713, BADLE); 24.95 (978-1-59710-370-1(5), 1597103705, BAD) Brilliance Audio.

Home Before Dark. unabr. ed. Susan Wiggs. Read by Tanya Eby. (Running Time: 12 hrs.). 2010. audio compact disk 89.97 (978-1-4418-3594-9(6), 9781441835949, BriAudCD Unabrid); audio compact disk 29.99 (978-1-4418-3593-2(8), 9781441835932, Bril Audio CD Unabri) Brilliance Audio.

Home Before Dark. unabr. ed. Susan Wiggs. Read by Tanya Eby. (Running Time: 10 hrs.). 2004. 24.95 (978-1-59335-092-5(9), 1593350929) Soulmate Audio Bks.

Home Before Dark. unabr. collector's ed. Susan Cheever. Read by Penelope Dellaporta. 8 cass. (Running Time: 12 hrs.). 1986. 64.00 (978-0-7366-0593-9(2), 1560) Books on Tape.
In "Home Before Dark" Cheever's daughter Susan uses his unpublished journals, letters & her own memories to tell the story of one of American literature's foremost writers. She gives us a moving chronicle of his successes & failures, his childhood, his stint in the army, his struggle to write a novel, his literary triumphs of the 1970's, the doubts & fears of his last years & finally the struggle with cancer that was his last.

Home Birth. Annie Finch. 2006. 4.00 (978-1-933675-05-3(5)) Dos Madres Pr.

Home Business Possibilities, Vol. I. Update Publicare Staff. 2 cass. (Running Time: 2 hrs.). 1992. 75.00 Set. (37SOR305CT) Sell Out Recordings.
Ideas & possibilities for home or small businesses.

Home Buying. 3rd rev. abr. ed. Eric Tyson & Ray Brown. Read by Brett Barry. (Running Time: 12600 sec.). (For Dummies Ser.). 2006. audio compact disk 14.95 (978-0-06-115273-3(0)) HarperCollins Pubs.

***Home Buying for Dummies 3rd Edition.** abr. ed. Eric Tyson & Ray Brown. Read by Brett Barry. (ENG.). 2006. (978-0-06-123043-1(X), Harper Audio); (978-0-06-123044-8(8), Harper Audio) HarperCollins Pubs.

Home Care in Obstetrics & Gynecology. Contrib. by John C. Morrison et al. 1 cass. (American College of Obstetrics & Gynecologists UPDATE: Vol. 21, No. 1). 1998. 20.00 Am Coll Obstetric.

Home Care Visual Rehabilitation Vol. 3: A Step-by-Step "How To" Sara Pazell. 1 cass. (Running Time: 42 min.). 1998. bk. 15.00 (978-1-58111-073-9(1)) Contemporary Medical.

Home Discipleship Hymnbook: Music Supplement CD Set. Perf. by Kathy Wessel. Ed. by Douglas Horne. Compiled by Douglas Horne. 5 CDs. 2004. audio compact disk 25.00 (978-0-9753133-1-2(2)) Home Discipleship.
Accompaniment Tracks for the Home Discipleship Hymnbook.

Home Energy Efficiency. Hosted by Nancy Pearlman. 1 cass. (Running Time: 28 min.). 10.00 (108) Educ Comm CA.

Home Fires. unabr. ed. Margaret Maron. Narrated by C. J. Critt. 5 cass. (Running Time: 8 hrs.). (Deborah Knott Mystery Ser.: No. 6). 1999. 46.00 (978-0-7887-3212-6(9), 95726E7) Recorded Bks.
Features the social & racial tension erupting in the sleepy North Carolina community.

Home Fires. unabr. ed. Luanne Rice. Read by Kate Reading. 7 cass. (Running Time: 10 hrs. 30 min.). 1996. 56.00 (978-0-7366-3288-1(3), 3943) Books on Tape.
Anne Davis has returned to the house where she grew up, trading the charmed life of her Manhattan penthouse & travel in France for a harsh winter on a windy New England island. In the wake of personal tragedy, she needs this home, with the security & love it has always meant. It is here she hopes to heal, holding onto treasured memories of the life she shared with her child & husband.

Home Fires Burning: Faith on the Home Front Trilogy. unabr. ed. Penelope J. Stokes. Narrated by Ruth Ann Phimister & C. J. Critt. 10 cass. (Running Time: 14 hrs. 30 mins.). 2001. 88.00 (978-0-7887-5285-8(5), K0051G7) Recorded Bks.
A stirring tale of love & faith, tested by World War II. When Libba Coltraine meets Link Winsome at a USO dance in Mississippi, she believes she has found someone to take her away from her domineering father. But suddenly, amidst a cloud of secrecy, Link is shipped to Europe.

Home for Chloe. K. S. Robeson. 2 CDs. (Running Time: 150 mins). (Tales from Wind Creek Ser.: Bk. 1). (J). (gr. 3-6). 2002. audio compact disk 11.95 (978-0-9723530-2-1(X)) Falcor Bks.
Forced to find a new home, Chloe joins the Animal Alliance of the Big Woods. But when she is captured by the animal control officer, who will save her? Audio version of the book - read by the author.

Home for Christmas. Contrib. by Amy Grant. Prod. by Brown Bannister & Ronn Huff. 2007. audio compact disk 9.99 (978-5-557-59288-8(1)) Pt of Grace Ent.

Home for Christmas. JoAnne Lower. Read by JoAnne Lower. Perf. by Martha Towey. 1 cass. (Running Time: 1 hr.). 1995. (978-1-888940-02-2(6)) J Lower Ent.
Personal stories of a young girl growing up on an Iowa farm.

Home for Christmas, Set. Anita Stansfield. 2 cass. 3.57 (978-1-57734-206-9(2), 07001592) Covenant Comms.

Home for Christmas: John 2:5. Ed Young. (J). 1981. 4.95 (978-0-7417-1205-9(9), A0205) Win Walk.

Home for Christmas: Luke 2:1-2- Ed Young. 1992. 4.95 (978-0-7417-1948-5(6), 948) Win Walk.

Home for the Holidays. 1 cass. 4.99 split cass. (978-1-55897-062-5(2), C 5161N); (978-1-55897-063-2(0), BK3080); audio compact disk 6.99 (978-1-55897-064-9(9), CD 5195J) Pub: Brentwood Music. Dist(s): Provident Mus Dist
Enjoy the celebration of our Savior's birth with these Christmas sing-along favorites. Includes: Noel Medley, Do You Hear What I Hear? & Good Christian Men Rejoice Medley.

Home for the Holidays. 2007. audio compact disk 12.98 (978-5-557-71865-3(6)) Madacy Ent Grp CAN.

Home for the Holidays. Perf. by Glen Campbell & Vince Gill. 1 cass. audio compact disk 15.99 CD. (D2023) Diamante Music Grp.
Home for the Holidays is a wonderful collection of carols blessed with Glen's smooth, soaring vocals.

Home for the Holidays. Contrib. by Elvis Presley. 2007. audio compact disk 29.98 (978-5-557-71833-2(8)) Madacy Ent Grp CAN.

Home for the Holidays. unabr. ed. Johanna Lindsey. Read by Laural Merlington. (Running Time: 5 hrs.). 2009. 24.99 (978-1-4233-6645-4(X), 9781423366454, Brilliance MP3); 24.99 (978-1-4233-6647-8(6), 9781423366478, BAD); 39.97 (978-1-4233-6646-1(8), 9781423366461, Brlnc Audio MP3 Lib); 39.97 (978-1-4233-6648-5(4), 9781423366485, BADLE); audio compact disk 24.99 (978-1-4233-6643-0(3), 9781423366430, Bril Audio CD Unabri); audio compact disk 69.97 (978-1-4233-6644-7(1), 9781423366447, BriAudCD Unabrid) Brilliance Audio.

Home for the Holidays. unabr. ed. Johanna Lindsey. 2000. 24.00 (978-0-694-52439-6(5)); 27.50 (978-0-694-52438-9(7)) HarperCollins Pubs.

Home for the Holidays - ShowTrax. Arranged by Mark Brymer. 1 CD. (Running Time: 5 mins.). 2000. audio compact disk 19.95 (08742135) H Leonard.
Just what you're looking for. A fun, swing arrangement of this holiday classic!.

***Home Free.** abr. ed. Fern Michaels. (Running Time: 3 hrs.). (Sisterhood Ser.). 2011. 9.99 (978-1-4558-0489-4(4), 9781455804894, BAD) Brilliance Audio.

Home Front: Seventeen Authentic Tunes of the Civil War. Perf. by Wayne Erbsen. 1 cass. (Running Time: 45 min.). 1992. 9.95 (978-0-9629327-8-6(7), NG006); audio compact disk 14.95 CD. (978-1-883206-20-8(0), NG-CD-006) Native Ground.
Captures the spirit of those who stayed at home. Includes both Union & Confederate patriotic tunes, minstrel songs, sentimental pieces & more.

Home Front: The Stirring Drama of the War Years in America, 1938-1945. William B. Williams. Narrated by Edward Brown & Frank Gorin. 4 cass. 1994. 21.95 Set. (978-1-55935-148-5(9)) Soundelux.
The war years 1938-1945 told through the voices, the songs & people who lived it.

Home Game: An Accidental Guide to Fatherhood. unabr. ed. Michael Lewis. Read by Dan John Miller. 1 MP3-CD. (Running Time: 4 hrs.). 2009. 39.97 (978-1-4233-8953-8(0), 9781423389538, Brlnc Audio MP3 Lib) Brilliance Audio.

Home Game: An Accidental Guide to Fatherhood. unabr. ed. Michael Lewis. Read by Dan john Miller. (Running Time: 4 hrs.). 2009. 39.97 (978-1-4233-8955-2(7), 9781423389552, BADLE) Brilliance Audio.

Home Game: An Accidental Guide to Fatherhood. unabr. ed. Michael Lewis. Read by Dan John Miller. (Running Time: 4 hrs.). 2009. 24.99 (978-1-4233-8952-1(2), 9781423389521, Brilliance MP3); 24.99 (978-1-4233-8954-5(9), 9781423389545, BAD); audio compact disk 69.97 (978-1-4233-8951-4(4), 9781423389514, BriAudCD Unabrid); audio compact disk 24.99 (978-1-4233-8950-7(6), 9781423389507, Bril Audio CD Unabri) Brilliance Audio.

Home Girls. unabr. ed. Short Stories. Olga Masters. Read by Natalie Bate. 5 cass. (Running Time: 7 hrs.). 2002. (978-1-86340-598-0(4), 560612) Bolinda Pubng AUS.
Each story in this collection is a study of the manifestations of power within the family. Twenty incisive domestic dramas are played out on the stage of poverty-stricken small town rural life where no-one's secrets are safe.

Home Health Care. (Running Time: 30 min.). 1989. 10.95 (I0130B090, HarperThor) HarpC GBR.

Home Improvement. 2004. 28.00 (978-1-57972-580-8(5)) Insight Living.

Home Improvement. 2004. audio compact disk 28.00 (978-1-57972-582-2(1)) Insight Living.

Home Improvement. unabr. ed. Keith A. Butler & Deborah L. Butler. 12 cass. (Running Time: 18 hrs.). 2001. 45.00 (A136) Word Faith Pubng.
The Bishop and his wife offer candid solutions from God's Word for marriages in crisis as well as marriage caught in the doldrums of old routines and the cares of everyday life.

Home Improvement. unabr. ed. Charles R. Swindoll. 4 cass. (Running Time: 4 hrs. 30 mins.). 1999. 20.95 (978-1-57972-318-7(7)) Insight Living.

Home Improvement, DIY, & Decorations Accessories in Malaysia: A Strategic Reference 2006. Compiled by Icon Group International, Inc. Staff. 2007. ring bd. 195.00 (978-0-497-82345-0(4)) Icon Grp.

Home Improvement Essential Skills 1-2-3. Meredith Books Staff. 2008. 14.95 (978-0-696-24110-9(2), Home Depot) Meredith Bks.

Home Improvements: The Chapman Guide to Negotiating Change with Your Spouse. unabr. ed. Gary Chapman. Narrated by Maurice England. (Marriage Savers Ser.). (ENG.). 2007. 9.79 (978-1-60814-237-8(X)) Oasis Audio.

***Home in Carolina.** abr. ed. Sherryl Woods. Read by Mary Robinette Kowal. 5 CDs. (Running Time: 5 hrs.). (Sweet Magnolias Ser.). 2010. audio compact disk 14.99 (978-1-4418-5402-5(9), 9781441854025, BACD) Brilliance Audio.

***Home in Carolina.** unabr. ed. Sherryl Woods. Read by Mary Robinette Kowal. 1 MP3-CD. (Running Time: 10 hrs.). (Sweet Magnolias Ser.). 2010. 19.99 (978-1-4418-5007-2(4), 9781441850072, Brilliance MP3); 39.97 (978-1-4418-5008-9(2), 9781441850089, Brlnc Audio MP3 Lib); 39.97 (978-1-4418-5010-2(4), 9781441850102, BADLE); 19.99 (978-1-4418-5009-6(0), 9781441850096, BAD); audio compact disk 29.99 (978-1-4418-5005-8(8), 9781441850058, Bril Audio CD Unabri); audio compact disk 79.97 (978-1-4418-5006-5(6), 9781441850065, BriAudCD Unabrid) Brilliance Audio.

Home in Tennessee. Sparky Rucker. 1 cass. (Running Time: 26 min.). (J). (gr. k up). 1981. 9.95 (978-0-939065-04-2(5), GW 1004) Gentle Wind.
Traditional songs for children.

Home in Tennessee. Perf. by Sparky Rucker. (J). 2001. audio compact disk 14.95 (978-0-939065-97-4(5)) Gentle Wind.

Home in That Rock: A Collection of Spirituals & Songs of Faith - ShowTrax. Perf. by Moses Hogan Singers, The. Arranged by Moses Hogan. Conducted by Moses Hogan. 1 CD. (Running Time: 90 mins.). 2000. audio compact disk 15.00 (08703287) H Leonard.
Features 11 Moses Hogan arrangements including "De Blin' Man Stood on de Road an' Cried" & "His Light Still Shines" featured in the excerpts above. Other selections include: "I Got a Home in-a Dat Rock," "Ride on King Jesus," "Little David Play on Your Harp," "He's Got the Whole World in His Hands," "Away in a Manger" & "Glory! Glory! Glory! to the Newborn King.

Home in Time for Christmas. abr. ed. Heather Graham. Read by Angela Dawe. (Running Time: 3 hrs.). 2009. audio compact disk 14.99 (978-1-4418-2547-6(9), 9781441825476, BACD) Brilliance Audio.

Home in Time for Christmas. abr. ed. Heather Graham. Read by Angela Dawe. (Running Time: 3 hrs.). 2010. audio compact disk 9.99 (978-1-4418-2548-3(7), 9781441825483, BCD Value Price) Brilliance Audio.

Home in Time for Christmas. unabr. ed. Heather Graham. Read by Angela Dawe. (Running Time: 7 hrs.). 2009. 24.99 (978-1-4233-9826-4(2), 9781423398264, BAD); 39.97 (978-1-4233-9825-7(4), 9781423398257, Brlnc Audio MP3 Lib); 39.97 (978-1-4233-9827-1(0), 9781423398271, BADLE); 24.99 (978-1-4233-9824-0(6), 9781423398240, Brilliance MP3); audio compact disk 74.97 (978-1-4233-9823-3(8), 9781423398233, BriAudCD Unabrid); audio compact disk 24.99 (978-1-4233-9822-6(X), 9781423398226, Bril Audio CD Unabri) Brilliance Audio.

***Home in Your Heart: A Meditation OnJohn 15:9.** Deborah Kukal. (ENG.). 2009. 14.98 (978-0-9801278-2-9(3)) Hydration.

Home Inspection Business from A to Z - Complete Kit: Real Estate Home Inspector, Homeowner, Home Buyer & Seller Survival Kit Series. 4th rev. ed. Guy Cozzi. 4 audio CD's. (Running Time: 10 hours). (Home Inspection from A to Z Ser.). 2003. pap. bk. (978-1-887450-03-4(3)) Nemmar Real Est.

Home Is the Sailor, Home from the Sea see Robert Louis Stevenson: His Poetry, Prose and the Story of His Life

Home Is Where the Heart Is, Set. unabr. ed. Joan Jonker. 8 cass. 1998. 83.95 (978-1-85903-114-8(5)) Pub: Magna Story GBR. Dist(s): Ulverscroft US

Home Is Where the Heart Is: Gen.45:1-28; Gen.46:29-30. Ed Young. 1988. 4.95 (978-0-7417-1687-3(9), 687) Win Walk.

Home Management In-Home Elderly Care. 11 cass. (Running Time: 30 min. per cass.). 99.00 Set. (978-1-877843-00-6(8)) Elder Care Solutions.
Focuses on a broad aspect of aging and its impact on the care required. Some specific topics addressed are: effective communication with the elderly, diet and exercise, psychological and physical aspects of aging, and care of specific illness.

Home Mountain. unabr. ed. Jeanne Williams. Read by Stephanie Brush. 12 cass. (Running Time: 12 hrs. 48 min.). 2001. 64.95 (978-1-55686-741-5(7)) Books in Motion.
In charge of three younger MacLeod children when their parents die, Katie Macleod pushes on to fulfill her father's dream to settle in the beautiful Chiricahua Mountains.

Home of the Blizzard. unabr. ed. Douglas Mawson. Read by James Condon. 12 cass. (Running Time: 20 hrs.). 1998. 96.00 (978-1-86442-233-7(5), 580539) Pub: Bolinda Pubng AUS. Dist(s): Lndmrk Audiobks
A detailed account of the Australian Antarctic Expedition's daily subsistence on the icy continent & its scientific endeavors.

Home on the Prairie. unabr. ed. Garrison Keillor. Perf. by Garrison Keillor. 4 CDs. (Running Time: 4 hrs.). (ENG.). 2003. audio compact disk 36.95 (978-1-56511-786-0(7), 1565117867) Pub: HighBridge. Dist(s): Workman Pub

Home on the Range: Kansas Pioneers & Their Music. Prod. by Kelly Werts. 1 cass. 1994. 10.95 (978-1-880652-57-2(9)); audio compact disk 15.95 CD. (978-1-880652-82-4(X)) Wichita Eagle.
Songs from Kansas history performed by Kansas folk musicians on traditional instruments.

Home Port see Twentieth-Century Poetry in English, No. 25, Recordings of Poets Reading Their Own Poetry

Home Rich. unabr. ed. Gerri Willis. (Running Time: 8 hrs. 0 mins.). 2008. 24.95 (978-1-4332-0980-2(2)) Blckstn Audio.

Home Rich: Increasing the Value of the Biggest Investment of Your Life. Gerri Willis. Read by Pam Ward. (Playaway Adult Nonfiction Ser.). 2008. 64.99 (978-1-60640-761-5(9)) Find a World.

Home Rich: Increasing the Value of the Biggest Investment of Your Life. unabr. ed. Gerri Willis. Read by Pam Ward. (Running Time: 30600 sec.). 2008. 54.95 (978-1-4332-0978-9(0)); audio compact disk 24.95 (978-1-4332-0981-9(0)); audio compact disk & audio compact disk 29.95 (978-1-4332-0982-6(9)); audio compact disk & audio compact disk 63.00 (978-1-4332-0979-6(9)) Blckstn Audio.

***Home Ruler: Traditional Irish Flute Music.** Catherine Mcevoy. (ENG.). 2008. audio compact disk 28.95 (978-0-8023-8172-9(3)) Pub: Clo Iar-Chonnachta IRL. Dist(s): Dufour

Home Run. unabr. ed. Gerald Seymour. Read by David Banks. 10 cass. (Running Time: 13 hrs. 32 min.). (Isis Ser.). (J). 1993. 84.95 (978-1-85695-405-1(6), 92083) Pub: ISIS Lrg Prnt GBR. Dist(s): Ulverscroft US

Home Run. unabr. ed. Gerald Seymour. Read by David Banks. 12 CDs. (Running Time: 13 hrs. 32 min.). (Isis Ser.). (J). 2001. audio compact disk

99.95 (978-0-7531-1210-6(8)) Pub: ISIS Lrg Prnt GBR. Dist(s): Ulverscroft US

Espionage in the Middle East is a dangerous business, and no one knows this better than Matthew Fumiss - for two decades, he has run the British agents in Iran. Meanwhile, Iranian exile Charlie Eashraq is pursuing the extermination of those responsible for the deaths of his father and sister and he smuggles into Britain raw intelligence for Fumiss. Furniss's dangerous journey into Iran builds up to a harrowing climax.

Home Run Heroes. John Bergez. (Overcoming the Odds Sports Biographies Ser.). 2000. audio compact disk 18.95 (978-1-4105-0143-1(4)) D Johnston Inc.

Home Run Heroes. John Bergez. Ed. by Jerry Stemach & Gail Portnuff Venable. Illus. by Jeff Ham. Narrated by Bernard Mixon. Contrib. by Ted S. Hasselbring. . (Running Time:). (Start-to-Finish Books). (J). (gr. 2-3). 2000. 35.00 (978-1-58702-465-8(9)) D Johnston Inc.

Home Run Heroes, Vol. 1. John Bergez. Ed. by Jerry Stemach & Gail Portnuff Venable. Illus. by Jeff Ham. Narrated by Bernard Mixon. Contrib. by Ted S. Hasselbring. (Start-to-Finish Books). (J). (gr. 2-3). 2002. 100.00 (978-1-58702-970-7(7)) D Johnston Inc.

Home Run Heroes, Vol. 1. unabr. ed. John Bergez. Ed. by Jerry Stemach et al. Illus. by Jeff Ham. Narrated by Bernard Mixon. Contrib. by Ted S. Hasselbring. 1 cass. (Running Time: 1 hr.). (Start-to-Finish Books). (J). (gr. 2-3). 2000. (978-1-893376-55-7(9), F16K2) D Johnston Inc.

Not only baseball fans will love this book. So will anyone who's ever wondered why baseball fans love to stand up and scream, "It's out'a here!" Explaining why hitting a home run is the hardest challenge in sports, the book tells about five all-time home run hitters, beginning with their early lives.

Home Run Kid Races On. unabr. ed. Matt Christopher. Read by Joshua Swanson. (Running Time: 2 hrs.). 2010. 9.98 (978-1-60788-306-7(6)); audio compact disk 12.98 (978-1-60788-305-0(8)) Pub: Hachet Audio. Dist(s): HachBkGrp

Home Safe: A Novel. unabr. ed. Elizabeth Berg. Read by Elizabeth Berg. 7 CDs. (Running Time: 8 hrs.). (ENG.). 2009. audio compact disk 34.95 (978-0-7393-2548-3(5), Random AudioBks) Pub: Random Audio Pubg. Dist(s): Random

Home School Vision of Victory. Speeches. Douglas W. Phillips. 1 cass. (Running Time: 1 hr.). 1999. 7.00 (978-0-9665233-8-6(5)) Pub: Vsn Forum. Dist(s): STL Dist NA

Home School Vision of Victory. Douglas W. Phillips. 1 CD. (Running Time: 1 hr.). 2003. audio compact disk 10.00 (978-1-929241-47-7(X)) Pub: Vsn Forum. Dist(s): STL Dist NA

Home Song. abr. ed. LaVyrle Spencer. Read by LaVyrle Spencer. 2 cass. (Running Time: 3 hrs.). 2002. 7.95 (978-1-57815-299-5(2), 1199, Media Bks Audio); audio compact disk 11.99 (978-1-57815-555-2(X), 1199CD3, Media Bks Audio) Media Bks NJ.

Are there sins of the heart beyond forgiving? The answer is revealed in this powerful novel of a family whose future is imperiled by the past.

Home Street Home, Set. unabr. ed. Elizabeth A. Webster. 8 cass. 1998. 83.95 (978-1-85903-076-9(9)) Pub: Magna Story GBR. Dist(s): Ulverscroft US

Home Study Course for Self-Esteem & Stress Control. 2nd unabr. rev. ed. Lilburn S. Barksdale. Illus. by E. Maxwell. 3 cass. 1989. pap. bk. 39.95 incl. 2 pap. bks., Daily Companion lesson cards, self-esteem, life style & stress evaluations. (978-0-918588-16-6(2), 115) NCADD.

Enables you to eliminate the root causes of low self-esteem & also of hurting emotions & destructive stress. Cassettes include: Basic Affirmations for Total & Unconditional Acceptance, Accepting My Own Authority/Getting Rid of Self-Condemnation & Guilt & Eliminating Destructive, Negative Emotions/Loving Myself & Others.

Home Study Tape Library. 6 cass. 125.00 set. Persuasive Comns.

Home, Sweet Home see Favorite American Poems

Home Sweet Home. Fisher-Price Staff. 1 cass. 1998. bk. 7.99 (978-1-56826-785-2(1)) Rhino Enter.

Home Sweet Home. Molly Jackel. (Room 202 Ser.). 2005. pap. bk. 69.00 (978-1-4105-0609-2(6)); audio compact disk 18.95 (978-1-4105-0607-8(X)) D Johnston Inc.

Home-Thoughts from Abroad see Browning's Last Duchess

Home to Big Stone Gap. unabr. ed. Adriana Trigiani. Read by Cassandra Campbell. 6 cass. (Running Time: 9 hrs. 15 mins.). (Big Stone Gap Ser.: Bk. 4). 2006. 81.00 (978-1-4159-3311-4(1)); audio compact disk 81.60 (978-1-4159-3312-1(X)) Pub: Books on Tape. Dist(s): NetLibrary CO

Home to Harmony. Philip Gulley. Narrated by Norman Dietz. 5 cass. (Running Time: 6 hrs. 45 mins.). 54.00 (978-1-4025-2154-6(5)); audio compact disk 58.00 (978-1-4025-3083-8(8)) Recorded Bks.

Home to Harmony. unabr. ed. Philip Gulley. Read by Philip Gulley. 2004. 19.95 (978-0-06-058483-2(1)) HarperCollins Pubs.

Home to Holly Springs: The First of the Father Tim Novels. Jan Karon. Contrib. by Scott Sowers. (Running Time: 12 hrs.). No. 1. (ENG.). (gr. 12 up). 2007. audio compact disk 39.95 (978-0-14-314254-6(2), PengAudBks) Penguin Grp USA.

Home to the High Fells. unabr. ed. Elizabeth Gill. Read by Rachel Bavidge. 7 cass. (Running Time: 9 hrs. 15 mins.). (Story Sound Ser.). 2007. 61.95 (978-1-85903-994-6(4)); audio compact disk 79.95 (978-1-85903-993-9(6)) Pub: Mgna Lrg Print GBR. Dist(s): Ulverscroft US

Home Tonight: Further reflection on the parable of the prodigal Son. unabr. ed. Henri J. M. Nouwen. (Running Time: 3 hrs. 42 mins. 0 sec.). (ENG.). 2009. audio compact disk 18.98 (978-1-59644-795-0(8), Hovel Audio) christianaud.

***Home Tonight: Further reflections on the parable of the prodigal Son.** unabr. ed. Henri J. M. Nouwen. Narrated by Arthur Morey. (ENG.). 2009. 10.98 (978-1-59644-796-7(6), Hovel Audio) christianaud.

Home Town. abr. ed. Tracy Kidder. Read by Daamien Krall. 2 cass. (Running Time: 3 hrs.). 1999. 17.95 (978-1-55935-297-0(3)) Soundelux.

Takes the listener inside the extraordinary & the ordinary lives that people live in Northampton, Massachusetts - to explore what makes a modern small city a success story.

Home Town. unabr. ed. Tracy Kidder. Read by Karen White. 10 cass. (Running Time: 15 hrs.). 1999. 80.00 (978-0-7366-4587-4(X), 5018) Books on Tape.

Hometown, U.S.A., the town of Northampton, Massachusetts & into the lives of people that live there. It is a place of startling complexity. Weaving together compelling stories of individual lives, delving into a rich & varied past, moving among all the levels of Northampton's social hierarchy, Kidder finds a great diversity contained within the town's narrow boundaries. Does the kind of small town that many Americans came from, & long for, still exist?.

Home Wrecker. unabr. ed. Allan Zullo. Read by John Ratzenberger. 2008. 1.37 (978-1-4233-8071-9(1), 9781423380719, BAD) Brilliance Audio.

Homebased Business - Your Guide to Success: How to Develop & Run Any Homebased Business. abr. ed. Thomas T. Beasley. Read by Thomas T. Beasley. 1 cass. pap. bk. 9.95 (978-0-9658763-0-8(6)); 14.95 (978-0-9658763-1-5(4)) Cedar Ridge.

How to choose a business, get customers, set-up production, how to start with small investment & grow with profits.

Homeboyz. Alan Lawrence Sitomer. Read by J. D. Jackson. 6. (Running Time: 7 hrs.). 2007. 51.75 (978-1-4281-5456-8(6)); audio compact disk 66.75 (978-1-4281-5461-2(2)) Recorded Bks.

Homecoming see Robert Lowell: A Reading

Homecoming. Elizabeth Gill. 9 cass. (Running Time: 12 hrs.). (Story Sound Ser.). (J). 2005. 76.95 (978-1-85903-784-3(4)) Pub: Mgna Lrg Print GBR. Dist(s): Ulverscroft US

Homecoming. Scripts. Dana Fuller Ross, pseud. 5 CDs. (Running Time: 6 hrs.). (Holts, an American Dynasty Ser.: Vol. 9). 2005. 30.00 (978-1-58943-027-3(1)) Am Pubng Inc.

1899, Michael Holt travels to Taos, New Mexico to film western adventures. Frank Holt returns to the U.S. to reconcile with his father who has chosen to abandon his military life and try to reunite his family. All of the surviving Holts and Blakes reunion in Taos where Frank discovers his destiny and love for his, now famous, artist step-cousin.

***Homecoming.** unabr. ed. Tonya Hurley. Narrated by Parker Posey. 1 Playaway. (Running Time: 5 hrs. 15 mins.). (YA). (gr. 7 up). 2009. 54.75 (978-1-4407-5060-1(2)); 51.75 (978-1-4407-5050-2(5)); audio compact disk 51.75 (978-1-4407-5054-0(8)) Recorded Bks.

Homecoming. unabr. ed. Bernhard Schlink. Read by Paul Michael. 8 CDs. (Running Time: 9 hrs.). 2008. audio compact disk 80.00 (978-1-4159-4715-9(5)) Random.

Homecoming. unabr. ed. Bernhard Schlink. Read by Paul Michael. 8 CDs. (Running Time: 9 hrs.). (ENG.). 2008. audio compact disk 34.95 (978-0-7393-5924-2(X), Random AudioBks) Pub: Random Audio Pubg. Dist(s): Random

Homecoming, unabr. ed. Cynthia Voigt. Narrated by Barbara Caruso. 10 pieces. (Running Time: 14 hrs. 15 mins.). (Tillerman Cycle Ser.: Bk. 1). (gr. 6 up). 1992. 87.00 (978-1-55690-586-5(6), 92123E7) Recorded Bks.

Tale of the Tillermans, four children abandoned by their parents, searching for a place to call home.

***Homecoming.** unabr. collector's ed. Tonya Hurley. Narrated by Parker Posey. 5 CDs. (Running Time: 5 hrs. 15 mins.). (YA). (gr. 7 up). 2009. audio compact disk 39.95 (978-1-4407-5055-7(6)) Recorded Bks.

***Homecoming: A Novel.** unabr. ed. Dan Walsh. Narrated by Roger Mueller. (Running Time: 8 hrs. 0 mins. 0 sec.). (ENG.). 2010. 18.19 (978-1-60814-673-4(1)); audio compact disk 25.99 (978-1-59859-722-6(1)) Oasis Audio.

Homecoming & Other Stories: A BBC Audio Exclusive. Maeve Binchy. (Running Time: 1 hr. 0 mins. 0 sec.). (ENG.). 2009. audio compact disk 24.95 (978-1-60283-775-1(9)) Pub: AudioGO. Dist(s): Perseus Dist

Homecoming Christmas: From South Africa. Contrib. by Bill & Gloria Gaither and Their Homecoming Friends & Bill Gaither. Prod. by Ben Speer. 2006. audio compact disk 17.99 (978-5-558-21035-4(4)) Gaither Music Co.

Homecoming for Murder. unabr. ed. John Armistead. Narrated by Mark Hammer. 8 cass. (Running Time: 10 hrs. 45 mins.). (Sheriff Bramlett Mystery Ser.). 1999. 70.00 (978-0-7887-3777-0(5), 95994E7) Recorded Bks.

The first murder was shocking. Why would anyone want to shoot a high school teacher? Then a second teacher was slain. As Sheriff Bramlett investigates, he will discover a dark legacy that threatens even his own family.

Homecoming Hymns. Contrib. by Lari Goss & William J. Gaither. Compiled by William J. Gaither. 2007. audio compact disk 16.98 (978-5-557-49212-6(7)); audio compact disk 15.00 (978-5-557-49211-9(9)) Gaither Music Co.

Homecoming Picnic. Contrib. by Bill & Gloria Gaither and Their Homecoming Friends & Bill Gaither. (Gaither Gospel Ser.). 2008. 12.99 (978-5-557-50363-1(3)) Gaither Music Co.

Homecoming: the Inner Child Workshop. John Bradshaw. (Running Time: 27000 sec.). 2008. audio compact disk 180.00 (978-1-57388-154-8(6)) J B Media.

Homecoming to Murder. unabr. ed. John Dellinger. Read by Jerry Sciarrio. 4 cass. (Running Time: 4 hrs. 42 min.). 2001. 26.95 (978-1-58116-095-6(X)) Books in Motion.

Marine Gunnery Sergeant Martin Mayfield meets a mysterious nun in a club car while traveling by train. The nun, a murder, and the Denver mob get Mayfield out of his marine clothes and back into his private investigator role.

Homecomings. unabr. ed. C. P. Snow. Read by John MacDonald. 8 cass. (Running Time: 12 hrs.). (Strangers & Brothers Ser.). 1985. 64.00 (1416) Books on Tape.

Lewis Eliot's unhappy marriage to a neurotic woman, her death, & his affair & eventual marriage to a woman more worthy of his love.

Homecooking with T. D. Jakes, Set. T. D. Jakes. 16 cass. 1997. 69.00 (978-1-57855-149-1(8)) T D Jakes.

Homefront. unabr. ed. Chuck Logan. 2005. 29.95 (978-0-7927-3685-1(0), CMP 820); 69.95 (978-0-7927-3683-7(4), CSL 820); audio compact disk 94.95 (978-0-7927-3684-4(2), SLD 820) AudioGO.

Homegrown Democrat: A Few Plain Thoughts from the Heart of America. unabr. ed. Garrison Keillor. 4 CDs. (Running Time: 5 hrs. 30 mins.). (ENG.). 2004. audio compact disk 22.95 (978-1-56511-928-4(2), 1565119282) Pub: HighBridge. Dist(s): Workman Pub

Homeland. E. V Thompson. Read by Joe Dunlop. 12 cass. (Running Time: 16 hrs.). (Soundings Ser.). (J). 2004. 94.95 (978-1-84283-568-5(8)) Pub: ISIS Lrg Prnt GBR. Dist(s): Ulverscroft US

Homeland. abr. ed. John Jakes. Read by Edward Herrmann. 4 cass. (Running Time: 6 hrs.). 2001. 25.00 (978-1-59040-115-6(8), Phoenix Audio) Pub: Amer Intl Pub. Dist(s): PerseuPGW

Homeland. unabr. ed. E. V. Thompson. Read by Joe Dunlop. 15 CDs. (Running Time: 57600 sec.). (Sound Ser.). 2003. audio compact disk 104.95 (978-1-84283-695-8(1)) Pub: ISIS Lrg Prnt GBR. Dist(s): Ulverscroft US

Homeland, Pt. 1. unabr. collector's ed. John Jakes. Read by Michael Kramer. 15 cass. (Running Time: 22 hrs. 30 min.). 1993. 120.00 (978-0-7366-2575-3(5), 3324-A) Books on Tape.

Spanning the turbulent 1890s, this is the first in Jake's new cycle about the Crown family of Chicago.

Homeland, Pt. 2. collector's ed. John Jakes. Read by Michael Kramer. 14 cass. (Running Time: 21 hrs.). 1993. 112.00 (978-0-7366-2576-0(3), 3324-B) Books on Tape.

Homeland: An Extraordinary Story of Hope & Survival. unabr. ed. George Obama. (Running Time: 8 hrs. 30 mins.). 2010. 29.95 (978-1-4417-3321-4(3)); 59.95 (978-1-4417-3317-7(5)); audio compact disk 29.95 (978-1-4417-3320-7(5)) Blckstn Audio.

Homeland: An Extraordinary Story of Hope & Survival. unabr. ed. George Obama. Narrated by Dion Graham. 8 CDs. (Running Time: 8 hrs. 30 mins.). 2010. audio compact disk 76.00 (978-1-4417-3318-4(3)) Blckstn Audio.

Homeland & Exile. Zalman Schachter. 2 cass. 18.00 set. (A0621-90) Sound Photosyn.

At the San Francisco Jewish Community Center.

***Homeland & Other Stories.** abr. ed. Barbara Kingsolver. Read by Barbara Kingsolver. (ENG.). 2005. (978-0-06-089461-0(X), Harper Audio); (978-0-06-089460-3(1), Harper Audio) HarperCollins Pubs.

Homeland & Other Stories. unabr. ed. Barbara Kingsolver. Read by Paula Parker. 6 vols. (Running Time: 9 hrs.). 2000. bk. 54.95 (978-0-7927-2233-5(7), CSL 122, Chivers Sound Lib) AudioGO.

Explores the twin themes of family ties and the life choices one must ultimately make alone.

Homeland & Other Stories. unabr. ed. Barbara Kingsolver. Read by Paula Parker. 8 CDs. (Running Time: 12 hrs.). 2001. audio compact disk 79.95 (978-0-7927-9978-8(X), SLD 029, Chivers Sound Lib) AudioGO.

Barbara Kingsolver creates a rich & emotionally resonant collection of twelve stories of hope, momentary joy & powerful endurance that explore the twin themes of family ties & the life choices one must ultimately make alone.

***Homeless.** Elsie Schmied Knoke. Read by Beverly Bremers & Tim Simmons. (Running Time: 55). (ENG.). 2009. 2.99 (978-1-61114-005-7(6)) Mind Wings Aud.

Homeless. Elsie Schmied Knoke. Read by Beverly Bremers & Tim Simmons. 2009. audio compact disk 5.49 (978-0-9821192-6-6(7)) Mind Wings Aud.

Homeless Bird. Gloria Whelan. Read by Sarita Choudhury. 3 CDs. (Running Time: 3 hrs. 15 mins.). (J). (gr. 5-9). 2004. audio compact disk 30.00 (978-0-8072-2013-9(2), Listening Lib) Random Audio Pubg.

Homeless Bird. unabr. ed. Gloria Whelan. Read by Sarita Choudhury. 2 vols. (Running Time: 3 hrs. 15 mins.). (J). (gr. 5-9). 2004. pap. bk. 29.00 (978-0-8072-8859-7(4), Listening Lib) Random Audio Pubg.

Homeless Bird. unabr. ed. Gloria Whelan. Read by Sarita Choudbury. 2 cass. (Running Time: 3 hrs. 15 mins.). (J). (gr. 5-9). 2004. 23.00 (978-0-8072-8858-0(6), Listening Lib) Random Audio Pubg.

Like many girls her age in India, thirteen-year-old-Koly is getting married. Full of hope and courage, she leaves home forever. But in a grim turn of events Koly finds herself cast out into a current of cruel tradition. Her future, it would seem, is lost. Yet this rare young woman, bewildered & brave, sets out to forge her own exceptional future.

Homeless Pooch. John R. Erickson. Read by John R. Erickson. 2 cass. (Running Time: Approx 2 hours). (Hank the Cowdog Ser.: A1). (J). 2004. 14.99 (978-1-59188-381-4(4)); audio compact disk 14.99 (978-1-59188-681-5(3)) Maverick Bks.

That?s right! It all starts with Hank as a puppy enjoying his family?s backyard home. But, feathers really fly when Hank the puppy defends his backyard against invading?Phantom Ducks? Hank?s mother says it?s a good time for him to go out on his own before the dogcatcher arrives! Hank makes his way to the Twitchell Livestock Auction. Will he join up with Slim, the cowboy he meets there? Or will the dogcatcher provide his new home?Hear Hank sing ?Leaving Home?.Bonus Stories: Included on this audio are the first two Hank the Cowdog short stories ever written!.

Homemade Band. Perf. by Hap Palmer. 1 cass. (J). 11.95 (EA 545C); lp 11.95 (EA 545) Kimbo Educ.

Beautiful Day - Play Your Sticks - Make a Pretty Sound - I'm a Little Wood Block & more.

Homemade Chopin: John Kane, piano. (Homemade Recordings by Pianist John Kane). 1994. audio compact disk (978-0-9706977-0-7(8)) Keynote Records.

Homemade Games & Activities: Make Your Own Rhythm Band! 1 cass. (J). (ps-2). 2001. pap. bk. 10.95 (KIM 9106C) Kimbo Educ.

Children will not only play games to music, but actually create their own fun. Turn household objects into newspaper balls, cardboard tube flutes, juice can rattles, sequined bean bags & more. Original lyrics set to favorite tunes gives this unique recording an extra fun twist. Together Again (Annie), A Spoonful of Sugar, Bear Necessities, Hi Ho, Whistle While You Work, Popeye the Sailor Man & more. Includes guide.

***Homemade Haunting: A Novel.** Zondervan. (ENG.). 2011. 14.99 (978-0-310-41270-0(6)) Zondervan.

Homemade Liszt: John Kane, Piano. (Homemade Recordings by Pianist John Kane). 2000. audio compact disk (978-0-9706977-5-2(9)) Keynote Records.

Homemade Love. J. California Cooper. 5 cass. (Running Time: 6 hrs. 45 mins.). 1998. 48.00 (978-0-7887-4834-9(3), F0002E7) Recorded Bks.

In one of her most popular volumes, the author writes with a warm, witty style that's definitely her own. Each of her short stories is a gem of downhome wisdom, polished with a bit of gossip, some heartbreak & lots of humor.

Homemade Mozart Vol. 1: Piano. Perf. by John Kane. 1994. audio compact disk (978-0-9706977-2-1(4)) Keynote Records.

Homemade Mozart Vol. 2: Piano. Perf. by John Kane. 1994. audio compact disk (978-0-9706977-4-5(0)) Keynote Records.

Homemade Rachmaninoff: Piano. Perf. by John Kane. 1994. audio compact disk (978-0-9706977-3-8(2)) Keynote Records.

Homemade 1994 Recital: Piano. Perf. by John Kane. 1994. audio compact disk (978-0-9706977-1-4(6)) Keynote Records.

Homenaje. Marcos Witt. 2003. audio compact disk 14.99 (978-0-8297-4372-2(3)) Zondervan.

Marcos Witt, together with Danilo Montero, Marcos Barriento and Jorge Lozano, participate in "Homecoming", the new project of CanZion Productions that was recorded live in a event with the same name October 14th, 1999 in the Aztec Stadium of Mexico. With a mix of music styles like "dance", pop, ballads, and pop-rock, this project talks about the identity of a Christian, evangelism and unity in the body of Christ. The production of "Homecoming" was directed by Coalo Zamorano, Emmanuel Espinosa y Marcos Witt. The first two, together with Isaac Escamilla y Juan Salinas, worked together in the musical arrangements. This event brought more than 95 thousand people together.

Homenaje. unabr. ed. Marcos Witt. (SPA.). 2003. 9.99 (978-0-8297-4374-6(X)) Pub: Vida Pubs. Dist(s): Zondervan

Homeopathy. Dana Ullman. 1 cass. (Roy Tuckman Interview Ser.). 9.00 (A0488-89) Sound Photosyn.

Homeopathy, Vol. 7. Jonathan Parker. 2 cass. (Running Time: 2 hrs.). 1998. 17.00 Set. (978-1-58400-006-8(6)) QuantumQuests Intl.

Homeopathy: Energy Medicine. Jane Cicchetti. 2 cass. (Running Time: 2 hrs.). 1992. 19.95 set. (978-1-57124-003-3(9)) Creat Seminars.

A natural system of health care.

Homeopathy: Medicine for the Twenty-First Century. Dana Ullman. 2 cass. 18.00 set. (A0692-90) Sound Photosyn.

Where it is useful & how it is done but not why it works just that it does.

Homeopathy, Chiropractic & Acupuncture. Andrew Weil. 1 cass. (Running Time: 1 hr.). (Integrated Consciousness & Health Ser.). 1976. 11.00 (3613) Big Sur Tapes.
Two hundred years ago, the medical profession enjoyed neither the prestige nor the monopoly on health care which it has today. With aseptic procedure & modern pharmacology far in the future, doctors killed as many people as they healed, leaving plenty of room in the health field for a variety of other healing systems. One of these systems, homeopathy, became an important alternative to allopathic (traditional) medicine & nearly became the dominant medical system in the United States. The basic premise of homeopathic medicine is that a substance which causes symptoms can be used to cure the very same symptoms, provided a small enough dosage is used. Even though science can't explain how homeopathy works, it does have a good cure rate & enjoyed much prominence in the 19th century.

Homeowners' Emergency Mortgage Assistance Act (HEMAP) Update. 1999. bk. 99.00 (AL-206) PA Bar Inst.
Guidelines, effective July 2, 1994, imposed new notice requirements & procedures & required the use of new model forms by lenders, among other changes. This package will give you a quick update on HEMAP.

Homeowners Guide to Basement & Crawlspace Waterproofing. Dale A. Pollard. 2005. audio compact disk 19.95 (978-1-59975-330-0(8)) Indep Pub IL.

Homepages im World Wide Web: Eine Interlinguale Untersuchung zur Textualitat in einem Globalen Medium. Daniela Schutte. Ed. by Albert Busch et al. (Germanistische Arbeiten zu Sprache und Kulturgeschichte Ser.: Vol. 44). (GER., 2004. bk. 76.95 (978-3-631-51326-2(7)) P Lang Pubng.

***Homeplace.** unabr. ed. Gilbert Morris. (Running Time: 12 hrs. 48 mins. 0 sec.). (Singing River Ser.). (ENG.). 2009. 12.99 (978-0-310-30525-5(X)) Zondervan.

***Homeport.** Nora Roberts. 2010. audio compact disk 9.99 (978-1-4418-5656-2(0)) Brilliance Audio.

Homeport. abr. ed. Nora Roberts. Read by Erika Leigh. 3 CDs. (Running Time: 3 hrs.). 2003. audio compact disk 14.99 (978-1-59086-518-7(9), 1590865189, BAU) Brilliance Audio.
The unseen assailant attacked Dr. Miranda Jones outside her Maine home as she returned from a busy lecture tour. After terrorizing her with a knife held to her throat, he stole her purse, slashed her tires, and disappeared. Shaken and bruised, Miranda was determined to put the assault out of her mind, and welcomed the distraction offered by a summons to Italy to verify the authenticity of a Renaissance bronze of a Medici courtesan known as The Dark Lady. However, instead of cementing Miranda's reputation as a leading authority in her field, the bronze nearly destroys it when her professional judgment is called into question and the bronze is declared a hoax. Desperate to restore her credibility and prove The Dark Lady is really a previously unknown work of Michelangelo, Miranda turns to Ryan Boldari, a seductive - and supposedly reformed - art thief. For Miranda, forced to rely on herself and a partner with his own hidden agenda, the only way home is filled with treachery, deception, and a danger that threatens everything she loves.

Homeport. unabr. ed. Nora Roberts. Read by Erika Leigh. 10 cass. (Running Time: 15 hrs.). 1998. 89.25 (978-1-56740-565-1(7), 1567405657, Unabridge Lib Edns) Brilliance Audio.

Homeport. unabr. ed. Nora Roberts. Read by Erika Leigh. (Running Time: 15 hrs.). 2004. 24.95 (978-1-59335-799-3(0), 1593357990, Brilliance MP3); 39.25 (978-1-59710-374-9(8), 1597103748, BADLE); 24.95 (978-1-59710-375-6(6), 1597103756, BAD); 39.25 (978-1-59335-933-1(0), 1593359330, Brlnc Audio MP3 Lib); 29.95 (978-1-59600-103-9(8), 1596001038) Brilliance Audio.

Homeport. unabr. ed. Nora Roberts. Read by Erika Leigh. (Running Time: 16 hrs.). 2008. audio compact disk 117.25 (978-1-4233-3406-4(X), 9781423334064, BriAudCD Unabrid); audio compact disk 38.95 (978-1-4233-3405-7(1), 9781423334057, Bril Audio CD Unabri) Brilliance Audio.

***Homer & Langley.** unabr. ed. E. L. Doctorow. Read by Arthur Morey. 6 CDs. (Running Time: 7 hrs.). 2009. audio compact disk 50.00 (978-1-4159-6563-4(3), BksonTape) Pub: Random Audio Pubg. Dist(s): Random

Homer & Langley. unabr. ed. E. L. Doctorow. Read by Arthur Morey. (ENG.). 2009. audio compact disk 32.00 (978-0-7393-3416-4(6), Random AudioBks) Pub: Random Audio Pubg. Dist(s): Random

Homer & the Birth of Tragedy. unabr. ed. Read by Walter Kaufmann. 1 cass. (Running Time: 1 hr. 25 mins.). (Sound Seminars Lectures on the Classics). 1963. 14.95 (C23115) J Norton Pubs.
A comparison of the "Iliad" with the works of Aeschylus. He discusses the similarities, the differences & the functions of the gods.

Homer Box Set: Iliad & Odyssey. Homer. Read by Anthony Heald. 2008. audio compact disk 29.95 (978-1-4332-4882-5(4)) Blckstn Audio.

Homer in Flight. abr. ed. Rabindranath Maharaj. Narrated by Luther Hansraj. Prod. by CBC Radio Staff. 3 cass. (Running Time: 4 hrs.). (Between the Covers Collection). (ENG.). 2005. 19.95 (978-0-86492-300-4(7)) Pub: BTC Audiobks CAN. Dist(s): U Toronto Pr

Homer Price. Robert McCloskey. Narrated by John McDonough. 3 CDs. (Running Time: 2 hrs. 45 mins.). (gr. 3 up). audio compact disk 29.00 (978-0-7887-6163-8(3)) Recorded Bks.

Homer Price. abr. ed. Robert McCloskey. 1 cass. (Running Time: 50 mins.). Dramatization. (J). (gr. 4-7). 1973. 9.95 (978-0-670-37732-9(5)) Live Oak Media.

Homer Price. unabr. ed. Robert McCloskey. Narrated by John McDonough. 2 pieces. (Running Time: 2 hrs. 45 mins.). (gr. 3 up). 2001. 20.00 (978-0-7887-4720-5(7), 96394E7) Recorded Bks.
Homer Price finds himself in the midst of a rib-tickling adventure. Like the time he tames a friendly skunk, then his new pet gets mixed up with dangerous robbers & other hilarious tales.

Homer Price. unabr. ed. Robert McCloskey. Narrated by John McDonough. 2 cass. (Running Time: 2 hrs. 45 mins.). (J). (gr. 3-5). 2001. pap. bk. & stu. ed. 34.24 Recorded Bks.
Homer Price always finds himself in the midst of a rib-tickling adventure. Like the time he tames a friendly skunk, then his new pet gets mixed up with dangerous robbers & other hilarious tales.

Homer Price. unabr. ed. Robert McCloskey. Narrated by John McDonough. 2 CDs. (Running Time: 2 hrs. 45 min.). (J). (gr. 3-5). 2001. audio compact disk 29.00 (C1387) Recorded Bks.

Homer Price, Set. abr. ed. Robert McCloskey. 11 vols. (Running Time: 50 mins.). Dramatization. (J). 1973. pap. bk. 15.95 incl. pap. bk. in bag. (978-0-670-37734-3(1)) Live Oak Media.

Homer Price, Set. abr. ed. Robert McCloskey. 11 vols. (Running Time: 50 mins.). Dramatization. (J). (gr. 4-7). 1973. bk. 24.95 incl. cloth bk. in bag. (978-0-670-37733-6(3)) Live Oak Media.

Homer Price Stories. Robert McCloskey. Read by Robert McCloskey. 1 cass. (J). pap. bk. 12.95 (PRA400); 8.95 (RAC400) Weston Woods.
Read-Along Cassette.

Homer's Daughter. unabr. collector's ed. Robert Graves. Read by Lindy Nettleton. 6 cass. (Running Time: 9 hrs.). 1986. 48.00 (978-0-7366-1051-3(0), 1979) Books on Tape.
Robert Graves recreates the Odyssey. He bases his story on Samuel Butler's argument that the author of the Odyssey was not the blind & bearded Homer of legend, but a young woman who calls herself Nausicaa in Graves' story.

Homer's Odyssey: A Fearless Feline Tale, or How I Learned about Love & Life with a Blind Wonder Cat. unabr. ed. Gwen Cooper. Read by Renée Raudman. (ENG.). 2009. audio compact disk 35.00 (978-0-307-70411-5(4), Random AudioBks) Pub: Random Audio Pubg. Dist(s): Random

***Homer's Odyssey: A Fearless Feline Tale, or How I Learned about Love & Life with a Blind Wonder Cat.** unabr. ed. Gwen Cooper. Read by Renée Raudman. 8 CDs. (Running Time: 9 hrs. 30 mins.). 2009. audio compact disk 80.00 (978-0-307-70413-9(0), BksonTape) Pub: Random Audio Pubg. Dist(s): Random

Homer's Sun Still Shines: Ancient Greece in Essays, Poems & Translations. Poems. Vera Lachmann. Ed. by Charles Miller. 1 cass. (Running Time: 32 min). 2004. per. 20.00 (978-0-9606522-3-5(X)) Trackaday.
Passages from Homer's Odyssey in English and Greek; poetry and excerpts from drama in English and Greek; musical setting by Tui St. George Tucker of a poem in German by Vera Lachmann.

Homer's the Iliad & the Odyssey. abr. unabr. ed. Alberto Manguel. Narrated by Michael Prichard. (Running Time: 7 hrs. 0 mins. 0 sec.). (Books That Changed the World Ser.). (ENG.). 2008. audio compact disk 59.99 (978-1-4001-3393-2(9)) Pub: Tantor Media. Dist(s): IngramPubServ

Homer's the Iliad & the Odyssey. unabr. ed. Alberto Manguel. Narrated by Michael Prichard. (Running Time: 7 hrs. 0 mins. 0 sec.). (Books That Changed the World Ser.). (ENG.). 2008. audio compact disk 19.99 (978-1-4001-5393-0(X)) Pub: Tantor Media. Dist(s): IngramPubServ

Homer's the Iliad & the Odyssey: A Biography. unabr. ed. Alberto Manguel. Narrated by Michael Prichard. (Running Time: 7 hrs. 0 mins. 0 sec.). (Books That Changed the World Ser.). (ENG.). 2008. audio compact disk 29.99 (978-1-4001-0393-5(2)) Pub: Tantor Media. Dist(s): IngramPubServ

Homer's the Odyssey. Stanley P. Baldwin. (Cliffs Notes (Playaway) Ser.). 2007. 34.99 (978-1-60252-891-8(8)) Find a World.

Homeschooling, the Solution to Our Education Problem. 2006. audio compact disk 7.20 (978-1-932012-69-9(9)) Apologia Educ.

Homesick, My Own Story. 2004. bk. 24.95 (978-0-7882-0655-9(9)); pap. bk. 14.95 (978-0-7882-0595-8(1)); 8.95 (978-1-56008-925-4(3)) Weston Woods.

Homespun. Perf. by Jenny Mahan. Music by Jenny Mahan. 2001. audio compact disk 15.50 (978-0-9659189-1-6(2)) Sweetwater Vis.

Homespun Songs of Faith, 1861-1865. Bobby Horton. 1 cass. (Running Time: 55 min.). 1991. 10.00 (978-1-882604-08-1(3), SRU 203 238) B Horton Mus.
Authentic Gospel songs & hymns presented as sung & played by Americans (North & South) during the War Between the States with historical written backgrounds for each tune.

Homespun Songs of Faith 1861-1865. Bobby Horton. 1 CD. 1991. audio compact disk 15.00 (978-1-882604-23-4(7)) B Horton Mus.

Homespun Songs of the C. S. A., Vol. 1. Bobby Horton. 1 cass. (Running Time: 55 min.). 1985. 10.00 (978-1-882604-00-5(8), SRU86 818); audio compact disk 15.00 CD. (978-1-882604-15-9(6)) B Horton Mus.
Authentic music of the Confederacy from The War Between the States played (on mostly "period" instruments) & sung in the style of the era; with written historical background for each tune presented.

Homespun Songs of the C. S. A., Vol. 2. Bobby Horton. 1 cass. (Running Time: 45 min.). 1986. 10.00 (978-1-882604-01-2(6), SRU99 761); audio compact disk 15.00 CD. (978-1-882604-16-6(4)) B Horton Mus.

Homespun Songs of the C. S. A., Vol. 3. Bobby Horton. 1 CD. 1987. audio compact disk 15.00 (978-1-882604-17-3(2)); 10.00 (978-1-882604-02-9(4), SR86-533) B Horton Mus.

Homespun Songs of the C. S. A., Vol. 4. Bobby Horton. 1 CD. 1988. audio compact disk 15.00 (978-1-882604-18-0(0)); 10.00 (978-1-882604-03-6(2), SR98-918) B Horton Mus.

Homespun Songs of the C. S. A., Vol. 5. Bobby Horton. 1 cass. (Running Time: 60 min.). 1993. 10.00 (978-1-882604-24-1(5), SR152 226) B Horton Mus.

Homespun Songs of the C. S. A., Vol. 5. Bobby Horton. 1 CD. 1996. audio compact disk 15.00 (978-1-882604-50-0(4)) B Horton Mus.

Homespun Songs of the Christmas Season. Bobby Horton. 1 cass. (Running Time: 40 min.). 10.00 (978-1-882604-07-4(5)) B Horton Mus.
Authentic songs of the Christmas Season played with (mostly) "period" instruments in the style of the Civil War period.

Homespun Songs of the Christmas Season, Vol. 1. Bobby Horton. 1 CD. audio compact disk 15.00 (978-1-882604-22-7(9)) B Horton Mus.

Homespun Songs of the Union Army, Vol. 1. Bobby Horton. 1 cass. (Running Time: 55 min.). 1987. 10.00 (978-1-882604-04-3(0), SR86-540); audio compact disk 15.00 CD. (978-1-882604-19-7(9)) B Horton Mus.
Authentic music of the Union Army from The War Between the States played (on mostly "period" instruments) & sung in the style of the period, with written historical backgrounds for each song presented.

Homespun Songs of the Union Army, Vol. 2. Bobby Horton. 1990. audio compact disk 15.00 (978-1-882604-20-3(2)); 10.00 (978-1-882604-05-0(9), SR114-583) B Horton Mus.

Homespun Songs of the Union Army, Vol. 3. Bobby Horton. 1 CD. 1991. audio compact disk 15.00 (978-1-882604-21-0(0)); 10.00 (978-1-882604-06-7(7), SR136 283) B Horton Mus.

Homespun Songs of the Union Army, Vol. 4. Bobby Horton. 1 cass. 1999. 10.00 (978-1-882604-53-1(9)); audio compact disk 15.00 (978-1-882604-54-8(7)) B Horton Mus.

Homespun Songs of Vicksburg: Soundtrack for the National Park Service. Bobby Horton. 1997. (978-1-882604-52-4(0)) B Horton Mus.

Homespun Songs of Vicksburg: Soundtrack for the NPS Film. Bobby Horton. 1 cass. 1997. 10.00 (978-1-882604-51-7(2)) B Horton Mus.

Homespun Tales. 1 cass. (Running Time: 41 min.). 1991. 11.95 (978-1-879991-03-3(9), 105C) Natl Storytlng Network.
A collection of stories told by America's best loved professional storytellers.

Homespun Tales: A Country-Flavored Collection. Short Stories. Perf. by Doc McConnell et al. Prod. by National Storytelling Press Staff. 1 CD. (Running Time: 48 mins.). 2002. audio compact disk 12.95 (978-1-879991-30-9(6), Natl Storytell) Natl Storytlng Network.
As new settlers made this land their own, they brought with them their most treasured possessions - including their stories. Homespun Tales: A Country-Flavored Collection presents tales, legends, and lore that reflect the roots and values of the American spirit. These timeless stories entertain and inspire, offering us courage, hope, and wisdom.This special collection, recorded live at the National Storytelling Festival, celebrates this country's favorite stories - from Jack tales and ghost stories to legends, folk and fairy tales, and personal remmbrances. Here for your enjoyment, is the best in American storytelling.

Homespun Tales: A Homecoming Collection from Napps. 1 cass. (Running Time: 48 min.). (J). 8.95 (WW743C) Weston Woods.

Homespun Tales: Homecoming Collection from Napps-the Snake & the Frog; the Farmer Who Vanished; the Crack of Dawn; Wiley & the Hairy Man; the Foolish Bet; the Peddler's Dream. 2004. 8.95 (978-1-56008-441-9(3)) Weston Woods.

***Homesteads.** Ernest Haycox. 2009. (978-1-60136-443-2(1)) Audio Holding.

Homesteads. Ernest Haycox. Read by Christopher Walker. (Running Time: 0 hr. 42 mins.). 1999. 10.95 (978-1-60083-500-1(7)) Iofy Corp.

Hometown Honeys. unabr. ed. Celeste Hamilton & Leslie Daniels. 1 cass. (Running Time: 90 min.). (Afterglow Romantic Walks Ser.). 1998. 10.99 (978-1-892026-00-2(7)) Afterglow.
Two short stories about finding love in your own backyard.

Hometown Legend. Jerry B. Jenkins. Read by Frank Muller. 4 cass. (Running Time: 6 hrs.). 2001. 24.98 Hachet Audio.
Cal Sawyer is raising a teenage daughter, Rachel, who is helping the coach keep the American Leather Football Company from going down the drain.

Hometown Legend. Jerry B. Jenkins. Narrated by Tom Stechschulte. 6 cass. (Running Time: 8 hrs. 45 mins.). 57.00 (978-1-4025-0246-0(X)) Recorded Bks.

Hometown Legend. abr. ed. Jerry B. Jenkins. Read by Frank Muller. (ENG.). 2005. 14.98 (978-1-59483-407-3(5)) Pub: Hachet Audio. Dist(s): HachBkGrp

Homeward Bound Two Soundtrack. Walt Disney Productions Staff. 1 CD. (J). audio compact disk 19.98 (978-0-7634-0041-5(6)) W Disney Records.

Homeward Bound Two Soundtrack. Prod. by Walt Disney Productions Staff. 1 cass. (J). 12.98 (978-0-7634-0039-2(4)) W Disney Records.

Homeward to an Open Door: Exploring Major Principles of "A Course in Miracles" unabr. ed. Carol Howe. 4 cass. (Running Time: 5 hrs.). 1993. 29.95 Set. (978-1-889642-18-5(5)) C Howe.
Designed for current students & those seeking a comprehensive introduction. Topics covered are: Belief systems to which we subscribe & their consequences. The physical body & its healing. Choices, decision-making & problem solving. Special vs. Holy relationships, our desire to be special, & the relationship of the ego to the world.

Homework Essentials Plus CD from Encyclopaedia Britannica: Reference & Learning for Grades 2 To 12. Compiled by Encyclopaedia Britannica, Inc. (gr. 2-12). 2004. audio compact disk 19.95 (978-1-59339-070-9(X), 032504 80 JCAS) Ency Brit Inc.

Homework Essentials Plus 2004 CD plus U. S. Presidents CD & Dinosaurs. Compiled by Encyclopaedia Britannica, Inc. 2004. audio compact disk (978-1-59339-082-2(3)); audio compact disk (978-1-59339-083-9(1)) Ency Brit Inc.

Homework Machine. Dan Gutman. 3. (Running Time: 3 hrs. 25 mins.). 2007. 33.75 (978-1-4281-4478-1(1)); audio compact disk 30.75 (978-1-4281-4483-5(8)) Recorded Bks.

Homework Review - The Syllogism. John Robbins. 1 cass. (Introduction to Logic Ser.: No. 7). 5.00 Trinity Found.

Homicidal Maniac see Escape, No. 2

Homicide Trinity. unabr. collector's ed. Rex Stout. Read by Michael Prichard. 8 cass. (Running Time: 8 hrs.). (Nero Wolfe Ser.). 1999. 64.00 (978-0-7366-4062-6(2), 4573) Books on Tape.
The orchid-growing gourmet Nero Wolfe & his confidential assistant, Archie Goodwin, dine on a three course feat of murder. The menu in the first case is a double helping of lethal instruments. In the second, an embarassing situation develops when Wolfe's own soup-stained tie becomes a deadly weapon. Finally, Rex Stout proves that one can indeed have too much money, when a healthy serving of greenbacks & a ham actor lead Archie to an unpleasant discovery: a poor dead soul who may or may not have gotten his just desserts.

Homicide: Understanding the Unique & Complex Challenges Survivors Face. Mary M. Wong. 1 cass. 1997. 12.00 (978-0-9645608-2-6(8)) ADM Pub.
Discusses the emotional, spiritual, physical, financial challenges the criminal justice system's effect on surviving family members categorized under subject headings - homocide, murder, grief, consolation, bereavement & law.

Homilias: Mensajes de Esperanza. P. Mariano de Blas. (SPA.). (YA). 2009. audio compact disk 18.95 (978-0-9674222-3-7(X)) Hombre Nuevo.

Hommage a Jean Moulin. André Malraux. 1 cass. (FRE.). 1992. 16.95 (1581-RF) Olivia & Hill.
The famous 20th-century writer & politician pays homage to the leader of the French Resistance when the latter's ashes were transported to the Pantheon.

Hommes Viennent de Mars, les Femmes Viennent de Venus. John Gray. Adapted by Jean-Louis Morgan. 1 cass. (Running Time: 90 mins.). (Collection Resources).Tr. of Men Are from Mars, Women are from Venus. (FRE.). 1998. cass. & audio compact disk 14.95 (978-2-921997-45-4(2)) Pub: Coffragants CAN. Dist(s): Penton Overseas
Recorded completely in international French language by well-known actors or speakers.

Homo Futurus (Readings From) Poems. Barbara Rosenthal. Read by Barbara Rosenthal. 1 CD. (Running Time: 30 mins.). 2005. audio compact disk 25.00 (978-0-9760793-4-7(8)) eMedialoft.
This spoken-word audio CD is digitally reamstered from the original NYC reading of her book "Homo Futurus" by Barbara Rosenthal, Surrealist Writer and Conceptual Artist, a keeper of ongoing journals for over 40 years, whose Literary Agent was Gunther Stuhlmann, editor of Anais Nin's "Diaries." This edited journal-text, in clipped, poetic phrases, covers the years of her early parenthood, the death of her mother, and the creation of some of her major mid-career works of art and philosophy.

Homo Politicus: The Strange & Scary Tribes That Run Our Government. unabr. ed. Dana Milbank. Read by Johnny Heller. (YA). 2008. 59.99 (978-1-60514-434-4(7)) Find a World.

Homo Politicus: The Strange & Scary Tribes That Run Our Government. unabr. ed. Dana Milbank. Read by Johnny Heller. 8 CDs. (Running Time: 10 hrs. 0 mins. 0 sec.). (ENG.). 2008. audio compact disk 34.99 (978-1-4001-0604-2(4)); audio compact disk 69.99 (978-1-4001-3604-9(0)); audio compact disk 24.99 (978-1-4001-5604-7(1)) Pub: Tantor Media. Dist(s): IngramPubServ

Homocystinuria - A Bibliography & Dictionary for Physicians, Patients, & Genome Researchers. Compiled by Icon Group International, Inc. Staff. 2007. ring bd. 28.95 (978-0-497-11374-2(0)) Icon Grp.

Homogeneous Catalysis. Instructed by Penny A. Chaloner. 7 cass. (Running Time: 6 hrs. 30 min.). 505.00 incl. 585pp. manual. (81) Am Chemical.
Provides an introduction to the field with examples from specialized laboratory procedures & large-scale industrial processes.

Homosexuality: Logos Feb. 20, 2000. Ben Young. 2000. 4.95 (978-0-7417-6170-5(X), B0170) Win Walk.

Homosexuality & the Renewal of Gender. John Beebe. Read by John Beebe. 1 cass. (Running Time: 98 min.). 1993. 10.95 (978-0-7822-0451-3(1), 529) C G Jung IL.
Homosexual development inevitably includes a serious engagement with the meaning of one's own gender. This can be a path with many windings, according to San Francisco analyst John Beebe, in which different lights are cast on the meaning of both masculinity & femininity of the individual person - leading to a renewal of traditional conceptions. Part of the conference set Who Do We Think We Are?: The Mystery & Muddle of Gender.

Homosexuality vs. Heterosexuality. Louise Fimlaid. 1 cass. 1992. 8.95 (1029) Am Fed Astrologers.

Homosexuals in History. unabr. ed. A. L. Rowse. Read by Ian Whitcomb. 12 cass. (Running Time: 18 hrs.). 1995. 96.00 (978-0-7366-3056-6(2), 3738) Books on Tape.
Public disdain for their lifestyle inspired prominent gays in history to great achievement. Fascinating from any point of view.

Hon. Sec. see Sir John Betjeman Reading His Poetry

Hondo. abr. unabr. ed. Louis L'Amour. Read by David Strathairn. 4 cass. (Running Time: 6 hrs.). (Louis L'Amour Ser.). (ENG.). 2004. audio compact disk 21.00 (978-0-7393-1092-2(5)) Pub: Random Audio Pubg. Dist(s): Random

Hondo & Fabian. unabr. ed. Peter McCarty. Narrated by Jeff Brooks. 1 CD. (Running Time: 6 mins.). (J). (ps-3). 2006. bk. 29.95 (978-0-439-84906-7(3), WHCD688); bk. 24.95 (978-0-439-84905-0(5), WHRA688) Weston Woods.
What happens when the dog of the house goes to the beach and leaves the cat at home with the baby? Find out in this gentle tale of the two very different days of house pets, Hondo the dog, and Fabian the cat.

Honest Christmas: Honesty Subliminals in Christmas Music. Tag Powell & Judith L. Powell. Music by Kay Blais. 1 cass. 1991. 12.95 (978-0-914295-97-6(7)) Top Mtn Pub.
You can make this Christmas selling season a merrier one - with fewer worries & more profits. One of the problems that comes with the rush of Christmas crowds is shoplifting. Now there's help for this challenge with this unique new subliminal, anti-shoplifting audiocassette "An Honest Christmas".

Honest Illusions. abr. ed. Nora Roberts. Read by Sandra Burr. (Running Time: 6 hrs.). 2007. audio compact disk 14.99 (978-1-4233-3206-0(7), 9781423332060, BCD Value Price) Brilliance Audio.

***Honest Illusions.** abr. ed. Nora Roberts. Read by Sandra Burr. (Running Time: 6 hrs.). 2010. audio compact disk 9.99 (978-1-4418-7686-7(3), 9781441876867, BCD Value Price) Brilliance Audio.

Honest Illusions. unabr. ed. Nora Roberts. Read by Sandra Burr. 10 cass. (Running Time: 14 hrs.). 1992. 89.25 Set. (978-1-56100-113-2(9), 1561001139, Unabridge Lib Edns) Brilliance Audio.
As the daughter of a world-renowned magician who is equally accomplished as a jewel thief, Roxy Nouvelle inherits her father's genius. Dashing escape artist Luke Callahan also possesses a gift for relieving the wealthy of their valuables. Brought up together, Roxy and Luke are partners first in illusion, then in crime, and finally in passion. But the shadow of his past stalks Luke, forcing him to vanish or see his loved one ruined. Years of hollow fame and lonely affluence pass before Roxy and Luke reunite to execute the most daring heist of their careers and to exact sweet revenge. The novels of Nora Roberts have earned her devoted fan around the world. Honest Illusions is a shimmering novel of magic, glamour, mystery, and intrigue.

Honest Illusions. unabr. ed. Nora Roberts. Read by Sandra Burr. (Running Time: 14 hrs.). 2005. 39.25 (978-1-59600-795-6(8), 9781596007956, BADLE); 24.95 (978-1-59600-794-9(X), 9781596007949, BAD); audio compact disk 24.95 (978-1-59600-792-5(3), 9781596007925, Brilliance MP3); audio compact disk 39.25 (978-1-59600-793-2(1), 9781596007932, Brlnc Audio MP3 Lib) Brilliance Audio.

Honest Illusions. unabr. ed. Nora Roberts. Read by Sandra Burr. (Running Time: 57600 sec.). 2008. audio compact disk 112.25 (978-1-4233-5606-6(3), 9781423356066, BriAudCD Unabrid); audio compact disk 38.95 (978-1-4233-5605-9(5), 9781423356059, Bril Audio CD Unabri) Brilliance Audio.

***Honest Illusions.** unabr. ed. Nora Roberts. Read by Sandra Burr. (Running Time: 16 hrs.). 2010. audio compact disk 24.99 (978-1-4418-7685-0(5), 9781441876850, Bril Audio CD Unabri); audio compact disk 79.97 (978-1-4418-7741-3(X), 9781441877413, BriAudCD Unabrid) Brilliance Audio.

Honest Is the Only Policy (Principle #9:See Yourself As a Service Center) Ephesians 6:12; 1 Peter 5:8. Ed Young. 1997. 4.95 (978-0-7417-2129-7(5), 1129) Win Walk.

***Honest John.** Anonymous. 2009. (978-1-60136-610-8(8)) Audio Holding.

Honest Money & Banking. Instructed by Stephen McDowell. 2000. 5.95 (978-1-887456-28-9(7)) Providence Found.

Honest President. H. Paul Jeffers. Narrated by Raymond Todd. (Running Time: 10 hrs.). 2001. 30.95 (978-1-59912-411-7(4)) Iofy Corp.

Honest President. unabr. ed. H. Paul Jeffers. Narrated by Raymond Todd. 7 cass. (Running Time: 10 hrs.). 2001. 49.95 (978-0-7861-2152-6(1), 2902) Blckstn Audio.
Today Grover Cleveland is mainly remembered as the only President to be elected to two non-consecutive terms. But in his day, Cleveland was a renowned reformer, an enemy of political machines who joined forces with Theodore Roosevelt to fight powerful party bosses, a moralist who vetoed bills he considered blatant raids on the Treasury, a vigorous defender of the Monroe Doctrine who resisted American imperialism, and a President who stood his ground against Wall Street robber barons in an era of big business. His real legacy, however, is his statesmanship. His time in office was plagued by scandal and a gossip-mongering press, but Grover Cleveland was a President of principle who never flinched from taking the high road.

Honest Thief & Other Stories see Great French & Russian Stories, Vol. 1, A Collection

Honest Thief & Other Stories. unabr. ed. Fyodor Dostoyevsky. Read by Walter Zimmerman. 1 cass. (Running Time: 88 min.). Incl. Long Exile. Leo Tolstoy. 1980. (N-52); Wedding. 1980. (N-52); 1980. 7.95 (N-52) Jimcin Record.
Best short works of a major Russian novelist.

Honestly. abr. ed. Sheila Walsh. (Running Time: 2 hrs. 0 mins. 0 sec.). (ENG.). 2003. 10.99 (978-0-310-26056-1(6)) Zondervan.

Honesty. 3 hrs. (Running Time: 3 cass.). (Adventures in Odyssey). (J). (gr. k-4). 2001. 12.99 Pub: Focus Family. Dist(s): Tommy Nelson
Adventures in Odyssey stories packaged by theme.

Honesty. Linda Eyre & Richard Eyre. 2 cass. (Running Time: 3 hrs.). (Teaching Your Children Values Ser.). (J). (ps-7). 2000. pap. bk. 16.95 (978-1-56015-785-4(2)) Penton Overseas.
Focuses on the values children need to become secure, confident & responsible people. Tape 1: coaching "how-to" program for parents. Tape 2: "Alexander's Amazing Adventures," features stories, songs, sound effects & background music. Helps them develop social skills, communication skills & life skills. Includes activity cards.

Honesty. Focus on the Family Staff. 3 cass. (Running Time: 3 hrs.). (Adventures in Odyssey). (J). (gr. 1-7). 2001. 9.99 (978-1-58997-019-9(5)) Pub: Focus Family. Dist(s): Tommy Nelson

Honesty, Vol. 7. AIO Team Staff. Created by Focus on the Family Staff. (Running Time: 1 hr. 10 mins. 0 sec.). (Adventures in Odyssey Life Lessons Ser.). (ENG.). (J). 2005. audio compact disk 5.99 (978-1-58997-224-7(4)) Pub: Focus Family. Dist(s): Tyndale Hse

Honesty: Easy. Eldon Taylor. Read by Eldon Taylor. Ed. by Leslie Brice. 1 cass. (Running Time: 1 hr.). 1992. 16.95 (978-1-56705-322-7(X)) Gateways Inst.
Self improvement.

Honesty & Positive Thinking: Lily's Big Lesson. unabr. ed. Trenna Daniells. Read by Trenna Daniells. 12 cass. (Running Time: 30 min.). (One to Grow On Ser.). (J). (gr. k-6). 1982. 9.95 (978-0-918519-08-5(X), 12007) Trenna Prods.
An impetuous young girl & a much desired pony teach children the invaluable lesson of cause & effect & that "what you put out in the world is what you get back".

Honesty & Positive Thinking - Lily's Big Lesson. Trenna Daniells. Narrated by Trenna Daniells. (ENG.). (J). 2009. (978-0-918519-54-2(3)) Trenna Prods.

Honesty, Simplicity & Revelation. Swami Amar Jyoti. 1 cass. 1979. 9.95 (K-22) Truth Consciousness.
Opening the heart to honestly see ourselves as we are. Being, not "trying to be." Touching the Divine.

Honey. unabr. ed. V. C. Andrews. 4 cass. (Isis Ser.). (J). 2003. 44.95 (978-0-7531-1604-3(9)); audio compact disk 51.95 (978-0-7531-1727-9(4)) Pub: ISIS Lrg Prnt GBR. Dist(s): Ulverscroft US

Honey: Lost on You. Perf. by Honey. Prod. by Dan Haseltine & Steven Mason. 1 cass., 1 CD. 1998. (978-0-7601-2208-2(3)); audio compact disk (978-0-7601-2209-9(1)) Provident Mus Dist.

Honey, Baby, Sweetheart. unabr. ed. Deb Caletti. Read by Amanda Ronconi. (Running Time: 8 hrs.). 2010. 39.97 (978-1-4233-9644-4(8), 9781423396444, Brlnc Audio MP3 Lib); 19.99 (978-1-4233-9643-7(X), 9781423396437, Brilliance MP3); 39.97 (978-1-4233-9646-8(4), 9781423396468, BADLE); 19.99 (978-1-4233-9645-1(6), 9781423396451, BAD); audio compact disk 54.97 (978-1-4233-9642-0(1), 9781423396420, BriAudCD Unabrid); audio compact disk 19.99 (978-1-4233-9641-3(3), 9781423396413, Bril Audio CD Unabri) Brilliance Audio.

Honey Buzz Principle. (Paws & Tales Ser.: Vol. 12). (J). 2001. 3.99 (978-1-57972-408-5(6)); audio compact disk 5.99 (978-1-57972-409-2(4)) Insight Living.

***Honey for a Child's Heart: The Imaginative Use of Books in Family Life.** Gladys Hunt. (Running Time: 4 hrs. 0 mins. 0 sec.). (ENG.). 2008. 14.99 (978-0-310-30456-2(3)) Zondervan.

Honey for Tea. unabr. ed. Elizabeth Cadell. Read by Diana Bishop. 5 cass. (Running Time: 6 hrs.). (Sound Ser.). 2004. 49.95 (978-1-86042-207-2(1), 22071) Pub: UlverLrgPrint GBR. Dist(s): Ulverscroft US
Jendy Marsh has been in love with Allen, a neighboring farmer, but he had eyes for only her sister Nancy. So when Nancy tells her that she is not going to marry Allen, Jendy cannot help feeling a tiny spark of hope. A rich, assorted group of people provide an entertaining drama of romance, intrigue & near tragedy.

Honey Moon. unabr. collector's ed. Susan Elizabeth Phillips. Read by Anna Fields. 10 cass. (Running Time: 15 hrs.). 1996. 80.00 (978-0-7366-3449-6(5), 4093) Books on Tape.
Hollywood discovers a South Carolina Orphan, Honey Jane Moon, & makes her a star. She lives a roller coaster life.

Honey, Mud, Maggots, & Other Medical Marvels: The Science Behind Folk Remedies & Old Wives' Tales. unabr. ed. Robert Root-Bernstein & Michele Root-Bernstein. Narrated by Nelson Runger. 8 cass. (Running Time: 11 hrs. 45 mins.). 1998. 70.00 (978-0-7887-2042-0(2), 95406E7) Recorded Bks.
Increasing contemporary interest in alternative medicine makes this well-written & detailed account of traditional healing practices & remedies timely. This well-paced, well-modulated reading is a surefire grabber, especially for those whose HMOs look askance at such therapeutic practices.

Honey on Hot Bread... & Other Heartfelt Wishes. Joni Hilton. 1 cass. 1995. 7.98 (978-1-57734-119-2(8), 06005578) Covenant Comms.
Warm, wise & witty thoughts.

Honey Trap. unabr. ed. Clive Egleton. Read by Christopher Kay. 12 cass. (Running Time: 18 hrs.). 2001. 94.95 (978-1-86042-897-5(5), 28975) Pub: Soundings Ltd GBR. Dist(s): Ulverscroft US

Honey Trap. unabr. ed. Clive Egleton. Read by Christopher Kay. 12 CDs. (Running Time: 13 hrs. 23 mins.). (Sound Ser.). 2002. audio compact disk 99.95 (978-1-86042-942-2(4)) Pub: UlverLrgPrint GBR. Dist(s): Ulverscroft US

Honeybees Help Flowers: Early Explorers Fluent Set A Audio CD. Benchmark Education Staff. (J). 2006. audio compact disk 10.00 (978-1-4108-7633-1(0)) Benchmark Educ.

Honeymoon. unabr. ed. James Patterson. Read by Campbell Scott & Hope Davis. (ENG.). 2005. 14.98 (978-1-59483-319-9(2)) Pub: Hachet Audio. Dist(s): HachBkGrp

Honeymoon. unabr. ed. James Patterson & Howard Roughan. Read by Campbell Scott & Hope Davis. (Running Time: 8 hrs.). (ENG.). 2009. 59.98 (978-1-60788-026-4(1)) Pub: Hachet Audio. Dist(s): HachBkGrp

Honeymoon House: A Selection from the Almost Home Anthology. unabr. ed. Mary Carter. (Running Time: 4 hrs.). 2009. 39.97 (978-1-4418-0086-2(7), 9781441800862, BADLE); 24.99 (978-1-4418-0085-5(9), 9781441800855, BAD) Brilliance Audio.

Honeymoon in Tehran: Two Years of Love & Danger in Iran. unabr. ed. Azadeh Moaveni. (Running Time: 11 hrs. 0 mins.). 2009. 29.95 (978-1-4332-6091-9(3)); audio compact disk 29.95 (978-1-4332-6090-2(5)); audio compact disk 65.95 (978-1-4332-6087-2(5)); audio compact disk 90.00 (978-1-4332-6088-9(3)) Blckstn Audio.

Honeymoon with Murder. Carolyn G. Hart. Read by Kate Reading. (Death on Demand Mystery Ser.: No. 4). 2000. audio compact disk 56.00 (978-0-7366-8051-6(9)) Books on Tape.

Honeymoon with Murder. unabr. ed. Carolyn G. Hart. Read by Kate Reading. 6 cass. (Running Time: 9 hrs.). (Death on Demand Mystery Ser.: No. 4). 2000. 48.00 (978-0-7366-4912-4(3)) Books on Tape.
Bookstore owner Annie Laurance's marriage to detective Max Darling is threatened when a bizarre murder occurs shortly after the wedding.

***Honeysuckle Summer.** abr. ed. Sherryl Woods. Read by Mary Robinette Kowal. (Running Time: 5 hrs.). (Sweet Magnolias Ser.). 2010. audio compact disk 14.99 (978-1-4418-5403-2(7), 9781441854032, BACD) Brilliance Audio.

***Honeysuckle Summer.** unabr. ed. Sherryl Woods. Read by Mary Robinette Kowal. (Running Time: 11 hrs.). (Sweet Magnolias Ser.). 2010. 19.99 (978-1-4418-5021-8(X), 9781441850218, BAD); 39.97 (978-1-4418-5020-1(1), 9781441850201, Brlnc Audio MP3 Lib); 39.97 (978-1-4418-5022-5(8), 9781441850225, BADLE); 19.99 (978-1-4418-5019-5(8), 9781441850195, Brilliance MP3); audio compact disk 79.97 (978-1-4418-5018-8(X), 9781441850188, BriAudCD Unabrid); audio compact disk 29.99 (978-1-4418-5017-1(1), 9781441850171, Bril Audio CD Unabri) Brilliance Audio.

Hong Kong. Stephen Coonts. Read by Michael Prichard. (Jake Grafton Novel Ser.: Vol. 8). 2000. audio compact disk 96.00 (978-0-7366-6300-7(2)) Books on Tape.

Hong Kong. unabr. ed. Stephen Coonts. Read by Michael Prichard. 10 cass. (Running Time: 15 hrs.). (Jake Grafton Novel Ser.: Vol. 8). 2000. 80.00 (978-0-7366-5629-0(4)) Books on Tape.
When the U.S. government sends Jake Grafton to Hong Kong to find out how deeply the U. S. consul-general is embedded in a political scandal, he takes his wife, Callie, along. The Graftons discover that Hong Kong is a powder keg ready to explode. When a rebel faction kidnaps Callie, Jake is pulled into the vortex of a high-tech civil war.

Hong Kong. unabr. ed. Stephen Coonts. Read by Michael Prichard. 12 CDs. (Running Time: 18 hrs.). (Jake Grafton Novel Ser.: Vol. 8). 2001. audio compact disk 96.00 Books on Tape.

***Hong Kong.** unabr. ed. Stephen Coonts. Read by Michael Prichard. (ENG.). 2007. (978-0-06-112601-7(2), Harper Audio); (978-0-06-112600-0(4), Harper Audio) HarperCollins Pubs.

Hong Kong. unabr. ed. Jan Morris. Read by Nadia May. 9 cass. (Running Time: 13 hrs.). 1996. 62.95 (978-0-7861-0917-3(3), 1720) Blckstn Audio.
Through firsthand reportage, Morris takes us through the crowded streets of the city; across the crowded floor of the Stock Exchange; to the Happy Valley racecourse, where taipans sip champagne in the owner's box; on the carnival-like ferry ride from Kowloon to Victoria. She also depicts a British opium port controlled by pirates, cutthroats, & scoundrel tycoons in the early days of Hong Kong. Finally, she looks ahead to July 1, 1997, the day when Britain's 99-year lease expires & Hong Kong is annexed to the People's Republic of China.

***Hong Kong Low Price.** abr. ed. Stephen Coonts. Read by Michael Cumpsty. (ENG.). 2005. (978-0-06-112602-4(0), Harper Audio); (978-0-06-112603-1(9), Harper Audio) HarperCollins Pubs.

Hongrois sans Peine. 1 cass. (Running Time: 1 hr., 30 min.). (FRE & HUN.). 2000. bk. 75.00 (978-2-7005-1315-8(0)) Pub: Assimil FRA. Dist(s): Distribks Inc

Honk & Holler Opening Soon. unabr. ed. Billie Letts. Read by Dick Hill. 6 cass. 1999. 57.25 (FS9-43187) Highsmith.

Honk, Honk, Rattle, Rattle. 1 CD. (Running Time: 25 min.). (J). 2005. audio compact disk 14.95 (978-0-9765887-5-7(7)) S Edu Res LLC.

Honky Tonk Kat. abr. ed. Karen Kijewski. Perf. by Harley J. Kozak. 4 cass. (Running Time: 5 hrs.). (Kat Colorado Mystery Ser.: No. 7). 1996. 23.00 Set. (978-1-56876-059-9(0)) Soundlines Ent.
When superstar country entertainer Dakota Jones begins receiving threatening letters, she turns to her childhood friend Private Eye Kat Colorado. Kat joins the tour, only to find the pranks escalate to murder.

Honky Tonk Singers. (Running Time: 30 mins.). 2006. audio compact disk 5.95 (978-1-59987-526-2(8)) Braun Media.

***Honolulu.** collector's unabr. ed. Alan Brennert. Narrated by Ali Ahn. 14 CDs. (Running Time: 15 hrs. 30 mins.). 2009. audio compact disk 69.95 (978-1-4361-7115-1(6)) Recorded Bks.

***Honolulu.** unabr. ed. Alan Brennert. Narrated by Ali Ahn. 1 Playaway. (Running Time: 15 hrs. 30 mins.). 2009. 64.75 (978-1-4361-9511-9(X)); 113.75 (978-1-4361-7113-7(X)); audio compact disk 123.75 (978-1-4361-7114-4(8)) Recorded Bks.

Honor! abr. ed. Dana Fuller Ross, pseud. Read by Lloyd James. 4 vols. (Wagons West: Bk. 1). 2003. (978-1-58807-645-8(8)) Am Pubng Inc.

Honor! abr. ed. Dana Fuller Ross, pseud. Read by Lloyd James. 4 vols. (Wagons West: Bk. 1). 2003. 25.00 (978-1-58807-392-1(0)) Am Pubng Inc.

Honor! abr. ed. Dana Fuller Ross, pseud. Read by Lloyd James. 5 vols. (Wagons West: Bk. 1). 2004. audio compact disk 30.00 (978-1-58807-395-2(5)); audio compact disk (978-1-58807-633-5(4)) Am Pubng Inc.

***Honor Among Enemies.** unabr. ed. David Weber. Read by Allyson Johnson. (Running Time: 19 hrs.). (Honor Harrington Ser.). 2011. 44.97 (978-1-61106-218-2(7), 9781611062182, BADLE); 44.97 (978-1-61106-217-5(9), 9781611062175, Brlnc Audio MP3 Lib); 29.99 (978-1-61106-216-8(0), 9781611062168, Brilliance MP3); audio compact disk 89.97 (978-1-61106-215-1(2), 9781611062151, BriAudCD Unabrid); audio compact disk 34.99 (978-1-61106-214-4(4), 9781611062144, Bril Audio CD Unabri) Brilliance Audio.

Honor among Thieves. abr. rev. ed. Jeffrey Archer. Read by Bill Roberts. Ed. by Kelley R. Ragland. 3 CDs. (Running Time: 3 hrs. 0 mins. 0 sec.). (ENG.). 2004. audio compact disk 14.95 (978-1-59397-522-7(8)) Pub: Macmill Audio. Dist(s): Macmillan

Honor among Thieves. unabr. ed. Jeffrey Archer. Narrated by George Guidall. 9 cass. (Running Time: 12 hrs. 45 mins.). 1994. 78.00 (978-1-55690-968-9(3), 94111E7) Recorded Bks.
It is known as Operation "Desert Calm" by the members of the Wall Street law firm's elite subsidiary. Assembling resources the CIA would envy, "Skills" prepares for its biggest & most outlandish job to date. For the sum of 100,000,000 dollars, the firm will steal an irreplaceable American treasure & sell it to Iraq's unforgiving president. Still smarting from his embarrassment in Operation Desert Storm, Saddam Hussein plans to burn the revered symbol on July 4th, live on CNN.

Honor & Glory. unabr. ed. Kim Murphy. Read by Dianna Dorman. (Running Time: 41400 sec.). (Civil War Ser.). 2006. 65.95 (978-0-7861-4898-1(5)); audio compact disk 81.00 (978-0-7861-5981-9(2)) Blckstn Audio.

Honor & Glory. unabr. ed. Kim Murphy. Read by Dianna Dorman. (Running Time: 41400 sec.). (Civil War Ser.). 2007. audio compact disk 29.95 (978-0-7861-7103-3(0)) Blckstn Audio.

***Honor Bar.** unabr. ed. Laura Lippman. Read by Linda Emond & Francois Battiste. (ENG.). 2008. (978-0-06-176307-6(1), Harper Audio); (978-0-06-176306-9(3), Harper Audio) HarperCollins Pubs.

Honor Bound. abr. ed. W. E. B. Griffin. Read by Dick Hill. 3 CDs, Library ed. (Running Time: 3 hrs.). (Honor Bound Ser.: Bk. 1). 2003. audio compact disk 62.25 (978-1-59086-571-2(5), 1590865715, BAU) Brilliance Audio.
Bestselling author W.E.B. Griffin has captivated readers with his electrifying saga of the Marine Corps. Now he presents his most powerful story of World War II - a desperate mission in the farthest reaching shadows of Nazi power... October 1942. At a secret rendezvous point off the coast of neutral

Argentina, a small merchant ship delivers supplies to Nazi submarines and raiders. The OSS is determined to sabotage the operation by any means necessary. But one of the key saboteurs they've enlisted - a young U.S. Marine - must fight his own private battle between duty and honor. Because he was chosen for a reason - to gain the trust and support of his own flesh and blood. A powerful Argentinian called "el Coronel." The father he never knew.

Honor Bound. abr. ed. W. E. B. Griffin. Read by Dick Hill. (Running Time: 3 hrs.). 2010. audio compact disk 9.99 (978-1-4418-0842-4(6), 9781441808424, BCD Value Price) Brilliance Audio.

Honor Bound. abr. ed. W. E. B. Griffin. Read by Dick Hill. 2 cass. (Running Time: 3 hrs.). (Honor Bound Ser.: No. 1). 2000. 7.95 (978-1-57815-012-0(4), 1002, Media Bks Audio) Media Bks NJ.
A wartime adventure, in which marine & army experts must sabotage the resupply of German ships & submarines in 1942 Nazi Germany.

Honor Bound. unabr. ed. W. E. B. Griffin. Read by Dick Hill. (Running Time: 22 hrs.). (Honor Bound Ser.: Bk. 1). 2008. audio compact disk 137.25 (978-1-4233-3833-8(2), 9781423338338, BriAudCD Unabrid); audio compact disk 39.95 (978-1-4233-3832-1(4), 9781423338321, Bril Audio CD Unabri) Brilliance Audio.

Honor Bound. unabr. ed. W. E. B. Griffin. Read by Dick Hill. (Running Time: 22 hrs.). (Honor Bound Ser.: Bk. 1). 2008. 44.25 (978-1-4233-3837-6(5), 9781423338376, BADLE); 44.25 (978-1-4233-3835-2(9), 9781423338352, Brlnc Audio MP3 Lib); 29.95 (978-1-4233-3834-5(0), 9781423338345, Brilliance MP3); 29.95 (978-1-4233-3836-9(7), 9781423338369, BAD) Brilliance Audio.

Honor Bound, Pt. 1. unabr. ed. W. E. B. Griffin. Read by Michael Russotto. 8 cass. (Running Time: 12 hrs.). (Honor Bound Ser.: No. 1). 64.00 (978-0-7366-2732-0(4), 3460-A/B) Books on Tape.
In 1942 Buenos Aires, a three-man team of Americans sabotages German ships & submarines.

Honor Bound, Pt. 2. unabr. ed. W. E. B. Griffin. Read by Michael Russotto. 8 cass. (Running Time: 12 hrs.). (Honor Bound Ser.: Bk. 1). 1994. 64.00 (978-0-7366-2733-7(2), 3460-B) Books on Tape.

Honor from God. Kenneth Copeland. 6 cass. 1990. 30.00 Set. (978-0-88114-912-8(8)) K Copeland Pubns.
Biblical teaching on honor.

Honor of Spies. unabr. ed. W. E. B. Griffin. Contrib. by Scott Brick. (Running Time: 22 hrs.). (ENG.). (gr. 12 up). 2009. audio compact disk 39.95 (978-0-14-314489-2(8), PengAudBks) Penguin Grp USA.

***Honor of Spies.** unabr. ed. W. E. B. Griffin & William E. Butterworth, IV. Read by Scott Brick. 17 CDs. (Running Time: 21 hrs. 30 mins.). 2009. audio compact disk 100.00 (978-0-307-57777-1(5), BksonTape) Pub: Random Audio Pubg. Dist(s): Random

Honor of the Big Snows. unabr. ed. James Oliver Curwood. Read by Laurie Klein. 6 cass. (Running Time: 6 hrs. 30 min.). Dramatization. 1992. 39.95 (978-1-55686-397-4(7), 397) Books in Motion.
A compelling adventure-romance set in the harsh lands of the frozen north, where passions run deep & a man's code of honor may bind him to secrecy, though it costs him everything.

Honor of the Clan. unabr. ed. John Ringo. Read by Marc Vietor & Julie Cochrane. (Running Time: 14 hrs.). (Posleen War Ser.: No. 10). 2009. audio compact disk 29.99 (978-1-4233-9513-3(1), 9781423395133, Bril Audio CD Unabri) Brilliance Audio.

Honor of the Clan. unabr. ed. John Ringo & Julie Cochrane. Read by Mark Vietor. (Running Time: 14 hrs.). (Posleen War Ser.: No. 10). 2009. 24.99 (978-1-4233-9515-7(8), 9781423395157, Brilliance MP3); 39.97 (978-1-4233-9517-1(4), 9781423395171, BADLE); audio compact disk 99.97 (978-1-4233-9514-0(X), 9781423395140, BriAudCD Unabrid) Brilliance Audio.

Honor of the Clan. unabr. ed. John Ringo & Cochrane Julie. Read by Mark Vietor. (Running Time: 14 hrs.). (Posleen War Ser.: No. 10). 2009. 39.97 (978-1-4233-9516-4(6), 9781423395164, Brlnc Audio MP3 Lib) Brilliance Audio.

Honor of the Maker. Joe Johnston. Read by J. M. Haggar. 1 cass. (Running Time: 38 min.). 1987. 4.95 (978-0-922067-03-9(1), JJA 8999) Johnston Mus Grp.
The story of J. M. Haggar, founder of Haggar Apparel Company, world's largest manufacturer of men's pants. In his own words, this Lebanese immigrant tells how his non-union company revolutionized the apparel business. Colorfully accented by 8 new songs that complete the story.

Honor of the Queen. unabr. ed. David Weber. Read by Allyson Johnson. (Running Time: 16 hrs.). (Honor Harrington Ser.: Bk. 2). 2009. 24.99 (978-1-4233-9530-0(1), 9781423395300, Brilliance MP3); 39.97 (978-1-4233-9532-4(8), 9781423395324, BADLE); 39.97 (978-1-4233-9531-7(X), 9781423395317, Brlnc Audio MP3 Lib); audio compact disk 29.99 (978-1-4233-9528-7(X), 9781423395287, Bril Audio CD Unabri); audio compact disk 99.97 (978-1-4233-9529-4(8), 9781423395294, BriAudCD Unabrid) Brilliance Audio.

Honor Parents: Exodus 20:12. Ed Young. 1999. 4.95 (978-0-7417-2222-5(4), 1222) Win Walk.

Honor Thyself. abr. ed. Danielle Steel. Read by Kyf Brewer. 5 CDs. (Running Time: 6 hrs.). 2008. audio compact disk 26.95 (978-1-4233-2026-5(3), 9781423320265, BACD) Brilliance Audio.

Honor Thyself. abr. ed. Danielle Steel. Read by Kyf Brewer. (Running Time: 6 hrs.). 2009. audio compact disk 14.99 (978-1-4233-2027-2(1), 9781423320272, BCD Value Price) Brilliance Audio.

Honor Thyself. unabr. ed. Danielle Steel. Read by Kyf Brewer. (Running Time: 9 hrs.). 2008. 39.25 (978-1-4233-2025-8(5), 9781423320258, BADLE); 24.95 (978-1-4233-2024-1(7), 9781423320241, BAD); 38.95 (978-1-4233-2018-0(2), 9781423320180, BAU); 92.25 (978-1-4233-2019-7(0), 9781423320197, BrilAudUnabridg); audio compact disk 38.95 (978-1-4233-2020-3(4), 9781423320203, Bril Audio CD Unabri); audio compact disk 24.95 (978-1-4233-2022-7(0), 9781423320227, Brilliance MP3); audio compact disk 97.25 (978-1-4233-2021-0(2), 9781423320210, BriAudCD Unabrid); audio compact disk 39.25 (978-1-4233-2023-4(9), 9781423320234, Brlnc Audio MP3 Lib) Brilliance Audio.

Honor Your Parents: Exodus 20:12. Ed Young. 1985. 4.95 (978-0-7417-1432-9(9), 432) Win Walk.

Honorable Brian Tobin, Canada's Minister of Fisheries & Oceans. Hosted by Nancy Pearlman. 1 cass. (Running Time: 29 min.). 10.00 (1306) Educ Comm CA.

Honorable Enemies. aber. ed. Joe Weber. Read by Bill Weideman. 2 cass. (Running Time: 3 hrs.). 2000. 7.95 (978-1-57815-013-7(2), 1039, Media Bks Audio) Media Bks NJ.
What would happen if the delicate & vital United States/Japanese relationship was sabotaged & stretched to the point of no return?.

Honorable Enemies. unabr. ed. Joe Weber. Read by Bill Weideman. (Running Time: 11 hrs.). 2009. 24.99 (978-1-4233-9150-0(0), 9781423391500, Brilliance MP3); 24.99 (978-1-4233-9152-4(7), 9781423391524, BAD); 39.97 (978-1-4233-9151-7(9), 9781423391517, Brlnc Audio MP3 Lib); 39.97 (978-1-4233-9153-1(5), 9781423391531, BADLE) Brilliance Audio.

Honorable Justice: The Life of Oliver Wendell Holmes. unabr. collector's ed. Sheldon M. Novick. Read by Michael Prichard. 11 cass. (Running Time: 16 hrs. 30 mins.). 1990. 88.00 (978-0-7366-1795-6(7), 2631) Books on Tape.
His book, The Common Law, still in print after 100 years, dominates the history of legal thought in America. He is still one of the best known justices of the Supreme Court. Born into mid-19th century Boston society, Holmes grew up knowing everyone. As a young man, he fought in the Civil War & was seriously wounded. He recovered & returned from the war to practice law & teach at Harvard Law School before his appointment to the bench. He lived to be 94.

Honorable Men. unabr. ed. Louis Auchincloss. Read by Grover Gardner. 8 cass. (Running Time: 12 hrs.). 1987. 64.00 (978-0-7366-1206-7(8), 2124) Books on Tape.
Moral tale of a successful & wealthy man who is forced to take sides on the Vietnam issue.

Honorary Consul. unabr. ed. Graham Greene. Read by Tim Pigott-Smith. 8 cass. (Running Time: 12 hrs.). 2000. 69.95 (978-0-7540-0552-0(6), CAB 1975) AudioGO.
A bungled kidnapping in a provincial Argentinian town. It tells of Charley Fortnum, a whiskey-sodden figure of dubious authority taken by a group of revolutionaries. A local doctor, negotiates with revolutionaries & authorities for Fortnum's release, the corruption of both becomes evident.

Honorary Consul. unabr. ed. Graham Greene. Read by Tim Pigott-Smith. 8 CDs. (Running Time: 12 hrs.). 2001. audio compact disk 79.95 (978-0-7540-5397-2(0), CCD088) Pub: Chivers Audio Bks GBR. Dist(s): AudioGO
A gripping tragicomedy of a bungled kidnapping in a provincial Argentinean town. It tells of Charley Fortnum, the "Honarary Consul", a whiskey-sodden figure of dubious authority taken by a group of revolutionaries. As Eduardo Plarr, a local doctor, negotiates with revolutionaries & authorities for Fortnum's release.

Honoring Self & Other. Paul Ferrini. Read by Paul Ferrini. 1 cass. (Running Time: 75 min.). (Christ Mind Talks & Workshops Ser.). 1997. audio compact disk 10.00 (978-1-879159-34-1(1)) Heartways Pr.
A workshop given at Pacific Church of Religious Science in November 1997.

Honoring the Earth. Angeles Arrien. 1 cass. 9.00 (A0629-90) Sound Photosyn.
An exploration of the sources of spiritual inspiration in ancient & modern stories that tell with humor & warmth of a balanced & harmonious relationship to the earth.

Honoring the Only Planet of Free Choice. abr. ed. Lee Carroll. Read by Lee Carroll. 1 cass. (Running Time: 1 hr. 03 min.). (Kryon Tapes Ser.). 1995. 10.00 (978-0-9636304-7-6(4)) Kryon Writings.
Live recording of channelled event.

Honor's Disguise. unabr. ed. Kristen Heitzmann. Read by Suzanne Niles. 8 CDs. (Running Time: 8 hrs. 36 min.). 2001. audio compact disk 52.00 (978-1-58116-122-9(0)) Books in Motion.
With Cole Jasper as foreman, Abbie dares to hope that his steady hand will bring serenity to the ranch. But trouble comes in the form of two bounty hunters trailing Cole for the murder of a saloon girl in Texas.

Honor's Disguise. unabr. ed. Kristen Heitzmann. Read by Suzanne Niles. 8 cass. (Running Time: 8 hrs. 36 min.). (Rocky Mountain Legacy Ser.: Bk. 4). 2001. 49.95 (978-1-58116-090-1(9)) Books in Motion.

Honor's Kingdom. unabr. ed. Owen Parry. 9 cass. (Running Time: 13 hrs. 30 mins.). 2002. 72.00 (978-0-7366-8725-6(4)); audio compact disk 88.00 (978-0-7366-8726-3(2)) Books on Tape.
Dispatched to London in the summer of 1862, as the Confederates secretly purchase warships to sweep the Union's commerce from the seas, Union Major Abel Jones arrives to discover the corpse of his predecessor in a basket of eels. The mystery deepens as Jones finds himself tangled in scandals in Parliament, grisly murders among Victorian England's poor, and the very real danger that Britain will be drawn into war with the U.S. once again.

Honor's Pledge. Kristen Heitzmann. Narrated by Kate Forbes. 6 cass. (Running Time: 9 hrs.). (Rocky Mountain Legacy Ser.). 59.00 (978-0-7887-9599-2(6)) Recorded Bks.

Honor's Pledge. unabr. ed. Kristen Heitzmann. Read by Suzanne Niles. 8 cass. (Running Time: 8 hrs. 30 min.). (Rocky Mountain Legacy Ser.: Bk. 1). 2001. 49.95 (978-1-58116-015-4(1)) Books in Motion.
Abigail Martin is a headstrong young woman who believes frontier life in the Colorado Rockies has everything she could ever want. Montgomery Farrel is a handsome, refined gentleman who sees in Abbie a reflection of his ideal. Their hopes suddenly collide when a debt must be paid... and honor is the price.

Honor's Price. Kristen Heitzmann. Narrated by Kate Forbes. 8 cass. (Running Time: 11 hrs. 30 mins.). (Rocky Mountain Legacy Ser.). 71.00 (978-0-7887-9603-6(8)) Recorded Bks.

Honor's Price. unabr. ed. Kristen Heitzmann. Read by Suzanne Niles. 8 cass. (Running Time: 10 hrs. 30 min.). (Rocky Mountain Legacy Ser.: Bk. 2). 2001. 49.95 (978-1-58116-016-1(X)) Books in Motion.
Montgomery Farrel believes his splintered world is about to heal when Abbie Martin accepts his love and offer of marriage. But Monte's need for revenge battles his sense of honor when the sabotage of others brings injury and devastation to the Farrel's new life.

Honor's Quest. Kristen Heitzmann. Narrated by Kate Forbes. 7 cass. (Running Time: 10 hrs.). (Rocky Mountain Legacy Ser.). 62.00 (978-0-7887-9601-2(1)) Recorded Bks.

Honor's Quest. unabr. ed. Kristen Heitzmann. Read by Suzanne Niles. 8 cass. (Running Time: 9 hrs. 18 min.). (Rocky Mountain Legacy Ser.: Bk. 3). 2001. 49.95 (978-1-58116-027-7(5)) Books in Motion.
Abigail and Montgomery Farrel take charge of their niece when Monty's sister dies. The Farrel's lives are filled with the joyful chaos that a child brings, when another tragedy strikes.

Honor's Splendour. abr. ed. Julie Garwood. Read by Anne Flosnik. (Running Time: 7 hrs.). 2010. audio compact disk 14.99 (978-1-4418-1225-4(3), 9781441812254, BACD) Brilliance Audio.

Honor's Splendour. unabr. ed. Julie Garwood. (Running Time: 14 hrs.). 2010. 24.99 (978-1-4418-1221-6(0), 9781441812216, Brilliance MP3); 24.99 (978-1-4418-1223-0(7), 9781441812230, BAD); 39.97 (978-1-4418-1222-3(9), 9781441812223, Brlnc Audio MP3 Lib); 39.97 (978-1-4418-1224-7(5), 9781441812247, BADLE) Brilliance Audio.

Honor's Splendour. unabr. ed. Julie Garwood. Read by Anne Flosnik. (Running Time: 14 hrs.). 2010. audio compact disk 29.99 (978-1-4418-1219-3(9), 9781441812193, Bril Audio CD Unabri); audio compact disk 87.97 (978-1-4418-1220-9(2), 9781441812209, BriAudCD Unabrid) Brilliance Audio.

Honor's Voice: The Transformation of Abraham Lincoln. abr. ed. Douglas L. Wilson. Read by Ed Asner. 2 cass. (Running Time: 3 hrs.). 1998. 17.95 (978-1-57453-254-8(5)) Audio Lit.
Traces Lincoln's early development, his friends & acquaintances in the Illinois of the 1830s & 40s.

Honor's Voice: The Transformation of Abraham Lincoln. unabr. collector's ed. Douglas L. Wilson. Read by Barrett Whitener. 11 cass. (Running Time: 16 hrs. 30 mins.). 1998. 88.00 (978-0-7366-4331-3(1), 4804) Books on Tape.
Lincoln's years as a boy & young man & how he came to greatness despite his often anguished personal life.

Honour & Empire. Philip McCutchan. 7 cass. (James Ogilvie Ser.). 2007. 61.95 (978-1-84283-759-7(1)) Pub: ISIS Lrg Prnt GBR. Dist(s): Ulverscroft US

Honour This Day. unabr. ed. Alexander Kent, pseud. Read by Michael Jayston. 8 cass. (Running Time: 8 hrs.). (Richard Bolitho Ser.: Bk. 17). 1993. 69.95 (978-0-7451-6093-1(X), CAB 529) AudioGO.

Honourable Company: A History of the English East India Company. unabr. collector's ed. John Keay. Read by Geoffrey Howard. 14 cass. (Running Time: 21 hrs.). 1995. 112.00 (978-0-7366-3048-1(1), 3730) Books on Tape.
Traces rise of East India Company. This mammoth international trading enterprise helped the Brits build their empire.

***Honourable Schoolboy.** John le Carré. Narrated by Simon Russell Beale. 2 CDs. (Running Time: 2 hrs. 0 mins. 0 sec.). (BBC Radio Ser.). (ENG.). 2010. audio compact disk 19.95 (978-1-60283-863-5(1)) Pub: AudioGO. Dist(s): Perseus Dist

***Honourable Schoolboy.** unabr. ed. John le Carré. Perf. by Simon Russell Beale. 3 CDs. (Running Time: 3 hrs.). 2010. audio compact disk 39.95 (978-0-7927-7265-1(2)) AudioGO.

Honourable Schoolboy. unabr. ed. John le Carré. Read by Frederick Davidson. 16 cass. (Running Time: 23 hrs. 30 mins.). 1991. 99.95 (978-0-7861-0270-9(5), 1236) Blckstn Audio.
George Smiley - who has assumed the unenviable job of restoring the health & reputation of his demoralized organization - goes on the offensive. Salvaging what he can of the Service's ravaged network of spies, summoning back a few trustworthy old colleagues, working them - & himself - around the clock, he searches for a whisper, a hint, a clue that will lead him back to his opposite number: Karla, the Soviet officer in Moscow Centre who masterminded the infamous treachery.

Honourable Schoolboy. unabr. ed. John le Carré. Read by Frederick Davidson. 2 pieces. (Running Time: 23 hrs.). 2000. 39.95 (978-0-7861-9004-1(3), 1236); audio compact disk 123.00 (978-0-7861-8136-0(2), 1236) Blckstn Audio.

***Honourable Schoolboy.** unabr. ed. John le Carré. (Running Time: 23 hrs.). 2010. audio compact disk 39.95 (978-1-4417-3565-2(8)) Blckstn Audio.

Honourable Schoolboy. unabr. collector's ed. John le Carré. Read by Wolfram Kandinsky. 15 cass. (Running Time: 22 hrs. 30 mins.). 1978. 120.00 (978-0-7366-0112-2(0), 1119) Books on Tape.
Traces the career of spychief George Smiley. Smiley sets out to rebuild the reputation of the British Secret Service, which has been shattered by a high level defection. Smiley recruits Jerry Westerby, the honourable schoolboy of the title, to help him trace funds flowing from Hong Kong to Communist China.

Honoured Society. unabr. collector's ed. Norman Lewis. Read by Richard Brown. 7 cass. (Running Time: 10 hrs. 30 min.). 1990. 56.00 (978-0-7366-1720-8(5), 2561) Books on Tape.
On July 10, 1943, the Allied armies landed in Sicily. When American forces sought & received help from the Mafia, opposition vanished. Within a week western Sicily was secure. The Honoured Society is a history of the Sicilian Mafia - its beginnings & particularly its role in the aftermath of WWII. The Sicilian political rebuilding after the war was guided, not always gently, by the firm hand of the families.

Honus & Me. unabr. ed. Dan Gutman. Narrated by Johnny Heller. 2 pieces. (Running Time: 2 hrs. 15 mins.). (Baseball Card Adventures Ser.). (gr. 4 up). 1997. 19.00 (978-0-7887-5445-6(9)) Recorded Bks.
Joe Stoshack may be an awkward kid, but he knows baseball - and baseball cards. Since he was seven, he has been collecting them. So when his mother tells him he can earn $5 by cleaning out an old lady's attic, Joe dreams of the cards he can buy. It's long, dusty work, and Joe is down to the last boxes when a piece of cardboard falls to the floor. With a shock, he recognizes the face of Honus Wagner, one of baseball's great early players. It is the most valuable baseball card in the world, and in mint condition! Before Joe can decide whether to tell the old woman or keep the card, he discovers it can carry him through time and space. Soon, he is with Honus in 1909!.

Honus Wagner. unabr. ed. Dennis De Valeria & Jeanne De Valeria. Read by Jonathan Reese. 10 cass. (Running Time: 15 hrs.). 1996. 52.00 (4263) Books on Tape.
Baseball's legendary "Flying Dutchman" joined the Louisville Colonels in 1897 & later became the game's first superstar.

Honus Wagner. unabr. ed. Dennis DeValeria & Jeanne B. DeValeria. Read by Ian Esmo. 10 cass. (Running Time: 16 hrs.). 1996. 69.95 (978-0-7861-0985-2(8), 1762) Blckstn Audio.
Honus Wagner, whose career in baseball (most of it with the Pittsburgh Pirates) stretched from 1895 to 1917, was the first American sports superstar of the twentieth century. One of the first five players to be inducted into the Baseball Hall of Fame in its first year (1939), he was probably the best shortstop in baseball's history. His great career & the dawn of baseball as a popular entertainment occurred simultaneously, & he has become a an icon of the early game; his 1909 baseball card, one of which sold four years ago for 451,000 dollars, is a holy grail of American memorabilia. This first major biography shows why Wagner was America's favorite image of the sport during baseball's transition to the modern era.

Hood: King Raven Trilogy. unabr. ed. Stephen R. Lawhead. Read by Adam Verner. (YA). 2007. 39.99 (978-1-60252-906-9(X)) Find a World.

Hood: The Legend Begins Anew. unabr. ed. Stephen R. Lawhead. Read by Adam Verner. (Running Time: 45000 sec.). (King Raven Trilogy: Bk. 1). 2006. audio compact disk 99.00 (978-0-7861-5949-9(9)) Blckstn Audio.

Hood: The Legend Begins Anew. unabr. ed. Stephen R. Lawhead. Narrated by Adam Verner. (Running Time: 12 hrs. 20 mins. 0 sec.). (King Raven Trilogy: Bk. 1). (ENG.). 2006. audio compact disk 34.99 (978-1-59859-162-0(2)) Oasis Audio.

Hood: The Legend Begins Anew. unabr. ed. Stephen R. Lawhead. Narrated by Adam Verner. (King Raven Trilogy). (ENG.). 2006. 24.49 (978-1-60814-238-5(8)) Oasis Audio.

Hoodoo Man: A Starletta Duvall Mystery. Judith Smith-Levin. Narrated by Marc Johnson. 6 cass. (Running Time: 8 hrs. 15 mins.). 55.00 (978-1-4025-2721-0(7)) Recorded Bks.

Hoogie Boogie: Louisiana French Music. Perf. by Michael Doucet & Sharon A. Doucet. 1 cass. (Running Time: 45 mins.). (J). (978-1-886767-24-9(6)); audio compact disk (978-1-886767-25-6(4)) Rounder Records.
"Here in French Louisiana, we love to sing & dance & make music & when family & friends get together, that's what we do. Sometimes it's a Cajun dance tune, sometimes a traditional song. Sometimes it's even a rocking Cajun-billy number or just a song that's fun to sing in French. We've even got a zydeco rap from right out of the bayous. You'll find songs full of colors, numbers, animals & clothing, along with lots of different musical sounds & rhythms for dancing. So allons a Lafayette & bring a friend. The party's getting started.".

Hoogie Boogie: Louisiana French Music for Children. Perf. by Michael Doucet. 1 cass. (Running Time: 46 min.). (Family Ser.). (J). (ps-9). 1992. 9.98 (8022); audio compact disk 14.98 (8022) Rounder Records.
The leading contemporary ambassador of cajun music displays his abilities on this recording (the cajun version of "The Hokey Pokey"). You'll find songs full of colors, numbers, animals & clothing, along with lots of different musical sounds for dancing & singing along.

Hook see Poetry & Voice of James Wright

Hook. unabr. ed. Donald E. Westlake. Read by William Dufris. 6 vols. (Running Time: 9 Hrs.). 2000. bk. 54.95 (978-0-7927-2416-2(X), CSL 305, Chivers Sound Lib) AudioGO.
Bryce Proctorr has a multimillion-dollar contract for his next novel, a trophy wife raking him over the coals of a protracted divorce, a bad case of writer's block & an impending deadline.

Hook. unabr. ed. Donald E. Westlake. Read by William Dufris. 8 CDs. (Running Time: 12 hrs.). 2001. audio compact disk 79.95 (978-0-7927-9954-2(2), SLD 005, Chivers Sound Lib) AudioGO.
Bryce Proctorr has a severe case of writer's block & an impending deadline. Wayne Prentice is a fading author in a world that no longer values his work.

Hook 'Em, Snotty! unabr. ed. Gary Paulsen. Narrated by Jeff Woodman. 1 cass. (Running Time: 1 hr.). (Gary Paulsen's World of Adventure Ser.: Bk. 5). (gr. 4 up). 1997. 10.00 (978-0-7887-0882-4(1), 95020E7) Recorded Bks.
Bobbie rounds up stray cattle on Grandpa's ranch each summer & this year her city cousin, Alex, is going to help.

***Hook, Line & Sinister: Mysteries to Reel You In.** unabr. ed. T. Jefferson Parker. (Running Time: 9 hrs. 0 mins.). 2010. 15.99 (978-1-4001-8661-7(7)) Tantor Media.

***Hook, Line & Sinister: Mysteries to Reel You In.** unabr. ed. T. Jefferson Parker. Narrated by Justine Eyre & John Allen Nelson. (Running Time: 9 hrs. 30 mins. 0 sec.). (ENG.). 2010. 24.99 (978-1-4001-6661-9(9)); audio compact disk 34.99 (978-1-4001-1661-4(9)); audio compact disk 69.99 (978-1-4001-4661-1(5)) Pub: Tantor Media. Dist(s): IngramPubServ

Hooked: A Thriller about Love & Other Addictions. abr. ed. Matt Richtel. Read by Jason Singer. (Running Time: 6 hrs.). (ENG.). 2007. 14.98 (978-1-59483-969-6(7), Twelve) Pub: GrandCentral. Dist(s): HachBkGrp

Hooked Generation. Jack Van Impe. 1977. 7.00 (978-0-934803-26-7(9)) J Van Impe.
Includes the testimony of the Van Impe family.

Hooked on Classical Walking One: (Beginner) Bruce Blackmon. 1 cass. (Running Time: 1 hr. 2 min.). 1991. 12.95 (978-1-56481-009-0(7)) Sports Music.
A one hour beginner level fitness walking program featuring well known classical works.

Hooked on Classical Walking Three: (Advanced) Bruce Blackmon. 1 cass. 1991. 12.95 (978-1-56481-011-3(9)) Sports Music.
A one hour advanced level fitness walking program featuring well known classical works.

Hooked on Classical Walking Two: (Intermediate) Bruce Blackmon. 1 cass. (Running Time: 1 hr. 2 min.). 1991. 12.95 (978-1-56481-010-6(0)) Sports Music.
A one hour intermediate level fitness walking program featuring well known classical works.

Hooked on Math. (J). 1989. cass. & flmstrp 149.95 HOP LLC.

Hooked on Math: Master the Facts. (J). (gr. 1-6). 1999. pap. bk. 229.95 (978-1-887942-77-5(7)) HOP LLC.

Hooked on Phonics. (J). 1985. 119.95 HOP LLC.

Hooked on Phonics - Learn to Read. (J). (ps-3). 1998. pap. bk. 229.95 (978-1-887942-88-1(2)) HOP LLC.

Hooked on Phonics - Learn to Read. deluxe ed. (J). (ps-3). 1998. pap. bk. 269.95 (978-1-887942-90-4(4)) HOP LLC.

Hooked on Phonics - Learn to Read: Classroom Edition. (J). (ps-3). 1999. pap. bk. 594.95 (978-1-887942-83-6(1)) HOP LLC.

Hooked on Phonics - Learn to Read: K-1st Grade. (J). (gr. k-1). 2000. pap. bk. 49.95 (978-1-887942-86-7(6)) HOP LLC.

Hooked on Phonics Classic. 1994. pap. bk. 269.95 (978-1-887942-89-8(0)) HOP LLC.

Hooked on Winning. Mark Pilarski. 2 cass. (Running Time: 2 hrs.). 1999. 14.95 Set. (978-0-9653214-0-2(1)) Winners Pubng.

Hookin' Up: An Unabridged Selection from with Ossie & Ruby. unabr. ed. Ruby Dee & Ossie Davis. Read by Ruby Dee & Ossie Davis. (Running Time: 6 hrs.). (ENG.). 2006. 14.98 (978-1-59483-491-2(1)) Pub: Hachet Audio. Dist(s): HachBkGrp

Ho'Oponopono: Energetic Forgiveness & Release. Short Stories. Dee Chips. 2 CDs. 2006. audio compact disk 29.95 (978-1-929661-25-1(8)) Transpersonal Pubng.

Ho'oponopono - Workshop. Morrnah Simeona. 6 cass. 54.00 (OC4W) Sound Horizons AV.

Hoopster. unabr. ed. Alan Lawrence Sitomer. Narrated by J. D. Jackson. 4 CDs. (Running Time: 5 hrs.). (YA). 2005. audio compact disk 48.75 (978-1-4193-5622-3(4), C3419); 41.75 (978-1-4025-7025-4(2), 97611) Recorded Bks.
Andre Anderson is a black teenager with a dream. Although he loves to play basketball and laugh with his friends, he also loves to write and wants to make his mark on the world. One summer when he is assigned to do a magazine article about race, he creates a passionate and explosive piece. Soon, he is the target of racists who brutally attack him, putting him in the hospital. With his hand and dream broken, he must figure out how to put his life back together in spite of the anger and injustice he now sees around him.

Hoopster: Read-Along/Homework Pack. unabr. ed. Alan Lawrence Sitomer. Narrated by J. D. Jackson. 4 cass. (Running Time: 5 hrs.). (YA). 2005. bk. 65.74 (978-1-4025-7027-8(9), 41853) Recorded Bks.

Hooray for Midsommar! (Greetings Ser.: Vol. 1). (gr. 2-3). 10.00 (978-0-7635-5865-9(6)) Rigby Educ.

Hooray for Reading Day! Margery Cuyler. Illus. by Arthur Howard. 1 CD. (Running Time: 12 mins.). (J). (gr. k-4). 2008. bk. 29.95 (978-0-8045-4194-7(9)) Spoken Arts.

Hooray for Reading Day! Margery Cuyler. Illus. by Arthur Howard. 1 cass. (Running Time: 12 mins.). (J). (gr. k-1). 2008. bk. 27.95 (978-0-8045-6969-9(X)) Spoken Arts.

Hooray for the Golly Sisters! unabr. ed. Betsy Byars. Narrated by C. J. Critt. 1 cass. (Running Time: 30 mins.). (I Can Read Bks.). (gr. 1 up). 1997. 10.00 (978-0-7887-0897-8(X), 95035E7) Recorded Bks.
The talented Golly sisters have driven their covered wagon across a wide river & into a new western town, where there's a big welcome banner flying just for them. Join May-May & Rose as they sing & dance their way through five lively adventures.

Hooray! 100 Days: Early Explorers Early Set A Audio CD. Benchmark Education Staff. (J). 2006. audio compact disk 10.00 (978-1-4108-7625-6(X)) Benchmark Educ.

Hoot. Carl Hiaasen. Read by Chad Lowe. 4 cass. (Running Time: 6 hrs. 29 mins.). (J). (gr. 3-6). 2004. 32.00 (978-0-8072-0923-3(6), Listening Lib) Random Audio Pubg.
Roy, the new kid in town, is intrigued by a boy he sees running away from the school bus with no books and no shoes. Roy is determined to uncover the mystery.

Hoot. unabr. ed. Carl Hiaasen. Read by Chad Lowe. (J). 2006. 39.99 (978-0-7393-7489-4(3)) Find a World.

Hoot. unabr. ed. Carl Hiaasen. Read by Chad Lowe. 6 CDs. (Running Time: 6 hrs. 29 mins.). (J). (gr. 3-6). 2004. audio compact disk 42.50 (978-0-8072-1595-1(3), S YA 395 CD, Listening Lib) Pub: Random Audio Pubg. Dist(s): NetLibrary CO

Hoot. unabr. ed. Carl Hiaasen. Read by Chad Lowe. 6 CDs. (Running Time: 6 hrs. 29 mins.). (ENG.). (J). (gr. 3). 2004. audio compact disk 29.95 (978-0-307-20697-8(1), Listening Lib) Pub: Random Audio Pubg. Dist(s): Random

Hoover Print. unabr. ed. Robert Bitterli. Read by M. J. Wilde. 8 cass. (Running Time: 12 hrs.). 2001. 35.00 (978-1-58807-078-4(6)) Am Pubng Inc.
Thirty years after his death, the search for J. Edgar Hoover's private files is once again at a fever pitch. Four high-profile assassinations, including that of a former President of the United States, bring Hoover's unquestioned power, neurotic need for secrecy, and compulsion to have something on everyone, back to the top of the desks of today's FBI. Especially since the only clue found at each murder was J. Edgar Hoover's right thumbprint. The race between the assassin and the FBI for Hoover's private files is on. The assassin needs the files to justify his actions to the world. The FBI must get to the files first to prevent worldwide outrage at the U.S. and to keep rivers of blood from flowing through the nation's city streets.

Hoover's FBI: The Inside Story by Hoover's Trusted Lieutenant. unabr. ed. Cartha D. DeLoach. Read by Jeff Riggenbach. 11 cass. (Running Time: 16 hrs.). 1996. 76.95 (978-0-7861-1011-7(2), 1789) Blckstn Audio.
Answers the questions that have plagued modern history most - the assassinations of John F. Kennedy, Jr. & Martin Luther King, Jr., the FBI crusades against organized crime & the Communist party, Hoover's disputed sexual orientation, & the "secret files" Hoover allegedly kept to blackmail hostile members of Congress. Sets the record straight about J. Edgar Hoover once & for all & provides a gripping narrative of a modern government agency caught on a tightrope between presidential administrations & the limits of the law.

Hop Frog see Tales of Terror & the Supernatural: A Collection

Hop Frog. rev. ed. Edgar Allan Poe. Ed. by Don Kisner. Adapted by Brenta Bruins. (Read-Along Radio Dramas Ser.). (YA). (gr. 7 up). 1998. ring bd. 38.00 (978-1-878298-13-3(5)) Balance Pub.

Hop, Hop, Hop! Sing-and-Dance Songs from Ladybug. 1 cass. (J). (ps-1). 2002. 10.95 (978-0-8126-0087-2(8)) Pub: Cricket Bks. Dist(s): PerseuPGW

Hop O' My Thumb see Sleeping Beauty & Other Stories

Hop on Pop. Dr. Seuss. (J). 1976. 14.00 (978-0-394-04145-2(3)) McGraw.

Hop, Skip, & a Jump: Activity Songs for the Very Young. Pam Donkin. 1 CD. (Running Time: 48 mins.). (J). (ps-k). 2006. audio compact disk 14.95 (978-1-58467-029-2(0)) Gentle Wind.

***Hop: the Chapter Book.** unabr. ed. Text by Annie Auerbach. (Running Time: 1 hr.). (Hop Ser.). (ENG.). 2011. 6.98 (978-1-60941-464-1(0)) Pub: Hachet Audio. Dist(s): HachBkGrp

Hop up & Jump Up! Sing & Dance Songs. Ladybug Magazine Editors. 1 cass. (J). 1998. 10.95 (978-0-8126-0217-3(X)) Open Ct Pub.

Hop up & Jump Up! Sing & Dance Songs. Ed. by Ladybug Magazine Staff. (J). (ps-1). 1998. bk. 19.95 (978-0-8126-0219-7(6)) Open Ct Pub.

Hopalong Cassidy. Contrib. by William Boyd. (Running Time: 10800 sec.). 2004. 9.98 (978-1-57019-619-5(2)) Radio Spirits.

Hopalong Cassidy. Perf. by William Boyd & Andy Clyde. (ENG.). 2009. audio compact disk 39.98 (978-1-57019-885-4(3)) Radio Spirits.

Hopalong Cassidy. Created by Radio Spirits. Contrib. by William Boyd. (Running Time: 10800 sec.). 2004. audio compact disk 9.98 (978-1-57019-620-1(6)) Radio Spirits.

Hopalong Cassidy. abr. ed. Clarence E. Mulford. Read by Stan Winiarski. Ed. by Jocelyn Kaye. 2 cass. (Running Time: 3 hrs.). 1995. 12.95 (978-1-882071-38-8(7)) B-B Audio.
Not that B-Western film character, but the intense hero of the original bestselling novel by Clarence Mulford. Rich in lore of Texas ranch life, Hopalong Cassidy revolves around the action on two neighboring spreads, Hopalongs Bar-20 and the H2.Th.

Hopalong Cassidy. collector's ed. Perf. by Radio Spirits & Joe Du Val. 6 cass. (Running Time: 9 hrs.). 2001. bk. 34.98 (4022) Radio Spirits.

Hopalong Cassidy: Adventures in the West. Created by Radio Spirits. (Running Time: 36000 sec.). 2007. audio compact disk 39.98 (978-1-57019-834-2(9)) Radio Spirits.

***Hopalong Cassidy: Bullets on the Range.** Perf. by William Boyd & Andy Clyde. 2010. audio compact disk 31.95 (978-1-57019-934-9(5)) Radio Spirits.

Hopalong Cassidy: Mystery at the Diamond & The Golden Lure. Perf. by William Boyd & Joe Du Val. 1 cass. (Running Time: 1 hr.). 2001. 6.98 (1508) Radio Spirits.

Hopalong Cassidy & The Cisco Kid: "The Boss of Vinegar Bend" & "The Phineas Boys" unabr. ed. 1 cass. (Running Time: 60 min.). Dramatization. 7.95 Norelco box. (WW 5327) Natl Recrd Co.
Hopalong Cassidy: William Boyd as Hoppy & Andy Clyde as California, while on their way back to Bar 20, meet widow Oats & her daughter Judy. The women have just been swindled by Mr. Scaggs on a land deal. Hoppy tries to get their money back...& he gets thrown in jail in the attempt. But justice prevails! The Cisco Kid: Here is adventure...here is romance...here is the famous O. Henry's Robin Hood of the old West...The Cisco Kid. This action packed story starts with a jailbreak & ends with a train robbery. Oh, Pancho...Oh, Cisco.

Hope. Executive Producer Donna Auguste. (YA). 2002. audio compact disk (978-0-9762377-3-0(3)) Leave a Little Room Found.

Hope. Perf. by Blackball Staff. 1 cass. 1997. audio compact disk 15.99 CD. (D0165) Diamante Music Grp.

Hope. Randy Houk. Read by Tom Chapin. Illus. by Walt Sturrock. Narrated by Tom Chapin. 1 cass. (Running Time: 10 min.). (Humane Society of the United States Animal Tales Ser.). (J). (gr. 1-5). 1996. pap. bk. 9.95 (978-1-882728-49-7(1)) Benefactory.
An injured pig is tossed into a dumpster, but is quickly rescued. She's brought to Farm Sanctuary, where a spotted fellow pig, Johnny, won't leave her side.

Hope. Ed. by Robert A. Monroe. 1 cass. (Running Time: 30 min.). (Meta Music Artist Ser.). 1989. 14.95 (978-1-56102-213-7(6)) Inter Indus.
A strikingly different composition that brings out conflicting shades of emotion. A portrayal in sound that evokes memories & pictures often different with each listening.

Hope. unabr. ed. Len Deighton. Read by James Faulkner. 8 cass. (Running Time: 12 hrs.). (Faith, Hope & Charity Trilogy: Bk. 2). 2000. 59.95 (978-0-7540-0014-3(1), CAB 1437) Pub: Chivers Audio Bks GBR. Dist(s): AudioGO
It is 1987, and Bernard Samson must reconcile with his wife, Fiona, and put his affair behind him. But the death of Tessa Kosinski on the night of Fiona's return casts a shadow over the Department. Bernard must uncover the truth behind Teresa's death and his wife's role in it before it's too late.

Hope, Pt. 1. unabr. ed. Herman Wouk. Read by Theodore Bikel. 9 cass. (Running Time: 13 hrs. 30 min.). 1994. 72.00 (3578-A) Books on Tape.
A tale of four Israeli army officers & the women they love in peace & war.

Hope, Pt. 2. unabr. ed. Herman Wouk. Read by Theodore Bikel. 9 cass. (Running Time: 13 hrs. 30 min.). 1994. 72.00 (3578-B) Books on Tape.

Hope, Vol. 2. unabr. ed. Chris Yaw. Perf. by Scott Hiltzik. 1 cass. (Running Time: 1 hr.). (Living Words Ser.). 1998. 9.98 (978-1-893613-01-0(1)); audio compact disk 11.98 (978-1-893613-05-8(4)) Living Wds.

***Hope! A Story of Change in Obama's America.** Eric Stevens. Illus. by Nick Derington. (Graphic Flash Ser.). (ENG.). 2010. audio compact disk 14.60 (978-1-4342-2581-8(X)) CapstoneDig.

Hope: Includes Plush Animal. Randy Houk. Read by Tom Chapin. Illus. by Walt Sturrock. Narrated by Tom Chapin. 1 cass. (Running Time: 10 min.). (Humane Society of the United States Animal Tales Ser.). (J). (gr. 1-5). 1995. bk. 34.95 (978-1-882728-24-4(6)) Benefactory.
An injured pig is tossed into a dumpster, but is quickly rescued. She's brought to Farm Sanctuary, where a spotted fellow pig, Johnny, won't leave her side.

Hope: Our Covenant with God. Kenneth Untener. 1 cass. (Running Time: 1 hr.). 2001. 8.95 (A6581) St Anthony Mess Pr.
Insights on hope with piano arrangements.

Hope: Songs for the Spirit. Compiled by Dean Diehl & Ed Kee. 1 CD. 2000. audio compact disk 9.99 (978-0-7601-3183-1(X), SO33438) Pub: Brentwood Music. Dist(s): Provident Mus Dist
Includes: "Let There Be Light," "A Little Stronger Every Day," "A Different Road," "Basics of Life," "Be the Word" & more.

Hope: Stories from the Collection More News from Lake Wobegon. unabr. ed. Garrison Keillor. (Running Time: 4380 sec.). (ENG.). 2008. audio compact disk 13.95 (978-1-59887-607-9(4), 1598876074) Pub: HighBridge. Dist(s): Workman Pub

Hope I: Includes Plush Animal. Randy Houk. Read by Tom Chapin. Illus. by Walt Sturrock. Narrated by Tom Chapin. 1 cass. (Running Time: 10 min.). (Humane Society of the United States Animal Tales Ser.). (J). (gr. 1-5). 1996. pap. bk. 19.95 (978-1-882728-39-8(4)) Benefactory.
An injured pig is tossed into a dumpster, but is quickly rescued. She's brought to Farm Sanctuary, where a spotted fellow pig, Johnny, won't leave her side.

Hope Again. Contrib. by Charles R. Swindoll. 1 cass. 1996. 15.99 Nelson.

Hope Again: When Life Hurts & Dreams Fade. 2005. 54.00 (978-1-57972-692-8(5)); audio compact disk 54.00 (978-1-57972-691-1(7)) Insight Living.

***Hope & Grace.** Prod. by Women of Faith. 2010. audio compact disk 11.99 (978-1-4261-0890-7(7)) Nelson.

Hope & Healing for Kids Who Cut: Learning to Understand & Help Those Who Self-Injure. unabr. ed. Marv Penner. (Running Time: 4 hrs. 33 mins. 0 sec.). (ENG.). 2009. 9.99 (978-0-310-77219-4(2)) Zondervan.

Hope & Help for OCD Sufferers: Help for Those Who Struggle with OCD. Featuring Mike Emlet. (ENG.). 2007. audio compact disk 11.99 (978-1-934885-13-0(4)) New Growth Pr.

Hope & Honor. Sid Shachnow & Jann Robbins. Read by Brian Emerson. (Running Time: 59400 sec.). 2005. audio compact disk 99.00 (978-0-7861-7799-8(3)); audio compact disk 29.95 (978-0-7861-8016-5(1)) Blckstn Audio.

Hope & Honor. Sid Shachnow & Jann Robins. Read by Brian Emerson. (Running Time: 13 hrs. 30 mins.). 2005. reel tape 72.95 (978-0-7861-3527-1(1)) Blckstn Audio.

Hope & Joy: Keys to a Balanced Life. Robert Morneau. 2 cass. (Running Time: 2 hrs.). 2001. 16.95 (A8120) St Anthony Mess Pr.
As adults, how do we restore hope and grow in joy as witnesses to our faith?.

Hope Anderson Case & The George Lane Case. Perf. by Larry Thor. 1 cass. (Running Time: 60 min.). Dramatization. (Broadway Is My Beat Ser.). 6.00 Once Upon Rad.
Radio broadcasts - mystery & suspense.

Hope at Work: For social service, non-profit, & faith-based Organizations. (ENG.). 2009. audio compact disk 18.00 (978-0-9773877-1-7(2)) Isld Press.

Hope Before Us. Elyse Larson. Read by Vanessa Benjamin. (Running Time: 54000 sec.). (Women of Valor Ser.). 2002. 79.95 (978-0-7861-3495-3(X)) Blckstn Audio.

Hope Before Us. Elyse Larson. Read by Vanessa Benjamin. (Running Time: 50400 sec.). (Women of Valor Ser.). 2006. audio compact disk 99.00 (978-0-7861-7885-8(X)) Blckstn Audio.

Hope Before Us. unabr. ed. Elyse Larson. Read by Vanessa Benjamin. (Running Time: 50400 sec.). (Women of Valor Ser.: No. 3). 2006. audio compact disk 29.95 (978-0-7861-8068-4(4)) Blckstn Audio.

***Hope Beyond Reason.** Dave Hess. 2010. audio compact disk 29.99 (978-0-7684-3215-2(4)) Destiny Image Pubs.

Hope Does More Than Float: Logos 11/15/87. Ben Youhg. 1997. 4.95 (978-0-7417-6105-7(X), B0105) Win Walk.

Hope-Filled Mind & a Peaceful Heart. unabr. ed. Dick Sutphen. Read by Dick Sutphen. 1 cass. (Running Time: 30 min.). (Quick Fix Meditations Ser.). 1998. 10.98 (978-0-87554-619-3(6), QF101) Valley Sun.
From this moment on, become confident about the future & the fulfillment of desires. Faith opens new doors & one forms a positive new perspective.

Hope for a Change: Commentaries by an Optimistic Realist. Michael Henderson. Contrib. by Susan Appelgate & Jerome Hart. 2 cass. (Running Time: 90 min. per cass.). 1992. 8.95 set. (978-1-85239-508-7(7)) Grosvenor USA.
Album of audio tapes of 42 radio commentaries previously published in book "Hope for a Change".

Hope for Adult Children of Alcoholics. 4 cass. Incl. Hope for Adult Children of Alcoholics: Reflections. (5629); Hope for Adult Children of Alcoholics: Side 1: Adult Relationships, Side 2: Stage of Growth. Robert Subby & Barbara Naiditch. (5629); Hope for Adult Children of Alcoholics: Side 1: Fulfillment in Recovery, Side 2: Decisions & Choices. Earnie Larsen & Elene Loecher. (5629); Hope for Adult Children of Alcoholics: Side 1: Grief & Loss, Side 2: The Twelve Steps & ACOA. Marty Kreuzer. (5629); 29.95 Set. (5629); 7.95 ea. Hazelden.
Workshop lectures & personal stories by some of the most respected speakers on adult children's issues today add new dimensions to understanding & overcoming the legacy of being the child of an alcoholic.

Hope for Adult Children of Alcoholics: Reflections see Hope for Adult Children of Alcoholics

Hope for Adult Children of Alcoholics: Side 1: Adult Relationships, Side 2: Stage of Growth see Hope for Adult Children of Alcoholics

Hope for Adult Children of Alcoholics: Side 1: Fulfillment in Recovery, Side 2: Decisions & Choices see Hope for Adult Children of Alcoholics

Hope for Adult Children of Alcoholics: Side 1: Grief & Loss, Side 2: The Twelve Steps & ACOA see Hope for Adult Children of Alcoholics

Hope for Africa: High Hope for Africa. Victorine Diakiese. (Running Time: 44:45).Tr. of Espoir Pour L'Afrique. (ENG.). 2009. audio compact disk 16.95 (978-0-9842842-0-7(6)) V Diakiese.

Hope for Africa (French) High Hope for Africa. Victorine Diakiese. (Running Time: 44:45).Tr. of Espoir Pour L'Afrique. (FRE.). 2009. audio compact disk 16.95 (978-0-9842842-1-4(4)) V Diakiese.

Hope for Animals & Their World: How Endangered Species Are Being Rescued from the Brink. unabr. ed. Jane Goodall. Read by Jane Goodall. Told to Thane Maynard & Gail Hudson. (Running Time: 12 hrs. 30 mins.). (ENG.). 2009. 26.98 (978-1-60024-870-2(5)) Pub: Hachet Audio. Dist(s): HachBkGrp

Hope for Animals & Their World: How Endangered Species Are Being Rescued from the Brink. unabr. ed. Jane Goodall. Read by Jane Goodall. Told to Thane Maynard & Gail Hudson. 11 CDs. (Running Time: 12 hrs. 30 mins.). (ENG., 2009. audio compact disk 39.98 (978-1-60024-868-9(3)) Pub: Hachet Audio. Dist(s): HachBkGrp

Hope for Broken Relationships 2006. Contrib. by CCEF Faculty Staff. (ENG.). 2006. 147.80 (978-1-934885-56-7(8)); audio compact disk 183.80 (978-1-934885-55-0(X)) New Growth Pr.

Hope for Compulsive Eaters. Judi Hollis. 12 cass. (Running Time: 60 min.). 1987. 90.00 Incl. wkbk. (5650G) Hazelden.

Hope for Every Moment Audio Devotional. T. D. Jakes. 2008. audio compact disk 24.99 (978-0-7684-2678-6(2)) Destiny Image Pubs.

Hope for Foster Children. Karen Jean Matsko Hood. 2006. 29.95 (978-1-59434-113-7(3)); audio compact disk 24.95 (978-1-59434-112-0(5)) Whspmg Pine.

***Hope for Our Troubled Times.** Charles R. Swindoll. 2009. audio compact disk 12.00 (978-1-57972-858-8(8)) Insight Living.

Hope for the Abused. Interview with Mary Wilkinson et al. 1 cass. (Running Time: 1 hr. 41 min.). (ICEL Three Ser.). 1996. 6.00 (978-1-57838-057-2(X)) CrossLife Express.
Abuse recovery.

Hope for the Flowers. Trina Paulus. 1 cass. (Running Time: 1 hr. 8 mins.). 1997. 12.95 (978-0-8091-8247-3(5)) Paulist Pr.
Audio version of Hope for the Flowers, a classic offering profound advice about making your way in a difficult world, one's calling and taking a road less traveled. Read by the author.

Hope for the Flowers. gif. ed. Trina Paulus. (Running Time: 1 hr. 8 mins.). 1997. bk. 19.95 (978-0-8091-8249-7(1), 8249-1) Paulist Pr.

Hope for the Flowers. unabr. ed. Trina Paulus. Read by Trina Paulus. 1 cass. (YA). 1997. 12.95 (978-0-8072-7884-0(X), Listening Lib) Random Audio Pubg.

Hope for the Future Family Through Pastoral Care. 1 cass. (Care Cassettes Ser.: Vol. 19, No. 4). 10.80 Assn Prof Chaplains.

Hope for the Separated: Wounded Marriages Can Be Healed. unabr. ed. Gary Chapman. Read by Gary Chapman. audio compact disk 19.99 (978-1-58926-902-6(0)) Oasis Audio.

Hope for the Separated: Wounded Marriages Can Be Healed. unabr. ed. Gary Chapman. Narrated by Gary Chapman. (ENG.). 2005. 13.99 (978-1-60814-239-2(6)); audio compact disk 27.99 (978-1-58926-901-9(2)) Oasis Audio.

Hope for the Troubled Heart. Billy Graham. Narrated by Jack Garrett. 5 cass. (Running Time: 7 hrs.). 50.00 (978-1-4025-0394-8(6)) Recorded Bks.

Hope for the Troubled Heart: Finding God in the Midst of Pain. Based on a book by Billy Graham. 1998. (978-0-913367-88-9(5)) Billy Graham Evangelistic Association.

Hope for Underachieving Kids. 2004. audio compact disk (978-1-930429-54-3(1)) Love Logic.

Hope from an Afghan Prison: The Dayna Curry & Heather Mercer Story. unabr. ed. Dayna Curry & Heather Mercer. 2 cass. (Running Time: 3 hrs..). 2002. 17.99 (978-1-58926-070-2(8), D52L-0100) Oasis Audio.
Two ordinary young women left the comforts of the United States to serve God by helping the poor in Afghanistan. They soon found themselves in the midst of an international war on terrorism-and in a Taliban prison.

Hope in a Jar. unabr. ed. Beth Harbison. Read by Orlagh Cassidy. 7 CDs. (Running Time: 9 hrs. 0 mins. 0 sec.). (ENG.). 2009. audio compact disk 29.95 (978-1-4272-0660-2(0), Rena Bks) Pub: St Martin. Dist(s): Macmillan

Hope in Christ & Growing Spiritually. Ed Pinegar. 1 cass. 1997. 9.98 (978-1-57734-081-2(7), 06005462) Covenant Comms.
Using the power of hope to enrich our lives.

Hope in God. Lynne Hammond. 1 CD. (Running Time: 1 hr). 2005. audio compact disk 5.00 (978-1-57399-269-5(0)) Mac Hammond.

Hope in God. Based on a movie by Lynne Hammond. 1 cass. (Running Time: 1 hr.). 2005. 5.00 (978-1-57399-217-6(8)) Mac Hammond.

Hope in Hurtful Times: A Study of 1 Peter. unabr. ed. Charles R. Swindoll. 9 cass. (Running Time: 7 hrs. 30 mins.). 1998. 44.95 (978-1-57972-273-9(3)) Insight Living.

Hope in the Lord. Composed by Paul Tate. 2001. audio compact disk 16.00 (978-1-58459-083-5(1)) Wrld Lib Pubns.

Hope in the Lord. Music by Paul Tate. 2001. 11.00 (978-1-58459-081-1(5)); audio compact disk 16.00 (978-1-58459-082-8(3)) Wrld Lib Pubns.

***Hope Is Contagious: Trusting God in the Face of Any Obstacle.** unabr. ed. Ken Hutcherson. (Running Time: 4 hrs. 57 mins. 29 sec.). (Letters to God Ser.). (ENG.). 2010. 16.99 (978-0-310-59740-7(4)) Zondervan.

Hope Is the Thing with Feathers see Poems & Letters of Emily Dickinson

***Hope of Man.** L. Ron Hubbard. (ENG.). 2002. audio compact disk 15.00 (978-1-4031-1042-8(5)) Bridge Pubns Inc.

***Hope of Man.** L. Ron Hubbard. (CHI.). 2010. audio compact disk 15.00 (978-1-4031-7380-5(X)); audio compact disk 15.00 (978-1-4031-7370-6(2)); audio compact disk 15.00 (978-1-4031-7367-6(2)); audio compact disk 15.00 (978-1-4031-7378-2(8)); audio compact disk 15.00 (978-1-4031-7376-8(1)); audio compact disk 15.00 (978-1-4031-7368-3(0)); audio compact disk 15.00 (978-1-4031-7366-9(4)); audio compact disk 15.00 (978-1-4031-7371-3(0)); audio compact disk 15.00 (978-1-4031-7365-2(6)); audio compact disk 15.00 (978-1-4031-7373-7(7)); audio compact disk 15.00 (978-1-4031-7374-4(5)); audio compact disk 15.00 (978-1-4031-7375-1(3)); audio compact disk 15.00 (978-1-4031-7369-0(9)); audio compact disk 15.00 (978-1-4031-7379-9(6)); audio compact disk 15.00 (978-1-4031-7377-5(X)); audio compact disk 15.00 (978-1-4031-7372-0(9)) Bridge Pubns Inc.

Hope of Prayer. 8 CDs. 2006. audio compact disk 59.00 (978-1-933207-15-5(9)) Ransomed Heart.

Hope Springs from Mended Places: Images of Grace in the Shadows of Life. bk. 14.99 Zondervan.

Hope Street. unabr. ed. Ken McCoy. Read by Ken McCoy. 8 cass. (Running Time: 10 hrs. 35 min.). (Storysound Ser.). (J). 2001. 69.95 (978-1-85903-452-1(7)) Pub: Mgna Lrg Print GBR. Dist(s): Ulverscroft US

Hope, the Blueprint of Faith. Kenneth Copeland. 8 cass. 1992. bk. 40.00 Set incl. study guide. (978-0-938458-19-7(1)) K Copeland Pubns.
Biblical teaching on faith.

Hope the Blueprint of Faith. Kenneth Copeland. 15 CDs. 2006. audio compact disk 40.00 (978-1-57562-840-0(6)) K Copeland Pubns.

Hope to Die. Lawrence Block. Read by Lawrence Block. (Matthew Scudder Mystery Ser.: No. 15). 1975. 9.99 (978-0-06-074334-5(4)) HarperCollins Pubs.

***Hope to Die.** abr. ed. Lawrence Block. Read by Lawrence Block. (ENG.). 2004. (978-0-06-078319-8(2), Harper Audio) HarperCollins Pubs.

***Hope to Die.** abr. ed. Lawrence Block. Read by Lawrence Block. (ENG.). 2004. (978-0-06-081399-4(7), Harper Audio) HarperCollins Pubs.

***Hope Unseen: The Story of the U. S. Army's First Blind Active-Duty Officer.** Scotty Smiley. Contrib. by Doug Crandall. Narrated by Dan John Miller. (ENG.). 2010. audio compact disk 39.99 (978-1-61120-006-5(7)) Dreamscap OH.

Hope Was Here. Joan Bauer. Read by Jenna Lamia. 4 CDs. (Running Time: 4 hrs. 31 mins.). (J). (gr. 7 up). 2004. audio compact disk 35.00 (978-1-4000-8615-3(9), Listening Lib) Random Audio Pubg.

Hope Was Here. unabr. ed. Joan Bauer. 3 vols. (Running Time: 4 hrs. 31 mins.). (J). (gr. 7 up). 2004. pap. bk. 36.00 (978-0-8072-1706-1(9), S YA 1013 SP, Listening Lib); 30.00 (978-0-8072-1698-9(4), Listening Lib) Pub: Random Audio Pubg. Dist(s): Random

Hope: When Life Hurts Most. Contrib. by Louie Giglio. 2008. audio compact disk 14.99 (978-5-557-44620-4(6)) Pt of Grace Ent.

Hope When You're Hurting: Answers to Four Questions Hurting People Ask. abr. ed. Larry Crabb & Dan B. Allender. (Running Time: 2 hrs. 0 mins. 0 sec.). (ENG.). 2003. 9.99 (978-0-310-26057-8(4)) Zondervan.

Hope You Need: From the Lord's Prayer. unabr. ed. Rick Warren. (ENG.). 2010. audio compact disk 39.99 (978-0-310-32873-5(X)) Zondervan.

***Hope You Need: From the Lord's Prayer.** unabr. ed. Rick Warren. (ENG.). 2010. 24.99 (978-0-310-55872-9(7)) Zondervan.

Hopes & Dreams. Dee Williams. Read by Kim Hicks. 2003. 69.95 (978-0-7540-8361-0(6)) Pub: Chivers Audio Bks GBR. Dist(s): AudioGO

Hopes & Expectations of Church for Religious & Religious Life. Fulton J. Sheen. 1 cass. 4.00 (76S) IRL Chicago.

Hopes & Fears for Art, Set. unabr. ed. William Morris. Read by Robert L. Halvorson. 5 cass. (Running Time: 450 min.). 35.95 (93) Halvorson Assocs.

Hopes & Prospects. unabr. ed. Noam Chomsky. Frwd. by Bill Moyers. (ENG.). 2010. audio compact disk 28.00 (978-1-931859-97-4(3)) Pub: Haymarket Bks. Dist(s): Consort Bk Sales

Hope's Boy. unabr. ed. Andrew Bridge. Read by David Drummond. 1 MP3-CD. (Running Time: 10 hrs. 30 mins. 0 sec.). (ENG.). 2008. 24.99 (978-1-4001-5606-1(8)); audio compact disk 34.99 (978-1-4001-0606-6(0)); audio compact disk 69.99 (978-1-4001-3606-3(7)) Pub: Tantor Media. Dist(s): IngramPubServ

Hope's Boy: A Memoir. unabr. ed. Andrew Bridge. Read by David Drummond. (YA). 2008. 59.99 (978-1-60252-928-1(0)) Find a World.

Hope's Cadillac. unabr. ed. Patricia Page. Narrated by C. J. Critt. 10 cass. (Running Time: 13 hrs. 45 mins.). 1997. 85.00 (978-0-7887-1148-0(2), 95118E7) Recorded Bks.
An affair, a divorce, a custody battle, usually the elements of a contemporary tragedy, begin a funny, savvy tale of how one woman rebuilds her life during the late 1960s.

Hope's Highway. Dorothy Garlock & Isabel Keating. 9 vols. 2004. 79.95 (978-0-7927-3133-7(6), CSL 629, Chivers Sound Lib); audio compact disk 94.95 (978-0-7927-3134-4(4), SLD 629, Chivers Sound Lib) AudioGO.

Hopi. Frank Waters. Read by Frank Waters. (Running Time: 28 min.). 13.95 (978-0-929402-04-8(9), LTS-2) Am Audio Prose.
Discusses the Hopi Prophecy, the special world of Kiva and the symbolism of the Corn Dance.

Hopi Prophesies. unabr. ed. Thomas Banyacya. 1 cass. (Running Time: 1 hr. 28 min.). 1982. 11.00 (12001) Big Sur Tapes.
In 1948, the elders of the Hopi tribe met to discuss the difficulties facing their people & the outside world. Thomas Banyacya, a young man at the time, was alarmed by what he heard, & has spent much of his life communicating the message of his people.

Hopi Snake Dance. unabr. ed. Joseph Henderson. 1 cass. (Running Time: 50 min.). 1989. 11.00 (06606) Big Sur Tapes.
A vivid description of Henderson's experience of the Hopi Snake Dance ceremony & the profound effect it had on him.

Hopi Turtle see Puss in Boots & Other Fairy Tales from Around the World

Hoping & Coping: The Parent-Teen Years: Proceedings of 45th Annual Convention National Association of Evangelicals Buffalo, New York. Read by Leroy Kettinger. 1 cass. (Running Time: 60 min.). 1987. 4.00 (326) Nat Assn Evan.

Hoping in Solitude see Desde la soledad y la Esperanza: Antonio, Fernando, Ramón, René, Gerardo

Hoping in Solitude: Antonio, Fernando, Ramón, René, Gerardo. 2008. pap. bk. 25.00 (978-959-211-317-6(3)) Pathfinder NY.

Hoppin' & Boppin' for Youngsters. Prod. by Angela Russ. Lyrics by Angela Russ. Arranged by Bill Burchell. 1 CD. (Running Time: 34 mins). (SPA.). (J). 2002. audio compact disk 13.99 (978-0-9660122-7-9(5)) Russ Invis.
Children sing and dance to this captivating music with easy, instructional, active lyrics that keep them stretching, snapping, giggling, bending, hopping, and skipping to kid's favorite songs and lullabies. Some songs are even sung with a bilingual twist. Before long, youngsters are singing original lyrics to familiar tunes. They are having so much fun, they don't even know they're learning about their body parts, following simple commands, identifying colors, counting, or scaling their ABCs. This CD is the second in the series and takes children Hoppin' & Boppin' through another 30-minutes of action-style songs. It begins with a stretch, gradually increases in motor skills, and finally cools children down to a restful calm. NO COUCH POTATOES HERE! Hoppin' & Boppin' for Youngsters will be available on video of DVD late 2002.

Hopping Freights: A Wild Sixties Adventure. Perf. by Doug Lipman. 1 cass. (Running Time: 1 hr.). Dramatization. (YA). (gr. 9 up). 1990. 9.95 (978-0-938756-30-9(3), 013) Yellow Moon.
Story about the beginning of a passage from boyhood to manhood. In the tradition of Jack Kerouac, Doug tells of a trip from Chicago to New York in a boxcar. Filled with humor, danger, & compassion.

Hora de Descanso. unabr. ed. John F. Taylor. Read by Marisela Rizik. Ed. by William Mosier. 1 cass. (Running Time: 25 min.). (J). 1994. 9.95 (978-1-883963-15-6(X)) ADD Plus.
A guided relaxation procedure for children in Spanish language.

Hora de Estrellas see Poesia y Drama de Garcia Lorca

Hora Es. unabr. ed. Mesianic Musica & Zondervan Publishing Staff. (SPA.). 2001. 9.99 (978-0-8297-3384-6(1)) Pub: Vida Pubs. Dist(s): Zondervan

Hora Es. unabr. ed. Zondervan Publishing Staff. 2001. audio compact disk 14.99 (978-0-8297-3382-2(5)) Zondervan.

Horace, Set. Corneille. 2 cass. (FRE.). 1991. 26.95 (1039-RF) Olivia & Hill.
Set during the war between Rome & Alba, Horace & his brothers are Roman, while Curiace & his brothers side with Alba. Horace, however, is married to Curiace's sister & Curiace is betrothed to Horace's sister Camille.

Horace & Morris, but Mostly Delores. James Howe. Read by Jason Harris. 11 vols. (Running Time: 8 mins.). (Live Oak Readalong Ser.). (J). 2003. pap. bk. 16.95 (978-1-59112-241-8(4)) Pub: Live Oak Media. Dist(s): AudioGO

Horace & Morris, but Mostly Dolores. James Howe. Illus. by Amy Waldrod. 14 vols. (Running Time: 8 mins.). 2003. pap. bk. 39.95 (978-1-59112-538-9(3)) Live Oak Media.

Horace & Morris, but Mostly Dolores. James Howe. Illus. by Amy Waldrod. 11 vols. (Running Time: 8 mins.). (J). 2003. pap. bk. 18.95 (978-1-59112-341-5(0)) Pub: Live Oak Media. Dist(s): AudioGO

Horace & Morris, but Mostly Dolores. James Howe. Illus. by Amy Waldrod. 11 vols. (Running Time: 8 mins.). 2003. bk. 25.95 (978-1-59112-242-5(2)); pap. bk. 37.95 (978-1-59112-243-2(0)) Live Oak Media.

Horace & Morris, but Mostly Dolores. James Howe. Illus. by Amy Waldrod. (Running Time: 8 mins.). (J). (gr. k-3). 2003. 12.95 (978-1-59112-340-8(2)) Live Oak Media.

Horace & Morris Join the Chorus. James Howe. Illus. by Amy Waldrod. 11 vols. pap. bk. 16.95 (978-1-59112-447-4(6)); 9.95 (978-1-59112-446-7(8)); audio compact disk 12.95 (978-1-59112-906-6(0)) Live Oak Media.

Horace & Morris Join the Chorus. James Howe. Illus. by Amy Waldrod. 11 vols. (J). 2005. bk. 25.95 (978-1-59112-448-1(4)); bk. 28.95 (978-1-59112-908-0(7)) Pub: Live Oak Media. Dist(s): AudioGO

Horary. Susan Horton. 1 cass. (Running Time: 1 hr. 30 min.). 8.95 (164) Am Fed Astrologers.

Horary: You Must Do the Bookkeeping First. Edward Helin. 1 cass. 8.95 (151) Am Fed Astrologers.
An AFA Convention workshop tape.

Horary Astrology. Sandy Dugan. Read by Sandy Dugan. 1 cass. (Running Time: 90 min.). 1994. 8.95 (1129) Am Fed Astrologers.

Horary Astrology. Eugene Moore. 1 cass. 8.95 (242) Am Fed Astrologers.
Completely modernized, brand new rules.

Horary Astrology. Gilbert Navarro. 5 cass. (Running Time: 60 min. per cass.). 1992. 8.95 ea. Am Fed Astrologers.

Horary Astrology. Joan Titsworth. 1 cass. (Running Time: 60 min.). 1992. 8.95 (1093) Am Fed Astrologers.

Horary Astrology. Joanne Wickenburg. 1 cass. (Running Time: 90 min.). 1986. 8.95 (598) Am Fed Astrologers.

Horary Astrology: An Introduction. Bobbye Bratcher-Hill. Read by Bobbye Bratcher-Hill. 1 cass. (Running Time: 90 min.). 1984. 8.95 (035) Am Fed Astrologers.

Horary Astrology: Group Sessions. Angela Gallo. 1 cass. 8.95 (522) Am Fed Astrologers.
Answer? on the spot before live audience.

Horary Astrology: Relationships & Missing Possessions. Gilbert Navarro. 1 cass. (Running Time: 90 min.). 1984. 8.95 (249) Am Fed Astrologers.

Horary Astrology: The Timing of the Horary Chart. Gilbert Navarro. 1 cass. (Running Time: 90 min.). 1990. 8.95 (853) Am Fed Astrologers.

Horary Odds & Ends. Gilbert Navarro. 1 cass. (Running Time: 90 min.). 1994. 8.95 (1159) Am Fed Astrologers.
Horary astrology tips & tricks.

Horary One & Two. Charles Dickenson. 1 cass. 8.95 (398) Am Fed Astrologers.
An AFA Convention workshop tape.

Horatio's Drive: America's First Road Trip. unabr. ed. Dayton Duncan & Ken Burns. 2 cass. (Running Time: 3 hrs.). 2003. 28.00 (978-0-7366-9480-3(3)) Books on Tape.

Horizon. unabr. ed. Helen MacInnes. Read by Eric Collinson. 4 cass. (Running Time: 6 hrs.). 2001. 44.95 (978-1-85496-143-3(8), 61438) Pub: Soundings Ltd GBR. Dist(s): Ulverscroft US

Horizon Storms. unabr. ed. Kevin J. Anderson. Narrated by George Guidall. 13 cass. (Running Time: 19 hrs.). (Saga of Seven Suns Ser.: Bk. 3). 2004. 99.75 (978-1-4025-3790-5(5)) Recorded Bks.

Horizon Storms. unabr. collector's ed. Kevin J. Anderson. Narrated by George Guidall. 16 CDs. (Running Time: 19 hrs.). (Saga of Seven Suns Ser.: Bk. 3). 2004. audio compact disk 59.95 (978-1-4025-9637-7(5)) Recorded Bks.

Horizons. unabr. ed. Robert A. Monroe. Read by Robert A. Monroe. (Running Time: 45 min.). (Gateway Experience - Exploring Ser.). 1984. 14.95 (978-1-56113-278-2(0)) Monroe Institute.
Look inward to memories, feelings & events.

Horizons. 2nd ed. Joan H. Manley et al. (C). bk. 111.95 (978-0-8384-7430-3(6)); bk. 152.95 (978-0-8384-8055-7(1)); bk. 103.95 (978-0-8384-6400-7(9)) Heinle.

Horizons. 2nd annot. ed. Joan H. Manley et al. (C). 2001. bk. & tchr. ed. 61.00 (978-0-8384-4474-0(1)) Heinle.

Horizons: Testbank. 2nd ed. Stuart Smith et al. (C). 2002. audio compact disk 29.50 (978-0-8384-1392-0(7)) Heinle.
A complete first-year French program, whose practical application allows students to connect their language skills to the global landscape. The truly francophone focus encourages students to compare their own cultures to the customs, perspectives and daily life of selected French-speaking communities.

Horizontes: Cuarta Edicion Instructor's Resource Manual. 4th ed. Gilman. Orig. Title: Horizontes 2e Gramatica Conversacion. 2002. pap. bk., tchr. ed., lab manual ed. 77.95 (978-0-470-00644-3(7), JWiley) Wiley US.

Horizontes: Repaso y Conversación. 6th ed. Graciela Ascarrunz Gilman et al. (C). 2008. 15.00 (978-0-470-04943-3(X), JWiley) Wiley US.

Horizontes, Lab Audio CDs: Repaso y Conversación. 5th ed. Graciela Ascarrunz Gilman et al. (SPA.). (C). 2004. audio compact disk 57.95 (978-0-471-69972-9(1)) Wiley US.

Horizontes 2e Gramatica Conversacion see Horizontes: Cuarta Edicion Instructor's Resource Manual

Horla see Tales of Terror & the Supernatural: A Collection

Horla. Guy de Maupassant. 1 cass. (FRE.). 1995. 13.95 (1080-OH) Olivia & Hill.
What causes a seemingly happy man to hallucinate? Are they hallucinations or are they real? It is this transformation & the ensuing horror that Maupassant, syphilitic & close to death, analyzes in this story.

Horla. unabr. ed. Guy de Maupassant. Read by Jim Killavey. 1 cass. (Running Time: 90 min.). Dramatization. Incl. Was It a Dream? 1981. (N-83); Wolf. 1981. (N-83); 1981. 7.95 (N-83) Jimcin Record.
Features strange creatures & terrifying dreams.

Hormone Replacement Therapy. Patricia Kelly. 1 cass. (Running Time: 43 min.). 1998. bk. 15.00 (978-1-58111-052-4(9)) Contemporary Medical.
Practical information on hormone dose & use & hormone use for women with family history of breast cancer. Discusses conflicting studies of risk.

Hormones & the Mind: Program from the Award Winning Public Radio Series. Interview. Hosted by Fred Goodwin. 1 CD. (Running Time: 1 Hour). 2001. audio compact disk 21.95 (978-1-932479-53-9(8), LCM 159) Lichtenstein Creat.
People often talk about being controlled by their hormones, but how do these chemicals really affect behavior? This week, we look at Hormones and the Mind. Guests include Dr. James McBride Dabbs, a Professor of Psychology who discusses testosterone and personality; Drs. Peter Schmidt and Catherine Roca from the National Institute of Mental Health, who explain the latest research on PMS; and Dr. Jeffrey Flier, an endocrinologist at Harvard Medical School, who explores the link between hormones and weight.

Hormones & Wheels. 3 CD Set. (Running Time: 202 Mins). 2003. audio compact disk 24.95 (978-1-930429-29-1(0)) Pub: Love Logic. Dist(s): Penton Overseas

Hormones & Wheels: Parent Survival Tips for Those Chaotic Teen Years. Jim Fay. Read by Jim Fay. Ed. by Bert Gurule Mizke. 3 cass. (Running Time: 3 hrs. 30 min.). 1994. 22.95 (978-0-944634-07-3(9)) Pub: Love Logic. Dist(s): Penton Overseas
Parenting expert, Jim Fay, takes a captivating look at the often harrowing job of parenting a teenager. With the proven techniques Jim shares with parents on these tapes, many desperate parents have actually survived the trying teen years - only to discover their teen has emerged a responsible, likeable young adult.

Hornblower. abr. gif. movie tie-in ed. C. S. Forester. Read by Ioan Gruffudd. 6 cass. (Hornblower Ser.). 1998. (978-1-84032-126-5(1), HoddrStoughton) Hodder General GBR.
Hornblower's wonderful adventures are set to meet a new & wider audience through the television.

Hornblower & the Atropos. C. S. Forester. Read by Geoffrey Howard. 2002. 56.00 (978-0-7366-8900-7(1)); audio compact disk 56.00 (978-0-7366-9127-7(8)) Books on Tape.

Hornblower & the Atropos. unabr. ed. C. S. Forester. Read by David Case. 7 cass. (Running Time: 10 hrs.). (Hornblower Ser.). 2001. 29.95 (978-0-7366-6760-9(1)) Books on Tape.
Hornblower hunts treasure & takes on a Spanish ship of battle twice his size.

Hornblower & the Atropos. unabr. collector's ed. C. S. Forester. Read by David Case. 7 cass. (Running Time: 10 hrs. 30 mins.). (Hornblower Ser.: No. 4). 1984. 56.00 (978-0-7366-0653-0(X), 1614) Books on Tape.
Hornblower, newly appointed to rank & responsibility, has more than his share of concerns when his ship "H.M.S. Atropos" springs a sizable leak during the processional ceremonies honoring the passing of Lord Nelson. But Hornblower skirts this disaster & plunges once more into his more natural habitat of hardship & battle. The "Atropos" sails off to retrieve a sunken treasure in Turkish waters...a task made all the more harrowing when he drives his outgunned sloop directly into battle with a great Spanish frigate.

Hornblower & the Crisis. unabr. ed. C. S. Forester. Read by Christian Rodska. 4 cass. (Running Time: 4 hrs. 20 mins.). (Hornblower Ser.: No. 11). 2000. 39.95 (978-0-7540-0482-0(1), CAB1905) Pub: Chivers Audio Bks GBR. Dist(s): AudioGO
It is 1805 & Napoleon prepares to invade England. Asked by the Admiralty to risk a shameful death, Hornblower agrees to a dangerous mission: turning spy to light a powder trail to Trafalgar. Contains two short stories featuring Hornblower & the Widow McCool & the Last Encounter.

Hornblower & the Hotspur. unabr. ed. C. S. Forester. Read by David Case. 8 cass. (Running Time: 12 hrs.). (Hornblower Ser.). 2001. (978-0-7366-6762-3(8)) Books on Tape.
Hornblower embarks on marriage & a new command. Both prove perilous.

Hornblower & the Hotspur. unabr. ed. C. S. Forester. Read by David Case. 8 cass. (Running Time: 12 hrs.). (Hornblower Ser.: Vol. 3). 2001. 64.00 (978-0-7366-8374-6(7)); audio compact disk 64.00 (978-0-7366-8394-4(1)) Books on Tape.
Hornblower is embarked on two ventures, both equally daunting and requiring his adherence to duty. The one is his marriage to Maria Ellen, contracted in a moment of absent-mindedness and weakness, and which he feels ill-equipped to endure. The marriage also comes with a redoubtable mother-in-law. As if this were not enough, the Peace of Amiens is dissolving, and Admiral William Cornwallis wants Hornblower to take the HOTSPUR, a small three-master, and prepare for action against "Boney" Napoleon. Naval action is more suited to Hornblower's constitution, and he performs brilliantly, aided by the utterly indispensable Mr. Bush. Hornblower may have a saturnine side to him, but there is a man of iron atop his feet of clay.

Hornblower & the Hotspur. unabr. collector's ed. C. S. Forester. Read by David Case. 8 cass. (Running Time: 12 hrs.). (Hornblower Ser.: No. 3). 1984. 64.00 (978-0-7366-0652-3(1), 1613) Books on Tape.
Hornblower is a hero with feet of clay, a man who grows beyond his limits & by example leads us in our imaginations to goals we otherwise would not seek. "Hornblower & the Hotspur" is the tenth in C. S. Forester's saga of the legendary commander. It sees him embarked on a marriage & a new command, adventures that requires equal resolution & stamina.

Hornblower & the Ship of the Line. C. S. Forester. Read by Geoffrey Howard. 2002. 48.00 (978-0-7366-8899-4(4)) Books on Tape.

Hornblower & the Ship of the Line. unabr. ed. C. S. Forester. Read by Bill Kelsey. 6 cass. (Running Time: 9 hrs.). (Hornblower Ser.). 2001. 29.95 (978-0-7366-6756-2(3)) Books on Tape.
Hornblower's first battleship command.

Hornblower & the Ship of the Line. unabr. collector's ed. C. S. Forester. Read by Bill Kelsey. 6 cass. (Running Time: 9 hrs.). (Hornblower Ser.: No. 6). 1987. 48.00 (978-0-7366-1228-9(9), 2146) Books on Tape.
Naval adventures of Horatio Hornblower in the Napoleonic Wars. This is the sixth volume in the eleven volume Hornblower series.

Hornblower During the Crisis. C. S. Forester. Read by Geoffrey Howard. 2002. audio compact disk 28.00 (978-0-7366-9116-1(2)) Books on Tape.

Hornblower During the Crisis. unabr. ed. C. S. Forester. Read by Gary Martin. 5 cass. (Running Time: 8 hrs.). (Hornblower Ser.). 2001. 24.95 (978-0-7366-6758-6(X)) Books on Tape.
Hornblower's last command & Forester's last book.

Hornblower During the Crisis. unabr. collector's ed. C. S. Forester. Read by Gary Martin. 5 cass. (Running Time: 5 hrs.). (Hornblower Ser.: No. 11). 1988. 30.00 (978-0-7366-1354-5(4), 2255) Books on Tape.
Captain Hornblower, after two hard years on blockade at Brest, has relinquished the helm of the Hotspur. He has no ship, only the promise of one. Meanwhile, there are battles to be fought.

Hornblower in the West Indies, Set. unabr. ed. 8 CDs. (Running Time: 36300 sec.). (Hornblower Ser.: No. 10). 2000. 84.95 (978-0-7540-5326-2(1), CCD 017) Pub: Chivers Audio Bks GBR. Dist(s): AudioGO
To be Commander-in-Chief of the West Indies, with nothing more to worry about than the suppression of the slave trade, the hunting down of piracy & the policing of the Caribbean, was pure joy to Rear Admiral Hornblower. However, during his command he is kidnapped by pirates & risks his life to prevent Europe from being plunged into war.

Hornblower West Indies. Jeff Archer. 2002. (978-1-84032-105-0(9), HoddrStoughton) Hodder General GBR.
Napoleon is finally defeated, but the world, far from falling into an easy rhythm of peace, seethes. France's empire is ripe for plucking, her citizens for revanche. Out of retirement and into this maelstrom comes Hornblower, assigned military and diplomatic chores for which only he is suited. The reader's anticipation is not disappointed, for where Hornblower sails, the law prevails, and in this final voyage with the Admiral, he has never been more engaging or in greater command.

Horne's Law. unabr. ed. Jory Sherman. Read by Kevin Foley. 4 cass. (Running Time: 5 hrs. 48 min.). (Horne Ser.: Bk. 2). 1996. 26.95 (978-1-55686-670-8(4)) Books in Motion.
Jack Horne was a man of courage & shunned the settlement. But he was hated by those in the settlement who appeared cowardly in his shadow.

Hornet Flight. Ken Follett. 2002. 88.00 (978-0-7366-8921-2(4)); 104.00 (978-0-7366-8922-9(2)) Books on Tape.

Hornet's Nest. Patricia Cornwell. Read by Kate Reading. (Andy Brazil Ser.: No. 1). 1997. audio compact disk 88.00 (978-0-7366-5968-0(4)) Books on Tape.

Hornet's Nest. unabr. ed. Patricia Cornwell. Read by Kate Reading. 9 cass. (Running Time: 13 hrs. 30 min.). (Andy Brazil Ser.: No. 1). 1997. 72.00 (978-0-913369-52-4(7), 4264) Books on Tape.
Dynamic trio of crime-solvers in Charlotte, North Carolina: Andy Brazil, an eager young reporter; Judy Hammer, the city's police chief; & Virginia West, Hammer's deputy & genuine head-turner. All are on the trail of a vicious serial killer.

Hornet's Nest. unabr. ed. Patricia Cornwell. Read by Kate Reading. 11 CDs. (Running Time: 13 hrs. 12 mins.). (Andy Brazil Ser.: No. 1). 2001. audio compact disk 44.00 Books on Tape.
Police & a reporter in Charlotte, NC track a serial killer who tortures, then shoots male tourists.

Hornets' Nest. unabr. ed. Paul Magrs. Narrated by Tom Baker. 5 CDs. (Running Time: 5 hrs. 0 mins. 0 sec.). (Doctor Who Ser.). (ENG.). 2010. audio compact disk 74.95 (978-1-60283-826-0(7)) Pub: AudioGO. Dist(s): Perseus Dist

Hornet's Nest: A Novel of the Revolutionary War. unabr. ed. Jimmy Carter. Narrated by John McDonough. 16 cassettes. (Running Time: 23 hrs). 2005. 99.75 (978-1-4025-6659-2(X)); audio compact disk 109.75 (978-1-4025-6684-4(0)) Recorded Bks.

Hornets' Nest: Circus of Doom. unabr. ed. Paul Magrs. Narrated by Tom Baker. (Running Time: 1 hr. 0 mins. 0 sec.). (ENG.). 2010. audio compact disk 24.95 (978-1-60283-868-0(2)) Pub: AudioGO. Dist(s): Perseus Dist

Hornets' Nest: Hive of Horror. unabr. ed. Paul Magrs. Narrated by Tom Baker. (Running Time: 1 hr. 0 mins. 0 sec.). (ENG.). 2010. audio compact disk 24.95 (978-1-60283-870-3(4)) Pub: AudioGO. Dist(s): Perseus Dist

Hornets' Nest: Sting in the Tale. Paul Magrs. Narrated by Tom Baker. (Running Time: 1 hr. 0 mins. 0 sec.). (ENG.). 2010. audio compact disk 24.95 (978-1-60283-869-7(0)) Pub: AudioGO. Dist(s): Perseus Dist

Hornets' Nest: The Dead Shoes. Paul Magrs. Narrated by Tom Baker. (Running Time: 1 hr. 0 mins. 0 sec.). (ENG.). 2010. audio compact disk 24.95 (978-1-60283-867-3(4)) Pub: AudioGO. Dist(s): Perseus Dist

***Hornet's Nest: The Stuff of Nightmares.** Paul Magrs. Read by Tom Baker & Richard Franklin. 1 CD. (Running Time: 1 hr.). (Doctor Who Ser.). 2010. audio compact disk 14.00 (978-1-4084-2673-9(0)) AudioGo GBR.

Horns. unabr. ed. Joe Hill. Read by Fred Berman. 2010. audio compact disk 39.99 (978-0-06-176802-6(2), Harper Audio) HarperCollins Pubs.

***Horns.** unabr. ed. Joe Hill. Read by Fred Berman. (ENG.). 2010. (978-0-06-196931-7(1), Harper Audio) HarperCollins Pubs.

***Horns: A Novel.** unabr. ed. Joe Hill. Read by Fred Berman. (ENG.). 2010. (978-0-06-196930-0(3), Harper Audio) HarperCollins Pubs.

Horns & Wrinkles. unabr. ed. Joseph Helgerson. Read by Jessica Almasy. 6 cass. (Running Time: 6 hrs. 45 mins.). (J). (gr. 4-7). 2007. 49.75 (978-1-4281-3367-9(4)); audio compact disk 66.75 (978-1-4281-3372-3(0)) Recorded Bks.

Hornswoggled. unabr. ed. Donis Casey & Pamela Ward. (Running Time: 32400 sec.). (Alafair Tucker Mysteries Ser.). 2007. audio compact disk 29.95 (978-1-4332-1089-1(4)) Blckstn Audio.

Hornswoggled: An Alafair Tucker Mystery. unabr. ed. Donis Casey. Read by Pam Ward. (Running Time: 32400 sec.). (Alafair Tucker Mysteries Ser.). 2007. 54.95 (978-1-4332-1087-7(8)) Blckstn Audio.

Hornswoggled: An Alafair Tucker Mystery. unabr. ed. Donis Casey. Read by Pamela Ward. (Running Time: 32400 sec.). (Alafair Tucker Mysteries Ser.). 2007. audio compact disk 63.00 (978-1-4332-1088-4(6)) Blckstn Audio.

Horoscope of Humanity. Eric A. Meece. 1 cass. 9.00 (A0779-90) Sound Photosyn.
Astrological conjunctions interestingly related to human historical events.

Horrible Big Black Bug. (gr. k-3). 10.00 (978-0-7635-6364-6(1)) Rigby Educ.

Horrible Harrry & the Purple People. unabr. ed. Suzy Kline. Narrated by Johnny Heller. 1 cass. (Running Time: 30 mins.). (J). 2000. pap. bk. 30.99 (41009X4) Recorded Bks.

Horrible Harry & the Ant Invasion. unabr. ed. Suzy Kline. Narrated by Johnny Heller. 1 cass. (Running Time: 45 mins.). (Horrible Harry Ser.: No. 2). (gr. 2 up). 1997. 10.00 (978-0-7887-1116-9(4), 95110E7) Recorded Bks.
Horrible Harry's teacher, Miss Mackle, is setting up an ant farm, & Harry hopes he will be chosen to take care of the creepy, crawly critters. But when Horrible Harry & his classmates send ants climbing up the stairs of the school, no one is shocked. Find out why & join Harry in three more adventures (including one with a deadly fish tank).

Horrible Harry & the Christmas Surprise. unabr. ed. Suzy Kline. Narrated by Johnny Heller. 1 cass. (Running Time: 45 mins.). (Horrible Harry Ser.). (gr. 2 up). 1998. 10.00 (978-1-4025-0919-3(7), 96707) Recorded Bks.
All the students in Room 2B are getting ready for Christmas. They are excited and filled with holiday spirit. But when their teacher, Miss Mackle, sits down in her chair, it breaks, and she gets hurt! Now Miss Mackle has to spend Christmas in the hospital. The students don't feel like celebrating any more. It's up to Harry to think of a present that will cheer her up and bring the holiday mood back. Will Harry find a gift that is wonderful - and horrible - enough?.

Horrible Harry & the Drop of Doom. Suzy Kline. Narrated by Johnny Heller. 1 cass. (Running Time: 45 mins.). (Horrible Harry Ser.). (gr. 2 up). 2001. 10.00 (978-0-7887-5495-1(5)) Recorded Bks.
Song Lee has invited Henry and some other classmates to an amusement park for a party. While Sydney raves about the newest ride, the Drop of Doom, Harry turns pale.

Horrible Harry & the Dungeon. Suzy Kline. Read by Johnny Heller. 1 cass. (Running Time: 45 mins.). (Horrible Harry Ser.: No. 7). (J). (gr. 2-4). 1999. stu. ed. 70.70 (978-0-7887-3220-1(X), 46876) Recorded Bks.
The school year is almost over & the students at South School are wild. Many are getting sent to the Suspension Room, where a big, hairy guy with a heavy bag guards students all day. But what does he do & what is in the bag? Horrible Harry is determined to find out, even if it means going there himself.

Horrible Harry & the Dungeon. unabr. ed. Suzy Kline. Narrated by Johnny Heller. 1 cass. (Running Time: 45 mins.). (Horrible Harry Ser.: No. 7). (gr. 2 up). 1999. 10.00 (978-0-7887-3155-6(6), 95828E7) Recorded Bks.

Horrible Harry & the Dungeon. unabr. ed. Suzy Kline. Narrated by Johnny Heller. 1 cass. (Running Time: 45 mins.). (Horrible Harry Ser.: No. 7). (J). (gr. 2-4). 2000. pap. bk. 22.24 (978-0-7887-3174-7(2), 40909X4) Recorded Bks.

Horrible Harry & the Green Slime. unabr. ed. Suzy Kline. Narrated by Johnny Heller. 1 cass. (Running Time: 45 mins.). (Horrible Harry Ser.: No. 3). (gr. 2 up). 1997. 10.00 (978-0-7887-0743-8(4), 94920E7) Recorded Bks.
In Room 2B, Horrible Harry is best at thinking up yukky ideas. But sometimes even Harry's most horrible plans turn out to be good. Horrible Harry & the rest of the South School gang are busy in four lively new adventures. The time spent in Room 2B is never dull with Horrible Harry around.

Horrible Harry & the Kickball Wedding. Suzy Kline. Narrated by Johnny Heller. (Running Time: 45 mins.). (Horrible Harry Ser.). (gr. 2 up). 10.00 (978-0-7887-9405-6(1)) Recorded Bks.

Horrible Harry & the Purple People. Suzy Kline. Read by Johnny Heller. 1 cass. (Running Time: 30 mins.). (Horrible Harry Ser.: No. 8). (J). (gr. 2-4). 1999. pap. bk. 30.99 (978-0-7887-3643-8(4), 41009); 158.20 (978-0-7887-3673-5(6), 46976) Recorded Bks.
Horrible Harry has finally gone too far. He keeps talking about purple people, even though he's the only one who can see them. When Harry promises to show one of the purple people to the class, his best friend, Doug, knows that Harry is heading for big trouble.

Horrible Harry & the Purple People. unabr. ed. Suzy Kline. Narrated by Johnny Heller. 1 cass. (Running Time: 45 mins.). (Horrible Harry Ser.: No. 8). (gr. 2 up). 2000. 10.00 (978-0-7887-3513-4(6), 95906E7) Recorded Bks.

Horrible Harry at Halloween. Suzy Kline. Narrated by Johnny Heller. 1 cass. (Running Time: 45 mins.). (Horrible Harry Ser.). (gr. 2 up). 2001. 10.00 (978-0-7887-5186-8(7)) Recorded Bks.
For Horrible Harry and the other students in Miss Mackle's third grade class, Halloween is the holiday with the most fun. Each year, Horrible Harry has the spookiest disguise.

Horrible Harry goes to Sea. Suzy Kline. Narrated by Johnny Heller. (Running Time: 45 mins.). (Horrible Harry Ser.). (gr. 2 up). 10.00 (978-1-4025-0937-7(5)) Recorded Bks.

Horrible Harry Goes to the Moon. unabr. ed. Suzy Kline. Narrated by Johnny Heller. 1 cass. (Running Time: 30 mins.). (Horrible Harry Ser.: No. 12). (J). (gr. 2-4). 2001. pap. bk. & stu. ed. 31.99 Recorded Bks.
When Horrible Harry & the other students in his class start gathering information about the moon, they also plan to buy a used telescope.

Horrible Harry Goes to the Moon. unabr. ed. Suzy Kline. Narrated by Johnny Heller. 1 cass. (Running Time: 5 hrs.). (Horrible Harry Ser.: No. 12). (gr. 2 up). 2001. 10.00 (978-0-7887-4706-9(1), 96388E7) Recorded Bks.

Horrible Harry in Room 2B. unabr. ed. Suzy Kline. Narrated by Johnny Heller. 1 cass. (Running Time: 45 mins.). (Horrible Harry Ser.: No. 1). (gr. 2 up). 1997. 10.00 (978-0-7887-0697-4(7), 94871E7) Recorded Bks.
Whether he's making Song Lee scream by showing her his pet snake, or playing a dead fish in the Thanksgiving play, Horrible Harry's not happy unless he's creating trouble.

Horrible Harry Moves up to Third Grade. unabr. ed. Suzy Kline. Narrated by Johnny Heller. 1 cass. (Running Time: 45 mins.). (Horrible Harry Ser.: No. 10). (gr. 2 up). 1998. 10.00 (978-0-7887-2215-8(8), 95514E7) Recorded Bks.
When Horrible Harry & his friend Doug start third grade, they discover that the first day of school is as strange as Mars. Six hilarious adventures, filled with the yucky, squirmy things that Harry & young people love.

Horrible Harry's Secret. unabr. ed. Suzy Kline. Narrated by Johnny Heller. 1 cass. (Running Time: 45 mins.). (Horrible Harry Ser.: No. 4). (gr. 2 up). 1997. 10.00 (978-0-7887-1341-5(8), 95190E7) Recorded Bks.
Harry's best friend Doug tells the story of how Horrible Harry falls in love with classmate Song Lee after meeting her frog, Bong & watching her feed it bits of liver on a toothpick.

Horrible Holiday. unabr. ed. Catherine Jinks. (Running Time: 35 mins.). (Aussie Bites Ser.). (YA). 2003. audio compact disk 39.95 (978-1-74030-966-0(9)) Pub: Bolinda Pubng AUS. Dist(s): Bolinda Pub Inc

Horror & Terror, Pt. 1. 1 cass. (Running Time: 1 hr.). 1999. (4058-4); audio compact disk CD. (4058-2) Audioscope.
Frightening sounds include: Bottomless Pit, Descent to Hell, Black Hole March, Boings, Bangs, Bats, Beeper Bats, Warped Chords, Crazy Cats (Musical Stings), Crematorium & more. Includes free bonus CD of sounds & effects.

Horror & Terror, Pt. 2. 1 cass. 1999. (4059-4); audio compact disk CD. (4059-2) Audioscope.
Frightening sounds include: Dragonsteps, Icy Cave, Lonely Fog, Ricoshet, Sinister Steps, Lost Control (car crash), Space Wars, Space Shots, Explosions, Superbomb & more.

Horror, Crime & Murder. 2003. bk. 15.99 (978-1-57815-561-3(4), Media Bks Audio) Media Bks NJ.

Horror House. unabr. ed. Mary Hooper. 2 CDs. (Running Time: 7560 sec.). (Mary Hooper's Haunted Ser.). (J). (gr. 3-6). 2007. audio compact disk 21.95 (978-1-4056-5582-8(8), Chivers Child Audio) AudioGO.

Horror in the Air: Tales of Terror, Weirdness, & the Occult. 8 CDs. (Running Time: 9 hrs). Dramatization. 2005. audio compact disk 26.95 (978-0-9770819-2-9(3)) Choice Vent.
Encounter the death who walks, rats, descents into madness, ghosts, mad scientists, gorillas, crimes against nature and much more in this classic collection of horror broadcasts from the Golden Age of Radio drama! Horror occupied a special place on radio during the 1940?s and 1950?s. Radio Again is pleased to present twenty-two tales of the supernatural featuring authors such as Mary Shelley, Bram Stoker, Charles Dickens and Ambrose

Bierce along with performances from Peter Lorre, Hal Holbrooke, Boris Karloff and the work of many other leading radio directors, writers and actors of the day. Also included are episodes from Strange, a rarely heard series narrated by Walter Gibson, creator and author of The Shadow. This anthology contains 9 hours of digitally mastered and restored episodes from 9 different series on 8 audio CD?s and a Program Booklet with photographs and background information by radio historian Anthony Tollin. Includes episodes from Dark Fantasy, Hall of Fantasy, Hermit?s Cave, Inner Sanctum, Lights Out, Murder At Midnight, Quiet Please, Strange, and Weird Circle.Includes the following episodes:Quiet Please ? Whence You Came 2/16/1948 === Quiet Please ? The Thing on the Fourble Board 8/9/1948 === Light?s Out ? Death Robbery 7/16/1947 === Light?s Out ? The Signalman 8/24/1946 === Strange ? Greenwood Acres 1955 === Strange ? Great Eastern 1955 === The Weird Circle ? Frankenstein 2/20/1944 === The Weird Circle ? The Middle Toe of the Right Foot 5/28/1944 === Hall of Fantasy ? He Who Follows Me 3/11/1950 === Hall of Fantasy ? The Shadow People 9/21/1953 === Hall of Fantasy ? The Judge?s House 4/3/1947 === Inner Sanctum ? The Black Seagull 3/7/1943 === Inner Sanctum ? The Unforgiving Corpse 5/28/1951 === Dark Fantasy ? The Demon Tree 12/5/1941 === Dark Fantasy ? Spawn of the Subhuman 2/27/1942 === Dark Fantasy ? Pennsylvania Turnpike 3/20/1942 === Murder At Midnight ? The Dead Come Back 11/18/1946 === Murder At Midnight ? The Kaballah 12/30/1946 === Strange ? Flying Dutchman 1955 === Strange ? The Ghost Train 1955 === The Hermit?s Cave ? Buried Alive === The Hermit?s Cave ? It Happened On Sunday.

Horror in the Air: Tales of Terror, Wierdness & the Occult. Perf. by Peter Lorre et al. (ENG.). 2008. audio compact disk 31.95 (978-1-57019-863-2(2)) Radio Spirits.

Horror Movie Madness. 1 cass. (Running Time: 1 hr.). 1999. (4248-4); audio compact disk CD. (4248-2) Audioscope.
Movie themes include: "The Exorcist," "Halloween," "Hellraiser," "Warlock," "Puppet Master," "Re-Animator," "The 7th Sign," "Jacob's Ladder," "Child's Play," "Twilight Zone" & more.

Horror Movie Madness. abr. ed. Tel K. 1999. audio compact disk 6.98 (978-1-57375-661-7(X)) Audioscope.

Horror Movies, the Monster Image, & Modern Children. unabr. ed. Dell Lebo. 1 cass. (Running Time: 21 min.). 1964. 12.95 (29156) J Norton Pubs.
An analysis of the ingredients that go into the making of a horror movie.

***Horror Stories of Robert E. Howard.** unabr. ed. Robert E. Howard. Narrated by Robertson Dean. (Running Time: 24 hrs. 0 mins. 0 sec.). (ENG.). 2010. 39.99 (978-1-4001-6229-1(7)); 26.99 (978-1-4001-8229-9(8)) Tantor Media.

***Horror Stories of Robert E. Howard.** unabr. ed. Robert E. Howard. Narrated by Robertson Dean & Dawkins Dean. (Running Time: 24 hrs. 0 mins. 0 sec.). 2010. audio compact disk 54.99 (978-1-4001-1229-6(X)); audio compact disk 109.99 (978-1-4001-4229-3(6)) Pub: Tantor Media. Dist(s): IngramPubServ

Horror Tales see Ruina de la Casa de los Ushers y Otros Cuentos Terrorificos

Horror Tales. Edgar Allan Poe. Read by Carlos J. Vega. (Running Time: 3 hrs.). 2002. 16.95 (978-1-60083-183-6(4), Audiofy Corp) Iofy Corp.

Horrors! abr. unabr. ed. Garrison Keillor. 2 CDs. (Running Time: 2 hrs.). (ENG.). 1996. audio compact disk 24.95 (978-1-56511-181-3(8), 1565111818) Pub: HighBridge. Dist(s): Workman Pub

Horrors of Matrimonial Litigation. Albert Momjian. 1 cass. (Running Time: 1 hr.). 1988. 20.00 PA Bar Inst.

Horse see Philip Levine

Horse. Dorling Kindersley Publishing Staff. (Eyewitness Videos Ser.). (ENG.). (J). (gr. 3). 2009. 12.99 (978-0-7566-5824-3(1)) DK Pub Inc.

Horse & His Boy see Complete Chronicles of Narnia

Horse & His Boy see Chronicles of Narnia Super-Soundbook

Horse & His Boy. Prod. by Paul Scofield. 2 cass. (Running Time: 2 hrs.). (Chronicles of Narnia Ser.: Vol. 5). 2001. 16.99 (BMDD015) Lodestone Catalog.

Horse & His Boy. Prod. by Paul Scofield. 2 cass. (Chronicles of Narnia Ser.: Bk.5). (J). (gr. 4-8). 1999. 16.99 (BMDD015, Random AudioBks) Random Audio Pubg.

Horse & His Boy. unabr. ed. C. S. Lewis. Read by Alex Jennings. Prod. by Paul Scofield. (Running Time: 014400 sec.). 2005. audio compact disk 29.95 (978-0-310-079330-2(9)) Zondkidz.

Horse & His Boy. abr. ed. Prod. by Paul Scofield. 2 cass. (Running Time: 3 cass.). (Chronicles of Narnia Ser.: Bk.5). (J). (gr. 4-8). 2002. 16.99 (D104) Blckstn Audio.
Shasta joins forces with Bree, the talking horse & flees north towards Narnia, where freedom reigns. For young Shasta, it is an adventure beyond his wildest dreams.

Horse & His Boy. adpt. ed. Read by Paul Scofield et al. C. S. Lewis. (Running Time: 240 hrs. 0 mins.). (Radio Theatre: Chronicles of Narnia Ser.). (ENG.). (J). (gr. 3). 2007. audio compact disk 14.97 (978-1-58997-510-1(3), Tyndale Ent) Tyndale Hse.

Horse & His Boy. unabr. ed. C. S. Lewis. Read by Alex Jennings. (Chronicles of Narnia Ser.: No. 3). (YA). 2006. 44.99 (978-1-59895-159-2(9)) Find a World.

***Horse & His Boy.** unabr. ed. C. S. Lewis. Read by Alex Jennings. 2005. (978-0-06-085450-8(2)); (978-0-06-085449-2(9)) HarperCollins Pubs.

Horse & His Boy. unabr. abr. ed. C. S. Lewis. Read by Alex Jennings. Prod. by Paul Scofield. 3 cass. (Running Time: 4 hrs. 0 mins. 0 sec.). (Chronicles of Narnia Ser.). (J). (gr. 6-8). 2002. 24.00 (978-0-06-051055-8(2)); audio compact disk 27.50 (978-0-06-051062-6(5)) HarperCollins Pubs.

Horse Before the Cart. Swami Amar Jyoti. 2 cass. 1979. 12.95 (B-6) Truth Consciousness.
Putting God First. 'Horse behind the cart' creates problems.

Horse Behind the Fireplace. (J). 2006. audio compact disk (978-1-933343-32-7(X), Pny) Staben Inc.

Horse Boy: A Father's Quest to Heal His Son. unabr. ed. Rupert Isaacson. Read by Rupert Isaacson. (Running Time: 10 hrs. 30 mins.). (ENG.). 2009. 19.98 (978-1-60024-544-2(7)) Pub: Hachet Audio. Dist(s): HachBkGrp

Horse Boy: A Father's Quest to Heal His Son. unabr. ed. Rupert Isaacson. Read by Rupert Isaacson. (Running Time: 10 hrs. 30 mins.). (ENG.). 2010. audio compact disk 19.98 (978-1-60788-191-9(8)) Pub: Hachet Audio. Dist(s): HachBkGrp

Horse Called Courage. Anne Schraff. 1 cass. (Running Time: 3710 sec.). (PageTurner Adventure Ser.). (J). 2002. 10.95 (978-1-56254-480-5(2), SP 4802) Saddleback Edu.
Word-for-word read-along of A Horse Called Courage.

Horse Chestnut Tree see Richard Eberhart Reading His Poetry

Horse Heaven. Jane Smiley. Narrated by Suzanne Toren. 18 cass. (Running Time: 26 hrs.). 2001. 151.00 (978-0-7887-4499-0(2), 96303E7) Recorded Bks.
From sudden spills to winner's circle presentations, the only thing predictable about horse racing - & life - is total unpredictability.

Horse Named Bill & Other Children's Songs. Perf. by Bluestein Family Staff. (J). Rounder Records.
In the 15 songs presented here, different instruments are featured in a wide variety of folk & traditional Styles, all with the warmth & virtuosity typical of the Bluestein Family. "A Horse Named Bill" is not only educational, but musically pleasing & fun to listen to for both children & adults. The Bluestein Family performs the songs of Woody Guthrie, Jean Ritchie & the Carter Family, as well as many traditional favorites.

Horse of a Different Killer. unabr. collector's ed. Jody Jaffe. Read by Frances Cassidy. 6 cass. (Running Time: 9 hrs.). 1997. 48.00 (978-0-913369-53-1(5), 4265) Books on Tape.
A show horse & its trainer have been killed, & Nattie Gold, reporter for the Charlotte Commercial Appeal & a horse owner herself, starts snooping for facts. The closer she gets to the truth, the more dangerous it gets for Nattie & her horse, Brenda Starr.

Horse Raid: An Arapaho Camp in the 1800s. Susan Korman. Illus. by Bill Farnsworth. 1 cass. (Smithsonian Odyssey Ser.). (ENG.). (J). (gr. 2-5). 1998. 7.95 (978-1-56899-621-9(7), C6011) Soundprints.
While visiting the Smithsonian Institution's Museum of Natural History, Kevin finds himself transported back in time to the Great Plains in the early 19th century. He must go on a horse raid & prove his bravery to the Arapaho tribe.

Horse Sense: For Kids & Other People. Perf. by Justin Bishop & Ted Smith. 1 cass. (J). (gr. k up). 9.98 (978-1-877737-91-6(7), 239) MFLP CA.
Performing around the world, Justin & Ted breathe new life into songs born on the great trail drives of the 1800s. Ten authentic favorites chosen for young'ns & accessible as a campfire sing-along, including "Git Along Little Dogies," "Red River Valley," " & Old Chisolm Trail.".

Horse Sense for Kids. Perf. by Horse Sense Staff. 1 cass. (Running Time: 39 min.). (J). 1994. 9.98 (978-1-56628-044-0(3), MLP 239B/WB 42558-4) MFLP CA.
Traditional cowboy music for kids.

Horse Sense for People: Use Gentle Wisdom to Enrich Relationships at Home & Work. abr. ed. Read by Monty Roberts. 4 cass. (Running Time: 6 hrs.). 2001. 24.95 (978-1-57270-239-4(7)) Audio Partners.
Month Roberts has spend his entire life working with horses. He's a real-life horse whisperer whose gentlemethods have yielded an unprecedented understanding of nonverbal communication between humans and animals.

Horse Snake. Short Stories. (5121) Am Audio Prose.

Horse Soldiers: The Extraordinary Story of a Band of U. S. Soldiers Who Rode to Victory in Afghanistan. abr. ed. Doug Stanton. Read by Dennis Boutsikaris. 6 CDs. (Running Time: 7 hrs. 0 mins. 0 sec.). (ENG.). 2009. audio compact disk 29.99 (978-0-7435-8081-6(8)) Pub: S&S Audio. Dist(s): S and S Inc

Horse Thief. unabr. ed. Loren Robinson. Read by Ron Varela. 6 cass. (Running Time: 7 hrs. 30 min.). (American Blend Ser.: Bk. 3). 2001. 39.95 (978-1-55686-797-2(2)) Books in Motion.
Young John Roberts escapes the Missouri border wars and a date with a rope, by joining a westward moving wagon train, forever changing his life.

Horse Thief: A Novel. unabr. ed. Robert Newton Peck. Narrated by Tom Stechschulte. 3 pieces. (Running Time: 5 hrs. 45 mins.). (gr. 7 up). 2002. 34.00 (978-1-4025-2270-3(3)) Recorded Bks.

Horse Whisperer. unabr. ed. Nicholas Evans. Read by Michael Kramer. 8 cass. (Running Time: 12 hrs.). 1996. 64.00 (978-0-7366-3215-7(8), 3878) Books on Tape.
When a 40-ton truck hits a girl & her horse, there can only be one winner. Luckily for Grace, the rider & her horse, Pilgrim, they weren't killed - just maimed & left in pain. The experts are not hopeful. But Annie Graves, Grace's mother, hears about Tom Booker, a cowboy with mystical gifts. He's called "The Whisperer." His soft voice can tame wild horses, like Pilgrim, who is mad with pain. And his touch can heal broken spirits, like Grace's. Guided by hope, Annie risks everything. With Grace & Pilgrim, she leaves her comfortable home in New York for the Booker ranch in Montana. Will she find redemption for those she loves & for herself?.

Horse Whisperer. unabr. ed. Nicholas Evans. Read by Frank Muller. 10 cass. 1999. 39.95 (FS9-43191) Highsmith.

Horse Whisperer. unabr. ed. Nicholas Evans. Narrated by Frank Muller. 9 cass. (Running Time: 12 hrs. 45 mins.). 1995. 78.00 (978-0-7887-0441-3(9), 94633E7) Recorded Bks.
When a family's life is shattered by a terrible accident, a mother's quest begins, to save her wounded daughter & a horse turned savage by pain. It is a journey that leads to the Horse Whisperer, a man with the ancient, mystical power to tame wild horses & heal broken spirits.

Horse Whisperer. unabr. ed. Nicholas Evans. Narrated by Frank Muller. 11 CDs. (Running Time: 12 hrs. 45 mins.). 1999. audio compact disk 98.00 (978-0-7887-3405-2(9), C1011E7) Recorded Bks.

Horse You Came in On. unabr. ed. Martha Grimes. Narrated by Patricia Conolly. 8 cass. (Running Time: 11 hrs. 45 mins.). (Richard Jury Novel Ser.). 1994. 70.00 (978-0-7887-0003-3(0), 94142E7) Recorded Bks.
British Chief Inspector Richard Jury uses his vacation to investigate a murder in Baltimore USA at the request of an old friend.

Horseman in the Sky. unabr. ed. Ambrose Bierce. Read by Walter Zimmerman & Jim Killavey. 1 cass. (Running Time: 56 min.). Incl. Man & the Snake. Ambrose Bierce. 1977. (N-4); Moonlit Road. Ambrose Bierce. 1977. (N-4); 1977. 7.95 (N-4) Jimcin Record.
Stories of war & ghostly happenings.

Horseman in the Sky, Vol. 7. unabr. ed. Ambrose Bierce. Narrated by Nelita B. Castillo. 1 cass. (Running Time: 38 min.). (Fantasies Ser.: Vol. VII). (J). 1984. 17.95 Incl. holder, scripts, lesson plans, & tchr's. guide. (978-0-86617-048-2(0)) Multi Media TX.
Comprehensive lesson plans that use classic short stories to develop skills in listening, reading, vocabulary, following details, making inferences, visualization, drawing conclusions, critical appreciation & comparison. This module's objective is to understand a way of life (or kind of person) different from our own (or from us).

Horseman, Pass By: A Novel. unabr. ed. Larry McMurtry. Narrated by Kerin McCue. 6 cass. (Running Time: 7 hrs. 45 mins.). 1993. 51.00 (978-1-55690-811-8(3), 93120E7) Recorded Bks.
A young man comes of age on his grandfather's Texas cattle ranch in the late 1950s.

Horseman, Pass By: A Novel. unabr. collector's ed. Larry McMurtry. Read by Wolfram Kandinsky. 7 cass. (Running Time: 7 hrs.). 1984. 42.00 (978-0-7366-0762-9(5), 1719) Books on Tape.
The story of Hud Bannon, the strong-willed son of an aging cattle rancher who finds himself trapped between the traditions of his father's cattle business & the restless yearnings dredged up by the new spirit of a land rapidly outgrowing its age-old customs & needs.

Horsemen. unabr. ed. Gary McCarthy. Read by Maynard Villers. 4 cass. (Running Time: 5 hrs. 30 min.). (Horsemen Ser.: Bk. 1). 1994. 26.95 (978-1-55686-530-5(9)) Books in Motion.
Here is the sprawling epic story of the Ballou family's brave struggle to fulfill a dream of raising the finest thoroughbred horses in the South. Their plans go astray as the Civil War intervenes.

Horses see Twentieth-Century Poetry in English, No. 23, Recordings of Poets Reading Their Own Poetry

Horses. unabr. ed. Ed. by Linda Spizzirri. 48 cass. (Running Time: 15 min.). Dramatization. (Educational Coloring Book & Cassette Package Ser.). (J). (gr. k-8). 1989. pap. bk. 6.95 (978-0-86545-162-9(1)) Spizzirri.
Discusses the prehistoric & wild horse plus many of the current famous breeds.

Horseshoer's Pen (Brown) Poems. Don Kennington. Read by Don Kennington. 1 cass. 1988. 8.00 (978-1-890672-05-8(X)) Phil Don.
Same poems as authored in "Trail Dust I".

Horseshoer's Pen (Gray), Vol. 4. Poems. Don Kennington. Read by Don Kennington. 1 cass. 1995. 8.00 (978-1-890672-08-9(4)) Phil Don.
Same poems as authored in "Trail Dust IV".

Horseshoer's Pen (Green), Vol. 5. Poems. Don Kennington. Read by Don Kennington. 1 cass. 1998. 8.00 (978-1-890672-09-6(2)) Phil Don.
Same poems as authored in "Trail Dust V".

Horseshoer's Pen (Red), Vol. 3. Poems. Don Kennington. Read by Don Kennington. 1 cass. 1992. 8.00 (978-1-890672-07-2(6)) Phil Don.
Same poems as authored in "Trail Dust III".

Horseshoer's Pen (Yellow), Vol. 2. Poems. Don Kennington. Read by Don Kennington. 1 cass. 1990. 8.00 Phil Don.
Same poems as authored in "Trail Dust II".

Horst Wessel. Short Stories. Charles Gusewelle. Read by Charles Gusewelle. 1 cass. (Running Time: 58 min). 13.95 (978-1-55644-072-4(3), 3071) Am Audio Prose.

Hortense Calisher. Interview. Interview with Hortense Calisher & Kay Bonetti. 1 cass. (Running Time: 40 min.). 13.95 (978-1-55644-096-0(0), 4032) Am Audio Prose.
Focuses on research structure of "Mysteries of Motion" & the scope of her long life career.

Horton Foote. unabr. ed. Horton Foote. 1 cass. (Running Time: 29 min.). 1988. 10.00 New Letters.
Playwright Horton Foote reads from "The Orphans' Home Cycle" & is interviewed.

Horton Hatches the Egg. Read by Marvin Miller. 1 cass. (J). 3.98 Clamshell. (978-1-55886-135-0(1), BB/PT 442) Smarty Pants.

Horton Hears a Who! And Other Sounds of Dr. Seuss. unabr. ed. Dr. Seuss. Read by Dustin Hoffman et al. 1 CD. (Running Time: 1 hr. 15 mins.). (ENG.). (J). (ps-3). 2008. audio compact disk 9.99 (978-0-7393-6265-5(8), Listening Lib) Pub: Random Audio Pubg. Dist(s): Random

***Horus Rising (Abridged)** Dan Abnett. (Horus Heresy Ser.). (ENG.). 2010. 29.95 (978-1-84970-016-0(8), Black Library) Pub: BL Pubng GBR. Dist(s): S and S Inc

Horzen's Original Oktoberfest Kit. J. Horzen. 1 cass. 1994. bk. 29.95 (978-1-886912-00-7(9)) H Pub.

Hosanna. Contrib. by Johnathan Crumpton & B. J. Davis. Prod. by Ed Kee. (ENG.). 2008. audio compact disk 24.99 (978-5-557-48382-7(9), Brentwood-Benson Music) Brentwood Music.

Hosanna to the King! A Worship Experience for Palm Sunday for Adult Choir, Children's Choir, Narrators & Congregation. Arranged by Bruce Greer. 1 cass. (Running Time: 9 min.). (J). 2001. 24.99 (MU-9293C); audio compact disk 29.99 (MU-9293T) Lillenas.
A wonderful worship experience for Palm Sunday - an occasion for which little is currently available. A creative blend of classic hymns & praise & worship songs. Provides an opportunity to include your children with the adult choir. Narrators are utilized also, as well as optional congregational participation. Accompaniment cassette includes vocal demo, split-channel & stereo trax mixes.

Hosanna! You Can! Stereo Acc. Greg Skipper. 1997. 10.98 (978-0-7673-3269-9(5)) LifeWay Christian.

Hosea: A Biblical Interpretation. Concept by Ermance Rejebian. (ENG.). 2007. 5.99 (978-1-60339-139-9(8)); audio compact disk 5.99 (978-1-60339-140-5(1)) Listenr Digest.

Hosea, Can You See? Hosea's Challenge to America! Chuck Missler. 2 CD's. (Running Time: 120 mins.). (Briefing Packages by Chuck Missler). 1999. audio compact disk 19.95 (978-1-57821-304-7(5)) Koinonia Hse.
Hosea's Challenge to America!Hosea, one of the most provocative prophets of the Old Testament, was called by God to declare God's impending judgment on the Northern Kingdom:They had been experiencing an unparalleled prosperity in their time; and yet they had sunk to the lowest moral depths of their two century history. It was the Best of Times and it was the Worst of Times.As a result, God was about to use their enemies as His instrument of judgment.America, too, is in a disturbingly comparable situation: Unparalleled prosperity on the one hand, and yet immorality unprecedented in our two century history.Is God also going to use our enemies as instruments of His judgment?Chuck Missler, internationally recognized Biblical authority, examines the predicament of Hosea and compares it with the present horizon confronting America.

***Hosea Commentary.** Chuck Missler. 2009. audio compact disk 44.95 (978-1-57821-433-4(5)) Koinonia Hse.

Hosea Commentary: Verse by verse with Chuck Missler. Chuck Missler. 1 CD Rom. (Running Time: 8 hours aprox). (Chuck Missler Commentaries). 2000. cd-rom (978-1-57821-105-0(0)) Koinonia Hse.
The book of Hosea is one of the most remarkable books of the Old Testament. No other messenger gives so complete an outline of the ways of God with His earthly people as does Hosea. This truly amazing book belongs in everyone's Bible study library.

Hospice Care for the Terminally Ill & Their Families. Edward Dobihal et al. 1986. 10.80 (0603) Assn Prof Chaplains.

Hospital: Man, Woman, Birth, Death, Infinity, Plus Red Tape, Bad Behavior, Money, God, & Diversity on Steroids. Julie Salamon. Read by Karen White. (Playaway Adult Nonfiction Ser.). (ENG.). 2009. 70.00 (978-1-60775-651-4(X)) Find a World.

Hospital: Man, Woman, Birth, Death, Infinity, Plus Red Tape, Bad Behavior, Money, God & Diversity on Steroids. unabr. ed. Julie Salamon. Narrated by Karen White. (Running Time: 15 hrs. 0 mins. 0 sec.). (ENG.). 2008. audio compact disk 75.99 (978-1-4001-3724-4(1)); audio compact disk 37.99 (978-1-4001-0724-7(5)); audio compact disk 24.99 (978-1-4001-5724-2(2)) Pub: Tantor Media. Dist(s): IngramPubServ

Hospital Care: Practical Missions of Mercy. 2007. audio compact disk 17.99 (978-1-934570-09-8(5)) Lanphier Pr.

Hospital Chaplaincy: A Ministry of Paradox. 1 cass. (Care Cassettes Ser.: Vol. 11, No. 5). 1984. 10.80 Assn Prof Chaplains.

Hospital Chaplaincy in Time of Constraints. 1 cass. (Care Cassettes Ser.: Vol. 12, No. 7). 1985. 10.80 Assn Prof Chaplains.

Hospital Circles. unabr. ed. Lucilla Andrews. Read by Christine Dawe. 4 cass. (Running Time: 6 hrs.). (Sound Ser.). 1987. 44.95 (978-1-85496-011-5(3), 60113) Pub: UlverLrgPrint GBR. Dist(s): Ulverscroft US

Hospital Ethics Committees. 1 cass. (Care Cassettes Ser.: Vol. 12, No. 9). 1985. 10.80 Assn Prof Chaplains.

Hospital Libraries & Public Services Sections - Product Enhancement: Value-Added Services in the Health Care Enterprise. 1 cass. (Medical Library Association 1998 Annual Meeting & Exhibit Ser.). 1998. 12.00 (18) Med Lib Assn.

Hospital Libraries Section & Research Policy Implementation Task Force - Empowerment through Benchmarking: Practical Tips in Design & Implementation of Benchmarking Studies. 1 cass. (Medical Library Association 1998 Annual Meeting & Exhibit Ser.). 1998. 12.00 (12) Med Lib Assn.

Hospital Ministries: A "Rational" Approach. R. S. Carpenter & John Serkland. 1986. 10.80 (0111) Assn Prof Chaplains.

Hospital Summer. unabr. ed. Lucilla Andrews. Read by Tracy Shaw. 4 cass. (Sound Ser.). 1985. 44.95 (978-1-85496-012-2(1), 60121) Pub: UlverLrgPrint GBR. Dist(s): Ulverscroft US

Hospitals & Clinics in Chile: A Strategic Reference 2007. Compiled by Icon Group International, Inc. Staff. 2007. ring bd. 195.00 (978-0-497-35857-0(3)) Icon Grp.

Hospitals in Germany: A Strategic Reference 2007. Compiled by Icon Group International, Inc. Staff. 2007. ring bd. 195.00 (978-0-497-35973-7(1)) Icon Grp.

Host see William Carlos Williams Reads His Poetry

Host. unabr. ed. Stephenie Meyer. Read by Kate Reading. (Running Time: 21 hrs.). (ENG.). 2008. 19.98 (978-1-60024-167-3(0)) Pub: Hachet Audio. Dist(s): HachBkGrp

Host. unabr. ed. Stephenie Meyer. Read by Kate Reading. (Running Time: 21 hrs.). (ENG.). 2010. audio compact disk 19.98 (978-1-60024-565-7(X)) Pub: Hachet Audio. Dist(s): HachBkGrp

Host. unabr. ed. Stephenie Meyer. Read by Kate Reading. 20 CDs. 2008. audio compact disk 129.00 (978-1-4159-5586-4(7), BksonTape) Pub: Random Audio Pubg. Dist(s): Random

***Hostage.** Don Brown. (Running Time: 11 hrs. 45 mins. 0 sec.). (Navy Justice Ser.). (ENG.). 2008. 14.99 (978-0-310-30486-9(5)) Zondervan.

Hostage. Robert Crais. Read by James Daniels. (Playaway Adult Fiction Ser.). 2008. 64.99 (978-1-60640-788-2(0)) Find a World.

Hostage. abr. ed. Robert Crais. Read by Robert Crais. (Running Time: 6 hrs.). 2004. audio compact disk 16.99 (978-1-59355-685-3(3), 1593556853, BCD Value Price) Brilliance Audio.
Jeff Talley was a good husband, a fine father, and a frontline negotiator with LAPD's SWAT unit. But the high stress, unforgiving job took an irreparable toll on his psyche. After a despondent father murders his wife and son and takes his own life, Talley hits bottom. His marriage ends, he resigns from SWAT, and he struggles to escape from his former life by taking the chief-of-police job in a sleepy, affluent bedroom community far from the chaos and crime of Los Angeles. But Talley's pursuit of peaceful small-town life is about to change when three young men, fleeing the robbery of a mini-mart, invade a tightly secured home, and take the family hostage. Plunged back into the high-pressure world that he has desperately been trying to put behind him, Talley finds his nightmare has barely begun, because this isn't just any house. It belongs to a brilliant white-collar criminal who launders money for L.A.'s renegade franchise of La Cosa Nostra. And the accountant's records of the incriminating money trail that lie within will put L.A.'s most lethal and volatile crime lord, Sonny Benza, behind bars. As Talley desperately tries to save the innocents inside, the full weight of Benza's wrath descends on him, putting Talley and his own family at risk. Soon, all involved are held hostage by the exigencies of fate and the only one capable of diffusing the crisis is the least stable of them all.

***Hostage.** abr. ed. Robert Crais & Suspense. Read by Robert Crais. (Running Time: 6 hrs.). 2010. audio compact disk 9.99 (978-1-4418-5651-7(X), 9781441856517) Brilliance Audio.

Hostage. abr. ed. W. E. B. Griffin. 5 CDs. (Running Time: 6 hrs.). No. 2. (ENG.). (gr. 8). 2005. audio compact disk 29.95 (978-0-14-305798-7(7), PengAudBks) Penguin Grp USA.

Hostage. abr. ed. W. E. B. Griffin. Read by Jay O. Sanders. (Running Time: 9 hrs.). Vol. 2. (ENG.). (gr. 8). 2006. audio compact disk 19.95 (978-0-14-314225-6(9), PengAudBks) Penguin Grp USA.

Hostage. unabr. ed. Charles Bukowski. Read by Charles Bukowski. 1 CD. (Running Time: 1 hr. 30 mins.). 1985. audio compact disk 16.98 (R2 71758) Rhino Enter.

Hostage. unabr. ed. Robert Crais. Read by James Daniels. 7 cass. Library ed. (Running Time: 9 hrs.). 2001. 78.25 (978-1-58788-501-3(8), 1587885018, Unabridge Lib Edns) Brilliance Audio.
"CRIMINALLY ENTERTAINING . . . THE TENSION BUILDS AS THE CHAOS ESCALATES INSIDE AND OUTSIDE THE HOUSE." - The New York Times Book Review In a sleepy suburb north of Los Angeles, a convenience-store robbery turns violent. With the police on their tail, three criminals flee the scene and invade a home in an exclusive gated community, taking captive a panicked father and his two children. Police chief Jeff Talley, a former hostage negotiator with the LAPD's SWAT unit, is now thrown back into the high-pressure world that he has so desperately tried to leave behind. But Talley's nightmare has barely begun, because this isn't just any house; it holds the dirty secrets of L.A.'s biggest crime lord. And the people inside aren't the only ones being held hostage. . . . "CAPTIVATING . . . A BLOCKBUSTER-READY TALE SO VIVID, YOU DON'T READ, YOU WATCH." - People.

Hostage. unabr. ed. Robert Crais. Read by James Daniels. (Running Time: 9 hrs.). 2004. 39.25 (978-1-59335-332-2(4), 1593353324, Brlnc Audio MP3 Lib) Brilliance Audio.

Hostage. unabr. ed. Robert Crais. Read by James Daniels. (Running Time: 9 hrs.). 2004. 39.25 (978-1-59710-377-0(2), 1597103772, BADLE); 24.95 (978-1-59710-376-3(4), 1597103764, BAD) Brilliance Audio.

Hostage. unabr. ed. Robert Crais. Read by James Daniels. (Running Time: 32400 sec.). 2008. audio compact disk 92.25 (978-1-4233-5604-2(7), 9781423356042, BriAudCD Unabrid); audio compact disk 34.95 (978-1-4233-5603-5(9), 9781423356035, Bril Audio CD Unabri) Brilliance Audio.

Hostage. unabr. ed. Robert Crais. Read by James Daniels. (Running Time: 9 hrs.). 2004. 24.95 (978-1-59335-004-8(X), 159335004X) Soulmate Audio Bks.

Hostage. unabr. ed. W. E. B. Griffin. Read by W. E. B. Griffin. 15 CDs. (Running Time: 64800 sec.). (Presidential Agent Ser.: No. 2). 2005. audio compact disk 42.95 (978-1-59737-119-3(X), 9781597371193, Bril Audio CD Unabri) Brilliance Audio.
By Order of the President, the first novel in Griffin's crackling new Presidential Agent series, won immediate acclaim from critics and fans alike. "True virtuosity," praised the Fort Worth Star-Telegram. "Cutting-edge," agreed Publishers Weekly. "The end leaves readers standing on the tarmac waiting for Castillo and his newly minted band of can-do compatriots to touch down and carry them away again on a new adventure." Charley Castillo works with the Department of Homeland Security, but more and more is the man to whom the President turns when he needs an investigation done discreetly. And no situation demands discretion more than the one before them now. An American diplomat's wife is kidnapped in Argentina, and her husband murdered before her eyes. Her children will be next, she is told, if she doesn't tell them where her brother is - a brother, as it turns out, who may know quite a bit about the burgeoning UN/Iraq oil-for-food scandal. There is an awful lot of money flying around, and an awful lot of hands are reaching up to grab it - and some of those hands don't mind shedding as much blood as it takes. Before the investigation is over . . . It might even be Castillo's blood.

Hostage. unabr. ed. W. E. B. Griffin. Read by Dick Hill. (Running Time: 18 hrs.). (Presidential Agent Ser.: No. 2). 2006. 44.25 (978-1-59737-124-7(6), 9781597371247, BADLE) Brilliance Audio.

Hostage. unabr. ed. W. E. B. Griffin. Read by Dick Hill. (Running Time: 18 hrs.). (Presidential Agent Ser.: Vol. 2). 2006. 29.95 (978-1-59737-123-0(8), 9781597371230, BAD) Brilliance Audio.

Hostage. unabr. ed. W. E. B. Griffin. Read by W. E. B. Griffin. 12 cass. (Running Time: 64800 sec.). (Presidential Agent Ser.: No. 2). 2006. 36.95 (978-1-59737-117-9(3), 9781597371179, BAU) Brilliance Audio.

Hostage. unabr. ed. W. E. B. Griffin. Read by W. E. B. Griffin. (Running Time: 64800 sec.). (Presidential Agent Ser.: Vol. 2). 2006. 107.25 (978-1-59737-118-6(1), 9781597371186, BrilAudUnabridg); audio compact disk 44.25 (978-1-59737-122-3(X), 9781597371223, Brlnc Audio MP3 Lib); audio compact disk 29.95 (978-1-59737-121-6(1), 9781597371216, Brilliance MP3); audio compact disk 127.25 (978-1-59737-120-9(3), 9781597371209, BriAudCD Unabrid) Brilliance Audio.

Hostage, unabr. ed. Theodore Taylor. Narrated by Johnny Heller. 3 cass. (Running Time: 4 hrs. 15 mins.). (gr. 7 up). 2001. 27.00 (978-0-7887-0430-7(3), 94622E7) Recorded Bks.
When 14-year-old Jamie Tidd traps a killer whale, he must decide what's more important: saving the animal's life or taking the reward money offered by a marine park.

Hostage. unabr. movie tie-in ed. Robert Crais. Read by James Daniels. (Running Time: 9 hrs.). 2005. 29.95 (978-1-59737-454-5(7), 9781597374545, BAU) Brilliance Audio.
"CRIMINALLY ENTERTAINING . . . THE TENSION BUILDS AS THE CHAOS ESCALATES INSIDE AND OUTSIDE THE HOUSE." - The New York Times Book Review In a sleepy suburb north of Los Angeles, a convenience-store robbery turns violent. With the police on their tail, three criminals flee the scene and invade a home in an exclusive gated community, taking captive a panicked father and his two children. Police chief Jeff Talley, a former hostage negotiator with the LAPD's SWAT unit, is now thrown back into the high-pressure world that he has so desperately tried to leave behind. But Talley's nightmare has barely begun, because this isn't just any house; it holds the dirty secrets of L.A.'s biggest crime lord. And the people inside aren't the only ones being held hostage. . . . "CAPTIVATING . . . A BLOCKBUSTER-READY TALE SO VIVID, YOU DON'T READ, YOU WATCH." - People.

Hostage Released Pt. 1: Psalms 51. Ed Young. 1989. 4.95 (978-0-7417-1752-8(2), 752) Win Walk.

Hostage Released Pt. 11: Psalms 51. Ed Young. 1989. 4.95 (978-0-7417-1753-5(0), 753) Win Walk.

Hostage to Death. unabr. ed. L. Ron Hubbard. Read by Kelly Ward et al. Narrated by R. F. Daley. 2 CDs. (Running Time: 2 hrs.). (Stories from the Golden Age Ser.). (ENG.). 2009. audio compact disk 10.95 (978-1-59212-386-5(4)) Gala Pr LLC.

Hostage to Murder. unabr. ed. Val McDermid. Read by Vari Sylvester. 7 cass. (Running Time: 9 hrs. 42 mins.). (Isis Cassettes Ser.). (J). 2004. 61.95 (978-0-7531-1801-6(7)); audio compact disk 79.95 (978-0-7531-2298-3(7)) Pub: ISIS Lrg Prnt GBR. Dist(s): Ulverscroft US

Hostages. Prod. by Laraim Associates. (Barclay Family Adventure Ser.). (J). 2003. audio compact disk (978-1-56254-981-7(2)) Saddleback Edu.

Hostile Hospital. unabr. ed. Lemony Snicket, pseud. Narrated by Tim Curry. 4 cass. (Running Time: 4 hrs. 30 mins.). (Series of Unfortunate Events Ser.: Bk. 8). 2003. 35.00 (978-1-4025-3744-8(1)) Recorded Bks.

Hostile Hospital. unabr. ed. Lemony Snicket, pseud. Narrated by Tim Curry. 4 cass. (Running Time: 4 hrs. 30 mins.). (Series of Unfortunate Events Ser.: Bk. 8). (YA). (gr. 5 up). 2003. 29.95 (978-1-4025-3745-5(X)) Recorded Bks.
There are many pleasant things to read about in this world, but instead of any of those agreeable things, this book contains yet another account of a dastardly plot by the evil Count Olaf to get his hands on the fortune belonging to Violet, Klaus, and Sunny Baudelaire. In their efforts to escape this particular plot, the unfortunate orphans encounter such truly frightening things as a burning building, unnecessary surgery, and heart-shaped balloons.

Hostile Hospital. unabr. abr. ed. Lemony Snicket, pseud. Read by Tim Curry. 3 cass. (Running Time: 4 hrs.). (Series of Unfortunate Events Ser.: Bk. 8). (J). (gr. 5 up). 2002. 20.00 (978-0-694-52625-3(8)) HarperCollins Pubs.

Hostile Hospital. unabr. abr. ed. Lemony Snicket, pseud. Read by Tim Curry. 4 CDs. (Running Time: 5 hrs.). (Series of Unfortunate Events Ser.: Bk. 8). (J). (gr. 3-8). 2003. audio compact disk 25.95 (978-0-06-056623-4(X)) HarperCollins Pubs.

Hostile Waters. unabr. collector's ed. Peter A. Huchthausen et al. Read by Geoffrey Howard. 6 cass. (Running Time: 9 hrs.). 1998. 48.00 (4763) Books on Tape.
In the fall of 1986, with the Cold War nearly over, an aging Soviet ballistic missile sub suffered a crippling accident, coming within moments of a nuclear meltdown.

***Hostile Witness.** abr. ed. William Lashner. Read by Ken Howard. (ENG.). 2007. (978-0-06-134434-3(6), Harper Audio); (978-0-06-134433-6(8), Harper Audio) HarperCollins Pubs.

Hostile Witness. unabr. ed. William Lashner. Narrated by Richard Ferrone. 14 cass. (Running Time: 19 hrs. 30 mins.). 1998. 112.00 (978-0-7887-1954-7(8), 95352E7) Recorded Bks.
Lashner creates an extraordinary world filled with corrupt politicians, gangland figures, & predatory attorneys.

Hosting the Kazimeer. unabr. ed. Christine Sales. Read by Ric Benson. 12 cass. (Running Time: 16 hrs. 36 min.). 2001. 64.95 (978-1-58116-019-2(4)) Books in Motion.
Young Landon has just been named Kazimeer among the village of presiding officer Taj. When the pending confrontation happens, Landon is forced to use his "morph powers," and takes over other beings, in order to survive to fight again, against the all powerful Taj.

Hot-Air Henry. Mary Calhoun. Read by Christina Moore. 1 cass. (Running Time: 15 mins.). (YA). 1999. stu. ed. 80.30 (978-0-7887-3871-5(2), 47036) Recorded Bks.
If you met Henry in "Cross Country Cat," you know he is no ordinary Siamese. Now he longs to go up in a hot-air balloon. He soon gets his wish & as much adventure as he can handle. Includes study guide.

Hot-Air Henry. unabr. ed. Mary Calhoun. Read by Peter Thomas. 1 cass. (Running Time: 15 mins.). (Picture Book Read-Along Ser.). (J). (gr. k-3). 1991. pap. bk. 17.00 (978-0-8072-6037-1(1), MR 27SP, Listening Lib) Random Audio Pubg.
When Henry, the sassy Siamese cat, stows away on a hot-air balloon, he has a fur-raising flight indeed.

Hot-Air Henry. unabr. ed. Mary Calhoun. Narrated by Christina Moore. 1 cass. (Running Time: 15 mins.). (YA). 2000. pap. bk. 23.20 (978-0-7887-3846-3(1), 41044X4) Recorded Bks.
If you met Henry in "Cross Country Cat," you know he is no ordinary Siamese. Now he longs to go up in a hot-air balloon. He soon gets his wish & as much adventure as he can handle. Includes study guide.

Hot-Air Henry. unabr. ed. Mary Calhoun. Narrated by Christina Moore. 1 cass. (Running Time: 15 mins.). (gr. 1 up). 2000. 10.00 (978-0-7887-3815-9(1), 96050E7) Recorded Bks.

Hot & Sweaty Rex. unabr. ed. Eric Garcia. Read by Jonathan Marosz. 8 cassettes. (Running Time: 12 hrs). 2005. 81.00 (978-0-7366-9860-3(4)) Books on Tape.

Hot & Thirsty. unabr. ed. Gail Taylor. Read by Gail Taylor. Ed. by James B. Kirgan. 1 cass. (Running Time: 1 hr. 30 min.). (Essence of Nature Ser.: Vol. 7). (J). 1989. 12.99 stereo. (978-1-878362-07-0(0)) Emerald Ent.
On this tape Thumper, the adventure dog, journeys through the Badlands National Park in South Dakota. This tape includes actual sounds of nature in the park & sounds from Native American rituals.

Hot Blood. Stephen Leather. 2007. 89.95 (978-0-7531-3768-0(2)); audio compact disk 99.95 (978-0-7531-2737-7(7)) Pub: ISIS Audio GBR. Dist(s): Ulverscroft US

Hot Blooded. Lisa Jackson. Narrated by Linda Skinner. 11 cass. (Running Time: 15 hrs. 45 mins.). (New Orleans Ser.: Bk. 1). 94.00 (978-1-4025-1368-8(2)) Recorded Bks.

Hot Box. abr. ed. Zane. 4 CDs. (Running Time: 44 hrs. 50 mins. 0 sec.). (ENG.). 2009. audio compact disk 25.00 (978-0-7435-5106-9(0)) Pub: S&S Audio. Dist(s): S and S Inc

***Hot Box.** unabr. ed. Zane. Comment by Zane. Read by Simi Howe & Krystal King. (Running Time: 9 hrs. 0 mins. 0 sec.). 2010. audio compact disk 29.99 (978-1-4423-3747-3(8)) Pub: S&S Audio. Dist(s): S and S Inc

Hot Fiddlin' Contrib. by Randy Howard. (Running Time: 2 hrs.). 2006. 24.95 (978-5-558-08941-7(5)) Mel Bay.

***Hot, Flat, & Crowded: Why We Need a Green Revolution - & How It Can Renew America.** abr. ed. Thomas L. Friedman. Read by Oliver Wyman. (Running Time: 9 hrs. 0 mins. 0 sec.). (ENG.). 2010. audio compact disk 14.99 (978-1-4272-1085-2(3)) Pub: Macmill Audio. Dist(s): Macmillan

Hot, Flat, & Crowded: Why We Need a Green Revolution - And How It Can Renew America. abr. ed. Thomas L. Friedman. Read by Oliver Wyman. 7 CDs. (Running Time: 9 hrs. 0 mins. 0 sec.). (ENG.). 2008. audio compact disk 29.95 (978-1-4272-0460-8(8)) Pub: Macmill Audio. Dist(s): Macmillan

Hot, Flat, & Crowded: Why We Need a Green Revolution - And How It Can Renew America. unabr. ed. Thomas L. Friedman. Read by Oliver Wyman. 1 MP3-CD. 2008. 74.95 (978-0-7927-5526-5(X), Chivers Sound Lib); 74.95 (978-0-7927-5587-6(1), Chivers Sound Lib); audio compact disk 124.95 (978-0-7927-5475-6(1), Chivers Sound Lib) AudioGO.

Hot, Flat, & Crowded: Why We Need a Green Revolution - And How It Can Renew America. unabr. ed. Thomas L. Friedman. Read by Oliver Wyman. 17 CDs. (Running Time: 21 hrs. 0 mins. 0 sec.). (ENG.). 2008. audio compact disk 59.95 (978-1-4272-0458-5(6)) Pub: Macmill Audio. Dist(s): Macmillan

Hot Hippo. 2004. bk. 24.95 (978-0-89719-776-2(3)); pap. bk. 14.95 (978-0-7882-0659-7(1)); 8.95 (978-1-56008-396-2(4)); cass. & flmstrp 30.00 (978-0-89719-582-9(5)) Weston Woods.

Hot Hippo. Mwenye Hadithi & Adrienne Kennaway. 1 cass. (J). (ps-3). pap. bk. 12.95 (PRA324) Weston Woods.
He longed to live in the water like the fishes instead of on dry land. But such a change required permission from Ngai, the god of Everything & Everywhere, who decided where the animals, fish & birds would live.

Hot Hippo. Mwenye Hadithi & Adrienne Kennaway. 1 cass. (J). (ps-3). 2004. 8.95 (978-0-89719-970-4(7), RAC324) Weston Woods.

Hot Ice. Nora Roberts. Read by Anna Fields. 2002. audio compact disk 80.00 (978-0-7366-8795-9(5)) Books on Tape.

Hot Ice. Madge Swindells. 2009. 69.95 (978-1-84559-625-5(0)) Pub: Soundings Ltd GBR. Dist(s): Ulverscroft US

Hot Ice. unabr. ed. Nora Roberts. 8 cass. (Running Time: 12 hrs.). 2002. 64.00 (978-0-7366-8670-9(3)) Books on Tape.
Whitney MacAllister has all the wealth, power and beauty anyone could ever wish for, and is therefore profoundly bored. Enter Douglas Lord, a good-looking, street-smart thief, who brings Whitney into his world of high adventure and murderous rivals. They come to a business agreement: Whitney will bankroll Douglas on an expedition to retrieve the legendary lost treasure of a long-dead Madagascar queen; in exchange, Whitney will get to come along and keep half the money once they have gained their prize. What neither of them bargains for is the growing attraction they feel for each other. Though they don't have much in common, they find that they are meant for each other. Now, they must keep each other alive both for business and for pleasure.

Hot Issues in Employment Law & Litigation: Highlighting the Supreme Court Term & Current Discrimination & Harassment Issues. 3 cass. (Running Time: 4 hrs.). 1999. 165.00 Set; incl. study guide. (VA994) Am Law Inst.

Hot Kid: A Novel. Elmore Leonard. 2005. audio compact disk 29.95 (978-0-06-078489-8(X)) HarperCollins Pubs.

Hot Kid: A Novel. unabr. ed. Elmore Leonard. Read by Arliss Howard. 7 CDs. (Running Time: 8 hrs.). 2005. audio compact disk 39.95 (978-0-06-078998-5(0)) HarperCollins Pubs.

***Hot Kid: A Novel.** unabr. ed. Elmore Leonard. Read by Arliss Howard. 2005. (978-0-06-079680-8(4), Harper Audio); (978-0-06-084590-2(2), Harper Audio) HarperCollins Pubs.

Hot Kid: A Novel. unabr. ed. Elmore Leonard. Narrated by Arliss Howard. 7 CDs. (Running Time: 8 hrs.). 2005. audio compact disk 89.75 (978-1-4193-4056-7(5), C3299); 69.75 (978-1-4193-4054-3(9), 98034) Recorded Bks.
Considered the undisputed master of the stylish crime caper, Elmore Leonard is one of America's most popular authors. The Hot Kid takes listeners back to the 1930s, when everyone dreamed of being a larger-than-life hero - or villain. Ultra-cool U.S. Marshal Carl Webster thrives on taking down notorious crooks. His latest adversary is the wicked Jack

Belmont, renegade son of an oil tycoon. Each time Carl and Jack meet, the tommy guns blaze - and their legend grows.

Hot Lead Payoff. 2 CDs. (Western Audiobooks Ser.). audio compact disk 14.95 (978-1-59212-226-4(4)) Gala Pr LLC.

Hot Lead Payoff. L. Ron Hubbard. Read by Geoffrey Lewis. 1 cass. 1995. 8.99 (978-0-88404-941-8(8)) Bridge Pubns Inc.
Tom Nolan & his brother, Bob, own the once most important ranch in Arizona. But the brothers are hard-pressed to keep their cattle & land, particularly when they become the only ones who can stop wealthy Texas carpetbagger Martin Graham from taking over the entire state.

Hot Lead Payoff. abr. ed. L. Ron Hubbard. Read by Geoffrey Lewis. 1 cass. (Running Time: 1 hr. 30 min.). 1994. 9.95 (978-0-88404-905-0(1)) Bridge Pubns Inc.

Hot Lead Payoff. abr. ed. L. Ron Hubbard. Illus. by Geoffrey Lewis. 1 cass. (Running Time: 1 hr. 30 min.). 2002. 9.95 (978-1-59212-016-1(4)) Gala Pr LLC.
Tom Nolan and his kid brother, Bob, own the Crazy N ranch, once the most important spread in Arizona. But the brothers are hard-pressed to keep their cattle and land, particularly when wealthy Texan carpetbagger Martin Graham arrives in town with plans to take over not only the Crazy N - but the rest of the state!.

Hot Mahogany. unabr. ed. Stuart Woods. Read by Tony Roberts. 7 CDs. (Running Time: 8 hrs.). No. 15. (ENG.). (gr. 8). 2008. audio compact disk 29.95 (978-0-14-314361-1(1), PengAudBks) Penguin Grp USA.

Hot Money. unabr. ed. Dick Francis. Read by Tony Britton. 8 cass. (Running Time: 12 hrs.). 2000. 59.95 (978-0-7451-4286-9(9), CAB 969) Pub: Chivers Audio Bks GBR. Dist(s): AudioGO
Millionaire Malcolm Pembroke had many enemies. Then his wife is murdered. The clues suggest the killer is from close to home, but after five marriages and nine children, who could it be? Pembroke entrusts his safety and money with his son, Ian, an amateur jockey. Soon he's gambling for incredible stakes, not the safest bet for a man on the run!.

Hot Money. unabr. ed. Dick Francis. Narrated by Simon Prebble. 8 cass. (Running Time: 11 hrs. 30 mins.). 1999. 71.00 (978-0-7887-4078-7(4), H1072E7) Recorded Bks.
When amateur jockey Ian Pembroke uncovers a dark secret from the past, he finds himself in a situation more dangerous than a high stakes horse race. Thirty-three-year-old Ian has had an unusual family life. His spectacularly wealthy father has been married five times. And the last Mrs. Pembroke was recently found smothered - with her head in a bag of potting soil. Now his father has become the target of mysterious "accidents." As Ian plunges into the role of bodyguard, deadly forces of greed, hate & vengeance swirl about him.

Hot Money. unabr. ed. Dick Francis. Narrated by Simon Prebble. 10 CDs. (Running Time: 11 hrs. 30 mins.). 2001. audio compact disk 94.00 (978-0-7887-3995-8(6), C1141E7) Recorded Bks.

Hot Money Caper. unabr. ed. Peter Chambers. Read by John Chancer. 3 cass. (Sound Ser.). 2004. 34.95 (978-1-85496-485-4(2)) Pub: UlverLrgPrint GBR. Dist(s): Ulverscroft US

Hot Money Caper. unabr. ed. Read by John Chancer. Perf. by Peter Chambers. 3 cass. (Running Time: 4 hrs. 30 min.). 1999. 34.95 (64852) Pub: Soundings Ltd GBR. Dist(s): Ulverscroft US

Hot Negative: Why Media Miss the Business Message. collector's ed. Jack Falvey. Read by Jonathan Marosz. 5 cass. (Running Time: 7 hrs. 30 min.). 1999. 40.00 (978-0-7366-4585-0(3), 4980) Books on Tape.
What's with the media? Why is it that when they report on a business or industry where we have knowledge or experience, they either get it wrong or just don't get it. Worse, why is it that when they report on an industry we don't know, we instinctively accept their version as gospel?.

Hot on Her Heels. unabr. ed. Susan Mallery. Read by Natalie Ross. (Running Time: 9 hrs.). (Lone Star Sisters Ser.). 2010. 19.99 (978-1-4418-3478-2(8), 9781441834782, Brilliance MP3); 19.99 (978-1-4418-3480-5(X), 9781441834805, BAD); 39.97 (978-1-4418-3479-9(6), 9781441834799, Brlnc Audio MP3 Lib); 39.97 (978-1-4418-3481-2(8), 9781441834812, BADLE); audio compact disk 79.97 (978-1-4418-3477-5(X), 9781441834775, BriAudCD Unabrid); audio compact disk 19.99 (978-1-4418-3476-8(1), 9781441834768, Bril Audio CD Unabri) Brilliance Audio.

Hot Pies on the Tramcar. Sheila Newberry & Julia Franklin. 2008. 54.95 (978-1-84652-276-5(5)); audio compact disk 71.95 (978-1-84652-277-2(3)) Pub: Magna Story GBR. Dist(s): Ulverscroft US

Hot Plastic. unabr. ed. Peter Craig. Read by Stephen Hoye. 7 cass. (Running Time: 10 hrs. 30 min.). 2004. 81.00 (978-0-7366-9755-2(1)) Books on Tape.
Can the father-son team of grifters and a female con artist who comes between them pull of the big score?.

Hot Potato. Joyce Holms. Read by Joe Dunlop. 7 cass. (Running Time: 8 hrs. 30 mins.). (Soundings Ser.). (J). 2005. 61.95 (978-1-84283-549-4(1)) Pub: ISIS Lrg Prnt GBR. Dist(s): Ulverscroft US

Hot Property. unabr. ed. Zoe Barnes. Read by Julia Franklin. 10 cass. (Running Time: 14 hrs.). 2001. 84.95 (978-0-7531-1225-0(6)) Pub: ISIS Audio GBR. Dist(s): Ulverscroft US
Dream home? Dream on. When Claire inherits a house, she thinks she?s struck it rich. But while the word cottage inspires images of a romantic idyll with roses round the door, there?s nothing remotely heavenly about Paradise Cottage. It?s a tumble-down wreck in the middle of nowhere more in need of a demolition expert than a decorator. Still, Claire?s not one to shirk a challenge. Much to the amusement of her hunky new neighbor, Aidan, she decides to renovate the cottage herself. After all, problem-solving, trouble-shooting it?s what she does best. She?s used to planning events for thousands of people. She can sort out one little cottage . . . can?t she.

Hot Pursuit. abr. ed. Suzanne Brockmann. Read by Renée Raudman & Patrick G. Lawlor. (Running Time: 6 hrs.). (Troubleshooter Ser.: No. 15). 2009. audio compact disk 26.99 (978-1-4233-4281-6(X), 9781423342816, BACD) Brilliance Audio.

Hot Pursuit. abr. ed. Suzanne Brockmann. Read by Renée Raudman & Patrick G. Lawlor. (Running Time: 6 hrs.). (Troubleshooter Ser.: No. 15). 2010. audio compact disk 14.99 (978-1-4233-4282-3(8), 9781423342823, BCD Value Price) Brilliance Audio.

***Hot Pursuit.** abr. ed. Suzanne Brockmann. Read by Renee Raudman and Patrick G. Lawlor. (Running Time: 6 hrs.). (Troubleshooters Ser.). 2011. audio compact disk 9.99 (978-1-4558-0042-1(2), 9781455800421, BCD Value Price) Brilliance Audio.

Hot Pursuit. unabr. ed. Suzanne Brockmann. Read by Renée Raudman & Patrick G. Lawlor. (Running Time: 13 hrs.). (Troubleshooter Ser.: No. 15). 2009. 24.99 (978-1-4233-4279-3(8), 9781423342793, BAD); 39.97 (978-1-4233-4278-6(X), 9781423342786, Brlnc Audio MP3 Lib) Brilliance Audio.

Hot Pursuit. unabr. ed. Suzanne Brockmann. Read by Renée Raudman & Renee Patrick G. Lawlor. (Running Time: 13 hrs.). (Troubleshooter Ser.: No. 15). 2009. 39.97 (978-1-4233-4280-9(1), 9781423342809, BADLE) Brilliance Audio.

Hot Pursuit. unabr. ed. Suzanne Brockmann. Read by Renée Raudman & Patrick G. Lawlor. (Running Time: 14 hrs.). (Troubleshooter Ser.: No. 15). 2009. audio compact disk 97.97 (978-1-4233-4276-2(3), 9781423342762, BriAudCD Unabrid); audio compact disk 38.99 (978-1-4233-4275-5(5), 9781423342755, Bril Audio CD Unabri) Brilliance Audio.

Hot Pursuit. unabr. ed. Suzanne Brockmann & Patrick G. Lawlor. Read by Renée Raudman. (Running Time: 13 hrs.). (Troubleshooter Ser.: No. 15). 2009. 24.99 (978-1-4233-4277-9(1), 9781423342779, Brilliance MP3) Brilliance Audio.

Hot Relationships. Tracey Cox. Read by Marie-Louise Walker. (Running Time: 19 hrs. 30 mins.). 2009. 114.99 (978-1-74214-218-0(4), 9781742142180) Pub: Bolinda Pubng AUS. Dist(s): Bolinda Pub Inc

Hot Relationships: How to Have One. unabr. ed. Tracey Cox. 2 CDs. (Running Time: 70200 sec.). 2005. audio compact disk 54.95 (978-1-74093-667-5(1)) Pub: Bolinda Pubng AUS. Dist(s): Bolinda Pub Inc

Hot Rock. unabr. collector's ed. Donald E. Westlake. Read by Michael Kramer. 7 cass. (Running Time: 7 hrs.). (Dortmunder Ser.). 1996. 56.00 (978-0-7366-3417-5(7), 4063) Books on Tape.
John Dortmunder, thief extraordinaire, wants nothing to do with the Balabomo Emerald. But when the African nation of Talabwo bids handsomely for his services, Dortmunder changes his tune. One thing after another goes wrong & the gem keeps slipping away.

Hot Rocks. unabr. ed. Nora Roberts. Read by Susan Ericksen. 7 CDs. (Running Time: 9 hrs.). 2010. audio compact disk 14.99 (978-1-4418-4265-7(9), 9781441842657, Bril Audio CD Unabri) Brilliance Audio.

***Hot Rocks.** unabr. ed. Nora Roberts. Read by Susan Ericksen. (Running Time: 8 hrs.). 2010. 14.99 (978-1-4418-4267-1(5), 9781441842671, Brilliance MP3); 14.99 (978-1-4418-4269-5(1), 9781441842695, BAD); 39.97 (978-1-4418-4268-8(3), 9781441842688, Brlnc Audio MP3 Lib); 39.97 (978-1-4418-4270-1(5), 9781441842701, BADLE); audio compact disk 49.97 (978-1-4418-4266-4(7), 9781441842664, BriAudCD Unabrid) Brilliance Audio.

Hot Sex: How to do It. Tracey Cox. Read by Fiona Macleod. (Running Time: 14 hrs. 25 mins.). 2009. 99.99 (978-1-74214-219-7(2), 9781742142197) Pub: Bolinda Pubng AUS. Dist(s): Bolinda Pub Inc

Hot Sex: How to Do It. unabr. ed. Tracey Cox. Read by Fiona MacLeod. (Running Time: 52200 sec.). 2005. audio compact disk 43.95 (978-1-74093-676-7(0)) Pub: Bolinda Pubng AUS. Dist(s): Bolinda Pub Inc

Hot Sex: How to Do It. unabr. ed. Tracey Cox. Read by Fiona Macleod. 12 CDs. (Running Time: 14 hrs. 25 mins.). 2005. audio compact disk 108.95 (978-1-74093-365-0(6)) Pub: Bolinda Pubng AUS. Dist(s): Bolinda Pub Inc

Hot Shot. unabr. collector's ed. Susan Elizabeth Phillips. Read by Anna Fields. 11 cass. (Running Time: 16 hrs. 30 min.). 1996. 88.00 (978-0-7366-3350-5(2), 4000) Books on Tape.
Her name is Susannah, but three men she brings together call her Hot Shot. She's the spark to a daring venture they start in a garage & build into an empire. For Sam, a rebel, the business is just the thrill he seeks; for Yank, an eccentric inventor, it's his vision fulfilled; & for Mitch, a starched marketing genius, it's a risk he has to take. But dreams can have a cruel price. For Susannah, daughter of a bigwig in a competing company, success means losing her family. The trade-off is unimagined courage & a passion that will enrich her dramatically. Is it worth it?.

Hot Six. Janet Evanovich. (Stephanie Plum Ser.: No. 6). 2001. (978-0-333-78251-4(8)) Macmillan UK GBR.

Hot Six. abr. ed. Janet Evanovich. Read by Debi Mazar. 3 CDs. (Running Time: 3 hrs. 0 mins. 0 sec.). (Stephanie Plum Ser.: No. 6). (ENG.). 2005. audio compact disk 19.95 (978-1-55927-965-9(6)) Pub: Macmill Audio. Dist(s): Macmillan

Hot Six. abr. ed. Janet Evanovich. (Stephanie Plum Ser.: No. 6). 2002. 7.95 (978-1-57815-265-0(8)); audio compact disk 11.99 (978-1-57815-546-0(0), 1111) Media Bks NJ.

Hot Six. unabr. ed. Janet Evanovich. Narrated by C. J. Critt. 7 cass. (Running Time: 9 hrs. 30 mins.). (Stephanie Plum Ser.: No. 6). 2000. 67.00 (978-0-7887-4848-6(3), 96103E7) Recorded Bks.
While trying to make an honest buck apprehending bond-skippers, Stephanie is shocked to learn her mentor-master bounty hunter Carols "Ranger" Manoso is suspected of murder. Digging through the local weapons & drug rackets, Stephanie hopes to get her man off the hook.But finding time for her other man, vice cop Joe Morelli, is getting harder each day & it doesn't help when Grandma moves in.

Hot Six. unabr. ed. Janet Evanovich. Narrated by C. J. Critt. 8 CDs. (Running Time: 9 hrs. 30 mins.). (Stephanie Plum Ser.: No. 6). 2001. audio compact disk 78.00 (978-0-7887-6173-7(0)) Recorded Bks.
Stephanie Plum, America's favorite bounty hunter, returns to the streets of Trenton, New Jersey for another rousing adventure. While trying to make an honest buck apprehending bond-skippers, Stephanie is shocked to learn her mentor, master bounty hunter Carlos Ranger Manoso, is suspected of murder. Digging through the local weapons & drug rackets, Stephanie hopes to get her man off the hook. But finding time for her other man, vice cop Joe Morelli, is getting harder each day. And it doesn't help when Grandma moves in, takes up driving lessons & dyes her hair pink.

Hot Smokey Burnout (c) 1990. Mark Robert Taeschner & Sean Thomas Taeschner. 1990. audio compact disk 15.00 (978-0-9708433-1-9(3)) Tesh Comics.

Hot Spot. unabr. collector's ed. Charles Williams. Read by Michael Russotto. 7 cass. (Running Time: 7 hrs.). 1993. 42.00 (978-0-7366-2388-9(4), 3159) Books on Tape.
Madox wasn't all bad, but his better nature doesn't stand a chance against these odds. Superb 1950s roman noir.

Hot Springs. unabr. ed. Stephen Hunter. Read by William Dufris. 14 vols. (Running Time: 21 hrs.). (Earl Swagger Ser.). 2001. bk. 110.95 (978-0-7927-2474-2(7), CSL 363, Chivers Sound Lib); audio compact disk 119.95 (978-0-7927-9917-7(8), SLD 068, Chivers Sound Lib) AudioGO.
In the summer of 1946, the most wide-open town in America is Hot Springs, Arkansas, a city of ancient, legendary corruption. While the pilgrims take the cure in the mineral-rich 142 degree water that bubbles from the earth, the brothels & casinos are the true source of the town's prosperity. It is run by an English-born gangster named Owney Maddox, who represents Hot Springs, packed with action, sex, sin & crime, is at once a relentlessly violent & deeply touching story.

Hot Stuff. Janet Evanovich & Leanne Banks. Read by Lorelei King. (Playaway Adult Fiction Ser.). (ENG.). 2009. 64.99 (978-1-60775-680-4(3)) Find a World.

Hot Stuff. unabr. ed. Janet Evanovich & Leanne Banks. (Running Time: 5 hrs.). 2007. 24.95 (978-1-4233-1875-0(7), 9781423318750, Brilliance MP3); audio compact disk 29.95 (978-1-4233-1873-6(0), 9781423318736, Bril Audio CD Unabri) Brilliance Audio.

Hot Stuff. unabr. ed. Janet Evanovich & Leanne Banks. Read by Lorelei King. 1 MP3-CD. (Running Time: 5 hrs.). 2007. 39.25 (978-1-4233-1876-7(5), 9781423318767, Brlnc Audio MP3 Lib); 39.25 (978-1-4233-1878-1(1), 9781423318781, BADLE); 24.95 (978-1-4233-1877-4(3), 9781423318774, BAD); 49.25 (978-1-4233-1872-9(2), 9781423318729, BrilAudUnabridg); audio compact disk 69.25 (978-1-4233-1874-3(9), 9781423318743, BriAudCD Unabrid) Brilliance Audio.

Hot Target. abr. ed. Suzanne Brockmann. Read by Melanie Ewbank. (Running Time: 28800 sec.). (Troubleshooter Ser.: No. 8). 2005. audio compact disk 16.99 (978-1-59737-666-2(3), 9781597376662, BCD Value Price) Brilliance Audio.
New York Times bestselling author Suzanne Brockmann knows exactly what makes hearts race and pulses pound: peril and passion. No one succeeds more brilliantly at blending these exhilarating elements in breathtaking novels of men and women forced to grapple with the deepest emotions and the highest risks. And there's no better proof than her new novel of suspense: Hot Target aims to thrill on every level. Like most men of action, Navy SEAL Chief Cosmo Richter has never learned how to take a vacation. So when he finds himself facing a month's leave, he offers his services to Troubleshooters Incorporated. Founded by a former SEAL, the private-sector security firm is a major player in the ongoing war against terrorism, carrying out covert missions too volatile for official U.S. military action. But the first case Richter takes on is anything but under the radar. High-profile maverick movie producer Jane Mercedes Chadwick hasn't quite completed her newest film, but she's already courting controversy. The World War II epic frankly portrays the homosexuality of a real-life hero - and the storm of media buzz surrounding it has drawn the fury of extremist groups. But despite a relentless campaign of angry e-mails, phone calls, and smear tactics, Chadwick won't be pressured into abandoning the project. Then the harassment turns to death threats. Though the FBI is on the scene, nervous Holly-wood associates call in Troubleshooters, and now Chadwick has an army of round-the-clock body-guards whether she likes it or not. And she definitely doesn't. But her stubbornness doesn't make FBI agent Jules Cassidy's job any easier. The fiercely independent filmmaker presents yet another emotional obstacle that Cassidy doesn't need - he's already in the midst of a personal tug-of-war with his ex-lover, and now he's also fighting a growing attraction to Chadwick's brother. Determined to succeed - and survive - on her own terms, Chadwick will face off with enemies and allies alike. And yet she hasn't counted on the bond she'll form with the quiet, capable Cosmo Richter. Even as the noose of deadly terror around them draws tighter, their feelings bring them closer. And when all hell erupts, desire and desperate choices will collide on a killing ground that may trap them both in the crossfire.

Hot Target. abr. ed. Suzanne Brockmann. Read by Patrick G. Lawlor & Melanie Ewbank. (Running Time: 8 hrs.). (Troubleshooter Ser.). 2009. audio compact disk 9.99 (978-1-4418-0838-7(8), 9781441808387, BCD Value Price) Brilliance Audio.

Hot Target. unabr. ed. Suzanne Brockmann. Read by Patrick G. Lawlor & Melanie Ewbank. (Running Time: 16 hrs.). (Troubleshooter Ser.: No. 8). 2004. 39.25 (978-1-59710-379-4(9), 1597103799, BADLE); 24.95 (978-1-59710-378-7(0), 1597103780, BAD); 39.25 (978-1-59335-876-1(8), 1593358768, Brlnc Audio MP3 Lib); 24.95 (978-1-59335-742-9(7), 1593357427) Brilliance Audio.
Like most men of action, Navy SEAL Chief Cosmo Richter never learned how to take a vacation. So when he finds himself facing a month's leave with little to do, he offers his services to Troubleshooters Incorporated. Founded by a former SEAL, the private-sector security firm is a major player in the ongoing war against terrorism, known for carrying out covert missions too volatile for official U.S. military action. But the first case Richter takes on is anything but under the radar. High-profile maverick movie producer Jane Mercedes Chadwick hasn't quite completed her newest film, but she's already courting controversy. The World War II epic frankly portrays the homosexuality of a real-life hero-and the storm of advance media buzz surrounding it has drawn the fury of extremist groups, including the neo-nazi Freedom Network. But despite a relentless campaign of angry e-mails, phone calls, and smear tactics, Chadwick won't be pressured into abandoning the project. Then the harassment turns to death threats, and her nervous Hollywood associates call in Troubleshooters. Now Jane has an army of round-the-clock bodyguards, whether she likes it or not. And she definitely doesn't, even after coming under fire. Determined to succeed - and survive - on her own terms, she's prepared to face off with enemies and allies alike. But she isn't ready for the bond she forms with the quiet, capable Cosmo Richter. Yet even as their feelings draw them closer, the noose of deadly terror all around them draws tighter. And when all hell erupts, desire and desperate choices will collide on a killing ground that may trap them both in the crossfire.

Hot Target. unabr. ed. Suzanne Brockmann. Read by Melanie Ewbank & Patrick G. Lawlor. 11 cass. (Running Time: 16 hrs.). (Troubleshooter Ser.: No. 8). 2004. 36.95 (978-1-59355-596-2(2), 1593555962, BAU) Brilliance Audio.
When Navy SEAL Chief Cosmo Richter's mother falls and breaks both of her wrists, he applies for a month of leave to care for her. Soon it becomes clear that she's comfortable and happy with her nursing care, and needs little from his besides a daily visit. Unused to idle time, Cosmo approaches former SEAL Tom Paoletti, founder of civilian security organization called Troubleshooters Incorporated. Tom eagerly signs him on. Cosmo has no idea that this temporary project will lead him deep into the life of movie producer and screenwriter Jane Mercedes Chadwick. Jane's latest project, American Hero - a World War II drama that dares to acknowledge homosexuality - has raised the ire of certain outspoken groups such as the so-called Freedom Network and she's been receiving horrifying death threats on a regular basis. On the surface, Hollywood writer Jane Chadwick and tough-as-nails Navy SEAL Cosmo Richter are polar opposites. But both have intricate facades in place, hiding their true selves from public scrutiny. When thrust together, they develop a tentative friendship and begin to let each other in. But neither has learned to trust, and they'll be many missteps before they can admit that what they've found is real love - and that their relationship is worth fighting for.

Hot Target. unabr. ed. Suzanne Brockmann. Read by Patrick G. Lawlor & Melanie Ewbank. 11 cass. (Running Time: 16 hrs.). (Troubleshooter Ser.: No. 8). 2004. 102.25 (978-1-59355-597-9(0), 1593555970, BrilAudUnabridg) Brilliance Audio.

Hot Target. unabr. ed. Suzanne Brockmann. Read by Melanie Ewbank & Patrick G. Lawlor. 13 CDs. (Running Time: 16 hrs.). (Troubleshooter Ser.: No. 8). 2004. audio compact disk 38.95 (978-1-59355-599-3(7), 1593555997, Bril Audio CD Unabri) Brilliance Audio.

Hot Target. unabr. ed. Suzanne Brockmann. Read by Patrick G. Lawlor & Melanie Ewbank. 13 CDs. (Running Time: 16 hrs.). (Troubleshooter Ser.: No. 8). 2004. audio compact disk 117.25 (978-1-59355-600-6(4), 1593556004, BriAudCD Unabrid) Brilliance Audio.

Hot Times: How to Eat Well, Live Healthy, & Feel Sexy During the Change. Ann Louise Gittleman. 2 cass. (Running Time: 1 hr. 30 min.). 1994. 14.95 set. (978-1-57124-011-8(X)) Creat Seminars.
Women health thorugh nutrition.

Hot Topics Flashcards, Fifth Edition: Flashcards for Passing the PMP Exam. Excerpts. Rita Mulcahy. 2 CDs. (Running Time: 3 Hours). 2005. audio compact disk 34.00 (978-1-932735-02-4(X)) RMC Pubns Inc.

Hot Topics in Charitable Giving. 1 cass. 1999. bk. 99.00 (ACS-1423) PA Bar Inst.
Do you have clients who need advice on the tax ramifications of charitable giving? This focuses on two important topics in this field: charitable remainder trusts & private foundations.

Hot Water. P. G. Wodehouse. Read by Jonathan Cecil. 6 cass. (Running Time: 9 hrs.). 2002. 54.95 (978-0-7540-0920-7(3), CAB 2342) Pub: Chivers Audio Bks GBR. Dist(s): AudioGO

Hot Water. unabr. ed. P. G. Wodehouse. Read by Jonathan Cecil. 6 CDs. (Running Time: 9 hrs.). 2003. audio compact disk 64.95 (978-0-7540-5555-6(8), CCD 246) AudioGO.

Hot Water. unabr. ed. P. G. Wodehouse. Read by Frederick Davidson. 6 cass. (Running Time: 8 hrs. 30 mins.). 1997. 44.95 (978-0-7861-1240-1(9), 1981) Blckstn Audio.
Engaged to the beautiful Beatrice Bracken, Patrick B. Franklyn believes himself the happiest American millionaire sportsman alive. Until he meets the delightful Jane Opal. Pursuing this enchantress to a chateau in Brittany, Packy finds himself navigating a maze of con-men, safe-blowers, & debauched French aristocrats, as the course of true love runs ever more whackily to its destination.

Hot Zone. Richard Preston. 2004. 10.95 (978-0-7435-4838-0(8)) Pub: S&S Audio. Dist(s): S and S Inc

Hot Zone. abr. ed. Richard Preston. 2 cass. 1996. 14.95 set. (50698) Books on Tape.
A biohazard SWAT team struggles in secret to stop the outbreak of a rare African virus in Washington D.C. suburbs. The virus kills nine out of 10 of its victims - at an alarming pace. More viruses, undetected in rain forests, could creep into human populations. Can they be stopped?.

Hot Zone, unabr. ed. Richard Preston. Narrated by Richard M. Davidson. 8 cass. (Running Time: 11 hrs.). 1995. 70.00 (978-0-7887-0266-2(1), 94475E7) Recorded Bks.
When research monkeys from a biomedical supply company begin dying of the Ebola virus, biohazard personnel from the Center for Disease Control & the U.S. Army began an urgent quest to contain the spread of the disease & determine the level of threat to human populations. Ratchets up the tension as scientists race to control the primate epidemic & prevent rumors that could lead to panic.

Hotel Alleluia. Lucinda Roy. Narrated by Peter Jay Fernandez. 10 cass. (Running Time: 14 hrs. 30 mins.). 88.00 (978-1-4025-1605-4(3)) Recorded Bks.

Hotel & Restaurant Equipment in Peru: A Strategic Reference 2007. Compiled by Icon Group International, Inc. Staff. 2007. ring bd. 195.00 (978-0-497-82381-8(0)) Icon Grp.

Hotel & Restaurant Equipment in Russia: A Strategic Reference 2006. Compiled by Icon Group International, Inc. Staff. 2007. ring bd. 195.00 (978-0-497-82401-3(9)) Icon Grp.

Hotel Casanova. Sue Leather. Read by Nigel Pilkington. (Running Time: 50 mins.). (Cambridge English Readers Ser.). (ENG., 2005. 9.00 (978-0-521-65053-3(4)) Cambridge U Pr.

Hotel du Lac. unabr. ed. Anita Brookner. Read by Anna Massey. 4 cass. (Running Time: 6 hrs.). 2000. 34.95 (978-0-7451-5810-5(2), CAB 217) Pub: Chivers Audio Bks GBR. Dist(s): AudioGO
Edith Hope is in disgrace and working out her probation on the shores of Lake Geneva. Friends and family have banished her to a Swiss solitude until she recovers her senses. Edith reminds herself that the hotel, at least, provides an excellent opportunity to finish writing her latest romantic novel. In the quiet opulence of the Swiss dining room, an irresistible diversion is provided to such an imaginative and compulsive observer.

Hotel du Lac. unabr. ed. Anita Brookner. Narrated by Alexandra O'Karma. 5 cass. (Running Time: 5 hrs. 30 mins.). 1988. 44.00 (978-1-55690-236-9(0), 88330E7) Recorded Bks.
Edith Hope takes refuge in a Swiss hotel from the admonishments of her friends. Then the worldly Mr. Neville broke into her circle of silence with a quaintly treacherous proposal of marriage.

Hotel for Dogs. Lois Duncan. Read by Katherine Kellgren. (Running Time: 3 hrs. 27 mins.). (Playaway Children Ser.). (J). (gr. 4-7). 2008. 49.99 (978-1-60640-955-8(7)) Find a World.

Hotel for Dogs. Lois Duncan & Katherine Kellgren. (J). (gr. 4-7). 2008. audio compact disk 19.95 (978-0-545-13373-9(4)) Scholastic Inc.

Hotel for Dogs. unabr. ed. Lois Duncan. Narrated by Katherine Kellgren. 3 CDs. (Running Time: 3 hrs. 27 mins.). (ENG.). (J). (gr. 4-7). 2008. audio compact disk 39.95 (978-0-545-13374-6(2)) Scholastic Inc.

Hotel Girl. unabr. ed. Anne Worboys. Read by Julia Sands. 6 cass. (Running Time: 8 hrs.). 1998. 69.95 Set. (978-1-85903-242-8(7)) Pub: Magna Story GBR. Dist(s): Ulverscroft US
Humiliated & betrayed by her fiance Martin Wingate on the eve of her wedding, Julie Creighton accepts a friend's offer of sanctuary in a villa overlooking the island of Crete. Under the influence of Greg Strathallan, Julie slowly begins to recover, but realises she has been used by her father & Oliver Wingate to merge their two powerful hotel empires. When her father suffers a heart attack, Julie must fight to save the family business. The bankers do not trust her, the employees are uncertain of her - & on top of everything else, Martin reappears promising to change.

Hotel Heaven: Confessions of a luxury hotel Addict. Matthew Brace. Read by Colin Moody. (Running Time: 10 hrs. 40 mins.). 2009. 84.99 (978-1-74214-169-5(2), 9781742141695) Pub: Bolinda Pubng AUS. Dist(s): Bolinda Pub Inc

Hotel Heaven: Confessions of a luxury hotel Addict. unabr. ed. Matthew Brace. Read by Colin Moody. (Running Time: 10 hrs. 40 mins.). 2008. audio compact disk 93.95 (978-1-921415-97-5(5), 9781921415975) Pub: Bolinda Pubng AUS. Dist(s): Bolinda Pub Inc

Hotel Honolulu. Paul Theroux. Narrated by George Guidall. 11 cass. (Running Time: 15 hrs. 45 mins.). 97.00 (978-1-4025-1600-9(2)) Recorded Bks.

Hotel Morgue. unabr. ed. Janet Laurence. 7 cass. 1998. 76.95 Set. (978-1-872672-82-3(5)) Pub: Magna Story GBR. Dist(s): Ulverscroft US

Hotel New Hampshire. unabr. collector's ed. John Irving. Read by Michael Prichard. 12 cass. (Running Time: 18 hrs.). 1988. 96.00 (978-0-7366-1290-6(4), 2197) Books on Tape.
Follows the Berry family across two continents & through three hotels. Family members attract friends who substitute lust, violence, laughter & tears for the standard bourgeois components.

Hotel on the Corner of Bitter & Sweet: A Novel. unabr. ed. Jamie Ford. Read by Feodor Chin. 9 CDs. (Running Time: 11 hrs.). 2009. audio compact disk 80.00 (978-1-4159-6209-1(X), BksonTape) Pub: Random Audio Pubg. Dist(s): Random

Hotel on the Corner of Bitter & Sweet: A Novel. unabr. ed. Jamie Ford. Read by Feodor Chin. (ENG.). 2009. audio compact disk 39.95 (978-0-7393-8283-7(7), Random AudioBks) Pub: Random Audio Pubg. Dist(s): Random

Hotel Oubliette. unabr. ed. Jane Anderson. Perf. by Edward Asner et al. 1 cass. (Running Time: 1 hr. 28 min.). 1993. 19.95 (978-1-58081-088-3(8)) L A Theatre.
Inspired by the recent rash of memoirs by released American hostages. A darkly comedic play that explores what happens when two emotionally disconnected men are chained to a post with an endless amount of time stretching before them. Deprived of both their freedom & the trappings of what has defined them as successful powerful males, they finally discover the art of meaningful conversation.

Hotel Paradise. unabr. ed. Martha Grimes. Read by Donada Peters. 9 cass. (Running Time: 13 hrs. 30 min.). (Emma Graham Mysteries Ser.). 1996. 72.00 (978-0-7366-3470-0(3), 4114) Books on Tape.
Here are the elements of tragedy: a neglected lake, covered with water lilies & rimmed by blowing grass; a once fashionable, now fading resort hotel; a derelict house full of dusty furnishings, uninhabited for almost 50 years; the death by drowning of a 12 year-old girl, 40 years in the past.

Hotel Pastis: A Novel of Provence. unabr. ed. Peter Mayle. Narrated by John Franklyn-Robbins. 9 cass. (Running Time: 12 hrs. 15 mins.). 1995. 78.00 (978-0-7887-0087-3(1), 94327E7) Recorded Bks.
An English advertising tycoon drops everything to open a small hotel in the French countryside. A merry tale of escape, romance & adventure.

Hotel Personnel & Restaurant Employees. J. Svatko. (Career English Ser.). 1984. (978-0-02-985260-6(9), Free Pr) S and S.

Hotel Regina, Set. Jean Nicol. Read by John Brand. 4 cass. 1999. 44.95 (61691) Pub: Soundings Ltd GBR. Dist(s): ISIS Pub

Hotel Riviera. unabr. ed. Elizabeth A. Adler. Read by Carrington MacDuffie. 9 CDs. (Running Time: 10 hrs.). 2004. audio compact disk 89.95 (978-0-7927-3197-9(2), SLD 647, Chivers Sound Lib); 59.95 (978-0-7927-3196-2(4), CSL 647, Chivers Sound Lib) AudioGO.
American Lola Laforet seems to have it all-a whirlwind romance that turned into "to have and to hold," a charmed life on the Cote d'Azur and ownership of the magnificent Hotel Riviera. Tragically the dream ends as abruptly as it begins when her beloved husband mysteriously disappears. Heartsick, confused, and lonely, her life is thrown into further turmoil when a handsome stranger, Jack Ferrar, an American ex-patriot living on his boat, drops anchor in Lola's harbor and teaches her the meaning of instant attraction. When various sinister people-all claiming ownership of the Hotel Riviera-and the police suddenly appear, Lola is forced to confront the past she left behind and track down her "vanished" husband, with only Jack-and her conflicted emotions-for company.

Hotel Spanish. 2003. ring bd. (978-0-9744783-2-6(6)) Spanish Acad Cu Inst.

Hotel Vendome. abr. ed. Danielle Steel. (Running Time: 6 hrs.). 2011. audio compact disk 19.99 (978-1-4233-8838-8(0), 9781423388388, BACD) Brilliance Audio.

Hotel Vendome. abr. ed. Danielle Steel. (Running Time: 6 hrs.). 2012. audio compact disk 14.99 (978-1-4233-8839-5(9), 9781423388395, BCD Value Price) Brilliance Audio.

Hotel Vendome. unabr. ed. Danielle Steel. (Running Time: 10 hrs.). 2011. 39.97 (978-1-4233-8835-7(6), 9781423388357, Brlnc Audio MP3 Lib); 39.97 (978-1-4233-8837-1(2), 9781423388371, BADLE); 24.99 (978-1-4233-8834-0(8), 9781423388340, Brilliance MP3); 24.99 (978-1-4233-8836-4(4), 9781423388364, BAD); audio compact disk 92.97 (978-1-4233-8833-3(X), 9781423388333, BriAudCD Unabrid); audio compact disk 38.99 (978-1-4233-8832-6(1), 9781423388326, Bril Audio CD Unabri) Brilliance Audio.

Hotels in Argentina: A Strategic Reference 2006. Compiled by Icon Group International, Inc. Staff. 2007. ring bd. 195.00 (978-0-497-35799-3(2)) Icon Grp.

***Hothead.** unabr. ed. Cal Ripken & Kevin Cowherd. (ENG.). (J). 2011. audio compact disk 27.00 (978-0-307-91644-0(8), Listening Lib) Pub: Random Audio Pubg. Dist(s): Random

***Hothouse Flower.** unabr. ed. Rose Impey. Read by Sophie Aldred. 4 CDs. (Running Time: 4 hrs. 33 mins.). (J). (gr. 4-7). 2009. audio compact disk 34.95 (978-1-4056-5981-9(5)) AudioGO.

Hothouse Flower & the Nine Plants of Desire: A Novel. unabr. ed. Margot Berwin. Read by Cassandra Campbell. (ENG.). 2009. audio compact disk 34.95 (978-0-7393-8393-3(0), Random AudioBks) Pub: Random Audio Pubg. Dist(s): Random

Hothouse Orchid. unabr. ed. Stuart Woods. Read by Carrington MacDuffie. 7 CDs. (Running Time: 8 hrs.). No. 5. (ENG.). (gr. 12 up). 2009. audio compact disk 29.95 (978-0-14-314486-1(3), PengAudBks) Penguin Grp USA.

Hottest State. abr. ed. Ethan Hawke. Read by Ethan Hawke. 2 cass. (Running Time: 3 hrs.). 1996. 17.00 set. (978-1-57042-399-4(7)) Hachet Audio.

Houdini!!! The Career of Ehrich Weiss. unabr. ed. Kenneth Silverman. Read by Lloyd James. 14 cass. (Running Time: 21 hrs.). 1997. 112.00 (978-0-7366-3806-7(7), 4476) Books on Tape.
Nearly three-quarters of a century after his death, Houdini remains synonymous with magic, a miracle worker of near mythic stature.

Houghton Mifflin English Vol. 9: Listening to Literature. (gr. 6-12). 1992. (978-0-395-59167-3(8), 2-22193) Holt McDoug.

Houghton Mifflin English Vol. 10: Listening to Literature. (gr. 6-12). 1992. tchr. ed. (978-0-395-59168-0(6), 2-22194) Holt McDoug.

Houghton Mifflin English Vol. 11: Listening to Literature. (gr. 6-12). 1992. tchr. ed. (978-0-395-59169-7(4), 2-22195) Holt McDoug.

Houghton Mifflin English Vol. 12: Listening to Literature. (gr. 6-12). 1992. tchr. ed. (978-0-395-59170-3(8), 2-22196) Holt McDoug.

Hound-Dog Man. unabr. ed. Fred Gipson. Read by Wolfram Kandinsky. 6 cass. (Running Time: 6 hrs.). (J). (gr. 4 up). 1990. 36.00 (978-0-7366-1768-0(X), 2607) Books on Tape.
Twelve-year-old Cotton Kinney had everything a boy could want - except a dog. For Christmas he bought his dad a dog collar & his mom an enameled pan just the right size for feeding a dog. But it didn't do any good. Christmas came & went, & Cotton was still without his dog. Then Blackie Scantling, best coon hunter in the country, & his two coon hounds, came by. Blackie took Cotton on a series of adventures that include a showdown with a bull, a wrestling match with a turkey gobbler, & Cotton's search for a dog to call his own.

Hound of Heaven see Famous Story Poems

Hound of Heaven: Luke 15:1-32. Ed Young. 1996. 4.95 (978-0-7417-2092-4(2), 1092) Win Walk.

***Hound of Rowan.** collector's unabr. ed. Henry H. Neff. Narrated by Jeff Woodman. 10 CDs. (Running Time: 11 hrs. 45 mins.). (Tapestry Ser.: Bk. 1). (YA). (gr. 5-8). 2009. audio compact disk 56.95 (978-1-4361-8690-2(0)) Recorded Bks.

***Hound of Rowan.** unabr. ed. Henry H. Neff. Narrated by Jeff Woodman. 1 Playaway. (Running Time: 11 hrs. 45 mins.). (Tapestry Ser.: Bk. 1). (YA). (gr. 5-8). 2009. 61.75 (978-1-4407-0375-1(2)); 97.75 (978-1-4361-8682-7(X)); audio compact disk 108.75 (978-1-4361-8686-5(2)) Recorded Bks.

Hound of the Baskervilles see Chien des Baskerville

Hound of the Baskervilles. Arthur Conan Doyle. Narrated by Grover Gardner. (ENG.). 2008. audio compact disk 24.95 (978-1-55685-992-2(9)) Audio Bk Con.

Hound of the Baskervilles. Arthur Conan Doyle. Read by Derek Jacobi. 4 cass. (Running Time: 6 hrs.). 2002. 39.95 (978-0-7540-0894-1(0), CAB 2316) Pub: Chivers Audio Bks GBR. Dist(s): AudioGO

Hound of the Baskervilles. Arthur Conan Doyle. 2008. audio compact disk 9.95 (978-1-60245-148-3(6)) GDL Multimedia.

Hound of the Baskervilles. Arthur Conan Doyle. Narrated by Walter Covell. (Running Time: 4 hrs. 30 mins.). 1980. 26.95 (978-1-59912-868-9(3)) Iofy Corp.

Hound of the Baskervilles. Arthur Conan Doyle. Read by David Timson. (Running Time: 3 hrs.). 1999. 31.95 (978-1-60083-774-6(3)) Iofy Corp.

Hound of the Baskervilles. Arthur Conan Doyle. Narrated by Tony Britton. (Running Time: 3 hrs.). 2006. 14.95 (978-1-59912-996-9(5)) Iofy Corp.

Hound of the Baskervilles. Arthur Conan Doyle. Narrated by Ralph Cosham. (Running Time: 19440 sec.). (Unabridged Classics in MP3 Ser.). (ENG.). (YA). 2008. audio compact disk 24.00 (978-1-58472-661-6(X), In Aud) Sound Room.

Hound of the Baskervilles. abr. ed. Arthur Conan Doyle. Narrated by Daniel Chodos. 2 cass. (Running Time: 3 hrs. 5 min.). 12.95 (978-0-89926-154-6(X), 842) Audio Bk.

Hound of the Baskervilles. abr. ed. Arthur Conan Doyle. Perf. by Nicol Williamson et al. 2 cass. (Running Time: 2 hrs. 50 mins.). (J). 1996. 17.00 (978-1-55994-073-3(5), CPN 505) HarperCollins Pubs.
This most renowned Sherlock Holmes mystery pits Holmes & Watson against a savage instrument of death, the "luminous, ghostly, spectral" hound that stalks the moors at night.

Hound of the Baskervilles. adpt. ed. Arthur Conan Doyle. (Bring the Classics to Life Ser.). (ENG.). 2008. audio compact disk 12.95 (978-1-55576-579-8(3)) EDCON Pubng.

Hound of the Baskervilles. unabr. ed. Arthur Conan Doyle. Read by Frederick Davidson. 4 cass. (Running Time: 5 hrs. 30 mins.). 1994. 32.95 (978-0-7861-0499-4(6), 1450) Blckstn Audio.
Dr. Mortimore looked strangely at us for an instant & his voice sank almost to a whisper as he answered, "Mr. Holmes, they were the footprints of a gigantic hound." The "luminous, ghostly, & spectral" hound of family legend has been seen roaming the moors at night. Sir Charles Baskerville has recently died, & it appears that the new baronet, Sir Henry, has inherited not only the vast wealth & property of his family, but a terrible destiny.

Hound of the Baskervilles. unabr. ed. Arthur Conan Doyle. Read by Gene Engene. 6 cass. (Running Time: 6 hrs. 30 mins.). 1986. 39.95 (978-1-55686-238-0(5), 692234) Books in Motion.
"Watson & I gazed out over the shadowy moor, half silver & half gloom. A distant howl arose from the shadowy depths, menacing, almost musical, rising & falling like the low constant murmur of the sea, the hound!".

Hound of the Baskervilles. unabr. ed. Arthur Conan Doyle. Read by David Case. 6 cass. (Running Time: 6 hrs.). 2001. 29.95 (978-0-7366-6802-6(0)) Books on Tape.
As a story of place & mood "The Hound of the Baskervilles" has few peers: unpopulated regions of bracken & bog, the fog sending its tendrils, chilly & cold, the cold stones of an isolated manor house & the terrifying prospect of the hound itself.

Hound of the Baskervilles, unabr. ed. Arthur Conan Doyle. Read by Frederick Davidson. 4 cass. 1999. 32.95 (FS9-34234) Highsmith.

Hound of the Baskervilles. unabr. ed. Arthur Conan Doyle. Read by Hugh Burden. 2 read-along cass. bk. 34.95 (S23928) J Norton Pubs.

Hound of the Baskervilles. unabr. ed. Arthur Conan Doyle. Read by Walter Covell. 4 cass. (Running Time: 5 hrs. 30 min.). 1979. 28.00 (C-28) Jimcin Record.
Gruesome beast stalks the moor & Sherlock Holmes stalks a mystery.

Hound of the Baskervilles. unabr. ed. Arthur Conan Doyle. Read by David Timson. 5 CDs. (Running Time: 6 hr. 17 min.). audio compact disk 34.98 (978-962-634-334-0(6), NA533412) Naxos.

Hound of the Baskervilles. unabr. ed. Arthur Conan Doyle. Narrated by David Ian Davies. 4 CDs. (Running Time: 8 hrs.). Dramatization. audio compact disk 39.50 (978-0-9708022-2-4(6)) One Voice.

Hound of the Baskervilles. unabr. ed. Arthur Conan Doyle. Narrated by Patrick Tull. 5 cass. (Running Time: 7 hrs.). (Sherlock Holmes Mystery Ser.). 1991. 44.00 (978-1-55690-237-6(9), 91333E7) Recorded Bks.
Sherlock Holmes, assisted by Dr. Watson, seeks to unravel the family curse that threatens the life of the last of the Baskervilles.

Hound of the Baskervilles. unabr. ed. Arthur Conan Doyle. 2005. audio compact disk 11.75 (978-1-4193-4119-9(7)) Recorded Bks.

Hound of the Baskervilles. unabr. ed. Arthur Conan Doyle. Read by Ralph Cosham. 1 cass. 24.95 (978-1-883049-[illegible]/2), Commuters Library) Sound Room.
Puts Holmes & Watson through their e[illegible] & provocative crime-solving paces.

Hound of the Baskervilles. unabr. ed. Arthur Conan Doyle. Narrated by David Case. (Running Time: 5 hrs. 30 mins. 0 sec.). (ENG.). 2008. 19.99 (978-1-4001-5897-3(4)); audio compact disk 22.99 (978-1-4001-0897-8(7)); audio compact disk 45.99 (978-1-4001-3897-5(3)) Pub: Tantor Media. Dist(s): IngramPubServ

Hound of the Baskervilles. unabr. ed. Arthur Conan Doyle. Narrated by Simon Prebble. (Running Time: 6 hrs. 30 mins. 0 sec.). (ENG.). 2009. 19.99 (978-1-4001-6515-5(6)); 14.99 (978-1-4001-8515-3(7)); audio compact disk 17.99 (978-1-4001-1515-0(9)); audio compact disk 55.99 (978-1-4001-4515-7(5)) Pub: Tantor Media. Dist(s): IngramPubServ

Hound of the Baskervilles. unabr. collector's ed. Arthur Conan Doyle. Read by David Case. 6 cass. (Running Time: 6 hrs.). (J). 1993. 48.00 (978-0-7366-2454-1(6), 3218) Books on Tape.
As a story of place & mood "The Hound of the Baskervilles" has few peers: unpopulated regions of bracken & bog, the fog sending its tendrils, chilly & cold, the cold stones of an isolated manor house & the terrifying prospect of the hound itself.

Hound of the Baskervilles, Set. unabr. ed. Arthur Conan Doyle. Narrated by Grover Gardner. 4 cass. (Running Time: 6 hrs.). 1986. 19.95 (978-1-55685-008-0(5)) Audio Bk Con.
Sherlock Holmes investigate a ghostly murderous hound on the moors. Is the fiend who plagues the Baskervilles family real or is it part of some deadly plot?.

***Hound of the Baskervilles: Bring the Classics to Life.** adpt. ed. Arthur Conan Doyle. (Bring the Classics to Life Ser.). 2008. pap. bk. 21.95 (978-1-55576-623-8(4)) EDCON Pubng.

Hound of the Baskervilles (A) abr. ed. Arthur Conan Doyle. (Running Time: 4 hrs.). 2009. audio compact disk 22.98 (978-962-634-948-9(4), Naxos AudioBooks) Naxos.

***Hounded.** unabr. ed. Kevin Hearn. (Running Time: 10 hrs.). (Iron Druid Chronicles Ser.). 2011. 39.97 (978-1-4418-7001-8(6), 9781441870018, Brinc Audio MP3 Lib); 39.97 (978-1-4418-7003-2(2), 9781441870032, BADLE); 14.99 (978-1-4418-7000-1(8), 9781441870001, Brilliance MP3); 24.99 (978-1-4418-7002-5(4), 9781441870025, BAD); audio compact disk 89.97 (978-1-4418-6999-9(9), 9781441869999, BriAudCD Unabrid); audio compact disk 29.99 (978-1-4418-6998-2(0), 9781441869982, Bril Audio CD Unabri) Brilliance Audio.

Hounded to Death. Rita Mae Brown. (Foxhunting Mysteries Ser.). 2008. audio compact disk 29.99 (978-1-4361-4141-3(9)) Recorded Bks.

Hounds & the Fury. unabr. ed. Rita Mae Brown. Narrated by Rita Mae Brown. (Running Time: 30600 sec.). (Foxhunting Mysteries Ser.). 2006. audio compact disk 34.99 (978-1-4193-9726-4(5)) Recorded Bks.

Hounds of Love. Poems. Mark Allen Gray. 1 case, 1 CD. (Running Time: 43 mins., 18 secs.). 2005. audio compact disk 9.95 (978-0-9761095-2-5(2), Gray Tech Pr) Gray Technolgies.
About the CDThe Hounds of Love compact disc contains the spoken-word recordings of the poems from the book The Hounds of Love. The author, Mark Allen Gray, introduces each of the four chapters from his book, then proceeds to take the listener through each poem in the tone, rhythm, and mood intended by the author.This collection of poems tells a familiar story in an unrestrained free verse form. This is a story of love discovered, love lived, love lost, and love resolved. In this story, love has no form, no rules, and no boundaries. It is free and it is loose and it is dogged by all of us, relentlessly. Like a pack of hounds on a hunt, it is a game, with one prize, and one loser.Love is a big subject to explore. Writers and artists of all types have been driven by its mystery, thrill, and madness for many millennia. It is the author?s hope that the listener will find some entertainment or healing value in this small story.Copyright ? 2005 by Gray Technologies Press. All Rights Reserved.

Hounds of the Baskervilles, abr. ed. Arthur Conan Doyle. Read by Michael J. Bennett. 4 cass. (Running Time: 6 hrs.). (Great Mysteries - Louis L'Amour Ser.). 2000. 12.99 (978-1-57815-158-5(9), 4407, Media Bks Audio) Media Bks NJ.

Houndsley & Catina. James Howe. Read by Peter Pamela Rose. Illus. by Marie-Louise Gay. 1 CD. (Running Time: 13 mins.). (Houndsley & Catina Ser.). (J). (gr. k-2). 2008. bk. 28.95 (978-1-4301-0300-4(0)); pap. bk. 18.95 (978-1-4301-0299-1(3)) Live Oak Media.

Houndsley & Catina & the Birthday Surprise. James Howe. Read by Peter Pamela Rose. Illus. by Marie-Louise Gay. 1 CD. (Running Time: 13 mins.). (Houndsley & Catina Ser.). (J). (gr. k-2). 2008. bk. 28.95 (978-1-4301-0308-0(6)); pap. bk. 18.95 (978-1-4301-0307-3(8)) Live Oak Media.

Hour Before Daylight: Memories of a Rural Boyhood. Jimmy Carter. Narrated by Tom Stechschulte. 7 CDs. (Running Time: 8 hrs. 30 mins.). audio compact disk 71.00 (978-0-7887-9933-4(9)) Recorded Bks.

Hour Before Daylight: Memories of a Rural Boyhood. abr. ed. Jimmy Carter. Read by Jimmy Carter. 2006. 18.95 (978-0-7435-6370-3(0), Audioworks) Pub: S&S Audio. Dist(s): S and S Inc

Hour Before Daylight: Memories of a Rural Boyhood. unabr. ed. Jimmy Carter. Narrated by Tom Stechschulte. 6 cass. (Running Time: 8 hrs. 30 mins.). 2001. 59.00 (978-0-7887-7248-1(1), 96696K8) Recorded Bks.
A timeless memoir & a powerful examination of a difficult time period in American history.

Hour Game. abr. ed. David Baldacci. Read by Ron McLarty. (Sean King & Michelle Maxwell Ser.: No. 2). (ENG.). 2005. 14.98 (978-1-59483-150-8(5)) Pub: Hachet Audio. Dist(s): HachBkGrp

Hour Game. abr. ed. David Baldacci. Read by Ron McLarty. (Running Time: 6 hrs.). No. 2. (ENG.). 2008. audio compact disk 14.98 (978-1-60024-218-2(9)) Pub: Hachet Audio. Dist(s): HachBkGrp

Hour Game. unabr. ed. David Baldacci. Read by Scott Brick. (Sean King & Michelle Maxwell Ser.: No. 2). (YA). 2007. 64.99 (978-1-60252-643-3(5)) Find a World.

Hour Game. unabr. ed. David Baldacci. Read by Scott Brick. (Sean King & Michelle Maxwell Ser.: No. 2). (ENG.). 2005. 16.98 (978-1-59483-149-2(1)) Pub: Hachet Audio. Dist(s): HachBkGrp

Hour Game. unabr. ed. David Baldacci. Read by Scott Brick. (Running Time: 11 hrs. 30 mins.). (ENG.). 2009. 59.98 (978-1-60788-072-1(5)) Pub: Hachet Audio. Dist(s): HachBkGrp

Hour I First Believed. unabr. ed. Wally Lamb. Read by George Guidall. 20 CDs. (Running Time: 25 hrs. 30 mins.). 2008. audio compact disk 75.00 (978-0-06-170303-4(6), Harper Audio) HarperCollins Pubs.

Hour I First Believed. unabr. ed. Wally Lamb. Read by George Guidall. (Running Time: 25 hrs. 30 mins.). 2008. 66.75 (978-1-4361-9851-6(8)); 113.75 (978-1-4361-5384-3(0)); audio compact disk 123.75 (978-1-4361-5386-7(7)) Recorded Bks.

***Hour I First Believed.** unabr. ed. Wally Lamb. Read by George Guidall. (ENG.). 2008. (978-0-06-177132-3(5), Harper Audio); (978-0-06-177133-0(3), Harper Audio) HarperCollins Pubs.

Hour I First Believed. unabr. collector's ed. Wally Lamb. Read by George Guidall. 20 CDs. (Running Time: 25 hrs. 30 mins.). 2008. audio compact disk 74.95 (978-1-4361-5387-4(5)) Recorded Bks.

Hour is Come. Kelley Varner. 4 cass. 1993. 25.00 Set. (978-0-938612-74-2(3)) Destiny Image Pubs.

Hour of Gospel Hymns. 1 cass. 10.98 (978-1-57908-238-3(6), 1191); audio compact disk 15.98 CD. (978-1-57908-237-6(8)) Platinm Enter.

Hour of No Impossibility. Lynne Hammond. 1 cass. (Running Time: 1 hr.). 2005. 5.00 (978-1-57399-252-7(6)); audio compact disk 5.00 (978-1-57399-274-9(7)) Mac Hammond.

Hour of No Impossibilty. Lynne Hammond. 2008. audio compact disk 6.00 (978-1-57399-403-3(0)) Mac Hammond.

Hour of Opportunity, Vol. 3. Richard Gorham & Orison Swett Marden. Narrated by Richard Gorham. (ENG.). 2006. audio compact disk 14.95 (978-0-9791934-2-2(7)) LshipTools.

Hour of the Cat. Peter Quinn. Read by Ned Schmidtke. (Running Time: 52200 sec.). 2005. 79.95 (978-0-7861-3515-8(8)); audio compact disk 29.95 (978-0-7861-8051-6(X)) Blckstn Audio.

Hour of the Cat. unabr. ed. Peter Quinn. Read by Ned Schmidtke. 12 CDs. (Running Time: 52200 sec.). 2005. audio compact disk 99.00 (978-0-7861-7836-0(1)) Blckstn Audio.

Hour of the Donkey. unabr. ed. Anthony Price. Read by Terry Wale. 10 cass. (Running Time: 15 hrs.). 2001. 84.95 (978-1-86042-721-3(9), 27219) Pub: Soundings Ltd GBR. Dist(s): Ulverscroft US
The nightmare of Dunkirk was appalling for the Prince Regent's Own South Downs Fusiliers, whose professional training had scarcely progressed beyond the parade ground.

Hour of the Hunter. unabr. ed. J. A. Jance. Read by Gene Engene. 12 cass. (Running Time: 14 hrs. 42 mins.). (Brandon Walker Ser.: Bk. 1). 1994. 64.95 (978-1-55686-470-4(1), 112714) Books in Motion.
Set in Arizona, this is the gripping story of Diana Ladd - the hunted. A brutal, psychopathic murderer is released from prison. He stalks Diana with intent to kill.

Hour of the Manatee. unabr. ed. E. C. Ayres. Read by John MacDonald. 7 cass. (Running Time: 10 hrs. 30 min.). 1994. 56.00 (978-0-7366-2875-4(4), 3579) Books on Tape.
An unlicensed private eye joins forces with the cops in a power struggle that doesn't flinch at murder.

Hour of the Olympics. unabr. ed. Mary Pope Osborne. Read by Mary Pope Osborne. 1 cass. (Running Time: 38 mins.). (Magic Tree House Ser.: No. 16). (J). (gr. k-3). 2004. pap. bk. 17.00 (978-0-8072-0785-7(3), LFTR 244 SP, Listening Lib) Random Audio Pubg.
In ancient Greece Jack and Annie witness the original Olympic games and are surprised to find what girls of the time were not allowed to do.

***Hour on Sunday: Creating Moments of Transformation & Wonder.** Nancy Beach. (Running Time: 6 hrs. 35 mins. 0 sec.). (ENG.). 2008. 24.99 (978-0-310-30457-9(1)) Zondervan.

Hour to Live, an Hour to Love: The True Story of the Best Gift Ever Given. unabr. ed. Richard Carlson. Read by Dick Hill & Susie Breck. (Running Time: 1 hr. 0 mins. 0 sec.). (ENG.). 2008. audio compact disk 35.99 (978-1-4001-3531-8(1)) Pub: Tantor Media. Dist(s): IngramPubServ

Hour to Live, an Hour to Love: The True Story of the Best Gift Ever Given. unabr. ed. Richard Carlson. Read by Dick Hill. Narrated by Susie Breck. (Running Time: 1 hr. 0 mins. 0 sec.). (ENG.). 2008. audio compact disk 17.99 (978-1-4001-0531-1(5)) Pub: Tantor Media. Dist(s): IngramPubServ

Hour to Live, an Hour to Love: The True Story of the Best Gift Ever Given. unabr. ed. Richard Carlson & Kristine Carlson. Narrated by Dick Hill & Susie Breck. (Running Time: 1 hr. 0 mins. 0 sec.). (ENG.). 2008. audio compact disk 17.99 (978-1-4001-5531-6(2)) Pub: Tantor Media. Dist(s): IngramPubServ

Hour to Live, an Hour to Love: The True Story of the Best Gift Ever Given. unabr. ed. Carlson et al. Read by Dick Hill & Susie Breck. (YA). 2008. 34.99 (978-1-60514-869-4(5)) Find a World.

Hourglass, Set. Will Brennan. Read by John Keyworth. 3 cass. 1999. 34.95 (60296) Pub: Soundings Ltd GBR. Dist(s): ISIS Pub

Hours. Michael Cunningham. Read by Alexander Adams. 1999. audio compact disk 40.00 (978-0-7366-5171-4(3)) Books on Tape.

Hours. collector's ed. Michael Cunningham. Read by Alexander Adams. 4 cass. (Running Time: 6 hrs.). 1999. 32.00 (978-0-7366-4496-9(2), 4932) Books on Tape.
An homage to Virginia Woolf. Opens with an evocation of Woolf's last days before her suicide in 1941 & moves to the stories of two modern American women who are trying to make rewarding lives for themselves in spite of the demands of friends, lovers, & family.

Hours. unabr. ed. Michael Cunningham. Read by Alexander Adams. 5 CDs. (Running Time: 6 hrs.). 2001. audio compact disk 29.95 (978-0-7366-5706-8(1)) Books on Tape.
A homage to Virginia Woolf. Opens with an evocation of Woolf's last days before her suicide in 1941 & moves to the stories of two modern American women who are trying to make rewarding lives for themselves in spite of the demands of friends, lovers & family.

Hours. unabr. ed. Michael Cunningham. 4 cass. (Running Time: 6 hrs.). 2003. 36.00 (978-0-7366-9849-8(3)) Books on Tape.

Hours. unabr. ed. Michael Cunningham. Read by Alexander Adams. 5 CDs. (Running Time: 6 hrs.). 2001. audio compact disk 29.95 Books on Tape.
On a gray suburban London morning in 1923, Virginia Woolf awakens from a dream that will soon lead to Mrs. Dalloway. In the present, on a beautiful June day in Greenwich Village, 52-year-old Clarissa Vaughan is planning a party for her oldest love, a poet dying of AIDS. And in Los Angeles in 1949, Laura Brown, pregnant & unsettled, does her best to prepare for her husband's birthday, but can't seem to stop reading Woolf. These women's lives are linked both by the 1925 novel & by the few precious moments of possibility each keeps returning to.

Hours. unabr. rev. ed. Michael Cunningham. 6 CDs. (Running Time: 7 hrs. 0 mins. 0 sec.). (ENG., 2003. audio compact disk 34.95 (978-1-55927-931-4(1)) Pub: Macmill Audio. Dist(s): Macmillan

Hours, Pt. 2. unabr. ed. Michael Cunningham. Read by Alexander Adams. 4 cass. (Running Time: 6 hrs.). 1999. 24.95 (978-0-7366-4520-1(9)) Books on Tape.
A homage to Virginia Woolf. Opens with an evocation of Woolf's last days before her suicide in 1941 & moves to the stories of two modern American women who are trying to make rewarding lives for themselves in spite of the demands of friends, lovers & family.

Hours Before Dawn, Set. unabr. ed. Celia Fremlin. 5 cass. 1998. 63.95 (978-1-85903-071-4(8)) Pub: Magna Story GBR. Dist(s): Ulverscroft US

House. Frank E. Peretti & Ted Dekker. Read by Frank E. Peretti. (Running Time: 34200 sec.). 2006. audio compact disk 81.00 (978-0-7861-7041-8(7)) Blckstn Audio.

House. abr. ed. Frank E. Peretti & Ted Dekker. (Running Time: 16200 sec.). 2006. audio compact disk 25.99 (978-1-59554-157-4(8)) Nelson.

House. abr. ed. Danielle Steel. Read by Erik Singer. (ENG.). 2008. audio compact disk 14.99 (978-0-7393-7603-4(9), Random AudioBks) Pub: Random Audio Pubg. Dist(s): Random

House. unabr. ed. Tracy Kidder. Read by Larry McKeever. 10 cass. (Running Time: 15 hrs.). 1986. 80.00 (978-0-7366-0786-5(2), 1739) Books on Tape.
Kidder follows the construction of a new house from gleam-in-the-eye to moving day. We get to know the ambitious owners, the architect who gives form to their dreams, the carpenters who pound the nails.

House, unabr. ed. Tracy Kidder. Narrated by Adrian Cronauer. 8 cass. (Running Time: 10 hrs. 30 mins.). 1986. 70.00 (978-1-55690-240-6(9), 86160E7) Recorded Bks.
Why on earth should the nail-by-nail building of a house hold any fascination for anyone? Because when you put a lawyer, an architect & a hippie builder together, that spells trouble. Kidder tells his story so well that you can't help but take sides.

House. unabr. ed. Frank E. Peretti & Ted Dekker. Narrated by Kevin King. (ENG.). 2006. 24.49 (978-1-60814-240-8(X)) Oasis Audio.

House. unabr. ed. Frank E. Peretti & Ted Dekker. Read by Frank E. Peretti. Narrated by Kevin King. (Running Time: 34200 sec.). (ENG.). 2006. audio compact disk 34.99 (978-1-59859-107-1(X)) Oasis Audio.

House. unabr. ed. Danielle Steel. 6 cass. (Running Time: 9 hrs.). 2006. 54.00 (978-1-4159-2684-0(0)); audio compact disk 72.00 (978-1-4159-2685-7(9)) Books on Tape.

House. unabr. ed. Danielle Steel. Read by Eric Singer. 8 CDs. (Running Time: 36000 sec.). (Danielle Steel Ser.). (ENG.). 2006. audio compact disk 39.95 (978-0-7393-2522-3(1), Random AudioBks) Pub: Random Audio Pubg. Dist(s): Random

House above the Bay. Ivy Preston. Read by Melissa Sinden. 4 cass. (Running Time: 6 hrs.). 1999. 44.95 (6240X) Pub: Soundings Ltd GBR. Dist(s): Ulverscroft US

House Arrest. unabr. ed. Mary Morris. Narrated by Alyssa Bresnahan. 6 cass. (Running Time: 7 hrs. 30 mins.). 51.00 (978-0-7887-2002-4(3), 95389E7) Recorded Bks.
Travel writer Maggie Conover is under house arrest at her hotel Onla Isla in the Caribbean because of her relationship with the revolutionary leader's missing daughter. Fearing for her life & longing for home, she reminisces about her own troubled past & about her last visit with the exotic, courageous Isabel. Available to libraries only.

House at Hemlock Farms-"Read-Along with Mimi" A Cool Chapterbook-Package. Mimi Morganstern. Illus. by Mimi Morganstern. (J). (gr. 3-6). 2000. per. 9.99 (978-0-9700522-4-7(3)) M Morganstern.

House at Pooh Corner. A. A. Milne. Read by Peter Dennis. 3 cass. (Running Time: 3 hrs.). 2005. 24.95 (978-0-7861-2926-3(3), 3404); audio compact disk 27.00 (978-0-7861-8197-1(4), 3404) Blckstn Audio.

House at Pooh Corner. A. A. Milne. (Running Time: 2 hrs.). (ENG.). audio compact disk 29.95 (978-1-84032-002-2(8), HoddrStoughton) Pub: Hodder General GBR. Dist(s): Trafalgar

House at Pooh Corner. A. A. Milne. Contrib. by David Benedictus. 2 cass. (Running Time: 3 hrs.). Dramatization. (J). 1998. (978-1-85998-651-6(X), HoddrStoughton) Hodder General GBR.

House at Pooh Corner. A. A. Milne. Narrated by Peter Dennis. (Running Time: 3 hrs.). (J). 2004. 20.95 (978-1-59912-671-5(0)) Iofy Corp.

House at Pooh Corner. unabr. ed. A. A. Milne. Read by Peter Dennis. 3 cass. (Running Time: 4 hrs.). (Winnie-the-Pooh Ser.). 2005. 14.95 (978-0-7861-2927-0(1)); audio compact disk 14.95 (978-0-7861-8198-8(2)) Blckstn Audio.

House at Pooh Corner. unabr. ed. A. A. Milne. Read by Peter Dennis. (J). 2006. 34.99 (978-1-59895-671-9(X)) Find a World.

House at Pooh Corner. unabr. ed. A. A. Milne. Perf. by Carol Channing. 1 cass. Incl. House at Pooh Corner: Piglet Does a Very Grand Thing. A. A. Milne. (J). (CP 1670); (J). 1984. 8.98 (978-0-89845-093-4(4), CP 1670) HarperCollins Pubs.

House at Pooh Corner. unabr. ed. A. A. Milne. Perf. by Carol Channing. 1 cass. (Running Time: 60 min.). (J). 1992. 11.00 (978-1-55994-582-0(6)) HarperCollins Pubs.
Channing reads all the characters with a British accent, except the narrator & the cranky, croaky Eeyore. She sings Pooh's made-up verses, such as "An Anxious Pooh Song," with great aplomb.

House at Pooh Corner. unabr. ed. A. A. Milne. Read by Stephen Fry et al. (ENG.). (J). (ps). 2009. audio compact disk 20.00 (978-0-307-70614-0(1), Listening Lib) Pub: Random Audio Pubg. Dist(s): Random

House at Pooh Corner. unabr. abr. ed. A. A. Milne. Read by Jim Broadbent. 2 CDs. (Running Time: 3 hrs.). (J). 2004. 22.00 (978-0-06-058253-1(7)) HarperCollins Pubs.

House at Pooh Corner, Set. A. A. Milne. Read by Peter Dennis. Illus. by Ernest H. Shepard. 4 cass. (Running Time: 4 hr.). (J). bk. (978-1-57375-653-2(9), 71524) Audioscope.

House at Pooh Corner, Set. A. A. Milne. Read by Charles Kuralt. 2 cass. (J). 13.58 Blisterpack. (PEN 8667) NewSound.
Tigger finds his way to the Hundred Acre Wood, & Pooh & his friends meet the bounciest creature they've ever seen. He can climb trees (but not down) & sometimes his bounces land Gloomy Donkeys in the water. Will the others succeed in unbouncing him?.

House at Pooh Corner, Set A. A. Milne. Read by Peter Dennis. Illus. by Ernest H. Shepard. 4 CDs. (Running Time: 4 hrs.). (J). bk. (978-1-57375-584-9(2), 71522) Audioscope.

House at Pooh Corner: Piglet Does a Very Grand Thing see House at Pooh Corner

House at Pooh Corner & Now We Are Six. unabr. ed. A. A. Milne. (J). 1997. 26.95 incl. wooden gift box. (978-1-55935-275-8(2)) Soundelux.

House at Pooh Corner & Now We Are Six, Set. unabr. ed. A. A. Milne. Read by Peter Dennis. 4 cass. (Running Time: 4 hrs.). (J). 1997. 22.95 (978-1-55935-249-9(3), 495290) Soundelux.
Here are the stories & poems which feature Winnie-the-Pooh, Christopher Robin & their friends.

House at Riverton. Kate Morton. Read by Caroline Lee. (Running Time: 69300 sec.). 2008. audio compact disk 128.00 (978-1-921334-86-3(X)) Bolinda Pubng AUS.

House at Riverton. Kate Morton. Read by Caroline Lee. (Running Time: 19 hrs. 15 mins.). 2009. 114.99 (978-1-74214-268-5(0), 9781742142685) Pub: Bolinda Pubng AUS. Dist(s): Bolinda Pub Inc

House at Riverton. unabr. ed. Kate Morton. Read by Caroline Lee. (Running Time: 19 hrs. 15 mins.). 2008. audio compact disk 123.95 (978-1-921415-02-9(9), 9781921415029) Pub: Bolinda Pubng AUS. Dist(s): Bolinda Pub Inc

***house at Riverton.** unabr. ed. Kate Morton. Read by Caroline Lee. (Running Time: 19 hrs. 15 mins.). 2008. 54.95 (978-1-74214-106-0(4), 9781742141060) Pub: Bolinda Pubng AUS. Dist(s): Bolinda Pub Inc

House at 2629 Woodland St. 1 cass. (Running Time: 90 min.). 2001. (978-1-893699-04-5(8)) AudioCraft.

House by Princes Park. unabr. ed. Maureen Lee. Read by Maggie Ollerenshaw. 12 cass. (Running Time: 18 hrs.). 2003. 96.95 (978-0-7540-0927-6(0), CAB 2349) AudioGO.

House by the Sea. Elvi Rhodes. 2009. 69.95 (978-1-4079-0453-5(1)); audio compact disk 84.95 (978-1-4079-0454-2(X)) Pub: Soundings Ltd GBR. Dist(s): Ulverscroft US

House by the Sea. unabr. ed. Nicola Thorne. 6 cass. (Running Time: 6 hrs. 35 mins.). (Isis Cassettes Ser.). (J). 2005. 54.95 (978-0-7531-2075-0(5)) Pub: ISIS Lrg Prnt GBR. Dist(s): Ulverscroft US

House by the Sea, Level 3. Patricia Aspinall. Contrib. by Philip Prowse. (Running Time: 1 hr. 54 mins.). (Cambridge English Readers Ser.). (ENG., 2000. 15.75 (978-0-521-77577-9(9)) Cambridge U Pr.

House by the Side of the Road see Classic American Poetry

House by the Side of the Road see Favorite American Poems

House Called Awful End. Philip Ardagh. Read by Martin Rayner. 2 cass. (Running Time: 2 hrs. 28 mins.). (Eddie Dickens Trilogy: Bk. 1). (J). (gr. 4 up). 2004. 23.00 (978-0-8072-1887-7(1), Listening Lib); audio compact disk 24.00 (978-0-8072-1999-7(1), Listening Lib) Random Audio Pubg.
Eddie finds himself incarcerated in St. Horrid's Home for Grateful Orphans, jailed for stealing a hot-air balloon, and sailing to America in a leaky boat.

House Calls & Hitching Posts. Sharp Hoover Dorcas. 2007. 29.95 (978-1-56148-583-3(7)) Good Bks PA.

***House Corrino.** unabr. ed. Brian Herbert & Kevin J. Anderson. Narrated by Scott Brick. (Running Time: 24 hrs. 0 mins.). (Prelude to Dune Ser.). 2009. 26.99 (978-1-4001-8363-0(4)) Tantor Media.

House Corrino. unabr. ed. Brian Herbert & Kevin J. Anderson. Narrated by Scott Brick. (Running Time: 24 hrs. 0 mins. 0 sec.). (Prelude to Dune Ser.).

(ENG.). 2010. 39.99 (978-1-4001-6363-2(3)); audio compact disk 109.99 (978-1-4001-4363-4(2)) Pub: Tantor Media. Dist(s): IngramPubServ

***House Divided.** unabr. ed. Pearl S. Buck. Narrated by Adam Verner. (Running Time: 18 hrs. 0 mins. 0 sec.). (Good Earth Trilogy). (ENG.). 2010. 27.99 (978-1-60814-718-2(5)); audio compact disk 39.99 (978-1-59859-763-9(9), SpringWater) Oasis Audio.

House Divided. unabr. ed. Catherine Cookson. Read by Susan Jameson. 10 CDs. (Running Time: 15 hrs.). 2000. audio compact disk 94.95 (978-0-7540-5331-6(8), CCD 022) Pub: Chivers Audio Bks GBR. Dist(s): AudioGO
It is the end of World War II & Matthew Wallingham is discharged from the army a decorated hero, but also a blind man. It seems the only person who can reach him is his nurse, Liz. After realizing his family is in disarray, he turns to Liz, but she has her own problems to deal with.

House Divided. unabr. ed. Catherine Cookson. Read by Susan Jameson. 10 cass. (Running Time: 15 hrs.). 2000. 84.95 (978-0-7540-0449-3(X), CAB 1872) Pub: Chivers Audio Bks GBR. Dist(s): AudioGO

House Dog's Grave see Poetry of Robinson Jeffers

House Floor Procedures. Ed. by TheCapitol.Net. 2006. 107.00 (978-1-58733-037-7(7)) TheCapitol.

House for Hermit Crab. unabr. ed. Eric Carle. Narrated by John McDonough. 1 cass. (Running Time: 15 mins.). (gr. 1 up). 1998. 10.00 (978-0-7887-2060-4(0), 95413E7) Recorded Bks.
Young children who are outgrowing their clothes or have to move away from their friends will be comforted to know that everyone has to grow or move on.

House for Me. Perf. by Fred Penner. 1 cass. (J). (ps-5). 1986. 10.98 (978-0-945267-58-4(4), YM087-CN); audio compact disk 13.98 (978-0-945267-59-1(2), YM087-CD) Youngheart Mus.
Songs include: "A Home Is a House for Me"; "Skip to My Lou"; "Camptown Races";" Oh, Susannah"; "Everything Is Ticketty-Boo"; "Hold 'Em Joe"; "Grandma's Glasses"; "Hush Little Baby"; "Jack Was Every Inch a Sailor";" The Sailor's Hornpipe" & more.

House for Sergin: Audiocassette. (Greetings Ser.: Vol. 2). (gr. 2-3). 10.00 (978-0-7635-5872-7(9)) Rigby Educ.

House for Sister Mary. unabr. ed. Lucilla Andrews. Read by Rebecca Wright. 4 cass. (Sound Ser.). 1986. 44.95 (978-1-85496-013-9(X), 6013X) Pub: UlverLrgPrint GBR. Dist(s): Ulverscroft US

House Harkonnen. unabr. ed. Brian Herbert & Kevin J. Anderson. Narrated by Scott Brick. (Running Time: 26 hrs. 30 mins. 0 sec.). (Prelude to Dune Ser.). (ENG.). 2009. audio compact disk 54.99 (978-1-4001-1362-0(8)) Pub: Tantor Media. Dist(s): IngramPubServ

House in Amalfi. unabr. ed. Elizabeth A. Adler. Read by Carrington MacDuffie. 2005. 29.95 (978-0-7927-3712-4(1), CMP 828); 54.95 (978-0-7927-3710-0(5), CSL 828); audio compact disk 79.95 (978-0-7927-3711-7(3), SLD 828) AudioGO.

House in the Middle of the Road see Zulu & Other African Folktales from Behind the Back of the Mountain

House in the Sunflowers. unabr. ed. Ruth Silvestre. 5 cass. (Isis Ser.). (J). 2003. 49.95 (978-0-7531-1606-7(5)) Pub: ISIS Lrg Prnt GBR. Dist(s): Ulverscroft US

House in the Sunflowers. unabr. ed. Ruth Silvestre. Read by Ruth Silvestre. 6 CDs. (Running Time: 6 hrs. 35 min.). (Isis Ser.). (J). 2003. audio compact disk 64.95 (978-0-7531-2232-7(4)) Pub: ISIS Lrg Prnt GBR. Dist(s): Ulverscroft US
Ruth Silvestre and her family found Bel-Air de Grezelongue, a house that had been left, deserted and uninhabited for ten years. They fell in love with it.A House in the Sunflowers tells of their affair with the house, from the search and initial frustrations, their euphoria when they finally bought it and the challenges of renovation and gradual assimilation into the local community.

House Is a House. 9.95 (978-1-59112-291-3(0)) Live Oak Media.

House Is a House for Me. Mary Ann Hoberman. Read by Linda Terheyden. Illus. by Betty Fraser. 1 cass. (Running Time: 30 mins.). (J). 2000. pap. bk. 19.97 (978-0-7366-9199-4(5)) Books on Tape.
Lilting rhyme & profuse illustrations put forth the premise that anything that contains something else can be considered a house.

House Is a House for Me. unabr. ed. Mary Ann Hoberman. Read by Linda Terheyden. Illus. by Betty Fraser. 11 vols. (Running Time: 8 mins.). (J). (gr. k-3). 1984. bk. 25.95 (978-0-941078-33-7(7)); pap. bk. 16.95 (978-0-941078-31-3(0)); pap. bk. & tchr. ed. 33.95 Reading Chest. (978-0-941078-32-0(9)) Live Oak Media.
Explores many different images of houses ranging from a "bird in a nest" to the more abstract "a throat is a house for a hum".

House Is a House for Me. Mary Ann Hoberman. Illus. by Betty Fraser. (Running Time: 8 mins.). 1984. 9.95 (978-1-59112-061-2(6)) Live Oak Media.

***House Justice.** unabr. ed. Mike Lawson. Read by Joe Barrett. (Running Time: 13 hrs. 0 mins.). 2010. 29.95 (978-1-4417-4799-0(0)); audio compact disk 32.95 (978-1-4417-4798-3(2)) Blckstn Audio.

***House Justice: A Joe Demarco Thriller.** unabr. ed. Mike Lawson. Read by Joe Barrett. (Running Time: 13 hrs. 0 mins.). 2010. 79.95 (978-1-4417-4795-2(8)); audio compact disk 109.00 (978-1-4417-4796-9(6)) Blckstn Audio.

House Lust: America's Obsession with Our Homes. unabr. ed. Daniel McGinn. Read by David Drummond. (Running Time: 9 hrs. 30 mins. 0 sec.). (ENG.). 2008. audio compact disk 34.99 (978-1-4001-0582-3(X)); audio compact disk 69.99 (978-1-4001-3582-0(6)); audio compact disk 24.99 (978-1-4001-5582-8(7)) Pub: Tantor Media. Dist(s): IngramPubServ

House Made of Dawn. N. Scott Momaday. Read by N. Scott Momaday. 1 cass. (Running Time: 39 min.). Incl. Names. 1983. (3091); 1983. 13.95 (978-1-55644-077-9(4), 3091) Am Audio Prose.
Momaday reads excerpts from his stories including "The Names" & work in progress.

House Made of Dawn. unabr. ed. N. Scott Momaday. Read by Scott Forbes. 7 cass. (Running Time: 7 hrs.). 1976. 42.00 (978-0-7366-0009-5(4), 1019) Books on Tape.
The story of Abel, a young American Indian living with his grandfather in the Pueblo of San Ysidro. The novel spans the 7 years from 1945 to 1952 during which Abel is an unassimilated Indian unable either to adapt to the white world or the find himself among the vestiges of his dying culture.

House Made of Dawn. unabr. ed. N. Scott Momaday. Narrated by George Guidall. 5 cass. (Running Time: 7 hrs.). 1999. 44.00 (978-0-7887-0849-7(X), 94995E7) Recorded Bks.
Carries you to the mysterious heart of the Southwest & to the soul of its ancient native people, weaving the story of a young mixed-blood torn between his tribal heritage & the poisonous enticements of the white world.

House Next Door. unabr. ed. Anne Rivers Siddons. Narrated by Barbara Rosenblat. 8 cass. (Running Time: 11 hrs.). 1996. 70.00 (978-0-7887-0472-7(9), 94665E7) Recorded Bks.
When a new house is built in a peaceful Southern neighborhood, terrifying things begin to happen. One woman summons the courage to stop its evil power.

House of a Thousand Lanterns. unabr. ed. Victoria Holt. Read by Eva Haddon. 10 cass. (Running Time: 15 hrs.). 2000. 69.95 (978-0-7451-6559-2(1), CAB 1175) Pub: Chivers Audio Bks GBR. Dist(s): AudioGO
Jane Lindsey was fascinated by the mere idea of the house, but it was a world away, in the oriental port of Kowloon, and she knew she'd never see it. Quite unbelievably her dream came true, altering her life forever. However, now the wife of a wealthy art dealer, Jane's life is shattered by a menacing secret.

House of a Thousand Lanterns. unabr. collector's ed. Victoria Holt. Read by Donada Peters. 8 cass. (Running Time: 12 hrs.). 1994. 64.00 (978-0-7366-2734-4(0), 102622) Books on Tape.
Jane Lindsay never imagined that she would be wealthy. Nor that she would fall in love with a man she couldn't trust. She is a young Englishwoman who finds a strange new world in the house that is both the one she dreamed of since childhood & the one where her worst nightmares are about to come true.

House of Abraham: Lincoln & the Todds, a Family Divided by War. unabr. ed. Stephen Berry. Read by Michael Prichard. (YA). 2008. 59.99 (978-1-60514-889-2(X)) Find a World.

House of Abraham: Lincoln & the Todds, a Family Divided by War. unabr. ed. Stephen Berry. Narrated by Michael Prichard. (Running Time: 10 hrs. 30 mins. 0 sec.). (ENG.). 2007. audio compact disk 24.99 (978-1-4001-5572-9(X)) Pub: Tantor Media. Dist(s): IngramPubServ

House of Abraham: Lincoln & the Todds, a Family Divided by War. unabr. ed. Stephen Berry. Read by Michael Prichard. (Running Time: 10 hrs. 30 mins. 0 sec.). (ENG.). 2007. audio compact disk 34.99 (978-1-4001-0572-4(2)); audio compact disk 69.99 (978-1-4001-3572-1(9)) Pub: Tantor Media. Dist(s): IngramPubServ

House of Arden. unabr. ed. E. Nesbit. Read by Flo Gibson. 5 cass. (Running Time: 6 hrs. 30 min.). (J). (gr. 1-3). 1998. 20.95 (978-1-55685-593-1(1)) Audio Bk Con.
A magical mole takes Edred & Elfrida through Tudor, Stuart & Napoleonic days in search of a treasure to save their castle.

House of Atreus & the Great Chain of Evil. unabr. ed. Narrated by Ralph Bates. 1 cass. (Running Time: 1 hr. 35 mins.). (Sound Seminars Lectures on the Classics). 1970. 14.95 (C23112) J Norton Pubs.
Aeschylus sees the House of Atreus story as the justification for law, which he declares to be divine. He peers deeper still, for this myth, one of the oldest of all, expresses the realities of man's being.

House of Barrymore. unabr. ed. Margot Peters. Read by Nadia May. (Running Time: 24 hrs. 30 mins.). 2010. 44.95 (978-1-4417-0974-5(6)); audio compact disk 140.00 (978-1-4417-0971-4(1)) Blckstn Audio.

House of Barrymore, Pt. 1. unabr. ed. Margot Peters. Read by Nadia May. 9 cass. (Running Time: 26 hrs.). 1999. 62.95 (978-0-7861-1649-2(8), 2477A, B) Blckstn Audio.
We see both the price & the privileges of their extraordinary fame. And, with the death of Ethel, the last of the three, we see the decline of the tradition that for some hundred years had sustained the Barrymores as America's first family of acting.

House of Barrymore, Pt. 2. unabr. ed. Margot Peters. Read by Nadia May. 9 cass. (Running Time: 26 hrs.). 1999. 62.95 (978-0-7861-1707-9(9), 2477A, B) Blckstn Audio.
Begins in the 1860s with Louise, Mrs. John Drew, the greatest comedienne of her time, mother of the brilliant Georgiana Drew Barrymore & mother-in-law of the vaudeville star & matinee idol Maurice Barrymore. Traces the intertwined lives, on & offstage, of the Barrymore triumvirate through the first half of this century.

House of Blue Leaves. unabr. ed. John Guare. Perf. by Ron Leibman & Sharon Gless. 2 CDs. (Running Time: 1 hrs. 32 mins.). 2008. audio compact disk 25.95 (978-1-58081-382-2(8)) L A Theatre.

House of Blue Leaves. unabr. ed. John Guare. Perf. by Sharon Gless et al. 1 cass. (Running Time: 1 hr. 34 mins.). 1996. 20.95 (978-1-58081-062-3(4), WTA4) L A Theatre.
This witty, poignant comedy unfolds in New York City on the day the Pope is expected to visit. Hearts are palpitating in the quiet borough of Queens, but not entirely on account of His Holiness. Bunny Flingus, a femme fatale from Flushing (or there abouts) is stirring things up in the quiet, unfulfilled life of aspiring songwriter, Artie Shaughnessy. Artie longs to leave his unhappy marriage, elope with Bunny & write a hit that will top the charts.

House of Blue Mangoes: A Novel. unabr. ed. David Davidar. Read by Robert Whitfield. 12 cass. (Running Time: 17 hrs. 30 mins.). 2002. 83.95 (978-0-7861-2190-8(4), 2937); audio compact disk 120.00 (978-0-7861-9528-2(2), 2937) Blckstn Audio.
A gripping family chronicle that spans nearly a half century and three generations of the Dorai family as they search for their place in rapidly changing society. Whether recruited into the burgeoning independence movement, apprenticed in ancient medical arts, or managing a British tea plantation, the Dorai men nevertheless find themselves drawn back to their ancestral land by profound emotional ties that transcend even the most powerful forces of history.

House of Bones. Short Stories. Robert A. Silverberg. Read by Jared Doreck. 1 CD. (Running Time: 1 hr). (Great Science Fiction Stories Ser.). 2005. audio compact disk 10.99 (978-1-884612-43-5(1)) AudioText.

House of Bush, House of Saud: The Secret Relationship Between the World's Two Most Powerful Dynasties. Craig Unger. Read by James Naughton. 2004. 15.95 (978-0-7435-3934-0(6)) Pub: S&S Audio. Dist(s): S and S Inc

House of Cards: A Tale of Hubris & Wretched Excess on Wall Street. unabr. ed. William D. Cohan. Narrated by Alan Sklar. 20 CDs. (Running Time: 25 hrs. 0 mins. 0 sec.). (ENG.). 2009. audio compact disk 99.99 (978-1-4001-4168-5(0)); audio compact disk 34.99 (978-1-4001-6168-3(1)) Pub: Tantor Media. Dist(s): IngramPubServ

House of Cards: A Tale of Hubris & Wretched Excess on Wall Street. unabr. ed. William D. Cohan. Read by Alan Sklar. Narrated by Alan Sklar. 20 CDs. (Running Time: 25 hrs. 0 mins. 0 sec.). (ENG.). 2009. audio compact disk 49.99 (978-1-4001-1168-8(4)) Pub: Tantor Media. Dist(s): IngramPubServ

***House of Cards: Promotional: A Tale of Hubris & Wretched Excess on Wall Street.** unabr. ed. William D. Cohan. Narrated by Alan Sklar. (Running Time: 25 hrs. 0 mins. 0 sec.). (ENG.). 2010. audio compact disk 14.95 (978-1-4001-2024-6(1)) Pub: Tantor Media. Dist(s): IngramPubServ

House of Correction: A Jack Flippo Mystery. unabr. ed. Doug Swanson. Narrated by Ron McLarty. 5 cass. (Running Time: 6 hrs. 15 mins.). 2002. 32.95 (978-1-4025-0961-2(8), RF688) Recorded Bks.
takes his hero Jack Flippo into the comically deceitful Texas underworld. Wesley Joy has a problem: he's been framed for drug running and murder. So, he calls on his old friend and pupil, Jack Flippo, to help him find the one person that can clear his name, Wesley's wife, the lovely Angelique. Wesley confides to Jack that she's hiding $200,000 but he's lost contact with her. Jack soon finds himself wrapped up in a confusing web of lies, where no one can be trusted. Armed with his wit and charm, he knows he won't be the one left holding the short end of the stick.

House of Corrections: A Jack Flippo Mystery. Doug Swanson. Narrated by Ron McLarty. 5 cass. (Running Time: 6 hrs. 15 mins.). 46.00 (978-1-4025-0960-5(X)); audio compact disk 58.00 (978-1-4025-3492-8(2)) Recorded Bks.

***House of Dark Shadows.** unabr. ed. Robert Liparulo. Read by Joshua Swanson. (Running Time: 9.5 hrs. NaN mins.). (Dreamhouse Kings Ser.). (ENG.). 2010. 29.95 (978-1-4417-7724-9(5)); 59.95 (978-1-4417-7721-8(0)); audio compact disk 90.00 (978-1-4417-7722-5(9)) Blckstn Audio.

***House of DBT.** 2010. 9.95 (978-1-933464-12-1(7)) Behavioral Tech.

House of Death: A Mystery of Alexander the Great. Paul C. Doherty. Read by Terry Wale. 10 cass. (Soundings Ser.). (J). 2005. 84.95 (978-1-84559-194-6(1)) Pub: ISIS Lrg Prnt GBR. Dist(s): Ulverscroft US

House of Dies Drear, unabr. ed. Virginia Hamilton. Narrated by Lynne Thigpen. 5 pieces. (Running Time: 7 hrs.). (gr. 6 up). 1995. 44.00 (978-0-7887-0329-4(3), 94521E7) Recorded Bks.
A family moves into a supposedly haunted house. The house was a station on the Underground Railroad, & local legend had it that the ghosts of its former owner, abolitionist Dies Drear & two slaves, all of whom were murdered in the house, still inhabit it. A valuable & serious history lesson is woven into a spooky mystery.

House of Dreams. unabr. ed. Brenda Joyce. Read by Laural Merlington. 9 cass. (Running Time: 14 hrs.). 2000. 37.95 (978-1-58788-057-5(1), 1587880571, BAU) Brilliance Audio.
In House of Dreams, two aristocratic families, one English, one Spanish, have been tragically destined to come together time and again over the centuries. Cassandra de Warenne spends her days in a quiet English manor, looking after her young neice, while her sister Tracey lives the glamorous life of a jet-setter. When Cass meets Tracey's newest conquest, Antonio de la Barca, she isn't prepared for the intense and immediate attraction - an attraction that heralds something deeper, more powerful, and more dangerous than Cass could ever imagine. For the de Warennes and the de la Barcas have a tangled history of horrendous heartbreak, bitter rivalry, and bloodshed that began 450 years ago, with one woman, Isabel, forsaken and betrayed by her family, her lover, and her friends. Today Isabel has summoned the two families together one final time - this time to complete a quest for vengeance from beyond the grave.

House of Dreams. unabr. ed. Brenda Joyce. Read by Laural Merlington. (Running Time: 14 hrs.). 2005. 39.25 (978-1-59600-680-5(3), 9781596006805, Brinc Audio MP3 Lib); 39.25 (978-1-59600-682-9(X), 9781596006829, BADLE); 24.95 (978-1-59600-681-2(1), 9781596006812, BAD); 24.95 (978-1-59600-679-9(X), 9781596006799, Brilliance MP3) Brilliance Audio.

House of Echoes. unabr. ed. Barbara Erskine. Narrated by Juanita McMahon. 13 cass. (Running Time: 18 hrs. 30 mins.). 1999. 108.00 (978-1-84197-010-3(7), H1010E7) Recorded Bks.
Joss Grant, adopted as a baby, decides to trace her natural parents & as a result discovers a letter from her mother leaving her the ancestral Belhaddon Hall. Moving into the house with her husband & young son. Joss soon discovers that Belhaddon Hall has been haunted for centuries by a malevolent spirit. Unable to convince her husband of the dangers they face, Joss must fight alone to solve the centuries old curse of the house & save her family & herself.

House of Echoes, Set. unabr. ed. Barbara Erskine. Narrated by Juanita McMahon. 13 cass. 1999. 108.00 (H1010K4, Clipper Audio) Recorded Bks.

House of Eliott. unabr. ed. Jean Marsh. Read by Stella Gonet. 8 cass. (Running Time: 8 hrs.). 1995. 69.95 Set. (978-0-7451-4364-4(4), CAB 1047) AudioGO.
The Eliott sisters' business would soon be much more than a genteel dress-making service during the 1920's & 1930's. Beatrice, the elder sister, considers herself plain & unmarriageable. Raffish society photographer, Jack Maddox, does not, but their relationship is seared with conflict. Evangeline, her younger sister, is the victim of rogues, philanderers, & her own desires. Regardless of their private turmoil, they strive to establish a fashion house in London that will rival any in Paris.

House of Fear, Set. Wadsworth Camp. Read by Flo Gibson. 5 cass. (Running Time: 7 hrs. 30 min.). 1996. 20.95 (978-1-55685-419-4(6)) Audio Bk Con.
Who or what evil spirits are causing terror & murder at Woodford's Theater? The cast of a revival is put in mortal fear.

House of God: Promised Blessings of the Temple, Talk on CD. Read by Truman G. Madsen. 2007. audio compact disk 13.95 (978-1-59038-732-0(5)) Desert Bks.

House of God: The Classic Novel of Life & Death in an American Hospital. unabr. collector's ed. Samuel Shem. Read by Bob Erickson. 9 cass. (Running Time: 13 hrs. 30 min.). 1983. 72.00 (978-0-7366-0633-2(5), 1594) Books on Tape.
Follows the internship of Roy Basch at the famous teaching hospital - "the House of God".

House of Green Turf. unabr. ed. Ellis Peters, pseud. Narrated by Simon Prebble. 5 cass. (Running Time: 7 hrs. 15 mins.). (Inspector George Felse Mystery Ser.: Vol. 8). 1993. 44.00 (978-1-55690-922-1(5), 93418E7) Recorded Bks.
Despite all evidence, world-class singer Maggie Tressider is convinced that she has killed someone. Her doctor suggests a psychiatrist, but Maggie hires a private investigator named Francis Killian to exorcise the demons that haunt her. But as Killian follows the paths that comprise Maggie's past, he begins to suspect the singer's fears are justified.

House of Hardie, Set. unabr. ed. Anne Melville. 8 cass. (Storysound Ser.). (J). 1996. 79.95 (978-1-85903-127-8(7)) Pub: Mgna Lrg Print GBR. Dist(s): Ulverscroft US

House of Horror. 1 CD. (Running Time: 30 min.). (Halloween Party Ser.). (J). (gr. k-5). 2001. pap. bk. 5.98 (9683-2) Peter Pan.
Spooky songs, sounds and stories with holiday spirit. Includes Halloween Party Tip Guide.

House of Israel: The Return. Robert Marcum. 9 cass. 2004. 29.95 (978-1-59156-068-5(3)); audio compact disk 29.95 (978-1-59156-069-2(1)) Covenant Comms.

House of Israel Vol. 2: A Land Divided. Robert Marcum. 10 cass. 2004. 29.95 (978-1-59156-308-2(9)) Covenant Comms.

House of Light. Joyce Carol Thomas. Narrated by Patricia R. Floyd. 6 cass. (Running Time: 8 hrs. 15 mins.). 59.00 (978-0-7887-8974-8(0)) Recorded Bks.

House of Love: Digitally Remastered. Contrib. by Amy Grant. Prod. by Keith Thomas & Michael Omartian. 2007. audio compact disk 13.99 (978-5-557-60487-1(1)) Pt of Grace Ent.

House of Lyall. unabr. ed. Doris Davidson. Read by Lesley Mackie. 14 cass. (Running Time: 21 hrs.). 2001. 99.95 (978-1-86042-747-3(2), 2-747-2) Pub: Soundings Ltd GBR. Dist(s): Ulverscroft US
Young Marion Cheyne comes from a humble background but her heart is full of ambition. Stealing a plate of gold sovereigns from her employer, she sets off for Aberdeen & changes her name to Marianne. Fortune smiles & a dream she thought impossible is fulfilled when she marries the heir of Castle Lyall. Marianne understands it is a business arrangement & life as lady of the glen suits her. Through the trials & triumphs of two world wars, Marianne will stop at nothing to guard her hard-won position. But there are many secrets in her past that refuse to stay safely buried. Nothing in the small community of the glen can remain hidden forever.

***House of Many Ways.** collector's unabr. ed. Diana Wynne Jones. Narrated by Jenny Sterlin. 7 CDs. (Running Time: 8 hrs.). (YA). (gr. 5-10). 2009. audio compact disk 41.95 (978-1-4361-6133-6(9)) Recorded Bks.

***House of Many Ways.** unabr. ed. Diana Wynne Jones. Narrated by Jenny Sterlin. 1 Playaway. (Running Time: 8 hrs.). (YA). (gr. 5-10). 2009. 56.75 (978-1-4407-0391-1(4)); 56.75 (978-1-4361-6124-4(X)); audio compact disk 77.75 (978-1-4361-6129-9(0)) Recorded Bks.

House of Meetings. unabr. ed. Martin Amis. 6 CDs. (Running Time: 6 hrs. 30 mins.). 2007. audio compact disk 64.95 (978-0-7927-4734-5(8), Chivers Sound Lib) AudioGO.
There were conjugal visits in the slave camps of the USSR. Valiant women would travel continental distances, over weeks and months, in the hope of spending a night, with their particular enemy of the people, in the House of Meetings. The consequences of these liaisons were almost invariably tragic. House of Meetings is about one such liaison. It is a triangular romance: two brothers fall in love with the same girl, a nineteen-year-old Jewess, in Moscow, which is poised for massacre in the gap between the war and the death of Stalin. Both brothers are arrested, and their rivalry slowly complicates itself over a decade in the slave camp above the Arctic Circle.

House of Mirrors. unabr. ed. Pierdomenico Baccalario. Read by Michael Page. (Running Time: 5 hrs.). (Ulysses Moore Ser.: Bk. 3). 2007. 39.25 (978-1-4233-1339-7(9), 9781423313397, BADLE); 24.95 (978-1-4233-1338-0(0), 9781423313380, BAD) Brilliance Audio.

House of Mirrors. unabr. ed. Pierdomenico Baccalario. Read by Michael Page. 4 cass. (Running Time: 18000 sec.). (Ulysses Moore Ser.: Bk. 3). (J). (gr. 4-7). 2007. 62.25 (978-1-4233-1333-5(X), 9781423313335, BrilAudUnabridg); audio compact disk 69.25 (978-1-4233-1335-9(6), 9781423313359, BriAudCD Unabrid); audio compact disk 39.25 (978-1-4233-1337-3(2), 9781423313373, Brinc Audio MP3 Lib); audio compact disk 24.95 (978-1-4233-1334-2(8), 9781423313342, Bril Audio CD Unabri) Brilliance Audio.

House of Mirrors. unabr. ed. Pierdomenico Baccalario & Michael Page. 1 MP3-CD. (Running Time: 18000 sec.). (Ulysses Moore Ser.: Bk. 3). (J). (gr. 4-7). 2007. audio compact disk 24.95 (978-1-4233-1336-6(4), 9781423313366, Brilliance MP3) Brilliance Audio.

House of Mirth. Edith Wharton. Read by Amy von Lecteur. 2009. 27.95 (978-1-60112-996-3(3)) Babblebooks.

House of Mirth. Edith Wharton. Narrated by Anna Fields. (Running Time: 14 hrs. 30 mins.). 2000. 41.95 (978-1-59912-672-2(9)) Iofy Corp.

House of Mirth. Edith Wharton. Narrated by Joanna Cassidy. (Running Time: 2 hrs. 30 mins.). 2006. 14.95 (978-1-59912-982-2(5)) Iofy Corp.

House of Mirth. abr. ed. (ENG.). 2006. 5.98 (978-1-59483-866-8(6)) Pub: Hachet Audio. Dist(s): HachBkGrp

House of Mirth. unabr. ed. Edith Wharton. Read by Eleanor Bron. 8 cass. (Running Time: 12 hrs.). (gr. 9-12). 1999. 34.95 (978-1-57270-119-9(6), F81119u) Pub: Audio Partners. Dist(s): PerseuPGW
High society in turn-of-the-century New York. Lily Bart, bright & 29 years old, moves in the glittering social circle. There, amongst the glib diversions of the nouveau riche, she seeks a husband who can both maintain & further her fairy-tale existence while providing unceasing admiration. Her world is shattered when Lily is accused of being the mistress of a wealthy married man.

House of Mirth. unabr. ed. Edith Wharton. Read by Anna Fields. 10 cass. (Running Time: 14 hrs. 30 mins.). 2001. 69.95 (978-0-7861-1961-5(6), 2732); audio compact disk 96.00 (978-0-7861-9762-0(5), 2732) Blckstn Audio.
Set among the elegant brownstones of New York City & opulent country houses like gracious Bellomont on the Hudson, it creates a satiric portrayal of "a society of irresponsible pleasure-seekers" with a precision comparable to that of Proust. The brilliant & complex characterization of the doomed Lily Bart, whose stunning beauty & dependence on marriage for economic survival reduce her to a decorative object, becomes an incisive commentary on the nature & status of women in that society.

House of Mirth, unabr. ed. Edith Wharton. Narrated by Barbara Caruso. 10 cass. (Running Time: 13 hrs. 30 mins.). 1989. 85.00 (978-1-55690-238-3(7), 89399E7) Recorded Bks.
Turn-of-the-century New York & a young woman of delicate tastes & moral sensibility is helplessly pitted against vulgarity & greed.

House of Mirth. unabr. ed. Edith Wharton. Narrated by Wanda McCaddon. (Running Time: 12 hrs. 30 mins. 0 sec.). (ENG.). 2008. audio compact disk 72.99 (978-1-4001-4035-0(8)); audio compact disk 27.99 (978-1-4001-6035-8(9)); audio compact disk 35.99 (978-1-4001-1035-3(1)) Pub: Tantor Media. Dist(s): IngramPubServ

House of Mirth. unabr. ed. Edith Wharton. Read by Anna Fields. (YA). 2008. 74.99 (978-1-60514-727-7(3)) Find a World.

House of Mirth. unabr. collector's ed. Edith Wharton. Read by Penelope Dellaporta. 10 cass. (Running Time: 15 hrs.). 1985. 80.00 (978-0-7366-0408-6(1), 1384) Books on Tape.
Stands as the work that established Wharton's literary reputation. In it she discovered her major subject: the fashionable New York society in which she had been raised.

House of Mirth, Set. unabr. ed. Edith Wharton. Narrated by Flo Gibson. 9 cass. (Running Time: 13 hrs. 30 min.). 1985. 28.95 (978-1-55685-009-7(3)) Audio Bk Con.
The haunting tale of Lily Bart, arrogant, brilliant & beautiful, who was envied & sought after by society until she broke one of its rules & started her decline.

House of Mondavi: The Rise & Fall of an American Wine Dynasty. unabr. ed. Julia Flynn Siler. Narrated by Alan Sklar. (Running Time: 17 hrs. 30 mins. 0 sec.). (ENG.). 2007. audio compact disk 79.99 (978-1-4001-3480-9(3)); audio compact disk 29.99 (978-1-4001-5480-7(4)) Pub: Tantor Media. Dist(s): IngramPubServ

House of Mondavi: The Rise & Fall of an American Wine Dynasty. unabr. ed. Julia Flynn Siler. Read by Alan Sklar. (Running Time: 17 hrs. 30 mins. 0 sec.). (ENG.). 2007. audio compact disk 39.99 (978-1-4001-0480-2(7)) Pub: Tantor Media. Dist(s): IngramPubServ

House of Morgan: An American Banking Dynasty & the Rise of Modern Finance, Pt. 1. collector's ed. Ron Chernow. Read by Jonathan Reese. 12 cass. (Running Time: 18 hrs.). 1991. 96.00 (978-0-7366-1890-8(2), 2718-A) Books on Tape.
This may be the most ambitious history ever written about an American banking dynasty. It is a rich, panoramic story of four generations of Morgans, of the firms they built, of their private alliances & public feuds & of a presence that continues to this day.

House of Morgan: An American Banking Dynasty & the Rise of Modern Finance, Pt. 2. unabr. collector's ed. Ron Chernow. Read by Jonathan Reese. 11 cass. (Running Time: 16 hrs. 30 min.). 1991. 88.00 (978-0-7366-1891-5(0), 2718-B) Books on Tape.

House of Mystery & Murder at Midnight: A Gift from the Dead & The Island of the Dead. unabr. ed. Perf. by John Griggs. 1 cass. (Running Time: 60 min.). Dramatization. 1947. 7.95 Norelco box. (MM-5800) Natl Recrd Co.
A Gift from the Dead: Roger Elliott, the Mystery Man, is summoned to investigate mysterious happenings in a Gothic Manor, involving a musical jewel box & a widow who receives rare gems from a ghostly benefactor. Sponsored by Post Corn Toasties. The Island of the Dead: A man sent to prison for a crime he did not commit, returns to seek revenge against those who put him there...after he has been sent to an island cemetery for burial.

House of Power. unabr. ed. Patrick Carman. Read by Jonathan Davis. (Running Time: 8 hrs.). (Atherton Ser.: No. 1). (ENG.). 2007. 9.98 (978-1-59483-967-2(0)) Pub: Hachet Audio. Dist(s): HachBkGrp

House of Prayer. Francis Frangipane. 1 cass. (Running Time: 90 mins.). (Strategies for our Cities Ser.: Vol. 5). 2000. 5.00 (FF06-005) Morning NC.
This series provides practical, biblical solutions that have been tested & have born fruit for those with a vision for their cities.

***House of Reckoning.** John Saul. Contrib. by Angela Dawe. (Playaway Adult Fiction Ser.). (ENG.). 2009. 69.99 (978-1-4418-2933-7(4)) Find a World.

House of Reckoning. unabr. ed. John Saul. Read by Angela Dawe. 1 MP3-CD. (Running Time: 11 hrs.). 2009. 39.97 (978-1-4418-0560-7(5), 9781441805607, Brinc Audio MP3 Lib); 24.99 (978-1-4418-0559-1(1), 9781441805591, Brilliance MP3); 24.99 (978-1-4418-0561-4(3), 9781441805614, BAD); 39.97 (978-1-4418-0562-1(1), 9781441805621, BADLE); audio compact disk 36.99 (978-1-4418-0557-7(5), 9781441805577, Bril Audio CD Unabri); audio compact disk 97.97 (978-1-4418-0558-4(3), 9781441805584, BriAudCD Unabrid) Brilliance Audio.

***House of Sand & Fog.** unabr. ed. Andre Dubus, III. Read by Andre Dubus, III. 2003. (978-0-06-073561-6(9), Harper Audio) HarperCollins Pubs.

***House of Sand & Fog.** unabr. ed. Andre Dubus, III. Read by Andre Dubus, III. (ENG.). 2003. (978-0-06-079949-6(8), Harper Audio) HarperCollins Pubs.

House of Sand & Fog. unabr. ed. Andre Dubus, III. Narrated by Andre Dubus, III. Narrated by Fontaine Dollas Dubus. 10 cass. (Running Time: 14 hrs.). 1999. 88.00 (978-0-7887-5989-5(2), 96665K8) Recorded Bks.
A once wealthy Iranian immigrant struggles for dignity in America. A troubled young woman strives to hold onto the lone remaining piece of her family's past. A sheriff is pulled by equally compelling obsessions of love & justice. The lives of these three very different people tragically converge around a small house in California.

House of Sand & Fog. unabr. abr. ed. Andre Dubus, III. Read by Andre Dubus, III. Read by Fontaine Dollas Dubus. 10 cass. (Running Time: 15 hrs.). 2001. 39.95 (978-0-694-52579-9(0)) HarperCollins Pubs.

House of Scorta. unabr. ed. Laurent Gaudé. Read by Daniel Oreskes & Barbara Caruso. Tr. by Stephen Sartarelli & Sophie Hawkes. (YA). 2007. 39.99 (978-1-60252-756-0(3)) Find a World.

House of Scorta. unabr. ed. Laurent Gaudé. Read by Barbara Caruso & Daniel Oreskes. Tr. by Stephen Sartarelli & Sophie Hawkes. 5 CDs. (Running Time: 6 hrs.). (ENG.). 2006. audio compact disk 26.95 (978-1-59887-014-5(9), 1598870149) Pub: Penguin-HghBrdg. Dist(s): Penguin Grp USA

House of Seven Gables. unabr. ed. Nathaniel Hawthorne. Read by Anthony Heald. (Running Time: 39600 sec.). 2008. 85.95 (978-1-4332-1194-2(7)); audio compact disk & audio compact disk 29.95 (978-1-4332-1198-0(X)); audio compact disk & audio compact disk 99.00 (978-1-4332-1195-9(5)) Blckstn Audio.

House of Stairs. unabr. ed. Barbara Vine, pseud. Read by Jane Asher. 8 cass. (Running Time: 10 hrs.). 1990. 69.95 set. (978-0-7451-6341-3(6), CAB 506) AudioGO.
It is the late 1960s, & Cosette has bought a rambling, run-down house in London. She invites her niece to visit, & when Elizabeth arrives she has a motley group of friends in tow. Most of them seem harmless enough, but there's something different about Bell.

House of Suns. unabr. ed. Alastair Reynolds. (Running Time: 18 hrs. 0 mins. 0 sec.). (ENG.). 2009. 34.99 (978-1-4001-5962-8(8)); audio compact disk 99.99 (978-1-4001-3962-0(7)); audio compact disk 49.99 (978-1-4001-0962-3(0)) Pub: Tantor Media. Dist(s): IngramPubServ

House of Tailors. Patricia Reilly Giff. Read by Blair Brown. 2 cass. (J). 2004. 23.00 (978-1-4000-9054-9(7), Listening Lib); audio compact disk 30.00 (978-1-4000-9491-2(7), Listening Lib) Random Audio Pubg.

House of the Dead. unabr. ed. Fyodor Dostoyevsky. Read by Walter Covell. 10 cass. (Running Time: 14 hrs. 30 mins.). 1987. 69.95 (978-0-7861-0606-6(9), 2096) Blckstn Audio.
The story is written in the form of a fictionalized memoir of a man serving a ten year prison sentence for murdering his wife.

House of the Dead. unabr. ed. Fyodor Dostoyevsky. Read by Walter Covell. 10 cass. (Running Time: 15 hrs.). 1986. 58.00 (C-162) Jimcin Record.
Prison life in Siberia.

House of the Dead. unabr. collector's ed. Fyodor Dostoyevsky. Read by Walter Covell. 10 cass. (Running Time: 15 hrs.). 1986. 80.00 (978-0-7366-3919-4(5), 9158) Books on Tape.
In 1849, at the age of 28, Dostoevsky was sentenced to four years at hard labor in Siberia. Among thieves & murderers, like Russians before him & since, he survived stupefying & mindless degradation. "The House of the Dead," presented in fictional form as the memoirs of a man condemned to ten years of penal servitude for murdering his wife, is in essence the account of this period of Dostoevsky's life.

House of the Mind. 1 cass. (Running Time: 45 mins.). 1980. 7.95 (978-1-58638-552-1(6)) Nilgiri Pr.
"One of Easwaran's classics, this funny and wise talk compares the mind to the interior of a Victorian house in complete disarray, with accumulated possessions and unruly tenants in every room. Gradually we make our way to the attic, where the real owner, the Self, resides.".

House of the Red Fish. unabr. ed. Graham Salisbury. Read by Jeff Woodman. 6 cass. (Running Time: 6 hrs. 39 mins.). (YA). (gr. 7 up). 2006. 59.75 (978-1-4281-2238-3(9)) Recorded Bks.
Continuing the story begun in Under the Blood-Red Sun, House of the Red Fish returns to Honolulu one year after the Japanese attack on Pearl Harbor. Thirteen-year-old Japanese American Tomi Nakaji must struggle to support his family after the arrest of his father and grandfather.

House of the Scorpion. Nancy Farmer. (J). audio compact disk 111.75 (978-1-4025-4556-6(8)) Recorded Bks.

House of the Scorpion. Nancy Farmer. 7 cass. (Running Time: 12 hrs. 30 mins.). (J). 2004. 29.99 (978-1-4025-4173-5(2), 70074) Recorded Bks.

House of the Scorpion. unabr. ed. Nancy Farmer. Narrated by Robert Ramirez. 9 pieces. (Running Time: 12 hrs. 30 mins.). (J). 2002. 80.75 (978-1-4025-3128-6(1)) Recorded Bks.

House of the Scorpion. unabr. ed. Nancy Farmer. Read by Raul Esparza. 9 CDs. (Running Time: 10 hrs. 0 mins. 0 sec.). (ENG.). (J). 2008. audio compact disk 39.99 (978-0-7435-7246-0(7)) Pub: S&S Audio. Dist(s): S and S Inc

***House of the Seven Gables.** Nathaniel Hawthorne. Narrated by Flo Gibson. 2010. audio compact disk 31.95 (978-1-60646-171-6(0)) Audio Bk Con.

House of the Seven Gables. Nathaniel Hawthorne. Read by Peter Marinker. (Running Time: 4 hrs.). 2000. 24.95 (978-1-60083-775-3(1)) Iofy Corp.

House of the Seven Gables. Nathaniel Hawthorne. Narrated by Donna Barkman. (Running Time: 12 hrs.). 2006. 56.95 (978-1-59912-143-7(3)) Iofy Corp.

House of the Seven Gables. Nathaniel Hawthorne. Read by Peter Marinker. (Running Time: 14240 sec.). 2006. audio compact disk 22.98 (978-962-634-381-4(8), Naxos AudioBooks) Naxos.

House of the Seven Gables. Nathaniel Hawthorne. Read by Donada Peters. (Running Time: 39600 sec.). (Unabridged Classics in Audio Ser.). (ENG.). 2006. audio compact disk 34.99 (978-1-4001-0206-8(5)); audio compact disk 24.99 (978-1-4001-5206-3(2)); audio compact disk 69.99 (978-1-4001-3206-5(1)) Pub: Tantor Media. Dist(s): IngramPubServ

House of the Seven Gables. abr. ed. Nathaniel Hawthorne. Read by Joan Allen. 4 cass. (Running Time: 6 hrs.). 2004. 25.00 (978-1-59007-119-9(0)) Pub: New Millenn Enter. Dist(s): PerseuPGW
a vivid depiction of American life and values, replete with brilliantly etched characters. The tale of a cursed house with a "mysterious and terrible past" and the generations linked to it, Hawthorne's chronicle of the Maule and Pyncheon families over two centuries reveals, in Mary Oliver's words, "lives caught in the common fire of history.

House of the Seven Gables. collector's ed. Nathaniel Hawthorne. Read by Donada Peters. 8 cass. (Running Time: 12 hrs.). 1993. 64.00 (978-0-7366-2530-2(5), 3282) Books on Tape.
An old New England family lives in a household that is for generations corrupted by a curse until it is removed at last by love.

House of the Seven Gables. unabr. ed. Nathaniel Hawthorne. Read by Anthony Heald. (Running Time: 43200 sec.). (Classic Collection (Blackstone Audio) Ser.). 2008. 19.95 (978-1-4332-1196-6(3)); audio compact disk 19.95 (978-1-4332-1197-3(1)) Blckstn Audio.

House of the Seven Gables. unabr. ed. Nathaniel Hawthorne. Read by Donna Barkman & Donada Peters. 8 cass. (Running Time: 12 hrs.). 1993. 64.00 (9110) Books on Tape.
An old mansion in Salem broods over the destiny of a New England family, the Pynchons: a haunting centuries-old curse, a forceful probing of national & personal guilt, a romance between the young heroine & an attractive stranger all intertwine.

House of the Seven Gables. unabr. ed. Nathaniel Hawthorne. Read by Buck Schirner. 8 cass. (Running Time: 11 hrs.). 2002. 29.95 (978-1-59086-299-5(6), 1590862996, BAU) Brilliance Audio.
When it was first erected, the House of Seven Gables typified the mechanical Colonel Pyncheon; but it developed through the years until, by Hepzibah's time, it has become humanized and almost organic. The history of the house is thus a record of continuity and change. Hawthorne's The House of the Seven Gables is a study of guilt and renewal from generation to generation. At the time of the Salem witch trials, the patriarch of the Pyncheons covets the property of a tradesman and manipulates public opinion so as to get Matthew Maule hanged for witchcraft and acquire the land. The dying man's curse on the Pyncheon family comes true generation upon generation and relationships between the families are colored forever by this "original sin." That is, until six generations later when the long-hidden truth is revealed. The House of the Seven Gables is Hawthorne's most humorous novel, it is also the work in which he is most serious in his devotion to the powers of beauty and imagination and his hatred of economic materialism and Philistinism.

House of the Seven Gables. unabr. ed. Nathaniel Hawthorne. Read by Buck Schirner. (Running Time: 11 hrs.). 2004. 39.25 (978-1-59335-370-4(7), 1593353707, Brinc Audio MP3 Lib) Brilliance Audio.

House of the Seven Gables. unabr. ed. Nathaniel Hawthorne. Read by Buck Schirner. (Running Time: 11 hrs.). 2004. 39.25 (978-1-59710-380-0(2), 1597103802, BADLE); 24.95 (978-1-59710-381-7(0), 1597103810, BAD) Brilliance Audio.

House of the Seven Gables. unabr. ed. Nathaniel Hawthorne. Read by Buck Schirner. 8 CDs. (Running Time: 39600 sec.). 2006. audio compact disk 97.25 (978-1-59737-134-6(3), 9781597371346, Unabridge Lib Edns); audio compact disk 38.95 (978-1-59737-133-9(5), 9781597371339, Bril Audio CD Unabri) Brilliance Audio.

House of the Seven Gables. unabr. ed. Nathaniel Hawthorne. Read by Donada Peters. (YA). 2007. 54.99 (978-1-60252-530-6(7)) Find a World.

House of the Seven Gables. unabr. ed. Nathaniel Hawthorne. Read by Donna Barkman. 8 cass. (Running Time: 12 hrs.). 1984. 56.00 (C-110) Jimcin Record.
Centuries-old curse casts a long shadow.

House of the Seven Gables. unabr. ed. Nathaniel Hawthorne. Narrated by Roslyn Alexander. 9 cass. (Running Time: 13 hrs.). 1993. 78.00 (978-1-55690-926-9(8), 93422E7) Recorded Bks.
A dark secret lurks in an old family mansion haunting each successive generation until it is finally brought to light.

House of the Seven Gables. unabr. ed. Nathaniel Hawthorne. Read by Buck Schirner. (Running Time: 11 hrs.). 2004. 24.95 (978-1-59335-093-2(7), 1593350937) Soulmate Audio Bks.
When it was first erected, the House of Seven Gables typified the mechanical Colonel Pyncheon; but it developed through the years until, by Hepzibah's time, it has become humanized and almost organic. The history of the house is thus a record of continuity and change. Hawthorne's The House of the Seven Gables is a study of guilt and renewal from generation to generation. At the time of the Salem witch trials, the patriarch of the Pyncheons covets the property of a tradesman and manipulates public opinion so as to get Matthew Maule hanged for witchcraft and acquire the land. The dying man's curse on the Pyncheon family comes true generation upon generation and relationships between the families are colored forever

by this "original sin." That is, until six generations later when the long-hidden truth is revealed. The House of the Seven Gables is Hawthorne's most humorous novel, it is also the work in which he is most serious in his devotion to the powers of beauty and imagination and his hatred of economic materialism and Philistinism.

House of the Seven Gables. unabr. ed. Nathaniel Hawthorne. Narrated by Donada Peters. (Running Time: 11 hrs. 0 mins. 0 sec.). (Tantor Unabridged Classics Ser.). (ENG.). 2009. 22.99 (978-1-4001-6079-2(0)); lab manual ed. 65.99 (978-1-4001-4079-4(X)); audio compact disk 32.99 (978-1-4001-1079-7(3)) Pub: Tantor Media. Dist(s): IngramPubServ

House of the Seven Gables, Set. unabr. ed. Nathaniel Hawthorne. Read by Flo Gibson. 7 cass. (Running Time: 10 hrs. 30 min.). 1989. 25.95 (978-1-55685-154-4(5)) Audio Bk Con.
The working out of a curse on the Pyncheon family of Salem, who have inhabited the house of the seven gables for generations is reviewed two centuries later by their descendants.

House of Thunder. Leigh Nichols, pseud. Read by Laural Merlington & Mel Foster. (Playaway Adult Fiction Ser.). (ENG.). 2009. 69.99 (978-1-60775-691-0(9)) Find a World.

House of Thunder. unabr. ed. Leigh Nichols, pseud. Read by Laural Merlington & Mel Foster. (Running Time: 10 hrs.). 2007. 39.25 (978-1-4233-3917-5(7), 9781423339175, BADLE); 24.95 (978-1-4233-3916-8(9), 9781423339168, BAD) Brilliance Audio.

House of Thunder. unabr. ed. Leigh Nichols, pseud. Read by Mel Foster & Laural Merlington. 7 cass. (Running Time: 36000 sec.). 2007. 82.25 (978-1-4233-3911-3(8), 9781423339113, BrilAudUnabridg); audio compact disk 97.25 (978-1-4233-3913-7(4), 9781423339137, BriAudCD Unabrid); audio compact disk 39.25 (978-1-4233-3915-1(0), 9781423339151, Brinc Audio MP3 Lib); audio compact disk 36.95 (978-1-4233-3912-0(6), 9781423339120, Bril Audio CD Unabri); audio compact disk 24.95 (978-1-4233-3914-4(2), 9781423339144, Brilliance MP3) Brilliance Audio.

***House of Tomorrow.** unabr. ed. Peter Bognanni. Narrated by Lloyd James. (Running Time: 10 hrs. 30 mins. 0 sec.). (ENG.). 2010. 24.99 (978-1-4001-6580-3(6)); 16.99 (978-1-4001-8580-1(7)); 34.99 (978-1-4001-9580-0(2)); audio compact disk 69.99 (978-1-4001-4580-5(5)); audio compact disk 34.99 (978-1-4001-1580-8(9)) Pub: Tantor Media. Dist(s): IngramPubServ

House of Wemyss: A Thousand Year History. Thomas Wemyss-Kessler. 2002. audio compact disk 12.00 (978-0-7884-2193-8(X)) Heritage Bk.

House of Whispering Shadows. Eugene Cunningham. (Running Time: 1 hr. 6 mins.). 1999. 10.95 (978-1-60083-486-8(8)) Iofy Corp.

***House of Whispering Shadows.** Eugene Cunningham. 2009. (978-1-60136-397-8(4)) Audio Holding.

House of Women. unabr. ed. Catherine Cookson. Read by Elizabeth Henry. 7 cass. (Running Time: 10 hrs. 30 mins.). (Sound Ser.). 2004. 61.95 (978-1-85496-610-0(3), 66103) Pub: UlverLrgPrint GBR. Dist(s): Ulverscroft US

House on Beartown Road. Elizabeth Cohen. Read by Bernadette Dunne. 6 cass. (Running Time: 8 hrs. 30 mins.). 2004. lib. bdg. 44.95 (978-0-7861-2627-9(2), 3235); audio compact disk 48.00 (978-0-7861-8785-0(9), 3235) Blckstn Audio.

House on Beartown Road. Elizabeth Cohen. Narrated by Bernadette Dunne. (Running Time: 7 hrs. 30 mins.). 2004. 27.95 (978-1-59912-673-9(7)) Iofy Corp.

House on Beartown Road. unabr. ed. Elizabeth Cohen. Read by Bernadette Dunne. 1 CD. (Running Time: 8 hrs. 30 mins.). 2004. lib. bdg. 24.95 (978-0-7861-8702-7(6), 3235) Blckstn Audio.
Elizabeth, a member of the ¿sandwich generation,¿ people caught in the middle of simultaneously caring for their children and for their aging parents, is the mother of Ava and the daughter of Daddy and responsible for both. Hers is the story of a woman¿s struggle to keep her family whole, to raise her child in a house of laughter and love, and to keep her father from hiding the house keys in his slip.

House on Beartown Road: A Memoir of Learning & Forgetting. unabr. ed. Elizabeth Cohen. Read by Bernadette Dunne. 7 CDs. (Running Time: 8 hrs. 30 mins.). 2004. audio compact disk 29.95 (978-0-7861-8728-7(X)); reel tape 29.95 (978-0-7861-2645-3(0)) Blckstn Audio.
Elizabeth, a member of the "sandwich generation," people caught in the middle of simultaneously caring for their children and for their aging parents, is the mother of Ava and the daughter of Daddy and responsible for both. Hers is the story of a woman's struggle to keep her family whole, to raise her child in a house of laughter and love, and to keep her father from hiding the house keys in his slippers. In this story full of everyday triumphs, Elizabeth, a suddenly single mother with a career and a mortgage and a hamper of laundry, finds her world spiraling out of control yet full of beauty.

House on East Eighty-Eighth Street see Lyle, Lyle, Crocodile

House on East 88th Street. 1 cass. (Running Time: 30 mins.). (J). 2000. pap. bk. 9.98 (T 6550 SP, Listening Lib) Random Audio Pubg.
With his clever tricks & engaging personality, Lyle wins the hearts of the Primm family & everyone else who has come to know him.

House on Fire. abr. ed. Denis Hamill. 2 cass. (Running Time: 3 hrs.). 1999. 16.95 Set. (978-1-882071-70-8(0)) B-B Audio.
Kevin Dempsey appeared to have it all: Polly, his beautiful wife, a former fashion model; Zoe, his beloved little girl; a rewarding job as a firefighter; the comfort of a close-knit Irish family. But as he sits one night in the new house he has bought as.

House on Fire. unabr. abr. ed. Denis Hamill & Max Allan Collins. Read by Danny Aiello & Max Allan Collins. 2 cass. (Running Time: 3 hrs.). (YA). 2001. 34.95 (978-0-929071-25-1(5)) B-B Audio.

House on Hope Street. unabr. ed. Danielle Steel. Read by Joseph Siravo. 4 cass. (Running Time: 6 hrs.). 2000. 31.95 (978-0-7366-5455-5(0), 5326) Books on Tape.
Liz and Jack Sutherland have the perfect life: happy marriage, successful joint law practice, and five wonderful children. It falls apart when a disgruntled client shoots Jack, on Christmas morning. Suddenly, Liz is alone, trying to both mother and father to the traumatized children, while struggling to keep the practice going. Then, a few weeks before Labor Day, the oldest child is in a devastating accident. The doctor, Bill Webster, becomes friends with Liz and soon she is starting to think of living again but her children fear she is forgetting their father.

House on Mango Street see Casa en Mango Street

House on Mango Street. unabr. ed. Sandra Cisneros. Read by Sandra Cisneros. 2 CDs. (Running Time: 7200 sec.). (ENG.). 2005. audio compact disk 14.99 (978-0-7393-2279-6(6), Random AudioBks) Pub: Random Audio Pubg. Dist(s): Random

House on Maple Street: And Other Stories. unabr. ed. Stephen King. Read by Stephen King. Read by Tabitha King et al. (Running Time: 5 hrs. 0 mins. 0 sec.). (ENG.). 2009. audio compact disk 14.99 (978-0-7435-9821-7(0)) Pub: S&S Audio. Dist(s): S and S Inc

House on the Cliff. abr. ed. Franklin W. Dixon. Read by Bill Irwin. 2 cass. (Running Time: 3 hrs. 29 mins.). (Hardy Boys Ser.: Vol. 2). (J). (gr. 4-7). 2004. 23.00 (978-0-8072-0770-3(5), Listening Lib) Random Audio Pubg.
Mr. Hardy disappears and it's up to the Hardy boys to discover the truth.

House on the Strand. Daphne Du Maurier. Read by Michael Maloney. (Running Time: 5 hrs.). 1999. 28.95 (978-1-60083-776-0(X)) Iofy Corp.

House on the Strand. abr. ed. Daphne Du Maurier. 4 CDs. 2005. audio compact disk 28.98 (978-962-634-341-8(9)) Naxos.

House on the Strand. unabr. ed. Daphne Du Maurier. Narrated by Ron Keith. 8 cass. (Running Time: 11 hrs.). 1990. 70.00 (978-1-55690-239-0(5), 90012E7) Recorded Bks.
Richard Young needs a change of scene. Though the Cornish town remains familiar, Richard finds himself flung back to the 14th century to medieval England.

House on Tradd Street. Karen White. Read by Aimee Bruneau. (Running Time: 43200 sec.). (Tradd Street Ser.: No. 1). 2008. audio compact disk 29.95 (978-1-59316-169-9(7)) Listen & Live.

House on Webster Street. Judith Michael. 2005. 25.95 (978-0-06-072516-7(8)) HarperCollins Pubs.

House on Winchester Lane. unabr. ed. Beverly Swerdlow Brown. 1 cass. (Running Time: 8 min.). (Kate & Tracy Series: We Love a Mystery!). (J). (gr. 4-8). 1989. pap. bk. 9.95 (978-0-87386-062-8(4)) Jan Prods.
The girls take a sightseeing tour of the home of Mrs. Winchester, widow of the inventor of the Winchester repeating rifle. Convinced that vengeful ghosts were likely to haunt her, she used her vast wealth to build a ghostproof house.

House on Winchester Lane. unabr. ed. Beverly Swerdlow Brown. 1 cass. (Running Time: 8 min.). (Kate & Tracy Series: We Love a Mystery!). (J). (gr. 4-8). 1989. bk. 16.99 (978-0-87386-058-1(6)) Jan Prods.

House or Home CD Series. 2004. audio compact disk 39.95 (978-1-59834-014-3(X)) Walk Thru the Bible.

***House Rules.** unabr. ed. Jodi Picoult. 1 Playaway. (Running Time: 20 hrs.). 2010. 64.75 (978-1-4407-7617-5(2)); 113.75 (978-1-4407-7614-4(8)); audio compact disk 123.75 (978-1-4407-7615-1(6)) Recorded Bks.

***House Rules.** unabr. ed. Jodi Picoult. Read by Mark Turetsky et al. 17 CDs. (Running Time: 20 hrs.). 2010. audio compact disk 44.99 (978-1-4407-8824-6(3)) Recorded Bks.

House Rules. unabr. ed. Rachel Sontag. Narrated by Nicole Poole. 7 cass. (Running Time: 8 hrs.). 2008. 61.75 (978-1-4361-0216-2(2)); audio compact disk 77.75 (978-1-4361-0218-6(9)) Recorded Bks.
Author Rachel Sontag recounts her dysfunctional childhood in this shocking memoir. On the surface, Rachel's physician father seemed perfect. He was well liked and equally respected in suburban Chicago. But home life was far different. An obsessive and manipulative man, he exercised complete control over everything, including the length of Rachel's hair and fingernails. Eventually, Rachel fought to break free and make some sense of her damaged life.

***House Rules: A Joe Demarco Thriller.** unabr. ed. Mike Lawson. (Running Time: 13 hrs. 30 mins.). (Joe Demarco Thriller Ser.). 2010. 29.95 (978-1-4417-5777-7(5)); 79.95 (978-1-4417-5773-9(2)); audio compact disk 32.95 (978-1-4417-5776-0(7)); audio compact disk 109.00 (978-1-4417-5774-6(0)) Blckstn Audio.

House Rules Committee: Gatekeeper to the Floor (CD) Featuring Chris Davis. Prod. by TheCapitol.Net. 2006. 107.00 (978-1-58733-042-1(3)) TheCapitol.

***House Secrets: A Joe Demarco Thriller.** unabr. ed. Mike Lawson. Read by Joe Barrett. (Running Time: 11 hrs. 30 mins.). (Joe Demarco Thrillers Ser.). 2010. 29.95 (978-1-4417-5769-2(4)); 65.95 (978-1-4417-5765-4(1)); audio compact disk 100.00 (978-1-4417-5766-1(X)); audio compact disk 29.95 (978-1-4417-5768-5(6)) Blckstn Audio.

House Sitter. Peter Lovesey. Read by Steve Hodson. (Chivers Audio Bks.). 2003. 84.95 (978-0-7540-8416-7(7)) Pub: Chivers Audio Bks GBR. Dist(s): AudioGO

House That I Built see Bienvenido Santos

House That Jack Built. 2004. 8.95 (978-1-56008-926-1(1)); cass. & flmstrp 30.00 (978-1-56008-685-7(8)) Weston Woods.

House That Jack Built. unabr. ed. Ed McBain, pseud. Read by Paul Shay. 6 cass. (Running Time: 9 hrs.). (Matthew Hope Mystery Ser.: No. 8). 1992. 48.00 (978-0-7366-2177-9(6), 2974) Books on Tape.
Matthew Hope defends an Indiana farmer accused of the murder of his gay brother. Hope knows that Ralph is no murderer. Can he prove his innocence?.

House That Sailed Away. unabr. ed. Pat Hutchins. Read by Brigit Forsyth. 2 cass. (Running Time: 2 hrs.). (J). 1995. 18.95 (978-0-7451-2501-5(8), CCA 3342, Chivers Child Audio) AudioGO.
It had rained every day since Grandma came to stay with Mom, Dad, Morgan, the baby, & Tailcat. Then the most amazing thing happened: the house started to shutter & rock, & then it just floated off down the street & into the sea! Before long, the whole family is surrounded by adventure: hungry cannibals, blood-thirsty pirates & buried treasure! But will they ever see dry land again?.

House That's Jack's/Animal Homes. Steck-Vaughn Staff. 1997. (978-0-8172-7378-1(6)) SteckVau.

House to House: A Soldier's Memoir. unabr. ed. David Bellavia. (Running Time: 34200 sec.). 2007. 44.95 (978-1-4332-0470-8(3)); audio compact disk 55.00 (978-1-4332-0471-5(1)) Blckstn Audio.

House to House: A Soldier's Memoir. unabr. ed. David Bellavia. Read by Ray Porter. Told to John Bruning. (Running Time: 34200 sec.). 2007. 24.95 (978-1-4332-0472-2(X)); audio compact disk 24.95 (978-1-4332-0473-9(8)) Blckstn Audio.

House to House: A Soldier's Memoir. unabr. ed. David Bellavia. Read by Ray Porter. Told to John R. Bruning. (Running Time: 34200 sec.). 2007. audio compact disk 29.95 (978-1-4332-0474-6(6)) Blckstn Audio.

House Unlocked. unabr. ed. Penelope Lively. 6 cass. (Isis Ser.). (J). 2003. 54.95 (978-0-7531-1351-6(1)) Pub: ISIS Lrg Prnt GBR. Dist(s): Ulverscroft US

House Unlocked. unabr. ed. Penelope Lively. Read by Sheila Mitchell. 7 CDs. (Isis Ser.). (J). 2003. audio compact disk 71.95 (978-0-7531-1408-7(9)) Pub: ISIS Lrg Prnt GBR. Dist(s): Ulverscroft US

House We Live In, Vol. 1. Perf. by Nancy Raven. 1 cass. (Running Time: 26 min.). (J). (ps-6). 1987. 10.00 (978-1-885292-05-6(8)) Lizards Rock.
Folk music for children, families, teachers.

House We Live In, Vol. 2. Perf. by Nancy Raven. 1 cass. (Running Time: 26 min.). (J). (ps-6). 1987. 10.00 (978-1-885292-06-3(6)) Lizards Rock.
Folk music for children, families & teachers.

House with a Clock in Its Walls. John Bellairs. Read by George Guidall. (Lewis Barnavelt Ser.: Bk. 1). 2000. audio compact disk 39.00 Recorded Bks.
You're guaranteed lots of laughs with this spine-tingling story about cozy fireplaces, wacky magic, chocolate chip cookies & spooky ghosts.

House with a Clock in its Walls. John Bellairs. Narrated by George Guidall. 4 CDs. (Running Time: 4 hrs. 30 mins.). (Lewis Barnavelt Ser.: Bk. 1). (gr. 5 up). audio compact disk 39.00 (978-0-7887-4739-7(8)) Recorded Bks.

House with a Clock in Its Walls. unabr. ed. John Bellairs. 1 read-along ccass. (Running Time: 61 min.). (Middle Grade Cliffhangers Ser.). (J). (gr. 4-6). 1986. 15.98 incl. bk. & guide. (978-0-8072-1148-9(6), SWR55SP, Listening Lib) Random Audio Pubg.
Lewis & his Uncle Jonathan, a wizard who practices white magic, live in an old house whose previous owner, an evil sorcerer, has devised a way to bring an end to the world & somewhere in the house is hidden a clock ticking off the minutes until doomsday.

House with a Clock in Its Walls, unabr. ed. John Bellairs. Narrated by George Guidall. 3 pieces. (Running Time: 4 hrs. 30 mins.). (Lewis Barnavelt Ser.: Bk. 1). (gr. 5 up). 1992. 27.00 (978-1-55690-587-2(4), 92124E7) Recorded Bks.
You're guaranteed lots of laughs with this spine-tingling story about cozy fireplaces, wacky magic, chocolate chip cookies & spooky ghosts.

Houseboat Mystery. unabr. ed. Jane Edwards. Read by Laurie Klein. 4 cass. (Running Time: 4 hrs. 6 min.). 1994. 26.95 (978-1-55686-564-0(3)) Books in Motion.
International intrigue & the threat of death face an ex-Navy Lieutenant who purchases a houseboat once owned by a famous newsman reported dead in an air crash in Hong Kong.

Household Appliances in Germany: A Strategic Reference 2006. Compiled by Icon Group International, Inc. Staff. 2007. ring bd. 195.00 (978-0-497-35974-4(X)) Icon Grp.

***household guide to Dying.** Debra Adelaide. Read by Heather Bolton. (Running Time: 11 hrs. 5 mins.). 2010. 94.99 (978-1-74214-627-0(9), 9781742146270) Pub: Bolinda Pubng AUS. Dist(s): Bolinda Pub Inc

household guide to Dying. unabr. ed. Debra Adelaide. Read by Heather Bolton. (Running Time: 11 hrs. 5 mins.). 2009. audio compact disk 98.95 (978-1-74214-069-8(6), 9781742140698) Pub: Bolinda Pubng AUS. Dist(s): Bolinda Pub Inc

***household guide to Dying.** unabr. ed. Debra Adelaide. Read by Heather Bolton. (Running Time: 11 hrs 5 mins.). 2010. 43.95 (978-1-74214-689-8(9), 9781742146898) Pub: Bolinda Pubng AUS. Dist(s): Bolinda Pub Inc

Household Spanish, Set. 2 cass. (Running Time: 2 hrs.). (SPA.). pap. bk. 29.95 (978-0-614-14764-3(6), S24400) J Norton Pubs.
For home managers who wish to communicate more effectively with their Spanish speaking domestic help. Included are common Spanish terms & instructions for each area of the house & for each appliance.

Household Spanish: How to Communicate with Your Spanish Employees. 2nd ed. William C. Harvey. 3 CDs. (SPA & ENG.). 2005. pap. bk. 16.95 (978-0-7641-7776-7(1)) Barron.

Householder & Monastic Life. Speeches. 1. (Running Time: 50). 2003. 9.95 (978-0-87481-352-4(2)) Vedanta Pr.
IN THE PRACTICE OF SPIRITUALUTY, THERE ARE DIFFERENT DUTIES FOR HOUSEHOLDERS AND MONASTICS. THIS LECTURE EXPLAINS THE DIFFERENT SPIRITUAL PRACTICES FOR EACH TYPE.

Householder Ethics. unabr. ed. Ann Ree Colton. 1 cass. 7.95 (978-0-917189-19-7(1)) A R Colton Fnd.

Housekeeping. Marilynne Robinson. Read by Marilynne Robinson. 1 cass. 1989. 13.95 (978-1-55644-328-2(5), 9031) Am Audio Prose.
The author reads excerpts from "Housekeeping & Mother Country".

Housekeeping. Marilynne Robinson. Read by Becket Royce. 2005. audio compact disk 49.95 (978-0-7927-3789-6(X)) AudioGO.

Housekeeping. Marilynne Robinson. Read by Becket Royce. 2005. 17.95 (978-1-59397-841-9(3)) Pub: Macmill Audio. Dist(s): Macmillan

Housekeeping. Marilynne Robinson. Read by Becket Royce. 2005. audio compact disk 29.95 (978-0-7927-3843-5(8)) Pub: Macmill Audio. Dist(s): Macmillan

Housekeeping. unabr. ed. Marilynne Robinson. Read by Becket Royce. 5 CDs. (Running Time: 5 hrs. 30 mins. 0 sec.). (ENG.). 2005. audio compact disk 29.95 (978-1-59397-786-3(7)) Pub: Macmill Audio. Dist(s): Macmillan

Housekeeping with Love. 1 CD. 1982. audio compact disk 19.98 (978-1-56001-701-1(5)) Potentials.
Spend twenty minutes with this program and you will find yourself motivated and activated. Housekeeping will become an act of love.The self-hypnosis is on track 1 and the subliminal is on track 2. The easy-listening music of the subliminal, together with the self-hypnosis, is the original format which most people love and with which they are most familiar.

Housekeeping with Love. Barrie Konicov. 1 cass. (Running Time: 79 min.). 11.98 (978-0-87082-631-3(X), 153) Potentials.
In the morning you are too rushed. In the evening you are too tired. On the weekends you are catching up on all the things you didn't do during the week. Spend 20 minutes with this tape and you will find yourself motivated.

Houses of Stone. unabr. ed. Barbara Michaels, pseud. Read by Kate Harper. 10 cass. (Running Time: 10 hrs.). 1995. 84.95 Set. (978-0-7451-6512-7(5), CAB 1128) AudioGO.
When young professor of English, Karen Holloway, comes upon an ancient manuscript with the name Ismene on it, she realizes it may be the important discovery that sparks her career. Karen immerses herself in a headlong search for the author's true identity. As she deciphers the charred pages, Karen begins to wonder whether the tale of horror that Ismene tells is not a novel but a memoir, the very possession of which may jeopardize her life.

Houses of Stone. unabr. ed. Barbara Michaels, pseud. Narrated by Barbara Rosenblat. 10 cass. (Running Time: 14 hrs.). 1995. 85.00 (978-0-7887-0261-7(0), 94470E7) Recorded Bks.
Professor Karen Holloway travels to Virginia to search for the grave of Ismene, the mysterious author of a battered 19th-century manuscript. But eerie, inexplicable coincidences make Karen wonder if Ismene is desperately trying to warn her from the grave.

Housewife's Guide to the Practical Striptease survival Kit. Miyoko Fujimori. (Running Time: 40 mins). 2006. per. 29.95 (978-0-9766505-1-5(7)) Indulgent Pr.
Survival Kit includes The Housewife's Guide to the Practical Striptease book, 30 minute Instructional CD, Four one time use shaving templates, 6ft Marabou Feather Boa, plus Miyoko will guide you through a 10-minute stripper workout!.

Housing Boom & Bust. unabr. ed. Thomas Sowell. Read by Robertson Dean. (Running Time: 4.5 hrs. 0 mins.). (ENG.). 2009. 44.95 (978-1-4332-9404-4(4)); audio compact disk 69.00 (978-1-4332-9405-1(2)) Blckstn Audio.

Housing Boom & Bust. unabr. ed. Thomas Sowell. (Running Time: 7 hrs.). (ENG.). 2009. audio compact disk 24.95 (978-1-4332-9407-5(9)) Blckstn Audio.

Housing Boom & Bust. unabr. ed. Thomas Sowell. Read by Robertson Dean. (Running Time: 7 hrs.). (ENG.). 2009. 29.95 (978-1-4332-9408-2(7)) Blckstn Audio.

Housing Cheap or on a Budget. Alfreda C. Doyle. Read by Sell Out Recordings Staff. 1 cass. (Running Time: 15 min.). 1991. 9.00 (S.O.R. 4002) Sell Out Recordings.
Possibilities for getting housing cheap or on a budget.

Housing Decisions. Evelyn L. Lewis & Carolyn S. Turner. (gr. 9-12). tchr. ed. 200.00 (978-1-59070-145-4(3)) Goodheart.

Houston Partner Conference. 2003. (978-1-59024-169-1(X)); audio compact disk (978-1-59024-170-7(3)) B Hinn Min.

Houston Regional Meeting, '96. 3 cass. 12.00 Set. (96A1-3) IRL Chicago.

Houstonians & Corinthians: 1 Cor. 1:1-3. Ed Young. 1985. 4.95 (978-0-7417-1479-4(5), 479) Win Walk.

Hover Car Racer. Matthew Reilly. Read by Sean Mangan. (Running Time: 10 hrs. 30 mins.). (Hover Car Racer Ser.). 2009. 94.99 (978-1-74214-278-4(8), 9781742142784) Pub: Bolinda Pubng AUS. Dist(s): Bolinda Pub Inc

Hover Car Racer. unabr. ed. Matthew Reilly. Read by Sean Mangan. 11 CDs. (Running Time: 37800 sec.). (Hover Car Racer Ser.). 2005. audio compact disk 103.95 (978-1-74093-645-3(0)) Pub: Bolinda Pubng AUS. Dist(s): Bolinda Pub Inc

Hover Car Racer. unabr. ed. Matthew Reilly. Read by Sean Mangan. (Running Time: 10 hrs. 30 mins.). (Hover Car Racer Ser.). 2008. 43.95 (978-1-921415-27-2(4), 9781921415272) Pub: Bolinda Pubng AUS. Dist(s): Bolinda Pub Inc

Hovering of Vultures. unabr. ed. Robert Barnard. Read by Frederick Davidson. 5 cass. (Running Time: 7 hrs.). 1995. 39.95 (978-0-7861-0718-6(9), 1596) Blckstn Audio.
What better victim in a Robert Barnard novel than a literary poseur? Not quite in the league of the Brontes, Susannah & Joshua Sneddon toiled at their creative tasks in a remote cottage in a tiny Yorkshire village in the early years of this century. Neither wrote great literature, but Susannah's work was always the more popular. Perhaps that's why Joshua one day killed his sister with an ax & shot himself in the head. Now, many years later, there's surprising new interest in the Sneddons, seemingly inspired by entrepreneur Gerald Suzman. Suzman has bought the Sneddon homestead, with plans to open it as a museum & to found a literary society known as the Sneddon Fellowship.

Hoverud Connections: Immigrant Ancestors from Valdres & Hallingdal, Norway & Their Descendants: 155 Years in America. Vivian Everson Sardeson. Ed. by Jean Sanders Ekern & Joan Ekern Axdal. 2003. audio compact disk 20.00 (978-0-9659896-3-3(1)) Asgard MN.

How A House Is Built: With 3D Construction Models. Dennis Fukai. (ENG.). 2009. pap. bk. 29.95 (978-0-9762741-4-8(0)) Insitebuilders.

How a Picture Book Is Made. 2004. 8.95 (978-1-56008-927-8(X)); cass. & flmstrp 30.00 (978-1-56008-686-4(6)) Weston Woods.

How a Picture Book Is Made; Island of the Skog. 2004. cass. & flmstrp 30.00 (978-0-89719-623-9(6)) Weston Woods.

***How a Second Grader Beats Wall Street: Golden Rules Any Investor Can Learn.** unabr. ed. Allan S. Roth. Read by Scott Peterson. (Running Time: 7 hrs.). (ENG.). 2010. 27.98 (978-1-59659-551-4(5), GildAudio) Pub: Gildan Media. Dist(s): HachBkGrp

How a Witch Tried to Kill a King see Spirits & Spooks for Halloween

How about Sex? unabr. ed. Howard B. Lyman. 1 cass. (Running Time: 24 min.). (Single Again Ser.). 12.95 (35021) J Norton Pubs.

How about Some Good News. Greg Skipper. 2001. 40.00 (978-0-633-01664-7(0)); 11.98 (978-0-633-01662-3(4)); audio compact disk 16.98 (978-0-633-01663-0(2)) LifeWay Christian.

How about Some Good News! Greg Skipper. 2001. audio compact disk 45.00 (978-0-633-01665-4(9)) LifeWay Christian.

How about You? John Farrell. (ENG.). (J). 2003. audio compact disk 15.95 (978-1-56397-832-6(6)) Boyds Mills Pr.

How about You? John Farrell. (ENG.). (J). (ps-3). 2003. reel tape 10.95 (978-1-56397-833-3(4)) Boyds Mills Pr.

How Administrators Can Improve Teaching: Moving from Talk to Action in Higher Education. Peter Seldin et al. Frwd. by Russell Edgerton. (Higher Education Ser.). 1990. bk. 34.45 (978-1-55542-277-6(2), Jossey-Bass) Wiley US.

How Anansi Brought Stories to Earth CD: Scripts for Young Readers. Read by Patrick Feehan. Retold by Heather McDonald. (J). 2009. 9.95 (978-1-60184-167-4(1)) Primry Concpts.

How & Why Stories: World Tales Kids Can Read & Tell. Martha Hamilton & Mitch Weiss. Illus. by Carol Lyon. 1 cass. (Running Time: 1 hr. 1 min.). (World Storytelling from August House Ser.). (gr. 1-7). 2000. 12.00 (978-0-87483-594-6(1)); audio compact disk 16.95 (978-0-87483-596-0(8)) Pub: August Hse. Dist(s): Natl Bk Netwk
Children and adults tell stories that answer the "How" and "Why" questions - collected with a global view.

***How Angel Peterson Got His Name.** unabr. ed. Gary Paulsen. (Running Time: 2 hrs.). 2011. 12.99 (978-1-4558-0156-5(9), 9781455801565, BAD); 39.97 (978-1-4558-0157-2(7), 9781455801572, BADLE); 12.99 (978-1-4558-0154-1(2), 9781455801541, Brilliance MP3); 39.97 (978-1-4558-0155-8(0), 9781455801558, Brinc Audio MP3 Lib); audio compact disk 12.99 (978-1-4558-0152-7(6), 9781455801527, Bril Audio CD Unabri); audio compact disk 39.97 (978-1-4558-0153-4(4), 9781455801534, BriAudCD Unabrid) Brilliance Audio.

How Angels Touch Our Lives: Logos 12/13/98. Ben Young. 1998. 4.95 (978-0-7417-6111-8(4), B0111) Win Walk.

How Angels Touch Your Life: Corinthians 15: 13-17. Ben Young. 1997. 4.95 (978-0-7417-6028-9(2), B0028) Win Walk.

How Animals Change & Grow Audio CD. Adapted by Benchmark Education Company Staff. Based on a work by Kira Freed. (Early Explorers Set C Ser.). (J). (gr. 2). 2008. audio compact disk 10.00 (978-1-60437-543-5(4)) Benchmark Educ.

How Archetypes Heal Us & Make Us Whole: The World of the Ideal. unabr. ed. Jacquelyn Small. 1 cass. (C). 1995. 11.00 (978-0-939344-09-3(2)) Eupsychian.
She teaches us how we enter into higher mind & merge with archetypal blueprints, the qualities of the soul. She clearly explains the archetypal level of consciousness as a psychological fact that transforms our consciousness.

How Arthur Was Crowned. unabr. ed. (Running Time: 20 min.). Dramatization. (J). (gr. 2-6). 1989. 9.95 (978-0-7810-0053-6(X), NIM-CW-131-4-C) NIMCO.
An English folk tale.

How Awesome Will It Be? A Teenager's Guide to Understanding & Preparing for the Second Coming. Roger McKenzie. (YA). 2005. audio compact disk 14.95 (978-1-59038-415-2(6)) Deseret Bk.

How Babies Grow. J. C. Willke. Read by J. C. Willke. 1 cass. (Running Time: 10 min.). 17.95 incl. 20 35mm slides. Hayes.

How Beautiful is Night. Perf. by George Shearing. 1 cass., 1 CD. 7.98 (TA 33325); audio compact disk 12.78 CD Jewel box. (TA 83325) NewSound.

How Blue Crane Taught Jackal to Fly see Zulu & Other African Folktales from Behind the Back of the Mountain

How Bright the Moon. (Running Time: 27 min.). 14.95 (23577) MMI Corp.
Discusses size, distance, brightness, other characteristics of our moon, in detail.

How Buyers Like to Be Sold: Sophisticated Sales Techniques Few Customers Can Resist. Jimmy Calano & Jeff Salzman. 4 cass. (Running Time: 4 hrs. 12 min.). 49.95 Set incl. 32p. wkbk. (V10143) CareerTrack Pubns.
In this insight-rich program, you'll hear straight talk on winning sales techniques - from the customer's point of view (the only view that matters). You get unconventional yet powerful strategies for every step of the sales process, from getting the buyer's attention to making the presentation, to "closing naturally," to following up & growing the account.

How Can I Be Healed? Elbert Willis. 1 cass. (Review of Divine Healing Ser.). 4.00 Fill the Gap.

How Can I Find the Right Love Partner? Lee Yelenics. 1 cass. 8.95 (372) Am Fed Astrologers.
Procedure to follow using personal planets.

How Can I Keep from Singing? Contrib. by Chris Tomlin. (Praise Hymn Soundtracks Ser.). 2007. audio compact disk 8.98 (978-5-557-71918-6(0)) Pt of Grace Ent.

How Can I Keep from Singing. Contrib. by Chris Tomlin. (Soundtraks Ser.). 2007. audio compact disk 8.99 (978-5-557-60870-1(2)) Christian Wrld.

How Can I Lower the Rising Number of Alcohol Related Birth Defects in My Community? unabr. ed. Linda Culbreth. Read by Linda Culbreth. 1 cass. (Running Time: 48 min.). 1998. 9.95 (978-1-893784-03-1(7)) Eagles Port.

How Can the Brain Transform Itself? J. Krishnamurti. 1 cass. (Running Time: 75 min.). (Brockwood Park Talks, 1983 Ser.: No. 1). 8.50 (ABT831) Krishnamurti.
Subjects examined: Is it possible to bring about a mutation in the very brain cells themselves, conditioned for thousands of years? Either one says that it is not possible & closes the door or one says I really don't know. Without any choice, am I aware that my brain is conditioned? What is the nature of conditioning? It is essentially experience & knowledge. Why is the structure of the psyche essentially based on knowledge? What am I without memory? Is it possible to live psychologically without memories? The division between memory & the observer creates conflict.

How Can This Be? John 3:5-9, 709. Ed Young. 1989. 4.95 (978-0-7417-1709-2(3), 709) Win Walk.

How Can We Sing. Joyce Landorf Heatherley. 1 cass. 1988. 7.95 (978-0-929488-21-9(0)) Balcony Pub Inc.
Whatever life has dealt us, we can sing because of "God, me & others." Healing, both emotional & spiritual, can come through these three working together.

How Can You Be in Two Places at Once. Perf. by Firesign Theatre Firesign Theatre Staff. 1 CD. (Running Time: 1 hr.). 2001. audio compact disk 15.95 Lodestone Catalog.
The Firesign Theatre's classic 1968 second album, where Babe buys a car with Climate Control & we meet Nick Danger, Third Eye, for the first time.

How Can You Sort? Early Explorers Early Set B Audio CD. Anna Lee. Adapted by Benchmark Education Staff. (J). 2007. audio compact disk 10.00 (978-1-4108-8241-7(1)) Benchmark Educ.

How Children Come to Faith in Christ. abr. ed. Jim Elliff & Dennis Rainey. Ed. by Keith Lynch. 3 cass. (Running Time: 3 hrs.). 1996. 14.95 Set. (978-1-57229-040-2(4)) FamilyLife.
How to bring your child to Christ.

How Children Raise Parents: The Art of Listening to Your Family. abr. ed. Dan Allender. Read by Dan Allender. 2 cass. (Running Time: 3 hrs.). 2003. 44.25 (978-1-59355-092-9(8), 1593550928); 17.95 (978-1-59355-091-2(X), 159355091X); audio compact disk 62.25 (978-1-59355-094-3(4), 1593550944); audio compact disk 19.95 (978-1-59355-093-6(6), 1593550936) Brilliance Audio.
Parents put their confidence in rules and principles and apply themselves to doing everything right. They believe that diligent application of the right methods will protect their kids from threatening influences and will assure that their kids succeed. But rather than building a healthy parent/child relationship, the rules-oriented approach places unreasonable demands and expectations on both parents and children. And the added pressure makes it more difficult for a child to feel loved by his parents - and by God. To reduce pressure and enjoy greater closeness, parents need to turn their approach upside-down by allowing God to use their children to lead them to spiritual maturity. How Children Raise Parents provides a bold new paradigm by showing that parenting is the process God uses to help parents grow up. This liberating approach helps parents learn to prize what they're being taught by their child's quirks, failures, and normal childhood dilemmas, rather than worrying about what their children will accomplish in life.

How Children Raise Parents: The Art of Listening to Your Family. abr. ed. Dan Allender. Read by Dan Allender. (Running Time: 3 hrs.). 2006. 39.25 (978-1-4233-0368-8(7), 9781423303688, BADLE); 24.95 (978-1-4233-0367-1(9), 9781423303671, BAD) Brilliance Audio.

How Children Raise Parents: The Art of Listening to Your Family. abr. ed. Dan B. Allender. Read by Dan B. Allender. (Running Time: 3 hrs.). 2006. 39.25 (978-1-4233-0366-4(0), 9781423303664, Brinc Audio MP3 Lib); 24.95 (978-1-4233-0365-7(2), 9781423303657, Brilliance MP3) Brilliance Audio.

***How Christ Came to Church.** unabr. ed. A. J. Gordon. Narrated by David Cochran Heath. (ENG.). 2004. 9.98 (978-1-59644-050-0(3), Hovel Audio) christianaud.

How Christ Came to Church. unabr. ed. A. J. Gordon. Narrated by David Cochran Heath. 2 CDs. (Running Time: 1 hr. 30 mins. 0 sec.). (ENG.). 2004. audio compact disk 15.98 (978-1-59644-052-4(X), Hovel Audio) christianaud.
How Christ Came To Church is an enlivening spiritual autobiography that grew out of a beleaguered pastorâ€(tm)s dream. This dream was the seminal event out of which blossomed a complete change in Gordonâ€(tm)s approach to ministry and a vivid transformation in his parishioners.

***How Christianity Changed the World.** Alvin J. Schmidt. (Running Time: 15 hrs. 41 mins. 0 sec.). (ENG.). 2009. 18.99 (978-0-310-30458-6(X)) Zondervan.

***How Could You Do That?!** abr. ed. Laura Schlessinger. Read by Laura Schlessinger. (ENG.). 2004. (978-0-06-081325-3(3), Harper Audio); (978-0-06-075567-6(9), Harper Audio) HarperCollins Pubs.

How Could You Do That?! The Abdication of Character, Courage, & Conscience. unabr. ed. Laura Schlessinger. Read by Mary Peiffer. 6 cass. (Running Time: 9 hrs.). 1996. 48.00 Set. (978-0-7366-3471-7(1), 4115) Books on Tape.
Excuses are what Laura Schlessinger doesn't want to hear. None justifies the selfish morality we find in today's society. As she does on her syndicated talk show, "Dr. Laura" here argues against quick, mindless pleasure & taking the easy way out to avoid consequences.

How Could You Do That?! The Abdication of Character, Courage, & Conscience. unabr. ed. Laura Schlessinger. Narrated by Barbara Caruso. 6 cass. (Running Time: 8 hrs. 30 mins.). 1996. 51.00 (978-0-7887-0676-9(4), 94855E7) Recorded Bks.
Based on the dialogues of the internationally syndicated radio program of a marriage & family therapist.

How Did I Get Here? Finding Your Way to Hope & Happiness When Life & Love Take Unexpected Turns. abr. ed. Barbara De Angelis. (Running Time: 3 hrs. 0 mins. 0 sec.). (ENG.). 2005. audio compact disk 19.95 (978-1-59397-510-4(4)) Pub: Macmill Audio. Dist(s): Macmillan

How Did I Get So Busy? The 28-Day Plan to Free Your Time, Reclaim Your Schedule, & Reconnect with What Matters Most. unabr. ed. Valorie Burton. Narrated by Valorie Burton. (ENG.). 2007. 17.49 (978-1-60814-241-5(8)); audio compact disk 24.99 (978-1-59859-333-4(1)) Oasis Audio.

How Did Our Lives Get So Cluttered? Jeff Davidson. 2002. audio compact disk 9.95 (978-1-60729-128-2(2)) Breath Space Inst.

How Did Our Lives Get So Cluttered? Jeff Davidson. 2002. 8.95 (978-1-60729-355-2(2)) Breath Space Inst.

How Did Our Lives Get So Cluttered? Mega Trends, Mega Reality & Mega Personal Power! Illus. by Angela Brown & Jeff Davidson. Prod. by Les Lingle. 1 cass. (Running Time: 30 mins.). (Words of Wellness - Your Show for Simple Solutions Ser.: Vol. 313). 2000. 12.95 (978-1-930995-05-5(9), LLP313) Life Long Pubg.
Feeling overwhelmed, pressed for time & overloaded with choices? Learn how to focus on your work at hand, finish what you start & make the most of your time.

How Did That Happen? Holding People Accountable for Results the Positive, Principled Way. unabr. ed. Roger Connors & Tom Smith. (Running Time: 10 hrs. 0 mins. 0 sec.). (ENG.). 2009. 24.99 (978-1-4001-6265-9(3)); audio compact disk 34.99 (978-1-4001-1265-4(6)); audio compact disk 69.99 (978-1-4001-4265-1(2)) Pub: Tantor Media. Dist(s): IngramPubServ

How Do Dinosaurs Eat Their Food? Jane Yolen. Narrated by Jane Yolen. Illus. by Mark Teague. (ENG.). (J). (ps-3). 2010. audio compact disk 9.95 (978-0-545-11755-5(0)) Scholastic Inc.

How Do Dinosaurs Eat Their Food? Narrated by Jane Yolen. 1 CD. (Running Time: 10 mins.). (J). (ps-2). 2007. bk. 29.95 (978-0-439-02746-5(2)); bk. 24.95 (978-0-439-02745-8(4)) Weston Woods.
With methods of eating and manners that are probably all too familiar to children and adults, these mischievous dinosaurs show in a big way that burping, spilling, playing with one¿s food and outright refusing to eat are not the best ways to enjoy a meal. An entertaining guide to table manners and a good reminder that positive and pleasant mealtime behavior gets the best results.

***How Do Dinosaurs Get Well Soon?** Jane Yolen. Narrated by Jane Yolen. Illus. by Mark Teague. (ENG.). 2010. audio compact disk 9.99 (978-0-545-24946-1(5)) Scholastic Inc.

How Do Dinosaurs Go to School? Jane Yolen. Narrated by Jane Yolen. Illus. by Mark Teague. (ENG.). (J). 2010. audio compact disk 9.99 (978-0-545-22594-6(9)) Scholastic Inc.

***How Do Dinosaurs Go to School?** Jane Yolen. 1 CD. (Running Time: 9 mins.). (J). (ps-3). 2009. audio compact disk 12.95 (978-0-545-19687-1(6)) Weston Woods.

***How Do Dinosaurs Go to School?** Jane Yolen. Illus. by Mark Teague. 1 CD. (Running Time: 9 mins.). (J). (ps-3). 2009. pap. bk. 18.95 (978-0-545-19707-6(4)) Weston Woods.

***How Do Dinosaurs Go to School?** Jane Yolen. Illus. by Mark Teague. 1 CD. (Running Time: 9 mins.). (J). (ps-3). 2009. bk. 29.95 (978-0-545-19700-7(7)) Weston Woods.

How Do Dinosaurs Say Good Night? Jane Yolen. Narrated by Jane Yolen. Illus. by Mark Teague. (How Do Dinosaurs... Ser.). (ENG.). (J). (ps-3). 2008. audio compact disk 9.95 (978-0-545-09319-4(8)) Scholastic Inc.

How Do Dinosaurs Say Good Night? Jane Yolen. 1 cass. (Running Time: 8 mins.). (J). (ps-1). 2004. bk. 24.95 (978-1-55592-099-9(3)); 8.95 (978-1-55592-958-9(3)) Weston Woods.
Story about bedtime rituals.

How Do Dinosaurs Say Good Night? abr. ed. Jane Yolen. 1 CD. (Running Time: 8 mins.). (J). (ps-1). 2004. audio compact disk 12.95 (978-1-55592-938-1(9)) Weston Woods.

How Do Dinosaurs Say Good Night & Other Dinosaur Tales: How Do Dinosaurs Get Well Soon?; How Do Dinosaurs Say Goodnight?; T Is for Terrible; Danny & the Dinosaur. unabr. ed. Jane Yolen et al. Read by Jane Yolen et al. (J). 2007. 44.99 (978-1-60252-607-5(9)) Find a World.

How Do Dinosaur's Say Goodnight? 2004. pap. bk. 38.75 (978-1-55592-632-8(0)); pap. bk. 14.95 (978-1-55592-170-5(1)) Weston Woods.

How Do Dinosaurs Say Goodnight? Jane Yolen. 2004. pap. bk. 32.75 (978-1-55592-368-6(2)) Weston Woods.

How Do I... In Visual Basic: 50 Tutorials. Carol Peterson. (C). 1999. audio compact disk 333.25 (978-1-57676-044-4(8)) Delmar.

How Do I Know God's Will? 2005. audio compact disk 27.95 (978-1-888992-88-5(3)) Catholic Answers.

How Do I Love Thee? see Classics of English Poetry for the Elementary Curriculum

How Do They Do It? (Hindu Dasas) Barbara Cameron. 1 cass. 8.95 (042) Am Fed Astrologers.
An AFA Convention workshop tape.

How Do Trees Grow? Early Explorers Fluent Set B Audio CD. Christina Riska. Adapted by Benchmark Education Staff. (J). 2007. audio compact disk 10.00 (978-1-4108-8245-5(4)) Benchmark Educ.

How Do We Get Sick? How Do We Get Well? Ralph Alan Dale. Read by Ralph Alan Dale. 1 cass. (Running Time: 2 hrs.). 1977. 9.00 (4) Dialectic Pubng.
Fourteen master keys to health.

How Do We Know Our Past Lives Are Real? Bettye B. Binder. Read by Bettye B. Binder. 2 cass. (Running Time: 2 hrs.). 1996. 16.95 SET. (978-1-879005-17-4(4)) Reincarnation Bks.
Contains exercises for distinguishing memory from imagination & past life regression which can be done at home.

How Do We Know When It's God? A Spiritual Memoir. abr. ed. Dan Wakefield. Read by Dan Wakefield. 2 cass. (Running Time: 3 hrs.). 2000. 18.00 (978-1-57453-347-7(9)) Audio Lit.
The author shares the triumphs and disasters of his spiritual pursuit as he stumbles through a minefield of failed marriages, painful career choices and alcohol. Exploring yoga, "a gift of God to my body and soul" and relying on Christianity, Wakefield is passionate and poetic about his dynamic, ever elusive faith.

How Do You Explain the Trinity? Logos January 25, 1998. Ben Young. 1998. 4.95 (978-0-7417-6070-8(3), B0070) Win Walk.

How Do You Spell - Como Se Deletrea. rev. ed. Bernetta Gresko. 2 cass. (Running Time: 3 hrs.). (ENG & SPA.). 1987. 14.50 (978-0-939755-04-2(1)) Sunset Prods.
For the non-English speaker to practice saying English words. Directions on tape in English.

How Do You Spell Geek? Julie Anne Peters. Read by Julie Dretzin. 3 cass. (Running Time: 3 hrs. 15 mins.). (YA). 1999. pap. bk. 40.24 (978-0-7887-2992-8(6), 40874); 88.70 (978-0-7887-3022-1(3), 46839) Recorded Bks.
Eighth-grader Kimberly & Ann are best friends. They spend every spare minute together, practicing for the National Spelling Bee. But when Ann is assigned to help a geeky new student, their plans & their friendship, go quickly awry.

How Do You Spell Geek?, unabr. ed. Julie Anne Peters. Narrated by Julie Dretzin. 3 cass. (Running Time: 3 hrs. 15 mins.). (gr. 7 up). 1999. 28.00 (978-0-7887-2962-1(4), 95736E7) Recorded Bks.

How Do You Spell God? The Risks & Blessings of Interfaith Dialogue. Marc Gellman & Thomas Hartman. 1 cass. (Running Time: 1 hr. 30 mins.). 2001. 9.95 (A8071) St Anthony Mess Pr.
Illustrates how we can explore another religion without destroying our own belief and that, in fact, dialogue can help us to appreciate our own faith more deeply.

How Do You Spell Sell? Richard Flint. 6 cass. Incl. How Do You Spell Sell? Plenty of Prospects. 1985.; How Do You Spell Sell? The Philosophy. 1985.; How Do You Spell Sell? The Power. 1985.; How Do You Spell Sell? To Persuade. 1985.; How Do You Spell Sell? To Purchase. 1985.; How Do You Spell Sell? Your Product at a Profit. 1985.; 1985. 70.00 (978-0-937851-05-0(1)) Pendelton Lane.
Explores the psychological understanding that sales people need.

How Do You Spell Sell?: Plenty of Prospects see How Do You Spell Sell?

How Do You Spell Sell?: The Philosophy see How Do You Spell Sell?

How Do You Spell Sell?: The Power see How Do You Spell Sell?

How Do You Spell Sell?: To Persuade see How Do You Spell Sell?

How Do You Spell Sell?: To Purchase see How Do You Spell Sell?

How Do You Spell Sell?: Your Product at a Profit see How Do You Spell Sell?

How Do You View Your body? Derek Prince. 1 cass. 5.95 (4402) Derek Prince.
Is America facing a cancer epidemic? Does God hold us accountable for how we treat our bodies? This challenging message could save your life.

How Do You Welcome a King. Mike Harland. 2000. 11.98 (978-0-633-02960-9(2)); audio compact disk 85.00 (978-0-633-00797-3(8)) LifeWay Christian.

How Do You Welcome a King? Mike Harland. 2000. 75.00 (978-0-633-00783-6(8)); audio compact disk 16.98 (978-0-633-02955-5(6)) LifeWay Christian.

How Doctors Think. unabr. ed. Jerome Groopman. Read by Michael Prichard. (YA). 2008. 59.99 (978-1-60252-969-4(8)) Find a World.

How Doctors Think. unabr. ed. Jerome Groopman. (Running Time: 10 hrs. 30 mins. 0 sec.). (ENG.). 2007. audio compact disk 69.99 (978-1-4001-3425-0(0)) Pub: Tantor Media. Dist(s): IngramPubServ

How Doctors Think. unabr. ed. Jerome Groopman. Narrated by Michael Prichard. 9 CDs. (Running Time: 10 hrs. 30 mins. 0 sec.). (ENG.). 2007. audio compact disk 34.99 (978-1-4001-0425-3(4)); audio compact disk 24.99 (978-1-4001-5425-8(1)) Pub: Tantor Media. Dist(s): IngramPubServ

How Does a Cactus Grow? Early Explorers Early Set B Audio CD. Clare O'Brien. Adapted by Benchmark Education Staff. (J). 2007. audio compact disk 10.00 (978-1-4108-8214-1(4)) Benchmark Educ.

***How does aspirin find a Headache.** abr. ed. David Feldman. Read by David Feldman. (ENG.). 2006. (978-0-06-088316-4(2), Harper Audio); (978-0-06-088315-7(4), Harper Audio) HarperCollins Pubs.

How Does God Lead? Psalms 32:8. Ed Young. 1989. 4.95 (978-0-7417-1755-9(7), 755) Win Walk.

How Does Man Know God? Gordon Clark. 1 cass. (Miscellaneous Lectures: No. 3). 5.00 Trinity Found.

How Everything Happens (Based on a Study of the Wave) see May Swenson

How Evil Works: Understanding & Overcoming the Destructive Forces That Are Transforming America. unabr. ed. David Kupelian. Narrated by Jon Gauger. (Running Time: 9 hrs. 11 mins. 40 sec.). (ENG.). 2010. 19.59 (978-1-60814-653-6(7)) Oasis Audio.

How Evil Works: Understanding & Overcoming the Destructive Forces That Are Transforming America. unabr. ed. David Kupelian. Narrated by Jon Gauger. 8 CDs. (Running Time: 9 hrs. 11 mins. 40 sec.). (ENG.). 2010. audio compact disk 27.99 (978-1-59859-710-3(8)) Oasis Audio.

How Excellent! Vol. 1: Songs for Teens. David Haas et al. 1996. audio compact disk 15.95 (377) GIA Pubns.

How Far from Austerlitz? Napoleon 1805-1815. collector's ed. Alistair Horne. Read by Bill Kelsey. 11 cass. (Running Time: 16 hrs. 30 min.). 2000. 88.00 (978-0-7366-5525-5(5)) Books on Tape.
Covering the pivotal decade of Napoleon's career. Starting with the victories at Ulm & Austerlitz & concluding with the defeat at Waterloo, we see that, once the conquering begins, it is hard to stop. One victory demands a second to protect it. Austerlitz was the last battle the Father of Modern Warfare would leave in absolute triumph. It marked the beginning of Napoleon's downfall.

How Fear Came. unabr. ed. Rudyard Kipling. Read by Walter Zimmerman & Walter Covell. 1 cass. (Running Time: 74 min.). Dramatization. (J). 1983. 8.95 (S-43) Jimcin Record.
More adventures with Mowgli & his friends in those two stories from "The Jungle Book".

***How Fear Came: A Story from the Jungle Books.** Rudyard Kipling. 2009. (978-1-60136-507-1(1)) Audio Holding.

How Fear Came & The Miracle of Purun Bhagat. Rudyard Kipling. 1 cass. 1989. 7.95 (S-43) Jimcin Record.
More adventure with Mowgli & friends.

How Federal Agencies Can Work Effectively with Congress & Its Staff (CD) Featuring Paul Powell. Prod. by TheCapitol.Net. 2006. 107.00 (978-1-58733-047-6(4)) TheCapitol.

How Fervent Catholic Families Are Needed. Mrs. Hitchcock. 1 cass. (National Meeting of the Institute, 1993 Ser.). 4.00 (93N6) IRL Chicago.

How Few Remain. collector's ed. Harry Turtledove. Narrated by George Guidall. 18 cass. (Running Time: 24 hrs. 30 mins.). (Great War Ser.: Bk. 2). 2002. 69.95 (978-1-4025-0630-7(9), 96607) Recorded Bks.
A generation after the South wins the Civil War, it annexes critical territory in Mexico. Outraged, the United States declares total war. This time the American army faces danger on all sides - Confederates, outlaws, Apaches, French, and even the British. George Custer and Teddy Roosevelt fight hard and give the Americans hope. But to win, they need a commander as brilliant as Stonewall Jackson, and they must stop Jeb Stuart's glorious cavalry.

How Few Remain. unabr. ed. Harry Turtledove. Narrated by George Guidall. 18 cass. (Running Time: 24 hrs. 30 mins.). (Great War Ser.: Bk. 2). 2002. 149.00 (978-1-4025-0629-1(5)) Recorded Bks.

How Fiction Works. unabr. ed. James Wood. (Running Time: 4 hrs. 0 mins.). (ENG.). 2009. 19.95 (978-1-4332-9122-7(3)); 24.95 (978-1-4332-9118-0(5)); audio compact disk 49.00 (978-1-4332-9119-7(3)) Blckstn Audio.

How Full Is Your Bucket? Positive Strategies for Work & Life. unabr. ed. Tom Rath. Told to Donald O. Clifton. 2005. 12.95 (978-0-7435-5113-7(3)) Pub: S&S Audio. Dist(s): S and S Inc

How Full Is Your Bucket? Positive Strategies for Work & Life. unabr. ed. Tom Rath. Read by Tom Rath. Told to Donald Clifton. 2 CDs. (Running Time: 20 hrs. 0 mins. 0 sec.). (ENG.). 2004. audio compact disk 20.00 (978-0-7435-4426-9(9)) Pub: S&S Audio. Dist(s): S and S Inc

How God Led Me into the Working of Miracles Pt. 1: How Spiritual Gifts Operate. Derek Prince. 1 cass. (B-2009) Derek Prince.

How God Led Me into the Working of Miracles Pt .2: Testimonies of Miraculous Healings. Derek Prince. 1 cass. (B-2010) Derek Prince.

How God Taught Me to Praise. 1986. 4.95 (C45) Carothers.

How Goes the Battle. Harry Binswanger. (Running Time: 60 min.). 14.95 (CB54C) Second Renaissance.
How far objectivism has come, how things stand today & what the prospects are for future victory.

How Good Is Good Enough? unabr. ed. Andy Stanley. 2 CDs. (Running Time: 2 hrs. 15 mins. 0 sec.). (ENG.). 2006. audio compact disk 15.98 (978-1-59644-274-0(3), Hovel Audio) christianaud.

***How Good Is Good Enough?** unabr. ed. Andy Stanley. Narrated by Paul Michael. (ENG.). 2006. 9.98 (978-1-59644-275-7(1), Hovel Audio) christianaud.

How Government Destroys Our Money. unabr. ed. Murray Newton Rothbard. 1 cass. (Running Time: 59 min.). 12.95 (429) J Norton Pubs.
Rothbard contends that government policies are to blame for inflation. He explains how this occurs through the excessive printing of paper money & the operation of the banking system.

How Great a Love Series. 2004. audio compact disk 22.00 (978-1-59834-051-8(4)) Walk Thru the Bible.

How Great Generals Win. unabr. ed. Bevin Alexander. Read by James Slattery. 8 cass. (Running Time: 11 hrs. 30 mins.). 1995. 56.95 (978-0-7861-0909-8(2), 1706) Blckstn Audio.
Throughout history great generals have done what their enemies have least expected. Instead of direct, predictable attack, they have deceived, encircled, outflanked, out-thought, & triumphed over often superior armies commanded by conventional thinkers. Collected here are the stories of the most successful commanders of all time - among them Hannibal, Genghis Khan, Napoleon, Stonewall Jackson, Sherman, Rommel, Mao Zedong - who have demonstrated at their own points in history, the strategic & tactical genius essential for victory. Ironically this virtue does not come naturally to military organizations, since more often than not the straight-ahead, narrow-thinking soldier will be promoted over his more lateral-minded, devious counterpart. Yet when the latter gets control, the results may be spectacular.

How Great Is Our God. Contrib. by Louie Giglio. 2008. audio compact disk 14.99 (978-5-557-44624-2(9)) Pt of Grace Ent.

How Great Is Our God. Contrib. by Passion. Prod. by Nathan Nockels. Contrib. by Louie Giglio. 2005. audio compact disk 16.98 (978-5-559-11298-5(4)) Pt of Grace Ent.

How Great Is Our God. Contrib. by Chris Tomlin. (Praise Hymn Soundtracks Ser.). 2005. audio compact disk 8.98 (978-5-559-07869-4(7)) Pt of Grace Ent.

How Great Is Our God. Contrib. by Chris Tomlin. (Mastertrax Ser.). 2006. audio compact disk 9.98 (978-5-558-01818-9(6)) Pt of Grace Ent.

How Great Is Our God. Contrib. by Chris Tomlin. (Worship Tracks (Word Tracks) Ser.). 2006. audio compact disk 8.98 (978-5-558-26895-9(6), Word Music) Word Enter.

How Great Our Joy. Tom Fettke. 1997. 75.00 (978-0-7673-3299-6(7)); 11.98 (978-0-7673-3298-9(9)); 8.00 (978-0-7673-3296-5(2)); audio compact disk 85.00 (978-0-7673-3300-9(4)) LifeWay Christian.

How Great Our Joy. Tom Fettke. 1997. audio compact disk 12.00 (978-0-7673-3439-6(6)); audio compact disk 16.98 (978-0-7673-3438-9(8)) LifeWay Christian.

How Great Thou Art. 1 cass. 7.98 (1000667); audio compact disk 14.95 (109114) Covenant Comms.
More great hymns from the New Hymn Book.

How Great Thou Art. Contrib. by Bill & Gloria Gaither and Their Homecoming Friends. (Gaither Gospel Ser.). 2007. audio compact disk 17.99 (978-5-557-62815-0(0)) Gaither Music Co.

How Great Thou Art. Bill Gaither & Gloria Gaither. (Gaither Gospel Ser.). 2007. 19.99 (978-5-557-62817-4(7)) Gaither Music Co.

How Great Thou Art. Perf. by Robert Kochis & Robin Kochis. 1 cass. (Running Time: 40 mins.). 1999. 10.95 (T8775); audio compact disk 15.95 (K5165) Liguori Pubns.
Songs include: "Kum Ba Yah," "Here I Am Lord," "Ave Maria," "On Eagle's Wings" & more.

How Great Thou Art. Warren W. Wiersbe. Read by Warren W. Wiersbe. 2 cass. (Running Time: 3 hrs.). 1987. 9.95 (978-0-8474-2315-6(8)) Back to Bible.
Features eight messages from Psalm 139, focusing on God's attributes.

How Great Thou Art: Gospel Favorites Live from the Grand Ole Opry. Contrib. by Steve Buchanan & Pete Fisher. 2008. audio compact disk 13.99 (978-5-557-47581-5(8)) Pt of Grace Ent.

How Green Was My Valley. unabr. ed. Richard Llewellyn. Read by Philip Madoc. 12 cass. (Running Time: 18 hrs.). 2000. 79.95 (978-0-7451-6106-8(5), CAB 650) Pub: Chivers Audio Bks GBR. Dist(s): AudioGO
Tells the dramatic tale of Huw Morgan, a coal miner, in a South Wales town during World War II. First there were green mountains and rich, fertile valleys. Then they discovered coal below the meadows and the people's lives changed. They learned to live with danger and disaster, and forgot how green their valley once was.

How Green Was My Valley, unabr. ed. Richard Llewellyn. Narrated by Patrick Tull. 14 cass. (Running Time: 21 hrs.). 1994. 112.00 (978-1-55690-981-8(0), 94120E7) Recorded Bks.
To young Huw Morgan, who lives with his large & boisterous family in a small village in South Wales, there seems no end to the bounty coal has brought to his valley. But as the shadow of the slag heap falls ominously over the land, destroying its beauty & embroiling the village in a controversy that pits brother against brother, Huw faces an uncertain future.

How Hackleburg Became a 13-Pie Church. 2005. audio compact disk 24.95 (978-1-885224-54-5(0), Bristol Bks) Bristol Hse.

How Happy I Would Be! Alma Flor Ada. Illus. by Viví Escrivá. (Stories for the Telling Ser.). (J). (gr. k-3). 4.95 (978-1-58105-322-7(3)) Santillana.

How He Cut His Stick see Classic Detective Stories, Vol. I, A Collection

How He Cut His Stick. unabr. ed. M. Bodkin. Read by Cindy Hardin. 1 cass. (Running Time: 56 min.). Dramatization. 1981. 8.95 (N-80) Jimcin Record.
Dora Myrl & Lovdday Brooks, Lady Detectives of the Victorian age.

How Hedley Hopkins Did a Dare, Robbed a Grave, Made a New Friend Who Might Not Really Have Been There at All & While He Was at It Committed a Terrible Sin Which Everyone Was Doing Even Though He Didn't Know It. unabr. ed. Paul Jennings. Read by Jerome Pride. (Running Time: 4 hrs.). (YA). 2006. audio compact disk 57.95 (978-1-74093-727-6(9)) Pub: Bolinda Pubng AUS. Dist(s): Bolinda Pub Inc

How High Is Heaven. Carolyn A. O'Riley. Illus. by Carolyn A. O'Riley. (J). (ps-2). 1998. spiral bd. 15.00 (978-1-891870-07-1(6), 00800) Archangels Pen.

How Hilda Hushed Her Hiccups. Tini Sisters Staff. Illus. by Erin Marie Mauterer. 1 CD. (Running Time: 15 min.). Dramatization. (Letter-Sound Listen & Retell Adventure Ser.). (J). (ps-2). 2000. bk. 18.95 (978-0-9678459-1-3(2)) Atori Pubng Inc.

How Hlakanyana Outwitted the Monster: A Story from Nelson Mandela's Favorite African Folktales. Read by Sean Hayes. Compiled by Nelson Mandela. Composed by Vusi Mahlasela. (Running Time: 7 mins.). (ENG.). 2009. 1.99 (978-1-60024-800-9(4)) Pub: Hachet Audio. Dist(s): HachBkGrp

How Humans Evolved. 2nd ed. Robert Boyd & Joan B. Silk. 1999. pap. bk. 60.29 (978-0-393-97477-5(4), Norton Paperbks) Norton.

How I Became a Pirate. Melinda Long. Narrated by Johnny Heller. (Running Time: 15 mins.). (J). 2003. audio compact disk 12.75 (978-1-4193-1765-1(2)) Recorded Bks.

***How I Changed My Mind about Women in Leadership: Compelling Stories from Prominent Evangelicals.** unabr. ed. Ed. by Alan F. Johnson. (Running Time: 12 hrs. 12 mins. 15 sec.). (ENG.). 2010. 16.99 (978-0-310-57747-8(0)) Zondervan.

How I Conquered Cancer. abr. ed. Excerpts. Eric Gardiner. Perf. by Eric Gardiner. 1 cass. (Running Time: 2 hrs.). Dramatization. 1998. bk. 14.95 Set. (978-1-885373-16-8(3)) Emerald Ink.
Describes a nauturopathic way to better health & conquering cancer without surgery.

How I Discovered the Basic Cause of Stress: "Feeling Good" unabr. ed. Lilburn S. Barksdale. Read by Lilburn S. Barksdale. Read by Mark Denis. 1 cass. (Running Time: 53 min.). 1980. 9.95 (978-0-918588-34-0(0), 176) NCADD.
L.S. Barksdale tells how three tragic events in his life led him to the basic cause of stress & how to overcome it. Side two presents the logic that allows you to return to your natural state of "feeling good".

How I Edited an Agricultural Paper see Man That Corrupted Hadleyburg & Other Stories

How I Edited an Agricultural Paper see Best of Mark Twain

How I Edited an Agricultural Paper see Favorite Stories by Mark Twain

How I Got Over. 1 cass., 1 CD. 10.98 (978-1-57908-355-7(2), 5308); audio compact disk 15.98 CD. (978-1-57908-354-0(4)) Platinm Enter.

How I Got the Hip Disc Jockey Blues. John B. Ryland & Johnson C. S. 3 CD's. (Running Time: 1 hrs. 47 mins.). 2003. 22.95 (978-0-9743985-1-8(9)) J B Ryland.

How I Got This Way. unabr. ed. Short Stories. Patrick F. McManus. Narrated by Norman Dietz. 5 cass. (Running Time: 7 hrs. 30 mins.). 1995. 44.00 (978-0-7887-0194-8(0), 94418E7) Recorded Bks.
A rib-tickling collection of stories about the outdoors. Join McManus & his pals on a venture into the Idaho wilderness that includes taking a hike with the President of the United States.

How I Helped O. J. Get Away with Murder: The Shocking Inside Story of Violence, Loyalty, Regret, & Remorse. unabr. ed. Mike Gilbert. Read by Mel Foster. (Running Time: 7 hrs. 0 mins. 0 sec.). (ENG.). 2008. audio compact disk 29.99 (978-1-4001-0759-9(8)) Pub: Tantor Media. Dist(s): IngramPubServ

How I Helped O. J. Get Away with Murder: The Shocking Inside Story of Violence, Loyalty, Regret, & Remorse. unabr. ed. Mike Gilbert. Read by Mel Foster. Narrated by Mel Foster. (Running Time: 7 hrs. 0 mins. 0 sec.). (ENG.). 2008. audio compact disk 19.99 (978-1-4001-5759-4(5)); audio compact disk 59.99 (978-1-4001-3759-6(4)) Pub: Tantor Media. Dist(s): IngramPubServ

How I Killed a Bear see Sampler of American Humor

How I Learned to Drive. unabr. ed. Paula Vogel. Perf. by Glenne Headly & Randall Arney. 2 CDs. (Running Time: 1 hr. 15 mins.). 2001. audio compact disk 25.95 (978-1-58081-188-0(4), CDTPT106) L A Theatre.

How I Lightened up. 1. 2004. audio compact disk 6.00 (978-1-932316-22-3(1)) Great C Pubng.

How I Live Now. Meg Rosoff. Read by Kim Mai. 4 CDs. (YA). 2005. audio compact disk 32.30 (978-0-307-20723-4(4)) Pub: Random Audio Pubg. Dist(s): NetLibrary CO

How I Live Now. unabr. ed. Meg Rosoff. Read by Kim Mai. 3 cass. (YA). 2005. 30.00 (978-0-307-20722-7(6)) Random.

How I Paid for College: A Novel of Sex, Theft, Friendship & Musical Theater. unabr. ed. Marc Acito. Narrated by Jeff Woodman. 10 CDs. (Running Time: 11 hrs.). 2004. audio compact disk 119.75 (978-1-4193-0740-9(1)) Recorded Bks.
It?s 1983, and 17-year-old Edward Zanni wants to study acting at Juilliard, but his newly remarried father who earns too much for Edward to claim scholarship money refuses to pay. So, Edward enlists the aid of his creative theater pals to swindle the money from his father.

How I Paid for College: A Novel of Sex, Theft, Friendship & Musical Theater. unabr. ed. Marc Acito. Narrated by Jeff Woodman. 8 cass. (Running Time: 11 hrs.). 2004. 79.75 (978-1-4193-0738-6(X), 97867MC) Recorded Bks.
From syndicated humor columnist Marc Acito comes a hysterically funny novel that is equal parts Ferris Bueller's Day Off, Fame, Risky Business, and The Catcher in the Rye. Edward Zanni is in a bind. He wants to study at Juilliard, but his father refuses to pay. So, while practicing for his high school's production of Grease, Edward enlists his theater pals to pose as priests and nuns and swindle the money from his father.

How I Paid for College: A Novel of Sex, Theft, Friendship & Musical Theater. unabr. ed. Marc Acito. 10 CDs. (Running Time: 11 hrs.). 2004. audio compact disk 29.99 (978-1-4193-0244-2(2), 01822) Recorded Bks.
Mix Ferris Bueller's Day Off with Fame and The Catcher in the Rye, and you might get this hilarious novel. Edward wants to study acting at Juilliard, but his wealthy father won't pay. So Edward gets his theater pals to pose as nuns and priests in an embezzlement and money laundering scheme.

How I Play Golf. abr. ed. Tiger Woods. Read by Walter Franks. (ENG.). 2005. 14.98 (978-1-59483-400-4(8)) Pub: Hachet Audio. Dist(s): HachBkGrp

How I Play Golf. abr. ed. Tiger Woods. Read by Tiger Woods. Read by Walter Franks. (Running Time: 4 hrs. 30 mins.). (ENG.). 2010. audio compact disk 17.98 (978-1-60788-206-0(X)) Pub: Hachet Audio. Dist(s): HachBkGrp

How I Quit My $100,000 A Year Job: The Audio Book Your BOSS Doesn't Want You to Hear. (ENG.). 2005. audio compact disk 29.99 (978-0-9787947-0-5(2)) Word Out.

How I Raised Myself from Failure to Success in Selling. Frank Bettger. 1 cass. (Running Time: 1 hr. 16 min.). 11.00 (978-0-89811-026-5(2), 5169) Meyer Res Grp.
Use Bettger's method to further your own career.

How I Raised Myself from Failure to Success in Selling. Frank Bettger. 1 cass. 10.00 SMI Intl.
The story of Bettger's experience has inspired thousands to achieve success in selling. Use this method to further your own career. Recommended for salespeople who want to grow.

How I Spent My Summer Holidays. abr. ed. W. O. Mitchell. Narrated by W. O. Mitchell. 3 cass. (Running Time: 10800 sec.). (Between the Covers Classics). (ENG.). 2005. 19.95 (978-0-86492-258-8(2)) Pub: BTC Audiobks CAN. Dist(s): U Toronto Pr
"Mitchell's ironically titled novel How I Spent My Summer Holidays tells the story of twelve-year-old Hugh, who loses his innocence during the hot prairie summer of 1924 when sexual passions explode into murder. Hearing this dark coming-of-age tale in Mitchell's own voice is an experience not to be missed.".

How I Spent My Summer Holidays. 3rd abr. ed. W. O. Mitchell. Narrated by W. O. Mitchell. (Running Time: 10800 sec.). (ENG.). 2008. audio compact disk 29.95 (978-0-86492-475-9(5)) Pub: BTC Audiobks CAN. Dist(s): U Toronto Pr

How I Write: Secrets of a Bestselling Author. unabr. ed. Janet Evanovich. Narrated by Janet Evanovich. 6 CDs. (Running Time: 15480 sec.). 2006. audio compact disk 64.95 (978-0-7927-4372-9(5), SLD 996) AudioGO.

How I Write: Secrets of a Serial Fiction Writer. unabr. ed. Janet Evanovich & Ina Yalof. Narrated by Alex Evanovich. 4 cass. 2006. 44.95 (978-0-7927-4530-3(2), CSL 996) AudioGO.

How I Write: Secrets of a Serial Fiction Writer. unabr. ed. Janet Evanovich & Ina Yalof. 6 CDs. (Running Time: 7 hrs. 30 mins.). (ENG.). 2006. audio compact disk 24.95 (978-1-59397-949-2(5)) Pub: Macmill Audio. Dist(s): Macmillan

How Intuition Is Born. Swami Amar Jyoti. 1 cass. 1980. 9.95 (K-34) Truth Consciousness.
Opening into the next reality. Peeling off our layers of darkness. Preparing the ground for grace. The Greatest prayer.

How It Ended. unabr. ed. Jay McInerney. (Running Time: 12 hrs. 0 mins.). 2009. 29.95 (978-1-4332-7110-6(9)); 79.95 (978-1-4332-7106-9(0)); audio compact disk 29.95 (978-1-4332-7109-0(5)); audio compact disk 99.00 (978-1-4332-7107-6(9)) Blckstn Audio.

How Lance Does It: Put the Success Formula of a Champion into Everything You Do. Brad Kearns. 2009. audio compact disk 28.00 (978-1-933309-70-5(9)) Pub: A Media Intl. Dist(s): Natl Bk Netwk

How Leaders Lead: The Essential Skills for Career & Personal Success. Ken Blanchard & Brian S. Tracy. Read by Ken Blanchard & Brian S. Tracy. 6 cass. (Running Time: 5 hrs.). 1989. 79.95 set incl. action guide. (2041) Dartnell Corp.
How-to guide for gaining the real-life management skills you need in the modern work place.

How Leaders Lead: The Essential Skills for Career & Personal Success. abr. ed. Ken Blanchard & Brian S. Tracy. Read by Ken Blanchard & Brian S. Tracy. Ed. by Vera Derr. 2 cass. (Running Time: 3 hrs.). 1995. pap. bk. & wbk. ed. 16.95 (978-0-85013-243-4(6), 393070) Dartnell Corp.
This is a how-to-guide for gaining the real-life management skills you need in the modern workplace. Learn how to get to the top & stay there, climb to the top faster & discover the leadership skills that you should be applying now.

How Life Imitates Chess. unabr. ed. Garry Kasparov. Read by Adam Grupper. (Running Time: 7 hrs. 0 mins. 0 sec.). (ENG.). 2007. audio compact disk 29.95 (978-1-4272-0228-4(1)) Pub: Macmill Audio. Dist(s): Macmillan

How Like a Winter Hath My Absence Been: Sonnet 97 see Palgrave's Golden Treasury of English Poetry

How Long Is Your Shadow? John 21:1-3; Acts 5:15. Ed Young. (J). 1979. 4.95 (978-0-7417-1095-6(1), A0095) Win Walk.

How Long Till Realization? Swami Amar Jyoti. 1 cass. 1981. 9.95 (C-31) Truth Consciousness.
No time factor is involved in Enlightenment. Using efforts to exhaust efforts till we surrender.

How long will you be on that Stuff? Education for those who love addicts taking Suboxone. Created by FDL Psychiatry. 2009. 39.99 (978-0-9840972-6-5(0)) Term Un Pub.

***How Loved.** Abundant Life Ministries , Abundant Life Ministries. (ENG.). 2006. audio compact disk 17.99 (978-92-822-5212-3(4)) Pub: Kingsway Pubns GBR. Dist(s): STL Dist NA

How Managers Make Things Happen. George Odiorne. 4 cass. (Running Time: 4 hrs.). 1988. pap. bk. 59.95 (978-0-13-397472-0(3)) P-H.
Features practical how-to information based on the proven principles & techniques developed by a national expert on management.

How Managers Make Things Happen. unabr. ed. George Odiorne. 4 cass. 59.95 set incl. 53-page wkbk. (S02070) J Norton Pubs.
This up-to-the-minute program will show you how to become a street-smart manager, take charge, & stay in control. You will learn specific ways to motivate people to act with scores of proven high-powered techniques for streamlining inefficient operations & eliminating careless slipshod work.

How Many? Sundance/Newbridge, LLC Staff. (Early Math Ser.). (gr. k-1). 2000. 12.00 (978-1-58273-306-7(6)) Sund Newbridge.

How Many? How Much? Audio. (Metro Reading Ser.). (J). (gr. k). 2000. 11.11 (978-1-58120-974-7(6)) Metro Teaching.

***How Many Fish?** unabr. ed. Caron Lee Cohen. (ENG.). 2008. (978-0-06-169470-7(3)); (978-0-06-171007-0(5)) HarperCollins Pubs.

How Many Muffins? Early Explorers Early Set A Audio CD. Benchmark Education Staff. (J). 2006. audio compact disk 10.00 (978-1-4108-7631-7(4)) Benchmark Educ.

How Many Vehicles Can You Name? I Can Name These Objects! Can You? What Animals Do You See? Gracie Middlebrooks-Hutcherson. Tr. by Earle D. Clowney. Illus. by Matthew Hutcherson, III. (ENG & SPA.). (J). 1992. (978-1-882485-06-2(8)) Enhance Your Chlds.

How Markets Fail: An Anatomy of Irrationality. unabr. ed. John Cassidy. (Running Time: 13 hrs. 30 mins.). 2009. audio compact disk 39.95 (978-1-4417-2308-6(0)) Blckstn Audio.

How Markets Fail: The Economics of Rational Irrationality. unabr. ed. John Cassidy. (Running Time: 13 hrs. 30 mins.). 2009. 79.95 (978-1-4417-2305-5(6)); audio compact disk 109.00 (978-1-4417-2306-2(4)) Blckstn Audio.

How Markets Fail: The Logic of Economic Calamities. unabr. ed. John Cassidy. (Running Time: 13 hrs. 30 mins.). 2009. 29.95 (978-1-4417-2309-3(9)) Blckstn Audio.

How Mary & the Rosary Can Change Your Life. Marcellino D'Ambrosio. 2004. audio compact disk 7.95 (978-1-932927-13-9(1)) Ascensn Pr.

How Men & Women Can Better Understand Each Other: How to Have a Healthy Sexual Life. Scripts. 2 cass. (Running Time: 60 mins.).Tr. of Hombre y la Mujer, Como Entenderse Mejor Hacia Una Vida Sexual Sana. (SPA.). 2003. 25.00 (978-0-9744786-4-7(4)) A Nogales.
Doctor Nogales is pleased to offer this important series of psychological self-help cassettes. Although they don't replace psychological therapy, they will give you the necessary information to find your own answers and possible solutions to common difficulties and life challenges. They also include practical exercises that can help to guide listeners to a healthier life. ?How Men and Women Can Better Understand Each Other??How to Have a Healthy Sexual Life?.

How Modern Churches Are Harming Families. John Thompson. 1 CD. (Running Time: 44 mins.). 2001. audio compact disk 10.00 (978-1-929241-53-8(4)) Pub: Vsn Forum. Dist(s): STL Dist NA

How Modern Churches Are Harming Families. John Thompson. 1 cass. (Running Time: 44 mins.). 2001. 7.00 (978-1-929241-40-8(2)) Pub: Vsn Forum. Dist(s): STL Dist NA

How Mother Nature Flowered the Fields. unabr. ed. Tom Schwartz. Read by Ron Knowles. (J). 2008. 34.99 (978-1-60514-645-4(5)) Find a World.

How Mother Nature Flowered the Fields. unabr. ed. Tom Schwartz. Narrated by Ron Knowles. (Running Time: 1 hr. 8 mins.). (ENG.). (J). 2006. 14.95 (978-1-57545-333-0(9), RP Audio Pubng) Pub: Reagent Press. Dist(s): OverDrive Inc

How Mrs. Claus Saved Christmas. Jeff Guinn. Read by Susan Denaker. Frwd. by Santa Claus. 7 CDs. (Running Time: 39600 sec.). 2005. audio compact disk 29.95 (978-1-59316-056-2(9), LL148) Listen & Live.
In this delightful follow-up to Jeff Guinn's "The Autobiography of Santa Claus," listeners hear the tale of jolly ol' Mrs. Claus and how she saved Christmas! Children, parents and entire families will enjoy this holiday classic!.

How Mrs. Claus Saved Christmas. unabr. ed. Jeff Guinn. Read by Susan Denaker. (YA). 2006. 39.99 (978-1-59895-203-2(X)) Find a World.

How Much Does Salvation Cost? Parables of Jesus. Ben Young. 2000. 4.95 (978-0-7417-6166-8(1), B0166) Win Walk.

How Much Is a Million? 2004. bk. 24.95 (978-1-55592-059-3(4)); pap. bk. 18.95 (978-1-55592-106-4(X)); pap. bk. 38.75 (978-1-55592-633-5(9)); pap. bk. 32.75 (978-1-55592-242-9(2)); pap. bk. 32.75 (978-1-55592-243-6(0)); pap. bk. 14.95 (978-1-55592-060-9(8)); audio compact disk 12.95 (978-1-55592-952-7(4)) Weston Woods.

How Much Is a Million. 2004. pap. bk. 14.95 (978-1-55592-659-5(2)) Weston Woods.

How Much Is a Million? Syd Hoff. Tr. by Teresa Mlawer. 1 cass. (Running Time: 1 hr. 30 mins.). (J). (gr. 1-2). 2004. 8.95 (978-1-55592-993-0(1), WW30944) Weston Woods.

How Much Is a Million? David M. Schwartz. Illus. by Steven Kellogg. 1 cass., 5 bks. (Running Time: 30 min.). (J). pap. bk. 32.75 Weston Woods.

How Much Is a Million? David M. Schwartz. Illus. by Steven Kellogg. 1 cass. (Running Time: 30 min.). (J). bk. 24.95; pap. bk. 12.95 Weston Woods.

How Much Is a Million? David M. Schwartz. Illus. by Steven Kellogg. Narrated by Bruce Johnson. Music by Bruce Zimmerman. 1 cass. (Running Time: 10 min.). (J). (gr. 1-4). 2000. pap. bk. 12.95 Weston Woods.
With the help of Marvelosissimo the Mathematical Magician, the concepts of a million, a billion & a trillion are not quite so intimidating. In fact they're fun for budding math students & for everyone with an imagination.

How Much Is Enough? David Freudberg. Perf. by Vicki Robin et al. 2 cass. (Running Time: 2 hrs.). 1991. 16.95 Set. (978-0-9640914-9-8(6)) Human Media.
Why people are consciously turning from materialism to a lifestyle relying more on inner fulfillment.

How much Is Enough? Harness the Power of Your Money Story-and Change Your Life. Pamela York Klainer. Narrated by Suzanne Toren. 7 cass. (Running Time: 9 hrs. 30 mins.). 64.00 (978-1-4025-3224-5(5)) Recorded Bks.

How Much Land Does a Man Need? 1 cass. (Running Time: 1 hr. 30 mins.). (SmartReader Ser.). (J). 1999. pap. bk. & tchr. ed. 19.95 (978-0-7887-2855-6(5), 79672T3) Recorded Bks.
An adaptation from the original text by Leo Tolstoi. Step back to 19th century Russia & discover what life was like for a hard-working farmer. Pahom finally buys some land of his own, but he still has problems. How much land does he need to be truly happy?.

How Much Wood Could a Woodchuck Chuck? unabr. ed. Danny Adlerman. 1 CD. (Running Time: 6 mins.). (J). (ps-k). 2007. bk. 17.00 (978-0-9705773-4-4(6)) Kids At Our House.

How Much Word Is in You? Jawanza Kunjufu. 1 cass. (Running Time: 60 mins.). 1999. 5.95 (AT22) African Am Imag.

How Musical Is Man? John Blacking. (Jessie & John Danz Lectures). 1990. 20.00 (978-0-295-75517-5(2)) U of Wash Pr.

How Not to Be a Fool: Making Wise Choices. Doug Fields. (Super-Ser.). 2007. audio compact disk 30.00 (978-5-557-78147-3(1)) Group Pub.

How Not to Be Irritated. 4.95 (C5) Carothers.

How Not to Do Apologetics: Evidentialism. John Robbins. 1 cass. (Blue Banner Lectures Ser.: No. 4). 5.00 Trinity Found.

How Not to Do Apologetics: Irrationalism. John Robbins. 1 cass. (Blue Banner Lectures Ser.: No. 3). 5.00 Trinity Found.

How Not to Do Apologetics: Rationalism. John Robbins. 1 cass. (Blue Banner Lectures Ser.: No. 2). 5.00 Trinity Found.

How Not to Get AIDS from Your Doctor. Robert Mendelsohn. 1 cass. (Running Time: 45 min.). 7.95 (AC25) Am Media.
Why it's no longer safe to go to one's doctor. Not only can one get AIDS, by many other doctor-transmitted or induced diseases as well.

How Not to Get Burned Set: Bible Truth Made Clear. Eugene Priddy. 10 CDs. (Running Time: 12 hrs.). Dramatization. 2003. audio compact disk 19.95 (978-0-9660012-7-3(3), BBI Pubns) Bible Basics.

***How Not to Get Fired Before You Get Hired: Job Interview Tactics & Strategies.** Kathy Pagana. (ENG.). 2010. audio compact disk 15.95 (978-1-933631-99-8(6)) Acanthus Pubg.

How not to Graduate into Poverty. Michael Brown. (ENG.). 2009. 14.95 (978-0-9818958-8-8(3)) Pub: Acanthus Pubg. Dist(s): AtlasBooks

How Not to Lose Heart. 2 CDs. 2007. audio compact disk 14.00 (978-1-933207-18-6(3)) Ransomed Heart.

How Not to Miss Christmas: Luke 2:6; Matt 2:2-5. Ed Young. 1994. 4.95 (978-0-7417-2041-2(8), 1041) Win Walk.

***How Now Shall We Live.** abr. ed. Charles Colson. Narrated by Wayne Shepherd. (ENG.). 2006. 14.98 (978-1-59644-102-6(X), Hovel Audio) christianaud.

How Now Shall We Live? abr. ed. Charles W. Colson & Nancy Pearcey. 6 CDs. (Running Time: 6 hrs. 48 mins. 0 sec.). (ENG.). 2006. audio compact disk 23.98 (978-1-59644-101-9(1), Hovel Audio) christianaud.
Christianity is more than a personal relationship with Jesus Christ. It is also a worldview that answers life's basic questions and shows us how we should live as a result of those answers. How Now Shall We Live? equips Christians to confront false worldviews and live redemptively in contemporary culture.True Christianity goes far beyond John 3:16a??beyond private faith and personal salvation. It is nothing less than a framework for understanding all of reality.It is a worldview. In How Now Shall We Live?, the 2000 Gold Medallion winner for best book about Christianity and society, Chuck Colson and Nancy Pearcey show that the great spiritual battle today is a cosmic struggle between competing worldviews. Through inspiring true stories and compelling teaching, they demonstrate how to A?Expose the false views and values of modern culture A?Live a more fulfilling life the way God created us to live A?Contend for the faith by understanding how nonbelievers think A?Build a society that reflects biblical principles.

How Now Shall We Live in the Face of Terrorism. Chuck Colson. 1 cass. (Running Time: 60 min.). (America Responds Ser.). 8.99 (978-1-58926-022-1(8)) Oasis Audio.

How One of You Can Bring the Two of You Together. abr. ed. Susan Page. 1 cass. (Running Time: 3 hrs.). 1999. 16.99 (70382) Courage-to-Change.
Learn how you can improve your marriage even if your partner is unwilling to help.

How Original Is Original Sin. unabr. ed. Aldous Huxley. 1 cass. (Running Time: 1 hr.). (Human Situation Ser.). 1959. 11.00 (01110) Big Sur Tapes.

How Our Past Lives Influence Us Now, Vol. 2. Bettye B. Binder. Contrib. by Mary Lynn Cullen. 6 cass. (Running Time: 6 hrs.). 1996. 19.95 SET. (978-1-879005-15-0(8)) Reincarnation Bks.
Lecture on identifying patterns of how past lives influence us now & how past life regression help people discover a joyful past life relationship. Questions & answers from audience reveals significant past life patterns influencing relationships now.

"How Paul Robeson Saved My Life" And Other Mostly Happy Stories. unabr. ed. Carl Reiner. Read by Carl Reiner. 2 cass. (Running Time: 3 hrs.). 2001. 18.00 (978-1-59040-027-2(5), Phoenix Audio) Pub: Amer Intl Pub. Dist(s): PerseuPGW
Filled with multi-dimensional tales, this short story collection is at once poignant, nostalgic and laugh-out-loud funny.

How People Change. Margaret Mead. 1 CD. (Running Time: 25 mins.). (Sound Seminars Ser.). 2006. audio compact disk 12.95 (978-1-57970-370-7(4), C35002D, Audio-For) J Norton Pubs.

How People Change. unabr. ed. Margaret Mead. 1 cass. (Running Time: 25 min.). 12.95 (35002) J Norton Pubs.
Our attitude toward change is crucial to our attitude toward the world as a whole; what is required to effect change in peoples & cultures.

How People Grow: What the Bible Reveals about Personal Growth. abr. ed. Henry Cloud. (Running Time: 2 hrs. 0 mins. 0 sec.). (ENG.). 2003. 10.99 (978-0-310-26058-5(2)) Zondervan.

How People Grow: What the Bible Reveals about Personal Growth. unabr. ed. Henry Cloud & John Townsend. 2001. 17.99 (978-0-310-24065-5(4)) Zondervan.

How Proust Can Change Your Life: Not a Novel. Alain de Botton. Read by Samuel West. 2 cass. (Running Time: 3 hrs.). 1999. 16.85 Set. (978-1-901768-34-3(1)) Pub: CSA Telltapes GBR. Dist(s): Ulverscroft US
Explores the nature of life, love, happiness & discontent.

How Proust Can Change Your Life: Not a Novel. abr. ed. Alain de Botton. Read by Samuel West. 2 cass. (Running Time: 3 hrs.). 1999. 17.95 (978-1-57270-097-0(1), L21097) Pub: Audio Partners. Dist(s): PerseuPGW
This unique, literary biography combines tongue-in-cheek self-help with insights gleaned from De Botton's reading of Proust's novels, letters & other writings.

How Rabbit Tricked Otter: And Other Cherokee Animal Stories. unabr. ed. Read by Gayle Ross. Music by Eddie Bushyhead. 1 cass. (Running Time: 1 hr.). (Native American Storytime Ser.). (J). (ps-5). 2001. 11.95 Parabola Bks.
Accompanied by traditional flute music, nine tales of Bear, Possum, Otter and the unforgettable trickster-hero, Rabbit. Includes "How Turtle's Back Was Cracked," "Why Possum's Tail Is Bare" and "The Origin of the Bear".

How RC Started, Side A. Harvey Jackins. 1 cass. 10.00 Rational Isl.
Side A: Describes the experiences that led to the development of re-evaluation counseling. Side B: A radio interview about re-evaluation counseling.

How Right You Are, Jeeves. unabr. ed. P. G. Wodehouse. Read by Ian Carmichael. 4 cass. (Running Time: 4 hrs. 49 min.). (Jeeves & Wooster Ser.). 2001. 24.95 (978-1-57270-237-0(0), C41237u) Pub: Audio Partners. Dist(s): PerseuPGW
The Times has announced, much to Bertie's astonishment, the news of his engagement to the beautiful Bobbie Wickham. But worse is yet to come - Uncle Tom's antique silver cow-creamer has gone missing. By a rare stroke of genius, Bertie finds a solution - which is to recall Jeeves from his annual holiday - & the incomparable manservant sorts everybody out in his usual imperturbable style.

How Right You Are, Jeeves. unabr. ed. P. G. Wodehouse. Read by Jonathan Cecil. Narrated by Ian Carmichael. 4 CDs. (Running Time: 17340 sec.). (Jeeves & Wooster Ser.). (ENG.). 2007. audio compact disk 25.95 (978-1-57270-833-4(6)) Pub: AudioGO. Dist(s): Perseus Dist

***How Ronald Reagan Changed My Life.** abr. ed. Peter Robinson. Read by Peter Robinson. (ENG.). 2004. (978-0-06-074634-6(3), Harper Audio); (978-0-06-079972-4(2), Harper Audio) HarperCollins Pubs.

How Satan Steals Finances. Elbert Willis. 1 cass. (Financial Prosperity Ser.). 4.00 Fill the Gap.

***How Sex Works.** unabr. ed. Sharon Moalem. Read by Oliver Wyman. (ENG.). 2009. (978-0-06-176870-5(7), Harper Audio); (978-0-06-176871-2(5), Harper Audio) HarperCollins Pubs.

How Shall We Escape? Nathaniel Holcomb. 2 cass. (Running Time: 3 hrs.). 1998. (978-1-930918-21-4(6)) Its All About Him.

How Shelley Died. unabr. ed. Gilbert Highet. Read by Gilbert Highet. 1 cass. (Running Time: 30 min.). 9.95 (23289-A) J Norton Pubs.

How Should We Then Live? The Rise & Decline of Western Thought & Culture. unabr. ed. Francis A. Schaeffer. Read by Kate Reading. (Running Time: 8 hrs. 0 mins. 0 sec.). (ENG.). 2007. audio compact disk 24.98 (978-1-59644-429-4(0)) christianaud.

***How Should We Then Live: The Rise & Decline of Western Thought & Culture.** unabr. ed. Francis A. Schaeffer. Narrated by Kate Reading. (ENG.). 2007. 14.98 (978-1-59644-430-0(4), Hovel Audio) christianaud.

***How Silver Fox & Coyote Came to Color the Butterfly.** Composed by Frances Rinaldi. (ENG.). (J). 2010. audio compact disk 9.97 (978-0-9826047-2-4(6)) Red FoxLLC FL.

How Sin Got Started: Romans 5:12-21. Ed Young. 1984. 4.95 (978-0-7417-1365-0(9), 365) Win Walk.

How Sinful Is Sin? Luke 15. Ed Young. 1985. 4.95 (978-0-7417-1460-2(4), 460) Win Walk.

***How Six Traveled the Wide World.** Anonymous. 2009. (978-1-60136-603-0(5)) Audio Holding.

How Some Animals Became As They Are see Chinese Fairy Tales

How Soon Hath Time... see Poetry of John Milton

How Spiders Got Eight Legs/Look at the Spider. Steck-Vaughn Staff. 1 cass. (Running Time: 30 min.). 1997. (978-0-8172-7375-0(1)) SteckVau.

How Starbucks Saved My Life: A Son of Privilege Learns to Live Like Everyone Else. unabr. ed. Michael Gates Gill. Read by Dylan Baker. 7 CDs. (Running Time: 8 hrs.). (ENG.). (gr. 8 up). 2007. audio compact disk 34.95 (978-0-14-314240-9(2), PengAudBks) Penguin Grp USA.

How Stella Got Her Groove Back. unabr. ed. Terry McMillan. Read by Tonya Jordan. 8 cass. (Running Time: 12 hrs.). 1996. 64.00 (978-0-7366-3418-2(5), 4064) Books on Tape.
Stella, age 42, has single-motherhood down to a science, maybe even an art. Look what she balances: an investment analyst job, a posh house, a BMW, a personal trainer & a great son. It's quite a life & at the same time, no life. Stella hasn't had romance in years.

How Stella Got Her Groove Back. unabr. ed. Terry McMillan. Narrated by Lynne Thigpen. 8 cass. (Running Time: 11 hrs. 30 mins.). 1996. 70.00 (978-0-7887-0755-1(8), 94653E7) Recorded Bks.
Stella Payne is a successful single mother. She vacations alone in Jamaica & finds something that has been missing from her life. The only problem is that he is half her age.

How Street Smart Is Your Family? unabr. ed. George S. Cleare. Ed. by Karl Mucker. 2 cass. (Running Time: 1 hr. 05 min.). Dramatization. 1994. 14.99 Set. (978-0-9643169-0-4(0)) Prsnl Security.
More than 50 life-saving tips are included. Tape One, "How to Raise Street-Smart Kids," offers the best ways to avoid situations that might lead to assault or child abuse. Tape Two, "How to Become a Street-Smart Senior," offers older adults dozens of practical ways to keep criminals away & stay safe. Topics covered include how to be safe on the street, in parking lots, & public buildings, as well as effective ways to avoid assault, rape, car jackings, kidnapping & robberies, among other crimes. Endorsed by public safety officials, teachers, & parents.

How Strong Is He? Logos September 26, 1999. Ben Young. 1999. 4.95 (978-0-7417-6149-1(1), B0149) Win Walk.

***How Success Happens.** unabr. ed. David Brooks. (Running Time: 7 hrs.). (ENG.). 2011. audio compact disk 35.00 (978-0-307-73900-1(7), Random AudioBks) Pub: Random Audio Pubg. Dist(s): Random

How Successful People Think: Change Your Thinking, Change Your Life. unabr. ed. John C. Maxwell. Read by John C. Maxwell. Read by Chris Sorenson. (Running Time: 3 hrs.). (ENG.). 2009. 16.98 (978-1-60024-610-4(9)) Pub: Center St. Dist(s): HachBkGrp

How Successful People Think: Change Your Thinking, Change Your Life. unabr. ed. John C. Maxwell. Read by John C. Maxwell. Read by Chris Sorensen. 3 CDs. (Running Time: 3 hrs.). (ENG.). 2009. audio compact disk 24.98 (978-1-60024-609-8(5)) Pub: Center St. Dist(s): HachBkGrp

How Successful Small Businesses Operate, Vol. 47. 1 cass. (Running Time: 45 min.). (Buisness Opportunities Ser.). 1987. 7.95 B & H Comm.
The key characteristics of successful small businesses, the skills needed for success & the reason why many successful small businesses are actually more profitable than their large corporate counterparts.

How Summer Came to Canada. 2004. 8.95 (978-1-56008-928-5(8)); cass. & flmstrp 30.00 (978-1-56008-687-1(4)) Weston Woods.

How Sweet It Is. 1 cass. (Running Time: 43 min.). (J). (ps-4). 1998. 9.98 (978-1-888795-09-7(3)); audio compact disk 12.98 CD. (978-1-888795-10-3(7)) Sugar Beats.
Thirteen songs from the 60's, 70's & 80's are remade info a fresh & lovely collection for children & their parents to enjoy.

How Sweet It Is: Fresh Versions of Retro Pop for Kids. Perf. by Sherry Goffin Kondor et al. 1 cass. (J). 1998. 9.98; 12.98 CD. Sugar Beats.
Includes favorite tunes from the '60s, '70s, & '80s, such as the Bee Gees, the Bangles, the Go-Gos & even the Archies. Listeners of all ages will find it hard to resist dancing around the house or bopping in the car to these catchy lyrics.

How Sweet the Sound Accompaniment. Cindy Berry. 1997. 75.00 (978-0-7673-3982-7(7)) LifeWay Christian.

How Sweet the Sound Cassette Promo Pak. Cindy Berry. 1997. 8.00 (978-0-7673-3986-5(X)) LifeWay Christian.

How Sweet the Sound Choir Cassette. Cindy Berry. 1997. 11.98 (978-0-7673-3984-1(3)) LifeWay Christian.

How Sweet the Sound Split Acc Cd. Cindy Berry. 1997. audio compact disk 85.00 (978-0-7673-3985-8(1)) LifeWay Christian.

How Teddy Bears Find Their Homes. David K. Waldman. 1 cass. (J). (gr. k-3). 1997. 7.95 (978-0-945522-00-3(2)) Rebecca Hse.
Teaching children through fantasy & song, values of love & self love.

How the Administrative Professional Changed When No One Was Looking Audio CD. 2005. audio compact disk 15.00 (978-0-9717456-4-3(1)) Office Dynamics.

How the Beetle Got Its Colors CD: Scripts for Young Readers. Read by Patrick Feehan. Retold by Heather McDonald. (J). 2009. 9.95 (978-1-60184-161-2(2)) Primry Concpts.

***How the Best Leaders Lead: Proven Secrets to Getting the Most Out of Yourself & Others.** unabr. ed. Brian Tracy. Read by Brian Tracy. (Running Time: 6 hrs.). (ENG.). 2009. 27.98 (978-1-59659-505-7(1), GildAudio) Pub: Gildan Media. Dist(s): HachBkGrp

How the Best Leaders Lead: Proven Secrets to Getting the Most Out of Yourself & Others. unabr. ed. Brian Tracy. Read by Brian Tracy. (Running Time: 6 hrs.). (ENG.). 2010. audio compact disk 29.98 (978-1-59659-358-9(X), GildAudio) Pub: Gildan Media. Dist(s): HachBkGrp

How the Camel Got His Hump see Just So Stories, Set, For Little Children

How the Camel Got His Hump. Rudyard Kipling. 1 read-along cass. (Running Time: 15 min.). (World of Just So Stories Ser.). (J). bk. 15.00 (SAC 6503B) Spoken Arts.

How the Camel Got His Hump. Rudyard Kipling. 1 cass. (J). 1989. bk. 14.00 Windham Hill.

How the Catholic Church Built Western Civilization. Thomas E. Woods, Jr. Read by Barrett Whitener. (Running Time: 7 mins.). 2005. 44.95 (978-0-7861-3668-1(5)); audio compact disk 55.00 (978-0-7861-7699-1(7)) Blckstn Audio.

How the Catholic Church Built Western Civilization. unabr. ed. Thomas E. Woods, Jr. 6 cass. (Running Time: 25200 sec.). 2005. 29.95 (978-0-7861-3655-1(3), E3523); audio compact disk 29.95 (978-0-7861-7744-8(6), ZE3523) Blckstn Audio.

How the Catholic Church Built Western Civilization. unabr. ed. Thomas E. Woods, Jr. 13 vols. (Running Time: 25200 sec.). 2005. audio compact disk 29.95 (978-0-7861-7970-1(8), ZM3523) Blckstn Audio.

How the Comb Gives a Fresh Meaning to the Hair. Short Stories. Walter Abish. Read by Walter Abish. (Running Time: 70 min.). 13.95 (978-1-55644-092-2(8), 4011) Am Audio Prose.
Performance by a leading experimental writer, winner of the 1982 Penn-Faulkner Award.

***How the Fox Cheated Two Bear Cubs.** Anonymous. 2009. (978-1-60136-599-6(3)) Audio Holding.

How the Garcia Girls Lost Their Accents. unabr. ed. Julia Alvarez. Narrated by Blanca Camacho & Anne Henk. 8 CDs. (Running Time: 34200 sec.). 2006. audio compact disk 19.99 (978-1-4193-7795-2(7), 03722) Recorded Bks.
Hailed by the Los Angeles Times as "simply wonderful," How the Garcia Girls Lost Their Accents captures the vivid lives of the Garcia sisters, four privileged and rebellious Dominican girls adapting to their new lives in America. In the 1960s, political tension forces the Garcia family away from Santo Domingo and toward the Bronx. The sisters all hit their strides in America, adapting and thriving despite cultural differences, language barriers, and prejudice. But Mami and Papi are more traditional, and they have far more difficulty adjusting to their new country. Making matters worse, the girls - frequently embarrassed by their parents - find ways to rebel against them. A touching coming-of-age tale, this enthralling book perfectly illuminates the intergenerational struggles and multicultural clashes so common to the American immigrant family.

***How the Government Got in Your Backyard: Superweeds, Frankenfoods, Lawn Wars, & the (Nonpartisan) Truth about Environmental Policies.** Jeff Gillman & Eric Heberlig. 2011. audio compact disk 39.99 (978-1-61120-005-8(9)) Dreamscap OH.

How the Grinch Stole Christmas! Dr. Seuss. Perf. by Boris Karloff. 1 cass. (J). 3.98 Clamshell. (978-1-55886-143-5(2), BB/PT 450) Smarty Pants.

How the Grinch Stole Christmas & Other Gifts from Dr. Seuss. unabr. ed. Dr. Seuss. Read by Walter Matthau. (ENG.). (J). (ps). 2008. audio compact disk 19.99 (978-0-7393-7856-4(2), Listening Lib) Pub: Random Audio Pubg. Dist(s): Random

How the Grouch Found Christmas. Dennis Allen. 1999. 75.00 (978-0-7673-9744-5(4)); 11.98 (978-0-7673-9714-8(2)); 8.00 (978-0-7673-9646-2(4)); audio compact disk 85.00 (978-0-7673-9724-7(X)); audio compact disk 16.98 (978-0-7673-9705-6(3)); audio compact disk 12.00 (978-0-7673-9656-1(1)) LifeWay Christian.

How the Hierarchy Communicates with Humans: Dreams & Visions That Changed the United States & History. Instructed by Manly P. Hall. 8.95 (978-0-89314-137-0(2), C820418) Philos Res.

How the Irish Saved Civilization: The Untold Story of Ireland's Heroic Role from the Fall of Rome to the Rise of Medieval Europe. unabr. ed. Thomas Cahill. Read by Donal Donnelly. 7 Cds. (Running Time: 8 hrs.). (Hinges of History Ser.: Vol. 1). (ENG.). 2003. audio compact disk 34.95 (978-0-7393-0965-0(X)) Pub: Random Audio Pubg. Dist(s): Random

How the Irish Saved Civilization: The Untold Story of Ireland's Heroic Role from the Fall of Rome to the Rise of Medieval Europe. unabr. ed. Thomas Cahill. Narrated by Donal Donnelly. 6 cass. (Running Time: 8 hrs.). 1996. 51.00 (978-0-7887-0570-0(9), 94747E7) Recorded Bks.
As Europe reaches intellectual stagnation & decline, Ireland bursts forth as a vigorous haven of scholarship in its first century of literacy.

***How the Left Swiftboated America.** unabr. ed. John Gibson. (ENG.). 2009. (978-0-06-200229-7(5), Harper Audio) HarperCollins Pubs.

***How the Left Swiftboated America: The Liberal Media Conspiracy to Make You Think George Bush Was the Worst President in History.** unabr. ed. John Gibson. (ENG.). 2009. (978-0-06-199913-0(X), Harper Audio) HarperCollins Pubs.

How the Leopard Got His Spots see Ten All Time Favorite Stories

How the Leopard Got His Spots see Just So Stories, Set, For Little Children

How the Leopard Got His Spots. 1 cass. (Running Time: 12 min.). (Talking Bear Tapes Ser.). (J). 1986. 4.95 (978-0-89926-201-7(5), 914D) Audio Bk.

How the Lonely Keep. Contrib. by Terminal. Prod. by Zack Hodges. 2005. audio compact disk 13.98 (978-5-559-05592-3(1)) Tooth & Nail.

How the Media Works & How to Work the Media: Capitol Learning Audio Course. Sheilah Kast. Prod. by TheCapitol.Net. (ENG.). 2007. 47.00 (978-1-58733-066-7(0)) TheCapitol.

***How the Mighty Fall.** unabr. ed. Jim Collins. Read by Jim Collins. (ENG.). 2009. (978-0-06-194090-3(9), Harper Audio); (978-0-06-195724-6(0), Harper Audio) HarperCollins Pubs.

How the Mighty Fall: And Why Some Companies Never Give In. unabr. ed. Jim Collins. Read by Jim Collins. 2009. audio compact disk 29.99 (978-0-06-193923-5(4), Harper Audio) HarperCollins Pubs.

How the Mind Works. Swami Amar Jyoti. 1 cass. 1978. 9.95 (J-14) Truth Consciousness.
The four compartments of mind. Conscience, the voice of true religion. Inner & outer Guru.

How the Ostrich Got Its Long Neck. unabr. ed. Verna Aardema. Narrated by John McDonough. 1 cass. (Running Time: 15 mins.). (gr. k up). 1997. 10.00 (978-0-7887-1086-5(9), 95090E7) Recorded Bks.
A young ostrich's compassion pays off in this delightful African folk tale. it comes to us from the Akamba people of Kenya, a word that means "the place where there are ostriches".

How the Other Half Lives. 1 cass. (Urban Problems Ser.). 10.00 (UP703) Esstee Audios.
A good hard look at how poverty affected the lives of those who had to scrimp through life.

How the Rainbow Came to Be see Como Nacio el Arco Iris

How the Rainbow Came to Be. Alma Flor Ada. (Stories for the Year 'Round Ser.). (J). (gr. k-3). 4.95 (978-1-58105-314-2(2)) Santillana.

How the Rattlesnake Got It's Rattle. Steck-Vaughn Staff. 1997. (978-0-8172-7374-3(3)) SteckVau.

How the Rhinoceros Got His Skin see Just So Stories, Set, For Little Children

How the Rhinoceros Got His Skin. Rudyard Kipling. 1 read-along cass. (World of Just So Stories Ser.). (J). bk. 15.00 (SAC 6503C) Spoken Arts.

How the Rhinoceros Got His Skin. Rudyard Kipling. 1 cass. (J). bk. 14.00 Windham Hill.

How the Snake Got Its Rattles see Your Own World

How the Special Needs Brain Learns. David A. Sousa. 2002. 99.95 (978-0-7619-4668-7(3), B7850XV) Pub: Corwin Pr. Dist(s): SAGE

How the Student Brain Learns (CD) Eric Jensen. 2006. 64.95 (978-1-890460-18-1(4)) Pub: Corwin Pr. Dist(s): SAGE

How the Swans Came to America. unabr. ed. Rick Fields & Elizabeth Gips. 1 cass. 1998. 11.00 (32002) Big Sur Tapes.

How the Tiger Got Its Stripes CD: Scripts for Young Readers. Read by Patrick Feehan. Retold by Heather McDonald. (J). 2009. 9.95 (978-1-60184-163-6(9)) Primry Concpts.

How the Toad Got Its Spots. Dorothy S. Bishop et al. 1 cass. (Bilingual Fables). (J). 12.00 (Natl Textbk Co); audio compact disk 69.95 (978-0-8442-7173-6(X), Natl Textbk Co) M-H Contemporary.
Features stories in Spanish & English.

How the Turtle Got Its Shell. Short Stories. Read by Jeff Olmsted. Adapted by Sandra Robbins. Illus. by Iku Oseki. (Running Time: 32 mins). (See-More's Stories Ser.). (J). 2001. pap. bk. 11.95 (978-1-882601-35-6(1)); pap. bk. 16.95 (978-1-882601-40-0(8)) See-Mores Wrkshop.

How the Turtle Got Its Shell: An African Tale. Sandra Robbins. Illus. by Iku Oseki. (See-More's Stories Ser.). (J). (ps-4). 1993. 5.50 (978-1-882601-04-2(1)) See-Mores Wrkshop.

How the Turtle Got Its Shell: An African Tale. unabr. ed. Sandra Robbins. Read by Jeff Olmsted et al. 1 cass. (Running Time: 32 min.). Dramatization. (See-More Ser.). (J). (gr. k-5). 1991. 5.00 (978-1-882601-11-0(4)) See-Mores Wrkshop.
Created for children based on Shadow Box Theatre's Production.

How the Universe Got Its Spots: Diary of a Finite Time in a Finite Space. unabr. ed. Janna Levin. Read by Christine Williams. (Running Time: 7 hrs. 30 mins.). 2010. 29.95 (978-1-4332-2969-5(2)); 54.95 (978-1-4332-2965-7(X)); audio compact disk 69.00 (978-1-4332-2966-4(8)) Blckstn Audio.

How the West Grew Rich. unabr. ed. Nathan Rosenberg & L. E. Birdzell, Jr. Read by Glenn Mitchell. 11 cass. (Running Time: 16 hrs.). 1989. 76.95 (978-0-7861-0274-7(8), 1240) Blckstn Audio.
Demonstrates that it was the break-up of centralized political & religious controls, rather than any one factor, that allowed an autonomous economic sphere to emerge.

***How the West was Read, Vol. 1.** Ed. by Robert J. Randisi. 2009. (978-1-60136-503-3(9)) Audio Holding.

***How the West was Read, Vol. 2.** Ed. by Robert J. Randisi. 2009. (978-1-60136-504-0(7)) Audio Holding.

***How the West Was Won.** unabr. ed. Louis L'Amour. (ENG.). 2011. audio compact disk 30.00 (978-0-307-91480-4(1), Random AudioBks) Pub: Random Audio Pubg. Dist(s): Random

How the Whale Got His Throat see Favorite Children's Stories: A Collection

How the Whale Got His Throat see Just So Stories, Set, For Little Children

How the Whale Got His Throat see Favorite Just So Stories

How the Whale Got His Throat. Rudyard Kipling. 1 read-along cass. (World of Just So Stories Ser.). (J). bk. 15.00 (SAC 6503A) Spoken Arts.

How the World Will End. Gary Arnold. (ENG.). 2009. audio compact disk 24.95 (978-1-57867-007-9(1)) Windhorse Corp.

How They Brought the Good News from Ghent to Aix see Browning's Last Duchess

How They Brought the Good News from Ghent to Aix see Classics of English Poetry for the Elementary Curriculum

How To. Elsevier USA.

How To. Nathaniel Holcomb. 3 cass. (Running Time: 4 hrs. 30 mins.). 1998. (978-1-930918-28-3(3)) Its All About Him.

How To: Flow in the Gifts of the Holy Spirit. unabr. ed. Andrew Wommack. Ed. by John Baker. 3 cass. (Running Time: 4 hrs. 30 mins.). 2001. 15.00 (978-1-881541-71-4(1), 1031) A Wommack.
Discusses how to flow in the gifts of the Holy Spirit, including, the importance of the gifts, knowing that the Lord is always "on," and understanding the divine flow.

How To: Volume 6. Created by Worship Together. (How to Worship Together Ser.). 2007. pap. bk. 21.95 (978-3-474-01170-3(7)) H Leonard.

How to Accompany. Duane Shinn. 1 cass. 19.95 (NS-4) Duane Shinn.
Teaches the basic principles of accompanying, which is different from playing solo piano.

***How to Ace Any US Military Exam: U. S. Navy Veteran & USA Memory Champion Reveals Secrets to Memorize Anything.** Ron White. (ENG.). 2010. audio compact disk 19.95 (978-0-9747212-5-5(5)) R White Train.

How to Achieve Healthy vs. Addictive Relationships. Theresa Exner. 1 cass. (Running Time: 72 min.). 9.95 (C051) A Ellis Institute.
Lively & engaging look at our assumptions about love. Learn to be a better friend to yourself & others by returning the focus of your love to personal growth.

How to Achieve Healthy vs. Addictive Relationships. Theresa Exner. 1 cass. (Running Time: 72 min.). 9.95 (C051) Inst Rational-Emotive.

How to Achieve Higher Consciousness. Jack Boland. 3 cass. 1980. 27.95 (978-0-88152-011-8(X)) Master Mind.
Learn to tap your reservoir of wisdom & power.

How to Achieve Material & Spiritual Success. Kriyananda, pseud. 1 cass. (Running Time: 75 min.). 9.95 (ST-47) Crystal Clarity.
Includes such topics as the human need to succeed; attitudes & qualities needed for success; dissolving obstacles through the power of concentration; measuring success by God's standards; how to obtain God's guidance.

How to achieve success in Sales see Como Lograr el Éxito: en Ventas, Edicion Empresarial

How to Achieve Total Prosperity. Mark Victor Hansen. 4 cass. 60.00 (1) M V Hansen.
Develop a "money consciousness" - earn, save, spend & invest money profitably.

How to Achieve True Prosperity. Kriyananda, pseud. 1 cass. (Running Time: 50 min.). 9.95 (SS-86) Crystal Clarity.
Topics include: Strengthening the energy flow as the main goal of any activity; why giving too much energy to "money & things" cuts you off from God; why working for the fun of it usually brings success; the importance of not thinking in terms of results; making God your partner.

How to Achieve Ultimate Success. Hosted by Paul Timm. 1 cass. (Running Time: 45 mins.). pap. bk. 99.95 (10011AV); pap. bk. 99.95 (1011AV) J Wilson & Assocs.

How to Acquire Dispassion. Swami Jyotirmayananda. Read by Swami Jyotirmayananda. 1 cass. (Running Time: 45 min.). 10.00 (800) Yoga Res Foun.

How to Acquire Peace of Mind. 1 cass. (Running Time: 1 hr.). 12.99 (606) Yoga Res Foun.

How to Acquire Spiritual Strength. (132) Yoga Res Foun.

How to Acquire Spiritual Strength, No. 1. Swami Jyotirmayananda. 1 cass. (Running Time: 1 hr.). 1990. 12.99 Yoga Res Foun.

How to Activate God's Power. Kenneth E. Hagin. 1 cass. 4.95 (SH05) Faith Lib Pubns.

How to Add Fills & Runs to Your Playing. Duane Shinn. 1 cass. 19.95 (NS-2) Duane Shinn.
Details how to put runs, echos & fillers in your piano playing to give it a full, professional sound. Uses the tune "Greensleaves" as a model.

How to Add Runs & Fills to Your Playing. Duane Shinn. Read by Duane Shinn. 1 cass. (Running Time: 60 min.). 19.95 incl. printed material. (NS-2) Duane Shinn.

How to Administer a Decedent's Estate. Read by John McDonnell, Jr. et al. (Running Time: 5 hrs. 30 min.). 1991. 97.00 Incl. 335p. tape materials. (ES-54170) Cont Ed Bar-CA.

How to Administer the Marital Deduction. Edward S. Schlesinger. 1 cass. (Running Time: 90 min.). 1995. 17.40 (M241) Am Law Inst.
Focuses on the strategies & techniques for taking the maximum allowable marital deduction & for decreasing the marital deduction. Mr. Schlesinger gives special attention to the surviving spouse's situation & to partial formula elections.

How to Advance Your Writing Career: An Audio Adaptation. Tracy St. John. 1 cass. (Running Time: 30 min.). 1988. 9.95 Reeder Pr.
Explains to would-be writers how to find a niche and market their work.

How to Age with Style. Albert Ellis. 1 cass. (Running Time: 70 min.). 9.95 (C045) A Ellis Institute.
This tape will appeal to people of all ages. It deals with the advantages of aging & helps you face the disadvantages straight-on. Octogenarian Ellis relates his own aging experiences - a lively, amusing, "no-baloney" approach.

How to Age with Style. Albert Ellis. 1 cass. (Running Time: 70 min.). 9.95 (C045) Inst Rational-Emotive.
Appeals to people of all ages. Deals with the advantages of aging & helps you face the disadvantages straight-on. Octogenarian Ellis relates his own aging experiences - a lively, amusing, "no-baloney" approach.

***How to amputate a Leg.** unabr. ed. Nathan Mullins. 2010. audio compact disk 77.95 (978-1-74214-885-4(9), 9781742148854) Pub: Bolinda Pubng AUS. Dist(s): Bolinda Pub Inc

How to Apply the Blood. Derek Prince. 1 cass. (Running Time: 60 min.). 5.95 (I-4255) Derek Prince.

How to Argue & Win Every Time: At Home, at Work, in Court, Everywhere, Every Day. unabr. ed. Gerry Spence. Read by Jonathan Marosz. 8 cass. (Running Time: 12 hrs.). 1995. 64.00 (978-0-7366-3079-5(1), 3760) Books on Tape.
Gerry Spence, one of America's most successful trial lawyers, tells you how to get your way every time. Strategy for the classroom, boardroom & bedroom.

How to Argue with Your Loved Ones see Como Pelear con sus Seres Queridos

How to Assert Yourself: Calmly & Confidently Get What You Want Without Hurting Others. unabr. ed. Cal LeMon. 2 cass. (Running Time: 3 hrs.). (Smart Audio Ser.). 2004. 19.99 (978-1-58926-333-8(2)) Oasis Audio.
Assertiveness is a choice you make for yourself - to stand up for your rights in a positive way...express anger and disagreement constructively, while preserving relationships. Learn to deal calmly and confidently with all kinds of people and get the results you want.

How to Assert Yourself: Calmly & Confidently Get What You Want Without Hurting Others. unabr. ed. Cal LeMon. Narrated by Cal LeMon. 3 CDs. (Running Time: 3 hrs.). (Smart Audio Ser.). (ENG.). 2004. audio compact disk 19.99 (978-1-58926-334-5(0)) Oasis Audio.

How to Attain Cosmic Consciousness. 1 cass. (Running Time: 1 hr.). 12.99 (200) Yoga Res Foun.

How to Attain Mental Serenity. 1 cass. (Running Time: 1 hr.). 12.99 (199) Yoga Res Foun.

How to Attain Peace. Swami Jyotirmayananda. Read by Swami Jyotirmayananda. 1 cass. (Running Time: 45 min.). 10.00 (812) Yoga Res Foun.

How to Attend a Prayer Meeting? Vincent M. Walsh. 1 cass. 1986. 4.00 Key of David.
Personal stories & examples told to promote a full understanding of the basic powers of the Renewal.

How to Attract a Soul Mate Relationship. Nina Atwood. (ENG.). 1999. 18.00 (978-0-9702809-0-9(4)) N Atwood Enter.

***How to Attract a Soul Mate Relationship.** Nina Atwood. (Running Time: 120). (ENG.). 2010. audio compact disk 18.00 (978-0-9702809-1-6(2)) N Atwood Enter.

How to Attract Inspiration in Any Field. Kriyananda, pseud. 1 cass. (Running Time: 80 min.). 9.95 (SC-5) Crystal Clarity.
How to listen inside yourself for inspiration; how to ask the Divine within you for answers; how to receive those answers; what to do if guidance doesn't come right away.

How to Attract Love. 2 CDs. 1981. audio compact disk 27.98 (978-1-56001-960-2(3)) Potentials.
Expand your "love awareness" and you will automatically draw to you the love you desire.This 2-CD program from our Super Consciousness series is our newest, most powerful format. On the self-hypnosis CD, SC programs have the Subliminal Persuasion soundtrack added under Barrie?s voice. And the 17th Century Baroque music on the Subliminal CD has the same beat as your body's natural rhythm, thereby allowing the suggestions to enter deeply and effortlessly.

How to Attract Love. Barrie Konicov. 1 cass. 11.98 (978-0-87082-332-9(9), 059) Potentials.
Through the mental processes contained in this program, your consciousness will be magnetized, & automatically draw you to love & desire. This will happen as a totally natural process when you expand your own "love awareness.".

How to Attract Love. Barrie Konicov. 1 CD. 2004. audio compact disk 19.98 (978-1-56001-667-0(1)) Potentials.
Expand your "love awareness" and you will automatically deaw to you the love you desire.You will find the self-hypnosis on track 1 and the subliminal on track 2. The easy-listening music of the subliminal, together with the self-hypnosis, is the original format which most people love and with which they are most familiar.

How to Attract Love: Atraiga el Amor. Barrie Konicov. 1 cass. (Running Time: 1 hr. 30 min.). (Spanish-Language Audios Ser.). (SPA.). 1995. 11.98 (978-0-87082-698-6(0), 059) Potentials.
Through the mental process taught on this tape, your consciousness can be magnetized, drawing to you the love you desire. You will also learn to deal with stressful people & events in a more loving way.

How to Attract Money. 1 CD. (Running Time: 40 minutes). 1998. 14.95 (978-0-9779472-7-0(0)) Health Wealth Inc.
This is a great hypnosis experience - no matter what your financial status! It is about prosperity. Perhaps you would like to enjoy the money you have, or not work so hard to get it. This helps to release blocks to your wealth by allowing them to surface and replacing them with what you would really like to experience. It helps you to picture and feel what it is you want so you can manifest it.

How to Attract Money. Bob Griswold. Read by Bob Griswold. 1 CD. (Running Time: 78 mins.). (Love Tapes Ser.). 2005. audio compact disk 15.98 (978-1-55848-158-9(3), Love Tapes) EffectiveMN.
Prosperity begins in the mind. This highly-effective and enjoyable CD will help you quickly break through your financial limitations and open the door to greater wealth. The most powerful program of its kind and it comes with a 100% satisfaction guarantee.This CD contains 3 programs. The first is a guided meditation with powerful imagery and techniques for achieving greater wealth. It also includes two excellent subliminal programs, one with the sound of ocean waves and the other with relaxing original music.

How to Attract Money. Robert E. Griswold. Read by Robert E. Griswold. 1 cass. 1992. 10.95 (978-1-55848-020-9(X)) EffectiveMN.
Prosperity begins in your mind, & this is your opportunity to use your mind to creatively produce more money.

How to Avoid & Overcome Depression: Winning Keys to Mental Wellness. abr. ed. Perf. by Angela Brown et al. 1 cass. (Running Time: 60 mins.). (Words of Wellness Ser.: Vol. 6). 2000. 14.95 (978-0-9673451-1-6(1), LLP306) Life Long Pubg.
How to recognize the symptoms of depression in you or a family member, simple steps to overcome depression naturally without medication, solutions to prevent depression from returning.

How to Avoid Communication Overload. Jeff Davidson. 2006. audio compact disk 9.95 (978-1-60729-123-7(1)) Breath Space Inst.

How to Avoid Communication Overload. jeff davidson. 2006. 8.95 (978-1-60729-338-5(2)) Breath Space Inst.

How to Avoid Environmental Liability: A Practical Guide for Corporations, Financial Institutions & Professionals. Randall Airst. Ed. by Susan Stann. 8 cass. pap. bk. Set.; Set. Marga Environ.

How to Avoid Getting Sued in Horse Matters: From Someone Who Has Learned the Hard Way. Karen Jean Matsko Hood. (Delights Ser.). 2006. 29.95 (978-1-59649-342-1(9)); audio compact disk 13.95 (978-1-59649-343-8(7)) Whsprng Pine.

How to Avoid Jetlag!, Set. Contrib. by Tyrrel Fairhead. 2 cass. (Running Time: 3 hrs.). 1999. pap. bk. 19.95 (978-1-875086-16-0(1)) Pub: J T Fairhead ZAF. Dist(s): Penton Overseas
Offers a mind & body approach to solving this usually predictable side-effect to our contemporary global lifestyle. Avoid the common symptoms: physical discomfort, dehydration, time distortion & sleep deprivation, physical & mental exhaustion & general debilitation.

How to Avoid Ripoffs. Bruce Williams. Read by Bruce Williams. 1 cass. (Insider's Report Ser.). 9.95 (978-0-944305-04-1(0)) Bonneville Media.
Features advice on avoiding being conned.

How to Avoid the Destructiveness of a Wrong Self-Image. As told by S. M. Davis. 1 CD. (Running Time: 1 hr.). 2003. audio compact disk 10.00 (978-1-929241-94-1(1)) Vsn Forum.

***How to Avoid the Most Common Mistakes New Managers Make.** PUEI. 2009. audio compact disk 199.00 (978-1-935041-63-4(0), CareerTrack) P Univ E Inc.

How to Awaken. Swami Amar Jyoti. 2 cass. 1978. 12.95 (P-22) Truth Consciousness.
Complaining in sleep vs. awakening; happiness vs. ecstasy. On magic & miracles, cleanliness & orderliness. The genesis of hope. The creation of time & space.

How to Balance Male & Female Energies. Kriyananda, pseud. (Running Time: 80 min.). (Relationships Ser.). 1986. 9.95 (ST-42) Crystal Clarity.
Includes: The heart's awakening as the first step towards balancing energies; why men & women need to serve each other; the ennobling qulity of the mother aspect of humanity.

***How to Balance Your Life: Practical Ways to Achieve Work/Life Balance.** unabr. ed. James O'Loghlin. Read by James O'Loghlin. 5 CDs. (Running Time: 5 hrs. 43 mins.). 2010. audio compact disk 63.95 (978-1-74214-644-7(9), 9781742146447) Pub: Bolinda Pubng AUS. Dist(s): Bolinda Pub Inc

How to Be a Ballerina. Perf. by Debra Bradnum. (Running Time: 45 min.). (J). 1997. cass. & video 9.98 (978-1-57330-716-1(5), Sony Wonder) Sony Music Ent.
Allows both aspiring ballerinas & children who have no dance experience to enjoy the elements of fantasy, dress-up play & creative movement.

***How to Be A Best Friend Forever: Making & Keeping Lifetime Relationships.** Zondervan. (ENG.). 2011. 14.99 (978-0-310-42925-8(0)) Zondervan.

How to Be a Better Coach. abr. ed. Curt Miller. Read by Curt Miller. 2 cass. (Running Time: 1 hrs. 55 min.). 1998. 19.95 Set; incl. wkbk. (978-1-57294-107-6(3), 11-0219) SkillPath Pubns.
Guide to handling conflicts, gaining commitment, motivating employees & offering praise & criticism.

How to Be a Better Receiver in Hypnosis. 1 cass. 14.98 (978-0-87554-415-1(0), NX502) Valley Sun.

How to Be a Billionaire: Proven Strategies from the Titans of Wealth. unabr. ed. Martin S. Fridson. Read by Johanna Ward. 8 cass. (Running Time: 11 hrs. 30 mins.). 2002. 56.95 (978-0-7861-2237-0(4), 2961); audio compact disk 80.00 (978-0-7861-9499-5(5), 2961) Blckstn Audio.
Looks at the careers, the methods, and the minds of self-made billionaires to distill the common keys to titanic accumulations of wealth. Each chapter explores a specific strategy and brings it to life through extended profiles of past and present masters of the art of making money.

How to Be a Cancer Victor. Ralph Alan Dale. Read by Ralph Alan Dale. 1 cass. (Running Time: 90 min.). 1979. 9.00 (6) Dialectic Pubng.
The main ways to treat & to prevent cancer.

How to Be a Champion! Winning Keys to Personal Wellness. abr. ed. Perf. by Angela Brown et al. 1 cass. (Running Time: 60 mins.). (Words of Wellness Ser.: Vol. 3). 2000. 14.95 (978-0-9673451-6-1(2), LLP303) Life Long Pubg.
How to be organized, set goals, set priorities, find balance & harmony in day-to-day-living. How to deal with pressure, end procrastination. How to live the life you've always dreamed of.

***How to Be a Christian in a Brave New World.** unabr. ed. Joni Eareckson Tada & Nigel M. de S. Cameron. (Running Time: 6 hrs. 21 mins. 0 sec.). (ENG.). 2009. 16.99 (978-0-310-77155-5(2)) Zondervan.

How to Be a Christian Without Being Religious Series. 2004. audio compact disk 32.00 (978-1-59834-022-8(0)) Walk Thru the Bible.

How to Be a Christian Without Being Ridiculous. abr. ed. Anthony Campolo. 1 cass. 1997. 10.99 (978-0-8499-6266-0(8)) Nelson.

How to Be a Complete & Utter Failure Live. Steve McDermott. 2003. audio compact disk 39.50 (978-0-273-66381-2(X)) Pub: Pearson Educ. Dist(s): Trans-Atl Phila

How to Be a Father. Derek Prince. 1 cass. (B-4050) Derek Prince.

How to Be a Father. Read by John Van Eenwyk. 1 cass. (Running Time: 2 hrs.). 1988. 10.95 (978-0-7822-0318-9(3), 331) C G Jung IL.

How to Be a Fearless Employee. unabr. ed. Pat Wagner. Read by Pat Wagner. Read by Alan Dumas. Ed. by Judy Byers. 1 cass. (Running Time: 55 min.). 1994. 12.95 (978-0-9642678-1-7(0)) Pattern Res.
Even without job security, you can take risks, make hard choices, increase your influence & stay employable.

How to Be a Fierce Competitor: What Winning Companies & Great Managers Do in Tough Times. unabr. ed. Jeffrey J. Fox. Read by Jeffrey J. Fox. 1 MP3-CD. (Running Time: 3 hrs.). 2010. 19.99 (978-1-4233-7630-9(7), 9781423376309, Brilliance MP3); 19.99 (978-1-4233-7632-3(3), 9781423376323, BAD); 39.97 (978-1-4233-7631-6(5), 9781423376316, Brinc Audio MP3 Lib); 39.97 (978-1-4233-7633-0(1), 9781423376330, BADLE); audio compact disk 19.99 (978-1-4233-7628-6(5), 9781423376286, Bril Audio CD Unabri); audio compact disk 62.97 (978-1-4233-7629-3(3), 9781423376293, BriAudCD Unabrid) Brilliance Audio.

How to Be a Friend of God. 2001. (978-0-940110-30-4(X)) Life Action Publishing.

How to Be a Friend of God Conf Audio. Nancy Leigh DeMoss. (ENG.). 2007. audio compact disk 27.99 (978-0-940110-77-9(6)) Life Action Publishing.

How to Be a Good Taekwon-Do Instructor. James S. Benko. Read by James S. Benko. 1986. 12.95 (TC-8) ITA Inst.
It takes more than simply a good technician to become a "good" Taekwon-Do instructor. Master Benko gives you the ingredients necessary for developing the attributes needed to become a good instructor.

How to Be a Great Communicator: In Person, on Paper & at the Podium. unabr. ed. Nido R. Qubein. Read by Nido R. Qubein. 4 CDs. (Running Time: 4 hrs.). (ENG., 2005. audio compact disk 19.98 (978-1-59659-025-0(4)) Pub: Gildan Media. Dist(s): HachBkGrp

How to Be a Great Communicator: In Person, on Paper, & on the Podium. Nido R. Qubein. Read by Nido R. Qubein. 6 cass. 59.95 Set. (472AD) Nightingale-Conant.
Acquire a rare & valuable skill.

How to Be a Great Dad: Eph. 6:4. Ed Young. 1996. 4.95 (978-0-7417-2103-7(1), 1103) Win Walk.

How to Be a Great Golfer. 2 CDs. 1981. audio compact disk 27.98 (978-1-56001-961-9(1)) Potentials.
The principles of relaxation, coordination, and concentration detailed in this program ensure a superb game of golf.This 2-CD program from our Super Consciousness series is our newest, most powerful format. On the self-hypnosis CD, SC programs have the Subliminal Persuasion soundtrack added under Barrie?s voice. And the 17th Century Baroque music on the Subliminal CD has the same beat as your body's natural rhythm, thereby allowing the suggestions to enter deeply and effortlessly.

How to Be a Great Golfer. Barrie Konicov. 1 cass. 11.98 (978-0-87082-420-3(1), 060) Potentials.
Great golf is the result of a well-coordinated body, working in harmony with a well-disciplined mind. The combination of these two things can produce terrific results. Details the principles of relaxation, coordination which add up to a superb game of golf.

How to Be a Great Golfer. Barrie Konicov. 1 CD. 2003. audio compact disk 16.98 (978-0-87082-978-9(5)) Potentials.
The principles of relaxation, coordination, and concentration detailed in this program ensure a superb game of golf.You will find the self-hypnosis on track 1 and the subliminal on track 2. The easy-listening music of the subliminal, together with the self-hypnosis, is the original format which most people love and with which they are most familiar.

How to Be a Great Lover. abr. ed. Lou Paget. Read by Lou Paget. (Running Time: 3 hrs.). (ENG.). 2006. audio compact disk 24.95 (978-1-59887-076-3(9), 1598870769) Pub: HighBridge. Dist(s): Workman Pub

How to Be a Great Mom: Luke 23:39-43, 46;John 19:25-27. Ed Young. 1996. 4.95 (978-0-7417-2098-6(1), 1097) Win Walk.

How to be a Karma Yoga. (166) Yoga Res Foun.

How to Be a No-Limit Person. Wayne W. Dyer. Read by Wayne W. Dyer. 6 cass. 49.95 Set. (858AD) Nightingale-Conant.
Break free & live.

How to Be a No-Limit Person. unabr. ed. Wayne W. Dyer. Read by Wayne W. Dyer. (Running Time: 4 hrs. 30 mins. 0 sec.). (ENG.). 2007. audio compact disk 29.95 (978-0-7435-6163-1(5), Nightgale) Pub: S&S Audio. Dist(s): S and S Inc

How to Be a People Magnet. abr. ed. Leil Lowndes. Narrated by Leil Lowndes. 2 cass. (Running Time: 3 hrs. 30 mins.). 2003. 17.95 (978-1-885408-95-2(1)); audio compact disk 23.95 (978-1-59316-005-0(4)) Listen & Live.

How to Be a Perfect Non-Perfectionist. Albert Ellis. 1 cass. (Running Time: 43 min.). 9.95 (C049) A Ellis Institute.
Demandingness is the downfall of the perfectionist - you're tough on yourself, on everyone else, & then tough on yourself again for being too tough! It is possible to achieve high goals & to aim at your personal best without hurting yourself in the process.

How to Be a Perfect Non-Perfectionist. Albert Ellis. 1 cass. (Running Time: 43 min.). 9.95 (C049) Inst Rational-Emotive.

How to Be a Pirate. unabr. ed. Cressida Cowell. Narrated by Gerard Doyle. 3 cass. (Running Time: 3 hrs. 45 mins.). (J). (gr. 4-7). 2005. 28.75 (978-1-4193-5085-6(4), 98117) Recorded Bks.

How to Be a Prayer Partner: A Guide to Becoming a Healing Companion. Carole Riley. 2 cass. (Running Time: 2 hrs.). 2001. vinyl bd. 18.95 (A6520) St Anthony Mess Pr.
A "prayer companion" is a person who is present to another and for another in a disciplined relationship of Christian love. Review guidelines and suggestions for the process of becoming a healing presence to another person on the journey of faith, and distinguish between being a prayer companion and being a spiritual director.

How to Be a Religious Person, No. 1. Swami Jyotirmayananda. (160) Yoga Res Foun.

How to Be a Religious Person, No. 2. Swami Jyotirmayananda. 1 cass. (Running Time: 1 hr.). 1990. 12.99 Yoga Res Foun.

How to Be a Solar Person in a Lunar World. Elayne J. Manago. 1 cass. 8.95 (220) Am Fed Astrologers.
Analysis of strength of Sun & Moon.

How to Be a Success in Life Series. Kenneth W. Hagin, Jr. 3 cass. 1992. 12.00 Set. (27J) Faith Lib Pubns.

How to Be a Successful Apartment Rental Consultant. 2 cass. (Running Time: 85 min.). 1981. pap. bk. 42.95 incl. workbook. (978-0-944298-13-8(3), NO. 838) Inst Real Estate.
Designed to train new rental agents & to help agents obtain better results when showing apartments.

How to Be a Successful Independent Medical Examiner Set: Practical Solutions to Problems & Challenges Facing Independent Medical Examiners. abr. ed. Christopher R. Brigham. 6 cass. 2000. 249.95 (978-1-892904-06-5(3)) SEAK.
Edited version of a SEAK, Inc. seminar.

How to Be a True Sadhaka. 1 cass. (Running Time: 1 hr.). 12.99 (193) Yoga Res Foun.

How to Be a Wild, Wise, & Witty Woman: Making the Most Out of Life Before You Run Out of It. Loretta LaRoche. 4 CDs. 2007. audio compact disk 23.95 (978-1-4019-1686-2(4)) Hay House.

How to Be a Winner. unabr. abr. ed. Zig Ziglar. Read by Zig Ziglar. 1 CD. (Running Time: 10 hrs. 0 mins. 0 sec.). (ENG.). 2002. audio compact disk 14.00 (978-0-7435-2505-3(1), Nightgale) Pub: S&S Audio. Dist(s): S and S Inc

How to Be Alone. unabr. ed. Jonathan Franzen. Read by Brian d'Arcy James. 2004. 23.95 (978-0-7435-4839-7(6)) Pub: S&S Audio. Dist(s): S and S Inc

How to Be an Adult. David Richo. 1 cass. (Running Time: 1 hr. 30 mins.). 1993. bk. 12.95 (978-0-8091-8133-9(9), 8133-9) Paulist Pr.
Shows the way to psychological and spiritual health.

***How to Be an American Housewife: A Novel.** unabr. ed. Margaret Dilloway. (Running Time: 8 hrs. 30 mins.). 2010. 29.99 (978-1-4001-9773-6(2)); 15.99 (978-1-4001-8773-7(7)) Tantor Media.

***How to Be an American Housewife: A Novel.** unabr. ed. Margaret Dilloway. Narrated by Emily Durante & Laural Merlington. (Running Time: 8 hrs. 0 mins. 0 sec.). (ENG.). 2010. 19.99 (978-1-4001-6773-9(6)); audio compact disk 71.99 (978-1-4001-4773-1(5)); audio compact disk 29.99 (978-1-4001-1773-4(9)) Pub: Tantor Media. Dist(s): IngramPubServ

How to Be an Awesome Sponsor & Keep Your Heap. Kim Klaver. (Running Time: 50 min.). 1997. 8.95 (978-1-891493-02-7(7)) Max Out Prodns.
How to attract & maintain a team of successful workers. Stories of the great empire builders.

How to Be an Effective Advocate in the Appellate Courts. 1996. bk. 99.00 (ACS-1195) PA Bar Inst.
What does it take to be a really outstanding advocate in the appellate courts? Learn helpful tips for making your oral & written advocacy more effective.

How to Be An Effective Speaker. 1 cass. (Running Time: 1 hr.). 12.99 (159) Yoga Res Foun.

How to Be an Effective Supervisor. (Running Time: 4 hrs.). pap. bk. & wbk. ed. 30.00 (978-0-7612-0617-0(5), 80215) AMACOM.
Supervisors learn how to: orient new employees quickly; train new employees to become productive more quickly; handle grievances & difficult employees; maintain good union relations; help formulate goals for their work units; communicate effectively with both superiors & subordinates; make faster decisions.

How to Be an Effective Supervisor, Set. 4 cass. (Running Time: 4 hrs.). Incl. How to Be an Effective Supervisor: Aspects of Leadership. (80214); How to Be an Effective Supervisor: Communication. (80214); How to Be an Effective Supervisor: Dealing with Conflict in the Workplace. (80214); How to Be an Effective Supervisor: Decision Making. (80214); How to Be an Effective Supervisor: Motivation, Working & the Supervisor. (80214); How to Be an Effective Supervisor: Planning & Productivity. (80214); How to Be an Effective Supervisor: Portrait of the Supervisor. (80214); How to Be an Effective Supervisor: Profile of the Successful Supervisor. (80214); How to Be an Effective Supervisor: Some Basics of Supervision. (80214); How to Be an Effective Supervisor: The Supervisor & the Organization. (80214); How to Be an Effective Supervisor: Understanding Your Employees. (80214); How to Be an Effective Supervisor: What Makes a Good Supervisor. (80214); 155.00 (978-0-7612-0616-3(7), 80214) AMACOM.

How to Be an Effective Supervisor: Aspects of Leadership see How to Be an Effective Supervisor

How to Be an Effective Supervisor: Communication see How to Be an Effective Supervisor

How to Be an Effective Supervisor: Dealing with Conflict in the Workplace see How to Be an Effective Supervisor

How to Be an Effective Supervisor: Decision Making see How to Be an Effective Supervisor

How to Be an Effective Supervisor: Motivation, Working & the Supervisor see How to Be an Effective Supervisor

How to Be an Effective Supervisor: Planning & Productivity see How to Be an Effective Supervisor

How to Be an Effective Supervisor: Portrait of the Supervisor see How to Be an Effective Supervisor

How to Be an Effective Supervisor: Profile of the Successful Supervisor see How to Be an Effective Supervisor

How to Be an Effective Supervisor: Some Basics of Supervision see How to Be an Effective Supervisor

How to Be an Effective Supervisor: The Supervisor & the Organization see How to Be an Effective Supervisor

How to Be an Effective Supervisor: Understanding Your Employees see How to Be an Effective Supervisor

How to Be an Effective Supervisor: What Makes a Good Supervisor see How to Be an Effective Supervisor

How to Be an Entrepreneur: The Six Secrets of Self-Made Success. Steve Parks. 2006. audio compact disk 39.50 (978-0-273-70996-1(8), FT Pren) Pearson EducLt GBR.

How to Be an Extraordinary Missionary. John Bytheway. (YA). 2005. audio compact disk 12.95 (978-1-59038-413-8(X)) Deseret Bk.

How to Be an Ideal Disciple II. 1 cass. (Running Time: 1 hr.). 12.99 (148) Yoga Res Foun.

How to Be an Inspiring Teacher. Kriyananda, pseud. (Running Time: 2 hrs.). 14.95 (ST-33) Crystal Clarity.
Explores: Inspiration as an inner feeling; the importance of experience; how to develop an intuitive flow; reading people on a soul level.

How to Be an Overcomer. Gloria Copeland. 4 cass. 1987. 20.00 Set incl. study guide. (978-0-88114-805-3(9)) K Copeland Pubns.
Biblical teaching on overcoming defeat.

How to be an Overcomer. Kenneth W. Hagin, Jr. 4 cass. 16.00 (21J) Faith Lib Pubns.

How to be Anointed. Steve Thompson. 1 cass. (Running Time: 90 mins.). (Power of Suffering Ser.: Vol. 2). 2000. 5.00 (ST04-002) Morning NC.
Steve's messages offer helpful instruction on an often misunderstood pathway which can release spiritual power in our lives.

How to Be Blessed by God. unabr. ed. Keith A. Butler. 3 cass. (Running Time: 4 hrs. 30 mins.). 2001. 15.00 (A132) Word Faith Pubng.
Most people want the blessings of God in their lives, but not as many know how to cooperate with God to experience His fullness. Many have the right heart to receive blessings; they just don't have the right instruction. Learn how you and your loved ones can be blessed by God!.

How to Be Booked by Speakers Bureaus. Dottie Walters. 1 cass. Orig. Title: Everything You Always Wanted to Know about Speakers Bureaus - but Didn't Know to Ask. 49.95 Audio Album. (978-0-934344-45-6(0)) Royal Pub.
Maximize your relationship with speakers bureaus & avoid costly mistakes. What bureaus expect from speakers. Do's/dont's, contracts, catalogs, exclusives, brokering, spin-off, I showcases, client-bureau-speaker relationships. How to have more speakers bureaus selling high fee bookings for you.

How to be Chaste While Being Chased. Curtis Jacobs. 2004. 9.95 (978-1-57734-621-0(1)); audio compact disk 10.95 (978-1-57734-633-3(5)) Covenant Comms.

How to Be Consistent in Your Life. Kenneth Copeland. 1 cass. 1988. 5.00 (978-0-88114-802-2(4)) K Copeland Pubns.
Biblical teaching on the power of patience.

How to Be Delivered. Derek Prince. 1 cass. 5.95 (4398) Derek Prince.
Deliverance from evil spirits is the one miracle which has no counterpart in the Old Testament. It is, therefore, the one distinctive sign that the kingdom of God has come & the first miracle of Jesus recorded in the Bible.

How to Be Delivered from Fear & Sickness. Tsea. 2008. DVD & audio compact disk (978-0-9797500-5-2(9)) TSEA.

***How to Be Evangelical without Being Conservative.** Roger E. Olson. (Running Time: 7 hrs. 2 mins. 0 sec.). (ENG.). 2009. 16.99 (978-0-310-77234-7(6)) Zondervan.

How to Be Excllent see Ser Excelente

How to Be Filled with the Spirit. Theodore H. Epp. Read by Theodore H. Epp. 1 cass. (Running Time: 60 min.). 1985. 4.95 (978-0-8474-2261-6(5)) Back to Bible.
Features messages explaining the prerequisites for the Spirit's filling.

How to Be Filled with the Spirit: Logos January 18, 1998. Ben Young. 1998. 4.95 (978-0-7417-6069-2(X), B0069) Win Walk.

How to Be Free from the Past, No. 1. Swami Jyotirmayananda. 1 cass. (Running Time: 1 hr.). 12.99 (156) Yoga Res Foun.

How to Be Free from the Past, No. 2. Swami Jyotirmayananda. 1 cass. (Running Time: 1 hr.). 12.99 (172) Yoga Res Foun.

How to Be Free from the Past, No. 3. Swami Jyotirmayananda. 1 cass. (Running Time: 1 hr.). 1990. 12.99 Yoga Res Foun.

How to Be Free of Bondage. 1 cass. (Running Time: 1 hr.). 12.99 (206) Yoga Res Foun.

How to Be Free of Guilt & Resentment. Bill Ferguson. Read by Bill Ferguson. 1 cass. 1990. 9.95 (978-1-878410-04-7(0)) Return Heart.
When you have guilt or resentment, you suffer. You lose your love, your aliveness & your peace of mind. You close down inside. This cassette will show you, step by step, how to be free of all guilt & resentment. You will learn how to release your upsets, heal your hurt & restore your inner peace.

How to Be Free of Upset & Stress. Bill Ferguson. Read by Bill Ferguson. 1 cass. 1990. 9.95 (978-1-878410-05-4(9)) Return Heart.
When you resist, you get upset & close down. You become ineffective & tend to make your situation worse. This cassette will show you how to be free of the fears & upsets that create stress & close you down. You will learn how to restore your inner peace & be naturally effective in any situation.

How to Be Good. unabr. ed. Nick Hornby. Narrated by Jenny Sterlin. 7 cass. (Running Time: 10 hrs.). 2002. 37.95 (978-0-7887-9046-1(3), 96787) Recorded Bks.
Katie is a doctor's wife, mother and all-around good person. David, on the other hand, is a bitter and sarcastic writer - that is until he is miraculously transformed into a sincere do-gooder with the need to help everyone and everything.

How to Be Happy. 6 cass. (Running Time: 6 hrs.). 2003. audio compact disk 42.00 (978-1-881541-92-9(4)) A Wommack.

How to Be Happy. Asha Praver. 1 cass. (Running Time: 90 min.). 9.95 (AP-4) Crystal Clarity.
Explains how you can turn a situation around simply by changing your energy flow, knowing how to concentrate that energy, & getting in touch with your inner self.

How to be Happy. unabr. ed. Andrew Wommack. Contrib. by John Baker. 6 cass. (Running Time: 7 hrs. 24 min.). 1997. 28.00 Set. (978-1-881541-30-1(4), 1019) A Wommack.
Discuss the topic of how to be happy especially if you are a christian.

How to Be Happy: Seven Steps to Understanding Yourself. unabr. ed. Benjamin Fry. (Running Time: 2 hrs. 0 mins. 0 sec.). (ENG., 2007. audio compact disk 19.95 (978-1-4055-0320-4(3)) Pub: Little BrownUK GBR. Dist(s): IPG Chicago

How to Be Happy Though Human. Albert Ellis. 1 cass. (Running Time: 62 min.). 9.95 (C008) A Ellis Institute.
Excellent discussion of the belief systems & lifestyles that interfere with happiness, & ways to overcome them. Shows you how to reduce apathy, anxiety, self-downing, & anger.

How to Be Happy Though Human. Albert Ellis. 1 cass. (Running Time: 62 min.). 9.95 (C008) Inst Rational-Emotive.

How to Be Happy Though Married. abr. ed. Tim LaHaye. Narrated by Wayne Shepherd. (ENG.). 2002. 13.99 (978-1-60814-242-2(6)) Oasis Audio.

How to Be Happy Though Married. abr. ed. Tim LaHaye. Read by Tim LaHaye. 2 cass. (Running Time: 150 mins.). 2002. 17.99 (978-1-58926-025-2(2)); audio compact disk 19.99 (978-1-58926-026-9(0)) Oasis Audio.

How to be Happy Though Married 20 Plus Years: Zech. 14:7. Ed Young. (J). 1981. 4.95 (978-0-7417-1169-4(9), A0169) Win Walk.

How to Be Led by God. Carol Crook. Read by Carol Crook. 4 cass. (Running Time: 5 hrs.). (YA). (gr. 5 up). 1999. bk. 20.00 Set. (978-0-939399-25-3(3)) Bks of Truth.
Tells why one should be led & gives pre-requisites for being led, types of leadings, confirmations & how to use, & one's responsibilities.

How to Be Led by the Holy Spirit. Derek Prince. 1 cass. (Running Time: 60 min.). (B-134) Derek Prince.

How to Be Led by the Holy Spirit, Vol. 2. Derek Prince. 1 cass. (Running Time: 60 min.). (B-135) Derek Prince.

How to Be Led by the Spirit, Vols. 1 & 2. Kenneth E. Hagin. 10 cass. 40.00 (46H, 47H) Faith Lib Pubns.

How to Be Magnanimous. (115) Yoga Res Foun.

How to be Magnanimous. Swami Jyotirmayananda. 1 cass. (Running Time: 1 hr.). 1990. 12.99 Yoga Res Foun.

How to Be Number One: Luke 18:9-14. Ed Young. (J). 1981. 4.95 (978-0-7417-1198-4(2), A0198) Win Walk.

How to Be Popular. 1 CD. 1982. audio compact disk Rental 19.98 (978-1-56001-702-8(3)) Potentials.
With this program you can make new friends, develop charm and charisma and be at ease wherever you go.The self-hypnosis is on track 1 and the subliminal is on track 2. The easy-listening music of the subliminal, together with the self-hypnosis, is the original format which most people love and with which they are most familiar.

How to Be Popular. Barrie Konicov. 1 cass. 11.98 (978-0-87082-433-3(3), 061) Potentials.
Develop the ease & the charm to make friends & be popular.

How to Be Popular. unabr. ed. Meg Cabot. Read by Kate Reinders. 5 CDs. (Running Time: 5 hrs. 35 mins.). (YA). (gr. 8 up). 2006. audio compact disk 38.25 (978-0-7393-3778-3(5), Listening Lib) Pub: Random Audio Pubg. Dist(s): NetLibrary CO

How to Be Positive. Read by Robert E. Griswold. 1 cass. 1992. 10.95 (978-1-55848-022-3(6)) EffectiveMN.
Helps you protect yourself from negativity; & to think feel, & be positive.

How to be Rational. Swami Jyotirmayananda. (154) Yoga Res Foun.

How to be Rational. Swami Jyotirmayananda. 1 cass. (Running Time: 1 hr.). 1990. 12.99 Yoga Res Foun.

How to Be Really Successful. George King. 2004. audio compact disk 12.50 (978-0-937249-18-5(1)) Aetherius Soc.

***How to Be Rich.** unabr. ed. Napoleon Hill et al. (Running Time: 4 hrs.). (ENG.). 2010. audio compact disk 25.95 (978-0-14-242858-0(2), PengAudBks) Penguin Grp USA.

How to Be Rich: Five Steps to Unlocking Your Inner Wealth. unabr. ed. Benjamin Fry. Read by Benjamin Fry. (Running Time: 2 hrs. 8 mins. 0 sec.). (ENG., 2008. audio compact disk 24.95 (978-1-4055-0365-5(3)) Pub: Little BrownUK GBR. Dist(s): IPG Chicago

How to Be Sincere. (139) Yoga Res Foun.

How to be Sincere. Swami Jyotirmayananda. 1 cass. (Running Time: 1 hr.). 1990. 12.99 Yoga Res Foun.

How to Be Successful Before You Are 25. unabr. ed. Christina Clement & Thomas Amshay. Read by Thomas Amshay. 1 cass. (Running Time: 45 min.). (YA). (gr. 10-12). 1989. 9.00 (978-0-939401-03-1(7)) RFTS Prod.
Simple rules of success that enables people to get what they want.

How to Be Successful in Christian Radio: National Association of Evangelicals, 47th Annual Convention, Columbus, Ohio, March 7-9, 1989. Mike Maddex. 1 cass. (Workshops Ser.: No. 13-Wednesd). 1989. 4.25 ea. 1-8 tapes.; 4.00 ea. 9 tapes or more. Nat Assn Evan.

How to Be the Parent You Always Wanted to Be. abr. ed. Adele Faber & Elaine Mazlish. 2004. 7.95 (978-0-7435-4840-3(X)) Pub: S&S Audio. Dist(s): S and S Inc

How to Be Treated Like a High Roller. abr. ed. Rob Renneisen. Read by Joe Burke. 1 cass. (Running Time: 1 hr. 30 min.). Dramatization. pap. bk. 16.95 (978-1-56703-022-8(X)) High-Top Sports.

How to Be Truly Awakened. 1 cass. (Running Time: 1 hr.). 12.99 (135) Yoga Res Foun.

How to Be Truly Prosperous. 1 cass. (Running Time: 1 hr.). 12.99 (122) Yoga Res Foun.

How to Be Unhappy at Work. Emmett Velten. 1 cass. (Running Time: 35 min.). 9.95 (C009) A Ellis Institute.
Lively talk on the benefits of unhappiness at work, how to make the worst of any situation, & how to decrease frustration tolerance. Those who want to be happier at work can do the opposite of what Velten advises.

How to Be Unhappy at Work. Emmett Velten. 1 cass. (Running Time: 35 min.). 9.95 (C009) Inst Rational-Emotive.

How to Be Unshaken by Adversity. Swami Jyotirmayananda. 1 cass. (Running Time: 45 min.). 1990. 10.00 Yoga Res Foun.

How to Be Used for God's Highest Purposes. Short Stories. Joel Osteen. 1 Cass. (Running Time: 30 Mins). 2001. 6.00 (978-1-59349-117-8(4), JA0117) J Osteen.

How to Beat the Cancer Odds. Rosemary Ross. 1 cass. 1987. 10.00 (978-0-9647382-0-1(1)) R Ross.
For cancer patients & those wishing to practice cancer prevention.

How to Beat the 80/20 Rule in Sales Team Performance: A Step-by-Step Guide to Building & Managing Top-Performing Sales Teams. Alan Rigg. Read by Alan Rigg. 2007. audio compact disk 49.95 (978-0-9745380-3-7(5)) EightTwenty Perf.

How to Beat the 80/20 Rule in Selling. Alan Rigg. Read by Alan Rigg. 2 CDs. (Running Time: 1 hr. 30 mins.). 2003. audio compact disk 49.95 (978-0-9745380-0-6(0)) EightTwenty Perf.
Are you considering a career in sales? Do you know whether you have what it takes to succeed?Are salespeople a mystery to you? Do you want to increase your understanding of the sales function?Does The 80/20 Rule describe your sales team?s performance? Do you want to increase the proportion of top performers on your sales team?Companies spend billions of dollars annually to recruit and train salespeople, only to see the majority leave, be terminated, or turn out to be mediocre producers. Why do only 20% of salespeople produce 80% of sales? How To Beat The 80/20 Rule In Selling solves this sales performance mystery.You will learn:? The financial impact of The 80/20 Rule? Why salespeople perform differently? The attributes required for sales success? Relationship preferences and selling styles? How sales manager style impacts sales performance? Why most sales training programs fail? Why incentives failThere are hundreds of books that have been written about sales. What is so special about this one? First, most books about sales are written from the standpoint of teaching someone how to sell. They don?t address the question of whether someone should pursue a career in sales. Second, information about sales is fragmented. If you take the time to read a lot of books and attend a lot of classes, you can build a broad base of knowledge?eventually. This book consolidates much of that information into one place. Third, despite the fact that companies spend billions of dollars annually to recruit and train salespeople, the majority leave, are terminated, or turn out to be mediocre producers. Clearly there are missing pieces to the sales puzzle. This book identifies the missing pieces.

How to Beat the 80/20 Rule in Selling: A Step-by-Step Guide to Achieving Top Sales Performance. Alan Rigg. Read by Alan Rigg. 2008. audio compact disk 39.95 (978-0-9745380-6-8(X), Perf Pr USA) EightTwenty Perf.

How to Become a Better Negotiator. abr. ed. Richard A. Luecke & James G. Patterson. Read by Jim Bond. (Running Time: 3 hrs.). (WorkSmart Ser.). 2008. 39.25 (978-1-4233-6384-2(1), 9781423363842, BADLE); 39.25 (978-1-4233-6382-8(5), 9781423363828, Brlnc Audio MP3 Lib); 17.95 (978-1-4233-6383-5(3), 9781423363835, BAD); 17.95 (978-1-4233-6381-1(7), 9781423363811, Brilliance MP3); audio compact disk 17.95 (978-1-4233-6379-8(5), 9781423363798, BACD); audio compact disk 55.25 (978-1-4233-6380-4(9), 9781423363804, BACDLib Ed) Brilliance Audio.

How to Become a Chick Magnet: A step-by-step guide to developing the subconscious mindset & practical skillset a man needs to effortlessly attract Women. Graham Stoney. (ENG.). 2009. 30.00 (978-0-9806453-2-3(8)) StoneyG AUS.

How to Become a Credit Repair Consultant. Speeches. Mervin Evans. Prod. by Lynette Bigelow. 3 Audio CD. (Running Time: 180 Minutes). 2006. audio compact disk 59.99 (978-0-914391-71-5(2)) Comm People Pr.

How to Become a Faithful Christian Pt. 1: The Benefits of Faithfulness. Alfred D. Harvey, Jr. 3 cass in album. (Running Time: 2 hrs. 45 mins.). 2003. 15.00 (978-1-932508-13-0(9)) Doers Pub.
becoming faithful.

How to Become a Faithful Christian Pt. 2: Hindrances to Faithfulness. Alfred D. Harvey, Jr. 10 cass in album. (Running Time: 9 hrs. 10 mins.). 2003. 50.00 (978-1-932508-14-7(7)) Doers Pub.

How to Become a Faithful Christian Pt. 3: What Is Faithfulness? Alfred D. Harvey, Jr. 4 cass in album. (Running Time: 3 hrs. 40 mins.). 2003. 20.00 (978-1-932508-15-4(5)) Doers Pub.

How to Become a Faithful Christian Pt. 4: How to Become Faithful. Alfred D. Harvey, Jr. 10 cass in album. (Running Time: 9 hrs. 10 mins.). 2003. 50.00 (978-1-932508-16-1(3)) Doers Pub.

How to Become a Great Boss: The Rules for Getting & Keeping the Best Employees. unabr. ed. Jeffrey J. Fox. Read by Jeffrey J. Fox. 2 CDs. (Running Time: 2 hrs. 30 mins.). 2002. audio compact disk 21.98 (978-1-4013-9671-8(2)) Pub: Hyperion. Dist(s): HarperCollins Pubs

How to Become a Marketing Superstar: Unexpected Rules That Ring the Cash Register. rev. abr. unabr. ed. Jeffrey J. Fox. Read by Jeffrey J. Fox. 2 CDs. (Running Time: 5 hrs.). 2002. audio compact disk 21.98 (978-1-4013-9748-7(4), Hyperion Audio) Pub: Hyperion. Dist(s): HarperCollins Pubs

How to Become a Master of Distribution Sales. Dave Kahle. 10 cass. 2000. ring bd. 139.50 (978-0-9647042-7-5(7)) DaCo.
If distributor salespeople are going to be effective in the 21st Century, they need to master these disciplines. Use this premium program to teach them the skills to give them a competitive edge. May also be used by individual salespeople as a stand-alone tool for improved performance. Help them learn to... 1. Organize Themselves Create powerful systems to operate at peak performance. Develop motivating goals. Manage information so it becomes a resource. 2. Build Relationships Understand the relationship building process. Master the seven rules for effective relationship building. Relate easily to different types of people. Make people comfortable with them. 3. Master Sales Skills Understand the levels of product that a distributor really sells. Effectively set appointments. Deal with voice mail. Organize a sales presentation for any product or service. Uncover a customer's deepest needs. Master the use of sales questions. Use features and benefits to your advantage. Close sales without jeopardizing relationships. Handle objections. Probe and clarify. 4. Manage Themselves Seven rules for effective time management . Deal effectively with fear, procrastination, depression, and adversity. Set motivating goals. 5. Work Smart by Planning and Preparing Master a planning process for any situation. Develop effective strategies for selling key accounts. Create effective territory plans. Plan each sales call. 6. Continually Improve Understand the ultimate competitive edge. Discover a system for continuous, life-long personal improvement. The package consists of: 10 audio-cassettes A 70 page resource guide that contains worksheets, templates and forms.

How to Become A MLM Rock Star. Randy Gage. 6 CD's. 2005. audio compact disk 97.00 (978-0-9744363-8-8(0)) Prime Concepts Grp.

How to Become a New Creation. Derek Prince. 1 cass. (B-4066) Derek Prince.

How to Become a Professional Photographer & Make Money Too! The Zen of Photography. Jeff Black. Read by Jeff Black. Read by Toni Blake-Cline. Des. by Gillian Conte. 3 cass. 1994. 39.95 Set, incl. bklt. in binder. (978-0-9652054-0-5(1)) Synergy Audio.
Information on setting up a business as a professional photographer with coverage on composition, equipment, film & marketing plus suggestions on working for & with the community & developing meditation disciplines.

How to Become a Rainmaker: The Rules for Getting & Keeping Customers & Clients. unabr. rev. ed. Jeffrey J. Fox. Read by Jeffrey J. Fox. 2 CDs. (Running Time: 2 hrs. 0 mins. 0 sec.). (ENG.). 2001. audio compact disk 20.00 (978-1-55927-674-0(6)) Pub: Macmill Audio. Dist(s): Macmillan

How to Become a Saint. Kriyananda, pseud. 1 cass. 9.95 (ST-60) Crystal Clarity.
Topics include: Getting clear on what it is we don't want; the importance of listening to others, yet detaching ourselves from their (& our own) opinions; sincerity as a necessary ingredient; why we must live life by deliberate choices; how this imperfect world aids sainthood.

How to Become a Star. Irene Hughes. 1 cass. 8.95 (810) Am Fed Astrologers.

How to Become a Superstar Sales Professional: Prospecting & Solution-Based Selling Skills for Business to Business Sales Professionals. Scripts. As told by Winnie Ary & Craig Rudesill. 3 CDs. (Running Time: 3 hrs. 30 mins). Dramatization. 2006. 24.95 (978-0-9774659-5-8(0), 1-866-372-2636) Cameo Pubns.
?Born? Salespeople Simply Don?t Exist!But You Can Discover the Secrets Superstar Sales Professionals Use to Reach the Top In How to Become a $uperstar $ales Professional, sales training expert Winnie Ary dispels the myth that good selling skills are a birthright rather than acquired skills. In her direct, right-to-the-point manner, she addresses many of the selling skills you must master in order to become a Superstar Sales Professional, while providing specific techniques and examples throughout each chapter.Now you can learn the high-impact selling strategies that lead to success, including how to:?Effectively prospect?Ask for the business?Address objections?Uncover needs?Listen for key messages that uncover customer needsAnd by using her ?Drills for Skills,? you can practice what you learn to develop both confidence and competency. Winnie?s clients often say she has a way of giving salespeople a ?map? that directs them to where they need go, and most important, shows them how to get there. Whether you are new to sales or a seasoned professional, after reading this book you will learn skills and techniques that will help you become a Superstar Sales Professional.

How to Become a True Disciple. (106) Yoga Res Foun.

How to Become A United States Citizen (Digital) Stacey Kammerman. 2007. audio compact disk 15.95 (978-1-934842-19-5(2)) KAMMS Consult.

How to Become a Venture Capital Consultant. Mervin Evans. 2 CD. (Running Time: 120 mins.). 2006. audio compact disk 99.99 (978-0-914391-73-9(9)) Comm People Pr.

How to Become a Water Walker. 3 cass. 2002. 15.00 (978-1-881541-79-0(7)) A Wommack.

How to Become a Water Walker. Created by AWMI. (ENG.). 2004. audio compact disk 20.00 (978-1-59548-038-5(2)) A Wommack.

How to Become CEO: The Rules for Rising to the Top of Any Organization. unabr. rev. ed. Jeffrey J. Fox. Read by Jeffrey J. Fox. 2 CDs. (Running Time: 1 hr. 30 mins. 0 sec.). (ENG.). 2001. audio compact disk 20.00 (978-1-55927-673-3(8)) Pub: Macmill Audio. Dist(s): Macmillan

How to Become Forever Thin. unabr. ed. Byron L. Wilt. Read by Byron L. Wilt. 4 cass. (Running Time: 2 hrs. 40 min.). (Be Free Ser.). 1993. bk. & stu. ed. 23.97 set. (978-0-9637814-0-6(5)); pap. bk. 39.97 Prof Human Being.
Teaches how to use the Magic within to become thin. Covers creating a possibility portrait image. The dangers of deprivation dieting. How to enjoy more food & weight loss.

How to Begin a Story. unabr. ed. Elizabeth R. Bills. 1 cass. (Running Time: 27 min.). (Secrets of Successful Writers Ser.). 1963. 12.95 (23021) J Norton Pubs.
Before beginning to write, certain preliminary decisions must be made, such as: What is the basic problem? With whom does the writer want to identify? What is the writer's purpose in writing the story.

How to Behave in the House of God. As told by Markus Bishop. 2 cass. (Running Time: 1 hr. 30 mins.). 2000. 10.00 (978-0-9628301-6-7(X)) M Bishop Minis.

How to Behave So Your Children Will Too: A Collection of Entertaining Stories & Practical Ideas Gathered from Real Pare. abr. ed. Sal Severe & Tim McCormick. Read by John Dossett. 2004. 10.95 (978-0-7435-4841-0(8)) Pub: S&S Audio. Dist(s): S and S Inc

How to Behave so your Preschooler will, Too! Sal Severe. Narrated by Brian Keeler. 8 CDs. 2002. audio compact disk 78.00 (978-1-4025-4398-2(0)) Recorded Bks.

How to Borrow Money from a Banker. Roger Bel Air. 4 cass. (Running Time: 2 hrs.). 1987. 59.95 R Bel Air.

How to Borrow Money from a Banker. unabr. ed. Roger Bel Air. 4 cass. 1989. 19.95 Aet incl. checklist. (S04100) J Norton Pubs.
Program for executives, business owners & investors on how to successfully negotiate financing with a bank.

How to Borrow Twice the Money. Somers H. White. 4 cass. 80.00 (C101) S White.
Helping individuals to better deal with lenders & investors, how to better present themselves for financing, how to tell their story to the bank in 90 seconds.

How to Break into Pharmaceutical Sales: A Headhunter's Strategy. Tom Ruff. Read by Chip Bolcik. 2008. audio compact disk 29.95 (978-0-9786070-0-5(7)) T Ruff.

How to Break Through Your Mental Barriers for Success, Vol. II. unabr. ed. David Essel. 1 cass. (Running Time: 1 hrs.). (David Essel's Dynamic Living Ser.). 1996. 9.95 (978-1-893074-00-2(5)) D Essel Inc.
Discover the action steps that will lead to your personal & professional breakthroughs: 1) Finding your focus, 2) Acknowledgement & commitment, 3) Accomplish morein less time, 4) Visualize your success, 5) Give to receive.

How to break your own Heart. unabr. ed. Maggie Alderson. Read by Catherine Milte. (Running Time: 12 hrs. 25 mins.). 2009. audio compact disk 103.95 (978-1-74214-362-0(8), 9781742143620) Pub: Bolinda Pubng AUS. Dist(s): Bolinda Pub Inc

How to Breathe Your Way Through Stess, Anxiety, & Anger. 1 CD. (Running Time: 32 mins.). 2005. audio compact disk 34.95 (978-0-9773181-0-0(9)) A Ahern.
Resurrect the Dream for Your Life!We are all born with a great dream for our lives; a dream which may have been submerged or derailed along the way by doing what we thought was ?right? and by suppressing that inner voice that urges us to listen to our souls longing. Dr. Ahern calls this self-hypnosis the ?conditioned mind? - the thought process that controls and limits us and prevents us from living our dreams. Dr. Ahern?s simple yet profound Snap Out of It Now Method takes just minutes to learn and will help you break free from the controlling limitations of your conditioned life and enable you to start living your dream. The Snap Out of It Now method will teach you the art of paying attention, of listening to your heart. It will help you enjoy life more fully, more effectively, and more peacefully.Breathe into Life.Most of us don?t know how to breathe properly and most of us are not even aware that we often hold our breath.By learning how to a few simple tools, you can reduce or eliminate stress, overwhelm, disease, low energy and bring back joy and enthusiasm in your life.In this Breathing Workshop, you?ll learn:1.How to Breathe to increase energy and improve your overall health and well-being.2.How to become aware of the feelings that arise in the body. If you are aware of what?s going on in your body you are in a healing state.3.How to become aware of the body breathing. Your body already knows how to heal itself ? it?s your thinking mind and conditioning that prevents it from doing its job!Learn How To:?Increase awareness of how your body communicates?Improve healing?Enhance athletic performance?Focus your thinking and enhance learning?Manage anxiety?Improve relationships?Experience more enjoyable sex.?Increase awareness of your feelings, wants, and needs.?Tap into richer levels of creativity and financial success.When we are aware of our breath we are connected with ourselves, others, and God.

How to Brighten Intellect. Swami Jyotirmayananda. 1 cass. (Running Time: 1 hr.). 1990. 12.99 Yoga Res Foun.

How to Build a Business Warren Buffett Would Buy: The R. C. Willey Story. Jeff Benedict. 2009. audio compact disk 19.95 (978-1-60641-116-2(0), Shadow Mount) Deseret Bk.

How to Build a Dinosaur: Extinction Doesn't Have to Be Forever. unabr. ed. Jack Horner & James Gorman. Read by Patrick G. Lawlor. (Running Time: 6 hrs. 30 mins. 0 sec.). (ENG.). 2009. audio compact disk 19.99 (978-1-4001-6141-6(X)); audio compact disk 24.99 (978-1-4001-1141-1(2)); audio compact disk 49.99 (978-1-4001-4141-8(9)) Pub: Tantor Media. Dist(s): IngramPubServ

How to Build a Giant Heap with or Without Your Friends, Family or Neighbors. Kim Klaver. 2 cass. (Running Time: 50 min.). 1996. 14.95 Set. (978-1-891493-01-0(9)) Max Out Prodns.
Humorous, yet practical instruction on how to market your business or product to the masses.

How to Build a Great Marriage: Matt. 19:4-6; Phil. 2:3-11. Ed Young. 1996. 4.95 (978-0-7417-2101-3(5), 1101) Win Walk.

How to Build a Happy Marriage & Keep It That Way. Robert Lauer. 2 cass. (Running Time: 3 hrs.). 1997. pap. bk. 15.95 (978-1-55977-701-8(X)) CareerTrack Pubns.

How to Build a House. unabr. ed. Dana Reinhardt. Read by Caitlin Greer. 5 CDs. (Running Time: 5 hrs. 24 mins.). (YA). (gr. 9 up). 2008. audio compact disk 45.00 (978-0-7393-6412-3(X), Listening Lib) Pub: Random Audio Pubg. Dist(s): Random
HARPER'S DAD IS getting a divorce from her beloved stepmother, Jane. Even worse, Harper has lost her stepsister, Tess; the divorce divides them. Harper decides to escape by joining a volunteer program to build a house for a family in Tennessee who lost their home in a tornado. Not that she knows a thing about construction. Soon she's living in a funky motel and working long days in blazing heat with a group of kids from all over the country. At the site, she works alongside Teddy, the son of the family for whom they are building the house. Their partnership turns into a summer romance, complete with power tools. Learning to trust and love Teddy isn't easy for Harper, but it's the first step toward finding her way back home.

How to Build a House. unabr. ed. Dana Reinhardt. Read by Caitlin Greer. (Running Time: 19440 sec.). (ENG.). (J). (gr. 9). 2008. audio compact disk 35.00 (978-0-7393-6410-9(3), Listening Lib) Pub: Random Audio Pubg. Dist(s): Random

How to Build a Network of Power Relationships. Harvey Mackay. 6 cass. (Running Time: 3 hrs.). 1995. bk. 59.95 Set. (12140AM) Nightingale-Conant.
Harvey Mackay teaches you to develop the contacts you need to get what you want - when you want it. Learn to get noticed by key decision makers...network with colleagues, clients & competitors...& identify the "hidden" market that accounts for 67 percent of all jobs. Discover eight ways to get a salary raise & 11 tips for successful negotiations. Let America's foremost networking authority show you how to use this tool to gain guidance, financial backing & other considerations.

How to Build a Praying Church. Tom Lovorn. 3 cass. bk. 89.95 Set. (418) Chrch Grwth VA.
Step-by-step planning necessary to successfully implement prayer ministries in your church.

How to Build a Profitable Business in Tough Economic Times. unabr. ed. Joan Sotkin. Read by Joan Sotkin. 2 cass. (Running Time: 2 hrs.). Dramatization. 1992. 19.95 set. (978-1-881002-89-5(6), T102) Build Your Busn.
This tape offers help to small business owners who are looking to increase their chance for survival. Tape includes: Value & Values - Musts for the 90's, Importance of Planning, Low Cost Marketing Tips, 30 Minutes a Day to Higher Profits.

How to Build a Successful Astrology Business. Sue Apitz-Upwall. Read by Sue Apitz-Upwall. 1 cass. (Running Time: 90 min.). 1994. 8.95 (1119) Am Fed Astrologers.

How to Build a Tin Canoe. Robb White. Narrated by Robb White. (Running Time: 6 hrs.). (C). 2005. 24.95 (978-1-59912-508-4(0)) Iofy Corp.

How to Build a Tin Canoe. Robb White. Read by Robb White. 4 cass. (Running Time: 6 hrs.). 2005. 44.95 (978-0-7861-2940-9(9), 3415); audio compact disk 45.00 (978-0-7861-8182-7(6), 3415) Blckstn Audio.

How to Build Collective Intelligence in Your Organization. Speeches. Seth Kahan. 1 CD. (Running Time: 1 hr 4 mins). 2004. audio compact disk 20.00 (978-0-9759206-1-9(8)) Prfmnce Dev Grp.
Topics include: Community: An Ancient Heritage* The World Bank's Collaboration Community* Frame of Mind as an Influence on Behavior* Bringing Care into Business* Business Performance Communities* Core Communication Constituencies.*

How to Build Fictional Characters. abr. ed. Dwight V. Swain. Read by Dwight V. Swain. 1 cass. (Running Time: 90 mins.). 1992. 12.95 (978-1-880717-26-4(3)) Writers AudioShop.
International fiction expert Dwight Swain tells how to create memorable heroes & villains, how to make your characters likable & give them purpose, the importance of putting story people in danger & how to discover their attitudes & motivation. Recorded at an Austin Writers' League seminar in Austin, Texas.

How to Build High Self-Esteem: A Practical Process for Personal Growth. Jack L. Canfield. 6 cass. 49.95 Set. (728AD) Nightingale-Conant.
This program works with both your conscious & your subconscious mind to enhance self-esteem & empower you to take positive action.

How to Build High Self-Esteem: A Practical Process for Personal Growth. Jack L. Canfield. 6 cass. 49.95 Set. (728AS) Pryor Resources.
No one needs to be stuck with low levels of self-esteem, especially in business. Here is a practical process for personal change.

How to Build Rapport. Tim Hallbom & Suzi Smith. Read by Tim Hallbom & Suzi Smith. 1 cass. (Running Time: 30 min.). 1986. 9.95 (978-1-55552-044-1(8)) Metamorphous Pr.
Introductory tape on using NLP to enhance rapport in relationships.

How to Build Team Skills in the Workplace, Set. 4 cass. (Essential Business Skills Ser.). 1999. 129.00 (80216CHDG); pap. bk. & wbk. ed. 30.00 (80217CHDG) AMACOM.
The Institute for Certification, a department of Professional Secretaries international, will grant points towards CPS recertification to qualified individuals who successfully complete this course. 1 CEU.

How to Build the Communication Bridge. Gary V. Whetstone. 6 cass. (Running Time: 9 hrs.). (Family & Relationships Ser.). 1995. bk. 50.00 (978-1-58866-225-5(X), VA006A) Gary Whet Pub.
Can two walk together less they be agreed? These teachings will help build your skills so that you can move to the highest expression of communication.

How to Build Your Child's Self-Esteem. Denis Waitley. Read by Denis Waitley. 6 cass. 49.95 Set. (699AD) Nightingale-Conant.

How to Build Your Firm Foundation. Kenneth Copeland. 4 cass. (Running Time: 4 hrs.). 1982. bk. 20.00 (978-0-938458-17-3(5), 020100) K Copeland Pubns.

How to Build Your Home & Save Thousands. Beverly Grisham & Wayne Clark. 1999. pap. bk. 16.95 (978-0-9673598-1-6(3)) Village Dev Corp.

How to Build Your Intuition. Pat Carroll. Read by Pat Carroll. Ed. by Tony Carroll. 1 cass. (Running Time: 30 min.). 10.00 Inner-Mind Concepts.
Explains how to relax & heighten the sense of awareness.

How to Build Your Net Worth: Buying Residential Real Estate with None of Your Own Money. C. Mark Leaphart. Read by C. Mark Leaphart. 6 cass. (Running Time: 3 hrs.). 1994. pap. bk. Set. (Leaphart) VCI Invest.
Self-help multi-media course, sold as an entire course or single-media pieces. Designed for personal financial improvement & gain through real estate acquisitions. Four paperback books, one booklet, six cassettes or three compact discs & one floppy disc.

How to Build Your Net Worth No 5 & 6: Buying Residential Real Estate with None of Your Own Money. C. Mark Leaphart & J. Kirk Leaphart, Jr. 2 cass. 1994. 14.95 Set. (978-1-890646-11-0(3)) Leaphart Prodns.

How to Build Your Net Worth Nos. 1-4: Buying Residential Real Estate with None of Your Own Money. C. Mark Leaphart & J. Kirk Leaphart, Jr. 4 cass. 1994. 14.95 Set. (978-1-890646-07-3(5)); audio compact disk 39.95 CD. (978-1-890646-06-6(7)) Leaphart Prodns.
Any person can go from zero experience in buying real estate to building a substantial net worth. Any person seeking to improve their financial position can benefit. Simple, but very detailed, with enough "how to" information for anyone or beginner or real estate buyer.

How to Buy a Car. 10.00 Esstee Audios.
How to select the car wanted & needed, either new or used. How to recognize flaws & how to best finance a purchase.

How to Buy a Love of Reading. unabr. ed. Tanya Egan Gibson. Narrated by Renée Raudman. (Running Time: 13 hrs. 30 mins. 0 sec.). 2009. 24.99 (978-1-4001-6246-8(7)); audio compact disk 75.99 (978-1-4001-4246-0(6)); audio compact disk 37.99 (978-1-4001-1246-3(X)) Pub: Tantor Media. Dist(s): IngramPubServ

How to Buy & Sell a Business: How You Can Win in the Business Quadrant. abr. unabr. ed. Garrett Sutton & Robert T. Kiyosaki. Read by Garrett Sutton. (Running Time: 6 hrs.). (ENG.). 2010. 16.98 (978-1-60024-884-9(5)); audio compact disk 24.98 (978-1-60024-882-5(9)) Pub: Hachet Audio. Dist(s): HachBkGrp

How to Buy Your First Home. Bill Galvin & Heather Kibbey. Read by Bill Galvin & Heather Kibbey. 1 cass. (Running Time: 1 hr. 23 min.). (Real Estate Ser.). 1987. 8.95 (978-0-9615067-1-1(7)) Panoply Pr.
A step-by-step guide for first time homebuyers, tips for choosing a good agent, researching the market, finding the best financing & understanding the closing process.

How to Call Upon Angels to Protect Yourself & Loved Ones: True Stories of Archangel Michael's Protection Elizabeth Clare Prophet. 1 cass. (Running Time: 1 hr.). 1995. 14.95 (978-0-922729-67-8(0)) Pub: Summit Univ. Dist(s): Natl Bk Netwk

How to Capture a First-Rate Mate: Attracting Beauty, Brains & Bucks. abr. ed. Leil Lowndes. Read by Leil Lowndes. (Running Time: 14400 sec.). 2006. audio compact disk 21.95 (978-1-59316-082-1(8)) Listen & Live.

How to Cha Cha Cha. unabr. ed. Conversa-Phone Institute Staff & Betty White. 1 cass. (Running Time: 55 min.). (Betty White's How to Ballroom Dance Ser.). 1990. 9.95 (978-1-56752-089-7(8)) Conversa-phone.
Teaches all of the most popular steps-breaks-turns - how to lead & how to follow. Fully illustrated instruction manual follows the audio tape. Learn today - dance tonight.

How to Challenge Psychological Evidence in Custody Cases. 1 cass. 1991. bk. 45.00 (AC-643) PA Bar Inst.

How to Change Anybody: Proven Techniques to Reshape Anyone's Attitude, Behavior, Feelings, or Beliefs. abr. ed. David J. Lieberman. Read by Bruce Sabath. 3 CDs. (Running Time: 3 hrs. 0 sec.). (ENG.). 2005. audio compact disk 19.95 (978-1-59397-603-3(8)) Pub: Macmill Audio. Dist(s): Macmillan

How to Change for the Better CD Series. 2006. audio compact disk 27.00 (978-1-59834-041-9(7)) Walk Thru the Bible.

How to Change, How to Take Risks. unabr. ed. Jennifer James. Read by Jennifer James. 1 cass. (Running Time: 1 hr.). 9.95 (978-0-915423-50-7(2)) Jennifer J.

How to Change Ideas CD. Edward De Bono. 1 CD. (Running Time: 55 mins.). 2006. audio compact disk 12.95 (978-1-57970-358-5(5), C33029D, Audio-For) J Norton Pubs.
The Yes-No system we use in our basic thinking is discussed and to what extent Lateral Thinking can be used as a third creative tool is examined.

How to Change Someone You Love: Four Steps to Help You Help Them. unabr. ed. Brad Lamm. Read by Brad Lamm. (Running Time: 7 hrs. 0 mins. 0 sec.). (ENG.). 2009. audio compact disk 29.99 (978-1-4272-0872-9(7)) Pub: Macmill Audio. Dist(s): Macmillan

How to Change Your Destiny. 1 cass. (Running Time: 50 min.). (Personal Growth Ser.). 9.95 (SS-83) Crystal Clarity.
Features: The relationship between destiny & karma; how to overcome karma or use it to best advantage; how spiritual tests speed personal growth; how to strengthen your aura.

How to Change Your Life with Astrology. Jeanne Avery. 1 cass. 1992. 8.95 (1007) Am Fed Astrologers.

How to Change Your Own Ideas. unabr. ed. Edward De Bono. 12.95 (978-0-88432-223-8(8), E33029) J Norton Pubs.
Explains how to develop your creativity & enable you to look at problems from totally new approaches.

How to Charleston. unabr. ed. Conversa-Phone Institute Staff & Betty White. 1 cass. (Running Time: 55 min.). (Betty White's How to Ballroom Dance Ser.). 1990. 9.95 (978-1-56752-093-4(6)) Conversa-phone.
Teaches all of the most popular steps-breaks-turns - how to lead & how to follow. Fully illustrated instruction manual follows the audio tape. Learn today - dance tonight.

How to Choose a College. Bruce Williams. Read by Bruce Williams. 1 cass. (Insider's Report Ser.). 9.95 (978-0-944305-08-9(3)) Bonneville Media.
Features advice for parent & student on how to choose a college.

How to Choose a Mate: Hebrews 11:20-21. Ed Young. 1992. 47.45 (978-0-7417-1920-1(7), 920) Win Walk.

How to Choose a Religion or Philosophy Most Appropriate to Your Own Needs. Instructed by Manly P. Hall. 8.95 (978-0-89314-138-7(0), C801019) Philos Res.

How to Choose a Therapist: Program from the Award Winning Public Radio Series. Interview. Hosted by Fred Goodwin. 1 CD. (Running Time: 1 hr). 2001. audio compact disk 21.95 (978-1-932479-54-6(6), LCM 187) Lichtenstein Creat.
In this hour, we explore How to Choose a Therapist. As tensions rise at home and abroad, more people than ever are seeking professional help.We'll hear from the nation's top mental health officials, including Dr. Steven Hyman, director of the National Institute of Mental Health and Dr. Bernard Arons, director of the nation's Center for Mental Health Services. We'll also speak with Dr. Susan Vaughan, an assistant professor of clinical psychiatry at Columbia University medical school and the author of The Talking Cure: The Science Behind Psychotherapy.

***How to Choose a Translation for All Its Worth: A Guide to Understanding & Using Bible Versions.** Zondervan. (Running Time: 6 hrs. 19 mins. 0 sec.). (ENG.). 2010. 9.99 (978-0-310-86922-1(6)) Zondervan.

How to Choose & Change Careers. Richard Nelson Bolles. Read by Richard Nelson Bolles. (Running Time: 1 hr.). 9.95 (I0080B090, HarperThor) HarpC GBR.

How to Choose Your True Lifetime Lover. Scripts. 1. (Running Time: 73 mins). Dramatization. 2006. audio compact disk 15.00 (978-0-9742164-1-6(0)) Smart Spouse.
It's a new era. This audio book shares with you the quality knowledge and advice which has been missing. It teaches you how to choose your true lifetime lover, and not an impostor. An impostor pretends to be the right one, and later ruins your quality of inner life with a painful divorce, domestic violence, or an empty shell marriage.Now it has been demystified. This audio teaches you how to use the new decision-making tool named the, 10 Step Smart Lover's Model, to empower you to foresee the future, and prevent a mismatch before wedlock. This model puts you in control to influence and create the future without unpleasant surprises. This model guides you to foresee and manage the risks and uncertainties in building your love relationship. You eliminate the odds of falling in love with a wrong person. This model teaches and guides you to make winning decisions that stand the test of time. So, are you dating? Do you have an important relationship decision to make? Do you want to put your mind at ease? Do you want to create a fulfilling love relationship? Now it's your time to decide.CONTENTS on this audio-book.Track 1: Introduction, and personal background.Track 2: Lessons from the failed marriagesTrack 3: Lessons from the successful marriages, and analysis.Track 4, Step #1: Self-awareness and preparation for success.Track 5, Step #2: Designing her/his Profile.Track 6, Step #3: Identifying and Proposing a Date.Track 7, Step #4: Your First Date - (making quality decisions)Track 8, Step #5: To-Do-Lists on Follow-up Dates.Track 9, Step #6: How to Talk and Evaluate Follow-up Dates.Track 10, Step #7: Timing Factor (last checklist)Track 11, Step #8: EngagementTrack 12, Step #9: Total CommitmentTrack 13, Step #10: The After Commitment Period.

How to Choose Your True Lifetime Lover. Alex Mugume. Read by Alex Mugume. 2006. 10.00 (978-0-9742164-2-3(9)) Smart Spouse.

***How to Clearly Communicate Employee Benefits.** PUEI. 2008. audio compact disk 199.00 (978-1-935041-06-1(1), CareerTrack) P Univ E Inc.

How to Clearly Hear from God. Alfred D. Harvey, Jr. 2 cass in album. (Running Time: 1 hr. 50 mins.). 2003. 10.00 (978-1-932508-23-9(6)) Doers Pub.
Hearing and obeying the voice of God is essential to your Christian walk. Discover clearly how to hear from God.

How to Close Every Sale. Joe Girard. Narrated by Richard M. Davidson. 6 CDs. (Running Time: 7 hrs. 15 min.). 2000. audio compact disk 58.00 (C1262E7) Recorded Bks.
Girard, who is also a best-selling author, reveals field-tested techniques, insider tips & useful common sense reminders that are guaranteed to give your sales career a boost.

How to close Every Sale. Joe Girard. Narrated by Richard M. Davidson. 6 CDs. (Running Time: 7 hrs. 15 mins.). audio compact disk 58.00 (978-0-7887-4769-4(X)) Recorded Bks.

How to Close Every Sale. Joe Girard & Robert L. Shook. Read by Joe Girard. 1 cass. (Running Time: 90 min.). 1990. 9.95 HarperCollins Pubs.

How to Close Every Sale, unabr. ed. Joe Girard. Narrated by Richard M. Davidson. 5 cass. (Running Time: 7 hrs. 15 mins.). 1989. 44.00 (978-0-7887-4073-2(3), 96165E7) Recorded Bks.

How to Close More Sales: Turbo-Charged Strategies. Kenneth R. Schock. (Running Time: 6 hrs.). 1988. 99.00 incl. hard binder. (978-0-923168-01-8(X)) Sales Focus.
Provides specific strategies on how to close more sales for the sales professional. These are special training sales tapes taught by award winning author & winner of Who's Who in Marketing & Sales Award in America in 1987. Covers all aspects of closing the sale - from behavioral styles to closing techniques. Specific closing strategies are stressed.

How to Close Sales & When. 1977. audio compact disk (978-0-89811-279-5(6)) Meyer Res Grp.

How to Close Sales & When. Paul J. Meyer. 1 cass. (Running Time: 20 min.). 11.00 (978-0-89811-019-7(X), 5156) Meyer Res Grp.
Learn these proven techniques for getting the order & for recognizing the right moment to close.

How to Close Sales & When. Paul J. Meyer. 1 cass. 10.00 (SP100017) SMI Intl.
Have you ever met a warm, friendly prospect but suddenly found yourself outside the client's door with no signature on the order? If so, master salesman Paul J. Meyer has some interesting ideas for you. Learn these proven techniques for getting the order - & for recognizing the right moment to close.

How to Collect Money for Your International Sales & How to Pay Your International Suppliers. Donald M. Gartrell. 1 cass. (Running Time: 30 min.). 1998. bk. 12.38 (978-1-893461-00-0(9)) Gartrell.
Discusses the pros & cons for buyer & seller of various international trade terms: cash in advance, letter of credit, standby letter of credit, documentary collection, & open account. Details how payment is assured.

How to Commence a Civil Litigation. (Running Time: 5 hrs. 30 min.). 1995. 92.00 Incl. 324p. coursebk. (20701) NYS Bar.
Reviews & analyzes the basics of handling a civil lawsuit up to the point of trial. The speakers focus on the practical aspects of handling the initial stages of a civil action from both plaintiff's & defendant's perspectives & highlight how to properly draft the early papers in a case.

How to Commit Monogamy: A Lighthearted Look at Long-Term Love. abr. ed. Elaine Viets. 2 cass. (Running Time: 3 hrs.). 1997. 17.95 (978-1-882467-22-8(1), Widstone Audio) Wildstone Media.
The author traces the historical changes in the perception & reality of monogamy from her childhood in the 1950s & through her college experiences during the turbulent 1960s & 1970s & her career to the present.

How to Communicate Better see Como Expresarse Mejor

How to Communicate Effectively with an Older Person. (Caregiving to the Elderly Ser.). 9.95 (978-1-877843-01-3(6)) Elder Care Solutions.
Listening, teaching self-care. Coping with speech & hearing problems. Verbal & non-verbal communication.

How to Communicate Like A Pro: In Person, on Paper & on the Podium. Nido Qubein. 6 CDs. 2005. audio compact disk 99.00 (978-0-939975-17-4(3)) Exec Pr NC.
Between business people, in group discussions and private conversations, communication means everything. Nido Qubein, consultant to the nation's top corporations, shares his techniques for successful communication in person, on paper, and on the podium. Your power to influence the lives of others in the world around you is as great as your ability to communicate. At home or at work, today's great communicators have more impact than ever before. This 12-session program is guaranteed to teach you how to communicate effectively in person, on paper and on the podium. You'll learn: 1. How to Become a Master Communicator2. How to Get People to Pay Attention to You3. How to Boost Your Audience Response Rating4. How to Help People Understand You Through Images5. How to Connect Through Stories6. How to Break Through Communication Barriers7. How to Listen Perceptively8. How to Target for Maximum Impact9. How to Target Results10. How to Give an Effective Speech11. How to Put More Power in Your Writing12. How to Communicate in the Information Age.

How to Communicate Political Ideas. unabr. ed. Nathaniel Branden. 1 cass. (Running Time: 55 min.). 12.95 (732) J Norton Pubs.
The techniques of political persuasion. Branden encouraged individuals to question their own motives for engaging in political conversion, & advised that they understand their own case.

How to Communicate with Animals. rev. ed. Penelope Smith. Read by Penelope Smith. 1 cass. (Running Time: 60 min.). (Interspecies Telepathic Connection Tape Ser.: No. 1). 1994. 9.95 (978-0-936552-13-2(1)) AnimaMundi.
A step-by-step guide through basic principles & techniques to show you how to get across to animals & help you remove your blocks to receiving telepathic communication from other species. A do-it-yourself workshop for those eager to get more in tune with animals.

How to Communicate with Your One to Six Year Old. unabr. ed. Christina Clement. Read by Thomas Amshay. 1 cass. (Running Time: 1 hr.). 1986. 5.00 (978-0-939401-09-3(6)) RFTS Prod.
Explains how to build a communication bridge that goes from childhood to adult friendship & teaches kids to be individuals.

How to "Comp" in a Combo. Duane Shinn. 1 cass. 19.95 (NS-5) Duane Shinn.
Explains how "comp" is short for "accompany," but comping in a combo is different than playing for a soloist.

How to Compete with Yourself & Win! The Art of Self-Motivation in the Workplace. 1992. (978-0-9633539-1-7(8)); (978-0-9633539-2-4(6)) D H Pavlakos & Assocs.

How to Conduct a Taekwon-Do Class. James S. Benko. 1986. 12.95 (TC-2) ITA Inst.
Gives you a detailed outline on how to correctly conduct a Taekwon-Do class.

How to Conduct a Taekwon-Do Promotional Examination. James S. Benko. 1986. 12.95 (TC-3) ITA Inst.
Covers the proper procedures for conducting a promotional examination. Also covers How to test & award ranks.

How to Conduct Effective Direct & Cross Examination. 1989. bk. 95.00 (AC-490) PA Bar Inst.

How to Conduct Successful Opportunity Meetings. Dave Johnson. 6 cass. (Dave Johnson Program of Sales Seminars). 65.00 D Johnson.
Shows how to quickly interest a few people or a large crowd in Network Marketing Opportunity.

How to Connect in Business in 90 Seconds or Less. Nicholas Boothman. Read by Nicholas Boothman. (Running Time: 3 hrs. 30 mins.). 2005. 21.95 (978-1-60083-127-0(3)) Iofy Corp.

How to Connect in Business in 90 Seconds or Less. abr. ed. Nicholas Boothman. Read by Nicholas Boothman. 2 cass. (Running Time: 3 hrs.). 2002. 16.95 (978-1-885408-82-2(X), LL074) Listen & Live.
An innovative system of forging instant connections into the workplace. Whether you're standing around the water cooler or giving a formal presentation, success in business depends on creating and maintaining effective relationships. Dig into the fundamentals and learn to mine the potential in every situation.

How to Connect in Business in 90 Seconds or Less. abr. ed. Nicholas Boothman. Read by Nicholas Boothman. 3 CDs. (Running Time: 12600 sec.). 2006. audio compact disk 19.95 (978-1-59316-075-3(5), LL167) Listen & Live.

How to Conquer Insomia see Como Vencer el Insomio

How to Conquer Test Anxiety & Achieve Higher Scores on Any Exam. unabr. ed. Neil Fiore. Read by Erik Synnestvedt. (Running Time: 1 hr. 17 mins.). (ENG.). 2008. 9.98 (978-1-59659-198-1(6), GildAudio) Pub: Gildan Media. Dist(s): HachBkGrp

How to Conquer the Four Ds of the Devil. Reed A. Benson. 1 cass. 7.98 (978-1-55503-669-0(4), 06004865) Covenant Comms.
Uplifting & inspirational talk.

How to Conquer the World with One Hand... & an Attitude. unabr. ed. Paul E. Berger & Stephanie Mensh. Read by Johnny Rodriguez. Frwd. by Julian M. Whitaker. 8 CDs. (Running Time: 547 minutes). 2007. audio compact disk 49.95 (978-0-9668378-8-9(6)) Positive Power.

How to Conquer Wall Street: An Introduction to Investing & Financial Planning. Scripts. Des. by T. Paxton. 1. (Running Time: 75 mins.). 2003. audio compact disk 18.00 (978-0-9742930-0-4(8)) Chicago Src.
Explains how to obtain financial information from publicly traded companies. Also, how to identify important traits of good companies. Gives examples.

How to Control Desires. Swami Jyotirmayananda. (140) Yoga Res Foun.

How to Control Desires, No. 1. Swami Jyotirmayananda. 1 cass. (Running Time: 1 hr.). 1990. 12.99 Yoga Res Foun.

How to Control Desires, No. 2. Swami Jyotirmayananda. 1 cass. (Running Time: 1 hr.). 1990. 12.99 Yoga Res Foun.

How to Control Desires, Vol. 2. Swami Jyotirmayananda. (141) Yoga Res Foun.

How to Control Imagination. Swami Jyotirmayananda. (109) Yoga Res Foun.

How to Control Imagination, No. 1. Swami Jyotirmayananda. 1 cass. (Running Time: 1 hr.). 1990. 12.99 Yoga Res Foun.

How to Control Imagination, No. 2. Swami Jyotirmayananda. (149) Yoga Res Foun.

How to Control Imagination, No. 3. Swami Jyotirmayananda. 1 cass. (Running Time: 1 hr.). 1990. 12.99 Yoga Res Foun.

How to Control Your Anger Before It Controls You. Albert Ellis & Chip Tafrate. 1 cass. 13.95 (C069) A Ellis Institute.
User-friendly instructions & exercises shows how to solve problems & assert yourself without becoming angry.

How to Control Your Anger Before It Controls You, abr. ed. Albert Ellis & Raymond C. Tafrate. Read by Stephen O'Hara. 2 cass. (Running Time: 3 hrs.). 1997. 17.95 (978-1-57453-118-3(2)) Audio Lit.
Practical, accessible, step-by-step program for understanding & controlling anger.

How to Control Your Anxiety Before It Controls You. Albert Ellis. 2 cass. (Running Time: 3 hrs.). 1999. 17.95 (978-1-57453-297-5(9)) Audio Lit.
Provides dozens of practical ways to control your behavior. Includes methods of thinking, feeling & acting & rational maxims to use to decrease anxiety & increase prospects for success & happiness.

How to Control Your Anxiety Before It Controls You, abr. ed. Albert Ellis. Read by Stephen O'Hara. 2 cass. (Running Time: 3 hrs.). 1999. 17.95 (978-1-57453-307-1(X)) Audio Lit.
Provides dozens of practical ways to stop sabotaging yourself by bringing the power of your rational mind to bear on the unreasonable anxieties that are controlling your behavior. Includes methods of thinking, feeling & acting & scores of rational maxims you can use to decrease your anxiety & increase your prospects for success & happiness.

How to Convince Other People see Como Convencer a los Demas

How to Convince Other People. Mario Elnerz. Read by Pedro Montoya. (Running Time: 3 hrs.). (C). 2001. 16.9[illegible]78-1-60083-264-2(4), Audiofy Corp) Iofy Corp.

How to Cook with Your Mate... And I Do[illegible]ean in the Kitchen! abr. ed. Kathleen Kryza. Read by Deidra Kelvin. 2 cass. (Running Time: 3 hrs.). (For Both Ser.). 1998. 16.95 (978-1-885408-19-8(6), LL012) Listen & Live.
A guide for pleasing the man or woman of your dreams with spicy recipes for romance.

How to Cooperate with Others. Swami Jyotirmayananda. 1 cass. (Running Time: 1 hr.). 12.99 (102) Yoga Res Foun.

How to Cooperate with Others, No. 2. Swami Jyotirmayananda. Read by Swami Jyotirmayananda. 1 cass. (Running Time: 60 min.). 12.99 (129) Yoga Res Foun.

How to Cooperate with Others, No. 3. Swami Jyotirmayananda. (170) Yoga Res Foun.

How to Cooperate with Others, No. 3. Swami Jyotirmayananda. 1 cass. (Running Time: 1 hr.). 1990. 12.99 Yoga Res Foun.

How to Count Crocodiles. unabr. ed. Margaret Mayo. Read by Nigel Anthony. 1 cass. (Running Time: 1 hrs., 30 min.). (J). (gr. 1-8). 1999. 9.95 (CTC 782, Chivers Child Audio) AudioGO.

An Asterisk (*) at the beginning of an entry indicates that the title is appearing for the first time.

How to Create a Life That Works. Bill Ferguson. Read by Bill Ferguson. 1 cass. 1990. 9.95 (978-1-878410-07-8(5)) Return Heart.

The more your life doesn't work, the more you suffer. In this cassette, you will discover how you create your own unworkability. You will discover why your life is the way it is & what you can do about it. You will learn how to clean up your life & live in a way that works.

How to Create a Magnetic Employer Brand (TM) David Lee. 1 CD. (Running Time: approximately 60 min.). 2006. audio compact disk 15.00 (978-0-9788911-3-8(9)) Hmn Nature.

How to Create a Story: Secrets of Successful Writers. unabr. ed. Elizabeth R. Bills. Read by Elizabeth R. Bills. Read by A. E. Van Vogt. 6 cass. 49.50 (S23350) J Norton Pubs.

Offers guides to writing & plotting a short story & novel as well as the writing of magazine articles. Other topics include getting started as a writer; beginning a story; the skeletal structure of a story; literary style; & the use of detail in a story. Also science fiction writer A. E. Van Vogt describes his writing system & how it has evolved throughout his career. He offers five steps to the writing of successful scenes of 800 words, the keystone of his system.

How to Create an Astrological Radio Show. Nancy Swanson. 1 cass. (Running Time: 90 min.). 1990. 8.95 (716) Am Fed Astrologers.

How to Create an Information Product in One Day or Less: The perfect guide or beginners & veteran business professionals who want to add information products to their product Offerings. Robert Imbriale. (ENG.). 2008. audio compact disk 19.95 (978-0-9777500-4-7(3)) Ultimate Wealth.

How to Create & Market Speaker Products. Dottie Walters et al. 8 cass. 125.00 Audio Album. (978-0-934344-48-7(5)) Royal Pub.

Sell thousands of dollars worth of your products at every performance. Why you should create products, how to do it, packaging, markets, lots more.

How to Create Intros & Endings. Duane Shinn. 1 cass. 19.95 (NS-3) Duane Shinn.

Explains how to create a "camouflage intro," "music box intro" & others. You'll learn a standard ending, a half-tone slide ending & others.

How to Create Power-Packed Ads, Brochures & Sales Letters That Make Money Now! The AdPOWER! Clinic Action Guide. unabr. ed. Drew Eric Whitman. Contrib. by Joseph Heier. 6 cass. (Running Time: 4 hrs. 30 min.). 1995. 89.95 Set. (978-0-9658104-1-8(0)) Whitman Stat.

Dozens of insider secrets used by top-agency advertising professionals to create powerfully effective print advertising of all kinds. Entertainingly presented with music & sound effects.

How to Create Prosperity. Bill Ferguson. Read by Bill Ferguson. 1 cass. 1990. 9.95 (978-1-878410-06-1(7)) Return Heart.

Prosperity is a choice. In this cassette, you will discover how you sabotage your own prosperity & set yourself up for financial suffering. You will learn why money is an issue for you & how to be free of money upsets forever. You will discover what creates prosperity & the key to abundance.

How to Cultivate Buds & Flowers. Read by Chogyam Trungpa. 3 cass. 1982. 31.50 (A030) Vajradhatu.

Three talks. This seminar deals with domestic & family situations. The first talk is by Chogyam Trungpa, Rinpoche, the second talk is by a panel of health professionals, & the last talk is by Mrs. Diana Mukpo, Chogyam Trungpa's wife.

How to Cultivate Buds & Flowers. Vajracarya. 3 cass. 1982. 31.50 Vajradhatu.

Deals with domestic & family situations.

How to Cultivate the Heart of Enlightenment. Vajracarya. Read by Chogyam Trungpa. 4 cass. 1980. 40.50 (A028) Vajradhatu.

Six talks. The topic of this seminar is enlightenment & how we can connect with it in our everyday lives.

How to Cut your Legal Costs. Somers H. White. 4 cass. (Running Time: 60 min. per cass.). 80.00 (C109) S White.

Learn how to secure the right attorney, how to control him, how to cut costs & avoid pitfalls.

How to Dad: Eph. 6:1-4. Ed Young. 2000. 4.95 (978-0-7417-2260-7(7), 1260) Win Walk.

How to Deal with Cultural Diversity in the Work Place. 1 cass. (Running Time: 30 mins.). pap. bk. 99.95 (1030AV); pap. bk. 99.95 (1030AV) J Wilson & Assocs.

How to Deal with Difficult Customers. PUEI. audio compact disk 199.00 (978-1-934147-76-4(1), CareerTrack) P Univ E Inc.

How to deal with difficult People see Como tratar con gente Dificil

How to Deal with Difficult People. Rick Brinkman. 2 cass. 1995. 15.95 Set. (978-0-943066-43-1(3)) CareerTrack Pubns.

How to Deal with Difficult People. Rick Brinkman & Rick Kirschner. 4 cass. (Running Time: 4 hrs. 26 min.). 59.95 (Q10015) CareerTrack Pubns.

Explains how to thwart the most frustrating types of negative behavior.

How to Deal with Difficult People. Albert Ellis. 1 cass. (Running Time: 70 min.). 9.95 (C043) A Ellis Institute.

Difficult people tend to be rigid, angry, critical, defensive, irresponsible - the list goes on & on. Learn how to deal with your own displeasure & frustration over the difficult people in your life so that you can deal more effectively with them.

How to Deal with Difficult People. Albert Ellis. 1 cass. (Running Time: 70 min.). 9.95 (C043) Inst Rational-Emotive.

How to Deal with Difficult People. PUEI. 2006. 69.95 (978-1-933328-82-9(7), CareerTrack); audio compact disk 89.95 (978-1-933328-81-2(9), CareerTrack) P Univ E Inc.

How to Deal with Difficult People. abr. ed. Barbara Braunstein. Read by Barbara Braunstein. 2 cass. (Running Time: 3 hrs.). 1996. bk. 21.95 (978-1-878542-68-7(0),) SkillPath Pubns.

How to Deal with Difficult People. unabr. ed. Rick Brinkman & Rick Kirschner. 4 cass. 59.95 set. (66263) Books on Tape.

Drs. Brinkman & Kirschner show you how to thwart the most frustrating types of behavior - quickly & confidently.

How to Deal with Grief. 4. 2004. audio compact disk 28.00 (978-1-59548-001-9(3)) A Wommack.

How To Deal with Grief. unabr. ed. Andrew Wommack. 4 cass. (Running Time: 6 hrs.). 2001. 20.00 (978-1-881541-72-1(X), 1032) A Wommack.

Explains how to deal with grief, and describes how Saton fights us, why problems come, and what the real source of grief is.

***How to Deal with Negativity in the Workplace.** PUEI. 2009. audio compact disk 199.00 (978-1-935041-80-1(0), CareerTrack) P Univ E Inc.

How to Deal with Negativity in the Workplace: Overcome & Eliminate Negative Attitudes & Behaviors at Work. 6 cass. 59.95 Set incl. wkbk. (12890AS) Pryor Resources.

Negativity in the workplace is an illness that has symptoms & is contagious. Productivity plummets, & absenteeism goes up. Learn to spot negative people before hiring them, stop office gossip, rebuild strained relationships, renew motivation & re-energize your team.

How to Deal with Sexual Abuse: A Child's Guide. 1 cass. (Running Time: 30 min.). 9.95 (I0720B090, HarperThor) HarpC GBR.

How to Deal with Temptation. 5 Cassette Tapes. 2005. (978-1-59548-051-4(X)); audio compact disk (978-1-59548-052-1(8)) A Wommack.

How to Decide Exactly What You Want. Dick Sutphen. 1 cass. (Running Time: 1 hr.). (RX17 Ser.). 1986. 14.98 (978-0-87554-316-1(2), RX125) Valley Sun.

You have the power & ability to decide what you want. You now develop clarity about your desires & goals. You now evaluate all the potentials & decide what you want. You dream of positive future directions when you sleep. You do best what you do naturally & joyfully. You have clarity of intent. You now have the courage to make life-changing decisions.

How to Deepen Your Spiritual Life. Kriyananda, pseud. 1 cass. 9.95 (ST-57) Crystal Clarity.

Includes: How to cooperate with God in achieving freedom; listening as a spiritual practice; ways to overcome doubt & indifference; conquering the ego's desire to express the lower self.

How to Defeat the E. R. A. unabr. ed. Phyllis Schlafly. 1 cass. (Running Time: 34 min.). 12.95 (329) J Norton Pubs.

How to Defrost Your Heart: Logos January 9, 2000. Ben Young. 2000. 4.95 (978-0-7417-6164-4(5), B0164) Win Walk.

How to Defuse the Dynamic in Dating. George W. Pace. 1 cass. 2004. 3.95 (978-1-57734-395-0(6), 34441360) Covenant Comms.

How to Defuse the Dynamite in Dating. George W. Pace. 1 cass. 5.98 (978-1-55503-268-5(0), 06004067) Covenant Comms.

Great message for youth & young adults.

How to Delegate. Alec R. Mackenzie. Intro. by A. E. Whyte. 1 cass. (Running Time: 39 min.). (Listen & Learn USA! Ser.). 1987. 8.95 (978-0-88684-065-5(1)) Listen USA.

Explains how to delegate responsibility to get more done.

How to Delegate Effectively. 4 cass. pap. bk. & wbk. ed. 155.00 (978-0-7612-0635-4(3), 80238NQ1) AMACOM.

This program will change your management thinking forever by helping you make that difficult transition from doer to leader. You'll learn how to: Use the five cardinal rules of delegating that guarantee success; Decide what to delegate & how to do it successfully; Utilize incentives to sustain employee motivation for completing delegated tasks & much more.

How to Delegate Effectively, Set. 4 cass. pap. bk. & wbk. ed. 30.00 (978-0-7612-0636-1(1), 80239NQ1) AMACOM.

How to Delegate Work & Ensure It's Done Right. 4 cass. 59.95 Set. (Q10017) CareerTrack Pubns.

In this program, Dick Lohr teaches you how to delegate intelligently from beginning to end. You'll find out what to delegate, to whom & how to supervise the process without meddling. You'll find out where delegation is (and isn't) & how not delegating hurts your career.

How to Delegate Work & Ensure It's Done Right. Dick Lohr. 1 cass. (Running Time: 175 min.). 1995. 15.95 (978-0-943066-46-2(8)) CareerTrack Pubns.

How to Delegate Work & Ensure It's Done Right. PUEI. 2006. audio compact disk 89.95 (978-1-933328-00-3(2), CareerTrack) P Univ E Inc.

How to Delineate Corporate Charts. Carol S. Mull. 1 cass. 8.95 (454) Am Fed Astrologers.

How to Deliver Exceptional Customer Service. 6 cass. pap. bk. 30.00 (978-0-7612-0638-5(8), 80089) AMACOM.

You'll learn to: Set up a new customer service department from scratch; Show your staff how to turn customer inquiries & orders into long-term relationships; Evaluate & update your existing customer service system; Teach staffers the five "Cs" of effective oral communication; Design a customer service system to efficiently handle inside sales, order processing, after-sale service, customer support, & technical service; Interview & select the most qualified job applicants, & train them for maximum efficiency; Train your staff to stay calm & polite when handling irate customers; Make a significant bottom-line contribution to your company.

How to Deliver Exceptional Customer Service, Set. 6 cass. pap. bk. & wbk. ed. 165.00 (978-0-7612-0637-8(X), 80088) AMACOM.

How to Design Your Mind for Greatness & Build Your Best You. Created by Blanche Williams-Corey. 2 CDs. (Running Time: 1 hr 33 mins). 2002. audio compact disk 29.95 (978-0-9722266-0-8(5)) Be Your Best You.

A step-by-step blueprint for designing, building and maintaining your greatness within.

How to Destroy Negative Influences see Destruir Influencias Negativas

How to Determine the Capital Necessary to Retire, Including Tax & Estate Planning Applications: A Survival Guide. 3 cass. (Running Time: 3 hrs. 30 min.). 1993. 155.00 Set; incl. study guide 214p. (M937) Am Law Inst.

Provides a framework for understanding determination & presents case studies to illustrate planning options.

How to Determine the Value of a Rental Property. Tom Lundstedt. Read by Tom Lundstedt. 2 cass. (Running Time: 2 hrs.). 1998. 49.95 set, incl. study guide. (978-1-881049-03-6(5)) Winding Brook.

A step-by-step guide to analyzing & pricing investment real estate quickly & easily.

How to Develop a Dynamic Vision for Your Organization. 2001. audio compact disk 13.95 (978-0-9700018-7-0(8)) D Anderson Corp.

How to Develop a Dynamic Vision for Your Organization, Vol. 2. unabr. ed. Dave Anderson. Read by Dave Anderson. 1 cass. 1999. 10.95 (978-0-9700018-2-5(7)) D Anderson Corp.

How to Develop a Family Mission Statement. unabr. ed. Stephen R. Covey. 2 cass. 1996. 15.95 Set. (83220) Books on Tape.

Help a family unite around a common purpose, develop self-discipline in children, eliminate bad family habits, &, most importantly, transform family life from a daily grind to a nurturing one, rich with meaningful relationships & fun.

How to Develop a Relationship with the Holy Spirit. Creflo A. Dollar. 3 cass. (Running Time: 4 hrs. 30 mins.). 2001. 15.00 (978-1-931172-98-1(6), TS223, Kidz Faith) Pub: Creflo Dollar. Dist(s): STL Dist NA

How to Develop a Winning Image. Nido R. Qubein. Read by Nido R. Qubein. 6 cass. (Professional Services Library). 69.95 Set. (496AD) Nightingale-Conant.

Discover key elements for distinguishing yourself in the marketplace, workable strategies for building yourself into a profitable entity, techniques for refining your professional image, & more.

How to Develop a Winning Image: Successfully Promoting Yourself. unabr. ed. Nido Qubein. Read by Nido Qubein. (Running Time: 4 hrs. 30 mins.). (ENG.). 2008. 19.98 (978-1-59659-226-1(5), GildAudio) Pub: Gildan Media. Dist(s): HachBkGrp

How to Develop Ahimsa (Nonviolence) (107) Yoga Res Foun.

***How to Develop & Administer Successful PTO Policies.** Created by CareerTrack. 2010. audio compact disk 199.95 (978-1-60959-004-8(X)) P Univ E Inc.

How to Develop Character in Your Children. As told by S. M. Davis. 1 CD. (Running Time: 1 hr. 4 min.). 2003. audio compact disk 10.00 (978-1-929241-90-3(9)) Vsn Forum.

Jesus was called the "express image" of God in Heb. 1:3. The Greek word for "express image" is charakter. Jesus had the mark, or character, of the Father on Him. In a different, yet similar way, you and I should have the mark of the character of Jesus upon our lives. An especially exciting study is noticing who Jesus praised and how He praised them.

How to Develop Cheerfulness. Swami Jyotirmayananda. 1 cass. (Running Time: 45 min.). 1990. 10.00 Yoga Res Foun.

How to Develop Cheerfulness, No. 2. Swami Jyotirmayananda. 1 cass. (Running Time: 1 hr.). 1990. 12.99 Yoga Res Foun.

How to Develop Cheerfulness, Vol. 2. Swami Jyotirmayananda. (162) Yoga Res Foun.

How to Develop Compassion. (145) Yoga Res Foun.

How to Develop Compassion, No. 1. Swami Jyotirmayananda. 1 cass. (Running Time: 1 hr.). 1990. 12.99 Yoga Res Foun.

How to Develop Compassion, No. 2. Swami Jyotirmayananda. 1 cass. (Running Time: 1 hr.). 1990. 12.99 Yoga Res Foun.

How to Develop Confidence & Esteem & How to Overcome Depression. Paul Stanyard. 1 cass. 12.50 Alpha Tape.

How to Develop Contentment. (161) Yoga Res Foun.

How to Develop Contentment. Swami Jyotirmayananda. 1 cass. (Running Time: 1 hr.). 1990. 12.99 Yoga Res Foun.

How to Develop Devotion. 2 cass. (Running Time: 2 hrs.). (Devotion Ser.). 14.95 (ST-32) Crystal Clarity.

Topics include: What is devotion; the eight "meannesses of the heart" which inhibit the flow of love & devotion; specific practices to aid the development of devotion; the intellect versus the heart as a means of knowing; keeping devotion in a state of reason.

How to Develop Devotion to God. Swami Jyotirmayananda. 1 cass. (Running Time: 45 min.). 1990. 10.00 Yoga Res Foun.

How to Develop Discrimination, No. 1. Swami Jyotirmayananda. 1 cass. (Running Time: 1 hr.). 1990. 12.99 Yoga Res Foun.

How to Develop Divine Virtues. Swami Jyotirmayananda. Read by Swami Jyotirmayananda. 1 cass. (Running Time: 45 min.). 10.00 (813) Yoga Res Foun.

How to Develop Effective Communication Skills. 1 cass. (Running Time: 34 mins.). pap. bk. 99.95 (1031AV); pap. bk. 99.95 (1031AV) J Wilson & Assocs.

How to Develop Endurance. Swami Jyotirmayananda. 1 cass. (Running Time: 1 hr.). 12.99 (107) Yoga Res Foun.

How to Develop Endurance, No. 2. Swami Jyotirmayananda. (180) Yoga Res Foun.

How to Develop Endurance, No. 2. Swami Jyotirmayananda. 1 cass. (Running Time: 1 hr.). 1990. 12.99 Yoga Res Foun.

How to Develop Endurance, No. 3. Swami Jyotirmayananda. (183) Yoga Res Foun.

How to Develop Endurance, No. 3. Swami Jyotirmayananda. 1 cass. (Running Time: 1 hr.). 1990. 12.99 Yoga Res Foun.

How to Develop Enthusiasm. (151) Yoga Res Foun.

How to Develop Enthusiasm. Swami Jyotirmayananda. 1 cass. (Running Time: 1 hr.). 1990. 12.99 Yoga Res Foun.

How to Develop Equal Vision. (194) Yoga Res Foun.

How to Develop Equal Vision. Swami Jyotirmayananda. 1 cass. (Running Time: 1 hr.). 1990. 12.99 Yoga Res Foun.

How to Develop Faith. 1 cass. (Running Time: 1 hr.). 12.99 (106) Yoga Res Foun.

How to Develop Foresight in Life. 1 cass. (Running Time: 1 hr.). 12.99 (130) Yoga Res Foun.

How to Develop Great Faith, Vol. 1. Bill Winston. 3 cass. (Running Time: 2hr.34min.). (C). 1996. 15.00 (978-1-931289-42-9(5)) Pub: B Winston Min. Dist(s): Anchor Distributors

How to Develop Great Faith, Vol. 2. Bill Winston. 4 cass. (Running Time: 3hr.48min.). (C). 1996. 20.00 (978-1-931289-43-6(3)) Pub: B Winston Min. Dist(s): Anchor Distributors

How to Develop Great Faith, Vol. 3. Bill Winston. 2 cass. (Running Time: 1hr.55min.). (C). 1996. 10.00 (978-1-931289-44-3(1)) Pub: B Winston Min. Dist(s): Anchor Distributors

How to Develop Inspiration. 1 cass. (Running Time: 1 hr.). 12.99 (128) Yoga Res Foun.

How to Develop Integrity. (155) Yoga Res Foun.

How to Develop Integrity. Swami Jyotirmayananda. 1 cass. (Running Time: 1 hr.). 1990. 12.99 Yoga Res Foun.

How to Develop Intuitional Knowledge. 1 cass. (Running Time: 1 hr.). 12.99 (174) Yoga Res Foun.

How to Develop Mental Health. (192) Yoga Res Foun.

How to Develop Mental Health, No. 2. Swami Jyotirmayananda. 1 cass. (Running Time: 1 hr.). 1990. 12.99 Yoga Res Foun.

How to Develop More Satisfying Relationships: A Time to Love, a Time to Hate - The Secret of Communication. Shmuel Irons. 2 cass. (Running Time: 3 hrs.). 19.95 Set. (978-1-889648-03-3(5)) Jwish Her Fdtn.

Rabbi Irons applies the timeless truths found in the Bible & Talmud to gain knowledge, peace of mind, & the practical tools to live a more fulfilled & happier life.

How to Develop Positive Imagination. 1 cass. (Running Time: 1 hr.). 12.99 (127) Yoga Res Foun.

How to Develop Presence of Mind. (137); 12.99 (151) Yoga Res Foun.

How to Develop Promptness. 1 cass. (Running Time: 1 hr.). 12.99 (154) Yoga Res Foun.

How to Develop Psychic Powers. (116) Yoga Res Foun.

How to Develop Psychic Powers II. 1 cass. (Running Time: 1 hr.). 12.99 (175) Yoga Res Foun.

How to Develop Purity of Intellect. Swami Jyotirmayananda. 1 cass. (Running Time: 45 min.). 1990. 10.00 Yoga Res Foun.

How to Develop Self-Confidence. 1 cass. (Running Time: 1 hr.). 12.99 (178); 12.99 (108) Yoga Res Foun.

How to Develop Self-Confidence, No. 2. Swami Jyotirmayananda. 1 cass. (Running Time: 1 hr.). 1990. 12.99 Yoga Res Foun.

How to Develop Self-Confidence & a Positive Self-Image Permanently & Forever. Michael S. Broder. 1 cassette. 1999. 19.95 (978-1-889577-05-0(7)) Media Psy Assocs.

How to Develop Self-Esteem in Your Child: Six Vital Ingredients. Bettie B. Youngs. 6 cass. 29.95 (6257) SyberVision.

Use it to help your child discover the satisfaction of setting & attaining worthwhile goals.

How to Develop Spirit of Renunciation. 1 cass. (Running Time: 1 hr.). 12.99 (188) Yoga Res Foun.

How to Develop Spiritual Aspiration. (123) Yoga Res Foun.

How to Develop Spiritual Aspiration. Swami Jyotirmayananda. 1 cass. (Running Time: 1 hr.). 1990. 12.99 Yoga Res Foun.

How to Develop Spiritual Strength. (159) Yoga Res Foun.

How to Develop Spiritual Strength, No. 2. Swami Jyotirmayananda. 1 cass. (Running Time: 1 hr.). 1990. 12.99 Yoga Res Foun.

How to Develop Surrender to God. 1 cass. (Running Time: 1 hr.). 12.99 (166) Yoga Res Foun.

How to Develop Surrender to God II. 1 cass. (Running Time: 1 hr.). 12.99 (190) Yoga Res Foun.

How to Develop the Art of Adaptability. 1 cass. (Running Time: 1 hr.). 12.99 (134) Yoga Res Foun.

How to Develop the Art of Listening. 1 cass. (Running Time: 1 hr.). 12.99 (111) Yoga Res Foun.

How to Develop the Art of Speaking. (111) Yoga Res Foun.

How to Develop the Art of Speaking, No. 1. Swami Jyotirmayananda. 1 cass. (Running Time: 1 hr.). 1990. 12.99 Yoga Res Foun.

How to Develop the Ingredients for Staying Together. Michael Broder. 1 cass. 14.95 (C062) Inst Rational-Emotive.
Proven methods for dealing with conflict are detailed, along with numerous exercises & techniques to help you improve communication so you can build a long-lasting & fulfilling relationship.

How to Develop the Ingredients for Staying Together Long-Term. Michael Broder. 1 cass. 1996. 12.95 (C062) A Ellis Institute.
This program begins by outlining the ingredients that studies have shown to be common to successful, longlasting relationships. Proven methods for dealing with conflict & negotiating mutually-beneficial solutions are detailed. Numerous exercises & techniques are provided to help you avoid the most common communication traps & build a long-lasting & fulfilling relationship.

How to Develop the Mind of a Strategist & Become a Trusted Advisor. Perf. by James E. Lukaszewski. (ENG.). 2007. audio compact disk 10.00 (978-1-883291-47-1(X)) Lukaszewski.

How to Develop the Power of Enthusiasm. 1964. audio compact disk (978-0-89811-286-3(9)) Meyer Res Grp.

How to Develop the Power of Enthusiasm. Paul J. Meyer. 1 cass. 10.00 (SP100006) SMI Intl.
Enthusiastic people change the world. Enthusiasm is the essential ingredient in all human achievement. Catch the contagious enthusiasm of Paul J. Meyer. Learn to feel & act more enthusiastic & influence others with the power of your enthusiasm.

How to Develop the Power of Enthusiasm. abr. ed. Paul J. Meyer. 1 cass. (Running Time: 29 min.). 11.00 (978-0-89811-010-4(6), 5139); Meyer Res Grp.
Think & act more enthusiastically & influence others with the power of your enthusiasm.

How to Develop the Spirit of Service. (122) Yoga Res Foun.

How to Develop the Spirit of Service, No. 2. Swami Jyotirmayananda. 1 cass. (Running Time: 1 hr.). 1990. 12.99 Yoga Res Foun.

How to Develop Trust in God. Creflo A. Dollar. 2 cass. (Running Time: 3 hrs.). 2000. 10.00 (978-1-931172-28-8(5), TS256, Kidz Faith) Pub: Creflo Dollar. Dist(s): STL Dist NA

How to Develop Vairagya (Dispassion) (103) Yoga Res Foun.

How To Develop Viveka (Discrimination) 1 cass. (Running Time: 1 hr.). 12.99 (120) Yoga Res Foun.

How to Develop Your Clairvoyant Powers. George King. 2006. audio compact disk (978-0-937249-26-0(2)) Aetherius Soc.

How to Develop Your Family Mission Statement. unabr. ed. Stephen R. Covey. Read by Stephen R. Covey. (Running Time: 2 hrs. 0 mins. 0 sec.). (ENG.). 2009. audio compact disk 19.99 (978-1-933976-82-2(9)) Pub: Franklin Covey. Dist(s): S and S Inc

How to Develop Your Heavenly Prayer Language. Alfred D. Harvey, Jr. 2 cass in album. (Running Time: 1 hr. 50 mins.). 2003. 10.00 (978-1-932508-19-2(8)) Doers Pub.

How to Develop Your Inner Magnetism. Asha Praver. 1 cass. (Meeting the Challenge of Living in the World Ser.). 9.95 (AT-64) Crystal Clarity.
Includes: How the world expresses magnetism; training your will power in small ways; the eyes & voice as mirrors of human consciousness; overcoming the fear of being dynamic.

How to Develop Your Personal Mission Statement. unabr. ed. Stephen R. Covey. Read by Stephen R. Covey. (Running Time: 2 hrs. 0 mins. 0 sec.). (ENG.). 2009. audio compact disk 19.99 (978-1-933976-81-5(0)) Pub: Franklin Covey. Dist(s): S and S Inc

How to Develop Your Talents. 1 cass. (Running Time: 1 hr.). 12.99 (113) Yoga Res Foun.

How to Dig a Hole to the Other Side of the World. (ENG.). (J). 1991. audio compact disk 12.95 (978-1-59519-307-0(3)) Live Oak Media.

How to Dig a Hole to the Other Side of the World. Faith McNulty. 1 cass. (Running Time: 13 min.). (J). (gr. 1-6). 1991. bk. 9.95 Live Oak Media.

How to Dig a Hole to the Other Side of the World. Faith McNulty. Illus. by Marc Simont. (Running Time: 13 mins.). 1991. 9.95 (978-1-59112-062-9(4)) Live Oak Media.

How to Dig a Hole to the Other Side of the World. Faith McNulty. Illus. by Marc Simont. 1 cass. (Running Time: 13 mins.). (J). (gr. 2-4). 1991. bk. 24.95 (978-0-87499-234-2(6)) Live Oak Media.

How to Dig a Hole to the Other Side of the World. Faith McNulty. Read by Peter Fernandez. Illus. by Marc Simont. 14 vols. (Running Time: 13 mins.). (J). 1991. pap. bk. & tchr. ed. 37.95 (978-0-87499-235-9(4)) Live Oak Media.

How to Dig a Hole to the Other Side of the World. Faith McNulty. Read by Peter Fernandez. Illus. by Marc Simont. 11 vols. (Running Time: 13 mins.). (J). (gr. 1-6). 1991. pap. bk. 16.95 (978-0-87499-233-5(8)) Live Oak Media.

How to Dig a Hole to the Other Side of the World. Faith McNulty. Read by Peter Fernandez. Illus. by Marc Simont. (Live Oak Readalong Ser.). (J). (ps-3). 2006. pap. bk. 18.95 (978-1-59519-308-7(1)) Live Oak Media.

How to Discipline Employees & Correct Performance Problems: Get the Results You Want Without Incurring Resentment, Making Enemies or Destroying Relationships. Walt Lacey. 4 cass. (Running Time: 4 hrs. 11 min.). 1994. 59.95 Set incl. 36p. wkbk. (V10168) CareerTrack Pubns.
Problem employees drag down morale, destroy productivity & drain your time & energy. With the skills you gain in this new program, you'll get problem employees back on track - or out of your hair. You'll learn to approach an employee about a problem...define expectations...encourage steady progress...& discipline, reassign or dismiss the person if necessary.

How to Discipline Employees & Correct Performance Problems: Get the Results You Want Without Incurring Resentment, Making Enemies or Detroying Relationships. Perf. by Walt Lacey. 4 cass. (Running Time: 6 hrs.). pap. bk. 59.95 CareerTrack Pubns.

How to Discipline in Our Turbulent Times. Dov Brezak. 1 cass. (Running Time: 90 mins.). 1999. 6.00 (W60FS) Torah Umesorah.

How to Discipline Your Flesh. Kenneth Copeland. 1 cass. 1984. 5.00 (978-0-88114-752-0(4)) K Copeland Pubns.
Biblical teaching on victorious living.

How to Disco. unabr. ed. Conversa-Phone Institute Staff & Betty White. 1 cass. (Running Time: 55 min.). (Betty White's How to Ballroom Dance Ser.). 1990. 9.95 (978-1-56752-103-0(7)) Conversa-phone.
Teaches all of the most popular steps-breaks-turns - how to lead & how to follow. Fully illustrated instruction manual follows the audio tape. Learn today - dance tonight.

How to Ditch Your Fairy. Justine Larbalestier. Read by Kate Atkinson. (Playaway Children Ser.). (ENG.). (J). 2009. 49.99 (978-1-4418-1028-1(5)) Find a World.

How to Ditch Your Fairy. unabr. ed. Justine Larbalestier. Read by Kate Atkinson. (Running Time: 7 hrs.). 2009. 24.99 (978-1-4418-0196-8(0), 9781441801968, Brilliance MP3); 39.97 (978-1-4418-0197-5(9), 9781441801975, Brlnc Audio MP3 Lib); 24.99 (978-1-4418-0198-2(7), 9781441801982, BAD); 39.97 (978-1-4418-0199-9(5), 9781441801999, BADLE); audio compact disk 29.99 (978-1-4418-0194-4(4), 9781441801944, Bril Audio CD Unabri) Brilliance Audio.

How to Ditch Your Fairy. unabr. ed. Justine Larbalestier. Read by Kate Atkinson. 6 CDs. (Running Time: 7 hrs.). (gr. 6-10). 2009. audio compact disk 69.97 (978-1-4418-0195-1(2), 9781441801951, BriAudCD Unabrid) Brilliance Audio.

How to Divorce As Friends. Bill Ferguson. Read by Bill Ferguson. 4 cass. (Running Time: 1 hrs. 50 min.). 1998. 25.00 Set. (978-1-878410-24-5(5)) Return Heart.
Learn how to take the conflict out of divorce. Learn how to heal your hurt, clean up your relationship & resolve issues and if necessary, part as friends.

How to Do a Men's Retreat Boot Camp. 13 CDs, 1 CD-ROM. 2007. audio compact disk 99.00 (978-1-933207-17-9(5)) Ransomed Heart.

How to Do Inadequacy Right & Faith & a Smorgasbord. Jack Marshall. 1 cass. 5.98 (978-1-55503-123-7(4), 06008901) Covenant Comms.
Humor, stories & insights.

How to Do Things Right: The Revelations of a Fussy Man. unabr. collector's ed. L. Rust Hills. Read by Jonathan Reese. 8 cass. (Running Time: 12 hrs.). 1995. 64.00 (978-0-7366-3036-8(8), 3718) Books on Tape.
Learn how to eat an ice cream cone properly, how to develop principles when you have none & why America needs a Leisure Ethic. These are among the topics the author explores in his leisurely & humorous ramble. The mission to turn chaos into order, to make fussiness respectable & to advance those passing fancies we have to get our stuff together. When you're not laughing out loud, you'll be thinking hard.

How to Double Your Self-Esteem. Jonathan Robinson. Read by Jonathan Robinson. 1 cass. (Running Time: 90 min.). 1995. 9.95 (978-1-57328-786-9(5)) Focal Pt Calif.
Self esteem refers to your internal sense of joy & self worth. Using simple but powerful techniques, it's possible to double your self esteem in just a few minutes. Recorded live at one of Jonathan Robinson's seminars, this 90 minute talk can lead to amazing changes in how you feel about yourself, & what you can accomplish.

How to Draw Divine Grace. 1 cass. (Running Time: 1 hr.). 12.99 (155) Yoga Res Foun.

How to Dress for Power, Money & Success. Somers H. White. 6 cass. (Running Time: 60 min. per cass.). 100.00 (C103) S White.
Teaches how to avoid mistakes & select the winning styles, fabric, colours & combinations based on research. Goes into detail for both men & women.

How to Dress up "Naked Music" on the Piano. 1 cass. bk. 39.95 (V-1) Duane Shinn.
Make your playing sound fuller & more exciting. If you read music to some degree, but don't know how to add to the written music, this is the ideal course. Every technique is demonstrated.

How to Dress up "Naked Music" on the Piano. Duane Shinn. 2 cass. 1987. pap. bk. 39.95 (978-0-912732-60-2(1)) Duane Shinn.

How to Dump a Guy: A Coward's Manual. Kate Fillion. Read by Laura Hamilton. 2 cass. (Running Time: 3 hrs.). 2000. pap. bk. 22.95 (LC024) Listen & Live.
If you're like most women, the mere thought of having to dump a guy makes you cringe. But don't despair, even the most cowardly women can master the subtle art of ditching. Offers helpful & hilarious advice on everything you need to know.

How to Dump a Guy: A Coward's Manual. abr. ed. Kate Fillion & Ellen Ladowsky. Read by Laura Hamilton. 2 cass. (Running Time: 3 hrs.). (For Women Ser.). 1999. 16.95 (978-1-885408-31-0(5), LL024) Listen & Live.
Advice on everything from how to know when to go, to choosing a great exit line, to surviving post-breakup hysteria.

How to Dump Your Wife: Practical Advice for the Good Man Trapped in a Bad Marriage. Lee Covington. Read by Catherine Landherr. 2005. audio compact disk (978-0-9762928-1-4(5)) KICK ASS Med.

How to Earn $100,000 for Your First Non-Fiction Book. 2000. 25.00 (978-1-930039-05-6(0)) Morgan Seminar.

How to Easily & Inexpensively Create Your Own Audio CD. Gordon Burgett. Read by Gordon Burgett. 1 CD. (Running Time: 75 mins.). 2005. 20.00 (978-0-910167-86-4(9)) Comm Unltd CA.
Gordon Burgett explains how a newcomer to the audio CD world can easily and inexpensively create their own products, whether it is audio alone or audio with an accompanying text workbook in CD downloadable format.

How to Easily Set up Your Website to Make Money While You Sleep. Kris Solie-Johnson. 2007. 49.95 (978-0-939069-07-1(5)) Amer Inst Small Bus.

How to Eat a Poem see **Gathering of Great Poetry for Children**

How to Eat an Elephant: Overcoming an Overwhelming Life. Wendy Y. Bailey. 1. (Running Time: 65 minutes). 2004. audio compact disk 18.95 (978-0-9749914-0-5(6)) Brilliance In Action.
How to Eat An Elephant will help you discover tips and tools to manage your life and work. You'll learn to discern when to delegate and how to communicate decisions coolly, calmly and proactively. Create certainty in the midst of confusion and change while creating new partnerships and alliances.

How to Eat Fried Worms. Thomas Rockwell. 2 cass. (Running Time: 132 min.). (J). 2001. audio compact disk 25.00 (978-0-8072-0507-5(9), Listening Lib) Random Audio Pubg.

How to Eat Fried Worms. unabr. ed. Thomas Rockwell. Read by Lionel Wilson. 2 cass. (Running Time: 2 hrs.). (J). 1997. 23.00 (LL 0002, Chivers Child Audio) AudioGO.

How to Eat Fried Worms. unabr. ed. Ed. by Thomas Rockwell. (J). 1991. (978-0-8072-8537-4(4), LB1SP, Listening Lib) Random Audio Pubg.
In this very humorous story, Billy takes on a bet, he will eat 15 worms in 15 days. His family and friends help devise ways to cook them.

How to Eat Fried Worms. unabr. ed. Thomas Rockwell. 2 cass. (Running Time: 3 hrs.). (J). (gr. 4-7). 1991. 15.95 (978-0-8072-8527-5(7), LBICX, Listening Lib) Random Audio Pubg.

How to Eat Fried Worms. unabr. ed. Thomas Rockwell. Read by Jay O. Sanders. 2 vols. (Running Time: 2 hrs. 12 mins.). (J). (gr. 3-7). 2004. pap. bk. 29.00 (978-0-8072-8797-2(0), Listening Lib); audio compact disk 20.40 (978-0-8072-1156-4(7), S YA 269 CD, Listening Lib) Pub: Random Audio Pubg. Dist(s): NetLibrary CO

How to Eat Fried Worms. unabr. ed. Thomas Rockwell & Christopher Reich. Read by Jay O. Sanders. 2 cass. (Running Time: 2 hrs. 12 mins.). (J). (gr. 3-7). 2004. 23.00 (978-0-8072-8796-5(2), Listening Lib) Random Audio Pubg.

How to Eat Fried Worms. unabr. movie tie-in ed. Thomas Rockwell. Read by Jay O. Sanders. (Running Time: 6780 sec.). (ENG.). (J). (gr. 1). 2006. audio compact disk 19.99 (978-0-7393-3656-4(8), Listening Lib) Pub: Random Audio Pubg. Dist(s): Random

How to Educate the Subconscious. Swami Jyotirmayananda. 1 cass. (Running Time: 1 hr.). 1990. 12.99 Yoga Res Foun.

How to Educate Your Children. (102) Yoga Res Foun.

How to Educate Your Children II. 1 cass. (Running Time: 1 hr.). 12.99 (170) Yoga Res Foun.

***How to Effectively Employ Online Training.** PUEI. 2009. audio compact disk 199.00 (978-1-935041-86-3(X), CareerTrack) P Univ E Inc.

How to Elevate the Mind, No. 1. Swami Jyotirmayananda. 1 cass. (Running Time: 1 hr.). 1990. 12.99 Yoga Res Foun.

How to Elevate Your Mind, No. 2. Swami Jyotirmayananda. (168) Yoga Res Foun.

How to Elevate Your Mind, No. 2. Swami Jyotirmayananda. 1 cass. (Running Time: 1 hr.). 1990. 12.99 Yoga Res Foun.

How to Embrace Challenge & Change in Business & Life. 1 CD. (Running Time: 42 min.). 2003. audio compact disk 14.99 (978-0-9744909-3-9(8)) Real Life Less.
This lively and inspirational presentation will give you practical and spiritual ways to deal with the daily difficulties of life and work to the sudden onslaught of a catastrophe or change. Debbie Gisonni will discuss her own struggle from tragedy to triumph, and then take you through her top ten real life lessons where she'll cover coping strategies, ways to find meaning in life, the power of humor, faith, optimism and more.

How to Empower Your Sales Force in a down Economy: Best Practices to Inspire & Enable Your Salespeople to Deliver, Track & Close More Leads. York Baur. 2009. 250.00 (978-1-59701-493-9(1)) ReedLogic.

How to End Migraine Pain: Using the Jackie Miller Method. Jackie Miller. Prod. by Jack Johnston. 2 CDs. (Running Time: 1 hr. 20 mins). 2001. audio compact disk 19.95 (978-1-882899-04-3(0), EMP-CD) J Johnston Seminars.
Jackie has been subject to migraine symptoms for over 35 years. She used to have to use codeine-based prescriptions and several days of bed rest to recover from the severe pain. Seeking a drug-free solution to the pain of migraines, she developed a simple method for avoiding the pain altogether. Although she continues to experience the precursor symptoms occasionally, by using the method detailed in this step-by-step guide, she has not experienced migraine pain in over 25 years!.

How to Enforce Civil Money Judgments. Read by Richard Enkelis et al. (Running Time: 2 hrs. 30 min.). 1992. 89.00 Incl. tape materials & Action Guide. (CP-55254) Cont Ed Bar-CA.
Experienced attorneys provide a step-by-step approach to locating assets & effectively executing on them. They explain the factors to consider before accepting a case; identifying property subject to enforcement; creating liens on judgment debtors' property; obtaining writs of execution; & levying on real & personal property.

How to Enhance Health & Vitality. 1 cass. (Running Time: 1 hr.). 12.99 (192) Yoga Res Foun.

How to Enhance Health & Vitality, No. 2. Swami Jyotirmayananda. 1 cass. (Running Time: 1 hr.). 1990. 12.99 Yoga Res Foun.

How to Enhance Passion & Sexual Satisfaction in Your Relationship. Michael Broder. 1 cass. 1996. 12.95 (C063) A Ellis Institute.
You will learn how to recognize your main obstacles to sexual enjoyment, & be given proven techniques for effectively overcoming them & expanding your range of sexual pleasure. The importance of clarifying specific sexual "turn-ons" is emphasized, along with explicit directions for helping you & your partner become more responsive to each other's unique desires.

How to Enhance Passion & Sexual Satisfaction in Your Relationship. Michael Broder. 1 cass. 14.95 (C063) Inst Rational-Emotive.
Teaches you how to recognize your main obstacles to sexual enjoyment, & presents proven techniques for effectively overcoming them. The importance of clarifying specific sexual "turn-ons" is emphasized, along with explicit directions for helping you & your partner to become more responsive to each other's unique desires.

How to Enhance Your Personal Magnetism. George King. 2006. audio compact disk (978-0-937249-27-7(0)) Aetherius Soc.

How to Enjoy Peace. (209) Yoga Res Foun.

How to Enjoy Peace. Swami Jyotirmayananda. 1 cass. (Running Time: 1 hr.). 1990. 12.99 Yoga Res Foun.

How to Enjoy Your Life & Your Job. unabr. ed. Dale Carnegie. Read by Rick Turner. (Running Time: 6 hrs. 0 mins. 0 sec.). (ENG.). 2010. audio compact disk 29.99 (978-1-4423-0315-7(8)) Pub: S&S Audio. Dist(s): S and S Inc

How to Enjoy Your Life Journey. 2005. audio compact disk 11.95 (978-0-911203-97-4(4)) New Life.

How to Enquire "Who Am I?", No. 1. Swami Jyotirmayananda. 1 cass. (Running Time: 1 hr.). 1990. 12.99 Yoga Res Foun.

How to Enrich Your Life. (131) Yoga Res Foun.

How to Enrich Your Life. Swami Jyotirmayananda. 1 cass. (Running Time: 1 hr.). 1990. 12.99 Yoga Res Foun.

How to Enter into Your Promised Land. Speeches. Told to Joel Osteen. 1 Cass. (Running Time: 30 Mins.). 2001. 6.00 (978-1-59349-125-3(5), JA0125) J Osteen.

How to Enter into Your Promised Land. Speeches. Joel Osteen. 1 Cass. (Running Time: 30 Mins.). 2001. 6.00 (978-1-59349-126-0(3), JA0126) J Osteen.

How to Enter into Your Promised Land, Pt. 3. Short Stories. Told to Joel Osteen. 1 Cass. (Running Time: 30 Mins.). 2001. 6.00 (978-1-59349-127-7(1), JA0127) J Osteen.

How to Enter the Soviet Market: Business Week Presents. Douglas Rosen. Ed. by Douglas Strouk. 1 cass. 1990. 99.00 (978-0-9626668-0-3(7)) How Enter Soviet Market.
Business leaders' personal experiences in doing business in the Soviet Union.

How to Enter the World of Paid Speaking. Dottie Walters & Lilly Walters. Read by Dottie Walters & Lilly Walters. 6 cass. (Running Time: 50 min. per cass.). 1986. 89.95 (978-0-934344-25-8(6)) Royal Pub.
Discusses specific information on how to set fees, work with audiences, sell products at back of room, find material, work with meeting planners in the world of paid speaking.

How to Establish a Professional Practice. Grace K. Morris. 1 cass. 8.95 (246) Am Fed Astrologers.
Location, image, fees, advertising, licensing, taxes, records.

How to Evaluate a Suitor. Douglas W. Phillips. 2 cass. (Running Time: 1 hr. 34 mins.). 2003. 14.00 (978-0-9744689-4-5(0)); audio compact disk 16.00 (978-0-9744689-3-8(2)) Pub: Vision Forum. Dist(s): STL Dist NA

How to Excel As a Professional Office Manager: The Audio "Instruction Manual" for Office Managers. Debra Smith. 4 cass. (Running Time: 4 hrs. 11 min.). 59.95 Set incl. 64p. wkbk. (V10166) CareerTrack Pubns.
This program is an easy-to-follow "instruction manual" for office managers. It's fast-paced, fun, & filled with tips & techniques you can use right away. Whether you're new to office management or an experienced pro, you'll gain new skills & valuable insights that will help you play the many roles of office manager with class, composure & confidence.

How to Exercise Vocal Gifts. Derek Prince. 1 cass. (I-3019) Derek Prince.

How to Expand Love: Widening the Circle of Loving Relationships. unabr. ed. Dalai Lama XIV. Read by Jeffrey Hopkins. Ed. by Jeffrey Hopkins. 5 CDs. (Running Time: 50 hrs. 0 mins. 0 sec.). (ENG.). 2005. audio compact disk 29.95 (978-0-7435-4440-5(4)) Pub: S&S Audio. Dist(s): S and S Inc

How to Experience Bliss. (202) Yoga Res Foun.

How to Experience Bliss. Swami Jyotirmayananda. 1 cass. (Running Time: 1 hr.). 1990. 12.99 Yoga Res Foun.

How to Experience the Extraordinary. Speeches. Joel Osteen. 1 Cass. (Running Time: 30 Mins.). 2001. 6.00 (978-1-59349-118-5(2), JA0118) J Osteen.

How to Experience the Good Life. Speeches. Creflo A. Dollar. 4 cass. (Running Time: 5 hrs.). 2002. 20.00 (978-1-59089-220-6(8)) Creflo Dollar.

How to Experience Your Spirituality. Bill Ferguson. Read by Bill Ferguson. 1 cass. 1990. 9.95 (978-1-878410-09-2(1)) Return Heart.
Spirituality is your life force. It's the essence of who you are. When you connect with your spirituality, you tap into the power of the universe. You experience total love & peace. You lose all limitation. This cassette will show you how to connect with your spirituality & how to experience yourself as one with God.

How to Express Your Creativity. Kriyananda, pseud. 1 cass. (Running Time: 90 min.). 9.95 (ST-45) Crystal Clarity.
Topics include: "Ever-newness" as the essence of the creative process; specific ways to develop creativity; creative activity as a route to attunement; pitfalls of the creative process.

How to Face Adversity. Swami Jyotirmayananda. (144) Yoga Res Foun.

How to Face Adversity, No. 1. Swami Jyotirmayananda. 1 cass. (Running Time: 1 hr.). 1990. 12.99 Yoga Res Foun.

How to Face Adversity, No. 2. Swami Jyotirmayananda. 1 cass. (Running Time: 1 hr.). 12.99 (162) Yoga Res Foun.

How to Face the Last Days Without Fear. Derek Prince. 1 cass. 5.95 (4382) Derek Prince.
"Fierce times" lie ahead, but this analysis of Revelation chapters 1 through 7 will inspire confidence & courage to face the future.

How to Face Unjust Criticism: Numbers 16:1-15. Ed Young. 1985. 4.95 (978-0-7417-1441-1(8), 441) Win Walk.

How to Fail a Business: The Mistakes Business Owners Make. abr. ed. Kevin S. Yorke. 1 cass. (Running Time: 1 hr. 30 min.). 1997. 17.95 (978-1-890958-07-7(7)) Gen Keeper.

How to Fall & Stay in Love with Jesus. 1998. (978-0-940110-33-5(4)) Life Action Publishing.

How to Fall & Stay in Love with Jesus Conf Audio. Nancy Leigh DeMoss. (ENG.). 2007. audio compact disk 27.99 (978-0-940110-78-6(4)) Life Action Publishing.

How to Feel & Look Nifty after 50! Jo Peddicord. (Running Time: 60 mins.). 2001. audio compact disk 8.00 (978-0-9654434-3-2(4)) Golden Aspen.

How to Feel Great All the Time: A Lifelong Plan for Unlimited Energy & Radiant Good Health. Valerie Saxion. 2005. 34.99 (978-1-932458-43-5(3)) Pub: Bronze Bow Pubng. Dist(s): STL Dist NA

How to Feel Great Twenty-Four Hours a Day. George Sheehan. Intro. by A. E. Whyte. 1 cass. (Running Time: 47 min.). 8.95 (978-0-88684-067-9(8), T-7) Listen USA.
Aging is a myth when you learn to feel great.

How to Fight a Girl. unabr. ed. Thomas Rockwell. Read by Ernie Sprance. 2 cass. (Running Time: 2 hrs.). (J). 1997. 23.00 (LL 0003, Chivers Child Audio) AudioGO.

How to Fight a Girl. unabr. ed. Thomas Rockwell. Read by Ernie Sprance. 2 cass. (J). 1991. pap. bk. 21.98 incl. pap. bk. & guide. (978-0-8072-7354-8(6), YA 835 SP, Listening Lib); 16.98 (978-0-8072-7353-1(8), YA 835 CX, Listening Lib) Random Audio Pubg.

How to Fight Fair in the Family. 1978. 4.95 (978-0-7417-1009-3(9)) Win Walk.

How to Fight for Your Family. Gary V. Whetstone. 8 cass. (Running Time: 12 hrs.). (Family & Relationships Ser.). 1996. bk. 65.00 (978-1-58866-228-6(4), VA001A) Gary Whet Pub.
This practical spiritual warfare teaching is a must for any family in conflict. Win every time! You will be taught how to see the demonic assignments against your family.

How to Finance a Home, Pt. 1. Bill Galvin & Heather Kibbey. Read by Bill Galvin & Heather Kibbey. 1 cass. (Running Time: 1 hr.). (Tapes Real Estate Ser.). 1987. 8.95 incl. worksheet. (978-0-9615067-2-8(5)) Panoply Pr.
Here's how to find the best new loan for you & your home. Learn about conventional and government financing, buydowns, discount points, qualifying, closing costs & more.

How to Finance a Home, Pt. 2. Bill Galvin & Heather Kibbey. Read by Bill Galvin & Heather Kibbey. 1 cass. (Running Time: 1 hr.). (Tapes Real Estate Ser.). 1987. 8.95 incl. glossary sheet. (978-0-9615067-3-5(3)) Panoply Pr.
Discover tips and techniques that make homebuying easier. Talks about assumptions, contracts, 2nd mortgages, sweat equity, 'no money down' & more.

How to Find a Job in Washington, DC: Capitol Learning Audio Course. Derrick Dortch. Prod. by TheCapitol.Net. (ENG.). 2008. 47.00 (978-1-58733-088-9(1)) TheCapitol.

How to Find a Love Relationship That Will Work for You. Michael Broder. 1 cass. 1996. 12.95 (C061) A Ellis Institute.
This program will help you determine the most important ingredients to look for (or avoid!) in your next relationship. Through imagery exercises you will visualize how to meet the kind of person you want & how to conquer your own emotional obstacles to involvement. Important information is provided on the nature of initial attraction, how to handle '90s dating issues, & how to overcome shyness & fear of rejection & make effective initial approaches.

How to Find a Love Relationship That Will Work for You. Michael Broder. 1 cass. 14.95 (C061) Inst Rational-Emotive.
Through imagery exercises you will visualize how to meet the kind of person you want & how to conquer your emotional obstacles to involvement. Important information is provided on how to handle 90's dating issues, & how to overcome shyness & fears of rejection & make effective initial approaches.

How to Find a Mate, Vol. 3. James T. Meeks. (Bad Boys-Bad Girls). 2000. 5.99 (978-1-931500-05-0(3)) J T M Minist.

How to Find & Keep a Mate. Rick Kirschner. 2 cass. (Running Time: 3 hrs.). 1995. 15.95 (978-1-55977-034-7(1)) CareerTrack Pubns.

How to Find Breathing Space. Jeff Davidson. 2009. audio compact disk 9.95 (978-1-60729-224-1(6)) Breath Space Inst.

How to Find God's Plan for Your Life. Derek Prince. 1 cass. 5.95 (014) Derek Prince.
Unconditional surrender is the door leading to true fulfillment as we discover & walk in God's plan for our lives.

How to Find God's Will. Created by AWMI. (ENG.). 2004. 20.00 (978-1-59548-043-9(9)) A Wommack.

***How to Find God's Will.** Created by Awmi. (ENG.). 2010. audio compact disk 35.00 (978-1-59548-196-2(6)) A Wommack.

How to Find Good Homes for the Elderly: Guide for Caseworkers & Public for Housing for Elderly. I.t. ed. W. W. Terry. 4 cass. 1998. pap. bk. 29.95 (978-0-9664903-1-2(2)) Thats Right SW.

How to Find Happiness Ideas & Advice about Finding the Perfect Partner, 4. Scripts. 2 cass. (Running Time: 60 mins).Tr. of Como Encontrar la Felicidad Ideas y Consejos Sobre la Pareja Ideal. (SPA.). 2003. 25.00 (978-0-9744786-3-0(6)) A Nogales.
Doctor Nogales is pleased to offer this important series of psychological self-help cassettes. Although they don't replace psychological therapy, they will give you the necessary information to find your own answers and possible solutions to common difficulties and life challenges. They also include practical exercises that can help to guide listeners to a healthier life. ?How to Find Happiness??Ideas and Advice About Finding the Perfect Partner?.

How to Find, Interview, Select & Hire a Good Salesperson. Dave Kahle. 4 cas. 2000. 97.50 (978-0-9647042-6-8(9)) DaCo.
*Hiring a good salesperson can be the most critical decisions you make. A good salesperson will make you money month after month, free up your time to do other things, and make life easier. But a mediocre performer can cause you sleepless nights, ruin hard-earned relationships with good customers, and waste thousands of dollars of your time and effort. This step-by-step guide directs you through this most crucial process. As you interact with this self-study program, you'll develop your own personalized action plan, learn how to attract exceptional performers, and weed out mediocre candidates. The program is full of crystal clear concepts that you can apply to your own situation, powerful practical application exercises, and proven secrets to attract good people. The package consists of: * Four audio-cassette tapes * A 70 page reference manual that's full of notes, text, illustrations, examples and exercises.*

How to Find Romance after Forty. unabr. ed. Julia Grice. Read by Ruth Stokesberry. 8 cass. (Running Time: 12 hrs.). 1988. 64.00 (978-0-7366-1270-8(X), 2180) Books on Tape.
Advice for the single over-40's on dating, relationships, & (re-) marriage.

How to Find the Cherries When Your Life Seems Like the Pits. unabr. ed. Jack N. Singer. 2 cass. (Running Time: 2 hrs.). (How to Change Your Life Ser.: Vol. 2). 1998. bk. 17.88 (978-0-9700694-1-2(3)) Psychologically Speak.
Listeners will learn how to stay positive & be winners, by recognizing their own attitude hardening behaviors. They'll master the five powerful secrets for successful thinking.

How to Find the Love of Your Life in 90 Days or Less. unabr. ed. Paul Hartunian. Read by Paul Hartunian. 2 cass. (Running Time: 3 hrs.). 1997. 17.95 Set. (978-0-939038-06-0(4)) Clifford Pubns.

How to Find the Perfect Mate: How to Meet the Right Person Not Just Someone You Are Attracted To. unabr. ed. Jonathan Robinson. Read by Jonathan Robinson. 1 cass. (Running Time: 1 hr.). 1996. 14.95 (978-1-57328-807-1(1)) Focal Pt Calif.
Motivation to go out there & meet women. Learn how to meet the right person not just someone you are attracted to.

How to Find the Right Job. Richard G. Hammes. Read by Richard G. Hammes. 1 cass. (Running Time: 1 hr. 10 min.). 16.95 (978-1-882561-50-6(3)) Hammes & Assocs.
Vital information to find a job, including networking, resume development, how to answer interview questions, writing effective letters, etc.

How to Find Time for God. Kriyananda, pseud. 1 cass. 9.95 (ST-76) Crystal Clarity.
The importance of realizing what it is that really fulfills us; what keeps us from devoting more time to God?; understanding how our emotions act as obstacles; the power of spiritual company; what we can do to crate additional time for God.

How to Find Your Mission in Life. Richard Nelson Bolles. Narrated by Robert O'Keefe. (Running Time: 1 hr. 15 mins.). 13.00 (978-1-4025-3222-1(9)) Recorded Bks.

How to Find Your Mission in Life. abr. ed. Richard Nelson Bolles. Read by Richard Nelson Bolles. 1 cass. (Running Time: 1 hr.). 1995. pap. bk. 9.95 (978-0-89815-702-4(1)) Audio Lit.
The author offers some very practical guidance toward answering such questions as: Why was I put here on earth? What does God want me to do with my life? What kind of goals should I keep ever before me?.

How to Find Your Place. Derek Prince. 1 cass. 1991. 5.95 (I-4333) Derek Prince.
If you are saved, God has a plan for your life. Discover the seven steps that will take you into that plan.

How to Find Your Purpose. Bill Ferguson. Read by Bill Ferguson. 1 cass. 1990. 9.95 (978-1-878410-08-5(3)) Return Heart.
Each person has a life purpose, a special gift, a job to do. A job that is so natural & enjoyable that you would pay to do it. Once you find your purpose, life takes on new meaning. You know you make a difference. This cassette will show you, step by step, how to find your purpose & how to put it into action.

How to Flow in the Gifts of the Spirit. 3. 2004. audio compact disk 21.00 (978-1-59548-002-6(1)) A Wommack.

***How to Follow God's Will: Cd Album.** Created by Awmi. (ENG.). 2010. audio compact disk 35.00 (978-1-59548-219-8(9)) A Wommack.

How to Follow His Leading. Elbert Willis. 1 cass. (Understanding the Holy Spirit Ser.). 4.00 Fill the Gap.

How to Forget Your Past & Believe in Your Future see Como Olvidar Tu Pasado Y Creer en Tu Futuro

How to Forgive an Enemy: 11 Samuel 19:16-23. Ed Young. 1982. 4.95 (978-0-7417-1244-8(X), 244) Win Walk.

How to Fox Trot. unabr. ed. Conversa-Phone Institute Staff & Betty White. 1 cass. (Running Time: 55 min.). (Betty White's How to Ballroom Dance Ser.). 1990. 9.95 (978-1-56752-087-3(1)) Conversa-phone.
Teaches all of the most popular steps-breaks-turns - how to lead & how to follow. Fully illustrated instruction manual follows the audio tape. Learn today - dance tonight.

***How to Fulfill God's Will: Cd Album.** Created by Awmi. (ENG.). 2010. audio compact disk 35.00 (978-1-59548-216-7(4)) A Wommack.

How to Fulfill Your Destiny. Created by AWMI. 3 CDs. 2005. 25.00 (978-1-59548-065-1(X)) A Wommack.

How to Fulfill Your Destiny. Created by AWMI. 2005. audio compact disk 25.00 (978-1-59548-064-4(1)) A Wommack.

How to Gain Power & Influence with People. Tony Alessandra. 6 cass. (Running Time: 6 hrs.). 1993. 39.95 set. (370A) Nightingale-Conant.

How to Get a Date. JoAnn Hibbert Hamilton. 1 cass. (Running Time: 55 min.). 1996. 7.98 Digital. (978-1-55503-832-8(8), 06005209) Covenant Comms.
Dating tips for young women.

How to Get a Date Worth Keeping. abr. ed. Henry Cloud. (Running Time: 2 hrs. 51 mins. 0 sec.). (ENG.). 2004. 12.99 (978-0-310-26580-1(0)) Zondervan.

How to Get a Date Worth Keeping. unabr. abr. ed. Henry Cloud. (ENG.). 2005. audio compact disk 19.99 (978-0-310-26577-1(0)) Zondervan.

How to Get a Job with the U. S. Federal Government. Derrick Dortch. Prod. by TheCapitol.Net. (ENG.). 2008. 47.00 (978-1-58733-128-2(4)) TheCapitol.

How to Get a New Husband: 1 Peter 3:1-12. Ed Young. 1983. 4.95 (978-0-7417-1279-0(2), 279) Win Walk.

How to Get & Keep Good Clients: The New Lawyer Editon Audio CD. Jay Foonberg. (ENG.). 2007. audio compact disk 79.95 (978-0-9795671-3-1(0)) Ntl Academy Law.

How to Get & Keep Good Clients: The 2007 Audio CD Series. Jay Foonberg. (ENG.). 2007. audio compact disk 179.95 (978-0-9795671-2-4(2)) Ntl Academy Law.

***How to Get Anointed.** Featuring Mason Betha. (ENG.). (YA). 2003. 49.00 (978-1-60989-001-8(9)) Born To Succee.

How to Get Appointments by Telephone. Mona Ling. 1 cass. 11.00 (978-0-89811-005-0(X), 5118) Meyer Res Grp.
Get appointments through the telephone with the prospects you want to see most.

How to Get Appointments by Telephone. Mona Ling. 1 cass. 10.00 (SP100002) SMI Intl.
The ability to get appointments with the prospects you most want to see will increase your earning power. The telephone can be your helper. Use these methods & ideas to improve your telephone ability.

How to Get Better Grades & Have More fun. Steve Douglass. 1 cass. (Running Time: 60 min.). (J). 1998. 3.00 (978-1-57902-004-0(6)) Integrtd Res.
Methods of study that are fun & beneficial at the same time.

How to Get God's Best for You: Luke 11:5-13. Ed Young. (J). 1980. 4.95 (978-0-7417-1124-3(9), A0124) Win Walk.

How to Get Happy, Stay Happy & Live Happily Ever After: Get Happy Now! 2nd ed. Chris Michaels. Ed. by Michele Blood. Illus. by Musivation International Staff. 1 cass. (Running Time: 1 hr.). 1996. 19.95 (978-1-890679-01-9(1), M007) Micheles.
Motivational program help improve one's life to the positive & towards success.

How to Get Hired. Clarke Kates. 1 cass. 1992. 11.95 (978-0-9631816-0-2(2)) See-R Pubns.

How to Get More Done with Less Time & Effort: A Streamlined Time Management Course. unabr. ed. Marty R. Foley. Read by Marty R. Foley. 1 cass. (Running Time: 59 min.). 1993. 15.00 (978-0-9637384-9-3(6)) Victory Vent.
A thorough yet simplified system for increasing productivity & gaining more free time at work & home. Reveals guaranteed, effective methods of setting & reaching goals, conquering procrastination, streamlining paperwork, & more. Favorably reviewed in Booklist.

How to Get More Sales Interviews. 1971. audio compact disk (978-0-89811-280-1(X)) Meyer Res Grp.

How to Get More Sales Interviews. Paul J. Meyer. 1 cass. (Running Time: 30 min.). 11.00 (978-0-89811-079-1(3), 7129) Meyer Res Grp.
Learn how to call & what to say to sell your prospect on granting you an interview.

How to Get More Sales Interviews. Paul J. Meyer. 1 cass. 10.00 (SP100026) SMI Intl.
Do you ever experience call reluctance? Do you have enough interviews to fill your sales day? Listen to master salesman Paul J. Meyer, & learn who to call & what to say to sell your prospect on granting you an interview.

How to Get on Oprah & Other Talk Shows. 2000. Rental 25.00 (978-1-930039-01-8(8)) Morgan Seminar.

How to Get on Radio Talk Shows All Across America. 2000. 25.00 (978-1-930039-09-4(3)) Morgan Seminar.

How to Get Organized for Your Business Success. unabr. ed. Kathryn R. Bechen. Read by Kathryn R. Bechen. 1 cass. (Running Time: 60 min.). 1994. 14.95 (978-0-9657248-0-7(8)) Orgzed With Ease.

How to Get Out of Debt God's Way. Creflo A. Dollar. (ENG.). 2001. reel tape 20.00 (978-1-59089-106-3(6)) Pub: Creflo Dollar. Dist(s): STL Dist NA

How to Get Out of Debt God's Way. Creflo A. Dollar. (ENG.). 2002. reel tape 50.00 (978-1-59089-107-0(4)) Pub: Creflo Dollar. Dist(s): STL Dist NA

How to Get Out of Marital Jams. Douglas A. Brinley. 1 cass. 1996. 9.98 (978-1-57734-002-7(7), 06005306) Covenant Comms.
Discover powerful ways to be a better spouse.

How to Get Peace of Mind. Swami Amar Jyoti. 1 cass. 1980. 9.95 (J-37) Truth Consciousness.
Peace is the door to higher consiousness; how we lose it. What occupies our mind most of the time?.

How to Get People to Think & Act Favorably with You. Millard Bennett. 1 cass. (Running Time: 1 hr. 4 min.). 11.00 (978-0-89811-025-8(4), 5167) Meyer Res Grp.
Tells how to attract the attention, cooperation & admiration of others.

How to Get People to Think & Act Favorably with You. Millard Bennett. 1 cass. 10.00 (SP100010) SMI Intl.
Persuasion gets things done. Millard Bennett, one of America's foremost experts on communication, tells how to attract the attention, cooperation, & admiration of others. If you work with people, persuasive skills make you more dynamic.

How to Get Results with People. Jeff Salzman. 4 cass. (Running Time: 2 hrs. 46 min.). 49.95 CareerTrack Pubns.
Discusses the techniques needed to get maximum results with bosses, co-workers, subordinates - friends & family.

How to Get Rich: 11 Cor. 8:1-9. Ed Young. 1990. 4.95 (978-0-7417-1791-7(3), 791) Win Walk.

How To Get Rich & Stay Rich. Fred J. Young. Read by Billy Nash. 2 cass. 1998. 17.95 Set. (978-1-57949-012-6(3)) Destination Success.

How to Get Rid of Evil Spirits & Restore Yourself to Sanity see Consciously Overcome Mental Illness

How to Get Right: Romans 2:17-29. Ed Young. 1983. 4.95 (978-0-7417-1352-0(7), 352) Win Walk.

How to Get Right with God: Logos December 14, 1997. Ben Young. 1997. 4.95 (978-0-7417-6060-9(6), B0060) Win Walk.

How to Get Special Effects on the Piano: Drums, Chimes, Bells, Music Box, Oriental Sounds, Etc. Duane Shinn. 1 cass. 19.95 (PS-1) Duane Shinn.
Demonstrates how to imitate the sound of a drum cadence; you'll learn to create a "music box" effect; you'll play chimes. You'll learn to sound like a bell; you'll create an "original" sound & other special effects.

How to Get Started. Elbert Willis. 1 cass. (Financial Prosperity Ser.). 4.00 Fill the Gap.

How to Get Started in Real Estate Investing. abr. ed. Robert Irwin. 3 cass. (Running Time: 4 hrs. 30 mins.). (McGraw Hill Audiobks.). 2003. 24.00 (978-0-9724462-6-6(5)); audio compact disk 28.00 (978-0-9724889-4-5(4)) Pub: A Media Intl. Dist(s): Natl Bk Netwk
Bestselling real estate author Bob Irwin walks readers through all the ins and outs of real estate investing.

How to Get the Best Possible Media Exposure for a Candidate at No Cost see Campaigning, Innovative: Four Case Studies

How to Get the Job You Want. 2nd ed. Bruno Vassel, III. (SPA & ENG.). 1989. pap. bk. & stu. ed. 39.95 (978-1-879002-01-2(9)) Vassel Enterprises.

How to Get the Job You Want, No. 1. Bruno Vassel, III. (Running Time: 36 min.). 1989. 9.95 Vassel Enterprises.
Teaches how to get a job.

How to Get the Job You Want, No. 2. Bruno Vassel, III. 1 cass. (Running Time: 36 min.). 1989. 9.95 (978-1-879002-04-3(3)) Vassel Enterprises.

How to Get the Job You Want, No. 3. Bruno Vassel, III. 1 cass. (Running Time: 36 min.). 1989. 9.95 Vassel Enterprises.

How to Get the Job You Want, No. 4. Bruno Vassel, III. 1 cass. (Running Time: 36 min.). 1990. 9.95 (978-1-879002-06-7(X)) Vassel Enterprises.

How to Get the Job You Want, No. 5. Bruno Vassel, III. 1 cass. (Running Time: 36 min.). 1989. 9.95 (978-1-879002-07-4(8)) Vassel Enterprises.

How to Get the Job You Want, No. 6. Bruno Vassel, III. 1 cass. (Running Time: 36 min.). 1989. 9.95 (978-1-879002-08-1(6)) Vassel Enterprises.

How to Get the Most in Marriage: Through Friendship. ed. Excerpts. Charles Rivers. 1 cass. (Running Time: 50 mins). 1998. 12.95 (978-0-9758984-1-3(8)) Falling Love.
This audio cassette is excerpted advice from the authors daily seminars for married couples. This cassette exist to help troubled marriages that are too busy for marital counsel.

How to Get the Most of Your Title Insurance Policy. Albert E. Pentecost. 1 cass. (Running Time: 1 hr.). 1983. 10.00 PA Bar Inst.

How to Get the Most Out of Mass. Scott Hahn. Read by Scott Hahn. 4 cass. 22.95 Set. (5232-C) Ignatius Pr.
Explains the many parts & elements of the Mass - from the entrance song, to the sign of the cross, to the final blessing.

How to Get the Most Out of Your Title Insurance Policy. Albert E. Pentecost. 1 cass. 1983. 10.00 PA Bar Inst.

How to Get Things Done: An Achiever's Guide to Better Time Management. 1 cass. (Running Time: 48 mins.). pap. bk. 99.95 (1010AV); pap. bk. 99.95 (1010AV) J Wilson & Assocs.

How to Get Things Done: An Achiever's Guide to Better Time Management. 1 cass. cass. & video 99.00 Incl. hdbk. (640-C47) Natl Seminars.
We all have the same amount of time. It's how we use it that makes the difference. This program provides you with a step-by-step approach to taking control of your time & using it wisely.

How to Get to Heaven in Twenty-One Days. unabr. ed. Gary Arnold. 1 cass. (Running Time: 1 hr.). 1997. pap. bk. 12.95 Windhorse Corp.
Experience with this pioneering work the dynamics of spiritual energy. Learn how to apply this energy to create heaven on earth.

How to Get to I Do Without the Jitters. Perf. by R. M. Peluso. Created by R. M. Peluso. 1 CD. 2006. audio compact disk 19.95 (978-0-9794674-1-7(1)) R M Peluso.

How to Get to the Top: Business Lessons Learned at the Dinner Table. abr. unabr. ed. Jeffrey J. Fox. Read by Jeffrey J. Fox. (Running Time: 9000 sec.). (ENG.). 2007. audio compact disk 19.95 (978-1-4272-0157-7(9)) Pub: Macmill Audio. Dist(s): Macmillan

How to Get What You Really, Really, Really, Really Want. Wayne W. Dyer & Deepak Chopra. 2 CDs. 2003. audio compact disk 18.95 (978-1-4019-0137-0(9), 1379) Hay House.

How to Get What You Really, Really, Really, Really Want. abr. ed. Wayne W. Dyer & Deepak Chopra. Read by Wayne W. Dyer & Deepak Chopra. 2 cass. (Running Time: 3 hrs.). (ENG.). 1998. 16.95 (978-1-56170-545-0(4), 447) Hay House.
How to use innate talents & wisdom to get all your desires.

How to Get What You Want. Zig Ziglar. 2004. 8.95 (978-0-7435-3914-2(1)) Pub: S&S Audio. Dist(s): S and S Inc

How to Get What You Want. abr. ed. Zig Ziglar. Read by Zig Ziglar. (Running Time: 10 hrs. 0 mins. 0 sec.). (ENG.). 2004. audio compact disk 15.00 (978-0-7435-3726-1(2), Sound Ideas) Pub: S&S Audio. Dist(s): S and S Inc

***How to Get what You Want & Want what You Have.** abr. ed. John Gray. Read by John Gray. (ENG.). 2005. (978-0-06-085650-2(5), Harper Audio); (978-0-06-085651-9(3), Harper Audio) HarperCollins Pubs.

***How to Get What You Want & Want What You Have.** unabr. ed. John Gray. Read by John Gray. (ENG.). 2005. (978-0-06-085647-2(5), Harper Audio); (978-0-06-085649-6(1), Harper Audio) HarperCollins Pubs.

How to Get What You Want on the Telephone Every Time! Bettye P. Zoller & Hugh Lampman. 1 cass. (Running Time: 1 hr.). 1996. 9.95 (978-1-884643-13-2(2)) Pub: Voicesvoices. Dist(s): Penton Overseas
Dynamic, proven new techniques & strategies for more effective verbal communication. Put dollars in your pocket by learning how to "nail the sale"; persuade & close like never before. How to cut through call screening to reach key decision-makers. New business/personal phone etiquette. The most effective answering machine messages & much, much more.

How to Get Your Book Published. unabr. ed. Hubert Bermont. 1 cass. 1989. 12.95 (978-0-88432-273-3(4), AF0730) J Norton Pubs.
Discusses how to find the right publisher & how to work with editors, illustrators, lawyers & agents; discusses contracts, money, & copyright protection.

How to Get Your Harvest. Creflo A. Dollar. 2008. audio compact disk 21.00 (978-1-59944-717-9(7)) Creflo Dollar.

How to Get Your Head Out of a Garbage Can: 11 Cor. 10:1-6. Ed Young. 1990. 4.95 (978-0-7417-1794-8(8), 794) Win Walk.

How to Get Your Kids into Modeling & TV Commercials. unabr. ed. Thomas T. Mosby. Read by Aaron Houseman et al. 2 cass. (Running Time: 1 hr.). 1991. pap. bk. 29.95 Set. (978-0-9631892-0-2(4)); 19.95 Set. (978-0-9631892-1-9(2)) Talent Scout.
A step by step course on 2 cassettes with 32 page supplementary workbook (illustrated) which teaches parents & their kids & also aspiring adult models & actors "How to Get into Modeling & TV Commercials." Covers: getting started, work available, finding representation, costs, terms, tips.

How to Get Your Point Across in 30 Seconds or Less. abr. ed. Milo O. Frank. Read by Milo O. Frank. 1 CD. (Running Time: 4 hrs. 50 mins. 0 sec.). (ENG.). 1999. audio compact disk 14.00 (978-0-671-58191-6(0), Sound Ideas) Pub: S&S Audio. Dist(s): S and S Inc
Milo Frank, former CBS television talent & casting head, who teaches communication skills to the top executives of such Fortune 500 companies as AT&T, IBM & Bank of America, shows you how easy it is to get your point across in 30 seconds, & get what you want. Media research proves it. Television commercials capitalize on it. People are only able to give their full undivided attention in 30 second "bites".

How to Get Your Song Out of Your Head & Down on Paper. Duane Shinn. 1 cass. 19.95 (S-8) Duane Shinn.

How to Get Yourself or Someone Else off to a Fast Start in Network Marketing. Dave Johnson. 6 cass. 65.00 D Johnson.
Challenges one to become a success by making a habit of regularly doing those things that failures refuse to do.

How to Get 1 Million Worth of Publicity... Free! Paul Hartunian. 6 audio CDs. (Running Time: approx 5 hours). 2006. spiral bd. 697.00 (978-0-614-13994-5(5)) Clifford Pubns.

How to Give: 11 Corinthians 8:1-9. Ed Young. 1995. 4.95 (978-0-7417-2083-2(3), 1083) Win Walk.

How to Give an Offering: 1 Cor. 16:1-4. Ed Young. 1986. 4.95 (978-0-7417-1523-4(6), 523) Win Walk.

How to Give Exceptional Customer Service. Lisa Ford. 6 cass. 89.95 set. (V10111); 79.95 Set, incl. wkbk., 43p. (Q10156) CareerTrack Pubns.
Pleasing today's demanding customers - so you stay foremost in their minds. Program highlights: What customers want - 7 essentials; Exceeding customer expectations; Developing an emotional connection with customers; Why customers leave - & how to keep them longer; Creating long-term "partnerships" with buyers, new & old; How do your customers see you? A quick self-assessment; How to establish rapport, convey support & build trust; & more.

How to Give Exceptional Customer Service. Lisa Ford. 2 cass. (Running Time: 2 hrs.). 1995. 15.95 (978-1-55977-051-4(1)) CareerTrack Pubns.

How to Give Her Absolute Pleasure: Totally Explicit Techniques Every Woman Wants Her Man to Know. abr. ed. Lou Paget. Read by Lou Paget. (Running Time: 3 hrs.). (ENG.). 2006. audio compact disk 24.95 (978-1-59887-077-0(7), 1598870777) Pub: HighBridge. Dist(s): Workman Pub

How to Give Your One-to-Six Year Old Self-Confidence. unabr. ed. Christina Clement. Read by Thomas Amshay. 1 cass. (Running Time: 1 hr.). 1986. 5.00 (978-0-939401-10-9(X)) RFTS Prod.
Examples & explanations of how parents can build confidence in their children.

How to Give Yourself the Power to Succeed: Recognizing the Things You're Doing That Keep You from the Things You Want. abr. ed. Sharon A. Michaels. 4 cass. (Running Time: 3 hrs.). 1996. 37.95 Set. (978-1-888972-01-6(7)) Empowering Publns.
Recognize the self-sabotaging things you're doing that hold you back from success & happiness.

How to Go Directly into Your Own Solo Law Practice & Succeed. into the New Millennium & Beyond. Gerald M. Singer. (ENG.). 2000. bk. 129.95 (978-1-58477-834-9(2)) Lawbk Exchange.

How to Go from Selling Residential to Commercial Real Estate, Set. Michael J. Lipsey. 4 cass. 29.95 (739AX) Nightingale-Conant.
Here's an invaluable program for moving into the highly competitive commercial real estate business. Mr. Lipsey translates the theories & forecasts into practical, day-to-day activities that virtually assure incomparable financial rewards.

How to Grow a Backbone. Susan Marshall. Narrated by Anna Fields. (Running Time: 8 hrs. 30 mins.). (C). 2000. 27.95 (978-1-59912-509-1(9)) Iofy Corp.

How to Grow a Backbone. unabr. ed. Susan Marshall. Read by Anna Fields. 6 cass. (Running Time: 8 hrs. 30 mins.). 2001. 44.95 (978-0-7861-2042-0(8), 2802) Blckstn Audio.
To succeed in business today, you must be strong, smart, competitive, resilient, tenacious and fearless. If you want to be heard at work, you must speak up. If you want to drive change, you need an action plan. If you want to keep your job in an increasingly competitive world, you must show on a daily basis how you add value to your company. In short, if you want to succeed, you need good, old-fashioned backbone.

How to Grow a Backbone: 10 Strategies for Gaining Power & Influence at Work. unabr. ed. Susan Marshall. Read by Anna Fields. 6 CDs. (Running Time: 8 hrs. 30 mins.). 2001. audio compact disk 56.00 (978-0-7861-9709-5(9), 2802) Blckstn Audio.
To succeed in business today, you must be strong, smart, competitive, resilient, tenacious and fearless. If you want to be heard at work, you must speak up. If you want to drive change, you need an action plan. If you want to keep your job in an increasingly competitive world, you must show on a daily basis how you add value to your company. In short, if you want to succeed, you need good, old-fashioned backbone.

How to Grow Old Disgracefully. unabr. ed. Hermione Gingold. Read by Gretel Davis. 7 cass. (Running Time: 8 hrs. 12 min.). 2001. 61.95 (978-1-85089-685-2(2), 91021) Pub: ISIS Audio GBR. Dist(s): Ulverscroft US
Hermione Gingold was the last of the great British eccentrics. Her acting career spanned seventy-eight years. This book is a hilarious self-portrait of the "funniest woman in the world".

How to Grow When Markets Don't. abr. ed. Adrian J. Slywotzky et al. Read by Richard Doyle. (ENG.). 2006. 14.98 (978-1-59483-190-4(4)) Pub: Hachet Audio. Dist(s): HachBkGrp

How to Handle a Tax Controversy at the IRS & in Court after the IRS Restructuring & Reform Act of 1998. 11 cass. (Running Time: 14 hrs.). 1998. 345.00 Set; incl. study guide_437p. (MD29) Am Law Inst.
Reviews the procedures & strategies for handling civil tax controversies during administrative audit & appeal & subsequent judicial proceedings in various trial courts with jurisdiction over federal tax cases.

How to Handle Adoptions in 1990. 1 cass. (Running Time: 90 min.). 1989. bk. 45.00 (AC-531) PA Bar Inst.

How to Handle Basic Copyright & Trademark Problems. 1 cass. (Running Time: 3 hrs. 30 min.). 85.00 three audiocass. (T7-9369) PLI.

How to Handle Basic Copyright & Trademark Problems. unabr. ed. Contrib. by Richard Dannay. 4 cass. (Running Time: 5 hrs. 30 min.). 1990. 50.00 course handbk. (T7-9281) PLI.
The faculty, consisting of experts with a wide range of knowledge & experience in the copyright & trademark areas, focuses on the handling of basic, everyday problems that practitioners in these areas & non-specialists most commonly encounter. The discussion in this February 1990 satellite program covers: the significant changes introduced in both copyright law by the Berne Convention Implementation Act of 1988 & in trademark law by the Trademark Law Revision Act of 1988, copyright & tradmark infringement litigation, licensing & ethical considerations, practice & procedures in the United States Copyright & the United States Patent & Trademark Offices.

How to Handle Conflict & Manage Anger. unabr. ed. Dennis Waitley. 2 cass. 13.95 (89481) Books on Tape.
Wherever there are involved, concerned people, there will be disagreements & tension. Life is too complex for anyone to expect to exist in a perennial state of harmony & bliss. Now Dennis Waitley shows us anger is a choice we make & not an event that happens. It's how we perceive & respond to the events in our lives that determines our success or failure.

How to Handle Conflict & Manage Anger, Set. Denis Waitley. 6 cass. 59.95 (10030AX) Nightingale-Conant.
This invaluable program will provide you with a conflict management "road map." In it, you'll listen as Denis Waitley teaches you how to stay calm, cool & collected even in emotionally charged situations. Discover ten conflict-resolution skills...four steps for keeping your control at all times...nine steps to living a hassle-free lifestyle...five styles of conflict management...& six rules that de-escalate tension. By identifying the early warning signs of conflict, you'll communicate more effectively with your spouse, family, friends & co-workers. You'll also save time, lower your organizational costs & improve productivity. Includes workbook.

How to Handle Confusion. Swami Amar Jyoti. 2 cass. 1978. 12.95 (J-17) Truth Consciousness.
Origin of confusion & getting clear. Being aware, starting with right attitude.

How to Handle Controversy: Acts 15:1-35. Ed Young. 1998. 4.95 (978-0-7417-2183-9(X), A1183) Win Walk.

How to Handle Controversy: Romans 12:9-21. Ed Young. 1984. 4.95 (978-0-7417-1398-8(5), 398) Win Walk.

How to Handle Controversy: Romans 12:9-21. Ed Young. 1997. 4.95 (978-0-7417-2139-6(2), 1139) Win Walk.

How to Handle Criticism. Barrie Konicov. 1 cass. 11.98 (978-0-87082-333-6(7), 062) Potentials.
Learn how to turn criticism into words of praise, by taking your reactions off automatic pilot.

How to Handle Difficult People. Joe Gilliam. 6 cass. 59.95 Set, incl. wkbk. (130-C47) Natl Seminars.
Learn to deal effectively with difficult people & touch situations through the powerful, effective principles taught in this series.

How to Handle Difficult People. unabr. ed. Joe Gilliam. 2004. 19.99 (978-1-58926-202-7(6)) Oasis Audio.

How to Handle Difficult People, Set. abr. ed. Joe Gilliam. 2 cass. (Running Time: 3 hrs.). 2000. 17.99 (978-1-886463-88-2(3)) Oasis Audio.

***How to Handle Employee Complaints & Concerns.** PUEI. 2009. audio compact disk 199.00 (978-1-935041-91-7(6), CareerTrack) P Univ E Inc.

How to Handle Money: 11 Corinthians 8:10-24. Ed Young. 1996. 4.95 (978-0-7417-2084-9(1), 1084) Win Walk.

How to Handle People Who Bring You Down. Adam Khan & J. Klassy Evans. 1 cass. 1990. 9.95 YouMe Works.

How to Handle Problems: James 1:2-12. Ed Young. (J). 1982. 4.95 (978-0-7417-1209-7(1), A0209) Win Walk.

***How to Handle the Management Problems of a Technical Specialist.** Created by Fred Pryor Seminars/CareerTrack. 2010. 199.95 (978-1-60959-007-9(4)) P Univ E Inc.

How to Handle the Personal Injury Case - Initial Client Interview to Jury Selection. 1990. 45.00 (AC-545) PA Bar Inst.

How to Harmonize with Yourself & Others. Duane Shinn. 1 cass. 19.95 (HAR-15) Duane Shinn.
Discusses the intervals that harmonize (consonant intervals) & the intervals that don't harmonize (dissonant intervals).

How to Harness Your Mind. Gary V. Whetstone. 4 cass. (Running Time: 6 hrs.). (Freedom Ser.). 1995. pap. bk. 35.00 (978-1-58866-215-6(2), VRO11A) Gary Whet Pub.
The mind of man with all of its complexities & conflicts can indeed be harnessed & put to good use to serve the Lord.

***How to Have a Beautiful Mind.** Edward De Bono. Read by Humphrey Bower. (Running Time: 5 hrs. 20 mins.). 2009. 64.99 (978-1-74214-546-4(9), 9781742145464) Pub: Bolinda Pubng AUS. Dist(s): Bolinda Pub Inc

How to Have a Beautiful Mind. unabr. ed. Edward De Bono. Read by Humphrey Bower. (Running Time: 5 hrs. 20 mins.). 2009. audio compact disk 63.95 (978-1-74214-006-3(8), 9781742140063) Pub: Bolinda Pubng AUS. Dist(s): Bolinda Pub Inc

***How to Have a Beautiful Mind.** unabr. ed. Edward De Bono. Read by Humphrey Bower. (Running Time: 5 hrs. 20 mins.). 2010. 43.95 (978-1-74214-512-9(4), 9781742145129) Pub: Bolinda Pubng AUS. Dist(s): Bolinda Pub Inc

How to Have a Grace - Filled Church. Frank Friedman et al. 1 cass. (Running Time: 1 hr. 43 min.). (ICEL Three Ser.). 1996. 6.00 (978-1-57838-056-5(1)) CrossLife Express.
Church growth.

How to Have a Happy Family. Marjorie Shaevitz & Morton Shaevitz. 4 cass. (Running Time: 4 hrs.). 1992. 44.95 set. (284A) Nightingale-Conant.

How to Have a Happy Relationship (Subliminal & Hypnosis), Vol. 38. Jayne Helle. 1 cass. (Running Time: 56 min. per cass.). 1998. 15.00 (978-1-891826-37-5(9)) Introspect.
Learn to develop an attitude of love, kindness & understanding, which creates the romance & happiness you deserve.

How to Have Confidence & Power in Dealing with People. Leslie T. Giblin. 4 cass. (Running Time: 4 hrs.). 1988. pap. bk. 49.95 (978-0-13-410697-7(0)) P-H.
Offers practical methods & tested techniques for adding power & confidence to interpersonal relationships.

How to Have Confidence & Power in Dealing with People. unabr. ed. Leslie T. Giblin. 2 cass. (Running Time: 3 hrs.). 2001. 18.00 (978-1-59040-091-3(7), Phoenix Audio) Pub: Amer Intl Pub. Dist(s): PerseuPGW

How to Have Fun & Make Money in Catering. Read by Kailin Gow. Created by Sparklesoup Studios Staff. (How to Have Fun & Make Money Ser.). 2003. audio compact disk 19.95 (978-1-932379-18-1(5)) Sparklesoup.

How to Have Great Laughing Sex. Steve Penny. Read by Steve Penny. 1 cass. (Running Time: 45 min.). 1995. 12.00 Lghng Sex Inst.
Link-up your libido with your funnybone & use the pelvic contractions of laughter for sexual pleasure with over 150 laughing sexercises.

How to Have Healthy, Happy Relationships. Denise Dudley. Read by Denise Dudley. 3 cass. (Running Time: 2 hrs. 41 min.). 1989. 29.95 incl. wkbk. (978-1-878542-49-6(4), 11-0301) SkillPath Pubns.
Provides information useful for finding, building, & maintaining harmonious relationships.

How to Have Love in Your Life. Bill Ferguson. Read by Bill Ferguson. 1 cass. 1990. 9.95 (978-1-878410-03-0(2)) Return Heart.
When you have love in your life, you are happy & alive. Life works. In this cassette, you will discover exactly what you do that creates or destroys love in your life & how to have love in abundance. You will learn the key to having all of your relationships work.

How to Have Purr-Fect Faith: Even at a Cat Show. Laura Thomas. 2004. audio compact disk 16.95 (978-0-9744284-3-7(4)) Abiding Bks.

***How to Have That Difficult Conversation You've Been Avoiding: With Your Spouse, Adult Child, Boss, Coworker, Best Friend, Parent, or Someone You're Dating.** abr. ed. Henry Cloud & John Townsend. (Running Time: 3 hrs. 0 mins. 0 sec.). (ENG.). 2008. 12.99 (978-0-310-27437-7(0)) Zondervan.

How to Heal a Painful Relationship. David Hartley. 1995. 15.95 (978-1-55977-281-5(6)) CareerTrack Pubns.

How to Heal a Painful Relationship: And If Necessary, How to Part As Friends. Bill Ferguson. Read by Bill Ferguson. 2 cass. (Running Time: 150 min.). 1999. 16.00 Set. (978-1-878410-26-9(1)) Return Heart.
Learn how to end the cycle of conflict & restore the love in any relationship. Learn how to heal the hurt, resolve issues, & if necessary, part as friends.

How to Heal Depression. Harold H. Bloomfield & Peter McWilliams. 3 cass. (Running Time: 4 hrs.). 1995. 15.95 Mary Bks.

How to Heal Depression. unabr. ed. Harold H. Bloomfield & Peter McWilliams. Read by Harold H. Bloomfield & Peter McWilliams. 6 cass. (Running Time: 9 hrs.). 1995. 19.95 set. (978-0-931580-37-6(4)) Mary Bks.

How to Heal the Sick. Gary V. Whetstone. 2 cass. (Running Time: 3 hrs.). (Empowerment Ser.). 1994. bk. 20.00 (978-1-58866-188-3(1), VE009A) Gary Whet Pub.
The cause of sickness is not what a man does but who the enemy is! This is a Step-By-Step teaching on how you can minister healing to others.

How to Heal Yourself & Others. Shivani Lucki. (Running Time: 105 min.). 14.95 (SL-1) Crystal Clarity.
Talks about the healing power of energy; attitudes as the main cause of energy blocks; how to free blocked energy; Yogananda's six principles for dynamic health.

How to Hear Far-Out Harmonies & Understand Them. Duane Shinn. 1 cass. bk. 19.95 (ET-4) Duane Shinn.
Explains how to listen for the root - the bass line - the tonal center, & how to determine whether the 3rd is major or minor, then determine whether the 5th is perfect, augmented, or diminished.

How to Hear from God. Creflo A. Dollar. 2009. audio compact disk 28.00 (978-1-59944-763-6(0)) Creflo Dollar.

How to Hear from God: Learn to Know His Voice & Make Right Decisions. abr. ed. Joyce Meyer. Read by Joyce Meyer. 5 CDs. (Running Time: 6 hrs.). (ENG.). 2004. audio compact disk 29.98 (978-1-58621-733-4(X)) Pub: Hachet Audio. Dist(s): HachBkGrp

How to Hear from God: Learn to Know His Voice & Make Right Decisions. abr. ed. Joyce Meyer. (ENG.). 2005. 14.98 (978-1-59483-290-1(0)) Pub: Hachet Audio. Dist(s): HachBkGrp

How to Hear from God: Learn to Know His Voice & Make Right Decisions. abr. ed. Joyce Meyer. (Running Time: 6 hrs.). (ENG.). 2009. 44.98 (978-1-60024-977-8(9)) Pub: Hachet Audio. Dist(s): HachBkGrp

***How to Hear God.** Benton Thompson, 3rd. 2010. audio compact disk 10.95 (978-0-9824755-3-9(5)) Bar Abba.

How to Hear God's Voice. 3. 2004. audio compact disk 21.00 (978-1-59548-003-3(X)) A Wommack.

How To Hear God's Voice. unabr. ed. Andrew Wommack. Ed. by John Baker. 3 cass. (Running Time: 4 hrs.). 2001. 15.00 (978-1-881541-70-7(3), 1030) A Wommack.
Three basic points on how to hear God's voice: God's sheep Do hear His voice, how God speaks, and God's Word is the ultimate test.

How to Hear Your Angels. unabr. ed. Doreen Virtue. 2010. audio compact disk 18.95 (978-1-4019-2659-5(2)) Hay House.

How to Help Someone Grieving. unabr. ed. Read by Dan Keeran & Jennie Keeran. 1 cass. 12.95 (978-0-88432-405-8(2), C29500) J Norton Pubs.
Each of us has innate skills that can be used to help others in our lives deal with the death of a loved one & ease their grief & psychological numbing. Dan & Jennie Keeran, practitioner therapists, teach what to say, what not to say, when to talk, & when to listen in the situation.

How to Help Your Child Succeed in School. WFD Staff. 1 cass. (Running Time: 40 min.). 1998. 18.00 (978-1-58373-008-9(7)) Ceridian Inc.
Practical advice on helping with homework, motivation, & working with child's school.

How to Help Your Husband Make More Money. Joanne Watson. Read by Kimberly Schraf. (Running Time: 3 hrs. 30 mins.). 2005. 19.95 (978-1-59912-919-8(1)) Iofy Corp.

How to Help Your Husband Make More Money So You Can Be a Stay-at-Home Mom. unabr. ed. Joanne Watson. 3 CDs. (Running Time: 3 hrs. 30 mins.). 2003. audio compact disk 23.95 (978-1-59316-004-3(6)); 17.95 (978-1-59316-003-6(8)) Listen & Live.
Shares secrets and, whether your husband is a car mechanic or a CEO, shows you how to help him: Build his confidence. Determine if he is underpaid. Negotiate a raise or promotion. Find high-paying job offers beyond the classifieds. Start his own business and become a self-employed success. Ace job interviews. Make sure he keeps that better-paying job. And much more!.

How to Help Yourself & Others with Personal Problems. unabr. ed. Peter Breggin. 1 cass. (Running Time: 56 min.). 12.95 (980) J Norton Pubs.
Self-oppression is the process in which children & adults give up self-determination, self-awareness & a belief in free will in their efforts to get along with oppressive authorities in society. Self-oppression must be replaced by a renewed love of personal freedom & applying more self-fulfilling principles to one's life. The principles of self-help & helping others are nearly identical.

How to Hide a Butterfly: And Other Insects. unabr. ed. Ruth Heller. 1 cass. (Running Time: 15 min.). (How to Hide Ser.). (J). (gr. k-3). 2001. pap. bk. 14.45 (978-0-8045-6573-8(2), 6573) Spoken Arts.
Tells the story of animal camouflage in nature while introducing new words to young readers.

How to Hide a Crocodile: And Other Reptiles. unabr. ed. Ruth Heller. 1 cass. (Running Time: 15 min.). (How to Hide Ser.). (J). (gr. k-3). 2001. pap. bk. 14.45 (6568) Spoken Arts.

How to Hide a Meadow Frog: And Other Amphibians. Ruth Heller. 1 cass. (Running Time: 15 min.). (How to Hide Ser.). (J). (gr. k-3). 2001. pap. bk. 14.45 (978-0-8045-6572-1(4), 6572) Spoken Arts.

How to Hide a Parakeet: And Other Birds. unabr. ed. Ruth Heller. 1 cass. (Running Time: 15 min.). (How to Hide Ser.). (J). (gr. k-3). 2001. pap. bk. 14.45 (978-0-8045-6570-7(8), 6570) Spoken Arts.

How to Hide a Polar Bear: And Other Mammals. unabr. ed. Ruth Heller. 1 cass. (Running Time: 15 min.). (How to Hide Ser.). (J). (gr. k-3). 2001. pap. bk. 14.45 (978-0-8045-6569-1(4), 6569) Spoken Arts.

How to Hide an Octopus & Other Sea Creatures. unabr. ed. Ruth Heller. 1 cass. (Running Time: 15 min.). (How to Hide Ser.). (J). (gr. k-3). 2001. pap. bk. 14.45 (978-0-8045-6571-4(6), 6571) Spoken Arts.

How to Hide Sin: 1 Peter 4:7-10. Ed Young. 1983. 4.95 (978-0-7417-1289-9(X), 289) Win Walk.

How to Hire: How to Fire. Brian S. Tracy. Read by Brian S. Tracy. 2 cass. (Effective Manager Seminar Ser.: No. 1). 95.00 Set, incl. 1-hr. videotape & 2 wkbks., program notes & study guide. (747VD) Nightingale-Conant.
Recruiting, selecting, staffing: & de-staffing; the right & wrong ways to do it.

How to Hire a Quality Staff. Dora C. Fowler. 1 cass. (Running Time: 60 min.). 9.95 (978-1-57323-008-7(1)) Natl Inst Child Mgmt.

How to Hire & Fire Without Incurring Discrimination Lawsuits. Read by Martin Wald. 1 cass. 1991. 20.00 (AL-118) PA Bar Inst.

***How to Hit a Curveball: Confront & Overcome the Unexpected in Business.** unabr. ed. Scott R. Singer & Mark Levine. Read by Don Hagen. (Running Time: 6 hrs. 30 mins.). (ENG.). 2010. 27.98 (978-1-59659-564-4(7), GildAudio) Pub: Gildan Media. Dist(s): HachBkGrp

How to Hit a Curveball: Confront & Overcome the Unexpected in Business. unabr. ed. Scott R. Singer & Mark Levine. Read by Walter Dixon & Don Hagen. (Running Time: 6 hrs. 30 mins.). (ENG.). 2010. audio compact disk 29.98 (978-1-59659-446-3(2), GildAudio) Pub: Gildan Media. Dist(s): HachBkGrp

How to Hold Successful Meetings. Hosted by Paul R. Timm. 1 cass. (Running Time: 30 mins.). pap. bk. 99.95 (1021AV); pap. bk. 99.95 (1021AV) J Wilson & Assocs.

How to Hustle. unabr. ed. Conversa-Phone Institute Staff & Betty White. 1 cass. (Running Time: 55 min.). (Betty White's How to Ballroom Dance Ser.). 1990. 9.95 (978-1-56752-100-9(2)) Conversa-phone.
Teaches all of the most popular steps-breaks-turns - how to lead & how to follow. Fully illustrated instruction manual follows the audio tape. Learn today - dance tonight.

How to Identify & Remove Curses! Gary V. Whetstone. 6 cass. (Running Time: 9 hrs.). (Freedom Ser.). 1993. pap. bk. 50.00 (978-1-58866-216-3(0), VROO5A) Gary Whet Pub.
Unseen words spoken by you or others have restricted & limited your success in life. This series helps you break the power of these curses that are working against you.

How to Immature for a Lifetime: Rev. 3:1-6. Ed Young. 1999. 4.95 (978-0-7417-2215-7(1), 1215) Win Walk.

How to Implement a Discipline Action Plan. Dora C. Fowler. 1 cass. (Running Time: 60 min.). 9.95 (978-1-57323-009-4(X)) Natl Inst Child Mgmt.

How to Impress Anyone. Leil Lowndes. Read by Leil Lowndes. 2009. audio compact disk 23.95 (978-1-59316-478-2(5)) Listen & Live.

How to Improve CEO Compensation & Bonus Structures in a down Economy: Specific Options, Case Studies, Tax Incentives & More. Klein Leslie. 2009. 250.00 (978-1-59701-503-5(2)) ReedLogic.

How to Improve Your Memory. 4 cass. (Running Time: 4 hrs.). pap. bk. 30.00 wkbk. (80227); 155.00 (80226) AMACOM.
Gives the listener a thorough grasp of general learning principles & specific mnemonic devices. Also helps implement these methods.

How to Improve Your Memory. Arthur Bornstein. Intro. by A. E. Whyte. 1 cass. (Running Time: 53 min.). (Listen & Learn USA! Ser.). 8.95 (978-0-88684-014-3(7)) Listen USA.
Provides practical techniques for memory enhancement.

How to Improve Your Memory: Absentmindedness, Acronyms & Acrostics & Vocabulary Words see How to Improve Your Memory

How to Improve Your Memory: Association & an Introductions to Mnemonics see How to Improve Your Memory

How to Improve Your Memory: Basic Learning Principles I see How to Improve Your Memory

How to Improve Your Memory: Basic Learning Principles II see How to Improve Your Memory

How to Improve Your Memory: Introducing Your Memory see How to Improve Your Memory

How to Improve Your Memory: Listening see How to Improve Your Memory

How to Improve Your Memory: Remembering Names & Faces see How to Improve Your Memory

How to Improve Your Memory: Remembering Numbers see How to Improve Your Memory

How to Improve Your Memory: The Nature of Memory see How to Improve Your Memory

How to Improve Your Memory: The Number Code & the One Hundred-Word Peg System see How to Improve Your Memory

How to Improve Your Memory: The Rhyming Peg, Loci & Picturing the Alphabet see How to Improve Your Memory

How to Improve Your Memory: The Word Replacement Method see How to Improve Your Memory

How to Improve Your Self Image. Jack Boland. 1 cass. 8.00 (BW01) Master Mind.

How to Increase & Retain Your Center's Enrollment Through Marketing. George B. Fowler. 4 cass. (Running Time: 6 hrs.). 29.00 Set. (2011) Natl Inst Child Mgmt.
Activities that are a major part of marketing a child care center.

How To Increase Your Faith: Romans 10: 14-21. Ben Young. 1997. 4.95 (978-0-7417-6030-2(4), B0030) Win Walk.

How to Increase Your Prayer Life. Creflo A. Dollar. 4 cass. (Running Time: 6 hrs.). 2000. 20.00 (978-1-931172-48-6(X), TS240, Kidz Faith) Pub: Creflo Dollar. Dist(s): STL Dist NA

How to Increase Your Sales Immediately Set: Interior Design, Kitchen, Bath & Remodeling. 2nd ed. Robert Oxley. 2 cass. (Running Time: 2 hrs. 15 mins.). 2000. pap. bk. & wbk. ed. 34.95 (978-0-9678289-1-6(0)) R Oxley Trng.

How to Increase Your Spiritual Effectiveness. Kenneth E. Hagin. 4 cass. 16.00 (21H) Faith Lib Pubns.

How to Inspire Spirituality in Others. Kriyananda, pseud. 1 cass. (Running Time: 90 min.). 9.95 (ST-34) Crystal Clarity.
Why we should try to inspire spirituality in others; the importance of an "offering" attitude; sharing with people on a heart level; the crucial role example; concentrating on those who are receptive.

How to Instantly Connect With Anyone. Leil Lowndes. 2009. audio compact disk 23.95 (978-1-59316-463-8(7)) Listen & Live.

How to Integrate Your Personality. 1 cass. (Running Time: 1 hr.). 12.99 (141) Yoga Res Foun.

How to Interview & Hire the Right People: A Step-by-Step Guide for Managers & Supervisors. Stephen Carline. 4 cass. (Running Time: 3 hrs. 18 min.). 59.95 Set incl. 40p. wkbk. (V10160) CareerTrack Pubns.
Developed by senior CareerTrack trainer Steve Carline, this program teaches you everything you need to know about successful hiring strategies & the thought-provoking right-way/wrong-way scenarios help drive home the specific hiring techniques you learn.

How to Keep America Number One in the World. unabr. ed. Spiro T. Agnew. 1 cass. (Running Time: 26 min.). 12.95 (149) J Norton Pubs.

How to Keep Children from Becoming Bitter. As told by S. M. Davis. 1 CD. (Running Time: 60 min.). 2003. audio compact disk 10.00 (978-1-929241-91-0(7)) Vsn Forum.
The first mention of bitterness in the Bible was a son: Esau, the child of Isaac and Rebekah. When he felt he had been done wrong, Esau cried out with a "bitter cry." Esau wound up rejecting the grace of God and becoming a profane fornicator. It is like God was saying to all parents: Protect your children from becoming bitter.

How to Keep from Being Lopsided: Luke 2:52. Ed Young. (J). 1981. 4.95 (978-0-7417-1192-2(3), A0192) Win Walk.

How to Keep from Feeling Bad: Removing the Roadblocks to Loving. unabr. ed. Lilburn S. Barksdale. Read by William Wolff & June Wolff. 1 cass. (Running Time: 1 hr. 01 min.). 1978. 9.95 (978-0-918588-37-1(5), 119) NCADD.
Side one reveals the three underlying causes of "feeling bad." Side two declares that love is our natural state, & shows how to avoid the trap of false ideas that are the roadblocks to experiencing it.

How to Keep from Going Bonkers. MGM and Associates Staff. Read by Maureen G. Mulvaney. 3 cass. (Running Time: 3 hrs.). 35.00 MGM & Assocs.
A fresh, dynamic approach to stress management. Relaxation & affirmation tape included.

How to Keep Spiritual Resolves, No. 2. Swami Jyotirmayananda. 1 cass. (Running Time: 1 hr.). 1990. 12.99 Yoga Res Foun.

How to Keep Your Dreams from Being Stolen see Como Evitar Que Te Roban Tus Suenos

How to Keep Your Lover Successfully. Alex Mugume. Read by Alex Mugume. 2006. 10.00 (978-0-9742164-4-7(5)); audio compact disk 15.00 (978-0-9742164-3-0(7)) Smart Spouse.

How to Kill Your Husband. unabr. ed. Kathy Lette. Read by Caroline Lee. (Running Time: 10 hrs. 45 mins.). 2009. audio compact disk 93.95 (978-1-74093-975-1(1), 9781740939751) Pub: Bolinda Pubng AUS. Dist(s): Bolinda Pub Inc

How to Know an Apostate: Jude 14-16. Ed Young. 1989. 4.94 (978-0-7417-1743-6(3), 743) Win Walk.

How to Know God. 1 cass. (Yoga & Christianity Ser.). 9.95 (ST-49) Crystal Clarity.
Includes: Outward ritual vs. inner communion; the importance of knowing Christ inwardly; pitfalls of too much humility & outward devotion; why spiritual aspirants need the right teacher, teachings, & technique.

How to Know God: The Soul's Journey into the Mystery of Mysteries. Deepak Chopra. Read by Deepak Chopra. 3 CDs. (Running Time: 5 hrs.). 2000. audio compact disk 29.95 (Random AudioBks) Random Audio Pubg.

How to Know God: The Soul's Journey into the Mystery of Mysteries. abr. ed. Deepak Chopra. Read by Deepak Chopra. 5 CDs. (Running Time: 5 hrs. 15 mins.). (Deepak Chopra Ser.). (ENG.). 2000. audio compact disk 24.95 (978-0-375-40950-9(5), Random AudioBks) Pub: Random Audio Pubg. Dist(s): Random

How to Know God's Will. Kriyananda, pseud. 1 cass. (Running Time: 105 min.). 14.95 (ST-43) Crystal Clarity.
Topics include: Personal & impersonal aspects of God's will; the importance of common sense; testing your actions against the feeling in your heart.

How to Know Higher Worlds. unabr. ed. Rudolf Steiner. Read by Marie Hubonette. Ed. by Brian Wright. 4 cass. (Running Time: 5 hrs. 30 min.). 1996. 24.95 (978-0-9650869-0-5(9)) Parzival.
One of four books that the turn-of-the-century philosopher & clairvoyant Rudolf Steiner emphasized as being of primary benefit for those individuals wishing to gain insight & experience from the spiritual world.

How to Land a Job. Bruce Williams. Read by Bruce Williams. 1 cass. (Insider's Report Ser.). 9.95 (978-0-944305-10-2(5)) Bonneville Media.
Features advice on getting a job.

How to Land Your Dream Job: No Resume! & Other Secrets to Get You in the Door. abr. ed. Jeffrey J. Fox. Read by Jeffrey J. Fox. (Running Time: 9000 sec.). (ENG.). 2007. audio compact disk 19.95 (978-1-4272-0180-5(3)) Pub: Macmill Audio. Dist(s): Macmillan

How to Latin Hustle. unabr. ed. Conversa-Phone Institute Staff & Betty White. 1 cass. (Running Time: 55 min.). (Betty White's How to Ballroom Dance Ser.). 1990. 9.95 (978-1-56752-101-6(0)) Conversa-phone.
Teaches all of the most popular steps-breaks-turns - how to lead & how to follow. Fully illustrated instruction manual follows the audio tape. Learn today - dance tonight.

How to Lead a Team: Training for the "Manager Turned Team Leader" Perf. by Sheila Paxton. 4 cass. (Running Time: 6 hrs.). pap. bk. 79.95 (V10294) CareerTrack Pubns.

How to Lead a Team: Training for the Manager Turned Team Leader. Sheila Paxton. 2 cass. (Running Time: 3 hrs.). 1997. 15.95 (978-1-55977-673-8(0)) CareerTrack Pubns.

How to Lead Successful Project Teams. 3 cass. pap. bk. 30.00 addtl. wkbks. (80173NQ1) AMACOM.
This program will show you how to move your own career forward by building teams that are consistently recognized for their achievements under your direction. You'll learn how to: Inspire commitment & contribution from each team member; Value & encourage differences of opinion; Identify & foster the eight characteristics of the high-performing team; Maintain the team's focus & help assure success; Delegate leadership to increase the commitment of members & move the team closer to its goal & much more.

How to Lead Successful Project Teams, Set. 3 cass. pap. bk. & wbk. ed. 155.00 (978-0-7612-0664-4(7), 80172NQ1) AMACOM.

How to Learn Anything Fast: Peak Performance for Your Brain. unabr. ed. Pat Wyman. Read by Pat Wyman. Read by James McGee. 6 cass. (Running Time: 6 hrs.). 1990. 59.95 Set, incl. manual. (978-1-890047-27-6(9)) Ctr New Discv Lrng.

How to Lease Office Space Profitably. Duane F. Roberts. 3 cass. (Running Time: 1 hr. 50 min.). 1981. pap. bk. 42.95 incl. workbook. (978-0-944298-08-4(7), NO. 841) Inst Real Estate.
Offers a step-by-step approach to strategies & tactics of leasing office space: analyzing the product & the competition, evaluating their needs, & negotiationg lease terms. The workbook is filled with useful study materials: a detailed outline, sample leasing forms & study questions.

***How to Legally Terminate Employees on Leave.** PUEI. 2009. audio compact disk 199.00 (978-1-935041-67-2(3), CareerTrack) P Univ E Inc.

How to Let Fear Serve You. abr. ed. Clay Nelson. 1 cass. (Running Time: 30 min.). 1998. 15.00 (978-0-9667411-1-7(0)) Consult Srvcs Network.

How to Let Go of Attachments. Swami Amar Jyoti. 1 cass. 1978. 9.95 (B-5) Truth Consciousness.
Attachment separates us from God & Master. Having courage to transcend it. Responsibility need not be a burden.

How to License Your Million Dollar Idea: Everything You Need to Know to Turn a Simple Idea into a Million Dollar Payday. 2nd unabr. rev. ed. Harvey Reese. Read by Harvey Reese. (Running Time: 6 hrs.). (ENG.). 2007. audio compact disk 29.98 (978-1-59659-081-6(5), GildAudio) Pub: Gildan Media. Dist(s): HachBkGrp

How to Lindy (Swing) unabr. ed. Conversa-Phone Institute Staff & Betty White. 1 cass. (Running Time: 55 min.). (Betty White's How to Ballroom Dance Ser.). 1990. 9.95 (978-1-56752-095-8(2)) Conversa-phone.
Teaches all of the most popular steps-breaks-turns - how to lead & how to follow. Fully illustrated instruction manual follows the audio tape. Learn today - dance tonight.

How to Listen. 1 cass. (Running Time: 50 min.). 9.95 (I0070B090, HarperThor) HarpC GBR.

How to Listen. unabr. ed. British Broadcasting Corporation Staff. 1 cass. (Running Time: 1 hr.). pap. bk. 19.95 incl. tapescript, comprehension activities & answer key. (978-0-88432-657-1(8), SEN220) J Norton Pubs.

How to Listen Powerfully. Lou Hampton. 4 cass. (Running Time: 4 hrs.). 49.95 CareerTrack Pubns.
Explains how to reduce mistakes, sharpen concentration & hear more of what people are really saying.

How to Listen to & Proclaim the Dharma. Read by Chogyam Trungpa & Osel Tendzin. 4 cass. 1979. 40.50 (A116) Vajradhatu.
Four talks. Dharma means things as they are. How do we relate to reality?.

How to Listen to & Understand Great Music. Instructed by Robert Greenberg. 6 cass. (Running Time: 36 hrs.). 2000. 349.95 Teaching Co.
Course 700, 6 parts, 48 lectures.

How to Listen to & Understand Great Music. 3rd ed. Instructed by Robert Greenberg. 24 cass. (Running Time: 36 hrs.). 2006. 349.95 (978-1-59803-268-0(2)); audio compact disk 179.95 (978-1-59803-269-7(0)) Teaching Co.

How to Listen to & Understand Great Music, Pts. 1-6. 3rd rev. ed. Instructed by Robert Greenberg. 24 cass. (Running Time: 36 hrs.). 1998. 134.95 (978-1-56585-195-5(1), 700) Teaching Co.

How to Listen to & Understand Great Music, Pts. I-VI. 3rd rev. ed. Instructed by Robert Greenberg. 48 CDs. (Running Time: 36 hrs.). 1998. bk. 179.95 (978-1-56585-371-3(7), 700) Teaching Co.

How to Listen to & Understand Great Music Vol. 2: The High Baroque. 3rd rev. ed. Instructed by Robert Greenberg. 4 cass. (Running Time: 6 hrs.). 1998. 399.95 (978-1-56585-196-2(X)) Teaching Co.

How to Listen to & Understand Great Music Vol. 3: The Classical Era I. 3rd rev. ed. Instructed by Robert Greenberg. 4 cass. (Running Time: 6 hrs.). 1998. 399.95 (978-1-56585-197-9(8)) Teaching Co.

How to Listen to & Understand Great Music Vol. 4: The Classical Era II & the Age of Revolution-Beethoven. 3rd rev. ed. Instructed by Robert Greenberg. 4 cass. (Running Time: 6 hrs.). 1998. 399.95 (978-1-56585-198-6(6)) Teaching Co.

How to Listen to & Understand Great Music Vol. 5: Nineteenth-Century Romanticism. 3rd rev. ed. Instructed by Robert Greenberg. 4 cass. (Running Time: 6 hrs.). 1998. 399.95 (978-1-56585-199-3(4)) Teaching Co.

How to Listen to & Understand Great Music Vol. 6: From Romanticism to Modernism: 1848 to 1913. 3rd rev. ed. Instructed by Robert Greenberg. 4 cass. (Running Time: 6 hrs.). 1998. 399.95 (978-1-56585-200-6(1)) Teaching Co.

How to Listen to & Understand Opera, Course 740. Instructed by Robert Greenberg. 16 cass. (Running Time: 24 hrs.). 2000. 249.95 (740) Teaching Co.
Features Monteverdi's "Orfeo," Verdi's "Otello" & Wagner's "Tristan & Isolde." Understand how musical & dramatic effects were achieved...what the composers were saying to their audiences...& why the differing social & political fortunes of the time were so important to each country's version of opera. Four parts, 32 lectures.

How to Listen to & Understand Opera, Vol. 2. Instructed by Robert Greenberg. 4 cass. (Running Time: 6 hrs.). 1997. 249.95 (978-1-56585-215-0(X)) Teaching Co.

How to Listen to & Understand Opera, Vol. 3. Instructed by Robert Greenberg. 4 cass. (Running Time: 6 hrs.). 1997. 249.95 (978-1-56585-216-7(8)) Teaching Co.

How to Listen to & Understand Opera, Vol. 4. Instructed by Robert Greenberg. 4 cass. (Running Time: 6 hrs.). 1997. 249.95 (978-1-56585-217-4(6)) Teaching Co.

How to Listen to & Understand Opera, Vols. I-IV. Instructed by Robert Greenberg. 32 CDs. (Running Time: 24 hrs.). 1997. bk. 129.95 (978-1-56585-375-1(X), 740); 99.95 (978-1-56585-214-3(1), 740) Teaching Co.

How to Listen to the Voice of Conscience. (146) Yoga Res Foun.

How to Listen to the Voice of Conscience. Swami Jyotirmayananda. 1 cass. (Running Time: 1 hr.). 1990. 12.99 Yoga Res Foun.

How to Live a Divine Life. 1 cass. (Running Time: 90 min.). (Devotion Ser.). 9.95 (82M) Crystal Clarity.
Explains how you are assisted by "currents of consciousness" (energy) once you decide to live for God; how the company of other devotees speeds your spiritual progress; importance of sharing your failures with God.

How to Live a Spiritual Life. (157) Yoga Res Foun.

How to Live a Spiritual Life. Swami Jyotirmayananda. 1 cass. (Running Time: 1 hr.). 1990. 12.99 Yoga Res Foun.

How to Live & Be Happy. Hugh Prather. 4 cass. 36.00 (OC95) Sound Horizons AV.

How to Live & Be Led by Your Spirit Man. Creflo A. Dollar. 25.00 (978-1-59089-074-5(4)) Pub: Creflo Dollar. Dist(s): STL Dist NA

How to Live & Not Die. Norvel Hayes. 6 cass. (Running Time: 6 hrs.). 2001. 30.00 (TNH-01) Harrison Hse.
A down-to-earth guide for getting rid of problem areas in your life by putting God's power to work for you. God doesn't want you to be sick... or to have any financial, emotional, social, spiritual or physical problem. But you've got to learn to do things His way! After you worship and praise God, you have the right to ask Him for any-thing. If you'll make up your mind, once and for all, that the life is in the Word of God, you won't have to suffer any longer. Your body doesn't care what God tells you. It will rise up and demand what it's craving. You have to tell your body to obey God's Word!.

How to Live Harmoniously with Your Children & Teens. unabr. ed. Peter H. Buntman. 4 cass. (Running Time: 40 min.). 1998. bk. 37.50 Ctr Fam Life.
Teaches parents detailed & specific learning skills on how to raise children & teens. After listening to the tapes, parents can readily put these skills into practice.

How to Live Harmoniously with Your Children & Teens Series. Peter H. Buntman & Eleanor M. Saris. 4 cass. 1990. pap. bk. 37.50 Set. (978-0-9623986-1-2(6)) Ctr Fam Life.
Teaches parents detailed & specific parenting skills on how to raise children & teens & immediately put these skills into practice.

How to Live in God's Best. Gloria Copeland. 6 cass. 1983. 30.00 Set incl. study guide. (978-0-938458-66-1(3)) K Copeland Pubns.
How to have God's best.

How to Live in God's Best. Gloria Copeland. 2008. audio compact disk 30.00 (978-1-57562-967-4(4)) K Copeland Pubns.

How to Live in Presence of God: Two Homilies - '78 Retreat. Fr. Hardon & P. Quay. 1 cass. 4.00 (78H) IRL Chicago.

How to Live in the Eighties. Kriyananda, pseud. 1 cass. (Running Time: 90 min.). 9.95 (ST-15) Crystal Clarity.
Discusses: Planetary causes of current world tensions; why the difficult times that lie ahead can also be times of opportunity; the individual's role in bringing about change; how the energy of the Eighties differs from that of the Sixties & Seventies.

How to Live in the Present. (110) Yoga Res Foun.

How to Live in the Present. Swami Jyotirmayananda. 1 cass. (Running Time: 1 hr.). 1990. 12.99 Yoga Res Foun.

How to Live in the World & Still Be Happy. Hugh Prather & Gayle Prather. 4 cass. 36.00 (OC135) Sound Horizons AV.
Designed for those who wish to begin developing enduring inner happiness and develop relationships with those around them.

***How to Live Joyously.** Barry Long. 2006. 24.95 (978-1-899324-24-8(0)) Pub: B Long Bks. Dist(s): AtlasBooks

How to Live Joyously: Being True to the Law of Life. Barry Long. 2 cass. (Running Time: 2 hrs. 36 min.). (ENG.). 1996. audio compact disk 17.95 (978-1-899324-07-1(0)) Pub: B Long Bks. Dist(s): AtlasBooks

How to Live the James Bond Lifestyle. Paul Kyriazi. Read by Paul Kyriazi. 1 cass. (Running Time: 1 hr., 30 min.). 1999. (978-0-9700677-9-1(8)) First Strike Prod.
A serious seminar. A course for men that shows you how to upgrade your life to the level of 007 no matter your age or financial level.

How to Live with Your Kids. Ken Davis. 1 cass. 1990. 14.99 (978-0-310-57638-9(5)) Zondervan.

How to Live with Your Kids When You've Already Lost Your Mind, Set. 2 cass. 2000. 12.95 (978-1-886463-95-0(6)) Oasis Audio.

How to Live with Your Parents Without Losing Your Mind, Set. 2 cass. 2000. 12.95 (978-1-886463-96-7(4)) Oasis Audio.

How to Live Worry-Free. Kenneth W. Hagin, Jr. 12.00 (C8129) Faith Lib Pubns.
A guide to the believer into God's safe haven of peace.

How to Lobby the Executive Branch & Independent Agencies: Capitol Learning Audio Course. James Bayless, Jr. Prod. by TheCapitol.Net. (ENG.). 2007. 47.00 (978-1-58733-068-1(7)) TheCapitol.

How to Lose Friends & Alienate People. abr. ed. Toby Young. Read by Toby Young. 4 cass. Library e. (Running Time: 6 hrs.). 2002. 62.25 (978-1-59086-444-9(1), 1590864441, Lib Edit) Brilliance Audio.
In 1995 high-flying British journalist Toby Young left London for New York to become a contributing editor at Vanity Fair. Other Brits had taken Manhattan - Alistair Cooke then, Anna Wintour now - so why couldn't he? But things didn't go quite according to plan. Within the space of two years he was fired from Vanity Fair, banned from the most fashionable bar in the city, and couldn't get a date for love or money. Even the local AA group wanted nothing to do with him. How to Lose Friends and Alienate People is Toby Young's hilarious account of the five years he spent looking for love in all the wrong places and steadily working his way down the New York food chain, from glossy magazine editor to crash-test dummy for interactive sex toys. But it's more than "the longest self-deprecating joke since the complete works of Woody Allen" (Sunday Times); it's also a seditious attack on the culture of celebrity from inside the belly of the beast. And there's even a happy ending as Toby Young marries - "for proper non-cynical reasons," as he puts it - the woman of his dreams. "Some people are lucky enough to stumble across the right path straight away; most of us only discover what the right one is by going down the wrong one first.".

How to Lose Friends & Alienate People. abr. ed. Toby Young. Read by Toby Young. (Running Time: 6 hrs.). 2006. 39.25 (978-1-4233-0108-0(0), 9781423301080, BADLE); 24.95 (978-1-4233-0107-3(2), 9781423301073, BAD); 39.25 (978-1-4233-0106-6(4), 9781423301066, Brlnc Audio MP3 Lib); 24.95 (978-1-4233-0105-9(6), 9781423301059, Brilliance MP3) Brilliance Audio.

How to Lose Friends & Alienate People. abr. ed. Toby Young. Read by Toby Young. (Running Time: 6 hrs.). 2008. audio compact disk 14.99 (978-1-4233-4466-7(9), 9781423344667, BCD Value Price) Brilliance Audio.

How to Love a Woman: On Intimacy & the Erotic Life of Women. Clarissa Pinkola Estes. 3 CDs. (Running Time: 10800 sec.). 2005. audio compact disk 24.95 (978-1-59179-398-4(X), AW00222D) Sounds True.

How to Love Difficult People: John 4: 17-21. Ben Young. 1997. 4.95 (978-0-7417-6018-0(5), B0018) Win Walk.

How to Love Your Teenager: Psalm 137:3-4; 11Samuel 13:1-39. Ed Young. 1996. 4.95 (978-0-7417-2102-0(3), 1102) Win Walk.

How to Love Yourself. Bill Ferguson. Read by Bill Ferguson. 1 cass. 1990. 9.95 (978-1-878410-02-3(4)) Return Heart.
Until you can love yourself, your life will be full of upset & ineffectiveness. In this cassette, you will discover what runs your life & keeps you from loving yourself. You will learn how to be free of self-invalidation & how to accept yourself just the way you are.

How to Love Yourself: Cherishing the Incredible Miracle That You Are. Louise L. Hay. Read by Louise L. Hay. 1 cass. (Running Time: 1 hr.). (Conversations on Living Lecture Ser.). (ENG.). 1994. 10.95 (978-1-56170-025-7(8), 252) Hay House.
In this lecture, Louise guides you through each of her ten steps to loving yourself. These ten steps are perfect for those who are looking for realistic, practical ways to feel good about themselves. She closes with a powerful meditation.

How to Love Yourself: Cherishing the Incredible Miracle That You Are. abr. ed. Louise L. Hay. 1 CD. 2005. audio compact disk 10.95 (978-1-4019-0437-1(8)) Hay House.

How to Make a Pot: Jeremiah 18:16. Ed Young. (J). 1981. 4.95 (978-0-7417-1170-0(2), A0170) Win Walk.

How to Make a Prediction. Calvin Hanes. 1 cass. 8.95 (140) Am Fed Astrologers.
How a successful prediction was made.

How to Make a Second Marriage Succeed. Lynn Scoresby. 2 cass. 9.98 (978-1-55503-287-6(7), 06004199) Covenant Comms.
A Practical help with all aspects of remarriage.

How to Make a Speech. unabr. ed. Steve Allen. 12.95 (1906) J Norton Pubs.
Allen reveals his own secrets for finding the right subject, grabbing & holding an audience's attention, overcoming stage fright & leaving the audience wanting more.

How to Make & Manage Million Dollar Media Reps. (ENG.). 2009. audio compact disk 20.00 (978-0-9766470-3-4(6)) Guld Resource.

How to Make Anyone Fall in Love with You. abr. ed. Leil Lowndes. Read by Leil Lowndes. 2 cass. (Running Time: 3 hrs.). 1999. 16.95 (978-1-882071-93-7(X)) B-B Audio.
In this fun, readable manual to finding and keeping love, renowned communications expert Lowndes offers a scientifically sound plan to capture the heart of Mr. or Ms. Right. This audiobook offers sure fire techniques based on scientific studies regarding.

How to Make Anyone Fall in Love with You. abr. ed. Leil Lowndes. Read by Leil Lowndes. (Running Time: 14400 sec.). 2007. audio compact disk 23.95 (978-1-59316-092-0(5)) Listen & Live.

How to Make Big Money in Your Own Small Business: Unexpected Rules Every Small Buiness Owner Needs to Know. abr. rev. ed. Jeffrey J. Fox. 2 CDs. (Running Time: 2 hrs. 30 mins.). 2004. audio compact disk 16.95 (978-1-59397-438-1(8)) Pub: Macmill Audio. Dist(s): Macmillan

How to Make Characters Live. unabr. ed. Elizabeth R. Bills. 1 cass. (Running Time: 29 min.). (Secrets of Successful Writers Ser.). 1964. 12.95 (23034) J Norton Pubs.
What determines the details the writer selects in delineating a character? What are the techniques for "showing" the reader what kind of person the character is?.

How to Make Cross-Functional Teams Work: What You Gain When Departments Collaborate. Instructed by Mark Howard. 4 cass. (Running Time: 3 hrs. 55 min.). 59.95 Set, incl. wkbk., 46p. (Q10161) CareerTrack Pubns.
Program highlights: Cross-functional teams - what they are; The 4 primary reasons to create teams; Where teams work best - some practical applications; The role of the project manager; The next step - how to propose forming a team to meet a particular need; The kinds of problems cross-functional teams solve best; Techniques to help teams solve problems, clarify objectives & reach solutions; & more.

How to Make Divorce Fun. Julie Collins et al. Illus. by Louie Collins. (ENG.). 2008. bk. 17.95 (978-0-9818015-0-6(1)) B N Inc.

How to Make Hymns & Gospel Songs Come Alive Through Evangelistic Embellishments. Duane Shinn. 6 cass. bk. 199.99 Duane Shinn.
Develops the concept of evangelistic playing by means of modern chords, runs, chord substitutions, rhythm development, etc. Includes printed lessons in a binder.

How to Make It into Your Promise Land. Speeches. Joel Osteen. 2 CDs. (J). 2002. audio compact disk 12.00 (978-1-931877-33-6(5), JCS012) J Osteen.

How to Make Lemonade When Life Hands You Lemons. unabr. ed. Jack N. Singer. 2 cass. (Running Time: 2 hrs.). (How to Change Your Life Ser.: Vol. 1). 1998. bk. 17.88 (978-0-9700694-0-5(5)) Psychologically Speak.
Listeners will learn how to overcome all of the obstacles to their success. They will learn how to maximize their self-confidence & rejuvenate their fun, joy & happiness. They will learn the best secret to overcoming stress.

***How to Make Love All Night.** abr. ed. Barbara Keesling. Read by Barbara Keesling. (ENG.). 2004. (978-0-06-081310-9(5), Harper Audio); (978-0-06-075225-5(4), Harper Audio) HarperCollins Pubs.

How to Make Love Like a Porn Star: A Cautionary Tale. Jenna Jameson. 2006. audio compact disk 22.95 (978-0-06-082347-4(X)) HarperCollins Pubs.

How to Make, Manage & Multiply a Fortune. Somers H. White. 8 cass. (Running Time: 60 min. per cass.). 200.00 (C123) S White.
Covers dealing with inflation and taxes, money flow, bond market, stock market, your portfolio, investing internationally, real estate and oil and gas, commodities, future planning, how trusts work, etc.

***How to Make Meetings Produce.** PUEI. 2009. audio compact disk 199.00 (978-1-935041-68-9(1), CareerTrack) P Univ E Inc.

How to Make Money from Home as a Freelancer: Work at Home As A Freelancer. Andy Anderson. (ENG.). 2007. 19.95 (978-0-9792582-2-0(7)) Payday Pubng.

How to Make Money in Stocks: A Winning System in Good Times or Bad. William J. O'Neil. Read by William J. O'Neil. 1 cass. (Running Time: 60 min.). 1988. 9.95 (978-0-07-047791-9(4)) Pub: McGraw-Hill Trade. Dist(s): McGraw
Explains how to make money reading the daily financial news pages, pick the best industry groups in the market, read charts like an expert & improve selection & timing, substantially reduce losses & mistakes, & turn profit from reading & analyzing the news.

How to Make Money in Stocks: A Winning System in Good Times or Bad. abr. ed. William J. O'Neil. 3 cass. (Running Time: 4 hrs. 30 mins.). (McGraw Hill Audiobks.). 2003. 24.00 (978-0-9724462-4-2(9)); audio compact disk 28.00 (978-0-9724889-2-1(8)) Pub: A Media Intl. Dist(s): Natl Bk Netwk
This bestseller has shown over one million investors the secrets to building stock market wealth.

How to Make Money Tomorrow Morning see Como Hacer Dinero Ya

How to Make Money with Your Camera. unabr. ed. Instructed by William Montaigne. 2 cass. 19.95 (S1527) J Norton Pubs.
Tells in detail how, when, where & what to photograph for spare-time dollars.

How to Make People Like You in 90 Seconds or Less. Nicholas Boothman. Read by Nicholas Boothman. (Running Time: 3 hrs.). 2005. 19.95 (978-1-59912-911-2(6)) Iofy Corp.

How to Make People Like You in 90 Seconds or Less. Nicholas Boothman. Narrated by Nicholas Boothman. 3 CDs. (Running Time: 3 hrs.). 2004. audio compact disk 19.95 (978-1-59316-042-5(9), LL134) Listen & Live.
Whether meeting a new client or bumping into a potential mate, you only have a few seconds to make a favorable impression. Is that really possible? Author Nicholas Boothman, a lecturer and licensed master practitioner of neurolinguistic programming, believes yes! He introduces a revolutionary approach to face-to-face communication that will help anyone succeed at making meaningful, and immediate, connections. Easily learned, it will help you make the best of any relationship?s most important moment?those first 90 seconds.Learn the power of a Really Useful Attitude, the secrets of voice tone and body language, the difference between ?opening up? words and ?closing down? words. And reinforcing all of these skills is knowing how to read another person?s sensory preference?most of us are Visual people,

some are Kinesthetic and a few are Auditory. So when you say, ?I see what you mean? to a Visual, you?re really speaking his or her language. And then you?re on your way!.

How to Make People Like You in 90 Seconds or Less. unabr. ed. Nicholas Boothman. Read by Nicholas Boothman. (YA). 2008. 39.99 (978-1-60514-691-1(9)) Find a World.

How to Make People Like You in 90 Seconds or Less. unabr. ed. Nicholas Boothman. 2 cass. (Running Time: 3 hrs.). 2001. 16.95 (978-1-885408-59-4(5), LL051) Listen & Live.
Introduces a revolutionary new approach to face-to-face communication that will help anyone succeed at making meaningful, & immediate connection.

How to Make Powerful Presentations. abr. ed. Interview. Read by Marjorie Brody. 1 mono. cass. (Running Time: 50 min.). 1984. 9.95 Newtown Psychological Ctr.
The Executive Director of Newtown interviews the guest expert, Marjorie Brody, a member of the Speech Department of a Pennsylvania community college. Focuses on specific steps to follow in preparing presentation, how to avoid problems when making a speech, helpful hints on how to use handouts & audio-visual devices, & a list of annoying habits to avoid.

How to Make Presentations with Confidence & Power, Set. Fred Pryor Seminars Staff. 6 cass. 1994. 59.95 (10870AX) Nightingale-Conant.
Gain the skills necessary to make polished presentations. Make a lasting impression on every client, committee & board you address. Learn to overcome stage fright & become an "audience-centered" speaker.

How to Make Presentations with Confidence & Power: Innovative Tips, Techniques, & Strategies to Empower You to Speak with Ease. Fred Pryor. 6 cass. 59.95 Set incl. wkbk. (10870AS) Pryor Resources.
Learn the presenting skills & speaking techniques that will have you off the sidelines & standing up with confidence & power.

How to Make Relationships Work: Winning Keys to Family & Relationship Wellness. abr. ed. Perf. by Angela Brown et al. 1 cass. (Running Time: 30 mins.). (Words of Wellness Ser.: Vol. 9). 2000. 12.95 (978-0-9673451-9-2(7), LLP309) Life Long Pubg.
How to work together in marriage, business & life, how to keep the spark alive in personal relationships after years of marriage. How to blend work & marriage for couples who work & live together.

How to Make Someone Love You Forever! in 90 Minutes or Less. abr. ed. Nicholas Boothman. Read by Nicholas Boothman. (Running Time: 14400 sec.). 2007. audio compact disk 23.95 (978-1-59316-102-6(6)) Listen & Live.

How to Make the Most of a Visit: To Your Loved One with Dementia. Interview. Sherril Bover & Nancy Graham. 1 CD. (Running Time: 24 mins). 2006. audio compact disk 12.95 (978-0-9771625-3-6(2)) SecondWind.
Conversations about caregiving.

How to Make Things Happen in Your Life. Lynne Palmer. 1 cass. (Running Time: 90 min.). 1986. 8.95 (575) Am Fed Astrologers.

How to Make Winning Presentations. Hosted by Paul R. Timm. 1 cass. (Running Time: 30 mins.). pap. bk. 99.95 (1022AV); pap. bk. 99.95 (1022AV) J Wilson & Assocs.

How to Make Your Dreams Come True. Tom Hopkins. Read by Tom Hopkins. 4 cass. (Running Time: 3 hrs. 30 min.). (J). 1992. 39.95 Set. (978-0-938636-26-7(X), 1300) T Hopkins Intl.
Pertaining to peer pressure, goal setting, bad habits & procrastination.

How to Make Your Faith Work More Effectively. Leroy Tompson, Sr. 2002. 30.00 (978-1-931804-16-5(8)) Ever Increase Wd Min.

How to Make Your Forecast Hot-Hot. Dee Wynne. 1 cass. 8.95 (726) Am Fed Astrologers.
An AFA Convention workshop tape.

How to Make Your Hands Do What Your Brain Tells Them to Do. Duane Shinn. 1 cass. 19.95 (TQ-1) Duane Shinn.
Presents techniques for training your hands & fingers so that they will be able to do what you tell them to.

How to Make Your Home, School & Work Place Less Toxic According to "Poisoning Our Children" Author Nancy Green. Hosted by Nancy Pearlman. 1 cass. (Running Time: 29 min.). 10.00 (1024) Educ Comm CA.

How to Make Your Kitchen Your Pharmacy. Rocco BenRoy. Read by Rocco BenRoy. 4 cass. (Running Time: 4 hrs. 30 mins.). 1999. 34.95 (978-0-9672359-2-9(8)) Eternal Way.
Foods have qualities that make them heating or cooling, drying or moisturizing, elevating or grounding. Learn the energetic properties & tastes of foods & which commonly used foods drain your vitality & affect your health & what you can do about it. Learn lifestyle habits & routines that support your program of change & renewal, so that you may reach your life's goals.

How to Make Your Playing Come Alive Through Pedaling & Dynamics. Duane Shinn. 1 cass. 19.95 (HAR-14) Duane Shinn.
Discusses how to use pedals correctly & then to use dynamics creatively.

How to Make Yourself Happy & Remarkably Less Disturbable. abr. ed. Albert Ellis. Read by Stephen O'Hara. 2 cass. (Running Time: 3 hrs.). 2001. 18.00 (978-1-57453-396-5(7)) Audio Lit.
Through anecdotes & a systematic approach, shows how to counter & conquer the pain of anxiety, depression, anger & self-pity.

How to Make $100k This Year as a Life Coach! abr. ed. Terri Levine. 2005. audio compact disk (978-0-9785426-5-8(7)) Ultimate Wealth.

How to Mambo. unabr. ed. Conversa-Phone Institute Staff & Betty White. 1 cass. (Running Time: 55 min.). (Betty White's How to Ballroom Dance Ser.). 1990. 9.95 (978-1-56752-091-0(X)) Conversa-phone.
Teaches all of the most popular steps-breaks-turns - how to lead & how to follow. Fully illustrated instruction manual follows the audio tape. Learn today - dance tonight.

How to Manage Change While Managing Yourself. Jack Pachuta. Read by Jack Pachuta. 6 cass. (Running Time: 3 hrs.). 1995. 69.00 set. (978-1-888475-03-6(X)) Mangmt Stratgies.
Complete 3-hour Change Management seminar recorded before a live audience. Topics include: Change as a natural process, Building a team while changing, Pitfalls to change, Stress, & Resistance.

How to Manage Conflict, Anger, & Emotion: Control, Confidence, & Composure in Even the Most Highly-Charged Situations. 6 cass. 59.95 Set incl. wkbk. (12841AS) Pryor Resources.
An innovative, solutions-driven approach to the inevitable conflicts that arise at work & at home. Discover practical, proven alternatives you can use in even the most difficult, frustrating situations.

***How to Manage Emotions in the Workplace.** PUEI. 2009. audio compact disk 199.00 (978-1-935041-60-3(6), CareerTrack) P Univ E Inc.

How to Manage Housework & Homemaking for an Older Person. 1989. 9.95 (978-1-877843-07-5(5)) Elder Care Solutions.
Keeping the older person safe & comfortable in his or her own home. Cleaning, shopping & laundry for the home- bound person.bound person. Organizing your work as a caregiver.

***How to Manage Multi-Generational Teams.** Created by CareerTrack. 2010. audio compact disk 199.95 (978-1-60959-019-2(8)) P Univ E Inc.

How to Manage Multiple Projects & Meet Deadlines. PUEI. 2006. audio compact disk 89.95 (978-1-933328-41-6(X), Fred Pryor) P Univ E Inc.

How to Manage Multiple Projects, Meet Deadlines, & Achieve Objectives: Get More Control over Your Time, Tasks, & Priorities Than You Ever Thought Possible. 6 cass. 59.95 Set incl. wkbk. (10510AS) Pryor Resources.
If you need to get more done in less time, recognize your real priorities, keep track of several projects, or establish & meet deadlines, this program is for you. It teaches you to easily handle the most impossible priorities & demands without long work days, stress-filled schedules, chaos, & panic.

How to Manage Priorities & Meet Deadlines, Set. Fred Pryor Seminars Staff. 6 cass. 59.95 (10510AX) Nightingale-Conant.
How can you deal with the increasing time demands today's workplace puts on you? This fact-filled seminar shows you how to identify your most important priorities, handle difficult or unexpected situations - even stay calm in the face of chaos. Includes workbook.

How to Manage Projects. Reich Gardner. Read by Reich Gardner. 6 cass. album. (Running Time: 4 hrs. 32 min.). 1990. 59.95 incl. wkbk. (978-1-878542-05-2(2), 11-0604) SkillPath Pubns.
Full-day seminar teaches planning fundamentals, how to keep projects on budget & on schedule, how to monitor & control to achieve specific goals, & how to solve problems & troubleshoot.

How to Manage Projects, Set. abr. ed. Troy Campbell. Read by Troy Campbell. 2 cass. (Running Time: 3 hrs.). 1996. bk. 21.95 (978-1-57294-074-1(3),) SkillPath Pubns.
Sharing the secrets of success.

How to Manage Projects & Priorities Using Effective Delegation Skills. PUEI. 2006. audio compact disk 199.00 (978-1-934147-65-8(6), Fred Pryor); audio compact disk 199.00 (978-1-934147-04-7(4), CareerTrack) P Univ E Inc.

How to Manage Projects, Priorities & Deadlines: The Art of Getting It Done. Jonathan Clark & Susan Clark. 8 cass. 79.95 Set, incl. wkbk. & tests. (132-C47) Natl Seminars.
The time crunch is on, & it's tough to keep up. You're pretty good at managing your daily priorities & ongoing workload. But when crisis erupts, watch out! Everything's different - new priorities, new deadlines, new pressures. It's easy to get buried. This series is full of practical tips to get you organized & back in control.

How to Manage Stress. Joseph Currier. 1 cass. (Running Time: 54 min.). (Listen & Learn USA! Ser.). 1982. 8.95 (978-0-88684-058-7(9)) Listen USA.
Includes Relaxation Techniques.

***How to Manage, Train & Motivate the Change-Resistant Employee.** PUEI. 2008. audio compact disk 199.00 (978-1-935041-19-1(3), CareerTrack) P Univ E Inc.

How to Manage Your Accounting Department. Andrew B. Titen. 6 cass. 159.00 Set, incl. textbk. & quizzer. (CPE3100) Bisk Educ.
How to successfully organize your department, train & supervise your staff & evaluate, monitor & tighten internal controls.

How to Manage Your Boss. unabr. ed. Christopher Hegarty. Read by Christopher Hegarty. 6 cass. (Running Time: 6 hrs.). 1986. 59.95 Set. (978-0-671-63473-5(9)) S&S Audio.

How to Manage Your Stress & Make It Work for You in the Shortest Period of Time. Michael Broder. 1 cass. 1999. 14.95 (C059) A Ellis Institute.
Rest & relaxation are not somewhere over the rainbow; they can be found right here in this program full of tips & techniques for making hard situations easier on yourself.

How to Manipulate the Press: A Study of How Reporters Work & Think. unabr. ed. Colonel Mason. Read by Colonel Mason. 2 cass. (Running Time: 3 hrs.). 1998. 16.95 Set. (978-0-9648046-4-7(6), LH-P98) Liv Hist Pub.
A basic "how to" book. Press traces the evolution of our modern day reporters & new agencies, tells how to deal with honest reporters & provides safeguards in dealing with the press in general, getting the news out.

How to Market & Sell Your Recruiting Services. Read by Bill Radin. 2 CDs. (Running Time: 100 minutes). (Professional Development Series for Recruiters: 1). 2002. audio compact disk 79.95 (978-1-929836-05-5(8)) Innovative Consulting.

How to Market & Sell Your Recruiting Services, Set. Bill Radin. Read by Bill Radin. 2 cass. (Running Time: 1 hr. 40 min.). (Professional Development Series for Recruiters: Vol. 1). 1999. wbk. ed. 79.95 (978-1-929836-00-0(7)) Innovative Consulting.
Sales training and performance improvement guide for executive recruiter and personnel consultants.

How to Market Financial Services to Women. unabr. ed. 1 cass. 1999. (978-1-930414-04-4(8)) L I M R A Intl.

How to Market Through Direct Mail. Nido R. Qubein. Read by Nido R. Qubein. 6 cass. (Professional Services Library). 69.95 Set. (497AD) Nightingale-Conant.
Discover key elements for distinguishing yourself in the marketplace, workable strategies for building yourself into a profitable entity, techniques for refining your professional image, & more.

How to Market Your Business with Little or No Money. Stephen Anderson. 2000. pap. bk. 24.95 (978-0-9702326-0-1(8)) Busin Success.

How to Market Your Professional Expertise. Nido R. Qubein. Read by Nido R. Qubein. 6 cass. (Professional Services Library). 69.95 Set. (495AD) Nightingale-Conant.

How to Market Your Professional Expertise: Marketing Professional Services. unabr. ed. Nido Qubein. Read by Nido Qubein. (Running Time: 4 hrs. 30 mins.). (ENG.). 2008. 19.98 (978-1-59659-227-8(3), GildAudio) Pub: Gildan Media. Dist(s): HachBkGrp

How to Market Your Web Site: More Hits More Money. abr. ed. Kevin S. Yorke. 1 cass. (Running Time: 1 hr. 30 min.). 1997. 17.95 cass. & box. (978-1-890958-10-7(7)) Gen Keeper.

How to Marry a King: 1 Samuel 25. Ed Young. 1982. 4.95 (978-0-7417-1235-6(0), 235) Win Walk.

How to Master Rhythm Problems - Once & for All!, Level 2. 4 cass. bk. 49.95 Set. (RP-2) Duane Shinn.
Learn to count & play the more advanced rhythms, such as the Shuffle, Gospel Waltz, Habanera, Pasa Doble, C & W, Tango, Fatback, Rhumba, Bolero, Bosa Nova, Cha Cha & Beguine.

How to Master the Art of Listing Real Estate. Tom Hopkins. Read by Tom Hopkins. 8 cass. 1986. bk. 125.00; 120.00 (978-0-938636-17-5(0), 1000) T Hopkins Intl.
Step by step methods for listing.

How to Master the Art of Selling Anything. Tom Hopkins. 12 cass. (Running Time: 12 hrs.). 1993. 180.00 set. (614AS) Nightingale-Conant.

How to Master the Art of Selling Anything. Tom Hopkins. bk. 165.00 (978-0-938636-15-1(4)) T Hopkins Intl.
Covers aspects of selling products from how & wherw to get customers through closing the sale & the necessary follow-up.

How to Master the Art of Selling Real Estate. Tom Hopkins. Read by Tom Hopkins. 8 cass. 1986. bk. 125.00; 120.00 (978-0-938636-18-2(9), 1018) T Hopkins Intl.
Presents steps required to meet quality, close & follow up with a buyer.

How to Master the Problems of Life. 1 cass. (Running Time: 30 min.). 1985. (0239) Evang Sisterhood Mary.
Subjects are: What Should I Do About My Difficult Personality?; Attacking Our Fear; Transformed Burdens; Is God For Us?.

How to Master Your Time. Brian S. Tracy. 6 CDs. (Running Time: 6 hrs.). audio compact disk 79.95 (978-1-55525-044-7(0), 7061cd) Nightingale-Conant.
Everyone starts the day with the same 24 hours...How will you use yours?.

How to Master Your Time. Brian S. Tracy. Read by Brian S. Tracy. 6 cass. (Running Time: 6 hrs.). 59.95 (978-1-55525-043-0(2), 7061A) Nightingale-Conant.
Applying his unique skills as a management & business consultant, Brian Tracy provides you with a concrete, step-by-step approach to making the best use of every minute of every day. You'll learn how to set goals & then achieve them quickly & most importantly, you'll find out why time is your most precious commodity & why time management is life management.

How to Match the Melody Notes of Any Song to a Chord in Your Left Hand. 2 cass. 39.95 Set, incl. printed material. (V-5) Duane Shinn.
Shows how you can tell which chords go with which melody notes. Learn how to go about matching the melody notes (the tune) of any song to the appropriate chords. It's really a simple process, once you understand it.

How to Maximize Your Potential as a Real Estate Professional: The 7 Keys to Instant & Long-Term Success. David Essel. (ENG.). 2006. audio compact disk 25.00 (978-1-893074-14-9(5)) D Essel Inc.

How to Meditate. 2002. 10.00 (978-0-9723861-1-1(4)); audio compact disk 15.00 (978-0-9723861-2-8(2)) Parah Pubns.

How to Meditate. Pat Carroll. Read by Pat Carroll. Ed. by Tony Carroll. 1 cass. (Running Time: 30 min.). 10.00 Inner-Mind Concepts.
Discusses how to communicate with the cosmic consciousness & receive messages while working through the white & golden light.

How to Meditate. Eternal Quest Staff & Kathleen McDonald. 1 cass. (Running Time: 60 min.). 1994. pap. bk. 5.95 (978-0-8356-1903-5(6), Quest) Pub: Theos Pub Hse. Dist(s): Natl Bk Netwk

How to Meditate. Kriyananda, pseud. 6 cass. (Running Time: 7 hrs.). 44.95 (LS-2) Crystal Clarity.
Detailed instructions in how to meditate, for both beginners & advanced students. Includes the Hong-Sau & Om Techniques, Kriya Prelocation & question-&-answer periods.

How to Meditate. Narrated by Dick Lutz. 1 cass. (Running Time: 15 min.). 1984. 7.95 (978-0-931625-16-9(5), 16) DIMI Pr.
Side A presents instructions for a simple, quick method of meditation. Side B is a relaxation narration to listen to as you begin meditating.

How to Meditate. abr. unabr. rev. ed. Lawrence LeShan. Read by Paul Michael. 3 CDs. (Running Time: 3 hrs. 0 mins. 0 sec.). (ENG.). 2004. audio compact disk 19.95 (978-1-59397-523-4(6)) Pub: Macmill Audio. Dist(s): Macmillan

How to Meditate - Shortened Version. Kriyananda, pseud. (Running Time: 90 min.). 1986. 9.95 (LS-25) Crystal Clarity.
Gives only Hong-Sau technique & includes basic information for both beginning & more advanced meditators but with less background information.

How to Meditate on God. 1 cass. (Running Time: 1 hr.). 12.99 (133) Yoga Res Foun.

How to Meditate with Pema Chodron: A Practical Guide to Making Friends with Your Mind. unabr. ed. Pema Chödrön. Read by Pema Chödrön. 5 CDs. (Running Time: 5 hrs. 30 mins.). 2008. audio compact disk 29.95 (978-1-59179-794-4(2)) Sounds True.

How to Meditate with Your Dog: An Introduction to Meditation for Dog Lovers. unabr. ed. James Jacobson & Kristine Chandler Madera. Read by James Jacobson. 4 CDs. 2005. audio compact disk 19.95 (978-0-9752631-3-6(7)) Pub: Maui Media. Dist(s): Midpt Trade

How to Meet Your Spirit Guides - Meet Your Spirit Guides - A Spiritual Experience in a Box! Claudia Coronado. 1. (Running Time: 60 mins.). 2004. audio compact disk 16.95 (978-0-9764153-8-1(0)) R James TV.
Claudia Coronado (Minister ULC), is a Soul-Empath, who does Psychic counseling and healing work in the US and Europe. She learned early in her life to trust her guides in adversary situations. Her main concern is to self-empower people into independence and to make them feel the power and guidance of being supported in every given moment.Trust the process, because you can connect too! Her guiding ones help to open and keep the space for each and everyone who wants to meet with their own guides through this CD. They supported her voice and let her find music, which works with both parts of the brain to support the process. The steps to follow are easy in this guides meditation and soon you will be able to contact your guides, angels or crossed over loved ones on your own! Be surprised!This CD is truly a product of Sedona:Idea and voice over by Claudia Coronado and her Guides.

How to Memorize Music. Duane Shinn. 1 cass. 19.95 (NS-7) Duane Shinn.
Discusses how to analyze the form of a song - ABA, AABA, ABAC, or whatever & explains how to practice by phrases to stimulate muscle memory to go along with brain cell memory.

***How to Memorize Names, Numbers, Speeches, Playing Cards & Everything Else: USA Record holder for fastest to memorize deck of cards shares Secrets.** Narrated by Ron White. (ENG.). 2010. audio compact disk 19.95 (978-0-9747212-7-9(1)) R White Train.

***How to Memorize the Presidents of US in 3 minutes, 14 Seconds: USA Memory Champion & Memory Record Holder.** Ron White. (ENG.). (J). 2010. audio compact disk 19.95 (978-0-9747212-6-2(3)) R White Train.

How to Mentally & Physically Toughen Yourself for Your Sport Season. 2 cass. 1999. 15.95 Set. (978-1-893353-11-4(7)) Peak Perf Pub.
Designed specifically for sports officials in all amateur & professional athletics, this program delivers cutting-edge information to utilize during pre-season, in-season & post season mental & physical training sessions.

How to Merengue & Samba. unabr. ed. Conversa-Phone Institute Staff & Betty White. 1 cass. (Running Time: 55 min.). (Betty White's How to Ballroom Dance Ser.). 1990. 9.95 (978-1-56752-096-5(0)) Conversa-phone.
Teaches all of the most popular steps-breaks-turns - how to lead & how to follow. Fully illustrated instruction manual follows the audio tape. Learn today - dance tonight.

How to Minister to the Lord. C. S. Lovett. Read by C. S. Lovett. 1 cass. (Running Time: 80 min.). 6.95 (549) Prsnl Christianity.
Your imagination & my voice combine to provide just the right emotion for enjoying the Lord's presence. Travel with me step-by-step as we enter the

"secret place" & behold the Lord waiting for you. Learn to bring words of comfort to Him & bless His heart as He enjoys your presence.

How to Mom. Ed Young. 2000. 4.95 (978-0-7417-2255-3(0), 1255) Win Walk.

How to Motivate People. David Merrill & Roger Reid. Intro. by A. E. Whyte. 1 cass. (Running Time: 45 min.). (Listen & Learn USA! Ser.). 8.95 (978-0-88684-005-1(8)) Listen USA.
Shows how to stimulate & motivate people.

How to Motivate People, Especially in the Workplace. Salenger Inc. Staff. 1 cass. (Running Time: 41 min.). 12.95 (201TP-W) Salenger.
Discusses major theories of motivation proposed by Maslow, Hertzberg, McClelland, Hersey & others.

How to Move from Rejection to Acceptance see Como Pasar Del Rechazo A la Aceptacion

How to Murder Your Mother-in-Law. unabr. ed. Dorothy Cannell. Read by Sharon Williams. (Running Time: 8 hrs.). (Ellie Haskell Mystery Ser.: No. 6). 2008. 24.95 (978-1-4233-5447-5(8), 9781423354475, Brilliance MP3); 24.95 (978-1-4233-5449-9(4), 9781423354499, BAD); 39.25 (978-1-4233-5448-2(6), 9781423354482, Brlnc Audio MP3 Lib); 39.25 (978-1-4233-5450-5(8), 9781423354505, BADLE) Brilliance Audio.

How to Negotiate Anything with Anyone Anywhere in the World. unabr. ed. Frank L. Acuff. 8 cass. (Running Time: 6 hrs.). 1993. 89.95 set, incl. action guide. (2042) Dartnell Corp.
Learn highly effective negotiating strategies that bring long-term success, as well as how to go head-to-head with the toughest negotiating opponents. Also included is a global tour of negotiating specifics for almost every region of the world.

How to Negotiate Computer Contracts. David F. Simon. 1 cass. (Running Time: 1 hr.). 1985. 15.00 cass. only. PA Bar Inst.

How to Negotiate the Sale from Start to Finish, Set. 4 cass. pap. bk. & wbk. ed. 155.00 (978-0-7612-0699-6(X), 80222QK1); pap. bk. & wbk. ed. 30.00 (978-0-7612-0700-9(7), 80223QK1) AMACOM.
Successful salespeople know almost instinctively how & when to negotiate. You'll learn how to: Apply the key steps involved in the sales negotiation process; Conduct buyer research to obtain the information needed for effective negotiations; Select & prepare members of the sales negotiating team & much more.

How to Negotiate Your Success! Jack Pachuta. Read by Jack Pachuta. 4 cass. (Running Time: 2 hrs.). 1992. 59.00 set. (978-1-888475-02-9(1)) Mangmt Stratgies.
Complete 2-hour negotiations seminar including: Power sources, strategies & tactics, Relationship strategies, Concessions, Alternatives at an Impasse, Questioning techniques, & other key concepts.

How to Never Be Hurt Again. Speeches. Creflo A. Dollar. 4 cass. (Running Time: 4 hrs. 45 min.). 2005. 20.00 (978-1-59089-992-2(X)); 28.00 (978-1-59089-993-9(8)) Creflo Dollar.

How to Obtain a Security Clearance from the U. S. Federal Government: Capitol Learning Audio Course. Derrick Dortch. Prod. by TheCapitol.Net. (ENG.). 2008. 47.00 (978-1-58733-090-2(3)) TheCapitol.

How to Obtain Healing. Creflo A. Dollar. (ENG.). 2000. 15.00 (978-1-59089-104-9(X)) Pub: Creflo Dollar. Dist(s): STL Dist NA

How to Oercome Religious Spirits. 2003. (978-1-59024-104-2(5)) B Hinn Min.

How to Open a Restaurant. Comment by Robert Krulwich. 1 cass. (Running Time: 40 min.). 10.95 (L0090B090, HarperThor) HarpC GBR.

How to Open Your Heart. 1 cass. (Love-Human & Divine Ser.). 9.95 (ST-55) Crystal Clarity.
Topics include: The liberating power of unconditional love; why we need to pray for devotion; the warmth & magnetism of impersonal love; meditation & service as ways to open your heart.

How to Operate With Others II. 1 cass. (Running Time: 1 hr.). 12.99 (129) Yoga Res Foun.

How to Operate Your Brain. Featuring Timothy Leary. 1994. 9.95 (978-1-59157-010-3(7)) Assn for Cons.

How to Organize a Capitol Hill Day. Ed. by TheCapitol.Net. 1 CD. (Running Time: 79 mins.). 2005. audio compact disk 107.00 (978-1-58733-016-2(4)) TheCapitol.
Knowing the in?s and out?s of organizing a Capitol Hill Day for your volunteers is essential to its success. Whether you are in DC or Omaha, our expert faculty will teach you how to organize an effective Capitol Hill Day. Learn how to maximize this day by combining training of volunteers with visits to congressional delegations.- What is the planning cycle- How to budget for the event- Planning tools necessary to create and produce an effective training event- Training your volunteers so they know what to expect, say, and do- How to follow up with your volunteers and keep them motivated after they leave Washington.

How to Organize Your Life & Get Rid of Clutter. Ab Jackson. 2 cass. (Running Time: 136 min.). 1996. 15.95 Set. (978-1-55977-566-3(1)) CareerTrack Pubns.
Topics: Two questions that decide the fate of every incoming piece of paper; How to create files that are easy to use; & Using the "4-boxes-and-a-list" system to tidy up messy areas.

How to Organize Your Life & Get Rid of Clutter. PUEI. 1995. audio compact disk 89.95 (978-1-933328-74-4(6), CareerTrack) P Univ E Inc.

How to Organize Your Life & Get Rid of Clutter. PUEI. 2007. audio compact disk 199.00 (978-1-934147-17-7(6), CareerTrack) P Univ E Inc.

How to Outperform Yourself Totally. Mark Victor Hansen. 4 cass. 60.00 (2) M V Hansen.
Create a positive self image, use your mind creatively & constructively.

How to Overcome Anxiety. (193) Yoga Res Foun.

How to Overcome Anxiety, No. 2. Swami Jyotirmayananda. 1 cass. (Running Time: 1 hr.). 1990. 12.99 Yoga Res Foun.

How to Overcome Battles. Taffi L. Dollar. 2008. audio compact disk 21.00 (978-1-59944-745-2(2)) Creflo Dollar.

How to Overcome Cowardliness. 1 cass. (Running Time: 1 hr.). 12.99 (145) Yoga Res Foun.

How to Overcome Craving. 1 cass. (Running Time: 1 hr.). 12.99 (179) Yoga Res Foun.

How to Overcome Depression. Earnie Larsen. 1 cass. (Running Time: 1 hr.). 1986. 10.95 (978-1-56047-002-1(X), A103) E Larsen Enterprises.
Discusses how to defeat depression.

How to Overcome Discouragement. J. Martin Kohe. 1 cass. 10.00 (SP100003) SMI Intl.
Everyone experiences problems & discouragement. Success requires meeting problems with confidence & assurance. Listen & learn to overcome discouragement through positive action.

How to Overcome Disruptive Workstyle Differences. PUEI. audio compact disk 199.00 (978-1-934147-96-2(6), CareerTrack) P Univ E Inc.

How to Overcome Dullness of Mind. 1 cass. (Running Time: 1 hr.). 12.99 (110) Yoga Res Foun.

How to Overcome Egoism. (108) Yoga Res Foun.

How to Overcome Egoism, No. 1. Swami Jyotirmayananda. 1 cass. (Running Time: 1 hr.). 1990. 12.99 Yoga Res Foun.

How to Overcome Evil. Derek Prince. 2 cass. 11.90 Set. (078-079) Derek Prince.
Evil is a being - Satan - whom we overcome when we learn to testify personally to what God's Word says about the Blood of Jesus.

How to Overcome Fear. (169); (706) Yoga Res Foun.

How to Overcome Fear. Swami Jyotirmayananda. 1 cass. (Running Time: 1 hr.). 1990. 12.99 Yoga Res Foun.

How to Overcome Fear & Live Life to the Fullest. abr. ed. Marcos Witt. Read by Marcos Witt. 2007. 17.95 (978-0-7435-6091-7(4)) Pub: S&S Audio. Dist(s): S and S Inc

How to Overcome Gossiping. 1 cass. 12.99 (157) Yoga Res Foun.

How to Overcome Greed. 1 cass. (Running Time: 1 hr.). 12.99 (185) Yoga Res Foun.

How to Overcome Hatred. 1 cass. (Running Time: 1 hr.). 12.99 (131) Yoga Res Foun.

How to Overcome Hatred, No. 2. Swami Jyotirmayananda. 1 cass. (Running Time: 1 hr.). 1990. 12.99 Yoga Res Foun.

How to Overcome Impossibilities. Creflo A. Dollar. 10.00 (978-1-59089-087-5(6)) Pub: Creflo Dollar. Dist(s): STL Dist NA

How to Overcome in Everyday Life. Read by Basilea Schlink. 1 cass. (Running Time: 30 min.). Incl. How to Overcome in Everyday Life: What Keeps Me from Being Happy? 1985. (0213); 1985. (0213) Evang Sisterhood Mary.
Focuses on coping with problems & difficulties & recognizing our spiritual blockades.

How to Overcome in Everyday Life: What Keeps Me from Being Happy? see How to Overcome in Everyday Life

How to Overcome Infatuation. 1 cass. (Running Time: 1 hr.). 12.99 (147) Yoga Res Foun.

How to Overcome Intolerance. 1 cass. (Running Time: 1 hr.). 12.99 (202) Yoga Res Foun.

How to Overcome Jealousy. Swami Jyotirmayananda. 1 cass. (Running Time: 45 min.). 1990. 10.00 Yoga Res Foun.

How to Overcome Jealousy II. 1 cass. (Running Time: 1 hr.). 12.99 (149) Yoga Res Foun.

How to Overcome Laziness. (190) Yoga Res Foun.

How to Overcome Laziness. Swami Jyotirmayananda. 1 cass. (Running Time: 1 hr.). 1990. 12.99 Yoga Res Foun.

How to Overcome Loneliness. (101); (210) Yoga Res Foun.

How to Overcome Loneliness, No. 2. Swami Jyotirmayananda. 1 cass. (Running Time: 1 hr.). 1990. 12.99 Yoga Res Foun.

How to Overcome Maya. (128) Yoga Res Foun.

How to Overcome Maya. Swami Jyotirmayananda. 1 cass. (Running Time: 1 hr.). 1990. 12.99 Yoga Res Foun.

How to Overcome Mental Stress. 1 cass. (Running Time: 1 hr.). 12.99 (191) Yoga Res Foun.

How to Overcome Mental Stress. Swami Jyotirmayananda. 1 cass. (Running Time: 45 min.). 1990. 10.00 Yoga Res Foun.

How to Overcome Negative Emotions. Kriyananda, pseud. 1 cass. (Running Time: 2 hrs.). 14.95 (78M) Crystal Clarity.
Methods for dealing with negativity, unwanted emotions, dislikes, misjudgements are discussed.

How to Overcome Negativity in the Workplace. PUEI. audio compact disk 89.95 (978-1-933328-27-0(4), CareerTrack) P Univ E Inc.

How to Overcome Negativity in the Workplace. PUEI. 2005. audio compact disk 89.95 (978-1-933328-28-7(2), CareerTrack) P Univ E Inc.

How to Overcome Negativity in the Workplace: Training to Help You Create a More Positive, Productive Work Environment. Perf. by Lani Arredondo. 4 cass. (Running Time: 4 hr.). 1997. 59.95 (V10300) CareerTrack Pubns.

How to Overcome Pain in Your Past Series. 2004. audio compact disk 40.00 (978-1-59834-003-7(4)) Walk Thru the Bible.

How to Overcome Pessimism. (156) Yoga Res Foun.

How to Overcome Pessimism. Swami Jyotirmayananda. 1 cass. (Running Time: 1 hr.). 1990. 12.99 Yoga Res Foun.

How to Overcome Pride. 1 cass. (Running Time: 1 hr.). 12.99 (181) Yoga Res Foun.

How to Overcome Pride, No. 2. Swami Jyotirmayananda. 1 cass. (Running Time: 1 hr.). 1990. 12.99 Yoga Res Foun.

How to Overcome Procrastination. (127) Yoga Res Foun.

How to Overcome Procrastination. Swami Jyotirmayananda. 1 cass. (Running Time: 1 hr.). 1990. 12.99 Yoga Res Foun.

How to Overcome Rajas. (207) Yoga Res Foun.

How to Overcome Rajas. Swami Jyotirmayananda. 1 cass. (Running Time: 1 hr.). 1990. 12.99 Yoga Res Foun.

How to Overcome Rejection & Betrayal. Derek Prince. 1 cass. (I-4037) Derek Prince.

How to Overcome Religious Spirits. 2003. audio compact disk (978-1-59024-103-5(7)) B Hinn Min.

How to Overcome Self-Pity. (164) Yoga Res Foun.

How to Overcome Self-Pity. Swami Jyotirmayananda. 1 cass. (Running Time: 1 hr.). 1990. 12.99 Yoga Res Foun.

How to Overcome Stress. 1 cass. (Running Time: 1 hr.). 12.99 (209) Yoga Res Foun.

How to Overcome Stress, No. 2. Swami Jyotirmayananda. 1 cass. (Running Time: 1 hr.). 1990. 12.99 Yoga Res Foun.

How to Overcome Stress & Fear. Kriyananda, pseud. 1 cass. (Running Time: 80 min.). 9.95 (ST-41) Crystal Clarity.
Ways to overcome fears; finding strength in devotion; the importance of enjoying our battles; how to strengthen the aura to ward off negative vibrations.

How to Overcome Tamas. 1 cass. (Running Time: 1 hr.). 12.99 (207) Yoga Res Foun.

How to Overcome the Doubting Mind. 1 cass. (Running Time: 1 hr.). 12.99 (167) Yoga Res Foun.

How to Overcome the Flesh. Gloria Copeland. 1 cass. 1986. 5.00 (978-0-88114-739-1(7)) K Copeland Pubns.
Biblical teaching on overcoming the flesh.

How to Overcome the Spirit of Lust. Creflo A. Dollar. 15.00 (978-1-59089-077-6(9)) Pub: Creflo Dollar. Dist(s): STL Dist NA

How to Overcome the Worrying Habit. Swami Jyotirmayananda. 1 cass. (Running Time: 45 min.). 1990. 10.00 Yoga Res Foun.

How to Overcome Vanity. 1 cass. (Running Time: 1 hr.). 12.99 (194) Yoga Res Foun.

How to Overcome Vanity, No. 2. Swami Jyotirmayananda. 1 cass. (Running Time: 1 hr.). 1990. 12.99 Yoga Res Foun.

How to Overcome Weakness. Swami Amar Jyoti. 2 cass. 1978. 12.95 (O-11) Truth Consciousness.
The source of weakness & ill health. Foods, medicines, holistic healing & the power within. On Enlightenment; the time of death; desire & the endless projection of creation.

How to Overcome Worrying. Read by Basilea Schlink. 1 cass. (Running Time: 30 min.). Incl. How to Overcome Worrying: On Fire for God. 1985. (0216); 1985. (0216) Evang Sisterhood Mary.
Topics are: God Intervenes; Don't Throw Away Your Trust; One Little Word Can Change Everything; Angels of God in Our Lives.

How to Overcome Worrying: On Fire for God see How to Overcome Worrying

How to Pachanga. unabr. ed. Conversa-Phone Institute Staff & Betty White. 1 cass. (Running Time: 55 min.). (Betty White's How to Ballroom Dance Ser.). 1990. 9.95 (978-1-56752-099-6(5)) Conversa-phone.
Teaches all of the most popular steps-breaks-turns - how to lead & how to follow. Fully illustrated instruction manual follows the audio tape. Learn today - dance tonight.

How to Parent So Children Will Learn. unabr. ed. Sylvia Rimm. Read by Sylvia Rimm. 3 cass. (Running Time: 2 hrs. 22 min.). 1989. 30.00 Set. (978-0-937891-05-6(3), SR106) Apple Pub Wisc.
Two-sided tapes include an interview with Dr. Sylvia Rimm & several parents about how to help their children become learners.

How to Party Dance. unabr. ed. Conversa-Phone Institute Staff & Betty White. 1 cass. (Running Time: 55 min.). (Betty White's How to Ballroom Dance Ser.). 1990. 9.95 (978-1-56752-098-9(7)) Conversa-phone.
Teaches all of the most popular steps-breaks-turns - how to lead & how to follow. Fully illustrated instruction manual follows the audio tape. Learn today - dance tonight.

How to Pass Appraiser Exam Ac. Ed. by Kaplan Publishing Staff. 2004. (978-1-4195-0776-2(1)) Dearborn Financial.

How to Pass on Convictions to Your Children. As told by S. M. Davis. 1 CD. (Running Time: 1 hr.). 2003. audio compact disk 10.00 (978-1-929241-95-8(X)) Vsn Forum.
When the Lord "appeared to Samuel in a dream by night" and said,"Ask what I shall give thee," Solomon wisely asked for an understanding heart. Knowledge is learning what God wants us to do. Wisdom is learning how to do it. Understanding is learning why to do it. When children ask the question, "Why?" it is not enough for parents to answer, "Because I said so." A key to passing beliefs, standards, and convictions onto the next generation is by giving them "understanding.".

How to PASS Tests. William Eaton. 1 cd. (Running Time: 30 min). 2003. audio compact disk 9.95 (978-0-9713693-6-8(4)); 6.95 (978-0-9713693-2-0(1)) W Eaton.
This book is the result of many years of study on why people fail tests. It is the owners manual on how to use your brain to help you pass the tests you are having trouble with.

How to Pass the Appraiser Ex C. Ed. by Kaplan Publishing Staff. 2004. (978-1-4195-0777-9(X)) Dearborn Financial.

How to Peabody. unabr. ed. Conversa-Phone Institute Staff & Betty White. 1 cass. (Running Time: 55 min.). (Betty White's How to Ballroom Dance Ser.). 1990. 9.95 (978-1-56752-102-3(9)) Conversa-phone.
Teaches all of the most popular steps-breaks-turns - how to lead & how to follow. Fully illustrated instruction manual follows the audio tape. Learn today - dance tonight.

How To Pick a Jury. 1986. bk. 60.00 incl. book.; 35.00 cass. only.; 25.00 book only. PA Bar Inst.

How to Pick Stocks Like Warren Buffett: Profiting from the Bargain Hunting Strategies of the World's Greatest Value Investor. Timothy P. Vick. Read by Timothy P. Vick. 3 CDs. (Running Time: 3 hrs.). 2004. audio compact disk 28.00 (978-1-932378-23-8(5)) Pub: A Media Intl. Dist(s): Natl Bk Netwk

How to Pick Stocks Like Warren Buffett: Profiting from the Bargain Hunting Strategies of the World's Greatest Value Investor. Timothy P. Vick. Read by Timothy P. Vick. 2 cass. (Running Time: 3 hrs.). 2004. 24.00 (978-1-932378-22-1(7)) Pub: A Media Intl. Dist(s): Natl Bk Netwk
Shows step by profitable step how any investor can follow Buffett's path and find consistent bargains regardless of the overall market.

How to Plant the Seeds of Your Happiness Tree. Instructed by Manly P. Hall. 8.95 (978-0-89314-139-4(9), C840909) Philos Res.

How to Play & Arrange. Duane Shinn. 29 cass. (Running Time: 60 min.). Incl. How to Play & Arrange: A Mighty Fortress; How to Play & Arrange: Abide with Me; How to Play & Arrange: Amazing Grace; How to Play & Arrange: Battle Hymn of the Republic; How to Play & Arrange: Beyond the Sunset; How to Play & Arrange: Bring Them In; How to Play & Arrange: Come Thou Fount; How to Play & Arrange: Face to Face; How to Play & Arrange: Fairest Lord Jesus; How to Play & Arrange: He Arose; How to Play & Arrange: Holy, Holy, Holy; How to Play & Arrange: How Great Thou Art; How to Play & Arrange: I Have Decided to Follow Jesus; How to Play & Arrange: I Surrender All; How to Play & Arrange: I'd Rather Have Jesus; How to Play & Arrange: In the Garden; How to Play & Arrange: In the Sweet By & By; How to Play & Arrange: Ivory Palace; How to Play & Arrange: Jesus Loves Me; How to Play & Arrange: Jesus Loves the Little Children; How to Play & Arrange: Just a Closer Walk; How to Play & Arrange: Just as I Am; How to Play & Arrange: Like A River Glorius; How to Play & Arrange: Morning Is Broken; How to Play & Arrange: My Faith Looks Up to Thee; How to Play & Arrange: Old Rugged Cross; How to Play & Arrange: There Is A Fountain; How to Play & Arrange: Turn Your Eyes Upon Jesus; How to Play & Arrange: What A Friend; 19.95 ea. Duane Shinn.
Discusses how to play the song as written, then how to arrange the song using a variety of arranging techniques.

How to Play & Arrange: A Mighty Fortress see How to Play & Arrange

How to Play & Arrange: Abide with Me see How to Play & Arrange

How to Play & Arrange: Amazing Grace see How to Play & Arrange

How to Play & Arrange: Battle Hymn of the Republic see How to Play & Arrange

How to Play & Arrange: Beyond the Sunset see How to Play & Arrange

How to Play & Arrange: Bring Them In see How to Play & Arrange

How to Play & Arrange: Come Thou Fount see How to Play & Arrange

How to Play & Arrange: Face to Face see How to Play & Arrange

How to Play & Arrange: Fairest Lord Jesus see How to Play & Arrange

How to Play & Arrange: He Arose see How to Play & Arrange

How to Play & Arrange: Holy, Holy, Holy see How to Play & Arrange

How to Play & Arrange: How Great Thou Art see How to Play & Arrange

How to Play & Arrange: I Have Decided to Follow Jesus see How to Play & Arrange

How to Play & Arrange: I Surrender All see How to Play & Arrange

How to Play & Arrange: I'd Rather Have Jesus see How to Play & Arrange

How to Play & Arrange: In the Garden see How to Play & Arrange

How to Play & Arrange: In the Sweet By & By see How to Play & Arrange

How to Play & Arrange: Ivory Palace see How to Play & Arrange

How to Play & Arrange: Jesus Loves Me see How to Play & Arrange

How to Play & Arrange: Jesus Loves the Little Children see How to Play & Arrange

How to Play & Arrange: Just a Closer Walk see How to Play & Arrange

How to Play & Arrange: Just as I Am see How to Play & Arrange

How to Play & Arrange: Like A River Glorius see How to Play & Arrange

How to Play & Arrange: Morning Is Broken see How to Play & Arrange

How to Play & Arrange: My Faith Looks Up to Thee see How to Play & Arrange

How to Play & Arrange: Old Rugged Cross see How to Play & Arrange

How to Play & Arrange: There Is A Fountain see How to Play & Arrange

How to Play & Arrange: Turn Your Eyes Upon Jesus see How to Play & Arrange

How to Play & Arrange: What A Friend see How to Play & Arrange

How to Play Blues & Boogie Woogie Piano. Robert Laughlin. 2 cass. 1986. pap. bk. 35.00 (978-0-929983-11-0(4)) New Schl Am Music.
Introduction to the basic elements of blues & boogie piano playing. Includes blues form, blues scale, rhythm, left hand patterns, right hand patterns, blues scale & "Blues Improvising Techniques" tape.

How to Play by Ear: A Guide to Chords & Progressions for Musicians, Songwriters, & Composers. Jack Hatfield. 1 cass. (Running Time: 1 hr. 32 min.). 1993. pap. bk. 8.00 (978-0-9651623-7-1(0)) Hatfield Mus.
Exercises & ear training examples that correspond with the text of "How to Play by Ear" book.

How to Play Chord Piano in Ten Days. Duane Shinn. 1 cass. bk. 39.95 (CP-1) Duane Shinn.
Learn how to play chord-style piano with this ten-day course in chording.

How to Play Country-Western Piano. Duane Shinn. 1 cass. 19.95 incl. bk. (PS-6) Duane Shinn.
Learn how to create a "country twang" & other western sounds.

How to Play Djembe: West African Rhythms for Beginners. Alan Dworsky & Betsy Sansby. 2000. bk. 24.95 (978-0-9638801-4-7(4)) Pub: Dancing Hands. Dist(s): SCB Distributors

How To Play Harmonica Instantly! Marcos Habif. 1985. pap. bk. (978-0-936601-77-9(9)) Harmonica Music.

How to Play Harmonica Instantly. Marcos Habif. 1 cass. (Running Time: 1 hr.). (J). 1985. incl. Hohner Harmonica. (978-0-936601-47-2(7)) Harmonica Music.
Complete How-to-play Harmonica for beginners to Blues style.

How to Play Harmonica Instantly! Piano/Keyboard. Marcos Habif. (How to Play Ser.). (J). 1985. bk. (978-0-936601-87-8(6)) Harmonica Music.

How to Play Lush, Modern, "Mood" Piano. Duane Shinn. 1 cass. bk. 39.95 (CP-4) Duane Shinn.
Teaches extended chords, chord substitutions, polytonality, chord prediction techniques & improvisation.

How to Play Piano by Ear. Duane Shinn. 1 cass. 39.95 (CP-5) Duane Shinn.
Teaches how to "chart" a tune so you can pick it out on the keyboard, all the types of chords & how they are used in playing by ear.

How to Play "Pop" Piano, Using the 2-Week Visualized Chording System. Duane Shinn. 1 cass. bk. 39.95 (CP-2) Duane Shinn.
Designed to teach playing "pop" piano, which means anything that can be played with "chording" in the left hand.

How to Play Rock Drums. Mary Hughes Shelton & Ruby T. Palmer. 1965. pap. bk. 18.95 (978-0-7390-1808-8(6), 176) Alfred Pub.

How to Play Rock Drums. Mary Hughes Shelton & Ruby T. Palmer. 1987. 8.95 (978-0-7390-1809-5(4), 171) Alfred Pub.

How to Play Roughly Half of All Songs Using Just Four Chords: I, IV, V, & I. Duane Shinn. 1 cass. 19.95 (HAR-13) Duane Shinn.
Discusses three chords in every key which are used more than any others. They are called the tonic (I), sub-dominant (IV) & dominant (V) chords. You'll also learn to match your melody note to these 3 chords, so you can harmonize simple songs. You'll learn the next-most-likely chord in each key. It's called the supertonic (II) chord.

How to Play Seven-String Guitar. Alan DeMause. 1999. pap. bk. 17.95 (978-0-7866-4115-4(0), 97113BCD) Mel Bay.

How to Play "Southern Style" Gospel Piano! 1 cass. pap. bk. 39.95 (PS-7) Duane Shinn.
This is more rhythmic than traditional gospel music, & uses a heavy tripletized beat. You can play any gospel song (or other music) in this style once you know how to create that special "Southern sound." You'll learn how to play Amazing Grace in this amazing style, & then apply the same technique to most any other gospel song.

How to Play the Finger Cymbals: Dallal's Tutorial for Belly Dancers. Perf. by Tamlyn Dallal. 1 cass. (Running Time: 1 hr.). 1996. pap. bk. 11.95 (978-1-890916-64-0(1)) Talion Pub.
Teaches basic rhythms & an excellent routine to music.

How to Play the Piano by Ear. Robert Laughlin. 5 cass. 1988. 99.00 Incl. textbk. & study guide. (978-0-929983-02-8(5)) New Schl Am Music.
Explains how to determine melodies & chord progressions to popular songs without the use of sheet music.

How to Play Twelve Christmas Carols on the Piano - This Christmas. Duane Shinn. 1 cass. bk. 39.95 (T-1) Duane Shinn.
Explains how to play "It Came Upon A Midnight Clear," "Joy to the World," "We Three Kings," "Silent Night," "Jingle Bells," "What Child is This?" (same as "Greensleeves"), "Away in a Manager," "Deck the Halls," "O Little Town of Bethlehem," "O Christmas Tree," "O Come All Ye Faithful," & "Good King Wenceslas".

How to Please a Woman in & Out of Bed. abr. ed. Daylle Deanna Schwartz. Read by Pamela Dillman. 2 cass. (Running Time: 3 hrs.). (For Men Ser.). 2001. 16.95 (978-1-885408-60-0(9), LL052) Listen & Live.
Provides you with new solutions for getting more from a woman - in & out of bed - without manipulating, arguing, or begging.

How to Please God. 1 cass. (Running Time: 60 min.). (Devotion Ser.). 9.95 (SC-7) Crystal Clarity.
Includes: Pleasing God as the sole reason for human life; how God blesses those who try to please Him; the diffemce between knowing & expressing God; why God's will, however inconvenient, is always right; how tests bring us closer to God.

How to Polka. unabr. ed. Conversa-Phone Institute Staff & Betty White. 1 cass. (Running Time: 55 min.). (Betty White's How to Ballroom Dance Ser.). 1990. 9.95 (978-1-56752-094-1(4)) Conversa-phone.
Teaches all of the most popular steps-breaks-turns - how to lead & how to follow. Fully illustrated instruction manual follows the audio tape. Learn today - dance tonight.

How to Position Yourself for Success: 12 Proven Strategies for Uncommon Achievement. rev. unabr. ed. Nido Qubein. Read by Nido Qubein. 4 CDs. (Running Time: 4 hrs. 30 mins.). (ENG.). 2008. audio compact disk 19.98 (978-1-59659-141-7(2), GildAudio) Pub: Gildan Media. Dist(s): HachBkGrp

How to Possess the Land Series. Kenneth E. Hagin. 5 cass. 1992. 20.00 Set. (68H) Faith Lib Pubns.

How to Practice: The Way to a Meaningful Life. unabr. ed. Dalai Lama XIV. Read by Jeffrey Hopkins. 2 cass. (Running Time: 50 hrs. 0 mins. 0 sec.). (ENG.). 2002. audio compact disk 30.00 (978-0-7435-0778-3(9), Sound Ideas) Pub: S&S Audio. Dist(s): S and S Inc
An instructional & inspirational guide broken down into the basic steps to enlightenment: how to practice morality, how to practice meditation & how to practice wisdom.

How to Practice: The Way to a Meaningful Life. unabr. ed. Dalai Lama XIV. Jeffrey Hopkins. 2006. 17.95 (978-0-7435-6373-4(5), Sound Ideas) Pub: S&S Audio. Dist(s): S and S Inc

How to Practice Adaptability, No. 2. Swami Jyotirmayananda. 1 cass. (Running Time: 1 hr.). 1990. 12.99 Yoga Res Foun.

How to Practice Adaptability II. (185) Yoga Res Foun.

How to Practice Austerity. (120) Yoga Res Foun.

How to Practice Discrimination. 1 cass. (Running Time: 1 hr.). 12.99 (210) Yoga Res Foun.

How to Practice Discrimination, No. 2. Swami Jyotirmayananda. 1 cass. (Running Time: 1 hr.). 1990. 12.99 Yoga Res Foun.

How to Practice Enquiry of "Who Am I?" 1 cass. (Running Time: 1 hr.). 12.99 (169) Yoga Res Foun.

How to Practice Integral Yoga. Swami Jyotirmayananda. 1 cass. (Running Time: 1 hr.). 1990. 12.99 Yoga Res Foun.

How to Practice Internal Yoga. 1 cass. (Running Time: 1 hr.). 12.99 (182) Yoga Res Foun.

How to Practice Introspection. 1 cass. (Running Time: 1 hr.). 12.99 (139) Yoga Res Foun.

How to Practice Japa. Swami Jyotirmayananda. (133) Yoga Res Foun.

How to Practice Japa, No. 1. Swami Jyotirmayananda. 1 cass. (Running Time: 1 hr.). 1990. 12.99 Yoga Res Foun.

How to Practice Japa, No. 2. Swami Jyotirmayananda. (172) Yoga Res Foun.

How to Practice Japa, No. 2. Swami Jyotirmayananda. 1 cass. (Running Time: 1 hr.). 1990. 12.99 Yoga Res Foun.

How to Practice Kundalini Yoga. Swami Jyotirmayananda. 1 cass. (Running Time: 1 hr.). 12.99 (116) Yoga Res Foun.

How to Practice Kundalini Yoga, No. 2. Swami Jyotirmayananda. (175) Yoga Res Foun.

How to Practice Kundalini Yoga, No. 2. Swami Jyotirmayananda. 1 cass. (Running Time: 1 hr.). 1990. 12.99 Yoga Res Foun.

How to Practice Meditation. (124) Yoga Res Foun.

How to Practice Meditation. Swami Jyotirmayananda. 1 cass. (Running Time: 1 hr.). 1990. 12.99 Yoga Res Foun.

How to Practice Moderation. 1 cass. (Running Time: 1 hr.). 12.99 (195) Yoga Res Foun.

How to Practice Relaxation. 1 cass. (Running Time: 1 hr.). 12.99 (132) Yoga Res Foun.

How to Practice Relaxation, No. 2. 1 cass. (Running Time: 1 hr.). 12.99 (160) Yoga Res Foun.

How to Practice Self-Discipline. (200) Yoga Res Foun.

How to Practice Self-Discipline. Swami Jyotirmayananda. 1 cass. (Running Time: 1 hr.). 1990. 12.99 Yoga Res Foun.

How to Practice Truth. 1 cass. (Running Time: 1 hr.). 12.99 (176) Yoga Res Foun.

How to Practice Truth, No. 2. Swami Jyotirmayananda. 1 cass. (Running Time: 1 hr.). 1990. 12.99 Yoga Res Foun.

How to Practice Truthfulness. 1 cass. (Running Time: 1 hr.). 12.99 (125) Yoga Res Foun.

How to Practice Vairagya (Dispassion), No. 2. Swami Jyotirmayananda. 1 cass. (Running Time: 1 hr.). 1990. 12.99 Yoga Res Foun.

How to Practice Vairagya (Dispassion), No. 3. Swami Jyotirmayananda. 1 cass. (Running Time: 1 hr.). 1990. 12.99 Yoga Res Foun.

How to Practice Vairagya (Dispassion) II. (182) Yoga Res Foun.

How to Practice Vedic Astrology: A Beginner's Guide to Casting Your Horoscope & Predicting Your Future. Andrew Bloomfield. 2003. bk. 29.95 (978-0-89281-085-7(8), Destiny Bks) Inner Tradit.

How to Pray. 2 cass. (Running Time: 3 hrs.). 2004. 19.99 (978-1-58602-210-5(5)); audio compact disk 39.99 (978-1-58602-211-2(3)) E L Long.

How to Pray. 1 cass. (Running Time: 1 hr.). 12.99 (201); (119) Yoga Res Foun.

***How to Pray.** unabr. ed. R. A. Torrey. Narrated by David Cochran Heath. (ENG.). 2005. 9.98 (978-1-59644-070-8(8), Hovel Audio) christianaud.

How to Pray. unabr. ed. R. A. Torrey. Narrated by David Cochran Heath. 2 CDs. (Running Time: 2 hrs. 30 mins. 0 sec.). (ENG.). 2005. audio compact disk 15.98 (978-1-59644-068-5(6), Hovel Audio) christianaud.
How to Pray is a gripping call to prayer. Pastor, educator, evangelist, and author R.A. Torrey delivers a no-nonsense handbook for praying correctly and receiving answers from God. The book is full of examples, stories and anecdotes that inwardly compel the listener to pray heartily. Topics covered include the importance of prayer, praying in the Spirit, constancy in prayer, and hindrances to prayer.

How to Pray, No. 2. 1 cass. (Running Time: 1 hr.). 12.99 (177) Yoga Res Foun.

How to Pray, No. 3. Swami Jyotirmayananda. 1 cass. (Running Time: 1 hr.). 1990. 12.99 Yoga Res Foun.

How to Pray: Matthew 6:5-8. Ed Young. (J). 1979. 4.95 (978-0-7417-1069-7(2), A0069) Win Walk.

How to Pray & Get What You Pray For. Derek Prince. 2 cass. 11.90 Set. (018-019) Derek Prince.
Successful prayer is positive confident access to God, bringing us unique joy as we see Him answer.

How to Pray for One Hour. Creflo A. Dollar. 15.00 (978-1-59089-094-3(9)) Pub: Creflo Dollar. Dist(s): STL Dist NA

How to Predict Which Chord Comes Next. Duane Shinn. 1 cass. 19.95 (CP-8) Duane Shinn.
Explains how to predict next chord to occur in a piece of music, popular, sacred, classical, or whatever.

How to Prepare a Winning Proposal: An Effective System to Sell Your Product, Project or Idea. Patricia Cramer. 2 cass. (Running Time: 2 hrs. 28 min.). 29.95 Set. (V10124) CareerTrack Pubns.
This program gives you a clear-cut system for writing compelling proposals - faster, more easily & with better results. You'll learn how to create irresistible proposals while saving yourself hours of frustration...gain the confidence that comes from knowing you've done a thorough, professional job...& get your proposals accepted enthusiastically.

How to Prepare an Initial Public Offering. unabr. ed. Contrib. by Candace K. Beinecki. 7 cass. (Running Time: 10 hrs.). 1989. 50.00 course handbk. (T7-9224) PLI.
An experienced faculty analyzes in depth the nuts & bolts of an initial public offering in the current market climate, with particular emphasis on the registration & underwriting process. Topics of discussion in this recording of PLI's July 1989 program include: selected current issues in IPOs, planning considerations & the corporate clean-up, drafting the registration statement & other aspects of accomplishing an initial registration, accounting issues, underwriting arrangements & documentation, SEC procedures & priorities, an overview of post-offering considerations & requirements.

How to Prepare & Use the Trial Notebook for Trial & Settlement. Contrib. by Thomas J. Vesper. (Running Time: 4 hrs.). 1985. 85.00 incl. program handbook. NJ Inst CLE.
Reveals how a trial notebook assists in meeting obligations under the court's civil case management theories, various approaches in preparing a trial notebook, step-by-step procedures in developing a trial notebook.

How to Prepare for a Malpractice Trial. Moderated by John E. Connolly. 2 cass. (General Sessions Ser.: Spring 1986). 1986. 15.00 (8608) Am Coll Surgeons.

How to Prepare for Marriage: 1 Cor. 7:12-16; Phil. 2:3-11. Ed Young. 1996. 4.95 (978-0-7417-2100-6(7), 1100) Win Walk.

How to Prepare for the Advanced Placement Test: Spanish. 2nd ed. Alice G. Springer. (SPA & ENG., 1997. pap. bk. 24.95 (978-0-7641-7022-5(8)) Barron.

How to Prepare for the Michigan Test Battery. Pamela J. Sharpe. 1982. suppl. ed. 8.95 (978-0-8120-2564-4(4)) Barron.

How to Prepare for the PRAXIS. 2nd rev. ed. Robert D. Postman. 1CD . 1999. pap. bk. 21.95 (978-0-7641-7140-6(2)) Barron.
Includes NTE corebattery, PPE professional skills (PPST) computer based test (CBT) & principles of leaming & teaching (PLT) a practice test & answers.

How to Prepare for the SAT II Spanish. 8th rev. ed. Christopher Kendris. 1 CD. (Running Time: 60 Min.). (SPA.). (C). 1999. pap. bk. 18.95 (978-0-7641-7142-0(9), BA897) Barron.
Listening Comprehension sections on compact disc & ten practice tests w/answers & explanations.

How to Prepare for the TOEFL: Test of English As a Foreign Language. 8th ed. Pamela J. Sharpe. 1996. 21.95 (978-0-8120-8422-1(5)) Barron.

How to Prepare for the TOEFL: Test of English As a Foreign Language. 9th ed. Pamela J. Sharpe. 1 CD. 1999. audio compact disk 19.95 (978-0-7641-7295-3(6)) Barron.

How to Prepare for the TOEFL: Test of English as a Foreign Language. 9th ed. Pamela J. Sharpe. 1 cass. 1999. Barron.

How to Prepare the Family Settlement Agreement & Final Account. 1 cass. 1990. bk. 45.00 (AC-555) PA Bar Inst.

How to Prepare the Federal Estate Tax Return. 1 cass. 1990. bk. 45.00 (AC-553) PA Bar Inst.

How to Prepare the Fiduciary & Decedent's Final Income Tax Returns. 1 cass. 1990. bk. 45.00 (AC-554) PA Bar Inst.

How to Prepare the Pennsylvania Inheritance Tax Return. 1998. bk. 99.00 (ACS-2014); bk. 99.00 (ACS-2014) PA Bar Inst.
Get "how-to-do-it" advice about how to prepare the Pennsylvania inheritance tax retum & accompanying schedules. Experienced estate planners & key representative from the Department of Revenue, Inheritance Tax Division, fill you in as authors on common traps & pitfalls & clear up the questions you may have.

How to Prepare the Pennsylvania Inheritance Tax Return. 1 cass. 1990. bk. 45.00 (AC-552) PA Bar Inst.

How to Prepare Your Heart. Created by AWMI. (ENG.). 2000. 20.00 (978-1-59548-089-7(7)); audio compact disk 20.00 (978-1-59548-090-3(0)) A Wommack.

How to Prepare Your Heart. Concept by AWMI. (ENG.). 2000. audio compact disk 20.00 (978-1-59548-024-8(2)) A Wommack.

How to Present a Professional Image: Build Your Personal Power & Professional Impact. Carol Price. 4 cass. (Running Time: 4 hrs. 5 min.). 59.95 Set. (V10097) CareerTrack Pubns.
Attention managers: Are the women in your organization moving up? This program will give them practical, career-boosting tips. They'll learn how to build a professional image that people notice, respect & respond to.

How to Present & Challenge Experts in Employment Cases: Persuading the Jury. 3 cass. (Running Time: 3 hrs. 30 min.). 1994. 155.00 Set; incl. study guide. (M130) Am Law Inst.
Using demonstrations of the cross examination of five expert witnesses in a hypothetical disability rights case, this program analyzes the current trends affecting the litigation of employment claims.

How to Prevent Crime in Our Society. (136) Yoga Res Foun.

How to Prevent Crime in Our Society. Swami Jyotirmayananda. 1 cass. (Running Time: 1 hr.). 1990. 12.99 Yoga Res Foun.

How to Prevent Drug Addiction. 1 cass. (Running Time: 1 hr.). 12.99 (138) Yoga Res Foun.

How to profit from today's rapid Changes. Robert Tucker. 2004. 7.95 (978-0-7435-4842-7(6)) Pub: S&S Audio. Dist(s): S and S Inc

How to Promote Cheerfulness. Swami Jyotirmayananda. Read by Swami Jyotirmayananda. 1 cass. (Running Time: 60 min.). 12.99 (104) Yoga Res Foun.

How to Promote English Correctly see Como Pronunciar Ingles Correctamente

How to Promote Mental Health. (147) Yoga Res Foun.

How to Promote Mental Health, No. 1. Swami Jyotirmayananda. 1 cass. (Running Time: 1 hr.). 1990. 12.99 Yoga Res Foun.

How to Promote Religious Unity. Swami Jyotirmayananda. 1 cass. (Running Time: 1 hr.). 1990. 12.99 Yoga Res Foun.

How to Promote Sattwa. 1 cass. (Running Time: 1 hr.). 12.99 (208) Yoga Res Foun.

How to Promote Sattwa. Swami Jyotirmayananda. 1 cass. (Running Time: 45 min.). 1990. 10.00 Yoga Res Foun.

How to Promote Self-Analysis. 1 cass. (Running Time: 1 hr.). 12.99 (163) Yoga Res Foun.

How to Promote Thought Power. (186) Yoga Res Foun.

How to Promote Thought Power. Swami Jyotirmayananda. 1 cass. (Running Time: 1 hr.). 1990. 12.99 Yoga Res Foun.

How to Promote True Culture. (134) Yoga Res Foun.

How to Promote True Culture. Swami Jyotirmayananda. 1 cass. (Running Time: 1 hr.). 1990. 12.99 Yoga Res Foun.

How to Promote Unity among Religions. 1 cass. (Running Time: 1 hr.). 12.99 (137) Yoga Res Foun.

How to Promote Unity of Man. Swami Jyotirmayananda. (148) Yoga Res Foun.

How to Promote Unity of Man. Swami Jyotirmayananda. 1 cass. (Running Time: 1 hr.). 1990. 12.99 Yoga Res Foun.

How to Promote Universal Love. 1 cass. (Running Time: 1 hr.). 12.99 (164) Yoga Res Foun.

How to Promote Wisdom. (121) Yoga Res Foun.

How to Promote Wisdom. Swami Jyotirmayananda. 1 cass. (Running Time: 1 hr.). 1990. 12.99 Yoga Res Foun.

***How to Promote Yourself & Your Business: Confessions of an Unashamed, Relentless Self Promoter.** Patricia Fripp. (ENG.). 2010. 40.00 (978-0-9815589-2-9(5)) Acanthus Pubg.

How to Promote Yourself Through Public Speaking. Nido R. Qubein. Read by Nido R. Qubein. 6 cass. (Professional Services Library). 69.95 Set. (498AD) Nightingale-Conant.
Discover key elements for distinguishing yourself in the marketplace, workable strategies for building yourself into a profitable entity, techniques for refining your professional image, & more.

How to Pronounce French Correctly. Stanley W. Connell & Dominique Poiriel. (How to Pronounce Ser.). (FRE.). 1995. audio compact disk 23.95 (978-0-8442-1518-1(X), 1518X, Contemporary) McGraw-Hill Trade.

How to Pronounce Japanese Correctly. Stanley W. Connell & Yoshio Satoh. 1 cass. (Running Time: 1 hr.). 1991. 19.95 (Passport Bks) McGraw-Hill Trade.

How to Pronounce Russian Correctly. unabr. ed. 1 cass. (Running Time: 55 mins.). (RUS.). bk. 24.95 (SRU125) J Norton Pubs.
Native speakers explain, illustrate & drill the basic sounds of Russian with emphasis on problem areas for English speakers.

How to Pronounce Spanish Correctly. Stanley W. Connell. (Running Time: 060 min.). (How to Pronounce Ser.). (SPA.). 1995. audio compact disk 19.95 (978-0-8442-7383-9(X), 7383X, Contemporary) McGraw-Hill Trade.

How to Prospect Your Way to Millions. 1971. audio compact disk (978-0-89811-281-8(8)) Meyer Res Grp.

How to Prospect Your Way to Millions. Paul J. Meyer. 1 cass. (Running Time: 30 min.). 11.00 (978-0-89811-077-7(7), 7128); Meyer Res Grp.
Learn to develop a prospect awareness.

How to Prospect Your Way to Millions. Paul J. Meyer. 1 cass. 10.00 (SP100025) SMI Intl.
If you spend hours driving aimlessly or drinking coffee because you have no one to call on, you'll welcome "How to Prospect Your Way to Millions". Listen & develop a prospect awareness. Fill your day with opportunity & your bank account with commissions.

How to Prosper in a Downturn: Your Path to Success & Fulfillment in the Next Ten Years. abr. ed. Harry S. Dent. Read by Harry S. Dent. (Running Time: 2 hrs. 0 mins. 0 sec.). (ENG.). 2010. audio compact disk 19.99 (978-1-4423-0064-4(7), Nightgale) Pub: S&S Audio. Dist(s): S and S Inc

How to Prosper in Hard Times. unabr. ed. Napoleon Hill & James Allen. (Running Time: 6 hrs.). (ENG.). (gr. 12 up). 2009. audio compact disk 29.95 (978-0-14-314482-3(0), PengAudBks) Penguin Grp USA.

***How to Prosper in the Age of Obamanomics: A Ruff Plan for Times Ahead.** Howard Ruff. (ENG.). 2010. 6.99 (978-0-9827081-2-5(2)) AuthorsDig.

How to Protect Your Child from Becoming a Missing Person. unabr. ed. Carolyn Anderson. Read by Carolyn Anderson. 1 cass. (Running Time: 30 min.). Dramatization. (J). (ps-7). 1992. pap. bk. & wbk. ed. 5.00 (978-1-883778-00-2(X)) Starlite Prods.
Tells parents how to spot potential kidnappers; shows parents how to get child to tell them problems that could be a danger to them.

How to Protect Your Child from Becoming a Missing Person. unabr. ed. Carolyn Anderson. Read by Carolyn Anderson. 1 cass. (Running Time: 30 min.). Dramatization. 1993. pap. bk. 12.00 Starlite Prods.

How to Protect Your Rights. Based on a book by W. Cleon Skousen, 1st. 2007. audio compact disk 11.95 (978-1-4276-3078-0(X)) AardGP.

How to Provide Excellent Customer Service. Linda Fracassi. Read by Linda Fracassi. 6 cass. (Running Time: 4 hrs. 21 min.). 1990. 59.95 Set, incl. wkbk. (978-1-878542-10-6(9), 11-0608) SkillPath Pubns.
Provides tips on how to provide quality customer service, including why customers leave, how to set customer service goals, improving listening skills, handling delicate situations, etc.

How to Psych Out Test Anxiety: A Revolutionary Cure for Test-A-Phobia. Frances M. Stern. Read by Frances Meritt Stern. 1 cass. (Running Time: 68 min.). 1992. 12.95 (978-1-884435-08-9(4)) Inst Behavior.
Self-help techniques to reduce test anxiety.

How to Publish Your Own Book & Earn a Fifty Thousand Dollar Profit. unabr. ed. Gordon Burgett. 2 cass. (Running Time: 2 hrs.). 1996. 30.00 Set, incl. wkbk. (978-0-910167-30-7(3)) Comm Unltd CA.
Explains how to publish a niche book.

How to Put More Time in Your Life. Dru Scott. 1 cass. (Running Time: 60 min.). 1999. 10.95 (978-0-9660527-8-7(1)) Bridgecross Pr.
Helps you find the time tools that fit your personality, your pressures & your priorities. This world-famous expert in success training helps you build a self-motivating, flexible program that works for you. It moves beyond traditional time management by combining classic time techniques with a new people-oriented approach.

How to Put Sell & Sales into Selling. Paul Stanyard. 1 cass. 12.50 Alpha Tape.

How to Put Undernotes under Your Right-Hand Melody. 1 cass. 19.95 Incl. summary sheet. (CP-18) Duane Shinn.
Teaches how to put harmonizing notes in your right hand, under the melody. Adds a great deal to the sound produced by your right hand, & applies to any & all styles.

How to Put Your Marriage under the Anointing. Leroy Tompson, Sr. 2002. 10.00 (978-1-931804-11-0(7)) Ever Increase Wd Min.

How to Qualify for the Marital Deduction. Edward S. Schlesinger. 1 cass. (Running Time: 90 min.). 1995. 17.40 (M226) Am Law Inst.
This tape examines ways to qualify for the marital deduction through outright dispositions & trusts.

How to quit smoking without gaining Weight. Martin Katahn. 2004. 9.95 (978-0-7435-4851-9(5)) Pub: S&S Audio. Dist(s): S and S Inc

How to Raise a Child of God (Selections) Tara Singh. Read by Charles Johnson. 2 cass. (Running Time: 3 hrs. 13 min.). (Books on Cassette Ser.). 1987. 17.95 (978-1-55531-184-1(9), #A153) Life Action Pr.
Explores marriage, conception, childhood through puberty, & education. Offers insight into the learning process & advises parents on how to deal with the issue of education in today's world.

How to Raise an Mvp: Most Valuable Person. abr. ed. Zondervan Publishing Staff et al. (Running Time: 2 hrs. 0 mins. 0 sec.). (ENG.). 2003. 8.99 (978-0-310-26061-5(2)) Zondervan.

How to Raise an MVP: Real World Advice to Help Your Children Be Winners in Life. Ambrose Robinson et al. 2 cass. (Running Time: 60 min. per cass.). 1996. 14.99 Set. (978-0-310-20967-6(6)) Zondervan.
The parents of David Robinson, the 1995 MVP for the NBA & off-the-court activist, philanthropist, & Christian role-model, detail David & his siblings' upbringings & share real-world advice on how to help your children be winners in life.

How to Raise Capital for a Growing Business. unabr. ed. Center for Entrepreneurial Management Staff. 1 cass. (Running Time: 1 hr. 17 min.). 12.95 (1362) J Norton Pubs.
How to obtain both types of capital - debt & equity. Specifics about SBA financing, bank loans & venture capital, where to obtain money.

How to raise emotionally healthy Children: Meeting the five critical needs of children & parents too! updated Edition. 2009. audio compact disk 29.95 (978-0-932767-16-5(8)) NMI Pubs.

How to Raise Happy, Confident Kids. Ed Bliss. 2 cass. 1995. 15.95 (978-1-55977-033-0(3)) CareerTrack Pubns.

How to Raise Happy, Healthy, Self-Confident Children. Brian S. Tracy & Bettie B. Youngs. 6 cass. 49.95 Set. (563PAB) Nightingale-Conant.
Learn how to talk to your kids so they'll listen & understand. Find ways to build a foundation of basic values for your children that will last a lifetime. And discover the keys to strengthening your children's self-confidence in everything they do.

How to Raise Healthy Achieving Children. Bruce A. Baldwin. Read by Bruce A. Baldwin. 1 cass. (Running Time: 40 min.). 1986. 7.95 (978-0-933583-05-4(2), PDC#875) Direction Dynamics.
Book on Tape: Chapter from "It's All in Your Head." Discusses the problems of achievement-oriented parents who often systematically reinforce children in ways that diminish the personal security needed to become a healthy achieving adult. The "3-P Method" of healthy parental response is defined along with seven new directions to build a solid base of personal security in children.

How to Raise Parents... in These Troubled Times. Clayton Barbeau. 2 cass. (Running Time: 1 hr. per cass.). 19.95 (9246) Franciscan Comns.
Discusses some do's & don'ts of interpersonal communication, adolescence vs. middlescence, premature sex & its consequences, Parental authority & the maturing teen, the right to privacy, the freedom to make mistakes.

How to Raise You Family. Narrated by John MacArthur, Jr. & Gary Ezzo. 4 cass. 13.95 (20131, HarperThor) HarpC GBR.

***How to Raise Your Adult Children: Because Big Kids Have Even Bigger Problems.** unabr. ed. Gail Parent & Susan Ende. (Running Time: 11 hrs. 0 mins.). 2010. 17.99 (978-1-4001-8830-7(X)) Tantor Media.

***How to Raise Your Adult Children: Because Big Kids Have Even Bigger Problems.** unabr. ed. Gail Parent & Susan Ende. Narrated by Karen White. (Running Time: 10 hrs. 0 mins. 0 sec.). (ENG.). 2010. 24.99 (978-1-4001-6830-9(9)); audio compact disk 83.99 (978-1-4001-4830-1(8)); audio compact disk 34.99 (978-1-4001-1830-4(1)) Pub: Tantor Media. Dist(s): IngramPubServ

How to Raise Your Family: Biblical Essentials for No-Regret Parenting. Interview with John MacArthur, Jr. & Gary Ezzo. 4 cass. 13.95 (20131, HarperThor) HarpC GBR.

How to Raise Your Fees & Get More Bookings with Publicity. 2000. 25.00 (978-1-930039-07-0(7)) Morgan Seminar.

How to Reach Baby Boomers. bk. 13.00 (978-0-687-76222-4(7)) Abingdon.

***How to Reach Your Full Potential for God: Never Settle for Less Than His Best.** unabr. ed. Charles F. Stanley. Read by Arthur Morey. (Running Time: 7 hrs. 48 mins. 0 sec.). (ENG.). 2010. audio compact disk 24.98 (978-1-59644-886-5(5)) christianaud.

***How to Reach Your Full Potential for God: Never Settle for Less Than His Best!** unabr. ed. Charles F. Stanley. Narrated by Arthur Morey. (ENG.). 2010. 14.98 (978-1-59644-887-2(3)) christianaud.

How to Reach Your Goals see Còmo Alcanzar Sus Metas

How to Reach Your Goals. Mario Elnerz. Read by Pedro Montoya. (Running Time: 3 hrs.). (C). 2001. 16.95 (978-1-60083-266-6(0), Audiofy Corp) Iofy Corp.

How to Read a Book. unabr. ed. Mortimer J. Adler & Charles Van Doren. Read by Patrick Cullen. 11 cass. (Running Time: 16 hrs.). 2004. 76.95 (978-0-7861-1286-9(7), 2184) Blckstn Audio.
Completely rewritten & updated, including a recommended reading list & supplied reading tests whereby the user can measure their own progress in reading skills, comprehension & speed.

How to Read a Book. unabr. ed. Mortimer J. Adler & Charles Van Doren. Read by Patrick Cullen. (Running Time: 16 hrs.). 1998. 76.95 (978-0-7861-1048-3(1)) Blckstn Audio.

How to Read a Chart. Doris C. Doane. 1 cass. 8.95 (514) Am Fed Astrologers.
Synthesize four basics.

How to Read & Decipher the Department of Defense (DoD) Budget: Capitol Learning Audio Course. Stephen Daggett. Prod. by TheCapitol.Net. (ENG.). 2008. 47.00 (978-1-58733-074-2(1)) TheCapitol.

How to Read & Understand Drama. audio compact disk 53.97 (978-0-13-435349-4(8)) P-H.

***How to Read & Understand Financial Statements.** PUEI. 2007. audio compact disk 199.00 (978-1-935041-89-4(4), CareerTrack) P Univ E Inc.

How to Read & Understand Poetry, Pts. I-II. Instructed by Willard Spiegelman. 12 cass. (Running Time: 12 hrs.). 1999. 129.95 (978-1-56585-051-4(3)); audio compact disk 69.95 (978-1-56585-305-8(9)) Teaching Co.

How to Read & Understand Poetry, Vol. 2. Instructed by Willard Spiegelman. 6 cass. (Running Time: 6 hrs.). 1999. 129.95 (978-1-56585-052-1(1)); audio compact disk 179.95 (978-1-56585-306-5(7)) Teaching Co.

How to Read & Why. Harold Bloom. Narrated by John McDonough. 8 cass. (Running Time: 11 hrs. 15 mins.). 2000. 74.00 (978-1-4025-0692-5(9), 96925) Recorded Bks.
The great scholar exhorts readers to consider the pleasures and benefits of reading well.

How to read & Why. Harold Bloom. Narrated by John McDonough. 10 CDs. (Running Time: 11 hrs. 15 mins.). audio compact disk 98.00 (978-1-4025-2089-1(1)) Recorded Bks.

How to Read Financial Statements. PUEI. 2007. audio compact disk 199.00 (978-1-934147-10-8(9), CareerTrack) P Univ E Inc.

How to Read for Everyday Living, Set 1. Eunice Insel & Ann Edson. 5 cass. (J). (gr. 5-6). 89.00 incl. 8 activity bks., manual incl. activity masters, manual. (978-0-89525-027-8(6), AMC 592) Ed Activities.
Teaches the necessary skills to read real-life materials & introduces a basic vocabulary dealing with a subject with which students must cope...from labels to pay checks. Includes reading, interpreting & following directions, lost & found ads, warranties, newspaper ads, recipes, menus, learner's permit, schedules, road signs, help-wanted ads, job applications, savings accounts, deposits, etc.

How to Read for Everyday Living, Set 2. Eunice Insel & Ann Edson. 5 cass. (YA). (gr. 5-6). 89.00 incl. 8 activity bks., manual. (AKC 593) Ed Activities.
Teaches the necessary skills to read real-life materials & introduces a basic vocabulary dealing with a subject with which students must cope...from labels to paychecks. Includes clothing care & food labels, appliances, coupons, train schedules, first aid, road maps, coin-operated machines, library cards, contracts, social security, driver's license, telephone directories, etc.

How to Read in the Content Areas, Set 1. Eunice Insel & A. N. Rabin. 5 cass. (J). (gr. 3-4). 79.00 incl. 10 activity bks., manual. (978-0-89525-624-9(X), AKC 590) Ed Activities.
Introduces vocabulary, reinforces words in context, has a relevant math, science, history & literature reading selection & a comprehensive skill-builder follow-up. Provides students with vocabulary development, structural & contextual application of reading skills in the subject matter areas.

How to Read Music . . . in One Evening. Duane Shinn. 1 cass. bk. 39.95 (MR-1) Duane Shinn.
Reduces music to its 3 basic elements: melody, rhythm, & harmony, & then shows how each element can be mastered almost overnight. Drawings make the book fun to read & act as "memory joggers" so that you won't forget what you've learned.

How to Read Tarot Cards. Marion Weinstein. 2006. audio compact disk 14.99 (978-1-890733-07-0(5)) Earth Magic.

How to Read Tarot Cards: A Live Workshop With Marion Weinstein. Marion Weinstein. 1 cass. (Running Time: 1 hrs.). (Dealing with the Future Ser.: Vol. 1). 1999. 10.00 (978-1-890733-01-8(6)) Earth Magic.
Learn to use one of the world's most powerful tools for self-understanding, personal growth & problem solving. You can read for yourself & for your friends.

How to Read Teresa & John: Interpretation of Religious Classics. Constance FitzGerald. 1 cass. (Voices of John & Teresa Ser.). 1987. 7.95 (TAH176) Alba Hse Comns.
Looks at interpretation using hermeneutics, exegesis, isogesis, along with personal & communal interpretation.

How to Read the Akashic Records: Accessing the Archive of the Soul & Its Journey. unabr. ed. Linda Howe. (Running Time: 6:27:59). 2009. audio compact disk 69.95 (978-1-59179-676-3(8)) Sounds True.

How to Read the Bible: A Guide to Scripture, Then & Now. unabr. ed. James L. Kugel. Read by Mel Foster. 2 MP3-CDs. (Running Time: 36 hrs.). 2008. 49.97 (978-1-4233-6580-8(1), 9781423365808, Brinc Audio MP3 Lib); 49.97 (978-1-4233-6582-2(8), 9781423365822, BADLE); 34.99 (978-1-4233-6581-5(X), 9781423365815, BAD); 34.99 (978-1-4233-6579-2(8), 9781423365792, Brilliance MP3); audio compact disk 119.97 (978-1-4233-6578-5(X), 9781423365785, BriAudCD Unabrid); audio compact disk 44.99 (978-1-4233-6577-8(1), 9781423365778, Bril Audio CD Unabri) Brilliance Audio.

How to Read the Natal Chart. Joan Titsworth. 1 cass. 8.95 (718) Am Fed Astrologers.
An AFA Convention workshop tape.

How to Realize 'Inaction' in Action. (187) Yoga Res Foun.

How to Realize "Inaction" in Action. Swami Jyotirmayananda. 1 cass. (Running Time: 1 hr.). 1990. 12.99 Yoga Res Foun.

How to Realize the Self. Swami Amar Jyoti. 1 cass. 1981. 9.95 (M-15) Truth Consciousness.
It is easy to realize the Self, but difficult to give up ego. Maintaining an inward gaze. Knowing the true nature of things.

How to Rebuild Your Broken World Series. 2005. audio compact disk 27.00 (978-1-59834-039-6(5)) Walk Thru the Bible.

How to Receive a Miracle. 3 CDs. 2004. audio compact disk 21.00 (978-1-59548-017-0(X)) A Wommack.

How to Receive a Miracle. Wommack, Andrew, Ministeries, Inc. Staff. 3 cass. (Running Time: 4 hrs. 40 min.). 14.00 Set. (978-1-881541-03-5(7), 1006) A Wommack.
There are times when we do need a miracle in our lives. This series goes beyond simply hoping for a miracle. The Bible tells us how to reach out & take hold of God's power.

***How to Receive a Miracle from God.** abr. ed. Reinhard Bonnke. (ENG.). 2010. audio compact disk (978-1-936081-04-2(0)) Casscomm.

How to Receive Blessings. Elbert Willis. 1 cass. (Financial Prosperity Ser.). 4.00 Fill the Gap.

How to Receive from God. Shuttlesworth. (ENG.). 2008. audio compact disk 5.00 (978-0-9820619-0-9(0), Faith Alive WV) TSEA.

How to Receive God's Best. Kenneth E. Hagin. 1 cass. 4.95 (SH24) Faith Lib Pubns.

How to Receive the Baptism in the Holy Spirit. 4.95 (C13) Carothers.

How to Receive the End of Your Faith. Creflo A. Dollar. 20.00 (978-1-59089-083-7(3)) Pub: Creflo Dollar. Dist(s): STL Dist NA

How to Receive the Holy Spirit. Derek Prince. 1 cass. (B-3018) Derek Prince.

How To Receive Your Father's Love: John 3: 1-10. Ben Young. 1996. 4.95 (978-0-7417-6013-5(4), B0013) Win Walk.

How to Recognize & Reward Employees. 4 cass. pap. bk. & wbk. ed. 30.00 (978-0-7612-0732-0(5), 80193NQ1) AMACOM.
Reveals how recognizing & rewarding employees can increase productivity, pride, & commitment. You'll learn how to: Plan for & develop a reward system; Structure a reward program to fit varying employee needs; Maximize the factors that lead to peak performance; Dispel "old-fashioned" workplace beliefs that may hinder development of an effective reward system & much more.

How to Recognize & Reward Employees, Set. 4 cass. pap. bk. & wbk. ed. 155.00 2 multiple choice tests. (978-0-7612-0731-3(7), 80192NQ1) AMACOM.

How to Recognize Spiritual Promptings. unabr. ed. Duane S. Crowther. 13.98 (978-0-88290-499-3(X)) Horizon Utah.

How to Recognize Spiritual Promptings. unabr. ed. Duane S. Crowther. Read by Duane S. Crowther. 1 cass. (Running Time: 60 min.). 13.98 (1834) Horizon Utah.
Emphasizes the importance of listening for & acting on the promptings of the Holy Ghost. An excellent guide to basic principles of personal revelation reception.

How to Reconcile Second Force. Jack Boland. 1 cass. (Super Ser.). 8.00 (BI09A) Master Mind.

How to Recreate Your World. unabr. ed. Jack Boland. Read by Jack Boland. 4 cass. (Running Time: 4 hrs.). 34.95 set. (978-0-88152-054-5(3), BA20) Master Mind.

How to Recruit, Interview, & Select the Right Employee, Set. 3 cass. pap. bk. & wbk. ed. 139.00 incl. 2 multiple choice tests. (978-0-7612-0733-7(3),

An Asterisk (*) at the beginning of an entry indicates that the title is appearing for the first time.

80188NQ1); pap. bk. & wbk. ed. 30.00 (978-0-7612-0734-4(1), 80189NQ1) AMACOM.
Presents a structured, skills-based system that will improve your chances of hiring the right person. You'll learn how to: Develop an effective five-part recruiting strategy; Screen job applicants & zero in on the right ones to interview; Develop an interview plan to save time & avoid costly mistakes; Get to know the candidate by making sure they do most of the talking; Close an interview on a positive note to keep the candidate interested & much more.

How to Reduce Pennsylvania Corporate Taxes. 1987. bk. 95.00 incl. book.; 50.00 cass. only.; 45.00 book only. PA Bar Inst.

How to Relax. Brian A. Johnson. Read by Brian A. Johnson. 1 cass. (Running Time: 1 hr.). (Toren Ser.). 1995. bk. 12.95 (978-0-9650204-1-1(X)) Neurotechtonics.
Outlines a step by step method of relaxation (i.e. breathing, music, imagery etc.). Title of music track for background "Journey of the Soul".

How to Remain Free & Prevent War. Read by Leonard Liggio et al. (Running Time: 60 min.). (Cal State Univ., Long Beach). 1984. 9.00 (F169) Freeland Pr.
Gives insights into, & advice on, this controversial topic. Panel discussion.

How to Remain Happy see Como Mantenerse Contento

How to Remember God. (105) Yoga Res Foun.

How to Remember God, No. 2. Swami Jyotirmayananda. 1 cass. (Running Time: 1 hr.). 1990. 12.99 Yoga Res Foun.

How to Remember God II. (143) Yoga Res Foun.

How to Remember Jokes Set: And a Whole Bunch of Drop Dead Jokes to Get You Started. unabr. ed. Philip Van Munching. Read by Philip Van Munching. 2 cass. (Running Time: 3 hrs.). 1999. 17.00 (978-0-9668567-3-6(2)) MediaBay Audio.
Combining a simple four step process, a former beer executive & ad man will turn listeners into better joke-tellers.

How to Remove Anxiety. (173) Yoga Res Foun.

How to Remove Anxiety, No. 1. Swami Jyotirmayananda. 1 cass. (Running Time: 1 hr.). 1990. 12.99 Yoga Res Foun.

How to Remove False Pride. 1 cass. (Running Time: 1 hr.). 12.99 (112) Yoga Res Foun.

How to Remove Ignorance. 1 cass. (Running Time: 1 hr.). 12.99 (123) Yoga Res Foun.

How to Remove Jealousy. 1 cass. (Running Time: 1 hr.). 12.99 (109) Yoga Res Foun.

How to Remove Mental Abnormalities. 1 cass. (Running Time: 1 hr.). 12.99 (113) Yoga Res Foun.

How to Remove Mental Conflicts. (188) Yoga Res Foun.

How to Remove Mental Conflicts. Swami Jyotirmayananda. 1 cass. (Running Time: 1 hr.). 1990. 12.99 Yoga Res Foun.

How to Remove Mental Depression. (113) Yoga Res Foun.

How to Remove Mental Depression. Swami Jyotirmayananda. 1 cass. (Running Time: 1 hr.). 1990. 12.99 Yoga Res Foun.

How to Remove Misunderstanding. 1 cass. (Running Time: 1 hr.). 12.99 (146) Yoga Res Foun.

How to Remove Pain. 1 cass. (Running Time: 1 hr.). 12.99 (607) Yoga Res Foun.

How to Remove Vanity. 1 cass. (Running Time: 1 hr.). 12.99 (168) Yoga Res Foun.

How to Renew Your Mind for Increase. Creflo A. Dollar. 2 cass. (Running Time: 3 hrs.). 2000. 10.00 (978-1-931172-30-1(7), TS254, Kidz Faith) Pub: Creflo Dollar. Dist(s): STL Dist NA

How to Repent. Blaine Yorgason & Brenton Yorgason. Read by Marvin Payne. 1 cass. (Gospel Power Ser.). 6.95 (978-0-929985-44-2(3)) Jackman Pubng.
A father writing a letter to his son to help him understand repentance.

How to Rescue At-Risk Students. 2nd rev. ed. Sharon L. Briggs & Ginny O. Sorrell. 2 cass. (J). (gr. 4-12). 1991. bk. 20.00 incl. hdbk. Set. (978-0-9627409-2-3(6)) Sound Reading.
Explains, demonstrates, models, & gives step-by-step instructions for implementing Briggs/Sorrell Recorded Book Method in content courses with academically at-risk, LD or ESL students to improve grades, raise reading fluency, increase self-esteem, & prevent school failure. Includes classroom, school, & district-wide organizational plans.

***How to Resolve Customer Complaints on the Spot.** PUEI. 2008. audio compact disk 199.00 (978-1-935041-15-3(0), CareerTrack) P Univ E Inc.

How to Respond Counterintuitively to Dependent & Dominant Gifted Underachievers. unabr. ed. Sylvia Rimm. Read by Sylvia Rimm. 1 cass. (Running Time: 52 min.). 1993. 10.95 (978-0-937891-24-7(X), SR34A) Apple Pub Wisc.
Dr. Rimm shares information on how to sensitize teachers & parents to understanding gifted underachievers' defensive patterns.

How to Respond to the Trials of Life. Speeches. Joel Osteen. 1 Cass. (Running Time: 30 Mins.). (J). 1999. Rental 6.00 (978-1-59349-036-2(4), JA0036) J Osteen.

How to Respond to the Trials of Life. Joel Osteen. 2 audio cass. (J). 2001. 10.00 (978-1-931877-07-7(6)); audio compact disk 8.00 (978-1-931877-24-4(6), JCS003) J Osteen.

How to Respond to the Trials of Life. Speeches. Joel Osteen. 1 cass. (Running Time: 30 mins.). (J). 1999. 6.00 (978-1-59349-030-0(5), JA0031) J Osteen.

How to Retain & Train Your Best Salespeople: Best Practices & Strategies to Motivate, Incentivize & Empower. Phil Harris. 2009. 250.00 (978-1-59701-471-7(0)) ReedLogic.

***How to Retain the Best & Brightest Employees.** PUEI. 2008. audio compact disk 199.00 (978-1-935041-03-0(7), CareerTrack) P Univ E Inc.

How to Retire Rich: Time-Tested Strategies to Beat the Market & Retire in Style. abr. ed. James P. O'Shaughnessy. Read by Steve Pietrofesa. 2 cass. (Running Time: 3 hrs.). 1998. 17.95 Set. (978-1-55935-302-1(3)) Soundelux.
Powerful strategies to turn as little as $20,000 into as much as $17 million over time.

How to Rhumba. unabr. ed. Conversa-Phone Institute Staff & Betty White. 1 cass. (Running Time: 55 min.). (Betty White's How to Ballroom Dance Ser.). 1990. 9.95 (978-1-56752-090-3(1)) Conversa-phone.
Teaches all of the most popular steps-breaks-turns - how to lead & how to follow. Fully illustrated instruction manual follows the audio tape. Learn today - dance tonight.

How to Ride a Donkey: Luke 19:28-47. Ed Young. 1996. 4.95 (978-0-7417-2093-1(0), 1093) Win Walk.

How to Ruin Your Life. Ben Stein. 1 CD. 2003. audio compact disk 10.95 (978-1-4019-0238-4(3), 2383) Hay House.

How to Rule the Kingdom of the Mind. Kriyananda, pseud. 1 cass. 9.95 (ST-68) Crystal Clarity.
Topics include: Understanding that the "citizens" of our kingdom - our personal qualities - are not us; how our negative qualities work against us; ways to "wear down" negative qualities that we can't overcome at once; God's role in changing you.

How to Rule the World from Your Couch. abr. unabr. ed. Laura Day. Read by Laura Day. (Running Time: 7 hrs. 30 mins. 0 sec.). (ENG.). 2009. audio compact disk 29.99 (978-0-7435-9789-0(3)) Pub: S&S Audio. Dist(s): S and S Inc

How to Run a More Productive Legal Practice. Prod. by Advantage Legal Seminars. 2008. 177.00 (978-0-9795737-5-0(0)) Anzman Publg.

How to Run a Radio Show. Eugene Moore. 1 cass. (Running Time: 90 min.). 1984. 8.95 (243) Am Fed Astrologers.

How to run a successful meeting in 1/2 the Time. abr. ed. Milo O. Frank. 2004. 7.95 (978-0-7435-4852-6(3)) Pub: S&S Audio. Dist(s): S and S Inc

How to Run the Successful Summer Camp Program in Child Care. Dora C. Fowler. 6 cass. (Running Time: 6 hrs.). 1987. pap. bk. 49.00 Set, incl. 45p. bk. (978-1-57323-010-0(3)) Natl Inst Child Mgmt.

How to Run Your Business So It Doesn't Run You see Run Your Business So It Doesn't Run You

How to satisfy a man every time... & have him beg for More! Naura Hayden. 2004. 10.95 (978-0-7435-4853-3(1)) Pub: S&S Audio. Dist(s): S and S Inc

How to Satisfy a Woman Every Time - and Have Her Beg for More! unabr. ed. Naura Hayden. Read by Naura Hayden. (ENG.). 2009. audio compact disk 19.95 (978-1-59887-917-9(0), 1598879170) Pub: HighBridge. Dist(s): Workman Pub

How to Save a Relationship. Earnie Larsen. 1 cass. (Running Time: 1 hr.). 1989. 10.95 (978-1-56047-014-4(3), A118) E Larsen Enterprises.
Discusses what can be done - ones own involvement & the involvement of partner.

How to Save Fity Percent of Your Lifetime Income. unabr. ed. Vernon K. Jacobs. 1 cass. (Running Time: 36 min.). 12.95 (963) J Norton Pubs.
Shows you how to save up to $100,000 during your lifetime on taxes, insurance, interest & uninvested money.

How to Save Free Enterprise. Ronald Reagan. 1 CD. (Running Time: 56 MIN.). 2005. audio compact disk 12.95 (978-1-57970-221-2(X), AF0276D) J Norton Pubs.

How to Save Free Enterprise. unabr. ed. Ronald Reagan. 1 cass. (Running Time: 56 min.). 12.95 (276) J Norton Pubs.
Reagan offers hope that bureaucratic interference in private industry & business can be reduced & that free enterprise might once again raise its head above the dark cloud of liberalism.

How to Save, Maintain & Improve a Couple Relationship see Como Salvar, Mantener y Mejorar la Relacion de Pareja

How to Save, Maintain & Improve A Couple Relationship. Mario Elnerz. Read by Hernando Iván Cano. (Running Time: 1 hr.). (C). 2002. 14.95 (978-1-60083-142-3(7), Audiofy Corp) Iofy Corp.

How to Save on Everything You Buy. unabr. ed. Vernon K. Jacobs. 1 cass. (Running Time: 24 min.). 12.95 (962) J Norton Pubs.
Covers comparison shopping, irregulars & seconds, credit, when to buy a house, saving money on cars & furniture, how to take advantage of sales & auctions.

How to Save Your Own Life: 15 Lessons on Finding Hope in Unexpected Places. unabr. ed. Michael Gates Gill. (Running Time: 5 hrs. 30 mins.). 2009. audio compact disk 29.95 (978-1-4417-2096-2(0)) Blckstn Audio.

How to Save Your Own Life: 15 Lessons on Finding Hope in Unexpected Places. unabr. ed. Michael Gates Gill. Read by Michael Gates Gill. (Running Time: 5 hrs. 30 mins.). 2009. 29.95 (978-1-4417-2097-9(9)); 34.95 (978-1-4417-2093-1(6)); audio compact disk 55.00 (978-1-4417-2094-8(4)) Blckstn Audio.

How to Say Goodbye. Contrib. by Michael W. Smith. (Praise Hymn Soundtracks Ser.). 2007. audio compact disk 8.98 (978-5-557-71917-9(2)) Pt of Grace Ent.

***How to Say Goodbye in Robot.** unabr. ed. Natalie Standiford. (Running Time: 7 hrs.). 2010. 39.97 (978-1-4418-5974-7(8), 9781441859747, BADLE); 24.99 (978-1-4418-5973-0(X), 9781441859730, BAD); 24.99 (978-1-4418-5971-6(3), 9781441859716, Brilliance MP3) Brilliance Audio.

***How to Say Goodbye in Robot.** unabr. ed. Natalie Standiford. Read by Kate Rudd. (Running Time: 7 hrs.). 2010. 39.97 (978-1-4418-5972-3(1), 9781441859723, Brlnc Audio MP3 Lib); audio compact disk 29.99 (978-1-4418-5969-3(1), 9781441859693, Bril Audio CD Unabri); audio compact disk 69.97 (978-1-4418-5970-9(5), 9781441859709, BriAudCD Unabrid) Brilliance Audio.

How to Screw up & Stay in Buiness Interview Series - the Jingle Jungle. Chris Le Roy. (ENG.). 2009. audio compact disk 29.00 (978-1-921183-10-2(1)) One-on-One AUS.

How to Secure Goodwill of Others. (150) Yoga Res Foun.

How to Secure Goodwill of Others. Swami Jyotirmayananda. 1 cass. (Running Time: 1 hr.). 1990. 12.99 Yoga Res Foun.

How to See a Bad Play see Middle-Aged Man on the Flying Trapeze

How to See Our Imperfections. Swami Amar Jyoti. 1 cass. 1976. 9.95 (K-72) Truth Consciousness.
In-depth look at various methods of seeing where we are wrong. Criteria of the right way.

How to See the Positive in Others. 1 cass. (Running Time: 1 hr.). 12.99 (196) Yoga Res Foun.

How to See Yourself As You Really Are. abr. unabr. ed. Dalai Lama XIV. Read by Jeffrey Hopkins. Ed. by Jeffrey Hopkins. 5 CDs. (Running Time: 6 hrs. 30 mins. 0 sec.). (ENG.). 2006. audio compact disk 29.95 (978-0-7435-6464-9(2), Sound Ideas) Pub: S&S Audio. Dist(s): S and S Inc

How to See Yourself As You Really Are. abr. unabr. ed. Read by Jeffrey Hopkins. Tr. by Jeffrey Hopkins. Illus. by Dalai Lama XIV. 2006. 17.95 (978-0-7435-6355-0(7), Audioworks) Pub: S&S Audio. Dist(s): S and S Inc

How to Seek the Gifts of the Spirit. unabr. ed. Duane S. Crowther. 13.98 (978-0-88290-498-6(1)) Horizon Utah.

How to Seek the Gifts of the Spirit. unabr. ed. Duane S. Crowther. Read by Duane S. Crowther. 1 cass. (Running Time: 60 min.). 13.98 (1833) Horizon Utah.
Answers questions about the nature & purpose of spiritual gifts. Twenty-six specific spiritual gifts are explained, & instructions given in the scriptures concerning how to petition for these choice gifts are related.

How to Self-Publish Your Own Book: Preparation & Production. unabr. ed. Gordon Burgett. Read by Gordon Burgett. 3 cass. (Running Time: 3 hrs.). 1993. 44.95 set incl. wkbk. (978-0-910167-23-9(0)) Comm Unltd CA.
Step-by-step explanation of how to prepare & produce a self-published book.

How to Sell. unabr. ed. 1 cass. 12.95 (1565) J Norton Pubs.
A real estate agent, a sales manager, & a personnel director share their insights & experiences in effective sales. Personnel specialists also identify many sales opportunities.

How to Sell. unabr. ed. Clancy Martin. (Running Time: 10 hrs. 0 mins.). 2009. 29.95 (978-1-4332-7577-7(5)); 59.95 (978-1-4332-7573-9(2)); audio compact disk 24.95 (978-1-4332-7576-0(7)); audio compact disk 80.00 (978-1-4332-7574-6(0)) Blckstn Audio.

How to Sell Seventy-Five Percent of Your Travel Writing. unabr. ed. Gordon Burgett. 2 cass. (Running Time: 2 hrs.). 1996. Set, incl. wkbk. (978-0-910167-29-1(X)) Freemn Assoc.
Explains how to enter the prosperous travel writing market.

How to Sell Well. Brian S. Tracy. Read by Brian S. Tracy. 2 cass. (Effective Manager Seminar Ser.: No. 11). 95.00 Set, incl. 1-hr. videotape & 2 wkbks., program notes & study guide. (754VD) Nightingale-Conant.
More than 100 practical ideas.

How to Sell When Nobody Is Buying: And How to Sell Even More When They Are. unabr. ed. Dave Lakhani. Read by Sean Pratt. (Running Time: 7 hrs.). (ENG.). 2009. 27.98 (978-1-59659-439-5(X), GildAudio) Pub: Gildan Media. Dist(s): HachBkGrp

How to Sell Your Book to General & Niche Markets. unabr. ed. Gordon Burgett. Read by Gordon Burgett. 3 cass. (Running Time: 3 hrs.). 1993. 44.95 set incl. wkbk. (978-0-910167-24-6(9)) Comm Unltd CA.
Shows how to sell self-published books to general & niche (tightly-targeted) markets.

How to Sell Your Home Without Paying a Real Estate Commission. Larry Fransen. Read by Dennis Gould. 6 cass. 1991. 69.95 Set. (978-0-9633635-0-3(6)) How-To Pubns.
Six cassette tapes & companion booklet in a shelf-ready album. Step by step presentation on selling your own home, supported by checklists & sample documents. Glossary.

How to Sell Your House When You Owe More Than What Buyers Are Willing to Pay. Jovan Roberts. 2008. audio compact disk 24.99 (978-1-4276-3109-1(3)) AardGP.

How to Sell Your Inventions for Cash! Everything You Need to Know to: Prepare Your Ideas & Inventions; Protect Them; Produce Prototypes Economically and; Present Them to Potential Licensees. Created by Mike Rounds. Narrated by Mike Rounds. 3 CDs. (Running Time: 3 hours). (ENG.). 2004. audio compact disk 39.95 (978-1-891440-28-1(4)) CPM Systems.

How to Sell Yourself. abr. ed. Joe Girard. Read by Joe Girard. 1 cass. (Running Time: 90 min.). 1992. 13.00 (978-1-55994-600-1(8), CPN 1938) HarperCollins Pubs.

How to Sell Yourself. abr. ed. Arch Lustberg. Read by Todd Licea. (Running Time: 14400 sec.). 2008. audio compact disk 23.95 (978-1-59316-107-1(7)) Listen & Live.

How to Sell 75% of Your Travel Writing. Gordon Burgett. Narrated by Gordon Burgett. 2 cass., 2 CDs. (Running Time: 45 mins.). 2005. cd-rom 29.95 (978-0-910167-85-7(0)) Comm Unltd CA.
Gordon Burgett explains the process by which professional writers sell more than 75% of their travel writing. This is a combination audio CD, with 45 minutes of how-to explanation, plus a text CD with 10 key documents that Gordon describes or suggests in the spoken message.

How to Serve Humanity. (177); 12.99 (119) Yoga Res Foun.

How to Serve Humanity, No. 3. Swami Jyotirmayananda. 1 cass. (Running Time: 1 hr.). 1990. 12.99 Yoga Res Foun.

How to Set & Achieve Goals. Bobbe Sommer. 4 cass. (Running Time: 4 hrs.). 39.95 Set. (Q10026) CareerTrack Pubns.
This program will help you & your people identify your goals - & map out steps to achieve them.

How to Set & Achieve Goals. Bobbe Sommer. 2 cass. (Running Time: 3 hrs.). 1995. 15.95 (978-1-55977-047-7(3)) CareerTrack Pubns.

How to Set & Really Achieve Your Goals. Hosted by Jeff Blackman. 1 cass. (Running Time: 35 mins.). pap. bk. 99.95 (1025AV); pap. bk. 99.95 (1025AV) J Wilson & Assocs.

How to Set Priorities. Alec R. Mackenzie. Intro. by A. E. Whyte. 1 cass. (Running Time: 51 min.). (Listen & Learn USA! Ser.). 1987. 8.95 (978-0-88684-062-4(7)) Listen USA.
Offers time saving steps to get more done.

How to Set up a Book-Signing Tour. As told by Thomas M. Ellis et al. Interview with Jo Condrill. 2004. audio compact disk 79.75 (978-0-9740970-2-2(0)) Pub: GoalMinds. Dist(s): AtlasBooks
Interview with experts who set up book-signing tours. They describe their process in detail and provide insightful comments on what to expect.An Action Planner is included.

How to Set up a Business Corporation. 1986. bk. 65.00 incl. book.; 35.00 cass. only.; 30.00 book only. PA Bar Inst.

How to Set up & Market Your Own Seminar. Gordon Burgett. Voice by Gordon Burgett. 3 CDs audio, 1 CD te. (Running Time: 155 min.). 2006. 44.95 (978-0-910167-87-1(7)) Comm Unltd CA.
Gordon Burgett offers a workshop nationally by this title, and it was earlier sold in audio cassette form. Here the three audio CDs, with the workbook on a downloadable text CD, are updated to mid-2006.

How to Set up & Market Your Own Seminar. unabr. ed. Gordon Burgett. Read by Gordon Burgett. 3 cass. 1996. 44.95 set incl. wkbk. (978-0-910167-08-6(7)) Comm Unltd CA.
Presents the steps one takes to set up & market a seminar.

How to Set up Your Astrological Practice. Jeanne D. Lawlor. 1 cass. (Running Time: 90 min.). 1990. 8.95 (738) Am Fed Astrologers.

How to Shoot an Amateur Naturalist. unabr. ed. Gerald Durrell. Read by Nigel Davenport. 6 cass. (Running Time: 6 hrs.). 1993. 54.95 set. (978-0-7451-4178-7(1), CAB 861, Chivers Child Audio) AudioGO.
Reminiscing about his successful TV series, The Amateur Naturalist, Durrell recalls giraffes hissing, a buffalo taking a snow bath, & lizards & caterpillars misbehaving. Durrell is characteristically hilarious & passionate about the natural world he knows so well.

How to Shop for a Husband: A Consumer Guide to Getting a Great Buy on a Guy. unabr. ed. Janice Lieberman. Read by Janice Lieberman. (Running Time: 5 hrs. 0 mins. 0 sec.). (ENG.). 2009. audio compact disk 24.95 (978-1-4272-0700-5(3)) Pub: Macmill Audio. Dist(s): Macmillan

How to Shout Without Screaming: Communicating God's Love Through Our Lifestyle. Doug Fields. (Super-Ser.). 2007. audio compact disk 30.00 (978-5-557-78139-8(0)) Group Pub.

How to Simplify Your Life. Jeff Cavins. 2004. audio compact disk 7.95 (978-1-932927-39-9(5)) Ascensn Pr.

How to Simplify Your Life. Mac Hammond. 13 cds. 2005. audio compact disk 52.00 (978-1-57399-279-4(8)) Mac Hammond.

How to Sing Your Part in a Group. Duane Shinn. 1 cass. bk. 19.95 (SG-2) Duane Shinn.
Teaches how to classify the voice & then learn to sing either soprano, alto, tenor, or bass, depending upon range.

How to Smell a Rat: The Five Signs of Financial Fraud. unabr. ed. Kenneth L. Fisher. Read by Scott Thomsen. Told to Lara Hoffmans. 5 CDs. (Running Time: 6 hrs.). 2009. audio compact disk 26.95 (978-1-61573-029-2(X), 161573029X) Pub: HighBridge. Dist(s): Workman Pub

How to Solve Our Human Problems: The Four Noble Truths. Geshe Kelsang Gyatso. Read by Glenn Fitzgerald. 3 CDs. (Running Time: 12600 sec.). 2007. audio compact disk 21.95 (978-0-9789067-2-6(1)) Tharpa NY.

How to Solve Problems. 1 cass. (Running Time: 1 hr.). 12.99 (150); 12.99 (618) Yoga Res Foun.

How to Solve the Prosperity Puzzle. Kenneth Copeland. 2 cass. 1987. 10.00 Set. (978-0-88114-918-0(7)) K Copeland Pubns.
Biblical teaching on prosperity.

How to Speak Dutch-ified English. Gary Gates. 2003. 18.00 (978-1-56148-314-3(1)) Good Bks PA.

How to Speak Dutchified English. unabr. ed. Gary Gates. Read by Gary Gates. Read by Tony Rose. 1 cass. (Running Time: 1 hr.). 1988. Toga Prodns.
Humorous lessons & comedy on a delightful accent of the American Tongue.

How to Speak English Without a Foreign Accent. Jack Catran. Read by Jack Catran. Ed. by Chuck Gordon. 20 cass. (Running Time: 2 hrs.). 49.95 set. Jade Pubns CAN.
Accent reduction.

How to Speak English Without a Foreign Accent. Jack Catran. 1986. (978-0-318-60713-9(1)) Jade Pubns CAN.

How to Speak English Without a Foreign Accent: Arabic. Jack Catran. 2 cass. (Running Time: 2 hrs.). 1986. bk. 49.95 incl. 50pp. bklet. (978-0-937399-04-0(3)) Jade Pubns CAN.

How to Speak English Without a Foreign Accent: Arabic Edition. Jack Catran. 1986. bk. (978-0-318-60986-7(X)) Jade Pubns CAN.

How to Speak English Without a Foreign Accent: Black English. Jack Catran. Read by Jack Catran. 2 cass. (Running Time: 2 hrs.). 1986. bk. 49.95 incl. 50pp. bklet. (978-0-937399-05-7(1)) Jade Pubns CAN.
Specializing exclusively on accent erasure. Approved by N. Y. City Board of Education & leading school & libraries.

How to Speak English Without A Foreign Accent: Black English Edition. Jack Catran. 1986. (978-0-318-60987-4(8)) Jade Pubns CAN.

How to Speak English Without a Foreign Accent: Chinese. Jack Catran. Read by Jack Catran. 2 cass. (Running Time: 60 min. per cass.). pap. bk. 49.95 (978-0-937399-21-7(3)) Jade Pubns CAN.
Designed to erase accents.

How to Speak English Without a Foreign Accent: Filipino. Jack Catran. Read by Jack Catran. 2 cass. (Running Time: 2 hrs.). 1986. bk. 49.95 incl. 50pp. bklet. (978-0-937399-12-5(4)) Jade Pubns CAN.
Specializing exclusively on accent erasure. Approved by N. Y. City Board of Education & leading schools & libraries.

How to Speak English Without a Foreign Accent: Filipino Edition. Jack Catran. 1986. bk. (978-0-318-60993-5(2)) Jade Pubns CAN.

How to Speak English Without a Foreign Accent: French. Jack Catran. Read by Jack Catran. 2 cass. (Running Time: 2 hrs.). 1986. bk. 49.95 incl. 50pp. bklet. (978-0-937399-14-9(0)) Jade Pubns CAN.

How to Speak English Without a Foreign Accent: French Edition. Jack Catran. 1986. (978-0-318-60996-6(7)) Jade Pubns CAN.

How to Speak English Without a Foreign Accent: German. Jack Catran. Read by Jack Catran. 2 cass. (Running Time: 2 hrs.). 1986. bk. 49.95 incl. 50pp. bklet. (978-0-937399-13-2(2)) Jade Pubns CAN.

How to Speak English Without a Foreign Accent: German Edition. Jack Catran. 1986. (978-0-318-60994-2(0)) Jade Pubns CAN.

How to Speak English Without a Foreign Accent: Hispanic. Jack Catran. 2 cass. (Running Time: 2 hrs.). 1986. bk. 49.95 incl. 50pp bklet. (978-0-937399-02-6(7)) Jade Pubns CAN.

How to Speak English without a Foreign Accent: Hispanic Edition. Jack Catran. 1986. (978-0-318-60860-0(X)) Jade Pubns CAN.

How to Speak English Without a Foreign Accent: Indian. Jack Catran. Read by Jack Catran. 2 cass. (Running Time: 2 hrs.). 1986. bk. 49.95 incl. 50pp. bklet. (978-0-937399-09-5(4)) Jade Pubns CAN.

How to Speak English Without a Foreign Accent: Indian Edition. Jack Catran. 1986. bk. (978-0-318-60991-1(6)) Jade Pubns CAN.

How to Speak English Without a Foreign Accent: Iranian. Jack Catran. Read by Jack Catran. 2 cass. (Running Time: 2 hrs.). 1986. bk. 49.95 (978-0-937399-08-8(6)) Jade Pubns CAN.
Designed to erase accesnts.

How to Speak English Without a Foreign Accent: Iranian Edition. Jack Catran. 1986. bk. (978-0-318-60990-4(8)) Jade Pubns CAN.

How to Speak English Without a Foreign Accent: Irish Edition. Jack Catran. 1986. bk. (978-0-318-60995-9(9)) Jade Pubns CAN.

How to Speak English Without a Foreign Accent: Israeli. Jack Catran. Read by Jack Catran. 2 cass. (Running Time: 60 min. per cass.). 1986. bk. 49.95 incl. 50 pp. bklet. (978-0-937399-06-4(X)) Jade Pubns CAN.
Specializing exclusively on accent erasure. Approved by N. Y. City Board of Education.

How To Speak English Without a Foreign Accent: Israeli Edition. Jack Catran. 1986. (978-0-318-60988-1(6)) Jade Pubns CAN.

How to Speak English Without a Foreign Accent: Italian. Jack Catran. Read by Jack Catran. 2 cass. (Running Time: 2 hrs.). 1986. bk. 49.95 incl. 50pp. bklet. (978-0-937399-10-1(8)) Jade Pubns CAN.
Specializing exclusively on accent erasure. Approved by N. Y. City Board of Education & leading schools & libraries.

How to Speak English Without a Foreign Accent: Italian Edition. Jack Catran. 1986. (978-0-318-60992-8(4)) Jade Pubns CAN.

How to Speak English Without a Foreign Accent: Japanese. Jack Catran. Read by Jack Catran. 2 cass. (Running Time: 60 min. per cass.). pap. bk. 49.95 (978-0-937399-20-0(5)) Jade Pubns CAN.
Designed to erase accents.

How to Speak English Without a Foreign Accent: Japanese Edition. Jack Catran. Read by Jack Catran. 2 cass. (Running Time: 60 min. per cass.). bk. 49.95 Jade Pubns CAN.

How to Speak English Without a Foreign Accent: Korean. Jack Catran. 2 cass. (Running Time: 2 hrs.). 1988. bk. 49.95 (978-0-937399-19-4(1)) Jade Pubns CAN.

How to Speak English Without a Foreign Accent: New York. Jack Catran. Read by Jack Catran. 2 cass. (Running Time: 2 hrs.). 1986. bk. 49.95 incl. 50pp. bklet. (978-0-937399-16-3(7)) Jade Pubns CAN.
Specializing exclusively on accent erasure. Approved by N. Y. City Board of Education & leading schools & libraries.

How to Speak English Without a Foreign Accent: New York Edition. Jack Catran. 2 cass. (Running Time: 1 hr. 30 min.). 1986. bk. (978-0-318-60998-0(3)) Jade Pubns CAN.

How to Speak English Without a Foreign Accent: Oriental. Jack Catran. 2 cass. (Running Time: 2 hrs.). 1986. bk. 49.95 incl. 50pp. bklet. (978-0-937399-03-3(5)) Jade Pubns CAN.

How to Speak English Without a Foreign Accent: Oriental Edition. Jack Catran. 1986. (978-0-318-60985-0(1)) Jade Pubns CAN.

How to Speak English Without a Foreign Accent: Pygmalion. Jack Catran. Read by Jack Catran. 2 cass. (Running Time: 2 hrs.). 1986. bk. 49.95 incl. 50pp. bklet. (978-0-937399-43-9(4)) Jade Pubns CAN.

How to Speak English Without a Foreign Accent: Russian. Jack Catran. Read by Jack Catran. 2 cass. (Running Time: 2 hrs.). 1986. bk. 49.95 incl. 50pp. bklet. (978-0-937399-07-1(8)) Jade Pubns CAN.
Specializing exclusively on accent erasure. Approved by N. Y. City Board of Education & leading schools & libraries.

How to Speak English Without a Foreign Accent: Russian Edition. Jack Catran. 2 cass. (Running Time: 1 hr. 30 min.). 1986. bk. (978-0-318-60989-8(4)) Jade Pubns CAN.

How to Speak English Without a Foreign Accent: Scandinavian. Jack Catran. Read by Jack Catran. 2 cass. (Running Time: 2 hrs.). 1986. bk. 49.95 incl. 50pp. bklet. (978-0-937399-15-6(9)) Jade Pubns CAN.
Specializing exclusively on accent erasure. Approved by N. Y. City Board of Education & leading schools & libraries.

How to Speak English Without a Foreign Accent: Scandinavian Edition. Jack Catran. 1986. bk. (978-0-318-60997-3(5)) Jade Pubns CAN.

How to Speak English Without a Foreign Accent: Vietnamese. Jack Catran. Read by Jack Catran. 2 cass. (Running Time: 2 hrs.). 1986. pap. bk. 49.95 incl. 50pp. bklet. (978-0-937399-17-0(5)) Jade Pubns CAN.

How to Speak English Without a Foreign Accent: Vietnamese Edition. Jack Catran. 1986. (978-0-318-61707-7(2)) Jade Pubns CAN.

How to Speak How to Listen. Mortimer J. Adler. Intro. by A. E. Whyte. 1 cass. (Running Time: 44 min.). (Listen & Learn USA! Ser.). 8.95 (978-0-88684-015-0(5)) Listen USA.
Provides valuable advice on how to improve your speaking skills.

How to Speak How to Listen. unabr. ed. Mortimer J. Adler. Read by Harold N. Cropp. 6 cass. (Running Time: 8 hrs. 30 mins.). 1995. 44.95 (978-0-7861-0851-0(7), 1649) Blckstn Audio.
Drawing on decades of experience as educator & philosopher, Adler gives the listener a short course in effective communication filled with the Adler wisdom & wit. Both instructive & practical, this tape will be invaluable to everyone: salespeople & executives involved in conferences & negotiations, politicians, lecturers & teachers, as well as families seeking to improve communication among themselves.

How to Speak in Public with Power, Enthusiasm & Effectiveness see Como Comunicarnos en Publico con Poder, Entusiasmo y Efectividad

How to Speak the Word of Audio. Thompson Leroy. 2002. 20.00 (978-1-931804-10-3(9)) Ever Increase Wd Min.

How to Speak up, Set Limits & Say No. Maria Arapakis. 4 cass. (Running Time: 4 hrs.). 49.95 CareerTrack Pubns.
With words & phrases to use in specific situations, this program helps get the treatment one wants from other people.

How to Speak Without an Accent. unabr. ed. Ellie Janow. 2 cass. bk. 29.95 Set. (SEN440) J Norton Pubs.

How to Spend Time with God. Speeches. Creflo A. Dollar. 2 cass. (Running Time: 3 hrs.). 1999. 10.00 (978-1-59089-163-6(5)) Creflo Dollar.

How to Spend Time with God. Creflo A. Dollar. 2009. audio compact disk 40.00 (978-1-59944-767-4(3)) Creflo Dollar.

How to Spiritualize a Marriage. 1 cass. (Running Time: 90 min.). (Relationship Ser.). 9.95 (ST-8S) Crystal Clarity.
Includes: Communicating on a level of silence; the need for space & solitude within marriage; treating marriage as fragile in order to make it strong; why marriages which lack a spiritual dimension often don't work; the importance of not taking your spouse for granted.

How to Spiritualize Business. Dennis Weaver. 1 cass. 1990. 8.50 (2514) Self Realization.
With sincerity, humor, & practical wisdom, Dennis Weaver shares down-to-earth advice based on the teachings of Paramahansa Yogananda & on his own efforts to balance outer accomplishments with inner peace.

How to Spiritualize Your Daily Life. Asha Praver. 1 cass. (Meeting the Challenge of Living in the World Ser.). 9.95 (AT-65) Crystal Clarity.
Topics include: Does God want us to be unhappy?; why we need to personalize God; How to view your accomplishments; the paramount importance of strong, dynamic energy.

How to Split a Church Pt. I: 1 Cor. 1:1-17. Ed Young. 1985. 4.95 (978-0-7417-1480-0(9), 480) Win Walk.

How to Split a Church Pt. II: 1 Cor. 1:1-17. Ed Young. 1985. 4.95 (978-0-7417-1481-7(7), 481) Win Walk.

How to Spot a Liar: Why People Don't Tell the Truth... & How You Can Catch Them. unabr. abr. ed. Gregory Hartley & Maryann Karinch. Read by Gregory Hartley & Maryann Karinch. (Running Time: 14400 sec.). 2007. audio compact disk 23.95 (978-1-59316-104-0(2)) Listen & Live.

How to Spot a No-Good Man - a Women's Credit Repair Guide. Mervin Evans. 2 CD / 2 Audiocasse. (Running Time: 160 Min). 2002. 29.99 (978-0-914391-39-5(9)) Comm People Pr.
A step by Step guide to restoring your credit after that NO-Good Man has Trashed your AAA= Credit!.

How to Spread Objectivism. Andrew Bernstein. 1 cass. (Running Time: 30 min.). 1995. 9.95 (978-1-56114-497-6(5), CB11C) Second Renaissance.
Concrete techniques to interest people in the ideas of objectivism.

How to Square Dance. unabr. ed. Conversa-Phone Institute Staff & Betty White. 1 cass. (Running Time: 55 min.). (Betty White's How to Ballroom Dance Ser.). 1990. 9.95 (978-1-56752-097-2(9)) Conversa-phone.
Teaches all of the most popular steps-breaks-turns - how to lead & how to follow. Fully illustrated instruction manual follows the audio tape. Learn today - dance tonight.

How to Stand in Faith. Creflo A. Dollar. 2009. audio compact disk 21.00 (978-1-59944-760-5(6)) Creflo Dollar.

How to Start a Business in California. Excerpts. Created by Entrepreneur Magazine. 2 CDs. (Running Time: 3600 sec.). (ENG.). 2005. audio compact disk 19.95 (978-1-932531-86-2(6), 1932531866) Pub: Entrepreneur Pr. Dist(s): McGraw

How to Start a Business in Florida. Excerpts. Created by Entrepreneur Magazine. 2 CDs. (Running Time: 3240 sec.). (ENG.). 2005. audio compact disk 19.95 (978-1-932531-87-9(4), 1932531874) Pub: Entrepreneur Pr. Dist(s): McGraw

How to Start a Business in New Jersey. Excerpts. Created by Entrepreneur Magazine. 2 CDs. (Running Time: 3000 sec.). (ENG.). 2005. audio compact disk 19.95 (978-1-932531-88-6(2), 1932531882) Pub: Entrepreneur Pr. Dist(s): McGraw

How to Start a Business in New York. Excerpts. Created by Entrepreneur Magazine. 2 CDs. (Running Time: 3120 sec.). (ENG.). 2005. audio compact disk 19.95 (978-1-932531-89-3(0), 1932531890) Pub: Entrepreneur Pr. Dist(s): McGraw

How to Start a Business in Texas. Excerpts. Created by Entrepreneur Magazine. 2 CDs. (Running Time: 3840 sec.). (ENG.). 2005. audio compact disk 19.95 (978-1-932531-90-9(4), 1932531904) Pub: Entrepreneur Pr. Dist(s): McGraw

How to Start a Career in Information Technology, 2nd Edition. 2nd rev. ed. Ian K. Fisher. (ENG.). 2007. audio compact disk 19.95 (978-0-9760052-2-3(0)) Pub: I Fisher. Dist(s): Lightn Source

***How to Start A Conversation & Make Friends.** abr. ed. Don Gabor. Read by Don Gabor. (ENG.). 2011. audio compact disk 20.00 (978-0-307-87886-1(4), Random AudioBks) Pub: Random Audio Pubg. Dist(s): Random

How to Start a Gift Basket Service Audio Guide. Excerpts. Entrepreneur Press. 4 CDs. (Running Time: 4 hrs). (ENG.). 2005. audio compact disk 59.95 (978-1-932531-81-7(5), 1932531815) Pub: Entrepreneur Pr. Dist(s): McGraw

How to Start a Hair Salon & Day Spa. Excerpts. Entrepreneur Press. 4 CDs. (Running Time: 4 Hrs). (ENG.). 2005. audio compact disk 59.95 (978-1-932531-83-1(1), 1932531831) Pub: Entrepreneur Pr. Dist(s): McGraw

How to Start a Home Business. unabr. ed. Gary Null. 1 cass. (Running Time: 58 min.). 12.95 (948) J Norton Pubs.
Mr. Null outlines dozens of successful, profitable home business ideas: specialized catering; raising small animals, flower & vegetable growing, & many others. Also included is a detailed, practical checklist to help you decide which home business idea is best for you, plus financing, government help & more.

How to Start a Medical Claims Billing Service Audio Guide. Excerpts. Entrepreneur Press. 4 CDs. (Running Time: 4 hrs). (ENG.). 2005. audio compact disk 59.95 (978-1-932531-82-4(3), 1932531823) Pub: Entrepreneur Pr. Dist(s): McGraw

How to Start a Successful Small Business Vol. 44: Eight Keys to Insure Profitability. Income Opportunities Editors. 2 cass. (Running Time: 1 hr. 45 min.). (Business Opportunities Ser.). 1987. 15.95 B & H Comm.
The principles, legalities & procedures for developing a profitable business, includes financial & pricing strategy, employee & customer relationships, business image building.

How to Start an Event Planning Service Audio Guide. Excerpts. 4 CDs. (Running Time: 4 hrs). 2005. audio compact disk 59.00 (978-1-932531-80-0(7)) Entrepreneur Pr.

How to Start & Build a Successful Speakers Bureau. Dottie Walters & Somers White. 1 cass. 125.00 Boxed Set, incl. bklt. (978-0-934344-34-0(5)) Royal Pub.
How to begin a bureau business, what to look out for, set fees. Ancillary income services to sell to speakers & meeting planner clients. How to broker celebrities. Bureaus all over the world have thanked us for this valuable information. Includes list of speaker qualifying questions.

How to Start & Manage Your Own Business, Set. unabr. ed. Arnold Van den Berg & Egon Van den Berg. 8 cass. (Running Time: 10 hrs.). 1995. pap. bk. 79.50 (978-0-88432-495-9(8), S01500, Audio-For) J Norton Pubs.
Examines goals & commitment & helps you decide whether you should buy or start a business. Also guides you through the maze of finding a product & pricing it, start-up costs, obtaining finacing, financial statements, & tax rules as well as marketing strategies. Cost sheets, balance sheets, & budgeting are all explained.

How to Start & Run Your Own Company -or- Sex, Money, & Power ... It's All the Same Thing. Speeches. Based on a book by Andrew C. Jacobs. Contrib. by Barry Frisch. 1. 2006. audio compact disk 14.95 (978-0-9726074-5-2(5)) Ideal Jacobs.

How to Start & Succeed in Your Own Business. Brian S. Tracy. Read by Brian S. Tracy. 6 cass. 54.95 Set. (451AD) Nightingale-Conant.

How to Start Personal Histories & Genealogy Journalism Businesses. Scripts. Anne Hart. 1 CD. (Running Time: 9 hours approximately). 2006. audio compact disk 5.00 (978-1-59971-232-1(6)) AardGP.
How to Start Personal Histories & Genealogy Journalism Businesses is a complete audio course consisting of 16 audio MP3 files (approximately 9 hours of listening) on a CD on how to interview, open, and operate personal histories and/or personal history journalism businesses. Combine with genealogy research, family history, or oral and personal history documentarian recording, time capsule making, interviewing, and presentation. Personal histories journalism and interviewing instruction also is helpful when presenting to selected media business or institutional success stories, recording memoirs of clients, or corporate histories as well as personal presentations of significant events, celebrations, and life stories.

How to Start Your Own Taekwon-Do Club. James S. Benko. 1986. 12.95 (TC-7) ITA Inst.
Finding a location for a building, designing advertising, how to get free advertising, how to get students, setting up the Dojang (school) & applying for the necessary documents to operate a business plus much more information is featured in this presentation. Even if you already have a school, this program will help you better run a club.

How to Stay Catholic in College. 2006. 5.95 (978-1-888992-72-4(7)) Catholic Answers.

How to Stay in Prosperity. Elbert Willis. 1 cass. (Financial Prosperity Ser.). 4.00 Fill the Gap.

How to Stay in the Power of God. Gloria Copeland. 1 cass. 1988. 5.00 (978-0-88114-803-9(2)) K Copeland Pubns.
Biblical teaching on prayer & meditation.

How to Stay Mentally Fit & Incredibly Productive, Vol. I. rev. unabr. ed. David Essel. 1 cass. (Running Time: 1 hr. 30 min.). (David Essel's Dynamic Living Ser.). 1998. 9.95 (978-1-893074-04-0(8)) D Essel Inc.
Discover the four keys to mental fitness: 1) Power of the open mind, 2) Greater Self acceptance, 3) Following your own journey, 4) Success through risk taking.

***How to Stay Positive in a Negative World: Cd Album.** Created by Awmi. (ENG.). 2010. audio compact disk 35.00 (978-1-59548-199-3(0)) A Wommack.

How to Stay up No Matter What Comes Down, Set. abr. ed. Mark Towers. Read by Mark Towers. 2 cass. (Running Time: 1 hr. 20 min.). 1996. bk. 21.95 (978-1-57294-038-3(7),) SkillPath Pubns.
Change. Too often, change is something that happens without warning. If you're prepared to cope with change, chances are much greater that you'll be among those who survive & succeed. Powerful strategies for keeping your skills, your self-esteem & your "self" up will help you endure no matter what befalls you.

How to Steal: Exodus 20:15. Ed Young. 1999. 4.95 (978-0-7417-2225-6(9), 1225) Win Walk.

How to Stop Being Teased & Bullied Without Really Trying. Israel C. Kalman. Read by Lola Kalman. Music [illegible]egg Breinberg. Contrib. by Yannai Kalman & Vanya Sebag. 2 cas[illegible]nning Time: 1 hr. 50 mins.). (J). (gr. 5 up). 2000. 20.00 (978-0-9706482[illegible])) TheWisdom.
Lessons for people who are teased & bullied. Teaches how to solve their problem.

How to Stop Procrastination Now! & Follow Through to Success. Joshua Bloom. 57 cass. (Running Time: 57 hrs.). 2001. ring bd. 129.95 (978-0-9710704-0-0(7)) Bloojay.

How to Stop Satan's Attack on God's Timing, Plans & Purposes. Gary V. Whetstone. (Practical Ministry Ser.: Vol. PM 203). (C). 1994. 90.00 (978-1-58866-044-2(3)) Gary Whet Pub.

How to Stop Smoking: And Stay Stopped for Good. unabr. ed. Gillian Riley. Read by Jerome Pride. (Running Time: 19200 sec.). 2008. audio compact disk 63.95 (978-1-921334-94-8(0), 9781921334948) Pub: Bolinda Pubng AUS. Dist(s): Bolinda Pub Inc

*__How to stop smoking & stay stopped for Good.__ Gillian Riley. Read by Jerome Pride. (Running Time: 5 hrs. 20 mins.). 2009. 64.99 (978-1-74214-279-1(6), 9781742142791) Pub: Bolinda Pubng AUS. Dist(s): Bolinda Pub Inc

How to Stop Worrying & Start Living. 2005. 39.99 (978-1-59895-033-5(9)) Find a World.

How to Stop Worrying & Start Living. unabr. ed. Dale Carnegie. Read by Andrew MacMillan & Andrew Macmillan. 9 CDs. (Running Time: 102 hrs. 50 mins. 0 sec.). (ENG.). 1999. audio compact disk 49.95 (978-0-671-57458-1(2), Sound Ideas) Pub: S&S Audio. Dist(s): S and S Inc

How to Stop Worrying & Start Living. unabr. ed. Dale Carnegie. Read by Andrew Macmillan. 2004. 23.95 (978-0-7435-4318-7(1)) Pub: S&S Audio. Dist(s): S and S Inc

How to Strengthen the Immune System, Set. Gary Null. 2 cass. 1995. 16.95 (978-1-879323-22-3(2)) Sound Horizons AV.
On these tapes nutritional expert Gary Null informs us that our environment has become polluted & that we are constantly bombarded by these toxins. Gary lays out a plan that guides you to repair your immune system & live your life with the vigor & vitality indicative of good health.

How to Stubbornly Refuse to Be Ashamed of Anything. Albert Ellis. 1 cass. (Running Time: 74 min.). 9.95 (C010) A Ellis Institute.
Learn humorous, practical ways to be less ashamed of your foibles & failings & overcome moralistic & perfectionistic standards.

How to Stubbornly Refuse to Be Ashamed of Anything. Albert Ellis. 1 cass. (Running Time: 74 min.). 9.95 (C010) Inst Rational-Emotive.

How to Study Ayn Rand's Writings. Harry Binswanger. 1 cass. (Running Time: 1 hr. 30 min.). 1995. 12.95 (978-1-56114-449-5(5), CB10C) Second Renaissance.
The general method & specific techniques to enhance the study of Ayn Rand's non-fiction writings.

How to Study Program. abr. ed. Ron Fry. Read by Beverly Butler & David Cooper. (YA). 2007. 59.99 (978-1-60252-838-3(1)) Find a World.

How to Study Program. abr. ed. Ron Fry. Read by Beverly Butler & David Cooper. Created by Highbridge Audio. 9 CDs. (Running Time: 36900 sec.). (ENG.). 2006. audio compact disk 34.95 (978-1-59887-034-3(3), 1598870343) Pub: HighBridge. Dist(s): Workman Pub

How to Study the Bible. 4 cass. 15.95 (2082, HarperThor) HarpC GBR.

How to Study the Bible. Chuck Missler. 2 cass. (Running Time: 2.5 hours plus). (Briefing Packages by Chuck Missler). 1994. vinyl bd. 14.95 Incls. notes. (978-1-880532-63-8(8)) Koinonia Hse.
Which translation is best? Which Study Bible? What are the secrets of resolving difficult or controversial passages?From forty years of intensive Bible study and teaching, Missler shares his favorite helps, secrets and practical suggestions on how to take the Bible seriously.Most Christians, although they want to do in-depth Bible study, know little of the types, philosophies and tools of study available. Is the Bible to be taken literally or figuratively? What study aids would be most helpful in beginning my own home study library?Going through the Bible book by book. "Eat the elephant one bite at a time." These studies produce the most lasting results. There is a balance in the "whole counsel of God." Emmaus Road in Luke 24:27.Where to Start?A good "first book" is the Gospel of John: "A child can wade in it and an elephant can bathe in it!" Other good starting points include Genesis, Acts, Matthew, Daniel, and Revelation (Which is the only book which unequivocally promises a blessing to the reader). You are unique; let the Spirit lead you.

How to Study the Bible. Chuck Missler. 2 CDs. (Running Time: 120 min. aprox.). (Briefing Packages by Chuck Missler). 2006. audio compact disk 19.95 (978-1-57821-336-8(3)) Koinonia Hse.

How to Study the Bible. Gary V. Whetstone. Instructed by June Austin. 9 cass. (Running Time: 13 hrs. 30 mins.). (Practics Ser.: PR102). 1996. pap. bk. 170.00 (978-1-58866-054-1(0), BR 102 A00) Gary Whet Pub.
When this course is completed, the student will know how to prove the Bible is true, why he should study the Bible, how to read the Bible & various study approaches to the Bible.

How to Study the "Miracle Course" unabr. ed. Carol Howe. 2 cass. (Running Time: 2 hrs. 45 min.). 1992. 17.95 Set. (978-1-889642-14-7(2)) C Howe.
Translates into simple, clear language the purpose & practice of "A Course in Miracles," a road map to the experience of happiness & peace of mind. In addition to providing an overview of its major concepts, this set covers: How it works, helpful hints & pitfalls to avoid for productive practice & understanding. The comforting message of "all's well" while we examine & release the limiting beliefs about ourselves & the world. Direct application of the principles to "real life".

How to Study the Scriptures. (Running Time: 1 hr.). 12.99 (115) Yoga Res Foun.

How to Study Your Bible, I. Dan Corner. 1 cass. 3.00 (40) Evang Outreach.

How to Study Your Bible, II. Dan Corner. 1 cass. 3.00 (41) Evang Outreach.

How to Study Your Bible, III. Dan Corner. 1 cass. 3.00 (42) Evang Outreach.

How to Subdue Ego II. (158) Yoga Res Foun.

How to Succeed: Your First Years in the Real World. Gloria G. Geary. Read by Gloria G. Geary. 1 cass. (Running Time: 45 min.). 1991. 9.95 (978-1-880529-01-0(7)) Pat Back.
Designed for the recent graduate; this cassette offers help in choosing the best career path, ways to increase your income & how to manage your money, secrets to successful job interviews & straight talk on having a happy & balanced life.

How to Succeed Against All Odds: Make Adversities Your Foot Mat. Margaret Dureke. 2002. audio compact disk (978-0-9701144-7-1(8)) Jahs.
Abridged version of the how to succeed book - motivational and inspirational - part I.

How to Succeed in Business without Working so Damn Hard: Rethinking the Rules, Reinventing the Game. Robert J. Kriegel. Narrated by L. J. Ganser. 5 cass. (Running Time: 7 hrs. 15 mins.). 48.00 (978-1-4025-1742-6(4)) Recorded Bks.

*__How to Succeed with NLP: Go from Good to Great at Work.__ unabr. ed. Anne Watson. Read by Erik Synnestvedt. (Running Time: 5 hrs. 30 mins.). (ENG.). 2010. 27.98 (978-1-59659-573-6(6), GildAudio) Pub: Gildan Media. Dist(s): HachBkGrp

How to Successfully Flirt, Date & Mate. Christine O'Keefe. Read by Christine O'Keefe. 6 cass. 1990. bk. & wbk. ed. 89.95 (978-0-9667974-0-4(X)) C OKeefe.

How to Successfully Use Technology As an Effective Teaching Tool. abr. ed. Debbie LaCoste. 6 cass. 1999. 75.00 Set, incl. resource handbk. (978-1-886397-27-9(9)) Bureau of Educ.

How to Supervise Bad Attitudes & Negative Behaviors. PUEI. audio compact disk 199.00 (978-1-934147-81-8(8), CareerTrack) P Univ E Inc.

How to Supervise Bad Attitudes & Negative Behaviors. PUEI. 2007. audio compact disk 199.00 (978-1-934147-54-2(0), CareerTrack) P Univ E Inc.

How to Supervise off-Site Employees. PUEI. audio compact disk 199.00 (978-1-934147-83-2(4), CareerTrack) P Univ E Inc.

How to Supervise off-Site Employees. PUEI. 2007. audio compact disk 199.00 (978-1-934147-53-5(2), CareerTrack) P Univ E Inc.

How to Supervise People. 1 cass. (Running Time: 48 mins.). pap. bk. 99.95 (1008AV); pap. bk. 99.95 (1008AV) J Wilson & Assocs.

How to Supervise People. Fred Pryor. 6 cass. (Running Time: 6 hrs.). 1995. 59.95 Set incl. wkbk. (11350AM) Nightingale-Conant.
Ideal for use as a training or reference tool.

How to Supervise People. PUEI. 2003. audio compact disk 89.95 (978-1-933328-42-3(8), Fred Pryor) P Univ E Inc.

How to Supervise People: Peak Performance in Motivating, Managing, & Taking Charge of Projects & People. Fred Pryor. 6 cass. 59.95 Set incls wkbk. (11350AS) Pryor Resources.
Learn to delegate, discipline, deliver praise & criticism, get others to work effectively under pressure, & organize people, projects, & schedules on an ongoing basis. Regardless of your previous experience in supervising, you can always work smarter & do your job better with fresh ideas & techniques. This powerful seminar will make you an even more productive, even better supervisor than you already are, one who consistently builds rapport, motivation, & pride in your emloyees.

How to Supervise People: Techniques for Getting Results Through Others. 1 cass. cass. & video 99.00 Incl. hdbk. (639-C47) Natl Seminars.
Leadership has been described as the art of making people want to do what needs to be done. Be a strong leader & get the best results by motivating others to achieve. You'll see "real life" examples of the principles of effective supervision at work & receive full explanations of the concepts behind each, so you can make them work for you.

How to Supervise People: Techniques for Getting Results Through Others. Eileen Parkinson. Read by Eileen Parkinson. 1 cass. bk. 95.00 incl. 1 45- min. videocassette. (5774PVD) Nightingale-Conant.
You'll learn the keys to building a successful team, how to deal positively with conflict, & how to improve overall operations.

How to Supplement Your Income. unabr. ed. Vernon K. Jacobs. 1 cass. (Running Time: 45 min.). 12.95 (966) J Norton Pubs.
A guide to the world of part-time work. How to find the jobs.

How to Survive a Major Earthquake. Libby Lafferty & Steven Sanders. 1 cass. (Running Time: 32 min.). 4.95 (978-0-929536-03-3(7)) Emb Cassettes.
Documents information on earthquake preparedness.

How to Survive a Robot Uprising: Tips on Defending Yourself Against the Coming Rebellion. Daniel H. Wilson. Read by Stefan Rudnicki. (Running Time: 10800 sec.). 2006. 24.95 (978-0-7861-4530-0(7)); audio compact disk 27.00 (978-0-7861-7148-4(0)) Blckstn Audio.

How to Survive a Robot Uprising: Tips on Defending Yourself Against the Coming Rebellion. abr. unabr. ed. Daniel H. Wilson. Exper. by Stefan Rudnicki. 4 CDs. (Running Time: 10800 sec.). 2006. audio compact disk 19.95 (978-0-7861-7290-0(8)) Blckstn Audio.

How to Survive a Robot Uprising: Tips on Defending Yourself Against the Coming Rebellion. abr. unabr. ed. Daniel H. Wilson. Read by Stefan Rudnicki. 3 cass. (Running Time: 10800 sec.). 2006. 19.95 (978-0-7861-4462-4(9)) Blckstn Audio.

How to Survive a Robot Uprising: Tips on Defending Yourself Against the Coming Rebellion. abr. unabr. ed. Daniel H. Wilson. (Running Time: 10800 sec.). 2006. audio compact disk 29.95 (978-0-7861-7712-7(8)) Blckstn Audio.

How to Survive (and Perhaps Thrive) on a Teacher's Salary. Danny Kofke. 2007. audio compact disk 17.99 (978-1-60247-653-0(5)) Tate Pubng.

How to Survive & Thrive Alongside the Superstores & Category Killers. unabr. ed. Rick Ott. Read by Rick Ott. 2 cass. (Running Time: 1 hr. 30 min.). 1997. 24.95 Set. (978-0-9663491-0-8(5)) Ocean View.
Strategies & techniques for small businesses that are tired of losing business to the big superstores.

*__How to Survive As a Minority on Campus.__ 2010. cd-rom 11.99 (978-0-9793927-3-3(X), RR&R) Posit Prints.

How to Survive Divorce. unabr. ed. Read by Larry Losoncy. 1 cass. 12.95 (978-0-88432-220-7(3), AF1900) J Norton Pubs.
Dr. Larry Losoncy describes emotional stages people experience after the divorce becomes final & gives positive suggestions for overcoming the painful effects of divorce.

How to Survive Divorce (audio CD) Grieving through Divorce. Larry Losoncy. (ENG.). 2007. audio compact disk 12.95 (978-1-57970-460-5(3), Audio-For) J Norton Pubs.

How to Survive in the U. S. A. English for Travelers & Newcomers. unabr. ed. 1 cass. bk. 34.50 (SEN157) J Norton Pubs.
Travelers to the United States for business, pleasure, or study often require help with the language needed in order to "survive." This intermediate-level program provides the American English required to get through customs at the airport, make telephone calls, mail letters, rent cars & hotle rooms, & understand transportation systems, as well as a wealth of other practical information about living in the United States.

How to Survive in the U.S.A. Audio Sampler: English for Travelers & Newcomers. Nancy Church & Ann Moss. 1 cass. (Running Time: 1 hr.). pap. bk. Cambridge U Pr.
This text presents the English needed for arriving in the United States: communicating by phone and mail, getting around, handling money, finding somewhere to stay, getting something to eat, and so on. Short recorded conversations in each unit help students understand a wide variety of American accents. Answers and notes for exercises appear at the back of the book.

How to Survive in Today's Economy. Larry A. Lackey, Sr. 1994. bk. & stu. ed. 207.00 (978-1-885102-01-0(1)) Busn Mgmt Inst.

How to Survive Rejection & Promote Acceptance. James R. Sherman. 1 cass. (Running Time: 41 min.). 11.00 (978-0-89811-214-6(1), 9450) Meyer Res Grp.
Techniques for getting rid of feelings of anxiety, guilt & rejection.

How to Survive Rejection & Promote Acceptance. James R. Sherman. 1 cass. 10.00 (SP100065) SMI Intl.
Rejection hurts. If you are ever rejected you can pick up the pieces & move ahead. This message will help you: get rid of feelings of anxiety; quit feeling guilty; develop immunity to feelings of rejection; promote acceptance.

How to Survive the End of the World As We Know It: Tactics, Techniques & Technologies for Uncertain Things. unabr. ed. James Wesley Rawles. Read by Dick Hill. (Running Time: 10 hrs.). 2009. 19.99 (978-1-4418-3061-6(8), 9781441830616, Brilliance MP3); 19.99 (978-1-4418-3063-0(4), 9781441830630, BAD); 39.97 (978-1-4418-3062-3(6), 9781441830623, Brlnc Audio MP3 Lib); 39.97 (978-1-4418-3064-7(2), 9781441830647, BADLE); audio compact disk 19.99 (978-1-4418-3059-3(6), 9781441830593, Bril Audio CD Unabri); audio compact disk 87.97 (978-1-4418-3060-9(X), 9781441830609, BriAudCD Unabrid) Brilliance Audio.

How to Survive the Happiest Day of Your Life: A Brand New Way to Look at Your Wedding. unabr. ed. Elaine Viets. Read by Elaine Viets. 1 cass. (Running Time: 50 min.). 9.95 (978-1-882467-07-5(8)) Wildstone Media.
Helpful & humorous guide to your wedding day. Topics covered include how to get the best deals on reception halls, advice on sensible places to register for gifts & exciting ways to "get away from it all" with the newest craze "Weddingmoons".

How to Survive the Loss of a Love. unabr. ed. Melba Colgrove et al. Read by Melba Colgrove et al. 2 cass. (Running Time: 3 hrs.). 2004. 11.95 (978-0-931580-47-5(1)) Pub: Mary Bks. Dist(s): APG

How to Survive Your Greatest Blessings. Emily Watts. 2005. audio compact disk 12.95 (978-1-59038-407-7(5)) Deseret Bk.

How to Survive Your Teenager's Years: An Audio Adaptation. Tracy St. John. 1 cass. (Running Time: 1 hr. 30 min.). 14.95 Reeder Pr.
Features humor about teenagers.

How to Take a Test. Stephen M. Foreman. Read by Steven C. Eggleston. 1 cass. (College Survival Ser.). 1988. 6.95 SCE Prod & List & Lrn.
Instructions on how to read carefully & answer test questions for optimum scores.

How to Take & Pass a Law School Examination. Irving Younger. 1981. 15.00 (978-1-55917-261-5(4)) Natl Prac Inst.

How to Take Charge of Our Lives, Set. Earnie Larsen. Read by Earnie Larsen. 6 cass. (Running Time: 6 hrs.). 1993. 45.95 (978-1-56047-080-9(1), A613) E Larsen Enterprises.
Discusses six keys to feeling better about ourselves, especially for those who have found themselves repeating self-defeating behaviors.

How to Take Standardized Tests. Charles Oliver. (YA). (gr. 10-12). 1981. pap. bk. 16.95 (978-0-89285-157-7(0), 1342) ELS Educ Servs.

How to Talk about Books You Haven't Read. unabr. ed. Pierre Bayard. Read by Grover Gardner. Tr. by Jeffrey Mehlman. (Running Time: 16200 sec.). 2007. 19.95 (978-1-4332-0797-6(4)); 44.95 (978-1-4332-0800-3(8)); audio compact disk 19.95 (978-1-4332-0798-3(2)); audio compact disk 29.95 (978-1-4332-0799-0(0)); audio compact disk 45.00 (978-1-4332-0801-0(6)) Blckstn Audio.

How to talk about sexual education Today see Como transmitir educacion sexual Hoy

How to Talk about Your Troubles. unabr. ed. O. Hobart Mowrer. 1 cass. (Running Time: 37 min.). 12.95 (978-0-88432-226-9(2), C29091) J Norton Pubs.
Admission of past wrongs to the significant people in one's life is presented as a basic therapeutic approach. Emphasis is placed on the relation of anxiety to guilt rather than to impulse.

How to Talk Minnesotan. unabr. abr. ed. Howard Mohr. Read by Howard Mohr. (Running Time: 1 hr.). (ENG.). 2001. audio compact disk 12.95 (978-1-56511-493-7(0), 1565114930) Pub: HighBridge. Dist(s): Workman Pub

How to Talk So Kids Can Learn: At Home & in School. abr. ed. Adele Faber. 2004. 9.95 (978-0-7435-4854-0(X)) Pub: S&S Audio. Dist(s): S and S Inc

How to Talk So Kids Can Learn: At Home & in School. abr. ed. Adele Faber & Elaine Mazlish. Read by Adele Faber & Elaine Mazlish. Told to Lisa Nyberg & Rosalyn Anstine Templeton. 2 CDs. (Running Time: 20 hrs. 0 mins. 0 sec.). (ENG.). 2005. audio compact disk 19.95 (978-0-7435-4474-0(9)) Pub: S&S Audio. Dist(s): S and S Inc

How to Talk So Kids Will Listen... & Listen So Kids Will Talk. abr. ed. Adele Faber & Elaine Mazlish. Read by Adele Faber & Elaine Mazlish. (Running Time: 10 hrs. 0 mins. 0 sec.). (ENG., 2002. audio compact disk 14.99 (978-0-7435-2508-4(6), Nightgale) Pub: S&S Audio. Dist(s): S and S Inc

How to Talk So Men Will Listen. abr. ed. Marian K. Woodall. Ed. by Kay Franklin. 1 cass. (Running Time: 1 hr.). 1993. 12.95 (978-0-941159-44-9(2)) Prof Busn Comns.
Teaches how to select an appropriate communications style for different communicating situations, with special emphasis on differences between "woman speak" & "man speak".

*__How to Talk So Teens Will Listen & Listen So Teens Will.__ abr. ed. Adele Faber. Read by Adele Faber. Read by Elaine Mazlish. (ENG.). 2005. (978-0-06-088325-6(1), Harper Audio); (978-0-06-088326-3(X), Harper Audio) HarperCollins Pubs.

How to Talk So Teens Will Listen & Listen So Teens Will Talk. abr. ed. Adele Faber. Read by Adele Faber. Read by Elaine Mazlish. 2005. audio compact disk 22.95 (978-0-06-082340-5(2)) HarperCollins Pubs.

How to Talk to a Liberal (If You Must) The World According to Ann Coulter. abr. ed. Ann Coulter. Read by Ann Coulter. 4 CDs. (Running Time: 18000 sec.). (ENG.). 2005. audio compact disk 14.99 (978-0-7393-2145-4(5), RH Aud Price) Pub: Random Audio Pubg. Dist(s): Random

How to Talk to a Widower. abr. ed. Jonathan Tropper. Read by Eric Ruben. (Running Time: 6 hrs.). 2008. audio compact disk 14.99 (978-1-4233-2849-0(3), 9781423328490, BCD Value Price) Brilliance Audio.

How to Talk to a Widower. unabr. ed. Jonathan Tropper. Read by Eric Rubenstein. (Running Time: 9 hrs.). 2007. 24.95 (978-1-4233-2844-5(2), 9781423328445, Brilliance MP3) Brilliance Audio.

How to Talk to a Widower. unabr. ed. Jonathan Tropper. Read by Eric Ruben. (Running Time: 9 hrs.). 2007. 39.25 (978-1-4233-2847-6(7), 9781423328476, BADLE); 24.95 (978-1-4233-2846-9(9), 9781423328469, BAD); 74.25 (978-1-4233-2841-4(8), 9781423328414, BrilAudUnabridg); audio compact disk 34.95 (978-1-4233-2842-1(6), 9781423328421, Bril Audio CD Unabri); audio compact disk 39.25 (978-1-4233-2845-2(0), 9781423328452, Brlnc Audio MP3 Lib); audio compact disk 92.25 (978-1-4233-2843-8(4), 9781423328438, BriAudCD Unabrid) Brilliance Audio.

How to Talk to Anyone. abr. ed. Leil Lowndes. Read by Leil Lowndes. 3 CDs. (Running Time: 4 hrs.). (What's New Ser.). 2004. audio compact disk 23.95 (978-1-59316-026-5(7), LL118) Listen & Live.
Leil Lowndes' How To Talk To Anyone offers 92 time-tested hints, tips, and techniques for confidently communicating with others. A best-selling author and renowned communications consultant, Lowndes focuses on ice-breaking skills and communication techniques that are proven successful when making a positive first impression, establishing instant rapport and credibility, and more. Packed with basic, no-nonsense advice and solid research evidence about which techniques work best in which areas, How To Talk To Anyone show readers how to: ?Make small talk not so small ?Use body language to captivate an audience ?Look like you know

what you're talking about - even when you don't How To Talk To Anyone is brimming with helpful hints, tips, and ideas for approaching, attracting and communicating with just about anyone. Whether you?re a shy guy or gal or you?re just looking for ways to improve your social skills.

How to Talk to Anyone, Anytime, Anywhere. unabr. abr. ed. Larry King. Read by Larry King. 2 CDs. (Running Time: 1 hr. 30 mins.). (ENG.). 2002. audio compact disk 19.95 (978-0-553-71372-5(8)) Pub: Random Audio Pubg. Dist(s): Random

How to Talk to Anyone, Anytime, Anywhere: The Secrets to Good Communication. Larry King. 5 cass. (Running Time: 5 hrs.). 1996. bk. 49.95 Set. (13400AY) Nightingale-Conant.
You'll discover the 8 traits common to all great conversationalists, master the fine art of active listening & identify the four secrets for selling yourself & your skills to others.

How to Talk to Women. 2nd ed. Eric Weber. 1 cass,. (Running Time: 1 hr. 30 min.). 1995. 23.95 (978-0-914094-68-5(8)) Symphony Pr.
Interpersonal relationships.

How to Talk to your Teens about Sex/Chastity. 2005. 16.95 (978-1-888992-85-4(9)); audio compact disk 21.95 (978-1-888992-84-7(0)) Catholic Answers.

How to Talk with Your Pet. Agnes J. Thomas. 2006. 12.99 (978-0-9770964-2-8(4)) Salty Cove Pr.

How to Talk Yankee: A Down East Foreign Language Record. Perf. by Robert Bryan & Tim Sample. 1 cass. 8.95 (978-0-9607546-8-7(7), 14) Bert and I Inc.
Lessons for talking like a native New Englander. To get across the right meanings & usage the performers act out comic situations & stories - all the while coaching you to try to imitate with the proper accent.

How to Tame Stage Fright & Be Your Best at the Podium. Read by Sharon Parish & Dick Goldberg. Ed. by Chuck Quirmback. 2 cass. (Running Time: 2 hrs.). 1984. 29.95 ArGee Prods.
Reveals a new approach to public speaking & proven methods to create a more persuasive & powerful speech.

How to Tame Your Thoughts. Creflo A. Dollar. 10.00 (978-1-59089-098-1(1)) Pub: Creflo Dollar. Dist(s): STL Dist NA

How to Tango. unabr. ed. Conversa-Phone Institute Staff & Betty White. 1 cass. (Running Time: 55 min.). (Betty White's How to Ballroom Dance Ser.). 1990. 9.95 (978-1-56752-092-7(8)) Conversa-phone.
Teaches all of the most popular steps-breaks-turns - how to lead & how to follow. Fully illustrated instruction manual follows the audio tape. Learn today - dance tonight.

How to Teach a Rape Defense Course. James S. Benko. Read by James S. Benko. 1986. 12.95 (TC-11) ITA Inst.
Too many well-meaning instructors attempt to teach women to defend themselves in a rape situation without any idea of how to properly structure such a course. Master Benko will teach you how to design an entire "realistic" program.

How to Teach a Self-Defense Course. James S. Benko. 1986. 12.95 (TC-12) ITA Inst.
A complete overview of how you can set up & teach a self-defense course.

How to Teach & Preach. Gary V. Whetstone. Instructed by June Austin. (Practics Ser.: Vol. PR 203). (C). 1996. 150.00 (978-1-58866-074-9(5)) Gary Whet Pub.

How to Teach Private Classes. James S. Benko. Read by James S. Benko. 1986. 12.95 (TC-10) ITA Inst.
Your students will learn faster & better, you will be able to increase your school's income. Master Benko teaches you how to teach private classes in order to develop each student's maximum potential.

How to Teach Your Voice to Sing. Duane Shinn. 1 cass. bk. 19.95 (SG-1) Duane Shinn.
Explains how to get tone, increase lung capacity, overcome nervousness, use the hands, & many other ingredients of singing.

How to Teach Yourself All about Chords. Duane Shinn. 1 cass. bk. 19.95 (HAR-1) Duane Shinn.
Shows how chords are formed, teaches about the various types of chords, & then shows how to predict which chord comes next in a song.

How to Teach Yourself Basic Harmony Fast. Duane Shinn. 1 cass. bk. 19.95 (HAR-1) Duane Shinn.
Takes you through key signatures, time signatures, note values, notation, & so forth.

How to Tell if Someone Loves You. unabr. ed. Christina Clement. Read by Thomas Amshay. 1 cass. (Running Time: 45 min.). 1986. 5.00 (978-0-939401-05-5(3)) RFTS Prod.
Rationalizations about what people do to each other in relationships - and why.

How to Tell You Mean Business for God: 1 Cor. 13:11; Acts 18:11; 11 Tim. 2:15. Ed Young. 1999. 4.95 (978-0-7417-2217-1(8), 1217) Win Walk.

How to Tell Your Friends from the Apes. Robert A. Wilson. 2 cass. 18.00 set. (A0320-89) Sound Photosyn.
Concise & funny, RAW fans should have this one - at the L.A. Whole Life Expo.

How to Think, Act, & Become a Millionaire. abr. ed. Robert Imbriale. 2006. audio compact disk (978-0-9785426-2-7(2)) Ultimate Wealth.

How to Think Creatively, Set. abr. ed. Pearl Rovaris-MacDonald. 2 cass. (Running Time: 1 hrs. 44 min.). 1998. bk. 21.95 (978-1-929874-02-6(2),) SkillPath Pubns.
Learn to respond to life in new ways, to suspend preconceived ideas, to step outside the familiar & access intuition, humor, imagination & playfulness & the many benefits they bring.

How to Think Creatively in the Workplace. (Essential Business Skills Ser.). 1999. pap. bk. & wbk. ed. 30.00 (80229CHDG); pap. bk. & wbk. ed. 129.00 (80228CHDG) AMACOM.
Improve the ability to generate new ideas & solve problems. The Institute for Certification, a department of Professional Secretaries International, will grant points towards CPS recertification to qualified individuals who successfully complete this course. 1 CEU.

How to Think Like a CEO: The 22 Vital Traits You Need to Be the Person at the Top. abr. ed. D. A. Benton. (Running Time: 1 hr. 30 mins.). (ENG.). 2006. 14.98 (978-1-59483-734-0(1)) Pub: Hachet Audio. Dist(s): HachBkGrp

How to Think Like a Christian. Perf. by Douglas W. Phillips. 1 CD. (Running Time: 1 hr.). 2001. audio compact disk 10.00 (978-1-929241-64-4(X)) Pub: Vision Forum. Dist(s): STL Dist NA

How to Think Like a Christian. Featuring Douglas W. Phillips. 1 cass. (Running Time: 1 hr.). 2001. 7.00 (978-1-929241-39-2(9)) Pub: Vsn Forum. Dist(s): STL Dist NA

How to Think Like Einstein. Thorpe. Read by Kerin McCue. 2009. audio compact disk 19.95 (978-1-59316-453-9(X)) Listen & Live.

How to Think Like Einstein. abr. ed. Scott Thorpe. Read by Kevin McCue. 2 cass. (Running Time: 3 hrs.). (Works the Mind Ser.). 2001. 16.95 (978-1-885408-57-0(9), LL049) Listen & Live.
In this totally accessible, ingenious audiobook, you will learn the tricks & techniques used by Albert Einstein & other great minds to solve bewildering problems. From business & parenting to becoming more creative & improving relationships. How to think like Einstein provides the tools to discovering breakthrough solutions to everyday challenges.

How to Think Like Leonardo da Vinci: Seven Steps to Genius Every Day. abr. ed. Michael J. Gelb. Read by Michael J. Gelb. 2 cass., 3 CDs. (Running Time: 3 hrs.). 1999. (Random AudioBks) Random Audio Pubg.
Teaches how to develop one's full potential, using the principles of Da Vincian thought identified by the author. Beginning with a brief historical biography of Da Vinci, Gelb illustrates the seven fundamental elements of Da Vinci's thought process.

How to Think Like Leonardo da Vinci: Seven Steps to Genius Every Day, unabr. ed. Michael J. Gelb. Narrated by Richard M. Davidson. 6 cass. (Running Time: 7 hrs. 45 mins.). 2000. 51.00 (978-0-7887-4074-9(1), 96166E7) Recorded Bks.
Let this world-renowned expert in innovative thinking show you that you don't have to be a genius to think like one. This revolutionary approach to learning & creativity will enrich every aspect of your life.

How to Think Positively. 1 cass. (Running Time: 1 hr.). 12.99 (121) Yoga Res Foun.

How to Torture an Author. (23332) J Norton Pubs.

How to Trade Options & Make Money. Robert Anderson. 2002. pap. bk. 59.95 (978-1-884350-80-1(1)) Alpha Pubng.

How to Train Singers: With Illustrated "Natural" Techniques & Taped Exercises. 2nd ed. Larra B. Henderson. 1991. bk., spiral bd., wbk. ed. 44.95 (978-0-13-441411-9(X), 710601) P-H.

How to Train Your Human Spirit. Creflo A. Dollar. 10.00 (978-1-59089-031-8(0)) Pub: Creflo Dollar. Dist(s): STL Dist NA

How to Train Your Parents. Pete Johnson. Read by Kris Marshall. 3 CDs. (J). 2003. audio compact disk 29.95 (978-0-7540-6614-9(2), Chivers Child Audio) AudioGO.

How to Transfer Your Closely Held Business. Irv Blackman & William Wallace. 2 cass. 99.00 set incl. wkbk. (740770KQ) Am Inst CPA.
This course guides you in helping your clients who own businesses. You can show them or their families how to avoid being clobbered with huge taxes when the business is eventually transferred.

How to Transform Your Life: Romans 12:1-2. Ed Young. 1997. 4.95 (978-0-7417-2138-9(4), 1138) Win Walk.

How to Transpose & Modulate. Duane Shinn. 1 cass. 19.95 (NS-1) Duane Shinn.
There are 12 major piano keys in which you can play, & each of these keys has 3 chords which occur more often than any others. You can transpose into any other key after your fingers get used to the configurations of that particular key. You'll also learn to modulate smoothly by finding the V7 chord in the new key, leading to the tonic chord.

***How to Trust God.** Benton Thompson, 3rd. 2010. audio compact disk 10.95 (978-0-9824755-4-6(3)) Bar Abba.

How to Trust Your Vibes at Work: And Let Them Work for You. Sonia Choquette. 4 CDs. 2006. audio compact disk 23.95 (978-1-4019-1151-5(X)) Hay House.

How to Try an Auto Accident Case. (Running Time: 5 hrs.). 1995. 92.00 Incl. 231p. coursebk. (20791) NYS Bar.
Designed to assist practitioners who are called upon to try automobile accident cases on behalf of plaintiffs or defendants. Both plaintiff's & defendant's perspectives are highlighted in the course of the presentations.

How to Tune Guitar. Brett Duncan. (Progressive Ser.). 2004. pap. bk. 5.95 (978-1-86469-209-9(X), 256-089) Kolala Music SGP.

How to Tune in to Higher Guidance. Kriyananda, pseud. 1 cass. 9.95 (ST-75) Crystal Clarity.
Topics include: Non-attachment as a prerequisite to receiving guidance; the danger of seeking guidance through psychic phenomena; attitudes that increase our receptivity; how to know whether our intuitions are God's will.

How to turn an interview into a Job. Jeffrey G. Allen. 2004. 5.95 (978-0-7435-4855-7(8)) Pub: S&S Audio. Dist(s): S and S Inc

How to Turn Disgustomers into Immediate Sales. Dave Johnson. (Dave Johnson Educational Library). 65.00 D Johnson.
Discusses how to never run out of energy & how to get an affirmative decision without making your prospect say 'yes'.

How to Turn Objections into Sales. 1971. audio compact disk (978-0-89811-282-5(6)) Meyer Res Grp.

How to Turn Objections into Sales. Paul J. Meyer. 1 cass. (Running Time: 45 min.). 11.00 (978-0-89811-078-4(5), 7130) Meyer Res Grp.
Learn to use a client's objection as the key that locks up the sale.

How to Turn Objections into Sales. Paul J. Meyer. 1 cass. 10.00 (SP100027) SMI Intl.
Does a prospect's first question or objection make you want to close your sample case & say good-bye?...or does it present a challenge that calls forth your best efforts? Listen to this cassette tape & learn to use a client's objection as the key that locks up the sale.

How to Turn off the TV in One Easy Lesson & Live Happily Ever After. Instructed by Manly P. Hall. 8.95 (978-0-89314-140-0(2), C840805) Philos Res.

How to Turn the Ordinary into Extraordinary. (Running Time: 48 mins.). audio compact disk (978-1-59076-205-9(3)) DscvrHlpPubng.

How to Turn Your Body into a Natural Healer. Adrianne Ahern. 2006. audio compact disk 24.95 (978-0-9773181-3-1(3)) A Ahern.

How to Turn Your Church Around. George Barna. 1 cass. 1996. 12.99 (978-7-5116-0053-0(0)) Gospel Lght.
Church administration.

How to Turn Your Expertise into A Multimedia Empire. Fran Harris. 2006. audio compact disk 1499.00 (978-1-59971-503-2(1)) AardGP.

How to Turn Your New Product Ideas into Cash. unabr. ed. Vernon Brabham. 1 cass. (Running Time: 1 hr. 05 min.). 1995. 19.95 (978-0-9646996-0-1(5)) Craftmark Prods.
Tells how a person can make money by producing, promoting & marketing their new product ideas - themselves.

How to Understand, Access, & Use the Internet: Master the Ultimate Communication Skill. 6 cass. 59.95 Set incl. wkbk. (13160AS) Pryor Resources.
An estimated 200 million people will soon be on-line, expanding their horizons & improving their bottom line, including your customers, clients & competition - why not you? Understand the hottest marketing tool in the easiest, most accessible, convenient way available.

***How to Understand & Administer a Budget.** PUEI. 2009. audio compact disk 199.00 (978-1-935041-78-8(9), CareerTrack) P Univ E Inc.

How to Understand & Listen to Great Music, Course No. 700. Robert Greenberg. 6 pts., 48 lectures. (Greenberg Lectures). 249.91 Set. Teaching Co.
The lectures in this series will enrich your life in a way that few other experiences can rival: with Professor Greenberg as your guide, you will suddenly be able to hear & understand an entire language of unmatched beauty, genius & power.

How to Unleash the Power Within & Attract Money: How Wealthy Do You Want to Be? As Wealthy As You Can IMANGINE. 4 cass. (Running Time: 6 hrs.). (ENG.). 2003. audio compact disk 129.00 (978-0-9741449-0-0(8)) Present Mem.

How to Update Your 12 & 24 Month Goals for Your Company. Deb Digregorio. 2009. 250.00 (978-1-59701-509-7(1)) ReedLogic.

How to Use Access for Windows 95. unabr. ed. Kimi Nance. Read by Lee McFadden. Ed. by Patricia A. Menges. 4 cass. (Running Time: 5 hrs. 20 min.). 1996. 225.00 set. (978-1-56562-071-1(2), 332) OneOnOne Comp Trng.

How to Use Cheap Postcards to Drive Massive Amounts of Traffic to Your Business. Kris Solie- Johnson. 2007. 49.95 (978-0-939069-02-6(4)) Amer Inst Small Bus.

How to Use Financial Data for More Effective Litigation Results. Laventhol & Horwath. (Running Time: 5 hrs.). 1985. 100.00 incl. program handbook. NJ Inst CLE.
Reveals how attorneys can work with accountants to use financial data for more effective results in commercial litigation, real estate, trial & settlement, bankruptcy, divorce litigation.

How to Use Free Publicity. Kris Solie-Johnson. 2007. 49.95 (978-0-939069-06-4(7)) Amer Inst Small Bus.

How to Use Microsoft Excel 7. unabr. ed. B. Alan August. Read by Lee McFadden. Ed. by Natalie B. Young. 4 cass. (Running Time: 5 hrs. 15 min.). 1996. pap. bk. 225.00 set. (978-1-56562-069-8(0), 292) OneOnOne Comp Trng.

How to Use Microsoft Windows 95. unabr. ed. Charles R. Wolf. Read by Lee McFadden. Ed. by Natalie B. Young. 4 cass. (Running Time: 5 hrs. 15 min.). 1995. cass. & disk 225.00 set. (978-1-56562-076-6(3), 160) OneOnOne Comp Trng.

How to Use Microsoft Word for Windows Version 2.X. unabr. ed. Christine Reid. Read by Lee McFadden. Ed. by Sally Hargrave. 4 cass. (Running Time: 4 hrs. 20 min.). 1992. pap. bk. 175.00 Set. (978-1-56562-011-7(9), 440) OneOnOne Comp Trng.
Self-paced training for Word for Windows 2.X.

How to Use PageMaker 5 for the Macintosh, Pt. I. unabr. ed. Natalie B. Young. Read by Lee McFadden. Ed. by Kim Clementz. 4 cass. (Running Time: 5 hrs. 18 min.). 1993. pap. bk. 175.00 (978-1-56562-037-7(2), 522) OneOnOne Comp Trng.
The hands-on course takes users step-by-step through PageMaker's desktop publishing capabilities. The course covers the basics - copying, cutting & pasting text, choosing a copy format & using templates & special effects. Document disk & reference guide included.

How to Use PageMaker 5 for the Macintosh, Pt. II. unabr. ed. Natalie B. Young. Read by Lee McFadden. Ed. by Kim Clementz. 4 cass. (Running Time: 5 hrs. 20 min.). 1993. pap. bk. 175.00 (978-1-56562-038-4(0), 524) OneOnOne Comp Trng.
The course advances the listener in the use of PageMaker's desktop publishing capabilities. Includes creating, editing & using style sheets, importing data from other applications & using the Story Editor. Document disk & reference guide included.

How to Use PageMaker 5 for Windows, Pt. II. unabr. ed. Linda K. Schwartz. Read by Lee McFadden. Ed. by Natalie B. Young. 4 cass. (Running Time: 5 hrs. 18 min.). pap. bk. 175.00 (978-1-56562-035-3(6), 520) OneOnOne Comp Trng.
The course advances the user in the use of PageMaker's desktop publishing capabilities. Includes creating, editing & using style sheets, importing data from other applications & using the Story Editor. Document disk & reference guide included.

How to Use Paradox 4.5 for Windows. 1994. tchr. ed. & wbk. ed. 29.00 (978-0-7402-0075-5(5), BLPDW451IG) Accelerated Comput Train.

How to Use PowerPoint for Windows 95. unabr. ed. Natalie B. Young. Read by Lee McFadden. Ed. by Kimi Nance. 4 cass. (Running Time: 5 hrs. 20 min.). 1995. pap. bk. 225.00 set. (978-1-56562-070-4(4), 622) OneOnOne Comp Trng.

How to Use Stories in Your Presentations. Robert S. Fish. Read by Robert S. Fish. 1 cass. (Running Time: 27 min.). 1993. 12.95 incl. script. (978-0-9660740-7-9(6)) Morgan Seminar.
Learn how to find, create & tell stories.

How to Use Tact & Skill in Handling People. Paul P. Parker. 1 cass. (Running Time: 36 min.). 11.00 (978-0-89811-009-8(2), 5130) Meyer Res Grp.
Offers ideas for getting things done through other people. Also available in Spanish.

How to Use Tact & Skill in Handling People. Paul P. Parker. 1 cass. 10.00 (SP100005) SMI Intl.
Listen to exciting ideas for getting things done through other people. Learn to make the basic qualities of human nature work for you, not against you. Learn & practice the art of handling people effectively.

How to Use the Circle of 4ths to Create Great Chord Progressions! 1 cass. 19.95 Incl. printed circle of 4ths. (CP-21) Duane Shinn.
The Circle of 4ths progresses through all twelve keys, & in it lies the secret of chord progressions. Learn how to move from major 7ths to minor 7ths; from suspensions to resolutions; & you'll learn how easy it is to develop your improvisations simply by breaking up the notes of the chord progressions within the circle.

How to Use the Course (How to) in Everyday Life (Basic Concepts) Diane B. Gusic. 2 cass. 1992. 18.00 set. (OC301&2-66) Sound Horizons AV.

How to Use the Hewlett-Packard 12-C Financial Calculator. Lonnie Scruggs. (ENG.). 2008. spiral bd. 49.00 (978-1-933553-03-0(0)) Atomic Sound.

How to Use the I Ching. unabr. ed. John Blofeld & Al Huang. 2 cass. (Running Time: 2 hrs.). 1978. 18.00 Set. (02904) Big Sur Tapes.
Explains how to "throw" the I Ching & entreats throwers to approach it intuitively. He talks about the differing approaches to translation: his, a modern interpretation to be used as a book of divination, & Wilhelm's, an historical reconstruction of what the I Ching meant at the time it was written. Huang opens the second tape with a meditation on allowing the self to be an open vehicle, to become what the Chinese commentary in the I Ching is saying.

How to Use the I Ching: A Live Workshop With Marion Weinstein. Marion Weinstein. 1 cass. (Running Time: 1 hrs.). (Dealing with the Future Ser.: Vol. 2). 1999. 10.00 (978-1-890733-02-5(4)) Earth Magic.
By means of aligning with the harmonious forces of the universe, this ancient Chinese system of divination is used for amazingly foolproof decision making.

How to Use the I Ching: A Live Workshop with Marion Weinstein. Featuring Marion Weintein. (Dealing with the Future Ser.). (ENG.). 2007. audio compact disk 14.99 (978-1-890733-11-7(3)) Earth Magic.

How to Use the Metronome. Duane Shinn. 1 cass. 19.95 (HAR-9) Duane Shinn.
Explains how to read tempo markings, such as M.M. 60; learn the continuum between largo & presto; learn the difference between a semibreve, a minim, crotchet, quaver, semi-quaver, & demi-semi-quaver.

How to Use the Phone in Your Job Search. Created by J. Barry Vanek. 2006. DVD & audio compact disk 39.95 (978-0-9767888-3-6(7)) So Pub.

How to Use the Science of Mind. abr. ed. Ernest Holmes. Read by Gene Ross. Ed. by John S. Niendorff. 2 cass. (Running Time: 2 hrs. 50 min.). 1986. 14.95 (978-0-917849-00-8(0), T208) Sci of Mind.
Discusses technique for spiritual healing, using universal power, the law of mind in action, & spiritual cause & physical effect.

How to Use the Tax Code to Facilitate Resolutions. 1998. bk. 99.00 (ACS-2094) PA Bar Inst.
How do the new tax changes affect family law? Should a couple file a joint return while a divorce is pending? Can alimony payments increase the funds available to a family? How can the tax credit for children be used to a family's best advantage? Will changes in the IRA law make any difference to the domestic relations practitioner?.

How to Use UNIX & Xenix. David S. Levin. Read by Lee McFadden. Ed. by Jacqueline Jonas & Patricia A. Menges. 4 cass. (Running Time: 4 hrs. 30 min.). (C). 1991. pap. bk. 245.00 set. (978-0-917792-49-6(1), 122) OneOnOne Comp Trng.

How to Use Words of Power: A Live Workshop With Marion Weinstein. Marion Weinstein. 2 cass. (Running Time: 1 hrs.). (Dealing with the Future Ser.: Vol. 3). 2000. 17.95 Set. (978-1-890733-03-2(2)) Earth Magic.
Explains the techniques upon which are based magic "spells," prayer & affirmations. Your own words will serve you better than someone else's eloquent incantations.

How to Use Words of Power: A Live Workshop with Marion Weinstein. Featuring Marion Weinstein. (Dealing with the Future Ser.). (ENG.). 2007. audio compact disk 24.99 (978-1-890733-10-0(5)) Earth Magic.

How to Use Your Emotions to Make Sound Decisions. 1 cass. 1998. (978-0-9661071-2-8(8)) Access Pr PA.

How to Use Your Personal Power to Promote Yourself: Making All the Right Professional Wellness Moves. abr. ed. Featuring Bob Janet. Interview with Angela Brown. Prod. by Les Lingle. 1 cass. (Running Time: 30 mins.). (Words of Wellness Ser.). 2000. 12.95 (978-1-930995-01-7(6), LLP301) Life Long Pubg.
Who could say no to you when you know all the right things to say, you know how to treat a customer & you execute your delivery with style & confidence?.

How to Utilize Your Time. (113) Yoga Res Foun.

How to Utilize Your Time. Swami Jyotirmayananda. 1 cass. (Running Time: 1 hr.). 1990. 12.99 Yoga Res Foun.

How to Value the Homemaker's Contribution in Personal Injury & Matrimonial Cases. Contrib. by Judith I. Avner et al. Comment by Geoffrey Gaulkin. (Running Time: 4 hrs.). 1984. 70.00 incl. program handbook. NJ Inst CLE.
Highlights include: how to utilize accepted theories for valuing the homemaker contribution, how to present these views in court, how to utilize the resource material available for determining a value.

How to Voice a Chord for a "Pro Sound" 1 cass. 19.95 Incl. summary sheet. (CP-20) Duane Shinn.
To "voice" means to arrange the notes of a chord on the keyboard so you get the sound you want. Since there are scores of ways to voice a chord, you need to know the principles involved.

How to Vote for a President: Habakkuk 2:1. Ed Young. 1992. 4.95 (978-0-7417-1939-3(8), 939) Win Walk.

How to Vote for a President: Habakkuk 2:1. Ed Young. 1996. 4.95 (978-0-7417-2120-4(1), 1120) Win Walk.

How to Vote for President: Lam.5:21. Ed Young. 1988. 4.95 (978-0-7417-1690-3(9), 690) Win Walk.

How to Waltz. unabr. ed. Conversa-Phone Institute Staff & Betty White. 1 cass. (Running Time: 55 min.). (Betty White's How to Ballroom Dance Ser.). 1990. 9.95 (978-1-56752-088-0(X)) Conversa-phone.
Teaches all of the most popular steps-breaks-turns - how to lead & how to follow. Fully illustrated instruction manual follows the audio tape. Learn today - dance tonight.

How to Want What You Have: Discovering the Magic & Grandeur of Ordinary Existence. unabr. collector's ed. Timothy Miller. Read by Jonathan Marosz. 6 cass. (Running Time: 9 hrs.). 1995. 48.00 (978-0-7366-3049-8(X), 3731) Books on Tape.
The simplest way to joy is treasuring what you have, says Dr. Timothy Miller. Anecdotal & thoughtful.

How to Watch TV News. unabr. ed. Neil Postman & Steve Powers. Read by Jeff Riggenbach. 4 cass. (Running Time: 5 hrs. 30 mins.). 1997. audio compact disk 32.95 Set. (978-0-7861-1062-9(7), 1833) Blckstn Audio.
Neil Postman, an author & academic, & Steve Powers, a television journalist, reveal the difference between what TV news says it is presenting & what it actually delivers - entertainment fodder versus genuine "news." For anyone who wants to control - not be controlled by - the powerful influence of TV, this book shows how to become a discerning viewer.

How to Wave Your Arms in Front of a Singing Crowd. Duane Shinn. 1 cass. 9.95 (G-3) Duane Shinn.
Explains how to: Gain & hold audience attention; Give a boost to a sagging accompianist; Hold hands correctly & naturally; & Lead songs in all standard beat patterns.

How to Weather the Storm. Taffi L. Dollar. 2008. audio compact disk 14.00 (978-1-59944-725-4(8)) Creflo Dollar.

How to Win a Cosmic War: God, Globalization, & the End of the War on Terror. abr. unabr. ed. Reza Aslan. Read by Sunil Malhotra. (ENG.). 2009. audio compact disk 35.00 (978-0-7393-8330-8(2), Random AudioBks) Pub: Random Audio Pubg. Dist(s): Random

How to Win a Lot More Business in Half the Time. Michael LeBoeuf. 6 cass. (Running Time: 6 hrs.). 1995. bk. 59.95 Set. (12860PA) Nightingale-Conant.
Dozens of proven strategies & tactics to help you swiftly adapt to changing customer needs & take advantage of new markets, trends & technology.

How to Win Any Argument: Without Raising Your Voice, Losing Your Cool, or Coming to Blows. abr. ed. Robert Mayer. Read by David Drummond. (Running Time: 14400 sec.). 2007. audio compact disk 23.95 (978-1-59316-106-4(9)) Listen & Live.

***How To Win Any Negotiation.** Robert Mayer. 2011. audio compact disk 23.95 (978-1-59316-575-8(7)) Listen & Live.

How to Win Arguments. unabr. ed. William A. Rusher. Read by Tory Hanson. 5 cass. (Running Time: 7 hrs.). 1989. 39.95 (978-0-7861-0044-6(3), 1043) Blckstn Audio.
This practical & highly entertaining book, will show you how to acquire the skills & techniques necessary to hold your own against even the best debaters.

How to Win at Monopoly. Armand Aronson. Read by Armand Aronson. 1 CD. (Running Time: 77min 31sec). 2003. audio compact disk 14.95 (978-1-932226-17-1(6)) Pub: Wizard Acdmy. Dist(s): Baker Taylor
Year after year Monopoly? is the biggest selling board game in the world. It has been a great gift for decades. It?s not going to go away. So, you might as well learn how to win, now. This book raises the bar as they say in high jumping. The competition will get better because everyone who learns what How to Win at Monopoly has to say will be a better player.Monopoly? can be an emotional game. Whenever emotions are heightened learning happens at a faster rate. So the educational benefits of Monopoly? and How to Win at Monopoly can be learned deeply and applied to other parts of life. Math, language and ?people skills? can all be enhanced. This book is a must for students of all ages, people in sales, people in management, and people in families. True learning is a gift that keeps on giving.Includes:77min 31sec Audio CD58 page booklet.

How to Win at the Healthcare Sales Game: A Successful Approach for Medical Salespeople & Buyers. John Jascoll. Read by John Jascoll. 1994. 10.00 (978-0-9643012-2-1(9)) Hazelwood Pr.

How to Win Customers & Keep Them for Life: An Action-Ready Blueprint for Achieving the Winner's Edge!, Set. Michael LeBoeuf. 6 cass. 59.95 (490AX) Nightingale-Conant.
Recent surveys indicate that it costs six times more to get a new customer than it does to keep one you already have. Discover can't-miss techniques for attracting qualified new customers & keys to keeping them happy. Protect your business' most valuable asset & transform your organization into a highly motivated, service-based team.

How to Win Friends & Influence People. unabr. ed. Dale Carnegie. Read by Andrew Macmillian. 8 CDs. (Running Time: 71 hrs. 50 mins. 0 sec.). (ENG.). 1999. audio compact disk 49.95 (978-0-671-57959-3(2)) Pub: S&S Audio. Dist(s): S and S Inc

How to Win Support Cases. 1985. bk. 65.00 incl. book.; 40.00 cass. only.; 25.00 book only. PA Bar Inst.

How to Win the Battle for Market Share. 1 cass. (America's Supermarket Showcase '96 Ser.). 1996. 11.00 (NGA96-004) Sound Images.

How to Win the Battle over the Flesh. Steve Hill. (ENG.). 2007. audio compact disk 25.00 (978-1-892853-80-6(9)) Togthr Hrvest.

***How to Win the Culture War.** Peter Kreeft. Read by Kevin Roberts. (ENG.). 2009. audio compact disk 21.95 (978-1-936231-04-1(2)) Cath Audio.

How to Win with People Package: Relationship Strategies. Tony Allessandra. 6 cass. (Running Time: 8 hrs.). 1995. 99.00 set, incl. wkbk. (710301EZ) Am Inst CPA.
Developing a successful accounting practice takes a client-service team capable of building solid relationships with its clients by reading & responding effectively to their unique needs. Through the fast-paced audio program, you'll learn to build profitable client relationships.

How to Win with Your Teen. Bob Lancer. (Running Time: 60 mins.). 9.95 (978-0-9628666-8-5(7)) Parent Sol.

How to Withdraw the Senses. Swami Jyotirmayananda. Read by Swami Jyotirmayananda. 1 cass. (Running Time: 60 min.). 12.99 (126) Yoga Res Foun.

How to Witness to Jehovah's Witnesses. Walter Ralston Martin. 1 cass. 1982. 23.99 (978-7-5116-0039-4(5)) Gospel Lght.

How to Witness to Mormons. Walter Ralston Martin. 1 cass. 1997. 23.99 (978-7-5116-0040-0(9)) Gospel Lght.
Evangelism.

***How to Woo A Reluctant Lady.** unabr. ed. Sabrina Jeffries. (Running Time: 11 hrs.). (Hellions of Halstead Hall Ser.). 2011. 19.99 (978-1-4418-3669-4(1), 9781441836694, BAD); 39.97 (978-1-4418-3670-0(5), 9781441836700, BADLE); 19.99 (978-1-4418-3667-0(5), 9781441836670, Brilliance MP3); 39.97 (978-1-4418-3668-7(3), 9781441836687, Brinc Audio MP3 Lib); audio compact disk 19.99 (978-1-4418-3665-6(9), 9781441836656, Bril Audio CD Unabri); audio compact disk 69.97 (978-1-4418-3666-3(7), 9781441836663, BriAudCD Unabrid) Brilliance Audio.

How to Work a Room: The Ultimate Guide to Savvy Socializing in Person & Online. abr. rev. ed. Susan RoAne. 3 CDs. (Running Time: 3 hrs. 0 mins. 0 sec.). (ENG.). 2004. audio compact disk 19.95 (978-1-59397-524-1(4)) Pub: Macmill Audio. Dist(s): Macmillan

How to Work Less & Make More: Practice & Wealth Management Solutions for Physicians. As told by David B. Mandell. Arranged by David B. Mandell. Based on a book by Christopher R. Jarvis. Christopher R. Stout. (ENG.). 2007. audio compact disk 9.95 (978-1-890415-22-8(7)) Guardian Pub.

How to Work the Hill Like a Pro. Ed. by TheCapitol.Net. 2005. audio compact disk 107.00 (978-1-58733-020-9(2)) TheCapitol.

How to Work the Hill Like a Pro: Capitol Learning Audio Course. Deanna Gelak. Prod. by TheCapitol.Net. (ENG.). 2007. 47.00 (978-1-58733-063-6(6)) TheCapitol.

How to Work with a Business Appraiser. 1 cass. (Running Time: 58 min.). (Business Valuation Discount Planning & Tax Dispute Techniques Ser.). 1995. 75.00 Incl. study guide. (M232) Am Law Inst.
This fundamental program explains the business appraiser's role, appraisal standards & methods, & active business methodology to help lawyers make the most of the attorney-appraiser partnership. Topics discussed include the burden of proof in transfer tax valuation; the business valuation appraiser as a source of evidence; confidentiality & attorney-client privilege issues; types of appraisers & selection of appraisers; & various appraisal "standards of value." Additional issues include active business methodology; appraiser reliance on data & assumptions; & valuation discounts. All attorneys & tax professionals who work with business appraisers in the preparation of tax returns, buy-sell agreements, & estate & gift planning in general will benefit from this presentation.

How to Work with People. Asha Praver. 1 cass. (Running Time: 90 min.). (Relationship Ser.). 9.95 (AT-52) Crystal Clarity.
The powerful magnetism of an uplifted consciousness; how to raise your consciousness to become more fully "yourself"; loyalty as the key to friendship & successful leadership; pitfalls in trying to achieve our ends at the expense of others.

How to Work with Spiritual Tests - Right Attitude for Devotees. 1 cass. (Running Time: 90 min.). (Devotion Ser.). 9.95 (SC-10) Crystal Clarity.
Why God tests us; does God want us to suffer?; love as the basis of faith; attitudes needed to find God; taking the difficult path.

How to Work with Your Emotions. 2 cass. (Running Time: 2 hrs.). (Personal Growth Ser.). 9.95 (ST-19) Crystal Clarity.
Why "releasing" your emotions is always a temporary solution; mistaken assumptions of psychology; why self-improvement approaches which exclude God don't work; how to turn your emotions Godward.

How to Write a Clinical Guide. Kathleen Anne McCarthy. (C). 2003. audio compact disk 9.95 (978-0-9672524-2-1(3)) Criticare Res.

How to Write a Curriculum That Works. Dora C. Fowler. 1 cass. (Running Time: 60 min.). 1990. 9.95 (978-1-57323-026-1(X)) Natl Inst Child Mgmt.
Staff training material for child care.

How to Write A Red Hot Busiiness Plan MAde EZ. Lynette Bigelow. 1-Audio CD. (Running Time: 40). 2006. audio compact disk 39.99 (978-0-914391-76-0(3)) Comm People Pr.

How to Write an Essay, Pt. A. unabr. ed. Gilbert Highet. 1 cass. (Running Time: 30 min.). (Gilbert Highet Ser.). 9.95 (23333) J Norton Pubs.
Gilbert Highet describes how he first learned to write & a comical diagnosis of the diseases that afflict a literary critic.

How to Write & Conduct Effective Performance Appraisals: And Use Them to Help Employees Develop & Improve. Jimmy Calano. 4 cass. (Running Time: 3 hrs. 42 min.). 59.95 Set incl. 48p. wkbk. (V10154) CareerTrack Pubns.
You'll learn ways to evaluate your people's performance fairly & objectively & you'll learn to prepare & deliver your appraisal so that it helps motivate & develop your people.

How to Write & Sell Your Travel Articles. abr. ed. Connie Sherley. Read by Connie Sherley. 1 cass. (Running Time: 90 mins.). 1987. 12.95 (978-1-880717-13-4(1)) Writers AudioShop.
Prolific travel writer covers getting started, the markets, what editors are looking for, photographs, press trips, getting several articles from one trip & selling to non-travel markets.

How to Write Astrology Books. Doris C. Doane. 1 cass. 8.95 (515) Am Fed Astrologers.
Basis for publishable manuscripts.

How to Write Best-Selling Romance. Brenda Wilbee. 6 cass. (Running Time: 5 hrs.). 1988. 24.95 (978-0-943777-07-8(0)) byBrenda.
Explains how to write romance novels.

***How to Write Comprehensive Policies & Procedures.** PUEI. 2009. audio compact disk 199.00 (978-1-935041-77-1(0), CareerTrack) P Univ E Inc.

How to Write for Everyday Living. Ann Edson & Eunice Insel. 5 cass. (YA). 89.00 incl. 8 activity bks., guide. (978-0-89525-210-4(4), AKC 359) Ed Activities.
Deals with the basic skills needed to function & communicate in the real world, on the job, & in school. Includes: Writing organized lists, arranging an address book, addressing envelopes & labels, writing orders, filling out an application, filling out an employment form, writing a resume, writing business letters, completing change of address forms, applying for rebates, sending a telegram, taking telephone messages, registering to vote, answering surveys.

How to Write for the Astrological Market. Elbert Wade. 1 cass. 8.95 (357) Am Fed Astrologers.
An AFA Convention workshop tape.

How to Write High-Profit Job Orders. Composed by Bill Radin. 2 CDs. (Running Time: 100 minutes). (Professional Development Series for Recruiters: Vol. 2). 2002. audio compact disk 79.95 (978-1-929836-06-2(6)) Innovative Consulting.
Sales training for recruiters.

How to Write High Profit Job Orders, Set. Bill Radin. Read by Bill Radin. 2 cass. (Running Time: 1 hr. 40 min.). (Professional Development Series for Recruiters: Vol. 2). 1999. pap. bk. & wbk. ed. 79.95 (978-1-929836-01-7(5)) Innovative Consulting.
Sales training & performance improvement guide for executive recruiter & personnel consultants.

How to Write Historical Fiction. abr. ed. Roberta Gellis. Read by Roberta Gellis. 1 cass. (Running Time: 90 mins.). (ENG.). 1988. 12.95 (978-1-880717-17-2(4),) Writers AudioShop.
One of the decade's most respected writers of this genre details the types of historical fiction, & gives basics of research to make the setting authentic, pin down the period & pick the key event.

How to Write Horoscope Columns. Elbert Wade. 1 cass. 8.95 (358) Am Fed Astrologers.
Prepare valid sunsign forecasts.

How to Write Humor. abr. ed. Mel Helitzer. Read by Mel Helitzer. 1 cass. (Running Time: 90 mins.). 1987. 12.95 (978-1-880717-15-8(8)) Writers AudioShop.
Author of three books on writing humor & university instructor explores the theory of humor, the 6 ingredients of good humor & the uses of humor for print, broadcast, speeches, ads & business.

How to Write Practically Any Business Document: Even If You Hate to Write. Ronnie Moore. 4 cass. (Running Time: 3 hrs. 27 min.). 49.95 Set incl. 32p. wkbk. (V10129) CareerTrack Pubns.
This program helps you write memos, letters, reports & proposals with the "Writing Roadmap" system that lets you get your ideas down on paper - fast. You'll gain confidence in your writing & save countless hours as you use your writing time more wisely.

How to Write, Publish & Sell Your Book & Turn it into a Never-ending Money Machine. Speeches. Jim Donovan. 4 CD's. (Running Time: 4 hours). 2007. audio compact disk 129.00 (978-0-9786891-2-4(7)) Austin Bay.

How to Write True Crime That Sells. unabr. ed. Gera-Lind Kolarik & Dolores Kennedy. Read by Gera-Lind Kolarik & Dolores Kennedy. 1 cass. (Running Time: 1 hr.). 1994. 7.95 (978-1-882071-44-9(1)) B-B Audio.
Two of todays top female true crime writers discuss how to write and sell true crime. Examples and dramatizations let you see behind the scenes as crimes occur. Then youll meet the people who bring the stories out in the open and learn the secrets of.

How to Write Your Own Life Story Set: Your Step-by-Step Guide to Turning Your Life Story into a Book. Patrika Vaughn. 4 cass. (Running Time: 6 hrs.). 1999. 45.00 Set. (978-0-9656309-5-5(1)) A Cappela Pub.

How to Write Your Own Short Plays & Skits. David C. Hon. 1 cass. 1977. 9.95 Incl. synopsis review. (C73) Meriwether Pub.
Professional playwright & director, David Hon, tells what he thinks about structuring a play for content, dialog, action & total appeal.

How to Write Your Own Ticket with God. Kenneth E. Hagin. 4 cass. 16.00 (38H) Faith Lib Pubns.

How Tracy Austin Broke My Heart. abr. ed. David Foster Wallace. Read by David Foster Wallace. (Running Time: 1 hr.). (ENG.). 2008. 2.98 (978-1-60024-313-4(4)) Pub: Hachet Audio. Dist(s): HachBkGrp

How Training Can Turn Strategy into Real Improvement. Ted Cocheu. (Management Ser.). 1993. bk. 29.95 (978-1-55542-521-0(6), Jossey-Bass) Wiley US.

How Vaccines Boost Resistance to Cancer. Virginia Livingston. (ENG.). 2008. audio compact disk Rental 12.95 (978-1-57970-531-2(6), Audio-For) J Norton Pubs.

How Vaccines Boost Resistance to Cancer. unabr. ed. Virginia Livingston. 1 cass. (Running Time: 32 min.). 12.95 (933) J Norton Pubs.

How We Came to the Fifth World: Como Vinimos Al Quinto Mundo. Mary Anchondo. Read by Harriet Rohmer. Ed. by Anna Olivarez. Illus. by Graciela Carillo. (J). (gr. 2-7). 1987. bk. 22.95 (978-0-89239-038-0(7)) Childrens Book Pr.

How We Create Our Own Reality. Jon Klimo. 1 cass. 9.00 (A0722-89) Sound Photosyn.
An exuberant culmination rap from the 1989 International Conference for the Study of Shamanism.

How We Decide. unabr. ed. Jonah Lehrer. Read by David Colacci. 1 MP3-CD. (Running Time: 10 hrs.). 2009. 39.97 (978-1-4233-7649-1(8), 9781423376491, Brlnc Audio MP3 Lib); 24.99 (978-1-4233-7650-7(1), 9781423376507, BAD); 24.99 (978-1-4233-7648-4(X), 9781423376484, Brilliance MP3); 39.97 (978-1-4233-7651-4(X), 9781423376514, BADLE); audio compact disk 87.97 (978-1-4233-7647-7(1), 9781423376477, BriAudCD Unabrid); audio compact disk 32.99 (978-1-4233-7646-0(3), 9781423376460, Bril Audio CD Unabri) Brilliance Audio.

How We Did It see Poetry & Voice of Muriel Rukeyser

How We Got Our Bible. Chuck Missler. 2 CDs. (Running Time: 120 min. aprox.). (Briefing Packages by Chuck Missler). 2006. audio compact disk 19.95 (978-1-57821-335-1(5)) Koinonia Hse.
Where did our Bible come from? How good are the texts? Why do we believe its origin is supernatural? How do we know that it really is the Word of God? How accurate are our translations? Which version is the best?Chuck Missler, an internationally recognized Biblical authority, reviews the origin of both the Old and New Testaments in light of recent discoveries and controversies.This product contains the complete How We Got Our Bible Briefing Package on two audio CD's, and as a bonus, we've included the never-seen-before Automated Multimedia Slideshow Presentation! (Windows only) Each Audio CD Briefing Pack contains two Compact Discs, with extensive supporting study notes, all packaged in a standard CD jewel case.

How We Got the Bible. Speeches. Douglas Jacoby. 4 CDs. (Running Time: 4 hours). 2005. audio compact disk 20.00 (978-0-9767583-5-8(0)) Illumination MA.

How We Group Animals Audio CD. Adapted by Benchmark Education Company Staff. Based on a work by Kira Freed. (Early Explorers Set C Ser.). (J). (gr. 2). 2008. audio compact disk 10.00 (978-1-60437-549-7(3)) Benchmark Educ.

How We Learn: Program from the Award Winning Public Radio Series. Interview. Hosted by Fred Goodwin. 1 CD. (Running Time: 1 Hour). 2000. audio compact disk 21.95 (978-1-932479-55-3(4), LCM 112) Lichtenstein Creat.
What happens in the brain when we learn? What do we know about learning, and how can it be applied in practical situations, like schools? In this hour, we talk to scientists and educators about applying research to learning. Guests include Dr. Kurt Fischer, the director of the Mind, Brain and Education program at the Harvard Graduate School of Education; Dr. William Greenough, chair of the Neuroscience Program at the University of Illinois; Dr. Ted Sizer, founder of the Coalition of Essential Schools; and Patmore Lewis, violinist with the New York Metropolitan Opera Orchestra.

How We Lost Our Freedom. Swami Amar Jyoti. 1 cass. 1980. 9.95 (K-33) Truth Consciousness.
What is freedom? How to be free again. The Soul & Its Relationships. Prayer, not bargaining with God.

How We Lost the Vietnam War. unabr. collector's ed. Nguyen Cao Ky. Read by Walter Zimmerman. 6 cass. (Running Time: 9 hrs.). 1988. 48.00 (978-0-7366-1445-0(1), 2328) Books on Tape.
Presents an account of the conflict - its origins, it realities & its end.

How We Think: Program from the Award Winning Public Radio Series. Interview. Hosted by Fred Goodwin. Comment by John Hockenberry. 1 CD. (Running Time: 1 hr). 2003. audio compact disk 21.95 (978-1-932479-56-0(2), LCM 296) Lichtenstein Creat.
In this hour, we explore How We Think.We ponder life and death; we write love poems and compose symphonies. What makes human beings so special?Guests include Dr. Mark Turner, who teaches both English and cognitive science at the University of Maryland and is the co-author of The Way We Think;. Dr. Kevin Dunbar of Dartmouth, who studies how people think, reason, and solve problems; and writer and poet Floyd Skloot, author of In the Shadow of Memory. We also examine how we make decisions and visit a small school in Wisconsin where students are being challenged to think like scientists. WIth commentary by John Hockenberry.

How We Think & Learn in Education. Tom Parent. 1 cass. (Running Time: 1 hr.). 2002. 5.00 (CLP89523) Christian Liberty.
Explains the fundamental difference between secular educators and Christian educators, in how they approach the teaching process.

How We Use Electricity. Sundance/Newbridge, LLC Staff. (Early Science Ser.). (gr. k-3). 2007. audio compact disk 12.00 (978-1-4007-6371-9(1)); audio compact disk 12.00 (978-1-4007-6372-6(X)); audio compact disk 12.00 (978-1-4007-6370-2(3)) Sund Newbrdge.

How Will I Know? Making the Marriage Decision. S. Michael Wilcox. 2005. audio compact disk 12.95 (978-1-59038-499-2(7)) Deseret Bk.

How Will the World End? Kenneth Wapnick. 2 CDs. 2007. audio compact disk 13.00 (978-1-59142-314-0(7), CD50) Foun Miracles.

How Will the World End? Kenneth Wapnick. 2007. 10.00 (978-1-59142-315-7(5)) Foun Miracles.

How Will You Make Yourself Known? John 14:22, 718. Ed Young. 1989. 4.95 (978-0-7417-1718-4(2), 718) Win Walk.

How William Became Shakespeare: A Light & Enlightening Lecture. Featuring Elliot Engel. 2000. bk. 15.00 (978-1-890123-17-8(X)) Media Cnslts.

How Winners Do It. Michael Mercer. 6 cass. 1992. 59.95 set. (263A) Nightingale-Conant.
Emulate & duplicate the success of the leaders of American business. Management psychology consultant Michael Mercer identifies the real skills behind success no matter what your career.

How Would Jesus Vote? A Christian Perspective on the Issues. abr. ed. D. James Kennedy & Jerry Newcombe. (ENG.). 2008. 6.99 (978-1-60814-243-9(4)) Oasis Audio.

How Would Jesus Vote? A Christian Perspective on the Issues. abr. ed. Jerry Newcombe & D. James Kennedy. Read by Jon Gauger. (Running Time: 3600 sec.). (ENG.). 2008. audio compact disk 9.99 (978-1-59859-314-3(5)) Oasis Audio.

How You Can Be More Creative. Roger Von Oech. 6 cass. 49.95 Set. (438AM) Nightingale-Conant.
Creativity is a skill you can learn. Roger von Oech, world-renowned authority on creative thinking, teaches you how to trigger the creativity within you. You'll solve problems faster & with more innovation. Great ideas will come more often because you'll know how your creativity works & you'll have a system for developing & using it to your full potential.

How You Can be more Interesting. Edward De Bono. Narrated by David Ackroyd. 4 cass. (Running Time: 5 hrs.). 38.00 (978-1-4025-0792-2(5)); audio compact disk 48.00 (978-1-4025-3475-1(2)) Recorded Bks.

How You Can Be More Interesting. abr. ed. Edward De Bono. Read by David Ackroyd. 4 cass. (Running Time: 6 hrs.). 2001. 25.00 (978-1-931056-36-6(6), N Millennium Audio) New Millenn Enter.
The key to being more interesting lies in developing a rich and lively mind that is full of possibilities and speculates about everything we encounter. But this doesn't mean we have to read about, analyze or study things we're not interested in. Interest derives primarily from playing with ideas. Becoming a more interesting person has never been so accessible or so much fun. Anyone can acquire this life-enhancing skill.

How You Can Change Your Life. (152) Yoga Res Foun.

How You Can Change Your Life. Swami Jyotirmayananda. 1 cass. (Running Time: 1 hr.). 1990. 12.99 Yoga Res Foun.

How You Can Know & Do the Will of God: Colossians. Robert A. Cook. 4 cass. (Running Time: 6 hrs.). 2000. 9.99 (978-7-902031-62-2(3)) Chrstn Dup Intl.

How You Can Know & Do the Will of God - Colossians. Narrated by Robert A. Cook. 4 cass. (Dr. Robert A. Cook's Teaching Ser.). 9.98 ea. (RC22) Chrstn Dup Intl.

How You Can Know the Will of God. Kenneth E. Hagin. (Running Time: 5539 sec.). (Faith Library). 2008. audio compact disk 14.00 (978-1-00-000176-1(8)) Faith Lib Pubns.

How You Can Know the Will of God. abr. ed. Kenneth E. Hagin. 2008. audio compact disk 14.00 (978-1-60616-021-3(4)) Faith Lib Pubns.

How You Leave Them Feeling - Audio Book. (ENG.). 2006. audio compact disk 36.95 (978-0-9778810-2-4(4)) J Ferrell.

How You Live. Contrib. by Point of Grace & Michael Blanton. Prod. by Brown Bannister. 2007. audio compact disk 16.99 (978-5-557-63608-7(0), Word Records) Word Enter.

How You Live. Contrib. by Point of Grace & Michael Blanton. Prod. by Brown Bannister. 2008. audio compact disk 17.99 (978-5-557-38474-2(X), Word Records) Word Enter.

How You Live (Turn up the Music) Contrib. by Point of Grace. (Soundtraks Ser.). 2007. audio compact disk 8.99 (978-5-557-52833-7(4)) Christian Wrld.

How YOU(tm) Are Like Shampoo: The Breakthrough Personal Branding System Based on Proven Big-Brand Marketing Methods to Help you Earn More, Do More, & be More at Work. Brenda Bence. (ENG.). 2008. 19.95 (978-0-9799010-7-2(3)) Global In Comm.

Howard Abell: The Innergame of Trading. Read by Howard Abell & Bob Koppel. 1 cass. 30.00 Dow Jones Telerate.
Books & seminars on trading historically assume that traders either possess innate psychological skills or they don't; that one has mental toughness or lacks the disposition necessary to trade. In truth, successful traders must identify, learn & practice certain skills. They must develop compelling personal motivation, goal setting skills, confidence, consistency, anxiety control, focus, estate management, positive & empowering self-talk & sustained mental conditioning. Howard's workshop provides serious traders with a sense of how it feels to trade successfully & an exciting opportunity to experience markets the same way some of the most renowned traders do.

Howard Alden: Live at the Smithsonian Jazz Cafe. Contrib. by Howard Alden. (Running Time: 1 hr. 44 mins.). 2006. 24.95 (978-5-558-09163-2(0)) Mel Bay.

Howard & Frances Karp, Pianists: Concert Performances from a Half-Century of Music-Making. UW Sch of Music Staff. Contrib. by Howard & Frances Karp. 2000. audio compact disk 45.00 (978-0-9658834-8-1(5)) Pub: U of Wis Pr. Dist(s): Chicago Distribution Ctr

Howard Bursen: Cider in the Kitchen. 1 cass. 9.98 (C-74) Folk-Legacy.
Outstanding 5-string banjo artist who can also sing.

Howard Hughes: The Life & Madness. unabr. ed. Donald L. Barlett & James B. Steele. Read by Christopher Hurt. 24 CDs. (Running Time: 34 hrs.). 2005. audio compact disk 69.95 (978-0-7861-7927-5(9), ZE1384) Blckstn Audio.

Howard Hughes: The Untold Story. Peter Brown & Pat Broeske. Read by Michael Prichard. 2000. audio compact disk 128.00 (978-0-7366-8013-4(6)) Books on Tape.

Howard Hughes: The Untold Story. unabr. collector's ed. Peter Brown & Pat Broeke. Read by Michael Prichard. 13 cass. (Running Time: 19 hrs. 30 mins.). 2000. 104.00 (978-0-7366-5439-5(9)) Books on Tape.
The story of Howard Hughes with particular attention to the glamorous, womanizing side of his life.

Howard Hughes Affair. unabr. ed. Stuart M. Kaminsky. Read by Christopher Lane. 4 cass. (Running Time: 5 hrs. 30 mins.). (Toby Peters Mystery Ser.: No. 4). 1995. audio compact disk 32.95 Set. (978-0-7861-0668-4(9), 1570) Blckstn Audio.
Toby Peters is a private detective with sore feet, a bad back, & a tendency to bruise easily. He lives on a strict diet of hot dogs, tacos, shredded wheat, & disaster, & spends most of his time at the wrong end of a gun. Peters can't get through the day without finding a corpse or losing his shoes or both, but he has a reputation for keeping his mouth shut...so when a nervous young billionaire finds a spy at his dinner party, he wants Peters on the job.

Howard Memerov Two. unabr. ed. Howard Nemerov. 1 cass. (Running Time: 29 min.). 1991. 10.00 (050490) New Letters.
War Stories.

Howard Moss, Pts. 1 & 11. unabr. ed. Howard Moss. 2 cass. (Running Time: 29 min.). 1985. 10.00 ea. One-sided cass.; 18.00 Two-sided cass. New Letters.
Two programs featuring National Book Award winner & poetry editor of "The New Yorker".

Howard Moss: A Retrospective Reading. Howard Moss. Read by Howard Moss. Ed. by Christopher King. 1 cass. (Running Time: 1 hr. 30 min.). 1987. 10.95 (978-0-8045-1171-1(3), SAC 1171) Spoken Arts.
Howard Moss, Poet, Playwright, Author, & Editor of Poetry at the New Yorker Magazine since 1948, Reads 35 Poems Spanning His Career.

Howard Nemerov. Interview with Howard Nemerov. 1 cass. (Running Time: 25 min.). 1978. 11.95 (L059) TFR.
The winner of the Pulitzer Prize for Poetry & The National Book Award talks about the meaninglessness of it all.

Howard Nemerov. unabr. ed. Howard Nemerov. 1 cass. (Author Speaks Ser.). 1991. 14.95 J Norton Pubs.
Archival recordings of 20th-century authors.

Howard Nemerov. unabr. ed. Howard Nemerov. Read by Howard Nemerov. 1 cass. (Running Time: 29 min.). 1986. 10.00 New Letters.

Howard Nemerov II. unabr. ed. Howard Nemerov. Interview with Rebekah Presson. 1 cass. (Running Time: 29 min.). 1990. 10.00 (050490) New Letters.
Nemerov was Poet Laureate of the United States until recently. He has also won the Pulitzer Prize & the National Book Award in poetry. Nemerov's most recent book, "War Stories", recalls his own World War II experience.

Howard Pyle's Book of Pirates. unabr. ed. Howard Pyle. Read by Simon Vance. 2006. 29.95 (978-0-7861-7755-4(1)) Blckstn Audio.

Howard Pyle's Book of Pirates. unabr. ed. Howard Pyle. Read by Robert Mansell. (J). 2007. 39.99 (978-1-60252-757-7(1)) Find a World.

Howard Pyle's Book of Pirates: Fiction, Fact & fancy Concerning the Buccaneers & Marooners of the Spanish Main from the Writing & Pictures of Howard Pyle Compiled by Merle Johnson. 2006. 54.95 (978-0-7861-4430-3(0)); audio compact disk 63.00 (978-0-7861-7380-8(7)) Blckstn Audio.

Howard Schwartz. unabr. ed. Howard Schwartz. 1 cass. (Running Time: 29 min.). 1991. 10.00 (051791) New Letters.
Lilith's Cave: Jewish Tales of the Supernatural.

Howard Stern: King of All Media. Paul D. Colford. 2 cass. 1996. 14.00 Set. (978-1-57375-422-4(6), 651345) Audioscope.
Everyone listens to Howard Stern, from trash collectors to CEOs. Stern's popularity knows no bounds - his radio show is syndicated nationwide, he is a best-selling author, & host of annual pay-per-view extravaganzas. Paul Colford chronicles the rise of the king of shock jocks from his humble beginnings to his battles with the FCC, his fascination with transcendental meditation & obsession with sex.

Howards End. E. M. Forster. Read by Amy von Lecteur. 2009. 27.95 (978-1-60112-976-5(9)) Babblebooks.

Howards End. unabr. ed. E. M. Forster. Read by Nadia May. 8 cass. (Running Time: 11 hrs. 30 mins.). 1992. 56.95 (978-0-7861-0376-8(0), 1331) Blckstn Audio.
Howards End is a charming country house which becomes the subject of a dispute between the Wilcox family & the Schlegel sisters. Through romantic entanglements, disappearing wills & sudden tragedy, the conflict over the house emerges as a symbolic struggle for England's very future.

Howards End. unabr. ed. E. M. Forster. 8 cass. (Running Time: 39600 sec.). 2006. 19.95 (978-0-7861-4615-4(X)) Blckstn Audio.

Howards End. unabr. ed. E. M. Forster. 9 CDs. (Running Time: 39600 sec.). 2007. audio compact disk 81.00 (978-0-7861-6847-7(1)); audio compact disk 24.95 (978-0-7861-7451-5(X)) Blckstn Audio.

Howards End. unabr. ed. E. M. Forster. Read by Nadia May. (YA). 2008. 64.99 (978-1-60514-728-4(1)) Find a World.

Howards End, unabr. ed. E. M. Forster. Narrated by John Franklyn-Robbins. 9 cass. (Running Time: 12 hrs. 45 mins.). 1993. 78.00 (978-1-55690-888-0(1), 93330E7) Recorded Bks.
The Schlegels (of old family money) meet the Wilcoxes (of the nouveau riche) in this portrait of the English upper classes in the years just prior to World War One.

***Howards End.** unabr. ed. E. M. Forster. Narrated by Steven Crossley. (Running Time: 12 hrs. 30 mins. 0 sec.). (ENG.). 2010. audio compact disk 78.99 (978-1-4001-4943-8(6)) Pub: Tantor Media. Dist(s): IngramPubServ

***Howards End.** unabr. ed. E. M. Forster. Narrated by Steven Crossley. (Running Time: 12 hrs. 30 mins. 0 sec.). (ENG.). 2010. 22.99 (978-1-4001-6943-6(7)) Pub: Tantor Media. Dist(s): IngramPubServ

***Howards End.** unabr. ed. E. m. Forster. Narrated by Steven Crossley. (Running Time: 12 hrs. 30 mins.). 2010. 18.99 (978-1-4001-8943-4(8)) Tantor Media.

***Howards End.** unabr. ed. E. M. Forster. Narrated by Steven Crossley. (Running Time: 12 hrs. 30 mins. 0 sec.). (ENG.). 2010. audio compact disk 32.99 (978-1-4001-1943-1(X)) Pub: Tantor Media. Dist(s): IngramPubServ

Howards End. unabr. collector's ed. E. M. Forster. Read by Jill Masters. 9 cass. (Running Time: 13 hrs. 30 min.). 1994. 72.00 (978-0-7366-2682-8(4), 3418) Books on Tape.
English country house passes from one family to another, influencing the lives of its present & would-be inhabitants.

Howard's End, Set. unabr. ed. E. M. Forster. Read by Flo Gibson. 8 cass. (Running Time: 11 hrs. 30 min.). 1992. 26.95 (978-1-55685-261-9(4)) Audio Bk Con.
The cultured, idealistic Schlegel sisters, the materialistic Wilcox family, & poor romantic Leonard Bast "only connect" (to quote the author's aphorism), sometimes in the deepest sense, in & around a charming country house in Hertfordshire. Who will inherit this cozy nest?.

Howards of Caxley. Miss Read Staff. Read by June Barrie. (Running Time: 22800 sec.). (Chivers Audio Bks.). 2003. audio compact disk 64.95 (978-0-7540-8779-3(4)) Pub: Chivers Audio Bks GBR. Dist(s): AudioGO

Howards of Caxley. Miss Read. Read by June Barrie. 2003. 54.95 (978-0-7540-8386-3(1)) Pub: Chivers Audio Bks GBR. Dist(s): AudioGO

Howie Mitchell: Folksongs & Ballads. 1 cass. 9.98 (C-5) Folk-Legacy.
The gentle art of a mountain dulcimer master.

Howie Mitchell: The Mountain Dulcimer, How to Make It & Play It. 1 cass. bk. 16.95 Set. (C-29) Folk-Legacy.

Howie Monroe & the Doghouse of Doom. James Howe. Read by Joe Grifasi. (Running Time: 48 mins.). (Tales from the House of Bunnicula Ser.). (J). (gr. 3-6). 2004. pap. bk. 17.00 (978-1-4000-8634-4(5), Listening Lib) Random Audio Pubg.

Howie Monroe & the Screaming Mummies of the Pharoah's Tomb II. James Howe. Read by Joe Grifasi. (Running Time: 50 mins.). (Tales from the House of Bunnicula Ser.). (J). (gr. 3-6). 2004. pap. bk. 17.00 (978-1-4000-8635-1(3), Listening Lib) Random Audio Pubg.

Howjadoo. Perf. by John McCutcheon. 1 cass. (J). (ps-5). 9.98 (235); audio compact disk 17.98 (D235) MFLP CA.
This is a wonderful mix of tunes using autoharp, hammered dulcimer, fiddle, mandolin, tin whistle, ocarina, Cajun accordion, tuba, viola, jaw harp & more. Rich harmonies & witty storyline introductions make this an especially fun, foot-stomping collection of folk tunes.

Howjadoo. Perf. by John McCutcheon. 1 cass. (Running Time: 41 min.). (Family Ser.). (J). (ps-7). 1983. 9.98 (978-1-886767-28-7(9), 8009); audio compact disk 14.98 (978-1-886767-29-4(7), 8009) Rounder Records.
John McCutcheon is the complete modern folk musician, a master of many instruments & traditions, whose compositions have become contemporary standards.

Howl, Growl, Moo, Whooo: A Book of Animal Sounds. Molly Carroll & Jeanne Sturm. (Rourke Discovery Library (CD-ROM) Ser.). (J). 2008. audio compact disk 24.95 (978-1-60472-777-7(2)) Rourke FL.

Howliday Inn. unabr. ed. James Howe. Read by Victor Garber. 2 vols. (Running Time: 3 hrs. 21 mins.). (Bunnicula Ser.). (J). (gr. 3-7). 2004. pap. bk. 29.00 (978-0-8072-8382-0(7), YA179SP, Listening Lib); 23.00 (978-0-8072-8381-3(9), YA179CX, Listening Lib) Random Audio Pubg.
Harold & Chester could hardly believe it. The Monroe family was going on vacation without them. Bunnicula, the family rabbit, would be boarded with a

neighbor. But they, the family's loyal dog & cat, were to be sent away with strangers; to a place called Chateau Bow-Wow. Chester observed, soon after they arrived, could more properly be called Howliday Inn. Though what was howling, neither of them knew. Chester had his suspicions however; only a werewolf could make that chilling sound.

Howlin' at the Moon. Sam Bush. 1 cass., 1 CD. 7.98 (SUH 3876); audio compact disk 12.78 CD Jewel box. (SUH 3876) NewSound.

Howling at the Moon: The Odyssey of a Monstrous Music Mogul in an Age of Excess. abr. ed. Walter Yetnikoff & David Ritz. Read by Walter Yetnikoff. (Running Time: 6 hrs.). (ENG.). 2004. audio compact disk 29.95 (978-0-7393-1162-2(X), RH AudioV) Pub: Random Audio Pubg. Dist(s): Random

Howling Dervishes of Turkey. unabr. ed. 1 cass. 1994. 12.95 (978-0-88432-385-3(4), C11127) J Norton Pubs.
Music.

Howling Dog: And Other Cases. unabr. ed. Seymour Simon. Narrated by Johnny Heller. 1 cass. (Running Time: 1 hr. 15 mins.). (Einstein Anderson, Science Detective Ser.). (gr. 3 up). 2000. 11.00 (978-0-7887-4199-9(3), 96278E7) Recorded Bks.
Adam "Einstein" Anderson enjoys telling bad jokes & solving problems using science. Whether the mystery involves space aliens, shrinking machines, or anything else, Einstein finds the solution.

Howling Dog & Other Cases. Seymour Simon. Read by Johnny Heller. 1 cass. (Running Time: 1 hrs. 15 mins.). (Einstein Anderson, Science Detective Ser.). (J). (gr. 3-6). 2000. pap. bk. 32.00 (978-0-7887-4457-0(7), 41148); wbk. ed. 159.30 (978-0-7887-4458-7(5), 47145) Recorded Bks.

Howling Harmonies. 1 cass. (Running Time: 60 min.). 1994. audio compact disk 15.95 CD. (2514, Creativ Pub) Quayside.
The chorus begins with a single howl lifting out of the darkness. One by one, the other wolves raise their voices, each in a different pitch, but in concert with the ones that came before.

Howling Harmonies. 1 cass. (Running Time: 60 min.). 1994. 9.95 (0251, NrthWrd Bks) TandN Child.

Howling House. Anne Schraff. Narrated by Larry A. McKeever. (Standing Tall 1 Mystery Ser.). (J). 2004. audio compact disk 14.95 (978-1-58659-269-1(6)) Artesian.

Howling House. unabr. ed. Anne Schraff. Narrated by Larry A. McKeever. 1 cass. (Running Time: 40 min.). (Standing Tall 1 Mystery Ser.). (J). 2004. 10.95 (978-1-58659-093-2(6), 54133) Artesian.

***Howling Man.** 2010. audio compact disk (978-1-59171-220-6(3)) Falcon Picture.

Hoy es Importante. unabr. ed. John C. Maxwell. (SPA.). 2005. audio compact disk 16.99 (978-987-557-054-2(0)) Pub: Vida Pubs. Dist(s): Zondervan

Hoy Mas Que Nunca. Miguel A. Guerra. 2002. 2.00 (978-0-8297-3775-2(8)); audio compact disk 3.60 (978-0-8297-3773-8(1)) Zondervan.

Hoy Mas Que Nunca. Miguel Angel Guerra. 1 CD. (Running Time: 1 hr. 30 min.). 2002. audio compact disk 9.99 (978-0-8297-3772-1(3)) Zondervan.

Hoy Nos Reunimos. Pedro Rubalcava. 1 cass. 2000. 16.00 (978-1-58459-017-0(3)); 11.00 (978-1-58459-016-3(5)) Wrld Lib Pubns.
Collection of Latin American religious text & music in the Latin American & Miriachi style.

Hoyden. 1 cass. (Running Time: 1 hr.). 2001. 11.95 (ARTC005) Lodestone Catalog.
Two country girls visit their matchmaking aunt in London.

HP Way: How Bill Hewlett & I Built Our Company. unabr. ed. David Packard. Narrated by Nelson Runger. 4 cass. (Running Time: 5 hrs. 15 mins.). 1995. 35.00 (978-0-7887-0342-3(0), 94534E7) Recorded Bks.
In 1938, two college friends decided to start a company out of a one-car garage. Today, that company, Hewlett-Packard, is universally acclaimed as the world's most admired technology corporation.

HP-41CX Systems Programming. Ed. by Marco A. V. Bitetto. 1 cass. 1999. (978-1-58578-095-2(2)) Inst of Cybernetics.

HP-48GX Systems Programming. Ed. by Marco A. V. Bitetto. 2000. (978-1-58578-098-3(7)) Inst of Cybernetics.

HR Detective. Doug Kalish. (Running Time: 16200 sec.). 2007. audio compact disk 29.95 (978-0-9765943-1-4(5)) Doug K.

HTML & JavaScript Programming Concepts: Electronic Instructor's Package. Barksdale & E. Shane Turner. 2000. tchr. ed. (978-0-538-68823-9(8)) South-West.

Hu-la-la Programs Booklet w/Music CD. Vicki Corona. Prod. by Vicki Corona. Hokili Lester. (Celebrate the Cultures Ser.: 2-36A). 2004. pap. bk. 24.95 (978-1-58513-150-1(4)) Dance Fantasy.

Huan Ching & the Golden Fish. Michael Reeser. Illus. by Dick Sakahara. (Publish-a-Book Ser.). (J). (gr. 1-6). 1988. lib. bdg. 22.83 (978-0-8172-2751-7(2)) Heinemann Rai.

Hubble & the Big Bang. unabr. ed. Paul Kupperberg. Read by Jay Snyder. (Running Time: 1 hr.). (Primary Sources of Revolutionary Scientific Discoveries & Theories Ser.). 2009. 19.99 (978-1-4233-9397-9(X), 9781423393979, Brilliance MP3); 39.97 (978-1-4233-9398-6(8), 9781423393986, Brinc Audio MP3 Lib); 39.97 (978-1-4233-9399-3(6), 9781423393993, BADLE); audio compact disk 19.99 (978-1-4233-9395-5(3), 9781423393955, Bril Audio CD Unabri); audio compact disk 39.97 (978-1-4233-9396-2(1), 9781423393962, BriAudCD Unabrid) Brilliance Audio.

Hubris. unabr. ed. Michael Isikoff & David Corn. Read by Stefan Rudnicki. 10 cass. (Running Time: 68400 sec.). 2006. 29.95 (978-0-7861-4630-7(3)) Blckstn Audio.

Hubris: The Inside Story of Spin, Scandal, & the Selling of the Iraq War. unabr. ed. Michael Isikoff. Read by Stefan Rudnicki. (Running Time: 68400 sec.). 2006. 95.95 (978-0-7861-4848-6(9)) Blckstn Audio.

Hubris: The Inside Story of Spin, Scandal, & the Selling of the Iraq War. unabr. ed. Michael Isikoff. Read by David Corn & Simon Vance. (Running Time: 68400 sec.). 2006. audio compact disk 29.95 (978-0-7861-7456-0(0)) Blckstn Audio.

Hubris: The Inside Story of Spin, Scandal, & the Selling of the Iraq War. unabr. ed. Michael Isikoff & David Corn. Read by Stefan Rudnicki. 11 CDs. (Running Time: 68400 sec.). 2006. audio compact disk 29.95 (978-0-7861-6842-2(0)) Blckstn Audio.

Hubris: The Inside Story of Spin, Scandal, & the Selling of the Iraq War. unabr. ed. Michael Isikoff & David Corn. Read by Stefan Rudnicki. (Running Time: 68400 sec.). 2006. audio compact disk 120.00 (978-0-7861-6090-7(X)) Blckstn Audio.

***Huck: The Remarkable True Story of How One Lost Puppy Taught a Family - and a Whole Town - about Hope & Happy Endings.** unabr. ed. Janet Elder. (Running Time: 7 hrs. 30 mins. 0 sec.). 2010. 24.99 (978-1-4001-6855-2(4)); 34.99 (978-1-4001-9855-9(0)); 16.99 (978-1-4001-8855-0(5)); audio compact disk 34.99 (978-1-4001-1855-7(7)); audio compact disk 83.99 (978-1-4001-4855-4(3)) Pub: Tantor Media. Dist(s): IngramPubServ

Huck Finn & Tom Sawyer among the Indians. unabr. ed. Mark Twain & Lee Nelson. Read by Grover Gardner. (Running Time: 8 hrs. 30 mins.). 2001. audio compact disk 24.95 (978-0-7861-8772-0(7), 3185) Blckstn Audio.

Huck Finn & Tom Sawyer among the Indians. unabr. ed. Mark Twain & Lee Nelson. Read by Grover Gardner. 7 CDs. (Running Time: 8 hrs. 30 mins.). 2004. audio compact disk 56.00 (978-0-7861-8986-1(X), 3185) Blckstn Audio.

Huck Finn & Tom Sawyer among the Indians. unabr. ed. Mark Twain & Lee Nelson. Read by Grover Gardner. 7 CDs. 2004. audio compact disk 35.95 (978-0-7861-8985-4(1)); reel tape 29.95 (978-0-7861-2582-1(9)) Blckstn Audio.
It is a story of adventure, wit, and wisdom in which Huck Finn, Tom Sawyer, and Jim head west on the trail of two white girls kidnapped by Sioux warriors. Tom and Huck seek true love while tramping through hostile Indian country, stealing from the United States Army, and facing a gunfight and hangman?s noose in California.

Huck Finn & Tom Saywer: Among the Indians. Mark Twain et al. 6 cass. (Running Time: 8 hrs. 30 mins.). 2002. 44.95 (978-0-7861-2580-7(2), 3185) Blckstn Audio.

Huckepack: Deutsch als Fremdsprache fuer die Grunds. Rotraud Cros & Doris Ladiges. 1 cass. (J). 1994. 29.25 (978-3-12-675095-0(8)) Intl Bk Import.

HUD Audit Guide. Betty A. King. 4 cass. 1995. bk. 199.00 set. (CPE0650) Bisk Educ.
A review of the provisions of the Consolidated Audit Guide of HUD programs. Discussion on the guidance for audits of projects funded under Section 8, subsidized housing, direct loans & capital advances.

Hudson River Wind Meditations. Lou Reed. 2 CDs. (Running Time: 2 hrs.). 2007. audio compact disk 17.98 (978-1-59179-554-4(0), M1117D) Sounds True.

Hudson Taylor: The Man Who Believed God. unabr. ed. Marshall Broomhall. Read by Frederick Davidson. 5 cass. (Running Time: 7 hrs.). 1996. 39.95 (978-0-7861-1005-6(8), 1782) Blckstn Audio.
Hudson Taylor is one of the most remarkable of Christianity's heroes. He is remembered both as the founder of the world-famous China Inland Mission & one of history's great men of faith. He left England on September 19, 1853, & did not reach China until the spring of 1894. The long & arduous voyage, persecution, poverty & the barriers of language & culture did not deter him from his mission. Throughout a life filled with trials of all sorts, Taylor remained confident in his knowledge of God's will & of His care, even in the shadow of death.

***Hudson Taylor's Spiritual Secret.** unabr. ed. Howard Taylor & Gregg Lewis. (Running Time: 7 hrs. 30 mins. 0 sec.). (ENG.). 2011. audio compact disk 24.98 (978-1-61045-040-9(X)) christianaud.

Huevo rojo y Jengibre. (Saludos Ser.: Vol. 1). (SPA.). (gr. 2-3). 10.00 (978-0-7635-5876-5(1)) Rigby Educ.

Huey Long, Pt. 1. unabr. collector's ed. Harry T. Williams. Read by Dick Estell. 9 cass. (Running Time: 13 hrs. 30 min.). (Christopher Enterprises Recording Ser.). 1988. 72.00 (978-0-7366-1382-8(X), 2275-A) Books on Tape.
Examines the career of one of the most extraordinary figures in American political history.

Huey Long, Pt. 2. unabr. collector's ed. T. Harry Williams. Read by Dick Estell. 9 cass. (Running Time: 13 hrs. 30 mins.). 1988. 72.00 (978-0-7366-1383-5(8), 2275-B) Books on Tape.

Huey Long, Pt. 3. unabr. collector's ed. Harry T. Williams. Read by Dick Estell. 8 cass. (Running Time: 12 hrs.). (Christopher Enterprises Recording Ser.). 1988. 64.00 (978-0-7366-1384-2(6), 2275-C) Books on Tape.

Huey Long: A Biography. unabr. ed. T. Harry Williams. (Running Time: 32 hrs. 0 mins.). (ENG.). 2009. 59.95 (978-1-4332-2313-6(9)); 79.95 (978-1-4332-9086-2(3)); 95.95 (978-1-4332-2309-9(0)); audio compact disk 169.00 (978-1-4332-2310-5(4)) Blckstn Audio.

Hug & a Kick & a Kick in the Pants. 2 cass. 1994. bk. 12.00 Set. (2001) Family Mtrs.
Creative approach to preventing disciplinary problems.

HUG Audio Gift Cards- Living the Dream: Living the Dream. Jennifer Yessler & Hug Audio Gift Cards. Read by Diane Burket. Ed. by Dave Bolick et al. Kristen Dewulf & Lisa Pavlock. (ENG.). 2008. audio compact disk 14.99 (978-0-9820704-2-0(X)) HUG.

HUG Audio Gift Cards -Relax, Renew & Energize: Relax, Renew & Energize. Jennifer Yessler & Hug Audio. Read by Diane Burket. Ed. by Dave Bolick & Tracy Dodson. Kristen Dewulf & Lisa Pavlock. 2008. audio compact disk 14.99 (978-0-9820704-3-7(8)) HUG.

Hug Me & Other Stories. abr. ed. Patti Stren. Read by Blythe Danner. 1 cass. Incl. I'm Only Afraid of the Dark at Night. (J). (CP 1715); Mountain Rose. (J). (CP 1715); Sloan & Philamena. (J). (CP 1715); (J). 1984. 8.98 (978-0-89845-139-9(6), CP 1715) HarperCollins Pubs.

Hug the Earth. Perf. by Tickle Tune Typhoon Staff. 1 cass. (J). 8.98 (236) MFLP CA.
Recycling, rhythm & responsibility for the planet are a few of the themes that weave through this wonderful recording.

Hug the Earth. Tickle Tune Typhoon Staff. 1 cass. (Running Time: 41 min.). (J). (gr. k-6). 1985. 9.98 (978-0-945337-03-4(5), SRU 84-488) Tickle Tune Typhoon.
Features a variety of musical styles and arrangements. Songs are up-tempo and inspire dance and movement participation; they celebrate the earth and care of the environment, and embrace the importance of all people.

Hug Your People: The Proven Way to Hire, Inspire & Recognize Your Employees & Achieve Remarkable Results. unabr. ed. Jack Mitchell. Read by James Boles. (Running Time: 6 hrs. 0 mins. 0 sec.). (ENG.). 2008. audio compact disk 59.99 (978-1-4001-3659-9(8)); audio compact disk 19.99 (978-1-4001-5659-7(9)) Pub: Tantor Media. Dist(s): IngramPubServ

Hug Your People: The Proven Way to Hire, Inspire, & Recognize Your Employees & Achieve Remarkable Results. unabr. ed. Jack Mitchell. Read by James Boles. (Running Time: 6 hrs. 0 mins. 0 sec.). (ENG.). 2008. audio compact disk 29.99 (978-1-4001-0659-2(1)) Pub: Tantor Media. Dist(s): IngramPubServ

***Huge: A Novel.** unabr. ed. James W. Fuerst. Read by Jeff Woodman. 1 Playaway. (Running Time: 11 hrs.). 2009. 59.99 (978-1-4417-2320-8(X)) Blckstn Audio.

Huge: A Novel. unabr. ed. James W. Fuerst. Narrated by Jeff Woodman. 8 CDs. (Running Time: 11 hrs.). 2009. audio compact disk 100.00 (978-1-4417-2314-7(5)) Blckstn Audio.

Huge: A Novel. unabr. ed. James W. Fuerst. Read by Jeff Woodman. (Running Time: 11 hrs. 0 mins.). 2009. 29.95 (978-1-4417-2317-8(X)); 65.95 (978-1-4417-2313-0(7)) Blckstn Audio.

Hugger Mugger. unabr. ed. Robert B. Parker. Read by Joe Mantegna. 4 cass. (Running Time: 6 hrs.). (Spenser Ser.). 2000. 32.00 (978-0-7366-4915-5(8), 5222) Books on Tape.
Someone has been killing racehorses at stables across the south, and Walter Clive, president of Three Fillies Stables, hires Spenser to find out who. Spencer goes to Georgia to protect Bugger Bugger, a two-year-old destined to become the next Secretariat. Despite the veneer of civility, Spenser encounters tensions beneath the surface old boy bonhomie. The case takes an even more deadly turn when the attacker claims a human victim, and Spenser must revise his impressions of the Three Fillies organization and watch his own back as well.

Hugger Mugger, Set. unabr. ed. Robert B. Parker. 6 cass. (Running Time: 10 hrs.). (Spenser Ser.). 2000. 29.95 (Random AudioBks) Random Audio Pubg.
Someone has been killing racehorses at stables across the south & the Boston P.I. (Spenser) travels to Georgia to protect the two-year old destined to become the next Secretariat.

Hugging the Shore Pt. 1: Essays & Criticism. unabr. collector's ed. John Updike. Read by John MacDonald. 9 cass. (Running Time: 13 hrs. 30 min.). 1984. 72.00 (978-0-7366-0993-7(8), 1930-A) Books on Tape.
Writing criticism is to writing fiction & poetry as hugging the shore is to sailing in the open sea, says Updike in his foreward to this collection of literary considerations.

Hugging the Shore Pt. 2: Essays & Criticism. collector's ed. John Updike. Read by John MacDonald. 8 cass. (Running Time: 12 hrs.). 1984. 64.00 (978-0-7366-0994-4(6), 1930-B) Books on Tape.

Hugging the Shore Pt. 3: Essays & Criticism. collector's ed. John Updike. Read by John MacDonald. 8 cass. (Running Time: 12 hrs.). 1984. 64.00 (978-0-7366-0995-1(4), 1930-C) Books on Tape.

Hughes: The Private Diaries, Memos, & Letters. unabr. ed. Richard Hack. Narrated by Dan Cashman. 12 cass. (Running Time: 18 hrs.). 2002. 99.00 (978-1-4025-1273-5(2), 96967) Recorded Bks.
Based on recently released personal letters, memos, notes, court testimony, declassified FBI files, and autopsy reports exposes the real story of Howard Hughes in this biography.

Hughes: The Private Diaries, Memos, & Letters: the Definitive Biography of the First American Billionaire. Richard Hack. Narrated by Dan Cashman. 15 CDs. (Running Time: 18 hrs.). audio compact disk 142.00 (978-1-4025-2917-7(1)) Recorded Bks.

Hughes: The Private Diaries, Memos & Letters: The Definitive Biography of the First American Billionaire. abr. ed. Richard Hack. Read by Daniel Cashman. 4 cass. (Running Time: 6 hrs.). 2004. 25.00 (978-1-59007-012-3(7)) Pub: New Millenn Enter. Dist(s): PerseuPGW
A biography of the legendary Howard Hughes based on newly uncovered personal letters, sealed court testimony, recently declassified FBI files & never-before-revealed autopsy findings with eight pages of rare & never before seen photographs.

Hughes: The Private Diaries, Memos & Letters: The Definitive Biography of the First American Billionaire. abr. ed. Richard Hack. Read by Richard Hack. 6 CDs. (Running Time: 6 hrs.). 2004. audio compact disk 39.95 (978-1-59007-041-3(0)) Pub: New Millenn Enter. Dist(s): PerseuPGW

Hughes: The Private Diaries, Memos & Letters: The Definitive Biography of the First American Billionaire. unabr. ed. Richard Hack. Read by Daniel Cashman. 12 cass. (Running Time: 18 hrs.). 2004. 39.95 (978-1-59007-040-6(2)) Pub: New Millenn Enter. Dist(s): PerseuPGW

Hugo Nominees 2002. Short Stories. Ursula K. Le Guin et al. Ed. by Jeremy Bloom. 2 CDs. (Running Time: 2 hrs 24 mins). 2002. audio compact disk 13.95 (978-0-9707056-8-6(9), 57-2) Frquency Pubng.
Four of the short stories nominated for the prestigeous Hugo Award (the equivalent, for the science fiction field, of the Grammies), read by talented voice actors.

Hugs for Little Ones. 2002. audio compact disk Provident Mus Dist.

Huichol Chant & The Deer Dance. unabr. ed. Prem Dass & Don Jose. 1 cass. 1977. 11.00 Big Sur Tapes.

Huichol Cosmology (Creation & Return) unabr. ed. Prem Dass. 2 cass. (Running Time: 2 hrs.). 1977. 18.00 Big Sur Tapes.

Huichol Journey. unabr. ed. Barbara Myerhoff. 1 cass. (Running Time: 1 hr. 32 min.). 1975. 11.00 (02001) Big Sur Tapes.
The poigniant tale of Myerhoff's meeting & apprenticeship with a Huichol medicine man, which led to her participation in the annual Huichol pilgrimage in search of peyote.

Huis Clos, Set. Jean-Paul Sartre. Perf. by Comedie Francaise. 2 cass. (FRE.). 1995. 26.95 (1713-RF) Olivia & Hill.
The famous quote, "L'Enfer c'est les autres," is the perfect summary for this play which reunites three former sinners in hell. Recorded in 1990.

Huit Contes, Set. Short Stories. Guy de Maupassant. Read by Madeleine Renaud. Anno. by René Olivier. Intro. by René Olivier. 2 cass. (Jenaer Romanische Texte Ser.: 3). (FRE.). 1991. 26.95 (1252-RF) Olivia & Hill.
A superb reading of eight Maupassant tales.

Hulagu's Web: The Presidential Pursuit of Senator Katherine Laforge. 2005. audio compact disk 34.95 (978-0-9755976-3-7(9)) Subterfuge Pubng.

Hulk 35-count Mix Ctr. (J). 2003. 167.65 (978-0-06-057458-1(5), HarperFestival) HarperCollins Pubs.

Hull down for Action. unabr. collector's ed. Armstrong Sperry. Read by Paul Shay. 6 cass. (Running Time: 6 hrs.). (J). 1989. 36.00 (978-0-7366-1570-9(9), 2437) Books on Tape.
A vintage boys' book about four youngsters set adrift in the South Pacific by a German undercover agent who commandeered their boat during WW II. But they make landfall on Guadalcanal, cross the island in a series of hair-raising escapades & finally gaze out on a hidden lagoon where the beautiful brigg that was taken from them, the Island Queen, lies anchored. How they get her back is the stuff legends are made of.

***Hull Zero Three.** unabr. ed. Greg Bear. (Running Time: 9 hrs.). 2010. 24.99 (978-1-4418-8677-4(X), 9781441886774, Brilliance MP3); audio compact disk 29.99 (978-1-4418-8675-0(3), 9781441886750, Bril Audio CD Unabri) Brilliance Audio.

***Hull Zero Three.** unabr. ed. Greg Bear. Read by Dan John Miller. (Running Time: 9 hrs.). 2010. 24.99 (978-1-4418-8679-8(6), 9781441886798, BAD); 39.97 (978-1-4418-8678-1(8), 9781441886781, Brinc Audio MP3 Lib); 39.97 (978-1-4418-8680-4(X), 9781441886804, BADLE); audio compact disk 79.97 (978-1-4418-8676-7(1), 9781441886767, BriAudCD Unabrid) Brilliance Audio.

Hullabaloo at Hunker Hill. (Paws & Tales Ser.: Vol. 21). (J). 2002. 3.99 (978-1-57972-426-9(4)); audio compact disk 5.99 (978-1-57972-427-6(2)) Insight Living.

Hullabaloo at the Zoo. (Sails Literacy Ser.). (gr. 1 up). 10.00 (978-0-7578-2661-0(X)) Rigby Educ.

Humaerobics. C. W. Metcalf & J. Mark Pearson. 1 cass. (Running Time: 37 min.). (Humor Exercises Set to Music Ser.). 1988. 9.95 (978-1-878365-01-9(0)) C W Metcalf.
Consultant C. W. Metcalf's unique mental & physical humor exercises with a background of original piano music by J. Mark Pearson.

***Human Action: A Treatise on Economics.** unabr. ed. Ludwig von Mises. Read by Bernard Mayes. (Running Time: 23 hrs. 30 mins.). 2010. 59.95 (978-1-4417-4559-0(9)); audio compact disk 160.00 (978-1-4417-4556-9(4)) Blckstn Audio.

Human Action: A Treatise on Economics, Part 1 Of 2, Vol. 1. unabr. ed. Ludwig von Mises. Read by Bernard Mayes. 16 cass. (Running Time: 44 hrs.). 1990. 99.95 (978-0-7861-0170-2(9), 1152A, B) Blckstn Audio.
A systematic study that covers every major topic in the science of economics. It is also one of the most convincing indictments of socialism & statism ever penned.

Human Action: A Treatise on Economics, Part 2 Of 2, Vol. 2. unabr. ed. Ludwig von Mises. Read by Bernard Mayes. 14 cass. (Running Time: 44 hrs.). 1990. 89.95 (978-0-7861-0171-9(7), 1152A, B) Blckstn Audio.

Human Anatomy & Physiology, Pt. 1. David Gantt. Read by Amy Bruce & Amanda Henkel. 3 CDs. (Running Time: 3 hrs.). 2005. audio compact disk 19.99 (978-1-884612-51-0(2)) AudioText.

Human Anatomy & Physiology, Pt. 1. unabr. ed. David G. Gantt. Read by Amy Bruce & Amanda Henkeel. Ed. by Denson K. McLain. 2 cass. (Running Time: 3 hrs.). (Biology-on-Tape Ser.). 1995. 19.99 Set. (978-1-884612-04-6(0)) AudioText.
A study guide covering anatomical positions, histology, bone growth & repair, the skeletal & muscular systems, the nervous system, the spinal cord, the brain, nerves & synapses, sensory receptors, & the endocrine system.

Human Anatomy & Physiology, Pt. 2. David Gantt. Read by Amy Bruce & Pat Bottino. 2005. audio compact disk 19.99 (978-1-884612-52-7(0)) AudioText.

Human Anatomy & Physiology, Pt. 2. unabr. ed. David G. Gantt. Read by Amy Bruce & Amanda Henkel. Ed. by Denson K. McLain. 2 cass. (Running Time: 3 hrs.). (Biology-on-Tape Ser.). 1996. 19.99 Set. (978-1-884612-06-0(7)) AudioText.
A study guide covering blood types, the heart, homeostasis, the circulatory system, the immune system, blood chemistry, energy metabolism, reproduction, & growth & aging.

Human Anatomy & Physiology: Instructor's Art/Lecture CD. 6th rev. ed. Marieb. audio compact disk 18.97 (978-0-8053-5465-2(4)) Addson-Wesley Educ.

Human Anatomy & Physiology: Student Replacement CD. 6th ed. Marieb. audio compact disk 14.97 (978-0-13-145503-0(6)) PH School.

***Human Anatomy Interactive Atlas/Interactive Lectures Flashcards on Cd.** 2nd rev. ed. Miller-Nielsen. (ENG.). 2010. audio compact disk 131.36 (978-0-7575-2946-7(1)) Kendall-Hunt.

Human Biological Machine As a Transformational Apparatus. E. J. Gold. 1 cass. (Running Time: 1 hr. 30 min.). 9.98 (TP115) Union Label.
This talk covers the machine as a 4-dimensional tunnel through creation, the soul as raw material, turning on the alchemical factory, the illusion of time, the Creation in higher dimensions.

***Human Blend.** unabr. ed. Alan Dean Foster. (Running Time: 7 hrs. 30 mins.). (Tipping Point Ser.). 2010. 29.99 (978-1-4001-9866-5(6)); 19.99 (978-1-4001-6866-8(X)); 14.99 (978-1-4001-8866-6(0)); audio compact disk 29.99 (978-1-4001-1866-3(2)); audio compact disk 71.99 (978-1-4001-4866-0(9)) Pub: Tantor Media. Dist(s): IngramPubServ

Human Body. Sundance/Newbridge, LLC Staff. (Early Science Ser.). (gr. k-3). 2007. audio compact disk 12.00 (978-1-4007-6163-0(8)); audio compact disk 12.00 (978-1-4007-6165-4(4)); audio compact disk 12.00 (978-1-4007-6164-7(6)) Sund Newbrdge.

Human Body audio CD: Fearfully & Wonderfully Made. Marilyn Shannon. Read by Candice Jones. (ENG.). 2007. 15.00 (978-1-932012-84-2(2)) Apologia Educ.

Human Body on File. Diagram Group. (gr. 6-12). 2004. audio compact disk 199.95 (978-0-8160-5400-8(2)) Facts On File.

Human Body, the Audio CD Theme Set: Set of 6 Set A. Adapted by Benchmark Education Staff. (English Explorers Ser.). (J). (gr. 3-6). 2007. audio compact disk 60.00 (978-1-4108-9837-1(7)) Benchmark Educ.

Human Body, the Audio CD Theme Set: Set of 6 Set B. Adapted by Benchmark Education Staff. (English Explorers Ser.). (J). (gr. 3-6). 2007. audio compact disk 60.00 (978-1-4108-9818-0(0)) Benchmark Educ.

Human Christ. Bartholomew. Read by Mary Margaret Moore. 1 cass. (Running Time: 42 min.). 10.00 High Mesa Pr.
Channeled info addresses: the discrepancy between the historical Christ & the human Christ through use of the Tarot.

Human Colonies in Orbit: Fact Verses Fiction. Ed. by Marco A. V. Bitetto. 1 cass. 1999. (978-1-58578-354-0(4)) Inst of Cybernetics.

Human Connection. Louise Jenkins. 1 cass. 8.95 (174) Am Fed Astrologers.
Analysis of chart based on early childhood through Saturn return.

Human Croquet, Set. unabr. ed. Kate Atkinson. Read by Susan Jameson. 8 cass. (Running Time: 8 hrs.). 1998. 69.95 (978-0-7540-0097-6(4), CAB1520) AudioGO.
It was once the great forest of Lythe: an impenetrable thicket shrouded with mystery, & home to the Fairfaxes. Over time, the forest became streets: Chestnut, Laurel & Sycamore; while the Fairfaxes dwindled. Isobel, born in the mid twentieth century, awaits the return of Eliza, her mother, whose disappearance is part of the mystery surrounding the great forest of Lythe.

Human Ecology: Wholeness in Action. Susan Kline et al. 1986. 10.80 (0807) Assn Prof Chaplains.

Human Energy Systems, 1990. Interview with Jack Schwarz & Will Noffke. 1980. 12.00 (#N1001) Aletheia Psycho.

Human Environment. Garry De Young. 1 cass. 5.00 De Young Pr.

Human Evolution. Phillip L. Walker. (C). 1998. audio compact disk (978-0-393-10211-6(4)) Norton.

Human Evolution & a New Psychology. unabr. ed. Colin Wilson. 4 cass. (Running Time: 3 hrs. 51 min.). 1968. 36.00 (05601) Big Sur Tapes.

Human Factor. unabr. ed. Graham Greene. Read by Tim Pigott-Smith. 8 cass. (Running Time: 12 hrss.). 2002. 69.95 (978-0-7540-0797-5(9), CAB 2219) AudioGO.

Human Future. Thomas Berry. 3 cass. 1992. 27.00 set. (OC310-68) Sound Horizons AV.

Human Genome Project: Program from the Award Winning Public Radio Series. Hosted by Fred Goodwin. Comment by John Hockenberry. Contrib. by Steven Moldin et al. 1 cass. (Running Time: 1 hr.). (Infinite Mind Ser.). 1999. audio compact disk 21.95 (978-1-888064-55-1(2), LCM 71) Lichtenstein Creat.
The Human Genome project has been working to map every gene in the human body. Scientists believe more than half of those genes relate to the mind. So what will all this information tell us about the way our brains work? Will we know who will become mentally ill and how to prevent that? And what will we do with that information?.

Human Intimacy. Victor L. Brown. 4 cass. 1998. 14.95 Set. (978-1-57008-543-7(9), Bkcraft Inc) Deseret Bk.

Human Intimacy & the Gospel. abr. ed. John L. Lund. 1 cass. (Running Time: 1 hr. 12 min.). 1997. bk. 9.95 (978-1-891114-29-8(8)) Commun Co.
Human intimacy viewed from three levels, physical, emotional, & spiritual.

Human Love in the Divine Plan. 2005. audio compact disk 79.99 (978-1-932927-54-2(9)) Ascensn Pr.

Human Meaning of Environmental Crisis. unabr. ed. Barry Commoner. 1 cass. 1971. 11.00 Big Sur Tapes.

Human Movement in the Rorschach Test. unabr. ed. Zygmunt A. Piotrowski. 1 cass. (Running Time: 20 min.). 1952. (29237) J Norton Pubs.
A detailed analysis of the difficult human movement response.

Human Nature, What Does It Mean? unabr. ed. Joseph Wood Krutch. 1 cass. (Running Time: 38 min.). 12.95 (25011) J Norton Pubs.
In an age which has lost faith in both divine revelation & a moral universe, the only defense against nihilistic relativism manners, morals, & the meaning of civilization is the concept of "human nature" as a constant.

Human Options. unabr. collector's ed. Norman Cousins. Read by Dan Lazar. 7 cass. (Running Time: 7 hrs.). 1981. 42.00 (978-0-7366-0662-2(9), 1624) Books on Tape.
Reflects the view that the test of freedom is represented by the type & range of options it makes available to people. Its conclusion is that the human race has not run out of options, however precarious or untidy the world may be or become.

Human Potential Movement. E. J. Gold & Claudio Naranjo. 3 cass. (Running Time: 4 hrs. 30 min.). 27.98 set. (TP222) Union Label.
An outrageously funny debate between Claudio Naranjo & E. J. Gold given at the Melia Foundation, in Berkeley, on the value of the human potential movement.

Human Potentialities. Aldous Huxley. 1 cass. (Running Time: 55 min.). 1961. 11.00 (01101) Big Sur Tapes.
The original field of choice is infinite; with latent potentials & untapped energies; the ultimate positive nature of man.

Human Potentialities. unabr. ed. Herbert A. Otto. 1 cass. (Running Time: 27 min.). 12.95 (35050) J Norton Pubs.

Human Prehistory & the First Civilizations, Parts I-III. Instructed by Brian M. Fagan. 18 cass. (Running Time: 18 hrs.). bk. 79.95 (978-1-56585-592-2(2), 380) Teaching Co.

Human Prehistory & the First Civilizations, Parts I-III. Instructed by Brian M. Fagan. 18 CDs. (Running Time: 18 hrs.). 2003. bk. 99.95 (978-1-56585-590-8(6), 380) Teaching Co.

Human Problem. Elbert Willis. 1 cass. (Victory of Surrender Ser.: Vol. 1). 4.00 Fill the Gap.

Human Relationship According to Teresa of Avila. Ernest E. Larkin. 1 cass. 1987. 7.95 (TAH195) Alba Hse Comns.
Focusing on chapters 4 through 7 of St. Teresa's Way of Perfection, Ernest Larkin addresses the key Christian command of love of God & neighbor. Teresa's tremendous insights & deep wisdom are here interpreted within a rich & broad field of contemporary understanding of human affectivity.

Human Resource Library. Ed. by Socrates Media Editors. 2005. audio compact disk 49.95 (978-1-59546-109-4(4)) Pub: Socrates Med LLC. Dist(s): Midpt Trade

Human Resource Management: Virtual Book. T. L. Amos & A. Ristow. 2002. audio compact disk 54.95 (978-0-7021-5540-6(3)) Pub: Juta & Co ZAF. Dist(s): Intl Spec Bk

Human Resources (HR) Library. Compiled by Don Morrison et al. 2005. audio compact disk 299.00 (978-0-927160-24-7(2)) Sound Resc Mgmt.

***Human Resources Law: 2010 Update.** PUEI. 2010. audio compact disk 199.00 (978-1-935041-93-1(2), CareerTrack) P Univ E Inc.

Human Rights & Civil Rights. unabr. ed. John Arthur. Read by Robert Guillaume. Ed. by John Lachs & Mike Hassell. 2 cass. (Running Time: 3 hrs.). Dramatization. (Morality in Our Age Ser.). 1995. 17.95 Set. (978-1-56823-034-4(6), 10513) Knowledge Prod.
Only a few hundred years ago there emerged the ideal of inalienable rights to life, liberty, property, free speech, freedom of conscience & religion, etc. Yet rights now are routinely claimed to include health care, employment, housing, & education; the Universal Declaration of Human Rights even lists paid vacations. Are rights bestowed by government, or do we possess them simply because we are human? Given the diversity of cultures, are there universal human rights? Do we have a "right" to all the things we need for a full & human life - even if it obligates others to provide them?.

Human Rights & Civil Rights. unabr. abr. ed. Read by Robert Guillaume. (Running Time: 10800 sec.). (Morality in Our Age Ser.). 2006. audio compact disk 25.95 (978-0-7861-6626-8(6)) Pub: Blckstn Audio. Dist(s): NetLibrary CO

Human Rights in the Administration of Justice: A Manual for Judges, Prosecutors & Lawyers (Includes CD-ROM) (Arabic Language) United Nations. (Professional Training Ser.). (ARA.). 2008. pap. bk. 95.00 (978-92-1-654015-9(X)) Untd Nat Pubns.

Human Sexuality Multimedia CDs: Multimedia Human Sexuality 2 CD (Windows/Macintosh) 2 CDs. (gr. 7-12). audio compact disk 126.00 (978-1-59070-358-8(3)) Goodheart.

Human Shadow. Robert Bly. 2 cass. 19.95 (OC126) Sound Horizons AV.
Discusses how to get such energy back from people to whom we have given it to.

Human Shadow. Robert Bly. 2 cass. (Running Time: 90 min. per cass.). 1986. 19.95 (978-1-879323-00-1(1), SET) Sound Horizons AV.
Two 90-minute cassette tapes on Bly's concept of the shadow. In this live presentation Bly expands on the core concepts that comprise his best selling book "A Little Book on the Human Shadow".

Human Side of Human-Beings: The Theory of Re-Evaluaton Counseling. Harvey Jackins. 1 cass. 10.00 (978-1-893165-45-8(0)) Rational Isl.
Introduction to re-evaluation counseling - a completely new theory of human behavior.

Human Side of Transformation. Innovation Groups Staff. 1 cass. (Running Time: 2 hrs.). (Transforming Local Government Ser.). 1997. 21.50 (978-1-882403-38-7(X)) Alliance Innov.
Training information for those working in local government.

Human Situation. Harvey Jackins. 4 cass.Tr. of Situacion Humana. 10.00 ea. cass. (978-1-893165-46-5(9)) Rational Isl.
Collection of writings on re-evaluation counseling.

Human Situation Series. unabr. ed. Aldous Huxley. 16 cass. 1959. 125.00 Set. (01122) Big Sur Tapes.
Series of lectures Aldous Huxley gave in 1959, illuminating not only the problems but also the potentialities of the modern world.

Human Smoke: The Beginnings of World War II, the End of Civilization. unabr. ed. Nicholson Baker. Narrated by Norman Dietz. (Running Time: 14 hrs. 0 mins. 0 sec.). (ENG.). 2008. audio compact disk 34.99 (978-1-4001-0789-6(X)); audio compact disk 24.99 (978-1-4001-5789-1(7)); audio compact disk 69.99 (978-1-4001-3789-3(6)) Pub: Tantor Media. Dist(s): IngramPubServ

Human Suffering & the Bible. Daniel Simundson. 1986. 10.80 (0612) Assn Prof Chaplains.

Human Technology: A Toolkit for Authentic Living. abr. ed. Ilchi Lee. Read by Franklin Belew. 4 CDs. (Running Time: 14400 sec.). 2005. audio compact disk 30.00 (978-1-932843-14-9(0)) Healing Society.

Human, the Orchid, & the Octopus: Exploring & Conserving Our Natural World. Jacques-Yves Cousteau & Susan Schiefelbein. Read by Stephen Hoye. Frwd. by Bill McKibben. (Playaway Adult Nonfiction Ser.). 2008. 69.99 (978-1-60640-703-5(1)) Find a World.

Human, the Orchid, & the Octopus: Exploring & Conserving Our Natural World. unabr. ed. Jacques Cousteau & Susan Schiefelbein. Read by Stephen Hoye. 2 MP3-CDs. (Running Time: 13 hrs. 0 mins. 0 sec.). (ENG.). 2008. 24.99 (978-1-4001-5608-5(4)); audio compact disk 75.99 (978-1-4001-3608-7(3)) Pub: Tantor Media. Dist(s): IngramPubServ

Human, the Orchid, & the Octopus: Exploring & Conserving Our Natural World. unabr. ed. Jacques Cousteau & Susan Schiefelbein. Read by Stephen Hoye. Frwd. by Bill McKibben. 11 CDs. (Running Time: 13 hrs. 0 mins. 0 sec.). (ENG.). 2008. audio compact disk 37.99 (978-1-4001-0608-0(7)) Pub: Tantor Media. Dist(s): IngramPubServ

Human to Horseman: A Journey of Discovery, Growth, & Celebration. 2009. audio compact disk 24.95 (978-0-9720122-8-7(1)) Horse Show.

Human Torpedo. Tim Winton. Read by Stig Wemyss. (Running Time: 3 hrs.). (Lockie Leonard Ser.). (YA). 2009. 54.99 (978-1-74214-356-9(3), 9781742143569) Pub: Bolinda Pubng AUS. Dist(s): Bolinda Pub Inc

Human Torpedo. unabr. ed. Tim Winton. Read by Stig Wemyss. 3 CDs. (Running Time: 3 hrs.). (Lockie Leonard Ser.). (YA). 2001. audio compact disk 54.95 (978-1-74030-597-6(3)) Pub: Bolinda Pubng AUS. Dist(s): Bolinda Pub Inc

***Human Traces.** Sebastian Faulks. Read by James Adams. (ENG.). 2009. 40.00 (978-1-4417-3613-0(1)) Blckstn Audio.

Human Traces. unabr. ed. Sebastian Falks. Read by James Adams. (Running Time: 20 hrs. 0 mins.). (ENG.). 2009. 44.95 (978-1-4332-2921-3(8)); 59.95 (978-1-4332-2917-6(X)); audio compact disk 123.00 (978-1-4332-2918-3(8)) Blckstn Audio.

Human Understanding, Set. unabr. ed. David Hume. Read by Robert L. Halvorson. 2 cass. (Running Time: 180 min.). 14.95 (37) Halvorson Assocs.

Human Understanding, Set. unabr. ed. John Locke. Read by Robert L. Halvorson. 2 cass. (Running Time: 180 min.). 14.95 (35) Halvorson Assocs.

Human Work of Transforming the Primitive. Read by Diane Martin. 5 cass. (Running Time: 6 hrs. 30 min.). 1990. 38.95 Set. (978-0-7822-0161-1(X), 426) C G Jung IL.
Centered on the psyche in everyday life & human relationships, this workshop considers subjects especially strong in transformative quality, such as the shamanistic ideal of metabolizing reality, encountering alchemical elements, the journey of returning to origin, the archetype of the trickster, & the nature of unconscious processes themselves. Martin is a faculty member of the C. G. Jung Institute of Chicago.

Humanae Vitae: Making Happier, Healthier People. Janet Smith. 4 cass. 1995. 22.95 Set. (6051-C) Ignatius Pr.
In a series of talks, Professor Janet Smith, editor of "Why Humanae Vitae Was Right," talks about the relationships between the 1968 papal encyclical "Humanae Vitae," which reaffirmed the Church's traditional ban on artificial methods of birth control, & the new papal encyclical on moral principles "Veritatis Splendor".

Humanist Tradition. Fiero. 1 cass. (C). 1992. 16.25 (978-0-697-14856-8(4)) McGrw-H Hghr Educ.

Humanistic Astrology. unabr. ed. Dane Rudhyar. 1 cass. (Running Time: 1 hr.). 1970. 11.00 (10106) Big Sur Tapes.
Addresses some of the basic questions about humanistic astrology. An excellent introduction to the topic.

Humanistic Psychology. unabr. ed. Charlotte Buhler. 1 cass. (Running Time: 51 min.). 12.95 (29002) J Norton Pubs.
Presentation & clarification of the concepts, cultural significance, & meaning of humanistic psychology to the individual.

Humanistic Tradition, Bks. 1-6. 4th ed. Gloria K. Fiero. 1 CD. (Running Time: 1 hr.). (C). 2001. 29.06 (978-0-07-238852-7(8), Mc-H Human Soc) Pub: McGrw-H Hghr Educ. Dist(s): McGraw
Compact Disc One 1 Ancient Greek: Epitaph for Seikilos 2 Gregorian Chant: Alleluya: Vidimus Stellam 3 Buddhist Chant: Morning Prayers 4 Islamic Call To Prayer 5 Arabo-Andalousian: Nouba Raml Al Maya 6 Troubadour Song: Ventadorn: Can vei la lauzeta mouver 7 Hildegard of Bingen: O Successores 8 The Play of Herod, Scene 2, "The Three Magi" 9 Early Medieval Polyphony: Rex Caeli, Domine 10 Early Medieval Polyphony: Agnus Dei 11 Early Medieval Polyphony: Benedicamus Domino 12 Perotin: Alleluya (Nativitas) 13 13th Century Motet: En non Diu! Quant voi 14 13th Century Dance: Estampie 15 The Music of India: Thumri 16 The Music of China: Ngoh Wai Heng Hong 17 Machaut: Notre Dame Mass, "Ite Missa Est" 18 English Round: Summer is Icumen In 19 Dufay: Missa, "L'Homme armé," Kyrie 20 Lasso: Matona Mia Cara 21 Morley: My Bonnie Lass She Smileth 22 Des Prez: Tulerant Dominum Meum 23 The Music of Africa-Senegal: Greetings from Podor 24 The Music of Africa-Angola: Gangele Song 25 Navajo: Night Chant Compact Disc Two 1 Gabrielli: Motet: In Ecclesiis 2 Monteverdi: Orfeo, Act II, "Vi recorda, o boschi ombros" 3 Handel: Messiah, "Hallelujah" Chorus 4 Bach: Cantata No. 80, Chorale: "Eine Feste Burg ist unser Gott 5 Vivaldi: The Four Seasons, "Spring," I 6 Bach: Brandenburg Concerto No. 4 in G Major, I 7 Bach: The Art of the Fugue, Canon in the 12th 8 Couperin: Ordre 22, Le Croc en Jambe 9 Haydn: Symphony No. 94 in G Major "Surprise," II 10 Mozart: Serenade In G Major, K. 525 "Eine Kleine Nachtmusik," I 11 Mozart: Marriage of Figaro, "Dove sono" 12 Beethoven: Symphony No. 3 in E-flat Major, I 13 Schubert: Erlkönig 14 Berlioz: Symphonie Fantastique, Op. 14, IV "March to the Scaffold" 15 Chopin: Etude in G-flat Major, Op. 10, No. 5 16 Debussy: Prélude a l'aprés midi d'un faune 17 Schoenberg: Pierrot Lunaire, "Heimweh" 18 Stravinsky: The Rite of Spring, "Sacrificial Dance" 19 Copland: Appalachian Spring, Variations on "Simple Gifts" 20 Cage: Sonata V 21 Handy: St. Louis Blues 22 Hardin: Hotter Than That 23 Parker: KoKo 24 Ligeti: Atmospheres 25 Babbitt: Ensembles for Synthesizer 26 Glass: Einstein on the Beach, Kneeplay 1.

Humanistic Tradition Music Listening CD: Volume 2. 5th ed. Gloria K. Fiero. 2005. audio compact disk 25.63 (978-0-07-291017-9(8), 9780072910179, Mc-H Human Soc) Pub: McGrw-H Hghr Educ. Dist(s): McGraw

***Humanitarian Jesus: Social Justice & the Cross.** unabr. ed. Ryan Dobson & Christian Buckley. Narrated by Johnny Heller. (ENG.). 2010. 14.98 (978-1-59644-699-1(4)); audio compact disk 24.98 (978-1-59644-698-4(6)) christianaud.

Humanities: Cultural Roots & Continuities. 6th ed. (gr. 6-12). 2001. audio compact disk (978-0-618-04547-1(3), 3-60775) CENGAGE Learn.

Humanities: Cultural Roots & Continuities, Vol. 2. 6th ed. (gr. 6-12). 2001. audio compact disk (978-0-618-04548-8(1), 3-60776) CENGAGE Learn.

Humanities in Western Culture. 4th rev. ed. Robert C. Lamm. (Eng.). (C). 2004. audio compact disk 27.50 (978-0-07-288014-4(7), 0072880147, Mc-H Human Soc) Pub: McGrw-H Hghr Educ. Dist(s): McGraw

Humanities Western Culture Vol. I: A Search for Human Values. 10th ed. Robert C. Lamm & Neal Cross. (C). 1995. (978-0-697-25428-3(3)) Brown & Benchmark.

Humanities Western Culture Vol. II: A Search for Human Values. 10th ed. Robert C. Lamm & Neal Cross. (C). 1995. (978-0-697-25430-6(5)) Brown & Benchmark.

Humanity & Divinity of Jesus, Pt. 1. Mother Angelica & Father Michael. 1 cass. (Running Time: 60 min.). (Mother Angelica Live Ser.). 1988. 10.00 (978-1-55794-110-7(6), T61) Eternal Wrd TV.
Explains the dual nature of Jesus, critizes "The Last Temptation of Christ," denounces the New Age Movement, & explains Gnosticism & reincarnation.

Humanity & Divinity of Jesus, Pt. 2. Mother Angelica & Father Michael. 1 cass. (Running Time: 60 min.). (Mother Angelica Live Ser.). 1988. 10.00 (978-1-55794-111-4(4), T62) Eternal Wrd TV.
Explains the Paraclete guidelines for knowing the action of the Holy Spirit in one's life, & how to identify the evils of the New Age Movement, blasphemy, reincarnation, magic & dark arts.

Humanity Mission. Marianne Williamson. Read by Marianne Williamson. 1 cass. (Running Time: 90 mins.). (Lectures on a Course in Miracles). 1999. 10.00 (978-1-56170-441-5(5), M824) Hay House.

Humanity of Christ: Logos October 26, 1997. Ben Young. 1997. 4.95 (978-0-7417-6053-1(3), B0053) Win Walk.

Humanity's Divinity. Helen M. Wright. Read by Alan Young. 6 cass. (Running Time: 8 hrs.). (Mary Baker Eddy - God's Great Scientist Ser.: Vol. 5). 1999. 19.95 (978-1-886505-11-7(X)) H M Wright.
Exploring Chapter V, "Prayer & Atonement," we continue to learn that our own right consciousness is God & that our physical body is only "a sensuous human concept," the product of wrong thinking. Rightly viewed, we are not mortals, but are divine; as Jesus said, "The kingdom of God is within you.".

Humanity's Divinity. abr. ed. Helen M. Wright. Read by Alan Young. Narrated by Michael Sutton. 6 cass. (Running Time: 8 hrs.). (God's Great Scientist Ser.: Vol. 5). 1998. 19.95 (978-1-886505-06-3(3)) H M Wright.
Through the teachings of Mary Baker Eddy, shows how one can find one's own true self, the "kingdom of God within you".

Humankind, Vol. 1. unabr. ed. 6 cass. (Running Time: 6 hrs. 30 min.). 1999. 24.95 (978-1-886373-10-5(8)) Human Media.
Examines the challenge all people face to develop personal ideals & values that uplift & strengthen our communities.

Humanoids & with Folded Hands. unabr. ed. Jack Williamson. Read by Stefan Rudnicki. 7 cass. (Running Time: 10 hrs.). 2002. 49.95 (978-0-7861-2332-2(X), 3040); audio compact disk 64.00 (978-0-7861-9346-2(8), 3040) Blckstn Audio.

Humble & Powerful. Eldon Taylor. 1 cass. (Running Time: 62 min.). (Inner Talk Ser.). 16.95 incl. script. (978-1-55978-021-6(5), 5421C) Progress Aware Res.
Soundtrack - Musical Themes with underlying subliminal affirmations.

Humble & Powerful: Environmental Theme. Eldon Taylor. 1 cass. 16.95 (978-1-55978-759-8(7), 5421F) Progress Aware Res.

Humble Approach to Truth. Swami Amar Jyoti. 1 cass. 1987. 9.95 (K-149) Truth Consciousness.
Truth won't be revealed by our experimentation; a reverent search is needed. The criterion of true wisdom. The Yogic approach to science.

Humbling. unabr. ed. Philip Roth. Read by Dick Hill. 1 MP3-CD. (Running Time: 3 hrs.). 2009. 39.97 (978-1-4418-0102-9(2), 9781441801029, Brlnc Audio MP3 Lib); 24.99 (978-1-4418-0101-2(4), 9781441801012, Brilliance MP3); 24.99 (978-1-4418-0103-6(0), 9781441801036, BAD); 39.97 (978-1-4418-0104-3(9), 9781441801043, BADLE); audio compact disk 24.99 (978-1-4418-0099-2(9), 9781441800992, Bril Audio CD Unabri); audio compact disk 62.97 (978-1-4418-0100-5(6), 9781441801005, BriAudCD Unabrid) Brilliance Audio.

Humbly Starting the Journey. Swami Amar Jyoti. 1 dolby cass. 1983. 9.95 (M-45) Truth Consciousness.
Starting from scratch on the inward journey. Simple & humble, vistas of Existence open. We are always loved.

Humboldt River. unabr. ed. Gary McCarthy. Read by Michael Taylor. 8 cass. (Running Time: 9 hrs. 54 min.). (Rivers West Ser.: Bk. 9). 2001. 49.95 (978-1-55686-768-2(9)) Books in Motion.
Stranded and in danger, Libby Pike stumbles upon help from a man with two sons. Together they would help him tame a harsh and savage wilderness.

Humboldt's Gift. unabr. ed. Saul Bellow. Read by Christopher Hurt. 13 cass. (Running Time: 19 hrs.). 1993. 85.95 set. (978-0-7861-0345-4(0), 1302) Blckstn Audio.
For many years Von Humboldt Fleisher & Charles Citrine were the best of friends - Humboldt a grand erratic figure, a great poet; Charlie a young man of frenzied & noble longings, straight out of the Middle West, his heart inflamed with literature. But by the 1970s, Humboldt has died a failure in New York & Charlie's success-ridden life in Chicago has taken various turns for the worse when Humboldt acts from the grave to change Charlie's life. He has left Charlie something in his will. Charlie comes into a legacy.

Humboldt's Gift. unabr. ed. Saul Bellow. Read by Christopher Hurt. (Running Time: 64800 sec.). 2008. audio compact disk 44.95 (978-0-7861-6256-7(2)); audio compact disk & audio compact disk 120.00 (978-0-7861-6255-0(4)) Blckstn Audio.

Humboldt's Gift, Set. unabr. ed. Saul Bellow. Read by Christopher Hurt. 13 cass. 1999. (FS9-51100) Highbridge Pr.

Hume in 90 Minutes. Paul Strathern. Read by Robert Whitfield. 2 CDs. (Running Time: 1 hr. 30 mins.). 2004. audio compact disk 17.00 (978-0-7861-8531-3(7), 3316) Blckstn Audio.

Hume in 90 Minutes. Paul Strathern. Read by Robert Whitfield. (Running Time: 5400 sec.). 2004. 15.95 (978-0-7861-2783-2(X), 3316) Blckstn Audio.

Hume in 90 Minutes. unabr. ed. Paul Strathern. Read by Robert Whitfield. (Running Time: 1 hr. 30 mins.). (Philosophers in 90 Minutes Ser.). 2004. reel tape 14.95 (978-0-7861-2788-7(0)); audio compact disk 14.95 (978-0-7861-8530-6(9)) Blckstn Audio.

Hume's Dialogues Concerning Natural Religion. Ed. by Albert A. Anderson. Lieselotte Anderson. 4 CDs. (Running Time: 5 hours). Dramatization. 2004. audio compact disk 30.00 (978-1-887250-40-5(9)) Agora Pubns.
Long before the current dispute in the USA about the teaching of evolution, Hume's dialogues presented and critically analyzed the idea of intelligent design. What should we teach our children about the creation of the world? What should we teach them about religion? The characters Demea, Cleanthes, and Philo passionately present and defend different answers to those questions. Demea opens the dialogue with a position derived from René Descartes and Father Malebranche - God's nature is a mystery, but God's existence can be proved logically. Cleanthes attacks that view, both because it leads to mysticism and because it attempts the impossible task of trying to establish existence on the basis pure reason, without appeal to sense experience. As an alternative, he offers intelligent design as proof of both God's existence and God's nature based on the same kind of scientific reasoning established by Copernicus, Galileo, and Newton. Taking a skeptical approach, Philo presents a series of arguments that question any attempt to use reason as a basis for religious faith. He suggests that human beings might be better off without religion.

***Humilitas: A Lost Key to Life, Love, & Leadership.** unabr. ed. John Dickson. (ENG.). 2011. 16.99 (978-0-310-57199-5(5)) Zondervan.

Humility. 1 cass. (Running Time: 1 hr.). 12.99 (712) Yoga Res Foun.

Humility. AIO Team Staff. Prod. by Focus on the Family Staff. (Running Time: 1 hr. 10 mins. 0 sec.). (Adventures in Odyssey Life Lessons Ser.). (ENG.). (J). (gr. 3-7). 2005. audio compact disk 5.99 (978-1-58997-182-0(5)) Pub: Focus Family. Dist(s): Tyndale Hse

Humility. Francis Frangipane. 1 cass. (Running Time: 90 mins.). (Strategies for our Cities Ser.: Vol. 7). 2000. 5.00 (FF06-007) Morning NC.
This series provides practical, biblical solutions that have been tested & have born fruit for those with a vision for their cities.

Humility: Mother of Meekness. Elbert Willis. 1 cass. (Might of Meekness Ser.). 4.00 Fill the Gap.

Humility: The Path to Glory. John MacArthur, Jr. 2 cass. pap. bk. 8.25 (HarperThor) HarpC GBR.

Humility: The Quiet Virtue. Everett L. Worthington & Everett L. Worthington, Jr. Read by Eileen Brady & Charles Roney. (Running Time: 5460 sec.). 2008. audio compact disk 19.95 (978-1-59947-131-0(0)) Pub: Templeton Pr. Dist(s): Chicago Distribution Ctr

***Humility: True Greatness.** unabr. ed. C. J. Mahaney. Narrated by Sean Runnette. (ENG.). 2009. 9.98 (978-1-59644-790-5(7), Hovel Audio) christianaud.

Humility: True Greatness. unabr. ed. C. J. Mahaney & Joshua Harris. (Running Time: 3 hrs. 42 mins. 0 sec.). (ENG.). 2009. audio compact disk 15.98 (978-1-59644-789-9(3), Hovel Audio) christianaud.

Humility Developers. Elbert Willis. 1 cass. (Humility of Heaven Ser.). 4.00 Fill the Gap.

Humility of Heaven Series. Elbert Willis. 4 cass. 13.00 Set. Fill the Gap.

Humility, the Beauty of Holiness. Prod. by InSpirit Tapes and CDs. 2 CDs. (Running Time: 1 hr., 45 mins.). 2007. audio compact disk 14.95 (978-1-932758-02-3(X)) InSpirit Tapes.

Humming Whispers. unabr. ed. Angela Johnson. Narrated by Michele-Denise Woods. 2 pieces. (Running Time: 2 hrs. 30 mins.). (gr. 6 up). 1997. 19.00 (978-0-7887-0437-6(0), 94629E7) Recorded Bks.
When her sister Nikki is well, fourteen-year-old Sophy shares magical days with her. But when Nikky hears the whispers, she withdraws, leaving Sophy alone & terrified that she, too, will begin to hear voices.

Hummingbirds. unabr. ed. Joshua Gaylord. Narrated by Cynthia Holloway. (Running Time: 11 hrs. 0 mins. 0 sec.). (ENG.). 2009. 24.99 (978-1-4001-6465-3(6)); audio compact disk 34.99 (978-1-4001-1465-8(9)); audio compact disk 69.99 (978-1-4001-4465-5(5)) Pub: Tantor Media. Dist(s): IngramPubServ

***Hummingbirds.** unabr. ed. Joshua Gaylord. Narrated by Cynthia Holloway. (Running Time: 11 hrs. 0 mins.). 2009. 17.99 (978-1-4001-8465-1(7)) Tantor Media.

Hummingbird's Daughter. unabr. ed. Luis Alberto Urrea. (Running Time: 15 hrs.). (ENG.). 2006. 14.98 (978-1-59483-816-3(X)) Pub: Hachet Audio. Dist(s): HachBkGrp

Hummingbird's Daughter. unabr. ed. Luis Alberto Urrea. (Running Time: 15 hrs.). (ENG.). 2009. 19.98 (978-1-60788-263-3(9)) Pub: Hachet Audio. Dist(s): HachBkGrp

Humor. 1 cass. (Running Time: 45 min.). (Relationship Ser.). 9.98 (978-1-55909-071-1(5), 60); 9.98 90 min. extended length stereo music. (978-1-55909-072-8(3), 60X) Randolph Tapes.
Uses laughter's healing power to promote happiness. Subliminal messages are heard 3-5 minutes before becoming ocean sounds or music.

Humor: Program from the Award Winning Public Radio Series. Featuring Phil Proctor & Peter Bergman. (Infinite Mind Ser.). 1998. audio compact disk 21.95 (978-1-888064-29-2(3), LCM 33) Lichtenstein Creat.
This week, The Infinite Mind looks at humor. What's involved in humor? What makes things funny? Where does funny live in our brains? Things are funny when they don't quite fit - when they're divorced from their normal context, or when they violate a pattern. There's often an element of discomfort in humor - maybe because we sense that violation. Humor can relieve anxiety, dissolve conflict, and be used as a tool for teaching. Dr. Fred Goodwin talks about humor with some of America's top comedians - including Margaret Cho, Peter Bergman and Phil Proctor of the Firesign Theater, Robert Klein, and Anne Beatts, an original writer for Saturday Night Live. They reveal how they generate their material, talk about secrets of comic timing, and discuss the relationship between humor and social commentary. Dr. Goodwin also interviews scientists who've researched humor in different cultures and found a spot in the brain that when stimulated generates laughter and feelings of amusement.

Humor: Week of October 21, 1998. Read by Fred Goodwin. Comment by John Hockenberry. Contrib. by Bill Fry et al. 1 cass. (Running Time: 1 hr.). (Infinite Mind Ser.). 15.00 Lichtenstein Creat.
What makes funny, well, - funny? And exactly where does funny "live" in your brain? Visit with top comics as well as serious researchers, who, strangely enough, have studied these things.

Humor Allies. C. W. Metcalf. Read by C. W. Metcalf. 1 cass. (Running Time: 54 min.). (Four Humor Visualizations Ser.). 1987. 9.95 (978-1-878365-02-6(9)) C W Metcalf.
Humor visualization exercises by consultant C. W. Metcalf with woodwind music.

Humor & Healing. Ann E. Weeks. 1 cass. 1994. 8.00 (978-1-886036-02-4(0)) Passages Pbg.
Healing aspects of humor.

Humor & Healing. unabr. ed. Bernie S. Siegel. 1 CD. (Running Time: 1 Hr 20 Mins). 2006. audio compact disk 14.95 (978-1-59179-389-2(0), AW00113D) Sounds True.
Humor and Healing is Bernie Siegel's sparkling conversation about the healing power of love and laughter. From how positive experiences help us lead longer, more productive lives ... to new findings about how laughter can heal ... to miracles of spontaneous remission in "terminally ill" patients ... you will find Humor and Healing to be a life-affirming house-call from this respected surgeon and speaker. "If you live in your heart, magic happens." This is the essence of Dr. Bernie Siegel's powerful approach to living in the present. Includes many examples of people who have turned their lives around against all odds. Recorded at the Fifth Annual Conference of the Humor Project in Sarasota Springs, New York.

Humor & Health: An Overview of Research, Literature, & Clinical Discoveries with Practical Applications & Recommendations. 2001. 38.00 (978-0-9655759-1-1(8)) J R Dunn.

Humor Goes a Long Way. Art Buchwald. Intro. by A. E. Whyte. 1 cass. (Running Time: 42 min.). (Listen & Learn USA! Ser.). 8.95 (978-0-88684-012-9(0)) Listen USA.
Art Buchwald offers answers to today's pressing questions.

Humor Happens. William Wait. 1 cass. 6.98 (06004202); 7.98 (978-1-55503-286-9(9), 06004202) Covenant Comms.
A hilarious talk on the place of humor in our lives.

Humor in Pastoral Care. 1 cass. (Care Cassettes Ser.: Vol. 12, No. 2). 1985. 10.80 Assn Prof Chaplains.

Humor in Religion. 1 cass. (Running Time: 25 min.). 12.00 (L320) MEA A Watts Cass.

Humor in the Local Government Workplace. unabr. ed. Innovation Groups Staff. Contrib. by Ralph Qualls, Jr. 1 cass. (Transforming Local Government Ser.: Vol. 6). 1999. 10.00 (978-1-882403-62-2(2), IG9906) Alliance Innov.

Humor Is a Laughing Matter. Perf. by Abe Wagner. 2 cass. (Running Time: 30 min.). 6.95 (978-0-926632-06-6(X)) A Wagner & Assocs.
Loaded with hysterical humor that charms audiences worldwide.

Humor Me, I'm Your Mother! unabr. ed. Barbara Johnson. Narrated by Carol Myers. (ENG.). 2006. 8.39 (978-1-60814-244-6(2)); audio compact disk 9.99 (978-1-59859-108-8(9)) Oasis Audio.

Humor of Mark Twain. unabr. ed. Mark Twain. Read by Thomas Becker. 2 CDs. (Running Time: 2 hrs. 30 mins.). 2000. audio compact disk 25.00 (978-1-58472-096-6(4), Commuters Library) Sound Room.

Humor of Mark Twain. unabr. ed. Short Stories. Mark Twain. Read by Thomas Becker. 2 cds. (Running Time: 2 hours 26 mins). (YA). 2002. audio compact disk 18.95 (978-1-58472-262-5(2), 009, In Aud) Pub: Sound Room. Dist(s): Baker Taylor
Contains The Notorious Jumping Frog of Calaveras County, The Story of the Old Ram, What Stumped the Bluejays, Tom Quartz, Cannibalism in the Cars, The Facts in the Great Beef Contract, Journalism in Tennessee, Punch, Brothers, Punch, The McWilliamses with Membranous Croup, and The Burglar Alarm.,.

Humor Power! Thomas R. Condon. 1 cass. (Creativity Unlimited Training Ser.). 12.95 (978-1-884305-83-2(0)) Changeworks.
"Helps tap the ability to see things differently, to stand reality on its ear!" - American Assn. of Therapeutic Humor.

Humor, Risk & Change. C. W. Metcalf. Read by C. W. Metcalf. 5 cass. (Running Time: 5 hrs.). (Survival Skills for People Over Five & Under Pressure Ser.). 1988. 49.95 (978-1-878365-00-2(2)) C W Metcalf.
Consultant & humorist C. W. Metcalf's exploration of humor skills that can be used as tools for healthy survival in the stress filled 1990s. Shows how humor can aid in productivity, risk taking, creativity & communication. Includes "Humor Allies.".

***Humorists: From Hogarth to Noël Coward.** unabr. ed. Paul Johnson. 1 MP3-CD. (Running Time: 9 hrs.). 2010. 29.95 (978-1-4417-5745-6(7)); 59.95 (978-1-4417-5741-8(4)); audio compact disk 90.00 (978-1-4417-5742-5(2)); audio compact disk 29.95 (978-1-4417-5744-9(9)) Blckstn Audio.

Humorous Chinese. Wang Hailong. 2 CDs. (Series of Practical Chinese Ser.). (CHI & ENG.). 2003. audio compact disk 9.95 (978-7-88703-209-6(1), HUCHCD) Pub: China Lang Univ CHN. Dist(s): China Bks

Humpback Goes North. Darice Bailer. 1 cass. (Running Time: 35 min.). (J). (ps-2). 2001. bk. 19.95 (SP 4001C) Kimbo Educ.
Little whale begins her first journey from warm waters to the Maine Coast. Includes book.

Humpback Goes North. Darice Bailer. Illus. by Stephen Marchesi. Narrated by Peter Thomas. 1 cass. (J). 1998. 5.00 (978-1-56899-533-5(4), BC4015) Soundprints.

Humphrey Bogart. unabr. ed. Read by Heywood Hale Broun. 1 cass. (Heywood Hale Broun Ser.). 12.95 (40204) J Norton Pubs.
Bogie's many friends try to outdo the other in relating yarns about Bogie's personality, his success, the many accidents that befell him, his wives, his roles & his legend.

Humphrey Bogart & Lauren Bacall: To Have & Have Not. unabr. ed. 1 cass. (Running Time: 60 min.). Dramatization. 7.95 Norelco box. (DD9340) Natl Recrd Co.
Bogart & Bacall recreate their roles as Harry Morgan & Marie Browning from the 1944 film based on the novel by Ernest Hemingway. Skipper-for-hire Bogart is tangled up in World War II intrigue. "Baby" Bacall repeats her now-famous line, "If you want me, just whistle...you know how to whistle, don't you Steve...you just put your lips together & blow!" In a sultry voice she also says, "I'm hard to get Steve, all you have to do is ask".

Humpty-Dumpty see Treasury of Lewis Carroll

Humpty Dumpty. Ed. by Mother Goose. (ENG., 2006. 15.95 (978-1-59249-576-4(1)) Soundprints.

Humpty Dumpty & Friends in the Southwest. unabr. ed. Poems. Esther L. Esparza et al. Illus. by Thomas Esparza, Jr. Contrib. by Esther La Madrid Esparza & Conrad Diesler. 1 cass. (Running Time: 20 min.). (J). (ps-9). 1990. 5.95 (978-1-879817-12-8(8)) Pub: Star Light Pr. Dist(s): iLeon
Twenty children's nursery rhymes in English & Spanish. Poems include: Jack Be Nimble-Juan, Se Listo, Little Jumping Joan-Saltadora Sarita, I Had a Little Pony-Yo Tenia un Caballito, Jack Spratt-Juan Ventura, Ride a Cock Horse-Voy al Barrio de Buenavina, The King of France-El Rey de Espana & Dame, Get Up-Doncella, Levantate.

Humpty Dumpty & Friends in the Southwest. unabr. ed. Poems. Esther L. Esparza et al. Illus. by Thomas Esparza, Jr. Contrib. by Esther La Madrid Esparza & Conrad Diesler. 1 cass. (Running Time: 20 min.). (J). (ps-9). 1991. 5.95 (978-1-879817-11-1(X), Bilingual) Pub: Star Light Pr. Dist(s): iLeon
Twenty children's nursery rhymes in English & Spanish. Poems include: Once I Saw a Little Bird-Una Vez Vi un Pajarito, This Little Bird-Este Pajarito, Little Redbird in the Tree-Pajarito, Can Tu, Simple Simon-Simonelo, For Every Evil-Para Cada Maldad, Christmas is a Coming-La Navidad Ya Viene, & Little Drops of Water-Gotitas de Agua.

Humpty Dumpty & Friends in the Southwest. unabr. ed. Poems. Esther L. Esparza et al. Read by Conrad Diesler. 1 cass. (Running Time: 20 min.). (J). (ps-9). 1991. 5.95 (978-1-879817-10-4(1), Bilingual) Pub: Star Light Pr. Dist(s): iLeon
Twenty children's nursery rhymes in English & Spanish. Poems include: Humpty Dumpty-Cocoloco, Old Mother Goose-Abuelita Gansa, Cocks Crow in the Morning-El Gallo Canta por la Manana, Rock-a-Bye-Baby-Duermete, Mi Hija, A Sunshiny Shower-Llovizna con Sol, Little Bo Peep-Betita Bonita, & Star Light, Star Bright-Estrellita, La Primera.

Humpty Dumpty & Friends in the Southwest. 3rd ed. Poems. Illus. by Robbie Miller. 1 CD, 1 Cass. (Running Time: 22 mins).Tr. of Coco Loco y Amigos en el Suroeste. (SPA & ENG.). (J). 2002. 12.95 (978-1-879817-27-2(6), Bilingual) Star Light Pr.
The audio CD and cassette follow the book with rythm and chant songs.

Humpty Dumpty at Sea. (J). (ps-3). 2000. 2.99 (978-1-85781-206-0(9)) Cimino Pub Grp.

Humpty Dumpty at Sea. 1 CD. 2004. audio compact disk 7.95 (978-0-8256-2762-0(1), AM975590) Pub: Music Sales. Dist(s): H Leonard

Humpty Dumpty's Fall Audio CD. Adapted by Benchmark Education Company Staff. Based on a work by Carrie Smith. (Reader's Theater Nursery Rhymes & Songs Ser.). (J). (gr. k-1). 2008. audio compact disk 10.00 (978-1-60437-982-2(0)) Benchmark Educ.

Humpty Jumpty. 1 CD. (Running Time: 39 min.). 2004. audio compact disk 16.98 (978-1-884273-31-5(9)) Rspberry Recs.

Hunchback Assignments. unabr. ed. Arthur G. Slade. Read by Jayne Entwistle. (ENG.). (J). (gr. 7). 2009. audio compact disk 34.00 (978-0-7393-8020-8(6), Listening Lib) Pub: Random Audio Pubg. Dist(s): Random

Hunchback in the Park see Dylan Thomas Reading On the Marriage of a Virgin, Over Sir John's Hill, In Country Sleep & Others

Hunchback in the Park see Dylan Thomas Reading His Poetry

Hunchback of Notre- Dame. Victor Hugo. Read by Bill Homewood. (Running Time: 2 hrs. 30 mins.). 1998. 20.95 (978-1-60083-777-7(8)) Iofy Corp.

Hunchback of Notre- Dame. Victor Hugo. Read by Carlos J. Vega. (Running Time: 3 hrs.). 2002. 16.95 (978-1-60083-203-1(2), Audiofy Corp) Iofy Corp.

Hunchback of Notre- Dame. Victor Hugo. Narrated by Jim Killavey. (Running Time: 19 hrs. 30 mins.). 2006. 67.95 (978-1-59912-814-6(4)) Iofy Corp.

Hunchback of Notre- Dame. Victor Hugo. Read by Bill Homewood. 2 cass. (Running Time: 2 hrs. 30 mins.). 1996. 34.98 (978-962-634-506-1(3), NA200614, Naxos AudioBooks) Naxos.
In the grotesque bell-ringer, Quasimodo, Hugo created one of the most vivid characters in classic fiction, in this tale peppered with humor but fuelled by the anguish which unfolds beneath the bells of the great cathedral of Paris.

Hunchback of Notre- Dame. abr. ed. Victor Hugo. Perf. by St. Charles Players. 2 cass. (Running Time: 2 hrs. 15 min.). Dramatization. (YA). (gr. 5-12). 2001. 16.95 (978-1-56994-529-2(2)) Monterey Media Inc.
Amidst the foreboding structure of Notre Dame Cathedral in Paris during medieval times, Quasimodo, the hunchbacked bell ringer, watches the city & it's people in awe, yet knowing that he can never belong among them because of his deformed shape. Through an odd turn of events, he finds himself cast in a struggle to save the beautiful gypsy dancer Esmaralda from being unjustly executed. Multicast dramatization uniquely tell this tragic tale of romance & intrigue. Music & background sounds are intertwined with dramatic character portrayals to result in a "radio theatre" style rendition of this classic tale.

Hunchback of Notre- Dame. unabr. ed. Victor Hugo. Read by Frederick Davidson. 13 cass. (Running Time: 19 hrs. 30 min.). 1996. 85.95 (978-0-7861-0988-3(2), 1765) Blckstn Audio.
Before the huge crowd that packed the cathedral square, Esmeralda stood between two executioners. Suddenly, Quasimodo, the hunchback of Notre Dame, rushed at the executioners & felled them with his enormous fists. He snatched the gypsy girl in one arm & ran with her into the church. A moment later he appeared at the top of the bell tower. Holding the girl above his head, he showed her triumphantly to all of Paris while his thunderous voice roared savagely to the sky: "Sanctuary! Sanctuary! Sanctuary!" Victor Hugo's masterful tale of heroism & adventure is set amid the riot, intrigue, & pageantry of medieval Paris.

Hunchback of Notre- Dame. unabr. ed. Victor Hugo. Read by Anthony Quayle. 2 read-along cass. bk. 34.95 (S23924) J Norton Pubs.

Hunchback of Notre- Dame. unabr. ed. Victor Hugo. Read by Jim Killavey. 14 cass. (Running Time: 20 hrs. 40 min.). 1991. 89.00 set. (C-218) Jimcin Record.
Great historical epic of the cathedral of Notre Dame & its deaf & dumb bell-ringer, Quasimodo.

Hunchback of Notre- Dame, unabr. ed. Victor Hugo. Narrated by George Guidall. 16 cass. (Running Time: 22 hrs. 45 mins.). 1991. 128.00 (978-1-55690-241-3(7), 91224E7) Recorded Bks.
The deformed bell-ringer of Notre Dame Cathedral in Paris opens the doors of the church & his heart to give sanctuary to a Gypsy girl.

Hunchback of Notre- Dame. unabr. collector's ed. Victor Hugo. Read by David Case. 13 cass. (Running Time: 19 hrs. 30 mins.). (J). 1992. 104.00 (978-0-7366-2281-3(0), 3068) Books on Tape.
The story of Esmeralda & Quasimodo set amid riot, intrique & pageantry of medieval Paris.

Hunchback of Notre- Dame, Set. Victor Hugo. Read by Flo Gibson. 11 cass. (Running Time: 16 hrs. 30 min.). 1995. 34.95 (978-1-55685-390-6(4)) Audio Bk Con.
The gallows, the torture wrack & angry mobs are part of the menace in this fantastic novel set in Paris in the fifteenth century. Quasimodo, the kind-hearted hunchback, & the lovely La Esmaralda are in a struggle to survive the brutality.

Hunchback of Notre Dame. 1 cass. (Read-Along Ser.). (J). bk. 7.99 (978-1-55723-992-1(4)); 11.99 Norelco. (978-1-55723-986-0(X)); audio compact disk 19.99 (978-1-55723-989-1(4)) W Disney Records.

Hunchback of Notre Dame. 1 cass. (J). 1996. 11.99 (978-1-55723-987-7(8)) W Disney Records.

Hunchback of Notre Dame. 1 cass. (J). (ps-3). 1996. audio compact disk 19.99 CD. (978-1-55723-988-4(6)) W Disney Records.

Hunchback of Notre Dame. Greg Rebis. Read by Bill Homewood. (Running Time: 9452 sec.). 2006. audio compact disk 17.98 (978-962-634-382-1(6), Naxos AudioBooks) Naxos.

Hunchback of Notre Dame. Greg Rebis. Read by David Case. (Running Time: 68400 sec.). (ENG.). 2006. audio compact disk 34.99 (978-1-4001-5211-7(9)); audio compact disk 99.99 (978-1-4001-3211-9(8)) Pub: Tantor Media. Dist(s): IngramPubServ

Hunchback of Notre Dame. abr. ed. Victor Hugo. Read by Julie Christie. 4 cass. (Running Time: 6 hrs.). 2004. 25.00 (978-1-59007-120-5(4)) Pub: New Millenn Enter. Dist(s): PerseuPGW
Step back into the 1400s, when life is full of superstition and mystery and a hunchback haunts Notre Dame Cathedral. As the Gypsy Girl enchants the heart of the hunchback and the priest vies for her love, the cast of The St. Charles Players brings the sights and sounds of medieval France to life.

Hunchback of Notre Dame. abr. adpt. ed. Victor Hugo. (Bring the Classics to Life: Level 2 Ser.). (ENG.). 2008. audio compact disk 12.95 (978-1-55576-462-3(2)) EDCON Pubng.

Hunchback of Notre-Dame. unabr. ed. Victor Hugo. Read by Frederick Davidson. (YA). 2006. 54.99 (978-1-59895-348-0(6)) Find a World.

Hunchback of Notre-Dame. unabr. ed. Victor Hugo. Narrated by David Case. (Running Time: 19 hrs. 0 mins. 0 sec.). (Tantor Unabridged Classics Ser.). (ENG.). 2009. audio compact disk 29.99 (978-1-4001-5903-1(2)) Pub: Tantor Media. Dist(s): IngramPubServ

Hunchback of Notre-Dame. unabr. ed. Victor Hugo. Read by David Case. (Running Time: 19 hrs. 0 mins. 0 sec.). (ENG.). 2009. audio compact disk 39.99 (978-1-4001-0903-6(5)) Pub: Tantor Media. Dist(s): IngramPubServ

***Hunchback of Notre Dame: Bring the Classics to Life.** adpt. ed. Victor Hugo. (Bring the Classics to Life Ser.). 2008. pap. bk. 21.95 (978-1-55576-499-9(1)) EDCON Pubng.

Hunchback of Notre Dame: My First Read along. 1 cass. (J). 1996. 6.98 (978-1-55723-999-0(1)) W Disney Records.

Hunchback of Notre Dame Sing-Along. 1 cass. (SPA & ENG.). (J). 1996. 7.98 (978-1-55723-997-6(5)) W Disney Records.

Hunchback of Notre Dame Sing-Along. 1 cass. (J). (ps-3). 1996. 12.98 (978-1-55723-990-7(8)); audio compact disk 22.50 (978-1-55723-991-4(6)) W Disney Records.

Hunchback of Notre Dame Soundtrack. Walt Disney Productions Staff. 1 CD. (J). (ps-3). 1996. audio compact disk 22.50 CD. (978-0-7634-0044-6(0)) W Disney Records.

Hunchback of Notre Dame Soundtrack. Prod. by Walt Disney Productions Staff. 1 cass. (SPA.). (J). (ps-3). 1996. 12.98 (978-0-7634-0043-9(2)) W Disney Records.

Hunchback of Notre Dame, with eBook. unabr. ed. Victor Hugo. Narrated by David Case. (Running Time: 19 hrs. 0 mins. 0 sec.). (ENG.). 2009. audio compact disk 79.99 (978-1-4001-3903-3(1)) Pub: Tantor Media. Dist(s): IngramPubServ

Hunches in Bunches. Dr. Seuss. (J). 1982. bk. 49.32 (978-0-676-30262-2(9)) SRA McGraw.

Hund und der Sperling. Jacob W. Grimm & Wilhelm K. Grimm. 1 cass. (Running Time: 60 min.). (Bruder Grimm Kinder & Hausmarchen Ser.). (GER.). 1996. pap. bk. 19.50 (978-1-58085-211-1(4), GR-06) Interlingua VA.

Hundred & One Days: A Baghdad Journal. unabr. ed. Asne Seierstad. Narrated by Josephine Bailey. (Running Time: 10 hrs. 0 mins. 0 sec.). (ENG.). 2005. audio compact disk 34.99 (978-1-4001-0158-0(1)); audio compact disk 22.99 (978-1-4001-5158-5(9)); audio compact disk 69.99 (978-1-4001-3158-7(8)) Pub: Tantor Media. Dist(s): IngramPubServ

Hundred Camels in the Courtyard. unabr. ed. Paul Bowles. 1999. audio compact disk 29.95 (978-0-932274-55-7(2)) Pub: Cadmus Eds. Dist(s): Natl Bk Netwk
Paul Bowles reads this classic suite of Moroccan kif stories that he recorded in Tangier, Morocco, in the Fall of 1978. Previously released as a 2 LP recording in 1981, and long sold out, these stories are now available again in this audiobook format. Bowles' accompanying essay for this recording is printed in the included booklet. It sets forth the method of writing employed in these stories - the selection of arbitrary incidents and phenomena factored into the kif-smoker's imperium of sensibility.

Hundred Days. 10.00 (HD417) Esstee Audios.

Hundred Days. Patrick O'Brian. Read by David Case. 7 cass. (Running Time: 10 hrs.). (Aubrey-Maturin Ser.). 1999. 29.95 (978-0-7366-4594-2(2), 4802) Books on Tape.
In this nineteenth installment of the Aubrey Maturin series, Napoleon escapes from Elba & the fate of Europe hinges on a secret mission.

Hundred Days. unabr. ed. Patrick O'Brian. (Running Time: 32400 sec.). (Aubrey-Maturin Ser.). 2007. 59.95 (978-1-4332-0122-6(4)) Blckstn Audio.

Hundred Days. unabr. ed. Patrick O'Brian. Read by Simon Vance. (Running Time: 32400 sec.). (Aubrey-Maturin Ser.). 2007. audio compact disk 72.00 (978-1-4332-0123-3(2)) Blckstn Audio.

Hundred Days. unabr. ed. Patrick O'Brian. Read by Simon Vance. (Running Time: 32400 sec.). (Aubrey-Maturin Ser.). 2008. 29.95 (978-1-4332-0911-6(X)); audio compact disk 29.95 (978-1-4332-0124-0(0)); audio compact disk 29.95 (978-1-4332-0912-3(8)) Blckstn Audio.

Hundred Days. unabr. ed. Patrick O'Brian. Read by David Case. 7 cass. (Running Time: 10 hrs. 30 mins.). (Aubrey-Maturin Ser.). 1999. 56.00 (978-0-7366-4356-6(7), 4802) Books on Tape.
Napoleon escapes from Elba and the face of Europe hinges on a desperate mission. Stephen Maturin must ferret out the French dictator's secret link to the powers of Islam, and Jack Aubrey must destroy it.

Hundred Days. unabr. ed. Patrick O'Brian. Narrated by Patrick Tull. 8 cass. (Running Time: 10 hrs. 30 mins.). (Aubrey-Maturin Ser.). 70.00 (978-0-7887-2490-9(8), 95565E7) Recorded Bks.
Napoleon is rumored to be joining forces with Muslim mercenaries. In an attempt to protect Europe, ship's doctor Maturin & Commodore Aubrey launch a daring mission. Available to libraries only.

Hundred Days. unabr. ed. Patrick O'Brian. Narrated by Patrick Tull. 9 CDs. (Running Time: 10 hrs. 30 mins.). (Aubrey-Maturin Ser.). 2000. audio compact disk 81.00 (978-0-7887-3404-5(0), C1010E7) Recorded Bks.

Hundred-Dollar Baby. unabr. ed. Robert B. Parker. Read by Joe Mantegna. 5 CDs. (Running Time: 6 hrs.). (Spenser Ser.). 2006. audio compact disk 38.25 (978-1-4159-3299-5(9)) Pub: Books on Tape. Dist(s): NetLibrary CO

Hundred-Dollar Baby. unabr. ed. Robert B. Parker. Read by Joe Mantegna. (Spenser Ser.). (YA). 2006. 44.99 (978-0-7393-7491-7(5)) Find a World.

Hundred-Dollar Baby. unabr. ed. Robert B. Parker. Read by Joe Mantegna. (Running Time: 21600 sec.). (Spenser Ser.). (ENG.). 2006. audio compact disk 29.95 (978-0-7393-1865-2(9)) Pub: Random Audio Pubg. Dist(s): Random

Hundred Dresses. Eleanor Estes. Narrated by Christina Moore. (Running Time: 1 hr.). (gr. 2 up). audio compact disk 12.00 (978-0-7887-9519-0(8)) Recorded Bks.

Hundred Dresses. unabr. ed. Eleanor Estes. Narrated by Christina Moore. 1 cass. (Running Time: 1 hr.). (gr. 2 up). 1998. 11.00 (978-0-7887-2631-6(5), 95635E7) Recorded Bks.
Every day Wanda Petronski wears the same faded blue dress to school & tells about her hundred dresses at home. Her classmates joke about her imaginary clothes, until they learn the wonderful secret of the dresses.

Hundred in the Hand. unabr. ed. Joseph M. Marshall & Joseph M. Marshall, III. Read by Joseph M. Marshall & Joseph M. Marshall, III. Read by John Terry. (Running Time: 36000 sec.). (Lakota Westerns (Blackstone Audio) Ser.). 2008. 59.95 (978-1-4332-2981-7(1)); audio compact disk 29.95 (978-1-4332-2985-5(4)); audio compact disk & audio compact disk 80.00 (978-1-4332-2982-4(X)) Blckstn Audio.

Hundred Penny Box. Sharon Bell Mathis. (J). 1988. 18.66 (978-0-394-76912-7(0)) SRA McGraw.

Hundred Secret Senses. unabr. ed. Amy Tan. Read by Amy Tan. 6 cass. (Running Time: 9 hrs.). 2001. 32.00 (978-1-59040-036-4(4), Phoenix Audio) Pub: Amer Intl Pub. Dist(s): PerseuPGW
A Chinese-American woman and her China-born half-sister undertake a journey toward the truth about our various selves as they rediscover the natural gifts of their hundred secret senses.

Hundred Secret Senses. unabr. ed. Amy Tan. Read by Frances Cassidy. 9 cass. (Running Time: 13 hrs. 30 min.). 1996. 72.00 (978-0-7366-3244-7(1), 3903); Rental 12.95 Set. (3903) Books on Tape.
Some things you can only know through the hundred secret senses...especially concerning matters of love. This trivia comes to Olivia when she travels from her home in San Francisco to a remote village of China where her half-sister, Kwan, grew up.

***Hundred Thousand Kingdoms.** unabr. ed. N. K. Jemisin. Read by Casaundra Freeman. (Running Time: 12 hrs.). (Inheritance Trilogy). 2010. 29.99 (978-1-4418-8647-7(8), 9781441886477, Brilliance MP3); 29.99 (978-1-4418-8649-1(4), 9781441886491, BAD); 44.97 (978-1-4418-8648-4(6), 9781441886484, Brinc Audio MP3 Lib); 44.97 (978-1-4418-8650-7(8), 9781441886507, BADLE); audio compact disk 34.99 (978-1-4418-8645-3(1), 9781441886453, Bril Audio CD Unabri); audio compact disk 89.97 (978-1-4418-8646-0(X), 9781441886460, BriAudCD Unabrid) Brilliance Audio.

Hundred Ways to Sunday Guided Drumming Journey. Robin Rice. Comment by Rosemarie Brown & Lyn Roberts-Herrick. 2001. audio compact disk 12.95 (978-0-9710876-5-1(2)) Be Who You Are Pr.

Hundredfold Life. Bill Winston. 6 cass. (Running Time: 5hr.09min.). (C). 1997. 25.00 (978-1-931289-65-8(4)) Pub: B Winston Min. Dist(s): Anchor Distributors

Hundredfold Principle. Kenneth Copeland. 6 cass. 1983. 30.00 Set incl. study guide. (978-0-938458-57-9(4)) K Copeland Pubns.
Biblical blessing.

Hundredth Dreamer. John Giannini. Read by John Giannini. 1 cass. (Running Time: 1 hr. 40 min.). 1994. 10.95 (978-0-7822-0461-2(9), 538) C G Jung IL.

Hundredth Man. abr. ed. J. A. Kerley. Read by Dick Hill. (Running Time: 4 hrs.). (Carson Ryder/Harry Nautilus Ser.). 2004. audio compact disk 69.25 (978-1-59355-582-5(2), 1593555822, BACDLib Ed) Brilliance Audio.
When bizarre and cryptic messages are found on a pair of corpses in Mobile, Alabama, junior police detective Carson Ryder and veteran cop Harry Nautilus find themselves in a mysterious public-relations quagmire pitting public safety against office politics. With the body count growing, Ryder must confront his family's terrifying past by seeking advice from his brother, a violent psychopath convicted of similarly heinous crimes. Ryder finds himself falling for Ava, the striking pathologist processing the gruesome corpses. But Ava's past holds its own nightmarish secrets. Ryder and Nautilus come to realize someone close to them is the killer's ultimate target-and time is running out before the killer plans to strike again.

Hundredth Man. abr. ed. J. A. Kerley. Read by Dick Hill. (Running Time: 4 hrs.). (Carson Ryder/Harry Nautilus Ser.). 2005. audio compact disk 14.99 (978-1-59737-425-5(3), 9781597374255, BCD Value Price) Brilliance Audio.

Hundredth Man. unabr. ed. J. A. Kerley. Read by Dick Hill. (Running Time: 9 hrs.). (Carson Ryder/Harry Nautilus Ser.). 2004. 24.95 (978-1-59335-328-5(6), 1593353286, Brilliance MP3); 29.95 (978-1-59355-578-8(4), 1593555784, BAU); 39.25 (978-1-59335-484-8(3), 1593354843, Brlnc Audio MP3 Lib); 74.25 (978-1-59355-579-5(2), 1593555792, BrilAudUnabridg) Brilliance Audio.

Hundredth Man. unabr. ed. J. A. Kerley. Read by Dick Hill. (Running Time: 9 hrs.). (Carson Ryder/Harry Nautilus Ser.). 2004. 39.25 (978-1-59710-383-1(7), 1597103837, BADLE); 24.95 (978-1-59710-382-4(9), 1597103829, BAD) Brilliance Audio.

Hungarian. 2 cass. (Running Time: 80 min.). (Language - Thirty Library). bk. 16.95 set in vinyl album. Moonbeam Pubns.
Using the proven method based on the famous U.S. Military accelerated language leaming program, Language/30 courses stress conversationally useful words & phrases.

Hungarian. Agnes Polgar et al. 1 cass. (Running Time: 1 hrs. 30 min.). (TravelWise Ser.). (ENG & HUN., 1998. pap. bk. 16.95 (978-0-7641-7107-9(0)) Barron.
Designed especially for international travelers, provides introductions to foreign destinations.

Hungarian. unabr. ed. Ed. by Charles Berlitz. 2 cass. (Running Time: 1 hr. 30 mins.). (Language/30 Brief Course Ser.). (HUN.). pap. bk. 21.95 (AF1062) J Norton Pubs.
Quick, highly condensed introduction to the words & phrases you'll need to communicate effectively in the country you're visiting. Cassettes & phrase guide book are in a vinyl album.

Hungarian: Language/30. rev. ed. Educational Services Corporation Staff. Intro. by Charles Berlitz. 2 cass. (HUN.). 1995. pap. bk. 21.95 (978-0-910542-87-6(2)) Educ Svcs DC.
Hungarian self-teaching language course.

Hungarian: Learn to Speak & Understand Hungarian with Pimsleur Language Programs. unabr. ed. Pimsleur. (Running Time: 16 hrs. 0 mins. 0 sec.). (Comprehensive Ser.). (ENG.). 2008. audio compact disk 345.00 (978-0-7435-6393-2(X), Pimsleur) Pub: S&S Audio. Dist(s): S and S Inc

Hungarian: Learn to Speak & Understand Hungarian with Pimsleur Language Programs. unabr. ed. Pimsleur Staff. (Running Time: 5 hrs. 0 mins. 0 sec.). (Basic Ser.). (ENG.). 2008. audio compact disk 24.95 (978-0-7435-6394-9(8), Pimsleur); audio compact disk 49.95 (978-0-7435-6396-3(4), Pimsleur) Pub: S&S Audio. Dist(s): S and S Inc

Hungarian Basic Course, Vol. 1. 24 CDs. (Running Time: 16 hrs.). (HUN.). 2005. audio compact disk 245.00 (978-1-57970-130-7(2), AFU500D) J Norton Pubs.

Hungarian Basic Course, Vol. 2. 20 CDs. (Running Time: 19 HRS.). (HUN.). 2005. audio compact disk 295.00 (978-1-57970-228-1(7), AFU550D) J Norton Pubs.

Hungarian Bible - New Testament (Spoken Word) Karolyl-Czegledy Version. Read by Joseph Steiner. 16 cass. 1994. 39.97 (978-1-58968-058-6(8), 9402A) Chrstn Dup Intl.

Hungarian Folk Music. unabr. ed. 1 cass. 1994. 12.95 (978-0-88432-355-6(2), C11144) J Norton Pubs.

Hungarian New Testament. Contrib. by J. Steiner. 16 cass. (HUN.). 1994. 39.98 Set. (978-7-902030-36-6(8)) Chrstn Dup Intl.
Bible.

Hungarian with Ease see Ungarisch Ohne Muhe

***Hunger for God: Desiring God Through Fasting & Prayer.** unabr. ed. John Piper. Narrated by Cris Obrien. (ENG.). 2006. 16.98 (978-1-59644-398-3(7), Hovel Audio) christianaud.

Hunger for God: Desiring God Through Fasting & Prayer. unabr. ed. John Piper. Narrated by David Cochran Heath. 5 CDs. (Running Time: 6 hrs. 30 mins. 0 sec.). (ENG.). 2006. audio compact disk 26.98 (978-1-59644-397-6(9), Hovel Audio) christianaud.

Hunger Games. Suzanne Collins. Read by Carolyn McCormick. (Hunger Games Ser.: No. 1). (J). 2008. 64.99 (978-1-60640-682-3(5)) Find a World.

Hunger Games. unabr. ed. Suzanne Collins. Narrated by Carolyn McCormick. (Hunger Games Ser.: No. 1). (J). (gr. 7). 2008. audio compact disk 39.95 (978-0-545-09102-2(0)); audio compact disk 84.95 (978-0-545-09106-0(3)) Scholastic Inc.

Hunger Point. abr. ed. Jillian Medoff. 2 cass. (Running Time: 3 hrs.). 1997. 18.00 Set. (978-0-694-51790-9(9), CPN 2632) HarperCollins Pubs.
A young woman struggling to come to terms with a younger sister afflicted with a serious eating disorder, parents who have grown apart, & her own ambivalence about growing up.

Hungerfield see Poetry of Robinson Jeffers

Hungry As the Sea. Wilbur Smith. 2 cass. (Running Time: 3 hrs.). (ENG., 2001. (978-0-333-78270-5(4)) Macmillan UK GBR.

Hungry As the Sea. unabr. collector's ed. Wilbur Smith. Read by Richard Brown. 12 cass. (Running Time: 18 hrs.). (Ballantyne Novels Ser.). 1988. 96.00 (978-0-7366-1453-5(2), 2335) Books on Tape.
The "Golden Prince" is deposed; once the flamboyant chairman of a huge shipping consortium, now the captain of a salvage tug - such is the revolution in the life of Nick Bereg. Then a cruise ship, stranded with 600 people in the frozen wastes of the Antarctic, could be his chance to fight back. His heroic salvage of the liner sweeps him back to even greater power

& even more deadly conflict with the man who has supplanted him as chairman.

Hungry for God? - Manna. Karl Coke. 3 cass. (Running Time: 3 hours). 2003. 15.00 (978-0-9743493-2-9(1)); audio compact disk 20.00 (978-0-9743493-3-6(X)) AndyBooks.

Hungry for Home. unabr. ed. Cole Moreton. Read by Gerry O'Brien. 8 cass. (Running Time: 12 hrs.). (Sound Ser.). (J). 2003. 69.95 (978-1-84283-419-0(3)) Pub: ISIS Lrg Prnt GBR. Dist(s): Ulverscroft US

Hungry for Home: A Journey from the Edge of Ireland. unabr. ed. Cole Moreton. 7 CDs. (Running Time: 39600 sec.). (Sound Ser.). 2003. audio compact disk 71.95 (978-1-84283-692-7(7)) Pub: ISIS Lrg Prnt GBR. Dist(s): Ulverscroft US

***Hungry for You.** unabr. ed. Lynsay Sands. (ENG.). 2010. (978-0-06-199891-1(5), Harper Audio) HarperCollins Pubs.

Hungry Ghost. Stephen Leather. 2008. 89.95 (978-0-7531-3816-8(6)); audio compact disk 99.95 (978-0-7531-2797-1(0)) Pub: ISIS Audio GBR. Dist(s): Ulverscroft US

Hungry Giant. Joy Cowley. 1 read-along cass. (J). 1986. 5.95 incl. bk. (978-0-86867-047-8(2)) Wright Group.
The Hungry Giant makes demands & the townspeople try & try to make him happy. They bring him what he wants & something he doesn't want, too.

Hungry Girl. unabr. ed. Lisa Lillien. Read by Lisa Lillien. 2 CDs. (Running Time: 2 hrs. 0 mins. 0 sec.). (ENG.). 2009. instr.'s gde. ed. 17.95 (978-1-4272-0752-4(6)) Pub: Macmill Audio. Dist(s): Macmillan

Hungry Hill. Daphne Du Maurier. Read by Maureen O'Brien. 12 cass. (Running Time: 18 hrs.). 2002. 96.95 (978-0-7540-0709-8(X), CAB 2131) AudioGO.

Hungry Hill. unabr. ed. Daphne Du Maurier. Read by Maureen O'Brien. 12 cass. (Running Time: 18 hrs.). 2002. 79.95 (CAB 2131) AudioGO.
This is a passionate story of five generations of an Irish family and the copper mine on Hungry Hill. Their fortunes and fates were closely bound with this copper mine, and the tale is told with all the magic and excitement.

Hungry Hill: A Memoir. (ENG.). 2009. audio compact disk 29.95 (978-0-9824807-0-0(9)) C Gaunt.

Hungry Ocean: A Swordboat Captain's Journey, unabr. ed. Linda Greenlaw. Read by Linda Greenlaw. 5 cass. (Running Time: 7 hrs.). 1999. 35.95 (978-1-56740-441-8(3), 1567404413, BAU); 57.25 (978-1-56740-667-2(X), 156740667X, Unabridge Lib Edns) Brilliance Audio.
In his number-one bestseller, The Perfect Storm, Sebastian Junger describes Linda Greenlaw as "one of the best sea captains, period, on the East Coast." Now Greenlaw tells her own riveting story of a thirty-day swordfishing voyage aboard one of the best-outfitted boats on the East Coast, complete with danger, humor, and characters so colorful they seem to have been ripped from the pages of Moby Dick. The excitement starts immediately, even before Greenlaw and her five-man crew leave the dock - and it doesn't stop until the last page. Under way, she must cope with nasty weather, equipment failure, and treachery aboard ship, not to mention the routinely backbreaking work of operating a fishing boat. Displaying a true fisherman's gift for storytelling and a true writer's flair for both drama and reflection, Greenlaw offers an exciting real-life adventure tale filled with the beauty and power of the sea.

Hungry Ocean: A Swordboat Captain's Journey. unabr. ed. Linda Greenlaw. Read by Linda Greenlaw. (Running Time: 7 hrs.). 2006. 39.25 (978-1-4233-1429-5(8), 9781423314295, BADLE); 24.95 (978-1-4233-1428-8(X), 9781423314288, BAD); audio compact disk 82.25 (978-1-4233-1425-7(5), 9781423314257, BriAudCD Unabrid); audio compact disk 39.25 (978-1-4233-1427-1(1), 9781423314271, Brinc Audio MP3 Lib); audio compact disk 29.95 (978-1-4233-1424-0(7), 9781423314240, Bril Audio CD Unabri); audio compact disk 24.95 (978-1-4233-1426-4(3), 9781423314264, Brilliance MP3) Brilliance Audio.

***Hungry Ocean: A Swordboat Captain's Journey.** unabr. ed. Linda Greenlaw. Read by Linda Greenlaw. (Running Time: 7 hrs.). 2010. audio compact disk 14.99 (978-1-4418-7805-2(X), 9781441878052, BCD Value Price) Brilliance Audio.

Hungry Ocean: A Swordboat Captain's Journey, Set. unabr. ed. Linda Greenlaw. Read by Linda Greenlaw. 5 cass. 1999. 35.95 (FS9-43910) Highsmith.

Hungry Planet Bible Project, The NT NLTse. Ed. by Hungry Planet Media Staff. 2009. audio compact disk 49.99 (978-1-4143-3462-2(1)) Tyndale Hse.

Hungry Tide: A Novel. unabr. ed. Amitav Ghosh. Read by Firdous Bamji. 14 CDs. (Running Time: 15.75 Hrs). 2005. audio compact disk 39.99 (978-1-4193-3694-2(0)) Recorded Bks.

Hunk-Ta-Bunk-Ta-Bed! Bed-time Bedlam & Lullabyes. unabr. ed. Katherine Dines et al. Read by Katherine Dines. 1 cass. (Running Time: 30 min.). (Hunk-Ta-Bunk-Ta Ser.: No. 3). (J). (gr. k-5). 1994. 10.00 (978-0-9631254-4-6(3), H-BED-3C); audio compact disk 16.00 (978-0-9631254-5-3(1), H-BED-3-CD) Hunk Ta Bunk.
12 original songs that feature 6 for the "I-don't-want-to-go-to-bed-yet" set, & 6 soothing tunes on the flip side. There's something for everyone on this recording, guaranteed to become a classic family favorite.

Hunk-Ta-Bunk-Ta-Boo! unabr. ed. Katherine Dines. Des. by Mathew McFarren. 1 CD. (Running Time: 32 min.). (Hunk-Ta-Bunk-Ta Ser.: No. 1). (J). (gr. k-5). 1991. audio compact disk 16.00 (978-0-9631254-7-7(8)) Hunk Ta Bunk.
An imaginative collection of 12 highly original & entertaining songs. Folk-style production using unusual instruments...the mandocello, tuba, Jew's harp, etc. The 170 page activity guide provides hours of fun educational activities for educators, home schoolers & parents.

Hunk-Ta-Bunk-Ta-Boo! unabr. ed. Katherine Dines. Read by Katherine Dines. 1 cass. (Running Time: 32 min.). (Hunk-Ta-Bunk-Ta Ser.: No. 1). (J). (gr. k-5). 1991. 12.00 (978-0-9631254-6-0(X)) Hunk Ta Bunk.

Hunk-Ta-Bunk-Ta-Boo-2! 12 Songs the Whole Family Will Enjoy. unabr. ed. Katherine Dines. Read by Katherine Dines. 1 cass. (Running Time: 35 min.). (Hunk-Ta-Bunk-Ta Ser.: No. 2). (J). (gr. k-5). 1994. 12.00 (978-0-9631254-8-4(6), H-BOO-2C); audio compact disk 16.00 (978-0-9631254-9-1(4), HBOO-2CD) Hunk Ta Bunk.
12 imaginative, up-beat, heart-felt original songs for children of all ages, especially those 4 to 10. The songs carry engaging messages about the world in which we live & motivate little minds & bodies to become the best they can be.

Hunk-Ta-Bunk-Ta Chants. Katherine Dines. 1 CD. (Running Time: 1 hr.). 2001. 15.95 Clckwrks.

Hunk-Ta-Bunk-Ta Chants: (Sayable Singable Phrases from Around the World) Katherine Dines. 1 CD. (Running Time: 30 min.). (J). (gr. k-5). 2001. audio compact disk 15.95 (978-1-892533-01-2(4)) Hunk Ta Bunk.
Explores some rich traditions in games and clapping chants, welcome and wave chants, nonsensical rhymes, rhythmic dialects, work chants, meditational chants and a story chant.

Hunk-Ta-Bunk-Ta Funsies. 1 CD. (Running Time: 60 min.). 2003. audio compact disk 15.99 (978-1-892533-02-9(2)) Hunk Ta Bunk.

Hunk-Ta-Bunk-Ta Funsies, Vol. 2. 1 CD. (Running Time: 54 min.). 2004. audio compact disk 15.99 (978-1-892533-03-6(0)) Hunk Ta Bunk.

Hunk-Ta-Bunk-Ta-GNU: Weird, Wild & Wacky Words. unabr. ed. Katherine Dines. Read by Katherine Dines. 1 cass. (Running Time: 35 min.). (Hunk-Ta-Bunk-Ta Ser.: No. 4). (J). (gr. k-5). 1996. 12.00 (978-0-9631254-2-2(7), H-GNU-1C); audio compact disk 16.00 (978-0-9631254-3-9(5), H-GNU-1-CD) Hunk Ta Bunk.
A gnu twist to an old subject, this recording focuses on English language & interesting words. There's even a song to learn in Sign language! Grammar, history, words, & meanings collide with great music to make learning English exciting & fun. "Pronoun Promenade"; "Pig Latino"; "Trey Tres Cliche"; & other songs bring language to life. 24 page fact filled book enclosed.

Hunk-Ta-Bunk-Ta-SPOOKY! Tunes & Tales to Chill Your Bones & Warm Your Spirits. Katherine Dines. Des. by Mathew McFarren. 1 CD. (J). (gr. k-5). 1997. audio compact disk 15.98 (978-0-9631254-1-5(9)) Hunk Ta Bunk.
Traditional folktales & original songs are artfully woven together by a spooky tale spinner who adds plenty of historical information & sound effects.

Hunk-Ta-Bunk-Ta-SPOOKY! Tunes & Tales to Chill Your Bones & Warm Your Spirits. Katherine Dines. Des. by Mathew McFarren. 1 cass. (J). (gr. k-5). 1998. 11.98 (978-0-9631254-0-8(0), HB-5) Hunk Ta Bunk.

Hunk-Ta-Bunk-Ta Wiggle, Vol. 1. unabr. ed. Katherine Dines. Contrib. by Hunk-Ta-Bunk-Ta Staff. 1 CD. (Running Time: 25 mins.). (J). (ps). 2007. audio compact disk 15.00 (978-1-892533-08-1(1)) Hunk Ta Bunk.

***Hunt.** (ENG.). 2010. audio compact disk (978-1-59171-300-5(5)) Falcon Picture.

Hunt. unabr. ed. Perf. by Boris Karloff. (Running Time: 53 min.). 12.95 (#754) J Norton Pubs.
"The Hunt" is a frightening story about the search for a werewolf. "The Walking Dead" is an eerie tale of voodoo & revenge in the tropics.

Hunt Ball. Rita Mae Brown. Narrated by Rita Mae Brown. (Running Time: 26100 sec.). (Foxhunting Mysteries Ser.). 2005. audio compact disk 34.99 (978-1-4193-5304-8(7)) Recorded Bks.

Hunt Ball. unabr. ed. Rita Mae Brown. Read by Rita Mae Brown. 6 CDs. (Running Time: 7 hrs.). (Foxhunting Mysteries Ser.). 2005. audio compact disk 69.75 (978-1-4193-4908-9(2), C3369); 49.75 (978-1-4193-4906-5(6), 98093) Recorded Bks.
When a faculty member of the local prep school is murdered, the headmistress and "Sister" Jane Arnold, master of the foxhounds at Virginia¿s Jefferson Hunt Club, work together to uncover a killer. It seems the slaying may have been politically motivated, as students were demonstrating to call attention to the role of slavery in the school¿s past. With the annual hunt ball approaching, the 70-something Sister already has plenty on her plate. Does she have time to catch a murderer?.

Hunt Club. abr. ed. John Lescroart. Read by Guerin Barry. (Running Time: 21600 sec.). (Wyatt Hunt Ser.). 2006. audio compact disk 16.99 (978-1-59600-881-6(4), 9781596008816, BCD Value Price) Brilliance Audio.
Please enter a Synopsis.

Hunt Club. abr. ed. Bret Lott. Read by Neil Patrick Harris. 4 cass. 2001. 12.99 (978-1-57815-208-7(9), Media Bks Audio) Media Bks NJ.

Hunt Club. unabr. ed. John Lescroart. Read by Guerin Barry. (Running Time: 13 hrs.). (Wyatt Hunt Ser.). 2006. 39.25 (978-1-59710-903-1(7), 9781597109031, BADLE); 24.95 (978-1-59710-902-4(9), 9781597109024, BAD); 34.95 (978-1-59355-365-4(X), 9781593553654, BAU); 92.25 (978-1-59355-391-3(9), 9781593553913, BrilAudUnabridg); audio compact disk 40.95 (978-1-59355-367-8(6), 9781593553678, Bril Audio CD Unabri); audio compact disk 107.25 (978-1-59355-368-5(4), 9781593553685, BriAudCD Unabrid); audio compact disk 39.25 (978-1-59335-851-8(2), 9781593358518, Brinc Audio MP3 Lib); audio compact disk 24.95 (978-1-59335-717-7(6), 9781593357177, Brilliance MP3) Brilliance Audio.
A federal judge is murdered, found shot to death in his home - together with the body of his mistress. The crime grips San Francisco. To homicide inspector Devin Juhle, it first looks like a simple case of a wife's jealousy and rage. But Juhle's investigation reveals that the judge had powerful enemies...some of whom may have been willing to kill to prevent him from meddling in their affairs. Meanwhile, private investigator Wyatt Hunt, Juhle's best friend, finds himself smitten with the beautiful and enigmatic Andrea Parisi. A lawyer who recently has become a celebrity as a commentator on Trial TV, Andrea has star power in spades, and seems bound for a national anchor job in New York City. Until Juhle discovers that Andrea, too, had a connection to the judge, along with a client that had everything to gain from the judge's death. And then she suddenly disappears.... Andrea becomes Juhle's prime suspect. Wyatt Hunt thinks she may be a kidnap victim, or worse...another murder victim. And far more than that, she's someone with whom he believes he may have a future. As the search for Andrea intensifies, Hunt gathers a loose band of friends and associates willing to bend and even break the rules, leading to a chilling confrontation from which none of them might escape.

Hunt, Dr X, the Walking Dead. Featuring Boris Karloff. 1950. audio compact disk 12.95 (978-1-57970-508-4(1), Audio-For) J Norton Pubs.

Hunt for a Man Killer. abr. ed. Read by Gary Alexander & Phil Tonken. 1 cass. (Running Time: 1 hr.). (Outdoor Life; Classic Stories of the Great Outdoors Ser.: Vol. 1). 1998. 9.95 (978-1-886463-42-4(5)) Oasis Audio.
A Colorado camper is dragged to his death & a local guide & his dogs are called on to track the rampaging bear. But who's hunting who? Includes three other stories.

***Hunt for Atlantis: A Novel.** unabr. ed. Andy McDermott. Narrated by Gildart Jackson. (Running Time: 16 hrs. 0 mins.). (Nina Wilde/Eddie Chase Ser.). 2010. 20.99 (978-1-4526-7017-1(X)); 29.99 (978-1-4526-5017-3(9)); audio compact disk 39.99 (978-1-4526-0017-8(1)) Pub: Tantor Media. Dist(s): IngramPubServ

***Hunt for Atlantis (Library Edition) A Novel.** unabr. ed. Andy McDermott. Narrated by Gildart Jackson. (Running Time: 16 hrs. 0 mins.). (Nina Wilde/Eddie Chase Ser.). 2010. 39.99 (978-1-4526-2017-6(2)); audio compact disk 95.99 (978-1-4526-3017-5(8)) Pub: Tantor Media. Dist(s): IngramPubServ

Hunt for Dark Infinity. James Dashner. (13th Reality Ser.: Bk. 2). 2009. audio compact disk 39.95 (978-1-60641-063-9(6), Shadow Mount) Deseret Bk.

Hunt for Red October. abr. ed. Tom Clancy. Read by Richard Crenna. 2 cass. (Running Time: 2 hrs. 41 mins.). 2004. 16.95 (978-0-88690-092-2(1), A20006) Pub: Audio Partners. Dist(s): PerseuPGW
A techno-thriller that pits the U.S.S.R. against the U.S.A. in the greatest submarine chase of all time.

Hunt for Red October. unabr. ed. Tom Clancy. Read by Frank Muller. 10 cass. (Running Time: 15 hrs.). 2004. 39.95 (978-0-945353-79-9(0), A90379u) Pub: Audio Partners. Dist(s): PerseuPGW
Silently, beneath the chill Atlantic waters, Russia's ultra-secret missile submarine, Red October, is heading west. The Americans want her. The Russians want her back. The most incredible chase in history is on!.

Hunt for Red October. unabr. ed. Tom Clancy. Read by J. Charles. (Running Time: 15 hrs.). 2004. 39.25 (978-1-59710-384-8(5), 1597103845, BADLE); 24.95 (978-1-59710-385-5(3), 1597103853, BAD) Brilliance Audio.

Hunt for Red October. unabr. ed. Tom Clancy. Read by J. Charles. (Running Time: 15 hrs.). 2004. audio compact disk 39.95 (978-1-59600-237-1(9), 1596002379) Brilliance Audio.
A deadly serious game of hide-and-seek is on. The CIA's brilliant young analyst, Jack Ryan, thinks he knows the reason for the sudden Red Fleet operation: the Soviets' most valuable ship, the Red October, is attempting to defect to the United States. The new ballistic-missile submarine's defection is high treason on an unprecedented scale and nearly the entire Soviet Atlantic Fleet has been ordered to find and destroy her at all costs. If the U.S. fleet can locate her first and get her safely to port, it will be the intelligence coup of all time. The nerve-wracking hunt goes on for eighteen days as the Red October tries to elude her hunters across 4000 miles of ocean. The rousing climax is one of the most thrilling underwater scenes ever written.

***Hunt for Red October.** unabr. ed. Tom Clancy. Read by J. Charles. (Running Time: 17 hrs.). 2010. 39.97 (978-1-4418-5056-0(2), 9781441850560, Brinc Audio MP3 Lib); 14.99 (978-1-4418-5055-3(4), 9781441850553, Brilliance MP3); audio compact disk 29.99 (978-1-4418-5053-9(8), 9781441850539); audio compact disk 89.97 (978-1-4418-5054-6(6), 9781441850546, BriAudCD Unabrid) Brilliance Audio.

Hunt for Red October. unabr. ed. Tom Clancy. Read by Frank Muller. (YA). 2008. 34.99 (978-1-60252-970-0(1)) Find a World.

Hunt for Red October, unabr. ed. Tom Clancy. Narrated by Frank Muller. 11 cass. (Running Time: 15 hrs.). 1987. 91.00 (978-1-55690-242-0(5), 87600E7) Recorded Bks.
A Russian submarine captain defects to the West with his vessel. The Americans want "Red October." The Soviets want her back. The hunt is on!.

Hunt for Red October. unabr. collector's ed. Tom Clancy. Read by John MacDonald. 12 cass. (Running Time: 18 hrs.). 1985. 96.00 (978-0-7366-0992-0(X), 1929) Books on Tape.
The Soviet's most valuable ship, a new ballistic-missile submarine with their most trusted & skilled naval officer at the helm, is attempting to defect to the United States. It is high treason on an unprecedented scale & the Soviet's mission is to seek & destroy her at any cost. If the U.S. fleet can locate the Red October & get her safely to port, it will be the intelligence coup of all time. But the submarine has a million square miles in which to hide & the deadly game of hide-&-seek is on.

Hunt the Tortoise. unabr. ed. E. X. Ferrars. Read by Julia Franklin. 6 CDs. (Running Time: 6 hrs. 20 min.). (Isis Ser.). (J). 2003. audio compact disk 64.95 (978-0-7531-2220-4(0)) Pub: ISIS Lrg Prnt GBR. Dist(s): Ulverscroft US
Lovely Celia Kent, a journalist from London, had so looked forward to a quiet vacation at Madame Oliver's gracious hotel on the French Riviera. It was disappointing to arrive and find Madame no longer in charge and the hotel itself inhabited by a group of very strange guests.Most disturbing of all was a stockbroker named Barre, whose strange entourage included a very temperamental tortoise. The sudden disappearance of this odd pet on a deserted quay provided a perfect portent of sinister things to come - including violent and cold-blooded murder.

Hunt the Tortoise. unabr. ed. E. X. Ferrars & Julia Franklin. 6 cass. (Isis Ser.). (J). 2003. 54.95 (978-0-7531-1183-3(7)) Pub: ISIS Lrg Prnt GBR. Dist(s): Ulverscroft US

Hunted, abr. ed. Dalton Walker. Read by Dick Wilkinson. 2 cass. (Running Time: 3 hrs.). (Shiloh: Bk. 4). 1999. Rental 16.95 (978-1-890990-29-9(9)) Otis Audio.
Shiloh vows revenge against the low-down vermin that killed his old war pal but gets tossed in jail for his friend's murder.

Hunted. unabr. ed. Wayne Barcomb. Read by Mark Deakins. 7 CDs. (Running Time: 8 hrs. 45 mins.). 2009. audio compact disk 90.00 (978-1-4159-4857-6(7), BksonTape) Pub: Random Audio Pubg. Dist(s): Random

***Hunted.** unabr. ed. P. C. Cast & Kristin Cast. (ENG.). (YA). 2009. 19.99 (978-1-4272-0608-4(2)) Pub: Macmill Audio. Dist(s): Macmillan

Hunted. unabr. ed. P. C. Cast & Kristin Cast. 9 CDs. (Running Time: 11 hrs. 0 mins. 0 sec.). No. 5. (ENG.). (YA). (gr. 9 up). 2009. audio compact disk 39.95 (978-1-4272-0607-7(4)) Pub: Macmill Audio. Dist(s): Macmillan

***Hunted.** unabr. ed. Brian Haig. Read by Scott Brick. 15 CDs. (Running Time: 18 hrs. 15 mins.). 2009. audio compact disk 100.00 (978-1-4159-6527-6(7), BksonTape) Pub: Random Audio Pubg. Dist(s): Random

***Hunted.** unabr. ed. Elmore Leonard. Read by Mark Hammer. (ENG.). 2010. (978-0-06-199369-5(7), Harper Audio); (978-0-06-199754-9(4), Harper Audio) HarperCollins Pubs.

Hunted. unabr. ed. Elmore Leonard. Narrated by Mark Hammer. 8 CDs. (Running Time: 8 hrs. 30 mins.). 1999. audio compact disk 65.00 (978-0-7887-3729-9(5), C1086E7) Recorded Bks.
Join Al Rosen in the holy land as he tries to evade a motley crew of Israelis, Arabs & Americans from Detroit.

Hunted. unabr. ed. Elmore Leonard. Narrated by Mark Hammer. 6 cass. (Running Time: 8 hrs. 30 mins.). 2000. 53.00 (978-0-7887-0838-1(4), 94983E7) Recorded Bks.

Hunted. unabr. collector's ed. Elmore Leonard. Read by Alexander Adams. 7 cass. (Running Time: 7 hrs.). 1995. 42.00 (978-0-7366-3161-7(5), 3832) Books on Tape.
Someone wants Al Rosen dead, & Al knows it better than anyone. But he thinks he's found refuge in Israel, & for three years, he's given danger the slip.

Hunter. Anne Schraff. 1 cass. (Running Time: 3580 sec.). (PageTurner Mystery Ser.). (J). 2002. 10.95 (978-1-56254-475-1(6), SP 4756) Saddleback Edu.
Word-for-word read-along of The Hunter.

Hunter. unabr. ed. James Byron Huggins. Read by Barrett Whitener. 14 cass. (Running Time: 21 hrs.). 1999. 112.00 (978-0-7366-4494-5(6), 4922) Books on Tape.
Hunter is the ultimate tracker, the world's best. If you're lost, Hunter can find you, whether you want him to or not. But he doesn't want to be involved in every search. particularly if it's the military asking and they are searching for a beast that no one's ever seen. But when Hunter learns it's now headed south for civilization, he reluctantly agrees to help. What he finds in the Arctic is a beast that is a half-human abomination, the result of outlaw genetic experiments that have given it a taste for human blood and may ha e made it immortal.

Hunter, unabr. ed. James Byron Huggins. Read by Barrett Whitener. 14 cass. (Running Time: 21 hrs.). 1999. 112.00 (4922) Books on Tape.
Hunter is the ultimate tracker, the world's best. If you're lost, Hunter can find you whether you want him to or not. But he doesn't want to be involved in every search, particularly if it's the military asking & they are searching for a beast that no one's ever seen. But when Hunter learns it's now headed south for civilization, he reluctantly agrees to help. What he finds in the Artic is a beast that is a half-human abomination, the result of outlaw genetic

experiments that have given it a taste for human blood & may have made it immortal.

***Hunter.** unabr. ed. L. J. Smith. Read by Khristine Hvam. (Running Time: 6 hrs.). (Forbidden Game Ser.: Bk. 1). 2010. audio compact disk 19.99 (978-1-4418-7539-6(5), 9781441875396, Bril Audio CD Unabri) Brilliance Audio.

Hunter. unabr. collector's ed. Richard Stark, pseud. Read by Michael Kramer. 4 cass. (Running Time: 6 hrs.). 1999. 24.95 (978-0-7366-4409-9(1), 4870) Books on Tape.
His partners had crossed him; his wife had emptied a .38 at his belly, & they'd left him in a burning house. Parker was tougher than they'd thought, but some business in the pen kept him busy for a while. Now he was out, & there was a matter of $45,000 & a matter of revenge that needed his immediate attention. Parker would have both, even if it meant going up against every man in the mob.

Hunter: A Chinese Folktale. Mary Casanova. Narrated by Richard Poe. 1 cass. (Running Time: 15 mins.). (gr. 2 up). 2001. 10.00 (978-0-7887-5499-9(8)) Recorded Bks.
Chinese folktale.

***Hunter: A Parker Novel.** Richard Stark. Narrated by Stephen Thorne. (Running Time: 5 hrs. 30 mins. 0 sec.). (ENG.). 2010. audio compact disk 19.95 (978-1-60998-106-8(5)) Pub: AudioGO. Dist(s): Perseus Dist

Hunter in My Heart: A Sportsman's Salmagundi. abr. ed. Robert F. Jones. Read by Dan Cashman. (Running Time: 16200 sec.). 2002. audio compact disk 28.00 (978-1-932378-78-8(2)) Pub: A Media Intl. Dist(s): Natl Bk Netwk

***Hunter Killer.** abr. ed. Patrick Robinson. Read by Simon Vance. (ENG.). 2005. (978-0-06-084568-1(6), Harper Audio); (978-0-06-084569-8(4), Harper Audio) HarperCollins Pubs.

***Hunter-Killer.** abr. ed. Patrick Robinson. Read by Simon Vance. (ENG.). 2005. (978-0-06-079673-0(1), Harper Audio) HarperCollins Pubs.

Hunter Killer. unabr. ed. Patrick Robinson. Read by Erik Steele. 11 cass. 2005. 89.95 (978-0-7927-3543-4(9), CSL 784); DVD, audio compact disk, audio compact disk 115.95 (978-0-7927-3627-1(3), SLD 784) AudioGO.

Hunters. W. E. B. Griffin. Read by Dick Hill. 2008. 129.99 (978-1-60640-921-3(2)) Find a World.

Hunters. unabr. ed. W. E. B. Griffin. (Running Time: 75600 sec.). (Presidential Agent Ser.: No. 3). 2007. audio compact disk 29.95 (978-1-4233-2353-2(X), 9781423323532, Brilliance MP3) Brilliance Audio.

Hunters. unabr. ed. W. E. B. Griffin. Read by Dick Hill. (Running Time: 21 hrs.). (Presidential Agent Ser.: Bk. 3). 2007. 44.25 (978-1-4233-2356-3(4), 9781423323563, BADLE); 29.95 (978-1-4233-2355-6(6), 9781423323556, BAD); 38.95 (978-1-4233-2349-5(1), 9781423323495, BAU); audio compact disk 44.25 (978-1-4233-2354-9(8), 9781423323549, Brlnc Audio MP3 Lib) Brilliance Audio.

Hunters. unabr. ed. W. E. B. Griffin. Read by Dick Hill. (Running Time: 21 hrs.). (Presidential Agent Ser.: No. 3). 2007. 117.25 (978-1-4233-2350-1(5), 9781423323501, BrilAudUnabridg); audio compact disk 42.95 (978-1-4233-2351-8(3), 9781423323518, Bril Audio CD Unabri) Brilliance Audio.

Hunters. unabr. ed. W. E. B. Griffin. Read by W. E. B. Griffin. Read by Dick Hill. 18 CDs. (Running Time: 75600 sec.). (Presidential Agent Ser.: No. 3). 2007. audio compact disk 137.25 (978-1-4233-2352-5(1), 9781423323525, BriAudCD Unabrid) Brilliance Audio.

***Hunters' Lodge.** Connie Monk & Tanya Myers. 2010. 79.95 (978-1-84652-854-5(2)); audio compact disk 84.95 (978-1-84652-855-2(0)) Pub: Magna Story GBR. Dist(s): Ulverscroft US

Hunter's Moon. collector's unabr. ed. Dana Stabenow. Read by Marguerite Gavin. 6 CDs. (Running Time: 8 hrs.). (Kate Shugak Ser.). 2000. audio compact disk 48.00 (978-0-7366-5192-9(6)) Books on Tape.
It's the height of hunting season in the bush. Experienced hunter Kate Shugak & her boyfriend volunteer to help out their friend & big-game outfitter George Perry with a hunting trip. The would be hunters are wealthy group of German executives. Used to pampering, the group has a style that clashes with Kate's selfsufficient ways. After successfully bagging a moose with two of her charges, Kate returns to camp to learn that a hunter has been shot. It appears to be an accident, until the body of a second hunter is discovered in even more gruesome circumstances. With no shortage of potential suspects, Kate realizes the moose & the bears aren't the only animals being hunted in the bush.

Hunter's Moon. unabr. ed. K. E. Soderberg. Read by Rusty Nelson. 4 cass. (Running Time: 5 hrs. 30 min.). 2001. 26.95 (978-1-58116-010-9(0)) Books in Motion.
A pale-skinned killer is roaming border settlements, taking whatever he wants. Tobe and Zack Ryker are called to find Klute Rayner, called the great white wolf by the Comanche who roam this dangerous wasteland.

Hunter's Moon. unabr. ed. Dana Stabenow. Read by Marguerite Gavin. 6 CDs. (Running Time: 7 hrs. 30 min.). (Kate Shugak Ser.). 2001. audio compact disk 29.95 (978-0-7366-5707-5(X)) Books on Tape.
It's the height of hunting season in the bush. Experienced hunter Kate Shugak & her boyfriend volunteer to help out their friend & big-game outfitter George Perry with a hunting trip. The would be hunters are wealthy group of German executives. Used to pampering, the group has a style that clashes with Kate's selfsufficient ways. After successfully bagging a moose with two of her charges, Kate returns to camp to learn that a hunter has been shot. It appears to be an accident, until the body of a second hunter is discovered in even more gruesome circumstances. With no shortage of potential suspects, Kate realizes the moose & the bears aren't the only animals being hunted in the bush.

Hunter's Moon. unabr. ed. Dana Stabenow. Read by Marguerite Gavin. 5 cass. (Running Time: 7 hrs. 30 min.). (Kate Shugak Ser.). 1999. 40.00 (978-0-7366-4590-4(X), 5007) Books on Tape.
A corporate hunting retreat turns into a deadly game of cat & mouse.

Hunter's Moon. unabr. collector's ed. Dana Stabenow. Read by Marguerite Gavin. 5 cass. (Running Time: 7 hrs. 30 min.). (Kate Shugak Ser.). 1999. 40.00 (978-0-7366-4635-2(3), 5007) Books on Tape.
It's the height of hunting season in the bush. Experienced hunter Kate Shugak & her boyfriend volunteer to help out their friend & big-game outfitter George Perry with a hunting trip. The would be hunters are wealthy group of German executives. Used to pampering, the group has a style that clashes with Kate's selfsufficient ways. After successfully bagging a moose with two of her charges, Kate returns to camp to learn that a hunter has been shot. It appears to be an accident, until the body of a second hunter is discovered in even more gruesome circumstances. With no shortage of potential suspects, Kate realizes the moose & the bears aren't the only animals being hunted in the bush.

Hunter's Moon: Poems from Boyhood to Manhood. Joseph Meredith. 1993. 12.95 (978-1-877770-85-2(X)) Time Being Bks.

Hunters of Dune. unabr. ed. Brian Herbert et al. Read by Scott Brick. 20 CDs. (Running Time: 73800 sec.). (Dune Ser.). (ENG.). 2006. audio compact disk 59.95 (978-1-59397-975-1(4)) Pub: Macmill Audio. Dist(s): Macmillan

Hunter's Road: A Journey with Gun & Dog Across the American Uplands. abr. ed. Jim Fergus. Narrated by Dick Hill. (Running Time: 16200 sec.). (Field & Stream Ser.). 2007. audio compact disk 28.00 (978-1-933309-50-7(4)) Pub: A Media Intl. Dist(s): Natl Bk Netwk

Hunters Trials see Sir John Betjeman Reading His Poetry

Hunting: The Southern Tradition. May Lamar & Rich Donnell. Ed. by Joe Johnston. (Running Time: 90 min.). 1988. 8.95 (978-0-922067-00-8(7)) Johnston Mus Grp.
Features a collection of hunting stories.

Hunting a Detroit Tiger, unabr. ed. Troy Soos. Narrated by Johnny Heller. 7 cass. (Running Time: 10 hrs. 15 mins.). (Mickey Rawlings Baseball Ser.: Vol. 4). 1999. 60.00 (978-0-7887-0926-5(7), 95066E7) Recorded Bks.
When Detroit Tigers utility player Mickey Rawlings discovers the body of a union leader at a 1920s organizational meeting, the members acuse him of the murder. Mickey suddenly finds himself in a dangerous squeeze play between the players union & the owners.

Hunting & Fishing from A to Zern. abr. unabr. ed. Ed Zern. Read by Randall James Stanton. 3 cass. (Running Time: 3 hrs.). 1996. 21.95 Set. (978-1-882071-31-9(X)) B-B Audio.
It takes a lifetime of outdoor adventure to build up a collection of hunting and fishing stories as entertaining as Ed Zerns. The grand old man of Field and Stream is at his best in A to Zern, with colorful stories, tall and true. This audio book comes.

Hunting Badger. abr. ed. Tony Hillerman. Read by George Guidall. 1 CD. (Running Time: 90 min.). (Joe Leaphorn & Jim Chee Novel Ser.). 2004. audio compact disk 14.95 (978-0-06-074682-7(3)) HarperCollins Pubs.

Hunting Badger. unabr. ed. Tony Hillerman. Narrated by George Guidall. 5 CDs. (Running Time: 6 hrs.). (Joe Leaphorn & Jim Chee Novel Ser.). 2000. audio compact disk 46.00 (978-0-7887-4201-9(9), C1130) Recorded Bks.
One year ago, Navajo policeman Jim Chee was part of a bungled FBI manhunt for two cop killers who were never captured. Now the killers may be at work again. Joined by retired officer Joe Leaphorn, Chee once again begins a search. Interweaves Navajo & Ute myths & history into a story based on actual events.

Hunting Badger. unabr. ed. Tony Hillerman. Narrated by George Guidall. 4 cass. (Running Time: 6 hrs.). (Joe Leaphorn & Jim Chee Novel Ser.). 1999. 35.00 (978-0-7887-3894-4(1), 96076) Recorded Bks.

Hunting Civil War Relics at Nimblewill Creek see James Dickey Reads His Poetry & Prose

Hunting down Amanda, Set. abr. ed. Andrew Klavan. 2 cass. (Running Time: 3 hrs.). 1999. 17.95 (978-1-55935-309-0(0)) Soundelux.
A jazz saxophonist finds himself drawn into the life of a woman in trouble. She's running - from him, from a disaster in Hunnicut, & from an ominous threat he can't even begin to understand.

***Hunting Eichmann: How a Band of Survivors & a Young Spy Agency Chased down the World's Most Notorious Nazi.** unabr. ed. Neal Bascomb. Narrated by Paul Hecht. 1 Playaway. (Running Time: 12 hrs. 45 mins.). 2009. 61.75 (978-1-4361-9512-6(8)); audio compact disk 123.75 (978-1-4361-7008-6(7)) Recorded Bks.

***Hunting Eichmann: How a Band of Survivors & a Young Spy Agency Chased down the World's Most Notorious Nazi.** unabr. ed. Neal Bascomb. Narrated by Paul Hecht. 11 cass. (Running Time: 12 hrs. 45 mins.). 2010. 92.75 (978-1-4361-7007-9(9)) Recorded Bks.

***Hunting Eichmann: How a Band of Survivors & a Young Spy Agency Chased down the World's Most Notorious Nazi.** unabr. collector's ed. Neal Bascomb. Narrated by Paul Hecht. 11 CDs. (Running Time: 12 hrs. 45 mins.). 2010. audio compact disk 54.95 (978-1-4361-7009-3(5)) Recorded Bks.

Hunting Evil: The Nazi War Criminals Who Escaped & the Quest to Bring Them to Justice. unabr. ed. Guy Walters. Read by Jonathan Cowley. (ENG.). 2010. audio compact disk 45.00 (978-0-307-71553-1(1), Random AudioBks) Pub: Random Audio Pubg. Dist(s): Random

Hunting Fear. Kay Hooper. Read by Dick Hill. (Fear Trilogy: Bk. 1). 2008. 64.99 (978-1-60640-803-2(8)) Find a World.

Hunting Fear. unabr. ed. Kay Hooper. Read by Dick Hill. (Running Time: 8 hrs.). (Fear Trilogy: Bk. 1). 2004. 24.95 (978-1-59335-757-3(5), 1593357575, Brilliance MP3); 39.25 (978-1-59335-891-4(1), 1593358911, Brlnc Audio MP3 Lib); 32.95 (978-1-59355-789-8(2), 1593557892, BAU); 82.25 (978-1-59355-790-4(6), 1593557906, BrilAudUnabridg); audio compact disk 36.95 (978-1-59355-792-8(2), 1593557922, Bril Audio CD Unabri); audio compact disk 92.25 (978-1-59355-793-5(0), 1593557930, BriAudCD Unabrid) Brilliance Audio.
He's no ordinary kidnapper. Not only does he strike again and again, but he collects the ransom, gets away safely, and leaves his helpless hostages dead. Now, after months of eluding the best that law enforcement can put against him, this monster has left nothing in his wake but a cold trail of unconnected victims. He's no ordinary cop. Lucas Jordan, a key agent and profiler in Noah Bishop's Special Crimes Unit, has an extraordinary skill: he locates missing people. But his uncanny ability comes with a price, and his methods rouse mistrust in the hard-nosed cops forced to call him into their investigations. Now Jordan has come to Clayton County, North Carolina, where the latest in a string of kidnapping victims has turned up dead. Complicating the situation is the presence - and predictions - of someone who's even more of an outsider than Jordan himself: carnival psychic Samantha Burke, a woman out of his own haunted past. Her warnings meet with skepticism from the local police but spur Jordan on to do what he does best: hunt fear. But the killer he is hunting is hunting Jordan - and he's already several moves ahead in a twisted game whose rules Jordan must learn in order to have a fighting chance. For his psychopathic opponent has extended a very personal challenge - and he's about to threaten the one life the profiler values even more than his own. . . .

Hunting Fear. unabr. ed. Kay Hooper. Read by Dick Hill. (Running Time: 8 hrs.). (Fear Trilogy: Bk. 1). 2004. 39.25 (978-1-59710-386-2(1), 1597103861, BADLE); 24.95 (978-1-59710-387-9(X), 159710387X, BAD) Brilliance Audio.

Hunting for Hoot Owls see Crimson Ramblers of the World, Farewell

Hunting from Home: A Year Afield in the Blue Ridge Mountains. abr. ed. Christopher Camuto. Narrated by Jeff Riggenbach. (Running Time: 14400 sec.). (Field & Stream Ser.). 2008. audio compact disk 28.00 (978-1-933309-34-7(2)) Pub: A Media Intl. Dist(s): Natl Bk Netwk

Hunting Ground. unabr. ed. Patricia Briggs. (Running Time: 10 hrs.). (Alpha & Omega Ser.: Bk. 2). 2009. 39.95 (978-1-4406-4463-4(2), PengAudBks) Penguin Grp USA.

Hunting of the Snark. Lewis Carroll, pseud. (J). (CDL5 1075) HarperCollins Pubs.

Hunting Party. Based on a book by Elizabeth Moon. (Serrano Legacy Ser.: Bk. 1). 2008. 12.99 (978-1-59950-542-8(8)) GraphicAudio.

Hunting Party. Based on a book by Elizabeth Moon. (Serrano Legacy Ser.: Bk. 1). 2008. 12.99 (978-1-59950-543-5(6)) GraphicAudio.

Hunting Party Part 1. Elizabeth Moon. (Serrano Legacy Ser.: Bk. 1). 2008. audio compact disk 19.99 (978-1-59950-431-5(6)) GraphicAudio.

Hunting Party Part 2. Elizabeth Moon. (Running Time: 21600 sec.). (Serrano Legacy Ser.: Bk. 1). 2008. audio compact disk 19.99 (978-1-59950-437-7(5)) GraphicAudio.

Hunting Season. Nevada Barr. 2009. audio compact disk 9.99 (978-1-4418-2658-9(0)) Brilliance Audio.

Hunting Season. Nevada Barr. Narrated by Barbara Rosenblat. 10 CDs. (Running Time: 11 hrs.). (Anna Pigeon Ser.: No. 10). audio compact disk 98.00 (978-1-4025-1570-5(7)) Recorded Bks.

Hunting Season. Nevada Barr. 7 cass. (Running Time: 11 hrs.). (Anna Pigeon Ser.: No. 10). 2004. 29.99 (978-1-4025-0861-5(1), 00974) Recorded Bks.

Hunting Season. abr. ed. Nevada Barr. Read by Joyce Bean. 4 cass. (Running Time: 6 hrs.). (Anna Pigeon Ser.: No. 10). 2002. 53.25 (978-1-59086-004-5(7), 1590860047, Lib Edit); audio compact disk 69.25 (978-1-59086-002-1(0), 1590860020, CD Lib Edit) Brilliance Audio.
When Anna answers a call to historic Mt. Locust, once a producing plantation and inn on Mississippi's Natchez Trace Parkway and now a tourist spot, the last thing she expects to encounter is murder. But the man Anna finds in the stand's old bedroom is no tourist in distress. He's nearly naked, and very dead, his body bearing marks consistent with an S & M ritual gone awry. On a writing table nearby is an open Bible, ominous passages circled in red. It seems the deceased is the brother of Raymond Barnette, local undertaker and a candidate for sheriff, who wants to keep any hint of kinkiness out of the minds of the God-fearing populace. Ray may be hiding a house full of secrets in the old family homestead, but before Anna can start her investigation, she's waylaid by malevolent poachers, peevish coworkers, and a suddenly turbulent romantic life. And when hidden agendas and old allegiances are revealed, it's suddenly Anna's life on the line.

Hunting Season. abr. ed. Nevada Barr. Read by Joyce Bean. (Running Time: 6 hrs.). (Anna Pigeon Ser.: No. 10). 2004. audio compact disk 16.99 (978-1-59355-696-9(9), 1593556969) Brilliance Audio.

Hunting Season. abr. ed. Nevada Barr. Read by Joyce Bean. (Running Time: 6 hrs.). (Anna Pigeon Ser.). 2006. 24.95 (978-1-4233-0607-8(4), 9781423306078, BAD) Brilliance Audio.

Hunting Season. abr. ed. Nevada Barr. Read by Joyce Bean. (Running Time: 6 hrs.). (Anna Pigeon Ser.: No. 10). 2006. 39.25 (978-1-4233-0608-5(2), 9781423306085, BADLE); audio compact disk 39.25 (978-1-4233-0606-1(6), 9781423306061, Brlnc Audio MP3 Lib); audio compact disk 24.95 (978-1-4233-0605-4(8), 9781423306054, Brilliance MP3) Brilliance Audio.

Hunting Season. unabr. ed. Nevada Barr. Narrated by Barbara Rosenblat. 8 cass. (Running Time: 11 hrs.). (Anna Pigeon Ser.: No. 10). 2002. 78.00 (978-1-4025-0748-9(8), 96913) Recorded Bks.
When Park Ranger Anna Pigeon answers a call to historic Mt. Locust, once a producing plantation and inn on Mississippi's Natchez Trace Parkway, the last thing she expects to encounter is a naked and very dead man. His body bears what looks like the brutal scars from an S&M ritual gone terribly wrong. When the deceased turned out to be the brother of a candidate for the office of local sheriff, a host of cover-ups, hidden agendas,old allegiances and buried secrets begins to emerge. follow Anna as she fights for her life.

Hunting Season. unabr. ed. P. T. Deutermann. Read by Dick Hill. 11 cass. (Running Time: 17 hrs.). 2001. 34.95 (978-1-58788-120-6(9), 1587881209); 118.25 (978-1-58788-121-3(7), 1587881217) Brilliance Audio.
When college kids hiking near an abandoned military industrial complex in West Virginia mysteriously disappear, special agent Janet Carter - earnest, honest, and fed up with the stifling chauvinistic environment at the Roanoke FBI headquarters - is called in to investigate. Unfortunately, there are no leads - it's as if the three just vanished into thin air. The authorities at the FBI are quick to write off the case as teenage runaways, and order Janet off the case - but not before she has the chance to speak with the father of one of the missing, Edwin Kriess. Kriess is an ex-"sweeper," a member of an elite CIA task force trained to track down and bring in rogue agents. To be a sweeper means to be expertly trained in the art of hunting and killing, and Kriess was not only a sweeper himself, but the agent in charge of training and leading the entire program. Only something went wrong - an assignment to track down an agent involved in a Chinese espionage plot ended in a bloody massacre, and threatened to reveal a monumental government cover-up. Kriess was quietly sacrificed to the scandal, and has since lived in solitude. But now his daughter is missing, and he knows that she didn't run away - and he will do anything to find her and bring her abductors to justice. His search brings him back to the abandoned industrial complex, where two right-wing religious fanatics - tied to the Waco disaster and inspired by the Oklahoma City bombing - are building a hydrogen bomb. When the FBI learns of Kriess' independent investigations, they fear the worst: he knows too many secrets already, and if his search efforts are successful, a scandal of epic proportions would unfold. They decide they need a plant, someone who has access to Kriess, and can win his trust. Someone who will report back what he knows, and what he finds - and that person is Janet Carter.

Hunting Season. unabr. ed. P. T. Deutermann. Read by Dick Hill. (Running Time: 17 hrs.). 2005. 44.25 (978-1-59600-711-6(7), 9781596007116, BADLE); 29.95 (978-1-59600-710-9(9), 9781596007109, BAD); audio compact disk 44.25 (978-1-59600-709-3(5), 9781596007093, Brlnc Audio MP3 Lib); audio compact disk 29.95 (978-1-59600-708-6(7), 9781596007086, Brilliance MP3) Brilliance Audio.

Hunting the Deceitful Turkey see Great American Essays: A Collection

Hunting the Devil. unabr. ed. Richard Lourie. Read by John MacDonald. 6 cass. (Running Time: 9 hrs.). 1994. 48.00 (978-0-7366-2627-9(1), 3367) Books on Tape.
Fifty-two dead. If it were war, you'd give him a medal. But when the victims are women & children & the killer a cannibal, you kill him - if you can catch him! For 12 years Russian police chased clues. Finally they closed in...on a nearsighted grandfather! Could it be? It could, & to prove it took ten days of fearsome interrogation, vividly reported here in mesmerizing detail.

Hunting the Wild Pineapple, unabr. ed. Thea Astley. Read by James Wright. 5 cass. (Running Time: 7 hrs. 30 min.). 1999. (978-1-876584-18-4(1), 590998) Bolinda Pubng AUS.
Leverson the narrator, at the center of these stories, calls himself a 'people freak'. Seduced by north Queensland's sultry beauty & unique strangeness, he is as fascinated by the invading hordes of misfits from the south as by the old established Queenslanders. Leverson's ironical yet compassionate view makes every story, every incident, a pointed example of human weakness or strength.

Hunting the wild Pineapple. unabr. ed. Thea Astley. Read by James Wright. (Running Time: 6 hrs. 5 mins.). 2009. audio compact disk 63.95 (978-1-74214-431-3(4), 9781742144313) Pub: Bolinda Pubng AUS. Dist(s): Bolinda Pub Inc

Hunting Trips. Theodore Roosevelt. 1998. pap. bk. 15.00 (978-0-676-54507-4(6)) SRA McGraw.

Hunting Unicorns. Bella Pollen. Read by Christopher Cazanove & Gabrielle de Cuir. (Running Time: 10 mins.). 2005. 59.95 (978-0-7861-3753-4(3)) Blckstn Audio.

Hunting Unicorns. Bella Pollen. Read by Christopher Cazanove & Gabrielle De Cuir. (Running Time: 36000 sec.). 2005. DVD, audio compact disk, audio compact disk 72.00 (978-0-7861-7642-7(3)) Blckstn Audio.

Hunting Unicorns. unabr. ed. Bella Pollen. Read by Christopher Cazanove & Gabrielle de Cuir. (Running Time: 10 mins.). 2005. 29.95 (978-0-7861-7908-4(2)) Blckstn Audio.

Hunting We Will Go Audio CD. Adapted by Benchmark Education Company Staff. Based on a work by Jeffrey B. Fuerst. (Reader's Theater Nursery Rhymes & Songs Ser.). (J). (gr. k-1). 2008. audio compact disk 10.00 (978-1-60437-998-3(7)) Benchmark Educ.

Hunting Wind. unabr. ed. Steve Hamilton. Read by Nick Sullivan. 6 vols. (Running Time: 9 hrs.). 2001. bk. 54.95 (978-0-7927-2501-5(8), CSL 390, Chivers Sound Lib) AudioGO.
Randy Wilkins is traveling two thousand miles to see Alex McKnight. They haven't seen each other in thirty years, but Randy is convinced that McKnight is the right man to help him on his quest. Randy has come back to Michigan to find Maria, the one true love of his life. he had walked away from her in 1971 and hasn't seen or heard from her since. McKnight agrees to help him and as the search for Maria deepens, he begins to realize that he is an unwilling player in a dangerous game.

***Hunting Wind.** unabr. ed. Steve Hamilton. Read by Dan John Miller. (Running Time: 9 hrs.). (Alex Mcknight Ser.). 2010. 24.99 (978-1-4418-3445-4(1), 9781441834454, Brilliance MP3); 24.99 (978-1-4418-3447-8(8), 9781441834478, BAD); 39.97 (978-1-4418-3446-1(X), 9781441834461, Brinc Audio MP3 Lib); 39.97 (978-1-4418-3448-5(6), 9781441834485, BADLE); audio compact disk 29.99 (978-1-4418-3443-0(5), 9781441834430, Bril Audio CD Unabri); audio compact disk 87.97 (978-1-4418-3444-7(3), 9781441834447, BriAudCD Unabrid) Brilliance Audio.

Huntington Disease - A Bibliography & Dictionary for Physicians, Patients, & Genome Researchers. Compiled by Icon Group International, Inc. Staff. 2007. ring bd. 28.95 (978-0-497-11235-6(3)) Icon Grp.

Huntington's Disease: Program from the Award Winning Public Radio Series. Interview. Hosted by Fred Goodwin. 1 CD. (Running Time: 1 hr.). 2000. audio compact disk 21.95 (978-1-932479-57-7(0), LCM 106) Lichtenstein Creat.
Huntington's Disease is a fatal genetic neurological illness that strikes in mid-life and affects mind, body and behavior. It is the disease that took Woody Guthrie's life. Recent advances in gene science are encouraging, but as the information hasn't yet brought an effective cure or treatment, the knowledge poses more questions than answers at this point. There is now a test that can tell you if you'll develop the disease, but there is little doctors can do for you if you test positive. In this program, we learn about the discovery of the gene mutation that causes the disease, and about exciting progress toward better treatment. We also talk to people who have agonized over whether or not to be tested for the disease that claimed their parent. Guests include Dr. Christopher Ross, the Director of the Baltimore Huntington's Disease Center at the Johns Hopkins School of Medicine, and Dr. Adam Rosenblatt, the clinical director of the Baltimore Huntington's Disease Center at the Johns Hopkins School of Medicine.

Huntress. unabr. ed. L. J. Smith. Read by Angela Dawe. (Running Time: 5 hrs.). (Night World Ser.: Vol. 7). 2010. 39.97 (978-1-4418-2064-8(7), 9781441820648, Brinc Audio MP3 Lib); 39.97 (978-1-4418-2066-2(3), 9781441820662, BADLE); 19.99 (978-1-4418-2063-1(9), 9781441820631, Brilliance MP3); 19.99 (978-1-4418-2065-5(5), 9781441820655, BAD); audio compact disk 59.97 (978-1-4418-2062-4(0), 9781441820624, BriAudCD Unabrid); audio compact disk 19.99 (978-1-4418-2061-7(2), 9781441820617, Bril Audio CD Unabri) Brilliance Audio.

***Hurlbut's Story of the Bible.** unabr. ed. Rev. Jesse, DD Hurlbut. Read by Robert Whitfield. (Running Time: 20 hrs. 30 mins.). 2010. 44.95 (978-1-4417-4609-2(9)); audio compact disk 123.00 (978-1-4417-4606-1(4)) Blckstn Audio.

Hurlbut's Story of the Bible. unabr. ed. Jesse Lyman Hurlbut. Read by Robert Whitefield. 14 cass. (Running Time: 20 hrs. 30 mins.). 1996. 89.95 (978-0-7861-1089-6(9), 1858) Blckstn Audio.
Contains 168 stories from the Bible, each one complete in itself, while together combining to form one narrative. It is the complete Bible story, running from Genesis to Revelation, written with language & style that will appeal to both children & adults.

Hurricane see Poetry of Hart Crane

Hurricane. Prod. by Laraim Associates. (Barclay Family Adventure Ser.). (YA). 2005. audio compact disk 10.95 (978-1-56254-993-0(6)) Saddleback Edu.

Hurricane. Alan Venable. Ed. by Jerry Stemach et al. Illus. by Jeff Ham & Susan Baptist. Narrated by Denise Jordan Walker. Contrib. by Ted S. Hasselbring. (Start-to-Finish Books). (J). (gr. 2-3). 2001. 35.00 (978-1-58702-531-0(0)) D Johnston Inc.

Hurricane! Alan Venable. (Natural Disasters Ser.). 2001. audio compact disk 18.95 (978-1-4105-0165-3(5)) D Johnston Inc.

Hurricane! Alan Venable. Ed. by Jerry Stemach. Narrated by Denise Jordan Walker. 2001. audio compact disk 200.00 (978-1-58702-530-3(2)) D Johnston Inc.

Hurricane. unabr. ed. Terry Trueman. Narrated by Ramon de Ocampo. 3 cass. (Running Time: 3 hrs. 15 mins.). (YA). (gr. 5-8). 2008. 30.75 (978-1-4361-1916-0(2)); audio compact disk 30.75 (978-1-4361-1921-4(9)) Recorded Bks.

Hurricane. unabr. collector's ed. Charles Nordhoff & James Norman Hall. Read by Jonathan Reese. 7 cass. (Running Time: 7 hrs.). 1979. 42.00 (978-0-7366-0261-7(5), 1256) Books on Tape.
A tale of the Polynesian life seen through the eyes of Dr. Kersaint, a French medical officer, climaxing with the force of a destructive, overpowering hurricane.

Hurricane, Vol. 2. Alan Venable. Ed. by Jerry Stemach et al. Illus. by Jeff Ham & Susan Baptist. Narrated by Denise Jordan Walker. Contrib. by Ted S. Hasselbring. (Start-to-Finish Books). (J). (gr. 2-3). 2002. 100.00 (978-1-58702-953-0(7)) D Johnston Inc.

Hurricane, Vol. 2. unabr. ed. Alan Venable. Ed. by Jerry Stemach et al. Illus. by Jeff Ham & Susan Baptist. Narrated by Denise Jordan Walker. Contrib. by Ted S. Hasselbring. 1 cass. (Running Time: 1 hr.). (Start-to-Finish Books). (J). (gr. 2-3). 2001. (978-1-58702-378-1(4), F38K2) D Johnston Inc.
This book combines exciting history with simple science to tell the story of hurricanes and their impact on people. Beginning with the tale of how Japan was twice saved from invasions by typhoons (as hurricanes are called in that part of the world), it describes Columbus' encounters with hurricanes and how we have borrowed the work hurricane from the original West Indian people. The book shows how, over the past 300 years, amateur and professional scientists have unravelled the secrets of these devastating storms.

Hurricane Gold. unabr. ed. Charlie Higson. Read by Gerard Doyle. (Running Time: 7 hrs. 0 mins.). (Young Bond Ser.: Bk. 4). 2010. 29.95 (978-1-4417-2764-0(7)); 54.95 (978-1-4417-2760-2(4)); audio compact disk 69.00 (978-1-4417-2761-9(2)) Blckstn Audio.

Hurricane Katrina: Self-Guided Tour. Pamela Pipes. (ENG.). 2007. audio compact disk (978-0-9801321-0-6(X)) Tours Bayou.

***Hurricane Punch.** abr. ed. Tim Dorsey. Read by Oliver Wyman. (ENG.). 2007. (978-0-06-126228-9(5), Harper Audio); (978-0-06-126229-6(3), Harper Audio) HarperCollins Pubs.

Hurricane Punch. unabr. ed. Tim Dorsey. Read by Oliver Wyman. 9 CDs. (Running Time: 37800 sec.). (Serge Storms Ser.: Bk. 9). 2007. audio compact disk 39.95 (978-0-06-122723-3(4)) HarperCollins Pubs.

Hurricane Season: A Coach, His Team, & Their Triumph in the Time of Katrina. unabr. ed. Neal Thompson. Read by David Drummond. 9 CDs. (Running Time: 11 hrs. 0 mins. 0 sec.). (ENG.). 2007. audio compact disk 34.99 (978-1-4001-0529-8(3)); audio compact disk 69.99 (978-1-4001-3529-5(X)); audio compact disk 24.99 (978-1-4001-5529-3(0)) Pub: Tantor Media. Dist(s): IngramPubServ

Hurricane Song. unabr. ed. Paul Volponi. Read by Jacob Norman. 1 MP3-CD. (Running Time: 2 hrs.). 2009. 39.97 (978-1-4233-8221-8(8), 9781423382218, Brinc Audio MP3 Lib); 39.97 (978-1-4233-8223-2(4), 9781423382232, BADLE); 24.99 (978-1-4233-8222-5(6), 9781423382225, BAD); 24.99 (978-1-4233-8220-1(X), 9781423382201, Brilliance MP3); audio compact disk 44.97 (978-1-4233-8219-5(6), 9781423382195, BriAudCD Unabrid); audio compact disk 24.99 (978-1-4233-8218-8(8), 9781423382188, Bril Audio CD Unabri) Brilliance Audio.

Hurricane Wills. unabr. ed. Sally Grindley. Narrated by Tom Lawrence. 4 CDs. (Running Time: 4 hrs. 23 mins.). (J). (gr. 5-7). 2007. audio compact disk 49.95 (978-1-4056-5724-2(3), Chivers Child Audio) AudioGO.

Hurricane Years, Pt. 1. unabr. collector's ed. Cameron Hawley. Read by John MacDonald. 8 cass. (Running Time: 12 hrs.). 1984. 64.00 (978-0-7366-0574-8(6), 1546A) Books on Tape.
Hawley addresses the question "why do men knock themselves out for a corporation?" & knock themselves out, particulary in mid-career, "the Hurricane Years", when stress takes its greatest toll.

Hurricane Years, Pt. 2. collector's unabr. ed. Cameron Hawley. Read by John MacDonald. 7 cass. (Running Time: 10 hrs. 30 mins.). 1984. 56.00 (978-0-7366-0575-5(4), 1546-B) Books on Tape.
Hawley addresses the question "why do men knock themselves out for a corporation? & knock themselves out they do, particulary in mid-career, "the hurricane years", when stress takes its greatest toll.

Hurricanes & Floods. Anne Schraff. Narrated by Larry A. McKeever. (Natural Disaster Ser.). (J). 2004. 10.95 (978-1-58659-118-2(5)); audio compact disk 14.95 (978-1-58659-352-0(8)) Artesian.

Hurried Children: Too Young to Learn so Much. Michelle Trudeau. Read by Michelle Trudeau. 1 cass. (Running Time: 19 min.). 9.95 (D0140B090, HarperThor) HarpC GBR.

Hurried Woman Syndrome: A Seven-Step Program to Conquer Fatigue, Control Weight, & Restore Passion to Your Relationship. abr. ed. Brent W. Bost. Read by Beth Richmond. (Running Time: 16200 sec.). 2006. audio compact disk 28.00 (978-1-932378-94-8(4)) Pub: A Media Intl. Dist(s): Natl Bk Netwk

Hurry down Sunshine: A Father's Memoir of Love & Madness. unabr. ed. Michael Greenberg. Read by Michael Greenberg. 5 CDs. (Running Time: 6 hrs. 30 mins.). (ENG.). 2008. audio compact disk 29.95 (978-0-7393-6883-1(4), Random AudioBks) Pub: Random Audio Pubg. Dist(s): Random

Hurry! Hurry! unabr. ed. Michele Sobel Spirn. 1 cass. (Running Time: 7 min.). (I Like to Read Ser.). (J). (ps-2). 1985. 16.99 incl. hardcover. (978-0-87386-002-4(0)) Jan Prods.
Everyone is always telling Alice to hurry. "Hurry! You'll be late for school," says her father. "Hurry! Dinner is ready," says her mother. "Can't you hurry?" ask her friends. "I am tired of hurrying," says Alice, "I will be slow today".

Hurry up & Meditate. unabr. ed. David Michie. Read by Nicholas Bell. (Running Time: 4 hrs. 45 mins.). 2009. audio compact disk 57.95 (978-1-74214-081-0(5), 9781742140810) Pub: Bolinda Pubng AUS. Dist(s): Bolinda Pub Inc

***Hurry up & Meditate.** unabr. ed. David Michie. Read by Nicholas Bell. (Running Time: 4 hrs. 45 mins.). 2010. 43.95 (978-1-74214-649-2(X), 9781742146492) Pub: Bolinda Pubng AUS. Dist(s): Bolinda Pub Inc

Hurry up, Franklin. Paulette Bourgeois. Illus. by Brenda Clark. Music by Bruce Cockburn. (Franklin Ser.). (ENG.). (J). (ps-3). 2000. 9.95 (978-1-55074-682-2(0)) Kids Can Pr CAN.

Hurst's the Heart. McGraw-Hill Staff et al. 1999. 195.00 (978-0-07-864185-5(3)) McGraw.

***Hurt Go Happy.** unabr. ed. Ginny Rorby. (Running Time: 8 hrs. NaN mins.). 2011. 29.95 (978-1-4417-7595-5(1)); 54.95 (978-1-4417-7592-4(7)); audio compact disk 76.00 (978-1-4417-7593-1(5)) Blckstn Audio.

Hurt Hawks see Poetry of Robinson Jeffers

***Hurtling Wings.** unabr. ed. L. Ron Hubbard. 2 CDs. (Running Time: 2 hrs.). (Stories from the Golden Age Ser.). (YA). (gr. 7 up). 2010. audio compact disk 9.95 (978-1-59212-303-2(1)) Gala Pr LLC.

Husband. unabr. ed. Dean Koontz. 10 cass. (Running Time: 15 hrs.). 2006. 90.00 (978-1-4159-3047-2(3)); audio compact disk 96.00 (978-1-4159-3048-9(1)) Books on Tape.

Husband, Lover, Spy. abr. ed. Janice Pennington & Carlos De Abreu. Read by Janice Pennington. 2 cass. 1995. 17.00 Set. (978-1-56876-036-0(1)) Soundlines Ent.
For seventeen years, "The Price is Right" hostess Janice Pennington was caught in a web of deceit. On September 27, 1975, her world was shattered when her husband disappeared in a restricted area along the Afghanistan, Pakistan & Russian Borders. Determined to find out what happened Janice embarked on a search from Los Angeles to the Kremlin.

Husband Material. unabr. ed. Maeve Haran. Read by Jacqueline King. 11 CDs. (Running Time: 11 hrs. 45 min.). (Isis Ser.). (J). 2003. audio compact disk 99.95 (978-0-7531-2237-2(5)); 76.95 (978-0-7531-1792-7(4)) Pub: ISIS Lrg Prnt GBR. Dist(s): Ulverscroft US
After sixteen years of marriage to the handsome but unfaithful Giles, Amanda is sure of one thing: she isn't going to make the same mistake twice. So when she - literally - bumps into charismatic Angus Day in his cobalt blue sports car, there's no way she's going to fall for all that charm baloney again. This time she's determined to choose someone suitable. Like Luke Knight, a caring, sharing new man who helps old ladies across the street. After all, it's obvious to anyone with a half a brain which one is better husband material, isn't it?.

Husband-Wife Relationship. Elbert Willis. 1 cass. (Relationship Ser.). 4.00 Fill the Gap.

Husbands & Fathers. Derek Prince. 2 cass. 1990. 5.95 ea. Derek Prince.
How should a man relate to his wife & children? How can he fulfill his God-given roles of prophet, priest & king?.

***Husbands & Wives Club: A Year in the Life of a Couples Therapy Group.** unabr. ed. Laurie Abraham. Narrated by Laural Merlington. (Running Time: 11 hrs. 30 mins.). 2010. 17.99 (978-1-4001-8630-3(7)); 24.99 (978-1-4001-6630-5(6)); audio compact disk 34.99 (978-1-4001-1630-0(9)); audio compact disk 69.99 (978-1-4001-4630-7(5)) Pub: Tantor Media. Dist(s): IngramPubServ

Husbands & Wives-tapes. Douglas Wilson. 4 cass. 1990. 12.00 (978-1-59128-208-2(X)) Canon Pr ID.

Hush. Jacqueline Woodson. audio compact disk (978-1-4025-5375-2(7)) Recorded Bks.

Hush. Jacqueline Woodson. Narrated by Sisi Aisha Johnson. 3 pieces. (Running Time: 3 hrs. 15 mins.). (gr. 6 up). 28.00 (978-1-4025-3130-9(3)) Recorded Bks.

***Hush: A Novel.** unabr. ed. Kate White. Read by Aimee Jolson. (ENG.). 2010. (978-0-06-200716-2(5), Harper Audio); (978-0-06-200044-6(6), Harper Audio) HarperCollins Pubs.

Hush, Hush. unabr. ed. Becca Fitzpatrick. Read by Caitlin Greer. 8 CDs. (Running Time: 9 hrs. 0 mins. 0 sec.). (ENG.). (YA). 2009. audio compact disk 34.99 (978-0-7435-9956-6(X)) Pub: S&S Audio. Dist(s): S and S Inc

Hush Little Baby see Gathering of Great Poetry for Children

Hush Little Baby. 2004. pap. bk. 14.95 (978-0-7882-0622-1(2)); 8.95 (978-1-56008-929-2(6)); cass. & flmstrp 30.00 (978-1-56008-688-8(2)) Weston Woods.

Hush Little Baby Carriage. 1 cass. 1995. 19.95 (978-1-55569-742-6(9)) Great Am Audio.

Hush Little Baby; Casey Jones; Billy Boy; Mommy, but Me a China Doll. 2004. (978-0-89719-827-1(1)) Weston Woods.

Hush Little Baby; Casey Jones; Billy Boy; Mommy, Buy Me a China Doll. 2004. cass. & flmstrp (978-0-89719-735-9(6)) Weston Woods.

Hush Money. unabr. ed. Robert B. Parker. Read by Burt Reynolds. 6 cass. (Running Time: 9 hrs.). (Spenser Ser.). 2001. 32.00 (978-1-59040-001-2(1), Phoenix Audio) Pub: Amer Intl Pub. Dist(s): PerseuPGW
Professor Robinson Nevins, the son of Hawk's boyhood mentor, asks Spenser to investigate why he was denied tenure. At the same time, Spenser's inamorata, Susan, asks him to come to the aid of an old college friend who is the victim of a stalker. Behind the ivy-covered walls of academe, political maneuverings take on deadly proportions.

Hush Money. unabr. ed. Robert B. Parker. Read by Burt Reynolds. 7 CDs. (Running Time: 9 hrs.). (Spenser Ser.). 2004. audio compact disk 45.00 (978-1-59007-549-4(8)); 34.95 (978-1-59007-206-6(5)) Pub: New Millenn Enter. Dist(s): PerseuPGW
Spenser and his buddy Hawk are helping a couple of troubled friends. The first case involves the denial of tenure for Professor Robinson Nevins. While tenure meetings are always closed-door affairs, Nevins assumes that the recent suicide of graduate student Prentice Lamont (who some claim was having an affair with Nevins) ruined his chances for a permanent position. Spenser and Hawk cut a path through the members of the tenure committee on their way to the truth of the Nevins case. The other investigation pits Spenser against the unknown stalker of K.C. Roth. Spenser's girlfriend, Susan, has known K.C. for a while, and while the PI is always eager to help a damsel in distress, the problem is that after he's resolved the case, K.C. begins a little stalking of her own - of Spenser.

Hush My Baby. Amanda Morter. (J). 2006. audio compact disk 14.99 (978-1-60247-056-9(1)) Tate Pubng.

Hush, My Baby. Amanda L. Morter. (ps). 2006. audio compact disk 12.99 (978-1-59886-725-1(3)) Tate Pubng.

Hushabye Trilogy; Dreamy Lullabyes to Ease Baby to Sleep. Andrew Stewart. 3 CDs. (Running Time: 3 hrs.). 1996. audio compact disk 19.95 (978-1-55961-411-5(0)) Relaxtn Co.

Hushabyes Trilogy. Andrew Stewart. 3 cass. (Running Time: 3 hrs.). (J). (ps-k). 1995. bk. 16.95 (978-1-55961-294-4(0)) Relaxtn Co.

Hushtown: Forest Community. Steck-Vaughn Staff. (J). 1999. (978-0-7398-0920-4(2)) SteckVau.

Husn-e-Jaana. Composed by Muzaffar Ali. 1 cass. 1997. (B97028); audio compact disk (CD B97028) Multi-Cultural Bks.

***Hustlin' Divas.** unabr. ed. De'nesha Diamond. (Running Time: 10 hrs.). 2010. 29.95 (978-1-4417-6579-6(4)); 59.95 (978-1-4417-6576-5(X)); audio compact disk 29.95 (978-1-4417-6578-9(6)); audio compact disk 90.00 (978-1-4417-6577-2(8)) Blckstn Audio.

***Hustling God: Why We Work So Hard for What God Wants to Give.** Zondervan. (Running Time: 6 hrs. 55 mins. 23 sec.). (ENG.). 2010. 9.99 (978-0-310-86943-6(9)) Zondervan.

Hustling on Gorky Street. unabr. ed. Yuri Brokhin. Read by Michael Prichard. 7 cass. (Running Time: 7 hrs.). 1976. 42.00 (978-0-7366-0006-4(X), 1016) Books on Tape.
The Soviet Union is generally perceived as a homogenous & uniform society. But this is not necessarily true. Within its confines, a whole universe of enterprise & opportunity abounds. Often delving into crime, prostitution & drugs, "Hustling on Gorky Street" is an expose of low-life in the Soviet Union.

Hutchinson-Gilford Progeria Syndrome - A Bibliography & Dictionary for Physicians, Patients, & Genome Researchers. Compiled by Icon Group International, Inc. Staff. 2007. ring bd. 28.95 (978-0-497-11236-3(1)) Icon Grp.

Huynh Quang Nhuong. Interview. Interview with Quang Nhuong Huynh & Kay Bonetti. 1 cass. (Running Time: 75 min.). 1985. 13.95 (978-1-55644-142-4(8), 5124) Am Audio Prose.
Talks about being drafted in the South Vietnamese Army. Although his sympathies lay with the North he felt he didn't have the "stuff of heroism" it took to live the life of a revolutionary. Wounded in battle five times & permanently paralyzed, he has lived in the U. S. since 1969.

Huysman's Pets. unabr. ed. Kate Wilhelm. (Running Time: 28800 sec.). 2007. 54.95 (978-1-4332-0718-1(4)); audio compact disk 29.95 (978-1-4332-0720-4(6)); audio compact disk 55.00 (978-1-4332-0719-8(2)) Blckstn Audio.

Hwyl a Hei Di Ho! Antur Penllyn & Y. Bala. 2005. audio compact disk 12.99 (978-88-88043-96-8(9)) Scuola Istruzione ITA.

Hwyl yr Wyl. Sain. 2005. audio compact disk 12.99 (978-88-88044-07-1(8)) Scuola Istruzione ITA.

Hyacinths to Feed the Soul: A Collection of Celtic. Trish Lindberg. 1 CD. 1999. audio compact disk 16.95 (978-1-893598-00-3(4)) Enfield Pubs NH.
A collection of celtic & contemporary songs.

Hyde. unabr. ed. Dan Mahoney. Read by Adams Morgan. 12 cass. (Running Time: 17 hrs. 30 mins.). 2000. 83.95 (978-0-7861-1755-0(9), 2559) Blckstn Audio.
NYPD Detective Brian McKenna is back where he belongs, hunting down a mysterious killer who preys upon the city's most forgotten members. At first blush, it seems as if these homeless men have frozen to death on the city streets. But this succession of deaths seems too suspicious for McKenna to ignore.

Hyde Park Headsman. unabr. ed. Anne Perry. Read by Terrence Hardiman. 12 vols. (Running Time: 54300 sec.). (Thomas Pitt Ser.). 2000. 96.95 (978-0-7927-2348-6(1), CSL 237, Chivers Sound Lib) AudioGO.
Not since the bloody deeds of Jack the Ripper have Londoners felt such terror as that aroused by the gruesome beheadings in Hyde Park. And if newly promoted Police Superintendent Thomas Pitt does not quickly apprehend the perpetrator, he is likely to lose his job. Yet even with the help of Charlotte Pitt's subtle investigation, the sinister violence continues. And in a shocking turn of events that nearly convinces the pair of sleuths that they have met their match, the case proves to be the Pitt's toughest ever.

Hyde Park Murder. unabr. ed. Elliott Roosevelt. Narrated by Frank Muller. 5 cass. (Running Time: 7 hrs.). (Eleanor Roosevelt Mystery Ser.: No. 2). 1986. 44.00 (978-1-55690-243-7(3), 86580E7) Recorded Bks.
Eleanor Roosevelt turns sleuth to solve the mystery of a dead stock-broker.

Hyderabad Brothers: Vocal. 1 cass. (Young Masters Ser.). 1992. (C92071) Multi-Cultural Bks.
Karnatic classical music.

Hyderabad Brothers: Vocal. 1 cass. (Dikshitar Masterpieces Ser.: Vol. 4). 1992. (C92051) Multi-Cultural Bks.

Hydraulic Measurements & Experimental Methods 2002: Proceedings of the Specialty Conference held in Estes Park, Colorado, July 28-August 1, 2002. Ed. by Tony L. Wahl & Clifford A. Pugh. 2002. audio compact disk 121.00 (978-0-7844-0655-7(3), 40655) Am Soc Civil Eng.

Hyena & the Moon: Stories to Listen to from Kenya. Heather McNeil. 1 cass. (Running Time: 60 min.). (World Folklore Ser.). (J). (gr. k-12). 11.00 (978-1-56308-397-6(3), X695) Libs Unl.
Selected tales recorded by the author in a shelf-ready case.

Hymn Before Battle. unabr. ed. John Ringo. Read by Marc Vietor. (Running Time: 14 hrs.). (Posleen War Ser.: No. 1). 2009. 24.99 (978-1-4233-9510-2(7), 9781423395102, Brilliance MP3); 39.97 (978-1-4233-9511-9(5), 9781423395119, Brlnc Audio MP3 Lib); 39.97 (978-1-4233-9512-6(3), 9781423395126, BADLE); audio compact disk 29.99 (978-1-4233-9508-9(5), 9781423395089, Bril Audio CD Unabri); audio compact disk 99.97 (978-1-4233-9509-6(3), 9781423395096, BriAudCD Unabrid) Brilliance Audio.

Hymn Festival. bk. 10.00 (978-0-687-04857-1(5)) Abingdon.

Hymn Makers 2. Created by Kingsway Music. 2007. audio compact disk 19.99 (978-5-557-90602-9(9)) Kingsway Pubns GBR.

Hymn of Creation. Joe Mattingly. 1 cass. 16.00 (978-1-58459-059-0(9)); 11.00 (978-1-58459-058-3(0)) Wrld Lib Pubns.
Contemporary collection of songs for Lent, Palm Sunday & the Trid.

Hymn Preludes for the Christmas Season. Composed by Robert E. Smith. 1 cass. 1998. audio compact disk 16.00 CD. (978-0-937690-51-2(1), 3024) Wrld Lib Pubns.
Religious music for the Christmas season.

Hymn to Adversity see Treasury of Oliver Goldsmith, Thomas Gray & William Collins

Hymn to Intellectual Beauty see Poetry of Shelley

Hymn to the Night see Treasury of Henry Wadsworth Longfellow

Hymned. Contrib. by Bart Millard. Prod. by Brown Bannister. 2005. audio compact disk 17.98 (978-5-558-93310-9(0)) INO Rec.

Hymns. Perf. by Cedarmont Kids. 1 cass. (J). 1999. 3.99 (978-0-00-504577-0(0)); audio compact disk 5.99 (978-0-00-507229-5(8)) Provident Music.

Hymns: 12 Songs. Perf. by Beth Neilsen Chapman. (Running Time: 35 mins.). 2004. audio compact disk (978-5-559-30407-6(7)) BNC Music.

Hymns & Bible Songs. 1 cass., 1 CD. (Running Time: 1 hr.). (Lullaby Ser.). (J). (TWIN 161); audio compact disk (TWIN 161) NewSound.

Hymns & Bible Songs. Compact Disc Staff. 1 cass.; 1 CD. (Running Time: 60 min.). (Growing Minds with Music Ser.). (J). 1998. audio compact disk 12.99 CD. (978-1-57583-065-0(5)) Twin Sisters.
Featuring the best-loved hymns & bible songs of all time, these thirty-three exquisitely arranged classics will bring joy to the soul & renew the mind.

Hymns & Bible Songs. Twin Sisters Productions Staff. 1 cass.; 1 CD. (Running Time: 60 min.). (Growing Minds with Music Ser.). (J). 1998. 8.99 (978-1-57583-066-7(3)) Twin Sisters.

Hymns & Carols for Worship: Vocal Solos for All Medium Range Voices. Ed. by James Curnow. 2007. pap. bk. 14.95 (978-90-431-2438-6(9), 9043124389) Pub: de Haske Pubns NLD. Dist(s): H Leonard

Hymns & Gospel Songs. Steve Amerson. 1999. 10.98 (978-7-83491-818-3(4)) Pub: Amerson Mus Min. Dist(s): STL Dist NA

Hymns & Gospel Songs. Steve Amerson. (Running Time: 30 min.). (ENG.). 2000. audio compact disk 15.98 (978-7-83491-821-3(4)) Pub: Amerson Mus Min. Dist(s): STL Dist NA

Hymns & Gospel Songs Tracks. Steve Amerson. (Running Time: 30 min.). (ENG.). 2007. audio compact disk 29.95 (978-7-83491-816-9(8)) Pub: Amerson Mus Min. Dist(s): STL Dist NA

Hymns & Gospel Tunes for Cello & Piano. Renata Bratt & Bert Ligon. (ENG.). 2009. pap. bk. 22.99 (978-0-7866-7755-9(4)) Mel Bay.

Hymns & Lullabies. 1 cass. (J). (978-0-7601-0179-7(5), C5578GP); audio compact disk (978-0-7601-0180-3(9), CD5578GP) Brentwood Music.
Beautiful songs of God's love softly lull your baby to sleep. Features: Brahms Lullaby, All Through the Night, Jesus Loves Me, Blessed Assurance & many more.

Hymns & Spiritual Songs, Set. Perf. by Cathedrals, The. 2 CDs. 1999. audio compact disk (978-0-7601-2733-9(6)) Brentwood Music.

Hymns & Spiritual Songs, Set. Perf. by Cathedrals, The. 2 cass. 1999. 16.99 (978-0-7601-2732-2(8)) Provident Music.

Hymns Collection. Contrib. by Anthony Burger & Luann Burger. (Gaither Gospel Ser.). 2008. audio compact disk 13.99 (978-5-557-42325-0(7)) Sprg Hill Music Group.

Hymns Continue. Perf. by Chicago Sings. 1 cass., 1 CD. 10.98 (978-1-57908-414-1(1), 1441); audio compact disk 15.98 CD. (978-1-57908-413-4(3), 1441) Platinm Enter.

Hymns for a Peaceful Sabbath. David Glen Hatch. 1 CD. audio compact disk 14.95 (2800926); 9.95 (10001271) Covenant Comms.
Hymns to enhance your family's Sabbath worship.

Hymns for a Peaceful Sabbath, No. 2. David Glen Hatch. 1 cass. 9.95 (10001425); audio compact disk 14.95 (28001087) Covenant Comms.

Hymns for Harmonica. Phil Duncan. 1 cass. pap. bk. 16.95 (93861P); 9.98 stereo. (93861C) Mel Bay.
Comprehensive collection of sacred songs, gospel songs, spirituals, & hymns arranged for solo performance by diatonic, chromatic, & cross-harp. All of the hymns are carefully arranged & flexible in usage.

Hymns for Living Vol. 1: Music for Courageous Living. 2002. audio compact disk 11.99 (978-1-57972-393-4(4)) Insight Living.

Hymns from the Bayou. 1 cd. audio compact disk 9.98 (978-1-57908-494-3(X), 5361) Platinm Enter.

Hymns From the Bayou, Set. unabr. ed. 1 cass., 1 CD. 7.98 (978-1-57908-495-0(8), 5361) Platinm Enter.

Hymns of Choice. Keith Christopher. 1997. 75.00 (978-0-7673-3122-7(2)); 11.98 (978-0-7673-3121-0(4)); audio compact disk 85.00 (978-0-7673-3123-4(0)) LifeWay Christian.

Hymns of Grace. Perf. by Choir of Grace Cathedral, San Francisco. 1 cass. 1998. 11.95 (MoreHse Pubng); audio compact disk 16.95 CD. (MoreHse Pubng) Church Pub Inc.
Organist John Fenstermaker & members of the Men & Boys choir perform favorite hymns including "Holy, Holy, Holy," "What Wondrous Love Is This," "Lift Every Voice" & more.

Hymns of Our Faith: St Paul's Church, Indianapolis, Indiana. Church Publishing. (ENG.). audio compact disk 18.00 (978-0-89869-284-6(9)) Church Pub Inc.

Hymns of the Faith. 2000. audio compact disk 50.00 (978-0-9707098-0-6(3)) B Hinn Min.

Hymns of the Faith. 2001. (978-1-59024-009-0(X)) B Hinn Min.

Hymns of the Faithful: Lent/Easter & Pentecost/Trinity. Richard Resch. audio compact disk 11.00 (978-0-570-07814-2(8), 20-2606) Concordia.

Hymns of the Faithful Series: CD of Advent/Christmas & Baptism/Communion. (Bible Studies). audio compact disk 11.00 (978-0-570-07940-8(3)) Concordia.

Hymns to Our Lady. Perf. by Mary Celeste & Mary Lyons. 1 cass. 5.25 (978-1-56036-033-9(X), 362735) AMI Pr.
"Fatima Ave" & other beautiful hymns.

Hymns We Love. 1 cass. (Running Time: 90 mins.). (Kidzup Ser.). (J). 2000. 8.99 (978-1-894281-51-5(9)) Pub: Kidzup CAN. Dist(s): Penton Overseas

Hymns We Love O/P. 1 CD. (Running Time: 90 mins.). (Kidzup Ser.). (J). 2000. audio compact disk 12.99 (978-1-894281-50-8(0)) Pub: Kidzup CAN. Dist(s): Penton Overseas

Hyp-No-Smoke: A self-hypnosis experiential smking cessation Program. Allen Chips. 1 CD. 2006. audio compact disk 14.95 (978-1-929661-26-8(6)) Transpersonal Pubng.

Hyper Javier Learns to Calm Down. Pamela M. Goldberg. Illus. by Jimmy Boring. (J). 2008. pap. bk. (978-0-9778941-6-1(9)) Camp MakeBelieve.

Hyperactive Children. Barrie Konicov. 1 cass. (YA). 11.98 (978-0-87082-334-3(5), 064) Potentials.
Shows how to improve the disposition of a hyperactive child.

Hyperbilirubinaemia & the Breastfeeding Infant, Module 2. Sally Page Goertz & Sarah McCamman. (Breastfeeding Management Ser.). (C). 2000. cd-rom 29.95 (978-0-7637-1131-3(4), 0763711314) Jones Bartlett.

Hypercard! Update & Trading Session. 2 cass. 1990. 16.00 set. Recorded Res.

Hypercoagulability in Prethrombotic States. Read by James L. Tullis. 1 cass. (Running Time: 90 min.). 1986. 12.00 (C8665) Amer Coll Phys.

Hyperdynamic Non-Dilated Cardiomyopathy: Diagnosis & Management. Read by William J. Powell, Jr. 1 cass. (Running Time: 90 min.). 1986. 12.00 (8608) Amer Coll Phys.

Hyperion. abr. ed. Dan Simmons. Read by Christopher Cazenove. 4 cass. (Running Time: 6 hrs.). 2001. 25.00 (978-1-57453-453-5(X)) Audio Lit.
On the world called Hyperion, beyond the law and the reach of twenty-eighth-century science, waits the creature called the Shrike. There are those who worship it. There are those who fear it. And there are those who have vowed to destroy it. In the Valley of the Time Tombs the Shrike waits for them all. On the eve of Armageddon, with the entire galaxy at war, seven pilgrims set forth on a final voyage to the Time Tombs. They seek the answers to the unsolved riddles of their lives and they have resolved to die before discovering anything less than the secrets of the universe itself.

Hyperion. unabr. ed. Dan Simmons. 2 MP3-CDs. (Running Time: 21 hrs.). (Hyperion Cantos Ser.). 2009. 44.97 (978-1-4233-8143-3(2), 9781423381433, Brlnc Audio MP3 Lib); 44.97 (978-1-4233-8144-0(0), 9781423381440, BADLE); 29.99 (978-1-4233-8142-6(4), 9781423381426, Brilliance MP3); audio compact disk 99.97 (978-1-4233-8141-9(6), 9781423381419, BriAudCD Unabrid); audio compact disk 49.99 (978-1-4233-8140-2(8), 9781423381402, Bril Audio CD Unabri) Brilliance Audio.

Hyperlipidemia: When & How to Treat for Prevention of Coronary Heart Disease. Read by Antonia M. Gotto, Jr. 1 cass. (Running Time: 90 min.). 1985. 12.00 (C852 8) Amer Coll Phys.

Hypersensitive Airways, Cough & Asthma. Moderated by E. R. McFadden, Jr. Contrib. by C. E. Reed et al. 1 cass. (Running Time: 90 min.). 1985. 12.00 (A8501) Amer Coll Phys.
Discussed by a moderator & experts who offer differing opinions.

Hypersexuality: Program from the Award Winning Public Radio Series. Hosted by Fred Goodwin. Comment by John Hockenberry. Contrib. by Julia T. Moore et al. 1 cass. (Running Time: 1 hr.). (Infinite Mind Ser.). 1998. audio compact disk 21.95 (978-1-888064-52-0(8), LCM 3) Lichtenstein Creat.
Why in her right mind would a 36-year-old school teacher have sex with a 13-year-old boy? And when she was released from prison on the strict condition that she never see him again, why would she go right back to him? Her doctor and her lawyer say there is good evidence that she was not in her right mind at all. Their position is that a mental illness, manic depressive illness, and a condition often related to manic depression - called hypersexuality - provides an explanation for her seemingly irrational behavior.

Hypershot. abr. ed. Trevor Scott. 2 cass. (Running Time: 3 hrs.). (Hot Pursuit Ser.). 2004. 18.00 (978-1-58807-337-2(8)) Am Pubng Inc.
In a time when the U.S. military is shrinking, our leaders are turning to high technology as a force equalizer. America has not had a new hand-held rifle since the M16 was introduced in the 1960s. Now there's a new gun ready to take its position as the NATO standard. A gun so sophisticated, so fast, so unbelievably accurate, it will turn the average shooter into an expert marksman instantly. The problem is, it was developed by a German company with no U.S. production contract. That's where Warfield Arms, a Denver gun company, enters the action. Warfield hires Chad Hunter, a private weapons designer who had worked for the German company, to go to Germany to convince the company that Warfield is the perfect partner. To sweeten the deal, Hunter must first convince Frank Baldwin, a struggling optics engineer from Wyoming, who has developed the most advanced rifle scope ever conceived, that his scope would be the perfect match for this new German rifle. With the scope as bait, the Germans would surely deal. What Hunter and Baldwin find in Germany during the middle of the Oktoberfest celebration, could just get them both killed. Other countries and private factions would like this new weapon, and some in Germany want it only for that country. There's murder, kidnapping, extortion, and shoot-outs.... Who said the end of the Cold War wouldn't be any fun?.

Hypersonic: Praise House Two. Contrib. by Ian Eskelin. 10.98 (978-0-7601-1155-0(3), C70009) Pub: Brentwood Music. Dist(s): Provident Mus Dist
Combines popular praise & worship choruses with modern sounds & textures that add new life to these beloved lyrics.

Hyperspace & Creation of the Universe. Michio Kaku. 2 cass. 1993. 18.00 set. (OC331-70) Sound Horizons AV.

Hypertension. Steven Gurgevich. (ENG.). 2002. audio compact disk 19.95 (978-1-932170-10-8(3), HWH) Tranceformation.

Hypertension. unabr. ed. Read by Robert A. Monroe. 1 cass. (Running Time: 30 min.). (Human Plus Ser.). 1990. 14.95 (978-1-56102-054-6(0)) Inter Indus.
Provides natural tool for listener to use for self regulation of blood pressure.

Hypertension or High Blood Pressure: Hipertension o Presion Arterial Alta. Lilly B. Gardner. Contrib. by Ann J. Gardner. 1 cass. (Running Time: 20 min.). 1997. 20.00 Incl. bklet, recipe cards, sample nutrition labels, boxed kit. (978-0-9659500-3-9(4)) Precepts.

Hyperwars: Eleven Strategies for Survival & Profit in the Era of on-Line Business. Bruce Judson. Told to Kate Kelly. 2004. 10.95 (978-0-7435-4856-4(6)) Pub: S&S Audio. Dist(s): S and S Inc

Hypno Music. Ormond McGill. 2000. (978-1-933332-22-2(0)) Hypnotherapy Train.

Hypno Music. Ormond McGill. 2003. audio compact disk (978-1-933332-29-1(8)) Hypnotherapy Train.

Hypno-Peripheral Processing Tapes, Set. Lloyd Glauberman. 12 cass. (Running Time: 30 min. per cass.). 34.95 (G851X); 175.00 set. Nightingale-Conant.
This breakthrough psychotechnology program combines the methods of hypnotherapy with the latest teachings of Neuro-Linguistic Programming. Each high-impact tape gently overloads your conscious mind with messages on two channels at once, creating a synergistic whole that unleashes both hemispheres of your brain. Includes The Quset for Excellence: A Personal Guide to High Performance, No.851PA-1X; Personal Ecology: The Complete Self-Esteem Program, No. 851PA-2X; Changing Emotions: A Stress-Management Program, No. 851PA-3X; Overcoming Procrastination: A Rhythmic Approach, No. 851PA-4X; Inside/Outside: The Motivational Weight-Loss Program, No. 851PA-5X; Feeling Better: The Mind/Body Connection, No. 851PA-6X.

Hypno Trips. Dean A. Montalbano. 4 cds. (Running Time: 5.5 hrs). (Hypnotic Sensory Response Audio Ser.). 2004. audio compact disk 89.95 (978-1-932086-19-5(6)) L Lizards Pub Co.

Hypno Trips: An HSR Trance Formation Tape. Dean A. Montalbano. 6 Cass. (Running Time: 6 hours). (C). 2002. 95.00 (978-1-932086-01-0(3)) L Lizards Pub Co.
This state of the art in recreational hypnosis allows you to experience hypnotic drugs states, astral travel, remote viewing and MUCH MUCH MORE!.

***Hypnodiet: The Mindful Way to Lose Weight - Forever.** Susan Hepburn. (Running Time: 2 hrs. 8 mins.). (ENG.). 2010. audio compact disk (978-1-4055-0778-3(0), HachetteDig UK) Little BrownUK GBR.

HypnoDreams 1: The Wisdom of the Water. Silvia Hartmann & Ananga Sivyer. 2002. audio compact disk 44.95 (978-1-873483-08-4(2)) DragonRising GBR.

HypnoDreams 2: Heart Healing. Silvia Hartmann & Ananga Sivyer. 2003. bk. 44.95 (978-1-873483-09-1(0)) DragonRising GBR.

HypnoDreams 3: Freedom. Silvia Hartmann & Ananga Sivyer. 2004. audio compact disk 44.95 (978-1-873483-10-7(4)) DragonRising GBR.

Hypnography. Sean Ryan. 2005. audio compact disk 14.99 (978-0-9663619-3-3(8), SE Pubng) Sophie Ent.

Hypnography: Spirit in the Night. Sean Ryan. 1 cass. (Running Time: 30 min.). 1997. audio compact disk 19.95 CD. (978-0-9663619-0-2(3)) Sophie Ent.
Improves a man's sexuality & can help impotence.

Hypnography for Men. Sean Ryan. 1999. 11.95 (978-1-886238-27-5(8)) Passion Press.

Hypnography for Men. unabr. ed. Sean Ryan. (Running Time: 60 min.). 1999. audio compact disk 16.95 (978-1-886238-25-1(1)) Passion Press.

Hypnography for Women. Sean Ryan. (Running Time: 60 min.). 1999. 11.95 (978-1-886238-29-9(4)); audio compact disk 16.95 (978-1-886238-28-2(6)) Passion Press.

Hypnomeditation / the Vital Energy of Life. Ormond McGill. 2 sided cassette. 2000. (978-1-933332-00-0(X)) Hypnotherapy Train.

Hypnomeditation / the Vital Energy of Life. Ormond McGill. 1 cassette - 2 sides. 2002. audio compact disk (978-1-933332-24-6(7)) Hypnotherapy Train.

Hypnomeditation for Activating the Chakras. Ormond McGill. 2000. (978-1-933332-15-4(8)) Hypnotherapy Train.

Hypnomeditation for Activating the Chakras. Ormond McGill. 2005. audio compact disk (978-1-933332-33-8(6)) Hypnotherapy Train.

HypnoSex. Created by Victoria Wizell. Voice by Victoria Wizell. 1 CD. 2001. audio compact disk 29.00 (978-0-9679176-7-2(0)) Hyptalk.
Utilize the power of your subconscious mind to stimulate your sexual senses! Hypnosis naturally allows you to tap into a great resource to stir up incredibly erotic sexual pleasure. In HypnoSex, you will create in your mind and stimulate within your physical body, an enlivened and heightened sexual response.

Hypnosis: Exploring Past Lives. unabr. ed. Osho Oshos. Read by Osho Oshos. 2 cass. (Running Time: 2 hrs.). 1992. 15.95 set. (DRC-042986A) Oshos.
The simple method of using hypnosis to explore past births, deaths & lives, the layers of collective & cosmic unconsciousness as well as the three peaks of superconsciousness.

Hypnosis: Program from the Award Winning Public Radio Series. Interview. Hosted by Fred Goodwin. Comment by John Hockenberry. 1 CD. (Running Time: 1hr). (Infinite Mind Ser.). 2002. audio compact disk 21.95 (978-1-888064-83-4(8), LCM 214) Lichtenstein Creat.
"You are growing verrrr-yyyyy sleeee-ppy." You may have heard Hollywood's version of hypnosis. This week, "The Infinite Mind" explores the science behind hypnosis and how it really works. We look at how and why medical doctors, dentists, therapists, and police investigators use this powerful tool to soothe pain, lose bad habits, reconstruct memories, and even solve crimes. Experts in hypnosis separate science fact from science fiction, answering questions like "Could a hypnotist make someone fall in love through hypnosis?" and "Could an unscrupulous person use hypnosis to make someone commit a crime?" Guests include Dr. David Spiegel, Professor and Associate Chair of Psychiatry and Behavioral Sciences at Stanford University School of Medicine; Jane Parsons-Fein, Director of the Parsons-Fein Institute for Hypnosis and Psychotherapy; Alan Scheflin, Professor of Law at Santa Clara University; and forensic psychologist Dr. Melvin Gravitz. Plus commentary - with a nod to Dick van Dyke - from John Hockenberry.

Hypnosis: Treasures & Dragons. unabr. ed. Osho Oshos. Read by Osho Oshos. 2 cass. (Running Time: 2 hrs.). 1992. 15.95 set. (DPA-051286A) Oshos.
Explains how to use hypnosis to unlock both the treasures of the superconscious & the dragons of the unconscious & how both can be used to support spiritual growth.

Hypnosis: Using the Mind-Body Connection. Steven Gurgevich. Prod. by Steven Gurgevich. 4 CDs. (Running Time: 5 hrs.). (ENG.). 2001. audio compact disk 59.95 (978-1-932170-00-9(6), Album1CD, HWH) Tranceformation.
An instructional seminar on hypnosis and autosuggestion that was created for you by Dr. Steven Gurgevich. It is not a recording of a previously live seminar... this one was made specifically for you. A full length practice tape is included. On this album, Dr. Gurgevich teaches you on a wide range of topics about hypnosis, including: hypnotic induction methods, myths and misconceptions, characteristics and levels of trance, the language of the subconscious mind, formulating autosuggestions, testing hypnotizability, use of tape recordings, clinical versus stage hypnosis, cautions of hypnosis, techniques of self-hypnosis, instruction in self-hypnosis and using hypnosis and autosuggestion for physical and mental health, mental conditioning, mental rehearsal, positive self-imaging, habit control, stress management, relaxation, and much more.

Hypnosis Alcohol Treatment: Staying Sober Through Hypnosis. Trevor H. Scott. 2005. audio compact disk 19.95 (978-0-9763138-8-5(X)) Beverly Hills CA.

Hypnosis Collection of Stories That Change: An HSR Trance Formation Tape. Dean A. Montalbano. 6. (Running Time: 4hrs 25 minutes). 2002. 95.00 (978-1-932086-03-4(X)) L Lizards Pub Co.

Hypnosis Demonstration. unabr. ed. George W. Kisker. 1 cass. (Running Time: 17 min.). 12.95 (29206) J Norton Pubs.
A complete hypnosis session for large or small groups. The recording demonstrates hypnosis induction by means of progressive relaxation. Induces hypnosis, tests for depth of hypnosis, & brings the subject out of hypnosis.

Hypnosis for a Good Night's Sleep. Ormond McGill. 1 cass. 1998. (978-1-933332-39-0(5)) Hypnotherapy Train.

Hypnosis for Anxiety Relief. Created by Victoria Wizell. Voice by Victoria Wizell. 2 CDs. 2001. audio compact disk 49.00 (978-0-9679176-8-9(9)) Hyptalk.
You will love the deep relaxation you will experience from each of these techniques and they will be useful in other situations in your life as well or just give you a nice feeling of peace within.

Hypnosis for Childbirth: Labor of Love. Created by Wendi Friesen. Prod. by Wendi.com Staff. 3 CDS. 2004. spiral bd. 149.00 (978-1-929058-80-8(2)) Wendicom.

Hypnosis for Confidence & Power. Based on a book by Wendi Friesen. 2 CDs. (Running Time: 5 Tracks). 2002. audio compact disk 49.00 (978-1-929058-03-7(9)) Wendicom.

Hypnosis for Coping Before & after Surgery. abr. ed. Josie Hadley. 1 cass. (Running Time: 1 hr.). (Health Ser.). 1997. 11.95 (978-1-57224-091-9(1)) New Harbinger.

Hypnosis for Cultivating Intuition. Perf. by Janet I. Decker. Created by Janet I. Decker. 1 CD. (Running Time: 46 min.). 2001. audio compact disk 16.95 (978-0-9709726-1-3(X)) Pub: Hypno Services. Dist(s): Baker Taylor
This Audio CD contains 2 programs. Program 1: "Hypnosis for Cultivating Intuition". Your intuition is your "inner guidance system". You can make it work for you. Verbal step-by-step instructions gently guide the listener into a hypnotic trance state. Positive suggestions are then given to the subconscious mind to help encourage and strengthen the listener's intuitive ability otherwise known as the "6th" sense and often referred to as that "gut feeling". With regular use the listener can learn to "feel" as well as see, hear, taste, touch and smell. Program 2: "Relax and Improve Your Intuition". Step-by-step instructions guide the listener into a deeply relaxed trance state. Deep relaxation is extremely beneficial to mind, body and spirit. Program 2 enhances the effects of program 1. Program 1 and program 2 may be used independently of each other. An enclosed booklet describes what hypnosis is and how best to use this CD to achieve the greatest results. Effects will vary from person to person. Hypnotherapy is considered "complimentary medicine" and is not intended to be used in place of medical or psychiatric care. (The Wolf on the cover of this audio CD represents what this hypnotic audio product can do for you. Wolf: Friendly, social, highly intelligent with a powerfully developed "intuitive" sense.).

Hypnosis for Health: Smoking Cessation & Weight Loss. Bo Sebastian. 1998. 9.99 (978-0-9646712-1-8(2)) B Sebastian.

Hypnosis for Hypnotists. Barrie Konicov. 1 cass. 11.98 (978-0-87082-300-8(0), 065) Potentials.
To become a truly outstanding hypnotist, you must take on the consciousness of a professional. This tape, will help anyone become interested in hypnosis as a profession.

Hypnosis for Overcoming Anger. Perf. by Janet I. Decker. Created by Janet I. Decker. 1 CD. (Running Time: 51 min.). 2001. audio compact disk 16.95 (978-0-9709726-6-8(0)) Pub: Hypno Services. Dist(s): Baker Taylor
This Audio CD contains 2 programs. Program 1: "Hypnosis for Overcoming Anger". Anger can become a thing of the past. Verbal step-by-step instructions gently guide the listener into a hypnotic trance state. Positive suggestions are then given to the subconscious mind to help calm the emotions so that life situations may be handled calmly, coolly and sensibly. Program 2: "Relax and Release Anger". Step-by-step instructions guide the listener into a deeply relaxed trance state. Deep relaxation is extremely beneficial to mind, body and spirit. Program 2 enhances the effects of program 1. Program 1 and program 2 may be used independently of each other. An enclosed booklet describes what hypnosis is and how best to use this CD to achieve the greatest results. Effects will vary from person to person. Hypnotherapy is considered "complimentary medicine" and is not intended to be used in place of medical or psychiatric care. (The deer on the cover of this audio CD represents what this hypnotic audio product can do for you. Deer: A gentle adaptable animal. The embodiment of serenity.).

Hypnosis for Overcoming Depression. abr. ed. Josie Hadley. Read by Josie Hadley. 1 cass. (Running Time: 60 min.). (Hypnosis Tape Ser.). 1997. 11.95 (978-1-57224-090-2(3), 63) New Harbinger.
Based on the book Hypnosis for Change. (HYP2). Approximately 60 minutes, no music.

Hypnosis for Pain Reduction - The Magic Pond. Michael Robinson. Narrated by Michael Robinson. Composed by Annie Schiola. Engineer Annie Schiola. 1 CD. (Running Time: 18 min.). 2003. audio compact disk 24.00 (978-0-9745230-2-6(X)) Loxias Audio Pub.
So the doctor tells you that you have to live with the pain. There are alternatives. Let Michael Robinson, SWA, help you to learn how to refocus your mind. Replace the pain with a more pleasant feeling by wading into the Magic Pond. The music and nature sounds by Annie Schiola travel along the same neuropathways to help synchronize your body with your mind to help you dilute the pain signal.

Hypnosis for Physical Improvement, Body Mastery Program. Wendi Friesen. 4 CDs. (Running Time: Nine Sessions). 2002. audio compact disk 99.00 (978-1-929058-08-2(X)) Wendicom.

Hypnosis for Psychic Development. Perf. by Janet I. Decker. Created by Janet I. Decker. 1 CD. (Running Time: 46 min.). 2001. audio compact disk 16.95 (978-0-9709726-2-0(8)) Pub: Hypno Services. Dist(s): Baker Taylor
This Audio CD contains 2 programs. Program 1: "Hypnosis for Psychic Development". Being Psychic is your brithright. Verbal step-by-step instructions gently guide the listener into a hypnotic trance state. Positive suggestions are then given to the subconscious mind to help encourage the "awakening" or "opening" of the "psychic center" otherwise known as the "third eye". With regular use the listener can discover just how incredible their mind really is. Program 2: "Relax and Develop Your Psychic Ability". Step-by-step instructions guide the listener into a deeply relaxed trance state. Deep relaxation is extremely beneficial to mind, body and spirit. Program 2 enhances the effects of program 1. Program 1 and program 2 may be used independently of each other. An enclosed booklet describes what hypnosis is and how best to use this CD to achieve the greatest results. Effects will vary from person to person. Hypnotherapy is considered "complimentary medicine" and is not intended to be used in place of medical or psychiatric care. (The black cat on the cover of this audio CD represents what this hypnotic audio product can do for you. Black Cat: Both the color and the animal denote mystery...that which is unrevealed. A powerfully psychic animal!).

Hypnosis for Relaxation. 2009. audio compact disk 30.00 (978-1-4276-3800-7(4)) AardGP.

Hypnosis for Relaxation - Peaceful Mountains. Michael Robinson. Narrated by Michael Robinson. Composed by Annie Schiola. Engineer Annie Schiola. 1 CD. (Running Time: 17 min.). 2003. audio compact disk 24.00 (978-0-9745230-0-2(3)) Loxias Audio Pub.
Take a break from all the tensions and worries of the day. Let Michael Robinson, SWA, be your personal tour guide to the deepest levels of relaxation and calm. The music and nature sounds by Annie Schiola will stimulate your imagination. You'll feel better than you have all day after you've visited the Peaceful Mountains.

Hypnosis for Remote Psychic Seduction. Wendi Johnson. Two cass. (Running Time: 2 sessions). 2002. audio compact disk 39.00 (978-1-929058-07-5(1)) Wendicom.

Hypnosis for Self-Confidence & Self-Esteem. Perf. by Janet I. Decker. Created by Janet I. Decker. 1 CD. (Running Time: 44 min.). 2001. audio compact disk 16.95 (978-0-9709726-7-5(9)) Pub: Hypno Services. Dist(s): Baker Taylor

Hypnosis for Sleep. abr. ed. Josie Hadley & Carol Staudacher. Read by Josie Hadley & Carol Staudacher. 1 cass. (Running Time: 44 min.). (Hypnosis Tape Ser.). 1987. 11.95 (978-0-934986-40-3(1), 21) New Harbinger.
Modifying your bedtime routine, turning off worry, using hypnosis for deep, restful sleep, awakening on time, and feeling refreshed. Voice only, no music.

Hypnosis for Stress Reduction. Perf. by Janet I. Decker. Created by Janet I. Decker. 1 CD. (Running Time: 48 min.). 2001. audio compact disk 16.95 (978-0-9709726-3-7(6)) Pub: Hypno Services. Dist(s): Baker Taylor
This Audio CD contains 2 programs. Program 1: "Hypnosis for Stress Reduction". Stress, and stress related illness, can be a thing of the past. Verbal step-by-step instructions gently guide the listener into a hypnotic trance state. Positive suggestions are then given to the subconscious mind to help relieve the accumulated stress and tension of everyday life. With regular use the listener can discover what it is like to be at peace with themselves and the world around them. Program 2: "Relax and Relieve Stress". Step-by-step instructions guide the listener into a deeply relaxed trance state. Deep relaxation is extremely beneficial to mind, body and spirit. Program 2 enhances the effects of Program 1 and Program 2 may be used independently of each other. An enclosed booklet describes what hypnosis is and how best to use this CD to achieve the greatest results. Effects will vary from person to person. Hypnotherapy is considered "complimentary medicine" and is not intended to be used in place of medical or psychiatric care. (The rabbit on the cover of this audio CD represents what this hypnotic audio product can do for you.Rabbit: Rabbits exude a sense of peacefulness and are very fertile creatures. Stress blocks creative fertility.).

Hypnosis for Therapists... Squeeze the Sponge. 2004. audio compact disk (978-1-932163-61-2(1)) Infinity Inst.

Hypnosis for Weight Loss: The Road of Decision. Michael Robinson. Narrated by Michael Robinson. Composed by Annie Schiola. Engineer Annie Schiola. 1 CD. (Running Time: 29 mins, 30 sec.). 2003. audio compact disk 24.00 (978-0-9745230-1-9(1)) Loxias Audio Pub.
Which ever diet you've chosen, reinforce your desire to stay on the right path with newer, healthier eating behaviors using The Road of Decision. Michael Robinson, SWA, guides you thru the decision making process on the unconscious level to help you to make the changes that you want to make. The music by Annie Schiola is composed to further stimulate the right hemisphere of the brain to strengthen your new decision pathways.

Hypnosis for Weight Loss, Weight Release. Wendi Friesen. 4 CDs. (Running Time: Eight Sessions). 2002. audio compact disk 89.00 (978-1-929058-06-8(3)) Wendicom.

Hypnosis to Help You Sleep Deeply. Perf. by Janet I. Decker. Created by Janet I. Decker. 1 CD. (Running Time: 40 min.). 2001. audio compact disk 16.95 (978-0-9709726-5-1(2)) Pub: Hypno Services. Dist(s): Baker Taylor
This Audio CD contains 2 programs. Program 1: "Hypnosis to Help You Sleep Deeply". Hypnotically induced sleep is a natural, restful sleep. Verbal step-by-step instructions gently consider the listener into a hypnotic trance state. Positive suggestions are then given to the subconscious mind to help induce a deep, sound, natural, and restful sleep. The listener will awaken fully rested and refreshed, at their desired time, ready to begin their day. Program 2: "Relax and Sleep Deeply". Step-by-step instructions guide the listener into a deeply relaxed trance state. Deep relaxation is extremely beneficial to mind, body and spirit. Program 2 enhances the effects of program 1. Program 1 and program 2 may be used independently of each other. An enclosed booklet describes what hypnosis is and how best to use this CD to achieve the greatest results. Effects will vary from person to person. Hypnotherapy is considered "complimentary medicine" and is not intended to be used in place of medical or psychiatric care. (The bear on the cover of this audio CD represents what this hypnotic audio product can do for you. Bear: Deep sleep (hibernation) comes naturally to bears. Bears give birth during their deep sleep period. Deep sleep enables productivity as well as creativity.).

Hypnosis to Improve Memory & Recall. Perf. by Janet I. Decker. Created by Janet I. Decker. 1 CD. (Running Time: 40 min). 2001. audio compact disk 16.95 (978-0-9709726-4-4(4)) Pub: Hypno Services. Dist(s): Baker Taylor
This Audio CD contains 2 programs. Program 1: "Hypnosis to Improve Memory and Recall". Give yourself the gift of an excellent memory. Verbal step-by-step instructions gently guide the listener into a hypnotic trance state. Positive suggestions are then given to the subconscious mind to help improve memory and recall. With regular use the listener can easily recall everything they ave seen, heard, smelled, touched, tasted and experienced. Program 2: "Relax and Improve Your Memory". Step-by-step instructions guide the listener into a deeply relaxed trance state. Deep relaxation is extremely beneficial to mind, body and spirit. Program 2 enhances the effects of program 1. Program 1 and 2 may be used independently of each other. An enclosed booklet describes what hypnosis is and how best to use this CD to achieve the greatest results. Effects will vary from person to person. Hypnotherapy is considered "complimentary medicine" and is not intended to be used in place of medical or psychiatric care. (The raven on the cover of this audio represents what this hypnotic audio product can do for you. Raven: Perhaps the most intelligent of all birds. Bearing an exceptional gift of memory.

Hypnotherapy: An Alternative Path to Health & Happiness. Kweethai Neill. Ed. by Steve Stork. (ENG.). 2009. audio compact disk 29.98 (978-0-9816385-2-2(X)) iChange.

Hypnotherapy: An Exploratory Casebook. Milton H. Erickson & Ernest L. Rossi. Intro. by Sidney Rosen. 1980. bk. 49.95 (978-0-8290-0347-5(9)) Ardent Media.

Hypnotherapy of Cosmic Love. Ormond McGill. 2000. (978-1-933332-16-1(6)) Hypnotherapy Train.

Hypnotic Awakening for Spirit Contact. Perf. by Janet I. Decker. Created by Janet I. Decker. 1 CD. (Running Time: 44 min.). 2001. audio compact disk 16.95 (978-0-9709726-0-6(1)) Pub: Hypno Services. Dist(s): Baker Taylor
This Audio CD contains 2 programs. Program 1: "Hypnotic Awakening for Spirit Contact". Open the door to other planes of existence. Verbal step-by-step instructions gently guide the listener into a hypnotic trance state. Positive suggestions are then given to the subconscious mind to help pierce the veil between the worlds. With regular use the listener can connect with their Angel, Spirit Guide, or loved ones who have crossed over. The veil is thinner than you think! Program 2: Relax and Experience Spirit Contact". Step-by-step instructions guide the listener into a deeply relaxed trance state. Deep relaxation is extremely beneficial to mind, body and spirit. Program 2 enhances the effects of program 1. Program 1 and program 2 may be used independently of each other. An enclosed booklet describes what hypnosis is and how best to use this CD to achieve the greatest results. Effects will vary from person to person. Hypnotherapy is considered "complimentary medicine" and is not intended to be used in place of medical or psychiatric care. (The owl on the cover of this audio CD represents what this hypnotic audio product can do for you. Owl: Bird of magic and darkness. Symbol of spirit and ghostly contact.).

Hypnotic Methods in Nonhypnotic Therapies. Aaron N. Hoorwitz. Frwd. by John J. O'Connor. 1989. bk. (978-0-318-61268-3(2)) Irvington.

Hypnotic Realities: The Induction of Clinical Hypnosis & Forms of Indirect Suggestion. Milton H. Erickson et al. 1976. reel tape 39.95 (978-0-8290-0112-9(3)) Ardent Media.

Hypnotic Sounds: Crickets - Woodland Birds. 1 cass. (Running Time: 60 min.). (YA). 11.98 (978-0-87082-853-9(3), 157) Potentials.
Soft trilling recalls the sounds of a sweet, summer evening. Relax & return to a twilight time & place. Enter a forest of audio delights. Cheerful twittering and chirping fill the woodland air. Designed to heighten your senses & improve your experience with self hypnosis.

Hypnotic Sounds: Heartbeat - Metronome. 1 cass. (YA). 11.98 (978-0-87082-850-8(9), 058) Potentials.
Tune into your body & feel, then hear the sound of your heart. Experience the constant rhythym of a metronome, set to move you into a deep state of self-hypnosis.

Hypnotic Sounds: Ocean - Thunder Storm. 1 cass. (YA). 11.98 (978-0-87082-851-5(7), 090) Potentials.
Close your eyes & picture waves crashing to shore, designed to heighten your senses & improve your experience with self-hypnosis.

Hypnotic Sounds: Summer Brook - Pattering Rain. 1 cass. (YA). 11.98 (978-0-87082-852-2(5), 155) Potentials.
The steady pattern of falling raindrops creates a totally relaxing atmosphere of gentleness. Rushing, falling, churning - the delightful sounds of a clear - running brook swirling down a mountainside. Designed to heighten your senses & improve your experience with self hypnosis.

Hypnotic Sounds: Windy Day - Seagulls. 1 cass. 11.98 (978-0-87082-854-6(1), 156) Potentials.
Blow away all cares, as running currents of wind carry you off to a vibrant place of your own. Recall the times of sand & shore, heightened by the sounds of a true seabird calling the seagull. Designed to heighten your senses & improve your experience with self hypnosis.

Hypnotic Techniques. unabr. ed. David Calof. 1 cass. (Running Time: 7 hrs.). 1988. 69.95 (978-1-884605-05-5(2)) Genesis II.
Direct & indirect inductions, hypnotic phenomena demonstrated, discussed & utilized. Pre-induction talk, client assessment, symptom utilization & history of hypnosis.

Hypnotic Time Travel CD Album. Bruce Goldberg. (ENG.). 2005. audio compact disk 75.00 (978-1-57968-023-7(2)) Pub: B Goldberg. Dist(s): Baker Taylor

Hypnotic Time Travel with Dr. Bruce Goldberg, Set. Bruce Goldberg. 6 cass. (ENG.). 2006. vinyl bd. 65.00 (978-1-885577-01-6(X)) Pub: B Goldberg. Dist(s): Baker Taylor
Self hypnosis program includes: Age Regression; Past Life Regression; Future Life Progression; Superconscious Mind; Out of Body Experience; Soul Plane Ascension.

Hypnotic Yoga. Created by Victoria Wizell. Voice by Victoria Wizell. 1 CD. 2003. audio compact disk 39.00 (978-0-9679176-4-1(6)) Hyptalk.
Become more in touch with your body. Hypnosis will help you to create a great sense of confidence in your abilities as well as enhance the strength and balance you feel during your Yoga practice as well as other times. Use the magical wisdom of your body to create more inner connection, inner quiet, and relaxation helping your stretching to go beyond old levels.

Hypnotist. unabr. ed. M. J. Rose. Read by Phil Gigante. 1 MP3-CD. (Running Time: 11 hrs.). (Reincarnationist Ser.). 2010. 24.99 (978-1-4233-9024-4(5), 9781423390244, Brilliance MP3); 24.99 (978-1-4233-9026-8(1), 9781423390268, BAD); 39.97 (978-1-4233-9025-1(3), 9781423390251, Brlnc Audio MP3 Lib); 39.97 (978-1-4233-9027-5(X), 9781423390275, BADLE); audio compact disk 34.99 (978-1-4233-9022-0(9), 9781423390220, Bril Audio CD Unabri); audio compact disk 99.97 (978-1-4233-9023-7(7), 9781423390237, BriAudCD Unabrid) Brilliance Audio.

Hypnotize Your Lover: Master the Art of Hypnotic Seduction, Set. Wendi Friesen. 2 cass. 1999. 39.95 (978-1-929058-01-3(2)) Wendicom.
Master the art of hypnotic sedction stimulate your lover with erotic hypnosis scripts. Release sexual dysfunction This is the second printing. This version is now being shipped, with many more scripts and stories, and ideas.

Hypnotize Your Lover... Deeper. Wendi Friesen. 2 cass. (Running Time: 2 hrs.). 2002. pap. bk. 49.00 (978-1-929058-15-0(2)) Wendicom.

***Hypnotize Yourself to a Worry-Free Life: America's #1 Self-Hypnosis Coach.** unabr. ed. Made for Success. Read by Crystal Dwyer. (Running Time: 4 hrs.). (Made for Success Ser.). 2010. audio compact disk 29.95 (978-1-4417-6784-4(3)) Blckstn Audio.

***Hypnotize Yourself to a Worry-Free Life (Library Edition) America's #1 Self-Hypnosis Coach.** unabr. ed. Made for Success. Read by Crystal Dwyer. (Running Time: 4 hrs.). (Made for Success Ser.). 2010. audio compact disk 90.00 (978-1-4417-6783-7(5)) Blckstn Audio.

Hypo & Hypernatremia. Read by Samuel O. Thier. 1 cass. (Running Time: 90 min.). 1986. 12.00 (C8668) Amer Coll Phys.

Hypochondria: Program from the Award Winning Public Radio Series. 1 CD. (Running Time: 60 mins). (Infinite Mind Ser.). 2003. audio compact disk 21.95 (978-1-932479-08-9(2), LCM 254) Lichtenstein Creat.
It's the butt of jokes and the bane of the medical community, but hypochondria is a real illness, and people with it suffer real pain. We'll explore everything from the history of the disorder to the latest treatments. Guests include: Dr. Arthur Barsky, a professor of psychiatry at Harvard Medical School and the director of psychosomatic research at Brigham and Women's Hospital in Boston; Carla Cantor, the author of Phantom Illness: Recognizing, Understanding, and Overcoming Hypochondria; Dr. Susan Baur, the author of Hypochondria: Woeful Imaginings; and Gene Weingarten, a humor columnist for The Washington Post and the author of The Hypochondriac's Guide to Life. And Death.

***Hypochondriacs: Nine Tormented Lives.** unabr. ed. Brian Dillon. Read by William Dufris. (Running Time: 9 hrs. 30 mins.). 2011. 29.95 (978-1-4417-5761-6(9)); 59.95 (978-1-4417-5757-9(0)); audio compact disk 90.00 (978-1-4417-5758-6(9)) Blckstn Audio.

Hypochondrogenesis - A Bibliography & Dictionary for Physicians, Patients, & Genome Researchers. Compiled by Icon Group International, Inc. Staff. 2007. ring bd. 28.95 (978-0-497-11237-0(X)) Icon Grp.

Hypochondroplasia - A Bibliography & Dictionary for Physicians, Patients, & Genome Researchers. Compiled by Icon Group International, Inc. Staff. 2007. ring bd. 28.95 (978-0-497-11238-7(8)) Icon Grp.

Hypocrisy. (712) Yoga Res Foun.

Hypocrisy. Swami Jyotirmayananda. 1 cass. (Running Time: 1 hr.). 1990. 12.99 Yoga Res Foun.

Hypocrisy. unabr. ed. Herman Kahn. 1 cass. (Running Time: 1 hr. 22 min.). 12.95 (217) J Norton Pubs.

Hypoglycemia? Good Food to the Rescue. Michael Klaper. 1 cass. (Running Time: 30 min.). (Help Yourself to Health Ser.). 7.00 (978-0-929274-07-2(5)) Gentle World.
One of a series of tapes discussing the relationship between a diet free of animal products & improving one's health or a particular disease.

Hypoglycemia: How to Recognize it, How to Control it. Read by Harvey M. Ross. 1 cass. (Running Time: 45 min.). 10.00 (AC23) Am Media.
A psychologist tells how he discovered that many of his patients' mental disorders were caused, not by psychological weakness or trauma, but by simple dietary deficiencies.

Hypohidrotic Ectodermal Dysplasia - A Bibliography & Dictionary for Physicians, Patients, & Genome Researchers. Compiled by Icon Group International, Inc. Staff. 2007. ring bd. 28.95 (978-0-497-11239-4(6)) Icon Grp.

Hysteria, Its Cause & Consequence. Instructed by Manly P. Hall. 8.95 (978-0-89314-142-4(9), C810830) Philos Res.

Hyungs: The Roots of Taekwon-Do. James S. Benko. 1986. 12.95 (TC-5) ITA Inst.
Outlines the hyungs (patterns) taught within the International Taekwon-Do Association. How to practice as well as how to teach hyungs is discussed. Also included are the meaning of all 24 hyungs.

I

I Ain't Got Time to Bleed. unabr. ed. Jesse Ventura. Read by Michael Kramer. 5 cass. (Running Time: 7 hrs. 30 mins.). 1999. 40.00 (5092) Books on Tape.
The author reveals the secrets of his electoral success & strategies for pioneering a new era in American government.

I Ain't Got Time to Bleed: Reworking the Body Politic from the Bottom Up. abr. ed. Jesse Ventura. Read by Jesse Ventura. 2 cass. (Running Time: 3 hrs.). 1999. audio compact disk 21.95 (978-0-375-40761-1(8), Random AudioBks) Random Audio Pubg.
Takes a look behind the scenes at one of the most controversial politicians, & his stand on the issues affecting his state Minneapolis, particularly tax reform & public education. It also covers his experience as a member of the U.S. Navy SEAL program & as a pro wrestler.

I Always Wondered yet Always Knew Move Right 21 AZ. Howard W. Gabriel, III. (J). (gr. k-12). 1987. 4.95 (978-0-936997-08-7(7), T87-06) M & H Enter.
In the First Story, Just about Everybody Abandoned the Old Retired School Teacher. He Realizes That Death Beckons & He Wonders if His Life's Work Has Really Meant Anything to Any of His Students. In the Second Story, a Family Becomes Fed up with Their Neighborhood & Get a Computer to Find a Better Place to Live.

I Am. Contrib. by Nicole C. Mullen. (Sound Performance Soundtracks Ser.). 2004. audio compact disk 5.98 (978-5-559-31804-2(3)) Pt of Grace Ent.

I Am: Awakening Self Acceptance. Emmett E. Miller. 1 cass. (Running Time: 90 min.). (Emmett Miller, M.D. Cassettes Ser.). 1989. 9.95 (978-1-55841-014-5(7)) Emmett E Miller.

I Am: Awakening Self-Acceptance. Emmett E. Miller. Read by Emmett E. Miller. 1 cass. (Running Time: 1 hr.). 1996. 10.00 (978-1-56170-370-8(2), 395) Hay House.
How to integrate the concepts of self-esteem & self-acceptance into your life.

I Am: The Nondual Teachings of Jesus. 3 Audio CDs. Featuring Adyashanti. (ENG.). 2007. audio compact disk 29.00 (978-1-933986-36-4(0)) Open Gate Pub.

***I Am: 123 Mango Tree.** Nadine Johnson. (Running Time: 15). (ENG.). 2010. audio compact disk 10.00 (978-0-9814874-5-8(9)) OneTMango.

I am - Awakening Self Acceptance. 1 CD. 1989. audio compact disk 16.95 (978-1-55841-107-4(0)) Emmett E Miller.
This tape helps you disvoer the answer to the all-important question, "who am I?" Self acceptance is the cornerstone of all self-esteem. with body and mind quiet, centered and focused, you awaken to that still, small voice within that speaks truthfully to you, "I Am." Two stimulating imagery experiences plus a one hour heart-to-heart talk.

I Am a Camera see Sound of Modern Drama: The Crucible

I Am a Camera. John Van Druten. (J). (SAC 7145) Spoken Arts.

I Am a Communicator. Eldon Taylor. 1 cass. (Running Time: 62 min.). (Inner Talk Ser.). 16.95 incl. script. (978-1-55978-489-4(X), 5366F) Progress Aware Res.
Soundtrack - Brook with underlying subliminal affirmations.

I Am a Communicator: Classics. Eldon Taylor. 1 cass. 16.95 (978-1-55978-567-9(5), 5366L) Progress Aware Res.

I Am a Confident Person. Richard J. Anderson. 1 CD. (Running Time: 60 mins.). 2005. audio compact disk 24.95 (978-0-9765897-2-3(9)) Sedona Wind Pub.
Love yourself and be as confident as you need to be to acheive what you want in life. Uses the power of affirmations and the latest in subliminal technology.

I Am a Falcon, Hooded... see Twentieth-Century Poetry in English, No. 28, Recordings of Poets Reading Their Own Poetry

I Am a Friendly Child. unabr. ed. Mary Richards. Read by Mary Richards. 1 cass. (Running Time: 45 min.). (Children's I Am Ser.). (J). 2007. audio compact disk 19.95 (978-1-56136-200-4(X)) Master Your Mind.
A lovely picnic in a sunny meadow where the child shares toys with others & makes new friends. Fantasy journey on both sides.

I Am a Gay Man (an Essay from Things I've Learned from Women Who've Dumped Me) abr. ed. Dan Savage. Read by Dan Savage. Ed. by Ben Karlin. (Running Time: 15 mins.). (ENG.). 2008. 1.98 (978-1-60024-340-0(1)) Pub: Hachet Audio. Dist(s): HachBkGrp

I Am a Genius. Eldon Taylor. 1 cass. (Running Time: 62 min.). (Inner Talk Ser.). 16.95 incl. script. (978-1-55978-627-0(2), 53786L) Progress Aware Res.
Soundtrack - Classics with underlying subliminal affirmations.

I Am a Genius: Peaceful Ocean. Eldon Taylor. 1 cass. 16.95 (978-1-55978-646-1(9), 53786O) Progress Aware Res.

I Am a Genius of Unspeakable Evil & I Want to Be Your Class President. unabr. ed. Josh Lieb. 4 CDs. (Running Time: 5 hrs.). (ENG.). (YA). (gr. 7). 2009. audio compact disk 29.95 (978-0-14-314506-6(1), PengAudBks) Penguin Grp USA.

I Am a Great Reader. Eldon Taylor. 1 cass. (Running Time: 62 min.). (Inner Talk Ser.). 16.95 incl. script. (978-1-55978-306-4(0), 5373A) Progress Aware Res.
Soundtrack - Tropical Lagoon with underlying subliminal affirmations.

I Am a Leader. Eldon Taylor. Read by Eldon Taylor. Ed. by Leslie Brice. 1 cass. (Running Time: 1 hr.). 1992. 16.95 (978-1-56705-325-8(4)) Gateways Inst.
Self improvement.

I Am a Leader. Eldon Taylor. 1 cass. (Running Time: 62 min.). (Inner Talk Ser.). 16.95 incl. script. (978-1-55978-018-6(5), 5418C) Progress Aware Res..
Soundtrack - Musical Themes with underlying subliminal affirmations.

I Am a Leader: Babbling Brook. Eldon Taylor. 1 cass. 16.95 (978-1-55978-538-9(1), 5418F) Progress Aware Res.

I Am a Lion! Short Stories. Carl Sommer. Narrated by Carl Sommer. 1 cass. Dramatization. (Another Sommer-Time Story Ser.). (J). (gr. 1-4). 2003. bk. 16.95 (978-1-57537-558-8(3)) Advance Pub.

I Am a Lion! Carl Sommer. Narrated by Carl Sommer. 1 cass. Dramatization. (Another Sommer-Time Story Ser.). (J). (gr. k-4). 2003. lib. bdg. 23.95 (978-1-57537-759-9(4)) Advance Pub.

***I Am A Lion! / ¡Yo Soy un Leon!** ed. Carl Sommer. Illus. by Greg Budwine. (Another Sommer-Time Story Bilingual Ser.). (ENG & SPA.). (J). 2009. bk. 26.95 (978-1-57537-178-8(2)) Advance Pub.

I Am a Lucky Person. Richard J. Anderson. 1 CD. (Running Time: 60 mins.). 2005. audio compact disk 24.95 (978-0-9765897-6-1(1)) Sedona Wind Pub.
Open yourself up to new possibilities and attract wonderful things into your life. Uses the power of affirmations and the latest in subliminal technology.

I Am a Non-Smoker. Prod. by Imagine. Created by Sharon Penchina & Stuart Hoffman. 1. (Running Time: 28.30). 2003. audio compact disk 14.95 (978-0-9740684-0-4(3)) Two Imagine.
Create a powerful mindset for success! After being safely guided into a state of complete mental and physical relaxation, your mind will very quickly get used to the idea that you don't smoke.The theory behind this approach is to provide reinforcement of the listener's motivation and determination to succeed, by enlisting the power of the subconscious mind in reducing physical or psychological withdrawal.

I Am a Reader: Music Theme. Eldon Taylor. 1 cass. 16.95 (978-1-55978-150-3(5), 5373C) Progress Aware Res.

I Am a Star. Inge Auerbacher. Read by Suzanne Toren. 2 cass. (Running Time: 1 hr. 45 mins.). (YA). 1999. stu. ed. 99.70 (978-0-7887-3872-2(0), 47037) Recorded Bks.
Inge is a happy seven-year-old German girl when the nightmare begins. As the Nazis gain power, her family is subjected to greater & greater horrors. Ample background material provides a helpful context for understanding Inge's experiences. But it is Inge's own story, told from a child's point of view & sprinkled liberally with her poems, that makes this chapter of world history personal & compelling.

I Am a Star: Child of the Holocaust. unabr. ed. Inge Auerbacher. Narrated by Suzanne Toren. 2 cass. (Running Time: 1 hr. 45 mins.). (YA). 2000. pap. bk. 33.24 (978-0-7887-3847-0(X), 41045X4) Recorded Bks.

I Am a Star: Child of the Holocaust, unabr. ed. Inge Auerbacher. Narrated by Suzanne Toren. 2 pieces. (Running Time: 1 hr. 45 mins.). (gr. 3 up). 2000. 19.00 (978-0-7887-2627-9(7), 95631E7) Recorded Bks.

I Am a Successful Person. Richard J. Anderson. 1 CD. (Running Time: 60 mins.). 2005. audio compact disk 24.95 (978-0-9765897-3-0(7)) Sedona Wind Pub.
Increase your belief in yourself, develope goal focus and achieve your highest financial goals. Uses the power of affirmations and the latest in subliminal technology.

I Am a Time Manager. Eldon Taylor. 1 cass. (Running Time: 62 min.). (Inner Talk Ser.). 16.95 incl. script. (978-1-55978-558-7(6), 5345L) Progress Aware Res.
Soundtrack - Classics with underlying subliminal affirmations.

I Am a Time Manager: Tropical Lagoon. Eldon Taylor. 1 cass. 16.95 (978-1-55978-321-7(4), 5345A) Progress Aware Res.

I Am America. unabr. ed. Mary Sheldon & Bob Van Dusen. Read by Gerald Ford et al. (Running Time: 5400 sec.). (J). (gr. 4-7). 2007. audio compact disk 19.95 (978-1-4332-0564-4(5)) Blckstn Audio.

I Am America. unabr. ed. Mary Sheldon & Bob VanDusen. 2 CDs. (Running Time: 1.5 hrs.). 2004. audio compact disk 17.95 (978-1-59007-157-1(3)) Pub: New Millenn Enter. Dist(s): PerseuPGW
This collection of stories about each state, told in the first person, introduces children to the most memorable facts about each state, with the different personality of each state reflected through dialects and stories. Features four former presidents.

I Am America. unabr. abr. ed. Mary Sheldon & Bob VanDusen. 1 cass. (Running Time: 1.5 hrs.). 2004. 14.95 (978-1-59007-156-4(5)) Pub: New Millenn Enter. Dist(s): PerseuPGW

I Am America: Classics Read by Celebrities Series. unabr. ed. Mary Sheldon & Bob Van Dusen. Read by President Ford et al. (Running Time: 5400 sec.). (J). (gr. 4-7). 2007. audio compact disk 24.00 (978-1-4332-0563-7(7)) Blckstn Audio.

I Am America (and So Can You!) Stephen Colbert. 2007. 34.99 (978-1-60252-228-2(6)) Find a World.

I Am America (and So Can You!) abr. ed. Stephen Colbert. Read by Stephen Colbert. (YA). 2007. 44.99 (978-1-60252-728-7(8)) Find a World.

I Am America (and So Can You!) abr. ed. Stephen Colbert. Read by Stephen Colbert. Read by David Pasquesi et al. (Running Time: 3 hrs. 30 mins.). (ENG.). 2007. 19.98 (978-1-60024-037-9(2)) Pub: Hachet Audio. Dist(s): HachBkGrp

I Am America (and So Can You!) abr. ed. Stephen Colbert. Read by Stephen Colbert. Read by Paul Dinello et al. 3 CDs. (Running Time: 3 hrs. 30 mins.). (ENG.). 2007. audio compact disk 24.98 (978-1-60024-036-2(4)) Pub: Hachet Audio. Dist(s): HachBkGrp

I Am An Oil Tanker. Fi Glover. 2 cass. (Running Time: 3 hrs.). 2002. 13.95 (978-1-85686-665-1(3), Audiobks) Pub: Random GBR. Dist(s): Trafalgar

I Am Anointed. Lynne Hammond. 2009. audio compact disk 6.00 (978-1-57399-420-0(0)) Mac Hammond.

I Am Assertive. Eldon Taylor. 1 cass. (Running Time: 62 min.). (Inner Talk Ser.). 16.95 incl. script. (978-1-55978-319-4(2), 5348A) Progress Aware Res.
Soundtrack - Tropical Lagoon with underlying subliminal affirmations.

I Am Assertive: Music Theme. Eldon Taylor. 1 cass. 16.95 (978-1-55978-133-6(5), 5348C) Progress Aware Res.

I Am Assertive: Ocean. Eldon Taylor. Read by Eldon Taylor. Ed. by Leslie Brice. 1 cass. (Running Time: 1 hr.). 1992. 16.95 (978-1-56705-319-7(X)) Gateways Inst.
Self improvement.

I Am Becoming the Woman I've Wanted. unabr. ed. Poems. Read by Ellen Burstyn et al. Ed. by Sandra H. Martz. 2 cass. (Running Time: 3 hrs.). 1998. 16.95 (978-1-57453-015-5(1)) Audio Lit.
Delves into the powerful feelings that women have about their bodies.

I Am Changed. Contrib. by Janet Paschal. (Studio Tracks Plus Ser.). 2006. audio compact disk 9.98 (978-5-558-32026-8(5)) Sprg Hill Music Group.

I Am Charismatic. Eldon Taylor. 1 cass. (Running Time: 62 min.). (Inner Talk Ser.). 16.95 incl. script. (978-1-55978-157-2(2), 5383C) Progress Aware Res.
Soundtrack - Musical Themes with underlying subliminal affirmations.

I Am Charlotte Simmons. Tom Wolfe. Read by Dylan Baker. 2004. 35.95 (978-1-59397-579-1(1)) Pub: Macmill Audio. Dist(s): Macmillan

I Am Charlotte Simmons. abr. ed. Tom Wolfe. Read by Dylan Baker. 2004. 17.95 (978-1-59397-578-4(3)) Pub: Macmill Audio. Dist(s): Macmillan

I Am Charlotte Simmons. unabr. ed. Tom Wolfe. Read by Dylan Baker. 3 pieces. 69.95 (978-0-7927-3354-6(1)) AudioGO.

I Am Charlotte Simmons. unabr. ed. Tom Wolfe. Read by Dylan Baker. 25 CDs. 2004. audio compact disk 139.95 (978-0-7927-3353-9(3)) AudioGO.

I Am Charlotte Simmons. unabr. rev. ed. Tom Wolfe. Read by Dylan Baker. 20 CDs. (Running Time: 31 hrs. 0 mins. 0 sec.). (ENG., 2004. audio compact disk 24.95 (978-1-59397-520-3(1)) Pub: Macmill Audio. Dist(s): Macmillan

I Am Colin see Secret Garden: A Young Reader's Edition of the Classic Story

I am Coming to You see Naja Kwako

I Am Cooperative. Eldon Taylor. 1 cass. (Running Time: 62 min.). (Inner Talk Ser.). 16.95 incl. script. (978-1-55978-755-0(4), 5358F) Progress Aware Res.
Soundtrack - Brook with underlying subliminal affirmations.

I Am Cooperative: Syntnesized Movements. Eldon Taylor. 1 cass. 16.95 (978-0-940699-07-6(9), 5358D) Progress Aware Res.

I Am Courageous. Eldon Taylor. Read by Eldon Taylor. Ed. by Leslie Brice. 1 cass. (Running Time: 1 hr.). 1992. 16.95 (978-1-56705-321-0(1)) Gateways Inst.
Self improvement.

I Am Courageous: Babbling Brook. Eldon Taylor. 1 cass. 16.95 (978-1-55978-766-6(X), 5417F) Progress Aware Res.

I Am Courageous: Music Theme. Eldon Taylor. 1 cass. 16.95 (978-1-55978-017-9(7), 5417C) Progress Aware Res.

I AM Course: The Instant Advanced Meditation Course. Created by Steven Sashen. (ENG.). 2007. (978-0-9785483-1-5(0)) Garuda, Inc.

I am Creative. Eldon Taylor. 1 cass. (Running Time: 62 min.). (Inner Talk Ser.). 16.95 (978-1-55978-361-3(3), 53788A) Progress Aware Res.
Soundtrack - Tropical Lagoon with underlying subliminal affirmations.

I Am Creative: Babbling Brook. Eldon Taylor. 1 cass. 16.95 (978-1-55978-511-2(X), 53788F) Progress Aware Res.

I Am Creative: Music Theme. Eldon Taylor. 1 cass. 16.95 (978-1-55978-139-8(4), 53788C) Progress Aware Res.

I Am Determined. David T. Demola. 1 cass. 4.00 (4-151) Faith Fellow Min.

I AM Discourses (Vol 3 Audio Cass. Tape) By the Ascended Master Saint Germain, Vol. 3. unabr. ed. Read by Gerald A. Craig. Godfre Ray King. 17 cass. (Running Time: 10 hrs. 24 min.). (Saint Germain Ser.: Vol. 3). (ENG.). 1986. 65.00 (978-1-878891-16-7(2), St Germain Ser) St Germain.
A series of thirty-three Discourses by Saint Germain & other Ascended Masters on the Law of Life & the use of the Words "I Am," God-in-Action.

***I AM Discourses (Vol 3-CD audio Book), vol 3.** Instructed by Saint Germain. (ENG.). 2008. audio compact disk 35.00 (978-1-878891-15-0(4), Ascend Mstr) St Germain.

I Am Fearfully & Wonderfully Made ! Carolyn Minor Daughtry. (J). 2003. pap. bk. 12.00 (978-0-9742796-0-2(9)) Blessings Unlimit.

I Am Free to Heal-Guided. unabr. ed. Mary Richards. Perf. by Brian Giorgi. Music by Charles Albert. 1 cass. (Running Time: 50 min.). (Guided Relaxation Ser.). 2007. audio compact disk 19.95 (978-1-56136-203-5(4)) Master Your Mind.
Imagine your body as a crystal-like figure - free of any impurities. A beautiful healing white light flows through you dispersing into a myriad of colors. Side 2: Be more loving to yourself. Select a thought stopping image that brings you joy.

I Am God - Not Man. 1 cass. (Running Time: 60 min.). 10.00 (978-1-55794-062-9(2), T13) Eternal Wrd TV.

I Am Healing Now. Read by Mary Richards. 1 cass. (Running Time: 50 min.). (Power Words of Affirmation Ser.). 2007. audio compact disk 19.95 (978-1-56136-195-3(X)) Master Your Mind.

I Am Honest. Eldon Taylor. 1 cass. (Running Time: 62 min.). (Inner Talk Ser.). 16.95 incl. script. (978-1-55978-754-3(6), 5333F) Progress Aware Res.
Soundtrack - Brook with underlying subliminal affirmations.

I Am Honest: Music Theme. Eldon Taylor. 1 cass. 16.95 (978-0-940699-59-5(1), 5333C) Progress Aware Res.

I Am Humble. Eldon Taylor. Read by Eldon Taylor. Ed. by Leslie Brice. 1 cass. (Running Time: 1 hr.). 1992. 16.95 (978-1-56705-323-4(8)) Gateways Inst.
Self improvement.

I am Hutterite: Audio Book on CD. unabr. ed. Mary-Ann Kirkby. 2010. audio compact disk 24.99 (978-1-4003-1628-1(6)) Nelson.

I Am, I Can, I Will. Charles B. Beckert. 1 cass. 2004. 9.95 (978-1-57734-485-8(5), 06006035) Covenant Comms.
Three keys to personal success.

I Am, I Can, I Will & How to Live With Yourself & Like It. Charles B. Beckert. 1 cass. 5.98 (978-1-55503-056-8(4), 0600776) Covenant Comms.
The power of positive thinking using gospel guidelines.

I Am Inheriting the Fullness of God's Names Audio Book. John Paul Jackson. Read by Carol Cavazos. 2004. audio compact disk 17.00 (978-1-58483-107-5(3)) Streams PubHse.
Are you reaping the benefits of your divine inheritance? Embark on the glorious adventure of knowing God and let Him show you the amazing mysteries and wonders reserved for those who bear His name. John Paul Jackson's I AM: Inheriting the Fullness of God's Names is read by Carol Cavazos.

I Am Intuitive. Eldon Taylor. 1 cass. (Running Time: 62 min.). (Inner Talk Ser.). 16.95 incl. script. (978-1-55978-767-3(8), 5424F) Progress Aware Res.
Soundtrack - Brook with underlying subliminal affirmations.

I Am Intuitive: Music Theme. Eldon Taylor. 1 cass. 16.95 (978-1-55978-587-7(X), 5424M) Progress Aware Res.

I Am Jack Boland - I Am an Alcoholic. Jack Boland. 1 cass. 8.00 (BW03) Master Mind.

I Am Jealous. Barrie Konicov. 1 cass. 11.98 (978-0-87082-335-0(3), 066) Potentials.
Designed to free your mind from the experience of jealousy so that you can then accept the other person in your life without jealous feelings.

I Am Jealous. Barrie Konicov. 1 CD. 2003. audio compact disk 16.98 (978-0-87082-979-6(3)) Potentials.
Free your mind from jealousy. You can accept the other person in your life without jealous feelings. You will find the self-hypnosis on track 1 and the subliminal on track 2. The easy-listening music of the subliminal, together with the self-hypnosis, is the original format which most people love and with which they are most familiar.

I Am Lavina Cumming. unabr. ed. Susan Lowell. Narrated by Barbara Caruso. 4 pieces. (Running Time: 4 hrs. 45 mins.). (gr. 4 up). 35.00 (978-0-7887-0527-4(X), 94722E5) Recorded Bks.
In 1905, 10-year-old Lavina hugs her father goodbye & boards a train headed north. She is leaving her father, her five brothers & her ranch in Arizona Territory to live with her rich aunt in California. Available to libraries only.

I Am Legend. unabr. ed. Richard Matheson. Read by Robertson Dean. (Running Time: 19800 sec.). 2007. audio compact disk 29.95 (978-1-4332-0332-9(4)) Blckstn Audio.

I Am Legend. unabr. ed. Richard Matheson. Read by Robertson Dean. (Running Time: 19800 sec.). 2007. 19.95 (978-1-4332-0330-5(8)); audio compact disk 19.95 (978-1-4332-0331-2(6)) Blckstn Audio.

I Am Legend. unabr. ed. Richard Matheson. Read by Dean Robertson. (YA). 2007. 74.99 (978-1-60252-869-7(1)) Find a World.

I Am Legend: And Other Stories. unabr. ed. Richard Matheson. Read by Robertson Dean & Yuri Rasovsky. 1 MP3-CD. 2007. 29.95 (978-1-4332-0864-5(4)); 65.95 (978-1-4332-0328-2(6)); audio compact disk 90.00 (978-1-4332-0329-9(4)) Blckstn Audio.

I Am Legend & the Shrinking Man. unabr. collector's ed. Richard Matheson. Read by Walter Lawrence. 9 cass. (Running Time: 13 hrs. 30 min.). 1992. 72.00 (978-0-7366-2147-2(4), 2946) Books on Tape.
The last man on earth must battle creatures of the night for mankind's survival. Riveting tale of terror.

I Am Madame X. Gioia Diliberto & Lorna Raver. 8 cass. (Running Time: 11 hrs. 30 mins.). 2002. 56.95 (978-0-7861-2602-6(7), 3198) Blckstn Audio.

I am Madame X. unabr. ed. Gioia Diliberto. Read by Lorna Raver. (Running Time: 11 hrs. 30 mins.). 2001. 24.95 (978-0-7861-8767-6(0), 3198) Blckstn Audio.

I am Madame X. unabr. ed. Gioia Diliberto. Read by Lorna Raver. 9 CDs. (Running Time: 11 hrs. 30 mins.). 2004. audio compact disk 72.00 (978-0-7861-8936-6(3), 3198) Blckstn Audio.

I Am Mellow. Eldon Taylor. 1 cass. (Running Time: 62 min.). (Inner Talk Ser.). 16.95 incl. script. (978-1-55978-129-9(7), 5368D) Progress Aware Res.
Soundtrack - Synthesized Moments with subliminal affirmations.

I Am Mordred: A Tale from Camelot. Nancy Springer. Read by Steven Crossley. 4 cass. (Running Time: 5 hrs.). (YA). 1999. stu. ed. 223.20 (978-0-7887-3036-8(3), 46853) Recorded Bks.
What would it be like to be born as Mordred, unwanted son of the great King Arthur, destined to kill his noble father? This imaginative fantasy tale, rich with Arthurian lore, lets you finally hear Mordred's side of the ageold story. Includes study guide.

I Am Mordred: A Tale from Camelot, unabr. ed. Nancy Springer. Narrated by Steven Crossley. 5 pieces. (Running Time: 5 hrs. 45 mins.). (gr. 7 up). 2000. 45.00 (978-0-7887-2976-8(4), 95686E7) Recorded Bks.

I Am Mordred: A Tale from Camelot. unabr. ed. Nancy Springer. Read by Steven Crossley. 4 cass. (Running Time: 5 hrs. 45 mins.). (YA). 2000. pap. bk. 68.99 (978-0-7887-3006-1(1), 40888X4) Recorded Bks.

I Am Morgan le Fay: A Tale from Camelot. Nancy Springer. Narrated by Jenny Sterlin. 6 pieces. (Running Time: 8 hrs. 30 mins.). (gr. 7 up). 2001. 56.00 (978-0-7887-5312-1(6)) Recorded Bks.

I Am Myself. unabr. ed. Phyllis U. Hiller. 1 cass. (Running Time: 21 min.). 1991. 12.95 (978-1-884877-11-7(7), 1992191C) Creat Mats Lib.
Therapeutic use for children & grown-ups who have experienced sex abuse.

***I Am Not a Serial Killer.** unabr. ed. Dan Wells. Narrated by John Allen Nelson. 1 MP3-CD. (Running Time: 7 hrs. 30 mins. 0 sec.). (John Cleaver Ser.). (ENG.). 2010. 24.99 (978-1-4001-6579-7(2)); 15.99 (978-1-4001-8579-5(3)); audio compact disk 34.99 (978-1-4001-1579-2(5)); audio compact disk 69.99 (978-1-4001-4579-9(1)) Pub: Tantor Media. Dist(s): IngramPubServ

***I Am Not A Serial Killer.** unabr. ed. Dan Wells. Narrated by John Allen Nelson. (Running Time: 9 hrs. 0 mins.). (John Cleaver Ser.). 2010. 34.99 (978-1-4001-9579-4(9)) Tantor Media.

I Am Not Ashamed. Contrib. by Janet Paschal. (Ultimate Tracks (Word Tracks) Ser.). 2006. audio compact disk 8.99 (978-5-558-26978-9(2), Word Music) Word Enter.

I Am Not, but I Know I Am: Welcome to the Story of God. unabr. ed. Louie Giglio. Narrated by Louie Giglio. (ENG.). 2005. 17.49 (978-1-60814-245-3(0)); audio compact disk 16.99 (978-1-59859-025-8(1)) Oasis Audio.

I Am Not Joey Pigza. unabr. ed. Jack Gantos. Read by Jack Gantos. (Running Time: 17160 sec.). (Joey Pigza Ser.: Bk. 4). (ENG.). (J). (gr. 5). 2007. audio compact disk 30.00 (978-0-7393-5628-9(3), Listening Lib) Pub: Random Audio Pubg. Dist(s): Random

I Am Not Joey Pigza. unabr. ed. Jack Gantos. Read by Jack Gantos. 4 CDs. (Running Time: 4 hrs. 47 mins.). (Joey Pigza Ser.: Bk. 4). (J). (gr. 4-7). 2007. audio compact disk 38.00 (978-0-7393-6147-4(3), Listening Lib) Pub: Random Audio Pubg. Dist(s): Random
Joey Pigza is knocked for a loop when his good-for-nothing dad shows up on his doorstep as a recycled person. After a lucky lotto win, Carter Pigza truly believes he's somebody else. He's even renamed himself Charles Heinz - and he insists that Joey and his mother join his happy Heinz family plan. "My head felt like it was full of bees, and they were busy in ways that were bad for me." Joey has little choice but to embrace a head-spinning series of changes, which include having to leave school to help out at the beat-up roadside diner his dad has purchased. But Joey is afraid that in going with the flow he will go over the falls and end up in a place far away from who he really is.

***I Am Number Four.** unabr. ed. Pittacus Lore. Read by Neil Kaplan. 2010. (978-0-06-204135-7(5)) HarperCollins Pubs.

I Am of Two Places: Children's Poetry. (Greetings Ser.: Vol. 2). (gr. 3-5). 10.00 (978-0-7635-1763-2(1)) Rigby Educ.

I Am Ozzy. abr. ed. Ozzy Osbourne. Read by Frank Skinner. Told to Chris Ayres. (Running Time: 3 hrs.). (ENG.). 2010. 16.98 (978-1-60788-369-2(4)) Pub: Hachet Audio. Dist(s): HachBkGrp

***I Am Ozzy.** abr. ed. Ozzy Osbourne. Read by Frank Skinner. Told to Chris Ayres. 3 CDs. (Running Time: 4 hrs.). 2010. audio compact disk 24.98 (978-1-60788-520-7(4)) Pub: Hachet Audio. Dist(s): HachBkGrp

I Am Persuaded. Bobby Hilton. 4 cass. 2002. 22.00 (978-1-930766-17-4(3)) Pub: Bishop Bobby. Dist(s): STL Dist NA

I Am Phoenix: Poems for Two Voices. Paul Fleischman. Narrated by Paul Fleischman. 1 cass. (Running Time: 15 mins.). (gr. 1 up). 2001. 10.00 (978-0-7887-2216-5(6), 96615E7) Recorded Bks.
Experience the magic & magnificence of the immortal phoenix, the fluttering elation of finches at dawn, & the loneliness of the last passenger pigeon as our talented narrators capture the beauty & vulnerability of the aviary kingdom.

I Am Potential: Eight Lessons on Living, Loving, & Reaching Your Dreams. unabr. ed. Patrick Henry Hughes et al. (Running Time: 6 hrs. NaN mins.). 2008. 44.95 (978-1-4332-4833-7(6)); audio compact disk 29.95 (978-1-4332-4836-8(0)); audio compact disk 50.00 (978-1-4332-4834-4(4)) Blckstn Audio.

I Am Potential: Eight Lessons on Living, Loving, & Reaching Your Dreams. unabr. ed. Patrick Henry Hughes et al. (Running Time: 6 hrs. 0 mins.). 2008. audio compact disk & audio compact disk 19.95 (978-1-4332-4835-1(2)) Blckstn Audio.

I Am Proud... My Bed is Dry. Read by Mary Richards. Music by Wayne Musgrave. (Children's I Am Ser.). (J). 10.95 Master Your Mind.
Discusses a magical trip into space where the child sends love to the planet Earth, & while up there hears "I am secure & safe. I feel a sense of comfort when I go to bed. I always wake up when I need to use the toilet. I then go back to sleep easily.".

I Am Reflective. Eldon Taylor. 1 cass. (Running Time: 62 min.). (Inner Talk Ser.). 16.95 incl. script. (978-1-55978-015-5(0), 5415C) Progress Aware Res.
Soundtrack with underlying subliminal affirmations.

I Am Reflective: Babbling Brook. Eldon Taylor. 1 cass. 16.95 (978-1-55978-765-9(1), 5415F) Progress Aware Res.

I Am Relaxed. Eldon Taylor. 1 cass. (Running Time: 62 min.). (Inner Talk Ser.). 16.95 (978-1-55978-354-5(0), 53798A) Progress Aware Res.
Soundtrack - Tropical Lagoon with underlying subliminal affirmations.

I Am Relaxed: Environmental Theme. Eldon Taylor. 1 cass. 16.95 (978-1-55978-517-4(9), 53798F) Progress Aware Res.

I Am Relaxed: Music Theme. Eldon Taylor. 1 cass. 16.95 (978-1-55978-209-8(9), 53798C) Progress Aware Res.

I Am Responsible. (Running Time: 45 min.). (Success Ser.). 9.98 (978-1-55909-140-4(1), 115) Randolph Tapes.
Taking responsibility for yourself is the most powerful action for positive change & success in your life.

I Am Rosa Parks. Rosa Parks & Jim Haskins. Narrated by Patricia R. Floyd. 1 cass. (Running Time: 15 mins.). (gr. 1 up). 2001. 10.00 (978-0-7887-5496-8(3)) Recorded Bks.
In her own words, Rosa Parks tells the story of her brave act and the events that followed.

I Am Secure & Confident. 1 cass. 12.98 (978-0-87554-509-7(2), 1107) Valley Sun.
Programming to be secure & confident, & filled with independence & determination. Also: You feel powerful & in control. You retain a calm, optimistic outlook. You are peaceful, balanced & harmonious. You project a positive self-image. You can do whatever you set your mind to. Your mind is calm & you have great inner courage. Every day, you feel more confident. Much, much more.

I Am Sleepy: Happy Dreams. Read by Mary Richards. Music by Wayne Musgrave. (Children's I Am Ser.). (J). 10.95 Master Your Mind.
A magical carpet ride to special places, encouraging nourishing sleep.

I Am Special. Maureen McElheron. 1 cass. (Running Time: 40 min.). (YA). (gr. 7-12). 1991. 12.00 (978-0-201-50347-0(6)) Longman.
Listening, speaking, reading, & writing activities for special-needs students entering the workplace.

I Am Special. Maureen McElheron. 1 cass. (Running Time: 40 min.). (YA). (gr. 7-12). 1991. pap. bk. 24.95 Pub: Wrld Lang Div. Dist(s): AddisonWesley

I Am Special Four Year Old Music Cassette: Songs for 4-Year Olds. Composed by Jack Miffleton. 2003. 13.95 (978-1-931709-21-7(1)) Our Sunday Visitor.
25 songs on audio-cassette to coordinate with the 5th Edition I Am Special Four-year Old Program.

I Am Special Kindergarten: Songs for Kindergarten. 5th ed. Composed by Jack Miffleton. 2001. audio compact disk 17.95 (978-0-87973-310-0(1)) Our Sunday Visitor.
All 25 songs in the I Am Special Kindergarten program, including 10 new ones written for the fifth edition, recorded by composer, Jack Miffleton.

I Am Special Kindergarten Music: Songs for Kindergarten. 5th ed. Composed by Jack Miffleton. 2001. 13.95 (978-0-87973-309-4(8)) Our Sunday Visitor.
All 25 songs in the I Am Special Kindergarten program, including 10 new ones written for the fifth edition, recored by composer, Jack Miffleton.

I Am Special Music: Songs for Four-year Olds. 5th ed. Composed by Jack Miffleton. 2003. audio compact disk 17.95 (978-1-931709-22-4(X)) Our Sunday Visitor.
25 songs on CD to coordinate with the I Am Special Four Year Old Program.

I Am Spock. abr. ed. Leonard Nimoy. Read by Leonard Nimoy. (Running Time: 4 hrs.). 2008. 39.25 (978-1-4233-5838-1(4), 9781423358381, BADLE); 39.25 (978-1-4233-5836-7(8), 9781423358367, Brinc Audio MP3 Lib); 24.95 (978-1-4233-5837-4(6), 9781423358374, BAD); 24.95 (978-1-4233-5835-0(X), 9781423358350, Brilliance MP3) Brilliance Audio.

I Am Thankful. Read by Mary Richards. 1 cass. (Running Time: 48 min.). (Children's I Am Ser.). (J). 2007. audio compact disk 19.95 (978-1-56136-121-2(6)) Master Your Mind.

***I Am that Woman How to be Sensational, Sexy & Fabulous Over 40: How to be Sensational, Sexy & Fabulous Over 40.** Rone de Beauvoir. (ENG.). 2010. bk. 25.95 (978-1-882682-14-0(9)) Omega Farm Pub.

I Am the Central Park Jogger: A Story of Hope & Possibility. abr. ed. Trisha Meili. 2004. 15.95 (978-0-7435-4857-1(4)) Pub: S&S Audio. Dist(s): S and S Inc

I Am the Cheese, unabr. ed. Robert Cormier. Narrated by Jeff Woodman & John Randolph Jones. 4 pieces. (Running Time: 5 hrs. 30 mins.). (gr. 8 up). 1993. 35.00 (978-1-55690-778-4(8), 93132E7) Recorded Bks.
A young man fights for his life against a mysterious enemy: his own memories of a family tragedy that lie buried in his subconscious.

I Am the Cute One. Perf. by Mary-Kate Olsen & Ashley Olsen. 1 cass. (Running Time: 1 hr.). (Mary-Kate & Ashley Series). (J). 2002. 8.98 (54245-4); audio compact disk 15.98 (978-1-56896-249-8(5), 54245-2) Lightyear Entrtnmnt.
America has watched the Olsen twins grow up from their TV series "Full House" to their current series "So Little Time". The whole family can enjoy this series of titles.

I Am the Cute One. Perf. by Mary-Kate Olsen & Ashley Olsen. 1 cass., 1 CD. (J). 7.18 (LIGHT 54245); audio compact disk 12.78 CD Jewel box. (LIGHT 54245) NewSound.
Includes: "Double up," "I Am the Cute One," "Ginger the Talking Horse," "Broccoli & Chocolate" & more.

I Am the Holy Ranger. 1 cass. 5.00 Lion Pub-Roar Rec.

I Am the Messenger. unabr. ed. Markus Zusak. Read by Marc Aden Gray. 7 CDs. (Running Time: 8 hrs. 40 mins.). (YA). (gr. 9 up). 2006. audio compact disk 46.75 (978-0-7393-3692-2(4), Listening Lib) Pub: Random Audio Pubg. Dist(s): NetLibrary CO

I Am the Messenger. unabr. ed. Markus Zusak. Read by Marc Aden Gray. 7 CDs. (Running Time: 31200 sec.). (ENG.). (J). (gr. 7-12). 2006. audio compact disk 45.00 (978-0-7393-3729-5(7), Listening Lib) Pub: Random Audio Pubg. Dist(s): Random

I Am the Mummy Heb-Nefert. unabr. ed. Eve Bunting. 1 cass. (Running Time: 15 min.). (J). 2001. pap. bk. 16.95 (978-0-8045-6849-4(9), 6849) Spoken Arts.
Heb-Nefert, a mummy encased in glass in a museum, recalls the days of long ago when she lived with her husband on the banks of the Nile.

I Am the New Black. abr. ed. Tracy Morgan & Anthony Bozza. (ENG.). 2009. audio compact disk 25.00 (978-0-7393-8194-6(6), Random AudioBks) Pub: Random Audio Pubg. Dist(s): Random

***I am the Night-Color Me Black.** 2010. audio compact disk (978-1-59171-184-1(3)) Falcon Picture.

I Am the Way, the Truth & the Life. unabr. ed. Fred Jelly. 2 cass. (Running Time: 2 hrs. 30 min.). 1993. 17.95 set. (TAH287) Alba Hse Comns.
Four excellent conferences on an extremely but rather neglected subject: Jesus as our Truth, our Way & our Life.

I Am Vallejo! Belén Garcia-Alvarado & Alan Venable. Ed. by Jerry Stemach. Narrated by Jos Saro Sol s. 2000. audio compact disk 200.00 (978-1-58702-479-5(2)) D Johnston Inc.

I Am Vallejo! Belén Garcia-Alvarado & Alan Venable. Ed. by Jerry Stemach et al. Illus. by Bob Stotts. Narrated by Jos Saro Sol s. Contrib. by Ted S. Hasselbring. (Start-to-Finish Books). (J). (gr. 2-3). 2000. 35.00 (978-1-58702-480-1(2)) D Johnston Inc.

I Am Vallejo! Belen Garcia-Alvarado & Alan Venable. (Step into History Ser.). 2000. audio compact disk 18.95 (978-1-4105-0148-6(5)) D Johnston Inc.

I Am Vallejo!, Vol. 4. Belén Garcia-Alvarado & Alan Venable. Ed. by Jerry Stemach et al. Illus. by Bob Stotts. Narrated by Jos Saro Sol s. Contrib. by Ted S. Hasselbring. (Start-to-Finish Books). (J). (gr. 2-3). 2002. 100.00 (978-1-58702-978-3(2)) D Johnston Inc.

I Am Vallejo!, Vol. 4. unabr. ed. Belén Garcia-Alvarado & Alan Venable. Ed. by Jerry Stemach et al. Illus. by Bob Stotts. Narrated by Jos Saro Sol s. Contrib. by Ted S. Hasselbring. 1 cass. (Running Time: 1 hr.). (Start-to-Finish Books). (J). (gr. 2-3). 2000. (978-1-893376-96-0(6), F21K2) D Johnston Inc.
More people should know about this astonishing Mexican-American hero of the Old West. This historical account begins with General Mariano Vallejo's childhood in Monterrey, California as the son of a Spanish soldier who had helped to found the mission at San Francisco in 1776. Mariano had some great adventures growing up on the wild California coast. When he was 14, Mexico won its independence from Spain.

I Am Wandering My Love. Barrie Konicov. 1 cass. 11.98 (978-0-87082-364-0(7), 067) Potentials.
The author has designed this program with the impact of the situation, to heal the separation & transform the relationship of the listener.

I Am Welcomed: Birthing Tape. Read by Mary Richards. (Children's I Am Ser.). 1987. 10.95 (079) Master Your Mind.

I Am Welcomed-Subliminal. Read by Mary Richards. 1 cass. (Running Time: 60 min.). (Children's I Am Ser.). (J). 2007. audio compact disk 19.95 (978-1-56136-120-5(8)) Master Your Mind.

I Am What I Am. unabr. ed. Swami Amar Jyoti. 1 cass. (Running Time: 1 hr. 30 min.). (Satsangs of Swami Amar Jyoti Ser.). 1998. 9.95 (978-0-933572-39-3(5), R113) Truth Consciousness.
In Subjective Oneness, there are no problems, only occurrences. To God there are no "others." Joy in Being.

I Am with You. Gloriae Dei Cantores Schola. audio compact disk 16.95 (978-1-55725-321-7(8), GDCD034) Paraclete MA.

I Am with You Always. 1 cass. (Running Time: 30 min.). 1985. (0282) Evang Sisterhood Mary.

I Am with You Always Series. 2005. audio compact disk 37.95 (978-1-59834-001-3(8)) Walk Thru the Bible.

I Am: 365 Names of God. John Paul Jackson. 2003. audio compact disk 16.00 (978-1-58483-081-8(6)) Streams PubHse.

I, Amber Brown. Paula Danziger. Read by Dana Lubotsky. (Running Time: 1 hr. 52 mins.). (Amber Brown Ser.: No. 8). (J). (gr. 2-4). 2004. pap. bk. 17.00 (978-0-8072-2064-1(7), Listening Lib) Random Audio Pubg.

I & My Chimney see Melville: Six Short Novels

I & Thou. unabr. ed. Milton Diamond. 1 cass. (Running Time: 1 hr.). (Human Sexuality Ser.). 12.95 (34016) J Norton Pubs.

***I Beat the Odds: My Amazing Journey from Foster Care to the NFL & Beyond.** Michael Oher. (ENG.). 2011. audio compact disk 29.95 (978-0-14-242886-3(8), PengAudBks) Penguin Grp USA.

I Beg to Differ with the Darwinian Theory. Instructed by Manly P. Hall. 8.95 (978-0-89314-143-1(7), C820725) Philos Res.

I Believe. Perf. by Marvin Sapp. 2002. audio compact disk 17.98 Provident Mus Dist.

I Believe. Excerpts. Thomas Junior Strawser. 1. (Running Time: 1-11-23 1-11-23). (ENG.). 2004. audio compact disk (978-0-9755695-0-4(3)) My Lvng Solutions.
I BELIEVE: The flagship of the Living Solutions series is a full length "easy-listening" CD with inspiring music and short remainders of the principles and results of the program. "I Believe" is a refreshing and relaxing material that has been called "Attitude Adjuster and a "Requirement for Relationships.".

I Believe: The Heart of the Catholic Faith. Marcellino D'Ambrosio. 2004. 12.95 (978-1-932927-17-7(4)); audio compact disk 19.95 (978-1-932927-16-0(6)) Ascensn Pr.

I Believe in Christ. David Glen Hatch. 1 cass. 7.98 (1000578); 9.95 (10001379); audio compact disk 15.95 (28001028) Covenant Comms.
This beautiful arrangement now comes with 6 additional new songs.

I Believe in Love. Contrib. by BarlowGirl. Prod. by Otto Price. (Studio Ser.). 2007. audio compact disk 9.99 (978-5-557-63569-1(6), Word Records) Word Enter.

I Believe in Myself. Read by Mary Richards. 1 cass. (Running Time: 50 min.). (Power Words of Affirmation Ser.). 12.95 (978-1-56136-194-6(1)) Master Your Mind.

I Believe in the Holy Spirit. 1985. (0229) Evang Sisterhood Mary.

I Believe in You. Contrib. by Joel Engle. (Sound Performance Soundtracks Ser.). 2007. audio compact disk 5.98 (978-5-557-71910-0(5)) Pt of Grace Ent.

I Believe in You & Me. Contrib. by Whitney Houston. (Wedding Traks Ser.). 2005. audio compact disk 8.99 (978-5-559-15688-0(4)) Christian Wrld.

I Belong. Contrib. by Kathryn Scott. 2007. audio compact disk 19.95 (978-5-557-57575-1(8)) Integrity Music.

I Belong. Contrib. by Kathryn Scott & Don Moen. Prod. by Brent Milligan. 2007. audio compact disk 13.99 (978-5-557-57578-2(2)) Integrity Music.

I Bless Your Name. Contrib. by Selah. 2006. audio compact disk 8.99 (978-5-558-26938-3(3), Word Music) Word Enter.

I Blow Minds for a Living. Jello Biafra. 2 cass. (Running Time: 2 hrs.). (AK Press Audio Ser.). 2000. 11.98 (978-1-902593-16-6(2), AK Pr San Fran) AK Pr Dist.
Includes "Was a Teenage Pacifist," " If Voting Changed Anything," "Running for Mayor," " Grow More Pot" & more, in the man's usual sarcastic, inimitable style.

I Blow Minds for a Living. Jello Biafra. 2 CDs. (AK Press Audio Ser.). (ENG.). 1999. audio compact disk 16.98 (978-1-902593-15-9(4)) Pub: AK Pr GBR. Dist(s): Consort Bk Sales

I Buy Low Set: How to Succeed in the Stock Market. Norman Jay Nowak. 4 cass. (Running Time: 3 hrs.). 2000. bk. (978-0-9700029-0-7(4)) Millionaire.
How to identify, evaluate & select common stocks traded in the U. S. markets. Includes chapters on researching financial & other corporate data.

I Call This Abandonment. Contrib. by Chasing Victory. Prod. by Nathan Dantzler. 2005. audio compact disk 13.98 (978-5-558-78005-5(3)) Mono Vs Ster.

I Call upon You, God! Leon C. Roberts. 1995. 10.95 (342); audio compact disk 15.95 (342) GIA Pubns.

I Can. 1 cass. (Young People Ser.). (J). (gr. 7 up). 12.98 (66) Randolph Tapes.
This age group faces many challenges. The tape helps strengthen self-esteem, determination, a sense of responsibility & self-confidence. Helps learning & retention.

I Can. 1 cass. (Young People Ser.). (J). (gr. 5-7). 2001. 12.98 (68) Randolph Tapes.
A must for pre-teens. Will help make things smoother & better. For self-esteem, habits, schoolwork, homework, etc.

I Can. 1 cass. (Running Time: 60 min.). (Young People Ser.). (J). (ps). 2001. 12.98 (69) Randolph Tapes.
Give every little person this program for increased learning & loving ability.

I Can. Ben Sweetland. 1 cass. (Running Time: 45 min.). 11.00 (978-0-89811-003-6(3), 5114); Meyer Res Grp.
Helps you find belief in your potential for success.

I Can. Ben Sweetland. 1 cass. 10.00 (SP100001) SMI Intl.
One of the classics in the self-improvement field. Ben Sweetland's timeless message helps you find belief in your potential for success.

I Can, No. 1. Betty L. Randolph. 1 cass. (Running Time: 45 min.). (I Can Ser.). (J). (gr. 1-4). 1989. bk. 9.98 (978-1-55909-198-5(3), 65S) Randolph Tapes.
Help self-esteem & learning habits. Subliminal messages are heard 3-5 minutes before becoming ocean sounds or music.

I Can, No. 2. Betty L. Randolph. 1 cass. (Running Time: 45 min.). (I Can Ser.). (J). (gr. 1). 1989. 9.98 (978-1-55909-200-5(9), 69S) Randolph Tapes.
A program for increased learning & loving ability. Subliminal messages are heard 3-5 minutes before becoming ocean sounds or music.

I Can, No. 3. 1 cass. (Running Time: 45 min.). (I Can Ser.). (J). (gr. 5-7). 9.98 (978-1-55909-081-0(2), 68) Randolph Tapes.
Help for self-esteem, habits, schoolwork, homework, etc. Subliminal messages are heard 3-5 minutes before becoming ocean sounds or music.

I Can, No. 4. Betty L. Randolph. 1 cass. (Running Time: 45 min.). (I Can Ser.). (YA). (gr. 8 up). 1989. bk. 9.98 (978-1-55909-199-2(1), 66S) Randolph Tapes.
Strengthens self-esteem, determination, responsibility, & helps learning & retention. Subliminal messages are heard 3-5 minutes before becoming ocean sounds or music.

I Can: Achieving Self-Empowerment. 1 cassette. (Running Time: 78 minutes, 22 seconds). 1989. 12.95 (978-1-55841-015-2(5)) Emmett E Miller.
Awaken and support confidence in your Self. Let feelings of achievement and success replace habits of self-doubt and self-criticism. Awaken and nurture the power within that can enable you to express your deepest truth. Two stimulating imagery experiences plus a one hour Heart-to-Heart talk.

I Can: Achieving Self-Empowerment. Emmett E. Miller. Read by Emmett E. Miller. 1 cass. (Running Time: 1 hr.). 1996. 10.95 (978-1-56170-367-8(2), 392) Hay House.
Learn about the importance of self-empowerment in your life & how your childhood experiences create it.

I Can / Achieving Self Empowerment. 1 CD. 1989. audio compact disk 16.95 (978-1-55841-108-1(9)) Emmett E Miller.
Awaken and support confidence in your Self. Let feelings of achievement and success replace habits of self-doubt and self-criticism. Awaken and nurture the power within that can enable you to express your deepest truth. Two stimulating experiences plus a one hour heart-to-heart talk.

I Can Be Anything. Steck-Vaughn Staff. 1996. (978-0-8172-6466-6(3)) SteckVau.

I Can Be Glad: The Music City Gospel Choir. Contrib. by Camp Kirkland. Conducted by Camp Kirkland. Created by Tom Fettke. Prod. by Tom Fettke. 1995. audio compact disk 90.00 (978-5-557-68288-6(0)) Allegis.

I Can Be Healthy. Richard J. Anderson. 1 CD. (Running Time: 60 mins.). 2005. audio compact disk 24.95 (978-0-9765897-4-7(5)) Sedona Wind Pub.
Increase your ability to feel more confident about your physical condition. Uses the power of affirmations and the latest in subliminal technology.

I Can (Birth-2 yrs) 1 cass. (Young People Ser.). (J). (ps). 12.98 (92) Randolph Tapes.
We now know that learning begins before birth & the young child's mind absorbs "like a sponge.".

I Can Dance! 1 cass., 1 CD. (Kidsongs Ser.). (J). 7.98 (SME 63481); audio compact disk 11.18 CD Jewel box. (SME 63481) NewSound.
Learn dance moves. Do the Charleston, the Twist, the Waltz, forming a Conga line & Barefootin' at the beach. Includes: "I Can Dance," "Dancing in the Street," "Charleston," "Don't You Just Love to Waltz?" & more.

I Can Do It! Barry Tesar. 1 cass. (Running Time: 1 hr.). (Subliminal Inspiration Ser.). 1992. 9.98 (978-1-56470-004-9(6)) Success Cass.
Subliminal program.

I Can Do It. Barry Tesar. 2 cass. 1998. 14.95 Set. (978-1-889800-16-5(3)) TNT Media Grp.

I Can Evangelism: Taking the I Can't Out of Sharing Your Faith. unabr. ed. Elisa Morgan. Narrated by Elisa Morgan. (Running Time: 3 hrs. 21 mins. 12 sec.). (ENG.). 2008. 9.79 (978-1-60814-246-0(9)); audio compact disk 19.99 (978-1-59859-421-8(4)) Oasis Audio.

***I Can Feel the Rhythm: 8 Rhythm-Teaching Chorals Using Vocal Speech.** Composed by Greg Gilpin. (ENG.). 2006. audio compact disk 34.99 (978-1-4234-9838-4(0), 1423498380) Pub: Shawnee Pr. Dist(s): H Leonard

I Can Go to the Rock. 1 cass., 1 CD. 10.98 (978-1-57908-341-0(2), 53014); audio compact disk 15.98 CD. (978-1-57908-340-3(4)) Platinm Enter.

I Can Hear the Mourning Dove. unabr. ed. James Bennett. Narrated by Barbara Rosenblat. 5 pieces. (Running Time: 7 hrs. 30 mins.). (gr. 9 up). 1992. 44.00 (978-1-55690-610-7(2), 92303E7) Recorded Bks.
Portrayal of a brilliant but disturbed young woman provides a deeply sensitive & perceptive exploration of some of the most devastating issues young adults face today, including suicide, rape & the death of a parent.

I Can Hear You. Perf. by Carolyn Arends & Rich Mullins. 1 cass. 1995. audio compact disk Brentwood Music.
Hailing from Vancouver, Canada, Dove Award winning songwriter Carolyn Arends mixes a rare blend of fresh, insightful lyrics with pop & folk musical influences. Features: Seize the Day, I Can Hear You & The Power of Love (with Rich Mullins).

I Can I Will. 1 cass. 1997. 7.95 (978-1-56253-424-0(6), Milady) Delmar.

I Can I Will. Frederick G. Elias. Read by Peter Bie. 6 cass. (Running Time: 59 min.). (Dynamics for Personal Success: Vol. 3). 1992. cass. & video 59.95 Set. ODC Pub.
The edited version of the book. Self-esteem & motivational messages.

I Can Lose Weight Now. Richard J. Anderson. 1 CD. (Running Time: 60 mins.). 2005. audio compact disk 24.95 (978-0-9765897-1-6(0)) Sedona Wind Pub.
Lose weight, increase your self esteem and develope your ideal body image using the power of affirmations and the latest in subliminal technology.

'I' Can Never be a Great Man see Twentieth-Century Poetry in English, No. 9, Recordings of Poets Reading Their Own Poetry

I Can Only Imagine. Contrib. by MercyMe. (Inoriginal Performance Trax Ser.). 2005. audio compact disk 9.98 (978-5-558-93080-1(2)) INO Rec.

I Can Only Imagine: Ultimate Power Anthems of the Christian Faith. 2008. audio compact disk 19.98 (978-5-557-51571-9(2)) INO Rec.

I Can Pray. Contrib. by Dove Brothers. (Soundtraks Ser.). 2007. audio compact disk 8.99 (978-5-557-56222-5(2)) Christian Wrld.

I Can (Pre-Birth-2 Yrs.) Betty L. Randolph. Read by Betty L. Randolph. Read by Leonard Baron. Ed. by Success Education Institute International Staff. 1 cass. (I Can Ser.). 1989. bk. 9.98 (978-1-55909-112-1(6), 92S) Randolph Tapes.
Features male-femal voice tracks with right-left brain - 3-5 minutes.

I Can Read You Like a Book: How to Spot the Messages & Emotions People Are Really Sending with Their Body Language. abr. ed. Gregory Hartley & Maryann Karinch. Read by Gregory Hartley & Maryann Karinch. 3 CDs. (Running Time: 4 hrs.). 2008. audio compact disk 23.95 (978-1-59316-109-5(3)) Listen & Live.

I Can Resist Everything But... Matthew 6:13. Ed Young. (J). 1979. 4.95 (978-0-7417-1085-7(4), A0085) Win Walk.

I Can See Myself in His Eyeballs. unabr. ed. Chonda Pierce. 2001. 17.99 (978-0-310-23839-3(0)) Zondervan.

I Can See Myself in His Eyeballs: God Is Closer Than You Think. abr. ed. Zondervan Publishing Staff & Chonda Pierce. (Running Time: 2 hrs. 0 mins. 0 sec.). (ENG.). 2003. 10.99 (978-0-310-26063-9(9)) Zondervan.

I Can See You. unabr. ed. Karen Rose. Read by Elisabeth S. Rodgers. (Running Time: 18 hrs. 30 mins.). (ENG.). 2009. 19.98 (978-1-60024-647-0(8)); audio compact disk 34.98 (978-1-60024-645-6(1)) Pub: Hachet Audio. Dist(s): HachBkGrp

I Can See You. unabr. ed. Karen Rose. Read by Elisabeth S. Rodgers. (Running Time: 18 hrs. 30 mins.). (ENG.). 2010. audio compact disk 19.98 (978-1-60788-214-5(0)) Pub: Hachet Audio. Dist(s): HachBkGrp

***I Can Take Tests - for Kids.** Jim Lohr. (Running Time: 30). (ENG.). 2010. 12.95 (978-0-9825720-1-6(8)) J Lohr Consult.

I Can (6-9 yrs) 1 cass. (Young People Ser.). (J). (ps-4). 12.98 (65) Randolph Tapes.
This tape is a must on your list. It is a lasting gift for a child. Helps self-esteem & learning habits. "Nothing of lasting strength can be built without a strong foundation.".

I Cannot Get You Close Enough. unabr. collector's ed. Ellen Gilchrist. Read by Mary Peiffer. 8 cass. (Running Time: 12 hrs.). 1993. 64.00 (978-0-7366-2432-9(5), 3197) Books on Tape.
Three novellas from American Book Award-winning author explore the human heart & its ties to family.

I Cannot Live with You see Poems & Letters of Emily Dickinson

I Can't Sleep - Insomnia & the Experience of the Night, Nos. 34-36, set. Carl Faber. Read by Roy Tuckman. 3 cass. (Running Time: 3 hrs. 45 min.). 1985. 28.00 (978-0-918026-41-5(5), SR 63-616) Perseus Pr.

I Can't Stay Long. unabr. ed. Laurie Lee. Read by Laurie Lee. 8 cass. (Running Time: 9 hrs. 30 min.). 2001. 69.95 (978-1-85089-603-6(8), 88081) Pub: ISIS Audio GBR. Dist(s): Ulverscroft US
Laurie Lee continues the story of his early life in a scrapbook of first loves & obsessions.

I Can!/¡Yo Puedo! abr. ed. Created by Mark Wesley & Gladys Rosa-Mendoza. (English Spanish Foundations Ser.). (J). 2008. audio compact disk 9.95 (978-1-931398-62-6(3)) Me Mi Pubng.

I Capture the Castle. Dodie Smith. Read by Emilia Fox. 4 cass. (Running Time: 6 hrs.). 2002. (978-1-901768-67-1(8)) CSA Telltapes GBR.

I Capture the Castle. Dodie Smith. Read by Emilia Fox. (Running Time: 5 hrs. 0 mins. 0 sec.). (ENG.). (gr. 5). 2009. audio compact disk 26.95 (978-1-934997-44-4(7)) Pub: CSAWord. Dist(s): PerseuPGW

I Capture the Castle. abr. ed. Dodie Smith. Read by Emilia Fox. 4 cass. (Running Time: 5 hrs.). (gr. 9-12). 2001. 24.95 (978-1-57270-224-0(9), M41224) Pub: Audio Partners. Dist(s): PerseuPGW
Tells the story of 17-year-old Cassandra & her family, who live in not-so-genteel poverty in the crumbling ruin of an old English castle.

I Capture the Castle. abr. ed. Dodie Smith. Read by Emilia Fox. 4 CDs. (Running Time: 5 hrs.). (gr. 9-12). 2001. audio compact disk 29.95 (978-1-57270-225-7(7), M45225) Pub: Audio Partners. Dist(s): PerseuPGW

I Capture the Castle. unabr. ed. Dodie Smith. Read by Jenny Agutter. 12 cass. (Running Time: 44280 sec.). 2001. 96.95 (978-0-7540-0644-2(1), CAB2066) AudioGO.
A story of love, sibling rivalry & a bohemian existence in a crumbling castle in the middle of nowhere. Cassandra Mortmain's journal records her fadingly glamorous stepmother, her beautiful, wistful older sister & the man to whom they both owe their isolation & poverty.

I Catch 'Em, God Cleans 'em. Contrib. by Gaither Vocal Band. (Gaither Homecoming Trax Ser.). 2006. audio compact disk 9.98 (978-5-558-11581-9(5)) Gaither Music Co.

I Cautiously Scanned My Little Life see Poems & Letters of Emily Dickinson

I Ching Symphony. Perf. by Frank Steiner, Jr. 1 cass., 1 CD. 7.98 (RM 8128); audio compact disk 14.38 CD Jewel box. (RM 8128) NewSound.

I Choose to Live. 2007. audio compact disk 19.95 (978-1-56136-125-0(9)) Master Your Mind.

I, Claudius. Robert Graves. Read by Nelson Runger. 10 Cass. (Running Time: 16.75 Hrs). 39.95 (978-1-4025-2370-0(X)) Recorded Bks.

I, Claudius. abr. ed. Robert Graves. Narrated by Derek Jacobi. Abr. by Sarah Kilgarriff. 4 CDs. (Running Time: 5 hrs. 0 mins. 0 sec.). (ENG.). 2008. audio compact disk 26.95 (978-1-934997-01-7(3)) Pub: CSAWord. Dist(s): PerseuPGW

I, Claudius. unabr. ed. Robert Graves. Read by Frederick Davidson. 12 cass. (Running Time: 17 hrs. 30 mins.). 1994. 83.95 (978-0-7861-0742-1(1), 1490) Blckstn Audio.
Tiberius Claudius Drusus Nero Germanicus lived from 10 B. C. to 54 A. D. Despised as a weakling & dismissed as an idiot because of his physical infirmities, Claudius survived the intrigues & poisonings that marked the reigns of Augustus, Tiberius, & the mad Caligula, to become Emperor of Rome in 41 A. D. "I, Claudius," the first part of Robert Graves's two-part account of the life of Tiberius Claudius, is written in the form of Claudius's autobiography & stands as one of the modern classics of historical fiction.

I, Claudius. unabr. ed. Robert Graves. Read by Frederick Davidson. 12 pieces. 2004. reel tape 44.95 (978-0-7861-2220-2(X)) Blckstn Audio.

I, Claudius. unabr. ed. Robert Graves. Read by Frederick Davidson. (Running Time: 17 hrs. 0 mins.). 2008. 44.95 (978-1-4332-1382-3(6)); audio compact disk 110.00 (978-1-4332-1380-9(X)) Blckstn Audio.

I, Claudius. unabr. ed. Robert Graves. Narrated by Nelson Runger. 12 cass. (Running Time: 16 hrs. 30 mins.). 1986. 97.00 (978-1-55690-245-1(X), 86990E7) Recorded Bks.
Lame, stammering Claudius, once a major embarrassment to the Imperial family & now Emperor of Rome, writes an eyewitness account of the reign of the first four Caesars. Filled with poisonings, betrayal & shocking excesses, this is history that rivals the most exciting contemporary fiction.

I, Claudius. unabr. collector's ed. Robert Graves. Read by David Case. 12 cass. (Running Time: 18 hrs.). 1993. 96.00 (978-0-7366-2389-6(2), 2059) Books on Tape.
Tiberius Claudius Drusus Nero Germanicus lived from 10 B.C. to 54 A.D. Physically weak, a stammerer, Claudius was ignored. He survived because of his infirmities. Imagine his agenda when he became emperor!.

I, Claudius: From the Autobiography of Tiberius Claudius. unabr. ed. Robert Graves. Read by Frederick Davidson. 12 CDs. (Running Time: 61200 sec.). 2008. audio compact disk & audio compact disk 19.95 (978-1-4332-1381-6(8)) Blckstn Audio.

I Come As A Brother: Bartholomew Revisited. Based on a book by High Mesa Press. (ENG.). 2009. audio compact disk 24.95 (978-0-9614010-8-5(7)) High Mesa Pr.

I Come As a Thief. unabr. ed. Louis Auchincloss. Read by Jonathan Reese. 7 cass. (Running Time: 7 hrs.). 1979. 42.00 (978-0-7366-0198-6(8), 1198) Books on Tape.
Tony Lowder, a promising New York lawyer, stands on the threshold of a successful social & professional career. The only barrier is money. Ethics give way to ambition, & Lowder accepts a bribe for delaying legal action against a brokerage firm.

I Confess/Mr. & Mrs. Smith/Rebecca. Perf. by Alfred Hitchcock. 2 CDs. (Running Time: 2 hrs.). 2002. audio compact disk 11.98 (7050); 9.98 (7000) Radio Spirits.
A Priest hears a killer's confession and can't tell the police, even after he becomes a suspect/A couple discovers their marriage license is invalid, with hilarious results/Mrs. de Winter is haunted by the memory of her husband's first wife.

I, Coriander. unabr. ed. Sally Gardner. Read by Juliet Stevenson. 5 cass. (Running Time: 7 hrs. 30 mins.). (J). (gr. 4-7). 2006. 40.00 (978-0-307-28461-7(1), Listening Lib); audio compact disk 42.50 (978-0-307-28462-4(X), Listening Lib) Pub: Random Audio Pubg. Dist(s): NetLibrary CO

I, Coriander. unabr. ed. Sally Gardner. Read by Juliet Stevenson. 6 CDs. (Running Time: 7 hrs. 28 mins.). (ENG.). (J). (gr. 5). 2006. audio compact disk 34.00 (978-0-307-28419-8(0), Listening Lib) Pub: Random Audio Pubg. Dist(s): Random

I Could Do That! Esther Morris Gets Women the Vote. unabr. ed. Linda Arms White. Narrated by Joan Allen. 1 CD. (Running Time: 16 mins.). (J). (gr. 2-4). 2006. bk. 29.95 (978-0-439-90582-4(6), WHCD692); bk. 24.95 (978-0-439-90576-3(1), WHRA692) Weston Woods.
This is the true story of Esther Morris, who started out life believing she could do anything, and then proved it, by building her own business, raising a family in the Wild West, working to get women the vote for the first time, AND becoming the first female judge and the first woman in the US to hold a political office!.

I Could Not Sleep for Thinking of the Sky see Gathering of Great Poetry for Children

I Could Sing of Your Love. Dennis Allen. 1999. audio compact disk 85.00 (978-0-633-00387-6(5)) LifeWay Christian.

I Could Sing of Your Love Forever. Dennis Allen. 1999. 11.98 (978-0-633-00391-3(3)); audio compact disk 16.98 (978-0-633-00389-0(1)) LifeWay Christian.

I Could Sing of Your Love forever Accompaniment Cassette. Dennis Allen. 1999. 75.00 (978-0-633-00388-3(3)) LifeWay Christian.

I Could Sing of Your Love forever Cassette Promo Pak. Dennis Allen. 1999. 8.00 (978-0-633-00386-9(7)) LifeWay Christian.

I Create Money in Abundance-Power Words. unabr. ed. Mary Richards. Music by Charles Albert. 1 cass. (Running Time: 50 min.). (Power Words

Ser.). 2007. audio compact disk 19.95 (978-1-56136-209-7(3)) Master Your Mind.
Short relaxation & visualization plus powerful power words that are audible.

I Cried Too: Grief Recovery CD of Songs, Story & Inspiration. Short Stories. Sheila Schmidt. 1 CD. (Running Time: 23 mins.). 2001. audio compact disk 12.99 (978-0-9716689-0-4(6)) Gold Faith.

I, Crocodile. 2004. bk. 24.95 (978-1-55592-073-9(X)); pap. bk. 18.95 (978-1-55592-432-4(8)); pap. bk. 38.75 (978-1-55592-434-8(4)); pap. bk. 32.75 (978-1-55592-436-2(0)); pap. bk. 14.95 (978-1-55592-435-5(2)); audio compact disk 12.95 (978-1-55592-914-5(1)) Weston Woods.

I, Crocodile. Fred Marcellino. 1 cass. (Running Time: 1 hr.). (J). 2001. bk. 24.95 (571) Weston Woods.

I, Crocodile. Fred Marcellino. 1 cass. (Running Time: 1 hr. 30 mins.). (J). (gr. 1-2). 2004. 8.95 (978-1-55592-982-4(6)) Weston Woods.

I Curse the Curse. Voice by Eddie Long. 2008. audio compact disk 15.99 (978-1-58602-380-5(2)) E L Long.

I Dare You. William H. Danforth. 1988. SMI Intl.

I Dare You. Thomas A. Harris. 1 cass. (Running Time: 32 min.). 11.00 (978-0-89811-028-9(9), 5171) Meyer Res Grp.
Look within yourself & your immediate surroundings for the success you desire. Also available in Spanish.

I Dare You. unabr. ed. William H. Danforth. 3 cass. (Running Time: 3 hrs.). 2001. 20.00 (978-0-9602416-2-0(X)) American Yth Found.
You have a four-fold life to live: a body, a brain, a heart and a soul-these are your living tools. To use and develop them is not a task. It is a golden opportunity." Founder of the Ralston Purina Company and one of the founders of the American Youth Foundation, lived his life by a four-fold philosophy - balancing one's mental, physical, social and spiritual capacities.

I Dare You: Embrace Life with Passion. abr. ed. Joyce Meyer. Read by Sandra McCollom. (Running Time: 6 hrs.). (ENG.). 2007. 24.98 (978-1-60024-012-6(7)) Pub: Hachet Audio. Dist(s): HachBkGrp

***I Dare You to Change!** unabr. ed. Bil Cornelius. Narrated by Bil Cornelius. (Running Time: 5 hrs. 25 mins. 10 sec.). (ENG.). 2010. 18.19 (978-1-60814-745-8(2)); audio compact disk 25.99 (978-1-59859-841-4(4)) Oasis Audio.

I Deal in Crime: William Davis Case & The Abigail Murray Case. Perf. by William Gargan. 1 cass. (Running Time: 1 hr.). 2001. 6.98 (2141) Radio Spirits.

I Deserve Better! Aim to Complete a Positive Circle in This Life! Rene Reyes. Prod. by Rene Reyes. Executive Producer Sweet Verse Publishers. (ENG., 2007. 25.00 (978-0-9796282-4-5(5)) Sweet Verse.

I Didn't Do It! Casey West. Narrated by Larry A. McKeever. (Standing Tall 3 Mystery Ser.). (J). 2003. 10.95 (978-1-58659-109-0(6)); audio compact disk 14.95 (978-1-58659-348-3(X)) Artesian.

I Didn't Know That: From Ants in the Pants to Wet Behind the Ears the Unusual Origins of the Things We Say. Karlen Evins. Read by Karlen Evins. (Running Time: 8520 sec.). 2007. audio compact disk 14.95 (978-0-9635474-2-2(9)) K Rose Pub.

I Didn't Know What Time It Was - ShowTrax. Arranged by Paris Rutherford. 1 CD. (Running Time: 5 mins.). 2000. audio compact disk 19.95 (08742293) H Leonard.
The Rodgers & Hart classic in an easy swing groove that will let your singers really show off their jazz style.

I Died for Beauty, but Was Scarce see Poems & Letters of Emily Dickinson

I Do CD #25105;#39000;#24847; CD: #23567;#32650;#21109;#20316;#35433;#27468;#38598; 4. (CHI.). 2005. audio compact disk 15.00 (978-0-9721862-2-3(0)) Lamb Music & Min.

I Don't Believe in Atheists. Chris Hedges. Read by Chris Hedges. (Playaway Adult Nonfiction Ser.). 2008. 54.99 (978-1-60640-513-0(6)) Find a World.

I Don't Believe in Atheists. unabr. ed. Chris Hedges. Read by Chris Hedges. (Running Time: 18000 sec.). (ENG., 2008. audio compact disk 26.95 (978-1-59887-623-9(6), 1598876236) Pub: HighBridge. Dist(s): Workman Pub

I Don't Care Who Started It. Rebecca Monley. 3 cass. (Running Time: 4 hrs.). 1995. Set. (AA2927) Credence Commun.
Rebecca Monley has been working with conflict resolution with families, business & schools. She is extremely practical with techniques on how to make your requests, stand your ground, & assert with love & forgive when that is called for.

***I Don't Have Enough Faith to be an Atheist.** unabr. ed. Norman Geisler & Frank Turek. Narrated by Kate Reading. (ENG.). 2006. 19.98 (978-1-59644-401-0(0), Hovel Audio) christianaud.

I Don't Have Enough Faith to Be an Atheist. unabr. ed. Frank Turek & Norman L. Geisler. Frwd. by David Limbaugh. 12 CDs. (Running Time: 15 hrs. 0 mins. 0 sec.). (ENG.). 2006. audio compact disk 34.98 (978-1-59644-399-0(5), Hovel Audio) christianaud.

I Don't Have Enough Faith to Be an Atheist. unabr. ed. Frank Turek & Norman L. Geisler. Narrated by Kate Reading. 2 MP3CDs. (Running Time: 15 hrs. 0 mins. 0 sec.). (ENG.). 2006. lp 24.98 (978-1-59644-400-3(2), Hovel Audio) christianaud.

I Don't Have to Make Everything All Better. abr. ed. Gary B. Lundberg & Joy S. Lundberg. 1 cass. (Running Time: 6 hrs.). 1999. 24.95 (20446) Courage-to-Change.
Learn how to walk emotionally with those you care about while empowering them to solve their own problems.

I Don't Have to Make Everything All Better: A Practical Approach to Walking Emotionally with Those You Care about While Empowering Them to Solve Their Own Problems. Gary B. Lundberg & Joy S. Lundberg. 4 cass. (Running Time: 6 hrs.). 24.95 (978-0-915029-03-7(0)) Riverpark Pub.
The authors read their book "I Don't Have to Make Everthing All Better" explaining the principles & how they improve relationships with children, teens, adult children, spouse, parents, blended families, friends, & on the job. Includes examples, anecdotes, & music.

***I Don't Know How She Does It: The Life of Kate Reddy, Working Mother.** abr. ed. Allison Pearson. Read by Emma Fielding. (ENG.). 2010. audio compact disk 14.99 (978-0-307-91419-4(4), Random AudioBks) Pub: Random Audio Pubg. Dist(s): Random

I Don't Know How She Does It: The Life of Kate Reddy, Working Mother. unabr. ed. Allison Pearson. 8 cass. (Running Time: 12 hrs.). 2002. 72.00 (978-0-7366-8826-0(9)) Books on Tape.
Kate Reddy must juggle her family and her aggressive career, while trying not to fall off life's treadmill.

I Don't Know Jack Audio Book: Poems in Search of Reason. Roger Huisinga. (ENG.). 2005. 12.95 (978-1-932278-16-3(8)) Pub: Mayhaven Pub. Dist(s): Baker Taylor

***I Don't Know What I Want but I Know It's Not This: A Step-by-Step Guide to Finding Gratifying Work.** unabr. ed. Julie Jansen. (Running Time: 7 hrs. 30 mins.). (ENG.). 2010. 34.98 (978-1-59659-621-4(X), GildAudio) Pub: Gildan Media. Dist(s): HachBkGrp

I Don't Regret. Contrib. by BarlowGirl. Prod. by Otto Price. (Studio Ser.). 2007. audio compact disk 9.99 (978-5-557-63570-7(X), Word Records) Word Enter.

I Don't Remember Dropping the Skunk, but I Do Remember Trying to Breathe. Ken Davis. Read by Ken Davis. 1 cass. (Running Time: 1 hr.). 1990. 12.99 (978-0-310-32348-8(7), 11792T) Zondervan.
A live presentation of Davis' book before an audience. Humorous advice on teenage survival skills.

I Don't Smoke. Eldon Taylor. 2 cass. 29.95 Set. (978-1-55978-740-6(6), 4405) Progress Aware Res.

I Don't Want Delilah; I Need You. 1996. 6.00 (978-1-58602-052-1(8)); audio compact disk 10.00 (978-1-58602-053-8(6)) E L Long.

***I Don't Want to Kill You.** unabr. ed. Dan Wells. (Running Time: 9 hrs. 0 mins.). (John Cleaver Ser.). 2011. 15.99 (978-1-4526-7054-6(4)); 24.99 (978-1-4526-5054-8(3)); audio compact disk 34.99 (978-1-4526-0054-3(6)) Pub: Tantor Media. Dist(s): IngramPubServ

***I Don't Want to Kill You (Library Edition)** unabr. ed. Dan Wells. (Running Time: 9 hrs. 0 mins.). (John Cleaver Ser.). 2011. 34.99 (978-1-4526-2054-1(7)); audio compact disk 83.99 (978-1-4526-3054-0(2)) Pub: Tantor Media. Dist(s): IngramPubServ

I Don't Want to Melt! Alma Flor Ada. (Stories for the Year 'Round Ser.). (J). (gr. k-3). 4.95 (978-1-58105-318-0(5)) Santillana.

***I Dream of Genie.** 2010. audio compact disk (978-1-59171-213-8(0)) Falcon Picture.

I Dreamt My Love A-Dying Lay see Twentieth-Century Poetry in English, No. 28, Recordings of Poets Reading Their Own Poetry

I, Dred Scott. unabr. ed. 1 cass. (Running Time: 1 hr. 15 mins.). (J). 2005. 12.85 (978-1-4193-2632-5(5)) Recorded Bks.

I Dreyfus. unabr. ed. Bernice Rubens. Read by Gareth Armstrong. 6 cass. (Running Time: 7 hrs. 39 mins.). (Isis Ser.). (J). 2002. 54.95 (978-0-7531-0630-3(2)); audio compact disk 71.95 (978-0-7531-1480-3(1)) Pub: ISIS Lrg Prnt GBR. Dist(s): Ulverscroft US
Sir Alfred Dreyfus, eminent headmaster of one of the greatest schools in England, is found guilty of a heinous crime. When Sam Temple, literary agent, visits Dreyfus in prison, he finds a man sunk beyond despair. As Dreyfus begins, reluctantly, the appalling narrative of his betrayal, he must confront, too, his own guilt for a lifetime's denial of his Jewish origins. Bernice Rubens has created a character of profound and moving humanity, in placing him at the end of the 20th century, she makes his story a tragedy, resonating with historical tragedy and bound in with the fate of six million others.

I Drink for a Reason. unabr. ed. David Cross. Read by David Cross. (Running Time: 7 hrs.). (ENG.). 2009. 24.98 (978-1-60024-649-4(4)); audio compact disk 29.98 (978-1-60024-648-7(6)) Pub: Hachet Audio. Dist(s): HachBkGrp

I Dwell in Possibility see Poems & Letters of Emily Dickinson

I Eat Kids & Other Songs for Rebellious Children. Barry Louis Polisar. Perf. by Barry Louis Polisar. 1 cass. (J). (gr. 1-6). 1975. 9.95 (978-0-9615696-3-1(8)) Pub: Rainbow Morn. Dist(s): IPG Chicago
Written about real kids & their concerns, this recording of original songs include: I've got a teacher, she's so mean, He eats asparagus, why can't you be that way?, I don't brush my teeth & I never comb y hair, I sneaked into the kitchen in the middle of the night, & I'm a 3-toed, triple-eyed, double jointed dinosaur.

I Excel in Exams: Babbling Brook. Eldon Taylor. 1 cass. 16.95 (978-1-55978-492-4(X), 5370F) Progress Aware Res.

I Excel in Exams: Classics. Eldon Taylor. 1 cass. 16.95 (978-1-55978-568-6(3), 5370L) Progress Aware Res.

I Feed a Flame Within see Poetry of John Dryden

I Feel Bad about My Neck: And Other Thoughts on Being a Woman. unabr. ed. Nora Ephron. Read by Nora Ephron. (ENG.). 2008. audio compact disk 14.99 (978-0-7393-6993-7(8), Random AudioBks) Pub: Random Audio Pubg. Dist(s): Random

I Feel Like a Giggle: God Made Me to Laugh & Sing. Perf. by Karyn Henley. Created by Karyn Henley. 1 CD. (Running Time: 30 minutes). (J). 2003. audio compact disk 8.99 (978-0-9743197-1-1(6), PLCD2) Child Sens Comm.
I Feel Like a Giggle celebrates the joy of being God's child. Children experience the comfort of knowing that God loves them and takes care of them. This music is age-appropriate, interactive and fun.

I Feel Like Praising: Big Songs for Little Kids. 2002. audio compact disk 9.99 Provident Music.

I Feel So Helpless - for Families of Ill Patients. Patricia O'Malley. Perf. by Barry Weiss. 1 cass. (Running Time: 50 min.). 1998. (978-1-892450-21-0(6), 119) Promo Music.
Guided imagery.

I Fell into a Box of Eggs see Gathering of Great Poetry for Children

I Felt a Funeral in My Brain see Poems & Letters of Emily Dickinson

I Follow Rules at School Audio CD. Adapted by Benchmark Education Company Staff. Based on a work by Cynthia Swain. (Early Explorers Set C Ser.). (J). (gr. k). 2008. audio compact disk 10.00 (978-1-60437-509-1(4)) Benchmark Educ.

I Forgive: Releasing Old Hurts Forever. Richard Jafolla & Mary-Alice Jafolla. Read by Richard Jafolla & Mary-Alice Jafolla. (Relationships Ser.). 1986. 12.95 (330) Stppng Stones.
Works on the Subconscious mind (subliminal) & conscious mind to bring about self-improvement.

I Found Her out There see Poetry of Thomas Hardy

I Free You from Jealousy. Barrie Konicov. 1 cass. 11.98 (978-0-87082-336-7(1), 068) Potentials.
Shows how to free the other person who is experiencing jealousy.

I Get along Without You Very Well. Music by Hoagy Carmichael. Arranged by Paris Rutherford. 1 CD. (Running Time: 5 mins.). 2000. audio compact disk 19.95 (08742499) H Leonard.
This 1938 standard is an easy accompanied ballad for jazz.

I, Gloria Gold, Set. unabr. ed. Judith Summers. 5 cass. 1989. 49.95 (978-1-85496-228-7(0)) Pub: UlverLrgPrint GBR. Dist(s): Ulverscroft US

I Goofed Again. Osho Oshos. Read by Osho Oshos. 1 cass. (Running Time: 90 min.). 10.95 (DBB-6004) Oshos.
Conveys a response to a question in which Osho shares a potent insight into personal transformation: "The moment you see your own faults, they drop like leaves." (Also known as the f - - tape.).

I Got a Bullfrog: Folksongs for the Fun of It. Perf. by David Holt. 1 cass. (Running Time: 39 min.). (gr. k up). 1994. audio compact disk 15.98 (978-0-942303-32-2(6)) Pub: August Hse. Dist(s): Natl Bk Netwk
David Holt brings to life the good old times with these great American Folksongs. He's performed for over one million children & these are the songs they like best. ALA Notable. Parents' Choice Silver.

I Got a Bullfrog: Folksongs for the Fun of It. Perf. by David Holt. 1 cass. (Running Time: 39 min.). (J). (gr. k up). 1994. 9.98 (978-0-942303-33-9(4), HW1255) Pub: High Windy Audio. Dist(s): August Hse

I Got a D in Salami. Henry Winkler & Lin Oliver. Read by Henry Winkler. 2 vols. (Running Time: 2 hrs. 54 mins.). (Hank Zipzer Ser.: No. 2). (J). (gr. 2-6). 2004. pap. bk. 29.00 (978-1-4000-9007-5(5), Listening Lib); 23.00 (978-0-8072-1945-4(2), ImaginStudio) Random Audio Pubg.

I Got It from the Cows: A Live Performance. Michael Perry. Perf. by Michael Perry. 1 CD. (Running Time: 74 mins). 2002. audio compact disk 10.00 (978-0-9631695-9-4(9)) Whist & Jugg.
Humorist Michael Perry recorded in live-audience setting discussing: The perfect cow; explaining the nurse thing to Dad; real firefighters don't wear tights; the dew is on the beer tent; faux pas avec Monster Truck; feather duster blues; celebrating the sewer snake; freaked at the Conoco; holy bumper sticker; fish squeezins; farmboy love; Greek love; Just Say Whoa. Material has been performed on Wisconsin and Minnesota public radio. More content info at www.sneezingcow.com.

I Got Shoes. Perf. by Sweet Honey in the Rock. 1 cass. (Running Time: 44 min.). (J). 1994. pap. bk. & act. bk. ed. 10.98 (978-1-56628-036-5(2), MLP 6102/WB 42552-4); 9.98 (978-1-56628-009-9(5), MFLP2838/WB42534-4) MFLP CA.
I Got Shoes, is a collection of 14 traditonal & new songs carefully selected to inspire, educate & empower youngsters growing up in troubled & confusing times.

I Gotta Be Me: Helping Children Be All They Can Be. Tim Jordan. Read by Tim Jordan. 1 cass. (Running Time: 40 mins.). 1996. 10.00 (978-0-9705335-1-7(9)); audio compact disk 10.00 (978-0-9705335-6-2(X)) Child & Families.
Helps parents with kids of all ages to create safe, close relationships & build self-esteem plus motivation.

I Gotta Praise. 2003. Pt of Grace Ent.

I Gotta Tell It. Perf. by Garnelle Spearman. 1 cass. 10.98 (978-1-57908-228-4(9), 1337); audio compact disk 15.98 CD. (978-1-57908-227-7(0)) Platinm Enter.

I Had a Dream. George Bloomer. audio compact disk Whitaker Hse.

I Had a Dream. unabr. ed. George Bloomer. 1 cass. (Running Time: 90 mins.). 2004. audio compact disk 14.99 (978-0-88368-870-0(0)) Pub: Whitaker Hse. Dist(s): Anchor Distributors
Join a life-changing journey and become a passenger in the caravan of God's liberating reality. See the plan of God for His people as spoken by Bishop Bloomer through seven nights of dreams revealed to him by the awesome presence of God.

I Had a Hippopotamus, Audiocassette. Hector Viverso Lee. (Metro Reading Ser.). (J). (gr. k). 2000. 8.46 (978-1-58120-984-6(3)) Metro Teaching.

I Hadn't Meant to Tell You This, unabr. ed. Jacqueline Woodson. Narrated by Lynne Thigpen. 2 pieces. (Running Time: 3 hrs.). (gr. 6 up). 1998. 21.00 (978-0-7887-2706-1(0), 95644E7) Recorded Bks.
Presumptuous, poorly dressed & unkempt, Lena steps uninvited into the tidy world of stylish, popular 12-year-old Marie, a leader among her circle of friends. Although Lena is a white outsider in this black community, she & Marie share a common bond. An honest exploration of abuse & incest.

I Hadn't Meant to Tell You This, Set, homework pack. unabr. ed. Jacqueline Woodson. 2 cass. (Running Time: 3 hrs.). (YA). 1998. 33.24 (40835) Recorded Bks.

I Hate People! Kick Loose from the Overbearing & Underhanded Jerks at Work & Get What You Want Out of Your Job. unabr. ed. Jonathan Littman & Marc Hershon. (Running Time: 6 hrs. 30 mins.). (ENG.). 2009. 24.98 (978-1-59659-407-4(1), GildAudio) Pub: Gildan Media. Dist(s): HachBkGrp

I Hate People! Kick Loose from the Overbearing & Underhanded Jerks at Work & Get What You Want Out of Your Job. unabr. ed. Jonathan Littman & Marc Hershon. Read by Jonathan Littman & Marc Hershon. (Running Time: 7 hrs.). (ENG.). 2009. audio compact disk 29.98 (978-1-59659-385-5(7), GildAudio) Pub: Gildan Media. Dist(s): HachBkGrp

I-Hate-Selling: The Audiocourse. Allan S. Boress. Read by Allan S. Boress. 8 cass. (Running Time: 8 hrs.). 1995. 119.00 set incl. study guide. (740080KQ) Am Inst CPA.
New business is what keeps a CPA firm going. And this fascinating audio course shows you how to methodically & effectively sell personal services; avoid mistakes; create personal chemistry & build trust; & maintain total control of the sale process. You'll discover the secrets of successful fee negotiation, & how to avoid the "haggling" trap; how to make compelling presentations; 10 techniques used by successful CPAs to sell more business; key steps for finding new business; methods for thoroughly qualifying prospective clients; tips to help you avoid wasting time, effort & energy. This course also demonstrates the major personality types & shows you how to quickly achieve rapport with each. And you'll find dynamic methods for positively & effortlessly influencing others.

***I Hate to Read!** Rita Marshall. Illus. by Etienne Delessert. Narrated by Asa Dorfman. 1 cass. (Running Time: 7 mins.). (J). (gr. k-3). 2008. bk. 27.95 (978-0-8045-6973-6(8)); bk. 29.95 (978-0-8045-4198-5(1)) Spoken Arts.

I Hate to Tell His Widow; Collect from a Corpse. abr. ed. Louis L'Amour. 2 cass. (Running Time: 3 hrs.). (Louis L'Amour Collector Ser.:). 2000. 7.95 (978-1-57815-102-8(3), 1073, Media Bks Audio) Media Bks NJ.
The brave men & women who settled the American frontier.

I Have a Coin: Early Explorers Emergent Set A Audio CD. Benchmark Education Staff. (J). 2006. audio compact disk 10.00 (978-1-4108-7605-8(5)) Benchmark Educ.

I Have a Dream. Margaret Dureke. Tr. by Margaret Dureke. 2003. audio compact disk (978-0-9701144-5-7(1)) Jahs.

I Have a Dream: The Life of Martin Luther King, Jr. Eric Metzgar. (Step into History Ser.). 2006. pap. bk. 69.00 (978-1-4105-0624-5(X)); audio compact disk 18.95 (978-1-4105-0622-1(3)) D Johnston Inc.

I Have a Hope. Contrib. by Tommy Walker & Randy Alward. Prod. by Ed Cash. 2008. audio compact disk 13.99 (978-5-557-45447-6(0)) Maranatha Music.

I Have a Song for You Vol. 1: About People & Nature. rev. ed. Janeen Brady. (J). (ps-4). pap. bk. & stu. ed. 9.95 (978-0-944803-01-1(6)) Brite Music.

I Have a Song for You Vol. 2: About Seasons & Holidays. Janeen Brady. (J). (ps-4). stu. ed. 9.95 (978-0-944803-04-2(0)) Brite Music.

I Have a Song for You Vol. 2: About Seasons & Holidays. Janeen Brady. Ed. by Ted Brady. Illus. by Phyllis Luch & Warren Luch. (J). (ps-4). 1979. 9.95 (978-0-944803-03-5(2)) Brite Music.

I Have a Song for You Vol. 2: About Seasons & Holidays. Janeen Brady. Illus. by Linda U. Howard. (J). (ps-4). 1987. pap. bk. & stu. ed. 9.95 (978-0-944803-05-9(9)) Brite Music.

I Have a Song for You Vol. 3: About Animals. Janeen Brady. Illus. by Linda U. Howard. (J). (ps-4). 1988. 9.95 (978-0-944803-07-3(5)) Brite Music.

I Have an Olive Tree. Eve Bunting. Read by Christina Moore. 1 cass. (Running Time: 15 mins.). (YA). 1999. stu. ed. 167.80 (978-0-7887-3674-2(4), 46977) Recorded Bks.
A beautiful tale of a child learning of her heritage. Sophia doesn't understand when her grandfather gives her an olive tree that grows on a small Greek island. But when she travels to Greece & sees her tree, everything makes sense.

I Have an Olive Tree. unabr. ed. Eve Bunting. Narrated by Christina Moore. 1 cass. (Running Time: 15 mins.). (YA). 2000. pap. bk. 31.95 (978-0-7887-3644-5(2), 41010X4) Recorded Bks.

I Have an Olive Tree. unabr. ed. Eve Bunting. Narrated by Christina Moore. 1 cass. (Running Time: 15 mins.). (ps up). 2000. 10.00 (978-0-7887-3512-7(8), 95865E7) Recorded Bks.

I Have No Mouth, & I Must Scream. Harlan Ellison. 2002. audio compact disk 29.95 (978-1-57453-537-2(4)) Audio Lit.

I Have No Mouth, & I Must Scream. unabr. ed. Audio Literature Staff. Read by Harlan Ellison. 4 cass. (Running Time: 6 hrs.). 2002. reel tape 25.00 (978-1-57453-422-1(X)) Audio Lit.
Contents include: an original introduction; "I Have No Mouth, and I Must Scream"; Laugh Track Grail"; "Repent, Harlequin!" said the Ticktockman; "The Very Last Day of a Good Woman"; "The Time of the Eye"; "Paladin of the Lost Hour"; "The Lingering Scent of Woodsmoke"; and "A Boy and His Dog".

I Have to give a Presentation, Now What?! Jude Westerfield. Narrated by Brian Keeler. 4 CDs. 2002. audio compact disk 39.00 (978-1-4025-3829-2(4)) Recorded Bks.

I Have 50 Cents: Early Explorers Early Set B Audio CD. Jamie A. Schroeder. Adapted by Benchmark Education Staff. (J). 2007. audio compact disk 10.00 (978-1-4108-8236-3(5)) Benchmark Educ.

I Hear a Rhapsody. Perf. by George Shearing. 1 cass., 1 CD. 7.98 (TA 33310); audio compact disk 12.78 CD Jewel box. (TA 83310) NewSound.

I Hear America Singing see Classic American Poetry

***I Hear Angels.** Sheila Walsh. Prod. by Women of Faith. 2010. audio compact disk 13.99 (978-1-4261-0908-9(3)) Nelson.

I Hear Memories! Beckie Karras. 1 cass. (Running Time: 34 min.). (J). 1991. pap. bk. 15.95 (978-1-879633-06-3(X)) Eldersong.
Side A has 14 familiar sound vignettes such as a baseball game & the zoo to stimulate reminiscences. Side B has a game of 25 "mystery sounds" to guess. Each cassette comes with an 18-page book containing discussion questions plus prop & music ideas.

I Hear the Angel's Singing-Music. 2007. audio compact disk 16.95 (978-1-56136-435-0(5)) Master Your Mind.

I Heard a Fly Buzz When I Died see Poems & Letters of Emily Dickinson

I Heard Him Come. Perf. by David Glen Hatch & Mormon Symphony. 1 cass. 1996. 9.95 Digitally Mastered. (101944); audio compact disk 14.95 CD Digitally Mastered. (109111) Covenant Comms.
Mormon Symphony joins with the talents of David Glen Hatch at the piano to perform captivating arrangements of ten well-known contemporary songs.

I Heard It with My Own Two Ears: A Corner to Grow In see I Heard It with My Own Two Ears: Listening Comprehension Skills

I Heard It with My Own Two Ears: A Visit to the Floor of the Ocean see I Heard It with My Own Two Ears: Listening Comprehension Skills

I Heard It with My Own Two Ears: Animals Get Scared Too see I Heard It with My Own Two Ears: Listening Comprehension Skills

I Heard It with My Own Two Ears: Are You Listening? see I Heard It with My Own Two Ears: Listening Comprehension Skills

I Heard It with My Own Two Ears: City Rhythm see I Heard It with My Own Two Ears: Listening Comprehension Skills

I Heard It with My Own Two Ears: If You Were a Street Light see I Heard It with My Own Two Ears: Listening Comprehension Skills

I Heard It with My Own Two Ears: Introduction to Listening Skills see I Heard It with My Own Two Ears: Listening Comprehension Skills

I Heard It with My Own Two Ears: Listening Comprehension Skills. unabr. ed. 12 cass. Incl. Lesson 1. I Heard It with My Own Two Ears: Introduction to Listening Skills. (J). (gr. k-6). (SAC 4003); Lesson 2. I Heard It with My Own Two Ears: Are You Listening? (J). (gr. k-6). (SAC 4003); Lesson 3. I Heard It with My Own Two Ears: Animals Get Scared Too. (J). (gr. k-6). (SAC 4003); Lesson 4. I Heard It with My Own Two Ears: If You Were a Street Light. (J). (gr. k-6). (SAC 4003); Lesson 5. I Heard It with My Own Two Ears: Where Do You Live? (J). (gr. k-6). (SAC 4003); Lesson 6. I Heard It with My Own Two Ears: Where Does Everybody Go? (J). (gr. k-6). (SAC 4003); Lesson 7. I Heard It with My Own Two Ears: Music Everywhere. (J). (gr. k-6). (SAC 4003); Lesson 8. I Heard It with My Own Two Ears: City Rhythm. (J). (gr. k-6). (SAC 4003); Lesson 9. I Heard It with My Own Two Ears: Ten Pound Boots plus Ten-Gallon Hat. (J). (gr. k-6). (SAC 4003); Lesson 10. I Heard It with My Own Two Ears: A Visit to the Floor of the Ocean. (J). (gr. k-6). (SAC 4003); Lesson 11. I Heard It with My Own Two Ears: Star Time. (J). (gr. k-6). (SAC 4003); Lesson 12. I Heard It with My Own Two Ears: A Corner to Grow In. (J). (gr. k-6). (SAC 4003); (J). (gr. k-6). 109.95 set, incl. tchr's. guide. (978-0-8045-4003-2(9), SAC 4003) Spoken Arts.
All are presented in story form to develop fundamental oral-aural skills of listening comprehension, thought organization, & verbal expression. Using familiar & not so familiar sounds, this series of cassette lessons may be presented in any order.

I Heard It with My Own Two Ears: Music Everywhere see I Heard It with My Own Two Ears: Listening Comprehension Skills

I Heard It with My Own Two Ears: Star Time see I Heard It with My Own Two Ears: Listening Comprehension Skills

I Heard It with My Own Two Ears: Ten Pound Boots plus Ten-Gallon Hat see I Heard It with My Own Two Ears: Listening Comprehension Skills

I Heard It with My Own Two Ears: Where Do You Live? see I Heard It with My Own Two Ears: Listening Comprehension Skills

I Heard It with My Own Two Ears: Where Does Everybody Go? see I Heard It with My Own Two Ears: Listening Comprehension Skills

I Heard That Song Before. unabr. ed. Mary Higgins Clark. Read by Jan Maxwell. 7 CDs. (Running Time: 8 hrs. 0 mins. 0 sec.). (ENG.). 2007. audio compact disk 39.95 (978-0-7435-6407-6(3)) Pub: S&S Audio. Dist(s): S and S Inc

I Heard That Song Before: A Novel. abr. ed. Mary Higgins Clark. Read by Jan Maxwell. (Running Time: 5 hrs. 0 mins. 0 sec.). (ENG.). 2009. audio compact disk 14.99 (978-0-7435-8329-9(9)) Pub: S&S Audio. Dist(s): S and S Inc

I Heard the Owl call My Name. Margaret Craven. Narrated by Frank Muller. 3 CDs. (Running Time: 3 hrs. 30 mins.). audio compact disk 29.00 (978-0-7887-4490-7(9)) Recorded Bks.

I Heard the Owl Call My Name. unabr. ed. Margaret Craven. Narrated by Frank Muller. 3 cass. (Running Time: 3 hrs. 30 mins.). 1987. 26.00 (978-1-55690-244-4(1), 87400E7) Recorded Bks.
A mortally ill young priest goes to the Pacific Northwest to serve a community of Kwakiutl Indians in British Columbia.

I Heard the Owl Call My Name. unabr. ed. Margaret Craven. Narrated by Frank Muller. 3 CD. (Running Time: 3 hrs. 30 min.). 2000. audio compact disk 29.00 (C1191E7) Recorded Bks.

I Heard You Paint Houses. Charles Demarco Brandt. 2003. 25.95 (978-0-06-059450-3(0)) HarperCollins Pubs.

I Heart Bloomberg. unabr. ed. Melody Carlson. Narrated by Brooke Sanford. (86 Bloomberg Place Ser.). (ENG.). 2008. 18.19 (978-1-60814-247-7(7)) Oasis Audio.

I Heart Bloomberg. unabr. ed. Melody Carlson. Read by Pam Turlow. Narrated by Brooke Sanford. (86 Bloomberg Place Ser.). (ENG.). 2008. audio compact disk 25.99 (978-1-59859-373-0(0)) Oasis Audio.

I Heart Revolution: With Hearts as One. Contrib. by Hillsong United et al. 2008. 14.98 (978-5-557-39781-0(7)) Integrity Music.

I Heart Revolution: with Hearts as One. Contrib. by Hillsong United. 2008. audio compact disk 17.98 (978-5-557-46350-8(X)) Hillsong Pubng AUS.

I Hide Away Your Word in My Heart Vol. 1: Scripture Songs for Kids. Scripture in Song, Ltd. Staff. 1 cass. (J). (gr. 8). 1995. (978-1-888191-05-9(8)) U of the Nations.
Collection of songs for preschoolers.

I Hide Away Your Word in My Heart Vol. 2: Scripture Songs for Kids. Scripture in Song, Ltd. Staff. 1 cass. (J). (gr. 8). 1995. (978-1-888191-06-6(6)) U of the Nations.

I Hide Away Your Word in My Heart Vol. 3: Scripture Songs for Kids. Scripture in Song, Ltd. Staff. 1 cass. (J). (gr. 8). 1995. (978-1-888191-07-3(4)) U of the Nations.

I Hide Away Your Word in My Heart Vols. 1-3: Scripture Songs for Kids. Scripture in Song, Ltd. Staff. 3 cass. (J). (gr. 8). 1995. set. (978-1-888191-09-7(0)) U of the Nations.

I Hope You Dance. gif. ed. Perf. by Lee Ann Womack. Illus. by Nicholson Aric. Lyrics by Mark D. Sanders & Tia Sillers. Prod. by Brighter Minds. 1 CD. (J). 2005. bds. 9.99 (978-1-57791-151-7(2), Little Melody Pr) Pub: Brighter Minds. Dist(s): Perseus Dist

I, Houdini: The Amazing Story of an Escape-Artist Hamster. unabr. ed. Lynne Reid Banks. 2 cass. (Running Time: 3 hrs.). (J). 1997. 23.00 (LL0084, Chivers Child Audio) AudioGO.

I, Houdini: The Amazing Story of an Escape-Artist Hamster. unabr. ed. Lynne Reid Banks. Read by Lynne Reid Banks. 2 cass. (Running Time: 2 hrs. 51 mins.). (J). (gr. 4-5). 1996. pap. bk. 28.00 (978-0-8072-7644-0(8), YA908SP, Listening Lib); 23.00 (978-0-8072-7643-3(X), YA908CX, Listening Lib) Random Audio Pubg.
A dauntless hamster lives up to the name Houdini by getting into & out of scrapes more daring than the great escape artist ever dreamed of.

I, Houdini: The Amazing Story of an Escape-Artist Hamster, Set. unabr. ed. Lynne Reid Banks. Read by Lynne Reid Banks. 2 cass. (J). (gr. 1-8). 1999. 16.98 (LL 0084, Chivers Child Audio) AudioGO.

I, Houdini: The Amazing Story of an Escape-Artist Hamster, Set. unabr. ed. Lynne Reid Banks. Read by Lynne Reid Banks. 2 cass. (YA). 1999. 16.98 (FS9-31418) Highsmith.

I in the Triangle. Robert A. Wilson. 1 cass. (Running Time: 1 hr. 25 min.). 1984. 11.00 (05502) Big Sur Tapes.

I in the Triangle. Robert A. Wilson. 2 cass. 18.00 set. (A0411-89) Sound Photosyn.
With an intro by John Lilly this is RAW at his most historically fascinating produced with video effects throughout.

I Is for Innocent. abr. ed. Sue Grafton. Read by Judy Kaye. 3 CDs. (Running Time: 3 hrs.). (Kinsey Millhone Mystery Ser.). (ENG.). 2004. audio compact disk 14.99 (978-0-7393-1417-3(3), RH Aud Price); audio compact disk 8.95 (978-0-7393-1418-0(1), Random Hse Audible) Pub: Random Audio Pubg. Dist(s): Random

I Is for Innocent. unabr. ed. Sue Grafton. Read by Mary Peiffer. 7 cass. (Running Time: 10 hrs. 30 min.). (Kinsey Millhone Mystery Ser.). 1993. 56.00 (978-0-7366-2433-6(3), 3198) Books on Tape.

***I, Isaac, Take You Rebekah.** Featuring Ravi Zacharias. 1986. audio compact disk 9.00 (978-1-61256-019-9(9)) Ravi Zach.

I-It & I-Thou Relationships: Inclusion, Control & Affection. Frank L. Natter. 1 cass. (Problem-Solving in Relationships Ser.). 1989. 10.00 (978-1-878287-68-7(0), ATA-11) Type & Temperament.
Anyone in a relationship about which they care deeply (good-shape relationships/difficult relationships) can learn of new insights & ways to appreciate & improve those relationships. Natter's comments on the work of Buber & others, & effects of motivation on relationships.

I, Juan de Pareja. Elizabeth Borton de Trevino. Read by Johanna Ward. (Playaway Children Ser.). (J). 2008. 39.99 (978-1-60640-749-3(X)) Find a World.

I, Juan de Pareja. unabr. ed. Elizabeth Borton De Trevino. Read by Johanna Ward. (Running Time: 18000 sec.). (J). 2006. audio compact disk 36.00 (978-0-7861-6640-4(1)); audio compact disk 19.95 (978-0-7861-7357-0(2)) Blckstn Audio.

I, Juan de Pareja. unabr. ed. Elizabeth Borton de Trevino. Read by Johanna Ward. 4 cass. (Running Time: 5 hrs. 30 mins.). (SPA.). 1998. 32.95 (978-0-7861-1422-1(3), 2298) Blckstn Audio.
In the era of Rembrandt, Rubens & Van Dyke, Spain had its own great painter - Diego Velasquez. His assistant: an African slave, Juan, by helping his master in his studio becomes an artist himself. Self-taught by watching his master's technique, he is torn between the need to keep his secret - for such work as the creation of art is forbidden to slaves - & the desire to reveal.

I, Judas. unabr. ed. Taylor Caldwell & Jess Stearn. Narrated by Grover Gardner. 9 cass. (Running Time: 13 hrs.). 1982. 78.00 (978-1-55690-246-8(8), 82040E7) Recorded Bks.
Caldwell & Stearn recreate the times, the politics & the persuasions of that greatest of times to bring to life the darkest & most infamous character of all: Judas Iscariot.

I Just Called to Say I Love You, Level 3. (Yamaha Clavinova Connection Ser.). 2004. disk 1.04 (978-0-634-09597-9(8)) H Leonard.

I Just Make Them up, See? see Science Fiction Favorites of Isaac Asimov

I Just Want You. Contrib. by Vicki Yohe. (Mastertrax Ser.). 2006. audio compact disk 9.98 (978-5-558-01815-8(1)) Pure SpringG.

***I Just Want You to Know: Letters to My Kids on Love, Faith, & Family.** unabr. ed. Kate Gosselin et al. (Running Time: 3 hrs. 39 mins. 7 sec.). (ENG.). 2010. 21.99 (978-0-310-41527-5(6)) Zondervan.

I Ka'u Moe'uhane. Laiana Wong. Illus. by Pelika Andrade & Makali'i Andrade. 1 cass. (HAW.). (J). (gr. 1-3). 1999. pap. bk. 5.95 (978-1-58191-072-8(X)) Aha Punana Leo.

I Kissed Dating Goodbye: A New Attitude Toward Romance & Relationships. Featuring Joshua Harris. 1996. 7.95 (978-1-56857-069-3(4)) Noble Pub Assocs.

I Knew Ellen White. Mem. of Alma Baker McKibben et al. (ENG.). 2007. audio compact disk 29.95 (978-1-930920-38-5(5)) L L T Prods.

I Knock at the Door: Life Is More Than Meat see Sean O'Casey Reading I Knock at the Door & Other Works

I Know. Perf. by Lori Wilke. 1 cass. (Running Time: 5 min.). 1998. 9.98 Sound track. (978-1-891916-35-9(1)) Spirit To Spirit.

I Know a Lot of Things; Sparkle & Spin. 2004. 8.95 (978-1-56008-930-8(X)); cass. & flmstrp 30.00 (978-1-56008-689-5(0)) Weston Woods.

I Know an Old Lady. 2004. 8.95 (978-1-56008-931-5(8)); cass. & flmstrp 30.00 (978-0-89719-553-9(1)) Weston Woods.

I Know an Old Lady. Perf. by Timmy Abell. 1 cass, 1 CD. (Running Time: 42 min.). (J). (ps-1). 1996. 10.00 (978-0-9665740-6-7(0), UP951); audio compact disk 16.00 CD. Upstream Prodns.
Collection of songs & stories ideal for the young listener. Enchanting in its simplicity, includes favorite traditional folk songs including "Little White Duck," "Go Tell Aunt Rhody" & one of Abell's most requested selections, an alphabet song called "A for the Ant." Timmy's famous "Bear Hunt" story is also included for an interactive playtime treat.

I Know I Am But Summer to Your Heart see Poetry of Edna St. Vincent Millay

I Know I Am, but What Are You? unabr. ed. Samantha Bee. Read by Samantha Bee. 6 CDs. (Running Time: 7 hrs.). 2010. audio compact disk 29.99 (978-0-7435-9988-7(8)) Pub: S&S Audio. Dist(s): S and S Inc

I Know I Can Climb the Mountain. unabr. ed. Poems. Dale S. Brown. Read by Bill Bradford. Ed. by Laura Fullen. 1 cass. (Running Time: 1 hr. 30 min.). (Learning Disability Ser.). 1995. 8.95 (978-1-881650-06-5(5)) Mntn Bks.
The author shares her experience with Attention Deficit Hyperactivity Disorder through her poetry.

***I know jesus loves me Too.** Kingsway. (ENG.). 2006. audio compact disk 17.99 (978-92-823-0392-4(6)) Pub: Kingsway Pubns GBR. Dist(s): STL Dist NA

I Know My Redeemer Liveth: Luke 24:13-30. Ed Young. (J). 1981. 4.95 (978-0-7417-1173-1(7), A0173) Win Walk.

I Know Some Lonely Houses Off the Road see Gathering of Great Poetry for Children

I Know That My Redeemer Lives. 1 cass. 7.98 (120022) Covenant Comms.

I know that you know that i Know: Narrating subjects from moll flanders To. George Butte. (Theory interpretation Narrativ Ser.). 2004. audio compact disk 9.95 (978-0-8142-9027-9(2)) Pub: Ohio St U Pr. Dist(s): Chicago Distribution Ctr

***I Know This Much Is True.** abr. ed. Wally Lamb. (ENG.). 2004. (978-0-06-075228-6(9), Harper Audio) HarperCollins Pubs.

***I Know This Much Is True.** abr. ed. Wally Lamb. Read by Ken Howard. (ENG.). 2004. (978-0-06-079998-4(6)) HarperCollins Pubs.

I Know This Much Is True. unabr. ed. Wally Lamb. Narrated by George Guidall. 24 cass. (Running Time: 32 hrs. 15 mins.). 1999. 177.00 (978-0-7887-2491-6(6), 95566E7) Recorded Bks.
A mystical, saga of personal growth & survival. All his life, Dominick Birdsey's schizophrenic identical twin has haunted his struggle for wholeness. Now his brother has committed an unthinkable act & middle-aged Dominick is in a tailspin.

I Know What the Caged Bird Feels. unabr. ed. Poems. Paul Laurence Dunbar. Read by Ameria Jones. 1 cass. (Running Time: 1 hr. 30 min.). 1997. 16.95 (978-0-9645593-6-3(6)) MasterBuy Audio Bks.
Consist of more than 30 poems, some in dialect, written by the noted African-American poet at the beginning of the 20th century. Also includes biographical information.

***I Know What You Did Last Summer.** unabr. ed. Lois Duncan. Read by Dennis Holland. (Running Time: 7 hrs. 30 mins.). (ENG.). (YA). 2010. 17.98 (978-1-60788-909-0(9)) Pub: Hachet Audio. Dist(s): HachBkGrp

I Know What You Look Like Naked: And Other Fictions. Roy Schneider. Read by Roy Schneider. 1 cass. (Running Time: 1 hr.). 1991. 12.50 (978-0-9618416-9-0(9)) Graffiti Comix.

I Know Where I'm Going, I Will Give My Love an Apple see Gathering of Great Poetry for Children

I Know Why the Caged Bird Sings. abr. ed. Maya Angelou. Read by Maya Angelou. 3 CDs. (Running Time: 3 hrs.). (ENG.). 1996. audio compact disk 23.00 (978-0-679-45173-0(0)) Pub: Random Audio Pubg. Dist(s): Random

I Know Why the Caged Bird Sings. abr. ed. Maya Angelou. Read by Maya Angelou. 3 CDs. (Running Time: 3 hrs.). 2001. audio compact disk 22.95 (978-0-375-45173-7(0), Random AudioBks) Random Audio Pubg.

I Know Why the Caged Bird Sings, unabr. ed. Maya Angelou. 3 CDs. (Running Time: 4 hrs. 30 mins.). 2001. audio compact disk 16.95 (51730) Books on Tape.
In this wrenching autobiographical story, Maya Angelou tells of her childhood in Stamps, Arkansas, where Maya & her brother, Bailey, lived with their grandmother, a remarkable woman. Amidst the joys, prejudices & violence intruded, causing Maya to close up. Learn how she rose above it all to become an accomplished author, poet & mother.

I Know Why the Caged Bird Sings, Set. abr. ed. Maya Angelou. Read by Maya Angelou. 2 cass. (Running Time: 3 hrs.). 1999. 16.85 (978-1-85686-048-2(5)) Ulvrscrft Audio.
In this first volume of her autobiography, the author beautifully evokes her childhood with her grandmother in the American south of the 1930's.

I Know You're There. Contrib. by Chandler. (Sound Performance Soundtracks Ser.). 2007. audio compact disk 5.98 (978-5-557-71909-4(1)) Pt of Grace Ent.

I Leap over the Wall. unabr. ed. Monica Baldwin. Read by Fleur Chandler. 8 cass. (Running Time: 11 hrs. 30 min.). 1995. 69.95 (978-1-85089-737-8(9), 89125) Pub: ISIS Audio GBR. Dist(s): Ulverscroft US
On October 26, 1941, Monica Baldwin left the convent, where for twenty-eight years she had lived in the strictest possible enclosure, & came out again into the world. This book is the story of what led her to leave & what happened after the doors closed behind her.

I Left My Heart in San Francisco, Level 2. (Yamaha Clavinova Connection Ser.). 2004. disk 1.04 (978-0-634-09588-7(9)) H Leonard.

I-Life: 5 Relational Rules to Help You Live Life to the Fullest. abr. ed. Doug Fields. (Super-Ser.). 2006. audio compact disk 50.00 (978-5-558-25707-6(5)) Group Pub.

I Light up Your Life. 1 cd. audio compact disk 15.98 Platinum Chrst Dist.

I Light up Your Life. Perf. by Phantasmic. 1 CD. audio compact disk 15.98 Platinum Chrst Dist.
Includes "Something about You," "Say Say Say," "Love is a Battlefield," "You Light up My Life," "Love Hurts," "I Turned into a Martian," "Chains of Love," "Could've Been," "Still Lovin' You," & Answers Don't Come Easy".

I Like Church, but...Audio Guidebook. abr. ed. J. Daniel Lupton. Read by J. Daniel Lupton. Intro. by David R. Mains. 2 cass. (50-Day Spiritual Adventure Ser.). 1996. 12.00 Set. (978-1-57849-005-9(7)) Chapel of Air.

I Like Gum. Amy Lowe. 1 cass. (Running Time: 45 min.). (J). (gr. 5-9). 1998. 9.98 (978-1-893967-11-3(5)); audio compact disk 14.98 (978-1-893967-10-6(7)) Emphasis Ent.
A variety of musical styles, including folk, blues, rock & country. A mixture of original songs that highlight environmental awareness, neighborhood diversity, & the ability of every child to make her or his own music.

I Like It Here. unabr. collector's ed. Kingsley Amis. Read by Barry Phillips. 7 cass. (Running Time: 7 hrs.). 1987. 42.00 (978-0-7366-1150-3(9), 2074) Books on Tape.
A literary gent from Wales, author of one obscure title, Garnet Bowen is equipped with a wife, three children & an abominable mother-in-law. Then he gets an offer that requires he leave London, which he can tolerate, for Portugal, which he can't. When he gets there he finds out why.

I Like Me! 2004. bk. 24.95 (978-1-56008-005-3(1)); pap. bk. 32.75 (978-1-55592-244-3(9)); pap. bk. 14.95 (978-1-56008-056-5(6)); 8.95 (978-0-7882-0057-1(7)); cass. & flmstrp 30.00 (978-0-89719-604-8(X)) Weston Woods.

I Like Me! Nancy Carlson. 1 cass., 5 bks. (Running Time: 4 min.). (J). 32.75 Weston Woods.
The story of a totally likeable pig who is delighted to be herself.

I Like Me! Nancy Carlson. 1 cass. (Running Time: 4 min.). (J). (ps-4). bk. 24.95 Weston Woods.

I Like Me! Nancy Carlson. 1 cass. (Running Time: 4 min.). (J). (ps-4). 1989. 12.95 Weston Woods.

I Like My Home Audio CD. Adapted by Benchmark Education Company Staff. Based on a work by Jeffrey B. Fuerst. (My First Reader's Theater Ser.). (J). (gr. k-1). 2008. audio compact disk 10.00 (978-1-60634-093-6(X)) Benchmark Educ.

I Like My Town Audio CD. Adapted by Benchmark Education Company Staff. Based on a work by Francisco Blane. (My First Reader's Theater Ser.). (J). (gr. k-1). 2008. audio compact disk 10.00 (978-1-60634-096-7(4)) Benchmark Educ.

I Like Myself - Inside & Out! Why? Just Because I'm ME! Karen Beaumont. 1 cass. (Running Time: 1 hr.). (J). 2001. pap. bk. 10.95 (KIM 0800C); pap. bk. & pupil's gde. ed. 11.95 (KIM 0800) Kimbo Educ.
Helps children develop a positive self-image & guides understanding of their personal feelings. Be My Friend, It's Not Easy When You're Small, Oh, I'm Angry & more. Includes manual.

I Like to Exercise. Rick Brown. Read by Rick Brown. Ed. by John Quatro. 1 cass. (Running Time: 30 min.). (Subliminal - Easy Listening Ser.). 1993. 10.95 (978-1-57100-023-1(2), E179); 10.95 (978-1-57100-047-7(X), J179); 10.95 (978-1-57100-071-2(2), N179); 10.95 (978-1-57100-095-8(X), S179); 10.95 (978-1-57100-119-1(0), W179); 10.95 (978-1-57100-143-6(3), H179) Sublime Sftware.
Makes a user want to work out.

I Like to See It Lap up Miles see Poems & Letters of Emily Dickinson

I Like to Smile. 1 cass. (J). 1988. 10.00 (978-0-9665740-8-1(7)) Upstream Prodns.
Includes ten original songs such as "I Have Feelings." "Life will still go on," "Life is getting better," "I like to smile" and "Dont bite me.".

I Like What I Like When I Do Not Worry see Gathering of Great Poetry for Children

I Like You: Hospitality under the Influence. unabr. ed. Amy Sedaris. (Running Time: 5 hrs.). (ENG.). 2006. 14.98 (978-1-59483-592-6(6)) Pub: Hachet Audio. Dist(s): HachBkGrp

I Like You: Hospitality under the Influence. unabr. ed. Amy Sedaris. (Running Time: 5 hrs.). (ENG.). 2009. 19.98 (978-1-60788-277-0(9)) Pub: Hachet Audio. Dist(s): HachBkGrp

I Listen Intently. Eldon Taylor. 1 cass. (Running Time: 62 min.). (Inner Talk Ser.). 16.95 incl. script. (978-1-55978-540-2(3), 5423F) Progress Aware Res.
Soundtrack - Brook with underlying subliminal affirmations.

***I Live in a Mad House.** unabr. ed. Kaye Umansky. Read by Tom Lawrence. 2 CDs. (Running Time: 1 hr. 51 mins.). (J). (gr. 3-5). 2009. audio compact disk 21.95 (978-1-4056-5452-4(X), Chivers Sound Lib) AudioGO.

I Look from Afar: Music from the Festival of Lessons & Carols & Evensong. (C). 2000. audio compact disk 16.99 (978-0-918769-48-0(5)) Univ South Pr.

I Look Young & Beautiful. Richard J. Anderson. 1 CD. (Running Time: 60 mins.). 2005. audio compact disk 24.95 (978-0-9765897-5-4(3)) Sedona Wind Pub.
You really can look younger, more attractive and increase your vitality. Uses the power of affirmations and the latest in subliminal technology.

I Lose Weight Now. Read by Mary Richards. 1 cass. (Running Time: 48 min.). (Power Words of Affirmation Ser.). 2007. audio compact disk 19.95 (978-1-56136-192-2(5)) Master Your Mind.

I Lost Everything in the Post-Natal Depression. Erma Bombeck. Narrated by Barbara Rosenblat. 4 CDs. (Running Time: 5 hrs. 15 mins.). 2001. audio compact disk 39.00 (978-0-7887-5173-8(5), C1335E7) Recorded Bks.
Erma takes a fun-filled look at what it's really like to be a modern wife & mother. She exposes threats to the most stable contemporary marriage & reveals what happens when a wife makes a dent in his car, couples cook over the hibachi & a woman expects romance from her worn out husband.

I Lost Everything in the Post-Natal Depression. unabr. ed. Erma Bombeck. Narrated by Barbara Rosenblat. 4 cass. (Running Time: 5 hrs. 15 mins.). 1970. 40.00 (978-0-7887-4381-8(3), 96189E7) Recorded Bks.
She takes a fun-filled look at what it's really like to be a modern wife & mother.

I Lost It at the Movies. unabr. ed. Pauline Kael. Read by Sheryl Dold. 11 cass. (Running Time: 16 hrs. 30 min.). 1988. 88.00 (978-0-7366-1422-1(2), 2308) Books on Tape.
The first collection of Pauline Kael's film reviews. Interwoven around reviews of such movies as On the Waterfront, Hud, West Side Story, Lolita and many others, are her views on the state of the film industry and the art of film criticism into the 1960s.

I Lost My Bear. 2004. bk. 29.95 (978-1-55592-704-2(1)) Weston Woods.

I Lost My Bear. 2004. bk. 24.95 (978-1-55592-694-6(0)); pap. bk. 18.95 (978-1-55592-707-3(6)); pap. bk. 38.75 (978-1-55592-714-1(9)); pap. bk. 32.75 (978-1-55592-710-3(6)); pap. bk. 14.95 (978-1-55592-698-4(3)); 8.95 (978-1-55592-547-5(2)); audio compact disk 12.95 (978-1-55592-553-6(7)) Weston Woods.

I Lost My Bear. Jules Feiffer. Read by Christina Moore. 1 cass. (Running Time: 15 mins.). (YA). 2000. pap. bk. 34.25 (978-0-7887-4095-4(4), 41091); 178.30 (978-0-7887-4096-1(2), 47084) Recorded Bks.
When a little girl looks for her favorite stuffed bear, she finds all sorts of things, but not her bear. Is it gone forever?.

I Lost My Bear. unabr. ed. Jules Feiffer. Narrated by Christina Moore. 1 cass. (Running Time: 15 mins.). (ps up). 2000. 10.00 (978-0-7887-4002-2(4), 96016E7) Recorded Bks.

I Lost My Grandfather's Brain. unabr. ed. Bruce Coville. Read by William Dufris. 2 vols. (Running Time: 2 hrs. 15 mins.). (I Was a Sixth Grade Alien Ser.: Vol. 3). (J). (gr. 3-6). 2004. pap. bk. 29.00 (978-0-8072-8385-1(1), YA180SP, Listening Lib); 23.00 (978-0-8072-8384-4(3), YA180CX, Listening Lib) Random Audio Pubg.

I Lost My Love in Baghdad: A Modern War Story. unabr. ed. Michael Hastings. Read by Michael Hastings. 6 CDs. (Running Time: 7 hrs. 30 mins. 0 sec.). (ENG.). 2008. audio compact disk 29.99 (978-1-4001-0735-3(0)); audio compact disk 19.99 (978-1-4001-5735-8(8)); audio compact disk 59.99 (978-1-4001-3735-0(7)) Pub: Tantor Media. Dist(s): IngramPubServ

I Love a Mystery. (Nostalgia Classics Ser.). 19.98 Moonbeam Pubns.
Includes "The Thing that Cries in the Night," "Bury Your Dead," & "Arizona".

I Love a Mystery. 6 cass. (Running Time: 60 min. per cass.). (Carlton E. Morse Collection). 1998. 24.98 Boxed gift set. (4302) Radio Spirits.
Includes: "The Thing That Cries in the Night" & "Bury Your Dead Arizona".

I Love A Mystery. 6 CDs. (Running Time: 6 hrs.). 2004. audio compact disk 29.95 (978-1-57816-215-4(7)) Audio File.

I Love a Mystery, Set. Perf. by Tony Randall et al. 6 cass. 24.95 (978-1-57816-037-2(5), 1016IL) Audio File.
Two complete adventures in one set starring Tony Randall as Reggie York, Jim Boles as Doc Long & Russell Thorsen as Jack Packard of the A-1 Detective Agency. Includes: "The Thing That Cries in the Night" & "Bury Your Dead, Arizona".

I Love a Mystery: Bury Your Dead, Arizona. Perf. by Tony Randall et al. 3 cass. (Running Time: 1 hr. ea.). 23.85 Set. (MM8050) Natl Recrd Co.
Jack (Russell Thorson), Doc (Jim Boles) & Reggie (Tony Randall) of the A-1 Detective Agency are in a freight yard in an empty box car trying to leave town so neither the police nor some small town hoods can find them. Doc lost their $25,000 reward money to hoods in a poker game, then drew a gun & took the money back when he discovered the game was crooked. The police want them to testify in a case & now trouble begins. Cast also includes Mercedes McCambridge.

I Love a Mystery: The Thing That Cries in the Night. Perf. by Tony Randall et al. 3 cass. (Running Time: 3 hrs.). 23.85 Set. (MM3363) Natl Recrd Co.
Grandma Martin asks Reggie (Tony Randall), Jack (Russell Thorson) & Doc (Jim Boles) of the A-1 Detective Agency to find the friend who is trying to murder her 3 granddaughters, Faith, Hope & Charity. They discover Faith has been blackmailed by the murdered family chauffeur, Hope discovered without a dress - "high" on something "decidedly not liquor," & Charity (Mercedes McCambridge) found with her arms & thighs slashed by a razor.

I Love Adventure. 6 cass. 24.98 Set. Moonbeam Pubns.

I Love Adventure. 13 episodes on 6 ca. (Running Time: 6 hrs. 30 min.). (Carlton E. Morse Collection). 1998. 26.98 Boxed set. (4300) Radio Spirits.
Jack Packard, Doc Long & Reggie Yorke battle the enemies of peace.

I Love Being Here with You. Perf. by Jeanie Bryson. 1 cass., 1 CD. 7.98 (TA 33336); audio compact disk 12.78 CD Jewel box. (TA 83336) NewSound.

I Love Lucy: Behind the Scenes. abr. ed. Perf. by Lucille Ball et al. Mem. of Jess Oppenheimer & Greg Oppenheimer. Narrated by Larry Dobkin. 2 cass. (Running Time: 3 hrs.). 2001. audio compact disk 12.98 (4406) Radio Spirits.
Inside look at how the show was conceived and developed. Jess Oppenheimer, the "brains" behind "My Favorite Husband" and "I Love Lucy, mixes backstage stories from both shows with Lucy's classic radio and TV comedy (including "Vitameatavegamin").

I Love Lucy: Behind the Scenes. abr. ed. Jess Oppenheimer et al. Read by Larry Dobkin. 2 cass. (Running Time: 180 min.). 1998. 17.95 Set. (978-1-55935-278-9(7)) Soundelux.
An 'insider's view' into the making of the most popular sitcom of all time.

I Love Lucy: Gen. 17:15-16. Ed Young. 1991. 4.95 (978-0-7417-1840-2(5), 840) Win Walk.

I Love My Body: Female. 1 cass. 10.00 (978-1-58506-027-6(5), 57) New Life Inst OR.
Feel happy with your body & be happier in everything you do!.

I Love My Body: Female. Barrie Konicov. 1 cass. 11.98 (978-0-87082-337-4(X), 069) Potentials.
Explains why you do not like your body, you do not like your life, & that this feeling is automatically & subconsciously projected to others who reflect those feelings back to you. The program shows that if you change your beliefs about your body you will change your entire world.

I Love My Body: Male. 1 cass. 10.00 (978-1-58506-026-9(7), 56) New Life Inst OR.
Feel happy with your body & be happier in everything you do!.

I Love My Body: Male. Barrie Konicov. 1 cass. 11.98 (978-0-87082-338-1(8), 070) Potentials.
Explains why you do not like your body, you do not like your life, & that this feeling is automatically & subconsciously projected to others who reflect those negative feelings back at you. Shows you that if you change your beliefs about your body, you will change your entire life.

I Love My Body - Female. Barrie Konicov. 1 CD. 2004. audio compact disk 19.98 (978-1-56001-673-1(6)) Potentials.
In working with thousands of people around the world, Barrie found that if we do not feel good about our bodies, we often do not like our life. Change your beliefs about your body and you will change your entire world. You will find the self-hypnosis on track 1 and the subliminal on track 2. The easy-listening music of the subliminal, together with the self-hypnosis, is the original format which most people love and with which they are most familiar.

I Love My Day School. Mary Lafleur et al. 1 cass. (Running Time: 30 min.). (J). 1996. cass. & video (978-0-9653809-8-0(X)) Eaho Prodns.
Fun, original, singable children's music.

I Love Seeds. unabr. ed. Burchie Green. 1 cass. (Running Time: 40 min.). (J). (gr. k-4). 1992. 9.98 (978-0-9649933-0-3(9)) Mud Pie Prods.
Original songs for children ages 3-12.

I Love to Laugh (from Mary Poppins) - ShowTrax. Arranged by Cristi Cary Miller. 1 CD. 2000. audio compact disk 19.95 H Leonard.
The fun never stops with this light-hearted song from Walt Disney's "Mary Poppins." It's a "smile-a-minute"!.

I Love to Sing! Songs for Babies & Toddlers. 1 cass., 1 CD. (J). 1999. 9.99 Reproducible. (607135001140607135001157); audio compact disk 14.99 CD. (607135001157) Gospel Lght.
Upbeat songs for active play & gentle, soothing lullabies for calming little ones at quiet time. Designed for use at home or with the Little Blessings Nursery Kit. Inc.

I Love to Sing: Songs for Babies & Toddlers. 1 cass.; 1 CD. (J). 9.99 (Regal Bks); audio compact disk 14.99 CD. Gospel Lght.
Tunes designed for use at home or with the Little Blessings Nursery Kit. Upbeat songs for active play & gentle, soothing lullabies for calming little ones.

I Love to Tell the Story. Prod. by Andy Griffith. 1 CD. audio compact disk Brentwood Music.
One of America's best-loved actors brings us a beautiful rendition of 25 classic hymns. General Market release only.

I Love to Tell the Story: A Hymns Collection. Contrib. by Mark Lowry & Paul Johnson. Prod. by Paul Johnson. (Gaither Gospel Ser.). 2007. 12.99 (978-5-557-67285-6(0)); audio compact disk 17.99 (978-5-557-67286-3(9)) Gaither Music Co.

I Love Toy Trains, Pt. 4, 5, 6. Score by Jim Coffey. 2003. audio compact disk 24.95 (978-0-937522-40-0(6)) Pub: TM Bks Video. Dist(s): MBI Dist Svcs

I Love Toy Trains, Pt. 7, 8, 9. Score by Jim Coffey. 2003. audio compact disk 24.95 (978-0-937522-41-7(4)) Pub: TM Bks Video. Dist(s): MBI Dist Svcs

I Love Toy Trains, Pt. 10, 11, 12. Score by Jim Coffey. 2003. audio compact disk 24.95 (978-1-932291-03-2(2)) Pub: TM Bks Video. Dist(s): MBI Dist Svcs

I Love Toy Trains, Pts. 1,2,3. Tm Books & Video Inc. 2004. DVD & audio compact disk 24.95 (978-0-937522-34-9(1)) Pub: TM Bks Video. Dist(s): MBI Dist Svcs

***I Love You, Beth Cooper.** unabr. ed. Larry Doyle. Read by Paul Rust. (ENG.). 2009. (978-0-06-190199-7(7), Harper Audio); (978-0-06-190198-0(9), Harper Audio) HarperCollins Pubs.

I Love You, Beth Cooper. unabr. movie tie-in ed. Larry Doyle. Read by Paul Rust. 6 CDs. (Running Time: 7 hrs. 30 mins.). 2009. audio compact disk 19.99 (978-0-06-177207-8(0), Harper Audio) HarperCollins Pubs.

I Love You Like Crazy Cakes. 2004. 8.95 (978-1-55592-962-6(1)); audio compact disk 12.95 (978-1-55592-936-7(2)) Weston Woods.

I Love You Like Crazy Cakes. (J). 2004. bk. 24.95 (978-1-55592-095-1(0)) Weston Woods.

I Love You Lord: Violin & Oboe. 1 cass. (Instrumental Praise Ser.). 1999. 7.99 (978-0-7601-2673-8(9), 83061-0504-483061-0504-2); audio compact disk 10.00 (978-0-7601-2674-5(7), 83061-0504-2) Provident Music.
Includes: "Abide with Me," "Amazing Grace," "As the Deer," "Beneath the Cross of Jesus," "Day by Day," "O How He Loves You & Me," "I Love You, Lord," "Morning Has Broken," "Sacred Head Now Wounded," "Savior, Like a Shepherd Lead Us," "The Lord Is My Shepherd," "The Old Rugged Cross," & more.

I Love You More: How Everyday Problems Can Strengthen Your Marriage. . Les and Leslie Parrott. (Running Time: 5 hrs. 58 mins. 0 sec.). (ENG.). 2009. 14.99 (978-0-310-30139-4(4)) Zondervan.

I Love You. Now What? Falling in Love Is a Mystery, Keeping It Isn't. abr. ed. Mabel Iam. (Running Time: 23400 sec.). 2008. audio compact disk 29.95 (978-1-4332-0841-6(5)); audio compact disk & audio compact disk 63.00 (978-1-4332-0843-0(1)) Blckstn Audio.

I Love You. Now What? Falling in Love Is a Mystery, Keeping It Isn't. abr. ed. Mabel Iam. Read by Traci Svendsgaard. (Running Time: 23400 sec.). 2008. 29.95 (978-1-4332-0839-3(3)); 54.95 (978-1-4332-0842-3(3)); audio compact disk 29.95 (978-1-4332-0840-9(7)) Blckstn Audio.

I Love You, Stinky Face. Lisa McCourt. Narrated by Kirsten Krohn. Illus. by Cyd Moore. 1 CD. (Running Time: 6 mins.). (J). (ps-3). 2009. pap. bk. 18.95 (978-0-545-11944-3(8)); audio compact disk 9.99 (978-0-545-11757-9(7)) Scholastic Inc.

I Loved, I Lost, I Made Spaghetti. unabr. ed. Giulia Melucci. Read by Giulia Melucci. 1 MP3-CD. (Running Time: 7 hrs.). 2009. 39.97 (978-1-4233-8935-4(2), 9781423389354, Brinc Audio MP3 Lib); 39.97 (978-1-4233-8937-8(9), 9781423389378, BADLE); 24.99 (978-1-4233-8934-7(4), 9781423389347, Brilliance MP3); 24.99 (978-1-4233-8936-1(0), 9781423389361, BAD); audio compact disk 87.97 (978-1-4233-8933-0(6), 9781423389330, BriAudCD Unabrid); audio compact disk 29.99 (978-1-4233-8932-3(8), 9781423389323) Brilliance Audio.

I Loved My Friend see Gathering of Great Poetry for Children

I Loved You Once see Classical Russian Poetry

I, Lucifer. Contrib. by Destroy the Runner. Prod. by Brian McTernan. 2008. audio compact disk 13.99 (978-5-557-47161-9(8)) Solid State MO.

I. M. A. G. E. Nan Allen & Dennis Allen. 10 cass. (Running Time: 10 hrs.). (YA). 2001. 54.99 (TA-9231PK) Lillenas.
Using imagination & humor, this musical beautifully expresses who we really are-in relationship to our Creator & in Jesus Christ. The drama portions are easily staged, yet pointed, fun & highly effective. Included are great new songs & several contemporary favorites, all arranged SAB with lots of unison & 2-part. Includes stereo trax & split-channel mixes. Cassette volume pack (10 unwrapped cassettes).

I. M. A. G. E. Nan Allen & Dennis Allen. 1 cass. (Running Time: 1 hr.). (YA). 1998. 12.99 (TA-9231C) Lillenas.

I. M. A. G. E. A Youth Musical about Who We Really Are. Created by Dennis Allen & Nan Allen. 1 cass. (Running Time: 45 min.). (YA). 2001. 80.00 (MU-9231C); audio compact disk 80.00 (MU-9213T) Lillenas.
Using imagination & humor, this musical beautifully expresses who we really are in relationship to our Creator & in Jesus Christ.The drama portions are easily staged, yet pointed, fun & highly effective. Included are great new songs & several contemporary favorites, all arranged SAB with lots of unison & 2-part. Accompaniment cassette with side 1, stereo trax & side 2, split-channel.

I Made It. 2001. 7.00 (978-0-9656062-3-3(6)); audio compact disk 12.00 (978-0-9656062-2-6(8)) OJU Min Assn.

I Make the Best of Every Situation. (Abraham-Hicks G-Ser.). 2004. audio compact disk 117.00 (978-1-935063-18-6(9)) Abraham-Hicks Pubs.

I Married a Communist. unabr. ed. Philip Roth. Read by Ron Silver. (YA). 2008. 54.99 (978-1-60514-840-3(7)) Find a World.

I Mea Aha Ke Kai? Lilinoe Andrews. Illus. by Brook Parker. 1 cass. (HAW.). (J). 1999. pap. bk. 6.95 (978-1-58191-080-3(0)) Aha Punana Leo.

I Met Murder. unabr. ed. Elizabeth Ferrars. Read by Frances Jeater. 5 cass. (Running Time: 6 hr. 30 min.). 1998. 49.95 (978-0-7531-0408-8(3), 970704) Pub: ISIS Audio GBR. Dist(s): Ulverscroft US
Whenever Felix, the light-fingered husband from whom Virginia Freer was semi-detached, reappeared in her life, it seemed murder did too. Holly, orphaned daughter of a famous actress had come to Rome to stay with Virginia's friends, the Brightwells. Holly disappeared, believed kidnapped & distraught Ann Brightwell was prepared to sell her valuables to meet the ransom demand. Felix thought there was something odd about the kidnapping & was convinced the ransom shouldn't be paid.

I Miss You, Stinky Face. Lisa McCourt. (ENG.). (J). (ps-3). 2009. audio compact disk 18.95 (978-0-545-13856-7(6)) Scholastic Inc.

I Motivate Me: How to Organize Your Life in 37 Minutes. Angela Tezeno. 2009. audio compact disk 19.95 (978-1-60743-827-4(5)) Indep Pub IL.

I Need a Hug. unabr. ed. Clara Barton Elementary School Staff. 1 cass. (Running Time: 5 min.). (J). (ps-3). 1993. pap. bk. 14.45 (978-0-8045-6755-8(7), 6755) Spoken Arts.

I Need a Job, Now What?! Janet Garber. Narrated by George Wilson. 3 CDs. 2001. audio compact disk 29.00 (978-0-7887-5180-6(8)) Recorded Bks.

I Need to Know (Dimelo) - ShowTrax. Perf. by Marc Anthony. Arranged by Alan Billingsley. 1 CD. (Running Time: 5 mins.). (SPA & ENG.). 2000. audio compact disk 19.95 (08201166) H Leonard.
This 1999 hit by Latin pop sensation Marc Anthony has an infectious vocal hook & cool dance beat that will add a spark to any show. Includes English & Spanish lyrics.

I Need You to Love Me. Contrib. by Barlow Girl. (Sound Performance Soundtracks Ser.). 2006. audio compact disk 5.98 (978-5-558-35305-1(8)) Pt of Grace Ent.

I Need Your Love - Is That True? How to Stop Seeking Love, Approval, & Appreciation & Start Finding Them Instead. abr. ed. Byron Katie. Read by Byron Katie. 4 CDs. (Running Time: 5 hrs.). (ENG.). 2005. audio compact disk 27.50 (978-0-7393-1699-3(0), RH-Aud Dim) Pub: Random Audio Pubg. Dist(s): Random

I Need Your Love - Is That True? How to Stop Seeking Love, Approval, & Appreciation & Start Finding Them Instead. unabr. ed. Byron Katie. 7 cass. (Running Time: 10 hrs. 30 min.). 2005. 63.00 (978-1-4159-1571-4(7)); audio compact disk 81.00 (978-1-4159-1658-2(6)) Books on Tape.

I Never Had It Made. abr. ed. Jackie Robinson. Read by Ossie Davis. (Running Time: 3 hrs.). 2008. 39.25 (978-1-4233-5862-6(7), 9781423358626, BADLE); 24.95 (978-1-4233-5859-6(7), 9781423358596, Brilliance MP3); 39.25 (978-1-4233-5860-2(0), 9781423358602, Brinc Audio MP3 Lib); 24.95 (978-1-4233-5861-9(9), 9781423358619, BAD) Brilliance Audio.

I Never Heard the Operetta: Selected Instrumentals. Composed by A. Wayne Jones. 1 CD. 2005. audio compact disk 18.95 (978-0-9763781-7-4(5)) Always Pubns.

I Never Lost As Much but Twice see Poems & Letters of Emily Dickinson

I Never Lost My Praise: Live. Contrib. by Tramaine Hawkins et al. Prod. by Kurt Carr & Jamie Hawkins. 2007. audio compact disk 17.98 (978-5-557-92865-6(0)) GospoCen.

I Never Promised You a Rose Garden. unabr. ed. Joanne Greenberg. 1 read-along cass. (Running Time: 4 hrs. 16 min.). (Young Adult Cliffhangers Ser.). (J). (gr. 6 up). 1985. 15.98 incl. bk. guide. (978-0-8072-1814-3(6), JRH107SP, Listening Lib) Random Audio Pubg.
The story of a young girl's journey from madness to reality.

I Never Saw a Moor see Poems & Letters of Emily Dickinson

I, Nigel Dorking. Mary-Anne Fahey. Read by Jasper Garner Gore. (Running Time: 7 hrs. 15 mins.). (J). 2009. 69.99 (978-1-74214-163-3(3), 9781742141633) Pub: Bolinda Pubng AUS. Dist(s): Bolinda Pub Inc

I, Nigel Dorking. unabr. ed. Mary-Anne Fahey. Read by Jasper Garner Gore. (Running Time: 7 hrs. 15 mins.). (J). 2008. audio compact disk 77.95 (978-1-74093-996-6(4), 9781740939966) Pub: Bolinda Pubng AUS. Dist(s): Bolinda Pub Inc

I "Noah" Friend. (J). pap. bk. 65.95 (522) Chrch Grwth VA.
The simple concept of each child inviting another child to church on a designated Sunday.

I. O. U. unabr. ed. Nancy Pichard. Read by Pamela Nyberg. 6 vols. (Running Time: 9 hrs.). (Jenny Cain Mystery Ser.). 2000. bk. 54.95 (978-0-7927-2225-0(6), CSL 114, Chivers Sound Lib) AudioGO.
It was a foggy day on her mother's funeral, and Jenny's pain and confusion was tremendous. Her mother had died of pneumonia after years in the Hampshire Psychiatric Hospital. As friends and family paid their condolences, Jenny began to wonder just what was really wrong with her mother. And how was it connected to the bankruptcy of the family business? When Jenny tries to find out, she is met with silence. Then someone shuts the garage door when exhausted Jenny falls asleep with the car's motor running.

***I. O. U. Why Everyone Owes Everyone & No One Can Pay.** unabr. ed. John Lanchester. Narrated by James Langton. 1 MP3-CD. (Running Time: 7 hrs. 30 mins. 0 sec.). (ENG.). 2010. 19.99 (978-1-4001-6543-8(1)); 14.99 (978-1-4001-8543-6(2)); audio compact disk 59.99 (978-1-4001-4543-0(0)); audio compact disk 29.99 (978-1-4001-1543-3(4)) Pub: Tantor Media. Dist(s): IngramPubServ

I. O. U. S. A. One Nation - Under Stress - In Debt. unabr. ed. Addison Wiggin & Kate Incontrera. Read by Sean Pratt. (ENG.). 2008. 29.98 (978-1-59659-289-6(3), GildAudio) Pub: Gildan Media. Dist(s): HachBkGrp

I, Omar: Instrumental. Donald Walters. 2002. audio compact disk 15.95 (978-1-56589-070-1(1)) Pub: Crystal Clarity. Dist(s): Natl Bk Netwk

I, Omar: Instrumental. J. Donald Walters. 2002. audio compact disk 15.95 (978-1-56589-071-8(X)) Pub: Crystal Clarity. Dist(s): Natl Bk Netwk

I Only Move Where There Is Fire. abr. ed. Da Avabhasa. 1 cass. (Method of the Siddhas Ser.). 1993. 11.95 (AT-IOM) Dawn Horse Pr.

I Only Say This Because I Love You: How the Way We Talk Can Make or Break Family Relationships Throughout Our Lives. unabr. ed. Deborah Tannen. Read by Patricia Mulholland. 10 vols. (Running Time: 15 hrs.). 2001. bk. 84.95 (978-0-7927-2518-3(2), CSL 407, Chivers Sound Lib) AudioGO.
Searching for signs of acceptance and belonging, we find sins of disapproval and rejection. Why do the seeds of family love so often yield a harvest of criticism and judgement.

I Only Say This Because I Love You: Talking in Families. Deborah Tannen. 2004. 15.95 (978-0-7435-4858-8(2)) Pub: S&S Audio. Dist(s): S and S Inc

I Open to You: Chants. Joyce Rupp. Composed by Joyce Rupp. Contrib. by Marlene Fitzpatrick et al. (Running Time: 47 mins.). 2004. audio compact disk 16.95 (978-1-59471-023-0(6)) Ave Maria Pr.

I Pledge Allegiance. June Swanson. Illus. by Rick Hanson. Narrated by Larry Robinson. (ENG.). (J). 1991. audio compact disk 12.95 (978-1-59519-310-0(3)) Live Oak Media.

I Pledge Allegiance. June Swanson. Illus. by Rick Hanson. (Running Time: 15 mins.). 1991. 9.95 (978-1-59112-063-6(2)) Live Oak Media.

I Pledge Allegiance. unabr. ed. June Swanson. 1 cass. (Running Time: 15 min.). (J). (gr. 2-6). 1991. 9.95 Live Oak Media.
A thorough examination of the history of the pledge of allegiance, its transitions to its present form, & its literal & figurative meanings.

I Pledge Allegiance. unabr. ed. June Swanson. Read by Larry Robinson. Illus. by Rick Hanson. 1 cass. (Running Time: 15 mins.). (J). (gr. 1-3). 1991. bk. 24.95 (978-0-87499-202-1(8)); pap. bk. 16.95 (978-0-87499-201-4(X)) Live Oak Media.

I Pledge Allegiance, Grades 1-3. unabr. ed. June Swanson. Read by Larry Robinson. Illus. by Rick Hanson. 14 vols. (Running Time: 15 mins.). 1991. pap. bk. & tchr. ed. 37.95 Reading Chest. (978-0-87499-203-8(6)) Live Oak Media.

I Promise: How 5 Commitments Determine the Destiny of Your Marriage. unabr. ed. Gary Smalley. Narrated by Nathan Larkin. (ENG.). 2006. 13.99 (978-1-60814-248-4(5)); audio compact disk 19.99 (978-1-59859-174-3(6)) Oasis Audio.

I. Q. Booster Kit. Simone Bibeau. 4 cass. 79.95 Set incl. wkbk. & 2 bonus cass. (545PAB) Nightingale-Conant.
Experts agree that 50 percent of your child's I.Q. level is formed by age seven. Ninety-eight percent is formed by age 13. In that time, your child's brain is actually growing. With the unique & easy-to-use kit, your child will establish the foundation for successful reading, increase his or her attention span, stimulate learning through games & be encouraged for both logical & abstract thinking.

I-Quest 2006 International Building Code: 5 users. ICC. 2006. audio compact disk 401.75 (978-1-58001-344-4(9)) Int Code Counc.

I-Quest 2006 International Fire Code Five User. ICC. 2006. audio compact disk 327.00 (978-1-58001-348-2(1)) Int Code Counc.

I-Quest 2009 IBC: Network Version, 10-Users. ICC. 2009. audio compact disk 830.00 (978-1-58001-802-9(5)) Int Code Counc.

I-Quest 2009 IBC: Network Version, 25-Users. ICC. 2009. audio compact disk 1946.00 (978-1-58001-803-6(3)) Int Code Counc.

I-Quest 2009 IBC: Network Version, 5-Users. ICC. 2009. audio compact disk 519.00 (978-1-58001-801-2(7)) Int Code Counc.

I-Quest 2009 IBC: Network Version, 50-Users. ICC. 2009. audio compact disk 3502.00 (978-1-58001-804-3(1)) Int Code Counc.

I-Quest 2009 IFC: Network Version, 25-Users. ICC. 2009. audio compact disk 1585.00 (978-1-58001-808-1(4)) Int Code Counc.

I-Quest 2009 IFC: Network Version, 5-Users. ICC. 2009. audio compact disk 423.00 (978-1-58001-806-7(8)) Int Code Counc.

I-Quest 2009 IFC: Network Version, 50-Users. ICC. 2009. audio compact disk 2853.00 (978-1-58001-809-8(2)) Int Code Counc.

***I Quit! Stop Pretending Everything Is Fine & Change Your Life.** unabr. ed. Geri Scazzero. Told to Peter Scazzero. (Running Time: 5 hrs. 3 mins. 8 sec.). (ENG.). 2010. 18.99 (978-0-310-32603-8(6)) Zondervan.

I Read Signs. 2004. 8.95 (978-1-56008-932-2(6)); cass. & flmstrp 30.00 (978-1-56008-690-1(4)) Weston Woods.

I Really Love Yiddish: A Mini Course in Yiddish. Emanuel S. Goldsmith. (YID.). 1998. pap. bk. 19.99 (978-1-877909-67-2(X)) Jwsh Bk Ctr Wrkmns Cir.

I Reason, Earth Is Short see Poems & Letters of Emily Dickinson

I Refuse to Raise a Brat: Straightforward Advice on Parenting in an Age of Overindulgence. abr. ed. Marilu Henner & Ruth V. Sharon. Read by Marilu Henner. 2 cass. (Running Time: 3 hrs.). 1999. 18.00 (978-0-694-52129-6(9), Harper Audio) HarperCollins Pubs.

I Relax & Let Go. Read by Mary Richards. 1 cass. (Running Time: 48 min.). (Power Words of Affirmation Ser.). 2007. audio compact disk 19.95 (978-1-56136-193-9(3)) Master Your Mind.

I Remember see Gathering of Great Poetry for Children

I Remember Duke, Hoagy & Strayhorn. Perf. by Ahmad Jamal. 1 cass., 1 CD. 7.98 (TA 33339); audio compact disk 12.78 CD Jewel box. (TA 83339) NewSound.

I Remember Heaven: Learning to Heal MySelf. Laurel Duran. Read by Laurel Duran. 1 cass. (Running Time: 1 hr. 25 mins.). 1998. 10.00 (978-0-9646909-1-2(8)) DuirSoul Bks.
The author gives an inspired account of her near-death experience visit to heaven & provides a detailed description of how she completely healed herself of quadriplegia.

I Remember, I Remember see Favorite American Poems

I Remember, I Remember... One Hundred Eighteen Favorite Poems. unabr. ed. Joan Duce. Read by Frances Jeater et al. 4 cass. (Running Time: 4 hrs. 20 min.). (Isis Ser.). (J). 1993. 44.95 (978-1-85089-725-5(5), 87115) Pub: ISIS Lrg Prnt GBR. Dist(s): Ulverscroft US

***I Remember Nothing: And Other Reflections.** unabr. ed. Nora Ephron. Read by Nora Ephron. (ENG.). 2010. audio compact disk 25.00 (978-0-307-87921-9(6), Random AudioBks) Pub: Random Audio Pubg. Dist(s): Random

I Remember Yule see Christmas with Ogden Nash

I Remember, 118 Favorite Poems. unabr. ed. Joan Duce. 4 cass. (Running Time: 6 hrs.). 2001. 44.95 (87115) Pub: ISIS Audio GBR. Dist(s): Ulverscroft US

I, Rhoda Manning, Go Hunting with My Daddy: And Other Stories. unabr. ed. Ellen Gilchrist. 6 cass. (Running Time: 9 hrs.). 2002. 56.00 (978-0-7366-8748-5(3)) Books on Tape.
Rhoda Manning had a wild if protected childhood and an extremely rebellious stint as a young adult. Here, a clutch of stories is told in the voice of Rhoda - as a child, as a divorced mother of three sons, and as an old woman, recalling the curse and blessing of being the only daughter of Big Dudley. There is a rich vein of sorrow here, but Gilchrist lightens the burden with a grasp of how both folly and grace are born of love; she proves once again that there is no other southern writer quite like her.

***I, Richard.** unabr. ed. Elizabeth George. Read by Derek Jacobi. (ENG.). 2004. (978-0-06-078431-7(8), Harper Audio) HarperCollins Pubs.

***I, Richard.** unabr. ed. Elizabeth George. Read by Derek Jacobi. (ENG.). 2004. (978-0-06-081437-3(3), Harper Audio) HarperCollins Pubs.

I Ride a Bucking Horse see Best of Mark Twain

I Rode with Stonewall. unabr. collector's ed. Henry Kyd Douglas. Read by Dick Estell. 10 cass. (Running Time: 15 hrs.). 1988. 80.00 (978-0-7366-1423-8(0), 2309) Books on Tape.
Stonewall Jackson depended on him; General Lee complimented him; Union soldiers admired him; and ladies everywhere adored him, this dashing, handsome, young Henry Kyd Douglas.

I Rule Dogsbottom School. Jon Blake. Read by Clare Corbett. (Running Time: 4920 sec.). (J). (gr. 1-4). 2006. audio compact disk 21.95 (978-1-4056-5576-7(3)) AudioGO GBR.

I. S. Ravdin Lecture in the Basic Sciences: From Cell to Surgery. 1 cass. (Named Lectures: C85-NL4). 1985. 7.50 (8534) Am Coll Surgeons.

I Said YES! Real Life Stories of Students, Teachers & Leaders Saying YES! to Youth Entrepreneurship in America's Schools. As told by Julie Kantor. 2006. audio compact disk 13.95 (978-0-9765823-7-3(6)) Gazelles Pubng.

I Saw Heaven! A Remarkable Visit to the Spirit World, Set. abr. ed. Lawrence E. Tooley. Read by Mark Van Wagoner. 2 cass. (Running Time: 2 hrs.). 1998. 16.98 (978-0-88290-645-4(3), 1871) Horizon Utah.
Describes paradise, spirit capabilities, & many other aspects of life after death from author's personal experience.

I Saw in Louisiana see Treasury of Walt Whitman

I Saw the Lord: A Wake-up Call for Your Heart. unabr. ed. Anne Graham Lotz. (Running Time: 4 hrs. 27 mins. 0 sec.). (ENG.). 2006. 14.99 (978-0-310-26970-0(9)) Zondervan.

I Say a Little Prayer. unabr. ed. E. Lynn Harris. Read by Mirron Willis. 6 cass. (Running Time: 7 hrs.). 2006. 54.00 (978-0-7366-9661-6(X), BksonTape); audio compact disk 72.00 (978-1-4159-0757-3(9), BksonTape) Pub: Random Audio Pubg. Dist(s): Random

I Say a Prayer for Me: One Woman's Life of Faith & Triumph. Stancie Anderson. Narrated by Susan Spain. 7 cass. (Running Time: 9 hrs. 30 mins.). 2002. 64.00 (978-1-4025-4408-8(1)) Recorded Bks.

I Searched the World. Perf. by Voices of Binghampton. 1 cass. 29.95 (V2028); audio compact disk 15.99 CD. (D2028) Diamante Music Grp.
Recorded in Memphis, a four star collection of 10 songs composed by Director, Kevin Davidson. Combines the traditional choir sound with a contemporary funky beat, resulting in a sure-to-be-hit.

I See Cubes: Early Explorers Emergent Set B Audio CD. Katherine Scraper. Adapted by Benchmark Education Staff. (J). 2007. audio compact disk 10.00 (978-1-4108-8197-7(0)) Benchmark Educ.

I See Grandma's House. unabr. ed. Betty Jo Goddard. Read by Betty Jo Goddard. 2 cass. (Running Time: 1 hr. 40 min.). Set. (978-0-9649863-0-5(2)) Manor Ln Prodns.
Short stories about growing up in rural Illinois in the 1930's. With music.

I See Jesus in You. Perf. by Lori Wilke. 1 cass. (Running Time: 5 min.). 1992. 9.98 Sound track. (978-1-891916-22-9(X)) Spirit To Spirit.

I See the Lord, Set. Bobby Hilton. 4 cass. (Running Time: 6 hrs.). 2000. 22.00 (978-1-930766-09-9(2)) Pub: Bishop Bobby. Dist(s): STL Dist NA
Religious ministry program.

I See the Moon. Perf. by Smith Sisters. 1 cass. (Running Time: 30 min.). (J). (gr. k-6). 1991. 9.98 incl. lyrics. (978-1-879305-12-0(7), AM-C-111) Am Melody.
Traditional & original folk & bluegrass songs performed by the Smith Sisters. Song lyrics included. ALA Notable Children's recording.

I See You Everywhere. unabr. ed. Julia Glass. Narrated by Mary Stuart Masterson. 10 CDs. (Running Time: 11 hrs. 30 mins.). 2008. audio compact disk 90.00 (978-1-4159-5692-2(8), BksonTape) Pub: Random Audio Pubg. Dist(s): Random

I See You Everywhere. unabr. ed. Julia Glass. Read by Julia Glass. Read by Mary Stuart Masterson. (Running Time: 12 hrs.). (ENG.). 2008. 22.50 (978-0-7393-7037-7(5)); audio compact disk 34.95 (978-0-7393-7036-0(7), Random AudioBks) Pub: Random Audio Pubg. Dist(s): Random

***I See, You Saw.** unabr. ed. Nurit Karlin. (ENG.). 2008. (978-0-06-169471-4(1)); (978-0-06-171005-6(9)) HarperCollins Pubs.

I Send a Voice. abr. ed. Evelyn Eaton. Read by Ellen Burstyn. 2 cass. (Running Time: 3 hrs.). 1995. 15.95 (978-0-944993-09-5(5)) Audio Lit.
An extraordinary journey into the heart of the Native American healing tradition.

I Sent a Letter to My Love. unabr. ed. Jeffrey Sweet. Perf. by Stephen Bogardus et al. Lyrics by Melissa Manchester. Music by Melissa Manchester. Based on a book by Bernice Rubens. 2 CDs. (Running Time: 1 hr. 51 mins.). 1998. audio compact disk 25.95 (978-1-58081-115-6(9), TPT109) Pub: L A Theatre. Dist(s): NetLibrary CO
Famed singer-songwriter Melissa Manchester performs in her new musical about romance & longing in small town America.

I Shall Be Made Thy Musique. Poems. Perf. by Garth Hewitt & Penelope Cave. 1 cass., 1 CD. (Running Time: 29 min.). 1997. 11.95 incl. script. (978-0-86347-086-8(6), MoreHse Pubng); audio compact disk 16.95 CD. (978-0-86347-091-2(2), MoreHse Pubng) Church Pub Inc.
Poems by John Donne, George Herbert, & Henry Vaughn set to music & sung by Garth Hewitt & Penelope Cave, with accompaniment from harpsichord, virginals, & portative organ. Script included.

I Shall Live: Surviving the Holocaust 1939-1945. unabr. ed. Henry Orenstein. Read by Henry Orenstein. 8 cass. (Running Time: 12 hrs.). 1996. 59.95 Set. (978-0-9644002-8-3(6)) Common Mode Hrmnic Wave.
Story of Orenstein's survival.

I Shall Live Forever see Secret Garden: A Young Reader's Edition of the Classic Story

***I Shall Not Hate: A Gaza Doctor's Journey on the Road to Peace & Human Dignity.** unabr. ed. Izzeldin Abuelaish. (Running Time: 7 hrs. 30 mins.). 2011. 14.99 (978-1-4526-7042-3(0)); 19.99 (978-1-4526-5042-5(X)); audio compact disk 29.99 (978-1-4526-0042-0(2)) Pub: Tantor Media. Dist(s): IngramPubServ

***I Shall Not Hate (Library Edition) A Gaza Doctor's Journey on the Road to Peace & Human Dignity.** unabr. ed. Izzeldin Abuelaish. (Running Time: 7 hrs. 30 mins.). 2011. 29.99 (978-1-4526-2042-8(3)); audio compact disk 71.99 (978-1-4526-3042-7(9)) Pub: Tantor Media. Dist(s): IngramPubServ

I Shall Not Want. unabr. ed. Julia Spencer-Fleming. Narrated by Suzanne Toren. 12 CDs. (Running Time: 14 hrs. 45 mins.). (Clare Fergusson/Russ Van Alstyne Mystery Ser.). 2008. audio compact disk 99.95 (978-0-7927-5454-1(9)) AudioGO.

***I Shall Wear Midnight.** Terry Pratchett. Read by Stephen Briggs. 2010. (978-0-06-206774-6(5)) HarperCollins Pubs.

***I Shall Wear Midnight.** unabr. ed. Terry Pratchett. Read by Stephen Briggs. 2010. (978-0-06-199680-1(7)) HarperCollins Pubs.

***I Shot an Arrow into the Air.** 2010. audio compact disk (978-1-59171-202-2(5)) Falcon Picture.

I Should Have Been Crucified. Contrib. by Don Marsh. 1997. 19.98 (978-0-7601-2067-5(6), 75700165) Pub: Brentwood Music. Dist(s): H Leonard

I Shouldn't Even Be Doing This. abr. ed. Bob Newhart. 2006. 24.98 (978-1-4013-8500-2(1)) Pub: Hyperion. Dist(s): HarperCollins Pubs

I Shouldn't Even Be Doing This! And Other Things That Strike Me as Funny. abr. ed. Bob Newhart. Read by Bob Newhart. (Running Time: 12600 sec.). 2007. audio compact disk 14.95 (978-1-4013-9023-5(4)) Pub: Hyperion. Dist(s): HarperCollins Pubs

***I Shudder.** unabr. ed. Paul Rudnick. Read by Paul Rudnick. (ENG.). 2009. (978-0-06-192872-7(0), Harper Audio); (978-0-06-196259-2(7), Harper Audio) HarperCollins Pubs.

I Sing Because I'm Happy. Perf. by Mahalia Jackson. Anno. by Jules Schwerin. 1 cass. 1979. (0-9307-90002-4-8) Smithsonian Folkways.
Interviews in the 1950s include Jackson reminiscing about her early childhood & her involvement with music. Includes four songs from concert performances.

I Sing the Body Electric!, unabr. collector's ed. Ray Bradbury. Read by Michael Prichard. 6 cass. (Running Time: 9 hrs.). 1990. 48.00 (978-0-7366-1737-6(X), 2577) Books on Tape.
Ray Bradbury's stories are songs of the strange, poems of a past that never was, whispers of a future that has yet to be. This collection includes a windup grandma on the Pinocchio plan, a humanoid Abe Lincoln, a baby born in the fifth dimension, & the ghost of Ernest Hemingway, among others. He weaves his own certain magic in these 18 gleaming tales of dimensions beyond our own.

***I Sing the Body Electric! And Other Stories.** unabr. ed. Ray Bradbury. Narrated by Dick Hill. (Running Time: 15 hrs. 0 mins. 0 sec.). (ENG.). 2010. 29.99 (978-1-4001-6819-4(8)); 20.99 (978-1-4001-8819-2(9)); audio compact disk 39.99 (978-1-4001-1819-9(0)) Pub: Tantor Media. Dist(s): IngramPubServ

***I Sing the Body Electric! (Library Edition) And Other Stories.** unabr. ed. Ray Bradbury. Narrated by Dick Hill. (Running Time: 15 hrs. 0 mins. 0 sec.). (ENG.). 2010. audio compact disk 95.99 (978-1-4001-4819-6(7)) Pub: Tantor Media. Dist(s): IngramPubServ

I Sing, You Sing. Jay Althouse & Sally K. Albrecht. Contrib. by Alan Billingsley. 1 CD. (ENG.). 1999. audio compact disk 29.95 (978-0-7390-0100-4(0), 18724) Alfred Pub.

I Sing, You Sing Holiday Songs. Jay Althouse. Composed by Sally K. Albrecht. (ENG.). 2002. audio compact disk 24.95 (978-0-7390-2711-0(5)) Alfred Pub.

I Sing, You Sing, Too! 30 Echo Songs for Young Singers. Composed by Sally K. Albrecht & Jay Althouse. (ENG.). 2008. audio compact disk 34.95 (978-0-7390-5258-7(6)) Alfred Pub.

***I Sit on My Tushi.** Yvonne Straus. Illus. by Yvonne Straus. Engineer Roger Stauss & Mark Greenberg. Voice by Bob Lisaius & Tracy Martin. Noteworthy Studios. 2010. audio compact disk 16.99 (978-0-9677376-1-4(3)) Y Straus.

I Sit on My Tushi: And Other Stories. unabr. ed. Yvonne Straus. Read by Tracy Martin & Bob Lisaius. Prod. by Roger Straus. 1 cass. (Running Time: 1 hr. 30 mins.). 2000. 9.95 (978-0-9677376-0-7(5)) Y Straus.
A collection of essays, many of them utilizing a wry sense of humor, commenting on our ways.

I, Sniper. abr. ed. Stephen Hunter. Read by Buck Schirner. 5 CDs. (Running Time: 6 hrs.). (Bob Lee Swagger Ser.). 2009. audio compact disk 26.99 (978-1-4233-6992-9(0), 9781423369929, BACD) Brilliance Audio.

I, Sniper. abr. ed. Stephen Hunter. Read by Buck Schirner. (Running Time: 6 hrs.). (Bob Lee Swagger Ser.). 2010. audio compact disk 14.99 (978-1-4233-6993-6(9), 9781423369936, BCD Value Price) Brilliance Audio.

I, Sniper. unabr. ed. Stephen Hunter. Read by Buck Schirner. 1 MP3-CD. (Running Time: 16 hrs.). (Bob Lee Swagger Ser.). 2009. 39.97 (978-1-4233-6989-9(0), 9781423369899, Brinc Audio MP3 Lib); 39.97 (978-1-4233-6991-2(2), 9781423369912, BADLE); 24.99 (978-1-4233-6988-2(2), 9781423369882, Brilliance MP3); 24.99 (978-1-4233-6990-5(4), 9781423369905, BAD); audio compact disk 92.97 (978-1-4233-6987-5(4), 9781423369875, BriAudCD Unabrid); audio compact disk 38.99 (978-1-4233-6986-8(6), 9781423369868, Bril Audio CD Unabri) Brilliance Audio.

I Spy e-Spy: PageTurner Spy. Janice Greene. 1 cass. (Running Time: 65 mins 49 secs). (PageTurner Spy Ser.). (YA). 2002. 10.95 (978-1-56254-492-8(6), SP 4926) Saddleback Edu.
Word-for-word read-along of I Spy e-Spy.

I Stand All Amazed. Curtis Jacobs. 2004. 9.95 (978-1-59156-075-3(6)); audio compact disk 11.95 (978-1-59156-076-0(4)) Covenant Comms.

***I Stand at the Door & Knock: Meditations by the Author of the Hiding Place.** Corrie ten Boom. (Running Time: 4 hrs. 0 mins. 0 sec.). (ENG.). 2008. 14.99 (978-0-310-30243-8(9)) Zondervan.

I Stand Here Ironing. Short Stories. Tillie Olsen. Read by Tillie Olsen. 1 cass. (Running Time: 1hr. 17 min.). Incl. Oh Yes. 1981. (1131); Yonnondio. 1981. (1131); 1981. 13.95 (978-1-55644-023-6(5), 1131) Am Audio Prose.
Olsen, as reader & interviewee, compels the listener like an ancient mariner until her tale is spun. The antiphonal passage from "Yonnondio" is equaled only by passages from "Dante's Inferno".

I Still Believe - ShowTrax. Perf. by Mariah Carey. Arranged by Ed Lojeski. 1 CD. (Running Time: 5 mins.). 2000. audio compact disk 19.95 (08201108) H Leonard.
Mariah Carey hits it big with this 1999 remake of the '80s pop ballad.

***I Still Dream about You: A Novel.** abr. unabr. ed. Fannie Flagg & Fannie Flagg. Read by Fannie Flagg. (ENG.). 2010. audio compact disk 40.00 (978-0-7393-5399-8(3), Random AudioBks) Pub: Random Audio Pubg. Dist(s): Random

***I Still Hate to Read!** Rita Marshall. Illus. by Etienne Delessert. Narrated by Asa Dorfman. 1 cass. (Running Time: 9 mins.). (J). (gr. k-3). 2008. bk. 27.95 (978-0-8045-6974-3(6)) Spoken Arts.

***I Still Hate to Read!** Rita Marshall. Illus. by Etienne Delessert. Narrated by Asa Dorfman. 1 CD. (Running Time: 9 mins.). (J). (gr. k-3). 2008. bk. 29.95 (978-0-8045-4199-2(X)) Spoken Arts.

I Still Hold On. Prod. by God Style Records Staff. (Running Time: 30 min.). 2004. audio compact disk 16.98 (978-5-559-59222-0(6)) Pub: Pt of Grace Ent. Dist(s): STL Dist NA

I Stink! 1 cass. 2004. bk. 24.95 (978-0-7882-0339-8(8)) Weston Woods.

I Stink. 2004. 8.95 (978-0-7882-0341-1(X)); audio compact disk 12.95 (978-0-7882-0342-8(8)) Weston Woods.

I Stink! & Other Stories about Our Town: I Stink!; Paperboy, the; Trashy Town; Dot the Fire Dog. unabr. ed. Kate McMullan et al. Read by Andy Richter et al. (J). 2008. 44.99 (978-1-60514-890-8(3)) Find a World.

I Succeed Now. Read by Mary Richards. 1 cass. (Running Time: 48 min.). (Power Words of Affirmation Ser.). 2007. audio compact disk 19.95 (978-1-56136-191-5(7)) Master Your Mind.

I Sure Am Glad to See You, Blackboard Bear. unabr. ed. Martha Alexander. 1 cass. (Running Time: 6 min.). (J). (ps-3). 1989. pap. bk. 14.45 (978-0-8045-6509-7(0), 6509) Spoken Arts.

I Surrender All. Perf. by Clay Crosse. 1 cass. 1999. (978-0-7601-2699-8(2)); audio compact disk (978-0-7601-2700-1(X)) Brentwood Music.

I Surrender All. Perf. by B. J. Thomas. 2006. audio compact disk 12.95 (978-1-59987-416-6(4)) Braun Media.

I Swear. Contrib. by Inhale Exhale. Prod. by Travis Wyrick. 2008. audio compact disk 13.99 (978-5-557-42214-7(5)) Solid State MO.

I T'ai Chi Music. Prod. by Valley Spirit Arts. (ENG.). 2006. audio compact disk 19.95 (978-1-889633-22-0(4)) Valley SpiritA.

I Taste a Liquor Never Brewed see Poems & Letters of Emily Dickinson

I Thank You God for Most This Amazing see Gathering of Great Poetry for Children

I the Jury. abr. ed. Mickey Spillane. Read by Stacy Keach. 2006. 9.95 (978-0-7435-6251-5(8)) Pub: S&S Audio. Dist(s): S and S Inc

I, the Jury. unabr. ed. Mickey Spillane. Read by Richard Wulf. 4 cass. (Running Time: 6 hrs.). (Mike Hammer Ser.). 1986. 32.00 (978-0-7366-0891-6(5), 1835) Books on Tape.
When Mike Hammer's best friend gets the business from a forty-five, he sets out to nail the killer.

I Thee Wed. Amanda Quick, pseud. Read by Mary Peiffer. 1999. audio compact disk 72.00 (978-0-7366-5181-3(0)) Books on Tape.

I Thee Wed. abr. ed. Amanda Quick, pseud. Read by Janet McTeer. 2 cass. 1999. 18.00 (FS9-43394) Highsmith.

I Thee Wed. unabr. ed. Amanda Quick, pseud. Read by Mary Peiffer. 7 cass. (Running Time: 10 hrs. 30 min.). 1999. 56.00 (978-0-7366-4564-5(0), 4971) Books on Tape.
Take one independent lady's companion. Add an enigmatic financier. Then mix in a volume of ancient lore & a ruthless killer & you have the recipe for this.

I Thee Wed. unabr. ed. Amanda Quick, pseud. Read by Mary Peiffer. 9 CDs. (Running Time: 13 hrs. 30 mins.). 2001. audio compact disk 72.00 Books on Tape.

I Thee Wed. unabr. ed. Amanda Quick, pseud. Narrated by Barbara Rosenblat. 7 cass. (Running Time: 10 hrs. 15 mins.). 1999. 60.00 (978-0-7887-3474-8(1), 95876E7) Recorded Bks.
Emma Greyson is a lady's companion. But when she meets a darkly handsome guest at her employer's estate, Emma is lured into his dangerous quest for an ancient book of potions.

I Thee Wed. unabr. ed. Amanda Quick, pseud. Narrated by Barbara Rosenblat. 9 CDs. (Running Time: 10 hrs. 15 mins.). 1999. audio compact disk 79.00 (978-0-7887-3978-1(6), C1097E7) Recorded Bks.

I Think Continually of Those see Caedmon Treasury of Modern Poets Reading Their Own Poetry

I think continually of those who were truly great see Twentieth-Century Poetry in English, No. 9, Recordings of Poets Reading Their Own Poetry

***I Think I Love You.** unabr. ed. Allison Pearson. (Running Time: 12 hrs.). (ENG.). 2011. audio compact disk 40.00 (978-0-307-74752-5(2), Random AudioBks) Pub: Random Audio Pubg. Dist(s): Random

I think im outta Here: A Memoir of All My Families. Carroll O'connor. 2004. 10.95 (978-0-7435-4859-5(0)) Pub: S&S Audio. Dist(s): S and S Inc

I Thought I Dealt with This! How to Free Yourself from Repetitive Patterns, Set. David Grudermeyer & Rebecca Grudermeyer. 2 cass. 18.95 INCL. HANDOUTS. (T-11) Willingness Wrks.

I Thought I Saw a Goonie Bird & Peace at Last. Howard W. Gabriel, III. (J). (gr. k-8). 1987. 2.95 (978-0-936997-05-6(2), T87-03) M & H Enter.
In the First Story a Real Mess Develops When Two Youngsters Try to Change the Bad Driving Habits of an Older Sibling. In the Second Story, One Spring, Two of Natures Most Important Creatures Find It Difficult to Understand & Accept Each Other. A Mighty Conflict Develops. Who Will Win?.

***I Thought My Father Was God.** abr. ed. Paul Auster. Read by Paul Auster. (ENG.). 2004. (978-0-06-078442-3(3), Harper Audio) HarperCollins Pubs.

***I Thought My Father Was God.** abr. ed. Paul Auster. Read by Paul Auster. (ENG.). 2004. (978-0-06-081432-8(2), Harper Audio) HarperCollins Pubs.

I Thought My Father Was God: And Other True Tales from NPR's National Story Project. abr. ed. Paul Auster. Read by Paul Auster. (Running Time: 32400 sec.). 2005. audio compact disk 34.95 (978-0-06-087411-7(2)) HarperCollins Pubs.

I Thought My Soul Would Rise & Fly: The Diary of Patsy, a Freed Girl. unabr. ed. Joyce Hansen. Read by Sisi Johnson. 3 cass. (Running Time: 3 hrs. 40 mins.). (Dear America Ser.). (J). (gr. 4-7). 2005. 25.95 (978-1-59519-469-5(X)) Live Oak Media.
Since she had secretly learned to read and write as a slave, 12-year-old Patsy is able to document her new life and dreams now that she is free. A time that isn't often written about, the Reconstruction Period offers a fascinating milieu for the reflections of a young girl as she determines what freedom means to her. An epilogue, historical notes, photos, and maps provide additional information.

I Thought My Soul Would Rise & Fly: The Diary of Patsy, a Freed Girl, Mars Bluff, South Carolina 1865. unabr. ed. Joyce Hansen. Read by Barbara Rosenblat. Directed By Robin Miles. 4 CDs. (Running Time: 15000 sec.). (Dear America Ser.). (J). (gr. 4-7). 2006. audio compact disk 28.95 (978-1-59519-476-3(2)) Live Oak Media.

***I Thought You Were Dead.** unabr. ed. Pete Nelson. Read by Josh Clark. (ENG.). 2010. audio compact disk 29.95 (978-1-61573-090-2(7), 1615730907) Pub: HighBridge. Dist(s): Workman Pub

I Told You So. abr. ed. Kate Clinton. (ENG.). 2009. audio compact disk (978-0-8070-4451-3(2)) Beacon Pr.

I, Tom Horn. unabr. ed. Will Henry. Narrated by Frank Muller. 9 cass. (Running Time: 13 hrs. 15 mins.). 1994. 78.00 (978-0-7887-0039-2(1), 94238E7) Recorded Bks.
Tom Horn sets the record straight on his legendary career as Pinkerton agent, cavalry scout & gunman. Tom Horn epitomized the blazing frontier spirit of the Old West. As a cavalry scouting & a Pinkerton detective running down cattle rustlers, the reckless gunslinger's exploits earned him notoriety & enemies. When he hired himself out as a manhunter, those enemies thought that the sharp-eyed shooter's long gun had dominated the West too long. But they couldn't have foretold the ironic destiny that would cage Tom Horn.

I, Too, Sing America: Three Centuries of African American Poetry. unabr. ed. Perf. by Renee Joshua-Porter & Ashley Bryan. Ed. by Catherine Clinton. 2 CDs. (Running Time: 2 hrs.). (YA). 2000. audio compact disk 28.95 (978-1-883332-57-0(5)) Audio Bkshelf.
From Lucy Terry to Rita Dove, this anthology features 25 poets & 35 poems with introductions to each poet & their work.

I, Too, Sing America: Three Centuries of African American Poetry. unabr. ed. Poems. Perf. by Renee Joshua-Porter & Ashley Bryan. Ed. by Catherine Clinton. 2 cass. (Running Time: 2 hrs.). (YA). (gr. 5 up). 2000. 21.95 Incl. vinyl bkpak. (978-1-883332-43-3(5)) Audio Bkshelf.

I Took My Frog to the Library. Eric A. Kimmel. Read by Deborah Brodie. Illus. by Blanche Sims. 1 cass. (J). 2000. pap. bk. 19.97 (978-0-7366-9223-6(1)) Books on Tape.
Havoc reigns when Bridgett's animal friends accompany her to the library.

I Took My Frog to the Library. Eric A. Kimmel. 1 cass. (Running Time: 35 min.). (J). (ps-4). 2001. pap. bk. 15.95 (VX-53C) Kimbo Educ.
Havoc reigns when Bridgett's animal friends go with her to the library. Includes book to read along with.

I Took My Frog to the Library. Eric A. Kimmel. Illus. by Blanche Sims. 14 vols. (Running Time: 4 mins.). 1997. pap. bk. 35.95 (978-1-59112-717-8(3)); 9.95 (978-1-59112-064-3(0)) Live Oak Media.

I Took My Frog to the Library. Eric A. Kimmel. Illus. by Deborah Brodie & Blanche Sims. 14 vols. (Running Time: 4 mins.). (J). (gr. k-3). 1997. pap. bk. & tchr. ed. 33.95 Reading Chest. (978-0-87499-404-9(7)) Live Oak Media.
Havoc reigns when Bridgett's animal friends accompany her to the library.

I Took My Frog to the Library. Eric A. Kimmel. Illus. by Blanche Sims. (Running Time: 4 mins.). (J). (ps-2). 1997. 12.95 (978-1-59112-715-4(7)) Live Oak Media.

I Took My Frog to the Library. unabr. ed. Eric A. Kimmel. Read by Deborah Brodie. Illus. by Blanche Sims. 11 vols. (Running Time: 4 mins.). (Live Oak Readalong Ser.). (J). (gr. k-3). 1997. pap. bk. 16.95 (978-0-87499-402-5(0)) AudioGO.

I Travelled among Unknown Men see Selected Poetry of William Wordsworth

I Two (EYE) Perf. by Michael W. Smith. Prod. by Wayne Kirkpatrick. 1 cass. 1988. audio compact disk Brentwood Music.
This now gold release features the hits, Secret Ambition & Pray for Me.

I Used to Be Fat. unabr. ed. Alyce P. Cornyn-Selby. Read by Alyce P. Cornyn-Selby. 1 cass. 1994. 8.95 (978-0-941383-24-0(5)) Beynch Pr.
Weight is a message from someone on the inside that "Wants Something". The message is written in code - crack the code. From Alyce who has lost 100 pounds & kept it off with a new method of inner talk.

I Used to Be Nice. Perf. by Rachel Bissex. 1 cass., 1 CD. 7.98 (ALC 132); audio compact disk 12.78 CD Jewel box. (ALC 132) NewSound.

I, Victoria. Cynthia Harrod-Eagles. Read by Diana Bishop. 16 cass. (Running Time: 18 hrs.). (Sound Ser.). (J). 2003. 104.95 (978-1-84283-397-1(9)) Pub: ISIS Lrg Prnt GBR. Dist(s): Ulverscroft US

I, Victoria. unabr. ed. Cynthia Harrod-Eagles. Read by Diana Bishop. 16 CDs. (Running Time: 21 hrs.). (Soundings (CDs) Ser.). (J). 2004. audio compact disk 109.95 (978-1-84283-787-0(7)) Pub: ISIS Lrg Prnt GBR. Dist(s): Ulverscroft US

I Visualize Successfully. Eldon Taylor. 1 cass. (Running Time: 62 min.). (Inner Talk Ser.). 16.95 (978-1-55978-580-8(2), 53787M) Progress Aware Res.
Soundtrack - Pastoral Themes with underlying subliminal affirmations.

I Visualize Successfully: Music Theme. Eldon Taylor. 1 cass. 16.95 (978-1-55978-059-9(2), 53787C) Progress Aware Res.

I Visualize Successfully: Ocean Theme. Eldon Taylor. 1 cass. 16.95 (978-1-55978-309-5(5), 53787A) Progress Aware Res.

I Walk by Faith: Believing in Christ & Yourself. David Glen Hatch. 1 cass. 7.98 (978-1-55503-937-0(5), 06005292) Covenant Comms.
A fireside with word & music.

I Walked out to the Graveyard to See the Dead see Richard Eberhart Reading His Poetry

I Walked Today Where Jesus Walked. Mormon Symphony. 1 cass. 9.95 (109404); audio compact disk 14.95 (289404) Covenant Comms.

I Walked Today Where Jesus Walked, Set, Vol. 1. Michael Ballam. 2 cass. 2004. 14.98 (978-1-57734-013-3(2), 1100785) Covenant Comms.
Musical tribute to the life & ministry of the Savior.

I Walked Today Where Jesus Walked, Set, Vol. 2. Michael Ballam. 2 cass. 14.98 (978-1-57734-014-0(0), 1100793) Covenant Comms.

I Wanna Be Me. Joanne Miller. Illus. by Gauss Rosanne. 1 CD. (ENG.). (J). 2009. audio compact disk 12.95 (978-0-9659072-7-9(9)) Forty-Eight Days.

I Wanna Be Your Shoebox. unabr. ed. Cristina Garcia. Read by Zinnia Su. 4 CDs. (Running Time: 4 hrs. 37 mins.). (J). (gr. 4-7). 2008. audio compact disk 38.00 (978-0-7393-6683-7(1), Listening Lib) Pub: Random Audio Pubg. Dist(s): Random

I Wanna Be Your Shoebox. unabr. ed. Illus. by Cristina García. (ENG.). (J). (gr. 5). 2008. audio compact disk 30.00 (978-0-7393-6515-1(0), Listening Lib) Pub: Random Audio Pubg. Dist(s): Random

I Wanna Go Home! Perf. by Bobby Collins. 1 CD. (Running Time: 1 hr.). 2003. audio compact disk 16.95 (978-1-929243-55-6(3)) Uproar Ent.
Bobby Collins is once again weaving a web of wit and observations, as he shares hilarious tales about marriage, kids and life in the merge lane. With the handsome good looks of Dean Martin, and the physical moves of Jerry Lewis, Bobby continues to be the "class clown extraordinaire!" The New York Times says, "Bobby Collins is the most natural comedian working today." Miami Herald labels him, "Funny, Funny, Funny, simply put: One of the Best!".

I Wanna Play: Songs by Bill Harley. Bill Harley. (J). 2006. audio compact disk 15.00 (978-1-878126-51-1(2), RRR 121) Round Riv Prodns.

I Wanna Sing! Scripture Songs: T & T-Book 3-Fifth Grade-NKJV Version. Contrib. by Melissa Woods. (I Wanna Sing! Ser.). (J). (gr. k-5). 2007. audio compact disk 13.95 (978-5-557-58253-7(3)) Nelson.

I Wanna Tickle the Fish. Lisa Atkinson. 1 cass. (Running Time: 40 min.). (J). (ps-1). 1987. 9.95 (978-0-939065-38-7(X), GW1042) Gentle Wind.
Bouncy songs about everyday life; includes songs for bathtime & bedtime.

I Wanna Tickle The Fish. Lisa Atkinson. (J). 1999. audio compact disk 14.95 (978-0-939065-65-3(7)) Gentle Wind.

I Want Burning. unabr. ed. Read by Coleman Barks. 1 CD. (Running Time: 1 hr. 15 mins.). 2001. audio compact disk 16.98 (978-1-56455-830-5(4), AW00488D) Sounds True.
An inspired evening featuring three literary legends of the 14th century Middle East: Jelaluddin Rumi, Hafiz, poet of the Persian world & Lalla, the astonishing Kashmiri woman poet, singer & dancer. Includes more than 50 poems, accompanied by vocals, pan flute, harmonium bells & hand drums.

I Want It Now. unabr. collector's ed. Kingsley Amis. Read by David Case. 8 cass. (Running Time: 8 hrs.). 1989. 48.00 (978-0-7366-1535-8(0), 2405) Books on Tape.
Ronnie Appleyard is a host for a TV panel-discussion show who meets Simon, a strange & moody girl whose family has money. Surely it's Simon's money he's after, but there is something about this erratic girl that threatens his cynicism.

I Want More Balloons. unabr. ed. Perf. by Heather H. Bacus. 1 cass. (Running Time: 40 min.). (J). (gr. 1-3). 1997. 10.00 (978-1-929050-06-2(2)) MW Prods.
A collection of kids songs.

I Want My Banana: English-French Version: Je Veux Ma Banane. Mary Risk & Jacqueline Jansen. Illus. by Alex De Wolf. 1 cass. (Running Time: 20 min.). (I Can Read Bks.). (ENG & FRE.). (J). (ps up). 1998. pap. bk. 9.95 (978-0-7641-7190-1(9)) Barron.
Repeats every word of the bilingual text in both languages so that children can hear exactly how the words sound.

I Want My House to Be a Home. T. D. Jakes. 1 cass. 1997. 20.00 (978-1-57855-010-4(6)) T D Jakes.

I Want My Mom! Grade K. abr. ed. Created by Rigby Staff. (Rigby Literacy Ser.). 2000. 9.70 (978-0-7635-7188-7(1), Rigby PEA) Pearson EdAUS AUS.

I Want the Peace of God. Kenneth Wapnick. 2 CDs. 2006. audio compact disk 10.00 (978-1-59142-267-9(1), CD41) Foun Miracles.

I Want the Peace of God. Kenneth Wapnick. 1 CD. (Running Time: 1 hr. 36 mins. 33 secs.). 2006. 8.00 (978-1-59142-268-6(X), 3m41) Foun Miracles.

I Want to Be Happy. Barrie Konicov. 1 cass. 2000. 16.98 (978-1-56001-314-3(1)) Potentials.

I Want to be Happy. Barrie Konicov. 1 CD. 2003. audio compact disk 16.98 (978-0-87082-972-7(6)) Potentials.
You have within you the power to be happy. This program will guide you to concentrate on harmonious, prosperous thoughts and bring you the happiness you earnestly seek.You will find the self-hypnosis on track 1 and the subliminal on track 2. The easy-listening music of the subliminal, together with the self-hypnosis, is the original format which most people love and with which they are most familiar.

I Want to be Happy. Barrie Konicov. 2 CDs. 2003. audio compact disk 27.98 (978-1-56001-978-7(6)) Potentials.

I Want to Be Like You. 1 cass. 1999. 7.98 (978-0-7601-2886-2(3)) Provident Music.

I Want to Go. Perf. by Larnelle Harris. 1 cass. 1998. 8.98 (978-0-7601-2696-7(8)) Brentwood Music.

I Want to Grow Hair, I Want to Grow up, I Want to Go to Boise: Children Surviving Cancer. unabr. ed. Erma Bombeck. Narrated by Barbara Rosenblat. 3 cass. (Running Time: 3 hrs. 30 mins.). 1997. 26.00 (978-0-7887-0653-0(5), 94830E7) Recorded Bks.
If you expect a book about children with terminal illness to be depressing, prepare to be pleasantly surprised. Despite struggling against incredible odds, these children are full of life, hope & humor. Bombeck's most touching & vibrantly funny book.

I want to Live see Quiero Vivir

I Want to Show Others I Love Jesus. (Junior Kids Church Ser.: Vol. 4). (J). 1998. bk. 134.99 (978-1-57405-353-1(1)) CharismaLife Pub.

I Want to Thank You. Jaden Bliss. 2008. audio compact disk 16.99 (978-1-59955-242-2(6)) CFI Dist.

I Want You! The Evolution of the All-Volunteer Force. Bernard Rostker. 2006. bk. 25.00 (978-0-8330-3895-1(8), MG-265) RAND Corp.

I Was a Communist for the FBI. Dana Andrews. 3 CDs. (Running Time: 3 hrs.). 2002. audio compact disk 19.98 (27632); 17.98 (27634) Radio Spirits.
Taken from the "actual records and authentic experiences" of real-life secret agent Matt Cvetic. Held listeners spellbound at the height of the Red Scare. Listen along for the murky and dangerous inner workings of the Party, all while trying to keep his mission a secret, even from his family.

I Was a Communist for the FBI. Contrib. by Dana Andrews. (Running Time: 10800 sec.). 2004. audio compact disk 9.98 (978-1-57019-523-5(4)) Radio Spirits.

***I Was A Communist for the FBI.** Perf. by Dana Andrews. 2009. audio compact disk 31.95 (978-1-57019-908-0(6)) Radio Spirits.

I Was a Communist for the FBI. Contrib. by Dana Andrews & Matt Cvetic. (Running Time: 10800 sec.). 2004. 9.98 (978-1-57019-522-8(6)) Radio Spirits.

I Was a Communist for the FBI: American Kremlin & Abby as in Abilgail. Perf. by Dana Andrews. 1 cass. (Running Time: 1 hr.). 2001. 6.98 (2460) Radio Spirits.

I Was a Communist for the FBI: Home Improvement & Red Gold. Perf. by Dana Andrews. 1 cass. (Running Time: 1 hr.). 2001. 6.98 (1677) Radio Spirits.

I Was a Communist for the FBI: Litle Boy Red & The Unwelcome Host. Perf. by Dana Andrews. 2001. 6.98 (1556) Radio Spirits.

I Was a Communist for the FBI: Trial by Fear & The Wrong Green. Perf. by Dana Andrews. 1 cass. (Running Time: 1 hr.). 2001. 6.98 (1678) Radio Spirits.

I Was A Pro-Life Atheist. Speeches. Steven Kellmeyer. 1. (Running Time: 1 hour). 2005. audio compact disk (978-0-9718128-2-6(9)) Bridegroom.

I Was a Sixth Grade Alien. Bruce Coville. Read by William Dufris. 2 cass. (Running Time: 4 hrs.). (I Was a Sixth Grade Alien Ser.: Vol. 1). (J). 2000. 64.00 (978-0-7366-9014-0(X)) Books on Tape.
Aliens have finally contracted Earth & have sent an ambassador, a single parent who brings along his kid, Pleskit. Because his father insists he attend public school, Pleskit becomes the world's first sixth grade alien. His attempts to fit in are hilariously catastrophic & only when his establishes tentative friendship with Tim Tompkins does Pleskit begin to understand that he is being sabatagoed But by whom?.

I Was a Sixth Grade Alien. unabr. ed. Bruce Coville. Read by William Dufris. 2 vols. (Running Time: 1 hr. 42 mins.). (I Was a Sixth Grade Alien Ser.: Vol. 1). (J). (gr. 3-6). 2004. pap. bk. 29.00 (978-0-8072-8201-4(4), S YA 138 SP, Listening Lib); 19.55 (978-0-8072-8200-7(6), YYA138CX, Listening Lib) Pub: Random Audio Pubg. Dist(s): NetLibrary CO
Aliens have finally contacted Earth and have sent an ambassador, a single parent who brings along his kid, Pleskit. Because his father insists he attend public school. Pleskit becomes the world's first sixth grade alien. His attempts to fit in are hilariously catastrophic and only when he establishes a tentative friendship with Tim Tompkins does Pleskit begin to understand that he is being sabotaged. But by whom?.

I Was a Spy for Joseph Stalin. Alexander Contract. Read by Alexander Contract. 1 cass. 1999. (978-0-912986-31-9(X)) Am Media.

I Was a Stranger. unabr. ed. John W. Hackett. Read by John MacDonald. 6 cass. (Running Time: 9 hrs.). 1986. 48.00 (978-0-7366-0919-7(9), 1862) Books on Tape.
In one of the most unusual true stories of escape to come out of W.W. II, General Hackett shares the long-held secret of his stay in the home of members of the Dutch resistance. When British troops were withdrawn after the Battle of Arnhem late in 1944, the general, badly wounded, had to be left behind. Hidden in the home of the de Nooij family, he recuperated until he was strong enough to make his escape.

I was Born to Be a Brother. Zaydek G. Michels-Gualtieri. Illus. by Daniel Liegey. (ENG.). 2006. bk. 18.95 (978-1-930775-10-7(5)) Pub: Platypus Media. Dist(s): Natl Bk Netwk

I was Born to be a Brother/I Was Born to be a Sister. Zaydek G. Michels-Gualtieri & Akaela S. Michels-Gualtieri. Illus. by Marcy Dunn Ramsey & Daniel Liegey. (ENG.). 2005. bk. 34.95 (978-1-930775-21-3(0)) Pub: Platypus Media. Dist(s): Natl Bk Netwk

I was Born to Be a Sister. Akaela S. Michels-Gualtieri. Illus. by Marcy Dunn Ramsey. (ENG.). 2006. bk. 18.95 (978-1-930775-11-4(3)) Pub: Platypus Media. Dist(s): Natl Bk Netwk

I was Born to Be a Sister. Akaela S. Michels-Gualtieri. Illus. by Marcy Dunn Ramsey. 2005. pap. bk. 9.95 (978-1-930775-24-4(5)) Pub: Platypus Media. Dist(s): Natl Bk Netwk

I Was in Prison & Ye Came unto Me. unabr. ed. Myrtle Smith. Prod. by David Keyston. 1 cass. (Running Time: 1 hrs. 4 min.). (Myrtle Smyth Audiotapes Ser.). 1998. , CD. (978-1-893107-05-2(1), M5, Cross & Crown) Healing Unltd.

I Was There see Monsarrat at Sea

I Was There see Ship That Died of Shame

I Was Told There'd Be Cake. unabr. ed. Sloane Crosley. Read by Sloane Crosley. 6 CDs. (Running Time: 6 hrs.). (ENG.). (gr. 12 up). 2008. audio compact disk 34.95 (978-0-14-314399-4(9), PengAudBks) Penguin Grp USA.

I Went Walking see Sali de Paseo, Grades K-3

I Went Walking see Sali de Paseo

I Went Walking. Sue Williams. 1 cass. (Running Time: 35 min.). (J). (ps-2). 2001. pap. bk. 15.95 (VX-663C) Kimbo Educ.
A walk around the farmyard becomes an exuberant event as we introduce a black cat, a red cow, a greedy duck & more. Includes book to read along with.

I Went Walking. Sue Williams. Illus. by Julie Vivas. 9.95 (978-1-59112-152-7(3)); 4.50 (978-1-59112-305-7(4)) Live Oak Media.

I Went Walking. Sue Williams. Illus. by Julie Vivas. (Running Time: 4 mins.). 2000. audio compact disk 12.95 (978-1-59112-718-5(1)) Live Oak Media.

I Went Walking. Sue Williams. Illus. by Julie Vivas. 41 vols. (Running Time: 4 mins.). (J). 2000. pap. bk. & tchr. ed. 37.95 Reading Chest. (978-0-87499-665-4(1)) Live Oak Media.
A walk around the farmyard becomes an exuberant event for the small child featured in this simple repetitive tale.

I Went Walking. Sue Williams. Illus. by Julie Vivas. 11 vols. (Running Time: 4 mins.). (J). (gr. k-3). 2000. bk. 25.95 (978-0-87499-664-7(3)); pap. bk. 16.95 (978-0-87499-663-0(5)) Pub: Live Oak Media. Dist(s): AudioGO
A sprightly, cumulative tale has extra child appeal with the use of an adult narrator questioning and a child responding in this playful readalong for very young listeners. As a boy walks along, one by one, different animals join in until there's quite a colorful parade following him!.

I Went Walking. Sue Williams. Tr. by Alma Flor Ada. (Running Time: 4 mins.). (J). 2000. 9.95 (978-0-87499-662-3(7)) Pub: Live Oak Media. Dist(s): Lectorum Pubns

I Went Walking. Sue Williams. Illus. by Julie Vivas. 14 vols. (Running Time: 4 mins.). 2003. pap. bk. 39.95 (978-1-59112-721-5(1)) Live Oak Media.

I Went Walking. Sue Williams. Read by Bonnie Kelly-Young & John Mazzoli. 11 vols. (Running Time: 4 mins.). (J). 2003. pap. bk. 18.95 (978-1-59112-719-2(X)) Pub: Live Oak Media. Dist(s): AudioGO

I Went Walking. unabr. ed. Sue Williams. Illus. by Julie Vivas. 22 vols. (Running Time: 8 mins.). (ENG & SPA.). (J). (gr. k-3). 2000. pap. bk. 33.95 (978-0-87499-666-1(X)) Live Oak Media.

I Will. 2002. audio compact disk (978-1-59250-075-8(7)) Gaiam Intl.

I Will Always Love You. 2008. audio compact disk 18.99 (978-5-557-49755-8(2), Word Records) Word Enter.

I Will Always Love You. unabr. ed. Cecily von Ziegesar. Read by Cassandra Morris. (Running Time: 10 hrs.). (Gossip Girl Ser.: No. 12). (ENG.). 2009. 22.98 (978-1-60024-845-0(4)) Pub: Hachet Audio. Dist(s): HachBkGrp

I Will Be Here. Contrib. by Steven Curtis Chapman. 2005. audio compact disk 8.99 (978-5-559-15690-3(6)) Christian Wrld.

I Will Be Married in a Year: The 10 Essential Steps to Finding Your Dream Mate & the Top 10 Pitfalls You Must Avoid. Janet Page. 2 cass. (Running Time: 2 hrs.). 2001. 79.99 (978-0-9726412-1-0(1)) Janet Page.

I Will Be Thine Always. 1984. 7.00 (2302) Self Realization.
Devotional chanting consists of simple prayers put to music, repeated over & over again with deep feeling until the consciousness becomes absorbed in the spiritual experience behind the words. In this recording, nuns of Paramahansa Yogananda's ashrams sing nine selections from his Cosmic Chants. These songs are performed in the traditional kirtan style of India - vocal chanting accompanied by harmonium, tabla, cymbals, bells & kartal.

I Will Be Your Friend. Perf. by Michael W. Smith. 1 cass. 1999. 8.98 (978-0-7601-3152-7(X)) Provident Music.

I Will Do Everything. Adi Da Samraj. 1 cass. (Classic Ser.). 11.95 (978-0-918801-65-4(6)) Dawn Horse Pr.
In this talk given in 1977, Sri Da Avabhasa proclaims His function as Sat-Guru ("Revealer of Truth") to all those who respond to Him. He makes it clear in His impassioned way that all you need to do is to resort to Him as your Sat-Guru.

I Will Exercise Regularly. unabr. ed. Dick Sutphen. Read by Dick Sutphen. 1 cass. (Running Time: 30 min.). (Quick Fix Meditations Ser.). 1998. 10.98 (978-0-87554-624-7(2), QF106) Valley Sun.
From this moment on, exercise regularly. Always fit exercises into the schedule & feel better.

***I Will Fear No Evil.** unabr. ed. Robert A. Heinlein. Read by Anthony Heald. (Running Time: 16 hrs. NaN mins.). (ENG.). 2011. 29.95 (978-1-4417-4057-1(0)); 89.95 (978-1-4417-4053-3(8)); audio compact disk 34.95 (978-1-4417-4056-4(2)); audio compact disk 118.00 (978-1-4417-4054-0(6)) Blckstn Audio.

I Will Fly Away. Marie Ketsia Theodore. (CRP., (J). 2005. 19.00 (978-1-58432-434-8(1)) Educa Vision.

I Will Follow Christ. Perf. by Clay Crosse et al. 1 cass. 1999. 7.98 (978-0-7601-2942-5(8)) Provident Music.

I Will Go. Contrib. by Starfield. Prod. by Allen Salmon & Ed Cash. 2008. audio compact disk 9.99 (978-5-557-47297-5(5)) Pt of Grace Ent.

I Will Go & Do - Soundtrack. Aaron Edson. 1 CD. (J). 2004. audio compact disk 9.95 (978-1-887938-47-1(8)) Snd Concepts.

I Will Go & Do - VHS. Read by Peace Mtn. Media Works Staff. Dramatization. (All Abouts Ser.). (J). (ps-3). 2003. 19.95 (978-1-887938-15-0(X)) Snd Concepts.
Teaches children about the importance of Baptism & Holy Ghost.

I Will Lift My Eyes. Contrib. by Bebo Norman. (Mastertrax Ser.). 2006. audio compact disk 9.98 (978-5-558-20096-6(0)) Essential Recs.

I Will Make You Fishers of Men. Dan Corner. 1 cass. 3.00 (43) Evang Outreach.

I Will Never Forget. Kay C. James & Jacquelline C. Fuller. 2 cass. (Running Time: 60 min.). 1993. 14.99 set. (978-0-310-48208-6(9)) Zondervan.
The riveting autobiography of one woman's journey from the projects to the corridors of power.

I Will Not Be Broken: Five Steps to Overcoming a Life Crisis. unabr. ed. Jerry White. Read by Jerry White. (Running Time: 6 hrs.). 2008. 39.95 (978-0-7927-5570-8(7), Chivers Sound Lib); audio compact disk 59.95 (978-0-7927-5482-4(4), Chivers Sound Lib) AudioGO.

I Will Remember You - ShowTrax. Arranged by Mac Huff. 1 CD. (Running Time: 5 mins.). (Pop Choral Ser.). 2000. audio compact disk 19.95 (08201126); audio compact disk 19.95 (08201126) H Leonard.
Originally recorded by Sarah McLachlan in 1995, the 1999 live recording was the main theme of the motion picture "The Brothers McMullen." With its gentle pop groove & message, it will be a great choral showcase for spring concert & graduation.

I Will Repay. unabr. ed. Emmuska Orczy. Read by Johanna Ward. 6 cass. (Running Time: 8 hrs. 30 mins.). 1994. 44.95 (978-0-7861-0778-0(2), 1506) Blckstn Audio.
It has been ten years since Juliette de Marny's father asked her to swear revenge upon Deroulede for the death of her brother in a duel. At last she finds herself in Deroulede's house with an easy opportunity to betray him to the Citizens of France for conspiring against the people. Juliette realizes, too late, that she is in love with Deroulede. Can the Scarlett Pimpernel rescue Deroulede from certain death by guillotine? Will Deroulede forgive Juliette for her betrayal of him? Romance & intrigue abound in this delightful swashbuckler.

I Will Repay. unabr. ed. Emmuska Orczy. Read by Johanna Ward. (Running Time: 27000 sec.). 2007. audio compact disk 29.95 (978-0-7861-7270-2(3)); audio compact disk & audio compact disk 55.00 (978-0-7861-6207-9(4)) Blckstn Audio.

I Will Rest in You. Perf. by Jaci Valazquez. 1 cass. 1999. (978-0-7601-2881-7(2)) Provident Music.

I Will Send My Song: Kammu Vocal Genres in the Singing of Kam Raw. Tr. by Hakan Lundstrom. Contrib. by Nordic Institute of Asian Studies Staff. 2005. bk. 28.00 (978-87-91114-32-8(2)) Pub: Nordic Institute DNK. Dist(s): UH Pr

I Will Shake All Things. Derek Prince. 2 cass. 11.90 Set. (4344-4345) Derek Prince.
Has the predicted final "shaking of all things" already begun? If so, you need to know how you can come through victoriously.

I Will Sing Thy Name. 1 cass. 1984. 8.50 (2206) Self Realization.
Over a thousand voices join Self-Realization Fellowship monks for "kirtan" - devotional chanting - creating a unique atmosphere of spiritual power & joy. Selections include: I Will Sing Thy Name; Jai Guru; Radha Govinda Jai; Spirit & Nature; He Bhagavan; Deliver Us From Delusion; Light the Lamp of Thy Love; Hare Krishna, Hare Ram; Aum Chant.

I Will Sing Thy Name: Chants. Paramhansa Yogananda. 2 CDs. audio compact disk 19.50 (978-0-87612-504-5(6)) Self Realization.

I Will Stay by You. 1985. (0280) Evang Sisterhood Mary.

I Will Survive. Dino Fekaris & Freddie Perren. 1996. audio compact disk 22.95 (978-0-634-09192-6(1)) H Leonard.

I Will Worship God. (Junior Kids Church Ser.: Vol. 1). (J). 1998. bk. 134.99 (978-1-57405-350-0(7)) CharismaLife Pub.

I Will Yet Choose Yerusalem Again: Zecharyah Chapter 2, Verse 12. 1 cass. (Running Time: 55 min.). 1996. 8.00 (978-0-9649618-4-5(9)) Hse of Yahweh.
Music inspired by the Creator, Yahweh, to show the tremendous love he has for His people in Yerusalem.

I Wish. Perf. by Billy Sprague. 1 cass. 1989. audio compact disk Brentwood Music.
Greatest hits, featuring: What Goes Around, Comes Around.

I Wish I Had a Red Dress. unabr. ed. Pearl Cleage. Narrated by Caroline S. Clay. 6 cass. (Running Time: 8 hrs. 45 mins.). 2002. 64.00 (978-0-7887-8930-4(9), F0048) Recorded Bks.
Focuses on Joyce, a social worker who counsels young black woman.

I Wish My Body Were. Byron Katie. 1 cass. (Running Time: 66 mins.). 2004. 12.00 (978-1-890246-20-4(4)); audio compact disk 15.00 (978-1-890246-18-1(2)) B Katie Int Inc.
What part of your body do you feel frustrated by or want to change? On this program, a woman investigates the size of her breasts and how it affects her relationship; a man does The Work on his penis's sexual performance, and a woman confronts her belief that her body is damaged.

I Wish This War Were Over & Poems. Poems. Diana O'Hehir. Read by Diana O'Hehir. 1 cass. (Running Time: 54 min.). 1991. 13.95 (978-1-55644-351-0(X), 10021) Am Audio Prose.
Poet & novelist O'Hehir reads selections from her first novel I Wish This War Were Over & four poems.

I Witness News, Vol. 1. Randy Benefield. Perf. by Brent Campbell. Music by Jon Von Seggen. 1 cass. (Running Time: 28 min.). Dramatization. 1996. 15.00 incl. script. (978-1-58302-033-3(0), STP-06A) One Way St.
Ten "news flash" puppet programs, each approximately two minutes long & features one male character.

I Witness News, Vol. 1. Randy Benefield. 2001. audio compact disk 15.00 (978-1-58302-181-1(7)) One Way St.
Fourteen pre-recorded puppet scripts.

I Witness News, Vol. 2. Randy Benefield. Perf. by Brent Campbell. Music by Jon Von Seggen. 1 cass. (Running Time: 29 min.). Dramatization. 1996. 15.00 incl. script. (978-1-58302-034-0(9), STP-06B) One Way St.
Ten "news flash" puppet programs from the New Testament, each approximately two minutes long, featuring one male character, plus four bonus Easter stories.

I Witness News, Vol. 2. Randy Benefield. 2001. audio compact disk 15.00 (978-1-58302-182-8(5)) One Way St.
contains all fourteen pre-recorded scripts.

I Witness News: Live from Jericho: A Children's Musical with Good News about God's Provision & Faithfulness. 1 cass. (Running Time: 50 min.). (J). 2001. 80.00 (MU-9287C); 54.99 (TA-9287PK); audio compact disk 80.00 (MU-9287T) Lillenas.
Musically suited to include all the kids in your church, this new offering allows participation by children of all ages in both the music & drama. A scriptural story line with a unique angle, presented as a news report on Joshua's victory at Jericho. Acccompaniment cassette with side 1, split-channel & side 2, stereo trax.

I Witness News: Live from Jericho: A Children's Musical with Good News about God's Provision & Faithfulness. 1 cass. (Running Time: 50 min.). (YA). 2001. 12.99 (TA-9287C) Lillenas.

I Wonder... What Would a Fish Wish For? unabr. ed. Marian L. Clish. Illus. by Lori Clish. 1 CD. (J). (gr. k-3). 1999. pap. bk. 14.95 (978-1-928632-06-1(8)) Writers Mrktpl.
Yellow is a small fish in a great, big fish bowl. So, she wished for more fish to be in the bowl with her. Unfortunately, she got more than she anticipated. Includes a parent reading guide at the end of the book.

I Wonder... What Would Happen If I Took an Elephant to School? unabr. ed. Marian L. Clish. Illus. by Jan Anderson. (J). (gr. k-3). 1999. bk. 18.95 (978-1-928632-36-8(X)) Writers Mrktpl.

I Wonder... What Would Happen If I Took an Elephant to School? unabr. ed. Marian L. Clish. Illus. by Jan Anderson. (J). (gr. k-3). 1999. pap. bk. 10.95 (978-1-928632-33-7(5)) Writers Mrktpl.

I Wonder Why: A Poem for Children. Connie Amarel. (Running Time: 420 sec.). (J). (ps-3). 2008. audio compact disk 9.99 (978-1-60604-253-3(X)) Tate Pubng.

I Wonder...What Would a Fish Wish For? unabr. ed. Marian L. Clish. Illus. by Lori Clish. 1 cass. (J). (gr. k-3). 1999. pap. bk. 10.95 (978-1-928632-05-4(X)) Writers Mrktpl.
A small fish in a big fish bowl wished there were more fish in her bowl, unfortunately she got more than she anticipated.

I Years Had Been from Home see Poems & Letters of Emily Dickinson

***I-9 & Immigration Law Compliance 2009.** PUEI. 2009. audio compact disk 199.00 (978-1-935041-66-5(5), CareerTrack) P Univ E Inc.

Iaccoca Tapes. Lee Iacocca. Read by Lee Iacocca. Read by William Novak. 6 cass. 49.95 Set. (123A) Nightingale-Conant.

Ian Fleming: The Man Behind James Bond. unabr. ed. Andrew Lycett. Read by Robert Whitfield. 16 cass. (Running Time: 23 hrs. 30 mins.). 1997. 99.95 (978-0-7861-1259-3(X), 2179) Blckstn Audio.
Sportsman, womanizer, naval commander, world-traveler, spy, this suave Old Etonian creator of the Cold War's archetypal secret agent was infinitely more complicated & interesting than his major fictional character, Agent 007. Fleming's wide-ranging & exciting life inevitably provided the plausible backdrop for the Bond novels.

***Ian Fleming: The Man behind James Bond.** unabr. ed. Andrew Lycett. Read by Robert Whitfield. (Running Time: 22 hrs.). 2010. 44.95 (978-1-4417-4695-5(1)); audio compact disk 39.95 (978-1-4417-4694-8(3)) Blckstn Audio.

Ian Rankin Inspector Rebus CD Collection: Resurrection Men, A Question of Blood, Fleshmarket Alley. abr. ed. Ian Rankin. Read by James MacPherson. (Running Time: 19 hrs.). (Inspector Rebus Ser.). 2007. audio compact disk 19.99 (978-1-4233-3429-3(9), 9781423334293, BACD) Brilliance Audio.

Ian Robb: From Different Angels. 1 cass., 1 CD. 9.98 (C-545); audio compact disk 14.98 CD. (CD-545) Folk-Legacy.
Songs from three friends: Bellamy, Rogers & MacColl.

Ian Robb: The Rose & Crown. 1 cass. 9.98 (C-106) Folk-Legacy.
A fine singer from Canada, backed by good friends.

Ian Robb & Hang the Piper. 1 cass. 9.98 (C-71) Folk-Legacy.
Songs & tunes by a fine singer & his friends.

Ias 3 year old Program. Paul Plum & Joan Plum. (J). 2005. 13.95 (978-1-59276-088-6(0)) Our Sunday Visitor.

Iatrogenic Illness in the Aged. Read by Knight Steel. 1 cass. (Running Time: 90 min.). 1986. 12.00 (C8627) Amer Coll Phys.

Iberia. James A. Michener. Read by Larry McKeever. 1994. 104.00 (978-0-7366-2877-8(0)) Books on Tape.

Iberia, Pt. 1. unabr. ed. James A. Michener. Read by Larry McKeever. 14 cass. (Running Time: 21 hrs.). 1994. 112.00 (978-0-7366-2876-1(2), 3580-A) Books on Tape.
More than bullfighters, warrior kings, cathedrals & orchards. An intimate, hidden land...Michener's Iberia.

Iberia, Pt. 2. James A. Michener. Read by Larry McKeever. 13 cass. (Running Time: 19 hrs. 30 min.). 1994. 104.00 (3580-B) Books on Tape.

IBM & the Holocaust: The Strategic Alliance Between Nazi Germany & America's Most Powerful Corporation. abr. ed. Edwin Black. As told by Edwin Black. 2008. audio compact disk 32.00 (978-0-914153-03-0(X)) Pub: Dialog. Dist(s): Natl Bk Netwk

Icarus. unabr. ed. Russell Andrews. Read by Patrick G. Lawlor. (Running Time: 13 hrs.). 2004. 39.25 (978-1-59335-359-9(6), 1593353596, Brinc Audio MP3 Lib) Brilliance Audio.

Icarus. unabr. ed. Russell Andrews. Read by Patrick G. Lawlor. (Running Time: 13 hrs.). 2004. 39.25 (978-1-59710-389-3(6), 1597103896, BADLE); 24.95 (978-1-59710-388-6(8), 1597103888, BAD) Brilliance Audio.

Icarus. unabr. ed. Russell Andrews. Read by Patrick G. Lawlor. (Running Time: 13 hrs.). 2004. 24.95 (978-1-59335-031-4(7), 1593350317) Soulmate Audio Bks.

Icarus Agenda, Pt. 1. unabr. collector's ed. Robert Ludlum. Read by Michael Prichard. 9 cass. (Running Time: 13 hrs. 30 min.). 1988. 72.00 (978-0-7366-1355-2(2), 2256-A) Books on Tape.
In dusty Masqat, Arab terrorists seize the American embassy. At the State Deptment in Washington, a freshman congressman who knows the Arab world makes a secret offer that may be the last remaining hope.

Icarus Agenda, Pt. 2. collector's ed. Robert Ludlum. Read by Michael Prichard. 9 cass. (Running Time: 13 hrs. 30 min.). 1988. 72.00 (978-0-7366-1356-9(0), 2256-B) Books on Tape.
In dusty Masqat, Arab terrorists seize the American embassy. At the State Department in Washington a freshman congressman, who knows the Arab world, makes a secret offer that may be the last remaining hope.

Icarus Hunt. collector's unabr. ed. Timothy Zahn. Read by Jonathan Marosz. 9 cass. (Running Time: 13 hrs. 30 min.). 2000. 72.00 (978-0-7366-4803-5(8), 5154) Books on Tape.
Jordan McKell, a renegade space pilot & his unusual alien partner, Ixil, incautiously agree to fly a ship & its special cargo to Earth. The ship, Icarus, turns out to be a ramshackle hulk with a ragtag crew & a cargo so secret it's sealed in a special container inside the ill-designed ship. As if that weren't bad enough, it looks like the authorities already suspect something is afoot, there's a saboteur aboard & the Icarus appears to be shaking apart at the seems. Things can, & do, get worse when McKell uncovers the true nature of the cargo. Their only chance to survive lies in staying one step ahead of their pursuers as they try to make it home.

Icarus Hunt. unabr. ed. Timothy Zahn. Read by Jonathan Marosz. 9 cass. (Running Time: 12 hrs.). 2001. 34.95 (978-0-7366-4957-5(3)) Books on Tape.

***Icarus Syndrome.** unabr. ed. Peter Beinart. Read by John Morgan. (ENG.). 2010. (978-0-06-201832-8(9), Harper Audio) HarperCollins Pubs.

***Icarus Syndrome: A History of American Hubris.** unabr. ed. Peter Beinart. Read by John Morgan. (ENG.). 2010. (978-0-06-201686-7(5), Harper Audio) HarperCollins Pubs.

Ice. unabr. ed. V. C. Andrews. Read by Laurel Lefkow. 4 cass. (Running Time: 5 hrs.). (Isis Ser.). (J). 2002. 44.95 (978-0-7531-1557-2(3)); audio compact disk 59.95 (978-0-7531-1586-2(7)) Pub: ISIS Lrg Prnt GBR. Dist(s): Ulverscroft US
Ice hides from the world behind a shield of silence. And that is what her mother hates about her. All she wants is a normal daughter who wears make-up and sexy clothes to attract boys. But Ice gets her chance to shine when she reveals her beautiful singing voice. And her extraordinary gift may become her saving grace when tragedy and deception almost destroy her dreams.

***Ice.** unabr. ed. Linda Howard. Read by Fred Sanders. 4 CDs. (Running Time: 5 hrs.). 2009. audio compact disk 30.00 (978-0-307-70266-1(9)) Random.

Ice. unabr. ed. Ed McBain, pseud. Read by Jonathan Marosz. 7 cass. (Running Time: 10 hrs. 30 min.). (87th Precinct Ser.: Bk. 36). 1995. 56.00 (978-0-7366-3180-8(1), 3849) Books on Tape.
Justice still applies to three low-life citizens who get murdered by the same brutal killer. McBain's most ambitious 87th Precinct novel.

Ice! unabr. collector's ed. Tristan Jones. Read by Richard Brown. 7 cass. (Running Time: 10 hrs. 30 mins.). 1990. 56.00 (978-0-7366-1796-3(5), 2632) Books on Tape.
Tristan Jones, described by Time magazine as "someone Lindbergh would have understood," wanted to sail a boat farther north than anyone else would ever attempt. Accompanied by Nelson, a one-eyed, three-legged Labrador, he set out from Iceland in the summer of 1959. The first winter he holed up in a Greenland fiord. Trapped by violent snowstorms, he nearly died. But he kept moving north, & by the second winter was solidly joined to an ice pack in the Arctic Ocean. For 366 days all he could do was hope the ice pack would drift far enough north for the record. His only certainty was the terrible ice, which finally won by crushing his boat. How could he & Nelson survive? But they did, & it makes us glad that intrepid men still live & write so the rest of us can share their remarkable adventures, of which this is certainly one.

***Ice: A Memoir of Gangster Life & Redemption-from South Central to Hollywood.** unabr. ed. Ice-T & Douglas Century. (Running Time: 10 hrs. NaN mins.). (ENG.). 2011. 29.95 (978-1-4417-7539-9(0)); 59.95 (978-1-4417-7536-8(6)); audio compact disk 29.95 (978-1-4417-7538-2(2)) Blckstn Audio.

***Ice: A Memoir of Gangster Life & Redemption-from South Central to Hollywood (Library Edition)** unabr. ed. Ice-T & Douglas Century. (Running Time: 10 hrs. NaN mins.). 2011. audio compact disk 90.00 (978-1-4417-7537-5(4)) Blckstn Audio.

Ice: A Novel. unabr. ed. Linda Howard. Read by Fred Sanders. (ENG.). 2009. audio compact disk 30.00 (978-0-307-57761-0(9), Random AudioBks) Pub: Random Audio Pubg. Dist(s): Random

Ice & Fire. (23313-A) J Norton Pubs.

Ice Bound: A Doctor. unabr. ed. Jerri Nielsen. Read by Jerri Nielsen. (Running Time: 13 hrs.). 2008. 39.25 (978-1-4233-3843-7(X), 9781423338437, Brlnc Audio MP3 Lib); 39.25 (978-1-4233-3845-1(6), 9781423338451, BADLE); 24.95 (978-1-4233-3842-0(1), 9781423338420, Brilliance MP3); 24.95 (978-1-4233-3844-4(8), 9781423338444, BAD) Brilliance Audio.

Ice Bound: A Doctor's Incredible Battle for Survival at the South Pole. abr. ed. Jerri Nielsen. Read by Jerri Nielsen. 3 cass. (Running Time: 6 hrs.). 2001. audio compact disk 57.25 (978-1-58788-186-2(1), 1587881861) Brilliance Audio.
The Antarctic winter, with temperatures 100 degrees below zero, shuts supply lines down completely; conditions are too treacherous for planes and boats and the only connection with the rest of the world is satellite hook-up. During the long winter of 1999, Dr. Nielsen, the only physician on a staff of forty-one people, discovered a lump in her breast. Consulting via satellite e-mail with doctors in the U.S., she was forced to perform a biopsy and in June began to treat herself with chemotherapy, in order to insure that she could survive until conditions permitted her rescue in October. A daring rescue by the Air National Guard ensued, who landed, dropped off a replacement physician, and in less than five minutes took off with Dr. Nielsen. Set in one of the most remote and desolate yet strikingly beautiful landscapes on earth, Jerri Nielsen's narrative of her transforming experiences is a thrilling adventure of researchers and scientists embattled by a hostile environment, a chronicle of marvels - and limits - of modern medical technology, and a penetrating exploration of the dynamics of an isolated, intensely connected community faced with adversity. But at its core this is a powerfully moving drama of one woman's voyage of self-discovery and courage and the fierce dedication of scores of colleagues - both known and unknown to her - whose aid proved to be her salvation.

Ice Bound: A Doctor's Incredible Battle for Survival at the South Pole. unabr. ed. Jerri Nielsen. Read by Jerri Nielsen. 6 cass. (Running Time: 11 hrs.). 2001. 89.25 (978-1-58788-013-1(X), 158788013X) Brilliance Audio.

Ice Bound: A Doctor's Incredible Battle for Survival at the South Pole. unabr. ed. Jerri Nielsen & Maryanne Vollers. Read by Jerri Nielsen. 8 cass. (Running Time: 11 hrs.). 2001. 35.95 (978-1-58788-012-4(1), 1587880121, BAU) Brilliance Audio.

Ice Brothers, Pt. 1. unabr. collector's ed. Sloan Wilson. Read by Dick Estell. 7 cass. (Running Time: 10 hrs. 30 min.). 1987. 56.00 (978-0-7366-1085-8(5), 2011-A) Books on Tape.
A Greenland patrol & the crew of the Coast Guard ice trawler Arluk are a microcoism of WW II & all wars because they transcend time & place.

Ice Brothers, Pt. 2. collector's ed. Sloan Wilson. Read by Dick Estell. 8 cass. (Running Time: 12 hrs.). 1987. 64.00 (978-0-7366-1086-5(3), 2011-B) Books on Tape.

Ice Child. Elizabeth McGregor. 2001. 29.99 (978-0-7887-8948-9(1)) Recorded Bks.

Ice Child. Elizabeth McGregor. Narrated by Davina Porter. 12 CDs. (Running Time: 14 hrs. 30 mins.). audio compact disk 116.00 (978-1-4025-2073-0(5)) Recorded Bks.

Ice Child. unabr. ed. Elizabeth McGregor. 12 cass. (Isis Ser.). (J). 2002. 94.95 (978-0-7531-1355-4(4)) Pub: ISIS Lrg Prnt GBR. Dist(s): Ulverscroft US

Ice Child. unabr. ed. Elizabeth McGregor. Narrated by Davina Porter. 10 cass. (Running Time: 14 hrs. 30 mins.). 2001. 94.00 (978-0-7887-9034-8(X)) Recorded Bks.
When London journalist Jo Harper loses her heart to maverick archaeologist Doug Marshall, she also takes on his obsession. Doug is determined to learn why two ships disappeared in the Arctic over 150 years ago. But a shocking accident forever changes their plans for the future. As Jo struggles to rebuild her life, she learns their young son Sam has contracted a life-threatening illness. The only suitable donor may be Doug's son by a previous marriage - and he is off somewhere in the Arctic on an expedition of his own.

***Ice Cold.** Tess Gerritsen. Contrib. by Tanya Eby. (Playaway Adult Fiction Ser.). 2010. (978-1-4418-7423-8(2)) Find a World.

***Ice Cold.** abr. ed. Tess Gerritsen. Read by Tanya Eby. 5 CDs. (Running Time: 6 hrs.). 2010. audio compact disk 24.99 (978-1-4233-9241-5(8), 9781423392415, BACD) Brilliance Audio.

***Ice Cold.** unabr. ed. Tess Gerritsen. (Running Time: 10 hrs.). 2010. 24.99 (978-1-4233-9209-5(4), 9781423392095, BAD); 39.97 (978-1-4233-9210-1(8), 9781423392101, BADLE) Brilliance Audio.

***Ice Cold.** unabr. ed. Tess Gerritsen. Read by Tanya Eby. 1 MP3-CD. (Running Time: 10 hrs.). 2010. 24.99 (978-1-4233-9207-1(8), 9781423392071, Brilliance MP3); 39.97 (978-1-4233-9208-8(6), 9781423392088, Brlnc Audio MP3 Lib); audio compact disk 36.99 (978-1-4233-9205-7(1), 9781423392057, Bril Audio CD Unabri); audio compact disk 97.97 (978-1-4233-9206-4(X), 9781423392064, BriAudCD Unabrid) Brilliance Audio.

***Ice Cold.** unabr. ed. Tess Gerritsen. Read by Tanya Eby. 1 Playaway. (Running Time: 10 hrs.). 2010. 39.99 (978-1-4418-7368-2(6)) Brilliance Audio.

Ice Cold Grave. unabr. ed. Charlaine Harris. Read by Alyssa Bresnahan. 8 cass. (Running Time: 8 hrs. 45 mins.). (Harper Connelly Ser.: No. 3). 2008. 61.75 (978-1-4281-8123-6(7)); audio compact disk 77.75 (978-1-4281-8125-0(3)) Recorded Bks.

Ice Continent. (J). (gr. 1-4). 2001. bk. 19.95 (SP 7005C) Kimbo Educ.
A story of Antarctica about penguins & seals. Includes book.

Ice Continent: A Story of Antarctica. Louise O. Young. Read by Randye Kaye. Illus. by Larry Elmore. 1 cass. (Running Time: 12 min.). (Habitat Ser.). (J). (gr. 1-4). 1997. 5.00 (978-1-56899-506-9(7), C7005) Soundprints.
On the frozen continent of Antarctica, a cold offshore wind blows. A single emperor penguin swims back towards her rookery, where her chick waits to be fed. But miles of frozen waste land & a stalking leopard seal stand between the emperor penguin & her hungry chick.

Ice Continent: A Story of Antarctica. Louise O. Young. Read by Randye Kaye. Illus. by Larry Elmore. Narrated by Randye Kaye. 1 cass. (Running Time: 12 min.). (Habitat Ser.). (ENG.). (J). (gr. 1-4). 1997. 19.95 (978-1-56899-502-1(4), BC7005) Soundprints.

Ice Cream. unabr. ed. Helen Dunmore. Read by Carole Boyd. 4 CDs. (Running Time: 4 hrs. 46 min.). (Isis Ser.). (J). 2003. audio compact disk 51.95 (978-0-7531-2242-6(1)) Pub: ISIS Lrg Prnt GBR. Dist(s): Ulverscroft US
Short stories ranging from Victorian tragedy to the tale of a dinner-lady's love, from the death of light-keeper's wife to the birth of babies from he Superstork catalogue.

Ice Cream. unabr. ed. Helen Dunmore & Carole Boyd. 4 cass. (Isis Ser.). (J). 2003. 44.95 (978-0-7531-0989-2(1)) Pub: ISIS Lrg Prnt GBR. Dist(s): Ulverscroft US

Ice Cream Show. unabr. ed. 1 cass. (Running Time: 55 min.). 1989. 12.95 (978-0-88432-271-9(8), C40115) J Norton Pubs.
Features anecdotes on the American craze for ice cream, its heyday, & the disappearance of the soda jerk.

Ice Diaries: The Untold Story of the Cold War's Most Daring Mission. unabr. ed. William Anderson. Narrated by Roger Mueller. (Running Time: 11 hrs. 0 mins. 0 sec.). (ENG.). 2008. audio compact disk 34.99 (978-1-59859-360-0(9)) Oasis Audio.

Ice Diaries: The Untold Story of the Cold War's Most Daring Mission. unabr. ed. William Anderson. Narrated by Roger Mueller. (Running Time: 11 hrs. 0 mins. 0 sec.). (ENG.). 2008. 24.49 (978-1-60814-249-1(3), SpringWater) Oasis Audio.

Ice Dragon. Jeffrey Lord. Read by Lloyd James. 2 vols. 2004. 18.00 (978-1-58807-365-5(3)) Am Pubng Inc.

Ice Dragon. Jeffrey Lord. Read by Lloyd James. 2 vols. No. 10. 2004. (978-1-58807-783-7(7)) Am Pubng Inc.

Ice Dragon. unabr. ed. George R. R. Martin. Read by Maggi-Meg Reed. 1 CD. (Running Time: 1 hr. 0 mins. 0 sec.). (ENG., (YA). (gr. 4-7). 2006. audio compact disk 12.95 (978-1-4272-0025-9(4)) Pub: Macmill Audio. Dist(s): Macmillan

Ice Dreams. Martin Fishman. 4 CDs. (Running Time: 6 hrs.). 2005. audio compact disk 24.95 (978-0-660-18317-6(X)) Pub: Canadian Broadcasting CAN. Dist(s): Georgetown Term

Ice Harvest. Scott Phillips. Narrated by Grover Gardner. (Running Time: 4 hrs. 30 mins.). 2005. 22.95 (978-1-59912-674-6(5)) Iofy Corp.

Ice Harvest. unabr. ed. Scott Phillips. 4 cass. (Running Time: 5.3 hrs. 0 mins.). 2005. 32.95 (978-0-7861-2923-2(9)); audio compact disk 32.00 (978-0-7861-8199-5(0)) Blckstn Audio.

Ice Harvest. unabr. movie tie-in ed. Scott Phillips. Read by Grover Gardner. 4 cass. (Running Time: 4 hrs. 30 mins.). 2005. 24.95 (978-0-7861-2739-9(2), E3308); audio compact disk 24.95 (978-0-7861-8576-4(7), ZE3308); audio compact disk 29.95 (978-0-7861-8511-5(2), ZM3308) Blckstn Audio.

Ice House. Minette Walters. Read by Simon Prebble. 6 Cass. (Running Time: 10.5 Hours). 29.95 (978-1-4025-5851-1(1)) Recorded Bks.

Ice House. unabr. ed. Michele Sobel Spirn. 1 cass. (Running Time: 7 min.). (I Like to Read Ser.). (J). (ps-2). 1985. bk. 16.99 (978-0-87386-001-7(2)) Jan Prods.
One day the Smith children wake up & find it has snowed. There is hard snow all over. "When I was little & it snowed like that," says their mother, "I made an ice house," & she explains how.

Ice House. unabr. ed. Minette Walters. Narrated by Simon Prebble. 9 CDs. (Running Time: 10 hrs. 30 mins.). 2001. audio compact disk 89.00 (978-0-7887-7170-5(1)) Recorded Bks.
A chilling story of love, loyalty & deadly intrigue. A small British village has long suspected that the three women living in a local manor house are witches or even worse. So when an unidentifiable body is found in the home's ice house, everyone is set to believe their guilt, especially police inspector Walsh. Ten years ago, Walsh suspected one of the women of murder, but was unable to make a case. Now he plans to do whatever it takes to untangle the women's secrets.

Ice House. unabr. ed. Minette Walters. Narrated by Simon Prebble. 7 cass. (Running Time: 10 hrs. 30 mins.). 2000. 61.00 (978-0-7887-4884-4(X), 96194E7) Recorded Bks.
A chilling story of love, loyalty & deadly intrigue. When a faceless corpse of uncertain vintage is discovered in the ice house of the home of three eccentric women, the village's chief police inspector can't wait to pin the murder on the home's owner, a woman whose husband mysteriously disappeared ten years earlier.

***Ice Hunt.** unabr. ed. James Rollins. Read by John Meagher. (ENG.). 2009. (978-0-06-195860-1(3), Harper Audio); (978-0-06-196156-4(6), Harper Audio) HarperCollins Pubs.

Ice Limit: News Reports on Recent Mysterious Events in the Antarctic Sea. abr. ed. Douglas Preston & Lincoln Child. Read by Scott Brick. (ENG.). 2005. 14.98 (978-1-59483-459-2(8)) Pub: Hachet Audio. Dist(s): HachBkGrp

Ice Limit: News Reports on Recent Mysterious Events in the Antarctic Sea. unabr. ed. Douglas Preston & Lincoln Child. Read by Scott Brick. (Running Time: 17 hrs. 30 mins.). (ENG.). 2010. 24.98 (978-1-60788-471-2(2)) Pub: Hachet Audio. Dist(s): HachBkGrp

Ice Maiden. Edna Buchanan. (Britt Montero Mystery Ser.). 2003. 56.00 (978-0-7366-9262-5(2)); audio compact disk 64.00 (978-0-7366-9263-2(0)) Books on Tape.

Ice Man: Confessions of a Mafia Contract Killer. unabr. ed. Philip Carlo. Read by Michael Prichard. (YA). 2008. 64.99 (978-1-60514-729-1(X)) Find a World.

Ice Man: Confessions of a Mafia Contract Killer. unabr. ed. Philip Carlo. Narrated by Michael Prichard. 14 CDs. (Running Time: 18 hrs. 30 mins. 0 sec.). (ENG.). 2006. audio compact disk 39.99 (978-1-4001-0262-4(6)); audio compact disk 79.99 (978-1-4001-3262-1(2)) Pub: Tantor Media. Dist(s): IngramPubServ

Ice Man: Confessions of a Mafia Contract Killer. unabr. ed. Philip Carlo. Read by Michael Prichard. (Running Time: 18 hrs. 30 mins. 0 sec.). (ENG.). 2006. audio compact disk 29.99 (978-1-4001-5262-9(3)) Pub: Tantor Media. Dist(s): IngramPubServ

Ice Mask. Richard Woodman. Read by Terry Wale. 8 cass. (Running Time: 10 hrs. 30 mins.). (Soundings Ser.). (J). 2004. 69.95 (978-1-84283-763-4(X)); audio compact disk 84.95 (978-1-84283-795-5(8)) Pub: ISIS Lrg Prnt GBR. Dist(s): Ulverscroft US

Ice Opinion, Set. abr. ed. Ice-T Staff. Read by Ice-T Staff. 2 cass. (Running Time: 3 hrs.). 1994. 16.95 (978-1-879371-66-8(9)); audio compact disk 29.95 (978-1-879371-69-9(3)) Pub Mills.
Controversial rap artist, Ice T examines violence, the ghetto, riots & his own reputation in this frank & very personal book about his life, on the streets & as a music star.

Ice Palace. unabr. ed. Edna Ferber. Read by Flo Gibson. 10 cass. (Running Time: 15 hrs.). (Classic Books on Cassettes Coll.). 1998. 80.00 Audio Bk Con.
Alaska before statehood in all its glory, beauty & bleakness.

Ice Palace. unabr. collector's ed. Edna Ferber. Read by Flo Gibson. 10 cass. (Running Time: 15 hrs.). 1984. 80.00 (978-0-7366-0668-4(8), 1630) Books on Tape.
This is the story of Alaska before statehood, where men pitted themselves against the elements & the wilds, only to find the greatest threat is from "outside".

***Ice Princess.** unabr. ed. Camilla Läckberg. (ENG.). 2010. audio compact disk 39.95 (978-1-61573-546-4(1), 1615735461) Pub: HighBridge. Dist(s): Workman Pub

Ice Queen. unabr. ed. Alice Hoffman. Read by Nancy Travis. 2005. 14.98 (978-1-59483-160-7(2)) Pub: Hachet Audio. Dist(s): HachBkGrp

Ice Queen. unabr. ed. Alice Hoffman. Read by Nancy Travis. (Running Time: 6 hrs.). (ENG.). 2009. 49.98 (978-1-60788-035-6(0)) Pub: Hachet Audio. Dist(s): HachBkGrp

Ice Run. abr. ed. Steve Hamilton. (Running Time: 4 hrs.). (Alex Mcknight Ser.: No. 6). 2004. audio compact disk 69.25 (978-1-59355-939-7(9), 1593559399) Brilliance Audio.
Alex McKnight is in love. Even though he met Natalie Reynaud, an officer from the Ontario Provincial Police, under difficult circumstances, they share a common bond of solitude, as well as the same nightmare - they're both cops who buried their partners. It's Alex's first real relationship in years, which in some ways is terrifying. But Natalie has her own fears to deal with - and her own secrets. They brave a violent snowstorm to spend the night together in a historic hotel in Sault Ste. Marie, Michigan. There, they meet a mysterious old man who seems to know a lot about Natalie - and about her family. But they won't be getting any answers from him - he'll be found frozen to death in a snowbank the very next morning. From this single incident, an old blood feud will be reignited, one going back decades to an event buried in her family's past - an event that even now can still drive men to kill each other. As much as Natalie doesn't want Alex to become entangled in this web of lies and hatred, there's no way he can let her face this danger alone. This is a man who has gotten beaten up, shot at, and

even dragged behind a snowmobile, all because he's a sucker for a friend in need. How much further will he go for love?.

Ice Run. unabr. ed. Steve Hamilton. Read by Jim Bond. 7 CDs. (Running Time: 9 hrs.). (Alex Mcknight Ser.). 2004. 24.95 (978-1-59335-321-6(9), 1593353219, Brilliance MP3); 39.25 (978-1-59335-482-4(7), 1593354827, Brlnc Audio MP3 Lib) Brilliance Audio.

Ice Run. unabr. ed. Steve Hamilton. Read by Jim Bond. 6 cass. Library ed. (Running Time: 9 hrs.). (Alex Mcknight Ser.: No. 6). 2004. 69.25 (978-1-59086-998-7(2), 1590869982, Unabridge Lib Edns); 29.95 (978-1-59086-997-0(4), 1590869974, BAU) Brilliance Audio.

Ice Run. unabr. ed. Steve Hamilton. Read by Jim Bond. (Running Time: 9 hrs.). (Alex Mcknight Ser.). 2004. 39.25 (978-1-59710-390-9(X), 159710390X, BADLE); 24.95 (978-1-59710-391-6(8), 1597103918, BAD) Brilliance Audio.

Ice Station. Matthew Reilly. Read by Sean Mangan. (Running Time: 15 hrs. 20 mins.). 2009. 109.99 (978-1-74214-276-0(1), 9781742142760) Pub: Bolinda Pubng AUS. Dist(s): Bolinda Pub Inc

Ice Station. unabr. ed. Matthew Reilly. Read by Sean Mangan. 9 cass. (Running Time: 15 hrs. 20 mins.). 2000. 72.00 (978-1-74030-109-1(9), 500321) Pub: Bolinda Pubng AUS. Dist(s): Bolinda Pub Inc

Ice Station. unabr. ed. Matthew Reilly. Read by Sean Mangan. 14 CDs. (Running Time: 15 hrs. 20 mins.). 2002. audio compact disk 118.95 (978-1-74030-893-9(X)) Pub: Bolinda Pubng AUS. Dist(s): Bolinda Pub Inc

Ice Station. unabr. ed. Matthew Reilly. Read by Sean Mangan. (Running Time: 55200 sec.). 2005. audio compact disk 43.95 (978-1-74093-679-8(5)) Pub: Bolinda Pubng AUS. Dist(s): Bolinda Pub Inc

Ice Station Zebra. unabr. ed. Alistair MacLean. Read by Steve Hodson. 8 cass. (Running Time: 10 hrs.). (Isis Ser.). (J). 2004. 69.95 (978-1-85089-751-4(4), 89065) Pub: ISIS Lrg Prnt GBR. Dist(s): Ulverscroft US

Ice Storm: And Other Poems Read by the Poet. Poems. George Scarbrough. 1 cass. (Running Time: 60 mins.). 1996. 10.00 (978-0-916078-11-9(6), Iris) Iris Pub Group.
31 poems read by the poet, George Scarbrough.

Ice Thief. Susan Gates. Read by Glen McCready. (Running Time: 5100 sec.). (J). 2001. audio compact disk 21.95 (978-0-7540-6789-4(0)) AudioGo GBR.

Iceberg. abr. ed. Clive Cussler. Read by Michael Prichard. 7 cass. (Running Time: 10 hrs. 30 min.). (Dirk Pitt Ser.). 1992. 56.00 (978-0-7366-2226-4(8), 3016) Books on Tape.
Frozen inside an ice mass are the charred remains of a long-missing yacht holding a priceless cargo. Dirk Pitt confronts a conspiracy to hijack a continent in a deadly Arctic confrontation.

Iceberg Slim: Reflections. abr. ed. Iceberg Slim. 2008. audio compact disk 18.98 (978-1-929243-81-5(2)) Uproar Ent.

Icebound. unabr. ed. Dean Koontz. Read by Paul Michael. 10 CDs. (Running Time: 32400 sec.). (Dean Koontz Ser.). (ENG.). 2007. audio compact disk 29.95 (978-0-7393-4141-4(3), Random AudioBks) Pub: Random Audio Pubg. Dist(s): Random

Icebound: The Jeannette Expedition's Quest for the North Pole. unabr. collector's ed. Leonard F. Guttridge. Read by John MacDonald. 8 cass. (Running Time: 12 hrs.). 1987. 64.00 (978-0-7366-0761-2(7), 1718) Books on Tape.
Details the perilous voyage to the North Pole made by 19th century American explorers.

Icebound Land. John Flanagan. Read by John Keating. 8. (Running Time: 8 hrs. 75 mins.). (Ranger's Apprentice Ser.: Bk. 3). 2007. 67.75 (978-1-4281-5562-6(7)); audio compact disk 87.75 (978-1-4281-5567-1(8)) Recorded Bks.

Icecrust & Snowflake see Poetry & Voice of Ted Hughes

Iced. Jenny Siler. Read by Betty Bobbitt. (Running Time: 7 hrs.). 2009. 74.99 (978-1-74214-285-2(0), 9781742142852) Pub: Bolinda Pubng AUS. Dist(s): Bolinda Pub Inc

Iced. unabr. ed. Jenny Siler. Read by Betty Bobbitt. 7 CDs. (Running Time: 25200 sec.). 2005. audio compact disk 83.95 (978-1-74093-666-8(3)) Pub: Bolinda Pubng AUS. Dist(s): Bolinda Pub Inc

Iced. unabr. ed. Jenny Siler. Read by Betty Bobbitt. 7 x CDs. (Running Time: 25200 sec.). 2006. audio compact disk 44.95 (978-1-74094-874-6(2)) Bolinda Pubng AUS.

Icefields. abr. ed. Thomas Wharton. Narrated by James MacDonald. 2 cass. (Running Time: 2 hrs. 30 mins.). (Between the Covers Collection). (ENG.). 1998. 14.95 (978-0-86492-238-0(8)) Goose Ln Eds CAN.
"In 1898, a doctor almost dies while exploring Alberta's Arcturus Glacier. Obsessed, he gives up his London practice to study the shining cathedral of ice that is at the heart of this powerfully evocative novel about the blend of science and mysticism that fuelled early twentieth-century exploration. Icefields won the Commonwealth Writers' Prize for Canada and the Caribbean.".

Icelandic Conversations. K. Chapman et al. 5 CDs. (Running Time: 5 hrs.). (ICE.). 2005. audio compact disk 85.00 (978-1-57970-258-8(9), AFIC10D, Audio-For) J Norton Pubs.
This course assumes a basic knowledge of Icelandic and is designed to give speech practice. Extensive Icelandic-English glossary.

Icelandic Conversations. unabr. ed. K. Chapman et al. 5 cass. (Running Time: 5 hrs.). (ICE & ENG.). (YA). (gr. 10-12). pap. bk. 85.00 (978-0-88432-515-4(6), AFIC10) J Norton Pubs.
Assumes a basic knowledge of Icelandic & is designed to give speech practice. The extensive glossary is Icelandic-English.

Icelandic Horses - A Basic Guide to This Rare Breed: Educational Book Series. Karen Jean Matsko Hood. 2006. audio compact disk 13.95 (978-1-59649-530-2(8)) Whsprng Pine.

Icelandic Sheepdog: A Basic Guide to this Canine Breed. 2005. 29.95 (978-1-59808-068-1(7)); audio compact disk 24.95 (978-1-59808-067-4(9)) Whsprng Pine.

Ice's Edge. Karen Young. 1 cass. (Running Time: 35 min.). (J). (ps-2). 2001. bk. 19.95 (SP 4011C) Kimbo Educ.
On the pack ice off the coast of Labrador, Little Harp Seal is born. Includes book.

Ice's Edge: The Story of a Harp Seal Pup. Karen Romano Young. Narrated by Peter Thomas. Illus. by Brian Shaw. 1 cass. (Smithsonian Oceanic Collection). (J). (ps-2). 1996. 5.00 (978-1-56899-319-5(6), C4011) Soundprints.
On the pack ice off the coast of Labrador, Little Harp Seal is born under a cloudy March sky. Here polar bears roam the ice pack looking for unsuspecting seals. Little Harp Seal's fluffy white fur hides him against the snow & ice as he grows bigger each day. Soon, his mother will leave him to migrate north. Little Harp Seal, his white baby fur turning gray, must learn to hunt & escape predators on his own.

Ice's Edge: The Story of a Harp Seal Pup. Karen Romano Young. Illus. by Brian Shaw. Narrated by Peter Thomas. 1 cass. (Smithsonian Oceanic Collection). (J). (ps-2). 1996. bk. 19.95 (978-1-56899-311-9(0), BC4011) Soundprints.

Ich bin ein Hamburger. Harry A. Walbruck & Eberhard Buser. 1 cass. (Wir Sprechen Deutsch Ser.). 20.00 (978-0-8442-2050-5(7), Natl Textbk Co) M-H Contemporary.
Features motivators for conversation & writing.

***Ichabod.** Featuring Ravi Zacharias. 1986. audio compact disk 9.00 (978-1-61256-010-6(5)) Ravi Zach.

Ichabod Crane see Legend of Sleepy Hollow

Ichi, Ni, San, Shi...Go! Harold Wright & Jonathan Wright. 1 CD. (Running Time: 1 hr.). 2003. audio compact disk 16.00 (978-0-9672234-2-1(3)) PRESTO & US.
Story selections from many books plus stories heard orally.

Iciest Sin. unabr. ed. H. R. F. Keating. Read by Sam Dastor. 5 cass. (Running Time: 6 hrs. 45 min.). (Inspector Ghote Mystery Ser.: No. 18). 1993. 42.00 set. (978-1-55690-891-0(1), 93333) Recorded Bks.
Inspector Ghoti witnesses the murder of a notorious Bombay blackmailer.

Icis 2002: Conference Proceedings. Ed. by M. A. Schmuckler et al. 2002. audio compact disk 49.95 (978-0-8058-4501-3(1)) Pub: L Erlbaum Assocs. Dist(s): Taylor and Fran

***Icon.** abr. ed. Neil Olson. Read by Eric Conger. (ENG.). 2005. (978-0-06-084582-7(1), Harper Audio); (978-0-06-079672-3(3), Harper Audio) HarperCollins Pubs.

Icon. unabr. ed. Frederick Forsyth. Read by David Case. 12 cass. (Running Time: 18 hrs.). 1997. 96.00 (978-0-913369-40-1(3), 4216) Books on Tape.
It's 1999 & Russia, wracked with famine & crime, nears anarchy. For Igor Komarov, a charismatic right-winger, opportunity knocks. He waits in the wings for the next election, promising a Russian reborn. Elder statesmen in the West want to know his agenda & hire the best man for the job, ex-CIA agent Jason Monk.

Icon. unabr. ed. Neil Olson. Read by Lewis Grenville. 10 CDs. (Running Time: 45000 sec.). 2005. DVD, audio compact disk, audio compact disk 94.95 (978-0-7927-3624-0(9), SLD 797) AudioGO.

Icon: A Novel. unabr. ed. Neil Olson. Read by Lewis Grenville. 2005. 29.95 (978-0-7927-3625-7(7), CMP 797); 69.95 (978-0-7927-3620-2(6), CSL 797) AudioGO.

Icon of Evil: Hitler's Mufti & the Rise of Radical Islam. David G. Dalin & John F. Rothmann. Read by Michael Prichard. (ENG.). 2009. 49.99 (978-1-60812-787-0(7)) Find a World.

Icon of Evil: Hitler's Mufti & the Rise of Radical Islam. unabr. ed. David G. Dalin & John F. Rothmann. Narrated by Michael Prichard. (Running Time: 7 hrs. 0 mins. 0 sec.). (ENG.). 2008. audio compact disk 24.99 (978-1-4001-0671-4(0)); audio compact disk 49.99 (978-1-4001-3671-1(7)); audio compact disk 19.99 (978-1-4001-5671-9(8)) Pub: Tantor Media. Dist(s): IngramPubServ

Icon of Gold. unabr. ed. Teresa Crane. Read by Phyllida Nash. 10 cass. (Running Time: 10 hrs.). 1998. 84.95 Set, Dolby Sound. (978-0-7540-0182-9(2), CAB 1605) AudioGO.
In the wake of World War II, a hasty marriage has become a clash of personalities for Cathy Kotsikas. Leon, her Greek husband, is charming, yet self-centered. In 1952, the death of his much-loved grandmother brings Nikos, Leon's son, to meet Cathy for the first time. Bereft & unhappy, Nikos is drawn to Cathy, & she to him. But neither sees the danger of the attraction until it is too late.

Icon, Rebel, Saint. Joan Chittister. 1 cass. (Running Time: 60 min.). 9.95 incl. study guide. Credence Commun.
Chittister uses three great women of scripture, Suzannah, Judith & Mary, to identify three roles women played then & still play now. The roles are dramatic, they are not pretty. Chittister uses her considerable biblical & historical learning to help women see what really happened then, is still happening now & must happen no longer.

Iconoclast see Twentieth-Century Poetry in English, No. 28, Recordings of Poets Reading Their Own Poetry

Icons of Evolution. 2004. DVD & audio compact disk 24.95 (978-0-01-222988-0(1)) Randolf Prod.

Icy Sparks. Gwyn Hyman Rubio. Narrated by Kate Forbes. 11 CDs. (Running Time: 13 hrs.). audio compact disk 114.00 (978-1-4025-2908-5(2)) Recorded Bks.

Icy Sparks. Gwyn Hyman Rubio. Narrated by Kate Forbes. 9 cass. (Running Time: 13 hrs.). 1998. 81.00 (978-0-7887-9926-6(6), 96858) Recorded Bks.
Takes you into the frightening world of a young girl struggling to live with Tourette's Syndrome. As Icy comes of age, she discovers that overcoming her handicap and leading a normal life is possible.

Icy Sparks. abr. ed. Gwyn Hyman Rubio. Read by Kate Miller. (YA). 2006. 44.99 (978-1-59895-539-2(X)) Find a World.

Icy Sparks. unabr. abr. ed. Gwyn Hyman Rubio. Read by Kate Miller. 6 CDs. (Running Time: 7 hrs.). (ENG.). 2001. audio compact disk 34.95 (978-1-56511-513-2(9), 1565115139) Pub: HighBridge. Dist(s): Workman Pub

***I'd Know You Anywhere.** unabr. ed. Laura Lippman. Read by Linda Emond. (ENG.). 2010. (978-0-06-204136-4(3), Harper Audio); (978-0-06-200694-3(0), Harper Audio) HarperCollins Pubs.

I'd Know You Anywhere. unabr. ed. Laura Lippman. Read by Linda Emond. 2010. audio compact disk 39.99 (978-0-06-198848-6(0), Harper Audio) HarperCollins Pubs.

I'd Like to Stop, But... Overcoming Addictions. Albert Ellis. 1 cass. (Running Time: 42 min.). 1999. 9.95 (C013) A Ellis Institute.
Especially helpful with problems of smoking & overeating, but applicable to all addictive behavior.

I'd Rather Have Jesus. Contrib. by Crabb Family. (Soundtraks Ser.). 2007. audio compact disk 8.99 (978-5-557-95423-5(6)) Christian Wrld.

I'd Rather Have Jesus. Perf. by Dallas Fort Worth Mass Choir. 1 cass., 1 CD. 9.98; audio compact disk 15.98 CD. Platinum Chrst Dist.

I'd Rather Laugh. abr. ed. Linda Richman. (ENG.). 2005. 14.98 (978-1-59483-430-1(X)) Pub: Hachet Audio. Dist(s): HachBkGrp

I'd Rather Laugh: How to Be Happy Even When Life Has Other Plans for You. Linda Richman. 2002. 17.98 (978-1-58621-127-1(7)) Hachet Audio.

***I'd Rather We Got Casinos.** Larry Wilmore. (ENG.). 2009. 14.99 (978-1-4013-9151-5(6)); 14.99 (978-1-4013-9152-2(4)) Pub: Hyperion. Dist(s): HarperCollins Pubs

I'd Rather We Got Casinos: And Other Black Thoughts. unabr. abr. ed. Larry Wilmore. Read by Larry Wilmore. 2009. audio compact disk 22.99 (978-1-4013-9150-8(8), Harper Audio) HarperCollins Pubs.

I'd Tell You I Love You, but Then I'd Have to Kill You. unabr. ed. Ally Carter. Read by Renée Raudman. (Running Time: 7 hrs.). (Gallagher Girls Ser.: No. 1). 2006. 39.25 (978-1-4233-1184-3(1), 9781423311843, BADLE); 24.95 (978-1-4233-1183-6(3), 9781423311836, BAD) Brilliance Audio.

I'd Tell You I Love You, but Then I'd Have to Kill You. unabr. ed. Ally Carter. Read by Renée Raudman. 5 cass. (Running Time: 25200 sec.). (Gallagher Girls Ser.: No. 1). (YA). (gr. 8-12). 2006. 69.25 (978-1-4233-1178-2(7), 9781423311782, BriAudUnabridg); audio compact disk 82.25 (978-1-4233-1180-5(9), 9781423311805, BriAudCD Unabrid); audio compact disk 39.25 (978-1-4233-1182-9(5), 9781423311829, Brlnc Audio MP3 Lib); audio compact disk 29.95 (978-1-4233-1179-9(5), 9781423311799); audio compact disk 24.95 (978-1-4233-1181-2(7), 9781423311812, Brilliance MP3) Brilliance Audio.
The Gallagher Academy for Exceptional Young Women is a fairly typical all-girls school - that is, if every school teaches advanced martial arts in PE, chemistry always consists of the latest in chemical warfare, and everyone breaks CIA codes for extra credit in computer class. So in truth, Gallagher Academy might posit itself as a school for geniuses but what they really mean is spies. But what happens when a Gallagher girl falls for a boy who doesn't have a code name? Cammie Morgan may be fluent in fourteen languages and capable of killing a man in seven different ways (three of which involve a piece of uncooked spaghetti), but the Gallagher Academy for Exceptional Young Women hasn't prepared her for what to do when she meets an ordinary boy who thinks she's an ordinary girl. Sure, she can tap his phone, hack into his computer, and track him through a mall without him ever being the wiser, but can she have a regular relationship with a regular boy who can never know the truth about her school (it's really not a last resort place for snooty heiresses with nowhere else to go), her family (her mother is a retired spy and headmistress of the school for goodness sake) or her life (daughter of spy royalty and destined for great things)? Cammie Morgan may be the next generation of an elite sisterhood of female spies, but in her sophomore year, she's doing something riskier than any Gallagher Girl has ever done before - she's falling in love.

Ida B. Katherine M. Hannigan. Read by Lili Taylor. 2 cass. (J). 2004. 23.00 (978-1-4000-9094-5(6), Listening Lib); audio compact disk 25.50 (978-1-4000-9483-7(6), Listening Lib) Pub: Random Audio Pubg. Dist(s): NetLibrary CO

Ida B. Wells. Prod. by Rex A. Barnett. 1 cass. (Running Time: 27 min.). 1993. 19.95 Hist Video.
Ida B. Wells spotlights a brave, selfless African-American woman who earned international acclaim for standing up against human rights abuses of Americans by Americans following slavery in 1865. Ida B. Wells was one of the foremost leaders of the era.

Idaho! abr. ed. Dana Fuller Ross, pseud. Read by Lloyd James. 4 vols. (Wagons West Ser.: No. 13). 2003. (978-1-58807-614-4(8)) Am Pubng Inc.

Idaho! abr. ed. Dana Fuller Ross, pseud. Read by Lloyd James. 4 cass. (Running Time: 360 mins.). (Wagon West Ser.: No. 13). 2003. 25.00 (978-1-58807-001-2(8)) Am Pubng Inc.

Idaho! abr. ed. Dana Fuller Ross, pseud. Read by Lloyd James. 5 vols. (Wagons West Ser.: No. 13). 2004. audio compact disk 30.00 (978-1-58807-380-8(7)); audio compact disk (978-1-58807-859-9(0)) Am Pubng Inc.

Idea de Lleana, EDL Level 8. (SPA.). 2003. 11.50 (978-0-7652-1004-3(5)) Modern Curr.

idea generator & Accelerator. unabr. ed. Ken Hudson. Read by Catherine Milte. (Running Time: 4 hrs. 45 mins.). 2009. audio compact disk 63.95 (978-1-74214-472-6(1), 9781742144726) Pub: Bolinda Pubng AUS. Dist(s): Bolinda Pub Inc

***Idea Hunter: How to Find the Best Ideas & Make Them Happen.** unabr. ed. Andy Boynton et al. Read by Erik Synnestvedt. (Running Time: 6 hrs.). (ENG.). 2011. 27.00 (978-1-59659-645-0(7), GildAudio); audio compact disk 29.98 (978-1-59659-634-4(1), GildAudio) Pub: Gildan Media. Dist(s): HachBkGrp

Idea of a University. unabr. ed. John Henry Newman. Read by Fred Williams. 14 cass. (Running Time: 20 hrs. 30 mins.). 1996. 89.95 (978-0-7861-0933-5(1), 1688) Blckstn Audio.
Newman masterfully defends his position that the duty of a university is instruction rather than research & to train the mind rather than to diffuse knowledge. He also defends theological teaching & the tutorial system.

Idea of Order at Key West see Caedmon Treasury of Modern Poets Reading Their Own Poetry

Idea of Perfection. Kate Grenville. Narrated by Odette Joannidis. 9 CDs. (Running Time: 11 hrs.). 1999. audio compact disk 101.00 (978-1-4025-4044-8(2)) Recorded Bks.

Idea of Perfection. unabr. ed. Kate Grenville. Narrated by Odette Joannidis. 8 cass. (Running Time: 11 hrs.). 2002. 72.00 (978-1-84197-373-9(4)) Recorded Bks.

Idea of Perfection. unabr. ed. Kate Grenville. Narrated by Odette Joannidis. 8 cass. (Running Time: 11 hrs.). 2002. 39.95 (978-1-4025-3196-5(6), RG208) Recorded Bks.
Set in the eccentric backwater town of Karakarook, New South Wales, this is the story of Douglas Cheeseman, a shy and clumsy engineer, and Harley Savage, a woman who is known for being rather large and abrupt. Douglas is there to pull down a quaint old bridge, and Harvey aims to foster heritage. They are clearly on a collision course-until they meet for the first time.

Idea of Progress: Science & Poetry. Joseph Mazzeo. 1 CD. (Running Time: 46 mins.). (Sound Seminars Ser.). 2006. audio compact disk 12.95 (978-1-57970-405-6(0), C25028D, Audio-For) J Norton Pubs.
Traces the development of the "progress" concept from early Aristotelian ideas of limited development to the gradual, continuous change espoused by Bacon, Hobbes, and others. Includes a brief discussion of present-day thought.

***Ideal Bride.** abr. ed. Stephanie Laurens. Read by Clare Higgins. (ENG.). 2004. (978-0-06-082453-2(0), Harper Audio); (978-0-06-078655-7(8), Harper Audio) HarperCollins Pubs.

Ideal Bride. unabr. ed. Stephanie Laurens. Narrated by Simon Prebble. 11 cass. (Running Time: 15 hrs.). (Cynster Family Ser.: Bk. 11). 2003. 99.75 (978-1-4025-9564-6(6), L1123MC, Griot Aud) Recorded Bks.

Ideal Chinese Dinner Party. Samain Bettina. (Running Time: 1 hr.). 2002. audio compact disk 15.99 (978-1-904972-06-8(3)) Global Jrny GBR GBR.

Ideal Day: Visualize & Manifest Your Desired Future. Mark Bancroft. Read by Mark Bancroft. 1 cass., bklet. (Running Time: 1 hr.). (Spirituality & Consciousness Ser.). 1999. 12.95 (978-1-58522-006-9(X), 710, EnSpire Aud) EnSpire Pr.
Two complete sessions plus printed instruction manual/guidebook. With healing music soundtrack.

Ideal Day: Visualize & Manifest Your Desired Future. Mark Bancroft. Read by Mark Bancroft. 1 CD, 1 bklet. (Running Time: 1 hr.). (Spirituality & Consciousness Ser.). 2006. audio compact disk 20.00 (978-1-58522-041-0(8)) EnSpire Pr.
Two complete sessions plus printed instructionmanual/guidebook. With healing music soundtrack.

Ideal French Dinner Party. Jordan Peters. (Running Time: 1 hr.). 2002. audio compact disk 15.99 (978-1-904972-04-4(7)) Global Jrny GBR GBR.

Ideal Greek Dinner Party. Samain Bettina. (Running Time: 1 hr.). 2002. audio compact disk 15.99 (978-1-904972-01-3(2)) Global Jrny GBR GBR.

Ideal Husband. Oscar Wilde. Narrated by Flo Gibson. (ENG.). 2007. audio compact disk 19.95 (978-1-55685-938-0(4)) Audio Bk Con.

Ideal Husband. Oscar Wilde. Read by Full Cast Production Staff. Contrib. by Rosalind Ayres et al. (Playaway Adult Fiction Ser.). (ENG.). 2008. 39.99 (978-1-60640-945-9(X)) Find a World.

Ideal Husband. unabr. ed. Oscar Wilde. Perf. by Rosalind Ayres et al. 1 cass. (Running Time: 1 hr. 42 mins.). 1997. 20.95 (978-1-58081-026-5(8), TPT80) L A Theatre.
A tender love story, a serpentine villainess, a glittering setting in London society & a shower of Wildean witticisms. This 1895 drama also seems eerily prescient, as it explores the plight of a promising young politician, desperate to hide a secret in his past. Explores the pitfalls of holding public figures to higher standards than the rest of us.

Ideal Husband. unabr. ed. Oscar Wilde. Perf. by Jacqueline Bisset et al. 2 CDs. (Running Time: 1 hr. 42 mins.). Dramatization. (L. A. Theatre Works). 2001. audio compact disk 25.95 (978-1-58081-215-3(5), CDTPT80) Pub: L A Theatre. Dist(s): NetLibrary CO

Ideal Husband. unabr. ed. Oscar Wilde. Perf. by Derek Jacobi et al. 2 cass. (Running Time: 3 hrs.). (Oscar Wilde Drama Ser.). 1997. Rental 16.95 (PengAudBks) Penguin Grp USA.

Ideal Husband, Set. unabr. ed. Oscar Wilde. Read by Flo Gibson. 3 cass. (Running Time: 3 hrs. 30 min.). 1997. 16.95 (978-1-55685-458-3(7), 458-7) Audio Bk Con.
In this wickedly funny play a seemingly ideal marriage & their charming, priveleged friends surmount such details as selling government secrets, theft, & bribery with love triumphant over all.

Ideal Indian Dinner Party. Samain Bettina. (Running Time: 1 hr.). 2002. audio compact disk 15.99 (978-1-904972-02-0(0)) Global Jrny GBR GBR.

Ideal Italian Dinner Party. Samain Bettina. (Running Time: 1 hr.). 2002. audio compact disk 15.99 (978-1-904972-07-5(1)) Global Jrny GBR GBR.

Ideal Mexican Dinner Party. Samain Bettina. (Running Time: 1 hr.). 2002. audio compact disk 15.99 (978-1-904972-03-7(9)) Global Jrny GBR GBR.

Ideal Mindset Personal Learning Course: How to Let Go of the Past & Prepare Your Mind for Profound Personal Growth. unabr. ed. Paul R. Scheele. Read by Paul R. Scheele. 8 cass. (Running Time: 5 hrs. 30 min.). 179.95 Set. (978-0-925480-39-2(8)) Learn Strategies.

Ideal Relationship CD Album. Bruce Goldberg. (ENG.). 2005. audio compact disk 75.00 (978-1-57968-056-5(9)) Pub: B Goldberg. Dist(s): Baker Taylor

Ideal Relationship Program Cassette Album, Set. Bruce Goldberg. Read by Bruce Goldberg. 6 cass. (Running Time: 3 hrs.). (ENG.). 2006. 65.00 (978-1-885577-76-4(1)) Pub: B Goldberg. Dist(s): Baker Taylor
Through self-hypnosis learn how to attract a soul mate and maintain a mutually fulfilling relationship for years to come.

Ideal Spanish Dinner Party. Samain Bettina. (Running Time: 1 hr.). 2002. audio compact disk 15.99 (978-1-904972-00-6(4)) Global Jrny GBR GBR.

Ideal Thai Dinner Party. Samain Bettina. (Running Time: 1 hr.). 2002. audio compact disk 15.99 (978-1-904972-05-1(5)) Global Jrny GBR GBR.

Ideal Weight. Paul R. Scheele. 1 cass. (Paraliminal Tapes Ser.). 1988. 24.95 (978-0-925480-03-3(7)) Learn Strategies.
Attain & maintain your natural, ideal weight without fad diets.

***Ideal Weight Hypnosis.** Voice by Paul Dale Anderson. (ENG.). 2010. audio compact disk 21.00 (978-0-937491-09-6(8)) TwoAM Pubns.

Idealistic Humanism: Right of the Individual to Be Right. Instructed by Manly P. Hall. 8.95 (978-0-89314-144-8(5), C850804) Philos Res.

IDEAS about Healing. Sara Wolch & Richard Handler. Contrib. by Sara Wolch & Richard Handler. Music by Andy McNeill. Contrib. by Kenneth Mason & Martin Vaillancourt. 3 CDs. (Running Time: 3 hrs.). 2005. audio compact disk 24.95 (978-0-660-19114-0(8)) Pub: Canadian Broadcasting CAN. Dist(s): Georgetown Term

Ideas & Revolution: Locke & America; Rousseau & France. unabr. ed. John Ridpath. 2 cass. (Running Time: 3 hrs.). 1997. 24.95 Set. (978-1-56114-475-4(4), ER52D) Second Renaissance.
A case study in the power of philosophical ideas.

Ideas for Better Living. unabr. ed. Merrill E. Douglass. 3 cass. (Running Time: 1 hr. 14 min.). pap. bk. 34.50 (978-0-88432-178-1(9), S13054); J Norton Pubs.
What about the time you don't work - that special, personal time that belongs to you alone? Wouldn't you like it to be more fulfilling, more meaningful, better for your health? This will help you to plan your time better.

Ideas for Parents. Jolene L. Roehlkepartain. (ENG., 2005. audio compact disk 69.95 (978-1-57482-873-3(8)) Pub: Search Inst. Dist(s): IPG Chicago

Ideas Have Consequences. unabr. ed. Richard M. Weaver. Read by Frederick Davidson. 5 cass. (Running Time: 7 hrs.). 1993. 39.95 (978-0-7861-0640-0(9), 1455) Blckstn Audio.
In what has become a classic work, Weaver unsparingly diagnoses the ills of our age & offers a realistic remedy. The world, he asserts, is intelligible, & man is free. The catastrophes of our age are the product not of necessity but of unintelligent choice. A cure, he submits, is possible. It lies in the right use of man's reason, in the renewed acceptance of an absolute reality, & in the recognition that ideas - like actions - have consequences. Robert Nisbet describes this work as, "one of the few authentic classics in the American political tradition".

Ideas Have Consequences. unabr. ed. Richard M. Weaver & Frederick Davidson. (Running Time: 7.5 hrs. NaN mins.). 2008. 29.95 (978-1-4332-5466-6(2)); audio compact disk 60.00 (978-1-4332-5465-9(4)) Blckstn Audio.

Ideas in Politics, Pts. I-II. Instructed by Jeremy Shearmur. 12 cass. (Running Time: 12 hrs.). 2001. 129.95 (978-1-56585-137-5(4)) Teaching Co.

Ideas in Politics, Pts. I-II, Vol. 1. Instructed by Jeremy Shearmur. 12 CDs. (Running Time: 12 hrs.). 2001. audio compact disk 179.95 (978-1-56585-718-6(6)) Teaching Co.

Ideas in Politics, Vol. 2. Instructed by Jeremy Shearmur. 6 cass. (Running Time: 6 hrs.). 2001. 129.95 (978-1-56585-138-2(2)); audio compact disk 179.95 (978-1-56585-719-3(4)) Teaching Co.

Ideas Leave not their Source: The heart of Nonduality. Gary Arnold. (ENG.). 2009. audio compact disk 24.95 (978-1-57867-010-9(1)) Windhorse Corp.

Ideas Library. unabr. ed. Youth Specialties Staff. 2002. audio compact disk 179.99 (978-0-310-23951-2(6)) Zondervan.

IDEAS of Donald Savoie. Donald Savoie. 2005. audio compact disk 15.95 (978-0-660-19289-5(6)) Canadian Broadcasting CAN.

Ideas, Synopsis, Research. Brenda Wilbee. 1 cass. (Running Time: 4 hrs. 30 min.). (Writing for Publication: Fiction that Sells Ser.: No. 6). 1987. 7.95 (978-0-943777-06-1(2)) byBrenda.
Getting ideas, writing the synopsis, doing research for fiction.

Ideas That Sing. Kim Brodey. 1 cass. 1995. 10.98 (978-1-896322-02-5(6)) Consort Bk Sales.

Ideas That Sing. Kim Brodey. 1 cass. (J). 1995. 18.95 Consort Bk Sales.

Ideas to Contemplate from Breaking Through. Short Stories. Based on a book by Barbara Stanny. 1. (Running Time: 70mins). 2006. audio compact disk 15.95 (978-1-934126-03-5(9)) Pwful Woman.
Hear a dozen different approaches to getting yourself out of any corner. The selections on this CD were especially chosen for listening while multi-tasking. These essays provide stimiulationg food for thought and can be enjoyed while driving, working out or walking your dog! They will definitely stimulate creative thinking and help you find a way out of your dilemma.

Ideas to Grow On, Set. unabr. ed. Trenna Daniells. 2 cass. (Running Time: 80 min.). Dramatization. (One to Grow On Ser.). (J). (gr. k-8). 1999. 19.95 (978-0-918519-22-1(5)) Trenna Prods.
Four stories that promote positive thinking & happiness. Action packed stories that promote self-esteem, self-responsibility, morals & values.

Identical. Ellen Hopkins. Read by Laura Flanagan. (Playaway Young Adult Ser.). (J). 2008. 39.99 (978-1-60640-514-7(4)) Find a World.

Identical. unabr. ed. Ellen Hopkins. Read by Laura M. Flanagan. 7 CDs. (Running Time: 8 hrs. 45 mins.). 2008. audio compact disk 29.95 (978-1-59887-735-9(6), 1598877356) Pub: HighBridge. Dist(s): Workman Pub

Identical Harvest. Neville Goddard. 1 cass. (Running Time: 62 min.). 1963. 8.00 (75) J & L Pubns.
Neville taught Imagination Creates Reality. He was a powerfully influential teacher of God as Consciousness.

Identical Strangers. Perf. by Andy Denton & Randy Thomas. 1 cass. 1997. audio compact disk 15.99 CD. (D 8150CD) Diamante Music Grp.
The Identical Strangers' style creates a new sound, with influences ranging from '60s Beatlesque pop to modern rock. This debut album captures a cohesive diversity musically, reflecting a stylistic versatility while maintaining a solid pop/roots-rock focus.

Identical Strangers: A Memoir of Twins Separated & Reunited. Elyse Schein & Paula Bernstein. Narrated by Alma Cuervo & Effie Johnson. (Running Time: 36000 sec.). 2007. audio compact disk 34.99 (978-1-4281-6997-5(0)) Recorded Bks.

Identidades: Student Activities Manual. Matilde O. Castells et al. 2005. audio compact disk 18.80 (978-0-13-111786-0(6)) Pearson Educ CAN CAN.

Identificando y Moviendo Barreras: Proceeding of the 45th Annual Convention National Association of Evangelicals Buffalo, New York. Read by Guillermo Luna. 1 cass. (Running Time: 60 min.). (SPA.). 1987. 4.00 (325) Nat Assn Evan.

Identification. Derek Prince. 4 cass. 23.80 Set. (071-072-073-074) Derek Prince.
Identification - of Jesus with us, of ourselves with Him - is the key that unlocks all He obtained for us by His death & resurrection.

Identification. unabr. ed. E. W. Kenyon. Read by Stephen Sobozenski. 1 cass. (Running Time: 1 hr. 15 min.). 1999. 8.50 (978-1-57770-024-1(4)) Kenyons Gospel.
An unveiling of the substitutionary sacrifice, showing what we are in Jesus Christ & how the Father sees us.

Identification of the Beloved. Adi Da Samraj. 1 cass. (Classic Ser.). 1992. 11.95 (978-0-918801-57-9(5)) Dawn Horse Pr.

Identifying & Analyzing User Needs: A Complete Handbook & Ready-to-Use Assessment Workbook with Disk. Lynn Westbrook. (Statistics & User Studies). 2000. wbk. ed. 79.95 (978-1-55570-388-2(7)) Neal-Schuman.

Identifying & Solving Key Workplace Issues in the 21st Century. 2006. audio compact disk (978-0-9777803-1-0(7)) Cabot Inst for Labor.

Identifying & Using Insurance Coverage in Business Litigation. Read by Thomas Johnson, Jr. & Kent Keller. (Running Time: 2 hrs. 45 min.). 1991. 70.00 Incl. 425p. tape materials. (CP-54114); 55.00 video rental. (CP-64114(63)) Cont Ed Bar-CA.

Identifying Christ. Featuring Bill Winston. 6 Cassetts. 2004. 30.00 (978-1-59544-003-7(8)) Pub: B Winston Min. Dist(s): Anchor Distributors

Identifying Strongholds. Francis Frangipane. 1 cass. (Running Time: 90 mins.). (Basics of Spiritual Warfare Ser.: Vol. 2). 2000. 5.00 (FF02-002) Morning NC.
Francis combines years of practical experience with a soundbiblical perspective in this popular & important series.

Identifying with Christ. Bill Winston. 6 CDs. 2004. audio compact disk 48.00 (978-1-59544-004-4(6)) Pub: B Winston Min. Dist(s): Anchor Distributors

Identity. unabr. collector's ed. Milan Kundera. Read by Barrett Whitener. 3 cass. (Running Time: 4 hrs. 30 mins.). 1998. 24.00 (978-0-7366-4282-8(X), 4780) Books on Tape.
There are situations in which we fail for a moment to recognize the person we are with, in which the identity of the other is erased while we simultaneously doubt our own. The author turns this into a love story.

Identity Affirmations. Read by Wayne Monbleau. 2 cass. (Running Time: 3 hrs.). 1994. 10.00 Set. (978-0-944648-32-2(0), LGT-1222) Loving Grace Pubns.
Religious.

Identity & Immortality. unabr. ed. Tom Schwartz. Narrated by Ron Knowles. (Running Time: 8 hrs. 30 mins.). 2009. audio compact disk 39.95 (978-1-57545-334-7(7), RP Audio Pubng) Pub: Reagent Press. Dist(s): OverDrive Inc

Identity Code. 2006. 59.95 (978-0-7861-4429-7(7)); audio compact disk 72.00 (978-0-7861-7381-5(5)) Blckstn Audio.

Identity Code: The 8 Essential Questions for Finding Your Purpose & Place in the World. unabr. ed. Larry Ackerman. 4 cass. (Running Time: 9 hrs. 30 mins.). (YA). 2006. 29.95 (978-0-7861-4390-0(8)) Blckstn Audio.

Identity Code: The 8 Essential Questions for Finding Your Purpose & Place in the World. unabr. ed. Larry Ackerman. Read by Brian Emerson. 5 CDs. (Running Time: 21600 sec.). 2006. audio compact disk 29.95 (978-0-7861-7448-5(X)) Blckstn Audio.

***Identity Economics: How Our Identities Shape Our Work, Wages, & Well-Being.** unabr. ed. George Akerlof & Rachel Kranton. Read by Sean Pratt. (Running Time: 4 hrs. 30 mins.). (ENG.). 2010. 27.98 (978-1-59659-508-8(6), GildAudio) Pub: Gildan Media. Dist(s): HachBkGrp

Identity in Conflict: Understanding of the Homosexual Condition. 1 CD. (Running Time: 1 hr.). 2003. audio compact disk 13.95 (978-1-932631-46-3(1)) Ascensn Pr.

Identity in Conflict: Understanding the Homosexual Condition. 1 cass. (Running Time: 1 hr.). 2003. 13.95 (978-1-932631-45-6(3)) Ascensn Pr.

***Identity Man.** Read by Andrew Klavan. (Running Time: 9 hrs. 0 mins. 0 sec.). (ENG.). 2010. audio compact disk 29.95 (978-1-60998-105-1(7)) Pub: AudioGO. Dist(s): Perseus Dist

Identity Theft. abr. ed. Ethan Pope. Narrated by Ethan Pope. (ENG.). 2007. 9.09 (978-1-60814-250-7(7)); audio compact disk 12.99 (978-1-59859-228-3(9)) Oasis Audio.

Identity Theft: And Other Stories. unabr. ed. Robert J. Sawyer. (Running Time: 13 hrs. 0 mins.). 2010. 19.95 (978-1-4417-1675-0(0)); 24.95 (978-1-4417-1671-2(8)); audio compact disk 30.00 (978-1-4417-1672-9(6)) Blckstn Audio.

Identity Theft - Prevention & Survival. unabr. ed. Mari J. Frank. Contrib. by Beth Givens & James E. Bauer. 6 cass. (Running Time: 4 hrs. 15 min.). 1997. 49.95 (978-1-892126-02-3(8)) Porpoise Pr.
Interviews with identity fraud experts to explain to you how to prevent further losses, & regain your financial security.

Identity Theft - Prevention & Survival. unabr. ed. Mari J. Frank. Ed. by Dale Fetherling. Contrib. by Beth Givens & James E. Bauer. 6 cass. (Running Time: 4 hrs. 15 min.). 1998. pap. bk. 79.95 (978-1-892126-00-9(1)) Porpoise Pr.

Identity Theft Risk & Recovery Manager. 2005. audio compact disk 29.95 (978-1-59546-270-1(8)) Socrates Med LLC.

***Ides: Caesar's Murder & the War for Rome.** unabr. ed. Stephen Dando-Collins. (Running Time: 10 hrs. 0 mins.). 2010. 29.95 (978-1-4417-5259-8(5)); 59.95 (978-1-4417-5255-0(2)); audio compact disk 29.95 (978-1-4417-5258-1(7)); audio compact disk 90.00 (978-1-4417-5256-7(0)) Blckstn Audio.

Ides of March see Richard Eberhart Reading His Poetry

Idiom Adventure: Fluency in Speaking & Listening. Dana Watkins. 2001. 19.95 (978-0-13-030965-5(6)) Longman.

Idiosyncratic Thinking. Richard Phillips Feynman. 8 cass. 72.00 set. (A0030-85) Sound Photosyn.
Workshop at Esalen with Ralph Leighton, Faustin Bray, & Brian Wallace. An extended dose of sensible, slightly off the wall thinking in anecdotes that leave 'em laughing & scratching their heads.

Idiot see Idiota

Idiot. Henry Carlisle. Read by Santiago Munévar. (Running Time: 3 hrs.). 2002. 16.95 (978-1-60083-256-7(3), Audiofy Corp) Iofy Corp.

Idiot. Read by Michael Sheen. Tr. by Henry Carlisle. (Running Time: 4 hrs.). 1999. 24.95 (978-1-60083-778-4(6)) Iofy Corp.

Idiot. Read by Michael Sheen. Tr. by Henry Carlisle from RUS. 3 cass. (Running Time: 4 hrs.). 1995. 17.98 (978-962-634-559-7(4), NA305914, Naxos AudioBooks) Naxos.
In his creation of Prince Muishkin, a character seeking perfection & yet fraught with ambiguity, Dostoyevsky anticipated the universal metaphysical unease of succeeding generations, & produced an unforgettable masterpiece.

Idiot. abr. ed. Read by Michael Sheen. Tr. by Henry Carlisle from RUS. 3 CDs. (Running Time: 4 hrs.). 1995. audio compact disk 22.98 (978-962-634-059-2(2), NA305912) Naxos.

Idiot. unabr. ed. Tr. by Henry Carlisle. Narrated by Robert Whitfield. 16 cass. (Running Time: 23 hrs. 30 mins.). 2002. 99.95 (978-0-7861-2170-0(X), 2920) Blckstn Audio.
A saintly man, Prince Myshkin, is thrust into the heart of a society more concerned with wealth, power, and sexual conquest than the ideals of Christianity. Myshkin soon finds himself at the center of a violent love triangle in which a notorious woman and a beautiful young girl become rivals for his affections. Extortion, scandal, and murder follow, testing the wreckage left by human misery to find "man in man.

***Idiot.** unabr. ed. Henry Carlisle. Narrated by Norman Dietz. (Running Time: 27 hrs. 0 mins. 0 sec.). 2010. 36.99 (978-1-4001-6977-1(1)); 28.99 (978-1-4001-8977-9(2)); audio compact disk 49.99 (978-1-4001-1977-6(4)) Pub: Tantor Media. Dist(s): IngramPubServ

Idiot. unabr. ed. Fyodor Dostoyevsky. Read by Robert Whitfield. (YA). 2008. 114.99 (978-1-60514-730-7(3)) Find a World.

***Idiot (Library Edition)** unabr. ed. Fyodor Dostoyevsky. Narrated by Norman Dietz. (Running Time: 27 hrs. 0 mins.). 2010. 49.99 (978-1-4001-9977-8(8)); audio compact disk 119.99 (978-1-4001-4977-3(0)) Pub: Tantor Media. Dist(s): IngramPubServ

Idiot Menagerie: Hallucinogens & Graphic Constructs. Jake Berry. 1 cass. 1988. 6.00 (978-0-944215-01-2(7)) Ninth St Lab.

Idiot Pride. unabr. ed. Matt Zurbo. Read by Dino Marnika. 3 cass. (Running Time: 2 hrs. 10 mins.). 2002. (978-1-86442-368-6(4), 590375) Bolinda Pubng AUS.
A story about cruising, & being on the run without going anywhere. It's about the claustrophobia of an inner city suburb, its dangers & pitfalls, & the salvation & humour found in the most solid of friendships. It's about being what you are, knuckles, passion, bullshit & all & about never forgetting you're an idiot.

Idiot Years. unabr. collector's ed. Brad A. Lewis. Read by Paul Shay. 7 cass. (Running Time: 10 hrs. 30 min.). 1995. 56.00 (978-0-7366-3029-0(5), 3711) Books on Tape.
A drifter finds commitment in the death of his sweetheart. Unexpectedly tender & touching.

Idiota. abr. ed. Fyodor Dostoyevsky. 3 CDs.Tr. of Idiot. (SPA.). 2002. audio compact disk 17.00 (978-958-8161-47-1(9)) YoYoMusic.

Idiots see Tales of Unrest

Idiots. unabr. ed. Joseph Conrad. Read by Walter Zimmerman. 1 cass. Dramatization. 1989. 7.95 (S-54) Jimcin Record.
Dramatization of a hideous tragedy.

Idiot's Guide to Chinese: Level I. 2003. audio compact disk 34.99 (978-1-58926-216-4(6), A22M-CH10) Oasis Audio.

Idiot's Guide to Chinese: Level II. 2003. audio compact disk 34.99 (978-1-58926-217-1(4), A22M-CH20) Oasis Audio.

Idiot's Guide to Chinese: Vocabulary. 2003. audio compact disk 34.99 (978-1-58926-277-5(8), A22M-CHVO) Oasis Audio.

Idiot's Guide to Italian: Level I. 2004. 34.99 (978-1-58926-212-6(3), A22M-IT10) Oasis Audio.

Idiot's Guide to Italian: Level II. 2004. audio compact disk 34.99 (978-1-58926-213-3(1), A22M-IT20) Oasis Audio.

Idiot's Guide to Italian: Vocabulary. 2004. audio compact disk 34.99 (978-1-58926-275-1(1), A22M-ITVO) Oasis Audio.

***Idiots Unplugged.** adpt. ed. Glenn Beck. Read by Glenn Beck. 1 CD. (Running Time: 1 hr. 15 mins.). 2010. audio compact disk 14.99 (978-1-4423-3396-3(0)) Pub: S&S Audio. Dist(s): S and S Inc

Iditarod: Story of the Last Great Race. Ian Young. (High Five Reading - Green Ser.). (ENG.). (gr. 3-4). 2007. audio compact disk 5.95 (978-1-4296-1420-7(X)) CapstoneDig.

Idle Days in Patagonia. unabr. collector's ed. W. H. Hudson. Read by John MacDonald. 7 cass. (Running Time: 7 hrs.). 1990. 42.00 (978-0-7366-1769-7(8), 2608) Books on Tape.
First published in 1893, W. H. Hudson's Idle Days in Patagonia is the narrative of his life's great adventure - a year in Patagonia. His time there climaxed 30 years as a naturalist, riding & roving in his native Argentina. His visit to this remote country fulfilled not only a private dream, but also a scientific mission. His collection of bird skins together with a brilliant report to the Zoological Society of London more than a century ago added greatly to his prestige as an ornithologist.

Idle Thoughts of an Idle Fellow. Jerome K. Jerome. 1996. pap. bk. 59.95 (978-1-86015-011-1(X)) Ulverscroft US.

***Idle Thoughts of an Idle Fellow.** Jerome K. Jerome. Read by Alfred von Lecteur. 2009. 27.95 (978-1-60112-974-1(2)) Babblebooks.

Idle Thoughts of an Idle Fellow. unabr. ed. Jerome K. Jerome. 4 cass. 1996. 44.95 (978-1-86015-430-0(1)) Pub: UlverLrgPrint GBR. Dist(s): Ulverscroft US
Being hard up, having the blues & being in love are just some aspects of the human condition in which Jerome K. Jerome reflects on his unique & whimsical fashion.

Idle Thoughts of an Idle Fellow, Set. unabr. ed. Jerome K. Jerome. Read by Richard Brown. 4 cass. (Running Time: 5 hrs.). 1991. 19.95 (978-1-55685-191-9(X)) Audio Bk Con.
One of England's most entertaining writers combines some light-hearted comments on serious matters with serious ones on light-hearted matters, forming a delightful picture of life among the leisured classes in 19th century England.

Idolatry of Doctrine: John 5:21. Ed Young. 1987. 4.95 (978-0-7417-1616-3(X), 616) Win Walk.

Idolatry of Emotionalism: John 5:21. Ed Young. 1987. 4.95 (978-0-7417-1617-0(8), 617) Win Walk.

Idoru, Set. abr. ed. William Gibson. Read by Jay O. Sanders. 2 cass. (Running Time: 3 hrs.). (gr. 8 up). 1996. 17.95 (978-0-399-14225-3(8), 394559, Putnam Adult) Penguin Grp USA.
Chia is rock star Rez's biggest fan. Laney is an info-wrangler with one freak talent & a dubious past. When Rez announces his intention to "marry" an idea idoru, a fully virtual Japanese celebrity construct, Chia & Laney find themselves on a collision course in post-quake tokyo. How "real" is the idoru? real enough to die for, in the neon rain of a media-drenched future.

Idyll of Red Gulch see Luck of Roaring Camp & Other Stories

Idyll of Red Gulch. 1979. (N-22) Jimcin Record.

Idyllwild. Mark Paul Sebar. (Wyler Scott Ser.: Vol. 2). 2009. (978-1-930246-33-1(1), 1930246331) Sebar Pubng.

IELTS Examination Papers. abr. ed. Created by Cambridge University Press. 5 Cass. (Running Time: 1 hr. 46 mins.). (IELTS Practice Tests Ser.). (ENG., 2006. 44.00 (978-0-521-67703-5(3)) Cambridge U Pr.

Ielts Masterclass Class Cassettes. Simon Haines & Peter May. (IELTS Masterclass Ser.). 2006. 39.95 (978-0-19-457537-9(3)) OUP.

IEnglish(r): The image-based audio-visual word, phrase & punctuation guide in english for your Ipod. David M. Horan & Rodney S. Horan. (ENG., 2008. 49.95 (978-0-9804178-9-0(9)) HoranLLSS AUS.

IEP Pro V. 1. Lawrence Steel. 2005. 39.95 (978-1-4129-1560-1(0)) Pub: Corwin Pr. Dist(s): SAGE

IExperience Access 2002 Course. audio compact disk 45.95 (978-0-7638-1726-8(0)) EMC-Paradigm.

IExperience Excel 2002 Course. audio compact disk 45.95 (978-0-7638-1725-1(2)) EMC-Paradigm.

IExperience Office XP Course. audio compact disk 55.95 (978-0-7638-1723-7(6)) EMC-Paradigm.

IExperience PowerPoint 2002 Course. audio compact disk 45.95 (978-0-7638-1727-5(9)) EMC-Paradigm.

IExperience Word 2002 Course. audio compact disk 45.95 (978-0-7638-1724-4(4)) EMC-Paradigm.

***If.** unabr. ed. Amy Carmichael. (Running Time: 1 hr. 0 mins. 0 sec.). (ENG.). 2011. audio compact disk 9.98 (978-1-61045-095-9(7), Hovel Audio) christianaud.

If a Tree Falls. 1 cass.; 1 CD. 1998. 10.98 (978-1-56628-106-5(7), 72495); audio compact disk 15.98 CD. (978-1-56628-105-8(9), 72495D) MFLP CA.

If a Tree Falls at Lunch Period. unabr. ed. Gennifer Choldenko. Read by Ariadne Meyers & Francois Battiste. 4 CDs. (Running Time: 4 hrs. 16 mins.). (YA). (gr. 7-10). 2007. audio compact disk 30.00 (978-0-7393-6120-7(1)) Pub: Random Audio Pubg. Dist(s): Random

If a Tree Falls at Lunch Period. unabr. ed. Gennifer Choldenko. Read by Francois Battiste & Ariadne Meyers. (Running Time: 15420 sec.). (ENG.). (J). (gr. 7). 2007. audio compact disk 28.00 (978-0-7393-4885-7(X), Listening Lib) Pub: Random Audio Pubg. Dist(s): Random

If All the Seas Were One Sea see Gathering of Great Poetry for Children

If Aristotle Ran General Motors: The New Soul of Business, unabr. ed. Tom Morris. Narrated by Nelson Runger. 7 cass. (Running Time: 9 hrs. 15 mins.). 1998. 60.00 (978-0-7887-1981-3(5), 95368E7) Recorded Bks.
Emphasizes openness, integrity, dignity & humanity as the means to achieving corporate as well as individual potential. Thousands of executives from such companies as Coca-Cola, Bayer & Merrill Lynch are profiting from his philosophy-based secrets.

If at First You Don't Succeed... Proceedings of the 45th Annual Convention National Association of Evangelicals Buffalo, New York. Read by Pamela Heim. 1 cass. (Running Time: 60 min.). 1987. 4.00 (329) Nat Assn Evan.

If Better Is Possible, Good Is No Longer an Option. (ENG.). 2004. audio compact disk 12.00 (978-0-9778921-3-6(1)) Dream Build.

If Death Ever Slept. unabr. ed. Rex Stout. Read by Michael Prichard. 4 cass. (Running Time: 6 hrs.). (Nero Wolfe Ser.). 2002. 24.95 (978-1-57270-252-3(4), Audio Editions) Pub: Audio Partners. Dist(s): PerseuPGW
Nero Wolfe is hired by millionaire Otis Jarrell to prove that his daughter-in-law is guilty of being a double-crossing snake. Archie, over Wolfe's objections, brashly agrees to perform as Jarrell's personal secretary to gather information about the possible misdeeds of the daughter-in-law.

If Death Ever Slept. unabr. ed. Rex Stout. Narrated by Michael Prichard. (Running Time: 21600 sec.). (Nero Wolfe Ser.). (ENG.). 2006. audio compact disk 27.95 (978-1-57270-531-9(0)) Pub: AudioGO. Dist(s): Perseus Dist

If Death Ever Slept. unabr. collector's ed. Rex Stout. Read by Michael Prichard. 7 cass. (Running Time: 7 hrs.). (Nero Wolfe Ser.). 1996. 56.00 (978-0-7366-3323-9(5), 3975) Books on Tape.
With Nero Wolfe on the job, you'd think murderers would take caution. But even the master detective can't stop a killing, especially if it's an inside job - right under the roof of his client, millionaire Otis Jarrell.

If Democrats Had Any Brains, They'd Be Republicans. abr. ed. Ann Coulter. Read by Ann Coulter. (Running Time: 12600 sec.). (ENG.). 2007. audio compact disk 24.95 (978-0-7393-6615-8(7), Random AudioBks) Pub: Random Audio Pubg. Dist(s): Random

If Dinosaurs Came Back. 1 cass. (Running Time: 35 min.). (J). (ps-3). 2001. pap. bk. 15.95 (VX-87C) Kimbo Educ.
Learn how dinosaurs could make significant contributions to today's society if they should return. Includes a read along book.

If Dinosaurs Came Back. Bernard Most. Illus. by Bernard Most. 9.95 (978-1-59112-165-7(5)) Live Oak Media.

If Ever I Return. Perf. by Connie Dover. 1 cass., 1 CD. 7.98 (TPM 301); audio compact disk 12.78 CD. (TPM 301) NewSound.

If Ever I Return, Pretty Peggy-O. unabr. ed. Sharyn McCrumb. Narrated by Sally Darling. 8 cass. (Running Time: 11 hrs. 30 mins.). (Ballad Ser.: No. 1). 1993. 70.00 (978-1-55690-921-4(7), 93417E7) Recorded Bks.
A once-famous folk singer returns to the small town of her birth, bringing with her a deadly mystery.

If Evolution Is Outlawed, Only Outlaws Will Evolve. Jello Biafra. 3 cass. (Running Time: 3 hrs.). (AK Press Audio Ser.). 2000. 14.98 (978-1-902593-05-0(7), AK Pr San Fran) AK Pr Dist.

If Evolution Is Outlawed, Only Outlaws Will Evolve. Jello Biafra. 3 CDs. (AK Press Audio Ser.). (ENG.). 2002. audio compact disk 19.98 (978-1-902593-04-3(9)) Pub: AK Pr GBR. Dist(s): Consort Bk Sales

If God Be for Us: A Musical Service Calling America Back to God. Narrated by Derric Johnson. Contrib. by Camp Kirkland. (ENG.). 1996. audio compact disk 12.00 (978-0-00-520082-7(2)) Allegis.

If God Is Good: Faith in the Midst of Suffering & Evil. abr. ed. Randy C. Alcorn. Read by Randy C. Alcorn. (ENG.). 2009. audio compact disk 25.00 (978-0-307-71438-1(1), Random AudioBks) Pub: Random Audio Pubg. Dist(s): Random

If Grant Had Been Drinking at Appomattox see Middle-Aged Man on the Flying Trapeze

If I Am Missing or Dead. unabr. ed. Janine Latus. Read by Shelly Frasier. (Running Time: 9 hrs. 0 mins. 0 sec.). (ENG.). 2007. audio compact disk 24.99 (978-1-4001-5401-2(4)) Pub: Tantor Media. Dist(s): IngramPubServ

If I Am Missing or Dead: A Sister's Story of Love, Murder, & Liberation. unabr. ed. Janine Latus. Read by Shelly Frasier. 8 CDs. (Running Time: 9 hrs. 0 mins. 0 sec.). (ENG.). 2007. audio compact disk 34.99 (978-1-4001-0401-7(7)); audio compact disk 69.99 (978-1-4001-3401-4(3)) Pub: Tantor Media. Dist(s): IngramPubServ

If I Could Fly. Jacqui LeBeau. Composed by Lawrence LeBeau. Voice by Clif Schindler & Sara Schindler. (ENG.). (J). 2008. audio compact disk 7.95 (978-0-9799640-1-5(6)) Fresh Con.

If I Could Only Live at the Pitch That Is Near Madness see Richard Eberhart Reading His Poetry

If I Did It: Confessions of the Killer. unabr. ed. O. J. Simpson. Read by Kim Goldman et al. Afterword by Dominick Dunne. 6. (Running Time: 25200 sec.). 2007. cass. & cass. 29.95 (978-1-4332-1181-2(5)) Blckstn Audio.

If I Did It: Confessions of the Killer. unabr. ed. O. J. Simpson. Read by G. Valmont Thomas et al. Afterword by Dominick Dunne. 7 CDs. (Running Time: 25200 sec.). 2007. audio compact disk & audio compact disk 29.95 (978-1-4332-1182-9(3)) Blckstn Audio.

If I Did It: Confessions of the Killer. unabr. ed. O. J. Simpson. Read by Kim Goldman et al. Afterword by Dominick Dunne. 1. (Running Time: 25200 sec.). 2007. audio compact disk & audio compact disk 29.95 (978-1-4332-1183-6(1)) Blckstn Audio.

If I Did It: Confessions of the Killer. unabr. ed. O. J. Simpson. Read by Kim Goldman & G. Valmont Thomas. Afterword by Dominick Dunne. Comment by Goldman Family Staff. Prologue by Pablo F. Fenjves. (Running Time: 25200 sec.). 2007. 54.95 (978-1-4332-1179-9(3)) Blckstn Audio.

If I Did It: Confessions of the Killer. unabr. ed. O. J. Simpson. Read by G. Valmont Thomas et al. Afterword by Dominick Dunne. Comment by Goldman Family Staff. Prologue by Pablo F. Fenjves. (Running Time: 25200 sec.). 2007. audio compact disk & audio compact disk 63.00 (978-1-4332-1180-5(7)) Blckstn Audio.

If I Die in a Combat Zone: Box Me up & Ship Me Home. unabr. ed. Tim O'Brien. Read by John MacDonald. 6 cass. (Running Time: 6 hrs.). 1985. 36.00 (978-0-7366-0896-1(6), 1840) Books on Tape.
O'Brien chronicles the dislocation a young American feels when he is yanked out of his Mom-&-apple pie midwestern home & thrown face first into the pit that was war-time Vietnam. O'Brien lived this tale twice-the first time in Nam, the second when he wrote it.

If I Don't Write It Nobody Else Will. abr. ed. Eric Sykes. Read by Eric Sykes. 2005. audio compact disk 18.00 (978-0-00-720669-8(0)) Pub: HarpC GBR. Dist(s): Trafalgar
The long awaited story of one of Britain_s greatest comic legends.

If I Get Out Alive. Hosted by Diane Keaton. 1 cass. (Running Time: 1 hr.). (978-1-888064-56-8(0)) Lichtenstein Creat.
This documentary, the result of a one-year investigation, exposes the systematic abuse & brutality faced by juveniles in the adult prison system. It features first-hand accounts from adolescents currently behind bars, rehabilitated youths who survived the system, parents of the children who died in adult prisons, legal experts, policy makers & correction officers. The program also addresses the abysmal mental health conditions in prison & jails faced by young people (fifty percent of whom, according to new research, are affected by a serious mental illness) as well as examining alternative sentencing programs that are successful in diverting young offenders from prison.

If I Had a Boat see Twentieth-Century Poetry in English, No. 30, Recordings of Poets Reading Their Own Poetry

***If I Had a Hammer: Building Homes & Hope with Habitat for Humanity.** unabr. ed. David Rubel. Read by Dan John Miller. (Running Time: 4 hrs.). 2010. 39.97 (978-1-4418-8921-8(3), 9781441889218, Candlewick Bril); 14.99 (978-1-4418-8920-1(5), 9781441889201, Candlewick Bril); audio compact disk 19.99 (978-1-4418-8916-4(7), 9781441889164, Candlewick Bril); audio compact disk 14.99 (978-1-4418-8918-8(3), 9781441889188, Candlewick Bril); audio compact disk 39.97 (978-1-4418-8919-5(1), 9781441889195, Candlewick Bril) Brilliance Audio.

***If I Had a Hammer: Stories of Building Homes & Hope with Habitat for Humanity.** unabr. ed. David Rubel. Read by Dan John Miller. (Running Time: 3 hrs.). 2010. audio compact disk 44.97 (978-1-4418-8917-1(5), 9781441889171, Candlewick Bril) Brilliance Audio.

If I Had a Pony: Animal Activity Songs. Sarah Barchas. Perf. by Sarah Barchas. Illus. by Elizabeth Gething. 1 cass.; 1 CD. (Running Time: 50 min.). (J). (gr. k-4). 1996. pap. bk. 12.95 (978-0-9632621-7-2(3)); pap. bk. 15.98 CD, paperback & lyric bk. (978-0-9632621-8-9(1)) High Haven Mus.

If I Had My Life to Live over I Would Pick More Daisies. unabr. ed. Read by Ellen Burstyn & Cch Pounder. Ed. by Sandra H. Martz. 2 cass. (Running Time: 3 hrs.). 1995. 16.95 (978-1-57453-000-1(3)) Audio Lit.
Like its companion volume, "When I Am an Old Woman I Shall Wear Purple," this anthology contains writings by women reflecting on the choices they have made, from childhood to old age.

If I Knew Then What I Know Now: CEO's & Other Smart Executives Share Wisdom They Wish They'd Been Told 25 Years Ago. unabr. ed. Richard Edler. Read by Brian Desmond. 2 cass. (Running Time: 2 hrs. 30 mins.). 1997. 17.95 (978-0-7861-1229-6(8), 1973) Blckstn Audio.
A compendium that will spare you years of saying "shoulda," "coulda" & "woulda.

If I Live to Be 100: Lessons from the Centenarians. abr. ed. Neenah Ellis. Read by Neenah Ellis. 5 CDs. (Running Time: 6 hrs.). (ENG.). 2002. audio compact disk 29.95 (978-1-56511-719-8(0), 1565117190) Pub: HighBridge. Dist(s): Workman Pub

If I Only Knew Then... Learning from Our Mistakes. unabr. ed. Read by Charles Grodin & Marion Grodin. Compiled by Charles Grodin. (Running Time: 3 hrs. 30 mins.). (ENG.). 2007. 19.98 (978-1-60024-111-6(5)) Pub: Hachet Audio. Dist(s): HachBkGrp

If I Ran the Circus. Dr. Seuss. (J). 1989. cass. & flmstrp 35.98 (978-0-676-30892-1(9)) SRA McGraw.

If I Ran the Zoo. Dr. Seuss. (J). 1985. 18.66 (978-0-394-07679-9(6)) SRA McGraw.

If I Stay. unabr. ed. Gayle Forman. Read by Kirsten Potter. (ENG.). (gr. 9 up). 2009. audio compact disk 29.95 (978-0-14-314445-8(6)) Penguin Grp USA.

***If I Stay.** unabr. ed. Gayle Forman. Read by Kirsten Potter. 4 CDs. (Running Time: 4 hrs. 48 mins.). (YA). (gr. 9 up). 2009. audio compact disk 45.00 (978-0-7393-8084-0(2), Listening Lib) Pub: Random Audio Pubg. Dist(s): Random

If I Told Him: A Completed Portrait of Picasso see Gertrude Stein Reads from Her Works

If I Told Him: A Completed Portrait of Picasso see Caedmon Treasury of Modern Poets Reading Their Own Poetry

If I Were a Bell (from Guys & Dolls) - ShowTrax. Score by Frank Loesser. Arranged by Mark Brymer. 1 CD. (Running Time: 90 mins.). 2000. audio compact disk 19.95 (08621143) H Leonard.
This classic song from Loesser's colorful musical is arranged in a swingin' style that will show your pop group at it's best.

If I Were in Charge of the World see Alexander & the Terrible, Horrible, No Good, Very Bad Day

If I Were Starting My Family over Again. 1978. 4.94 (978-0-7417-1011-6(0)) Win Walk.

If I Were Tickled by the Rub of Love see Dylan Thomas Reading: And Death Shall Have No Dominion and Other Poems

If I Were Tickled By the Rub of Love see Dylan Thomas Reading His Poetry

If I Were You. Perf. by Sandi Patty & Daryl Coley. 1 cass. 1999. 8.98 (978-0-7601-3151-0(1)) Provident Music.

If I Were You. Steck-Vaughn Staff. 2003. (978-0-7398-8428-7(X)) SteckVau.

If I Were You. unabr. ed. L. Ron Hubbard. Read by Nancy Cartwright. 2 CDs. (Running Time: 2 hrs.). (Stories from the Golden Age Ser.). 2008. audio compact disk 9.95 (978-1-59212-290-5(6)) Gala Pr LLC.

If I'd Killed Him When I Met Him. unabr. ed. Sharyn McCrumb. Narrated by Barbara Rosenblat. 6 cass. (Running Time: 7 hrs. 45 mins.). (Elizabeth MacPherson Ser.: No. 8). 1996. 51.00 (978-0-7887-0506-9(7), 94699E7) Recorded Bks.
Elizabeth MacPherson, a young forensic anthropologist, searches for her missing husband, while she tries to solve two baffling cases of murder.

If I'd Never Had a Teacher: A Song Tribute to Teachers. Barry Lane. 1 CD. 2002. audio compact disk 5.00 (978-1-931492-04-1(2)) Discover Writing.
Barry wrote this song tribute for his 4th grade teacher, Miss Carolyn Foley. It is a persuasive essay on how we need to improve our attitude towards teachers.

***If I'm Forgiven, Why Does My Past Still Bother Me? Recognizing the Blessings of the Continuous Atonement.** Brad Wilcox. 2011. 14.99 (978-1-60641-961-8(7)) Deseret Bk.

If I'm so Wonderful, Why Am I Still Single? Susan Page. 4 cass. (Running Time: 6 hrs.). 1995. 19.95 (978-1-55977-016-3(3)) CareerTrack Pubns.

If It Moves, Kiss It. unabr. collector's ed. Joni Moura & Jackie Sutherland. Read by Nancy Dannevik. 7 cass. (Running Time: 7 hrs.). 1979. 42.00 (978-0-7366-0221-1(6), 1219) Books on Tape.
There was a time when to be a female member of the armed services was a great adventure. This book is about those times. A sequel to "Tender Loving Care," this volume carries forward the adventures of two nurses who confound the rules of an impersonal military establishment.

If It's Not Yours, Let It Go! Set: How to Stop Taking on Other People's Stuff. David Grudermeyer & Rebecca Grudermeyer. 2 cass. 18.95 INCL. HANDOUTS. (T-42) Willingness Wrks.

If Jesus Can't Fix It. Contrib. by Mighty Clouds of Joy et al. Prod. by Sanchez Harley et al. 2007. audio compact disk 5.99 (978-5-557-67283-2(4)) Pt of Grace Ent.

If Life Is a Bowl of Cherries - What Am I Doing in the Pits? Erma Bombeck. Narrated by Barbara Rosenblat. 4 CDs. (Running Time: 3 hrs. 45 mins.). audio compact disk 39.00 (978-0-7887-4762-5(2)) Recorded Bks.

If Life Is a Bowl of Cherries - What Am I Doing in the Pits? Erma Bombeck. Narrated by Barbara Rosenblat. 4 CDs. (Running Time: 3 hrs. 45 min.). 2000. audio compact disk 39.00 (C1255E7) Recorded Bks.
America's enchanting lady of humor pondered what it takes to survive modern life. Whether she's poking fun at the joys of motherhood or taking a poignant look at the difficulties of aging, she will have you laughing out loud till the tears stream down your face.

If Life Is a Bowl of Cherries - What Am I Doing in the Pits? unabr. ed. Erma Bombeck. Narrated by Barbara Rosenblat. 3 cass. (Running Time: 3 hrs. 45 mins.). 2000. 26.00 (978-0-7887-4086-2(5), 96171E7) Recorded Bks.

If Looks Could Kill. Kate White. 9 cass.l. (Running Time: 13 hrs.). 2002. 72.00 (978-0-7366-8840-6(4)); audio compact disk (978-0-7366-8841-3(2)) Books on Tape.

If Looks Could Kill. abr. ed. M. William Phelps. Read by J. Charles. (Running Time: 6 hrs.). 2009. audio compact disk 14.99 (978-1-4233-4922-8(9), 9781423349228, BCD Value Price) Brilliance Audio.

If Looks Could Kill. abr. ed. Kate White. Read by Parker Posey. (ENG.). 2005. 14.98 (978-1-59483-364-9(8)) Pub: Hachet Audio. Dist(s): HachBkGrp

If Looks Could Kill. unabr. ed. M. William Phelps. Read by J. Charles. (Running Time: 12 hrs.). 2008. 39.25 (978-1-4233-4920-4(2), 9781423349204, BADLE); 24.95 (978-1-4233-4919-8(9), 9781423349198, BAD); 97.25 (978-1-4233-4914-3(8), 9781423349143, BrilAudUnabridg); audio compact disk 102.25 (978-1-4233-4916-7(4), 9781423349167, BriAudCD Unabrid); audio compact disk 39.25 (978-1-4233-4918-1(0), 9781423349181, Brinc Audio MP3 Lib); audio compact disk 38.95 (978-1-4233-4915-0(6), 9781423349150, Bril Audio CD Unabri); audio compact disk 24.95 (978-1-4233-4917-4(2), 9781423349174, Brilliance MP3) Brilliance Audio.

If Mama Goes South, We're All Going with Her. abr. ed. (Running Time: 10800 sec.). 2006. audio compact disk 24.95 (978-1-4233-0353-4(9), 9781423303534, Brilliance MP3) Brilliance Audio.
With all that women have to do and the many "hats" they wear, it's easy for them to feel like they are "going south" physically, emotionally, or spiritually. And yet, others are depending on them and being influenced by them. So for those women who are running on empty, feeling lonely or weary, Lindsey O'Connor offers an invigorating dose of hope. If Mama Goes South, We're All Going with Her looks at five biblical principles from Galatians for overcoming problems that weigh women down and dilute their influence on others. What does it really look like to "not grow weary in well doing"? Am I really making a difference? Why do I feel alone? These questions, and more, are touched upon with splashes of humor and plenty of personal

depth. O'Connor includes a chapter about the delivery of her fifth child, an event that forced her into a ten-week coma, from which she is currently and miraculously recovering.

If Mama Goes South, We're All Going with Her. abr. ed. Lindsey O'Connor. Read by Lindsey O'Connor. 2 cass. (Running Time: 3 hrs.). 2003. 17.95 (978-1-59355-243-5(2), 1593552432); 44.25 (978-1-59355-244-2(0), 1593552440); audio compact disk 19.95 (978-1-59355-245-9(9), 1593552459); audio compact disk 62.25 (978-1-59355-246-6(7), 1593552467) Brilliance Audio.

If Mama Goes South, We're All Going with Her. abr. ed. Lindsey O'Connor. Read by Lindsey O'Connor. (Running Time: 3 hrs.). 2006. 39.25 (978-1-4233-0356-5(3), 9781423303565, BADLE); 24.95 (978-1-4233-0355-8(5), 9781423303558, BAD); 39.25 (978-1-4233-0354-1(7), 9781423303541, Brinc Audio MP3 Lib) Brilliance Audio.

If Marriages Are Made in Heaven, Why Can't They Be Endured on Earth? Richard Flint. 4 cass. Incl. If Marriages Are Made in Heaven, Why Can't They Be Endured on Earth? Earthly People with Earthly Problems. 1984.; If Marriages Are Made in Heaven, Why Can't They Be Endured on Earth? Heavenly Terms with Earthly Definitions. 1984.; If Marriages Are Made in Heaven, Why Can't They Be Endured on Earth? If. 1984.; If Marriages Are Made in Heaven, Why Can't They Be Endured on Earth? Testing Your Relationship. 1984.; 1984. 50.00 (978-0-937851-07-4(8)) Pendelton Lane.
Contains Flint's research into personal & family relationships. Based on the philosphy that the number one drain of energy from people is created by problems in personal relationships,it takes a look at four types of relationships, & defines the ten common struggles that all couples have in common.

If Marriages Are Made in Heaven, Why Can't They Be Endured on Earth?: Earthly People with Earthly Problems see If Marriages Are Made in Heaven, Why Can't They Be Endured on Earth?

If Marriages Are Made in Heaven, Why Can't They Be Endured on Earth?: Heavenly Terms with Earthly Definitions see If Marriages Are Made in Heaven, Why Can't They Be Endured on Earth?

If Marriages Are Made in Heaven, Why Can't They Be Endured on Earth?: If see If Marriages Are Made in Heaven, Why Can't They Be Endured on Earth?

If Marriages Are Made in Heaven, Why Can't They Be Endured on Earth?: Testing Your Relationship see If Marriages Are Made in Heaven, Why Can't They Be Endured on Earth?

If Mary Baker Eddy's Manual Were Obeyed, Vol. 1. abr. ed. Helen M. Wright. Read by Alan Young. 4 cass. (Running Time: 2 hrs. 45 mins.). 1997. pap. bk. 15.50 (978-1-886505-08-7(X)) H M Wright.
Covers important ground surrounding the hidden history of Eddy's Church Manual.

If Men Were Angels. unabr. ed. Reed Karaim. Read by James Daniels. (Running Time: 9 hrs.). 2008. 39.25 (978-1-4233-7148-9(8), 9781423371489, Brinc Audio MP3 Lib); 24.95 (978-1-4233-7147-2(X), 9781423371472, Brilliance MP3); 24.95 (978-1-4233-7149-6(6), 9781423371496, BAD); 39.25 (978-1-4233-7150-2(X), 9781423371502, BADLE) Brilliance Audio.

If Morning Ever Comes: A Novel. unabr. ed. Anne Tyler. Read by Jeanne Hopson. 8 cass. (Running Time: 8 hrs.). 1989. 48.00 (978-0-7366-1495-5(8), 2371) Books on Tape.
His family, that known & mysterious universe of women, was less surprised by Ben Joe's homecoming that he was himself. They were the center that welcomed but that didn't include him. Only Shelley was love past, love present...& love unforeseen.

If My Head Hurt a Hair's Foot see Dylan Thomas Reading His Poetry

If My Head Hurt a Hair's Foot see Evening with Dylan Thomas

If Nobody Loves You Create the Demand: A Powerful Jolt of Entrepreneurial Energy & Wisdom. Joel A. Freeman. Read by Joel A. Freeman. (ENG.). 2007. audio compact disk 24.99 (978-1-934068-29-8(2), AuthLifestyle) Pub: AuthenticMedia. Dist(s): STL Dist NA

If Not Now, When? Duty & Sacrifice in America's Time of Need. unabr. ed. (ret.) Jack Jacobs & Douglas Century. (Running Time: 9.5 hrs. 0 mins.). (ENG.). 2009. audio compact disk 29.95 (978-1-4332-8985-9(7)) Blckstn Audio.

If not Now, When? Duty & Sacrifice in America's Time of Need. unabr. ed. Jack Jacobs (Ret.) & Douglas Century. (Running Time: 9.5 hrs. 0 mins.). (ENG.). 2009. 29.95 (978-1-4332-8986-6(5)) Blckstn Audio.

If not Now, When? Duty & Sacrifice in America's Time of Need. unabr. ed. Jack Jacobs (Ret.) & Douglas Century. (Running Time: 9.5 hrs. 0 mins.). (ENG.). 2009. 59.95 (978-1-4332-8982-8(2)); audio compact disk 90.00 (978-1-4332-8983-5(0)) Blckstn Audio.

If Only I Were. . Short Stories. Carl Sommer. Narrated by Carl Sommer. 1cass. Dramatization. (Another Sommer-Time Story Ser.). (J). (gr. 1-4). 2003. bk. 16.95 (978-1-57537-551-9(6)) Advance Pub.

If Only I Were. Carl Sommer. Narrated by Carl Sommer. 1 cass. Dramatization. (Another Sommer-Time Story Ser.). (J). (gr. k-4). 2003. lib. bdg. 23.95 (978-1-57537-752-0(7)) Advance Pub.

***If Only I Were... / Si Sólo Pudiera Ser.** ed. Carl Sommer. Illus. by Kennon James. (Another Sommer-Time Story Bilingual Ser.). (ENG & SPA.). (J). 2009. bk. 26.95 (978-1-57537-179-5(0)) Advance Pub.

If Only It Were True Unabridged. unabr. ed. Marc Levy. Read by Michael McGlone. 2004. 15.95 (978-0-7435-4860-1(4)) Pub: S&S Audio. Dist(s): S and S Inc

If Only They Could Talk. unabr. ed. James Herriot. Read by Christopher Timothy. 8 cass. (Running Time: 12 hrs.). (Vet Ser.: Bk. 1). 2000. 59.95 (978-0-7451-4272-2(9), CAB 955) Pub: Chivers Audio Bks GBR. Dist(s): AudioGO
When newly-qualified vet James Herriot arrives in the Yorkshire village of Darrowby, he has no idea what to expect. How will he get along with his new boss, the local farmers, and what will the animals think? If only they could talk!.

If Perfect in Christ, Why Are We Judged?; The Enemy Within. C. S. Lovett. 1 cass. 6.95 (7029) Prsnl Christianity.
Expands on truths of the book, "Jesus Is Coming - Get Ready".

***If the Buddha Dated: A Handbook for Finding Love on a Spiritual Path.** unabr. ed. Charlotte Kasl. Narrated by Renée Raudman. (Running Time: 6 hrs. 0 mins.). (Buddha Guides). 2010. 13.99 (978-1-4001-8541-2(6)) Tantor Media.

***If the Buddha Dated: A Handbook for Finding Love on a Spiritual Path.** unabr. ed. Charlotte Kasl. Narrated by Renée Raudman. (Running Time: 6 hrs. 0 mins. 0 sec.). (Buddha Guides). (ENG.). 2010. 19.99 (978-1-4001-6541-4(5)); audio compact disk 24.99 (978-1-4001-1541-9(8)); audio compact disk 49.99 (978-1-4001-4541-6(4)) Pub: Tantor Media. Dist(s): IngramPubServ

***If the Buddha Got Stuck: A Handbook for Change on a Spiritual Path.** unabr. ed. Charlotte Kasl. Narrated by Renée Raudman. (Running Time: 8 hrs. 30 mins.). (Buddha Guides). 2010. 15.99 (978-1-4001-8539-9(4)); 19.99 (978-1-4001-6539-1(3)); audio compact disk 59.99 (978-1-4001-4539-3(2)); audio compact disk 29.99 (978-1-4001-1539-6(6)) Pub: Tantor Media. Dist(s): IngramPubServ

***If the Buddha Married: Creating Enduring Relationships on a Spiritual Path.** unabr. ed. Charlotte Kasl. Narrated by Renée Raudman. (Running Time: 7 hrs. 30 mins. 0 sec.). (Buddha Guides). (ENG.). 2010. 19.99 (978-1-4001-6540-7(7)); 14.99 (978-1-4001-8540-5(8)); audio compact disk 29.99 (978-1-4001-1540-2(X)); audio compact disk 59.99 (978-1-4001-4540-9(6)) Pub: Tantor Media. Dist(s): IngramPubServ

If the Dinosaurs Came Back. Bernard Most. Read by Rick Adamson. (J). (ps-3). 2006. bk. 28.95 (978-1-59519-316-2(2)) Live Oak Media.

If the Dinosaurs Came Back. unabr. ed. Bernard Most. Illus. by Bernard Most. Read by Rick Adamson. 11 vols. (Running Time: 6 mins.). (J). (gr. k-3). 1991. bk. 25.95 (978-0-87499-237-3(0)); pap. bk. 16.95 (978-0-87499-236-6(2)) Live Oak Media.
This book suggests ways in which dinosaurs could make significant contributions to today's society if they should ever return.

If the Dinosaurs Came Back, Grades K-3. unabr. ed. Bernard Most. Read by Rick Adamson. 14 vols. (Running Time: 6 mins.). (J). 1991. pap. bk. & tchr. ed. 37.95 Reading Chest. (978-0-87499-238-0(9)) Live Oak Media.

***If the Foundations Are Being Destoryed, What Can the Righteous Do?** Featuring Ravi Zacharias. 1993. audio compact disk 9.00 (978-1-61256-048-9(2)) Ravi Zach.

If the Shoe Fits... Cinderella Stories from Around the World. Perf. by Milbre Burch. Adapted by Milbre Burch. (ENG.). 2005. audio compact disk 15.00 (978-0-9795271-3-5(9)) Kind Crone.

If the Shoe Fits... (A Novel in Three Parts for the Adult Children of Divorced Parents & Their Parents)... or... A Patchwork of a Woman... from... the Chronicles of a Crazy Girl. 21 cass. (Running Time: 30 hrs. 1 min.). 2005. audio compact disk (978-0-9770947-9-0(0)) SOS P.

If the Shoe Fits... (A Novel in Three Parts for the Adult Children of Divorced Parents & Their Parents)... or... A Patchwork of a Woman... from the Chronicles of a Crazy Girl. (Running Time: 30 hrs. 1 min.). 2005. (978-0-9770947-0-7(7)) SOS P.

If the Shoe Fits... Don't Wear It. Susan Sullivan. 2006. (978-0-9770947-1-4(5)) SOS P.

If the Tooth Be Known. (Paws & Tales Ser.: Vol. 25). (J). 2002. audio compact disk 5.99 (978-1-57972-415-3(9)) Insight Living.

If the Tooth Be Known. (Paws & Tales Ser.: Vol. 25). (YA). 2002. 3.99 (978-1-57972-414-6(0)) Insight Living.

If There Be Thorns. unabr. ed. V. C. Andrews. Read by Donada Peters. 9 cass. (Running Time: 13 hrs. 30 mins.). (Dollanganger Ser.). 1989. 72.00 (978-0-7366-1483-2(4), 2359) Books on Tape.
Chris & Cathy make a loving home for 14-year old Jory, & for Bart, who has quite a dazzling imagination for a nine year old. Then the lights come on in the house next door. Soon the Old Lady in Black is there, watching them, guarded by her strange old butler. Bart's transformation begins, fed by hints about his past. These revelations unhinge him & Bart totters on the edge of madness. His parents can only wait for the climax to a horror that flowered in an attic whose thorns are still tipped with fire.

If Thine Eye Offend Thee: Fighting the Plague of Pornography. Steven A. Cramer. 1 cass. 1999. 9.95 (978-1-57734-459-9(6), 06005977) Covenant Comms.
A powerful talk with real solutions.

***If This Bed Could Talk.** abr. ed. Liz Maverick & Kimberly Dean. Read by Erica Bell et al. (ENG.). 2006. (978-0-06-123554-2(7), Harper Audio); (978-0-06-121507-0(4), Harper Audio) HarperCollins Pubs.

If This Was Happiness: A Biography of Rita Hayworth. unabr. ed. Barbara Leaming. Read by Anna Fields. 9 cass. (Running Time: 13 hrs.). 1997. 62.95 (978-0-7861-1072-8(4), 1842) Blckstn Audio.
Rita Hayworth was the epitome of 1940s Hollywood glamour - the legendary "Love Goddess." Yet behind the smoldering image lay a tragic secret that wrecked her private life. She suffered sexual & physical abuse at her father's hands that would scar her for life.

If Walls Could Talk. 2000. 12.95 (978-0-9666484-8-5(X)) Dimby Co Inc.

If We Don't Pray. Contrib. by Johnathan Crumpton & Russell Mauldin. Prod. by Ed Kee. (ENG.). 2008. audio compact disk 24.99 (978-5-557-48381-0(0), Brentwood-Benson Music) Brentwood Music.

***If Wishes Were Horses: A Novel.** unabr. ed. Robert Barclay. (ENG.). 2011. (978-0-06-201296-8(7), Harper Audio); (978-0-06-206371-7(5), Harper Audio) HarperCollins Pubs.

If You Believe in... True Love! With True Love. Marlene A. Ryan. Ed. by Carrie-Anne Ryan. Contrib. by John P. Ryan. 1999. pap. bk. 24.95 (978-1-929327-00-3(5)) Ashly Pubns.

If You Can Give It Up...Have It All. T. D. Jakes. 1 cass. 2001. 6.00 (978-1-57855-267-2(2)) T D Jakes.

If You Can Pronounce It, You Can Read It. If You Can Read It, You Can Speak It. 2nd ed. Created by Donna Lynn Smith. 1CD or 1 cass. (SPA.). 2007. stu. ed. 11.95 (978-0-9793655-1-5(1), 6851) R Language.

If You Can Talk You Can Write. abr. ed. Joel Saltzman. Read by Joel Saltzman. 2 cass. (Running Time: 3 hrs.). 1999. 17.95 (978-1-57270-106-9(4), L21106) Pub: Audio Partners. Dist(s): PerseuPGW
Take the anxiety out of writing & learn how to "talk" on paper. Will help to conquer the killer P's - Perfectionism, Paralysis & Procrastination - & get you writing.

If You Can't Rock Me (from Stuart Little) - ShowTrax. Perf. by Brian Setzer Orchestra Staff. Arranged by Roger Emerson. 1 CD. (Running Time: 1 hr. 30 mins.). 2000. audio compact disk 19.95 (08201175) H Leonard.
The fun is in full swing with this zesty hit. A show choir spectacle!.

If You Could Be Calm about Being Angry, What Would It Be Like? Anger Management by Positive Imaging & Music. Music by Thomas Tamalonis-Olofsson. (ENG.). 2008. audio compact disk 15.00 (978-0-9771008-5-9(5)) A M Tamalonis.

***If You Could Hear What I See.** abr. ed. Kathy Buckley. Read by Kathy Buckley. (ENG.). 2008. (978-0-06-179916-7(5), Harper Audio); (978-0-06-174461-7(1)) HarperCollins Pubs.

If You Could See Me Now. abr. ed. Cecelia Ahern. Read by Rupert Degas & Susan Lynch. 5 CDs. (Running Time: 21600 sec.). 2006. audio compact disk 29.98 (978-1-4013-8332-9(7), Hyperion Audio) Pub: Hyperion. Dist(s): HarperCollins Pubs

If You Could See What I Hear. Kathy Buckley. Read by Kathy Buckley. 3 cass. (Running Time: 4 hrs. 30 min.). 2001. 24.00 HarperCollins Pubs.

If You Could See What I See: The Tenets of Novus Spiritus. abr. ed. Sylvia Browne. 2 CDs. (Running Time: 7200 sec.). 2006. audio compact disk 18.95 (978-1-4019-0894-2(2)) Hay House.

If You Don't Have Big Breasts, Put Ribbons on Your Pigtails. abr. ed. Barbara Corcoran & Bruce Littlefield. Narrated by Barbara Corcoran. 3 CDs. (Running Time: 4 hrs.). 2004. audio compact disk 23.95 (978-1-59316-019-7(4), LL111) Listen & Live.
In "If You Don't Have Big Breasts...," Barbara shares her hilarious stories about growing up, getting into trouble, failing miserably, and then starting over again. In each chapter, she comes back to one of her mom's unconventional lessons, and how it applies in the real world of business. Whatever your calling, the homespun lessons that work for Barbara will help you use what you've got to create success in your life. Whether you're just starting out, fighting your way up the career ladder, or reentering the workforce, Use What You've Got is an owner's manual to your most valuable asset.

If You Give a Moose a Muffin. Laura Joffe Numeroff. Read by Robby Benson. Interview with Felicia Bond. 1 cass. (J). (gr. 2 up). 1997. 11.95 (HarperChildAud) HarperCollins Pubs.

If You Give a Mouse a Cookie. Laura Joffe Numeroff. (J). 1986. 18.66 (978-0-676-31656-8(5)) SRA McGraw.

If You Give a Mouse a Cookie, Vol. 9. unabr. ed. Laura Joffe Numeroff. Read by Carol Kane. Illus. by Felicia Bond. 1 cass. (Running Time: 30 mins.). (J). 1998. bk. 14.98 (t5759SMH, Listening Lib) Random Audio Pubg.
A fun game & gigglesome song.

If You Give a Pig a Pancake. Laura Joffe Numeroff & Felicia Bond. Read by David Hyde. 1 cass. (Running Time: 30 mins.). (J). 2000. bk. 11.98 (T 6543 SMH, Listening Lib) Random Audio Pubg.
Story about a demanding pig & an accommodating little girl. Includes mini-book.

If You HAve God You Have Everything: A Faith Adventure of a Young Bulgarian Woman. Ceitci Demirkova. 2006. audio compact disk 20.00 (978-1-4276-0181-0(X)) AardGP.

If you haven't got the time to do it right when will you find the time to do It. Jeffrey J. Mayer. 2004. 7.95 (978-0-7435-4861-8(2)) Pub: S&S Audio. Dist(s): S and S Inc

If You Listen. unabr. ed. Charlotte Zolotow. (J). 2005. audio compact disk 13.95 (978-0-06-059788-7(7), HarperChildAud) HarperCollins Pubs.

If You Made a Million. 2004. pap. bk. 18.95 (978-1-55592-178-1(7)); pap. bk. 38.75 (978-1-55592-634-2(7)); pap. bk. 32.75 (978-1-55592-365-5(8)); pap. bk. 32.75 (978-1-55592-364-8(X)); pap. bk. 14.95 (978-1-55592-166-8(3)) Weston Woods.

If You Made a Million. (J). (gr. k-4). 2004. bk. 24.95 (978-1-55592-096-8(9)); pap. bk. 14.95 (978-1-55592-097-5(7)); pap. bk. 18.95 (978-1-55592-136-1(1)); 8.95 (978-1-55592-964-0(8)); audio compact disk 12.95 (978-1-55592-935-0(4)) Weston Woods.
Marvelosissimo the mathematical magician teaches kids about various forms of money and how it can be used to buy things, pay off debt, and build interest.

If You Really Loved Me. Ann Rule. 2004. 10.95 (978-0-7435-4862-5(0)) Pub: S&S Audio. Dist(s): S and S Inc

If You Should Meet a Crocodile see Gathering of Great Poetry for Children

If You Survive. George Wilson. Narrated by Brian Keller. 8 CDs. (Running Time: 8 hrs. 30 min.). 2000. audio compact disk 78.00 Recorded Bks.
A startling first-person account of the final year of World War II. Wilson was the only man from his original company to finish the war. As a Second Lieutenant, he went ashore at Utah Beach after the D-Day invasion amidst burned vehicles, sunken landing craft, and broken fortifications. From the breakthrough at Saint-Lo, to the Battle of the Bulge, to the final push on Germany, Wilson survived ferocious battles and bitter weather. After earning several decorations and a promotion to First Lieutenant, Wilson was wounded. But he healed quickly and returned to duty. Wilson's account is an incredibly moving, continuous stream of devastating combat experiences that will make readers wonder how any infantryman could have survived this war.

If You Survive. unabr. ed. George Wilson. Narrated by Brian Keeler. 6 cass. (Running Time: 8 hrs. 45 mins.). 2000. 57.00 (978-0-7887-4422-8(4), 96231E7) Recorded Bks.
First-person account of WWII from just after the D-Day invasion to Germany's surrender. Fighting unimaginable hardships & fears, Wilson is the only man from his original company to finish the war.

If You Survive. unabr. ed. George Wilson. Narrated by Brian Keeler. 6 cass. (Running Time: 8 hrs. 45 mins.). 2002. 34.95 (978-0-7887-6516-2(7), RD060) Recorded Bks.

If You Want God's Best. Derek Prince. 2 cass. 11.90 Set. (110-111) Derek Prince.
Do you want to become a hundredfold person? Then decide not to settle for less than God's best.

If You Want Joy. 7.00 (CJY) J Van Impe.
Features messages of love & hope, reconciliation & restoration.

If You Want Me To: The Best of Ginny Owens. Contrib. by Ginny Owens & Don Donahue. 2006. 13.99 (978-5-558-26041-0(6)) Rocket.

If You Want to Hear from God. Derek Prince. 1 cass. 5.95 (4341) Derek Prince.
God's agenda for Derek & Ruth's sabbatical was altogether different than anticipated. Derek describes unsuspected barriers that had to be dealt with before they could receive God's direction.

If You Want to Walk on Water, You've Got to Get Out of the Boat. abr. ed. Zondervan Publishing Staff & John Ortberg. (Running Time: 2 hrs. 0 mins. 0 sec.). (ENG.). 2004. 9.99 (978-0-310-26064-6(7)) Zondervan.

***If You Want to Walk on Water, You've Got to Get Out of the Boat.** unabr. ed. Zondervan. (Running Time: 7 hrs. 51 mins. 22 sec.). (ENG.). 2010. 18.99 (978-0-310-87517-8(X)) Zondervan.

If You Were a Bat/Slowpoke Snail. Created by Steck-Vaughn Staff. (Running Time: 390 sec.). (Primary Take-Me-Home Books Level A Ser.). 1998. 9.80 (978-0-8172-8666-8(7)) SteckVau.

If You Were Coming in the Fall see Poems & Letters of Emily Dickinson

If You Wish to Become a Writer. unabr. ed. Elizabeth R. Bills. 1 cass. (Running Time: 26 min.). (Secrets of Successful Writers Ser.). 1963. 12.95 (23019) J Norton Pubs.
Why write? Where does the writer get his material? What does it take to become a writer?.

If You're Not Called to Stay, Then Go!, Set. George Verwer. 4 cass. (Running Time: 6 hrs.). 2000. 12.99 (978-1-886463-76-9(X)) Oasis Audio.

***If You're Not First, You're Last: Sales Strategies to Dominate Your Market & Beat Your Competition.** unabr. ed. Grant Cardone. Narrated by Richard Allen. 1 MP3-CD. (Running Time: 5 hrs. 30 mins. 0 sec.). 2010. 19.99 (978-1-4001-6879-8(1)); 24.99 (978-1-4001-9879-5(8)); 13.99 (978-1-4001-8879-6(2)); audio compact disk 24.99 (978-1-4001-1879-3(4)); audio compact disk 59.99 (978-1-4001-4879-0(0)) Pub: Tantor Media. Dist(s): IngramPubServ

If You're Not Here, Please Raise Your Hand: Poems about School. unabr. ed. Poems. Kalli Dakos. Narrated by Christina Moore et al. 1 cass. (Running

Time: 1 hr.). (gr. 2 up). 1998. 10.00 (978-0-7887-1789-5(8), 95261E7) Recorded Bks.
Dakos blends clever wit & insight with her experience as a former elementary reading specialist to make poetry fun for students.

If You're Not Here, Please Raise Your Hand: Poems about School, Homework. Poems. Kalli Dakos. 1 cass. (Running Time: 1 hr.). (J). 1997. bk. 22.20 (978-0-7887-1830-4(4), 40610) Recorded Bks.

If You're Not Here, Please Raise Your Hand Class Set: Poems about School. Poems. Kalli Dakos. 1 cass., 10 bks. (Running Time: 1 hr.). (J). 1997. bk. 70.30 (978-0-7887-3151-8(3), 46271) Recorded Bks.
Dakos blends clever wit & insight with her experience as a former elementary reading specialist to make poetry fun for students.

Igbo Basic Course. unabr. ed. Foreign Service Institute Staff. 12 cass. (Running Time: 12 hrs. 30 mins.). (YA). (gr. 10-12). 1946. pap. bk. 295.00 (978-0-88432-375-4(7), AF1G10) J Norton Pubs.
One of the major languages of western Africa, Igbo is spoken principally in the east-central part of Nigeria. Course includes tone drills, dialogs, short narratives & vocabulary.

Igbo Basic Course: Multilingual Books Language Course. FSI Staff. 12 CDs. (Multilingual Books Intensive Language Courses). (IBO.). 2006. per. 199.00 (978-1-58214-325-5(0)) Language Assocs.
Ther Foreign Service Institute course of this West African Language of the Congo-Niger family. It is basen on classroom experience in the teaching of complex tonal systems.

Igbo Basic Course (FSI) 14 CDs. (Running Time: 12 hrs. 30 mins.). (IBO.). 2005. audio compact disk 295.00 (978-1-57970-131-4(0), AFIG10D) J Norton Pubs.

***Iggie's House.** unabr. ed. Judy Blume. (ENG.). (J). 2011. audio compact disk 25.00 (978-0-307-74764-8(6), Listening Lib) Pub: Random Audio Pubg. Dist(s): Random

Iggy Pop: Open up & Bleed. unabr. ed. Paul Trynka. (Running Time: 52200 sec.). 2007. 85.95 (978-1-4332-0294-0(8)); audio compact disk 108.00 (978-1-4332-0295-7(6)) Blckstn Audio.

Iggy Pop: Open up & Bleed. unabr. ed. Paul Trynka. Read by William Dufris. (Running Time: 52200 sec.). 2007. 32.95 (978-1-4332-0186-8(0)); audio compact disk 32.95 (978-1-4332-0187-5(9)); audio compact disk 29.95 (978-1-4332-0188-2(7)) Blckstn Audio.

***Iggy the Iguana Audio Book, Vol. 1.** 2nd ed. Melissa Williams. (ENG.). (J). 2010. audio compact disk 14.99 (978-0-9818054-4-3(2)) Long Tale TX.

Ignatian Prayer in the Marketplace. Thomas Green. 1 cass. (Running Time: 1 hr. 25 min.). 1995. 8.95 (TAH353) Alba Hse Comns.
You are invited to discover how to bring this highly honored spirituality into all areas of your life, & learn to apply the methods of Ignatian discernment to your decision making. Truly rewarding material for everyone, whether you have been introduced to the exercises of St. Ignatius or are as yet unfamiliar with them.

Ignatian Retreat. Donald McGuire. 9 cass. 1995. 45.00 Set. (149-C) Ignatius Pr.
Fr. McGuire, one of the premier retreat masters in the country & the Spiritual Director for Mother Teresa & for her Missionaries of Charity, gives a powerful & life-changing retreat on the Spiritual Exercises of St. Ignatius. He helps the retreatant to delve deeply into the profound mysticism of the Spiritual Exercises, & to grasp the key principles of the spiritual life.

Ignatius MacFarland: Frequenaut! unabr. ed. Paul Feig. Read by Paul Feig. (Running Time: 6 hrs.). 2008. 39.25 (978-1-4233-7675-0(7), 9781423376750, BADLE); 39.25 (978-1-4233-7673-6(0), 9781423376736, Brinc Audio MP3 Lib); 24.95 (978-1-4233-7674-3(9), 9781423376743, BAD); 24.95 (978-1-4233-7672-9(2), 9781423376729, Brilliance MP3); audio compact disk 74.25 (978-1-4233-7671-2(4), 9781423376712, BriAudCD Unabrid); audio compact disk 26.95 (978-1-4233-7670-5(6), 9781423376705, Bril Audio CD Unabri) Brilliance Audio.

Ignatius New Testament RSV-CE. Read by Mark Taheny. 14 CDs. (Running Time: 14 hrs.). 2003. audio compact disk 58.95 (978-1-57058-556-2(3), rc02-cd) St Joseph Communs.
Available on CD for the first time, here is the audio version of the New Testament that was chosen by the Holy See for use in the Catechism of the Catholic Church and all official English translations of Church Documents. Perfect for serious study and apologetics, the Revised Standard Version?Catholic Edition (a.k.a. The Ignatius Bible) is also the translation of choice for Dr. Scott Hahn, Fr. Benedict Groeschel, Fr. Mitch Pacwa and a host of others.Produced by special arrangement with Ignatius Press this digitally re-mastered audio recording of the Ignatius New Testament?RSV-CE comes in an attractive album of CDs and is available exclusively from St. Joseph Communications. Brought vividly to life by Mark Taheny?s word-for-word narration, this superb audio presentation lets you listen to God?s Word at home or on-the-go and provides a great way to add a dramatic new dimension to personal or group Bible study.

***Ignited: Learn the secrets of an artist burned alive who went on to create a life she never dreamed Possible.** Allison Massari. (Running Time: 277). (ENG.). 2010. 47.00 (978-0-615-37427-7(1)) Massari Fine.

Igniting Enthusiasm & Motivation: Classic. Eldon Taylor. Read by Eldon Taylor. Ed. by Leslie Brice. 1 cass. (Running Time: 1 hr.). 1992. 16.95 (978-1-56705-089-9(1)) Gateways Inst.
Self improvement.

Igniting Enthusiasm & Motivation: Easy. Eldon Taylor. Read by Eldon Taylor. Ed. by Leslie Brice. 1 cass. (Running Time: 1 hr.). 1992. 16.95 (978-1-56705-090-5(5)) Gateways Inst.

Igniting Enthusiasm & Motivation: Harmonies. Eldon Taylor. Read by Eldon Taylor. Ed. by Leslie Brice. 1 cass. (Running Time: 1 hr.). 1992. 16.95 (978-1-56705-091-2(3)) Gateways Inst.

Igniting Enthusiasm & Motivation: Ocean. Eldon Taylor. Read by Eldon Taylor. Ed. by Leslie Brice. 1 cass. (Running Time: 1 hr.). 1992. 16.95 (978-1-56705-092-9(1)) Gateways Inst.

Igniting Enthusiasm & Motivation: Stream. Eldon Taylor. Read by Eldon Taylor. Ed. by Leslie Brice. 1 cass. (Running Time: 1 hr.). 1992. 16.95 (978-1-56705-093-6(X)) Gateways Inst.

Igniting Intuition: Unearthing Body Genius. Christiane Northrup & Mona Lisa Schulz. Read by Christiane Northrup & Mona Lisa Schulz. 6 cass. (Running Time: 6 hrs.). (ENG.). 1999. 59.95 (978-1-56170-599-3(3), 474) Hay House.
Connecting emotional problems with physical ones.

Igniting Intuition: Unearthing Body Genius. Christiane Northrup & Mona Lisa Schulz. 2 CDs. 2005. audio compact disk 18.95 (978-1-4019-0652-8(4)) Hay House.

Igniting Intuition: Unearthing Body Genius. Christiane Northrup & Mona Lisa Schulz. 6 CDs. (ENG.). 2005. audio compact disk 23.95 (978-1-4019-0655-9(9)) Hay House.

Igniting Intuition Set: Unearthing Body Genius. Christiane Northrup & Mona Lisa Schulz. Read by Christiane Northrup & Mona Lisa Schulz. 2 cass. (Running Time: 2 hrs.). 2000. 18.95 (978-1-56170-769-0(4), 4068) Hay House.
How healing is related to intuition.

Igniting the Embers. Andrew Cusack. 1 cass. (Running Time: 51 min.). 1995. 8.95 (TAH341) Alba Hse Comns.
Msgr. Cusack demonstrates how to restructure the personal journey toward the whole dimension of love, directing the listener through the "4 T's", Time - Talk - Tenderness - Trust. Developing the God event in oneself allows the priest to lead others to a profound understanding of God's love as well.

Igniting Your Soul Life. Gary Zukav & Michael Toms. 1 cass. (Running Time: 1 hr.). (New Dimensions Ser.). 1999. 10.95 (978-1-56170-726-3(0), 4033) Hay House.
Discover how to live your passion once you find it, how to develop your intuitive powers, and techniques that help your personality become aligned with your soul.

Ignition. unabr. ed. Kevin J. Anderson & Doug Beason. Read by Roger Dressler. (Running Time: 8 hrs.). 2008. 39.25 (978-1-4233-5322-5(6), 9781423353225, BADLE); 24.95 (978-1-4233-5321-8(8), 9781423353218, BAD); audio compact disk 39.25 (978-1-4233-5320-1(X), 9781423353201, Brinc Audio MP3 Lib); audio compact disk 24.95 (978-1-4233-5319-5(6), 9781423353195, Brilliance MP3) Brilliance Audio.

Ignorance, Natural or Acquired. Instructed by Manly P. Hall. 8.95 (978-0-89314-145-5(3), C860413) Philos Res.

Ignorance of Blood. Robert Wilson. 2009. 84.95 (978-0-7531-4499-2(9)); audio compact disk 99.95 (978-0-7531-4500-5(6)) Pub: Isis Pubng Ltd GBR. Dist(s): Ulverscroft US

Ignore Everybody: And 39 Other Keys to Creativity. unabr. ed. Hugh MacLeod. Narrated by William Dufris. (Running Time: 2 hrs. 0 mins. 0 sec.). (ENG.). 2009. 19.99 (978-1-4001-6339-7(0)); audio compact disk 19.99 (978-1-4001-1339-2(3)); audio compact disk 39.99 (978-1-4001-4339-9(X)) Pub: Tantor Media. Dist(s): IngramPubServ

Ignored Health Hazards for Pilots & Drivers: The A-B-C-D-E-F-G-H File; with Emphasis on Aspartame (Nutrasweet) Disease. unabr. ed. H. J. Roberts. Read by H. J. Roberts. 2 cass. (Running Time: 2 hrs. 25 min.). 1998. bk. 19.95 Set. (978-1-884243-08-0(8)) Sunshine Sentinel.
A summary of common medical disorders & nutritional problems that are conducive to pilot error, driver error, & accidents, but infrequently considered accidents.

Igor Kipnis: His First Solo Recordings. Perf. by Igor Kipnis. Composed by Johann Sebastian Bach et al. 1 CD. 1999. audio compact disk 16.99 (VAIA 1185) VAI Audio.
Perhaps the most celebrated harpsichordist of our time, Kipnis is heard here in his historic debut disc, recorded in 1962 & originally released on the Golden Crest label. Program features Bach: French Suite No. 6 (BWV 817), Fantasia in G Minor (BWV 917), Prelude, Fugue, & Allegro in E flat Major (BWV 998), Toccata in E Minor (BWV 914); Handel: Suite No. 5 in E Major, Bk. 1 (HWV430); Soler (attrib.): Fandango in D Minor; Dussek: The Sufferings of the Queen of France.

Igraine the Brave. unabr. ed. Cornelia Funke. Read by Xanthe Elbrick. 4 CDs. (Running Time: 15900 sec.). (ENG.). (J). (gr. 3-7). 2007. audio compact disk 28.00 (978-0-7393-5618-0(6), Listening Lib) Pub: Random Audio Pubg. Dist(s): Random

Igraine the Brave. unabr. ed. Cornelia Funke & Anthea Bell. Narrated by Xanthe Elbrick. 4 CDs. (Running Time: 4 hrs. 25 mins.). (J). (gr. 4-6). 2007. audio compact disk 38.00 (978-0-7393-6101-6(5), Random AudioBks) Pub: Random Audio Pubg. Dist(s): Random

Igrok see Jugador

Igual Que Mi Amiga Grande Vol. 4: Level 4. (Fonolibros Ser.). 2003. 11.50 (978-0-7652-0991-7(8)) Modern Curr.

Il Vino: La Vite e la Viticoltura. 1 cass. (Running Time: 45 mins.). (ITA.). pap. bk. 16.95 (SIT255) J Norton Pubs.
Intermediate-level readings with accompanying cassettes can improve both reading & listening comprehension. Texts include exercises & answer key.

Ike: His Life & Times. unabr. ed. Piers Brendon. Narrated by Nelson Runger. 14 cass. (Running Time: 19 hrs. 45 mins.). 1987. 112.00 (978-1-55690-247-5(6), 87450E7) Recorded Bks.
The life & times of President Eisenhower.

'Il Canzoniere of Fransesco Petrarca: Multilingual Books Literature. Ed. by Maurizio Falyhera & Cristina Giocometti. 1 CD. (Running Time: 90). (Audio Anthology of Italian Literature Ser.: 2). (ITA.). 1999. spiral bd. 29.95 (978-1-58214-103-9(7)) Language Assocs.

Ile au Tresor, Set. Robert Louis Stevenson. Read by A. D. Bouzina et al. 5 cass.Tr. of Treasure Island. (FRE.). 1992. 39.95 (1628-VSL) Olivia & Hill.
Famous tale of mutiny, piracy & buried treasure.

Ile aux Trente Cerceuils, Set. Maurice Leblanc. 6 cass. (FRE.). 1991. 46.95 (1474-LV) Olivia & Hill.
An Arsene Lupin adventure.

Ileo-Anal Anastomoses & Reservoir Procedures. 2 cass. (Colon & Rectal Surgery Ser.: C85-CR3). 15.00 (8557) Am Coll Surgeons.

Iliad. Robert Fagles. Read by Derek Jacobi. (Playaway Young Adult Ser.). 2009. 64.99 (978-1-60775-733-7(8)) Find a World.

Iliad. Robert Fagles. Read by Anton Lesser. (Running Time: 4 hrs.). 1999. 24.95 (978-1-60083-779-1(4)) Iofy Corp.

Iliad. Robert Fagles. Read by Daniel Quintero. (Running Time: 3 hrs.). 2003. 16.95 (978-1-60083-285-7(7), Audiofy Corp) Iofy Corp.

Iliad. Robert Fagles. Read by Anton Lesser. Tr. by William Cowper from GRE. 3 cass. (Running Time: 4 hrs.). 1995. 17.98 (978-962-634-562-7(4), NA306214, Naxos AudioBooks) Naxos.

Iliad. Robert Fagles. Tr. by Robert Fitzgerald. Narrated by George Guidall. 14 CDs. (Running Time: 16 hrs. 45 mins.). audio compact disk 134.00 (978-1-4025-1758-7(0)) Recorded Bks.

Iliad. Homer. Read by Stanley Lombardo. Tr. by Stanley Lombardo. 12 CDs. 2006. audio compact disk 42.00 (978-1-930972-08-7(3)) Pub: Parmenides Pub. Dist(s): Chicago Distribution Ctr
Elizabeth A. Kaye specializes in communications as part of her coaching and consulting practice. She has edited Requirements for Certification since the 2000-01 edition.

Iliad. Homer & Stanley Lombardo. (ENG.). 2007. 29.40 (978-1-930972-22-3(9)) Parmenides Pub.

Iliad. abr. ed. Robert Fagles. Perf. by Anthony Quayle. Tr. by Richmond A. Lattimore. 1 cass. (J). 1984. 12.95 (978-0-694-50147-2(6), SWC 1196) HarperCollins Pubs.

Iliad. abr. ed. Robert Fagles. Read by Anton Lesser. Tr. by William Cowper from GRE. 3 CDs. (Running Time: 4 hrs.). (J). (gr. 9-12). 1995. audio compact disk 22.98 (978-962-634-062-2(2), NA306212) Naxos.

Iliad. abr. ed. Robert Fagles. Read by Anton Lesser. 4. (Running Time: 18600 sec.). 2007. audio compact disk 28.98 (978-962-634-458-3(X), Naxos AudioBooks) Naxos.

Iliad. abr. ed. Homer. Read by Roger Rees. 4 cass. (Running Time: 6 hrs.). 2004. 25.00 (978-1-59007-004-8(6)) Pub: New Millenn Enter. Dist(s): PerseuPGW
Set against the backdrop of the final days of the Trojan War, the Iliad tells the story of Achilles, a model warrior & paragon of all qualities the Greeks prized most in a young hero. Retired from the war in response to real & imagined insults from his commander & king, Agamemnon, Achilles is pulled back into the conflict by the death of his friend, Patroclus. Achilles' wrath knows no bounds as he exacts bloody vengeance & brings the proud city of Troy to ruins. It is only by the command of Zeus, chief of the gods, that Achilles permits the body of the slain Trojan champion, Hector, to be returned to his mourning father, King Priam.

Iliad. unabr. ed. Robert Fagles. Read by John Lescault. (YA). 2006. 49.99 (978-1-59895-170-7(X)) Find a World.

Iliad, unabr. ed. Poems. Robert Fagles. Tr. by Robert Fitzgerald. Narrated by George Guidall. 12 cass. (Running Time: 16 hrs. 45 mins.). 1994. 97.00 (978-1-55690-971-9(3), 94201E7) Recorded Bks.
The story of the Greek warrior Achilles, who withdraws from the battle for Troy in anger at his general Agamemnon; he is convinced to rejoin the fight to avenge the death of his friend Patrocles, ultimately killing the Trojan prince, Hector.

Iliad. unabr. ed. Homer. Read by Anton Lesser. 13 CDs. (Running Time: 59610 sec.). 2006. audio compact disk 81.98 (978-962-634-428-6(8), NAX42812, Naxos AudioBooks) Naxos.

Iliad. unabr. ed. Homer. 2005. audio compact disk 14.25 (978-1-4193-2353-9(9)) Recorded Bks.

***Iliad.** unabr. ed. Null Homer. Narrated by Michael Page. (Running Time: 16 hrs. 0 mins.). 2010. 20.99 (978-1-4001-8706-5(0)) Tantor Media.

***Iliad.** unabr. ed. Null Homer. Narrated by Michael Page. (Running Time: 20 hrs. 0 mins. 0 sec.). (ENG.). 2010. 27.99 (978-1-4001-6706-7(X)); audio compact disk 35.99 (978-1-4001-1706-2(2)); audio compact disk 85.99 (978-1-4001-4706-9(9)) Pub: Tantor Media. Dist(s): IngramPubServ

Iliad. unabr. ed. Read by Ennis Rees. 10.95 (978-0-8045-0848-3(8), SAC 848) Spoken Arts.

Iliad, Set. abr. ed. Robert Fagles. Read by Roger Rees. Tr. by Samuel Butler. 4 cass. (Running Time: 6 hrs.). 1999. 24.95 (978-1-57453-323-1(1)) Audio Lit.
Tells how Achilles's wrath brought about the fall of Troy. It conveys the essence of ancient Greece, implacable, metaphysical, heroic & tragic. The grandeur & tragedy of the human condition resonate in this great epic, which can once again be enjoyed in its original oral form.

Iliad, Set. unabr. ed. Robert Fagles. Read by Nadia May. 9 cass. 1999. 62.95 (FS9-51125) Highsmith.

Iliad: The Story of Achilles. unabr. ed. Homer. Read by Anthony Heald. (Running Time: 13 hrs. 50 mins.). (ENG.). 2009. 29.95 (978-1-4332-8907-1(5)); 79.95 (978-1-4332-8903-3(2)); audio compact disk 109.00 (978-1-4332-8904-0(0)) Blckstn Audio.

Iliad & Odyssey. Homer. Read by Anthony Heald. Tr. by W. H. D. Rouse. (Running Time: 90000 sec.). 2008. audio compact disk 44.95 (978-1-4332-4883-2(2)) Blckstn Audio.

"Iliad" & "Odyssey" of Homer, Course 3000. Instructed by Elizabeth Vandiver. 12 cass. (Running Time: 12 hrs.). 2000. 129.95 Teaching Co.
Twenty-four lectures explaining the cultural assumptions that lie behind Homer's lines & probes the relationship of the epics to traditional orally transmitted poetry & surveys the archaeological evidence for an actual conflict.

Iliad & The Odyssey. unabr. ed. Homer. Read by John Lescault. 1CD. (Running Time: 20 hrs 49 mins). 2002. audio compact disk 18.95 (978-1-58472-404-9(8), In Aud) Pub: Sound Room. Dist(s): Baker Taylor
MP3 format.

Iliad of Homer. Instructed by Elizabeth Vandiver. 6 CDs. (Running Time: 6 hrs.). 1999. bk. 39.95 (978-1-56585-317-1(2), 301); 29.95 (978-1-56585-066-8(1), 301) Teaching Co.

Iliad of Homer, Set. unabr. ed. Read by Stephen G. Daitz. 24 cass. (Running Time: 24 hrs.). 1994. pap. bk. 199.00 (978-0-88432-766-0(3), S23840) J Norton Pubs.
Daitz has recreated one of the oldest poems of Western literature in a manner which approximates the original performance. Complete program consists of 4 parts, each with corresponding Greek text with English translation.

Iliad of Homer Audiobook. Homer. Read by Peter Jay Fernandez. 12 cass. 2005. 19.95 (978-1-56585-992-0(8)); audio compact disk 29.95 (978-1-59803-008-2(6)) Teaching Co.

Iliad of Sandy Bar & Other Stories, Set. unabr. ed. Bret Harte. Read by Grover Gardner. 3 cass. (Running Time: 4 hrs 30 min.). (gr. 3 up). 1992. 16.95 (978-1-55685-236-7(3)) Audio Bk Con.
This amusing & moving collection also includes "How Santa Claus Came to Simpson's Bar," "An Heiress of Red Dog," "Uncle Jim & Uncle Billy," "The Convalescence of Jack Hamlin" & "Chu Chu".

***Iliada.** abr. ed. Homero. Read by Daniel Quintero. (SPA.). 2003. audio compact disk 17.00 (978-958-28-1822-7(0)) Pub: Yoyo Music COL. Dist(s): YoYoMusic

Iliada & la Odisea: The Iliad & the Odyssey. unabr. ed. Homer. Read by Daniel Quintero. (YA). 2007. 39.99 (978-1-60252-533-7(1)) Find a World.

I'll Be Seeing You. abr. ed. Mary Higgins Clark. Read by Ellen Parker. 2004. 9.95 (978-0-7435-4511-2(7)) Pub: S&S Audio. Dist(s): S and S Inc

I'll Be Seeing You. unabr. ed. Mary Higgins Clark. Read by Mary Peiffer. 7 cass. (Running Time: 10 hrs. 30 min.). 1994. 56.00 (978-0-7366-2628-6(X), 3368) Books on Tape.
Imagine staring into the face of an unidentified murder victim & finding that the face staring back is your own! It shocks Meghan Collins, a reporter who thought herself unflappable. Searching first to identify the Jane Doe, then to uncover her murderer, Meghan finds that truths once exposed can never be denied, unless death steps in to erase the traces.

I'll Be Seeing You. unabr. ed. Mary Higgins Clark. Read by Kate Skinner. 8 cass. (Running Time: 11 hrs.). 2004. 79.75 (978-1-4025-3527-7(9)) Recorded Bks.
Meghan Collins is a young reporter covering a story about a female stabbing victim. The victim bears a striking resemblance to Meghan. What?s really strange is that it seems this killing might be connected to an explosion in which Meghan?s father died four months earlier. The investigation of these deaths takes Meghan down a treacherous path.

I'll Be There for You: Songs of Friendship, Brotherhood & Sisterhood. 1 cass. 1998. 7.98 (978-1-56826-949-8(8)) Rhino Enter.

I'll Be Watching You. Andrea Kane. 2005. 25.95 (978-0-06-076332-9(9)) HarperCollins Pubs.

***I'll Be Watching You.** abr. ed. Andrea Kane. Read by Linda Emond. (ENG.). 2005. (978-0-06-083504-0(4), Harper Audio); (978-0-06-083503-3(6), Harper Audio) HarperCollins Pubs.

I'll Be Watching You. unabr. ed. Andrea Kane. Read by Kathleen McNenny. 2005. 29.95 (978-0-7927-3443-7(2), CMP 737); 59.95 (978-0-7927-3425-3(4), CSL 737); audio compact disk 89.95 (978-0-7927-3426-0(2), SLD 737) AudioGO.

I'll Be Watching You. unabr. ed. M. William Phelps. Read by J. Charles. 1 MP3-CD. (Running Time: 14 hrs.). 2008. 24.95 (978-1-4233-6186-2(5), 9781423361862, Brilliance MP3); 39.25 (978-1-4233-6187-9(3),

9781423361879, Brinc Audio MP3 Lib); 39.25 (978-1-4233-6189-3(X), 9781423361893, BADLE); 24.95 (978-1-4233-6188-6(1), 9781423361886, BAD); audio compact disk 107.25 (978-1-4233-6185-5(7), 9781423361855, BriAudCD Unabrid); audio compact disk 38.95 (978-1-4233-6184-8(9), 9781423361848, Bril Audio CD Unabri) Brilliance Audio.

I'll Be with You Always: The Farewell. Perf. by Jimmy Orion Ellis. Selected by Peter Herbert. (I'll Be With You Always - The Farewell CD). 1999. audio compact disk 15.00 (978-1-877858-87-1(0)) Amer Focus Pub.

I'll Be Your Best Friend - Book & Audio Cassette. 1 read-along cass. (J). (ps-3). 1986. bk. 9.98 (978-0-89544-156-0(X), NO. 156) Silbert Bress.
Stewart discovers who his real friends are & what real friendship is all about.

I'll Catch the Moon. Nina Crews. (Metro Reading Ser.). (J). (gr. k). 2000. 8.46 (978-1-58120-991-4(6)) Metro Teaching.

I'll Find You. Clair M. Poulson. 6 cass. 2004. 24.95 (978-1-57734-802-3(8)) Covenant Comms.

I'll Fly Away. Lisa Pertillar Brevard. Perf. by Lisa Pertillar Brevard. Photos by Frank Lynn Brevard. (ENG & SPA.). 2010. audio compact disk 12.95 (978-0-9749499-4-9(9), Blk Butterfly Rec) Monarch Baby.

I'll Follow You. Perf. by Thomison, Lawrence and The Voices of Bridgehampton. Prod. by David Curry. 1 cass. 29.95 (V2026) Diamante Music Grp.
The eclectic choice of material will appeal to both traditional & contemporary fans.

I'll Lead You Home. Perf. by Michael W. Smith. 1 cass. 1995. audio compact disk Brentwood Music.
I'll Lead You Home achieved gold status in under 2 months, garnered a Grammy award & brought Michael a Dove Award for Songwriter of the Year. Features: Cry for Love, Straight to the Heart & I'll Lead You Home.

Ill Mannered Killer. unabr. ed. W. Bartow Wright. Read by Rusty Nelson. 6 cass. (Running Time: 6 hrs. 30 min.). (Bucky Dolan Ser.: Bk. 2). 2001. 39.95 (978-1-55686-957-0(6)) Books in Motion.
Bucky is stalked by a half-mad East German assassin who mistakenly believes Bucky cheated him out of millions of dollars during the Cold War.

I'll Mature When I'm Dead: Amazing Tales of Adulthood. unabr. ed. Dave Barry. 4 CDs. (Running Time: 5 hrs.). (ENG.). 2010. audio compact disk 29.95 (978-0-14-242777-4(2), PengAudBks) Penguin Grp USA.

Ill Met by Moonlight. Sarah A. Hoyt. Narrated by Jason Carter. 8 CDs. (Running Time: 8 hrs. 40 mins.). 2003. audio compact disk 47.95 (978-0-9657255-3-8(7)) Buzzy Multimed.
A young Williams Shakespeare crosses fates with those of the Fae...The result a struggle for life and love and the inspiration for the most celebrated of all English language authors.

Ill Never Be Broke Another Aud. L. Thompson. 2002. 15.00 (978-1-931804-21-9(4)) Ever Increase Wd Min.

I'll Never Be Young Again. Daphne Du Maurier. Read by Jonathan Firth. 10 vols. (Running Time: 15 hrs.). 2003. 84.95 (978-0-7540-8379-5(9)) Pub: Chivers Audio Bks GBR. Dist(s): AudioGO

***I'll Never do it Again: And Other Broken Promises That Need the Continuous Atonement.** Brad Wilcox. 2010. audio compact disk 14.99 (978-1-60641-256-5(6)) Deseret Bk.

I'll Never Find Anything in Here. Susan Attiyah. 2001. audio compact disk 10.00 (978-1-893108-31-8(7), 123513) Neighbrhd Pr Pubng.

I'll Sail upon the Dog-star see Gathering of Great Poetry for Children

I'll Say Yes. Contrib. by Brooklyn Tabernacle Choir et al. 2008. 14.98 (978-5-557-38679-1(3)) Integrity Music.

I'll Say Yes. Contrib. by Brooklyn Tabernacle Choir & Carol Cymbala. Prod. by Carol Cymbala. 2008. audio compact disk 16.98 (978-5-557-51578-8(X)) Integrity Music.

I'll Say Yes: She Said Yes. Perf. by Rick Altizer. 1 cass. 1999. Provident Music.

I'll Take Manhattan. unabr. ed. Judith Krantz. Read by Jami Castell. 14 cass. (Running Time: 18 hrs. 52 min.). (Isis Ser.). (J). 1994. 99.95 (978-1-85695-863-9(9), 941006) Pub: ISIS Lrg Prnt GBR. Dist(s): Ulverscroft US

I'll Take You There. unabr. ed. Joyce Carol Oates. Read by Kate Fleming. 8 vols. (Running Time: 12 hrs.). 2002. bk. 69.95 (978-0-7927-2710-1(X), CSL 496, Chivers Sound Lib); audio compact disk 94.95 (978-0-7927-2737-8(1), SLD 496, Chivers Sound Lib) AudioGO.
As the novel opens, Anellia looks back on her first years in college at Syracuse University in the 1960s. She's haunted by her mother's early death, and by the guilt her brothers and father cast upon her. She is then swept away by an intense love affair with an extremely gifted Black philosophy student. In an era when interracial relationships were deemed unseemly in mainstream society, her torturous affair can only lead to Anellia's further alienation. Anellia's sense of rejection reaches a turning point in the final section, when her father unexpectedly reappears in her life, and she makes the journey from upstate New York to the Midwest to be with him in his final days. In her search for acceptance and truth, she discovers the power of her own survival.

I'll Tell Them I Remember You. William Peter Blatty. Read by William Peter Blatty. 2 cass. (Running Time: 3 hrs.). 1995. 17.50 (978-1-886392-06-9(4), Parrot Bks) Walberg Pubng.
The author of The Exorcist tells a wonderful story about his mother, The Exorcist, & life after death. This is a jewel!.

I'll Tell You How the Sun Rose see Gathering of Great Poetry for Children

I'll Tell You How the Sun Rose see Poems & Letters of Emily Dickinson

I'll Wait for You, My Darling. (ENG.). (YA). 2008. audio compact disk (978-1-931856-02-7(8)) Adelante Bks.

***I'll Walk Alone.** abr. ed. Mary Higgins Clark. (Running Time: 5 hrs. 0 mins. 0 sec.). (ENG.). 2011. audio compact disk 29.99 (978-1-4423-3753-4(2)) Pub: S&S Audio. Dist(s): S and S Inc

***I'll Walk Alone.** unabr. ed. Mary Higgins Clark. (Running Time: 9 hrs. 0 mins. 0 sec.). (ENG.). 2011. audio compact disk 39.99 (978-1-4423-3755-8(9)) Pub: S&S Audio. Dist(s): S and S Inc

Ill Wind. 18.00 (978-1-59040-206-1(5)) Pub: Amer Intl Pub. Dist(s): PerseuPGW

Ill Wind. unabr. ed. Nevada Barr. Narrated by Barbara Rosenblat. 7 cass. (Running Time: 9 hrs. 45 mins.). (Anna Pigeon Ser.: No. 3). 1999. 62.00 (978-0-7887-2932-4(2), 95717E7) Recorded Bks.
When ranger Anna Pigeon investigates medical emergencies in Mesa Verde Park, she uncovers a dangerous plan threatening innocent tourists & Mother Nature.

Ill Wind. unabr. collector's ed. Kevin J. Anderson & Doug Beason. Read by Larry McKeever. 13 cass. (Running Time: 19 hrs. 30 min.). 1996. 104.00 (978-0-7366-3713-8(3), 4397) Books on Tape.
A supertanker crashes off the shores of San Francisco, producing the largest oil spill in history.

Illegal Man. abr. ed. Jerry Ahern & Sharon Ahern. Read by Alan Zimmerman. 4 cass. (Running Time: 360 min.). 2000. 25.00 (978-1-58807-000-5(X)) Am Pubng Inc.
To his friends and neighbors in Atlanta, John Benson was a solid citizen - owner of a successful sporting goods store and a devoted family man. Then a car bomb meant for him destroyed that carefully crafted life and set Benson off on a frantic search to find out what had happened to his missing wife and daughter, and for the people who wanted him dead.

Illegal Possession. unabr. ed. Kay Hooper. Narrated by Deanna Hurst. 5 CDs. (Running Time: 5 hrs. 10 mins.). (ENG.). 2008. audio compact disk 19.95 (978-1-60283-406-4(7)) Pub: AudioGO. Dist(s): Perseus Dist

Illegitimate: How a Loving God Rescued a Son of Polygamy. unabr. ed. Brian Mackert. Narrated by Jon Gauger. (Running Time: 7 hrs. 35 mins. 41 sec.). (ENG.). 2008. 19.59 (978-1-60814-251-4(5)); audio compact disk 27.99 (978-1-59859-497-3(4)) Oasis Audio.

Illini Legends, Lists & Lore: 100 Years of Big Ten Heritage. 2nd ed. Mike Pearson. 1 CD. (Running Time: 1 hr.). 2002. bk. 34.95 (978-1-58261-347-5(8)) Pub: Sports Pub. Dist(s): IngramPubServ

Illinois! abr. ed. Dana Fuller Ross, pseud. Read by Lloyd James. Abr. by Mary Bevoni. 4 vols. (Wagons West Ser.: No. 18). 2004. 25.00 (978-1-58807-150-7(2)); (978-1-58807-619-9(9)) Am Pubng Inc.

Illinois Real Estate: Principles & Practices. 3rd ed. Illus. by Tim Rice. (C). 2007. audio compact disk 38.95 (978-0-324-17880-7(8)) Pub: South-West. Dist(s): CENGAGE Learn

Illness: A Spiritual Crisis. Chaplain C. Holland. 2 cass. 21.95 Self-Control Sys.
A preparation for pastors & pastoral care professionals in the training of laymen for hospital visitation.

Illuminated. unabr. ed. Matt Bronleewe. Read by Rob Lamont. (YA). 2007. 39.99 (978-1-60252-839-0(X)) Find a World.

Illuminated. unabr. ed. Matt Bronleewe. Narrated by Rob Lamont. (ENG.). 2007. 17.49 (978-1-60814-252-1(3)) Oasis Audio.

Illuminated Door: Journeys into Your Soul. (ENG.). 2009. audio compact disk 16.00 (978-0-9799617-3-1(4)) Heart N.

Illuminated Path. unabr. ed. Dane Rudhyar. 2 cass. (Running Time: 2 hrs.). 1969. 18.00 Set. (10103) Big Sur Tapes.
Describes the goal of a transformative journey as "the building of a completely new & immortal organism of conscious selfhood, which is attuned to cosmic rhythms & which becomes a permanent factor in the universe".

Illuminating the Afterlife: Your Soul's Journey Through the Worlds Beyond. Cyndi Dale. (Running Time: 12600 sec.). 2008. audio compact disk 24.95 (978-1-59179-951-1(1)) Sounds True.

Illuminating the Dark Night: Three Strategies for Converting Our Culture. 2003. 13.95 (978-1-932631-47-0(X)); audio compact disk 13.95 (978-1-932631-48-7(8)) Ascensn Pr.

Illuminating Your Heart. 1998. 95.00 (978-1-893027-34-3(1)) Path of Light.

Illuminating Your Heart's Desire: Sankalpa. Swami Shankardev Saraswati & Jayne Stevenson. (ENG.). 2007. audio compact disk 22.00 (978-0-9803496-0-3(5)) Big Shakti AUS.

Illumination. unabr. ed. Jill Gregory and Karen Tintori. Read by Sandra Burr. (Running Time: 10 hrs.). 2009. 39.97 (978-1-4233-4356-1(5), 9781423343561, BADLE) Brilliance Audio.

Illumination. unabr. ed. Jill Gregory & Karen Tintori. (Running Time: 9 hrs.). 2008. 39.97 (978-1-4233-4354-7(9), 9781423343547, Brinc Audio MP3 Lib); 24.99 (978-1-4233-4353-0(0), 9781423343530, Brilliance MP3); audio compact disk 87.97 (978-1-4233-4352-3(2), 9781423343523, BriAudCD Unabrid); audio compact disk 34.99 (978-1-4233-4351-6(4), 9781423343516, Bril Audio CD Unabri) Brilliance Audio.

Illumination. unabr. ed. Jill Gregory & Karen Tintori. Read by Sandra Burr. (Running Time: 10 hrs.). 2009. 24.99 (978-1-4233-4355-4(7), 9781423343554, BAD) Brilliance Audio.

Illumination Night. unabr. ed. Alice Hoffman. Read by Agnes Herrmann. 6 vols. (Running Time: 6 hrs.). 1999. bk. 54.95 (978-0-7927-2305-9(8), CSL 194, Chivers Sound Lib) AudioGO.
A little boy who wants to grow. An elderly woman at the end of her life. A teenage girl with a ruthless passion. A young couple wrenched apart by desire & fear. A blond giant who hides his terrifying height & beauty. These are the fascinating people's featured. Set on Martha's Vineyard, this story weaves together the lives of six wonderfully realized people who possess a quiet understanding & a willful determination.

Illuminations see Fantastic Tales of Ray Bradbury

Illuminations. Poems. Arthur Rimbaud. Read by G. Bejean & C. Deis. 1 cass. (FRE.). 1991. 22.95 (1423-VSL) Olivia & Hill.
The famous collection of poems by this 19th-century Symbolist.

Illuminati's New World Order. Ed. by Alan H. Peterson. As told by Doc Marquis. (American Focus on Satanic Crime Ser.: Vol. 14). 1999. 45.00 (978-1-877858-84-0(6)) Amer Focus Pub.

Illuminator. unabr. ed. Brenda Rickman Vantrease. Read by Simon Jones. 10 cass. 2005. 84.95 (978-0-7927-3495-6(5), CSL 763); audio compact disk 115.95 (978-0-7927-3496-3(3), SLD 763) AudioGO.

Illuminatus! Leviathan, Part III. Robert Shea & Robert Anton Wilson. 2008. 34.95 (978-0-9796694-3-9(X)) Deepleaf Prod.

Illuminatus! Part I: The Eye in the Pyramid. Robert Shea. 2007. 34.95 (978-0-9796694-1-5(3)) Deepleaf Prod.

Illuminatus! Part II: The Golden Apple. Robert Shea & Robert Anton Wilson. (ENG.). 2007. 29.95 (978-0-9796694-2-2(1)) Deepleaf Prod.

Illusion. unabr. ed. Denise Robertson. Read by Anne Dover. 6 cass. (Running Time: 8 hrs.). 1999. 54.95 (978-0-7531-0586-3(1), 990607) Pub: ISIS Audio GBR. Dist(s): Ulverscroft US
Returning home, Rachel senses a familiar tension in the air. This is not the first affair her father has had, but along with the revelation of his latest adultery comes even more shocking news. The very foundations of her childhood shaken, Rachel is also horrified to find out that she is pregnant. As cracks begin to appear in her relationship with her boyfriend & her family, she feels the need to find out more about her own mysterious past. But it seems there are even more surprises in store for her.

Illusion of Achievement. unabr. ed. R. D. Laing. 1 cass. (Running Time: 55 min.). 1967. 11.00 (07002) Big Sur Tapes.
Relates schizophrenia - seen as the voyage backward to discover the uncontaminated self - to his Zen-like philosophy.

Illusion of Desire. Swami Amar Jyoti. 2 cass. 1989. 12.95 (B-16) Truth Consciousness.
Freedom from desire, living by His will, all is provided. "Where to draw the line" is desire speaking.

Illusion of Eternity see Richard Eberhart Reading His Poetry

Illusion of Limitation: The Liberation of Self. Guy Finley. (ENG.). 2005. 24.95 (978-1-929320-43-1(4)) Life of Learn.

Illusion of Limitation: The Liberation of Self. Guy Finley. 2005. reel tape 27.95 (978-1-929320-21-9(3)); audio compact disk 39.95 (978-1-929320-22-6(1)) Life of Learn.

Illusion of Space, Time & Ego. Swami Amar Jyoti. 1 cass. 1986. 9.95 (R-84) Truth Consciousness.
All conceptions are superimpositions upon Reality, illusory dreams only. Dissolving the basic illusion. Vedantic meditation.

Illusion of World-Process. Swami Jyotirmayananda. Read by Swami Jyotirmayananda. 1 cass. (Running Time: 45 min.). 10.00 (808) Yoga Res Foun.

Illusion, Reality & the New Age. Swami Amar Jyoti. 1 cass. 1991. 9.95 (R-103) Truth Consciousness.
All darkness is but the absence of Light. Rebuilding the foundation for really alive, conscious living.

***Illusions.** abr. ed. Janet Dailey. Read by Allison Janney. (ENG.). 2005. (978-0-06-089424-5(5), Harper Audio); (978-0-06-089425-2(3), Harper Audio) HarperCollins Pubs.

Illusions: The Adventures of a Reluctant Messiah. abr. ed. Richard Bach. Read by Richard Bach. 1 cass. 1984. 8.98 (CDL5 1585) HarperCollins Pubs.

Illusion's Game. Vajracarya. Read by Chogyam Trungpa. 1 cass. 1976. 10.00 Vajradhatu.
A seminar by the scholar & meditation master trained in the philosophical & meditative traditions of Buddhism in Tibet.

Illusionst: L-Book. Fran Heckrotte. Sheri. (ENG.). 2007. 14.95 (978-0-9800846-9-6(5)) Lbook Pub.

Illustrated London News: 1905-1907. unabr. ed. G. K. Chesterton. Read by Helen Stoltzfus et al. 20 cass. 79.95 set. (325) Ignatius Pr.
Chesterton's columns from the years 1905-1907 offer a feast of the great man's insight & wit. Subjects range from "Cardboard Noses" & "The Millionaire's Freak Dinner on Community Sharing" to "The Political Instincts of Women" & "English Ideas about the French.".

Illustrated London News: 1908-1910. unabr. ed. G. K. Chesterton. Read by Josephine Bellacomo et al. 23 cass. 91.95 set. (326) Ignatius Pr.
Chesterton's columns from the years 1908-1910 offer a feast of the great man's insight & will. Subjects range from "Cardboard Noses" & "Millionaire's Freak Dinner on Community Sharing" to "Political Instincts of Women" & "English Ideas about the French.".

Illustrated Man see Fantastic Tales of Ray Bradbury

Illustrated Man. Ray Bradbury. Narrated by Paul Hecht. 8 CDs. (Running Time: 8.25 hrs.). audio compact disk 39.95 (978-1-4025-3934-3(7)) Recorded Bks.

Illustrated Man. abr. ed. Ray Bradbury. Read by Leonard Nimoy. 1 cass. 1984. 8.98 (CP 1479) HarperCollins Pubs.

Illustrated Man. unabr. ed. Ray Bradbury. (Running Time: 1 hr. 0 mins.). (ENG.). 2009. 29.95 (978-1-4332-9720-5(5)); 59.95 (978-1-4332-9716-8(7)); audio compact disk 90.00 (978-1-4332-9717-5(5)); audio compact disk & audio compact disk 24.95 (978-1-4332-9719-9(1)) Blckstn Audio.

Illustrated Man. unabr. ed. Ray Bradbury. Read by Paul Hecht. 5 Cass. (Running Time: 8.25 Hrs.). 24.95 (978-1-4025-3933-6(9)) Recorded Bks.

Illustrated Man, unabr. ed. Ray Bradbury. Narrated by Paul Hecht. 7 cass. (Running Time: 8 hrs. 15 mins.). (gr. 10). 1998. 62.00 (978-0-7887-2725-2(7), 95665E7) Recorded Bks.
A hiker meets a man whose upper body is covered with illustrations so vivid & beautiful that they literally come to life. One by one the images quiver with fantastic tales guaranteed to stir the imagination.

***Illustrated Man.** unabr. ed. Ray Bradbury. (Running Time: 8 hrs. 0 mins.). 2010. 15.99 (978-1-4001-8826-0(1)) Tantor Media.

***Illustrated Man.** unabr. ed. Ray Bradbury. (Running Time: 9 hrs. 30 mins. 0 sec.). (ENG.). 2010. audio compact disk 71.99 (978-1-4001-4826-4(X)); audio compact disk 29.99 (978-1-4001-1826-7(3)) Pub: Tantor Media. Dist(s): IngramPubServ

***Illustrated Man.** unabr. ed. Ray Bradbury & Ray Bradberry. (Running Time: 9 hrs. 30 mins. 0 sec.). (ENG.). 2010. 19.99 (978-1-4001-6826-2(0)) Pub: Tantor Media. Dist(s): IngramPubServ

Illustrated Man. unabr. collector's ed. Ray Bradbury. Read by Michael Prichard. 8 cass. (Running Time: 8 hrs.). 1988. 48.00 (978-0-7366-1291-3(2), 2198) Books on Tape.
The tattooed man moves, & in the arcane designs scrawled upon his skin swirl tales beyond imagining - tales of love & laughter, darkness & death, of mankind's glowing, golden past & dim, haunted future.

Illustrated Mum. Jacqueline Wilson. Read by Josie Lawrence. 5 CDs. (Running Time: 8 hrs. 30 mins.). (J). 2002. audio compact disk 49.95 (978-0-7540-6583-8(9), CHCD 083) AudioGO.

Illustrated Mum. unabr. ed. Jacqueline Wilson. Read by Josie Lawrence. 4 cass. (Running Time: 4 hrs.). 2001. 32.95 (CTC871) AudioGO.

ILM Homework Student Version for Stewart's Calculus. 5th ed. (C). 2003. audio compact disk 19.95 (978-0-534-39382-3(9)) Pub: Brooks-Cole. Dist(s): CENGAGE Learn

Ilokano Newspaper Reader. Pamela Johnstone-Moguet. 1988. 13.00 (978-0-931745-49-2(7)) Dunwoody Pr.

Ilokano Newspaper Reader, Set. Pamela Johnstone-Moguet & R. David Zorc. 2 cass. (Running Time: 60 min. per cass.). (ILO.). 1988. 13.00 (3070) Dunwoody Pr.
Twenty-five selections provide a broad range of articles together with necessary lexical & grammatical information to make the link between spoken language & the various genres of the media.

Ilrn Stdt Ver-Mathematics: Practical Odyssey. 6th ed. (C). 2006. audio compact disk 10.95 (978-0-495-12669-0(1)) Pub: Brooks-Cole. Dist(s): CENGAGE Learn

Ilrn Student Tutorial for Hirsch/Goodman's Understanding Elementary Algebra with Geometry: A Course for College Students. 6th ed. (C). 2005. audio compact disk 12.95 (978-0-534-99973-5(5)) Pub: Brooks-Cole. Dist(s): CENGAGE Learn

Ilrn Student Vers-Elem/Intermediate Algebra: Combined App. 4th ed. (C). 2005. audio compact disk 10.95 (978-0-495-00999-3(7)) Pub: Brooks-Cole. Dist(s): CENGAGE Learn

ILrn Tutorial for Hurley's a Concise Introduction to Logic. 9th ed. Patrick J. Hurley. (C). 2005. audio compact disk 16.95 (978-0-495-00027-3(2)) Pub: Wadsworth Pub. Dist(s): CENGAGE Learn

Ilrn Tutorial Student Version for Precalculus, 6th. 5th ed. (C). 2005. audio compact disk 11.95 (978-0-534-40217-4(8)) Pub: Brooks-Cole. Dist(s): CENGAGE Learn

Ilse's Journey. 2002. pap. bk. 19.95 (978-0-9729712-0-1(3)) R Klampert.

ILT Customcourse 40 3/05. 5th ed. 2005. audio compact disk (978-1-4188-8613-4(0)) Course Tech.

***Ilustrado.** unabr. ed. Miguel Syjuco. Narrated by William Dufris. (Running Time: 12 hrs. 0 mins.). 2010. 17.99 (978-1-4001-8720-1(6)); 34.99 (978-1-4001-9720-0(1)); 24.99 (978-1-4001-6720-3(5)); audio compact disk

69.99 (978-1-4001-4720-5(4)); audio compact disk 34.99 (978-1-4001-1720-8(8)) Pub: Tantor Media. Dist(s): IngramPubServ

I'm a Believer. (Paws & Tales Ser.: Vol. 29). (J). 2002. 3.99 (978-1-57972-459-7(0)); audio compact disk 5.99 (978-1-57972-460-3(4)) Insight Living.

I'm a Can Do Kid & Other Self-Esteem Building Songs & Activities. John Archambault & David Plummer. Ed. by Kim Cernek. Illus. by Marek-Janci Design Staff. (Happy Song Sing-Alongs Ser.: Vol. 2357). 1999. pap. bk. & tchr. ed. 13.99 (978-1-57471-638-2(7), 2357) Creat Teach Pr.

I'm a Champion. Mac Huff & John Jacobson. 1 CD. 2000. audio compact disk 19.95 (09970205) H Leonard.
Help your students feel confident & celebrate the fact that everyone shines in their own special way.

I'm a Jet Pilot. Geoffrey T. Williams. 1. (Running Time: 18 mins). Dramatization. (J). 2005. audio compact disk 24.95 (978-1-59971-067-9(6)) AardGP.
A young boy wants to become a jet pilot. He rides in the cockpit of a giant 737 airliner, learning about the physics of flight and details of flying a commercial airliner, then he visits the Top Gun Navy pilot school where he learns about flying fighter jets.

I'm a Pleasure to Shop For see Christmas with Ogden Nash

I'm a Stranger Here Myself: Notes on Returning to America after Twenty Years Away. abr. ed. Bill Bryson. Read by Bill Bryson. 5 CDs. (Running Time: 6 hrs.). (ENG.). 1999. audio compact disk 29.95 (978-0-553-45650-9(4)) Pub: Random Audio Pubg. Dist(s): Random

I'm a Stranger Here Myself: Notes on Returning to America after Twenty Years Away. abr. ed. Bill Bryson. 4 cass. (Running Time: 6 hrs.). 2000. 25.00 (Random AudioBks); audio compact disk 29.95 (Random AudioBks) Random Audio Pubg.

I'm a Teacher. Michael Popkin. 1 cass. (Running Time: 10 min.). 1994. 5.00 (K1424) Active Parenting.
Original theme song from the video discussion program - Active Parenting.

I'm a Very Special Person. Dale Baroni. (J). 1982. 11.95 Ed Activities.

I'm An Animal: Songs of the Earth as the Animals See It. Sarah Weeks. Perf. by Sarah Weeks. 1 cass. (YA). 1998. 15.98 (978-1-56896-295-5(9)); audio compact disk 8.98 CD. (978-1-56896-296-2(7)) Lightyear Entrtnmnt.
Sixteen catchy tunes poking fun at the similiarities between humans & animals. Will appeal to listeners of all age, & the lyrics are sure to inspire young environmentalists.

I'm Blessed. Prod. by Soul West Records Staff. Featuring Alvin Willis & Praise Alive. 1 CD. (Running Time: 30 min.). 2004. audio compact disk 17.98 (978-5-559-49499-9(2)) Pub: Pt of Grace Ent. Dist(s): STL Dist NA

I'm Dirty! Kate McMullan & Jim McMullan. Read by Steve Buscemi. 1 CD. (Running Time: 8 mins.). (J). (ps-2). 2008. bk. 29.95 (978-0-545-09456-6(9)); audio compact disk 12.95 (978-0-545-09449-8(6)) Weston Woods.
Meet a backhoe loader reporting for duty and find out just how dirty it can get while doing its job.

I'M Down. unabr. ed. Mishna Wolff. 1 MP3-CD. (Running Time: 8 hrs. 30 mins. 0 sec.). (ENG.). 2009. 19.99 (978-1-4001-6278-9(5)); audio compact disk 59.99 (978-1-4001-4278-1(4)); audio compact disk 29.99 (978-1-4001-1278-4(8)) Pub: Tantor Media. Dist(s): IngramPubServ

***I'm Dreaming of a Black Christmas.** unabr. ed. Lewis Black. 4 CDs. (Running Time: 5 hrs.). (ENG.). 2010. audio compact disk 25.95 (978-0-14-242855-9(8), PengAudBks) Penguin Grp USA.

I'm Dying Laughing. unabr. ed. Christina Stead. Read by Anna Fields. 15 cass. (Running Time: 22 hrs. 30 min.). 1998. 95.95 (1910) Blckstn Audio.
Recreates the political turbulence of the American Left & the clamor & menace of the McCarthy Right. Mirrors the times of its memorable characters - the heady revolutionary fervor of the Depression, the short collaborative effort of wartime America, & the fracturing, fractious Cold War years.

I'm Dying Laughing. unabr. ed. Christina Stead. Read by Anna Fields. 15 cass. (Running Time: 22 hrs.). 2006. 95.95 (978-0-7861-1141-1(0), 1910) Blckstn Audio.

I'm Dying up Here: Heartbreak & High Times in Stand-up Comedy's Golden Era. unabr. ed. William Knoedelseder. Narrated by William Dufris. (Running Time: 8 hrs. 30 mins. 0 sec.). (ENG.). 2009. audio compact disk 69.99 (978-1-4001-3184-6(7)); audio compact disk 24.99 (978-1-4001-5184-4(8)); audio compact disk 34.99 (978-1-4001-0184-9(0)) Pub: Tantor Media. Dist(s): IngramPubServ

I'm Easy (an Essay from Things I've Learned from Women Who've Dumped Me) abr. ed. Paul Simms. Read by Paul Simms. Ed. by Ben Karlin. (Running Time: 15 mins.). (ENG.). 2008. 1.98 (978-1-60024-345-5(2)) Pub: Hachet Audio. Dist(s): HachBkGrp

I'm Glad I Did, I Wish I Had, Set. Daryl Hoole. 2 cass. 13.95 (978-1-57734-432-2(4), 06005950) Covenant Comms.
A treasure chest of practical ideas for women.

I'm Glad You Asked That. Derek Prince. 1 cass. 1990. 5.95 (I-4319) Derek Prince.
Derek Prince personally responds to questions dealing with such critical current issues as: predestination vs. free will, Christian reaction to abortion, is the Church the new Israel?, & will the church be a remnant?.

I'm Going to Be Famous. unabr. ed. Tom Birdseye. Narrated by Jeff Woodman. 3 pieces. (Running Time: 3 hrs. 15 mins.). (gr. 3 up). 27.00 (978-0-7887-0593-9(8), 94770E7) Recorded Bks.
When fifth-grader Arlo Moore sets his mind to becoming famous, his first thought is to try to break a world record. He likes to eat bananas & he loves to read the "Guinness Book of World Records," so he decides to try to break the banana-eating record. Soon, Arlo & three of his friends are practicing like mad & driving their parents & school principal crazy. Available to libraries only.

I'M Going to Be Famous, Set. unabr. ed. Tom Birdseye. Narrated by Jeff Woodman. 3 cass. (Running Time: 3 hrs. 50 min.). (J). 1996. 27.00 (94770) Recorded Bks.

I'm Going to Write a Book, Pt. 1. unabr. ed. Gilbert Highet. 1 cass. (Running Time: 30 min.). (Gilbert Highet Ser.). 9.95 (23332) J Norton Pubs.
Writing a novel: its dangers & reward. A whimsical account of ways of making authors miserable without actually taking them into a torture chamber.

I'm Gonna Keep on Singin' A Soulful Celebration Collection. Contrib. by Bradley Knight. (Jubilation Ser.). (ENG.). 2008. audio compact disk 16.99 (978-5-557-46528-1(6), Brentwood-Benson Music) Brentwood Music.

I'm Gonna Keep on Singin' Satb. Contrib. by Bradley Knight. (Jubilation Ser.). (ENG.). 2008. audio compact disk 10.00 (978-5-557-46526-7(X), Brentwood-Benson Music) Brentwood Music.

I'm Gonna Keep on Singin' The Songs of Andrae Crouch: Bass. Contrib. by Johnathan Crumpton & Bradley Knight. Prod. by Bradley Knight. (Jubilation Ser.). (ENG.). 2008. audio compact disk 5.00 (978-5-557-46523-6(5), Brentwood-Benson Music) Brentwood Music.

I'm Gonna Keep on Singin' The Songs of Andrae Crouch: Soprano. Contrib. by Johnathan Crumpton & Bradley Knight. Prod. by Bradley Knight. (Jubilation Ser.). (ENG.). 2008. audio compact disk 5.00 (978-5-557-46525-0(1), Brentwood-Benson Music) Brentwood Music.

I'm Gonna Keep on Singin' The Songs of Andrae Crouch: Tenor. Contrib. by Johnathan Crumpton & Bradley Knight. Prod. by Bradley Knight. (Jubilation Ser.). (ENG.). 2008. audio compact disk 5.00 (978-5-557-46524-3(3), Brentwood-Benson Music) Brentwood Music.

I'm Gonna Keep on Singing: The Songs of Andrae Crouch: A Soulful Celebration Collection. Contrib. by Johnathan Crumpton & Bradley Knight. Prod. by Bradley Knight. (Jubilation Ser.). (ENG.). 2008. audio compact disk 95.00 (978-5-557-46527-4(8), Brentwood-Benson Music) Brentwood Music.

***I'm Gonna Like Me: Letting off a Little Self-Esteem.** abr. ed. Jamie Lee Curtis. Read by Jamie Lee Curtis. 2006. (978-0-06-128535-6(8)) HarperCollins Pubs.

***I'm Gonna Like Me: Letting off a Little Self-Esteem.** abr. ed. Jamie Lee Curtis. Read by Jamie Lee Curtis. 2007. (978-0-06-123237-4(8)) HarperCollins Pubs.

***I'm Hosting as Fast as I Can!** unabr. ed. Tom Bergeron. Read by Tom Bergeron. (ENG.). 2009. (978-0-06-189650-7(0), Harper Audio); (978-0-06-184547-5(7), Harper Audio) HarperCollins Pubs.

I'm in Charge of Celebrations. unabr. ed. Byrd Baylor. Read by Byrd Baylor. 1 cass. (Running Time: 12 min.). (Byrd Baylor: Storyteller Ser.). (J). (gr. k-6). 1990. 5.95 (978-0-929937-17-5(1)) SW Series.
Byrd Baylor tells about her own special celebrations.

I'm in Marsport Without Hilda see Asimov's Mysteries

I'm Just a DJ but... It Makes Sense to Me. abr. ed. Tom Joyner. (ENG.). 2005. 14.98 (978-1-59483-249-9(8)) Pub: Hachet Audio. Dist(s): HachBkGrp

I'm Just a DJ but... It Makes Sense to Me. abr. ed. Tom Joyner. Read by Tom Joyner Enterprises. Contrib. by Mary Flowers Boyce. (Running Time: 4 hrs.). (ENG.). 2009. 39.98 (978-1-60788-059-2(8)) Pub: Hachet Audio. Dist(s): HachBkGrp

I'm Just a Kid. Rory. Perf. by Rory. 1 cass. (Running Time: 30 min.). (J). 1992. 8.98 (978-1-56406-556-8(1)); 8.98 Incl. sleeve pack. (978-1-56406-582-7(0)); audio compact disk 13.98 CD. (978-1-56406-569-8(3)) Sony Music Ent.

I'm Learning to Multiply. Kidzup Productions Staff. (Running Time: 54 min.). (J). (gr. 1-3). 2004. audio compact disk 18.99 (978-1-894677-65-3(X)) Pub: Kidzup Prodns. Dist(s): Penton Overseas

I'm Looking Through You: Growing up Haunted: A Memoir. unabr. ed. Jennifer Finney Boylan. Read by Jennifer Finney Boylan. (Running Time: 9 hrs. 30 mins. 0 sec.). (ENG.). 2008. audio compact disk 34.99 (978-1-4001-0596-0(X)); audio compact disk 24.99 (978-1-4001-5596-5(7)); audio compact disk 69.99 (978-1-4001-3596-7(6)) Pub: Tantor Media. Dist(s): IngramPubServ

I'm Nobody! Who Are You?: Poems of Emily Dickinson for Young People see Poems & Letters of Emily Dickinson

I'm Not Alone. 2003. audio compact disk (978-0-9747117-0-6(5)) Ben Williams.

I'm Not an Insect. 2008. audio compact disk 3.99 (978-0-9802359-5-1(2)) Abena Pub.

I'm Not Being Fed. 1 cass. (Running Time: 1 hr.). 2003. 13.95 (978-1-932631-19-7(4)); audio compact disk 13.95 (978-1-932631-21-0(6)) Ascensn Pr.

I'm Not Cindy Brady. Perf. by Suzanne Westenhoefer. 2000. audio compact disk 16.98 (978-1-929243-24-2(3)) Uproar Ent.

I'm Not Crazy, I'm Singercising! see I'm Not Crazy, I'm Vocalizing: Singing Exercises in or Out of Your Car

I'm Not Crazy, I'm Vocalizing. rev. ed. Karen Oleson. 1 cass. (Running Time: 40 min.). (Vocalizing Ser.). (J). 1991. bk. 15.95 (978-1-886789-06-7(1), 1214-41); bk. 19.95 CD. (978-1-886789-07-4(X), 1214-41) VoiceTech WA.
Singing warmups & instruction. Eight fully orchestrated exercises - one size fits all - fun & lively. Popular with music teachers & commuters. Warm-up kit includes bumper sticker & instructional booklet.

I'm Not Crazy, I'm Vocalizing: Singing Exercises in or Out of Your Car. 2nd rev. ed. 1 cass. Orig. Title: I'm Not Crazy, I'm Singercising!. 1991. 15.95 Incl. bklt. (1214-41); audio compact disk 19.95 CD Incl. bklt. (1214-41) VoiceTech WA.
Singing exercise warm-up kit includes bumper sticker that declares "I'm Not Crazy, I'm Vocalizing". Booklet contains information about voice development & care plus lead sheet for each exercise.

I'm Not in the Mood Set: What Every Woman Should Know about Improving Her Libido. abr. ed. Judith Reichman. Read by Judith Reichman. 2 cass. (Running Time: 180 min.). 1998. 17.95 (978-1-55935-293-2(0)) Soundelux.
Reveals how small doses of testosterone can dramatically revive sexual desire & pleasure in women. Offers answers to many sexuality-related questions for women, from the medical correspondent for "The Today Show.".

I'm Not Ok! Is It Just Me? Like New & Somewhat Improved. unabr. ed. Ken Davis. Narrated by Ken Davis. (Running Time: 9000 sec.). (ENG.). 2006. audio compact disk 12.99 (978-1-59859-128-6(2)) Oasis Audio.

I'm Not Okay! Ken Davis. 1 cass. (Running Time: 1 hr. 30 min.). 2000. 9.99 (978-1-886463-91-2(3)) Oasis Audio.
Hilarious stories & observations make for some of the best comedy you've ever experienced & it's all wrapped up in a message of hope that can change your life forever.

I'm Not Okay/ Is It Just Me. unabr. ed. Ken Davis. Narrated by Ken Davis. (ENG.). 2006. 9.09 (978-1-60814-253-8(1)) Oasis Audio.

I'm off to Montana for to Throw the Hoolihan. abr. ed. Stephen A. Bly. 2 cass. (Running Time: 3 hrs.). (Code of the West Ser.: No. 6). 2001. 17.99 (978-1-58926-016-0(3)) Oasis Audio.
Tap Andrews is no longer an escaped fugitive. Or a lawman backing down a mob. Or a brand inspector dodging rustlers' ambushes. He's a rancher and family man, moving his very pregnant wift and their eleven-year-old ward to a new life in Montana.

I'm off to Montana for to Throw the Hoolihan. unabr. ed. Stephen A. Bly. Read by Jerry Sciarrio. 6 CDs. (Running Time: 6 hrs. 30 min.). 2001. audio compact disk 39.00 (978-1-58116-124-3(7)) Books in Motion.
Tap and a very expecting Pepper set out for a new life on the Slash-Bar-4 in Montana. But outlaws, and a possible range war, force Tap to use his gun skills, and at the same time, to strengthen his trust in God.

I'm off to Montana for to Throw the Hoolihan. unabr. ed. Stephen A. Bly. Read by Jerry Sciarrio. 6 cass. (Running Time: 6 hrs. 30 min.). (Code of the West Ser.: No. 6). 2001. 39.95 (978-1-58116-104-5(2)) Books in Motion.

I'm OK but You Need Professional Help! David Granirer. 1 cass. (Running Time: 65 min.). 1999. 10.95 (978-0-9641310-0-2(5)) Tune-In Counsel.
Laugh your way to sanity with Psychotherapist/Stand-up Comic David Granirer's routine satirizing therapy, personal growth, spirituality, & the New Age. Also included is a keynote presentation on how laughter reduces stress, & increases wellness & personal empowerment.

I'm OK, You're Not, A Journey in Personal Discovery. James Tippett. Read by James Tippett. Tipson Enterprises. (ENG.). 2009. 32.00 (978-0-9822181-0-5(9)) Tipson Ent.

I'm on a Mission (Cassette) Compiled by Sunday School Publishing Board. (J). 2006. 7.95 (978-1-932972-55-9(2)) Townsnd-Pr.

I'm on a Mission (CD) Compiled by Sunday School Publishing Board. (J). 2006. audio compact disk 13.95 (978-1-932972-54-2(4)) Townsnd-Pr.

I'm on the Potty. Fritzie Locke. 1 cass. (Running Time: 30 min.). (J). 2003. 7.95 (978-0-9650258-0-5(2), Persnickety Pr) Pub: DBP & Assocs. Dist(s): Penton Overseas
A delightful collection of 14 sing along songs set to classic Nursery Rhyme melodies. A fun & entertaining approach to the often stressful experience, for both child & parent, of potty training. The use of repetitive lyrics & recognizable melodies make a positive connection between the child & the training process. Includes progress chart & stickers.

I'm Only a Man. Contrib. by Emery. Prod. by Matt Boesch & Matt Carter. 2007. 18.99 (978-5-557-59281-9(4)) Tooth & Nail.

I'm Only a Man. Contrib. by Emery. Prod. by Ryan Boesch & Matt Carter. 2007. audio compact disk 13.99 (978-5-557-59282-6(2)) Tooth & Nail.

I'm Only Afraid of the Dark at Night see Hug Me & Other Stories

I'm Reading...All by Myself! 1 cass. (J). (ps-2). 1982. 12.95 (978-0-88679-249-7(5)) Educ Insights.

I'm Rich. Contrib. by Gold City. (Soundtraks Ser.). 2007. audio compact disk 8.99 (978-5-557-56224-9(9)) Christian Wrld.

I'm Sorry I Haven't a Clue: The Award-Winning BBC Radio Comedy. unabr. ed. Created by Humphrey Lyttelton. Narrated by Full Cast. (Running Time: 2 hrs. 0 mins. 0 sec.). (ENG.). 2010. audio compact disk 24.95 (978-1-60283-842-0(9)) Pub: AudioGO. Dist(s): Perseus Dist

***I'm Sorry I Haven't a Clue Two Vol. 2: The Award-Winning BBC Radio Comedy.** Told to Humphrey Lyttelton. 2 CDs. (Running Time: 1 hr. 50 mins. 0 sec.). 2010. audio compact disk 24.95 (978-0-563-52969-9(5)) Pub: AudioGO. Dist(s): Perseus Dist

I'm Still Here. Perf. by Highway QCs. 1 cass. 1997. 10.98 (978-1-57908-171-3(1), 1288) Platinm Enter.

***I'm Still Here in the Bathtub: Brand New Silly Dilly Songs: Brand New Silly Dilly Songs.** unabr. ed. Alan Katz. (Running Time: 1 hr.). (J). 2010. audio compact disk 9.99 (978-1-4418-5939-6(X), 9781441859396, Bril Audio CD Unabri) Brilliance Audio.

***I'm Still Here in the Bathtub: Brand New Silly Dilly Songs: Brand New Silly Dilly Songs.** unabr. ed. Alan Katz. (Running Time: 1 hr.). 2010. 4.99 (978-1-4418-5941-9(1), 9781441859419, BAD); 19.97 (978-1-4418-5942-6(X), 9781441859426, BADLE); audio compact disk 19.97 (978-1-4418-5940-2(3), 9781441859402, BriAudCD Unabrid) Brilliance Audio.

I'm Still Standing: From Captive U. S. Soldier to Free Citizen - My Journey Home. unabr. ed. Shoshana Johnson. (Running Time: 9 hrs. 30 mins.). 2010. 29.95 (978-1-4417-2906-4(2)); 59.95 (978-1-4417-2902-6(X)); audio compact disk 29.95 (978-1-4417-2905-7(4)); audio compact disk 90.00 (978-1-4417-2903-3(8)) Blckstn Audio.

I'm Tired of the Pain: A Guide for Peace. Joseph Bordes-Kohn, Sr. (ENG.). 2008. 15.95 (978-0-9766654-0-3(9), Now I See) Now I See & Assocs.

I'm Too Big. Lone Morton & Mary Risk. 1 cass. (Running Time: 20 min.). (I Can Read Bks.).Tr. of Je Suis Mucho Grande. (ENG & FRE., (J). (ps up). 1998. pap. bk. 9.95 (978-0-7641-7189-5(5)) Barron.
Repeats every word of the bilingual text in both languages so that children can hear exactly how the words sound.

I'm Too Big. Lone Morton & Mary Risk. 1 cass. (Running Time: 20 min.). (I Can Read Bks.).Tr. of Je Suis Mucho Grande. (ENG & SPA., (J). (ps up). 1998. 9.95 (978-0-7641-7193-2(3)) Barron.

I'm Too Busy to Talk Now. 1 cass. Incl. Balladeer Burl Ives. Interview with Burl Ives. (1722); Composer John Cage. Interview with John M. Cage. (1722); (Conversations with American Artists Over 70 Series). 12.95 (1722); 12.95 (1723); 12.95 (1726) J Norton Pubs.
Discover what the creative life means to an older person & how aging can nourish creativity. The artists tell how they overcame career frustrations & personal tragedies & talk about the sources of their artistic inspiration.

I'm Too Busy to Talk Now. unabr. ed. 1 cass. Incl. I'm Too Busy to Talk Now: Artist Alice Neel. Interview with Alice Neel. (1724); I'm Too Busy to Talk Now: Artist Louise Nevelson. Interview with Louise Nevelson. (1724); (Conversations with American Artists Over 70 Series). 12.95 (1724) J Norton Pubs.

I'm Too Busy to Talk Now: Artist Alice Neel see I'm Too Busy to Talk Now

I'm Too Busy to Talk Now: Artist Louise Nevelson see I'm Too Busy to Talk Now

I'm Too Busy to Talk Now: Conversations with American Artists Over 70. unabr. ed. 6 cass. 55.00 Set. (S1720) J Norton Pubs.

I'm Too Busy to Talk Now: Conversations with American Artists Over 70 Series. unabr. ed. 1 cass. Incl. Poet Josephine Miles. Interview with Josephine Miles. (1721); Poet Stanley Kunitz. Interview with Stanley Kunitz. (1721); 12.95 (1721) J Norton Pubs.

I'm Too Fond of My Fur Bks. 4-6: Four Mice Deep in the Jungle - Paws Off, Cheddarface! unabr. ed. Geronimo Stilton. Read by Edward Herrmann. 3 CDs. (Running Time: 3 hrs.). (ENG.). (J). (gr. 1). 2005. audio compact disk 25.00 (978-0-307-20639-8(4), ImaginStudio) Pub: Random Audio Pubg. Dist(s): Random

I'm Your Friend & My Name Is Spinoza. unabr. ed. Read by Peter Himmelman. Perf. by Peter Himmelman. 1 cass. (Running Time: 30 min.). Dramatization. (J). 1984. 8.95 (978-1-58452-010-8(8), 4390); 8.95 Spanish version. (978-1-58452-019-1(1), 5390) Spinoza Co.

Image: A Guide to Pseudo-Events in America. unabr. ed. Daniel J. Boorstin. Read by Frederick Davidson. 7 cass. (Running Time: 10 hrs.). 1993. 49.95 (978-0-7861-0449-9(X), 1401) Blckstn Audio.
First published in 1962, this wonderfully provocative book introduced the notion of "pseudo-events" - events such as press conferences & presidential debates, which are manufactured solely in order to be reported - & the contemporary definition of celebrity as "a person who is known for his well-knownness." Since then Daniel J. Boorstin's prophetic vision of an America inundated by its own illusions has become essential for any reader who wants to distinguish the manifold deceptions of our culture from its few enduring truths.

Image & Reality. Aldous Huxley. 1 cass. 1999. 11.00 (01129) Big Sur Tapes.
1961 Radio Interview.

Image & Reality of the Child Conference. 7 cass. (Running Time: 10 hrs. 30 min.). 1990. 64.95 Set. (978-0-7822-0006-5(0), IRC) C G Jung IL.

Image & Self-Projection. Julie White. 4 cass. (Running Time: 3 hrs. 53 min.). 49.95 CareerTrack Pubns.
Discusses the secrets behind the professional style & personal power of today's most successful women.

Image & Self-Projection for Women: How to Come Across As the Capable, Confident Professional You Are. Julie White. 4 cass. (Running Time: 4 hrs. 16 min.). 49.95 Set incl. 24p. wkbk. (V10147) CareerTrack Pubns.
If you're like many professional women, you're running so hard to keep up, you sometimes forget to look where you're going. This program gives you the chance to put yourself back on track. Consider it a crucial investment in your confidence, your motivation & your career.

Image Management Systems in Pharmaceutical Applications: Image Processing System for Pharmaceutical R&D. 1 cass. 1990. 8.50 Recorded Res.

Image of Conspiracy: A Mystery Adventure. abr. ed. Margo Power. 2 cass. (Running Time: 120 min.). 1999. 10.95 (978-1-894188-03-6(9)) APG.

Image of God: Psalm 8:4-6. Ed Young. 1990. Rental 4.95 (978-0-7417-1828-0(6), 828) Win Walk.

Image-of-God Genetics. Jonathan Murro. 1 cass. 1990. 7.95 A R Colton Fnd.

Image of God in You. Kenneth Copeland. 6 cass. 1982. bk. 30.00 Set incl. study guide. (978-0-938458-24-1(8)) K Copeland Pubns.
Biblical study on changing your self-image.

Image of Mary. Short Stories. Perf. by Myranda Summers. As told by David Lee Summers. 1 CD. (Running Time: 57 mins). 2003. audio compact disk 6.95 (978-1-885093-32-5(2)) Hadrosaur Pr.

Image of the New Age. Swami Amar Jyoti. 1 cass. 1987. 9.95 (K-88) Truth Consciousness.
What will the new age be like; something totally new or a big jump in evolution? Conscious living. Removing the impositions to hear the voice of God.

Imager. L. E. Modesitt, Jr. Read by William Dufris. (Imager Portfolio Ser.: Bk. 1). 2009. 89.99 (978-1-60847-917-7(X)) Find a World.

Imager. unabr. ed. L. E. Modesitt, Jr. Narrated by William Dufris. 2 MP3-CDs. (Running Time: 18 hrs. 0 mins. 0 sec.). (Imager Portfolio Ser.: Bk. 1). (ENG.). 2009. audio compact disk 34.99 (978-1-4001-6180-5(0)); audio compact disk 99.99 (978-1-4001-4180-7(X)); audio compact disk 49.99 (978-1-4001-1180-0(3)) Pub: Tantor Media. Dist(s): IngramPubServ

Imager's Challenge. unabr. ed. L. E. Modesitt, Jr. Narrated by William Dufris. (Running Time: 18 hrs. 30 mins. 0 sec.). (Imager Portfolio Ser.: Bk. 2). (ENG.). 2009. 34.99 (978-1-4001-6181-2(9)); audio compact disk 49.99 (978-1-4001-1181-7(1)); audio compact disk 99.99 (978-1-4001-4181-4(8)) Pub: Tantor Media. Dist(s): IngramPubServ

***Imager's Challenge.** unabr. ed. L. E. Modesitt, Jr. Narrated by William Dufris. (Running Time: 18 hrs. 30 mins.). (Imager Portfolio Ser.: Bk. 2). 2009. 22.99 (978-1-4001-8181-0(X)) Tantor Media.

***Imager's Intrigue.** unabr. ed. L. E. Modesitt, Jr. (Running Time: 18 hrs. 0 mins.). (Imager Portfolio Ser.: Bk. 3). 2010. 49.99 (978-1-4001-9182-6(3)); 22.99 (978-1-4001-8182-7(8)) Tantor Media.

***Imager's Intrigue.** unabr. ed. L. E. Modesitt, Jr. Narrated by William Dufris. (Running Time: 22 hrs. 30 mins. 0 sec.). (Imager Portfolio Ser.: Bk. 3). 2010. 34.99 (978-1-4001-6182-9(7)); audio compact disk 95.99 (978-1-4001-4182-1(6)); audio compact disk 49.99 (978-1-4001-1182-4(X)) Pub: Tantor Media. Dist(s): IngramPubServ

Images of Christ: A Celebration. Crossroads Staff. 1996. 7.95 (978-0-8245-1570-6(6)) Pub: Crossroad NY. Dist(s): IPG Chicago

Images of Initiation. James Hillman et al. Read by James Hillman et al. Ed. by Richard Chelew. 2 cass. (Running Time: 2 hrs. 45 min.). 1992. 19.95 Bookpack, set. (978-1-880155-05-9(2), OTA 105) Oral Trad Arch.
Stories, poems, & song punctuate straight-talk dialogue between author/psychologist James Hillman, mythologist/storyteller Michael Meade, & initiated West African tribesman Malidoma Some as they work together to connect our lost rituals of initiation to the crises that modern men & modern culture face today.

Images of Life: Stories As Portraits of Human Development Vol. 1: Childhood. Lois Khan. Read by Lois Khan. 10 cass. (Running Time: 14 hrs.). 1994. 66.95 (978-0-7822-0442-1(2), 520) C G Jung IL.
Using myth, folktales, legends, & fairy tales, Lois Khan's three-volume course examines stages of development from child to adult through the psychological tasks these stories present to us.

Images of Life: Stories As Portraits of Human Development Vol. 2: Adolescence. Lois Khan. Read by Lois Khan. 9 cass. (Running Time: 12 hrs. 20 min.). 1994. 61.95 (978-0-7822-0460-5(0), 537) C G Jung IL.

Images of Life: Stories As Portraits of Human Development Vol. 3: Adulthood. Lois Khan. Read by Lois Khan. 9 cass. (Running Time: 13 hrs.). 1994. 61.95 (978-0-7822-0465-0(1), 542) C G Jung IL.
The third & final part of Jungian analyst Lois Khan's course examines the psychology of adulthood through fairy tales & other stories. Khan explores how adults actualize the lessons of earlier phases of life: caretaking, claiming one's power, & enriching the life of the family, nation, & world at large - politically, ecologically, & spirtually.

Images of the Self in Dreams. Read by Diane Martin. 2 cass. (Running Time: 2 hrs. 30 min.). 1988. 18.95 Set. (978-0-7822-0158-1(X), 345) C G Jung IL.

Imaginable Future. Bill Gates. 1 cass. (Running Time: 58 mins.). 2001. 12.95 Smithson Assocs.

Imaginary Conversations see Cambridge Treasury of English Prose: Austen to Bronte

Imaginary Invalid. unabr. ed. Molière. Perf. by Molly Bryant et al. Tr. by John Wood from FRE. 1 cass. (Running Time: 1 hrs. 32 min.). 1997. 19.95 (978-1-58081-114-9(0), TPT107) L A Theatre.
France's master comic playwright has a field day with the subjects of hypochondria & our blind obedience to doctors. Moliere's witty attack on the medical profession has more than a little resonance today.

***Imaginary Jesus: A Not-Quite True Story.** unabr. ed. Matt Mikalatos. (Running Time: 5 hrs. 45 mins. 0 sec.). (ENG.). 2010. audio compact disk 21.98 (978-1-59644-249-8(2), christaudio) christianaud.

***Imaginary Jesus: A Not-Quite True Story.** unabr. ed. Matt Mikalatos. (Yasmin Peace Ser.). (ENG.). 2010. 12.98 (978-1-59644-250-4(6), christaudio) christianaud.

Imaginary Journey. Diane Snowball. Perf. by Mark Vineis. Illus. by Randy Glusac et al. (J). (gr. 1-7). 10.95 (978-1-879531-55-0(0)) Mondo Pubng.

Imaginary Window. Perf. by Jack Grunsky. 1 cass. (J). (gr. 4 up). 10.98 (YM031-CN); lp 12.98 (YM031-R); audio compact disk 13.98 (YM031-CD) Youngheart Mus.
Songs include: "Hot Hot Hot"; "Victoria Village School"; "My Window"; "The Lion Sleeps Tonight"; "The Lion's Yawn"; "The Tutor"; "The Bamboo Flute"; "Bamboo"; "Our School Rap"; "Listen"; "Land of the Silver Birch" & more.

Imaginate. 2nd ed. Chastain. 1 cass. stu. ed. 12.75 (978-0-8384-2081-2(8)) Heinle.

Imaginate. 3rd ed. Chastain & Guntermann. (SPA.). (C). 2001. pap. bk. 40.00 (978-0-8384-1645-7(4)) Heinle.

Imagination. Neville Goddard. 1 cass. (Running Time: 62 min.). 1969. 8.00 (58) J & L Pubns.
Neville taught Imagination Creates Reality. He was a powerfully influential teacher of God as Consciousness.

Imagination: Program from the Award Winning Public Radio Series. Interview. Hosted by Fred Goodwin. Comment by John Hockenberry. 1 CD. (Running Time: 1 hr.). (Infinite Mind Ser.). 2001. audio compact disk 10.00 (978-1-888064-65-0(X), LCM 193) Lichtenstein Creat.
In this hour, we explore Imagination. A great new job, a bigger home, a romantic evening. We all conjure up possibilities in our minds. But just what is imagination? Guests include Dr. Jerome Singer, a professor of psychology at Yale University and one of the pioneers in the study of imagination; Dr. Alan Leslie, professor of psychology and director of the Cognitive Development Laboratory at Rutgers University; Dr. Paul Harris, developmental psychologist and professor at the Harvard Graduate School of Education and author of The Work of the Imagination; Dr. Marjorie Taylor, professor of psychology at the University of Oregon and author of Imaginary Companions and the Children Who Create Them; and children's book writer and artist Maira Kalman.

Imagination & Science, East & West. Robert Thurman & Arthur Zajonc. 5 cass. 45.00 (OC150) Sound Horizons AV.

Imagination Cruise. Read by Chris Holder. (J). 1999. audio compact disk 14.95 (978-0-939065-87-5(8)) Gentle Wind.

Imagination Cruise. Read by Chris Holder. 1 cass. (Running Time: 50 min.). (J). (gr. 2-6). 1987. 9.95 (978-0-939065-39-4(8), GW 1043) Gentle Wind.
Visit a spider, bee & frog talking in a field, travel the Erie Canal & meet a wizard.

Imagination of Class: Masculinity & the Victorian Urban Poor. Daniel Bivona & Roger B. Henkle. 2006. audio compact disk 9.95 (978-0-8142-9096-5(5)) Pub: Ohio St U Pr. Dist(s): Chicago Distribution Ctr

Imagination Theatre: Bauman & the Box. Jim French. 1 CD. (Running Time: 1 hr.). 2001. audio compact disk 12.95 (ITCD094) Lodestone Catalog.
Harry Anderson stars as a magician with a new trick. The Haunted Plumbing of Harold Poole: Murder isn't always the answer.

Imagination Theatre: Sherlock Holmes' Adventure of the Blind Man. Jim French. 1 CD. (Running Time: 1 hr.). 2001. audio compact disk 12.95 (ITCD135) Lodestone Catalog.
New Holmes? It's true! The Unmasking: Ever felt you've known someone before? It can happen.

Imagination Theatre: The Bouganville Giant. Jim French. 1 CD. (Running Time: 1 hr.). 2001. audio compact disk 12.95 (ITCD008) Lodestone Catalog.
An inactive volcano houses giant moths. Nightmare: Afraid of heights? A Skydiver dreams his 'chute won't open.

Imagination Theatre: The Procedure. Jim French. 1 CD. (Running Time: 1 hr.). 2001. audio compact disk 12.95 (ITCD030) Lodestone Catalog.
A plastic surgeon must disguise an alien as a human. The Door of Lotim: An archaeologist buys an artifact that send him elsewhere!.

Imagination Theatre: The Thing in the Woods. Jim French. 1 CD. (Running Time: 1 hr.). 2001. audio compact disk 12.95 (ITCD123) Lodestone Catalog.
Post-WW III invasions have nothing on this unknown terror.The House on Brookside Lane: A million bucks for a house where two were killed.

Imagination Theatre: Trial at Wolftrap. Jim French. 1 CD. (Running Time: 1 hr.). 2001. audio compact disk 12.95 (ITCD088) Lodestone Catalog.
Patty Duke & John Astin, stranded in Canadian wilderness. Lesser of Two Evils: The doctor of a famous mob boss faces a decision.

Imagination vs. Reason: William Blake's Dilemma. Read by June Singer. 1 cass. (Running Time: 1 hr.). 1986. 9.95 (978-0-7822-0261-8(6), 221) C G Jung IL.

Imagination Your Only Creative Faculty. George King. 2006. audio compact disk (978-0-937249-25-3(4)) Aetherius Soc.

Imaginative Experience. unabr. ed. Mary Wesley. Read by Samuel West. 6 cass. (Running Time: 9 hrs.). 2000. 49.95 (978-0-7451-4383-5(0), CAB 1067) Pub: Chivers Audio Bks GBR. Dist(s): AudioGO
A traveler on a London train sees the train stop on the countryside, and a white-faced woman leap off to help a sheep stranded on his back. When she turns back towards the train, he sees her face is full of tragedy. Considering tragedies of his own, he recognizes hers: a strange but familiar despair, unable to ignore the desperation in others.

Imaginative Life see Poetry of Geoffrey

Imaginative Woman see Thomas Hardy: Selected Short Stories

Imagine Hearing the Goddess Prophecies: The Last Princess & the Cup of Immortality. Executive Producer D. R. Whitney. Based on a book by D. R. Whitney. Therese McLaughlin et al. Executive Producer James Whitney. Engineer Chris Hastings. (ENG.). (YA). 2009. 69.95 (978-0-9822508-1-5(9)) Isle of Avln.

Imagine No Religions. Stephen F. Uhl. Based on a book by Stephen F. Uhl. 2008. 3.95 (978-0-9793169-1-3(X)) Golden Rule AZ.

Imagine That: Intelligent Songs for Kids. (Running Time: 40 min.). (J). (ps-3). 1996. 11.00; audio compact disk 16.00 CD. Monty Harper.
Song recordings are intelligent & creative.

***Imagine This.** Featuring The cast of the London Production of Imagine This. 2010. audio compact disk 18.98 (978-1-60883-217-0(1)) PublicMedia.

Imagine Yourself Slim. 1 cassette. (Running Time: 76:21 mins.). 1980. 12.95 (978-1-55841-019-0(8)) Emmett E Miller.
Four experiences teach you how to relax thoroughly, create the positive image you want your body to achieve and visualize the pounds falling away. Imprint this image in your deeper mind, where eating behavior begins. A new way to enjoy food and reward yourself. A perfect companion to any exercise/dietary plan.

Imagine Yourself Slim. 1 CD. 1980. audio compact disk 16.95 (978-1-55841-111-1(9)) Emmett E Miller.
Four experiences teach you how to relax thoroughly, crete the positive image you want your body to achieve and visualize the pounds falling away. Imprint this image in your deeper mind, where eating behavior begins. A new way to enjoy food and reward yourself. A perfgect companion to any exercise/dietary plan.

Imagine Yourself to Sleep Vol.1: A Getting to Sleep Tape for Kids. Bett Sanders & Chuck Cummings. 1 cass. (Be a Bird & Fly & Be a Ball & Bounce Ser.). (J). (ps-5). 1988. 9.98 (978-0-9620824-1-2(4)) Audio Outings.
Uses guided imagery & soothing nature sounds to help children ease into sleep while cultivating their imagination.

Imagine Yourself to Sleep Vol.2: Guided Imagery & Nature Sounds for Kids (Be a Horse-Be a Cat) Bett Sanders & Chuck Cummings. Read by Bett Sanders & Chuck Cummings. 1 cass. (Running Time: 1 hr.). (J). (ps-5). 1990. 9.98 (978-0-9620824-2-9(2), AO 20C) Audio Outings.
Two psychologists offer a delightful & soothing way for children to get to sleep - guided imagery & nature sounds. Helps reduce stress.

Imagined Environment & Releasing Stress & Pain. Patricia Yu & Diane Harlowe. Read by Patricia Yu. 1 cass. (Running Time: 22 min.). 1984. 9.95 (978-1-877950-03-2(3)) Uncharted Ctry Pub.
A relaxation tape using imagery. "Imagine a place that's just the way you want it to be. Let pain wash away, feeling refreshed & renewed".

Imagineering. Michael Leboeuf. 2004. 7.95 (978-0-7435-4863-2(9)) Pub: S&S Audio. Dist(s): S and S Inc

Imaging. Barrie Konicov. 1 cass. 11.98 (978-0-87082-435-7(X), 071) Potentials.
Close your eyes & create the image of your world coming to light. Imagine, picture & even dream in color.

Imaging. Barrie Konicov. 1 CD. 2004. audio compact disk 19.98 (978-1-56001-669-4(8)) Potentials.
In every self-improvement book, you are told to imagine, imagine, imagine. Close your eyes and create the image of your world coming to light. You will find the self-hypnosis on track 1 and the subliminal on track 2. The easy-listening music of the subliminal, together with the self-hypnosis, is the original format which most people love and with which they are most familiar.

Imaging for Fine Art & Salon Photography: OCR for Automatic Indexing of Large Image Databases. 1 cass. 1990. 8.50 Recorded Res.

Imaging in Obstetrics & Gynecology. Contrib. by John W. Seeds et al. 1 cass. (American College of Obstetrics & Gynecologists UPDATE: Vol. 23, No. 2). 1998. 20.00 Am Coll Obstetric.

Imagining Don Giovanni. unabr. ed. Anthony J. Rudel. 6 cass. (Running Time: 9 hrs.). 2001. 24.00 (978-1-57511-099-8(7)) Pub Mills.
In October 1787 Giacomo Casanova and Wolfgang Mozart are believed to have met in a Prague coffeehouse to discuss a new opera based on the life of Don Juan. From this minor episode, Anthony Rudel has spun a tale in which the two, along with the poet Lorenzo Da Ponte, work to complete the operatic masterpiece.

***Imam's Daughter: My Desperate Flight to Freedom.** Hannah Shah. (Running Time: 6 hrs. 52 mins. 11 sec.). (ENG.). 2010. 14.99 (978-0-310-32576-5(5)) Zondervan.

Imhotep: Developing Your Talents. Gwendolyn J. Crenshaw & Aesop Enterprise Inc. Staff. 1 cass. (Heroes & Sheroes Ser.). (J). (gr. 3-12). 1991. (978-1-880771-07-5(1)) AESOP Enter.

Imitatio Christi see Imitation of Christ

Imitation in Death. abr. ed. J. D. Robb, pseud. Read by Susan Ericksen. (Running Time: 21600 sec.). (In Death Ser.). 2007. audio compact disk 14.99 (978-1-4233-1760-9(2), 9781423317609, BCD Value Price) Brilliance Audio.

Imitation in Death. unabr. ed. J. D. Robb, pseud. Narrated by Susan Ericksen. 8 cass. (Running Time: 11 hrs.). (In Death Ser.). 2003. 30.95 (978-1-59086-723-5(8), 1590867238, BAU) Brilliance Audio.

Imitation in Death. unabr. ed. J. D. Robb, pseud. Read by Susan Ericksen. 7 cass. (Running Time: 11 hrs.). (In Death Ser.). 2003. 87.25 (978-1-59086-724-2(6), 1590867246) Brilliance Audio.

Imitation in Death. unabr. ed. J. D. Robb, pseud. Read by Susan Ericksen. (Running Time: 11 hrs.). (In Death Ser.). 2004. 39.25 (978-1-59335-613-2(7), 1593356137, Brlnc Audio MP3 Lib) Brilliance Audio.
Summer, 2059. A man wearing a cape and a top hat approaches a prostitute on a dark, New York City street. Minutes later, the woman is dead. Left at the scene is a letter addressed to Lieutenant Eve Dallas, inviting her to play his game and unveil his identity. He signs it, "Jack." Now Dallas is in pursuit of a murderer who knows as much about the history of serial killers as she does. He has studied the most notorious and the most vicious slayings in modern times. But he also wants to make his own mark. He has chosen his victim: Eve Dallas. And all Eve knows is that he plans to mimic the most infamous murderers of all - starting with Jack the Ripper... "Robb's energetic prose and hard-edged dialogue will keep readers engrossed." -Publishers Weekly "Edgy and raw." -Booklist.

Imitation in Death. unabr. ed. J. D. Robb, pseud. Read by Susan Ericksen. (Running Time: 11 hrs.). (In Death Ser.). 2004. 39.25 (978-1-59710-393-0(4), 1597103934, BADLE); 24.95 (978-1-59710-392-3(6), 1597103926, BAD) Brilliance Audio.

Imitation in Death. unabr. ed. J. D. Robb, pseud. Read by Susan Ericksen. (Running Time: 39600 sec.). (In Death Ser.). 2007. audio compact disk 36.95 (978-1-4233-1757-9(2), 9781423317579, Bril Audio CD Unabri); audio compact disk 102.25 (978-1-4233-1758-6(0), 9781423317586, BriAudCD Unabrid) Brilliance Audio.

Imitation in Death. unabr. ed. J. D. Robb, pseud. Read by Susan Ericksen. (Running Time: 11 hrs.). (In Death Ser.). 2004. 24.95 (978-1-59335-223-3(9), 1593352239) Soulmate Audio Bks.

Imitation of Christ. Thomas à Kempis. 6 cass. (Running Time: 9 hrs.). 1994. 14.95 (978-0-89942-325-8(6), 325/00) Cathlic Bk Pub.

Imitation of Christ. Thomas à Kempis. Read by Al Covaia. Tr. by Paul Zomberg. 6 cass. 1987. 24.95 Set. (927-C) Ignatius Pr.

Imitation of Christ. Thomas à Kempis. 1. 2005. 7.00 (978-0-9772747-1-0(3)) Tree City.

Imitation of Christ. Thomas à Kempis.Tr. of Imitatio Christi. (ENG.). 2008. 19.99 (978-1-4245-0812-9(6)) Tre Med Inc.

***Imitation of Christ.** Thomas à Kempis. Read by Joe McClane.Tr. of De Imitatio Christi. (ENG.). 2010. audio compact disk 19.95 (978-1-936231-05-8(0)) Cath Audio.

Imitation of Christ. unabr. ed. Thomas A. Kempis. Narrated by David Cochran Heath. 1 MP3CD. (Running Time: 6 hrs. 6 mins. 0 sec.).Tr. of Imitatio Christi. (ENG.). 2004. lp 19.98 (978-1-59644-021-0(X), Hovel Audio) christianaud.
Thomas A. Kempis' collection of meditative writings from the Bretheren of the Common Life is the most widely read book in the world after the Bible. The reflective devotions have been a heartening friend to great men such as Thomas More, St. Ignatius Loyola, Thomas Merton, Pope John Paul I, and John Wesley. Learning to live live Jesus is the central task that A. Kempis explores in this classic devotional. This book provides comfort and counsel to every person who seeks to live a more connected and whole life.

***Imitation of Christ.** unabr. ed. Thomas A. Kempis. Narrated by David Cochran Heath. (Running Time: 6 hrs. 6 mins. 0 sec.). (ENG.). 2004. 14.98 (978-1-59644-022-7(8), Hovel Audio) christianaud.

Imitation of Christ. unabr. ed. Thomas à Kempis. 5 CDs. (Running Time: 6 hrs. 6 mins. 0 sec.). (Mystics Ser.).Tr. of Imitatio Christi. (ENG.). 2004. audio compact disk 23.98 (978-1-59644-020-3(1), Hovel Audio) christianaud.
Thomas A. Kempis' collection of meditative writings from the Bretheren of the Common Life is the most widely read book in the world after the Bible. The reflective devotions have been a heartening friend to great men such as Thomas More, St. Ignatius Loyola, Thomas Merton, Pope John Paul I, and John Wesley. Learning to live live Jesus is the central task that A. Kempis explores in this classic devotional. This book provides comfort and counsel to every person who seeks to live a more connected and whole life.

Imitation of Christ, Set. unabr. ed. Thomas à Kempis. Read by Robert L. Halvorson. 6 cass. (Running Time: 540 min.). 42.95 (91) Halvorson Assocs.

Immanuel: An Advent Collection. Created by Marty Parks. 2007. audio compact disk 10.00 (978-5-557-69908-2(2)); audio compact disk 59.99 (978-5-557-63279-9(4)) Lillenas.

Immanuel: John 1:14. Ed Young. 1996. 4.95 (978-0-7417-2126-6(0), 1126) Win Walk.

***Immanuel: Praying the Names of God through the Christmas Season.** unabr. ed. Ann Spangler. (Running Time: 2 hrs. 14 mins. 0 sec.). (ENG.). 2009. 14.99 (978-0-310-77203-3(6)) Zondervan.

***Immanuel: The Deity of the Messiah.** Chuck Missler & Mark Eastman. (ENG.). 2009. audio compact disk 19.95 (978-1-57821-441-9(6)) Koinonia Hse.

Immanuel: The Transcendent Nature & Deity of Messiah. Chuck Missler & Mark Eastman. 2 cass. (Running Time: 2.5 hours). (Creator Ser.). 1996. vinyl bd. 14.95 Set, incl. study notes. (978-1-880532-36-2(0)) Koinonia Hse.
** Why do we believe that Jesus is the Messiah? * What is the probability that even 8 of the messianic prophecies in the Old Testament would be fulfilled in one man?* Do both the Old and New Testaments claim the deity of the Messiah?As part of their recent series on The Creator Beyond Time and Space, Chuck Missler and Dr. Mark Eastman explore the historical evidence, claims, attributes, and authentication of Immanuel - God with us.*

Immanuel Kant: Germany (1724-1804) A. J. Mandt. Read by Charlton Heston. Ed. by George H. Smith & Wendy McElroy. 2 cass. (Running Time: 3 hrs.). (Giants of Philosophy Ser.). 1995. 17.95 (978-0-938935-23-0(2), 10307) Pub: Knowledge Prod. Dist(s): APG
Kant believed that reason, the most fundamental human faculty, creates a world where all events are casually connected; it enables us to act morally, to enjoy beauty & to appreciate nature's magnificence. Kant forecast the possibility of a purely rational religion & believed that the international rule of reason might lead to permanent peace.

Immanuel Kant: Germany (1724-1804) abr. ed. Narrated by Charlton Heston. (Running Time: 8268 sec.). (Audio Classics: the Giants of Philosophy Ser.). 2006. audio compact disk 25.95 (978-0-7861-6943-6(5)) Pub: Blckstn Audio. Dist(s): NetLibrary CO

Immanuel Kant: Germany (1724-1804), Set. unabr. ed. Read by Charlton Heston. 2 cass. (Giants of Philosophy Ser.). 17.95 (K123) Blckstn Audio.
See how one of the world's most important philosophers created a complete system of thought, including his views on ethics, metaphysics, politics & aesthetics. Learn about his epistemology - how we know what we know.

Immanuel Kant's Gimmick. unabr. ed. Adam Mossoff. 1 cass. (Running Time: 1 hrs. 40 min.). 1998. 12.95 (978-1-56114-314-6(6), CM50C) Second Renaissance.
Presents the philosophic context in which Kant's subversion of reason arose.

Immanuel Velikovsky: Cosmos Of Catastrophe. 1 cass. (Running Time: 1 hr.). 14.95 (CBC582) MMI Corp.
Covers the fight between "science & scientism".

***Immanuel's Veins.** unabr. ed. Ted Dekker. 2010. audio compact disk 29.99 (978-1-4003-1674-8(X)) Nelson.

Immediate Action: The True Story of His Life in the SAS. unabr. ed. Andy McNab. Read by Steven Pacey. 12 cass. (Running Time: 12 hrs.). 1996. 96.95 Set. (978-0-7451-6671-1(7), CAB 1287) AudioGO.
This is the extraordinary account of Andy McNab's life, from his days as a young soldier fighting the IRA, to his stint as a member of the world's most highly trained Special Forces Unit. Told with grim humor & riveting detail, McNab sweeps us into a blistering first-hand account of life at the edge of the battle.

Immediate Breast Reconstruction. 2 cass. (Plastic & Maxillofacial Surgery Ser.: C85-PL2). 1985. 15.00 (8581) Am Coll Surgeons.

Immediate Inference, Validity, Euler Circles - Logic & Theology: Empirical Apologetics. John Robbins. 1 cass. (Introduction to Logic Ser.: No. 6). 5.00 Trinity Found.

Immediate Stress Management. Created by Randall Maynard. 1 CD. (Running Time: 40 mins). 1999. audio compact disk (978-0-9633737-5-5(7)) Nordique.

Immense Design of Things: Light & Dark in Willa Cather, Carl Jung, & Ourselves. Lucia Woods & Daniel Lindley. 1 cass. (Running Time: 1 hr.). 1995. 9.95 (978-0-7822-0498-8(8), 574) C G Jung IL.
This presentation joins readings from Jung & Cather with photographs, commentary, & amplification to explore the ways in which the artist & the psychologist illuminate our lives & deepen awareness of our own journey.

Immensity. J. Krishnamurti. 1 cass. (Running Time: 75 min.). (Krishnamurti & Professor David Bohm - 1980 Ser.: No. 8). 8.50 (ABD808) Krishnamurti.
Krishnamurti & Prof. Bohm offer penetrating, in-depth dialogues which shed light on the fundamental issues of existence.

Immerse: Deeper Worship from Today's Top Female Artists. Contrib. by Don Moen. 2008. audio compact disk 13.99 (978-5-557-47916-5(3)) Integrity Music.

Immersed in the Spirit. Derek Prince. 1 cass. (B-3013) Derek Prince.

Immersed in the Splendor of God: Resources for Worhsip Renewal. F. Russell Mitman. 2005. pap. bk. 25.00 (978-0-8298-1614-3(3)) Pilgrim OH.

Immigrant. Perf. by Urban "D". (Running Time: 30 min.). 2004. audio compact disk 16.98 (978-5-559-43839-9(1)) Pub: Pt of Grace Ent. Dist(s): STL Dist NA

Immigrant Son I: An Armenian Boyhood. unabr. ed. Harry Chinchinian. Read by James Soyk, Sr. 2 cass. (Running Time: 2 hrs.). (YA). (gr. 6 up). 1997. 12.95 Set. (978-0-9653535-5-7(9)) Plum Tree.
About growing up during the depression & the people who left lasting impressions on the life of a child.

Immigrant Son II: Refusing to Grow Up. unabr. ed. Harry Chinchinian. Read by James Soyk, Sr. 2 cass. (Running Time: 3 hrs.). (YA). (gr. 6 up). 1998. 16.95 Set. (978-1-892476-01-2(0)) Plum Tree.
Describes predicaments while working in an uncle's grocery store during the Great Depression; camping with the precocious gang leader, Antranik; traveling in Europe during & after World War II; & attending school to become a physician-pathologist.

Immigrants. ed. 6 CDs. (Running Time: 6 hrs.). 2005. audio compact disk 29.50 (978-1-57970-351-6(8), S19500D, Audio-For) J Norton Pubs.
10 immigrants to the United States tell their stories. Most came during the peak decades of immigration, 1900 to 1920. It is fortunate that many who came so long ago were still alive when recorded in the 1940s and eager to share their experiences. They cam from countries all over the world. Some achieved success and wealth, some neither. People interviewed include: Robert Fritz, born in Sweden in 1885; Frank Gallucci, born in Italy in 1899; Albert Abrahamian, born in Armenia in 1906; Jacob Potofsky, born in Russia in 1894; Daniel Dzabadoz, born in Hungary in 1896; Charles T. Rice, born in Ireland in 1893; William D. Lee, born in China in 1897; Alfonso Aréchiga, born in Mexico in 1913; Victoria Lemanski, born in Poland in 1901; and Fanny Loria, born in Germany in 1933. In each life story, important events of history are seen from a human perspective: the breakup of political and social structures, the upheavals of war, the Russian Revolution, the Irish struggles, the rise of Hitler and Mussolini. (Reissue in CD format of programs previously available as audio cassettes.).

Immigrants. unabr. ed. 6 cass. (Running Time: 5 hrs. 45 min.). 29.50 (S19500) J Norton Pubs.
Eleven immigrants to the U. S. tell the stories of their lives in a series of taped, informal conversations. These men & women relate what they remember of the towns where they grew up, their families & schooling, the reasons that impelled them to emigrate, the journey by land & sea & the begining of life in the new country.

Immigrants. unabr. ed. Howard Fast. Read by Multivoice Production Staff. (Running Time: 13 hrs.). 2008. 39.25 (978-1-4233-7210-3(7), 9781423372103, BADLE); 24.95 (978-1-4233-7207-3(7), 9781423372073, Brilliance MP3); 24.95 (978-1-4233-7209-7(3), 9781423372097, BAD); 39.25 (978-1-4233-7208-0(5), 9781423372080, Brinc Audio MP3 Lib) Brilliance Audio.

Immigrant's Daughter. unabr. ed. Howard Fast. Read by Sandra Burr. (Running Time: 10 hrs.). 2008. 24.95 (978-1-4233-7125-0(9), 9781423371250, BAD); 39.25 (978-1-4233-7124-3(0), 9781423371243, Brinc Audio MP3 Lib) Brilliance Audio.

Immigrant's Daughter. unabr. ed. Howard Fast. Read by Sandra Burr. (Running Time: 10 hrs.). 2008. 39.25 (978-1-4233-7126-7(7), 9781423371267, BADLE); 24.95 (978-1-4233-7123-6(2), 9781423371236, Brilliance MP3) Brilliance Audio.

Immigrate to the U. S. A. by Purchasing a Business or Real Estate. Ramon Carrion & Georgette Gillis. 3 cass. 1995. 159.00 Set. (978-0-937387-12-2(6)) Am Advisory.
Legal reference.

Immigrating, Traveling, & Internationally Adopted Children. Contrib. by Margaret K. Hostetter et al. 1 cass. (American Academy of Pediatrics UPDATE: Vol. 17, No. 1). 1998. 20.00 Am Acad Pediat.

Immigration: Debating the Issues. Ed. by Nicholas Capaldi. (Contemporary Issues Ser.). (ENG., 1997. 23.98 (978-1-57392-142-8(4)) Prometheus Bks.

Immigration Act of Nineteen Ninety. 1991. 70.00 (AC-616) PA Bar Inst.

Immigration & A Look at: "Silent Explosion" Hosted by Nancy Pearlman. 1 cass. (Running Time: 29 min.). 10.00 (413) Educ Comm CA.

Immigration Law. 7 cass. (Running Time: 9 hrs.). (C). 1998. 235.00 Incl. course materials. (MC38) Am Law Inst.

Immigration Reform & Your Business Client. H. Ronald Klasko. 1 cass. (Running Time: 1 hr.). 1987. 20.00 PA Bar Inst.

Immobilized Cells & Enzymes. David R. Walt. 5 cass. (Running Time: 5 hrs. 12 min.). 430.00 incl. manual. (978-0-8412-1254-1(6), C-90); 22.00 manual. (978-0-8412-1256-5(2)) Am Chemical.
Teaches you what immmobilization is & when to use immobilization by discussing various methods of immobilization, including many examples.

Immoral. Brian Freeman. Read by Joe Barrett. (Running Time: 18 mins.). 2005. 89.95 (978-0-7861-3669-8(3)); audio compact disk 108.00 (978-0-7861-7698-4(9)) Blckstn Audio.

Immoral. unabr. ed. Brian Freeman. 13 vols. (Running Time: 18 mins.). 2005. 29.95 (978-0-7861-8001-1(3), ZM3516); 32.95 (978-0-7861-3546-2(8), E3516) Blckstn Audio.

Immoral. unabr. ed. Brian Freeman. Read by Joe Barrett. 11 CDs. (Running Time: 48600 sec.). 2005. audio compact disk 34.95 (978-0-7861-7778-3(0), ZE3516) Blckstn Audio.

Immoral Certainty. unabr. ed. Robert K. Tanenbaum. Read by Connor O'Brien. 8 cass. (Running Time: 12 hrs.). (Butch Karp Mystery Ser.). 1997. 64.00 (978-0-7366-3689-6(7), 4368) Books on Tape.
A killer is roaming New York with the "immoral certainty" that he won't be caught. When they investigate three savage murders, A.D.A. Butch karp & his colleague Marlene Ciampi pick up his trail. At the top of the list of suspects is a vicious sociopath, whose past leads to a posh day-care center, to the Mafia & finally, most chillingly, to a monstrous figure whose child victims call him "the Bogeyman." Just as the pieces are falling into place in this murderous puzzle, a kidnapping occurs. It will jeopardize everything at stake in the case & threaten all that Butch Karp holds dear.

Immoraliste, Set. André Gide. 3 cass. (FRE.). 1991. 34.95 (1353-LV) Olivia & Hill.
Michel, a quiet historian, marries his cousin in order to please his father. During the honeymoon, he discovers that his sexual tendencies are not directed toward women.

Immoraliste: Introductory Chapters. André Gide. Read by Monique Lebreton-Savigny. 2 cass. (Running Time: 2 hrs.). (FRE.). 1997. pap. bk. 29.50 Set. (978-1-58085-370-5(6)) Interlingua VA.

Immortal. unabr. ed. Angela Elwell Hunt. Narrated by Christina Moore. 9 cass. (Running Time: 12 hrs.). 2000. 78.00 (978-0-7887-4956-8(0), K0011E7) Recorded Bks.
An ancient legend that offers some surprising new insights on the nature of life, love & Christian trust, Cluadia Fisher understands people. Lawyers pay her exorbitant fees to read potential jurors & help pick people who will find their clients innocent whether they are or not. But when she takes a job in Europe with an organization dedicated to world peace, she meets a man she can't quite read, a man, she soon learns, who may be much more than he seems.

***Immortal.** unabr. ed. Gillian Shields. Read by Emily Durante. (ENG.). 2010. (978-0-06-201429-0(3), KTegenBooks); (978-0-06-201604-1(0), KTegenBooks) HarperCollins Pubs.

Immortal Bard see Science Fiction Favorites of Isaac Asimov

***Immortal Beloved.** unabr. ed. Cate Tiernan. Read by Kelly Lintz. (Running Time: 9 hrs. 30 mins.). (Immortal Beloved Ser.: No. 1). (ENG.). (YA). 2010. 22.98 (978-1-60788-713-3(4)) Pub: Hachet Audio. Dist(s): HachBkGrp

Immortal Gregorian Chant, Pt. 1. Perf. by Religious Monks. 1988. audio compact disk 15.95 (183) GIA Pubns.

Immortal Gregorian Chant, Pt. 2. Perf. by Religious Monks. 1988. audio compact disk 15.95 (184) GIA Pubns.

Immortal Highlander. unabr. ed. Karen Marie Moning. Read by Phil Gigante. (Running Time: 10 hrs.). (Highlander Ser.). 2008. 39.25 (978-1-4233-4164-2(3), 9781423341642, Brinc Audio MP3 Lib); 39.25 (978-1-4233-4166-6(X), 9781423341666, BADLE); 24.95 (978-1-4233-4165-9(1), 9781423341659, BAD); audio compact disk 97.25 (978-1-4233-4162-8(7), 9781423341628, BriAudCD Unabrid); audio compact disk 24.95 (978-1-4233-4163-5(5), 9781423341635, Brilliance MP3); audio compact disk 29.95 (978-1-4233-4161-1(9), 9781423341611, Bril Audio CD Unabri) Brilliance Audio.

***Immortal Hunter.** unabr. ed. Lynsay Sands. Read by Victoria Mcgee. (ENG.). 2010. (978-0-06-196756-6(4), Harper Audio) HarperCollins Pubs.

***Immortal Hunter: A Rogue Hunter Novel.** unabr. ed. Lynsay Sands. Read by Victoria Mcgee. (ENG.). 2010. (978-0-06-195867-0(0), Harper Audio) HarperCollins Pubs.

Immortal in Death. J. D. Robb, pseud. Narrated by Cristine McMurdo-Wallis. 10 CDs. (Running Time: 11 hrs. 45 mins.). (In Death Ser.). audio compact disk 97.00 (978-1-4025-1538-5(3)) Recorded Bks.

Immortal in Death. J. D. Robb, pseud. Narrated by Cristine McMurdo-Wallis. 8 cass. (Running Time: 11 hrs. 45 mins.). (In Death Ser.). 1996. 71.00 (978-0-7887-5447-0(5), 96126) Recorded Bks.
When a glamorous model on her quest to the top winds up dead, police lieutenant Eve Dallas is on the case. Suspicion points toward Eve's best friend, the other woman in a fatal love triangle. Now Eve must infiltrate New York City's drug-infested underworld in her search for the truth.

Immortal in Death. J. D. Robb, pseud. Narrated by Cristine McMurdo-Wallis. 8 CDs. (Running Time: 11 hrs. 45 mins.). (In Death Ser.). 2002. audio compact disk 97.00 (96126) Recorded Bks.

Immortal in Death. abr. ed. J. D. Robb, pseud. Read by Susan Ericksen. 4 cass. Library ed. (Running Time: 6 hrs.). (In Death Ser.:). 2001. 53.25 (978-1-58788-198-5(5), 1587881985, Lib Edit) Brilliance Audio.

Immortal in Death. abr. ed. J. D. Robb, pseud. Read by Susan Ericksen. (Running Time: 6 hrs.). (In Death Ser.). 2007. audio compact disk 14.99 (978-1-4233-3659-4(3), 9781423336594, BCD Value Price) Brilliance Audio.

Immortal in Death. unabr. ed. J. D. Robb, pseud. Read by Susan Ericksen. (Running Time: 10 hrs.). (In Death Ser.). 2004. 39.25 (978-1-59710-395-4(0), 1597103950, BADLE); 24.95 (978-1-59710-394-7(2), 1597103942, BAD); 24.95 (978-1-59335-759-7(1), 1593357591, Brilliance MP3); 39.25 (978-1-59335-893-8(8), 1593358938, Brinc Audio MP3 Lib); 29.95 (978-1-59355-821-5(X), 159355821X, BAU); 82.25 (978-1-59355-822-2(8), 1593558228, BrilAudUnabridg); audio compact disk 33.95 (978-1-59355-823-9(6), 1593558236, Bril Audio CD Unabri); audio compact disk 92.25 (978-1-59355-824-6(4), 1593558244, BriAudCD Unabrid) Brilliance Audio.
Beauty and Youth are Desperate Matters for Some . . . She was one of the most sought after women in the world. A top model who would stop at nothing to get what she wanted - even another woman's man. And now she was dead, the victim of a brutal murder. Police lieutenant Eve Dallas put her professional life on the line to take the case when suspicion fell on her best friend, the other woman in the fatal love triangle. Beneath the façade of glamour, Eve found that the world of high fashion thrived on an all-consuming obsession for youth and fame. One that led from the runway to the dark underworld of New York City where drugs could be found to fulfill any desire - for a price . .

Immortal Life of Henrietta Lacks. unabr. ed. Rebecca Skloot. Read by Cassandra Campbell & Bahni Turpin. 2010. audio compact disk 35.00 (978-0-307-71250-9(8), Random AudioBks) Pub: Random Audio Pubg. Dist(s): Random

Immortal Sherlock Holmes. Arthur Conan Doyle. 1 cass. (Running Time: 1 hr.). (Radiobook Ser.). 1987. 4.98 (978-0-929541-20-4(0)) Radiola Co.

Immortal Strangeness see Savagery of Love: Brother Antoninus Reads His Poetry

Immortal Wife: The Biographical Novel of Jessie Benton Fremont, Pt. 1 & 2. unabr. ed. Irving Stone. Read by Penelope Dellaporta. 17 cass. (Running Time: 25 hrs. 30 mins.). Incl. Pt. 1. Immortal Wife: The Biographical Novel of Jessie Benton Fremont. 10 cass. (Running Time: 15 hrs.). Irving Stone. Read by Penelope Dellaporta. 1983. 80.00 (1633-A); Pt. 2. Immortal Wife: The Biographical Novel of Jessie Benton Fremont. 7 cass. (Running Time: 10 hrs. 30 mins.). Irving Stone. Read by Penelope Dellaporta. 1983. 56.00 (1633-B); 1984. 136.00 (978-0-7366-0671-4(8), 1633 A&B) Books on Tape.
Jessie Benton was the spirited daughter of a powerful western expansionist senator, Thomas Hart Benton of Missouri. At 16 she met her match, John C. Fremont, then a lieutenant in the U.S. Topographical Corps. Immersed at an early age in the political battles of her father's career. Her loyalty & strong will sustained Fremont through his court-martial; her inspiration helped him become the first senator from California & a candidate for the U.S. presidency.

Immortalists: Charles Lindbergh, Dr. Alexis Carrel, & Their Daring Quest to Live Forever. unabr. ed. David M. Friedman. Narrated by Todd McLaren. (Running Time: 11 hrs. 30 mins. 0 sec.). (ENG.). 2007. audio compact disk 34.99 (978-1-4001-0526-7(9)); audio compact disk 69.99 (978-1-4001-3526-4(5)); audio compact disk 24.99 (978-1-4001-5526-2(6)) Pub: Tantor Media. Dist(s): IngramPubServ

Immortality. Ed. by Paul Edwards. (ENG.). 1997. 24.98 (978-1-57392-130-5(0)) Prometheus Bks.

Immortality: How Science Is Extending Your Life Span - And Changing the World. abr. ed. Ben Bova. Read by Christian Noble. 2 cass. (Running Time: 3 hrs.). 2001. 18.00 (978-1-59040-128-6(X), Phoenix Audio) Pub: Amer Intl Pub. Dist(s): PerseuPGW

Immortality & the World of the Supernatural: Life after Death - The World of the Supernatural. unabr. ed. Shmuel Irons. Read by Shmuel Irons. 2 cass. (Running Time: 3 hrs.). 19.95 Set. (978-1-889648-04-0(3)) Jwish Her Fdtn.
Applies the timeless truths found in the Bible & Talmud to gain knowledge, peace of mind, & the practical tools to live a happier life.

Immortality Poems. Mary M. Slappey. Read by Mary M. Slappey. 1986. 10.00 Interspace Bks.

Immortality Tape: Life Beyond Death. Ormond McGill. 2000. (978-1-933332-17-8(4)) Hypnotherapy Train.

Immortality Tape: Life Beyond Death. Ormond McGill. 2002. audio compact disk (978-1-933332-25-3(5)) Hypnotherapy Train.

Immortals. Michael Korda. 2004. 10.95 (978-0-7435-4864-9(7)) Pub: S&S Audio. Dist(s): S and S Inc

***Immortals.** unabr. ed. J. T. Ellison. Read by Joyce Bean. (Running Time: 11 hrs.). (Taylor Jackson Ser.). 2010. 24.99 (978-1-4418-3865-0(1), 9781441838650, Brilliance MP3); 24.99 (978-1-4418-3867-4(8), 9781441838674, BAD); 39.97 (978-1-4418-3866-7(X), 9781441838667, Brinc Audio MP3 Lib); 39.97 (978-1-4418-3868-1(6), 9781441838681, BADLE); audio compact disk 29.99 (978-1-4418-3863-6(5), 9781441838636, Bril Audio CD Unabri); audio compact disk 79.97 (978-1-4418-3864-3(3), 9781441838643, BriAudCD Unabrid) Brilliance Audio.

Immortals. unabr. ed. As told by Tracy Hickman. Based on a book by Tracy Hickman & Laura Hickman. 2007. 12.95 (978-0-9799725-0-8(7)) Scribes Forge.

Immortals: The Redeeming. Jennifer Ashley. 2008. audio compact disk 43.95 (978-1-897304-64-8(1)) Pub: AudioRealms CN CAN. Dist(s): Natl Bk Netwk

Immune - Young. Eldon Taylor. 1 cass. (Running Time: 62 min.). (Neurophonics Ser.). 16.95 (978-1-55978-659-1(0), 1010) Progress Aware Res.
Sound patterns for Altered States of Consciousness with underlying subliminal affirmations & frequency response signals. Use with headphones only.

Immune Booster. Steven Gurgevich. (ENG.). 2005. audio compact disk 19.95 (978-1-932170-29-0(4), HWH) Tranceformation.

Immune System: Why It's a Problem in the 90s. Don Partridge. 1 cass. 9.00 (A780-90) Sound Photosyn.
Entertaining & instructive, from SJ New Age Renaissance Fair.

Immunity & Longevity - Spiritual Healing. Robert E. Griswold. Read by Robert E. Griswold. 1 cass. (Super Strength Ser.). 1993. 10.95 (978-1-55848-313-2(6)) EffectiveMN.
Two complete non-subliminal programs to help let the power of your mind & spirit activate the body's ability to help & maximize the quality & length of life.

Immunity Through Herbs. David Christopher. 1 cass. (Running Time: 44 min.). 1989. 4.95 (AHY101) Christopher Pubns.
Live lecture discussing use of herbs to aid the immune system, detailing herbs for different systems of the body.

Immunization. Contrib. by Stephen R. Wells et al. 1 cass. (American College of Obstetrics & Gynecologists UPDATE: Vol. 22, No. 2). 1998. 20.00 Am Coll Obstetric.

Immunization Practices. Contrib. by Neal A. Halsey et al. 1 cass. (American Academy of Pediatrics UPDATE: Vol. 18, No. 4). 1998. 20.00 Am Acad Pediat.

Immunizing. abr. ed. Robert A. Monroe. Read by Robert A. Monroe. (Running Time: 30 min.). (Human Plus Ser.). 1989. 14.95 (978-1-56102-014-0(1)) Inter Indus.
Alert immune system to seek out & destroy disease producing organisms.

Immunochemistry. unabr. ed. Read by Julian B. Fleishman. 4 cass. (Running Time: 4 hrs. 30 min.). 465.00 Set, incl. 111p. manual. (96) Am Chemical.

Immunodeficiency - Office Presentation & Workup. Contrib. by Jerry Winkelstein et al. 1 cass. (American Academy of Pediatrics UPDATE: Vol. 17, No. 3). 1998. 20.00 Am Acad Pediat.

Immunology for the Surgeon. Moderated by John A. Mannick. 2 cass. (General Sessions Ser.: GS-4). 1986. 19.00 (8632) Am Coll Surgeons.

Immunotherapy of Diabetes. Moderated by Arthur H. Rubenstein. Contrib. by Fritz H. Bach & George S. Eisenbarth. 1 cass. (Running Time: 90 min.). 1986. 12.00 (D8646) Amer Coll Phys.

Immutability of God: Psalms 112:6-8. Ed Young. 1982. 4.95 (978-0-7417-1265-3(2), 265) Win Walk.

Imogene's Antlers. 1 cass. (Running Time: 35 min.). (J). (ps-3). 2001. pap. bk. 15.95 (VX-50C) Kimbo Educ.
Imogene wakes up to discover she has sprouted a huge set of antlers. Includes read along book.

Imogene's Antlers. 9.95 (978-1-59112-284-5(8)) Live Oak Media.

Imogene's Antlers. David Small. Read by Randye Kaye. 1 cass. (J). 2000. pap. bk. 19.97 (978-0-7366-9207-6(X)) Books on Tape.
Imogene wakes up one morning to discover she has sprouted a tremendous set of antlers. She accepts this calamity with grace while others around her panic & overreact. Her patience is eventually rewarded when the antlers vanish as suddenly as they appeared only to be replaced by another surprise.

Imogene's Antlers. David Small. Illus. by David Small. 14 vols. (Running Time: 5 mins.). 1994. pap. bk. 39.95 (978-1-59112-725-3(4)) Live Oak Media.

Imogene's Antlers. David Small. Illus. by David Small. (Running Time: 5 mins.). (J). (gr. k-3). 1994. 12.95 (978-1-59112-722-2(X)) Live Oak Media.

Imogene's Antlers. David Small. Illus. by David Small. Read by Randye Kaye. 11 vols. (Running Time: 5 mins.). (J). (gr. 1-6). 1994. bk. 25.95 (978-0-87499-323-3(7)) Live Oak Media.
Imogene wakes up one morning to discover she has sprouted a tremendous set of antlers. She accepts & bears this calamity with great grace while others around her panic & overreact. Her patience is eventually rewarded when the antlers vanish as suddenly as they appeared - only to be replaced by another surprise.

Imogene's Antlers. David Small. Illus. by David Small. Read by Randye Kaye. 11 vols. (Running Time: 5 mins.). (J). (gr. 1-6). 2005. pap. bk. 16.95 (978-0-87499-322-6(9)) Pub: Live Oak Media. Dist(s): AudioGO
Imogene wakes up one morning to discover she has sprouted a tremendous set of antlers. She accepts this calamity with grace while others around her panic and overreact. Her patience is eventually rewarded when the antlers vanish as suddenly as they appeared-only to be replaced by another surprise!.

Imogene's Antlers. unabr. ed. David Small. Illus. by David Small. Read by Randye Kaye. 14 vols. (Running Time: 5 mins.). (J). 1994. pap. bk. & tchr. ed. 37.95 Reading Chest. (978-0-87499-324-0(5)) Live Oak Media.
Imogene wakes up one morning to discover she has sprouted a tremendous set of antlers. She accepts & bears this calamity with great grace while others around her panic & overreact. Her patience is eventually rewarded when the antlers vanish as suddenly as they appeared - only to be replaced by another surprise.

***Impact.** unabr. ed. Douglas Preston. Read by Scott Sowers. 1 Playaway. (Running Time: 11 hrs.). 2010. 89.95 (978-0-7927-6876-0(0)); 54.95 (978-0-7927-6875-3(2)); audio compact disk 89.95 (978-0-7927-6874-6(4)) AudioGO.

Impact. unabr. ed. Douglas Preston. Read by Scott Sowers. 9 CDs. (Running Time: 11 hrs. 0 mins. 0 sec.). (ENG.). 2010. audio compact disk 39.99 (978-1-4272-0681-7(3)) Pub: Macmill Audio. Dist(s): Macmillan

Impact: Anti-Bullying Posters for Teens & Twenties. Sarah Jones. 2003. 27.95 (978-1-904315-19-3(4)) Pub: P Chapman GBR. Dist(s): SAGE

Impact Fee Legislation, 1991. 1 cass. 1991. 65.00 (AC-614) PA Bar Inst.

Impact Listening 1, Classroom Set. Ellen Kisslinger. 2002. 34.00 (978-962-00-5139-5(4)); audio compact disk 34.00 (978-962-00-5142-5(4)) Longman Far East HKG.

Impact Listening 2, Classroom Set. Jill Robbins & Andrew MacNeill. 2002. 34.00 (978-962-00-5140-1(8)) Longman Far East HKG.

Impact Listening 2, Classroom Set, Level 2. Jill Robbins et al. 2002. audio compact disk 34.00 (978-962-00-5143-2(2)) Longman Far East HKG.

Impact Listening 3, Classroom Set. Kenton Harsch & Kate Wolfe-Quintero. 2002. 34.00 (978-962-00-5141-8(6)) Longman Far East HKG.

Impact Listening 3, Classroom Set, Level 3. Kenton Harsch & Kate Wolfe-Quintero. 2002. audio compact disk 34.00 (978-962-00-5144-9(0)) Longman Far East HKG.

***Impact of a Faithful Father.** Charles R. Swindoll. 2010. audio compact disk 12.00 (978-1-57972-892-2(8)) Insight Living.

Impact of Asbestos & Radon on Real Estate Practice. David G. Mandelbaum. 1 cass. (Running Time: 1 hr.). 1988. 20.00 PA Bar Inst.

Impact of Asbestos on Real Estate. unabr. ed. Contrib. by Stanley J. Levy. 4 cass. (Running Time: 5 hrs.). 1989. 50.00 course handbk. (T7-9250) PLI.
In this recording of PLI's November 1989 program, the many ways in which asbestos impacts on real estate are explored & practical solutions for dealing with the problems it creates are offered. A distinguished faculty considers how asbestos affects buyers, sellers, landlords, tenants, building staff, tenants' employees, outside maintenance workers & contractors. Regulatory, health & insurance issues are also discussed.

Impact of Divine Love. Robert F. Morneau. 8 cass. 1990. 59.95 (TAH217) Alba Hse Comns.
Bishop Morneau examines the autobiographies of Augustine, Thomas Merton, John of the Cross, Teresa of Avila, C. S. Lewis, Simone Weil, Etty Hillesum & John Henry Newman to show how the grace of God consistently has transformed lives throughout the centuries & affects each one of us today.

Impact of DRG's, PPO's & Contract Medicine in Surgery. 2 cass. (Colon & Rectal Surgery Ser.: C84-GS3). 1984. 15.00 (8407) Am Coll Surgeons.

Impact of Environmental Law on Real Estate & Other Commercial Transactions. 8 cass. 275.00 Incl. course materials. (MC18) Am Law Inst.
Explores the multifaceted transactional & redevelopment dilemmas posed by environmental laws, negotiation strategies necessary to protect commercial clients, post-closing liabilities & regulatory obstacles to development, as well as disclosure requirements & ethical duties.

Impact of Environmental Regulations on Business Transactions. unabr. ed. Contrib. by A. Patrick Nucciarone. 4 cass. (Running Time: 5 hrs. 30 min.). 1988. pap. bk. 60.00 (T6-9093) PLI.
This recording of PLI's September 1988 satellite program explores: significant environmental statues, business transactions that must address environmental issues, i.e., acquisitions & operations management, cleanup responsibilities & liability limitations, potential liabilities, including Superfund remedial liabilities, liabilities of the parties including lenders, insurance coverage, remediation & litigation expenses, bankruptcy protection & protecting the client through an environmental audit.

Impact of Islam on the Collective Psyche. Lois Khan. Read by Lois Khan. 5 cass. (Running Time: 7 hrs.). 1992. 39.95 set. (978-0-7822-0346-2(9), 448) C G Jung IL.
As we are well aware from recent times, the Middle East challenges us to come to terms with very different ways of being. The countries which have most profoundly impacted America & the West - Iran & Iraq - are the seats of two major Islamic sects, the Shiites & Suuni. Holding great archetypal significance, the ancient religions of Iran & Iraq have deeply influenced the collective psyche of the region & the world. Indeed, it could be argued that this geographic area is the cradle of patriarchal civilization. This course looks closely at the psychology of Islam & aims toward a clearer understanding of the cultures that challenge us to learn new ways of being human.

***Impact of Social Media Within Your Organization.** Puei. 2010. 199.95 (978-1-60959-002-4(3)) P Univ E Inc.

Impact of the New ALI REstatement on Suretyship & Guaranty Issues in Modern Business Practice. 3 cass. (Running Time: 3 hrs. 30 min.). 1995. 160.00 incl. study materials. (D240) Am Law Inst.

Impact of the Swine Flu (H1N1 Flu) on Health Care Lawyers & Their Clients: Instant Impact Seminar with Jack Fernandez, Jr. Viewable on Your Computer or IPod. Fernandez Jack. 2009. 299.95 (978-1-59701-466-3(4)) ReedLogic.

***Impartial Witness.** Charles Todd. Narrated by Rosalyn Landor. (Running Time: 10 hrs. 54 mins. 0 sec.). (Bess Crawford Mystery Ser.: No. 2). (ENG.). 2010. audio compact disk 29.95 (978-1-60998-097-9(2)) Pub: AudioGO. Dist(s): Perseus Dist

Imparting the Blessing to Your Children. unabr. ed. William T. Ligon, Sr.. Read by William T. Ligon, Sr. Read by Dorothy J. Ligon & William T. Ligon, Jr. 4 cass. (Running Time: 4 hrs. 30 min.). 1989. 16.00 Set. (978-1-886327-01-6(7)) Fathers Blessing.
Religious.

Impasse a la Dame. 1 cass. (Running Time: 60 mins.). Dramatization. (Maitres du Mystere Ser.). (FRE.). 1996. 11.95 (1834-MA) Olivia & Hill.
Popular radio thriller, interpreted by France's best actors.

Impassioned Heart. George Maloney. 7 cass. (Running Time: 5 hrs. 20 min.). 1992. 27.95 set. (TAH263) Alba Hse Comns.
Father Maloney says that an "intellectual" faith is not enough for our faithless age. If he is right, then these cassettes are the perfect corrective.

Impatience of Job: Job 4:5;5-6. Told to Ed Young. 1983. 4.95 (978-0-7417-1316-2(0), 316) Win Walk.

Impeachment of Andrew Johnson. Kenneth Bruce. 1 cass. (Running Time: 1 hr.). Dramatization. (Excursions in History Ser.). 12.50 Alpha Tape.

Impending Death of the Democratic Party. Ephraim Lindsey. 2007. audio compact disk 17.99 (978-1-60462-108-2(7)) Tate Pubng.

Imperatrice, Vol. 1. I.t. ed. Nicole Avril. (French Ser.). 1994. bk. 30.99 (978-2-84011-091-0(1)) Pub: UlverLrgPrint GBR. Dist(s): Ulverscroft US

Imperatrice, Vol. 2. I.t. ed. Nicole Avril. (French Ser.). 1994. bk. 30.99 (978-2-84011-092-7(X)) Pub: UlverLrgPrint GBR. Dist(s): Ulverscroft US

Imperfect Birds. unabr. ed. Anne Lamott. Contrib. by Susan Denaker. (Running Time: 12 hrs.). (ENG.). (gr. 12 up). 2010. audio compact disk 39.95 (978-0-14-314536-3(3), PengAudBks) Penguin Grp USA.

***Imperfect Endings: A Daughter's Tale of Life & Death.** unabr. ed. Zoe FitzGerald Carter. Narrated by Karen White. (Running Time: 9 hrs. 0 mins. 0 sec.). 2010. 19.99 (978-1-4001-6624-4(1)); 15.99 (978-1-4001-8624-2(2)); audio compact disk 29.99 (978-1-4001-1624-9(4)); audio compact disk 59.99 (978-1-4001-4624-6(0)) Pub: Tantor Media. Dist(s): IngramPubServ

***Imperfect Strangers.** abr. ed. Stuart Woods. Read by Anthony Heald. (ENG.). 2005. (978-0-06-084211-6(3), Harper Audio); (978-0-06-084210-9(5), Harper Audio) HarperCollins Pubs.

Imperial Ambitions: Conversations with Noam Chomsky on the Post-9/11 World [American Empire Project] (tt) abr. ed. Noam Chomsky & David Barsamian. 2005. 14.95 (978-1-59397-845-7(6)) Pub: Macmill Audio. Dist(s): Macmillan

Imperial Bedrooms. unabr. ed. Bret Easton Ellis. Read by Andrew McCarthy. 4 CDs. (Running Time: 4 hrs.). 2010. audio compact disk 25.00 (978-0-307-73505-8(2), Random AudioBks) Pub: Random Audio Pubg. Dist(s): Random

Imperial Cruise: A Secret History of Empire & War. unabr. ed. James Bradley. Read by Richard Poe. (Running Time: 9 hrs.). (ENG.). 2009. 26.98 (978-1-60024-396-7(7)) Pub: Hachet Audio. Dist(s): HachBkGrp

***Imperial Cruise: A Secret History of Empire & War.** unabr. ed. James Bradley. Read by Richard Poe. 1 MP3-CD. (Running Time: 9 hrs.). 2009. 54.99 (978-1-60788-003-5(2)) Pub: Hachet Audio. Dist(s): HachBkGrp

***Imperial Cruise: A Secret History of Empire & War.** unabr. ed. James Bradley. Read by Richard Poe. 8 CDs. (Running Time: 9 hrs.). 2009. audio compact disk 89.99 (978-1-60788-002-8(4)) Pub: Hachet Audio. Dist(s): HachBkGrp

***Imperial Cruise: A Secret History of Empire & War.** unabr. ed. James Bradley. Read by Richard Poe. (Running Time: 9 hrs.). (ENG.). 2010. audio compact disk 19.98 (978-1-60788-670-9(7)) Pub: Hachet Audio. Dist(s): HachBkGrp

***Imperial Leader: The Life of Winston Churchill.** RadioArchives.com. (Running Time: 780). (ENG.). 2009. audio compact disk 29.98 (978-1-61081-156-9(9)) Radio Arch.

Imperial Life in the Emerald City. unabr. ed. Rajiv Chandrasekaran. 10 CDs. (Running Time: 12 mins.). (YA). 2007. audio compact disk 90.00 (978-0-7861-5830-0(1)) Blckstn Audio.

Imperial Life in the Emerald City. unabr. ed. Rajiv Chandrasekaran. Read by Ray Porter. (YA). 2007. 69.99 (978-1-60252-562-7(5)) Find a World.

Imperial Life in the Emerald City: Inside Iraq's Green Zone. unabr. ed. Rajiv Chandrasekaran. Read by Ray Porter. (Running Time: 37800 sec.). 2006. audio compact disk 29.95 (978-0-7861-5837-9(9)) Blckstn Audio.

Imperial Life in the Emerald City: Inside Iraq's Green Zone. unabr. ed. Rajiv Chandrasekaran. Read by Ray Porter. (Running Time: 37800 sec.). 2007. 72.95 (978-0-7861-4966-7(3)) Blckstn Audio.

Imperial Life in the Emerald City: Inside Iraq's Green Zone. unabr. ed. Rajiv Chandrasekaran & Roy Porter. (Running Time: 12 hrs. 45 mins.). (YA). 2006. 29.95 (978-0-7861-4956-8(6)) Blckstn Audio.

Imperial Presidency. Noam Chomsky. (Running Time: 1 hr. 10 mins.). (AK Press Audio Ser.). (ENG.). 2005. audio compact disk 14.98 (978-1-904859-43-7(7)) Pub: AK Pr GBR. Dist(s): Consort Bk Sales

Imperial Presidency. unabr. ed. Arthur M. Schlesinger, Jr. 1 cass. (Running Time: 56 min.). 12.95 (40048) J Norton Pubs.
Discusses the growth of presidential power from George Washington to the Nixon administration, which nearly succeeded in creating a presidential dictatorship.

***Imperial Woman: The Story of the Last Empress of China.** unabr. ed. Pearl S. Buck. Narrated by Kirsten Potter. (Running Time: 14 hrs. 0 mins. 0 sec.). (ENG.). 2011. audio compact disk 39.99 (978-1-59859-850-6(3), SpringWater) Oasis Audio.

Imperials Hall of Fame Series. Perf. by Imperials, The. 1 cass., 1 CD. (Imperials Hall of Fame Series). 1998. 16.99; audio compact disk 19.99 CD. Provident Mus Dist.

Imperials: the Definitive Collection. Contrib. by Imperials. 2007. audio compact disk 7.97 (978-5-558-14541-0(2), Word Records) Word Enter.

Imperium. abr. ed. Robert Harris. Read by Oliver Ford Davies. 2006. 17.95 (978-0-7435-6183-9(X)) Pub: S&S Audio. Dist(s): S and S Inc

Imperium. unabr. ed. Robert Harris. Read by Oliver Ford Davies. 2006. 29.95 (978-0-7435-6184-6(8)) Pub: S&S Audio. Dist(s): S and S Inc

Imperium: A Novel of Ancient Rome. abr. ed. Robert Harris. Read by Oliver Ford Davies. (Running Time: 6 hrs. 0 mins. 0 sec.). 2010. audio compact disk 14.99 (978-0-7435-7649-9(7)) Pub: S&S Audio. Dist(s): S and S Inc

Imperium: A Novel of Ancient Rome. unabr. ed. Robert Harris. Read by Simon Jones. (Running Time: 13 hrs. 30 mins. 0 sec.). (ENG.). 2006. audio compact disk 49.95 (978-0-7435-5515-9(5)) Pub: S&S Audio. Dist(s): S and S Inc

Impersonator, Set. unabr. ed. Mary I. Taylor. Read by Flo Gibson. 6 cass. (Running Time: 8 hrs.). 1998. bk. 24.95 (978-1-55685-532-0(X)) Audio Bk Con.
When beautiful Mary Lang pretends to be Mary Haddon, she enters D.C. society as Mrs. Whiting's niece & surmounts many awkward situations. The discovery of who she really is comes as a shock to all, including herself.

Impetus for New Life from the Synod. Eva M. Ackerman. 1 cass. (National Meeting of the Institute, 1995 Ser.). 4.00 (95N2) IRL Chicago.

Implement, Engage, Press: How to Receive God's Promises for Your Life. Gloria Copeland. (ENG.). 2009. audio compact disk 20.00 (978-1-57562-987-2(9)) K Copeland Pubns.

Implementing a Collaborative Practice. Contrib. by Hal C. Lawrence, III et al. 1 cass. (American College of Obstetrics & Gynecologists UPDATE: Vol. 23, No. 6). 1998. 20.00 Am Coll Obstetric.

Implementing Ongoing Transition Plans for the IEP: A Student-Driven Approach to IDEA Mandates. Pat McPartland. Ed. by Tom Kinney. Des. by Sherry Pribbenow. 2005. spiral bd. 49.00 (978-1-57861-534-6(8), IEP Res) Attainment.

Implementing Self-Directed Work Teams: The Breakthrough Method for Increasing Productivity, Sparking Innovation & Reducing Costs. Loren Ankarlo. 4 cass. (Running Time: 3 hrs. 20 min.). 59.95 Set incl. 64p. wkbk. (V10167) CareerTrack Pubns.
You'll learn proven strategies from Loren Ankarlo - one of the nation's leading experts on self-directed teams - & you'll hear first-hand accounts of how other organizations have utilized self-directed teams to address projects & problems.

Implementing Total Quality Management, Set. Mark Towers. Read by Mark Towers. 2 cass. (Running Time: 3 hrs.). 1996. bk. 21.95 (978-1-878542-74-8(5),) SkillPath Pubns.
Motivating & starting a total quality strategy.

Implementing Total Quality Management: How to Make TQM Work in Your Organization. Verne Hamish. 4 cass. (Running Time: 3 hrs. 43 min.). 79.95 Set incl. 48p. wkbk. & 86p. Memory Jogger. (V10177) CareerTrack Pubns.
TQM authority Verne Hamish gives you hard numbers & case studies to back up every principle he teaches & sample scenarios show you how to put TQM principles into action with your team, in your workplace.

Implementing Your Client's Right to Die. Edward S. Schlesinger. 1 cass. (Running Time: 90 min.). 1990. 17.40 (M792) Am Law Inst.
With the U.S. Supreme Court's 1990 "Cruzan" decision as the backdrop, this tape: Addresses the multitude of issues estate planners face regarding a client's wishes on life-prolonging procedures; Encourages estate planners to prepare a health care document as part of a client's overall estate plan; Explains how to draft a health care document.

Implications of Brain Research for Ministry. 1 cass. (Care Cassettes Ser.: Vol. 21, No. 6). 1994. 10.80 Assn Prof Chaplains.

Import-Export: How to Get Started in International Trade. Carl A. Nelson. 6 cass. 1995. 34.95 (978-0-945493-04-4(5)) Global Busn Trade.
How to start import-export.

Importance of a True Guru. Brother Anandamoy. 1984. 8.50 (2504) Self Realization.
Discusses the seldom-understood distinctions between a spiritual teacher & a true guru; degrees of spiritual evolution; personal stories about Paramahansa Yogananda's life & training of disciples; how to deepen one's attunement with the guru.

Importance of Being Earnest. 2009. audio compact disk 16.95 (978-1-60646-076-4(5)) Audio Bk Con.

Importance of Being Earnest. Oscar Wilde. 1 cass. 18.95 (CART003) CA Artists.

Importance of Being Earnest. Oscar Wilde. 1 CD. (Running Time: 30 min.). 2004. audio compact disk 15.95 (978-1-895837-93-3(6)) Pub: Insomniac CAN. Dist(s): Natl Bk Netwk
An audio version of Oscar Wilde's most enduring play; originally produced by the CBC.

Importance of Being Earnest. Oscar Wilde. Read by Evans Gielgud. (Running Time: 1 hr. 45 mins.). (C). 2006. 20.95 (978-1-60083-780-7(8)) Iofy Corp.

Importance of Being Earnest. Oscar Wilde. 1 cass. (Running Time: 90 mins.). 2001. 18.95 Lodestone Catalog.

Importance of Being Earnest. Oscar Wilde. Read by Edith Evans. Perf. by John Gielgud. 2 CDs. (Running Time: 1 hr. 50 min.). audio compact disk 17.98 (978-962-634-342-5(7), NA234212) Naxos.

Importance of Being Earnest. Oscar Wilde. 1 cass. (Running Time: 30 min.). 2001. 8.95 (978-1-895837-68-1(5)) Pub: StoneFox Pubg CAN. Dist(s): StackpoleBks
Jack Worthing & Algernon Moncrieff begin to bend the truth in hopes of adding a bit of excitement to their lives. Each invents an imaginary friend as an excuse to escape from the dull life of the country to the excitement of the town. Their deceptions eventually converge, resulting in a series of crises that threaten to spoil their romantic pursuits. The play is well-known for its witty comedy & its satire of institutions like class, marriage & romantic love.

Importance of Being Earnest. abr. ed. 2 cass. (Running Time: 3 hrs.). (Oscar Wilde Drama Ser.). 1998. 16.95 (PengAudBks) Penguin Grp USA.

Importance of Being Earnest. unabr. ed. Oscar Wilde. 2 CDs. (Running Time: 3 hrs.). (gr. 9-12). 2005. audio compact disk 15.95 (978-0-660-18536-1(9)) Canadian Broadcasting CAN.
To mark the centenary of Wilde's death, the Stratford Festival of Canada stages this unique production of the original, complete four-act version of his famous play. This does not replace the well-known three-act version, but does give the audience an opportunity to enjoy the play that Wilde originally wrote, with its extra characters, more pointed social commentary, additional scenes and new dialogue. This play remains perhaps Wilde's wittiest and most loved romantic comedy.

Importance of Being Earnest. unabr. ed. Oscar Wilde. Read by Full Ensemble Cast. (YA). 2006. 34.99 (978-1-59895-638-2(8)) Find a World.

Importance of Being Earnest. unabr. abr. ed. Oscar Wilde. 2 CDs. (Running Time: 2 hrs.). (ENG.). 2002. audio compact disk 22.95 (978-1-56511-677-1(1), 1565116771) Pub: HighBridge. Dist(s): Workman Pub
Attacks Victorian manners and morals in what can only be described as the most maliciously delicious way. A witty satire of Victorian social hyposcrisy, Wilde pulls the strings on his cast of late-Victorian characters making them appear, first and foremost, exactly as they are - superficial, upper class Englishmen bound and cinched by an artificial code of manners.

Importance of Being Earnest, Set. unabr. ed. Oscar Wilde. Narrated by Christopher Hurt. 2 cass. (Running Time: 3 hrs.). 1984. 14.95 (978-1-55685-010-3(7)) Audio Bk Con.
The classic 19th century comedy of manners. Jack Worthing & Algernon Moncrief masquerade under the name of Ernest to win the love of Gwendolyn & Cecily.

***Importance of Being Earnest: Classic Radio Theatre Series.** Oscar Wilde. Told to Jeremy Clyde & Richard Pasco. (Running Time: 2 hrs. 20 mins. 0 sec.). (ENG.). 2010. audio compact disk 24.95 (978-1-4084-2693-7(5)) Pub: AudioGO. Dist(s): Perseus Dist

Importance of Being Ernest Hemingway No. 28: A Light & Enlightening Lecture. Featuring Elliot Engel. 2000. bk. 15.00 (978-1-890123-28-4(5)) Media Cnslts.

Importance of Decision. Derek Prince. 1 cass. (B-4018) Derek Prince.

Importance of Developing a Strong Will. Speeches. Told to Joel Osteen. 1 Cass. (Running Time: 30 Mins.). 2001. 6.00 (978-1-59349-105-5(0), JA0105) J Osteen.

Importance of Duty. unabr. ed. David Barton. Read by David Barton. 1 cass. (Running Time: 1 hrs.). 1996. bk. 4.95 (978-0-925279-54-5(4), A17) Wallbuilders.
"Duty" was one of the strongest words in early America. Today we have lost its true meaning & thus the benefits which come from accepting our duty. Discover this character trait in our Founding Fathers & their words about our duties today.

Importance of Early Identification & Early Intervention with NLD: An Occupational Therapists' Perspective. Rondalyn Whitney. 1 cass. (Running Time: 1 hr. 19 min.). 1998. bk. 20.00 (978-1-58111-057-9(X)) Contemporary Medical.
NLD description, occupation therapists' perspective choosing schools & sensory integration.

Importance of Fairy Tales for Children. Read by Bruno Bettelheim. 1 cass. (Running Time: 1 hr.). 10.95 (F0470B090, HarperThor) HarpC GBR.

Importance of Follow-Up. Dan Corner. 1 cass. 3.00 (44) Evang Outreach.

Importance of Having a Strong Will, Pt. 2. Speeches. Joel Osteen. 1 Cass. (Running Time: 30 Mins.). 2001. 6.00 (978-1-59349-106-2(9), JA0106) J Osteen.

Importance of Human Relationships. 1 cass. (Love-Human Divine Ser.). 9.95 (ST-54) Crystal Clarity.
Explores: Why we need human relationships; why we inevitably experience what we condemn in others; the importance of respect; accepting criticism without defensiveness.

Importance of Jesus. Kenneth Wapnick. 2 CDs. 2004. audio compact disk 14.00 (978-1-59142-146-7(2), CD51) Foun Miracles.
In this workshop, the importance of Jesus in the ego's plan of atonement is contrasted with his importance in the Holy Spirit's plan. It is shown how the ego's Jesus-the biblical Jesus- validates the centrality of individual and bodily existence, thereby ensuring the ego's continuation; whereas the Jesus of A Course in Miracles is shown to symbolize the thought of God's Love in our minds that gently leads us out of the dream of specialness and individuality. The Jesus of A Course in Miracles thus replaces the image of the biblical Jesus portrayed throughout history, who was so thoroughly rooted in the world's dream of the body.

***Importance of Jesus.** Kenneth Wapnick. 2010. 11.00 (978-1-59142-483-3(6)) Foun Miracles.

Importance of Jesus' Resurrection. Dan Corner. 1 cass. 3.00 (45) Evang Outreach.

Importance of Laughter. Speeches. Joel Osteen. 1 Cass. (Running Time: 30 Mins.). (J). 2000. 6.00 (978-1-59349-060-7(7), JA0060) J Osteen.

Importance of People. unabr. ed. Clarence B. Randall. 1 cass. (Running Time: 22 min.). 12.95 (13029) J Norton Pubs.

Importance of Pluto. K. Hamaker-Zondag. 1 cass. 8.95 (671) Am Fed Astrologers.
An AFA Convention workshop tape.

Importance of Policy & Theory, Side A. Harvey Jackins. 1 cass. 10.00 Rational Isl.
Side A: Talks about the importance of policy & theory, particularly in relation to re-evaluation counseling communities. Side B: Outlines a policy for the ending of anti-semitism.

Importance of Thought Forms. unabr. ed. Robert A. Monroe. Read by Robert A. Monroe. Ed. by Robert A. Moroe. (Running Time: 45 min.). (Explorer Ser.). 1985. 12.95 (978-1-56113-024-5(9), 25) Monroe Institute.
How thoughts can manifest, affecting you & those around you.

Important Changes to the Pa. Securities Act. 1999. bk. 99.00 (ACS-2291) PA Bar Inst.
On January 25,1999, Act 109 became effective & substantially changed important provisions in the Pennsylvania Securities Act of 1972. This features both the legal & policy changes emanating from these amendments. The focus is on "cutting edge" issues that give your clients the advantage in a competitive business environment.

Important Family. unabr. ed. Dorothy Eden. Read by Anne Dover. 7 cass. (Running Time: 10 hrs. 30 min.). (Sound Ser.). 2004. 61.95 (978-1-85496-670-4(7), 66707) Pub: UlverLrgPrint GBR. Dist(s): Ulverscroft US
Sir John, Lady Iris Devenish & their daughter Celina set out in 1862 for New Zealand, to take their place in the creation of an ideal colony there. But colonizing a wild, unfriendly terrain is far more difficult than Sir John imagined. A sudden storm & drugs play their parts in a story that climaxes in intrigue & murder.

Important Issues in Drafting Tax Apportionment Provisions. 1 cass. (Running Time: 50 min.). 1993. 95.00 Incl. study guide. (Y507) Am Law Inst.
Examines the pitfalls of poorly drafted clauses & offers guidance on structuring them to prevent the government from becoming the biggest beneficiary.

Important Men Of Tomorrow: 1 Chron. 17:1-5, 22:5-11. Ed Young. (J). 1980. 4.95 (978-0-7417-1133-5(8), A0133) Win Walk.

Importing As a Small Business. John W. Spiers. 1 cass. 1988. 99.50 (978-0-9621814-0-5(4)) Five Star WA.

Impossible. Nancy Werlin. Read by Emily Durante. (Playaway Young Adult Ser.). (J). 2009. 54.99 (978-1-60812-656-9(0)) Find a World.

Impossible. unabr. ed. Danielle Steel. Read by David Garrison. 9 CDs. (Running Time: 9 hrs. 30 mins.). 2005. audio compact disk 81.00 (978-1-4159-1661-2(6)); 63.00 (978-1-4159-1575-2(X)) Books on Tape.
A typical Steel love story about a successful, glamorous art gallery owner who meets an outrageously offbeat artist. Sasha, 48 years old, recently widowed with two grown children, was married to the most fantastic man in the world. Griefstricken, she continues to work nonstop to build her Paris gallery into an international success; she is conservative and driven by tradition, always insisting on having things her own way. Liam is a "wacky" artist who is nine years her junior. His marriage has collapsed because of his intolerable, reckless behavior; a nonconformist, he lives for the moment. The couple meeting coincidentally when Sasha's son Xavier introduces Liam as an up-and-coming talent. Steel takes the listener into the worlds of glamour, art, and plush settings from the Hamptons to Paris.

Impossible. unabr. ed. Nancy Werlin. Read by Emily Durante. (Running Time: 9 hrs.). 2008. 39.97 (978-1-4233-7863-1(6), 9781423378631, Brlnc Audio MP3 Lib); 39.97 (978-1-4233-7865-5(2), 9781423378655, BADLE); 24.99 (978-1-4233-7864-8(4), 9781423378648, BAD); 24.99 (978-1-4233-7862-4(8), 9781423378624, Brilliance MP3); audio compact disk 72.97 (978-1-4233-7861-7(X), 9781423378617, BriAudCD Unabrid); audio compact disk 29.99 (978-1-4233-7860-0(1), 9781423378600, Bril Audio CD Unabri) Brilliance Audio.

Impossible - Who Said So? Elbert Willis. 1 cass. (Learning Lordship Ser.). 4.00 Fill the Gap.

Impossible Journey. unabr. ed. 4 cass. (Running Time: 4 hrs. 45 min.). 2003. 37.00 (978-1-4025-4255-8(0)) Recorded Bks.
Shows the hardships and horrors of 1930s communist Russia, through the eyes of two brave, resourceful young heroes. When Marya and Georgi learn that their parents have been sent thousands of miles away to separate camps in Siberia, their lives seem hopeless. Faced with the prospect of orphanages and separation from each other, the children decide they must do whatever it takes to make the impossible journey in search of their parents.

Impossible Takes Longer. Art E. Berg. 1 cass. 1992. (978-1-883437-02-2(4)) Invictus Comm.

Impostor. unabr. ed. June Drummond. 7 cass. 1998. 76.95 Set. (978-1-85903-001-1(7)) Pub: Magna Story GBR. Dist(s): Ulverscroft US

***Impostor.** unabr. ed. Damon Galgut. Read by Humphrey Bower. (Running Time: 8 hrs. 21 mins.). 2010. audio compact disk 83.95 (978-1-74214-550-1(7), 9781742145501) Pub: Bolinda Pubng AUS. Dist(s): Bolinda Pub Inc

Impotence Conquered Now. Norman J. Caldwell. Read by Norman J. Caldwell. Ed. by Achieve Now Institute Staff. 1 cass. (Running Time: 20 min.). (Health-Imaging Ser.). 1988. 9.97 (978-1-56273-073-4(8)) My Mothers Pub.
We help give a boost to natural recovery.

Impotent: No More. Barrie Konicov. 1 cass. 11.98 (978-0-87082-339-8(6), 072) Potentials.
Experience increased physical desire & address those patterns that cause impotence by a series of physical, mental, & emotional factors.

Impress Them on Your Children: Practical Lessons for Instilling the Word of God in the Hearts of Children. Al Baird et al. 4 cass. 1998. 21.99 Set. (978-1-57782-059-8(2)) Discipleshp.
It is not enough for parents to give their children head knowledge. They need to have god's word impressed on their hearts. Now parents can sit at the feet of men who have done it.

Impression of Solitude. Ed. by Robert A. Monroe. 1 cass. (Running Time: 30 min.). (Meta Music Artist Ser.). 1992. 14.95 (978-1-56102-246-5(2)) Inter Indus.
Expresses the impact of Czechoslovakia's sudden freedom on the composer.

Impressionist Poets. unabr. ed. Poems. Arthur. Read by Philippe De Montebello. 1 cass. (Running Time: 1 hr.). 1996. 16.95 (978-1-885608-05-5(5)) Airplay.
The director of the Metropolitan Museum of Art reads the poety of Baudelaire, Rimbaud, Mallarme & others in French with English translation.

Impressions of Theophrastus Such. George Eliot. Read by Anais 9000. 2008. 27.95 (978-1-60112-172-1(5)) Babblebooks.

Imprint. abr. ed. Robert A. Monroe. Read by Robert A. Monroe. (Running Time: 30 min.). (Human Plus Ser.). 1989. 14.95 (978-1-56102-015-7(X)) Inter Indus.
Use for full retention of materials in day-to-day memory applications.

***Imprint of a Faithful Mother.** Charles R. Swindoll. 2010. audio compact disk 12.00 (978-1-57972-888-5(X)) Insight Living.

Improbable Adventures of Sherlock Holmes. unabr. ed. John Joseph Adams. Read by Anne Flosnik & Simon Vance. (Running Time: 24 hrs.). 2010. 29.99 (978-1-4418-3911-4(9), 9781441839114, BAD); audio compact disk 99.97 (978-1-4418-3908-4(9), 9781441839084, BriAudCD Unabrid) Brilliance Audio.

Improbable Adventures of Sherlock Holmes. unabr. ed. Read by Anne Flosnik & Simon Vance. Ed. by John Joseph Adams. (Running Time: 21 hrs.). 2010. 44.97 (978-1-4418-3910-7(0), 9781441839107, Brlnc Audio MP3 Lib); 29.99 (978-1-4418-3909-1(7), 9781441839091, Brilliance MP3); audio compact disk 29.99 (978-1-4418-3907-7(0), 9781441839077, Bril Audio CD Unabri) Brilliance Audio.

Improbable Adventures of Sherlock Holmes. unabr. ed. Read by Simon Vance and Anne Flosnik. Ed. by John Joseph Adams. (Running Time: 24 hrs.). 2010. 44.97 (978-1-4418-3912-1(7), 9781441839121, BADLE) Brilliance Audio.

Improbable Cause. unabr. ed. J. A. Jance. Read by Gene Engene. 6 cass. (Running Time: 7 hrs. 48 min.). Dramatization. (J. P. Beaumont Mystery Ser.). 1993. 39.95 (978-1-55686-462-9(0), 752414) Books in Motion.
The dentist was sitting bolt upright, mouth opened wide, stone cold dead. There was no lack of suspects - the brutalized wife, the pretty, sexually abused dental assistant & the ex-con who was a very intimate friend of the widow.

Improbable Cause. unabr. collector's ed. J. A. Jance. Read by Connor O'Brien. 6 cass. (Running Time: 9 hrs.). (J. P. Beaumont Mystery Ser.). 1997. 48.00 (978-0-7366-3609-4(9), 4266) Books on Tape.
The dentist was found sitting upright, mouth agape, stone-cold dead. J.P. Beaumont quickly tagged his main suspects.

***Improper Life of Bezellia Grove.** unabr. ed. Susan Gregg Gilmore. (Running Time: 8 hrs. 30 mins.). 2010. 15.99 (978-1-4001-8834-5(2)); 19.99 (978-1-4001-6834-7(1)); audio compact disk 71.99 (978-1-4001-4834-9(0)); audio compact disk 29.99 (978-1-4001-1834-2(4)) Pub: Tantor Media. Dist(s): IngramPubServ

Improve Athletic Abilities. 1 cass. (Running Time: 60 min.). 10.95 (026) Psych Res Inst.
Mental sport performance conditioning.

Improve Creativity. Bruce Goldberg. (ENG.). 2005. audio compact disk 17.00 (978-1-57968-094-7(1)) Pub: B Goldberg. Dist(s): Baker Taylor

Improve Creativity. Bruce Goldberg. Read by Bruce Goldberg. 1 cass. (Running Time: 25 min.). (ENG.). 2007. 13.00 (978-1-885577-59-7(1)) Pub: B Goldberg. Dist(s): Baker Taylor
Through self-hypnosis turn creative projects from writing to music & artistic pursuits into a successful reality.

Improve Study Habits (Hypnosis), Vol. 5. Jayne Helle. 1 cass. (Running Time: 56 min.). 1996. 15.00 (978-1-891826-04-7(2)) Introspect.
Learning is easy with the right mental outlook.

Improve Your Concentration. Read by Robert E. Griswold. 1 cass. 1992. 10.95 (978-1-55848-005-6(6)) EffectiveMN.
Many people find the harder they concentrate, the more difficult it is & the more frustrated they become. This will help you focus your attention where you want it.

Improve Your German. Ruth Rach. (Improve Your... Ser.). (GER.). 1995. pap. bk. 79.95 (978-0-8442-2572-2(X), Natl Textbk Co) M-H Contemporary.

Improve Your Italian: The Practice & Improve Method. Paola Tite. 8 cass. (Running Time: 480 min.). (Improve Your... Ser.). (ITA.). 1995. pap. bk. 79.95 (978-0-8442-8551-1(X), Natl Textbk Co) M-H Contemporary.

Improve Your Memory. 2 cass. (Running Time: 60 min. per cass.). (Self Hypnosis & Subliminal Reinforcement Ser.). 14.95 (978-1-55569-235-3(4), SUB-8011) Great Am Audio.
Presents tools for positive self-change.

Improve Your Memory. Lee Pulos. Read by Lee Pulos. 1 cass. (Running Time: 60 min.). 9.95 (978-1-55569-429-6(2), 4015) Great Am Audio.
Subliminal self-help.

Improve Your Memory. Gary Small. 1 CD. (Running Time: 1 hr.). (Guided Self-Healing Ser.). 2006. audio compact disk 15.95 (978-1-59179-179-9(0), W814D) Sounds True.
Learn how to instantly improve your memory skills, whether you're a student trying to order and retain a blizzard of new and often confusing information, a busy professional trying to keep up with your constantly changing career and home life, a harried parent juggling too many tasks in too little time, or someone concerned that as we age we can no longer retain information the way we could when we were younger.

Improve Your Memory: Hypnotic & Subliminal Learning. David Illig. 2000. 14.99 (978-0-86580-021-2(9)) Success World.

Improve Your Memory: Mind Power Techniques That Get Results! unabr. ed. Amy J. Mews. Perf. by John Schneeman. 1 cass. (Running Time: 60 min.). (Mind Power Ser.). 1994. 11.99 (978-1-892654-02-1(4), BET030) FutureLife.
Mental exercises, techniques, & guided relaxation sessions for improving visual & auditory recall.

Improve Your Memory, Improve Your Productivity. PUEI. audio compact disk 199.00 (978-1-934147-99-3(0), CareerTrack) P Univ E Inc.

Improve Your Memory Now: Tools & Exercise to Maximize Your Barin. unabr. ed. Gary Small. Read by Gary Small. 2 CDs. (Running Time: 2 hrs.). 2003. audio compact disk 24.95 (978-1-59179-081-5(6)) Sounds True.
Breakthrough nutrition and lifestyle recommendations for keeping your brain healthy for life. A memory self-assessment exercise to gauge the memory improvements you will gain during this course. The Look, Snap, and Connect technique for remembering names, faces, information and anything else better.

Improve Your Mood. abr. ed. Matthew McKay & Patrick Fanning. Read by Jerry Landis. 1 cass. (Running Time: 20 min.). (Daily Relaxer Audio Ser.). 1998. 7.95 (978-1-57224-099-5(7)) New Harbinger.

Improve Your Performance for Bass Guitar & Guitar Players. Christopher Love. Read by Christopher Love. 1 cass. (Running Time: 30 min.). 1997. 10.95 (978-1-891820-27-4(3)) World Sangha Pubg.
Self-hypnosis meditation for healing, self-improvement & realizing our full & powerful potential as spiritual beings.

Improve Your Performance for Drummers. Christopher Love. Read by Christopher Love. 1 cass. (Running Time: 30 min.). 1997. 10.95 (978-1-891820-25-0(7)) World Sangha Pubg.

Improve Your Performance for Keyboard & Piano Players. Christopher Love. Read by Christopher Love. 1 cass. (Running Time: 30 min.). 1997. 10.95 (978-1-891820-26-7(5)) World Sangha Pubg.

Improve Your Performance for Singers. Christopher Love. Read by Christopher Love. 1 cass. (Running Time: 30 min.). 1997. 10.95 (978-1-891820-24-3(9)) World Sangha Pubg.

Improve Your Quality of Life Set: Fifteen Ways to Make Your Life Better! David Grudermeyer & Rebecca Grudermeyer. 2 cass. 18.95 INCL. HANDOUTS. (T-40) Willingness Wrks.

Improve Your Relationship. Bruce Goldberg. (ENG.). 2005. audio compact disk 17.00 (978-1-57968-078-7(X)) Pub: B Goldberg. Dist(s): Baker Taylor

Improve Your Relationship. Bruce Goldberg. Read by Bruce Goldberg. 1 cass. (Running Time: 25 min.). (ENG.). 2007. 13.00 (978-1-885577-45-0(1)) Pub: B Goldberg. Dist(s): Baker Taylor
Transform any existent relationship into one of positivity and fulfillment through self-hypnosis.

Improve Your Self-Image. Bob Griswold. Read by Bob Griswold. 1 CD. (Running Time: 78 mins.). (Love Tapes Ser.). Orig. Title: Self-Image II. 2005. audio compact disk 15.98 (978-1-55848-153-4(2), Love Tapes) EffectiveMN.
Enhance you ability to learn, grow, and make positive changes in your life. This highly-effective and enjoyable CD will help you build self-esteem and succeed in all areas of life.. This is one of the most popular self-improvement programs of all times and comes with a 100% satisfaction guarantee.This CD contains 3 programs. The first is a guided meditation with powerful imagery and techniques for improving your self-image. It also includes two excellent subliminal programs, one with the sound of ocean waves and the other with relaxing original music.

Improve Your Self-Image II. Read by Robert E. Griswold. 1 cass. 1992. 10.95 (978-1-55848-043-8(9)) EffectiveMN.
Additional powerful methods for self-image developing.

Improve Your Study Habits. Stephen M. Foreman. Ed. by Steven C. Eggleston. 1 cass. (College Survival Ser.). 1988. 6.95 SCE Prod & List & Lrn.
Instructions to college students on time management & study skills.

Improve Your Typing Speed & Accuracy. John B. Morgan. 2 cass. 8.95 incl. drill sheets, scorecard in box. (978-0-917551-01-7(X)) Incentive Learn.
For those with basic typing ability, specially designed drills are recorded & correlated with a booklet of 20 exercises.

Improved Learning. 1998. 24.95 (978-1-58557-016-4(8)) Dynamic Growth.

Improved Self-Esteem, Empowerment & Achievement. Scripts. Marjorie Baker Price. Perf. by Marjorie Baker Price. 3 cassettes. (Running Time: 90 minutes). 1990. 26.95 (978-0-9713013-7-5(9)) Centering Pubns.
"Feel Good About Yourself", "Create Your Own Future" and "Achieve Peak Performance Through Your Own Best Self". These are the titles of three audiotapes in this transformational set for improved self-esteem, empowerment and self-directed forcus and creation, which will allow you to find your own chosen purpose and achieve your dreams. Each 30 minute self-hypnosis listening exercise will move you into a space of deep relaxation and heightened clarity. Here you can envision and direct from a restored sense of belief, trust and determination yourself and your life.

Improving Accounts Receivable Collections. Jane K. Cleland. 6 cass. (Running Time: 60 min. per cass.). 1991. 165.90 Set. (978-1-877680-06-9(0)) Tiger Pr.
This series is intended to provide specific tips, recommendations & inspiration for accounts receivable collectors. Learn to negotiate, listen, handle excuses & love your job!.

Improving Audit Efficiency & Effectiveness. G. William Glezen & Professional Development Institute Staff. 1 cass. (Running Time: 8 hrs.). 1995. bk. 119.00 (752902EZ) Am Inst CPA.
This highly rated course provides you with a wealth of innovative ideas to improve your auditing practice. To retain current clients & attract new ones, your firm must adopt efficient procedures for conducting effective audits. This thorough course identifies opportunities that can help you improve audit efficiency; reduce excess & nonproductive audit procedures; & save you money on your overall audit costs.

Improving Aural Comprehension. Joan Morley. (C). (gr. 10-12). 1984. bk. 150.00 (978-0-472-00200-9(7), 00200) U of Mich Pr.

Improving College Management: An Integrated Systems Approach. Thomas E. Tellefsen. (Higher & Adult Education Ser.). 1990. bk. 62.00 (978-1-55542-182-3(2), Jossey-Bass) Wiley US.

Improving Communication. John Gray. Read by John Gray. 2 cass. (Running Time: 3 hrs.). (Secrets of Successful Relationships Ser.). 1994. 17.95 (978-1-886095-01-4(9)) Genesis Media Grp.
A seminar series helping people understand the opposite sex.

Improving Corporate Donations: New Strategies for Grantmakers & Grantseekers. Vic Murray. (Nonprofit Sector-Public Administration Ser.). 1991. bk. 42.00 (978-1-55542-394-0(9), Jossey-Bass) Wiley US.

Improving Defective Eyesight. Matthew Manning. Music by Ben Horne. 1 cass. 11.95 (MM-110) White Dove NM.
The tape describes a three-part program to help improve eyesight. It includes eye exercises, mental healing techniques, & adopting a new attitude towards seeing. This tape is intended only to help near- & far-sightedness & astigmatism. For other eye problems see Fighting Back.

Improving Guest Relations in the Nursing Home. unabr. ed. Charlotte Eliopoulos. Read by Charlotte Eliopoulos. 1 cass. (Running Time: 25 min.). 1991. 15.00 (978-1-882515-15-8(3)) Hlth Educ Netwk.
Describes factors influencing guest relations in the nursing home & measures to improve guest relations.

Improving Patient Safety: Lessons from American, Australian & British Healthcare. Ed. by Stuart Emslie. 1 CD. 2002. audio compact disk 40.00 (978-0-941417-76-1(X)) ECRI.

Improving People & Performance. Bob Burgess & Jim Savage. 6 cass. 1987. 89.95 (978-1-56207-212-4(9)) Zig Ziglar Corp.
This program is a non-intimidating method of identifying personality traits in yourself, your family & employees. Your improved understanding will lead to better relationships.

Improving Personal Relationships. Shad Helmstetter. 1 cass. (Self-Talk Cassettes Ser.). 10.95 (978-0-937065-30-3(7)) Grindle Pr.

***Improving Reading: Interventions Strategies & Resources Cd.** 5th rev. ed. Johns-Lenski. (ENG.). 2010. audio compact disk 53.96 (978-0-7575-6839-8(4)) Kendall-Hunt.

Improving Relationships: Old & New. Read by Robert E. Griswold. 1 cass. 1992. 10.95 (978-1-55848-023-0(4)) EffectiveMN.
Designed to help you make friends easily, develop better understanding & communication with others & enjoy many great relationships.

Improving Self-Esteem. 1998. 24.95 (978-1-58557-019-5(2)) Dynamic Growth.

Improving Spoken American English. Rosalie H. Smith. 1 cass. (978-1-883834-13-5(9)) Dynamic Comun.

Improving Spoken English: An Intensive Personalized Program in Perception, Pronunciation, Practice in Context. Joan Morley. (C). 1979. bk. 150.00 (978-0-472-00206-1(6), 00206) U of Mich Pr.

Improving Study Habits. Norman J. Caldwell. Read by Norman J. Caldwell. Arranged by Achieve Now Institute Staff. 1 cass. (Running Time: 20 min.). (Childrens' Self-Help Ser.). (J). 1988. 9.97 (978-1-56273-090-1(8)) My Mothers Pub.
Positive ways to organize, persever & feel confidence of remembering.

Improving Vision. Barrie Konicov. 1 cass. 11.98 (978-0-87082-313-8(2), 073) Potentials.
Shows how through the proper course of exercise & applied suggestion, you could improve your eyesight significantly.

Improving Your Athletic Performance. 1997. 24.95 (978-1-58557-007-2(9)) Dynamic Growth.

Improving Your Career. Shad Helmstetter. 1 cass. (Self-Talk Cassettes Ser.). 10.95 (978-0-937065-07-5(2)) Grindle Pr.

Improving Your Concentration. Shad Helmstetter. 1 cass. (Self-Talk Cassettes Ser.). 10.95 (978-0-937065-14-3(5)) Grindle Pr.

Improving Your Kicks. 1 cass. (Martial Arts Programming Ser.). 12.50 (978-0-87554-191-4(7), K101) Valley Sun.
You react instantly & accurately. Everyday you improve your kicking ability. Everyday you kick faster & harder. You now perfect your snap & speed kicks. You now perfect your power kicks. You now coordinate your strikes & kicks for maximum effectiveness. You now accomplish your martial arts goals.

Improving Your Personal Problem-Solving. Frank L. Natter. 12 cass. (Running Time: 18 hrs.). 1989. 99.95 set. (978-1-878287-91-5(5), ATA-O) Type & Temperament.
Set of 12 tapes includes Solving Personal Problems using psychological type & temperament, including vocational choice & life cycles; solving relationship problems, including Love Triangles/Love Class, Buber's I-It & I-Thou relationship; Inclusion, Control & Affection; Listening/Transactional Analysis & Rational Living, & Legal Problem-Solving.

Improving Your Personal Problem-Solving, Pts. 1 & 2. Frank L. Natter. 7 cass. (Running Time: 90 min. per cass.). 1989. 54.95 Set. (978-1-878287-71-7(0), ATAF-I & II) Type & Temperament.

Improving Your Personal Problem-Solving, Pt. 2: Relationships. Frank L. Natter. Read by Frank L. Natter. 3 cass. 1989. 24.95 Set. (978-1-878287-66-3(4)) Type & Temperament.
Like Leo Buscaglia, Natter has taught classes on love & relationships, & much of the best is distilled here. He covers the principles of Buber's "I-Thou" relationships, & the Inclusion-Control-Affection motivational approach popular in organizations, but powerful also for couples. Tips on the art of listening & T.A. (transactional analysis) round out this exceptional series. Includes: Love Triangles/Love Class (ANA-10); ANA-11 I-It & I-Thou Relationships/Inclusion-Control-Affection; ANA-12 Listening/Transactional Analysis & Rational Living.

Improving Your Relationship with Money. unabr. ed. Joan Sotkin. Read by Joan Sotkin. 2 cass. (Running Time: 2 hrs.). Dramatization. 1992. 19.95 set. (978-1-881002-91-8(8), T103) Build Your Busn.
How to release blocks that keep you from prosperity, How to step into the MoneyFlow & stay there, How to develop your money muscles, How to stop worrying & obsessing about money, How to replace money vagueness with money clarity.

Improving Your Serve: The Art of Unselfish Living. unabr. ed. Charles R. Swindoll. 8 cass. (Running Time: 6 hrs. 30 mins.). 1999. 39.95 (978-1-57972-314-9(4)) Insight Living.

Improving Your Strikes & Punches. 1 cass. (Martial Arts Programming Ser.). 12.50 (978-0-87554-192-1(5), K102) Valley Sun.
Everyday you strike with more power & speed. You react instantly & accurately. You now coordinate your strikes, punches & kicks for maximum effectiveness. You now draw upon all of your past awareness to perfect your techniques. You are a martial artist with incredible punching & striking ability.

Improvisation Course & Chord Studies. Jerry Hahn. (Jerry Hahn Contemporary Guitar Ser.: Vol. 3). 1998. spiral bd. 17.95 (978-0-7866-3219-0(4), 94185BCD) Mel Bay.

Improvisation, Inc. unabr. ed. Robert Lowe. Read by David Hilder. 7 cass. (Running Time: 10 hrs.). 2001. 49.95 (978-0-7861-2072-7(X), 2833); audio compact disk 64.00 (978-0-7861-9695-1(5), 2833) Blckstn Audio.
Performers have been doing it for centuries. Now, for the first time, Robert Lowe, a pioneer in the field of improvisation, hands you the techniques you need to think on your feet and shows you how to apply these techniques in your workplace or classroom.

Improvisation Step by Step: Improvising Classical Music on Piano. Misha Stefanuk. 2008. lib. bdg. 22.95 (978-0-7866-6106-0(2)) Mel Bay.

***Improvisational Cook 1.** abr. ed. Sally Schneider. (ENG.). 2006. (978-0-06-135552-3(6), Harper Audio) HarperCollins Pubs.

***Improvisational Cook 2.** abr. ed. Sally Schneider. (ENG.). 2006. (978-0-06-135553-0(4), Harper Audio) HarperCollins Pubs.

Improvisation/Bridging the Gap. Ron Nairn. 2001. per. 19.95 (978-0-7866-5859-6(2)) Mel Bay.

Improvisation/Bridging the Gap Treble Clef Edition. Ron Nairn. 2001. per. 19.95 (978-0-7866-5860-2(6)) Mel Bay.

Improvise with Eric Nagler. Perf. by Eric Nagler. 1 cass. (Running Time: 45 min.). (Family Ser.). (J). (ps-5). 1989. 9.98 (8018); audio compact disk 14.98 (8018) Rounder Records.
Nagler showcases the extent of his talents & resourcefulness. In addition to playing conventional instruments (guitar, banjo, mandolin, autoharp & fiddle) he also uses some less conventional ones (musical saw, bones, & sewerphone).

Improvising Blues Harmonica. David Barrett & John Garcia. 2008. pap. bk. 19.95 (978-0-7866-7321-6(4)) Mel Bay.

Improvising Jazz Piano. John Mehegan. 1985. 9.95 (978-0-318-70317-6(3), AM72844) Music Sales.

Impulse. abr. ed. Michael Weaver. Read by Stacey Keach. (ENG.). 2006. 9.99 (978-1-59483-830-9(5)) Pub: Hachet Audio. Dist(s): HachBkGrp

Impulse. abr. ed. Michael Weaver. Read by Stacy Keach. 2001. 7.95 (978-1-57815-216-2(X), Media Bks Audio) Media Bks NJ.

Impulse. unabr. ed. Catherine Coulter. Read by Valerie Leonard. 10 vols. (Running Time: 15 hrs.). 2000. bk. 84.95 (978-0-7927-2385-1(6), CSL 274, Chivers Sound Lib) AudioGO.
When wealthy, beautiful Rafaella Holland puts her dazzling newspaper career on hold to care for her ailing mother, she learns of a long-held family secret: the true identity of her real father, whom she never knew. Wanting to exact revenge upon this notorious, world-famous man who wronged her mother, she is determined to find him. Her search takes her to an exclusive Caribbean island, a protected sanctuary for the rich & powerful.

Impulse. unabr. ed. Ellen Hopkins. Read by Jeremy Guskin et al. (ENG., 2009. audio compact disk 29.95 (978-1-59887-756-4(9), 1598877569) Pub: HighBridge. Dist(s): Workman Pub

Impulse Control. Eldon Taylor. 1 cass. (Running Time: 62 min.). (Inner Talk Ser.). 16.95 incl. script. (978-1-55978-164-0(5), 53872C) Progress Aware Res.
Soundtrack - Musical Themes with underlying subliminal affirmations.

Impulse Control: Easy. Eldon Taylor. Read by Eldon Taylor. Ed. by Leslie Brice. 1 cass. (Running Time: 1 hr.). 1992. 16.95 (978-1-56705-224-4(X)) Gateways Inst.
Self improvement.

Impulse Control: Ocean. Eldon Taylor. Read by Eldon Taylor. Ed. by Leslie Brice. 1 cass. (Running Time: 1 hr.). 1992. 16.95 (978-1-56705-225-1(8)) Gateways Inst.

Impulse Control: Peaceful Ocean. Eldon Taylor. 1 cass. 16.95 (978-1-55978-647-8(7), 53782O) Progress Aware Res.

Impulse Factor: The Hidden Force Behind the Choices We Make. unabr. ed. Nick Tasler. Read by Buck Schirner. (Running Time: 8 hrs.). 2008. 24.95 (978-1-4233-7516-6(5), 9781423375166, BAD); 24.95 (978-1-4233-7514-2(9), 9781423375142, Brilliance MP3); 39.25 (978-1-4233-7515-9(7), 9781423375159, Brinc Audio MP3 Lib); 39.25 (978-1-4233-7517-3(3), 9781423375173, BADLE); audio compact disk 87.25 (978-1-4233-7513-5(0), 9781423375135, BriAudCD Unabrid) Brilliance Audio.

Impulse Factor: Why Some of Us Play It Safe & Others Risk It All. unabr. ed. Nick Tasler. Read by Buck Schirner. 7 CDs. (Running Time: 8 hrs.). 2008. audio compact disk 29.95 (978-1-4233-7512-8(2), 9781423375128, Bril Audio CD Unabri) Brilliance Audio.

iMusica para todo el mundo! see Music, Music for Everyone

Imzadi. Peter David. Read by Jonathan Frakes. (Running Time: 4 hrs.). 2000. 19.95 (978-1-60083-423-3(X), Audiofy Corp) Iofy Corp.

Imzadi II: Triangle. Peter David. Read by Robert O'Reilly. 2 cass. (Running Time: 3 hrs.). (Star Trek Ser.). 1999. 15.00 (978-0-671-03343-9(3)) S and S Inc.
Events which broke up commander Worf from his beloved Deanna Troy.

In a Class by Itself. 2 LPs. pupil's gde. ed. 15.00 (KIM 3006); 15.00 incl. guide. (KIM 3006C) Kimbo Educ.
Barre & centre floor techniques to the music of the 1890's.

In a Class by Itself, Set. abr. ed. Sandra Brown. 2 cass. 1999. 18.00 (FS9-50994) Highsmith.

In a Dark, Dark Room & Other Scary Stories. abr. ed. Alvin Schwartz. Illus. by Dirk Zimmer. 1 cass. (Running Time: 90 min.). (I Can Read Bks.). (J). (ps-3). 1990. 8.99 (978-1-55994-233-1(9), TBC 2339) HarperCollins Pubs.

In a Dark, Dark Room & Other Scary Stories. abr. ed. Alvin Schwartz. Illus. by Dirk Zimmer. (I Can Read Bks.). (J). (gr. 1-3). 2008. 9.99 (978-0-06-133613-3(0), HarperFestival) HarperCollins Pubs.

In a Dark House. Deborah Crombie. Read by Michael Deehy. 8 cass. (Duncan Kincaid/Gemma James Novel Ser.). 69.95 (978-0-7927-3341-6(X), CSL 702); audio compact disk 94.95 (978-0-7927-3342-3(8), SLD 702) AudioGO.

In a Dark Wood: A Novel. unabr. ed. Amanda Craig. Read by Daniel Hill. 8 cass. (Running Time: 12 hrs.). 2001. 69.95 (978-0-7540-0649-7(2), CAB 2071) Pub: Chivers Audio Bks GBR. Dist(s): AudioGO
Benedick Hunter is a man who has lost everything, but his life takes on a new direction when he finds a book of his mother's in which real people and their stories are strangely interwoven with traditional fairy tales.

In a Dry Season. Peter Robinson. Narrated by Ron Keith. 14 CDs. (Running Time: 17 hrs.). (Inspector Banks Mystery Ser.). audio compact disk 134.00 (978-1-4025-3494-2(9)) Recorded Bks.

In a Dry Season. unabr. ed. Peter Robinson. Narrated by Ron Keith. 12 cass. (Running Time: 17 hrs.). (Inspector Banks Mystery Ser.). 2002. 99.00 (978-0-7887-9499-5(X)) Recorded Bks.
An insufferable drought ravages the Yorkshire countryside, depleting the Thornfield Reservoir, revealing the remnants of the flooded town of Hobb's End and the terrible secrets kept safe within its watery tomb. Amongst the ruins, the remains of a woman's body are discovered. Detective Banks deduces that the woman was strangled and repeatedly stabbed more than 50 years ago. His investigation takes him on a treacherous quest to bring a killer, who has escaped detection for over a half a century, to justice.

In a Family Way. Tana Reiff. 1 cass. (That's Life Ser.: Bk. 4). 1994. 10.95 (978-0-7854-1098-0(8)) Am Guidance.

In a Far Country see Son of the Wolf

In a Far Country. 1984. (S-51) Jimcin Record.

In a German Pension, Set. unabr. ed. Katherine Mansfield. Read by Flo Gibson. 2 cass. (Running Time: 3 hrs.). 1989. 14.95 (978-1-55685-143-8(X)) Audio Bk Con.
A British lady seeks "The Cure". amog an assorted group of germans, in such tales as "Germans at Meat", "The Baron", "The Sister of the Baroness", "Fran Fisher", "The Modern Seul", "A Life Bad", "The Child-Who-Was Tired" & "The Advanced Lady".

In a Heart Beat - Dracula. Paul Christian & Bram Stoker. 1 cass. (J). (gr. 1-12). 1996. 4.95 (978-1-57555-007-7(5)) Cedar Bay Pr.
"In a Heartbeat" is a novella for those who fancy themselves as vampires. Bundled with the classic "Dracula" by Bram Stoker.

***In a Heartbeat: How Cheerful Giving Changed Our Lives.** unabr. ed. Leigh Anne Tuohy et al. (Running Time: 7 hrs. 0 mins. 0 sec.). (ENG.). 2010. audio compact disk 29.99 (978-1-4272-1098-2(5)) Pub: Macmill Audio. Dist(s): Macmillan

In a League of His Own: Pop Standards Played by Ron Odrich & You: Clarinet Play-along Pack. Ron Odrich. 2008. pap. bk. 24.98 (978-1-4234-6882-0(1), 1423468821) Pub: Music Minus. Dist(s): H Leonard

In a Narrow Grave: Essays on Texas. unabr. collector's ed. Larry McMurtry. Read by Wolfram Kandinsky. 7 cass. (Running Time: 7 hrs.). 1988. 42.00 (978-0-7366-1446-7(X), 2329) Books on Tape.
Collection of essays on what it means to come from Texas.

In a Nutshell: Afghanistan: A History. unabr. ed. (Running Time: 1 hr. 20 mins.). 2009. audio compact disk 14.98 (978-962-634-961-8(1), Naxos AudioBooks) Naxos.

In a Nutshell: Karma & Rebirth. unabr. ed. Jinananda. (Running Time: 1 hr. 20 mins.). 2009. audio compact disk 14.98 (978-962-634-945-8(X), Naxos AudioBooks) Naxos.

In a Nutshell: Tibet: A History. unabr. ed. Jonathan Gregson. (Running Time: 1 hr. 20 mins.). 2009. audio compact disk 14.98 (978-962-634-962-5(X), Naxos AudioBooks) Naxos.

In a Pig's Eye: Reflections on the Police State, Repression & Native America. Ward Churchill. (Running Time: 2 hrs.). (AK Press Audio Ser.). (ENG.). 2002. audio compact disk 19.98 (978-1-902593-50-0(2)) Pub: AK Pr GBR. Dist(s): Consort Bk Sales

***In a Pit with a Lion on a Snowy Day: How to Survive & Thrive When Opportunity Roars.** unabr. ed. Mark Batterson. (ENG.). 2008. 12.98 (978-1-59644-586-4(6), Hovel Audio) christianaud.

In a Pit with a Lion on a Snowy Day: How to Survive & Thrive When Opportunity Roars. unabr. ed. Mark Batterson. Read by Mark Batterson. (Running Time: 5 hrs. 12 mins. 0 sec.). (ENG.). 2008. audio compact disk 21.98 (978-1-59644-585-7(8)) christianaud.

In a Place Called Gethsemane. Truman G. Madsen. 1 cass. 1990. 7.95 (978-1-57008-036-4(4), Bkcraft Inc) Deseret Bk.

In a Small Small Pond. 2004. bk. 24.95 (978-1-55592-081-4(0)); pap. bk. 32.75 (978-1-55592-246-7(5)); pap. bk. 32.75 (978-1-55592-247-4(3)); pap. bk. 14.95 (978-1-55592-082-1(9)) Weston Woods.

In a Spring Garden; Attic of the Wind; Casey at the Bat; Custard the Dragon; Owl & the Pussy-Cat; Wynken, Blynken & Nod. 2004. (978-0-89719-812-7(3)); cass. & flmstrp (978-0-89719-721-2(6)) Weston Woods.

In a Strange City. unabr. ed. Laura Lippman. Read by Laurence Bouvard. 8 cass. (Running Time: 11 hrs.). (Tess Monaghan Ser.: No. 6). (J). 2002. 69.95 (978-0-7531-1521-3(2)); audio compact disk 89.95 (978-0-7531-1584-8(0)) Pub: ISIS Lrg Prnt GBR. Dist(s): Ulverscroft US
Every year on January 19th the grave of Edgar Allan Poe in Baltimore is visited by the Poe Toaster, also known as the Visitor, who leaves three red roses and a half-empty bottle of cognac. He has remained anonymous for fifty years and his visit is one of Baltimore's best-loved rituals. Then, early one January, Tess is asked to find out his identity. Refusing the assignment, she goes to the January vigil anyway.

In a Strange Land. Margaret Thomson Davis. 6 cass. (Running Time: 8 hrs.). (Story Sound Ser.). (J). 2005. 54.95 (978-1-85903-785-0(2)) Pub: Mgna Lrg Print GBR. Dist(s): Ulverscroft US

In a Summer Season. unabr. ed. Elizabeth Taylor. Read by Gretel Davis. 7 cass. (Running Time: 8 hrs. 45 min.). 1994. 61.95 (978-1-85089-727-9(1), 9003X) Pub: ISIS Audio GBR. Dist(s): Ulverscroft US
Kate Heron is a wealthy widow who married a man ten years her junior. Their love arms them against the disapproval of conservative friends, until the return of Kate's old friend Charles.

In a Sunburned Country. Bill Bryson. Read by Bill Bryson. 7 cass. (Running Time: 10 hrs. 30 min.). 2000. 39.95 (H557) Blckstn Audio.
The authors' previous excursion up, down & over the Appalachian Trail resulted in the sublime bestseller "A Walk in the Woods." Now he has traveled around the world & all the way "Down Under" to Australia, a shockingly under-discovered country with the friendliest inhabitants, the driest weather & the most peculiar & lethal wildlife to be found on this planet. A deliciously funny, fact-filled & adventurous performance that combines humor, wonder & unflagging curiosity.

In a Sunburned Country. unabr. ed. Bill Bryson. Read by Bill Bryson. 7 cass. (Running Time: 10 hrs. 30 mons.). 2002. 56.00 (978-0-7366-5434-0(8), 5305) Books on Tape.
The author takes us on an adventure-filled tour of Australia, a land with the friendliest people, the hottest, driest weather, and the most peculiar wildlife to be found on the planet. Taking us far beyond the beaten tourist path. He introduces us to Australians who are cheerful, extroverted and unfailingly obliging, the beaming products of a land with clean, safe cities, cold beer and constant sunshine. Australia is an immense and fortunate land.

In a Sunburned Country. unabr. ed. Bill Bryson. Read by Bill Bryson. 9 CDs. (Running Time: 12 hrs.). (ENG.). 2000. audio compact disk 49.95 (978-0-553-50259-6(X)) Pub: Random Audio Pubg. Dist(s): Random

In a Tropical Rain Forest Audio CD. Adapted by Benchmark Education Company Staff. Based on a work by Katherine Scraper. (Early Explorers Set C Ser.). (J). (gr. 1). 2008. audio compact disk 10.00 (978-1-60437-541-1(8)) Benchmark Educ.

In a Vision of the Night. Neville Goddard. 1 cass. (Running Time: 62 min.). 1964. 8.00 (15) J & L Pubns.
Neville taught Imagination Creates Reality. He was a powerfully influential teacher of God as Consciousness.

In Adoration of the King of Kings. Nan Gurley. Contrib. by Camp Kirkland. Created by Camp Kirkland. Contrib. by Tom Fettke. Created by Tom Fettke. (ENG.). 1995. audio compact disk 12.00 (978-0-00-509174-6(8)) Allegis.

***In Adoration of the King of Kings.** Nan Gurley. Contrib. by Camp Kirkland. Created by Camp Kirkland. Contrib. by Tom Fettke. Created by Tom Fettke. (ENG.). 1995. audio compact disk 16.99 (978-0-00-509172-2(1)) Allegis.

In Alaska with Shipwreck Kelly. abr. ed. Dan Cushman. Read by Dick Hill. (Running Time: 10800 sec.). (Five Star Westerns Ser.). 2007. audio compact disk 24.95 (978-1-4233-3571-9(6), 9781423335719, Brilliance MP3); audio compact disk 39.25 (978-1-4233-3572-6(4), 9781423335726, Brlnc Audio MP3 Lib) Brilliance Audio.

In Alaska with Shipwreck Kelly. abr. ed. Dan Cushman. Read by Dick Hill. (Running Time: 3 hrs.). (Five Star Westerns Ser.). 2007. 39.25 (978-1-4233-3574-0(0), 9781423335740, BADLE); 24.95 (978-1-4233-3573-3(2), 9781423335733, BAD) Brilliance Audio.

In Alaska with Shipwreck Kelly. unabr. ed. Dan Cushman. Read by Rob McQuay. 5 cass. (Running Time: 7 hrs. 30 min.). 2000. Rental 13.50 30 day. Books on Tape.
All the excitement of the Gold Rush unfolds as two men race to establish the first gambling casino in the Yukon.

In All Kinds of Weather, Kids Make Music! Sunny, Stormy, & Always Fun Music Activities for You & Your Child. Lynn Kleiner. (ENG.). 2001. audio compact disk 14.95 (978-0-7579-0001-3(1)) Alfred Pub.

***In an Antique Land: History in the Guise of a Traveler's Tale.** unabr. ed. Amitav Ghosh. Read by Simon Vance. (Running Time: 9 hrs.). 2010. 24.99 (978-1-4418-3502-4(4), 9781441835024, Brilliance MP3); 39.97 (978-1-4418-3503-1(2), 9781441835031, Brlnc Audio MP3 Lib); audio compact disk 29.99 (978-1-4418-3500-0(8), 9781441835000, Bril Audio CD Unabri); audio compact disk 89.97 (978-1-4418-3501-7(6), 9781441835017, BriAudCD Unabrid) Brilliance Audio.

In an Eastern Rose Garden. abr. ed. Khan Inayat. Read by Jay Sheridan & Jan Sheridan. 2 cass. (Running Time: 3 hrs.). Dramatization. 1994. 24.95 set. (978-1-883388-01-0(5)) Add Venture.
A selection of readings from the hardcover book, In an Eastern Rose Garden. To enhance comprehension, brief musical interludes have been interspersed with the readings.

In an Edinburgh Drawing Room. Lucilla Andrews. 2009. 49.95 (978-1-84559-942-3(X)); audio compact disk 59.95 (978-1-84559-943-0(8)) Pub: Soundings Ltd GBR. Dist(s): Ulverscroft US

In an Evil Time. unabr. ed. Bill Pronzini. Read by William Dufris. 6 vols. (Running Time: 9 hrs.). 2002. bk. 54.95 (978-0-7927-2531-2(X), CSL 420, Chivers Sound Lib) AudioGO.
Jack Hollis had finally steeled himself for what had to be done: When a man is threatening your daughter and grandson, when reason can't stop it, when restraining orders don't work and the police can't help, then a father's choices are limited. David Rakubian was vicious, abusive, powerful, deadly and Angela's husband. Everyone Hollis knew all wanted to help save Angela. But this was something jack knew he had to do himself. Failure would be costly: success just as risky. and Jack must hurry, before he loses his nerve.

In an Instant: A Family's Journey of Love & Healing. unabr. ed. Bob Woodruff. Narrated by Bob Woodruff. Narrated by Lee Woodruff. 8 cass. (Running Time: 9 hrs. 45 mins.). 2007. 72.75 (978-1-4281-5761-3(1)); audio compact disk 92.75 (978-1-4281-5763-7(8)) Recorded Bks.

In an Instant: A Family's Journey of Love & Healing. unabr. ed. Lee Woodruff & Bob Woodruff. Narrated by Lee Woodruff & Bob Woodruff. 8 CDs. (Running Time: 10 hrs.). 2007. audio compact disk 34.99 (978-1-4281-5760-6(3)) Recorded Bks.

In & Out of the Forest. unabr. ed. Winifred Foley. Read by Sarah Sherborne. 4 cass. (Running Time: 6 hrs.). 1999. 34.95 (978-0-7531-0493-4(8), 990317) Pub: ISIS Audio GBR. Dist(s): Ulverscroft US
To anyone born after World War II, Foley's account of her childhood, domestic service, early married life with Syd, & final return to her beloved Forest of Dean must seem incredible. Throughout a life which might have broken many a brave spirit, her sense of humor, sheer courage, affection for her family & friends kept her going.

In & Out the Windows: My Life as a Psychic. unabr. ed. Dilys Gater. Read by Dilys Gater. 4 cass. (Running Time: 6 hrs.). 2001. 44.95 (978-1-898670-05-6(6), 750056) Pub: ISIS Audio GBR. Dist(s): ISIS Pub
Dilys Gater is a top-selling author, a practicing "Wise Woman," a psychic, a medium & a healer. This is her warm, informal account of how she became a professional psychic & how it affected her life. She presents rare glimpses into personal cases including ghosts & hauntings, regression to past lives, animal angels, mischievious spirits & reveals what it is like to live & work on an everyday basis with one foot in the spirit world.

In at the Kill. unabr. ed. Alexander Ferguson. Read by Graham Roberts. 14 cass. (Running Time: 18 hrs.). 2000. 99.95 (978-1-86042-693-3(X), 2693X) Pub: Soundings Ltd GBR. Dist(s): Ulverscroft US
A captured agent is shot by Gestapo & left for dead, but has been nursed back to health at a farmhouse in Alsace. And now she has a score to settle.

***In Aunt Giraffe's Green Garden: & Frogs Wore Red Suspenders.** unabr. ed. Jack Prelutsky. Read by Jack Prelutsky. (ENG.). 2007. (978-0-06-145119-5(3), GreenwillowBks); (978-0-06-145120-1(7), GreenwillowBks) HarperCollins Pubs.

In Aunt Giraffe's Green Garden & the Frogs Wore Red Suspenders. unabr. ed. Jack Prelutsky. Read by Jack Prelutsky. 2 CDs. (Running Time: 1 hr.). (J). (ps-3). 2007. 17.95 (978-0-06-125456-7(8), HarperChildAud) HarperCollins Pubs.

In Aunt Lucy's Kitchen. Cynthia Rylant. Narrated by Suzanne Toren. 1 cass. (Running Time: 30 mins.). (Cobble Street Cousins Ser.: No. 1). (gr. 2 up). 2002. 10.00 (978-0-7887-9584-8(8)) Recorded Bks.
Lily, Rosie, and Tess are spending the summer with Aunt Lucy and decide to start a cookie company. Soon they have baked dozens of cookies and have made some wonderful new friends, including a shy man who has a crush on Aunt Lucy! Now the cousins are cooking up plans to get them together.

In Beauty May I Walk: Restoring Life to the Sacred, Medications on Misplaced Identity. unabr. ed. Linley Solari et al. 2 cass. (Running Time: 3 hrs). 2002. 19.95 (978-0-9714130-0-9(2)) L Solari.
A collage of teaching, meditation, poetry, and chant that explores the truth of being within the theme of "walking in beauty" from Navajo cosmology. Meditations are designed to help the listener shift out of negative mind states in just a minute.

In Berkeley, California. Perf. by Ali A. Khan. 1 cass. 9.98 (A0055-0) Sound Photosyn.
With Pranesh Khan on tabla. Ragas: Darbari Kanara, Madan Manjari.

In Better Hands. Contrib. by Natalie Grant. (Sound Performance Soundtracks Ser.). 2007. audio compact disk 5.98 (978-5-557-51416-3(3)) Pt of Grace Ent.

In Big Trouble. unabr. ed. Laura Lippman. Read by Deborah Hazlett. (Tess Monaghan Ser.: No. 4). (YA). 2008. 74.99 (978-1-60514-646-1(3)) Find a World.

In Big Trouble. unabr. ed. Laura Lippman. 2009. audio compact disk 39.99 (978-0-06-195501-3(9), Harper Audio) HarperCollins Pubs.

***In Big Trouble: A Tess Monaghan Novel.** Laura Lippman. Narrated by Deborah Hazlett. (Running Time: 10 hrs. 15 mins. 0 sec.). (ENG.). 2010. audio compact disk 29.95 (978-1-60998-134-1(0)) Pub: AudioGO. Dist(s): Perseus Dist

In Bondage to Freedom. Instructed by Manly P. Hall. 8.95 (978-0-89314-146-2(1), C800140) Philos Res.

In Case of Emergency. unabr. collector's ed. Georges Simenon. Read by Michael Prichard. 5 cass. (Running Time: 5 hrs.). 1983. 30.00 (978-0-7366-0536-6(3), 1510) Books on Tape.
In this novel of obsession, Lucien Gobillot, a respected & brilliant criminal lawyer, makes a perverse & sordid liaison with a prostitute who celebrates infidelity like a virtue. Driven by forces he cannot control, Gobillot plumbs the depths of degradation. It is logical he should find murder waiting there.

In Case You Missed It. Tracy St. John. Comment by Bruce Ryan. 1 cass. (Running Time: 30 min.). 9.95 Reeder Pr.
Features kicker stories aired on WLTF Radio and comments by Tracy St. John & Bruce Ryan.

In Celebration of Women. Nancy Stewart. 1 cass. (Running Time: 40 min.). 1991. 9.95 (978-1-885430-09-0(4), FS104) Frnds St Music.
Songs for & about women.

In Chancery. John Galsworthy. Read by David Case. (Running Time: 39600 sec.). (Forsyte Saga Ser.). 2006. audio compact disk 29.95 (978-0-7861-7404-1(8)) Blckstn Audio.

In Chancery. unabr. ed. John Galsworthy. Read by David Case. (Running Time: 39600 sec.). (Forsyte Saga Ser.). 2006. 72.95 (978-0-7861-4667-3(2)); audio compact disk 29.95 (978-0-7861-6740-1(8)) Blckstn Audio.

In Chancery, unabr. ed. John Galsworthy. Narrated by Neil Hunt. 8 cass. (Running Time: 11 hrs. 30 mins.). (Forsyte Saga Ser.: Vol. 2). 1988. 70.00 (978-1-55690-182-9(8), 88040E7) Recorded Bks.

In Chancery, Vol. 2. John Galsworthy. Read by Flo Gibson. 9 cass. (Running Time: 12 hrs. 30 min.). (Forsyte Saga Ser.: Bk. II). 1996. 28.95 (978-1-55685-428-6(5)) Audio Bk Con.
"Indian Summer of a Forsyte," an interlude, recounts the lyrical last days of old Jolyon as he basks in the glow of his visits with beautiful Irene. "In Chancery" deals with Soames' divorce & marriage to a French woman, Annette, & the love story of Irene & young Joylon.

In Chancery & Awakening, unabr. ed. John Galsworthy. Read by David Case. 8 cass. (Running Time: 12 hrs.). (Forsyte Saga Ser.). 1998. 64.00 (978-0-7366-4195-1(5), 4693) Books on Tape.
This epic sweeps from the 1880s through the 1920s, recounting the lives & loves of an upper-middle-class English family, the Forsyte's. Tied to the waning values of Victorianism, this privileged clan is shaken to its core when the First World War shatters the English social order. Chronicling the brave new world into which the family is thrown, Galsworthy's tale brings to life an unforgettable cast of characters: Soames Forsyte, the rigid family patriarch; Irene, his beautiful, seductive wife; Cousin Jolyon, an artist committed to freedom & creativity & a host of other.

***In Cheap We Trust: The Story of a Misunderstood American Virtue.** unabr. ed. Lauren Weber. Read by Marguerite Gavin. (Running Time: 9 hrs.). (ENG.). 2010. 34.98 (978-1-59659-535-4(3), GildAudio) Pub: Gildan Media. Dist(s): HachBkGrp

In Christ Alone. Contrib. by Avalon. (Mastertrax Ser.). 2006. audio compact disk 9.98 (978-5-558-16190-8(6)) Pt of Grace Ent.

In Christ Alone. Contrib. by Adrienne Liesching & Geoff Moore. (Mastertrax Ser.). 2006. audio compact disk 9.98 (978-5-558-01805-9(4)) FF Rcds.

In Christ Alone: Modern Hymns of Worship. Contrib. by Bethany Dillon & Matt Hammitt. Prod. by John Mark Painter. 2008. audio compact disk 13.99 (978-5-557-48823-5(5)) Pt of Grace Ent.

In Christ Alone (Medley) Contrib. by Phillips Craig & Dean. (Praise Hymn Soundtracks Ser.). 2005. audio compact disk 8.98 (978-5-558-93073-3(X)) Pt of Grace Ent.

In Christ Alone with the Solid Rock. Contrib. by Travis Cottrell. 2008. audio compact disk 24.95 (978-5-557-47839-7(6)) Hosanna NM.

In Cold Blood. unabr. ed. Truman Capote. Read by Scott Brick. 12 CDs. (Running Time: 14 hrs.). 2006. audio compact disk 84.15 (978-1-4159-3092-2(9)); 81.00 (978-1-4159-3091-5(0)) Books on Tape.
On November 15, 1959, in the small town of Holcomb, Kansas, four members of the Clutter family were savagely murdered by blasts from a shotgun held a few inches from their faces. There was no apparent motive for the crime, and there were almost no clues. As Truman Capote reconstructs the murder and the investigation that led to the capture, trial, and execution of the killers, he generates both mesmerizing suspense and astonishing empathy. In Cold Blood is a work that transcends its moment, yielding poignant insights into the nature of American violence.

In Cold Blood. unabr. ed. Truman Capote. Read by Wolfram Kandinsky. 11 cass. (Running Time: 16 hrs. 30 mins.). 1993. 88.00 (978-0-7366-2476-3(7), 133539) Books on Tape.
In Kansas in the 1960s you didn't slaughter innocent people & then cop a plea. Finally we're given an illuminating account of the story of Hickock & Smith, who didn't plan on killing a family of four.

In Cold Blood. unabr. ed. Truman Capote. Read by Scott Brick. 12 CDs. (Running Time: 14 hrs. 30 mins.). (ENG.). 2006. audio compact disk 34.95 (978-0-7393-3364-8(X), Random AudioBks) Pub: Random Audio Pubg. Dist(s): Random

In Cold Pursuit. unabr. ed. Ursula Curtiss. 5 cass. 1998. 63.95 Set. (978-1-872672-78-6(7)) Pub: Magna Story GBR. Dist(s): Ulverscroft US

In Colt Blood. collector's ed. Jody Jaffe. Read by Bernadette Dunne. 7 cass. (Running Time: 10 hrs. 30 min.). 1999. 56.00 (978-0-7366-4787-8(2), 5134) Books on Tape.
When Natalie Gold's boss at "The Charlotte Commercial Appeal" orders her to find a local horse whisperer to interview, she knows just the person: Sarah Jane Lowell, but before she can set up a meeting, Sarah Jane vanishes along with her newfound friend: Nattie's eccentric father. Their disappearance coincides with the murder of Fuzzy McMahon, whose bludgeoned body was found at the very stable where Nattie was supposed to meet Sarah Jane. Who could the killer be?.

In Concert at St. John's. Perf. by Ali A. Khan. 1 cass. 8.98 (A0053-0) Sound Photosyn.
With Zakir Hussain on tabla. Raga: Kirwani.

In Connection with Kilshaw. unabr. collector's ed. Peter Driscoll. Read by Chris Winfield. 8 cass. (Running Time: 8 hrs.). 1977. 48.00 (978-0-7366-0067-5(1), 1078) Books on Tape.
British intelligence veteran Harry Finn is sent to Ireland to kill James Campbell Kilshaw, a Protestant extremist leader. This decision, reluctantly arrived at, is expected to defuse a highly inflammable situation & avert a full-scale civil war. Finn soon realizes that even he as an outsider must prepare to fight for his life.

In Constant Prayer. unabr. ed. Robert Benson. Frwd. by Phyllis Tickle. Narrated by Robertson Dean. (Running Time: 3 hrs. 30 mins. 0 sec.). (ENG.). 2008. audio compact disk 24.98 (978-1-59644-635-9(8), Hovel Audio) christianaud.

***In Constant Prayer.** unabr. ed. Robert Benson. Narrated by Robertson Dean. (ENG.). 2008. 14.98 (978-1-59644-636-6(6), Hovel Audio) christianaud.

In Contact, Bk. 2. 2nd ed. Jane Sturtevant. 3 cass. (Scott Foresman English Ser.). 2002. 50.10 (978-0-201-66408-9(9)); audio compact disk 50.10 (978-0-201-66410-2(0)) AddisonWesley.

In Contempt. abr. ed. Christopher A. Darden. 2 cass. (Running Time: 2 hrs.). 15.95 (17240) Books on Tape.
Criticized as an "Uncle Tom," Darden stood up & argued that "no one is above the law; not the police, not the rich, not O.J. Simpson." His memoir is the rare story of one man who refused to choose between his heritage & his humanity.

In Contempt. unabr. ed. Christopher A. Darden. Read by Howard Weinberger. 10 cass. (Running Time: 15 hrs.). 1996. 80.00 (978-0-913369-29-6(2), 4182) Books on Tape.
For more than a year Christopher Darden argued passionately & tirelessly, giving voice to the victims in the O. J. Simpson murder trial.

In Contempt. unabr. ed. Christopher A. Darden. Contrib. by Jess Walter. 1 cass. (Running Time: 1 hr.). 2002. 18.00 (978-0-7881-6613-6(1)) DIANE Pub.

In Conversation With: Capital Radio. (Running Time: 1 hr. 30 mins.). 2005. 16.95 (978-1-59912-928-0(0)) Iofy Corp.

In Country. Bobbie Ann Mason. Read by Bobbie Ann Mason. 1 cass. (Running Time: 58 min.). 1985. 13.95 (978-1-55644-128-8(2), 5041) Am Audio Prose.
The author reads excerpts from "In Country".

In Country Sleep see Dylan Thomas Reading On the Marriage of a Virgin, Over Sir John's Hill, In Country Sleep & Others

In Country Sleep see Dylan Thomas Reading His Poetry

In Creativity's Wake. Sujantra G. McKeever. Read by Sujantra G. McKeever. Ed. by Joe Statt. 1 cass. (Running Time: 40 min.). 1994. 10.00 (978-1-885479-04-4(2)) McKeever Pubng.
A tape of original poetry & music which emerges from the mystical realms of experience.

In Crisis Lies the Seed of Change. Tom Rusk. Read by Tom Rusk. 1 cass. (Running Time: 50 min.). 1991. 10.95 (978-1-56170-028-8(2), 255) Hay House.
Explains personal crises & teaches how you can find your own way to handle them.

In Custody. unabr. ed. Anita Desai. Read by Garard Green. 6 cass. (Running Time: 7 hrs. 15 min.). 2001. 54.95 (978-1-85089-717-0(4), 90024) Pub: ISIS Audio GBR. Dist(s): Ulverscroft US
Deven is a lecturer in a college & had resigned himself to a safe & mediocre life. However, when his long-time friend Murad suddenly comes to see him, Deven sees a chance to change all that & achieve fame & fulfill his many dreams. Murad suggests that they go to Delhi to interview the greatest living Urdu poet, Nur. After a while Deven realizes that Nur is no longer a great poet, but a weak grasping old man whose creative days are long since over. By then though, it is too late to turn back as his dreams rapidly start turning into disasters.

In Daddy's Arms, I Am Tall. Contrib. by Angela Johnson & Davida Adedjouma. 1 cass. (Running Time: 16 mins.). (J). (ps). 2002. bk. 25.95 (978-0-87499-895-5(6)) Live Oak Media.
This collection of poetry honoring African-American fathers melds a variety of visual images with poems.

In Daddy's Arms, I Am Tall. Contrib. by Angela Johnson & Davida Adedjouma. 41 vols. (Running Time: 16 mins.). (J). 2002. pap. bk. & tchr.'s planning gde. ed. 37.95 (978-0-87499-896-2(4)) Live Oak Media.

In Daddy's Arms I Am Tall. Javaka Steptoe. Illus. by Javaka Steptoe. (Running Time: 16 mins.). 2002. 9.95 (978-0-87499-893-1(X)); audio compact disk 12.95 (978-1-59112-315-6(1)) Live Oak Media.

In Daddy's Arms I Am Tall. Javaka Steptoe. Illus. by Javaka Steptoe. 14 vols. (Running Time: 16 mins.). 2004. pap. bk. 39.95 (978-1-59112-539-6(1)) Live Oak Media.

In Daddy's Arms I Am Tall. Javaka Steptoe. Illus. by Javaka Steptoe. 11 vols. (Running Time: 16 mins.). (J). 2004. pap. bk. 18.95 (978-1-59112-316-3(X)) Pub: Live Oak Media. Dist(s): AudioGO

In Daddy's Arms, I Am Tall. abr. ed. Contrib. by Angela Johnson & Davida Adedjouma. 11 vols. (Running Time: 16 mins.). (Live Oak Readalong Ser.). (J). 2002. pap. bk. 16.95 (978-0-87499-894-8(8)) Pub: Live Oak Media. Dist(s): AudioGO

In Danger's Hour. unabr. ed. Douglas Reeman. Read by David Rintoul. 8 cass. (Running Time: 8 hrs.). 1993. bk. 69.95 (978-0-7451-6225-6(8), CAB 424) AudioGO.

In Danger's Path, Pt. 1. unabr. ed. W. E. B. Griffin. Read by Michael Russotto. 9 cass. (Running Time: 13 hrs. 30 mins.). (Corps Ser.: Bk. 8). 1999. 72.00 (978-0-7366-4541-6(1), 4890-A) Books on Tape.
The mission of Brigadier General Fleming Pickering in the Gobi Desert, as he attempts a daring rescue and espionage.

In Danger's Path, Pt. 2. unabr. ed. W. E. B. Griffin. Read by Michael Russotto. 8 cass. (Running Time: 12 hrs.). (Corps Ser.: Bk. 8). 1999. 64.00 (978-0-7366-4542-3(X), 4890-B) Books on Tape.

In Danger's Path, Set. abr. ed. W. E. B. Griffin. Read by Stephen Lang. 4 cass. (Corps Ser.: No. 8). 1999. 24.95 (FS9-43324) Highsmith.

In Darwin We Trust: Creed. Ben Young. (Faith Worth Dying for Ser.). 2000. 4.95 (978-0-7417-6218-4(8), B0218) Win Walk.

In Death Divided see Dylan Thomas Reading

***In Deep Water: The Anatomy of a Disaster, the Fate of the Gulf, & How to End Our Oil Addiction.** unabr. ed. Peter Lehner & Bob Deans. (Running Time: 7.5 hrs. NaN mins.). (ENG.). 2010. 29.95 (978-1-4417-7364-7(9)); 54.95 (978-1-4417-7361-6(4)); audio compact disk 24.95 (978-1-4417-7363-0(0)); audio compact disk 69.00 (978-1-4417-7362-3(2)) Blckstn Audio.

In Defense of America. unabr. ed. Spiro T. Agnew. 1 cass. (Running Time: 20 min.). 12.95 (148) J Norton Pubs.

In Defense of Financial Markets. Yaron Brook. 7 cass. (Running Time: 8 hrs. 30 min.). 1997. 69.95 Set. (978-1-56114-407-5(X), DR46D) Second Renaissance.
An instructive defense of financial markets, financiers & the profit motive.

In Defense of Food: An Eater's Manifesto. unabr. ed. Michael Pollan. Read by Scott Brick. Contrib. by Scott Brick. 5 CDs. (Running Time: 7 hrs.). (ENG.). (gr. 12 up). 2008. audio compact disk 29.95 (978-0-14-314274-4(7), PengAudBks) Penguin Grp USA.

In Defense of Nuclear Power. unabr. ed. Peter Beckmann & Robert White-Stevens. 1 cass. (Running Time: 55 min.). 12.95 (418) J Norton Pubs.

In Defense of Our America: The Fight for Civil Liberties in the Age of Terror. unabr. ed. Anthony D. Romero & Dina Temple-Raston. Narrated by Michael Prichard. (Running Time: 7 hrs. 30 mins. 0 sec.). (ENG.). 2007. audio compact disk 19.99 (978-1-4001-5478-4(2)) Pub: Tantor Media. Dist(s): IngramPubServ

In Defense of Our America: The Fight for Civil Liberties in the Age of Terror. unabr. ed. Anthony D. Romero & Dina Temple-Raston. Read by Michael Prichard. (Running Time: 7 hrs. 30 mins. 0 sec.). (ENG.). 2007. audio compact disk 59.99 (978-1-4001-3478-6(1)) Pub: Tantor Media. Dist(s): IngramPubServ

In Defense of Our America: The Fight for Civil Liberties in the Age of Terror. unabr. ed. Dina Temple-Raston & Anthony D. Romero. Narrated by Michael Prichard. (Running Time: 7 hrs. 30 mins. 0 sec.). (ENG.). 2007. audio compact disk 29.99 (978-1-4001-0478-9(5)) Pub: Tantor Media. Dist(s): IngramPubServ

***In Defense of the Helpless.** Charles R. Swindoll. 2010. audio compact disk 18.00 (978-1-57972-899-1(5)) Insight Living.

In Defense of Women. unabr. ed. H. L. Mencken. Read by Fred Williams. 4 cass. (Running Time: 5 hrs. 30 mins.). 2000. 32.95 (978-0-7861-1791-8(5), 2590) Blckstn Audio.
Find me an obviously intelligent man, a man free from sentimentality & illusion, a man hard to deceive, a man of the first class & I'll show you a man with a wide streak of woman in him. Bonaparte had it; Goethe had it; Bismarck & Lincoln had it. The truth is neither sex, without some fertilization by the complementary characters of the other, is capable of the highest reaches of human endeavor. The wholly manly man lacks the wit necessary to give objective form to his soaring & secret dreams.

***In Defense of Women.** unabr. ed. H.L. Mencken. Read by Fred Williams. (Running Time: 5.5 hrs. NaN mins.). (ENG.). 2011. 29.95 (978-1-4417-8518-3(3)); audio compact disk 55.00 (978-1-4417-8516-9(7)) Blckstn Audio.

In-Depth Analysis of South African Gold Shares. unabr. ed. Michael West. 1 cass. (Running Time: 26 min.). 12.95 (1110) J Norton Pubs.
West offers a comprehensive look at the industry. He points out that 1 ounce of gold is recovered from every three & one-half tons of rock brought to the surface, & that the only sound investment to be made today is in medium grade, medium or long-life mines.

In-Depth Study of Noah's Ark. 2001. 8.95 (978-1-930514-20-1(4), DWDDNA) Diana Waring.

In-Depth Study of the Seven Wonders of the Ancient World. Short Stories. 1 cass. (Running Time: 80 mins.). 2001. 8.95 (978-1-930514-21-8(2), DWDDSW) Diana Waring.

In Detail Bk 2-Audio Tapes. Rainey. 2003. (978-0-8384-4605-8(1)) Heinle.

***In Dreams.** unabr. ed. Nora Roberts. (Running Time: 3 hrs.). 2011. 19.99 (978-1-4418-6742-1(2), 9781441867421, Brilliance MP3); 19.99 (978-1-4418-6744-5(9), 9781441867445, BAD); 39.97 (978-1-4418-6745-2(7), 9781441867452, BADLE) Brilliance Audio.

***In Dreams.** unabr. ed. Nora Roberts. Read by Justine Eyre. (Running Time: 3 hrs.). 2011. 39.97 (978-1-4418-6743-8(0), 9781441867438, Brlnc Audio MP3 Lib); audio compact disk 19.99 (978-1-4418-6740-7(6), 9781441867407, Bril Audio CD Unabri); audio compact disk 62.97 (978-1-4418-6741-4(4), 9781441867414, BriAudCD Unabrid) Brilliance Audio.

In Dubious Battle. John Steinbeck. Narrated by Tom Stechschulte. 7 cass. (Running Time: 10 hrs. 15 mins.). 1936. 61.00 (978-1-4025-1049-6(7), 95786) Recorded Bks.
In California apple country, a group of migrant workers decides to strike against landowners. The situation quickly spirals out of control as Jim Nolan responds to urgent emotional pressures around him.

In Dubious Battle, unabr. collector's ed. John Steinbeck. Read by Michael Keenan. 7 cass. (Running Time: 10 hrs. 30 mins.). 1994. 56.00 (978-0-7366-2878-5(9), 3581) Books on Tape.
In the California apple country, 900 migratory workers rise up "in dubious battle" against the landowners. The group takes on a life of its own, stronger than its individual members & more frightening.

In Eugene, Oregon. Perf. by Ali A. Khan. 1 cass. 8.98 (A0054-0) Sound Photosyn.
With Swapan Chaudhuri on tabla. Ragas: Bihag, Hem Bihag.

In Every Pew Sits a Broken Heart: Hope for Every Believer. abr. ed. Zondervan Publishing Staff & Ruth Graham. Told to Stacy Mattingly. (Running Time: 4 hrs. 24 mins. 0 sec.). (ENG.). 2004. 10.99 (978-0-310-26065-3(5)) Zondervan.

In Every Pew Sits a Broken Heart: Hope for the Hurting. unabr. abr. ed. Ruth Graham. Told to Stacy Mattingly. (Running Time: 4 hrs. 44 mins. 0 sec.). (ENG.). 2004. audio compact disk 24.99 (978-0-310-25669-4(0)) Zondervan.

In Every Tongue: Spanish for Latter-Day Saints. Robert W. Blair. 1 cass. 1994. 39.95 (978-0-87579-759-5(8)) Deseret Bk.

In Exile from the Land of Snows. John Avedon. 1 cass. 9.00 (OC28L) Sound Horizons AV.

In Explanation of Our Times see Poetry & Reflections

***In Fifty Years We'll All Be Chicks... And Other Complaints from an Angry Middle-Aged White Guy.** abr. ed. Adam Carolla. Read by Adam Carolla. 2010. audio compact disk 30.00 (978-0-307-75136-2(8), Random AudioBks) Pub: Random Audio Pubg. Dist(s): Random

In Flanders Fields see Classic American Poetry

In Flanders Fields see Favorite American Poems

In Flanders Fields & Other Poems about War. John McCrae & Wilfred Owen. Read by Ralph Cosham. (YA). 2008. pap. bk. 38.00 (978-1-58472-579-4(6), In Aud) Sound Room.

In Flanders Fields & Other Poems about War. John McCrae & Wilfred Owens. Read by Ralph Cosham. (Running Time: 2 hrs.). (C). 2003. 15.95 (978-1-59912-082-9(8), Audiofy Corp) Iofy Corp.

In-Flight Arabic: Learn Before You Land. abr. unabr. l.t. ed. Living Language Staff. Ed. by Suzanne E. McGrew. 1 cass. (Running Time: 1 hr.). (In-Flight Ser.). (ENG.). 2001. audio compact disk 13.95 (978-0-609-81064-4(2), LivingLang) Pub: Random Info Grp. Dist(s): Random

In-Flight Chinese: Learn Before You Land. abr. unabr. l.t. ed. Living Language Staff. Ed. by Suzanne E. McGrew. 1 CD. (Running Time: 1 hr.). (In-Flight Ser.). (ENG.). 2001. audio compact disk 13.95 (978-0-609-81074-3(X), LivingLang) Pub: Random Info Grp. Dist(s): Random

In-Flight Croatian. unabr. l.t. ed. Living Language Staff. (In-Flight Ser.). (ENG.). 2006. audio compact disk 13.95 (978-1-4000-2279-3(7), LivingLang) Pub: Random Info Grp. Dist(s): Random

In-Flight Czech: Learn Before You Land. abr. unabr. l.t. ed. Living Language Staff. Ed. by Suzanne E. McGrew. 1 cass. (Running Time: 1 hr.). (In-Flight Ser.). (ENG.). 2001. audio compact disk 13.95 (978-0-609-81065-1(0), LivingLang) Pub: Random Info Grp. Dist(s): Random

In-Flight German: Learn Before You Land. abr. unabr. l.t. ed. Living Language Staff. Ed. by Suzanne E. McGrew. 1 cass. (Running Time: 1 hr.). (In-Flight Ser.). 2001. audio compact disk 13.95 (978-0-609-81067-5(7), LivingLang) Pub: Random Info Grp. Dist(s): Random

In-Flight Greek: Learn Before You Land. abr. unabr. l.t. ed. Living Language Staff. Ed. by Suzanne E. McGrew. 1 cass. (Running Time: 1 hr.). (In-Flight Ser.). (ENG.). 2001. audio compact disk 13.95 (978-0-609-81097-2(9), LivingLang) Pub: Random Info Grp. Dist(s): Random

In-Flight Italian: Learn Before You Land. unabr. l.t. ed. Living Language Staff. Ed. by Suzanne E. McGrew. 1 cass. (Running Time: 1 hr.). (In-Flight Ser.). (ENG.). 2001. audio compact disk 13.95 (978-0-609-81071-2(5), LivingLang) Pub: Random Info Grp. Dist(s): Random

In-Flight Japanese: Learn Before You Land. unabr. l.t. ed. Living Language Staff. Ed. by Suzanne E. McGrew. 1 cass. (Running Time: 1 hr.). (In-Flight Ser.). 2001. audio compact disk 13.95 (978-0-609-81072-9(3), LivingLang) Pub: Random Info Grp. Dist(s): Random

In-Flight Polish: Learn Before You Land. unabr. l.t. ed. Living Language Staff. Ed. by Suzanne E. McGrew. 1 cass. (Running Time: 1 hr.). (In-Flight Ser.). (ENG.). 2001. audio compact disk 13.95 (978-0-609-81075-0(8), LivingLang) Pub: Random Info Grp. Dist(s): Random

In-Flight Portuguese: Learn Before You Land. abr. unabr. l.t. ed. Living Language Staff. Ed. by Suzanne E. McGrew. 1 cass. (Running Time: 1 hr.). (In-Flight Ser.). (ENG.). 2001. audio compact disk 13.95 (978-0-609-81076-7(6), LivingLang) Pub: Random Info Grp. Dist(s): Random

In-Flight Spanish: Learn Before You Land. abr. unabr. l.t. ed. Living Language Staff. Ed. by Suzanne E. McGrew. 1 cass. (Running Time: 1 hr.). (In-Flight Ser.). (ENG.). 2001. audio compact disk 13.95 (978-0-609-81078-1(2), LivingLang) Pub: Random Info Grp. Dist(s): Random

In-Flight Swedish: Learn Before You Land. abr. unabr. l.t. ed. Living Language Staff. Ed. by Suzanne E. McGrew. 1 cass. (Running Time: 1 hr.). (In-Flight Ser.). (ENG.). 2001. audio compact disk 13.95 (978-0-609-81096-5(0), LivingLang) Pub: Random Info Grp. Dist(s): Random

In-Flight Thai: Learn Before You Land. abr. unabr. l.t. ed. Living Language Staff. Ed. by Christopher A. Warnasch. 1 cass. (Running Time: 1 hr.). (In-Flight Ser.). 2001. audio compact disk 13.95 (978-0-609-81099-6(5), LivingLang) Pub: Random Info Grp. Dist(s): Random

In Freedom's Cause. Abr. by Jim Weiss. (ENG.). (YA). 2006. audio compact disk 32.95 (978-1-882513-92-5(4)) Pub: Greathall Prods. Dist(s): Allegro Dist

In Freedom's Cause: A Story of Wallace & Bruce. unabr. ed. G. A. Henty. Read by Jim Hodges. 8 cass. (Running Time: 11 hrs.). (YA). (gr. 5 up). 1999. 35.00 (978-1-929756-02-5(X)) J Hodges.
William Wallace and Robert the Bruce struggle and war for freedom from England.

In Gallant Company. unabr. ed. Alexander Kent, pseud. Narrated by Steven Crossley. 8 cass. (Running Time: 11 hrs. 15 mins.). (Richard Bolitho Ser.: Bk. 3). 1998. 70.00 (978-0-7887-2607-1(2), 95618E7) Recorded Bks.
Listeners who relish the dashing sea tales of Patrick O'Brian will love the adventures of the 20-year-old British Lieutenant Richard Bolitho in the perilous early days of the Revolutionary War.

In Giro per la Letteratura: Scivere e Leggere nei Corsi Intermedi d'Italiano. Elizabeth Giansiracusa & Kenneth Berri. (C). tchr. ed. 30.50 (978-0-8384-4971-4(9)) Heinle.

In Giro per l'Italia: Listening Comprehension Audiocassette. Graziana Lazzarino & Maria Cristina Peccianti. (C). 2002. 15.00 (978-0-07-248991-0(X), Mc-H Human Soc) Pub: McGrw-H Hghr Educ. Dist(s): McGraw

In Glory of Spirit. Param Yogananda. 2008. audio compact disk 14.00 (978-0-87612-526-7(7)) Self Realization.

In God We Trust. Mark Bradford. Prod. by One Way Street Staff. (Running Time: 38 minutes and 24 seconds). (Target Trax Ser.). 2002. audio compact disk 15.00 (978-1-58302-214-6(7)) One Way St.
One Way Street and parody writer Mark Bradford have teamed up again to bring you another spectacular Traget Trax CD. It is all patriotic music and includes the "Star-spangled Banner" sung acapella. The lyrics and instrumental sound tracks are included.

In God We Trust: Compact Disc. 2008. audio compact disk 14.00 (978-1-59548-130-6(3)) A Wommack.

In God We Trust: From Tragedy to Triumph. unabr. ed. Keith A. Butler. 5 cass. (Running Time: 7 hrs. 30 mins.). 2002. 25.00 (A23) Word Faith Pubng.

In God's Army: Christ's Cadets. C. C. Martindale. 4 cass. 18.95 (721) Ignatius Pr.
Character studies of St. Aloysius Gonzaga, St. Stanislaus Kostka, & St. John Berchmans.

In God's School. 1 cass. (Running Time: 30 min.). 1985. (0264) Evang Sisterhood Mary.
"...that he may exalt you in due time." A lesson from the children of Israel.

In Good Taste! Cannibalism - Who Did It, Where, How & Why. Carole Marsh. (Extreme History). 1994. 14.95 (978-0-7933-7367-3(0)) Gallopade Intl.

In Grandma's Kitchen. Eileen Comstock. (Running Time: 1 hr. 20 mins.). (ENG.). 2003. audio compact disk 11.95 (978-1-894856-00-3(7)) Pub: Fifth Hse Publ CAN. Dist(s): IngramPubServ

In Guilty Night. unabr. ed. Alison Taylor. Narrated by Gareth Potter. 10 cass. (Running Time: 12 hrs. 30 mins.). 2000. 89.00 (978-1-84197-076-9(X), H1070E7) Recorded Bks.
Fourteen-year-old Arwel Thomas' body, abused & battered, is found by a railway line in the beautiful Welsh mountains. A notorious runaway from the local welfare home, even his parents think he got what he deserved. Or did he? Several discrepancies that raise doubts about Arwel's life. Someone knows the full story; the problem is finding out who it is. Meanwhile, Arwel's beautiful, wretched sister won't talk about him, other children at the home vanish in the night, willingly or unwillingly & the man who befriended him has his own troubles. Clues are scarce, but persistence suddenly starts to pay off.

In Guilty Night. unabr. ed. Alison Taylor. Narrated by Gareth Potter. 11 CDs. (Running Time: 12 hrs. 30 mins.). 2000. audio compact disk 115.00 (978-1-84197-088-2(3), C1180E7) Recorded Bks.

In Harmony. Perf. by James Taylor et al. 1 cass. (J). (ps up). 9.98 (243) MFLP CA.
Rock with your kids to this star-studded collection from well-known entertainers doing their favorite children's songs.

In Harmony, Vol. 2. Perf. by Billy Joel et al. 1 cass. (J). (ps up). 9.98 (290); audio compact disk 16.98 (D290) MFLP CA.
Includes: "Nobody Knows But Me" by Billy Joel, "Sunny Skies" by James Taylor, "Splish Splash" by Dr. John, "Some Kitties Don't Care" by Kenny Loggins, "Santa Claus is Comin' to Town" by Bruce Springsteen & many more.

In Harmony with God. Andre Huynh. 2007. audio compact disk 24.99 (978-1-60247-184-9(3)) Tate Pubng.

***In Harm's Way.** unabr. ed. Ridley Pearson. Read by Phil Gigante. (Running Time: 11 hrs.). (Sun Valley Ser.). 2010. audio compact disk 29.99 (978-1-4233-8355-0(9), 9781423383550, Bril Audio CD Unabri) Brilliance Audio.

***In Harm's Way.** unabr. ed. Ridley Pearson. Read by Phil Gigante & Christopher Lane. (Running Time: 11 hrs.). (Sun Valley Ser.). 2010. audio compact disk 82.97 (978-1-4233-8356-7(7), 9781423383567, BriAudCD Unabrid) Brilliance Audio.

In Harm's Way: The Sinking of the USS Indianapolis & the Extraordinary Story of Its Survivors. unabr. ed. Doug Stanton. Read by Grover Gardner. 6 vols. (Running Time: 9 hrs.). 2001. bk. 54.95 (978-0-7927-2511-4(5), CSL 400, Chivers Sound Lib); audio compact disk 79.95 (978-0-7927-9926-9(7), SLD 077, Chivers Sound Lib) AudioGO.
On July 30, 1945, the battle cruiser USS Indianapolis was torpedoed in the South Pacific. An estimated 300 men were killed upon impact; close to 900 sailors were cast into the Pacific Ocean, where they remained, undetected by the navy, for nearly five days. They struggled to survive, fighting off hypothermia, sharks, physical and mental exhaustion, and, finally, hallucinatory dementia.

In Her Defense. Stephen Horn. Read by Scott Brick. 2000. audio compact disk 88.00 (978-0-7366-7133-0(1)) Books on Tape.

In Her Defense. unabr. ed. Stephen Horn. Read by Scott Brick. 9 cass. (Running Time: 13 hrs. 30 mins.). 2000. 72.00 (978-0-7366-5457-9(7), 5328); audio compact disk 44.00 Books on Tape.
Frank O'Connell fights to defend Ashley Bronson from a murder both believe she was justified in committing.

In Her Shoes. Jennifer Weiner. Narrated by Barbara McCulloh. 11 cass. (Running Time: 15 hrs. 30 mins.). 2002. 99.00 (978-1-4025-3947-3(9)) Recorded Bks.

In Her Shoes. movie tie-in abr. ed. Jennifer Weiner. Read by Karen Ziemba. 5 CDs. (Running Time: 50 hrs. 0 mins. 0 sec.). (ENG.). 2005. audio compact disk 14.95 (978-0-7435-4011-7(5), Audioworks) Pub: S&S Audio. Dist(s): S and S Inc
Meet Rose Feller. She's thirty years old and a high-powered attorney with a secret passion for romance novels. She dreams of a man who will slide off her glasses, gaze into her eyes, and tell her that she's beautiful. She also dreams of getting her fantastically screwed-up little sister to get her life. together. Meet Rose's sister, Maggie. Twenty-eight years old, drop-dead gorgeous and only occasionally employed. Although her dreams of big-screen stardom haven't progressed, Maggie dreams of fame and fortune - and of getting her dowdy big sister to stick to a skin-care regime. These two women with nothing in common but childhood tragedy, shared DNA, and the same size feet, are about to learn that their family is more different than they ever imagine, and that they're more alike, than they'd ever believe. In Her Shoes observes Rose and Maggie, the brain and the beauty, as they make journeys of discovery. Along the way, the'll encounter a wild cast of characters and they'll borrow shoes and clothes and boyfriends, and make peace with their most intimate enemies - each other. Funny and poignant, In Her Shoes will speak to anyone who has endured the bonds of big - or little - sisterhood, or longed for a life different from the one the world has dictated, and dreamed of trying something else on for size.

In His Care: Releasing Concern for a Loved One. Richard Jafolla & Mary-Alice Jafolla. Read by Richard Jafolla & Mary-Alice Jafolla. (Special Spiritual Ser.). 1986. 12.95 (380) Stppng Stones.
Motivational tapes that work on the subconscious mind (subliminal) & conscious mind to bring about self-improvement.

In His Compassion. Elbert Willis. 1 cass. (Christ Like Living Series). 4.00 Fill the Gap.

In His Eyes. Perf. by Tim Greene. Prod. by Ronnie Brookshire. 1 cass. 1999. (978-0-7601-3139-8(2)); audio compact disk (978-0-7601-3138-1(4)) Brentwood Music.
Includes "Come Away with Me" which was written for his mother.

In His Footsteps. Elbert Willis. 1 cass. (Christ Like Living Series). 4.00 Fill the Gap.

In His Forgiving Love. Elbert Willis. 1 cass. (Christ Like Living Series). 4.00 Fill the Gap.

***In His Image.** 2010. audio compact disk (978-1-59171-249-7(1)) Falcon Picture.

In His Image. James BeauSeigneur. Narrated by Pete Bradbury. 9 cass. (Running Time: 13 hrs.). (Christ Clone Trilogy: Bk. 1). 84.00 (978-1-4025-0392-4(X)); audio compact disk 111.00 (978-1-4025-2926-9(0)) Recorded Bks.

In His Image. James BeauSeigneur. 2003. 34.99 (978-1-4025-3724-0(7)) Recorded Bks.

In His Image. unabr. ed. David Rorvik. Read by Edmund Stoiber. 7 cass. 41.65 (B-104) Audio Bk.
An account of the events leading up to the cloning of a man.

In His Image, Set. Steven A. Cramer. 2 cass. 2004. 13.95 (978-1-57734-531-2(2), 07002203) Covenant Comms.

In His Image: God's Master Creation. abr. ed. Linda R. Gray. Read by Linda R. Gray. 1 cass. (Running Time: 60 min.). 1998. 5.00 (978-0-9668661-1-7(8)); cass. & video 20.00 (978-0-9668661-2-4(6)) Centuries Past.
A parallel between the physical & spiritual births; two units of hereditary materials are used to express likeness of cellular activity in the human body to the work of the Trinity in the body of Christ, the Church.

In His Own Voice: Multiple Personality. Ed. by Milton H. Erickson et al. 1 cass. (In His Own Voice Ser.). (ENG.). 1991. 14.95 (978-0-931513-07-7(3), 51307) Pub: Triang Pr. Dist(s): Norton

In His Own Voice: Problem Drinkers. Milton H. Erickson. Ed. by Madeleine Richeport-Haley. Contrib. by Jay Haley. Narrated by Jay Haley. 1 cass. (In His Own Voice Ser.). (ENG.). 1991. 19.95 (978-0-931513-10-7(3), 51310) Pub: Triang Pr. Dist(s): Norton

In His Own Voice: Sex Therapy: The Female. Milton H. Erickson. Ed. by Madeleine Richeport-Haley. Contrib. by Jay Haley. Narrated by Jay Haley. 2 cass. (In His Own Voice Ser.). (ENG.). 1991. 29.95 (978-0-931513-09-1(X), 51309) Pub: Triang Pr. Dist(s): Norton

In His Own Voice: Sex Therapy: The Male. Milton H. Erickson. Contrib. by Jay Haley. Narrated by Jay Haley. 2 cass. (In His Own Voice Ser.). (ENG.). 1991. 29.95 (978-0-931513-08-4(1), 51308) Pub: Triang Pr. Dist(s): Norton

In His Own Words: Robert F. Kennedy. Ed. by Pent. 1 cass. (Running Time: 39 min.). 1995. audio compact disk 10.98 (978-1-885959-12-6(5), JRCS 7037) Jerden Recs.
Historical compilation of edited speeches includes RFK's dramatic address to the Democratic National Convention, his feelings on violence & the murder of MLK, his victory speech in Los Angeles - the night of his assassination - & much more.

In His Presence. E. W. Kenyon. Read by Stephen Sobozenski. 6 cassettes. (Running Time: 5 hrs. 30 mins.). 2004. 28.00 (978-1-57770-031-9(7)) Kenyons Gospel.
The secret of prayer.

In His Presence. E. W. Kenyon. Read by Stephen Sobozenski. 6 CDs. (Running Time: 5 hrs. 30 mins.). 2004. audio compact disk 32.00 (978-1-57770-036-4(8)) Kenyons Gospel.

In His Presence. Prod. by Maranatha! Music. 1 cass. (Running Time: 60 min.). 1991. 9.95 (978-0-927992-40-4(X)) Questar.
A celebration of the peace, love, & promises of God in word & song.

In His Resurrection Power. Elbert Willis. 1 cass. (Christ Like Living Series). 4.00 Fill the Gap.

In His Steps. Charles Monroe Sheldon. Read by Lloyd James. 6 CDs. (Running Time: 8 hrs. 30 mins.). 2004. audio compact disk 55.00 (978-0-7861-8141-4(9), 1121) Blckstn Audio.

In His Steps. unabr. ed. Charles M. Sheldon. Read by Rob Gregory. 6 cass. (Running Time: 8 hrs. 30 mins.). 2006. 44.95 (978-0-7861-0136-8(9), 1121) Blckstn Audio.
This timeless classic, written at the turn of century, has blessed millions of people who have asked the vital question, "What does it really mean to be a Christian?".

In His Steps. unabr. ed. Charles M. Sheldon. Narrated by Nelson Runger. 6 cass. (Running Time: 9 hrs.). 1999. 51.00 (978-0-7887-0582-3(2), 94760E7) Recorded Bks.
Over one 100 years ago, Reverend Sheldon delivered a sermon to his congregation. Little did he know that his humble parable would evolve into a novel that would be published in 45 languages & affect the lives of 15 million people. Asking the question, "What would Jesus do?", this inspirational classic's simple message transcends literature, theology & religion.

In His Steps. unabr. ed. Charles M. Sheldon. 7 CDs. (Running Time: 8 hrs. 18 mins. 0 sec.). (ENG.). 2006. audio compact disk 26.98 (978-1-59644-352-5(9), Hovel Audio) christianaud.
One hundred years ago Christians read Charles Sheldon's In His Steps with runaway enthusiasm. Sheldon's story traces the account of the fictional Reverend Maxwell who challenges himself and his congregation to constantly ask, "What would Jesus do?"? This question puts all of life's circumstances in a new light. Those characters in Sheldon's book who take the challenge of this question seriously live dramatically changed lives.But a changed life responding to Jesus' example of compassion and grace does not always make things easier. People in Sheldon's story learn that acting like Jesus can alienate others who prefer status quo comfort and social respectability. The real challenge of the question, "What would Jesus do?" is not the initial fervor it evokes but the sustained devotion it can produce.

***In His Steps.** unabr. ed. Charles M. Sheldon. Narrated by Simon Vance. (ENG.). 2006. 16.98 (978-1-59644-353-2(7), Hovel Audio) christianaud.

In Honor of Eyak: The Art of Anna Nelson Harry. Ed. by Michael E. Krauss. (C). 1982. 9.00 (978-0-933769-08-3(3)) Alaska Native.

In Honor of St. Francis: Music for the Little Poor Man of Assisi. Schola Cantorum of St. Peter the Apostle Staff. Directed By J. Michael Thompson. 2005. audio compact disk 16.95 (978-0-8146-7948-7(X)) Liturgical Pr.

In Honor of Take Back the Night: A Collection of Poetry & Thoughts about Take Back the Night. 2005. 29.95 (978-1-59649-041-3(1)) Whsprng Pine.

In Honor of Take Back the Night: A Collection of Poetry & Thoughts about Take Back the Night. Karen Jean Matsko Hood. 2006. audio compact disk 24.95 (978-1-59649-044-4(6)) Whsprng Pine.

***In Honor of Take Back the Night, Fundraiser Reflection Book: A Collection of Bible Verses, Prayers, & Inspirational Poetry for Reflection & Healing.** Karen Jean Matsko Hood. 2011. 24.95 (978-1-59434-927-0(4)) Whsprng Pine.

In Hot Pursuit. unabr. ed. Focus on the Family Staff & AIO Team Staff. 4 CDs. (Running Time: 6 hrs.). (Adventures in Odyssey Ser.). (ENG.). (J). 2004. audio compact disk 24.99 (978-1-58997-240-7(6)) Pub: Focus Family. Dist(s): Tyndale Hse

In-House & Service Bureau Conversion: Converting Documents to Digital Images. 1 cass. 1990. 8.50 Recorded Res.

In-House Training: Maximizing Your Lawyers' Professional Potential. 4 cass. (Running Time: 5 hrs.). 1994. 175.00 incl. study materials. (M128) Am Law Inst.
This program teaches successful methods for systematic implementation of lawyer training programs in the law office, designed as a practical workshop for lawyers & legal managers & administrators from all types of organizations who are seeking to develop an effective training systen or looking to improve an existing training program.

In Just One Night. 1996. 7.00 (978-0-9656062-6-4(0)); audio compact disk 12.00 (978-0-9656062-5-7(2)) OJU Min Assn.

In KPFK Studios on Something's Happening! Rupert Sheldrake. 2 cass. (Roy Tuckman Interview Ser.). 18.00 Set. (A0297-88) Sound Photosyn.

In-Law Relationships: The Chapman Guide to Becoming Friends with Your In-Laws. unabr. ed. Gary Chapman. Narrated by Maurice England. (Running Time: 2 hrs. 44 mins. 48 sec.). (Marriage Savers Ser.). (ENG.). 2008. 10.49 (978-1-60814-255-2(8)) Oasis Audio.

In-Law Relationships: The Chapman Guide to Becoming Friends with Your In-Laws. unabr. ed. Gary Chapman. Read by Gary Chapman. Narrated by Maurice England. (Running Time: 2 hrs. 44 mins. 48 sec.). (Marriage Savers Ser.). (ENG.). 2008. audio compact disk 14.99 (978-1-59859-439-3(7)) Oasis Audio.

In Love & War. unabr. ed. Jim Stockdale & Sybil Stockdale. Read by Christopher Hurt & Mary Woods. 12 cass. (Running Time: 18 hrs.). 1985. 96.00 (978-0-7366-0492-5(8), 1466) Books on Tape.
On September 9, 1965, James Stockdale was shot down on a bombing run over North Vietnam. Captured, he remained in a Hanoi prison for seven years as the highest ranking POW. Two struggles began - one was his battle to survive, one was Sybil Stockdale's - trying to raise a family alone & live without her husband. Both rose to the challenge. The Commander called up all his reserves of strength & faith, while Sybil attacked government inertia as head of the League of POW/MIA Families. She was as confrontational with our government as she was with the Vietnamese.

In Love for Life: The Four Secrets an Incredible Christian Marriage. 1 cass. (Running Time: 1 hr.). 2003. 13.99 (978-1-932631-55-5(0)) Ascensn Pr.

In Love for Life: The Four Secrets of an Incredible Christian Marriage. 2003. audio compact disk 13.95 (978-1-932631-56-2(9)) Ascensn Pr.

In Love for Long see Twentieth-Century Poetry in English, No. 23, Recordings of Poets Reading Their Own Poetry

In Love with Shining Truth. Swami Amar Jyoti. 1 cass. 1982. 9.95 (R-41) Truth Consciousness.
Loving detachment from personality & self-image. Sat-Chit-Ananda, Truth, Consciousness & Bliss. The greatest service to mankind.

In Love's Shadow. collector's ed. Catherine Lanigan. Read by Anna Fields. 7 cass. (Running Time: 10 hrs. 30 min.). 2000. 56.00 (978-0-7366-4846-2(1)) Books on Tape.
On a cold December evening, a shot rang out in a wealthy Chicago suburb & the lives of three women were forever changed. Bud Pulaski, successful businessman, committed suicide, leaving behind a shattered wife, an estranged sister, a bitter mistress & many unanswered questions. Roya, the faithful wife, struggles to keep her family together & the business afloat while falling in love for the very first time. Daria, the younger sister, must step out from behind Bud's shadow & face her own mistakes. Kitt, the mistress, can't admit to the truth about her role in Bud's death. They are three women searching for a ray of hope in love's shadow.

In Love's Shadow. collector's ed. Catherine Lanigan. Read by Anna Fields. 8 CDs. (Running Time: 12 hrs.). 2000. audio compact disk 64.00 (978-0-7366-5215-5(9)) Books on Tape.

In Memoriam see Treasury of Alfred Lord Tennyson

In Memory of Junior. unabr. ed. Clyde Edgerton. Narrated by Sally Darling & Norman Dietz. 6 cass. (Running Time: 7 hrs. 30 mins.). 1993. 51.00 (978-1-55690-789-0(3), 93101E7) Recorded Bks.
As an elderly husband & wife hover on the brink of death, their families & neighbors speculate, sometimes angrily, sometimes with insight & humor, on their various inheritances.

In Memory of W. B. Yeats see Caedmon Treasury of Modern Poets Reading Their Own Poetry

In Memory Yet Green: The Autobiography of Isaac Asimov, 1920-1954 see In Memory Yet Green, Pts. 1-2, The Autobiography of Isaac Asimov, 1920-1954

In Memory Yet Green Pts. 1-2: The Autobiography of Isaac Asimov, 1920-1954. unabr. ed. Isaac Asimov. Read by Dan Lazar. 20 cass. (Running Time: 30 hrs.). Incl. Pt. 1. In Memory Yet Green: The Autobiography of Isaac Asimov, 1920-1954. 10 cass. (Running Time: 15 hrs.). Isaac Asimov. Read by Dan Lazar. 1998. 80.00 (1300-A); Pt. 2. In Memory Yet Green: The Autobiography of Isaac Asimov, 1920-1954. 10 cass. (Running Time: 15 hrs.). Isaac Asimov. Read by Dan Lazar. 1998. 80.00 (1300-B); 1998. 160.00 (978-0-7366-0312-6(3), 1300A&B) Books on Tape.
Asimov tells how he got it all together. Ranging through human history & thought. Asimov is a perfect guide as we travel with him on his numerous voyages of discovery.

In Midlife. Read by Murray Stein. 2 cass. (Running Time: 2 hrs.). 1991. 16.95 Set. (978-0-7822-0297-7(7), 430) C G Jung IL.

In Morocco. unabr. ed. Edith Wharton. Read by Anna Fields. 4 cass. (Running Time: 5 hrs. 30 mins.). 1999. 32.95 (978-0-7861-1518-1(1), 2368) Blckstn Audio.
Edith Wharton's account of the country's cities & deserts.

In Morocco. unabr. ed. Edith Wharton. Read by Anna Fields. 4 cass. (Running Time: 6 hrs.). 1999. audio compact disk 24.95 (978-0-7861-1551-8(3)) Blckstn Audio.
Recounts the author's fascinating journey through a strangely medieval land that at the time (1917) still carried the fragrance of its romantic past. See the country of the Crusades, Saladin & the Caliphate of Baghdad through her eyes.

In Morocco. unabr. ed. Edith Wharton & Anna Fields. (Running Time: 6 hrs. NaN mins.). 2008. 19.95 (978-1-4332-5432-1(8)); audio compact disk 50.00 (978-1-4332-5431-4(X)) Blckstn Audio.

In Morocco, Set. unabr. ed. Edith Wharton. Read by Anna Fields. 4 cass. 1999. 32.95 (FS9-50912) Highsmith.

In Mortal Combat Pt. 1: Korea, 1950-1953. unabr. collector's ed. John Toland. Read by John MacDonald. 9 cass. (Running Time: 13 hrs. 30 min.). 1993. 72.00 (978-0-7366-2577-7(1), 3325-A) Books on Tape.
Brilliant examination of America's first limited war. Vast & gripping.

In Mortal Combat Pt. 2: Korea, 1950-1953. collector's ed. John Toland. Read by John MacDonald. 8 cass. (Running Time: 12 hrs.). 1993. 64.00 (978-0-7366-2578-4(X), 3325-B) Books on Tape.

In Motion / Posture Works: The Alexander Technique. 1. (Running Time: 77 minutes). 2004. audio compact disk 23.00 (978-0-615-12656-2(1)) Somatic Ed.

In My Craft of Sullen Art see Dylan Thomas Reading His Poetry

In My Craft or Sullen Art see Evening with Dylan Thomas

In My Father's Court. unabr. ed. Isaac Bashevis Singer. Read by Wolfram Kandinsky. 7 cass. (Running Time: 10 hrs. 30 min.). 1986. 56.00 (978-0-7366-0391-1(3), 1368) Books on Tape.
An account of a time & place now lost to us - a Jewish ghetto in rural Poland in the three years prior to World War I.

In my father's Den. Maurice Gee. Read by Humphrey Bower. (Running Time: 6 hrs. 20 mins.). 2009. 69.99 (978-1-74214-229-6(X), 9781742142296) Pub: Bolinda Pubng AUS. Dist(s): Bolinda Pub Inc

In My Father's Den. unabr. ed. Maurice Gee. Read by Humphrey Bower. (Running Time: 22800 sec.). 2007. audio compact disk 77.95 (978-1-74093-955-3(7), 9781740939553) Pub: Bolinda Pubng AUS. Dist(s): Bolinda Pub Inc

In My Father's House. Contrib. by Kyle Bielfield. 2001. pap. bk. 48.90; audio compact disk 22.95 Ellis Family Mus.

In My Father's House. unabr. ed. Ernest J. Gaines. Narrated by Peter Francis James. 5 cass. (Running Time: 7 hrs. 3[illegible] mins.). 1994. 44.00 (978-0-7887-0041-5(3), 94240E7) Rec[illegible] Bks.
A successful minister & civil rights lead[illegible] small Louisiana town is suddenly confronted with the son he aba[illegible]oned years before. When his guilty past bursts forth, Phillip spirals in an emotional whirlwind that threatens to destroy his family, his parish & the man he has worked to become.

In My Father's House. unabr. collector's ed. Ernest J. Gaines. Read by Dan Lazar. 6 cass. (Running Time: 6 hrs.). 1982. 36.00 (978-0-7366-0514-4(2), 1488) Books on Tape.

In My Hands: Memories of a Holocaust Rescuer. Irene Gut Opdyke & Jennifer Armstrong. Read by Hope Davis. 4 cass. (Running Time: 7 hrs.). (J). 2000. 30.00 (978-0-7366-9012-6(3)) Books on Tape.
First-person account of one young woman's courageous & successful efforts to protect Jews from the Nazis during the Holocaust makes for a vivid listening experience.

In My Hands: Memories of a Holocaust Rescuer. unabr. ed. Irene Gut Opdyke & Jennifer Armstrong. Read by Hope Davis. 4 vols. (Running Time: 7 hrs. 7 mins.). (J). (gr. 5 up). 2004. pap. bk. 42.00 (978-0-8072-0867-0(1), LYA 150 SP, Listening Lib); 32.00 (978-0-8072-8343-1(6), LL0182, Listening Lib) Random Audio Pubg.
First-person account of one young woman's courageous & successful, efforts to protect Jews from the Nazis during the Holocaust makes for a vivid listening experience.

In My Hometown. Tom Chapin. 1 cass. 1998. 9.98 Blisterpk avail. (978-1-57330-871-7(4), Sony Wonder) Sony Music Ent.
Memorable characters, special places & a joyful celebration of the everyday events that make up life in a typical American town. Features 15 brand new, original songs in a wide range of musical styles...with witty lyrics that touch on issues important to us all.

In My Mother's Eyes. Perf. by Cathy Ellis & Esther Ellis. 1 cass. 1999. 15.95 (978-1-879542-71-6(4), EFMME1); audio compact disk 15.95 Ellis Family Mus.
Songs include: "In My Mother's Eyes", "My Best Friend Here On Earth", "Child", "Friend", "The First to Give", "Psalm 91", "The Love in His Eyes", "Still Small Voice", "I Keep My Promise", "Apple of God's Eye", "Oh, The Lord is Faithful", & "Always Have A Dream".

In My Own Backyard. unabr. ed. Judi Kurjian. 1 cass. (Running Time: 11 min.). (SPA.). (J). (gr. k-4). 1994. pap. bk. 17.90 (6815S) Spoken Arts.

In My Own Backyard. unabr. ed. Judi Kurjian. 1 cass. (Running Time: 11 min.). (J). (gr. k-4). 1994. bk. 27.90 (978-0-8045-6815-9(4), 6815) Spoken Arts.
Did you ever wonder who used to live in a typical backyard? Introduces students to agrarian America, pioneers, North American pre-Columbus, cavemen, dinosaurs and more.

In My Pocket/Beads. Created by Steck-Vaughn Staff. (Running Time: 352 sec.). (Primary Take-Me-Home Books Level K Ser.). 1998. 9.80 (978-0-8172-8651-4(9)) SteckVau.

In My Rear View Mirror. unabr. ed. Scripts. Sal Marchiano. Read by Sal Marchiano. 6 cass. (Running Time: 9 hrs.). 2003. 29.95 (978-1-59007-373-5(8), N Millennium Audio); audio compact disk 49.95 (978-1-59007-374-2(6), N Millennium Audio) Pub: New Millenn Enter. Dist(s): PerseuPGW

In My Two Hands. Betsy Rose. 1 cass. (Running Time: 60 min.). 1988. 11.00 (978-0-938077-18-3(X), 7718X) Parallax Pr.
Features a collection of hymns chants & "country-eastern" ballads based on the teachings of Thich Nhat Hanh & Creation Spirituality.

***In-N-Out Burger.** unabr. ed. Stacy Perman. Read by Loren Lester. (ENG.). 2009. (978-0-06-196158-8(2), Harper Audio); (978-0-06-195856-4(5), Harper Audio) HarperCollins Pubs.

In Navajoland see May Swenson

In Nixon's Web: A Year in the Crosshairs of Watergate. unabr. ed. Ed Gray & L. Patrick Gray. Read by Michael Prichard. (YA). 2008. 59.99 (978-1-60514-436-8(3)) Find a World.

In Nixon's Web: A Year in the Crosshairs of Watergate. unabr. ed. L. Patrick Gray, III & Ed Gray. Narrated by Michael Prichard. (Running Time: 11 hrs. 30 mins. 0 sec.). (ENG.). 2008. audio compact disk 24.99 (978-1-4001-5673-3(4)); audio compact disk 69.99 (978-1-4001-3673-5(3)); audio compact disk 34.99 (978-1-4001-0673-8(7)) Pub: Tantor Media. Dist(s): IngramPubServ

In No Time Flat! Audio CD. Karen Blanchard & Christine Root. 2003. audio compact disk 10.95 (978-1-887744-36-2(3), DeltPubng) Delta Systems.

***In Office Hours.** Lucy Kellaway. Narrated by Alison Reid. (Running Time: 10 hrs. 0 mins. 0 sec.). (ENG.). 2011. audio compact disk 29.95 (978-1-60998-152-5(9)) Pub: AudioGO. Dist(s): Perseus Dist

In Our Time see Poetry & Voice of Muriel Rukeyser

In Our Time; The Torrents of Spring; Men Without Women. unabr. collector's ed. Ernest Hemingway. Read by Wolfram Kandinsky. 9 cass. (Running Time: 13 hrs. 30 min.). 1989. 72.00 (978-0-7366-1614-0(4), 2473) Books on Tape.
In Our Time marked the American debut of the young Ernest Hemingway. A selection of 14 short stories & 15 vignettes, it was praised for its simple use of language to convey complex emotions. Now recognized as one of the most original short story collections in 20th-century literature, it also provides a key to Hemingway's later work. The Torrents of Spring is a parody of the Chicago school of literature. Poking fun at the "great race" of writers, it depicts a vogue that Hemingway refused to follow. According to The New York Times, it "reveals Hemingway's gift for high-spirited nonsense...it contributes to that thoughtful gaiety which true wit should inspire." Men Without Women is Hemingway's third book of short stories. It includes "The Undefeated," "In Another Country," "Hills Like White Elephants," "The Killers" & 10 others.

In Papua New Guinea. unabr. collector's ed. Christina Dodwell. Read by Donada Peters. 7 cass. (Running Time: 10 hrs. 30 mins.). 1988. 56.00 (978-0-7366-1313-2(7), 2219) Books on Tape.
Account of travels by a young British explorer with a reputation for going unprepared.

In Partnership with Roy of Hollywood. Riane Eisler. 1 cass. (Roy Tuckman Interview Ser.). 9.00 (A0496-89) Sound Photosyn.
A short background & update on partnership studies & the impact of "The Chalice & the Blade" on anthropology & social models.

In Patagonia. unabr. ed. Bruce Chatwin. Read by David Case. 6 cass. (Running Time: 9 hrs.). 1988. 48.00 (978-0-7366-1314-9(5), 2220) Books on Tape.
Travel book from the isolated southernmost tip of South America, by the author of "On the Black Hill".

In Patagonia. unabr. ed. Bruce Chatwin. Read by Christian Rodska. 6 cass. (Running Time: 9 hrs.). 2000. 49.95 (978-0-7540-0100-3(8), CAB 1523) Pub: Chivers Audio Bks GBR. Dist(s): AudioGO
Patagonia: the name calls to mind giants, outlaws and Magellan's dog-headed monsters. Called 'the utmost place of the earth', Patagonia is the stretch of the land at the southern tip of South America. Bruce Chatwin travels to the remote country to uncover the myths and meet the people whose stories delay him on his journey.

In Perfect Stillness. Swami Amar Jyoti. 1 dolby cass. 1985. 9.95 (R-66) Truth Consciousness.
The goal of meditation, Samadhi, that perfect stillness from which Oneness emerges. Rising above ordinariness. Lessons of earth consciousness must be learned.

In Pharaoh's Army: Memories of the Lost War. unabr. collector's ed. Tobias Wolff. Read by Michael Kramer. 6 cass. (Running Time: 6 hrs.). 1995. 36.00 (978-0-7366-3057-3(0), 3739) Books on Tape.
A first-person account that traces the day-to-day drudgery of the horror called Vietnam.

In Play: Having a Life That Becomes. Read by Leland Roloff. 1 cass. (Running Time: 90 min.). 1990. 10.95 (978-0-7822-0236-6(5), 408) C G Jung IL.

In Praise of Ancestors. Poems. Lisa Pertillar Brevard. Perf. by Lisa Pertillar Brevard. Photos by Frank Lynn Brevard. 1 Enhanced CD. (Running Time: 46 mins.). 2004. audio compact disk 15.95 (978-0-9749499-3-2(0)) Monarch Baby.
"Lisa Pertillar Brevard's In Praise Of Ancestors, an enhanced English/Spanish debut CD on her own New Orleans-based Black Butterfly Records. Delivering a message of healing, the CD features spirituals, gospels, a cappella ballads and spoken word poetry in honor of her deceased parents." - Steppin' Out - "Released." (ASCAP Playback Magazine, Volume 11 Issue 3 / Summer 2004).

In Praise of Imperfection. unabr. ed. Rita Levi-Montalcini. Read by Diane Gnagnarelli. 8 cass. (Running Time: 9 hrs. 40 min.). 1991. 39.00 set. (978-1-879884-02-1(X)) Sound Writs.
A remarkable memoir by the fourth woman to receive a Nobel Prize in Medicine.

In Praise of Old Age: The Chinese Elderly. 1 cass. (Running Time: 30 min.). 9.95 (I0580B090, HarperThor) HarpC GBR.

***In Praise of Pip.** (ENG.). 2010. audio compact disk (978-1-59171-259-6(9)) Falcon Picture.

***In Praise of Plan B: Moving from 'What Is' to 'What Can Be'** Zondervan. (ENG.). 2010. 14.99 (978-0-310-42770-4(3)) Zondervan.

In Praise of Simplicity. Irving Younger. 1 cass. (Running Time: 20 min.). 1988. 12.95 PEG MN.

In Praise of Stay-at-Home Moms. unabr. ed. Laura Schlessinger. Read by Laura Schlessinger. (Running Time: 4 hrs. 30 mins.). 2009. audio compact disk 29.99 (978-0-06-171197-8(7), Harper Audio) HarperCollins Pubs.

***In Praise of Stay-at-Home Moms.** unabr. ed. Laura Schlessinger. Read by Laura Schlessinger. (ENG.). 2009. (978-0-06-180564-6(5), Harper Audio); (978-0-06-180563-9(7), Harper Audio) HarperCollins Pubs.

In Praise of Wisdom. Neville Goddard. 1 cass. (Running Time: 62 min.). 1965. 8.00 (106) J & L Pubns.
Neville taught Imagination Creates Reality. He was a powerfully influential teacher of God as Consciousness.

In Private: Music for Ballet Class. Perf. by L. Stanford et al. 1 cass, 1 CD. 15.00 (BOD8403C); audio compact disk 18.00 CD. (BOD8403CD) Kimbo Educ.
A unique collection with 19 compositions for a complete ballet class.

In Pursuit: Training Exercise. 1 CD. (Running Time: 1 hr.). wbk. ed. 49.00 Prof Pride.
This training package is well put together. Each chase is followed on an actual map. Students will love this exercise.

In Pursuit: Training Exercise. 1 cass. 2000. 24.95 Prof Pride.
Each chase is followed on an "actual map".

In Pursuit of Elegance: Why the Best Ideas Have Something Missing. unabr. ed. Matthew E. May. (Running Time: 8 hrs. 0 mins.). (ENG.). 2009. 29.95 (978-1-4332-9233-0(5)); 54.95 (978-1-4332-9229-3(7)); audio compact disk 69.00 (978-1-4332-9230-9(0)) Blckstn Audio.

In Pursuit of Happiness & Good Government. unabr. ed. Charles Murray. Read by Phillip J. Sawtelle. 7 cass. (Running Time: 10 hrs.). 1989. 49.95 (978-0-7861-0061-3(3), 1058) Blckstn Audio.
Develops a strong argument calling for a return to the Jeffersonian ideals of community, local government & individualism.

In Pursuit of Peace: 21 Ways to Conquer Anxiety, Fear, & Discontentment. abr. ed. Joyce Meyer. Read by Joyce Meyer. Read by Pat Lentz. 5 CDs. (Running Time: 6 hrs.). (ENG.). 2004. audio compact disk 29.98 (978-1-58621-730-3(5)) Pub: Hachet Audio. Dist(s): HachBkGrp

In Pursuit of Peace: 21 Ways to Conquer Anxiety, Fear, & Discontentment. abr. ed. Joyce Meyer. Read by Pat Lentz. (ENG.). 2005. 14.98 (978-1-59483-152-2(1)) Pub: Hachet Audio. Dist(s): HachBkGrp

In Pursuit of Peace: 21 Ways to Conquer Anxiety, Fear, & Discontentment. abr. ed. Joyce Meyer. Read by Pat Lentz. (Running Time: 6 hrs.). (ENG.). 2009. 44.98 (978-1-60024-633-3(8)) Pub: Hachet Audio. Dist(s): HachBkGrp

In Pursuit of Reason: The Life of Thomas Jefferson, unabr. ed. Noble E. Cunningham, Jr. Read by Phillip J. Sawtelle. 12 cass. (Running Time: 17 hrs. 30 mins.). 1989. 83.95 (978-0-7861-0031-6(1), 1030) Blckstn Audio.
The focus of this work is upon Jefferson's dedication to reason, natural law & the rights of man.

In Pursuit of Reason: The Life of Thomas Jefferson. unabr. ed. Noble E. Cunningham, Jr. Narrated by Nelson Runger. 12 cass. (Running Time: 18 hrs.). 1988. 97.00 (978-1-55690-250-5(6), 88600E7) Recorded Bks.
Biography of Jefferson encourages its readers to see the administrator, diplomat, party leader, plantation owner, architect &, educational reformer.

***In Pursuit of Silence: Listening for Meaning in a World of Noise.** unabr. ed. George Prochnik. Read by Don Hagen. (Running Time: 9 hrs. 30 mins.). (ENG.). 2010. 34.98 (978-1-59659-571-2(X), GildAudio) Pub: Gildan Media. Dist(s): HachBkGrp

In Pursuit of Success, Eight Strategies to the Top! Joe B. Hill. Read by Joe B. Hill. 1 cass. (Running Time: 47 min.). 1996. 12.95 (978-1-890262-00-6(5)) Total Power Pubg.
Motivational-inspirational content that will help you realize & attain all of your dreams & goals.

In Pursuit of the Almighty's Dollar: A History of Money & American Protestantism. James Hudnut-Beumler. (ENG.). 2007. 29.95 (978-0-8078-8337-2(9)); audio compact disk 34.95 (978-0-8078-8339-6(5)) U of NC Pr.

In Pursuit of the Green Lion. abr. ed. Judith M. Riley. Read by Juliet Mills. 2 cass. (Running Time: 3 hrs.). 1990. 15.95 set. (978-0-9627187-4-8(2), 40000) Pub Mills.
The adventures of fourteenth century heroine Margaret of Ashbury as she finds love in her marriage of convenience to Gregory, the would-be monk who has been her tutor & censor. When Gregory becomes entangled in the Hundred Years' War & disappears in France, Margaret marshals her friends & goes off in search of the husband she is coming to love.

In Pursuit of the Proper Sinner, Pt. 1. Elizabeth George. Read by Donada Peters. 8 cass. (Running Time: 12 hrs.). (Inspector Lynley Ser.). 1999. 64.00 (978-0-7366-4652-9(3), 5033-A) Books on Tape.
Investigating a grisly crime, two English detectives learn neither the victims nor the suspects are who they appear to be.

In Pursuit of the Proper Sinner, Pt. 2. Elizabeth George. Read by Donada Peters. 8 cass. (Running Time: 12 hrs.). (Inspector Lynley Ser.). 1999. 64.00 (978-0-7366-4722-9(8), 5033-B) Books on Tape.

In Pursuit of the Proper Sinner, Set. abr. ed. Elizabeth George. Read by Derek Jacobi. 4 cass. (Inspector Lynley Ser.). 1999. 25.95 (FS9-51012) Highsmith.

In Quest of the Pearl. rev. ed. Sydney Banks. Read by Sydney Banks. 2003. audio compact disk (978-1-55105-413-1(2)) Lone Pine Publ CAN.

In Quest of the Universe. 3rd ed. Karl F. Kuhn et al. (C). 2001. audio compact disk 101.00 (978-0-7637-1674-5(X), 1674-X) Jones Bartlett.

In Quest of Universe. 2nd ed. Kuhn. (C). 1999. stu. ed. 18.75 (978-0-7637-0989-1(1), 0989-1) Jones Bartlett.

In Quest Universe. 3rd ed. Karl F. Kuhn et al. (C). 2001. stu. ed. 19.95 (978-0-7637-1675-2(8), 1675-8) Jones Bartlett.

In Quiet Silence: Christmas in a Cloister. Perf. by Society of Saint John the Evangelist. 1 CD. (Running Time: 1 hr. 12 mins.). 2003. audio compact disk 14.95 (978-1-56101-218-3(1)) Pub: Cowley Pubns. Dist(s): Natl Bk Netwk

In Real Life. Charlayne Woodard. Perf. by Charlayne Woodard. 2 CDs. (Running Time: 1 hr. 49 mins.). 2005. audio compact disk 25.95 (978-1-58081-276-4(7), CDTPT187) Pub: L A Theatre. Dist(s): NetLibrary CO

In Remembrance of Me: Matthew 26:26-29. Ed Young. 1984. 4.95 (978-0-7417-1370-4(5), 370) Win Walk.

In Remembrance of Me: Matthew 26:26-29. Ed Young. 1984. 4.95 (978-0-7417-1414-5(0), 414) Win Walk.

In Retrospect: The Tragedy & Lessons of Vietnam. unabr. ed. Robert S. McNamara. Read by Alexander Adams. 8 cass. (Running Time: 12 hrs.). 1995. 64.00 (3843) Books on Tape.
How America "stumbled" into the war, how the Vietnam policy grew & how it quickly became impossible to withdraw, as told by the man who strategized the unpopular war on a daily basis.

In Search of a City. Ruth Prince. 1 cass. (Running Time: 60 min.). 5.95 (B-8001) Derek Prince.

In Search of America. abr. ed. Peter Jennings & Todd Brewster. Read by Peter Jennings. 4 cass. (Running Time: 6 hrs.). 2002. 25.98 (978-0-7868-6951-0(8)) Pub: Hyperion. Dist(s): HarperCollins Pubs

In Search of an Eagle. 1997. 59.95 Set. (978-1-56253-430-1(0), Milady) Delmar.

In Search of Bill Clinton: A Psychological Biography. unabr. ed. John D. Gartner. Read by Stephen Hoye. (Running Time: 17 hrs. 0 mins. 0 sec.). (ENG.). 2008. audio compact disk 99.99 (978-1-4001-3998-9(8)); audio compact disk 34.99 (978-1-4001-5998-7(9)); audio compact disk 49.99 (978-1-4001-0998-2(1)) Pub: Tantor Media. Dist(s): IngramPubServ

In Search of Black America. David J. Dent. Narrated by Dion Graham. 12 cass. (Running Time: 16 hrs. 30 mins.). 98.00 (978-0-7887-5120-2(4)) Recorded Bks.

In Search of Burningbush: A Story of Golf, Friendship, & the Meaning of Irons. abr. ed. Michael Konik. Read by Lloyd James. (Running Time: 16200 sec.). 2005. audio compact disk 28.00 (978-1-932378-86-3(3)) Pub: A Media Intl. Dist(s): Natl Bk Netwk

In Search of Captain Zero: A Surfer's Road Trip beyond the End of the Road. unabr. ed. Allan C. Weisbecker & Joe Barrett. (Running Time: 10 hrs. NaN mins.). 2008. 29.95 (978-1-4332-2561-1(1)); 59.95 (978-1-4332-2557-4(3)); audio compact disk 80.00 (978-1-4332-2558-1(1)) Blckstn Audio.

In Search of Churchill: A Historian's Journey, unabr. collector's ed. Martin Gilbert. Read by David Case. 9 cass. (Running Time: 13 hrs. 30 min.). 1996. 72.00 (978-0-7366-3392-5(8), 4041) Books on Tape.
Martin Gilbert, Winston Churchill's official biographer, has devoted nearly 30 years to his subject. It's taken that long to track down every scrap of information about this twentieth-century titan.

In Search of Enemies: A CIA Story. unabr. ed. John Stockwell. Narrated by Tom West. 7 cass. (Running Time: 9 hrs. 30 mins.). 1981. 60.00 (978-1-55690-251-2(4), 81070E7) Recorded Bks.
An ex-task force commander breaks silence on U. S. involvement in Angola in 1975.

In Search of Excellence. Tom Peters. Intro. by A. E. Whyte. 1 cass. (Running Time: 52 min.). (Listen & Learn USA! Ser.). 8.95 (978-0-88684-055-6(4)) Listen USA.
Explains eight principles used by the most successful corporations.

In Search of Excellence. unabr. ed. Tom Peters & Robert H. Waterman, Jr. Read by Michael Prichard. 11 cass. (Running Time: 16 hrs. 30 min.). 1984. 88.00 (1923) Books on Tape.

In Search of Excellence, unabr. ed. Tom Peters & Robert H. Waterman, Jr. Narrated by James Hamilton. 9 cass. (Running Time: 13 hrs. 30 mins.). 1984. 78.00 (978-1-55690-252-9(2), 84021E7) Recorded Bks.
Eight companies are analyzed for qualities that define their excellence. It's especially interesting in light of current events, as America falls further & further behind.

In Search of Filmwallahs. unabr. ed. Julian C. Hollick. 1 cass. (Running Time: 60 min.). 1991. 15.00 (978-1-56709-013-0(3), 1013) Indep Broadcast.
An exploration of the Indian cinema, which is the largest in the world with over 800 new films every year & over 11 million filmgoers every day.

In Search of Heart. Richard Rohr. Read by Richard Rohr. 1 cass. (Running Time: 61 min.). 1993. 9.95 (978-7-900784-26-1(8), AA2671) Credence Commun.
Rohr talks about our culture's deficiencies & our own possibilities of finding our heart of flesh.

In Search of History, Pt. 1. unabr. collector's ed. Theodore H. White. Read by Dan Lazar. 8 cass. (Running Time: 12 hrs.). 1980. 64.00 (978-0-7366-0451-2(0), 1425-A) Books on Tape.
Theodore White was a correspondent for "Time" magazine. In his autobiography we meet Douglas MacArthur, both as outcast & conqueror, listen to a troubled Eisenhower preparing to lay aside his uniform & plunge into politics; visit Mao Tse Tung in his cave in Hunan & trace the power-curve of America's greatness across the glory years at home & abroad.

In Search of History, Pt. 2. collector's ed. Theodore H. White. Read by Dan Lazar. 9 cass. (Running Time: 13 hrs. 30 min.). 1980. 72.00 (978-0-7366-0452-9(9), 1425-B) Books on Tape.

In Search of Israel (Audio) Batya Ruth Wootten. Voice by Batya Ruth Wootten. (ENG.). 2009. 14.95 (978-1-886987-35-7(1)) KeyofDavid.

In Search of L. L. Bean, unabr. ed. M. R. Montgomery. Narrated by Nelson Runger. 6 cass. (Running Time: 9 hrs.). 51.00 (978-1-55690-904-7(7), 86620E7) Recorded Bks.
Montgomery, originally set out to write an "expose" of the nationally famous mail order clothing & outdoors catalog business, but it never materialized. Try as he might, Montgomery came away with a grudging respect for the business & the people he encountered. Along the way we are treated to bits on salmon fishing, float planes & Maine humor. Available to libraries only.

In Search of Ladura. unabr. ed. Robert Cawley. Read by Maynard Villers. 4 cass. (Running Time: 4 hrs. 30 min.). 1995. 26.95 (978-1-55686-624-1(0)) Books in Motion.
Arizona, 1994. In the turbulent 90's the long lost medallion of LaDura comes into the possession of a young woman on the brink of financial disaster. It's the key to a lost treasure.

In Search of Mockingbird. unabr. ed. Loretta Ellsworth. Narrated by Jessica Almasy. 4 CDs. (Running Time: 4 hrs. 15 mins.). (YA). (gr. 7-10). 2008. audio compact disk 46.75 (978-1-4361-1606-0(6)); 33.75 (978-1-4361-1601-5(5)) Recorded Bks.
The touching story of one girl's journey to find herself, In Search of Mockingbird is Loretta Ellsworth's heartfelt novel. It's 1986, and 15-year-old Erin is none too pleased by her widowed father's announcement that he's getting married. When she discovers her late mother's diary, she learns that she wanted to be a writer just like Erin does. So she runs away from home on a Greyhound bus, determined to track down Harper Lee - the author of both her and her mother's favorite book. What unfolds is a poignant quest of self-discovery and the making of a strong young woman.

In Search of Normal: Moving Life from Chaos to Clarity. Cindy Kubica. 6 CDs. (Running Time: 5 hours). 2003. audio compact disk 99.95 (978-0-9745157-0-0(1), ISON-A) Studio Ten.
Are you in search of a new normal? If the stress in your life is stealing your energy, disrupting your sleep, and fogging your mind then it?s time to make some serious life changes. This program gives you a step-by-step approach to gain control of your chaos and create the life you are longing for. With raw honesty, professional speaker and author, Cindy Kubica, shares what went wrong in her life and how she gained control by taking responsibility for her own happiness, creating the life she truly desired.You can, too! It?s time to stop waiting for others to change to be happy; you have no control over what they do. Take control over what you have the power to change?yourself. If you are not living the life you desire then it?s time to begin your journey to ?redefine your normal??one step at a time.

In Search of Stones: A Pilgrimage of Faith, Reason, & Discovery. abr. ed. M. Scott Peck. (ENG.). 2006. 14.98 (978-1-59483-828-6(3)) Pub: Hachet Audio. Dist(s): HachBkGrp

In Search of Stones: A Pilgrimage of Faith, Reason, & Discovery. unabr. collector's ed. M. Scott Peck. Read by Jonathan Reese. 11 cass. (Running Time: 16 hrs. 30 min.). 1997. 88.00 (978-0-913369-63-0(2), 4302) Books on Tape.
A three-week tour through the countryside of Wales, England & Scotland. It is a trip that takes Peck & his wife Lily to a land strewn with megalithic stones of past cultures, silent monuments to human achievement.

In Search of the Beloved. unabr. ed. Perf. by Eknath Easwaran. 1 cass. (Running Time: 1 hr.). 1983. 7.95 (978-1-58638-553-8(4)) Nilgiri Pr.

In Search of the Mighty Reptar: Songs & Stories. 1 cass., 1 CD. (Rugrats Ser.). (J). 6.38 Blisterpack. (KID 72980); audio compact disk 9.58 CD Jewel box. NewSound.

In Search of the Miraculous. abr. ed. P. D. Ouspensky. Read by Laurence Rosenthal. 1 cass. (Running Time: 1 hr. 30 min.). 1995. 10.95 (978-0-944993-88-0(5)) Audio Lit.

In search of the Obvious: The Antidote for Today?s Marketing Mess. unabr. ed. Jack Trout. Read by Sean Pratt. (Running Time: 6 hrs. 30 mins.). (ENG.). 2009. 24.98 (978-1-59659-328-2(8), GildAudio) Pub: Gildan Media. Dist(s): HachBkGrp

In Search of the Ruby Sword. unabr. ed. Michele Sobel Spirn. 1 cass. (Running Time: 20 min.). (Time Traveler Ser.). (J). (gr. 3-6). 1984. bk. 16.99 (978-0-934898-62-1(6)); pap. bk. 9.95 (978-0-934898-74-4(X)) Jan Prods.
Diana & Tom travel back to Camelot, King Arthur's Court. Their mission is to find a magic sword before it falls into the hands of the evil wizard, Cronin.

In Search of the Spirit. (Running Time: 60 mins.). 2002. audio compact disk 15.99 (978-1-904972-25-9(X)) Global Jrny GBR GBR.

In Search of the Trojan War. Michael Wood. Read by Gordon Dulieu. 8 cass. (Running Time: 12 hrs.). 2001. 69.95 (89123) Pub: Soundings Ltd GBR. Dist(s): Ulverscroft US

In Search of Tiger. unabr. ed. Tom Callahan. Read by Buck Schirner. 5 cass. (Running Time: 7 hrs.). 2003. 27.95 (978-1-59086-653-5(3), 1590866533, BAU); audio compact disk 82.25 (978-1-59086-656-6(8), 1590866568, CD Unabrid Lib Ed); 69.25 (978-1-59086-654-2(1), 1590866541, CD Unabrid Lib Ed); audio compact disk 29.95 (978-1-59086-655-9(X), 159086655X, BAU) Brilliance Audio.
Tom Callahan has written the seminal book on golfing great Tiger Woods. Woods, who has gone out of his way to protect his privacy, has never allowed himself to get close enough to a writer to be properly examined on the page. Callahan, commonly regarded as one of the best all-round sports writers in the country, has followed Tiger around the world of golf for more than seven years, enjoying a certain access to the man and his family. He even went so far as to travel to Vietnam to learn the fate of the South Vietnamese soldier who was Earl Wood's best friend during the war - and his son's namesake. Tiger is twenty years old when the book opens and twenty-seven when it closes. During those years, Callahan covered Woods at all the Majors, including the Masters, the U.S. Open, and the British Open, culminating in Tiger's heart-stopping race to make history by clinching the string of Majors affectionately nicknamed the Tiger Slam. Along the way, Tom Callahan hears from everyone who is anyone in the world of Tiger Woods, including Phil Mickelson, Jack Nicklaus, David Duval, Butch Harmon, Ernie Els, and, of course, Tiger's rather ubiquitous mother and father. As much as we learn about Tiger - how he sees himself in relation to the courses he plays on and the players he has learned from and competed with - we also enjoy a bird's-eye view of golf as it is now with Tiger on the scene, and as it was for centuries before.

In Search of Tiger. unabr. ed. Tom Callahan. Read by Buck Schirner. (Running Time: 7 hrs.). 2004. 39.25 (978-1-59335-382-7(0), 1593353820, Brlnc Audio MP3 Lib) Brilliance Audio.

In Search of Tiger. unabr. ed. Tom Callahan. Read by Buck Schirner. (Running Time: 7 hrs.). 2004. 39.25 (978-1-59710-396-1(9), 1597103969, BADLE); 24.95 (978-1-59710-397-8(7), 1597103977, BAD) Brilliance Audio.

In Search of Tiger. unabr. ed. Tom Callahan. Read by Buck Schirner. (Running Time: 7 hrs.). 2004. 24.95 (978-1-59335-094-9(5), 1593350945) Soulmate Audio Bks.

In Search of Wisdom. Ernest Kurtz. 1 cass. 1986. 7.95 (1698) Hazelden.
The popular author of "Not-God" & "Shame & Guilt" describes an AA approach to spirituality.

***In Serena's Web.** Kay Hooper. Narrated by Emily Woo Zeller. (Running Time: 5 hrs. 0 mins. 0 sec.). (ENG.). 2010. audio compact disk 19.95 (978-1-60283-910-6(7)) Pub: AudioGO. Dist(s): Perseus Dist

***In Serena's Web.** unabr. ed. Kay Hooper. Narrated by Emily Woo Zeller. 1 Playaway. 2010. 64.95 (978-0-7927-7060-2(9)); audio compact disk 49.95 (978-0-7927-6968-2(6)) AudioGO.

In-Service Reviews in Clinical Laboratory Science. 12 cass. (Clinical Laboratory Science Ser.). 225.00 set, 1 cass. per month with 1 yr. subscript., individual pkg. (1042-7430); 295.00 set, 1 cass. per month with 1 yr. subscript., department pkg. (1042-7430) Ed Reviews.
Reviews & updates covering topics of practical importance in Bacteriology, Blood Banking, Chemistry, Hematology, Mycology, Serology, Toxicology, Urinalysis, Safety/First Aid, Office Testing, Instruments/Equipment, Diseases/Syndromes & Human Relations.

In-Service Reviews in Diagnostic Medical Sonography. 12 cass. (Diagnostic Medical Sonography Ser.). 225.00 set, 1 cass. per month with 1 yr. subscript., individual pkg. (1041-0104); 295.00 set, 1 cass. per month with 1 yr. subscript., department pkg. (1041-0104) Ed Reviews.
Reviews & updates covering all areas of diagnostic medical sonography.

In-Service Reviews in Nuclear Medicine. 12 cass. 225.00 set, 1 cass. per month with 1 yr. subscript., individual pkg. (1041-0090); 295.00 set, 1 cass. per month with 1 yr. subscript., department pkg. (1041-0090) Ed Reviews.
Includes reviews & updates on imaging & function studies of the heart, thyroid, liver, gallbladder, G.I. tract & scrotum, bones, etc. Also covers therapy.

In-Service Reviews in Radiologic Technology. 12 cass. (Radiologic Technology Ser.). 225.00 set, 1 cass. per month with 1 yr. subscript., individual pkg. (1041-0082); 295.00 set, 1 cass. per month with 1 yr. subscript., department pkg. Ed Reviews.
Reviews & updates covering all areas of radiologic technology: Conventional, CT, MRI, special studies, ultrasound & more.

In-Service Reviews in Respiratory Care. 12 cass. (Respiratory Care Ser.). 225.00 set, 1 cass. per month with 1 yr. subscript., individual pkg.; 295.00 set, 1 cass. per month with 1 yr. subscript., department pkg. Ed Reviews.
Reviews & updates covering important clinical topics in respiratory care.

In Session - The Divas. bk. 24.95 (978-1-85909-693-2(X), Warner Bro) Alfred Pub.

In Session with Chuck Berry. 2001. bk. 24.95 (978-1-85909-702-1(2), Warner Bro) Alfred Pub.

In Session with George Benson. George Benson. 2001. bk. 24.95 (978-1-85909-646-8(8), Warner Bro) Alfred Pub.

In Session with Peter Green. Peter Green. 2001. bk. 24.95 (978-1-85909-645-1(X), Warner Bro) Alfred Pub.

In Siberia. unabr. ed. Colin Thubron. Read by Stephen Thorne. 10 CDs. (Running Time: 10 hrs. 35 min.). 2001. audio compact disk 89.95 (978-0-7531-0895-6(X), 10895X) Pub: ISIS Audio GBR. Dist(s): Ulverscroft US
Describes Colin Thubron's 15,000-mile journey - from the site of the last Czar's murder, to the ice-bound graves of ancient Scythians, to Baikal, deepest and oldest of the world's lakes. Exquisitely written, compassionate, underpinned with humour, it is the account of a people moving through the ruins of Communism into more private, diverse and often stranger worlds.

In Siberia. unabr. ed. Colin Thubron. Read by Stephen Thorne. 8 cass. (Running Time: 10 hrs. 35 min.). (Isis Ser.). (J). 2001. 69.95 (978-0-7531-0860-4(7), 000611) Pub: ISIS Lrg Prnt GBR. Dist(s): Ulverscroft US

In Some Quiet Place & Follow Another Star. Jim Metcalf. Narrated by Jim Metcalf. 1 cass. (Running Time: 33 hrs. NaN mins.). (ENG.). 2000. 15.95 (978-1-56554-851-0(5)) Pelican.

In Souls There Is No Sex: Building a Peace Movement see In Souls There Is No Sex: The Quaker Testimony on Gender Equality

In Souls There Is No Sex: One Reform & Another see In Souls There Is No Sex: The Quaker Testimony on Gender Equality

In Souls There Is No Sex: Pioneers in Antislavery & Women's Rights see In Souls There Is No Sex: The Quaker Testimony on Gender Equality

In Souls There Is No Sex: Quaker Women Today see In Souls There Is No Sex: The Quaker Testimony on Gender Equality

In Souls There Is No Sex: Status of Quaker Women in the Eighteenth & Nineteenth Centuries see In Souls There Is No Sex: The Quaker Testimony on Gender Equality

In Souls There Is No Sex: The Adventures of the Traveling Quaker Women Ministers see In Souls There Is No Sex: The Quaker Testimony on Gender Equality

In Souls There Is No Sex: The Alice Paul Story see In Souls There Is No Sex: The Quaker Testimony on Gender Equality

In Souls There Is No Sex: The Quaker Testimony on Gender Equality. 9 cass. Incl. In Souls There Is No Sex: Building a Peace Movement. Mildred Olmstead. 1985.; In Souls There Is No Sex: One Reform & Another. Margaret Bacon. 1985.; In Souls There Is No Sex: Pioneers in Antislavery & Women's Rights. Margaret Bacon. 1985.; In Souls There Is No Sex: Quaker Women Today. Demi Kurz & Cynthia Taylor. 1985.; In Souls There Is No Sex: Status of Quaker Women in the Eighteenth & Nineteenth Centuries. Margaret Bacon. 1985.; In Souls There Is No Sex: The Adventures of the Traveling Quaker Women Ministers. Margaret Bacon. 1985.; In Souls There Is No Sex: The Alice Paul Story. Amelia R. Fry. 1985.; In Souls There Is No Sex: Were Fox & Fell Feminists? Margaret Bacon. 1985.; In Souls There Is No Sex: Women's Business Meetings: Training for Leadership. Margaret Bacon. 1985.; 1985. 28.00 Set.; 4.50 ea. Pendle Hill.

In Souls There Is No Sex: Were Fox & Fell Feminists? see In Souls There Is No Sex: The Quaker Testimony on Gender Equality

In Souls There Is No Sex: Women's Business Meetings: Training for Leadership see In Souls There Is No Sex: The Quaker Testimony on Gender Equality

In Sound & Sight of the Sea. Gwenda Ledbetter. Read by Gwenda Ledbetter. 1 cass. (Running Time: 1 hr. 09 min.). (J). (gr. 3 up). 1992. 10.00 (978-0-9617007-1-3(8), BE5072) G LedBetter.
Personal stories of growing up on Virginia's Eastern Shore, during the 30's & 40's. Each story contains an element of change. Looking back the changes shine like sparks from a beach fire in a summer night sky.

In Spirit & Truth. Megan McKenna. 6 cass. (Running Time: 6 hrs.). 1995. Set. Credence Commun.
This retreat is based on John's gospel & most of it is about the woman at the well.

In Spirit & Truth. abr. ed. Contrib. by W. Clifford Petty. 2006. audio compact disk 17.00 (978-1-58459-282-2(6)) Wrld Lib Pubns.

In Step with the Master Teacher. David Zimmerman & Esther Zimmerman. 2004. audio compact disk 149.00 (978-0-86508-266-3(9)) Pub: BCM Pubns. Dist(s): STL Dist NA

In Storm & in Calm. unabr. ed. Lucilla Andrews. Read by Jane Jermyn. 4 cass. (Running Time: 6 hrs.). 2001. 44.95 (60148) Pub: Soundings Ltd GBR. Dist(s): Ulverscroft US

In Storm & in Calm, Set. Lucilla Andrews. Read by Jane Jermyn. 4 cass. 1999. 44.95 (60148) Pub: Soundings Ltd GBR. Dist(s): ISIS Pub

In Storm & In Calm, Set. unabr. ed. Lucilla Andrews. Read by Jane Jermyn. 4 cass. (Sound Ser.). 1986. 44.95 (978-1-85496-014-6(8), US0054) Pub: UlverLrgPrint GBR. Dist(s): Ulverscroft US

In Sunlight, in a Beautiful Garden. unabr. ed. Kathleen Cambor. Read by James Daniels. (Running Time: 10 hrs.). 2005. 39.25 (978-1-59600-713-0(3), 9781596007130, Brlnc Audio MP3 Lib); 24.95 (978-1-59600-712-3(5), 9781596007123, Brilliance MP3); 39.25 (978-1-59600-715-4(X), 9781596007154, BADLE); 24.95 (978-1-59600-714-7(1), 9781596007147, BAD) Brilliance Audio.

In Suspect Terrain. unabr. ed. John McPhee. Read by Walter Zimmerman. 6 cass. (Running Time: 6 hrs.). 1991. 36.00 Set. (978-0-7366-2060-4(5), 2869) Books on Tape.
A composite of travels through ancient terrains with an internationally known geologist.

In Suspect Terrain: From Annals of the Former World. unabr. ed. John McPhee. Narrated by Nelson Runger. 5 cass. (Running Time: 6 hrs. 45 mins.). 1998. 44.00 (978-0-7887-4060-2(1), 96021E7) Recorded Bks.
Geology is the fascinating subject of this Pulitzer Prize-winning collection. In its first book, "Basin & Range," McPhee traveled across the U.S. with a proponent of plate tectonics. Now he covers some of the same terrain with a geologist who seriously questions plate tectonics.

In Sweet Rejoicing - Music for Christmas Vol. 3: Ars Antiqua Choralis. Perf. by Cathedral Singers. 1994. 10.95 (323); audio compact disk 15.95 (323) GIA Pubns.

In Tall Grass see Carl Sandburg Reading Cool Tombs & Other Poems

In Tara's Halls see Evening with Dylan Thomas

In Tenebris I see Poetry of Thomas Hardy

In That Wonderful Year Of 1944. (Running Time: 2 hrs.). 2004. 10.95 (978-1-57816-206-2(8)); audio compact disk 12.95 (978-1-57816-205-5(X)) Audio File.

In That Wonderful Year Of 1948. (Running Time: 2 hrs.). 2004. audio compact disk 12.95 (978-1-57816-207-9(6)) Audio File.

In the Absence of Angels. unabr. ed. Elizabeth Glaser & Palmer. Read by Sheila Hart. (Running Time: 11 hrs.). 2009. 24.99 (978-1-4233-9699-4(5), 9781423396994, BAD); 39.97 (978-1-4233-9700-7(2), 9781423397007, BADLE) Brilliance Audio.

In the Absence of Angels. unabr. ed. Elizabeth Glaser & Laura Palmer. Read by Sheila Hart. (Running Time: 11 hrs.). 2009. 24.99 (978-1-4233-9697-0(9), 9781423396970, Brilliance MP3); 39.97 (978-1-4233-9698-7(7), 9781423396987, Brlnc Audio MP3 Lib) Brilliance Audio.

In the Arms of God. Thomas Merton. 1 cass. (Running Time: 54 min.). 1993. 8.95 Credence Commun.
Bernard says we must do the will of God. God will take care of the results.

In the Arms of His Love. Steven A. Cramer. 1 cass. 7.98 (978-1-55503-367-5(9), 069106) Covenant Comms.
A touching fireside talk with ideas from his great book.

In the Backyard Audio CD. Adapted by Benchmark Education Company Staff. Based on a work by Kira Freed. (Early Explorers Set C Ser.). (J). (gr. 2). 2008. audio compact disk 10.00 (978-1-60437-547-3(7)) Benchmark Educ.

In the Beginning see Twentieth-Century Poetry in English, No. 28, Recordings of Poets Reading Their Own Poetry

In the Beginning. Lyrics by Debbie Friedman. Music by Debbie Friedman. 3 CDs. (ENG & HEB.). 1994. audio compact disk 39.95 (978-1-890161-08-8(X)) Sounds Write.

In the Beginning. abr. ed. Read by Alister E. McGrath. 4 cass. (Running Time: 6 hrs.). 2002. 24.95 (978-1-57270-249-3(4)) Pub: Audio Partners. Dist(s): PerseuPGW
Woven into this story are murder, deceit, bitter political feuds, and religious conflicts so intense that they threatened the unity of England. McGrath provides details about the Bible's global influence, inspiration that continues to this day. It has profoundly shaped English-speaking culture since its original publication in the 17th century.

In the Beginning: Biblical Creation & Science. Nathan Aviezer. Read by Michael Jarmus. Prod. by Alden Films Staff. (Running Time: 3 hrs. 18 mins. 0 sec.). (ENG.). 2010. audio compact disk 29.95 (978-1-877684-73-9(2)) Pub: Alden Films. Dist(s): Perseus Dist

In the Beginning: Fundamentalism, the Scopes Trial, & the Making of the Antievolution Movement. Michael Lienesch. (ENG., 2007. 34.95 (978-0-8078-8430-0(8)); audio compact disk 39.95 (978-0-8078-8432-4(4)) U of NC Pr.

In the Beginning: John's Gospel About God. Eugene LaVerdiere. 3 cass. (Running Time: 3 hrs.). 2001. 24.95 (A6610) St Anthony Mess Pr.
Focuses on the series of signs in the first 12 chapters of John and then explains how the signs are brought to fulfillment through the Last Supper, the Passion and the Resurrection.

In the Beginning: The Book of Genesis. abr. ed. Zondervan Publishing Staff. (Running Time: 3 hrs. 0 mins. 0 sec.). (NIV Audio Bible Ser.). (ENG.). 2003. 8.99 (978-0-310-26066-0(3)) Zondervan.

In the Beginning: The Book of Genesis. unabr. rev. ed. 2002. audio compact disk 14.99 (978-0-310-94488-1(0)) Zondervan.

In the Beginning (Getting Pregnant) unabr. ed. Milton Diamond. 1 cass. (Running Time: 1 hr.). (Human Sexuality Ser.). 12.95 (34010) J Norton Pubs.

In the Beginning There Was... Information. Chuck Missler & Stephen Meyer. 2 CDs. (Running Time: 2 hrs.). (Briefing Packages by Chuck Missler). 2000. audio compact disk 19.95 (978-1-57821-289-7(8)) Koinonia Hse.
"Although the tiniest bacterial cells are incredibly small, each is in effect a veritable microminiaturized factory containing thousands of exquisitely designed pieces of intricate molecular machinery, made up of 100,000,000,000 atoms, far more complicated than any machine built by man and absolutely without parallel in the nonliving world."-Biochemist Michael DentonWhat is the most absurd myth of our culture?Are we really the result of a series of cosmic accidents?Can we explain the origin of design information in our DNA? Darwinists cannot explain; they can only assert. Darwinists cannot account for the origin of information. In this Briefing Pack, Dr. Stephen Meyer joins Chuck Missler in reviewing some of the revealing insights from microbiology and the information sciences on the evidences of design in the origin of life and their implications for our destiny.

In the Belly of the Bloodhound: Being an Account of a Particularly Peculiar Adventure in the Life of Jacky Faber. L. A. Meyer. Read by Katherine Kellgren. (Bloody Jack Adventures Ser.: Bk. 4). (YA). (gr. 7). 2009. 59.99 (978-1-60812-754-2(0)) Find a World.

In the Belly of the Bloodhound: Being an Account of a Particularly Peculiar Adventure in the Life of Jacky Faber. unabr. ed. L. A. Meyer. Read by Katherine Kellgren. 13 CDs. (Running Time: 15 hrs.). (Bloody Jack Adventures Ser.: Bk. 4). (YA). (gr. 7 up). 2008. audio compact disk 29.95 (978-1-59316-142-2(5)) Listen & Live.

In the Best Families: A Nero Wolfe Mystery. unabr. ed. Rex Stout. Narrated by Michael Prichard. (ENG.). 2009. audio compact disk 29.95 (978-1-60283-563-4(2)) Pub: AudioGO. Dist(s): Perseus Dist

In the Best of Families. unabr. ed. Rex Stout. Read by Michael Prichard. 6 cass. (Running Time: 8 hrs.). (Nero Wolfe Ser.). 2000. 29.95 (978-1-57270-146-5(3), N61146u) Pub: Audio Partners. Dist(s): PerseuPGW
Nero Wolfe is asked to help a rich old woman whose husband is getting money in a mysterious way. When the woman & her favorite dog are murdered, the case leads Wolfe to a direct confrontation with the most dangerous racketeer in the U.S. & Wolfe must hide out from everyone, including Archie. Has the career of the world's most famous sleuth ended?.

In the Best of Families. unabr. collector's ed. Rex Stout. Read by Michael Prichard. 8 cass. (Running Time: 8 hrs.). (Nero Wolfe Ser.). 1995. 64.00 (978-0-7366-3058-0(9), 3740) Books on Tape.
Nero & Archie collide with America's most dangerous man. If they don't run & hide, the man may have their hides.

In the Best Possible Taste. abr. ed. Kenny Everett. Read by Kenny Everett. 2 cass. (Running Time: 2 hrs.). 1998. 16.85 Set. (978-0-563-55711-1(7)) BBC WrldWd GBR.
Totally unique humour.

In the Big Country. unabr. collector's ed. John Jakes. Read by Michael Kramer. 7 cass. (Running Time: 10 hrs. 30 min.). 1994. 56.00 (978-0-7366-2822-8(3), 3532) Books on Tape.
Eleven of Jakes' finest stories capture the humor, violence & adventure of America's great frontier.

In the Bleak Midwinter. 2007. audio compact disk 15.00 (978-1-931569-06-4(1)) Pub: U of Wis Pr. Dist(s): Chicago Distribution Ctr

In the Bleak Midwinter. Julia Spencer-Fleming. Read by Suzanne Toren. 9 cass. (Clare Fergusson/Russ Van Alstyne Mystery Ser.). 2004. 79.95 (978-0-7927-3179-5(4), CSL 641, Chivers Sound Lib); audio compact disk 99.95 (978-0-7927-3180-1(8), SLD 641, Chivers Sound Lib) AudioGO.

***In the Blink of an Eye.** Hasso Von Bredow. 2010. 71.95 (978-1-4450-0288-0(4)); audio compact disk 79.95 (978-1-4450-0289-7(2)) Pub: Isis Pubng Ltd GBR. Dist(s): Ulverscroft US

In the Blink of an Eye: The FBI Investigation of TWA Flight 800. unabr. ed. Pat Milton. Narrated by Richard Poe. 13 cass. (Running Time: 19 hrs.). 1999. 104.00 (95979E7) Recorded Bks.
In the evening of July 17, 1996, TWA flight 800 fell out of the sky, claiming the lives of all 230 people aboard. Associated Press reporter Pat Milton offers a rare inside look at the investigation of the mysterious explosion & the experts who struggled to find the truth behind the most disturbing aviation disaster. Includes an exclusive interview with the author.

In the Blue Light of African Dreams. unabr. ed. Paul Watkins. Narrated by Richard Poe. 9 cass. (Running Time: 12 hrs. 15 mins.). 1991. 78.00 (978-1-55690-625-1(0), 91410E7) Recorded Bks.
An American flyer, doing time in the French Foreign Legion seeks an escape.

In the Break. unabr. ed. Jack Lopez. Read by Ramon de Ocampo. 5 CDs. (Running Time: 5 hrs. 30 mins.). (YA). (gr. 9 up). 2006. audio compact disk 49.75 (978-1-4281-0468-6(2)); 39.75 (978-1-4281-0463-1(1)) Recorded Bks.
A championship surfer, Jack Lopez accurately depicts the art of surfing in this tale described as The Outsiders for a new age. In the Break tells the story of fifteen year-old Jamie and Juan, best friends who live and breathe surfing. They don't have a care in the world when they're out on the water. But when an argument between Jamie and his abusive step-father comes to blows, Jamie turns to the one person who can help. Together the two (plus Jamie's sister Amber) head for Mexico - surfboards stowed in the back.

In the Castle of the Flynns. unabr. ed. Michael Raleigh. Read by Patrick G. Lawlor. 8 cass. (Running Time: 11 hrs.). 2002. 34.95 (978-1-59086-057-1(8), 1590860578, BAU); 87.25 (978-1-59086-058-8(6), 1590860586, Unabridge Lib Edns) Brilliance Audio.
The year is 1954 and Daniel Dorsey learns at the age of eight the intimate meaning of death when his parents are killed in a car crash. Taken in by his colorful, at times mad, and always tender and caring extended family, Daniel learns that even the deepest sorrows and hurt can be healed. Michael Raleigh's In the Castle of the Flynns is about a young boy growing up Irish in a vibrant 1950s Chicago neighborhood. Now grown and looking back on those years, Daniel recalls his bouts with grief and fear of abandonment as he learns to adjust to his new surroundings amidst his oddball family. It is a time of wakes and weddings, conflicts and romance. Above all, it is a time when Daniel comes to understand both his own loss and the dark places in the lives of his loved ones. In the Castle of the Flynns is a poignant, often hilarious story of hope, passions and unforgettable memories.

In the Castle of the Flynns. unabr. ed. Michael Raleigh. Read by Patrick G. Lawlor. (Running Time: 11 hrs.). 2004. 39.25 (978-1-59335-337-7(5), 1593353375, Brlnc Audio MP3 Lib) Brilliance Audio.

In the Castle of the Flynns. unabr. ed. Michael Raleigh. Read by Patrick G. Lawlor. (Running Time: 11 hrs.). 2004. 39.25 (978-1-59710-398-5(5), 1597103985, BADLE); 24.95 (978-1-59710-399-2(3), 1597103993, BAD) Brilliance Audio.

In the Castle of the Flynns. unabr. ed. Michael Raleigh. Read by Patrick G. Lawlor. (Running Time: 11 hrs.). 2004. 24.95 (978-1-59335-021-5(X), 159335021X) Soulmate Audio Bks.

In the Chambers of the Sea. unabr. ed. Susan Rendell & Anita Best. Read by Joel Hynes & Deirdre Gillard-Rowlings. 1 CD. (Running Time: 32400 sec.). 2004. audio compact disk 24.95 (978-0-9734223-6-8(X)) Rattling Bks CAN.

In the Clap Shack. unabr. collector's ed. William Styron. Read by Grover Gardner. 3 cass. (Running Time: 3 hrs.). 1988. 18.00 (978-0-7366-1315-6(3), 2221) Books on Tape.
Aimed at adult audiences, this is a reading of the play set in the urological ward of a U. S. Naval Hospital in 1943.

***In the Company of Angels: True Stories of Angelic Encounters.** unabr. ed. Robert Strand. Narrated by Maurice England. (ENG.). 2010. 8.98 (978-1-59644-947-3(0)); audio compact disk 10.98 (978-1-59644-946-6(2)) christianaud.

In the Company of Cheerful Ladies. Alexander McCall Smith. Read by Lisette Lecat. 8 CDs. (Running Time: 9.5 Hrs). (No. 1 Ladies' Detective Agency Ser.: No. 6). audio compact disk 29.99 (978-1-4193-1174-1(3)) Recorded Bks.

In the Company of Eagles. unabr. ed. Ernest K. Gann. Narrated by George Guidall. 7 cass. (Running Time: 10 hrs. 30 mins.). 1991. 60.00 (978-1-55690-248-2(4), 91218E7) Recorded Bks.
Sebastian Kupper, Oberleutnant in a German Jasta Squadron & Paul Chamay, a sergeant in one of France's Escadrille forces are WWI ace fighter pilots. But Kupper is growing tired. His nerves are on edge; he thinks too often of death.

In the Company of Heroes: The True Story of Black Hawk Pilot Michael Durant & the Men Who Fought & Fell at Mogadishu. abr. ed. Michael Durant & Steven Hartov. 2004. 15.95 (978-0-7435-4865-6(5)) Pub: S&S Audio. Dist(s): S and S Inc

In the Company of Liars. abr. ed. David Ellis. Read by Dick Hill & Susie Breck. (Running Time: 6 hrs.). 2005. audio compact disk 74.25 (978-1-59737-001-1(0), 9781597370011, BACDLib Ed) Brilliance Audio.
In the Company of Liars is that rare animal - a truly original thriller, strikingly fresh and unpredictable. Told chronologically in reverse, from its enigmatic end to its brilliant beginning, it's centered around a woman on trial for murder - Allison Pagone, who is caught between competing forces, each represented by someone who may not care if the pressure kills her in the end. A prosecutor wants Allison convicted and put on death row. An FBI agent believes she can squeeze her into ratting on her family. A daughter and an ex-husband need to save their own skins. And circling them all, a group who would prefer to kill her quietly and anonymously, but who also are not what they seem. Our first picture of Allison is in the moments after her death. Then the story moves backward in time like the acclaimed film Memento: an hour before, then a day, back and back until we're at the beginning and can see what's really happened - and most shocking, what has not. At every turn, Allison knows what she sees may not be what's real. The only sure thing is her place in a vortex of half-truths, threat, and suspicion. When her nightmare is over, where will she be? In the company of friends - or the company of liars?.

In the Company of Liars. abr. ed. David Ellis. Read by Dick Hill & Susie Breck. (Running Time: 21600 sec.). 2006. audio compact disk 16.99 (978-1-59737-002-8(9), 9781597370028, BCD Value Price) Brilliance Audio.

In the Company of Liars. unabr. ed. David Ellis. Read by Dick Hill & Susie Breck. (Running Time: 10 hrs.). 2005. 39.25 (978-1-59710-543-9(0), 9781597105439, BADLE); 24.95 (978-1-59710-542-2(2), 9781597105422, BAD); 39.25 (978-1-59335-815-0(6), 9781593358150, Brlnc Audio MP3 Lib) Brilliance Audio.

In the Company of Liars. unabr. ed. David Ellis. Read by Susie Breck & Dick Hill. (Running Time: 10 hrs.). 2005. 24.95 (978-1-59335-681-1(1), 9781593356811, Brilliance MP3) Brilliance Audio.

In the Company of Liars. unabr. ed. David Ellis. Read by Dick Hill & Susie Breck. 10 cass. (Running Time: 10 hrs.). 2005. 32.95 (978-1-59086-773-0(4), 9781590867730, BAU); 82.25 (978-1-59086-774-7(2), 9781590867747, BrilAudUnabridg) Brilliance Audio.

***In the Company of Others.** Jan Karon. Read by Erik Singer. (Running Time: 14 hrs.). (ENG.). 2010. audio compact disk 39.95 (978-0-14-242840-5(X), PengAudBks) Penguin Grp USA.

In the Company of Soldiers: A Chronicle of Combat in Iraq. abr. ed. Rick Atkinson. 2004. 15.95 (978-0-7435-3931-9(1)) Pub: S&S Audio. Dist(s): S and S Inc

In the Company of the Courtesan. abr. ed. Sarah Dunant. Read by Richard Thomas. (YA). 2006. 49.99 (978-0-7393-7493-1(1)) Find a World.

In the Company of the Courtesan. unabr. ed. Sarah Dunant. Read by Stephen Hoye. 12 CDs. (Running Time: 15 hrs.). 2006. audio compact disk 81.60 (978-1-4159-2681-9(6)); 90.00 (978-1-4159-2680-2(8)) Books on Tape.
Escaping the sack of Rome in 1527, with their stomachs churning on the jewels they have swallowed, the courtesan Fiammetta and her dwarf companion, Bucino, head for Venice, the shimmering city born out of water to become a miracle of east-west trade: rich and rancid, pious and profitable, beautiful and squalid. With a mix of courage and cunning they infiltrate Venetian society. Together they make the perfect partnership: the sharp-tongued, sharp-witted dwarf, and his vibrant mistress, trained from birth to charm, entertain, and satisfy men who have the money to support her. Yet as their fortunes rise, this perfect partnership comes under threat, from the searing passion of a lover who wants more than his allotted nights to the attentions of an admiring Turk in search of human novelties for his sultan's court. But Fiammetta and Bucino's greatest challenge comes from a young crippled woman, a blind healer who insinuates herself into their lives and hearts with devastating consequences for them all.

In the Company of Writers: A Life in Publishing. unabr. collector's ed. Charles Scribner, Jr. Read by Grover Gardner. 5 cass. (Running Time: 5 hrs.). 1991. 30.00 (978-0-7366-2061-1(3), 2870) Books on Tape.
This memoir of a life in one of America's great publishing houses is a rare treat for all lovers of books & the people who make them. The third publishing Scribner did not enshrine the past, & neither does this candid, thoroughly engaging account of how he upheld the Scribner tradition while guiding it into the modern world & grappling with legends such as Ernest Hemingway, Edmund Wilson, & Charles Lindbergh.

In the Cook's Hands see En Manos de la Cocinera & Other Short Stories

In the Country of Men. unabr. ed. Hisham Matar. Read by Stephen Hoye. (YA). 2008. 54.99 (978-1-60514-891-5(1)) Find a World.

In the Country of Men. unabr. ed. Hisham Matar. (Running Time: 8 hrs. 0 mins. 0 sec.). (ENG.). 2007. audio compact disk 59.99 (978-1-4001-3418-2(8)) Pub: Tantor Media. Dist(s): IngramPubServ

In the Country of Men. unabr. ed. Hisham Matar. Read by Stephen Hoye. (Running Time: 8 hrs. 0 mins. 0 sec.). (ENG.). 2007. audio compact disk 29.99 (978-1-4001-0418-5(1)); audio compact disk 19.99 (978-1-4001-5418-0(9)) Pub: Tantor Media. Dist(s): IngramPubServ

In the Courts of the Crimson Kings. unabr. ed. S. M. Stirling. Read by Todd McLaren. (YA). 2008. 59.99 (978-1-60514-437-5(1)) Find a World.

In the Courts of the Crimson Kings. unabr. ed. S. M. Stirling. Narrated by Todd McLaren. (Running Time: 12 hrs. 0 mins. 0 sec.). (Lords of Creation Ser.). (ENG.). 2008. audio compact disk 34.99 (978-1-4001-0610-3(9)); audio compact disk 69.99 (978-1-4001-3610-0(5)) Pub: Tantor Media. Dist(s): IngramPubServ

In the Courts of the Crimson Kings. unabr. ed. S. M. Stirling. Narrated by Todd McLaren. (Running Time: 12 hrs. 0 mins. 0 sec.). (Lords of Creation Ser.). (ENG.). 2008. audio compact disk 24.99 (978-1-4001-5610-8(6)) Pub: Tantor Media. Dist(s): IngramPubServ

In the Courts of the Sun. unabr. ed. Brian D'Amato. (Running Time: 27 hrs. 30 mins. 0 sec.). (ENG.). 2009. audio compact disk 109.99 (978-1-4001-4140-1(0)); audio compact disk 39.99 (978-1-4001-6140-9(1)); audio compact disk 54.99 (978-1-4001-1140-4(4)) Pub: Tantor Media. Dist(s): IngramPubServ

In the Cow's Backyard. Alma Flor Ada. (Stories for the Year 'Round Ser.). (J). (gr. k-3). 4.95 (978-1-58105-315-9(0)) Santillana.

In the Dark see Whistler

In the Dark. unabr. ed. Mark Billingham. Narrated by Stephen Hoye. (Running Time: 11 hrs. 30 mins. 0 sec.). (ENG.). 2009. lab manual ed. 75.99 (978-1-4001-4034-3(X)); audio compact disk 37.99 (978-1-4001-1034-6(3)); audio compact disk 24.99 (978-1-4001-6034-1(0)) Pub: Tantor Media. Dist(s): IngramPubServ

In the Dark. unabr. ed. Brian Freeman. Read by Joe Barrett. (Running Time: 13 hrs. 0 mins.). 2009. 29.95 (978-1-4332-6205-0(3)); audio compact disk 32.95 (978-1-4332-6204-3(5)); audio compact disk 99.00 (978-1-4332-6202-9(9)); audio compact disk 72.95 (978-1-4332-6201-2(0)) Blckstn Audio.

In the Dark of the Night. abr. ed. John Saul. Read by Mel Foster. (Running Time: 21600 sec.). 2007. audio compact disk 14.99 (978-1-4233-0442-5(X), 9781423304425, BCD Value Price) Brilliance Audio.

In the Dark of the Night. unabr. ed. John Saul. Read by Mel Foster. (Running Time: 11 hrs.). 2006. 39.25 (978-1-4233-0440-1(3), 9781423304401, BADLE); 24.95 (978-1-4233-0439-5(X), 9781423304395, BAD); 82.25 (978-1-4233-0434-0(9), 9781423304340, BrilAudUnabridg); audio compact disk 97.25 (978-1-4233-0436-4(5), 9781423304364, BriAudCD Unabrid); audio compact disk 39.25 (978-1-4233-0438-8(1), 9781423304388, Brlnc Audio MP3 Lib); audio compact disk 36.95 (978-1-4233-0435-7(7), 9781423304357, Bril Audio CD Unabri); audio compact disk 24.95 (978-1-4233-0437-1(3), 9781423304371, Brilliance MP3) Brilliance Audio.
The latest novel from the New York Times bestselling author of Suffer the Children, The Right Hand of Evil, and Black Creek Crossing - for his legion of fans, and all readers of mainstream thrillers. This latest tour de force is a summertime chiller that climaxes in horrific Fourth of July mayhem. An exercise in fright-packed suspense that asks what happens when a teenage boy discovers a collection of serial-killer memorabilia - and becomes possessed by the spirits of the objects' original owners. "[Saul is] one of America's favorite fright writers." - Fort Worth Star Telegram.

***In the Dark of the Night, the Devil's Labyrinth, Faces of Fear.** abr. ed. John Saul & 3-In-1 Cd Coll. (Running Time: 17 hrs.). 2010. audio compact disk 29.99 (978-1-4418-5050-8(3), 9781441850508) Brilliance Audio.

In the Days of the Comet. unabr. ed. H. G. Wells. Read by Jack Sondericker. 8 cass. (Running Time: 10 hrs.). Dramatization. 1991. 49.95 (978-1-55686-368-4(3), 368) Books in Motion.
People began to take the approaching comet for granted, until an awakening mist covered the earth.

In the Days of the Comet. unabr. ed. H. G. Wells. Read by Walter Covell. 6 cass. (Running Time: 9 hrs.). Dramatization. 1982. 39.00 (C-80) Jimcin Record.
Strange changes on earth due to the approach of a mysterious comet.

In the Deep End. unabr. ed. Kate Cann. Read by Nicky Talacko. (Running Time: 20700 sec.). (Diving In Ser.). (YA). (gr. 9-16). 2006. audio compact disk 63.95 (978-1-74093-786-3(4)) Pub: Bolinda Pubng AUS. Dist(s): Bolinda Pub Inc

In the Deep Midwinter. unabr. ed. Robert Clark. Narrated by George Guidall. 8 cass. (Running Time: 10 hrs. 30 mins.). 1997. 70.00 (978-0-7887-0812-1(0), 94962E7) Recorded Bks.
Late in the 1940s, midwestern lawyer Richard MacEwan sorts through his brother's papers. He discovers intimate details about those closest to him that will shake the foundations of his relationships with his family.

In the Desert/Buildings That Go. Steck-Vaughn Staff. 2002. (978-0-7398-5984-1(6)) SteckVau.

In the Dinosaur's Paw. unabr. ed. Patricia Reilly Giff. Read by Suzanne Toren. 1 cass. (Running Time: 1 hr. 10 mins.). (Follow the Reader Ser.). (J). (gr. 1-2). 1985. pap. bk. 17.00 incl. bk. & guide. (978-0-8072-0098-8(0), FTR104SP, Listening Lib) Random Audio Pubg.
Follow the kids in Ms. Rooney's second grade class as they learn & grow through an entire year filled with fun & surprises.

In the Driver's Seat. unabr. ed. Perf. by Eknath Easwaran. 1 cass. (Running Time: 1 hr.). 1985. 7.95 (978-1-58638-554-5(2)) Nilgiri Pr.

In the Drivers Seat: Emotions. Scripts. Gaaren Anderson. 3 CDs. (Running Time: 3 hrs). 2005. audio compact disk 38.00 (978-0-9767712-0-3(9)) Therapy Integration.
Our society seems fairly sophisticated in its understanding of the cause-effect relationships in physics, finances, and transportation. But we seem to still think emotions are magic. Examples of this are everywhere, such as, " I fell in love", "I got depressed", or "You made me mad". Like they just happen to us. Recent research has opened up a wealth of information on brain chemistry, which is starting to turn the magic into science. However, most of the explanations are in highly technical terms, which leave most people cold and confused. This course is designed turn science into common sense.This 3-CD set pulls together recent brain chemistry research findings & 7 years of application with clients in therapy, & presents them in an easy-to-understand format. It uses common-sense analogies & every-day examples to which most people can easily relate. It shows you specific mechanics of how the Situation, Thoughts, & Body interact, & gives very specific suggestions & exercises to do.One of my clients, who uses them successfully calls them "Mind Tricks" to gain mastery.

In the Electric Mist with Confederate Dead. unabr. ed. James Lee Burke. Narrated by Mark Hammer. 10 cass. (Running Time: 14 hrs.). (Dave Robicheaux Ser.). 1993. 85.00 (978-1-55690-886-6(5), 93328E7) Recorded Bks.
Dave Robicheaux is back on the Louisiana police force, contending with a besotted Hollywood movie star, a New Orleans mobster & a 30 year old corpse.

In the Electric Mist with Confederate Dead. unabr. collector's ed. James Lee Burke. Read by Michael Kramer. 9 cass. (Running Time: 13 hrs. 30 min.). (Dave Robicheaux Ser.). 1995. 72.00 (978-0-7366-2940-9(8), 3636) Books on Tape.
Small town Louisiana detective Dave Robicheaux grapples with past-&-present unsolved murders, one of which haunts him through the ghost of a famed Civil War officer.

In the evil Day. Peter Temple. Read by Nicholas Bell. (Running Time: 10 hrs. 10 mins.). 2009. 84.99 (978-1-74214-288-3(5), 9781742142883) Pub: Bolinda Pubng AUS. Dist(s): Bolinda Pub Inc

In the Evil Day. unabr. ed. Peter Temple. Read by Nicholas Bell. 9 CDs. (Running Time: 10 hrs. 10 mins.). 2007. audio compact disk 93.95 (978-1-74030-952-3(9)) Pub: Bolinda Pubng AUS. Dist(s): Bolinda Pub Inc

In the evil Day. unabr. ed. Peter Temple. Read by Nicholas Bell. (Running Time: 10 hrs. 10 mins.). 2008. 43.95 (978-1-74214-072-8(6), 9781742140728) Pub: Bolinda Pubng AUS. Dist(s): Bolinda Pub Inc

In the Eye of the Storm. John H. Groberg. 4 cass. 1998. 24.95 Set. (978-1-57008-575-8(7), Bkcraft Inc) Deseret Bk.

In the Fall. unabr. ed. Jeffrey Lent. Narrated by Tom Stechschulte. 18 cass. (Running Time: 24 hrs. 45 mins.). 2000. 151.00 (978-0-7887-4854-7(8), 96432E7) Recorded Bks.
As the Civil War ends, Norman Pelham, a wounded Yankee soldier is rescued by Leah, a runaway slave. When he is well enough to travel, they walk north to his family's farm in Vermont but Leah's bitter history, laced with cruelty, quickly begins to color their union. The violence that compelled Leah to flee her birthplace will later drive her son to a life of crime & her grandson back to the South in search of the lost links to his heritage. The Generations of the Pelham find that they can go home again but the results are far darker than they expect.

In the Fifth. Enid Blyton. 1 cass. (Running Time: 1 hr.). (J). 1999. (978-1-84032-061-9(3), HoddrStoughton) Hodder General GBR.
Darrell Rivers finally has to say goodbye to Malory Towers forever.

In the Firezone: Firesign LIVE 1999. Perf. by Firesign Theatre Firesign Theatre Staff. 2 CDs. (Running Time: 2 hrs.). 2001. audio compact disk 24.95 Lodestone Catalog.
One of the climactic performances of their Give Me Mortality tour.

In the Firezone: Firesign LIVE, 1999. Firesign Theatre Firesign Theatre Staff. 2 CDs. (Running Time: 2 cass.). 2000. 24.95 (978-1-57677-145-7(8)) Lodestone Catalog.
One of the climactic performances of their Give Me Immortality tour, with updated earlier material and unique pieces like Spamlet and Shakespeare In Heat, all digitally recorded in living mono. Some of their classic material is revived and given a fresh spin, and the new 1998 album, with its new characters, is introduced for live performance. A treat for fans and collectors, and a great time for anyone!.

***In the Footsteps of the Band of Brothers: A Return to Easy Company's Battlefields with Sergeant Forrest Guth.** unabr. ed. Larry Alexander. (Running Time: 12 hrs. 0 mins.). 2010. 34.99 (978-1-4001-9625-8(6)); 17.99 (978-1-4001-8625-9(0)) Tantor Media.

***In the Footsteps of the Band of Brothers: A Return to Easy Company's Battlefields with Sergeant Forrest Guth.** unabr. ed. Larry Alexander. Narrated by Norman Dietz. (Running Time: 11 hrs. 30 mins. 0 sec.). (ENG.). 2010. 24.99 (978-1-4001-6625-1(X)); audio compact disk 69.99 (978-1-4001-4625-3(9)); audio compact disk 34.99 (978-1-4001-1625-6(2)) Pub: Tantor Media. Dist(s): IngramPubServ

In the Forest. 2004. 8.95 (978-1-56008-933-9(4)); cass. & flmstrp 30.00 (978-1-56008-691-8(2)) Weston Woods.

In the Forest. unabr. ed. Marie Hall Ets. 1 read-along cass. (Running Time: 7 min.). (J). 1978. 9.95 Live Oak Media.
A small boy, with his paper hat & new horn, uses his imagination & plays with animals while on a walk through the forest.

In the Forest Audio CD. Adapted by Benchmark Education Company Staff. Based on a work by Cynthia Swain. (Early Explorers Set C Ser.). (J). (gr. k-1). 2008. audio compact disk 10.00 (978-1-60437-517-6(5)) Benchmark Educ.

In the Frame. unabr. ed. Dick Francis. Read by Geoffrey Howard. 5 cass. (Running Time: 7 hrs.). 1996. 39.95 (978-0-7861-1021-6(X), 1799) Blckstn Audio.
Charles Todd is an English artist who is well known & respected for his renderings of sleek & athletic horses. What he now faces at his cousin Donald's house is also art - the art of a perfectly brutal murderer. Donald's home has been burglarized & his wife, Regina, is lying on her back dead, her face the color of cream. Donald is shattered, shocked, & a prime suspect. And Todd suddenly finds himself involved in a dangerous manhunt as he searches, against all odds, for an elusive killer & some murderous answers.

In the Frame. unabr. ed. Dick Francis. Read by Geoffrey Howard. 6 CDs. (Running Time: 7 hrs.). 2006. audio compact disk 48.00 (978-0-7861-8783-6(2), 1799) Blckstn Audio.

***In the Frame.** unabr. ed. Dick Francis. Read by Geoffrey Howard. (Running Time: 6 hrs. 0 mins.). 2010. 29.95 (978-1-4417-5557-5(8)) Blckstn Audio.

In the Frame. unabr. ed. Dick Francis. Read by Tony Britton. 6 cass. (Running Time: 9 hrs.). 2000. 49.95 (978-0-7451-5952-2(4), CAB 137) Pub: Chivers Audio Bks GBR. Dist(s): AudioGO
The house had been stripped of all its treasures: the furniture, family silver and antique china were gone. And if it were a shock to Charles Todd, painter of horses, it was even more harrowing to his cousin Donald, whose house it was and whose young wife Regina lay on the floor bloody and dead. A coincidental meeting with a widow who has also lost her worldly goods sends Charles off to Australia on a trail of tremendous risks where villians will stop at nothing to achieve their ends.

In the Frame. unabr. ed. Dick Francis. Narrated by Peter Gerald. 5 cass. (Running Time: 7 hrs.). 1990. 44.00 (978-1-55690-253-6(0), 90026E7) Recorded Bks.
Regina's death plunges Charles Todd into a violent manhunt, as he stays one jump ahead of the police, who want to arrest him for murder & a murderous gang of art thieves.

In the Fullness of Time: Luke 2:1-7,3:1-6. Ed Young. 1989. 4.95 (978-0-7417-1770-2(0), 770) Win Walk.

In the Fullness of Time: 2002 Holiday Messages. 2002. 11.95 (978-1-57972-516-7(3)); audio compact disk 20.00 (978-1-57972-517-4(1)) Insight Living.

In the Garden see Secret Garden: A Young Reader's Edition of the Classic Story

In the Garden: 36 Favorite Piano Hymns. Contrib. by Eric Wyse. 2007. audio compact disk 19.95 (978-1-59856-264-4(9)); audio compact disk 19.95 (978-5-558-11380-8(4)); audio compact disk 13.97 (978-1-59856-602-4(4)) Hendrickson MA.

In the Garden CD Collection: Blue Dahlia; Black Rose; Red Lily. abr. ed. Nora Roberts. Read by Susie Breck. (Running Time: 18 hrs.). (In the Garden Trilogy: Bks. 1-3). 2007. audio compact disk 34.95 (978-1-4233-2314-3(9), 9781423323143, BACD) Brilliance Audio.

***In the Garden of Beasts: Love, Terror, & an American Family in Hitler's Berlin.** unabr. ed. Erik Larson. (ENG.). 2011. audio compact disk 45.00 (978-0-307-91457-6(7), Random AudioBks) Pub: Random Audio Pubg. Dist(s): Random

***In the Garden of Iden: A Novel of the Company.** unabr. ed. Kage Baker. (Running Time: 11 hrs. NaN mins.). (Company Novels Ser.). (ENG.). 2011. 29.95 (978-1-4417-7434-7(3)); 65.95 (978-1-4417-7431-6(9)); audio compact disk 29.95 (978-1-4417-7433-0(5)); audio compact disk 100.00 (978-1-4417-7432-3(7)) Blckstn Audio.

In the Garden of the Lord. 1 cass. (Running Time: 36 min.). 7.95 (978-1-58169-001-9(0), GDS102) Genesis Comm Inc.
Designed for today's busy women to listen to & meditate as the spoken word, with original musical backgrounds, leads you through 24 sets of Scriptures, reflections, & prayers to renew spirit and soul.

In the Goddess' Name, I Summon You see George Seferis

***In the Graveyard of Empires: America's War in Afghanistan.** unabr. ed. Seth G. Jones. Read by William Hughes. (Running Time: 16 hrs.). 2010. 29.95 (978-1-4417-6976-3(5)); 85.95 (978-1-4417-6973-2(0)); audio compact disk 34.95 (978-1-4417-6975-6(7)); audio compact disk 118.00 (978-1-4417-6974-9(9)) Blckstn Audio.

In the Grip of Official Treason. Jello Biafra. (AK Press Audio Ser.). 2007. audio compact disk 19.98 (978-1-904859-62-8(3)) Pub: AK Pr GBR. Dist(s): Consort Bk Sales

In the Hand of the Goddess. unabr. ed. Tamora Pierce. Read by Trini Alvarado. 3 cass. (Running Time: 4 hrs. 59 mins.). (Song of the Lioness Ser.: Bk. 2). (J). (gr. 6 up). 2004. pap. bk. 36.00 (978-0-8072-0665-2(2), S YA 338 SP, Listening Lib); 30.00 (978-0-8072-0605-8(9), Listening Lib) Random Audio Pubg.
Disguised as a boy, Alanna of Trebond becomes a squire - to none other than the prince of the realm. But Prince Jonathan is much more to Alanna; he is her ally, her best friend and one of the few who knows that she's really a girl. Now it will take all of Alanna's awesome skill, strength and growing magical powers to protect him from the mysterious evil sorcerer who is bent on his destruction - and hers.

In the Hand of the Goddess. unabr. ed. Tamora Pierce. Read by Trini Alvarado. (Song of the Lioness Ser.: Bk. 2). (ENG.). (J). (gr. 6). 2009. audio compact disk 30.00 (978-0-7393-8105-2(9), Listening Lib) Pub: Random Audio Pubg. Dist(s): Random

In the Hands of Providence. unabr. ed. Alice Rains Trulock. Read by Tom Parker. 9 cass. (Running Time: 13 hrs. 30 mins.). 1996. 62.95 (1817) Blckstn Audio.
Story of Joshua Lawrence Chamberlain of Maine, who as a lieutenant colonel of the Twentieth Maine Volunteer Infantry Regiment, fought at Antietam & Fredericksburg, & then led his regiment to glory at Gettysburg. Promoted to brigadier general, he received the formal Confederate surrender at Appomattox, endearing himself to future generations with his unforgettable salute to Robert E. Lee's defeated army. After the war he was elected four times as Maine's governor.

In the Hands of Providence: Joshua L. Chamberlain & the American Civil War. unabr. ed. Alice Rains Trulock. Read by Tom Parker. 9 cass. (Running Time: 13 hrs.). 2006. 62.95 (978-0-7861-1045-2(7), 1817) Blckstn Audio.

***In the Hands of Providence: Joshua L. Chamberlain & the American Civil War.** unabr. ed. Alice Rains Trulock. Read by Tom Parker. (Running Time: 13 hrs.). 2010. 29.95 (978-1-4417-4523-1(8)); audio compact disk 109.00 (978-1-4417-4520-0(3)) Blckstn Audio.

In the Heart of the Canyon. unabr. ed. Elisabeth Hyde. Read by Mark Deakins & Cassandra Campbell. (ENG.). 2009. audio compact disk 34.95 (978-0-7393-8365-0(5), Random AudioBks) Pub: Random Audio Pubg. Dist(s): Random

In the Heart of the Country. unabr. ed. H. E. Bates. Read by Martyn Read. 4 cass. (Running Time: 6 hrs.). 2000. 34.95 (978-0-7531-0676-1(0), 991215) Pub: ISIS Audio GBR. Dist(s): Ulverscroft US
Describes the spring of 1941, the coldest for a hundred years, June days as grey as January; a reassuring mid-summer of foxgloves & fishing trips; an autumn of kingfishers & trees heavy with fruit; & the rural isolation of a harsh winter with bushes still laden with berries in December.

In the Heart of the Sea: The Tragedy of the Whaleship Essex. Nathaniel Philbrick. Read by Scott Brick. 2000. audio compact disk 72.00 (978-0-7366-5972-7(2)) Books on Tape.

In the Heart of the Sea: The Tragedy of the Whaleship Essex. unabr. ed. Nathaniel Philbrick. Read by Scott Brick. 7 cass. (Running Time: 10 hrs. 30 mins.). 2000. 56.00 (978-0-7366-5504-0(2), 5344) Books on Tape.
In 1821, in the farthest reaches of the South Pacific, the whaleship Essex was rammed and sunk by an eighty-ton bull sperm whale. Fearing cannibals on the islands to the west, the twenty-men crew made for the coast of South America, 3,000 miles away, in three tiny boats. During ninety days at sea, they clung to life and, one by one, succumbed to hunger, thirst, disease and fear. When eight survivors were retrieved off the coast of Chile, they had sailed almost 4,500 nautical miles across the Pacific.

In the Heart of the Sea: The Tragedy of the Whaleship Essex. unabr. ed. Nathaniel Philbrick. 7 cass. (Running Time: 10 hrs.). 2001. 14.95 Books on Tape.
In 1820, the Essex set sail from Nantucket on a routine voyage for whales. Fifteen months later, in the farthest reaches of the South Pacific, it was rammed and sunk by an eighty-ton bull sperm whale. Its twenty-man crew, fearing cannibals on the islands to the west, made for the 3,000-mile-distant coast of South America in three tiny boats. During ninety days at sea under horrendous conditions, they clung to life and, one by one, succumbed to hunger, thirst, disease and fear. When eight survivors were retrieved off the coast of Chile, they had sailed almost 4,500 nautical miles across the Pacific.

In the Heart of the Sea: The Tragedy of the Whaleship Essex. unabr. ed. Nathaniel Philbrick. Read by Scott Brick. 9 CDs. (Running Time: 13 hrs. 30 mins.). 2001. audio compact disk 72.00 Books on Tape.
The first sinking of a ship by a whale and the extraordinary struggle to survive that followed.

In the Heart of the Sea: The Tragedy of the Whaleship Essex. unabr. ed. Nathaniel Philbrick. Read by Jonathan Oliver. 9 CDs. (Running Time: 13 hrs. 30 min.). 2001. audio compact disk 84.95 (978-0-7531-1033-1(4), 110334) Pub: ISIS Audio GBR. Dist(s): Ulverscroft US

In the Heart of the Sea: The Tragedy of the Whaleship Essex. unabr. ed. Nathaniel Philbrick. Read by Jonathon Oliver. 8 cass. (Running Time: 12 hrs.). (Isis Ser.). (J). 2001. 69.95 (978-0-7531-1004-1(0), 001105) Pub: ISIS Lrg Prnt GBR. Dist(s): Ulverscroft US

In the Heart of the Spirit. Perf. by Jeannie Perrington. 1 cass. (Running Time: 46 min.). 1997. (978-0-9652802-3-5(3)) Timeless Prods.
Inspirational piano arrangements.

In the Highlander's Bed. unabr. ed. Cathy Maxwell. Read by Anne Flosnik. (Running Time: 28800 sec.). 2008. 54.95 (978-1-4332-1328-1(1)); audio compact disk & audio compact disk 70.00 (978-1-4332-1329-8(X)); audio compact disk & audio compact disk 29.95 (978-1-4332-1330-4(3)) Blckstn Audio.

In the Hospital. Perf. by Peter Alsop. 1 CD. (Running Time: 1 hr., 07 min.). (J). (gr. k-6). pap. bk. Moose Schl Records.
Features songs & stories for children in the hospital. Comes with a bound, fully annotated book for medical professionals & parents.

In the Hospital. Perf. by Peter Alsop & Bill Harley. 1 cass. (J). (ps-7). 9.98 (2180) MFLP CA.
Two of the funniest people in children's music show how to deal with a strange & confusing place. Inspiring songs & insights answer children's questions with sensitivity & respect.

In the Hospital. Peter Alsop & Bill Harley. Perf. by Peter Alsop. 1 cass. (Running Time: 1 hr. 07 min.). (J). (gr. k-6). 1989. pap. bk. 15.00 (MS503) Moose Schl Records.
Features songs & stories for children in the hospital. Comes with a bound, fully annotated book for medical professionals & parents.

In the Hotel of Lost Light see Poetry & Voice of Galway Kinnell

In the Hour Before Midnight. unabr. ed. Jack Higgins. Read by Stephen Rhea. 4 cass. (Running Time: 6 hrs.). 2000. 34.95 (978-0-7451-6021-4(2), CAB 337) Pub: Chivers Audio Bks GBR. Dist(s): AudioGO
Behind the beautiful, sun-soaked facade of Sicily, lurks a dark and barren place where the Mafia reign supreme. Stacey Wyatt's job is to free the beautiful daughter of a local millionaire from Sicily's biggest Mafia man. But only after the deaths of many men does he locate the girl in question, and realize that his own life is now in grave danger.

In the Hour Before Midnight. unabr. collector's ed. Jack Higgins. Read by Ian Whitcomb. 6 cass. (Running Time: 6 hrs.). 1984. 36.00 (978-0-7366-0481-9(2), 1456) Books on Tape.
Stacey Wyatt is a gifted pianist, also a competent mercenary soldier. But at the moment, he is sojourning in an Egyptian prison. A story of foreign intrigue.

In the House of the Lord. unabr. ed. Robert Flynn. Narrated by Norman Dietz. 7 cass. (Running Time: 10 hrs.). (Tcu Press Texas Tradition Ser.). 1969. 69.75 (978-1-4193-1205-2(7), S1069MC); audio compact disk 99.75 (978-1-4193-1207-6(3), CS019MC) Recorded Bks.

In the House of the Lord: Live in Houston. Contrib. by Mighty Clouds of Joy. Prod. by Sanchez Harley. Contrib. by Ken Pennell & Larry Blackwell. Prod. by Ay'ron Lewis. 2005. audio compact disk 16.98 (978-5-559-10073-9(0)) Pt of Grace Ent.

In the House of the Riddle Mother. Clarissa Pinkola Estes. 2 CDs. (Running Time: 2 Hrs 30 Mins). 2005. audio compact disk 19.95 (978-1-59179-320-5(3), AW00152D) Sounds True.
From the bestselling author of Women Who Run With the Wolves comes this compelling audio seminar about the dream lives of women. Each night of our lives, we experience between five and seven dreams, each reflecting our most intimate passions and conflicts. A dream is like a riddle, Dr. Estes teaches. Once solved, it can provide a surprising answer to an unresolved question buried within the psyche. On In the House of the Riddle Mother, Dr. Estes, one of the seminal thinkers of our time, surveys the most common patterns of women?s dreams. Based on 26 years of work and research in the field of Jungian psychology, this session is a dense, poetic storehouse of information about women, their dreams, and their destinies. Instructive sections analyze 17 archetypal dream motifs, including: dreams about relationships ? dreams about birth ? ?dark man? dreams ? animal dreams ? dreams about treasure ? disaster dreams ? and 12 others.Join Dr. Estes beyond the gates of the conscious mind, where each place, each face, each drama is a fertile symbol waiting for interpretation in the house of the riddle mother.

In the Huddle with... Steve Young. unabr. ed. Matt Christopher. Narrated by Richard M. Davidson. 3 cass. (Running Time: 3 hrs. 15 mins.). (gr. 4 up). 1997. 27.00 (978-0-7887-0952-4(6), 95078E7) Recorded Bks.
Puts you on the football field with San Francisco-49ers superstar quarterback.

In the Image of God. Thomas Merton. 1 cass. (Running Time: 60 min.). (St. Bernard Ser.). 8.95 (AA2135) Credence Commun.
Merton explains the great Cistercian mystics' rich & complex notion of pure love.

In the Key of Earth. Marjorie de Muynck. 2007. audio compact disk 17.98 (978-1-59179-620-6(2)) Sounds True.

In the Key of Healing. Steven Halpern. 1 CD. (Running Time: 1 hr.). (Healing Music Ser.). 1996. audio compact disk 14.95 (978-1-55961-376-7(9)) Relaxtn Co.

In the Land Beyond My Dreams. (Running Time: 1 hr. 11 mins.). audio compact disk 14.00 (978-0-87612-499-4(6)) Self Realization.

In the Land Beyond My Dreams. 1984. 7.00 (2232) Self Realization.
Twelve selections from Cosmic Chants, arranged for organ & played by a monk of the Self-Realization Order. Selections include: "In the Land Beyond My Dreams," "From This Sleep, Lord," "Do Not Dry the Ocean of My Love," "In the Valley of Sorrow," "They Have Heard Thy Name," "Deliver Us from Delusion," "When Thy Song Flows Through Me" & "Thou Art My Life.".

***In the Land of Believers: An Outsider's Extraordinary Journey into the Heart of the Evangelical Church.** unabr. ed. Gina Welch. (Running Time: 12 hrs. 0 mins.). 2010. 17.99 (978-1-4001-8642-6(0)) Tantor Media.

***In the Land of Believers: An Outsider's Extraordinary Journey into the Heart of the Evangelical Church.** unabr. ed. Gina Welch. Narrated by Judith Brackley. (Running Time: 13 hrs. 30 mins. 0 sec.). (ENG.). 2010. 24.99 (978-1-4001-6642-8(X)); audio compact disk 69.99 (978-1-4001-4642-0(9)); audio compact disk 34.99 (978-1-4001-1642-3(2)) Pub: Tantor Media. Dist(s): IngramPubServ

In the Land of Difficult People: 24 Timeless Tales Reveal How to Tame Beasts at Work. unabr. ed. Terrence L. Gargiulo & Gini Graham Scott. (Running Time: 4 hrs.). (ENG.). 2009. 24.98 (978-1-59659-369-5(5), GildAudio) Pub: Gildan Media. Dist(s): HachBkGrp

In the Land of Dreamy Dreams. unabr. collector's ed. Ellen Gilchrist. Read by Ruth Stokesberry. 7 cass. (Running Time: 7 hrs.). 1989. 42.00 (978-0-7366-1542-6(3), 2411) Books on Tape.
A collection of 14 short stories which Ellen Gilchrist wrote after being selected for a grant from the National Endowment for the Arts.

In the Land of the Mound Builders. unabr. ed. Fred R. Hoffman. Read by Maynard Villers. 4 cass. (Running Time: 6 hrs.). (Mound Builders Ser.: Bk. 2). 1995. 26.95 (978-1-55686-615-9(1)) Books in Motion.
The story continues with modern man Billy Buck still trapped in the Mound Builders world & searching for the portal to a modern dimension.

In the Life of the Believer Faith Tape Pack. 2002. (978-1-931713-18-4(9)) Word For Today.

In the Life of the Believer Fruit Tape Pack. 2002. (978-1-931713-23-8(5)) Word For Today.

In the Life of the Believer Grace Tape Pack. 2002. (978-1-931713-22-1(7)) Word For Today.

In the Life of the Believer Service Tape Pack. 2002. (978-1-931713-20-7(0)) Word For Today.

In the Life of the Beliver Foundations Tape Pack. 2002. (978-1-931713-21-4(9)) Word For Today.

In the Line of Duty, 443. Interview. Hosted by Fred Goodwin. 1 CDs. (Running Time: 59 mins). 2006. 21.95 (978-1-933644-34-9(6)) Lichtenstein Creat.
Dr. Wayne Fenton was as comfortable on the streets as he was in the lab; a sort of a Renaissance psychiatrist who bridged the gap between research, treatment and public policy. But over the Labor Day weekend, Wayne Fenton?s efforts to care for a critically ill young man went tragically awry. The eminent psychiatrist, deputy director for clinical affairs at the National Institute of Mental Health, was found beaten to death in his office. The patient, a bright, 19-year old college-bound ice hockey player, confessed to police and was charged with first-degree murder. In this special edition of The Infinite Mind, we?ll speak with the nation?s top mental health policy makers and advocates about the life and work of Dr. Wayne Fenton, hear an interview with Dr. Fenton himself about his work with seriously ill patients and his efforts to understand the nature of psychosis, and we'll try to make some sense of his death, a death that came in the line of duty. Host Dr. Fred Goodwin's guests include: Thomas Insel, M.D., director of the National Institute of Mental Health (NIMH), who worked closely with Dr. Wayne Fenton for the past six years at NIMH, where Dr. Fenton helped develop new diagnostic tools and treatments for servere mental illnesses such as schizophrenia; Tom Bernard, Co-President and Co-founder of Sony Pictures Classics, who was a close friend of Wayne Fenton; and David L. Shern, Ph.D., the CEO and president of the National Mental Health Association, the nation?s oldest and largest mental health advocacy group. The program also includes excerpts from Lichtenstein Creative Media's Peabody Award-winning "Voices of an Illness" series, narrated by Jason Robards, that provides a window on the interaction between Dr. Fenton and one of his seriously ill patients, a young woman who had been suffering from schizophrenia; both Dr. Fenton and the patient, who had since recovered, explain what happened when she was first brought to Dr. Fenton's office while she was in a severely psychotic state. We also hear the first-person story of a New York City accountant, who has recovered from schizophrenia, and describes living with the stigma of the mental illness.

In the Line of Fire, Set. abr. ed. Max Allan Collins. Read by Gary Cole. 4 cass. (Running Time: 4 hrs.). 1993. 22.95 (978-1-56876-009-4(4)) Soundlines Ent.
This suspense-drama locks onto the trail of an assassin out to kill the President of the United States. Only Frank Horrigan, a thirty year veteran, has the instinct & the intuition to keep him from succeeding.

In the Meadow (Don't Feed Our Bears) Don't Feed Our Bears. (ENG.). (J). 2008. pap. bk. 14.95 (978-0-615-23968-2(4)) KRussell Prods.

In the Middle of Nowhere. unabr. ed. Terry Underwood. Read by Terry Underwood. 7 cass. (Running Time: 9 hrs.). 2004. 56.00 (978-1-74030-105-3(6), 500324) Pub: Bolinda Pubng AUS. Dist(s): Lndmrk Audiobks

In the middle of Nowhere. unabr. ed. Terry Underwood. Read by Terry Underwood. (Running Time: 11 hrs. 10 mins.). 2009. 43.95 (978-1-74214-073-5(4), 9781742140735) Pub: Bolinda Pubng AUS. Dist(s): Bolinda Pub Inc

In the Middle of the Night. (Language of Mathematics Ser.). 1989. 7.92 (978-0-8123-6486-6(4)) Holt McDoug.

In the Midnight Hour. unabr. ed. Michelle Spring. Read by Julia Sands. 9 CDs. (Running Time: 10 hrs. 36 min.). (Isis Ser.). (J). 2003. audio compact disk 84.95 (978-0-7531-2236-5(7)); 69.95 (978-0-7531-1671-5(5)) Pub: ISIS Lrg Prnt GBR. Dist(s): Ulverscroft US
A four-year-old child vanishes without a trace from a wild stretch of shoreline in North Norfolk. His body is never found. Liam is busking quietly away on a street in Cambridge when a wealthy woman befriends him, daring to hope that he is the son who vanished twelve years ago. Laura Principal is called in to settle the question of identity. As she searches for answers Laura comes face to face with a loss that threatens to shatter her own world.

In the Midnight Rain. Ruth Wind. Narrated by Cristine McMurdo-Wallis. 9 cass. (Running Time: 12 hrs.). 81.00 (978-1-4025-0954-4(5)); audio compact disk 97.00 (978-1-4025-2099-0(9)) Recorded Bks.

In the Midst of Death. unabr. ed. Lawrence Block. Read by Alan Sklar. 4 vols. (Running Time: 6 hrs.). (Matthew Scudder Mystery Ser.: No. 3). 2000. bk. 39.95 (978-0-7927-2367-7(8), CSL 256, Chivers Sound Lib) AudioGO.
Jerry Broadfield is a cop who has been charged with extortion. His former buddies in the NYPD would like to see him dead. And when a dead hooker turns up in his apartment he is saddled with a murder rap as well. Broadfield screams "frame-up" but nobody believes him, except Matthew Scudder, an ex-policeman-turned-private-investigator. But finding a killer among Jerry's sleazebag connections is going to be difficult & dangerous.

In the Month of Kislev. 2004. 8.95 (978-1-56008-352-8(2)); cass. & flmstrp 30.00 (978-1-56008-804-2(4)) Weston Woods.

In the Month of Kislev. unabr. ed. 1 cass. (Running Time: 12 min.). (J). (ps-3). 2004. pap. bk. 14.95 (978-0-7882-0685-6(0), PRA357); 8.95 (978-0-7882-0500-2(5), RAC357) Weston Woods.
A wealthy arrogant merchant learns the true meaning of Hanukkah when he takes a poor family to court for smelling his wife's pancakes.

In the Month of Kislev. unabr. ed. Nina Jaffe. Illus. by Louise August. Narrated by Theodore Bikel. 1 cass. (Running Time: 12 min.). (J). (ps-3). 2004. bk. 24.95 (978-0-7882-0660-3(5), HRA357) Weston Woods.

In the Mood, Leve 3. (Yamaha Clavinova Connection Ser.). 2004. disk 1.04 (978-0-634-09594-8(3)) H Leonard.

In the Mood: The Kings of the Big Bands. Colin King. 2004. audio compact disk 14.99 (978-1-84067-472-9(5)) Pub: Caxton Editions GBR. Dist(s): Bk Sales Inc

In the Mood Again: Use the Power of Healthy Hormones to Reboot Your Sex Life at Any Age. unabr. ed. Genie, MMSC James. (Running Time: 11 hrs.). 2009. audio compact disk 39.95 (978-1-4417-2104-4(5)) Blckstn Audio.

In the Mood Again: Use the Power of Healthy Hormones to Reboot Your Sex Life at Any Age. unabr. ed. Genie James. Read by Pam Ward. (Running Time: 11 hrs. 0 mins.). 2009. 29.95 (978-1-4417-2105-1(3)) Blckstn Audio.

In the Mood Again: Use the Power of Healthy Hormones to Reboot Your Sex Life-at Any Age. unabr. ed. Genie James M.M.SC. Read by Pam Ward. (Running Time: 11 hrs. 0 mins.). 2009. 65.95 (978-1-4417-2101-3(0)); audio compact disk 100.00 (978-1-4417-2102-0(9)) Blckstn Audio.

In the Moon of Red Ponies. abr. ed. James Lee Burke. Read by Will Patton. (Billy Bob Holland Ser.). 2004. 15.95 (978-0-7435-4237-1(1)) Pub: S&S Audio. Dist(s): S and S Inc

In the Moon of Red Ponies. unabr. ed. James Lee Burke. Read by Will Patton. (Billy Bob Holland Ser.). 2004. 23.95 (978-0-7435-3942-5(7)) Pub: S&S Audio. Dist(s): S and S Inc

In the Moon of Red Ponies. unabr. abr. ed. James Lee Burke. Read by Will Patton. (Running Time: 6 hrs. 0 mins. 0 sec.). (Billy Bob Holland Ser.). 2007. audio compact disk 14.95 (978-0-7435-6660-5(2)) Pub: S&S Audio. Dist(s): S and S Inc

In the Moonlight see Great French & Russian Stories, Vol. 1, A Collection

In the Moonlight see De Maupassant Short Stories

In the Moonlight see Maupassant's Best Known Stories

In the Moonlight see Favorite Stories by Guy de Maupassant

In the Morning. Perf. by Steve Green. 1 cass. 1999. Provident Music.

In the Mysteries of the Female Body: Midwifery in the 21st Century. Ina M. Gaskin. 2 cass. 18.00 set. (A0636-90) Sound Photosyn.
Her storytelling & dedication to her craft is an inspiring eye-opener. Gaskin brings new light to the possibilities & far-reaching benefits for a society that accepts & encourages the practice of midwifery.

***In the Name of Honor.** unabr. ed. Richard North Patterson. Narrated by John Bedford Lloyd. 1 Playaway. (Running Time: 15 hrs.). 2010. 104.95 (978-0-7927-7218-7(0)); 59.95 (978-0-7927-7217-0(2)); audio compact disk 99.95 (978-0-7927-7150-0(8)) AudioGO.

***In the Name of Honor.** unabr. ed. Richard North Patterson. Read by John Bedford Lloyd. 12 CDs. (Running Time: 15 hrs.). (ENG.). 2010. audio compact disk 39.99 (978-1-4272-0947-4(2)) Pub: Macmill Audio. Dist(s): Macmillan

In the Name of Ishmael. Giuseppe Genna. Narrated by Grover Gardner. (Running Time: 14 hrs. 30 mins.). 2003. 41.95 (978-1-59912-510-7(2)) Iofy Corp.

In the Name of Ishmael. unabr. ed. Giuseppe Genna. Read by Grover Gardner. (Running Time: 14 hrs. 30 mins.). 2000. audio compact disk 24.95 (978-0-7861-8810-9(3), 3168) Blckstn Audio.

In the Name of Ishmael. unabr. ed. Giuseppe Genna. Read by Grover Gardner. Tr. by Ann Goldstein. 10 pieces. 2004. reel tape 39.95 (978-0-7861-2570-8(5)); audio compact disk 49.95 (978-0-7861-9083-6(3)) Blckstn Audio.

In the Name of Ishmael. unabr. ed. Giuseppe Genna. Read by Grover Gardner. Tr. by Ann Goldstein. 12 CDs. (Running Time: 14 hrs. 30 mins.). 2006. audio compact disk 96.00 (978-0-7861-8982-3(7), 3168) Blckstn Audio.

In the Name of Ishmail. Giuseppe Genna & Grover Gardner. 10 cass. (Running Time: 14 hrs. 30 mins.). 2002. 69.95 (978-0-7861-2584-5(5), 3168) Blckstn Audio.

In the Name of Jesus: Reflections on Christian Leadership. unabr. ed. Henri J. M. Nouwen. Read by Paul Smith. 1 CD. (Running Time: 3600 sec.). 2006. audio compact disk 16.95 (978-0-86716-812-9(9)) St Anthony Mess Pr.

In the Name of Security. Peter Goodchild. Perf. by John De Lancie et al. 1 cass. (Running Time: 3 hrs. 2 min.). 1997. 27.95 (978-1-58081-127-9(2), RDP27) L A Theatre.
Three spy cases rocked America between 1948 & 1954: the trial of Alger Hiss; the trial of Julius & Ethel Rosenberg & the case of J. Robert Oppenheimer. Combines re-enactments that are based on transcripts, archival material & new evidence, as well as the latest assessments by American historians, scientists & relatives & friends of the accused.

In the Name of Security. abr. ed. Peter Goodchild. 3 CDs. (Running Time: 10860 sec.). (L. A. Theatre Works Audio Theatre Collections). 1997. audio compact disk 29.95 (978-1-58081-326-6(7)) Pub: L A Theatre. Dist(s): NetLibrary CO

In the Name of the Father: Washington's Legacy, Slavery & the Making of a Nation. Francois Furstenberg. Read by Michael Prichard. (Playaway Adult Nonfiction Ser.). 2008. 64.99 (978-1-60640-998-5(0)) Find a World.

In the Name of the Father: Washington's Legacy, Slavery, & the Making of a Nation. unabr. ed. Francois Furstenberg. Read by Michael Prichard. 8 CDs. (Running Time: 10 hrs. 0 mins. 0 sec.). (ENG.). 2006. audio compact disk 34.99 (978-1-4001-0278-5(2)) Pub: Tantor Media. Dist(s): IngramPubServ
In the Name of the Father is filled with vivid stories of American print culture, including a wonderful consideration of the first great American hack biographer cum bookseller, Parson Weems, author of the first blockbuster Washington biography. But François Furstenberg's achievement is not limited to showing what all these civic texts were and how they infused Americans with a national spirit: how they created what Abraham Lincoln so famously called "the mystic chords of memory." He goes further to show how the process of defining the good citizen in America was complicated and compromised by the problem of slavery. Ultimately, we see how reconciling slavery and republican nationalism would have fateful consequences that haunt us still, in attitudes toward the socially powerless that persist in America to this day.

In the Name of the Father: Washington's Legacy, Slavery & the Making of a Nation. unabr. ed. Francois Furstenberg. Read by Michael Prichard. (Running Time: 10 hrs. 0 mins. 0 sec.). (ENG.). 2006. audio compact disk 24.99 (978-1-4001-5278-0(X)); audio compact disk 69.99 (978-1-4001-3278-2(9)) Pub: Tantor Media. Dist(s): IngramPubServ

In the Name of the Lord. Contrib. by Sandi Patty. (Ultimate Tracks (Word Tracks) Ser.). 2006. audio compact disk 8.99 (978-5-558-14520-5(X), Word Music) Word Enter.

In the Nick of Time. unabr. ed. Robert E. Swindells. Read by Clare Corbett. 2 CDs. (Running Time: 1 hr. 41 mins.). (J). (gr. 4-7). 2008. audio compact disk 29.95 (978-1-4056-5750-1(2)) AudioGO.

In the Night Kitchen. 2004. bk. 24.95 (978-0-89719-777-9(1)); pap. bk. 32.75 (978-1-55592-245-0(7)); 8.95 (978-1-56008-390-0(5)); cass. & flmstrp 30.00 (978-0-89719-561-4(2)) Weston Woods.

In the Night Kitchen. Maurice Sendak. 1 cass., 5 bks. (Running Time: 30 min.). (J). pap. bk. 32.75 Weston Woods.
Aroused by noises in the night, Mickey falls out of bed & into the night kitchen, where three Oliver Hardy-like bakers prepare to bake him a cake.

In the Night Kitchen. Maurice Sendak. Illus. by Maurice Sendak. 1 cass. (Running Time: 30 min.). (J). (gr. k-5). bk. 24.95 Weston Woods.

In the Night Kitchen. Maurice Sendak. Narrated by Peter Schickele. 1 cass. (Running Time: 6 min.). (J). (ps-3). 2004. pap. bk. 8.95 (978-0-89719-949-0(9), RAC302) Weston Woods.

In the Night Kitchen. Maurice Sendak. Illus. by Maurice Sendak. 1 cass. (J). (gr. k-5). 2004. pap. bk. 14.95 (978-0-89719-776-6(X), PRA302) Weston Woods.

In the Night Kitchen; Brother to the Wind; Emperor's New Clothers, the; Beauty & the Beast. 2004. cass. & flmstrp (978-0-89719-761-8(5)) Weston Woods.

In the Night Kitchen; Brother to the Wind; Emperor's New Clothes, the; Beautyand the Beast. 2004. (978-1-56008-824-0(9)) Weston Woods.

In the Orchard see Gathering of Great Poetry for Children

In the Palomar Arms. 1983. (3141) Am Audio Prose.

***In the Path of Falling Objects.** unabr. ed. Andrew Smith. Read by Mike Chamberlain. 9 CDs. (Running Time: 10 hrs. 31 mins.). (YA). (gr. 9 up). 2009. audio compact disk 60.00 (978-0-307-57974-4(3), Listening Lib) Pub: Random Audio Pubg. Dist(s): Random

In the Path of Falling Objects. unabr. ed. Andrew Smith. Read by Mike Chamberlain. (J). (gr. 9). 2009. 44.00 (978-0-7393-8652-1(2), Listening Lib) Pub: Random Audio Pubg. Dist(s): Random

In the Path of God: Islam & Political Power. Daniel Pipes. 1986. 3.00 (152) ISI Books.

In the Pines - Mandolin Edition. Transcribed by Matt Flenner. 1999. pap. bk. 24.95 (978-0-7866-4308-0(0), 97320CDP) Mel Bay.

In the Place of Justice: A Story of Punishment & Deliverance. unabr. ed. Wilbert Rideau. Read by Dominic Hoffman. (ENG.). 2010. audio compact disk 40.00 (978-0-307-73671-0(7), Random AudioBks) Pub: Random Audio Pubg. Dist(s): Random

In the Presence of a Great Mystery. unabr. ed. Eckhart Tolle. 3 CDs. (Running Time: 2 hrs. 50 mins. 0 sec.). (ENG.). 2006. audio compact disk 21.95 (978-1-57731-557-5(X)) Pub: New Wrld Lib. Dist(s): PerseuPGW

In the Presence of Angels. Joy Yoxall. 2006. audio compact disk 17.95 (978-1-901923-80-3(0), 247-046) Pub: Divinit Pubing GBR. Dist(s): Bookworld

***In the Presence of My Enemies: A Gripping Account of the Kidnapping of American Missionaries in the Philippine Jungle.** unabr. ed. Gracia Burnham & Dean Merrill. Narrated by Pam Ward. (Running Time: 11 hrs. 30 mins. 0 sec.). (ENG.). 2010. audio compact disk 26.98 (978-1-59644-251-1(4)) christianaud.

***In the Presence of My Enemies: A Gripping Account of the Kidnapping of American Missionaries in the Philippine Jungle.** unabr. ed. Gracia Burnham & Dean Merrill. Narrated by Pam Ward. (ENG.). 2010. 16.98 (978-1-59644-252-8(2)) christianaud.

In the Presence of the Enemy. unabr. ed. Elizabeth George. Read by Donada Peters. 15 cass. (Running Time: 22 hrs. 30 min.). (Inspector Lynley Ser.). 1996. 120.00 (978-0-7366-3278-2(6), 3934) Books on Tape.
Dennis Luxford, tabloid editor, receives a letter saying that someone has kidnapped Charlotte Bowen, 10, & if Luxford doesn't publicly admit that he fathered her, the girl will die. But revealing this secret could devastate the career of the girl's mother as well. The closer New Scotland Yard inspectors draw to a grim solution, the more danger they find.

In the Presence of the Enemy. unabr. ed. Elizabeth George. Narrated by Davina Porter. 16 cass. (Running Time: 22 hrs. 45 mins.). (Inspector Lynley Ser.). 2000. 128.00 (978-0-7887-0523-6(7), 94718E7) Recorded Bks.

In the President's Secret Service: Behind the Scenes with Agents in the Line of Fire & the Presidents They Protect. unabr. ed. Ronald Kessler. Narrated by Alan Sklar. 1 MP3-CD. (Running Time: 9 hrs. 0 mins. 0 sec.). (ENG.). 2009. 19.99 (978-1-4001-6312-0(9)); audio compact disk 59.99 (978-1-4001-4312-2(8)); audio compact disk 29.99 (978-1-4001-1312-5(1)) Pub: Tantor Media. Dist(s): IngramPubServ

In the Quiet. John G. Elliott. 2000. audio compact disk 14.95 (978-1-930864-15-3(9)) Galestorm.

In the Quiet. John G. Elliott. Read by John G. Elliott. 2000. 10.95 (978-1-930864-16-0(7)) Galestorm.

In the Ravine & Other Short Stories. Anton Chekhov. Read by Kenneth Branagh. 3 cass. (Running Time: 3 hrs. 30 min.). 2002. 17.98 (978-962-634-761-4(9), NA326114, Naxos AudioBooks); audio compact disk 22.98 (978-962-634-261-9(7), NA326112, Naxos AudioBooks) Naxos.
Here are eleven short stories, Oh! The Public, The Chorus Girl, The Trousseau Without a Title, Children, Misery, The Beggar Fat and Thin, Hush, The Orator, In The Ravine.

In the Ravine & Other Short Stories. unabr. ed. Anton Chekhov. Read by Kenneth Branagh. (YA). 2008. 54.99 (978-1-60514-892-2(X)) Find a World.

In the Red, unabr. ed. Clive Egleton. Narrated by Simon Prebble. 8 cass. (Running Time: 11 hrs.). 70.00 (978-0-7887-0566-3(0), 94743E7) Recorded Bks.
Follows British intelligence agent Harry Freeland as he zeros in on a deadly double agent who is threatening his career & his life. Available to libraries only.

In the Reign of Terror. Short Stories. Read by Jim Weiss. Prod. by Greathall Productions. 8 CDs. (Running Time: 9 hrs.). Dramatization. (YA). 2004. audio compact disk 32.95 (978-1-882513-97-0(5)) Greathall Prods.
Nine hous of breathtaking adventure during the French Revolution. As the revolution begins, we meet harry Sandwith, a yong Englishman hired to be a companion to the sons of a nobleman. At first considered by the aristocratic family to be beneath their class, Harry soon proves his worth by saving the lives of the girls in the family. Throughout the story, Harry is called upon to summon his courage as he rescues his French friends from the perils of war-torn France.

In the Reign of Terror: The Adventures of a Westminster Boy. unabr. ed. Read by Stuart Langton. (Running Time: 28800 sec.). (J). 2007. 54.95 (978-0-7861-4743-4(1)); audio compact disk 63.00 (978-0-7861-5876-8(X)); audio compact disk 29.95 (978-0-7861-7008-1(5)) Blckstn Audio.

In the Ruins of Empire: The Japanese Surrender & the Battle for Postwar Asia. unabr. ed. Ronald H. Spector. Narrated by Michael Prichard. (Running Time: 12 hrs. 30 mins. 0 sec.). (ENG.). 2007. audio compact disk 24.99 (978-1-4001-5417-3(0)); audio compact disk 69.99 (978-1-4001-3417-5(X)) Pub: Tantor Media. Dist(s): IngramPubServ

In the Ruins of Empire: The Japanese Surrender & the Battle for Postwar Asia. unabr. ed. Ronald H. Spector. Narrated by Michael Prichard. (Running Time: 12 hrs. 30 mins. 0 sec.). (ENG.). 2007. audio compact disk 34.99 (978-1-4001-0417-8(3)) Pub: Tantor Media. Dist(s): IngramPubServ

***In the Rundown.** unabr. ed. Joe Hill. (ENG.). 2007. (978-0-06-155225-0(9)); (978-0-06-155226-7(7)) HarperCollins Pubs.

In the Sea Audio CD. Adapted by Benchmark Education Company Staff. Based on a work by Cynthia Swain. (My First Reader's Theater Ser.). (J). (gr. k-1). 2008. audio compact disk 10.00 (978-1-60634-084-4(0)) Benchmark Educ.

In the Service of Dragons. unabr. ed. Robert Stanek, pseud. Read by Karl Fehr. (J). 2008. 54.99 (978-1-60514-586-0(6)) Find a World.

In the Service of Dragons: In the Service of Dragons, Book 1. unabr. ed. Robert Stanek, pseud. Narrated by Karl Fehr. (Running Time: 5 hrs. 58 mins.). (YA). 2009. 16.95 (978-1-57545-335-4(5), RP Audio Pubng) Pub: Reagent Press. Dist(s): OverDrive Inc

In the Service of Dragons - Book 2: In the Service of Dragons Book 2. unabr. ed. Robert Stanek, pseud. Read by Karl Fehr. (J). 2008. 54.99 (978-1-60514-647-8(1)) Find a World.

In the Service of Dragons II: In the Service of Dragons, Book 2. unabr. ed. Robert Stanek, pseud. Narrated by Karl Fehr. (Running Time: 6 hrs. 4 mins.). (ENG.). (YA). 2009. 19.95 (978-1-57545-336-1(3), RP Audio Pubng) Pub: Reagent Press. Dist(s): OverDrive Inc

In the Service of Dragons III: In the Service of Dragons, Book 3. unabr. ed. Robert Stanek, pseud. Read by Karl Fehr. (J). 2008. 54.99 (978-1-60514-682-9(X)) Find a World.

In the Service of Dragons III: In the Service of Dragons, Book 3. unabr. ed. Robert Stanek, pseud. Narrated by Karl Fehr. (Running Time: 5 hrs. 35 mins.). (ENG.). (YA). 2009. 19.95 (978-1-57545-337-8(1), RP Audio Pubng) Pub: Reagent Press. Dist(s): OverDrive Inc

In the Service of Dragons IV: In the Service of Dragons, Book 4. unabr. ed. Robert Stanek, pseud. Narrated by Karl Fehr. (Running Time: 6 hrs. 12 mins.). (ENG.). (YA). 2009. 19.95 (978-1-57545-338-5(X), RP Audio Pubng) Pub: Reagent Press. Dist(s): OverDrive Inc

In the Service of Dragons IV: In the Service of Dragons Book 4. unabr. ed. Robert Stanek, pseud. Read by Karl Fehr. (J). 2008. 54.99 (978-1-60514-893-9(8)) Find a World.

In the Service of Gaia: The Call. George Drake. (Running Time: 16 mins). 2006. pap. bk. 14.95 (978-0-9788246-1-7(X)) CSTM.
Sixteen minute example of the meditation technique known as Trumpeting, two tracks overlaid, both performed by the author. Two bells, one initiating and the other ending the performance are the only instruments used.

In the Service of Gaia: The Call. George W. Drake. Perf. by George W. Drake. 2006. audio compact disk 10.95 (978-0-9788246-0-0(1)) CSTM.

In the Shade of the Saguaro. Patty Horn. Perf. by Arizona Children's Choir. Illus. by Susan Mrosek. 1 cass. (Running Time: 30 min.). (J). (gr. k-6). 1994. pap. bk. 15.95 (978-0-9644105-0-3(8)) Two Geckos Mus.
Children's songs about the desert with guitar & vocals.

In the Shade of the Saguaro. Perf. by Patty Horn & Arizona Children's Choir. 1 cass. (Running Time: 30 min.). (J). (gr. k-5). 1994. 8.95 (978-0-9644105-1-0(6)) Two Geckos Mus.

In the Shadow of Fame. Sue Erikson Bloland. Read by Celeste Lawson. (Running Time: 6 hrs.). 2005. 24.95 (978-1-59912-511-4(0)) Iofy Corp.

In the Shadow of Fame: A Memoir by the Daughter of Erik H. Erikson. Sue Erikson Bloland. 5 CDs. (Running Time: 6 hrs.). 2005. DVD & audio compact disk 55.00 (978-0-7861-8230-5(X), 3400) Blckstn Audio.

In the Shadow of Fame: A Memoir by the Daughter of Erik H. Erikson. unabr. ed. Sue Erickson Bloland. Read by Celeste Lawson. 5 cass. (Running Time: 7 hrs.). 2005. reel tape 29.95 (978-0-7861-2917-1(4), E3400); audio compact disk 29.95 (978-0-7861-8231-2(8), ZE3400); audio compact disk 29.95 (978-0-7861-8313-5(6), 3400) Blckstn Audio.

In the Shadow of Fame -Lib. Sue Erikson Bloland. Read by Celeste Lawson. 5 cass. (Running Time: 6 hrs.). 2005. 44.95 (978-0-7861-2918-8(2), 3400) Blckstn Audio.

In the Shadow of the Ark. Anne Provoost. Ed. by Marguerite Gavin. 7 cass. (Running Time: 10 hrs.). 2004. 49.95 (978-0-7861-2823-5(2), 3297); audio compact disk 64.00 (978-0-7861-8440-8(X), 3297) Blckstn Audio.

In the Shadow of the Ark. Anne Provoost. Narrated by Marguerite Gavin. (Running Time: 8 hrs.). 2004. 30.95 (978-1-59912-512-1(9)) Iofy Corp.

In the Shadow of the Ark. unabr. ed. Anne Provoost. 13 pieces. (Running Time: 10 hrs.). 2005. audio compact disk 24.95 (978-0-7861-8522-1(8), 3297); audio compact disk 39.95 (978-0-7861-8587-0(2), ZE3297); reel tape 32.95 (978-0-7861-2728-3(7), E3297) Blckstn Audio.
The rumor of the flood to come was too terrible to be true, and like most, Re Jana does not believe it. How could a god-anyone's god-determine who deserves to live and who to die? It was the rising waters that chased Re Jana's family from their home in the marshes. To the desert they fled, following the trail of animals and people who had gone before them. And there, in the dry center of the desert, rose the frame of a boat of unprecedented proportions, Noah's ark. Even as she falls in love with the builder's son, Ham, and panic spreads in the gathered tribes, Re Jana questions all that she hears and believes her family will be saved, even as the deluge begins and the doors to the ark are sealed.

In the Shadow of the Crown. unabr. ed. Jean Plaidy. Read by Anne White. 14 cass. (Running Time: 19 hrs.). 1996. 99.95 (978-1-85695-227-9(4), 960806) Pub: ISIS Audio GBR. Dist(s): Ulverscroft US
As the cherished & only surviving child of Henry VIII's marriage to Katherine of Argon, Mary Tudor faced an assured future until her father decided to rid himself of her mother, & so brought devastating changes not only to Mary, but to the entire country. Young & inexperienced, Mary was left alone to face the dangers of those who lived in the shadow of the crown.

***In the Shadow of the Cypress: A Novel.** unabr. ed. Thomas Steinbeck. Read by Jeff Harding. 1 MP3-CD. (Running Time: 8 hrs.). 2010. 39.97 (978-1-4418-3823-0(6), 9781441838230, Brlnc Audio MP3 Lib); 24.99 (978-1-4418-3822-3(8), 9781441838223, Brilliance MP3); 24.99 (978-1-4418-3824-7(4), 9781441838247, BAD); 39.97 (978-1-4418-3825-4(2), 9781441838254, BADLE); audio compact disk 29.99 (978-1-4418-3820-9(1), 9781441838209); audio compact disk 89.97 (978-1-4418-3821-6(X), 9781441838216, BriAudCD Unabrid) Brilliance Audio.

In the Shadow of the Glacier. unabr. ed. Vicki Delany. Read by Carrington MacDuffie. (Running Time: 36000 sec.). 2007. 59.95 (978-1-4332-1093-8(2)) Blckstn Audio.

In the Shadow of the Glacier. unabr. ed. Vicki Delany & Carrington MacDuffie. (Running Time: 36000 sec.). 2007. audio compact disk 63.00 (978-1-4332-1094-5(0)); audio compact disk 29.95 (978-1-4332-1095-2(9)) Blckstn Audio.

In the Shadow of the Glen. (SAC 8046) Spoken Arts.

In the Shadow of the Moons. unabr. ed. Nansook Hong. Read by Anna Fields. 6 cass. (Running Time: 8 hrs. 30 mins.). 2001. 44.95 (978-0-7861-1939-4(X), 2710) Blckstn Audio.
Born in South Korea to religious parents, Nansook was picked at age fifteen by the Reverend Moon to marry his son, Hyo Jin.

In the Shadow of the Moons: My Life in the Reverend Sun Myung Moon's Family. unabr. ed. Nansook Hong. Read by Anna Fields. 6 CDs. (Running Time: 8 hrs. 30 mins.). 2006. audio compact disk 55.00 (978-0-7861-8147-6(8), 2710) Blckstn Audio.

In the Skin of a Lion. abr. ed. Michael Ondaatje. Read by Wilem Dafoe. 2 cass. 1998. 15.00 Set. (978-0-333-72603-7(0)) Ulvrscrft Audio.
Set in Toronto in the 1920s & 30s. It blends real & invented histories with a moving love story. Tunnellers, bridge builders, the rich, immigrants & those who dreamed the city are all figures in Ondaatje's imaginative canvas.

In the Skin of a Lion & Running in the Family. unabr. ed. Excerpts. Michael Ondaatje. Read by Michael Ondaatje. 1 cass. (Running Time: 83 min.). 1993. 13.95 (978-1-55644-385-5(4), 13021) Am Audio Prose.

In the Small Small Pond. 2004. pap. bk. 18.95 (978-1-55592-107-1(8)); pap. bk. 38.75 (978-1-55592-635-9(5)); audio compact disk 12.95 (978-1-55592-951-0(6)) Weston Woods.

In the Small, Small Pond. Denise Fleming. 1 cass. (Running Time: 5 min.). (J). (ps-1). 2004. 8.95 (978-1-55592-976-3(1)) Weston Woods.
Cheerful introduction to the seasons.

In the Small, Small Pond & Other Stories That Rhyme: In the Small, Small Pond; Stars! Stars! Stars!; Wild about Books; Come on, Rain!; Zin! Zin! Zin! A Violin! unabr. ed. Denise Fleming et al. Read by Laura Dem et al. (J). 2008. 44.99 (978-1-60514-943-1(8)) Find a World.

In the Spirit. 1986. 4.95 (C12) Carothers.

In the Spirit. Morningstar Inc. Staff. 1998. 10.99 (978-7-5124-0183-9(3)) Destiny Image Pubs.

In the Spirit. abr. ed. Susan L. Taylor. (ENG.). 2006. 9.99 (978-1-59483-780-7(5)) Pub: Hachet Audio. Dist(s): HachBkGrp

In the Spirit of Crazy Horse: The Story of Leonard Peltier & the FBI's War on the American Indian Movement. unabr. ed. Peter Matthiessen. (Running Time: 23 hrs. 50 mins.). (ENG.). 2009. 44.95 (978-1-4332-8862-3(1)); 79.95 (978-1-4332-8858-6(3)); 59.95 (978-1-4332-9082-4(0)); audio compact disk 123.00 (978-1-4332-8859-3(1)) Blckstn Audio.

In the Spirit of Leadership. Cheryl Esposito. 2008. audio compact disk 14.95 (978-0-9799252-1-4(5)) Pub: Plumb Road. Dist(s): AtlasBooks

In the SpotLight: Guided Exercises to Create a Calm & Confident State of Mind, Body, & Spirit While Speaking or Performing. Scripts. Janet Esposito. Featuring Diane Bahr-Groth. 1 CD. (Running Time: 77:29 mins.). 2003. audio compact disk 21.95 (978-0-9742966-1-6(9)) Janet E Esp.

In the Station of the Metro (A Poem from the Poets' Corner) The One-and-Only Poetry Book for the Whole Family. unabr. ed. Ezra Pound & John Lithgow. Read by John Lithgow. (Running Time: 10 mins.). (ENG.). 2008. 0.99 (978-1-60024-326-4(6)) Pub: Hachet Audio. Dist(s): HachBkGrp

In the Still of the Night: The Strange Death of Ronda Reynolds. abr. ed. Ann Rule. Read by Blair Brown. 5 CDs. (Running Time: 6 hrs. 0 mins. 0 sec.). 2010. audio compact disk 29.99 (978-0-7435-9973-3(X)) Pub: S&S Audio. Dist(s): S and S Inc

In the Swim. Douglas Florian. 1 cass. (Running Time: 15 min.). (J). (gr. k-3). 1998. pap. bk. 26.95 (978-0-8045-6851-7(0), 6851) Spoken Arts.

In the Tall, Tall Grass. unabr. ed. Denise Fleming. 1 cass. (Running Time: 6 min.). (J). (gr. k-3). 1993. pap. bk. 17.90 (978-0-8045-6683-4(6), 6683) Spoken Arts.
If you were a fuzzy caterpillar crawling through the tall, tall grass on a sunny afternoon, what would you see? This backyard nature tour is one no child

will want to miss. Ala Notable Children's Book. School Library Journal Best Books of the Year. IRA/CBC Children's Choice Award.

In the Teeth of the Evidence: And Other Mysteries. unabr. ed. Dorothy L. Sayers. Read by Ian Carmichael. 10 cass. (Running Time: 15 hrs.). (Lord Peter Wimsey Mystery Ser.). 2000. 59.95 (978-0-7451-4398-9(9), CAB 1082) Pub: Chivers Audio Bks GBR. Dist(s): AudioGO
All that remained of the garage was a heap of charred and smoldering beams. In the drivers seat of the car were the remains of a body. An accident said the police and the widow. She had been warning her husband for months about the dangers of the car. Murder, said the famous detective, Lord Peter Wimsey, who proceeded to track down the killer.

In the Tidal Marshes see Twentieth-Century Poetry in English, No. 25, Recordings of Poets Reading Their Own Poetry

In the Time of the Americans, Pt. 1. unabr. collector's ed. David Fromkin. Read by Dick Estell. 9 cass. (Running Time: 13 hrs. 30 min.). 1996. 72.00 (978-0-7366-3393-2(6), 4042-A) Books on Tape.

In the Time of the Americans, Pt. 2. collector's ed. David Fromkin. Read by Dick Estell. 9 cass. (Running Time: 13 hrs. 30 min.). 1996. 72.00 (978-0-7366-3394-9(4), 4042-B) Books on Tape.
An improbable fraternity of leaders moved the U.S. from isolationism to the top world player. What inspired their policy.

In the Time of the Pharaohs. unabr. ed. Michele Sobel Spirn. 1 cass. (Running Time: 20 min.). (Time Traveler Ser.). (J). (gr. 3-6). 1984. bk. 16.99 (978-0-934898-61-4(8)); pap. bk. 9.95 (978-0-934898-73-7(1)) Jan Prods.
Tom & Diana use the magic ring to travel back to the days of the ancient pharaohs in Egypt. Their mission is to protect Queen Hat-Shepsut from the jealous Prince Thut-mose who wants to take over the throne.

In the Tree House at Night see James Dickey Reads His Poetry & Prose

In the Upper Room: John 15:12-17. Ed Young. 1983. 4.95 (978-0-7417-1290-5(3), 290) Win Walk.

***In the Valley of the Shadow: The Authenticity of Religious Belief & What Matters Most in Our Lives.** unabr. ed. James L. Kugel. (Running Time: 8 hrs. 0 mins. 0 sec.). 2011. 19.99 (978-1-4526-5048-7(9)); 15.99 (978-1-4526-7048-5(X)); audio compact disk 29.99 (978-1-4526-0048-2(1)) Pub: Tantor Media. Dist(s): IngramPubServ

***In the Valley of the Shadow (Library Edition) The Authenticity of Religious Belief & What Matters Most in Our Lives.** unabr. ed. James L. Kugel. (Running Time: 8 hrs. 0 mins.). 2011. 29.99 (978-1-4526-2048-0(2)); audio compact disk 71.99 (978-1-4526-3048-9(8)) Pub: Tantor Media. Dist(s): IngramPubServ

In the Wake of the Plague: The Black Death & the World It Made. Norman F. Cantor. Narrated by John McDonough. 5 cass. (Running Time: 6 hrs. 30 mins.). 49.00 (978-0-7887-9608-1(9)) Recorded Bks.

In the Wake of the Storm: A Special Report. Interview. Hosted by Peter Kramer. 1CD. (Running Time: 1hr). 2005. 21.95 (978-1-933644-18-9(4), LCM 391) Lichtenstein Creat.
It's the story of the hurricane that?s as yet untold. When one million people evacuated the Gulf Coast, they left behind the regions most vulnerable residents, poor people, and people with multiple physical and mental disabilities. They are finally escaping... but to what? And of the one million people who fled, experts say we can also expect to see increased long-term rates of post-traumatic stress disorder, depression, and anxiety.Particularly damaged by these budget cuts is the state of Texas, now the new home to hundreds of thousands of refugees suffering from severe trauma reactions as well as a whole range of severe and persistent mental illnesses. How will states cope? Can we expect that mental health disaster relief will receive the same attention and funding as housing, food and other medical needs?Mental health experts have been warning for years of the consequences a disaster of the scope of Katrina on the nations already under-funded and over-stressed mental health system. But much like the warnings about New Orleans fragile levees, these cautions have been disregarded; the mental health infrastructure in much of the country gutted by deep cuts in community mental health programs.We'll hear from leading trauma experts on the scene in Houston about efforts to cope with the demands that the disaster has placed on the mental health care system, including an exclusive report from the Astrodome, where a psychiatrist struggles to provide medication and counseling for thousands of refugees, some of whom arrived so disturbed that they were tearing their hair and skin and actively trying to take their own lives. And we will speak with Thom Bornemann, director of the Carter Center Mental Health Program, who says that the nation is ill-equipped to handle a crisis of this magnitude.Plus why does disaster bring out the best in some people while others are just crushed? Well present some of the most pertinent information from our award-winning program on Resilience, produced in the weeks following the September 11th attacks, including an interview with Dr. Robert Sapolsky (author of "Why Zebras Don't Get Ulcers") who discusses how people can recover following trauma.

In the Web of Ideas. unabr. collector's ed. Charles Scribner, Jr. Read by Alexander Adams. 6 cass. (Running Time: 6 hrs.). 1994. 36.00 (978-0-7366-2779-5(0), 3498) Books on Tape.
Armchair journey through the books, places & intellectual realms that shaped the head of Charles Scribner's Sons, Publishers.

In the Wet. unabr. ed. Nevil Shute. Read by Stephen Thorne. 8 cass. (Running Time: 12 hrs.). 2003. 69.95 (978-0-7540-0986-3(6), CAB 2408) AudioGO.

In the Wet. unabr. ed. Nevil Shute. Narrated by Norman Dietz. 8 cass. (Running Time: 12 hrs.). 1988. 70.00 (978-1-55690-254-3(9), 88650E7) Recorded Bks.
An old man lies dying during the rainy season in the Queensland outback. And in the night, slipping in & out of an opium sleep that drifts him towards death, he draws his listener into a tale that opens onto incredible horizons.

In the Wet. unabr. collector's ed. Nevil Shute. Read by Stuart Courtney. 9 cass. (Running Time: 13 hrs. 30 min.). 1984. 72.00 (978-0-7366-0828-2(1), 1778) Books on Tape.
An elderly clergyman stationed in the Australian bush is called to the bedside of a dying derelict.

In the White Giant's Thigh see Child's Christmas in Wales

In the Winter Dark. unabr. ed. Tim Winton. Read by James Wright. 5 cass. (Running Time: 4 hrs.). 1999. 40.00 (978-1-876584-02-3(5), 590480) Bolinda Pubng AUS.
Night falls. In a lonely valley called the Sink, four people prepare for a quiet evening. Then in his orchard, Murray Jacob sees a moving shadow. Across the swamp, his neighbor Ronnie watches her lover leave and feels her baby roll inside her. And on the verandah of the Stubbses house, a small dog is torn screaming from its leash by something unseen. Nothing will ever be the same again.

In the Winter Dark. unabr. ed. Tim Winton. Read by James Wright. 4 CDs. (Running Time: 4 hrs.). 2005. audio compact disk 57.95 (978-1-74093-112-0(2)) Pub: Bolinda Pubng AUS. Dist(s): Bolinda Pub Inc

In the Woods. Tana French. Read by Steven Crossley. (Running Time: 21 hrs.). Bk. 1. (ENG.). (gr. 12 up). 2007. audio compact disk 39.95 (978-0-14-314218-8(6), PengAudBks) Penguin Grp USA.

In the Year of the Boar & Jackie Robinson. unabr. ed. Bette Bao Lord. Read by Melissa Hughes. 3 CDs. (Running Time: 3 hrs. 15 mins.). (J). (gr. 3-6). 2008. audio compact disk 39.95 (978-0-9814890-0-1(1)) Audio Bkshelf.

In the Year of the Boar & Jackie Robinson. unabr. ed. Bette Bao Lord. Narrated by Christina Moore. 3 pieces. (Running Time: 3 hrs. 30 mins.). (gr. k up). 1998. 27.00 (978-0-7887-1794-9(4), 95266E7) Recorded Bks.
Not only is this a wonderful glimpse at American life in the 1940s, but it is also an opportunity for young listeners to learn about life in China & what it's like to be an immigrant.

In the Year of the Boar & Jackie Robinson. unabr. ed. Bette Bao Lord. Narrated by Christina Moore. 3 CDs. (Running Time: 3 hrs. 30 mins.). (gr. k up). 2000. audio compact disk 27.00 (978-0-7887-4220-0(5), C1159E7) Recorded Bks.

In the Year of the Boar & Jackie Robinson, Homework Set. unabr. ed. Bette Bao Lord. Read by Christina Moore. 3 cass. (Running Time: 3 hrs. 30 min.). (J). 1997. bk. 40.20 (978-0-7887-1837-3(1), 40617) Recorded Bks.
Learn about life in China, American life in the 1940s & what it's like to be an immigrant.

In the Zone: Where the Holy Ghost Roams. Poems. Based on a poem by Charles Morton. Voice by Mary Morton. 1 cass. (Running Time: 54 mins.). 2004. audio compact disk 15.00 (978-0-9677079-7-6(8)) B I T S.
The most exciting time in all of history to be alive is right now, because God said "In the last days I will pour out my Spirit upon all ﬂesh!" The CD project consists of spoken word and songs for the soul that the Holy Spirit inspired me to write and perform! The title of this CD "In The Zone" in based on Galatians 5:16 "This I say then, walk in the Spirit and you will not fulﬁll the lust of the ﬂesh." It is our desire to live in the zone where the Holy Ghost roams.

In Their Own Voices: A Century of Recorded Poetry. Poems. Compiled by Rebekah Presson. 4 cass. (Running Time: 6 hr.). 1998. bk. 39.98 (978-1-56826-694-7(4), R4 72408); bk. 59.98 (978-1-56826-693-0(6), R2 72408) Rhino Enter.

In Their Wisdom. unabr. ed. C. P. Snow. Read by John MacDonald. 8 cass. (Running Time: 12 hrs.). (Strangers & Brothers Ser.). 1984. 64.00 (978-0-7366-0450-5(2), 1424) Books on Tape.
It was as a member of the House of Lords that C. P. Snow conceived the idea for this portrait of judicial corruption.

In This Land. Perf. by Sweet Honey in the Rock. 1 cass. (Running Time: 68 min.). 9.98 (978-1-877737-14-5(3), EB2756/WB4-42522) MFLP CA.
A capella songs in the African-American traditions of gospel, congregational, jazz, folk, R & B, & rap. Messages of love & positive social change.

In This Mountain. Jan Karon. Narrated by John McDonough. 11 cass. (Running Time: 15 hrs. 30 mins.). (Mitford Ser.: Bk. 7). 102.00 (978-1-4025-2388-5(2)) Recorded Bks.

In This Mountain. abr. ed. Jan Karon. 1 CD. (Running Time: 7 hrs.). (Mitford Ser.: Bk. 7). (gr. 12 up). 2002. audio compact disk 29.95 (978-0-14-280004-1(X), PengAudBks) Penguin Grp USA.
All is placid in Mitford after Father Tim returns from Whitecap Island, but events are looming that will challenge everyon'e faith.

In This Mountain. unabr. ed. Jan Karon. Narrated by John McDonough. 11 cass. (Running Time: 15 hrs. 30 mins.). (Mitford Ser.: Bk. 7). 2002. 49.95 (978-1-4025-2389-2(0), RG085) Recorded Bks.
Father Tim and Cynthia again living in Mitford. Though Father Tim dislikes change, he dislikes retirement even more. Staring at a blank page in a proposed book of essays, waging a losing battle against moles, and filling an occasional pulpit, he decides to take on a unique and difficult ministry. He even begins to think he likes change-until an unexpected event propels him on a painful journey that shakes his faith, his marriage, and the whole town of Mitford.

In This Rain. unabr. ed. S. J. Rozan. Read by Susan Ericksen. 1 MP3-CD. (Running Time: 11 hrs.). 2007. 54.95 (978-0-7927-4746-8(1), Chivers Sound Lib); audio compact disk 89.95 (978-0-7927-4672-0(4), Chivers Sound Lib) AudioGO.
Three years ago, a child's death sent one innocent man to prison and blew open a vortex of corruption at the heart of Manhattan's lucrative construction industry. Joe Cole was that innocent man. A former Buildings Department inspector, the ex-con now lives a broken life, cut off from his wife and daughter, and from the city he loves. But a woman's murder and the death of a young man rip open old wounds - plunging Joe and his former partner, a beautiful, hard-charging investigator, into the darkest corners of the city and into a desperate race to expose the secrets that help the powerful hide their crimes.

In Time of War: Hitler's Terrorist Attack on America. unabr. ed. Read by Raymond Todd. (Running Time: 52200 sec.). 2006. 89.95 (978-0-7861-4658-1(3)); audio compact disk 120.00 (978-0-7861-6748-7(3)); audio compact disk 44.95 (978-0-7861-7408-9(0)) Blckstn Audio.

In Times of Trouble: Psalm 42-43. Ed Young. 1989. 4.95 (978-0-7417-1748-1(4), 748) Win Walk.

***In Too Deep.** Jude Watson. Read by David Pittu. (39 Clues (Playaway) Ser.). (ENG.). (J). 2009. 49.99 (978-1-61587-711-9(8)) Find a World.

***In Too Deep.** abr. ed. Jayne Ann Krentz. (Running Time: 6 hrs.). (Arcane Society Ser.). 2010. 9.99 (978-1-4418-9402-1(0), 9781441894021, BAD) Brilliance Audio.

***In Too Deep.** abr. ed. Jayne Ann Krentz. Read by Joyce Bean. (Running Time: 6 hrs.). (Arcane Society Ser.). 2010. audio compact disk 24.99 (978-1-4233-7401-5(0), 9781423374015, BACD) Brilliance Audio.

***In Too Deep.** unabr. ed. Jayne Ann Krentz. (Running Time: 10 hrs.). (Arcane Society Ser.). 2010. 24.99 (978-1-4233-7399-5(5), 9781423373995, BAD); 39.97 (978-1-4233-7400-8(2), 9781423374008, BADLE); 24.99 (978-1-4233-7397-1(9), 9781423373971, Brilliance MP3) Brilliance Audio.

***In Too Deep.** unabr. ed. Jayne Ann Krentz. Read by Joyce Bean. (Running Time: 10 hrs.). (Arcane Society Ser.). 2010. 39.97 (978-1-4233-7398-8(7), 9781423373988, Brinc Audio MP3 Lib); audio compact disk 36.99 (978-1-4233-7395-7(2), 9781423373957, Bril Audio CD Unabri); audio compact disk 87.97 (978-1-4233-7396-4(0), 9781423373964, BriAudCD Unabrid) Brilliance Audio.

In Too Deep, Bk. 6. Jude Watson. (39 Clues Ser.). (ENG.). (J). (gr. 3-7). 2009. audio compact disk 49.95 (978-0-545-16088-9(X)) Scholastic Inc.

In Too Deep, Bk. 6. Jude Watson. Narrated by David Pittu. (39 Clues Ser.: Bk. 6). (ENG.). (J). (gr. 3-7). 2009. audio compact disk 19.95 (978-0-545-16025-4(1)) Scholastic Inc.

In-Training Examination: Use & Abuse. 2 cass. (General Sessions Ser.: C84-SP1). 1984. 15.00 (8416) Am Coll Surgeons.

In Tune with the Divine. Swami Amar Jyoti. 2 cass. 1978. 12.95 (C-13) Truth Consciousness.
How to know God's Will. Playing our role selflessly with devotion to the Cosmic Engineer. Finding our fittest position.

In Turbation. Poems. John M. Bennett. Read by John M. Bennett. Perf. by Dick Metcalf. Music by Dick Metcalf & Mr. Painful. 1 cass. (Running Time: 60 min.). 1996. 6.00 (978-0-935350-60-9(8)) Luna Bisonte.
Avant-garde poetry with improvizational music.

In Turkish Waters. Charles Whiting & Charles Whitting. Read by Michael Wade. 5 cass. (Storysound Ser.). (J). 2003. 49.95 (978-1-85903-510-8(8)) Pub: Mgna Lrg Print GBR. Dist(s): Ulverscroft US

In View of Eternity. Read by Basilea Schlink. 1 cass. (Running Time: 30 min.). Incl. In View of Eternity: The Hour Is Near. 1985. (0276); 1985. (0276) Evang Sisterhood Mary.
Seeing life from the perspective of eternity - God's paths of chastening & their marvelous outcome; Pressing on to attain the supreme goal - the Marriage Supper of the Lamb.

In View of Eternity: The Hour Is Near see In View of Eternity

In Vitro Diagnostics (IVD) Products in Italy: A Strategic Reference 2006. Compiled by Icon Group International, Inc. Staff. 2007. ring bd. 195.00 (978-0-497-36040-5(3)) Icon Grp.

In Vitro Fertilization - Facts & Fantasies. 2 cass. (Gynecology & Obstetrics Ser.: C84-GO6). 1984. 15.00 (8437) Am Coll Surgeons.

In Vitro Fertilization, Embryo Transfer & Beyond. 2 cass. (Gynecology & Obstetrics Ser.: C85-GO2). 15.00 (8560) Am Coll Surgeons.

In Which a House Is Built at Pooh Corner for Eeyore. unabr. ed. A. A. Milne. Read by Peter Dennis. Illus. by Ernest H. Shepard. 1 cass. (Classic Pooh Treasury Ser.). (J). bk. (978-1-57375-527-6(3), 71394) Audioscope.
It once occurred to our mildly muddled bear friend (that being Winnie-the-Pooh), that he had a house, Piglet had a house, Owl had a house but, Eeyore had nowhere to live. it can be frightfully frigid in the Hundred Acre Wood. A house must be built for Eeyore. Includes 3 stories.

In Which Christopher Robin Gives Pooh a Party. unabr. ed. A. A. Milne. Read by Peter Dennis. Illus. by Ernest H. Shepard. 1 cass. (Winnie-the-Pooh Ser.). (J). bk. (978-1-57375-046-2(8), 70554) Audioscope.
Pooh plans for fun & games with Christopher & friends, but knowing our lovable bear, anything can happen. Includes bonus stories on Side B.

In Which Everyone Has a Birthday & Gets Two Presents. unabr. ed. A. A. Milne. Read by Peter Dennis. Illus. by Ernest H. Shepard. 1 cass. (Running Time: 90 mins.). (Winnie-the-Pooh Ser.). (J). bk. (978-1-57375-015-8(8), 70134) Audioscope.
What will Pooh, Christopher Robin & friends do to celebrate this special day?.

In Which It Is Shown That Tiggers Don't Climb Trees. unabr. ed. A. A. Milne. Read by Peter Dennis. Illus. by Ernest H. Shepard. 1 cass. (Classic Pooh Treasury Ser.). (J). bk. Incl.Keepsake bk. (978-1-57375-529-0(X), 71414) Audioscope.
Tiggers are good flyers. They can jump farther than Kangas. Tiggers can swim. They can do everything (or so Tigger says). Tigger proves that, what goes up does NOT necessarily come down (easily, that is). Includes 4 stories.

In Which Piglet Meets a Heffalump. unabr. ed. A. A. Milne. Read by Peter Dennis. Illus. by Ernest H. Shepard. 1 cass. (Winnie-the-Pooh Ser.). (J). bk. (978-1-57375-014-1(X), 70124) Audioscope.
Piglet has something to tell his friends about the Horrible Heffalump! But who does it turn out to be? Includes bonus stories on Side B.

In Which Pooh Goes Visiting & Gets into a Tight Place & in Which Pooh & Piglet Go Hunting & Nearly Catch a Woozle. unabr. ed. A. A. Milne. Read by Peter Dennis. Illus. by Ernest H. Shepard. 1 cass. (Winnie-the-Pooh Ser.). (J). bk. (978-1-57375-001-1(8), 70014) Audioscope.

In Which Tigger Is Unbounced. unabr. ed. A. A. Milne. Read by Peter Dennis. Illus. by Ernest H. Shepard. 1 cass. (Classic Pooh Treasury Ser.). (J). bk. (978-1-57375-528-3(1), 71404) Audioscope.
Even a Tigger can get too bouncy for one's own good. When Pooh & his pals try to "unbounce" him, their well-thought-out plan backfires. Includes 3 stories.

In Which We Are Introduced to Winnie the Pooh & Some Bees, & the Stories Begin. unabr. ed. A. A. Milne. Read by Peter Dennis. Illus. by Ernest H. Shepard. 1 cass. (Winnie-the-Pooh Ser.). (J). bk. (978-1-57375-000-4(X), 70004) Audioscope.
Includes bonus stories on Side B.

***In with the Devil: A Fallen Hero, a Serial Killer, & a Dangerous Bargain for Redemption.** unabr. ed. James Keene & Hillel Levin. (Running Time: 9 hrs.). 2010. 29.95 (978-1-4417-5641-1(8)); 59.95 (978-1-4417-5637-4(X)); audio compact disk 29.95 (978-1-4417-5640-4(X)); audio compact disk 90.00 (978-1-4417-5638-1(8)) Blckstn Audio.

In Your Dreams. Tom Holt. 12 cass. (Isis Cassettes Ser.). (J). 2005. 94.95 (978-0-7531-2120-7(4)); audio compact disk 99.95 (978-0-7531-2380-5(0)) Pub: ISIS Lrg Prnt GBR. Dist(s): Ulverscroft US

In Your Garden. 1 cass. (Running Time: 1 hr.). (J). (gr. k up). 2001. 10.95 (XB 10017C) Kimbo Educ.
Slap-happy songs offer food hints, house-cleaning tips & even pet care suggestions. A terrific recording filled with positive messages. Lessons & laughter.

In Your Garden. 1 CD. (Running Time: 1 hr.). (YA). (gr. k up). 2001. audio compact disk 14.95 (XB 10017CD) Kimbo Educ.

In Your Hands. 1 cass. (Running Time: 35 min.). 2001. 5.95 (KIM 9150C) Kimbo Educ.

In Your Mind's Eye Set: Relaxation Techniques for Rejuvenating Your Life. Eli Bay. 5 cass. 1994. 49.95 (10920AX) Nightingale-Conant.
Enter a deeply meditative state of relaxation. In it, you'll listen as Eli Bay - host of the award-winning television series Beyond Stress & director of Toronto's Relaxation Response Institute - guides you to a deeply meditative state that can make you calmer & more relaxed while simultaneously enhancing your mental & physical performance. His holistic approach - which blends yoga, transcendental meditation, Zen, Soviet sports psychology & various ancient philosophies - is widely considered one of the most practical & effective "hands-on" relaxation methods today. It will empower you with the ability to excel in a world of unprecedented change & stress.

In Your Wildest Dreams. Focus on the Family Staff & AIO Team Staff. 4 CDs. (Running Time: 6 hrs.). (Adventures in Odyssey Ser.: No. 34). (ENG.). (J). 2005. audio compact disk 24.99 (978-1-56179-887-2(8)) Pub: Focus Family. Dist(s): Tyndale Hse

***In Zanesville.** Jo Ann Beard. 2011. audio compact disk 44.99 (978-1-61120-016-4(4)) Dreamscap OH.

Inadmissible Evidence, Pt. 1. unabr. ed. Philip Friedman. Read by Alexander Adams. 8 cass. (Running Time: 12 hrs.). 1993. 64.00 (3237-A) Books on Tape.
Young D.A. faces the prosecutor's ultimate question: Did the defendant actually commit the crime?.

Inadmissible Evidence, Pt. 2. unabr. ed. Philip Friedman. Read by Alexander Adams. 8 cass. (Running Time: 12 hrs.). 1993. 64.00 (3237-B) Books on Tape.
Young D.A. faces the prosecutor's ultimate question: Did the defendant actually commit the crime?.

Inaugural Address of Barack Obama. Barack Obama. (JPN., 2009. pap. bk. 24.00 (978-4-255-00457-0(9)) Asahi Shu JPN.

Inaugural Celebration: The Center for Studies in Science & Spirituality. Brian Swimme & Thomas Berry. 1 cass. 9.00 (A0607-90) Sound Photosyn.
Great event & whopper talks by Swimme & Berry.

Inauguration of President Bush & Vice President Quayle, 1989. 1 cass. (Running Time: 60 min.). 1989. 11.95 (K0840B090, HarperThor) HarpC GBR.

***Inbound Marketing: Get Found Using Google, Social Media, & Blogs.** unabr. ed. Brian Halligan & Dharmesh Shah. Read by Erik Synnestvedt. (Running Time: 5 hrs.). (ENG.). 2009. 24.98 (978-1-59659-492-0(6), GildAudio) Pub: Gildan Media. Dist(s): HachBkGrp

***Inc. Yourself.** Judith H. McQuown. 2011. audio compact disk 23.95 (978-1-59316-569-7(2)) Listen & Live.

Inca Gold. unabr. ed. Clive Cussler. Read by Michael Prichard. 15 cass. (Running Time: 22 hrs. 30 min.). (Dirk Pitt Ser.). 1995. 120.00 (978-0-7366-2896-9(7), 3596) Books on Tape.
On a marine expedition in the Peruvian Andes, Dirk Pitt & his companions, including the beautiful archaeologist Dr. Shannon Kelsey, find themselves in a no-holds-barred struggle against cut-throat smugglers out to uncover the lost Inca treasure. In this subterranean world of darkness, they race against time & the threat of death, for the real key to the mystery lies beneath the ancient treasure chamber.

Inca World. Compiled by Benchmark Education Staff. 2005. audio compact disk 10.00 (978-1-4108-5502-2(3)) Benchmark Educ.

Incantation. Alice Hoffman. Read by Jenna Lamia. (ENG.). (YA). (gr. 8-12). 2009. 44.99 (978-1-60775-670-5(6)) Find a World.

Incantation. unabr. ed. Alice Hoffman. Read by Jenna Lamia. (Running Time: 3 hrs.). 2006. 39.25 (978-1-4233-2364-8(5), 9781423323648, BADLE); 24.95 (978-1-4233-2363-1(7), 9781423323631, BAD) Brilliance Audio.

Incantation. unabr. ed. Alice Hoffman. Read by Jenna Lamia. 2 cass. (Running Time: 10800 sec.). (YA). (gr. 8-12). 2006. 44.25 (978-1-4233-2358-7(0), 9781423323587, BrilAudUnabridg); audio compact disk 62.25 (978-1-4233-2360-0(2), 9781423323600, BriAudCD Unabrid); audio compact disk 39.25 (978-1-4233-2362-4(9), 9781423323624, Brinc Audio MP3 Lib); audio compact disk 24.95 (978-1-4233-2361-7(0), 9781423323617, Brilliance MP3); audio compact disk 19.95 (978-1-4233-2359-4(9), 9781423323594, Bril Audio CD Unabri) Brilliance Audio.
Estrella is a Marrano: During the time of the Spanish Inquisition, she is one of a community of Spanish Jews living double lives as Catholics. And she is living in a house of secrets, raised by a family who practices underground the ancient and mysterious way of wisdom known as kabbalah. When Estrella discovers her family's true identity - and her family's secrets are made public - she confronts a world she's never imagined, where new love burns and where friendship ends in flame and ash, where trust is all but vanquished and betrayal has tragic and bitter consequences.

***Incarceron.** unabr. ed. Catherine Fisher. Narrated by Kim Mai Guest. 10 CDs. (Running Time: 11 hrs. 37 mins.). (YA). (gr. 7 up). 2010. audio compact disk 65.00 (978-0-307-70709-3(1), Listening Lib) Pub: Random Audio Pubg. Dist(s): Random

Incarceron. unabr. ed. Catherine Fisher. Read by Kim Mai Guest. (ENG.). (J). (gr. 7). 2010. audio compact disk 48.00 (978-0-307-70707-9(5), Listening Lib) Pub: Random Audio Pubg. Dist(s): Random

***Incarnate Leadership: 5 Leadership Lessons from the Life of Jesus.** Zondervan. (Running Time: 4 hrs. 4 mins. 18 sec.). (ENG.). 2010. 9.99 (978-0-310-86932-0(3)) Zondervan.

Incarnation & Sexuality. James Nelson & Eugene Jaberg. 1986. 10.80 (0712) Assn Prof Chaplains.

Incarnation Crosses - 1. The Realm of Alcyone: The Global Incarnation Index. Ra Uru Hu. 4 CDs. (Running Time: 4 hrs. 27 mins.). 2000. audio compact disk (978-0-9671115-9-9(5)) zc design.
Describes the Incarnation Crosses humans are born with. Related to the Human Design System.

Incarnation Crosses - 2: The Realm of Dhube: The Global Incarnation Index. Ra Uru Hu. 3 CDs. (Running Time: 2 hrs. 47 mins.). (Global Incarnation Index). 2000. audio compact disk (978-1-931164-00-9(2)) zc design.

Incarnation Crosses - 3. The Realm of Jupiter Vol. 3: The Global Incarnation Index. Ra Uru Hu. (Global Incarnation Index). 2000. audio compact disk 48.00 (978-1-931164-11-5(8)) zc design.

Incarnation Crosses - 4. The Realm of Sirius Vol. 4. Ra Uru Hu. (Global Incarnation Index). 2000. audio compact disk 48.00 (978-1-931164-12-2(6)) zc design.

Incendiary. Chris Cleave. Narrated by Susan Lyons. (Running Time: 29700 sec.). 2005. audio compact disk 29.99 (978-1-4193-5626-1(7)) Recorded Bks.

Incentives for Grace Giving: 11 Corinthians 9:1-15. Ed Young. 1996. 4.95 (978-0-7417-2085-6(X), 1085) Win Walk.

Incest & Physical Abuse. Stephanie Ennis. 1 cass. 8.95 (108) Am Fed Astrologers.
Measuring potential for abuse in natal chart.

Incest & Sexual Addiction. John Bradshaw. (Running Time: 10800 sec.). 2008. audio compact disk 100.00 (978-1-57388-156-2(2)) J B Media.

Inch by Inch. unabr. ed. Leo Lionni. Narrated by Ron McLarty. 1 cass. (Running Time: 7 mins.). (J). (ps-1). 2006. 8.95 (978-0-439-93521-0(0), WRAC699); audio compact disk 12.95 (978-0-439-93522-7(9), WCD699RA) Weston Woods.

Inch by Inch. unabr. ed. Leo Lionni. Illus. by Leo Lionni. Narrated by Ron McLarty. 1 cass. (Running Time: 7 mins.). (J). (ps-1). 2006. pap. bk. 14.95 (978-0-439-90584-8(2), WPRA699); pap. bk. 18.95 (978-0-439-90585-5(0), WPCD699) Weston Woods.
To keep from being eaten, a resourceful inchworm measures a robin's tail, a flamingo's neck, a toucan's beak, a heron's legs, and a nightingale's song.

Inchon: the Music of Robert W. Smith, Volume 2: Featuring Inchon & Other Concert Band Works. Contrib. by Houston Symphonic Band. Conducted by Robert W. Smith. (ENG.). 2002. audio compact disk 19.95 (978-0-7579-9723-5(6)) Alfred Pub.

Incident see Poetry of Countee Cullen

Incident at Lancaster. 1 cass. 10.00 Esstee Audios.
American espionage in the Revolution.

Incident at Niagara. Henry Hughes. Tr. by Repertory Theatre Staff. 1 cass. (Running Time: 24 min. per cass.). 1985. 10.00 (RAH912) Esstee Audios.
Tale of a gentleman sailor who led a mutiny against gunrunning Captain Gore in the U.S. - Canadian waters during Martin Van Buren's administration.

Incident at Owl's Creek. Ambrose Bierce. 10.00 (LSS1111) Esstee Audios.

Incident at Vichy. Arthur Miller. Contrib. by Lawrence Pressman et al. (Running Time: 4320 sec.). 2002. audio compact disk 25.95 (978-1-58081-254-2(6), CDTPT170) Pub: L A Theatre. Dist(s): NetLibrary CO

Incident of the French Camp see Classics of English Poetry for the Elementary Curriculum

Incidents in the Life of a Slave Girl. Linda Brent. Read by Anais 9000. 2008. 27.95 (978-1-60112-012-0(5)) Babblebooks.

Incidents in the Rue Laugier. Anita Brookner. Read by Lindsay Sandison. 7 CDs. (Running Time: 10 hrs. 30 mins.). 2001. audio compact disk 62.96 (978-0-7531-1052-2(0), 110520) Pub: ISIS Audio GBR. Dist(s): Ulverscroft US

Incidents in the Rue Laugier. unabr. ed. Anita Brookner. Read by Lindsay Sandison. 6 cass. (Running Time: 9 hrs.). (Isis Ser.). (J). 2004. 54.95 (978-1-85695-232-3(0), 951002) Pub: ISIS Lrg Prnt GBR. Dist(s): Ulverscroft US

Incline Thine Ear: God's Prescription for Divine Health. Kenneth E. Hagin. 6 cass. 24.00 (52H) Faith Lib Pubns.

Inclusion Ideas That Really Work: Practical Classroom Strategies, Set. Linda Tilton. Read by Linda Tilton. 6 cass. (Running Time: 3 hr. 41 min.). (J). (gr. k-6). 1997. 75.00 Incl. resource hdbk. (978-1-886397-10-1(4)) Bureau of Educ.
Live audio seminar.

Incognito Mosquito: Private Insective. abr. ed. E. A. Hass. Perf. by Don Adams. 1 cass. (Running Time: 52 min.). (J). (gr. 4-6). 1984. 8.98 (978-0-89845-305-8(4), CP1749) HarperCollins Pubs.
Four solve-it-yourself mini-mysteries utilizing puns. Includes: "The Mysterious Case of the Unsafe Safe," "The Waterbug Scandal," "The Case of the Vanishing Magician" & "Whatever Happened to Mickey".

Income for Life from Real Estate: How the Tortoise Got Rich. Al Lee. 2001. bk. & wbk. ed. 49.95 (978-0-9711738-0-4(X)) Pub: A Lee. Dist(s): Book Pub Co

Income Tax Changes As a Result of the Revenue Conciliation Act of 1990. Read by Dennis G. Hursh. 1 cass. 1991. 20.00 (AL-105) PA Bar Inst.

Income Tax Planning for Everyone. unabr. ed. David K. Luhman. Read by David K. Luhman. 1 cass. (Running Time: 1 hr. 30 min.). (Personal Finance for Everyone Ser.: Vol. 4). 1996. 9.00 (978-1-889297-14-9(3)) Numen Lumen.
Overview of the income tax system, record keeping, filing a return, picking the right form, filing status, exemptions, taxable income, other taxable income, business income, capital gains & losses, rents, Social Security, adjustments to income, itemized deductions, paying your taxes, tax credits.

***Incomparable Christ.** unabr. ed. John Stott. (ENG.). 2006. 10.98 (978-1-59644-267-2(0), Hovel Audio) christianaud.

Incomparable Light see Richard Eberhart Reading His Poetry

Incomparable Rex: The Last of the High Comedians. unabr. ed. Patrick Garland. Narrated by Paul Matthews. 7 cass. (Running Time: 9 hrs.). 1999. 62.00 (978-1-84197-019-6(0), H1019E7) Recorded Bks.
An affectionate & witty memoir of one of Britian's greatest theatrical & cinematic talents: Rex Harrison was famed for his urbane style, his wit, his numerous wives & his appalling temper, quite apart from his legendary & much loved performance as Professor Higgins in "My Fair Lady".

Incomparable Rex: The Last of the High Comedians. unabr. ed. Patrick Garland. Based on a novel by Patrick Garland. Narrated by Paul Matthews. 8 CDs. (Running Time: 9 hrs.). 2001. audio compact disk 75.00 (978-1-84197-097-4(2), C1140E7) Recorded Bks.
An affectionate & witty memoir of one of Britain's greatest theatrical & cinematic talents.

Incomplete & Inaccurate History of Sport. unabr. ed. Kenny Mayne. Narrated by David A. Drummond. (Running Time: 6 hrs. 0 mins. 0 sec.). (ENG.). 2008. audio compact disk 29.99 (978-1-4001-0753-7(9)) Pub: Tantor Media. Dist(s): IngramPubServ

Incomplete & Inaccurate History of Sport: And Other Random Thoughts from Childhood to Fatherhood. unabr. ed. Kenny Mayne. Narrated by David Drummond. (Running Time: 6 hrs. 0 mins. 0 sec.). (ENG.). 2008. audio compact disk 19.99 (978-1-4001-5753-2(6)); audio compact disk 59.99 (978-1-4001-3753-4(5)) Pub: Tantor Media. Dist(s): IngramPubServ

Incomplete Revenge. unabr. ed. Jacqueline Winspear. Narrated by Orlagh Cassidy. 8 CDs. (Running Time: 11 hrs.). (Maisie Dobbs Mystery Ser.: Bk. 5). 2008. audio compact disk 79.95 (978-0-7927-5244-8(9)) AudioGO.
With the country in the grip of economic malaise, and worried about her business, Maisie Dobbs is relieved to accept an apparently straightforward assignment from an old friend to investigate a potential land purchase. Her inquiries take her to a picturesque village in Kent during the hop-picking season, but beneath its pastoral surface she finds evidence that something is amiss. Mysterious fires erupt in the village with alarming regularity, and a series of petty crimes suggests a darker criminal element at work. As Maisie discovers, the villagers are bitterly prejudiced against outsiders who flock to Kent at harvest-time - even more troubling, they seem possessed by the legacy of a war-time Zeppelin raid. Maisie grows increasingly suspicious of a peculiar secrecy that shrouds the village, and ultimately she must draw on all her finely honed skills of detection to solve one of her most intriguing cases.

Incomplete Revenge. unabr. ed. Jacqueline Winspear. Read by Orlagh Cassidy. 8 CDs. (Running Time: 9 hrs. 15 mins. 0 sec.). (Maisie Dobbs Mystery Ser.: Bk. 5). (ENG.). 2008. audio compact disk 39.95 (978-1-4272-0301-4(6)) Pub: Macmill Audio. Dist(s): Macmillan

Incomprehensivility: Romans 11:27-36. Ben Young. 1997. 4.95 (978-0-7417-6032-6(0), B0032) Win Walk.

***Inconceivable: A Medical Mistake, the Baby We Couldn't Keep, & Our Choice to Deliver the Ultimate Gift.** unabr. ed. Carolyn Savage & Sean Savage. (ENG.). 2011. (978-0-06-202739-9(5), Harper Audio) HarperCollins Pubs.

Inconjuncts. Alan Epstein. 1 cass. 8.95 (402) Am Fed Astrologers.
Psychological chart analysis using inconjuncts.

Incontinentia Pigmenti - A Bibliography & Dictionary for Physicians, Patients, & Genome Researchers. Compiled by Icon Group International, Inc. Staff. 2007. ring bd. 28.95 (978-0-497-11240-0(X)) Icon Grp.

Inconvenient Book: Real Solutions to the World's Biggest Problems. unabr. abr. ed. Glenn Beck. Read by Glenn Beck. (Running Time: 6 hrs. 0 mins. 0 sec.). (ENG.). 2007. audio compact disk 29.95 (978-0-7435-6953-8(9)) Pub: S&S Audio. Dist(s): S and S Inc

Inconvenient Corpse. abr. ed. Philip Daniels. Read by Peter Joyce. 4 cass. (Running Time: 6 hrs.). (Sound Ser.). 2004. 44.95 (978-1-85496-286-7(8), 62868) Pub: UlverLrgPrint GBR. Dist(s): Ulverscroft US

Inconvenient Truth: The Planetary Emergency of Global Warming & What We Can Do about It. abr. ed. Al Gore. Read by Blair Underwood et al. (Running Time: 3 hrs. 0 mins. 0 sec.). (ENG.). 2008. audio compact disk 19.95 (978-0-7435-7202-6(5)) Pub: S&S Audio. Dist(s): S and S Inc

Inconvenient Wife. unabr. ed. Megan Chance. Read by Kathe Mazur. 9 cass. (Running Time: 13 hrs. 30 mins.). 2004. 81.00 (978-1-4159-0102-1(3)) Books on Tape.
In 1880s New York high society, a restless and passionate wife breaks through social conventions.

Inconvenient Woman. unabr. ed. Dominick Dunne. Read by Michael Kramer. 12 cass. (Running Time: 18 hrs.). 1999. 96.00 (978-0-7366-3280-5(8), 3936) Books on Tape.
A high society man gets caught between his wife & his mistress. Which one becomes inconvenient? A tale of love & betrayal.

Incorporate Your Business: The National Corporation Kit. 3rd ed. Daniel Sitarz. (Small Business Library Ser.). 2001. audio compact disk 24.95 (978-0-935755-88-6(8)) Pub: Nova Pub IL. Dist(s): Natl Bk Netwk

***Incorrigible Children of Ashton Place: The Hidden Gallery.** unabr. ed. Maryrose Wood. (ENG.). 2011. (978-0-06-201255-5(X)) HarperCollins Pubs.

***Incorrigible Children of Ashton Place: Book I.** unabr. ed. Maryrose Wood. Read by Katherine Kellgren. (ENG.). 2010. (978-0-06-199165-3(1)) HarperCollins Pubs.

***Incorrigible Children of Ashton Place: Book I: The Mysterious Howling.** unabr. ed. Maryrose Wood. Read by Katherine Kellgren. (ENG.). 2010. (978-0-06-198832-5(4)) HarperCollins Pubs.

Increase Athletic Performance. Bruce Goldberg. (ENG.). 2005. audio compact disk 17.00 (978-1-57968-099-2(2)) Pub: B Goldberg. Dist(s): Baker Taylor

Increase Athletic Performance. Bruce Goldberg. Read by Bruce Goldberg. 1 cass. (Running Time: 25 min.). (ENG.). 2007. bk. 13.00 (978-1-885577-63-4(X)) Pub: B Goldberg. Dist(s): Baker Taylor
Through self-hypnosis connect with the subconscious mind, & become physically & mentally fit.

Increase Concentration & Energy. (Martial Arts Programming Ser.). 12.50 (978-0-87554-194-5(1), K104) Valley Sun.
You now concentrate better than ever. You have more energy than ever before. You relax when you are training & performing drills. You eliminate distractions when kicking & punching. Your concentration becomes sharper & more focused. You draw on your total body & mind in kicking & punching.

Increase Confidence: Guided Meditation. Concept by Vicky Thurlow. Voice by Vicky Thurlow. (ENG.). 2008. audio compact disk 14.95 (978-0-9817055-2-1(9)) DVT Invest.

Increase Creativity: Ignite imagination & Insight. unabr. ed. Kelly Howell. 1 CD. (Running Time: 60 min.). (ENG.). 2003. audio compact disk 14.95 (978-1-881451-50-1(X)) Brain Sync.
Experience a quantum leap in your ability to image, create and execute new ideas with this groundbreaking program. Completely free of spoken words or subliminal messages, Increase Creativity delivers 60 minutes of soothing music mixed with theta sound waves to trigger the remarkable mental state known as hemispheric synchronization. As intellect and creativity integrate, your mind soars to lucid heights of awareness. Creative blocks dissolve. New ideas and insights spontaneously flash into consciousness. The results are profound.

Increase Creativity: Open Channels to Inspiration. unabr. ed. Kelly Howell. Contrib. by Robert Schwimmer. 1 cass. (Running Time: 1 hr.). 1994. 11.95 (978-1-881451-26-6(7)) Brain Sync.
In a pleasant state of relaxation, your mind generates new perceptions, ideas & knowledge that effortlessly integrate into your work, your play & your life.

Increase Creativity & Self-Expression: Guided Meditation. Concept by Vicky Thurlow. Voice by Vicky Thurlow. (ENG.). 2008. audio compact disk 14.95 (978-0-9817055-4-5(5)) DVT Invest.

Increase Energy+Conquer Procrastination. 2004. audio compact disk 14.95 (978-1-55848-108-4(7)) EffectiveMN.

Increase Love, Faith, & Trust: Guided Meditation. Concept by Vicky Thurlow. Voice by Vicky Thurlow. (ENG.). 2008. audio compact disk 14.95 (978-0-9817055-3-8(7)) DVT Invest.

Increase Sales. Betty L. Randolph. 1 stereo cass. (Running Time: 45 min.). (Self-Hypnosis Ser.). 9.98 (978-1-55909-152-7(5), 812) Randolph Tapes.
Describes how to think big & sell successfully. Music background & spoken word.

Increase Sales. Betty L. Randolph. Read by Betty L. Randolph. Read by Leonard Baron. Ed. by Success Education Institute International. 1 cass. (Running Time: 60 min.). (Success Ser.). 1989. bk. 9.98 90 min. extended length stereo music. (978-1-55909-022-3(7), 31X); 9.98 (978-1-55909-192-3(4), 31B) Randolph Tapes.
Teaches how to Think Big & helps you "close the deal!" Subliminal messages are heard for 3-5 minutes before becoming ocean sounds or music.

Increase Self-Discipline. Dick Sutphen. 1 cass. (Running Time: 1 hr.). (RX17 Ser.). 14.98 (978-0-87554-349-9(9), RX166) Valley Sun.

Increase Self-Discipline. Dick Sutphen. 1 cass. (Running Time: 1 hr.). (Only Subliminals Ser.). 1990. 12.98 (978-0-87554-449-6(5), T209) Valley Sun.
One hour of soothing, digitally mastered stereo music with positive subliminal suggestions phrased for maximum acceptance by your subconscious mind.

Increase Self-Discipline & Accomplish Your Goals. 1 cass. 10.49 (978-0-87554-429-8(0), SS106) Valley Sun.
There is no easier, more convenient way to program your mind, any time, any place. No distracting ocean waves or music, Silent Subliminals contain just pure subliminals that bypass your conscious hearing to go directly to your brain.

Increase Self-Esteem. Dick Sutphen. 1 cass. (Running Time: 1 hr.). (Only Subliminals Ser.). 1990. 12.98 (978-0-87554-450-2(9), T210) Valley Sun.
One hour of soothing, digitally mastered stereo music with positive subliminal suggestions phrased for maximum acceptance by your subconscious mind.

Increase Vitality. Michael Reed Gach. (Running Time: 1 hr. 15 mins.). 2006. audio compact disk 15.95 (978-1-59179-085-3(9), W718D) Sounds True.

Increase Vitality: Optimal Classical Compositions for Invigoration & Activity. Andrew Weil & Joshua Leeds. (Running Time: 60 mins.). 2006. audio compact disk 17.98 (978-1-59179-541-4(9), M1100D) Sounds True.

Increase Your Brain Power. Bruce Goldberg. (ENG.). 2005. audio compact disk 17.00 (978-1-57968-098-5(4)) Pub: B Goldberg. Dist(s): Baker Taylor

Increase Your Brain Power. Bruce Goldberg. Read by Bruce Goldberg. 1 cass. (Running Time: 25 min.). (ENG.). 2007. 13.00 (978-1-885577-62-7(1)) Pub: B Goldberg. Dist(s): Baker Taylor
Through self-hypnosis learn how to maximize thought processes, & vastly increase knowledge & memory.

Increase Your Confidence. abr. ed. Gael Lindenfield. Read by Polly Adams. 1 cass. (Running Time: 90 mins.). (Successful Living Ser.). 1998. 9.95 (978-0-694-51906-4(5), CPN10134) HarperCollins Pubs.

Increase Your Dollar Income. 1 cass. (Sleep Programming Tapes Ser.). 12.98 (978-0-87554-542-4(4), 1115) Valley Sun.

Increase Your Energy - Conquering Procrastination. Robert E. Griswold. Read by Robert E. Griswold. 1 cass. (Super Strength Ser.). 1993. 10.95 (978-1-55848-308-8(X)) EffectiveMN.
Two complete non-subliminal programs to help become energized & motivated.

Increased Capacity for God. Elbert Willis. 1 cass. (Increasing Spiritual Assurance Ser.). 4.00 Fill the Gap.

Increased Love & Caring. Read by Mary Richards. (Subliminal Impact Ser.). 12.95 (606) Master Your Mind.
Any relationship can flourish with constant communication.

Increasing Communication. 1 CD. (Running Time: 1 hour 15 minutes). 1980. 14.95 (978-0-9779472-6-3(2)) Health Wealth Inc.
Whether in love relationships, work relationships, family relationships, etc. - it seems so easy to get caught up in negative emotions and personality conflicts. Communication with ?difficult? people, or people we resist can become an unpleasant, destuctive downward spiral.Marc Reymont, in his clear and entertaining style, will capture your attention as he makes sense of how we get ourselves tangled up in unpleasant relationships with others. He shares the incredibly powerful, yet simple antidote to open the lines of communication without any effort. The technique applies equally as well to situations and conditions. Take the time to use this information - you will be astounded at the results!Without a doubt, one of the most comprehensive, practical and useful recordings ever! No matter what the "problems" seem to be, the realizations you will make with this lecture will turn those problems into their own solutions. Take control over your ability to positively interact and effectively communicate with others! A perfect introduction into truth teachings!"You don't have to feel trapped in any situation. You don't have to feel trapped in any habit or any circumstance. Right now you can gian your Spiritual Freedom with this meditation, as you turn within. You can reverse ANY situation, you can reposition yourself now in consciousness, where it all begins..." - Marc Reymont, New Age Awareness Foundation.

***Increasing Efficiency.** L. Ron Hubbard. (ENG.). 2002. audio compact disk 15.00 (978-1-4031-1431-0(5)) Bridge Pubns Inc.

***Increasing Efficiency.** L. Ron Hubbard. (RUS.). 2010. audio compact disk 15.00 (978-1-4031-7392-8(3)); audio compact disk 15.00 (978-1-4031-7384-3(2)); audio compact disk 15.00 (978-1-4031-7385-0(0)); audio compact disk 15.00 (978-1-4031-7387-4(7)); audio compact disk 15.00 (978-1-4031-7394-2(X)); audio compact disk 15.00 (978-1-4031-7388-1(5)); audio compact disk 15.00 (978-1-4031-7396-6(6)); audio compact disk 15.00 (978-1-4031-7383-6(4)); audio compact disk 15.00 (978-1-4031-7391-1(5)); audio compact disk 15.00 (978-1-4031-7395-9(8)); audio compact disk 15.00 (978-1-4031-7390-4(7)); audio compact disk 15.00 (978-1-4031-7389-8(3)); audio compact disk 15.00 (978-1-4031-7382-9(6)); audio compact disk 15.00 (978-1-4031-7386-7(9)); audio compact disk 15.00 (978-1-4031-7393-5(1)); audio compact disk 15.00 (978-1-4031-7381-2(8)) Bridge Pubns Inc.

Increasing Faith's Effectiveness. Elbert Willis. 1 cass. (Faith School Ser.: Vol. 2). 4.00 Fill the Gap.

Increasing Negotiating Skills Without Manipulation. Somers H. White. 8 cass. (Running Time: 60 min. per cass.). 200.00 (C122) S White.
Learn how to negotiate so both parties win.

Increasing Self-Confidence - Self-Esteem. Norman J. Caldwell. Read by Norman J. Caldwell. Ed. by Achieve Now Institute Staff. 1 cass. (Running Time: 20 min.). (Self-Directed Improvement Ser.). 1988. 9.97 (978-1-56273-058-1(4)) My Mothers Pub.
Build confidence & self-esteem rapidly.

Increasing Self-Esteem: By Transforming Critical Voices. Linda L. Fudold. 1 cass. 1997. 12.95 (978-1-884605-06-2(0)) Genesis II.

Increasing Self-Esteem: Echotech. Eldon Taylor. Read by Eldon Taylor. Ed. by Leslie Brice. 1 cass. (Running Time: 1 hr.). 1992. 19.95 (978-1-56705-001-1(8)) Gateways Inst.
Self improvement.

Increasing Spiritual Assurance Series, Set. Elbert Willis. 4 cass. 13.00 Fill the Gap.

Increasing Student Spelling Achievement, Set. Rebecca Sitton. Read by Rebecca Sitton. 6 cass. (Running Time: 7 hr.). (J). (gr. 1-8). 1994. 75.00 (978-1-886397-03-3(1)) Bureau of Educ.
Live audio workshop including 6 cassettes & a comprehensive resource handbook.

Increasing Student Spelling Achievement Not Just on Test, but in Daily Writing Across the Curriculum, Set. Rebecca Sitton. 6 cass. (Running Time: 4 hr. 47 min.). (J). (gr. 1-8). 1998. 75.00 Incl. handbk. (978-1-886397-20-0(1)) Bureau of Educ.

Increasing the Effectiveness of paraprofessionals & Classroom Teachers Working Together: Highly Effective Strategies for Inclusive Classrooms. Susan Fitzell. 2007. audio compact disk 95.00 (978-1-886397-82-8(1)) Bureau of Educ.

Increasing the Flow of Favor see Aumentando el Fluir del Favor

Increasing the Success of Your Title I Students Using Integrated Reading & Writing Strategies, Set. Mary B. Seaborg. Read by Mary B. Seaborg. 6 cass. (Running Time: 3 hr. 42 min.). (J). (gr. 1-5). 1997. 75.00 Incl. resource hdbk. (978-1-886397-11-8(2)) Bureau of Educ.
Live audio seminar.

Increasing Your Energy Level. Norman J. Caldwell. Read by Norman J. Caldwell. Ed. by Achieve Now Institute Staff. 1 cass. (Running Time: 20 min.). (Better Health Ser.). 1988. 9.97 (978-1-56273-052-9(5)) My Mothers Pub.
Not more energy - tap your highest energy source - inner-mind high energy. It's so close you can feel it!.

Increasing Your Persuasive Power. Mac Hammond. 1 CD. (Running Time: 1 hr). 2005. audio compact disk 5.00 (978-1-57399-258-9(5)) Mac Hammond.

Increasing Your Speed & Accuracy. 1 cass. (Martial Arts Programming Ser.). 12.50 (978-0-87554-193-8(3), K103) Valley Sun.
You react instantly & accurately. You draw upon your total awareness in kicking & punching. Your perception becomes sharper & more focused. You make progress with each training session. Your techniques are focused & accurate now. You relax & your speed & accuracy increase greatly.

Increasing Your Students' Science Achievement. Perf. by Jack Hassard. 6 cass. (Running Time: 4 hrs. 1 min.). (YA). (gr. 6-12). 2000. pap. bk. & wbk. ed. 85.00 (978-1-886397-35-4(X)) Bureau of Educ.
Live workshop.

Increasing Your Success. John Gray. 2 cass. (Running Time: 2 hrs.). 1996. 17.95 (978-1-886095-13-7(2)) Genesis Media Grp.

Incredible Adventures of Jack Flanders. Meatball Fulton. Read by Robert Lorick. Music by Tim Clark. 5 cass. (Running Time: 5 hrs.). (Jack Flanders Ser.). 30.00 set. (JFS) ZBS Ind.

Incredible Adventures of Jack Flanders. unabr. ed. Meatball Fulton. Read by Robert Lorick et al. 5 cass. (Running Time: 5 hrs.). Dramatization. 1981. 29.95 Set. (978-1-881137-11-5(2)); audio compact disk 35.00 (978-1-881137-44-3(9)) ZBS Found.
Seated in the comfortable arms of a green velvet chair, Jack is transported to a strange, other-world of magic, pirates & sorcery.

Incredible Bath Time Revue. Perf. by Brooks Caldwell et al. 1 cass. (Running Time: 30 min.). (Live! from Possumtrot, USA Ser.: No. 1). (J). (ps-2). 1994. 10.95 (978-1-888137-01-9(0)) LuvTwoLisn.
"Live! from Possumtrot, USA" audio adventures are positive, supportive tapes for kids ages 3-7. While the songs & stories entertain, they encourage imagination, friendship & caring. "The Incredible Bath Time Revue" (Songs for tubbing or anytime). Children join Professor Pip & the Possumtrot Players in the Possumtrot Theater for a wet & wonderful show about the joys of taking a bath.

Incredible Bongo Band. unabr. ed. 2004. audio compact disk 19.95 (978-1-59007-408-4(4)) New Millenn Enter.

Incredible Creatures That Defy Evolution Audio Special. Interview. Executive Producer Steve Greisen. Prod. by Reel Productions. Narrated by Jobe Martin. 1 CD. (Running Time: 30 mins.). 2002. audio compact disk 9.95 (978-0-9707422-4-7(X)) Reel Prodns.
30-minute CD Audio Special Fast paced and professionally produced this audio special looks into the remarkable designs of animals that cannot possible by explained by evolution. Learn about a bird that as a non-swimmer flies over 4000 miles of ocean and lands right on target everytime NEVER getting lost.Learn about a beattle that can produce fire to defend itself.Learn about some evolutionary ideas that are still in the public school textbooks even though long ago they were debunked as frauds!.

Incredible First Six Years. Thomas Amshay & Christina Clement. Read by Thomas Amshay. 4 cass. (Running Time: 4 hrs.). 1987. 40.00 (978-0-939401-00-0(2)) RFTS Prod.

Incredible Gospel. Contrib. by Various Artists. 2008. audio compact disk 11.99 (978-5-557-41366-4(9)) Maranatha Music.

Incredible Journey. Sheila Burnford. Read by Megan Follows. 2 cass. (Running Time: 3 hrs. 10 mins.). (J). 2000. 18.00 (978-0-7366-9027-0(1)) Books on Tape.
A Labrador retriever, an English bull terrier & a Siamese cat trek 300 miles across Canada to reunite with their family. With instinct & love as their only guides, these pets face all kinds of peril as they try to make their way home.

Incredible Journey. Sheila Burnford. 3 cass. (Running Time: 187 min.). (J). (gr. 3-5). 2001. audio compact disk 28.00 (978-0-8072-0508-2(7), Listening Lib) Random Audio Pubg.

Incredible Journey. Laura Simms. As told by Laura Simms. 1 cass. (Running Time: 42 min.). (J). (gr. k-5). 1981. 9.95 (978-0-939065-01-1(0), GW 1001) Gentle Wind.
Folktales from around the world for young children. Includes "Mouse's Children," "The Gollywolf," "Delgadina," "The Squeaky Door," "Sunman," "Little Burned Face," "Brolga".

Incredible Journey. Read by Laura Simms. (J). (gr. k-5). 1981. audio compact disk 14.95 (978-0-939065-82-0(7)) Gentle Wind.

Incredible Journey. unabr. ed. Sheila Burnford. Read by Megan Follows. 3 CDs. (Running Time: 3 hrs. 7 mins.). (Middle Grade Cassette Librariestm Ser.). (J). (gr. 5-9). 2004. audio compact disk 30.00 (978-0-8072-1168-7(0), S YA 162 CD, Listening Lib); pap. bk. 29.00 (978-0-8072-8322-6(3), YA162SP, Listening Lib); 23.00 (978-0-8072-8321-9(5), LL0181, Listening Lib) Random Audio Pubg.
A Labrador retriever, an English bull terrier & a Siamese cat trek 300 miles across Canada to reunite with their family. With instinct & love as their only guides, these pets face all kinds of peril as they try to make their way home.

Incredible Journey. unabr. ed. Sheila Burnford. Read by Megan Follows. 3 CDs. (Running Time: 3 hrs 7 mins.). (ENG.). (J). (gr. 3). 2006. audio compact disk 14.99 (978-0-307-28402-0(6), Listening Lib) Pub: Random Audio Pubg. Dist(s): Random

Incredible Journey CD Series. 2003. audio compact disk 48.00 (978-1-59834-027-3(1)) Walk Thru the Bible.

Incredible Self-Confidence. Dick Sutphen. 1 cass. (Running Time: 1 hr.). (RX17 Ser.). 14.98 (978-0-87554-318-5(9), RX127); cass. & video 59.95 incl. 4 audio cass. & 1 video cass. (978-0-87554-332-1(4), PK105) Valley Sun.
Includes: Incredible Self-Confidence Video Hypnosis; Instruction/Motivation Tape; The 25 Best Ways to Negotiate What You Want; Powerful Person; & Incredible Self-Confidence.

Incredible Shrinking Kid. unabr. ed. Megan McDonald. Read by Nancy Cartwright. (Running Time: 45 mins.). (Stink Ser.). (ENG.). (J). (gr. 1). 2005. audio compact disk 16.00 (978-0-307-20638-1(6), ImaginStudio) Pub: Random Audio Pubg. Dist(s): Random
Every morning, Judy measures Stink, and it's always the same: 3 feet, 8 inches tall. Stink feels like even the class newt is growing faster than he is. Then one day, the ruler reads - 3 feet, 7 and three-quarter inches! Can it be? Is Stink shrinking? Stink tries everything to look like he's growing, but wearing up-and-down stripes and spiking his hair don't seem to be fooling anybody into thinking he's taller. What would James Madison, Stink's hero (and the shortest person to ever serve as President of the United States) do?.

Incredible Shrinking Man. unabr. ed. Richard Matheson. Read by Yuri Rasovsky. 6 cass. 2006. 54.95 (978-0-7861-3792-3(4)); audio compact disk 63.00 (978-0-7861-7576-5(1)) Blckstn Audio.

Incredible Shrinking Man. unabr. ed. Richard Matheson. Read by Yuri Rasovsky. 1 MP3-CD. (Running Time: 8 hrs.). 2008. 29.95 (978-0-7861-7851-3(5)); 19.95 (978-1-4332-1259-8(5)); audio compact disk 19.95 (978-1-4332-1260-4(9)) Blckstn Audio.

Incredible Voyage. unabr. collector's ed. Tristan Jones. Read by Richard Brown. 10 cass. (Running Time: 15 hrs.). 1990. 80.00 (978-0-7366-1826-7(0), 2662) Books on Tape.
In a daring six-year voyage by sail, Tristan Jones traveled from the Dead Sea, the lowest body of water in the world, to the Andes Mountains & Lake Titicac, the highest - an epic & singular journey of exploration & discovery. Along the way he was thrown in jail, attacked by Arabs, rescued by Ethiopians, nearly killed by a rat, saved by a crocodile. He found a desolate island off Colombia, full of political prisoners. In Cartagena, it was drug dealers, in Zanzibar assassins...& thieves almost everywhere.

Incredible Westward Movement. Scripts. 1 cass. or 1 CD. (Running Time: 25 mins.). 2000. pap. bk. & tchr. ed. 29.95 Bad Wolf Pr.
Takes you westward across the ever-expanding frontier, from life in the wilderness of Kentucky, to farming on the prairies, to trapping & trading in the far west. Meet familiar friends (e.g. Daniel Boone, Lewis & Clark & Sacagawea) & make new ones (e.g. Susan Shelly Magath & Stagecoach Mary). Also includes the excitement of the Louisiana Purchase, the challenges of the Oregon, Santa Fe & Old Spanish Trails, the mixed blessings of the Transcontinental Railroad & the misery of the Trail of Tears. Sheet music available.

***Incredible World of Horace Ford.** 2010. audio compact disk (978-1-59171-185-8(1)) Falcon Picture.

Incredibles: Audio Story Adventure. Created by Walt Disney Records Staff. 2004. (978-0-7634-2155-7(3)) Walt Disney.

Incredibly Revolting Ghost! Ghosthunters & the Incredibly Revolting Ghost! unabr. ed. Cornelia Funke. Read by John Beach. 2 CDs. (Running Time: 2 hrs. 3 mins.). (Ghosthunters Ser.: No. 1). (J). (ps-3). 2006. audio compact disk 24.00 (978-0-7393-3577-2(4), Listening Lib); 23.00 (978-0-7393-3576-5(6), Listening Lib) Pub: Random Audio Pubg. Dist(s): Random
Look out for ghost goo! Dripping sticky green slime wherever it goes, an "ASG" (that's Averagely Spooky Ghost) is hiding out in Tom's cellar. Why? Because it's being haunted, too - by a much bigger, way badder Incredibly Revolting Ghost ("IRG," for anyone new to ghouls). And the IRG is the kind of ghost that uses its head - as a ginormous bellowing bowling ball, gross! Good thing for Tom his grandma's best friend just happens to be a world-famous ghosthunter.

Incredibly Revolting Ghost! Ghosthunters & the Incredibly Revolting Ghost! unabr. ed. Cornelia Funke. Read by John Beach. (Running Time: 7380 sec.). (Ghosthunters Ser.: No. 1). (ENG.). (J). (gr. 1). 2006. audio compact disk 19.95 (978-0-7393-3103-3(5), Listening Lib) Pub: Random Audio Pubg. Dist(s): Random

Incredibly Strange Music. A. Juno & V. Vale. 1 CD. (Running Time: 1 hr.). audio compact disk 12.95 (978-0-940642-34-8(4)) Greatapes.

Incredulity of Father Brown. unabr. ed. G. K. Chesterton. Read by Frederick Davidson. 6 cass. (Running Time: 8 hrs. 30 mins.). (Father Brown Mystery Ser.). 1992. 44.95 (978-0-7861-0126-9(1), 1112) Blckstn Audio.
Father Brown's powers of detection allow him to sit beside the immortal Holmes but he is also, to quote Rufus King, "in all senses a most pleasantly fascinating human being". You will be enchanted by the scandalously innocent man of the cloth, with the umbrella, who exhibits such uncanny insight into ingeniously tricky human problems.

Incredulity of Father Brown. unabr. collector's ed. G. K. Chesterton. Read by Richard Green. 8 cass. (Running Time: 8 hrs.). (Father Brown Mystery Ser.). 1986. 48.00 (978-0-7366-0893-0(1), 1837) Books on Tape.
Sent to officiate a dispute in South America, Father Brown lands in the middle of a revolution, recognized, attacked & left for dead. In fact, everyone thinks he is dead, until he rises from his coffin, creating no end of trouble with the natives... for they certainly know a resurrection when they see one!.

Increment. unabr. ed. David Ignatius. Narrated by Dick Hill. 11 CDs. (Running Time: 13 hrs. 30 mins. 0 sec.). (ENG.). 2009. audio compact disk 34.99 (978-1-4001-1069-8(6)); audio compact disk 24.99 (978-1-4001-6069-3(3)); audio compact disk 69.99 (978-1-4001-4069-5(2)) Pub: Tantor Media. Dist(s): IngramPubServ

Incubus Dreams. unabr. ed. Laurell K. Hamilton. Read by Cynthia Holloway. (Running Time: 30 hrs.). (Anita Blake, Vampire Hunter Ser.: No. 12). 2004. 44.25 (978-1-59710-400-5(0), 1597104000, BADLE); 29.95 (978-1-59710-401-2(9), 1597104019, BAD); 44.25 (978-1-59335-812-9(1), 1593358121, Brlnc Audio MP3 Lib); 29.95 (978-1-59335-678-1(1), 1593356781, Brilliance MP3); audio compact disk 155.25 (978-1-59086-274-2(0), 1590862740, BriAudCD Unabrid); audio compact disk 59.95 (978-1-59600-324-8(3), 1596003243) Brilliance Audio.
As consultant to the Regional Preternatural Crime Investigation Unit, Anita's called in on what appears to be a case involving a serial killer - a vampire serial killer - who may be preying on strippers. She's sure that none of the local vamps are responsible - but her judgment may be clouded by a conflict of interest. For she is, after all, the consort of Jean-Claude, the ever-intoxicating Master Vampire of the City - something that both her human friends and her ex, the alpha werewolf Richard, are quick to point out. Surrounded by suspicion, overwhelmed by her attempts to control the primal lusts that continue to wrack her as a result of her passionate contacts with vampire, werewolf, and the shapeshifter Micah, Anita does something unprecedented. She calls for help.

Incubus Dreams. unabr. abr. ed. Laurell K. Hamilton. Read by Cynthia Holloway. 8 cass. (Running Time: 12 hrs.). (Anita Blake, Vampire Hunter Ser.: No. 12). 2004. 87.25 (978-1-59086-205-6(8), 1590862058, BrilAudUnabridg); 32.95 (978-1-59086-204-9(X), 159086204X, BAU); audio compact disk 38.95 (978-1-59086-273-5(2), 1590862732, Bril Audio CD Unabri) Brilliance Audio.

***Incurable.** John Marsden. Read by Mikaela Martin. (Running Time: 7 hrs.). (Ellie Chronicles). (YA). 2009. 59.99 (978-1-74214-336-1(9), 9781742143361) Pub: Bolinda Pubng AUS. Dist(s): Bolinda Pub Inc

Incurable. unabr. ed. John Marsden. Read by Mikaela Martin. (Running Time: 25200 sec.). (Ellie Chronicles: Bk. 2). (YA). (gr. 7). 2006. audio compact disk 83.95 (978-1-74093-765-8(1)) Pub: Bolinda Pubng AUS. Dist(s): Bolinda Pub Inc

Incurable. unabr. ed. John Marsden. Read by Mikaela Martin. (Running Time: 7 hrs.). (Ellie Chronicles). (YA). 2009. 43.95 (978-1-74214-114-5(5), 9781742141145) Pub: Bolinda Pubng AUS. Dist(s): Bolinda Pub Inc

Indecent Exposure. unabr. ed. Tom Sharpe. Read by David Case. 7 cass. (Running Time: 10 hrs. 30 min.). 1992. 56.00 (978-0-7366-2178-6(4), 2975) Books on Tape.
Sharpe's second South African novel following "Riotous Assembly." No faction is safe from Sharpe's tongue. "Two of the funniest books in modern fiction." (B-O-T Editorial Review Board).

Indecent Obsession. unabr. ed. Colleen McCullough. Read by Wanda McCaddon. 8 cass. (Running Time: 12 hrs.). 1982. 64.00 (978-0-7366-0579-3(7), 1549) Books on Tape.
The time is 1945, the setting Base Fifteen, a military hospital in the Pacific. The war is over & the remaining staff & patients await evacuation. In the smallest & most remote ward 5 men - human flotsam the war has thrown together - cling like a pracarious family around the strong & caring figure of their nurse, Sister Honour Langtry. Into this uneasy equilibrium comes a sixth patient. Aiming only to avoid involvement, he ironically falls in love with Langtry. Love means commitment, & he must choose between laying down & picking up responsibilities.

Indelible. Karin Slaughter. Read by Deborah Hazlett. 8 cass. (Grant County Ser.: Bk. 4). 69.95 (978-0-7927-3292-1(8), CSL 683); audio compact disk 94.95 (978-0-7927-3293-8(6), SLD 683); audio compact disk 29.95 (978-0-7927-3294-5(4), CMP 683) AudioGO.

***Indelible.** abr. ed. Karin Slaughter. Read by Becky Ann Baker. (ENG.). 2004. (978-0-06-078274-0(9), Harper Audio); (978-0-06-081377-2(6), Harper Audio) HarperCollins Pubs.

Indemnity Only. unabr. ed. Sara Paretsky. Read by Donada Peters. 8 cass. (Running Time: 8 hrs.). (V. I. Warshawski Novel Ser.). 1992. 64.00 (978-0-7366-2282-0(9), 3069) Books on Tape.
It's July in Chicago & all V. I. Warshawski wants is to go home & beat the heat. But she can't. She's got a late night meeting with a potential client, the

head of Chicago's biggest bank. The job seems simple enough: find his son's missing girlfriend.

Independence see Poems from Black Africa

Independence! abr. ed. Dana Fuller Ross, pseud. Read by Sambrook Erickson. 4 cass. (Running Time: 6 hrs.). (Wagon West Ser.: No. 1). 2002. 25.00 (978-1-58807-006-7(9)) Am Pubng Inc.
In 1837, a fiery young widow, Claudia Humphries, and a bold wagon master, Sam Brentwood, discover that it is their destiny to command the first leg of the remarkable journey to Independence, Missouri. Traveling under secret orders from President Andrew Jackson, Brentwood's task is to win a desperate race against England and Russia in order to bring the promised land of the Pacific Northwest under the American flag.

Independence! abr. ed. Dana Fuller Ross, pseud. Read by Sambrook Erikson. 5 vols. (Wagons West Ser.: No. 1). 2003. audio compact disk (978-1-58807-821-6(3)) Am Pubng Inc.

Independence! abr. ed. Dana Fuller Ross, pseud. Read by Sambrook Erikson. 5 vols. (Wagon West Ser.: No. 1). 2003. audio compact disk 30.00 (978-1-58807-343-3(2)) Am Pubng Inc.

Independence! abr. ed. Dana Fuller Ross, pseud. Read by Phil Gigante. (Running Time: 5 hrs.). (Wagons West Ser.: No. 1). 2009. audio compact disk 14.99 (978-1-4418-1661-0(5), 9781441816610, BACD) Brilliance Audio.

Independence. unabr. ed. Nathaniel Branden. 1 cass. (Running Time: 44 min.). 12.95 (812) J Norton Pubs.
Authentic independence does not entail indifference to the response of others, & no one can achieve it in all areas of their lives. The true independent strives to understand the world through his own eyes, rather than the opinions of others.

Independence! unabr. ed. Dana Fuller Ross, pseud. Read by Phil Gigante. (Running Time: 11 hrs.). (Wagons West Ser.: No. 1). 2009. 24.99 (978-1-4418-1657-3(7), 9781441816573, Brilliance MP3); 24.99 (978-1-4418-1659-7(3), 9781441816597, BAD); 39.97 (978-1-4418-1658-0(5), 9781441816580, Brinc Audio MP3 Lib); 39.97 (978-1-4418-1660-3(7), 9781441816603, BADLE); audio compact disk 29.99 (978-1-4418-1655-9(0), 9781441816559, Bril Audio CD Unabri); audio compact disk 82.97 (978-1-4418-1656-6(9), 9781441816566, BriAudCD Unabrid) Brilliance Audio.

Independence Day. unabr. ed. Richard Ford. Read by Richard Poe. 12 Cass. (Running Time: 20 Hrs). 44.95 (978-1-4025-2816-3(7)) Recorded Bks.

Independence Day. unabr. ed. Richard Ford. Narrated by Richard Poe. 14 cass. (Running Time: 20 hrs.). 1998. 112.00 (978-0-7887-2601-9(3), 95506E7) Recorded Bks.
Relentlessly thoughtful, heart-wrenching, yet hilarious portrait of an ordinary American man.

Independence Day in the United States. unabr. ed. Maria Latona. Ed. by Marybeth Hageman. 3 cass. (English for You! Ser.). 1998. 39.95 Set, incl. tchr's. guide, student texts, worksheets. (48003) Recorded Bks.
ESL students will understand & enjoy celebrations along with their native speaker friends. Student texts contain key vocabulary & a wide range of exercises including: conversation practice, comprehension, discussion, writing, grammar, & critical thinking.

Independence Day: The Biblical Foundation of a Free Nation: Lamentations 5:21. Ed Young. (J). 1979. 4.95 (978-0-7417-1068-0(4), A0068) Win Walk.

Independence of Miss Mary Bennet. unabr. ed. Colleen McCullough. Narrated by Jen Taylor. 11 CDs. (Running Time: 13 hrs. 45 mins.). 2009. audio compact disk 99.95 (978-0-7927-6018-4(2), Chivers Sound Lib) AudioGO.

Independence of Miss Mary Bennet. unabr. ed. Colleen McCullough. Read by Jen Taylor. (Running Time: 13 hrs. 45 mins.). 2009. 59.95 (978-0-7927-6169-3(3), Chivers Sound Lib); 59.95 (978-0-7927-6168-6(5), Chivers Sound Lib) AudioGO.

Independent American. unabr. ed. Walt Whitman. 1 cass. (Running Time: 30 min). (Gilbert Highet Ser.). 9.95 (23303) J Norton Pubs.
Walt Whitman's poem on the Fourth of July is read & discussed & how "The Gettysburgh Address" was written & delivered is also analyzed.

Independent Fluency Practice Passages: Fiction & Nonfiction. Newmark Learning, LLC. (Fluency Instruction Practice Ser.). (gr. 1). 2009. audio compact disk (978-1-60719-084-4(2)) Newmark Learn.

Independent Fluency Practice Passages: Fiction & Nonfiction. Newmark Learning, LLC. (Fluency Instruction Practice Ser.). (gr. 2). 2009. audio compact disk (978-1-60719-085-1(0)) Newmark Learn.

Independent Fluency Practice Passages: Fiction & Nonfiction. Newmark Learning, LLC. (Fluency Instruction Practice Ser.). (gr. 3). 2009. audio compact disk (978-1-60719-086-8(9)) Newmark Learn.

Independent Fluency Practice Passages: Monologues & Dialogues. Newmark Learning, LLC. (Fluency Instruction Practice Ser.). (gr. 1). 2009. audio compact disk (978-1-60719-081-3(8)) Newmark Learn.

Independent Fluency Practice Passages: Monologues & Dialogues. Newmark Learning, LLC. (Fluency Instruction Practice Ser.). (gr. 2). 2009. audio compact disk (978-1-60719-082-0(6)) Newmark Learn.

Independent Fluency Practice Passages: Monologues & Dialogues. Newmark Learning, LLC. (Fluency Instruction Practice Ser.). (gr. 3). 2009. audio compact disk (978-1-60719-083-7(4)) Newmark Learn.

Independent Scholars. 1 cass. (Running Time: 1 hr.). 10.95 (F0320B090, HarperThor) HarpC GBR.

Independents. (Running Time: 55 min.). 2003. audio compact disk 9.99 (978-5-559-97626-6(1)) Pub: Pt of Grace Ent. Dist(s): STL Dist NA

Independents Day: Awakening the American Spirit. Lou Dobbs. (Running Time: 5 hrs.). (ENG.). (YA). (gr. 12). 2007. audio compact disk 29.95 (978-0-14-314257-7(7), PengAudBks) Penguin Grp USA.

Indescribable. Contrib. by Louie Giglio. 2008. audio compact disk 14.99 (978-5-557-44623-5(0)) Pt of Grace Ent.

Indestructible: The Unforgettable Story of a Marine Hero at the Battle of Iwo Jima. Jack Lucas. Read by Lloyd James. Told to D. K. Drum. Frwd. by Bob Dole. (Running Time: 19800 sec.). 2006. 44.95 (978-0-7861-4560-7(9)) Blckstn Audio.

Indestructible: The Unforgettable Story of a Marine Hero at the Battle of Iwo Jima. unabr. ed. Jack Lucas. Read by Lloyd James. Frwd. by Bob Dole. 5 cass. (Running Time: 19800 sec.). 2006. 29.95 (978-0-7861-4389-4(4)); audio compact disk 29.95 (978-0-7861-7478-2(1)) Blckstn Audio.

Indestructible: The Unforgettable Story of a Marine Hero of Iwo Jima. Jack Lucas. Read by Lloyd James. Told to Drum D K. Frwd. by Bob Dole. (Running Time: 19800 sec.). 2006. audio compact disk 55.00 (978-0-7861-7078-4(6)) Blckstn Audio.

Indestructible: The Unforgettable Story of a Marine Hero of Iwo Jima. unabr. ed. Jack Lucas. Read by Lloyd James. Told to D. K. Drum. Frwd. by Bob Dole. (Running Time: 19800 sec.). 2006. audio compact disk 29.95 (978-0-7861-7809-4(4)) Blckstn Audio.

Indestructible Relationships/Real Liberation. Marianne Williamson. Read by Marianne Williamson. 1 cass. (Running Time: 90 mins.). (Lectures on a Course in Miracles). 1999. 10.00 (978-1-56170-233-6(1), M736) Hay House.

India & Pakistan. abr. ed. Gregory Kozlowski. Read by Peter Hackes. Ed. by Mike Hassell. 2 cass. (Running Time: 3 hrs.). Dramatization. (World's Political Hot Spots Ser.). (YA). (gr. 11 up). 1992. 17.95 (978-0-938935-96-4(8), 10361) Knowledge Prod.
As one of the world's most ancient civilizations, India presents a rich mosaic of political, religious, & cultural influences. In 1947, this vast nation was split into two nations, Pakistan & India, to separate battling Hindus & Moslems.

India & Pakistan. unabr. ed. Gregory Kozlowski. Read by Peter Hackes. Ed. by Mike Hassell. Prod. by Pat Childs. (Running Time: 10800 sec.). (World's Political Hot Spots Ser.). 2006. audio compact disk 25.95 (978-0-7861-6449-3(2)) Pub: Blckstn Audio. Dist(s): NetLibrary CO

India & the Saints. Frederick Spiegelberg. 2 cass. (Running Time: 49 min.). 1964. 18.00 set. (08801) Big Sur Tapes.

India Fan. unabr. collector's ed. Victoria Holt. Read by Donada Peters. 9 cass. (Running Time: 13 hrs. 30 min.). 1991. 72.00 (978-0-7366-2010-9(9), 2826) Books on Tape.
Framling, a grand estate, stands on a hill dominating the village, just as Lady Harriet Framling, the occupant, reigns over the villagers. Farmers & workers stand aside to let her carriage pass. Close by lives Drusilla Delany, the vicar's daughter. Though impoverished, she is often invited to Framling for tea. The Framling children do not like Drusilla & resent her being forced on them. They arrange for her to receive a beautiful jeweled fan. Drusilla is thrilled - until she learns the fan carries a curse that travels with it from owner to owner.

India, Folk Music. unabr. ed. 1 cass. 1994. 12.95 (978-0-88432-389-1(7), C11131) J Norton Pubs.

India, Pakistan, Urdu New Testament. (URD.). 2002. 35.00 (978-1-57449-199-9(7), 107716) Pub: Hosanna NM. Dist(s): Am Bible

Indian Boyhood. unabr. ed. Charles Alexander Eastman. 4 cass. (Running Time: 6 hrs.). 2003. audio compact disk 34.95 (978-1-58472-588-6(5), In Aud) Sound Room.

Indian Boyhood, Set. unabr. ed. Charles A. Eastman. Read by Jim Killavey. 5 cass. (Running Time: 7 hrs. 30 min.). (J). (gr. 6 up). 1994. 35.00 in vinyl album. (C-260) Jimcin Record.
A first-hand account of the life of a young Sioux boy until the age of fifteen.

Indian Control of Indian Education. 1 cass. (Running Time: 30 min.). 8.00 (HO-80-05-14, HarperThor) HarpC GBR.

Indian Country: A Novel. Philip Caputo. Read by Philip Caputo. 2 cass. (Running Time: 1 hr. 46 min.). 1988. 13.95 (978-1-55644-289-6(0), 8031) Am Audio Prose.
Caputo reads the concluing chapters of Indian Country, in which Christian Starkmann, a Vietnam veteran suffering from post-traumatic stress disorder begins to find his way forward into mental & spiritual health.

Indian Creek Chronicles: A Winter in the Bitterrrot Wilderness. unabr. collector's ed. Peter Fromm. Read by Michael Kramer. 7 cass. (Running Time: 7 hrs.). 1995. 42.00 (978-0-7366-3017-7(1), 3701) Books on Tape.
A winter in the wilderness makes a man out of the author. True life adventure.

Indian Elections Heat Up; The Indian Elections. unabr. ed. Julian C. Hollick. 1 cass. (Running Time: 60 min.). 1989. 15.00 (978-1-56709-026-0(5), 1055) Indep Broadcast.
Four reports on the dominant issues of the November 1989 general elections in India.

Indian Elephant Tea. Prod. by Big Kidz Band Staff. 1 CD. (Running Time: 40 min.). 2003. audio compact disk 14.98 (978-1-57940-086-6(8)) Rounder Records.

Indian Heroes & Great Chieftains. abr. ed. Charles A. Eastman. Read by Lorenzo Baca. 2 cass. (Running Time: 3 hrs.). 1995. 16.95 (978-0-944993-82-8(6)) Audio Lit.
Biographical portraits of great Indian leaders, Red Cloud, Spotted Tail, Crazy Horse, Sitting Bull & Chief Joseph - from the pen of Charles Eastman, a Santee Sioux born in 1858. Eastman was raised by his Indian family & eventually followed his converted Christian father along "the white man's trail," attending Dartmouth & becoming a government physician at the Pine Ridge Indian Agency. Eastman provides insights & vignettes about these leaders which allow us to see the human reality behind their legendary Indian names.

Indian Hills Horror. Anne Schraff. Narrated by Larry A. McKeever. (Horror Ser.). (J). 2001. 10.95 (978-1-58659-077-2(4)); audio compact disk 14.95 (978-1-58659-335-3(8)) Artesian.

Indian in the Cupboard. Lynne Reid Banks. Read by Lynne Reid Banks. 3 cass. (Running Time: 4 hrs. 8 mins.). (Indian in the Cupboard Ser.: No. 1). (J). (gr. 4-7). 2000. 24.00 (978-0-7366-9075-1(1)) Books on Tape.
Something is magical about the cupboard Omri's brother gave him for his birthday.

Indian in the Cupboard. unabr. ed. Lynne Reid Banks. Read by Lynne Reid Banks. 3 cass. (Running Time: 3 hrs.). (Indian in the Cupboard Ser.: No. 1). (J). (gr. 4-7). 1997. 30.00 (LL 3075) AudioGO.

Indian in the Cupboard. unabr. ed. Lynne Reid Banks. Read by Lynne Reid Banks. 8 cass. (Running Time: 8 hrs.). (Indian in the Cupboard Ser.). (J). (gr. 4-7). 1996. 38.00 (3957) Books on Tape.
Includes "The Secret of the Indian": When Omri's friend Patrick returns from a trip back in time to the Wild West, he brings with him a deadly cyclone that threatens to level London; & "The Mystery of the Cupboard": Omri discovers an old journal with clues that can help him solve the mystery of the cupboard's magic.

Indian in the Cupboard. unabr. ed. Lynne Reid Banks. Read by Lynne Reid Banks. 8 cass. (Running Time: 12 hrs.). (Indian in the Cupboard Ser.). (J). (gr. 4-7). 1996. 48.00 (3944) Books on Tape.
The two titles that are part of the series: "the Indian in the cupboard", when Omri discovers he can bring his toys to life & "the Return of the Indian" when he sends his indian off to fight in the French & Indian War.

Indian in the Cupboard. unabr. ed. Lynne Reid Banks. Read by Lynne Reid Banks. 3 cass. (Running Time: 4 hrs. 22 mins.). (Indian in the Cupboard Ser.). (J). (gr. 3-7). 1990. 30.00 (978-0-8072-7236-7(1), YA809CX, Listening Lib) Random Audio Pubg.

Indian in the Cupboard. unabr. ed. Lynne Reid Banks. Read by Lynne Reid Banks. 3 vols. (Running Time: 4 hrs. 22 mins.). (Indian in the Cupboard Ser.). (J). (gr. 3-7). 2004. pap. bk. 36.00 (978-0-8072-7308-1(2), YA809SP, Listening Lib) Random Audio Pubg.

Indian in the Cupboard, Set. Lynne Reid Banks. 11 cass. (Indian in the Cupboard Ser.). (J). (gr. 4-7). 1996. 59.95 Set. (978-0-8072-7781-2(9), Listening Lib) Random Audio Pubg.

Indian in the Cupboard, Set. unabr. ed. Lynne Reid Banks. Read by Lynne Reid Banks. 3 cass. (Running Time: 4 hrs. 30 min.). (Indian in the Cupboard Ser.). (J). (gr. 4-7). 1992. 23.95 (L176) Blckstn Audio.
Omri locks his little plastic Indian in an old medicine cabinet. The next morning, he opens his cupboard, &, to his astonishment, there inside, crouching in the darkest comer with knife raised in terror & defiance, is a miniature, live Indian brave.

Indian Killer. abr. ed. Sherman Alexie. Read by Sherman Alexie. 3 cass. (Running Time: 4 hrs. 30 min.). 1996. 21.95 (978-1-57453-119-0(0), 494447) Audio Lit.

Indian Melodies: For Violin. Created by Hal Leonard Corporation Staff. Candida Connolly. 2004. pap. bk. 19.95 (978-1-84761-154-3(0), 1847611540) Pub: Schott Music Corp. Dist(s): H Leonard

Indian Music. Leela Floyd. Ed. by Kenneth McLeish & Valerie McLeish. (Oxford Topics in Music Ser.). 1985. 14.95 (978-0-19-321340-1(0)) OUP.

Indian Pipes: A Martha's Vineyard Mystery. unabr. ed. Cynthia Riggs. Read by Davina Porter. (Running Time: 8 hrs. 30 mins.). 2009. 29.95 (978-1-4332-2873-5(4)); 54.95 (978-1-4332-2869-8(6)); audio compact disk 76.00 (978-1-4332-2870-4(X)) Blckstn Audio.

Indian Reorganization Act. 1 cass. (Running Time: 30 min.). 9.95 (G0180B090, HarperThor) HarpC GBR.

Indian Rhythms for Drumset. Pete Lockett. 2008. pap. bk. 24.95 (978-1-4234-5678-0(5), 1423456785) Pub: Hudson Music. Dist(s): H Leonard

Indian Summer. unabr. ed. Louise Brindley. Read by Marie McCarthy. 7 cass. (Running Time: 9 hrs. 15 min.). 1999. 76.95 (978-1-85903-261-9(3)) Pub: Magna Story GBR. Dist(s): Ulverscroft US
When her husband's affair with artist Francesca Delgado threatens to become headline news, Caroline Fraser rents a cottage on the north-east coast of Yorkshire, which local legend says is haunted by a woman in white. Intent on restoring the cottage to its former glory despite attempts by the enigmatic owner, Cameron McCauley to prevent her Caroline regains a sense of purpose & identity. Just as her resentment of McCauley turns more to understanding, her husband Felix reappears, desperate to save their marriage. Caroline must decide whether to rebuild the past, or hold on to her new future.

Indian Summer, Set. unabr. ed. William Dean Howells. Read by Flo Gibson. 6 cass. (Running Time: 9 hrs.). 1989. 24.95 (978-1-55685-126-1(X)) Audio Bk Con.
In Florence Italy a middle-aged american architect returns to resume his studies, recapture his past & to sort out his relationships with Mrs. Bowen & her Charge Imagene.

Indian Summer of an Uncle see Jeeves

Indian Wars. 1 cass. 10.00 Esstee Audios.
The troubled Great Plains & how the Indians fought the U.S.

Indiana Jones & the Kingdom of the Crystal Skull. movie tie-in unabr. ed. James Rollins. Read by L. J. Ganser. 7 CDs. (Running Time: 8 hrs. 30 mins.). (ENG.). 2008. audio compact disk 31.95 (978-0-7393-5898-6(7)) Pub: Random Audio Pubg. Dist(s): Random

Indians. Rick Steber. Illus. by Don Gray. 1 cass. (Tales of the Wild West Ser.: Vol. 3). 1987. bk. 9.95 (978-0-945134-53-4(3)) Bonanza Pub.

Indications & Values of Nuclear Cardiology Stress Testing. Read by George A. Beller. 1 cass. (Running Time: 90 min.). 1986. 12.00 (C8620) Amer Coll Phys.

Indictment. unabr. ed. Barry Reed. Narrated by George Guidall. 10 cass. (Running Time: 14 hrs. 45 mins.). 1994. 85.00 (978-0-7887-0157-3(6), 94379E7) Recorded Bks.
When a beautiful young woman is found dead on the outskirts of Boston, the District Attorney, who is running a Senatorial campaign, will stop at nothing to get an indictment. But soon police officers are hiding crucial evidence & FBI agents are listening in on conversations.

Indictment. unabr. collector's ed. Barry Reed. Read by Christopher Lane. 13 cass. (Running Time: 19 hrs. 30 min.). 1994. 104.00 (978-0-7366-2914-0(9), 3611) Books on Tape.
A prominent Boston surgeon, with no alibi for murder, is the prime target of an ambitious DA with an eye on the U.S. Senate.

Indigenous Strains in America Literature: Romanticism. unabr. ed. Elizabeth R. Bills. 1 cass. (Running Time: 25 mins.). 1963. 12.95 (23061) J Norton Pubs.
A discussion of the romantic ideals expressed by Cooper, Whitman, Hemingway, Thoreau & Emerson.

Indigenous Wisdom: A Peace Project Talking Circle. 2006. audio compact disk 15.00 (978-0-9771907-1-3(4)) Chanting Pr AK.

Indignation. Philip Roth. Read by Dick Hill. (Playaway Adult Fiction Ser.). (ENG.). 2009. 54.99 (978-1-60775-862-4(8)) Find a World.

Indignation. unabr. ed. Philip Roth. Read by Dick Hill. 1 MP3-CD. (Running Time: 5 hrs.). 2008. 39.25 (978-1-4233-6975-2(0), 9781423369752, Brinc Audio MP3 Lib); 39.25 (978-1-4233-6977-6(7), 9781423369776, BADLE); 24.95 (978-1-4233-6974-5(2), 9781423369745, Brilliance MP3); 24.95 (978-1-4233-6976-9(9), 9781423369769, BAD); audio compact disk 74.25 (978-1-4233-6973-8(4), 9781423369738, BriAudCD Unabrid); audio compact disk 26.95 (978-1-4233-6972-1(6), 9781423369721, Bril Audio CD Unabri) Brilliance Audio.

Indigo. Perf. by Ray Mitchell & Mike Harris. Created by Matthew Manning. Prod. by Stuart Wilde. 1 cass. 10.95 (CN612) White Dove NM.
A sensuous yet relaxing tape with the feel of a coral sunset over a slow moving river in the indigo time of night. Ray Mitchell is a jazz pianist & Mike Harris an acoustic bass player both with the ability to create a sultry relaxed mood.

Indigo, Crystal, & Rainbow Children: A Guide to the New Generations of Highly Sensitive Young People. Doreen Virtue. 2 CDs. (Running Time: 3 hrs.). 2005. audio compact disk 17.95 (978-1-4019-0564-4(1), 5641) Hay House.

Indigo Dreaming: Meditations for Children. Amy Hamilton. Contrib. by Christine Morrison. (Running Time: 3480 sec.). 2006. audio compact disk 15.95 (978-0-9802984-0-6(7)) Joshua Bks AUS.

Indigo Dreams: Garden of Wellness. unabr. abr. ed. Short Stories. Lori Lite. 1 CD. (Running Time: 1 hr. 7 mins.). (Indigo Dreams Ser.). (J). (gr. k-5). 2006. audio compact disk 15.95 (978-0-9787781-0-1(3)) LiteBooks.

Indigo Dreams: 4 Children's Stories Designed to Decrease Stress & Anxiety While Increasing Self-Esteem & Self-Awareness. abr. ed. Lori Lite. (Running Time: 3600 sec.). (J). (ps-4). 2003. audio compact disk 15.95 (978-0-9708633-4-8(9)) LiteBooks.

Indigo Dreams: Adult Relaxation: Real Techniques for Real People Feeling Real Stress & Anxiety. abr. ed. Lori Lite. 1. (Running Time: 60 min.). (Indigo Dreams Ser.). (YA). (gr. 12). 2006. audio compact disk 15.95 (978-0-9708633-3-1(0)) LiteBooks.

Indigo King. unabr. ed. James A. Owen. Read by James Langton. (Running Time: 9 hrs. 30 mins. 0 sec.). (Chronicles of the Imaginarium Geographica Ser.). (ENG.). (YA). 2008. audio compact disk 34.99 (978-0-7435-7471-6(0)) Pub: S&S Audio. Dist(s): S and S Inc

***Indigo Notebook.** unabr. ed. Laura Resau. Read by Justine Eyre. 7 CDs. (Running Time: 8 hrs. 25 mins.). (YA). (gr. 8-11). 2009. audio compact disk 55.00 (978-0-307-57981-2(6), Listening Lib) Pub: Random Audio Pubg. Dist(s): Random

Indigo Notebook. unabr. ed. Laura Resau. Read by Justine Eyre. (ENG.). (J). (gr. 5). 2009. audio compact disk 37.00 (978-0-307-57979-9(4), Listening Lib) Pub: Random Audio Pubg. Dist(s): Random

Indigo Ocean Dreams: 4 Children's Stories Designed to Decrease Stress, Anger & Anxiety While Increasing Self-Esteem & Self-Awareness. abr. ed. Lori Lite. (Running Time: 60 min.). (Indigo Dreams Ser.). (J). (gr. 1-7). 2004. audio compact disk 15.95 (978-0-9708633-6-2(5)) LiteBooks.

Indigo Slam. abr. ed. Robert Crais. Read by David Stuart. (Running Time: 10800 sec.). (Elvis Cole Ser.). 2006. audio compact disk 14.99 (978-1-4233-1956-6(7), 9781423319566, BCD Value Price) Brilliance Audio.

Indigo Slam. unabr. ed. Robert Crais. Read by Michael Prichard. 6 cass. (Running Time: 9 hrs.). (Elvis Cole Ser.). 1997. 48.00 for sale to libraries only. (978-0-7366-3833-3(4), 4553) Books on Tape.
Private detective Elvis Cole is back & he's involved in a missing-person case.

Indigo Slam. unabr. ed. Robert Crais. Read by David Stuart. 6 cass. (Running Time: 7 hrs.). (Elvis Cole Ser.). 1997. 57.25 (978-1-56100-827-8(3), 1561008273, Unabridge Lib Edns) Brilliance Audio.
When a 15-year-old girl shows up to plead with Elvis to find her errant father, his first impulse is to hand the case over to Social Services. But he sees how hard the kid is working to keep her two siblings together and afloat. The father sounds like an angel; the case should be a cinch. But as Elvis investigates, he finds the dad seems to be a mover in the criminal underworld who is on the verge of a grand scheme. Could this be the right guy? As Elvis and sidekick Joe Pike try their hand at babysitting, events are set in motion that will pit them against a scary group of counterfeiters - and the even scarier U.S. Marshals.

Indigo Slam. unabr. ed. Robert Crais. Read by David Stuart. (Running Time: 7 hrs.). (Elvis Cole Ser.). 2006. 39.25 (978-1-4233-1413-4(1), 9781423314134, BADLE); 24.95 (978-1-4233-1412-7(3), 9781423314127, BAD); audio compact disk 39.25 (978-1-4233-1411-0(5), 9781423314110, Brlnc Audio MP3 Lib); audio compact disk 87.25 (978-1-4233-1409-7(3), 9781423314097, BriAudCD Unabrid); audio compact disk 34.95 (978-1-4233-1408-0(5), 9781423314080, Bril Audio CD Unabri); audio compact disk 24.95 (978-1-4233-1410-3(7), 9781423314103, Brilliance MP3) Brilliance Audio.

Indigo Teen Dreams: Guided Meditation - Relaxation Techniques Designed to Decrease Stress, Anger & Anxiety While Increasing Self-Esteem & Self-Awareness. abr. ed. Lori Lite. 1. (Running Time: 60 min.). (Indigo Dreams Ser.). 2005. audio compact disk 15.95 (978-0-9708633-9-3(X)) LiteBooks.

Indigo's Star. Hilary McKay. Read by Helen Lederer. 3 cass. (Casson Family Ser.: Bk. 2). (J). 2004. 30.00 (978-1-4000-9024-2(5), Listening Lib) Random Audio Pubg.

Indigo's Star. Hilary McKay. Read by Helen Lederer. 4 CDs. (Casson Family Ser.: Bk. 2). (J). (gr. 3-6). 2004. audio compact disk 38.00 (978-1-4000-9485-1(2), Listening Lib) Random Audio Pubg.

Indio. Sherry Garland. Read by Alyssa Bresnahan. 5 cass. (Running Time: 7 hrs.). (YA). (gr. 7 up). 1999. pap. bk. & stu. ed. 57.25 (978-0-7887-3008-5(8), 40890) Recorded Bks.
Fourteen-year-old Ipa-tah-chi has survived the Apache raid that took her grandmother & brother. But the strange, pale warriors who ride into her village on magnificent four-legged creatures pose a much greater threat. Chronicles the virtual extinction of the native "indio" & the birth of the Mexican race.

Indio, unabr. ed. Sherry Garland. Narrated by Alyssa Bresnahan. 5 pieces. (Running Time: 7 hrs.). (gr. 7 up). 1999. 44.00 (978-0-7887-2978-2(0), 95748E7) Recorded Bks.

Indio, Class set. Sherry Garland. Read by Alyssa Bresnahan. 5 cass. (Running Time: 7 hrs.). (YA). (gr. 7 up). 1999. wbk. ed. 114.80 (978-0-7887-3038-2(X), 46855) Recorded Bks.
Fourteen year old Ipa-tah-chi has survived the Apache raid that took her grandmother & brother. But the strange, pale warriors who ride into her village on magnificent four legged creatures pose a much greater threat. Chronicles the virtual extinction of the native "Indio" & the birth of the Mexican race.

Indirect Effect of Direct Legislation: How Institutions Shape Interest Group Systems. Frederick J. Boehmke. 2005. audio compact disk 9.95 (978-0-8142-9074-3(4)) Pub: Ohio St U Pr. Dist(s): Chicago Distribution Ctr

Indiscreet Letter. Based on a story by Eleanor Hallowell Abbott. (ENG.). 2007. 5.00 (978-1-60339-085-9(5)); audio compact disk 5.00 (978-1-60339-086-6(3)) Listenr Digest.

Indiscretion. Judith Ivory. Narrated by Barbara Rosenblat. 9 cass. (Running Time: 13 hrs. 15 mins.). 88.00 (978-0-7887-9548-0(1)) Recorded Bks.

Indiscretions. collector's ed. Carol Doumani. Read by Mary Peiffer. 7 cass. (Running Time: 10 hrs. 30 min.). 1999. 56.00 (978-0-7366-4634-5(5), 5000) Books on Tape.
This wickedly sardonic tale sneaks a peek behind the sunglasses of four L.A. archetypes - the socialite, the financier, the Hollywood star & the journalist who writes about them all.

Indiscretions. unabr. ed. Carol Doumani. Read by Mary Peiffer. 6 cass. (Running Time: 9 hrs.). 1999. 29.95 (978-0-7366-4480-8(6)) Books on Tape.
This wickedly sardonic tales sneaks a peek behind the sunglasses of four L.A. archetypes - the socialite, the financier, the Hollywood star & the journalist who writes about them all.

Indiscretions of Archie. P. G. Wodehouse. Read by Alfred von Lecteur. 2009. 27.95 (978-1-60112-989-5(0)) Babblebooks.

Indiscretions of Archie, unabr. ed. P. G. Wodehouse. Read by Frederick Davidson. 6 cass. (Running Time: 7 hrs.). 1997. 44.95 (978-0-7861-1175-6(5), 1921) Blckstn Audio.
Having made a bitter enemy of Daniel Brewster, owner of New York's Hotel Cosmopolis, Archie Moffam (fresh from England) checks out & heads south where he woos & weds one Lucille Brewster. Back at the hotel, Archie once again finds himself confronted by Mr. Brewster. Then the fun begins.

Indispensable Assistant, Set. abr. ed. Lesley Bissett. Read by Lesley Bissett. 2 cass. (Running Time: 3 hrs.). 1996. bk. 21.95 (978-1-878542-70-0(2),) SkillPath Pubns.
Regaining control over your day & your job.

Indispensable You! abr. ed. Ed. by Kim Anderson & Scott Pemberton. 2 cass. (Running Time: 3 hrs.). 1997. 15.95 Set. (978-0-85013-265-6(7)) Dartnell Corp.
A straightforward program that tells you how to: See every function as ultimately providing service to an internal or external customer; Develop a "continuous learning" mindset that prevents you from ever becoming obsolete; Strengthen the skills that help you gain cooperation from others so you & coworkers can get more done in less time. You will also learn winning strategies for building your personal motivation & leadership style & tips for keeping cool, calm & collected when "the heat is on".

"Indispensables" German Vocabulary Builder. 1 cass. (Running Time: 22 mins.). 9.95 (CGE104) J Norton Pubs.
A basic vocabulary of 50 words & phrases, recorded by native speakers, that will help you deal with most common situations.

"Indispensables" Italian Vocabulary Builder. unabr. ed. 1 cass. (Running Time: 22 mins.). 1996. 9.95 (978-0-88432-949-7(6), CIT104) J Norton Pubs.
Includes 50 words & phrases, recorded by native speakers, that will help you deal with most common situations.

Individual & History. Aldous Huxley. 1 cass. (Running Time: 52 min.). 1961. 11.00 Big Sur Tapes.

Individual & the World. 4 cass. 45.00 set. (9915) MEA A Watts Cass.

Individual Income Tax Refresher Course, 1997. Sidney Kess. 6 cass. (Running Time: 6 hrs.). 1996. pap. bk. 165.00 (0913) Toolkit Media.
Reviews the fundamentals for completing federal income tax forms & schedules, & points out ways to help eliminate costly errors & take advantage of tax-saving possibilities.

Individual Income Tax Refresher Course 2003. rev. ed. Sidney Kess. 6 cass. 2002. pap. bk. 175.00 (978-0-8080-0910-8(9)) Toolkit Media.

Individual Income Taxation. Douglas A. Kahn & Totaltape Editorial Board. 3 cass. 1995. bk. 159.00 set. (CPE0145) Bisk Educ.
An excellent overview of complex federal income tax laws, a concise blueprint of the federal income tax structure & how it works plus explains & interprets the major principles of income taxation.

Individual Intelligence Testing. unabr. ed. Elizabeth R. Miller. 1 cass. (Running Time: 31 min.). (Testing in the Schools Ser.). 1969. (29233) J Norton Pubs.
This program is part of Dr. Howard Lyman's series "Testing in the Schools." It stresses the value of the general mental test & offers a critical evaluation of individual intelligence testing.

Individual Life of Man. unabr. ed. Aldous Huxley. 1 cass. (Running Time: 56 min.). (Human Situation Ser.). 1959. 11.00 (01105) Big Sur Tapes.

Individual Replacement Audio CDs. Created by Candyce Ihnot. 1991. audio compact disk 9.00 (978-1-59621-313-5(2)) Read Naturally.

Individual Replacement Cassettes. Created by Candyce Ihnot. 1991. 8.00 (978-1-59621-312-8(4)) Read Naturally.

Individual Uses of Positive Substitution & Problem Solutions, Set-IP. Russell E. Mason. 1 cass. 1975. pap. bk. 35.00 (978-0-89533-007-9(5)) F I Comm.

Individual Values vs. Corporate Culture. Somers H. White. 4 cass. (Running Time: 60 min. per cass.). 80.00 (C105) S White.
Examines the roots of values, significant changes in personal values over the past 50 years, the impact of those changes at work, on health & happiness, the interaction between corporate culture and individual values, which values work best, which corporate cultures work best, etc.

Individualist: Power of the Enneagram Individual Type Audio Recording. Scripts. Based on a work by Enneagram Institute Staff. 1 CD. (Running Time: 60 mins.). 2005. audio compact disk 10.00 (978-0-9755222-3-3(X)) Enneagr.
Type Four Individual Type Audio Recording (ITAR) in CD format from the audio tapeset The Power of the Enneagram. Includes a 25 minute introduction to the system as a whole, as well as a 35 minute exposition on Type Four. An excellent way for therapists or business consultants to introduce the Enneagram to clients, or to work with the Enneagram in ongoing situations.

Individualized Stress Management. 1982. 15.00 (455) Inst Personality & Ability.
Designed to teach you two skills: How to achieve a special level of deep muscle relaxation; how to be sensitive to early stages of muscular tension throughout your body. The skill of deep muscle relaxation can be learned in ten sessions & should take place on a daily basis. Once the technique has been learned, it should be used on a daily basis by anyone experiencing stress-related illnesses.

Individualizing Instruction: Making Learning Personal, Empowering & Successful. Roger Hiemstra & Burton Sisco. (Higher Education Ser.). 1990. bk. 37.95 (978-1-55542-255-4(1), Jossey-Bass) Wiley US.

Individual's Relation to Himself. Nathaniel Branden. 2 CDs. (Running Time: 83 mins.). 2005. audio compact disk 11.95 (978-1-57970-246-5(5), AF0559D, Audio-For) J Norton Pubs.

Individual's Relation to Himself. unabr. ed. Nathaniel Branden. 1 cass. (Running Time: 1 hr. 23 min.). 12.95 (559) J Norton Pubs.
Branden focuses on the repression of emotions - such as pain, excitement & anger. He analyzes the causes & consequences of emotional repression, & suggests techniques for overcoming this problem & learning to express feelings in a healthy manner.

Individuating in Marriage Through Wounding & Healing. Read by Murray Stein. 1 cass. (Running Time: 1 hr.). 1981. 9.95 (978-0-7822-0264-9(0), 080) C G Jung IL.

Indochina's Children: Coming of Age in America. 1 cass. (Running Time: 30 min.). 10.95 (D0290B090, HarperThor) HarpC GBR.

Indonesia Update. 2005. audio compact disk 24.90 (978-981-230-309-7(X), CD3) ISEAS SGP.

Indonesian: Language/30. rev. ed. Educational Services Corporation Staff. Intro. by Charles Berlitz. 2 cass. (IND.). 1994. pap. bk. 21.95 set. (978-0-910542-68-5(6)) Educ Svcs DC.
Indonesian self-teaching language course.

Indonesian: Learn to Speak & Understand Indonesian with Pimsleur Language Programs. Pimsleur Staff. 5 CDs. (Running Time: 500 hrs. 0 mins. NaN sec.). (Compact Ser.). (KOR & ENG.). 2003. audio compact disk 115.00 (978-0-7435-0626-7(X), Pimsleur) Pub: S&S Audio. Dist(s): S and S Inc

Indonesian: Learn to Speak & Understand Indonesian with Pimsleur Language Programs. unabr. ed. Pimsleur. 5 CDs. (Running Time: 50 hrs. 0 mins. 0 sec.). (Compact Ser.). (IND & ENG.). 2006. audio compact disk 49.95 (978-0-7435-5059-8(5)) Pub: S and S. Dist(s): S and S Inc

***Indonesian, Basic: Learn to Speak & Understand Indonesian with Pimsleur Language Programs.** Pimsleur. (Running Time: 5 hrs. 0 mins. 0 sec.). (Basic Ser.). (ENG.). 2010. audio compact disk 24.95 (978-0-7435-9883-5(0), Pimsleur) Pub: S&S Audio. Dist(s): S and S Inc

***Indonesian, Comprehensive: Learn to Speak & Understand Indonesian with Pimsleur Language Programs.** Pimsleur. (Running Time: 16 hrs. 0 mins. 0 sec.). (Comprehensive Ser.). (ENG.). 2010. audio compact disk 345.00 (978-0-7435-9886-6(5), Pimsleur) Pub: S&S Audio. Dist(s): S and S Inc

***Indonesian, Conversational: Learn to Speak & Understand Indonesian with Pimsleur Language Programs.** Pimsleur. (Running Time: 8 hrs. 0 mins. 0 sec.). (Conversational Ser.). (ENG.). 2010. audio compact disk 49.95 (978-0-7435-9884-2(9), Pimsleur) Pub: S&S Audio. Dist(s): S and S Inc

Indonesian for Speakers of English, Compact. unabr. ed. 5 cass. (Running Time: 5 hrs.). (Pimsleur Tapes Ser.). 1997. 129.00 Set. (18510, Pimsleur) S&S Audio.
A ten-lesson-unit program based upon the Pimsleur Spoken Language Programmed Instructional Method, providing basic beginning language training to the ACTFL Novice Level.

Indonesian Popular Music: Kroncong Dangdut & Langgam Jawa. Anno. by Philip Yampolsky. 1 cass. (Running Time: 68 min.). (Music of Indonesia Ser.: Vol. 2). 1991. (0-9307-400560-9307-40056-2-0); audio compact disk (0-9307-40056-2-0) Smithsonian Folkways.
Kroncong & dangdut both began as music of the urban poor. These studio recordings of some of the stars of each tradition, is an excellent introduction to Indonesiam popular music.

Indonesian Sans Peine. M. Beck Hurault. 1 cass. (Running Time: 1 hr., 30 min.). (FRE & IND.). 2000. bk. 75.00 (978-2-7005-1366-0(5)) Pub: Assimil FRA. Dist(s): Distribks Inc

Indonesian Speakers: Learning the Sounds of American English. unabr. ed. 4 cass. (Accent English Ser.). bk. 89.50 incl. 144-pg bk, 42 visual aid cards, mirror. (SEN190) J Norton Pubs.

Indonesian, Survival. unabr. ed. 3 cass. (Running Time: 2 hrs. 30 mins.). (IND.). (J). (gr. 10-12). 1992. pap. bk. 75.00 (978-0-88432-398-3(6), AFIN10) J Norton Pubs.
Mini-course with pronunciation, vocabulary & basic sentence structure on colloquial Indonesian for travel & daily topics. Reference cards help reinforce newly acquired vocabulary.

Indoor Mobility: Self Study Course. 2nd ed. William Allen et al. 1 cass. 1997. 22.00 (978-1-890786-02-1(0)) Visions-Srvs.
Teaching skills to visually impaired persons.

***Indulgence in Death.** abr. ed. J. D. Robb, pseud. Read by Susan Ericksen. (Running Time: 6 hrs.). (In Death Ser.). 2010. 14.99 (978-1-4418-9236-2(2), 9781441892362, BAD); audio compact disk 26.99 (978-1-4418-3621-2(7), 9781441836212, BACD) Brilliance Audio.

***Indulgence in Death.** unabr. ed. J. D. Robb, pseud. Read by Susan Ericksen. 1 MP3-CD. (Running Time: 13 hrs.). (In Death Ser.). 2010. 24.99 (978-1-4418-3617-5(9), 9781441836175, Brilliance MP3); 39.97 (978-1-4418-3618-2(7), 9781441836182, Brlnc Audio MP3 Lib); audio compact disk 38.99 (978-1-4418-3615-1(2), 9781441836151, Bril Audio CD Unabri); audio compact disk 99.97 (978-1-4418-3616-8(0), 9781441836168, BriAudCD Unabrid) Brilliance Audio.

***Indulgence in Death.** unabr. ed. J. D. Robb, pseud. Read by J. D. Robb, pseud. (Running Time: 11 hrs.). (In Death Ser.). 2010. 39.97 (978-1-4418-3620-5(9), 9781441836205, BADLE) Brilliance Audio.

***Indulgence in Death.** unabr. ed. J. D. Robb, pseud. Read by Susan Ericksen. (Running Time: 11 hrs.). (In Death Ser.). 2010. 24.99 (978-1-4418-3619-9(5), 9781441836199, BAD) Brilliance Audio.

Industrial Air Quality Management in Vietnam: A Strategic Reference 2007. Compiled by Icon Group International, Inc. Staff. 2007. ring bd. 195.00 (978-0-497-82474-7(4)) Icon Grp.

Industrial Cleaning Products & Machinery in Italy: A Strategic Reference 2007. Compiled by Icon Group International, Inc. Staff. 2007. ring bd. 195.00 (978-0-497-36041-2(1)) Icon Grp.

Industrial Magic. unabr. ed. Kelley Armstrong. Read by Laural Merlington. Narrated by Laural Merlington. (Running Time: 14 hrs. 0 mins. 0 sec.). (Women of the Otherworld Ser.: Bk. 4). (ENG.). 2008. audio compact disk 29.99 (978-1-4001-5743-3(9)); audio compact disk 79.99 (978-1-4001-3743-5(8)); audio compact disk 39.99 (978-1-4001-0743-8(1)) Pub: Tantor Media. Dist(s): IngramPubServ

***Industrial Minerals & Rocks: Commodities, Markets, & Uses.** 7th ed. Ed. by Jessica Elzea Kogel et al. (ENG.). 2006. audio compact disk (978-0-87335-249-9(1)) SMM&E Inc.

Industrial Non-Broadcast: Track Three. 2 cass. 1990. 17.00 set. Recorded Res.

Industrial Relations in Canada Instructor's Resource Cd. McQuarrie. 2003. bk. 156.76 (978-0-470-83230-1(4)) Wiley US.

Industrial Revolution, the Great Depression. unabr. ed. Robert LeFevre. 1 cass. (Running Time: 1 hr. 52 min.). 12.95 (1008) J Norton Pubs.
Insights into the "Roaring Twenties," the Federal Reserve System.

Industrial Robots in Japan: A Strategic Reference 2007. Compiled by Icon Group International, Inc. Staff. 2007. ring bd. 195.00 (978-0-497-82328-3(4)) Icon Grp.

Industrial Surfacants Electronic Handbook. Michael Ash & Irene Ash. 1994. audio compact disk 325.00 (978-0-566-07506-3(7), Gower Pubng) Pub: Ashgate Pub GBR. Dist(s): Ashgate Pub

Indwelling: An Experience in Sound & Drama. adpt. ed. Tim LaHaye & Jerry B. Jenkins. 4 CDs. (Left Behind Ser.: Bk. 7). (ENG., 2002. audio compact disk 19.99 (978-0-8423-4340-4(7)) Tyndale Hse.

Indwelling: An Experience in Sound & Drama. unabr. ed. Tim LaHaye & Jerry B. Jenkins. Read by Jack Sondericker. 8 cass. (Running Time: 10 hrs.). 2001. 49.95 Books in Motion.
The question of who killed Nicolae will be answered, as Rayford, Buck, Chloe, and the rest of the Tribulation Force are faced with continued peril in a world turned upside down by cataclysmic events.

Indwelling: The Beast Takes Possession. Tim LaHaye & Jerry B. Jenkins. Narrated by Richard Ferrone. 8 cass. (Running Time: 10 hrs. 30 mins.). (Left Behind Ser.: Bk. 7). 2000. 76.00 (978-0-7887-4670-3(7), 96381E7) Recorded Bks.
It has been three & a half years since the Rapture took up the bodies of the innocent to Heaven. Scripture foretells that the seven-year tribulation will now become the Great Tribulation. As the world mourns the death of a renowned leader, the Tribulation Force looks for the next predicted sign that Satan will take possession of the Antichrist & raise him from the dead.

Indwelling: The Beast Takes Possession. Tim LaHaye & Jerry B. Jenkins. Narrated by Richard Ferrone. 9 CDs. (Running Time: 10 hrs. 30 mins.). (Left Behind Ser.: Bk. 7). 2001. audio compact disk 89.00 (978-0-7887-5156-1(5), C1319E7) Recorded Bks.

Indwelling: The Beast Takes Possession. Tim LaHaye & Jerry B. Jenkins. Read by Richard Ferrone. 6 cass. (Running Time: 10 hrs. 30 mins.). (Left Behind Ser.: Bk. 7). 2004. 29.95 (978-0-7887-5129-5(8), 00084); audio compact disk 39.95 (978-0-7887-5138-7(7), 00092) Recorded Bks.
Creating a thrilling scenario of the end times upon planet Earth, with the ultimate battle between good and evil being waged, the series combines Biblical prophecy with current events. It has been three and a half years since the Rapture took up the bodies of the innocent to Heaven. The prophecies foretell that this is the point when the seven-year Tribulation shall become the Great Tribulation, with the forces of evil tightening their grip on humanity in preparation for the final battle.

Indwelling: The Beast Takes Possession. abr. ed. Tim LaHaye & Jerry B. Jenkins. Read by Frank Muller. 3 CDs. (Running Time: 3 hrs.). (Left Behind Ser.: Bk. 7). (ENG., 2000. audio compact disk 19.99 (978-0-8423-3966-7(3)) Tyndale Hse.

Indwelling: The Beast Takes Possession. unabr. ed. Tim LaHaye & Jerry B. Jenkins. Read by Jack Sondericker. 9 CDs. (Running Time: 10 hrs.). (Left Behind Ser.: Bk. 7). 2001. audio compact disk 58.50 (978-1-58116-131-1(X)) Books in Motion.
The question of who killed Nicolae will be answered, as Rayford, Buck, Chloe, and the rest of the Tribulation Force are faced with continued peril in a world turned upside down by cataclysmic events.

Inertial Propulsion Systems. Interview with Bob Cook et al. Hosted by Bruce Stephen Holmes. 1 cass. (Running Time: 2 hrs.). 16.95 (AT5335) Lghtwrks Aud & Vid.
Two interviews with inventor Bob Cook reveal details about his amazing non-fossil fuel propulsion engine - one of the first motion causing machines to defy Sir Isaac Newton's third law of motion!.

Inés del Alma Mía see Inés of My Soul

***Inés del Alma Mía.** Isabel Allende. Prod. by FonoLibro Inc. Narrated by Isabel Varas. (SPA.). 2010. audio compact disk 17.95 (978-1-61154-005-5(4)) Fonolibro Inc.

Inés del Alma Mía. abr. ed. Isabel Allende. Read by Isabel Varas. (SPA.). 2009. 59.99 (978-1-60775-713-9(3)) Find a World.

Inés del Alma Mía. abr. ed. Isabel Allende. 4. (Running Time: 18000 sec.). (SPA.). 2007. audio compact disk 24.95 (978-1-933499-10-9(9)) Fonolibro Inc.

Inés of My Soul. unabr. ed. Isabel Allende. Read by Blair Brown. 8 cass. (Running Time: 12 hrs. 45 mins.).Tr. of Inés del Alma Mía. 2006. 64.00 (978-1-4159-3620-7(X)); audio compact disk 80.00 (978-1-4159-3602-3(1)) Books on Tape.
Born into a poor family in Spain, Inés, a seamstress, finds herself condemned to a life of hard work without reward or hope for the future. It is the sixteenth century, the beginning of the Spanish conquest of the Americas, and when her shiftless husband disappears to the New World, Inés uses the opportunity to search for him as an excuse to flee her stifling homeland and seek adventure. After her treacherous journey takes her to Peru, she learns that her husband has died in battle. Soon she begins a fiery love affair with a man who will change the course of her life: Pedro de Valdivia, war hero and field marshal to the famed Francisco Pizarro.

Inés of My Soul. unabr. ed. Isabel Allende. Read by Blair Brown. 10 CDs. (Running Time: 45000 sec.).Tr. of Inés del Alma Mía. 2006. audio compact disk 39.95 (978-0-06-118545-8(0)) HarperCollins Pubs.

Inevitable States in the Development of Co-Counseling, Side B. Rational Isl.

Inevitable Word: 1 Cor.15:55. Ed Young. (J). 1980. 4.95 (978-0-7417-1130-4(3), A0130) Win Walk.

Inexplicable. Contrib. by Don Friesen. 2007. audio compact disk 16.98 (978-1-929243-75-4(8)) Uproar Ent.

Inextinguishable Symphony: A True Story of Music & Love in Nazi Germany. unabr. ed. Martin Goldsmith. Read by Martin Goldsmith. 8 cass. (Running Time: 11 hrs. 30 mins.). 2001. 56.95 (978-0-7861-2091-8(6), 2853) Blckstn Audio.
Set amid the growing tyranny of Germany's Third Reich, here is the riveting and emotional tale of Gunther Goldschmidt and Rosemarie Gumpert, two courageous Jewish musicians who struggled to perform under unimaginable circumstances and found themselves falling in love in a country bent on destroying them. A poignant testament to the enduring vitality of music and love even in the harshest times, The Inextinguishable Symphony gives us a compelling look at an important piece of Holocaust history that has heretofore gone largely untold.

***Inextinguishable Symphony: A True Story of Music & Love in Nazi Germany.** unabr. ed. Martin Goldsmith. Read by Martin Goldsmith. (Running Time: 12 hrs.). 2010. 29.95 (978-1-4417-1894-5(X)); audio compact disk 105.00 (978-1-4417-1891-4(5)) Blckstn Audio.

Infallible Effects of Karma. Contrib. by Tsering Everest. 2 cass. (Running Time: 1 hr. 30 mins.). 1998. 14.00 (978-1-881847-22-9(5)) Padma Pub CA.
Lama Tsering discusses the idea of Karma & how it affects our lives. She gives practical advice on how to change our habits & accumulate merit & wisdom.

***Infamous.** unabr. ed. Ace Atkins. (Running Time: 15 hrs. 30 mins.). 2010. 39.99 (978-1-4001-9566-4(7)); 20.99 (978-1-4001-8566-5(1)) Tantor Media.

***Infamous.** unabr. ed. Ace Atkins. Narrated by Dick Hill. (Running Time: 14 hrs. 0 mins. 0 sec.). (ENG.). 2010. 29.99 (978-1-4001-6566-7(0)); audio compact disk 39.99 (978-1-4001-1566-2(3)); audio compact disk 79.99 (978-1-4001-4566-9(X)) Pub: Tantor Media. Dist(s): IngramPubServ

***Infamous.** unabr. ed. Suzanne Brockmann. Read by Angela Dawe and Patrick Lawlor. (Running Time: 15 hrs.). 2010. 24.99 (978-1-4418-5063-8(5), 9781441850638, Brilliance MP3); 39.97 (978-1-4418-5064-5(3), 9781441850645, Brinc Audio MP3 Lib); 24.99 (978-1-4418-5065-2(1), 9781441850652, BAD); 39.97 (978-1-4418-5066-9(X), 9781441850669, BADLE) Brilliance Audio.

***Infamous.** unabr. ed. Suzanne Brockmann. Read by Angela Dawe & Patrick G. Lawlor. (Running Time: 16 hrs.). 2010. audio compact disk 24.99 (978-1-4418-5061-4(9), 9781441850614, Bril Audio CD Unabri) Brilliance Audio.

***Infamous.** unabr. ed. Suzanne Brockmann. Read by Angela Dawe and Patrick Lawlor. (Running Time: 16 hrs.). 2010. audio compact disk 79.97 (978-1-4418-5062-1(7), 9781441850621, BriAudCD Unabrid) Brilliance Audio.

Infamous. unabr. ed. Joan Collins. Read by Erika Leigh. (Running Time: 10 hrs.). 2009. 39.97 (978-1-4233-8603-2(5), 9781423386032, Brinc Audio MP3 Lib); 24.99 (978-1-4233-8602-5(7), 9781423386025, Brilliance MP3); 39.97 (978-1-4233-8605-6(1), 9781423386056, BADLE); 24.99 (978-1-4233-8604-9(3), 9781423386049, BAD) Brilliance Audio.

Infamy: Pearl Harbor & Its Aftermath. unabr. collector's ed. John Toland. Read by John MacDonald. 8 cass. (Running Time: 12 hrs.). 1986. 64.00 (978-0-7366-1041-4(3), 1971) Books on Tape.
The events of Sunday morning, December 7, 1941, have always been shrouded in mystery. The bombs had scarcely stopped falling before Americans of every stripe were calling for an investigation.

Infancy Narratives of the Gospels. Raymond E. Brown. 2004. 32.50 (978-1-904756-06-4(9)) STL Dist NA.

Infant: Acts 2:37-41; John 3:3-4. Ed Young. 1998. 4.95 (978-0-7417-2196-9(1), 1196) Win Walk.

Infant CPR Anytime: Personal Learning Program. Created by American Academy of Pediatrics. 2007. 34.95 (978-1-58110-263-5(1)); 34.95 (978-1-58110-262-8(3)) Am Acad Pediat.

Infant Development. Robert Stone. 1 cass. 1986. 10.00 (978-0-938137-13-9(1)) Listen & Learn.
Historical perspective issues, development theories, prenatal development, birth & neonatal stages, physical growth. Language, social & emotional development & more.

Infant Holy: Christmas Music for Guitar & Other Instruments. Stephen Petrunak. 1 cass. 1999. 10.95 (CS-466); audio compact disk 15.95 (CD-466) GIA Pubns.

Infant Mind: Program from the Award Winning Public Radio Series. Hosted by Fred Goodwin. Comment by John Hockenberry. Contrib. by Peter W. Jusczyk et al. 1 cass. (Running Time: 1 hr.). (Infinite Mind Ser.). 1998. audio compact disk 21.95 (978-1-888064-38-4(2), LCM 17) Lichtenstein Creat.
How important is a child's environment to the fateful first year of life? What are the respective roles of genes, and the way we treat an infant, in defining the type of person they become? Researchers report how babies respond to nurturing and learn languages. Plus the trials of a child prodigy, John Hockenberry, and your calls.

Infant Psychiatry: Crying, Feeding, & Sleeping Problems. Contrib. by Klaus K. Minde et al. 1 cass. (American Academy of Pediatrics UPDATE: Vol. 16, No. 1). 1998. 20.00 Am Acad Pediat.

Infantile-Onset Ascending Hereditary Spastic Paralysis - A Bibliography & Dictionary for Physicians, Patients, & Genome Researchers. Compiled by Icon Group International, Inc. Staff. 2007. ring bd. 28.95 (978-0-497-11241-7(8)) Icon Grp.

Infantile States in Adolescents. Read by Gustav Bovensiepen. 1 cass. (Running Time: 90 min.). 1990. 10.95 (978-0-7822-0026-3(5), 410) C G Jung IL.

Infected. unabr. ed. Scott Sigler. Read by Scott Sigler. 9 CDs. 2008. audio compact disk 80.00 (978-1-4159-4952-8(2), BksonTape) Pub: Random Audio Pubg. Dist(s): Random

Infected. unabr. ed. Scott Sigler. Read by Scott Sigler. (Running Time: 43200 sec.). (ENG.). 2008. audio compact disk 34.95 (978-0-7393-2885-9(9), Random AudioBks) Pub: Random Audio Pubg. Dist(s): Random

Infections from Animals. Contrib. by Edgar K. Marcuse et al. 1 cass. (American Academy of Pediatrics UPDATE: Vol. 17, No. 7). 1998. 20.00 Am Acad Pediat.

Infectious Complications. Jonathan Gold. (AIDS: The National Conference for Practitioners). 1986. 9.00 (978-0-932491-49-7(9)) Res Appl Inc.

***Infernal Affairs.** Jane Heller. 2009. (978-1-60136-494-4(6)) Audio Holding.

Infernal Glove, Chronicle 2. unabr. ed. Malcolm Muggeridge. Read by Frederick Davidson. 9 cass. (Running Time: 1 hr. 30 min. per cass.). 62.95 Set. (1042) Blckstn Audio.
Opens with the author in Geneva preparing a survey, the purpose of which then escaped him. Thence, back to India as assistant editor of the "Calcutta Statesman." Next, home to England, working on the "Evening Standard" & living in rural Sussex on a base income of five pounds a week. These "happiest years" of his life ended with the coming of World War II, the events of which provide the focus of this book.

Infernal Grove. unabr. ed. Malcolm Muggeridge. Read by Frederick Davidson. 9 cass. (Running Time: 13 hrs.). (Chronicles of Wasted Time Ser.: 2). 1989. 62.95 (978-0-7861-0043-9(5), 1042) Blckstn Audio.
The son of a pioneer socialist, as a youth the author embraced utopian socialism & Soviet communism. Later, serving as the Manchester Guardian's man in Moscow, his leftest verve vanished. When his editor refused to print his expose of the Russian famine in which millions were to perish, he left Russia. His descriptions are vibrant & his criticism of modern phenomena is severe.

Infernal Serpent. Perf. by John Thaw. 2 cass. (Running Time: 1 hr. 50 min.). (Inspector Morse Mystery Ser.). 1998. 14.95 (978-1-56938-258-5(1), AMP-2581) Acorn Inc.
Facing the might of Oxford University, Inspector Morse tackles a particularly unsavory case involving child abuse & a respected academic family.

Inferno. Dante Alighieri. Ed. by Dante Alighieri. Read by Heathcote Williams. Tr. by Benedict Flynn. 3 cass. (Running Time: 4 hrs.). (Divine Comedy Ser.: Pt. 1). 1996. 17.98 (978-962-634-599-3(3), NA309914, Naxos AudioBooks) Naxos.
The first part of Dante's epic trilogy...The poet Virgil is sent to rescue Dante, a soul lost in the gloomy wood of spiritual torment.

Inferno. abr. ed. Troy Denning. Read by Marc Thompson. (Running Time: 23400 sec.). (Star Wars Ser.). (ENG.). 2007. audio compact disk 29.95 (978-0-7393-2399-1(7), Random AudioBks) Pub: Random Audio Pubg. Dist(s): Random

Inferno. abr. unabr. ed. Dante Alighieri. Ed. by Dante Alighieri. Read by Heathcote Williams. Tr. by Benedict Flynn. 3 CDs. (Running Time: 4 hrs.). (Divine Comedy Ser.: Pt. 1). 1996. audio compact disk 19.98 (978-962-634-099-8(1), NA309912, Naxos AudioBooks) Naxos.

Inferno. unabr. ed. Dante Alighieri. Ed. by Dante Alighieri. Read by Heathcote Williams. Tr. by Benedict Flynn. 4 CDs. (Running Time: 4 hr. 10 min.). audio compact disk 28.98 (978-962-634-317-3(6), NA431712) Naxos.

Inferno. unabr. ed. Larry Niven & Jerry Pournelle. Read by Tom Weiner. (Running Time: 6 hrs. NaN mins.). 2008. 29.95 (978-1-4332-5908-1(7)); audio compact disk 44.95 (978-1-4332-5904-3(4)); audio compact disk 50.00 (978-1-4332-5905-0(2)) Blckstn Audio.

Inferno: From the Divine Comedy. unabr. ed. Dante Alighieri. Read by Heathcote Williams. (YA). 2007. 34.99 (978-1-60252-531-3(5)) Find a World.

Inferno of Dante. Dante Alighieri. 2005. audio compact disk 19.95 (978-1-4193-2926-5(X)) Recorded Bks.

Inferno of Dante. abr. ed. Read by John Cleese. Tr. by Robert Pinsky. 2 cass. (Running Time: 3 hrs.). 1997. 17.95 (978-1-57453-132-9(8)) Audio Lit.

Inferno of Dante. unabr. ed. Dante Alighieri. Tr. by Robert Pinsky. Narrated by George Guidall. 4 cass. (Running Time: 5 hrs. 15 mins.). 35.00 (978-0-7887-0393-5(5), 94585E7) Recorded Bks.
Pinsky, the distinguished American poet, preserves the burning clarity & universal relevance of this 13th century literary masterpiece in a triumphant new translation for our times. Available to libraries only.

Inferno of Dante. unabr. ed. Dante Alighieri. 2005. audio compact disk 6.00 (978-1-4193-4118-2(9)) Recorded Bks.

Inferno of Dante. unabr. ed. Dante Alighieri. Read by George Guidall. Tr. by Robert Pinsky. 3 Cass. (Running Time: 5.25 Hrs.). 19.95 (978-1-4025-2792-0(6)) Recorded Bks.

Infertility Manual. 2nd ed. Rao. 2004. bk. 75.00 (978-81-8061-251-0(1)) Jaypee Brothers IND.

Infidel. Ayaan Hirsi Ali. Narrated by Ayaan Hirsi Ali. (Running Time: 61200 sec.). 2007. audio compact disk 39.99 (978-1-4281-5658-6(5)) Recorded Bks.

Infidel. unabr. ed. Ted Dekker. Narrated by Adam Verner. (Books of History Chronicles: Bk. 2). (ENG.). 2008. 16.09 (978-1-60814-457-0(7)) Oasis Audio.

Infidel. unabr. ed. Ted Dekker. Narrated by Adam Verner. (Running Time: 5 hrs. 5 mins. 31 sec.). (Books of History Chronicles: Bk. 2). (ENG.). (gr. 8-13). 2008. audio compact disk 22.99 (978-1-59859-271-9(8)) Oasis Audio.

Infidel. unabr. ed. Ayaan Hirsi Ali. Narrated by Ayaan Hirsi Ali. 14 cass. (Running Time: 17 hrs.). 2007. 113.75 (978-1-4281-5659-3(3)); audio compact disk 123.75 (978-1-4281-5661-6(5)) Recorded Bks.

Infidelidad. Lupita Venegas.Tr. of Infidelity. (SPA.). 2009. audio compact disk 15.00 (978-1-935405-39-9(X)) Hombre Nuevo.

Infidelity see Infidelidad

***Infidelity Pact: Unabridged Value-Priced Edition.** Carrie Karasyov. Narrated by Isabel Keating. (Running Time: 8 hrs. 46 mins. 0 sec.). (ENG.). 2010. audio compact disk 14.95 (978-1-60283-989-2(1)) Pub: AudioGO. Dist(s): Perseus Dist

Infiltrator. Jerry Ahern. Read by Carol Eason. 2 vols. No. 3. 2004. 18.00 (978-1-58807-491-1(9)); (978-1-58807-943-5(0)) Am Pubng Inc.

Infinite Awakening see Integrative Restoration: The ancient practice of Yoga Nidra for easing stress, healing trauma & awakening to your timeless Presence

Infinite Awakening: The Principles & Practice of Yoga Nidra Audiocassette Tape Set. Richard (C.) Miller. 3 cassettes. (Running Time: 4 hrs). 1995. 24.95 (978-1-893099-01-2(6)) Anahata Pr.
Yoga Nidra is the ancient 12-step process of Self-inquiry that awakens you to your true nature as radiant, unqualified Presence. Five guided meditations help you explore and transcend core beliefs. Guided practices cover: the physical and energy bodies, the bodies of emotion and intellect, the blissful sheath of consciousness, and the sheath of personal 'ego-I' identity.

Infinite Crisis: Part 1 Of 2, Vol. 1. unabr. ed. Based on a novel by Greg Cox. 6 CDs. (Running Time: 6 hrs.). 2007. audio compact disk 19.99 (978-1-59950-301-1(8)) GraphicAudio.

Infinite Crisis: Part 2 Of 2, Vol. 2. unabr. ed. Based on a novel by Greg Cox. 6 CDs. (Running Time: 7 hrs.). 2007. audio compact disk 19.99 (978-1-59950-302-8(6)) GraphicAudio.

***Infinite Days.** unabr. ed. Rebecca Maizel. Narrated by Justine Eyre. (Running Time: 9 hrs. 0 mins. 0 sec.). (Vampire Queen Ser.). (ENG.). 2010. 24.99 (978-1-4001-6890-3(2)); 16.99 (978-1-4001-8890-1(3)); audio compact disk 34.99 (978-1-4001-1890-8(5)); audio compact disk 83.99 (978-1-4001-4890-5(1)) Pub: Tantor Media. Dist(s): IngramPubServ

Infinite Grace. Contrib. by Women of Faith et al. Prod. by Chance Scoggins & Chance Scoggins. 2008. audio compact disk 13.99 (978-5-557-47089-6(1)) MyrrhR.

Infinite Horizon. Swami Amar Jyoti. 1 cass. 1985. 9.95 (R-74) Truth Consciousness.
Cutting asunder the knots of bondage. The unknown regions of our ancient heritage. Education which enlightens. Language of the birds. Meditation on the Absolute.

Infinite Man see Infinitud Humana

Infinite Mind: in Any Language: Program from the Award Winning Public Radio Series. Interview. Hosted by Peter Kramer. 1 CD. (Running Time: 1 hr). (Infinite Mind Ser.). 2003. audio compact disk 21.95 (978-1-932479-01-0(5), LCM 265) Lichtenstein Creat.
In this hour, we explore Mental Health Care for Immigrants, with guest host Dr. Peter Kramer. Guests include Dr. Arthur Kleinman, professor of medical anthropology and psychiatry at Harvard Medical School and one of the world's leading experts in medical anthropology and cross-cultural psychiatry; Dr. Jane Delgado, a clinical psychologist and the president and CEO of the National Alliance for Hispanic Health; Dr. Mohamed Farrag, a psychologist and the clinical director of ACCESS: the Arab Community Center for Economic and Social Services in Dearborn, Michigan; and Dr. Yinka Akinsulure-Smith a psychologist from Sierra Leone who works at the Bellevue /NYU Program for Survivors of Torture.

Infinite Mind: Parenting: Program from the Award Winning Public Radio Series: the Best of the Infinite Mind. Interview. Hosted by John Goodwin. 1 CD. (Running Time: 1 hr). (Infinite Mind Ser.). 2003. audio compact disk 21.95 (978-1-932479-00-3(7), LCM 267) Lichtenstein Creat.
In this hour we delve into our archives to bring you some of the best of The Infinite Mind segments on Parenting. We'll find out how to deal with the toddler who won't let you talk on the phone, and the teenager who won't listen. Guests include, Dr. Stanley Greenspan, a clinical professor of psychiatry and pediatrics at George Washington University and author of The Growth of the Mind; Annie Lamott, best-selling author of Bird by Bird: Some Instructions on Writing and Life; Adele Faber and Elaine Mazlish, authors of How to Talk So Kids Will Listen and Listen So Kids Will Talk; Debbie and Lisa Ganz, who run the website www.twinsworld.com; Dr. Harold Koplewicz, director and founder of the New York University Child Study Center and the director of the Division of Child and Adolescent Psychiatry at New York University Medical Center and Bellevue Hospital Center; and Laurie Berkner, children's songwriter and performer.

Infinite Mind Update: Program from the Award Winning Public Radio Series. Interview. Hosted by Fred Goodwin. 1 CD. (Running Time: 1 hr). (Infinite Mind Ser.). 2003. audio compact disk 21.95 (978-1-932479-10-2(4), LCM 252) Lichtenstein Creat.
In this hour, we do something a little different. Since the pace of progress in neuroscience and psychiatry is staggering, we revisit some of our past topics and fill you in on the latest discoveries. We'll hear about the latest in autism research with Dr. Fred Volkmar of Yale University, and we'll take another look at the deadly interaction between chemical dependence and mental illness with Charles Curie, who leads SAMHSA, the Substance Abuse and Mental Health Services Administration. Turning to mood disorders - which, over a lifetime, affect one in five Americans - we'll speak with Dr. Andrew Leuchter of UCLA about a simple technique that could provide us with an early test for the effectiveness of antidepressants. We'll also discuss encouraging research into suicide prevention with Dr. Ross Baldessarini of Harvard University, and visit a small school in Texas designed specifically for children with bipolar disorder.

Infinite Mind's Most Humorous Moments. Interview. Hosted by Peter Kramer. 1 CD. (Running Time: 1 hr). 2005. 21.95 (978-1-933644-17-2(6), LCM 390) Lichtenstein Creat.
Why are chickens funnier than ducks? Can humor help us cope with tragedy? And what makes funny, well, funny? To answer such questions we look back at some of the most humorous moments from The Infinite Mind, with guests including stand-up comedians, humor columnists, and a surprise visit from Jonathan Katz, the voice of Dr. Katz: Professional Therapist and Dr. Harold Stein on the new IFC TV series ?Hopeless Pictures.? We listen to past interviews with star comedians Robert Klein, Lewis Black, and Margaret Cho as they relate their experiences in the comedy industry, and the knowledge they?ve gleaned. We hear a clinical explanation of how humor can help assuage fear and pain from Stanford University?s Dr. David Spiegel, and humorist Al Franken relates a very sobering example of this and its relevance during the aftermath of September 11th. Other guests include author, columnist, and professional hypochondriac, Gene Weingarten, BrainBanker and singer, Dr. Jill Bolte Taylor, and two of the original members of the Firesign Theater, Phil Proctor and Peter Bergman. With commentary by John Hockenberry.

Infinite Possibilities: The Art of Living Your Dreams. Mike Dooley. 12 CDs. (Running Time: 12 hrs.). 2001. audio compact disk 129.40 (978-0-9642168-6-0(8)) Totally Unique.

Infinite Possibilities: The Art of Living Your Dreams. abr. unabr. ed. Mike Dooley. Read by Mike Dooley. (Running Time: 11 hrs. 0 mins. 0 sec.). (ENG.). 2009. audio compact disk 39.99 (978-0-7435-8233-9(0)) Pub: S&S Audio. Dist(s): S and S Inc

Infinite Possibilities: The Art of Living Your Dreams. unabr. ed. Mike Dooley. 12 cass. (Running Time: 12 hrs.). 2001. 119.40 (978-0-9642168-5-3(X)) Totally Unique.

***Infinite Quest: Develop Your Psychic Intuition to Take Charge of Your Life.** unabr. ed. John Edward. Read by John Edward. (Running Time: 11 hrs.). 2010. 24.99 (978-1-4418-9153-2(6), 9781441891532, BAD); 39.97 (978-1-4418-9154-9(4), 9781441891549, BADLE); 24.99 (978-1-4418-9151-8(X), 9781441891518, Brilliance MP3); 39.97 (978-1-4418-9152-5(8), 9781441891525, Brlnc Audio MP3 Lib); audio compact disk 24.99 (978-1-4418-9149-5(8), 9781441891495, Bril Audio CD Unabri); audio compact disk 59.97 (978-1-4418-9150-1(1), 9781441891501, BriAudCD Unabrid) Brilliance Audio.

***Infinite Reality: Avatars, Eternal Life, Universal Consciousness, & the Dawn of the Virtual Age.** unabr. ed. Jim Blascovich & Jeremy Bailenson. (ENG.). 2011. (978-0-06-202715-3(8), Harper Audio) HarperCollins Pubs.

Infinite Self: 33 Steps to Reclaiming Your Inner Power. unabr. ed. Stuart Wilde. 6 cass. (Running Time: 6 hrs.). 1995. pap. bk. 59.95 (978-1-55525-013-3(0), 13390A) Nightingale-Conant.
If you genuinely have the desire to experience the realm of consciousness beyond your everyday, business-as-usual life-to 'transcend'- then Stuart Wilde wants to help you learn.

Infinities. unabr. ed. John Banville. Read by Julian Rhind-Tutt. (ENG.). 2010. audio compact disk 35.00 (978-0-307-70665-2(6), Random AudioBks) Pub: Random Audio Pubg. Dist(s): Random

Infinitud Humana. Miguel Angel Cornejo. 2 cass. (Running Time: 2 hrs.).Tr. of Infinite Man. (SPA.). 2002. (978-968-6210-51-4(2)) Taller del Exito.
A full work of pedagogy, human values and messages that elevate the spirit, as well as the secrets that allow us to obtain personal excellence.

InFINity. Trout Fishing in America Staff. 1 CD. 2001. audio compact disk 15.98 Trout Record.

Infinity. unabr. ed. Sherrilyn Kenyon. 9 CDs. (Running Time: 9 hrs. 0 mins. 0 sec.). (ENG.). (YA). 2010. audio compact disk 17.99 (978-1-4272-0909-2(X)) Pub: Macmill Audio. Dist(s): Macmillan

Infinity Affair. unabr. ed. James H. Cobb & Robert Ludlum. 12 CDs. (Running Time: 13 hrs.). (Covert-One Ser.). 2010. audio compact disk 39.98 (978-1-60024-411-7(4)) Pub: Hachet Audio. Dist(s): HachBkGrp

Infinity Affair. unabr. ed. Robert Ludlum & James Cobb. (Running Time: 13 hrs.). (Covert-One Ser.). 2009. 26.98 (978-1-60024-412-4(2)) Pub: Hachet Audio. Dist(s): HachBkGrp

Infinity of Mirrors. unabr. collector's ed. Richard Condon. Read by Penelope Dellaporta. 8 cass. (Running Time: 12 hrs.). 1980. 64.00 (978-0-7366-0168-9(6), 1170) Books on Tape.
A beautiful young French Jew, Paula Bernheim & a Prussian officer, Wilhelm von Rhode, meet & fall in love. They are married & settle in Berlin just as Hitler's rise to power begins.

Infinity Welcomes: Seven Better Than Life. Grant Naylor. 1 cass. 1998. 18.70 (978-1-897774-64-9(8)) Ulvrscrft Audio.

Infinity's Child. unabr. ed. Harry Stein. Read by Laural Merlington. (Running Time: 10 hrs.). 2009. 39.97 (978-1-4233-8567-7(5), 9781423385677, Brlnc Audio MP3 Lib); 39.97 (978-1-4233-8569-1(1), 9781423385691, BADLE); 24.99 (978-1-4233-8566-0(7), 9781423385660, Brilliance MP3); 24.99 (978-1-4233-8568-4(3), 9781423385684, BAD) Brilliance Audio.

Inflammatory Disease of the Small & Large Bowel. 3 cass. (Spring Meeting Philadelphia, PA Ser.: S87-GS2). 1987. 28.50 (8702) Am Coll Surgeons.
Includes screening & dysplasia, restorative procedures, sexually transmitted colon diseases, precautions for the surgeon, etc.

Inflammatory Diseases of the Pleura & Lung. 2 cass. (Thoracic Surgery Ser.: C85-TH1). 1985. 15.00 (8585) Am Coll Surgeons.

Inflatable Globe see Twentieth-Century Poetry in English, No. 5, Recordings of Poets Reading Their Own Poetry

Inflation: How to Stop It & Its Destruction of Capital Markets. unabr. ed. Hans F. Sennholz & Henry Hazlitt. 1 cass. (Running Time: 1 hr. 23 min.). 12.95 (344) J Norton Pubs.

Inflation: Made & Manufactured in Washington, D.C. unabr. ed. William E. Simon. 1 cass. (Ludwig von Mises Lecture Ser.). 12.95 (M 32) J Norton Pubs.

Inflation, an "Addiction" & How to "Kick the Habit" unabr. ed. Arthur Kemp. 1 cass. (Running Time: 43 min.). 12.95 (287) J Norton Pubs.

Inflation & Our Economic Crisis. unabr. ed. Howard E. Kershner. 1 cass. (Running Time: 1 hr. 24 min.). 12.95 (712) J Norton Pubs.

Inflation, Deflation, Oil & Gold. unabr. ed. Donald J. Hoppe. 1 cass. (Running Time: 52 min.). 12.95 (371) J Norton Pubs.

Inflation or Deflation? unabr. ed. John Exter. 1 cass. (Running Time: 1 hr. 3 min.). 12.95 (343) J Norton Pubs.

Inflationary Book of the 1920s CD Set. ed. Murray N. Rothbard. 2 CDs. (Running Time: 86 mins.). 2006. audio compact disk 14.95 (978-1-57970-395-0(X), AF0214D, Audio-For) J Norton Pubs.
Dr. Rothbard analyzes the economic build-up to the Crash and indicts the Federal Reserve System policies, rather than the free market. (From the series "Cornell Lectures on 20th-Century American Economic History.").

Inflationary Boom of the 1920's. unabr. ed. Murray Newton Rothbard. 2 cass. (Running Time: 2 hrs. 12 min.). 19.95 (214) J Norton Pubs.
Analysis of the economic build-up to the Crash & Federal Reserve System policies.

Influence: Exodus 2:1-10. Ed Young. 1984. 4.95 (978-0-7417-1411-4(6), 411) Win Walk.

Influence Factor: Growing in Leadership, Changing Your World. Mac Hammond. 7 Cds. (Running Time: 6 hours). 2002. audio compact disk 35.00 (978-1-57399-175-9(9)) Mac Hammond.
Influence. Whether you're a housewife, a pastor or a CEO, you can benefit from an increase in influence. This series will show you the way.

Influence Factor: Growing in Leadership, Changing Your World. Mac Hammond. 7 cass. (Running Time: 6 hrs.). 2005. 17.50 (978-1-57399-227-5(5)) Mac Hammond.
Influence. Whether you're a housewife, a pastor, or a CEO, you can benefit from an increase in influence.

Influence of Darwin on Philosophy & Other Essays. unabr. ed. John Dewey. (Great Books in Philosophy). (ENG.). 1997. 16.98 (978-1-57392-137-4(8)) Prometheus Bks.

Influence of Natal House Rulers. Edward Helin. 1 cass. (Running Time: 90 min.). 1994. 8.95 (1106) Am Fed Astrologers.
Horoscope houses & their planetary rulers.

Influence of Sea Power upon History. unabr. collector's ed. Alfred Thayer Mahan. Read by Jonathan Reese. 14 cass. (Running Time: 21 hrs.). 1995. 112.00 (978-0-7366-3148-8(8), 3822) Books on Tape.
In 1886, the U.S. had no navy to speak of. But it did have Alfred Mahan, a captain in the U.S. Navy, who had spent much of his career observing a real navy: the British Empire's. At 46, Mahan was 10 years short of retirement when the newly formed Naval & War College at Newport, Rhode Island, asked him to lecture on naval history & tactics. Out of his lectures grew a book that would change the world. It's no exaggeration that "The Influence of Seapower upon History" affected the outcome of both great world wars. When it was first published in 1890, prime ministers, presidents, kings, admirals & chancellors eagerly studied its strategies, which England first employed to rule the seas. All the major powers have used it to shape imperial policies.

Influence of the Bible in America. 2002. 4.95 (978-0-925279-90-3(0)) Wallbuilders.

Influencer: The Power to Change Anything. unabr. ed. Kerry Patterson et al. Read by Eric Conger. (Running Time: 30600 sec.). (ENG.). 2007. audio compact disk 34.95 (978-1-59887-576-8(0), 1598875760) Pub: HighBridge. Dist(s): Workman Pub

Influential Selling. 2005. audio compact disk 19.95 (978-0-9772257-2-9(0)) CornerStone Leader.

Influential Women in History: A Collection of Biographies. Katherine Krohn et al. (Playaway Children Ser.). (ENG.). (J). 2009. 39.99 (978-1-60775-754-2(0)) Find a World.

Influenza: A Guide for the Public & Healthcare Staff on Diagnosis, Treatment, & Epidemics. Ed. by Daniel Farb. 2007. 49.95 (978-1-59491-292-4(0), U HlthCare-U Bus) Pub: UnivofHealth. Dist(s): AtlasBooks

Influx of the Array. Jeri Massi. Interview with Del Thompson. 2 cass. (Running Time: 2 hrs.). (YA). 1996. 15.00 Set. (978-0-9657977-0-2(8)) Gold Cuff.
Science Fiction. Jennifer Knightly is rescued from a crooked lawyer by her uncle. His involvement in laser research brings them both into contact with a creature that lives on light energy & threatens to reverse the entire ecosystem at Earth.

Info Bytes: An Introduction to World Evangelization. Prod. by UnveilinGlory. (ENG.). 2001. audio compact disk 24.99 (978-1-930924-20-8(8), ACMC) Caleb Res.

InfoFount Bonus & Sample Disk V1: Samples from Martial Strategists, Transformational Greats, & Antecedent Wisdom Titles. Excerpts. Narrated by Ross M. Armetta. 1 CD. (Running Time: 72 Mins. Aprox.). 2005. audio compact disk 2.99 (978-1-59733-000-8(0)) InfoFount.
Features a complete short story and descriptions and highlights from Martial Strategists series titles including The Art of War, Bushido, and The Book of 5 Rings with information about other series titles. Also included are descriptions and highlights from Transformational Greats series titles including As a Man Thinketh, As a Man Thinketh 2, Acres of Diamonds, The Majesty of Calmness, The Path of Prosperity, The Way of Peace, and the Kingship of Self- Control. It also has short samples from the Antecedent Wisdom series Greatest Americans of the Early Republic including George Washington, Benjamin Franklin, Early American Inventors, and Early American Women's Education etc. More information on titles at www. InfoFount.com.

Informal Afternoon of Reflection on Jungian Psychology. Read by Marie-Louise Von Franz. 1 cass. (Running Time: 2 hrs.). 1984. 12.95 (978-0-7822-0066-9(4), ND7505) C G Jung IL.

Informal Discussion of Biocentric Therapy. unabr. ed. Nathaniel Branden. 1 cass. (Running Time: 1 hr. 10 min.). 12.95 (556) J Norton Pubs.
Branden discusses the understanding of the mind & body as an integrated whole, & gives a clear presentation of his theory of neurosis.

Informal Esalen Lectures (1975-1980) Gregory Bateson. 16 cass. (Running Time: 18 hrs.). (Twelve Tape Ser.). 1980. 119.00 (02815) Big Sur Tapes.
Ten informal talks, discussing: metaphors, schizophrenia, patterns which connect, boundaries and interfaces, complexity and unifying simplicity, epistemology, civilization and addictions, etc.

Informal Fallacies - Logic & Theology Pt. 2: Christ's Use of Logic. John Robbins. 1 cass. (Introduction to Logic Ser.: No. 3). 5.00 Trinity Found.

Informal Hour with Dorothy Parker. unabr. ed. Dorothy Parker. Read by Dorothy Parker. 1 cass. (Running Time: 60 min.). 10.95 (978-0-8045-0726-4(0), SAC 726) Spoken Arts.
Author reads her story "Horsie" & recites twenty-six of her poems.

Informal Talk with Reb Zalman Schachter-Shalomi. Read by Zalman Schachter-Shalomi & Eve Ilsen. 1 cass. (Running Time: 1 hr. 30 min.). 9.98 (TP225) Union Label.
Reb Zalman Schachter-Shalomi talks about the Creation, interchanges between esoteric schools, & traveling between microcosmic & macrocosmic viewpoints in the Work. Teaching stories are used to illustrate the ideas.

***Informant.** abr. ed. James Grippando. Read by James Naughton. (ENG.). 2004. (978-0-06-082395-5(X), Harper Audio) HarperCollins Pubs.

Informant. unabr. ed. James Grippando. Narrated by George Guidall. 8 cass. (Running Time: 11 hrs. 30 mins.). 1997. 75.00 (978-0-7887-0908-1(9), 95007E7) Recorded Bks.
An unknown informant demands payment from the press for predictions of grisly murders. When his prophecies come true, a reporter secretly collaborates with the FBI to stop the killings.

Informant. unabr. ed. James Grippando. Narrated by George Guidall. 8 cass. (Running Time: 11 hrs. 30 mins.). 2002. 39.95 (978-0-7887-8261-9(4), RD742) Recorded Bks.
In this tale, he creates a sadistic serial killer who is so disturbingly real, he will make your skin crawl. An unknown informant sends reporter Michael Posten a woman's name. The day after the postmark she becomes a murder victim. Now the informant is demanding payment for predictions of more grisly murders. Shocked by the first prophecy, Michael secretly collaborates with FBI agent Victoria Santos to uncover the source and stop future killings. James Grippando's experience as a trial lawyer enables him to create incidents that could step straight from the front page. Yet his characters are so real, they could live next door.

Informant: A True Story. Kurt Eichenwald. Narrated by George Wilson. 18 cass. (Running Time: 24 hrs. 30 mins.). 2001. 141.00 (978-1-4025-1241-4(4)) Recorded Bks.

Informant: A True Story. abr. ed. Kurt Eichenwald. Read by Arthur Morey. (ENG.). 2009. audio compact disk 25.00 (978-0-7393-2491-2(8), Random AudioBks) Pub: Random Audio Pubg. Dist(s): Random

Informant: A True Story. abr. ed. Kurt Eichenwald. 2 cass. (Running Time: 3 hrs.). 2000. 18.00 (978-1-55935-349-6(X)) Soundelux.
Government informant Archer Daniels Midland, a senior executive within one of America's most politically powerful companies, reveals a vast criminal conspiracy.

***Informant, the Low Price.** abr. ed. James Grippando. Read by James Naughton. (ENG.). 2004. (978-0-06-082394-8(1), Harper Audio) HarperCollins Pubs.

Informateur. pap. bk. 16.95 (978-88-8148-816-2(7)) Pub: Europ Lang Inst ITA. Dist(s): Distribks Inc

Information. unabr. ed. Martin Amis. Read by Stuart Langton. 11 cass. (Running Time: 16 hrs. 30 min.). 1998. 88.00 (978-0-7366-4163-0(7), 4666) Books on Tape.
Professional jealousy leads a failed novelist to plan a successful friend's downfall.

***Information: A History, a Theory, a Flood.** unabr. ed. James Gleick. (Running Time: 18 hrs.). (ENG.). 2011. audio compact disk 50.00 (978-0-307-91496-5(8), Random AudioBks) Pub: Random Audio Pubg. Dist(s): Random

Information Age/The Return of the Self. Marianne Williamson. Read by Marianne Williamson. 1 cass. (Running Time: 90 mins.). (Lectures on a Course in Miracles). 1999. 10.00 (978-1-56170-320-3(6), M803) Hay House.

Information & Communication Technology (ICT) & Broadcasting Equipment in Egypt: A Strategic Reference 2007. Compiled by Icon Group International, Inc. Staff. 2007. ring bd. 195.00 (978-0-497-35930-0(8)) Icon Grp.

Information & Communication Technology (ICT) in South Africa: A Strategic Reference 2007. Compiled by Icon Group International, Inc. Staff. 2007. ring bd. 195.00 (978-0-497-35874-7(3)) Icon Grp.

Information & Image Management: End-User Requirements for the Next Generation of ODS. 1 cass. 1990. 8.50 Recorded Res.

Information Entrepreneur Intensive Home Study Course. Randy Gage et al. (ENG.). 2005. audio compact disk 1997 (978-0-9762299-3-3(5)) Prime Concepts Grp.

Information Management Compliance Warrior. Based on a book by Randolph Kahn. Adapted by Atdoc. (ENG.). 2006. audio compact disk (978-0-9793071-1-9(2)) Atdoc.

Information Officer. unabr. ed. Mark Mills. (Running Time: 10 hrs. 30 mins.). 2010. audio compact disk 39.95 (978-1-4417-2128-0(2)) Blckstn Audio.

Information Officer. unabr. ed. Mark Mills. Read by Gerard Doyle. (Running Time: 10 hrs. 30 mins.). 2010. 29.95 (978-1-4417-2129-7(0)); 65.95 (978-1-4417-2125-9(8)); audio compact disk 100.00 (978-1-4417-2126-6(6)) Blckstn Audio.

***Information Overload! Get a Grip on Workplace Communication.** PUEI. 2009. audio compact disk 199.00 (978-1-935041-81-8(9), CareerTrack) P Univ E Inc.

Information Security (IS) Equipment & Services in India: A Strategic Reference 2007. Compiled by Icon Group International, Inc. Staff. 2007. ring bd. 195.00 (978-0-497-36014-6(4)) Icon Grp.

Information Systems Today: Why IS Matters. 2nd ed. Leonard Jessup & Joseph Valacich. 2005. bk. 148.67 (978-0-13-199708-0(4)) Pearson Educ CAN CAN.

Information Technology. Eric Glendinning & John McEwan. 2006. 24.25 (978-0-19-457494-5(6)) OUP.

Information Technology (IT) Equipment & Services in Greece: A Strategic Reference 2007. Compiled by Icon Group International, Inc. Staff. 2007. ring bd. 195.00 (978-0-497-35993-5(6)) Icon Grp.

Information Technology (IT) Hardware in India: A Strategic Reference 2006. Compiled by Icon Group International, Inc. Staff. 2007. ring bd. 195.00 (978-0-497-36015-3(2)) Icon Grp.

Information Technology (IT) Security Software in Hong Kong: A Strategic Reference 2006. Compiled by Icon Group International, Inc. Staff. 2007. ring bd. 195.00 (978-0-497-35999-7(5)) Icon Grp.

Information Technology (IT) Security Software in Singapore: A Strategic Reference 2006. Compiled by Icon Group International, Inc. Staff. 2007. ring bd. 195.00 (978-0-497-82414-3(0)) Icon Grp.

Information Technology (IT) Security Software in South Africa: A Strategic Reference 2007. Compiled by Icon Group International, Inc. Staff. 2007. ring bd. 195.00 (978-0-497-35875-4(1)) Icon Grp.

Information Technology (IT) Services & E-commerce in Ecuador: A Strategic Reference 2006. Compiled by Icon Group International, Inc. Staff. 2007. ring bd. 195.00 (978-0-497-35923-2(5)) Icon Grp.

Information Technology (IT) Training Services in China: A Strategic Reference 2006. Compiled by Icon Group International, Inc. Staff. 2007. ring bd. 195.00 (978-0-497-35881-5(6)) Icon Grp.

Informational Guides for Groups, Communication, Living & Change: Guides for Groups & Personal Change, Set-GL. Russell E. Mason. 1975. pap. bk. 35.00 (978-0-89533-019-2(9)) F I Comm.

***Informationist: A Thriller.** unabr. ed. Taylor Stevens. (Running Time: 11 hrs.). (ENG.). 2011. audio compact disk 40.00 (978-0-307-87824-3(4), Random AudioBks) Pub: Random Audio Pubg. Dist(s): Random

Informer. Perf. by Victor McLaglen. 1 cass. (Running Time: 60 min.). 1935. 7.95 (DD-8870) Natl Recrd Co.
"The Informer" takes place in Dublin, Ireland during the time of the Irish rebellion. Turning in a friend for reward money, the informer suffers the pangs of his conscience. "Watch on the Rhine" is the story of a German refugee & underground leader who came to America with his wife & family. He finds he is still being hunted by the Nazi's in the U.S.

Informers. unabr. ed. Bret Easton Ellis. Read by Christian Rummel & Therese Plummer. (Running Time: 8 hrs.). 2009. 39.97 (978-1-4233-9586-7(7), 9781423395867, Brlnc Audio MP3 Lib) Brilliance Audio.

Informers. unabr. ed. Bret Easton Ellis. Read by Christian Rummel & Plummer Therese. (Running Time: 8 hrs.). 2009. 39.97 (978-1-4233-9587-4(5), 9781423395874, BADLE) Brilliance Audio.

Informers. unabr. ed. Bret Easton Ellis. Read by Christian Rummel & Therese Plummer. 7 CDs. (Running Time: 8 hrs.). (Audible Modern Classic Ser.). 2009. audio compact disk 29.99 (978-1-4233-9583-6(2), 9781423395836, Bril Audio CD Unabri); audio compact disk 82.97 (978-1-4233-9584-3(0), 9781423395843, BriAudCD Unabrid) Brilliance Audio.

Informers. unabr. ed. Bret Easton Ellis. Read by Christian Rummel et al. (Running Time: 8 hrs.). 2009. 24.99 (978-1-4233-9585-0(9), 9781423395850, Brilliance MP3) Brilliance Audio.

Infotech Audio CD. 4th ed. Santiago Remancha Esteras. (Running Time: 1 hr. 16 mins.). (ENG.). 2008. audio compact disk 25.00 (978-0-521-70301-7(8)) Cambridge U Pr.

Infusing Research into Practice: NACADA Webinar Series 21. Featuring Joshua Smith & Wendy Troxel. (ENG.). 2008. audio compact disk 140.00 (978-1-935140-62-7(0)) Nat Acad Adv.

Ingenu, Set. Francois Voltaire, pseud. Read by Bernard Merle. 2 cass. (FRE.). 1995. 26.95 (1755-KFP) Olivia & Hill.
The tormented love of an Indian for a young French woman. Biting social satire which questions the myth of the noble savage.

Ingestion-Toxicology-Meningitis. Fred Henretig & Roger Barkin. (Pediatric Emergencies: The National Conference for Practitioners Ser.). 1986. 9.00 (978-0-932491-78-7(2)) Res Appl Inc.

Ingles. Pimsleur Staff. 4 CDs. (Running Time: 4 hrs. 30 min.). 2002. audio compact disk 19.95 (978-0-7435-2976-1(6), Pimsleur); audio compact disk 19.95 (978-0-7435-2984-6(7), Pimsleur) Pub: S&S Audio. Dist(s): S and S

Ingles. abr. ed. Ed. by Berlitz Publishing Staff. (Running Time: 1 hr.). (Berlitz Rush Hour Express Ser.). (ESP & ENG.). 2004. audio compact disk 9.95 (978-981-246-596-2(0), 465960) Pub: APA Pubns Serv SGP. Dist(s): IngramPubServ

Ingles. abr. ed. Berlitz Publishing Staff. (Berlitz Guaranteed Ser.). (ENG.). 2008. audio compact disk 19.95 (978-981-268-232-1(5)) Pub: APA Pubns Serv SGP. Dist(s): IngramPubServ

Ingles. 2nd rev. ed. Howard Beckerman. Created by Langenscheidt Publishers Staff. 3 CDs. (Running Time: 1 hr.). (Rush Hour Ser.). (ENG & SPA.). 2003. audio compact disk 24.95 (978-981-246-275-6(9), 462759) Pub: Berlitz Pubng. Dist(s): Langenscheidt

Ingles, Set. Jessica Langemeier. (SPA.). 2009. audio compact disk 19.99 (978-0-470-38977-5(X), For Dummies) Wiley US.

Ingles al Espanol. unabr. ed. Mark R. Nesbitt. Read by David Rojas & Cindy Rojas. (Running Time: 3600 sec.). 2007. audio compact disk 17.00 (978-1-4332-1100-3(9)) Blckstn Audio.

Ingles al Espanol: English for Spanish Speakers. abr. unabr. ed. Mark R. Nesbitt. Narrated by David Rojas. (Running Time: 1 hr. 16 mins. 29 sec.). (SPA & ENG.). 2007. audio compact disk 9.99 (978-1-59859-179-8(7)) Oasis Audio.

Ingles al Espanol: English for Spanish Speakers. unabr. ed. Mark R. Nesbitt. Narrated by David Rojas. (SPA.). 2007. 6.99 (978-1-60814-254-5(X)) Oasis Audio.

Ingles Americano Para Hispanohablantes. Mark Frobose. 8 CDs. 2004. 59.00 (978-1-893564-09-1(6)) Macmill Audio.

Ingles Basico: Curso Completo en CDs. Cortina Language Institute Staff. 4 CDs. (ENG.). 2005. audio compact disk 29.95 (978-0-8050-7875-6(4), Cort) Pub: H Holt & Co. Dist(s): Macmillan

Ingles Callejero: Las Frases Mas Utiles para ENAMORAR. A. P. Pacheco. Read by Claudia Pacheco.Tr. of Most Useful Phrases for Courting. (SPA., 2008. audio compact disk 10.95 (978-0-9754939-4-6(9), DB Bks USA) Pub: Dragonbean. Dist(s): Giron Bks

Ingles Callejero: Las Frases Mas Utiles para SOLICITAR TRABAJO. A. P. Pacheco. Read by Claudia Pacheco.Tr. of Most Useful Phrases for Finding a Job. (SPA., 2008. audio compact disk 10.95 (978-0-9754939-3-9(0), DB Bks USA) Pub: Dragonbean. Dist(s): Giron Bks

Ingles Callejero: Vulgaridades y coloquialismos que todo hispano debe aprender para vivir y trabajar en Estados Unidos. Text by A. P. Pacheco. Des. by C. V. Pacheco.Tr. of Expletives & coloquialisms all Hispanics should learn to live & work in the United States. (SPA.). 2005. per. 22.50 (978-0-9754939-1-5(4), DB Bks USA) Pub: Dragonbean. Dist(s): Giron Bks

Ingles Callejero: Vulgaridades y coloquialismos que todo hispano debe aprender para vivir y trabajar en Estados Unidos. Read by Claudia Pacheco. Des. by Claudia Pacheco. Text by A. P. Pacheco. A. P. Pacheco.Tr. of Expletives & coloquialisms all Hispanics should learn to live & work in the United States. (SPA.). 2005. audio compact disk 12.95 (978-0-9754939-2-2(2), DB Bks USA) Pub: Dragonbean. Dist(s): Giron Bks

Ingles de cada Dia. (SPA.). 2002. bk. 8.90 (978-84-494-2378-9(3), 1402) Oceano Grupo ESP.

Ingles de Los Negocios. Richard Pratt. Tr. by Francisco J. Anton from FRE. Contrib. by Leslie Rofe & Dominique De Beauregard. 3 cass. (Running Time: 3 hrs.). 1984. bk. 75.00 (978-2-7005-1307-3(X)) Pub: Assimil FRA. Dist(s): Distribks Inc

Ingles en EspaÑol: Auvifon, Vol. 1116. (SPA & ENG., 2005. pap. bk. 69.95 (978-0-9647863-0-1(3)) Audio Vis Lang.

Ingles en EspaÑol: Auvifon, Vol.2, Bk.2, CD. 7-12. (SPA & ENG., 2005. pap. bk. 69.95 (978-0-9647863-1-8(1)) Audio Vis Lang.

Ingles en Marcha. unabr. ed. Howard Beckerman. (Berlitz Audio for Kids Ser.). (SPA.). 2007. audio compact disk 12.95 (978-981-268-077-8(2)) Pub: Berlitz Pubng. Dist(s): Langenscheidt

Ingles en Tres Meses see Fast & Easy: English for Spanish Speakers

Ingles en Tres Meses, Vol. 1. 8 cass. (Running Time: 12 hrs.). J Norton Pubs. *Features the Granadies Method for learning English as a second language.*

Ingles en Tres Meses: English in Three Months, Courses 1-3. unabr. ed. Joseph N. Granados & Mary P. Granados. 40 cass. (Running Time: 34 hrs. 49 min.). (SPA & ENG.). 1982. pap. bk. 395.00 Set. (978-1-879090-00-2(7), E100) Granados Schl.
3 volume Comprehensive English language course for the Spanish-speaker. Course work covers basic, intermediate & advanced levels.

Ingles en Tres Meses, Curso 1: Ingles Basico: English in Three Months Course One: Basic English. unabr. ed. Joseph N. Granados & Mary P. Granados. 8 cass. (Running Time: 10 hrs. 02 min.). (SPA & ENG.). (YA). 1977. pap. bk. 115.00 (978-1-879090-01-9(5), AFE300) J Norton Pubs. *Comprehensive basic English course for the Spanish-speaker.*

Ingles en Tres Meses, Curso 2: Ingles Intermedio: English in Three Months Course Two: Intermediate English. unabr. ed. Joseph N. Granados & Mary P. Granados. 16 cass. (Running Time: 11 hrs. 05 min.). (SPA & ENG.). (YA). 1981. pap. bk. 135.00 (978-1-879090-02-6(3), AFE320) J Norton Pubs.
Comprehensive intermediate English course for the Spanish-speaker.

Ingles en Tres Meses, Curso 3: Ingles Avanzado: English in Three Months Course Three: Advanced English. unabr. ed. Joseph N. Granados & Mary P. Granados. 16 cass. (Running Time: 13 hrs. 42 min.). (SPA & ENG.). (YA). 1982. pap. bk. 145.00 (978-1-879090-03-3(1), AFE340) J Norton Pubs. *Comprehensive advanced English course for the Spanish-speaker.*

Ingles en 100 Dias: English in 100 Days. Aguilar Staff. 2007. pap. bk. 19.99 (978-1-59820-968-6(X)) Santillana.

Ingles Facil para Todos con. Yara Marrase. 1 cass. (SPA & ENG.). 1985. 12.00 (978-1-884249-04-4(3)) Pub Especiales.

Ingles Para Ciudadania Americana. Yara Marrase. 1 cass. (SPA & ENG.). 1989. 12.00 (978-1-884249-09-9(4), TX2-507-729) Pub Especiales.

Ingles para Construccion. Stacey Kammerman. (SPA.). 2006. audio compact disk 15.98 (978-0-9785424-0-5(1)) NPG Music FL.

Ingles para Construccion: English for Construction. Created by Kamms. (Running Time: 3600 sec.). (Ingles en el Trabajo Ser.). (ENG.). 2006. audio compact disk 10.98 (978-1-934842-43-0(5)) KAMMS Consult.

Inglés para Construcción (Digital) Stacey Kammerman. 2006. audio compact disk 15.95 (978-0-9788099-5-9(5)) KAMMS Consult.

Ingles para Construccion Jewel Case. Kamms.Tr. of English for Construction Jewel Case. 2007. audio compact disk (978-0-9795000-2-2(8)) NPG Music FL.

Ingles para Conversacion. abr. ed. Stacey Kammerman. (Running Time: 3600 sec.). (Ingles en el Trabajo Ser.). 2008. audio compact disk 15.95 (978-1-934842-66-9(4)) Pub: KAMMS Consult. Dist(s): Natl Bk Netwk

Ingles para Dummies. Jessica Langemeier. (Para Dummies (Playaway) Ser.). (SPA.). 2009. 39.99 (978-1-60812-591-3(2)) Find a World.

Ingles para Educadores. Stacey Kammerman. 2007. audio compact disk 15.98 (978-0-9785424-7-4(9)) NPG Music FL.

Ingles para Educadores: English for Educators: Maestros, Profesores, Instructores. Created by Kamms. (Running Time: 3600 sec.). (Ingles en el Trabajo Ser.). 2007. audio compact disk 10.98 (978-1-934842-49-2(4)) KAMMS Consult.

Inglés para Educadores (Digital) Stacey Kammerman. 2007. audio compact disk 15.95 (978-1-934842-02-7(8)) KAMMS Consult.

Ingles para Educadores Jewel Case. Kamms.Tr. of English for Educators Jewel Case. (SPA.). 2007. audio compact disk (978-0-9795000-7-7(9)) NPG Music FL.

Inglés para el Hispanohablante Libro 1 see English for the Spanish Speaker Book 1

Inglés para el Hispanohablante Libro 2 see English for the Spanish Speaker Book 2

Inglés para el Hispanohablante Libro 3 see English for the Spanish Speaker Book 3

Inglés para el Hispanohablante Libro 4 see English for the Spanish Speaker Book 4

Ingles para el Trabajo Domestico. Stacey Kammerman. (SPA.). 2006. audio compact disk 15.98 (978-0-9785424-4-3(4)) NPG Music FL.

Ingles para el Trabajo Domestico: English for Housekeeping. Created by Kamms. (Running Time: 3600 sec.). (Ingles en el Trabajo Ser.). 2006. audio compact disk 10.98 (978-1-934842-44-7(3)) KAMMS Consult.

Inglés para el Trabajo Doméstico (Digital) Stacey Kammerman. 2006. audio compact disk 15.95 (978-0-9788099-6-6(3)) KAMMS Consult.

Ingles para el Trabajo Domestico Jewel Case. Kamms.Tr. of English for Housekeeping Jewel Case. (SPA.). 2007. audio compact disk (978-0-9795000-6-0(0)) NPG Music FL.

Ingles Para Emergencias: English for Emergencies. unabr. ed. Joseph N. Granados & Mary P. Granados. 1 cass. (Running Time: 35 min.). (SPA & ENG.). 1983. pap. bk. 15.00 (978-1-879090-04-0(X), E104) Granados Schl. *Emergency English for the Spanish speaker, for communication with police, paramedics, hospitals, etc., in emergency situations.*

Ingles Para Enamorar. Yara Marrase. 1 cass. (SPA & ENG.). 1995. 12.00 (978-1-884249-13-6(2)) Pub Especiales.

Ingles para Entrevistas de Trabajo. Stacey Kammerman. 2007. audio compact disk 15.98 (978-0-9785424-8-1(7)) NPG Music FL.

Ingles para Entrevistas de Trabajo: English for Job Interviews. Created by Kamms. (Running Time: 3600 sec.). (Ingles en el Trabajo Ser.). 2007. audio compact disk 10.98 (978-1-934842-52-2(4)) KAMMS Consult.

Inglés para Entrevistas de Trabajo (Digital) Stacey Kammerman. 2007. audio compact disk 15.95 (978-1-934842-05-8(2)) KAMMS Consult.

Ingles para Entrevistas de Trabajo Jewel Case. Kamms.Tr. of English for Job Interviews Jewel Case. (SPA.). 2007. audio compact disk (978-0-9795000-8-4(7)) NPG Music FL.

Ingles para Hospitalidad. Stacey Kammerman. (SPA.). 2006. audio compact disk 15.98 (978-0-9785424-2-9(8)) NPG Music FL.

Ingles para Hospitalidad: English for Hospitality. Created by Kamms. (Running Time: 3600 sec.). (Ingles en el Trabajo Ser.). 2006. audio compact disk 10.98 (978-1-934842-45-4(1)) KAMMS Consult.

Inglés para Hospitalidad (Digital) Stacey Kammerman. 2006. audio compact disk 15.95 (978-0-9788099-7-3(1)) KAMMS Consult.

Ingles para Hospitalidad Jewel Case. Kamms.Tr. of English for Hospitality Jewel Case. (SPA.). 2007. audio compact disk (978-0-9795000-4-6(4)) NPG Music FL.

Inglés para Industrias Manufactureras. Stacey Kammerman.Tr. of English for Manufacturing (Single). (SPA.). 2008. audio compact disk 15.95 (978-1-934842-36-2(2)) Pub: KAMMS Consult. Dist(s): Natl Bk Netwk

Inglés para Industrias Manufactureras (Double) Stacey Kammerman.Tr. of English for Manufacturing (Double). (SPA.). 2008. audio compact disk 15.95 (978-1-934842-21-8(4)) KAMMS Consult.

Ingles para Jardineria. Stacey Kammerman. (SPA.). 2006. audio compact disk 15.98 (978-0-9785424-3-6(6)) NPG Music FL.

Inglés para Jardinería (Digital) Stacey Kammerman. 2006. audio compact disk 15.95 (978-0-9788099-8-0(X)) KAMMS Consult.

Ingles para Jardineria Jewel Case. Kamms.Tr. of English for Landscaping Jewel Case. (SPA.). 2007. audio compact disk (978-0-9795000-5-3(2)) NPG Music FL.

Ingles para Jardineria/English for Landscaping. Created by Kamms. (Running Time: 3600 sec.). (Ingles en el Trabajo Ser.). 2009. audio compact disk 10.98 (978-1-934842-46-1(X)) KAMMS Consult.

Ingles Para la Mujer con. Yara Marrase. 1 cass. (SPA & ENG.). 1988. 12.00 (978-1-884249-07-5(8)) Pub Especiales.

Ingles para la Oficina Medica: English for the Medical Office. Created by Kamms. (Running Time: 3600 sec.). (Ingles en el Trabajo Ser.). 2007. audio compact disk 10.98 (978-1-934842-50-8(8)) KAMMS Consult.

Inglés para la Oficina Médica (Digital) Stacey Kammerman. 2007. audio compact disk 15.95 (978-1-934842-03-4(6)) KAMMS Consult.

Ingles para la Oficina Medica Jewel Case. Kamms.Tr. of English for the Medical Office Jewel Case. (SPA.). 2007. audio compact disk (978-0-9795000-9-1(5)) NPG Music FL.

***Ingles para Limpieza y Mantenimiento.** Stacey Kammerman.Tr. of English for Cleaning & Maintenance. 2007. audio compact disk & audio compact disk 15.95 (978-0-9798427-0-2(0)) Pub: KAMMS Consult. Dist(s): Natl Bk Netwk

Inglés para Limpieza Y Mantenimiento (Digital) Stacey Kammerman. 2007. audio compact disk 15.95 (978-1-934842-01-0(X)) KAMMS Consult.

Inglés para Limpieza y Mantenimiento (single) Stacey Kammerman. 2008. audio compact disk 10.98 (978-1-934842-48-5(6)) KAMMS Consult.

Ingles para los Negocios. abr. ed. Stacey Kammerman. (Running Time: 3600 sec.). (Ingles en el Trabajo Ser.). (SPA.). 2008. audio compact disk 15.95 (978-1-934842-38-6(9)) Pub: KAMMS Consult. Dist(s): Natl Bk Netwk

Ingles Para los Trabajadores. Yara Marrase. 1 cass.Tr. of English for the Work Place. (SPA & ENG.). 1993. 18.95 (978-1-884249-11-2(6), TXU572-393) Pub Especiales.

Ingles para los Trabajos. abr. ed. Stacey Kammerman. (Running Time: 3600 sec.). (Ingles en el Trabajo Ser.). (SPA.). 2008. audio compact disk 15.95 (978-1-934842-37-9(0)) Pub: KAMMS Consult. Dist(s): Natl Bk Netwk

Inglés para Los Trabajos (Double) Stacey Kammerman. (SPA.). 2008. audio compact disk 15.95 (978-1-934842-22-5(2)) KAMMS Consult.

Ingles para Mantenimiento y Limpieza Amaray Case. Voice by Kamms. (SPA.). 2007. audio compact disk (978-0-9795000-0-8(1)) NPG Music FL.

Inglés para Negocios (Double) Stacey Kammerman.Tr. of English for Business (Double). (SPA.). 2008. audio compact disk 15.95 (978-1-934842-23-2(0)) KAMMS Consult.

Ingles Para Ninos - English for Spanish Children. unabr. ed. Conversa-Phone Institute Staff. 1 cass. (Running Time: 50 min.). (Round the World Basic Language Programs Ser.). (ENG & SPA.). (J). 1988. 9.95 (978-1-56752-037-8(5), COCB-1375) Conversa-phone.
Conversational lessons teaching basic English sentences, words & phrases through the day in the life of two fun loving children, Peter & Alice. An illustrated manual is included with the program.

Ingles para Oficina Medica. Stacey Kammerman. 2007. audio compact disk 15.98 (978-0-9785424-9-8(5)) NPG Music FL.

Ingles para Restaurante. Stacey Kammerman. (SPA.). 2006. audio compact disk 15.98 (978-0-9785424-1-2(X)) NPG Music FL.

Ingles para Restaurante Jewel Case. Kamms.Tr. of English for Construction Jewel Case. (SPA.). 2007. audio compact disk (978-0-9795000-3-9(6)) NPG Music FL.

Ingles para Restaurantes: English for Restaurants. Created by Kamms. (Running Time: 3600 sec.). (Ingles en el Trabajo Ser.). 2006. audio compact disk 10.98 (978-1-934842-47-8(8)) KAMMS Consult.

Inglés para Restaurantes (Digital) Stacey Kammerman. 2006. audio compact disk 15.95 (978-1-934842-00-3(1)) KAMMS Consult.

Ingles Para Todos. Joann Peters et al. 3 cass. (Running Time: 3 hrs.).Tr. of English for Everyone. (ENG & SPA.). pap. bk. 29.95 (978-970-607-051-7(6)) Pub: Plaza ESP. Dist(s): Distribks Inc
Teaching English to Spanish speaking students.

***Ingles para Vendedores y Cajeros.** Stacey Kammerman.Tr. of English for Sales People & Cashiers. 2007. audio compact disk & audio compact disk 15.95 (978-0-9798427-1-9(9)) Pub: KAMMS Consult. Dist(s): Natl Bk Netwk

Ingles para Vendedores y Cajeros: English for Salespeople & Cashiers. Created by Kamms. (Running Time: 3600 sec.). (Ingles en el Trabajo Ser.). 2007. audio compact disk 10.98 (978-1-934842-51-5(6)) KAMMS Consult.

Ingles para Vendedores y Cajeros Amaray Case. Kamms.Tr. of English for Sales & Cashiers. 2007. audio compact disk (978-0-9795000-1-5(X)) NPG Music FL.

Inglés para Vendedores y Cajeros (Digital) Stacey Kammerman. 2007. audio compact disk 16.00 (978-1-934842-04-1(4)) KAMMS Consult.

Ingles Perfeccionamento. Assimil Staff.Tr. of Using English. 1999. pap. bk. 75.00 (978-2-7005-1306-6(1)) Pub: Assimil FRA. Dist(s): Distribks Inc

Ingles Practico: Practical English for Spanish Speakers. rev. ed. Educational Services Corporation Staff. 2 cass. 1994. pap. bk. 21.95 incl. pap. text. (978-0-910542-66-1(X)) Educ Svcs DC.
English self-teaching language course for Spanish speakers.

Ingles Practico Sin Maestro. Robert James Dixson. (SPA.). (C). (gr. 9 up). 1972. 70.00 (978-0-685-73420-9(X)) Prentice ESL.

Ingles Primario. Yara Marrase. 1 cass.Tr. of Primary English. (SPA & ENG.). 1989. 12.00 (978-1-884249-01-3(9), TX2-705-779) Pub Especiales.

Ingles Rush Hour Express Cd Berlitz. (RUSH HOUR EXPRESS Ser.). 2008. audio compact disk 9.95 (978-981-268-237-6(6)) Pub: Berlitz Pubng. Dist(s): Langenscheidt

Ingles sin Barreras, Set. 12 cass. (Running Time: 8 hrs. 48 mins.). (ENG & SPA.). 130.00 (978-1-59172-123-9(7)) Lexicon Mark.
Helps Spanish speakers learn English while driving, cleaning, working, or just relaxing. This on-the-go course features audiocassettes and 2 study guides.

Inglese I. unabr. ed. Pimsleur Staff & Pimsleur. 16 cass. (Running Time: 160 hrs. 0 mins. 0 sec.). (Comprehensive, English As a Second Langu Ser.). (ITA.). 2002. 295.00 (978-0-7435-2528-2(0), Pimsleur) Pub: S&S Audio. Dist(s): S and S Inc

Ingmar Bergman Archives. Ed. by Paul Duncan & Bengt Wanselius. Intro. by Erland Josephson. (ENG., 2008. 200.00 (978-3-8365-0023-4(X)) Pub: Taschen DEU. Dist(s): IngramPubServ

Ingredients for Perfect Love. Don J. Black. Read by Don J. Black. 1 cass. 1993. 7.98 (978-1-55503-590-7(6), 06004792) Covenant Comms.
Learn how to increase your love.

Ingredients for Success: Faith, Patience & Love. Gloria Copeland. Perf. by Gloria Copeland. 4 cass. (Running Time: 4 hrs.). 1996. cass. & video 20.00 (978-1-57562-016-9(2)) K Copeland Pubns.
Biblical teaching on faith, patience & love.

Ingredients of Leadership. Perf. by James E. Lukaszewski. (ENG.). 2007. audio compact disk 10.00 (978-1-883291-48-8(8)) Lukaszewski.

Inhabitant of Carcosa see Classic Ghost Stories, Vol. 2, A Collection

Inherent Vice. unabr. ed. Thomas Pynchon. Read by Ron McLarty. 12 CDs. (Running Time: 15 hrs.). (ENG.). (gr. 12 up). 2009. audio compact disk 39.95 (978-0-14-314476-2(6), PengAudBks) Penguin Grp USA.

Inheritance. Joyce Landorf Heatherley. 1 cass. 1988. 7.95 (978-0-929488-04-2(0)) Balcony Pub Inc.
What is your true inheritance?.

Inheritance. unabr. ed. Tamera Alexander. (Running Time: 11 hrs. 0 mins. 0 sec.). (ENG.). 2009. audio compact disk 28.98 (978-1-59644-700-4(1), christaudio) christianaud.

***Inheritance.** unabr. ed. Tamera Alexander. Narrated by Tavia Gilbert. (ENG.). 2009. 16.98 (978-1-59644-701-1(X), christaudio) christianaud.

Inheritance. unabr. ed. Keith Baker. 10 CDs. (Isis (CDs) Ser.). (J). 2005. audio compact disk 89.95 (978-0-7531-2292-1(8)) Pub: ISIS Lrg Prnt GBR. Dist(s): Ulverscroft US

Inheritance. unabr. ed. Keith Baker. Read by Stephen Armstrong. 9 cass. (Running Time: 10 hrs. 45 mins.). (Isis Cassettes Ser.). (J). 2005. 76.95 (978-0-7531-1911-2(0)) Pub: ISIS Lrg Prnt GBR. Dist(s): Ulverscroft US

Inheritance. unabr. ed. Susan Ferrier. Narrated by Flo Gibson. 15 cass. (Running Time: 22 hrs. 30 mins.). 2003. 43.95 (978-1-55685-744-7(6)) Audio Bk Con.
Gertrude, a charming young countess and heiress, deals with a turbulent romance and a shocking discovery that deprives her of her birthright. Some good laughs and melodrama.

Inheritance. unabr. ed. Simon Tolkien. Read by Simon Tolkien. (Running Time: 12 hrs.). 2010. 39.97 (978-1-4233-9031-2(8), 9781423390312, Brinc Audio MP3 Lib); 39.97 (978-1-4233-9033-6(4), 9781423390336, BADLE); 24.99 (978-1-4233-9032-9(6), 9781423390329, BAD); 24.99 (978-1-4233-9030-5(X), 9781423390305, Brilliance MP3); audio compact disk 87.97 (978-1-4233-9029-9(6), 9781423390299, BriAudCD Unabrid); audio compact disk 29.99 (978-1-4233-9028-2(8), 9781423390282, Bril Audio CD Unabri) Brilliance Audio.

***Inheritance & Rewards.** Chuck Missler. (ENG.). 2009. audio compact disk 19.95 (978-1-57821-457-0(2)) Koinonia Hse.

Inheritance of God's Son. Kenneth Wapnick. 2 CDs. 2007. audio compact disk 11.00 (978-1-59142-327-0(9), CD45) Foun Miracles.

Inheritance of God's Son. Kenneth Wapnick. 2007. 9.00 (978-1-59142-328-7(7)) Foun Miracles.

Inheritance of Loss. Kiran Desai. Read by Meera Simhan. (Running Time: 13 hrs.). (ENG.). (gr. 12 up). 2007. audio compact disk 39.95 (978-0-14-314230-0(5), PengAudBks) Penguin Grp USA.

Inheritance of Our Salvation. Creflo A. Dollar. 25.00 (978-1-59089-090-5(6)) Pub: Creflo Dollar. Dist(s): STL Dist NA

Inheritance of the Heart. 2001. 10.00 (978-1-58602-076-7(5)) E L Long.

Inheriting the Trade: A Northern Family Confronts Its Legacy as the Largest Slave-Trading Dynasty in U. S. History. unabr. ed. Thomas Norman DeWolf. (Running Time: 9 hrs.). 2008. 39.25 (978-1-4233-5069-9(3), 9781423350699, BADLE); 24.95 (978-1-4233-5068-2(5), 9781423350682, BAD) Brilliance Audio.

Inheriting the Trade: A Northern Family Confronts Its Legacy as the Largest Slave-Trading Dynasty in U. S. History. unabr. ed. Thomas Norman DeWolf. Read by Thomas Norman DeWolf. 8 cass. (Running Time: 9 hrs.). 2008. 87.25 (978-1-4233-5063-7(4), 9781423350637, BrilAudUnabridg) Brilliance Audio.

Inheriting the Trade: A Northern Family Confronts Its Legacy as the Largest Slave-Trading Dynasty in U. S. History. unabr. ed. Thomas Norman Dewolf. Read by Thomas Norman Dewolf. 8 CDs. (Running Time: 32400 sec.). 2008. audio compact disk 92.25 (978-1-4233-5065-1(0), 9781423350651, BriAudCD Unabrid); audio compact disk 39.25 (978-1-4233-5067-5(7), 9781423350675, Brlnc Audio MP3 Lib); audio compact disk 34.95 (978-1-4233-5064-4(2), 9781423350644, Bril Audio CD Unabri); audio compact disk 24.95 (978-1-4233-5066-8(9), 9781423350668, Brilliance MP3) Brilliance Audio.

Inhuman Bondage: The Rise & Fall of Slavery in the New World. David Brion Davis. Read by Raymond Todd. (Running Time: 61200 sec.). 2007. 85.95 (978-1-4332-0134-9(8)); audio compact disk 99.00 (978-1-4332-0135-6(6)); audio compact disk 29.95 (978-1-4332-0136-3(4)) Blckstn Audio.

Iniciacion al Euskara (Basque) 1 cass. (Running Time: 1 hr.). (FRE & SPA.). 2000. bk. 75.00 (978-2-7005-1386-8(X)) Pub: Assimil FRA. Dist(s): Distribks Inc

***Inimitable Jeeves.** P. G. Wodehouse. Narrated by Richard Briers & Michael Hordern. 3 CDs. (Running Time: 3 hrs. 30 mins. 0 sec.). (ENG., 2010. audio compact disk 29.95 (978-0-563-52552-3(5)) Pub: AudioGO. Dist(s): Perseus Dist

Inimitable Jeeves. P. G. Wodehouse. Read by Martin Jarvis. (ENG.). 2009. audio compact disk 33.07 (978-1-906147-37-2(X), CSAW) CSA Telltapes GBR.

Inimitable Jeeves. P. G. Wodehouse. Narrated by Frederick Davidson. (Running Time: 7 hrs.). 1999. 27.95 (978-1-59912-675-3(3)) Iofy Corp.

Inimitable Jeeves. abr. ed. P. G. Wodehouse. Read by Martin Jarvis. Abr. by Neville Teller. 3 CDs. (Running Time: 3 hrs. 0 mins. 0 sec.). (ENG.). 2009. audio compact disk 22.95 (978-1-934997-24-6(2)) Pub: CSAWord. Dist(s): PerseuPGW

Inimitable Jeeves. unabr. ed. P. G. Wodehouse. Read by Jonathan Cecil. 6 cass. (Running Time: 6 hrs. 20 mins.). 2000. 29.95 (978-1-57270-150-2(1), C61150u) Pub: Audio Partners. Dist(s): PerseuPGW
Bertie is in trouble again! His lovesick pal Bingo Little falls in love with every girl he lays eyes on. Bertie's real problem begins when Bingo decides to marry one of the girls & enlists Bertie's help. Luckily, Jeeves, as usual, comes to the rescue.

Inimitable Jeeves. unabr. ed. P. G. Wodehouse. Narrated by Jonathan Cecil. (Running Time: 22620 sec.). (ENG.). 2006. audio compact disk 29.95 (978-1-57270-542-5(6)) Pub: AudioGO. Dist(s): Perseus Dist

Inimitable Jeeves. unabr. ed. P. G. Wodehouse. Read by Frederick Davidson. 5 cass. (Running Time: 7 hrs. 30 min.). 2000. 27.95 (978-0-7861-1775-8(3)) Pub: Blckstn Audio. Dist(s): Penton Overseas

Inimitable Jeeves. unabr. ed. P. G. Wodehouse. Read by Frederick Davidson. 5 cass. (Running Time: 7 hrs.). 2000. 39.95 (978-0-7861-1740-6(0), 2545); audio compact disk 48.00 (978-0-7861-9903-7(2), 2545) Blckstn Audio.
When Bingo Little falls in love at a Camberwell subscription dance & Bertie Wooster drops into the mulligatawny, there's work for a wet-nurse. Who better than Jeeves? This is the first Jeeves & Wooster story Plum ever wrote. There's a wide collection of terrifying aunts, miserly uncles, love-sick friends & unwanted fiances that make the plot really witty.

Inimitable Jeeves. unabr. ed. P. G. Wodehouse. Read by Jonathan Cecil. 6 cass. (Running Time: 9 hrs.). (Jeeves & Wooster Ser.). 2000. 49.95 (978-0-7451-6373-4(4), CSL 061) Pub: Chivers Audio Bks GBR. Dist(s): AudioGO
When Bingo Little falls in love with a waitress at the town dance, and Bertie falls into the mulligatawny, there's work for a wet-nurse. Who better than Jeeves? With his usual savoir-faire, Jeeves saves the day in his unflappable and inimitable way.

Inimitable Jeeves. unabr. ed. P. G. Wodehouse. Read by Frederick Davidson. 5 cass. (Running Time: 7 hrs.). 2000. 27.95 Penton Overseas.

***Inimitable Jeeves, Vol. 2.** P. G. Wodehouse. Read by Martin Jarvis. (Running Time: 5 hrs. 0 mins. 0 sec.). (ENG.). 2010. audio compact disk 22.95 (978-1-934997-63-5(3)) Pub: CSAWord. Dist(s): PerseuPGW

Inimitable Winston Churchill: A Light & Enlightening Lecture, Featuring Elliot Engel. 2000. bk. 15.00 (978-1-890123-24-6(2)) Media Cnslts.

Inishfallen, Fare Thee Well: The Death of Mrs. Casside see Sean O'Casey Reading Juno & the Paycock & Other Works

Initial Care of the Trauma Patient. (Postgraduate Programs Ser.: C84-PG5). 1984. 85.00 (8485) Am Coll Surgeons.
Provides review of the latest concepts & techniques in resuscitation & management of the injury victim.

Initial Pastoral Call. Bruce Hartung. 1986. 10.80 (0104A) Assn Prof Chaplains.

Initial Post Mortem Estate Planning Steps. Edward S. Schlesinger. 1 cass. (Running Time: 90 min.). 1986. 17.40 (M651) Am Law Inst.
Do you always remember everything that needs to be done immediately after a client has died? Listen to this audiotape & be confident that you have taken the necessary initial post mortem estate planning steps.

Initiate. Louise Cooper. 10 CD. (Running Time: 6 hrs, 30 mins). Dramatization. 2006. audio compact disk 29.99 (978-1-59426-454-2(6), MundPr) Mundania Pr.
The seven gods of Order had ruled unchallenged for centuries, served by the adepts of the Circle in their bleak northern castle on the Star Peninsula. But for Tarod?the most enigmatic and formidable sorcerer in Circle?s ranks?a darker affinity had begun to call. Threatening his beliefs, even his sanity, it rose unbidden from beyond time; an ancient and deadly adversary that could plunge the world into madness and chaos?and whose power might rival that of the gods themselves.And though Tarod?s mind and heart were pledged to Order, his soul was another matter.

Initiating Pastoral Relationships. Lawrence Holst. 1986. 10.80 (0607) Assn Prof Chaplains.

Initiation. Govinda. Read by Karen Petrella. Ed. by Dietmar R. Rittner. 1 cass. (Running Time: 1 hr. 30 min.). (ViViD-Process Ser.). 1993. 14.95 (978-1-884027-05-5(9)) Magic Sunrise.
A guided visualization with relaxing music. Travel with your light body into a crystal & from there to the realms of the spiritual masters to receive your initiation.

Initiation. Perf. by Roth, Gabrielle, and the Mirrors. 1 cass. 9.95 (SA610) White Dove NM.
An invitation to dance, INITIATION is a movement ritual designed to free your body & all of its parts. This music is a map. It can take you from inertia to ecstasy if you surrender to its pulse.

Initiation Vol. I: Meditation-Relaxation. Barbara Stone. Read by Barbara Stone. 1 cass. (Running Time: 1 hrs. 21 min.). 1994. bk. 10.95 (978-1-893129-01-6(2), 002) Stonepower.
Side 1: guided body scan relaxation with chakra attunement. Side 2: guided meditation.

Initiation au Breton Sans Peine. 3 cass. (Running Time: 1 hr., 30 min.). (BRE & FRE.). 2000. cass. & audio compact disk 75.00 (978-2-7005-1345-5(2)) Pub: Assimil FRA. Dist(s): Distribks Inc

***Initiation, Human & Solar: Mp3.** Alice A. Bailey. (ENG.). 2009. audio compact disk 15.00 (978-0-85330-210-0(3)) Lucis Pr GBR.

Initiation into Dynamic & Soul Mantra. George King. 2007. audio compact disk (978-0-937249-40-6(8)) Aetherius Soc.

Initiation into the Mysteries. Michael P. Marshall. Read by Michael P. Marshall. Ed. by Jonathan C. Renaud. Music by Ted Crook. 1 cass. (Running Time: 52 min.). 1995. 9.00 (978-0-912403-12-0(8)) Prod Renaud.
Ancient rites, their meanings & symbols & how they apply to today's world.

Initiation of the Awakening Heart Centre-A Guided Meditation for Beginners: Eagle Heart & Spirit. Mel Brand. 2007. audio compact disk 39.99 (978-1-4276-2319-5(8)) AardGP.

Initiation Rediscovered. Read by Louise Bode. 1 cass. (Running Time: 1 hr.). 1983. 9.95 (978-0-7822-0018-8(4), 119) C G Jung IL.

Initiation to the Andean Orchid Flower Essences: An Extraordinary Workshop Given by Roger Valencia Espinosa & Star Riparetti. unabr. ed. Instructed by Star Riparetti & Roger Valencia. 4 cass. (Running Time: 4 hrs.). (Evolutionary Flower Essences from Orchids in Peru: Vol. 1). 1996. 33.00 Set. (978-1-892457-02-8(4)) Laughng Star Pr.

Initiative: A Course for Advanced Learners. Richard Walton & Mark Bartram. (Running Time: 1 hr. 31 mins.). (ENG.). 2000. 26.24 (978-0-521-57580-5(X)) Cambridge U Pr.

Injunctions: Why, When, How. Read by Stuart Pollak et al. (Running Time: 2 hrs. 45 min.). 1991. 89.00 Incl. 127p. tape materials. (CP-55225) Cont Ed Bar-CA.

Injury Time: A Comedy of Middle-Aged Passion. unabr. ed. Beryl Bainbridge. Read by Timothy West. 4 cass. (Running Time: 6 hrs.). 2002. 39.95 (978-0-7540-0733-3(2), CAB 2155) AudioGO.

Injustice for All. unabr. ed. J. A. Jance. Read by Gene Engene. 6 cass. (Running Time: 8 hrs. 30 min.). Dramatization. (J. P. Beaumont Mystery Ser.). 1992. 39.95 (978-1-55686-415-5(9), 415) Books in Motion.
The blonde on the beach was screaming. A dead man lay at her feet. That murder was only the first ingredient Beaumont discovered in a deadly mixture of politics & passion.

Injustice for All. unabr. collector's ed. J. A. Jance. Read by Connor O'Brien. 7 cass. (Running Time: 10 hrs. 30 min.). (J. P. Beaumont Mystery Ser.). 1997. 56.00 (978-0-7366-3568-4(8), 4217) Books on Tape.
The blonde on the beach was screaming. A dead man lay at her feet. It turns out that both the lady & the corpse served on the State Parole Board. Can J. P. Beaumont wade through the politics to get at a killer?.

***Ink Exchange.** unabr. ed. Melissa Marr. Read by Nick Landrum. (ENG.). 2008. (978-0-06-169179-9(8)); (978-0-06-170225-9(0)) HarperCollins Pubs.

Ink Exchange. unabr. ed. Melissa Marr. Narrated by Nick Landrum. 8 cass. (Running Time: 9 hrs.). (Wicked Lovely Ser.: No. 2). (YA). (gr. 9 up). 2008. 67.75 (978-1-4361-3765-2(9)); audio compact disk 87.75 (978-1-4361-3770-6(5)) Recorded Bks.

Ink on His Fingers. Louise Vernon. Narrated by Fern Ebersole. (ENG.). (J). 2008. audio compact disk 15.95 (978-0-9801244-6-0(8)) IG Publish.

Ink Truck. William Kennedy. Read by William Kennedy. 1 cass. (Running Time: 77 min.). Incl. Billy Phelan's Greatest Game; Ironweed. William Kennedy. (Albany Cycle Ser.).; Legs; 13.95 (978-1-55644-107-3(X)) Am Audio Prose.

Inkdeath. unabr. ed. Cornelia Funke. Read by Allan Corduner. 16 CDs. (Running Time: 19 hrs. 46 mins.). (Inkheart Trilogy: Bk. 3). (J). (gr. 4-7). 2008. audio compact disk 90.00 (978-0-7393-6302-7(6), Listening Lib) Pub: Random Audio Pubg. Dist(s): Random

Inkdeath. unabr. ed. Cornelia Funke. Read by Allan Corduner. (Inkheart Trilogy: Bk. 3). (ENG.). (J). (gr. 5). 2008. audio compact disk 67.00 (978-0-7393-6300-3(X), Listening Lib) Pub: Random Audio Pubg. Dist(s): Random

Inkheart. unabr. ed. Cornelia Funke. Read by Lynn Redgrave. (YA). 2006. 59.99 (978-0-7393-7495-5(8)) Find a World.

Inkheart. unabr. ed. Cornelia Funke. Read by Lynn Redgrave. 10 cass. Library ed. (Running Time: 13 hrs. 15 min.). (Inkheart Trilogy: Bk. 1). (J). (gr. 4-7). 2004. 55.00 (978-0-8072-1951-5(7), Listening Lib); audio compact disk 72.25 (978-0-8072-2010-8(8), Listening Lib) Pub: Random Audio Pubg. Dist(s): NetLibrary CO

Inkheart. unabr. ed. Cornelia Funke. Read by Lynn Redgrave. 14 CDs. (Running Time: 56160 sec.). (Inkheart Trilogy: Bk. 1). (ENG.). (J). (gr. 4-7). 2005. audio compact disk 34.99 (978-0-307-28227-9(9), Listening Lib) Pub: Random Audio Pubg. Dist(s): Random

Inklings. unabr. ed. Humphrey Carpenter. Read by Bernard Mayes. 9 cass. (Running Time: 13 hrs.). 1990. 62.95 (978-0-7861-0103-0(2), 1096) Blckstn Audio.
During the 1930's at Oxford, C. S. Lewis, J. R. R. Tolkien, & Charles Williams - remarkable friends & scholars - met regularly to discuss philosophy & read aloud from their works. Carpenter's account brings to life those warm & enchanting evenings in Lewis's room at Magdalen College where their imaginations ran wild.

Inkspell. collector's unabr. ed. Cornelia Funke. Read by Brendan Fraser. 11 cass. (Running Time: 16 hrs. 30 mins.). (Inkheart Trilogy: Bk. 2). (J). (gr. 4-7). 2005. 65.00 (978-0-307-28291-0(0), Listening Lib); audio compact disk 72.25 (978-0-307-28292-7(9), Listening Lib) Pub: Random Audio Pubg. Dist(s): NetLibrary CO

Inkspell. unabr. ed. Cornelia Funke. Read by Brendan Fraser. 16 CDs. (Running Time: 67800 sec.). (Inkheart Trilogy: Bk. 2). (ENG., (J). (gr. 5-7). 2005. audio compact disk 60.00 (978-0-307-28162-3(0), Listening Lib) Pub: Random Audio Pubg. Dist(s): Random

Inktomi & the Ducks: And Other Assiniboin Trickster Stories. unabr. ed. Read by Ron Evans. 1 cass. (Running Time: 1 hr.). (Native American Storytime Ser.). (ps-7). 1994. 11.00 (978-0-930407-33-9(4)) Parabola Bks.
Inktomi, selfish bumbler, troublemaker, and one of the liveliest characters in Assiniboin mythology, is brought to life in these stories by native storyteller Ron Evans. Inktomi's unlikely and humorous approaches to relationships, telling the truth and problem-solving are always the children's favorites.

Inland Voyage. unabr. collector's ed. Robert Louis Stevenson. Read by Walter Zimmerman. 5 cass. (Running Time: 5 hrs.). 1998. 30.00 (978-0-7366-3964-4(0), 9502) Books on Tape.
Inspired by a canoe trip the author made with a friend in 1876 on the rivers of nothern France. As we travel with him, we meet a rich variety of characters, portrayed with relish by the vivacious & energetic young author.

***Inn at Eagle Point.** unabr. ed. Sherryl Woods. Read by Christina Traister. (Running Time: 12 hrs.). (Chesapeake Shores Ser.). 2010. 39.97 (978-1-4418-4990-8(4), 9781441849908, Brlnc Audio MP3 Lib); 19.99 (978-1-4418-4991-5(2), 9781441849915, BAD); 39.97 (978-1-4418-4992-2(0), 9781441849922, BADLE); 19.99 (978-1-4418-4989-2(0), 9781441849892, Brilliance MP3); audio compact disk 19.99 (978-1-4418-4987-8(4), 9781441849878, Bril Audio CD Unabri); audio compact disk 79.97 (978-1-4418-4988-5(2), 9781441849885, BriAudCD Unabrid) Brilliance Audio.

Inn at Lake Devine. unabr. ed. Elinor Lipman. Read by Beth Fowler. 8 vols. (Running Time: 12 hrs.). 2000. bk. 69.95 (978-0-7927-2292-2(2), CSL 181, Chivers Sound Lib) AudioGO.
It is the 1960's and Natalie Marx is stunned when her mother inquires about vacationing at a Vermont hotel and is refused because their family is Jewish. So begins Natalie's fixation with the Inn and the family who owns it. And when Natalie finagles an invitation to join a friend on vacation there, she sets herself upon a path that will inextricably link her adult life to this peculiar family and their hotel.

Inner Affair. Miss Dee. 1 cass. 1992. 8.95 (1026) Am Fed Astrologers.

Inner Alchemy. 1 cass. (Running Time: 1 hr.). 1990. 8.95 (978-0-8356-1914-1(1)) Theos Pub Hse.
Examines equilibrium, transformation, & synchronicity.

Inner & Outer Poverty. Thomas Merton. 1 cass. (Running Time: 60 min.). (Poverty Ser.). 4.50 (AA2104) Credence Commun.
Discusses sins against poverty in our society & the demands of poverty in the monastery.

Inner Art of Mediation. Jack Kornfield. 6 CDs. 2004. audio compact disk 39.95 (978-1-59179-144-7(8), AF00777D) Sounds True.

Inner Art of Meditation. Jack Kornfield. 6 cass. 49.95 Set. (11760PAM) Nightingale-Conant.
Cultivate a stronger spirituality, a deeper serenity & heightened awareness of yourself with this calming, enriching program. Author, psychologist, therapist & meditation instructor Jack Kornfield teaches you the four foundations of mindfulness..how emotions affect your experience...how to find freedom in truth...& much more. Ideal for anyone seeking serenity, The Inner Art of Meditation provides a path for creating a Zen-like simplicity & balance in all aspects of your life.

Inner Awakening & Transformation. E. J. Gold. 1 cass. (Running Time: 90 min.). 1986. 9.98 (TP109) Union Label.
E. J. Gold discusses the human biological machine, its defense mechanisms against the waking state, methods of awakening the machine, his practical approach to transformation & the background for his ideas & where they came from, with comments by interviewer Mary Houston of WBAI radio.

Inner Awareness. John F. Barnes. 2 cass. (Running Time: 3 hrs.). 2000. (978-1-929894-01-7(5)) M F R Treatment Ctrs.
This tape series provides the reasons why slowing one's breathing diaphragmatically is important for developing the relaxation necessary to break the "flight or fight alarm".

Inner Balance: Outer Harmony. Patricia J. Crane. Read by Patricia J. Crane. 1 cass. (Running Time: 56 min.). 1986. 10.00 (978-1-893705-01-2(3)) Hlth Horiz.
Four deep relaxation exercises with soothing music to reduce stress & tension.

Inner Beauty. 1 cass. (Running Time: 60 min.). 10.95 (051) Psych Res Inst.

Inner Bhagavad Gita: In the Light of Sri Nisargadatta Maharaj. Stephen Wolinsky. Prod. by maurizio benazzo et al. (ENG.). 2009. audio compact disk 19.95 (978-0-9786608-7-1(0)) Neti Neti Films.

Inner Bitch Guide to Men, Relationships, Dating, Etc. unabr. ed. Elizabeth Hilts. Read by Alyssa Bresnahan. 2 cass. (Running Time: 3 hrs.). (For Women Ser.). 1999. 16.95 (978-1-885408-26-6(9), LL019) Listen & Live.
This is the end of Toxic Niceness as we know it! No more two-week wonders, no more romantic cul-de-sacs, no more saying "yes" when you mean "no".

Inner Bliss. As told by R.E.Y. L.M.T. 2003. audio compact disk 18.99 (978-0-9727097-0-5(3)) REY.

Inner Child Healing. 1 cassette. 1986. 12.95 (978-1-55841-017-6(1)) Emmett E Miller.
A truly beautiful and pwerful work of art, perhaps the most relaxing tape of all. There are no challenges on this tape; it is a pure invitation to come and be taken care of, a chance for your Inner Child to be honored and loved the way it deserves to be. Dr. Miller and Margot Forrest gently guide you to relax deeply. Your Inner Child is then invited forth to hear the words of healing and love spoken by Dr. Miller's 11 year old daughter, Lauren. The lovely background music was composed and performed by Dr. Miller. Side 2 features a heart-to-heart talk on the true meaning and value of the child part of you that dwells within.

Inner Child Healing. 1 CD. 1996. audio compact disk 16.95 (978-1-55841-112-8(7)) Emmett E Miller.
A truly beautiful and powerful work of art. There are no challenges on this tape. it is a pure invitation to come and be taken care of, a chance for your Inner Child to be honored and loved the way it deserves to be.

Inner Child (Hypnosis), Vol. 28. Jayne Helle. 1 cass. (Running Time: 28 min.). 1996. 15.00 (978-1-891826-27-6(1)) Introspect.
By healing the inner child, you help the adult you have become.

Inner Christianity: A Guide to the Esoteric Tradition. Richard Smoley. Read by Richard Smoley. 8 CDs. (Running Time: 10 hours). 2004. audio compact disk 35.00 (978-0-9663401-5-0(9)) BMA Studios.

Inner Circle. unabr. ed. T. C. Boyle. 2004. 99.00 (978-1-4159-0318-6(2)); audio compact disk 104.00 (978-1-4159-0319-3(0)) Books on Tape.

***Inner Circle.** unabr. ed. Kate Brian, pseud. Narrated by Cassandra Campbell. (Running Time: 5 hrs. 30 mins. 0 sec.). (Private Ser.). (ENG.). 2010. 19.99 (978-1-4001-6235-2(1)); audio compact disk 29.99 (978-1-4001-1235-7(4)) Pub: Tantor Media. Dist(s): IngramPubServ

***Inner Circle.** unabr. ed. Kate Brian, pseud. Narrated by Cassandra Campbell. (Running Time: 5 hrs. 30 mins.). (Private Ser.). 2010. 13.99 (978-1-4001-8235-0(2)) Tantor Media.

***Inner Circle.** unabr. ed. Brad Meltzer. (Running Time: 14 hrs.). (ENG.). 2011. audio compact disk 39.98 (978-1-60788-676-1(6)) Pub: Hachet Audio. Dist(s): HachBkGrp

***Inner Circle.** unabr. ed. Brad Meltzer. Read by Scott Brick. (Running Time: 14 hrs.). (ENG.). 2011. 26.98 (978-1-60788-677-8(4)) Pub: Hachet Audio. Dist(s): HachBkGrp

***Inner Circle (Library Edition)** unabr. ed. Kate Brian, pseud. Narrated by Cassandra Campbell. (Running Time: 5 hrs. 30 mins. 0 sec.). (Private Ser.). (ENG.). 2010. audio compact disk 59.99 (978-1-4001-4235-4(0)) Pub: Tantor Media. Dist(s): IngramPubServ

Inner City Blues. unabr. ed. Paula L. Woods. Read by Fran L. Washington. (Running Time: 11 hrs.). 2008. 39.25 (978-1-4233-7144-1(5), 9781423371441, Brlnc Audio MP3 Lib); 39.25 (978-1-4233-7146-5(1), 9781423371465, BADLE); 24.95 (978-1-4233-7143-4(7), 9781423371434, Brilliance MP3); 24.95 (978-1-4233-7145-8(3), 9781423371458, BAD) Brilliance Audio.

Inner City Blues, Set. abr. ed. Paula L. Woods. Read by Fran L. Washington. 2 cass. 1999. 17.95 (FS9-43326) Highsmith.

Inner Connections Series. Arleen Lorrance. Hosted by Diane K. Pike. 11 cass. (Running Time: 48 min. per cass.). 1999. 106.00 Set. Teleos Inst.
Taken from a talk show broadcast out of Phoenix, Arizona, & Providence, Rhode Island. Guests include: Richard Moss, Nicole LaVoie, Marion Nelson,

Ram Dass, Howard Cutler, Scott Miller, Barbara Marx Hubbard, John Vasconcellos, Michael Murphy & Matthew Fox.

Inner Connections Series No. 1: Guest - Richard Moss. 1 cass. (Running Time: 48 min.). 1998. 7.00 Teleos Inst.
The author of "The Second Miracle" helps people to touch their deeper essence & transform their lives. Theme: Consciousness as Relationship. Love Principle: Receive All People as Beautiful Exactly as They Are.

Inner Connections Series No. 2: Guest - Nicole LaVoie. 1 cass. (Running Time: 48 min.). 1998. 7.00 Teleos Inst.
Pioneer in healing sounds & founder of Sound Wave Energy. Author of "Return to Harmony." Theme: Taking Conscious Responsibility for Our Health & Well-Being. Love Principle: Have No Expectations, but Rather Abundant Expectancy.

Inner Connections Series No. 3: Guest - Marion Nelson. 1 cass. (Running Time: 48 min.). 1998. 7.00 Teleos Inst.
Entrepreneur who provides a bridge between Asia & the United States through her business, Global View. Theme: Expressing Gratitude. Love Principle: Problems Are Opportunities.

Inner Connections Series No. 4: Guest - Ram Dass. 1 cass. (Running Time: 48 min.). 1998. 7.00 Teleos Inst.
Author of "Be Here Now" & teacher of consciousness at large for over 30 years. Theme: The Self As a Spiritual Laboratory. Love Principle: Create Your Own Reality Consciously.

Inner Connections Series No. 5: Guest - Howard Cutler. 1 cass. (Running Time: 48 min.). 1998. 7.00 Teleos Inst.
Psychologist & author of "The Art of Happiness," written with the Dalai Lama. Theme: Beyond Suffering. Love Principle: Be the Change You Want to See Happen.

Inner Connections Series No. 6: Theme - Life As a Waking Dream. Contrib. by Arleen Lorrance & Diane K. Pike. 1 cass. (Running Time: 48 min.). 1998. 7.00 Teleos Inst.
Introduction of the method. Love Principle: Provide Others with Opportunities to Give.

Inner Connections Series No. 7: Guest - Scott Miller. 1 cass. (Running Time: 48 min.). 1998. 7.00 Teleos Inst.
Senior Associate with Move the Mountain Leadership Center in Iowa whose work is helping families move out of poverty. Theme: The Joy of Giving. Love Principle: Choice Is the Life Process.

Inner Connections Series No. 8: Guest - Barbara Marx Hubbard. 1 cass. (Running Time: 48 min.). 1998. 7.00 Teleos Inst.
Noted author, futurist, speaker & social architect, whose new book "Conscious Evolution" addresses the power of our social potential. Theme: Consciously Creating the Future. Love Principle: Create Your Own Reality Consciously.

Inner Connections Series No. 9: Guest - John Vasconcellos. 1 cass. (Running Time: 48 min.). 1999. 7.00 Teleos Inst.
California State Senator, who has been called the conscience of the legislature & the Johnny Appleseed of self-esteem. Theme: Integrity in Politics. Love Principle: Problems are Opportunities.

Inner Connections Series No. 10: Guest - Michael Murphy. 1 cass. (Running Time: 48 min.). 1999. 7.00 Teleos Inst.
Founder of Esalen Institute, leader in the human potential movement, & author of "Golf in the Kingdom." Theme: Sports as a Spiritual Pathway. Love Principle: Have No Expectations, but Rather Abundant Expectancy.

Inner Connections Series No. 11: Guest - Matthew Fox. 1 cass. (Running Time: 48 min.). 1999. 7.00 Teleos Inst.
Director of the Institute in Culture & Creation Spirituality & author of "Original Blessing" & "The Reinvention of Work." Theme: Creative Spirituality. Love Principle: Provide Others with Opportunities to Give.

Inner Counselor. Ann Nunley. 1999. bk. 39.95 (978-1-58501-011-0(1)) SterlingHse.

Inner Dance. 1 cass. bk. (978-1-55961-336-1(X)) Relaxtn Co.

Inner Dance. Jeffrey Thompson. 1 CD. (Running Time: 1hr.). audio compact disk 13.95 (978-1-55961-303-3(3)) Relaxtn Co.

Inner Dance of the Martial Arts Master. Barrie Konicov. 1 cass. (Running Time:). 11.98 (978-0-87082-824-9(X), 154) Potentials.
There is a moment of time that escapes all description. A moment that is best described as the inner dance. It is this inner dance you seek as you move upon your path to master the martial art of your choice.

***Inner Development Process.** Ira Progoff. 2010. audio compact disk 15.00 (978-1-935859-10-9(2)) Dialogue Assoc.

Inner Ear, Pt. 1. 1 cass. (Running Time: 1 hr.). Incl. Pt. 1. Inner Ear: Carl Sandburg. (C062AB090); Pt. 2. William Carlos Williams. (C062AB090); 11.95 (C062AB090, HarperThor) HarpC GBR.

Inner Ear, Pt. 3. 1 cass. (Running Time: 1 hr.). Incl. Pt. 3. Inner Ear: Emily Dickinson & Marianne Moore. (C062BB090); Pt. 4. Poetry of Wallace Stevens. (C062BB090); 11.95 (C062BB090, HarperThor) HarpC GBR.

Inner Ear, Pt. 5. 1 cass. (Running Time: 1 hr.). Incl. Pt. 5. Inner Ear: e. e. cummings. (C062CB090); Pt. 6. Gary Snyder. (C062CB090); 11.95 (C062CB090, HarperThor) HarpC GBR.

Inner Ear: Carl Sandburg see Inner Ear

Inner Ear: e. e. cummings see Inner Ear

Inner Ear: Emily Dickinson & Marianne Moore see Inner Ear

Inner Eating: Cultivate Conscious Eating & a Healthy Relationship to Food. Mark Bancroft. Read by Mark Bancroft. 1 cass., bklet. (Running Time: 1 hr.). (Health & Fitness Ser.). 1999. 12.95 (978-1-58522-037-3(X), 406) EnSpire Pr.
Two complete sessions plus printed instructionmanual/guidebook. With healing music soundtrack.

Inner Eating: Cultivate Conscious Eating & a Healthy Relationship to Food. Mark Bancroft. Read by Mark Bancroft. 1 CD, 1 bklet. (Running Time: 1 hr.). (Health & Fitness Ser.). 2006. audio compact disk 20.00 (978-1-58522-053-3(1)) EnSpire Pr.

Inner Fitness: Supercharge Mind & Body. unabr. ed. Read by Kelly Howell. 1 cass. (Running Time: 60 min.). 1993. 11.95 (978-1-881451-09-9(7)) Brain Sync.
"Inner Fitness" guides the listener through advanced relaxation & meditation techniques. Within minutes daily pressures & fears are lifted. Precision-engineered tones & chanting that resonates with the seven energy centers are used to energize & balance the chakra system. The endocrine glands in turn become stimulated, which positively influences behavior & one's physical condition. Guided imagery & powerful breathing exercises free the mind to ascend to higher levels of awareness & understanding. The results are astonishing & positively life-changing.

Inner Frontier. Featuring Timothy Leary & Robert Anton Wilson. 1989. 9.95 (978-1-59157-008-0(5)) Assn for Cons.

Inner Game of Golf. unabr. collector's ed. Timothy W. Gallwey. Read by Ron Shoop. 6 cass. (Running Time: 9 hrs.). 1987. 48.00 (978-0-7366-1244-9(0), 2159) Books on Tape.
Psychological approach to improving one's game.

Inner Game of Selling: Discovering the Hidden Forces that Determine Your Success. abr. ed. Ron Willingham. Read by Ron Willingham. 2006. 11.95 (978-0-7435-6527-1(4)) Pub: S&S Audio. Dist(s): S and S Inc

Inner Game of Selling - Business Success. Robert E. Griswold. Read by Robert E. Griswold. 1 cass. (Super Strength Ser.). 1994. 10.95 (978-1-55848-316-3(0)) EffectiveMN.
Two complete non-subliminal programs that help unleash natural abilities for unlimited success in sales & all areas of business.

Inner Game of Tennis. unabr. collector's ed. Timothy W. Gallwey. Read by Ron Shoop. 5 cass. (Running Time: 5 hrs.). 1987. 30.00 (978-0-7366-1136-7(3), 2060) Books on Tape.
Explores the limitless potential of mind & body through the media of tennis. Also teaches you how to play the inner game on & off the court.

Inner Game of Winning. Timothy Gallwey. Intro. by A. E. Whyte. (Listen & Learn USA! Ser.). 8.95 (978-0-88684-064-8(3)) Listen USA.
Shows how to win both inner & outer "games".

Inner Game of Work, Set. abr. ed. W. Timothy Gallwey. 2 cass., 3 CDs. (Running Time: 3 hrs.). 1999. 18.00 (978-0-375-40895-3(9), Random AudioBks) Random Audio Pubg.
The author has spent the last twenty years as a lecturer & business consultant to some of America's top corporations, including AT&T, Apple, Coca-Cola, & IBM. His transition from sports to business was a natural, because the Inner Game has never just been about learning a better backhand. It's about learning to learn.

Inner Harbor. Nora Roberts. Read by Guy Lemonier. (Chesapeake Bay Ser.: Bk. 3). 2008. 64.99 (978-1-60640-789-9(9)) Find a World.

Inner Harbor. abr. ed. Nora Roberts. Read by Guy Lemonier. (Running Time: 3 hrs.). (Chesapeake Bay Ser.: Bk. 3). 2005. audio compact disk 14.99 (978-1-59600-093-3(7), 9781596000933, BCD Value Price); audio compact disk 62.25 (978-1-59600-094-0(5), 9781596000940, BACDLib Ed) Brilliance Audio.
This is the third novel in a best-selling trilogy featuring three young men bound by the love of an extraordinary couple who took them in and raised them as brothers. Phillip's brothers, Cameron and Ethan, are now happily married. The family boat building business is starting to thrive. And the Quinn's are closer than ever to keeping Seth permanently protected from his errant mother who would sell her own son rather than loving him the way the Quinns do. Phillip Quinn understands Seth's troubled past. He has the scars from his own rough and tumble childhood on the streets of Boston. He spent his days stealing and his nights doing anything to make a fast buck. Now he's a high-powered advertising executive who favors Armani suits and rare wines. When he meets educated, cultured Sybill, he figures he's found his perfect match. And when he discovers she has a family connection to young Seth, they join forces to secure the boy's future. Look for the other titles in this series: Book One: Sea Swept and Book Two: Rising Tides.

Inner Harbor. abr. ed. Nora Roberts. Read by Guy Lemonier. 2 cass. (Chesapeake Bay Ser.: Bk. 3). 1999. 17.95 (FS9-43315) Highsmith.

Inner Harbor. unabr. ed. Nora Roberts. Read by Guy Lemonier. 6 cass. (Running Time: 9 hrs.). (Chesapeake Bay Ser.: Bk. 3). 1998. 57.25 (978-1-56740-559-0(2), 1567405592, Unabridge Lib Edns) Brilliance Audio.

Inner Harbor. unabr. ed. Nora Roberts. Read by Guy Lemonier. (Running Time: 9 hrs.). (Chesapeake Bay Ser.: Bk. 3). 2005. 39.25 (978-1-59710-403-6(5), 9781597104036, BADLE); 24.95 (978-1-59710-402-9(7), 9781597104029, BAD); 24.95 (978-1-59335-794-8(X), 9781593357948, Brilliance MP3); 39.25 (978-1-59335-928-7(4), 9781593359287, Brlnc Audio MP3 Lib) Brilliance Audio.

Inner Harbor. unabr. ed. Nora Roberts. Read by Guy Lemonier. (Running Time: 9 hrs.). (Chesapeake Bay Ser.: Bk. 3). 2008. audio compact disk 92.25 (978-1-4233-5650-9(0), 9781423356509, BriAudCD Unabrid); audio compact disk 34.95 (978-1-4233-5649-3(7), 9781423356493, Bril Audio CD Unabri) Brilliance Audio.

Inner Harbor. unabr. ed. Nora Roberts. Read by Guy Lemonier. 6 cass. (Chesapeake Bay Ser.: Bk. 3). 1999. 73.25 (FS9-43284) Highsmith.

Inner Harmony. Miss Dee. 1 cass. (Running Time: 1 hr. 30 min.). 8.95 (1025) Am Fed Astrologers.

Inner Healer Vol. 30: Accelerate Natural Healing. Jonathan Parker. 2 cass. (Running Time: 1 hr. 45 min.). 1992. 17.00 Set. (978-1-58400-029-7(5)) QuantumQuests Intl.

Inner Healing. Read by Mary Richards. 12.95 (619) Master Your Mind.
Presents subliminal suggestions to become more forgiving, loving, & positive.

Inner Healing. D.A. Tubesing. 1 cass. (Running Time: 40 min.). (Guided Meditation Ser.: No. 3). 11.95 (978-0-938586-80-7(7), IH) Whole Person.
Side A: Inner Healing. Integrate your conscious & unconscious mind to unlock your body's own healing process. Inner Healing guides the listener through relaxation techniques to find spiritual strength & renewal. Use it as a daily wellness meditation or when needed for self-healing. Side B: Peace with Pain. When physical or emotional pain is overwhelming - when other techniques fail to provide effective relief - learn to make peace with pain. This tape guides the listener through the raging storm of pain to peace & serenity at the eye of the hurricane. Use again & again to achieve a sense of inner tranquility & acceptance.

Inner Healing: What it Is & what it Is Not. Henry W. Wright. (ENG.). 2008. audio compact disk 24.95 (978-1-934680-50-6(8)) Be in Hlth.

Inner Journey. 1 cass. (Running Time: 30 min.). (Meta Music Artist Ser.). 1991. 14.95 (978-1-56102-241-0(1)) Inter Indus.
Free-form composition uses sounds as undefinable as the level of consciousness they dramatize. There is Hemi-Sync as the background.

Inner Journey: Sleeping Through the Rain. unabr. ed. Mohannad Sadigh et al. Read by Mohannad Sadigh et al. 1 cass. (Running Time: 1 hr.). (Metamusic Artist Ser.: Vol. 1). 1993. 24.95 (978-1-56113-551-6(8)) Inter Indus.
Music with hemi-sync background.

Inner Journeys ... Outer Mastery, Vol. 1. Created by Bill Bauman. 2007. audio compact disk 15.00 (978-0-9765138-7-2(0)) Ctr Soulful.

Inner Journeys ... Outer Mastery, Vol. 2. Created by Bill Bauman. (ENG.). 2007. audio compact disk 15.00 (978-0-9765138-8-9(9)) Ctr Soulful.

Inner Journeys Relaxation Tape: A Relaxation Tape to Help Heal Food, Weight & Body Image Issues. unabr. ed. Andrea LoBue & Marsea Marcus. Read by Andrea LoBue & Marsea Marcus. Music by Ken Bweick. 1 cass. (Running Time: 90 min.). Dramatization. 1994. 10.00 (978-0-9655733-0-6(3)) InnerSolutions.
A relaxation tape for people with food, weight & body issues.

Inner Journey/Spiritual Cleansing & Healing. Created by Anne H. Spencer-Beacham. 1. 2003. audio compact disk (978-1-932163-46-9(8)) Infinity Inst.

Inner Joy. Read by Mary Richards. 12.95 (205) Master Your Mind.
Describes a way to relax & experience feelings of peace & inner joy.

Inner King & Queen. Michael Meade & Robert Bly. 2 cass. 16.95 set. (978-1-879323-04-9(4)) Sound Horizons AV.

Inner Kingdom; Christ Jesus. Jonathan Murro & Ann Ree Colton. 1 cass. 7.95 A R Colton Fnd.
Discusses the goal of God-Realization.

Inner Life Series. unabr. ed. Allan Blumenthal & Jean M. Blumenthal. Read by Allan Blumenthal & Jean M. Blumenthal. 1 cass. (Running Time: 1 hr.). 1996. 14.95 (978-1-57724-004-4(9), Prncpal Srce Audio) Objectivist Ctr.
The authors argue that the achievement of happiness & self-esteem requires us to defeat the guilt & repression that are the great enemies of our inner lives.

Inner Light of Consciousness. Swami Amar Jyoti. 1 cass. 1989. 9.95 (M-98) Truth Consciousness.
Disciplining our life to discover the inner world. "Go deeper, you'll find the answer".

Inner Mastery Series. unabr. ed. Krs Edstrom. Read by Krs Edstrom. 6 cass. (Running Time: 40 min. per cass.). (YA). 1994. 49.75 Norelco size. (978-1-886198-07-4(1)) Soft Stone Pub.
Includes: "Relax Mind & Body", "Defeat Pain", "Conquer Stress", "Sleep Through Insomnia", "Everyday Meditation" & "Instrumentals I". Effective guided meditation techniques designed for mainstream America. Based on 20 years experience & research.

Inner Meaning of Dharma. Swami Amar Jyoti. 1 cass. 1989. 9.95 (K-113) Truth Consciousness.
Dharma keeps us on the path. Becoming a whole integrated person.

Inner Meaning of the Ramayana. Swami Amar Jyoti. 2 cass. 1987. 12.95 (K-100) Truth Consciousness.
The glorious epic of Ramayana. Its intrinsic philosophy, applicable any time, anywhere. The mystery of good & evil explained. Misfortunes of the machine age.

Inner Mechanism of Healing. Masud Karim. 1 cass. 9.00 (A0392-88) Sound Photosyn.
ICSS '88.

Inner Paths. David Freudberg. Perf. by Dalai Lama XIV et al. 6 cass. (Running Time: 6 hrs.). (Kindred Spirits Ser.: Vol. 1). 1982. 24.95 Set. (978-0-9640914-4-3(5)) Human Media.
A listening library of spiritual wisdom from the world's great traditions. Contains such wisdom from The Dalai Lama & photographer/author Jane English.

Inner Peace. Music by Steven Halpern. 1 cass. 9.95 (LA125); audio compact disk 14.95 (LA125D) Lghtwrks Aud & Vid.
Deeply meditational piano & electronic music that creates an oasis of serenity. With titles like "Awakening", "Angel Song" & "Oneness", Halpern sets the mood for a spiritually guided journey from which you emerge feeling relaxed, recharged & renewed.

Inner Peace. Read by Mary Richards. (Subliminal Impact Ser.). 12.95 Master Your Mind.
Presents subliminal messages to love oneself & others.

Inner Peace: Cultivate & Experience Deep Inner Peace. Mark Bancroft. Read by Mark Bancroft. 1 cass., bklet. (Running Time: 60 min.). (Spirituality & Consciousness Ser.). 1998. 12.95 (978-0-9665539-3-2(4), EnSpire Aud) EnSpire Pr.
Two complete sessions plus printed instructionmanual/guidebook. With healing music soundtrack.

Inner Peace: Cultivate & Experience Deep Inner Peace. Mark Bancroft. Read by Mark Bancroft. 1 CD, bklet. (Running Time: 60 min.). (Spirituality & Consciousness Ser.). 2006. audio compact disk 20.00 CD & bklet. (978-0-9665539-2-5(6)) EnSpire Pr.

Inner Peace & Relaxation. Liah Kraft-Kristaine. Read by Liah Kraft-Kristaine. 1 cass. (Running Time: 62 min.). 1988. 9.95 (978-1-878095-02-2(1)) LMI Prodns.
Coping more easily with life. Dynamic relaxation.

Inner Peace for Busy People: Simple Strategies for Transforming Your Life. Joan Borysenko. (ENG.). 2001. 24.95 (978-1-56170-911-3(5)) Hay House.

Inner Peace for Busy People: Simple Strategies for Transforming Your Life. abr. ed. Joan Borysenko. 2 CDs. (Running Time: 3 hrs.). 2005. audio compact disk 18.95 (978-1-4019-0425-8(4)) Hay House.

Inner Peace for Busy Women: Balancing Work, Family, & Your Inner Life. abr. ed. Joan Z. Borysenko. 2 CDs. 2003. audio compact disk 18.95 (978-1-4019-0123-3(9), 1239) Hay House.

Inner Peace, Security, & Spiritual Awakening: Guided Meditation. Concept by Vicky Thurlow. Voice by Vicky Thurlow. 2008. audio compact disk 14.95 (978-0-9817055-6-9(1)) DVT Invest.

Inner Realms. Alexandra Delis-Abrams. Read by Alexandra Delis-Abrams. Music by Tony Selvage. 1 cass. (Running Time: 1 hr. 2 min.). 1992. 11.00 (978-1-879889-07-1(2)) Adage Pubns.
How intuition affects your life & guides meditation to energize & relax, softly spoken with electric violin background.

Inner Rhythm. Randy Crafton. 1 cass. (Running Time: 1 hr.). 1996. 9.95 (978-1-55961-353-8(X)); audio compact disk 14.95 (978-1-55961-352-1(1)) Relaxtn Co.

Inner Sanctuary. Read by Mary Richards. 12.95 (507) Master Your Mind.
Presents methods to create an inner place of sanctuary.

Inner Sanctum. 1 cass. (Running Time: 60 min.). Incl. Musical Score. (MM-7050); Wailing Wall. (MM-7050); 7.95 (MM-7050) Natl Recrd Co.

Inner Sanctum. 1 cass. (Running Time: 1 hr.). Dramatization. Incl. Black Art. 1945. (MM8415); Till Death Do Us Part. 1945. (MM8415); 1945. 7.95 (MM8415) Natl Recrd Co.
Host Raymond opens the squeaking door to the story of Larry Gifford who gets involved in a murder he didn't commit, is arrested & sentenced to hang. A wealthy, beautiful & very strange French woman helps him escape. Then Larry discovers he cannot escape from her unusual powers. In "Till Death Do Us Part" honey-mooners witness a murder being committed & have to start running from the murderer.

Inner Sanctum. Perf. by Raymond Johnson & Paul McGrath. 9 CDs. (Running Time: 9 hrs.). 2002. audio compact disk 39.98; 34.98 Radio Spirits.
Welcomes you through the creaking door for nine thrilling hours of mystery and suspense. If you like twisted tales of the macabre, you'll love this collection, featuring the best episodes from one of the most-popular shows from the Golden Age of Radio.

Inner Sanctum. Perf. by Boris Karloff. 1 cass. (Running Time: 60 min.). Incl. Musical Score. (MM-7050); Wailing Wall. (MM-7050); 7.95 (MM-7050) Natl Recrd Co.
In "The Wailing Wall", Boris Karloff murders his wife & seals her in a wall of his home. He plasters & wallpapers the wall, but continues to hear unnatural wailing moans from the hidden tomb. In "Musical Score", a ship hit by a stray mine leaves five people on a life-raft. For 17 days one constantly hums a musical score to his injured wife. Then murder takes place, but the humming of the song continues.

Innocence Soundtrack. (YA). 2005. 14.98 (978-1-59409-520-7(5)) Bandai Ent.

Innocent. unabr. ed. Ian McEwan. Narrated by John Franklyn-Robbins. 7 cass. (Running Time: 10 hrs.). 1994. 60.00 (978-1-55690-937-5(3), 93433E7) Recorded Bks.
War-weary Berlin has much to offer Leonard Markham, a young, naive postal engineer - first the arts of sophisticated intrigue then the delights of sexual pleasure. But Leonard's new knowledge carries a heavy price, dragging him & the listener into a new type of story that is exhaustively suspenseful & utterly irresistible.

***Innocent.** unabr. ed. Scott Turow. Narrated by Edward Herrmann. 2 MP3-CDs. (Running Time: 14 hrs.). 2010. 69.99 (978-1-60788-529-0(8)); audio compact disk 114.99 (978-1-60788-528-3(X)) Pub: Hachet Audio. Dist(s): HachBkGrp

Innocent. unabr. ed. Scott Turow. Read by Edward Herrmann. (Running Time: 13 hrs.). (ENG.). 2010. 26.98 (978-1-60024-920-4(5)); audio compact disk 39.98 (978-1-60024-921-1(3)) Pub: Hachet Audio. Dist(s): HachBkGrp

Innocent Ambassadors. unabr. collector's ed. Philip Wylie. Read by Charles Garst. 10 cass. (Running Time: 15 hrs.). 1983. 80.00 (978-0-7366-0547-2(9), 1521) Books on Tape.
What began as a flight to Hawaii to see their first grandchild expands to nearly a 3-month trip around the world for Wylie & his wife. Among the countries they visit are China, Japan, India, Turkey & the Middle East.

Innocent as Sin. unabr. ed. Elizabeth Lowell. Read by Carol Monda. 9 CDs. (Running Time: 39600 sec.). 2007. audio compact disk 39.95 (978-0-06-125654-7(4), Harper Audio) HarperCollins Pubs.

***Innocent as Sin.** unabr. ed. Elizabeth Lowell. Read by Carol Monda. (ENG.). 2007. (978-0-06-147292-3(1), Harper Audio); (978-0-06-147291-6(3), Harper Audio) HarperCollins Pubs.

Innocent Blood. unabr. ed. P. D. James. Read by Penelope Dellaporta. 9 cass. (Running Time: 13 hrs. 30 min.). 1992. 72.00 (978-0-7366-2252-3(7), 3041) Books on Tape.
Adopted as a child, Philippa Palfrey always had the best of everything. But at 18, she wanted more: the identity of her real parents. Having fantasized endlessly that she was the illegitimate daughter of an aristocrat & a parlor maid, Philippa wasn't prepared for the startling truth.

Innocent Blood. unabr. ed. P. D. James. Read by Michael Jayston. 10 cass. (Running Time: 15 hrs.). 2000. 69.95 (978-0-7451-6068-9(9), CAB 487) Pub: Chivers Audio Bks GBR. Dist(s): AudioGO
Now 18 and well-educated, the adopted daughter of Maurice Palfrey, Philippa, has made a terrible discovery upon reviewing her birth certificate. Some things are better left alone. In another part of London, Norman Scase is steeling himself to meet Philippa's mother: the murderess who, years ago, strangled and buried his little daughter.

***Innocent by Association.** unabr. ed. Lisa Jackson. (Running Time: 6 hrs.). 2011. audio compact disk 19.99 (978-1-4418-8448-0(3), 9781441884480, Bril Audio CD Unabri) Brilliance Audio.

Innocent Diversion. Kathleen Rowntree. Read by Patricia Gallimore. 8 cass. (Running Time: 12 hrs.). 2001. 69.95 (990908) Pub: ISIS Audio GBR. Dist(s): Ulverscroft US

Innocent Eye. unabr. ed. Philip Hook. Narrated by Christopher Kay. 8 cass. (Running Time: 11 hrs. 15 min.). 2000. 71.00 (H1200L8, Clipper Audio) Recorded Bks.
When a man is gunned down in an exclusive London hotel room, the killer leaves only one clue: a photograph of a landscape by Monet. Only Daniel Stern knows the connection. His bitter quest for family justice has led him on a journey across Europe. But just as he approaches his goal, he encounters one final, terrible dilemma.

Innocent Graves. abr. ed. Peter Robinson. Read by Ian Abercrombie. 2 cass. (Running Time: 3 hrs.). (Inspector Banks Mystery Ser.). 1997. 17.00 (978-1-56876-060-5(4), 394919) Soundlines Ent.
Chief Inspector Alan Banks is shocked when a school girl is found murdered in a local Eastvale graveyard. When the girl turns out to be the daughter of a powerful businessman, the questions surrounding her death become more complicated.

Innocent in Death. J. D. Robb, pseud. Read by Susan Ericksen. (In Death Ser.). 2008. 74.99 (978-1-60640-804-9(6)) Find a World.

Innocent in Death. unabr. ed. J. D. Robb, pseud. Read by Susan Ericksen. (Running Time: 21600 sec.). (In Death Ser.). 2007. audio compact disk 14.99 (978-1-4233-1607-7(X), 9781423316077, BCD Value Price) Brilliance Audio.

Innocent in Death. unabr. ed. J. D. Robb, pseud. Read by Susan Ericksen. (Running Time: 12 hrs.). (In Death Ser.). 2007. 39.25 (978-1-4233-1605-3(3), 9781423316053, BADLE); 24.95 (978-1-4233-1604-6(5), 9781423316046, BAD); 87.25 (978-1-4233-1599-5(5), 9781423315995, BrilAudUnabridg); audio compact disk 102.25 (978-1-4233-1601-5(0), 9781423316015, BriAudCD Unabrid); audio compact disk 39.25 (978-1-4233-1603-9(7), 9781423316039, Brlnc Audio MP3 Lib); audio compact disk 38.95 (978-1-4233-1600-8(2), 9781423316008, Bril Audio CD Unabri); audio compact disk 24.95 (978-1-4233-1602-2(9), 9781423316022, Brilliance MP3) Brilliance Audio.

***Innocent Mage.** unabr. ed. Karen Miller. Narrated by Kirby Heyborne. (Running Time: 18 hrs. 30 mins. 0 sec.). (Kingmaker, Kingbreaker Ser.). 2010. 34.99 (978-1-4001-6984-9(4)); 22.99 (978-1-4001-8984-7(5)); audio compact disk 49.99 (978-1-4001-1984-4(7)) Pub: Tantor Media. Dist(s): IngramPubServ

***Innocent Mage (Library Edition)** unabr. ed. Karen Miller. Narrated by Kirby Heyborne. (Running Time: 18 hrs. 30 mins.). (Kingmaker, Kingbreaker Ser.). 2010. 49.99 (978-1-4001-9984-6(0)); audio compact disk 119.99 (978-1-4001-4984-1(3)) Pub: Tantor Media. Dist(s): IngramPubServ

Innocent Man: Murder & Injustice in a Small Town. abr. ed. John Grisham. Read by Dennis Boutsikaris. (Running Time: 21600 sec.). (John Grisham Ser.). (ENG.). 2008. audio compact disk 19.99 (978-0-7393-6567-0(3), Random AudioBks) Pub: Random Audio Pubg. Dist(s): Random

Innocent Man: Murder & Injustice in a Small Town. unabr. ed. John Grisham. 8 cass. (Running Time: 12 hrs.). 2006. 72.00 (978-1-4159-3306-0(5)); audio compact disk 76.50 (978-1-4159-3307-7(3)) Pub: Books on Tape. Dist(s): NetLibrary CO

Innocent Man: Murder & Injustice in a Small Town. unabr. ed. John Grisham. Read by Dennis Boutsikaris. (YA). 2006. 54.99 (978-0-7393-7497-9(4)) Find a World.

Innocent Man: Murder & Injustice in a Small Town. unabr. ed. John Grisham. Read by Craig Wasson. 10 CDs. (Running Time: 45000 sec.). (John Grisham Ser.). (ENG.). 2006. audio compact disk 44.95 (978-0-7393-4048-6(4), Random AudioBks) Pub: Random Audio Pubg. Dist(s): Random

Innocent Traitor: A Novel of Lady Jane Grey. Alison Weir. Narrated by Stina Nielsen. (Running Time: 65700 sec.). 2007. audio compact disk 39.99 (978-1-4281-2052-5(1)) Recorded Bks.

Innocent Traitor: A Novel of Lady Jane Grey. unabr. ed. Alison Weir. 16 cass. (Running Time: 18 hrs. 25 mins.). 2007. 133.75 (978-1-4281-2028-0(9)); audio compact disk 123.75 (978-1-4281-2030-3(0)) Recorded Bks.

Innocent Versus Significant Systolic Murmurs. Read by W. Proctor Harvey. 1 cass. (Running Time: 90 min.). 1985. 12.00 (C8543) Amer Coll Phys.

Innocents Abroad. Mark Twain. Narrated by Flo Gibson. (ENG.). 2009. audio compact disk 48.95 (978-1-60646-121-1(4)) Audio Bk Con.

Innocents Abroad. unabr. ed. Mark Twain. Narrated by Flo Gibson. 14 cass. (Running Time: 19 hrs. 20 mins.). 2003. 42.95 (978-1-55685-691-4(1)) Audio Bk Con.
An hilarious, sometimes biting account of Mark Twain's travels through France, Italy, Greece, Russia, Palestine & Egypt. Warning: some racism.

***Innocents Abroad.** unabr. ed. Mark Twain. Narrated by Robin Field. (ENG.). 2010. 34.98 (978-1-59644-976-3(4), MissionAud); audio compact disk 39.98 (978-1-59644-975-6(6), MissionAud) christianaud.

Innocents Abroad. unabr. collector's ed. Mark Twain. Read by Michael Prichard. 14 cass. (Running Time: 21 hrs.). 1986. 112.00 (978-0-7366-0912-8(1), 1855) Books on Tape.
Mark Twain's story of his encounter with the "Old-World." Twain used his travelogue to search out the archetypal differences between Americans & Europeans to define the American identity.

Innocents of Broadway see Best of O. Henry

Innovate Like Edison: The Success System of America's Greatest Inventor. abr. ed. Sarah Miller Caldicott. 5 CDs. (Running Time: 5 hrs.). 2007. audio compact disk 27.95 (978-1-59316-111-8(5)) Listen & Live.

Innovation & Entrepreneurship. unabr. ed. Peter F. Drucker. Read by Michael Wells. 7 cass. (Running Time: 10 hrs.). 1990. 49.95 (978-0-7861-0198-6(9), 1174) Blckstn Audio.
Presents innovations & entrepreneurship as a purposeful & systematic discipline. It clearly explains & analyzes the challenges & opportunities of America's new entrepreneurial economy.

Innovation Exchange: City/County Managers Staff Share Ideas That Work in Their Jurisdictions. unabr. ed. Innovation Groups Staff. 1 cass. (Transforming Local Government Ser.: Vol. 5). 1999. 10.00 (978-1-882403-61-5(4), IG9905) Alliance Innov.

Innovation Millionaires. unabr. collector's ed. Gene Bylinsky. Read by Daniel Grace. 6 cass. (Running Time: 9 hrs.). 1977. 48.00 (978-0-7366-0051-4(5), 1063) Books on Tape.
Surveys the career, both personal & corporate, of today's entrepreneurs & how their ingenious blending of technology & finance produced fortunes for themselves & their backers.

Innovation Revolution. Tom Peters. 6 cass. (Running Time: 6 hrs.). 1997. (978-1-55525-047-8(5), 16780A); audio compact disk (978-1-55525-051-5(3), 16780CD) Nightingale-Conant.
Lead the business revolution.

***Innovations Elementary.** Andrew Walkley & Hugh Dellar. (ENG.). (C). 2005. 63.95 (978-1-4130-1273-6(6)) Pub: Heinle. Dist(s): CENGAGE Learn

Innovations in Cement Manufacturing. 2004. audio compact disk 100.00 (978-0-89312-235-5(1)) Portland Cement.

Innovations in Health Care Delivery: Insights for Organization Theory. Stephen S. Mick et al. (Health Management Ser.). 1990. bk. 45.00 (978-1-55542-281-3(0), Jossey-Bass) Wiley US.

Innovations in Portland Cement Manufacturing. Javed I. Bhatty et al. 2004. pap. bk. 295.00 (978-0-89312-234-8(3), RP400) Portland Cement.

Innovative Selling: Your Edge to Accellerate Your Selling Success. Keith Rosen. Read by Keith Rosen. 6 cass. 1998. 149.00 Set. (978-0-9666036-0-6(5)) Profit Bldrs.
A complete selling system that delivers, step-by-step, the skills tools & techniques to dramatically increase your selling performance & income. Learn the essential communication skills including effective questioning & active listening to make selling a natural conversation in order to attract clients as opposed to pushing or using generic selling strategies.

Innovative Strategies in Risk Management. Speeches. David Hulett. 1 CD. (Running Time: 68 mins). 2005. audio compact disk 14.87 (978-1-895186-48-2(X)) Multi-Media ON CAN.
Qualitative risk analysis is a way to rank project risks in low, moderate and high ?bins? based on their probability of occurring and their impact on project objectives if they do occur. The main question is how to determine probability and impact scores of very low, low, moderate, high, or very high. Many risk analyses fail to define what these scores mean or fail to be consistent across project objectives. Controversy also exists concerning whether we can use cardinal (numerical) or ordinal (relative) scores, or both. Quantitative schedule risk analysis involves quantifying possible values for activity durations, constructing continuous probability distributions, and simulating the schedule. Topics covered include: the quality of the schedule?s construction, the use of constraints and resources, parallel paths and the ?merge bias,? the three promises of schedule risk analysis, and probabilistic and conditional branching.

Innovative Techniques for Building Positive Client Self-Esteem. Dennis Butts. 7 cass. 109.00 Set. (74207); 55.00 exam. (74208) Am Coun Assn.
How many times have you wondered how to deal with what you know is at the root of many client problems - low self- esteem? Improved self-esteem will give your clients greater happiness & increased chances of success & fulfillment. You will learn a whole person approach, conditions for creating self- esteem, & the use of imagery & music in counseling, along with practical applications for any client settings.

Innovator's Dilemma: When New Technologies Cause Great Firms to Fall. abr. ed. Clayton M. Christensen. 2 CDs. (Running Time: 2 hrs. 30 min.). (ENG.). 2001. audio compact disk 24.95 (978-1-56511-415-9(9), 1565114159) Pub: HighBridge. Dist(s): Workman Pub

Input - Output. John R. Boyd & Mary Ann Boyd. (YA). (gr. 7-12). 1989. 29.95 (978-0-933759-16-9(9)) Abaca Bks.

Inquebrantable Ley de Siembra Y Cosecha. Tr. of Unchangeable Law of Seedtime & Harvest. (SPA.). 2008. audio compact disk 21.00 (978-0-944129-18-0(8)) High Praise.

***Inquest: A Detective Story from the Strand.** Loel Yeo. 2009. (978-1-60136-497-5(0)) Audio Holding.

Inquiring Brain. J. Krishnamurti. 1 cass. (Running Time: 75 min.). (Madras - the Last Talks 1986 Ser.: No. 3). 8.50 (AMT863) Krishnamurti.
Krishnamurti traveled to India in November, 1985, for the last time. These, his final public talks, were given a little over a month before his death. He addresses the fact that despite the amazing technological achievements of modern times, man has remained, psychologically, the barbarian he was when he first appeared on earth. Krishnamurti maintains that each of us is responsible for the brutality & divisiveness of the society in which we live, a society which is only a reflection of ourselves & as such, incapable of being saved from chaos except through a profound change in each human psyche. His lifelong work is the foundation for his insistence that such a change is possible.

Inquiry into the Impact of Public Land Management Practices on Bushfires in Victoria. Environment and Natural Resources Committee. 2008. pap. bk. 0.00 (978-0-9757811-3-5(8)) VicnatRes AUS.

Inquiry into True Identity. Swami Amar Jyoti. 1 cass. 1985. 9.95 (R-75) Truth Consciousness.
Removing the last layer of ego. With what light do we see the darkness? Yogic understanding of the body. Meditation on Awareness.

Ins & Outs of Cricket. unabr. ed. 2 cass. 15.95 (SCN 115) J Norton Pubs.
Provides the truth about the game of Cricket.

Ins & Outs of Therapy: A Consumer's Guide. unabr. ed. Miriam Ehrenberg & Otto Ehrenberg. 1 cass. (Running Time: 51 min.). 12.95 (35210) J Norton Pubs.
The authors discuss which psychotherapy is for you, how you choose a therapist & more.

Insanity see Twentieth-Century Poetry in English, No. 24, Recordings of Poets Reading Their Own Poetry

Insanity Defense: Program from the Award Winning Public Radio Series. Interview. Hosted by Fred Goodwin. Comment by John Hockenberry. 1 CD. (Running Time: 1 hr.). (Infinite Mind Ser.). 2001. audio compact disk 21.95 (978-1-932479-58-4(9), LCM 150) Lichtenstein Creat.
Everyone knows about the insanity defense, but not everyone realizes just how uncommon this verdict is. Nor do they understand the scrupulous and lengthy process that follows most acquittals by reason of insanity. This show explores the legal ins and outs of the rare insanity defense. Guests include law professor Richard Bonnie and forensic psychiatrist Dr. Philip Resnick. Commentary by John Hockenberry.

Insatiable. unabr. ed. Meg Cabot. Read by Emily Bauer. 2010. audio compact disk 39.99 (978-0-06-198851-6(0), Harper Audio) HarperCollins Pubs.

***Insatiable.** unabr. ed. Meg Cabot. Read by Emily Bauer. (ENG.). 2010. (978-0-06-200892-3(7), Harper Audio); (978-0-06-201605-8(9), Harper Audio) HarperCollins Pubs.

Insatiable: Tales from a Life of Delicious Excess. abr. ed. Gael Greene. (Running Time: 3 hrs.). (ENG.). 2006. 14.98 (978-1-59483-504-9(7)) Pub: Hachet Audio. Dist(s): HachBkGrp

Inscription. Daniel Weissbort. Ed. by Stanley H. Barkan. (Review Jewish Writers Chapbook Ser.: No. 3). 1991. 10.00 (978-0-89304-339-1(7)) Cross-Cultrl NY.

Inscriptions see Twentieth-Century Poetry in English, No. 17, Walt Whitman Speaks for Himself

Inscrutable Charlie Muffin. unabr. ed. Brian Freemantle. Read by Steven Crossley. 4 cass. (Running Time: 5 hrs.). (Sound Ser.). 2002. 44.95 (978-1-84283-066-6(X)) Pub: UlverLrgPrint GBR. Dist(s): Ulverscroft US
Charlie Muffin is dead. Because he exposed them as amateur blunderers, British Intelligence had him murdered, with a little help from the Americans. But if charlie Muffin is dead, who is the unkempt, unprepossessing man cautiously making his way to Hong Kong, mainland China, and into the back pocket of the CIA? Is Charlie Muffin trouble-shooting for someone? Or is he just looking for trouble.

Insec in Amsterdam:Insecurities in European Cities: Crime-Related Fear Within the Context of New Anxieties & Community-Based Crime Prev. Irene Sagel-Grande & Manuela du Bois-Reymond. (C). 2005. audio compact disk 23.00 (978-90-5170-799-1(1)) Pub: Purdue U Pr. Dist(s): AtlasBooks

Insect. Dorling Kindersley Publishing Staff. Narrated by Martin Sheen. (DK Eyewitness Bks.). (ENG.). (J). (gr. 1). 2006. 12.99 (978-0-7566-2828-4(8)) DK Pub Inc.

Insect Life Cycles: Audio Edition Plus Book. Bobbie Kalman & Molly Aloian. (World of Insects Ser.). (ENG.). (J). 2005. audio compact disk 10.00 (978-0-7787-7622-2(0)) CrabtreePubCo CAN.

Insect Ninja. Aaron Reynolds. (Tiger Moth Ser.). (J). (gr. 3-5). 2007. audio compact disk 14.60 (978-1-59889-998-6(8)) CapstoneDig.

Insectos/Insects EBooks. Created by Rourke Publishing Group. (Rourke Discovery Library). (J). 2008. audio compact disk 39.95 (978-1-60472-086-0(7)) Rourke FL.

Insects Vol. 122: Get Kids Excited About Insects! unabr. ed. Kim Mitzo Thompson & Karen Mitzo Hilderbrand. 1 CD. (Running Time: 32 min.). (Get Kids Excited about Ser.). (J). (ps-4). 1999. audio compact disk 12.99 (978-1-57583-202-9(X)) Twin Sisters.
Whether singing about metamorphosis or learning about "true bugs" children will gain an understanding of the importance of insects.

Insects & Spiders Activity B. 2004. audio compact disk 13.99 (978-1-57583-358-3(1)) Twin Sisters.

Insects, Spiders, & a Visit from the Bugman. Hosted by Nancy Pearlman. 1 cass. (Running Time: 27 min.). 10.00 (230) Educ Comm CA.

Insects That Work Together. Bobbie Kalman & Molly Aloian. (World of Insects Ser.). (ENG.). (J). 2005. audio compact disk 10.00 (978-0-7787-7620-8(4)) CrabtreePubCo CAN.

Inside. Excerpts. Erika Hammerschmidt. 1CD. (Running Time: 40 mins). 2005. audio compact disk 11.00i (978-0-9748570-8-4(4)) Tyborne Hill Pubs.

Inside - Outside: The Motivational Weight-Loss Program. Lloyd Glauberman. 2 cass. (Hypno-Peripheral Processing Tapes Ser.). 34.95 Set. (851PA-5M) Nightingale-Conant.
This breakthrough psychotechnology program combines the methods of hypnotherapy with the latest teachings of Neuro-Linguistic Programming. Each high-impact tape gently overloads your conscious mind with messages on two channels at once, creating a synergistic whole that unleashes both hemispheres of your brain.

Inside Adobe Indesign. Integrated Technologies, Inc. Staff. 1 CD. (Running Time: 1 hr.). 1999. pap. bk. 49.99 (978-0-7357-0948-5(3)) Alpha Pearson.

Inside Advantage: A Self-Paced Program to Make Managers More Effective. Roger Fritz. 6 cass. (Running Time: 6 hrs.). 1987. 49.95 incl. wkbk. & Meeting Leaders Guide. (2003) Dartnell Corp.
A complete self-paced management training program designed to give new & veteran managers the skill they need to succeed.

Inside Advantage, 4-CD Set: The Strategy that Unlocks the Hidden Growth in Your Business. Robert H. Bloom. 2009. audio compact disk 28.00 (978-1-933309-76-7(8)) Pub: A Media Intl. Dist(s): Natl Bk Netwk

Inside America's Toughest Prison. Hosted by Jackie Lyden. 1 cass. (Running Time: 40 min.). 10.95 (G0530B090, HarperThor) HarpC GBR.

Inside Aubrey. unabr. ed. Gilbert Highet. Read by Gilbert Highet. 1 cass. (Running Time: 30 min.). 9.95 (23287-A) J Norton Pubs.

Inside Camp X. abr. ed. Lynn P. Hodgson. Read by Michael Booth. 4 pieces. (Running Time: 4 hrs. 30 mins.). 2004. reel tape 24.99 (978-1-894003-27-8(6)) Pub: Scenario Prods CAN. Dist(s): PerseuPGW

Inside Congress: The Shocking Scandals, Corruption, & Abuse of Power Behind the Scenes on Capitol Hill. unabr. ed. Ronald Kessler. Read by Barrett Whitener. 7 cass. (Running Time: 10 hrs.). 1997. 49.95 (978-0-7861-1248-7(4), 2156) Blckstn Audio.
Sent shock waves through the most powerful institutions of our government. Kessler goes to the very heart of our democratic system, Congress, & finds it's rotten to the core.

without falling under his hypnotic power. It is up to Smith and his faithful companion, Dr. Petrie, to foil Dr. Fu-Manchu's diabolical plot. In The Insidious Dr. Fu-Manchu, the lethal "Zayat Kiss", a red mark resembling the imprint of painted lips, is found among cocaine needle tracks on the dead body of Sir Chrichton Davey. The power of Fu-Manchu is far reaching as he employs a giant poisonous centipede, deadly toadstools and lethal green mists to murder and kidnap the great minds of the West. Is the beautiful Karamaneh the key to uncovering the evil Doctor's lair, or is she a pawn leading Smith and Petrie to their deaths?.

Insidious Dr. Fu-Manchu. unabr. ed. Sax Rohmer, pseud. Narrated by John Bolen. (Running Time: 8 hrs. 0 mins. 0 sec.). (Fu-Manchu Ser.). (ENG.). 2009. audio compact disk 27.99 (978-1-4001-0939-5(6)); audio compact disk 55.99 (978-1-4001-3939-2(2)); audio compact disk 19.99 (978-1-4001-5939-0(3)) Pub: Tantor Media. Dist(s): IngramPubServ

Insidious Dr. Fu-Manchu. unabr. collector's ed. Sax Rohmer, pseud. Read by Gary Martin. 6 cass. (Running Time: 9 hrs.). (J). 1990. 48.00 (978-0-7366-3954-5(3), 9204) Books on Tape.
Here is the first of the adventures of Nayland Smith, a civilized Englishman who pits all his logic & experience against a cunning & malevolent crime lord, the inscrutable & sinister celestial, Dr. Fu Manchu.

Insieme: Student Program. 2nd ed. Romana Habekovic. 1 cass. (Running Time: 90 min.). (ENG.). (C). 1998. stu. ed. 81.56 (978-0-07-913222-2(7), 0079132227, Mc-H Human Soc) Pub: McGrw-H Hghr Educ. Dist(s): McGraw

Insight. 12 cass. 84.00 incl. script Set incl. binder. (60012AB) Nightingale-Conant.
The foundation of Insight is a dynamic monthly cassette/magazine concept. Each edition of Insight contains segments by two Speakers-of-the-Month addressing vital issues in self-development, motivation, goal achievement & much more.

Insight. Read by Wayne Monbleau. 2 cass. (Running Time: 2 hrs. 30 min.). 1993. 10.00 Set. (978-0-944648-17-9(7), LGT-1186) Loving Grace Pubns.
Religious.

Insight: Case Files from the Psychic World. abr. ed. Sylvia Browne. Read by Jeannie Hackett. Told to Lindsay Harrison. (Running Time: 18000 sec.). (ENG.). 2006. audio compact disk 26.95 (978-1-59887-031-2(9), 1598870319) Pub: HighBridge. Dist(s): Workman Pub

Insight & Precognition. unabr. ed. Gary Arnold. 1 cass. (Running Time: 1 hr.). 1997. pap. bk. 12.95 (978-1-57867-289-9(9)) Windhorse Corp.
Learn the rules & syntax by which the spirit communicates itself to the conscious mind.

Insight & the Structure of Being. J. Krishnamurti. 1 cass. (Running Time: 75 min.). (Krishnamurti & Professor David Bohm - 1980 Ser.: No. 11). 8.50 (ABD8011) Krishnamurti.
Krishnamurti & Prof. Bohm offer penetrating, in-depth dialogues which shed light on the fundamental issues of existence.

Insight into Austerity, No. 1. Swami Jyotirmayananda. Read by Swami Jyotirmayananda. 1 cass. (Running Time: 45 min.). 10.00 (822) Yoga Res Foun.

Insight into Austerity, No. 2. Swami Jyotirmayananda. 1 cass. (Running Time: 45 min.). 1990. 10.00 Yoga Res Foun.

Insight into Bondage & Release. Swami Jyotirmayananda. 1 cass. (Running Time: 45 min.). 1990. 10.00 Yoga Res Foun.

Insight into Destruction of Vasanas. Swami Jyotirmayananda. 1 cass. (Running Time: 45 min.). 1990. 10.00 Yoga Res Foun.

Insight into Devotion (Bhakti) Swami Jyotirmayananda. 1 cass. (Running Time: 45 min.). 1990. 10.00 Yoga Res Foun.

Insight into Dharma. Swami Jyotirmayananda. 1 cass. (Running Time: 45 min.). 1990. 10.00 Yoga Res Foun.

Insight into Education. Swami Jyotirmayananda. 1 cass. (Running Time: 45 min.). 1990. 10.00 Yoga Res Foun.

Insight into Ego. Swami Jyotirmayananda. 1 cass. (Running Time: 45 min.). 1990. 5.00 Yoga Res Foun.

Insight into Energy. Swami Jyotirmayananda. 1 cass. (Running Time: 45 min.). 1990. 10.00 Yoga Res Foun.

Insight into Faith. Swami Jyotirmayananda. 1 cass. (Running Time: 45 min.). 1990. 10.00 Yoga Res Foun.

Insight into Freedom. Swami Jyotirmayananda. 1 cass. (Running Time: 45 min.). 1990. 10.00 Yoga Res Foun.

Insight into Grace. Swami Jyotirmayananda. 1 cass. (Running Time: 45 min.). 1990. 10.00 Yoga Res Foun.

Insight into Happiness. Swami Jyotirmayananda. 1 cass. (Running Time: 45 min.). 1990. 10.00 Yoga Res Foun.

Insight into Hinduism. Swami Jyotirmayananda. 1 cass. (Running Time: 45 min.). 1990. 10.00 Yoga Res Foun.

Insight into IELTS Cassette China Edition. Vanessa Jakeman & Clare McDowell. 2002. (978-7-88012-140-7(4)) Cambridge U Pr.

Insight into IELTS Extra, with Answers South Asia Edition: The Cambridge IELTS Course Workbook. Vanessa Jakeman & Clare McDowell. 2003. pap. bk. (978-0-521-54692-8(3)) Cambridge U Pr.

Insight into Inspiration. Swami Jyotirmayananda. 1 cass. (Running Time: 45 min.). 1990. 10.00 Yoga Res Foun.

Insight into Intuition. Swami Jyotirmayananda. Read by Swami Jyotirmayananda. 1 cass. (Running Time: 45 min.). 10.00 (814) Yoga Res Foun.

Insight into Kleshas. Swami Jyotirmayananda. Read by Swami Jyotirmayananda. 1 cass. (Running Time: 45 min.). 10.00 (820) Yoga Res Foun.

Insight into Knowledge. Swami Jyotirmayananda. 1 cass. (Running Time: 45 min.). 1990. 10.00 Yoga Res Foun.

Insight into Knowledge of Truth. Swami Jyotirmayananda. 1 cass. (Running Time: 45 min.). 1990. 10.00 Yoga Res Foun.

Insight into Memory. Swami Jyotirmayananda. 1 cass. (Running Time: 45 min.). 1990. 10.00 Yoga Res Foun.

Insight into Non-Duality. Swami Jyotirmayananda. Read by Swami Jyotirmayananda. 1 cass. (Running Time: 45 min.). 10.00 (809) Yoga Res Foun.

Insight into Non-Violence. Swami Jyotirmayananda. 1 cass. (Running Time: 45 min.). 1990. 10.00 Yoga Res Foun.

Insight into Optimism. Swami Jyotirmayananda. 1 cass. (Running Time: 45 min.). 1990. 10.00 Yoga Res Foun.

Insight into Peace. Swami Jyotirmayananda. 1 cass. (Running Time: 45 min.). 1990. 10.00 Yoga Res Foun.

Insight into PET. Helen Naylor & Stuart Hagger. (Running Time: 2 hrs. 8 mins.). (ENG.). 2004. 44.10 (978-0-521-52756-9(2)) Cambridge U Pr.

Insight into Prosperity. Swami Jyotirmayananda. 1 cass. (Running Time: 45 min.). 1990. 10.00 Yoga Res Foun.

Insight into Religion. Swami Jyotirmayananda. 1 cass. (Running Time: 45 min.). 1990. 10.00 Yoga Res Foun.

Insight into Sadhana (Spiritual Discipline) Swami Jyotirmayananda. 1 cass. (Running Time: 45 min.). 1990. 10.00 Yoga Res Foun.

Insight into Self-Effort. Swami Jyotirmayananda. 1 cass. (Running Time: 45 min.). 1990. 10.00 Yoga Res Foun.

Insight into Sleep, No. 1. Swami Jyotirmayananda. 1 cass. (Running Time: 45 min.). 1990. 10.00 Yoga Res Foun.

Insight into Sleep, No. 2. Swami Jyotirmayananda. 1 cass. (Running Time: 45 min.). 1990. 10.00 Yoga Res Foun.

Insight into Spiritual Aspiration. Swami Jyotirmayananda. 1 cass. (Running Time: 45 min.). 1990. 10.00 Yoga Res Foun.

Insight into Spiritual Progress. Swami Jyotirmayananda. 1 cass. (Running Time: 45 min.). 1990. 10.00 Yoga Res Foun.

Insight into Spirituality. Swami Jyotirmayananda. 1 cass. (Running Time: 45 min.). 1990. 10.00 Yoga Res Foun.

Insight into the New Age. Willis Harman. 6 cass. (Running Time: 60 min. per cass.). (Insight Ser.). 1988. 49.95 (978-0-945093-12-1(8)) Enhanced Aud Systs.
Lectures on mind-body research, history of consciousness, & creativity enhancement.

Insight into the New Age. Willis Harman. 2 cass. (Running Time: 60 min. per cass.). (Insight Ser.). 1989. 16.95 (978-0-945093-11-4(X)) Enhanced Aud Systs.

Insight into the Study of Scriptures. Swami Jyotirmayananda. 1 cass. (Running Time: 45 min.). 1990. 10.00 Yoga Res Foun.

Insight into Upasana (Devout Meditation) Swami Jyotirmayananda. 1 cass. (Running Time: 45 min.). 1990. 10.00 Yoga Res Foun.

Insight into Vrittis, No. 1. Swami Jyotirmayananda. 1 cass. (Running Time: 45 min.). 1990. 10.00 Yoga Res Foun.

Insight into Vrittis, No. 2. Swami Jyotirmayananda. Read by Swami Jyotirmayananda. 1 cass. (Running Time: 45 min.). 10.00 (821) Yoga Res Foun.

Insight into Vrittis, No. 3. Swami Jyotirmayananda. 1 cass. (Running Time: 45 min.). 1990. 10.00 Yoga Res Foun.

Insight into Willpower, No. 1. Swami Jyotirmayananda. 1 cass. (Running Time: 45 min.). 1990. 10.00 Yoga Res Foun.

Insight into Willpower, No. 2. Swami Jyotirmayananda. 1 cass. (Running Time: 45 min.). 1990. 10.00 Yoga Res Foun.

Insight into Willpower, No. 3. Swami Jyotirmayananda. 1 cass. (Running Time: 45 min.). 1990. 10.00 Yoga Res Foun.

Insight into Yoga Ethics. (191) Yoga Res Foun.

Insight into Yoga Ethics. Swami Jyotirmayananda. 1 cass. (Running Time: 1 hr.). 1990. 12.99 Yoga Res Foun.

Insight Meditation Kit. unabr. ed. Sharon Salzberg. 2 CDs. (Running Time: 2 hrs. 30 mins.). 2006. audio compact disk 29.95 (978-1-56455-906-7(8), W553) Sounds True.

Insights from Gurdjieff. unabr. ed. Ralph Metzner. 1 cass. (Running Time: 1 hr. 30 min.). 1968. 11.00 (01602) Big Sur Tapes.
Speaks of Gurdjieff's life & the basic structure of the Gurdjieffian system.

***Insights f/Today 3e-Audio.** 3rd ed. Richard G. Smith. (C). 2003. audio compact disk 34.95 (978-0-7593-9819-1(4)) Pub: Heinle. Dist(s): CENGAGE Learn

Insights into... Addictions: Prevention, eradication, Healing. Henry W. Wright. (ENG.). 2008. audio compact disk (978-1-934680-48-3(6)) Be in Hlth.

Insights into... Allergies. Henry W. Wright. (ENG.). 2008. audio compact disk 14.95 (978-1-934680-21-6(4)) Be in Hlth.

Insights into... Cancer: Prevention, eradication, Healing. Henry W. Wright. (ENG.). 2008. audio compact disk 14.95 (978-1-934680-22-3(2)) Be in Hlth.

Insights into... Pain: Prevention, eradication, Healing. Henry W. Wright. (ENG.). 2008. audio compact disk 24.95 (978-1-934680-42-1(7)) Be in Hlth.

***Insights on Romans Volume 1: The Christian's Constitution.** Charles R. Swindoll. 2010. audio compact disk 62.00 (978-1-57972-886-1(3)) Insight Living.

***Insights on Romans Volume 2: The Christian's Constitution.** Charles R. Swindoll. 2010. audio compact disk 62.00 (978-1-57972-890-8(1)) Insight Living.

Insights on the Book of Mormon, Set. 6 cass. 19.95 Set. (978-1-55503-827-4(1), 0900125) Covenant Comms.
An inspiring collection.

Insights to Help You Survive the Peaks & Valleys Audio Book: Can You Stand to Be Blessed? T. D. Jakes. 2008. audio compact disk 29.99 (978-0-7684-2714-1(2)) Destiny Image Pubs.

Insights to Help Your Survive the Peaks & Valleys: Can You Stand to Be Blessed. T. D. Jakes. Read by Carey Conley. (ENG.). 2008. 24.99 (978-1-4245-0870-9(3)) Tre Med Inc.

Insomnia. 1 cass. (Running Time: 60 min.). 10.95 (030) Psych Res Inst.
Elimination of poor sleeping patterns by positive feedback.

Insomnia. Deepak Chopra. 4 cass. 49.95 Set incl. wkbk. (11370PAM) Nightingale-Conant.
Imagine being able to sleep deeply, soundly & peacefully every night without taking medication! Dr. Deepak Chopra provides proven techniques to help you eliminate the underlying causes of insomnia - & create a balanced mind & body. Learn to integrate biological rhythms to improve sleep...use music, massage & aromatherapy for deeper rest...select the right visual stimuli before bed...& much more.

Insomnia. Read by Robert S. Friedman & Kelly Howell. 1 cass. (Running Time: 60 min.). (Sound Techniques for Healing Ser.). 11.95 (978-1-881451-20-4(8)) Brain Sync.
The body's biorhythms are regulated while being eased into the oceanic depths of the delta frequency. Here refreshing & restorative sleep is experienced.

Insomnia. Bruce Goldberg. (ENG.). 2005. audio compact disk 17.00 (978-1-57968-081-7(X)) Pub: B Goldberg. Dist(s): Baker Taylor

Insomnia. Bruce Goldberg. 1 cass. (ENG.). 2006. 13.00 (978-1-885577-13-9(3)) Pub: B Goldberg. Dist(s): Baker Taylor
Self hypnosis program that allows you to go to sleep faster and obtain a better night's rest.

Insomnia. Barrie Konicov. 1 CD. 2003. audio compact disk 16.98 (978-0-87082-969-7(6)) Potentials.
Let Barrie assist you to sleep deeply throughout the night. Enjoy peaceful dreams and wake at the time of your choice. Have a restful sleep, for a change. You will find the self-hypnosis on track 1 and the subliminal on track 2. The easy-listening music of the subliminal, together with the self-hypnosis, is the original format which most people love and with which they are most familiar.

Insomnia. Barrie Konicov. 2 CDs. 2003. audio compact disk 27.98 (978-1-56001-979-4(4)) Potentials.

Insomnia. unabr. ed. Richard R. Bootzin. 1 cass. (Running Time: 57 min.). 12.95 (29352) J Norton Pubs.

Insomnia. unabr. ed. Stephen King. Eli Wallach. (ENG., 2008. audio compact disk 59.95 (978-1-59887-763-2(1), 1598877631) Pub: HighBridge. Dist(s): Workman Pub

Insomnia, Set. Barrie Konicov. 2 cass. 14.98 (978-1-56001-318-1(4), ACII 074) Potentials.
Suggests that if you are properly motivated you can sleep & sleep deeply, throughout the night with peaceful dreams & you can awaken at the time of your choice.

Insomnia: Combata el Insomnia. Barrie Konicov. 1 cass. (Running Time: 1 hr. 30 min.). (Spanish-Language Audios Ser.). (SPA.). 1995. 11.98 (978-0-87082-759-4(6), 074) Potentials.
This tape can help you to sleep & sleep deeply throughout the night with peaceful dreams.

Insomnia: Program from the Award Winning Public Radio Series. Read by John Updike. Hosted by Fred Goodwin. Contrib. by John Hockenberry et al. 1 cass. (Running Time: 1 hr.). (Infinite Mind Ser.). 1999. audio compact disk 21.95 (978-1-888064-15-5(3), LCM 56) Lichtenstein Creat.
One-third of Americans, in a recent survey, reported experiencing a bout of insomnia in the past year. One-sixth of Americans rated their insomnia as "serious." This program looks at the role of sleep and the causes and treatments of insomnia, including a new Harvard program that attacks insomnia through behavior modification. We will travel to the Amazon rain forest to learn about "dream-change" with native shamans. Also, author John Updike reads a poem on his own sleeplessness and John Hockenberry speculates about the two kinds of sleepers.

Insomnia Cured. abr. ed. Roger W. Breternitz. 1 cass. (Running Time: 45 min.). 1985. pap. bk. 9.95 (978-1-893417-12-0(3)) Vector Studios.
Hypnosis: Side A is introduction to whys & wherefores of insomnia. Side B has relaxation & reprogramming scripts with suggestions to aid in deep relaxation to induce deep sleep & rest.

Insomnia Relief / Sleep Tonight. Created by Anne H. Spencer-Beacham. 1. 2003. audio compact disk (978-1-932163-48-3(4)) Infinity Inst.

Insomniac. Lewis Winokur. 1 cass. (Running Time: 40 min.). 1995. 14.95 (978-0-9650854-0-3(6)) L Winokur.

Insomnio. Carlos González. Read by Carlos González. Ed. by Dina Gonzalez. 1 cass. (Running Time: 32 min.). (SPA.). 1990. 10.00 (978-1-56491-016-5(4)) Imagine Pubs.
In Spanish. It helps people to relax & sleep better. Easy to do mental drills.

***Inspector Alleyn Mysteries: A Man Lay Dead & A Surfeit of Lampreys: A BBC Radio Crimes Full-Cast Drama.** Ngaio Marsh. Narrated by Jeremy Clyde & Full Cast. (Running Time: 2 hrs. 0 mins. 0 sec.). (ENG.). 2010. audio compact disk 24.95 (978-1-4084-6693-3(7)) Pub: AudioGO. Dist(s): Perseus Dist

Inspector Ghote Goes by Train. unabr. ed. H. R. F. Keating. Read by Sam Dastor. 8 cass. (Running Time: 12 hrs.). (Inspector Ghote Mystery Ser.: No. 7). 2002. 69.95 (978-0-7540-0799-9(5), CAB 2221) AudioGO.

Inspector Ghote Hunts the Peacock. H. R. F. Keating. Read by Sam Dastor. 6 cass. (Running Time: 9 hrs.). (Inspector Ghote Mystery Ser.: No. 4). 2002. 54.95 (978-0-7540-0885-9(1), CAB 2307) Pub: Chivers Audio Bks GBR. Dist(s): AudioGO

Inspector Ghote Plays a Joker. unabr. ed. H. R. F. Keating. Read by Sam Dastor. 6 cass. (Running Time: 9 hrs.). (Inspector Ghote Mystery Ser.: No. 5). 2002. 54.95 (978-0-7540-0753-1(7), CAB 2175) AudioGO.
Inspector Ghote embarks on one of his strangest cases when he is ordered to prevent a murder, the killing of a precious flamingo in the Bombay zoo. And then there is the racehorse fancied to win the local Derby, which gets replaced by a donkey. Ghote finds things going disastrously as bit by bit he unearths the traces of a monstrous practical joker. But then the fun stops and inspector Ghote has a more serious murder on his hands.

Inspector Ghote's Good Crusade. unabr. ed. H. R. F. Keating. Read by Sam Dastor. 6 cass. (Running Time: 9 hrs.). (Inspector Ghote Mystery Ser.: No. 2). 2003. 54.95 (978-0-7540-0925-2(4), CAB 2347) AudioGO.

***Inspector Hopper.** unabr. ed. Doug Cushman. (ENG.). 2008. (978-0-06-169472-1(X)); (978-0-06-171321-7(X)) HarperCollins Pubs.

Inspector Logan: Level 1. Richard MacAndrew. As told by Hilary Maclean. Contrib. by Philip Prowse. (Running Time: 41 mins.). (Cambridge English Readers Ser.). (ENG., 2003. 9.45 (978-0-521-75081-3(4)) Cambridge U Pr.

Inspector Maigret & the Strangled Stripper. unabr. ed. Georges Simenon. Read by Michael Prichard. 4 cass. (Running Time: 5 hrs.). 2001. 17.95 (978-0-7366-5725-9(8)) Books on Tape.
The legendary Parisian detective enters the underworld of Montmartre to search out a maniacal killer.

Inspector Maigret & the Strangled Stripper. unabr. collector's ed. Georges Simenon. Read by Michael Prichard. 5 cass. (Running Time: 5 hrs.). 1983. 30.00 (978-0-7366-0533-5(9), 1507) Books on Tape.

Inspector Mclevy Mysteries: A BBC Radio Full-Cast Dramatization. David Ashton. (Running Time: 2 hrs. 0 mins. 0 sec.). (ENG.). 2009. audio compact disk 24.95 (978-1-60283-750-8(3)) Pub: AudioGO. Dist(s): Perseus Dist

Inspector Morse Series. Perf. by John Thaw. 8 cass. (Running Time: 12 hrs.). 1998. 59.80 (978-1-56938-255-4(7), AMP-2557) Acorn Inc.
A brilliant, romantic & solitary detective is drawn to solving brutally sordid crimes. Morse probes human weakness in the academic environs of Oxford, where his unconventional investigative methods raise many eyebrows.

Inspector West Alone. unabr. collector's ed. John Creasey. Read by Stuart Courtney. 7 cass. (Running Time: 10 hrs. 30 min.). 1984. 56.00 (978-0-7366-0343-0(3), 1329) Books on Tape.
The inspector has been framed for murder. He is found by the police in an empty house with the body of a dead girl near him, battered with an axe bearing West's fingerprints. The identification in his wallet is not his own. He risks career, life, & the safety of everyone close to him as he untangles this set-up.

Inspiración para el Éxito. unabr. ed. Read by Pedro Montoya.Tr. of Inspiration to Success. (SPA.). 2002. audio compact disk 13.00 (978-958-43-0139-0(X)) YoYoMusic.

Inspiration! Vivienne Verdon-Roe. 1 cass. 9.00 (A0291-88) Sound Photosyn.
At Women in the World Conference.

Inspiration: Songs & Wisdom from the Holy Bible. Narrated by George Vafiadis. (Running Time: 25200 sec.). (Unabridged Classics in MP3 Ser.). (ENG.). 2008. audio compact disk 24.00 (978-1-58472-652-4(0), In Aud) Sound Room.

Inspiration: Songs & Wisdom from the Holy Bible: Psalms, Proverbs, Ecclesiastes, & Song of Solomon. Read by George Vafiadis. (Playaway Adult Nonfiction Ser.). 2008. 74.99 (978-1-60640-837-7(2)) Find a World.

Inspiration: Was That a Prompting of the Spirit or Just Me? Read by Jack Marshall. 1 cass. 1993. 7.98 (978-1-55503-560-0(4), 06004725) Covenant Comms.
General inspiration.

Inspiration: Your Ultimate Calling. abr. ed. Wayne W. Dyer. Read by Wayne W. Dyer. (Playaway Adult Nonfiction Ser.). 2008. 59.99 (978-1-60640-621-2(3)) Find a World.

Inspiration: Your Ultimate Calling. abr. ed. Wayne W. Dyer. 4 CDs. 2006. audio compact disk 23.95 (978-1-4019-0725-9(3)) Hay House.

Inspiration for Today, Vol. 2. unabr. ed. Narrated by Michael York. 2 CDs. (Running Time: 7200 sec.). (Word of Promise Ser.). 2008. audio compact disk 17.99 (978-1-4185-3321-2(1)) Nelson.

***Inspiration for Your Day: Poems & Messages to Lift Your Heart.** Ilchi Lee. (Running Time: 49 mins.). 2010. audio compact disk 17.95 (978-1-935127-45-1(4)) Pub: BEST Life. Dist(s): SCB Distributors

Inspiration to Excercise. Barry Tesar. 1 cass. (Running Time: 1 hr.). (Subliminal Inspiration Ser.). 1992. 9.98 (978-1-56470-023-0(2)) Success Cass.
Subliminal program.

Inspiration to Success see Inspiración para el Éxito

Inspiration to Success. Read by Pedro Montoya. (Running Time: 1 hr.). (C). 2002. 14.95 (978-1-60083-141-6(9), Audiofy Corp) Iofy Corp.

Inspirational Gifts of the Spirit. Kenneth E. Hagin. 4 cass. 16.00 (07H) Faith Lib Pubns.

Inspirational Songs. Paul Sybert. 1 CD. (Running Time: 45 mins). 2005. audio compact disk 15.00 (978-0-9767842-1-0(1)) Paul Syb.

Inspirational Thoughts. Wayne W. Dyer. 1 CD. 2007. audio compact disk 10.95 (978-1-4019-1175-1(7)) Hay House.

Inspirational Words of Abraham Lincoln. abr. ed. Gene Griessman. 1 cass. (Running Time: 1 hr. 30 min.). 1999. 11.95 (978-0-9652831-4-4(3)) Soundelux.

Inspirations - The "I Am" Presence: The Geometry of Being - Geometry in Motion. Eldon Taylor. Directed By Eldon Taylor. 1 cass. (Running Time: 30 min.). (Sacred Geometry Ser.). 1997. cass. & video 29.95 (978-1-55978-671-3(X), V109) Progress Aware Res.
Geometry in motion developing from fractals, forming mandalas, absolutely mesmerizing with tones & frequencies.

Inspire Any Audience: Proven Secrets of the Pros. abr. ed. Tony Jeary. Read by Tony Jeary. Frwd. by Zig Ziglar. 2 cass. (Running Time: 3 hrs.). 1999. 17.95 (978-1-57270-102-1(1), K21102) Pub: Audio Partners. Dist(s): PerseuPGW
Offers proven secrets of the pros for powerful presentations. Learn what to do before a presentation, how to win your audience in the first three minutes, master the tools of the trade & close a presentation with 100% audience buy-in.

***Inspired: The Secrets of Bob Proctor.** unabr. ed. Linda Proctor. Read by Victoria Velenosi. (Running Time: 2 hrs. 30 mins.). (ENG.). 2010. 19.98 (978-1-59659-583-5(3), GildAudio) Pub: Gildan Media. Dist(s): HachBkGrp

Inspired Bach: Music to Enhance Your Spirit. (Running Time: 3347 sec.). (Inspired Ser.). 2004. audio compact disk 11.99 (978-5-553-96345-3(1)) Royal Art GBR.

Inspired by ... the Bible Experience: A Dramatic Audio Bible Performed by 400 of Today's Biggest Starts. unabr. ed. Zondervan Publishing Staff. Read by Angela Bassett & Samuel L. Jackson. 18 CDs. (Running Time: 21 hrs.). (ENG.). 2006. audio compact disk 49.99 (978-0-310-92631-3(9)) Zondervan.

Inspired by ... the Bible Experience#8482;: Complete Old Testament. unabr. ed. (Running Time: 65 hrs. 30 mins. 0 sec.). (ENG.). 2007. 49.99 (978-0-310-93813-2(9)) Zondervan.

Inspired by ... the Bible Experience#8482;: OT downloadable bundle Book 10. unabr. ed. (Running Time: 3 hrs. 57 mins. 0 sec.). (ENG.). 2007. 3.60 (978-0-310-93822-4(8)) Zondervan.

Inspired by ... the Bible Experience#8482;: OT downloadable bundle Book 11. unabr. ed. (Running Time: 3 hrs. 25 mins. 0 sec.). (ENG.). 2007. 3.60 (978-0-310-93823-1(6)) Zondervan.

Inspired by ... the Bible Experience#8482;: OT downloadable bundle Book 12. unabr. ed. (Running Time: 2 hrs. 35 mins. 0 sec.). (ENG.). 2007. 3.60 (978-0-310-93824-8(4)) Zondervan.

Inspired by ... the Bible Experience#8482;: OT downloadable bundle Book 13. unabr. ed. (Running Time: 3 hrs. 23 mins. 0 sec.). (ENG.). 2007. 3.60 (978-0-310-93825-5(2)) Zondervan.

Inspired by ... the Bible Experience#8482;: OT downloadable bundle Book 14. unabr. ed. (Running Time: 3 hrs. 13 mins. 0 sec.). (ENG.). 2007. 3.60 (978-0-310-93826-2(0)) Zondervan.

Inspired by ... the Bible Experience#8482;: OT downloadable bundle Book 15. unabr. ed. (Running Time: 1 hr. 53 mins. 0 sec.). (ENG.). 2007. 3.60 (978-0-310-93827-9(9)) Zondervan.

Inspired by ... the Bible Experience#8482;: OT downloadable bundle Book 16. unabr. ed. (Running Time: 2 hrs. 1 mins. 0 sec.). (ENG.). 2007. 3.60 (978-0-310-93828-6(7)) Zondervan.

Inspired by ... the Bible Experience#8482;: OT downloadable bundle Book 17. unabr. ed. (Running Time: 2 hrs. 23 mins. 0 sec.). (ENG.). 2007. 3.60 (978-0-310-93829-3(5)) Zondervan.

Inspired by ... the Bible Experience#8482;: OT downloadable bundle Book 18. unabr. ed. (Running Time: 2 hrs. 10 mins. 0 sec.). (ENG.). 2007. 3.60 (978-0-310-93830-9(9)) Zondervan.

Inspired by ... the Bible Experience#8482;: OT downloadable bundle Book 19. unabr. ed. (Running Time: 2 hrs. 29 mins. 0 sec.). (ENG.). 2007. 3.60 (978-0-310-93831-6(7)) Zondervan.

Inspired by ... the Bible Experience#8482;: OT downloadable bundle Book 2. unabr. ed. (Running Time: 2 hrs. 26 mins. 0 sec.). (ENG.). 2007. 3.60 (978-0-310-93814-9(7)) Zondervan.

Inspired by ... the Bible Experience#8482;: OT downloadable bundle Book 20. unabr. ed. (Running Time: 2 hrs. 42 mins. 0 sec.). (ENG.). 2007. 3.60 (978-0-310-93832-3(5)) Zondervan.

Inspired by ... the Bible Experience#8482;: OT downloadable bundle Book 21. (Running Time: 2 hrs. 42 mins. 0 sec.). (ENG.). 2007. 3.60 (978-0-310-93833-0(3)) Zondervan.

Inspired by ... the Bible Experience#8482;: OT downloadable bundle Book 22. unabr. ed. (Running Time: 0 hr. 51 mins. 0 sec.). (ENG.). 2007. 3.60 (978-0-310-93834-7(1)) Zondervan.

Inspired by ... the Bible Experience#8482;: OT downloadable bundle Book 23. unabr. ed. (Running Time: 1 hr. 12 mins. 0 sec.). (ENG.). 2007. 3.60 (978-0-310-93835-4(X)) Zondervan.

Inspired by ... the Bible Experience#8482;: OT downloadable bundle Book 24. unabr. ed. (Running Time: 0 hr. 37 mins. 0 sec.). (ENG.). 2007. 3.60 (978-0-310-93836-1(8)) Zondervan.

Inspired by ... the Bible Experience#8482;: OT downloadable bundle Book 25. unabr. ed. (Running Time: 1 hr. 56 mins. 0 sec.). (ENG.). 2007. 3.60 (978-0-310-93837-8(6)) Zondervan.

Inspired by ... the Bible Experience#8482;: OT downloadable bundle Book 26. unabr. ed. (Running Time: 5 hrs. 16 mins. 0 sec.). (ENG.). 2007. 3.60 (978-0-310-93838-5(4)) Zondervan.

Inspired by ... the Bible Experience#8482;: OT downloadable bundle Book 27. unabr. ed. (Running Time: 1 hr. 52 mins. 0 sec.). (ENG.). 2007. 3.60 (978-0-310-93839-2(2)) Zondervan.

Inspired by ... the Bible Experience#8482;: OT downloadable bundle Book 28. unabr. ed. (Running Time: 1 hr. 0 mins. 0 sec.). (ENG.). 2007. 3.60 (978-0-310-93840-8(6)) Zondervan.

Inspired by ... the Bible Experience#8482;: OT downloadable bundle Book 3. unabr. ed. (Running Time: 4 hrs. 14 mins. 0 sec.). (ENG.). 2007. 3.60 (978-0-310-93815-6(5)) Zondervan.

Inspired by ... the Bible Experience#8482;: OT downloadable bundle Book 4. unabr. ed. (Running Time: 4 hrs. 53 mins. 0 sec.). (ENG.). 2007. 3.60 (978-0-310-93816-3(3)) Zondervan.

Inspired by ... the Bible Experience#8482;: OT downloadable bundle Book 5. unabr. ed. (Running Time: 3 hrs. 36 mins. 0 sec.). (ENG.). 2007. 3.60 (978-0-310-93817-0(1)) Zondervan.

Inspired by ... the Bible Experience#8482;: OT downloadable bundle Book 6. unabr. ed. (Running Time: 1 hr. 14 mins. 0 sec.). (ENG.). 2007. 3.60 (978-0-310-93818-7(X)) Zondervan.

Inspired by ... the Bible Experience#8482;: OT downloadable bundle Book 7. unabr. ed. (Running Time: 1 hr. 26 mins. 0 sec.). (ENG.). 2007. 3.60 (978-0-310-93819-4(8)) Zondervan.

Inspired by ... the Bible Experience#8482;: OT downloadable bundle Book 8. unabr. ed. (Running Time: 0 hr. 39 mins. 0 sec.). (ENG.). 2007. 3.60 (978-0-310-93820-0(1)) Zondervan.

Inspired by ... the Bible Experience#8482;: OT downloadable bundle Book 9. unabr. ed. (Running Time: 0 hr. 43 mins. 0 sec.). (ENG.). 2007. 3.60 (978-0-310-93821-7(X)) Zondervan.

***Inspired by â€¦ the Bible Experienceâ„¢: the Easter Story: The Death & Resurrection of Jesus.** Zondervan. (Running Time: 0 hr. 25 mins. 0 sec.). (ENG.). 2009. 1.99 (978-0-310-56678-6(9)) Zondervan.

***Inspired by â€¦ the Bible Experienceâ„¢: Zechariah - Malachi.** (Running Time: 0 hr. 53 mins. 0 sec.). (ENG.). 2007. 3.60 (978-0-310-93899-6(6)) Zondervan.

Inspired by... the Bible Experience, Galatians - Colossians. unabr. ed. (Running Time: 1 hr. 24 mins. 0 sec.). (ENG.). 2007. 3.60 (978-0-310-93795-1(7)) Zondervan.

Inspired by... the Bible Experience, Hebrews - James. unabr. ed. (Running Time: 1 hr. 4 mins. 0 sec.). (ENG.). 2007. 3.60 (978-0-310-93797-5(3)) Zondervan.

Inspired by... the Bible Experience, New Testament. unabr. ed. (Running Time: 20 hrs. 32 mins. 0 sec.). (ENG.). 2007. 34.99 (978-0-310-93800-2(7)) Zondervan.

Inspired by... the Bible Experience, Revelation. unabr. ed. (Running Time: 1 hr. 24 mins. 0 sec.). (ENG.). 2007. 3.60 (978-0-310-93799-9(X)) Zondervan.

Inspired by... the Bible Experience, 1 Peter - Jude. unabr. ed. (Running Time: 1 hr. 18 mins. 0 sec.). (ENG.). 2007. 3.60 (978-0-310-93798-2(1)) Zondervan.

Inspired by... the Bible Experience, 1 Thessalonians - Philemon. unabr. ed. (Running Time: 1 hr. 19 mins. 0 sec.). (ENG.). 2007. 3.60 (978-0-310-93796-8(5)) Zondervan.

Inspired by... the Bible Experience, 1-2 Corinthians. unabr. ed. (Running Time: 1 hr. 51 mins. 0 sec.). (ENG.). 2007. 3.00 (978-0-310-93794-4(9)) Zondervan.

Inspired by... the Bible Experience#8482;: Acts. unabr. ed. (Running Time: 2 hrs. 25 mins. 0 sec.). (ENG.). 2007. 3.60 (978-0-310-93637-4(3)) Zondervan.

Inspired by... the Bible Experience#8482;: John. unabr. ed. (Running Time: 2 hrs. 5 mins. 0 sec.). (ENG.). 2007. 3.60 (978-0-310-93605-3(5)) Zondervan.

Inspired by... the Bible Experience#8482;: Luke. unabr. ed. (Running Time: 2 hrs. 41 mins. 0 sec.). (ENG.). 2007. 3.60 (978-0-310-93638-1(1)) Zondervan.

Inspired by... the Bible Experience#8482;: Matthew. unabr. ed. (Running Time: 2 hrs. 26 mins. 0 sec.). (ENG.). 2007. 3.60 (978-0-310-93639-8(X)) Zondervan.

Inspired by... the Bible Experience#8482;: Romans. unabr. ed. (Running Time: 1 hr. 5 mins. 0 sec.). (ENG.). 2007. 3.60 (978-0-310-93700-5(0)) Zondervan.

Inspired by... the Bible Experience#8482;, Romans to Revelation. unabr. ed. Zondervan Publishing Staff. (Running Time: 1 hr. 34 mins. 0 sec.). (ENG.). 2007. 3.60 (978-0-310-93630-5(6)) Zondervan.

Inspired by...the Bible Experience: New Testament. 2006. audio compact disk 64.99 (978-0-310-60856-1(2)) Zondervan.

Inspired by...the Bible Experience: New Testament. Zondervan Publishing Staff. 2006. audio compact disk 64.99 (978-0-310-60831-8(7)) Zondervan.

Inspired by...the Bible Experience: New Testament. unabr. ed. Created by Zondervan Publishing Staff. (Running Time: 0 hr. 20 mins. 11 sec.). (ENG.). 2006. 34.99 (978-0-310-92633-7(5)) Zondervan.

Inspired by...the Bible Experience: Old Testament. unabr. ed. Media Group Productions Staff. Read by Forest Whitaker et al. (ENG.). 2007. audio compact disk 84.99 (978-0-310-93857-6(0)) Zondervan.

Inspired Imagery. 1 CD. 1989. audio compact disk 16.95 (978-1-55841-120-3(8)) Emmett E Miller.
This CD offers a lecture presentation to health professionals at the "Power of Imagination" conference sponsored by the Institute for the Advancement of Human Behavior.

Inspired Imagery: Finding Inner Direction for Your Life. 1 cassette. 1989. 12.95 (978-1-55841-036-7(8)) Emmett E Miller.
A cassette to help you understand "little imagery" - used to work with specific symptoms or problems; visualize "big imagery" - life direction, meaning, purpose, self-esteem; and to refocus daily thoughts and bring new energy and possibilities into your life.

Inspired Marketing: The Astonishing Fun New Way to Create More Profits for Your Business by Following Your Heart. unabr. ed. Joe Vitale, Jr. & Craig Perrine. Read by Joe Vitale, Jr. & Craig Perrine. (Running Time: 12 hrs.). (ENG.). 2008. 24.98 (978-1-59659-232-2(X), GildAudio) Pub: Gildan Media. Dist(s): HachBkGrp

Inspired Success/Love vs. Judgment. Marianne Williamson. Read by Marianne Williamson. 1 cass. (Running Time: 90 mins.). (Lectures on a Course in Miracles). 1999. 10.00 (978-1-56170-234-3(X), M737) Hay House.

***Inspired to Worship.** Sammy Horner. (ENG.). 2006. audio compact disk 17.99 (978-92-822-5912-2(9)) Pub: Kingsway Pubns GBR. Dist(s): STL Dist NA

Inspiring Presentations from the National Rosary Congress. 16 cass. 35.00 Set. (978-1-56036-102-2(6)) AMI Pr.

Inspiring Stories of Courage from Christians Serving Around the World, Bk. 2. unabr. ed. Compiled by Kim P. Davis. (Running Time: 14 hrs. 43 mins. 20 sec.). (Voices of the Faithful Ser.). 2009. 13.99 (978-1-60814-596-6(4)) Oasis Audio.

Installing & Managing Microsoft Exchange Server 2007 (5047) Training Course. Created by K-Alliance Staff. 2007. 995.00 (978-1-60540-017-4(3)) K Alliance.

Instant Bass: Play Right Now! Danny Morris. CD. (Instant Ser.). 2000. pap. bk. 14.95 (978-0-634-01667-7(9), 0634016679) H Leonard.

Instant Blues Harmonica, Vol. 2. 12.95 Musical I Pr.

Instant Blues Harmonica for the "Musical Idiot" David Harp. 1 cass. (Running Time: 96 min.). (YA). (gr. k up). bk. 12.95 Musical I Pr.

Instant Calm: Meditations to Train Your Brain & Calm Your Emotions in an Instant. Perf. by Rebecca Ann Nagy. Created by Rebecca Ann Nagy. Arranged by Richard Shulman. Music by Richard Shulman. 2007. (978-0-9796531-0-0(X)) Extra Potential.

Instant Conversation English for Spanish: Learn to Speak & Understand English for Spanish with Pimsleur Language Programs. 2nd ed. Pimsleur Staff. (Running Time: 800 hrs. 0 mins. NaN sec.). (Conversational Ser.). (JPN & SPA.). 2002. audio compact disk 49.95 (978-0-7435-2910-5(3), Pimsleur) Pub: S&S Audio. Dist(s): S and S Inc

Instant Conversational Advanced German - Module Four. AMR Staff. 1 cass. (AMR Language Ser.). 46.95 Vinyl Album. (978-1-55536-315-4(6)) Oasis Audio.
Designed to build on a basic knowledge of a language & bring you to a high level of conversational ability. Complex sentence structure & grammar are taught within the context of practical everyday situations.

Instant Conversational Chinese, Set. 4 cass. (Running Time: 4 hrs. 30 min.). (AMR Language Ser.). Oasis Audio.
An additional 2000 words to expand your Chinese vocabulary.

Instant Conversational Chinese Vocabulary, Set. AMR Staff. 4 cass. (Running Time: 6 hrs.). (AMR Language Ser.). (CHI.). 2004. 46.99 (978-1-886463-69-1(7)) Oasis Audio.

Instant Conversational French - Advanced, Set. 2nd ed. AMR Staff. 4 cass. (Instant Language Courses Ser.). (FRE.). 2004. pap. bk. 46.99 (978-1-886463-60-8(3)) Oasis Audio.

Instant Conversational French - Advanced Plus, Set. 2nd ed. AMR Staff. 4 cass. (Instant Language Courses Ser.). (FRE.). 2004. pap. bk. 46.99 (978-1-886463-61-5(1)) Oasis Audio.
A team of memory and linguistic experts have designed this world class foreign language self-study course. International travelers, students, and business people can now learn to converse in a new language in less than half the time they expect. Instant Language is guaranteed to work for beginners, as a refresher course, and even for people who have been frustrated in other attempts to learn a new language.

Instant Conversational French - Basic. 2002. instr.'s gde. ed. 46.99 (978-1-55678-081-3(8), Lrn Inc) Oasis Audio.

Instant Conversational French - Basic. 2nd ed. AMR Staff. 4 cass. (Instant Language Courses Ser.). (FRE.). 1998. pap. bk. 46.99 (978-1-886463-28-8(X)) Oasis Audio.
Learn to greet a friend, use the telephone, navigate your way around the airport, get through customs, exchange money, check into your hotel, go shopping & a great deal more.

Instant Conversational French - Basic: Intermediate. 4 CDs. (Running Time: 6 hrs.). 2002. instr.'s gde. ed. 46.99 (978-1-55678-082-0(6), Lrn Inc) Oasis Audio.
A team of memory and linguistic experts has designed the world's most effective foreign language self-study course. International travelers, students and business people can now learn to converse in half the time they expect. Instant Language is guaranteed to work for beginners, as a refresher course, and even for people who have been frustrated in other attempts to learn a new language. With these instant Language courses, you can actually start learning today. Includes guidebook.

Instant Conversational French - Intermediate, Set. AMR Staff. 4 cass. (AMR Language Ser.). (FRE.). 1999. pap. bk. 46.99 (978-1-886463-34-9(4)) Oasis Audio.
You'll learn how to make friends, schedule a business appointment, arrange transportation & eat at a restaurant. Plus you will review verbs, language patterns & much more.

Instant Conversational French Vocabulary, Set. 2nd ed. AMR Staff. 4 cass. (Running Time: 3 hrs. 30 mins.). (Instant Language Courses Ser.). (FRE.). 1999. pap. bk. 46.99 (978-1-886463-65-3(4)) Oasis Audio.
An additional 2000 words to expand your French vocabulary.

Instant Conversational German - Advanced, Set. 2nd ed. AMR Staff. 4 cass. (Running Time: 60 mins. per cass.). (Instant Language Courses Ser.). (GER.). 1999. bk. 46.99 (978-1-886463-62-2(X)) Oasis Audio.
The equivalent of four years of college conversational language instruction. Subject material business related, politics, family relations, health care, schooling, traffic accidents & more. A concentration on grammar instruction.

Instant Conversational German - Advanced Plus, Set. 2nd ed. AMR Staff. 4 cass. (Running Time: 5 hrs. 45 mins.). (Instant Language Courses Ser.). (GER.). 2004. pap. bk. 46.99 (978-1-886463-63-9(8)) Oasis Audio.
A team of memory and linguistic experts have designed this world class foreign language self-study course. International travelers, students, and business people can now learn to converse in a new language in less than half the time they expect. Instant Language is guaranteed to work for beginners, as a refresher course, and even for people who have been frustrated in other attempts to learn a new language.

Instant Conversational German - Basic. 2002. instr.'s gde. ed. 46.99 (978-1-55678-083-7(4), Lrn Inc) Oasis Audio.

Instant Conversational German - Basic. 2nd ed. AMR Staff. 4 cass. (Running Time: 6 hrs.). (Instant Language Courses Ser.). (GER.). 1998. bk. 46.99 (978-1-886463-29-5(8)) Oasis Audio.
Learn to greet a friend, use the telephone, navigate your way around the airport, get through customs, exchange money, check into your hotel, go shopping & a great deal more.

Instant Conversational German - Intermediate, Set. AMR Staff. 4 cass. (AMR Language Ser.). (GER.). 1998. bk. 46.99 (978-1-886463-35-6(2)) Oasis Audio.
You'll learn how to make friends, schedule a business appointment, arrange transportation & eat at a restaurant. Plus you will review verbs, language patterns & much more.

Instant Conversational German Vocabulary, Set. AMR Staff. 4 cass. (AMR Language Ser.). (GER.). 1999. pap. bk. 46.99 (978-1-886463-66-0(2)) Oasis Audio.
Designed to provide you with a wealth of words not in Modules 1-4. Boost your language vocabulary by 2000 words.

Instant Conversational Italian Set: Vocabulary. 4 cass. (Running Time: 3 hrs. 30 min.). 46.95 Oasis Audio.
An additional 2000 words to expand your Italian vocabulary.

Instant Conversational Italian - Basic. 2002. instr.'s gde. ed. 46.99 (978-1-55678-085-1(0), Lrn Inc) Oasis Audio.

Instant Conversational Italian - Basic. 2nd ed. AMR Staff. 4 cass. (Instant Language Courses Ser.). (ITA.). 1998. bk. 46.99 (978-1-886463-30-1(1)) Oasis Audio.
Learn to greet a friend, use the telephone, navigate your way around the airport, get through customs, exchange money, check into your hotel, go shopping & a great deal more.

Instant Conversational Italian - Intermediate, Set. 2nd ed. AMR Staff. 4 cass. (Instant Language Courses Ser.). (ITA.). 1998. bk. 46.99 (978-1-886463-36-3(0)) Oasis Audio.
You'll learn how to make friends, schedule a business appointment, arrange transportation & eat at a restaurant. Plus you will review verbs, language patterns & much more.

Instant Conversational Italian Vocabulary, Set. 2nd ed. AMR Staff. 4 cass. (Running Time: 60 mins. per cass.). (Instant Language Courses Ser.). (ITA.). 1999. pap. bk. 46.99 (978-1-886463-67-7(0)) Oasis Audio.
Vocabulary words provide you with a wealth of Italian words not covered in the basis course (200 words).

Instant Conversational Japanese: Intermediate. 4 CDs. (Running Time: 6 hrs.). 2002. pap. bk. 46.99 (978-1-55678-088-2(5), Lrn Inc) Oasis Audio.
A team of memory and linguistic experts has designed the world's most effective foreign language self-study course. International travelers, students and business people can now learn to converse in half the time they expect. Instant Language is guaranteed to work for beginners, as a refresher course, and even for people who have been frustrated in other attempts to learn a new language. With these instant Language courses, you can actually start learning today. Includes guidebook.

Instant Conversational Japanese - Basic. 2002. audio compact disk 46.99 (978-1-55678-087-5(7), Lrn Inc) Oasis Audio.

Instant Conversational Japanese - Basic. 2nd ed. AMR Staff. 4 cass. (Instant Language Courses Ser.). (JPN.). 1998. bk. 46.99 (978-1-886463-31-8(X)) Oasis Audio.
Learn to greet a friend, use the telephone, navigate your way around the airport, get through customs, exchange money, check into your hotel, go shopping & a great deal more.

Instant Conversational Japanese - Intermediate, Set. 2nd ed. AMR Staff. 4 cass. (Instant Language Courses Ser.). (JPN.). 1998. 46.99 (978-1-886463-37-0(9)) Oasis Audio.
You'll learn how to make friends, schedule a business appointment, arrange transportation, & eat at a restaurant. Plus you will review verbs, language patterns & much more.

Instant Conversational Japanese Vocabulary, Set. AMR Staff. 4 cass. (Running Time: 4 hrs.). (AMR Language Ser.). (JPN.). 1999. pap. bk. 46.99 (978-1-886463-68-4(9)) Oasis Audio.
An additional 2000 words to expand your Japanese vocabulary.

Instant Conversational Mandarin Chinese: Intermediate. 4 CDs. (Running Time: 6 hrs.). 2002. pap. bk. 46.99 (978-1-55678-090-5(7), Lrn Inc) Oasis Audio.
A team of memory and linguistic experts has designed the world's most effective foreign language self-study course. International travelers, students and business people can now learn to converse in half the time they expect. Instant Language is guaranteed to work for beginners, as a refresher course, and even for people who have been frustrated in other attempts to learn a new language. With these instant Language courses, you can actually start learning today. Includes guidebook.

Instant Conversational Mandarin Chinese - Basic. 2002. audio compact disk 46.99 (978-1-55678-089-9(3), Lrn Inc) Oasis Audio.

Instant Conversational Mandarin Chinese - Basic. AMR Staff. 4 cass. (AMR Language Ser.). (CHI.). 1998. 46.99 (978-1-886463-32-5(8)) Oasis Audio.
Learn to greet a friend, use the telephone, navigate your way around the airport, get through customs, exchange money, check into your hotel, go shopping & a great deal more.

Instant Conversational Mandarin Chinese - Intermediate, Set. AMR Staff. 4 cass. (AMR Language Ser.). (CHI.). 1999. 46.99 (978-1-886463-38-7(7)) Oasis Audio.
You'll learn how to make friends, schedule a business appointment, arrange transportation, & eat at a restaurant. Plus you will review verbs, language patterns & much more.

Instant Conversational Spanish: Intermediate. 4 CDs. (Running Time: 6 hrs.). 2002. pap. bk. 46.99 (978-1-55678-080-6(X)) Oasis Audio.
A team of memory and linguistic experts has designed the world's most effective foreign language self-study course. International travelers, students and business people can now learn to converse in half the time they expect. Instant Language is guaranteed to work for beginners, as a refresher course, and even for people who have been frustrated in other attempts to learn a new language. With these instant Language courses, you can actually start learning today. Includes guidebook.

Instant Conversational Spanish - Advanced Plus, Set. AMR Staff. 4 cass. (Running Time: 4 hr. 30 mins.). (AMR Language Ser.). (SPA.). 1999. bk. 46.99 (978-1-886463-59-2(X)) Oasis Audio.

Instant Conversational Spanish - Basic. 2002. audio compact disk 46.99 (978-1-55678-079-0(6), Lrn Inc) Oasis Audio.

Instant Conversational Spanish - Basic. 2nd ed. AMR Staff. 4 cass. (Instant Language Courses Ser.). (SPA.). 1998. vinyl bd. 46.99 (978-1-886463-27-1(1)) Oasis Audio.
Learn to greet a friend, use the telephone, navigate your way around the airport, get through customs, exchange money, check into your hotel, go shopping & a great deal more.

Instant Conversational Spanish - Intermediate, Set. 2nd ed. AMR Staff. 4 cass. (Instant Language Courses Ser.). (SPA.). 1998. bk. 46.99 (978-1-886463-33-2(6)) Oasis Audio.
You'll learn how to make friends, schedule a business appointment, arrange transportation & eat at a restaurant. Plus you will review verbs, language patterns & much more.

Instant Conversational Spanish Vocabulary, Set. 2nd ed. AMR Staff. 4 cass. (Running Time: 3 hrs. 30 mins.). (AMR Language Ser.). (SPA.). 2004. pap. bk. 46.99 (978-1-886463-64-6(6)) Oasis Audio.
A team of memory and linguistic experts have designed this world class foreign language self-study course. International travelers, students, and business people can now learn to converse in a new language in less than half the time they expect. Instant Language is guaranteed to work for beginners, as a refresher course, and even for people who have been frustrated in other attempts to learn a new language.

Instant Converstional Advanced English Vocabulary, Set. AMR Staff. 4 cass. (Running Time: 60 min. per cass.). (AMR Language Ser.). bk. 46.95 Oasis Audio.
Teaches approximately 500 words in specialized categories such as: Business, Economics, Diplomacy, Debate, Politics, Medicine, Religion, & Computer Science. The student will learn definitions, spelling, pronunciations, & the use of these words in the proper context.

Instant English Vocabulary, Vol. 1, Set. AMR Staff. 4 cass. (Running Time: 60 mins. per cass.). (AMR Language Ser.). 1999. bk. 46.95 (978-1-886463-70-7(0)) Oasis Audio.
Vocabulary words are presented in blocks of synonyms. The student learns a word as well as the synonyms to the word. Then the course explains the subtle differences between these synonyms to ensure that the word is used correctly. Teaches approximately 500 vocabulary words.

Instant English Vocabulary, Vol. 2, Set. AMR Staff. 4 cass. (Running Time: 6 hrs.). (AMR Language Ser.). 1999. 46.95 (978-1-886463-71-4(9)) Oasis Audio.

Instant English Vocabulary, Vol. 3, Set. AMR Staff. 4 cass. (Running Time: 60 mins. per cass.). (AMR Language Ser.). 1999. bk. 46.95 VINYL ALBUM. (978-1-886463-72-1(7)) Oasis Audio.
Teaches approximately 500 words in specialized categories such as: Business, Economics, Diplomacy, Debate, Politics, Medicine, Religion & Computer Science. The student will learn definitions, spelling, pronunciations & the use of these words in the proper context.

Instant English Vocabulary, Vol. 4, Set. AMR Staff. 4 cass. (AMR Language Ser.). 1999. 46.95 (978-1-886463-73-8(5)) Oasis Audio.
Provides you with approximately 250 primary words & an additional 750 secondary words, placed in the text to teach you these words & their relationship to the primary words.

Instant Flute: Includes Block-Style Flute. 3rd rev. ed. David Harp. 1 cass. (Running Time: 1 hr. 38 min.). (ENG., (gr. k up). 1992. 14.95 (978-0-918321-22-0(0)) Pub: Musical I Pr. Dist(s): PerseuPGW

Instant Genius the Constitution: The Cheat Sheets of Culture. Alan R. Hirsch. 1 cass. (Running Time: 060 min.). (Instant Genius Ser.). 1998. 12.00 (978-1-891115-05-9(7)) Good Think.

Instant Genius: The Constitution Vol. 1: The Cheat Sheets of Culture. Alan R. Hirsch. Read by Melissa Leebaert. 1 cass. (Running Time: 55 min.). (Instant Genius Ser.: Vol. 7). 1998. Good Think.
An introduction to the history, structure & content of the Constitution, & its influence on American politics.

Instant Guitar! Pat Conway. 1995. audio compact disk 12.95 (978-0-8256-2266-3(2), AM32517) Pub: Music Sales. Dist(s): H Leonard

Instant Guts! How to Take a Risk & Win in Every Area of Your Life. Joan G. Frank. 1 cass. (Running Time: 70 min.). 1993. bk. 14.95 (978-1-882940-00-4(8)) Big Mouth.

Instant IELTS: Ready-to-Use Tasks & Activities. Guy Brook-Hart. (Running Time: 59 mins.). (Cambridge Copy Collection). (ENG.). 2004. tchr. ed. 25.00 (978-0-521-75535-1(2)) Cambridge U Pr.

Instant IELTS: Ready-to-Use Tasks & Activities. Guy Brook-Hart. (Running Time: 55 mins.). (Cambridge Copy Collection). 2004. tchr. ed. 25.00 (978-0-521-75536-8(0)) Cambridge U Pr.

Instant Immersion Chinese I-DVD. Topics Entertainment Staff. 2009. audio compact disk 19.99 (978-1-60077-447-8(4)) TOPICS Ent.

Instant Immersion Chinese Mandarin Crash Course. Created by Topics Entertainment. (Instant Immersion Ser.). 2007. audio compact disk 9.95 (978-1-60077-116-3(5)) TOPICS Ent.

***Instant Immersion Deployment Pack: Afganistan.** Topics Entertainment Staff. 2010. audio compact disk 39.99 (978-1-60077-632-8(9)) TOPICS Ent.

***Instant Immersion Deployment Pack: Germany.** Topics Entertainment Staff. 2010. audio compact disk 39.99 (978-1-60077-633-5(7)) TOPICS Ent.

***Instant Immersion Deployment Pack: Iraq.** Topics Entertainment Staff. 2010. audio compact disk 39.99 (978-1-60077-629-8(9)) TOPICS Ent.

***Instant Immersion Deployment Pack: Japan.** Topics Entertainment Staff. 2010. audio compact disk 39.99 (978-1-60077-631-1(0)) TOPICS Ent.

***Instant Immersion Deployment Pack: Korea.** Topics Entertainment Staff. 2010. audio compact disk 9.99 (978-1-60077-630-4(2)) TOPICS Ent.

Instant Immersion English. unabr. ed. Topics Entertainment Staff. 2006. audio compact disk 19.95 (978-1-59150-850-2(9)) TOPICS Ent.

Instant Immersion French. unabr. deluxe ed. Topics Entertainment Staff. 2006. audio compact disk 29.95 (978-1-59150-834-2(7)) TOPICS Ent.

Instant Immersion French Crash Course. Created by Topics Entertainment. (Instant Immersion Ser.). 2007. audio compact disk 9.95 (978-1-60077-112-5(2)) TOPICS Ent.

Instant Immersion French I-DVD. Topics Entertainment Staff. 2009. audio compact disk 19.99 (978-1-60077-443-0(1)) TOPICS Ent.

Instant Immersion German Crash Course: Essential Vocabulary, Phrases & Pronunciation for Quick & Easy Mastery. Created by Topics Entertainment. (Instant Immersion Ser.). 2007. audio compact disk 9.95 (978-1-60077-349-5(4)) TOPICS Ent.

Instant Immersion German I-DVD. Topics Entertainment Staff. 2009. audio compact disk 19.99 (978-1-60077-445-4(8)) TOPICS Ent.

Instant Immersion Ingles Crash Course. 3 cd's. 2003. audio compact disk 9.95 (978-1-59150-375-0(2)) TOPICS Ent.
Millones de personas en el ambito mundial han descubierto el valor de Instant Immersion?. El programa mas efectivo y profundo para aprendizaje de lenguajes que utiliza personas cuya lengua materna es el ingles y expresiones culturales para hacer que hables un idioma extranjero facilmente. Ahora, turistas, estudiantes y viajeros de negocios pueden emplear este mismo metodo; pero en un modo mas rapido y condensado con Curso Rapido de Ingles Instant Immersion?. Este audio es un conjunto de esenciales del lenguaje extranjero en 3 CD. Desde saludos hasta los sonidos del alfabeto, el curso rapido enfatiza lo basico para tener una comunicacion en tu nuevo lenguaje, ayudandote a conversar en ingles.

Instant Immersion Ingles I-DVD. Topics Entertainment Staff. 2009. audio compact disk 19.99 (978-1-60077-448-5(2)) TOPICS Ent.

Instant Immersion Italian Crash Course. Created by Topics Entertainment. (Instant Immersion Ser.). 2007. audio compact disk 9.95 (978-1-60077-113-2(0)) TOPICS Ent.

Instant Immersion Italian I-DVD. Topics Entertainment Staff. 2009. audio compact disk 19.99 (978-1-60077-444-7(X)) TOPICS Ent.

Instant Immersion Japanese Audio Deluxe. unabr. deluxe ed. Created by Topics Entertainment. (Instant Immersion Ser.). 2006. audio compact disk 29.95 (978-1-59150-837-3(1)) TOPICS Ent.

Instant Immersion Japanese Crash Course. Created by Topics Entertainment. (Instant Immersion Ser.). 2007. audio compact disk 9.95 (978-1-60077-115-6(7)) TOPICS Ent.

Instant Immersion Japanese I-DVD. Topics Entertainment Staff. 2009. audio compact disk 19.99 (978-1-60077-446-1(6)) TOPICS Ent.

Instant Immersion Spanish Audio Deluxe. unabr. deluxe ed. Topics Entertainment Staff. 2006. audio compact disk 29.95 (978-1-59150-833-5(9)) TOPICS Ent.

Instant Immersion Spanish Audio Learning System: 8 CD Audio Set. Topics Entertainment. (ENG.). 2008. audio compact disk 19.99 (978-1-60077-435-5(0)) TOPICS Ent.

Instant Immersion Spanish Crash Course. 3 cd's. 2003. audio compact disk Rental 9.95 (978-1-59150-374-3(4)) TOPICS Ent.
Millions of people worldwide have discovered the value of Instant Immersion?, the effective, in-depth program of language learning that uses native speakers and cultural notes to make speaking a foreign language easy. Now, tourists on the go, students, and business travelers in a hurry, can employ these same celebrated methods in a quicker, condensed format with the Instant Immersion? Spanish Crash Course, the audio suite of foreign-language fundamentals on 3 CDs. From salutations to sounds of the alphabet, the Crash Course emphasizes the basics of spoken communication in your new language, enabling you to converse in Spanish. Instant Immersion? Spanish Crash Course is your fast track to Spanish proficiency!.

Instant Immersion Spanish I-DVD. Topics Entertainment Staff. 2009. audio compact disk 19.99 (978-1-60077-442-3(3)) TOPICS Ent.

Instant Impact: How the Carlyle Group¿s Settlement on New Rules of Conduct Will Immediately Impact PE Firms & Their Employees. Heather Stone. 2009. 250.00 (978-1-59701-484-7(2)) ReedLogic.

Instant Impact: How the EU Fine on Intel Will Immediately Impact Antitrust Lawyers & Their Clients. John Cove & Steve Holtzman. 2009. 250.00 (978-1-59701-483-0(4)) ReedLogic.

Instant Impact: Understanding Facebook's Username Cybersquatting Risks to Your Clients. Michael Hobbs. 2009. 250.00 (978-1-59701-520-2(2)) ReedLogic.

Instant Impact: Understanding the Impact of New U. S. Antitrust Efforts & the Immediate Ramifications on Lawyers & Their Clients. Mark Popofsky. 2009. 250.00 (978-1-59701-479-3(6)) ReedLogic.

Instant Impact: What Board Members Need to Know about the SEC Proposal for New Investor Powers. Davis Kaufman. 2009. 250.00 (978-1-59701-490-8(7)) ReedLogic.

Instant Impact: What HR Professionals Need to Know about the Ricci V. Destefano Supreme Court Verdict ¿ Immediately Updating Testing & Interviewing Policies that Could Cause Workplace Discrimination Lawsuits. Jay Zweig. 2009. 250.00 (978-1-59701-537-0(7)) ReedLogic.

Instant Impact: What Ricci V. Destefano Means for Civil Rights Lawyers, Their Clients & Workplace Discrimination Issues. Lynne Bernabai. 2009. 250.00 (978-1-59701-533-2(4)) ReedLogic.

Instant Impact: What Ricci V. Destefano Means for Labor & Employment Lawyers, Their Clients & Workplace Discrimination Issues. Paul Garry. Anna Wermuth. 2009. 250.00 (978-1-59701-534-9(2)) ReedLogic.

Instant Impact: What the Climate Change Bill Means for Environmental Lawyers & Their Clients. Mark Johnson. 2009. 250.00 (978-1-59701-524-0(5)) ReedLogic.

Instant Impact: What Venture Capital & Private Equity Professionals Need to Know about the Overhaul of the Financial Regulatory System. Jim Dugan. 2009. 250.00 (978-1-59701-526-4(1)) ReedLogic.

Instant Influence. Robert B. Cialdini. Read by Robert B. Cialdini. 6 cass. (Running Time: 5 hrs.). 1991. 69.95 Set, incl. Action Guide. (2004) Dartnell Corp.
Dr. Cialdini explains how to harness the Six Powerful Principles of Influence to get what you ask for in any business situation. Program focuses on ethical persuasion techniques.

Instant Influence. abr. ed. Robert B. Cialdini. Read by Robert B. Cialdini. Ed. by Vera Derr. 2 cass. (Running Time: 3 hrs.). 1996. 15.95 Set. (978-0-85013-245-8(2)) Dartnell Corp.
Tells you how to ask for - & receive - approval, cooperation, & compliance in any business situation. By learning how to harness the effective & ethical powers of instant influence you'll: convince your superiors to go along with your plans & proposals, motivate your employees & co-workers to cooperate with you, persuade customers to make the right buying decisions.

***Instant Influence.** unabr. ed. Michael Pantalon. Read by Walter Dixon. (Running Time: 6 hrs.). (ENG.). 2011. 27.00 (978-1-59659-651-1(1), GildAudio); audio compact disk 29.98 (978-1-59659-650-4(3), GildAudio) Pub: Gildan Media. Dist(s): HachBkGrp

Instant Inspiration. Calvin Williams, Sr. 2003. audio compact disk (978-0-9740513-2-1(2)) Confidnce Build Pub.

Instant Meditation. 1 cass. 10.00 (978-1-58506-043-6(7), 83) New Life Inst OR.
Melt your tensions away & feel a total relaxation you never dreamed possible.

Instant Meditation. Scripts. Diane L. Ross. 1 CD. (Running Time: 20 mins.). 2005. audio compact disk 16.90 (978-0-9765740-0-2(4)) Parsley Pr FL.
This unique recording combines the age-old benefits of meditation with the speed and effectiveness of modern self-hypnosis techniques. Learn this simple meditation and experience the profound benefits of achieving expanded states of consciousness, without years of study! This guided meditation will allow you to develop the powers within to obtain h igher levels of consciousness where deep inner wisdom and understanding are waiting to unfold. Develop a deeper level of awareness than you ever thought possible. It's easier than you think!.

Instant Motivation: Thirty-One Pep Talks. 1 cass. 7.95 (1637, Lrn Inc) Oasis Audio.

Instant Negotiator Successpak. Frank D'Alessandro. 1 cass.,1 CD,1 vid. (Running Time: 1 hr.). 2000. pap. bk. & wbk. ed. 79.95 (978-1-930307-01-8(2)) Amer Negotiation.
One on one instruction from a Master Negotiator. Watch effective negotiators in action & use their dialogue for your negotiations. Learn how to use 13 illustrated defenses that give you the power against tough negotiators.

Instant PET: Ready-to-Use Tasks & Activities. Martyn Ford. (Running Time: 1 hr. 17 mins.). (Cambridge Copy Collection). (ENG., 2007. audio compact disk 25.20 (978-0-521-61126-8(1)) Cambridge U Pr.

Instant PET Audio Cassette: Ready-to-Use Tasks & Activities. Martyn Ford. (Running Time: 1 hr. 50 mins.). (Cambridge Copy Collection). (ENG.). 2007. 25.20 (978-0-521-61125-1(3)) Cambridge U Pr.

Instant Piano. Les Horan & Linda Ekblad. 1 cass. (Play by Ear Ser.). 1986. pap. bk. 10.95 (978-0-312-41875-5(2), St Martin Griffin) Pub: St Martin. Dist(s): Macmillan

Instant Rapport. Michael Brooks. Read by Michael Brooks. 1 cass. (Running Time: 1 hr.). 1999. (978-0-671-03340-8(9)) S and S Inc.
Discover that special combination of confidence & chemistry that all winners share.

Instant Rapport. abr. ed. Michael Brooks. 1 CD. (Running Time: 10 hrs. 0 mins. 0 sec.). (ENG., 2002. audio compact disk 14.00 (978-0-7435-2070-6(X), Nightgale) Pub: S&S Audio. Dist(s): S and S Inc

Instant Rock Lead Guitar. Austin Sicard, Jr. 1997. bk. 9.95 (978-0-7866-2489-8(2), 95054BCD) Mel Bay.

Instant Spanish. (ENG., (YA). 2008. pap. bk. 49.95 (978-0-942168-14-3(3)) Dean Vaughn Learning Systems Inc.

Instant Warnings to Avoid Poor Decisions. 1 cass. 1998. (978-0-9661071-0-4(1)) Access Pr PA.

Instant Zen. unabr. ed. Jim McMullan. Read by Jim McMullan. 1 cass. (Running Time: 1 hr. 30 min.). 1998. 10.95 (978-1-57511-042-4(3)) Pub Mills.
Zen sayings for daily living.

Instant Zen: Waking up in the Present Lectures of Zen Master Foyan. abr. ed. Read by Mitchell Ryan. Tr. by Thomas Cleary. 2 cass. (Running Time: 3 hrs.). 1996. 17.95 (978-1-57453-077-3(1)) Audio Lit.
Simple exercises designed to lead to the awakening of insight.

Instantaneous Personal Magnetism. Paul R. Scheele. Read by Paul R. Scheele. 1 cass. (Running Time: 24 min.). (Paraliminal Tapes Ser.). 1990. 14.95 (978-0-925480-12-5(6)) Learn Strategies.
Helps listener create a presence of personal power.

Instantaneous Transformation: An Honest Look at Self-Realization. Ariel Kane & Shya Kane. 2 CDs. (Running Time: 1 hr. 48 mins.). 2002. audio compact disk (978-1-888043-10-5(5)) ASK Prodns.
"Listening to this audio may be the only workshop you ever need experience." Dayna Cole, NAPRA ReVIEWWhen you hear Ariel and Shya Kane's Instantaneous Transformation audio workshop, it could dramatically change your life. The Kanes have found that the slightest shift in one's reality can produce a quantum shift in one's life. When that instant occurs, it is hard to say. You just suddenly realize that you feel lighter, freer, more alive and you are interacting naturally and effectively with your present environment. By listening to this CD you can discover fulfillment without working on yourself.

Instantaneous Transformation Set: An Honest Look at Self Realization. Ariel Kane & Shya Kane. Contrib. by Helene DeLillo. 2 cass. (Running Time: 1 hrs. 48 min.). 1995. (978-1-888043-03-7(2)) ASK Prodns.
Investigates the Kanes' revolutionary technology which allows the listener to discover fulfillment without working on problems.

Instantaneous Transformation Set: An Honest Look at Self Realization. Ariel Kane & Shya Kane. 2 cass. 1995. 16.95 (978-1-879323-28-5(1)) Sound Horizons AV.
When you hear Shya & Ariel Kane's Instantaneous Transformation it could dramatically change your life. By listening to these tapes you can discover fulfillment without working on yourself. The Kanes have found that the slightest shift in one's perception can produce a quantum shift in one's life.

Instincts: Program from the Award Winning Public Radio Series. Interview. Hosted by Fred Goodwin. 1 CD. (Running Time: 1 hr.). (Infinite Mind Ser.). 2000. audio compact disk 21.95 (978-1-932479-59-1(7), LCM 107) Lichtenstein Creat.
Instincts are among the very earliest influences on human behavior. These primitive motivations that we share with animals are being unlocked by modern neuroscience. To find out more, we visit with a Harvard University researcher who looks at animal instincts in order to advance our knowledge of human instincts. Plus the researcher who found the location of the maternal instinct in the brain. We'll also hear from a geographer, whose life work has focused how we move through the world, was challenged ... by sudden blindness. Plus - the latest from Nature Neuroscience magazine as we ask the age-old question: "Why won't men ask for directions?".

Institute of Self-Worth: A Curriculum for Life. Vic M. Porter. Voice by Vic M. Porter. (ENG.). 2004. ring bd. (978-0-9822185-1-8(6)) Vic Porter.

Instructing a Child's Heart: Audio Book. Tedd Tripp & Margy Tripp. (ENG.). 2008. audio compact disk 35.00 (978-0-9815400-3-0(1)) Shepherd Pr PA.

Instructional Coaching School-Based Staff Development for Improved Teacher & Student Learning, Vol. 1501. (Enabling Teachers & Students to Thrive Ser.: Vol. 1500). (C). 2005. video 675.00 (978-1-58740-152-7(5)) SchImprove.

Instructional Strategies Designed for Block Schedules, Set. unabr. ed. Louis Mangione. Read by Louis Mangione. 6 cass. (Running Time: 3 hr. 37 min.). (J). (gr. 6-12). 1998. 75.00 (978-1-886397-16-3(3)) Bureau of Educ.

***Instructions.** unabr. ed. Neil Gaiman. Read by Neil Gaiman. (ENG.). 2010. (978-0-06-199166-0(X)); (978-0-06-198395-5(0)) HarperCollins Pubs.

Instructions for Developing Devotion. Swami Jyotirmayananda. 1 cass. (Running Time: 45 min.). 1990. 10.00 Yoga Res Foun.

Instructive Moments with the Savior. Ken Gire. 1 cass. 1992. 14.99 (978-0-310-54978-9(7)) Zondervan.

Instructor Resource Cd for Fundamentals of Physics , Seventh Edition. 7th ed. M. A. K. Halliday. (YA). 2005. tchr. ed. (978-0-471-47060-1(0)) Wiley US.

Instructor Resources. instr.'s gde. ed. 340.95 (978-0-7638-2307-8(4)) EMC-Paradigm.

Instructor Resources. instr.'s gde. ed. 69.00 (978-0-7638-2229-3(9)); instr.'s gde. ed. 69.95 (978-0-7638-2267-5(1)); 225.00 (978-0-7638-0141-0(0)); audio compact disk 225.00 (978-0-7638-2904-9(8)) Paradigm MN.

Instructor Resources. Brian Shmaefsky. instr.'s gde. ed. 69.95 (978-0-7638-2341-2(4)) EMC-Paradigm.

Instructor Resources: Instructor Resource CD. audio compact disk 69.00 (978-0-7638-2260-6(4)) Paradigm MN.

Instructor Resources: Instructor Resources on CD. audio compact disk 54.95 (978-0-7638-2203-3(5)) Paradigm MN.

Instructor Resources: MarketPlace(r) Audio Lessons. audio compact disk 99.95 (978-0-8219-3409-8(0)) EMC-Paradigm.

Instructor Resources: Print Instructor's Guide with CD. instr.'s gde. ed. 69.95 (978-0-7638-2280-4(9)) EMC-Paradigm.

Instructor Resources: Spanish Audio Summaries. audio compact disk 49.95 (978-0-8219-3408-1(2)) EMC-Paradigm.

Instructor Resources: Test Generator. audio compact disk 169.95 (978-0-8219-3407-4(4)) EMC-Paradigm.

Instructor Resources: Test Generator on CD. audio compact disk 129.00 (978-0-7638-2261-3(2)) Paradigm MN.

Instructor Resources: Working with Graphics & Charts. audio compact disk 49.95 (978-0-8219-3414-2(7)) EMC-Paradigm.

Instructor Resources: 1-29 with Instructor's Solutions & Resources CD. annot. ed. instr.'s gde. ed. 79.95 (978-0-7638-1998-9(0)) Paradigm MN.

Instructor's CD. Contrib. by Open University Staff. audio compact disk 165.00 (978-0-7167-0999-2(6)) Pub: W H Freeman. Dist(s): Macmillan

Instructor's Manual & Test Bank Cd to Accompany Nutrition: A Culinary Approach. Mary Anne Eaton & Janet Rouslin. (C). 2005. audio compact disk (978-0-7575-2518-6(0), 0757525180) Kendall-Hunt.

Instructor's Media Library. 6 vols. DVD & audio compact disk 164.80 (978-0-7167-5814-3(8)) Pub: W H Freeman. Dist(s): Macmillan

Instructors Music Cassette. Eduardo Zayas-Bazan. (YA). 1999. (978-0-13-087045-2(5)) P-H.

Instructor's Resource CD. Paul R. Ehrlich & Anne H. Ehrlich. audio compact disk 212.10 (978-0-7167-0680-9(6)) Pub: W H Freeman. Dist(s): Macmillan

Instructor's Resource CD to Accompany SPSS for Introductory Statistics: Use & Interpretation. 3rd rev. ed. George A. Morgan. 2007. audio compact disk (978-0-8058-6440-3(7), Pysch Press) Tay Francis Ltd GBR.

Instrument of Peace: An Inspirational Book of Healing, Comfort & Consolation Through the Music of the Harp. Malinda Gerke. 2008. bk. 22.95 (978-1-935122-08-1(8)) K&B Products.

Instrument Pilot FAA Written Exam Test Prep. Irvin N. Gleim. 2001. 60.00 (978-1-58194-141-8(2)) Gleim Pubns.

Instrument Rated Christians. Nathaniel Holcomb. 8 cass. (Running Time: 12 hrs.). 1998. (978-1-930918-27-6(5)) Its All About Him.

Instrumental. 2004. 7.99 (978-0-8297-4172-8(0)) Zondervan.

Instrumental Dreams. Compiled by Robert Gass. (Running Time: 53 hrs. 52 mins.). 2004. audio compact disk (978-1-891319-80-8(9)) Spring Hill CO.

Instrumental Moods. 1 cass., 1 CD. 8.78 (VIR 45397); audio compact disk 12.78 CD Jewel box. (VIR 45397) NewSound.

***Instrumental Solotrax Volume 3: Sacred Solos for Trombone & Orchestra.** (ENG.). 1989. 12.99 (978-5-557-45486-5(1)) Lillenas.

***Instrumental Solotrax, Volume 8, B-Flat Trumpet, B-Flat Clarinet.** Contrib. by Marty Parks. (Instrumental Solotrax Ser.). (ENG.). 1999. audio compact disk 29.99 (978-5-552-48592-5(0)) Lillenas.

Instrumentals I. unabr. ed. Krs Edstrom. Read by Krs Edstrom. 1 cass. (Running Time: 40 min.). (Inner Mastery Ser.). 1994. 12.95 Bk. box size. (978-1-886198-05-0(5), IMS06) Soft Stone Pub.
Celestially flavored music designed to calm and center. Play in your car, during a hot bath, dinner or any time you want an auditory massage. Endorsed by hospitals, airlines and psychologists. The music for each tape in the series was created in a unique and memorable way. I sat with engineering/composing wonder Jeff Silverman in his private recording studio while he played my voice tracks. I don't think we even realized it at first, but the (meditation) tracks brought us into a meditation so that the whole process became quite ethereal. It WAS a meditation. I decided to devote one tape in the series to the wonderful sounds that were created during this meditation.Too often we "go through the motions" of life, not tuned in to what is happening internally - how our mind and body interrelate and how the outside world and our inside world interrelate. The purpose of these tapes is not only that you feel results after each listen, but that you develop increasingly deeper skills to serve you in all of life's challenges and excursions. Commonly considered negatives such as pain, stress and insomnia are experienced in a new, non-judgmental way that invites insight and is both growth-promoting and freeing. Once perceived enemies turn into welcome teachers. Similarly, positive and everyday events such as watching a bird soar, hitting a ball or conducting business are experienced in a more complete way; a way that enriches your relationship to self and thus the outside world.

Instrumentos. 1 cass. (Primeros Pasos en Ciencia Ser.). (SPA.). (J). 12.00 (7455-9, Natl Textbk Co) M-H Contemporary.
Helps children in grades 1-4 discover the process of scientific investigation. Part of the First Steps in Science Program.

Instruments in the Redeemer's Hands: People in Need of Change Helping People in Need of Change. Paul David Tripp. (ENG.). 2002. audio compact disk 49.95 (978-1-934885-61-1(4)) New Growth Pr.

***Instruments of Darkness: A Novel.** unabr. ed. Imogen Robertson. (Running Time: 13 hrs. 30 mins.). 2011. 18.99 (978-1-4526-7046-1(3)); 24.99 (978-1-4526-5046-3(2)); audio compact disk 37.99 (978-1-4526-0046-8(5)) Pub: Tantor Media. Dist(s): IngramPubServ

***Instruments of Darkness (Library Edition) A Novel.** unabr. ed. Imogen Robertson. (Running Time: 13 hrs. 30 mins.). 2011. 37.99 (978-1-4526-2046-6(6)); audio compact disk 90.99 (978-1-4526-3046-5(1)) Pub: Tantor Media. Dist(s): IngramPubServ

Instruments of Night. unabr. ed. Thomas H. Cook. Narrated by George Guidall. 7 cass. (Running Time: 9 hrs. 15 mins.). 1999. 60.00 (978-0-7887-2929-4(2), 95610E7) Recorded Bks.
When a novelist is asked to write an ending to an unsolved murder case, he begins to find the borders between memory & madness growing precipitously narrow.

Instruments of Peace, Vol. 2. Marty Haugen. 1994. 10.95 (326); audio compact disk 15.95 (326) GIA Pubns.

Instruments of the Orchestra. Read by Jeremy Siepmann. 7 CDs. (Running Time: 8 hrs.). 2003. pap. bk. 39.99 (978-1-84379-042-6(4)) Naxos.
This is a set of portraits in depth, featuring individual instruments in many contexts and in pieces from the Middle Ages to the present.

Instruments of the Orchestra 1. Roy Bennett. Contrib. by Roy Bennett. (Cambridge Assignments in Music Ser.). (ENG., 1982. 38.99 (978-0-521-23860-1(9)) Cambridge U Pr.

Instruments of the Orchestra 2. Roy Bennett. Contrib. by Roy Bennett. (Cambridge Assignments in Music Ser.). (ENG.). 1985. 38.99 (978-0-521-26830-1(3)) Cambridge U Pr.

Insurance Coverage for Pollution. 1 cass. 1990. bk. 45.00 (AC-579) PA Bar Inst.

Insurance Coverage Issues & Applications. (Running Time: 5 hrs. 30 min.). 1994. 92.00 Incl. 216p. coursebk. (20441) NYS Bar.
Addresses many of the practical issues that arise on a recurring basis in insurance practice. The presentations address coverage issue questions & are aimed at improving the lawyer's advocacy in this area of law.

Insurance Coverage Issues in Employment Law. 11 cass. (Running Time: 16 hrs. 30 min.). 1997. 395.00 Set; incl. study guide 150p. (MB96) Am Law Inst.
New advanced course also covers insurance fundamentals for the uninitiated.

Insurance, Excess & Reinsurance Coverage Disputes, 1990. unabr. ed. Contrib. by Thomas R. Newman & Barry R. Ostrager. 7 cass. (Running Time: 10 hrs.). 1990. 50.00 course handbk. (T7-9258) PLI.
This recording of PLI's January 1990 program examines recent developments, new trends & court decisions in insurance coverage litigation. Designed for lawyers, brokers, risk managers & other professionals involved with insurance, topics discussed include: rules of policy construction, choice of law-forum considerations, occurrence, policy coverage for mass tort claims, coverage for asbestos property damage claims, special problems involving excess insurance, coverage issues arising out of insured's knowledge of risks, special problems in hazardous waste coverage litigation, broker liability, current problems involving reinsurance, alternative dispute resolution: controlling conflict & its costs, reinsurance issues arising out of insurer insolvency, bad faith liability & disputes between primary & excess insurers, punitive damages: recovery & insurance coverage.

Insurance Law. 2nd ed. John F. Dobbyn. 6 cass. (Running Time: 8 hrs.). (Outstanding Professors Ser.). 1996. 39.95 Set. (978-1-57793-019-8(3)) Sum & Substance.
Lecture given by a prominent American law school professor on the subjects of Civil Procedure, Contracts, Criminal, Real Property, Torts, and Exam Skills:Essay Writing.

Insurance Law. 3rd rev. ed. John F. Dobbyn. 1 cass. (Running Time: 90 mins.). (Audio Tape Ser.). 1999. 57.00 (978-0-314-24295-2(3), 29959, West Lglwrks) West.

Insurance Practice & Litigation. 1990. 45.00 (AC-572) PA Bar Inst.

Insurance Problems in Real Estate Development & Construction. 1986. bk. 80.00 incl. book.; 45.00 cass. only.; 35.00 book only. PA Bar Inst.

Insurance Sales: Music or Ocean Format. Betty L. Randolph. (Specialazed Sales Ser.). 1989. bk. 14.98 (978-1-55909-220-3(3), 130P) Randolph Tapes.
Doing a great job for your clients & set records in earnings for yourself & your company!.

Insurance Services in China: A Strategic Reference 2006. Compiled by Icon Group International, Inc. Staff. 2007. ring bd. 195.00 (978-0-497-35882-2(4)) Icon Grp.

Insurer vs. Insurer Disputes. 8 cass. (Running Time: 6 hrs.). 1990. bk. 55.00 incl. 261-page course handbook. (T6-9152) PLI.

Insurge, Set. Jules Valles. 6 cass. (FRE.). 1996. 52.95 (1816-LQP) Olivia & Hill.
Novel set during the Commune, the revolt of Parisian workers after the Franco-Prussian War (1871), which resulted in 100,000 dead, 3,500 rebels executed without trial & 40,000 imprisoned or exiled. Paris lost 50% of its workers. Valles was a witness of these events.

Insurgent Mexico. unabr. ed. John Reed. Narrated by Frank Muller. 5 cass. (Running Time: 7 hrs.). 1985. 44.00 (978-1-55690-256-7(5), 85480E7) Recorded Bks.
In 1913, at the height of the Mexican Revolution, the author, a magazine correspondent headed South to cover the story of the year. His travels with a group of rebels that included the legendary Pancho Villa earned him everlasting fame as a reporter & left behind a series of unmatched portraits of a people, a place & a time.

Insurrection. J. M. Dillard. 2004. 10.95 (978-0-7435-4636-2(9)) Pub: S&S Audio. Dist(s): S and S Inc

***Int Korean Beg 2.** 2nd rev. ed. Klear. 2010. audio compact disk 195.00 (978-0-8248-3518-7(2)) UH Pr.

Integral Tarot CD Treasure Chest. Suzanne Wagner. 5. 2005. audio compact disk 49.95 (978-0-9763331-1-1(2)) S Winds Pubns.

Integral Tarot Meditation CD Set. Speeches. Suzanne Wagner. 4 CDs. (Running Time: 4 hrs. 40 mins). 2005. audio compact disk 39.95 (978-0-9763331-3-5(9)) S Winds Pubns.

Integral Trees. unabr. ed. Larry Niven. Read by Pat Bottino. 6 cass. (Running Time: 8 hrs. 30 mins.). 1996. 44.95 (978-0-7861-0967-8(X), 1744) Blckstn Audio.
For a long time the State used slower-than-light spacecraft to prepare star systems for colonization by Man. Normally the ramseeders traveled centuries-long circuits which began & ended at Earth. Normally the mixed crew of citizens & "corpsicle" convicts remained with their ship. Normally ultimate control of the mission was exercised by a built-in cyborg "adviser," the true despot of the tiny State microcosm that was the ship. But little happened normally when Discipline reached the double-star system of T3 & LeVoy's Star. There, an immense doughnut-shaped gaseous envelope had formed around a neutron star - & a vast volume of that nearly empty cloud was comfortably habitable to Man. Though it has very little usable land, the Smoke Ring had evolved a huge variety of free-fall life-forms, most of which were edible & all of which could fly.

Integrate Education. unabr. ed. Aldous Huxley. 1 cass. (Running Time: 43 min.). (Human Situation Ser.). 1959. 11.00 (01127) Big Sur Tapes.

Integrated Advocacy: Utilizing Your Strengths As a Trial Lawyer. William A. Barton. 6 cass. (Running Time: 6 hrs.). 2001. pap. bk. 185.00 (978-0-943380-63-6(4)) PEG MN.

Integrated Advocacy: Utilizing Your Strengths As a Trial Lawyer. William A. Barton. 6 CDs. (Running Time: 6 hrs.). 2002. pap. bk. 205.00 (978-0-943380-62-9(6)) PEG MN.

Integrated Approach: Surgery, Radiation & Chemotherapy in Urologic Malignancy. 2 cass. (Urologic Surgery Ser.: C85-UR2). 1985. 15.00 (8589) Am Coll Surgeons.

Integrated Approach to ER. 1 cass. (Care Cassettes Ser.: Vol. 11, No. 6). 1984. 10.80 Assn Prof Chaplains.

Integrated Chinese. audio compact disk 125.00 (978-0-88727-560-9(5)); audio compact disk 250.00 (978-0-88727-561-6(3)) Cheng Tsui.

Integrated Chinese. Told to Tao-chung Yao. 1 cass. (CHI.). 1997. wbk. ed. 10.95 (978-0-88727-286-8(X)) Cheng Tsui.

Integrated Chinese. Tao-chung Yao. 1 cass. (CHI.). 1997. wbk. ed. 10.95 (978-0-88727-283-7(5)) Cheng Tsui.

Integrated Chinese. Tao-chung Yao et al. 3 cass. (Running Time: 4 hrs.). (CHI & ENG.). (gr. 13 up). 2003. pap. bk. 110.00 (978-0-88727-405-3(6)) Cheng Tsui.
"Ideal for: High school, college and adult learners with no prior knowledge of Chinese. This acclaimed, bestselling series is successful because it integrates all four language skills-listening, speaking, reading, and writing. Integrated Chinese helps you ".

Integrated Chinese. Tao-chung Yao et al. 6 CDs. (Running Time: 9 hrs.). (CHI & ENG., (gr. k up). 2003. pap. bk. 62.95 (978-0-88727-406-0(4)) Cheng Tsui.

Integrated Chinese. 2nd ed. audio compact disk 125.00 (978-0-88727-469-5(2)) Cheng Tsui.

Integrated Chinese. 3rd rev. ed. Liu & Yuehua Liu. (C). 2000. audio compact disk 34.95 (978-0-88727-686-6(5)) Cheng Tsui.

Integrated Chinese. 3rd rev. ed. Liu & Tao-chung Yao. (C). 2008. audio compact disk 43.95 (978-0-88727-642-2(3)) Cheng Tsui.

***Integrated Chinese.** 3rd rev. ed. Cheng & Tsui & Yuehua Liu. (C). 2010. audio compact disk 34.95 (978-0-88727-695-8(4)) Cheng Tsui.

Integrated Chinese: Level 1. Tao-chung Yao et al. 2005. audio compact disk 43.95 (978-0-88727-467-1(6)); audio compact disk 125.00 (978-0-88727-468-8(4)); audio compact disk 43.95 (978-0-88727-470-1(6)); audio compact disk 125.00 (978-0-88727-471-8(4)) Cheng Tsui.

Integrated Chinese: Level 2. 2nd ed. Tao-chung Yao et al. 2005. audio compact disk 76.95 (978-0-88727-472-5(2)); audio compact disk (978-0-88727-473-2(0)) Cheng Tsui.

Integrated Chinese Level 1, Pt. 1: Language Lab for Textbook. Tao-chung Yao et al. 3 cass. (Running Time: 4 hrs. 30 mins.). (CHI.). 1997. 65.00 (978-0-88727-288-2(6)) Cheng Tsui.

Integrated Chinese Level 1, Pt. 1: Language Lab for Workbook. Tao-chung Yao et al. 1 cass. (Running Time: 1 hr. 30 mins.). 1997. 20.00 (978-0-88727-289-9(4)) Cheng Tsui.

Integrated Chinese Level 1, Pt. 2: Language Lab for Textbook. Tao-chung Yao et al. 2 cass. (Running Time: 3 hrs.). (CHI.). 1997. 45.00 (978-0-88727-290-5(8)) Cheng Tsui.

Integrated Chinese Level 1, Pt. 2: Language Lab for Workbook. Tao-chung Yao et al. 1 cass. (Running Time: 1 hr. 30 mins.). 1997. 20.00 (978-0-88727-291-2(6)) Cheng Tsui.

Integrated Chinese Level 2: Language Lab for Textbook. Tao-chung Yao et al. 5 cass. (Running Time: 7 hrs. 30 mins.). (CHI.). 1997. 110.00 (978-0-88727-292-9(4)) Cheng Tsui.

Integrated Chinese Level 2: Language Lab for Workbook. Tao-chung Yao et al. 1 cass. (Running Time: 1 hr. 30 mins.). 1997. 20.00 (978-0-88727-293-6(2)) Cheng Tsui.

Integrated Chinese 1/1. Tao-chung Yao et al. 4 vols. (Running Time: 193 mins.). (CHI & ENG., (gr. 13 up). 2003. pap. bk. 43.95 (978-0-88727-404-6(8)) Cheng Tsui.

Integrated Chinese 1/2 Audio CDs. 3rd rev. ed. Tao-chung Yao. (C). 2009. 29.95 (978-0-88727-677-4(6)) Cheng Tsui.

Integrated Consciousness & Health: Mann Ranch Seminar. Andrew Weil. 6 cass. (Running Time: 5 hrs. 57 min.). 1976. 56.00 Vinyl Album Set. (02605) Big Sur Tapes.
A weekend seminar at the Mann Ranch in Ukiah, California. Exploring the nature of whole consciousness & methods of promoting integration of elements that seem separate. Topics are: Plants, Drugs & Health; Healthy & Altered States of Consciousness; Homeopathy, Chiropractic & Acupuncture; On Nutrition; On Coca & Other Natural Drugs; & Altered States Without Drugs.

Integrated English. Victoria F. Kimbrough & Irene Frankel. 1997. audio compact disk 39.95 (978-0-19-434860-7(1)); audio compact disk 39.95 (978-0-19-434874-4(1)) OUP.

Integrated English. Victoria F. Kimbrough & Irene Frankel. 1998. 39.95 (978-0-19-434617-7(X)) OUP.

Integrated English. Linda Lee. 1998. audio compact disk 39.95 (978-0-19-434929-1(2)) OUP.

Integrated English. Linda Lee. 1999. audio compact disk 39.95 (978-0-19-434949-9(7)) OUP.

Integrated English: Explorations 2. Linda Lee. 2001. audio compact disk 39.95 (978-0-19-435041-9(X)) OUP.

Integrated English No. 1: Gateways. Victoria F. Kimbrough & Irene Frankel. 1997. 39.95 (978-0-19-434609-2(9)) OUP.

Integrated Healthcare Information Systems: How to Develop, Design, Program & Implement. A. Laurence Smith. Contrib. by William R. McCreight et al. 2007. per. 87.50 (978-0-9797236-0-5(4)) A L Smith.

Integrated Hospital Information Systems: Hospital Based Systems, Vol. 6. A. Laurence Smith. 2007. per. 85.00 (978-0-9797236-4-3(7)) A L Smith.

Integrated Korean: Advanced Intermediate Level 1. Ho-min Sohn & Eun-Joo Lee. (Klear Textbooks in Korean Language Ser.). (KOR & ENG., 2002. bk. 29.00 (978-0-8248-2568-3(3)) UH Pr.

Integrated Korean: Advanced Intermediate Level 2, Vol. 2. Ho-min Sohn & Eun-Joo Lee. (Klear Textbooks in Korean Language Ser.). (KOR & ENG., 2002. bk. 29.00 (978-0-8248-2526-3(8)) UH Pr.

Integrated Korean: Advanced Intermediate 1. KLEAR (Korean Language Education and Research Center) Staff. (Korean Language Education & Research Center/Korea Foundation Ser.). 2003. audio compact disk 27.00 (978-0-8248-2831-8(3)) UH Pr.

Integrated Korean: Advanced Intermediate 2. KLEAR (Korean Language Education and Research Center) Staff. (Korean Language Education & Research Center/Korea Foundation Ser.). 2003. audio compact disk 27.00 (978-0-8248-2832-5(1)) UH Pr.

Integrated Korean: Beginning Level 1. Korean Language Education and Research Center Staff. 2000. audio compact disk 197.00 (978-0-8248-2514-0(4), Kolowalu Bk) UH Pr.

Integrated Korean: Beginning Level 1. Carol Schulz. 7 vols. (Klear Textbooks in Korean Language Ser.). 2000. bk. & wbk. ed. 20.00 (978-0-8248-2175-3(0)) UH Pr.

Integrated Korean: Beginning Level 2. Korean Language Education and Research Center Staff. 2000. audio compact disk 197.00 (978-0-8248-2515-7(2), Kolowalu Bk) UH Pr.

Integrated Korean: Intermediate Level 1. Carol Schulz. 4 vols. (Klear Textbooks in Korean Language Ser.). (ENG & KOR., 2001. bk. & wbk. ed. 20.00 (978-0-8248-2420-4(2)) UH Pr.

Integrated Korean: Intermediate Level 2, Vol. 2. Jiha Hwang & Young-Geun Lee. 5 vols. (Klear Textbooks in Korean Language Ser.). (ENG & KOR., 2001. bk. & wbk. ed. 20.00 (978-0-8248-2423-5(7)) UH Pr.

Integrated Korean: Intermediate 1. Korean Language Education and Research Center Staff. 2001. audio compact disk 102.00 (978-0-8248-2604-8(3), Kolowalu Bk) UH Pr.

Integrated Korean: Intermediate 2. Korean Language Education and Research Center Staff. 2001. audio compact disk 127.00 (978-0-8248-2605-5(1), Kolowalu Bk) UH Pr.

Integrated Korean Vol. 2: Beginning Level 2. Sung-Ock Sohn. 8 vols. (Klear Textbooks in Korean Language Ser.). (ENG & KOR., 2000. bk. & wbk. ed. 20.00 (978-0-8248-2184-5(X)) UH Pr.

Integrated Life. Douglas Wilson. (ENG.). 2008. audio compact disk 24.00 (978-1-59128-358-4(2)) Canon Pr ID.

Integrated Online Library Services Pt. I: Changing Systems. 2 cass. 1990. 16.00 set. Recorded Res.

Integrated Online Library Services Pt. II: Changing Systems. 2 cass. 1990. 16.00 set. Recorded Res.

Integrated Online Library Services Pt. III: The Library of Tomorrow. 2 cass. 1990. 16.00 set. Recorded Res.

Integrated Online Library Services Pt. IV: Expanding Access to Information. 2 cass. 1990. 16.00 set. Recorded Res.

Integrated Physics & Chemistry: Talking Textbooks. 2002. audio compact disk (978-1-928629-95-5(4)) Paradigm Accel.

Integrating Commodities into a Balanced Financial Plan. R. Stoker. 1 cass. (Commodities Investing Through Managed Accounts Ser.). 15.00 (Mngd Acct Reprts) Futures Pub.

Integrating Evil in Society & Politics. unabr. ed. Stephan Hoeller. 1 cass. (Running Time: 1 hr. 30 min.). 1981. 11.00 (40006) Big Sur Tapes.
Hoeller says that when individuals or societies lack self-knowledge & interior integration, they project the evil or shadow content of the unconscious & make the presence of an evil & loathsome enemy a veritable psychic necessity.

Integrating Mind & Body for Better Golf Vol. 1: Putting. unabr. ed. M. Rosa Nicholas. 1 cass. (Running Time: 1 hr. 11 min.). 1998. 19.95 (978-1-892673-01-5(0)) Peak Per Psych.
Empowers golfers to be in a "short game zone." Improves confidence, focus, relaxation & reads on the fringe or green. Enhances the ability to putt consistently well.

Integrating Mind & Body for Better Golf Vol. 2: Overcoming the Yips. unabr. ed. M. Rosa Nicholas. 1 cass. (Running Time: 1 hr. 04 min.). 1998. 19.95 (978-1-892673-02-2(9)) Peak Per Psych.
Empowers golfers to overcome anxious reactions known as the yips. Eliminates the yips & restores confidence on the fringe or green. Enhances putting potential.

Integrating Mind & Body for Better Golf Vol. 3: Meditation. unabr. ed. Nicholas M. Rosa. 1 cass. (Running Time: 55 min.). 1998. 19.95 (978-1-892673-03-9(7)) Peak Per Psych.
Teaches golfers how to meditate in order to relax, regulate emotional reactions, enhance stamina & feeling of well-being. Enhances overall game play.

Integrating Mind & Body for Better Tennis: Serving. Nick Rosa & Jeanne Craft. Executive Producer Stephen McWilliams. Voice by Joseph Primavera. 1 CD. 2004. audio compact disk 19.95 (978-1-892673-05-3(3)) Peak Per Psych.
Integrating Mind & Body for Better Tennis: Serving -A Revolutionary CD will enable you to: Serve with More Power & Accuracy* Maximize Muscle Memory for Excellent Technique* Be Naturally Relaxed & Focused* Enhances Confidence in Your Serve.*

Integrating Parish Ministry in a Dynamic World. Joseph M. Champlin. 2 cass. (Running Time: 3 hrs. 26 min.). 1998. 19.95 Set. (TAH398) Alba Hse Comns.
Effective methods to deal with prioritizing personal, pastoral & ministerial expectations at a time when time itself seems to be extended to the breaking point. Developed by Fr. Champlin as material for personal & group retreats.

Integrating Psychology & Politics. unabr. ed. Peter Breggin. 1 cass. (Running Time: 1 hr. 3 min.). 12.95 (747) J Norton Pubs.
"Voluntary servitude" is Breggin's topic; why people don't break free of their oppressors. The model for oppression, Breggin contends, is childhood.

Integrating Science & Mysticism. unabr. ed. John C. Lilly & Toni Lilly. 1 cass. (Running Time: 90 min.). 1981. 11.00 (03904) Big Sur Tapes.

Integrating Spiritual Disciplines in Our Daily Life. Susan Muto. 4 cass. (Running Time: 4 hrs.). 2001. 34.95 (A6620) St Anthony Mess Pr.

Integrating the Daemonic. Hal Stone. 1 cass. (Running Time: 1 hrs.). 1982. 10.95 (978-1-56557-058-0(8), T70) Delos Inc.
Hal Stone has made a significant contribution to our understanding of the role of disowned instinctual energies in our lives & in our society. This is a live recording of his memorable lecture.

Integrating Your Many Parts Set: How to Win the War Between Your Selves. David Grudermeyer & Rebecca Grudermeyer. 2 cass. 18.95 INCL. HANDOUTS. (T-18) Willingness Wrks.

Integration: The Dynamo of Reason. unabr. ed. Gary Hull. 4 cass. (Running Time: 5 hrs.). 1995. 49.95 Set. (978-1-56114-275-0(1), CH49D) Second Renaissance.
Identification of this crucial thinking skill with exercises designed to make it an automatized habit.

Integration & Human Life: Say's Law. John Ridpath. 2 cass. (Running Time: 3 hrs. 15 min.). 1996. 24.95 Set. (978-1-56114-383-2(9), DR15D) Second Renaissance.
A discussion of this most fundamental integration in economics.

Integration by Essentials. unabr. ed. Peter Schwartz. 1 cass. (Running Time: 1 hrs. 30 min.). 1997. 12.95 (978-1-56114-312-2(X), CS50C) Second Renaissance.
A detailed analysis of the crucial role of essentials in the mental act of integration.

Integration Marketing: How Small Businesses Become Big Businesses? & Big Businesses Become Empires. unabr. ed. Mark Joyner. Read by Erik Synnestvedt. (Running Time: 2 hrs.). (ENG.). 2009. 14.98 (978-1-59659-405-0(5), GildAudio) Pub: Gildan Media. Dist(s): HachBkGrp

Integration of Head & Heart. Swami Amar Jyoti. 1 cass. 1978. 9.95 (K-18) Truth Consciousness.
Following Dharma, the integrating force. A living approach to Truth & Bliss. Going step by step or in a flash. The Yoga teachings.

Integration of the Ageless, Timeless, Spiritual Laws. Instructed by Manly P. Hall. 8.95 (978-0-89314-149-3(6), C800142) Philos Res.

Integrative Restoration: The ancient practice of Yoga Nidra for easing stress, healing trauma & awakening to your timeless Presence. Richard Cushing Miller. 6 CDs. (Running Time: 270 Minutes). Orig. Title: Infinite Awakening. (ENG.). 2007. audio compact disk 49.95 (978-1-893099-04-3(0)) Anahata Pr.

Integrative Spirituality. David Spangler. 6 cass. 54.00 (OC1) Sound Horizons AV.

Integrity. Speeches. Joel Osteen. 1 Cass. (Running Time: 30 Mins). 2001. 6.00 (978-1-59349-090-4(9), JA0090) J Osteen.

Integrity. Emmet L. Robinson. Read by Emmet L. Robinson. 1 cass. (Running Time: 48 min.). 1994. 13.95 King Street.
How to do well by doing what's right.

***Integrity: The Courage to Meet the Demands of Reali.** abr. ed. Henry Cloud. Read by Henry Cloud. (ENG.). 2006. (978-0-06-113465-4(1), Harper Audio); (978-0-06-113466-1(X), Harper Audio) HarperCollins Pubs.

Integrity: The Courage to Meet the Demands of Reality - How Six Essential Qualities Determine Your Success in Business. abr. ed. Henry Cloud. Read by Henry Cloud. (Running Time: 21600 sec.). 2006. audio compact disk 29.95 (978-0-06-088671-4(4)) HarperCollins Pubs.

Integrity: The Way to God's Best. unabr. ed. Keith A. Butler. 5 cass. (Running Time: 7 hrs. 30 mins.). 2001. 10.00 (A141) Word Faith Pubng.
The way to God's best lies along the path of integrity. In order to live a life of integrity; you have to have faith in God and a fear of God, a faith that acknowledges that His way is the best way, and a fear of disobeying the truth.

Integrity Day. unabr. ed. R. Buckminster Fuller. 4 cass. (Running Time: 3 hrs. 54 min.). 1983. 36.00 (00702) Big Sur Tapes.

***Integrity Is Everything.** John Lavenia. 2009. 24.95 (978-1-61584-542-2(9)) Indep Pub IL.

Integrity of God's Word. Kenneth Copeland. 6 cass. 1983. 30.00 Set incl. study guide. (978-0-938458-52-4(3)) K Copeland Pubns.
Integrity of God's word.

Integrity Selling. unabr. ed. Ron Willingham. Read by Larry McKeever. 5 cass. (Running Time: 5 hrs.). 1988. 30.00 (978-0-7366-1316-3(1), 2222) Books on Tape.
Sales techniques are analysed & suggestions made for improving customer relations.

Integrity, the Endangered Virtue. Instructed by Manly P. Hall. 8.95 (978-0-89314-150-9(X), C830717) Philos Res.

Integrity's Impact: Your Practical Guide to Integrity's Power, Benefits, & Use. Be More. Expect More. Achieve More, Right Now! Mark A. Willson. (Troubleshooter's Ser.: Vol. 1). 2005. audio compact disk 75.00 (978-0-9749658-1-9(2)) Uncommon Tech.

Integrity's IWORSHIP: A Total Worship Experience: volume N. Contrib. by Don Moen. (iWorship Ser.). 2007. 29.98 (978-5-557-72178-3(9)) Integrity Music.

Integrity's Iworship: Resource system Dvd. (iWorship Ser.). 2003. 29.98 (978-5-552-36340-7(X)) Integrity Music.

Integrity's Iworship @Home: Volume 7. Contrib. by Don Moen. Created by Integrity Music. Prod. by Adrienne Gray. (iWorship Ser.). 2007. 14.98 (978-5-557-72177-6(0)) Integrity Music.

Integrity's Iworship: No Boundaries. Contrib. by Don Moen. 2005. 21.98 (978-5-558-78805-1(4)) Pt of Grace Ent.

Integrity's Iworship Platinum. Contrib. by Don Moen. 2006. audio compact disk 19.98 (978-5-558-11374-7(X)) Integrity Music.

Intellectual Bankruptcy of Our Age. Ayn Rand. Read by Ayn Rand. 1 cass. (Running Time: 55 min.). 12.95 (978-1-56114-071-8(6), AR11C) Second Renaissance.
Ayn Rand's first talk at Ford Hall Forum, addressed to a predominantly liberal audience. The treason of today's intellectuals against the nineteenth century ideal of liberalism. Their abandonment of reason & capitalism in favor of mysticism & statism.

Intellectual Bankruptcy of Our Age. Comment by Ayn Rand. 1 cass. (Running Time: 55 min.). (Ford Hall Forum Ser.). 1961. 12.95 (AR11C) Second Renaissance.
Treason of today's intellectuals against the nineteenth century ideal of genuine liberalism.

Intellectual Bankruptcy of Our Age - Q & A. Ayn Rand. 1 cass. (Running Time: 30 min.). 1993. 12.95 (978-1-56114-290-3(5), AR47C) Second Renaissance.

Intellectual Devotional: American History. unabr. ed. David S. Kidder & Noah D. Oppenheim. Read by Helen Litchfield & Jeff Woodman. (Running Time: 18 hrs. 45 mins. 0 sec.). (ENG.). 2007. audio compact disk 59.95 (978-1-4272-0264-2(8)) Pub: Macmill Audio. Dist(s): Macmillan

Intellectual Devotional: Modern Culture. unabr. ed. David S. Kidder & Noah D. Oppenheim. Read by Oliver Wyman & Helen Litchfield. 1 MP3-CD. 2008. 74.95 (978-0-7927-5822-8(6)); audio compact disk 117.95 (978-0-7927-5837-2(4)) Pub: AudioGO. Dist(s): Perseus Dist

Intellectual Devotional: Revive Your Mind, Complete Your Education, & Roam Confidently with the Cultured Class. unabr. ed. David S. Kidder & Noah D. Oppenheim. Narrated by Oliver Wyman & Helen Litchfield. 2 MP3-CDs. (Running Time: 20 hrs.). 2008. 74.95 (978-0-7927-5816-7(1), Chivers Sound Lib); audio compact disk 117.95 (978-0-7927-5657-6(6), Chivers Sound Lib) AudioGO.

Intellectual Devotional: Revive Your Mind, Complete Your Education, & Roam Confidently with the Cultured Class. unabr. ed. David S. Kidder & Noah D. Oppenheim. Narrated by Oliver Wyman & Helen Litchfield. (Running Time: 20 hrs.). 2008. 29.95 (978-1-4272-0167-6(6)) Pub: Macmill Audio. Dist(s): Macmillan

Intellectual Devotional: Revive Your Mind, Complete Your Education, & Roam Confidently with the Cultured Class. unabr. ed. David S. Kidder & Noah D. Oppenheim. Read by Oliver Wyman & Helen Litchfield. 16 CDs. (Running Time: 20 hrs. 0 mins. 0 sec.). (ENG.). 2008. audio compact disk 59.95 (978-1-4272-0545-2(0)) Pub: Macmill Audio. Dist(s): Macmillan

Intellectual Devotional Modern Culture: Converse Confidently about Society & the Arts. unabr. ed. David S. Kidder & Noah D. Oppenheim. Read by Oliver Wyman & Helen Litchfield. 16 CDs. (Running Time: 20 hrs. 0 mins. 0 sec.). (ENG.). 2008. audio compact disk 59.95 (978-1-4272-0536-0(1)) Pub: Macmill Audio. Dist(s): Macmillan

Intellectual Property. Kenneth W. Thomas. (Sum & Substance Ser.). 2003. 63.00 (978-0-314-24294-5(5), West Lglwrks) West.

Intellectual Property Antitrust Interface: Advising Clients in an Uncertain Area. 1997. bk. 99.00 (ACS-1217); bk. 99.00 (ACS-1217) PA Bar Inst.
In the intellectual property domain, practitioners must know when appropriate development & protection of an interest ends & antitrust violations begin. The dividing line wavers back & forth, depending on the most recent case law.

Intellectual Property Leadership Conference: Top Partners on Best Practices & Strategies for Success in the Realm of Intellectual Property. Speeches. ReedLogic Conference Staff. (Running Time: 4 hrs). 2006. audio compact disk 499.00 (978-1-59701-054-2(5)) Aspatore Bks.
*The Intellectual Property Leadership Conference features eleven speeches totaling approximately four hours of authoritative, insider?s perspectives on the best practices and keys to success in the Intellectual Property arena. Featuring attorneys representing some of the industry?s top 200 law firms, this conference provides a broad yet comprehensive overview of implementing dynamic strategies to provide clients with superior intellectual property counsel. Each speaker shares their insight for successful strategies and industry expertise in a format similar to a radio address, with graphics displayed in the background. Simply insert the CD-ROM into your computer, sit back, and watch and learn from the top professionals in the field as they discuss their specific processes for working with clients and best practices for ensuring success. The breadth of perspectives presented enable attendees to get inside some of the great minds of the ADR world without leaving the office. The Conference has been produced on CD-ROM and can be viewed in PowerPoint by any PC-based computer.Conference Features Speeches by:1. Karen Artz Ash, Partner; Katten Muchin Zavis Rosenman - ?Do Your Research?2. Paul Berman, Partner; Covington & Burling - ?Practice and Learn?3. Ivor Elrifi, Member; Mintz, Levin, Cohn, Ferris, Glovsky and Popeo - ?Dedication?4. Gary Frischling, Partner; Irell & Manella - ?Strategic Planning?5. Kenneth Hautman, Partner; Hogan & Hartson - ?Every Company in America is an Intellectual Property Company?6. Albert Jacobs, Shareholder; Greenberg Taurig - ?Be Aware?7. Grant Kang, Member; Husch & Eppenberger - ?Be Realistic? 8. Joel Lutzker, Partner; Schulte Roth & Zabel LLP - ?Get to Know the Client?9. Fabio Marino, Partner; Bingham McCutchen - ?Create & Protect?10. Chun Ng, Partner; Perkins Coie LLP - ?Understand Your Client.?In This CD You Will Learn: *The 3 ?golden rules? of Intellectual Property Law*Where IP attorneys add the most direct value for a client*The biggest misconceptions in IP Law and how to overcome them*How IP attorneys establish the best type of relationship with a client*Tips on remaining innovative and preparing for change in the industry.*

Intellectual Property Opportunities Brought about by Companies Going Through Bankruptcy or Reorganization. Thomas Hemnes. 2009. 250.00 (978-1-59701-497-7(4)) ReedLogic.

Intellectual Understanding of Enlightenment. Sai Maa Lakshmi Devi. 1. 2005. audio compact disk 16.00 (978-0-9766664-4-8(8)) HIU Pr.

Intellectual World of Our Founding Fathers. Forrest McDonald. 1 cass. (Running Time: 50 min.). 10.95 (NI-87-09-04, HarperThor) HarpC GBR.

Intellectuals. unabr. ed. Paul Johnson. Read by Frederick Davidson. 13 cass. (Running Time: 19 hrs.). 1989. 85.95 (978-0-7861-0052-1(4), 1050) Blckstn Audio.
This sketch of the minds that have shaped the modern world is an assessment of the moral & judgmental credentials of intellectuals who have advised the human race.

Intellectuals. unabr. ed. Paul Johnson. Read by Frederick Davidson. (Running Time: 18 hrs. 50 mins.). 2008. 44.95 (978-1-4332-4992-1(8)); audio compact disk 120.00 (978-1-4332-4991-4(X)) Blckstn Audio.

Intellectuals. unabr. ed. Paul Johnson. Read by Richard Brown. 14 cass. (Running Time: 21 hrs.). 1992. 112.00 (978-0-7366-2148-9(2), 2947) Books on Tape.
An examination of the credentials of those intellectuals who shaped the modern world.

Intellectuals & Society. unabr. ed. Thomas Sowell. Read by Weiner Tom. (Running Time: 12 hrs. 30 mins.). 2010. 29.95 (978-1-4417-1566-1(5)) Blckstn Audio.

Intellectuals & Society. unabr. ed. Thomas Sowell. Read by Tom Weiner. (Running Time: 12 hrs. 30 mins.). 2010. 72.95 (978-1-4417-1562-3(2)); audio compact disk 39.95 (978-1-4417-1565-4(7)); audio compact disk 105.00 (978-1-4417-1563-0(0)) Blckstn Audio.

Intelligence. Osho Oshos. 1 cass. 9.00 (A0654-89) Sound Photosyn.

Intelligence: Program from the Award Winning Public Radio Series. Hosted by Fred Goodwin. Comment by John Hockenberry. Contrib. by Jay McLelland et al. 1 cass. (Running Time: 1 hr.). (Infinite Mind Ser.). 1999. audio compact disk 21.95 (978-1-888064-10-0(2), LCM 66) Lichtenstein Creat.
Intelligence is a word we use everyday. But what does it really mean? Is it a single, measurable factor, or a combination of factors? In this hour, Dr. Goodwin talks to experts about what we mean when we talk about intelligence, how we measure it, and how it relates to performance in school, work and life. Plus, a special report from the White House Conference on Mental Health. We hear from President Clinton, First Lady Hillary Rodham Clinton, Al and Tipper Gore and others at this summit meeting on care for people with mental illnesses.

Intelligence, Experience, & Evolution. Gregory Bateson. 1 cass. 1975. 10.00 Vajradhatu.
With illustrations ranging from the story of Job, to the evolutionary relationship between horses & grass, the author describes the correspondence between natural evolution & the equilibrium of intelligence.

Intelligence in War: Knowledge of the Enemy from Napoleon to Al-Qaeda. abr. ed. John Keegan. Read by Simon Prebble. 10 CDs. (Running Time: 9 hrs.). (ENG.). 2003. audio compact disk 37.95 (978-0-7393-0755-7(X)) Pub: Random Audio Pubg. Dist(s): Random

Intelligence Matters: The CIA, the FBI, Saudi Arabia, & the Failure of America's War on Terror. abr. ed. Bob Graham & Jeff Nussbaum. 4 CDs. (Running Time: 5 hrs.). 2004. audio compact disk 29.95 (978-0-7393-1783-9(0), Random AudioBks) Pub: Random Audio Pubg. Dist(s): Random

Intelligence Matters: The CIA, the FBI, Saudi Arabia, & the Failure of America's War on Terror. unabr. abr. ed. Bob Graham & Jeff Nussbaum. 3 cass. (Running Time: 5 hrs.). 2004. 25.95 (978-0-7393-1782-2(2), Random AudioBks) Pub: Random Audio Pubg. Dist(s): Random
For ten years, Senator Graham served on the Senate Intelligence Committee, where he had access to some of the nation?s most closely guarded secrets. Following the attacks of September 11, 2001, Graham co-chaired a historic joint House-Senate inquiry into the intelligence community?s failures. From that investigation and his own personal fact-finding, Graham discovered disturbing evidence of terrorist activity and a web of complicity:.

Intelligence of the Heart. Joseph C. Pearce. 2 cass. 1991. 18.00 set. (OC277-62) Sound Horizons AV.

Intelligence of the Heart. unabr. ed. Joseph C. Pearce. 1 cass. (Running Time: 90 min.). 1992. 11.00 (01902) Big Sur Tapes.
Presents a compelling case for seeing our lives as a process in which evolution fulfills itself through our growing understanding. He describes a feeling of hidden greatness common in adolescence that signals a profound transformation &, if supported, puts us in touch with the very purpose of creation.

Intelligencer. abr. ed. Leslie Silbert. Read by Jan Maxwell & Alfred Molina. 2004. 15.95 (978-0-7435-3930-2(3)) Pub: S&S Audio. Dist(s): S and S Inc

Intelligent Asset Allocator: How to Build Your Portfolio to Maximize Returns & Minimize Risk. William Berstein. 3 cass. 2004. 24.00 (978-1-932378-48-1(0)) Pub: A Media Intl. Dist(s): Natl Bk Netwk

Intelligent Asset Allocator: How to Build Your Portfolio to Maximize Returns & Minimize Risk. William Berstein. 4 CDs. 2004. audio compact disk 28.00 (978-1-932378-49-8(9)) Pub: A Media Intl. Dist(s): Natl Bk Netwk

Intelligent Body, Vol. 3. Frank Wildman. Read by Frank Wildman. 6 cass. (Running Time: 9 hrs.). 1993. 70.00 Set. (978-1-889618-52-4(7)) Feldenkrais Move.
Movement education - 12 Feldenkrais awareness through movement lessons.

Intelligent Body, Vols. 1 & 2. Frank Wildman. Read by Frank Wildman. 12 cass. (Running Time: 18 hrs. 33 min.). 1984. 130.00 Set. (978-1-889618-51-7(9)) Feldenkrais Move.
Movement education - 24 Feldenkrais awareness through movement lessons.

***Intelligent Investor.** abr. ed. Benjamin Graham. Read by Bill Mcgowan. (ENG.). 2005. (978-0-06-085430-0(8), Harper Audio); (978-0-06-085429-4(4), Harper Audio) HarperCollins Pubs.

Intelligent Investor: The Classic Text on Value Investing. abr. ed. Benjamin Graham. Read by Bill McGowan. 2005. audio compact disk 22.95 (978-0-06-079383-8(X)) HarperCollins Pubs.

Intelligent Living: Ecc. 10:1-11. Ed Young. 1994. 4.95 (978-0-7417-2002-3(7), 1002); 19.95 (978-0-7417-4002-1(8), AV01002) Win Walk.

Intelligent Mindlessness. unabr. ed. Alan Watts. 4 cass. (Running Time: 5 hrs. 33 min.). 1970. 36.00 Set. (02511) Big Sur Tapes.
A practical workshop using sound in guided meditations, with entertaining introductory talks.

Intelligent Organization: Complexity & Change in Today's Workplace. Speeches. Featuring David Whyte. single CD in Jewel C. 2004. audio compact disk 15.00 (978-1-932887-09-9(1)) Pub: Many Rivers Pr. Dist(s): Partners-West
On The Intelligent Organization, David Whyte speaks about the phenomenon of change in turbulent times of our organizations. Combining the recitation of poems with insightful commentary, he shows the remarkable precision of poetry to illuminate steps that human beings as well as organizations need to take in order to adapt to the newly emerging workplace.

Intelligent Person's Guide to Dating & Mating. Albert Ellis. 1 cass. (Running Time: 59 min.). 9.95 (C014) A Ellis Institute.
Delightful, down-to-earth tape full of helpful tips. Learn how to feel good about yourself, survive rejection, & become assertive without being aggressive.

Intelligent Person's Guide to Dating & Mating. Albert Ellis. 1 cass. (Running Time: 59 min.). 9.95 (C014) Inst Rational-Emotive.
Learn how to feel good about yourself, survive rejection, & become assertive without being aggressive.

Intelligent Transport Systems Standards. Bob Williams. (Intelligent Transportation Systems Ser.). 2008. audio compact disk 159.00 (978-1-59693-291-3(0)) Artech Hse.

Intemperies. Poems. Jacques Prevert. Read by Jacques Prevert. Read by Arletty. 1 cass. (FRE.). 1991. 21.95 (1389-LQP) Olivia & Hill.
A selection of Prevert's poems.

Intensify Creative Ability. Dick Sutphen. 1 cass. (Running Time: 1 hr.). (RX17 Ser.). 1986. 14.98 (978-0-87554-319-2(7), RX128) Valley Sun.
You now release the unlimited power of your creative ability. You now utilize the unlimited powers of your subconscious mind. The wisdom of the universe is within you & you draw upon the awareness. You feel creative & you are creative. You easily generate creative solutions. You now draw unlimited creative inspiration from life experiences.

Intensity. unabr. ed. Dean Koontz. Read by Kate Burton. (Running Time: 11 hrs. 30 mins.). (Dean Koontz Ser.). (ENG.). 2006. audio compact disk 29.95 (978-0-7393-3425-6(5), Random AudioBks) Pub: Random Audio Pubg. Dist(s): Random

Intensity for the Goal. unabr. ed. Swami Amar Jyoti. 1 cass. (Satsangs of Swami Amar Jyoti). 1997. 9.95 (978-0-933572-28-7(X), M-107) Truth Consciousness.
First-hand knowledge of the Goal requires serious effort. Finding a solid, living Presence of the Lord.

Intensity of Longing. Swami Amar Jyoti. 1 cass. 1977. 9.95 (C-7) Truth Consciousness.
Dedication & devotion to the Goal. Why we forget God. Letting go of unconsciousness. 'Not me, God Thou'.

Intensity of Our Warfare. Dan Corner. 1 cass. 3.00 (46) Evang Outreach.

***Intensive Bulgarian 1 Audio Supplement [SPOKEN-WORD CD]: To Accompany Intensive Bulgarian 1, a Textbook & Reference Grammar.** Ronelle Alexander. (ENG.). 2010. audio compact disk 29.95 (978-0-299-25034-8(2)) Pub: U of Wis Pr. Dist(s): Chicago Distribution Ctr

***Intensive Bulgarian 2 Audio Supplement [SPOKEN-WORD CD]: To Accompany Intensive Bulgarian 2, a Textbook & Reference Grammar.** Ronelle Alexander. (ENG.). 2010. audio compact disk 29.95 (978-0-299-25044-7(X)) Pub: U of Wis Pr. Dist(s): Chicago Distribution Ctr

Intensive Care & Surgery on the Pregnant Patient. 2 cass. (Gynecology & Obstetrics Ser.: C84-GO2). 1984. 15.00 (8433) Am Coll Surgeons.

Intensive Consonant Pronunciation Practice. Joan Morley. (C). 1993. 250.00 (978-0-472-00235-1(X)) U of Mich Pr.

Intensive Geriatric Board Review, Vol. A225. unabr. ed. University Of North Texas Health Science Center At Fort Worth Staff. 21 cass. (Running Time: 27 hrs. 50 min.). 1995. 595.00 set. (978-1-57664-363-1(8)) CME Info Svcs.
Continuing medical education home-study. Complete package contains audiotapes, syllabus, self-assessment examination to earn CME Category 1 credit.

Intensive Group. unabr. ed. Carl Ransom Rogers. 1 cass. (Running Time: 59 min.). 1966. 18.00 (4010) Big Sur Tapes.
Describes the factors that constitute an encounter group.

Intensive Overview of Analytical Psychology. 16 cass. (Running Time: 14 hrs.). 1991. 83.95 Set. (978-0-7822-0000-3(1), OVERVIEW) C G Jung IL.

Intensive Review of Internal Medicine, Vol. A197. 4th unabr. ed. 52 cass. (Running Time: 50 hrs.). 1995. 950.00 set. (978-1-57664-361-7(1)) CME Info Svcs.
Continuing medical education home-study. Complete package contains audiotapes, syllabus, self-assessment examination to earn CME Category 1 credit.

Intensive Review of Pediatric Emergency Medicine. Ed. by Christopher King & Brent R. King. 24 cassettes. (Running Time: 36 hours). 2000. 550.00 (978-0-9720467-9-4(8)) TPEM.
Twenty-four 90-minute audiotapes and text summaries designed as a comprehensive self-study course for board preparation.

Intensive Review of Pediatrics, Vol. A198. unabr. ed. 35 cass. (Running Time: 41 hrs.). 1995. 875.00 set. (978-1-57664-362-4(X)) CME Info Svcs.
Continuing medical education home-study. Complete package contains audiotapes, syllabus, self-assessment examination to earn CME Category 1 credit.

Intensive Training Session on Meditation. Read by Chogyam Trungpa. 2 cass. 1986. 22.50 (A094) Vajradhatu.
An introduction to meditation practice. One of the last seminars done by the Vidyadhara before his death.

***Intent to Kill.** abr. ed. James Grippando. Read by Jonathan Davis. (ENG.). 2009. (978-0-06-180626-1(9), Harper Audio); (978-0-06-180627-8(7), Harper Audio) HarperCollins Pubs.

Intent to Kill. unabr. ed. Emma Page. Read by Terry Wale. 6 cass. (Running Time: 8 hrs.). 1999. 54.95 (978-1-86042-605-6(0), 26050) Pub: Soundings Ltd GBR. Dist(s): Ulverscroft US
Even though he had been diagnosed with a fatal illness, the apparent suicide of Robert Anstey, sole owner of the highly successful Paragon Tools, came as a shock to those who knew him. Why would he bother to take his prescribed medicine in the correct quantity before overdosing on sleeping pills? Ten-year-old Billy Coleman, his stepmother off on holiday with her new boyfriend, has disappeared after being left alone at home. Evidence begins to emerge which suggest he has been in the Anstey's house. Is there a link between the two cases? Robert Anstey's death touches the lives of wide network of people & reveals the darker sides of many of them as a web of lies, corruption & greed come to light.

Intent to Kill. unabr. ed. Emma Page. Read by Terry Wale. 8 CDs. (Running Time: 7 hrs. 30 mins.). (Sound Ser.). 2002. audio compact disk 79.95 (978-1-84283-176-2(3)) Pub: UlverLrgPrint GBR. Dist(s): Ulverscroft US
Even though he had been diagnosed with a fatal illness, the apparent suicide of Robert Anstey, came as a shock to those who knew him. Why would he bother to take his prescribed medicine in the correct quantity before overdosing on sleeping pills? Ten-year-old Billy Coleman, his stepmother off on holiday with her new boyfriend. has disappeared after being left alone at home. Evidence begins to emerge which suggest the has been in the Anstey's house. Is there a link between the two cases? Robert Anstey's death touches the lives of numerous people and reveals the darker sides of many of them as a web of lies, corruption and greed comes to light.

Intent to Kill: Accidents Happen, but This Was No Accident. unabr. ed. James Grippando. Read by Jonathan Davis. 2009. audio compact disk 39.99 (978-0-06-176805-7(7), Harper Audio) HarperCollins Pubs.

Intention & Choice in Shamanic Practice. Shelly Thompson. 1 cass. 9.00 (A0394-88) Sound Photosyn.
ICSS '88.

Intentional Healing: Consciousness & Connection for Health & Well-Being. abr. ed. Jeanne Achterberg. (Running Time: 21600 sec.). 2008. audio compact disk 69.95 (978-1-59179-807-1(8)) Sounds True.

Intentional Women of Influence Leadership Series. 2004. audio compact disk (978-0-9749306-2-6(8)) Giant Impact.

Inter-Dimensional Communication. unabr. ed. Dianthus. 1 cass. (Running Time: 1 hr. 17 min.). (ENG.). 1996. 11.00 (978-1-890372-02-6(1)) Dianthus.
Nine methods: telepathy; clairaudience, impression; clairvoyance; living a visual experience; intuition; assisting critical life situations; storytelling; transpiration; a visit.

Interacciones. 4th ed. Emily Spinelli. (C). bk. 70.95 (978-0-8384-6481-6(5)); bk. 57.95 (978-0-8384-6482-3(3)); bk. 124.70 (978-0-8384-7066-4(1)); bk. 110.95 (978-0-8384-7975-9(8)) Heinle.

Interacciones 5e-Text+Audio Cd Package-School Version. 5th ed. Emily Spinelli et al. (C). 2005. bk. 74.95 (978-1-4130-2976-5(0)) Pub: Heinle. Dist(s): CENGAGE Learn

Interact. Guy Aston. 1 cass. 1983. 13.00 incl. tapescript. Alemany Pr.
This gives intermediate students practice in developing oral fluency. Units center around activities such as games & the planning of outings that require students to communicate among themselves.

Interaction. Susan S. St. Onge et al. 2003. bk. & wbk. ed. 89.75 (978-0-8384-1041-7(3)); bk. & stu. ed. 73.35 (978-0-8384-1049-3(9)) Heinle.
Interaction continues to offer a systematic and unified presentation of intermediate structures and functions. A complete program offering unparalleled support for the study of culture, literature, and language at the intermediate level.

Interaction. Susan S. St. Onge et al. (C). 2003. bk. & wbk. ed. 65.95 (978-0-8384-1040-0(5)) Heinle.

Interaction. 5th ed. St. Onge. stu. ed. 5.00 (978-0-8384-8115-8(9)) Heinle.

Interaction. 5th ed. St. Onge. (C). bk. 107.95 (978-0-8384-8312-1(7)); bk. 91.95 (978-0-8384-8319-0(4)) Heinle.

Interaction. 5th ed. Susan S. St. Onge et al. bk., wbk. ed., lab manual ed. 97.20 (978-0-8384-1050-9(2)) Heinle.

Interaction. 6th ed. St. Onge & Kulick. (C) ... 94.95 (978-0-8384-7071-8(8)) Heinle.

Interaction. 6th ed. Susan S. St. Onge et al. 2002. stu. ed. (978-0-8384-0600-7(9)) Heinle.

Interaction, Set. Edwin T. Cornelius. Illus. by John Odam. (New Technology English Ser.: Vol. 8). 1984. 17.00 (978-0-89209-160-7(6)) Pace Grp Intl.

Interaction of Spirituality & Ministry. Bernard R. Bonnot. 2 cass. (Running Time: 2 hrs.). 14.95 incl. shelf-case. (TAH084) Alba Hse Comns.
Shows that ministry is a prime source of spiritual growth for all who minister.

Interactions I & II. Margaret Mian Yan & Jennifer Li-Chia Liu. (Chinese in Context Language Learning Ser.). (ENG.). 1998. 125.00 (978-0-253-33416-9(0)) Ind U Pr.

Interactions 1: Listening/Speaking. 4th rev. ed. Created by McGraw-Hill Staff. 2001. 65.00 (978-0-07-233064-9(3), 9780072330649, ESL/ELT) Pub: McGrw-H Hghr Educ. Dist(s): McGraw

Interactions 1 L/S Assess AC. 4th rev. ed. Judith Tanka et al. (C). 2001. 23.13 (978-0-07-255612-4(9), 9780072556124, ESL/ELT) Pub: McGrw-H Hghr Educ. Dist(s): McGraw

Interactions 2 Listening/Speaking. 4th abr. ed. Created by McGraw-Hill Companies Staff. i cass. (Running Time: 1 hr.). (ENG.). (C). 1996. 45.63 (978-0-07-013330-3(1), 0070133301, Mc-H Human Soc) Pub: McGrw-H Hghr Educ. Dist(s): McGraw

Interactions/Mosaic: Silver Edition - Interactions 1 (High Beginning to Low Intermediate) - Listening/Speaking Class Audio CD. 5th ed. Judith Tanka & Paul Most. (Interactions Ser.). (C). 2007. cd-rom 61.25 (978-0-07-329421-6(7), 0073294217, ESL/ELT) Pub: McGrw-H Hghr Educ. Dist(s): McGraw

Interactions/Mosaic: Silver Edition - Interactions 1 (High Beginning to Low Intermediate) - Listening/Speaking Class Audio Tapes. 5th ed. Judith Tanka & Paul Most. (Interactions Ser.). (C). 2007. 49.38 (978-0-07-329420-9(9), 0073294209, ESL/ELT) Pub: McGrw-H Hghr Educ. Dist(s): McGraw

Interactions/Mosaic: Silver Edition - Interactions 2 (Low Intermediate to Intermediate) - Listening/Speaking Class Audio CD. 5th ed. Judith Tanka & Lida Baker. (Interactions Ser.). (C). 2007. cd-rom 80.00 (978-0-07-329424-7(1), 0073294241, ESL/ELT) Pub: McGrw-H Hghr Educ. Dist(s): McGraw

Interactions/Mosaic: Silver Edition - Interactions 2 (Low Intermediate to Intermediate) - Listening/Speaking Class Audio Tapes. 5th ed. Judith Tanka & Lida Baker. (Interactions Ser.). (C). 2007. 80.00 (978-0-07-329423-0(3), 0073294233, ESL/ELT) Pub: McGrw-H Hghr Educ. Dist(s): McGraw

Interactions/Mosaic: Silver Edition - Mosaic 1 (Intermediate to High Intermediate) - Listening/Speaking Audio CDs (6) 5th ed. Jami Hanreddy & Elizabeth Whalley. (Mosaic Ser.). (C). 2007. cd-rom 80.00 (978-0-07-329411-7(X), 007329411X, ESL/ELT) Pub: McGrw-H Hghr Educ. Dist(s): McGraw

Interactive Animal Kit: Bears. (Running Time: 10 min.). (J). (gr. 1-3). 1996. pap. bk. 10.95 2 posters. Scholastic Inc.
Bears from the massive grizzly to the lumbering giant panda & the diminutive sun bear are the subject of this interactive animal kit.

Interactive Approaches to Teaching: A Framework for INSET. Mark Collis & Penny Lacey. 1996. audio compact disk 39.95 (978-1-85346-366-2(3)) Pub: David Fulton GBR. Dist(s): Taylor and Fran

Interactive Babysitter Training Course to Accompany: Blast. Natl Safety Council. (C). 2003. audio compact disk 26.50 (978-0-7637-3160-1(9), 0763731609) Jones Bartlett.

Interactive Diagrams CD for Use with College Algebra. 6th ed. Raymond A. Barnett et al. 1999. audio compact disk 22.50 (978-0-07-013593-2(2)) McGrw-H Hghr Educ.

Interactive Dictations: A listening / speaking / writing Text. Judy DeFilippo & Catherine Sadow. 1 CD. (Running Time: 78 MINS). 2006. audio compact disk Rental 18.00 (978-0-86647-240-1(1)) Pro Lingua.

Interactive Dictations: A listening / speaking / writing Text. Judy DeFilippo & Catherine Sadow. 1 CD. (Running Time: 78 MINS). (gr. 8-12). 2006. pap. bk. 28.00 (978-0-86647-241-8(X)) Pro Lingua.

Interactive Directory of Learning Resources 2nd Edition. Harvey. 1998. audio compact disk 139.95 (978-0-566-08130-9(X)) Ashgate Pub Co.

Interactive First Responder: A Scenario-Based Approach. AAOS Staff & National Safety Council (NSC) Staff. (C). 1999. stu. ed. 44.95 (978-0-7637-0525-1(X), 076370525X) Jones Bartlett.

Interactive Home Shopping - It's Here! 1 cass. (America's Supermarket Showcase '96 Ser.). 1996. 11.00 (NGA96-042) Sound Images.

Interactive Japanese Bk. 1: An Introductory Course, Set. Takako Tomoda & Brian May. (International Ser.). (JPN., 1996. 30.00 (978-4-7700-2063-5(5)) Kodansha.

Interactive Musician. Alfred Publishing Staff. (ENG.). 2004. tchr. ed. 99.95 (978-0-7390-3531-3(2)); stu. ed. 39.95 (978-0-7390-3530-6(4)) Alfred Pub.

Interactive Oral & Mental Starters: For the Key Stage 3 Mathematics Framework. Mary Pardoe. 2005. audio compact disk 455.00 (978-0-340-88472-0(X), HodderMurray) Pub: Hodder Edu GBR. Dist(s): Trans-Atl Phila

Interactive Oral & Mental Starters for the Key Stage 3 Mathematics Framework Year 8. Mary Pardoe. 2005. audio compact disk 455.00 (978-0-340-88471-3(1), HodderMurray) Pub: Hodder Edu GBR. Dist(s): Trans-Atl Phila

Interactive Organic Chemistry CD-ROM: Version 2.0. Vining. 2000. audio compact disk 63.95 (978-0-03-021969-6(8)) Brooks-Cole.

Interactive Writing & Beyond: Practical Strategies for Beginning Writers (Grades K-2) Narrated by Patricia Calabrese. 6 cass. (Running Time: 4 hrs. 27 mins.). 2001. 89.00 (978-1-886397-42-2(2)) Bureau of Educ.
Live audio program & a comprehensive resource handbook.

Intercambios. 4th ed. Guiomar Borras Alvarez. 2002. audio compact disk 10.00 (978-0-8384-2511-4(9)) Heinle.

***Intercept.** unabr. ed. Patrick Robinson. Narrated by Charles Leggett. 2 MP3-CDs. (Running Time: 15 hrs. 23 mins.). 2010. 69.95 (978-0-7927-7208-8(3)); audio compact disk 110.95 (978-0-7927-7133-3(8)) AudioGO.

***Intercept: A Novel of Suspense.** Patrick Robinson. Narrated by Charles Leggett. (Running Time: 15 hrs. 23 mins. 0 sec.). (ENG.). 2011. audio compact disk 29.95 (978-1-60998-144-0(8)) Pub: AudioGO. Dist(s): Perseus Dist

Intercepted Signs: Environment vs. Destiny. Joanne Wickenburg. 1 cass. 8.95 (363) Am Fed Astrologers.
How intercepted signs & planets influence order of chart.

Interceptions. Helen Garrett. 1 cass. (Running Time: 90 min.). 1990. 8.95 (835) Am Fed Astrologers.

Intercession. Derek Prince. 1 cass. (I-4033) Derek Prince.

Intercession: By Precept & Example. Kenneth E. Hagin. 6 cass. 24.00 (22H) Faith Lib Pubns.

Intercession Brings the Outpouring. Kenneth Copeland. 1 cass. (Outpouring of the Spirit Ser.: No. 2). 1983. 5.00 (978-0-88114-290-7(5)) K Copeland Pubns.
Biblical study on Spirit-filled living.

Intercessor. Perf. by Bill Murk. 1 Tape. 2002. 9.99 (978-0-9725443-7-5(2)); audio compact disk 14.99 (978-0-9725443-6-8(4)) Pub: Myrrh Pub. Dist(s): STL Dist NA
Bill Murk (violin) and Richard Drexler (jazz keyboard) team up to create Bill's most exciting violin recording yet! Together they provide a contemplative musical environment for intercession.

Intercessor's Breakdown Point. Elbert Willis. 1 cass. (Developing an Interceding Life Ser.). 4.00 Fill the Gap.

Intercessor's Motive. Elbert Willis. 1 cass. (Developing an Interceding Life Ser.). 4.00 Fill the Gap.

Intercessor's Operation Sphere. Elbert Willis. 1 cass. (Developing an Interceding Life Ser.). 4.00 Fill the Gap.

Intercessor's Warfare. Elbert Willis. 1 cass. (Developing an Interceding Life Ser.). 4.00 Fill the Gap.

Intercessory Prayer. Kenneth Copeland. 4 cass. 1983. 20.00 Set incl. study guide. (978-0-938458-60-9(4)) K Copeland Pubns.
Biblical prayer.

Intercessory Prayer. Kenneth E. Hagin. 4 cass. 16.00 (03H) Faith Lib Pubns.

***Intercessory Prayer: How God Can Use Your Prayers to Move Heaven & Earth.** unabr. ed. Dutch Sheets. Narrated by Robertson Dean. (ENG.). 2008. 16.98 (978-1-59644-554-3(8), Hovel Audio) christianaud.

Intercessory Prayer: How God Can Use Your Prayers to Move Heaven & Earth. unabr. ed. Dutch Sheets. Read by Robertson Dean. (Running Time: 8 hrs. 18 mins. 0 sec.). (ENG.). 2008. audio compact disk 26.98 (978-1-59644-553-6(X)) christianaud.

Interchange. 3rd ed. Jack C. Richards. (Interchange Third Edition Ser.). (ENG.). 2005. lab manual ed. 70.00 (978-0-521-61341-5(8)) Cambridge U Pr.

Interchange: English for International Communication, Levels 1-3. 1 cass. (Running Time: 60 min.). 1991. 14.95 ea. Cambridge U Pr.

Interchange: Intro Lab CDs. 3rd ed. Jack C. Richards. (Interchange Third Edition Ser.). (ENG.). 2005. lab manual ed. 70.00 (978-0-521-61339-2(6)) Cambridge U Pr.

Interchange Class, Vol. 1. 3rd rev. ed. Jack C. Richards et al. (Interchange Third Edition Ser.). (ENG.). 2004. 59.00 (978-0-521-60185-6(1)) Cambridge U Pr.

Interchange Class, Vol. 2. 3rd rev. ed. Jack C. Richards et al. 2 Cass. (Interchange Third Edition Ser.). (ENG.). 2004. 59.00 (978-0-521-60207-5(6)) Cambridge U Pr.

Interchange Class, Vol. 3. 3rd rev. ed. Jack C. Richards et al. 3 Cass. (Interchange Third Edition Ser.). (ENG.). 2004. 59.00 (978-0-521-60229-7(7)) Cambridge U Pr.

Interchange Class Audio: Includes Student Self-Study Audio. 3rd rev. ed. Jack C. Richards et al. 2 CDs. (ENG.). 2004. audio compact disk 59.00 (978-0-521-60206-8(8)) Cambridge U Pr.

Interchange Class Audio CDs, Level 1, Vol. 1. 3rd rev. abr. ed. Jack C. Richards et al. Told to Jonathan Hull & Susan Proctor. (ENG.). 2004. audio compact disk 59.00 (978-0-521-60184-9(3)) Cambridge U Pr.

Interchange Class Audio CDs, Level 3, Vol. 3. 3rd rev. abr. ed. Jack C. Richards et al. Told to Jonathan Hull & Susan Proctor. 3 CDs. (ENG.). 2005. audio compact disk 59.00 (978-0-521-60228-0(9)) Cambridge U Pr.

Interchange: Intro. 3rd rev. ed. Jack C. Richards. (Interchange Third Edition Ser.). (ENG.). 2004. audio compact disk 59.00 (978-0-521-60164-1(9)) Cambridge U Pr.

Interchange Intro Class. 3rd rev. ed. Jack C. Richards. (Interchange Third Edition Ser.). (ENG.). 2004. 59.00 (978-0-521-60163-4(0)) Cambridge U Pr.

Interchange 1. 3rd ed. Jack C. Richards. (Interchange Third Edition Ser.). (ENG.). 2005. lab manual ed. 70.00 (978-0-521-61340-8(X)) Cambridge U Pr.

Interchange 3. 3rd rev. ed. Jack C. Richards. (Interchange Third Edition Ser.). (ENG.). 2005. audio compact disk 70.00 (978-0-521-61342-2(6)) Cambridge U Pr.

Intercom 2000, Level 1. 3rd ed. Anna Uhl Chamot et al. 5 cass. (Running Time: 7 hrs.). 40.95 (978-0-8384-8937-6(0)) Heinle.

Intercom 2000: Duplicating Package, Level 3. Anna Uhl Chamot. 99.95 (978-0-8384-1849-9(X)) Heinle.

Intercom 2000: Tape Duplicating Package, Level 3. 3rd ed. Anna Uhl Chamot. 2000. pap. bk. 99.95 (978-0-8384-1848-2(1)) Heinle.
Intercom 2000 is a four-level basic course featuring a spiraled approach to language learning with presentation, reinforcement, expansion, and regular review of communication forms and structures.

Intercom 2000: Tape Duplicating Package, Level 4. 3rd ed. Anna Uhl Chamot. pap. bk. 99.95 (978-0-8384-1867-3(8)) Heinle.

Intercom 2000 3E: Tape Duplicating Package, Level 3. Anna Uhl Chamot. 99.95 (978-0-8384-1866-6(X)) Heinle.

Interdependence of Mind & Body. Trogawa Rinpoche. 2 cass. 1993. 18.00 set. (OC353-74) Sound Horizons AV.

Interdimensional Astrology. Pamela Crane. 2 cass. (Running Time: 60 min. per cass.). 1992. 8.95 ea. Am Fed Astrologers.

Interdisciplinary Out-Patient Care. Granger Westburg. 1986. 10.80 (0106B) Assn Prof Chaplains.

Interest & Capitalization. unabr. ed. Murray Newton Rothbard. 1 cass. (Running Time: 1 hr. 6 min.). (Introduction to Free Market Economics Ser.). 12.95 (311) J Norton Pubs.
Time preference; capitalization; the stock market; the economics of slavery.

Interest of Justice. unabr. ed. Nancy Taylor Rosenberg. Read by Frances Cassidy. 10 cass. (Running Time: 15 hrs.). 1996. 80.00 (978-0-913369-20-3(9), 4169) Books on Tape.
Laura Sanderstone's future can't get much brighter. At 38, she's a judge in Orange County, California, with no place to go but up. Then someone butchers her younger sister & brother-in-law.

Interest Rates & Money Markets Made Easy. Ed. by Robert Krulwich. 1 cass. (Running Time: 20 min.). 9.95 (I0110B090, HarperThor) HarpC GBR.

Interesting Life. abr. ed. Bailey White. Read by Bailey White. 1 cass. (Running Time: 1 hr. 30 min.). 2001. 13.00 (978-1-59040-167-5(0), Phoenix Audio) Pub: Amer Intl Pub. Dist(s): PerseuPGW

Interesting Times. Terry Pratchett. Read by Tony Robinson. 2 cass. (Running Time: 3 hrs. 0 mins. 0 sec.). (Discworld Ser.). (ENG.). 1996. 16.99 (978-0-552-14425-4(8)) Pub: Transworld GBR. Dist(s): IPG Chicago

Interesting Times. unabr. ed. Terry Pratchett. Read by Nigel Planer. 6 cass. (Running Time: 9 hr. 45 min.). (Discworld Ser.). (J). 2001. 54.95 (978-1-85695-814-1(0), 950603) Pub: ISIS Lrg Prnt GBR. Dist(s): Ulverscroft US

Interesting Times. unabr. ed. Terry Pratchett. Read by Nigel Planer. 9 CDs. (Running Time: 10 hrs.). (Discworld Ser.). (J). 2002. audio compact disk 84.95 (978-0-7531-0738-6(4)) Pub: ISIS Lrg Prnt GBR. Dist(s): Ulverscroft US
The oldest and most inscrutable empire on the Discworld is in turmoil, brought about by the revolutionary treatise, What I Did on My Holidays. Workers are uniting, with nothing to lose but their water buffaloes. Warlords are struggling for power. And all that stands in the way of terrible doom for everyone is Rincewind the Wizard, who can't even spell the word "wizard". Cohen the barbarian hero, five foot tall in his surgical sandals, who has had a lifetime's experience of not dying...and a very special butterfly.

Interfaces - Boundaries Which Connect. unabr. ed. Gregory Bateson. 1 cass. (Running Time: 1 hr. 31 min.). (Informal Esalen Lectures). 1980. 11.00 (02809) Big Sur Tapes.
Bateson considers the whole of our mental life as a dance of complicated interfaces, & sees interfaces as boundaries which connect rather than as barriers between two active areas.

Intergenerational Cell Groups. Lorna Jenkins. 6 cass. (Running Time: 9 hrs.). 2001. 29.95 (CLCA) Touch Pubns.
Solid advice for discipline, prayer & more.

Interior Castle. Saint Teresa of Avila. (Pure Gold Classics Ser.). (ENG., 2008. pap. bk. 14.99 (978-0-88270-464-7(8)) Bridge-Logos.

***Interior Castle.** St. Teresa of Avila. Read by Karen Savage. (ENG.). 2009. audio compact disk 18.95 (978-1-936231-06-5(9)) Cath Audio.

***Interior Castle.** unabr. ed. Teresa of Avila. Narrated by Susan Denaker. (ENG.). 2007. 16.98 (978-1-59644-480-5(0), Hovel Audio) christianaud.

Interior Castle. unabr. ed. Teresa of Avila. Read by Susan Denaker. 7 CDs. (Running Time: 7 hrs. 30 mins. 0 sec.). (ENG.). 2007. audio compact disk 26.98 (978-1-59644-479-9(7), Hovel Audio) christianaud.

Interior Design Process: New Directions. unabr. ed. Walter Kleeman, Jr. 1 cass. (Running Time: 25 min.). 1969. 12.95 (11012) J Norton Pubs.
Discusses the psychological stresses resulting from limitation & faulty arrangement of space.

Interior Design Process: Psychosocial Factors. unabr. ed. Walter Kleeman, Jr. 1 cass. (Running Time: 24 min.). 1969. 12.95 (11013) J Norton Pubs.
Discusses the environmental design of dormitories, libraries, hospitals & business research & committee rooms, & suggests arrangements for maximun functioning.

Interior Life. Mrinalini Mata. 1984. 6.50 (2404) Self Realization.
An informal talk by the author on the teachings of Paramahansa Yogananda showing why the interior life is unique to each seeker - a relationship with God that gradually becomes more intimate & complete, satisfying all desires of heart & soul. Emphasis is given to understanding the divine purpose of our outer circumstances - relationships with family & friends, work, health, etc. - so that we can respond to them in a way that hastens our spiritual development.

Interior Textiles in Belgium: A Strategic Reference 2006. Compiled by Icon Group International, Inc. Staff. 2007. ring bd. 195.00 (978-0-497-35827-3(1)) Icon Grp.

Interior Textiles in Brazil: A Strategic Reference 2006. Compiled by Icon Group International, Inc. Staff. 2007. ring bd. 195.00 (978-0-497-35840-2(9)) Icon Grp.

Interlopers. Alan Dean Foster. Narrated by Ben Browder. 8 CDs. (Running Time: 8 hrs 45 mins). 2004. audio compact disk 47.95 (978-0-9657255-4-5(5)) Buzzy Multimed.

Interlopers, Vol. 1. unabr. ed. Saki. Narrated by Amato Petale. 1 cass. (Running Time: 42 min.). Incl. Cask of Amontillado. Edgar Allan Poe. (J). 1984.; Last Lesson. Alphonse Daudet. (J). 1984.; (Fantasies Ser.). (J). 1984. 17.95 Incl. holder, scripts, lesson plans, & tchr's. guide. (978-0-86617-042-0(1)) Multi Media TX.
Comprehensive lesson plans that use classic short stories to develop skills in listening, reading, vocabulary, following details, making inferences, visualization, drawing conclusions, critical appreciation & comparison. This module's object is to identify elements that provide the dramatic interest in plot: expectation, suspense, surprise & revelation.

Interlude see Twentieth-Century Poetry in English, No. 29, Recordings of Poets Reading Their Own Poetry

Interlude in Death. J. D. Robb, pseud. Read by Susan Ericksen. (In Death Ser.). 2008. 44.99 (978-1-60640-595-6(0)) Find a World.

Interlude in Death. unabr. ed. J. D. Robb, pseud. Read by Susan Ericksen. (Running Time: 3 hrs.). (In Death Ser.). 2006. 39.25 (978-1-4233-0998-7(7), 9781423309987, BADLE); 24.95 (978-1-4233-0997-0(9), 9781423309970, BAD); audio compact disk 62.25 (978-1-4233-0993-2(6), 9781423309932, BriAudCD Unabrid); audio compact disk 39.25 (978-1-4233-1175-1(2), 9781423311751, Brlnc Audio MP3 Lib); audio compact disk 19.95 (978-1-4233-0992-5(8), 9781423309925, Bril Audio CD Unabri); audio compact disk 24.95 (978-1-4233-1174-4(4), 9781423311744, Brilliance MP3) Brilliance Audio.
In early spring of 2059, Lieutenant Eve Dallas is called off planet to face a grueling ordeal - giving a seminar at the largest police conference of the year, to be held in a swanky resort. A resort which just happens to be owned by her husband, Roarke, of course. Even though Eve can't quite see it that way, it's supposed to be at least partly a vacation. But work intrudes in the form of a bloody homicide, and Eve is off and running. The case is complicated by Eve's personal history with the victim - and by the killer's history with Roarke. As danger closes in and the body count rises, Eve must find a way to stop the cycle of violence and revenge, and shove the past back where it belongs.

Interludes. Great American Audio. 3 cass. (Running Time: 3 hrs.). 1990. 19.95 (978-1-55569-410-4(1), 7156) Great Am Audio.
Contains 3-60 minute digitally mastered cassettes.

Interludes, Vol. 1. abr. ed. Nina Mattikow. 3 cass. (Running Time: 3 hrs.). (Interludes Music Ser.). 1992. 19.95 Set. (978-1-55569-538-5(8), 43100) Great Am Audio.
Features sounds of nature & music.

Interludes, Vol. 2. abr. ed. Nina Mattikow. 3 cass. (Running Time: 3 hrs.). (Interludes Music Ser.). 1992. 19.95 Set. (978-1-55569-539-2(6), 43101) Great Am Audio.

Interludes 4-Crate. 4 cass. (Running Time: 4 hrs.). 1989. 17.95 (978-1-55569-298-8(2), 5770-13) Great Am Audio.
Features sounds of nature and music.

Intermediario. abr. ed. Scripts. John Grisham. Narrated by Karl Hoffman. 6 CDs. (Running Time: 21600 sec.).Tr. of Broker. (SPA.). 2006. audio compact disk 29.95 (978-1-933499-02-4(8)) Fonolibro Inc.
FonoLibro les trae, en una magnifica produccion, el audiolibro en espa?ol del mas reciente exito del famoso escritor John Grisham, autor de los bestsellers ?La Firma?, ?El Informe Pelicano?, ?Tiempo para Matar?, ?El Rey de los Pleitos? y ?El Cliente?, Gracias a un indulto presidencial, Joel Backman es liberado tras seis a?os de confinamiento por uso indebido de una informacion altamente confidencial. Backman habia obtenido un programa capaz de poner en peligro el sistema de vigilancia por via satelite mas sofisticado del mundo, cuando dirigia un poderoso bufete de abogados, y era conocido como ?El Intermediario.? En vez de informar sobre el descubrimiento a las autoridades de su pais, decidio hacer el negocio de su vida vendiendo dicha informacion, pero las cosas salieron mal y fue condenado por traicion a veinte a?os de carcel. A pesar de la gravedad del asunto, la CIA logra que Backman sea liberado mucho antes y, argumentando que son muchos los que desearian acabar con su vida, lo saca del pais oculto en un avion militar. Su destino es Italia donde podra empezar una nueva vida bajo una identidad oculta y la proteccion de la CIA. Sin embargo, Backman, no solo desconfia de las buenas intenciones de esta, sino que sospecha que todo pueda ser una trampa.Un emocionante thriller que aborda con realismo los intereses que mueven las altas esferas y el enorme poder que tienen las principales agencias de espionaje del mundo.

Intermediate: Emergency Care & Transportation of the Sick & Injured Student Review Manual. American Academy of Orthopaedic Surgeons Staff. (C). 2005. audio compact disk 51.95 (978-0-7637-3466-4(7), 0763734667) Jones Bartlett.

Intermediate Acoustic Guitar. Greg Horne. 1 CD. (Running Time: 1 hr. 30 mins.). (ENG.). 2000. audio compact disk 11.00 (978-0-7390-0428-9(X), 19339) Alfred Pub.

Intermediate Algebra. Created by Pearson/Prentice Hall. (Math XL Ser.). 2006. audio compact disk 26.67 (978-0-13-134606-2(7)) Not Available.

Intermediate Algebra. 3rd ed. Elayn Martin-Gay. 2006. audio compact disk 36.80 (978-0-13-188759-6(9)) Pearson Educ CAN CAN.

Intermediate Algebra. 9th ed. Lial et al. (Math XL Ser.). 2004. audio compact disk 26.67 (978-0-321-29376-3(2)) AddisonWesley.

Intermediate Algebra: A Graphing Approach. 3rd ed. Created by Pearson/Prentice Hall. (Math XL Ser.). 2004. audio compact disk 26.67 (978-0-13-168004-3(8)) Pearson Educ CAN CAN.

Intermediate Algebra: Chapter Test Prep. 4th ed. K. Elayn Martin-Gay. 2004. audio compact disk 17.80 (978-0-13-148790-1(6)) Pearson Educ CAN CAN.

Intermediate Anecdotes in American English. Leslie A. Hill. (Anecdotes in American English Ser.). 1981. 17.50 (978-0-19-502829-4(5)) OUP.

Intermediate Arabic Three: A Reading Course. Mahdi Alosh. 2 cass. 10.00 (978-0-87415-218-0(6), 86B) Foreign Lang.

Intermediate Arabic 1 Pt. 1: Our Living Language. Mahdi Alosh. 2 cass. 1992. 10.00 (978-0-87415-212-8(7), 84B) Foreign Lang.

Intermediate Arabic 2 Pt. 2: Our Living Language. Mahdi Alosh. 1 cass. 1992. 5.00 (978-0-87415-215-9(1), 85B) Foreign Lang.

Intermediate Autism - Focus on Treatment: Sponsored by the Occupational Therapy Association of California. Valerie Adams & Sandra Greene. 3 cass. (Running Time: 4 hrs.). 1997. bk. 150.00 (978-1-58111-016-6(2)) Contemporary Medical.
Reviews of definition of Pervasive Developmental Disorders; delivery models; supporting theories; treatment approaches & interventions.

Intermediate Belly Dance Bklt with Music CD. Vicki Corona. (ENG., 1990. audio compact disk 24.95 (978-1-58513-173-0(3)) Dance Fantasy.

Intermediate Blues Guitar. Workshop Arts Staff & M. Smith. 1994. pap. bk. 8.95 (978-0-7390-1811-8(6), 4481) Alfred Pub.

Intermediate Bulgarian 1. Charles Gribble & Lyubomira P. Gribble. 1 cass. 1984. 5.00 (978-0-87415-021-6(3), 14B) Foreign Lang.

Intermediate Bulgarian 2. Lyubomira P. Gribble & Charles Gribble. 3 cass. 1985. 15.00 (978-0-87415-024-7(8), 15B) Foreign Lang.

Intermediate Cherokee, Module I & II, Set. 2 cass. (Running Time: 2 hrs.). pap. bk. 49.95 (AFCK20) J Norton Pubs.
Pronunciation, vocabulary & syntax are stressed in everyday situations.

Intermediate Cherokee, Module III & IV, Set. 2 cass. (Running Time: 2 hrs.). pap. bk. 49.95 (AFCK30) J Norton Pubs.

Intermediate Clarinet Solos - Vol. II. Jerome Bunke. 2008. pap. bk. 24.98 (978-1-4234-6147-0(9), 1423461479) Pub: Music Minus. Dist(s): H Leonard

Intermediate Clarinet Solos - Volume 3. Stanley Drucker. 2008. pap. bk. 24.98 (978-1-4234-6148-7(7), 1423461487) Pub: Music Minus. Dist(s): H Leonard

Intermediate Czech 1. Charles E. Townsend & Elaine McKee. 5 cass. 1984. 25.00 (978-0-87415-033-9(7), 18B) Foreign Lang.

Intermediate Czech 2. Charles E. Townsend et al. 3 cass. 1985. 15.00 (978-0-87415-036-0(1), 19B) Foreign Lang.

Intermediate Electric Bass. David Overthrow. (ENG.). 2000. audio compact disk 10.00 (978-0-7390-0687-0(8), 19360) Alfred Pub.

Intermediate English for Spanish Speakers, Set. unabr. ed. Conversa-Phone Institute Staff. 3 cass. (Running Time: 2 hrs. 30 min.). (Modern Method Language Ser.). 1994. 23.95 (978-1-56752-078-1(2)) Conversa-phone.
Continuation of Basic English Course, teaching more verbs & conversation. Includes 96 page manual & 16 page Verbs Booklet.

Intermediate Fingerstyle for Guitar. Lou Manzi & Nat Gunod. 1 CD. (Running Time: 1 hr. 30 mins.). (ENG.). 1998. audio compact disk 10.95 (978-0-7390-0596-5(0), 17824) Alfred Pub.

Intermediate French Horn Solos - Volume II. Mason Jones. 2008. pap. bk. 24.98 (978-1-59615-213-7(3), 1596152133) Pub: Music Minus. Dist(s): H Leonard

Intermediate French Horn Solos - Volume III. Mason Jones. 2008. pap. bk. 24.98 (978-1-59615-216-8(8), 1596152168) Pub: Music Minus. Dist(s): H Leonard

Intermediate German Through Fairy Tales. 1 cass., bklet. (Running Time: 50 mins.). (GER.). pap. bk. 32.95 (978-1-57970-002-7(0), SGE120) J Norton Pubs.

Consists of 5 Grimm Brothers fairy tales spoken in precise & excellent German. Allows the learner to anticipate what is being said on the tape & concentrate on correct pronunciation. The booklet is a verbatim transcript so that the learner can follow along to build listening skills & vocabulary. Exercises cover vocabulary, grammar & comprehension.

Intermediate Gypsy Jazz Guitar. John Jorgenson. 2005. pap. bk. 39.95 (978-0-7866-7420-6(2)) Mel Bay.

Intermediate Jazz Guitar. Jody Fischer. 1 CD. (FRE.). Date not set. pap. bk. (978-0-7390-0830-0(7), 19378) Alfred Pub.

***Intermediate Listening Comprehension.** 3rd ed. Phyllis L. Lim & Patricia A. Dunkel. (ENG.). (C). 2005. 242.95 (978-1-4130-0595-0(0)) Pub: Heinle. Dist(s): CENGAGE Learn

Intermediate Listening Comprehension: Understanding & Recalling Spoken English. 2nd ed. Patricia A. Dunkel & Phyllis L. Lim. 5 cass. 54.00 (978-0-8384-4839-7(9), 6321285, Newbury) Heinle.

Differentiates between various rhetorical cues, & develops aural English fluency at the intermediate level.

Intermediate Mandarin Chinese. (Intermediate Ser.). (CHI & ENG., 2009. audio compact disk 29.95 (978-981-268-509-4(X)) Pub: Berlitz Pubng. Dist(s): Langenscheidt

***Intermediate Mezzo Soprano Solos.** Fay Kittelson. 2009. pap. bk. 24.98 (978-1-4234-5926-2(1), 1423459261) Pub: Music Minus. Dist(s): H Leonard

Intermediate Modern Standard Arabic. Peter F. Abboud et al. 4 cass. 1983. 49.06 Set. U MI Lang Res.

Intermediate Pilates Matwork: Flowing Fitness Challenge: 35 Exercises. Instructed by Aliesa George. (ENG.). 2006. 12.00 (978-0-9771576-5-5(2)) Ctr Pilates.

Intermediate Polish One, Jerzy R. Krzyzanowski et al. 7 cass. (Running Time: 9 hr.). (OSU Foreign Language Publications). (POL.). (C). 1986. 35.00 (978-0-87415-103-9(1), 43B) Foreign Lang.

Polish language tapes.

Intermediate Polish Two. Jerzy R. Krzyzanowski et al. 5 cass. (Running Time: 7 hrs.). (OSU Foreign Language Publications). (POL.). (C). 1986. 25.00 set. (978-0-87415-106-0(6), 44B) Foreign Lang.

Polish language tapes.

Intermediate Serbo-Croatian 1. Biljana Sljivic-Simsic & Krinka Vidakovic. 5 cass. 1986. 25.00 (978-0-87415-070-4(1), 30B) Foreign Lang.

***Intermediate Soprano Solos: Kate Hurney.** Kate Hurney. 2009. pap. bk. 24.98 (978-1-4234-5932-3(6), 1423459326) Pub: Music Minus. Dist(s): H Leonard

Intermediate Spanish. 3rd rev. ed. Created by Berlitz Publishing Staff. 3 CDs. (Berlitz Intermediate Ser.). 2008. audio compact disk 29.95 (978-981-268-410-3(7)) Pub: Berlitz Pubng. Dist(s): Langenscheidt

Intermediate Spanish Series. 7th ed. John G. Copeland et al. (SPA.). 2001. lab manual ed. (978-0-03-029611-6(0)); lab manual ed. (978-0-03-029636-9(6)) Harcourt Coll Pubs.

Intermediate Stories for Children of All Ages. Narrated by Dale Bulla. 1 cass. (Running Time: 59 min.). (J). (gr. 2 up). 1990. 9.95 (978-1-884197-02-4(7)) N Horizon Educ.

Four tales told by Dale Bulla, storyteller. Nos. 1 & 3 are growing up stories, No. 4 is historical fiction, No. 2 is a folktale. No. 1: The Kids in the Car; No. 2: Jack & the North Wind; No. 3: My Pet Rattlesnake; No. 4: Dick Whittington & His Cat.

Intermediate Swahili Newspaper Reader. 1984. 24.00 (978-0-931745-14-0(4)) Dunwoody Pr.

Intermediate Swahili Newspaper Reader, Set. John B. Rutayuga & John D. Murphy. 4 cass. (Running Time: 1 hr. 30 min. per cass.). (SWA.). 1984. 29.00 (3075) Dunwoody Pr.

Twenty readings provide the student with a broad selection of articles together with the necessary lexical & grammatical aids. The subject matter covers a variety of fields, including discussions of political, economic, military, & human interest topics.

Intermediate TOEFL Test Practices. Keith S. Folse. 4 cass. 1997. 40.00 Set. U of Mich Pr.

Intermediate TOEFL Test Practices. rev. ed. Keith S. Folse. 4 cass. (Running Time: 6 hrs.). (C). 1997. 40.00 (978-0-472-00270-2(8), 00270) U of Mich Pr.

Intermediate Trumpet Solos - Vol. 1. Robert Nagel. 2008. pap. bk. 24.98 (978-1-59615-428-5(4), 1596154284) Pub: Music Minus. Dist(s): H Leonard

Intermediate Ukranian 1. Assya Humesky & Val Bolen. 1 cass. 1984. 5.00 (978-0-87415-061-2(2), 26B) Foreign Lang.

Intermediate Workbook Audio Word ESL. Molinsky. 2002. wbk. ed. 43.85 (978-0-13-434507-9(X)) Longman.

Intermission to the Moon. Contrib. by Dream Too Late. Prod. by Steve Wilson. 2007. audio compact disk 13.99 (978-5-557-56808-1(5)) Tooth & Nail.

Intermissions, Vol. 2. Dameans, The. Perf. by Gary Ault et al. 1997. 10.95 (407); audio compact disk 15.95 (407) GIA Pubns.

Intern at Provident Hospital see Poetry & Reflections

Internal Combustion: How Corporations & Governments Addicted the World to Oil & Derailed the Alternatives. Edwin R. Black. Read by Stephen Hoye. (Playaway Adult Nonfiction Ser.). (ENG.). 2009. 69.99 (978-1-60775-786-3(9)) Find a World.

Internal Combustion: How Corporations & Governments Addicted the World to Oil & Derailed the Alternatives. unabr. ed. Edwin Black. Read by Stephen Hoye. (Running Time: 15 hrs. 30 mins. 0 sec.). (ENG.). 2006. audio compact disk 37.99 (978-1-4001-0324-9(X)); audio compact disk 24.99 (978-1-4001-5324-4(7)) Pub: Tantor Media. Dist(s): IngramPubServ

Internal Combustion: How Corporations & Governments Addicted the World to Oil & Subverted the Alternatives. unabr. ed. Edwin Black. Read by Stephen Hoye. (Running Time: 15 hrs. 30 mins. 0 sec.). (ENG.). 2006. audio compact disk 75.99 (978-1-4001-3324-6(6)) Pub: Tantor Media. Dist(s): IngramPubServ

Internal Control Structure: The Auditor's Responsibilities. Don Pallais. 2 cass. 1994. 119.00 incl. wkbk. (749726VC) Am Inst CPA.

This course thoroughly examines SAS No. 55, Consideration of the Internal Control Structure in a Financial Statement Audit, & SAS No. 60 Communication of Internal Control Structure Related Matters Noted in an Audit. SAS No. 55 decrees that you must understand the control structure when planning & performing an audit, & SAS No. 60 provides you with guidance in identifying & reporting internal control structure conditions. Other topics include: audit planning, minimum level of work required, documenting your work, how to test controls, designing substantive tests, & control weaknesses & how to report them.

Internal Marketing (for Dentists) Marsha Freeman. 2 cass. (Running Time: 90 min.). 1997. Set. (978-0-910167-39-0(7)) Freemn Assoc.

Explains how dentists can provide ideal internal marketing.

Internal Revenue Service vs. the Single Taxpayer. unabr. ed. Vivien Kellems. 1 cass. (Running Time: 57 min.). 12.95 (125) J Norton Pubs.

Internal Teacher/The Principles of Forgiveness. Marianne Williamson. Read by Marianne Williamson. 1 cass. (Running Time: 90 mins.). (Lectures on a Course in Miracles). 1999. 10.00 (978-1-56170-235-0(8), M738) Hay House.

International Baby: A Gentle African Journey. (Baby Tunes Ser.). (J). (ps). 1998. audio compact disk 10.98 (978-1-56826-889-7(0)) Masquerade.

International Baby Vol. 1: A Gentle African Journey. 1 cass., 1 CD. (Baby Tunes Ser.: Vol. 1). (J). 4.78 (KID 72954); audio compact disk 7.98 CD Jewel box. (KID 72954) NewSound.

An exotic journey through the sounds & music of equatorial Africa; across the savanna, along gentle rivers, into tropical jungles & through small villages where children sing.

International Building Code: Code & Commentary CD 2006. ICC. 2006. audio compact disk 150.75 (978-1-58001-491-5(7)) Int Code Counc.

International Building Code Commentary 2003. ICC. 2003. audio compact disk 148.00 (978-1-58001-214-0(0)) Int Code Counc.

International Building Code 2006 Single. ICC. 2006. audio compact disk 83.50 (978-1-58001-377-2(5)) Int Code Counc.

International Carols for Alto Saxophone. Costel Puscoiu. 1998. pap. bk. 19.95 (978-0-7866-3821-5(4), 97528BCD) Mel Bay.

International Carols for Dulcimer. Laurel Benedict. 1994. pap. bk. 16.95 (978-0-7866-1142-3(1), 95309P) Mel Bay.

International Carols for Pan Flute: Beginning-Intermediate Level. Costel Puscoiu. 1996. pap. bk. 19.95 (978-0-7866-2077-7(3), 95978BCD) Mel Bay.

International Carols for Recorder: Beginning-Intermediate Level. Costel Puscoiu. 1996. pap. bk. 19.95 (978-0-7866-2078-4(1), 95971BCD) Mel Bay.

International Christmas: Seasonal Stories & Poems from Canada & Around the World. Margaret Atwood et al. 2 CDs. (Running Time: 2 hrs. 30 mins.). (ENG.). 2004. audio compact disk 19.95 (978-0-86492-343-1(0)) Pub: BTC Audiobks CAN. Dist(s): U Toronto Pr

International Code Commentaries Complete Collection 2003. ICC. 2003. audio compact disk 455.50 (978-1-58001-289-8(2)) Int Code Counc.

International Codes: Spanish Edition CD-ROM 2003. ICC. 2006. audio compact disk 305.00 (978-1-58001-722-0(3)) Int Code Counc.

International Codes: Spanish Edition CD-ROM 2006. ICC. 2006. audio compact disk 310.00 (978-1-58001-723-7(1)) Int Code Counc.

International Codes the Designer Collection 2006 Single. ICC. 2006. audio compact disk 198.00 (978-1-58001-376-5(7)) Int Code Counc.

***International Criminal Tribunal for Rwanda: Basic Documents & Case Law 2007-2008 (CD-ROM)** International Criminal Tribunal for Rwanda Staff. (ENG & FRE.). 2009. audio compact disk 15.00 (978-92-1-056728-2(5)) Untd Nat Pubns.

International Crisis Updates: National Association of Evangelicals, 47th Annual Convention, Columbus, Ohio, March 7-9, 1989. Jerry Ballard. 1 cass. (Workshops Ser.: No. 35-Thursda). 1989. 4.25 ea. 1-8 tapes. Nat Assn Evan.

International Educational Services in Romania: A Strategic Reference 2007. Compiled by Icon Group International, Inc. Staff. 2007. ring bd. 195.00 (978-0-497-82396-2(9)) Icon Grp.

International Employee Benefits, 1990. Moderated by James P. Klein. 1 cass. 1990. 20.00 (T7-9300) PLI.

International Encyclopedia of Ergonomics & Human Factors. 2nd rev. ed. Waldemar Karwowski. 2006. audio compact disk 944.00 (978-0-8493-9244-3(6)) Pub: CRC Pr. Dist(s): Taylor and Fran

International Energy Conservation Code: Code & Commentary CD 2006. ICC. 2006. audio compact disk 38.25 (978-1-58001-498-4(4)) Int Code Counc.

International Existing Building Code: Code & Commentary CD 2006. ICC. 2006. audio compact disk 57.00 (978-1-58001-499-1(2)) Int Code Counc.

International Film Buyers Directory, Vol. 1. Hollywood Creative Directory Staff. 1999. pap. bk. 54.95 (978-1-878989-97-0(9)) Hollywood Creat Dir.

International Fire Code: Code & Commentary on CD 2006. ICC. 2006. audio compact disk 73.75 (978-1-58001-493-9(3)) Int Code Counc.

International Fire Code 2006 Single User. ICC. 2006. audio compact disk 68.00 (978-1-58001-380-2(5)) Int Code Counc.

International Folk Songs for Solo Singers: Medium Low Voice. Ed. by Jay Althouse. (For Solo Singers Ser.). (ENG.). 1997. audio compact disk 11.95 (978-0-7390-2011-1(0)) Alfred Pub.

International Fuel Gas Code: Code & Commentary CD 2006. ICC. 2006. audio compact disk 62.50 (978-1-58001-496-0(8)) Int Code Counc.

International HDTV Production: Track One. 2 cass. 1990. 17.00 set. Recorded Res.

International Herald Tribune: On the Record. Ethel Tiersky & Robert Hughes. 1999. pap. bk. 39.95 (978-0-8442-0311-9(4), 03114) M-H Contemporary.

International Herald Tribune Set: Morning Edition - Mastering Reading & Language Skills with the Newspaper. Ethel Tiersky & Robert Hughes. 3 cass. (Running Time: 3 hrs.). 1996. pap. bk. 39.95 (978-0-8442-0580-9(X), 0580X) M-H Contemporary.

Collection of 30 authentic articles helps students develop English skills through a current, real-life medium.

International Library Topics: Commonwealth Library Association (COMLA) Interview with K. C. Harrison & Mary Casteleyn. 50.00 St Mut.

International Library Topics: International Federation of Library Associations (IFLA) Interview with K. C. Harrison & Mary Casteleyn. 50.00 St Mut.

Interviews between K.C. Harrison & Mary Casteleyn.

International Library Topics: Libraries in Scandinavia. Interview with K. C. Harrison & Mary Casteleyn. 80.00 St Mut.

International Library Topics: The Library Association. Interview with K. C. Harrison & Mary Casteleyn. 80.00 St Mut.

International Library Topics: Westminster City Libraries. Interview with K. C. Harrison & Mary Casteleyn. 50.00 St Mut.

International Marketing - Creativity & Innovation see Marketing Internacional - Creatividad E Innovacion

International Marketing - Creativity & Innovation. Basilio Balli Morales. Read by Basilio Balli Morales. (Running Time: 1 hr.). 2003. 14.95 (978-1-60083-304-5(7), Audiofy Corp) Iofy Corp.

International Mechanical Code: Code & Commentary CD 2006. ICC. 2006. audio compact disk 62.50 (978-1-58001-494-6(1)) Int Code Counc.

***International Miracle Institute Correspondence Program Year 3: IMICP (94 Cd's & Manual with Tests)** Christian Harfouche. (ENG.). (C). 2006. ring bd. 399.00 (978-1-888966-21-3(1)) MEDIAGrp.

***International Miracle Institute Correspondence Program Year 4: IMICP (106 Cd's & Manual with Tests)** Christian Harfouche. (ENG.). (C). 2006. ring bd. 439.00 (978-1-888966-22-0(X)) MEDIAGrp.

International Narcotics Control Board Publications 2008: Report & Supplement, Narcotic Drugs, Psychotropic Substances, Precursors. United Nations. 2009. audio compact disk 35.00 (978-92-1-148235-5(6)) Untd Nat Pubns.

International Peace Academy. Indar J. Rikhye. 1 cass. 9.00 (A0107-86) Sound Photosyn.

On side B, Ruth Young, founder of the Peace Academy, speaks.

International Plumbing Code: Code & Commentary CD 2006. ICC. 2006. audio compact disk 62.50 (978-1-58001-495-3(X)) Int Code Counc.

International Politics with Power Web. 8th ed. John T. Rourke. 2000. pap. bk. 51.88 (978-0-07-246104-6(7), Dshkn McG-Hill) McGrw-H Hghr Educ.

International Relations Panel Discussion: A Worldwide Perspective of Carcinoma of the Stomach. 2 cass. (General Sessions Ser.: C85-SP4). 15.00 (8546) Am Coll Surgeons.

International Residential Code: Code & Commentary on CD 2006. ICC. 2006. audio compact disk 150.75 (978-1-58001-492-2(5)) Int Code Counc.

International Residential Code 2006 Single User. ICC. 2006. audio compact disk 64.00 (978-1-58001-379-6(1)) Int Code Counc.

International Surgical Education: Panel Discussion Sponsored by the Committee on Surgical Education in Medical Schools. Moderated by Glenn W. Geelhoed. 2 cass. (Spring Sessions Ser.: SP-5). 1986. 19.00 (8676) Am Coll Surgeons.

International Symposia on Experimental Methods for Microgravity Materials Research. 1 cd. audio compact disk 99.00 (4038CD) TMS.

International Trust & Estate Planning. 9 cass. (Running Time: 12 hrs.). 1998. 345.00 Set; incl. study guide 643p. (MB45) Am Law Inst.

New advanced course deals with estate planning both for the foreign client with U.S. connections, which may include family members or active or passive investments, & for the U.S. client with foreign connections.

International Trust & Estate Planning. 1 cass. (Running Time: 12 hrs.). 1999. 345.00 Incl. study guide. (AE26) Am Law Inst.

International Who's Who. 2nd rev. ed. Ingrid Monson. 2000. cd-rom 580.00 (978-1-85743-083-7(2)) Pub: Routledge. Dist(s): Taylor and Fran

Internet: Systems & Applications. John Marshall Baker. 2006. audio compact disk 43.95 (978-0-7638-2259-0(0)) Paradigm MN.

***Internet Bullies.** Cerebellum Academic Team. (Running Time: 14 mins.). (Lesson Booster Ser.). 2008. cd-rom 79.95 (978-1-59443-695-6(9)) Cerebellum.

Internet Explained Short & Sweet. unabr. ed. Julian Padowicz. Read by Julian Padowicz. 1 cass. (Running Time: 1 hr. 07 min.). 1995. 12.95 (978-1-881288-10-7(2), BFI AudioBooks) BusnFilm Intl.

Explains what Internet is all about for people not necessarily planning to go "on line".

Internet Explorer 7 Classroom-to-Go. unabr. ed. William Stanek. Read by Ron Knowles. (YA). 2008. 34.99 (978-1-60514-587-7(4)) Find a World.

Internet Explorer 7 Classroom-to-Go: Self-paced Instructional Training Course. abr. ed. William Stanek. Narrated by Ron Knowles. (Running Time: 1 hr. 32 mins.). (ENG.). 2007. 14.95 (978-1-57545-339-2(8), Classroom) Pub: Reagent Press. Dist(s): OverDrive Inc

Internet for Dummies. abr. ed. J. Berendt. 1 cass. 9.95 (69450) Books on Tape.

A simple, clear & fun guide that takes the horror out of meeting the Internet for the first time, & provides more tips if you know the basics. Fast & friendly learning.

Internet for Physicians. 2nd ed. Roger P. Smith & Margaret J. a. Edwards. 1999. pap. bk. 34.95 (978-0-387-98724-8(X)) Spri.

Internet for Practical Litigators: Your Guide to Effective Research & Investigation on the "Web" 3 cass. (Running Time: 3 hrs. 30 min.). 1997. 160.00 Set; incl. study guide 140p. (D256) Am Law Inst.

Discussion supplemental by actual Internet screen images provides information on how to use the Internet efficiently & effectively in legal & factual research. Explains legal & technical problems relating to the use of digitized information.

Internet Law Update. (Running Time: 6 hrs.). 1999. bk. 99.00 (ACS-2232); bk. 99.00 (ACS-2232) PA Bar Inst.

The Internet changing the face of world commerce & creating opportunities no lawyer can afford to overlook. Internet law is evolving as fast as the number of clients who conduct their business in this new medium. Designed for practitioners who want all of the latest developments.

Internet Market in Venezuela: A Strategic Reference 2006. Compiled by Icon Group International, Inc. Staff. 2007. ring bd. 195.00 (978-0-497-82469-3(8)) Icon Grp.

Internet Office Suite. 13 cass. 99.00 Set. (3300-C47) Natl Seminars.

In this comprehensive training pack, top experts explain step-by-step how to harness the power of the Internet in your organization. Get insider tips & techniques for finding tons of information & locating exactly what you need - fast!.

Internet Riches: The Simple Money-Making Secrets of Online Millionaires. unabr. ed. Scott Fox. Read by Scott Fox. 1 MP3-CD. (Running Time: 8 hrs.). 2008. 39.25 (978-1-4233-6389-7(2), 9781423363897, Brlnc Audio MP3 Lib); 39.25 (978-1-4233-6391-0(4), 9781423363910, BADLE); 24.95 (978-1-4233-6390-3(6), 9781423363903, BAD); 24.95 (978-1-4233-6388-0(4), 9781423363880, Brilliance MP3); audio compact disk 82.25 (978-1-4233-6387-3(6), 9781423363873, BriAudCD Unabrid); audio compact disk 29.95 (978-1-4233-6386-6(8), 9781423363866, Bril Audio CD Unabri) Brilliance Audio.

***Internet Safety 101: Educate, Equip, Empower.** Donna Rice Hughes. (Internet Safety 101 Ser.). (ENG.). 2010. pap. bk. 24.95 (978-0-578-04097-4(2)) Enough.

***Internet Safety 101 Workbook & Resource Guide.** Donna Rice Hughes. Told to Cris Clapp Logan. (Internet Safety 101 Ser.). (ENG.). 2010. pap. bk. 39.95 (978-0-578-04098-1(0)) Enough.

Internet Searches: Sales Skills Development Program on the Use of the Internet for Optimal Searching, with an Emphasis on Healthcare. Daniel Farb & Bruce Gordon. 2004. audio compact disk 74.95 (978-1-932634-45-7(2)) Pub: UnivofHealth. Dist(s): AtlasBooks

Internet Services in China: A Strategic Reference 2006. Compiled by Icon Group International, Inc. Staff. 2007. ring bd. 195.00 (978-0-497-35883-9(2)) Icon Grp.

Interpersonal Communication Skill. Debra Sutch. 2 cass. (Running Time: 3 hrs.). 1996. 15.95 (978-1-55977-488-6(6)) CareerTrack Pubns.

Interpersonal Communication Skills. Instructed by Debra Sutch. 4 cass. (Running Time: 4 hrs. 19 min.). 59.95 Set, incl. wkbk., 42p. (Q10178) CareerTrack Pubns.

Training to minimize conflict & build collaboration in today's team-oriented workplace. These tapes will show you how to: Express yourself clearly the first time - without overexplaining or repeating yourself; Be more influential in achieving team goals; Gain other people's attention & support, & make a good impression on everyone; & "Take the floor" comfortably in meetings.

Interpersonal Communication Skills: Dramatically Improve Your Ability to Build Winning Working Relationships with Everyone, Everyday. Fred Pryor. 6 cass. 59.95 Set incl. wkbk. (14490AR) Pryor Resources.
Learn to understand & deal with the four basic personality types while reducing the stress that difficult people bring. Work with everyone smoothly & productively. Handle criticism, complaints, & mistakes with ease. Send clearer messages, increase feedback, & understand non-verbal signals.

Interpersonal Relationships. 1 cass. (Running Time: 60 min.). 10.95 Psych Res Inst.
Plant the seeds of harmony toward relationships with others.

Interplanetary Jammin' A Kids-Eye View of the Solar System. Donna Amorosia. 1992. audio compact disk 35.00 (978-0-7935-2894-3(1)) H Leonard.

Interplay of Mind & Body Realities. Andrew Weil. 2 cass. (Running Time: 3 hrs.). 1982. 18.95 Dolphin Tapes.
A wide-ranging discussion of what we experience as reality in both mind and body.

Interpret the Rays. Mae R. Wilson-Ludlam. 1 cass. 8.95 (602) Am Fed Astrologers.
Focus them for spiritual life potential.

Interpret Your Rays Through the Planets. Mae R. Wilson-Ludlam. 1 cass. 8.95 (369) Am Fed Astrologers.
Past life & present linked, rays discussed.

Interpret Your Rays Using Astrology. Mae R. Wilson-Ludlam. 1 cass. 8.95 (370) Am Fed Astrologers.
Set up your soul chart, blend rays & planets.

***Interpretation of Dreams.** unabr. ed. Sigmund Freud. Read by Robert Whitfield. (Running Time: 19 hrs.). 2010. 44.95 (978-1-4417-4689-4(7)); audio compact disk 123.00 (978-1-4417-4686-3(2)) Blckstn Audio.

Interpretation of Dreams: The Complete & Definitive Text. unabr. ed. Sigmund Freud. Read by Robert Whitfield. 13 cass. (Running Time: 19 hrs.). 2001. 85.95 (978-0-7861-2080-2(0), 2841) Blckstn Audio.
Freud revealed his discoveries about why we dream, what we dream and what our dreams mean. In this volume, Freud further demonstrated that it is in the treatment of abnormal mental states that dream analysis is the most valuable. For dreams not only reveal to us the cryptic mechanisms of phobias, obsessions and delusions, they are also the most potent tools in healing them.

Interpretation of Infrared Spectra. 2nd ed. Instructed by Norman B. Colthup. 4 cass. (Running Time: 4 hrs.). 435.00 set, incl. manual, 152p. (1) Am Chemical.
Interprets infrared spectra of organic compounds.

Interpretation of Murder: A Novel. unabr. ed. Jed Rubenfeld. Narrated by Kirby Heyborne. 9 cass. (Running Time: 13 hrs.). 2006. 81.00 (978-1-4159-3140-0(2)); audio compact disk 81.60 (978-1-4159-3141-7(0)) Pub: Books on Tape. Dist(s): NetLibrary CO

Interpretation of NMR Spectra. Instructed by Leroy F. Johnson & Roy H. Bible. 8 cass. (Running Time: 5 hrs. 54 min.). 215.00 incl. 117pp. manual. (34) Am Chemical.
Provides an introduction to the theory & methodology of interpreting NMR spectra.

Interpretations in Physics, No. 1. Read by Werner Heisenberg & David Bohm. 1 cass. (Running Time: 56 min.). 14.95 (CBC1002) MMI Corp.
Discusses Human concepts behind scientific discoveries.

Interpretations in Physics, No. 2. Read by Leon Rosenfeld & David Bohm. 1 cass. (Running Time: 56 min.). 14.95 (CBC1003) MMI Corp.
Interpretations of quantum theory - lingering problems of matter, space & time.

Interpretations in Physics, No. 3. Read by Gerhard Herzberg. 1 cass. (Running Time: 55 min.). 14.95 (CBC1004) MMI Corp.
Discusses experiments in measurement. What is a thing? Discusses some gaps between the quantum theory & lab practice.

Interpretations in Physics, No. 4. Read by F. David Peat et al. 1 cass. (Running Time: 54 min.). 14.95 (CBC1005) MMI Corp.
Intuition & intellect in the creation of scientific theories. The interpretation of the quantum theory is the subject under discussion.

Interpreter of Maladies. abr. ed. Jhumpa Lahiri. 4 cass. (Running Time: 6 hrs.). 2000. 24.95 (978-1-55935-346-5(5)) Soundelux.

Interpreter of Maladies. unabr. ed. Jhumpa Lahiri. Read by Matilda Novak. (YA). 2006. 44.99 (978-1-59895-541-5(1)) Find a World.

Interpreter of Maladies. unabr. ed. Jhumpa Lahiri & Matilda Novak. Read by Matilda Novak. 5 CDs. (Running Time: 6 hrs.). (ENG.). 2005. audio compact disk 26.95 (978-1-56511-932-1(0), 1565119320) Pub: HighBridge. Dist(s): Workman Pub

Interpreter's Edge. 5 cass. (Running Time: 5 hrs.). 1999. pap. bk. 70.00 (EDGE) Sign Enhancers.
Improve your interpreting skills with 47 lessons in simultaneous interpreting, consecutive interpreting & memory lessons. Prepare for the legal setting with fascinating expert witness testimony, actual court proceedings & jury instructions.

Interpreter's RX: A Training Program for Spanish/English Medical Interpreting. Holly M. Mikkelson. Illus. by Jim Willis. 3 cass. (Running Time: 3 hrs.). (SPA & ENG.). (C). 1994. pap. bk. 69.95 (978-1-880594-11-7(0), ACE012) Pub: ACEBO. Dist(s): Continental Bk

Interpreter's Toolbelt: It's Just the Beginning. (ENG.). 2009. audio compact disk 15.00 (978-0-9840517-0-0(8)) Lanker Assocs.

Interpreting Asc-MC Arcs. Richard Nolle. 1 cass. 8.95 (257) Am Fed Astrologers.
ASC-MC arc as key to understanding natal & progressed charts.

Interpreting Aspects in a Right Brain Way. Barbara Nowak. 1 cass. 8.95 (263) Am Fed Astrologers.
Merge separate parts of the chart into unified whole.

Interpreting Dreams. Jack Deere. 1 cass. (Running Time: 90 mins.). (Hearing God's Voice Ser.: Vol. 4). 2000. 5.00 (JD04-004) Morning NC.
These messages are an outstanding collection that lay a solid & practical foundation for discerning God's voice.

***Interpreting Dreams & Visions for Your Soul.** Katie Souza. (ENG.). 2011. audio compact disk 25.00 (978-0-7684-0268-1(9)) Pub: Expected End. Dist(s): Destiny Image Pubs

***Interpreting Failures, Conserving Victories.** Featuring Ravi Zacharias. 1990. audio compact disk 9.00 (978-1-61256-043-4(1)) Ravi Zach.

Interpreting Great Legends of the World. Manly P. Hall. 5 cass. 40.00 Set. Philos Res.
Includes: "Mystery of the Iron Tower" (India); "The Gesar Khan" (Tibet); "The Court of the Sea King" (Japan); "The Queen of Heaven" (China); & "The Gold Legend" (Europe).

Interpreting Great Legends of the World. Narrated by Manly P. Hall. (Running Time: 150 min.). 1999. 40.00 (978-0-89314-151-6(8)) Philos Res.

Interpreting Kant's Political Philosophy. John Ridpath. 2 cass. (Running Time: 3 hrs.). 1991. 24.95 Set. (978-1-56114-129-6(1), CR06D) Second Renaissance.

Interpreting the Book of Revelation. unabr. ed. Duane S. Crowther. Read by Duane S. Crowther. 1 cass. (Running Time: 90 min.). 1992. 13.98 (978-0-88290-440-5(X), 1831) Horizon Utah.
This tape details Book of Revelation events extending from before the creation of the earth to the end of the earth's temporal existence. Accompanying the tape is a written documentation for all passages cited.

Interpreting the Prophetic. Steve Thompson. 1 cass. (Running Time: 90 mins.). (Prophetic Ministry Ser.: Vol. 3). 2000. 5.00 (ST01-003) Morning NC.
Now updated & expanded, this popular series combines insights from the Scriptures & personal experience to explain how we can more effectively hear from God & minister prophetically.

Interpreting the 20th Century I-IV: The Struggle over Democracy. Instructed by Pamela Radcliff. 24 CDs. (Running Time: 24 hrs.). 2004. bk. 129.95 (978-1-56585-886-2(7), 8090) Teaching Co.

Interpreting the 20th Century I-IV: The Struggle over Democracy, I-IV. Instructed by Pamela Radcliff. 24 cass. (Running Time: 24 hrs.). 2004. bk. 99.95 (978-1-56585-855-8(7), 8090) Teaching Co.

Interpreting Types & Shadows. Rick Joyner. 1 cass. (Running Time: 90 mins.). (Foundation Ser.: Vol. 4). 2000. 5.00 (RJ04-004) Morning NC.
Firmly establishing basic Christian principles, these messages also illuminate some of the primary enemies of truth, such as legalism & the control spirit.

Interracial Couples. Mark Paul Sebar. 2009. (978-1-930246-30-0(7), 1930246307) Sebar Pubng.

Interrogating Orientalism: Contextual Approaches & Pedagogical Practices. Diane Long Hoeveler & Jeffrey Cass. (C). 2006. audio compact disk 9.95 (978-0-8142-9109-2(0)) Pub: Ohio St U Pr. Dist(s): Chicago Distribution Ctr

Interrogation. Thomas H. Cook. Narrated by George Guidall. 6 cass. (Running Time: 8 hrs.). 48.00 (978-1-4025-1867-6(6)); audio compact disk 69.00 (978-1-4025-3501-7(5)) Recorded Bks.

Interrogation. Thomas H. Cook. Narrated by George Guidall. 5 cass. (Running Time: 8 hrs.). 2004. 24.99 (978-1-4025-0874-5(3), 01104) Recorded Bks.
Journeys into the darkest corners of the human heart to tell a mesmerizing story of crime and retribution, and the forces that push even good people to the breaking point. Two inner-city cops discover the body of 10-year-old Cathy Lake in a public park. A homeless suspect, Albert Jay Smalls, is arrested and interrogated. It's 1952, before Miranda and Gideon, a time when the police had more latitude in dealing with a suspect involved in a heinous crime. Officers Norman Cohen and Jack Pierce have only 24 hours to make Smalls talk before he's released.

Interruption in Your Bloodline. Voice by Eddie Long. (YA). 2006. audio compact disk 9.99 (978-1-58602-352-2(7)) E L Long.

Interruption of Everything. Terry McMillan. 2005. 72.00 (978-0-7366-9609-8(1)); audio compact disk 90.00 (978-0-7366-9610-4(5)) Books on Tape.

Intersecting Realities & Fictions of Virginia Woolf & Colette. Helen Southworth. 2004. audio compact disk 9.95 (978-0-8142-9041-5(8)) Pub: Ohio St U Pr. Dist(s): Chicago Distribution Ctr

Intersection of Joy & Money on the Radio. Mackey Miriam McNeill. 2005. audio compact disk 16.99 (978-0-9723563-1-2(2)) Prosp Pub KY.

Interspace Cassettes for Culture. 7 cass. (Running Time: 30 min. per cass.). 7.00 ea. pap. bk.; 45.00 Amethyst Remembrance, VHS or Beta video. Interspace Bks.
Immortality Poems, 30 or 60 mins.; Poetry Power - A Giant Lies Sleeping, 60 mins.; Heartbeats, 30 or 60 mins.; or Amethyst Remembrance (in memory of the New England poet of the last century - Emily Dickinson), 30 min.

Interspecies Telepathic Connection. rev. unabr. ed. Penelope Smith. 1 cass. (Running Time: 48 min.). 1994. 6.95 (978-0-936552-11-8(5)) AnimaMundi.
A spirited introduction to the subject of communication with animals.

Interspecies Telepathic Connection Tape Series. rev. ed. Penelope Smith. 6 cass. (Running Time: 6 hrs.). 1994. 59.95 set. (978-0-936552-12-5(3)) AnimaMundi.
This series covers the theory & practice of directly communicating mind-to-mind & heart-to-heart with other species.

Interstate Audio - Adventure Volume 1. Short Stories. 2 CDs. (Running Time: 2 hrs). Dramatization. 2006. audio compact disk 9.95 (978-1-60245-011-0(0)) GDL Multimedia.

Interstate Audio - Comedy Volume 1. Short Stories. 2 CDs. (Running Time: 2 hrs.). Dramatization. 2006. audio compact disk 9.95 (978-1-60245-009-7(9)) GDL Multimedia.

Interstate Audio - Comedy Volume 2. Scripts. 2 CDs. (Running Time: 2 hrs.). 2006. audio compact disk 9.95 (978-1-60245-010-3(2)) GDL Multimedia.

Interstate Audio - Mysteries Volume 1. Short Stories. 2 CDs. (Running Time: 2 hrs.). Dramatization. 2006. audio compact disk 9.95 (978-1-60245-012-7(9)) GDL Multimedia.

Interstate Audio - Sci Fi Volume 1. Short Stories. 2 CDs. (Running Time: 2 hrs.). Dramatization. 2006. audio compact disk 9.95 (978-1-60245-007-3(2)) GDL Multimedia.

Interstate Audio - Sci Fi Volume 2. Short Stories. 2 CDs. (Running Time: 2 hrs.). Dramatization. 2006. audio compact disk 9.95 (978-1-60245-008-0(0)) GDL Multimedia.

Interstate Audio - Westerns Volume 1. Short Stories. 2 CDs. (Running Time: 2 hrs.). Dramatization. 2006. audio compact disk 9.95 (978-1-60245-005-9(6)) GDL Multimedia.

Interstate Audio - Westerns Volume 2. Scripts. 2 CDs. (Running Time: 2 hrs.). 2006. audio compact disk 9.95 (978-1-60245-006-6(4)) GDL Multimedia.

Interstate Audio- Civil War Volume 1. Jules Verne & Jerry Robbins. (ENG.). 2008. audio compact disk 14.95 (978-1-60245-177-3(X)) GDL Multimedia.

Interstate Audio- Gettysburg. Jerry Robbins. (ENG.). 2008. audio compact disk 14.95 (978-1-60245-178-0(8)) GDL Multimedia.

Interstate Audio- Old Time Radio Volume 1 - Detectives. Scripts. 2 CDs. (Running Time: 2 hrs.). 2006. audio compact disk 9.95 (978-1-60245-016-5(1)) GDL Multimedia.

Interstate Audio- Old Time Radio Volume 2- Radio Classics. Scripts. 2 CDs. (Running Time: 2 hrs.). 2006. audio compact disk 9.95 (978-1-60245-017-2(X)) GDL Multimedia.

Interstate Audio- OTR Volume 3- Crime Fighting & the Blues. Nostalgia Ventures. (ENG.). 2008. audio compact disk 9.95 (978-1-60245-103-2(6)) GDL Multimedia.

Interstate Audio- Road to Revolution. Jerry Robbins. (ENG.). 2008. audio compact disk 9.95 (978-1-60245-173-5(7)) GDL Multimedia.

Interstate Audio- Shiloh. Jerry Robbins. (ENG.). 2008. audio compact disk 9.95 (978-1-60245-179-7(6)) GDL Multimedia.

Interstate Audio- Suspense Volume 1. Short Stories. 2 CDs. (Running Time: 2 hrs.). Dramatization. 2006. audio compact disk 9.95 (978-1-60245-013-4(7)) GDL Multimedia.

Interstate Audio- Thrillers Volume 1. Short Stories. 2 CDs. (Running Time: 2 hrs.). Dramatization. 2006. audio compact disk 9.95 (978-1-60245-014-1(5)) GDL Multimedia.

Interstate Audio- Thrillers Volume 2. Short Stories. 2 CDs. (Running Time: 2 hrs.). Dramatization. 2006. audio compact disk 9.95 (978-1-60245-015-8(3)) GDL Multimedia.

Interstate 5 North Heritage Tour: Seattle to Blaine. Text by Jens Lund. (ENG., 2004. spiral bd. 17.95 (978-1-891466-06-9(2)); spiral bd. 12.00 (978-1-891466-05-2(4)) NW Heritage.

Interstate 5 South Heritage Tour: Seattle to Vancouver, Washington. Interview. Text by Jens Lund. 2 CDs. (Running Time: 110 mins.). (Washington Heritage Tours Ser.: Vol. 5). (ENG., 2002. spiral bd. 17.95 (978-1-891466-04-5(6)); spiral bd. 12.00 (978-1-891466-03-8(8)) NW Heritage.

***Interstate 69: The Unfinished History of the Last Great American Highway.** unabr. ed. Matt Dellinger. (Running Time: 9 hrs. 0 mins.). 2010. 15.99 (978-1-4001-8792-8(3)); 24.99 (978-1-4001-6792-0(2)); audio compact disk 83.99 (978-1-4001-4792-2(1)); audio compact disk 34.99 (978-1-4001-1792-5(5)) Pub: Tantor Media. Dist(s): IngramPubServ

Interstate 90 East Heritage Tour: Seattle to Spokane. Willie Smyth. (ENG., 2007. spiral bd. 17.95 (978-1-891466-07-6(0)) NW Heritage.

Interstellar Pig. unabr. ed. William Sleator. 1 cass. (Running Time: 55 min.). (Young Adult Cliffhangers Ser.). (YA). (gr. 4-6). 1995. pap. bk. 15.98 (978-0-8072-1856-3(1), JRH128SP, Listening Lib) Random Audio Pubg.
While staying at the seashore, Barney befriends a woman & two men who move in next door. He realizes that they are searching for information about the captain who once lived in Barney's room & that they endanger the world with their game of Interstellar Pig.

Interstitial Nephritis. Read by Ralph A. DeFronzo. 1 cass. (Running Time: 9 min.). 1986. 12.00 (C8635) Amer Coll Phys.

Intervals: The Key to Big Ears! 1 cass. 19.95 Incl. summary sheet. (HAR-10) Duane Shinn.
An interval is the distance between any two notes. When you hear a melody, can you hear what intervals are being used? This tape will teach you when a singer is moving up a minor 6th, or down a perfect 4th. It will drill you on intervals from unisoms to octaves. Learn the difference between consonant & dissonant intervals, major, minor, & perfect intervals & how they invert.

Intervals: The Key to Perfect Intonation. Duane Shinn. 1 cass. 19.95 (HAR-10) Duane Shinn.
Presents drills on intervals from unisons to octaves (1 through 8) & discusses the difference between consonant & dissonant intervals, major, minor, & perfect intervals & how they invert.

***Intervention.** Terri Blackstock. (Running Time: 9 hrs. 8 mins. 0 sec.). (Intervention Ser.). (ENG.). 2009. 19.99 (978-0-310-28906-7(8)) Zondervan.

Intervention. Robin Cook. (Running Time: 11 hrs.). No. 9. (ENG.). (gr. 12 up). 2009. audio compact disk 39.95 (978-0-14-314457-1(X), PengAudBks) Penguin Grp USA.

Intervention. unabr. ed. Terri Blackstock. (Running Time: 9 hrs. 8 mins. 0 sec.). (Intervention Ser.). (ENG.). 2009. audio compact disk 19.99 (978-0-310-28905-0(X)) Zondervan.

Intervention Information Systems: Smoking Cessation. George R. Lesmes & Margo R. Hearst. (C). 1993. (978-1-882953-05-9(3)) Intervent Info.

Intervention Strategies for Sexual Abuse. Robert H. Rencken. 5 cass. bk. 109.00 Set. (74201); 79.00 Set. (74202); 55.00 exam. (74203) Am Coun Assn.
This program covers the dimensions & treatment of child sexual abuse & offers practical intervention strategies for counselors, social workers, & other caregivers in any professional setting.

Interventions Audio: Collaborative Planning for Students at Risk. 9. 2005. audio compact disk 75.00 (978-1-59909-001-6(5)) Pac North Pub.

Interventions Audio Second Edition: Evidence-Based Behavioral Strategies for Individual Students. Randy Sprick. 2008. audio compact disk (978-1-59909-018-4(X)) Pac North Pub.

Interview. Ole Nydahl. 1 cass. 9.00 (A0266-87) Sound Photosyn.
A personal look at the Danish born Tibetan Buddhist yogi.

Interview. Zeke the Sheik. 1 cass. (Roy Tuckman Interview Ser.). 9.00 (A0190-85) Sound Photosyn.

Interview: Are You from the Fourth Dimension? Rudolf V. B. Rucker. 1 cass. 9.00 (A0112-87) Sound Photosyn.
Dr. Rudolf von Bitter Rucker, Professor of Mathematics & Computer Science, is his official academic persona, but to Science Fiction fans he is one of the orginal cyberpunks. Brian taped. Some of Faustin's interview has appeared on Mondo 2000, No. 7.

Interview: Listening Comprehension for the High Intermediate & Advanced Students/Book & Cassette. Edwin T. Cornelius. (English As a Second Language Bk.). 1981. 37.99 (978-0-582-79782-6(9), 75036) Longman.

Interview: Mary Lee Settle. Interview. Interview with Mary Lee Settle & Kay Bonetti. 1 cass. (Running Time: 56 min.). 13.95 (978-1-55644-058-8(8), 2132) Am Audio Prose.
Interview focuses on "The Beulah Quintet," its history of research & composition, internal structure & intellectual surroundings.

Interview: On the Road Again. Stephen Gaskin. 1 cass. 9.00 (A0446-89) Sound Photosyn.
The two interviews take us back 20 years to the present. Who & what's down on the Farm, the trials & triumphs of community living. A lot of real wisdom, midwifery & general right living going on.

Interview: Stephen Gaskin Today. Stephen Gaskin. 2 cass. 18.00 set. (A0399-88) Sound Photosyn.

Interview & Science Fiction Poetry Readings. Bruce Boston. Read by Bruce Boston. Music by Alfred Rucker. 1 cass. 9.00 (A0017-87) Sound Photosyn.
Enjoyable listening with a good reader, reading his own material.

Interview at Her Home in Berkeley. Helen Palmer. 1 cass. 9.00 (A0398-88) Sound Photosyn.
Casual, hospitable & informative, Helen discusses Enneagrams, & her work as a psychic.

Interview on KPFK. Allen Ginsberg. 1 cass. (Roy Tuckman Interview Ser.). 9.00 (A0196-85) Sound Photosyn.

Interview on Nixon & the Conservatives. unabr. ed. M. Stanton Evans. 1 cass. (Running Time: 40 min.). 12.95 (AFO176) J Norton Pubs.

Interview Power. 6 cass. (J). (gr. 10-12). 1986. 39.95 (978-0-913286-76-0(1), 1339, Lrn Inc) Oasis Audio.

Interview Tapes. Arthur Young. 5 cass. 45.00 set. (A0157-83) Sound Photosyn.
These excellent introductions to Arthur's theory & processes can also be purchased individually. Faustin interviews, Brian records.

Interview Tapes, Vol. 1: Introduction to the Reflexive Universe. Arthur Young. 1 cass. 9.00 (A0158-83) Sound Photosyn.

Interview Tapes, Vol. 2: Theory of the Reflexive Universe. Arthur Young. 1 cass. 9.00 (A0159-83) Sound Photosyn.

Interview Tapes, Vol. 3: The Geometry of Meaning. Arthur Young. 1 cass. 9.00 (A0160-83) Sound Photosyn.

Interview Tapes, Vol. 4: "Why Seven?" Arthur Young. 1 cass. 9.00 (A0161-83) Sound Photosyn.

Interview Tapes, Vol. 5: Shakespeare-Bacon Controversy. Arthur Young. 1 cass. 9.00 (A0162-83) Sound Photosyn.

Interview with a Lemming see My World & Welcome to It

Interview with a Lemming see World of James Thurber

Interview with a Lemming see Great American Short Stories

Interview with a Lemming see Fourteen American Masterpieces

Interview with Amanda Foulger. E. J. Gold & Amanda Foulger. 1 cass. (Running Time: 1 hr.). 9.98 (TP064) Union Label.
A radio interview in Los Angeles. Amanda Foulger interviews E. J. Gold.

Interview with Amy Hempel & Jo Sapp. Amy Hempel. 1 cass. (Running Time: 65 min.). 1992. 13.95 (978-1-55644-379-4(X), 12032) Am Audio Prose.
With just two published volumes, Hempel is revered by readers & other writers alike for her genuinely distinctive voice & fictional territory. Here she discusses several of her stories & her traumatic 20s, which she says served as "research" for many of her short fictions.

Interview with Ann Beattie & Kay Bonetti. Ann Beattie. 1 cass. (Running Time: 57 min.). 1987. 13.95 (978-1-55644-178-3(9), 7022) Am Audio Prose.
Beattie offers commentary on several short stories & her novels, plus excellent talk about a variety of related issues, including direct response to her critics.

Interview with Ayn Rand. Ayn Rand. 1 cass. (Running Time: 22 min.). 1992. 12.95 (978-1-56114-110-4(0), AR24C) Second Renaissance.

Interview with Chinua Achebe & Kay Bonetti. Chinua Achebe. 1 cass. (Running Time: 85 min.). 1988. 13.95 (978-1-55644-284-1(X), 8012) Am Audio Prose.
Achebe explains what is uniquely African, or at least non-Western, in his viewpoint regarding the role of the artist in the community & the function of art.

Interview with Clenora Hudson-Weems & Kay Bonetti. Clenora Hudson-Weems. Hosted by Kay Bonetti. 1 cass. (Running Time: 1 hr. 30 min.). 1995. 10.00 (978-1-55644-407-4(9), 407-9) Am Audio Prose.
Discussion with African-American scholar about her two books: Africana Womanism: Reclaiming Ourselves & Emmett Till: Sacrificial Lamb of the Civil Rights Movement.

Interview with David Bradley & Kay Bonetti. David Bradley. 1 cass. (Running Time: 80 min.). 1992. 13.95 (978-1-55644-373-2(0), 12012) Am Audio Prose.
Bradley discusses The Chaneysville Incident & South Street, his first novel. Also talks about his family, growing up a preacher's kid, & the limiting aspects of race on how he is perceived both as an individual & as a writer.

Interview with Elizabeth Spencer & Kay Bonetti. Elizabeth Spencer. 1 cass. (Running Time: 76 min.). 1993. 13.95 (978-1-55644-389-3(7), 13032) Am Audio Prose.

Interview with Gladys Swan & Kay Bonetti. Gladys Swan. 1 cass. (Running Time: 60 min.). 1993. 13.95 (978-1-55644-392-3(7), 13042) Am Audio Prose.

Interview with Granger Westberg. abr. ed. 1 cass. (Care Cassettes Ser.: Vol. 14, No. 8). 1987. 10.80 Assn Prof Chaplains.

Interview with Jamaica Kincaid & Kay Bonetti. Jamaica Kincaid. 1 cass. (Running Time: 59 min.). 1991. 13.95 (978-1-55644-363-3(3), 11022) Am Audio Prose.
Kincaid tells her story of "lighting out" for America at the age of 17 from the tiny West Indian island of Antigua, & speaks of the process of writing her way through the influences of her British Colonial education to find her own writing voice.

Interview with James Crumley & Kay Bonetti. James Crumley. 1 cass. (Running Time: 62 min.). 1992. 13.95 (978-1-55644-376-3(5), 12022) Am Audio Prose.
Crumley discusses the context of his work, the development of his writing voice, & the evolution of his career, including his screen-writing. He also talks about many of the things he is interested in, including the American West, the current social & political climate, even his life long love of cars.

Interview with Janet Lewis & Kay Bonetti. Janet Lewis. 1 cass. (Running Time: 57 min.). 1988. 13.95 (978-1-55644-302-2(1), 8072) Am Audio Prose.
Lewis discusses her early interest in Native American culture, the composition & themes of her three famous historical novels, her work as librettist, historian & poet, & her long & happy life.

Interview with Jessica Hagedorn. Interview with Kay Bonetti. 1 cass. (Running Time: 58 min.). 1995. 13.95 (978-1-55644-405-0(2), 14032); 25.00 reading & interview set. (978-1-55644-406-7(0), 14033) Am Audio Prose.
Readings include Prose & Poetry from the works, Dogeaters & Danger & Beauty.

Interview with Jim Wilkinson. John C. Nash. 2002. 19.95 (978-0-89871-512-5(1)) Soc Indus-Appl Math.

Interview with John Hersey & Kay Bonetti. John Hersey. 1 cass. (Running Time: 82 min.). 1988. 13.95 (978-1-55644-293-3(9), 8052) Am Audio Prose.
A rare interview with the late highly distinguished author & journalist.

Interview with Josephine Humphreys & Kay Bonetti. Josephine Humphreys. 1 cass. (Running Time: 57 min.). 1988. 13.95 (978-1-55644-296-4(3), 8062) Am Audio Prose.
In this intimate conversation, Humphreys discusses her interest in language, humor, the effects of emotion on human actions, & the essential mystery of the writer's craft.

Interview with Kenneth Thurston Hurst. Contrib. by Paul Brunton. 1 cass. (Running Time: 1 hr.). 9.95 Larson Pubns.
A personal interview with Paul Brunton's son about PB. Hightlight a 10-minute message about meditation spoken in Paul Brunton's voice to members of Wisdom's Goldenrod study center.

Interview with Larry Brown & Kay Bonetti: Author Interview Ser. Larry Brown. 1 cass. (Running Time: 1 hr.). 1995. 13.95 (978-1-55644-412-8(5), 15022); 19.95 set. (978-1-55644-413-5(3), 15023) Am Audio Prose.
Lively & informative discussion with leading southern writer, conducted by Kay Bonetti.

Interview with Larry Heinemann & Kay Bonetti. Larry Heinemann. 1 cass. (Running Time: 78 min.). 1988. 13.95 (978-1-55644-299-5(8), 8042) Am Audio Prose.
Winner of the 1987 National Book Award talks about the award's impact on his life & career, & discusses his aesthetic stance.

Interview with Leonard Peikoff. Interview with Leonard Peikoff. 1 cass. (Running Time: 35 min.). 14.95 (LP53C) Second Renaissance.
Addresses the basics of Objectivism, the cultural barriers it faces, & its future place in history.

Interview with Lillian Hellman. unabr. ed. Lillian Hellman. Read by Lillian Hellman. 1 cass. (Running Time: 46 min.). 1969. 12.95 (23059) J Norton Pubs.
The author discusses her plays & other writings & reminisces.

Interview with Lynne Cheney, Author. Interview with Lynne Cheney & Leonard Peikoff. 1 cass. (Philosophy: Who Needs It? Ser.). 1998. 12.95 (LPXXC49) Second Renaissance.

Interview with Marc N. Weiss at Cornell, 1970 see Berrigan Raps

Interview with Margaret Walker & Kay Bonetti. Margaret Walker. 1 cass. (Running Time: 86 min.). 1991. 13.95 (978-1-55644-369-5(2), 11042) Am Audio Prose.
A frank & engaging conversation with vintage poet, novelist, essayist & biographer. Walker talks about the continuum of African American literature, her arduous work on Jubilee, her close working relationship with Richard Wright & her critical biography, as well as her legal tangles with the Wright Estate & with author Alex Haley.

Interview with Mario Vargas Llosa & Elsbieta Sklodowska. Mario Vargas Llosa. 1 cass. (Running Time: 87 min.). 1993. 13.95 (978-1-55644-395-4(1), 13052) Am Audio Prose.

Interview with Mark Harris & Kay Bonetti. Mark Harris. 1 cass. (Running Time: 86 min.). 1987. 13.95 (978-1-55644-181-3(9), 7032) Am Audio Prose.
Harris talks about his life & how he transmutes it into fiction, saying that all his narrators are in some way himself, disguised.

Interview with Michael Ondaatje & Len Scher. Michael Ondaatje. 1 cass. (Running Time: 58 min.). 1993. 13.95 (978-1-55644-386-2(2), 13022) Am Audio Prose.

Interview with Mona Simpson & Kay Bonetti. Mona Simpson. 1 cass. (Running Time: 44 min.). 1987. 13.95 (978-1-55644-196-7(7), 7072) Am Audio Prose.
Author discusses her response to every young writer's dream come true, publishing a first novel to critical acclaim & bestsellerdom as well.

Interview with Ntozake Shange & Kay Bonetti. Ntozake Shange & Kay Bonetti. 1 cass. 1989. 13.95 (978-1-55644-335-0(8), 9052) Am Audio Prose.

Interview with Paulette Jiles & Kay Bonetti. Paulette Jiles. 1 cass. (Running Time: 60 min.). 1993. 13.95 (978-1-55644-383-1(8), 13012) Am Audio Prose.

Interview with Peter Matthiessen & Kay Bonetti. Peter Matthiessen. 1 cass. (Running Time: 58 min.). 1987. 13.95 (978-1-55644-184-4(3), 7042) Am Audio Prose.
Matthiessen examines the tension in his writing life between the pull to fiction, which he calls his true calling, & the time-consuming demands of his non-fiction, a product of his social & environmental advocacy.

Interview with Philip Caputo & Kay Bonetti. Philip Caputo. 1 cass. (Running Time: 75 min.). 1988. 13.95 (978-1-55644-290-2(4), 8032) Am Audio Prose.
Caputo proves himself a vigorous, sensitive & articulate spokesperson for the writer's craft & vision. He addresses the war novel & the literature of Vietnam with thoughtfulness.

Interview with Richard Avedon. unabr. ed. Connie Goldman. 1 cass. 1985. 12.95 J Norton Pubs.
The photographer discusses his life & work.

Interview with Richard Currey & Kay Bonetti. Richard Currey. 1 cass. (Running Time: 60 min.). 1991. 13.95 (978-1-55644-360-2(9), 11012) Am Audio Prose.
Currey talks candidly about his thematic concerns, the process of transforming data from one's own experience into fiction, & poetry & music as elements in his work.

Interview with Roy at the Phoenix Bookstore in L. A. Riane Eisler. 1 cass. 9.00 (A0458-89) Sound Photosyn.

Interview with Roy at the Phoenix Bookstore in L.A. Riane Eisler. 1 cass. (Roy Tuckman Interview Ser.). 9.00 (A0458-89) Sound Photosyn.

Interview with Sheila Ballantyne & Kay Bonetti. Sheila Ballantyne. 1 cass. (Running Time: 57 min.). 1988. 13.95 (978-1-55644-287-2(4), 8022) Am Audio Prose.
This O. Henry Prize-winner discusses the relationship of fiction to autobiography, & talks about her emergence as an artist after many years of traditional wife & motherhood.

Interview with the Author of Storming Heaven. Jay Stevens. 1 cass. 9.00 (A0245-87) Sound Photosyn.
Faustin interviews & Brian records Jay's articulated odyssey.

Interview with the Filmmaker. Karil Daniels. 1 cass. 9.00 (A0244-87) Sound Photosyn.
Producer/Director of Water Baby: Experiences of Underwater Birthing.

***Interview with the Vampire.** unabr. ed. Anne Rice. (ENG.). 2011. audio compact disk 25.00 (978-0-307-91400-2(3), Random AudioBks) Pub: Random Audio Pubg. Dist(s): Random

Interview with the Vampire. unabr. ed. Anne Rice. Narrated by Frank Muller. 10 cass. (Running Time: 14 hrs. 45 mins.). (Vampire Chronicles: Bk. 1). 1994. 85.00 (978-0-7887-0065-1(0), 94321E7) Recorded Bks.
Provides an evocative & erotic introduction to the nightime world of the vampire. The vampire Louis becomes uncannily real as he shares his story with a terrified boy reporter.

Interview with the Vampire. unabr. ed. Anne Rice. Narrated by Frank Muller. 13 CDs. (Running Time: 14 hrs. 45 mins.). (Vampire Chronicles: Bk. 1). 1999. audio compact disk 114.00 (978-0-7887-3442-7(3), C1048E7) Recorded Bks.

Interview with Toni Morrison. Interview. Interview with Toni Morrison & Kay Bonetti. 1 cass. (Running Time: 1 hr. 18 min.). 1987. 13.95 (978-1-55644-080-9(4), 3112) Am Audio Prose.
Interview with one of America's finest writers covers her Midwestern roots in an integrated mill town & their influence on her choice of themes & subject matter; her search for a craft & voice which would adequately embody her vision & address a black audience; & a variety of issues surrounding the "black female writer question" including her reputation as "Superwoman".

Interview with Wallace Stegner & Kay Bonetti. Wallace Stegner. 1 cass. (Running Time: 74 min.). 1987. 13.95 (978-1-55644-199-8(1), 7082) Am Audio Prose.
This informative interview covers topics ranging from the origins of his characters & themes to a discussion of regionalism in American literature.

Interview with William Maxwell. Interview with William Maxwell & Kay Bonetti-Callison. 1 cass. (Running Time: 90 min.). 1996. 13.95 (978-1-55644-446-3(X)) Am Audio Prose.

Interviewed by Albert Hofmann. unabr. ed. Albert Hofmann. 1 cass. (Running Time: 1 hr. 25 min.). 1984. 11.00 (03502) Big Sur Tapes.

Interviewed by Allen Watts. unabr. ed. Alan Watts. 1 cass. (Running Time: 1 hr. 10 min.). 1964. 11.00 (02503) Big Sur Tapes.
An informal conversation on Watts' houseboat in Sausalito discussing many topics including concentration, technology, nature, & materialism, with Watts drawing in many rather provocative perspectives.

Interviewed by Mike Hodel. Roy Tuckman. 1 cass. (Roy Tuckman Interview Ser.). 9.00 (A0183-87) Sound Photosyn.

Interviewed by Wilson Van Dusen. Wilson Van Dusen. 2 cass. (Running Time: 2 hrs.). 1963. 18.00 set. (05401) Big Sur Tapes.

Interviewing, Hiring & Firing. abr. ed. Keith Shannon. Read by Keith Shannon. 2 cass. (Running Time: 2 hrs. 5 min.). 1998. 19.95 Set; incl. wkbk. (978-1-57294-113-7(8), 11-0223) SkillPath Pubns.
Compilation of the must-have tools required by today's changing, challenging workplace.

Interviewing Strategies: Moving from Survival to Success. Janet Hauter. 3 cass. (Running Time: 2 hrs. 30 min.). 25.00 Set. (5010) Natl Inst Child Mgmt.
Focuses on the cost of turnover & implications for staff stability & cohesion; a clear step-by-step process of defining the best candidate for a position; what can & cannot be said in an interview; & aligning the candidate to the center's culture, values & skill sets.

Interviewing the Client. James McElhaney et al. 1 cass. (Running Time: 54 min.). (Training the Advocate: The Pretrial Stage Ser.). 1985. 20.00 (FAPTA01) Natl Inst Trial Ad.

Interviewing Your Daughter's Date: 8 Steps to No Regrets. abr. ed. Dennis Rainey. Read by Dennis Rainey. (Running Time: 4740 sec.). 2007. audio compact disk 14.99 (978-1-60200-046-9(8)) FamilyLife.

Interviews - Artists: Recordings from Cv/Visual Arts Research Archive 1988-96. 2007. audio compact disk 40.00 (978-1-901161-74-8(9)) Cv Pubns GBR.

Interviews in French (Femmes et Metiers), Series I Complete Set. unabr. ed. Judith Frommer & Margaret C. Weitz. 4 cass. (Running Time: 45 min. per cass.). (YA). (gr. 10 up). ring bd. 41.95 (978-0-88432-146-0(0), AFF400) J Norton Pubs.
Features intermediate level taped conversations with 3 contemporary French women: J. Benoite, Elisabeth Hoche & Dominique Dupuis. Each program includes a listener's guide & vocabulary list.

Interviews in French (Femmes et Metiers), Series II Complete Set. unabr. ed. 3 cass. (Running Time: 3 hrs.). (YA). (gr. 10-12). 1994. ring bd. 41.95 (978-0-88432-255-9(6), AFF405) J Norton Pubs.
Advanced-level conversations with six contemporary French women: Danielle Delfour, Corinne Monod & Anne-Marie Bailly. Each program includes a listener's guide & vocabulary list.

Interviews in French (Femmes et Metiers) Anne-Marie Bailly, Nurse. unabr. ed. 1 cass. (Running Time: 45 mins.). (Series II). pap. bk. 14.95 (AFF408) J Norton Pubs.
Conversation providing interesting insights into various aspects of French life & culture as well as perspectives on the experience & attitude of the French woman professional. Includes vocabulary list.

Interviews in French (Femmes et Metiers) Corinne Monod, Secretary. unabr. ed. 1 cass. (Running Time: 45 mins.). (Series II). pap. bk. 14.95 (AFF407) J Norton Pubs.

Interviews in French (Femmes et Metiers) Danielle Delfour, Dentist. unabr. ed. 1 cass. (Running Time: 45 mins.). (Series II). pap. bk. 14.95 (AFF406) J Norton Pubs.

Interviews in French (Femmes et Metiers) Dominique Dupuis, Executive. unabr. ed. 1 cass. (Running Time: 45 mins.). (Series I). pap. bk. 14.95 (AFF403) J Norton Pubs.

Interviews in French (Femmes et Metiers) Elisabeth Hoche, Engineer. unabr. ed. 1 cass. (Running Time: 45 mins.). (Series I). pap. bk. 14.95 (AFF402) J Norton Pubs.

Interviews in French (Femmes et Metiers) J. Benoite, Politician. unabr. ed. 1 cass. (Running Time: 45 mins.). (Series I). pap. bk. 14.95 (AFF401) J Norton Pubs.

Interviews with Impact: Proven Techniques for Minimizing the Risks & Maximizing the Rewards of Media Interviews. unabr. ed. 1 cass. (Running Time: 45 min.). (Meet the Media with Your Agenda Ser.: Vol. 2). 1998. 12.00 (978-1-893039-02-5(1), Speechmasters) Integratd Commns Inc.
Get your messages, stated your way, into the news with this insiders approach to interviews. From the reporter's call, to the preparation, to the interview, this will help you master every aspect of interviews.

Interviews with the Frazzled Entrepreneur. Hosted by H. Les Brown. (ENG.). 2009. audio compact disk 14.95 (978-0-9798668-3-8(9)) Life Pilot.

***InterWorld.** unabr. ed. Neil Gaiman. Read by Christopher Evan Welch. 2007. (978-0-06-147584-9(X)); (978-0-06-147583-2(1)) HarperCollins Pubs.

InterWorld. unabr. ed. Neil Gaiman & Michael Reaves. Read by Christopher Evan Welch. (J). 2008. 39.99 (978-1-60514-973-8(X)) Find a World.

InterWorld. unabr. ed. Neil Gaiman & Michael Reaves. Read by Christopher Evan Welch. (Running Time: 19800 sec.). (J). (gr. 5-9). 2007. audio compact disk 19.95 (978-0-06-125460-4(6), HarperChildAud) HarperCollins Pubs.

Intimacy. Clayton Barbeau. 4 cass. (Running Time: 3 hrs.). 34.95 (9212) Franciscan Comns.
Explores some of the common cultural expectations & attitudes towards intimacy including some of the structures in society that make intimacy difficult.

Intimacy. Jack Deere. 1 cass. (Running Time: 90 mins.). (Intimacy with God & the End-Time Church Ser.: Vol. 6). 2000. 5.00 (JD09-006) Morning NC.
Oneness with the Father is essential for every believer in these last days & the teaching in this six-tape series will impart a heartfelt hunger for intimate fellowship with Him.

Intimacy. Shad Helmstetter. 1 cass. (Self-Talk Cassettes Ser.). 10.95 (978-0-937065-32-7(3)) Grindle Pr.

Intimacy: My Journal. Poems. Paul Sybert. 1 CD. (Running Time: 30 mins). 2005. audio compact disk 15.00 (978-0-9767842-0-3(3)) Paul Syb.

Intimacy & Personal Relationships. 1 cass. (Explore, Strengthen & Renew: Healthy Relationships Ser.). 8.95 (1523G) Hazelden.

Intimacy & Relationships. Eldon Taylor. 1 cass. (Running Time: 62 min.). (Inner Talk Ser.). 16.95 (978-1-55978-068-1(1), 5329A) Progress Aware Res.
Soundtrack - Tropical Lagoon with underlying subliminal affirmations.

Intimacy & Relationships: Babbling Brook. Eldon Taylor. 1 cass. 16.95 (978-1-55978-543-3(8), 5329F) Progress Aware Res.

Intimacy & Relationships: Easy. Eldon Taylor. Read by Eldon Taylor. Ed. by Leslie Brice. 1 cass. (Running Time: 1 hr.). 1992. 16.95 (978-1-56705-113-1(8)) Gateways Inst.
Self improvement.

Intimacy & Relationships: Harmonies. Eldon Taylor. Read by Eldon Taylor. Ed. by Leslie Brice. 1 cass. (Running Time: 1 hr.). 1992. 16.95 (978-1-56705-114-8(6)) Gateways Inst.

Intimacy & Relationships: Music Theme. Eldon Taylor. 1 cass. 16.95 (978-1-55978-070-4(3), 5329C) Progress Aware Res.

Intimacy & Relationships: Ocean. Eldon Taylor. Read by Eldon Taylor. Ed. by Leslie Brice. 1 cass. (Running Time: 1 hr.). 1992. 16.95 (978-1-56705-115-5(4)) Gateways Inst.

Intimacy & Relationships: Stream. Eldon Taylor. Read by Eldon Taylor. Ed. by Leslie Brice. 1 cass. (Running Time: 1 hr.). 1992. 16.95 (978-1-56705-326-5(2)) Gateways Inst.

Intimacy in Marriage: 1 Peter 3:1-9, 732. Ed Young. 1989. 4.95 (978-0-7417-1732-0(8), 732) Win Walk.

Intimacy of Conflict. Sam Keen & Ofer Zur. 1 cass. 9.00 (A0426-89) Sound Photosyn.
You & the significant other have to be tight to fight is the concept Sam & Ofer are arguing about...so put up yer dukes, partner.

Intimacy with God: Daniel 9:1-19. Ed Young. 1995. 4.95 (978-0-7417-2077-1(9), 1078) Win Walk.

Intimacy with God & the End-Time Church Series. Jack Deere. 6 cass. (Running Time: 9 hrs.). 2000. 30.00 (JD09-000) Morning NC.
Oneness with the Father is essential for every believer in these last days & the teaching in this six-tape series will impart a heartfelt hunger for intimate fellowship with Him.

Intimacy with the Almighty see Intimidad con el Todopoderoso

Intimacy with the Almighty. 2004. 14.00 (978-1-57972-594-5(5)); audio compact disk 14.00 (978-1-57972-595-2(3)) Insight Living.

Intimacy with the Almighty: Four Spiritual Disciplines for Cultivating Closeness with God. Charles R. Swindoll. 1 cass. (Running Time: 1 hr.). 1997. 10.95 (978-1-57972-014-8(5)); audio compact disk 16.95 (978-1-57972-013-1(7)) Insight Living.
Offers all new insights to guide people on a journey of intimacy with God.

Intimacy with the Almighty Series: Four Spiritual Disciplines for Cultivating Closeness with God. Charles R. Swindoll. 2 cass. (Running Time: 5 hrs.). 1996. 11.95 (978-1-57972-034-6(X)) Insight Living.
Bible study on spiritual disciplines to grow closer to God.

Intimacy/Reborn in Spirit. Marianne Williamson. Read by Marianne Williamson. 1 cass. (Running Time: 90 mins.). (Lectures on a Course in Miracles). 1999. 10.00 (978-1-56170-236-7(6), M739) Hay House.

Intimate Encounters Audio Series. 2000. (978-1-893307-21-6(2)) Intimacy Pr.

Intimate Issues: 21 Questions Christian Women Ask about Sex. Linda Dillow & Lorraine Pintus. (ENG.). 2010. 26.99 (978-1-934384-27-5(5)) Pub: Treasure Pub. Dist(s): STL Dist NA

Intimate Kill. unabr. ed. Margaret Yorke. Read by Trevor Nichols. 6 cass. (Running Time: 9 hrs.). 2001. 54.95 (978-0-7540-0587-2(9), CAB2010) Pub: Chivers Audio Bks GBR. Dist(s): AudioGO
After serving ten years of a life sentence for murder, Stephen Dawes was released to start a new life. Stephen knew that he could not let the past bury itself, for he knew he had not killed his wife Marcia, so he set out to reconstruct her last hours.

Intimate Letters. unabr. ed. Bel Mooney. Read by Diana Quick. 8 cass. (Running Time: 12 hrs.). 1998. 69.95 (978-0-7540-0206-2(3), CAB 1629) AudioGO.
Rosa's husband Simon, died a few days after forgetting their anniversary. While learning to use his computer, she discovers intimate letters to an anonymous mistress. Rosa decides to discover the identity of this mysterious person, & have revenge on her dead husband.

***Intimate Lives of the Founding Fathers.** unabr. ed. Thomas Fleming. (Running Time: 16 hrs. 30 mins.). 2010. 44.95 (978-1-4417-5657-2(4)); 89.95 (978-1-4417-5653-4(1)); audio compact disk 34.95 (978-1-4417-5656-5(6)); audio compact disk 118.00 (978-1-4417-5654-1(X)) Blckstn Audio.

Intimate Marriage: The Keys to Building a Closer, Deeper Relationship. Jimmy Evans. 1996. 5.00 (978-0-00-519066-1(5)) Majestic Mda.

***Intimate Moments with the Savior: Learning to Love.** Zondervan. (Running Time: 12 hrs. 38 mins. 8 sec.). (Moments with the Savior Ser.). (ENG.). 2010. 14.99 (978-0-310-86435-6(6)) Zondervan.

Intimate Portrait: Women with Soul. Contrib. by Rhino Records Staff. (Running Time: 1 hr. 3 mins.). 1999. audio compact disk 11.98 (978-0-7379-0085-9(7)) Rhino Enter.

Intimate Touch of Prayer. 2006. audio compact disk 12.95 (978-1-59038-675-0(2)) Deseret Bk.

Intimates Through Time: Edgar Cayce's Mysteries of Reincarnation. unabr. collector's ed. Jess Stearn. Read by John MacDonald. 8 cass. (Running Time: 12 hrs.). 1994. 64.00 (978-0-7366-2879-2(7), 3582) Books on Tape.
Reincarnation through seven successive lives. Based on the psychic readings of Edgar Cayce.

Intimations of Hergalya: Coming Ashore to a Larger Earth. Kieth Thompson. 1 cass. (AA & A Symposium Ser.). 9.00 (A0259-87) Sound Photosyn.
The final, often humorous, summation at the AA&A Symposium.

Intimations of Immortality. Kenneth Ring. 2 cass. 1993. 18.00 set. (OC334-71) Sound Horizons AV.

***Intimidad con el Todopoderoso.** Charles R. Swindoll.Tr. of Intimacy with the Almighty. 2010. audio compact disk 12.00 (978-1-57972-898-4(7)) Insight Living.

Intimo Padre. Read by Ladoración. (SPA.). 2008. audio compact disk 14.99 (978-0-8297-6110-8(1)) Pub: Vida Pubs. Dist(s): Zondervan

Intitled Walter Mosley, Vol. 2. abr. ed. Walter Mosley. 4 cass. (Running Time: 6 hrs.). 2002. 25.98 (978-1-58621-281-0(8)) Hachet Audio.

Into His Presence. 1999. 8.00 (978-0-7673-9843-5(2)); 11.98 (978-0-7673-9835-0(1)); 75.00 (978-0-7673-9790-2(8)); audio compact disk 12.00 (978-0-7673-9845-9(9)); audio compact disk 16.98 (978-0-7673-9813-8(0)); audio compact disk 85.00 (978-0-7673-9811-4(4)) LifeWay Christian.

Into His Presence: The Joy & Power of Holy Spirit Inspired Prayer. 4 cass. (Running Time: 4 hrs.). 2003. 20.00 (978-1-57399-170-4(8)) Mac Hammond.
In this series, you'll learn how to transform your prayer life from drudgery to delight by following the flow of the Holy Spirit.

Into His Presence: The Joy & Power of Holy Spirit Inspired Prayer, 1 of Prayer Series. Lynne Hammond. 4 CDs. 2006. audio compact disk 20.00 (978-1-57399-302-9(6)) Mac Hammond.

Into Intuition. Jack Boland. 1 cass. 8.00 (BW02) Master Mind.

Into Love & Out Again. Elinor Lipman. Read by Paula Parker. 5 CDs. 2004. audio compact disk 59.95 (978-0-7927-3147-4(6), SLD 290, Chivers Sound Lib) AudioGO.

Into Love & Out Again. unabr. ed. Elinor Lipman. Read by Paula Parker. 4 vols. (Running Time: 6 hrs.). 2000. bk. 39.95 (978-0-7927-2401-8(1), CSL 290, Chivers Sound Lib) AudioGO.
These wry & sassy tales illustrate the vulnerable heartbeat beneath the brash style of the eighties.

Into That Darkness Peering: Nightmarish Tales of the Macabre, Vol. 1. unabr. ed. Edgar Allan Poe. Narrated by Wayne June. 1 CD. (Running Time: 56). 2008. audio compact disk 14.95 (978-0-9778453-0-9(3)) AudioBkCase.

Into That Darkness Peering: Nightmarish Tales of the Macabre, Vol. 2. unabr. ed. Short Stories. Edgar Allan Poe. Narrated by Wayne June. 1 CD. (ENG.). 2008. audio compact disk 14.95 (978-0-9778453-1-6(1)) AudioBkCase.

***Into That Darkness Peering: Nightmarish Tales of the Macabre, Vol. 3.** Edgar Allan Poe. Narrated by Wayne June. 3. (ENG.). 2010. audio compact disk 14.99 (978-0-9778453-2-3(X)) AudioBkCase.

Into the Beautiful North. unabr. ed. Luis Alberto Urrea. Narrated by Susan Ericksen. 1 MP3-CD. (Running Time: 11 hrs. 30 mins. 0 sec.). (ENG.). 2009. 24.99 (978-1-4001-6206-2(8)); audio compact disk 69.99 (978-1-4001-4206-4(7)); audio compact disk 34.99 (978-1-4001-1206-7(0)) Pub: Tantor Media. Dist(s): IngramPubServ

Into the Bermuda Triangle: Pursuing the Truth Behind the World's Greatest Mystery. abr. ed. Gian J. Quasar. Read by Michael Prichard. (Running Time: 16200 sec.). 2007. audio compact disk 28.00 (978-1-933309-15-6(6)) Pub: A Media Intl. Dist(s): Natl Bk Netwk

Into the Black Hole. 2 cass. (Running Time: 1 hr. 30 mins.). (SmartReader Ser.). (J). 1999. pap. bk. & tchr. ed. 19.95 (978-0-7887-0279-2(3), 79319T3) Recorded Bks.
When a 13-year-old girl accompanies her parents on a space voyage to view a black hole, she has an exciting chance to learn the latest information about these cosmic mysteries.

Into the Blue. unabr. ed. Robert Goddard. Read by Frederick Davidson. 13 cass. (Running Time: 19 hrs 30 min.). 1995. 85.95 (978-0-7861-0651-6(4), 1563) Blckstn Audio.
As caretaker of the villa belonging to Alan Dysart, M.P., on the Greek Island of Rhodes, Harry Barnett had come to the last shabby stop in a life punctuated by failure. Yet lately he had been genuinely, innocently happy: buoyed by the friendship of a young woman, Heather Mallender. Then, on a cold & silent mountain path, Heather vanished without a trace. Suspected of her murder although no body was found, Harry remains convinced that she is alive - somewhere.

Into the Blue. unabr. ed. Robert Goddard. Read by Paul Shelley. 14 cass. (Running Time: 21 hrs.). 2000. 110.95 (978-0-7540-0524-7(0), CAB 1947) Pub: Chivers Audio Bks GBR. Dist(s): AudioGO
A middle-aged failure, leading a shabby existence, Harry Barnet, is reduced to caretaking a friend's villa on the island of Rhodes & working in a bar to earn his keep. Then a guest at the villa, a young woman he had instantly warmed up to disappears, on a mountain peak. Harry becomes obsessed by the mystery that has changed his life & begins to trace back the movements & encounters that led to the moment when she vanished into the blue.

Into the Blue. unabr. ed. Robert Goddard. Read by Paul Shelley. 14 CDs. (Running Time: 21 hrs.). 2000. audio compact disk 115.95 (978-0-7540-5388-0(1), CCD 079) Pub: Chivers Audio Bks GBR. Dist(s): AudioGO
Harry Bennett, a middle-aged failure, leading a shabby existence, is reduced to caretaking a friend's villa on the island of Rhodes & working in a bar to earn his keep. Then a guest at the villa, a young woman he had instantly warmed to, disappears on a mountain peak.

Into the Dark: An Echo Falls Mystery. unabr. ed. Peter Abrahams. Narrated by Julie Dretzin. 6 CDs. (Running Time: 7 hrs.). (YA). (gr. 5-8). 2008. audio compact disk 67.75 (978-1-4361-0634-4(6)); 56.75 (978-1-4361-0629-0(X)) Recorded Bks.
Edgar-nominated author Peter Abrahams' Echo Falls mysteries have been honored with an Agatha Award. Starring amateur sleuth Ingrid Levin-Hill, these tales are filled with thrills and suspense. Out snowshoeing, Ingrid finds a body buried in the drifts. Her discovery sets off a firestorm revealing long-hidden secrets that get her Grampy sent to jail.

Into the Deeper Pools. unabr. ed. Poems. Lawrence Ferlinghetti. Read by Lawrence Ferlinghetti. 1 cass. (Running Time: 58 min.). 1984. 12.95 (23650) J Norton Pubs.
Poems from 1955 through to his most recent volume.

Into the Fire. Jeffrey S. Savage. 3 cass. 2004. 7.48 (978-1-59156-043-2(8)); audio compact disk 7.48 (978-1-59156-044-9(6)) Covenant Comms.

Into the Fire. abr. ed. Suzanne Brockmann. Read by Patrick G. Lawlor & Renée Raudman. 5 CDs. (Running Time: 6 hrs.). (Troubleshooter Ser.: No. 13). 2008. audio compact disk 26.95 (978-1-4233-4263-2(1), 9781423342632, BACD) Brilliance Audio.

Into the Fire. abr. ed. Suzanne Brockmann. Read by Patrick G. Lawlor & Renée Raudman. (Running Time: 6 hrs.). (Troubleshooter Ser.: No. 13). 2009. audio compact disk 14.99 (978-1-4233-4264-9(X), 9781423342649, BCD Value Price) Brilliance Audio.

Into the Fire. abr. ed. Linda Davies. Read by Isla Blair. 2 cass. (Running Time: 3 hrs.). 1999. 16.85 Set. (978-0-00-105582-7(8)) Ulvrscrft Audio.
Helen Jencks is beautiful & confident & a brilliant trader at the top City bank. Now Helen has been implicated in a multi-million-dollar scam in London. Fast-paced about how Helen escapes to Peru & discovers the truth behind her father's disappearance, then returns triumphantly to outscam the insider dealers who had set her up for the fall.

Into the Fire. unabr. ed. Suzanne Brockmann. Read by Patrick G. Lawlor & Renée Raudman. 2 MP3-CDs. (Running Time: 19 hrs.). (Troubleshooter Ser.: No. 13). 2008. 29.95 (978-1-4233-4259-5(3), 9781423342595, Brilliance MP3); 44.25 (978-1-4233-4260-1(7), 9781423342601, Brinc Audio MP3 Lib) Brilliance Audio.

Into the Fire. unabr. ed. Suzanne Brockmann. Read by Renée Raudman & Patrick G. Lawlor. (Running Time: 19 hrs.). (Troubleshooter Ser.: No. 13). 2008. 44.25 (978-1-4233-4262-5(3), 9781423342625, BADLE) Brilliance Audio.

Into the Fire. unabr. ed. Suzanne Brockmann. Read by Patrick G. Lawlor & Renée Raudman. (Running Time: 19 hrs.). (Troubleshooter Ser.: No. 13). 2008. 29.95 (978-1-4233-4261-8(5), 9781423342618, BAD); audio compact disk 38.95 (978-1-4233-4257-1(7), 9781423342571, Bril Audio CD Unabri); audio compact disk 117.25 (978-1-4233-4258-8(5), 9781423342588, BriAudCD Unabrid) Brilliance Audio.

Into the Fire. unabr. ed. Alexander Fullerton. Read by Jacqueline King. 10 cass. (Running Time: 15 hrs.). 2001. 84.95 (21555) Pub: Soundings Ltd GBR. Dist(s): Ulverscroft US

Into the Fire. unabr. ed. Mary Pat Kanaley. Read by Kris Faulkner. 8 cass. (Running Time: 8 hrs. 6 min.). 2001. 49.95 (978-1-58116-156-4(5)) Books in Motion.
In the 1880's Kathryn Reichart flees an abusive life among the wealthy upper class in New York City. She heads West in order to establish a new identity and safe haven for herself and the child she carries. Mere chance lends a hand on the streets of frontier town Spokane Falls. Kathryn is accidentally knocked down in the street and then rescued by Chase Austin, a man hiding the dark secrets of his own past. Both find solace and redemption in a hesitant romance and wilderness life that defies the society of the day. Looming over their fate is Kathryn's tormenter, and husband, seeking her, his child, and revenge.

Into the Forest. unabr. ed. Jean Hegland. Narrated by Alyssa Bresnahan. 7 cass. (Running Time: 10 hrs. 15 mins.). 1998. 60.00 (978-0-7887-1989-9(0), 95376E7) Recorded Bks.
Sometime in the future, as America collapses in the chaos of war, pollution & bankruptcy, two sisters pool their resources to survive in the hills above San Francisco.

***Into the Gauntlet.** Margaret Peterson Haddix. Contrib. by Scholastic, Inc. Staff. (ENG.). 2010. audio compact disk 49.99 (978-0-545-22630-1(9)) Scholastic Inc.

***Into the Gauntlet, Bk. 10.** unabr. ed. Margaret Peterson Haddix. Contrib. by Scholastic, Inc. Staff. Narrated by David Pittu. (39 Clues Ser.: Bk. 10). (J). 2010. audio compact disk 19.99 (978-0-545-22629-5(5)) Scholastic Inc.

Into the Genius Zone. Deepak Chopra & Edward Strachar. 8 cass. (Running Time: 8 hrs.). 1996. cass. & video (978-1-55525-048-5(3), 18950PAV) Nightingale-Conant.
Maximize your inborn genius.

Into the Genius Zone. Edward Strachar. 1996. (978-0-9717185-4-8(7)) InGenius Inc.

Into the Harvest. Derek Prince. 1 cass. 5.95 (4380) Derek Prince.
The "latter rain" of the Holy Spirit is given to equip us for the brief "weeks of harvest" that will close this age. Then each of us must give an account of the "talents" committed to us.

Into the Heart of Breast Cancer Vol. 1: For Women Who Fear & for Women Who Have Breast Cancer. Terry Bienkowski. 2 cass. (Running Time: 2 hrs.). 1998. bk. 16.95 Set. (978-0-9666678-0-6(8)) One Heart Prod.
Includes Side A: Aspects & healing tools & women's breast cancer stories; Side B: A & B, guided imagery for fear of & healing breast cancer.

Into the Labyrinth, 3rd ed. Gerald W. Page. Featuring Thomas E. Fuller et al. 1 cass. (Running Time: 90 min.). Dramatization. 2002. 9.95 (978-0-929483-12-2(X)) Centauri Express Co.

Into the Land of the Unicorns. unabr. ed. Bruce Coville. Read by Full Cast Production Staff. 2 cass. (Running Time: 3 hrs.). (Unicorn Chronicles: Bk. 1). (J). (gr. 4-7). 1999. 23.00 (LL 0125, Chivers Child Audio) AudioGO.

Into the Land of the Unicorns. unabr. ed. Bruce Coville. Narrated by Bruce Coville. 4 CDs. (Running Time: 4 hrs.). (Unicorn Chronicles: Bk. 1). (J). (gr. 4-6). 2009. audio compact disk 38.00 (978-1-934180-83-9(1)) Full Cast Audio.

Into the Land of the Unicorns. unabr. ed. Bruce Coville. 2 cass. (Unicorn Chronicles: Bk. 1). (J). (gr. 4-7). 1999. 16.98 (FS9-43235) Highsmith.

Into the Land of the Unicorns. unabr. ed. Bruce Coville. Read by Words Take Wing Repertory Company Staff. 2 cass. (Running Time: 3 hrs. 19 mins.). (Unicorn Chronicles: Bk. 1). (J). (gr. 3-7). 1998. pap. bk. 29.00 (978-0-8072-7963-2(3), YA952SP, Listening Lib) Random Audio Pubg.
Follow young Cara on the adventure of a lifetime when she jumps off a church roof to escape a mysterious stranger & enters the world of the unicorns.

Into the Land of the Unicorns. unabr. ed. Bruce Coville. Read by Bruce Coville. Read by Words Take Wing Repertory Company Staff. 2 cass. (Running Time: 3 hrs. 19 mins.). (Unicorn Chronicles: Bk. 1). (J). (gr. 3-7). 1998. 23.00 (978-0-8072-7962-5(5), YA952CX, Listening Lib) Random Audio Pubg.

Into the Light. Keith Terry. 3 CDs. 2004. audio compact disk 14.95 (978-1-59156-403-4(4)) Covenant Comms.

Into the Light, Set. Keith C. Terry. 2 cass. 2004. 11.98 (978-1-55503-865-6(4), 07001258) Covenant Comms.
The captivating sequel of "Out of Darkness".

Into the Light: Mindfulness Meditation for Relaxation, Healing, & Staying Well. Anne Milligan. (ENG.). 2007. audio compact disk 18.95 (978-0-9773158-9-5(4)) Sing Rock.

Into the Light: 12 Stories On - Trusting God, Facing Fear & More! Focus on the Family & AIO Team Staff. (Running Time: 5 hrs.). (Adventures in Odyssey Ser.). (ENG.). (J). (gr. 1-7). 2007. audio compact disk 24.99 (978-1-58997-446-3(8), Tyndale Ent) Tyndale Hse.

***Into the Mirror.** abr. ed. Lawrence Schiller. Read by Sam Tsoutsouvas. (ENG.). 2006. (978-0-06-113532-3(1), Harper Audio); (978-0-06-113533-0(X), Harper Audio) HarperCollins Pubs.

Into the Mist. Patrick Carman. Read by Ron McLarty. (Running Time: 24960 sec.). (Land of Elyon Ser.: Bk. 4). (J). (gr. 4-7). 2007. audio compact disk 28.95 (978-0-545-02464-8(1)); audio compact disk 64.95 (978-0-545-02490-7(0)) Scholastic Inc.

Into the Mist. unabr. ed. Patrick Carman. Read by Ron McLarty. (Land of Elyon Ser.: Bk 4). (J). 2007. 49.99 (978-1-60252-758-4(X)) Find a World.

Into the Napping House. unabr. ed. Audrey Wood. Read by Carl Shaylen & Jennifer Shaylen. Ed. by Liz Van Doren. Illus. by Don Wood. 1 cass. (Running Time: 21 min.). (J). (ps-2). 1990. 8.00 (978-0-15-256712-5(7)) Harcourt CAN CAN.
Don & Audrey Wood's best-selling book is brought to life by experienced children's musicians Carl & Jennifer Shaylen. Side One of the tape is "The Sleepy Side" for nap or bedtime. It opens with a lovely, restful reading of The Napping House, followed by two peaceful lullabies. Side Two, "The Awake Side," begins with the new "Napping House Song," performed exclusively for this recording.

Into the Region of Awe: Mysticism in C. S. Lewis. unabr. ed. David C. Downing. Read by Simon Vance. (Running Time: 6 hrs. NaN mins.). 2008. 29.95 (978-1-4332-5773-5(4)); audio compact disk 44.95 (978-1-4332-5769-8(6)); audio compact disk 50.00 (978-1-4332-5770-4(X)) Blckstn Audio.

Into the Rising Sun. Patrick O'Donnell. Read by Jeff Riggenbach. (Running Time: 10 hrs.). 2002. 30.95 (978-1-59912-513-8(7)) Iofy Corp.

Into the Rising Sun. unabr. ed. Patrick K. O'Donnell. Read by Jeff Riggenbach. 8 CDs. (Running Time: 11 hrs. 30 mins.). 2002. audio compact disk 64.00 (978-0-7861-9537-4(1), 2951); audio compact disk 24.95 (978-0-7861-9215-1(1), 2951); 49.95 (978-0-7861-2201-1(3), 2951) Blckstn Audio.
Presents an unvarnished look at the war on the ground, a final gift from aging warriors who have already given so much.

Into the Rising Sun. unabr. ed. Patrick K. O'Donnell. Read by Jeff Riggenbach. 8 pieces. 2004. reel tape 35.95 (978-0-7861-2206-6(4)) Blckstn Audio.

Into the Rising Sun: In Their Own Words, World War II's Pacific Veterans Reveal the Heart of Combat. unabr. ed. Read by Jeff Riggenbach. 9 CDs. (Running Time: 34200 sec.). 2005. audio compact disk 32.95 (978-0-7861-7693-9(8), ZE2951) Blckstn Audio.
Patrick O'Donnell has made a career of uncovering the hidden history of World War II by tracking down and interviewing its most elite troops: the Rangers, Airborne, Marines, and First Special Service Force, forerunners to America's Special Forces. These veterans were often the first in and the last out of every conflict, from Guadalcanal and Burma to the Philippines and the black sands of Iwo Jima. Heroes among heroes, they include many recipients of the Navy Cross, the Distinguished Service Cross, the Silver Star and other medals of battlefield valor, but none bragged about it. As one

soldier put it, "When somebody gets decorated, it's because a lot of other men died." By at last telling their stories, these men present an unvarnished look at the war on the ground, a final gift from aging warriors who have already given so much. Only with such accounts as these can the true horror of the war in the Pacific be fully known.

Into the Silence. Janet Dian. Read by Janet Dian. 1 cass. (Running Time: 45 min.). 1992. 10.00 (978-0-9626446-4-1(1)) Expan Pub Co.
Meditation; Developing communication between self, Oversoul & God.

Into the Storm. Taylor Anderson. Read by William Dufris. (Destroyermen Ser.). (ENG.). 2009. 69.99 (978-1-60812-809-9(1)) Find a World.

Into the Storm. abr. ed. Suzanne Brockmann. Read by Melanie Ewbank & Patrick G. Lawlor. (Running Time: 21600 sec.). (Troubleshooter Ser.: No. 10). 2007. audio compact disk 14.99 (978-1-59737-360-9(5), 9781597373609, BCD Value Price) Brilliance Audio.
Please enter a Synopsis.

Into the Storm. unabr. ed. Taylor Anderson. Narrated by William Dufris. (Running Time: 16 hrs. 0 mins. 0 sec.). (Destroyermen Ser.). (ENG.). 2008. audio compact disk 39.99 (978-1-4001-0806-0(3)); audio compact disk 29.99 (978-1-4001-5806-5(0)) Pub: Tantor Media. Dist(s): IngramPubServ

Into the Storm. unabr. ed. Taylor Anderson. Narrated by William Dufris. (Running Time: 16 hrs. 0 mins. 0 sec.). (Destroyermen Ser.: Bk. 1). (ENG.). 2008. audio compact disk 79.99 (978-1-4001-3806-7(X)) Pub: Tantor Media. Dist(s): IngramPubServ

Into the Storm. unabr. ed. Suzanne Brockmann. Read by Patrick G. Lawlor & Melanie Ewbank. (Running Time: 15 hrs.). (Troubleshooter Ser.: No. 10). 2006. 44.25 (978-1-59710-835-5(9), 9781597108355, BADLE); 29.95 (978-1-59710-834-8(0), 9781597108348, BAD) Brilliance Audio.

Into the Storm. unabr. ed. Suzanne Brockmann. Read by Melanie Ewbank & Patrick G. Lawlor. (Running Time: 15 hrs.). (Troubleshooter Ser.: No. 10). 2006. 92.25 (978-1-59600-154-1(2), 9781596001541, BrilAudUnabridg); audio compact disk 107.25 (978-1-59600-156-5(9), 9781596001565, BriAudCD Unabrid); audio compact disk 38.95 (978-1-59600-155-8(0), 9781596001558, Bril Audio CD Unabri); audio compact disk 44.25 (978-1-59335-949-2(7), 9781593359492, Brinc Audio MP3 Lib); audio compact disk 29.95 (978-1-59335-948-5(9), 9781593359485, Brilliance MP3) Brilliance Audio.

***Into the Storm: Violent Tornadoes, Killer Hurricanes, & Death-Defying Adventures in Extreme Weather.** unabr. ed. Reed Timmer & Andrew Tilin. (Running Time: 10 hrs. 0 mins.). 2010. 16.99 (978-1-4001-8789-8(3)); 34.99 (978-1-4001-9789-7(9)); 24.99 (978-1-4001-6789-0(2)); audio compact disk 34.99 (978-1-4001-1789-5(5)); audio compact disk 83.99 (978-1-4001-4789-2(1)) Pub: Tantor Media. Dist(s): IngramPubServ

Into the Storm Pt. 1: A Study in Command. unabr. ed. Tom Clancy & Fred Franks, Jr. Read by Michael Prichard. 10 cass. (Running Time: 15 hrs.). 1997. 80.00 (4409-A) Books on Tape.
Focusing on General Frederick M. Franks, Jr., who led the armor & infantry of VII Corps, the main coalition force that broke the back of Saddam Hussein's Republican Guard during Operation Desert Storm.

Into the Storm Pt. 2: A Study in Command. Tom Clancy & Fred Franks, Jr. Read by Michael Prichard. 1997. 64.00 (978-0-7366-3731-2(1)) Books on Tape.

Into the Storm Pt. 2: A Study in Command. unabr. ed. Tom Clancy & Fred Franks, Jr. Read by Michael Prichard. 8 cass. (Running Time: 12 hrs.). 1997. 80.00 (978-0-7366-3730-5(3), 4409-B) Books on Tape.

Into the Wild. Jon Krakauer. Read by Philip Franklin. 1999. audio compact disk 48.00 (978-0-7366-7498-0(5)) Books on Tape.

Into the Wild. unabr. ed. Jon Krakauer. Read by Philip Franklin. 6 CDs. (Running Time: 7 hrs.). (ENG.). 2007. audio compact disk 19.99 (978-0-7393-5804-7(9), Random AudioBks) Pub: Random Audio Pubg. Dist(s): Random

Into the Wild. unabr. collector's ed. Jon Krakauer. Read by Philip Franklin. 5 cass. (Running Time: 7 hrs. 30 mins.). 1999. 40.00 (978-0-7366-4726-7(0), 5064) Books on Tape.
A dramatic story of a twenty-four-year-old man who vanished in the Alaskan wilderness.

Into the Wilderness. Sara Donati. Read by Kate Reading. (Wilderness Ser.: No. 1). 1999. 88.00 (978-0-7366-4396-2(6)); 88.00 (978-0-7366-4397-9(4)) Books on Tape.

Into the Wilderness, Pt. 1. unabr. ed. Sara Donati. Read by Kate Reading. 11 cass. (Running Time: 16 hrs. 30 min.). (Wilderness Ser.: No. 1). 1998. 88.00 (4858-A) Books on Tape.
When Elizabeth Middleton leaves England to join her father at the edge of the New York wilderness, she does so with a strong will & an unwavering purpose: to teach school to children of all races. It is December when she arrives in a cold climate unlike any she has ever experienced. And she has encountered Nathaniel Bonner.

Into the Wilderness, Pt. 2. unabr. ed. Sara Donati. Read by Kate Reading. 11 cass. (Running Time: 16 hrs. 30 min.). (Wilderness Ser.). 1998. 88.00 (4858-B) Books on Tape.

Into the Woods. unabr. ed. Lyn Gardner. Read by Phyllida Nash. 8 CDs. (Running Time: 8 hrs. 51 mins.). (J). (gr. 4-7). 2008. audio compact disk 69.95 (978-1-4056-5812-6(6), Chivers Child Audio) AudioGO.
Three young sisters must defeat the evil Dr. DeWilde before he takes control of the whole land with his wicked wolves and monstrous magic - but at what cost?.

Into Thin Air. Jon Krakauer. Read by Philip Franklin. 1997. audio compact disk 64.00 (978-0-7366-5136-3(5)) Books on Tape.

Into Thin Air. unabr. ed. Jon Krakauer. Read by Philip Franklin. 7 cass. (Running Time: 10 hrs. 30 mins.). 1997. 56.00 (978-0-7366-3754-1(0), 4429) Books on Tape.
When asked why he wanted to attempt Everest, the British mountaineer George Mallory explained, "Because it's there." Everest is still there for the climbing, and it's as deadly as ever. In 1996 Jon Krakauer was sent to report on the Everest industry, the high-priced expeditions that take novices and experts alike into the most forbidding terrain on the planet. The experienced climber got more than he bargained for. On May 10th, an unexpected blizzard hit the summit just as two American teams were descending. Eight people, including the two professional leaders, were lost and another terribly injured. This is one man's reflection on risk and tragedy.

Into Thin Air. unabr. ed. Jon Krakauer. Read by Philip Franklin. 8 CDs. (Running Time: 12 hrs.). 2001. audio compact disk 64.00 Books on Tape.
This is the eye-witness account of the May 1996 tragedy on Mount Everest, in which several climbers were killed in a blizzard.

Into Thin Air: A Personal Account of the Mt. Everest Disaster. unabr. ed. Jon Krakauer. Read by Jon Krakauer. (Running Time: 28800 sec.). (ENG.). 2007. audio compact disk 29.95 (978-0-7393-4379-1(3), Random AudioBks) Pub: Random Audio Pubg. Dist(s): Random

Into Your Presence. Mike Atkins. 2005. audio compact disk 12.95 (978-0-9759218-4-5(3)) M Atkins Min.

Intolerance of Tolerance. D. A. Carson. 2009. audio compact disk 21.98 (978-1-59644-759-2(1), Hovel Audio) christianaud.

Intonation in Context: Intonation Practice for Upper-Intermediate & Advanced Learners of English. Barbara Taylor Bradford. (Running Time: 1 hr. 10 mins.). (ENG., 1988. 24.00 (978-0-521-26490-7(1)) Cambridge U Pr.

***Intonation in Context Audio CD: Intonation Practice for Upper-intermediate & Advanced Learners of English.** Barbara Bradford. (Running Time: 1 hr. 8 mins.). (ENG.). 2010. audio compact disk 23.00 (978-0-521-18745-9(1)) Cambridge U Pr.

Intonation Patterns in Tyrolean. Geoffrey Barker. (Berkeley Insights in Linguistics & Semiotics Ser.: Vol. 57). 2005. bk. 61.95 (978-0-8204-6837-2(1)) P Lang Pubng.

Intonation Patterns of American English Cassette Series see Intonation Patterns of American English CD Series

Intonation Patterns of American English CD Series. 4th ed. Lorna D. Sikorski. 4 CDs. (Running Time: 4 hrs. 25min.). (Mastering Effective English Communication Ser.). Orig. Title: The Intonation Patterns of American English Cassette Series. (gr. 7 up). 2004. spiral bd. & wbk. ed. 94.95 (978-1-883574-07-9(2), 5312) LDS & Asocs.
No other audio program we know of tackles this key element of true fluency in American English so practically. Here are more than 100 workbook pages and 4 cds of audio practice, with exercises for developing control of the nebulous elements of intonation: word lists for the eight major word patterns, basic falling and rising sentence rules, unique word reduction guidelines and drills for emphatic intonation. NOTE: Everything on CD is in the workbook, but more activities are included in print.

Intoxicating Grace. Ben Young. 2000. 4.95 (978-0-7417-6192-7(0), B0192) Win Walk.

Intra-Aortic Balloon Pump. unabr. ed. Instructed by April Kimball. 3 cass. (Running Time: 6 hrs.). 1990. 79.00 cass. & soft-bound bk. (HT13) Ctr Hlth Educ.
Actual case studies, balloon tracings & explicit diagrams will give you the necessary skills & confidence to perform balloon pump procedures quickly & accurately. It's the perfect course for ICU-CCU nurses who must use IABP's frequently.

Intra-Op, Tape 2. abr. ed. Robert A. Monroe. Read by Robert A. Monroe. 6 cass. (Emergency Ser.). 1983. 69.00 Set. (978-1-56102-701-9(4)); Inter Indus.
Use during surgery procedure.

Intransigence of Higher Beings. Arthur Young. 1 cass. 9.00 (A0286-88) Sound Photosyn.

Intraoperative & Perioperative Complications of Urologic Surgery. Moderated by W. Scott McDougall. 2 cass. (Urologic Surgery Ser.: UR-4). 1986. 19.00 (8671) Am Coll Surgeons.

Intrauterine Fetal Assessment, 1986. Moderated by Robert J. Luby. 2 cass. (Gynecology & Obstetrics Ser.: GO-6). 1986. 19.00 (8645) Am Coll Surgeons.

Intrauterine "Surgery" on the Fetus. 2 cass. (Gynecology & Obstetrics Ser.: C84-GO4). 1984. 15.00 (8435) Am Coll Surgeons.

Intravenous Therapy for Prehospital Providers. AAOS Staff. (Ems Continuing Education Ser.). (C). 2001. tchr. ed. 146.95 (978-0-7637-1940-1(4), 1940-4) Jones Bartlett.

Intrepid. Bill White. 2008. audio compact disk 29.95 (978-1-4332-4888-7(3)) Blckstn Audio.

Intrepid: The Epic Story of America's Most Legendary Warship. unabr. ed. Bill White & Robert Gandt. (Running Time: 11 hrs. 5 mins.). 2008. 29.95 (978-1-4332-4889-4(1)); 72.95 (978-1-4332-4886-3(7)); audio compact disk 90.00 (978-1-4332-4887-0(5)) Blckstn Audio.

Intrepid Aging & Self Renewal. unabr. ed. Frank Barron. 1 cass. 1987. 9.00 (978-1-56964-607-6(4), A0008-87) Sound Photosyn.
An invigorating discussion about artist heroes & personal heroics.

Intricacies of Prayer: Exploring the Essentials of Spirit-Inspired Prayer. Lynne Hammond. (ENG.). 2007. audio compact disk 30.00 (978-1-57399-338-8(7)) Mac Hammond.

Intricate Balance. Perf. by Michael Gettel. 1 cass. 9.98 (MPC2702); audio compact disk 14.98 CD. Miramar Images.
Expanding on themes of his first album, San Juan Suite, Gettel again explores the beauty & intrigue of the Pacific Northwest. Incorporating jazz characteristics into his writing makes Intricate Balance an innovative & unique compilation.

Intricate Lives. unabr. ed. Shirley Kaufman. 1 cass. (Running Time: 59 min.). (Watershed Tapes of Contemporary Poetry Ser.). 1980. 12.95 (23643) J Norton Pubs.
A retrospective of the American poet now living & writing in Jerusalem.

Intrigue. Marion Chesney. Narrated by Jill Tanner. 4 cass. (Running Time: 5 hrs. 30 mins.). (Daughters of Mannerling Ser.: Vol. 2). 37.00 (978-1-4025-0972-8(3)); audio compact disk 48.00 (978-1-4025-3076-0(5)) Recorded Bks.

Intrigue Langue, Culture et Mystere dans le Monde Francophone: Audio Program on CDs. Blood & Yasmina Mobarek. (FRE.). 38.47 (978-0-13-184428-5(8)) PH School.

Intrigues. abr. ed. Mercedes Lackey. (Running Time: 6 hrs.). 2009. audio compact disk 14.99 (978-1-4233-0807-2(7), 9781423308072, BCD Value Price) Brilliance Audio.

Intrigues. unabr. ed. Mercedes Lackey. Read by Nick Podehl. (Running Time: 10 hrs.). (Valdemar Ser.). 2010. 24.99 (978-1-4233-0802-7(6), 9781423308027, Brilliance MP3); audio compact disk 29.99 (978-1-4233-0800-3(X), 9781423308003, Bril Audio CD Unabri) Brilliance Audio.

***Intrigues.** unabr. ed. Mercedes Lackey. Read by Nick Podehl. (Running Time: 11 hrs.). (Valdemar Ser.). 2010. 24.99 (978-1-4233-0804-1(2), 9781423308041, BAD); 39.97 (978-1-4233-0805-8(0), 9781423308058, BADLE); audio compact disk 79.97 (978-1-4233-0801-0(8), 9781423308010, BriAudCD Unabrid) Brilliance Audio.

***Intrigues.** unabr. ed. Mercedes Lackey. Read by Nick Podehl. (Running Time: 10 hrs.). (Collegium Chronicles: Bk. 2). 2010. 39.97 (978-1-4233-0803-4(4), 9781423308034, Brlnc Audio MP3 Lib) Brilliance Audio.

Intro Focus Ten. unabr. ed. Robert A. Monroe. Read by Robert A. Monroe. (Running Time: 45 min.). (Gateway Experience - Discovery Ser.). 1981. 14.95 (978-1-56113-251-5(9)) Monroe Institute.
Establish the Mind Awake - Body Asleep.

Intro Focus 12. unabr. ed. Robert A. Monroe. Read by Robert A. Monroe. (Running Time: 45 min.). (Gateway Experience - Threshold Ser.). 1983. 14.95 (978-1-56113-256-0(X)) Monroe Institute.
Establish the higher energy state.

Intro to Blues Keyboard. Vinnie Martucci. (ENG.). 1997. audio compact disk 9.95 (978-0-7390-2571-0(6)) Alfred Pub.

Intro to Conversation Confidence. abr. ed. Leil Lowndes. Read by Leil Lowndes. 1 CD. (Running Time: 72 mins.). 2001. audio compact disk 29.95 Books on Tape.
Make great first impressions! Learn how to establish a rapport with anyone, and how to know if you are making a good impression. Recognize the 10 common phrases you should never use in everyday conversation.

Intro to Conversation Confidence. unabr. ed. Read by Leil Lowndes. 2 cass. (Running Time: 2 hrs.). 2001. 26.96 Books on Tape.

Intro to Conversation Confidence. unabr. ed. Leil Lowndes. Read by Leil Lowndes. 2 cass. (Running Time: 2 hrs.). 2000. (978-1-931187-11-4(8), CC1) Word Success.

Intro to Jazz Keyboard. Vinnie Martucci. (ENG.). 1997. audio compact disk 9.95 (978-0-7390-2574-1(0)) Alfred Pub.

Intro to Living Body Map. unabr. ed. Robert A. Monroe. Read by Robert A. Monroe. (Running Time: 45 min.). (Gateway Experience - Threshold Ser.). 1983. 14.95 (978-1-56113-261-4(6)) Monroe Institute.
Create your living-body map to balance physical body.

Intro to Rock Keyboard. Vinnie Martucci. (ENG.). 1997. audio compact disk 9.95 (978-0-7390-2577-2(5)) Alfred Pub.

Intro to the Guitar for the Visually Impaired, Vol. 1, Set. unabr. ed. William M. Brown, Jr. 4 cass. (Running Time: 4 hrs.). (YA). (gr. 3 up). 1997. 37.00 (978-0-9700478-0-9(0)) Valdosta Mus.
A music instruction course for beginning guitarists who are visually impaired or blind.

Intro to Verbal Advantage. unabr. ed. Charles Harrington Elster. Read by Charles Harrington Elster. 2 cass. (Running Time: 2 hrs.). 2000. (978-1-931187-25-1(8), VA1); audio compact disk 29.95 (978-1-931187-06-0(1), CDVA1) Word Success.

Intro to Verbal Advantage, Level 1. abr. ed. Charles Harrington Elster. 1 CD. (Running Time: 72 mins.). 2001. audio compact disk 29.95 Books on Tape.
This program will provide you the word power and English skills you need for success. It is also perfect for the SAT.

Introducing a Life of All Possibilities. unabr. ed. Stan Kendz. Read by Stan Kendz. 1 cass. (Running Time: 60 min.). 1995. 10.00 (978-1-57582-004-0(8)) HAPPE Progs.
Learn skills like levitation, invisibility, perfect health, immortality, & more.

Introducing All Around the Drums. Steve Sher. (Progressive Ser.). 2004. pap. bk. 19.95 (978-1-875726-03-5(9), 256-090) Kolala Music SGP.

Introducing Alternate Tunings. Mark Dziuba. (ENG.). 1996. audio compact disk 10.95 (978-0-7390-2566-6(X)) Alfred Pub.

Introducing Bar Chords. Stephen Carter & Brett Duncan. (Progressive Ser.). 1997. pap. bk. 24.95 (978-1-875726-91-2(8), 256-092) Kolala Music SGP.

Introducing Beats, Fills & Solos for Drums. Steven Sher. (Progressive Ser.). 1997. pap. bk. 19.95 (978-1-875726-05-9(5), 256-093) Kolala Music SGP.

Introducing Blues Guitar. Brett Duncan. 1 CD. (Running Time: 1 hr. 30 min.). (Progressive Ser.). 1997. pap. bk. 24.95 (978-1-875726-29-5(2), 256-094) Kolala Music SGP.

Introducing Classical Guitar, Bk. 1. Stephen Carter. (Progressive Ser.). 1997. pap. bk. 19.95 (978-1-875726-23-3(3), 256-095) Kolala Music SGP.

Introducing Dewayne Woods & When Singers Meet. Contrib. by Dewayne Woods et al. 2006. audio compact disk 17.98 (978-5-558-16002-4(0), Verity) Brentwood Music.

Introducing Discipleship Evangelism. Based on a work by Andrew Wommack & Don Krow. 2004. 20.00 (978-1-59548-036-1(6)) A Wommack.

Introducing Drums. Peter Gelling. (Progressive Ser.). 2004. pap. bk. 19.95 (978-1-875691-19-7(7), 256-097) Pub: Kolala Music SGP. Dist(s): Bookworld

Introducing Guitar, Bk. 1. Andrew Scott. (Progressive Ser.). 1997. pap. bk. 9.95 (978-1-875726-11-0(X), 256-099) Kolala Music SGP.

Introducing Guitar Supplementary Songbook A. Andrew Scott. (Progressive Ser.). 1997. pap. bk. 19.95 (978-1-875726-14-1(4), 256-103) Kolala Music SGP.

Introducing Guitar Supplementary Songbook B. Andrew Scott. (Progressive Ser.). 1997. pap. bk. 19.95 (978-1-875726-15-8(2), 256-104) Kolala Music SGP.

Introducing Guitar Supplementary Songbook C. Andrew Scott. (Progressive Ser.). 1997. pap. bk. 19.95 (978-1-875726-16-5(0), 256-105) Kolala Music SGP.

Introducing Guitar Young Beginner. Andrew Scott. (Progressive Ser.). 2004. pap. bk. 9.95 (978-1-86469-241-9(3), 256-110) Kolala Music SGP.

Introducing Jazz for the Rock Guitarist. Mark Brown. (ENG.). 1996. audio compact disk 10.95 (978-0-7390-2568-0(6)) Alfred Pub.

Introducing Keyboard Young Beginner. Andrew Scott. (Progressive Ser.). 2004. pap. bk. 9.95 (978-1-86469-243-3(X), 256-111) Kolala Music SGP.

Introducing Normal Speech & Language Development: Milestones Across the Lifespan see Milestones: Normal Speech & Language Development Across the Lifespan

Introducing Objectivism: Conflicts of Men's Interests. Ayn Rand. 1 cass. (Running Time: 55 min.). 1962. 12.95 (978-1-56114-114-2(3), AR29C) Second Renaissance.

Introducing Piano Young Beginner. Andrew Scott. (Progressive Ser.). 2004. pap. bk. 9.95 (978-1-86469-244-0(8), 256-112) Kolala Music SGP.

Introducing Postmodernism. Richard Appignanesi. Read by Richard Appignanesi. (Running Time: 2 hrs.). (C). 2005. 20.95 (978-1-60083-785-2(9)) Iofy Corp.

Introducing Postmodernism. abr. ed. Richard Appignanesi. 2 CDs. audio compact disk 17.98 (978-962-634-363-0(X), NA236312) Naxos.

Introducing Recorder Young Beginner. Andrew Scott. (Progressive Ser.). 2004. pap. bk. 9.95 (978-1-86469-248-8(0), 256-113) Kolala Music SGP.

Introducing Robert Stanek's Ruin Mist: Special Edition for in the Service of Dragons. abr. ed. Robert Stanek, pseud. Narrated by Gary Ryan. (Running Time: 10 mins.). (ENG.). (YA). 2008. 1.95 (978-1-57545-321-7(5), RP Audio Pubng) Pub: Reagent Press. Dist(s): OverDrive Inc

Introducing Voice Dialogue. Hal Stone & Sidra Stone. 1 cass. 1990. 10.95 (978-1-56557-008-5(1)) Delos Inc.
Provides a clear & comprehensive step-by-step introduction to the Voice Dialogue method, an incomparable tool for contacting & learning about the many selves. This is a must for people who are interested in using Voice Dialogue either personally or professionally!.

Introducing Well-Being. unabr. ed. Stan Kendz. Read by Stan Kendz. 1 cass. (Running Time: 60 min.). 1994. 10.00 (978-1-57582-010-1(2)) HAPPE Progs.
Learn to prevent or cure disease & produce total well-being.

Introduction: Your Relationship with the Energy of the Universe. Loy Young. 1993. 9.95 (978-1-882888-12-2(X)) Aquarius Hse.

Introduction - God's Greatest Purpose. Read by Lee Lefebre. 1 cass. (Running Time: 1 hr. 25 min.). (GraceLife Conference Ser.: Vol. 1). 1993. 6.00 (978-1-57838-106-7(1)); 6.00 (978-1-57838-005-3(7)) CrossLife Express.
Christian living.

Introduction & Overview of "What Color Is Your Parachute?" abr. ed. Richard Nelson Bolles & Carol Christen. 1 cass. (Running Time: 1 hr.). 1995. bk. 9.95 (978-0-89815-701-7(3)) Audio Lit.
In an illuminating question & answer session with Carol Christen, Richard Bolles tells the story behind the book & how it came to be written. Along the way, he talks in personal terms about the factors which influenced him & his thoughts about the consequences of the book's popularity.

Introduction au Thai. 1 cass. (Running Time: 1 hr. 30 min.).Tr. of Introduction to Thai. (FRE & THA.). 2000. bk. 75.00 (978-2-7005-1327-1(4)) Pub: Assimil FRA. Dist(s): Distribks Inc

***Introduction by Nick Hornby: Selection from Things I've Learned from Women Who've Dumped Me.** abr. ed. Ben Karlin. (Running Time: 3 mins.). (ENG.). 2010. 1.98 (978-1-60788-803-1(3)) Pub: Hachet Audio. Dist(s): HachBkGrp

Introduction to Accounting Requirements for Government Contracts. rev. ed. Norman J. Lorch. 1 cass. 1994. 119.00 incl. wkbk. (740513VC) Am Inst CPA.
This course explains the federal procurement process, takes you through cost principles & the latest rulings of the Cost Accounting Standards Board, finance considerations, & the Federal Acquisition Regulations (FAR) requirements, & covers the AICPA audit guide for federal contractors (included in your course package). The course also discusses OMD Circular A-122. A comprehensive case study & numerous exhibits enhance your understanding. As a refresher or as an introduction to accounting for government contracts, this course eases you over the hurdles.

Introduction to Acupuncture. Ralph Alan Dale. Read by Ralph Alan Dale. 1 cass. (Running Time: 90 min.). 1980. 9.00 (12) Dialectic Pubng.
What is acupuncture, how it works, what are its uses.

Introduction to Acupuncture for Podiatrists. Ralph Alan Dale. Read by Ralph Alan Dale. 1 cass. (Running Time: 90 min.). 1979. 9.00 (13) Dialectic Pubng.
What is acupuncture, how it works, special uses in podiatry.

Introduction to Administrative Process: Cases & Materials. Thomas G. Field, Jr. (Carolina Academic Press Law Casebook Ser.). 2004. bk. 75.00 (978-1-59460-009-8(0)) Carolina Acad Pr.

Introduction to Analytical Psychology. Kenneth James. Read by Kenneth James. 1 cass. (Running Time: 46 min.). 1994. 9.95 (978-0-7822-0466-7(X), 543) C G Jung IL.
C. G. Jung's contributions to the understanding of the human psyche are compelling & practical for those interested in personal development. His concepts of persona & shadow, psychological types, the archetypes, the collective unconscious, & the self are fundamental to our current understanding of the psyche, & his methods of dream interpretation & active imagination are valuable keys to unlocking its mysteries. Analyst Kenneth James brings these concepts to life in this delightful introduction to Jungian psychology.

Introduction to Apologetics; Historical Apologetics: The Early Church. John Robbins. 1 cass. (Introduction to Apologetics Ser.: No. 1). 5.00 Trinity Found.

Introduction to Apologetics Series. John Robbins. 10 cass. 50.00 Set. Trinity Found.

Introduction to Applied Phonetics: A Laboratory Workbook. Mary Louise Edwards. 2001. (978-0-205-27749-0(7)) Allyn.

Introduction to Archaeology, Pts. I-II, Vol. 1. Instructed by Susan McCarter. 12 cass. (Running Time: 12 hrs.). 1996. 129.95 (978-1-56585-012-5(2)) Teaching Co.

Introduction to Archaeology, Vol. 2. Instructed by Susan McCarter. 6 cass. (Running Time: 6 hrs.). 1996. 129.95 (978-1-56585-013-2(0)) Teaching Co.

Introduction to Artificial Intelligence. unabr. ed. William R. Parks. Read by William R. Parks. 2 cass. (Running Time: 2 hrs.). (Artificial Intelligence Ser.). 1989. 49.95 Tape Text.
An introduction to artificial intelligence, history, expert systems, applications & survey of AI languages.

Introduction to Bailey Astrology. Gayle Garrison. 1 cass. 1992. 8.95 (1034) Am Fed Astrologers.

Introduction to Bankruptcy Practice. Read by Thomas E. Carlson et al. (Running Time: 5 hrs. 45 min.). 1991. 115.00 Incl. 284p. tape materials. (BU-55214) Cont Ed Bar-CA.

Introduction to Bashkir. Karen Jean Matsko Hood. (Gaited Horse Breed Ser.: 2). 2002. 24.95 (978-1-59210-060-6(0), 1-59210-060-0) Whsprng Pine.

Introduction to Biomedical Polymers. unabr. ed. Read by Michael Szycher. 5 cass. (Running Time: 4 hrs. 36 min.). 485.00 Set, incl. 155p. manual. (B2) Am Chemical.

Introduction to Brahms: Piano Concerto No. 2. Narrated by Jeremy Siepmann. 2 CDs. (Running Time: 2 hrs.). 2002. pap. bk. 17.99 (978-1-930838-16-1(6), 8.558030-31) Naxos.
There is perhaps no great piano concerto grander than the Brahms 13 flat. With the spaciousness of a symphony, the drama of an opera, the intimacy of a lullaby and the intertwining raptures of the greatest love songs, it touches an almost every emotion with extraordinary immediacy and power. Its virtuosity is spellbinding, yet always substantial. But how is made? How does it grow? What holds it together? Here we explore the music from the inside out, and hear how the mightiest of musical oaks can grow from the smallest of musical acorns.

Introduction to Buddhism: An Explanation of the Buddhist Way of Life. Geshe Kelsang Gyatso. (Running Time: 4 hrs. 30 mins. 0 sec.). (ENG., 2011. audio compact disk 19.95 (978-0-9789067-8-8(0)) Pub: Tharpa Pubns GBR. Dist(s): IPG Chicago

Introduction to Buddhism: An Explanation of the Buddhist Way of Life. 2nd unabr. ed. Geshe Kelsang Gyatso. Narrated by Michael Sington. 4 CDs. (Running Time: 4 hrs. 30 mins. 0 sec.). (ENG., 2005. audio compact disk 24.95 (978-0-948006-95-1(1)) Pub: Tharpa Pubns GBR. Dist(s): IPG Chicago

Introduction to Chant. Monks of Solesmes. 1 cass. (Running Time: 1 hr. 30 mins.). 1995. 24.95 (978-1-55725-143-5(6)); audio compact disk 29.95 (978-1-55725-142-8(8)) Paraclete MA.

Introduction to Chinese Pronunciation & the Pinyin Romanization. Hugh M. Stimson. 1 cass. 1975. 8.95 incl. suppl. materials. (978-0-88710-035-2(X)) Yale Far Eastern Pubns.

Introduction to Chinese Pronunciation (Yale Romanization) 1 cass. 1957. 8.95 incl. suppl. materials. (978-0-88710-037-6(6)) Yale Far Eastern Pubns.

Introduction to Christianity. 6 cass. 19.95 (2037, HarperThor) HarpC GBR.

Introduction to Christianity, Vol. 2. John MacArthur, Jr. 6 cass. 19.95 (20137, HarperThor) HarpC GBR.

Introduction to Church Fathers. Thomas Merton. 1 cass. (Running Time: 60 min.). (Early Christian Spirituality Ser.). 8.95 (AA2081) Credence Commun.
Commentary on early Christianity, specifically the early Christian fathers.

Introduction to Church History. Rick Joyner. 1 cass. (Running Time: 90 mins.). (Church History & the Coming Move of God Ser.: Vol. 1). 2000. 5.00 (RJ11-001) Morning NC.
Church history is brought to life with practical applications & insights into how the enemy uses the same strategy against every new move of God.

Introduction to Classical Education: A Guide for Parents. unabr. ed. Christopher Perrin. Read by Christopher Perrin. 1 CD. (Running Time: 80 mins.). 2004. audio compact disk 3.25 (978-1-60051-021-2(3)) Classical Acad.
This book is an ideal introduction to classical education written by the headmaster of an established classical academy. It traces the history of classical education and describes its modern renaissance. The book also highlights the distinctive elements of the movement including its emphasis on teaching grammar, logic and rhetoric (the Trivium), and the extraordinary achievements of students who are receiving a classical education. Other sections address the role and benefit of classical language study (Latin and Greek) and integrated learning through a study of the great books of western civilization. The book is written in a colloquial, engaging style, with several anecdotes, diagrams and charts. This book is especially recommended to parents just beginning their examination of classical education. We have priced this booklet (and the Audio CD) very low so that schools and co-ops can affordably distribute it to parents. We encourage homeschoolers to give this booklet to other parents who may wish to consider classical education.The Audio CD contains the same text(unabridged) as the book on one 80 minute CD, divided by Subject Headings.

Introduction to Community Health. 3rd ed. James F. McKenzie et al. (C). 1999. audio compact disk 35.95 (978-0-7637-1088-0(1), 1088-1) Jones Bartlett.

Introduction to Community Health: Instructor CD. 3rd ed. James McKenzie et al. (C). 1999. audio compact disk 49.95 (978-0-7637-0974-7(3), 0974-3) Jones Bartlett.

Introduction to Community Health Web. James McKenzie & Robert Pinger. (C). 1998. audio compact disk 99.00 (978-0-7637-0749-1(X), 0749-X) Jones Bartlett.

Introduction to Computer-Based Image Databases. 2 cass. 1990. 17.00 set. Recorded Res.

Introduction to Computer Modeling of Chemical Processes. unabr. ed. Read by Bruce A. Finlayson. 3 cass. (Running Time: 3 hrs. 30 min.). 1988. 435.00 Set, incl. 152p. manual. (978-0-8412-1508-5(1), A6) Am Chemical.
Find out how to use a computer to design chemical processes. This practical new ACS Audio Course will give you the training you need to use computer modeling to suggest simple process improvements to save both energy - & dollars.

Introduction to Computers CD Course: Student Courseware; CD Course. audio compact disk 28.50 (978-0-7638-1077-1(0)) EMC-Paradigm.

Introduction to Conscious Dying. Bruce Goldberg. (ENG.). 2005. audio compact disk 17.00 (978-1-57968-036-7(4)) Pub: B Goldberg. Dist(s): Baker Taylor

Introduction to Conscious Dying. Bruce Goldberg. Read by Bruce Goldberg. 1 cass. (Running Time: 25 min.). (ENG.). 2006. 13.00 (978-1-885577-22-1(2)) Pub: B Goldberg. Dist(s): Baker Taylor
Overviews the process and prepares one to use the meditation and hypnosis programs.

Introduction to Continuum Movement. Emile Conrad Da'oud. 1 cass. 9.00 (OC15L) Sound Horizons AV.

Introduction to Cosmobiology. Laura Des Jerdins. 1 cass. 8.95 (797) Am Fed Astrologers.

Introduction to Cosmobiology. Eleonora Kimmel. 1 cass. 8.95 (195) Am Fed Astrologers.
Discusses the basics of cosmobiology.

Introduction to Curing the Cause & Preventing Disease. 2007. audio compact disk (978-0-9796135-6-2(6)) Curing the Cause.

Introduction to Database & dBase III & III Plus. P.C. Elite Software Services, Inc. Staff. 1 cass. (MicroMastery - Database Management, dBase III, III Plus, IV Ser.). 149.95 incl. wkbk., disk, reference guide, exam. (103424KQ) Am Inst CPA.
This course will help you understand database concepts, differentiate spreadsheets & databases, & learn to identify & design simple programs.

Introduction to Database & dBASE III & III Plus (CVE) P.C. Elite Software Services, Inc. Staff. (Running Time: 10 hrs.). (DBASE III, III Plus, IV Ser.). 1995. 149.95 incl. study guide & disk. (103424EZ) Am Inst CPA.

Introduction to Databases & dBase IV. P.C. Elite Software Services, Inc. Staff. 1 cass. (MicroMastery - Database Management, dBase III, III Plus, IV Ser.). 149.95 incl. wkbk. & disk. (103440) Am Inst CPA.
Learn to understand database concepts & to identify & design simple applications.

Introduction to Databases & dBASE IV (CVE) P.C. Elite Software Services, Inc. Staff. (Running Time: 10 hrs.). (DBASE III, III Plus, IV Ser.). 1995. 149.95 incl. study guide & disk. (103440EZ) Am Inst CPA.

***Introduction to Dianetics.** L. Ron Hubbard. (ENG.). 2002. audio compact disk 15.00 (978-1-4031-0869-2(2)) Bridge Pubns Inc.

***Introduction to Dianetics.** L. Ron Hubbard. (HEB.). 2010. audio compact disk 15.00 (978-1-4031-7402-4(4)); audio compact disk 15.00 (978-1-4031-7408-6(3)); audio compact disk 15.00 (978-1-4031-7398-0(2)); audio compact disk 15.00 (978-1-4031-7399-7(0)); audio compact disk 15.00 (978-1-4031-7407-9(5)); audio compact disk 15.00 (978-1-4031-7401-7(6)); audio compact disk 15.00 (978-1-4031-7409-3(1)); audio compact disk 15.00 (978-1-4031-7412-3(1)); audio compact disk 15.00 (978-1-4031-7404-8(0)); audio compact disk 15.00 (978-1-4031-7411-6(3)); audio compact disk 15.00 (978-1-4031-7400-0(8)); audio compact disk 15.00 (978-1-4031-7410-9(5)); audio compact disk 15.00 (978-1-4031-7397-3(4)); audio compact disk 15.00 (978-1-4031-7405-5(9)); audio compact disk 15.00 (978-1-4031-7406-2(7)); audio compact disk 15.00 (978-1-4031-7403-1(2)) Bridge Pubns Inc.

Introduction to Dianetics. abr. ed. L. Ron Hubbard. Read by Lloyd Sherr. 1 CD. (Running Time: 1 hr.). 2002. audio compact disk 13.95 (978-1-4031-0549-3(9)) Bridge Pubns Inc.

Introduction to Dianetics. abr. ed. L. Ron Hubbard. Read by Lloyd Sherr. 1 cass. (Running Time: 1 hr.). 2002. 10.00 (978-1-4031-0552-3(9)) Bridge Pubns Inc.

Introduction to Digital Compositing & Visual Effects. Walker. 2005. pap. bk. 44.95 (978-0-240-51944-9(2), FocalSci) Sci Tech Bks.

Introduction to Don Quixote. (23315-A) J Norton Pubs.

Introduction to Donizetti: "L'Elisir d'Amore" (The Elixir of Love) Thomson Smillie. Read by David Timson. audio compact disk 8.99 (978-1-84379-079-2(3), 8.558120) NaxMulti GBR.

Introduction to Dream Yoga. H. E. Rinpoche. Contrib. by Lisa Leghorn. 2 cass. (Running Time: 2 hrs.). (Archival Ser.). 12.00 Set. (PP-AVADY) Padma Pub CA.
The foundational aspects of Tibetan dream yoga practice.

Introduction to Economics. unabr. ed. George J. Viksnins. 10 cass. (Running Time: 9 hrs. 30 min.). 88.00 (781-790) J Norton Pubs.
Discusses a survey of the economic policies of the past decade serves as a framework within which the management & mismanagement of the economy.

Introduction to Economics Series. John Robbins. 12 cass. 60.00 Set. Trinity Found.

Introduction to Egyptian Arabic. Ernest T. Abdel-Massih. 12 cass. 1981. 92.61 Set. U MI Lang Res.

Introduction to Electional Astrology. Gilbert Navarro. 1 cass. 8.95 (250) Am Fed Astrologers.
Elect a time to accomplish your objectives.

Introduction to Environmental Law. 8 cass. (Running Time: 9 hrs.). bk. 75.00 incl. 708-page course handbook. (T6-9142) PLI.

Introduction to Environmental Law Practice: Navigating the Federal System. James A. Rogers et al. 1 cass. (Running Time: 90 min.). (Environmental Law Ser.). 1995. 59.00 incl. study materials, 136p. (M238) Am Law Inst.
Seasoned faculty pulls it all together for practitioners who must understand how the system works to successfully represent clients & their interest. Includes: common features of Superfund, RCRA, CWA, & CAA - federal-state partnership, permit programs, challenges to EPA rulemaking, public interest groups; EPA information gathering & inspection authority; EPA regulations & rulemaking - types of processes, interpretation, & keeping up with developments; enforcement programs; EPA & Department of Justice enforcement activities & how to respond.

Introduction to Esoteric Astrology. Beverly J. Farrell. Read by Beverly J. Farrell. 1 cass. (Running Time: 90 min.). 1994. 8.95 (1160) Am Fed Astrologers.

Introduction to Esoteric Astrology. Donna Van Toen. 1 cass. 8.95 (594) Am Fed Astrologers.
Signs, etc. symbolize reasons for being here.

Introduction to Evidence. 1 cass. (Running Time: 1 hr.). (Basic Concepts in the Law of Evidence Ser.). 1975. 15.00 (EYX01) Natl Inst Trial Ad.

Introduction to Expert Systems. unabr. ed. William R. Parks. Read by William R. Parks. 2 cass. (Running Time: 2 hrs.). (Artificial Intelligence Ser.). 1989. 49.95 Tape Text.
Introduction to knowledge engineering, knowledge representation, tools & applications.

Introduction to Feng Shui. Created by Linda Binns. 2003. audio compact disk 9.95 (978-0-9748331-0-1(X)) Hrm Ins Out.
An introduction to the principles and concepts of Feng Shui and how it can help you in your life.

Introduction to Free Market Economics. unabr. ed. Murray Newton Rothbard. 16 cass. (Running Time: 22 hrs.). 153.00 (S00301) J Norton Pubs.
Consists of 16 one-hour lectures on basic free market economics presented by one of the leading economic philosophers of this century.

Introduction to Greek Philosophy, Pts. 1-2. Instructed by David Roochnik. 12 cass. (Running Time: 12 hrs.). 2002. bk. 54.95 (978-1-56585-111-5(0), 4477) Teaching Co.

Introduction to Greek Philosophy, Pts. I-II. Instructed by David Roochnik. 12 CDs. (Running Time: 12 hrs.). 2002. bk. 69.95 (978-1-56585-352-2(0), 4477) Teaching Co.

Introduction to Greek Philosophy, Vol. 2. Instructed by David Roochnik. 6 cass. (Running Time: 6 hrs.). 2002. 129.95 (978-1-56585-112-2(9)) Teaching Co.

Introduction to HDTV Pt. 1: Workshop One. 2 cass. 1990. 17.00 set. Recorded Res.
Topics covered include history of high definition, HDTV technology, & HDTV production.

Introduction to HDTV Pt. 2: Workshop Three. 2 cass. 1990. 17.00 set. Recorded Res.
Topics covered include distribution, sets & receivers, & nonbroadcast overview.

Introduction to Ho'Oppnopono - Lecture. Morrnah Simeona. 2 cass. 18.00 (OC4L) Sound Horizons AV.

Introduction to Horary Astrology. Gilbert Navarro. 1 cass. (Running Time: 90 min.). 1990. 8.95 (807) Am Fed Astrologers.

Introduction to Human Disease. 5th ed. Leonard V. Cowley. (C). 2001. audio compact disk 99.00 (978-0-7637-1728-5(2), 1728-2) Jones Bartlett.

Introduction to Human Geography the Cultural Landscape: Instructor's CD-ROM. 8th rev. ed. Rubenstein. audio compact disk 18.97 (978-0-13-142943-7(4)) PH School.

Introduction to Human Sexuality. unabr. ed. Milton Diamond. 1 cass. (Running Time: 1 hr.). (Human Sexuality Ser.). 12.95 (34001) J Norton Pubs.

Introduction to India. unabr. ed. Julian C. Hollick & Marilyn Turkovich. 1 cass. (Running Time: 60 min.). 1985. pap. bk. 40.00 (978-1-56709-024-6(9), 1028) Indep Broadcast.
Three distinct programs offered on one tape & one booklet are designed to introduce Middle & High School student to the people & land of India. 1. Listening to India 2. One the Shores of Vast Humanity; presents the diversity of land, religion, & language poetry & song; 3. Beneath the Surface, offers conversations with six Indian teenagers about their values & life goals.

Introduction to Intellectual History. John Ridpath. 1 cass. (Running Time: 40 min.). 1992. 7.95 (978-1-56114-128-9(3), CR06C) Second Renaissance.

Introduction to Intellectual Property: Cases & Materials. Thomas G. Field, Jr. (Carolina Academic Press Law Casebook Ser.). 2003. bk. 70.00 (978-0-89089-236-7(9)) Carolina Acad Pr.

Introduction to ISO 9002 Registration. 1 cass. (Running Time: 75 min.). 39.00 (310111) Am Assn Clinical Chem.
AACC's informative introduction to ISO 9002 & a case study from a laboratory director whose lab is ISO registered.

Introduction to Jewish Mysticism. Zalman Schachter. 5 cass. Incl. Introduction to Jewish Mysticism: Hasidic Masters & Teaching. 1978.; Introduction to Jewish Mysticism: Hasidic Prayer. 1978.; Introduction to Jewish Mysticism: Hasidic Song & Dance. 1978.; Introduction to Jewish Mysticism: The Concepts of the Kaballah. 1978.; Introduction to Jewish Mysticism: The Yet Unresolved. 1978.; 1978. 17.50 Set.; 4.50 ea. Pendle Hill.

Introduction to Jewish Mysticism: Hasidic Masters & Teaching see Introduction to Jewish Mysticism

Introduction to Jewish Mysticism: Hasidic Prayer see Introduction to Jewish Mysticism

Introduction to Jewish Mysticism: Hasidic Song & Dance see Introduction to Jewish Mysticism

Introduction to Jewish Mysticism: The Concepts of the Kaballah see Introduction to Jewish Mysticism

Introduction to Jewish Mysticism: The Yet Unresolved see Introduction to Jewish Mysticism

Introduction to Judaism, Vol. I-II. Instructed by Shai Cherry. 12 cass. (Running Time: 12 hrs.). bk. 54.95 (978-1-56585-922-7(7), 6423) Teaching Co.

Introduction to Judaism, Vol. I-II. Instructed by Shai Cherry. 12 CDs. (Running Time: 12 hrs.). 2004. bk. 69.95 (978-1-56585-924-1(3), 6423) Teaching Co.

Introduction to Jung's Life & Work. Murray Stein. Read by Murray Stein. 1 cass. (Running Time: 90 min.). 1992. 10.95 (978-0-7822-0408-7(2), 498) C G Jung IL.

Author & analyst Murray Stein presents an historical overview of Jung's life & work, detailing his relationship with Freud, & discussing reasons for Jung's increasing popularity & relevance for contemporary society.

Introduction to Leading under Pressure: At CCFL: Live. Speeches. Gabriela Cora-Locatelli. (Running Time: 45 mins.). 2004. 27.00 (978-0-9766645-5-0(0)) Exe H & W Inc.

Audio download of a live presentation on Introduction to Leading under Pressure.

Introduction to Leading under Pressure: At NAWBO: Live. Gabriela Cora-Locatelli. (Running Time: 45 mins). 2004. 27.00 (978-0-9766645-6-7(9)) Exe H & W Inc.

Introduction to Leading under Pressure, audiovisual download, is based on a presentation given to a group of successful women business owners.

Introduction to Leading under Pressure: At NAWBO: Live. Gabriela Cora-Locatelli. (Running Time: 45 mins.). 2005. cass. & DVD 117.00 (978-0-9766645-9-8(3)) Exe H & W Inc.

Introduction to LISP. unabr. ed. William R. Parks. Read by William R. Parks. 2 cass. (Running Time: 2 hrs.). (Artificial Intelligence Ser.). 1989. 49.95 Tape Text.

A tutorial covering beginning key concepts of LISP programming. Topics include: lists, functions, predicates, conditionals & recursion.

Introduction to Listening: How to Increase Awareness of Your Inner Guide. Lee Coit. 1 cass. 1989. 10.95 (978-0-936475-01-1(3)) Las Brisas.

Discusses how to listen to one's intuition.

Introduction to Literature. 8th ed. Alison Booth. 2 vols. (YA). 2002. pap. bk. 56.80 (978-0-393-97743-1(9)) Norton.

Introduction to Logic. Leonard Peikoff. 20 cass. (Running Time: 27 hrs.). 1993. 225.00 Set. (978-1-56114-176-0(3), LP30D) Second Renaissance.

Introduction to Logic - Definition of Terms. John Robbins. 1 cass. (Introduction to Logic Ser.: No. 1). 5.00 Trinity Found.

Introduction to Logic Series. John Robbins. 9 cass. 45.00 Set. Trinity Found.

Introduction to Logic with Elogic CD Rom. 12th ed. COPI. 2005. audio compact disk 86.67 (978-0-13-168950-3(9), Prentice Hall) Pub: P-H. Dist(s): Pearson Educ

Introduction to Lotus 1-2-3. Edward Harms. (Running Time: 12 hrs.). (MicroMastery Lotus Ser.). 1995. 149.95 incl. wkbk. & disk. (103430EZ) Am Inst CPA.

Introduction to Lotus 1-2-3 Macros 2.0. Linda Stanley. 1 cass. (MicroMastery Lotus Ser.). 149.95 incl. wkbk. & disk. (103450KQ) Am Inst CPA.

This new course will teach you to design, test, & debug macros such as those which automate common Lotus tasks: save, print, titles, sort, etc.

Introduction to Lotus 1-2-3 Macros 2.0 (CVE) Linda Stanley. (Running Time: 10 hrs.). (MicroMastery Lotus Ser.). 1995. 149.95 incl. wkbk. & disk. (103450EZ) Am Inst CPA.

Introduction to Medical Astrology. Nancy Kahn. 1 cass. 8.95 (185) Am Fed Astrologers.

Overview of chart and using diet as preventive medicine.

Introduction to Meditation. Eknath Easwaran. Read by Eknath Easwaran. 1 cass. (Running Time: 1 hr.). 1989. 7.95 (978-1-58638-555-2(0)) Nilgiri Pr.

Features summary of Easwaran's method of meditation.

Introduction to Meditation & Yoga Nidra: Relaxation & Stress Reduction, Healing & Rejuvenation. Swami Shankardev Saraswati & Jayne Stevenson. 2004. audio compact disk 22.00 (978-0-9803496-5-8(6)) Big Shakti AUS.

Introduction to Metaphysics. Michael P. Marshall. Read by Michael P. Marshall. Ed. by Jonathan C. Renaud. Music by Ted Crook. 1 cass. (Running Time: 52 min.). 1995. 9.00 (978-0-912403-13-7(6)) Prod Renaud.

A basic understanding of how our thoughts & emotions create our lives. We recommend that you also listen to "Initiation into the Mysteries" to supplement this tape.

Introduction to Mideast Business. unabr. ed. George Olmstead. 1 cass. (Running Time: 40 min.). 12.95 (452) J Norton Pubs.

Introduction to Miranon. unabr. ed. Robert A. Monroe. Read by Robert A. Monroe. (Running Time: 45 min.). (Explorer Ser.). 1983. 12.95 (978-1-56113-004-7(4), 5) Monroe Institute.

The story of Leona & Lemuria.

Introduction to Modern Standard Arabic Pronunciation & Writing. Ernest N. McCarus & Raji Mahmud Rammuny. 1 cass. 14.25 U MI Lang Res.

Introduction to Mozart: "Don Giovanni" Thomson Smillie. Read by David Timson. audio compact disk 8.99 (978-1-84379-078-5(5), 8.558115) NaxMulti GBR.

Introduction to Mundane Astrology. Glenn Malec. 1 cass. 8.95 (693) Am Fed Astrologers.

An AFA Convention workshop tape.

Introduction to New Age Awareness. Dean Marshall & Marie Kirkendoll. 3 cass. (Running Time: 3 hrs.). (New Age Ser.). 29.95 Quest NW Pub.

Introduction to NLP. 2004. audio compact disk (978-1-932163-59-9(X)) Infinity Inst.

Introduction to NLP: Psychological Skills for Understanding & Influencing People. Joseph O'Connor & Ian McDermott. 2 cass. 1998. (978-0-7225-3415-1(9), HarperThor) HarpC GBR.

Introduction to Objectivism. unabr. ed. Nathaniel Branden. 1 cass. (Running Time: 1 hr. 27 min.). 12.95 (560) J Norton Pubs.

Branden provides a clear overview of the objectivist philosophy, with special emphasis on ethics & social philosophy. Branden presents & illuminates the central ideas of Ayn Rand as portrayed in her famous novel, "Atlas Shrugged".

Introduction to Old Occitan. William D. Paden. (Introduction to Older Languages Ser.: No. 4). 1998. bk. 35.00 (978-0-87352-293-9(1), Z103C) Modern Lang.

Introduction to Option Trading Success. Instructed by James Bittman. 1 cass. (Running Time: 90 mins.). (Trade Secrets Audio Ser.). 2002. 19.95 (978-1-931611-63-3(7)) Marketplace Bks.

The CBOE's top options trainer, James Bittman, introduces first-timers and fledgling traders to the exciting options arena. Bittman explains in concise, step-by-step terms exactly how options work, providing clear explanations and examples of the most common - and valuable - option strategies. You'll discover how to develop a solid options trading plan - and tailor it to your own goals and risk limitations. Learn what it takes to start trading options profitably with the critical "two D's" - discipline and decision making. Other revealing insights include the 3 key steps to any successful options investment and learning to "think" like an options investor. With Bittman's basic strategies, this comprehensive video-and its complete online support materials - your entry into the options market will be far more focused and effective.

Introduction to Organization. Mac Hammond. 2 cass. (Running Time: 2 hrs.). (Simplify Your Life Ser.: Vol. 1). 1997. 12.00 Set. (978-1-57399-057-8(4)) Mac Hammond.

The importance of organizing all the areas of your life by simplifying it.

Introduction to Orthopaedic Nursing. Contrib. by JoAn Blink et al. 1 CD. (Running Time: 1 hr.). 2001. audio compact disk 99.00 (978-1-892665-12-6(3)) Natl Assn Ortho Nurse.

Introduction to Parapsychology. unabr. ed. Gardner Murphy. 1 cass. (Running Time: 25 min.). 12.95 (29112) J Norton Pubs.

Non-technical discussion of the problems & experimental techniques in the field of extra-sensory perception.

Introduction to Past Life. Pat Carroll. Read by Pat Carroll. Ed. by Tony Carroll. 1 cass. (Running Time: 30 min.). 10.00 Inner-Mind Concepts.

Discusses how to tap into the subconscious memories of other lives.

Introduction to Patents. unabr. ed. Read by C. Kenneth Bjork & Richard B. Racine. 3 cass. (Running Time: 3 hrs.). 350.00 Set, incl. 60p. manual. (B7) Am Chemical.

Introduction to Persian. rev. ed. Wheeler M. Thackston. 9 cass. (Running Time: 13 hrs.). (C). 1993. 90.00 (978-0-936347-30-1(9)) IBEX.

Introduction to Persian Tape & Book. W. M. Thackston. 1995. pap. bk. 110.00 (978-0-936347-71-4(6)) IBEX.

Introduction to Persian 3rd Edition Book & 9 CDs. Wheeler M. Thackston. (ENG.). 2007. pap. bk. 120.00 (978-1-58814-059-3(8)) IBEX.

Introduction to Personal Computers Audio. Specialized Systems Consultants Inc., Staff. 1 cass. 1992. pap. bk. 19.95 (978-0-916151-56-0(5)) Specialized Systs.

Introduction to Personal Computing. Janice S. Rinehart & Sharon Touhy Cook. Ed. by Natalie B. Young. 2 cass. 1997. bk. & stu. ed. 125.00 Set. (978-0-917792-97-7(1), 130) OneOnOne Comp Trng.

Offers learners carefully tailored instruction in understanding each of the common software categories such as word processing, databases, spreadsheets, integrated packages, presentation software, desktop publishing, CAD & drawing packages, communication software & much more.

Introduction to Personal Power: The First Four Days of the 30 Day Program. unabr. ed. Anthony Robbins. Read by Anthony Robbins. Ed. by John Paul Zahody. Prod. by John Paul Zahody. 4 cass. (Running Time: 3 hrs. 10 min.). 1992. 29.95 Set. (978-0-9632802-0-6(1)) Guthy-Renker.

Anthony Robbins offers methods for self improvement & fulfillment.

Introduction to Praise. Read by Ruth Collingridge. 1 cass. (Running Time: 1 hr.). 9.00 (978-0-932305-69-5(5), 581006) Aglow Communs.

Arranged for optional use with the "Introduction to Praise" workbook. Its purpose is to enhance individual or group worship & assist in establishing praise as part of devotional time.

Introduction to Principals & Practices, Vol. 1. Charles Muir & Caroline Muir. Read by Charles Muir & Caroline Muir. 1 cass. (Running Time: 72 min.). (Tantra: The Art of Conscious Loving Ser.). 1989. 12.00 (978-1-882570-00-3(6)) HI Goddess.

Charles & Caroline Muir reveal the secrets of this age-old science which will enable your sexual sharing to heal, energize, awaken consciousness & unfold the depths of Love & Joy. An excellent introduction to ancient Tantric concepts & how they are necessary in today's western world. This recording presents crucial information & will leave you with a complete overview of Tantric practice.

Introduction to Prophetic Ministry. Rick Joyner. 1 cass. (Running Time: 90 mins.). (Prophetic Ministry & Gifts Ser.: Vol. 1). 2000. 5.00 (RJ06-001) Morning NC.

These messages contain advanced teaching on the prophetic ministry, including discussion of strongholds & hindrances.

Introduction to Puccini: "Turandot" Thomson Smillie. audio compact disk 8.99 (978-1-84379-097-6(1)) NaxMulti GBR.

Introduction to Quaker Practice; Money & Personal Wealth. 10 cass. Incl. Introduction to Quaker Practice; Money & Personal Wealth: Implications of Membership on a Friends Meeting. 1977.; Introduction to Quaker Practice; Money & Personal Wealth: Investing Our Money Responsibly. Martha B. Savio. 1977.; Introduction to Quaker Practice; Money & Personal Wealth: Modern Quaker Philanthropy - Folklore & Fact. Wilmer L. Tjossem. 1977.; Introduction to Quaker Practice; Money & Personal Wealth: Private Wealth - Bane or Blessing. Alan R. Hunt & Richard K. Taylor. 1977.; Introduction to Quaker Practice; Money & Personal Wealth: Quaker Group Decision-Making. Matthais C. Drake. 1977.; Introduction to Quaker Practice; Money & Personal Wealth: Silence & the Vocal Ministry. Helen G. Hole. 1977.; Introduction to Quaker Practice; Money & Personal Wealth: The Changing Aspects of Friends Testimonies. Lyle Tatum. 1977.; Introduction to Quaker Practice; Money & Personal Wealth: The Exercise of Authority in the Society of Friends. Colin W. Bell. 1977.; Introduction to Quaker Practice; Money & Personal Wealth: The World Peace Tax Fund. Edward F. Snyder. 1977.; Introduction to Quaker Practice; Money & Personal Wealth: We Are What We Do: Reflections on Work, Power & Powerlessness in a Wealthy Society. John R. Coleman. 1977.; 1977. 30.00 Set.; 4.50 ea. Pendle Hill.

Introduction to Quaker Practice; Money & Personal Wealth: Implications of Membership on a Friends Meeting see Introduction to Quaker Practice; Money & Personal Wealth

Introduction to Quaker Practice; Money & Personal Wealth: Investing Our Money Responsibly see Introduction to Quaker Practice; Money & Personal Wealth

Introduction to Quaker Practice; Money & Personal Wealth: Modern Quaker Philanthropy - Folklore & Fact see Introduction to Quaker Practice; Money & Personal Wealth

Introduction to Quaker Practice; Money & Personal Wealth: Private Wealth - Bane or Blessing see Introduction to Quaker Practice; Money & Personal Wealth

Introduction to Quaker Practice; Money & Personal Wealth: Quaker Group Decision-Making see Introduction to Quaker Practice; Money & Personal Wealth

Introduction to Quaker Practice; Money & Personal Wealth: Silence & the Vocal Ministry see Introduction to Quaker Practice; Money & Personal Wealth

Introduction to Quaker Practice; Money & Personal Wealth: The Changing Aspects of Friends Testimonies see Introduction to Quaker Practice; Money & Personal Wealth

Introduction to Quaker Practice; Money & Personal Wealth: The Exercise of Authority in the Society of Friends see Introduction to Quaker Practice; Money & Personal Wealth

Introduction to Quaker Practice; Money & Personal Wealth: The World Peace Tax Fund see Introduction to Quaker Practice; Money & Personal Wealth

Introduction to Quaker Practice; Money & Personal Wealth: We Are What We Do: Reflections on Work, Power & Powerlessness in a Wealthy Society see Introduction to Quaker Practice; Money & Personal Wealth

Introduction to Radiological Imaging of Human Gross Anatomy. 2003. audio compact disk 39.85 (978-0-9741245-2-0(4)) P Sarai.

Introduction to Ravel: Bolero & Ma Mere L'oye. Narrated by Jeremy Siepmann. 2 CDs. (Running Time: 1 hr. 30 mins.). 2002. pap. bk. 17.99 (978-1-930838-17-8(4), 8.558032-33) Naxos.

The famous Bolero and the enchanting Mother Goose Suite give us Ravel, the orchestral sorcerer, at the peak of his unsurpassed powers. From the fierce vitality of sun-baked Spain to the most poignant evocations of childhood and innocence, he captures the immediacy of experience as we feel it. Behind his every work was a craftsman of amazing skill so astonishing that we can examine his artistic workshop in the minutes detail without dispelling any of the magic.

Introduction to Re-evaluation Counseling. Harvey Jackins. 1 cass. 10.00 (978-1-893165-48-9(5)) Rational Isl.

Discusses the theory of Re-evaluation Counseling.

Introduction to Rossini: The Barber of Seville. Thomson Smillie. Narrated by David Timson. 1 CD. (Running Time: 1 hr. 15 mins.). 2002. audio compact disk 8.99 (978-1-930838-19-2(0), 8.558008) Naxos.

Most popular opera. Its effervescent overture presents a perfect platform for the amusing plot in which the barber, Figaro, state-manages a romance between Count Almaviva and Rosina and puts to flight the old suitor, Dr. Bartolo. In this introduction, we explore the facets of this opera that make it a favorite for everyone form opera houses and symphonies to Bugs Bunny.

Introduction to Rossini: Trancredi. Read by David Timsom. audio compact disk 8.99 (978-1-84379-080-8(7), 8.558121) NaxMulti GBR.

Introduction to Rudolph Steiner. Robert McDermott. 1 cass. 9.00 (OC18L); 54.00 (OC61) Sound Horizons AV.

Introduction to Sensory Awareness. unabr. ed. Charlotte Selver. 1 cass. (Running Time: 1 hr. 25 min.). 1969. 11.00 (05001) Big Sur Tapes.

Explores sensory awareness, its philosophy & practice, through experiential sessions. She describes sensory awareness as a study into our own nature reached by very simple activities, & suggests that we should take seriously every manifestation of our living organism.

Introduction to Simulation. Thomas C. Goldsmith. 1 cass. (Running Time: 30 min.). 10.95 (13044) J Norton Pubs.

A discussion of simulation as a concept & technique in human engineering - what simulating is, what it is used for & the general attributes of a simulator.

Introduction to Soulcollage. Speeches. Seena B. Frost. Voice by Seena B. Frost. 1. (Running Time: 60). 2003. 12.95 (978-0-9643158-7-7(4)) Pub: Hanford Mead. Dist(s): Baker Taylor

This audiotape describes the process of SoulCollage from author, Seena B. Frost's book, "SoulCollage". SoulCollage is deeply satisfying art that anyone can do. With intuition and images we make personal tarot-like cards. Frost encourages us to use our own sense of inner direction and gives practical information that helps us use SoulCollage to connect more to self, others, and Spirit. On Side two, Frost leads a guided relaxation, set to music, through the chakras to identify animal images-allies for the Companion suit of your SoulCollage Deck.

Introduction to Spirit World Realities. Henry W. Wright. (ENG.). 2008. audio compact disk 17.95 (978-1-934680-35-3(4)) Be in Hlth.

Introduction to Spiritual Gifts: Logos 01/10/99. Ben Young. 1999. 4.95 (978-0-7417-6114-9(9), B0114) Win Walk.

Introduction to Swing-Style Drumming. Joe Maroni. 2008. spiral bd. 19.95 (978-0-7866-0559-0(6)) Mel Bay.

Introduction to Teaching: Becoming a Professional. 2nd ed. Donald Kauchak & Paul Eggen. 2005. pap. bk. & pap. bk. 100.00 (978-0-13-169865-9(6)) P-H.

Introduction to Thai see Introduction au Thai

Introduction to the Art of Influence. unabr. ed. Linda L. Fudold. 1 cass. 1998. 14.95 (978-1-884605-09-3(5)) Genesis II.

Four key methods introduce the art of influence. Learn to influence & how to detect & defend against uninvited influence.

Introduction to the Bible. Michael P. Marshall. Read by Michael P. Marshall. Ed. by Jonathan C. Renaud. Music by Ted Crook. 1 cass. (Running Time: 52 min.). 1995. 9.00 (978-0-912403-09-0(8)) Prod Renaud.

New, refreshing material not revealed elsewhere. The Bible seen symbolically & mythically, with interpretations going far beyond, yet including, the literal meanings.

Introduction to the Croatian & Serbian Languages. 3 cass. (Running Time: 3 hrs.). (SER & CRO.). pap. bk. 79.50 (S15365) J Norton Pubs.

Gives equal treatment to the two principal variants, Serbian (Eastern) & Croatian (Western), of the language commonly called Serbo-Croatian. Book contains 31 lesson units, 12 reading passages, a comprehensive grammar & glossaries. Dialogs are recorded separately in Serbian & Croatian.

Introduction to the Deva Method: A Non-Classical Approach for Singers. Jeannie Deva. (Running Time: 60 min.). 1995. pap. bk. 24.95 (978-1-882224-14-2(0)) Jeannie Deva.

Eighty page method book & cassette containing singing instruction & exercises in the Deva Method for contemporary music.

Introduction to the Devout Life. St. Francis De Sales. Read by Al Covaia. Tr. by John K. Ryan. 7 cass. (Running Time: 10 hrs. 30 min.). 1987. 28.95 (934-C) Ignatius Pr.

Devotional advice for people living in the world.

***Introduction to the Devout Life.** St. Francis DeSales. Read by Paul Wilkinson. 2009. audio compact disk 24.95 (978-1-936231-07-2(7)) Cath Audio.

Introduction to the Dwelling Place of God. Rick Joyner. 1 cass. (Running Time: 90 mins.). (Foundation Ser.: Vol. 1). 2000. 5.00 (RJ05-001) Morning NC.

As an overview of God's plan for His church, this series contains essential truths for everyone who wants to see the church become all that she is called to be.

Introduction to the Enneagram. unabr. ed. Helen Palmer. 1 cass. (Running Time: 1 hr. 9 min.). 1991. 11.00 (08601) Big Sur Tapes.

Describes the relationship between personality type & higher mental & emotional potentials that develop from the preoccupations of the nine Enneagram types. She presents an introduction to the Enneagram, an ancient system of personality types with roots in centuries-old Sufi traditions.

Introduction to the Gospel of Luke. Jude Winkler. 1994. 7.50 (978-0-89942-832-1(0)) Cathlic Bk Pub.

Introduction to the HP-15C. Chris Palmer. 1 cass. 8.95 (273) Am Fed Astrologers.

Improve your calculation capabilities.

Introduction to the Human Design System. Ra Uru Hu. 2000. audio compact disk 12.00 (978-1-931164-10-8(X)) zc design.

Introduction to the Kaballah. Warren Kenton. 2 cass. (OC58L) Sound Horizons AV.
Described as a map depicting the many paths to spiritual growth. It helps the aspirant to find the way to his or her destination without becoming diverted by the many byways.

Introduction to the Mass. F. X. Lasance. Narrated by Charles A. Coulombe. 3 cass. (Running Time: 3 hrs.). 2000. 21.00 (20229) Cath Treas.
Taken from the explanatory notes by the beloved priest-writer Fr. Lasance, for his edition of the Roman Missal. For lovers of the Traditional Mass, this is a thrilling explanation not only of the parts of the Mass, but of its history & folklore. Covers the Mass in Medieval life & a capsule "Mass-tour" around the world.

Introduction to the "Miracle Course" unabr. ed. Carol Howe. 1 cass. (Running Time: 1 hr. 30 min.). 1992. 9.95 (978-1-889642-12-3(6)) C Howe.
Excellent for newcomers & current students alike. It is brief, clear, practical, & addresses the questions most frequently asked.

Introduction to the New You Technique. Bruce Goldberg. (ENG.). 2005. audio compact disk 17.00 (978-1-57968-088-6(7)) Pub: B Goldberg. Dist(s): Baker Taylor

Introduction to the New You Technique. Bruce Goldberg. Read by Bruce Goldberg. 1 cass. (Running Time: 25 min.). (ENG.). 2007. 13.00 (978-1-885577-55-9(9)) Pub: B Goldberg. Dist(s): Baker Taylor
Dr. Goldberg overviews this exciting field & instructs how to use the other programs to take charge of one's life.

Introduction to the Piano for the Visually Impaired, Vol. 1, set. unabr. ed. William M. Brown, Jr. 4 cass. (Running Time: 4 hrs.). (YA). (gr. 3 up). 1997. 37.00 (978-0-9700478-1-6(9)) Valdosta Mus.
A music instruction course for beginning pianists who are blind or visually impaired.

Introduction to the Practice of Red Tara, Set. Tr. by Tsering Everest. Contrib. by Chagdud Tulku. 3 cass. (Running Time: 4 hrs. 30 mins.). 1998. 18.00 (978-1-881847-26-7(8)) Padma Pub CA.
Tulku leads the listener through contemplations & meditations that detail the stages of visualization, offering insight into the purpose of deity practice.

***Introduction to the Shoshoni Language: Dammen Daigwape.** Drusilla Gould & Christopher Loether. (ENG.). 2010. audio compact disk 20.00 (978-1-60781-126-8(X)) Pub: U of Utah Pr. Dist(s): Chicago Distribution Ctr

Introduction to the Spiritual Life Series. 4 cass. 32.00 incl. vinyl storage album. Crystal Clarity.
Includes: What is the Spiritual Path?; Attitudes of a Devotee; New Age Spiritual Values: Simplicity, Moderation, Cooperation; Signs of Spiritual Progress - Finding a True Teaching.

Introduction to the Study of Religion. Instructed by Charles B. Jones. 2007. 129.95 (978-1-59803-372-4(7)); audio compact disk Rental 69.95 (978-1-59803-373-1(5)) Teaching Co.

Introduction to the Study of the Bible. Joseph A. Grassi. 6 cass. 42.95 incl. shelf-case. (TAH137) Alba Hse Comns.
Provides background to the author's work on "The Spiritual Message of the Gospels" & "The Spiritual Message of the New Testament".

Introduction to the Tabernacle of God. Rick Joyner. 1 cass. (Running Time: 90 mins.). (Foundation Ser.: Vol. 2). 2000. 5.00 (RJ05-002) Morning NC.
As an overview of God's plan for His church, this series contains essential truths for everyone who wants to see the church become all that she is called to be.

Introduction to the Theology of the Body. 2003. 24.95 (978-1-932631-63-0(1)); audio compact disk 24.95 (978-1-932631-62-3(3)) Ascensn Pr.

Introduction to the Tree of Life. Warren Kenton. 2 cass. 18.00 (2 CASS.) Sound Horizons AV.

Introduction to Thinking. unabr. ed. Barbara Branden. 1 cass. (Running Time: 1 hr. 41 min.). (Principles of Efficient Thinking Ser.). 12.95 (701) J Norton Pubs.
Why a science of thinking is necessary; consequences of faulty thinking methods; the relation between efficient thinking & intelligence; the philosophy presuppositions of efficient thinking.

Introduction to Thomas Hardy see Evening with Dylan Thomas

Introduction to Tibetan Buddhism. unabr. ed. Lama A. Govinda. 1 cass. (Running Time: 1 hr. 15 min.). 1998. 11.00 (06304) Big Sur Tapes.
Talks of the mutual exchange & understanding now emerging between East & West, which leads to a deepening of religious consciousness in general.

Introduction to Trading Futures Online. Instructed by Russell Wasendorf. 1 cass. (Running Time: 90 mins.). 2002. 19.95 (978-1-931611-71-8(8)) Marketplace Bks.
Get started trading futures online with this brand new audio training course from expert futures trader Russ Wasendorf. Russ knows the futures game inside and out - and the online arena is where it's being played today. Learn all the ropes quickly.

Introduction to Trumpet. Rainer Auerbach. 2004. pap. bk. 22.95 (978-3-89922-014-8(5)) AMA Verlag DEU.

Introduction to Trusts. Dearborn Staff. 1999. pap. bk. 37.00 (978-0-7931-3176-1(6)) Kaplan Pubng.

Introduction to Upasana. Swami Jyotirmayananda. Read by Swami Jyotirmayananda. 1 cass. (Running Time: 60 min.). 12.99 (715) Yoga Res Foun.

Introduction to Verdi: Aida. Thomson Smillie. Narrated by David Timson. 1 CD. (Running Time: 1 hr.). 2002. audio compact disk 8.99 (978-1-930838-20-8(4), 8.558009) Naxos.
Ancient Egypt and the war with Ethiopia is the setting for Verdi's grandest opera. It is the story of the love between Rhadames, the Egyptian general and Aida, an Ethiopian slave, and the jealousy of Amneris, daughter of the King of Egypt. It was written in 1871 for a commission from the Khedive of Egypt to inaugurate the new opera house in Cairo. One hundred-thirty years after its premier, Aida continues to intrigue its audiences with an ancient story that resonates beautifully even today, where it is a worldwide standard.

Introduction to Verdi: 'Falstaff' Thomson Smillie. Read by David Timson. audio compact disk 8.99 (978-1-84379-098-3(X), 8.558158) NaxMulti GBR.

Introduction to Verdi: "Il Trovatore" Thomson Smillie. Read by David Timson. audio compact disk 8.99 (978-1-84379-082-2(3)) NaxMulti GBR.

Introduction to Vivaldi: The Four Seasons. Narrated by Jeremy Siepmann. 2 CDs. (Running Time: 2 hrs.). 2002. pap. bk. 17.99 (978-1-930838-18-5(2), 8.558028-29) Naxos.
The Four Seasons is one of the most popular classical works ever written, four violin concertos, each capturing moods and illustrating stories related to a specific time of year. After 300 years, their melodies continue to thrill and seduce, their harmonies to haunt and excite, their tone painting to ravish the ear and inspire the imagination. But how do they work their particular magic? Why have they succeeded where others have failed? In this voyage of discovery, each movement is preceded by a lively exploration of its means, with the help of many examples and useful analogies.

Introduction to WordPerfect 5.1. Joan Singer. 1 cass. 149.95 incl. study guide & disk. (103420KQ) Am Inst CPA.
System requirements: IBM or compatible computer with hard disk drive & printer. Requires WordPerfect Version 5.1.

Introduction to WordPerfect 5.1 (CVE) Joan Singer. (Running Time: 10 hrs.). (Micromastery-Word Processing Ser.). 1995. 149.95 incl. study guide & disk. (103420EZ) Am Inst CPA.

Introduction to Written Discovery. James McElhaney et al. 1 cass. (Running Time: 52 min.). (Training the Advocate: The Pretrial Stage Ser.). 1985. 20.00 (FAPTA04) Natl Inst Trial Ad.

Introductory Algebra: Chapter Test Prep. 4th ed. Blitzer. 2005. audio compact disk 17.80 (978-0-13-133076-4(4)) Pearson Educ CAN CAN.

Introductory & Intermediate Algebra. 2nd ed. Marvin L. Bittinger. (Interact Math Ser.). 2003. audio compact disk 26.67 (978-0-201-79519-6(1)) AddisonWesley.

Introductory & Intermediate Algebra for College Students/Essentials of Introductory & Intermediate Algebra. 2nd ed. Blitzer. (Math XL Ser.). 2005. audio compact disk 26.67 (978-0-13-192176-4(2)) Pearson Educ CAN CAN.

Introductory Chemistry. Eva M. Bushman. (J). 1984. 165.95 (978-0-89420-216-2(2), 236000) Natl Book.

Introductory Guide to Relaxation. Howard Eisenberg. Read by Howard Eisenberg. Read by Edward Ullman. Contrib. by Neil Eisenberg. 1 cass. (Running Time: 45 min.). 1997. Bienestar.
Take control of the situations that lead to stress in your life.

Introductory Lakota. unabr. ed. 15 cass. (Running Time: 12 hrs.). (J). (gr. 10-12). 1989. pap. bk. 225.00 (978-0-88432-448-5(6), AFLK10) J Norton Pubs.
The Lakota language today is spoken by thousands of Sioux people living primarily in South Dakota, west of the Missouri River. All recordings are by native speakers. Developed at Oglala Lakota College, Rosebud Reservation, South Dakota, the emphasis is on sound & meaning. Exercises for written practice are included, using the Roman alphabet, because Lakota was never written until recently. Includes 9p. final test.

Introductory Lakota CDs & Text. 15 CDs. (Running Time: 12 hrs.). (SIO.). 2005. audio compact disk 225.00 (978-1-57970-193-2(0), AFLK10D) J Norton Pubs.

Introductory Lectures on Psychoanalysis. abr. ed. Sigmund Freud. Read by Sydney Walker. 2 cass. (Scholarly Works on Audiotape Ser.). 1993. 17.95 set, in vinyl pkg. (978-1-879557-01-7(0)) Audio Scholar.
Our therapy works by transforming what is unconscious into what is conscious. In these words Sigmund Freud (1856-1939) explains the basis of psychoanalysis. The Introductory Lectures were first presented as a series of 28 lectures given by Freud at the University of Vienna beginning in 1915. While World War I raged just hundreds of miles away, the sixty year old Freud explained his theories to students & lay persons anxious to understand the hidden forces of human conflict. To the uninitiated, the Introductory Lectures provide an easy to follow first hand introduction to Freud's ideas. To Freud, the Introductory Lectures were not just a summing up of his life's work - they were the opportunity to break new ground. The Introductory Lectures can be regarded as the textbook of psychoanalysis, as Freud's clearest accounting of his theories on Dreams & the Unconscious. His exposition is a pedagogic tour de force.

Introductory Module. Ed. by American Association for Medical Transcription Staff. 16 cass. (Exploring Transcription Practices Ser.). (C). 1993. pap. bk. & stu. ed. 495.00 Set, incl. handbk. (978-0-935229-16-5(7)) Am Assoc Med.
For medical transcription students, fulfills the recommendation for Fundamentals of Medical Transcription as defined in AAMT's Model Curriculum for Medical Transcription.

Introductory Oceanography: Instructor's Resource CD. 10th rev. ed. Trujillo Thurman. audio compact disk 18.97 (978-0-13-143882-8(4)) PH School.

Introductory Personal Finance for Everyone. unabr. ed. David K. Luhman. Read by David K. Luhman. 1 cass. (Running Time: 1 hr. 30 min.). (Personal Finance for Everyone Ser.: Vol. 1). 1996. 9.00 (978-1-889297-11-8(9)) Numen Lumen.
Financial goals, managing debt, bankruptcy, budgeting, net worth, emergency funds, insurance, disability insurance, life insurance, long-term care insurance, financial advisors, home ownership, mortgage strategies, tangible assets, securities investing, estate planning.

Introductory Physics: Syllabus. Norman H. Crowhurst. (J). 1974. pap. bk. 164.70 (978-0-89420-158-5(1), 230000) Natl Book.

Introductory Talk on Ear-Training. David L. Burge. 1 cass. (Running Time: 90 min.). 4.00 EarTraining.
Talk on relative & perfect pitch. For all musicians, beginning & advanced.

Introductory Topics: Intermediate Listening Comprehension, Set. Helen Sophia Solorzano & Laurie Leach Frazier. 2002. 51.00 (978-0-8013-1513-8(1)) Longman.

Intros & Endings. Robert Laughlin. Read by Robert Laughlin. 1 cass. (Running Time: 1 hr.). 1989. pap. bk. 23.00 (978-0-929983-14-1(9), 170) New Schl Am Music.
Features techniques for adding introductions & endings to pop songs.

INTRUDER. Peter Blauner. 2004. 10.95 (978-0-7435-4870-0(1)) Pub: S&S Audio. Dist(s): S and S Inc

Intruder. abr. ed. Peter Blauner. Read by Michael Gross. 2 cass. (Running Time: 3 hrs.). 1999. (394045) S&S Audio.
The stability of a successful couple is broken when Jacob's wife Dana, a psychiatric social worker, is stalked by a homeless patient of hers. Jake is driven to the snapping point & takes a fatal step that could destroy everything he cares about.

Intruder. unabr. ed. Peter Blauner. Narrated by George Guidall. 8 cass. (Running Time: 11 hrs. 50 min.). Rental 16.50 Set. (94801) Recorded Bks.

Intruder, unabr. ed. Peter Blauner. Narrated by George Guidall. 8 cass. (Running Time: 11 hrs. 30 mins.). 1999. 70.00 (978-0-7887-0627-1(6), 94801E7) Recorded Bks.
Successful Manhattan lawyer Jacob Schiff cherishes his wife & teenaged son. but when one of his wife's psychiatric patients starts stalking her, Jacob feels his family's security slipping away. One night, Jacob takes a fatal step to end the harrassment.

Intruder in the Dust. unabr. ed. William Faulkner. Read by Wolfram Kandinsky. 7 cass. (Running Time: 10 hrs. 30 mins.). (YA). 1994. 56.00 (978-0-7366-2735-1(9), 3462) Books on Tape.
Lucas Beauchamp, a black man, is accused of murdering a white man & threatened with lynching at the hands of a mob. The only person in Jefferson who believes in Lucas' innocence is Charles (Chick) Mallison, a 16-year-old white boy. To prove it he enlists the help of a young black friend & a 70-year-old white spinster in digging up the corpse of the supposed victim & leading the authorities to the real murderer.

Intruders. unabr. ed. Stephen Coonts. Read by Michael Prichard. 11 cass. (Running Time: 16 hrs. 30 min.). (Jake Grafton Novel Ser.: Vol. 6). 1995. 88.00 Set. (978-0-7366-2915-7(7)) Books on Tape.
A Navy ace teaches Marines new tricks in A-6 intruders. Jake Grafton is back, better than ever.

Intruders. unabr. ed. Michael Marshall. (Running Time: 15 hrs. 0 mins.). (ENG.). 2009. 29.95 (978-1-4332-4943-3(X)); 85.95 (978-1-4332-4940-2(5)); audio compact disk 110.00 (978-1-4332-4941-9(3)) Blckstn Audio.

Intruders from Outer Space. Read by Brian Mason. 1 cass. (Running Time: 36 min.). 14.95 (13596) MMI Corp.
Tektites & meteorites are examined. Discusses approximately 150 objects which fall to the earth each year.

Intrusions of Dr. Czissar. unabr. ed. Eric Ambler. 2 cass. (Running Time: 2 hrs.). 21.95 (978-1-55656-012-5(5)) Pub: Dercum Audio. Dist(s): APG
Mr. Jones' wife is dead! His third wife and the third one to die! His alibi is rock solid. Dr. Czissar must first prove that Jones did not murder his wife before he can prove how he, in fact, did.

Intuition. Stuart Wilde. Read by Stuart Wilde. 1 cass. (Running Time: 1 hr.). 1996. 10.95 (978-1-56170-284-8(6), 296) Hay House.

Intuition. Stuart Wilde. One CD. 2007. audio compact disk 10.95 (978-1-4019-0674-0(5)) Hay House.

Intuition: How to Use Your Gut Instinct for Greater Personal Power. Marcia Emery. 6 cass. (Running Time: 6 hrs.). 1995. 59.95 Set, incl. guidebk. (12940AS) Nightingale-Conant.
This program will teach you how to recognize this untapped resource that will awaken the most creative forces in you, & sharpen your strategic vision.

Intuition & the Mystical Life. unabr. ed. Caroline Myss & Clarissa Pinkola Estes. 3 CDs. (Running Time: 4 hrs.). 2003. audio compact disk 24.95 (978-1-59179-105-8(7)) Sounds True.
Two of the country's leading intuitives and authors are together for the first time on audio with Intuition and the Mystical Life, where listeners join them to explore: The difference between instinct and intuition: when to use each of these powerful decision-making tools. Spiritual emergencies using the power of prayer for empowerment during these initiations into the next level of divine awakening.

Intuition in the Clinical Setting. unabr. ed. Helen Palmer. 3 cass. (Running Time: 3 hrs. 50 min.). 1987. 21.00 Set. (HP003) Big Sur Tapes.
Palmer discusses applying the practices of sacred traditions to the theapist's task of forming a reliable intuitive connection with clients.

Intuition Medicine - The Science of Energy, Francesca McCartney. Ed. by Edward Mills. Illus. by Magnus Design Staff. Photos by Irene H. Young. 8 cass. (Running Time: 8 hrs.). 2000. pap. bk. 90.00 (978-0-9677861-0-0(X)) Intuition.

Intuition Medicine - The Science of Energy Vol. 2: Grounding Meditation. unabr. ed. Francesca McCartney. 1 cass. (Running Time: 1 hr.). 2000. 10.00 Intuition.
Principles of Grounding presented & guided visualizations for emotional well-being, mental clarity, enhanced physical health meditation.

Intuition Medicine - The Science of Energy Vol. 3: Aura, Life Force, Earth Energy Meditation. unabr. ed. Francesca McCartney. 1 cass. (Running Time: 1 hr.). 2000. 10.00 (978-0-9677861-2-4(6)) Intuition.
Information presented & guided visualization to strengthen nervous system, enhance sense of identity & create protection & emotional boundaries.

Intuition Medicine - The Science of Energy Vol. 4: Chakra Meditation. unabr. ed. Francesca McCartney. 1 cass. (Running Time: 1 hr.). 1990. 10.00 (978-0-9677861-4-8(2)) Intuition.
Descriptions, functions & guided visualizations to raise health of immune system & enhance psychometry & clairvoyance.

Intuition Medicine - The Science of Energy Vol. 5: Color Meditation. unabr. ed. Francesca McCartney. 1 cass. (Running Time: 1 hr.). 1990. 10.00 (978-0-9677861-5-5(0)) Intuition.
Energy & color concepts presented & guided visualizations for enhanced clairvoyance, moods control & self healing.

Intuition Medicine - The Science of Energy Vol. 6: Kundalini Energy Meditation. unabr. ed. Francesca McCartney. 1 cass. (Running Time: 40 mins.). 1990. 10.00 (978-0-9677861-6-2(9)) Intuition.
Guided visualization to enhance creativity, vitality, intuition & expand personal spiritual awareness.

Intuition Medicine - The Science of Energy Vol. 7: Male/Female Energy Meditation. unabr. ed. Francesca McCartney. 1 cass. (Running Time: 1 hr.). 2000. 10.00 (978-0-9677861-7-9(7)) Intuition.
Male - Female concepts in our society & guided visualization to increase self identity/self love, enhanced perception of all relationships, reproductive system healing.

Intuition Medicine - The Science of Energy Vol. 8: Creating Healthy Relationships. unabr. ed. Francesca McCartney. 1 cass. (Running Time: 1 hr.). 2000. 10.00 (978-0-9677861-8-6(5)) Intuition.
How to use your intuition in sensing relationships with others. Benefits clairvoyance, knowing, compassion with increased relationship intimacy & integrity.

Intuition Medicine - The Science of Energy Vol. 9: Prosperity Meditation. unabr. ed. Francesca McCartney. 1 cass. (Running Time: 1 hr.). 1990. 10.00 (978-0-9677861-9-3(3)) Intuition.
How to recognize your prosperous nature. Meditations to enhance clarity for major & minor decisions & increase abundance in all areas of your life.

Intuition Training. Helen Palmer. Read by Helen Palmer. 2 cass. (Running Time: 2 hrs. 30 min.). 1992. 17.95 Set. (978-7-900783-34-9(2), AA2551) Credence Commun.
How to practice & develop your intuitive state of mind.

Intuition Training. unabr. ed. Helen Palmer. 2 cass. (Running Time: 3 hrs.). 1990. 18.00 Set. (HP002) Big Sur Tapes.
Details the placement of intuition, the capacities of the inner observer; & discrimination between projections & accurate intuitive impressions.

Intuitionist. Colson Whitehead. Narrated by Peter Jay Fernandez. 8 CDs. (Running Time: 9 hrs. 45 mins.). 2001. audio compact disk 78.00 (978-0-7887-5356-5(8), C1374E7) Recorded Bks.
Lila Mae Watson - the first black female inspector in the world's tallest city - has the highest performance rating of anyone in the Department of Elevator Inspectors. This upsets her superiors, because Lila is an Intuitionist: she inspects elevators simply by the feelings she gets riding in them. When a brand new elevator crashes, Lila becomes caught in the conflict between her Intuitionist methods & the beliefs of the power-holding Empiricists. Her only hope for clearing her name lies in finding the plans of an eccentric elevator genius for the 'black boxO: a perfect elevator.

Intuitionist. unabr. ed. Colson Whitehead. Narrated by Peter Jay Fernandez. 7 cass. (Running Time: 9 hrs. 45 mins.). 2000. 65.00 (978-0-7887-4323-8(6), 96229E7) Recorded Bks.

Intuitive Eating: A Practical Guide to Freedom from Chronic Dieting. Evelyn Tribole & Elyse Resch. 2009. audio compact disk 29.95 (978-1-59179-682-4(2)) Sounds True.

Intuitive Healing. Judith Orloff. 6 CDs. 2002. audio compact disk 59.95 (978-1-4019-0029-8(1)) Hay House.

Intuitive Listening: How Intuition Talks Through Your Body. unabr. ed. Christiane Northrup & Mona Lisa Schulz. 6 CDs. (Running Time: 6 hrs.). 2006. audio compact disk 29.95 (978-1-4019-0669-6(9)) Hay House.

Intuitive Manager. Roy Rowan & Tony Whyte. (Running Time: 40 min.). 8.95 Listen USA.
Results from extensive studies of decision-making practices of CEO's from major corporations. Provides clues to the workings of "managing by intuition" by developing the ability to combine past experience with an estimate of the future & the ability to fuse together future instincts with current knowledge.

Intuitive Power: Your Natural Resource. Caroline Myss. 4 CDs. 2004. audio compact disk 23.95 (978-1-4019-0529-3(3)) Hay House.

***Intuitive Security.** unabr. ed. Lloyd Vaughan. (Running Time: 3 hrs.). (ENG.). 2010. 24.98 (978-1-59659-657-3(0), GildAudio) Pub: Gildan Media. Dist(s): HachBkGrp

Intuitive You with the Answer Technique: The Answer Technique. Excerpts. Diane L. Golz. 1. (Running Time: 60). 2002. pap. bk. 32.00 (978-0-9717957-2-3(X)) Abundance Harm Joy.
This audio tape includes exerpts from Diane L. Golz's Seminar, "The Answer Technique". Based on her book, "Intuitive You", the tape teaches how you can communicate with spirituat guidance for life enriching answers. Diane teaches the step by step method so you will immediately know the answers to your urgent "yes" and "no" questions, in the privacy of your own home. Achieve clarity and relieve anxiety and stress, today and forever. Enjoy inner balance, love, peace and harmony in every day life using your own intuition.

Inuit Legends, Vol. 1. Contrib. by Barbara Worthy. 2 CDs. (Running Time: 2 hrs.). 2005. audio compact disk 19.95 (978-0-660-18983-3(6)) Pub: Canadian Broadcasting CAN. Dist(s): Georgetown Term

Inuit Legends, Vol. 2. Contrib. by Barbara Worthy. 2 CDs. (Running Time: 2 hrs.). 2005. audio compact disk 19.95 (978-0-660-19049-5(4)) Pub: Canadian Broadcasting CAN. Dist(s): Georgetown Term

Inupiaq Phrase & Conversation Lessons. Lawrence Kaplan & Lorena Williams. 2 cass. (Running Time: 2 hrs.). 2000. 26.00 (978-1-55500-073-8(8)) Pub: Alaska Native. Dist(s): Chicago Distribution Ctr

***Invaders.** (ENG.). 2010. audio compact disk (978-1-59171-311-1(0)) Falcon Picture.

Invaders from the Great Goo Galaxy. unabr. ed. Blake A. Hoena. 1 CD. (Eek & Ack Ser.). (J). (gr. 3-5). 2007. audio compact disk 14.60 (978-1-59889-995-5(3)) CapstoneDig.

Invader's Plan. L. Ron Hubbard. 2 cass. (Running Time: 3 hrs.). Dramatization. (Mission Earth Dekalogy Ser.: Vol. 1). 2000. 15.95 Set. (978-0-88404-685-1(0)) Bridge Pubns Inc.
Brilliantly blends science fiction & action/adventure on a vast interstellar scale with stinging satire - in the literary tradition of Voltaire, Swift & Orwell - on the world's foibles & fancies.

Invader's Plan. L. Ron Hubbard. 2 cass. (Running Time: 3 hrs.). (Mission Earth Ser.: No. 1). 2001. 19.95 (LRON001) Lodestone Catalog.

Invader's Plan. abr. ed. L. Ron Hubbard. 2 cass. (Running Time: 3 hrs.). (Mission Earth Ser.: Vol. 1). 2002. 15.95 (978-1-59212-057-4(1)) Gala Pr LLC.
Earth. Present day. Danger looms over the human race when a secret mission from another planet is sent to prevent mankind from destroying itself and the planet. Why? Because Earth is a stopover station between galaxies and must be prepared for invasion a hundred years from now at all costs.

Invalid's Story see $30,000 Bequest & Other Stories

Invalid's Story see Best of Mark Twain

***Invasion.** unabr. ed. Jon S. Lewis. Narrated by John Haag. (Running Time: 8 hrs. 0 mins. 0 sec.). (C. H. A. O. S. Novel Ser.). (ENG.). 2011. audio compact disk 27.99 (978-1-59859-848-3(1)) Oasis Audio.

***Invasion.** unabr. ed. Jon S. Lewis. Narrated by John Haag. (Running Time: 8 hrs. 0 mins. 0 sec.). (C. H. A. O. S. Novel Ser.). (ENG.). 2011. 19.59 (978-1-60814-792-2(4)) Oasis Audio.

Invasion de la Normandie. R. de Roussy De Sales. (Drole d'Equipe Ser.). 15.00 (978-0-8442-1352-1(7), Natl Textbk Co) M-H Contemporary.
Features short dialogues designed for intermediate students.

Invasion of Privacy. abr. ed. Read by Laural Merlington. (Running Time: 21600 sec.). (Nina Reilly Ser.). 2006. audio compact disk 39.25 (978-1-4233-0110-3(2), 9781423301103, Brinc Audio MP3 Lib); audio compact disk 24.95 (978-1-4233-0109-7(9), 9781423301097, Brilliance MP3) Brilliance Audio.
Twelve years ago, a young girl disappeared. Now a filmmaker has made a movie about it. The girl's parents call it invasion of privacy. A woman lawyer calls it murder. The bloodstains on the courtroom floor belong to attorney Nina Reilly. Months earlier she'd been shot during a heated murder trial. She should have died that day. Instead, Nina has returned to the same Lake Tahoe court. Her only concession to her lingering fear is to give up criminal law. She figures an invasion of privacy lawsuit is a nice, safe civil action that will help her support her young son and pay the bills for her one-woman law office. She figures wrong. Nina's client is Terry London, a filmmaker whose documentary about a missing girl is raising disturbing questions. The girl's distraught parents believe the film invades their privacy. But Terry's brutal murder changes everything. Breaking her promise to herself, Nina decides to defend Terry's accused murderer, a man she'd known years before and hoped never to see again. Suddenly the secrets of Nina's past are beginning to surface in a murder case that gets more dangerous every day. The evidence against her client is shocking and ironclad - a video of Terry's dying words. The only chance Nina has to save the man may be illegal. And if it fails, Nina may lose the case, her practice...and even her life.

Invasion of Privacy. abr. ed. Perri O'Shaughnessy. Read by Laural Merlington. 4 cass. (Running Time: 6 hrs.). (Nina Reilly Ser.). 2001. 53.25 (978-1-58788-471-9(2), 1587884712) Brilliance Audio.

Invasion of Privacy. abr. ed. Perri O'Shaughnessy. Read by Laural Merlington. (Running Time: 6 hrs.). (Nina Reilly Ser.). 2006. 39.25 (978-1-4233-0112-7(9), 9781423301127, BADLE); 24.95 (978-1-4233-0111-0(0), 9781423301110, BAD) Brilliance Audio.

Invasion of Privacy. unabr. ed. Perri O'Shaughnessy. Read by Laural Merlington. (Running Time: 14 hrs.). (Nina Reilly Ser.). 2010. 24.99 (978-1-4418-3679-3(9), 9781441836793, Brilliance MP3); 24.99 (978-1-4418-3681-6(0), 9781441836816, BAD); 39.97 (978-1-4418-3680-9(2), 9781441836809, Brinc Audio MP3 Lib); 39.97 (978-1-4418-3682-3(9), 9781441836823, BADLE); audio compact disk 29.99 (978-1-4418-3677-9(2), 9781441836779, Bril Audio CD Unabri); audio compact disk 89.97 (978-1-4418-3678-6(0), 9781441836786, BriAudCD Unabrid) Brilliance Audio.

Invasion of the Body Snatchers. unabr. ed. Jack Finney. Read by Kristoffer Tabori. (Running Time: 23400 sec.). 2007. 19.95 (978-0-7861-4982-7(5)) Blckstn Audio.

Invasion of the Body Snatchers. unabr. ed. Jack Finney. Read by Kristoffer Tabori. (Running Time: 23400 sec.). 2007. 44.95 (978-0-7861-6801-9(3)); audio compact disk 29.95 (978-0-7861-6955-9(9)); audio compact disk 55.00 (978-0-7861-6800-2(5)) Blckstn Audio.

Invasion of the Body Snatchers. unabr. ed. Jack Finney. Narrated by George Wilson. 5 cass. (Running Time: 7 hrs. 15 mins.). 1999. 44.00 (978-0-7887-2935-5(7), 95718E7) Recorded Bks.
Dr. Miles Bennell's account of an insidious alien plot to take over the minds & bodies of his family & friends.

Invasion of the Body Snatchers. unabr. ed. Jack Finney. Read by Kristoffer Tabori. 6 CDs. (Running Time: 23400 sec.). 2007. audio compact disk 19.95 (978-0-7861-5781-5(X)) Blckstn Audio.
On a quiet fall evening in the small, peaceful town of Mill Valley, California, Dr. Miles Bennell discovered an insidious, horrifying plot. Silently, subtly, almost imperceptibly, alien life-forms were taking over the bodies and minds of his neighbors, his friends, his family, the woman he loved - the world as he knew it.

Invasion of the Body Snatchers. unabr. ed. Jack Finney. Read by Kristoffer Tabori. (YA). 2007. 49.99 (978-1-60252-611-2(7)) Find a World.

Invasion of the Mind Swappers from Asteroid 6! James Howe. Read by Joe Grifasi. (Running Time: 43 mins.). (Tales from the House of Bunnicula Ser.). (J). (gr. 3-6). 2004. pap. bk. 17.00 (978-1-4000-8633-7(7), Listening Lib) Random Audio Pubg.

Invasion of the Vampire Spiders. unabr. ed. Susan Gates. Read by Russell Boulter. 3 CDs. (Running Time: 3 hrs. 43 mins.). (J). (gr. 4-7). 2007. audio compact disk 29.95 (978-1-4056-5609-2(3)) AudioGo GBR.

Invasion U. S. A., 1942. unabr. ed. Loren Robinson. Read by Michael Taylor. 6 cass. (Running Time: 6 hrs. 12 min.). 1994. 39.95 (978-1-55686-503-9(1)) Books in Motion.
World War II, fiction. What if the Japanese won the war in the Pacific & actually mounted an invasion on the beaches of the West Coast? Here is a believable scenario.

Invasive Procedures. unabr. ed. Orson Scott Card & Aaron Johnston. Read by Stefan Rudnicki. (Running Time: 43200 sec.). 2007. 72.95 (978-1-4332-1057-0(6)); audio compact disk 90.00 (978-1-4332-1058-7(4)); audio compact disk 29.95 (978-1-4332-1059-4(2)) Blckstn Audio.

Invent & Grow Richer! An Inventor's Guide. unabr. ed. 2 cass. (Running Time: 1 hr. 42 min.). 1999. 27.00 incl. script Set. (978-0-9646996-1-8(3)) Craftmark Prods.
How to take an idea for a new product, develop it, manufacture, promote and market it.

Inventing a Nation: Washington, Adams, Jefferson. unabr. ed. Gore Vidal. Narrated by Gore Vidal. Narrated by Paul Hecht. 4 cass. (Running Time: 5 hrs. 15 mins.). 2004. 24.99 (978-1-4025-6574-8(7), 03814); audio compact disk 24.99 (978-1-4025-6575-5(5), 01282) Recorded Bks.
The three men most responsible for the shaping of America come to life as never before. Volumes have been written about George Washington, John Adams, and Thomas Jefferson, but no previous work captures the intimate and vital details the way Inventing a Nation does. Vidal's consummate skill takes you into the minds and private rooms of these great men, illuminating their opinions of one another and their concerns about crafting a workable democracy.

Inventing A to Z. Com, Volume 1, Vol. 1. Read by Phil Bertolo & Lisa Ascolese. (Running Time: 43 mins). 2007. audio compact disk 19.95 (978-0-9790948-0-4(1)) Wrld Innovatns.
Enjoy listening to Phil Bertolo and Lisa Ascolese as they have an open and clear discussion on how to get started in the business of inventing. Gain insight and experience as this CD explains all of the basic points and requirements to get yourself started in the business. As Vendors for National Television Networks as well as Retail, Phil and Lisa will give you clear comprehensive and priceless information. They will take you from your original idea, all the way to manufacturing and beyond on this easy to understand CD. Let Phil Bertolo and Lisa Ascolese walk you through the process as they do what they do best! Get your business started with "INVENTING A-to-Z" "Volume-1".

Inventing Dinosaurs. Interview. 2 CDs. (Running Time: 7200 sec.). (Ideas Ser.). (ENG.). 2006. audio compact disk 19.95 (978-0-660-19542-1(9), CBC Audio) Pub: Canadian Broadcasting CAN. Dist(s): Georgetown Term

Inventing Elliot. unabr. ed. Graham Gardner. Read by Dominic Taylor. 4 cass. (Running Time: 6 hrs.). (YA). 2004. 32.00 (978-0-8072-2320-8(4), Listening Lib) Pub: Random Audio Pubg. Dist(s): Random
Elliot was the target of bullies at his old school, but when he moves to a new school he takes the opportunity to reinvent himself.

Inventing for the Clueless(TM) Narrated by Mike Rounds. (Running Time: 46 mins., 53 seconds). (ENG.). 2004. audio compact disk 19.95 (978-1-891440-32-8(2)) CPM Systems.

Inventing Niagara: Beauty, Power, & Lies. unabr. ed. Ginger Strand. Read by Karen White. Narrated by Karen White. (Running Time: 13 hrs. 30 mins. 0 sec.). (ENG.). 2008. audio compact disk 24.99 (978-1-4001-5771-6(4)); audio compact disk 69.99 (978-1-4001-3771-8(3)); audio compact disk 34.99 (978-1-4001-0771-1(7)) Pub: Tantor Media. Dist(s): IngramPubServ

Inventing the Dream: California Through the Progressive Era. collector's ed. Kevin Starr. Read by Lloyd James. 15 cass. (Running Time: 22 hrs. 30 min.). 2000. 120.00 (978-0-7366-5594-1(8)) Books on Tape.
Focuses on the turn of the century years &, in particular, the emergence of Southern California as a regional culture in its own right.

Inventing the Middle Ages. unabr. ed. Norman F. Cantor. Read by Frederick Davidson. 14 cass. (Running Time: 20 hrs. 30 mins.). 1994. 89.95 (978-0-7861-0699-8(9), 1457) Blckstn Audio.
Cantor focuses on the lives & works of twenty of the great medievalists of this century, demonstrating how the events of their lives, & their spiritual & emotional outlooks, influenced their interpretations of the Middle Ages. He makes their scholarship an intensely personal & passionate exercise, full of color & controversy, displaying the strong personalities & creative minds that brought new insights about the past.

Invention & Motive. J. Krishnamurti. 1 cass. (Running Time: 1 hr.). (Ojai Public Talks - 1984 Ser.: No. 3). 8.50 (AJT843) Krishnamurti.
In the idyllic setting of the oak grove in Ojai, California, Krishnamurti began giving talks in 1922. Over the years, hundreds of thousands of people have heard Krishnamurti explore every aspect of our lives, his language & expression constantly changing, as he strove to communicate to each successive generation those profound truths which he had come upon, & which he maintained were accessible to all.

Invention of Air: A Story of Science, Faith, Revolution, & the Birth of America. unabr. ed. Steven Johnson. (Running Time: 6 hrs.). (ENG.). (gr. 8). 2008. audio compact disk 29.95 (978-0-14-314370-3(0), PengAudBks) Penguin Grp USA.

Invention of Childhood. unabr. ed. Read by Hugh Cunningham & Michael Morpurgo. (Running Time: 6 hrs. 0 mins. 0 sec.). (ENG.). 2010. audio compact disk 49.95 (978-1-60283-806-2(2)) Pub: AudioGO. Dist(s): Perseus Dist

Invention of Everything Else. unabr. ed. Samantha Hunt. Read by Marguerite Gavin. (Running Time: 36000 sec.). 2008. 29.95 (978-1-4332-0940-6(3)); 59.95 (978-1-4332-0938-3(1)); audio compact disk 29.95 (978-1-4332-0941-3(1)); audio compact disk & audio compact disk 29.95 (978-1-4332-0942-0(X)); audio compact disk & audio compact disk 72.00 (978-1-4332-0939-0(X)) Blckstn Audio.

Invention of Gods. J. Krishnamurti. 1 cass. (Running Time: 1 hr.). (Ojai Public Talks - 1984 Ser.: No. 2). 8.50 (AJT842) Krishnamurti.

Invention of Hugo Cabret. unabr. ed. Brian Selznick. Read by Jeff Woodman. (J). 2007. 44.99 (978-1-60252-612-9(5)) Find a World.

Invention of Hugo Cabret. unabr. ed. Brian Selznick. Read by Jeff Woodman. 3 CDs. (ENG.). (J). (gr. 4-7). 2007. audio compact disk 49.95 (978-0-545-00387-2(3)) Scholastic Inc.

Invention of Hugo Cabret. unabr. ed. Brian Selznick. Read by Jeff Woodman. Narrated by John Curless. 3 CDs. (Running Time: 3 hrs. 30 mins.). (J). (gr. 4-7). 2007. audio compact disk 29.95 (978-0-545-00363-6(6)) Scholastic Inc.

Inventions. Steck-Vaughn Staff. 1 cass. (Running Time: 1 hr. 30 min.). 2002. 9.00 (978-0-7398-6211-7(1)) SteckVau.

Inventions. Sundance/Newbridge, LLC Staff. (Early Science Ser.). (gr. k-3). 2007. audio compact disk 12.00 (978-1-4007-6634-5(6)); audio compact disk 12.00 (978-1-4007-6632-1(X)); audio compact disk 12.00 (978-1-4007-6633-8(8)) Sund Newbrdge.

Inventions: Great Ideas & Where They Came From. Sarah Houghton. (High Five Reading - Green Ser.). (ENG.). (gr. 3-4). 2007. audio compact disk 5.95 (978-1-4296-1421-4(8)) CapstoneDig.

***Inventions & Discovery Collection: Isaac Newton & the Laws of Motion/Jonas Salk & the Polio Vaccine/Louis Pasteur & Pasteurization/Marie Curie & Radioactivity.** Andrea Gianopoulos et al. (Playaway Children Ser.). (ENG.). (J). 2009. 39.99 (978-1-61545-860-8(3)) Find a World.

Inventions Rock: SoundTrax. Lois Brownsey & Marti Lunn Lantz. (ENG.). 2003. audio compact disk 29.95 (978-0-7390-3058-5(2)) Alfred Pub.

***Inventors: A Century of Flight.** Cerebellum Academic Team. (Running Time: 30 mins.). (Just the Facts Ser.). 2010. 24.95 (978-1-59163-253-5(6)) Cerebellum.

***Inventors: Benjamin Franklin.** Cerebellum Academic Team. (Running Time: 30 mins.). (Just the Facts Ser.). 2010. 24.95 (978-1-59163-269-6(2)) Cerebellum.

***Inventors: Famous Inventors & Inventions.** Cerebellum Academic Team. (Running Time: 30 mins.). (Just the Facts Ser.). 2010. 24.95 (978-1-59163-261-0(7)) Cerebellum.

***Inventors: Henry Ford.** Cerebellum Academic Team. (Running Time: 30 mins.). (Just the Facts Ser.). 2010. 24.95 (978-1-59163-266-5(8)) Cerebellum.

***Inventors: The Life & Mind of Albert Einstein.** Cerebellum Academic Team. (Running Time: 30 mins.). (Just the Facts Ser.). 2010. 24.95 (978-1-59163-263-4(3)) Cerebellum.

***Inventors: Thomas Edison.** Cerebellum Academic Team. (Running Time: 30 mins.). (Just the Facts Ser.). 2010. 24.95 (978-1-59163-268-9(4)) Cerebellum.

Inventrepreneurship: Intellectual Property Strategy for the Inventor. unabr. ed. S. Pal Asija. Read by S. Pal Asija. 1 cass. (Running Time: 6 hrs.). 1997. 50.00 (978-1-891325-06-9(X)) Our Pal.
All aspects of inventrepreneurship including intellectual property strategy & what, where, when, why & how can we learn from natural systems for better inventrepreneurship.

Inverness Square. unabr. ed. Rose Boucheron. Read by Julia Franklin. 5 cass. (Running Time: 6 hrs. 35 mins.). (Storysound Ser.). (J). 2002. 49.95 (978-1-85903-490-3(X)) Pub: Mgna Lrg Print GBR. Dist(s): Ulverscroft US

Inverse Condemnation & Related Government Liability. 10 cass. (Running Time: 14 hrs.). 1996. 315.00 Incl. course materials. (MB14) Am Law Inst.
Covers the recent case law developments & explores the legal standards & analysis for determining regulatory takings. Also considers the practical aspects of litigating regulatory cases as well as questions concerning the calculation of taking damages.

Inverse Condemnation & Related Government Liability. 1 cass. (Running Time: 16 hrs. 30 min.). 1999. 395.00 Incl. study guide. (AE18) Am Law Inst.

Inversion Magic. Duane Shinn. 1 cass. 19.95 (HAR-17) Duane Shinn.
Teaches how to turn chords upside down in a hurry.

Invest in Yourself & Enjoy the Sweet Smell of Success. Jack E. Strauser. Read by Stanley Johnson & Karen E. Koogler. 1 cass. (Invest in Yourself Success Ser.). 19.95 (978-0-9629668-2-8(7)) Jesco Corp.
Part of the Invest in Yourself Success Series, particularly Enjoy the Sweet Smell of Success, a question & answer format dealing with setting up a flower vending business.

Investigacion de Mercados. unabr. ed. Flavio Vera.Tr. of Market Research. (SPA.). audio compact disk 13.00 (978-958-43-0227-4(2)) YoYoMusic.

Investigating Geography B. Jackie Arundale et al. 2003. tchr. ed. 168.50 (978-0-340-81080-4(7), HodderMurray) Pub: Hodder Edu GBR. Dist(s): Trans-Atl Phila

Investigating Geography C: Teacher's Resource CD-ROM. Chris Durbin et al. 2004. tchr. ed. 168.50 (978-0-340-81081-1(5), HodderMurray) Pub: Hodder Edu GBR. Dist(s): Trans-Atl Phila

Investigating History: Britain 1500-1750. David Lozell Martin et al. 2005. audio compact disk 152.50 (978-0-340-86908-6(9), HodderMurray) Pub: Hodder Edu GBR. Dist(s): Trans-Atl Phila

Investigating History: Britain 1750-1900. John D. Clare. 2004. tchr. ed. 152.50 (978-0-340-86911-6(9), HodderMurray) Pub: Hodder Edu GBR. Dist(s): Trans-Atl Phila

Investigating History: Medieval Britain 1066-1500. Martyn Whittock & John D. Clare. 2004. tchr. ed. 152.50 (978-0-340-86907-9(0), HodderMurray) Pub: Hodder Edu GBR. Dist(s): Trans-Atl Phila

Investigating Musical Styles. Roy Bennett. Contrib. by Roy Bennett. (Running Time: 1 hr. 22 mins.). (Cambridge Assignments in Music Ser.). (ENG., 1992. 106.00 (978-0-521-40955-1(1)) Cambridge U Pr.

Investigating the Scientific Method with Max Axiom, Super Scientist. Donald B. Lemke. Illus. by Tod Smith & Al Milgram. Contrib. by Dennis Spears & Colleen Buckman. (Graphic Science Ser.). (ENG.). (gr. 3-4). 2008. audio compact disk 6.95 (978-1-4296-3192-1(9)) CapstoneDig.

Investigations of Quentin Nickles. Contrib. by John Richard Wright. 1 CD. (Running Time: 2 hrs.). 2005. audio compact disk 19.95 (978-0-660-19045-7(1)) Pub: Canadian Broadcasting CAN. Dist(s): Georgetown Term

Investigator: Power of the Enneagram Individual Type Audio Recording. Scripts. Based on a work by Enneagram Institute Staff. 1 CD. (Running Time: 60 mins.). 2004. audio compact disk 10.00 (978-0-9755222-4-0(8)) Enneagr.
Type Five Individual Type Audio Recording (ITAR) in CD format from the audio tapeset The Power of the Enneagram. Includes a 25 minute

introduction to the system as a whole, as well as a 35 minute exposition on Type Five. An excellent way for therapists or business consultants to introduce the Enneagram to clients, or to work with the Enneagram in ongoing situations.

Investigators. unabr. ed. W. E. B. Griffin. Read by Michael Russotto. 13 cass. (Running Time: 19 hrs. 30 min.). (Badge of Honor Ser.: Vol. 7). 1998. 104.00 (978-0-7366-4084-8(3), 4593) Books on Tape.
Dirty cops & urban terrorists fill this exciting police drama. A story of police who put their lives on the line.

Investing. 4th rev. abr. ed. Eric Tyson. Read by Brett Barry. (Running Time: 12600 sec.). 2006. audio compact disk 14.95 (978-0-06-115323-5(0)) HarperCollins Pubs.

Investing: An Objective Approach. unabr. ed. Yaron Brook. 6 cass. (Running Time: 7 hrs.). 1998. 79.95 Set. (978-1-56114-478-5(9), DB52D) Second Renaissance.
Explanation of how financial markets work - & how they can work for you.

Investing & the Personal Computer, Vol. 55. Derek Anderson. 1 cass. (Running Time: 30 min.). (Personal Computing Ser.). 1986. 7.95 B & H Comm.
Answers how much knowledge a person needs to handle stock market strategies on a PC & obtain advice, research, prices & values of your holdings.

***Investing for Dummies 4th Edition.** abr. ed. Eric Tyson. Read by Brett Barry. (ENG.). 2006. (978-0-06-123042-4(1), Harper Audio); (978-0-06-123041-7(3), Harper Audio) HarperCollins Pubs.

Investing in Gold & Silver: Everything You Need to Know to Profit from Precious Metals Now. abr. ed. Michael Maloney. Read by Christian Rummel. (Running Time: 3 hrs. 30 mins.). (Rich Dad's Advisors Ser.). (ENG.). 2008. instr.'s gde. ed. 16.98 (978-1-60024-508-4(0)) Pub: Hachet Audio. Dist(s): HachBkGrp

Investing in Gold & Silver: Everything You Need to Profit from Precious Metals Now. abr. ed. Michael Maloney. Read by Christian Rummel. 3 CDs. (Running Time: 3 hrs. 30 mins.). (ENG.). 2008. audio compact disk 24.98 (978-1-60024-507-7(2)) Pub: Hachet Audio. Dist(s): HachBkGrp

Investing in Mutual Funds. abr. ed. Lita Epstein. Narrated by Grover Gardner & Jonathon Marosz. (Pocket Idiot Guides). (ENG.). 2007. audio compact disk 15.99 (978-1-59859-220-7(3)) Oasis Audio.

Investing in One Lesson. unabr. ed. Mark Skousen. Read by Jeff Riggenbach. (Running Time: 18000 sec.). 2008. 34.95 (978-1-4332-2845-2(9)); audio compact disk & audio compact disk 40.00 (978-1-4332-2846-9(7)); audio compact disk & audio compact disk 19.95 (978-1-4332-2849-0(1)) Blckstn Audio.

Investing in the Fine Arts. unabr. ed. Sigmund Rothschild. Read by Sigmund Rothschild. 3 cass. 29.95 Set. (S941) J Norton Pubs.
Surveys the field of fine arts. Includes "Auction Buying Techniques", "How to Buy Paintings" & "Investing in Gems & Jewelry".

Investing in the Fine Arts: Auction Buying Techniques. unabr. ed. Sigmund Rothschild. Read by Sigmund Rothschild. 1 cass. 12.95 (947) J Norton Pubs.
Surveys the field of fine arts, gems & antiquities & explains the type of bidding used, as well as the "secret" auction practices of the dealer.

Investing in the Fine Arts: How to Buy Paintings. unabr. ed. Sigmund Rothschild. Read by Sigmund Rothschild. 1 cass. 12.95 (950) J Norton Pubs.
Surveys the field of fine arts, explains how the value of a piece is determind & how authenticity can be assured. Also discusses the pitfalls to be avoided in fine arts investing & offers sources of information for the buyer.

Investing in the Fine Arts: Investing in Gems & Jewelry. Sigmund Rothschild. Read by Sigmund Rothschild. 1 cass. 12.95 (967) J Norton Pubs.
Surveys the field of gems & show how the value of a piece is determined & how authenticity can be assured. Also discusses the pitfalls to be avoided in such investing & offers sources of information for the buyer.

Investing in the Troubled Company. unabr. ed. Contrib. by Steven R. Gross. 8 cass. (Running Time: 12 hrs. 30 min.). 1989. 50.00 course handbk. (T7-9235) PLI.
This recording of PLI's September 1989 course focuses on the evolving corporate strategies involved in the financial restructuring of troubled companies. The panelists deal with the tensions created by the interplay of corporate, securities & mergers & acquisitions law on the one hand & the Bankruptcy Code on the other. Topics include fiduciary obligations; selling & buying assets in bankruptcy; & the problems relating to trading claims & attempted takeovers, analyzed in each case from the points of view of management & directors, existing creditors & investors.

Investing in the Troubled Company 1990. 9 cass. (Running Time: 11 hrs. 30 min.). bk. 95.00 incl. 691-page course handbook. (T6-9138) PLI.

Investing Internationally: Stocks, Commodities, Options. unabr. ed. James E. Sinclair. 1 cass. (Running Time: 32 min.). 12.95 (1111) J Norton Pubs.
The strategy of international banking interests is outlined in the light of their effects on the currency, equality & commodity markets of the future.

Investing Secrets of John Templeton, Vol. 38. John Templeton. 1 cass. (Running Time: 60 min.). (Money Talk Ser.). 1986. 7.95 B & H Comm.
One of the most successful money managers reveals his opinions on the stock market.

Investment Adviser Regulation. 8 cass. (Running Time: 11 hrs. 30 min.). 1998. 275.00 Set; incl. study guide. (MC49) Am Law Inst.
Advanced course presents a comprehensive, integrated program on all of the regulatory areas of concern to investment professionals.

Investment-Attractive Russian Companies. 6th rev. ed. BIA. (J). 2006. audio compact disk 289.00 (978-1-4187-5244-6(4)) Bus Info Agency.

Investment-Attractive Russian Companies. 6th rev. ed. BIA. (J). 2006. audio compact disk 249.00 (978-1-4187-5243-9(6)) Bus Info Agency.

Investment Company Regulation & Compliance. 10 cass. (Running Time: 14 hrs. 30 min.). 1999. 345.00 Set; incl. study guide 473p. (AD87) Am Law Inst.
Basic course provides comprehensive training in mutual fund law. Explains in depth all of the core concepts of the operation of an investment company & the practical application of those concepts under the Investment Company Act of 1940.

Investment Economics. Richard Sylvester. 11 cass. 1981. 219.45 (978-0-932010-39-1(3)) AcademiaPub.
Insider explanations of real property rental, estate tax planning, the tax-deferred exchange & technology impacts.

Investment Management Regulation. 1 cass. (Running Time: 10 hrs. 30 min.). 1999. 345.00 Incl. study guide. (AE25) Am Law Inst.

Investment Management Regulation: Thursday-Friday, October 16-17, 1997, Loews L'Enfant Plaza Hotel, Washington, D. C. 8 cass. (Running Time: 10 hrs. 50 min.). 1997. 345.00 Incl. course materials. (MC23) Am Law Inst.
Designed for private practitioners, corporate counsel, & compliance personel who deal with mutual funds & related investment vehicles. Covers developments in investment management regulation &, in particular, recent regulatory initiatives concerning the mutual fund industry & cross-industry activities of banks & insurance companies.

Investment Open Forum: Nineteen Eighty-Five. Contrib. by Dick James et al. 1 cass. (Running Time: 60 min.). 6.25 (#A-IF) CAR LA.
Presents information about what a residential real estate agent should expect when first approaching the commercial, industrial, investment or office space areas of the real estate industry.

Investment Opportunities in Uranium. unabr. ed. Ira U. Cobleigh. 1 cass. (Running Time: 20 min.). 12.95 (1106) J Norton Pubs.
Cobleigh claims uranium is one of the great phenomena that have changed our lives in the past 40 years, & considers it as a solution in part of our fuel & inflation problems, & as an avenue of investment.

Investment Philosophers & Financial Economists. unabr. ed. Joanne Skousen. Read by Louis Rukeyser. (Running Time: 9000 sec.). (Secrets of the Great Investors Ser.). 2006. audio compact disk 25.95 (978-0-7861-6488-2(3)) Pub: Blckstn Audio. Dist(s): NetLibrary CO

Investment Strategy. unabr. ed. James Dines. 1 cass. (Running Time: 1 hr. 12 min.). 12.95 (393) J Norton Pubs.

Investment Timing from Personal Horoscope. Bill Sarrubi. 1 cass. (Running Time: 1 hr. 30 min.). 8.95 (228) Am Fed Astrologers.

Investments Outside Stock & Commodities in an Inflationary Depression. unabr. ed. John Kamin & Jerome Smith. 1 cass. (Running Time: 1 hr. 12 min.). 12.95 (362) J Norton Pubs.

Investors Definitive HOW to Short Sales Course. Mike Cheatwood. (ENG.). 2008. ring bd. 269.00 (978-1-933553-05-4(7)) Atomic Sound.

Investors' Handbook for Russia. 6th rev. ed. BIA. (J). 2006. audio compact disk 389.00 (978-1-4187-5378-8(5)) Bus Info Agency.

Investors' Handbook for the Central Federal District of Russia. 6th rev. ed. BIA. (J). 2006. audio compact disk 389.00 (978-1-4187-5376-4(9)) Bus Info Agency.

Investors' Handbook for the Far Eastern Federal District of Russia. 6th rev. ed. BIA. (J). 2006. audio compact disk 389.00 (978-1-4187-5374-0(2)) Bus Info Agency.

Investors' Handbook for the Northwestern Federal District of Russia. 6th rev. ed. BIA. (J). 2006. audio compact disk 389.00 (978-1-4187-5379-5(3)) Bus Info Agency.

Investors' Handbook for the Siberian Federal District of Russia. 6th rev. ed. BIA. (J). 2006. audio compact disk 389.00 (978-1-4187-5377-1(7)) Bus Info Agency.

Investors' Handbook for the Southern Federal District of Russia. 6th rev. ed. BIA. (J). 2006. audio compact disk 389.00 (978-1-4187-5375-7(0)) Bus Info Agency.

Investors' Handbook for the Urals Federal District of Russia. 6th rev. ed. BIA. (J). 2006. audio compact disk 389.00 (978-1-4187-5380-1(7)) Bus Info Agency.

Investors' Handbook for the Volga Federal District of Russia. 6th rev. ed. BIA. (J). 2006. audio compact disk 389.00 (978-1-4187-5381-8(5)) Bus Info Agency.

***Investors Manifesto: Preparing for Prosperity, Armageddon, & Everything in Between.** unabr. ed. William Bernstein. Read by Scott Peterson. (Running Time: 6 hrs.). (ENG.). 2009. 27.98 (978-1-59659-495-1(0), GildAudio) Pub: Gildan Media. Dist(s): HachBkGrp

Invictus see Favorite American Poems

Invigorating. Ed. by Peter Samuels. (Running Time: 60 mins.). 2002. audio compact disk 15.99 (978-1-904451-28-0(4)) Global Jrny GBR GBR.

Invincible see Twentieth-Century Poetry in English, No. 1, Recordings of Poets Reading Their Own Poetry

Invincible. abr. ed. Troy Denning. Read by Marc Thompson. (Running Time: 21600 sec.). (Star Wars Ser.). (ENG.). 2008. audio compact disk 29.95 (978-0-7393-2402-8(0), Random AudioBks) Pub: Random Audio Pubg. Dist(s): Random

Invincible: My Journey from Fan to NFL Team Captain. abr. ed. Vince Papale. Read by Mel Foster. Told to Chad Millman. (Running Time: 10800 sec.). 2007. audio compact disk 14.99 (978-1-4233-2416-4(1), 9781423324164, BCD Value Price) Brilliance Audio.

Invincible: My Journey from Fan to NFL Team Captain. abr. ed. Vince Papale. Read by Mel Foster. (Running Time: 3 hrs.). 2010. audio compact disk 9.99 (978-1-4418-0841-7(8), 9781441808417, BCD Value Price) Brilliance Audio.

Invincible: My Journey from Fan to NFL Team Captain. unabr. ed. Vince Papale. Read by Mel Foster. (Running Time: 25200 sec.). 2006. audio compact disk 24.95 (978-1-4233-2411-9(0), 9781423324119, Brilliance MP3); audio compact disk 29.95 (978-1-4233-2409-6(9), 9781423324096, Bril Audio CD Unabri) Brilliance Audio.
Soon to be a major Disney film, Invincible is the true story of Philadelphia Eagles fan Vince Papale, who, at 30 years old, tried out for the Eagles during an open call in 1976, and made the team. Papale was a school-teacher and bartender who showed up at the tryout, ran a 4.5 second 40-yard dash, and won a contract on the spot. Papale's never-say-die attitude became the inspiration for turning the Eagles into a Super Bowl team. This is an underdog story that will inspire others to pursue their dreams. In the film, Mark Wahlberg will star as Papale, with Greg Kinnear as coach Dick Vermeil.

Invincible: My Journey from Fan to NFL Team Captain. unabr. ed. Vince Papale & Chad Millman. Read by Mel Foster. (Running Time: 7 hrs.). 2006. 39.25 (978-1-4233-2414-0(5), 9781423324140, BADLE); 24.95 (978-1-4233-2413-3(7), 9781423324133, BAD); 39.25 (978-1-4233-2412-6(9), 9781423324126, Brlnc Audio MP3 Lib); audio compact disk 82.25 (978-1-4233-2410-2(2), 9781423324102, BriAudCD Unabrid) Brilliance Audio.

***Invincible: The Chronicles of Nick.** unabr. ed. Sherrilyn Kenyon. Read by Holter Graham. (Running Time: 11 hrs. 0 mins. 0 sec.). (ENG.). (YA). 2011. audio compact disk 29.99 (978-1-4272-1124-8(8)) Pub: Macmill Audio. Dist(s): Macmillan

Invincible Slave-Owners see Winter's Tales

Invisible! Robert Swindells. Read by Kim Hicks. (Running Time: 13020 sec.). (J). 2001. audio compact disk 29.95 (978-0-7540-6773-3(4)) AudioGo GBR.

Invisible. abr. ed. Andrew Britton. Read by J. Charles. (Running Time: 6 hrs.). (Ryan Kealey Ser.). 2009. audio compact disk 14.99 (978-1-4233-0756-3(9), 9781423307563, BCD Value Price) Brilliance Audio.

***Invisible.** unabr. ed. Paul Auster. Read by Paul Auster. 6 CDs. (Running Time: 8 hrs. 30 mins.). 2009. audio compact disk 74.95 (978-0-7927-6707-7(1)) AudioGO.

Invisible. unabr. ed. Paul Auster. Read by Paul Auster. 6 CDs. (Running Time: 7 hrs. 30 mins. 0 sec.). (ENG.). 2009. audio compact disk 34.99 (978-1-4272-0805-7(0)) Pub: Macmill Audio. Dist(s): Macmillan

Invisible. unabr. ed. Andrew Britton. Read by J. Charles. (Running Time: 15 hrs.). (Ryan Kealey Ser.). 2008. 39.25 (978-1-4233-0754-9(2), 9781423307549, BADLE); 24.95 (978-1-4233-0753-2(4), 9781423307532, BAD); 112.25 (978-1-4233-0748-8(8), 9781423307488, BrilAudUnabridg); audio compact disk 24.95 (978-1-4233-0751-8(8), 9781423307518, Brilliance MP3); audio compact disk 39.95 (978-1-4233-0749-5(6), 9781423307495, Bril Audio CD Unabri); audio compact disk 39.25 (978-1-4233-0752-5(6), 9781423307525, Brlnc Audio MP3 Lib); audio compact disk 117.25 (978-1-4233-0750-1(X), 9781423307501, BriAudCD Unabrid) Brilliance Audio.

Invisible. unabr. ed. Pete Hautman. Read by Norm Lee. 3 CDs. (Running Time: 3 hrs. 34 mins.). (YA). 2006. audio compact disk 44.75 (978-1-4193-8456-1(2), C3661); 29.75 (978-1-4193-8451-6(1), 98324) Recorded Bks.
National Book Award-winning author Pete Hautman crafts a powerful tale of one tormented boy's troubled life in Invisible. Seventeen-year-old Doug Hanson is obsessed - with his best friend Andy, with pretty Melissa Haverman, and with his model railroad town. Doug also has terrible secrets from his past, and he isn't taking the medication his psychiatrist prescribed.

Invisible Acts of Power: The Divine Energy of a Giving Heart. Caroline Myss. 4 CDs. (Running Time: 5 hrs.). 2006. audio compact disk 29.95 (978-1-59179-135-5(9), W833D) Sounds True.

Invisible Barriers to Healing. Derek Prince. 1 cass. (Running Time: 60 min.). 5.95 (I-4258) Derek Prince.

Invisible Bodies of Men in Hindu Philosphy. Manly P. Hall. 5 cass. (Running Time: 150 min.). 1999. 40.00 Set. (978-0-89314-152-3(6)) Philos Res.
Includes: The Sthula Sharira - Physical Body & Its Attributes; The Living Shariri - The Etheric & Vital Bodies - Their Function; The Kamarupa; The Rupa & Arupa Manas; & The Buddhic Sheath.

Invisible Bridge. unabr. ed. Julie Orringer. Read by Arthur Morey. 2010. audio compact disk 50.00 (978-0-307-71354-4(7), Random AudioBks) Pub: Random Audio Pubg. Dist(s): Random

Invisible City: A Portrait of Turin. Kevin Sylvester. Contrib. by Paul Kennedy. (Running Time: 3600 sec.). 2006. audio compact disk 16.95 (978-0-660-19567-4(4), CBC Audio) Canadian Broadcasting CAN.

Invisible Cord. unabr. ed. Catherine Cookson. Read by Elizabeth Henry. 9 cass. (Running Time: 13 hrs. 30 mins.). 2001. 79.95 (978-1-85496-407-6(0), 64070) Pub: Soundings Ltd GBR. Dist(s): Ulverscroft US

Invisible Employee: Realizing the Hidden Potential in Everyone. unabr. ed. Chester Elton. (Running Time: 3 hrs. 0 mins. 0 sec.). (ENG.). 2006. audio compact disk 19.99 (978-1-4001-0222-8(7)) Pub: Tantor Media. Dist(s): IngramPubServ

Invisible Employee: Realizing the Hidden Potential in Everyone. unabr. ed. Chester Elton. Read by Alan Aklar. (Running Time: 3 hrs. 0 mins. 0 sec.). (ENG.). 2006. audio compact disk 39.99 (978-1-4001-3222-5(3)) Pub: Tantor Media. Dist(s): IngramPubServ

Invisible Employee: Realizing the Hidden Potential in Everyone. unabr. ed. Adrian Gostick & Chester Elton. Narrated by Alan Sklar. (Running Time: 3 hrs. 0 mins. 0 sec.). (ENG.). 2006. audio compact disk 19.99 (978-1-4001-5222-3(4)) Pub: Tantor Media. Dist(s): IngramPubServ

Invisible Friend, Marene P. Fassina. 1 cass. (Running Time: 1 hr.). (J). 1991. 3.95 (978-1-892996-02-2(2)) M Fassina.

Invisible Garment Audio CD Set: 30 Spiritual Principles that Weave the Fabric of Human Life. 8 CDs. 2006. audio compact disk 32.95 (978-0-9786239-8-2(3)) Generosity Inc.

Invisible Gorilla: And Other Ways Our Intuitions Deceive Us. unabr. ed. Daniel Simons & Christopher Chabris. Read by Dan Woren. (ENG.). 2010. audio compact disk 35.00 (978-0-307-73575-1(3), Random AudioBks) Pub: Random Audio Pubg. Dist(s): Random

Invisible Hand Comes to Life: Economics in "Atlas Shrugged" unabr. ed. Richard Salsman. 2 cass. (Running Time: 3 hrs.). 1997. 24.95 Set. (978-1-56114-520-1(3), DS51D) Second Renaissance.
The role of the creative, uncoerced mind in capitalism's productiveness.

Invisible Hands: The Making of the Conservative Movement from the New Deal to Reagan. unabr. ed. Kim Phillips-Fein. Narrated by Lorna Raver. (Running Time: 12 hrs. 30 mins. 0 sec.). (ENG.). 2009. audio compact disk 69.99 (978-1-4001-4075-6(7)); audio compact disk 24.99 (978-1-4001-6075-4(8)) Pub: Tantor Media. Dist(s): IngramPubServ

Invisible Hands: The Making of the Conservative Movement from the New Deal to Reagan. unabr. ed. Kim Phillips-Fein. Read by Lorna Raver. (Running Time: 12 hrs. 30 mins. 0 sec.). (ENG.). 2009. audio compact disk 34.99 (978-1-4001-1075-9(0)) Pub: Tantor Media. Dist(s): IngramPubServ

Invisible Hunters - Los Cazadores Invisibles. Read by Harriet Rohmer et al. As told by Octavio Chow & Morris Vidaure. Illus. by Joe Sam. 1 cass. (Running Time: 30 min.). (Tales of the Americas Ser.). (ENG & SPA.). (J). (gr. 1 up). 9.95 (978-0-89239-054-0(9)) Pub: Childrens Book Pr. Dist(s): PerseuPGW
Miskito Indians of Nicaragua vow to the magic Dar vine that they will never sell the animals they hunt. A metaphor for what happens when native cultures meet with the outside world.

Invisible Hunters (Los Cazadores Invisibles) Read by Harriet Rohmer. As told by Harriet Rohmer. As told by Octavio Chow. Illus. by Joe Sam. 1 cass. (YA). (gr. 1 up). bk. 25.95 (978-0-89239-036-6(0)) Childrens Book Pr.

Invisible Man see Hombre Invisible

Invisible Man. Ralph Ellison. 4 cass. 1999. 25.95 Set. (Random AudioBks) Random Audio Pubg.

Invisible Man. H. G. Well. Retold by John Bergez. (Classic Literature Ser.). 2005. pap. bk. 69.00 (978-1-4105-0113-4(2)); audio compact disk 18.95 (978-1-4105-0114-1(0)) D Johnston Inc.

Invisible Man. H. G. Wells. Read by Alfred von Lecteur. 2009. 27.95 (978-1-60112-986-4(6)) Babblebooks.

Invisible Man. H. G. Wells. Narrated by Walter Covell. (Running Time: 5 hrs.). 1986. 30.95 (978-1-59912-815-3(2)) Iofy Corp.

Invisible Man. H. G. Wells. Read by Guillermo Piedrahita. (Running Time: 3 hrs.). 2002. 16.95 (978-1-60083-200-0(8), Audiofy Corp) Iofy Corp.

Invisible Man. H. G. Wells. Read by Scott Brick. (Running Time: 6 hrs. 24 mins.). 2003. 27.95 (978-1-60083-634-3(8), Audiofy Corp) Iofy Corp.

Invisible Man. H. G. Wells. Perf. by Leonard Nimoy et al. 2 cass. (Running Time: 2 hrs.). 2001. 17.95 (ALEN007); audio compact disk 19.95 (ALEN008) Lodestone Catalog.
A chilling tale of the mad scientist who falls victim to his own diabolical scheme.

Invisible Man. abr. ed. H. G. Wells. Read by Edward Herman. 4 cass. (Running Time: 6 hrs.). (Ultimate Classics Ser.). 2004. 25.00 (978-1-931056-74-8(9), N Millennium Audio) New Millenn Enter.
A strange man, wrapped up from head to foot, arrives at a village inn on a wintry day seeking, in the name of human charity, a room & fire. His

readiness to pay wins him the quick attendance of his hostess, but from that moment on nothing about him bespeaks business as usual.

Invisible Man. abr. adpt. ed. H. G. Wells. (Bring the Classics to Life: Level 3 Ser.). (ENG.). 2008. audio compact disk 12.95 (978-1-55576-449-4(5)) EDCON Pubng.

Invisible Man. unabr. ed. Ralph Ellison. Read by Joe Morton. 16 CDs. (Running Time: 1 hr. 51 mins.). (ENG.). 2005. audio compact disk 34.95 (978-0-7393-2207-9(9), Random AudioBks) Pub: Random Audio Pubg. Dist(s): Random

Invisible Man. unabr. ed. Ralph Ellison. Read by Joe Morton. 11 cass. 1999. 39.95 (FS9-43909) Highsmith.

Invisible Man. unabr. ed. Ralph Ellison. Narrated by Peter Francis James. 15 cass. (Running Time: 22 hrs.). 1947. 122.00 (978-0-7887-4366-5(X), 96072E7) Recorded Bks.
Chronicling a young black man's search for identity through a maze of American intolerance, it is a story of racial prejudice. Even more, it reflects upon humanity's search for what is right & true in an increasingly devious & complex world.

Invisible Man. unabr. ed. H. G. Wells. Read by James Adams. (Running Time: 5.5 hrs. 0 mins.). (ENG.). 2009. 29.95 (978-1-4332-7755-9(7)); 34.95 (978-1-4332-7751-1(4)); audio compact disk 55.00 (978-1-4332-7752-8(2)) Blckstn Audio.

Invisible Man. unabr. ed. H. G. Wells. Read by Tim Behrens. 4 cass. (Running Time: 5 hrs. 30 min.). 26.95 (978-1-55686-158-1(3), 158) Books in Motion.
The sometimes humorous, sometimes eerie story of a man rendered invisible by a chemical process he labored to develop and to which he can't find the antidote.

Invisible Man. unabr. ed. H. G. Wells. Read by Scott Brick. (YA). 2007. 64.99 (978-1-60252-563-4(3)) Find a World.

Invisible Man. unabr. ed. H. G. Wells. Read by Jim Killavey. 4 cass. (Running Time: 5 hrs. 30 mins.). 1979. 27.00 (C-12) Jimcin Record.
Discovers the secret of invisibility & plans a reign of terror.

Invisible Man. unabr. ed. H. G. Wells. Narrated by Vicki Morgan. 4 cass. (Running Time: 4 hrs. 45 mins.). 1986. 35.00 (978-1-55690-257-4(3), 86590E7) Recorded Bks.
A chemist invents a means to make himself invisible.

Invisible Man. unabr. ed. H. G. Wells. Narrated by Scott Brick. (Running Time: 6 hrs. 30 mins. 0 sec.). (ENG.). 2008. 19.99 (978-1-4001-5857-7(5)); audio compact disk 55.99 (978-1-4001-3857-9(4)) Pub: Tantor Media. Dist(s): IngramPubServ

Invisible Man. unabr. ed. H. G. Wells. Read by Peter Joyce. 4 cass. (Running Time: 5 hrs. 40 min.). 1998. 44.95 (978-1-86015-452-2(2)) Pub: UlverLrgPrint GBR. Dist(s): Ulverscroft US
The experiments of a demented scientist bring disaster to himself & those around him.

Invisible Man. unabr. ed. H. G. Wells. Narrated by Scott Brick. (Running Time: 6 hrs. 30 mins. 0 sec.). (ENG.). 2008. audio compact disk 27.99 (978-1-4001-0857-2(8)) Pub: Tantor Media. Dist(s): IngramPubServ

Invisible Man: Abridged. (ENG.). 2007. (978-1-60339-061-3(8)); cd-rom & audio compact disk (978-1-60339-062-0(6)) Listenr Digest.

***Invisible Man: Bring the Classics to Life.** adpt. ed. H. g. Wells. (Bring the Classics to Life Ser.). 2008. pap. bk. 21.95 (978-1-55576-504-0(1)) EDCON Pubng.

Invisible Man - A Father Brown Mystery. G. K. Chesterton. Narrated by James Arthur. (Running Time: 2 hrs. 30 mins.). 2006. 14.95 (978-1-59912-999-0(X)) Iofy Corp.

Invisible Man & other Cases. Seymour Simon. Narrated by Johnny Heller. (Running Time: 1 hr.). (Einstein Anderson Ser.). (gr. 3 up). 10.00 (978-1-4025-2699-2(7)) Recorded Bks.

Invisible Man & Selected Short Stories of Edgar Allan Poe. unabr. ed. H. G. Wells. Read by William Shephard. 8 cass. (Running Time: 8 hrs.). Incl. Black Cat. Edgar Allan Poe. 1984. (1082); Cask of Amontillado. Edgar Allan Poe. 1984. (1082); Fall of the House of Usher & Other Writings. Edgar Allan Poe. 1984. (1082); Ligeia. Edgar Allan Poe. 1984. (1082); Pit & the Pendulum. Edgar Allan Poe. 1984. (1082); Tell-Tale Heart. Edgar Allan Poe. 1984. (1082); 1977. 48.00 (978-0-7366-0072-9(8), 1082) Books on Tape.
Great tales from two masters of science fiction & horror.

Invisible Man Read Along. (Saddleback's Illustrated Classics Ser.). (YA). 2006. (978-1-56254-911-4(1)) Saddleback Edu.

Invisible Monsters. unabr. ed. Chuck Palahniuk. Read by Fields Anna. (Running Time: 21600 sec.). 2007. 24.95 (978-0-7861-4799-1(7)) Blckstn Audio.

Invisible Monsters. unabr. ed. Chuck Palahniuk. Read by Anna Fields. (Running Time: 21600 sec.). 2007. 44.95 (978-0-7861-4803-5(9)) Blckstn Audio.

Invisible Monsters. unabr. ed. Chuck Palahniuk. Read by Fields Anna. 5 CDs. (Running Time: 21600 sec.). 2007. audio compact disk 24.95 (978-0-7861-6238-3(4)) Blckstn Audio.

Invisible Monsters. unabr. ed. Chuck Palahniuk. Read by Anna Fields. (Running Time: 21600 sec.). 2007. audio compact disk 29.95 (978-0-7861-7201-6(0)); audio compact disk 45.00 (978-0-7861-6234-5(1)) Blckstn Audio.

Invisible Mountain. unabr. ed. Carolina De Robertis. (ENG.). 2009. audio compact disk 45.00 (978-0-7393-8446-6(5), Random AudioBks) Pub: Random Audio Pubg. Dist(s): Random

***Invisible Order, Book One, the: Rise of the Darklings: Rise of the Darklings.** unabr. ed. Paul Crilley. (Running Time: 8 hrs.). (Invisible Order Trilogy). 2010. 39.97 (978-1-4418-8869-3(1), 9781441888693, BADLE) Brilliance Audio.

***Invisible Order, Book One, the: Rise of the Darklings: Rise of the Darklings.** unabr. ed. Paul Crilley. Read by Katherine Kellgren. (Running Time: 7 hrs.). (Invisible Order Trilogy). (YA). 2010. 39.97 (978-1-4418-8868-6(3), 9781441888686, Brinc Audio MP3 Lib) Brilliance Audio.

Invisible Prey. unabr. ed. John Sandford. Read by Richard Ferrone. 9 CDs. (Running Time: 11 hrs.). (ENG.). (gr. 8). 2007. audio compact disk 39.95 (978-0-14-314206-5(2), PengAudBks) Penguin Grp USA.

Invisible Road. unabr. ed. Elizabeth Knox. Read by Caroline Lee & Edwina Wren. (Running Time: 23 hrs. 55 mins.). (YA). 2008. 54.95 (978-1-74214-047-6(5), 9781742140476) Pub: Bolinda Pubng AUS. Dist(s): Bolinda Pub Inc

Invisible Support... Delivering a Differentiated Curriculum. rev. ed. Jean Jameson et al. 1995. 74.95 (978-1-873942-90-1(7)) Pub: P Chapman GBR. Dist(s): SAGE

***Invisible Terror Collection.** unabr. ed. Bill Myers. (Running Time: 8 hrs. 40 mins. 1 sec.). (Forbidden Doors Ser.). (ENG.). (YA). 2010. 12.99 (978-0-310-42634-9(0)) Zondervan.

***Invisible Terror Collection: the Encounter.** Bill Myers. (Running Time: 2 hrs. 31 mins. 0 sec.). (Forbidden Doors Ser.). (ENG.). (YA). 2009. 4.99 (978-0-310-72032-4(X)) Zondervan.

***Invisible Terror Collection: the Guardian.** Bill Myers. (Running Time: 3 hrs. 0 mins. 0 sec.). (Forbidden Doors Ser.). (ENG.). (YA). 2009. 4.99 (978-0-310-72031-7(1)) Zondervan.

***Invisible Terror Collection: the Haunting.** Bill Myers. (Running Time: 3 hrs. 10 mins. 0 sec.). (Forbidden Doors Ser.). (ENG.). (YA). 2009. 4.99 (978-0-310-77261-3(3)) Zondervan.

Invisible Touch: The Four Keys to Modern Marketing. Harry Beckwith. Narrated by George Wilson. 4 cass. (Running Time: 5 hrs. 45 mins.). 38.00 (978-0-7887-5502-6(1)) Recorded Bks.

Invisible Touch: The Four Keys to Modern Marketing. abr. ed. Harry Beckwith. Read by Jim Ward. (ENG.). 2005. 14.98 (978-1-59483-472-1(5)) Pub: Hachet Audio. Dist(s): HachBkGrp

Invisible Touch: The Four Keys to Modern Marketing. unabr. ed. Harry Beckwith. 2001. 37.00 (T1003L8) Recorded Bks.
Beckwith takes a more in-depth look at the principles outlined in his bestselling debut, "Selling the Invisible," to build on the importance of effective communication with consumers.

Invisible Wall. unabr. ed. Harry Bernstein. Read by John Lee. (Running Time: 34200 sec.). 2007. 59.95 (978-0-7861-4991-9(4)); audio compact disk 72.00 (978-0-7861-5756-3(9)) Blckstn Audio.

Invisible Wall: A Love Story That Broke Barriers. unabr. ed. Harry Bernstein. Read by John Lee. (Running Time: 34200 sec.). 2007. 26.95 (978-0-7861-4868-4(3)); audio compact disk 26.95 (978-0-7861-6080-8(2)) Blckstn Audio.

Invisible Wall: A Love Story That Broke Barriers. unabr. ed. Harry Bernstein. Read by John Lee. (Running Time: 34200 sec.). 2007. audio compact disk 29.95 (978-0-7861-7158-3(8)) Blckstn Audio.

Invisible War CD Series. 2005. audio compact disk 22.00 (978-1-59834-019-8(0)) Walk Thru the Bible.

Invisible Woman: The Story of Charles Dickens & Nelly Ternan. unabr. ed. Claire Tomalin. 8 cass. (Running Time: 12 hrs.). 2001. 64.00 (978-0-7366-6183-6(2)) Books on Tape.
When Ellen Ternan met Charles Dickens, she was 18 & he was 45. She was a hard-working actress in a society that equated her profession with prostitution, or something close to it. Dickens was the most lionized writer in England, the great bard of domestic virtue.

Invitation. Contrib. by Meredith Andrews & Conor Farley. Prod. by Jason Ingram & Rusty Varenkamp. 2008. audio compact disk 11.99 (978-5-557-44757-7(1), Word Records) Word Enter.

***Invitation.** abr. ed. Oriah. Read by Oriah. (ENG.). 2006. (978-0-06-113052-6(4), Harper Audio); (978-0-06-113051-9(6), Harper Audio) HarperCollins Pubs.

Invitation. unabr. ed. Catherine Cookson. Read by Susan Jameson. 8 cass. (Running Time: 8 hrs.). 1993. 69.95 (978-0-7451-5863-1(3), CAB 474) AudioGO.

Invitation. 4th ed. Ana C. Jarvis. 1993. 57.00 (978-0-03-072406-0(6)) Harcourt.

Invitation: A Simple Guide to the Bible. unabr. ed. Eugene H. Petersen. Narrated by Eugene H. Petersen. (ENG.). 2008. 16.09 (978-1-60814-256-9(6)) Oasis Audio.

Invitation: A Simple Guide to the Bible. unabr. ed. Eugene H. Peterson. (Running Time: 21600 sec.). (ENG.). 2008. audio compact disk 22.99 (978-1-59859-322-8(6)) Oasis Audio.

Invitation: Billy Graham & the Lives God Touched. unabr. ed. Aram Tchividjian & Basyle Tchividjian. Narrated by Basyle Tchividjian. Music by Pat Boone. (Running Time: 2 hrs. 0 mins. 0 sec.). (ENG.). 2008. audio compact disk 15.98 (978-1-59644-655-7(2), christianSeed) christianaud.

***Invitation: Billy Graham & the Lives God Touched.** unabr. ed. Basyle Tchividjian. (ENG.). 2008. 9.98 (978-1-59644-656-4(0), christianSeed) christianaud.

Invitation au Monde Francophone. A. Jarvis. (C). bk. 111.95 (978-0-8384-7966-7(9)) Heinle.

Invitation Au Monde Francophone. Gilbert A. Jarvis. bk. 119.25 (978-0-8384-6440-3(8)) Heinle.

Invitation au Monde Francophone. Gilbert A. Jarvis et al. (FRE.). 2000. lab manual ed. (978-0-03-031006-5(7)) Harcourt Coll Pubs.

Invitation au Monde Francophone: Testing Program. Gilbert A. Jarvis et al. (C). 2000. (978-0-03-030971-7(9)) Harcourt Coll Pubs.

Invitation Essentials. Gilbert A. Jarvis et al. (ENG & FRE.). (C). 1991. bk. (978-0-318-69147-3(7)) Harcourt Coll Pubs.

Invitation Essentials. 2nd ed. Gilbert A. Jarvis et al. (C). 1995. bk. 74.00 (978-0-03-010382-7(7)) Harcourt.

Invitation Only. unabr. ed. Kate Brian, pseud. Narrated by Cassandra Campbell. (Running Time: 6 hrs. 30 mins. 0 sec.). (Private Ser.: No. 2). (ENG.). (J). (gr. 9-12). 2009. 19.99 (978-1-4001-6232-1(7)); audio compact disk 59.99 (978-1-4001-4232-3(6)); audio compact disk 29.99 (978-1-4001-1232-6(X)) Pub: Tantor Media. Dist(s): IngramPubServ

***Invitation to a Beheading.** Vladimir Nabokov. 2010. audio compact disk 29.99 (978-1-4418-7310-1(4)) Brilliance Audio.

Invitation to Awaken: Selected Talks & Dialogues with Adyashanti. 7 Audio CDs. Featuring Adyashanti. (ENG.). 2007. audio compact disk 75.00 (978-1-933986-35-7(2)) Open Gate Pub.

Invitation to Celebrate Recovery: Freedom from Your Hurts, Hang-Ups & Habits. Narrated by John Baker. (Invitation (Maranatha) Ser.). 2008. audio compact disk 9.99 (978-5-557-46572-4(3)) Maranatha Music.

Invitation to Comfort. Narrated by Tim Clinton. (Invitation (Maranatha) Ser.). 2008. audio compact disk 9.99 (978-5-557-46573-1(1)) Maranatha Music.

Invitation to Easter: Matthew 28:1-8; Mark 15:46. Ed Young. 1997. 4.95 (978-0-7417-2134-1(1), 1134) Win Walk.

Invitation to Freedom: A Journey from Brokenness to Wholeness. Narrated by Beth Moore. (Invitation (Maranatha) Ser.). 2008. audio compact disk 9.99 (978-5-557-46574-8(X)) Maranatha Music.

Invitation to Hope. Narrated by Kay Warren. (Invitation (Maranatha) Ser.). 2008. audio compact disk 9.99 (978-5-557-46575-5(8)) Maranatha Music.

Invitation to Insight. Instructed by Manly P. Hall. 8.95 (978-0-89314-153-0(4), C830814) Philos Res.

Invitation to Oceanography. 2nd ed. Paul Pinet. (C). 1999. audio compact disk 101.00 (978-0-7637-1249-5(3), 1249-3) Jones Bartlett.

Invitation to Provence. Elizabeth A. Adler. Read by Carrington MacDuffie. 6 cass. 54.95 (978-0-7927-3305-8(3), CSL 688); audio compact disk 79.95 (978-0-7927-3306-5(1), SLD 688) AudioGO.

Invitation to Psychology. 3rd ed. Wade & Carol Tavris. tchr. ed. 18.97 (978-0-13-178713-1(6)) PH School.

Invitation to Shabbat: A Beginner's Guide to Weekly Celebration. Ruth Perelson & Union of American Hebrew Congregations Department Staff. 1997. pap. bk. 18.00 (978-0-8074-0632-8(5), 386501) URJ Pr.

Invitation to Solitude & Silence: Experiencing God's Transforming Presence. unabr. ed. Ruth Haley Barton. Narrated by Ruth Haley Barton. (Running Time: 4 hrs. 8 mins. 10 sec.). (ENG.). 2009. 13.99 (978-1-60814-548-5(4)); audio compact disk 19.99 (978-1-59859-604-5(7)) Oasis Audio.

Invitation to the Ishaya's Ascension. unabr. ed. MSI Staff. 1 cass. (Running Time: 1 hr.). 1998. (978-0-931783-66-1(6)) SFA Pubns.

Invitation to the Married Life. unabr. ed. Angela Huth. Read by Angela Huth. 8 cass. (Running Time: 10 hrs. 30 min.). (Isis Ser.). (J). 1996. 69.95 (978-0-7531-0080-6(0), 960705) Pub: ISIS Lrg Prnt GBR. Dist(s): Ulverscroft US
Explores the affairs, imaginary & real, of middle-aged married couples. Deals with the varieties of love & boredom that flourish between a husband & a wife.

Invitation to the Opera. unabr. ed. John L. DiGaetani. Read by Nadia May. 7 cass. (Running Time: 10 hrs.). 1996. 49.95 (978-0-7861-1064-3(3), 1835) Blckstn Audio.
This invaluable primer will introduce the uninitiated to the mysteries of opera & help more experienced buffs to expand their understanding & deepen their appreciation of the art form.

Invocation of the Angels. Joan Borysenko. Read by Joan Borysenko. Ed. by Jill Kramer. 1 cass. (Running Time: 60 min.). 1995. 10.00 (978-1-56170-120-9(3), 276) Hay House.
Treatments & meditations to help you in your appeal to the angels around you.

Invocation of the Angels. Joan Z. Borysenko. 1 CD. 2005. audio compact disk 10.95 (978-1-4019-0434-0(3)) Hay House.

Invocation of the Holy Name, A Prayer for All Seasons. Contrib. by Kallistos T. Ware. 4 cass. (Running Time: 240 mins.). 15.95 (978-1-891295-07-2(1), OakPubns) St Vladimirs.

Invocations. (Running Time: 61 min.). 1981. 12.00 (978-0-932360-48-9(3)) Archae Edns.
An audio-art piece about the sound of the language of prayer in 25 languages. Available with openings in German, English, Scandinavian languages, Latin, & Italian-Yugoslav languages.

Invocations: Sacred Music from World Traditions. 1 cass., 1 CD. 7.98 (MOW 151); audio compact disk 12.78 CD Jewel box. (MOW 15188) NewSound.

Invocations for Health, Longevity & Healing a Broken Heart. Hua-Ching Ni. Read by Maoshing Ni. 1 cass. (Running Time: 30 min.). 1992. 9.95 (AINVO, Shrine Eternal) SevenStar Comm.
A series of invocations (positive affirmations) from an ancient natural spiritual tradition for cultivating health & longevity & healing a broken heart.

Invoking His Help. Swami Amar Jyoti. 1 cass. 1982. 9.95 (M-32) Truth Consciousness.
How did we get into this 'bottle' of ego? End of all evolutions: the ultimate awakening into full Consciousness.

Invoking the Magnificence of the I AM. Sai Maa Lakshmi Devi. 2002. audio compact disk 16.00 (978-1-933488-09-7(3)) HIU Pr.
Sai Maa Lakshmi Devi leads us in a profound meditation capturing the essence of Her work - transforming the density of our physical matter into Light. Progressively flooding the physical and subtle bodies with the radiance of the I AM Self, Sai Maa guides us step by step to connect with the God Presence within and step into our own Mastery.Excellent for use with daily spiritual practice.Recorded in San Rafael, CA June 2002.

Invoking the Muse. Layne Redmond. 1 CD. (Running Time: 55 mins.). 2006. audio compact disk 16.98 (978-1-59179-181-2(2), M816D) Sounds True.
While researching the ancient music of Greece, Layne Redmond discovered the beautiful "Hymn to the Muse" written in 157 A.D., and was inspired to create a musical tribute to each of the Nine Muses. On Invoking the Muse, Layne Redmond offers listeners a landscape of haunting melodies and mesmerizing layers of rhythm and harmony dedicated to the power of the Muse.

Invoking the Sacred: For Healing, Guidance, Abundance & Relationships. Caroline Myss & Ron Roth. (Invoking The Sacred). 1995. 55.00 (978-1-893869-51-6(2)) Celbrtng Life.

Involvement with Life. Ram Dass. 1 cass. (Running Time: 1 hr. 32 min.). 1974. 11.00 (00604) Big Sur Tapes.

Inward Journey: More Music from Health Journeys. Perf. by Steven Mark Kohn. Composed by Steven Mark Kohn. 1 CD. (Running Time: 75 Minutes). (Health Journeys Ser.: No. 2144). 2003. audio compact disk 17.98 (978-1-881405-67-2(2)) Hlth Jrnys.
Three tracks of music to explore, energize, calm and uplift. Inward Journey was initially written to accompany the Health Journeys audio program Healing Trauma, taking the listener on a deep journey down into the layers of the heart, from pain to transcendence. Breaking Free is the energizing, motivating and empowering music from the Cardiac Rehab program. And Dreamwaves, scored to end-of-life care, has an evocative, gentle sweetness that quiets the body, touches the heart and settles the spirit.

Inward or True Beauty. J. Krishnamurti. 1 cass. (Running Time: 1 hr.). (Krishnamurti with Dr. Allan W. Anderson Ser.: No. 9). 8.50 (APA749) Krishnamurti.
These 1974 dialogues cover the entire spectrum of Krishnamurti's teaching in a series highly regarded for its depth of inquiry into each particular subject.

Iodine. unabr. ed. Haven Kimmel. (ENG.). 2008. audio compact disk 29.95 (978-1-60283-457-6(1)) Pub: AudioGO. Dist(s): Perseus Dist

Ion-Exchange Chromatography. Instructed by Harold F. Walton. Prod. by American Chemical Society Staff. 5 cass. (Running Time: 5 hrs.). 25.00 manual. Am Chemical.
Overviews the highly diverse field of ion chromatography. It teaches the basic theory behind semingly complicated processes. Lessons provide a wealth of information on the nature of ion exchange, its uses, basic, techniques, & future applications of this valuable analytical tool. Filled with practical examples & helpful practice exercises, this course provides a fascinating insight into the theories & applications involved in ion-exchange chromatography.

Ionia: A Quest. unabr. collector's ed. Freya Stark. Read by Donada Peters. 8 cass. (Running Time: 8 hrs.). 1991. 48.00 (978-0-7366-1922-6(4), 2746) Books on Tape.
Ionia is a travel book unlike any other that the author has written, for when she went to Asia Minor it was on an exploration into history with Herodotus as her companion. Ionia & Aeolis, Heracleia & Aphrodisias - these are names that for many have only the sound of familiarity. Through the author's discoveries we experience them too, & in doing so find a world which, in spite of harshness, conflict & insecurity, contains much beauty & happiness.

Ionian Mission. Patrick O'Brian. (Running Time: 12 hrs. 0 mins.). (Aubrey-Maturin Ser.). 2005. 72.95 (978-0-7861-3448-9(8)); audio compact disk 90.00 (978-0-7861-7933-6(3)) Blckstn Audio.

Ionian Mission. Patrick O'Brian. Narrated by Simon Vance. (Running Time: 12 hrs.). (Aubrey-Maturin Ser.). 2005. 34.95 (978-1-59912-676-0(1)) Iofy Corp.

Ionian Mission. Patrick O'Brian. Narrated by Patrick Tull. 13 CDs. (Running Time: 15.25 hrs). (Aubrey-Maturin Ser.). 1981. audio compact disk 49.95 (978-1-4025-6287-7(X)) Recorded Bks.

Ionian Mission. unabr. ed. Patrick O'Brian. Read by Simon Vance. 10 CDs. (Running Time: 43200 sec.). (Aubrey-Maturin Ser.). 2005. audio compact disk 32.95 (978-0-7861-7783-7(7), ZE3457) Blckstn Audio.

Ionian Mission. unabr. ed. Patrick O'Brian. Read by Richard Brown. 10 cass. (Running Time: 15 hrs.). (Aubrey-Maturin Ser.). 1993. 80.00 (978-0-7366-2336-0(1), 3115) Books on Tape.
A sudden turn of events take Jack Aubrey & Stephen Maturin on a hazardous mission to the Greek Islands. Eighth in series.

Ionian Mission. unabr. ed. Patrick O'Brian. Narrated by Patrick Tull. 11 cass. (Running Time: 15 hrs. 15 mins.). (Aubrey-Maturin Ser.: No. 8). 1994. 91.00 (978-1-55690-985-6(3), 94124E7) Recorded Bks.
Shoved into a temporary command in "that rotten old Worcester," Aubrey is off to the Mediterranean to join the Royal Navy's blockade of the French port of Toulon, where he will eventually be dispatched by Admiral Harte (unfortunately the same Admiral Harte he cuckolded years ago) on a secret mission that promises to embroil Aubrey in political conflict. His friend Stephen's help notwithstanding, Aubrey faces some of the choppiest waters of his career.

Ionian Mission. unabr. ed. Patrick O'Brian & Simon Vance. 13 vols. (Running Time: 12 hrs.). (Aubrey-Maturin Ser.). 2005. audio compact disk 29.95 (978-0-7861-8109-4(5), ZM3457) Blckstn Audio.

Ionian Mission. unabr. ed. Patrick O'Brian & Simon Vance. 9 cass. (Running Time: 12 hrs.). (Aubrey-Maturin Ser.). 2005. 29.95 (978-0-7861-3541-7(7), E3457) Blckstn Audio.

Ionych. Anton Chekhov. 1 cass. (Running Time: 1 hr. 30 min.). (RUS.). 1996. pap. bk. 24.50 (978-1-58085-566-2(0)) Interlingua VA.
Includes Russian text. The combination of written text & clarity & pace of diction will open the door for intermediate & advanced students to genuine comprehension & the use of literary texts for advancement in rapid understanding of written & oral language materials. The audio text plus written text concept makes foreign languages accessible to a much wider range of students than books alone.

Iosepa Kaho'oluhi Nawahiokalani'opu'u. Ku'ulei Higashi. 1 cass. (HAW., (J). (gr. 2-3). 1999. pap. bk. 5.95 (978-1-58191-081-0(9)) Aha Punana Leo.

Iowa Baseball Confederacy: A Novel see W. P. Kinsella

Iowa Baseball Confederacy: A Novel. unabr. ed. W. P. Kinsella. Read by Tom Parker. 6 cass. (Running Time: 9 hrs.). 1994. 44.95 (978-0-7861-0475-8(9), 1353) Blckstn Audio.
Gideon Clarke is a man on a quest. He is out to prove to the world, as his father tried before him, that the world-champion Chicago Cubs traveled to Onamata, Iowa, in the summer of 1908 for an exhibition game against all-stars from the Iowa Baseball Confederacy, an amateur league. Gideon's life is further complicated by the unpredictable comings & goings of his wife, Sunny, who often heads for the interstate, bag in hand, to hitch to God-knows-where, leaving Gideon to his lonely baseball obsession. On one such lonely evening, Gideon & his best friend, Stan, an aging bush-league outfielder, follow an old train roadbed, the Baseball Spur, to a rendezvous with time & destiny.

Iowa Baseball Confederacy: A Novel. unabr. ed. W. P. Kinsella. Read by Tom Parker. 6 cass. (Running Time: 8 hrs. 30 mins.). 2006. 44.95 (978-0-7861-0401-7(5), 1353) Blckstn Audio.

Iowa Baseball Confederacy: A Novel. unabr. ed. W. P. Kinsella. Read by W. P. Kinsella. 1 cass. (Running Time: 29 min.). 1991. 10.00 (051686) New Letters.

Iowa Senate Race see Campaigning, Innovative: Four Case Studies

Ipcress File. unabr. ed. Len Deighton. Read by Robert Whitfield. 1 CD. (Running Time: 7 hrs.). 2001. audio compact disk 19.95 (zm2447) Blckstn Audio.
For the working-class narrator, an apparently straightforward mission to find a missing biochemist becomes a journey to the heart of a dark & deadly conspiracy.

Ipcress File. unabr. collector's ed. Len Deighton. Read by Paul Daneman. 7 cass. (Running Time: 7 hrs.). 1990. 42.00 (978-0-7366-1827-4(9), 2663) Books on Tape.
What would happen if the Kremlin could bring off a plot to put its operatives in controling positions in Her Majesty's government? Subjects, with the highest security clearance, who feed top level secrets directly to the East? It would mean, for England, almost certain destruction! This gripping novel of international intrigue & espionage is not only a fascinating adventure but a superb close-up of the inner workings of a shadowy & fantastic profession. And because the Russians enjoyed such success in real life in penetrating British security, Len Deighton's fiction mirrors fact.

Ipi No. 59: Maria Del Sol. 2003. audio compact disk 3.99 (978-0-8297-3859-9(2)) Zondervan.

IPocketBible New Living Translation Edition: For your IPod. Narrated by Mike Kellogg. 5 CDs. (Running Time: 73 hrs 33 minutes). Dramatization. 2005. 49.97 (978-0-9753761-2-6(8)) Laridian Inc.
Complete text and audio of New Living Translation Bible for reading and listening to on iPod mobile digital devices.

***IPocketBible the Message Remix Edition: For your IPod.** Narrated by Kelly Ryan Nolan. (Running Time: 4500). (ENG.). 2007. audio compact disk 49.97 (978-0-9753761-3-3(6)) Laridian Inc.

IPower: 4 Keys to Download the Power. Perf. by Patrick Ondrey. (ENG.). 2007. audio compact disk (978-0-9795480-2-4(0)) Palm Tree.

Ipupiara: Rainforest Shaman. Interview. Ipupiara & Cleicha. As told by Ipupiara & Cleicha. Interview with Laura Lee. Prod. by Paul Robear. Contrib. by Scott Sanders. 3 cass. (Running Time: 3 hrs.). 2001. 24.95 (978-1-889071-21-3(8), 6325) Radio Bookstore.
In this audio presentation, Ipupiara, a shaman of the Uru-e-wau-wau tribe of the Brazilian Amazon shares the story of his life, his training as a shaman, as well as: Why his tribe call themselves "The People of the Stars" and the legend of their ET visitation. The Tribal Elders? Message. The world's impact on the Amazon Rainforest. A simple technique for purifying and protecting the home. Why the world is as you dream it. Focusing one's intent. Why "we are all shamans" in training and hold this promise in our very DNA. Our need for symbols. A reminder that shamans are human beings, not saints, nor magicians. Reconnecting to the Great Spirit and to Mother Earth. The role and tools of shamans. Where and how healing occurs.Ipu?s wife Cleicha performs these traditional chants: Calling upon the Spirits, Honoring Mother Earth, and Chanting for Community.

IQ Booster Kit Vols. 1-4: Designed to Increase Your Child's Learning Potential. unabr. ed. Simone Bibeau. Read by Simone Bibeau. 4 cass. (Running Time: 6 hrs.). (Developing the Early Learner Ser.). (J). (ps-2). 1984. pap. bk. 99.00 incl. 4 bks. (978-0-940406-05-6(5), 012) Perception Pubns.
Designed to teach parents how to understand & increase their child's learning potential.

Iqbal. 2 cass. (Running Time: 3 hrs.). 2004. 19.75 (978-1-4025-8487-9(3)) Recorded Bks.

Ira Says Goodbye. Bernard Waber. Read by Larry Robinson. 1 cass. (J). 2000. pap. bk. 19.97 (978-0-7366-9204-5(5)) Books on Tape.
Ira deals with a common crisis of childhood when he is confronted with the news that his neighbor & closest friend, Reggie, is moving to another town.

Ira Says Goodbye. Bernard Waber. Illus. by Bernard Waber. 14 vols. (Running Time: 18 mins.). 1991. pap. bk. 35.95 (978-1-59519-048-2(1)); 9.95 (978-1-59112-067-4(5)); audio compact disk 12.95 (978-1-59519-046-8(5)) Live Oak Media.

Ira Says Goodbye. Bernard Waber. Illus. by Bernard Waber. 11 vols. (Running Time: 18 mins.). (J). 1991. pap. bk. 18.95 (978-1-59519-047-5(3)) Pub: Live Oak Media. Dist(s): AudioGO

Ira Says Goodbye. unabr. ed. Bernard Waber. Illus. by Bernard Waber. Read by Larry Robinson. 11 vols. (Running Time: 18 mins.). (J). (gr. k-3). 2005. pap. bk. 16.95 (978-0-87499-138-3(2)) AudioGO.
Ira deals with a common crisis of childhood when he is confronted with the news that his neighbor and closest friend, Reggie, is moving to another town.

Ira Says Goodbye. unabr. ed. Bernard Waber. Illus. by Bernard Waber. Read by Larry Robinson. 14 vols. (Running Time: 18 mins.). (J). 1991. pap. bk. & tchr. ed. 33.95 Reading Chest. (978-0-87499-140-6(4)) Live Oak Media.
This story deals with a common crisis of childhood when Ira, first introduced in "Ira Sleeps Over", is confronted with the news that his neighbor & closest friend, Reggie, is moving to another town.

Ira Says Goodbye. unabr. ed. Bernard Waber. Illus. by Bernard Waber. Read by Larry Robinson. 11 vols. (Running Time: 18 mins.). (J). (gr. k-3). 1991. bk. 25.95 (978-0-87499-139-0(0)) Live Oak Media.

Ira Series. Bernard Waber. Illus. by Bernard Waber. 22 vols. (Running Time: 32 mins.). 1991. pap. bk. 30.95 (978-0-87499-473-5(X)) Live Oak Media.

Ira Sleeps Over. Bernard Waber. Read by Larry Robinson. 1 cass. (J). 2000. pap. bk. 19.97 (978-0-7366-9206-9(1)) Books on Tape.
A small boy who, is invited to sleep at a friend's house, faces a dilemma. Does he take his teddy bear along & be embarrassed or leave the bear home & sleep without his constant bedtime companion?.

Ira Sleeps Over. Bernard Waber. 1 read along cass. (Running Time: 14 min.). (J). 1984. 9.95 Live Oak Media.
The story of a small boy who, when invited to sleep at a friend's house, faces the dilemma of taking his teddy bear along & being embarrassed or leaving the bear home & sleeping without his constant bedtime companion.

Ira Sleeps Over. Bernard Waber. Read by Larry Robinson. 11 vols. (Running Time: 14 mins.). (J). (gr. k-3). 1984. pap. bk. 16.95 (978-0-941078-34-4(5)) Pub: Live Oak Media. Dist(s): AudioGO
Everyone's favorite story of a small boy who, when invited to sleep at a friend's house, faces a dilemma. Does he take his teddy bear along and be embarrassed or leave the bear home and sleep without his constant bedtime companion?.

Ira Sleeps Over. Bernard Waber. Illus. by Bernard Waber. (Running Time: 14 mins.). 1984. 9.95 (978-1-59112-068-1(3)); audio compact disk 12.95 (978-1-59519-050-5(3)) Live Oak Media.

Ira Sleeps Over. Bernard Waber. Illus. by Bernard Waber. 11 vols. (Running Time: 14 mins.). (J). 1984. pap. bk. 18.95 (978-1-59519-051-2(1)) Pub: Live Oak Media. Dist(s): AudioGO

Ira Sleeps Over. unabr. ed. Bernard Waber. Read by Larry Robinson. 14 vols. (Running Time: 14 mins.). (J). 1984. pap. bk. & tchr. ed. 33.95 Reading Chest. (978-0-941078-35-1(3)) Live Oak Media.
The story of a small boy who, when invited to sleep at a friend's house, faces the dilemma of taking his teddy bear along & being embarrassed or leaving the bear home & sleeping without his constant bedtime companion.

Ira Sleeps Over. unabr. ed. Bernard Waber. Read by Larry Robinson. 11 vols. (Running Time: 14 mins.). (J). (gr. k-3). 1984. bk. 25.95 (978-0-941078-36-8(1)) Live Oak Media.

IRad: Interactive Radiology Review & Assessment. Felix S. Chew et al. (ENG.). 2000. audio compact disk 199.00 (978-0-683-30382-7(1)) Lppncott W W.

Iran: The Untold Story. unabr. collector's ed. Mohamed Heikal. Read by Bob Erickson. 6 cass. (Running Time: 9 hrs.). 1984. 48.00 (978-0-7366-0737-7(4), 1694) Books on Tape.
Heikal tells us what happened in the last days of the Shah's regime. He discloses for the first time what Khomeini's forces knew about American intentions & how they uncovered top U.S. secrets.

Iraq: The Forever War. Noam Chomsky. (Running Time: 1 hr. 0 mins. 0 sec.). (PM Audio Ser.). (ENG.). 2010. audio compact disk 14.95 (978-1-60486-100-6(2)) Pub: Pm Pre. Dist(s): IPG Chicago

Iraq & Biblical Prophecy CD Series. 2004. audio compact disk 17.00 (978-1-59834-031-0(X)) Walk Thru the Bible.

Iraq War. John Keegan. Narrated by Simon Vance. (Running Time: 8 hrs. 30 mins.). (C). 2004. 27.95 (978-1-59912-677-7(X)) Iofy Corp.

Iraq War. unabr. ed. John Keegan. 6 cass. (Running Time: 8 hrs.). 2004. 44.95 (978-0-7861-2777-1(5), 3299); audio compact disk 56.00 (978-0-7861-8541-2(4), 3299) Blckstn Audio.

Iraq War. unabr. ed. John Keegan. Read by Geoffrey Howard. (Running Time: 8 hrs.). 2005. audio compact disk 24.95 (978-0-7861-8520-7(1), 3299); audio compact disk 32.95 (978-0-7861-8585-6(6), ZE3299); reel tape 29.95 (978-0-7861-2730-6(9), E3299) Blckstn Audio.
From the best-selling author of The First World War and Intelligence in War comes the most up-to-date and informed study yet of the Iraq War. John Keegan, whom the New York Review of Books calls "the best historian of our day," now brings his extraordinary expertise to bear on perhaps the most controversial war of our time. In exclusive interviews with Secretary of Defense Donald Rumsfeld and General Tommy Franks, John Keegan has gathered information about the war that adds immeasurably to our grasp of its causes, complications, costs, and consequences. The Iraq War is authoritative, timely, and vitally important to our understanding of a conflict whose ramifications are as yet unknown.

Iraqi Arabic Dialect Orientation Course CDs & Text. 4 CDs. (Running Time: 2 hrs.). (ARA.). 2005. audio compact disk 85.00 (978-1-57970-163-5(9), AFA550D) J Norton Pubs.

Iraqi Dialect Orientation Course. Prod. by Defense Language Institute Staff. 4 cass. (Running Time: 2 hrs.). 2001. pap. bk. 65.00 (AFA550) J Norton Pubs.
Presumes a rudimentary knowledge of Arabic & is designed to supplement existing texts. Lesson 1 stresses pronunciation & Iraqi dialect sounds, thereafter Lessons 2-11 are grouped by topic. Typical situations include greetings, use of courtesy phrases, expressions of time & weather.

Iraqi Dialect Orientation Course: Mdultilingual Books Language Course. Joe Kallu et al. 4 CD's. (Multilingual Books Intensive Language Courses). (ARA.). (C). 2003. per. 79.00 (978-1-58214-198-5(3)) Language Assocs.

Iraqi Dialect Orientation Course: Multilingual Books Language Course. Joe Kallu. 4 cass. (Multilingual Books Intensive Cassette Foreign Language Ser.). (ARA.). (C). 2003. per. 69.00 (978-1-58214-193-0(2)) Language Assocs.

***Ireland.** unabr. ed. Frank Delaney. Read by Frank Delaney. (ENG.). 2005. (978-0-06-083884-3(1), Harper Audio); (978-0-06-083883-6(3), Harper Audio) HarperCollins Pubs.

Ireland. unabr. ed. Paul Johnson. Read by Nadia May. 6 cass. (Running Time: 8 hrs. 30 mins.). 1995. 44.95 (978-0-7861-0717-9(0), 1595) Blckstn Audio.
No one will gainsay that Ireland is a beautiful, enchanted place. But Ireland has a history more varied, turbulent, fascinating & terrible than any other. From the first English presence in Ireland in the twelfth century, through siege, rebellion & civil war, to Irish Ascendancy, Home Rule & the present-day troubles, bestselling author Paul Johnson tells, with remarkable clarity & concision, the compelling story of this most remarkable island.

Ireland. unabr. ed. Wendy McElroy. Read by Harry Reasoner et al. 2 cass. (Running Time: 3 hrs.). (World's Political Hot Spots Ser.). 1991. 17.95 Set. (978-0-938935-90-2(9), 10355) Knowledge Prod.
This "isle of poets & scholars" has known almost constant warfare for centuries. In 1920, it was divided into North & South; yet this purely political solution left a religious & cultural schism intact.

Ireland. unabr. ed. Read by Harry Reasoner. Created by Blackstone Audiobooks. (Running Time: 10800 sec.). (World's Political Hot Spots Ser.). 2006. audio compact disk 25.95 (978-0-7861-6695-4(9)) Pub: Blckstn Audio. Dist(s): NetLibrary CO

Ireland. unabr. novel ed. Frank Delaney. Read by Frank Delaney. 2005. audio compact disk 39.95 (978-0-06-074189-1(9)) HarperCollins Pubs.

Ireland: A Concise History from the Twelfth Century to the Present Day. unabr. ed. Paul Johnson. Read by Nadia May. (Running Time: 28800 sec.). 2007. audio compact disk 63.00 (978-0-7861-5813-3(1)); audio compact disk 29.95 (978-0-7861-5814-0(X)) Blckstn Audio.

Ireland: Cork to Shannon, Tape 3. 1 cass. (Running Time: 90 min.). (Guided Auto Tape Tour). 12.95 (I3); Comp Comms Inc.

Ireland: Shannon to Sligo, Tape 1. 1 cass. (Running Time: 90 min.). (Guided Auto Tape Tour). 12.95 (I1); Comp Comms Inc.

Ireland: Sligo to Cork, Tape 2. 1 cass. (Running Time: 90 min.). (Guided Auto Tape Tour). 12.95 (I2); Comp Comms Inc.

Ireland's Best Fiddle Tunes. Compiled by Paul McNevin. 2000. audio compact disk 27.95 (978-0-7866-5681-3(6)) Waltons Manu IRL.

Ireland's Best Fiddle Tunes, Volume 1. Compiled by Paul McNevin. (Ireland's Best Collection). 2003. audio compact disk 34.95 (978-1-85720-105-5(1)) Waltons Manu IRL.

Ireland's Best Polkas & Slides. Created by Mel Bay Publications Inc. 2000. audio compact disk 26.95 (978-0-7866-5680-6(8)) Mel Bay.

Ireland's Best Session Tunes, Volume 1. Created by Walton Manufacturing Ltd. 2000. audio compact disk 26.95 (978-0-7866-5683-7(2)) Waltons Manu IRL.

Ireland's Best Session Tunes, Volume 1. Created by Waltons Publishing. (Ireland's Best Collection). 2003. audio compact disk 34.95 (978-1-85720-107-9(8)) Waltons Manu IRL.

Ireland's Best Session Tunes, Volume 2. John Canning. (Ireland's Best Collection). 2003. audio compact disk 34.95 (978-1-85720-144-4(2)) Waltons Manu IRL.

Ireland's Best Slow Airs. Created by Mel Bay Publications Inc. 2001. audio compact disk 27.95 (978-0-7866-5682-0(4)) Waltons Manu IRL.

Ireland's Best Tin Whistle Tunes. Compiled by Clare McKenna. 2000. audio compact disk 27.95 (978-0-7866-5679-0(4)) Waltons Manu IRL.

Ireland's Best Tin Whistle Tunes, Volume 1. Compiled by Claire McKenna. (Ireland's Best Collection). 2003. audio compact disk 29.95 (978-1-85720-106-2(X)) Waltons Manu IRL.

Ireland's Own see Sir John Betjeman Reading His Poetry

Irene at Large. unabr. ed. Carole Nelson Douglas. Narrated by Virginia Leishman & Patrick Tull. 10 cass. (Running Time: 13 hrs. 30 mins.). 2000. 91.00 (978-0-7887-2492-3(4), 95567E7) Recorded Bks.
Mystery that begins in the rugged afghanistani wilderness & ends in bustling Victorian London. As flamboyant diva & amateur detective Irene Adler protects a stranger form an unnamed foe, she finds herself matching wits with both a vicious killer & Sherlock Holmes. The only woman known to have earned the admiration of Sherlock Holmes, Irene reveals new information about this famous sleuth.

Irene, la Valiente. William Steig. 1 cass. (Running Time: 35 min.). (SPA.). (J). 2001. 15.95 (VXS-44C) Kimbo Educ.

Irene, la Valiente. William Steig. Illus. by William Steig. (Running Time: 20 mins.). 1997. 9.95 (978-1-59112-069-8(1)) Live Oak Media.

Irene, la Valiente. William Steig. Illus. by William Steig. Read by Susan Rybin. 14 vols. (Running Time: 20 mins.). (SPA.). 1997. pap. bk. & tchr. ed. 33.95 Reading Chest. (978-0-87499-416-2(0)) Live Oak Media.
Despite a raging snowstorm, Irene, a dressmaker's daughter offers to deliver the duchess's newly finished ball gown. This story follows her journey through the storm.

Irene la Valiente. William Steig. Illus. by William Steig. 14 vols. (Running Time: 20 mins.). 1997. pap. bk. 35.95 (978-1-59519-171-7(2)); audio compact disk 12.95 (978-1-59519-169-4(0)) Live Oak Media.

Irene la Valiente. William Steig. Illus. by William Steig. 11 vols. (Running Time: 20 mins.). (SPA.). (J). (gr. k-4). 1997. 12.95 (978-1-59519-170-0(4)) Live Oak Media.

Irene, la Valiente. unabr. ed. William Steig. Illus. by William Steig. Read by Susan Rybin. 1 cass. (Running Time: 20 mins.). (SPA.). (J). (gr. k-3). 1997. bk. 24.95 (978-0-87499-415-5(2)); pap. bk. 16.95 (978-0-87499-414-8(4)) Pub: Live Oak Media. Dist(s): AudioGO

Irene's Last Waltz. unabr. ed. Carole Nelson Douglas. Narrated by Virginia Leishman. 12 cass. (Running Time: 16 hrs.). 2000. 97.00 (978-0-7887-2493-0(2), 95568E7) Recorded Bks.
After her last case, diva & amateur detective Irene Adler, the only woman ever to have outwitted Sherlock Holmes, recuperates at her home in Paris. But rest is fleeting when a royal princess approaches her about a loveless husband & a puzzling dilemma that threatens to destroy whole sections of Europe.

Iris: A Memoir of Iris Murdoch. unabr. ed. John Bayley. Narrated by Tony Haygarth. 5 cass. (Running Time: 7 hrs.). 1998. 48.00 (978-1-84197-413-2(7)) Recorded Bks.
Iris Murdoch and John Bayley were inseparable for over 40 years. She was one of Britain's most distinguished authors, he a respected Oxford professor. This moving yet unsentimental memoir chronicles their life together in the heady atmosphere of academia, her immense achievements as a writer, and her eventual tragic decline after succumbing to Alzheimer's Disease.

Iris & Walter & Cousin Howie. Elissa Haden Guest. Narrated by Barbara McCulloh. (Running Time: 30 mins.). (J). 2003. 10.75 (978-1-4025-9418-2(6)) Recorded Bks.

Iris Johansen: Pandora's Daughter; Quicksand; Dark Summer. abr. ed. Iris Johansen. (Running Time: 18 hrs.). 2009. audio compact disk 34.99 (978-1-4418-0150-0(2), 9781441801500, BACD) Brilliance Audio.

***Iris Johansen CD Collection 2: Deadlock; Blood Game.** abr. ed. Iris Johansen. Read by Jennifer Van Dyck. (Running Time: 12 hrs.). 2010. audio compact disk 19.99 (978-1-4418-6163-4(7), 9781441861634, BACD) Brilliance Audio.

Irish see Acting with an Accent

Irish. 2 cass. (Running Time: 80 min.). (Language - Thirty Library). bk. 16.95 set in vinyl album. Moonbeam Pubns.

Using the proven method based on the famous U.S. Military accelerated language learning program, Language/30 courses stress conversationally useful words & phrases.

Irish. unabr. ed. Ed. by Charles Berlitz. 2 cass. (Language/30 Brief Course Ser.). (IRI.). pap. bk. 21.95 (AF1059) J Norton Pubs.

Quick, highly condensed introduction to the words & phrases you'll need to communicate effectively in the country you're visiting. Cassettes & phrase guide book are in a vinyl album.

Irish: Language 30. Educational Services Corporation Staff. 2004. audio compact disk 21.95 (978-1-931850-04-9(6)) Educ Svcs DC.

Irish: Language/30. rev. ed. Educational Services Corporation Staff. Intro. by Charles Berlitz. 2 cass. (IRI.). 1994. pap. bk. 21.95 (978-0-910542-85-2(6)) Educ Svcs DC.

Irish self-teaching language course.

Irish: Learn to Speak & Understand Gaelic Irish with Pimsleur Language Programs. unabr. ed. Pimsleur Staff. (Running Time: 5 hrs. 0 mins. 0 sec.). (Basic Ser.). (ENG.). 2007. audio compact disk 49.95 (978-0-7435-6401-4(4), Pimsleur) Pub: S&S Audio. Dist(s): S and S Inc

Irish: Learn to Speak & Understand Irish (Gaelic) unabr. ed. Pimsleur Staff. 4 CDs. (Running Time: 400 hrs. 0 mins. NaN sec.). (Pimsleur Language Program Ser.). (ENG.). 2001. audio compact disk 19.95 (978-0-7435-0015-9(6), Pimsleur) Pub: S&S Audio. Dist(s): S and S Inc

Irish-American - Scandinavian-American. Joe Giordano. Narrated by George Guidall. Contrib. by Monica McGoldrick & Beth Erickson. 6 cass. (Running Time: 30 min.). (Growing Up in America Ser.: Vol. 1). 1997. 12.00 Set. (978-1-891207-01-3(6)) Ethnic Prods.

Irish Button Accordion Techniques. Contrib. by Peter Browne. (Running Time: 50 mins.). (ENG.). 2006. 32.95 (978-5-558-08920-2(2)) Waltons Manu IRL.

Irish Country Christmas. unabr. ed. Patrick Taylor. Narrated by John Keating. 13 CDs. (Running Time: 16 hrs. 30 mins. 0 sec.). (Irish Country Bks.). (ENG.). 2008. audio compact disk 44.95 (978-1-4272-0520-9(5)) Pub: Macmill Audio. Dist(s): Macmillan

***Irish Country Courtship.** unabr. ed. Patrick Taylor. (Running Time: 14 hrs. 0 mins. 0 sec.). (Irish Country Bks.). (ENG.). 2010. audio compact disk 39.99 (978-1-4272-1059-3(4)) Pub: Macmill Audio. Dist(s): Macmillan

Irish Country Doctor. unabr. ed. Patrick Taylor. Read by John Keating. (Running Time: 11 hrs. 0 mins. 0 sec.). (ENG.). 2009. audio compact disk 39.95 (978-1-4272-0704-3(6), Rena Bks) Pub: St Martin. Dist(s): Macmillan

Irish Country Girl. unabr. ed. Patrick Taylor. Read by Terry Donnelly. (Running Time: 10 hrs. 30 mins. 0 sec.). (Irish Country Bks.). (ENG.). 2010. audio compact disk 39.99 (978-1-4272-0890-3(5)) Pub: Macmill Audio. Dist(s): Macmillan

Irish Country Village. unabr. ed. Patrick Taylor. Read by John Keating. (Running Time: 14 hrs. 0 mins. 0 sec.). (ENG.). 2008. audio compact disk 39.95 (978-1-4272-0276-5(1)) Pub: Macmill Audio. Dist(s): Macmillan

Irish Dadgad Guitar. Sarah McQuaid. 1996. audio compact disk 19.95 (978-0-946005-93-2(1)) Pub: Ossian IRL. Dist(s): H Leonard

Irish Fairy Tales. unabr. ed. Perf. by Cyril Cusack. 1 cass. Incl. Cucullin & the Legend of Knockmany. (J). (CDL5 1349); Guleesh. (J). (CDL5 1349); (J). 1972. 11.00 (978-0-694-50710-8(5), CDL5 1349) HarperCollins Pubs.

Irish Fairy Tales & Legends. Una Leavy. 1998. 9.95 (978-1-57098-240-8(6)) Robs Rinehart.

Irish Favorites. Perf. by Dennis Day. 1 cass., 1 CD. 7.18 (RAN 8262); audio compact disk 11.98 CD Jewel box. (RAN 8262) NewSound.

Irish Fiddle Book. Matt Cranitch. 2006. pap. bk. 34.95 (978-1-900428-67-5(9)) Pub: Ossian IRL. Dist(s): H Leonard

Irish Fiddle Book: The Art of Traditional Fiddle-Playing. rev. ed. Matt Cranitch. 1988. audio compact disk 34.95 (978-1-900428-90-3(3)) Pub: Ossian IRL. Dist(s): Music Sales

Irish Fiddle Playing, Volume 2: A Guide for the Serious Player. Philip John Berthoud. 2008. lib. bdg. 19.95 (978-0-7866-0752-5(1)) Mel Bay.

Irish Folk Tales for Children. Perf. by Sharon Kennedy. 1 cass. (Running Time: 1 hr.). (Family Ser.). (J). (ps-7). 1996. 9.98 (978-1-886767-15-7(7), 8040); audio compact disk 14.98 (978-1-886767-14-0(9), 8040) Rounder Records.

Tales of wizards & leprechauns, of seal kings & magic transformations. Interwoven with the stories is the music of harper Barbara Russell, fiddler Johnny Cunningham & accordionist Evan Harlan.

Irish for Beginners. Angela Wilkes & J. Shackell. 1 cass. (Passport's Languages for Beginners Ser.). (IRI., 1999. pap. bk. 14.95 (978-0-8442-1390-3(X), 1390X, Passport Bks) McGraw-Hill Trade.

Irish Gold. abr. ed. Andrew M. Greeley. 2 cass. (Running Time: 3 hrs.). (Nuala Anne McGrail Ser.). 2001. 18.00 (978-1-59040-153-8(0), Phoenix Audio) Pub: Amer Intl Pub. Dist(s): PerseuPGW

Irish Isle: New Irish Cuisine, Traditional Irish Music. Sharon O'Connor. (Sharon O'Connor's Menus & Music Ser.). 1996. bk. 24.95 (978-1-883914-15-8(9)) Menus & Music.

Irish Isle: New Irish Cuisine, Traditional Irish Music. Sharon O'Connor. (Sharon O'Connor's Menus & Music Ser.: Vol. XI). 1999. pap. bk. 24.95 (978-1-883914-29-5(9)) Menus & Music.

Irish Music for Fiddle Made Easy. Philip John Berthoud. 2008. pap. bk. 14.95 (978-0-7866-7568-5(3)) Mel Bay.

Irish Music for Flatpicking Guitar Made Easy. Philip John Berthoud. 2008. pap. bk. 14.95 (978-0-7866-7692-7(2)) Mel Bay.

Irish Music for Mandolin Made Easy. Philip John Berthoud. 2008. pap. bk. 14.95 (978-0-7866-7567-8(5)) Mel Bay.

Irish Night Before Christmas, an/A Leprechaun's St. Patrick's Day. Read by Sarah Blazek. (Running Time: 23 mins.). (Night Before Christmas Ser.). (ENG.). (J). 2010. audio compact disk 15.95 (978-1-58980-730-3(8)) Pelican.

Irish Poetry, Stories & Songs. 1 CD. (Running Time: 60 mins.). (Abbey Theatre Reads Ser.).Tr. of Aisteoirí na Mainistreach ag Léamh. (IRI.). 2006. audio compact disk 15.95 (978-1-57970-374-5(7), ABB003D, Audio-For) J Norton Pubs.

The musical Irish language is purely spoken by actors, most of whom have Irish as their first language. Poetry ranges from works of modern writers to old poems which have survived through the ages.

Irish Reel Book. Patrick Steinbach. 2005. pap. bk. 24.95 (978-3-89922-023-0(4)) AMA Verlag DEU.

Irish Short Stories. John B. Keane. 1 cass. 1998. 11.95 (978-1-57098-239-2(2)) Robs Rinehart.

Irish Tale: Tom Moore & the Seal Woman. Michael R. Kasony_O'Malley. Retold by Michael R. Kasony_O'Malley. Illus. by Michael J. Rowland. (J). 2007. lib. bdg. 19.95 (978-0-9776170-3-6(3)) Green Igric.

Irish Tenor Banjo Complete Techniques. Gerry O'Connor. (Running Time: 1 hr.). (ENG.). 2006. 32.95 (978-5-558-08923-3(7)) Waltons Manu IRL.

***Irish Thunder: The Hard Life & Times of Micky Ward.** unabr. ed. Bob Halloran. (Running Time: 9.5 hrs. NaN mins.). (ENG.). 2010. 29.95 (978-1-4417-7665-5(6)); 59.95 (978-1-4417-7662-4(1)); audio compact disk 29.95 (978-1-4417-7664-8(8)); audio compact disk 90.00 (978-1-4417-7663-1(X)) Blckstn Audio.

Irish Tradition of Mysticism. Thomas Merton. 1 cass. 8.95 (AA2268) Credence Commun.

Irish Traditional Guitar Accompaniment. Contrib. by Gavin Ralston. (Running Time: 50 mins.). 2006. 29.95 (978-5-558-08917-2(2)) Mel Bay.

Irish Traditional Guitar Accompaniment. Gavin Ralston. 1999. pap. bk. 35.95 (978-0-7866-5308-9(6)) Waltons Manu IRL.

***Irish Treasures & Originals 2.** Marie O'Reilly. (ENG.). 1992. 11.95 (978-0-8023-7083-9(7)) Pub: Clo Iar-Chonnachta IRL. Dist(s): Dufour

***Irish Trilogy: Jewels of the Sun, Tears of the Moon,Heart of the Sea.** abr. ed. Nora Roberts. Read by Patricia Daniels. (Running Time: 15 hrs.). (Irish Trilogy: Vols. 1-3). 2010. audio compact disk 29.99 (978-1-4418-5091-1(0), 9781441850911, BACD) Brilliance Audio.

Irish Verse & Ballads. unabr. ed. Read by Siobhan McKenna. 1 cass. (Running Time: 45 min.). 10.95 (978-0-8045-0707-3(4), SAC 46-2) Spoken Arts.

Poems by Yeats, James Stephens, James Joyce, Padraic Colum.

Irish Whistle. Tom Maguire. 1 cass. 1997. pap. bk. 12.95 (978-0-8023-9064-6(1)) Dufour.

Irish Whistle Book. Tom Maguire. 1996. audio compact disk 11.95 (978-0-946005-90-1(7)) Pub: Ossian IRL. Dist(s): H Leonard

***Irish Whistle Book Demo Cd.** Tom Maguire. (ENG.). 2000. audio compact disk 15.95 (978-0-8023-9077-6(3)) Pub: Ossian IRL. Dist(s): Dufour

Irish Whistle Tune. Tom Maguire. 1 cass. (ENG.). 1996. 14.95 (978-0-8023-9063-9(3)) Dufour.

Irish Whistle Tune Book. Tom Maguire. 1996. audio compact disk 11.95 (978-0-946005-91-8(5)) Pub: Ossian IRL. Dist(s): H Leonard

Irma Quarterdeck Reports. unabr. ed. Harley L. Sachs. Illus. by Peter Wells. 5 cass. (Running Time: 5 hrs.). 2001. 20.00 (978-0-9705390-5-2(3)) I D E V C O.

Iron & Silk. unabr. ed. Mark Salzman. Read by Bill Whitaker. 4 cass. (Running Time: 6 hrs.). 1990. 32.00 (978-0-7366-1860-1(0), 2691) Books on Tape.

Mark Salzman graduated from Yale with a major in Chinese studies & in 1982 left the United States to teach English in Hunan. This is the story of his adventures there. Salzman was unusual, not only for his command of the language, but also for his grasp of the culture. Among other things, he had a black belt in karate. Through the sport he developed a powerful friendship with Pan Quingfu, China's premier martial art expert. Salzman trained with him & reports on the experience.

Iron & Silk. unabr. ed. Mark Salzman. Read by Barry Carl. 4 Cass. (Running Time: 6 Hours). 19.95 (978-1-4025-2806-4(X)) Recorded Bks.

Iron & Silk, unabr. ed. Mark Salzman. Narrated by Barry Carl. 4 cass. (Running Time: 6 hrs.). 1989. 35.00 (978-1-55690-258-1(1), 89710E7) Recorded Bks.

Mark Salzman graduated "summa cum laude" from Yale University in 1982. With his degree in his pocket, he took his cello & himself to China for a two-year stint teaching English. This is his portrait of the people & places he encountered.

Iron Duke. unabr. ed. L. Ron Hubbard. Read by Michael Yurchak. 2 CDs. (Running Time: 2 hrs.). (Stories from the Golden Age Ser.). (ENG.). (gr. 6). 2009. audio compact disk 9.95 (978-1-59212-173-1(X)) Gala Pr LLC.

Iron Facade. unabr. ed. Catherine Cookson. Read by Geraldine Somerville. 6 cass. (Running Time: 6 hrs.). 1994. 54.95 (978-0-7451-4282-1(6), CAB 965) AudioGO.

Successful novelist Prudence Dudley seems to have everything but due to a dysfunctional childhood, she suffers a nervous breakdown. She flees with her aunt to a peaceful lake cottage & is unwittingly drawn into Davie McVeigh's life, the owner of the cottage. There, she finds his past was as unhappy as her own.

Iron Giant: Original Motion Picture Soundtrack. Michael Kamen. Perf. by Tyrones, The et al. 1 cass. (Running Time: 1 hr.). (J). 2002. 10.98 (978-0-7379-0082-8(2), 75942); 10.98 (75943); audio compact disk 16.98 (978-0-7379-0083-5(0), 75943) Rhino Enter.

The soundtrack to the highly acclaimed Warner Bros. animated feature film, featuring classic pop songs and an original score. Songs include Blast off, Rockin in the Orbit, Kookie's Mad Pad, Salt Peanuts, Comin' Home Baby, Cha hua-hua, Let's Do the Cha Cha, Blues Walk, I Got a Rocket in My Pocket, Seachin, Honeycomb, Destination Moon, You Can Be, Who You Choose To Be.

Iron Hand of Mars. unabr. ed. Lindsey Davis. Narrated by Donal Donnelly. 10 cass. (Running Time: 14 hrs.). (Marcus Didius Falco Ser.). 2000. 85.00 (978-0-7887-0226-6(2), 94451E7) Recorded Bks.

***Iron Hand of Mars: A BBC Full-Cast Radio Drama.** Lindsey Davis. Narrated by Full Cast Production Staff & Anton Lesser. (Running Time: 3 hrs. 0 mins. 0 sec.). (ENG., 2010. audio compact disk 29.95 (978-1-4056-8795-9(9)) Pub: AudioGO. Dist(s): Perseus Dist

Iron Horse: Lou Gehrig in His Time. unabr. collector's ed. Ray Robinson. Read by Jay Robertson. 6 cass. (Running Time: 9 hrs.). 1991. 48.00 (978-0-7366-1983-7(6), 2800) Books on Tape.

Lou Gehrig, the New York Yankees great, is best known for having played in a record 2130 consecutive games & for having died at 37 of ALS, to which he gave his name - Lou Gehrig's disease. Gehrig was a case of the boy finding himself through sports. He had a remarkable talent for baseball, almost an intuition. He was a great competitor, never greater than in his final bout with illness. His death made him an immortal American hero.

Iron Horses of the Santa Fe Southwest. Sonja Howle. 2 CDs. (Running Time: 1hour 37min 19sec). 2004. pap. bk. 12.95 (978-1-932226-35-5(4)) Pub: Wizard Acdmy. Dist(s): Baker Taylor

When the Santa Fe Railway followed the path of least resistance across the ?great American desert? they encountered a world like no other.This book will introduce you to the team of leading men and women who helped create a vision and an empire.Iron Horses like Cyrus Holliday, the engine and father of the Atchison, Topeka and Santa Fe Railway; Fred Harvey, the steam; Mary Colter, the architect of the Southwest; and of William Haskell Simpson, the wise poet and advertising director of the railway for over 30 years who became an Iron Horse in art, advertising and public relations.Then, one of the Iron Horses of today, bold enough to share the visions of the Railway's artists and of other artists, with the world ... Philip Anschutz.It's our Southwest?s story of love, passion and betrayal, of not giving up even when betrayed and ignored. It's the story of warriors brave enough to create a new vision.It will inspire and encourage you ? to be an Iron Horse in your life, your company and your industry.Cover Art, ?Un Cavallo Nero? by Santa Fe?s Antony CorsoIncludes:1hour 37min 19sec on 2 Audio CDs86 page booklet.

Iron House: Stories from the Yard, abr. ed. Jerome Washington. Read by Jerome Washington. 2 cass. (Running Time: 3 hrs.). 1996. 17.95 (978-1-57453-029-2(1), 330098) Audio Lit.

Reveals the ghastly ineptitude of American "prison reform." But most important, it depicts prisoners & guards alike simply as the human beings they are, people who must face, every day, often violently, one of the most inhuman & corrupt communities in history, where individuals are driven necessarily to brutality, insanity, & death as well as to desperate brotherhood & savage enlightenment.

Iron Hunt. unabr. ed. Marjorie M. Liu. (Running Time: 9 hrs. 30 mins. 0 sec.). (ENG.). 2008. audio compact disk 34.99 (978-1-4001-1003-2(3)); audio compact disk 24.99 (978-1-4001-6003-7(0)); audio compact disk 69.99 (978-1-4001-4003-9(X)) Pub: Tantor Media. Dist(s): IngramPubServ

Iron John. Robert Bly. Narrated by Richard Ferrone. 7 cass. (Running Time: 12.5 hrs.). 29.95 (978-1-4025-5596-1(2)) Recorded Bks.

Iron John: A Book about Men, unabr. ed. Robert Bly. Narrated by Richard Ferrone. 9 cass. (Running Time: 12 hrs. 30 mins.). 1992. 78.00 (978-1-55690-627-5(7), 92104E7) Recorded Bks.

Explores the idea of the missing father in contemporary society & encourages men in their pursuit of the "inner warrior.".

Iron John & the Male Mode of Feeling. Robert Bly. Read by Robert Bly. 1 cass. (Running Time: 1 hr. 36 min.). 1991. 11.00 Bookpack. (978-1-880155-01-1(X), 766) Oral Trad Arch.

Live performance from a men's gathering Bly tells the "Iron John" story & discusses 10 ways in which the male mode of feeling differs from the female mode with Michael accompanying on drum. Library edition packaging.

Iron Man: The Cal Ripken, Jr., Story. unabr. ed. Harvey Rosenfeld. Read by Ian Esmo. 8 cass. (Running Time: 11 hrs. 30 mins.). 2000. 56.95 (978-0-7861-1123-7(2), 1888) Blckstn Audio.

Iron Man: The Cal Ripkin Jr. Story. unabr. ed. Harvey Rosenfeld. Read by Ian Esmo. 8 cass. (Running Time: 12 hrs.). 1997. 56.95 (1888) Blckstn Audio.

Chronicles Junior's ascent to super stardom. What was it like playing baseball with a father as manager & a brother as a double-play combination? How did his father's firing & his brother's trade affect him? Captures the grit & determination of the greatest shortstop ever to play the game of baseball.

Iron Mountain. Prod. by Laraim Associates. (Barclay Family Adventure Ser.). (YA). 2005. audio compact disk 10.95 (978-1-56254-994-7(4)) Saddleback Edu.

Iron Orchid. Stuart Woods. Read by Carrington MacDuffie. (Holly Barker Ser.: No. 4). 2005. audio compact disk 81.00 (978-1-4159-2319-1(1)) Books on Tape.

Iron Pirate. unabr. ed. Douglas Reeman. Read by David Rintoul. 10 cass. (Running Time: 15 hrs.). 2000. 59.95 (978-0-7451-4302-6(4), CAB 985) Pub: Chivers Audio Bks GBR. Dist(s): AudioGO

The German cruiser Prinz Luitpold was always lucky in battle. To the beleaguered German army in the Baltic Sea, she was a symbol of hope. When the order comes to lead an attack in the Atlantic, Kapitan Hechler knows it's only a matter of time before their luck runs out. But Hechler's problems worsen, as a glory-seeking admiral arrives on board.

Iron Ring, unabr. ed. Lloyd Alexander. Narrated by Ron Keith. 7 pieces. (Running Time: 9 hrs. 15 mins.). (gr. 6 up). 1998. 63.00 (978-0-7887-2264-6(6), 95507E7) Recorded Bks.

Inspired by the mythology of India, Alexander tells an epic tale of high adventure as Tamar, the boy-king, takes an enchanted journey.

Iron Ring, Class Set. unabr. ed. Lloyd Alexander. Read by Ron Keith. 7 cass., 10 bks. (Running Time: 9 hrs. 15 min.). (J). 1998. bk. 133.70 (978-0-7887-2555-5(6), 46725) Recorded Bks.

Iron Ring, Homework Set. unabr. ed. Lloyd Alexander. Read by Ron Keith. 7 cass. (Running Time: 9 hrs. 15 min.). (J). 1998. bk. 76.24 (978-0-7887-2251-6(4), 40735) Recorded Bks.

Iron River. abr. ed. T. Jefferson Parker. Read by David Colacci. (Running Time: 6 hrs.). (Charlie Hood Novel Ser.: Bk. 3). 2010. audio compact disk 24.99 (978-1-4418-2542-1(8), 9781441825421) Brilliance Audio.

Iron River. abr. ed. T. Jefferson Parker. Read by David Colacci. (Running Time: 6 hrs.). (Charlie Hood Novel Ser.: Bk. 3). 2011. audio compact disk 14.99 (978-1-4418-2546-9(0), 9781441825469, BCD Value Price) Brilliance Audio.

Iron River. unabr. ed. T. Jefferson Parker. Read by David Colacci. (Running Time: 11 hrs.). (Charlie Hood Novel Ser.: Bk. 3). 2010. 24.99 (978-1-4233-7917-1(9), 9781423379171, BAD); 39.97 (978-1-4233-7916-4(0), 9781423379164, Brlnc Audio MP3 Lib); 39.97 (978-1-4233-7918-8(7), 9781423379188, BADLE); 24.99 (978-1-4233-7915-7(2), 9781423379157, Brilliance MP3); audio compact disk 38.99 (978-1-4233-7913-3(6), 9781423379133, Bril Audio CD Unabri); audio compact disk 92.97 (978-1-4233-7914-0(4), 9781423379140, BriAudCD Unabrid) Brilliance Audio.

Iron Road. unabr. ed. Jane Jackson. Read by Patricia Gallimore. 7 cass. (Running Time: 10 hrs.). (Sound Ser.). (J). 2003. 61.95 (978-1-84283-514-2(9)) Pub: ISIS Lrg Prnt GBR. Dist(s): Ulverscroft US

Iron Rose. unabr. ed. Peter Temple. Read by Marco Chiappi. 4 cass. (Running Time: 6 hrs.). 2001. (978-1-74030-164-0(1), 500952) Bolinda Pubng AUS.

***Iron Rose.** unabr. ed. Peter Temple. Read by Marco Chiappi. (Running Time: 7 hrs. 12 mins.). 2010. audio compact disk 87.95 (978-1-74214-662-1(7), 9781742146621) Pub: Bolinda Pubng AUS. Dist(s): Bolinda Pub Inc

Iron Staircase. (1153) Books on Tape.

***Iron Thorn.** unabr. ed. Caitlin Kittredge. (Iron Codex Ser.). (ENG.). (J). 2011. audio compact disk 54.00 (978-0-307-74728-0(X), Listening Lib) Pub: Random Audio Pubg. Dist(s): Random

Iron Tiger. unabr. ed. Jack Higgins. Read by Barry Foster. 6 cass. (Running Time: 6 hrs.). 1993. bk. 54.95 (978-0-7451-6022-1(0), CAB 173) AudioGO.

Iron Tiger. unabr. collector's ed. Jack Higgins. Read by Ian Whitcomb. 6 cass. (Running Time: 6 hrs.). 1984. 36.00 (978-0-7366-0503-8(7), 1477) Books on Tape.

Jack Drummond, an adventurer, is suddenly caught up in a bloody border war. To survive he must take on the entire Chinese Communist army. Against them he has only one very desperate plan.

Iron Tongue of Midnight: A Tito Amato Mystery. unabr. ed. Beverle Graves Myers. Read by Geoffrey Blaisdell. (Running Time: 36000 sec.). (Baroque Mystery Ser.). 2008. audio compact disk & audio compact disk 90.00 (978-1-4332-1155-3(6)) Blckstn Audio.

Iron Tongue of Midnight: A Tito Amato Mystery. unabr. ed. Beverle Graves Myers & Geoffrey Blaisdell. (Running Time: 36000 sec.). (Baroque Mystery Ser.). 2008. 72.95 (978-1-4332-1154-6(8)); audio compact disk 29.95 (978-1-4332-1156-0(4)) Blckstn Audio.

Iron Trail. unabr. ed. Max Brand. Read by Wade Bryce. 8 vols. (Running Time: 12 hrs.). 1997. 69.95 (978-0-7927-2210-6(8), CSL 099, Chivers Sound Lib) AudioGO.

Young Eddie Larned earned a hero's welcome for gunning down the two most violent & feared outlaws in the Valley & for returning the money they

stole from the bank. With his reward money, it looked like he would be set for life. But there were two men who knew about the hero's past & they were going to make him pay for it. One of them was a lawman & the other a crook. The only question was which one could get to Eddie first.

Ironclad: The Epic Battle, Calamitous Loss, & Historic Recovery of the USS Monitor. abr. ed. Paul Clancy. Read by Grover Gardner. (Running Time: 16200 sec.). 2006. audio compact disk 28.00 (978-1-932378-98-6(7)) Pub: A Media Intl. Dist(s): Natl Bk Netwk

Ironfire. unabr. ed. David Ball. Narrated by George Guidall. 22 cass. (Running Time: 32 hrs.). 2004. 99.75 (978-1-4025-1723-5(8)) Recorded Bks.
In the 16th century, only the Knights of Malta stand against the Ottoman Empire of Suleiman the Magnificent and his 40,000 brutal warriors.

Ironhand. Charlie Fletcher. Narrated by Jim Dale. (Running Time: 34680 sec.). (Stoneheart Trilogy: Bk. 2). (ENG.). (J). (gr. 4-7). 2008. audio compact disk 39.95 (978-0-545-02746-5(2)) Scholastic Inc.

Ironhand. unabr. ed. Charlie Fletcher. Read by Jim Dale. (Stoneheart Trilogy: Bk. 2). (J). 2008. 44.99 (978-1-60514-925-7(X)) Find a World.

Ironhand. unabr. ed. Charlie Fletcher. Read by Jim Dale. 8 CDs. (Running Time: 9 hrs. 38 mins.). (Stoneheart Trilogy: Bk. 2). (ENG.). (J). (gr. 4-7). 2008. audio compact disk 79.95 (978-0-545-03320-6(9)) Scholastic Inc.

Ironing Man, Level 3. Colin B. Campbell. Contrib. by Philip Prowse. (Running Time: 1 hr. 53 mins.). (Cambridge English Readers Ser.). (ENG.). 1999. 15.75 (978-0-521-66494-3(2)) Cambridge U Pr.

Ironman. unabr. ed. Chris Crutcher. Narrated by George Guidall et al. 5 pieces. (Running Time: 6 hrs. 15 mins.). (YA). (gr. 8 up). 44.00 (978-0-7887-0428-4(1), 94620E7) Recorded Bks.
Story of Bo Brewster, a high school athlete & a survivor of child abuse, who joins an anger management group. In a series of letters to his hero, Larry King, Bo reveals how the other members of the group help him prepare for his greatest challenge ever: an ironman triathlon. Available to libraries only.

Ironman. unabr. ed. Chris Crutcher. Narrated by George Guidall & Johnny Heller. 6 CDs. (Running Time: 6 hrs. 15 mins.). (YA). (gr. 8 up). 2000. audio compact disk 48.00 (978-0-7887-3739-8(2), C1110E7) Recorded Bks.

Irons in the Fire. unabr. ed. John McPhee. Narrated by Nelson Runger. 6 cass. (Running Time: 7 hrs. 30 mins.). 1998. 51.00 (978-0-7887-1879-3(7), 95301E7) Recorded Bks.
Contains six wonderfully observant & entertaining slices of life ranging from a present-day cattle brand inspector to a mason who works on Plymouth Rock.

Ironweed see Ink Truck

Ironweed. abr. ed. William Kennedy. Read by Jason Robards. 2 cass. (Running Time: 3 hrs.). (Albany Cycle Ser.). 1993. 15.95 (978-0-88690-130-1(8), M20138) Pub: Audio Partners. Dist(s): PerseuPGW
The story of Francis Phelan's return to Albany to make peace with his ghosts.

Ironweed. abr. ed. William Kennedy. Read by Jason Robards. 2 cass. (Running Time: 3 hrs.). (Albany Cycle Ser.). 2000. 7.95 (978-1-57815-186-8(4), 1126, Media Bks Audio); audio compact disk 11.99 (978-1-57815-513-2(4), 1126 CD3, Media Bks Audio) Media Bks NJ.

Ironweed. unabr. collector's ed. William Kennedy. Read by Wolfram Kandinsky. 8 cass. (Running Time: 8 hrs.). (Albany Cycle Ser.). 1987. 48.00 (978-0-7366-1081-0(2), 2008) Books on Tape.
Francis Phelan, ex-ballplayer, part-time gravedigger, full-time drunk, has hit bottom. Years ago he left Albany in a hurry after killing a scab during a trolley workers' strike. He ran away again after accidentally & fatally-dropping his infant son. Now, in 1938, Francis is back in town, roaming the old familiar streets with a hobo pal, trying to make peace with the ghosts of the past & the present.

***Ironwood Tree.** unabr. ed. Holly Black & Tony DiTerlizzi. Read by Mark Hamill. (Running Time: 1 hr. 3 mins.). (Spiderwick Chronicles: Bk. 4). (ENG.). (J). 2007. 7.50 (978-0-7393-6244-0(5), Listening Lib) Pub: Random Audio Pubg. Dist(s): Random

Iroquois Diplomacy on the Early American Frontier. unabr. ed. Timothy J. Shannon. Narrated by George K. Wilson. (Running Time: 9 hrs. 30 mins.). 2008. 56.75 (978-1-4361-6518-1(0)); audio compact disk 72.75 (978-1-4361-2377-8(1)) Recorded Bks.

Irrational Fear. Donald Davis. 2006. audio compact disk 14.95 (978-0-87483-820-6(7)) Pub: August Hse. Dist(s): Natl Bk Netwk

Irrational Fear. unabr. ed. Donald Davis. Read by Donald Davis. (J). 2008. 34.99 (978-1-60252-972-4(8)) Find a World.

Irrational Season. l.t. ed. Madeleine L'Engle. (Crosswicks Journal: Bk. 3). 1986. bk. (978-0-7089-6258-9(0)) UlverLrgPrint GBR.

Irrationalism. Gordon Clark. 1 cass. (Lectures on Apologetics: No. 10). 5.00 Trinity Found.

Irrationality. J. Krishnamurti. 1 cass. (Running Time: 75 min.). (Krishnamurti & Professor David Bohm - 1980 Ser.: No. 3). 8.50 (ABD803) Krishnamurti.
Krishnamurti & Prof. Bohm offer penetrating, in-depth dialogues which shed light on the fundamental issues of existence.

Irregular People. Joyce Landorf Heatherley. 1 cass. 1988. 7.95 (978-0-929488-05-9(9)) Balcony Pub Inc.
How to forgive & relate to your irregular person.

Irregulars: Roald Dahl & the British Spy Ring in Wartime Washington. Jennet Conant. Read by Simon Prebble. (Playaway Adult Nonfiction Ser.). 2008. 54.99 (978-1-60640-629-8(9)) Find a World.

Irregulars: Roald Dahl & the British Spy Ring in Wartime Washington. unabr. ed. Jennet Conant. Read by Simon Prebble. 10 CDs. (Running Time: 11 hrs. 30 mins.). (ENG., 2008. audio compact disk 34.95 (978-1-59887-693-2(7), 1598876937) Pub: HighBridge. Dist(s): Workman Pub

Irreligion: A Mathematician Explains Why the Arguments for God Just Don't Add Up. unabr. ed. John Allen Paulos. Narrated by Dick Hill. (Running Time: 4 hrs. 0 mins. 0 sec.). (ENG.). 2008. audio compact disk 24.99 (978-1-4001-0630-1(3)) Pub: Tantor Media. Dist(s): IngramPubServ

Irreligion: A Mathematician Explains Why the Arguments for God Just Don't Add Up. unabr. ed. John Allen Paulos. Read by Dick Hill. (Running Time: 4 hrs. 0 mins. 0 sec.). (ENG.). 2008. audio compact disk 19.99 (978-1-4001-5630-6(0)); audio compact disk 49.99 (978-1-4001-3630-8(X)) Pub: Tantor Media. Dist(s): IngramPubServ

Irreparable Harm. abr. ed. Lee Gruenfeld. Read by Angie Dickinson. 2 cass. (Running Time: 3 hrs.). 1993. 16.95 set. (978-1-879371-55-2(3), 40230) Pub Mills.
Pamela Jacoby is a police officer; the man questioning her is an innovative psychiatrist. The interrogation is crucial because it involves the brutal murder of Pamela's lover. The explosive revelation that results shocks the police department & reveals the depths of Pamela's torment.

Irreparable Harm. abr. ed. Randy Singer. Read by Ross Ballard, II. 2 cass. (Running Time: 3 hrs.). 2003. 44.25 (978-1-59355-097-4(9), 1593550979); 17.95 (978-1-59355-096-7(0), 1593550960); audio compact disk 62.25 (978-1-59355-099-8(5), 1593550995); audio compact disk 19.95 (978-1-59355-098-1(7), 1593550987) Brilliance Audio.
Bright but inexperienced attorney Mitchell Taylor is torn between warring personal and professional interests. Can he help his client - a young surrogate mother - and save the child she carries without sealing the fate of others? When Dr. Nathan Brown and his wife, Cameron, undergo a controversial method of in vitro fertilization, some of their cloned embryos are used to achieve a pregnancy in surrogate Maryna Sareth while the others are cryogenically preserved. Dr. Brown's premature death, however, and mounting evidence that the baby has Down's Syndrome unleash a legal, ethical, and moral firestorm. Dr. Brown's dying wish is that the remaining embryos be used for stem cell research. His wife wants to force the abortion of the baby Maryna carries in hopes that one of the remaining embryos can produce a "healthy" child. Meanwhile, Mitchell wrestles with an agonizing ethical dilemma: Can he protect the embryos, which requires that a federal legislative ban on cloning be overturned, while at the same time helping the beautiful young surrogate save the child she carries - possible only if the ban is upheld? With time running out, Mitchell and Maryna must run the gauntlet of bioethical nightmares, corporate treachery, and life-threatening confrontations if they are to save the unborn and avoid irreparable harm.

Irreparable Harm. abr. ed. Randy Singer. Read by Ross Ballard II. (Running Time: 3 hrs.). 2006. 39.25 (978-1-4233-0376-3(8), 9781423303763, BADLE); 24.95 (978-1-4233-0375-6(X), 9781423303756, BAD) Brilliance Audio.

Irreparable Harm. abr. ed. Randy D. Singer. Read by Ross Ballard, II. (Running Time: 3 hrs.). 2006. 39.25 (978-1-4233-0374-9(1), 9781423303749, Brlnc Audio MP3 Lib); 24.95 (978-1-4233-0373-2(3), 9781423303732, Brilliance MP3) Brilliance Audio.

Irreplaceable. unabr. ed. Stephen Lovely. Read by Phil Gigante & Tanya Eby Sirois. 1 MP3-CD. (Running Time: 12 hrs.). 2009. 24.99 (978-1-4233-8304-8(4), 9781423383048, Brilliance MP3); 39.97 (978-1-4233-8305-5(2), 9781423383055, Brlnc Audio MP3 Lib); 39.97 (978-1-4233-8307-9(9), 9781423383079, BADLE); 24.99 (978-1-4233-8306-2(0), 9781423383062, BAD); audio compact disk 89.97 (978-1-4233-8303-1(6), 9781423383031, BriAudCD Unabrid); audio compact disk 36.99 (978-1-4233-8302-4(8), 9781423383024, Bril Audio CD Unabri) Brilliance Audio.

***Irresistible.** unabr. ed. Susan Mallery. Read by Cecelia Frontero. (Running Time: 8 hrs.). 2011. 19.99 (978-1-4418-7618-8(9), 9781441876188, Brilliance MP3); 39.97 (978-1-4418-7620-1(0), 9781441876201, BADLE); 39.97 (978-1-4418-7619-5(7), 9781441876195, Brlnc Audio MP3 Lib); audio compact disk 19.99 (978-1-4418-7616-4(2), 9781441876164, Bril Audio CD Unabri); audio compact disk 79.97 (978-1-4418-7617-1(0), 9781441876171, BriAudCD Unabrid) Brilliance Audio.

***Irresistible.** unabr. ed. Karen Robards. Read by Anne Flosnik. (Running Time: 12 hrs.). (Banning Sisters Trilogy). 2010. 24.99 (978-1-4418-6439-0(3), 9781441864390, Brilliance MP3); 39.97 (978-1-4418-6440-6(7), 9781441864406, Brlnc Audio MP3 Lib); 24.99 (978-1-4418-6441-3(5), 9781441864413, BAD); 39.97 (978-1-4418-6442-0(3), 9781441864420, BADLE); audio compact disk 29.99 (978-1-4418-6437-6(7), 9781441864376, Bril Audio CD Unabri); audio compact disk 89.97 (978-1-4418-6438-3(5), 9781441864383, BriAudCD Unabrid) Brilliance Audio.

Irresistible Forces, Set. abr. ed. Danielle Steel. 4 cass. 1999. 26.95 (FS9-50992) Highsmith.

Irresistible Impulse. unabr. ed. Robert K. Tanenbaum. Read by Connor O'Brien. 8 cass. (Running Time: 12 hrs.). (Butch Karp Mystery Ser.). 1998. 64.00 (978-0-7366-4134-0(3), 4639) Books on Tape.
As head of the District Attorney's homicide bureau, Butch Karp knows two things inside out: the legal system & the ean streets of New York. Now he's going to learn about obsession, as in the obsession of a man stalking a world-famous musician or the obsession of lawyers in his own office, some of whom would kill for a high-profile case, or of his wife, Marlene, who heads her own detective agency & packs a Cold. 380 for protection. Neither Butch nor Marlene realize that they are about to become flash points in the hottest controversy to rock the city in years.

Irresistible Offer: How to Sell Your Product or Service in 3 Seconds or Less. unabr. rev. ed. Mark Joyner. Read by Mark Joyner. (Running Time: 6 hrs.). (ENG.). 2006. audio compact disk 19.98 (978-1-59659-069-4(6), GildAudio) Pub: Gildan Media. Dist(s): HachBkGrp

Irresistible Revolution: Living As an Ordinary Radical. unabr. ed. Shane Claiborne. (ENG.). 2007. 19.99 (978-0-310-27667-8(5)) Zondervan.

Irresistible Revolution: Living as an Ordinary Radical. unabr. ed. Shane Claiborne. (Running Time: 7 hrs. 50 mins. 0 sec.). (ENG.). 2007. 14.99 (978-0-310-27668-5(3)) Zondervan.

Irresponsible People: How to Stay Responsible When Others Aren't, Set. David Grudermeyer & Rebecca Grudermeyer. 2 cass. 18.95 INCL. HANDOUTS. (T-27) Willingness Wrks.

Irreverent Introduction see Evening with Dylan Thomas

Irreverent Observer. Paul Krassner. 1 cass. 9.00 (A0768-90) Sound Photosyn.
Faustin chats with the humorist, publisher & political gadfly.

Irrevocable Trust. unabr. ed. David R. Addleman. Read by Rusty Nelson. 6 cass. (Running Time: 6 hrs. 30 min.). (David R. Addleman Mystery Ser.). 2001. 39.95 (978-1-55686-848-1(0)) Books in Motion.
Professional thief Paul Morrison accepts the assignment to recover a young woman's fortune robbed from the victim's trust account by a bank executive. Paul discovers a mob operation.

Irrigation Equipment in Argentina: A Strategic Reference 2006. Compiled by Icon Group International, Inc. Staff. 2007. ring bd. 195.00 (978-0-497-35800-6(X)) Icon Grp.

Irrisistable You. Wendi Friesen. 1 CD. 2002. audio compact disk 29.00 (978-1-929058-11-2(X)) Wendicom.
By amplifying your best qualities and creating an AURA of charisma, you will feel more attractive, confident and irresistable. The best part is... that you will notice others take more interest in you and seem to want to be closer to you. One man from New York called me every week to tell me about all the women that were suddenly calling him and wanting him... in a big way! He said it just kept getting better and better. For men or women, this will make you magnetic!.

Irritable Bowel Syndrome. Read by Norton J. Greenberger. 1 cass. (Running Time: 90 min.). 1986. 12.00 (C8603) Amer Coll Phys.

Irritable Bowel Syndrome. Steven Gurgevich. (ENG.). 2002. audio compact disk 19.95 (978-1-932170-14-6(6), HWH) Tranceformation.

I.R.S. Man (Matthew) Matthew 9:9-12. Ed Young. 1985. 4.95 (978-0-7417-1474-9(4), 474) Win Walk.

Irving Babbitt: An Overview. Read by Russell Kirk. 1 cass. 3.00 (113) ISI Books.

Irving Berlin: A Daughter's Memoir. unabr. collector's ed. Mary E. Barrett. Read by Mary Peiffer. 8 cass. (Running Time: 12 hrs.). 1995. 64.00 (978-0-7366-3059-7(7), 3741) Books on Tape.
Berlin composed more than 1,000 popular songs & influenced generations of music-minded. Daughter Ellin confirms his life was as charming as his music.

Irving Berlin: An American Legacy. Michael Ballam. 2 cass. (Running Time: 3 hrs.). 14.98 (978-1-55503-336-1(9), 119115); 12.98 (119115) Covenant Comms.
Talk plus music-the life & legacy of a great man.

Irving Berlin & Ragtime America. unabr. collector's ed. Ian Whitcomb. Read by Ian Whitcomb. 7 cass. (Running Time: 10 hrs. 30 min.). 1988. 56.00 (978-0-7366-1447-4(8), 2330) Books on Tape.
Focuses on the creation of American popular music in the early years of this century, the music which in its many guises - from ragtime to foxtrot, to boogie-woogie to rock n' roll, from swing to Rhythm & Blues - has provided the pulse & beat of Western civilization. At the center of that creative turmoil that gave rise to this music was Irving Berlin.

Irving Berlin's America - ShowTrax. Music by Irving Berlin. Arranged by Roger Emerson & Paul Murtha. 1 CD. (Running Time: 7 mins.). 2000. audio compact disk 35.00 (08742392) H Leonard.
With a musical career spanning a century, the 20th century was Irving Berlin's own & his music was America's music. This spectacular choir, band & opt. string medley of some of Berlin's classic songs offers a variety of entertaining performance options. Includes: "Alexander's Ragtime Band," "There's No Business Like Show Business," "Puttin' on the Ritz," "Always," "Blue Skies" & "God Bless America.".

Irving Younger's Classic Speeches on Law & Life. Irving Younger. 1988. 95.00 (978-0-943380-55-1(3)) PEG MN.

Irwin Schiff: The Untax Movement. (Running Time: 90 min.). (Long Beach City College). 1983. 10.00 (F156) Freeland Pr.
Shares methods by which to keep more of our income away from the IRS.

Irwin the Sock. Jamie DeWitt & David J. Klein. Illus. by Julie Brickloe. (Publish-a-Book Ser.). (J). (gr. 1-6). 1987. lib. bdg. 22.83 (978-0-8172-3157-6(9)) Heinemann Rai.

Is a Pharmacy Right for Me? 1 cass. (America's Supermarket Showcase '96 Ser.). 1996. 11.00 (NGA96-024) Sound Images.

Is Adoption the Right Choice for You? Hosted by Mardie Caldwell. (ENG.). 2008. audio compact disk 12.95 (978-0-9705734-9-0(9)) Pub: Am Carrage Hse Pubng. Dist(s): STL Dist NA

Is America A Christian Nation? unabr. ed. David Barton. Read by David Barton. 1 cass. (Running Time: 1 hr.). 1990. 4.95 (978-0-925279-56-9(0)) Wallbuilders.
An examination of Supreme Court rulings, official government documents, writings, & statements of the Founding Fathers concerning the important role that Christian principles were to play in public, educational, & governmental affairs.

Is America Utopian? Read by John Rao. 1 cass. Incl. Pt. 1. Is America Utopian? Discussion. (130); 3.00 (130) ISI Books.

Is America Utopian?: Discussion see Is America Utopian?

Is America Utopian? Discussion, Pt. 2. 1 cass. 3.00 (131) ISI Books.

Is Anybody Out There? Locating & Contacting Extraterrestrial Beings. Read by Bernard Oliver. 1 cass. (Running Time: 43 min.). 14.95 (35035) MMI Corp.
Discusses current thinking in this area - why it is now possible for us to contact other beings in the Universe.

Is Anybody There? Jean Ure. Read by Finty Williams. (Running Time: 11220 sec.). (J). 2001. audio compact disk 29.95 (978-0-7540-6763-4(7)) AudioGo GBR.

Is Anyone Listening? A Primer to Change Your Life Forever: Audio CD. Gloria J. Sterling. Read by Gloria J. Sterling. 1 CD. 2007. 20.00 (978-0-9790467-3-5(4)) Intuitions Multi-Media.

Is Anyone Really Normal? Perspectives on Abnormal Psychology. Drew Westen. 4 cass. (Running Time: 12 hrs.). 19.95 Set; 8 lectures; incl. course guide. (658) Teaching Co.
Brings the clash of perspectives into the open & suggests ways in which they might inform each other & afford a more comprehensive understanding of ourselves & others. Includes examples of individual disasters & disorders, as well as the therapies that addressed them.

Is Anyone Really Normal? Perspectives on Abnormal Psychology. Instructed by Drew Westen. 4 cass. (Running Time: 6 hrs.). 1991. 39.95 (978-1-56585-184-9(6)) Teaching Co.

Is Aspartame (Nutrasweet) Safe? A Medical, Public Health & Legal Overview - 1995. unabr. ed. H. J. Roberts. Read by H. J. Roberts. 2 cass. (Running Time: 2 hrs.). 1995. 19.95 Set. (978-1-884243-04-2(5)) Sunshine Sentinel.
Dr. Roberts is widely recognized as the authority on aspartame disease. He reviews the background of aspartame, the numerous features of reactions to such products, the challenges to high risk groups, the FDA & health professionals.

Is Bankruptcy for Your Client? Read by Kenneth E. Aaron. 1 cass. 1991. 20.00 (AL-116) PA Bar Inst.

Is Belief Necessary? 1 cass. (Running Time: 29 min.). 8.50 (AIA70) Krishnamurti.
This is an interview with Krishnamurti by the Australian Broadcasting Commission.

Is Big Brother Still Watching? The George Orwell Legacy. Contrib. by George Woodcock & Paul Kennedy. 2 CDs. (Running Time: 5 hrs.). 2005. audio compact disk 39.95 (978-0-660-19036-5(2)) Pub: Canadian Broadcasting CAN. Dist(s): Georgetown Term

Is Calvinism Biblical?-mp3. Read by Douglas Wilson & Steve Gregg. 2001. 12.00 (978-1-59128-326-3(4)) Canon Pr ID.

Is Calvinism Biblical?-tape. Read by Douglas Wilson & Steve Gregg. 6 cass. 2001. 15.00 (978-1-59128-328-7(0)) Canon Pr ID.

Is Capitalism or Socialism the Moral System? (Debate) John Ridpath & Bob Rae. 2 cass. (Running Time: 2 hrs.). 1992. 19.95 Set. (978-1-56114-138-8(0), HR04D) Second Renaissance.

Is Causation Imaginable? Neville Goddard. 1 cass. (Running Time: 62 min.). 1964. 8.00 (110) J & L Pubns.
Neville taught Imagination Creates Reality. He was a powerfully influential teacher of God as Consciousness.

Is Christianity a Religion?, Pt. 1. Gordon Clark. 1 cass. (Lectures on Apologetics: No. 2). 5.00 Trinity Found.

Is Christianity a Religion?, Pt. 2. Gordon Clark. 1 cass. (Lectures on Apologetics: No. 3). 5.00 Trinity Found.

Is Christianity a Religion?, Pt. 3. Gordon Clark. 1 cass. (Lectures on Apologetics: No. 4). 5.00 Trinity Found.

Is Christianity Good for Women? Zsuzsanna E. Budapest. 3 cass. 27.00 set. (A0402-87) Sound Photosyn.
She's cookin' on many burners.

***Is Duitse A Bheirin Gra.** Sile Ni Fhlaithearta. Sile Ni Fhlaithearta. (ENG.). 2010. audio compact disk 25.95 (978-0-8023-8181-1(2)) Pub: Clo Iar-Chonnachta IRL. Dist(s): Dufour

Is Economic Freedom Possible? Benjamin A. Rogge. (106) J Norton Pubs.

Is Economic Interventionism Ever Justified? Read by Ronald H. Nash. 1 cass. 3.00 (135) ISI Books.

Is Eternity in Your Heart? Ecclesiastes 3:11. Ed Young. 1982. 4.95 (978-0-7417-1226-4(1), 226) Win Walk.

Is Evolution Fit to Survive? 2001. 29.95 (978-1-931812-00-9(4)) Nat Parents.

Is Exact Forecasting Possible? Julie Baum. 1 cass. 8.95 (027) Am Fed Astrologers.
Experiences based on writings of renown astrologers.

Is for America. Devin Scillian. (J). audio compact disk 13.95 (978-1-58536-086-4(4)) Pub: Sleepng Bear. Dist(s): Gale

Is for Apple, B Is for Bike, C Is for Cat Book 1 Audio CD: ELT - English Language Teaching. Waldyr Lima. 2000. audio compact disk (978-0-7428-0602-3(2)) CCLS Pubg Hse.

Is for Apple, B Is for Bike, C Is for Cat Book 2 Audio CD: ELT - English Language Teaching. Waldyr Lima. 2000. audio compact disk (978-0-7428-0603-0(0)) CCLS Pubg Hse.

Is for Apple, B Is for Bike, C Is for Cat Book 3 Audio CD: ELT - English Language Teaching. Waldyr Lima. 2000. audio compact disk (978-0-7428-0604-7(9)) CCLS Pubg Hse.

Is God's Word Relevant to My Life? Logos 10/04/98. Ben Young. 1998. 4.95 (978-0-7417-6101-9(7), B0101) Win Walk.

Is Government Necessary? unabr. ed. Jarret B. Wollstein & Lawrence Burns. 1 cass. (Running Time: 56 min.). 12.95 (440) J Norton Pubs.

Is Half a Sextile Better Than None? Donna Van Toen. 1 cass. 8.95 (356) Am Fed Astrologers.

Is He Popenjoy? unabr. ed. Anthony Trollope. Narrated by Flo Gibson. 14 cass. (Running Time: 23 hrs.). 2003. 42.95 (978-1-55685-690-7(3),) Audio Bk Con.
Who is to be the next Marquis of Brotherton & who will inherit the title of Lord Popenjoy? Will it be Lord George Germain's nephew born of mysterious parentage or will it be his own son? A very amusing book full of colorful characters.

Is History Out of Control? Daniel 7:1-12. Ed Young. 1995. 4.95 (978-0-7417-2075-7(2), 1075) Win Walk.

Is It Alive? Sundance/Newbridge, LLC Staff. (Early Science Ser.). (gr. k-3). 2007. audio compact disk 12.00 (978-1-4007-6156-2(5)); audio compact disk 12.00 (978-1-4007-6155-5(7)); audio compact disk 12.00 (978-1-4007-6154-8(9)) Sund Newbrdge.

***Is It Because I'm Black?** 2010. cd-rom 11.99 (978-0-9793927-2-6(1), RR&R) Posit Prints.

Is It Dangerous to Pray: Matthew 6:10. Ed Young. (J). 1979. 4.95 (978-0-7417-1077-2(3), A0077) Win Walk.

Is It Just Me? abr. ed. Wayne R. Davis. 1 cass. (Running Time: 90 mins.). 2002. 9.99 (978-1-58926-056-6(2)) Oasis Audio.
Pays tribute to veterans, explores the differences between men and women and ponders the questions: "It is just me?".

Is It Love or Is It Addiction? 1 cass. (Running Time: 60 min.). (Discovery Ser.). 9.95 (978-0-89486-600-5(1), 5623G) Hazelden.

Is It Love or Is It Addiction? abr. ed. Brenda Schaeffer. Read by Karesa McElheny. 2 cass. (Running Time: 3 hrs.). 1999. 17.95 (978-1-57453-299-9(5)) Audio Lit.
Provides tools to sort out the aspects of relationships that stem from fear & lack of trust & move from love addiction to real love.

Is It Possible to End All Sorrow? J. Krishnamurti. 1 cass. (Running Time: 75 min.). (Brockwood Park Talks - 1984 Ser.: No. 3). 8.50 (ABT843) Krishnamurti.
Is there a morality that is not relative, not limited? Is there a freedom per se, for itself, not away from something? Are wer all aware of the great suffering of humanity, of each one of us?.

Is It Possible to Live with Total Lucidity? J. Krishnamurti. 1 cass. (Running Time: 62 min.). (Krishnamurti & Prof. Huston Smith - 1968 Ser.). 8.50 (AHS68) Krishnamurti.

Is It Possible to Rest the Brain? Tara Singh. 1 cass. (Running Time: 40 min.). (Exploring a Course in Miracles Ser.). 9.95 (978-1-55531-233-6(0), #A185) Life Action Pr.
Deals with freeing the brain from pressure so that it can rest in God.

Is It Really Not a Coincidence? Read by Basilea Schlink. 1 cass. (Running Time: 30 min.). Incl. Is It Really Not a Coincidence? The New Creation. 1985. (0278); 1985. (0278) Evang Sisterhood Mary.
The frustrations of daily life - no longer just a coincidence, but part of the wise plan of God; Not a theory, but a testimony from life experience.

Is It Really Not a Coincidence?: The New Creation see Is It Really Not a Coincidence?

Is It Simple Forgetfulness or the Real Thing. AgeWiseLiving LLC. (ENG.). 2007. 14.95 (978-0-9796879-0-7(X)) AgeWiseLiving.

Is Jesus Divine? Matt. 26:57-65. Ed Young. 1992. 4.95 (978-0-7417-1947-8(9), 947); 19.95 (978-0-7417-3947-6(X), AV0947) Win Walk.

Is Jesus Present Now? Neville Goddard. 1 cass. (Running Time: 62 min.). 1964. 8.00 (104) J & L Pubns.
Neville taught Imagination Creates Reality. He was a powerfully influential teacher of God as Consciousness.

Is Kissing a Girl Who Smokes Like Licking an Ashtray?, unabr. ed. Randy Powell. Narrated by Ed Sala. 4 cass. (Running Time: 5 hrs. 30 mins.). (gr. 6 up). 1997. 35.00 (978-0-7887-0201-3(7), 94426E7) Recorded Bks.
Powell captures the real-life anxieties of teenagers in this account of the friendship that develops between two offbeat high schoolers - beautiful, brash Heidi & weird, wild-haired Biff. Filled with smart & sassy dialogue, this unusual book will ring true for any teenager.

Is Life Arranged Backwards? Genesis 13:1-18. Ed Young. 1994. 4.95 (978-0-7417-2027-6(2), 1027) Win Walk.

Is Meditation on God Compatible with Modern Life? Daya Mata. 1984. 8.50 (2102) Self Realization.
Presents the author's conviction that meditation, combined with the right activity, can bring complete fulfillment to every man & woman. Topics include: Principles of balanced living; Achieving success in personal & business life; Overcoming negative thinking; How to develop devotion; Getting along with others.

Is Neptune Masking Your True Potential? Doris Kaye. 1 cass. (Running Time: 90 min.). 1988. 8.95 (681) Am Fed Astrologers.

Is Paris Burning?, unabr. ed. Larry Collins & Dominique Lapierre. Read by Frederick Davidson. 11 cass. (Running Time: 16 hrs.). 1994. 76.95 (978-0-7861-0740-7(5), 1492) Blckstn Audio.
"Is Paris burning?" is the question Hitler asked over & over as the French Second & American Fourth Divisions battered their way into the city. Bestselling authors & renowned journalists Larry Collins & Dominique Lapierre drew on French Resistance radio messages, German military records & secret correspondence between de Gaulle, Churchill, Roosevelt & Eisenhower. They interviewed countless people: soliders, civilians, Allied generals & even the Nazi commandant who helped Paris fight for her life.

Is Peace Possible in Today's World? Brother Anandamoy. 1985. 8.50 (2512) Self Realization.
Topics include: Why God does not stop war; Is there a time when it is right to fight; War & peace in relation to the Cosmic Plan; Understanding the deeper meaning of nonviolence; Free will, karma & evolution; The real causes of war & peace.

Is Prediction in Astrology Possible? ACT Staff. 1 cass. 8.95 (479) Am Fed Astrologers.
Accurate prediction possible? Desirable?.

Is Religion a Dedication or a Commitment? Instructed by Manly P. Hall. 8.95 (978-0-89314-154-7(2), C860629) Philos Res.

Is Ritalin Necessary? The Ritalin Report. Billie Jay Sahley. (Running Time: 58 min.). 1996. 10.00 (978-1-889391-03-8(4)) Pain & Stress.

Is Ritalin Wrong for Our Hyperactive Kids? Interview with Michelle Trudeau. 1 cass. (Running Time: 21 min.). 9.95 (I0540B090, HarperThor) HarpC GBR.

Is Romance Biblical? Song of Sol. 1:8-11. Ed Young. 1986. 4.95 (978-0-7417-1532-6(5), 532) Win Walk.

Is Success Within Your Control? The Philosophy of Success Two. Leonard Peikoff. 1998. 12.95 (LPXXC82) Second Renaissance.

Is That the Reason I Get Abused? Learn How to Create & Maintain Healthy Boundaries in Your Relationships. Jef Gazley. 1 CD. 2005. audio compact disk 24.95 (978-1-933154-22-0(5), asktheinternet) Int Therapist.
To be able to have high self-esteem it is imperative that a person knows what personal healthy boundaries are and how to defend them without offending other people. This self-improvement book on appropriate boundaries is a great resource for information and education about personal boundaries. It describes what healthy boundaries are and how to apply them in the every day life. Learn how to identify abuse and gain the self-esteem to stop it. By Jef Gazley, M.S., LMFT (c)2005.

Is That the Reason I Have a Substance Abuse Problem? Treatment Options & Tips on How to Become Drug & Alcohol Free. Jef Gazley. 1 CD. 2005. audio compact disk 24.95 (978-1-933154-23-7(3), asktheinternet) Int Therapist.
Do you wonder if you have a drug problem or suffer from alcohol addiction or substance abuse? When is "one more drink" one too many? Is yours an alcoholic or substance dependent family? What is the difference between substance abuse and chemical dependence? "Is that the reason I have a substance abuse problem" describes how the drug problem starts and how the substance abuse cycle continues. It is a self-help tool for self-improvement. By Jef Gazley, M.S., LMFT (c)2005.

Is That the Reason I Try to Take Care of People too Much & Cannot Say No? Learn What Codependency Is & How to Treat it to Develop Healthy Relationships. Jef Gazley. 1 CD. 2005. audio compact disk 24.95 (978-1-933154-24-4(1), asktheinternet) Int Therapist.
Are the feelings of others more important than your own? Do you tend to suppress your feelings? Do you place the unhealthy needs of your alcoholic teen or spouse before your own? Are you an enabler? When is help really help? You may be subject to the tendency of codependency. This informative mental health book gives insight to the symptoms and origins of codependence and allows you to develop healthy relationships. Let this educational book be your first step toward better health and wellness! By Jef Gazley, M.S., LMFT (c)2005.

Is That the Reason My Relationships Fail? Learn How to Develop Healthy Relationships without Becoming Addicted to Love. Jef Gazley. 1 CD. 2005. audio compact disk 24.95 (978-1-933154-27-5(6), asktheinternet) Int Therapist.
Is it real love? Do you need love or relationship advice? Do you feel like half a person without sex or a relationship? Are you afraid of abandonment? Do you feel you might die without your partner? Love addiction and Sex addiction is much more common than people usually think. This self-improvement book describes the cycle of love addiction that is common in this type of relationship and compares healthy love to unhealthy love. By Jef Gazley, M.S., LMFT (c)2005.

Is That the Reason Our Children Don't Mind? Tips & Advice to Learn Effective Parenting Skills. Jef Gazley. 1 CD. 2005. audio compact disk 24.95 (978-1-933154-28-2(4), asktheinternet) Int Therapist.
Take the stress out of parenting! This self-improvement and educational book for parents describes the basic principles of effective parenting in a simple and straight forward format. Competent and caring parenting is essential for the well being of any child and a prerequisite for effective adult mental health when the child grows up. However, most parents are not taught the essential building blocks of effective parenting and often put too much stress on themselves. This actually decreases good parenting creates undo stress for the whole family. Learn the secrets of good parenting now from this educational book! By Jef Gazley, M.S., LMFT (c)2005.

Is That the Reason Why I Cannot Communicate Well? Learn How to Avoid Conflict, Increase Communication Skills, & How to Become Assertive. Jef Gazley. 1 CD. 2005. audio compact disk 24.95 (978-1-933154-25-1(X), asktheinternet) Int Therapist.
In the heat of an argument, do you feel as if no one is listening? Do you ever feel like you are talking, but not being heard in your relationships? Do you have a hard time expressing how you feel? Learn how to avoid conflict, communicate well, and become assertive. This self-improvement book teaches the art of effective communication, assertiveness, conflict resolution, and how to express feelings appropriately. These are essential skills for relationships and mental health. By Jef Gazley, M.S., LMFT (c)2005.

Is That the Reason Why I Cannot Deal with Stress after a Traumatic Experience? Learn to Identify the Symptoms & Dynamics of PTSD & How to Resolve Them. Jef Gazley. 1 CD. 2005. audio compact disk 24.95 (978-1-933154-29-9(2), asktheinternet) Int Therapist.
This self-improvement book explains the causes and development of Post-Traumatic Stress Disorder. Over a period of time, overwhelming shock and/or shocking experiences can cripple your ability to deal effectively in the present day. This problem often develops when people grow up in dysfunctional families. You will see yourself here, and discover that Post-Traumatic Stress Disorder (PTSD) is not something mysterious, and is curable. By Jef Gazley, M.S., LMFT (c)2005.

Is That the Reason Why Our Family Does Not Communicate Well? Learn How to Overcome the Effects of a Dysfunctional Family. Jef Gazley. 1 CD. 2005. audio compact disk 24.95 (978-1-933154-26-8(8), asktheinternet) Int Therapist.
Did you come from a dysfunctional family? Could you benefit from family counseling? What is a dysfunctional family, how do the family members interact, and what kind of damage is the result? This educational self-improvement book gives you a blueprint of a dysfunctional family, the dynamics involved, how shame develops and how to overcome the effects of a dysfunctional family. It is a map to greater self- esteem and wellness for the whole family. By Jef Gazley, M.S., LMFT (c)2005.

Is the Bible Reliable? 12 cass. 35.95 (2065, HarperThor) HarpC GBR.

***Is the Father of Jesus the God of Muhammad? Understanding the Differences between Christianity & Islam.** Timothy George. (Running Time: 5 hrs. 35 mins. 0 sec.). (ENG.). 2009. 14.99 (978-0-310-30462-3(8)) Zondervan.

Is the "New Catechism" a Source of Hope? Perf. by John Vennari. 1 cass. (Running Time: 90 mins.). 7.00 (20204) Cath Treas.
Explains why the New Universal Cathechism, hailed to be "an answer to a prayer" will actually further the post-Vatican II crisis.

Is The President Still Alive? 10.00 Esstee Audios.
Examines how for the first time in American history, a president was incapacitated & the nation wondered about George Washington & who was running the nation.

Is the Rooster Crowing? Matt. 26:74. Ed Young. 1988. 4.95 (978-0-7417-1695-8(X), 695) Win Walk.

Is the Water Safe to Drink? Hosted by Renee Montagne. 1 cass. (Running Time: 30 min.). 9.95 (I0450B090, HarperThor) HarpC GBR.

Is the World Getting Better? Asha Praver. 1 cass. (Change the World or Change Yourself Ser.). 9.95 (AP-9) Crystal Clarity.
Topics include: The meaning of the "New Age"; the spiritual implications of planetary evolution; why planetary (material) perfection is impossible; spiritual evolution as the purpose of life.

Is There a Guardian Angel? Instructed by Manly P. Hall. 8.95 (978-0-89314-155-4(0), C831211) Philos Res.

Is There a Space Without End? J. Krishnamurti. 1 cass. (Running Time: 1 hr.). (Krishnamurti & Pupul Jayakar - 1983 Ser.: No. 2). 8.50 (APJ832) Krishnamurti.

Is There a Word from the Lord? Mark Chironna. 1 cass. 1992. 7.00 (978-1-56043-922-6(X)) Destiny Image Pubs.

Is There an Eastern Mind & a Western Mind? J. Krishnamurti. 1 cass. (Running Time: 1 hr.). (Krishnamurti & Pupul Jayakar - 1983 Ser.: No. 1). 8.50 (APJ831) Krishnamurti.

Is There Another Way of Communicating? J. Krishnamurti. 1 cass. (Running Time: 75 min.). (Krishnamurti & Professor David Bohm - 1980 Ser.: No. 15). 8.50 (ABD8015) Krishnamurti.
Krishnamurti & Prof. Bohm offer penetrating, in-depth dialogues which shed light on the fundamental issues of existence.

Is There Human Freedom Without Economic Freedom? Read by Tibor R. Machan. 1 cass. 3.00 (133) ISI Books.

Is There Life after Death? Elisabeth Kubler-Ross. 2 CDs. (Running Time: 8100 sec.). 2005. audio compact disk 19.95 (978-1-59179-378-6(5), W974D) Sounds True.
In 1969, Dr. Elisabeth Kubler-Ross changed the way we think about the fi nal stage of our lives with her revolutionary book, On Death and Dying. Now, in this landmark recording, this revered researcher speaks about her largely private revelations, observations, and conclusions on life after death. Dr. Kubler-Ross, the first scientist to embark upon a genuine inquiry on the similarities between near-death experiences of people all over the world, gathered empirical data and personal impressions from countless studies that informed her opinions on what awaits us all when we leave this life. From her family archives comes a rare published audio of this trailblazing author speaking in her own words, as she engages the oldest question of all: Is There Life After Death?.

Is There Life after Housework? 2 cass. 14.95 Bonneville Media.
Features tips on how to save time on house work.

Is There Not A Cause? Achieving the Impossible Through Vision, Faith, & Passion. Mac Hammond. 3 cass. (Running Time: 3 hrs). 2005. (978-1-57399-235-0(6)) Mac Hammond.
Discover the three elements that make up a godly cause and how faith and passion work together to make your God-given vison a reality.

***Is There Not a Cause? Achieving the Impossible Through Vision, Faith & Passion.** Mac Hammond. 2010. audio compact disk 18.00 (978-1-57399-457-6(X)) Mac Hammond.

***Is There Not a Cost?** Featuring Ravi Zacharias. 2009. audio compact disk 9.00 (978-1-61256-017-5(2)) Ravi Zach.

Is There Order to the Universe? Dianthus. (ENG.). 1999. 19.95 (978-0-9622160-6-0(2)) Dianthus.

Is There Really a God? Rom. 2:18-22. Ed Young. 1992. 4.95 (978-0-7417-1946-1(0), 946) Win Walk.

***Is There Really a Human Race?** abr. ed. Jamie Lee Curtis. (ENG.). 2006. (978-0-06-124362-2(0)) HarperCollins Pubs.

***Is There Really a Human Race?** abr. ed. Jamie Lee Curtis. Read by Jamie Lee Curtis. 2006. (978-0-06-128536-3(6)) HarperCollins Pubs.

Is There Something Beyond Thought? J. Krishnamurti. Read by J. Krishnamurti. 1 cass. (Running Time: 90 min.). 1985. 8.50 (978-1-55994-326-0(2), AJT852) Krishnamurti.

Is There Something Beyond Thought? abr. ed. J. Krishnamurti. Read by J. Krishnamurti. 1 cass. (Running Time: 60 min.). (Ojai Talks Ser.). 1988. bk. 9.95 (978-0-06-250476-0(2)) HarperCollins Pubs.
Krishnamurti explores the relatedness of all human problems & the nature of time & thought. He offers no simple answers to questions & the origins of fear & desire, but examines the depth & breadth of these long-standing problems.

Is This An Important Day? Arlene Kramer. 1 cass. 8.95 (687) Am Fed Astrologers.
An AFA Convention workshop tape.

Is This You? 2004. 8.95 (978-1-56008-934-6(2)); cass. & flmstrp 30.00 (978-1-56008-692-5(0)) Weston Woods.

Is Vasectomy Safe? Medical Risks & Legal Implications. unabr. ed. H. J. Roberts. Read by H. J. Roberts. 2 cass. (Running Time: 2 hrs.). 1992. 19.95 set. (978-0-9633260-3-4(1)) Sunshine Sentinel.
A medical, public health & legal overview of the potential long-term complications following vasectomy including severe autoimmune reactions & cancer by a renowned clinician & researcher.

Is Your All on the Altar? Perf. by C. L. Fairchild & Voices of Greater Faith. 1 cass. 1997. audio compact disk 15.98 CD. (D2203) Diamante Music Grp.
Brimming with traditional Gospel flavor as can be heard on the title cut, as well as "Be Still & Know" & "I'm a Witness".

Is Your Child Autistic? Hosted by Mardie Caldwell. Featuring Ron Huff. (ENG.). 2008. audio compact disk 12.95 (978-0-9705734-0-7(5)) Pub: Am Carrage Hse Pubng. Dist(s): STL Dist NA

Is Your Dream God's Vision. 1. 2004. audio compact disk 6.00 (978-1-932316-24-7(8)) Great C Pubng.

Is Your God Worthy of Love? John 14:7-10. Ed Young. (J). 1980. 4.95 (978-0-7417-1116-8(8), A0116) Win Walk.

Is Your House Really a Home? Kenneth W. Hagin, Jr. 4 cass. 1997. 16.00 (C718) Faith Lib Pubns.
Rev. Kenneth Hagin, Jr. provides rich, practical teaching on how you can turn your house into a home where God is reverenced, His principles are practiced, & His character is demonstrated.

Is Your Mama a Llama? 2004. bk. 24.95 (978-1-55592-084-5(5)); pap. bk. 32.75 (978-1-55592-248-1(1)); audio compact disk 12.95 (978-1-55592-950-3(8)) Weston Woods.

Is Your Mama a Llama? 2004. pap. bk. 14.95 (978-1-55592-085-2(3)) Weston Woods.

Is Your Mama a Llama. 2004. pap. bk. 18.95 (978-1-55592-141-5(8)) Weston Woods.

Is Your Mama a Llama? Deborah Guarino. 1 cass. (Running Time: 6 min.). (J). (ps-1). 2004. 8.95 (978-1-55592-978-7(8)) Weston Woods.
Lloyd the llama is looking for his mama. "Is your mama a llama?" he asks a bat, a swan, a cow, a seal and a kangaroo.

Is Your Mama a Llama -Spanish. 2004. pap. bk. 38.75 (978-1-55592-636-6(3)); pap. bk. 32.75 (978-1-55592-712-7(2)); 8.95 (978-1-55592-546-8(4)) Weston Woods.

Is Your Miracle Passing You By? Kenneth W. Hagin, Jr. 1 cass. 4.95 (SJ05) Faith Lib Pubns.

Is Your Problem a Stumbling-block or a Stepping-stone? unabr. ed. Myrtle Smyth. Prod. by David Keyston. 1 cass. (Running Time: 61 mins.). (Myrtle Smyth Audiotape Ser.). 2000. 8.95 (978-1-893107-35-9(3), M27) Healing Unltd.
Lecture on the metaphysical content of the subject.

Isaac Asimov. Interview with Isaac Asimov. 1 cass. (Running Time: 30 min.). 1980. 12.95 (L005) TFR.
Charming & immodest, Asimov welcomes the fact that his major reputation is in science fiction. But he also calls attention to his books on science fact as well as his novels, short stories, mysteries, histories, biographies, autobiographies & various works on human satire, literature & religion.

Isaac Asimov Library. unabr. ed. Isaac Asimov. Read by Isaac Asimov. 6 cass. Incl. Feeling of Power. (C-407); Last Question. (C-407); Satisfaction Guaranteed. (C-407); Someday. (C-407); (C-407); 7.95 rental. Audio Bk.

Isaac Asimov on The Future of Man. 1 cass. (Running Time: 30 min.). 14.95 (CBC595) MMI Corp.
Continuance of man's evolution, genetics, importance of space exploration are some topics discussed.

Isaac Bashevis Singer. Interview with Isaac Bashevis Singer. 1 cass. (Running Time: 45 min.). 1968. 12.95 (L069) TFR.
Responding to Saul Bellow's statement that there is no such thing as a Jewish writer, Singer says "So maybe I don't exist." It's a playful remark, but it also says something about his fascination with ghosts & dybbuks, the sphere of the supernatural.

Isaac Bashevis Singer. abr. ed. Isaac Bashevis Singer. Read by Isaac Bashevis Singer. Tr. by Cecil Hemley from YID. 1 cass. Incl. Gimpel the Fool & Other Stories. Isaac Bashevis Singer. (SWC 1200); Man Who Came Back. (SWC 1200); 1984. 12.95 (978-0-694-50151-9(4), SWC 1200) HarperCollins Pubs.

Isaac Bashevis Singer Reader. unabr. ed. Isaac Bashevis Singer. Read by Wolfram Kandinsky. 10 cass. (Running Time: 15 hrs.). Incl. Black Wedding. (1369); Blood. (1369); Feast. (1369); Friend of Kafka. Isaac Bashevis Singer. (1369); Getzel the Monkey. (1369); Gimpel the Fool & Other Stories. Isaac Bashevis Singer. (1369); Lecture. (1369); Man Who Came Back. (1369); Mirror. (1369); Seance. (1369); Short Friday. (1369); Slaughterer. (1369); Spinoza of Market Street. Isaac Bashevis Singer. (1369); Unseen. (1369); Yentyl the Yeshiva Boy. Isaac Bashevis Singer. (1369); (J). 1987. 80.00 (978-0-7366-0392-8(1), 1369) Books on Tape.

Isaac Newton. unabr. ed. James Gleick. Read by Allan Corduner. 4 cass. (Running Time: 6 hrs.). 2003. audio compact disk 29.95 (978-0-06-055486-6(X)) HarperCollins Pubs.

***Isaac Newton.** unabr. ed. James Gleick. Read by Allan Corduner. (ENG.). 2005. (978-0-06-084631-2(3), Harper Audio); (978-0-06-084632-9(1), Harper Audio) HarperCollins Pubs.

Isaac Newton: The Last Sorcerer. unabr. collector's ed. Michael White. Read by Stuart Langton. 10 cass. (Running Time: 15 hrs.). 1999. 80.00 (978-0-7366-4487-7(3), 4926) Books on Tape.
Issac Newton, one of the greatest scientific minds of all time was an individual of surprising qualities. The man whose observations formed the basis of modern thinking in physics was also an astrologer & alchemist, embedded in the superstitions of his time.

Isaac Newton & the Laws of Motion. Andrea Gianopoulos & Charles Barnett III. Illus. by Phil Miller. (Inventions & Discovery Ser.). (ENG.). (gr. 3-4). 2007. audio compact disk 6.95 (978-1-4296-1115-2(4)) CapstoneDig.

Isaac Newton & the Laws of Motion (INK Audiocassette) (Inventions & Discovery Ser.). (ENG.). 2007. audio compact disk 5.95 (978-0-7368-7990-3(0)) CapstoneDig.

Isaac Newton's New Physics. unabr. ed. Gordon Brittan. Read by Edwin Newman. (Running Time: 10800 sec.). (Audio Classics: Science & Discovery Ser.). 2006. audio compact disk 25.95 (978-0-7861-6435-6(2)) Pub: Blckstn Audio. Dist(s): NetLibrary CO

Isaac Newton's New Physics. unabr. ed. Gordon Brittan. Read by Edwin Newman. Ed. by Jack Sommer & Mike Hassell. 2 cass. (Running Time: 2 hrs. 45 min.). Dramatization. (Science & Discovery Ser.). (YA). (gr. 11 up). 1993. 17.95 set. (978-0-938935-70-4(4), 10405) Knowledge Prod.
Newton was a natural philosopher (the word "scientist" had not yet been coined) who described a planetary system held together by gravitational forces. His "Principia" changed science forever; gravity not only explained the orbits of stars - it explained common earthly events as well. Newton established a way of thinking that still shapes our everyday understanding of how the world works.

Isaacs Live: Live from Norway. Contrib. by Isaacs et al. Prod. by Lily Isaacs et al. 2008. 19.99 (978-5-557-48889-1(8)) Gaither Music Co.

Isaac's Storm: A Man, a Time, & the Deadliest Hurricane in History. abr. ed. Erik Larson. Read by Edward Herrmann. (Running Time: 21600 sec.). (ENG.). 2006. audio compact disk 19.99 (978-0-7393-4036-3(0), Random AudioBks) Pub: Random Audio Pubg. Dist(s): Random

Isaac's Storm: A Man, a Time, & the Deadliest Hurricane in History. unabr. ed. Erik Larson. Narrated by Richard M. Davidson. 8 cass. (Running Time: 9 hrs.). 2000. 67.00 (978-0-7887-4304-7(X), 96221E7) Recorded Bks.
In 1900 a storm moved across Galveston, Texas. As the director of its weather station watched, Galveston's security & its future washed away. Includes an exclusive interview with the author.

Isabeau. unabr. ed. Ann de Lisle. Read by Richard Aspel. 8 cass. (Running Time: 12 hrs.). 1999. (978-1-876584-34-4(3), 590996) Bolinda Pubng AUS.
Bent on delivering a treasonous letter to save her cause, Jacobite rebel Isabeau Macpherson is captured mid-flight by the enemy. Her captors are not the English but more despised still, fellow Scots fighting against Bonnie Prince Charlie. Despite her obvious hatred for him & all that he represents, Alistair Campbell is bewitched by her fearless & beautiful charge. When Isabeau escapes & is captured by the English & tortured, he risks everything to free her. Torn between loyalty to her cause & love for a man who is her sworn enemy, Isabeau is forced to take sides in a battle that threatens to destroy them both.

Isabella Gardner. unabr. ed. Isabella Gardner. 1 cass. (Author Speaks Ser.). 1991. 14.95 J Norton Pubs.
Archival recordings of 20th-century authors.

Isabella Gardner. unabr. ed. Isabella Gardner. Read by Isabella Gardner. 1 cass. (Running Time: 29 min.). 1981. 10.00 (121181) New Letters.

Isabella Moon. unabr. ed. Laura Benedict. Read by Renée Raudman. (Running Time: 14 hrs.). 2007. 39.25 (978-1-4233-3436-1(1), 9781423334361, BADLE); 24.95 (978-1-4233-3435-4(3), 9781423334354, BAD); 97.25 (978-1-4233-3430-9(2), 9781423334309, BrilAudUnabridg); audio compact disk 36.95 (978-1-4233-3431-6(0), 9781423334316, Bril Audio CD Unabri); audio compact disk 24.95 (978-1-4233-3433-0(7), 9781423334330, Brilliance MP3); audio compact disk 112.25 (978-1-4233-3432-3(9), 9781423334323, BriAudCD Unabrid); audio compact disk 39.25 (978-1-4233-3434-7(5), 9781423334347, Brlnc Audio MP3 Lib) Brilliance Audio.

Isabel's Bed. unabr. ed. Elinor Lipman. Read by Grace Conlin. 7 cass. (Running Time: 10 hrs.). 1995. 49.95 (978-0-7861-0810-7(X), 1633) Blckstn Audio.
Harriet Mahoney, an unpublished, fortyish & recently jilted writer, moves in with Isabel Krug, a sexy blonde with a tabloid past, to ghostwrite her story. Unusually talented in the man department, Isabel revamps & inspires Harriet as they gear up to tell all. Life according to Isabel is a soap-opera extravaganza, an experience to be swallowed whole & the attitude is catching.

Isabel's Bed, Set. abr. ed. Elinor Lipman. Read by Elinor Lipman. 2 cass. (Running Time: 3 hrs.). 1996. 16.95 (978-1-57511-002-8(4), 394405) Pub Mills.
When writer Harriet Mahoney answered an ad to ghostwrite a book based on the life of Isabel Krug, a sexy blonde with a tabloid past, little did she know that her escape from New York would end up a free-fall into happiness. After Harriet moves into Isabel's Cape Cod retreat she is drawn into Isabel's freewheeling soap opera of a life. Soon, Harriet's memories of her bagel-baking ex-boyfriend fade into oblivion as the two women write Isabel's louder than life memoir & Harriet wins the affection of a gentle man who appreciates in her what other men have failed to see.

Isabel's Texas Two-Step. unabr. ed. Annie Bryant. Read by Roxanne Hernandez. (Beacon Street Girls Special Adventure Ser.: No. 5). (ENG.). (J). (gr. 4). 2008. audio compact disk 19.95 (978-0-7393-7334-7(X), Listening Lib) Pub: Random Audio Pubg. Dist(s): Random

Isaiah: A Biblical Interpretation. Concept by Ermance Rejebian. (ENG.). 2007. 5.99 (978-1-60339-157-3(6)); audio compact disk 5.99 (978-1-60339-158-0(4)) Listenr Digest.

Isaiah & the Book of Mormon. Terry Ball. 4 cass. 2004. 19.95 (978-1-59156-312-9(7)); audio compact disk 19.95 (978-1-59156-313-6(5)) Covenant Comms.

Isaiah Commentary. Chuck Missler. 1 MP3 CD-ROM. (Running Time: 24 hrs.). (Chuck Missler Commentaries). 2001. cd-rom 44.95 (978-1-57821-143-2(3)) Koinonia Hse.
Isaiah was the most comprehensive of all prophets: his writing spans the entirety of history, from the creation of the world to the creation of "a new heavens and new earth." No other prophet matches his majestic eloquence on the glory of God and the redemptive work and sufferings of the Coming Messiah, all the while making us clearly aware of God's abounding Grace. This MP3 CD-ROM (compatible with both Windows and Macintosh operating systems) is self-contained and includes: Over 28 hours of Verse-by-Verse audio teaching through the book of Isaiah as MP3 files.

Isaiah Commentary. deluxe ed. Chuck Missler. 24 cass. (Running Time: 24 hrs.). (Heirloom Edition Ser.). 1996. im. lthr. 89.95 Incl. notebk. & notes. (978-1-880532-32-4(8)) Koinonia Hse.

Isaiah Effect. Gregg Braden. 2 CDs. (Running Time: 2 Hrs 30 Mins). 2005. audio compact disk 19.95 (978-1-59179-304-5(1), AW00493D) Sounds True.
In Jerusalem, within the Shrine of the Book Museum, resides the Great Isaiah Scroll - the most precious artifact of the famed Dead Sea Scrolls. Why is this single document, lost to humanity for more than 2,000 years, so crucial to modern scholars and mystics today? On The Isaiah Effect, the bestselling author of Awakening to Zero Point takes us on an investigation into this ancient Essene scripture - to reveal a set of inner tools capable of altering the destiny of human civilization. "Prayer and prophecy have the power to heal our bodies and spirits 'shift the course of nations' and even influence the ebbs and flows of weather and geology," teaches Braden. Yet today, few of us know how to harness the awesome potential of these two spiritual technologies. Now, drawing on new insights into the physics of time and prophecy, Gregg Braden shows us how to decode the true meaning of the Great Isaiah Scroll and other prophetic scriptures - how prayer can change the outcome of those predictions - and how these two spiritual practices, together, create The Isaiah Effect.

Isaiah I. (LifeLight Bible Studies: Course 16). 13.95 Set. (20-2532) Concordia.

Isaiah 2. (LifeLight Bible Studies: Course 17). bk. & stu. ed. 0.55 (978-0-570-09379-4(1), 20-2536) Concordia.

Isak Dinesen: The Life of a Storyteller. unabr. ed. Judith Thurman. Narrated by Davina Porter. 15 cass. (Running Time: 21 hrs. 30 mins.). 1997. 120.00 (978-0-7887-0719-3(1), 94895E7) Recorded Bks.
Biography twines together a carefully researched narrative of Isak Dinesen's fabled life & a perceptive portrait of her literary art.

Isak Dinesen Feast: A Performance Anthology. unabr. abr. ed. Isak Dinesen. Read by Isak Dinesen. Read by Julie Harris & Colleen Dewhurst. 6 cass. (Running Time: 7 hrs. 35 mins.). 2004. 29.95 (978-1-57270-029-1(7), M61029) Pub: Audio Partners. Dist(s): PerseuPGW
Includes Dinesen's "Out of Africa," "Babette's Feast," Bill Luce's "Lucifer's Child" & the author herself telling two stories.

Isak Dinesen Herself. unabr. ed. Isak Dinesen. Read by Isak Dinesen. 1 cass. (Running Time: 1 hr. 15 mins.). 2004. 10.95 (978-0-945353-31-7(6), M10331a) Pub: Audio Partners. Dist(s): PerseuPGW
Historic recording features two complete stories: "The King's Letter," which connects Dinesen's life in Denmark with her life in Africa, & "The Wine of the Tetrarch," the story of the Apostle Peter on the Wednesday after Easter.

Ischemic Leg. 2 cass. (General Sessions Ser.: C85-GS7). 15.00 (8542) Am Coll Surgeons.

Ish. Peter H. Reynolds. Illus. by Peter H. Reynolds. Narrated by Chester Gregory. Music by Joel Goodman. 1 CD. (Running Time: 7 minds.). (J). (ps-4). 2005. bk. 29.95 (978-0-439-80429-5(9), WHCD676) Scholastic Inc.

Ish. unabr. ed. Peter H. Reynolds. Illus. by Peter H. Reynolds. Narrated by Chester Gregory. Music by Joel Goodman. 1 cass. (Running Time: 7 mins.). (J). (ps-4). 2005. bk. 24.95 (978-0-439-80428-8(0), WHRA676) Scholastic Inc.
With a little encouragement from his sister, Ramon discovers that creativity is about a lot more than getting things just "right." Combining the spareness of fable with the potency of parable, the creator of The Dot shines a bright beam of light on the need to kindle and tend our creative flames with care.

Ishbane Conspiracy. Angela Alcorn et al. Read by Frank Muller. (Running Time: 24000 sec.). (ENG.). 2007. audio compact disk 26.99 (978-1-934384-03-9(8)) Pub: Treasure Pub. Dist(s): STL Dist NA

Ishi: The Last Yahi. Bernie Krause. 1 cass. (Running Time: 34 min.). (Music & Word Ser.). 1994. 9.95 (2315, NrthWrd Bks) TandN Child.
These rare, re-mastered recordings of Ishi speaking & singing in his native Yahi language were originally recorded in 1911-1914.

Ishi in Two Worlds: A Biography of the Last Wild Indian in North America. unabr. ed. Theodora Kroeber & Karl (Foreword by) Kroeber. Read by Lorna Raver. (Running Time: 11 hrs. 0 mins.). (ENG.). 2009. 29.95 (978-1-4332-5388-1(7)); 65.95 (978-1-4332-5385-0(2)); audio compact disk 100.00 (978-1-4332-5386-7(0)) Blckstn Audio.

Ishi in Two Worlds: A Biography of the Last Wild Indian in North America. unabr. collector's ed. Theodora Kroeber. Read by Mary Woods. 6 cass. (Running Time: 9 hrs.). 1990. 48.00 (978-0-7366-1689-8(6), 2536) Books on Tape.
Ishi was literally a Stone Age man, the last of a "lost" tribe, when in 1911 he stumbled into 20th century California. In the following five years thousands of visitors watched him chip arrowheads, shape bows & make fire in the halls of the museum where he made his home. Theodora Kroeber puts together two necklaces: first, the story of a tribe that survived undisturbed for hundreds of years along the streams of Mount Lassen. The second necklace is the story of Ishi's adjustment to the trolley-world of San Francisco.

Ishmael Reed: "Flight to Canada" unabr. ed. Ishmael Reed. Read by Ishmael Reed. 1 cass. (Running Time: 29 min.). 1984. 10.00 New Letters.
The story of a recently escaped modern black slave who makes his way to freedom via jumbo jet & probes the contemporary American psyche along the way.

Ishmael Reed II. unabr. ed. Ishmael Reed. Read by Ishmael Reed. 1 cass. (Running Time: 29 min.). 1989. 10.00 New Letters.
Reed reads poetry & is interviewed.

ISing: Praise & Worship: Ready-to-Sing Vocal Solos. Created by Shawnee Press. (ENG.). 1999. pap. bk. 14.95 (978-1-59235-263-0(4)) Shawnee Pr.

Isis Reminiscence Selection. unabr. ed. 16 cass. (Running Time: 20 hrs. 55 min.). 2001. ISIS Audio GBR.
Comprises a range of biographies & autobiographies from the British Isles.

Isla Bajo el Mar see Island Beneath the Sea

Isla Bajo el Mar see Island Beneath the Sea: A Novel

Isla de Abel. unabr. ed. William Steig. Narrated by Gonzalo Madruga. 2 cass. (Running Time: 2 hrs. 45 min.).Tr. of Abel's Island. (SPA.). (J). (gr. 2). 1997. 14.00 bk. (978-1-55690-878-1(4), 93320) Recorded Bks.
Share a children's classic with Spanish-speaking children in this delightful audio production. Abel, a rich & silly mouse, has never had to work for anything until he is stranded on a deserted island.

Isla Del Skog. Tr. of Island of the Skog, the. (SPA.). 2004. 8.95 (978-0-7882-0294-0(4)) Weston Woods.

Isla Del Tesoro. abr. ed. Abuelo Historias Del. (SPA.). 2007. audio compact disk 13.00 (978-958-8318-08-0(4)) Pub: Yoyo Music COL. Dist(s): YoYoMusic

Isla del Tesoro. abr. ed. Robert Louis Stevenson. 2 cds. (Running Time: 7200 sec.).Tr. of Treasure Island. (SPA.). 2007. audio compact disk 16.95 (978-1-933499-50-5(8)) Fonolibro Inc.

Isla del Tesoro. abr. ed. Robert Louis Stevenson. Read by Guillermo Piedrahita. 3 CDs.Tr. of Treasure Island. (SPA.). 2002. audio compact disk 17.00 (978-958-9494-66-0(8)) YoYoMusic.

Islam. Malise Ruthven. Read by Malise Ruthven. 3 cds. 2004. audio compact disk 22.98 (978-962-634-321-0(4), Naxos AudioBooks) Naxos.

Islam. unabr. ed. Charles Adams. Read by Ben Kingsley. (Running Time: 10800 sec.). (Religion, Scriptures, & Spirituality Ser.). 2006. audio compact disk 25.95 (978-0-7861-6482-0(4)) Pub: Blckstn Audio. Dist(s): NetLibrary CO

Islam. unabr. ed. Charles Adams. Read by Ben Kingsley. Ed. by Walter Harrelson & Mike Hassell. 2 cass. (Running Time: 3 hrs.). Dramatization. (Religion, Scriptures & Spirituality Ser.). 1994. 17.95 (978-1-56823-011-5(7), 10454) Pub: Knowledge Prod. Dist(s): APG
Islam today is a rapidly growing religion: Indonesia, the most populous Islamic land, has well over 100 million Muslims. Islam began in the seventh century, & has evolved into various forms - Sunni, Shi'ah, Sufi mysticism, etc. Also described are the backgrounds & connections of related groups like the Druse, Baha'i, the Nation of Islam, & others.

Islam: A Complete Way of Life; The Five Pillars of Islam. unabr. ed. Julian C. Hollick. 1 cass. (Running Time: 60 min.). (World of Islam Ser.). 1985. 15.00 (978-1-56709-053-6(2), 1025) Indep Broadcast.
Islam claims to be a blueprint for politics, economics & social behavior to a far greater extent than other religions. This program examines the basic elements of Islam & explains why it is not just a religion, but a complete way of life. Side B: This program explores what it means to be a Muslim, a total cultural experience far more encompassing than anything we know in the West.

Islam: A Short History. unabr. ed. Karen Armstrong. Narrated by Richard M. Davidson. 5 cass. (Running Time: 6 hrs. 45 mins.). 2002. 48.00 (978-1-4025-1283-4(X)) Recorded Bks.
A comprehensive guide to Islam.

Islam, a History. unabr. ed. 2 cds. 2002. pap. bk. (978-1-58472-378-3(5), In Aud) Sound Room.
Documentary.

Islam, a History. unabr. ed. 2 cds. 2002. audio compact disk 18.95 (978-1-58472-376-9(9), In Aud) Pub: Sound Room. Dist(s): Baker Taylor

Islam: A Very Short Introduction: A Very Short Introduction. Malise Ruthven. Read by Malise Ruthven. (Running Time: 4 hrs.). (C). 2005. 24.95 (978-1-60083-786-9(7)) Iofy Corp.

***Islam & Christianity.** Featuring Ravi Zacharias. 1991. audio compact disk 9.00 (978-1-61256-046-5(6)) Ravi Zach.

Islam & Democracy in North Africa. unabr. ed. Julian C. Hollick. 1 cass. (Running Time: 45 min.). (Islam Revisited Ser.). 1992. spiral bd. 12.50 transcript. (978-1-56709-040-6(0), 1038); 15.00 (978-1-56709-041-3(9), 1081) Indep Broadcast.
The five individual program titles are: Algeria Goes Fundamentalist; Are Islam & Democracy Incompatible?; Islamic Fundamentalism & Human Rights in Tunisia; Islam & Democracy: The West's Dilemma; Hassan Turabi: The Next Ayatollah.

Islam & Modern Science see Muhammad: The Truth Exposed: the Prophet of Islam

Islam & the Arab Empire Series: World Events over Time Collection. Eugene Lieber. (ENG.). 2006. audio compact disk 20.00 (978-1-935069-13-3(6)) IAB Inc.

Islam & the West. Seyyed Hossein Nasr. 2008. audio compact disk 29.99 (978-1-4361-7437-4(6)) Recorded Bks.

Islam in America: The Other Face of Eve. unabr. ed. Julian C. Hollick. 1 cass. (Running Time: 1 hr.). (World of Islam Ser.). 1985. 15.00 (978-1-56709-058-1(3), 1035) Indep Broadcast.
Side A (Islam in America: The Black Muslims): This Program Looks at the growth of Islam among Afro-Americans & the radical divisions within existing "Black Islam" between the Nation of Islam & the American Muslim Mission. Side B (The Other Face of Eve): This Program examines the many different human conditions within the Muslim world, the effect of Islam of women & their rights & the influence of traditional patriarchal values throughout the Islamic world.

Islam Unveiled. unabr. ed. Robert Spencer. Read by Nadia May. 6 pieces. 2004. reel tape 29.95 (978-0-7861-2401-5(6)); audio compact disk 32.95 (978-0-7861-9332-5(8)) Blckstn Audio.

Islam Unveiled: Disturbing Questions about the World's Fastest Growing Faith. unabr. ed. Robert Spencer. Read by Nadia May. 6 cass. (Running Time: 8 hrs. 30 min.). 2003. 44.95 (978-0-7861-2340-7(0)); audio compact disk 48.00 (978-0-7861-9376-9(X)) Blckstn Audio.
In this captivating, carefully researched book, Robert Spencer asks the hard questions about Islam and gives the hard answers, providing a profoundly needed antidote to the wishful thinking and willful distortions that have swamped the media since the September 11 attacks. As noted observer of the Arab world David Pryce-Jones says in his introduction, "In its own lively style, Islam Unveiled puts down a strong and significant marker to what lies ahead, as Islam and the rest of the world strive to come to terms.".

Islam Unveiled: Disturbing Questions about the World's Fastest Growing Faith. unabr. ed. Robert Spencer. Read by Nadia May. 1 CD. (Running Time: 8 hrs. 30 mins.). 2003. audio compact disk 24.95 (978-0-7861-9068-3(X)) Blckstn Audio.

Islamic Civilization. Akram Zahoor. 2002. audio compact disk 65.00 (978-0-9702389-3-1(2)) ZMD.

Islamic Terrorists vs. America. Hosted by Leonard Peikoff. 2 cass. (Philosophy: Who Needs It? Ser.). 1998. 25.95 Set. (LPXXC69) Second Renaissance.

Island. Jay O'Callahan. Perf. by Jay O'Callahan. 1 CD. (Running Time: 46 min 12 sec). Dramatization. (YA). 2004. audio compact disk 15.00 (978-1-877954-45-0(4)) Pub: Artana Prodns. Dist(s): Yellow Moon
Good and evil castaways on an island where strange creatures roam. A story of enchantment and romance. Winner of the Parents' Choice Award.

Island. abr. ed. Heather Graham. Read by Joyce Bean. (Running Time: 6 hrs.). 2010. audio compact disk 9.99 (978-1-4418-0819-6(1), 9781441808196, BCD Value Price) Brilliance Audio.

Island. unabr. ed. Heather Graham. Read by Joyce Bean. (Running Time: 32400 sec.). 2006. audio compact disk 36.95 (978-1-4233-0759-4(3), 9781423307594) Brilliance Audio.
Please enter a Synopsis.

Island. unabr. ed. Heather Graham. Read by Joyce Bean. (Running Time: 9 hrs.). 2006. 39.25 (978-1-4233-0764-8(X), 9781423307648, BADLE); 24.95 (978-1-4233-0763-1(1), 9781423307631, BAD); 74.25 (978-1-4233-0758-7(5), 9781423307587, BrilAudUnabridg); audio compact disk 39.25 (978-1-4233-0762-4(3), 9781423307624, Brlnc Audio MP3 Lib); audio compact disk 92.25 (978-1-4233-0760-0(7), 9781423307600, BriAudCD Unabrid); audio compact disk 24.95 (978-1-4233-0761-7(5), 9781423307617, Brilliance MP3) Brilliance Audio.

Island. unabr. ed. Elin Hilderbrand. Read by Denice Hicks. (Running Time: 15 hrs.). (ENG.). 2010. 24.98 (978-1-60788-241-1(8)); audio compact disk 34.98 (978-1-60788-240-4(X)) Pub: Hachet Audio. Dist(s): HachBkGrp

Island, unabr. ed. Gary Paulsen. Narrated by Jeff Woodman. 4 pieces. (Running Time: 6 hrs.). (gr. 5 up). 1994. 35.00 (978-0-7887-0130-6(4), 94355E7) Recorded Bks.
A young man seeks solitude & contact with nature on an island in a northern lake, but his parents are unable to understand why he spends more & more time there. Young adults will identify with him as he grapples with the sensitive issues of coming-of-age.

***Island: A Novel.** Elin Hilderbrand. Read by Denice Hicks. (Running Time: 15 hrs.). (ENG.). 2011. audio compact disk & audio compact disk 19.98 (978-1-60941-268-5(0)) Pub: Hachet Audio. Dist(s): HachBkGrp

Island: The Collected Stories. unabr. collector's ed. Alistair MacLeod. Read by John Lee. 9 cass. (Running Time: 13 hrs. 30 min.). 2001. 72.00; audio compact disk 88.00; audio compact disk 19.99 Books on Tape.
Sixteen short stories, masterworks, from one of Canada's most important writers.

Island Apart. unabr. ed. Lillian Beckwith. Read by Vivien Heilbron. 4 cass. (Running Time: 4 hrs.). (Mini-CAB Audio Bks.). 1994. 39.95 (978-0-7451-4329-3(6), CAB 1012) AudioGO.
When Ruari MacDonald goes to the small Scottish island of Islay to find a wife, he returns with Kristy MacLennan. The two return to Westisle where they adapt to the mysteries of marriage & discover the harsh realities of life.

Island Apart. unabr. ed. Lillian Beckwith. Read by Vivien Heilbron. 4 cass. (Running Time: 6 hrs.). 1999. 34.95 (CAB 1012) Pub: Chivers Audio Bks GBR. Dist(s): AudioGO
When Ruari MacDonald goes to the small Scottish island of Islay to find a wife, he returns with Kirsty MacLennan. The two return to Westisle where they adapt to the mysteries of marriage and discover the harsh realities of life.

Island at the Center of the World: The Epic Story of Dutch Manhattan & the Forgotten Colony That Shaped America. Russell Shorto. 11 CDs. (Running Time: 13 hrs.). 2004. audio compact disk 34.99 (978-1-4193-0044-8(X), 01862) Recorded Bks.

***Island Beneath the Sea.** unabr. ed. Isabel Allende. Read by S. Epatha Merkerson.Tr. of Isla Bajo el Mar. (ENG.). 2010. (978-0-06-199756-3(0), Harper Audio) HarperCollins Pubs.

Island Beneath the Sea. unabr. ed. Isabel Allende. Read by S. Epatha Merkerson. 13 CDs. (Running Time: 16 hrs.).Tr. of Isla Bajo el Mar. 2010. audio compact disk 39.99 (978-0-06-199362-6(X), Harper Audio) HarperCollins Pubs.

***Island Beneath the Sea: A Novel.** unabr. ed. Isabel Allende. Read by S. Epatha Merkerson.Tr. of Isla Bajo el Mar. 2010. (978-0-06-199755-6(2), Harper Audio) HarperCollins Pubs.

Island Boy & Miss Rumphius. unabr. ed. Barbara Cooney. Read by Tracy Lord. Music by Bruce Boege. 1 CD. (Running Time: 32 min.). (YA). (ps up). 1996. audio compact disk 15.95 (978-1-883332-66-2(4)) Audio Bkshelf.
Two cherished stories by favorite children's author Barbara Cooney transport listeners of all ages to the magic of the Maine coast.

***Island Christmas: A Kids' Musical about Giving.** Contrib. by Jukka Palonen. Created by Shelby Haun et al. (ENG.). 2008. 29.99 (978-5-557-40964-3(5)) Lillenas.

Island Dreams: Songs & Lullabies Carried on the Wind. Perf. by Aiko Shimada et al. Composed by Aiko Shimada. 1 CD. (Running Time: 55 min.). (ENG & JPN.). 2004. audio compact disk 15.00 (978-0-9770499-7-4(3)) Koto World.
Winner of three national awards. Acoustic music from Japan, Okinawa, Hawai'i, and beyond; as uplifting and nurturing as an ocean breeze. Performed by Dragonfly: Aiko Shimada , vocals and guitars; Elizabeth Falconer, koto; and introducing Mako, Okinawan sanshin, vocals, and ukulele. The songs on this CD are sung in Okinawan, English, and Japanese, and include: Tinsagu nu Hana (Balsam Flowers), Pupu Hinuhinu (Shiny Shell Lullaby), MAHALO, Warabi Gami (Blessings from Heaven), Tsukinu Kaisha (Ocean Moon), Tanabata no Uta (Song of the Star Festival), Ku'u Pua I Paoakalani (My Flowers at Paoakalani), Migumi (One), When Pueo Flies, Akata Sundunchi (My Heart, My Home), Kojo no Tsuki (Moonlit Castle Reflections), Hatachi Miyarabi (Youthful Beauty), Dreaming~Yume.

***Island Eddy.** Island Eddy. (ENG.). 2008. audio compact disk 28.95 (978-0-8023-8170-5(7)) Pub: Clo Iar-Chonnachta IRL. Dist(s): Dufour

Island Fantasies. 1 CD. (Running Time: 30 min). (Luau Celebration Ser.: 3). 1994. audio compact disk 16.95 (978-1-58513-975-0(0)) Dance Fantasy.

Island Fantasies. Michael Perkins. 1 cass. (Running Time: 1 hr. 30 min.). 9.98 (978-0-89334-135-0(5)) Humanics Pub Grp.

Island Fling. unabr. collector's ed. Ian Skidmore. Read by Rodney Fay. 7 cass. (Running Time: 7 hrs.). 1986. 42.00 (978-0-7366-0728-5(5), 1685) Books on Tape.
When a tiny Welsh island declares independence from Great Britain, the government of England is shaken to its depths & plans an invasion to subjugate the unruly islanders. The new nation puts up its defenses knowing this will be their finest hour.

Island Girl. Perf. by Meeka. Contrib. by Art Halperin. 1 cass. (J). 1999. 10.98 (978-1-57471-489-0(9), YM113-CN); audio compact disk 13.98 (978-1-57471-490-6(2), YM113-CD) Youngheart Mus.
Songs include: "Are We There Yet?"; "Have Some Fun"; "Meeka Meets Sally"; "Island Girl"; "Thirsty Island"; "Sisters"; "U.F.O. Tonight"; "Kazoo?"; "Wiggle & Pull"; "Sam the Monkey"; "Drop It Jake"; "Down by the Sea" & "Every Day Is Carnival.".

Island in the Sea of Time. unabr. ed. S. M. Stirling. Read by Todd McLaren. Narrated by Todd McLaren. (Running Time: 26 hrs. 0 mins. 0 sec.). (Nantucket Ser.). (ENG.). 2008. audio compact disk 34.99 (978-1-4001-5679-5(3)); audio compact disk 99.99 (978-1-4001-3679-7(2)); audio compact disk 49.99 (978-1-4001-0679-0(6)) Pub: Tantor Media. Dist(s): IngramPubServ

Island Interlude. unabr. ed. Jane Edwards. Read by Laurie Klein. 4 cass. (Running Time: 5 hrs.). 1994. 26.95 Set. (978-1-55686-554-1(6)) Books in Motion.
Denise O'Shea takes a job at Hotel Caribe Azure, a luxury hotel in the Caribbean & is shocked by the poverty of the natives in contrast to the conspicuous consumption of the hotel guests.

Island Lullaby. 1 cass. (Running Time: 1 hr.). 9.95 (978-1-55961-624-9(5)) Relaxtn Co.

Island Madness. unabr. ed. Tim Binding. Read by Sean Barrett. 12 CDs. (Running Time: 12 hrs.). 2000. audio compact disk 89.95 (978-0-7531-0979-3(4), 109794) Pub: ISIS Audio GBR. Dist(s): Ulverscroft US
It is 1943 & the German army has been defeated at Stalingrad. The tide is beginning to turn. But on Guernsey & the rest of the Channel Islands, the only British territory to have been occupied by German troops, such a reversal is unimaginable.

Island Madness. unabr. ed. Tim Binding. Read by Sean Barrett. 10 cass. (Running Time: 13 hrs. 30 mins.). (Isis Ser.). (J). 2001. 84.95 (978-0-7531-0646-4(9), 990906) Pub: ISIS Lrg Prnt GBR. Dist(s): Ulverscroft US
1943, the German Army has been defeated at Stalingrad. The tide is beginning to turn. But on Guernsey & the rest of the Channel Islands, the only British territory to have been occupied, such a reversal is unimaginable. The reality of war seems a lifetime away, yet resentment & the debilitating effects of food shortages undercut the picturesque calm. However, life goes on, parties are held, love affairs blossom & the Guernsey Amateur Dramatic & Operatic Players continue to stage their productions. When a young local woman is found murdered, both the islanders & the occupiers are forced to acknowledge that this most civilized of wars conceals a more bitter & darker struggle than anyone cares to recognize.

Island Magic. unabr. collector's ed. Elizabeth Goudge. Read by Donada Peters. 8 cass. (Running Time: 12 hrs.). 1991. 64.00 (978-0-7366-1951-6(8), 2772) Books on Tape.
The Channel Islands were divided in allegiance between France & England. Of French blood & yet subjects of Queen Victoria, the Islanders were curious hybrid creatures. But now, in 1888, England was slowly stretching out her arms to them. Colin du Frocq was eight years old at the time & his dreams were of the sea that surrounded his home. By day he stole away & took to the sea in any boat that was sailing. At night he lay in bed & listened to the waves beat against the shore. Then one night, in a wild storm, a ship drove onto the nearby cliffs & a strange man entered Colin's life, changing Colin's course forever.

Island of Doctor Death & Other Stories & Other Stories. Short Stories. Gene Wolfe. Read by Gene Wolfe. 1 cass. (Running Time: 48 min.). 13.95 (978-1-55644-119-6(3), 4151) Am Audio Prose.
Wolfe reads his short stories including "Solar Labyrinth".

Island of Doctor Moreau, with EBook. unabr. ed. H. G. Wells. Narrated by Jonathan Kent. (Running Time: 5 hrs. 0 mins. 0 sec.). (ENG.). 2009. audio compact disk 19.99 (978-1-4001-1114-5(5)); audio compact disk 19.99 (978-1-4001-6114-0(2)) Pub: Tantor Media. Dist(s): IngramPubServ

Island of Doctor Moreau, with eBook. unabr. ed. H. G. Wells. Narrated by Jonathan Kent. (Running Time: 5 hrs. 0 mins. 0 sec.). (ENG.). 2009. audio compact disk 39.99 (978-1-4001-4114-2(1)) Pub: Tantor Media. Dist(s): IngramPubServ

Island of Dr. Moreau. H. G. Wells. Read by Jonathan Kent. (Running Time: 5 hrs.). 2005. 25.95 (978-1-60083-622-0(4), Audiofy Corp) Iofy Corp.

Island of Dr. Moreau. H. G. Wells. Read by Jonathan Kent. (Running Time: 14400 sec.). (Unabridged Classics in Audio Ser.). (ENG.). 2005. audio compact disk 49.99 (978-1-4001-3053-5(0)) Pub: Tantor Media. Dist(s): IngramPubServ

Island of Dr. Moreau. H. G. Wells. Perf. by Atlanta Radio Theatre Company Staff. 1 cass. (Running Time: 1 hr.). 2001. 12.95 (ARTC001) Lodestone Catalog.
A live production of a classic horror tales of all time. Unspeakable tortures inflicted on innocent people & beasts in the name of science gone mad.

Island of Dr. Moreau. unabr. ed. H. G. Wells. Read by Flo Gibson. 3 cass. (Running Time: 4 hrs. 30 mins.). (YA). (gr. 9 up). 1996. 16.95 (978-1-55685-602-0(4)) Audio Bk Con.
Edward Prendick is ship-wrecked on an island where a mad vivisectionist tries to transform animals into human beings with monstrous results.

Island of Dr. Moreau. unabr. ed. H. G. Wells. Read by Robin Lawson. 4 cass. (Running Time: 5 hrs. 30 mins.). (gr. 9-12). 1994. 32.95 (978-0-7861-0732-2(4), 1485) Blckstn Audio.
Living in the nineteenth century & facing the impact of Darwin's theory of evolution, H.G. Wells wrote this haunting masterpiece, an evolutionary fantasy. It is about a shipwrecked naturalist who becomes involved in an experiment to "humanize" animals by surgery. Dr. Moreau, a scientist expelled from his homeland for performing cruel vivisection experiments, finds an isolated island that provides him the freedom to continue torturous transplantations & create hideous creatures with manlike intelligence. But as the cruelly enforced order on Moreau's island dissolved, the true consequences of his meddling emerge.

Island of Dr. Moreau. unabr. ed. H. G. Wells. Read by Jack Sondericker. 4 cass. (Running Time: 4 hrs. 30 min.). 1989. 26.95 (978-1-55686-292-2(X), 292) Books in Motion.
Narrowly missing death in a shipwreck, Pendrick finds a risky sanctuary on a remote island as the invited guest of Dr. Moreau. Dr. Moreau filled with worthy or mad ambitions succeeds in achieving only the grotesque. When Pendrick discovers the ghastly experiments, he is horrified by what he sees.

Island of Dr. Moreau. unabr. ed. H. G. Wells. Featuring T. E. Fuller et al. 1 cass. (Running Time: 90 min.). Dramatization. 2002. 12.95 (978-0-929483-14-6(6)) Centauri Express Co.
Moreau, misunderstood and hounded by the London medical community, retreats to a Pacific island to continue his experiments. The goal: Nothing less than to surgically rebuild animals into the shape of men - and to teach them the meaning of humanity.

Island of Dr. Moreau. unabr. ed. H. G. Wells. Read by Jonathan Kent. (YA). 2007. 44.99 (978-1-60252-564-1(1)) Find a World.

Island of Dr. Moreau. unabr. ed. H. G. Wells. Read by Jim Killavey. 4 cass. (Running Time: 4 hrs. 30 min.). 1979. 21.00 (C-9) Jimcin Record.
Scientific experiments gone amok lead to the horror of half-man, half animal creatures on a remote island.

Island of Dr. Moreau, unabr. ed. H. G. Wells. Narrated by Simon Prebble. 4 cass. (Running Time: 5 hrs. 15 mins.). (gr. 7). 36.00 (978-0-7887-0539-7(3), 94734E7) Recorded Bks.
One man boldly takes evolution into his own hands for the first time. Available to libraries only.

Island of Dr. Moreau. unabr. collector's ed. H. G. Wells. Read by Jonathan Kent. 5 cass. (Running Time: 5 hrs.). 1997. 30.00 (978-0-7366-3648-3(X), 4313) Books on Tape.
Moreau's experiments needed seclusion & victims.

Island of Enchantment. Ivy Preston. Read by Diana Bishop. 4 cass. (Running Time: 6 hrs.). 1999. 44.95 (65743) Pub: Soundings Ltd GBR. Dist(s): Ulverscroft US

Island of Sheep. unabr. ed. John Buchan. Read by Edmund Dehn. 7 cass. (Running Time: 8 hrs. 45 min.). (Isis Ser.). (J). 2004. 61.95 (978-1-85695-769-4(1), 940503) Pub: ISIS Lrg Prnt GBR. Dist(s): Ulverscroft US

Island of the Blue Dolphins. Scott O'Dell. Read by Tantoo Cardinal. 3 cass. (Running Time: 4 hrs.). (J). 2000. 38.25 (978-0-7366-9050-8(6)) Pub: Books on Tape. Dist(s): NetLibrary CO
Portrait of life in the natural world glistens with new light. When the young Karana loses her family, her instinct for survival carries her through the years she spends on a deserted island, living by her wits.

Island of the Blue Dolphins. Scott O'Dell. Read by Tantoo Cardinal. 4 CDs. (Running Time: 3 hrs. 51 mins.). (J). (gr. 5-9). 2004. audio compact disk 32.30 (978-0-8072-1779-5(4), Listening Lib) Pub: Random Audio Pubg. Dist(s): NetLibrary CO

Island of the Blue Dolphins. unabr. ed. Scott O'Dell. Read by Tantoo Cardinal. (J). 2006. 39.99 (978-0-7393-7499-3(0)) Find a World.

Island of the Blue Dolphins. unabr. ed. Scott O'Dell. 2 cass. (Running Time: 3 hrs). (YA). 2002. 17.99 (978-0-8072-0877-9(9), Listening Lib) Random Audio Pubg.

Island of the Blue Dolphins. unabr. ed. Scott O'Dell. Read by Tantoo Cardinal. 3 vols. (Running Time: 3 hrs. 51 mins.). (J). (gr. 5-9). 2004. pap. bk. 36.00 (978-0-8072-8326-4(6), YA163SP, Listening Lib); 30.00 (978-0-8072-8325-7(8), LL0177, Listening Lib) Random Audio Pubg.
When the young Karana loses her family, her instinct for survival carries her through the years she spends on a deserted island, living by her wits.

Island of the Blue Dolphins. unabr. ed. Scott O'Dell. Read by Tantoo Cardinal. 4 CDs. (Running Time: 3 hrs. 41 mins.). (ENG.). (J). (gr. 5). 2005. audio compact disk 19.95 (978-0-307-24316-4(8), Listening Lib) Pub: Random Audio Pubg. Dist(s): Random

Island of the Blue Dolphins. unabr. ed. Scott O'Dell. Narrated by Christina Moore. 4 CDs. (Running Time: 4 hrs. 30 min.). (J). (gr. 5). 2001. audio compact disk 39.00 (C1054E7) Recorded Bks.
Classic tale of a Ghalas-At Indian girl stranded on an island off the coast of 19th-century California.

Island of the Blue Dolphins, unabr. ed. Scott O'Dell. Narrated by Christina Moore. 3 pieces. (Running Time: 4 hrs. 30 mins.). (gr. 5 up). 1994. 27.00 (978-1-55690-467-7(3), 92321E7) Recorded Bks.
Karana, a Ghalas-At Indian & her tribe live peacefully on their island until the arrival of a Russian otter-hunting ship. When the hunters prove treacherous, killing most of the tribe, Karana & her younger brother, Ramo, are all that is left of her family. Abandoned, Karana must draw on reserves of intelligence, resourcefulness & courage in order to survive.

Island of the Blue Dolphins. unabr. ed. Scott O'Dell. Read by Tantoo Cardinal. 3 cass. (Running Time: 3 hrs.). (J). pap. bk. 29.00 (LL1035AC) Weston Woods.

Island of the Day Before. unabr. ed. Umberto Eco. Read by Michael Russotto. 11 cass. (Running Time: 16 hrs. 30 mins.).Tr. of Isola del Giorno Prima. 1996. 88.00 (3879) Books on Tape.
An eclectic, esoteric blend of science, metaphysics & romance create a kind of lyrical tale that only Umberto Eco can tell. By moving us back to the 17th century, the author points us toward an understanding of our own place in the universe & in time. An Italian nobleman, Roberto, finds himself shipwrecked just beyond an island bisected by the international date line. If he can only get to the island, Roberto thinks he might be able to rewrite his past. He might even be able to alter the destiny of humankind. But alas, he can't swim.

Island of the Grass King, unabr. ed. Nancy Willard. Narrated by Barbara Rosenblat. 2 cass. (Running Time: 3 hrs.). (gr. 4). 1992. 19.00 (978-1-55690-603-9(X), 92208E7) Recorded Bks.
Anatole climbs on the back of a winged horse & flies to a far away island.

Island of the Sequined Love Nun. unabr. ed. Christopher Moore. (Running Time: 11 hrs. 0 mins.). 2009. 29.95 (978-1-4332-9321-4(8)); 65.95 (978-1-4332-9317-7(X)); audio compact disk 100.00 (978-1-4332-9318-4(8)) Blckstn Audio.

Island of the Sequined Love Nun. unabr. ed. Christopher Moore. Read by Oliver Wyman. 2009. audio compact disk 24.99 (978-0-06-177063-0(9), Harper Audio) HarperCollins Pubs.

***Island of the Sequined Love Nun.** unabr. ed. Christopher Moore. Read by Oliver Wyman. (ENG.). 2009. (978-0-06-190257-4(8), Harper Audio); (978-0-06-190255-0(1), Harper Audio) HarperCollins Pubs.

Island of the Skog. 2004. bk. 24.95 (978-0-89719-883-7(2)); pap. bk. 32.75 (978-1-55592-249-8(X)); pap. bk. 14.95 (978-1-56008-057-2(4)); 8.95 (978-1-56008-935-3(0)); 8.95 (978-1-56008-142-5(2)); cass. & flmstrp 30.00 (978-0-89719-624-6(4)) Weston Woods.

Island of the Skog. Steven Kellogg. 1 cass., 5 bks. (Running Time: 11 min.). (J). pap. bk. 32.75 Weston Woods.
One side with page turn signals, one side without.

Island of the Skog. Steven Kellogg. 1 cass. (Running Time: 11 min.). (J). (ps-7). bk. 24.95 Weston Woods.

Island of the Skog. Steven Kellogg. 1 read-along cass. (Running Time: 11 min.). (J). (ps-7). 2000. pap. bk. 12.95 (QPRA174) Weston Woods.
In pursuit of freedom & happiness, a band of extraordinary mice & their leader set sail to an island inhabited by a seemingly hostile Skog with seemingly gigantic feet. But when the two parties meet face to face, they find they have a lot in common.

Island of the Skog, the see Isla Del Skog

Island of the Swans, Pt. 1. unabr. collector's ed. Ciji Ware. Read by Penelope Dellaporta. 10 cass. (Running Time: 15 hrs.). 1989. 80.00 (978-0-7366-1662-1(4), 2512-A) Books on Tape.
Jane Maxwell can't remember a time when Thomas Fraser was not at her side when she was growing up in 18th-century Scotland. Only when Jane believes him dead in the American colonies does she respond to the handsome Duke of Gordon. But Fraser is not dead & he returns to find Jane a bride. Her marriage becomes a turbulent dance of tender wooing & clashing wills as the Duke seeks to win her once & for all.

Island of the Swans, Pt. 2. collector's ed. Ciji Ware. Read by Penelope Dellaporta. 9 cass. (Running Time: 13 hrs. 30 min.). 1989. 72.00 (978-0-7366-1663-8(2), 2512-B) Books on Tape.

Island Pharisees, unabr. ed. John Galsworthy. Read by Flo Gibson. 5 cass. (Running Time: 7 hrs. 30 min.). 1986. 20.95 (978-1-55685-011-0(5)) Audio Bk Con.
Shelton, a member of the English landed gentry in the early 1900's opens his eyes & clearly sees the plight of the underprivileged & of downtrodden women. This causes his fiancee some distress.

Island Race. abr. ed. Winston L. S. Churchill. Read by Edward De Souza & Edward Heath. 3 cass. (Running Time: 4 hrs.). 1995. 17.98 (978-962-634-547-4(0), NA304714, Naxos AudioBooks); audio compact disk 22.98 (978-962-634-047-9(9), NA304712, Naxos AudioBooks) Naxos.
Adaptation of Churchill's four-volume "A History of the English-Speaking Peoples," takes the listener from Caesar's invasion of 55BC to the close of Victoria's reign. An ideal guide through the facts and underlying spirit of British history.

Island Raiders WWII. unabr. ed. William Carmer. Read by Michael Taylor. 3 cass. (Running Time: 3 hrs. 12 min.). 1994. 21.95 (978-1-55686-502-2(3)) Books in Motion.
The Marine Raiders were one of the most elite military units in WWII. Based on fact, here is a fictionalized version of a Raider attack on a Japanese held island.

Island Serenity. (Running Time: 60 mins.). 2002. audio compact disk 15.99 (978-1-904972-66-2(7)) Global Jmy GBR GBR.

Island Wife. unabr. ed. Jessica Stirling. Read by Kara Wilson. 12 cass. (Running Time: 12 hrs.). 1998. 96.95 (978-0-7540-0235-2(7), CAB 1658) AudioGO.
The arrival of the new owners of the Fetternish estate, the Baverstock brothers, brings unwelcome changes to a young woman & her daughters who have known no other life than living on a farm.

Island Within. abr. ed. Richard Nelson. Read by Richard Nelson. 2 cass. (Running Time: 3 hrs.). 1991. 16.95 (978-0-939643-35-6(9)) Audio Pr.
Essays from the author's book, "The Island Within," winner of the 1991 John Burroughs Medal for outstanding nature writing.

Islands see Twentieth-Century Poetry in English, No. 28, Recordings of Poets Reading Their Own Poetry

Islands. Anne Rivers Siddons. Read by Kate Fleming. 8 vols. 2004. bk. 69.95 (978-0-7927-3213-6(8), CSL 653, Chivers Sound Lib); bk. 94.95 (978-0-7927-3214-3(6), SLD 653, Chivers Sound Lib) AudioGO.

***Islands.** abr. ed. Anne Rivers Siddons. Read by Dana Ivey. (ENG.). 2005. (978-0-06-087932-7(7), Harper Audio); (978-0-06-087933-4(5), Harper Audio) HarperCollins Pubs.

***Islands.** unabr. ed. Di Morrissey. Read by Kate Hood. (Running Time: 15 hrs.). 2010. audio compact disk 108.95 (978-1-74214-066-7(1), 9781742140667) Pub: Bolinda Pubng AUS. Dist(s): Bolinda Pub Inc

Islands. unabr. ed. Anne Rivers Siddons. Read by Dana Ivey. 8 cass. (Running Time: 12 hrs.). 2004. 39.95 (978-0-06-055459-0(2)) HarperCollins Pubs.

***Islands.** unabr. ed. Anne Rivers Siddons. Read by Dana Ivey. (ENG.). 2005. (978-0-06-087920-4(3), Harper Audio); (978-0-06-087921-1(1), Harper Audio) HarperCollins Pubs.

Islands Calling. Perf. by Magical Strings. 1 cass.; 1 CD. 1998. 10.98 (978-1-56628-091-4(5), 72535); audio compact disk 15.98 CD. (978-1-56628-090-7(7), 72535D) MFLP CA.

Islands in the Stream. unabr. ed. Ernest Hemingway. 9 cass. (Running Time: 12 hrs.). 2001. 34.95 (978-0-7366-5676-4(6)) Books on Tape.
An alienated & isolated artist, who lives in solitude on an island, has his fragile paradise shattered by the arrival of three sons - one of whom is subsequently killed in battle.

Islands in the Stream. unabr. ed. Ernest Hemingway. Read by Bruce Greenwood. 2006. 29.95 (978-0-7435-6515-8(0), Audioworks); audio compact disk 49.95 (978-0-7435-6440-3(5), Audioworks) Pub: S&S Audio. Dist(s): S and S Inc

Islands in the Stream. unabr. collector's ed. Ernest Hemingway. Read by Alexander Adams. 9 cass. (Running Time: 13 hrs. 30 mins.). 1992. 72.00 (978-0-7366-2179-3(2), 2976) Books on Tape.
This major novel, published posthumously, traces the complex life of Thomas Hudson. "An exquisite finale to a brilliant career" (Publisher's Source).

***Islands of Profit in a Sea of Red Ink: Why 40% of Your Business Is Unprofitable, & How to Fix It.** unabr. ed. Jonathan L. S. Byrnes. Read by Erik Synnestvedt. (Running Time: 9 hrs.). (ENG.). 2010. 34.98 (978-1-59659-667-2(8), GildAudio) Pub: Gildan Media. Dist(s): HachBkGrp

***Islands of Profit in a Sea of Red Ink: Why 40% of Your Business Is Unprofitable, & How to Fix It.** unabr. ed. Jonathan L. S. Byrnes. Read by Erik Synnestvedt. (Running Time: 9 hrs.). (ENG.). 2010. audio compact disk & audio compact disk 29.98 (978-1-59659-531-6(0), GildAudio) Pub: Gildan Media. Dist(s): HachBkGrp

Islands of the Blessed. unabr. ed. Nancy Farmer. Read by Gerard Doyle. 12 CDs. (Running Time: 13 hrs. 30 mins. 0 sec.). No. 3. (ENG.). (YA). 2009. audio compact disk 39.99 (978-0-7435-8368-8(X)) Pub: S&S Audio. Dist(s): S and S Inc

***Islands of the Damned: A Marine at War in the Pacific.** unabr. ed. R. V. Burgin & William Marvel. Narrated by Sean Runnette. (Running Time: 6 hrs. 30 mins. 0 sec.). (ENG.). 2010. 24.99 (978-1-4001-6464-6(8)); 34.99 (978-1-4001-9464-3(4)); 14.99 (978-1-4001-8464-4(9)); audio compact disk 69.99 (978-1-4001-4464-8(7)); audio compact disk 34.99 (978-1-4001-1464-1(0)) Pub: Tantor Media. Dist(s): IngramPubServ

Isle of Dogs. unabr. ed. Patricia Cornwell. Read by Michele Hall. 10 cass. (Running Time: 15 hrs.). (Andy Brazil Ser.: No. 3). 2001. 80.00 (978-0-7366-8087-5(X)); 96.00 (978-0-7366-8272-5(4)) Books on Tape.
The Governor of Virginia has ordered that speed traps be painted on all roads, and that speeders are to be detected by low-flying aircraft. An island off the coast of Virginia, the nonconformist Isle of Tangier, decides that it cannot abide by this decree, and revolts against the government in Richmond, cementing its act of defiance by kidnapping a dentist. Police superintendent Judy Hammer and her right-hand man, Andy Brazil, must surmount some mysteriously blocked channels of communication in the state government to untangle this, as well as some other sticky situations.

***Isle of Fire.** unabr. ed. Wayne Thomas Batson. (Running Time: 13 hrs. 0 mins. 0 sec.). (ENG.). 2011. audio compact disk 39.99 (978-1-59859-873-5(2)) Oasis Audio.

Isle of Magnus. unabr. ed. Chief Little Summer. Contrib. by Warm Night Rain. 1 CD. (J). (gr. k-4). 1999. audio compact disk 11.95 CD. (978-1-880440-19-3(9)) Piqua Pr.
Mysterious volcano crater where children learn & play with unusual toys.

Isle of Masks. unabr. ed. Pierdomenico Baccalario. Read by Michael Page. (Running Time: 4 hrs.). (Ulysses Moore Ser.: Bk. 4). 2008. 24.95 (978-1-4233-1344-1(5), 9781423313441, Brilliance MP3); 39.25 (978-1-4233-1345-8(3), 9781423313458, Brinc Audio MP3 Lib); 39.25 (978-1-4233-1347-2(X), 9781423313472, BADLE); 24.95 (978-1-4233-1346-5(1), 9781423313465, BAD); audio compact disk 24.95 (978-1-4233-1342-7(9), 9781423313427, Bril Audio CD Unabri); audio compact disk 48.97 (978-1-4233-1343-4(7), 9781423313434, BriAudCD Unabrid) Brilliance Audio.

Isle of Octavia: Gross Darkness. Christopher Lawson. 2007. audio compact disk 24.99 (978-1-60462-010-8(2)) Tate Pubng.

Isle of Orleans. Tom McDermott. 2004. pap. bk. 34.98 (978-1-59615-108-6(0), 586-036) Pub: Music Minus. Dist(s): Bookworld

***Isle of Swords.** unabr. ed. Wayne Thomas Batson. (Running Time: 13 hrs. 0 mins. 0 sec.). (ENG.). 2011. audio compact disk 39.99 (978-1-59859-872-8(4)) Oasis Audio.

Isle of Venus. unabr. ed. Tom E. Neet. Read by Lynda Evans. 6 cass. (Running Time: 6 hrs. 54 min.). (Mel Tippet Mystery Ser.: Bk. 1). 1996. 39.95 (978-1-55686-641-8(0)) Books in Motion.
A wealthy woman of advanced age is found dead in the Isle of Venus health spa. Mel is hired to find the killer.

Ismail & Isaac; Resurgent Islam Today. unabr. ed. Julian C. Hollick. 1 cass. (Running Time: 60 min.). (World of Islam Ser.). 1985. 15.00 (978-1-56709-056-7(7), 1031) Indep Broadcast.
Side A: In this program, Muslims express their viewpoint on the often-strained relationship between Christians & Muslims & what might be done to improve it. Side B: In the past few years there has been another worldwide resurgence in the Islamic world. This program explores what is happening in the islamic world, what the real causes of this resurgence are & what it means for us in the West.

***Isn't It Romantic.** Peter Straub. 2009. (978-1-60136-493-7(8)) Audio Holding.

Isn't That the Truth. Thompson et al. 2001. 75.00 (978-0-633-01519-0(9)) LifeWay Christian.

Isnt That the Truth. Hal Wright. 2001. 8.00 (978-0-633-01510-7(5)); audio compact disk 85.00 (978-0-633-01533-6(4)) LifeWay Christian.

Isn't That the Truth. Hal Wright. 2001. 11.98 (978-0-633-01524-4(5)); audio compact disk 16.98 (978-0-633-01529-9(6)) LifeWay Christian.

ISO 9001:2000: An Audio Workshop & Master Slide Presentation. 2nd ed. Jack West & Charles A. Cianfrani. (Running Time: 1 hr. 49 mins.). 2001. 150.00 (978-0-87389-514-9(2), H1109) ASQ Qual Pr.

Isobel Gunn. abr. ed. Audrey Thomas & Audrey Thomas. Narrated by Duncan Fraser. 3 cass. (Running Time: 4 hrs.). (ENG.). 2002. 24.95 (978-0-86492-331-8(7)) Pub: BTC Audiobks CAN. Dist(s): U Toronto Pr
"Weaving together fact and fiction, Isobel Gunn tells the tale of a young Orkney woman who disguises herself as a man and travels with the Hudson's Bay Company in 1806. Well-known film and television actor Duncan Fraser lends his resonant voice and rich Scottish accent to this superb audio adaptation.".

Isobutyryl-CoA Dehydrogenase Deficiency - A Bibliography & Dictionary for Physicians, Patients, & Genome Researchers. Compiled by Icon Group International, Inc. Staff. 2007. ring bd. 28.95 (978-0-497-11242-4(6)) Icon Grp.

Isola del Giorno Prima see Island of the Day Before

Ison Method. unabr. ed. David Ison. Read by David Ison. (Running Time: 2:00:00). 2009. audio compact disk 19.98 (978-1-60297-009-0(2)) Sounds True.

Ison Pain Management System: Music & Meditation to Release Pain & Anxiety. unabr. ed. David Ison. Read by David Ison. (Running Time: 2:00:00). 2009. audio compact disk 19.98 (978-1-60297-011-3(4)) Sounds True.

Ison Sleep System: Relax & Sleep - Easily & Naturally. David Ison. Read by David Ison. (ENG.). 2009. 39.99 (978-1-61574-923-2(3)) Find a World.

Isovaleric Acidemia - A Bibliography & Dictionary for Physicians, Patients, & Genome Researchers. Compiled by Icon Group International, Inc. Staff. 2007. ring bd. 28.95 (978-0-497-11243-1(4)) Icon Grp.

Israel. 2001. (978-1-931713-01-6(4)) Word For Today.

Israel. unabr. ed. Zondervan Publishing Staff. 1998. 9.99 (978-0-8297-2681-7(0)) Zondervan.

Israel, Bk. 3. 2001. 8.99 (978-0-8297-2579-7(2)) Pub: Vida Pubs. Dist(s): Zondervan

Israel: Past, Present & Future. Duane S. Crowther. Read by Duane S. Crowther. 1 cass. (Running Time: 90 min.). 1990. 13.98 (978-0-88290-404-7(3), 1830) Horizon Utah.
A thorough explanation of the history & prophetic destiny of the House of Israel. It summarizes the Old Testament history telling of Abraham, Isaac & Jacob, but also focuses on the many prophecies of future events which will involve Israel.

Israel: Past, Present & Future. Derek Prince. 6 cass. 29.95 Set. (IP1) Derek Prince.
The name Israel occurs about 2,600 times in the Bible. The clear picture of God's dealings with Israel, provided in this series, is essential to a full understanding of the Bible.

Israel Pt. 1: A History. unabr. collector's ed. Martin Gilbert. Read by David Case. 12 cass. (Running Time: 18 hrs.). 1999. 96.00 (978-0-7366-4500-3(4), 4936-A) Books on Tape.
The author traces Israel's history from the struggle of its pioneers in the nineteenth century up to the present day. Israel is often at the center of world attention - usually because of wars, political & social divisions, conflict with her Arab neighbors & the Palestinians in her midst, & the stark intrusion of acts of terror into daily life. But even though conflict, has been so much a part of everyday existence, the history of Israel ultimately uplifts & inspires.

Israel Pt. 2: A History. unabr. collector's ed. Martin Gilbert. Read by David Case. 12 cass. (Running Time: 18 hrs.). 1999. 96.00 (978-0-7366-4715-1(5), 4936-B) Books on Tape.

Israel & New Breed - A Deeper Level: Worship Tools Book/CD/DVD Pack. Israel Houghton. 2009. pap. bk. 29.95 (978-1-4234-3526-6(5), 1423435265) H Leonard.

Israel & Palestine: A History of the Conflict. unabr. ed. 2 cds. 2002. audio compact disk 18.95 (978-1-58472-265-6(7), In Aud) Pub: Sound Room. Dist(s): Baker Taylor

Israel & Palestine, a History of the Conflict. unabr. ed. 2 cds. 2002. audio compact disk (978-1-58472-267-0(3), In Aud) Sound Room.

Israel & the Church. Derek Prince. 3 cass. 14.95 (I-IC1) Derek Prince.

Israel II. unabr. ed. Zondervan Publishing Staff. (SPA.). 1998. 9.99 (978-0-8297-2787-6(6)) Pub: Vida Pubs. Dist(s): Zondervan

Israel in the Headlines. Derek Prince. 1 cass. 5.95 (4403) Derek Prince.
The news reports are unreliable & often biased; much of the Church is asleep. Only the prophetic Scriptures uncover the real issues.

Israel Lobby & U. S. Foreign Policy. unabr. ed. John J. Mearsheimer & Stephen M. Walt. Read by Jason Culp. (Running Time: 20 hrs. 0 mins. 0 sec.). (ENG.). 2007. audio compact disk 49.95 (978-1-4272-0212-3(5)) Pub: Macmill Audio. Dist(s): Macmillan

Israel, My Beloved. Contrib. by Karen Davis. Prod. by Gabriel Alonso. 2006. audio compact disk 16.98 (978-5-558-43591-7(7)) Pt of Grace Ent.

Israeli Folk Dancing Booklet w/Audio CD. Vicki Corona. (Celebrate the Cultures Ser.: 1-24A). 1990. pap. bk. 24.95 (978-1-58513-128-0(8)) Dance Fantasy.

Israel's Bible Bloc: A Judio-Christian Movement in the Knesset. Avi Lipkin. 2 CDs. (Running Time: 120 mins.). 2005. audio compact disk 19.95 (978-1-57821-286-6(3)) Koinonia Hse.
Fifteen years of extensive travel in the U.S., Canada, Europe and Israel and countless speaking engagements in churches, synagogues and political forums have led to the belief that Israel cannot survive the Islamic juggernaut out to destroy it unless Jews and Christians march in lockstep both globally and in God's city, Jerusalem. Avi brings us up-to-date on this growing realization within Israel's governing body, the Knesset. This exciting trend is important to all who love Israel.

Israel's Story: Part One. abr. ed. Read by Clifford M. Yeary et al. (Little Rock Scripture Study Ser.). 2007. audio compact disk 39.00 (978-0-8146-8636-2(2)) Liturgical Pr.

Issue of Abortion in America. Robert Cavalier et al. (C). (gr. 13). 1998. audio compact disk (978-0-415-18450-2(9), Rout) Tay Francis Ltd GBR.

Issue of Justice: Origins of the Israel/Palestine Conflict. Norman Finkelstein. (AK Press Audio Ser.). (ENG.). 2005. audio compact disk 14.98 (978-1-904859-23-9(2)) Pub: AK Pr GBR. Dist(s): Consort Bk Sales

Issues & Answers. 7.00 (CIA) J Van Impe.
Features messages of love & hope, reconciliation & restoration.

Issues & Answers in Jesus' Day. Charles R. Swindoll. 1998. 44.95 (978-1-57972-292-0(X)) Insight Living.

Issues & Answers in Jesus's Day. 2005. (978-1-57972-683-6(6)); audio compact disk 54.00 (978-1-57972-682-9(8)) Insight Living.

Issues in Biomedical Ethics. Donnie Self. 1986. 10.80 (0302A) Assn Prof Chaplains.

Issues in Construction Law: New Perspectives on Liabilities & Contracts. 3 cass. (Running Time: 3 hrs.). 1987. pap. bk. 49.00; 36.00 (543-0090-01) Amer Bar Assn.
A recording of two 1987 Annual Meeting programs on construction law. Topics cover A201-1987, construction disputes, site safety & bonds in real estate construction.

Issues in Intimacy in Pediatrics. 1986. 10.80 (0312) Assn Prof Chaplains.

Issues in Mariology. Father Kricek. 6 cass. 24.00 Set. (92I) IRL Chicago.

Issues in Pastoral Care Advocacy & Administration. 1 cass. (Care Cassettes Ser.: Vol. 16, No. 4). 1989. 10.80 Assn Prof Chaplains.

Issues in Self-Improvement: Sixth House. Jeff Green. 1 cass. 8.95 (528) Am Fed Astrologers.
Creative strategies for self-improvement.

Issues in the Conceptualization of Music. Ed. by James Porter & Attila J. Racz. (Selected Reports in Ethnomusicology: Vol. 7). 1988. bk. 22.95 (978-0-318-36431-5(X)) UCLA Dept Ethnom.

Issues on Pain Management. Elliott Krames. 1 cass. (Running Time: 62 min.). (C). 1997. bk. 20.00 (978-1-58111-026-5(X)) Contemporary Medical.
Discusses different pain treatment modalities, worker's compensation, how to evaluate & treat pain, medicine addiction.

Istanbul Express. unabr. ed. T. Davis Bunn. Read by Ron Varela. 4 cass. (Running Time: 4 hrs. 48 min.). (Destiny Ser.: Bk. 5). 2001. 26.95 (978-1-55686-990-7(8)) Books in Motion.
Now assigned to relief efforts in the Eastern Mediterranean, Col. Jake Burnes finds the growing presence of a grand power scheme in the former Byzantine Empire, activity lead by an allied power.

ISTFA 2001 Microelectronics Seminar Slides. 2001. bk. 75.00 (978-0-87170-767-3(5)) ASM.

Isthmus. unabr. ed. Alan R. Walden. Read by Charlie O'Dowd. 6 cass. (Running Time: 10 hrs.). 2001. 30.00 (978-1-58807-080-7(8)) Am Pubng Inc.
Confronted with guerilla warfare and assassins, the brothers, wives, lovers, and assorted players pursue an intricate plan for a Central American peace treaty and fight for the independence of five oppressed nations. With militant forces determined to sabotage the plans for a peace treaty, a failutre during any step of the plan could bring instant death to the brothers Mendoza and their allies.

Istwa ak Kont Kreyol (Book & Tape) Maude P. Fontus. (CRP.). (J). 2005. lib. bdg. 16.00 (978-1-58432-308-2(6)) Educa Vision.

Istwa Chat ak Sourit. Maude Heurtelou. Illus. by Louis Louissaint. 1 cass. (Running Time: 1 hr.).Tr. of Cat & Mouse. (CRP.). (J). (gr. 3-5). 1999. pap. bk. 19.00 (978-1-881839-90-3(7)) Educa Vision.

Istwa Ti Zwazo Ble a. Maude Heurtelou. Illus. by Louis Louissaint. 1 cass. (Running Time: 1 hr.).Tr. of Blue Bird. (CRP.). (J). (gr. 3-5). 1999. pap. bk. 19.00 (978-1-881839-91-0(5)) Educa Vision.

Istwa Tipoul. Maude Heurtelou. Illus. by Louis Louissaint. 1 cass. (Running Time: 1 hr.).Tr. of Four Friends. (CRP.). (J). (gr. 3-5). 1999. pap. bk. 19.00 (978-1-881839-95-8(8)) Educa Vision.

It! Paula Froelich. Narrated by Anna Fields. (Running Time: 12 hrs. 5 mins.). 2005. 35.95 (978-1-59912-514-5(5)) Iofy Corp.

***It.** unabr. ed. Stephen King. (Running Time: 42 hrs. 0 mins.). 2010. 59.95 (978-1-4417-3873-8(8)); 105.95 (978-1-4417-3910-0(6)); 105.95 (978-1-4417-3869-1(X)); audio compact disk 99.00 (978-1-4417-3870-7(3)) Blckstn Audio.

It. unabr. ed. Stephen King. Read by Steven Weber. 35 CDs. (Running Time: 45 hrs.). (ENG.). 2010. audio compact disk 59.95 (978-0-14-242787-3(X), PengAudBks) Penguin Grp USA.

***It: How Churches & Leaders Can Get It & Keep It.** Craig Groeschel. (Running Time: 6 hrs. 0 mins. 0 sec.). (ENG.). 2008. 16.99 (978-0-310-30244-5(7)) Zondervan.

It! Nine Secrets of the Rich & Famous That'll Take you to the Top. unabr. ed. Paula Foelich. Read by Anna Fields. 5 cass. (Running Time: 8 hrs. 30 mins.). 2005. 29.95 (978-0-7861-3044-3(X)) Blckstn Audio.

It! 9 Secrets of the Rich & Famous That Will Take You to the Top. Paula Froelich. Read by Anna Fields. (Running Time: 18000 sec.). 2005. cass., cass., DVD 34.95 (978-0-7861-3028-3(8)); DVD, audio compact disk, audio compact disk 36.00 (978-0-7861-7976-3(7)) Blckstn Audio.

It! 9 Secrets of the Rich & Famous That Will Take You to the Top. unabr. ed. Paula Froelich. Read by Anna Fields. 13 vols. (Running Time: 18000 sec.). 2005. DVD & audio compact disk 29.95 (978-0-7861-8153-7(2)); audio compact disk 29.95 (978-0-7861-7996-1(1)) Blckstn Audio.

It Ain't As Easy As It Looks. abr. ed. Porter Bibb. Read by Porter Bibb. 2 cass. (Running Time: 3 hrs.). Dramatization. bk. 16.95 set. (978-1-56703-020-4(3)) High-Top Sports.

It All Adds up Home Connection Kit. Created by Music Movement and Magination. (ENG.). 2009. audio compact disk 19.95 (978-1-935572-14-5(8)) MMnM Bks.

It All Adds up Home Connection Kit - Bilingual. Created by Music Movement and Magination. 2009. spiral bd. 19.95 (978-1-935572-15-2(6)) MMnM Bks.

It All Adds up Supplemental Curriculum Kit. Created by Music Movement and Magination. (ENG.). 2009. spiral bd. 179.95 (978-1-935572-06-0(7)) MMnM Bks.

***It All Began in Monte Carlo.** Elizabeth Adler. Narrated by Susan Boyce. (Running Time: 11 hrs. 9 mins. 0 sec.). (ENG.). 2011. audio compact disk 29.95 (978-1-60998-140-2(5)) Pub: AudioGO. Dist(s): Perseus Dist

It All Comes Together Right Here. unabr. ed. Joe Romano. Perf. by Non-Toxic Band. 1 cass. (Running Time: 33 min.). (J). (gr. k-6). 1993. bk. 12.95 (978-0-9640675-0-9(1), SR 185-117) Non-Toxic Music.
Twelve original songs for children ages 2-10 years with a full color, illustrated lyric booklet. Some environmental themes.

It All Fits Together, Pack. Willow Creek Association. (J). 2002. audio compact disk 64.95 (978-0-310-64384-5(8)) Zondervan.

It All Fits Together Full Year & Music CD Pack. Zondervan Publishing Staff. (J). 2004. audio compact disk 909.99 (978-0-310-64419-4(4)) Zondervan.

It All Started When. AIO Team Staff. Created by Focus on the Family Staff & Marshal Younger. (Running Time: 5 hrs. 30 mins.). (Adventures in Odyssey Gold Ser.). (ENG.). (J). 2006. audio compact disk 24.99 (978-1-58997-288-9(0)) Pub: Focus Family. Dist(s): Tyndale Hse

It Came from Beneath the Bed! James Howe. Read by Joe Grifasi. (Running Time: 42 mins.). (Tales from the House of Bunnicula Ser.). (J). (gr. 3-6). 2004. pap. bk. 17.00 (978-1-4000-8632-0(9), Listening Lib) Random Audio Pubg.

It Came from Within. Andy Stanley. 2006. audio compact disk 24.99 (978-1-59859-091-3(X)) Oasis Audio.

It Came to Pass: Expecting God's Promises in Your Life. 3. (Running Time: 3 hrs.). 2001. 15.00 (978-1-57399-117-9(1)) Mac Hammond.
In this celebratory series, Mac Hammond examines the special phease "it came to pass" and how it relates to stagaes of progression we must go through if God's high prupose is truly going to be born through us.

It Came upon a Midnight Clear. D. M. Gregg. 2009. audio compact disk 29.99 (978-1-60799-004-8(0)) Tate Pubng.

It Can't Happen Here. unabr. ed. Sinclair Lewis. Read by Christopher Hurt. (Running Time: 46800 sec.). 2008. 79.95 (978-1-4332-2205-4(1)); audio compact disk & audio compact disk 99.00 (978-1-4332-2206-1(X)) Blckstn Audio.

It Can't Happen Here. unabr. ed. Sinclair Lewis. Read by Christopher Hurt. (Running Time: 46800 sec.). (Classic Collection Ser.). 2008. audio compact disk 29.95 (978-1-4332-2209-2(4)); audio compact disk & audio compact disk 19.95 (978-1-4332-2208-5(6)) Blckstn Audio.

It Cost All He Had. Derek Prince. 1 cass. (Running Time: 60 min.). 5.95 (I-4254) Derek Prince.

It Couldn't Be Done see Favorite American Poems

It Couldn't Matter Less. unabr. ed. Peter Cheyney. Read by David Wade. 5 cass. (Running Time: 7 hrs. 30 mins.). 1999. 49.95 (6352X) Pub: Soundings Ltd GBR. Dist(s): Ulverscroft US

It Couldn't Matter Less. unabr. ed. Peter Cheyney. 5 cass. (Sound Ser.). 2004. 49.95 (978-1-85496-352-9(X)) Pub: UlverLrgPrint GBR. Dist(s): Ulverscroft US

It Doesn't Take a Hero: The Autobiography. H. Norman Schwarzkopf & Peter Petre. (Running Time: 6 hrs.). 2004. 20.00 (978-0-7567-6664-1(8)) DIANE Pub.

It Doesn't Take a Hero: The Autobiography of General H. Norman Schwarzkopf. unabr. ed. Peter Petre. Read by John MacDonald. Illus. by Norman Schwarzkopf. Norman Schwarzkopf. 15 cass. (Running Time: 22 hrs. 30 mins.). 1994. 120.00 (978-0-7366-2579-1(8), 3326) Books on Tape.
Candid, outspoken autobiography of "Stormin' Norman's" life & career.

IT Equipment & Services in Russia: A Strategic Reference 2007. Compiled by Icon Group International, Inc. Staff. 2007. ring bd. 195.00 (978-0-497-82402-0(7)) Icon Grp.

It Grows on You: And Other Stories. unabr. ed. Stephen King. Read by Stephen King. Read by Gary Sinese et al. (Running Time: 4 hrs. 30 mins. 0 sec.). (ENG.). 2009. audio compact disk 14.99 (978-0-7435-9824-8(5)) Pub: S&S Audio. Dist(s): S and S Inc

It Had to Be You. abr. unabr. ed. Cecily von Ziegesar. Read by Cassandra Morris. (Running Time: 11 hrs.). (Gossip Girl Ser.). (ENG.). 2009. 16.98 (978-1-60024-071-3(2)) Pub: Little Brn Bks. Dist(s): HachBkGrp

It Had to Be You. unabr. ed. Jill Churchill. Read by Wendy Dillon. 4 cass. (Grace & Favor Mystery Ser.: No. 5). 2005. 39.95 (978-0-7927-3524-3(2), CSL 776); audio compact disk 59.95 (978-0-7927-3525-0(0), SLD 776) AudioGO.

It Had to Be You. unabr. ed. Patricia Cornwell. Read by Kate Reading. 3 cass. (Win Garano Ser.: No. 2). 2008. 60.00 (978-1-4159-3816-4(4), BksonTape); audio compact disk 60.00 (978-1-4159-3817-1(2), BksonTape) Pub: Random Audio Pubg. Dist(s): Random

It Had to Be You. unabr. collector's ed. Susan Elizabeth Phillips. Read by Anna Fields. 9 cass. (Running Time: 13 hrs. 30 min.). (Chicago Stars Bks.: No. 1). 1996. 72.00 (978-0-7366-3217-1(4), 3880) Books on Tape.
It's Dan Calebow's worst nightmare: Phoebe Somerville, a trendy New York knockout, inherits the Chicago Stars, the football team he coaches & she wants to help him run it. Phoebe's sure he needs her. He's a sexist, good-ol'-boy jock with a one-track mind. She can straighten him out. So why should each find the other attractive? Call it the competitive urge, but these two stubborn people play the game for keeps.

It Happened Like This see Erskine Caldwell

***It Happened One Autumn.** unabr. ed. Lisa Kleypas. Read by Rosalyn Landor. (Running Time: 11 hrs.). (Wallflower Ser.: Bk. 2). 2010. 24.99 (978-1-4418-5185-7(2), 9781441851857, Brilliance MP3); 39.97 (978-1-4418-5186-4(0), 9781441851864, Brlnc Audio MP3 Lib); 24.99 (978-1-4418-5187-1(9), 9781441851871, BAD); 39.97 (978-1-4418-5188-8(7), 9781441851888, BADLE); audio compact disk 29.99 (978-1-4418-5183-3(6), 9781441851833, Bril Audio CD Unabri); audio compact disk 79.97 (978-1-4418-5184-0(4), 9781441851840, BriAudCD Unabrid) Brilliance Audio.

It Happened One Night. Perf. by Clark Gable & Claudette Colbert. Based on a story by Samuel Hopkins Adams. 1 cass. (Running Time: 60 min.). 7.95 (CD-8820) Natl Recrd Co.
It's a fast-moving story of a pampered society girl who is running away from a wealthy father & her fiancee. A glib wise-cracking newspaper reporter recognizes her, & together they take a cross-country bus back to New York.

***It Happened One Season.** unabr. ed. Stephanie Laurens. Read by To be Announced. (Running Time: 13 hrs. NaN mins.). (ENG.). 2011. 29.95 (978-1-4417-7490-3(4)); 72.95 (978-1-4417-7487-3(4)); audio compact disk 105.00 (978-1-4417-7488-0(2)) Blckstn Audio.

It Happens Every Spring. Perf. by Ray Milland et al. 1 cass. (Running Time: 1 hr.). 1999. 6.98 (4182) Radio Spirits.

It Happens Every Spring. unabr. ed. Gary Chapman & Catherine Palmer. Read by Jill Shellabarger. (Running Time: 36000 sec.). (Seasons of Marriage Ser.). (ENG.). 2007. audio compact disk 24.99 (978-1-59859-198-9(3)) Oasis Audio.

It Happens Every Spring. unabr. ed. Catherine Palmer & Gary Chapman. (Seasons of Marriage Ser.). (ENG.). 2007. 17.49 (978-1-60814-258-3(2)) Oasis Audio.

It Has Come! see Secret Garden: A Young Reader's Edition of the Classic Story

It Is a Beauteous Evening, Calm & Free see Selected Poetry of William Wordsworth

It Is a Living Coral see Twentieth-Century Poetry in English, No. 4, Recordings of Poets Reading Their Own Poetry

It Is Almost the Year Two Thousand see Robert Frost in Recital

It Is Brain Surgery: Program from the Award Winning Public Radio Series. Hosted by Fred Goodwin. Contrib. by John Hockenberry et al. 1 cass. (Running Time: 1 hr.). (Infinite Mind Ser.). 1999. audio compact disk 21.95 (978-1-888064-22-3(6), LCM 48) Lichtenstein Creat.
This week we explore the latest developments in brain surgery, that most delicate of arts. Learn about the history of brain surgery from the Renaissance to the present day as Dr. Goodwin hosts top surgeons and a pioneer in 'split-brain' studies who explains what "left-brained" and "right-brained" really mean. Plus we go inside the operating room, hear the sound of neurons firing in the brain, and hear from both doctor and patient during surgery. Also, commentary from John Hockenberry.

It Is Done! Miracles Still Happen! unabr. ed. Kathy Lewis. 5 CDs. (Running Time: 4 hrs. 9 mins). 2002. audio compact disk 13.95 (978-0-9728293-1-1(8)) Capstone Institute.
Autobiographical- based on author's life full of one incredible miracle after another, including miraculous healing, incredible business opportunities leading to multi million dollar business, and much more.

It Is Finished see Twentieth-Century Poetry in English, No. 25, Recordings of Poets Reading Their Own Poetry

It Is Finished. Kenneth E. Hagin. (Spiritual Life & Scriptual Healing Ser.). 24.00 Faith Lib Pubns.

It Is Finished. Gary Rhodes. 1997. 11.98 (978-0-7673-3998-8(3)); 75.00 (978-0-7673-3997-1(5)); 8.00 (978-0-7673-3994-0(0)); audio compact disk 85.00 (978-0-7673-3996-4(7)); audio compact disk 12.00 (978-0-7673-3568-3(6)); audio compact disk 16.98 (978-0-7673-3567-6(8)) LifeWay Christian.

It Is Finished: The Passion of Christ According to John. Bert Polman. (Running Time: 30 mins.). (Scripture Alive Ser.). 1998. 15.95 (978-1-56212-338-3(6), 415101) FaithAliveChr.

It Is Good to Have Been Young in Youth see Robert Louis Stevenson: His Poetry, Prose and the Story of His Life

It Is Mine to Avenge, I Will Repay, Says the Lord. Dan Corner. 1 cass. 3.00 (47) Evang Outreach.

It Is No Secret. Contrib. by Bill & Gloria Gaither and Their Homecoming Friends. (Gaither Homecoming Classics Ser.). 2005. audio compact disk 17.98 (978-5-559-05762-0(2)) Gaither Music Co.

It Is Time. Vance Havner. 2009. audio compact disk 13.95 (978-0-578-01984-0(1)) Sapphire Dig.

It Is Time! Audio CD. Adapted by Benchmark Education Company Staff. Based on a work by Francisco Blane. (My First Reader's Theater Ser.). (J). (gr. k-1). 2008. audio compact disk 10.00 (978-1-60634-099-8(9)) Benchmark Educ.

It Is Well. 1 cass., 1 CD. 10.98 (978-1-57908-347-2(1), 5304); audio compact disk 15.98 CD. (978-1-57908-346-5(3)) Platinm Enter.

It Is Well: 11 Kings 4:8-37. Ed Young. 1984. 4.95 (978-0-7417-1388-9(8), 388) Win Walk.

It Is Well with My Soul. Contrib. by Sandi Patty. (Inoriginal Performance Trax Ser.). 2004. audio compact disk 9.98 (978-5-559-38077-3(6)) INO Rec.

It Is Well with My Soul. Contrib. by 4Him Staff. (iWorship Ser.). 2004. audio compact disk 9.98 (978-5-559-38186-2(1)) Integrity Music.

It Is Well with My Soul: Selections from Lift Every Voice & Sing II. Carl Haywood. (ENG.). audio compact disk 18.00 (978-0-89869-290-7(3)) Church Pub Inc.

It Is Within. Neville Goddard. 1 cass. (Running Time: 62 min.). 1965. 8.00 (7) J & L Pubns.
Neville taught Imagination Creates Reality. He was a powerfully influential teacher of God as Consciousness.

It Looked Like Forever. unabr. collector's ed. Mark Harris. Read by Christopher Hurt. 6 cass. (Running Time: 9 hrs.). 1989. 48.00 (978-0-7366-1543-3(1), 2412) Books on Tape.
Henry Wiggen, a pitcher on the comeback trail, is now 39, a fading veteran with a floating fastball, a finnicky prostrate & other intimations of mortality. Released from his team after 19 years, he rebels against retirement.

It Looked Like Spilt Milk. 9.95 (978-1-59112-153-4(1)) Live Oak Media.

It Looked Like Spilt Milk. Charles Shaw. (J). (gr. k-4). 2001. bk. 15.95 (VX-98C) Kimbo Educ.
Simple white shapes on a blue background look like many things, but only on the last page is identity of the ever-changing shape revealed, a cloud. Includes book.

It Looked Like Spilt Milk. Charles G. Shaw. Narrated by Peter Fernandez. (J). 1998. audio compact disk 12.95 (978-1-59519-317-9(0)) Live Oak Media.

It Looked Like Spilt Milk. Charles Green Shaw. Illus. by Charles Green Shaw. (Running Time: 4 mins.). 1988. 9.95 (978-1-59112-070-4(5)) Live Oak Media.

It Looked Like Spilt Milk. abr. ed. Charles G. Shaw. Read by Peter Fernandez. (J). (ps-3). 2006. bk. 28.95 (978-1-59519-320-9(0)) Live Oak Media.

It Looked Like Spilt Milk. unabr. ed. Charles Green Shaw. 1 cass. (Running Time: 4 min.). (J). (gr. k-3). 1988. 9.95 Live Oak Media.

It Looked Like Spilt Milk. unabr. ed. Charles Green Shaw. Illus. by Charles Green Shaw. Read by Peter Fernandez. 11 vols. (Running Time: 4 mins.). (J). (gr. 1-3). 1988. bk. 25.95 (978-0-87499-110-9(2)); pap. bk. 16.95 (978-0-87499-109-3(9)) Live Oak Media.

It Looked Like Spilt Milk, Grades 1-3. unabr. ed. Charles Green Shaw. Illus. by Charles Green Shaw. Read by Peter Fernandez. 14 vols. (Running Time: 4 mins.). 1988. pap. bk. & tchr. ed. 33.95 Reading Chest. (978-0-87499-111-6(0)) Live Oak Media.
A constantly changing white silhouette assumes the shapes of well known objects before revealing its true identity as a fluffy cloud.

It Looked Like Split Milk; Sleepy Book. 2004. 8.95 (978-1-56008-936-0(9)); cass. & flmstrp 30.00 (978-1-56008-693-2(9)) Weston Woods.

It Must Be Grace. Contrib. by Women of Faith. 2008. audio compact disk 11.99 (978-5-557-47088-9(3)) MyrrhR.

It Must Be Love. unabr. ed. Rachel Gibson. Narrated by Richard Ferrone. 7 cass. (Running Time: 10 hrs.). 2001. 59.00 (978-0-7887-5982-6(5), L1007L8) Recorded Bks.
When a very unlikely pair cross paths in It Must Be Love, the result is captivating. Undercover cop Joe Shanahan thinks he's doing a bang-up job of keeping his robbery suspect under surveillance - until she blows his cover and brings him down with a can of hairspray. Now the beautiful Gabrielle Breedlove has agreed to help him catch the real thief by letting him pose as her boyfriend.

***It Only Takes a Moment.** unabr. ed. Mary Jane Clark. Read by Isabel Keating. (ENG.). 2008. (978-0-06-170240-2(4)); (978-0-06-170242-6(0)) HarperCollins Pubs.

It Only Takes a Moment. unabr. ed. Mary Jane Clark. Read by Isabel Keating. 2008. audio compact disk 34.95 (978-0-06-155761-3(7), Harper Audio) HarperCollins Pubs.

It Only Takes a Spark: Acts 9:32-43. Ed Young. 1998. 4.95 (978-0-7417-2165-5(1), A1165) Win Walk.

It Pays to Be Ignorant. unabr. ed. Perf. by Tom Howard et al. 2 cass. (Running Time: 2 hrs.). Dramatization. 1997. 10.95 (978-1-57816-151-5(7), IP2401) Audio File.
Comedy spoof on panel quiz shows.

It Pays to Be Ignorant & Can You Top This? unabr. ed. 1 cass. (Running Time: 60 min.). Dramatization. 7.95 Norelco box. (CC1919) Natl Recrd Co.
It Pays to Be Ignorant: Tom Howard - Master of Ceremonies. Panelists - Harry McNaughton, George Shelton & Lulu McConnell. The comedy panel show that was a spoof on all the "intelligent" panel shows on radio. "Why is a watchdog smaller in the daytime?" "Because he's let out at night." Correct! Pay that man nine dollars...because, "it pays to be ignorant!" Can You Top This: Panelists - Ward Wilson, Joe Laurie, Jr., Harry Hirschfield & Peter Donald. This is an "unrehearsed & spontaneous" comedy panel show...with the panelists all trying for laughs on the Colgate-Palmolive Laugh Meter with jokes galore...some new, some old...but all of them funny! Excellent way for speakers & comedians to add some clever, funny & clean jokes to their act.

It Pays to Talk: How to have the Essential Conversations with your Family. Carrie Schwab-Pomerantz & Charles Schwab. Read by Anna Fields. 2002. 90.00 (978-0-7366-8932-8(X)) Books on Tape.

It Pleased the Lord to Crush Him. Jack Deere. 1 cass. (Running Time: 90 mins.). (Cross Ser.: Vol. 4). 2000. 5.00 (JD01-004) Morning NC.
These are outstanding messages on the work & power of the most important truths of our faith.

***It Screams at Night.** Michael Dahl. Illus. by Yap Kun Rong. (Dragonblood Ser.). (ENG.). 2010. audio compact disk 14.60 (978-1-4342-2569-6(0)) CapstoneDig.

It Shouldn't Happen to a Vet. unabr. ed. James Herriot. Read by Christopher Timothy. 8 cass. (Running Time: 12 hrs.). (Vet Ser.: Bk. 2). 2000. 59.95 (978-0-7451-4226-5(5), CAB 909) Pub: Chivers Audio Bks GBR. Dist(s): AudioGO
How on earth did James Herriot come to be sitting on a high Yorkshire moor, smelling vaguely of cows? Now firmly settled into the Darrowby-based practice, James isn't sure. But he still loves it, and still has plenty to learn.

It Sleeps in Me. unabr. ed. Kathleen O'Neal Gear. 7 cass. (Running Time: 10 hrs. 30 mins.). 2005. 63.00 (978-1-4159-0766-5(8)); audio compact disk 81.00 (978-1-4159-0767-2(6)) Books on Tape.

It Take Brains, No Brawn Set: New Opportunities for Power & Leadership. Linda Cline Chandler. 6 cass. (Leadership & Empowerment Ser.). 1994. (978-0-9639400-2-5(3)) Lrning Two-Thousand.
Focuses on new opportunities for power & leadership in the coming new century. Describes the new kind of leadership that is necessary to lead our companies, cities, our organizations & our nation.

It Takes a Family: Conservatism & the Common Good. abr. ed. Rick Santorum. Read by Rick Santorum. (Running Time: 25200 sec.). 2006. audio compact disk 27.99 (978-1-59859-125-5(8)) Oasis Audio.

It Takes a Family: Conservatism & the Common Good. unabr. ed. Rick Santorum. Narrated by Rick Santorum. (ENG.). 2006. 19.59 (978-1-60814-259-0(0)) Oasis Audio.

It Takes a Lot of People: Tribute to Woody Guthrie. Perf. by Larry Long & Children of Oklahoma Staff. 1 cass. (J). 1999.; audio compact disk; audio compact disk Rounder Records.
All of the songs on this album were collectively written by Larry Long & children of Oklahoma (some 60 of whom join Larry in concert), with the exception of Woody's works & Shirley Davis' "Song of Thanks." In each Oklahoma town, children gathered oral history from their parents & grandparents. In school they shared their favorite thoughts & memories of home. These songs express the history & hopes of the children of the state. The album was recorded live at the Crystal Theatre in Okema, Oklahoma (the home of Woody Guthrie) on December 1, 1988. It was Okema's first tribute to Woody. Songs include "Bound for Glory," "Talking Fishing Blues," "Oklahoma Hills," "This Land Is Your Land" & recitations excerpted from Guthrie's writings on love, kids, freedom, "Bound for Glory" & "This Is Our World.".

It Takes an Angel, Set. Dan Yates. 2 cass. 1999. 13.95 (978-1-57734-472-8(3), 07002084) Covenant Comms.
Sometimes only Heaven can help! Romantic sequel to "An Angel in the Family.".

It Takes Courage! Drama Series #1: Magogo's Village. (YA). 2006. audio compact disk (978-0-9752917-4-0(2)) Kerus Global.

It Takes Faith. Jack Christianson. 2004. 9.95 (978-1-57734-886-3(9)); audio compact disk 11.95 (978-1-57734-930-3(X)) Covenant Comms.

It Takes One to Know One. Gervase Phinn. 1 cass. (Running Time: 1 hr. 30 mins.). (ENG., (J). 2001. (978-0-14-180280-0(4), PengAudBks) Penguin Grp USA.
A collection of poems based around the familiar themes of school & family.

It Takes Two! Jay Althouse. Composed by Sally K. Albrecht. (ENG.). 2004. audio compact disk 34.95 (978-0-7390-3490-3(1)) Alfred Pub.

It Takes Two: Making Relationships Work. Speeches. Creflo A. Dollar. 6 CDs. (Running Time: 5 hrs.). 2000. audio compact disk 34.00 (978-1-59089-946-5(6)) Creflo Dollar.

It Takes Two: Making Relationships Work. Creflo A. Dollar. 5 cass. (Running Time: 7 hrs. 30 mins.). 2001. 25.00 (978-1-931172-16-5(1), TS295, Kidz Faith) Pub: Creflo Dollar. Dist(s): STL Dist NA

It Takes Two to Know One. unabr. ed. Gregory Bateson. 2 cass. (Running Time: 2 hrs. 20 min.). (Informal Esalen Lectures). 1980. 18.00 Set. (02813) Big Sur Tapes.

It Took a Miracle. Contrib. by Don Marsh. 1996. 11.98 (978-0-7601-0569-6(3), 75602054) Pub: Brentwood Music. Dist(s): H Leonard

It Took a Miracle. Contrib. by Don Marsh. 1996. 85.00 (978-0-7601-0654-9(1), 75606439); 85.00 (978-0-7601-0655-6(X), 75606284); 4.00 (978-0-7601-0656-3(8), 75602055); 4.00 (978-0-7601-0657-0(6), 75602052); 4.00 (978-0-7601-0658-7(4), 75602053) Pub: Brentwood Music. Dist(s): H Leonard

It Took a Miracle: 1 Kings 17:17-24. Ed Young. 1987. 4.95 (978-0-7417-1596-8(1), 596) Win Walk.

It Used to Matter. unabr. ed. Gregory Bateson. 1 cass. (Running Time: 1 hr. 28 min.). (Informal Esalen Lectures). 1980. 11.00 (02810) Big Sur Tapes.
Referring to Accidie, the medieval devil representing sloth that arises from hopelessness, Bateson contrasts modern-day society to the 19th Century, particularly in relation to the "lustiness" or enthusiasm of the 19th Century & its activities.

It Was a Dark & Stormy Night: 101 Funniest Openings from the Worst Novels Never Written. abr. ed. Perf. by Marni Webb et al. Compiled by Scott Rice. 1 cass. (Running Time: 1 hr. 30 mins.). 1997. 10.95 (978-1-57270-045-1(9), C11045, Audio Editions) Pub: Audio Partners. Dist(s): PerseuPGW
A wonderful antidote to writer's block, this collection features winners from the famous Bulwer-Lytton contest, complete with music & sound effects.

It Was a Lover & His Lass: From "As You Like It" see Palgrave's Golden Treasury of English Poetry

It Was Cruel see Monsarrat at Sea

It Was You, Set. Perf. by Mighty Clouds of Joy. 1 cass., 1 CD. (Running Time: 57 mins.). 10.98 (978-1-57908-499-8(0), 5362); audio compact disk 16.98 (978-1-57908-498-1(2), 5362) Platinm Enter.

It Wasn't Me. Contrib. by Suni Paz. (Stories for the Year 'Round Ser.). (J). (gr. k-3). 2000. 3.95 (978-1-58105-312-8(6)) Pub: Santillana. Dist(s): Lectorum Pubns

It Wasn't Me, It Was Her (an Essay from Things I've Learned from Women Who've Dumped Me) abr. ed. Rick Marin. Read by Rick Marin. Ed. by Ben Karlin. (Running Time: 15 mins.). (ENG.). 2008. 1.98 (978-1-60024-352-3(5)) Pub: Hachet Audio. Dist(s): HachBkGrp

It Went Too Far - Beyond the End of the Drama, Nos. 28, 29 & 30. Carl Faber. 3 cass. (Running Time: 3 hrs. 45 min.). 1984. 28.50 (978-0-918026-42-2(3), SR 60-182) Perseus Pr.

It Won't Hurt Forever: Guiding Your Child Through Trauma. Peter Levine. 2 CDs. 2004. audio compact disk 19.95 (978-1-59179-302-1(5), AW00490D) Sounds True.
How do you help your child recover from life's painful experiences? Dr. Levine offers his 35 years of expertise to show parents and caretakers how to help children recover from accidents and other traumatic events - using the body's own healing mechanisms.

Ita Ford: Missionary Martyr. Phyllis Zagano. Perf. by Phyllis Zagano. 1 cass. pap. bk. (AA3020) Credence Commun.
Murdered & martyred trying to help the poor in Central America.

Italian see Acting with an Accent

Italian. Created by Berlitz. (Berlitz Hide This CD Ser.). (ITA & ENG., 2007. audio compact disk 9.95 (978-981-268-055-6(1)) Pub: APA Pubns Serv SGP. Dist(s): IngramPubServ

Italian. Ed. by Berlitz Publishing Staff. (Running Time: 1 hr.). (Berlitz Rush Hour Express Ser.). (ITA & ENG.). 2004. audio compact disk 9.95 (978-981-246-597-9(9), 465979) Pub: APA Pubns Serv SGP. Dist(s): IngramPubServ

Italian. Berlitz Publishing Staff. (Berlitz Guaranteed Ser.). (ENG.). 2007. audio compact disk 19.95 (978-981-268-233-8(3)) Pub: APA Pubns Serv SGP. Dist(s): IngramPubServ

Italian. Contrib. by Berlitz Publishing Staff. (NOVA PREMIER Ser.). (ENG.). 2008. audio compact disk 49.95 (978-0-8416-0043-0(0)) Pub: APA Pubns Serv SGP. Dist(s): IngramPubServ

Italian. Ed. by Berlitz Publishing Staff. 3 CDs. (ADVANCED Ser.). (ENG.). 2008. audio compact disk 34.95 (978-981-268-321-2(6)) Pub: APA Pubns Serv SGP. Dist(s): IngramPubServ

Italian. Ed. by Berlitz Publishing Staff. (Berlitz iPhrase Ser.). (ENG.). 2008. audio compact disk 12.95 (978-981-268-486-8(7)) Pub: APA Pubns Serv SGP. Dist(s): IngramPubServ

Italian. Berlitz Publishing Staff. (Berlitz for Your Trip Ser.). 2007. audio compact disk 9.95 (978-981-268-046-4(2)) Pub: Berlitz Pubng. Dist(s): Langenscheidt

Italian. Collins UK. Prod. by Clelia Boscolo. Contrib. by Rosi McNab. (Running Time: 3 hrs. 0 mins. 0 sec.). (Collins Easy Learning Audio Course Ser.). (ENG.). 2009. audio compact disk 13.95 (978-0-00-727174-0(3)) Pub: HarpC GBR. Dist(s): IPG Chicago

***Italian.** Kristine K. Kershul. ([i]10 minutes a day[/i][sup]R[/sup] AUDIO CD Ser.). (ENG.). 2007. audio compact disk 42.95 (978-1-931873-27-7(5)) Pub: Bilingual Bks. Dist(s): Midpt Trade

Italian. Lonely Planet Publications Staff. 2 cass. (Running Time: 80 min.). (Language - Thirty Library). bk. 16.95 set in vinyl album. Moonbeam Pubns.
Using the proven method based on the famous U.S. Military accelerated language learning program, Language/30 courses stress conversationally useful words & phrases.

Italian. Lonely Planet Publications Staff. 1 cass. (Running Time: 1 hr.). (Listen & Learn a Language Ser.). (ITA.). (J). bk. (TWIN 412) NewSound.

Italian. Lydia Vellaccio & Maurice Elston. 1 cass. (Running Time: 60 min.). (Language Complete Course Packs Ser.). 1993. 17.95 (Passport Bks) McGraw-Hill Trade.

Italian. rev. ed. Berlitz Editors. 1 cass. (Running Time: 1 hr. 30 min.). (Cassettepack Ser.). (ITA., 1998. pap. bk. 18.95 (978-2-8315-6332-9(1)) Berlitz Intl Inc.
For travelers.

Italian. rev. ed. Berlitz Publishing Staff. 1 CD. (Running Time: 1 hr.). (Berlitz Kids Language Pack Ser.). (ITA & ENG., 2003. audio compact disk 26.95 (978-981-246-367-8(4), 463674) Pub: Berlitz Pubng. Dist(s): Langenscheidt

Italian. unabr. ed. Ed. by Charles Berlitz. 2 cass. (Running Time: 1 hr. 30 mins.). (Language/30 Brief Course Ser.). pap. bk. 21.95 (AF1026) J Norton Pubs.
Quick, highly condensed introduction to the words & phrases you'll need to communicate effectively in the country you're visiting. Cassettes & phrase guide book are in a vinyl album.

Italian. unabr. ed. Linguistics Staff. Created by Oasis Audio Staff. (Complete Idiot's Guide Ser.). (ENG.). 2005. audio compact disk 19.99 (978-1-59859-058-6(8)) Oasis Audio.

Italian. unabr. ed. Linguistics Staff. Created by Oasis Audio Staff. 2 cass. (Running Time: 3 hrs.). (Complete Idiot's Guide to Languages Ser.). (ENG & ITA.). 2005. audio compact disk 9.99 (978-1-59859-120-0(7)) Oasis Audio.

Italian. unabr. ed. Oasis Audio Staff & Linguistics Staff. Narrated by Linguistics Staff. (Complete Idiot's Guides). (ENG.). 2005. audio compact disk 39.99 (978-1-59859-064-7(2)) Oasis Audio.

Italian. 2nd ed. Collins Publishers Staff. Prod. by Clelia Boscolo. Contrib. by Rosi McNab. (Running Time: 3 hrs. 0 mins. 0 sec.). (Collins Easy Learning Audio Course Ser.). (ITA & ENG.). 2009. audio compact disk 17.95 (978-0-00-728755-0(0)) Pub: HarpC GBR. Dist(s): IPG Chicago

Italian. 2nd rev. ed. Howard Beckerman. Ed. by Berlitz Publishing Staff. 3 CDs. (Running Time: 1 hr.). (Rush Hour Ser.). (ITA.). 2003. audio compact disk 24.95 (978-981-246-273-2(2), 462732) Pub: Berlitz Pubng. Dist(s): Langenscheidt

Italian. 2nd rev. ed. Berlitz Publishing Staff. (Berlitz Deluxe Language Pack Ser.). (ITA & ENG., 2008. audio compact disk 79.95 (978-981-268-405-9(0)) Pub: Berlitz Pubng. Dist(s): Langenscheidt

Italian. 3rd rev. ed. Created by Berlitz Publishing Staff. 6 CDs. (Berlitz Basic Ser.). (ITA & ENG., 2007. audio compact disk 29.95 (978-981-268-228-4(7)) Pub: APA Pubns Serv SGP. Dist(s): Langenscheidt

Italian. 3rd rev. ed. Created by Berlitz Publishing Staff. 3 CDs. (Berlitz Intermediate Ser.). 2008. audio compact disk 29.95 (978-981-268-409-7(3)) Pub: Berlitz Pubng. Dist(s): Langenscheidt

Italian, Pack. deluxe ed. Created by Berlitz Guides Staff. 12. (Berlitz Deluxe Language Ser.). (ENG & ITA., 2005. audio compact disk 79.95 (978-981-246-706-5(8), 467068) Pub: Berlitz Pubng. Dist(s): Langenscheidt

***Italian, Set.** Clelia Boscolo. Contrib. by Rosi McNab. (Running Time: 7 hrs. 5 mins.). (Collins Easy Learning Audio Course Ser.). (ITA & ENG.). 2010. audio compact disk 24.95 (978-0-00-734779-7(0)) Pub: HarpC GBR. Dist(s): IPG Chicago

Italian: Language 30. Educational Services Corporation Staff. 2004. audio compact disk 21.95 (978-1-931850-05-6(4)) Educ Svcs DC.

Italian: Language/30. rev. ed. Educational Services Corporation Staff. Intro. by Charles Berlitz. 2 cass. (ITA.). 1992. pap. bk. 21.95 (978-0-910542-60-9(0)) Educ Svcs DC.
Italian self-teaching language course.

Italian: Learn to Speak & Understand Italian with Pimsleur Language Programs. Pimsleur Staff. (Running Time: 11 hrs. 50 mins. 0 sec.). (Express Ser.). (ENG.). 2003. audio compact disk 11.95 (978-0-7435-3391-1(7), Pimsleur) Pub: S&S Audio. Dist(s): S and S Inc

Italian: Learn to Speak & Understand Italian with Pimsleur Language Programs. 2nd unabr. ed. Pimsleur Staff. Created by Simon and Schuster Staff. 5 CDs. (Running Time: 50 hrs. 0 mins. 0 sec.). (Basic Ser.). (ITA & ENG.). 2005. audio compact disk 24.95 (978-0-7435-5068-0(4), Pimsleur) Pub: S&S Audio. Dist(s): S and S Inc

Italian: Living Language Complete Course. rev. ed. Contrib. by Barry Leonard. 2000. 22.00 (978-0-7881-9684-3(7)) DIANE Pub.

Italian: Quick & Simple. 2nd rev. ed. Pimsleur Staff. 4 CDs. (Running Time: 400 hrs. 0 mins. NaN sec.). (Quick & Simple Ser.). (ITA & ENG.). 2002. audio compact disk 19.95 (978-0-7435-0955-8(2), Pimsleur) Pub: S&S Audio. Dist(s): S and S Inc

Italian: Speak & Read the Pimsleur Way. Pimsleur Staff. (Running Time: 7 hrs. 30 mins. 0 sec.). (Go Ser.). (ENG.). 2009. audio compact disk 29.99 (978-0-7435-9657-2(9)) Pub: S&S Audio. Dist(s): S and S Inc

Italian Set: Basic I. 4 cass. (Learn While You Drive Ser.). (ITA.). 1995. bk. 47.95 (6001-AMR) Olivia & Hill.
Language course designed specifically for use in your car. The sentence in the foreign language is always followed by an English translation. Subjects covered: travel, shopping, ordering meals, placing telephone calls, telling time, counting money, using postal system, sightseeing, theater, arranging & attending business meetings & above all, making friends.

Italian Set: Basic II. 4 cass. (Learn While You Drive Ser.). (ITA.). 1995. bk. 44.95 (6002-AMR) Olivia & Hill.

Italian - English. 1 cass. (Lyric Language Ser.). (ITA & ENG.). (J). 7.98 Blisterpack. (POI 503) NewSound.

Italian - English, Level 3. Penton Overseas, Inc. Staff. 2 cass. (Running Time: 9 min. per cass.). (VocabuLearn Ser.). (ENG & ITA.). 1989. 15.95 (978-0-939001-27-9(6)) Penton Overseas.

Italian Affair, Set. unabr. ed. Julie Ellis. Read by Liza Ross. 6 vols. (Running Time: 8 hr.). 1999. bk. 54.95 (978-0-7927-2308-0(2), CSL 197, Chivers Sound Lib) AudioGO.
Upon her mother's dying request, Lisa came to Italy to find her half-brother. She arrives at the Villa Como, a tourist hotel run by the Contessa Menotti & her daughter-in-law. However, Lisa's brother is nowhere to be found, & the only clue is an oil painting of a young boy she discovers in the closed wing of the house. Then she meets fellow-American Scott Anderson, who is looking for a friend who disappeared from Paris two weeks ago. Scott claims his friend bears a remarkable resemblance to Lisa herself.

Italian American - German American. Joe Giordano. Narrated by George Guidall. Contrib. by Hinda Winawer & Norbert Wetzel. 6 cass. (Running Time: 30 min.). (Growing Up in America Ser.: Vol. 6). 1997. 12.00 Set. (978-1-891207-06-8(7)) Ethnic Prods.

Italian Arias of the Baroque & Classical Eras: High Voice. Ed. by John Glenn Paton. (ITA.). 1994. audio compact disk 11.95 (978-0-7390-2705-9(0)) Alfred Pub.

Italian Art Songs of the Romantic Era: Medium High. John Glenn Paton & Patricia A. Chiti. 1 CD. (ITA.). 1994. audio compact disk 16.95 (978-0-7390-0247-6(3), 4975) Alfred Pub.

Italian Backgrounds, Set. Edith Wharton. Read by Flo Gibson. 3 cass. (Running Time: 4 hrs.). 1996. 16.95 (978-1-55685-412-5(9)) Audio Bk Con.
Glorious descriptions of Italy as the author travels through the Pennine Alps, Tuscany, Rome, & Milan & often uses the backgrounds of great paintings & the work of sculptors to enhance the effect.

Italian Bible - New Testament (Spoken Word) Riveduta Version. Read by Elio Milazzo. 16 cass. 1994. 39.97 (978-1-58968-052-4(9), 4001A) Chrstn Dup Intl.

Italian Business Situations: A Spoken Language Guide. Vincent Edwards & Gianfranca G. Shepheard. (Languages for Business Ser.). 1995. 34.95 (978-0-415-12852-0(8)) Pub: Routledge. Dist(s): Taylor and Fran

Italian, Conversational: Learn to Speak & Understand Italian with Pimsleur Language Programs. 2nd unabr. ed. Pimsleur Staff & Pimsleur. 8 CDs. (Running Time: 80 hrs. 0 mins. 0 sec.). (Instant Conversation Ser.). (ITA & ENG.). 2005. audio compact disk 49.95 (978-0-7435-5043-7(9), Pimsleur) Pub: S&S Audio. Dist(s): S and S Inc

Italian Culture Capsules. unabr. ed. 1 cass. (Running Time: 1 hr.). 12.95 (978-0-88432-506-2(7), CCIT01) J Norton Pubs.
The brief culture capsules recorded in English at the end of each lesson unit of the introductory courses are available as separate cassettes.

Italian Dialogs. 1 cass. (Running Time: 1 hr.). 1991. pap. bk. & tchr. ed. 42.50 (978-1-57970-005-8(5), SIT115) J Norton Pubs.
Learners at all levels will enjoy the 30 brief, humorous dialogs illustrating characteristics of Italian culture. Presented in basic Italian with a vocabulary of high-frequency words & expressions & exercises. Includes instructor's guide.

Italian Education. unabr. ed. Tim Parks. Read by Stuart Langton. 10 cass. (Running Time: 15 hrs.). 2001. 80.00 (978-0-7366-8387-6(9)) Books on Tape.
Tim Parks has already had the Peter Mayle experience of becoming initiated into the social life of a different country - in his case, the labyrinthine codes of behavior in Italy. Now, he examines what it will be like for his bilingual children to learn to become Italian - how Italians teach their little Italians how to be Italian. He finds the same quirks and oddities among the young ones as among their parents - the same perverse love of theatricality in all personal relationships, the same mixture of sentimentality and calculation.

Italian for Dimwits: 6 One Hour Audio Cassette Tapes/ Complete Listening Guide & Tapescript. 1999. 59.00 (978-1-893564-29-9(0)) Macmill Audio.

Italian for Dummies. unabr. ed. Teresa L. Picarazzi. Read by Becky Wilmes & Gian Luca Ferme. (YA). 2008. 34.99 (978-1-60252-973-1(6)) Find a World.

Italian for Dummies Audio Set. Teresa L. Picarazzi. (For Dummies Ser.). (ITA & ENG.). 2007. audio compact disk 19.99 (978-0-470-09586-7(5), For Dummies) Wiley US.

Italian for Modern Living. Robert A. Hall, Jr. 6 dual track cass. (Spoken Language Ser.). (J). (gr. 9-12). 1974. bk. 80.00 (978-0-87950-321-5(1)); pap. bk. & stu. ed. 100.00 (978-0-87950-322-2(X)) Spoken Lang Serv.

Italian for Speakers of English, Three. unabr. ed. 16 cass. (Running Time: 15 hrs.). (Pimsleur Tapes Ser.). (ITA & ENG.). 1997. 345.00 Set. (18703, Pimsleur) S&S Audio.
An additional thirty-lesson-unit program, for a total of ninety lesson units. Will allow the learner to achieve the ACTFL Intermediate-High Spoken Proficiency Level.

Italian I, Set, study guide. Paul Pimsleur. 16 cass. (Pimsleur Language Learning Ser.). 1995. 345.00 Set, incl. study guide. (0671-52156-X) SyberVision.

Italian I: Learn to Speak & Understand Italian with Pimsleur Language Programs. 2nd rev. ed. Pimsleur Staff. 16 CDs. (Running Time: 160 hrs. 0 mins. 0 sec.). (Comprehensive Ser.). (ENG.). 2002. audio compact disk 345.00 (978-0-7435-1837-6(3), Pimsleur) Pub: S&S Audio. Dist(s): S and S Inc

Italian I Basic. Paul Pimsleur. 8 lessons on 4 cass. (Pimsleur Language Learning Ser.). 1995. 29.95 (52165-1) SyberVision.

Italian II, Set, study guide. Paul Pimsleur. 16 cass. (Pimsleur Language Learning Ser.). 1996. 345.00 Set, incl. study guide. (0671-57074-9) SyberVision.

Italian II: Learn to Speak & Understand Italian with Pimsleur Language Programs. 2nd ed. Pimsleur Staff. (Running Time: 160 hrs. 0 mins. 0 sec.). (Comprehensive Ser.). (ENG.). 2004. audio compact disk 345.00 (978-0-7435-2879-5(4), Pimsleur) Pub: S&S Audio. Dist(s): S and S Inc

Italian III, Set, study guide. Paul Pimsleur. 16 cass. (Pimsleur Language Learning Ser.). 1998. 345.00 Set, incl. study guide. (0671-58120-1) SyberVision.

Italian III: Learn to Speak & Understand Italian with Pimsleur Language Programs. 2nd ed. Pimsleur Staff. (Running Time: 160 hrs. 0 mins. 0 sec.). (Comprehensive Ser.). (ENG.). 2004. audio compact disk 345.00 (978-0-7435-2881-8(6), Pimsleur) Pub: S&S Audio. Dist(s): S and S Inc

Italian in a Minute. 1 cass. (Language in a Minute Cassette Ser.). 5.95 (978-0-943351-16-2(2), XC1003) Cimino Pub Grp.
Feel at home in any foreign country with these 101 esssential words & phrases. Hear each word introduced in English, hear them pronounced by a Voice of America instructor. Practice at your own pace, you can check yourself with the wallet sized dictionary included.

Italian in 30 Days. 2nd rev. abr. ed. Created by Berlitz Guides. (Berlitz in 30 Days Ser.). 2007. audio compact disk 19.95 (978-981-268-222-2(8)) Pub: APA Pubns Serv SGP. Dist(s): Langenscheidt

Italian Intermezzo: Recipes by Celebrated Italian Chefs, Romantic Italian Music. Sharon O'Connor. (Sharon O'Connor's Menus & Music Ser.). (ENG., 2000. pap. bk. 24.95 (978-1-883914-22-6(1)) Menus & Music.

Italian Language. 2005. 44.99 (978-1-59895-002-1(9)) Find a World.

Italian Lo Dica in Italian: Levels One & Two. Giovanni Cavagna. 10 cass. 175.00 Set. (Natl Textbk Co) M-H Contemporary.
Develops the conversational & reading ability students need to get along comfortably in Italian.

Italian Music. Kim Mitzo Thompson & Karen Mitzo Hilderbrand. Arranged by Hal Wright. (J). 1994. pap. bk. 13.99 (978-1-57583-274-6(7), Twin 412CD); audio compact disk 12.99 (978-1-57583-304-0(2), Twin 112CD) Twin Sisters.

Italian New Testament. Narrated by Elio Milazzo. 16 cass. (Running Time: 24 hrs.). (ITA.). 1994. 39.99 (978-7-902033-01-5(4)) Chrstn Dup Intl.

Italian on the Go. 1 cass. (Languages on the Go Ser.). (ITA.). 1992. bk. 14.95 (978-0-8120-7831-2(4)) Barron.

Italian on the Go. 2nd unabr. ed. Marcel Danesi. 2 cass. (Running Time: 3 hrs.). (On the Go Ser.). 2001. 14.95 (978-0-7641-7350-9(2)) Barron.
Foreign language-learning series features updated dialogue that closely reflect the contemporary scene in Italy.

Italian on the Go: A Level One Language Program. 3rd ed. Marcel Danesi. (On the Go/Level 1 Ser.). (ENG & ITA., 2004. bk. 18.99 (978-0-7641-7756-9(7)) Barron.

Italian on the Road, Level 2. Marcel Danesi. 2 cass. (Running Time: 90 min. per cass.). (Languages on the Road Ser.). (ENG & ITA.). 1992. pap. bk. 11.95 incl. script set. (978-0-8120-7936-4(1)) Barron.
The perfect steps forward for those who already know some language basics but want to learn more. They're designed primarily for travelers, but are good ways for everybody to learn a new language - with a minimum of drudgery & a maximum of enjoyment. Because these programs stress the

spoken word, they're ideal for use while the learner is driving a car, jogging with a Walkman, or doing any routine chores.

Italian Part A (Modern Spoken Italian) CDs & Text. Elaine Vertucci Baran. 8 CDs. (Running Time: 8 hrs.). (ITA.). 2005. audio compact disk 225.00 (978-1-57970-132-1(9), AFZ501D) J Norton Pubs.

Italian Phonetics, Diction & Intonation. Pierina B. Castiglione. 2 cass. (Running Time: 3 hrs. 30 min.). (ITA.). 1997. 23.95 Set, bk. avail. (978-0-913298-77-0(8)) S F Vanni.
Features conversation & reading exercises.

Italian Phonology, unabr. ed. 10 cass. (Running Time: 10 hrs. 30 mins.). (ITA.). (J). (gr. 10-12). 1992. pap. bk. 245.00 (978-0-88432-456-0(7), SIT230) J Norton Pubs.
The study of Italian sounds, stresses, & intonation. Although the course may be used at any stage of learning, it is especially valuable for those who have already have some familiarity with the language but wish to pronounce it more authentically.

Italian Phonology CDs & Text. 10 CDs. (Running Time: 10 hrs.). (ITA.). 2005. audio compact disk 245.00 (978-1-57970-189-5(2), SIT230D) J Norton Pubs.

Italian Phrase Book Pack. rev. ed. Collins Publishers Staff. (ENG & ITA.). 2003. pap. bk. 13.99 (978-0-00-765097-2(3)) Pub: HarpC GBR. Dist(s): Trafalgar

Italian Phrasebook & Dictionary. Collins Publishers Staff. (ITA & ENG., bk. 19.99 (978-0-00-768269-0(7)) Pub: HarpC GBR. Dist(s): Trafalgar

Italian Plus: Learn to Speak & Understand Italian with Pimsleur Language Programs. Pimsleur. (Running Time: 5 hrs. 0 mins. 0 sec.). (Compact Ser.). (ENG.). 2008. audio compact disk 115.00 (978-0-7435-7164-7(9), Pimsleur) Pub: S&S Audio. Dist(s): S and S Inc

Italian Programmatic Course Level 1 Cd: Multilingual Books Language Course. FSI Staff. Ed. by Augustus Koski & Marianne Lehr Adams. 15 CD's. (Multilingual Books Intensive Language Courses). (ITA.). (C). 2003. per. 199.00 (978-1-58214-136-7(3)) Language Assocs.
Units 1 -15.

Italian Quarter. unabr. ed. Domenica De Rosa. Read by Aileen Gonsalves. 6 cass. (Running Time: 7 hrs. 5 mins.). (Isis Cassettes Ser.). 2006. 54.95 (978-0-7531-3537-2(X)) Pub: ISIS Lrg Prnt GBR. Dist(s): Ulverscroft US

Italian Quartet. Jane Candia Coleman. Read by Gabrielle De Cuir. 2002. 40.00 (978-0-7366-8571-9(5)) Books on Tape.

Italian Renaissance, I-III. Instructed by Kenneth Bartlett. 18 cass. (Running Time: 18 hrs.). 2005. 199.95 (978-1-59803-057-0(4)) Teaching Co.

Italian Renaissance, Vol. I-III. Instructed by Kenneth Bartlett. 18 CDs. (Running Time: 18 hrs). 2005. audio compact disk 99.95 (978-1-59803-059-4(0)) Teaching Co.

Italian Rush Hour Express Cd Berlitz. (RUSH HOUR EXPRESS Ser.). 2008. audio compact disk 9.95 (978-981-268-238-3(4)) Pub: Berlitz Pubng. Dist(s): Langenscheidt

Italian Savvy Traveler Food & Dining: CDs & Booklet. 2 CDs. (Running Time: 1 hr. 39 min.). (ITA.). 2005. audio compact disk 21.95 (978-1-57970-133-8(7), SIT580D) J Norton Pubs.

Italian Secretary. unabr. ed. Caleb Carr. Read by Simon Prebble. 2005. 15.95 (978-0-7435-5158-8(3)) Pub: S&S Audio. Dist(s): S and S Inc

Italian Vocabulary, Set. 4 cass. (Learn While You Drive Ser.). (ITA.). 1995. 47.95 (6003-AMR) Olivia & Hill.
A wealth of words not covered in the basic courses (2000 words). Specifically designed to increase vocabulary without opening a book.

Italian with Ease see Italienisch Ohne Muhe Heute

Italian with Ease see Nuevo Italiano sin Esfuerzo

Italian with Michel Thomas. (Delux Language Ser.). 2000. 69.95 (978-0-658-00825-2(0), 008250) M-H Contemporary.

Italiano e i Dialetti. 1 cass. (Running Time: 55 mins.). (ITA.). pap. bk. 16.95 (SIT250) J Norton Pubs.
Intermediate-level readings with accompanying cassettes can improve both reading & listening comprehension. Texts include exercises & answer key.

Italiano in Diretta Pt. 1: Student Program. 2nd ed. Antonella Pease. 6 cass. (Running Time: 9 hrs.). (C). 1993. 53.13 (978-0-07-911279-8(X), 9780079112798, Mc-H Human Soc) Pub: McGrw-H Hghr Educ. Dist(s): McGraw

Italians. unabr. ed. Luigi Barzini. Read by Fred Williams. 10 cass. (Running Time: 14 hrs. 30 mins.). 1995. 69.95 (978-0-7861-0720-9(0), 1601) Blckstn Audio.
Luigi Barzini explores his country with all its paradoxes, privacies & delights intact. An Italian deeply immersed in politics, a deputy, a distinguished journalist & a cosmopolitan, perceptive man, Barzini has written this book in English. It may well become the standard work on the Italians for travelers, enthusiasts, & students. Barzini touches on nearly every aspect of Italian hopes, failures & achievements past, present, & future.

Italians before Italy: Conflict & Competition in the Mediterranean. Instructed by Kenneth R. Bartlett. 2007. 129.95 (978-1-59803-346-5(8)); audio compact disk 69.95 (978-1-59803-347-2(6)) Teaching Co.

Italienisch Ohne Muhe Heute. 1 CD. (Running Time: 1 hr. 30 min.).Tr. of Italian with Ease. (GER & ITA.). 2000. bk. 95.00 (978-2-7005-1053-9(4)); bk. 75.00 (978-2-7005-1016-4(X)) Pub: Assimil FRA. Dist(s): Distribks Inc

Italo Calvino - le Litta Invisibili: Multilingual Books Literature. Excerpts. Italo Calvino. Ed. by Maurizio Falyhera & Cristiana Grocometti. 1 cass. (Running Time: 90 mins.). (Audio Anthology of Italian Literature Ser.: 13). (ITA.). 1999. spiral bd. 19.95 (978-1-58214-124-4(X)) Language Assocs.

Italo Calvino - le Litta Invisibili: Multilingual Books Literature, Excerpts. Italo Calvino. Ed. by Maurizio Falyhera & Cristiana Grocometti. 1 CD. (Running Time: 90 mins.). (Audio Anthology of Italian Literature Ser.: 13). (ITA.). 1999. spiral bd. 29.95 (978-1-58214-149-7(5)) Language Assocs.

Italo Suevo - from Raccorti: Multilingual Books. Excerpts. Ed. by Maurizio Falyhera & Cristina Giocometti. 1 CD. (Running Time: 90 mins.). (Audio Anthology of Italian Literature Ser.: Vol. 10). (ITA.). 1999. audio compact disk 29.95 (978-1-58214-119-0(3)) Language Assocs.

Italo Suevo - from Raccorti: Multilingual Books Literature on Tape/cd, Excerpts. Ed. by Maurizio Falyhera & Cristina Giocometti. 1 cass. (Running Time: 90 mins.). (Audio Anthology of Italian Literature Ser.: 10). (ITA.). 1999. spiral bd. 19.95 (978-1-58214-118-3(5)) Language Assocs.

Italy. Robert S. Kane. 1 cass. (Passport's Travel Paks Ser.). bk. & pap. bk. 29.95 incl. vinyl case & map. (978-0-8442-9277-9(X), Passport Bks) McGraw-Hill Trade.
An introduction to the country's culture & customs, plus brief language orientation of common words, phrases & expressions.

Italy: Arts of Florence. (Running Time: 50 min.). 1990. 12.95 (CC483) Comp Comms Inc.
Starting at the Ponte Vecchio, your tour winds through the "new market" & an extensive visit to the Uffizi Museum & Galley. Your walk continues to the Palazzo Strozzi & down the elegant Tornabuoni, ending at Santa Maria Novella.

Italy: Churches of Rome (Walking Tour) 1 cass. (Running Time: 60 min.). 12.95 (CC476) Comp Comms Inc.
Eight of Rome's most sacred shrines: Chiesa del Gesu, Santa Maria in Aracoeli, Santa Maria Sopra Minerva, San Giovanni in Laterano, Scala Santa, San Clemente, Santa Maria Maggiore, San Pietro in Vincoli.

Italy: Classical Rome (Walking Tour) 1 cass. (Running Time: 60 min.). 12.95 (CC472) Comp Comms Inc.
From the overwhelming Colosseum, through the most ancient part of the city centered on the Roman Forum.

Italy: Heart of Rome (Walking Tour) 1 cass. (Running Time: 60 min.). 12.95 (CC474) Comp Comms Inc.
Takes you through the center of Rome, visit the Piazza Colonna where the Roman Stock Exchange is located, pass by boutiques & salons on the Via Condotti, see the Spanish Steps, Mausoleum of Augustus Caesar, ending your tour at the Piazza del Popolo.

Italy: Historic Venice. (Running Time: 50 min.). 1990. 12.95 (CC482) Comp Comms Inc.
Tour the Doge's Palace, stroll by the Church of San Moise, the Teatro Fenice, & the Accademia, the great art museum of Venice. After a short visit to Santa Maria della Salute, return on a boatride to San Marco.

Italy: Modern Rome (Walking Tour) 1 cass. (Running Time: 60 min.). 12.95 (CC475) Comp Comms Inc.
Takes you through elegant shopping areas, famous churches, piazzas, & the Museum of Rome.

Italy: Rome - A Traveler's Companion (Overview) 1 cass. (Running Time: 60 min.). 11.95 (CC480) Comp Comms Inc.
Introduces you to Rome of yesterday & today, ancient ruins & robust food. Suggests where to stop for the Cappuccino, Cornetto & Gelatto.

Italy: Rome of the Popes & People (Walking Tour) 1 cass. (Running Time: 60 min.). 12.95 (CC473) Comp Comms Inc.
Starts in the Piazza della Rotonda, where the Pantheon is located, see the priceless art & sculpture in churches, visit the Piazza Navona, the Via dei Coronari & more.

Italy: Ruins of Pompeii. (Running Time: 50 min.). 1990. 12.95 (CC484) Comp Comms Inc.
The civic Forum, Temple of Jupiter, the Macellu, the Basilica, the Stabian Baths, the commercial enterprises along the Via dell'Abbondanza, the House of Menander, Villa of Julia Felix, Amphitheater, Teatro Piccolo & Teatro Grande, House of the Faun, House of the Labyrinth, House of the Vetii, Via del Sepolchri & the Villa dei Misteri.

Italy: This Is Italy (Overview) 1 cass. (Running Time: 60 min.). 12.95 (CC471) Comp Comms Inc.
Basic facts of the Italian nation: its history, music, art, architecture, government, economy & cuisine, plus a language study , & shopping hints.

Itazuke Tower. Dick Jonas. 1 cass. . 10.00; audio compact disk 15.00 EROSONIC.
Includes: "Itazuke Tower," "DaNang Lullabye," "Korean Waterfall," "And the Band Played Waltzing Matilda," "Strike Eagle," "Crack Went the Rifle," "Grunt," "Another Old Soldier," "Stand to Your Glasses," "Man Who Flies the Back Seat," "Heinz E. Coordes," "Let's Get Away with It All," "Strafing 'Round the Mountain," & "Fireball.".

***Itch.** collector's unabr. ed. Michelle D. Kwasney. Narrated by Angela Jayne Rogers. 6 CDs. (Running Time: 6 hrs. 15 mins.). (YA). (gr. 5-8). 2009. audio compact disk 66.75 (978-1-4361-4831-3(6)) Recorded Bks.

***Itch.** unabr. ed. Michelle D. Kwasney. Narrated by Angela Jayne Rogers. 6 cass. (Running Time: 6 hrs. 15 mins.). (YA). (gr. 5-8). 2009. 51.75 (978-1-4361-4822-1(7)); audio compact disk 66.75 (978-1-4361-4827-6(8)) Recorded Bks.

Itch. unabr. ed. Benilde Little. Narrated by Caroline S. Clay. 5 cass. (Running Time: 7 hrs. 15 mins.). 1998. 46.00 (978-0-7887-5121-9(2), F0015L8) Recorded Bks.
Abra Dixon is well educated, fashionable & married to the perfect man. She also runs a film production company with her childhood friend, Natasha. But Abra's perfect life suddenly comes to a crashing halt when her husband leaves her for a sexy young model. Now, in a world where everyone seems so confident, Abra will need to develop her new resources & strength.

Itch. unabr. ed. Benilde Little. Narrated by Caroline S. Clay. 6 CDs. (Running Time: 7 hrs. 15 mins.). 2001. audio compact disk 69.00 (978-1-4025-1009-0(8), C1588) Recorded Bks.
Abra Dixon is well educated, fashionable, and married to the perfect man. She also runs a film production company with her childhood friend, Natasha. Abra's perfect life is suddenly thrown off course when her husband leaves her for a sexy young model. As Abra and Natasha try to find a backer for their latest film, they must navigate the opulent world of directors and investors. But now Abra must learn to be single and strong again. In a world where everyone seems so confident, Abra will need to develop her own definition of success.

ITE 2003 Technical Conference & Exhibit-Transportation's Role in Successful Communities. Institute of Transportation Engineers Staff. (Publication Ser.). 2003. audio compact disk (978-0-935403-75-6(2)) Inst Trans Eng.

ITE 2005 Annual Meeting & Exhibit Compendium of Technical Papers. 2005. audio compact disk 60.00 (978-1-933452-08-1(0), CD-038) Inst Trans Eng.

Item Analysis, Pt. 1. Patricia Hoefler. 1991. (978-1-56533-176-1(1)) MEDS Pubng.

Item Analysis, Pt. 2. Patricia Hoefler. 1991. (978-1-56533-177-8(X)) MEDS Pubng.

ITK - To Accompany Human Biology. 3rd ed. Daniel D. Chiras. (C). 1999. audio compact disk 99.00 (978-0-7637-0961-7(1), 0961-1) Jones Bartlett.

***Itk- Emergency Medical Responder 5E Instructor's Toolkit Cd.** 5th rev. ed. AAOS. 2010. audio compact disk 319.95 (978-0-7637-9272-5(1)) Jones Bartlett.

***Itk- Tactical Medicine Essentials Instructor's Toolkit.** ACEP. 2011. audio compact disk 154.95 (978-0-7637-9444-6(9)) Jones Bartlett.

ITK for Health & Wellness. 6th ed. Gordon Edlin et al. (C). 1999. audio compact disk 99.00 (978-0-7637-0963-1(8), 0963-8) Jones Bartlett.

ITK to Accompany Essential Genetics. 2nd ed. Dan Hartl & Elizabeth Jones. (C). 1999. audio compact disk 99.00 (978-0-7637-0945-7(X), 0945-X) Jones Bartlett.

It's a Baby Shower! 1 CD. (Running Time: 90 mins.). 2000. 7.95 (978-0-9650258-5-0(3), Persnickety Pr) Pub: DBP & Assocs. Dist(s): Penton Overseas
The perfect shower gift for the future mom-to-be. Humorous songs will make the baby shower one to remember for many years to come. Also includes lullabies for the little one's arrival.

It's a Beautiful Day. George Bloomer. 2001. audio compact disk 13.99 (978-1-892352-31-6(1)) Blooming Bks.

Its a Beautiful Day. George Bloomer. 2005. audio compact disk 14.99 (978-0-88368-935-6(9)) Whitaker Hse.

It's a Dog's Life. John R. Erickson. 2 cass. (Running Time: 2 hrs.). (Hank the Cowdog Ser.: No. 3). (J). (gr. 2-5). 1989. 16.95 (978-0-87719-071-4(2)) Lone Star Bks.

It's a Dog's Life. unabr. ed. John R. Erickson. Read by John R. Erickson. Illus. by Gerald L. Holmes. 2 cass. (Hank the Cowdog Ser.: No. 3). (J). (gr. 2-5). 1985. pap. bk. 13.95 (978-0-916941-03-1(5)) Maverick Bks.

It's a Dog's Life. unabr. ed. John R. Erickson. Read by John R. Erickson. 2 cassettes. (Running Time: approx. 3 hours). (Hank the Cowdog Ser.: No. 3). (J). 2002. 17.99 (978-1-59188-303-6(2)) Maverick Bks.

It's a Dog's Life. unabr. ed. John R. Erickson. Read by John R. Erickson. 3 CDs. (Running Time: Approx. 3 hours). (Hank the Cowdog Ser.: No. 3). (J). 2002. audio compact disk 19.99 (978-1-59188-603-7(1)) Maverick Bks.

It's a Dog's Life. unabr. ed. John R. Erickson. 2 cass. (Running Time: 2 hrs. 30 mins.). (Hank the Cowdog Ser.: No. 3). (J). (gr. 2-5). 2000. 18.00 (978-0-8072-8262-5(6), Listening Lib) Random Audio Pubg.
Hank hitches a ride into town to visit his sister, Maggie, who never really took to ranch life. Maggie doesn't like swimming in the sewer, chewing on old bones, or digging in the mud. So, it's up to Uncle Hank to teach Maggie's four pups the basics of their cowdog heritage, beginning with Garbage Patrol.

It's a Dog's Life. unabr. collector's ed. John R. Erickson. 3 CDs. (Running Time: 4 hrs. 30 mins.). (Hank the Cowdog Ser.: No. 3). (J). (gr. 2-5). 2001. audio compact disk 28.00 Books on Tape.
Hank's third adventure opens with Hank in trouble again, so he decides to make a visit to town to see his sister. Sounds innocent enough, but then Hank takes his nieces and nephews on a garbage patrol and gets captured by the dog catcher. Will he find a way out?.

It's a Dog's Life. unabr. collector's ed. John R. Erickson. Read by John R. Erickson. 2 cass. (Running Time: 3 hrs.). (Hank the Cowdog Ser.: No. 3). (J). (gr. 2-5). 2001. 16.95 (978-0-7366-6892-7(6)) Books on Tape.
Hank must teach his nephews the basics of their Cowdog heritage, beginning with the garbage pail.

It's a Dog's Life, Set. unabr. ed. John R. Erickson. 2 cass. (Hank the Cowdog Ser.: No. 3). (J). (gr. 2-5). 1998. 17.00 (21645) Recorded Bks.

It's a Dog's Life & Murder in the Middle Pasture. unabr. ed. John R. Erickson. Read by John R. Erickson. 4 cass. (Running Time: 6 hrs.). (Hank the Cowdog Ser.: Nos. 2-3). (J). 2002. 26.99 (978-0-916941-62-8(0)); audio compact disk 31.99 (978-0-916941-82-6(5)) Maverick Bks.
It's been a busy few days for the head of ranch security, what with routine patrols and not-so-routine combat with headless monsters. When the dust settles, Hank decides to take a break from duty and visit his sister in town. There, he enjoys the garbage patrol of a lifetime and faces down a brood of sassy town cats'and the plot thickens.

It's a Dulcimer Life. Neal Hellman. 1993. 9.98 (978-1-56222-683-1(5), 94881C) Mel Bay.

It's a Fair Day, Amber Brown. Paula Danziger. Illus. by Tony Ross. (Running Time: 18 mins.). audio compact disk 12.95 (978-1-59112-361-3(5)) Live Oak Media.

It's a Fair Day, Amber Brown. Paula Danziger. Illus. by Tony Ross. 14 vols. (Running Time: 18 mins.). 2003. pap. bk. 31.95 (978-1-59112-564-8(2)) Live Oak Media.

It's a Fair Day, Amber Brown. Paula Danziger. Illus. by Tony Ross. 11 vols. (Running Time: 18 mins.). (Readalongs for Beginning Readers Ser.). (J). 2003. bk. 25.95 (978-1-59112-246-3(5)); pap. bk. 16.95 (978-1-59112-245-6(7)); pap. bk. 29.95 (978-1-59112-247-0(3)); pap. bk. 18.95 (978-1-59112-362-0(3)) Pub: Live Oak Media. Dist(s): AudioGO

It's a Fair Day, Amber Brown. Paula Danziger. Illus. by Tony Ross. (Running Time: 18 mins.). (J). (gr. k-3). 2003. 9.95 (978-1-59112-244-9(9)) Live Oak Media.

It's a Girl's World. Lynn Glazier. 2005. audio compact disk 24.95 (978-0-660-19308-3(6)) Canadian Broadcasting CAN.

***It's A Good Life.** 2010. audio compact disk (978-1-59171-214-5(9)) Falcon Picture.

It's a Great Day to Praise the Lord. Created by Hal Leonard Corporation Staff. 1997. 11.98 (978-0-7601-0769-0(6), 75602105) Pub: Brentwood Music. Dist(s): H Leonard

It's a Great Day to Praise the Lord. Created by Hal Leonard Corporation Staff. 1997. 85.00 (978-0-7601-1403-2(X), 75606320); audio compact disk 85.00 (978-0-7601-1034-8(4), 75606321) Pub: Brentwood Music. Dist(s): H Leonard

It's a Meaningful Life: It Just Takes Practice, abr. ed. Bo Lozoff. Read by Bo Lozoff. 2 cass. (Running Time: 3 hrs.). 2000. 25.00 (978-1-57453-351-4(7)) Audio Lit.
Happiness is not found by striving for self-improvement but by combining spiritual practice with a devotion to community & service. Addresses the difficulties & blessings of a life focused on the well-being of others.

It's a New Day. 2003. 10.00 (978-1-58602-131-3(1)); audio compact disk 20.00 (978-1-58602-132-0(X)) E L Long.

It's a New Life! Perf. by Tom Barabas. 1 cass., 1 CD. 7.98 (SOP 7173); audio compact disk 11.98 CD Jewel box. (SOP 7173) NewSound.

It's a Party: Planning a Successful Retail Sales Event. Deborah Chaddock Brown. 2006. spiral bd. 20.00 (978-0-9789054-0-8(7)) D Chaddock Brown.

It's a Purl Thing. unabr. ed. Elizabeth Lenhard. Narrated by Liz Morton. 7 cass. (Running Time: 9 hrs. 30 mins.). 2005. 61.75 (978-1-4193-6188-3(0), 98194) Recorded Bks.
Elizabeth Lenhard makes knitting cool for teens with Chicks with Sticks (It's a purl thing). The knitting bug has spread from Scottie Shearer to popular Amanda, free-sprited Bella, and Tay, the anti-girl. The four become an unlikely group of friends with an even more unlikely hobby. But will the pressures of conformity at Stark High keep them from remaining pals? Young listeners will want to take up their own sticks as they listen along to the animated narration of Liz Morton.

It's a Rainbow World. Romper Room staff. (J). 1987. 9.95 (978-0-89845-282-2(1), HarperChildAud) HarperCollins Pubs.

It's a Ska Ska Ska Ska World. Perf. by Bunch of Believers Staff. 1 cass. (J). 1999. (978-5-551-88166-7(0), KMGC8689); audio compact disk 16.99 (978-5-551-88182-7(2), KMGD8689) Provident Mus Dist.
A fun, unique approach to youth ministry, this bunch of believers offers songs that make you laugh & think at the same time. Songs about home schooling, mission trips & trips to the Goodwill store are combined with lyrics that celebrate miracles, witnessing & the salvation message.

It's A Slippery Slope. Spalding Gray. 1 cass. (Running Time: 73 min.). 1998. (978-0-9662042-2-3(0)) Mouth Almighty.

It's a Small World. 1 cass. (J). 1991. bk. 6.98 (978-1-55723-492-6(2)) W Disney Records.

It's a Sound-Byte Life! A Matchbox Mystery. abr. ed. Neville DeAngelou-George. Narrated by Neville DeAngelou-George. Perf. by Jeremy Schwab et al. Music by Josh Hendrik. Engineer Chuck Snapp. 2

CDs. (Running Time: 2 hrs 17 mins). 2005. audio compact disk 27.00 (978-0-9769121-0-1(4)) BMT Audio.
It's a SOUND-BYTE Life (A Dramatized Matchbox Mystery) by Timberwolf Award winner, Neville DeAngelou-George. You've lost the golden touch. Eighteen hours of your life has just gone blank. You remember the strange things your soul-mate told you, which you had dismissed as an outcrop of his endearing personality and peculiar sense of humor. You remember them because they are unfolding just like he said they would: the Handsome Riddler, the Mother Cupboard Syndrome, the Sound-Byte Life! Your incredible lover with a penchant for mind-bending riddles has inexplicably dropped out of sight and no one around recalls you having such a lover, such a soul-mate.. You're absolutely certain this is no dream. You still dream.Someone is trying to assassinate you but you have no proof and you don?t know who. 363 households are depending on you for rescue. What would you do? Can you reclaim your golden life? Does anyone ever escape the SOUND-BYTE Life in tact or just survive as a permanent riddle?Peena is about to find out. This inspiring and hilarious dramatization is the kind of hell ride you'd want to take time and again. But is it all a deft trick of an imaginer or is this you in a box desperately trying to get out? There is only one way to know. Take the ride.

It's a Swing Thing: Andrew Carlton & the Swing Doctors. Perf. by Andrew Carlton. Prod. by Wysh Productions. 1 cass., 1 CD. 1998. 10.98; audio compact disk 15.98 CD. Provident Mus Dist.

It's a Thin Line. Kimberla Lawson Roby. Narrated by Susan Spain. 7 cass. (Running Time: 9 hrs. 30 mins.). 64.00 (978-0-7887-9001-0(3)); audio compact disk 78.00 (978-1-4025-2937-5(6)) Recorded Bks.

It's a Wonder-Full Life. Contrib. by John DeVries. Created by Pam Andrews & Luke Gambill. 2008. audio compact disk 16.98 (978-5-557-40846-2(0), Brentwood-Benson Music) Brentwood Music.

It's a Wonder-Full Life: Unison/2-Part. Contrib. by John DeVries. Created by Pam Andrews & Luke Gambill. 2008. audio compact disk 90.00 (978-5-557-40845-5(2), Brentwood-Benson Music) Brentwood Music.

It's a Wonderful Christmas. Contrib. by Michael W. Smith & Michael Blanton. Prod. by David Hamilton. 2007. audio compact disk 13.99 (978-5-557-58779-2(9)) Pt of Grace Ent.

It's a Wonderful Christmas. Perf. by Andy Williams. 1 CD. 1997. audio compact disk 15.98 (978-1-57511-037-0(7)) Pub Mills.

It's a Wonderful Christmas. unabr. ed. Perf. by Andy Williams. 1 CD. (Running Time: 30 mins.). 2004. audio compact disk 15.98 (978-1-59007-448-0(3)) Pub: New Millenn Enter. Dist(s): PerseuPGW

It's a Wonderful Christmas. unabr. ed. Perf. by Andy Williams. 1 CD. (Running Time: 40 min.). 1997. audio compact disk 12.98 CD. Pub Mills.
A charming holiday performance from the legendary Andy Williams featuring the actor-singer narrating the story "The Greatest Gift" & performing his classic song, "It's the Most Wonderful Time of the Year".

It's a Wonderful Christmas: 22 Holiday Vocal & Instrumental Classics. 2007. audio compact disk 5.99 (978-5-557-59236-9(9)) Maranatha Music.

It's a Wonderful Hope: 22 Inspirational Vocal & Instrumental Classics. 2008. audio compact disk 5.99 (978-5-557-47074-2(3)) Maranatha Music.

It's a Wonderful Life. Frank Capra, Jr. Based on a story by Philip Van Doren Stern. 1999. pap. bk. 13.10 (978-1-900912-66-2(X)) Mr Punch Prodns GBR.
The heart warming story of George Bailey, who is prevented from committing suicide the night before Christmas by the apprentice angel Clarence, who takes him on a journey back through his life to show him how the town of Bedford Falls would have been had he never lived.

It's a Wonderful Life. Perf. by Jimmy Stewart. 1 cass. (Running Time: 60 min.). 1947. 7.95 (DC-7950) Natl Recrd Co.
Explains the problems, the fun, the accomplishments & the love of a good man. When despair becomes great it takes an elf-like apprentice angel to make Jimmy realize how full & meaningful his life has been.

It's a Wonderful Life. collector's adpt. ed. Perf. by James Stewart & Donna Reed. 1 CD. (Running Time: 1 hr.). (Christmas at Radio Spirits Ser.). 1999. audio compact disk 4.98 (978-1-57019-343-9(6), OTR7012) Pub: Radio Spirits. Dist(s): AudioGO
Starring James Stewart (George Bailey), Donna Reed (Mary Hatch), Victor Moore (Clarence), Bill Johnstone (Mr. Bailey), John McIntire (Joseph), Leo Cleary (Uncle Billy), Edwin Maxwell (Potter) and Janet Scott (Mrs. Bailey). A Lux Radio Theatre hour-long radio adaptation of Frank Capra's 1946 Liberty/RKO film fantasy about a man who thinks his life has had no meaning until an angel shows him differently.

It's a Wonderful Life. collector's adpt. ed. Perf. by James Stewart & Donna Reed. 1 cass. (Running Time: 1 hr.). (Adventures in Old-Time Radio Ser.). 2002. 4.98 (978-1-57019-172-5(7), OTR4159) Pub: Radio Spirits. Dist(s): AudioGO

It's a Wonderful World (Countries A-Z) Listening (Sing & Learn) Composed by Sally K. Albrecht & Jay Althouse. (ENG.). 2005. audio compact disk 13.99 (978-0-7390-3655-6(6)) Alfred Pub.

It's a Wonderful World (Countries A-Z) SoundTrax. Composed by Sally K. Albrecht & Jay Althouse. (ENG.). 2005. audio compact disk 39.95 (978-0-7390-3657-0(2)) Alfred Pub.

It's a Zoo Out There - Animals A to Z (27 Unison Songs for Young Singers) Jay Althouse. Composed by Sally K. Albrecht. (ENG.). 2004. audio compact disk 34.95 (978-0-7390-3459-0(6)) Alfred Pub.

It's a Zoo Out There - Animals A to Z (27 Unison Songs for Young Singers) Sing & Learn. Composed by Sally K. Albrecht & Jay Althouse. (ENG.). 2005. audio compact disk 13.99 (978-0-7390-3634-1(3)) Alfred Pub.

It's a...Bundle. 2001. audio compact disk 129.00 (CZW11505) Am Guidance.

It's All about Cats. Donald Davis. 2007. audio compact disk 14.95 (978-0-87483-873-7(1)) Pub: August Hse. Dist(s): Natl Bk Netwk

It's All about Faith: Rediscovering the Building Blocks of Christianity. Mac Hammond. 2008. audio compact disk 18.00 (978-1-57399-340-1(9)) Mac Hammond.

It's All about Love. Perf. by Gina. 1 cass. 1997. audio compact disk 15.99 CD. (D9951) Diamante Music Grp.
Expands on the themes of God's love & healing that occur when we are in a relationship with Him.

It's All about the Blood with There Is a Fountain. Created by Lillenas Publishing. 2007. audio compact disk 24.99 (978-5-557-54326-2(0)) Lillenas.

It's all Good. unabr. ed. Andrew Daddo. Read by Andrew Daddo. (Running Time: 6 hrs.). 2007. audio compact disk 63.95 (978-1-74093-851-8(8)) Pub: Bolinda Pubng AUS. Dist(s): Bolinda Pub Inc

It's All Good - Positive Thinking Skills: Susan Hite's Train Your Brain Series. Susan Hite. 1 CD. (Running Time: 58 min.). 2002. bk. 15.00 (978-1-890123-54-3(4)) Media Cnslts.
In this inspiring & motivational presentation, Susan Hite teaches you to consciously recognize positive signals and to find the good in all situations at any level.

It's All Made Up: 7 Ideas You Must Know to Create Your Life. Rick Tamlyn. 1 cass. (Running Time: 1 hr. 10 mins.). 2002. 10.00 (978-0-9723130-0-1(1)) Its All Made.
We get to make up our lives however we want! This tape gives you 7 ideas to help you get started!.

It's All Right with Me: An Evening of Cole Porter. Bradford B. Newquist. 1 cass. 1996. 15.00 (978-0-9655404-1-4(3)); audio compact disk 10.00 CD. (978-0-9655404-0-7(5)) Prism Studio.

It's All up to Youth. Larry Johnson. 1 cass. 6.98 (978-1-55503-298-2(2), 06004261) Covenant Comms.
Five guidelines for avoiding pitfalls & being happy in the teen years.

It's All Within Your Reach: How to Live Your Dreams. Michael Wickett. Read by Michael Wickett. 6 cass. 34.95 Set. (450AD) Nightingale-Conant.
Your dreams can come true.

It's Always Darkest Before the Fun Comes Up. Chonda Pierce. 1 cass. 1998. 16.99 (978-0-310-22553-9(1)) Zondervan.

It's always Something. abr. ed. Gilda Radner. 2004. 10.95 (978-0-7435-4871-7(X)) Pub: S&S Audio. Dist(s): S and S Inc

It's Another Fine Day. abr. ed. Created by Focus on the Family. 4 cass. (Adventures in Odyssey Gold Ser.). (ENG.). (J). (gr. 3-7). 2005. audio compact disk 24.99 (978-1-58997-287-2(2)) Pub: Focus Family. Dist(s): Tyndale Hse

***It's Beginning to Look a Lot Like Zombies! The Book of Zombie Christmas Carols.** unabr. ed. Michael P. Spradlin. (Running Time: 2 hrs.). 2010. audio compact disk 12.99 (978-1-4418-5312-7(X), 9781441853127, Bril Audio CD Unabri) Brilliance Audio.

IT's Better to Laugh... Life Good Luck Bad Hair Days & QVC: America's Top Learning Expert Shows How Every Child Can Succeed. Kathy Levine. 2004. 10.95 (978-0-7435-4872-4(8)) Pub: S&S Audio. Dist(s): S and S Inc

It's Called a Breakup Because It's Broken: The Smart Girl's Breakup Buddy. abr. ed. Greg Behrendt & Amiira Ruotola-Behrendt. Read by Greg Behrendt & Amiira Ruotola-Behrendt. (Running Time: 10800 sec.). (ENG.). 2005. audio compact disk 21.95 (978-0-7393-2184-3(6)) Pub: Random Audio Pubg. Dist(s): Random

It's Called Work for a Reason! Your Success Is Your Own Damn Fault. unabr. ed. Larry Winget. Read by Larry Winget. (Running Time: 21600 sec.). (ENG.). (gr. 8 up). 2006. audio compact disk 34.95 (978-0-14-314180-8(5), PengAudBks) Penguin Grp USA.

It's Campmeeting Time: ... in the Choir Loft. Contrib. by Joseph Linn. Prod. by Joseph Linn & Mosie Lister. (ENG.). 1995. audio compact disk 90.00 (978-0-00-506373-6(6)) Lillenas.

It's Christmas. Mormon Tabernacle Choir. 1 cass. 4.98 (120030); audio compact disk 8.98 (140363) Covenant Comms.

It's Christmas Time. Perf. by City on a Hill. 2002. audio compact disk (Essential Records) Brentwood Music.

It's Christmas Time Story CD (Babytown Storybook) Short Stories. Created by Queen Lane. Prod. by Queen Lane. Voice by Jaina Lane. 1 CD. (Running Time: 22 mins). Dramatization. (BABYTOWN Ser.: Bk. 4). (J). 2005. audio compact disk 10.00 (978-0-9772738-6-7(5)) Quebla.
Can you imagine what life would be like if you were born able to talk? Well, Baby can! Considered the town?s most ambitious under-one-nager, Baby is proud to be like-a-girl as she ventures through life dissecting the who, what, and whys of everything in sight. Baby is the littlest prodigy with the biggest imagination, always ready to save the day. Children of all ages will be delighted to see just how silly things can be through the eyes of an infant.It?s Baby?s first Christmas and she has lots to learn about trees, presents, and even Santa Clause. But in IT'S CHRISTMAS TIME, Dad has a special surprise for the family. He wants to share in the Christmas spirit and give some of their presents away. Will Baby give a gift?.

It's Christmastime. Steve Amerson. 2000. 10.98 (978-5-551-04543-4(9)) Pub: Amerson Mus Min. Dist(s): STL Dist NA

It's Christmastime. Steve Amerson. (ENG.). 2004. 15.98 (978-5-551-04542-7(0)) Pub: Amerson Mus Min. Dist(s): STL Dist NA

It's Christmastime Tracks. Steve Amerson. 1 cass. (Running Time: 30 mins.). (ENG.). 2007. 29.95 (978-5-551-04544-1(7)) Pub: Amerson Mus Min. Dist(s): STL Dist NA

It's Cool in the Furnace. Contrib. by Joseph Linn et al. (J). (ps-3). 2007. audio compact disk 16.98 (978-5-557-49267-6(4), Word Music); audio compact disk 8.00 (978-5-557-49261-4(5), Word Music) Word Enter.

It's Earth Day! Early Explorers Fluent Set A Audio CD. Benchmark Education Staff. (J). 2006. audio compact disk 10.00 (978-1-4108-7635-5(7)) Benchmark Educ.

It's Easier Than You Think: The Buddhist Way to Happiness. abr. ed. Sylvia Boorstein. Read by Sylvia Boorstein. 2 cass. (Running Time: 3 hrs.). 1997. 17.95 (978-1-57453-120-6(4)) Audio Lit.

***It's Easy Being Green! A Songbook or Program Teaching Us Ways to Save Our Planet.** Composed by Sally K. Albrecht & Jay Althouse. Contrib. by Tim Hayden. (ENG.). 2010. audio compact disk (978-0-7390-6913-4(6)) Alfred Pub.

***It's Easy Being Green: One Student's Guide to Serving God & Saving the Planet.** Emma Sleeth. (Running Time: 3 hrs. 8 mins. 0 sec.). (Invert Ser.). (ENG.). (YA). 2009. 12.99 (978-0-310-77225-5(7)) Zondervan.

It's Enough to Make a Grown Man Cry. abr. ed. Ken Davis. 1 cass. (Running Time: 1 hr.). 2001. 9.99 (978-1-58926-008-5(2)) Oasis Audio.
A look at the clues around the shortest verse in the Bible to give us a new perspective on why Jesus wept. But he doesn't stop there. "If you know what makes God cry, then you know how to make Him dance with joy!" This wonderfully entertaining audiobook is filled with hope & encouragement for believers of all ages.

It's Fun to Clap. Perf. by William Janiak. 1 cass. (Running Time: 1 hr.). (J). 2001. 10.95 (KIM 70189C) Kimbo Educ.
The LaSong, Shrug Your Shoulders, It's Time for Music, Boom! Boom! Boom!, Shirt, Shirt, Here Comes the Cow, Hop Like a Bunny, The Body Care Song, Make Your Eyes, Hands Go up & Down, I Like to Dance & more. Includes guide.

It's Got to Be Easier Than This. Bill Caskey. 2 CDs. (Running Time: 1 hr 30 mins). 2003. audio compact disk 59.95 (978-0-9722587-4-6(4)) Caskey Ach Strat.

It's Got to Be Easier Than This: New Ideas to Change the Way You Think about Business. 2nd ed. Bill Caskey. 2 CD's and 1 workbo. Orig. Title: It's Got to Be Easier Than This: New Ideas to Change the Way You Think about Business. 2004. audio compact disk 59.95 (978-0-9758510-6-7(3)) Caskey Ach Strat.
Have you ever wondered how to make business easier? Or, how to work the same number of hours and get better results?Caskey is the man who can help you get to the top.How you think determines how you act. And how you act determines your results. So to change results?over a long period of time?you must change thought. And that?s what this program does.? learn how to change your patterns of focus & belief?discover techniques that yield higher results with less stressThese 22 Principles of Thought ? about the market, about your self, about your customer?will dramatically change how you think about selling.And, make it easier. Discover these Rules, Tools and Attitudes that yield higher results with less stress.Bill Caskey is founder of Caskey Achievement Strategies and has been a professional development leader for over 16 years. Professionals across the country practice his strategies to intelligently grow their businesses.It?s Got To Be Easier Than This includes 2 audio CDs, a companion workbook, and a Personal Power card that will serve as a daily reminder of the Fundamental Shifts necessary in selling.

It's Got to Be Easier Than This: New Ideas to Change the Way You Think about Business see It's Got to Be Easier Than This: New Ideas to Change the Way You Think about Business

It's Halloween! Lois Zucek & Gary Earl. 1 cass. (J). (ps-5). 1995. 9.98 incl. text. (978-1-887074-01-8(5)); audio compact disk 12.98 CD. (978-1-887074-00-1(7)) Rainbow Waterfall TM.

***It's Hard to Be Five: Learning How to Work My Control Panel.** abr. ed. Jamie Lee Curtis. Read by Jamie Lee Curtis. 2006. (978-0-06-128537-0(4)) HarperCollins Pubs.

***It's Hard to Be Five: Learning How to Work My Control Panel.** abr. ed. Jamie Lee Curtis. 2007. (978-0-06-123239-8(4)) HarperCollins Pubs.

***It's How You Play the Game & the Games Do Count.** abr. ed. Brian Kilmeade. Read by Brian Kilmeade. (ENG.). 2007. (978-0-06-145083-9(9), Harper Audio) HarperCollins Pubs.

It's How You Play the Game & the Games Do Count CD. abr. ed. Brian Kilmeade. Read by Kilmeade Brian. (ENG.). 2007. (978-0-06-145084-6(7), Harper Audio) HarperCollins Pubs.

It's How You Play the Game/the Games Do Count: The Powerful Sports Moments That Taught Lasting Values to America's Finest/America's Best & Brightest on the Power of Sports. abr. ed. Brian Kilmeade. Read by Brian Kilmeade. (Running Time: 21600 sec.). 2007. audio compact disk 29.95 (978-0-06-125667-7(6), Harper Audio) HarperCollins Pubs.

***It's in His Kiss: the Epilogue II.** unabr. ed. Julia Quinn. Read by Kevan Brighting. (ENG.). 2007. (978-0-06-153702-8(0), Harper Audio); (978-0-06-147272-5(7), Harper Audio) HarperCollins Pubs.

It's in the News. C. Badger & S. H. Hartman. 1 cass. (C). 1981. 75.00 (978-0-7175-0986-7(9)) St Mut.

It's in the Noise. Rita Twiggs. 1 cass. (Running Time: 60 mins.). 2001. 5.99 (978-0-88368-742-0(9), 777429) Pub: Whitaker Hse. Dist(s): Anchor Distributors

It's Just Like Heaven. 2005. audio compact disk 9.99 (978-5-559-07877-9(8)) Pt of Grace Ent.

It's Just the Way I Am Set: What to Do When Temperaments Differ. David Grudermeyer & Rebecca Grudermeyer. 2 cass. 18.95 INCL. HANDOUTS. (T-50) Willingness Wrks.

It's Justin Time, Amber Brown. Paula Danziger. Illus. by Tony Ross. (Running Time: 17 mins.). (J). (gr. k-3). 2002. 12.95 (978-1-59112-365-1(8)) Live Oak Media.

It's Justin Time, Amber Brown. Paula Danziger. 14 vols. (Running Time: 17 mins.). (J). 2002. pap. bk. & tchr.'s planning gde. ed. 29.95 (978-0-87499-908-2(1)) Live Oak Media.
This easy-reader goes back to when Amber is turning seven and wants nothing more than a watch. Her best friend, Justin, has no regard for keeping time, much to Amber's dismay.

It's Justin Time, Amber Brown. Paula Danziger. Illus. by Tony Ross. 14 vols. (Running Time: 17 mins.). 2002. pap. bk. 31.95 (978-1-59112-566-2(9)) Live Oak Media.

It's Justin Time, Amber Brown. abr. ed. Paula Danziger. 11 vols. (Running Time: 17 mins.). (J). (ps-2). 2002. bk. 25.95 (978-0-87499-907-5(3)); pap. bk. 16.95 (978-0-87499-906-8(5)) Pub: Live Oak Media. Dist(s): AudioGO

Its Love 101:Is Jesus Really God? 1 John 1: 1-3. Ben Young. 1996. 4.95 (978-0-7417-6008-1(8), B0008) Win Walk.

It's Magic: Doris Day's Early Years at Warner Brothers. 1 cass. 1998. 11.98 (978-1-56826-970-2(6)) Rhino Enter.

It's Mine! Leo Lionni. (J). 1986. 18.66 SRA McGraw.

It's Murder Going Home. unabr. ed. Marlys Millhiser. Read by Lynda Evans. 8 cass. (Running Time: 9 hrs. 30 min.). (Charlie Greene Mystery Ser.: Bk. 4). 2001. 49.95 (978-1-55686-796-5(4)) Books in Motion.
Charlie returns home for her mother's surgery, only to face the case of a missing neighbor, and the forgotten father of Charlie's own daughter.

***It's My America Too.** abr. ed. Ben Ferguson. Read by Ben Ferguson. (ENG.). 2004. (978-0-06-078549-9(7), Harper Audio); (978-0-06-081498-4(5), Harper Audio) HarperCollins Pubs.

It's Never Crowded along the Extra Mile. Wayne W. Dyer. 6 cass. (ENG.). 2002. reel tape 59.95 (978-1-4019-0171-4(9), 1719) Hay House.

It's Never Too Late: Leading Adolescents to Lifelong Literacy. unabr. ed. Janet Allen. Narrated by Ruth Ann Phimister. 6 cass. (Running Time: 7 hrs. 45 mins.). 1999. 51.00 (978-0-7887-2390-2(1), 95546E7) Recorded Bks.
An inside look at some of the problems faced by teenagers in the classroom. This practical "how-to" program will appeal to teachers, parents & anyone else concerned about indifferent or hostile students.

It's Never Too Late to Be Friends. David Christensen & Michael Christensen. 11.95 (978-1-56236-711-4(0)) Pub: Aspen Bks. Dist(s): Origin Bk Sales

It's Never Too Late to Be Great! Bernadette Greggory. Narrated by Bernadette Greggory. Music by Tracy Collins. (ENG.). 2008. 11.00 (978-0-9662049-1-9(5)) B Greggory Assocs.

It's Never Too Late to be Great. unabr. ed. Bernadette Greggory. Read by Bernadette Greggory. 1 cass. (Running Time: 1 hr.). 1997. 13.95 (978-0-9662049-0-2(5)) B Greggory Assocs.
Explores the inner path to self discovery. The greatness that lies within each of us, lighting our way & giving us the courage to live our dreams.

It's Not about Me. Perf. by Ametria. 1 cass. 2000. 11.98 (978-0-7601-3449-8(9), SO36143); audio compact disk (978-0-7601-3448-1(0), SO36143) Brentwood Music.
Songs include: "God Is So Good," "Prayer Changes Things," "Wait," "No Weapon," "His Love" & more.

It's Not about Me: Rescue from the Life We Thought Would Make Us Happy. abr. unabr. ed. Max Lucado. 2 cass. 2004. 15.99 (978-1-59145-162-4(0)) Nelson.

It's Not about the Bike: My Journey Back to Life. abr. ed. Lance Armstrong & Sally Jenkins. Read by Oliver Wyman. 4 CDs. (Running Time: 4 hrs.). (ENG.). 2000. audio compact disk 29.95 (978-1-56511-449-4(3), 1565114493) Pub: HighBridge. Dist(s): Workman Pub

Its Not about the Coffee: Leadership Lessons from a Life at Starbucks. unabr. ed. Howard Behar. Read by Malcolm Hillgartner. Told to Janet Goldstein. Frwd. by Howard Schultz. (Running Time: 16200 sec.). 2007. 19.95 (978-1-4332-0802-7(4)) Blckstn Audio.

It's Not about the Coffee: Leadership Principles from a Life at Starbucks. unabr. ed. Howard Behar. Read by Malcolm Hillgartner. Told to Janet Goldstein. Frwd. by Howard Schultz. (Running Time: 16200 sec.). 2007. audio compact disk 19.95 (978-1-4332-0803-4(2)) Blckstn Audio.

It's Not about the Coffee: Leadership Principles from a Life at Starbucks. unabr. ed. Howard Behar. Read by Malcolm Hillgartner. Told to Janet Goldstein. Frwd. by Howard Schultz. (Running Time: 16200 sec.). 2008. 24.95 (978-1-4332-0805-8(9)); audio compact disk 19.95 (978-1-4332-0804-1(0)); audio compact disk & audio compact disk 27.00 (978-1-4332-0806-5(7)) Blckstn Audio.

It's Not about the Money. unabr. ed. Bob Proctor. Read by Bob Proctor. (Running Time: 6 hrs.). (ENG.). 2009. 24.98 (978-1-59659-370-1(9), GildAudio) Pub: Gildan Media. Dist(s): HachBkGrp

It's Not about the Money. unabr. ed. Bob Proctor. Read by Bob Proctor. (Running Time: 6 hrs.). (ENG.). 2009. audio compact disk 29.98 (978-1-59659-376-3(8), GildAudio) Pub: Gildan Media. Dist(s): HachBkGrp

It's Not about the Truth: The Untold Story of the Duke Lacrosse Case & the Lives It Shattered. unabr. ed. Don Yaeger & Mike Pressler. Narrated by Dick Hill. (Running Time: 11 hrs. 0 mins. 0 sec.). (ENG.). 2007. audio compact disk 34.99 (978-1-4001-0520-5(X)); audio compact disk 69.99 (978-1-4001-3520-2(6)); audio compact disk 24.99 (978-1-4001-5520-0(7)) Pub: Tantor Media. Dist(s): IngramPubServ

***It's Not as Bad as You Think: Why Capitalism Trumps Fear & the Economy Will Thrive.** unabr. ed. Brian S. Wesbury. Read by Sean Pratt. (Running Time: 7 hrs. 30 mins.). (ENG.). 2009. 26.98 (978-1-59659-489-0(6), GildAudio) Pub: Gildan Media. Dist(s): HachBkGrp

It's not Easy being a Goddess. Barbara McBride-Smith. (Running Time: 1 hr.). 1998. audio compact disk 14.95 (978-0-87483-761-2(8)) Pub: August Hse. Dist(s): Natl Bk Netwk

It's Not Easy Being Green: And Other Things to Consider. abr. ed. Jim Henson et al. Read by Jerry Nelson et al. 1 CD. (Running Time: 3600 sec.). 2005. audio compact disk 17.98 (978-1-4013-8329-9(7)) Pub: Hyperion. Dist(s): HarperCollins Pubs

It's Not Fair! Short Stories. Carl Sommer. Narrated by Carl Sommer. 1 cass. Dramatization. (Another Sommer-Time Story Ser.). (J). 2003. bk. 16.95 (978-1-57537-569-4(9)) Advance Pub.

It's Not Fair! Narrated by Carl Sommer. 1 cass. Dramatization. (Another Sommer-Time Story Ser.). (J). (gr. k-4). 2003. lib. bdg. 23.95 (978-1-57537-770-4(5)) Advance Pub.

Karacter Kidz Song included with narration by the author Carl Sommer.

***It's Not Fair! / ¡No Es Justo!** ed. Carl Sommer. Illus. by Greg Budwine. (Another Sommer-Time Story Bilingual Ser.). (ENG & SPA.). (J). 2009. bk. 26.95 (978-1-57537-180-1(4)) Advance Pub.

It's Not Fair, Jeremy Spencer's Parents Let Him Stay up All Night! A Guide to the Tougher Parts of Parenting. unabr. ed. Anthony E. Wolf. Narrated by George Guidall. 5 cass. (Running Time: 7 hrs.). 44.00 (978-0-7887-0625-7(X), 94799E7) Recorded Bks.

The Author of "Get Out of My Life, but First Could You Drive Me & Cheryl to the Mall," focuses on parenting's most difficult challenges: setting limits & making children behave. Available to libraries only.

It's Not Just Who You Know: Transform Your Life (And Your Organization) by Turning Colleagues & Contacts into Lasting, Genuine Relationships. unabr. ed. Thomas Spaulding & Tommy Spaulding. Read by Dustin Rubin. Frwd. by Ken Blanchard. 2010. audio compact disk 30.00 (978-0-307-73612-3(1), Random AudioBks) Pub: Random Audio Pubg. Dist(s): Random

It's Not My Fault: The No-Excuse Plan to Put You in Charge of Your Life. unabr. ed. Henry Cloud & John Townsend. Narrated by Henry Cloud & John Townsend. (ENG.). 2007. 16.09 (978-1-60814-260-6(4)); audio compact disk 22.99 (978-1-59859-183-5(5)) Oasis Audio.

It's Not My Turn to Look for Grandma! And Other Stories. unabr. ed. Short Stories. April Halprin Wayland. Read by April Halprin Wayland. Perf. by Barney Saltzberg et al. Illus. by George Booth. 1 CD. (Running Time: 40 mins.). 2000. audio compact disk (978-0-9666277-1-8(7)) April H Wayland.

5 stories & 17 poems that include "Chickadilla Song," accompanied by fiddle, banjo & spoons. Title story is a brand new hill tale with lots of pep.

It's Not My Turn to Look for Grandma! And Other Stories. unabr. ed. April Halprin Wayland. Read by April Halprin Wayland. Perf. by Barney Saltzberg et al. 1 cass. (Running Time: 40 min.). (gr. k-12). 1997. (978-0-9666277-0-1(9), EAN:90000) April H Wayland.

Includes 5 stories, 17 poems: "Chickadilla Song," accompanied by fiddle, banjo, spoons.

It's Not Odd - It's GOD!! God's Miracles & Other Stories of His Grace & Mercy in the Lifetime of an Old Lady. Lo-Dee Hammock. 2007. audio compact disk 19.95 (978-0-9800625-1-9(9)) Sun King Media.

It's Not over until You Win! How to Become the Person You Always Wanted to Be - No Matter What the Obstacles. Les Brown. 2004. 7.95 (978-0-7435-1886-4(1)) Pub: S&S Audio. Dist(s): S and S Inc

It's Not over until You Win! How to Become the Person You Always Wanted to Be - No Matter What the Obstacles. abr. ed. Les Brown. Read by Les Brown. 2 CDs. (Running Time: 13 hrs. 0 mins. 0 sec.). (ENG.). 2005. audio compact disk 19.95 (978-0-7435-5035-2(8)) Pub: S&S Audio. Dist(s): S and S Inc

Les Brown is one of the most popular motivational speakers in the world today. In It's Not Over Until You Win!, Brown offers a powerful and inspirational plan to help people overcome any obstacle in their lives. Les Brown himself has been through countless ups and downs, suffering through personal and career crises including the cancellation of his television show and the death of his beloved mother. In this unique audio program, Brown tells you how he rose from those depths and how you can, too. It's Not Over Until You Win! will demonstrate: How to cope with the loss of a loved one How to recover self-esteem when you lose your job How to keep away from self-destructive behavior Filled with the passion and exuberance that will empower you to overcome any obstacle, It's Not Over Until You Win! captures the amazing spirit of Brown's electric speaking style in a sure-fire empowerment audiobook that will galvanize anyone to take their lives to a higher level of satisfaction and fulfillment.

It's Not the Big That Eat the Small... It's the Fast That Eat the Slow: How to Use Speed As a Competitive Tool in Business. abr. ed. Jason Jennings & Laurence Haughton. Read by Jason Jennings & Laurence Haughton. 5 CDs. (Running Time: 7.5 hrs.). 2004. audio compact disk 34.95 (978-1-59007-039-0(9)) Pub: New Millenn Enter. Dist(s): PerseuPGW

If you want to think quicker & act faster, all the information you need is here. You'll find real-life lessons from the speediest international business people & companies on how to become faster than anyone else in today's ever-changing business world.

It's Not the Big That Eat the Small... It's the Fast That Eat the Slow: How to Use Speed As a Competitive Tool in Business. unabr. ed. Jason Jennings & Laurence Haughton. Read by Jason Jennings & Laurence Haughton. 6 cass. (Running Time: 7.5 hrs.). 2004. 29.95 (978-1-59007-017-8(8)) Pub: New Millenn Enter. Dist(s): PerseuPGW

It's Not the Dress, It's the Girl in the Dress. Elizabeth Craig. 2008. audio compact disk 14.95 (978-1-60641-085-1(7)) Deseret Bk.

It's Not the End of the World. unabr. ed. Judy Blume. 1 cass. (Running Time: 1 hr. 22 min.). (Young Adult Cliffhangers Ser.). (YA). (gr. 5 up). 1985. 15.98 incl. bk. & guide. (978-0-8072-1820-4(0), JRH110SP, Listening Lib) Random Audio Pubg.

Somehow Karen must keep her parents together...forever! That is, if she can figure out a way for them to talk to each other face to face. When her parents finally do meet, Karen isn't prepared for the outcome.

***It's Not the End of the World.** unabr. ed. Judy Blume. (ENG.). (J). 2011. audio compact disk 28.00 (978-0-307-74768-6(9), Listening Lib) Pub: Random Audio Pubg. Dist(s): Random

It's Not the Fall That Kills You: Laughing All the Way to That Sudden Stop at the End. unabr. ed. Joe Malarkey. Read by Joe Malarkey. 2 cass. (Running Time: 1 hr. 40 min.). 1998. 24.95 Set. (978-1-892447-08-1(8)) Laten Print.

It's Not Too Late. David Minazian. Music by William Drews. 1 cass. (Running Time: 42 min.). 9.95 (978-1-878993-87-8(9)); audio compact disk 11.95 (978-1-878993-86-1(0)) Jeremiah Films.

Collection of ten songs.

It's Not What You Sell, It's What You Stand For: Why Every Extraordinary Business Is Driven by Purpose. unabr. ed. Roy M. Spence, Jr. & Haley Rushing. Read by Bill Weideman. (Running Time: 9 hrs.). 2009. 39.97 (978-1-4233-8139-6(4), 9781423381396, BADLE); 24.99 (978-1-4233-8138-9(6), 9781423381389, BAD); 24.99 (978-1-4233-8136-5(X), 9781423381365, Brilliance MP3) Brilliance Audio.

It's Not What You Sell, It's What You Stand For: Why Every Extraordinary Business Is Driven by Purpose. unabr. ed. Roy M. Spence, Jr. & Haley Rushing. Read by Bill Weideman. 1 MP3-CD. (Running Time: 9 hrs.). 2009. 39.97 (978-1-4233-8137-2(8), 9781423381372, Brlnc Audio MP3 Lib); audio compact disk 87.97 (978-1-4233-8135-8(1), 9781423381358, BriAudCD Unabrid); audio compact disk 29.99 (978-1-4233-8134-1(3), 9781423381341, Bril Audio CD Unabri) Brilliance Audio.

It's Not What You're Eating, It's What's Eating You. abr. ed. Janet Greeson. 2004. 7.95 (978-0-7435-4885-4(X)) Pub: S&S Audio. Dist(s): S and S Inc

It's Not What You're Eating, It's What's Eating You: The 28-Day Plan to Heal Hidden Food Addiction. abr. ed. Janet Greeson. Read by Janet Greeson. Ed. by Simon and Schuster Staff. 1 cass. (Running Time: 90 min.). 1994. Rental 4.00 S&S Audio.

The audio program will teach listeners: How to recognize food addiction & overeating, How to use psychological techniques to banish depression, Vitamin & mineral therapies to reduce stress & cravings, How to break the dieting & binge-purge cycles & learn to eat normally. A powerful audio work that addresses the physical, emotional & spiritual causes of food addiction, this will help any food addict discover the keys to reshape their body & mind.

It's Not Your Fault. 2001. 6.00 (978-1-58602-099-6(4)) E L Long.

It's Ok - Say "No"! Betty L. Randolph. (Running Time: 45 min.). (Educational Ser.). 1989. bk. 15.98; 9.98 (978-1-55909-103-9(7), 85S) Randolph Tapes.

It's Ok If You're Clueless: And 23 More Tips for the College Bound. unabr. ed. Terry McMillan. (Running Time: 2700 sec.). 2006. audio compact disk 19.95 (978-1-4193-9733-2(8)) Recorded Bks.

It's Ok to Be Different: Olliver's Adventures on Monkey Island. unabr. ed. Trenna Daniells. 12 cass. (Running Time: 30 min.). (One to Grow On Ser.). (J). (gr. k-6). 1982. 9.95 (978-0-918519-03-0(9), 12002) Trenna Prods.

Offers a good example of how to deal with the peer pressures of being different.

It's Ok to Be Different - Olliver's Adventures on Monkey Island. Trenna Daniells. Narrated by Trenna Daniells. (J). 2009. (978-0-918519-27-6(6)) Trenna Prods.

It's Ok to Be Yourself: Frog's Magic Journey. Trenna Sutphen. Read by Trenna Sutphen. 1 cass. (Running Time: 30 min.). (One to Grow On! Ser.). (J). (gr. 4 up). 7.95 (12011) Trenna Prods.

It's Only a Game. Terry Bradshaw & David Fisher. 2004. 10.95 (978-0-7435-4887-8(6)) Pub: S&S Audio. Dist(s): S and S Inc

It's Only a Game. abr. ed. Terry Bradshaw. Read by Terry Bradshaw. 3 CDs. (Running Time: 3 hrs.). 2001. audio compact disk 24.00 S&S Audio.

From his humble beginnings in Shreveport, Louisiana, to his success as the centerpiece of the highest rated football studio show in television history, Terry has always understood the importance of hard work. A veritable jack-of-all-trades, he has probably held more jobs than any other football Hall of Famer ever, from being a pipeline worker, a youth minister, a professional singer, actor, television and radio talk show host, to one of the nation's most popular speakers.

It's Only Me: The Ted Williams We Hardly Knew. John Underwood. 2005. bk. 27.95 (978-1-57243-695-4(6)) Triumph Bks.

It's Our Ship: The No-Nonsense Guide to Leadership. abr. ed. D. Michael Abrashoff. Read by D. Michael Abrashoff. (Running Time: 3 hrs. 30 mins.). (ENG.). 2008. 16.98 (978-1-60024-158-1(1)); audio compact disk 24.98 (978-1-60024-157-4(3)) Pub: Hachet Audio. Dist(s): HachBkGrp

It's Our World. unabr. ed. Cake and Candle Cassettes, Inc. Staff. Read by Ron Trigilio & Mary Camire. 1 cass. (Running Time: 26 min.). (J). (gr. k-8). 1993. 7.95 (978-0-9649745-4-8(1)) Cake & Candle.

Personalized audio cassette tape which narrates & sings a child's first name, encouraging the child to dream, imagine, plan & unite with children throughout the world.

It's Raining in Mango. unabr. ed. Thea Astley. Read by Jan Friedl. 7 cass. (Running Time: 10 hrs. 30 mins.). 1998. (978-1-86442-301-3(3), 580951) Bolinda Pubng AUS.

Tale of one Australian family traced from the 1860's to the 1980's, beginning with Cornelius Laffey, an Irish-born journalist who wrestled his kin from the easy living of 19th century Sydney, to take them to Northern Queensland where thousands of hopefuls are digging for gold in the mud.

***It's Raining Pigs & Noodles.** unabr. ed. Jack Prelutsky. Read by Jack Prelutsky. (ENG.). 2008. (978-0-06-162967-9(7)); (978-0-06-162968-6(5)) HarperCollins Pubs.

It's Raining Pigs & Noodles. unabr. abr. ed. Jack Prelutsky. Read by Jack Prelutsky. 1 CD. (Running Time: 1 hr.). (J). (gr. k-5). 2008. 14.95 (978-0-06-145135-5(5), HarperChildAud) HarperCollins Pubs.

It's So Good: Fun English Songs for Children. Lyrics by Alain Le Lait. Music by Alain Le Lait. Des. by Christy Pitts. 1CD & 1bk. (Running Time: 30 minutes). (J). 2003. audio compact disk 15.95 (978-0-9747122-0-8(5), ENG100) Yadeeda.

Original songs by Alain Le Lait, great for ESL programs.

It's Story Telling Time with Linda Goss. Read by Linda Goss. 1 cass. (Running Time: 60 mins.). (J). 1999. 12.95 (F-45034) African Am Imag.

It's Superman! unabr. ed. Tom De Haven. Read by Scott Brick. (Running Time: 59400 sec.). 2006. 29.95 (978-0-7861-4724-3(5)); 79.95 (978-0-7861-4838-7(1)); audio compact disk 29.95 (978-0-7861-6547-6(2)); audio compact disk 29.95 (978-0-7861-7317-4(3)); audio compact disk 99.00 (978-0-7861-6133-1(7)) Blckstn Audio.

It's Thanksgiving. unabr. ed. Jack Prelutsky. Read by Jack Prelutsky. 1 read-along cass. (Running Time: 12 min.). (Follow the Reader Ser.). (J). (gr. 1-3). 1985. 15.98 incl. bk. & guide. (978-0-8072-0082-7(4), FTR96SP, Listening Lib) Random Audio Pubg.

Twelve humorous, nostalgic and fanciful poetic reminiscences.

***It's the Best Day Ever, Dad!** unabr. ed. Brooke Shields. Read by Brooke Shields. (ENG.). 2009. (978-0-06-177594-9(0)); (978-0-06-180595-0(5)) HarperCollins Pubs.

It's the Miracle. 1 cass. (Running Time: 36 min.). 1998. 9.95; 14.98 CD. Baker Taylor.

Collection of melodic, catchy, & singable songs will inspire joyful Hanukkah singing.

It's the Most Wonderful Time of the Year. Contrib. by Point of Grace. (Studio Ser.). 2005. audio compact disk 9.98 (978-5-558-82758-3(0), Word Records) Word Enter.

It's the Truth. Rosenshontz. Perf. by Gary Rosen & Bill Shontz. 1 cass. (Running Time: 38 min.). (Rosenshontz Ser.). (J). (ps-6). 1992. 8.98 (978-1-879496-53-8(4)); audio compact disk 13.98 CD. (978-1-56896-039-5(5)) Lightyear Entrtnmnt.

A two-man duo singing delightful children's songs.

It's the Truth. Rosenshontz. Perf. by Gary Rosen & Bill Shontz. 1 cass. (Running Time: 38 min.). (Rosenshontz Ser.). (J). (ps-6). 1993. pap. bk. 8.98 Incl. Long Box. (978-1-879496-54-5(2)) Lightyear Entrtnmnt.

It's Time! Sundance/Newbridge, LLC Staff. (Early Math Ser.). (gr. k-1). 2000. 12.00 (978-1-58273-314-2(7)) Sund Newbrdge.

It's Time: Calling Forth God's Gift. Lisa Bevere. 2004. audio compact disk 14.99 (978-1-933185-46-0(5)) Messengr Intl.

It's Time CD. 2007. audio compact disk 14.99 (978-1-933185-20-0(1)) Messengr Intl.

It's Time for Music. Merrill Staton Entertainment Staff et al. (ENG.). 1995. audio compact disk 9.95 (978-0-7390-1680-0(6), 14067) Alfred Pub.

It's Time for Saturn. E. Pacetti. 1 cass. (Running Time: 60 min.). 1992. 8.95 (1080) Am Fed Astrologers.

***It's Time Life Message Series.** Lisa Bevere. 2010. audio compact disk 0.00 (978-1-933185-67-5(8)) Messengr Intl.

It's Time Now to Break Your Box. Rita Twiggs. 1 cass. (Running Time: 60 mins.). 2001. 5.99 (978-0-88368-744-4(5), 777445) Pub: Whitaker Hse. Dist(s): Anchor Distributors

It's Time to Believe God. Creflo A. Dollar. 2 cass. (Running Time: 3 hrs.). 2001. 10.00 (978-1-931172-86-8(2), TS66, Kidz Faith) Pub: Creflo Dollar. Dist(s): STL Dist NA

It's Time to Pray! Creflo A. Dollar. 2 cass. (Running Time: 3 hrs.). 2000. 10.00 (978-1-931172-56-1(0), TS236, Kidz Faith) Pub: Creflo Dollar. Dist(s): STL Dist NA

It's Time to Rally! Mark Crow. 2 cass. (Running Time: 2 hrs.). 2001. (978-1-931537-19-3(4)) Vision Comm Creat.

It's Time to Receive. Speeches. Creflo A. Dollar. 2 cass. (Running Time: 3 hrs.). 2002. 10.00 (978-1-59089-224-4(0)) Creflo Dollar.

It's Time to Rest: Living in the Goodness of God. Speeches. Creflo A. Dollar. 3 cass. (Running Time: 4 hrs.). 2001. 15.00 (978-1-59089-144-5(9)) Creflo Dollar.

It's Time to Reveal What God Longs to Heal Audio Book: Naked & Not Ashamed. T. D. Jakes. 2008. audio compact disk 29.99 (978-0-7684-2721-9(5)) Destiny Image Pubs.

It's Time To Seek The Lord. Gary V. Whe[illegible]e. 4 cass. (Running Time: 6 hrs.). (Empowerment Ser.). 1996. pap[illegible].00 (978-1-58866-190-6(3), VE012A) Gary Whet Pub.

Are you frustrated because what you planned for your life hasn't happened yet?.

It's Time to Sleep, My Love & On the Night You Were Born: The You Are Loved Collection. unabr. ed. Nancy Tillman & Eric Metaxas. 1 CD. (Running Time: 1 hr. 0 mins. 0 sec.). (ENG., (J). (ps-7). 2008. audio compact disk 14.95 (978-1-4272-0553-7(1)) Pub: Macmill Audio. Dist(s): Macmillan

It's Time to Straighten Up. 2 CASS. 2004. 9.99 (978-1-58602-198-6(2)); audio compact disk 19.99 (978-1-58602-199-3(0)) E L Long.

It's Time to Wake up (Niki Davies) Niki Davies. bk. 17.95 (978-1-85909-669-7(7), Warner Bro) Alfred Pub.

It's Toddler Time. Created by Carol Hammett & Elaine Bueffel. 1 CD. (Running Time: 1 hr.). (J). 2001. pap. bk. 14.95 (KIM 0815CD) Kimbo Educ.

Here's the record you've been asking for. Activities & exercises created specifically for toddler fitness & development. Top of the Morning, Head, Shoulders, Knees & Toes, Itsy, Bitsy Spider, If You're Happy & You Know It & 15 more. Includes guide with lyrics & activities.

It's Toddler Time. Created by Carol Hammett & Elaine Bueffel. 1 cass. (Running Time: 1 hr.). (J). (ps). 2001. 10.95 (KIM 0815C) Kimbo Educ.

It's Too Frightening for Me. unabr. ed. Shirley Hughes. Read by John Bennett. 1 cass. (Running Time: 1 hr.). (J). 1995. 9.95 (978-1-85549-246-2(6), CTC 078, Chivers Child Audio) AudioGO.

It's You. Interview with Donna Lander. Prod. by Yaron Gershovsky. 1 cass. (Running Time: 59 min.). (C). 1998. 9.95 (978-1-890161-34-7(9), SWP615C); audio compact disk 15.95 (978-1-890161-35-4(7), SWP615CD) Sounds Write.

Thirteen English songs based on Judaic texts & life cycle events. Arranged by Gershovsky, musical director of "Manhattan Transfer".

***It's Your Call: What Are You Doing Here?** unabr. ed. Gary Barkalow. Narrated by Gary Barkalow. (Running Time: 5 hrs. 9 mins. 23 sec.). (ENG.). 2010. 13.99 (978-1-60814-771-7(1)); audio compact disk 19.99 (978-1-59859-805-6(8)) Oasis Audio.

It's Your Career - Power It. Scripts. David J. Bowman. 1 cass, 1 CD. (Running Time: 40 mins). Dramatization. 2002. pap. bk. 24.99 (978-0-9742258-0-7(0)) TTG Consultants.

Contains a 40 minute Audio Cassette and an Audio CD. It provides the easy way to a better, higher paying job. The fast track to extra quality in life. This "career insurance" is a permanent investment in your future. This audio will show you the way to a rewarding career that will increase your financial security.

It's Your Misfortune & None of My Own. abr. ed. Stephen A. Bly. 2 cass. (Running Time: 3 hrs.). (Code of the West Ser.: No. 1). 2001. 17.99 (978-1-58926-005-4(8)) Oasis Audio.

A Colorado rancher & a Kentucky lady have agreed to marry sight unseen. Both die & two other individuals with dubious pasts, unknown to one another, take up their identities & their destinies.

It's Your Misfortune & None of My Own. unabr. ed. Stephen A. Bly. Read by Jerry Sciarrio. 6 cass. (Running Time: 6 hrs. 6 min.). (Code of the West Ser.: Bk. 1). 2001. 39.95 (978-1-58116-035-2(6)) Books in Motion.

When a stagecoach wreck forces dance hall girl Pepper Paige to care for an injured woman, Pepper sees her big chance when the "mail order bride" dies from her injuries. Pepper sets off to meet this "successful" rancher.

It's Your Money (Isn't It?) Narrated by Edward Reid. 6 CDs. (Running Time: 6 hrs). 2004. audio compact disk 29.95 (978-0-9711134-1-1(6)) Review & Herald.

Audio track from the video seminar by the same title.

It's Your Move! Kenneth W. Hagin, Jr. 2 cass. 1995. 8.00 Set. (33J) Faith Lib Pubns.

It's Your Move! Transform Your Dreams from Wishful Thinking to Reality. Scripts. Dannye Williamsen. Perf. by John Dean Williamsen. 5 CDs. (Running Time: 4 hrs. 30 mins.). (ENG.). 2004. audio compact disk 34.95 (978-0-9726058-0-9(0), 770-438-0889) Williamsen Pubns.
IT'S YOUR MOVE! is designed to provide not only an understanding of the creative process that is taking place in your life and ours, but also to offer information about the tools you have for working with this process. Just as important is the heads-up it provides about the pitfalls you may encounter on your efforts toward personal growth and the strategies that can help you work through these obstacles. It is a no-frills approach to the work of change.

It's Your Ship: Management Techniques from the Best Damn Ship in the Navy. abr. ed. D. Michael Abrashoff. (Running Time: 3 hrs.). (ENG.). 2006. 14.98 (978-1-59483-496-7(2)); audio compact disk 24.98 (978-1-59483-196-6(3)) Pub: Hachet Audio. Dist(s): HachBkGrp

It's Your Ship: Management Techniques from the Best Damn Ship in the Navy. abr. ed. D. Michael Abrashoff. (Running Time: 3 hrs.). (ENG.). 2009. 39.98 (978-1-60788-109-4(8)) Pub: Hachet Audio. Dist(s): HachBkGrp

It's Your Ship: Managing Techniques from the Best Damn Ship in the Navy. D. Michael Abrashoff. Narrated by George Wilson. 5 cass. (Running Time: 6 hrs. 30 mins.). 47.00 (978-1-4025-3216-0(4)) Recorded Bks.

It's Your Time: Activate Your Faith, Achieve Your Dreams, & Increase in God's Favor. abr. ed. Joel Osteen. Read by Joel Osteen. 5 CDs. (Running Time: 6 hrs. 0 mins. 0 sec.). (ENG.). 2009. audio compact disk 29.99 (978-0-7435-9685-5(4)) Pub: S&S Audio. Dist(s): S and S Inc

It's Your Turn to Be Blessed, Pts. 1-2. C. S. Lovett. 1 cass. (Running Time: 60 min.). 6.95 (556) Prsnl Christianity.
Relax & soak up the teachings of Dr. Lovett. Hear the truths of the blessing book presented in a different light.

It's Your Turn to Be Blessed, Pts. 3-4. C. S. Lovett. 1 cass. (Running Time: 60 min.). 6.95 (557) Prsnl Christianity.
A continuation of the teaching by Dr. Lovett, covering all four sections of the book.

Its Zoo Out There. Sally Albrecht. (ENG.). 2005. audio compact disk 14.95 (978-0-7390-3994-6(6)) Alfred Pub.

Itsy Bitsy Spider. unabr. ed. Iza Trapani. Read by Brownie Macintosh & Julie Thompson. 1 cass. (Running Time: 8 min.). (J). (gr. k-4). 1994. pap. bk. 17.90 (978-0-8045-6767-1(0), 6767) Spoken Arts.
American Bookseller Pick of the Lists.

Itsy Bitsy Spider Climbs Again Audio CD. Adapted by Benchmark Education Company Staff. Based on a work by Jeffrey B. Fuerst. (Reader's Theater Nursery Rhymes & Songs Ser.). (J). (gr. k-1). 2008. audio compact disk 10.00 (978-1-60437-992-1(8)) Benchmark Educ.

Itsy Bitsy Spider's Heroic Climb. unabr. ed. David Novak. Read by David Novak. 1 cass. (Running Time: 1 hr. 3 mins.). (American Storytelling Ser.). (J). (ps-3). 1994. bk. 12.00 (978-0-87483-346-1(9)) August Hse.
Recorded live with children's laughter & participation.

Itty Bitty Phonics Readers. Short Stories. Rozanne Lanczak Williams. Prod. by Steven Traugh. 2 CDs. (Running Time: 3 hrs.). (J). (ps-2). 2002. audio compact disk 18.99 (978-1-57471-993-2(9), 3265) Creat Teach Pr.
2 CDs that contain 36 book title readings with an echo and narration reading of each title. Coordinates with book assortment CTP 3258.

Itty-Bitty Songs for Itty-Bitty Folks. Perf. by Victor Cockburn et al. 1 cass. (Running Time: 42 min.). (J). (ps up). 1992. 10.00 (978-0-944941-07-2(9)) Talking Stone Pr.
Traditional & original songs for young children.

Ivan el Imbecil y Otros Cuentos. unabr. ed. Leon Tolstoi. Read by Guillermo Piedrahita. 3 CDs.Tr. of Ivan the Idiot, & Other Tales. (SPA.). 2001. audio compact disk 17.00 (978-958-9494-37-0(4)) YoYoMusic.

Ivan Takes a Wife see Love Overboard

Ivan the Idiot, & Other Tales see Ivan el Imbecil y Otros Cuentos

Ivan the Idiot, & Other Tales. Leo Tolstoy. Read by Guillermo Piedrahita. (Running Time: 3 hrs.). 2001. 16.95 (978-1-60083-173-7(7), Audiofy Corp) Iofy Corp.

Ivan the Not-So Terrible: Getting to Yesterday/the Coffin Caper/Where There's a Will. Rich Stim. Read by Peter Rofé. (Running Time: 4080 sec.). (J). (gr. k-6). 2007. audio compact disk 12.95 (978-1-933781-07-5(6)) TallTales Aud.

Ivan the Terrible. unabr. ed. Henri Troyat. Read by John MacDonald. 6 cass. (Running Time: 9 hrs.). 1986. 48.00 Set. (978-0-7366-1059-9(6), 1986) Books on Tape.
By the time of his coronation at age 17, Ivan's hunger for blood was matched only by his other sensual appetites. He was the first Russian ruler to call himself Czar, to gain for himself the power of an autocrat & to leave behind a record that would make Stalin blush.

Ivanhoe. Walter Scott, Sr. Narrated by Flo Gardner. (ENG.). 2007. audio compact disk 44.95 (978-1-55685-944-1(9)) Audio Bk Con.

Ivanhoe. Walter Scott, Sr. Narrated by Christopher Lee. 2004. audio compact disk 39.95 (978-0-563-52482-3(0)) AudioGO.

Ivanhoe. Walter Scott, Sr. Read by Carlos Zambrano. (Running Time: 3 hrs.). 2001. 16.95 (978-1-60083-167-6(2), Audiofy Corp) Iofy Corp.

Ivanhoe. Walter Scott, Sr. Read by Jim Killavey. 14 cass. (Running Time: 21 hrs.). 1986. 69.00 incl. album. (C-159) Jimcin Record.
Gallant knight fights evil.

Ivanhoe. Walter Scott, Sr. Read by Jonathan Oliver. 2 cass. (Running Time: 2 hrs. 30 mins.). 1994. 13.98 (978-962-634-525-2(X), NA202514, Naxos AudioBooks) Naxos.
The brave knight comes from the Crusades to claim the Anglo-Saxon princess, Rowena, as his bride. But he becomes caught up in the fued between Prince John & his brother, Richard the Lionheart, who has returned to England incognito.

Ivanhoe. abr. ed. Walter Scott, Sr. Perf. by Douglas Fairbanks, Jr. 2 cass. 1977. 19.95 (978-0-694-50430-5(0), SWC 2076) HarperCollins Pubs.

Ivanhoe. abr. ed. Walter Scott, Sr. Read by Jonathan Oliver. 2 CDs. (Running Time: 2 hrs. 30 mins.). (Classic Fiction Ser.). 1994. audio compact disk 15.98 (978-962-634-025-7(8), NA202512, Naxos AudioBooks) Naxos.

Ivanhoe. abr. ed. Walter Scott, Sr. Read by David Warner. 4 cass. (Running Time: 6 hrs.). 2004. 25.00 (978-1-59007-007-9(0)) Pub: New Millenn Enter. Dist(s): PerseuPGW
Ivanhoe, a trusted ally of Richard-the-Lion-Hearted, returns from the Crusades to reclaim the inheritance his father denied him. Ivanhoe defends Rebecca, a vibrant, beautiful Jewish woman, against a charge of witchcraft - but it is Lady Rowena who is Ivanhoe's true love. The wicked Prince John plots to usurp England's throne, but Richard-the-Lion-Hearted and Robin Hood team up to defeat the Normans and regain the castle.

Ivanhoe. abr. ed. Walter Scott, Sr. Read by Carlos Zambrano. 3 CDs. (SPA.). 2001. audio compact disk 17.00 (978-958-9494-22-6(6)) YoYoMusic.

***Ivanhoe.** adpt. ed. Walter Scott. (Bring the Classics to Life Ser.). (ENG.). 2008. audio compact disk 12.95 (978-1-55576-583-5(1)) EDCON Pubng.

Ivanhoe. unabr. ed. Walter Scott, Sr. Read by Frederick Davidson. 17 CDs. (Running Time: 20 hrs. 30 mins.). 2001. audio compact disk 136.00 (978-0-7861-9711-8(0), 2338) Blckstn Audio.
Unforgettable scenes include: the thrilling rescue of Sir Wilfred of Ivanhoe & his fellow captives from Templar's castle by Robin Hood; Richard the Lion-Hearted's aid in Ivanhoe's triumph at evil King John's tournament; & the wounded Ivanhoe's duel to save the fair Jewess, Rebecca, from the dreaded stake.

Ivanhoe. unabr. ed. Walter Scott, Sr. Read by Frederick Davidson. 14 cass. (Running Time: 20 hrs. 30 mins.). 1999. 89.95 (978-0-7861-1486-3(X), 2338) Blckstn Audio.

Ivanhoe. unabr. ed. Walter Scott, Sr. Read by Michael Page. (Running Time: 18 hrs.). 2005. 44.25 (978-1-59737-014-1(2), 9781597370141, BADLE); 29.95 (978-1-59737-013-4(4), 9781597370134, BAD); audio compact disk 44.25 (978-1-59737-012-7(6), 9781597370127, Brlnc Audio MP3 Lib); audio compact disk 29.95 (978-1-59737-011-0(8), 9781597370110, Brilliance MP3); audio compact disk 112.25 (978-1-59737-010-3(X), 9781597370103, BriAudCD Unabrid); audio compact disk 44.95 (978-1-59737-009-7(6), 9781597370097, Bril Audio CD Unabri) Brilliance Audio.

Ivanhoe. unabr. ed. Walter Scott, Sr. Read by Frederick Davidson. (YA). 2008. 119.99 (978-1-60514-732-1(X)) Find a World.

***Ivanhoe.** unabr. ed. Walter Scott, Sr. Narrated by Simon Prebble. (Running Time: 18 hrs. 30 mins. 0 sec.). (ENG.). 2010. 34.99 (978-1-4001-6606-0(3)); audio compact disk 91.99 (978-1-4001-4606-2(2)); audio compact disk 45.99 (978-1-4001-1606-5(6)) Pub: Tantor Media. Dist(s): IngramPubServ

***Ivanhoe.** unabr. ed. Walter Scott, Sr. Narrated by Simon Prebble. (Running Time: 20 hrs. 0 mins.). 2010. 23.99 (978-1-4001-8606-8(4)) Tantor Media.

Ivanhoe, Pt. A. unabr. collector's ed. Walter Scott, Sr. Read by Jim Killavey. 7 cass. (Running Time: 10 hrs. 30 min.). (Jimcin Recording Ser.). (J). 1986. 56.00 (978-0-7366-3921-7(7), 9160-A) Books on Tape.
The disinherited knight Ivanhoe, his fair lady Rowena, Richard the Lion-Hearted & Robin Hood, these are people shaped by the forces of tradition, molded by their nation's history.

Ivanhoe, Pt. B. collector's ed. Walter Scott, Sr. Read by Jim Killavey. 7 cass. (Running Time: 10 hrs. 30 min.). (J). 1986. 56.00 (978-0-7366-3922-4(5), 9160-B) Books on Tape.
The disinherited knight Ivanhoe, his fair lady Rowena, Richard the Lion-Hearted & Robin Hood - these are people shaped by the forces of tradition, molded by their nation's history.

Ivanhoe, Set. Walter Scott, Sr. Read by Flo Gibson. 12 cass. (Running Time: 17 hrs. 30 min.). (YA). (gr. 4-10). 1997. 39.95 (978-1-55685-455-2(2)) Audio Bk Con.
The Norman Saxon conflict is vividly described with battle scenes, medieval pageantry & romantic escapades. The hero Sir Wilfred Ivanhoe, the lovely brave Jewess Rebecca, Richard the Lion-Hearted, Robin Hood & his merry band are just a few of the chivalrous characters.

***Ivanhoe: Bring the Classics to Life.** adpt. ed. Walter Scott. (Bring the Classics to Life Ser.). 2008. pap. bk. 21.95 (978-1-55576-653-5(6)) EDCON Pubng.

Ivanhoe Readalong. Walter Scott, Sr. (Illustrated Classics Collection). 1994. pap. bk. 14.95 (978-0-7854-0765-2(0), 40502) Am Guidance.

I've Always Wanted to Play Piano, Bk. 1. Susan Ogilvy. Illus. by Judy Cantwell Gelfert & Robert Patrick. 1996. bk. 39.95 (978-0-9717954-0-2(1)) Ogilvy Music.

I've Been Born Again. Bridgestone Staff. 2004. audio compact disk 7.98 (978-1-56371-037-7(4)) Brdgstn Multimed Grp.

Ive Been Born Again. Bridgestone Staff. 2004. 5.98 (978-1-56371-001-8(3)) Brdgstn Multimed Grp.

I've Been Delivered. 1 cass. (Running Time: 90 mins.). (Best of Contemporary Christian Ser.). 1999. 9.95 (978-1-56015-728-1(3)); audio compact disk 16.95 (978-1-56015-727-4(5)) Penton Overseas.
Includes: "Love Me Good," Christopher Marks; "Lucky One," Marie Evans; "The Great Adventure," Christian B. Jackson; "Pray for Me," David Walker.

I've Been Redeemed. Contrib. by Dale Mathews. 1996. audio compact disk 55.00 (978-0-7601-1259-5(2), 75606305) Pub: Brentwood Music. Dist(s): H Leonard

I've Been Tested, & Now I'm Ready. 2001. audio compact disk 19.99 (978-1-58602-083-5(8)) E L Long.

I've Been Tested, & Now I'm Ready. 2001. 10.00 (978-1-58602-072-9(2)) E L Long.

I've Been Thinking: About Living, Loving & Learning. Carol Goodman Heizer. Read by Carol Goodman Heizer. 1 cass. (Running Time: 1 hr. 30 min.). 1997. 9.95 (978-0-9656402-2-0(1)) Alpha Pub KY.
Stories from author's life & perspective that all people can relate to. It will make the listener laugh, cry, & shout "Bravo" - contemplating what life is all about.

I've Been to the Mountaintop: An Unabridged selection from A Call to Conscience - the Landmark Speeches of Dr. Martin Luther King, Jr. unabr. ed. Read by Andrew Young & Martin Luther King, Jr. (Running Time: 1 hr.). (ENG.). 2006. 1.98 (978-1-59483-488-2(1)) Pub: Hachet Audio. Dist(s): HachBkGrp

I've Been Working on the Railroad. (Song Box Ser.). (gr. 1-2). bk. 8.50 (978-0-7802-0938-1(9)) Wright Group.

I've Been Working on the Railroad: 1 Big Book, 6 Each of 1 Student Book, & 1 Cassette. (Song Box Ser.). (gr. 1-2). 68.95 (978-0-7802-0939-8(7)) Wright Group.

I've Fallen & I Can Get up! Dave Fitzgerald Live. unabr. ed. Perf. by Dave Fitzgerald & John Docimo. 1 cass. (Running Time: 44 min.). 1998. 10.95 (978-0-9669309-2-4(4)) Humor Inst.
Comedian Dave Fitzgerald performs live his inspiring material about weight loss, coffee addiction & his bout with cancer.

I've Got a Yo-Yo. Tom Paxton. 1 cass. (Running Time: 52 min.). (J). 1997. 9.98; 14.98 (978-1-57940-012-5(4)) Rounder Records.
Since the early years of children's music, one of the genre's leading songwriters & performers has been folksinger Tom Paxton. "I've Got a Yo-Yo", the second volume of Tom Paxton's classic songs for children, is geared toward older children. This collection finds Tom exploring some of the milestones of childhood - things like bike riding, measles & the games children play. From the rollicking title track to the uplifting "The Crow that Wanted to Sing", Tom's skills as a first-rate folksinger make this an essential celebration of growing up. Older children will relate to the subterranean urban adventure of "The Subway Song", to the Saturday morning ball-game of "Baseball Kids", or to the joys of learning to ride a bike. Many of these songs feature the participation of a children's chorus, complementing Tom's own vocals. This recording also incorporates elements of some regional styles, such as polka, bluegrass & calypso.

I've Got Imagination. Perf. by Rachel Sumner. 1 cass., 1 CD. (Running Time: 45 min.). (Rachel's Fun Time Ser.: Vol. 3). (J). (ps-5). 1997. 9.98 (978-1-886673-06-9(3), RR-05, Songs by Rachel); audio compact disk 14.98 (978-1-886673-07-6(1), RR-CD5, Songs by Rachel) Rachels Recs.

I've Got My Love to Keep Me Warm (Medley) - ShowTrax. Arranged by Ed Lojeski. 1 CD. (Running Time: 7 mins.). 2000. audio compact disk 35.00 (08742339) H Leonard.
The cold wind may be blowing but your audience will feel warm & cozy with this medley of all-time great standards. Includes: "Button up Your Overcoat"; "I've Got My Love to Keep Me Warm" & "Let It Snow! Let It Snow! Let It Snow".

I've Got Rainbows! Ladybug Magazine Editors. 1 cass. (J). (ps-1). 1998. 10.95 (978-0-8126-0067-4(3)) Open Ct Pub.

I've Got Rainbows! Songbook. Ladybug Magazine Staff. (ps-1). 1998. bk. 19.95 (978-0-8126-0138-1(6)) Open Ct Pub.

I've Got Sixpence see Sound of Modern Drama: The Crucible

I've Got Sixpence. (J). (SAC 7145) Spoken Arts.

I've Got Super Power. Charette. (J). 11.95 Ed Activities.

I've Got the Power. unabr. ed. Keith A. Butler, II. 1 cass. (Running Time: 1 hrs. 30 mins.). 2001. 5.00 (A81) Word Faith Pubng.

I've Got to Be Me. 1979. 4.95 (978-0-7417-1002-4(1)) Win Walk.

I've Got to Know. Utah Phillips. 2003. audio compact disk (978-1-902593-84-5(7)) AK Pr Dist.

I've Got You under My Skins. Irv Cottler. 1986. pap. bk. 19.95 (978-0-7390-0772-3(6), 173) Alfred Pub.

I've Got You under Skins. Irv Cottler. (ENG.). 2000. audio compact disk 10.95 (978-0-7390-1707-4(1), 19629) Alfred Pub.

I've Got Your Back. T. D. Jakes. 1 cass. 1997. 15.00 (978-1-57855-203-0(6)) T D Jakes.

I've Had It with That Kid. Effective Behavior Solutions. (ENG.). 2004. audio compact disk 19.95i (978-0-9822057-1-6(6)) Eff Behav Sol.

I've Had It with You. Effective Behavior Solutions. (ENG.). 2004. audio compact disk 19.95i (978-0-9822057-0-9(8)) Eff Behav Sol.

I've Seen Jesus: Encountering the Risen Christ. Contrib. by Robert Sterling. Created by Robert Sterling. Created by Deborah Craig-Claar. (Running Time: 2400 sec.). 2007. audio compact disk 59.95 (978-5-557-53126-9(2), Word Music) Word Enter.

Ivory. unabr. ed. Tony Park. Read by Mark Davis. (Running Time: 15 hrs. 40 mins.). 2009. audio compact disk 118.95 (978-1-74214-482-5(9), 9781742144825) Pub: Bolinda Pubng AUS. Dist(s): Bolinda Pub Inc

***Ivory Dagger.** Patricia Wentworth. 2010. 61.95 (978-0-7531-3135-0(8)); audio compact disk 79.95 (978-0-7531-3136-7(6)) Pub: Isis Pubng Ltd GBR. Dist(s): Ulverscroft US

***Ivory Grin: A Lew Archer Novel.** unabr. ed. Ross Macdonald. Read by Grover Gardner. (Running Time: 8 hrs. 30 mins.). 2010. 29.95 (978-1-4332-7871-6(5)); 54.95 (978-1-4332-7867-9(7)); audio compact disk 76.00 (978-1-4332-7868-6(5)) Blckstn Audio.

Ivory Swing. unabr. ed. Janette Turner Hospital. Read by Lise Rodgers. 6 cass. (Running Time: 9 hrs.). 1998. (978-1-86340-715-1(4), 570422) Bolinda Pubng AUS.
The conflict between Juliet's love of husband & children, & her own passionate need for expression is intensified by her move from small town Canada to Southern India. The stifling restrictions on her freedom are magnified in the plight of her young widowed neighbor. The beautiful Yashoda longs to embrace the Western values that would release her from the strictures of Indian tradition.

Ivory Tower. unabr. ed. Henry James. Read by Flo Gibson. 5 cass. (Running Time: 7 hrs.). 1996. 20.95 (978-1-55685-404-0(8)) Audio Bk Con.
This unfinished late novel is complex & convoluted & is for Henry James scholars. He explores the reactions of a naive young British heir to his inheritance of an American fortune, as well as the reactions of members of this new community.

Ivory's Ghosts: The White Gold of History & the Fate of Elephants. unabr. ed. John Frederick Walker. Read by David Colacci. (Running Time: 11 hrs.). 2009. 39.97 (978-1-4233-7801-3(6), 9781423378013, Brlnc Audio MP3 Lib); 39.97 (978-1-4233-7803-7(2), 9781423378037, BADLE); 24.99 (978-1-4233-7800-6(8), 9781423378006, Brilliance MP3); 29.99 (978-1-4233-7802-0(4), 9781423378020, BAD); audio compact disk 92.97 (978-1-4233-7799-3(0), 9781423377993, BriAudCD Unabrid); audio compact disk 34.99 (978-1-4233-7798-6(2), 9781423377986, Bril Audio CD Unabri) Brilliance Audio.

Ivs Cd Beg & Inter Alg 2e. 2nd ed. (C). 2004. audio compact disk 15.95 (978-0-534-46316-8(9)) Pub: Brooks-Cole. Dist(s): CENGAGE Learn

Ivy Appleton: Prop Widow. 2001. 19.95 (978-0-9714779-0-2(6)) Tape Escapes.

Ivy Chronicles. Karen Quinn. 2005. audio compact disk 34.99 (978-1-4193-2027-9(0)) Recorded Bks.

***IWant: My Journey from Addiction & Overconsumption to a Simpler, Honest Life.** Jane Velez-Mitchell. Narrated by Jane Velez-Mitchell. (ENG.). 2009. audio compact disk 29.95 (978-0-7573-1525-1(9)) Health Comm.

Iwo Jima. unabr. collector's ed. Richard F. Newcomb. Read by Arthur Addison. 7 cass. (Running Time: 10 hrs. 30 min.). 1996. 56.00 (978-0-7366-3324-6(3), 3976) Books on Tape.
It's only a tiny atoll some 700 miles from the Japanese capital, but it was considered vital to the war effort i the Pacific. On February 19, 1945, six months before the war's end, the largest Marine force ever sent into battle, backed by the greatest fighting fleet ever assembled in those waters, launched a bloody assault on Iwo Jima. The brutal, five-week campaign that followed was one of the costliest (more than 5,000 lives lost). To most, the battle was a famous photograph of a flag-raising, but to the men of the Fifth Amphibious Corps, it was a matter of life & death.

Iwo Jima: World War II Veterans Remember the Greatest Battle of the Pacific. unabr. ed. Larry Smith. Read by Dick Hill. Narrated by Dick Hill. (Running Time: 13 hrs. 0 mins. 0 sec.). (ENG.). 2008. audio compact disk 24.99 (978-1-4001-5721-1(8)); audio compact disk 34.99 (978-1-4001-0721-6(0)); audio compact disk 69.99 (978-1-4001-3721-3(7)) Pub: Tantor Media. Dist(s): IngramPubServ

IWorship: A Total Worship Experience. 2 cass. (Running Time: 3 hrs.). 2003. audio compact disk 24.95 (978-0-634-06104-2(6)) H Leonard.
Features well-known worship artists with 33 powerful songs, such as: Above All · As the Deer · Awesome God · Breathe · God of Wonders · I Can Only Imagine · Lord, I Lift Your Name on High · My Redeemer Lives · Shout to the Lord · We All Bow Down · and more.

Iworship: A Total Worship Experience. Contrib. by Various Artists. (Iworship Ser.). 2008. audio compact disk & audio compact disk 19.98 (978-5-557-43326-6(0)) Integrity Music.

IWoz: Computer Geek to Cult Icon. unabr. ed. Steve Wozniak. Told to Gina Smith. 9 CDs. (Running Time: 9 hrs. 0 mins. 0 sec.). (ENG.). 2007. audio compact disk 34.99 (978-1-4001-0328-7(2)) Pub: Tantor Media. Dist(s): IngramPubServ

Iwoz: How I Invented the Personal Computer & Had Fun along the Way. unabr. ed. Steve Wozniak. Read by Patrick G. Lawlor. (Running Time: 9 hrs. 0 mins. 0 sec.). (ENG.). 2007. audio compact disk 24.99 (978-1-4001-5328-2(X)) Pub: Tantor Media. Dist(s): IngramPubServ

IWoz: How I Invented the Personal Computer, Co-Founded Apple, & Had Fun Doing It. Gina Wozniak Smith. Read by Patrick G. Lawlor. Told to Gina Smith. (Playaway Adult Nonfiction Ser.). 2008. 64.99 (978-1-60640-858-2(5)) Find a World.

IWoz: How I Invented the Personal Computer, Co-Founded Apple, & Had Fun Doing It. unabr. ed. Steve Wozniak. Read by Patrick G. Lawlor. Told to Gina Smith. (Running Time: 9 hrs. 0 mins. 0 sec.). (ENG.). 2007. audio compact disk 69.99 (978-1-4001-3328-4(9)) Pub: Tantor Media. Dist(s): IngramPubServ

Iyanla Live! Faith, Vol. 2. Iyanla Vanzant. Read by Iyanla Vanzant. 1 cass. (Running Time: 90 mins.). 1999. 12.00 S&S Audio.

Izaak Walton League's "Save Our Streams" Program. Hosted by Nancy Pearlman. 1 cass. (Running Time: 29 min.). 10.00 (816) Educ Comm CA.

Izzy, Willy-Nilly. unabr. ed. Cynthia Voigt. 4 cass. (Running Time: 5 hrs.). (J). 2000. 30.00 (Random AudioBks) Random Audio Pubg.
Izzy's never been one to complain. Izzy's the nice girl, from a family that believes good manners & a stiff upper lip are key to facing any situation. Even after a car accident leaves her disabled, she's determined not to show how much she's hurting, it takes Rosamunde, a girl who seems to care nothing about good manners, to forcibly disrupt Izzy's life & help her face her changed existence.

Izzy, Willy-Nilly. unabr. ed. Cynthia Voigt. 6 vols. (Running Time: 8 hrs. 18 mins.). (J). (gr. 7 up). 2004. pap. bk. 46.00 (978-0-8072-8763-7(6), YA260SP, Listening Lib) Random Audio Pubg.
Izzy's never been one to complain. Izzy's from a family that believes good manners & a stiff upper lip are key to facing any situation. Even after a car accident leaves her disabled, she's determined not to show how much she's hurting. It takes Rosamunde, a girl who seems to care nothing about good manners, to forcibly disrupt Izzy's life & help her face her changed existence.

Izzy, Willy-Nilly. unabr. ed. Cynthia Voigt. Read by Mandy Siegfried. 6 cass. (Running Time: 8 hrs. 18 mins.). (J). (gr. 7 up). 2004. 40.00 (978-0-8072-8762-0(8), YA260CX, Listening Lib) Random Audio Pubg.

J

J. B. Priestley. J. B. Priestley. Read by J. B. Priestley. 1 cass. (Running Time: 42 min.). Incl. Delight. (SAC 7048); Long Trousers. (SAC 7048); Many Others. (SAC 7048); Mineral Water in Bedrooms of Foreign Hotels. (SAC 7048); Smoking in a Hot Bath. (SAC 7048); 10.95 (978-0-8045-0716-5(3), SAC 7048) Spoken Arts.

J. D. Edwards OneWorld: A Beginner's Guide. Eric Fisher. 2001. cd-rom & audio compact disk 50.00 (978-0-07-212313-5(3)) M-H Sch Educ Grp.

J. D. Robb CD Collection 1: Naked in Death, Glory in Death, Immortal in Death. abr. ed. Read by Susan Ericksen. (Running Time: 18 hrs.). (In Death Ser.). 2008. audio compact disk 34.95 (978-1-4233-4647-0(5), 9781423346470, BACD) Brilliance Audio.

***J. D. Robb CD Collection 10: Promises in Death, Kindred in Death.** abr. ed. J. D. Robb, pseud. Read by Susan Ericksen. (Running Time: 12 hrs.). (In Death Ser.). 2010. audio compact disk 19.99 (978-1-4418-6165-8(3), 9781441861658, BACD) Brilliance Audio.

J. D. Robb CD Collection 3: Holiday in Death; Conspiracy in Death; Loyalty in Death. abr. ed. J. D. Robb, pseud. Read by Susan Ericksen. (Running Time: 18 hrs.). (In Death Ser.). 2008. audio compact disk 34.95 (978-1-4233-4649-4(1), 9781423346494, BACD) Brilliance Audio.

J. D. Robb CD Collection 4: Witness in Death; Judgment in Death; Betrayal in Death. abr. ed. J. D. Robb, pseud. Read by Susan Ericksen. (Running Time: 18 hrs.). (In Death Ser.). 2008. audio compact disk 34.95 (978-1-4233-4650-0(5), 9781423346500, BACD) Brilliance Audio.

J. D. Robb CD Collection 5: Seduction in Death; Reunion in Death; Purity in Death. abr. ed. J. D. Robb, pseud. Read by Susan Ericksen. (Running Time: 18 hrs.). (In Death Ser.). 2009. audio compact disk 34.99 (978-1-4233-4651-7(3), 9781423346517, BACD) Brilliance Audio.

J. D. Robb CD Collection 6: Portrait in Death; Imitation in Death; Divided in Death. abr. ed. J. D. Robb, pseud. Read by Susan Ericksen. (Running Time: 18 hrs.). (In Death Ser.). 2009. audio compact disk 34.99 (978-1-4233-4652-4(1), 9781423346524, BACD) Brilliance Audio.

J. D. Robb CD Collection 7: Visions in Death; Survivor in Death; Origin in Death. abr. ed. J. D. Robb, pseud. Read by Susan Ericksen. (Running Time: 19 hrs.). (In Death Ser.). 2009. audio compact disk 34.99 (978-1-4233-4653-1(X), 9781423346531) Brilliance Audio.

J. D. Robb CD Collection 8: Memory in Death; Born in Death; Innocent in Death. abr. ed. J. D. Robb, pseud. Read by Susan Ericksen. (Running Time: 18 hrs.). (In Death Ser.). 2009. audio compact disk 34.99 (978-1-4233-4654-8(8), 9781423346548, BACD) Brilliance Audio.

J. D. Robb CD Collection 9: Creation in Death, Strangers in Death, Salvation in Death. abr. ed. J. D. Robb, pseud. Read by Susan Ericksen. (Running Time: 18 hrs.). (In Death Ser.). 2009. audio compact disk 34.99 (978-1-4418-1654-2(2), 9781441816542, BACD) Brilliance Audio.

J. D. Sumner & the Stamps: Final Sessions. Perf. by J. D. Sumner and the Stamps. 1 cass. 1999. 10.98 (978-0-7601-2874-9(X)); audio compact disk 16.98 (978-0-7601-2873-2(1)) Provident Music.

J. D. Sumner & the Stamps Quartet. Perf. by J. D. Sumner and the Stamps. 1 cass. (Gospel Music Hall of Fame Ser.: Vol. 1). 1999. 16.99 (978-0-7601-2797-1(2)); audio compact disk 19.99 (978-0-7601-2796-4(4)) Provident Music.

J. Edgar! unabr. ed. Tom Leopold & Harry Shearer. Perf. by John Goodman et al. Music by Peter Matz. 2 cass. (Running Time: 1 hr. 45 mins.). 2001. 23.95 (978-1-58081-021-0(7), TPT36) L A Theatre.
A musical comedy about one of the most powerful men in the 20th century America, about his love life & his obsession to keep that life a secret by knowing the secrets of everyone else's love life.

J Edgar! unabr. ed. Tom Leopold & Harry Shearer. Perf. by Harry Shearer et al. Music by Peter Matz. 2 CDs. (Running Time: 1 hr. 45 mins.). 2001. audio compact disk 25.95 (978-1-58081-175-0(2), CDTPT36) Pub: L A Theatre. Dist(s): NetLibrary CO

J. Edgar! unabr. ed. Tom Leopold et al. Read by John Goodman. (YA). 2008. 34.99 (978-1-60514-983-7(7)) Find a World.

J. Edgar Hoover: The Man & the Secrets. collector's ed. Curt Gentry. Read by Dick Estell. 13 cass. (Running Time: 19 hrs. 30 min.). 1992. 104.00 (978-0-7366-2283-7(7), 3070-A) Books on Tape.
For almost 50 years, J. Edgar Hoover held virtually unchecked public power. He manipulated every president from FDR to Nixon but shrank from human contact. He was a mass of contradictions...a hypochondriac who became a national hero, a bachelor obsessed with sexual slander, a federal official with a web of connections to organized crime.

J. Edgar Hoover: The Man & the Secrets. unabr. collector's ed. Curt Gentry. Read by Dick Estell. 13 cass. (Running Time: 19 hrs. 30 min.). 1992. 104.00 (978-0-7366-2284-4(5), 3070B) Books on Tape.

J. Golden. James Arrington. 1 CD. 2004. audio compact disk 10.98 (978-1-57734-113-0(9), 2500787) Covenant Comms.
The life & legend of J. Golden Kimball.

J. Golden, Set. James Arrington. 2 cass. 2004. 11.95 (978-1-55503-373-6(3), 0700428) Covenant Comms.
A one-man play explores the life & legend of J. Golden Kimball.

J. Habakuk Jephson's Statement see Tales of the Supernatural

J Is for Judgment. unabr. ed. Sue Grafton. Read by Mary Peiffer. 7 cass. (Running Time: 10 hrs. 30 min.). (Kinsey Millhone Mystery Ser.). 1994. 56.00 (978-0-7366-2736-8(7), 3463) Books on Tape.
When real-estate scam artist Wendell Jaffe disappeared at sea, he was declared dead. However, Jaffe soon was spotted in Mexico & Kinsey was hired to investigate. Oddly enough, the con man's past converges with Kinsey's own family history.

J. J.'s Story. unabr. ed. J. J. Rameriz. 1 cass. 1995. 5.00 (978-1-57892-038-9(8)) Prayer Pt Pr.
A testimony.

J. M. Hurst Cycles Trading & Trading Course, Set. J. M. Hurst. 2 cass. 1998. ring bd. 495.00 (978-0-934380-46-1(5), 1400) Traders Pr.

J. M. Roberts' History of the World, Pt. I. unabr. ed. J. M. Roberts. Read by Frederick Davidson. 16 cass. (Running Time: 24 hrs.). 1999. 99.95 (1945-A) Blckstn Audio.
Covers the forgotten experiences of ordinary men as well as chronicling the acts of men in power.

J. M. Roberts' History of the World, Pt. II. unabr. ed. J. M. Roberts. Read by Frederick Davidson. 13 cass. (Running Time: 19 hrs. 30 min.). 1999. 85.95 (1945-B) Blckstn Audio.

J. M. Roberts' History of the World, Pt. III. unabr. ed. J. M. Roberts. Read by Frederick Davidson. 8 cass. (Running Time: 12 hrs.). 1999. 56.95 (1926-C) Blckstn Audio.

J. N. Loughborough & the 3 Cent Silver. C. Mervyn Maxwell. (J). (gr. 1-6). 2005. DVD & audio compact disk (978-0-9705169-5-4(9)) Petra Pubng Co.

J. Neil Schulman: Picturing Libertarian Futures. (Running Time: 60 min.). 1980. 9.00 (F105) Freeland Pr.
The author begins with a "story" to illustrate the theme of his talk.

J. P. Donleavy. Interview with J. P. Donleavy. 1 cass. (Running Time: 30 min.). 1980. 11.95 (L018) TFR.
Author of "The Ginger Man" talks in a surprisingly reserved way about his lusty, bawdy, irreverent writing. He refuses to get excited about Princess Margaret's reference to the Irish as "pigs" saying that the word is an appropriate description of agricultural people.

J. P. Landers - Solve a Mystery, Bk. 1. unabr. ed. Short Stories. Marian L. Clish. Read by Marian L. Clish. Illus. by Steven Crombie. 1 cass. (Running Time: 20 min.). (J). (gr. 2-7). 1999. bk. 15.95 (978-1-928632-26-9(2)) Writers Mrktpl.
Fourteen mini-mysteries to solve. Answers in back of the book. Match wits with the famous master detective.

J. P. Landers - Solve a Mystery, Bk. 2. unabr. ed. Short Stories. Marian L. Clish. Read by Marian L. Clish. Illus. by Steven Crombie. 1 cass. (J). (gr. 2-7). 1999. bk. 15.95 (978-1-928632-28-3(9)) Writers Mrktpl.

J. Q. Adams & the Gag Rule. 10.00 Esstee Audios.
An ex-president fights for the people's rights.

J. R. R. Tolkien. J. R. R. Tolkien. 1 cass. (Author Speaks Ser.). 1991. 14.95 J Norton Pubs.
Archival recordings of 20th-century authors.

J. R. R. Tolkien: Myth, Morality & Religion. Richard Purthill. 5 CDs. (Running Time: 5 hrs.). 2003. audio compact disk 30.95 (978-1-57058-546-3(6), rc13-cd) St Joseph Communs.
J.R.R. Tolkien has been voted the "Greatest Writer of the 20th Century" and the first two movies in an epic trilogy based on his The Lord of the Rings have broken box-office records around the world. But what makes his sweeping fantasy such a compelling and enduring work? Could it be Tolkien's own devotion to his Catholic Faith?In the new audio version of Richard Purthill's book J.R.R. Tolkien: Myth, Morality & Religion, you'll discover how Tolkien's fantasy stories creatively incorporate profound religious and ethical ideas. Professor Purthill's scholarly approach reveals the moral depth of Tolkien's work and cuts through current subjectivism and cynicism regarding morality and religion.According to Peter Kreeft, Purthill is "both a clear and commonsensical philosopher? Discovering him is like meeting Strider in the Inn at Bree: we have found a Ranger, a reliable guide through middle-earth.".

J. R. R. Tolkien Audio CD Collection. unabr. abr. ed. J. R. R. Tolkien. Read by J. R. R. Tolkien. Read by Christopher Tolkien. 4 CDs. (Running Time: 4 hrs.). 2001. audio compact disk 25.00 (978-0-694-52570-6(7)) HarperCollins Pubs.

J. R. R. Tolkien Collection. unabr. ed. J. R. R. Tolkien. Narrated by Full Cast Production Staff. Brian Sibley. (Running Time: 20 hrs. 0 mins. 0 sec.). (ENG.). 2009. audio compact disk 99.95 (978-1-60283-661-7(2)) Pub: AudioGO. Dist(s): Perseus Dist

J. Robert Oppenheimer: Shatterer of Worlds. unabr. collector's ed. Peter Goodchild. Read by Jonathan Reese. 8 cass. (Running Time: 12 hrs.). 1995. 64.00 (978-0-7366-3000-9(7), 3688) Books on Tape.
J. Robert Oppenheimer's behavior led the FBI to brand "Father of the Nuclear Age" a communist spy. Astonishing revelations.

J. S. Bach: Sonatas & Partitas for Unaccompanied Violin. CD-UW Music School Staff. Contrib. by Vartan Manoogian. 2005. audio compact disk 25.00 (978-1-931569-05-7(3)) Pub: U of Wis Pr. Dist(s): Chicago Distribution Ctr
In thisnbsp; new recording,Vartan Manoogian’s elegant artistry brings to lifenbsp; J.S. Bach’s unsurpassed masterwork for unaccompanied violin. nbsp;nbsp;nbsp;nbsp;The violin used for this recording was made by J. B. Guadagnini in Piacenza, Italy in 1747.nbsp;According to records dated 1956 in the archives of violin maker William E. Hill of London, England, "the earliest connection which we had with this instrument was when it was in the possession of Lady Kingston at the beginning of this century, who was a well-known amateur player, the pupil of Emil Sauret.nbsp; It subsequently passed into the possession of a well-known professional, Miss Blaha, who emanated from Germany and from whose heirs the instrument was purchased by us in 1929. It was then sold to Mr. Robert Bower, a well-known collector, and from him passed into the hadns of Mr. Harry Blech, formerly a well-known soloist and now the conductor of the Mozart Players (in London)." In 1956 it was sold to M. Paolo Peterlango of Milano, Italy, from whom the eminent Italian violinist Franco Gulli purchased it in 1960.nbsp; Mr. Manoogian obtained the Guadagnini in the 1980s 2 CD Compact Disc set.

J. S. Bach Pt. 1: Two-Part Inventions for Two Basses. Bunny Brunel. 1999. pap. bk. 22.95 (978-0-7866-3224-4(0), 96978BCD) Mel Bay.

J. S. Bach - Double Concerto in D Minor, BWV1043. Composed by Johann Sebastian Bach. 2006. pap. bk. 34.98 (978-1-59615-132-1(3), 1596151323) Pub: Music Minus. Dist(s): H Leonard

J. S. Bach - Violin Concerto No. 1 in A Minor, BWV1041; Violin Concerto No. 2 in E Major, BWV1042. Composed by Johann Sebastian Bach. 2006. pap. bk. 34.98 (978-1-59615-133-8(1), 1596151331) Pub: Music Minus. Dist(s): H Leonard

J. T. unabr. ed. Jane Wagner. 1 read-along cass. (Running Time: 25 min.). (Middle Grade Cliffhangers Ser.). (J). (gr. 3-5). 1983. 15.98 (978-0-8072-1100-7(1), SWR 31 SP, Listening Lib); (Listening Lib) Random Audio Pubg.
J. T. Gamble is just "turnin' bad," in the worst way an urban ghetto has to offer. But J. T. turns sensitive, responsible, & loving when he adopts a sick alley cat.

J. W. Rivers. unabr. ed. J. W. Rivers. Read by J. W. Rivers. 1 cass. (Running Time: 29 min.). 1986. 10.00 New Letters.
A sequence from "When Owls Cry, Indians Die," about Mexican history & effects on the Indian population.

J. Wrap A & A Naciones Cantaran. Montero Y Sigueme. (SPA.). 2000. 30.00 (978-0-8297-3005-0(2)) Pub: Vida Pubs. Dist(s): Zondervan

J. Wrap Animah Min. Jonathan Settel. (SPA.). 2000. 30.00 (978-0-8297-3107-1(5)) Pub: Vida Pubs. Dist(s): Zondervan

J. Wrap Musica Cristiana Tropical. Tropical. (SPA.). 2000. 30.00 (978-0-8297-2773-9(6)) Pub: Vida Pubs. Dist(s): Zondervan

J Wrap Paz en la Tierra. René González. (SPA.). 2000. 30.00 (978-0-8297-2541-4(5)) Pub: Vida Pubs. Dist(s): Zondervan

J Wrap por la Vida. (SPA.). 2000. 30.00 (978-0-8297-2578-0(4)) Pub: Vida Pubs. Dist(s): Zondervan

J. Wrap Quiero Alabarte, Vol. 3. Maranatha Singers. (SPA.). 2000. 30.00 (978-0-8297-3345-7(0)) Pub: Vida Pubs. Dist(s): Zondervan

J Wrap Soldados de Jesus. Miguel Cassina. (SPA.). 2000. 30.00 (978-0-8297-2680-0(2)) Zondervan.

J. Wrap Vida. (SPA.). 1999. 30.00 (978-0-8297-2970-2(4)) Pub: Vida Pubs. Dist(s): Zondervan

J. Wrapub de la Aventura. Nathan Aanderud. (SPA.). 2000. 30.00 (978-0-8297-3276-4(4)) Pub: Vida Pubs. Dist(s): Zondervan

Jabberwocky see Treasury of Lewis Carroll

Jabez the Story: Why God's Heart Was Moved. 1 cass. (Running Time: 1 hr. 30 mins.). 2001. 9.95 (978-1-929753-09-3(8)) Spirit of Hope.

Jabo. unabr. ed. Robert B. Hamilton. Read by Rusty Nelson. 12 cass. (Running Time: 11 hrs. 24 min.). 2001. 64.95 (978-1-55686-866-5(9)) Books in Motion.
Millionaire Private Eye Nick Jabo accepts the typical "observe activities of" case, leading to attempts on Nick's life by a stalker with a murderous sense of humor.

Jacaranda Blue. unabr. ed. Joy Dettman. Read by Deidre Rubenstein. (Running Time: 11 hrs. 45 mins.). 2009. audio compact disk 98.95 (978-1-921334-67-2(3), 9781921334672) Pub: Bolinda Pubng AUS. Dist(s): Bolinda Pub Inc

Jacaranda Tree. unabr. ed. H. E. Bates. Read by Sam Dastor. 8 cass. (Running Time: 8 hrs.). 1993. 69.95 (978-0-7451-4209-8(5), CAB 892) AudioGO.
Burma had been a wonderful home to its citizens before World War II. But with the invasion of the Japanese, they were thrown into a deadly inferno of war & feared for their lives.

***Jacinto's Remnant.** unabr. ed. Karen Traviss. Narrated by David Colacci. (Running Time: 16 hrs. 0 mins.). (Gears of War Ser.). 2010. 39.99 (978-1-4001-9471-1(7)) Tantor Media.

***Jacinto's Remnant.** unabr. ed. Karen Traviss. Narrated by David Colacci. (Running Time: 16 hrs. 0 mins. 0 sec.). (Gears of War Ser.). (ENG.). 2010. audio compact disk 79.99 (978-1-4001-4471-6(X)) Pub: Tantor Media. Dist(s): IngramPubServ

Jack. unabr. ed. Judy Johnson. Read by Alan King. (Running Time: 3 hrs. 5 mins.). 2009. audio compact disk 54.95 (978-1-921415-51-7(7), 9781921415517) Pub: Bolinda Pubng AUS. Dist(s): Bolinda Pub Inc

Jack: A Life Like No Other. abr. ed. Geoffrey Perret. Read by Dick Hill. 6 cass. (Running Time: 9 hrs.). 2001. 29.95 (978-1-58788-969-1(2), 1587889692, Nova Audio Bks); 69.25 (978-1-58788-972-1(2), 1587889722, Lib Edit); audio compact disk 37.95 (978-1-58788-970-7(6), 1587889706, CD); audio compact disk 96.25 (978-1-58788-971-4(4), 1587889714, CD Lib Edit) Brilliance Audio.
There has been no complete biography like this one. Jack deals with the full scope of Kennedy's life - his family, his friends, his infidelities. There's much new to say, much culled from hundreds of hours of tapes from the Oval Office that were unavailable until now. Through painstaking research, Geoffrey Perret located thousands of revealing documents on national security issues and foreign affairs, subjects to which Kennedy devoted most of his time and energy. All of the documents from the Assassination Records Review Board are now available as well, and Perret has mined the Kennedy Library in a way few others have, finding letters and diaries that have never before seen the light of day. But perhaps most important here is the narrative ability of Perret. With style and substance, he brings to life again the man who left such an indelible impression on our century.

Jack: A Life Like No Other. abr. ed. Geoffrey Perret. Read by Dick Hill. (Running Time: 8 hrs.). 2008. 39.25 (978-1-4233-6209-8(8), 9781423362098, Brinc Audio MP3 Lib); 39.25 (978-1-4233-6211-1(X), 9781423362111, BADLE); 24.95 (978-1-4233-6210-4(1), 9781423362104, BAD); 24.95 (978-1-4233-6208-1(X), 9781423362081, Brilliance MP3) Brilliance Audio.

Jack: C. S. Lewis & His Times. unabr. ed. George Sayer. Read by Frederick Davidson. 10 cass. (Running Time: 14 hrs. 30 mins.). 1990. 69.95 (978-0-7861-0188-7(1), 1165) Blckstn Audio.
Sayer helps us see clearly Lewis's early years hinting at the flashes of childhood brilliance & eccentricity that would later become Lewis's hallmarks. He sheds new light on Lewis's academic career, discusses his transforming Christian experience & objectively assesses the role of religion in his life, deals frankly with his controversial relationship with Mrs. Moore & provides a revealing, passionate account of his marriage to Joy Davidman.

Jack: Straight from the Gut. Jack Welch & John A. Byrne. Narrated by Mike Barnicle. 10 cass. (Running Time: 14 hrs.). 2001. 88.00 (978-1-4025-0190-6(0), 96852) Recorded Bks.
The story behind the man Business Week called "the most impressive CEO of his time." A true American icon, Jack Welch tells the people who shaped his life and of his highly publicized successes and failures with General Electric.

Jack: Straight from the Gut. Jack Welch & John A. Byrne. Narrated by Mike Barnicle. 12 CDs. (Running Time: 14 hrs.). 2001. audio compact disk 116.00 (978-1-4025-0481-5(0), C1537) Recorded Bks.
The author tells of the people who shaped his life and of his highly publicized successes and failures with General Electric.

Jack: Straight from the Gut. abr. ed. Jack Welch & John A. Byrne. Read by Jack Welch. (ENG.). 2005. 14.98 (978-1-59483-191-1(2)) Pub: Hachet Audio. Dist(s): HachBkGrp

Jack: Straight from the Gut. abr. ed. Jack Welch & John A. Byrne. Read by Jack Welch. (Running Time: 6 hrs.). (ENG.). 2009. 44.98 (978-1-60024-547-3(1)) Pub: Hachet Audio. Dist(s): HachBkGrp

Jack: Straight from the Gut. unabr. ed. Jack Welch. Narrated by Mike Barnicle. 12 CDs. (Running Time: 14 hrs. 15 mins.). 2001. audio compact disk 116.00 Recorded Bks.
A true American icon, Jack Welch tells of the people who shaped his life and of his highly publicized successes and failures with general Electric. Narrator Mike Barnicle voices the straight-shooting legacy of a candid, engaging man.

Jack: Straight from the Gut. unabr. ed. Jack Welch & John A. Byrne. Read by Mike Barnicle. (ENG.). 2005. 16.98 (978-1-59483-401-1(6)) Pub: Hachet Audio. Dist(s): HachBkGrp

Jack Alive. Read by Ray Hicks. 1 cass. 8.00 (JA0052); audio compact disk 15.00 CD. (JA0052C) Appalshop.
Master storyteller Ray Hicks of Beech Mountain, North Carolina, known for his "Jack" tales, mixes songs, & "just talk" with stories from his own life. Recorded live at his home.

Jack & Granny Ugly. Read by Donald Davis. 1 cass. (Running Time: 1 hr.). (YA). (gr. 1-4). 1997. 12.00 (978-0-87483-507-6(0)) Pub: August Hse. Dist(s): Natl Bk Netwk
Jack, the adolescent Everyman, confronts the adult world in these tales of courage & wit. In "Granny Ugly" Jack relies on his common sense & several odd companions; in "Something Old, Something New" he discovers that things aren't always what they seem.

***Jack & Harry.** unabr. ed. Tony McKenna & Mervyn Davis. Read by David Tredinnick. (Running Time: 14 hrs.). 2009. audio compact disk 103.95 (978-1-74214-539-6(6), 9781742145396) Pub: Bolinda Pubng AUS. Dist(s): Bolinda Pub Inc

Jack & Jill. 2000. (978-1-57042-750-3(X)) Hachet Audio.

Jack & Jill. James Patterson. Read by Michael Kramer. (Alex Cross Ser.: No. 3). 1997. audio compact disk 80.00 (978-0-7366-8519-1(7)) Books on Tape.

Jack & Jill. abr. ed. James Patterson. Read by Blair Underwood & John Rubinstein. (Running Time: 3 hrs.). (Alex Cross Ser.: No. 3). (ENG.). 2006. 14.98 (978-1-59483-605-3(1)); audio compact disk 17.98 (978-1-59483-604-6(3)) Pub: Hachet Audio. Dist(s): HachBkGrp

Jack & Jill. abr. ed. James Patterson. Read by Blair Underwood & John Rubinstein. (Running Time: 3 hrs.). (Alex Cross Ser.: No. 3). (ENG.). 2009. 24.98 (978-1-60788-284-8(1)) Pub: Hachet Audio. Dist(s): HachBkGrp

Jack & Jill. unabr. ed. Louisa May Alcott. Narrated by Flo Gibson. (Running Time: 8 hrs. 59 mins.). (J). (gr. 3-6). 2006. 24.95 (978-1-55685-764-5(0)) Audio Bk Con.

Jack & Jill. unabr. ed. James Patterson. Read by Michael Kramer. 8 cass. (Running Time: 12 hrs.). (Alex Cross Ser.: No. 3). 1997. 64.00 (978-0-913369-41-8(1), 4218) Books on Tape.
In the middle of the night, a U. S. senator is found murdered in his Georgetown home. The only clue: a mysterious rhyme signed "Jack & Jill" promising more murders. Meanwhile, in Washington D. C., the beaten body of a little girl turns up in front of an elementary school. Is there a connection in the killings.

Jack & Jill. unabr. ed. James Patterson. Narrated by Richard Ferrone & George Guidall. 12 CDs. (Running Time: 13 hrs. 30 mins.). (Alex Cross Ser.: No. 3). 1999. audio compact disk 99.00 (978-0-7887-3415-1(6), C1021E7) Recorded Bks.
Alex Cross must follow a trail of nursery rhymes to find out who's murdering politicians & children in our nation's capital.

Jack & Jill. unabr. ed. James Patterson. Narrated by George Guidall & Richard Ferrone. 10 cass. (Running Time: 13 hrs. 30 mins.). (Alex Cross Ser.: No. 3). 1997. 85.00 (978-0-7887-0804-6(X), 94953E7) Recorded Bks.

Jack & Jill Play on the Hill Audio CD. Adapted by Benchmark Education Company Staff. Based on a work by Brooke Harris. (Reader's Theater Nursery Rhymes & Songs Ser.). (J). (gr. k-1). 2008. audio compact disk 10.00 (978-1-60437-988-4(X)) Benchmark Educ.

Jack & the Bean Stalk see Jacques et le Haricot Magique

Jack & the Bean Tree. 2004. bk. 24.95 (978-0-89719-779-3(8)); cass. & flmstrp 30.00 (978-0-89719-577-5(9)) Weston Woods.

Jack & the Beanstalk see Three Little Pigs & Other Fairy Tales

Jack & the Beanstalk see Stories Children Love to Hear

Jack & the Beanstalk. Scripts. 1 cass. or 1 CD. (Running Time: 20 mins.). (J). (gr. 1-5). 2000. pap. bk. & tchr. ed. 29.95 Bad Wolf Pr.
Developed specifically for "first time" musical producers & performers, it has been performed successfully by all kinds of students: big kids, little kids, gifted, ESL. The familiar story of Jack, a beanstalk, a nasty Giant & a very special goose. Sheet music available.

Jack & the Beanstalk. 1 cass. (J). 3.98 Clamshell. (978-1-55886-110-7(6), BB/PT 437) Smarty Pants.

***Jack & the Beanstalk.** Anonymous. 2009. (978-1-60136-576-7(4)) Audio Holding.

Jack & the Beanstalk. Arlene Capriola & Rigmor Swenson. Ed. by Cherisse Mastry. Illus. by Kathy Burns. 1 cass. (Once upon a Time Ser.). (J). (gr. k-2). 1998. 6.95 (978-1-57022-163-7(4), ECS1634) ECS Lrn Systs.

Jack & the Beanstalk. Arlene Capriola & Rigmor Swenson. Ed. by Cherisse Mastry. Illus. by Kathy Burns. 1 cass. (Once upon a Time Ser.). (J). (gr. k-2). 1998. pap. bk. & wbk. ed. 12.95 (978-1-57022-174-3(X)) ECS Lrn Systs.

Jack & the Beanstalk. As told by Michael Palin. Music by David A. Stewart. 1 cass. (Running Time: 1 hr.). 9.95 Weston Woods.
Foolish young Jack sells his family's cow for a handful of magic beans. Follow Jack up beyond the blue sky into a hilarious series of misadventures with a dimwitted ogre & his extra-large spouse.

Jack & the Beanstalk. Pocketaudio. 1 cass. (Running Time: 50 min.). (J). 2002. pap. bk. 12.95 (978-2-89558-084-3(7)) Pub: Al Stanke CAN. Dist(s): Penton Overseas

Jack & the Beanstalk. Ed. by George Rose. 1 cass. (J). 1986. 5.95 incl. bk. Scholastic Inc.

Jack & the Beanstalk. Adapted by Claudie Stanke. Illus. by Andre Pijet. 1 cass., bk. (Running Time: 15 mins.). (Classic Stories Ser.). (J). (ps-3). audio compact disk 9.95 (978-2-921997-82-9(7)) Pub: Coffragants CAN. Dist(s): Penton Overseas
Will help children understand that they cannot solve all their problems with magic. Time & patience are often more effective.

Jack & the Beanstalk. Composed by David A. Stewart. Narrated by Michael Palin. (Running Time: 30 mins.). (Rabbit Ears Collection). (J). (gr. k-4). 1998. 9.95 (PRE944AC) Weston Woods.
Foolish young Jack sells his family's cow for a handful of magic beans. Follow Jack up beyond the blue sky into a hilarious series of misadventures with a dimwitted ogre & his extra-large spouse.

Jack & the Beanstalk. Narrated by Bryan White. Adapted by Lisa Silver & Alan R. Schulman. 1 cass. (Running Time: 30 min.). (Froggy's Country Storybook Ser.: Vol. 2). (J). (gr. k-3). 1997. pap. bk. 12.98 Incl. full color follow-along bk. & autographed photo of narrator with Froggy, the host. (978-1-890818-75-3(5)) Virginia Recs.
Classic children's story told with a country adaptation with excerpts of hit country songs.

Jack & the Beanstalk. unabr. ed. Richard Caudle & Melissa Caudle. Read by Brad Caudle. Illus. by Anthony Guerra. 1 cass. (Running Time: 22 min.). (Rock 'N Read Ser.). (J). (gr. 1 up). 1996. pap. bk. 7.95 (978-1-878489-66-1(6), RL966) Rock N Learn.
Educator-developed approach teaches reading skills by using familiar stories & a cassette that presents both a slow version & a faster version for kids to follow along. Stories have a happy ending & teach an important lesson about life.

Jack & the Beanstalk. unabr. ed. Read by Julie Harris. 1 read-along cass. (Running Time: 12 min.). (World of Words Ser.). (J). (gr. k-3). bk. 15.00 (SAC 6500I) Spoken Arts.

Jack & the Beanstalk. unabr. ed. Ed McBain, pseud. Read by Michael Prichard. 6 cass. (Running Time: 9 hrs.). (Matthew Hope Mystery Ser.: No. 4). 1985. 48.00 (1965) Books on Tape.
On a steamy August day, Jack McKinney plunked down $4,000 on a farm, promised the remaining $36,000 in cash, & ordered Matthew Hope to push the deal through. Four days later McKinney was dead - no sign of the cash. As Hope is drawn deeper into his affairs he runs into a far-from-grieving mother, a sexually provoking sister, & a prostitute who's come into a sudden windfall.

Jack & the Beanstalk, Set. (ARA., (J). (gr. 2-5). 1987. 12.95 (978-0-86685-662-1(5), LDL162) Pub: Librairie du Liban FRA. Dist(s): Intl Bk Ctr

Jack & the Beanstalk & Other Children's Favorites. (J). 2005. audio compact disk (978-1-933796-30-7(8)) PC Treasures.

Jack & the Beanstalk & Other Classics of Childhood. unabr. ed. Various Authors. Read by Celebrity Narrators. (Running Time: 2 hrs.). 2009. 19.95 (978-1-4417-1138-0(4)); audio compact disk 14.95 (978-1-4417-1137-3(6)) Blckstn Audio.

Jack & the Beanstalk Audio CD. Benchmark Education Company. Based on a work by Brenda Parkes. (Shared Reading Classics Ser.). (J). (gr. k-2). 2009. audio compact disk 10.00 (978-1-60634-770-6(5)) Benchmark Educ.

Jack & the Beanstalk, the Stubborn Witch, Rapuzel, Betsy, the Magic Bus. EDCON Publishing Group Staff. (ENG.). 2008. audio compact disk 12.95 (978-0-8481-0418-4(8)) EDCON Pubng.

Jack Armstrong see Great Kid's Shows

Jack Armstrong the All American Boy: The Mystery of the Sunken Reef, Set. unabr. ed. Perf. by Charles Flynn et al. 3 cass. (Running Time: 3 hrs.). Dramatization. 1997. 15.95 (978-1-57816-144-7(4), JA303) Audio File.
Old time radio broadcast adventure serial.

Jack Benny. 1 cass. (Running Time: 60 min.). 5.99 (5230) Great Am Audio.
Radio classics. Radio's perennial 39 year old in "Charlie's Aunt" with Ronald Coleman & "The Cheapest Hotel in Town.".

Jack Benny. 2 cass. (Running Time: 2 hrs.). (Double Value Packs Ser.). 1991. (978-1-55569-377-0(6), 7109) Great Am Audio.
Radio's perennial 39 years-old featured in: "Jack Hires Rochester, Jack Discovers his Cast Members", "A Lover's Triangle" & "The Hospital Skit".

Jack Benny. Perf. by Jack Benny. 3 CDs. (Running Time: 3 hrs.). 2002. audio compact disk 34.98 (27582); 34.98 (4690); 17.98 (27584) Radio Spirits.
More than four decades after the last broadcast, this program still stands out as one of the greatest comedy shows ever. this special three-hour collectors addition brings together six of Benny's funniest shows and features previously unreleased episodes. Celebrate Jack's 39th birthday, again, take a ride to Cuc...amonga and sit back and enjoy as jack and the gang dish out the laughs.

Jack Benny. Created by Radio Spirits. (Running Time: 10800 sec.). 2004. 9.98 (978-1-57019-752-9(0)); audio compact disk 9.98 (978-1-57019-751-2(2)) Radio Spirits.

Jack Benny. unabr. ed. 4 cass. (Running Time: 4 hrs.). (Cassette Crates Ser.). 1991. (978-1-55569-458-6(6), 7300) Great Am Audio.
Contains: "Murder at Romanoff's", "Cowboys & Indians", "A Lover's Triangle", "Joe Visits the Doctor", "On the Golf Course", "Murder at the Racket Club", "Jack Hires Rochester" & "Jack Plans to go Abroad".

Jack Benny, Vol. 2. Read by Jack Benny. 3 cass. (Running Time: 3 hrs.). (3-Hour Collectors' Editions Ser.). 2002. 9.98 (978-1-57019-512-9(9), 27584) Radio Spirits.

Jack Benny, Vol. 2. Radio Spirits Staff. Read by Jack Benny. 3 CDs. (Running Time: 3 hrs.). (3-Hour Collectors' Editions Ser.). 2005. audio compact disk 9.98 (978-1-57019-513-6(7), 27582) Radio Spirits.

Jack Benny: Jack's Birthday & Treasure of the Sierra Madre. Perf. by Jack Benny. 1 cass. (Running Time: 1 hr.). 2001. 6.98 (2579) Radio Spirits.

***Jack Benny: Maestro.** Perf. by Jack Benny. 2010. audio compact disk 27.95 (978-1-57019-921-9(3)) Radio Spirits.

***Jack Benny: Neighbors.** Perf. by Jack Benny & Ronald Colman. 2010. audio compact disk 31.95 (978-1-57019-946-2(9)) Radio Spirits.

Jack Benny: Picture Parodies. Perf. by Jack Benny et al. (ENG.). 2009. audio compact disk 24.95 (978-1-57019-900-4(0)) Radio Spirits.

***Jack Benny: The Gang's All Here.** Perf. by Jack Benny et al. 2009. audio compact disk Rental 39.98 (978-1-57019-892-2(6)) Radio Spirits.

Jack Benny: The Holiday Shows. 6 cass. 24.95 Set in vinyl bookstyle album. (978-1-57816-034-1(0), JBH601) Audio File.
Celebrate a year's worth of holidays with Jack & the gang: Mary Livingston, Phil Harris, Dennis Day, Eddie "Rochester" Anderson, Don Wilson, Bob Crosby, plus Mel Blanc, Frank Nelson, Sheldon Leonard & others.

Jack Benny: The Horn Blows at Midnight. unabr. ed. Perf. by Claude Rains et al. 1 cass. (Running Time: 60 min.). Dramatization. 7.95 Norelco box. (CC-5730) Natl Recrd Co.
Jack Benny as a minor angel, Athaniel, from the 3rd Phalanx, 15th Cohort, is sent to Earth with Gabriel's trumpet...his mission is to destroy the planet by blowing his horn at precisely midnight. Naturally, complications arise with Jack Benny, supplying the laughter. Claude Rains is the chief, Mercedes MacCambridge is the chief's secretary, & Hans Conreid plays the part of Beethovan. Presented by Ford Motor Company. The commercials are nostalgic...the selling of the "new fashion winning" 1949 Ford cars. Ford Theatre broadcast of March 4, 1949 is based on the classic 1945 movie of the same name.

Jack Benny: World War II. 6 cass. 24.95 Set. (978-1-57816-033-4(2), 1008JB) Audio File.
The big star...& the big war. Jack & the regulars, Don Wilson, Phil Harris, Rochester, Dennis Day & Mary Livingstone in specially selected shows during World War II.

Jack Benny & Fred Allen see Great Christmas Comedy: Selected Sketches

Jack Benny Christmas Show of 1950 & The Jimmy Durante Christmas Show of 1947. unabr. ed. 1 cass. (Running Time: 60 min.). Dramatization. 7.95 Norelco box. (CC-9843) Natl Recrd Co.
Jack Benny: Jack's on his annual Christmas shopping trip with Mary Livingston. Jack buys a pair of cuff links for his announcer, Don Wilson, & drives the clerk, Mel Blanc, crazy. Phil Harris, Dennis Day & Mr. Kitzel are also buying gifts in the same store. Dennis buys his mother a corset! The Sportsmen sing a Lucky Strike commercial. Jimmy Durante: Ten year old movie star, Margaret O'Brien, joins the Schnoz in this fun-filled show. Jimmy, as Santa Claus, takes little Margaret along with him as he makes his rounds on this night before Christmas. The cast includes Arthur Treacher, Candy Candido, & Rexall sportscaster Tommy Harmon.

Jack Benny Christmas Show of 1952. 1 cass. (Running Time: 1 hr.). 7.95 (CC8060) Natl Recrd Co.

Jack Benny Christmas Show of 1953. Perf. by Bob Crosby & Jack Benny. 1 cass. (Running Time: 60 min.). 1953. 7.95 (CC-8070) Natl Recrd Co.
On the Jack Benny show, we find Jack on his annual Christmas shopping trip with Mary in Palm Springs. Jack decides to buy Don a Christmas gift of dates, but he is undecided, plain dates or with nuts. Cast also includes Mary Livingston & Don Wilson. On the Red Skelton show, "Deadeye" goes into the woods to cut Christmas trees to sell in the city. "Clem Kadiddlehopper" is a Christmas tree salesman. Red is also "Junior, the mean little kid," starring as "The Little Christmas Tree" in a holiday pageant, where he & Santa have quite a dicussion.

Jack Benny Christmas Show of 1954. Perf. by Mel Blanc. 1 cass. (Running Time: 1 hr.). 1954. 7.95 (CC-8080) Natl Recrd Co.
Mel Blanc is the harrassed departmemt store clerk when Jack goes to the art department to buy a Chritsmas gift of water colors for Don Wilson; or should he get oils? This time Mrs. Mel Blanc is there to help & Jack runs into problems. Cast also includes Mary Livingston, Don Wilson, Dennis Day, & Rochester. On the Phil Harris-Alice Faye Christmas Show, Phil & Frank Remley (Elliot Lewis) discover there isn't going to be a Christmas tree this year in the Town Square so they decide to go into "snow country" & cut down a 30 foot tree. Includes Walter Tetley as Julius & Robert North as Willie.

Jack Benny Holiday Show. (Running Time: 6 hrs.). 2004. audio compact disk 29.95 (978-1-57816-191-1(6)) Audio File.

Jack Benny Program. 6 cass. (Running Time: 6 hrs.). 24.95 (978-1-57816-036-5(7), 1015JB) Audio File.
A dozen classic comedy broadcasts featuring Jack, the regulars, & a host of great guests provide nonstop laughs. Complete with commercials.

Jack Benny Program. 1 CD. (Running Time: 1 hr.). (Old-Time Radio Blockbusters Ser.). 2002. audio compact disk 4.98 (978-1-57019-395-8(9), OTR7706) Pub: Radio Spirits. Dist(s): AudioGO
"Jesse James," pts. 1 and 2.

Jack Benny Program. 6 CDs. (Running Time: 6 hrs.). 2004. audio compact disk 29.95 (978-1-57816-213-0(0)) Audio File.

Jack Benny Program. Perf. by Jack Benny et al. 10 CDs. (Running Time: 10 hrs). 2002. pap. bk. 39.98 (4334); pap. bk. 34.98 (4333); 34.98 (4333) Radio Spirits.
Jack Benny delighted audiences on radio and television for more than 30 years. One of the secrets to Benny's longevity was his ability to attract America's brightest stars as guests to his program, where they knew Benny would always let them have the last laugh.

Jack Benny Program. Perf. by Phil Harris & Louella Parsons. 1 cass. (Running Time: 60 min.). 7.95 (CC-2939) Natl Recrd Co.
Listeners are reacting to the "I can't stand Jack Benny because..." contest; cast also includes Mary Livingston, Don Wilson, Dennis Day, & Rochester. In "Life of Riley," before the big football game, Riley sees a man give some money to Junior & suspects his son of accepting a bribe to throw the game.

Jack Benny Program. Chuck Schaden. 2 cass. (Speaking of Radio Ser.: Vol. 1). 10.95 (978-1-57816-020-4(0), SR101) Audio File.
Not just Old Time Radio...but a "behind the scenes" documentary featuring interviews, recollections & anecdotes from conversations with the stars & people who made this program one of America's best-loved shows for over 23 years! Hear Jack himself, Dennis Day, Phil Harris, Don Wilson, Sheldon Leonard & others talk about the good old days of radio...then hear excerpts from the shows...highlights from 23 years of Classic Radio comedy.

Jack Benny Program. Chuck Schaden. 2 cass. (Speaking of Radio Ser.: Vol. 2). 10.95 (978-1-57816-021-1(9), SR102) Audio File.

Jack Benny Program. Chuck Schaden. 2 cass. (Speaking of Radio Ser.: Vol. 3). 10.95 (978-1-57816-022-8(7), SR103) Audio File.

Jack Benny Program. Chuck Schaden. 6 cass. (Speaking of Radio Ser.: Vols. 1-3). 29.95 (978-1-57816-023-5(5), SRJB) Audio File.

Jack Benny Program. unabr. ed. Perf. by Ed Sullivan et al. 10 vols. (Running Time: 10 hrs.). (10-Hour Collections). 2002. bk. 34.98 (978-1-57019-485-6(8), OTR4333) Pub: Radio Spirits. Dist(s): AudioGO
Jack Benny delighted audiences on radio and television for more than 30 years. One of the secrets to Benny's longevity was his ability to attract America's brightest stars as guests to his program-where they knew Benny would always let them have the last laugh. Radio Spirits and the Smithsonian present 20 classic episodes of The Jack Benny Program, featuring a list of guest stars that reads like a Who's Who of Hollywood. Ed Sullivan, Don Ameche, Jimmy Stewart, Bob Hope, Bing Crosby, Orson Welles, Danny Kaye, Al Jolson and Red Skelton are just some of the big names included in this hilarious collection of 20 Benny favorites.

Jack Benny Program, Vol. 1. Perf. by Phil Harris et al. 6 cass. (Running Time: 1 hr. 30 mins. per cass.). (Golden Age of Radio Ser.). 1998. 44.95 (Q102) Blckstn Audio.
Includes such escapades as: "The Frightwig Murder Case," featuring Lauren Bacall & Humphrey Bogart; "Halloween" with Basil Rathbone; "The Egg & I"; " The Lost Weekend" with Ray Milland & others.

Jack Benny Program, Vol. 2. Perf. by Phil Harris et al. 6 cass. (Running Time: 1 hr. 30 mins. per cass.). (Golden Age of Radio Ser.). 34.98 (Q104) Blckstn Audio.
1944 - 1949 were the air dates for these 18 classic episodes. The high jinx included Jack, his entourage, Bing Crosby, Jane Wyman, Hoagy Carmichael, Amos 'n' Andy, James Stewart, Edgar Bergen, Red Skelton & other "thespians.".

Jack Benny Program, Vol. 2. collector's ed. Perf. by Mary Livingstone et al. 6 cass. (Running Time: 9 hrs.). 1998. bk. 34.98 (4104) Radio Spirits.
Collection of 18 classic episodes from 1944 to 1949 includes Hollywood Canteen, Jack Has Problems Buying a Cigar, I Can't Stand Jack Benny contest, Weekend at the Waldorf, A Ride in Jack's Maxwell, The Killer with

Edward G. Robinson, Jack Tries to Get Sportsmen Quartet Back, Jack's Double Date and 10 more.

Jack Benny Program, Vol. 3. Perf. by Phil Harris et al. 6 cass. (Running Time: 1 hr. 30 mins. per cass.). (Golden Age of Radio Ser.). 34.98 (Q105) Blckstn Audio.

Programs aired 1938-1940 featured guests such at screen legends Barbara Stanwyck & Joan Bennett.

Jack Benny Program, Vol. 3. collector's ed. Perf. by Mary Livingstone et al. 6 cass. (Running Time: 9 hrs.). 1998. bk. 34.98 (4145) Radio Spirits.

18 classic comedy programs from 1938 through early 1940, including Jack Films a Love Scene, Play: "The Hound of the Baskervilles", Jack is Late for the Show, Play: "Murder in the Library", Christmas at Jack's House, Everyone Wants a Raise, Dennis Day's First Show, Skiing at Yosemite, Birthday party for Jack and 9 more.

Jack Benny Program, Vol. 4. collector's ed. Perf. by Mary Livingstone et al. 6 cass. (Running Time: 9 hrs.). 2001. bk. 29.98 (4551) Radio Spirits.

18 classic broadcasts that aired between 1939 and 1948. Features episodes of Jack's infamous feud with Fred Allen and wartime remotes entertaining the troops.

Jack Benny Program: Al Jolson & Frank Fontaine. Perf. by Al Jolson et al. 1 cass. (Running Time: 1 hr.). 2001. 6.98 (2397) Radio Spirits.

Jack Benny Program: Alexander Graham Bell & Loretta Young. Perf. by Jack Benny & Loretta Young. 1 cass. (Running Time: 1 hr.). 2001. 6.98 Radio Spirits.

Jack Benny Program: Annual New Year's Party & Fred Allen. Perf. by Jack Benny & Fred Allen. 1 cass. (Running Time: 1 hr.). 2001. 6.98 (2438) Radio Spirits.

Jack Benny Program: Beverly Hills Beavers' Theater & Violin Lesson. Perf. by Jack Benny. 1 cass. (Running Time: 1 hr.). 2001. 6.98 (2346) Radio Spirits.

Jack Benny Program: Buck Benny & Buck Benny Rides Again. Perf. by Jack Benny. 1 cass. (Running Time: 1 hr.). 2001. 6.98 (2353) Radio Spirits.

Jack Benny Program: Buck Benny Rides Again & Again & Money Ain't Everything. Perf. by Jack Benny. 1 cass. (Running Time: 1 hr.). 2001. 6.98 (2354) Radio Spirits.

Jack Benny Program: Buck Benny's New Year & Fresh Eggs. Perf. by Jack Benny. 1 cass. (Running Time: 1 hr.). 2001. 6.98 (2356) Radio Spirits.

Jack Benny Program: Buck Shot & The Diamond Watch. Perf. by Jack Benny. 1 cass. (Running Time: 1 hr.). 2001. 6.98 (2355) Radio Spirits.

Jack Benny Program: Buckingham Benny & Buck's Mexican Adventure. Perf. by Jack Benny. 1 cass. (Running Time: 1 hr.). 2001. 6.98 (2357) Radio Spirits.

Jack Benny Program: Camping with Kids & N.Y. or Bust. Perf. by Jack Benny. 1 cass. (Running Time: 1 hr.). 2001. 6.98 (2341) Radio Spirits.

Jack Benny Program: Chicago Here We Come & Chicago Conga. Perf. by Jack Benny. 1 cass. (Running Time: 1 hr.). 2001. 6.98 Radio Spirits.

Jack Benny Program: Christmas Spirit & Shocking. Perf. by Jack Benny. 1 cass. (Running Time: 1 hr.). 2001. 6.98 (2340) Radio Spirits.

Jack Benny Program: Dennis Loves Barbara & Easter Parade. Perf. by Jack Benny. 1 cass. (Running Time: 1 hr.). 2001. 6.98 (2342) Radio Spirits.

Jack Benny Program: Don's Contract & Jack is at His Wits End with Don. Perf. by Jack Benny. 1 cass. (Running Time: 1 hr.). 2001. 6.98 (1565) Radio Spirits.

Jack Benny Program: Foggy Knight in London & UCLA vs. USC. Perf. by Jack Benny. 1 cass. (Running Time: 1 hr.). 2001. 6.98 (2352) Radio Spirits.

Jack Benny Program: Goodbye 47, Hello 48 & Rose Bowling. Perf. by Jack Benny. 1 cass. (Running Time: 1 hr.). 2001. 6.98 (2335) Radio Spirits.

Jack Benny Program: Hints to Jack about Christmas Gift & Problems with Jack's Tree Lights. Perf. by Jack Benny. 1 cass. (Running Time: 1 hr.). 2001. 6.98 (2221) Radio Spirits.

Jack Benny Program: House in Palm Springs & Doo Wah Ditty. Perf. by Jack Benny. 1 cass. (Running Time: 1 hr.). 2001. 6.98 (2337) Radio Spirits.

Jack Benny Program: I Can't Stand Jack Benny Contest & Ronald & Benita Colman. Perf. by Ronald Colman et al. 1 cass. (Running Time: 1 hr.). 2001. 6.98 (2121) Radio Spirits.

Jack Benny Program: Jack & the Gang Vacation in Palm Springs & Jack to Paints His House. Perf. by Jack Benny. 1 cass. (Running Time: 1 hr.). 2001. 6.98 (2420) Radio Spirits.

Jack Benny Program: Jack is Christmas Shopping & Gang Travels to Palm Springs. Perf. by Jack Benny. 1 cass. (Running Time: 1 hr.). 2001. 6.98 (1755) Radio Spirits.

Jack Benny Program: Jack Is Mad about Dennis' & Phil's Radio Show & Academy Awards. Perf. by Jack Benny. 1 cass. (Running Time: 1 hr.). 2001. 6.98 (2262) Radio Spirits.

Jack Benny Program: Jack Loses Him Memory & Results of Jack's Memory Loss. Perf. by Jack Benny. 1 cass. (Running Time: 1 hr.). 2001. 6.98 (1982) Radio Spirits.

Jack Benny Program: Jack's Birthday is Tomorrow & Treasure of the Sierra Madre. Perf. by Jack Benny. 1 cass. (Running Time: 1 hr.). 2001. 6.98 (2579) Radio Spirits.

Jack Benny Program: Leaving Town & That's a Lot of Bull. Perf. by Jack Benny. 1 cass. (Running Time: 1 hr.). 2001. 6.98 (2336) Radio Spirits.

Jack Benny Program: Leo Durocher & Tax Man. Perf. by Jack Benny & Leo Durocher. 1 cass. (Running Time: 1 hr.). 2001. 6.98 (1931) Radio Spirits.

Jack Benny Program: Naval Air Station, Livermore, CA & Dennis Daydreams. Perf. by Jack Benny. 1 cass. (Running Time: 1 hr.). 2001. 6.98 (1754) Radio Spirits.

Jack Benny Program: New NBC Studios in San Francisco & Ice Skating in Central Park. Perf. by Jack Benny. 1 cass. (Running Time: 1 hr.). 2001. 6.98 (2244) Radio Spirits.

Jack Benny Program: New Year's Eve & USC vs. Alabama. Perf. by Jack Benny. 1 cass. (Running Time: 1 hr.). 2001. 6.98 (2333) Radio Spirits.

Jack Benny Program: Operation: Option & Momentous Meetings. Perf. by Jack Benny. 1 cass. (Running Time: 1 hr.). 2001. 6.98 (2348) Radio Spirits.

Jack Benny Program: Operation Recuperation & Don's Day. Perf. by Jack Benny. 1 cass. (Running Time: 1 hr.). 2001. 6.98 (2344) Radio Spirits.

Jack Benny Program: Orson Welles & Joe Louis. Perf. by Jack Benny. 1 cass. (Running Time: 1 hr.). 2001. 6.98 (1753) Radio Spirits.

Jack Benny Program: Philzie Lamb & Stinky Pie & Nightmares of Fred Allen. Perf. by Jack Benny. 1 cass. (Running Time: 1 hr.). 2001. 6.98 (2358) Radio Spirits.

Jack Benny Program: Public Insect #1 & Feud with Fred Allen. Perf. by Jack Benny. 1 cass. (Running Time: 1 hr.). 2001. 6.98 (2361) Radio Spirits.

Jack Benny Program: Publicity Pigeons & Like a Mother to Me. Perf. by Jack Benny. 1 cass. (Running Time: 1 hr.). 2001. 6.98 (2347) Radio Spirits.

Jack Benny Program: Riding a Horse & George Washington Slept Here. Perf. by Jack Benny. 1 cass. (Running Time: 1 hr.). 2001. 6.98 (2521) Radio Spirits.

Jack Benny Program: Sage-brush Soap Jingle & Jack the Champ. Perf. by Jack Benny. 1 cass. (Running Time: 1 hr.). 2001. 6.98 (2345) Radio Spirits.

Jack Benny Program: Snow White & the Seven Dwarfs & Jack Tells How He Saved Fred Allen's Life. Perf. by Jack Benny. 1 cass. (Running Time: 1 hr.). 2001. 6.98 (2480) Radio Spirits.

Jack Benny Program: Stolen Violin & Ben Bernie's Disappearance. Perf. by Jack Benny. 1 cass. (Running Time: 1 hr.). 2001. 6.98 (2359) Radio Spirits.

Jack Benny Program: Stop the Bus & Edward, My Son. Perf. by Jack Benny. 1 cass. (Running Time: 1 hr.). 2001. 6.98 (2343) Radio Spirits.

Jack Benny Program: The Champion Set-up & Last Show of the Season. Perf. by Jack Benny. 1 cass. (Running Time: 1 hr.). 2001. 6.98 (1962) Radio Spirits.

Jack Benny Program: The Gold Rush & Missing Maxwell. Perf. by Jack Benny. 1 cass. (Running Time: 1 hr.). 2001. 6.98 (2349) Radio Spirits.

Jack Benny Program: The Happy Hour Tea Room & Gary Cooper. Perf. by Jack Benny. 1 cass. (Running Time: 1 hr.). 2001. 6.98 (2017) Radio Spirits.

Jack Benny Program: The Seventh Hole at Hillcrest Country Club & Cleaning Jack's Den. Perf. by Jack Benny. 1 cass. (Running Time: 1 hr.). 2001. 6.98 (2497) Radio Spirits.

Jack Benny Program: Train Leaving on Track 5 Routine & After a Show. Perf. by Jack Benny. 1 cass. (Running Time: 1 hr.). 2001. 6.98 (1547) Radio Spirits.

Jack Benny Program: TV Show Trek & Wrong Jack. Perf. by Jack Benny. 1 cass. (Running Time: 1 hr.). 2001. 6.98 (2351) Radio Spirits.

Jack Benny Program: Unjust Reward & Jack Plays "The Bee" Perf. by Jack Benny. 1 cass. (Running Time: 1 hr.). 2001. 6.98 (2360) Radio Spirits.

Jack Benny Program: Walking Man Contest & And the Winner is. Perf. by Jack Benny. 1 cass. (Running Time: 1 hr.). 2001. 6.98 (2338) Radio Spirits.

Jack Benny Program: Where's Jack & The Egg & I. Perf. by Jack Benny. 1 cass. (Running Time: 1 hr.). 2001. 6.98 (2339) Radio Spirits.

Jack Benny Program: Yukon Jack & Journey to the Surface of the Earth. Perf. by Jack Benny. 1 cass. (Running Time: 1 hr.). 2001. 6.98 (2372) Radio Spirits.

Jack Benny Program Pts. 1-2: Jesse James. Perf. by Jack Benny. 1 CD. (Running Time: 1 hr.). (Old-Time Radio Blockbusters Ser.). 2001. audio compact disk 4.98 (7706) Radio Spirits.

Jack Benny Show. Perf. by Bing Crosby et al. 1 cass. (Running Time: 60 min.). 1948. 7.95 (CC-5070) Natl Recrd Co.

Jack visits the Colmans as he wants Ronald to appear in a movie with him. While there he borrows Ronald's Academy Award Oscar. On the way home he is held up & the Oscar is stolen. In the next show Jack goes to Bing's home to borrow an Oscar from him to give to Ronald Colman. Cast also includes Benita Colman, Phil Harris, Rochester, Dennis Day, Don Wilson, Mary Livingston, & the Ink Spots.

Jack Benny Show. unabr. ed. Perf. by Groucho Marx & Eddie Cantor. 1 cass. (Running Time: 60 min.). Dramatization. (Jack Benny Special Edition Ser.: No. 1). 1944. 7.95 Norelco box. (CC8501) Natl Recrd Co.

Groucho Marx: Jack & Groucho are playing checkers, as they need the exercise. Groucho wants to double the stakes they are playing for, but Jack thinks 5 cents is enough. Everyone then joins in on a melodrama, "The Gilroy Murder Case." Grapenuts. Eddie Cantor: Broadcast from the Hollywood Canteen. The whole gang is working there...Mary is dancing, Rochester is trying to sing, & Butterfly is also entertaining. They meet Larry Adler who plays "Begin the Beguine" on his harmonica. Eddie Cantor is also working there, & he & Jack get into an argument over who is the older. Lucky Strike.

Jack Benny Show: Broadcast from Chicago & Broadcast from New York. unabr. ed. Perf. by Al Jolson. 1 cass. (Running Time: 60 min.). Dramatization. (Jack Benny Special Edition Ser.: No. 4). 1947. 7.95 Norelco box. (CC8504) Natl Recrd Co.

Broadcast from Chicago: Jack is performing at the Chicago Theatre, & he says that 5,000 people came to meet him at the train. He leads them in a Congo line for two miles that finally ends at the Chicago Theatre box office! A lot of local Chicago & Waukegan gags. Dennis Day is his usual funny self with some great lines. Lucky Strike. Broadcast from New York: Al Jolson sings two fine songs in the inimitable Al Jolson style..."April Showers" & "You Made Me Love You." Mr. Kitzel has a funny skit, & the Sportsman Quartet sing a commercial. Phil Harris says he is the toast of New York..."Rye" toast. Lucky Strike.

Jack Benny Show: Departing for New York & Larry Adler - Harmonica Virtuoso. unabr. ed. 1 cass. (Running Time: 60 min.). Dramatization. 7.95 Norelco box. (CC8506) Natl Recrd Co.

Departing for New York: Jack is to appear on TV in New York, & the preparations for the trip are quite disorganized. A ride to the train station in his Maxwell, buying magazines from Mr. Kitzel, meeting Phil Harris & his piano player, & finally Dennis Day's mother, produce enough laughs for anyone. Lucky Strike, 1951. Larry Adler - Harmonica Virtuoso: Broadcast live from the army air base at Marshfield, California. It is Jack's birthday, & he offers a prize to anyone that can guess his age...they are fired. He gets a birthday gift - a can of K-rations. Larry Adler plays a very fine rendition of "Blues in the Night." Grapenuts, 1944.

Jack Benny Show: Jack's Birthday & A "Nice, Sweet" Program. unabr. ed. 1 cass. (Running Time: 60 min.). Dramatization. (Jack Benny Special Edition Ser.: No. 3). 1946. 7.95 Norelco box. (CC8503) Natl Recrd Co.

Jack's Birthday: Once again Jack is still not age 40...when happy with something, why change it? Skits with Jack taking violin lessons from Professor LeBlanc, & Rochester's boating accident are funny. An Indian Reservation commercial is thoroughly enjoyable. Lucky Strike. A "Nice, Sweet" Program: Jack has been criticized by a writer who has written an article saying that Jack's show consists of sarcastic humor & insulting jokes. Jack does a nice, sweet program, "Life Can Be Beautiful Type," for the writer. Don Wilson even sings the commercial. Lucky Strike.

Jack Benny Show: The IRS Visits Jack & The IRS Re-Visits Jack. unabr. ed. Perf. by Ronald Colman. 1 cass. (Running Time: 60 min.). Dramatization. (Jack Benny Special Edition Ser.: No. 5). 1951. 7.95 Norelco box. (CC8505) Natl Recrd Co.

The IRS Visits Jack: Jack receives a telephone call from the IRS. They want to discuss his 1950 income tax return. Jack tells Rochester to "get me an Alcatraz, I mean an Alka Seltzer!" Jack tells the two IRS agents he earned 375,000 dollars. His expenses for entertainment were 17.00 dollars. The IRS agents are dumbfounded. Lucky Strike. The IRS Re-Visits Jack: The IRS agents still can't believe that anyone earning 375,000 dollars a year can only spend 17.00 dollars a year on entertainment. They check this out with Ronald & Bonita Colman & learn that Jack took them, & Mary, out to an expensive restaurant, yet, spent only 3.90. The explanation is really hilarious. Lucky Strike.

Jack Benny Show: The Lost Weekend & Fred Allen & Jack Paar. unabr. ed. Perf. by Ray Milland. 1 cass. (Running Time: 60 min.). Dramatization. (Jack Benny Special Edition Ser.: No. 2). 7.95 Norelco box. (CC8502) Natl Recrd Co.

The Lost Weekend Sketch: This is one hilarious Lost Weekend sketch (their version) with Jack & Ray playing twin brothers...both alcoholics. Phil Harris is funny as the elder brother who frowns on drinking & wants them to stay away from liquor! Lots of laughs & gags. Lucky Strike, 1946. Fred Allen & Jack Paar: This is their last show of the season, & Jack decides to go down Jack Benny's Alley & ask the questions, "Who is the better comedian...Jack or Fred Allen?" Allen appears on the show...to louse-up Jack's show. Parr is introduced as the kid that will be Jack's summer replacement. He gets "some-kind-of" advice from Jack & Fred. Lucky Strike, 1947.

Jack Benny Show: "Your Money or Your Life!" unabr. ed. Perf. by Ronald Coleman et al. 1 cass. (Running Time: 1 hr.). 4.95 (978-1-57816-110-2(X), JB219) Audio File.

Two consecutive radio show on 3/28/48 & 4/4/48.

Jack Benny Show No. 2. Perf. by Phil Harris et al. 1 cass. (Running Time: 60 min.). Incl. Jack Benny Show No. 2: Jack Goes into His Vault. (CC-8420); Jack Benny Show No. 2: Jack's First Time on CBS. (CC-8420); 7.95 (CC-8420) Natl Recrd Co.

Jack gets a violin lesson from Professor LaBlanc & goes down to his vault to get the dollar & fifty cents for the fee. On his first show for CBS, Jack drives everyone crazy with his constant worry. Cast also includes Don Wilson, Mel Blanc, & Mary Livingston.

Jack Benny Show No. 2: Jack Goes into His Vault see Jack Benny Show No. 2

Jack Benny Show No. 2: Jack's First Time on CBS see Jack Benny Show No. 2

Jack Benny, Special Edition. 2 CDs. (Running Time: 2 hrs.). 2004. audio compact disk 12.95 (978-1-57816-220-8(3)) Audio File.

Jack Benny Special Edition: Jack's Famous Vault & Jack's Quartet: The Sportsmen. unabr. ed. Perf. by Jack Benny. 2 cass. (Running Time: 2 hrs.). 10.95 Set. (978-1-57816-152-2(5), JBA201) Audio File.

Jack Benny Spoofs. Created by Radio Spirits. (Running Time: 10800 sec.). 2004. 9.98 (978-1-57019-756-7(3)); audio compact disk 9.98 (978-1-57019-755-0(5)) Radio Spirits.

Jack Benny Visits & Kingfish Wins a TV. 1 cass. (Running Time: 60 min.). Dramatization. (Amos 'n' Andy Ser.). 1949. 6.00 Once Upon Rad.

Radio broadcasts - humor.

Jack Benny, WW II. 6 CDs. (Running Time: 6 hrs.). 2004. audio compact disk 29.95 (978-1-57816-214-7(9)) Audio File.

Jack Blank & the Imagine Nation. unabr. ed. Matt Myklusch. Read by Norbert Leo Butz. (Running Time: 9 hrs. 30 mins. 0 sec.). (ENG.). (J). 2010. audio compact disk 34.99 (978-1-4423-0478-9(2)) Pub: S&S Audio. Dist(s): S and S Inc

Jack Buck: Voice of the Cardinals. Janell Hughes. (ENG.). 2006. audio compact disk 16.00 (978-0-9818365-0-8(X)) Baseball Voice.

Jack Conroy: Reading & Interview. Interview. 1 cass. (Running Time: 1 hr. 4 min.). Incl. Disinherited. (1043); 14.95 (978-1-55644-007-6(3), 1043) Am Audio Prose.

Selections from the classic novel of the Great Depression vividly depict the world of manual labor for men, women & children of that time. Conroy's interview covers his career as editor of three highly influential left-wing literary journals during the Thirties, including the story of the "Partisan Review Anvil".

Jack Conroy: The Fields of Golden Glow. unabr. ed. Jack Conroy. Read by Jack Conroy. 1 cass. (Running Time: 29 min.). 1991. 10.00 (110478) New Letters.

Jack Conroy Memorial. unabr. ed. Jack Conroy. Read by Jack Conroy. 1 cass. (Running Time: 29 min.). 1990. 10.00 (033090) New Letters.

Conroy was one of the most important writers of the Proletariat Movement of the 1930's. This program features a 1978 recording of Conroy reading from his autobiography.

Jack Gilbert. unabr. ed. Ed. by Jim McKinley. Prod. by Rebekah Presson. 1 cass. (Running Time: 29 min.). (New Letters on the Air Ser.). 1994. 10.00 (011794) New Letters.

The San Francisco poet publishes his first book in 11 years this month. Gilbert reads from "The Great Fires" & talks about his work, which has been called the "stoniest & most ascetic Romanticism in American poetry." Gilbert says his poetry is about "ideas & perceptions," which he tries to express "with the least means possible".

Jack Higgins: Dark Justice, the Killing Ground. abr. unabr. ed. Jack Higgins. (Running Time: 15 hrs.). 2010. audio compact disk 19.99 (978-1-4418-4959-5(9), 9781441849595, BACD) Brilliance Audio.

Jack Higgins: The White House Connection, Dark Justice, & Without Mercy. unabr. ed. Jack Higgins. (Running Time: 20 hrs.). 2006. audio compact disk 36.95 (978-1-4233-1677-0(0), 9781423316770, Bril Audio CD Unabri) Brilliance Audio.

The White House Connection: Someone is killing off the members of a splinter group known as the Sons of Erin, normally not a cause for much concern, but the consequences are much greater than anyone realizes. For in these actions lie the seeds of disaster: the fall of two governments, the derailing of the Irish peace process. Dillon and Johnson must stop this unknown assassin, the heads of state agree, quickly, quietly, before all hell breaks loose... Dark Justice: Someone is recruiting a shadowy network of agents with the intention of creating terror. White House operative Blake Johnson and his opposite number in British intelligence, Sean Dillon, set out to trace the source of the havoc, but behind the first man they find another, and behind him another still. And that man is not pleased by the interference. Soon he will target them all: Johnson, Dillon, Dillon's colleagues. And one of them will fall... Without Mercy: As Detective Superintendent Hannah Bernstein of Special Branch lies recuperating in the hospital, a dark shadow sent by a figure from the past steals across the room and finishes the job. Consumed by grief and rage, Dillon, Blake, Ferguson, and all who loved Hannah swear vengeance, no matter where it takes them.

Jack in the Pulpit. unabr. ed. Cynthia Riggs. Read by Davina Porter. (Running Time: 28800 sec.). (Martha's Vineyard Mystery Ser.). 2007. 54.95 (978-1-4332-0227-8(1)); audio compact disk 29.95 (978-1-4332-0229-2(8)); audio compact disk 63.00 (978-1-4332-0228-5(X)) Blckstn Audio.

Jack Introduces Staff & Filming Jack's Life. Perf. by Jack Benny. 1 cass. (Running Time: 60 min.). Dramatization. (Jack Benny Show Ser.). 1949. 6.00 Once Upon Rad.

Radio broadcasts - humor.

Jack Jouett's Ride. 2004. 8.95 (978-1-56008-937-7(7)); cass. & flmstrp 30.00 (978-1-56008-694-9(7)) Weston Woods.

Jack Kerouac. 1 cass. (Running Time: 60 min.). 10.95 (OP-79-01-02, HarperThor) HarpC GBR.

Jack Kerouac Collection. Jack Kerouac. 4 cass. 1990. 39.98 Set. (978-0-930589-03-5(3)) Rhino Enter.

Jack Kerouac Collection. Jack Kerouac. 1 cass. 1998. bk. 39.98 (978-1-56826-199-7(3)) Rhino Enter.

Jack Kerouac Collection. deluxe ed. Jack Kerouac. 4 CDs. (Running Time: 6 hrs.). 2001. bk. 49.98 (R2 70939) Rhino Enter.

Jack, Knave & Fool. unabr. ed. Bruce Alexander. Read by Stuart Langton. 8 cass. (Running Time: 12 hrs.). (Sir John Fielding Mystery Ser.). 1999. 64.00 (4889); 64.00 (978-0-7366-4444-0(X), 4889) Books on Tape.
In the fifth Sir John Fielding mystery, the legendary eighteenth-century London judge takes on his most difficult case to date. A lord dies suddenly while attending a concert. A disembodied head washes up on the banks of the Thames. While investigating both, Sir John and Jeremy learn more than they ever cared to about families, greed, deception and the peculiar nature of homicide.

Jack London: Short Stories. Jack London. Read by Richard Rohan et al. (Playaway Young Adult Ser.). 2008. 39.99 (978-1-60640-842-1(9)) Find a World.

Jack London: White Fang/the Call of the Wild. unabr. ed. Jack London. Read by John Lee. (Running Time: 41400 sec.). 2006. audio compact disk & audio compact disk 19.95 (978-0-7861-6681-7(9)) Blckstn Audio.

Jack London Collection. Jack London. Ed. by Jerry Stemach et al. Retold by John Matern. Illus. by Karyl Shields. Narrated by Ed Smaron. Contrib. by Ted S. Hasselbring. 1 cass. (Running Time: 1 hr.). (Start-to-Finish Books: Vol. 2). 1999. (978-1-893376-47-2(8), F08K2) D Johnston Inc.
Two prospectors have stayed out in the wild Yukon until both are starving and lost. The stronger man abandons the weaker. The weak man keeps moving. Every hour of the day, every step is pain. Hunting minnows and birds to eat is torturous frustration. Finally, pursued by a starving wolf the man comes in sight of the sea and a ship is his only chance of rescue.

Jack London Collection. Jack London. Ed. by Jerry Stemach et al. Retold by John Matern. Illus. by Karyl Shields. Narrated by Ed Smaron. 1 cass. (Running Time: 1 hr.). (Start-to-Finish Books: Vol. 2). 2000. 35.00 (978-1-58702-441-2(1)) D Johnston Inc.

Jack London Collection. Jack London. Retold by John Matern. Illus. by Karyl Shields. (Start-to-Finish Books: Vol. 2). 2002. 100.00 (978-1-58702-962-2(6)) D Johnston Inc.

Jack London Collection. Retold by John Matern. Jack London. (Famous Short Stories Ser.). 1999. audio compact disk 18.95 (978-1-4105-0135-6(3)) D Johnston Inc.

Jack London Short Stories. Jack London. Narrated by Flo Gibson. 2009. audio compact disk 16.95 (978-1-60646-093-1(5)) Audio Bk Con.

Jack London Short Stories. unabr. ed. Jack London. Read by Tim Behrens. 4 cass. (Running Time: 4 hrs.). 1986. 26.95 (978-1-55686-233-5(4), 233) Books in Motion.
Nine classic Jack London short stories. The stories are: To Build a Fire, Up the Slide, The Sun Dog Trail, The Law of Life, Love of Life, Husky-Wolf Dog of the North, Housekeeping in the Klondike, To the Man on Trail, The Priestly Perogative.

Jack London Short Stories, Set. unabr. ed. Jack London. Read by Flo Gibson. 2 cass. (Running Time: 3 hrs.). 1994. 14.95 (978-1-55685-306-7(8)) Audio Bk Con.
Man's inhumanity to man, as well as man pitted against nature & the violence of the elements, are vividly exposed in the following stories: "Love of Life", "Batard", "The House of Mapuhi", & "Mauki".

Jack Maggs. unabr. ed. Peter Carey. Narrated by Steven Crossley. 9 cass. (Running Time: 13 hrs. 30 mins.). 1998. 80.00 (978-0-7887-2185-4(2), 95481E7) Recorded Bks.
In the 1830s, risking execution if he is discovered, Jack Maggs returns to England from Australia. Hiring on as a servant of a wealthy London household, he insinuates himself into their affairs, secure in the knowledge that they cannot guess his ultimate goal.

Jack Matonis: A Radical, New Approach to Opposing Government: The Weapons for Liberty. (Running Time: 60 min.). (Cal State Univ., Long Beach). 1982. 9.00 (F131) Freeland Pr.
Discusses his experiences with the IRS & offers suggestions to the audience on how to help themselves in tax matters.

Jack Matonis: A Technological Rebellion Against Government. (Running Time: 60 min.). (Cal State Univ., Long Beach). 1981. 9.00 (F118) Freeland Pr.
Discusses & gives answers to questions that many tax-payers (& non-tax-payers) are interested in.

Jack Matonis: Constitutional Law & the Tax Revolt. 2 cass. (Running Time: 3 hrs.). (Remanent Tapes). 1979. 19.00 (R302A & B) Freeland Pr.
Tells about events that government has caused in legal proceeding & taxes, & he suggests certain investment alternatives that might help the investor avoid high taxes.

Jack Matonis: Individual Counter-Government Action As a Means to Future Liberty. (Running Time: 60 min.). (Cypress College). 1980. 9.00 (F100) Freeland Pr.
Jailed for his refusal to pay income tax, this Attorney-at-Law talks about "Monkey Wrench Law," describing ways that citizens can achieve justice, & suggests various methods for obtaining favorable court decisions.

Jack Matonis Pt. 2: Workshop Talk. (Running Time: 60 min.). (Cal State Univ., Long Beach). 1982. 9.00 (F144A & B) Freeland Pr.
Talks about his battle with the tax collectors & suggests things one can do to save themselves from the pitfalls of tax-paying.

Jack Matonis: Workshop Talk Pt. 1: New Approaches to Opposing Government. (Running Time: 60 min.). (Cal State Univ., Long Beach). 1982. 9.00 (F143) Freeland Pr.
Talks about his battle with the tax collectors & suggest things one can do to save themselves from the pitfalls of tax-paying.

Jack Matthews. unabr. ed. Jack Matthews. Read by Jack Matthews. 1 cass. (Running Time: 29 min.). 1990. 10.00 (012690) New Letters.
Novelist, poet & short story writer is interviewed & reads from his story, "Ghostly Populations".

Jack Nicklaus: My Story. unabr. ed. Jack Nicklaus & Ken Bowden. Read by Ian Esmo. 13 cass. (Running Time: 19 hrs.). 1998. 85.95 (978-0-7861-1429-0(0), 2315) Blckstn Audio.
Inside, in-depth account of legendary major triumphs, along with many other competition highlights - & some lowlights, too - of one of the greatest sports careers of all time.

Jack Prelutsky Holiday Audio Collection. abr. ed. Jack Prelutsky. Read by Jack Prelutsky. (J). 2005. 13.95 (978-0-06-082065-7(9), HarperChildAud) HarperCollins Pubs.

***Jack Prelutsky Holiday Audio Collection.** unabr. ed. Jack Prelutsky. Read by Jack Prelutsky. (ENG.). 2006. (978-0-06-135546-2(1), GreenwillowBks); (978-0-06-135545-5(3), GreenwillowBks) HarperCollins Pubs.

Jack Prelutsky's Big Collection. Jack Prelutsky. Read by Jack Prelutsky. 2 cass. (Running Time: 1 hr. 28 mins.). (J). (gr. k-3). 2004. 23.00 (978-0-8072-8428-5(9), Listening Lib) Random Audio Pubg.

Jack Prelutsky's Fantasy Festival. Jack Prelutsky. Read by Jack Prelutsky. 2 cass. (Running Time: 1 hr. 38 mins.). (J). (gr. k-3). 2004. 23.00 (978-0-8072-8429-2(7), Listening Lib) Random Audio Pubg.

Jack Russell: Dog Detective Dog Den Mystery. unabr. ed. Darrel Odgers & Sally Odgers. Read by Alan King. (Running Time: 2700 sec.). (Jack Russell: Dog Detective Ser.). (J). (gr. 3-7). 2006. audio compact disk 39.95 (978-1-74093-763-4(5)) Pub: Bolinda Pubng AUS. Dist(s): Bolinda Pub Inc

Jack Tales. Read by Maud Long. 8.95 (L47); 8.95 (L48) Lib Congress.
Includes Jack in the Giants' New Ground & Jack & the Varmints.

Jack Tales: More Than a Beanstalk. Read by Donald Davis. 1 cass. (Running Time: 43 min.). (J). (ps-4). 1984. 8.95 (978-0-89719-934-6(0), WW727C) Weston Woods.
Collection includes "Jack & Old Bluebeard," "Jack Tells a Story," & "Jack & the Silver Sword".

Jack Welch & the GE Way: Management Insights & Leadership Secrets of the Legendary CEO. Robert Slater. 4 cass. (Running Time: 6 hrs.). 2004. 24.00 (978-1-932378-42-9(1)); audio compact disk 28.00 (978-1-932378-43-6(X)) Pub: A Media Intl. Dist(s): Natl Bk Netwk
A brilliant portrait that tells you how he dismatled the boundaries betweenmanagement layers, between engineers and marketers, and between GE and its customers to streamline the process of getting products and services to market.

Jack Wheeler: The New Revolution in the Third World. (Running Time: 60 min.). (Cal State Univ., Long Beach). 1984. 9.00 (F168) Freeland Pr.
Wheeler, who started his world-wide exploring at age 14, takes us to Afghanistan, Angola, Asia & Central America. His first-hand knowledge of the freedom movements in the Third World reflects his philosophy.

Jack Wilkins: A Merry Christmas. Jack Wilkins. 2002. audio compact disk (20257CD) Mel Bay.

Jackalope. Janet Stevens & Susan Stevens Crummel. Narrated by Tom Stechschulte. (Running Time: 30 mins.). (J). 2003. audio compact disk 12.75 (978-1-4193-1753-8(9)) Recorded Bks.

Jackal's Head. unabr. ed. Elizabeth Peters, pseud. Read by Grace Conlin. 5 cass. (Running Time: 7 hrs.). 1995. 39.95 (978-0-7861-0657-8(3), 1553) Blckstn Audio.
Althea Tomlinson came back to Egypt as just another tourist. That's what she told herself, anyway. Really, though, what drove her was a desire to discover the truth behind her father's disgrace & subsequent death. That she knew something was unquestionable. But what? Finding out would clear her father's name, certainly. It could also lead to Althea's death...because the secret is centuries old - as old as the treasure of Nerfertiti.

Jackal's Head. unabr. ed. Elizabeth Peters, pseud. Read by Grace Conlin. (Running Time: 23400 sec.). 2008. audio compact disk & audio compact disk 60.00 (978-1-4332-3414-9(9)); audio compact disk & audio compact disk 29.95 (978-1-4332-3415-6(7)) Blckstn Audio.

Jackdaws. unabr. ed. Ken Follett. Read by Kate Reading. 10 cass. (Running Time: 15 hrs.). 2001. 80.00 (978-0-7366-8313-5(5)) Books on Tape.
Picture the Dirty Dozen as six women, operating behind Nazi lines, and you'll have the premise of this propulsive thriller. Felicity "Flick" Clairet is an officer in the British Special Operations Executive, responsible for crippling German communications before D-Day. Her first plan to destroy a German telephone exchange fails. Her backup "Hail Mary" plan must be carried out immediately. For it, she must recruit from the cream of SOE rejects, a shooting aristocrat, and the odd prisoner or two. Eventually, she assembles a team of six, including two lesbians and a German transvestite. They must infiltrate the exchange as cleaning women, and dismantle it in six hours. To add to the difficulty, the Germans are waiting for them.

Jackdaws. unabr. ed. Ken Follett. 12 CDs. (Running Time: 14 hrs. 40 mins.). 2001. audio compact disk 96.00 (978-0-7366-8456-9(5)) Books on Tape.
An unlikely, motley team of six women must invade and destroy a German telephone exchange in World War II.

Jacki Sorensen's Aerobic Club for Kids. Instructed by Jacki Sorensen. 1 cass. (Running Time: 1 hr.). (J). 2001. pap. bk. 10.95 (KIM 1230C); pap. bk. & pupil's gde. ed. 11.95 (KIM 1230C) Kimbo Educ.
The professional who designed the first aerobics record now offers a fitness sport anyone can play - a club any kid can join! Includes warm-up, strength exercises, aerobics, & stretching exercises. Follow Jacki through Ghostbusters, Footloose, The A-Team & lots more high spirited, motivating routines. Includes guide.

Jacki Sorensen's Aerobic Workout: On Location. Jacki Sorensen. 2 cass. (Running Time: 20 min.). 2001. pap. bk. 18.95 (KIM1235C); pap. bk. & stu. ed. 20.95 (KIM1235) Kimbo Educ.
A complete Aerobic Workout for men & women that gives every muscle group expert attention! There's a step-by-step illustrated booklet, & Jackie's own cues to guide you. Includes a complete floor workout & over 20 minutes of aerobic conditioning. As you workout to How Will I Know, Living in America, The Heat Is On & other hot songs, you'll end up feeling exhilarated, not exhausted.

Jackie & Me. unabr. ed. Dan Gutman. 2 cassettes. (Running Time: 2 hrs). (Baseball Card Adventures Ser.). (J). 2004. 19.75 (978-1-4193-0384-5(8)) Recorded Bks.

Jackie, Ari & Jack: The Tragic Love Triangle. Read by January Jones. 2 cass. (Running Time: 2 hrs.). 2000. 17.95 (978-0-9662951-1-5(0)) Pub: P J Pubng. Dist(s): Penton Overseas
Conspiracy theory of the Kennedy assassination.

Jackie, Ari & Jack: The Tragic Triangle. unabr. ed. January Jones. Read by January Jones. 2 cass. (Running Time: 2 hrs.). 2000. 17.95 Penton Overseas.

Jackie Conoce al Monstrun de Enojo see Jackie Meets the Anger Monster

Jackie, Ethel, Joan: Women of Camelot. abr. ed. J. Randy Taraborrelli. Read by Beth Fowler. (ENG.). 2005. 14.98 (978-1-59483-474-5(1)) Pub: Hachet Audio. Dist(s): HachBkGrp

Jackie Kennedy Poems. unabr. ed. Caroline Kennedy Schlossberg. 1 cass. (Running Time: 90 mins.). 2001. 12.98 (978-1-58621-183-7(8)) Hachet Audio.

Jackie Mason's Favorite Comedy Hits. 10 vols. (Running Time: 10 hrs.). bk. 39.98 (978-1-57019-698-0(2), OTR40082) Pub: Radio Spirits. Dist(s): AudioGO

Jackie Mason's Favorite Comedy Hits. Read by Jackie Mason. 10 vols. (Running Time: 10 hrs.). 2004. bk. 34.98 (978-1-57019-699-7(0), OTR40084) Pub: Radio Spirits. Dist(s): AudioGO

Jackie Meets the Anger Monster. Gretchen L. Randolph & Wanda H. Appleton. Composed by Peter A. Appleton. 1 cass. (Running Time: 12 min.).Tr. of Jackie Conoce al Monstrun de Enojo. (ENG & SPA., (J). (ps-6). 1996. pap. bk. 26.95 Incl. bk. (978-1-890239-52-7(6)) Healthy Assn.
A new baby in the house arouses many feelings in Jackie. The Anger Monster helps her sift through conflicting emotions & recognize what's most important - she's missing her mom. Educational materials on how to work with feelings.

Jackie Meets the Anger Monster. Gretchen L. Randolph & Wanda H. Appleton. Composed by Peter A. Appleton. 1 cass. (Running Time: 12 min.).Tr. of Jackie Conoce al Monstrun de Enojo. (J). (gr. k-6). 1996. pap. bk. 26.95 Incl. bk. (978-1-890239-51-0(8)) Healthy Assn.

Jackie Meets the Anger Monster: Jackie Conoce al Monstrun de Enojo. Gretchen L. Randolph & Wanda H. Appleton. Composed by Peter A. Appleton. 1 cass. (Running Time: 12 min.). (ENG & SPA., (J). (ps-6). 1997. pap. bk. 19.95 (978-1-890239-53-4(4)) Healthy Assn.

Jackie Robinson, Level 1. 2 cass. (Running Time: 1 hr. 30 mins.). (SmartReader Ser.). (J). 1999. pap. bk. & tchr. ed. 19.95 (978-0-7887-1156-5(3), 79417T3) Recorded Bks.
Jackie Robinson became a hero on two playing fields. He was the first African American to play in Major League Baseball & he was a major figure in the battle for civil rights.

Jackie Robinson, Level 2. 2 cass. (Running Time: 1 hr. 30 mins.). (SmartReader Ser.). (J). 1999. pap. bk. & tchr. ed. 19.95 (978-0-7887-0280-8(7), 79320T3) Recorded Bks.

Jackie Robinson: A Biography. unabr. ed. Arnold Rampersad. Read by Michael Prichard. 19 cass. (Running Time: 28 hrs. 30 mins.). 1998. 80.00 (978-0-7366-4201-9(3), 4698-A); 80.00 (978-0-7366-4202-6(1), 4698-B) Books on Tape.
The life of Jackie Robinson, first man to break the color barrier in major league baseball is explored as never before.

Jackie Robinson: Baseball's Great Pioneer. Jason Glaser. Illus. by Cynthia Martin et al. (Graphic Biographies Ser.). (ENG.). (gr. 3-4). 2007. audio compact disk 6.95 (978-1-4296-1472-6(2)) CapstoneDig.

Jackie Robinson & the American Dream. John Bergez. (Overcoming the Odds Sports Biographies Ser.). 2001. audio compact disk 18.95 (978-1-4105-0168-4(X)) D Johnston Inc.

Jackie Robinson & the American Dream, Vol. 5. John Bergez. Ed. by Jerry Stemach et al. Illus. by Jeff Ham. Narrated by Bernard Mixon. Contrib. by Ted S. Hasselbring. (Start-to-Finish Books). (J). (gr. 2-3). 2001. 35.00 (978-1-58702-540-2(X)) D Johnston Inc.

Jackie Robinson & the American Dream, Vol. 5. John Bergez. Ed. by Jerry Stemach et al. Illus. by Jeff Ham. Narrated by Bernard Mixon. Contrib. by Ted S. Hasselbring. (Start-to-Finish Books). (J). (gr. 2-3). 2002. 100.00 (978-1-58702-956-1(1)) D Johnston Inc.

Jackie Robinson & the American Dream, Vol. 5. unabr. ed. John Bergez. Ed. by Jerry Stemach et al. Illus. by Jeff Ham. Narrated by Bernard Mixon. Contrib. by Ted S. Hasselbring. 1 cass. (Running Time: 1 hrs.). (Start-to-Finish Books). (J). (gr. 2-3). 2001. (978-1-58702-381-1(4), F41K2) D Johnston Inc.
In 1947, Jackie Roosevelt Robinson, the grandson of a slave, shattered baseball's "color barrier" by becoming the first African-American to play in the major leagues in the 20th century. At a time when segregation still prevailed in much of the United States, Jackie braved insults, bean balls, and death threats to become one of baseballs greatest players.

Jackie Robinson (INK Audiocassette) Baseball's Great Pioneer. (Graphic Library Biographies I Ser.). (ENG.). 2006. audio compact disk 5.95 (978-0-7368-7453-3(4)) CapstoneDig.

Jackie Torrence: Ountain Magic-Jack Tales I-Jack & the Northwest Wind: Jack & the Three Sillies; Jack & the King's New Ground. 2004. 8.95 (978-1-56008-443-3(X)) Weston Woods.

Jackie Torrence: Ountain Magic-Jack Tales Ii-Soldier Jack;Jack Goes Out to Seek His Fortune. 2004. 8.95 (978-1-56008-444-0(8)) Weston Woods.

Jackie's Wild Seattle. Will Hobbs. Narrated by Stina Nielsen. 5 CDs. (Running Time: 6 hrs.). (YA). 2003. audio compact disk 49.75 (978-1-4025-8079-6(7)) Recorded Bks.

Jackie's Wild Seattle. unabr. ed. 4 cass. (Running Time: 6 hrs.). 2003. 38.00 (978-1-4025-6713-1(8)) Recorded Bks.
Fourteen-year-old Shannon and her little brother Cody have the time of their lives when they spend the summer rescuing animals for a little-known wildlife shelter, Jackie¿s Wild Seattle. Their parents away in Pakistan, Shannon and Cody are left with their Uncle Neal. What transpires when this odd team sets off to save beasts of many furs and feathers is an often hilarious tale of healing and growth that will capture listeners¿ hearts. Will Hobbs is an ALA award-winning author of young adult fiction. His many celebrated novels include Beardance.

Jacknife. William W. Johnstone. 2008. audio compact disk 19.99 (978-1-59950-177-2(5)) GraphicAudio.

Jacko: The Great Intruder. unabr. ed. Thomas Keneally. Read by James Wright. 10 cass. (Running Time: 15 hrs.). 1998. (978-1-86442-326-6(9), 581053) Bolinda Pubng AUS.
Jacko Emptor, Northern Territory born, brings Australia to the television screens of America. Is America ready for him? Is he ready for America? Jacko, investigative reporter, exploits American innocence to break into living rooms & penetrate the heart's secrets but these secrets make their claim on him too.

Jackrabbit Factor: Why You Can. Leslie Householder. Read by Trevan Householder. Pref. by Trevan Householder. (ENG.). 2007. audio compact disk 29.95 (978-0-9765310-4-3(6)) Thoughts A.

Jack's First Job: And Other Appalachian Jack Tales. Donald Davis. 1 cass. (Running Time: 60 mins.). (American Storytelling Ser.). (gr. 1-7). 1994. 12.00 (978-0-87483-322-5(1)) Pub: August Hse. Dist(s): Natl Bk Netwk

Jack's Journey. Mark Miller & Laurie Zellman. 2004. bk. 65.00 (978-0-687-08670-2(1)) Abingdon.

Jack's Journey. Mark Miller & Laurie Zellman. 2007. bk. 60.00 (978-0-687-06661-2(1)); bk. 15.00 (978-0-687-06651-3(4)) Abingdon.

Jack's Last Call: Say Goodbye to Kerouac. Based on a play by Patrick Fenton. Adapted by Sue Zizza. Directed By Sue Zizza. Featuring Len Cariou. Engineer David Shinn. 2008. audio compact disk 14.95 (978-0-9816706-0-7(1)) SueMedia Prod.

Jackson. unabr. ed. Max Byrd. Narrated by George Guidall. 12 cass. (Running Time: 17 hrs. 15 mins.). 1998. 97.00 (978-0-7887-1999-8(8), 95386E7) Recorded Bks.
Despite being called a crude backwoods barbarian, Jackson's fiery speeches & status as a legend of the Battle of New Orleans secured his party's nomination - & the presidency.

Jackson-Weiss Syndrome - A Bibliography & Dictionary for Physicians, Patients, & Genome Researchers. Compiled by Icon Group International, Inc. Staff. 2007. ring bd. 28.95 (978-0-497-11244-8(2)) Icon Grp.

Jackson Years. (Presidency Ser.). 10.00 Esstee Audios.
Examine's Jacksonian democracy & how it changed America's outlook.

Jackson's Dilemma. Iris Murdoch. Narrated by Juliet Mills. 8 cass. (Running Time: 10 hrs. 45 mins.). 72.00 (978-1-84197-464-4(1)) Recorded Bks.

Jackson's Dilemma. abr. unabr. ed. Iris Murdoch. Perf. by Juliet Mills. 8 cass. (Running Time: 18 hrs.). 2004. 25.00 (978-1-931056-91-5(9), N Millennium Audio) Pub: New Millenn Enter. Dist(s): PerseuPGW
The tale begins on the eve of a wedding. Edward of Hatting Hall is to marry the lovely Marian. Benet, his rather fussy & reclusive friend & neighbor, is in charge of the proceedings. He's also the one who finds Marian's hasty note calling the whole thing off. Everyone is thrown into a tizzy. As they all wait for further word & worry about suicide & abduction, we learn their painful secrets in scenes notable for their dramatic intensity.

Jacky Boy. unabr. ed. Ken McCoy. Read by Ken McCoy. 8 cass. (Running Time: 10 hrs. 35 mins.). (Story Sound Ser.). (J). 2006. 69.95 (978-1-85903-867-3(0)) Pub: Mgna Lrg Print GBR. Dist(s): Ulverscroft US

Jaco Pastorius: Modern Electric Bass. rev. ed. Jaco Pastorius & Jerry Jemmott. Ed. by Dan Thress. Intro. by Mark Egan. Contrib. by Lincoln Goines & Ebet Roberts. 1 cass. (Video Transcription Ser.). bk. 21.95 DCI Music Video.
Teaches the serious musician the art of electric bass playing & improvisation by the late great Jaco Pastorius. Featured are transcriptions of Jaco's examples & solos.

Jacob & Esau - the Restless Heart. David T. Demola. 1 cass. 4.00 (A-1074-9) Faith Fellow Min.

Jacob Have I Loved. Lisa French. (Focus on Reading (Saddleback) Ser.). (ENG.). (YA). 2009. audio compact disk 23.99 (978-1-59905-510-7(4)) Saddleback Edu.

Jacob Have I Loved. abr. ed. Katherine Paterson. Read by Moira Kelly. (J). 2007. 34.99 (978-1-60252-759-1(8)) Find a World.

***Jacob Have I Loved.** abr. ed. Katherine Paterson. Read by Moira Kelly. (ENG.). 2009. (978-0-06-112604-8(7)); (978-0-06-088746-9(X)) HarperCollins Pubs.

Jacob Have I Loved, unabr. ed. Katherine Paterson. Narrated by Christina Moore. 4 pieces. (Running Time: 5 hrs. 45 mins.). (gr. 5 up). 1998. 35.00 (978-0-7887-2080-2(5), 95433E7) Recorded Bks.
Life on a small fishing island in the Chesapeake Bay sounds like a peaceful existence, but it isn't for Sara Louise Bradshaw. She has spent her entire young life in the shadow of her beautiful & talented twin, Caroline. A look at the pangs involved in growing up to be independent & strong.

Jacob Have I Loved. unabr. ed. Katherine Paterson. Narrated by Christina Moore. 5 CDs. (Running Time: 5 hrs. 45 mins.). (gr. 5 up). 2000. audio compact disk 45.00 (978-0-7887-4217-0(5), C1156E7) Recorded Bks.

Jacob Two-Two & the Dinosaur. Mordecai Richler. 1 CD. (Running Time: 1 hr. 30 mins.). (Jacob Two-Two Ser.). 2005. audio compact disk 12.95 (978-0-660-18926-0(7)) Pub: Canadian Broadcasting CAN. Dist(s): Georgetown Term

Jacob Two-Two's First Spy Case. Mordecai Richler. (Jacob Two-Two Ser.). 2005. audio compact disk 12.95 (978-0-660-18924-6(0)) Pub: Canadian Broadcasting CAN. Dist(s): Georgetown Term

Jacob's Hands. unabr. ed. Aldous Huxley & Christopher Isherwood. Read by Burt Reynolds. 2 cass. (Running Time: 3 hrs.). 2001. 18.00 (978-1-59040-086-9(0), Phoenix Audio) Pub: Amer Intl Pub. Dist(s): PerseuPGW

Jacob's House. Dott Clarke Koch. Ed. by William Koch. (J). 2006. bk. (978-0-9789043-4-0(6)) Wildot.

Jacob's Ladder. abr. ed. Donald McCaig. 2002. 12.99 (978-1-57815-262-9(3)) Media Bks NJ.

Jacob's Ladder. unabr. ed. Donald McCaig. Narrated by George Guidall. 16 cass. (Running Time: 22 hrs. 30 mins.). 1999. 130.00 (978-0-7887-2184-7(4), 95480E7) Recorded Bks.
The Civil War made wrenching changes in the lives of all who lived on the Virginia plantation, Gatewood. Traces the families of Gatewood's masters & slaves through a passionate & dramatic era of American history.

Jacob's Ladder That Leads to the Stars. Manly P. Hall. 1 cass. 8.95 (978-0-89314-156-1(9), C870503) Philos Res.

Jacob's Room. Virginia Woolf. Narrated by Flo Gibson. 2008. audio compact disk 24.95 (978-1-60646-019-1(6)) Audio Bk Con.

Jacob's Room, unabr. ed. Virginia Woolf. Read by Nadia May. 5 cass. (Running Time: 7 hrs.). 1998. 39.95 (978-0-7861-1338-5(3), 2233) Blckstn Audio.
Attempts to evoke the inner life of Jacob Flanders & his social milieu during the first decade & a half of the 20th century.

***Jacob's Room.** unabr. ed. Virginia Woolf. Read by Nadia May. (Running Time: 6 hrs. 0 mins.). 2010. 29.95 (978-1-4417-6232-0(9)); audio compact disk 55.00 (978-1-4417-6230-6(2)) Blckstn Audio.

Jacob's Room, Set. Virginia Woolf. Read by Flo Gibson. 4 cass. (Running Time: 6 hrs.). 1996. 19.95 (978-1-55685-410-1(2)) Audio Bk Con.
We meet Jacob as a small boy, follow him through Cambridge, sharing thoughts on philosophy & literature with his colleagues, & enjoy his travels & romances in Greece. Then we learn how others see him. The remarkable imagery makes some sections almost poetical.

Jacqou le Croquant. unabr. ed. Eugène Leroy. Read by Vincent Graal. (YA). 2007. 84.99 (978-2-35569-025-9(1)) Find a World.

Jacqueline Kennedy Onassis. Prod. by A&E Television Network Staff. 1 cass. 1998. 9.95 (978-0-7670-0439-8(6)) A & E Home.
Historical - U.S.

Jacqueline Susann's Shadow of the Dolls. abr. ed. Rae Lawrence. Read by Melanie Ewbank. 4 CDs Library ed. (Running Time: 4 hrs.). 2001. audio compact disk 61.25 (978-1-58788-484-9(4), 1587884844, CD Lib Edit) Brilliance Audio.

Jacqueline Susann's Shadow of the Dolls. unabr. ed. Rae Lawrence. Read by Melanie Ewbank. 6 cass. (Running Time: 9 hrs.). 2001. 29.95 (978-1-58788-480-1(1), 1587884801, BAU); 69.25 (978-1-58788-481-8(X), 158788481X, Unabridge Lib Edns) Brilliance Audio.
Valley of the Dolls was sexy, shocking, and unrelenting in its revelations of the dangers facing women who dare to chase their most glamorous dreams. It shot to the top of the bestseller lists in 1966 and made Jacqueline Susann a superstar. It remains the quintessential big, blockbuster, must-read, can't-put-down bestseller. Before her death in 1974, Susann spent many months working on a draft for a sequel that continued the stories of Anne Welles, Neely O'Hara, and Lyon Burke. Now, after thirty years, the perfect writer has been found to turn Susann's deliciously ambitious ideas into a novel that matches the original shock for shock and thrill for thrill. In Jacqueline Susann's Shadow of the Dolls, Rae Lawrence picks up the story in the late '80s and brings it right into the next century. Long a devoted "Valley" girl herself, Rae has re-imagined the original characters in a contemporary reality (and adjusted their ages just a bit), exactly as Jackie would have wanted her to. And if you've never read Valley of the Dolls, no matter. Sometimes the present is even more surprising and fun when you don't remember the past. And what a story! Neely's golden voice has brought her fame and success, but now she craves acceptance in social circles where her kind of success means nothing at all. Anne, born and bred in those very circles, must choos between returning home or pursuing a fabulous television career - and the kind of passion she once knew with Lyon. And Lyon, who loses everything including Anne, looks for happiness in the most unexpected of places. Taking us behind the closed doors of New York, East Hampton, and Los Angeles, whetting our appetites for more with a new generation of young women and men who grow up far too fast, and spicing the whole story with a generous sprinkling of sex, drugs, and cosmetic surgery, Jacqueline Susann's Shadow of the Dolls is the ultimate beach read for our time. But feel free to devour it any time of the year, wherever you are. It's been a long time since readers had this much fun between the covers. It's time to jump back in.

Jacqueline Susann's Shadow of the Dolls. unabr. ed. Rae Lawrence. Read by Melanie Ewbank. (Running Time: 9 hrs.). 2004. 39.25 (978-1-59335-405-3(3), 1593354053, Brinc Audio MP3 Lib) Brilliance Audio.

Jacqueline Susann's Shadow of the Dolls. unabr. ed. Rae Lawrence. Read by Melanie Ewbank. (Running Time: 9 hrs.). 2004. 39.25 (978-1-59710-404-3(3), 1597104043, BADLE); 24.95 (978-1-59710-405-0(1), 1597104051, BAD) Brilliance Audio.

Jacqueline Susann's Shadow of the Dolls. unabr. ed. Rae Lawrence. Read by Melanie Ewbank. (Running Time: 9 hrs.). 2004. 24.95 (978-1-59335-154-0(2), 1593351542) Soulmate Audio Bks.

Jacques et le Haricot Magique. Tr. of Jack & the Bean Stalk. (FRE.). (J). pap. bk. 12.95 (978-2-89558-069-0(3)) Pub: Coffragants CAN. Dist(s): Penton Overseas

Jacques et le Haricot Magique. Richard Leduc. 1 cass. (Running Time: 50 mins.). (Best-Sellers Ser.).Tr. of Jack & the Bean Stalk. (FRE., (J). (ps-2). audio compact disk 9.95 (978-2-921997-80-5(0)) Pub: Coffragants CAN. Dist(s): Penton Overseas
Features classic children's fables recorded completely in French by well-known artists.

Jacques Hetu. Jacques Hetu. 2004. audio compact disk 15.95 (978-0-662-33322-7(5)) Pub: Canadian Broadcasting CAN. Dist(s): Georgetown Term

Jacques le Fataliste, Pt. 2, set. Denis Diderot. 3 cass. (FRE.). 1992. 31.95 (1550-VSL) Olivia & Hill.
Jacques, an inveterate fatalist, recounts his love affairs to his master in the course of their random travels. This 18th-century classic is read by a cast of actors.

Jacques le Fataliste, Pts. 1 & 2, set. Denis Diderot. 7 cass. (FRE.). 1992. 34.95 (1549-VSL) Olivia & Hill.

Jacques le Fataliste, Set. Denis Diderot. 7 cass. (FRE.). 1991. 59.95 (1549-50) Olivia & Hill.
Jacques, an inveterate fatalist, recounts his love affairs to his master in the course of their random travels.

Jacques Marquette. Joseph P. Donnelly. 6 cass. 24.95 (303) Ignatius Pr.
Life of the Jesuit missionary to the North American Indians.

Jacques-Yves Cousteau. Interview. Interview with Jacques Cousteau. 1978. (L010) TFR.

Jacquou le Croquant: Level 1. E. Le Roy. bk. 14.95 (978-2-09-032980-3(7), CL9807E) Pub: Cle Intl FRA. Dist(s): Continental Bk

Jade & Jeopardy. Lynn Gardner. 5 cass. 2004. 19.95 (978-1-57734-651-7(3)) Covenant Comms.

Jade & the Blessed Mysteries of Life see Jade et les Sacres Mysteres de la Vie

Jade et les Sacres Mysteres de la Vie. 1 CD. (Running Time: 1 hr.).Tr. of Jade & the Blessed Mysteries of Life. 2001. bk. 14.95 Pub: Coffragants CAN. Dist(s): Penton Overseas

***Jade Island.** unabr. ed. Elizabeth Lowell. Read by Robin Rowan. (ENG.). 2009. (978-0-06-196712-2(2), Harper Audio); (978-0-06-182978-9(1), Harper Audio) HarperCollins Pubs.

Jade Island. unabr. ed. Elizabeth Lowell. Read by Laural Merlington. 8 cass. 1999. 73.25 (FS9-43244) Highsmith.

Jade Palace Vendetta. collector's ed. Dale Furutani. Read by Jonathan Marosz. 5 cass. (Running Time: 7 hrs. 30 min.). 1999. 40.00 (978-0-7366-4656-7(6), 5038) Books on Tape.
The saga's hero is noble ronin Matsuyama Kaze, a warrior whose sense of honor is as keen as his deadly sword. Kaze continues the search to find his lord's missing child. This time out, Kaze is waylaid when he saves a helpless merchant from a vicious gang of killers & soon discovers that everything is not what it appears. He finds himself trapped in a web of deceit & violence, where a veneer of propriety hides great evil. Only Kaze's quick wit & martial skills can save him & keep him on his quest to find the kidnapped child.

Jade Tiger. Jenn Reese. (Running Time: 9 mins.). 2009. audio compact disk 33.95 (978-1-897304-60-0(9)) Dorch Pub Co.

***Jade Tiger.** Jenn Reese. (Running Time: 9 mins.). 2009. 19.95 (978-1-897331-10-1(X), AudioRealms) Dorch Pub Co.

Jade Tiger. Jenn Reese. Read by Stephanie Riggio. Prod. by Fred Godsmark. (Running Time: 30600 sec.). 2006. audio compact disk 19.95 (978-0-8095-6223-7(5)) Pub: Wildside. Dist(s): Diamond Book Dists

Jade Tiger. abr. ed. Jenn Reese. Read by Stephanie Riggio. (Running Time: 30600 sec.). 2006. audio compact disk 37.95 (978-0-8095-6224-4(3)) Pub: Wildside. Dist(s): Diamond Book Dists

Jade Warrior. abr. ed. Jeffrey Lord. Read by Lloyd James. 2 vols. No. 2. 2003. 18.00 (978-1-58807-357-0(2)); (978-1-58807-775-2(6)) Am Pubng Inc.

Jade Warrior. abr. ed. Jeffrey Lord. Read by Carol Eason. Abr. by Ted McClure. 3 CDs. (Running Time: 3 hrs.). (Richard Blade Adventure Ser.: No. 2). 2004. audio compact disk 25.00 (978-1-58807-493-5(5)) Am Pubng Inc.
British secret agent Richard Blade is propelled into a parallel dimension. He finds himself in mortal danger. The land is in peril. The Mongs, a cruel people, attack the aristocratic Caths. Into this maelstrom comes Blade, the man who can help change the outcome. But only if he can trust someone to help him and time doesn't run out first. Blade's trials continue in this second book of the series.

Jades Garden. Sandi Johnson. Perf. by Dora Saad. 1 cass. (J). 2000. 4.99 (978-1-929063-54-3(7), 153); audio compact disk 9.99 (978-1-929063-55-0(5), 154) Moons & Stars.

Jaet Evanovich. bk. 15.99 (978-1-57815-558-3(4), Media Bks Audio) Media Bks NJ.

Jafar Husain Khan Badauni & Party, Vol. 1. 1 cass. (Qawwali Ser.). 1992. (D92052) Multi-Cultural Bks.

Jafar Husain Khan Badauni & Party, Vol. 2. 1 cass. (Qawwali Ser.). 1992. (D92053) Multi-Cultural Bks.

Jagai & Madhai Redeemed. 1 cass. (Spiritual Stories Ser.). 5.00 Bhaktivedanta.

Jaguar see Poetry & Voice of Ted Hughes

Jaguar. unabr. ed. Roland Smith. Narrated by Johnny Heller. 4 pieces. (Running Time: 5 hrs. 30 mins.). (gr. 5 up). 1999. 38.00 (978-0-7887-3828-9(3), 96065E7) Recorded Bks.
Fourteen-year-old Jacob Lansa is leaving New York to spend his spring break in Brazil. He will help his father, a field biologist, set up a jaguar preserve in the rain forest. But soon he finds himself in a life-&-death struggle against lawless opportunists & the perils of nature.

Jaguar. unabr. ed. Roland Smith. Narrated by Johnny Heller. 4 cass. (Running Time: 5 hrs. 30 mins.). (YA). (gr. 5 up). 1999. pap. bk. & stu. ed. 52.50 (978-0-7887-3848-7(8), 41046X4) Recorded Bks.

Jaguar, Class set. Roland Smith. Read by Johnny Heller. 4 cass. (Running Time: 5 hrs. 30 mins.). (YA). (gr. 5 up). 1999. wbk. ed. 118.30 (978-0-7887-3873-9(9), 47038) Recorded Bks.
Fourteen year old Ipa-tah-chi has survived the Apache raid that took her grandmother & brother. But the strange, pale warriors who ride into her village on magnificent four legged creatures pose a much greater threat. Chronicles the virtual extinction of the native "Indio" & the birth of the Mexican race.

Jaguar Woman & the Wisdom of the Butterfly Tree. Lynn V. Andrews. Read by Lynn V. Andrews. 2 cass. (Running Time: 60 min. per cass.). (J). (gr. 5 up). 1989. 14.95 HarperCollins Pubs.

Jaguars Ripped My Flesh. Tim Cahill. Read by Tim Cahill. 2 cass. (Running Time: 3 hrs.). 1992. 16.95 (978-0-939643-43-1(X), NrthWrd Bks) TandN Child.
In eight essays from his books, "Jaguars Ripped My Flesh" and "A Wolverine Is Eating My Leg," Cahill explores the near and far corners of the earth. Filled with fun, adventure and all-too-frequent encounters with danger and the unknown, his stories provide a fascinating portrait of the wild sides of both the natural and human worlds.

Jai Ma. 2 CDs. (Running Time: 1 hr. 33 mins.). audio compact disk 19.50 (978-0-87612-501-4(1)) Self Realization.

Jai Ma: A Concert of Devotional Song from India. Perf. by Sri Sen & Srimati Sen. 2 cass. 1978. 14.00 set. (2902) Self Realization.
Simple, hauntingly beautiful Bengali bhajans, performed by Sri & Srimati S. N. Sen & their students from the Yogoda School of Indian Music, convey the devotional fervor & heightened spiritual awareness that is the soul of Indian music.

Jail Break Spells Double the Trouble: Jake the Beagle's Crazy Adventures. Based on a book by Regina Hernandez. 1 CD. (Running Time: 74 mins). (Jake the Beagle Crazy Adventure Ser.: 5). (J). 2003. audio compact disk 14.99 (978-0-9727771-9-3(9)) Regal Enter.

Jail Ministry. 1 cass. (Care Cassettes Ser.: Vol. 20, No. 5). 1993. 10.80 Assn Prof Chaplains.

***Jailhouse Lawyer.** unabr. ed. Phillip Margolin. Read by Austin Cooper. (ENG.). 2008. (978-0-06-136554-6(8), Harper Audio); (978-0-06-172671-2(0)) HarperCollins Pubs.

Jailhouse Stories. Neil Haugerud. 2002. audio compact disk (978-0-9726524-0-7(X)) Ford Soundesign.

Jails & Detention Centers: Care Behind Bars. 2007. audio compact disk 17.99 (978-1-934570-06-7(0)) Lanphier Pr.

Jaja, Jiji, Cuac. Doreen Cronin. Illus. by Betsy Lewin.Tr. of Giggle, Giggle, Quack. (SPA.). (J). (gr. 1-2). 8.95 (978-0-439-73609-1(9), WW32926) Lectorum Pubns.

***Jake & Dinos Chapman: from Hell to Hell.** Ed. by Robert Eikmeyer. Dinos Chapman & Jake Chapman. (Running Time: 1 hr.). (ENG.). 2010. audio compact disk 35.00 (978-3-941185-45-6(4)) Pub: Verlag fur Moderne DEU. Dist(s): Dist Art Pubs

Jake & Pete. unabr. ed. Gillian Rubinstein. Read by Alan King. 2 cass. (Running Time: 2 hrs.). (J). 2004. 24.00 (978-1-74093-215-8(3)) Bolinda Pubng AUS.

Jake & Pete. unabr. ed. Gillian Rubinstein. Read by Alan King. 3 CDs. (Running Time: 2 hrs.). 2004. audio compact disk 54.95 (978-1-74093-520-3(9)) Pub: Bolinda Pubng AUS. Dist(s): Bolinda Pub Inc

Jake & the Migration of the Monarch with CD. Crystal Ball O'Connor. Illus. by Valerie Bunch Hollinger. Composed by Sharon Kazee. (J). 2005. audio compact disk 18.95 (978-0-9774038-3-7(1)) Monarch Pubs.

Jake Drake, Bully Buster. unabr. ed. Andrew Clements. Narrated by Johnny Heller. 1 cass. (Running Time: 1 hr.). (Jake Drake Ser.: Bk. 1). (gr. 2 up). 2002. 10.00 (978-1-4025-0929-2(4)) Recorded Bks.
Jake Drake has always been a bully magnet. Ever since nursery school, bigger kids have been giving him tons of trouble. When Link Baxter and his family move in down the street, and Link joins Jake's class in school, Jake finds out right away that he's not just a bully - he's a Superbully! Link makes fun of Drake at every available opportunity and even gets Drake sent to the principle's office. What can Jake do to stop these attacks?.

Jake Drake, Know-it-All. abr. ed. Andrew Clements. Narrated by Johnny Heller. 1 cass. (Running Time: 1 hr. 30 mins.). (Jake Drake Ser.). (gr. 2 up). 2002. 10.00 (978-1-4025-0931-5(6)) Recorded Bks.
Third-grader Jake Drake has always been good with computers. The Local computer store is sponsoring his elementary school's science fair, and the grand prize is a new computer. Jake needs an idea and a partner.

Jake Drake, Teacher's Pet. Andrew Clements. Narrated by Johnny Heller. (Running Time: 1 hr. 45 mins.). (Jake Drake Ser.). (gr. 2 up). 10.00 (978-1-4025-0933-9(2)) Recorded Bks.

Jake Finds a Penny. unabr. ed. Barbara Sobel. Illus. by Louise Ziffer. 1 cass. (Running Time: 7 min.). (Friends & Neighbors Ser.). (J). (gr. k-2). 1986. lib. bdg. 16.99 incl. hardcover. (978-0-87386-019-2(5)) Jan Prods.
Jake is very happy that he has found a penny. He knows that a penny is money & has big plans for spending it. Poor Jake is in for a big surprise.

Jake Ransom & the Skull King's Shadow. unabr. ed. James Rollins. Read by Pedro Pascal. (J). 2009. audio compact disk 27.99 (978-0-06-176103-4(6), HarperChildAud) HarperCollins Pubs.

***Jake Ransom & the Skull King's Shadow.** unabr. ed. James Rollins. Read by Pedro Pascal. (ENG.). 2009. (978-0-06-180596-7(3)); (978-0-06-180601-8(3)) HarperCollins Pubs.

Jake, Reinvented. unabr. ed. 3 cass. (Running Time: 4 hrs. 30 min.). (J). 2004. 28.00 (978-1-4025-7030-8(9)) Recorded Bks.

Jake's Thing, unabr. collector's ed. Kingsley Amis. Read by David Case. 7 cass. (Running Time: 10 hrs. 30 mins.). 1988. 56.00 (978-0-7366-1385-9(4), 2276) Books on Tape.
"Jake's thing" has quit working & the psychiatrist isn't much help.

Jala. Sounds True Staff. 2005. audio compact disk 16.98 (978-1-59179-465-3(X)) Sounds True.

Jali Kunda: Griot Music of West Africa & Beyond. Foday M. Suso. 1 CD. (Running Time: 1 hr.). 1996. pap. bk. 28.95 (978-1-55961-381-1(5), Ellipsis Arts) Relaxtn Co.

Jam Plastic: Now You Can Play Lead Guitar with a Live Band. Richard J. Zerbey. (YA). (gr. 7 up). 1986. bk. (978-0-318-60147-2(8)); pap. bk. 21.95 (978-0-935565-07-2(8), JPHV-I); pap. bk. 15.95 (978-0-935565-04-1(3)) Sound Ent.

Jam Plastic Heavy Metal. Richard J. Zerby. Perf. by Richard J. Zerby. 1 cass. (Running Time: 45 min.). (Now You Can Play Lead Guitar with a Live Band Ser.). (YA). (gr. 6-12). bk. 21.95; pap. bk. 15.95 Sound Ent.
Contains a heavy metal band for guitarist to play along with. Also contains verbal & musical instruction & demonstration which are printed in the accompanying book.

Jam Plastic Heavy Metal. Richard J. Zerby & Richard J. Zerbey. Perf. by Richard J. Zerby. 1 cass. (Running Time: 45 min.). (Now You Can Play Lead Guitar with a Live Band Ser.). (YA). (gr. 7 up). 1985. 7.99 (978-0-935565-10-2(8)) Sound Ent.

Jam Plastic Punk. Richard J. Zerbey. 1 cass. (Running Time: 45 min.). (Now You Can Play Lead Guitar with a Live Band Ser.). (YA). (gr. 7 up). 1986. pap. bk. 15.95 (978-0-935565-05-8(1)) Sound Ent.
Contains a punk band for guitarist to play along with. Also contains verbal & musical demonstration & instruction which are printed in the accompanying book.

Jam Plastic Punk. Richard J. Zerby & Richard J. Zerbey. Perf. by Richard J. Zerby. 1 cass. (Running Time: 45 min.). (Now You Can Play Lead Guitar with a Live Band Ser.). (YA). (gr. 7 up). 1986. bk. 21.95 (978-0-935565-08-9(6)); 7.99 (978-0-935565-11-9(6)) Sound Ent.

Jam Plastic Rock. Richard J. Zerby & Richard J. Zerbey. 1 cass. (Running Time: 45 min.). (Now You Can Play Guitar with a Live Band Ser.). (YA). (gr. 7 up). 1986. bk. 21.95 (978-0-935565-06-5(X)); pap. bk. 15.95 (978-0-935565-03-4(5)); 7.99 (978-0-935565-09-6(4)) Sound Ent.
Contains a rock band for guitarist to play along with. Also contains verbal and musical instruction and demonstrations which are printed in the accompanying book.

Jam Trax Guitar Method, Bk. 1. 1 CD. (Running Time: 1 hr.). 1997. bk. 12.95 (978-0-8256-1585-6(2), AM 940346) Music Sales.

Jam Trax Guitar Method, Bk. 2. 1 CD. (Running Time: 1 hr.). 1997. bk. 12.95 (978-0-8256-1586-3(0), AM 940357) Music Sales.

Jam Trax Guitar Method Book. 1997. pap. bk. 21.95 (978-0-8256-1587-0(9), AM 940368) Omnibus NY.

Jam with Bon Jovi Tab. Bon Jovi. audio compact disk 24.95 (978-0-7119-7197-4(8), AM953931) Music Sales.

Jam with Carlos Santana. Perf. by Carlos Santana. 1 CD. (Running Time: 60 mins.). 1997. bk. 24.95 (978-1-85909-487-7(2), Warner Bro) Alfred Pub.

Jam with Gary Moore. 1998. bk. 26.95 (978-1-85909-440-2(6), Warner Bro) Alfred Pub.

Jam with the Blues Masters. bk. 21.95 (978-1-85909-679-6(4), Warner Bro) Alfred Pub.

Jam with the Eagles. 2005. pap. bk. 29.95 (978-1-84328-677-6(7), Warner Bro) Alfred Pub.

Jam with Whitesnake. 2000. bk. 26.95 (978-1-85909-609-3(3), Warner Bro) Alfred Pub.

Jamaica & Brianna, unabr. ed. Juanita Havill. Narrated by Lynne Thigpen. 1 cass. (Running Time: 15 mins.). (ps up). 1999. 10.00 (978-0-7887-3506-6(3), 95900E7) Recorded Bks.
Jamaica is unhappy about wearing her brother's old hand-me-down boots, especially when her friend Brianna has beautiful fuzzy pink ones. Expresses the pangs of young children learning valuable lessons about jealousy & friendship.

Jamaica & Brianna. unabr. ed. Juanita Havill. Narrated by Lynne Thigpen. 1 cass. (Running Time: 15 mins.). (J). (ps up). 2000. pap. bk. 24.20 (978-0-7887-3645-2(0), 41011X4) Recorded Bks.

Jamaica & Brianna, Class set. Juanita Havill. Read by Lynne Thigpen. 1 cass. (Running Time: 15 mins.). (J). (ps up). 1999. wbk. ed. 90.30 (978-0-7887-3675-9(2), 46978) Recorded Bks.

Jamaica Blue. unabr. ed. Donn Bruns. 6 CDs. (Running Time: 7 hrs.). 2003. audio compact disk 48.00 (978-0-7861-9131-4(7), 3155); 39.95 (978-0-7861-2522-7(5), 3155) Blckstn Audio.
Against the exotic backdrop of Jamaica and Florida, charismatic rock reporter Mick Sever investigates a reggae band's involvement with the violent deaths of young girls in this gripping mystery of music and murder.

Jamaica Inn. unabr. ed. Daphne Du Maurier. Read by Wanda McCaddon. 8 cass. (Running Time: 12 hrs.). 1984. 64.00 (978-0-7366-0936-4(9), 1879) Books on Tape.
When Mary Yellan finds herself marooned in a mouldering inn on the bleak Cornish moors it takes all her wits & courage to survive.

Jamaica Inn. unabr. ed. Daphne Du Maurier. Read by Tony Britton. 8 cass. (Running Time: 12 hrs.). 2000. 59.95 (978-0-7451-4065-0(3), CAB 762) Pub: Chivers Audio Bks GBR. Dist(s): AudioGO
Jamaica Inn stands alone on Bodmin Moor, stark and forbidding, its walls tainted with corruption. Mary Yellon soon learns of her uncle's strange trade there. But does he deal in darker secrets still?.

Jamaica Inn. unabr. ed. Daphne Du Maurier. Read by Tony Britton. 10 CDs. 2000. audio compact disk 94.95 (978-0-7540-5351-4(2), CCD 042) Pub: Chivers Audio Bks GBR. Dist(s): AudioGO
Jamaica Inn stands alone on Bodmin Moor., stark & forbidding, its walls tainted with corruption. Mary Yellon soon learns of her uncle's strange trade there. But does he deal in darker secrets still?.

Jamaica Inn. unabr. ed. Daphne Du Maurier. Narrated by Barbara Rosenblat. 8 cass. (Running Time: 11 hrs.). 1989. 70.00 (978-1-55690-259-8(X), 89320E7) Recorded Bks.
Mary Yellan, young & innocent, suspects nothing until she walks inside the cold embrace of Jamaica Inn. What evil has turned her aunt into a frightened crone?.

Jamaican Patwa No Problem: A Tourist's Guide to Jamaican Language & Culture. Janice Samuels. (ENG.). 2009. audio compact disk 18.95 (978-0-615-32819-5(9)) JustuwaitnSee.

Jamaica's Find. unabr. ed. Juanita Havill. Narrated by Kim Staunton. 1 cass. (Running Time: 15 mins.). (gr. k up). 1998. 10.00 (978-0-7887-2062-8(7), 95415E7) Recorded Bks.
When Little Jamaica finds a dirty & worn stuffed dog in the park, she takes it home. Having a crisis of conscience, she decides to do the right thing & gets a very happy surprise.

Jamais de Jasmin. Des Marguerite. pap. bk. 19.95 (978-88-7754-783-5(9)) Pub: Cideb ITA. Dist(s): Distribks Inc

Jambalaya! And Other Tasty Food Songs from Around the World. Perf. by Nancy Raven. 1 cass. (Running Time: 40 min.). (J). (ps-6). 1992. 10.00 (978-1-885292-03-2(1)) Lizards Rock.
Folk music for children, families & teachers.

Jambalaya: The Natural Woman's Book of Personal Charms & Practical Rituals. Luisay Teisch. Read by Luisay Teisch. 2 cass. (Running Time: 2 hrs.). 1988. bk. 14.95 (978-0-06-250863-8(6)) HarperCollins Pubs.

Jambalaya (On the Bayou) - ShowTrax. Arranged by Kirby Shaw. 1 CD. (Running Time: 5 mins.). 2000. audio compact disk 19.95 (08201213) H Leonard.
This is the ragin'-est-cajunest arrangement you'll ever find of this great Hank Williams classic! Easy to learn & tons of fun to sing, the middle section opens up for a road-house style piano solo & a foot-stompin' dance break.

Jamberry. 1 cass. (Running Time: 35 min.). (J). (ps-4). 2001. pap. bk. 15.95 (VX-71C) Kimbo Educ.
In rocking rhyme & action a young boy is lead by a larger-than-life bear on a breathtaking berry-picking adventure. Includes read along book.

Jamberry. Bruce Degen. 1 read-along cass. (Running Time: 4 min.). (I Can Read Bks.). (J). (ps-3). 1986. 9.95 Live Oak Media.
In rocking rhyme & rollicking action a young boy is led by a larger-than-life bear on a breathtaking berry-picking adventure.

Jamberry. Bruce Degen. Narrated by Peter Fernandez. (J). 1986. audio compact disk 12.95 (978-1-59519-321-6(9)) Live Oak Media.

Jamberry. Bruce Degen. Illus. by Bruce Degen. (Running Time: 4 mins.). 1986. 9.95 (978-1-59112-071-1(3)) Live Oak Media.

Jamberry. Bruce Degen. Illus. by Bruce Degen. Read by Peter Fernandez. 11 vols. (Running Time: 4 mins.). (I Can Read Bks.). (J). (gr. k-3). 1986. bk. 25.95 (978-0-87499-028-7(9)); pap. bk. 16.95 (978-0-87499-026-3(2)) Live Oak Media.

Jamberry. Bruce Degen. Read by Peter Fernandez. (J). (ps-3). 2006. bk. 28.95 (978-1-59519-362-9(6)); pap. bk. 39.95 (978-1-59519-323-0(5)) Live Oak Media.

Jamberry Board Book & Tape. abr. ed. Bruce Degen. Illus. by Bruce Degen. (Share a Story Ser.). (J). (ps up). 1998. 9.99 (978-0-694-70096-7(7)) HarperCollins Pubs.

Jamberry cassette LC-613CT. 9.95 (978-1-59112-500-6(6)) Live Oak Media.

Jamberry, Grades K-3. Bruce Degen. Illus. by Bruce Degen. Read by Peter Fernandez. 14 vols. (Running Time: 4 mins.). (J). 1986. pap. bk. & tchr. ed. 37.95 Reading Chest. (978-0-87499-027-0(0)) Live Oak Media.

Jambo. Ella Jenkins. 1 CD. (Running Time: 1 hr.). (J). 2001. audio compact disk 15.00 (FC 45017CD) Kimbo Educ.

Jambo & Other Call & Response Songs & Chants. Perf. by Ella Jenkins. 1 cass. (Running Time: 32 min.). (J). (ps-4). 1990. (0-9307-450170-9307-45017-2-4); audio compact disk (0-9307-45017-2-4) Smithsonian Folkways.
Twelve call & response songs with simple rhythmic sounds & lyrics in English & Swahili. Includes "On Safari," "Counting in Swahili" & "Yemayah".

Jamela's Dress. Niki Daly. Narrated by Lyn M. Brown. 1 cass. (Running Time: 9 min.). (J). (ps-2). 2001. bk. 26.95 (978-0-8045-6878-4(2), 6878) Spoken Arts.
Mama is pleased with the dress material she has bought for a friend's wedding. So is Jamela, who can't resist letting it wrap around her and parading through the township. Unfortunately, Mama's prized fabric is ruined during the escapade, but in the end Jamela earns an unexpected reward for her antics and the day is saved.

James: Hands-on Christianity. 2003. 54.00 (978-1-57972-546-4(5)); audio compact disk 54.00 (978-1-57972-545-7(7)) Insight Living.

James: Practical & Authentic Living. 1998. 57.95 (978-1-57972-272-2(5)) Insight Living.

James Agee: A Portrait. abr. ed. James Agee. Perf. by James Agee. Perf. by James Flye. 2 cass. 1985. 19.95 (978-0-694-50398-8(3), SWC 2042) HarperCollins Pubs.

James Alan McPherson. unabr. ed. James Alan McPherson. Prod. by Rebekah Presson. 1 cass. (Running Time: 29 min.). 1991. 10.00 (022291) New Letters.

***James & Karen Hood Foundation, Fundraiser Poetry Book.** Karen Jean Matsko Hood & James G. Hood. 2011. 24.95 (978-1-59434-939-3(8)) Whspmg Pine.

James & the Giant Peach see Roald Dahl

James & the Giant Peach see James et la Grosse Peche

James & the Giant Peach. Prod. by Walt Disney Productions Staff. 1 CD. (J). 1996. audio compact disk 22.50 (978-0-7634-0055-2(6)) W Disney Records.

***James & the Giant Peach.** abr. ed. Roald Dahl. Read by Jeremy Irons. (ENG.). 2004. (978-0-06-079978-6(1)); (978-0-06-074606-3(8)) HarperCollins Pubs.

James & the Giant Peach. unabr. ed. Roald Dahl. Read by Jeremy Irons. (Running Time: 9000 sec.). (J). 2007. audio compact disk 14.95 (978-0-06-136535-5(1), HarperChildAud) HarperCollins Pubs.

James & the Giant Peach Soundtrack. Prod. by Myattic Studio. (YA). 2000. audio compact disk 89.95 (978-0-7365-3275-4(7)) Films Media Grp.

James & the Giant Peach Soundtrack. Prod. by Walt Disney Productions Staff. 1 cass. (J). 1996. 12.98 (978-0-7634-0054-5(8)) W Disney Records.

James B. Hall. Interview. Interview with James B. Hall & Kay Bonetti. 1 cass. (Running Time: 51 min.). 13.95 (978-1-55644-015-1(4), 1082) Am Audio Prose.
Contends that all writers are "taught," & discusses questions of fame, commercial success as a taing, & place of the "university writer"; good stories about the Iowa Writer's Workshop immediately after W. W. II & some of his famous classmates like Flannery O'Connor.

James B. Hall, Pts. 1 & 11. Read by James B. Hall. 2 cass. (Running Time: 1 hr.). 1985. 10.00 ea. New Letters.
California author James B. Hall reads poems about farm scenes & others.

James Baldwin. Interview with James Baldwin. 1 cass. (Running Time: 30 min.). 1980. 12.95 (L007) TFR.
Talks about his voyages of self-discovery in Harlem, Europe, Africa & the American South. He explains his special insights into three contemporary upheavals: the Black, women's & gay movements.

James Baldwin. Interview. Interview with James Baldwin & Kay Bonetti. 1 cass. (Running Time: 1 hr.). 13.95 (978-1-55644-094-6(4), 4022) Am Audio Prose.
Interview focuses on Baldwin's current stands on many racial & aesthetic issues discussed in his essays & his response to the criticisms leveled at him during the 60's by Cleaver & Baraka.

James Baldwin. unabr. ed. James Baldwin. 1 cass. (Author Speaks Ser.). 1991. 14.95 J Norton Pubs.
Archival recordings of 20th-century authors.

James Baldwin: The View from Here. James Baldwin. 1 cass. (Running Time: 60 mins.). (J). 1999. 12.95 (SPA 1182) African Am Imag.

James Baldwin: The View from Here. Narrated by James Baldwin. 1 cass. (Running Time: 60 min.). 10.95 (K0290B090, HarperThor) HarpC GBR.

James Baldwin: The View from Here. unabr. ed. 1 cass. (Running Time: 45 min.). 1989. 10.95 (978-0-8045-1182-7(9), SAC 1182) Spoken Arts.

James Baldwin Reading. 20.97 (978-0-13-090267-2(5)) P-H.

James Bertolino. James Bertolino. Read by James Bartolino. 1 cass. (Running Time: 29 min.). 1986. 10.00 New Letters.
James Bertolino, a poet from Washington State, reads from his book, "First Credo".

James Bogan. unabr. ed. James Bogan. Read by James Bogan. 1 cass. (Running Time: 29 min.). 1986. 10.00 New Letters.
James Bogan, poet & folk-humorist of the Missouri Ozarks, reads litanies & lists in Whitman style.

James Bond Box Set (from Russia with Love & Moonraker) Casino Royale Is being released as a movie on 11/17/06. It will bring interest in Ian Fleming's Works. unabr. ed. Ian Fleming. Read by Robert Whitfield. 11 cass. (Running Time: 15 hrs. 30 mins.). 2006. 24.95 (978-0-7861-4607-9(9)) Blckstn Audio.

James Boys: A Novel Account of Four Desperate Brothers. unabr. ed. Richard Liebmann-Smith. (Running Time: 10 hrs. 0 mins.). 2008. 29.95 (978-1-4332-1539-1(X)); audio compact disk 29.95 (978-1-4332-1540-7(3)) Blckstn Audio.

James Boys: A Novel Account of Four Desperate Brothers. unabr. ed. Richard Liebmann-Smith. Read by Malcolm Hillgartner. (Running Time: 9.5 hrs. 0 mins.). 2008. 29.95 (978-1-4332-1541-4(1)); 59.95 (978-1-4332-1537-7(3)); audio compact disk 80.00 (978-1-4332-1538-4(1)) Blckstn Audio.

James Buchanan: Politics & Economics. Narrated by James Buchanan. 1 cass. (Running Time: 60 min.). 10.95 (K0300B090, HarperThor) HarpC GBR.

James Clavell. Interview with James Clavell. 1 cass. (Running Time: 35 min.). 1981. 12.95 (L014) TFR.
Clavell talks about his novel & TV series, "Shogun." He traces his fascination with the Orient to the fact that he was a Japanese prisoner of war during W.W.II. All of his novels, he says, combine to make a history of the Anglo Saxon in the Orient. E. G. Seidensticker talks on his translation of The Tale of Genji which concerns the amours of a young Japanese prince 1,000 years ago.

James Commentary. Chuck Missler. 8 CD's. (Running Time: 8 hours). (Chuck Missler Commentaries). 2006. audio compact disk 44.95 (978-1-57821-353-5(3)) Koinonia Hse.
The Book of James focuses on the believer's justification before men. His robust epistle focuses on the practical Christian walk rather than on doctrine; it is directed toward a living faith. Faith is not believing in spite of the evidence; Faith is obeying in spite of the consequences. This collection of 8 individual audio CDs contains more than 8 hours of verse-by-verse commentary on the book of James coupled with extensive study notes. Plus, as an added bonus, this package also includes the fully automated MP3 CD-ROM for a total of 9 CDs! James One: James 1:1-12 - Introduction. Victorious faith. Crown of life. James Two: James 1:13-27 - Temptation. Doers of the Word. "Religion." James Three: James 2:1-13 - Gossip. Manifested faith. Lack of justice. Judgment. James Four: James 2:14-26 - 3 kinds of faith. Justified. Faith without works is dead. James Five: James 3:1-12 - Controlling faith. The tongue. Know a tree by its fruit. James Six: James 3:13 - Chapter 4 - Wisdom. Evidences of true wisdom. Submissive faith. The World, the Flesh, the Devil. James Seven: James 5 - The rich. Straight talk. The power of patience. Prayer. James Eight:Conclusion - Shroud of Turin. The Knights Templar. Freemasonry.

James Commentary: Verse-by-Verse with Chuck Missler. Chuck Missler. 1 MP3 CD-ROM. (Running Time: 10 hrs.). (Chuck Missler Commentaries). 2000. cd-rom 29.95 (978-1-57821-116-6(6)) Koinonia Hse.

James Crenner. Read by James Crenner. 1 cass. (Running Time: 29 min.). 1985. 10.00 New Letters.
One of a weekly half-hour radio program with authors talking & presenting their own works. James Crenner here reads from "My Head Flies on Again".

James Dean: A Concise Biography. unabr. ed. William Hall. Read by William Roberts. 2 cass. (Running Time: 2 hrs.). (Isis Ser.). (J). 2001. 24.95 (978-0-7531-0723-2(6)) Pub: ISIS Lrg Prnt GBR. Dist(s): Ulverscroft US
His death on September 30, 1955, at the age of twenty-four, made James Dean an icon of the rebellious youth culture that he had symbolized in "Rebel Without a Cause". Born in 1931 in Indiana, he began acting while at university. His screen roles in "East of Eden" and "Giant" brought him nominations for Academy Awards. Behind the cameras his private life was just as turbulent and unpredictable as any of the characters he portrayed.

James Dickey. Read by James Dickey. 1 cass. (Running Time: 45 min.). 12.95 (L016) TFR.
Talks about his long poem, "Zodiac" & his novel, "Deliverance." He discusses that southern living produces strong writing & that violence is a necessary, even desirable part of life.

James Dickey. unabr. ed. James Dickey. Read by James Dickey. 1 cass. (Running Time: 29 min.). 1987. 10.00 (120487) New Letters.
Interview with author of the novel "Deliverance." Dickey is also the former poetry consultant to the Library of Congress.

James Dickey Reads His Poetry & Prose. abr. ed. Poems. James Dickey. Read by James Dickey. 1 cass. Incl. Celebration. (SWC 1333); Deliverance. (SWC 1333); Diabetes Mellitus. (SWC 1333); Encounter in the Cage Country. (SWC 1333); Falling. (SWC 1333); For the Last Wolverine. (SWC 1333); Hunting Civil War Relics at Nimblewill Creek. (SWC 1333); In the Tree House at Night. (SWC 1333); Mercy. (SWC 1333); Messages. (SWC 1333); Scarred Girl. (SWC 1333); 1984. 12.95 (978-0-694-50213-4(8), SWC 1333) HarperCollins Pubs.

James Earl Jones Reads the Bible - New Testament. unabr. ed. American Bible Society Staff. Read by James Earl Jones. (YA). 2007. 59.99 (978-1-60252-644-0(3)) Find a World.

James Earl Jones Reads the Bible New Testament-KJV. Read by James Earl Jones. (Running Time: 68400 sec.). 2007. audio compact disk 29.95 (978-1-59150-974-5(2)) TOPICS Ent.

James et la Grosse Peche, Set. Roald Dahl. Read by Genevieve Lezy et al. 2 cass.Tr. of James & the Giant Peach. (FRE.). (J). 1992. bk. 35.95 (1GA064) Olivia & Hill.
Young James lives with his aunt isolated from children his own age. A bored & dull child until the discovery of the giant peach & the magical world it holds within.

James Gallagher: Independence Movement for California's Coastal Islands. (Running Time: 60 min.). Incl. Anthony Hargis: Individual Secession. 1983. (FL2); (Freeland Ser.). 1983. 7.00 (FL2) Freeland Pr.
On side one James Gallagher discusses the actions he has taken to convince the residents of Catalina Island to secede from California. On side two Anthony Harris presents solutions for those who need to make some positive moves toward freedom & taking charge of their lives.

James Galvin. unabr. ed. James Galvin. Read by James Galvin. 1 cass. (Running Time: 29 min.). 1989. 10.00 (112689) New Letters.
Galvin reads several poems from his latest book, "Elements," & talks about the idea of being a "Western Writer".

James Hall & Worship & Praise - Live from New York. Perf. by James Hall & Worship and Praise. 1 cass., 1 CD. 10.98 (978-1-57908-336-6(6), 1402); audio compact disk 15.98 CD. (978-1-57908-335-9(8)) Platinm Enter.

James Herriot: The Life of a Country Vet. unabr. ed. Graham Lord. Read by Stuart Langton. 7 cass. (Running Time: 10 hrs. 30 mins.). 1998. 56.00 (978-0-7366-4193-7(9), 896054) Books on Tape.
An affectionate biography that follows Alf Wight, better known as James Herriot, from his childhood in a Glasgow slum, to veterinary college, to life as a vet in Yorkshire. Along the way, we encounter some extraordinary events & hidden tragedies in this seemingly magical life.

James Herriot Collection. unabr. ed. 44 CDs. 2006. audio compact disk 380.00 (978-0-7927-4510-5(8), SLD1040) AudioGO.

James Herriot Collection, Set. unabr. ed. James Herriot. Read by Christopher Timothy. 35 CDs. (Running Time: 40 hrs. 0 mins. 0 sec.). (ENG.). 2006. audio compact disk 89.95 (978-1-4272-0026-6(2)) Pub: Macmill Audio. Dist(s): Macmillan

James Herriot's Cat Stories. unabr. rev. abr. ed. James Herriot & James Herriot. Read by Christopher Timothy. 3 CDs. (Running Time: 3 hrs. 0 mins. 0 sec.). (ENG.). 2004. audio compact disk 19.95 (978-1-59397-525-8(2)) Pub: Macmill Audio. Dist(s): Macmillan

James Herriot's Favorite Dog Stories. unabr. rev. ed. James Herriot. Read by Christopher Timothy. 3 CDs. (Running Time: 3 hrs. 0 mins. 0 sec.). (ENG.). 2004. audio compact disk 19.95 (978-1-59397-526-5(0)) Pub: Macmill Audio. Dist(s): Macmillan

James Herriot's Treasury for Children: Warm & Joyful Animal Tales. unabr. ed. James Herriot. Read by Jim Dale. 2 CDs. (Running Time: 1 hr. 30 mins. 0 sec.). (ENG.). (J). (ps-3). 2008. audio compact disk 14.95 (978-1-4272-0524-7(8)) Pub: Macmill Audio. Dist(s): Macmillan

James Joyce. Edna O'Brien. Read by Donada Peters. 2000. audio compact disk 40.00 (978-0-7366-5212-4(4)) Books on Tape.

James Joyce. Edna O'Brien. Read by Donada Peters. 4 cass. (Running Time: 6 hrs.). 2000. Rental 24.95 (978-0-7366-4941-4(7)) Books on Tape.
A concise biography of one of the greatest & most complex novelists of the twentieth century.

James Joyce. unabr. ed. Brendan Behan. 1 cass. (Running Time: 36 min.). 1962. 12.95 (23071) J Norton Pubs.
A whimsical talk about Joyce, a short reading, & the rendition of an impromptu folksong by Behan before the James Joyce Society.

James Joyce. unabr. ed. Edna O'Brien. Read by Donada Peters. 5 CDs. (Running Time: 7 hrs. 30 mins.). 2001. audio compact disk 40.00 Books on Tape.
O'Brien traces Joyce's early days as a rambunctious young Jesuit student; his falling in love with a tall, red-haired Galway girl named Nora Barnacle on Bloomsday; and his exile to Trieste where he found success, love, and finally, despair. Joyce's raucous life as well as thoughtful commentary on his major writings is presented without the academic accoutrements that have made other Joyce biographies so difficult to read. O'Brien captures with simplicity the brilliance and complexity of this great master.

James Joyce. unabr. collector's ed. Edna O'Brien. Read by Donada Peters. 4 cass. (Running Time: 6 hrs.). 1999. 32.00 (978-0-7366-4824-0(0), 5169) Books on Tape.
A concise biography of one of the greatest & most complex novelists of the twentieth century.

James Joyce, Pt. 1. unabr. collector's ed. Richard Ellmann. Read by David Case. 15 cass. (Running Time: 22 hrs. 30 min.). 1994. 120.00 (978-0-7366-2823-5(1), 3533 A/B) Books on Tape.
Revision of Ellmann's 1959 classic brings "the greatest literary biography of the century" up-to-date for a new generation.

James Joyce, Pt. 2. unabr. collector's ed. Richard Ellmann. Read by David Case. 13 cass. (Running Time: 19 hrs. 30 min.). 1994. 104.00 (978-0-7366-2824-2(X), 3533-A) Books on Tape.
The most superb literary biography of the century for a new generation.

James Joyce: The Complete Recordings. Read by James Joyce. Mem. of Eugene Jolas. 1 Compact Disc plus . 2003. audio compact disk 27.99 (978-0-9748452-0-3(5)) Rnwnd Unboun.

James Joyce: The Dead & Other Stories from Dubliners. Read by T. P. McKenna. 1 cass. 12.00 (978-1-878427-20-5(2), XC415) Cimino Pub Grp.

James Joyce Collection. unabr. ed. James Joyce. Perf. by Gabriel Byrne. 4 cass. (Running Time: 6 hrs.). 2004. 25.00 (978-1-59007-002-4(X)) Pub: New Millenn Enter. Dist(s): PerseuPGW
In these short stories from Dubliners & selections from A Portrait of the Artist as a Young Man, esthetic & alienated sensibilities suffer & survive the paralysis & stifling conventions of everyday life & family. On these tender yet uncompromising portraits, the affection & understanding of the artist for his fellow countrymen & for the city & culture that both define & hold them captive cast a luminous glow.

James Joyce in 90 Minutes. unabr. ed. Paul Strathern. Read by Robert Whitfield. (Running Time: 2 hrs. NaN mins.). 2009. audio compact disk 22.95 (978-1-4332-1781-4(3)); audio compact disk 27.00 (978-1-4332-1782-1(1)) Blckstn Audio.

James Joyce Reads. unabr. ed. James Joyce. Read by James Joyce. 1 cass. (Running Time: 46 mins.). 11.95 (H116) Blckstn Audio.
The only recording ever made of Joyce himself reading from "Ulysses." Also includes him reading from "Finnegan's Wake" & Cyril Cusack reading selections from Joyce's poetry.

James Joyce Reads James Joyce see James Joyce Soundbook

James Joyce Reads James Joyce. abr. ed. James Joyce. Perf. by James Joyce. Perf. by Cyril Cusack. 1 cass. Incl. Chamber Music. (CPN 1340); Ecce Puer. Lyrics by James Joyce. Music by Stephen Albert. (CPN 1340); Finnegans Wake & Anna Livia Plurabelle. James Joyce. (CPN 1340); Pomes Penyeach. James Joyce. (CPN 1340); Ulysses. (CPN 1340); 1984. 9.95 (978-0-89845-778-0(5), CPN 1340) HarperCollins Pubs.

James Joyce Soundbook. unabr. ed. James Joyce. Read by Cyril Cusack et al. 4 cass. (Running Time: 1 hr.). 1989.; 25.00 (978-0-89845-039-2(X), SBC 112) HarperCollins Pubs.

James Joyce's Stephen Hero. unabr. ed. Joseph Prescott. 1 cass. (Running Time: 27 min.). 1970. 12.95 (23070) J Norton Pubs.
Part of an early draft of "A Portrait of the Artist as a Young Man", "Stephen Hero" is interesting in itself & revealing about the evolution of Joyce as a craftsman.

James Leo Herlihy. Interview. Interview with James L. Herlihy & Kay Bonetti. 1 cass. (Running Time: 1 hr. 30 min.). 13.95 (978-1-55644-047-2(2), 2072) Am Audio Prose.
A wide-ranging discussion of Herlihy's career in the theatre as actor & playwright, his friendship with Anais Nin, his involvement in the anti-war movement, & his reasons for leaving writing behind.

James Longstreet: Lee's War Horse. unabr. collector's ed. Bryan Conrad & H. J. Eckenrode. Read by Michael Prichard. 8 cass. (Running Time: 12 hrs.). 1992. 64.00 (978-0-7366-2253-0(5), 3042) Books on Tape.
James Longstreet was one of the great Confederate generals. He fought from First Manassas through Appomattox & commanded the First Corps of Lee's army from its creation in 1862 to the surrender in April 1865. Lee held him in high regard & relied heavily on him after Stonewall Jackson's death.

James Madison: The Founding Father. unabr. ed. Robert A. Rutland. Read by John MacDonald. 8 cass. (Running Time: 11 hrs. 30 mins.). 1989. 56.95 (978-0-7861-0089-7(3), 1082) Blckstn Audio.
Provides a revealing portrait of a prolific human being - the man Thomas Jefferson called "the greatest man in the world." Madison is shown to be adept as a legislator, writer, Secretary of State, President, elder statesman & perhaps most importantly, as a man who believed most implicitly in the mutual dependence of democracy & individual freedom.

James Madison & the Struggle for the Bill of Rights. unabr. ed. Richard Labunski. Read by Richard Poe. 10 CDs. (Running Time: 41400 sec.). 2006. audio compact disk 39.99 (978-1-4193-9613-7(7)) Recorded Bks.

James Madison & the Struggle for the Bill of Rights. unabr. ed. Richard E. Labunski. Read by Richard Poe. 10 cass. (Running Time: 11 hrs. 50 mins.). 2006. 92.75 (978-1-4281-0297-2(3)); audio compact disk 123.75 (978-1-4281-0299-6(X)) Recorded Bks.

James Marshall's Favorite Fairy Tales: Red Riding Hood; Goldilocks & the Three Bears; Three Little Pigs, the; Cinderella; Hansel & Gretel. unabr. ed. James Marshall. Read by Donal Donnelly et al. (J). 2007. 44.99 (978-1-60252-645-7(1)) Find a World.

James Mason: Odd Man Out. unabr. ed. Sheridan Morley. Read by John Rye. 7 cass. (Running Time: 7 hrs.). 2001. 61.95 (978-1-85089-803-0(0), 10991) Pub: ISIS Audio GBR. Dist(s): Ulverscroft US
Sheridan Morley tells the story of James Mason, one of Britain's best loved film stars.

James McConkey. unabr. ed. Read by James McConkey. 1 cass. (Running Time: 29 min.). 1985. 10.00 New Letters.
Reads from "The Tree House Confessions" & discusses his work.

James McKinley. Interview. Interview with James McKinley & Kay Bonetti. 1 cass. (Running Time: 56 min.). 13.95 (978-1-55644-075-5(8), 3082) Am Audio Prose.
Accomplished parajournalist, essayist, & fiction writer discusses issues surrounding the practice of balancing the world of non-fiction & fiction writing & implications on one's craft & vision.

James McKinley: Robert Graves. unabr. ed. James McKinley. Read by James McKinley. 1 cass. (Running Time: 29 min.). 1991. 10.00 (010778) New Letters.

James McKinley I. Read by James McKinley. 1 cass. (Running Time: 29 min.). Incl. Assassination in America; 1987. 10.00 New Letters.
Reads selections concerning John Kennedy, Martin Luther King & Robert Kennedy.

James Mellow. Interview with James R. Mellow. 1 cass. (Running Time: 50 min.). 1974. 11.95 (L050) TFR.
Talks about the Stein-Toklas salon & its lasting effect on contempory literature.

James Michener. Interview with James A. Michener. 1 cass. (Running Time: 45 min.). 1978. 13.95 (L051) TFR.
Talks about his writing from "Tales of the South Pacific" to "Chesapeake" & discusses what influence his being a foundling may have had on his work.

James Monroe. Linda R. Wade. (J). 1993. 9.95 (978-0-87386-088-8(8)) Jan Prods.

James Pike: Prayer in Public Schools see Buckley's Firing Line

James Ragan. unabr. ed. James Ragan. Read by James Ragan. 1 cass. (Running Time: 29 min.). 1986. 10.00 New Letters.
James Ragan, screenwriter as well as poet, reads from "In the Talking Hours" & "Womb Weary".

James Reiss. unabr. ed. James Reiss. Read by James Reiss. 1 cass. (Running Time: 29 min.). 1986. 10.00 New Letters.
James Reiss, who commutes weekly between Ohio & New York, reads poems from "The Breathers".

James Robison: Envy. unabr. ed. James Robison. Read by James Robison. 1 cass. (Running Time: 29 min.). 1987. 10.00 (091887) New Letters.
Robison reads the story "Envy," & talks about how he maintains his own voice.

James Schevill. unabr. ed. Read by James Schevill. 1 cass. (Running Time: 29 min.). 1985. 10.00 New Letters.
James Schevill reads from "The American Fantasies: Collected Poems 1945-1981".

James Stewart. unabr. ed. Donald Dewey. Read by Tom Parker. 13 cass. (Running Time: 19 hrs.). 1997. 85.95 (978-0-7861-1201-2(8), 1965) Blckstn Audio.
Drawn from nearly 200 interviews with childhood neighbors, fellow workers, old loves, airmen who worked with Stewart during World War II, as well as with close & estranged family members & friends.

James Stewart. unabr. ed. Donald Dewey. (Running Time: 66600 sec.). 2007. audio compact disk 44.95 (978-0-7861-6004-4(7)); audio compact disk 120.00 (978-0-7861-6003-7(9)) Blckstn Audio.

James Still & Randy Wilson: Heritage. Perf. by James Still & Randy Wilson. 1 cass. 10.00 (JA0068) Appalshop.
Poetry, music, & interview with James Still on his life & work. "Appalachia: A Definition," River of Earth (poem) "I Was Born Humble"; from Afterword "The Run for the Elbertas," "Wolfpen Creek," "Leap Minnows, Leap," "Dance on Pushback"; from River of Earth "Those I Want in Heaven" with "Should There Be Such a Place," & "Heritage." Traditional music performed by Randy Wilson on lap dulcimer, hammer dulcimer & fretless banjo.

James Tate. unabr. ed. Read by James Tate. 1 cass. (Running Time: 29 min.). 1985. 10.00 New Letters.
James Tate's book, "The Lost Pilot", won the Yale Series of Younger Poets.

James Tate Two. unabr. ed. James Tate. 1 cass. (Running Time: 29 min.). 1991. 10.00 (060791) New Letters.

James to Revelation: New International Version. abr. ed. Read by Sarah Finch. 2 cass. (Running Time: 0 hr. 60 mins. 0 sec.). (Hodder Christian Audiobooks Ser.). (ENG.). 1995. 16.99 (978-1-85998-212-9(3), HoddrStoughton) Pub: Hodder General GBR. Dist(s): IPG Chicago

James Welch. Interview. Interview with James Welch & Kay Bonetti. 1 cass. (Running Time: 54 min.). 1985. 13.95 (978-1-55644-135-6(5), 5072) Am Audio Prose.
Examines the author's books in Native American context.

James Whitcomb Riley: Young Poet. Minnie Belle Mitchell & Montrew Dunham. Read by Patrick G. Lawlor. (Running Time: 7200 sec.). (Young Patriots Ser.). (J). 2007. 22.95 (978-1-4332-0151-6(8)) Blckstn Audio.

James Whitcomb Riley: Young Poet. unabr. ed. Minnie Belle Mitchell & Montrew Dunham. Read by Patrick G. Lawlor. (Young Patriots Ser.). (J). 2007. 34.99 (978-1-60252-708-9(3)) Find a World.

Jamestown Community. Compiled by Benchmark Education Staff. 2005. audio compact disk 10.00 (978-1-4108-5501-5(5)) Benchmark Educ.

Jamestown Education: English, Yes! Level 3: Beginning, Learning English Through Literature, Vol. 3. rev. ed. Burton Goodman. (Jamestown Education: English, Yes! Ser.). 2003. audio compact disk 43.96 (978-0-07-861508-5(9), 9780078615085) Pub: Jamestown. Dist(s): McGraw
Level 3 Wolf based on a story by Jack London Crucita based on a story by Manuela Williams Crosno The Last Leaf based on a story by O. Henry The Hero based on a story by Stephen Crane Land based on a story by Leo Tolstoy Irregular Verbs Present and Past Tenses Score Chart.

Jamestown Education: English, Yes! Level 5: Intermediate B, Learning English Through Literature, rev. ed. Burton Goodman. (Jamestown Education: English, Yes! Ser.). 2003. audio compact disk 43.96 (978-0-07-861510-8(0), 9780078615108) Pub: Jamestown. Dist(s): McGraw
Level 5 The Boy Who Drew Cats based on a story by Lafcadio Hearn The Open Window based on a story by Saki Shoes for Hector based on a story by Nicholasa Mohr The Necklace based on a story by Guy de Maupassant Kaddo's Wall based on an African Folktale retold by Harold Courlander and George Herzog The Comeback based on a story by Elizabeth Van Steenwyk God Sees the Truth, but Waits based on a story by Leo Tolstoy Irregular Verbs Score Chart.

Jamestown Education: English, Yes! Level 7: Transitional, Learning English Through Literature, rev. ed. Burton Goodman. (Jamestown Education: English, Yes! Ser.). 2003. audio compact disk 43.96 (978-0-07-861512-2(7), 9780078615122) Pub: Jamestown. Dist(s): McGraw
Level 7 Unit 1: TheTeacher by Alma Flor Ada Unit 2: TheTiger based on a story by Lin Yutang Magic Words (poem) by a Netsilik Inuit Unit 3: After Twenty Years based on a story by O. Henry Unit 4: The Stove based on a story by Marjorie Pickthall Unit 5: Early Autumn The City (poem) Lonely House (song lyrics) Declaration (poem) Dreams (poem) by Langston Hughes Unit 6: An Occurrence at Owl Creek Bridge based on a story by Ambrose Bierce Unit 7: Ta-Na-E-Ka based on a story by Mary Whitebird Grandfather (poem) by James K. Cazalas Unit 8: The Circuit based on a story by Francisco Jimenez Unit 9: A Boy's Best Friend based on a story by Isaac Asimov Moco Limping (poem) by David Nava Monreal Score Chart.

Jamestown Education: Reading Fluency: Level A, Level A. Camille L. Z. Blachowicz. (ENG.). 2004. audio compact disk 43.96 (978-0-07-869117-1(6), 0078691176) Pub: Glencoe. Dist(s): McGraw

Jamestown Education: Reading Fluency: Level B, Level B. Camille L. Z. Blachowicz. (ENG.). 2004. audio compact disk 43.96 (978-0-07-869118-8(4), 0078691184) Pub: Glencoe. Dist(s): McGraw

Jamestown Education: Reading Fluency: Level C, Level C. Camille L. Z. Blachowicz. (ENG.). 2004. audio compact disk 43.96 (978-0-07-869119-5(2), 0078691192) Pub: Glencoe. Dist(s): McGraw

Jamestown Education: Reading Fluency: Level D, Level D. Camille L. Z. Blachowicz. (ENG.). 2004. audio compact disk 43.96 (978-0-07-869120-1(6), 0078691206) Pub: Glencoe. Dist(s): McGraw

Jamestown Education: Reading Fluency: Level E, Level E. Camille L. Z. Blachowicz. (ENG.). 2004. audio compact disk 43.96 (978-0-07-869121-8(4), 0078691214) Pub: Glencoe. Dist(s): McGraw

Jamestown Education: Reading Fluency: Level G, Level G. Camille L. Z. Blachowicz. (ENG.). 2004. audio compact disk 43.96 (978-0-07-869123-2(0), 0078691230) Pub: Glencoe. Dist(s): McGraw

Jamestown Education: Reading Fluency: Level H, Level H. Camille L. Z. Blachowicz. (ENG.). 2004. audio compact disk 43.96 (978-0-07-869124-9(9), 0078691249) Pub: Glencoe. Dist(s): McGraw

Jamestown Education: Reading Fluency: Level I, Level I. Camille L. Z. Blachowicz. (ENG.). 2004. audio compact disk 43.96 (978-0-07-869125-6(7), 0078691257) Pub: Glencoe. Dist(s): McGraw

Jamestown Education: Reading Fluency: Level J, Level J. Camille L. Z. Blachowicz. (ENG.). 2004. audio compact disk 43.96 (978-0-07-869126-3(5), 0078691265) Pub: Glencoe. Dist(s): McGraw

Jamgon Kongtrul. Read by Chogyam Trungpa. 6 cass. 1974. 63.00 (A046) Vajradhatu.
Six talks. Jamgon Kongtrul of Sechen was Chogyam Trungpa's root guru. The basic theme of this seminar is the importance of commitment to one tradition before encompassing other traditions.

***Jamie Lee Curtis Audio Collection.** unabr. ed. Jamie Lee Curtis. Read by Jamie Lee Curtis. 2006. (978-0-06-122998-5(9)); (978-0-06-122997-8(0)) HarperCollins Pubs.

Jamie Lee Curtis Audio Collection: Is There Really a Human Race? - When I Was Little - Tell Me about the Night I Was Born - Today I Feel Silly - Where Do Balloons Go? - I'm Gonna Like Me - It's Hard to Be Five. unabr. ed. Jamie Lee Curtis. Read by Jamie Lee Curtis. Illus. by Laura Cornell. Contrib. by David Nichtern. (Running Time: 3600 sec.). (J). (ps-3). 2006. 14.95 (978-0-06-121528-5(7), HarperChildAud) HarperCollins Pubs.

Jamie Lee Curtis Audio Collection: When I was Little; Tell Me Again About the Night I Was Born; Today I Feel Silly; Where Do Balloons Go?; I'm Gonna Like Me. unabr. ed. Jamie Lee Curtis. 1 cass. (Running Time: 1 hr. 30 mins.). (gr. k-2). 2002. 12.00 (978-0-06-051311-5(X)) HarperCollins Pubs.

Jamie Lee Curtis CD Audio Collection: When I Was Little; Tell Me Again About the Night I Was Born; Today I Feel Silly; Where Do Balloons Go?; I'm Gonna Like Me; It's Hard to Be Five. unabr. ed. Jamie Lee Curtis. 1 CD. (Running Time: 1 hr.). 2004. audio compact disk 13.95 (978-0-06-052233-9(X), HarperChildAud) HarperCollins Pubs.

Jamie Murrell. unabr. ed. Jaime Murrell. 2003. 9.99 (978-0-8297-3564-2(X)) Vida Pubs.

Jammin' with the Alphabet. Ricki Korey Birnbaumi. 1 CD. (Running Time: 25 mins.). (J). 2005. audio compact disk 15.95 (978-0-9706094-3-4(4)) Effective Lit Meth.
Jammin' With The Alphabet is a wonderful CD which teaches the foundational skills needed to learn to read and spell. Songs are catchy and up-beat and children ages 3 through 8 years will love to learn them and sing them over and over again. This CD helps make learning to read fun and even exciting.

Jan Renfrow Sings Her Own. Jan Renfrow. 1 cass. (Running Time: 30 min.). 1993. Jan Renfrow.
A back-to-basics folk cassette featuring eight original songs written & performed exclusively by Jan Renfrow, aka, The Folktress. These songs have never before been released, except for "Sad-Eyed Suzie," which was released previously on "Yours in Song".

Jane & the Genius of the Place. Stephanie Barron, pseud. Read by Kate Reading. (Jane Austen Mystery Ser.: No. 4). 2000. audio compact disk 80.00 (978-0-7366-8049-3(7)) Books on Tape.

Jane & the Genius of the Place. collector's ed. Stephanie Barron, pseud. Read by Kate Reading. 8 cass. (Running Time: 12 hrs.). (Jane Austen Mystery Ser.: No. 4). 2000. 64.00 (978-0-7366-4844-8(5)) Books on Tape.
In the waning days of summer, Jane Austen is off to the Canterbury Races, where the rich & fashionable go to gamble away their fortunes. She is unprepared for the shocking drama that ensues when Francoise Grey, a raven-haired wanton, recklessly leaps the rail on her fleet black horse & joins the race. Only hours after Mrs. Grey has departed the race grounds in triumph, her lifeless body (minus her ruby riding habit) is found, gruesomely strangled. As rumors spread that Napoleon's fleet is bound for Kent, Jane begins to suspect that Grey's murder was an act of war rather than a crime of passion.The peaceful fields of Kent have become a very dangerous place & Jane's thirst for justice may exact the steepest price of all, her life.

Jane & the Man of the Cloth, unabr. collector's ed. Stephanie Barron, pseud. Read by Kate Reading. 8 cass. (Running Time: 12 hrs.). (Jane Austen Mystery Ser.: No. 2). 1997. 64.00 (978-0-7366-3683-4(8), 4362) Books on Tape.
The vacationing Austen family must seek shelter at High Down Grange when their carriage overturns.

Jane & the Prisoner of Wool House. unabr. ed. Stephanie Barron, pseud. Read by Kate Reading. 7 cass. (Running Time: 10 hrs. 30 mins.). (Jane Austen Mystery Ser.: No. 6). 2001. 56.00 (978-0-7366-8483-5(2)) Books on Tape.
Jane Austen investigates the alleged murder of a French sea captain by her brother's friend, a captain himself.

Jane & the Stillroom Maid. Stephanie Barron, pseud. Read by Kate Reading. (Jane Austen Mystery Ser.: No. 5). 2000. audio compact disk 64.00 (978-0-7366-7069-2(6)) Books on Tape.

Jane & the Stillroom Maid. Stephanie Barron, pseud. 6 cass. (Running Time: 9 hrs.). (Jane Austen Mystery Ser.: No. 5). 2000. 29.95 (978-0-7366-5682-5(0)) Books on Tape.
Jane Austen as a sleuth continues to delight as she solves a murder mystery while visiting her relatives in Derbyshire.

Jane & the Stillroom Maid. collector's ed. Stephanie Barron, pseud. Read by Kate Reading. 6 cass. (Running Time: 9 hrs.). (Jane Austen Mystery Ser.: No. 5). 2000. 48.00 (978-0-7366-5589-7(1)) Books on Tape.
While out on a walk in the hills during a visit to her relatives in Derbyshire, Jane finds a terribly mutilated body. It turns out to be Tess Arnold, a stillroom maid at a local estate known for her skill as an herbalist. Was Tess suspected of witchcraft? Was she thought to be a traitor to the secret rites of the Freemasons? What was her relationship with the Duke's family? Was the killing the work of a madman? When the wrong person is accused of murder, Jane Austen becomes an innocent victim's only hope in a friendishly clever & breathlessly diverting mystery.

Jane & the Stillroom Maid. unabr. ed. Stephanie Barron, pseud. Read by Kate Reading. 8 CDs. (Running Time: 12 hrs.). (Jane Austen Mystery Ser.: No. 5). 2001. audio compact disk 64.00 Books on Tape.
Jane Austen as a sleuth continues to delight as she solves a murder mystery while visiting her relatives in Derbyshire.

Jane & the Unpleasantness at Scargrave Manor. unabr. collector's ed. Stephanie Barron, pseud. Read by Kate Reading. 8 cass. (Running Time: 12 hrs.). (Jane Austen Mystery Ser.: No. 1). 1997. 64.00 (978-0-7366-3569-1(6), 4219) Books on Tape.
Stephanie Barron imagines Jane Austen had used her wit & powers of observation as a sleuth before becoming an author. In her first case, Jane has scarcely arrived at the estate of her friend, Isobel Payne, when a mysterious ailment fellsIsobel's husband, the Earl of Scargrave. Worse yet, Isobel gets a letter accusing her of the murder & adultery to boot. Wisely, Isobel turns to Jane, who starts sifting through the motives of the Scargrave Manor's guest.

Jane & the Wandering Eye. unabr. collector's ed. Stephanie Barron, pseud. Read by Kate Reading. 7 cass. (Running Time: 10 hrs. 30 min.). (Jane Austen Mystery Ser.: No. 3). 1998. 56.00 (978-0-7366-4164-7(5), 4667) Books on Tape.
As Christmas of 1804 approaches, Jane Austen finds herself in Bath, England & bored to death. Thus, she welcomes an assignment from a titled friend: keep a discreet watch over his niece. But at a masquerade thronged with the fashionable & the notorious, Jane's diversion turns deadly, someone kills a guest. Standing by the body, knife in hand, is Simon, Marquis of Kinsfel. Jane knows he's innocent, but must learn who did the deed & why. A bewildering array of suspects emerge. Stephanie Barron weaves manners, mayhem & murder into a captivating novel of intrigue & suspense.

Jane Austen. Helena Leroy. Read by Anita Wright. 2 cass. (Running Time: 3 hrs.). 2001. 24.95 (980515) Pub: Soundings Ltd GBR. Dist(s): Ulverscroft US

Jane Austen. Carol Shields. 4 cass. (Running Time: 6 hrs.). 2001. 32.00 (978-0-7366-6185-0(9)) Books on Tape.
In Jane Austen, Shields follows this superb novelist from her early family life in Steventon to her later years in Bath, her broken engagement, & her intense relationship with her sister Cassandra. She reveals both the very private woman & the acclaimed author.

Jane Austen. Carol Shields. Read by Donada Peters. 2001. audio compact disk 40.00 (978-0-7366-7508-6(6)) Books on Tape.

Jane Austen. unabr. ed. Carol Shields. Read by Donada Peters. 4 cass. (Running Time: 6 hrs.). 2001. 24.95 (978-0-7366-6815-6(2)) Books on Tape.
Carol Shields reveals the very private woman & acclaimed author behind the enduring classics, "Sense & Sensibility," "Pride & Prejudice," & "Emma".

Jane Austen: A Biography. Elizabeth Jenkins. Read by Teresa Gallagher. 2 cass. (Running Time: 2 hrs. 30 mins.). (YA). (gr. 9 up). 2000. 13.98 (978-962-634-701-0(5), NA220114, Naxos AudioBooks); audio compact disk 17.98 (978-962-634-201-5(3), NA220112, Naxos AudioBooks) Naxos.
Highly prized not only for their light irony, humor and deception of contemporary English country life, but also for their underlying serious qualities.

Jane Austen: A Life. David Nokes. Read by Donada Peters. 15 cass. (Running Time: 22 hrs. 30 mins.). 2000. 120.00 (978-0-7366-4441-9(5), 4886) Books on Tape.
In an intimate portrait of Jane Austen, the author reveals the disturbing family secrets & conflicts that formed her character.

Jane Austen: A Life, unabr. collector's ed. Claire Tomalin. Read by Donada Peters. 9 cass. (Running Time: 13 hrs. 30 mins.). 1998. 72.00 (978-0-7366-4185-2(8), 4683) Books on Tape.
Captures & portrays Jane Austen with a clarity never before achieved in a brilliant biography describing the much-loved writer who showed unfailing bravery when it came to the challenges of her own life.

Jane Austen: Her Life. unabr. ed. Park Honan. Narrated by Davina Porter. 12 cass. (Running Time: 18 hrs.). 1989. 97.00 (978-1-55690-260-4(3), 89450E7) Recorded Bks.
Closely observed domestic life against backdrop of the events of the day (Trafalgar - The War of 1812) - an examination of Jane Austen's life.

***Jane Austen: The Complete Novels.** unabr. ed. Jane Austen. Read by Juliet Stevenson & Emilia Fox. 69 CDs. (Running Time: 83 hrs.). 2009. audio compact disk 250.00 (978-962-634-274-9(9), Naxos AudioBooks) Naxos.

Jane Austen Set: A Concise Biography. unabr. ed. Helen Lefroy. Read by Anita Wright. 2 cass. (Running Time: 2 hrs., 15 min.). (Pocket Biography Ser.). 1998. 24.95 (978-0-7531-0335-7(4), 980515) Pub: ISIS Audio GBR. Dist(s): Ulverscroft US
Draws from Jane Austen's letters to describe her life in vicarage at Steventon & later at Bath & Chawton, her relationships with family & friends - especially her beloved sister, Cassandra, the society which she inhabited & the detail of Nineteenth-century life which she sharply observed.

Jane Austen: A Biography: A Biography. Elizabeth Jenkins. Read by Gallagher Gallagher. (Running Time: 2 hrs. 30 mins.). (C). 2004. 20.95 (978-1-60083-788-3(3)) Iofy Corp.

Jane Austen Book Club. Karen Joy Fowler. Read by Kimberly Schraf. (Running Time: 9 hrs.). 2005. 23.95 (978-1-60083-327-4(6)) Iofy Corp.

Jane Austen Book Club. unabr. ed. Karen Joy Fowler. Read by Kimberly Schraf. 7 CDs. (Running Time: 9 hrs.). (What's New Ser.). 2004. audio compact disk 34.95 (978-1-59316-027-2(5), LL119) Listen & Live.
A sublime comedy of contemporary manners, this is the novel Jane Austen might well have written had she lived in twenty-first- century California. Nothing ever moves in a straight line in Karen Joy Fowler's fiction, and in her latest, the complex dance of modern love has never been so devious or so much fun. Six Californians join to discuss Jane Austen's novels. Over the six months they meet, marriages are tested, affairs begin, unsuitable arrangements become suitable, and love happens. With her finely sighted eye for the frailties of human behavior and her finely tuned ear for the absurdities of social intercourse, Fowler has never been wittier nor her characters more appealing. The result is a delicious dissection of modern relationships. Dedicated Austenites will delight in unearthing the echoes of Austen that run through the novel, but most readers will simply enjoy the vision and voice that, despite two centuries of separation, unite two great writers of brilliant social comedy.

Jane Austen CD Collection: Pride & Prejudice, Persuasion, Emma. unabr. ed. Jane Austen. (Running Time: 35 hrs.). 2008. audio compact disk 39.99 (978-1-4233-8656-8(6), 9781423386568) Brilliance Audio.

Jane Austen Collection. abr. ed. Jane Austen. Narrated by Joanna Lumley et al. 12 CDs. (Running Time: 15 hrs. 0 mins. 0 sec.). (ENG.). 2009. audio compact disk 42.95 (978-1-934997-40-6(4)) Pub: CSAWord. Dist(s): PerseuPGW

Jane Austen Collection Vol. 1: Emma, Mansfield Park, Northanger Abbey, The Biography. Jane Austen & Elizabeth Jenkins. Read by Teresa Gallagher & Juliet Stevenson. 10 cass. (Running Time: 12 hrs. 45 min.). 2000. 52.98 (978-962-634-702-7(3), NAX20214, Naxos AudioBooks) Naxos.
"Emma," "Mansfield Park," "Northanger Abbey," "Jane Austen - A Biography".

Jane Austen Collection Vol. 1: Emma, Mansfield Park, Northanger Abbey, The Biography. Jane Austen & Elizabeth Jenkins. Read by Teresa Gallagher & Juliet Stevenson. Prod. by Nicolas Soames. 10 CDs. (Running Time: 12 hrs. 45 mins.). 2000. audio compact disk 62.98 (978-962-634-202-2(1), NAX20212, Naxos AudioBooks) Naxos.

Jane Austen Collection Vol. 2: Sense & Sensibility, Persuasion, Pride & Prejudice, Lady Susan. Jane Austen. Read by Juliet Stevenson et al. 11 cass. (Running Time: 13 hrs. 15 min.). 2001. 54.98 (978-962-634-729-4(5), NAX23014, Naxos AudioBooks); audio compact disk 67.98 (978-962-634-229-9(3), NAX23012, Naxos AudioBooks) Naxos.

Jane Austen Quintet. Jane Austen. Narrated by Flo Gibson. (ENG.). 2008. 74.95 (978-1-60646-033-7(1)) Audio Bk Con.

Jane Austen Sampler Set: Pride & Prejudice & Sense & Sensibility. abr. ed. Jane Austen. Read by Claire Bloom. 2 cass. (Running Time: 3 hrs.). 1996. 18.00 (978-0-694-51759-6(3)) HarperCollins Pubs.
The perfect introduction to Austen's two best-known works.

Jane Austen's Charlotte. unabr. ed. Julia Barrett, pseud. Read by Johanna Ward. 6 cass. (Running Time: 8 hrs. 30 mins.). 2001. 44.95 (978-0-7861-2044-4(4), 2804); audio compact disk 64.00 (978-0-7861-9706-4(4), 2804) Blckstn Audio.
In completing Jane Austen's last novel, Julia Barrett has emerged with a literary treasure, holding true to the characters and theme designed by Ms. Austen. Set in the developing seaside town of Sanditon, it portrays a young woman from the countryside who is exposed to the sophistication and cynicism of resort life.

Jane Boleyn: The True Story of the Infamous Lady Rochford. abr. ed. Julia Fox. Read by Jenny Sterlin. (Running Time: 21600 sec.). (ENG.). 2007. audio compact disk 29.95 (978-0-7393-5879-5(0), Random AudioBks) Pub: Random Audio Pubg. Dist(s): Random

Jane Cooper. Read by Jane Cooper. 1 cass. (Running Time: 29 min.). Incl. Scaffolding: New & Selected Poems; Threads: Rosa Luxemburg from Prison; 1987. 10.00 New Letters.
Reads from two books.

Jane Eyre. Charlotte Brontë. Narrated by Flo Gibson. 2009. audio compact disk 44.95 (978-1-60646-090-0(0)) Audio Bk Con.

Jane Eyre. Charlotte Brontë. Narrated by Maureen O'Brien. (Running Time: 18 hrs. 0 mins. 0 sec.). (Cover to Cover Ser.). (ENG.). 2010. audio compact disk 29.95 (978-1-60283-570-2(5)) Pub: AudioGO. Dist(s): Perseus Dist

Jane Eyre. Charlotte Brontë. Read by Maureen O'Brien. 15 cass. (Running Time: 21 hrs. 40 min.). 87.95 (CC/008) C to C Cassettes.

Jane Eyre. Charlotte Brontë. Narrated by Donna Barkman. (Running Time: 21 hrs.). 1986. 27.95 (978-1-59912-376-9(2)) Iofy Corp.

Jane Eyre. Charlotte Brontë. Read by Yadira Sánchez. (Running Time: 3 hrs.). 2001. 16.95 (978-1-60083-160-7(5), Audiofy Corp) Iofy Corp.

Jane Eyre. Charlotte Brontë. Read by Betsy Hershberg. 13 cass. (Running Time: 19 hrs. 30 min.). 1993. 73.80 Set. (978-1-56544-020-3(X), 350007); Rental 12.00 30 day rental Set. (350007) Literate Ear.
A precursor of feminist novels. Jane Eyre is an orphan when her protective uncle dies & her cold aunt sends her away. Full of courage & spirit, Jane secures a position as a governess. Her employer is Edward Rochester, a brooding melancholy man. Their passion & its demise revolutionized the scope of romantic fiction.

Jane Eyre. Charlotte Brontë. Read by Emma Fielding. 3 cass. (Running Time: 4 hrs.). 1996. 17.98 (978-962-634-586-3(1), NA308614, Naxos AudioBooks) Naxos.
Tale of a young woman entangled with the powerful Mr. Rochester. Battling inside Jane are passion & prudence; she struggles to survive the turmoil they cause.

Jane Eyre. Charlotte Brontë. 2 CDs. (Running Time: 2 hrs. 30 mins.). (J). audio compact disk 17.99 (978-1-58926-326-0(X), Oasis Kids) Oasis Audio.

Jane Eyre. Charlotte Brontë. 2005. audio compact disk 39.95 (978-1-4193-6525-6(8)) Recorded Bks.

Jane Eyre. abr. ed. Charlotte Brontë. Read by Emma Fielding. (Running Time: 4 hrs.). 2000. 24.95 (978-1-60083-789-0(1)) Iofy Corp.

Jane Eyre. abr. ed. Charlotte Brontë. (Classics Collection). 2001. 7.95 (978-1-57815-241-4(0), Media Bks Audio) Media Bks NJ.

Jane Eyre. abr. ed. Charlotte Brontë. Read by Emma Fielding. 3 CDs. (Running Time: 4 hrs.). (J). (gr. 9-12). 1996. audio compact disk 22.98 (978-962-634-086-8(X), NA308612) Naxos.

Jane Eyre. abr. ed. Charlotte Brontë. Perf. by Juliet Mills. 4 cass. (Running Time: 6 hrs.). (Ultimate Classics Ser.). 2004. 25.00 (978-1-931056-49-6(8), N Millennium Audio) New Millenn Enter.
As a penniless orphan, Jane Eyre had to endure many adversities in order to secure her status as a governess in the home of a Mr. Rochester, a temperamental man with a dark secret - a secret so powerful it could destroy the powerful bond he had created with Jane Eyre.

Jane Eyre. abr. ed. Charlotte Brontë. Read by Juliet Mills. 4 cass. (Running Time: 6 hrs.). 2001. 25.00 Olive LLC.

Jane Eyre. abr. ed. Charlotte Brontë. Contrib. by Joanna David. Abr. by Carol Rosen. 4 cass. (Running Time: 6 hrs.). (ENG.). (gr. 12 up). 2003. 16.95 (978-0-14-086187-7(4), PenGlobal) Penguin Grp USA.
The spirited Jane Eyre secures a job as governess at Thornfield Hall, home of the capricious & sardonic Rochester. But there is something in the Hall, something in Rochester himself, that must remain hidden away. When it is disclosed, Jane's moral fortitude is put to a test that almost destroys her. In this haunting work, Bronte explores human psychology with a clarity of vision that remains unmatched.

Jane Eyre. abr. ed. Charlotte Brontë. Read by Joanna David. (Running Time: 6 hrs.). (ENG.). (gr. 12 up). 2005. audio compact disk 16.95 (978-0-14-305812-0(6), PengAudBks) Penguin Grp USA.

Jane Eyre. abr. ed. Charlotte Brontë. Read by Yadira Sánchez. 3 CDs. (SPA.). 2001. audio compact disk 17.00 (978-958-9494-38-7(2)) YoYoMusic.

Jane Eyre. unabr. ed. Charlotte Brontë. Read by Maureen O'Brien. 16 cass. (Running Time: 21 hrs. 40 mins.). (gr. 9-12). 1999. 49.95 (978-1-57270-100-7(5), F91100u) Pub: Audio Partners. Dist(s): PerseuPGW
Bronte's unconventional love story pairs the plain-looking Jane & her passionate intensity with the reserved & gruff Rochester.

Jane Eyre, unabr. ed. Charlotte Brontë. Read by Nadia May. 13 cass. (Running Time: 19 hrs.). 1994. 85.95 (978-0-7861-0648-6(4), 1452) Blckstn Audio.
Jane Eyre, a plain yet spirited governess, was a new kind of heroine - one whose virtuous integrity, sharp intellect & tireless perseverance broke through class barriers to win equal stature with the man she loved. Hailed by William Makepeace Thackeray as "the masterwork of a great genius," this impassioned love story is still regarded, over a century after it first appeared, as one of the finest novels in literature.

Jane Eyre. unabr. ed. Charlotte Brontë. Read by Juliet Mills. (Running Time: 70200 sec.). 2008. audio compact disk 29.95 (978-1-4332-0956-7(X)) Blckstn Audio.

***Jane Eyre.** unabr. ed. Charlotte Brontë. Read by Nadia May. (Running Time: 19 hrs.). 2010. audio compact disk 123.00 (978-1-4332-5393-5(3)) Blckstn Audio.

***Jane Eyre.** unabr. ed. Charlotte Brontë. Read by Nadia May. (Running Time: 19 hrs. NaN mins.). 2011. 44.95 (978-1-4332-5394-2(1)); audio compact disk 29.95 (978-1-4417-1039-0(6)) Blckstn Audio.

Jane Eyre. unabr. ed. Charlotte Brontë. 14 cass. (Running Time: 21 hrs.). 2002. 112.00 (978-0-7366-8682-2(7)); audio compact disk 144.00 (978-0-7366-8683-9(5)) Books on Tape.
Jane Eyre's love for the haunted Mr. Rochester rescues him from a life of vast unhappiness and solitude.

Jane Eyre. unabr. ed. Charlotte Brontë. Read by Susan Ericksen. 14 cass. (Running Time: 20 hrs.). (Bookcassette Classic Collection). 1997. 64.25 (978-1-56740-562-0(2), 1567405622, Unabridge Lib Edns) Brilliance Audio.
After a sad and neglected childhood as an orphan, Jane Eyre was hired by Edward Rochester as governess for his ward. Jane was pleased with the quiet country life at Thornfield, with the beautiful old manor house and gardens, with the book-filled library, and with her own comfortable room. But there were stories of a strange tenant, a woman who laughed like a maniac, and who stayed in rooms on the third floor. The moody Rochester, however, rebuffed her attempts to find out about the woman, and ordered her to keep quiet about strange noises she heard at night. One night in the garden, Edward Rochester embraced Jane and proposed marriage. But the quiet ceremony in the village church was shockingly halted by a stranger who claimed that Rochester was already married - to the raving maniac Jane had heard crying in the house. Grief-stricken, Jane left Thornfield, feeling that her life was over before it had really begun. But life had many surprises in store for our heroine, and among them there just might be a happily-ever-after.

Jane Eyre. unabr. ed. Charlotte Brontë. Read by Susan Ericksen. (Running Time: 20 hrs.). 2005. 44.25 (978-1-59600-944-8(6), 9781596009448, BADLE); 29.95 (978-1-59600-943-1(8), 9781596009431, BAD); audio compact disk 44.95 (978-1-59600-939-4(X), 9781596009394, Bril Audio CD Unabri); audio compact disk 44.25 (978-1-59600-942-4(X), 9781596009424, Brlnc Audio MP3 Lib); audio compact disk 29.95 (978-1-59600-941-7(1), 9781596009417, Brilliance MP3); audio compact disk 112.25 (978-1-59600-940-0(3), 9781596009400, BriAudCD Unabrid) Brilliance Audio.

Jane Eyre. unabr. ed. Charlotte Brontë. Read by Amanda Root. (YA). 2007. 84.99 (978-1-60252-532-0(3)) Find a World.

Jane Eyre. unabr. ed. Charlotte Brontë. Read by Amanda Root. (Running Time: 20 hrs. 30 mins.). 2006. 90.95 (978-1-60083-790-6(5)) Iofy Corp.

Jane Eyre. unabr. ed. Charlotte Brontë. Perf. by Meg W. Owen & Patrick Allen. Adapted by Barbara Couper. 5 cass. 25.95 (SCN 205) J Norton Pubs.
Over a hundred years after its first publication, the story of the sympathetic Jane & the forceful & magnetic Rochester still elicits a mixed reception.

Jane Eyre. unabr. ed. Charlotte Brontë. Read by Donna Barkman. 15 cass. (Running Time: 23 hrs.). 1982. 79.00 (C-92) Jimcin Record.
Tempestuous novel of love & loss.

Jane Eyre. unabr. ed. Charlotte Brontë. 17 CDs. bk. 98.98 (978-962-634-357-9(5), Naxos AudioBooks) Naxos.

Jane Eyre, unabr. ed. Charlotte Brontë. Narrated by Flo Gibson. 12 cass. (Running Time: 17 hrs. 30 mins.). 1980. 97.00 (978-1-55690-261-1(1), 80170E7a) Recorded Bks.
Jane Eyre, an impoverished governess strives to reveal the secret that locks the door to her employer's heart.

Jane Eyre. unabr. ed. Charlotte Brontë. Narrated by Wanda McCaddon. 15 CDs. (Running Time: 18 hrs. 30 mins. 0 sec.). (Tantor Unabridged Classics Ser.). (ENG.). 2008. audio compact disk 89.99 (978-1-4001-3635-3(0)); audio compact disk 44.99 (978-1-4001-0635-6(4)) Pub: Tantor Media. Dist(s): IngramPubServ

Jane Eyre. unabr. ed. Charlotte Brontë. Read by Wanda McCaddon. (Running Time: 18 hrs. 30 mins. 0 sec.). (ENG.). 2008. 34.99 (978-1-4001-5635-1(1)) Pub: Tantor Media. Dist(s): IngramPubServ

Jane Eyre. unabr. ed. Charlotte Brontë. Read by Juliet Mills. (Running Time: 70200 sec.). 2008. audio compact disk & audio compact disk 120.00 (978-1-4332-1355-7(9)) Blckstn Audio.

Jane Eyre. unabr. ed. Jayne Lewis. (Running Time: 30 mins.). (ENG.). 2006. 5.98 (978-1-59483-711-1(2)) Pub: Hachet Audio. Dist(s): HachBkGrp

Jane Eyre. unabr. ed. Read by Joseph Prescott. 1 cass. (Running Time: 29 min.). 1970. 12.95 (23079) J Norton Pubs.
Presents a study of the peculiar aspects of the novel "Jane Eyre" including adherence to romantic convention, didacticism, & exempla.

Jane Eyre. unabr. abr. ed. Charlotte Brontë. Perf. by Juliet Mills. 13 cass. (Running Time: 19.50 hrs.). 2004. 46.95 (978-1-59007-121-2(2)) Pub: New Millenn Enter. Dist(s): PerseuPGW
In early nineteenth-century England, an orphaned young woman accepts employment as a governess at Thornfield Hall, a country estate owned by the mysteriously remote Mr. Rochester.

Jane Eyre, Pt. 1. unabr. collector's ed. Charlotte Brontë. Read by Penelope Dellaporta. 8 cass. (Running Time: 12 hrs.). 1988. 64.00 (978-0-7366-1448-1(6), 2331-A) Books on Tape.
Jane Eyre is an orphan child who knows only abuse & misery from her mistress. As a young girl she is sent off to boarding school where her good character & diligent habits win her friends & respect. In time Jane herself becomes a teacher at the school.

Jane Eyre, Pt. 2. collector's ed. Charlotte Brontë. Read by Penelope Dellaporta. 8 cass. (Running Time: 12 hrs.). 1988. 64.00 (978-0-7366-1449-8(4), 2331-B) Books on Tape.

Jane Eyre, Set. Charlotte Brontë. Narrated by Flo Gibson. 12 cass. (Running Time: 18 hrs.). 1986. 39.95 (978-1-55685-012-7(3)) Audio Bk Con.
The trials of the orphaned Jane & the eventual tribulations as she assumes the duties of governess to the ward of Rochester in an old English manor, which also houses a strange dark secret.

Jane Eyre, Set. Excerpts. Charlotte Brontë. Read by Fanny Ardant. 2 cass. 1992. 34.95 (1528-EF) Olivia & Hill.
Excerpts from the passionate tale of the orphaned young woman who comes to Thornfield castle to become a governess & falls in love with the moody Mr. Rochester.

Jane Eyre, Set. unabr. ed. Charlotte Brontë. Read by Nadia May. 13 cass. 1999. 85.95 (FS9-50919) Highsmith.

Jane Eyre (A) abr. ed. Charlotte Brontë. (Running Time: 4 hrs.). 2009. audio compact disk 22.98 (978-962-634-947-2(6), Naxos AudioBooks) Naxos.

Jane Fairfax: The Secret Story of the Second Heroine in Jane Austen's Emma. unabr. ed. Joan Aiken. Read by Marlene Sidaway. 8 cass. (Running Time: 10 hrs. 30 min.). 1997. 69.95 (978-1-85695-527-0(3), 93067) Pub: ISIS Audio GBR. Dist(s): Ulverscroft US
Jane Fairfax was musical, accomplished & elegant. But what of her childhood friendship with Emma Woodhouse & her summer visit to Weymouth?.

Jane Field. unabr. ed. Mary E. Wilkins Freeman. Read by Flo Gibson. 3 cass. (Running Time: 3 hrs.). 1998. 16.95 (978-1-55685-560-3(5)) Audio Bk Con.
Jane Field leaves Green River to go to Elliot to make a small claim on her sister's will which was sent to her in error. When she is mistaken for her sister, she decides to pretend she is Esther in order to gain the whole estate. Conscience takes its toll.

Jane Goodall: Animal Scientist. Katherine Krohn. Illus. by Cynthia Martin & Anne Timmons. (Graphic Biographies Ser.). (ENG.). (gr. 3-4). 2007. audio compact disk 6.95 (978-1-4296-1471-9(4)) CapstoneDig.

Jane Goodall: Finding Hope in the Wilds of Africa. (High Five Reading - Purple Ser.). (ENG.). (gr. 4-5). 2007. audio compact disk 5.95 (978-1-4296-1445-0(5)) CapstoneDig.

Jane Goodall: Finding Hope in the Wilds of Africa. Diana Briscoe. (High Five Reading Ser.). (ENG.). (gr. 4 up). 2004. audio compact disk 5.95 (978-0-7368-3856-6(2)) CapstoneDig.

Jane Goodall: Human Beings & Chimpanzees. Narrated by Jane Goodall. 1 cass. (Running Time: 1 hr.). 10.95 (K0190B090, HarperThor) HarpC GBR.

Jane Goodall & the Chimpanzees of Gombe. Helen Sillett. (World Around Us Ser.). 2003. pap. bk. 69.00 (978-1-4105-0012-0(8)); audio compact disk 18.95 (978-1-4105-0197-4(3)) D Johnston Inc.

Jane Goodall (INK Audiocassette) Animal Scientist. (Graphic Library Biographies I Ser.). (ENG.). 2006. audio compact disk 5.95 (978-0-7368-7454-0(2)) CapstoneDig.

Jane Goodall/From Wheels to Wings. Steck-Vaughn Staff. 2002. (978-0-7398-5992-6(7)) SteckVau.

Jane Hirshfield. unabr. ed. Ed. by Jim McKinley. Prod. by Rebekah Presson. 1 cass. (Running Time: 29 min.). (New Letters on the Air Ser.). 1994. 10.00 (030794) New Letters.
Hirshfield reads from her new book of poems "The October Palace" & talks about the newly-published anthology she edited, "Women in Praise of the Sacred: 43 Centuries of Spiritual Poetry by Women." The San Francisco Bay Area writer also discusses the spiritual journeys of women in literary history.

Jane Kenyon. Jane Kenyon. Read by Jane Kenyon. 1 cass. (Running Time: 29 min.). Incl. Boat of Quiet Hours. 1987. (20); 1987. 10.00 (20) New Letters.
Kenyon reads from her second volume of poetry & talks about life & gardenning at Eagle Pond Farm.

***Jane Slayre: The Literary Classic... with a Blood-Sucking Twist.** unabr. ed. Charlotte Brontë. Read by Kate Reading. (Running Time: 14 hrs.). 2010. audio compact disk 32.95 (978-1-4417-5218-5(8)) Blckstn Audio.

***Jane Slayre: The Literary Classic... with a Blood-Sucking Twist.** unabr. ed. Charlotte Brontë & Sherri Browning Erwin. Read by Kate Reading. (Running Time: 14 hrs. 0 mins.). 2010. 29.95 (978-1-4417-5219-2(6)) Blckstn Audio.

***Jane Slayre: The Literary Classic...with a Blood-Sucking Twist.** unabr. ed. Sherri Browning Erwin. (Running Time: 14 hrs. 0 mins.). 2010. 79.95 (978-1-4417-5215-4(3)); audio compact disk 109.00 (978-1-4417-5216-1(1)) Blckstn Audio.

Jane Smiley. unabr. ed. Jane Smiley. Read by Jane Smiley. 1 cass. (Running Time: 29 min.). 1991. 10.00 (062891) New Letters.
The author of the acclaimed "The Age of Grief" reads from her last book, "Ordinary Love & Good Will" & talks about her writing.

***Jane's Fame: How Jane Austen Conquered the World.** unabr. ed. Claire Harman. Narrated by Wanda McCaddon. (Running Time: 9 hrs. 30 mins. 0 sec.). (ENG.). 2010. 24.99 (978-1-4001-6693-0(4)); 16.99 (978-1-4001-8693-8(5)); audio compact disk 34.99 (978-1-4001-1693-5(7)); audio compact disk 69.99 (978-1-4001-4693-2(3)) Pub: Tantor Media. Dist(s): IngramPubServ

Janet Beeler. unabr. ed. Janet Beeler. Read by Janet Beeler. Prod. by Rebekah Presson. 1 cass. (Running Time: 29 min.). 1978. 10.00 (121678) New Letters.

Janet Burroway I: Poetry. unabr. ed. Read by Janet Burroway. 1 cass. (Running Time: 29 min.). 1986. 10.00 New Letters.
Janet Burroway reads from "Material Goods" & talks about writing.

Janet Burroway II: "Winn Dixie" unabr. ed. Read by Janet Burroway. (Running Time: 29 min.). 1986. 10.00 New Letters.
A short story set in a Florida Laundromat.

Janet Dailey's Americana II. unabr. ed. Janet Dailey. 4 cass. (Running Time: 6 hrs.). 2002. 25.00 (978-1-59040-185-9(9)) Audio Lit.
This is the second trilogy in the Americana romance series. Fire and Ice tells of a California woman who must marry to meet the demands of her mother's will. After the Storm features Coloradan Lanie MacLeod, who pays a heavy price when she asks her estranged husband for financial help for her ailing mother. In Difficult Decision, set in Connecticut, Deborah Holland becomes intimately involved with her very handsome and very married boss.

Janet Dailey's Americana III. unabr. ed. Janet Dailey. 6 cass. (Running Time: 9 hrs.). 2002. 32.00 (978-1-59040-235-1(9)) Audio Lit.
Features appearances by detectives Lew Fonesca, Abraham Lieberman, Inspector Porfiry Petrovich Rostnikov and Toby Peters. Contents include: "The Man Who Beat the System", "Snow Birds "(Edgar-nominated story), "Bitter Lemons", "Dead Cat On Gila Street", "Amnesia", "Punishment", "The Man Who Hated Books", "Busted Blossoms" and "The Final Toast".

Janet Evanovich: Full Bloom, Full Scoop, Hot Stuff. unabr. ed. Janet Evanovich. Read by Lorelei King. (Running Time: 21 hrs.). 2009. audio compact disk 39.99 (978-1-4233-8655-1(8), 9781423386551) Brilliance Audio.

Janet Kauffman. unabr. ed. Janet Kauffman. Read by Janet Kauffman. 1 cass. (Running Time: 29 min.). 1986. 10.00 New Letters.
The Michigan writer reads poems from "The Weather Book".

Janet Waking see Twentieth-Century Poetry in English, No. 5, Recordings of Poets Reading Their Own Poetry

Janey: A Little Plane in a Big War. unabr. ed. Alfred W. Schultz. Read by Gerry Whitman. Ed. by Kirk Neff. 7 cass. (Running Time: 10 hrs.). 2001. 45.00 (978-0-913337-45-5(5)) Southfarm Pr.
Janey was Alfred W. Schultz's World War II artillery spotter plane, an L-4B Piper Cub. Both Janey and Schultz participated in the fighting from North Africa through Sicily, Italy, and southern France to Germany. Janey was the only L-4B Piper Cub to survive the entire European War intact. In August 1945, Janey was exhibited in Paris at the Eiffel Tower along with the bigger, fiercer, and sexier World War II fighters and bombers.

Janey Crane. Created by Kane Press. (Let's Read Together Ser.). 2005. audio compact disk 4.25 (978-1-57565-175-0(0)) Kane Pr.

Jango. William Nicholson. Read by Michael Page. (Noble Warriors (Playaway) Ser.). (ENG.). (J). 2008. 64.99 (978-1-60640-596-3(9)) Find a World.

Jango. unabr. ed. William Nicholson. Read by Michael Page. 8 CDs. (Running Time: 36000 sec.). (Noble Warriors Trilogy: Bk. 2). (YA). (gr. 7-12). 2007. audio compact disk 29.95 (978-1-4233-1844-6(7), 9781423318446, Bril Audio CD Unabri); audio compact disk 24.95 (978-1-4233-1845-3(5), 9781423318453, Brilliance MP3); audio compact disk 92.25 (978-1-4233-1849-1(8), 9781423318491, BriAudCD Unabrid); audio compact disk 39.25 (978-1-4233-1850-7(1), 9781423318507, Brinc Audio MP3 Lib) Brilliance Audio.

Jango: Book Two of the Noble Warriors. unabr. ed. William Nicholson. Read by Michael Page. (Running Time: 10 hrs.). (Noble Warriors Ser.). 2007. 39.25 (978-1-4233-1852-1(8), 9781423318521, BADLE); 24.95 (978-1-4233-1851-4(X), 9781423318514, BAD) Brilliance Audio.

Jango: Book Two of the Noble Warriors. unabr. ed. William Nicholson. Read by Michael Page. 6 cass. (Running Time: 36000 sec.). (Noble Warriors Trilogy: Bk. 2). (YA). (gr. 7-12). 2007. 74.25 (978-1-4233-1848-4(X), 9781423318484, BrilAudUnabridg) Brilliance Audio.

***Janice the Original.** abr. ed. Janice Dickinson. Read by Janice Dickinson. (ENG.). 2006. (978-0-06-114322-9(7), Harper Audio); (978-0-06-114323-6(5), Harper Audio) HarperCollins Pubs.

Janice the Original: Dating, Mating, & Extricating. abr. ed. Janice Dickinson. Read by Dickinson Janice. 2 CDs. (Running Time: 3 hrs.). 2006. audio compact disk 22.95 (978-0-06-077876-7(8)) HarperCollins Pubs.

Janice's Attic Songs for Kids. 1 CD. (Running Time: 1 hr.). (J). 2002. audio compact disk (978-0-9722848-0-6(X)) Morn-Time Min.
These catchy favorites from the Janice's Attic video series will keep your children singing along about important lessons on thoughtfulness, obedience, nature, how to keep their body machines in tip-top shape, and much more!.

Janis Allen on Recognition. unabr. ed. Janis Allen. Read by Janis Allen. Read by Michael McCarthy. Ed. by Susan Palmer. 1 cass. (Running Time: 1 hr. 03 min.). 1993. pap. bk. 10.00 (978-1-882944-03-3(8)) Creat Sound.
Management - Self-help in giving & receiving positive recognition with employee.

Janissary Tree. unabr. ed. Jason Goodwin. Read by Stephen Hoye. (YA). 2007. 59.99 (978-1-60252-841-3(1)) Find a World.

Janissary Tree. unabr. ed. Jason Goodwin. Read by Stephen Hoye. (Running Time: 11 hrs. 0 mins. 0 sec.). (Yashim the Eunuch Ser.). (ENG.). 2007. audio compact disk 37.99 (978-1-4001-0504-5(8)); audio compact disk 24.99 (978-1-4001-5504-0(5)); audio compact disk 75.99 (978-1-4001-3504-2(4)) Pub: Tantor Media. Dist(s): IngramPubServ

Janitor's Boy. Andrew Clements. Read by B. D. Wong. 2 vols. (Running Time: 2 hrs. 48 mins.). (J). (gr. 3-7). 2004. pap. bk. 29.00 (978-0-8072-8360-8(6), Listening Lib) Random Audio Pubg.

Janitor's Boy. unabr. ed. Andrew Clements. Read by B. D. Wong. 2 cass. (Running Time: 2 hrs. 48 mins.). (J). (gr. 3-7). 2004. 23.00 (978-0-8072-8359-2(2), LL 0193, Listening Lib) Random Audio Pubg.
Jack Rankin is embarrassed to attend the school where his father is a janitor, until an enlightening punishment forces him to learn surprising secrets about his old man and the old building.

Janner on Speechmaking. Greville Janner. 1990. 61.95 (978-0-566-02835-9(2), Gower Pubng) Pub: Ashgate Pub GBR. Dist(s): Ashgate Pub

***Jan's Story: Love Lost to the Long Goodbye of Alzheimer's.** unabr. ed. Barry Petersen. (Running Time: 7 hrs. 0 mins.). 2010. 14.99 (978-1-4001-8916-8(0)) Tantor Media.

***Jan's Story: Love Lost to the Long Goodbye of Alzheimer's.** unabr. ed. Barry Petersen. 1 MP3-CD. (Running Time: 7 hrs. 30 mins. 0 sec.). 2010. 19.99 (978-1-4001-6916-0(X)); audio compact disk 29.99 (978-1-4001-1916-5(2)) Pub: Tantor Media. Dist(s): IngramPubServ

***Jan's Story (Library Edition) Love Lost to the Long Goodbye of Alzheimer's.** unabr. ed. Barry Petersen. 6 CDs. (Running Time: 7 hrs. 30 mins. 0 sec.). 2010. audio compact disk 71.99 (978-1-4001-4916-2(9)) Pub: Tantor Media. Dist(s): IngramPubServ

***Janson Command.** Robert Ludlum. 2010. audio compact disk 39.98 (978-1-60788-643-3(X)) Pub: Hachet Audio. Dist(s): HachBkGrp

Janson Directive. abr. ed. Robert Ludlum. Read by Paul Michael. 5 CDs. (Running Time: 6 hrs. 0 mins. 0 sec.). (ENG.). 2008. audio compact disk 14.95 (978-1-4272-0567-4(1)) Pub: Macmill Audio. Dist(s): Macmillan

Janson Directive. unabr. ed. Robert Ludlum. Read by Paul Michael. 14 vols. (Running Time: 18 hrs.). 2002. bk. 110.95 (978-0-7927-2711-8(8), CSL 497, Chivers Sound Lib); audio compact disk 129.95 (978-0-7927-2738-5(X), SLD 497, Chivers Sound Lib); audio compact disk 49.95 (978-0-7927-2763-7(0), CMP 497, Chivers Child Audio) AudioGO.
Paul a Janson has a difficult past, which includes a shadowy, notorious career in U.S. Consular Operations. Now living a quiet life, nothing could lure him back into the field. Nothing, except Peter Novak, a man who once saved Janson's life, who has been kidnapped by terrorists and is set to be executed. Hanson hastily assembles a team of former colleagues and proteges to rescue Novak but the operation goes horribly wrong. Now Janson finds himself marked for death and his only hope is to uncover the truth behind these events, a truth that has the power to foment wars, topple governments, and change the very course of history.

Janson Directive. unabr. rev. ed. Robert Ludlum. Read by Paul Michael. 18 CDs. (Running Time: 22 hrs. 0 mins. 0 sec.). (ENG., 2002. audio compact disk 60.00 (978-1-55927-763-1(7)) Pub: Macmill Audio. Dist(s): Macmillan

January Dancer. unabr. ed. Michael Flynn. (Running Time: 11 hrs. 5 mins.). 2008. 29.95 (978-1-4332-5099-6(3)); 65.95 (978-1-4332-5096-5(9)); audio compact disk 90.00 (978-1-4332-5097-2(7)) Blckstn Audio.

January Gladsong see Brian Patten Reading His Poetry

Janus Man. unabr. ed. Colin Forbes. Read by Steven Pacey. 12 cass. (Running Time: 15 hrs. 24 min.). (Isis Ser.). (J). 2004. 94.95 (978-1-85089-709-5(3), 90092) Pub: ISIS Lrg Prnt GBR. Dist(s): Ulverscroft US

Japa Yoga: The Instructional Audio CD. Prod. by Richard Esquinas. 2002. audio compact disk 20.00 (978-0-9721757-3-9(3)) R Esquinas.

Japa Yoga: The Learning Kit. Richard Esquinas. Prod. by Richard Esquinas. (Running Time: 50 minutes). 2002. per. 69.00 (978-0-9721757-4-6(1)) R Esquinas.

Japa Yoga Learning Kit II. Richard Esquinas. Prod. by Richard Esquinas. (Running Time: 50 minutes). 2002. per. 69.00 (978-0-9721757-5-3(X)) R Esquinas.

Japan. unabr. ed. Edwin O. Reischauer. 6 cass. (Running Time: 6 hrs.). 49.50 (S19040); J Norton Pubs.
A tour through Japanese civilization, its history, culture & heritage.

Japan: Its History, Culture & Heritage. Edwin O. Reischauer. 6 cass., pamphlet. (Running Time: 6 hrs.). pap. bk. 69.95 (S19040) J Norton Pubs.
An informal tour through Japanese civilization. Begins with the early influence of China, through Japan's 700 years of feudalism & into the "economic miracle" that began in the 1950s.

Japan: Its History, Culture & Heritage 6-CD Set. Edwin O. Reischauer. 6 CDs. (Running Time: 6 hrs.). 2005. audio compact disk 69.95 (978-1-57970-190-1(6), S19040D) J Norton Pubs.

Japan at War Pt. 1: An Oral History. unabr. collector's ed. Haruko Taya Cook & Theodore F. Cook. Read by Dick Estell. 9 cass. (Running Time: 13 hrs. 30 min.). 1994. 72.00 (978-0-7366-2880-8(0), 3583-A) Books on Tape.
How WWII looked to the Japanese. Based on oral interviews, it's a fascinating story.

Japan at War Pt. 2: An Oral History. collector's ed. Haruko Taya Cook & Theodore F. Cook. Read by Dick Estell. 8 cass. (Running Time: 12 hrs.). 1994. 64.00 (978-0-7366-2881-5(9), 3583-B) Books on Tape.

Japan, Land of the Rising Sun. Cerebellum Academic Team Staff. Executive Producer Ronald M. Miller. (Running Time: 2 hrs.). (Just the Facts Ser.). 2010. 39.95 (978-1-59163-603-8(5)) Cerebellum.

Japan Smarts by Dancing Beetle. Perf. by Eugene Ely. 1 cass. (Running Time: 86 min.). (J). 1994. 10.00 Erthviibz.
Japanese science, myth, ecology & nature sounds come together when Ms. Goldcarp & the spunky musical humans read & sing with Dancing Beetle.

Japan Today. Theodore F. Welch & Hiroki Kato. 1 cass. (Running Time: 1 hr.). (J). 1985. 12.00 (978-0-8442-8502-3(1), Natl Textbk Co) M-H Contemporary.
Introduction to Japanese language & expressions on tape, provides a look at Japanese culture.

Japanese. 2 cass. (Running Time: 80 min.). (Language - Thirty Library). bk. 16.95 set in vinyl album. Moonbeam Pubns.
Using the proven method based on the famous U.S. Military accelerated language learning program, Language/30 courses stress conversationally useful words & phrases.

Japanese. 1 cass. (Running Time: 90 min.). (TravelTalk Ser.). 1993. 15.00 incl. script incl. 288-page phrasebook-dictionary. (LivingLang) Random Info Grp.

Japanese. Nobuo Akiyama & Carol S. Flamm. 10 cass. 150.00 (Natl Textbk Co) M-H Contemporary.
Motivates beginning students toward mastery of Japanese.

Japanese. H. Ballhatchet & S. Kaiser. 1 cass. (Running Time: 60 min.). (Language Complete Course Packs Ser.). 1993. 17.95 (Passport Bks) McGraw-Hill Trade.

Japanese. Barron's Educational Editorial Staff. 1 cass. (Running Time: 1 hrs. 30 min.). (TravelWise Ser.). (ENG & JPN., 1998. pap. bk. 16.95 (978-0-7641-7095-9(3)) Barron.
Designed especially for international travelers, provides introductions to foreign destinations.

Japanese. Fumitsugu Enokida et al. Contrib. by Rosi McNab. (Running Time: 3 hrs. 0 mins. 0 sec.). (Collins Easy Learning Audio Course Ser.). (JPN & ENG.). 2009. audio compact disk 19.95 (978-0-00-731366-2(7)) Pub: HarpC GBR. Dist(s): IPG Chicago

Japanese. Pimsleur Staff. 2000. 295.00 (978-0-671-31604-4(4), Pimsleur) S&S Audio.

Japanese. Pimsleur Staff. 8 lessons. 2001. 29.95 (978-0-671-31649-5(4), Pimsleur) S&S Audio.

Japanese. Eriko Sato. (Running Time: 10800 sec.). (For Dummies Ser.). (JPN & ENG.). 2008. audio compact disk 19.99 (978-0-470-17813-3(2), For Dummies) Wiley US.

Japanese. rev. ed. 2 cass. (Running Time: 90 min. per cass.). (Basic Courses Ser.). 1993. bk. 30.00 CD editions. (LivingLang) Random Info Grp.

Japanese. unabr. ed. Ed. by Charles Berlitz. 2 cass. (Running Time: 1 hr. 30 mins.). (Language/30 Brief Course Ser.). pap. bk. 21.95 (AF1027) J Norton Pubs.
Quick, highly condensed introduction to the words & phrases you'll need to communicate effectively in the country you're visiting. Cassettes & phrase guide book are in a vinyl album.

Japanese. unabr. ed. Linguistics Staff. Created by Oasis Audio Staff. (Complete Idiot's Guide Ser.). (ENG.). 2005. audio compact disk 19.99 (978-1-59859-057-9(X)) Oasis Audio.

Japanese. unabr. ed. Linguistics Staff. Narrated by Linguistics Staff. Created by Oasis Audio Staff. 2 cass. (Running Time: 3 hrs.). (Complete Idiot's Guide to Languages Ser.). (ENG & JPN.). 2005. audio compact disk 9.99 (978-1-59859-122-4(3)) Oasis Audio.

Japanese. unabr. ed. Oasis Audio Staff & Linguistics Staff. Narrated by Linguistics Staff. (Complete Idiot's Guides). (ENG.). 2005. audio compact disk 39.99 (978-1-59859-063-0(4)) Oasis Audio.

Japanese. unabr. ed. Harold Stearns. 4 cass. (Running Time: 6 hrs.). (Accent English Ser.). (ENG.). 1991. bk. 89.50 set, incl. visual aids cards. J Norton Pubs.
English as a second language instructional program.

Japanese. 2nd unabr. ed. Pimsleur Staff. 2001. 295.00 (978-0-671-04780-1(9), Pimsleur) S&S Audio.
English as a second language.

Japanese: Language 30. Educational Services Corporation Staff. 2004. audio compact disk 21.95 (978-1-931850-06-3(2)) Educ Svcs DC.

Japanese: Language/30. rev. ed. Educational Services Corporation Staff. Intro. by Charles Berlitz. 2 cass. (JPN.). 1992. pap. bk. 21.95 (978-0-910542-57-9(0)) Educ Svcs DC.
Japanese self-teaching language course.

Japanese: Learn Japanese While You Drive. abr. unabr. l.t. ed. Living Language Staff. (All-Audio Courses Ser.). (JPN & ENG.). 2006. audio compact disk 21.95 (978-1-4000-2128-4(6), LivingLang) Pub: Random Info Grp. Dist(s): Random

Japanese: Learn to Speak & Understand Japanese. 3rd unabr. ed. Pimsleur Staff. 5 CDs. (Running Time: 50 hrs. 0 mins. 0 sec.). (Basic Ser.). (JPN & ENG.). 2005. audio compact disk 24.95 (978-0-7435-5072-7(2), Pimsleur) Pub: S&S Audio. Dist(s): S and S Inc

Japanese: Learn to Speak & Understand Japanese with Pimsleur Language Programs. Pimsleur Staff. (Running Time: 11 hrs. 50 mins. 0 sec.). (Express Ser.). (ENG.). 2003. audio compact disk 11.95 (978-0-7435-3388-1(7), Pimsleur) Pub: S&S Audio. Dist(s): S and S Inc

Japanese: The Spoken Language, Pt. 1. unabr. ed. Eleanor Harz Jorden & Mari Noda. 9 cass. (Running Time: 9 hrs.). 1988. bk. 127.45; pap. bk. 95.90 Cheng Tsui.
Beginning Japanese language learning through the spoken medium. Hundreds of drills, incorporating thousands of exchanges, are all in a response format so that each exchange constitutes a mini-conversation. For High School, College & adult learners.

Japanese: The Spoken Language, Pt. 2. unabr. ed. Eleanor Harz Jorden & Mari Noda. 12 cass. (Running Time: 12 hrs.). 1988. bk. 154.95; pap. bk. 117.90 Cheng Tsui.
Beginning Japanese language learning for high school students & adults through the spoken medium. Hundreds of drills, incorporating thousands of exchanges, are all in a response format so that each exchange constitutes a mini-conversation.

Japanese: The Spoken Language, Vol. 2. unabr. rev. ed. Eleanor Harz Jorden & Mari Noda. 12 cass. (Running Time: 12 hrs.). (Japanese Ser.). (JPN & ENG.). (C). (gr. 13 up). 1997. 95.00 (978-0-88727-131-1(6)) Cheng Tsui.
These audio cassette recordings are designed to accompany the Japanese: The Spoken Language textbook and include Drills, Core Conversations, and Eavesdropping Exercises. Japanese: The Spoken Language textbook includes brief and natural core conversations, drills, and explanations of linguistic analysis and of how the language is used within Japanese society today. The core conversations cover situations in which foreigners typically find themselves interacting with Japanese. Hundreds of drills are presented in a response format, so that each exchange constitutes a mini-conversation. Instead of overwhelming students with the unfamiliar Japanese writing system, the authors intentionally use romaji, or alphabetized Japanese, throughout the texts so students can concentrate on developing their Japanese communication skills.

Japanese: The Spoken Language, Vol. 3. rev. ed. Eleanor Harz Jorden & Mari Noda. 6 cass. (Japanese Ser.). (JPN & ENG.). (C). (gr. 13 up). 1997. 54.95 (978-0-88727-158-8(8)) Cheng Tsui.

Japanese - English. 1 cass. (Lyric Language Ser.). (JPN & ENG.). (J). 7.98 Blisterpack. (POI 505); 7.98 Blisterpack. (POI 505) NewSound.

Japanese Americans: Prisoners at Home. Godwin Chu. (Step into History Ser.). 2000. audio compact disk 18.95 (978-1-4105-0163-9(9)) D Johnston Inc.

Japanese Americans: Prisoners at Home. Godwin Chu. Ed. by Jerry Stemach. Illus. by Jeff Ham. 2001. audio compact disk 200.00 (978-1-58702-524-2(8)) D Johnston Inc.

Japanese-Americans: The Redress Effort. 1 cass. (Running Time: 30 min.). 9.95 (G0210B090, HarperThor) HarpC GBR.

Japanese Americans: Prisoners at Home, Vol. 9. Godwin Chu. Ed. by Jerry Stemach et al. Illus. by Jeff Ham. Narrated by Joe Sikora. Contrib. by Ted S. Hasselbring. (Start-to-Finish Books). (J). (gr. 2-3). 2001. 35.00 (978-1-58702-525-9(6)) D Johnston Inc.

Japanese Americans: Prisoners at Home, Vol. 9. unabr. ed. Godwin Chu. Ed. by Jerry Stemach et al. Illus. by Jeff Ham. Narrated by Joe Sikora. Contrib. by Ted S. Hasselbring. 1 cass. (Running Time: 1 hr.). (Start-to-Finish Books). (J). (gr. 2-3). 2001. (978-1-58702-376-7(8), F36) D Johnston Inc.
Johnny Ohashi was living in San Francisco, California, when, in 1942, President Roosevelt's Executive Order 9066 mandated the internment of the Japanese Americans. The Ohashi family was taken to a work camp in the remote desert town of Topaz, Utah. Life at the camp was hard. Stripped of their most basic rights, the Ohashi family struggled to keep their courage in the face of great adversity. Based on actual experiences of Japanese American during World War II.

Japanese Basic. Paul Pimsleur. 8 lessons on 4 cass. (Pimsleur Language Learning Ser.). 1995. 29.95 (52164-1) SyberVision.

Japanese, Beginning Level 1. Eleanor H. Jorden. (Multilingual Books Intensive Cassette Foreign Language Ser.). 1965. spiral bd. 199.00 (978-1-58214-035-3(9)) Language Assocs.

Japanese, Beginning Level 2. Eleanor H. Jorden. 1965. spiral bd. 225.00 (978-1-58214-036-0(7)) Language Assocs.

Japanese, Beginning Levels 1 & 2. Eleanor H. Jorden. 1965. spiral bd. 395.00 (978-1-58214-163-3(0)) Language Assocs.

Japanese Bible - New Testament (Spoken Word) Colloquial Version. Read by Koichi Sakai & Hiromasa Doida. 24 cass. (Running Time: 36 hrs.). (JPN.). 1994. 49.97 Set. (978-1-58968-067-8(7), 9701A) Chrstn Dup Intl.
Taken from the Colloquial Version.

Japanese Brush Mind. Kazuaki Tanahashi. 1 cass. 9.00 (A0316-88) Sound Photosyn.
In this workshop, see the wielding of the biggest sumi brush in the world - poetry in motion.

Japanese Corporate Affiliate Directory USA. 2004. pap. bk. 2995.00 (978-0-7605-4736-6(X)) Rector Pr.

JApanese Corporate Affiliate Directory USA Canada Mexico. 11th ed. 2002. pap. bk. 2995.00 (978-0-7605-4734-2(3)) Rector Pr.

Japanese Culture Capsules. unabr. ed. 1 cass. (Running Time: 1 hr.). 12.95 (978-0-88432-507-9(5), CCJA01) J Norton Pubs.
Practical information (in English) for the traveler to Japan on vacation or on business. These culture capsules cover Japanese Customs, traditions, manners & language usage including: greeting & bows, the tea ceremony, miyage (gift giving) & dining out.

Japanese for Busy People, Vol. II. rev. ed. Association for Japanese Language, Teaching Staff. 1995. 50.00 (978-4-7700-1885-4(1)) Kodansha.

Japanese for College Students, Vol. 1. ICU Staff. 3 cass. (Running Time: 4 hrs. 20 mins.). (Japanese for College Student Ser.). 1996. 50.00 (978-4-7700-2108-3(9)) Pub: Kodansha Intl JPN. Dist(s): OUP

Japanese for College Students, Vol. 2. ICU Staff. 3 cass. (Running Time: 3 hrs.). (Japanese for College Student Ser.). 1997. cass. & cass. 50.00 (978-4-7700-2109-0(7)) Pub: Kodansha Intl JPN. Dist(s): OUP

Japanese for College Students, Vol. 3. ICU Staff. 3 cass. (Running Time: 2 hrs. 50 mins.). (Japanese for College Student Ser.). 1997. 50.00 (978-4-7700-2110-6(0)) Pub: Kodansha Intl JPN. Dist(s): OUP

Japanese for Dummies. unabr. ed. Eriko Sato. Read by Becky Wilmes & Hiro Tsuchiya. (YA). 2008. 34.99 (978-1-60514-588-4(2)) Find a World.

Japanese for Everyone: A Functional Approach to Daily Communications. Nagara Susumu. 1990. 80.00 (978-0-87040-857-1(7)) Pub: Japan Pubns USA. Dist(s): OUP

Japanese for Fun: Make Your Stay in Japan More Enjoyable. Taeko Kamiya. (JPN., 1990. 15.95 (978-0-8048-1691-5(3)) Tuttle Pubng.

Japanese for Speakers of English, Three. unabr. ed. 16 cass. (Running Time: 15 hrs.). (Pimsleur Tapes Ser.). (JPN & ENG.). 1997. 345.00 Set. (18529, Pimsleur) S&S Audio.
An additional thirty-lesson-unit program, for a total of ninety lesson units. Will allow the learner to achieve the ACTFL Intermediate-High Spoken Proficiency Level.

Japanese, for Speakers of English Two. unabr. ed. 16 cass. (Running Time: 15 hrs.). (Pimsleur Tapes Ser.). 1996. 345.00 set. (18528, Pimsleur) S&S Audio.
An additional thirty-lesson unit program, accomplished at the same rate as a Pimsleur I. Will enable the learner to achieve the ACTFL Intermediate-Mid Spoken Proficiency Level.

Japanese for Two Shakuhachi (Bamboo Flutes) unabr. ed. 1 cass. 12.95 (7386) J Norton Pubs.

Japanese for Young People, Set. Ajalt. 48.00 (978-4-7700-2497-8(5)) Pub: Kodansha Intl JPN. Dist(s): Kodansha

Japanese for Young People, Vol. I. Association for Japanese Language, Teaching Staff. 3 cass. (Running Time: 5 hrs.). 1998. wbk. ed. 48.00 (978-4-7700-2179-3(8)) Pub: Kodansha Intl JPN. Dist(s): Kodansha

Japanese for Young People, Vol. 3. AJALT. 3 CDs. (Running Time: 2 hrs. 40 mins.). (Japanese for Young People Ser.). 2001. audio compact disk 65.00 (978-4-7700-2810-5(5)) Pub: Kodansha Intl JPN. Dist(s): OUP

Japanese Guaranteed. Kayo Nonaka & Berlitz Publishing Staff. (Berlitz Guaranteed Ser.). (JPN & ENG., 2007. audio compact disk 19.95 (978-981-268-185-0(X)) Pub: APA Pubns Serv SGP. Dist(s): IngramPubServ

Japanese I, Set, study guide. Paul Pimsleur. 16 cass. (Pimsleur Language Learning Ser.). 1995. 345.00 Set, incl. study guide. (0671-52155-1) SyberVision.

Japanese I: Learn to Speak & Understand Japanese with Pimsleur Language Programs. 3rd ed. Pimsleur Staff. (Running Time: 400 hrs. 0 mins. NaN sec.). (Quick & Simple Ser.). (ITA & ENG.). 2002. audio compact disk 19.95 (978-0-7435-2351-6(2), Pimsleur) Pub: S&S Audio. Dist(s): S and S Inc

Japanese I: Learn to Speak & Understand Japanese with Pimsleur Language Programs. 3rd unabr. ed. Pimsleur Staff. 16 CDs. (Running Time: 160 hrs. 0 mins. 0 sec.). (Comprehensive Ser.). (ENG.). 2002. audio compact disk 345.00 (978-0-7435-2353-0(9), Pimsleur) Pub: S&S Audio. Dist(s): S and S Inc

Japanese II, Set, study guide. Paul Pimsleur. 16 cass. (Pimsleur Language Learning Ser.). 1998. 345.00 Set, incl. study guide. (0671-57076-5) SyberVision.

Japanese II: Learn to Speak & Understand Japanese with Pimsleur Language Programs. 2nd ed. Pimsleur Staff & Pimsleur. 16 CDs. (Running Time: 160 hrs. 0 mins. 0 sec.). (Comprehensive Ser.). (ENG.). 2004. audio compact disk 345.00 (978-0-7435-2883-2(2), Pimsleur) Pub: S&S Audio. Dist(s): S and S Inc

Japanese III, Set. Paul Pimsleur. 16 cass. (Pimsleur Language Learning Ser.). 1998. 345.00 Set, incl. study guide. (0671-57958-4) SyberVision.

Japanese III: Learn to Speak & Understand Japanese with Pimsleur Language Programs. 2nd ed. Pimsleur Staff & Pimsleur. (Running Time: 160 hrs. 0 mins. 0 sec.). (Comprehensive Ser.). (ENG.). 2005. audio compact disk 345.00 (978-0-7435-2885-6(9), Pimsleur) Pub: S&S Audio. Dist(s): S and S Inc

Japanese in a Minute. 1 cass. (Language in a Minute Cassette Ser.). 5.95 (978-0-943351-26-1(X), XC1010) Cimino Pub Grp.
Feel at home in any foreign country with these 101 esssential words & phrases. Hear each word introduced in English, hear them pronounced by a Voice of America instructor. Practice at your own pace, you can check yourself with the wallet sized dictionary included.

Japanese in 30 Days. 2nd rev. abr. ed. Created by Berlitz Guides. (Berlitz in 30 Days Ser.). 2007. audio compact disk 21.95 (978-981-268-223-9(6)) Pub: APA Pubns Serv SGP. Dist(s): Langenscheidt

Japanese in 60 Minutes. Created by Berlitz. (Berlitz in 60 Minutes Ser.). (JPN & ENG., 2007. audio compact disk 9.95 (978-981-268-206-2(6)) Pub: APA Pubns Serv SGP. Dist(s): Langenscheidt

Japanese Koto Music. unabr. ed. 1 cass. 12.95 (7131) J Norton Pubs.

Japanese Koto Orchestra. unabr. ed. 1 cass. 12.95 (7167) J Norton Pubs.

Japanese New Testament. Sakai & Doida. 24 cass. (Running Time: 36 hrs.). (JPN.). 1994. 49.98 (978-7-902032-74-2(3)) Chrstn Dup Intl.

Japanese on Location. Yasuko Izaki. 1 cass. (Languages on Location Ser.). (JPN., (YA). (gr. 10-12). 1992. bk. 10.95 (978-0-8120-7902-9(7)) Barron.

Japanese Say Hello. rev. ed. Louis Aarons. 4 cass. (Running Time: 4 hrs. 75 min.). (WordMate Ser.). (JPN.). (J). (gr. 9 up). 1996. spiral bd. 49.95 (978-1-887447-03-4(2)) WordMate.
Basic Japanese for native speakers of English includes pronunciation guide, word lists, study & review tests, interactive dialogs for communication, essential grammar, & glossary with correlated workbook. Requires stereo headphones.

Japanese Shakuhachi Music. unabr. ed. 1 cass. 12.95 (7176) J Norton Pubs.

Japanese Temple Music. unabr. ed. 1 cass. 12.95 (7117) J Norton Pubs.

Japanese the Spoken Language, Vol. 1. rev. ed. Eleanor H. Jordan & Mari Noda. Read by Mari Noda. 14 cass. (Japanese Ser.). (JPN & ENG.). (C). (gr. 13 up). 1997. 145.00 Set. (978-0-88727-247-9(9)) Cheng Tsui.

Japanese the Spoken Language Vol. 1. unabr. rev. ed. Eleanor H. Jorden & Mari Noda. 9 cass. (Running Time: 9 hrs.). (Japanese Ser.). (JPN & ENG.). (C). (gr. 13 up). 1997. 75.00 (978-0-88727-130-4(8)) Cheng Tsui.
These audio cassette recordings are designed to accompany the Japanese: The Spoken Language textbook and include Drills, Core Conversations, and Eavesdropping Exercises. This revised edition contains 14 cassettes with built-in pauses for students to repeat after the model. Japanese: The Spoken Language textbook includes brief and natural core conversations, drills, and explanations of linguistic analysis and of how the language is used within Japanese society today. The core conversations cover situations in which foreigners typically find themselves interacting with Japanese. Hundreds of drills are presented in a response format, so that each exchange constitutes a mini-conversation. Instead of overwhelming students with the unfamiliar Japanese writing system, the authors intentionally use romaji, or alphabetized Japanese, throughout the texts so students can concentrate on developing their Japanese communication skills.

Japanese Vocabulary, Set. AMR Staff. 4 cass. (Running Time: 60 min.). (AMR Language Ser.). 1980. vinyl bd. 46.95 (978-1-55536-149-5(8)) Oasis Audio.
Vocabulary words provide additional words not covered in the basis program. Boosts your language vocabulary by 2,000 words.

Japanese Vocabulary Builder. unabr. ed. 1 cass. 14.95 (SJA010) J Norton Pubs.
Recorded dictionary provides 101 essential words & phrases for the traveler.

Japanese Vol 2 Earworms. (EARWORMS Ser.). 2009. audio compact disk 24.95 (978-0-8416-1071-2(1)) Pub: Earworms Pubng. Dist(s): Langenscheidt

Japanese with Ease see Giapponese Senza Sforzo

Japanese with Ease see Japanisch Ohne Muhe Heute

Japanese Word Book. Yuko Green. Read by Fumiteru Nitta. 1 cass. (Rainbow International Word Book Ser.). 1989. 7.95 Bess Pr.
A native speaker pronounces each word in the accompanying book twice.

Japanese Word Book. unabr. ed. 1 cass. (Running Time: 52 mins.). (YA). (gr. 10-12). 1994. pap. bk. & wbk. ed. 24.95 (SJA350) J Norton Pubs.
Illustrates Japanese life & culture with 200 words & phrases, captioned using romanized spellings, kanji, hiragana, katakana & English. Book includes a writing & pronunciation guide & Japanese-English & English-Japanese glossaries.

Japanese/Chinese: Includes Wordlist, Level 3. Vocabuleam. 2 cass. (Running Time: 90 min. ea.). (VocabuLearn Ser.). (CHI.). (J). 1995. 15.95 (978-957-9330-76-3(X)) Penton Overseas.

Japanese/Chinese Level I, Level 1. Vocabuleam. 2 cass. (Running Time: 90 mins. ea.). (VocabuLearn Ser.). (CHI.). 1995. 15.95 (978-957-9330-74-9(3)) Penton Overseas.

Japanese/Chinese Level II, Level 2. Vocabuleam. 1 cass. (VocabuLearn Ser.). (CHI.). 1995. 15.95 (978-957-9330-75-6(1)) Penton Overseas.

Japanisch Ohne Muhe Heute, Level 1. 1 cass. (Running Time: 1 hr. 30 min.).Tr. of Japanese with Ease. (GER & JPN., 1997. pap. bk. 75.00 (978-2-7005-1013-3(5)) Pub: Assimil FRA. Dist(s): Distribks Inc

Japanisch Ohne Muhe Heute, Level 2. 1 cass. (Running Time: 1 hr. 30 min.).Tr. of Japanese with Ease. (GER & JPN., 1997. pap. bk. 75.00 (978-2-7005-1014-0(3)) Pub: Assimil FRA. Dist(s): Distribks Inc

Japji Sahib. unabr. ed. Poems. 1 cass. 1994. 14.95 (978-0-88432-589-5(X), S04055) J Norton Pubs.
Guru Nanak's 15th century poem including 31-page booklet.

Japonais sans Peine, Vol. 1. 1 cass. (Running Time: 1 hr., 30 min.). (FRE & JPN.). 2000. bk. 95.00 (978-2-7005-2007-1(6)) Pub: Assimil FRA. Dist(s): Distribks Inc

Japonais sans Peine, Vol. 2. 1 CD. (Running Time: 1 hr., 30 min.). (FRE & JPN.). 2000. bk. 95.00 (978-2-7005-2008-8(4)) Pub: Assimil FRA. Dist(s): Distribks Inc

Jar: A Tale from the East. (J). 2000. bk. 9.99 (978-0-9716826-6-5(6)) Fine Media Grp.

Jar: A Tale from the East. (ARA.). (J). 2002. bk. 9.99 (978-1-932008-00-5(4)) Fine Media Grp.

Jarabon. 1985. (AS001) Audio Saga.

Jardin del Eden, Vol. 2. Orlando Rodriguez. 1 cass. (Running Time: 1 hr. 30 mins.). (Sabio Y Prudente Ser.).Tr. of Garden of Eden. (SPA.). (J). (ps-2). 2000. 5.99 (978-0-8254-0981-3(0), Edit Portavoz) Kregel.

Jared Carter. unabr. ed. Ed. by Jim McKinley. Prod. by Rebekah Presson. 1 cass. (Running Time: 29 min.). (New Letters on the Air Ser.). 1994. 10.00 (092494) New Letters.
Carter won the prestigious Walt Whitman Award for his poetry in 1980 & was the winner of the New Letters Literary Award in 1992. Carter's poetry celebrates the history & culture of the American middle-west & much of it is set in the fictious Mississinewa County, located not far from Carter's own home town in Indiana. He reads from his new book, "After the Rain".

Jargan. unabr. ed. Max Brand. Read by Tom Weiner. (Running Time: 7200 sec.). 2007. 22.95 (978-0-7861-4890-5(X)); audio compact disk 27.00 (978-0-7861-5990-1(1)); audio compact disk 19.95 (978-0-7861-7110-1(3)) Blckstn Audio.

Jarhead: A Marine's Chronicle of the Gulf War & Other Battles. unabr. ed. Anthony Swofford. 6 cass. (Running Time: 8 hrs.). 2003. 59.00 (978-1-4025-5922-8(4)) Recorded Bks.

Jarhead: A Marine's Chronicle of the Gulf War & Other Battles. unabr. ed. Anthony Swofford. Narrated by Anthony Swofford. 7 CDs. (Running Time: 8 hrs.). 2003. audio compact disk 78.00 (978-1-4025-6175-7(X), C2324) Recorded Bks.

Jarhead: A Marine's Chronicle of the Gulf War & Other Battles. unabr. ed. Anthony Swofford. 2004. 21.95 (978-0-7435-4888-5(4)) Pub: S&S Audio. Dist(s): S and S Inc

Jarhead: A Marine's Chronicle of the Gulf War & Other Battles. unabr. collector's ed. Anthony Swofford. Narrated by Anthony Swofford. 6 cass. (Running Time: 8 hrs.). 2003. 34.95 (978-1-4025-5923-5(2)) Recorded Bks.
Anthony Swofford served in a U.S. Marine Corps Surveillance and Target Acquisition/Scout-Sniper platoon during the Gulf War. His fiction and nonfiction have appeared in The New York Times, Harper?s, Men?s Journal, and The Iowa Review. In Jarhead, a New York Times best-seller, he offers a devastating account of the war from the viewpoint of one who experienced it firsthand and lived to tell his story in all its horror.

Jarka Ruus. unabr. ed. Terry Brooks. 9 cass. (Running Time: 13 hrs.). (High Druid of Shannara Ser.: Bk. 1). 2003. 80.00 (978-0-7366-9420-9(X)) Books on Tape.
A new hero arises to save the reformed Ilse Witch from her deadly prison.

Jars of Clay: If I Left the Zoo. Perf. by Jars of Clay. 1 cass. 1999. (978-0-7601-2910-4(X)); audio compact disk (978-0-7601-2909-8(6)) Brentwood Music.
Rare blend of innovation, artistry, ministry & simple, good-natured fun. The band's distinctive style shines through on a project that genuinely captures the total personality of Jars of Clay like never before.

Jars of Clay: Greatest Hits. Contrib. by Jars of Clay. 2008. audio compact disk 17.98 (978-5-557-46348-5(8)) Essential Recs.

Jascha Heifitz - Favorite Encores: Violin Play-along 2-CD Set. Jascha Heifitz. 2007. pap. bk. 29.98 (978-1-59615-193-2(5), 1596151935) Pub: Music Minus. Dist(s): H Leonard

Jasmine. Randy Houk. Illus. by Randy Houk. Read by Tom Chapin. Narrated by Tom Chapin. 1 cass. (Running Time: 9 min.). (Humane Society of the United States Animal Tales Ser.). (J). (gr. 1-5). 1993. pap. bk. 9.95 (978-1-882728-47-3(5)) Benefactory.
How does a courageous cat survive months alone in a locked apartment? (Hint: birdseed & a leaky faucet). True story of Jasmine's rescue & adoption by a large family.

Jasmine. Randy Houk. Read by Tom Chapin. 1 cass. (Running Time: 9 min.). (Humane Society of the United States Animal Tales Ser.). (J). (gr. k-4). 1998. pap. bk. 19.95 Incl. plush animal. Benefactory.

Jasmine. Bharati Mukherjee. (Running Time: 30 min.). 8.95 (AMF-226) Am Audio Prose.
Talks about India, Iowa, & the American character.

Jasmine, Incl. plush animal. Randy Houk. Illus. by Randy Houk. Read by Tom Chapin. Narrated by Tom Chapin. 1 cass. (Running Time: 9 min.). (Humane Society of the United States Animal Tales Ser.). (J). (gr. 1-5). 1993. bk. 34.95 (978-1-882728-16-9(5)) Benefactory.
How does a courageous cat survive months alone in a locked apartment? (Hint: birdseed & a leaky faucet). True story of Jasmine's rescue & adoption by a large family.

Jasmine & Stars: Reading More Than Lolita in Tehran. Fatemeh Keshavarz. (ENG.). 2007. 24.95 (978-0-8078-8396-9(4)); audio compact disk 29.95 (978-0-8078-8398-3(0)) U of NC Pr.

Jasmine Flower. 1 cass. (Running Time: 45 mins.). (J). audio compact disk 16.95 (978-1-57606-243-2(0)) Pub: Wind Recs. Dist(s): Shens Bks

Jason & the Golden Fleece see Tanglewood Tales

***Jason & the Golden Fleece.** Benny Fuentes. Illus. by Gerardo Sandoval. Retold by Nel Yomtov. (Mythology Ser.). (ENG.). 2010. audio compact disk 14.60 (978-1-4342-2572-6(0)) CapstoneDig.

Jason's Dominion. unabr. ed. Aileen Armitage. Read by Laura Brattan. 5 cass. (Running Time: 6 hrs. 43 min.). (Isis Ser.). (J). 2001. 49.95 (978-0-7531-0551-1(9)) Pub: ISIS Lrg Prnt GBR. Dist(s): Ulverscroft US

Ruth Steadman comes to a small village in the Yorkshire Moors to do some research for a TV series. She finds that the people of Jacob's Well seem bitterly hostile towards her. What do they have to hide? Why is the vicar leaving? Is there really a curse shadowing the family at Blackledge Hall? The truth is so haunting and unique that Ruth's life will never be quite the same again.

Jason's Gold. collector's ed. William Hobbs. Read by Boyd Gaines. 4 cass. (Running Time: 6 hrs.). (J). 2000. 30.00 (978-0-7366-9023-2(9)) Books on Tape.

Fifteen-year-old Jason Hawthorn is heading west with a bad case of Klondike fever. Racing to catch up to his brothers in the gold fields, Jason meets an adventurous girl named Jamie & the not-yet famous Jack London. But mostly he travels alone with King, a husky he's rescued from a madman.

Jason's Gold. unabr. ed. Will Hobbs. Read by Boyd Gaines. (ENG.). (J). (gr. 5). 2009. audio compact disk 35.00 (978-0-7393-8231-8(4), Listening Lib) Pub: Random Audio Pubg. Dist(s): Random

Jason's Gold. unabr. ed. William Hobbs. Read by Boyd Gaines. 4 vols. (Running Time: 5 hrs. 41 mins.). (J). (gr. 5-9). 2004. pap. bk. 38.00 (978-0-8072-8229-8(4), Listening Lib); 32.00 (978-0-8072-8228-1(6), LL0168, Listening Lib) Random Audio Pubg.

Fifteen-year Jason Hawthorn is heading west with a bad case of Klondike fever. Racing to catch up to his brothers in the gold fields, Jason meets an adventurous girl named Jamie & the not-yet-famous Jack London. But mostly he travels alone with King, a husky he's rescued from a madman.

Jasper & his Friends. 1CD. 2005. audio compact disk 16.99 (978-1-928624-21-9(9)) Lucky Three Ranch.

Jasper Dash & the Flame-Pits of Delaware. unabr. ed. M. T. Anderson. Read by Marc Cashman. (M. T. Anderson's Thrill Tales Ser.). (J). (gr. 3). 2009. 39.00 (978-0-7393-5619-7(4), Listening Lib) Pub: Random Audio Pubg. Dist(s): Random

***Jasper Dash & the Flame-Pits of Delaware: A Pals in Peril Tale.** unabr. ed. M. T. Anderson. Read by Marc Cashman. 6 CDs. (Running Time: 6 hrs. 57 mins.). (YA). (gr. 5-8). 2009. audio compact disk 45.00 (978-0-7393-6194-8(5), Listening Lib) Pub: Random Audio Pubg. Dist(s): Random

Jasper National Parks: Columbia Icefield to Jasper. 1 cass. (Running Time: 90 min.). (Guided Auto Tape Tour). 12.95 (P6); Comp Comms Inc.

Jataka Tales. abr. ed. Noor I. Khan. Read by Ellen Burstyn. Music by Alauddin Mathieu. 1 cass. (Running Time: 1 hr. 30 min.). 1995. 10.95 (978-0-944993-27-9(3)) Audio Lit.

Delightful & profound stories from ancient India that have guided & entertained millions throughout the ages.

Jaula Dorada. Contrib. by Suni Paz & Sam Glaser. (Cuentos Para Todo el Ano Ser.). (SPA., (J). (gr. k-3). 2000. 4.95 (978-1-58105-250-3(2)) Santillana.

Jaures. Henri Guillemin. 1 cass. (FRE.). 1991. 22.95 (1206-VSL) Olivia & Hill.

***Java: The True Story of a Shelter Dog Who Rescued a Woman.** Sage Lewis. 2010. audio compact disk (978-1-4507-0326-0(7)) Indep Pub IL.

Java: an Introduction to Problem Solving & Programming: Instructor's Resource CD. 4th ed. Savitch. audio compact disk 18.97 (978-0-13-149221-9(7)) PH School.

Java Jems. Poems. Cindi R. Maciolek. 1 cass. (Running Time: 50 min.). (Five Minute Inspirations for Busy People). 1998. 10.00 (978-0-9647911-1-4(0)) Grand Arbor Pr.

Java Spider. unabr. ed. Geoffrey Archer. Read by Christian Rodska. 10 cass. (Running Time: 10 hrs.). 1998. 84.95 (978-0-7540-0064-8(8), CAB1487) AudioGO.

A British minister is a pawn in a deadly game played out in Indonesia. Authorities in Jakarta claim that he has been seized by a guerrilla movement. And when horrific satellite pictures of him are released on national television, the government sends Nick Randall to rescue him. With the aid of a woman TV reporter, he penetrates a remote island, where an armed local rebellion is threatening to explode.

Java Swing: Version 2.0.2. 2001. audio compact disk (978-1-929366-06-4(X)) SkillBuilders.

Java 2 SDK: Standard Edition. Sun Microsystems Staff. (C). 2001. audio compact disk 12.95 (978-0-7637-1890-9(4), 1890-4) Jones Bartlett.

Jawbreaker: The Attack on Bin Laden & Al Qaeda: A Personal Account by the CIA's Key Field Commander. abr. ed. Ralph Pezzullo & Gary Berntsen. (Running Time: 21600 sec.). (ENG.). 2005. audio compact disk 29.95 (978-0-7393-2348-9(2), Random AudioBks) Pub: Random Audio Pubg. Dist(s): Random

Jaws. unabr. ed. Peter Benchley. Narrated by Erik Steele. 8 CDs. (Running Time: 9 hrs. 30 mins.). (ENG.). 2009. audio compact disk 29.95 (978-1-60283-583-2(7)) Pub: AudioGO. Dist(s): Perseus Dist

Jaws: Making a Best Seller. unabr. ed. Read by Heywood Hale Broun et al. 1 cass. (Heywood Hale Broun Ser.). 12.95 (40064) J Norton Pubs.

Discussion with Peter Benchley ("Jaws"), Tom Congdon & David Brown.

Jay Kinney. Interview with Elizabeth Gips. 1 cass. 1999. 11.00 (32011) Big Sur Tapes.

Kinney is the founder of Gnosis Magazine - 1996 Santa Cruz.

Jay Mcgraw's Life Strategies for Dealing with Bullies. Jay McGraw. Read by Jay McGraw. (Playaway Young Adult Ser.). (ENG.). (J). 2009. 40.00 (978-1-60775-615-6(3)) Find a World.

Jay Snelson: Attenuation of War, Optimization of Peace. (Running Time: 60 min.). (Cal State Univ., Long Beach). 1984. 9.00 (F161) Freeland Pr.

Shares his experience as a teacher, while he informs us with his scientific knowledge & conclusions.

Jay Stevens on KPFK. Jay Stevens. 1 cass. (Roy Tuckman Interview Ser.). 9.00 (A0080-87) Sound Photosyn.

Jay interviews the author of "Storming Heaven: LSD & the American Dream".

Jaya Radhe Jaya Krishna. 1 cass.; 1 CD. 4.95 (CD-9); audio compact disk 14.95 CD. Bhaktivedanta.

Jayanta Mahapatra. Read by Jayanta Mahapatra. 1 cass. (Running Time: 29 min.). 1985. 10.00 New Letters.

One of India's foremost poets writing in English, reads from "Relationship".

Jayber Crow. unabr. ed. Wendell Berry. Read by Paul Michael. 12 CDs. (Running Time: 15 hrs. 0 mins. 0 sec.). (ENG.). 2007. audio compact disk 34.98 (978-1-59644-444-7(4), christaudio) christianaud.

***Jayber Crow.** unabr. ed. Wendell Berry. Narrated by Paul Michael. (Yasmin Peace Ser.). (ENG.). 2007. 19.98 (978-1-59644-445-4(2), christaudio) christianaud.

Jayne Ann Krentz: Light in Shadow, Truth or Dare, Falling Awake. abr. ed. Jayne Ann Krentz. (Running Time: 18 hrs.). 2007. audio compact disk 34.95 (978-1-4233-2316-7(5), 9781423323167, BACD) Brilliance Audio.

Jayne Ann Krentz CD Collection: Lost & Found; Smoke in Mirrors. abr. ed. Jayne Ann Krentz. 9 CDs. (Running Time: 10 hrs.). 2005. audio compact disk 29.95 (978-1-59737-703-4(1), 9781597377034, BACD) Brilliance Audio.

Lost and Found (Narrator: Sandra Burr, Director: Joyce Bean) Cady Briggs is very useful to Mack Easton - her expertise in art and antiques helps his shadowy, low-profile company, Lost and Found, find missing treasures for high-paying clients. But as Cady's beloved Aunt Vesta warns her, being useful to a client is one thing - being used is another. Still, Cady finds it hard to resist the magnetic pull Mack exerts, an attraction she felt from the first time she heard his voice on the phone. And as their work together puts them in an explosive situation, Cady wonders just how much she'd risk for the thrill of being with this man. Smoke in Mirrors (Narrator: Aasne Vigesaa and James Daniels, Director: Laura Grafton) A con artist and seductress, Meredith Spooner lived fast - and died young. Now it seems Meredith's last scam is coming back to haunt Leonora Hutton. An email just arrived in which Meredith explains that the embezzled money is waiting for Leonora in an offshore account ... and a safe-deposit key is on the way. Lenora's already been accused of being in on the theft by Thomas Walker. Eager to prove him wrong, she sets out to collect the cash and hand it over. But she discovers two other items in the safe-deposit box. One is a book about Mirror House - a mansion filled with antique mirrors, where Meredith engineered her final deception. The other is a set of newspaper stories about a thirty-year-old murder that occurred there - unsolved to this day.

Jayne Ann Krentz Collection: Eclipse Bay; Dawn in Eclipse Bay; Summer in Eclipse Bay. abr. ed. Jayne Ann Krentz. Read by Joyce Bean. 12 cass. (Running Time: 18 hrs.). (Eclipse Bay Ser.). 2003. 29.95 (978-1-59086-539-2(1), 1590865391, Nova Audio Bks) Brilliance Audio.

Eclipse Bay (Luann Kindem, engineer) Their grandfathers hated each other. Their fathers hated each other. And as the next generation of Hartes and Madisons, Hannah and Rafe are expected to hate each other too. But Hannah Harte - a successful wedding consultant with a skeptical view of marriage - remembers the long-ago night on the beach that revealed Rafe as much more than just "that disreputable Madison boy." And Rafe remembers the heroic gesture that proved Hannah's fierce spirit was stronger than any feud - and saved him from near-certain imprisonment. Now - reunited by a surprising inheritance after years of living their separate lives - Rafe and Hannah return to Eclipse Bay, and the hostilities that still divide, and bind, their families. And they are discovering something that is at once delightful and deeply disturbing . . . They don't hate each other. Not at all. . . Dawn in Eclipse Bay (Melissa Coates, engineer) Nothing was ever simple between a Madison and a Harte. The feud that had divided their families still simmered. Now, only months after their siblings' wedding, Lillian Harte and Gabe Madison are at each other's throats. Successful CEO Gabe had insisted on becoming a client of Lillian's matchmaking service. And after five disastrous dates, Lillian is at her wit's end. If she hadn't already decided to close her business and move home to Eclipse Bay, Gabe would have been the final straw. But when she finds Gabe at her door demanding she fulfill their business contract, the sparks between them suddenly turn personal. Once again, Eclipse Bay will witness a showdown - between a relentless Madison and irresistible Harte... Summer in Eclipse Bay (Melissa Coates, engineer) Word gets around fast in Eclipse Bay. Nick Harte should know - his family's legendary feud with the Madisons fueled the local gossip mill for years before finally cooling off. But people are still talking - and rumor has it Nick's involved with someone new... Art gallery owner Octavia Brightwell doesn't take chances - especially on handsome, charming men. But that's only part of the reason why she turned Nick down six times before - finally - agreeing to a date. Octavia's related to the woman who sparked the long-time family feud - and fears that falling hard for Nick would only ignite the flames again. Octavia knows her family's past is best kept hidden. But her secret isn't safe in Eclipse Bay - and neither is her heart.

Jayne Anne Phillips. unabr. ed. Jayne Anne Phillips. Read by Jayne Anne Phillips. 1 cass. (Running Time: 29 min.). 1989. 10.00 (120389) New Letters.

Here she reads from fast lanes & talks about moving from young writer of promise to established writer.

Jayne Anne Phillips Interview with Kay Bonetti. Jayne Anne Phillips. 1 cass. (Running Time: 53 min.). 1991. 13.95 (978-1-55644-366-4(8), 11032) Am Audio Prose.

Thoughtful & articulate conversation. Phillips discusses her fascination with the ways in which people find & make family for themselves in a world in which traditional structures are increasingly dying back.

***Jayne Castle CD Collection: Dark Light, Obsidian Prey.** abr. ed. Jayne Castle, pseud. Read by Joyce Bean. (Running Time: 10 hrs.). 2011. audio compact disk 19.99 (978-1-4418-7865-6(3), 9781441878656, BACD) Brilliance Audio.

Jazayer. 1 cass. 1989. 9.98 incl. Norelco pkg. (978-1-877737-39-8(9), EB 2549); audio compact disk 12.98 CD. (978-1-877737-50-3(X)) MFLP CA.

Traditional & contemporary Middle Eastern dance music.

Jazz. Walter Dean Myers. Read by James Williams & Vaneese Thomas. Illus. by Christopher A. Myers. 1 cass. (Running Time: 43 mins.). (YA). (gr. 4-9). 2007. bk. 25.95 (978-1-4301-0019-5(2)) Live Oak Media.

***Jazz.** Walter Dean Myers. Read by James 'D Train' Williams. Illus. by Christopher Myers. (ENG.). (J). 2008. pap. bk. 18.95 (978-1-4301-0021-8(4)) Live Oak Media.

Jazz. unabr. ed. Toni Morrison. Narrated by Lynne Thigpen. 6 cass. (Running Time: 7 hrs. 45 mins.). 1993. 51.00 (978-1-55690-842-2(3), 93215E7) Recorded Bks.

A young couple's journey from the rural south to the thriving Harlem of the 1920's leads to exhilaration, followed by confusion, tragedy & ultimately, redemption.

Jazz. unabr. ed. Toni Morrison. Narrated by Lynne Thigpen. 7 CDs. (Running Time: 7 hrs. 45 mins.). 2000. audio compact disk 63.00 (978-0-7887-3967-5(0), C1122E7) Recorded Bks.

Jazz. unabr. ed. Walter Dean Myers. Read by James Williams & Vaneese Thomas. Illus. by Christopher A. Myers. 1 CD. (Running Time: 43 mins.). (YA). (gr. 4-9). 2007. bk. 28.95 (978-1-4301-0022-5(2)) Live Oak Media.

Jazz: A History. 2nd ed. Frank Tirro. 1 CD. (Running Time: 1 hr.). (C). 1993. cass. & cd-rom (978-0-393-99734-7(0)) Norton.

Jazz: A History of America's Music. abr. ed. Ken Burns & Geoffrey C. Ward. Read by LeVar Burton. (Running Time: 32400 sec.). (ENG.). 2007. audio compact disk 24.99 (978-0-7393-5732-3(8), Random AudioBks) Pub: Random Audio Pubg. Dist(s): Random

Jazz: A History of America's Music. abr. ed. Geoffrey C. Ward & Ken Burns. 2000. audio compact disk 39.95 (978-0-375-74277-4(8), Random AudioBks) Random Audio Pubg.

Jazz-A-Ma-Tazz. 1 cass. (Running Time: 48 min.). 1998. 10.98; 15.98 CD. Baby Music.

Jazz-A-Ma-Tazz. Perf. by Hayes Greenfield. 1 cass., 1 CD. (Running Time: 47 min.). (J). 1998. 10.98 (3010-4); audio compact disk 15.98 CD. (3010-2) Baby Music.

Teaches jazz to children through familiar songs (traditional) put in a jazz context.

Jazz & Poetry & Other Reasons: Opus One: the Beat Goes On. (ENG.). 2008. audio compact disk 14.00 (978-0-931191-23-7(8)) Rob Briggs.

Jazz & the Classical Guitar Theory & Application. Ken Hatfield. (ENG.). 2005. spiral bd. 29.95 (978-0-7866-7236-3(6), 99986BCD) Mel Bay.

Jazz Anyone Compact Disc (3) Composed by Willie Thomas. (Jazz Anyone... . . ? Ser.). (ENG.). 1997. audio compact disk 24.95 (978-0-7692-1668-3(4), Warner Bro) Alfred Pub.

Jazz Chants. Carolyn Graham. (Jazz Chants Ser.). 1978. 24.50 (978-0-19-502410-4(9)) OUP.

Jazz Chants. Carolyn Graham. (Jazz Chants Ser.). 2000. audio compact disk & audio compact disk 24.50 (978-0-19-436699-1(5)) OUP.

Jazz Chants. Carolyn Graham. (Jazz Chants Ser.). 2000. 24.50 (978-0-19-436698-4(7)) OUP.

Jazz Chants. Carolyn Graham. (Jazz Chants Ser.). 2003. audio compact disk 24.50 (978-0-19-438605-0(8)) OUP.

Jazz Chants for Children. Carolyn Graham. (Jazz Chants Ser.). 2003. audio compact disk 24.50 (978-0-19-438607-4(4)) OUP.

Jazz Chops for Guitar. Ed. by Alfred Publishing. (ENG.). 2001. audio compact disk 10.95 (978-1-929395-36-1(1)) Pub: Workshop Arts. Dist(s): Alfred Pub

Jazz Classics with Easy Changes, Vol. 6. Created by Hal Leonard Corporation Staff. 2002. pap. bk. 16.99 (978-0-634-04405-2(2), 0634044052) H Leonard.

Jazz Combo Drumming. Contrib. by Danny Gottlieb et al. (Running Time: 1 hr. 10 mins.). 2005. 24.95 (978-5-558-09172-4(X)) Mel Bay.

Jazz Composition & Orchestration. William Russo. 1 CD. 1996. audio compact disk 17.00 (978-0-226-73215-2(0)) Pub: U Ch Pr. Dist(s): Chicago Distribution Ctr

Jazz Duets. Friedman. (CD Ser.). 2001. bk. 16.98 (978-1-56799-360-8(5), Friedman-Fairfax) M Friedman Pub Grp Inc.

Jazz Fantasia see Carl Sandburg's Poems for Children

Jazz Fingerpicking Guitar: For Beginners. Brett Duncan. 2008. pap. bk. 24.95 (978-1-86469-376-8(2)) Kolala Music SGP.

Jazz Fly. Matthew Gollub. Perf. by Matthew Gollub. Illus. by Karen Hanke. (J). (ps-1). 2000. bk. 17.95 (978-1-889910-17-8(1)) Pub: Tortuga Pr. Dist(s): Baker Taylor

Jazz Fly. Matthew Gollub. Perf. by Matthew Gollub. 1 CD. (Running Time: 1 hr. 30 mins.). (J). (gr. k-4). 2001. audio compact disk 8.95 (978-1-889910-19-2(8)) Tortuga Pr.

Jazz Fly 2: The Jungle Pachanga. Matthew Gollub. Illus. by Karen Hanke. (ENG.). (J). 2010. bk. 17.95 (978-1-889910-44-4(9)) Tortuga Pr.

Jazz Greats: Duke Ellington; Ella Fitzgerald; Ellington Was Not A Street. unabr. ed. Brian Pinkney & Kadir Nelson. Read by Forest Whitaker et al. (J). 2007. 44.99 (978-1-60252-610-5(9)) Find a World.

Jazz Guitar Cameos: Intermediate Level. Adrian Ingram. 1998. pap. bk. 17.95 (978-0-7866-3081-3(7), 96750BCD) Mel Bay.

Jazz Guitar Duets: Intermediate-Advanced Level. Jimmy Wyble & Jim Hershman. 1997. pap. bk. 19.95 (978-0-7866-2472-0(8), 96305BCD) Mel Bay.

Jazz Guitar for Classical Cats. Andrew York. 1 CD. (Running Time: 1 hr. 30 mins.). (ENG.). 2001. audio compact disk 10.00 (978-0-7390-0922-2(2), 19384) Alfred Pub.

Jazz Guitar for Classical Cats - Harmony. Andrew York. 1 CD. (ENG.). 1999. audio compact disk 10.00 (978-0-7390-0112-7(4), 18472) Alfred Pub.

Jazz Guitar Handbook. Alan DeMause. 1997. pap. bk. 9.95 (978-0-7866-2702-8(6), 94170BCD) Mel Bay.

Jazz Guitar Licks in Tablature. Jay Umb... 97. pap. bk. 17.95 (978-0-7866-1618-3(0), 95884BCD) M...

Jazz Guitar Sight-Reading. Adam Levy. (ENG.). 1997. audio compact disk 9.95 (978-0-7390-2583-3(X)) Alfred Pub.

Jazz Guitar Workshop. Charlie Byrd & John Griggs. 2002. lib. bdg. 24.95 (978-0-7866-5986-9(6), 97517BCD) Mel Bay.

Jazz Hits: Volume 1. Contrib. by Mb3. 2006. audio compact disk 14.95 (978-5-558-04669-4(4)) Mel Bay.

Jazz in Praise of the Lord. unabr. ed. Owen Dodson. Read by Owen Dodson. 1 cass. (Running Time: 40 min.). (Watershed Tapes of Contemporary Poetry). 1979. 12.95 (23618) J Norton Pubs.

A retrospective of the black poet & playwright.

Jazz Intermediate Guitar. Workshop Arts Staff. 1 CD. (Running Time: 1 hr. 30 mins.). (ENG.). 1995. audio compact disk 10.95 (978-0-7390-1278-9(9), 14124) Alfred Pub.

Jazz Jam Trax for Guitar. Ralph Agresta. 1997. audio compact disk 12.95 (978-0-8256-1606-8(9)) Pub: Music Sales. Dist(s): H Leonard

Jazz Keyboard Harmony. Noah Baerman. (ENG.). 2001. audio compact disk 10.00 (978-0-7390-1108-9(1)) Alfred Pub.

Jazz Lead Guitar Method. Peter Gelling. (Progressive Ser.). 2004. pap. bk. 19.95 (978-1-86469-174-0(3), 256-116) Kolala Music SGP.

Jazz Legends. Bunny Crumpacker & Chick Crumpacker. 1995. bk. 19.95 (978-0-87905-683-4(5)) GibbsSmith Pub.

Jazz Licks Encyclopedia. Jody Fisher. (ENG.). 2001. audio compact disk 10.00 (978-0-7390-1119-5(7)) Alfred Pub.

Jazz Loon. 1 cass. (Running Time: 60 min.). 1994. audio compact disk 15.95 CD. (2704, Creativ Pub) Quayside.

Combination of uninhibited human musicianship & the passionate calls of loons.

Jazz Loon. 1 cass. (Running Time: 60 min.). 1994. 9.95 (2702, NrthWrd Bks) TandN Child.

Jazz Philharmonic. Bob Phillips & Randy Sabien. (ENG.). 2000. audio compact disk 10.95 (978-0-7390-1043-3(3)) Alfred Pub.

Jazz Philharmonic Second Set. Bob Phillips & Randy Sabien. (ENG.). 2004. audio compact disk 10.95 (978-0-7390-3623-5(8)) Alfred Pub.

Jazz Piano - Improvisation Concepts: Jazz Workbooks. Philipp Moehrke. (Jazz Piano Concepts Ser.). 2009. pap. bk. 29.95 (978-3-89922-118-3(4)) AMA Verlag DEU.

Jazz Play-Along: For Guitar, Wind Instruments, & Piano. Joe Diorio et al. 2001. audio compact disk 19.95 (978-0-7866-5967-8(X)) Mel Bay.

Jazz Revival. Perf. by Brentwood Music Staff. 1 CD. 1999. audio compact disk 16.98 (978-0-7601-2686-8(0)) Pub: Brentwood Music. Dist(s): Provident Mus Dist

Jazz Riffs for Piano. 1995. bk. 17.95 (978-0-89524-963-0(4)) Pub: Cherry Lane. Dist(s): H Leonard

Jazz Riffs for Piano. 1 cass., 1 CD. (Great Riffs Ser.). bk. 14.95 (02503619); audio compact disk 17.95 CD & bk. (02503620) H Leonard.

Learn the hottest tags, patterns, turnarounds, & solos in the style of the jazz world's legendary talents, such as Bud Powell, Thelonious Monk, George

Shearing, Red Garland, Erroll Garner, Chick Corea, Bill Evans, & Keith Jarrett.

Jazz, Rock Adult. Bert Konowitz. 1 CD. (Running Time: 1 hr. 30 mins.). (Alfred's Basic Piano Library Ser.). (ENG.). 1995. audio compact disk 10.95 (978-0-7390-1335-9(1), 14519) Alfred Pub.

Jazz-Rock & RandB: Clarinet. James L. Hosay. 2006. pap. bk. 15.95 (978-90-431-2273-3(4), 9043122734) H Leonard.

Jazz-Rock & RandB: Trombone. James L. Hosay. 2006. pap. bk. 15.95 (978-90-431-2274-0(2), 9043122742) H Leonard.

Jazz-Rock & RandB: Trumpet. James L. Hosay. 2006. pap. bk. 15.95 (978-90-431-2275-7(0), 9043122750) H Leonard.

Jazz Rock in the U. S. A. Clarinet - Grade 3-4. Composed by James Hosay. 2001. pap. bk. 15.95 (978-90-431-0974-1(6), 9043109746) H Leonard.

Jazz Singer. Perf. by Al Jolson & Gail Patrick. 1 cass. (Running Time: 60 min.). 1947. 7.95 (DD-6000) Natl Recrd Co.
The story of a cantor's son who became a superstar. This film brought sound to the movies for the first time.

Jazz Skills-Filling the Gaps for the Serious Guitarist. Jody Fisher. (ENG.). 2000. audio compact disk 10.95 (978-1-929395-12-5(4)) Pub: Workshop Arts. Dist(s): Alfred Pub

Jazz Sonatas for Solo Guitar. Ivor Mairants. 1997. pap. bk. 19.95 (978-0-7866-1376-2(9), 95634BCD) Mel Bay.

Jazz Standards for Solo Jazz Guitar. Created by Hal Leonard Corporation Staff. 2008. pap. bk. 19.99 (978-1-4234-3043-8(3), 1423430433) H Leonard.

Jazz Styles. 6th ed. Mark C. Gridley. 1 cass. (Running Time: 1 hr.). 1996. bk. 46.53 (978-0-13-268343-2(1)) P-H.

Jazz Styles: History & Analysis, with Jazz Styles Demonstration. 6th ed. Mark C. Gridley. 1996. audio compact disk 11.33 (978-0-614-14925-8(8)) P-H.

Jazz Trio: Eubie Blake, Bix Beiderbeck & Duke Ellington. unabr. ed. 3 cass. (Running Time: 55 min. per cass.). 1989. 18.95 Set. (978-0-88432-270-2(X), S40100) J Norton Pubs.
Biographers' narrative of three musical geniuses & their contributions to the history of American Jazz.

Jazz Tunes. William Bay. (QwikGuide Ser.). 2000. pap. bk. 5.95 (978-0-7866-5297-6(7), 98628BCD) Mel Bay.

Jazz Up Your Life Music. Tag Powell & Peter Abood. 1 cass. 1988. 12.95 (978-0-914295-74-7(8)) Top Mtn Pub.
Jazz music designed to increase energy, happiness, enthusiasm & stamina.

Jazz Violin Studies. Usher Abell. 1986. 9.98 (978-1-56222-612-1(6), 93954C) Mel Bay.

Jazz Wolf. 1 cass. (Running Time: 60 min.). 1994. audio compact disk 15.95 CD. (2334, Creativ Pub) Quayside.
Cry of the wolf. Wails of the saxophone & the spontaneous quality of modern jazz. Music & nature blend.

Jazz Wolf. 1 cass. (Running Time: 60 min.). 1994. 9.95 (2332, NrthWrd Bks) TandN Child.

Jazz Workbooks. Philipp Moehrke. (Solo Jazz Piano Concepts Ser.). 2009. audio compact disk 26.95 (978-3-89922-117-6(6)) AMA Verlag DEU.

Jazz Works. Ann Collins. 1 CD. (Running Time: 1 hr. 30 mins.). 2000. audio compact disk 14.95 (978-0-7390-0913-0(3), 18545) Alfred Pub.

Jazz 101. John F. Szwed. Narrated by Grover Gardner. (Running Time: 8 hrs. 30 mins.). 2003. 27.95 (978-1-59912-515-2(3)) Iofy Corp.

Jazz 101: A Complete Guide to Learning & Loving Jazz. unabr. ed. John F. Szwed. Read by Grover Gardner. 7 CDs. (Running Time: 8 hrs. 30 mins.). 2003. audio compact disk 56.00 (978-0-7861-9126-0(0), 3166); 44.95 (978-0-7861-2538-8(1), 3166); audio compact disk 24.95 (978-0-7861-8868-0(5), 3166) Blckstn Audio.
Jazz 101 is a fascinating entrée into the world of jazz, for the beginner, novice, or jazz enthusiast. Szwed takes listeners on a tour of the varied and nonlinear history of jazz, exploring how it developed from an ethnic music to become America's most popular music and then part of the avant-garde in less than fifty years. Szwed's complete overview includes the major types of jazz and significant jazz musicians of the twentieth century; the roots of jazz, including its European and African influences; and recommended listening, plus appendices on jazz singers, record guides, and more.

Jazz 101: A Complete Guide to Learning & Loving Jazz. unabr. ed. John F. Szwed. Read by Grover Gardner. 6 pieces. 2004. reel tape 29.95 (978-0-7861-2567-8(5)); audio compact disk 35.95 (978-0-7861-9086-7(8)) Blckstn Audio.

Jazzabilities, Book 1 - Book/CD: Later Elementary Level. Eric Baumgartner. (ENG.). 2008. pap. bk. 10.99 (978-1-4234-8606-0(4), 1423486064) Pub: Willis Music Co. Dist(s): H Leonard

Jazzing up Instruction. Peter Aleshkovsky. 2002. pap. bk. 36.95 (978-1-931596-00-8(X)) Pub: Scarecrow. Dist(s): Rowman

Jazziz Chronicles: The Guitarist - A Collection of Interviews & Features from the Award-Winning Magazine. Cherry Lane Music Staff. 2002. bk. 19.95 (978-1-57560-440-4(X), HL02500354) Pub: Cherry Lane. Dist(s): H Leonard

JazzKids Vocal Swing. Composed by Willie Myette. 1 CD. (Running Time: 39 mins.). 2002. audio compact disk 14.95 (978-1-891679-10-0(4), JKVS01) JazzKids.
Original JazzKids songs performed by professional jazz musicians and vocalist. The whole family will find themselves singing these catchy tunes. This CD is a great introduction to jazz music for kids!.

Jazzmatazz: Bb Clarinet. Stephen Bulla. (ENG.). 2005. pap. bk. 15.95 (978-90-431-2148-4(7), 9043121487) H Leonard.

Jazzmatazz: Bb Trumpet. Stephen Bulla. 2005. pap. bk. 15.95 (978-90-431-2150-7(9), 9043121509) H Leonard.

Jazzmatazz: C Instruments. Stephen Bulla. 2005. pap. bk. 15.95 (978-90-431-2152-1(5), 9043121525) H Leonard.

Jazzmatazz: Eb Alto Saxophone. Stephen Bulla. (ENG.). 2005. pap. bk. 15.95 (978-90-431-2149-1(5), 9043121495) H Leonard.

Jazzmatazz: Trombone. Stephen Bulla. 2005. pap. bk. 15.95 (978-90-431-2151-4(7), 9043121517) H Leonard.

Jazzplay. 2 CDs. (Running Time: 2 hrs.). 2001. audio compact disk 25.95 (EXIT002) Lodestone Catalog.
To name just a few "the Horn of Gabriel", "Finish Your Sentence", "Moods for Jazz" & "Trick the Devil".

Jazztastic. bk. 14.95 (978-1-85909-785-4(5), Warner Bro) Alfred Pub.

Jazztastic: Clt Inter Level B. bk. 14.95 (978-1-85909-782-3(0), Warner Bro) Alfred Pub.

Jazztastic: Flt Inter Level B. bk. 14.95 (978-1-85909-781-6(2), Warner Bro) Alfred Pub.

Jazztastic: Pno Inter Level B. bk. 14.95 (978-1-85909-786-1(3), Warner Bro) Alfred Pub.

Jazztastic - Tenor Sax Intermediate Level B. bk. 14.95 (978-1-85909-784-7(7), Warner Bro) Alfred Pub.

Jazzy Classix: Alto Saxophone. (Pop Instrumental Ser.). 2005. audio compact disk 17.95 (978-0-7579-1641-0(4), ED9586, Warner Bro) Alfred Pub.

Jazzy Classix: Clarinet. (Pop Instrumental Ser.). 2005. audio compact disk 17.95 (978-0-7579-1642-7(2), ED9587, Warner Bro) Alfred Pub.

Jazzy Classix: Flute. (Pop Instrumental Ser.). 2005. audio compact disk 17.95 (978-0-7579-1643-4(0), ED9589, Warner Bro) Alfred Pub.

Jazzy Classix: Tenor Saxophone. (Pop Instrumental Ser.). 2005. audio compact disk 17.95 (978-0-7579-1644-1(9), ED9598, Warner Bro) Alfred Pub.

Jazzy Classix: Trumpet. (Pop Instrumental Ser.). 2005. audio compact disk 17.95 (978-0-7579-1645-8(7), ED9588, Warner Bro) Alfred Pub.

Jazzy Classix: Violin. (Pop Instrumental Ser.). 2005. audio compact disk 17.95 (978-0-7579-1646-5(5), ED9599, Warner Bro) Alfred Pub.

Je Mange Donc je Maigris. Perf. by Michel Montignac. 1 cass., bklet. (Running Time: 50 mins.).Tr. of Eat & Lose Weight. (FRE.). cass. & audio compact disk 14.95 (978-2-921997-55-3(X)) Pub: Coffragants CAN. Dist(s): Penton Overseas
Recorded completely in international French language by well-known actors or speakers.

Je Suis Mucho Grande see I'm Too Big

Je Veux Bien! 2nd ed. Jeannette D. Bragger & Donald Rice. (C). 2001. bk. 57.75 (978-0-8384-4745-1(7)) Heinle.

Je Voudrais Pas Crever. Poems. Boris Vian. Read by Pierre Brasseur. 1 cass. (FRE.). 1991. 21.95 (1494-LQP) Olivia & Hill.
A series of poems.

Jealous God. unabr. collector's ed. John Braine. Read by Christopher Hurt. 9 cass. (Running Time: 13 hrs. 30 mins.). 1984. 72.00 (978-0-7366-0494-9(4), 1468) Books on Tape.
Braine's fourth novel is the censorious conscience of a young schoolmaster, Vincent Durgarven, who struggles to fulfill his mother's wish that he become a priest.

Jealousy. 1 cass. (Running Time: 60 min.). 10.95 (039) Psych Res Inst.
Substitution of love, trust & understanding for destructive fears & possessiveness.

Jealousy of God Series. Paul Cain. 3 cass. (Running Time: 4 hrs. 30 mins.). 2000. 15.00 (PC05-000) Morning NC.
"Trembling at his Word," "Who Will Ascend to the Lord's Hill?" & "Recapturing the Jealousy of God." God is jealous for his people & Paul issues a prophetic call for believers to be equally jealous for God & his glory.

Jean & Johnny. unabr. ed. Beverly Cleary. 1 cass. (Running Time: 75 min.). (Young Adult Cliffhangers Ser.). (YA). (gr. 7 up). 1986. 15.98 incl. bk. & guide. (978-0-8072-1846-4(4), JRH125SP, Listening Lib) Random Audio Pubg.
Johnny asks Jean to dance. Soon, Jean is doing all the things that seemed so silly to her before, like casually strolling by Johnny's locker, nervously calling him up & then hanging up & not wearing her glasses in an attempt to look better.

Jean Auel. unabr. ed. Jean M. Auel. Read by Jean M. Auel. (Running Time: 29 min.). Incl. Clan of the Cave Bear. Jean M. Auel. (Earth's Children Ser.: Vol. 1).; Valley of Horses. Jean M. Auel. (Earth's Children Ser.: Vol. 2).; 1987. 10.00 New Letters.
Reads & talks about her work.

Jean Coulthard. Jean Coulthard. 2004. audio compact disk 15.95 (978-0-662-33320-3(9)) Pub: Canadian Broadcasting CAN. Dist(s): Georgetown Term

Jean de la Lune, Set. Marcel Achard. Perf. by Madeleine Renaud & Michel Simon. 2 cass. Dramatization. (FRE.). 1996. 28.95 (1817-LQP) Olivia & Hill.
Achard's 1929 tender comedy: an unfaithful wife manages to convince her husband, who refuses to see the truth, that she has always been faithful to him. Performance includes two French leading actors.

Jean Fritz: Eleven Pb/Racpkg. 2004. pap. bk. (978-1-55592-660-1(6)) Weston Woods.

Jean Fritz: Six Revolutionary Ware Figures. 2004. cass. & flmstrp 30.00 (978-0-89719-526-3(4)) Weston Woods.

Jean Fritz: Six Revolutionary War Figures-What's the Big Idea, Ben Franklin?; Where Was Patrick Henry on the 29Th of May?; & Then What Happened, Paul Revere?; Why Don't You Get a Horse, Sam Adams?; Will You Sign Here, John Hancock?; Can't You Make Them Behave, King George? 2004. 8.95 (978-0-89719-926-1(X)) Weston Woods.

Jean Moulin et la resistance apres l'occupation, Set. Henri Amouroux. 2 cass. (Francais sous l'occupation Ser.). (FRE.). 1991. 26.95 (1236-RF) Olivia & Hill.

Jean Papineau-Couture. Jean Papineau-Couture. 2004. audio compact disk 15.95 (978-0-662-33316-6(0)) Pub: Canadian Broadcasting CAN. Dist(s): Georgetown Term

Jean-Paul Sartre: France (1905-1980) abr. ed. Narrated by Charlton Heston. (Running Time: 7966 sec.). (Audio Classics: the Giants of Philosophy Ser.). 2006. audio compact disk 25.95 (978-0-7861-6942-9(7)) Pub: Blckstn Audio. Dist(s): NetLibrary CO

Jean-Paul Sartre: France (1905-1980) abr. ed. Narrated by Charlton Heston. 2 CDs. (Running Time: 2 hrs. 16 mins.). (Giants of Philosophy Ser.). 1999. audio compact disk 16.95 (978-1-56823-079-5(6)) Pub: Knowledge Prod. Dist(s): APG
Jean-Paul Sartre (1905-1980), a French philosopher, is perhaps the best known advocate of existentialism. This view says that in the face of the meaninglessness of life and the finality of death, we must establish our own authentic existence. In this way, he believed, we can attain dignity by our own efforts.

Jean-Paul Sartre: France (1905-1980) unabr. ed. John Compton. Read by Charlton Heston. Ed. by George H. Smith & Wendy McElroy. 2 cass. (Running Time: 3 hrs.). (Giants of Philosophy Ser.). 1991. 17.95 Set. (978-0-938935-29-2(1), 10313) Knowledge Prod.
A leading advocate of existentialism, the view that we must establish our own existence & individual dignity, despite a meaningless life & a final death.

Jean-Paul Sartre: France (1905-1980) unabr. ed. Read by Charlton Heston. 2 cass. (Giants of Philosophy Ser.). 17.95 (K129) Blckstn Audio.
See how one of the world's most important philosophers created a complete system of thought, including his views on ethics, metaphysics, politics & aesthetics. Learn about his epistemology - how we know what we know.

Jean Piaget - Cognitive Development. Robert Stone. 1 cass. 1986. 10.00 (978-0-938137-12-2(3)) Listen & Learn.
Accomodation, assimilation, equilibration, egocentricity, operation, concrete operations, formal operations, intelligence, space, time, causality, language, & more.

Jean Redpath: Frae My Ain Countrie. 1 cass. 9.98 (C-49) Folk-Legacy.
All the beauty & simplicity of the Scots tradition.

Jean Shepherd: Don't Be a Leaf. Perf. by Jean Shepherd. 4 CDs. (Running Time: 3 hrs). 2006. audio compact disk 16.95 (978-0-9770819-4-3(X)) Choice Vent.
Radio Again is pleased to present 4 classic radio performances on audio compact disc by raconteur Jean Shepherd from the archives of Hartwest Productions.In Don?t Be A Leaf, Jean Shepherd muses on the impact of dirty glasses on life, shopping for cars with the old man, fly swatters, growing up with the White Sox and the great divide between Southside and Northside baseball fans. Shepherd asks the questions; are you the rider or the ridden? A leaf or a tree? What is the Master Plan Illusion and what is your Master Plan? So friends, enjoy this collection. Keep smiling, keep your knees loose, and don?t give them a sitting target! Includes liner notes with excerpts from the biography EXCELSIOR, YOU FATHEAD! The Art and Enigma of JEAN SHEPHERD By Eugene B. Bergmann.4 Audio CDs - Digitally remastered and restored. Each program is approximately 44 minutes. Total running time approximately 3 hours.Programs in this collection:CD 1 Hero of the Great Drama of LifeCD 2 Southside Chicago Baseball CD 3 The Master Plan IllusionCD 4 Don?t Be A LeafHumorist Jean Shepherd (1921-1999), creator/narrator of the holiday movie favorite A Christmas Story and author of numerous other works of fiction and television, had a long and stellar career on radio and was heard most days during the period of 1955-1977 on WOR radio in New York, a clear-channel station heard along the Eastern seaboard and points west. Shepherd?s radio work was both unique and transitional in the development of today?s talk radio. Shepherd could talk, and talk he did, touching his listeners intimately as if speaking to an audience of one. Shepherd was inducted into the Radio Hall of Fame in 2005.The radio programs in this collection, long lost and forgotten, were created in the mid 1960?s by Shepherd for radio and television syndicator Hartwest Productions in the format heard on Shepherd?s WOR shows of the day, right down to his familiar Bahn Frei theme music.

Jean Shepherd: Kicks. Jean Shepherd. (ENG.). 2008. audio compact disk 18.95 (978-1-57019-853-3(5), Radio Again USA) Radio Spirits.

Jean Shepherd: Pomp & Circumstance. Jean Shepherd. (ENG.). 2008. audio compact disk 31.95 (978-1-57019-852-6(7), Radio Again USA) Radio Spirits.

Jean Shepherd: The Fatal Flaw. Perf. by Jean Shepherd. 2009. audio compact disk 31.95 (978-1-57019-893-9(4), Radio Again USA) Radio Spirits.

Jean Shepherd: The X Random Factor. Perf. by Jean Shepherd. 8 CDs. (Running Time: 6 hrs). 2006. audio compact disk 27.95 (978-0-9770819-3-6(1)) Choice Vent.
Radio Again is pleased to present 8 classic radio performances by raconteur Jean Shepherd on audio compact disc from the archives of Hartwest Productions.The X Random Factor contains all the classic elements of Shepherd?s brilliant radio work, combining humor, story telling, kazoo playing, and general musings on everyday life the nature of man; from being yanked into the world, why every kid needs a swamp, the quicksand myth, to being left behind by the world around you. So listen and enjoy The X Random Factor. Learn why there?s a turtle on the cover, and remember there are 9 to 5 odds against anything in life. Keep your knees loose! Includes liner notes with excerpts from the biography EXCELSIOR, YOU FATHEAD! The Art and Enigma of JEAN SHEPHERD By Eugene B. Bergmann.8 Audio CDs - Digitally remastered and restored. Each program is approximately 44 minutes. Total running time approximately 6 hours.Programs in this collection:CD 1 Yanked Into the World CD 5 What Man IsCD 2 Receptacles of Uncharted Passions CD 6 Living in CirclevilleCD 3 Commitment to Adulthood CD 7 Gradually Being Phased OutCD 4 The Grandstand Syndrome CD 8 The X Random FactorHumorist Jean Shepherd (1921-1999), creator/narrator of the holiday movie favorite A Christmas Story and author of numerous other works of fiction and television, had a long and stellar career on radio and was heard most days during the period of 1955-1977 on WOR radio in New York, a clear-channel station heard along the Eastern seaboard and points west. Shepherd?s radio work was both unique and transitional in the development of today?s talk radio. Shepherd could talk, and talk he did, touching his listeners intimately as if speaking to an audience of one. Shepherd was inducted into the Radio Hall of Fame in 2005.The radio programs in this collection, long lost and forgotten, were created in the mid 1960?s by Shepherd for radio and television syndicator Hartwest Productions in the format heard on Shepherd?s WOR shows of the day, right down to his familiar Bahn Frei theme music.

Jean Shepherd Ticket to Ride. Perf. by Jean Shepherd. 2008. audio compact disk 18.95 (978-1-57019-877-9(2), Radio Again USA) Radio Spirits.

Jean Stafford: A Letter see Robert Lowell: A Reading

Jean Vilar: Ses Grandes Roles. unabr. ed. 1 cass. (FRE.). 15.95 (CFR458) J Norton Pubs.

Jean Vilar: "Ses Grands Roles" unabr. ed. Read by Jeanne Provost. 1 cass. (French Literature Ser.). (FRE.). 1987. 11.95 (978-0-8045-0924-4(7), SAC 924) Spoken Arts.

Jeanne d'Arc see Treasury of French Prose

Jeanne d'Arc. Lucia Bonato. pap. bk. 19.95 (978-88-7754-637-1(9)) Pub: Cideb ITA. Dist(s): Distribks Inc

Jeanne Jugan: Humble So As to Love More. Paul Milcent. 6 cass. 24.95 (302) Ignatius Pr.
Life of Blessed Jeanne Jugan, Foundress of the Little Sisters of the Poor.

Jeanne Long: Natural Price Reversal Points for All Stocks & Commodities World-Wide. Read by Jeanne Long. 1 cass. 30.00 Dow Jones Telerate.
The lecture will illustrate how prices stop & reverse at the channel lines, & then bounce off one line to go to the opposite line. The movement from one channel line to the next facilitates ease of trading the channels. Simple technical tools will demonstrate where & when to take profits. The techniques can be used alone or combined with your favorite technical tools for added confidence & profits. The channels, derived from astronomical mathematical calculations, are easily inserted on graphs using CompuTrac's SNAP module or Jeanne's personal software, the Universal Clock. Jeanne will include the manual calculations with the class notes allowing anyone to calculate the channels. She will demonstrate the value of the moving channel lines on DJIA, World Markets, Currencies, Gold, Silver, Oil, Soybeans & Wheat.

***Jeannie Out of the Bottle.** unabr. ed. Barbara Eden. (ENG.). 2011. audio compact disk 35.00 (978-0-307-91434-7(8), Random AudioBks) Pub: Random Audio Pubg. Dist(s): Random

Jeb Stuart: The Last Cavalier. unabr. ed. Burke Davis. Read by Barrett Whitener. 13 CDs. (Running Time: 16 hrs.). 2002. audio compact disk 104.00 (978-0-7861-9389-9(1), 3021); 76.95 (978-0-7861-2362-9(1), 3021) Blckstn Audio.
A full and definitive biography of the dashing and enigmatic Confederate hero of the Civil War, General J.E.B. Stuart.

Jeb Stuart: The Last Cavalier. unabr. ed. Burke Davis. Read by Barrett Whitener. (Running Time: 15 hrs. 50 mins.). (ENG.). 2009. 29.95 (978-1-4332-9749-6(3)) Blckstn Audio.

Jeb Stuart: The Last Cavalier. unabr. collector's ed. Burke Davis. Read by Dick Estell. 11 cass. (Running Time: 16 hrs. 30 mins.). 1987. 88.00 (978-0-7366-1208-1(4), 2126) Books on Tape.
Biography of James Ewell Brown Stuart, the 'flawed hero' of the Confederate Army during the Civil War.

***Jed Mckenna's Notebook Audio: All Bonus Content from the Enlightenment Trilogy, Final Edition.** Jed McKenna. 2010. cd-rom 24.95 (978-0-9801848-9-1(4)) Wisefool Pr.

Jedburghs. unabr. ed. Will Irwin. Read by Patrick G. Lawlor. (Running Time: 10 hrs. 0 mins. 0 sec.). (ENG.). 2005. audio compact disk 34.99 (978-1-4001-0183-2(2)) Pub: Tantor Media. Dist(s): IngramPubServ

Jedburghs: The Secret History of the Allied Special Forces, France 1944. unabr. ed. Will Irwin. Read by Patrick G. Lawlor. (Running Time: 10 hrs. 0 mins. 0 sec.). (ENG.). 2005. audio compact disk 22.99 (978-1-4001-5183-7(X)); audio compact disk 69.99 (978-1-4001-3183-9(9)) Pub: Tantor Media. Dist(s): IngramPubServ

Jeeves. abr. ed. P. G. Wodehouse. Read by Terry Thomas & Roger Livesey. 1 cass. (Running Time: 52 min.). Incl. Indian Summer of an Uncle. (CPN 1137); Jeeves Takes Charge. (CPN 1137); (Jeeves & Wooster Ser.). 1998. 12.00 (978-1-55994-004-7(2), CPN 1137) HarperCollins Pubs.

***Jeeves: Joy in the Morning.** P. G. Wodehouse. Narrated by Michael Hordern & Richard Briers. (Running Time: 3 hrs. 5 mins. 0 sec.). (ENG., 2010. audio compact disk 29.95 (978-1-84607-137-9(2)) Pub: AudioGO. Dist(s): Perseus Dist

Jeeves: Short Stories. unabr. ed. Short Stories. P. G. Wodehouse. Read by Flo Gibson. 3 cass. (Running Time: 4 hrs. 30 min.). (gr. 8 up). 1998. 16.95 (978-1-55685-571-9(0)) Audio Bk Con.
Takes Bertie Wooster to America where his old reliable valet Jeeves rescues him & his cohorts from various predicaments.

Jeeves & the Feudal Spirit: A BBC Full-Cast Radio Drama. P. G. Wodehouse. Narrated by Jonathan Cecil. (Running Time: 20400 sec.). (Jeeves & Wooster Ser.). (ENG.). 2007. audio compact disk 27.95 (978-1-57270-834-1(4)) Pub: AudioGO. Dist(s): Perseus Dist

***Jeeves & the Feudal Spirit: A BBC Full-Cast Radio Drama.** P. G. Wodehouse. Narrated by Richard Briers & Michael Hordern. 2 CDs. (Running Time: 3 hrs. 0 mins. 0 sec.). (ENG.). 2010. audio compact disk 29.95 (978-0-563-49439-3(5)) Pub: AudioGO. Dist(s): Perseus Dist

Jeeves & the Feudal Spirit: A BBC Full-Cast Radio Drama. P. G. Wodehouse et al. 2 cass. Dramatization. (Jeeves & Wooster Ser.). 1991. 14.95 set. Minds Eye.
Dramatizations produced by the BBC.

Jeeves & the Feudal Spirit: A BBC Full-Cast Radio Drama. unabr. ed. P. G. Wodehouse. Read by Jonathan Cecil. (Jeeves & Wooster Ser.). 2003. 24.95 (978-1-57270-299-8(0)) Pub: Audio Partners. Dist(s): PerseuPGW

Jeeves & the Feudal Spirit: A BBC Full-Cast Radio Drama. unabr. ed. P. G. Wodehouse. 2 vols. (Running Time: 2 hrs). Dramatization. (Jeeves & Wooster Ser.). 2003. audio compact disk 29.95 (978-0-563-49674-8(6)) BBC Worldwide.

Jeeves & the Feudal Spirit: A BBC Full-Cast Radio Drama. unabr. ed. P. G. Wodehouse. Read by Frederick Davidson. 5 cass. (Running Time: 7 hrs.). (Jeeves & Wooster Ser.). 1996. 39.95 (978-0-7861-0916-6(5), 1723) Blckstn Audio.
It was Bertie Wooster's opinion that his new mustache would do something for him. It was Jeeve's opinion that it did indeed do something for him. Something unmentionable. A certain coolness between them was bound to result. Against this stormy, "Wuthering Heights" sort of background a giant drama begins to unfold, involving, among other things, Bertie's possession of a stolen necklace & the soul-shattering prospect of a trip to the marriage altar. The imperturbable Jeeves rallies to the cause & preempts the part usually reserved for the United States Marines, thus aiding Bertie, who gets himself out of more than one complication in his feckless life.

Jeeves & the Feudal Spirit: A BBC Full-Cast Radio Drama. unabr. ed. P. G. Wodehouse. Read by Frederick Davidson. 6 CDs. (Running Time: 7 hrs.). (Jeeves & Wooster Ser.). 2000. audio compact disk 48.00 (978-0-7861-9825-2(7), 1723) Blckstn Audio.
A certain coolness between Bertie & Jeeves results from a mustachet. Against this stormy, Wuthering Heights sort of background a giant drama begins to unfold.

Jeeves & the Feudal Spirit: A BBC Full-Cast Radio Drama. unabr. ed. P. G. Wodehouse. Read by Jonathan Cecil. 6 cass. (Running Time: 9 hrs.). (Jeeves & Wooster Ser.). 2000. 49.95 (978-0-7451-6549-3(4), CAB 1165) Pub: Chivers Audio Bks GBR. Dist(s): AudioGO
How fortunate that Stilton Cheesewright drew Bertie Wooster, the favorite, in the Drones Club annual Dart Tournament. Stilton had just about had it with Bertie, he didn't like men trifling with his fiancee Florence Cray's affections! Besides, Florence seemed to prefer Percy Gorringe over Stilton. And on top of it all, Bertie was growing a mustache that Jeeves disapproved of strongly!.

Jeeves & the Mating Season. unabr. ed. P. G. Wodehouse. Read by Jonathan Cecil. 6 cass. (Running Time: 7 hrs.). 2003. 29.95 (978-1-57270-318-6(0)) Pub: Audio Partners. Dist(s): PerseuPGW

Jeeves & the Mating Season. unabr. ed. P. G. Wodehouse. Read by Jonathan Cecil. 6 CDs. (Running Time: 6 hrs. 51 mins.). (Audio Editions Ser.). (ENG.). 2003. audio compact disk 29.95 (978-1-57270-319-3(9)) Pub: AudioGO. Dist(s): Perseus Dist

Jeeves & the Old School Chum. P. G. Wodehouse. Read by Alexander Spencer. 2 Cass. (Running Time: 3.5 Hrs.). 14.95 (978-1-4025-2371-7(8)) Recorded Bks.

Jeeves & the Old School Chum, unabr. ed. Short Stories. P. G. Wodehouse. Narrated by Alexander Spencer. 3 cass. (Running Time: 3 hrs. 30 mins.). 1985. 26.00 (978-1-55690-262-8(X), 85150E7) Recorded Bks.
Bertie Wooster's friend, Bingo Little, suffers pangs of hunger for the longings of his heart.

Jeeves & the Song of Songs, unabr. ed. Short Stories. P. G. Wodehouse. Narrated by Alexander Spencer. 3 cass. (Running Time: 4 hrs.). 1988. 26.00 (978-1-55690-263-5(8), 85140E7) Recorded Bks.
Includes: "The Inferiority Complex of Old Sippy"; "The Kid Clementina"; "Indian Summer of an Uncle"; "The Yuletide Spirit" & "The Impending Doom".

Jeeves & the Tie That Binds. unabr. ed. P. G. Wodehouse. Read by Frederick Davidson. 4 cass. (Running Time: 5 hrs. 30 mins.). 1992. 32.95 (978-0-7861-0291-4(8), 1255) Blckstn Audio.
Jeeves belongs to a club for butlers in London's fashionable West End, & one of the rules there is that every member must contribute to the club book everything about the fellow he is working for; the idea being that such information will help those seeking new employment. If a member is contemplating signing up with someone, he looks him up in the club book. Some dull employers are given only a few lines in the club book, but Jeeves has penned eighteen pages about his employer, Bertie Wooster. And Bertie, quite understandably, is perturbed. Suppose the book falls into unscrupulous hands? The imagination boggles. Here is not only a gripping drama, but seventeen chapters of unadulterated delight.

Jeeves & the Tie That Binds, Set. unabr. ed. P. G. Wodehouse. Read by Frederick Davidson. 4 cass. 1999. 32.95 (FS9-43176) Highsmith.

Jeeves Collection. P. G. Wodehouse. 8 CDs. (Running Time: 12 hrs.). 2002. audio compact disk 79.95 (978-0-563-53051-0(0), BBCD 004) BBC Worldwide.

Jeeves in the Morning. unabr. ed. P. G. Wodehouse. Read by Jonathan Cecil. 2004. 27.95 (978-1-57270-434-3(9)) Pub: Audio Partners. Dist(s): PerseuPGW
Bertie desperately wants to avoid the rural town of Steeple Bumpleigh, where his fearsome Aunt Agatha and her husband Lord Worplesdon (Uncle Percy) live, along with Bertie's ex-fiancée Florence Cray and her troubled younger brother. Nonetheless, Jeeves talks Bertie into visiting his Uncle Percy and mayhem ensues: Florence's younger brother accidentally sets fire to the cottage where Bertie is to stay, but Uncle Percy accuses Bertie of arson. Florence is now betrothed to "Stilton" Cheesewright, an old school chum of Bertie's who is now a town constable - and when Florence threatens to ditch him, he decides Bertie's up to no good. Meanwhile, Bertie promises Cousin Nobby to talk to Uncle Percy, who won't accept her engagement to a young writer. Can Bertie reconcile the family? Only Jeeves can help him weather the storm.P.G. Wodehouse first introduced the upper class twit, Bertie Wooster, and his astonishing valet, Jeeves, in a 1915 short story entitled "Extricating Young Gussie." Many more stories and full-length novels followed. Whereas Bertie's appraisals of a given predicament are often feeble and impetuous, Jeeves possesses great aplomb and common sense, married to a cool intelligence and ability to express himself with precision and economy.

Jeeves in the Morning. unabr. ed. P. G. Wodehouse. Read by Jonathan Cecil. (ENG.). 2004. audio compact disk 29.95 (978-1-57270-435-0(7)) Pub: AudioGO. Dist(s): Perseus Dist

Jeeves in the Morning. unabr. ed. P. G. Wodehouse. Read by Frederick Davidson. 5 cass. (Running Time: 7 hrs.). 2003. 39.95 (978-0-7861-0963-0(7), 1740) Blckstn Audio.
Featuring the inimitable gentleman's gentleman, Jeeves, & his master, Bertie Wooster, "Jeeves in the Morning" reflects the glories & absurdities of a vanished era as Jeeves & Bertie frolic through a series of outrageous & nightmarish doings.

Jeeves in the Morning. unabr. ed. P. G. Wodehouse. Read by Frederick Davidson. 7 CDs. (Running Time: 7 hrs.). 2000. audio compact disk 56.00 (978-0-7861-9941-9(5), 1740) Blckstn Audio.

Jeeves in the Offing. P. G. Wodehouse. Read by Simon Callow. 3 CDs. (Jeeves & Wooster Ser.). 2002. audio compact disk (978-0-14-180392-0(4)) Pnguin Bks Ltd GBR.
Taking a trip to Brinkley Court should be a joy for Bertie. When, however, he discovers that his fellow guests are to include his former fiancée Bobbie Wickham, Mrs Cream the crime writer, Bertie's favourite brain specialist Sir Roderick Glossop and his equally popular ex-headmaster, prize-stinker Aubrey Upjohn, Bertie looks set to have a troublesome time.

Jeeves in the Offing. unabr. ed. P. G. Wodehouse. Read by Frederick Davidson. 4 cass. (Running Time: 7 hrs.). (Jeeves & Wooster Ser.). 2006. 32.95 (978-0-7861-2604-0(3), 3200); audio compact disk 48.00 (978-0-7861-8934-2(7), 3200) Blckstn Audio.

Jeeves Takes Charge see Jeeves

Jeeves Takes Charge. unabr. ed. P. G. Wodehouse. Narrated by Alexander Spencer. 3 cass. (Running Time: 4 hrs. 30 mins.). 1984. 26.00 (978-1-55690-264-2(6), 84068E7) Recorded Bks.
Bertie Wooster finds life with the perfect "gentleman's gentleman" can be less than ideal.

Jeeves Takes Charge & Bertie Changes His Mind. unabr. ed. P. G. Wodehouse. Read by Edward Duke. 1 cass. (Running Time: 1 hr.). Dramatization. 1988. 7.95 (978-1-882071-20-3(4), 022) B-B Audio.
The rare pleasure of a long laugh with an old friend is common place. Through his lively wit we meet Bertie Wooster: young, British and rich. Bertie has a particular way of acting and fortunately, an extraordinary gentleman's gentleman. jeeves, to extricate him from his particular sort of troubles.

Jeff Davis & Jeff Warner: Two Little Boys. 1 cass., 1 CD. (J). 9.98 (C-573); audio compact disk 14.98 CD. (CD-573) Folk-Legacy.
An excellent collection of folksongs for youngsters.

Jeff Green Collection. Jeff Green. 6 cass. 39.95 (978-1-57677-011-5(7), MAXM126) Lodestone Catalog.

***Jeff in Venice, Death in Varanasi: A Novel.** unabr. ed. Geoff Dyer. Read by Simon Vance. (Running Time: 9 hrs. 30 mins.). 2010. 29.95 (978-1-4417-5339-7(7)); 59.95 (978-1-4417-5335-9(4)); audio compact disk 29.95 (978-1-4417-5338-0(9)); audio compact disk 90.00 (978-1-4417-5336-6(2)) Blckstn Audio.

Jeff Regan, Investigator: The Diamond Quartet & The Man Who Came Back. Perf. by Jack Webb. 1 cass. (Running Time: 1 hr.). 2001. 6.98 (2539) Radio Spirits.

Jeff Regan, Investigator: The Lady Who Wanted to Live & The Little Man's Lament. Perf. by Jack Webb. 1 cass. (Running Time: 1 hr.). 2001. 6.98 (2603) Radio Spirits.

Jeff Regan, Investigator: The Lonesome Lady, The Lady with the Golden Hair. Jack Webb. 1 cass. (Running Time: 1 hr.). 2001. 6.98 (2398) Radio Spirits.

Jeff Regan Investigator: The Lyon's Eye. Perf. by Jack Webb et al. 2008. audio compact disk 31.95 (978-1-57019-873-1(X)) Radio Spirits.

Jeff Regan, Investigator: The Man in the Door & The House by the Sea. Perf. by Jack Webb. 1 cass. (Running Time: 1 hr.). 2001. 6.98 (2580) Radio Spirits.

Jeff Riggenbach: Decadence & the Ideology of Freedom. (Running Time: 60 min.). (Cal State Univ., Long Beach). 1982. 9.00 (F138) Freeland Pr.
Presents a history of decadence in correlation with the advances of technology.

Jeff Shaara's Civil War Battlefields: Discovering America's Hallowed Ground. abr. ed. Jeff Shaara. Read by Robertson Dean. (Running Time: 25200 sec.). (ENG.). 2007. audio compact disk 29.95 (978-0-7393-4120-9(0), Random AudioBks) Pub: Random Audio Pubg. Dist(s): Random

Jefferson: A Novel. unabr. ed. Max Byrd. Narrated by George Guidall. 12 cass. (Running Time: 16 hrs. 45 mins.). 1999. 99.00 (978-0-7887-3243-0(9), 95651E7) Recorded Bks.
Based on careful research & written to be enjoyed, this is a masterful fictional portrait of an enigmatic & powerful personality. As Jefferson functions as American ambassador to Paris, he faces daunting political & personal challenges.

Jefferson: And the Ordeal of Liberty. unabr. ed. Dumas Malone. Read by Anna Fields. 14 cass. (Running Time: 20 hrs. 30 mins.). (Jefferson & His Time Ser.: Vol. 3). 2006. 89.95 (978-0-7861-1378-1(2), 2262) Blckstn Audio.
Includes the story of the final & most crucial phase of Jefferson's secretaryship of state; his retirement to Monticello; his assumption of the leadership of the opposition party; & the crisis during the half-war with France when the existence of political expression was threatened & the freedom of individuals imperiled.

Jefferson: And the Rights of Man. unabr. ed. Dumas Malone. Read by Anna Fields. 13 cass. (Running Time: 19 hrs.). (Jefferson & His Time Ser.: Vol. 2). 1998. 85.95 (978-0-7861-1323-1(5), 2248) Blckstn Audio.
Tells the story of the eventful middle years in the life of Thomas Jefferson: including his ministry to France in the years just before the French Revolution & much more.

Jefferson: The President, First Term 1801-1805. unabr. ed. Dumas Malone. Read by Anna Fields. 13 cass. (Running Time: 19 hrs.). (Jefferson & His Time Ser.: Vol. 4). 1998. 85.95 (978-0-7861-1362-0(6), 2271) Blckstn Audio.
Jefferson's first years in office find him confronting a nation deeply divided following the administrations of Washington & Adams & many subsequent conflicts. He acquires the vast territory of Louisiana for the United States, challenges the growing power of the federal judiciary, continues to press his opposition to the Hamiltonian doctrine of an overriding central government, assumes the unchallenged leadership of his party, & is universally acknowledged as the preeminent American patron of science & general learning.

Jefferson: The Sage of Monticello. unabr. ed. Dumas Malone. Read by Anna Fields. 13 cass. (Running Time: 19 hrs.). (Jefferson & His Time Ser.: Vol. 6). 1998. 85.95 (978-0-7861-1419-1(3), 2295) Blckstn Audio.
Recounts the accomplishments, friendships & family difficulties of Jefferson's last seventeen years - including his retirement from the presidency, his personal tribulations & his major role in founding the Library of Congress & the University of Virginia.

Jefferson: The Virginian. unabr. ed. Dumas Malone. Read by Anna Fields. 12 cass. (Running Time: 17 hrs. 30 mins.). (Jefferson & His Time Ser.: Vol. 1). 1998. 83.95 (978-0-7861-1339-2(1), 2234) Blckstn Audio.
Covers Jefferson's ancestry, youth, education & legal career; his marriage & the building of Monticello; the drafting of the Declaration of Independence & the "Notes on Virginia" his rich, fruitful legislative career; his highly controversial governorship; & his early services to the development of the West.

Jefferson & Monticello. unabr. ed. Jack McLaughlin. Read by Christopher Hurt. 9 cass. (Running Time: 13 hrs.). 1990. 62.95 (978-0-7861-0189-4(X), 1166) Blckstn Audio.
The portrait that emerges focuses on the domestic life as seen through the prism of his love affair with Monticello. Close up, this is an absorbing portrayal of a towering, complex figure whose energies & interests remain a source of awe & delight.

Jefferson & the Ordeal of Liberty. unabr. ed. Dumas Malone. Read by Anna Fields. (Running Time: 70200 sec.). (Jefferson & His Time (Blackstone Audio) Ser.). 2007. audio compact disk 44.95 (978-0-7861-6166-9(3)); audio compact disk 120.00 (978-0-7861-6165-2(5)) Blckstn Audio.

Jefferson & the Rights of Man. unabr. ed. Dumas Malone. Read by Anna Fields. (Running Time: 68400 sec.). (Jefferson & His Time Ser.). 2007. audio compact disk 120.00 (978-0-7861-6163-8(9)); audio compact disk 44.95 (978-0-7861-6164-5(7)) Blckstn Audio.

Jefferson & Vaccination. 1 cass. 10.00 Esstee Audios.
The great genius brings a medical advance.

Jefferson Bible: The Life & Morals of Jesus of Nazareth. unabr. ed. Thomas Jefferson. Read by Sam Gray. 1 cass. (Running Time: 2 hrs. 30 min.). 1995. 16.95 (978-1-887094-01-6(6)) Palisades Pr.
Thomas Jefferson's interpretation of the Bible.

Jefferson Davis, Pt. 1. unabr. ed. William C. Davis. Read by Jeff Riggenbach. 9 cass. (Running Time: 26 hrs.). 1994. 62.95 (978-0-7861-0790-2(1), 1546A,B) Blckstn Audio.
This book paints a vivid picture of Davis as a multifaceted, often charismatic man, a man who mirrored the turbulent times in which he lived & who stood solidly for the South that he loved. It shows him as a loyal son of Mississippi from his earliest childhood; hardworking planter; compassionate slave owner, & a staunch defender of the institution; hero of the Mexican War; impassioned spokesman for the Southern position in the antebellum U.S. Senate; & able Secretary of War under Franklin Pierce.

Jefferson Davis, Pt. 2. unabr. ed. William C. Davis. Read by Jeff Riggenbach. 13 cass. (Running Time: 26 hrs.). 1994. 85.95 (978-0-7861-0845-9(2), 1546A,B) Blckstn Audio.
Ranging over the complete span of Jefferson Davis's long life, this book paints a vivid picture of Davis as a multifaceted , often charismatic man, a man who mirrored the turbulent times in which he lived & who stood solidly for the South that he loved. But it is on the years of the Civil War & Davis' performance as President of the Confederacy that the book naturally focuses. The author shows clearly why no one was ever neutral toward Jefferson Davis. Loved by many for his eloquence, personal courage, intense loyalty & devotion, Davis was disliked & even vilified by many more for his well-known obstinacy & vanity, adherence to failed generals, feuds with his best commanders & inability or unwillingness to delegate responsibility to others.

Jefferson the President Vol. 5, Pt. 1: Second Term, 1805-1809. unabr. ed. Dumas Malone. Read by Anna Fields. 10 cass. (Running Time: 24 hrs. 30 mins.). (Jefferson & His Time Ser.: Vol. 5). 1998. 69.95 (978-0-7861-1374-3(X), 2282-A,B) Blckstn Audio.
Completes the story of his presidency - carrying him through his troubled second term, but also to the end of an official career that spanned some forty years. A vibrant account of his disparate activities & finally, retiring to his beloved haven at Monticello.

Jefferson the President Vol. 5, Pt. 2: Second Term, 1805-1809. unabr. ed. Dumas Malone. Read by Anna Fields. 7 cass. (Running Time: 10 hrs. 30 min.). (Jefferson & His Time Ser.: Vol. 5, Pt. 2). 1998. 49.95 (978-0-7861-1413-9(4), 2282-B) Blckstn Audio.
Completes the story of his presidency - carrying him through his troubled second term, but also to the end of an official career that spanned some forty years.

Jefferson the President, First Term, 1801-1805. unabr. ed. Dumas Malone. Read by Anna Fields. (Running Time: 68400 sec.). (Jefferson & His Time Ser.). 2007. audio compact disk 120.00 (978-0-7861-6167-6(1)) Blckstn Audio.

Jefferson the President, First Term 1801-1805. unabr. ed. Dumas Malone. Read by Anna Fields. (Running Time: 68400 sec.). (Jefferson & His Time (Blackstone Audio) Ser.). 2007. audio compact disk 44.95 (978-0-7861-6168-3(X)) Blckstn Audio.

Jefferson the President, Second Term, 1805-1809. unabr. ed. Dumas Malone. Read by Anna Fields. 7 cass. (Running Time: 24 hrs. 30 mins.). (Thomas Jefferson & His Time Ser.: Vol. 5). 2006. 49.95 (978-0-7861-1427-6(4), 2282-A,B) Blckstn Audio.

Jefferson the President, Second Term, 1805-1809. unabr. ed. Dumas Malone. Read by Anna Fields. (Running Time: 88200 sec.). (Jefferson & His Time (Blackstone Audio) Ser.). 2007. audio compact disk 130.00 (978-0-7861-6169-0(8)) Blckstn Audio.

Jefferson the President, Second Term 1805-1809. unabr. ed. Dumas Malone. Read by Anna Fields. (Running Time: 88200 sec.). (Jefferson & His Time (Blackstone Audio) Ser.). 2007. audio compact disk 44.95 (978-0-7861-6171-3(X)) Blckstn Audio.

Jefferson the Virginian. unabr. ed. Dumas Malone. Read by Anna Fields. (Running Time: 57600 sec.). (Jefferson & His Time Ser.). 2007. audio compact disk 108.00 (978-0-7861-6161-4(2)); audio compact disk 29.95 (978-0-7861-6162-1(0)) Blckstn Audio.

Jeffersons: Gen. 13:11. Ed Young. 1991. 4.95 (978-0-7417-1842-6(1), 842) Win Walk.

Jefferson's Demons: Portrait of a Restless Mind. unabr. ed. Michael Knox Beran. Read by Dan Cashman. 7 cass. (Running Time: 10 hrs. 30 min.). 2004. 32.95 (978-1-59007-433-6(5)); audio compact disk 55.00 (978-1-59007-434-3(3)) Pub: New Millenn Enter. Dist(s): PerseuPGW

Jefferson's Secrets: Death & Desire at Monticello. unabr. ed. Andrew Burnstein. Narrated by Simon Vance. 12 CDs. (Running Time: 14 hrs. 30 mins. 0 sec.). (ENG.). 2005. audio compact disk 39.99 (978-1-4001-0148-1(4)) Pub: Tantor Media. Dist(s): IngramPubServ

Jefferson's Secrets: Death & Desire at Monticello. unabr. ed. Andrew Burstein. Narrated by Simon Vance. (Running Time: 14 hrs. 30 mins. 0 sec.). (ENG.). 2005. audio compact disk 79.99 (978-1-4001-3148-8(0)); audio compact disk 22.99 (978-1-4001-5148-6(1)) Pub: Tantor Media. Dist(s): IngramPubServ

Jefferson's War. Joseph Wheelan. Narrated by Patrick Cullen. (Running Time: 12 hrs. 30 mins.). 2005. 34.95 (978-1-59912-516-9(1)) Iofy Corp.

Jefferson's War: America's First War on Terror, 1801-1805. Joseph Wheelan. Read by Patrick Cullen. (Running Time: 45000 sec.). 2005. cass., cass., DVD 12.30 (978-0-7861-3498-4(4)); DVD & audio compact disk 12.30 (978-0-7861-8065-3(X)); DVD, audio compact disk, audio compact disk 12.30 (978-0-7861-7882-7(5)) Blckstn Audio.

Jeffery Deaver Suspense Collection. abr. ed. Jeffery Deaver. (Running Time: 17 hrs. 0 mins. 0 sec.). (ENG.). 2008. audio compact disk 19.99 (978-0-7435-8154-7(7)) Pub: S&S Audio. Dist(s): S and S Inc

Jeffrey Combs Reads H. P. Lovecraft's Herbert West - Re-Animator. Short Stories. Narrated by Jeffrey Combs. Prod. by Beyond Books. 1. (Running Time: 72 mins.). 1999. audio compact disk 12.00 (978-0-9745103-9-2(4), BBCD-01, Beyond Bks OR) Lurker.

Jehoshaphat & the People of Judah. Speeches. Joel Osteen. 1 Cass. (Running Time: 30 Min.). (J). 2000. 6.00 (978-1-59349-046-1(1), JA0046) J Osteen.

Jehovah Reigns. John Stevenson. 1 cass. 10.98 (978-7-900606-18-1(1)); audio compact disk 14.98 CD. (978-7-900606-20-4(3)) Destiny Image Pubs.

Jehovah's Witnesses. Walter Ralston Martin. 1 cass. 1997. 6.99 (978-7-5116-0030-1(1)) Gospel Lght.
Evangelism.

Jehovah's Witnesses at the Door, Set. Contrib. by Gospel Light Publications Staff. 2 cass. 1997. 11.99 (978-7-5116-0043-1(3)) Gospel Lght.
Evangelism.

Jehovah's Witnesses, Witnessing To. Dan Corner. 1 cass. 3.00 (48) Evang Outreach.

Jellicoe Road. unabr. ed. Melina Marchetta. Read by Rebecca Macauley. (YA). 2009. audio compact disk 87.95 (978-1-74214-464-1(0), 9781742144641) Pub: Bolinda Pubng AUS. Dist(s): Bolinda Pub Inc

Jelly Belly. unabr. ed. Robert Kimmel Smith. 1 cass. (Running Time: 85 min.). (Middle Grade Cliffhangers Ser.). (J). (gr. 4-6). 1984. 15.98 (978-0-8072-1106-9(0), SWR 34 SP, Listening Lib); (Listening Lib) Random Audio Pubg.
Ned wants to resist the joys of junk food, but it's easier said than done. Isn't there some way to keep eating the goodies & still lose weight?.

Jelly Pie. Roger McGough & Brian Patten. 1 cass. (Running Time: 35 min.). (J). (gr. 1 up). 9.00 (978-0-14-088127-1(1), CC/042) C to C Cassettes.
Jelly Pie is a selection of verse taken from Pattern's Gargling with Jelly & McGough's Sky in the Pie, two best selling collections of poetry.

Jelly Roll Morton Vol. I: The Library of Congress Recordings. Jelly Roll Morton. 1 cass. (Sandy Hook Release Ser.: No. 111). 1989. 7.98 (CSH-2111) Radiola Co.
Recorded in 1938 in Washington, D.C., Ferdinand "Jelly Roll" Morton combined commentary, playing, singing, exaggeration & autobiography to create this important documentary - a colorful & personalized history of New Orleans Jazz.

Jemima J. unabr. ed. Jane Green. Narrated by Barbara Rosenblat. 9 cass. (Running Time: 13 hrs. 30 mins.). 2002. 82.00 (978-1-4025-1945-1(1)) Recorded Bks.
There's a beautiful, funny, bright woman behind all Jemima's fat, and not even she has an inkling how wonderful she can be. When an Internet liaison spurs her to dive headlong into diet and exercise, Jemima finds doors open to her as if by magic.

Jemima Shore's First Case & Other Stories. unabr. ed. Antonia Fraser. Read by Patricia Hodge. 6 cass. (Running Time: 9 hrs.). 2000. 49.95 (CAB 340) Pub: Chivers Audio Bks GBR. Dist(s): AudioGO
There are 13 stories in all, including the case of a missing bride on a Venetian honeymoon, the murder at Arcangelo's Salon where Jemima has her hair done, and the tale of the ghostly visitor to the bedroom of two children.

Jennie. unabr. ed. Douglas Preston. Read by Multivoice Production Staff. (Running Time: 12 hrs.). 2009. 39.97 (978-1-4233-8631-5(0), 9781423386315, Brlnc Audio MP3 Lib); 39.97 (978-1-4233-8633-9(7), 9781423386339, BADLE); 24.99 (978-1-4233-8630-8(2), 9781423386308, Brilliance MP3); 24.99 (978-1-4233-8632-2(9), 9781423386322, BAD) Brilliance Audio.

Jennie Vol. 1: The Life of Lady Randolph Churchill. unabr. collector's ed. Ralph G. Martin. Read by Dick Estell. 9 cass. (Running Time: 13 hrs. 30 mins.). 1991. 72.00 (978-0-7366-1892-2(9), 2719) Books on Tape.
If she had simply been the mother of Winston Churchill, her place in history would have been assured. But the Brooklyn-born Jennie was also the most fascinating & desirable woman of her age, the toast & the scandal of two continents throughout her long life. Volume I, The Romantic Years, follows Jennie as she leaves her wealthy American home to marry Lord Randolph Churchill. Lord Randolph was a rising young politician whom she helped shape into one of the most important men in the British Empire. His career was cut short by his early death in 1895 at age 46. Volume II, The Dramatic Years, tells the second half of her life with its many love affairs, two later marriages & numerous business ventures. Through it all she remained if not a devoted mother, then one who encouraged the aspirations of her two sons, one of whom was destined to greatness.

Jennie Vol. 2: The Life of Lady Randolph Churchill. unabr. collector's ed. Ralph G. Martin. Read by Dick Estell. 10 cass. (Running Time: 15 hrs.). 1991. 80.00 (978-0-7366-1893-9(7), 2720) Books on Tape.

Jennie Gerhardt. Theodore Dreiser. Read by Anais 9000. 2008. 27.95 (978-1-60112-194-3(6)) Babblebooks.

Jennifer, Hecate, MacBeth, William McKinley, & Me, Elizabeth. unabr. ed. E. L. Konigsburg. Read by Carol Stewart. 2 cass. (Running Time: 3 hrs.). (J). (gr. 1-8). 1999. 23.00 (LL 0129, Chivers Child Audio) AudioGO.

Jennifer, Hecate, MacBeth, William McKinley, & Me, Elizabeth. unabr. ed. E. L. Konigsburg. 1 read-along cass. (Running Time: 83 min.). (Children's Cliffhangers Ser.). (J). (gr. 3-6). 1986. 15.98 incl. bk. & guide. (978-0-8072-1144-1(3), SWR49SP, Listening Lib) Random Audio Pubg.
When Elizabeth moves to a new town, she never expects to meet Jennifer, a real witch. Their friendship grows with their shared craft & spells, until they argue over a special flying potion.

Jennifer, Hecate, MacBeth, William McKinley, & Me, Elizabeth. unabr. ed. E. L. Konigsburg. Read by Carol Jordan Stewart. 2 vols. (Running Time: 2 hrs. 32 mins.). (J). (gr. 4-7). 1998. pap. bk. 29.00 (978-0-8072-8001-0(1), YA963SP, Listening Lib); 19.55 (978-0-8072-8000-3(3), YA963CX, Listening Lib) Pub: Random Audio Pubg. Dist(s): NetLibrary CO
Being the new kid in town isn't easy for ten-year-old Elizabeth until she meets Jennifer - an honest to goodness witch.

Jennifer, Hecate, MacBeth, William McKinley, & Me, Elizabeth. unabr. ed. E. L. Konigsburg. Read by Carol Jordan Stewart. (J). (gr. 3). 2008. audio compact disk 14.99 (978-0-7393-5016-4(1), Listening Lib) Pub: Random Audio Pubg. Dist(s): Random

Jennifer, Hecate, MacBeth, William McKinley, & Me, Elizabeth, Set. unabr. ed. E. L. Konigsburg. Read by Carol Stewart. 2 cass. (YA). 1999. 16.98 (FS9-43239) Highsmith.

Jennifer Murdley's Toad. Bruce Coville. Perf. by Bruce Coville. 2 cass. (Running Time: 2 hrs. 45 mins.). (Magic Shop Bks.). (J). 2000. 18.00 (978-0-7366-9089-8(1)) Books on Tape.
Jennifer Murdley has just stumbled into Mr. Elives' Magic Shop, where she buys a toad named Bufo. Of course, the odds of buying a normal toad in that shop are zero, as Jennifer finds out when Bufo starts to talk.

Jennifer Murdley's Toad. unabr. ed. Bruce Coville. Read by Bruce Coville. Read by Words Take Wing Repertory Company Staff. 2 vols. (Running Time: 2 hrs. 52 mins.). Dramatization. (Magic Shop Bks.). (J). (gr. 3-6). 1996. pap. bk. 29.00 (978-0-8072-7604-4(9), YA895SP, Listening Lib) Random Audio Pubg.
How do you handle a talking toad you bought from a magic shop. Jennifer is in for some very strange surprises from her new amphibian friend.

Jennifer Murdley's Toad. unabr. ed. Bruce Coville. Read by Bruce Coville. Read by Words Take Wing Repertory Company Staff. 2 cass. (Running Time: 2 hrs. 52 mins.). Dramatization. (Magic Shop Bks.). (J). (gr. 3-6). 1996. 23.00 (978-0-8072-7603-7(0), YA895CX, Listening Lib) Random Audio Pubg.

Jennifer Murdley's Toad, Set. unabr. ed. Bruce Coville. 2 cass. (Magic Shop Bks.). (YA). 1999. 16.98 (FS9-26776) Highsmith.

Jennifer Tapes, Vol. 1. Barrie Konicov & Cynthia P. Oullette. 4 cass. (Running Time: 1 hr. 29 min. per cass.). (J). 1989. 11.98 (978-0-87082-925-3(4)) Potentials.

Jennifer Tapes, Vol. 2. Barrie Konicov. 1 cass. (J). 1989. 11.98 (978-0-87082-926-0(2)) Potentials.

Jennifer Tapes, Vol. 3. Barrie Konicov. 1 cass. (J). 1989. 11.98 (978-0-87082-927-7(0)) Potentials.

Jennifer Tapes, Vol. 4. Barrie Konicov. 1 cass. (J). 1989. 11.98 (978-0-87082-928-4(9)) Potentials.

Jennifer's Ingenuity & Santa Will Never Find Orlando's House. Howard W. Gabriel, III. (J). (gr. k-8). 1987. 2.95 (978-0-936997-06-3(0), T87-04) M & H Enter.
In the First Story, a Stubborn Old Man Meets More Than His Match in the Love & Determination of This Youngster. In the Second Story, Lucky Larry Almost Loses Everything in His Daring Effort to Help His New Friends.

Jenny & the Cornstalk: Early Fluency Stage 3. Created by Steck-Vaughn Staff. (Running Time: 1207 sec.). (Pair-It Bks.). (J). (gr. 2). 1997. (978-0-8172-7377-4(8)) SteckVau.

Jenny Gets Glasses. unabr. ed. Roni S. Denholtz. 1 cass. (Running Time: 7 min.). (Read It Alone Ser.). (J). (ps-3). 1985. 16.99 incl. hardcover. (978-0-87386-005-5(5)) Jan Prods.
Jenny goes to the eye doctor & finds out she needs glasses. But she keeps forgetting to wear them. Her sister helps out.

Jenny Giraffe Discovers the French Quarter/Jenny Giraffe's Mardi Gras Ride. Narrated by Cecilia Dartez. 1 cass. (Running Time: 24 hrs. NaN mins.). (Jenny Giraffe Ser.). (ENG.). (J). (ps-3). 1997. 9.95 (978-1-56554-264-8(9)) Pelican.

***Jenny Giraffe Discovers the French Quarter/Jenny Giraffe's Mardi Gras Ride CD.** Cecilia Dartez. Narrated by Cecilia Dartez. (Running Time: 24 hrs. NaN mins.). (ENG.). (J). 2010. audio compact disk 15.95 (978-1-58980-803-4(7)) Pelican.

Jenny McCarthy's Uncensored Hollywood Diary. abr. ed. Jenny McCarthy. Read by Jenny McCarthy. 2 cass. (Running Time: 3 hrs.). 1997. 18.00 (978-0-694-51867-8(0)) HarperCollins Pubs.

Jenny Wren. Dawn L. Watkins. 1 cass. (J). 1990. 10.75 (978-0-00-140625-4(6)) BJUPr.

Jenny Wren. Dawn L. Watkins. 2 cass. (J). (gr. 3-7). 2000. pap. bk. 14.98 (978-0-89084-909-5(9), 100065) BJUPr.

Jenny Wren. abr. ed. Dawn L. Watkins. 2 cass. (Running Time: 2 hrs. 25 mins.). (J). (gr. 3-7). 1990. 10.95 (978-0-89084-908-8(0), 045930) BJUPr.

Jenny Wren. unabr. ed. E. H. Young. Narrated by Flo Gibson. 7 cass. (Running Time: 10 hrs. 30 mins.). 2003. 25.95 (978-1-55685-723-2(3)) Audio Bk Con.
Lovely, lively young Jenny learns about life and love in this charming bucolic tale.

Jenny's Adopted Brothers. (J). (CDL5 1608) HarperCollins Pubs.

Jenny's Birthday Book see Cumpleanos de Minina Timida

Jenny's Birthday Book. 2004. 8.95 (978-1-56008-938-4(5)); cass. & flmstrp 30.00 (978-1-56008-695-6(5)) Weston Woods.

Jenny's Corner. unabr. ed. Frederic Bell. Narrated by Alyss Bresnahan. 1 cass. (Running Time: 1 hr. 25 min.). (J). (gr. 1). 1996. 10.00 (94815) Recorded Bks.

Jenny's Corner. unabr. ed. Frederic Bell. Narrated by Alyssa Bresnahan. 1 cass. (Running Time: 1 hr. 15 mins.). (gr. 1 up). 1996. 10.00 (978-0-7887-0610-3(1), 94815E7) Recorded Bks.
One girl's struggle to save the deer who live in the woods near her home from the guns of the local hunters.

Jenny's First Party. (J). (CDL5 1577) HarperCollins Pubs.

Jentezen Franklin Presents Moving Foward. Contrib. by Free Chapel. Told to Ricardo Sanchez. 2007. audio compact disk 13.99 (978-5-557-72183-7(5)) Integrity Music.

Jeopardy. unabr. ed. Sarah Lacey. Read by Tessa Gallagher. 5 cass. (Running Time: 6 hrs. 35 min.). 63.95 (978-1-85903-173-5(0)) Pub: Magna Story GBR. Dist(s): Ulverscroft US
Determined to find her friend who has disappeared, tax inspector Leah Hunter is led down a dangerous trail of drugs & blackmail where her own life is in jeopardy.

***Jeopardy Room.** 2010. audio compact disk (978-1-59171-237-4(8)) Falcon Picture.

Jeremiah Commentary: Verse-by-Verse with Chuck Missler. Chuck Missler. 1 MP CD-ROM. (Running Time: 20 hrs.). 2000. cd-rom 44.95 (978-1-57821-128-9(X)) Koinonia Hse.
Here is one of the bravest, most tender, yet most pathetic figures in all history: a patriot as well as a prophet. He is known as the "Weeping Prophet" as he watched his nation decline and finally fall under God's judgment. During Jeremiah's 40 years of ministry, he never received a hint of gratitude. As one of the most important of the "Major Prophets," Jeremiah is a rich, rewarding study. It is full of surprises, deeply touching episodes and extremely moving reading. It is also, in many ways, profoundly timely for us today!.

Jeremiah in the Dark Woods. unabr. ed. Allan Ahlberg. Read by Johnny Morris. 1 cass. (Running Time: 1 hr.). (J). (gr. 1-8). 1995. 9.95 (978-1-85549-236-3(9), CTC 073, Chivers Child Audio) AudioGO.

Jeremiah Was a Bullfrog! (Running Time: 60 min.). 10.98; audio compact disk 10.98 CD. Creat Teach Pr.
Kids & parents will be singing along with this lighthearted recording.

Jeremiah Was a Bullfrog! Perf. by Hoyt Axton. 1 cass. (J). (ps-4). 1995. 10.98 (978-0-945267-10-2(X), YM041-CN); audio compact disk 13.98 (978-0-945267-08-9(8), YM041-CD) Youngheart Mus.
Songs include: "Joy to the World"; "Oh! Susanah"; "Don't Push Me down"; "I Had a Rooster"; "Goin' to the Zoo"; "On Top of Spaghetti"; "It's a Small World"; "Straighten up & Fly Right"; "Pet Parade"; "Big Rock Candy Mountain" & more.

Jeremy: The Tale of an Honest Bunny. Jan Karon. Narrated by John McDonough. (Running Time: 1 hr. 15 mins.). (gr. 2 up). audio compact disk 20.00 (978-1-4025-1485-2(9)) Recorded Bks.

Jeremy: The Tale of an Honest Bunny. unabr. ed. Jan Karon. Narrated by John McDonough. 1 cass. (Running Time: 1 hr. 15 mins.). (gr. 2 up). 2002. 14.00 (978-1-4025-0786-1(0)) Recorded Bks.
Putting the finishing touches on her latest creation, Lydia sews the last silver button on the handsome blue suitcoat and gives the little bunny a name - Jeremy. Then he comes to life! As much as she would love to keep him, she has promised him to a little girl in America named Candace. During his journey to his new home, Jeremy draws strength from the note Lydia tucked in his pocket. It is a Bible verse: "He will give his angels charge over you, to keep you in all your ways.".

Jeremy - a Christmas Story. Jay O'Callahan. Perf. by Jay O'Callahan. 1 cass. (Running Time: 49 min.). (J). (gr. 1 up). 1991. 10.00 (978-1-877954-21-4(7)) Pub: Artana Prodns. Dist(s): Yellow Moon
A mischievous boy dreams of carving beautiful wooden presents for everyone in the world. He finally gets his wish, but in a way that is surprisingly bigger & better than he imagined.

Jeremy, A Christmas Story. Jay O'Callahan. Perf. by Jay O'Callahan. 1 CD. (Running Time: 48 min 40 sec). Dramatization. (YA). 2005. audio compact disk 15.00 (978-1-877954-51-1(9)) Artana Prodns.
Jeremy had a twinkle in his eye: it came from his dream of making toys and giving them to children. As he grew older, Jeremy thought more about how he could make money from selling the toys than of the joy of giving them away, and his twinkle disappeared. Would he ever get it back? Also, on the CD, Christmas Candles, a Pill Hill Story.

Jeremy Brown: Secret Agent. Simon Cheshire. 3 CDs. (Running Time: 10800 sec.). (J). 2005. audio compact disk 29.95 (978-0-7540-6698-9(3)) AudioGo GBR.

Jeremy Davenport. 1 cass., 1 CD. 7.98 (TA 33376); audio compact disk 12.78 CD. (TA 83376) NewSound.

Jeremy Fink & the Meaning of Life. unabr. ed. Wendy Mass. Read by Andy Paris. 8 CDs. (Running Time: 9 hrs. 25 mins.). (J). (gr. 5-7). 2007. audio compact disk 87.75 (978-1-4281-3402-7(6)) Recorded Bks.

Jeremy Poldark. unabr. ed. Winston Graham. Read by Tony Britton. 8 cass. (Running Time: 8 hrs.). (Poldark Ser.: Vol. 3). 1996. 69.95 (978-0-7451-6612-4(1), CAB1228) AudioGO.
Ross Poldark has been charged with plundering two ships. And against his wishes, Ross's wife Demelza attends the trial, knowing that he could face the death sentence. Meanwhile, the elopement of Verity Poldark has caused her brother Francis to quarrel with his cousin, Ross, who he holds responsible. And because of this quarrel, Ross believes Francis has betrayed his business plans to the Warleggans, a family of bankers who are quickly gaining control of the commercial life in Cornwall.

Jeremy Poldark. unabr. ed. Winston Graham. Read by Tony Britton. 8 cass. (Running Time: 12 hrs.). (Poldark Ser.: Bk. 3). 2000. 59.95 (CAB 1228) Pub: Chivers Audio Bks GBR. Dist(s): AudioGO
Ross Poldark is charged with plundering two ships. His wife Demelza attends the trial, knowing that he could face the death sentence. Meanwhile, the elopement of Verity Poldark causes her brother Francis to quarrel with Ross, who he holds responsible. And because of this quarrel, Ross believes Francis has betrayed his business plans in favor of the Warleggans, a family of bankers who are quickly gaining control of the commercial life in Cornwell.

Jeremy Thatcher, Dragon Hatcher. Bruce Coville. Perf. by Bruce Coville. 2 cass. (Running Time: 1 hrs. 40 mins.). (Magic Shop Bks.). (J). 2000. 18.00 (978-0-7366-9090-4(5)) Books on Tape.
Young Jeremy Thatcher buys a mysterious, shining ball at a magic shop that turns out to be a dragon's egg. Jeremy takes the responsibility of hatching the egg & caring for the baby dragon.

Jeremy Thatcher, Dragon Hatcher. unabr. ed. Bruce Coville. Read by Bruce Coville. Read by Words Take Wing Repertory Company Staff. 2 vols. (Running Time: 2 hrs. 40 mins.). Dramatization. (Magic Shop Bks.). (J). (gr. 3-6). 1995. pap. bk. 29.00 (978-0-8072-7532-0(8), YA873SP, Listening Lib); 23.00 (978-0-8072-7531-3(X), YA873CX, Listening Lib) Random Audio Pubg.
When Jeremy Thatcher follows the strange instructions given to him by the weird old man who runs Elives' Magic Shop, he finds himself raising a tiny, mischief-loving dragon named Taimat. But as Jeremy soon learns even a tiny dragon can mean big trouble.

Jeremy Thatcher, Dragon Hatcher, Set. unabr. ed. Bruce Coville. 2 cass. (Magic Shop Bks.). (YA). 1999. 16.98 (FS9-26777) Highsmith.

Jericho Files. unabr. ed. Alan Gold. Read by Stanley McGeagh. 13 cass. (Running Time: 19 hrs.). 2004. 104.00 (978-1-876584-72-6(6), 591106) Pub: Bolinda Pubng AUS. Dist(s): Lndmrk Audiobks
One small, yellowed photograph of a man on horseback. Old files from Stalin's time, molding in the Kremlin archives. An Israeli Prime Minister who seems determined to throw his people into further war. A trail of murder & terrorism across Australia, the Middle East & Europe. Whoever holds the photograph holds the key to unlock many secrets.

Jericho Point. unabr. ed. Meg Gardiner. Read by Tanya Eby Sirois. (Running Time: 10 hrs.). (Evan Delaney Ser.). 2008. 39.25 (978-1-4233-6134-3(2), 9781423361343, Brlnc Audio MP3 Lib); 39.25 (978-1-4233-6136-7(9), 9781423361367, BADLE); 24.95 (978-1-4233-6133-6(4), 9781423361336, Brilliance MP3); 24.95 (978-1-4233-6135-0(0), 9781423361350, BAD);

audio compact disk 97.25 (978-1-4233-6132-9(6), 9781423361329, BriAudCD Unabrid); audio compact disk 36.95 (978-1-4233-6131-2(8), 9781423361312, Bril Audio CD Unabri) Brilliance Audio.

Jericho Sanction: A Novel. abr. ed. Oliver North & Joe Musser. 8 CDs. (Running Time: 6 hrs.). 2003. audio compact disk 29.99 (978-0-8054-3033-2(4)) BH Pubng Grp.
Oliver North follows his New York Times bestselling novel, Mission Compromised, with a suspenseful, action-packed sequel set in Israel and Iraq.

Jericho Years, unabr. ed. Aileen Armitage. Read by Anne Dover. 10 cass. (Running Time: 13 hrs. 30 min.). (Isis Ser.). (J). 1997. 84.95 (978-0-7531-0261-9(7), 970711) Pub: ISIS Lrg Prnt GBR. Dist(s): Ulverscroft US
Widower James Hemingway is thinking of breaking with tradition & selling Jericho Farm, the Family home, high in the Pennines. Then David, this beloved & only son, is struck by a fatal illness, & returns to Jericho, with Lisa, the girl he wants to marry. As the family copes with fresh tragedy & begins to weld together once more, an entirely unexpected & unconventional relationship explodes into their lives, one that offers hope to James, to Lisa & to Jericho Farm.

Jerome Camps Out. unabr. ed. Eileen Christelow. Narrated by Johnny Heller. 1 cass. (Running Time: 15 mins.). (gr. k up). 1998. 10.00 (978-0-7887-3205-8(6), 95764E7) Recorded Bks.
Jerome Alligator is going on a camping trip with the Swamp School. But, he must share a tent with the class bully. This is turning out to be his worst weekend ever! When Jerome comes up with a clever solution to his problem, the result surprises everyone.

Jerome Camps Out. unabr. ed. Eileen Christelow. Read by Johnny Heller. 1 cass. (Running Time: 15 min.). (J). (gr. 2). 1999. 178.30 CLASS SET . (978-0-7887-3216-4(1), 46872) Recorded Bks.
Jerome Alligator is going on a camping trip with the Swamp School. But he must share a tent with the class bully. When Jerome comes up with a clever solution, the result surprises everyone.

Jerome Camps Out. unabr. ed. Eileen Christelow. Narrated by Johnny Heller. 1 cass. (Running Time: 15 min.). (J). 2000. pap. bk. 33.00 (40905X4) Recorded Bks.

Jerome Charyn. Interview. Interview with Jerome Charyn & Kay Bonetti. 1 cass. (Running Time: 59 min.). 13.95 (978-1-55644-004-5(9), 1022) Am Audio Prose.
Discussion of Charyn's novels about Isaac Sidel & the author's use of street language & pop culture in his fiction.

Jerome Rothenberg. unabr. ed. Read by Jerome Rothenberg. 1 cass. (Running Time: 29 min.). 1985. 10.00 New Letters.
Jerome Rothenberg believes in "poetry as performance" & includes chanting with Seneca Indian horn rattles.

Jeronimo's House see Twentieth-Century Poetry in English, No. 9, Recordings of Poets Reading Their Own Poetry

Jerry & the Jannans. unabr. ed. Elly Brewer. Read by Glen McCready. 8 CDs. (Running Time: 8 hrs. 10 mins.). (YA). (gr. 5-8). 2007. audio compact disk 69.95 (978-1-4056-5716-7(2), Chivers Child Audio) AudioGO.

Jerry Epstein: Time Has Made a Change in Me. 1 cass., 1 CD. 9.98 (C-607); audio compact disk 14.98 CD. (CD-607) Folk-Legacy.
Folksongs from various sources, well sung.

Jerry Falwell's: God Save America. Perf. by Jerry Falwell et al. 1 cass., 1 CD. 1998. 10.98 (978-0-7601-2307-2(1)); audio compact disk 15.98 CD. (978-0-7601-2308-9(X)) Provident Mus Dist.

Jerry Hendrick's Essential Twelve-Bar Blues. Contrib. by Jerry Hendricks. 1994. bk. 14.95 (978-0-7119-3455-9(X), AM91211) Omnibus NY.

Jerry Peyton's Notched Inheritance. unabr. collector's ed. Max Brand. Read by Jonathan Marosz. 5 cass. (Running Time: 5 hrs.). 1994. 30.00 (978-0-7366-2683-5(2), 3419) Books on Tape.
Horse thief steals a rancher's gun, unleashing a surprising chain of events.

Jerry Rasmussen: Get Down Home. 1 cass. 9.98 (C-77) Folk-Legacy.
Fine singer & songmaker from Janesville, Wisconsin.

Jerry Rasmussen: The Secret Life of Jerry Rasmussen. 1 cass. 9.98 (C-101) Folk-Legacy.
Jerry's second Folk-Legacy recording.

Jerry Rasmusssen: Handful of Songs. 1 cass. 9.98 (C-516) Folk-Legacy.
More excellent songs by this Wisconsin songmaker.

Jerry Robinson. (Running Time: 40 min.). (From the Source Ser.). 1987. 9.95 (978-0-944831-12-0(5)) Health Life.

Jerry Snyder's Guitar School, Method Book, Bk 1, Bk. 1. Jerry Snyder. 1 CD. (ENG.). 1998. audio compact disk 9.00 (978-0-7390-0815-7(3), 17881) Alfred Pub.

Jerusalem see Poetry of William Blake

Jerusalem. Contrib. by Bill & Gloria Gaither and Their Homecoming Friends. (Gaither Gospel (Video) Ser.). (ENG.). 2005. 19.98 (978-5-559-20597-7(4)) Gaither Music Co.

Jerusalem: One City, Three Faiths. abr. ed. Karen Armstrong. Read by Karen Armstrong. 2004. audio compact disk 29.95 (978-0-06-059186-1(2)) HarperCollins Pubs.

Jerusalem - The Lord's City. Richard Hebertson & Barbara Hebertson. 1 cass. 7.98 (978-1-55503-863-2(8), 06005098) Covenant Comms.
Memories & impressions of the Holy City.

Jerusalem Countdown. John Hagee. Read by Eric Martin. (ENG.). 2007. audio compact disk 29.99 (978-1-930034-74-7(1)) Casscomm.

Jerusalem Creek: Journeys into Driftless Country. abr. ed. Ted Leeson. Read by Lloyd James. (Running Time: 16200 sec.). 2005. audio compact disk 28.00 (978-1-932378-73-3(1)) Pub: A Media Intl. Dist(s): Natl Bk Netwk

Jerusalem Diet. abr. ed. Ted Haggard. Read by Ted Haggard. Frwd. by Larry Gee. (Running Time: 12600 sec.). 2005. audio compact disk 19.99 (978-1-59859-115-6(0)) Oasis Audio.

Jerusalem in Herod's Day. 10.00 (RME106) Esstee Audios.

Jerusalem Interlude. abr. ed. Bodie Thoene & Brock Thoene. Read by Aimee Lilly. 4 cass. (Running Time: 6 hrs.). (Zion Covenant Ser.: Bk. 4). 2001. 22.99 (978-1-58926-018-4(X)) Oasis Audio.
In Jerusalem Interlude Leah and Shimon Feldstein, two Jews in prewar Europe, face the terrigying truth that they must either escape of perish. When the two finally do reach the Promised Land, they find a long, sinister shadow casting its darkness over the Holy Land. Will they ever find true peace? Will their time in Jerusalem be merely a brief interlude in their ongoing struggle for a homeland?.

Jerusalem Interlude. unabr. ed. Bodie Thoene & Brock Thoene. Read by Susan O'Malley. 12 cass. (Running Time: 17 hrs. 30 mins.). (Zion Covenant Ser.: Bk. 4). 2002. 83.95 (978-0-7861-2195-3(5), 2942); audio compact disk 120.00 (978-0-7861-9534-3(7), 2942) Blckstn Audio.
Leah and Shimon Feldstein finally reach the Promised Land. They enter their new life under the shadow of the Western Wall, only to find that a longer, more sinister shadow is casting its darkness over the Holy Land. Will they ever find true peace, a resting place for their spirits? Or will their time in Jerusalem be only a brief interlude in the ongoing struggle for a homeland?.

Jerusalem, Shining Still. unabr. ed. Karla Kuskin. Perf. by Theodore Bikel. 1 cass. (Running Time: 39 min.). (J). (ps-3). 1987. 11.00 (978-0-89845-775-9(0), HarperChildAud) HarperCollins Pubs.
A retelling of Jerusalem's 4,000-year history, revealing its majesty & importance...from the story of David to its present.

Jerusalem Vigil. Bodie Thoene & Brock Thoene. Narrated by Edward Petherbridge. 11 CDs. (Running Time: 12 hrs. 30 mins.). (Zion Legacy Ser.: Bk. 1). audio compact disk 111.00 (978-1-4025-1534-7(0)) Recorded Bks.

Jerusalem Vigil. unabr. ed. Bodie Thoene & Brock Thoene. Narrated by Edward Petherbridge. 9 cass. (Running Time: 12 hrs. 30 mins.). (Zion Legacy Ser.: Bk. 1). 2001. 82.00 (978-0-7887-4632-1(4)) Recorded Bks.

Jerusalem 1913: The Origins of the Arab-Israeli Conflict. unabr. ed. Amy Dockser Marcus. (Running Time: 7 hrs. 0 mins. 0 sec.). (ENG.). 2007. audio compact disk 29.99 (978-1-4001-0361-4(4)) Pub: Tantor Media. Dist(s): IngramPubServ

Jerusalem 1913: The Origins of the Arab-Israeli Conflict. unabr. ed. Amy Dockser Marcus. (Running Time: 7 hrs. 0 mins. 0 sec.). (ENG.). 2007. audio compact disk 19.99 (978-1-4001-5361-9(1)); audio compact disk 59.99 (978-1-4001-3361-1(0)) Pub: Tantor Media. Dist(s): IngramPubServ

Jerusalem's Heart: A Novel of the Struggle for Jerusalem. unabr. ed. Bodie Thoene & Brock Thoene. Narrated by Paul Hecht. 10 cass. (Running Time: 14 hrs.). (Zion Legacy Ser.: Bk. 3). 2002. 89.75 (978-1-4025-4426-2(X), K0076MC, Griot Aud) Recorded Bks.

Jervell & Lange-Nielsen Syndrome - A Bibliography & Dictionary for Physicians, Patients, & Genome Researchers. Compiled by Icon Group International, Inc. Staff. 2007. ring bd. 28.95 (978-0-497-11245-5(0)) Icon Grp.

***Jess-Belle.** (ENG.). 2010. audio compact disk (978-1-59171-275-6(0)) Falcon Picture.

Jesse. Gary Soto. Narrated by Robert Ramirez. 4 CDs. (Running Time: 4 hrs. 15 mins.). (gr. 10 up). audio compact disk 42.00 (978-1-4025-2309-0(2)) Recorded Bks.

Jesse, unabr. ed. Gary Soto. Narrated by Robert Ramirez. 3 pieces. (Running Time: 4 hrs. 15 mins.). (gr. 10 up). 2000. 29.00 (978-0-7887-3166-2(1), 95839E7) Recorded Bks.
Jesse & his brother are working as fieldhands to pay for their community college courses. But the path to a good education isn't going to be an easy one for these two young Mexican-Americans. Filled with wry humor & realism, reflecting Soto's own experiences growing up in California. Includes study guide.

Jesse, unabr. ed. Gary Soto. Read by Robert Ramirez. 3 cass. (Running Time: 4 hrs. 15 mins.). (YA). 2000. pap. bk. 42.24 (978-0-7887-3188-4(2), 40923X4) Recorded Bks.

Jesse, Class set. unabr. ed. Gary Soto. Read by Robert Ramirez. 3 cass. (Running Time: 4 hrs. 15 mins.). (YA). (gr. 10 up). 1999. 99.70 (978-0-7887-3234-8(X), 46890) Recorded Bks.

Jesse: A Lesson in Dealing with Your Anger & Other Troublesome Feelings. unabr. ed. Julian Padowicz. (Running Time: 45 min.). (YA). (gr. 4-12). 1998. (978-1-881288-18-3(8), BFI AudioBooks) BusnFilm Intl.
Teenager gets into difficulty by mishandling his anger towards a classmate - learns that we are not responsible for what we feel, but for how we act out feelings.

Jesse Bear, What Will You Wear? unabr. ed. Nancy White Carlstrom. Narrated by John McDonough. 1 cass. (Running Time: 15 mins.). (ps up). 1998. 10.00 (978-0-7887-1951-6(3), 95349E7) Recorded Bks.
What does a little bear wear as he dances & plays his way through a sunny summer day? Pants that dance, sun on his legs that run, rice in his hair from lunch & bear hugs & kisses at bedtime.

Jesse James & the James-Younger Gang. Dave Southworth. 2 cass/. (Running Time: 1 hr. 25 min.). (Library of Concise Audio Histories). 13.95 Set. (978-1-890778-08-8(7)) Wld Horse Pub.

***Jesse Stone #10.** unabr. ed. Robert B. Parker. (ENG.). 2011. audio compact disk 32.00 (978-0-7393-8489-3(9), Random AudioBks) Pub: Random Audio Pubg. Dist(s): Random

Jesse Ventura. Keith Elliot Greenberg. Read by Doug Ordunio. 1 cass. (Running Time: 1 hr. 30 min.). 2000. 9.95 (978-0-7366-4711-3(2)) Books on Tape.
On November 3, 1998, the state of Minnesota elected former professional wrestler Jesse "The Body" Ventura as its governor. The only Reform Party candidate ever elected to a major office, his election shocked the country & even the world.

Jesse Ventura. collector's ed. Keith Elliot Greenberg. Read by Doug Ordunio. 2 cass. (Running Time: 3 hrs.). 2000. 12.95 (978-0-7366-5224-7(8)) Books on Tape.

Jesse Ventura. unabr. ed. Keith Elliot Greenberg. Read by Doug Ordunio. 2 CDs. (Running Time: 3 hrs.). (Biography Ser.). (YA). 2000. audio compact disk 24.00 (5230-CD) Books on Tape.

Jesse Ventura. unabr. collector's ed. Keith Elliot Greenberg. Read by Doug Ordunio. 1 cass. (Running Time: 90 mins.). (Biography Ser.). (YA). (gr. 5-12). 2000. 9.95 (978-0-7366-5035-9(0), 5230) Books on Tape.

Jessica. Bryce Courtenay. Read by Humphrey Bower. (Running Time: 19 hrs.). 2009. 114.99 (978-1-74214-204-3(4), 9781742142043) Pub: Bolinda Pubng AUS. Dist(s): Bolinda Pub Inc

Jessica. unabr. ed. Bryce Courtenay. Narrated by Humphrey Bower. 10 cass. (Running Time: 19 hrs.). 2001. 80.00 (978-1-74030-441-2(1)) Pub: Bolinda Pubng AUS. Dist(s): Bolinda Pub Inc

Jessica. unabr. ed. Bryce Courtenay. Read by Humphrey Bower. (Running Time: 68400 sec.). 2007. audio compact disk 54.95 (978-1-921334-33-7(9), 9781921334337) Pub: Bolinda Pubng AUS. Dist(s): Bolinda Pub Inc

Jessica. unabr. ed. Bryce Courtenay. Read by Humphrey Bower. (Running Time: 19 hrs.). 2008. audio compact disk 123.95 (978-1-74214-021-6(1), 9781742140216) Pub: Bolinda Pubng AUS. Dist(s): Bolinda Pub Inc

Jessica Hagedorn. Jessica Hagedorn. Read by Jessica Hagedorn. 1 cass. (Running Time: 68 min.). 1995. 13.95 (978-1-55644-404-3(4), 14031) Am Audio Prose.
Author reads Prose & Poetry from her works, Dogeaters & Danger & Beauty.

Jessica Powers: Landscapes of the Sacred. Robert F. Morneau. 1 cass. (Running Time: 52 min.). 1991. 7.95 (TAH257) Alba Hse Comns.
The Bishop speaks about the importance of having a companion on life's journey & one of his is Jessica. The voice of the spirit, he remarks, must find its expression & as St. John of the Cross showed, poetry is ideal for this.

Jessica's Girl. unabr. ed. Josephine Cox. Read by Maggie Ollerenshaw. 12 cass. (Running Time: 12 hrs.). 1993. 96.95 (978-0-7451-4207-4(9), CAB 890) AudioGO.
On her deathbed, Jessica Mulligan warned her daughter, Phoebe, to stay away from her uncle. Phoebe goes to his house, however, where she is banished to a bare attic & treated with malice. What is the dark secret that causes him to mistreat her this way?.

***Jessica's Guide to Dating on the Dark Side.** unabr. ed. Beth Fantaskey. Narrated by Katherine Kellgren & Jeff Woodman. 1 Playaway. (Running Time: 11 hrs.). (YA). (gr. 7 up). 2009. 64.75 (978-1-4407-3898-2(X)); 67.75 (978-1-4407-3888-3(2)); audio compact disk 97.75 (978-1-4407-3892-0(0)) Recorded Bks.

***Jessica's Guide to Dating on the Dark Side.** unabr. collector's ed. Beth Fantaskey. Narrated by Katherine Kellgren & Jeff Woodman. 9 CDs. (Running Time: 11 hrs.). (YA). (gr. 7 up). 2009. audio compact disk 51.95 (978-1-4407-3896-8(3)) Recorded Bks.

Jessie. unabr. ed. Lori Wick. Narrated by Jill Shellabarger. (Running Time: 8 hrs. 22 mins. 9 sec.). (Big Sky Dreams Ser.). (ENG.). 2008. 19.59 (978-1-60814-261-3(2)); audio compact disk 27.99 (978-1-59859-430-0(3)) Oasis Audio.

Jessie Bear, What Will You Wear? unabr. ed. Nancy White Carlstrom. Read by John McDonough. 1 cass. (Running Time: 15 min.). (J). (gr. 2). 1998. 79.00 CLASS SET . (978-0-7887-3579-0(9), 46285); 23.20 HMWK SET . (978-0-7887-1950-9(5), 40657) Recorded Bks.
What does a little bear wear as he dances & plays his way through a summer day?.

Jest & Die. Stella Whitelaw. 2009. 54.95 (978-1-84559-617-0(X)) Pub: Soundings Ltd GBR. Dist(s): Ulverscroft US

Jester. abr. ed. James Patterson. (ENG.). 2005. 14.98 (978-1-59483-277-2(3)) Pub: Hachet Audio. Dist(s): HachBkGrp

Jester. unabr. ed. James Patterson & Andrew Gross. Read by Neil Dickson. (ENG.). 2005. 16.98 (978-1-59483-278-9(1)) Pub: Hachet Audio. Dist(s): HachBkGrp

Jester. unabr. ed. James Patterson & Andrew Gross. Read by Neil Dickson. (Running Time: 13 hrs.). (ENG.). 2009. 79.98 (978-1-60024-957-0(4)) Pub: Hachet Audio. Dist(s): HachBkGrp

Jesucristo Es el Mismo. (SPA.). (J). 2009. audio compact disk 12.99 (978-1-933172-53-8(3)) Jayah Producc.

Jesucristo Es Vida. unabr. ed. Nelson Ned. (SPA.). 2001. 9.99 (978-0-8297-3464-5(3)) Pub: Vida Pubs. Dist(s): Zondervan

Jesuit & the Skull. PH.D., Amir D Aczel. Read by Barrett Whitener. (Playaway Adult Nonfiction Ser.). (ENG.). 2008. 64.99 (978-1-60640-999-2(9)) Find a World.

Jesuit & the Skull. unabr. ed. Aczel Aczel. (Running Time: 8 hrs. 0 mins. 0 sec.). (ENG.). 2007. audio compact disk 34.99 (978-1-4001-0491-8(2)) Pub: Tantor Media. Dist(s): IngramPubServ

Jesuit & the Skull: Teilhard de Chardin, Evolution, & the Search for Peking Man. unabr. ed. Amir D. Aczel. Read by Barrett Whitener. (Running Time: 8 hrs. 0 mins. 0 sec.). (ENG.). 2007. audio compact disk 24.99 (978-1-4001-5491-3(X)); audio compact disk 69.99 (978-1-4001-3491-5(9)) Pub: Tantor Media. Dist(s): IngramPubServ

Jesus. abr. ed. James Bell. Narrated by Chris Fabry. (Complete Idiot's Guides). (ENG.). 2004. audio compact disk 27.99 (978-1-58926-837-1(7), 6837) Oasis Audio.

Jesus. abr. ed. James Bell. 2005. 25.99 (978-1-58926-836-4(9), 6836) Pub: Oasis Audio. Dist(s): TNT Media Grp

Jesus: A Life. unabr. collector's ed. A. N. Wilson. Read by David Case. 8 cass. (Running Time: 12 hrs.). 1993. 64.00 (978-0-7366-2580-7(1), 3327) Books on Tape.
An unconventional examination of the historical reality of Jesus. Warning: the author is an ex-Christian.

Jesus: A Meditation on His Stories & His Relationships with Women. unabr. ed. Andrew M. Greeley. (Running Time: 5 hrs. 0 mins. 0 sec.). (ENG.). 2007. audio compact disk 49.99 (978-1-4001-3404-5(8)) Pub: Tantor Media. Dist(s): IngramPubServ

Jesus: A Meditation on His Stories & His Relationships with Women. unabr. ed. Andrew M. Greeley. Read by Dick Hill. (Running Time: 5 hrs. 0 mins. 0 sec.). (ENG.). 2007. audio compact disk 24.99 (978-1-4001-0404-8(1)); audio compact disk 19.99 (978-1-4001-5404-3(9)) Pub: Tantor Media. Dist(s): IngramPubServ

Jesus: A Novel. unabr. ed. Walter Wangerin, Jr. (Running Time: 12 hrs. 45 mins. 0 sec.). (ENG.). 2005. 16.29 (978-0-310-26909-0(1)) Zondervan.

Jesus: A Story of Enlightenment. unabr. ed. Deepak Chopra. Read by Deepak Chopra. 6 CDs. (Running Time: 7 hrs.). (ENG.). 2008. audio compact disk 29.95 (978-1-60283-495-8(4)) Pub: AudioGO. Dist(s): Perseus Dist

Jesus: A Story of Enlightenment. unabr. ed. Deepak Chopra. 1 MP3-CD. 2008. 39.95 (978-0-7927-5823-5(4)); audio compact disk 74.95 (978-0-7927-5646-0(0)) AudioGO.

Jesus: A 21st Century Biography. unabr. ed. Paul Johnson. (Running Time: 7 hrs.). 2010. audio compact disk 34.95 (978-1-4417-2196-9(7)) Blckstn Audio.

Jesus: A 21st Century Biography. unabr. ed. Paul Johnson. Read by Ralph Cosham. (Running Time: 7 hrs. 0 mins.). 2010. 29.95 (978-1-4417-2197-6(5)); 44.95 (978-1-4417-2193-8(2)); audio compact disk 69.00 (978-1-4417-2194-5(0)) Blckstn Audio.

Jesus: Forgiving Victim, Transforming Savior. Richard Rohr. 1 cass. (Running Time: 1 hr.). 2001. 8.95 (A6931) St Anthony Mess Pr.
Suggests that if we understand the way Jesus lives the position of victim, we have been truly initiated into the Christian mystery.

Jesus: God's Plan of Salvation. Neville Goddard. 1 cass. (Running Time: 62 min.). 1964. 8.00 (40) J & L Pubns.
Neville taught Imagination Creates Reality. He was a powerfully influential teacher of God as Consciousness.

Jesus: His Life. Read by Jack Perkins. 1 cass. (Running Time: 90 min.). 1997. 9.95 (978-0-7670-0002-4(1)) A & E Home.

Jesus: His Life & Teachings. Joseph F. Girzone. Read by Raymond Todd. 3 cass. (Running Time: 4 hrs.). 2001. 23.95 (978-0-7861-1878-6(4), 2677); audio compact disk 32.00 (978-0-7861-9807-8(9), 2677) Blckstn Audio.
A retelling of the life & work of Jesus based on the accounts in the Gospels of Matthew, Mark, Luke, & John.

Jesus: His Life & Teachings. Joseph F. Girzone. Ed. by Joseph F. Girzone. Narrated by John McDonough. 4 cass. (Running Time: 5 hrs. 30 mins.). 38.00 (978-1-4025-3254-2(7)) Recorded Bks.

Jesus: Is He God, Man or Both? 2004. audio compact disk 7.95 (978-1-932927-02-3(6)) Ascensn Pr.

Jesus: Is He God, Man, or Both? 2004. 6.95 (978-1-932927-04-7(2)) Ascensn Pr.

Jesus: Man, Myth or Messiah CD Series. 2006. audio compact disk 24.95 (978-1-59834-126-3(X)) Walk Thru the Bible.

Jesus: Songs of Gratitude & Love. Kenneth Wapnick. 32 CDs. 2004. audio compact disk 126.00 (978-1-59142-158-0(6), CD100) Foun Miracles.

Jesus: Teacher Extraordinaire! John Shea. 1 cass. (Running Time: 90 min.). 1990. 8.95 (978-0-914070-70-2(3), 327) ACTA Pubns.
An analysis of the teaching methods of Jesus, using both biblical & contemporary stories to explain why Jesus was so effective as a teacher & what people can learn from him about sharing the Good News today.

Jesus: The Name above Every Name. Kenneth Copeland. 6 cass. 1991. 30.00 Set incl. study guide. (978-0-88114-837-4(7)) K Copeland Pubns.
Study on the authority of Jesus Name.

Jesus: Why the World Is Still Fascinated by Him. unabr. ed. Tim LaHaye & David Minasian. Narrated by Wayne Shepherd. (Running Time: 5 hrs. 45 mins. 11 sec.). (ENG.). 2009. 18.19 (978-1-60814-513-3(1)); audio compact disk 25.99 (978-1-59859-574-1(1)) Oasis Audio.

Jesus: 90 Days with the One & Only. unabr. ed. Beth Moore. Narrated by Renee Ertl. (Running Time: 7 hrs. 58 mins. 40 sec.). (Personal Reflections Ser.). (ENG.). 2007. audio compact disk 24.99 (978-1-59859-263-4(7)) Oasis Audio.

Jesus Set: When God Became a Man. Charles R. Swindoll. 2 cass. 1998. 11.95 (978-1-57972-144-2(3)) Insight Living.

Jesus Vol. II: El Mejor Amigo. (Heroes de la Fe Ser.). 2000. (978-1-57697-783-5(8)) Untd Bible Amrcas Svce.

Jesus Vol. III: El Salvador del Mundo. (Heroes de la Fe Ser.). 2000. (978-1-57697-784-2(6)) Untd Bible Amrcas Svce.

Jesus - Man of Authority. 1 cass. (J). 1995. 5.99 (978-1-886858-28-2(4)) Shepherds Tales.

Jesus - The Spirit of Prophecy; Antichrist & the Jewish Dream. C. S. Lovett. 1 cass. 6.95 (7025) Prsnl Christianity.
Expands on truths of the book, "Latest Word on the Last Days".

Jesus - Worthy of Our First Love! 1985. (0205) Evang Sisterhood Mary.

***Jesus among Other Gods.** Featuring Ravi Zacharias. 1990. audio compact disk 9.00 (978-1-61256-037-3(7)) Ravi Zach.

Jesus & Family. unabr. ed. Read by Gayle D. Erwin. 1 cass. (Running Time: 1 hr.). 1992. 4.95 (978-1-56599-525-3(2), C-25) Yahshua Pub.

Jesus & His Aloneness; Liturgy in the Life of a Christian. Joseph F. Girzone. Read by Joseph F. Girzone. 1 cass. (Running Time: 90 min.). 1992. 7.95 (978-0-911519-19-8(X)) Richelieu Court.
Girzone's public talk on these topics.

Jesus & Me: The Collection. Perf. by Glen Campbell et al. 1 cass. 1997. audio compact disk 15.99 CD. (D2037) Diamante Music Grp.
A compilation of ten of Glen's most popular Contemporary Christian songs, plus two new songs. Features many of the inspirationsl songs that earned Glen a Dove Award, & a name recognized in the Christian music market all across America.

Jesus & Our Hopeless Situations. 1 cass. (Running Time: 30 min.). 1985. (0286) Evang Sisterhood Mary.
Talks about: The Victory Has Been Won; Live in Reconcilliation; He Is Here; Redeemed To Love.

Jesus & the Gospels, Vol. I-III. Instructed by Luke Timothy Johnson. 18 cass. (Running Time: 18 hrs.). 2004. bk. 79.95 (978-1-56585-940-1(5), 6240); bk. 99.95 (978-1-56585-942-5(1), 6240) Teaching Co.

Jesus & the Human Factor: Proceedings of the 45th Annual Convention National Association of Evangelicals Buffalo, New York. Read by Anthony Campolo. 1 cass. (Running Time: 60 min.). 1987. 4.00 (301) Nat Assn Evan.

Jesus & the Modern Crisis. Swami Amar Jyoti. 1 cass. 1987. 9.95 (K-103) Truth Consciousness.
Jesus, the "meek revolutionary." The central theme of his message, applicable to today's complexity.

Jesus & the Quiet Revolution. Swami Amar Jyoti. 1 cass. 1989. 9.95 (K-116) Truth Consciousness.
In simplicity & humility, inner revolution is born. Prophets look to true deliverance, ultimate solution of life as a whole.

Jesus & the Twelve. Tom Seims. Illus. by Scott Arbuckle. (In the Picture with Jesus Ser.). (J). 1994. 12.99 (3-1222) David C Cook.

Jesus & Women. Rosemary Haughton. 4 cass. (Running Time: 4 hrs.). 1983. 29.95 incl. shelf-case. (TAH104) Alba Hse Comns.
Series of meditative reflections on the women in the life of Jesus & His very special relationship with them.

***Jesus As They Saw Him.** Featuring Ravi Zacharias. 1982. audio compact disk 9.00 (978-1-61256-033-5(4)) Ravi Zach.

Jesus, Bright Stranger. Kenneth Wapnick. 4 CDs. 2004. audio compact disk 22.00 (978-1-59142-143-6(8), CD97) Foun Miracles.
This 2002 workshop discusses Helen Schucman's poem, "Bright Stranger," which describes her-and our- attempt to keep Jesus' love away, and the futility of such attempts. Because our real fear is not of crucifixion but redemption, we try to bring Jesus into the world in order to deny that he is in our mind, love's source. It is explained how the ego's fear, along with its defenses of hate and judgment, ultimately has no power over love. Although we cover it with "locks and keys"-representing our need to protect ourselves-these defenses lack the power to succeed. Jesus-our "bright stranger"-is the light that shines in the dream, dissolving its fear into its own nothingness as our defenses fall away before his gentle coming.

***Jesus, Bright Stranger.** Kenneth Wapnick. 2010. 18.00 (978-1-59142-491-8(7)) Foun Miracles.

Jesus [Broken]. 2004. audio compact disk 16.99 (978-7-5124-0093-1(4)) Destiny Image Pubs.

***Jesus Calling: Enjoying Peace in His Presence.** unabr. ed. Sarah Young. Narrated by Pam Ward. (ENG.). 2009. 14.98 (978-1-59644-738-7(9), christianSeed) christianaud.

Jesus Calling: Seeking Peace in His Presence. unabr. ed. Sarah Young. Read by Pam Ward. (Running Time: 8 hrs. 0 mins. 0 sec.). (ENG.). 2009. audio compact disk 24.98 (978-1-59644-737-0(0), christianSeed) christianaud.

Jesus, CEO: Using Ancient Wisdom for Visionary Leadership. Laurie Beth Jones. 2004. 11.95 (978-0-7435-3917-3(6)) Pub: S&S Audio. Dist(s): S and S Inc

Jesus, CEO: Using Ancient Wisdom for Visionary Leadership. abr. ed. Laurie Beth Jones. Read by Laurie Beth Jones. (Running Time: 13 hrs. 0 mins. 0 sec.). (ENG.). 2003. audio compact disk 19.95 (978-0-7435-3599-1(5), Sound Ideas) Pub: S&S Audio. Dist(s): S and S Inc
A revolutionary new audio program that will guide business leaders into the next century! He gave them a vision of something larger than themselves. The world is changing at almost breakneck speed, and the leaders who succeed will be those who can marshal their most powerful resources in the most effective ways. With principles embedded in spirituality, ethics and strength, acclaimed motivator Laurie Beth Jones brings us Jesus, CEO - a bold yet sensitive inspirational guide for leadership success. After years in business, Jones was struck by the notion that Jesus' leadership approach ran counter to most of today's management styles. In Jesus, CEO, she explains that by harnessing the three strengths behind Jesus' leadership techniques (the strengths of self-mastery, action, and relationships), we can become the empowered leaders that the next millenium will require. Following the example of Jesus - a "CEO" who took a disorganizied "staff" of twelve and built a thriving "enterprise" - Jesus, CEO details a simple, profound, fresh, and often humor-filled approach to motivating and managing others.

Jesus Christ: High Priest of the New Covenant. Read by Wayne Monbleau. 3 cass. (Running Time: 4 hrs.). 1993. 15.00 Set. (978-0-944648-25-4(8), LGT-1207) Loving Grace Pubns.

Jesus Christ: Our Savior. Creflo A. Dollar. 2009. audio compact disk 21.00 (978-1-59944-772-8(X)) Creflo Dollar.

Jesus Christ, Forever, Amen. Created by Lillenas Publishing Company. 2007. audio compact disk 24.99 (978-5-557-54316-3(3)) Lillenas.

Jesus Christ in the Writings of St. John of the Cross. Regis Jordan. 1 cass. (Running Time: 40 min.). 8.95 I C S Pubns.
Fr. Regis Jordan, O.C.D. explores the Christocentric nature of St. John of the Cross's life, experience & writings.

Jesus Christ, Son of God, Savior. Voice by Brian Brodersen. 3 cassettes. 2001. reel tape 13.99 (978-1-931667-00-5(4)) Calvar ChalPub.

Jesus, Companion on Our Journey. Kenneth Wapnick. 4 CDs. 2004. audio compact disk 29.00 (978-1-59142-149-8(7), CD99) Foun Miracles.
Choosing Jesus as our companion helps us to understand the nature of the journey, without which it is meaningless. We had traveled from the light to the darkness, and then, with Jesus as our guide, we return through the darkness to the light that was always there. However, while our journey from the light was taken alone with the ego, we return with our former special love and hate partners, which is what it means to join with Jesus in forgiveness. Thus do we all return together to the light, with the light, as the light.

***Jesus, Companion on Our Journey.** Kenneth Wapnick. 2010. 18.00 (978-1-59142-489-5(5)) Foun Miracles.

Jesus' Concept of the Church; Jesus' Life As It Reflects His Message. Joseph F. Girzone. Read by Joseph F. Girzone. 1 cass. (Running Time: 90 min.). 1992. 7.95 (978-0-911519-13-6(0)) Richelieu Court.
Girzone's public talk on these topics.

***Jesus Died for This? A Satirist's Search for the Risen Christ.** unabr. ed. Becky Garrison. (Running Time: 6 hrs. 4 mins. 35 sec.). (ENG.). 2010. 14.99 (978-0-310-77354-2(7)) Zondervan.

***Jesus Drives Me Crazy! Lose Your Mind, Find Your Soul.** Zondervan. (Running Time: 5 hrs. 22 mins. 0 sec.). (ENG.). 2010. 9.99 (978-0-310-86939-9(0)) Zondervan.

Jesus Dynasty: The Hidden History of Jesus, His Royal Family, & the Birth of Christianity. abr. ed. James D. Tabor. Read by James D. Tabor. 2006. 17.95 (978-0-7435-5421-3(3)) Pub: S&S Audio. Dist(s): S and S Inc

Jesús, el mejor amigo - Jesús, el salvador del Mundo. (SPA.). (J). 2004. audio compact disk (978-1-933218-00-7(2)) Untd Bible Amrcas Svce.

Jesus Endures the Sorrows of Life with Us. Benedict J. Groeschel. 2 cass. (Running Time: 2 hrs. 9 min.). 1993. 16.95 Set. (TAH293) Alba Hse Comns.
Fr. Groeschel spiritually & emotionally relates the cross of Jesus to the suffering, agony & death experienced in this life. Not exclusively a Lenten program. Meditational & Devotional. Deals realistically with failure, pain, sickness, (terminal & other) & death.

***Jesus Family Tomb: The Discovery, the Investigation, & Th.** unabr. ed. Simcha Jacobovici & Charles Pellegrino. Read by Michael Ciulla. (ENG.). 2007. (978-0-06-143294-1(6), Harper Audio); (978-0-06-143293-4(8), Harper Audio) HarperCollins Pubs.

Jesus, Fantasy or Truth. Kenneth Wapnick. 2 CDs. 2004. audio compact disk 11.00 (978-1-59142-164-1(0), CD103) Foun Miracles.

***Jesus, Fantasy or Truth?** Kenneth Wapnick. 2010. 9.00 (978-1-59142-504-5(2)) Foun Miracles.

Jesus for President: Politics for Ordinary Radicals. unabr. ed. Shane Claiborne & Chris Haw. 1 CD. (Running Time: 2 hrs. 0 mins. 0 sec.). (ENG.). 2008. audio compact disk 22.99 (978-0-310-29287-6(5)) Zondervan.

***Jesus for President: Politics for Ordinary Radicals.** unabr. ed. Shane Claiborne & Chris Haw. (Running Time: 8 hrs. 21 mins. 0 sec.). (ENG.). 2008. 12.99 (978-0-310-29288-3(3)) Zondervan.

Jesus for the Non-Religious. unabr. ed. John Shelby Spong. Read by Alan Sklar. 10 CDs. (Running Time: 43200 sec.). 2007. audio compact disk 39.95 (978-0-06-123074-5(X)) HarperCollins Pubs.

***Jesus for the Non-Religious.** unabr. ed. John Shelby Spong. Read by Alan Sklar. (ENG.). 2007. (978-0-06-126255-5(2), Harper Audio); (978-0-06-126256-2(0), Harper Audio) HarperCollins Pubs.

Jesus Freak: 10th Anniversary. Contrib. by dcTalk. 2006. audio compact disk 19.99 (978-5-558-55062-7(7)) FF Rcds.

Jesus Gave Gifts, Set. Interview with James T. Barbarossa. Featuring Willie Coates et al. 10 cass. (Running Time: 60 mins. per cass.). 1998. 49.00 (978-0-9676380-4-1(6)) Step By Step Min.

Jesus His Power Unleashed: Easter. abr. ed. Narrated by Kailey Bell. (Kidz Rock Ser.). (ENG.). (J). 2008. 6.29 (978-1-60814-007-7(5)) Oasis Audio.

Jesus Hopped the a Train. Stephen Adly Guirgis. Contrib. by Joe Quintero & Charlie Robinson. (Running Time: 5700 sec.). 2007. audio compact disk 25.95 (978-1-58081-366-2(6)) Pub: L A Theatre. Dist(s): NetLibrary CO

Jesus I Never Knew. Philip Yancey. Read by Bill Richards. (Running Time: 10 hrs. 20 mins. 0 sec.). (ENG.). (gr. 11). 2006. audio compact disk 29.99 (978-0-310-27359-2(5)) Zondervan.

Jesus I Never Knew. abr. ed. Philip Yancey. (Running Time: 2 hrs. 0 mins. 0 sec.). (ENG.). 2003. 10.99 (978-0-310-26069-1(8)) Zondervan.

Jesus I Never Knew. unabr. ed. Compiled by Philip Yancey. 2 cass. (Running Time: 60 min. per cass.). 1995. 17.99 (978-0-310-20418-3(6)) Zondervan.

Jesus I Never Knew. unabr. ed. Philip Yancey. 4 cass. (Running Time: 6 hrs.). 1999. 29.99 (978-0-310-23227-8(9)) Zondervan.
Introduces you to a new perspective on the Jesus of the Bible. You will find someone you've never known who is capable of turning your life completely around.

Jesus I Never Knew. unabr. ed. Zondervan Publishing Staff & Philip Yancey. (Running Time: 10 hrs. 20 mins. 0 sec.). (ENG.). 2003. 14.99 (978-0-310-26157-5(0)) Zondervan.

Jesus I Trust in You. George Maloney. 4 cass. (Running Time: 6 hrs.). 1990. 32.95 set. (TAH230) Alba Hse Comns.
A blend of Western thought, Eastern mysticism & Irish humor in this retreat about trusting in our loving God.

Jesus in Blue Jeans: A Practical Guide to Everyday Spirituality. Laurie Beth Jones. 2004. 7.95 (978-0-7435-4889-2(2)) Pub: S&S Audio. Dist(s): S and S Inc

Jesus in India: The soundtrack music score of the motion Picture. Score by Brian Thomas Lambert. Prod. by Paul Davids. 1 CD. (Running Time: 1 hr. 37 mins.). 2008. audio compact disk 16.95 (978-0-9819244-7-2(6)) YELLOW HAT PRO.

***Jesus in Present Tense: The I AM Statements of Christ.** unabr. ed. Warren W. Wiersbe. (Running Time: 7 hrs. 0 mins. 0 sec.). (ENG.). 2011. audio compact disk 21.98 (978-1-61045-034-8(5)) christianaud.

Jesus in the Gospels. unabr. ed. Samuel Sandmel. 1 cass. (Running Time: 27 min.). 12.95 (31008) J Norton Pubs.
Points out that the Gospels were not a biography, but a tract motivated by piety & necessarily brief.

***Jesus, Interrupted.** unabr. ed. Bart D. Ehrman. Read by Jason Culp. (ENG.). 2009. (978-0-06-186720-0(9), Harper Audio); (978-0-06-188265-4(8), Harper Audio) HarperCollins Pubs.

Jesus Is All the World to Me. Stan Pethel. 1998. 75.00 (978-0-7673-9957-9(9)); 11.98 (978-0-7673-9939-5(0)); audio compact disk 16.98 (978-0-7673-9942-5(0)); audio compact disk 85.00 (978-0-7673-9935-7(8)) LifeWay Christian.

Jesus Is All the World to Me Promo Pack. Stan Pethel. 1998. 8.00 (978-0-7673-9884-8(X)); audio compact disk 12.00 (978-0-7673-9888-6(2)) LifeWay Christian.

Jesus Is As Good As It Gets. William G. Rowland. 2001. bk. 5.00 (978-0-687-03502-1(3)) Abingdon.

Jesus Is God's Son. (Junior Kids Church Ser.: Vol. 2). (J). 1998. bk. 134.99 (978-1-57405-351-7(5)) CharismaLife Pub.

Jesus Is Here. Charles M. Sheldon. Narrated by Adams Morgan. (Running Time: 10 hrs.). 2002. 30.95 (978-1-59912-517-6(X)) Iofy Corp.

Jesus Is Here. unabr. ed. Charles M. Sheldon. Read by Adams Morgan. 7 cass. (Running Time: 10 hrs.). 2002. 49.95 (978-0-7861-2299-8(4), 2988) Blckstn Audio.

Jesus Is Lord. Vincent M. Walsh. 1 cass. 1986. 4.00 Key of David.
Personal stories & examples that promote a full understanding of the basic powers of the Renewal.

Jesus Is Lord! 1 Cor. 12:1-6. Ed Young. 1986. 4.95 (978-0-7417-1507-4(4), 507) Win Walk.

Jesus Is My All in All: Praying with the Saint of Calcutta. Mother Teresa of Calcutta. Read by Brian Patrick & Julie O'Neill. Ed. by Brian Kolodiejchuk. (Running Time: 3600 sec.). 2009. audio compact disk 14.95 (978-0-86716-934-8(6)) St Anthony Mess Pr.

Jesus Is: Remix. Contrib. by Hillsong London. 2007. audio compact disk 9.99 (978-5-557-57573-7(1)) Hillsong Pubng AUS.

Jesus Is So Much Better. unabr. ed. Keith A. Butler. 7 cass. (Running Time: 10 hrs. 30 mins.). 2001. 35.00 (A133) Word Faith Pubng.

Jesus Is Watching: Mark 12:42-44 Pledge Sunday. Ben Young. 2000. 4.95 (978-0-7417-6220-7(X), B0220) Win Walk.

Jesus Is Wonderful. (Junior Kids Church Ser.: Vol. 3). (J). 1998. bk. 134.99 (978-1-57405-352-4(3)) CharismaLife Pub.

Jesus Knows I'm a Christian. Elspeth Young. 2009. audio compact disk 14.95 (978-1-59038-977-5(8)) Deseret Bk.

Jesus I Vol. I: Un Rey ha Nacido. (Heroes de la Fe Ser.). 2000. (978-1-57697-782-8(X)) Untd Bible Amrcas Svce.

Jesus, Light in the Dream. Kenneth Wapnick. 2 CDs. 2004. audio compact disk 14.00 (978-1-59142-118-4(7), CD91) Foun Miracles.
Using Freud's theory of dreams as the framework, this half-day workshop focuses on Jesus being the light of truth in the world's illusory dream. His love is the call to us-then and now-from outside the dream to take his hand as we walk through the ego's dreams-mind and body-of victim and victimizer. Emphasis is placed not only on the fear of leaving behind our specialness, but also on the desire to be the perfect thought of love that Jesus exemplifies. This desire makes it possible for us ultimately to take his hand and leave the dream entirely.

***Jesus, Light in the Dream.** Kenneth Wapnick. 2010. 11.00 (978-1-59142-506-9(9)) Foun Miracles.

Jesus Lives! Tom Siems. Illus. by Scott Arbuckle. (In the Picture with Jesus Ser.). (J). 1994. 12.99 (3-1223) David C Cook.

Jesus Lives. Tom Siems & Scott Arbuckle. 1 cass. (In the Picture with Jesus Ser.). (J). (ps-3). 1994. 12.99 (3-1223) David C Cook.

Jesus' Love Leads to Victory. 1 cass. (Running Time: 30 min.). Incl. Jesus' Love Leads to Victory: He Will Lift Us Up. 1985. (0291); 1985. (0291) Evang Sisterhood Mary.
Reveals the assurance of victory in an age of defeat & the way to heavenly glory.

Jesus' Love Leads to Victory: He Will Lift Us Up see Jesus' Love Leads to Victory

Jesus Love Me. 1 cass. (Wee Sing Ser.). (J). bk. 7.98 Blisterpack. (PSS 7853) NewSound.

Jesus Loves Me. Perf. by Toni Rose. 2006. audio compact disk 9.95 (978-1-59987-423-4(7)) Braun Media.

Jesus Loves the Little Children. Prod. by Twin Sisters Productions Staff. 1 CD. (Running Time: 30 mins). (J). 2005. audio compact disk 6.99 (978-1-57583-811-3(7)) Twin Sisters.
Jesus loves the little children, all the children of the world. Lead preschoolers and young children in celebration of such amazing love with these classic songs and choruses arranged for today's kids. Watch their tender hearts open wide with praise and worship as you sing these all-time favorite Bible songs together at home, church, and school. BONUS! The ENHANCED CD includes 58 pages of sheet music that can be printed from your own computer!.

***Jesus Loves You... This I Know.** unabr. ed. Craig Gross & Jason Harper. Narrated by Lloyd James. (ENG.). 2009. 12.98 (978-1-59644-750-9(8), christianSeed) christianaud.

Jesus Loves You... This I Know. unabr. ed. Craig Gross & Harper Jason. (Running Time: 4 hrs. 30 mins. 0 sec.). (ENG.). 2009. audio compact disk 21.98 (978-1-59644-749-3(4), christianSeed) christianaud.

Jesus Makes All Things New! 1 cass. (Running Time: 30 min.). 1985. (0268) Evang Sisterhood Mary.
Includes: One in the Lord: War on My Ego; Make Love Your Aim.

***Jesus Manifesto: It's Time to Restore the Supremacy of Jesus Christ.** unabr. ed. Leonard Sweet & Frank Viola. Narrated by Sean Runnette. (ENG.). 2010. 16.98 (978-1-59644-386-0(3)); audio compact disk 26.98 (978-1-59644-385-3(5)) christianaud.

Jesus of Nazareth. Truman G. Madsen. 16 cass. 1998. 39.95 Set. (Bkcraft Inc) Deseret Bk.

Jesus of Nazareth. Truman G. Madsen. 2006. audio compact disk 39.95 (978-1-59038-639-2(6)) Deseret Bk.

Jesus of Nazareth. Narrated by Orson Welles. 4 cass. (Running Time: 6 hrs.). 2001. 29.95 (AMER001) Lodestone Catalog.

Jesus of Nazareth. unabr. ed. Benedict XVI, pseud. Read by Don Leslie. (Running Time: 50400 sec.). (ENG.). 2007. audio compact disk 34.95 (978-0-7393-5697-5(6), Random AudioBks) Pub: Random Audio Pubg. Dist(s): Random

Jesus of Nazareth. unabr. ed. Joseph Ratzinger. 2001. 25.00 (978-1-58807-037-1(9)) Am Pubng Inc.
Audio drama is the account of Jesus based on stories and scripture taken from the Holy Bible. Orson Welles narrates the story, along with an international cast of actors from the Actors Workshop in Lisbon, Portugal.

Jesus of Nazareth, Vol. 1. Truman G. Madsen. 4 cass. 1990. 20.95 Set. (978-1-57008-038-8(0), Bkcraft Inc) Deseret Bk.

Jesus of Nazareth, Vol. 2. Truman G. Madsen. 4 cass. 1991. 20.95 Set. (978-1-57008-039-5(9), Bkcraft Inc) Deseret Bk.

Jesus of Nazareth, Vol. 3. Truman G. Madsen. 4 cass. 1992. 20.95 set. (978-1-57008-040-1(2), Bkcraft Inc) Deseret Bk.

Jesus of Nazareth: The Heart of Catechesis. Virgilio Elizondo. 1 cass. (Running Time: 1 hr.). 2001. 8.95 (A6861) St Anthony Mess Pr.
The catechetical core of the Church is knowing, living, remembering, proclaiming and celebrating Jesus of Nazareth who becomes alive in each one of us as our Savior.

Jesus of Nazareth Vol. 4: The Last Week. Truman G. Madsen. 4 cass. 1994. 20.95 set. (978-1-57008-089-0(5), Bkcraft Inc) Deseret Bk.

Jesus' Offer in the Last Times. 1985. (0279) Evang Sisterhood Mary.

Jesus on Trial. John MacArthur, Jr. 8 cass. 24.95 (20160, HarperThor) HarpC GBR.

Jesus or Barabas. Neville Goddard. 1 cass. (Running Time: 62 min.). 1964. 8.00 (31) J & L Pubns.
Neville taught Imagination Creates Reality. He was a powerfully influential teacher of God as Consciousness.

Jesus Our Joy. George Maloney. 4 cass. (Running Time: 3 hrs. 58 min.). 1994. 3.95 Set. (TAH308) Alba Hse Comns.
Fr. Maloney deepens our understanding of "joy" & explores the important causes of joy that mystically center in our relationship with God & others. For Father Maloney, joy comes from accepting the love of God that abounds in our hearts.

Jesus Our Jubilee. Kenneth Copeland. 6 cass. 1982. 30.00 Set incl. study guide. (978-0-938458-55-5(8)) K Copeland Pubns.
Jesus, our total well-being.

Jesus Our Lord. 4 cass. (Running Time: 6 hrs.). 1998. 20.95 (978-1-57972-296-8(2)) Insight Living.

Jesus, Our Reedemer: Logos November 9, 1997. Ben Young. 1997. Rental 4.95 (978-0-7417-6055-5(X), B0055) Win Walk.

Jesus Paid the Highest Price. Contrib. by Robert Sterling. Created by David M. Edwards & Regi Stone. 2007. audio compact disk 24.98 (978-5-557-53093-4(2), Word Music) Word Enter.

***Jesus Papers: Exposing the Greatest Cover-up in Histor.** abr. ed. Michael Baigent. Read by Michael Baigent. (ENG.). 2006. (978-0-06-113489-0(9), Harper Audio); (978-0-06-113488-3(0), Harper Audio) HarperCollins Pubs.

Jesus Parables. 1 cass. (Running Time: 59 min.). 1996. (978-0-9665138-1-3(9)) Jesus Pubs.

Jesus Prayer. Albert Rossi. 2005. audio compact disk 12.00 (978-0-88141-291-8(0)) St Vladimirs.

Jesus Prayer. Bartholomew. 1 cass. (Running Time: 58 min.). 7.95 (TAH010) Alba Hse Comns.
Explains how the simple "Lord Jesus, have mercy," is actually a complete prayer & can become a perfect prayer as one focuses completely on the words one is reciting.

Jesus Prayer. George Maloney. Read by George Maloney. 1 cass. (Running Time: 63 min.). 8.95 (AA0362) Credence Commun.
Explains how to use this ancient yet contemporary form of prayer to meditate & feel God's presence.

Jesus' Promise: If You but Knew. Kenneth Wapnick. 1 CD. (Running Time: 3 hrs. 46 mins. 54 secs.). 2006. 18.00 (978-1-59142-291-4(4), 3m133); audio compact disk 23.00 (978-1-59142-290-7(6), CD133) Foun Miracles.

Jesus, Prophets, Male & Female Imagery. Carolyn Osiek. 2 cass. (Running Time: 2 hrs. 45 min.). 1991. 18.95 set. (TAH238) Alba Hse Comns.
An accurate perception of Pentecost & appreciation of the way that the church needs to be constantly renewed to overcome culturally imposed limitations.

Jesus: Psychic or Prophet? Alarming Propaganda or Astonishing Predictions. 3 cass. 7.00 set. (978-0-934803-96-0(X)) J Van Impe.

Jesus Rediscovered, unabr. ed. Malcolm Muggeridge. Read by Frederick Davidson. 6 cass. (Running Time: 8 hrs. 30 mins.). 1989. 44.95 (978-0-7861-0065-1(6), 1062) Blckstn Audio.
This work includes his thoughts & reflections upon the Christian religion.

Jesus' Reliance on Prayer. Dan Corner. 1 cass. 3.00 (49) Evang Outreach.

Jesus Reveals His Heart of Love to Us. Read by Mother Basilea Schlink. 1 cass. (Running Time: 30 min.). 1985. (0236) Evang Sisterhood Mary.
Subjects are: Lord, Look on Me; Jesus Enters Jerusalem; The Great Offer of the Living Lord.

Jesus Says . . . I Am. Edd Anthony. Read by Edd Anthony. 2007. audio compact disk 16.95 (978-1-881586-14-2(6)) Canticle Cass.

Jesus, Shepherd of the FLock. Megan McKenna. 1 cass. (Running Time: 1 hr.). 2001. 8.95 (A6951) St Anthony Mess Pr.
Better understand the image of sheep and appreciate the role of a shepherd as well as appropriate the words of Jesus: "I am the Good Shepherd and I know my sheep".

Jesus Silences His Critics. 4 cass. 15.95 incl. study guide. (20146, HarperThor) HarpC GBR.

Jesus' Son. unabr. ed. Denis Johnson. Read by Will Patton. 3 CDs. (Running Time: 3 hrs. 0 mins. 0 sec.). (ENG.). 2009. audio compact disk 19.99 (978-1-4272-0571-1(X)) Pub: Macmill Audio. Dist(s): Macmillan

Jesus Stills the Storm. 1 cass. (J). (978-0-944391-74-7(5)) DonWise Prodns.
Narrates biblical story designed especially for children.

***Jesus Storybook Bible: Every story whispers his Name.** unabr. ed. Sally Lloyd-Jones. (Running Time: 3 hrs. 22 mins. 0 sec.). (ENG.). (J). 2009. 16.99 (978-0-310-29429-0(0)) Zondervan.

Jesus Style. unabr. ed. Gayle D. Erwin. Read by Gayle D. Erwin. 4 cass. (Running Time: 4 hrs.). 1992. 24.95 Set. (978-1-56599-066-1(8)) Yahshua Pub.

Jesus Style of Leadership. unabr. ed. Read by Gayle D. Erwin. 1 cass. (Running Time: 1 hr.). 1992. 4.95 (978-1-56599-511-6(2), C-11) Yahshua Pub.

Jesus, Symbol & Reality. Kenneth Wapnick. 4 CDs. 2004. audio compact disk 22.00 (978-1-59142-152-8(7), CD66) Foun Miracles.
While a seemingly abstract and intellectual exercise, distinguishing between symbol and reality is shown in this workshop to be crucial to one's spiritual growth as a student of A Course in Miracles. Missing this aspect of what is taught in the Course ensures that one remain a spiritual child. This means that one could never develop a relationship with Jesus that would lead to joining with him in the love and peace that is outside the world's dream, and that alone is our true reality.

***Jesus, Symbol & Reality.** Kenneth Wapnick. 2010. 18.00 (978-1-59142-490-1(9)) Foun Miracles.

Jesus, Take the Wheel. Contrib. by Carrie Underwood. (Sound Performance Soundtracks Ser.). 2006. audio compact disk 5.98 (978-5-558-43571-9(2)) Pt of Grace Ent.

Jesús Te Ama. unabr. ed. Nelson Ned. (SPA.). 1998. 9.99 (978-0-8297-2717-3(5)) Pub: Vida Pubs. Dist(s): Zondervan

Jesus, Teacher of Forgiveness, Model of Resurrection. Kenneth Wapnick. 10 CDs. 2004. audio compact disk 59.00 (978-1-59142-162-7(4), CD21) Foun Miracles.
This workshop focuses on Jesus-who he is and how we can develop a relationship with him, as he asks of us in A Course in Miracles. Hindrances to this relationship are discussed, specifically our grievances against him which are rooted, sometimes secretly, in traditional notions of the crucifixion and resurrection-the belief our sins have indeed had an effect. Correcting these erroneous beliefs, Jesus helps us to demonstrate his message of Atonement in our own lives: that our seeming sins against both him and God have had no effect, and so guilt and fear are completely unjustified.

Jesus' Teaching on Divorce: Matthew 5:31-32. Ed Young. 1979. 4.95 (978-0-7417-1058-1(7), A0059) Win Walk.

Jesus, the Ancient Love. Kenneth Wapnick. 4 CDs. 2004. audio compact disk 26.00 (978-1-59142-134-4(9), CD94) Foun Miracles.
Formerly entitled "Walking with Jesus," this workshop combines poems of Helen Schucman with readings from "A Course in Miracles" in discussing our love-hate relationship with Jesus. Our hate is born of the fear of growing up to become like him, thereby turning away from our specialness. This need to keep Jesus in our own image and likeness is reflected in "the dream of mockery" the world has made of him. Accepting our ultimate oneness with him is foreshadowed by the recognition of our inherent oneness with all the Sonship. In that vision is our ascent up the ladder assured, as we grow to awaken to the truth of our Identity as God's one Son.

***Jesus, the Ancient Love.** Kenneth Wapnick. 2010. 21.00 (978-1-59142-501-4(8)) Foun Miracles.

Jesus the Book. Frank Eickermann & Durga Holzhauser. (ENG.). 2009. pap. bk. 24.80 (978-1-936060-26-9(4)) CLP FLorida.

Jesus the Christ. James E. Talmage. Narrated by Charles Freed. 22 CDs. 2004. audio compact disk 39.95 (978-1-57734-840-5(0)) Covenant Comms.

Jesus the Christ, Set. James E. Talmage. Narrated by Charles Freed. 20 CDs. audio compact disk 49.95 (978-1-57734-321-9(2), 0300160) Covenant Comms.

Jesus the Christ, Set. James E. Talmage. Narrated by Charles Freed. 14 cass. 2004. 49.95 (978-1-55503-546-4(9), 030023) Covenant Comms.

***Jesus the Early Years.** Narrated by Tsea. 2010. audio compact disk 5.00 (978-0-9819971-5-5(5)) TSEA.

Jesus, the Great Hunter. unabr. ed. Read by Gayle D. Erwin. 1 cass. (Running Time: 1 hr.). 1992. 4.95 (978-1-56599-512-3(0), C-12) Yahshua Pub.
Luke 19: 1-10.

Jesus the Healer. E. W. Kenyon. Read by Stephen Sobozenski. 3 CDs. (Running Time: 2 hrs. 46 mins.). 2005. audio compact disk 24.00 (978-1-57770-039-5(2)) Kenyons Gospel.
Multitudes have been healed while reading this book. A revelation of the Father's will for the sick.

Jesus the Healer. unabr. ed. E. W. Kenyon. Read by Stephen Sobozenski. 2 cass. (Running Time: 2 hrs. 50 min.). 1998. 13.00 Set. (978-1-57770-023-4(6)) Kenyons Gospel.
Multitudes have been healed while reading this book. A Revelation of the Father's will for the sick.

Jesus, the Manifestation of the Holy Spirit. Kenneth Wapnick. 6 CDs. 2005. audio compact disk 40.00 (978-1-59142-163-4(2), CD31) Foun Miracles.

Jesus, The Mention of Your Name. Perf. by Donnie McClurkin. 1 cass. 1999. 7.98 (978-0-7601-2753-7(0)) Brentwood Music.

Jesus the One & Only. Travis Cottrell. 2000. 40.00 (978-0-633-01493-3(1)); 11.98 (978-0-633-01491-9(5)) LifeWay Christian.

Jesus the One & Only. Genevox Music Staff. 2000. audio compact disk 16.98 (978-0-633-01492-6(3)) LifeWay Christian.

Jesus the One & Only. Contrib. by Ed Kee. 1994. 11.98 (978-1-55897-410-4(5), 75602263) Pub: Brentwood Music. Dist(s): H Leonard

Jesus, the One & Only. abr. ed. Beth Moore. Read by Laural Merlington. 2 cass. (Running Time: 3 hrs.). 2002. 17.95 (978-1-59086-675-7(4), 1590866754, Nova Audio Bks); 44.25 (978-1-59086-676-4(2), 1590866762, CD Lib Edit); audio compact disk 24.95 (978-1-59086-677-1(0), 1590866770, CD Unabridged); audio compact disk 62.25 (978-1-59086-678-8(9), 1590866789, CD Lib Edit) Brilliance Audio.
In Jesus, the One and Only, Beth Moore introduces you to an intimate God in an up-close and personal portrait of the life of Jesus the Messiah. This is far more than just a work on the life of Christ. Jesus, the One and Only is a romance, and you are invited to become part of it. As He has done in the past, God will use Beth's words to woo you into falling in love with Jesus of Nazareth. Come to know Christ personally. Watch and listen as He breaks up a funeral by raising the dead, confronts conniving religious leaders of His day, teaches on a Galilean hillside, or walks on the waves and calms the storm. Like a ragtag band of followers nearly two thousand years ago, you will not be the same.

Jesus, the One & Only. abr. ed. Beth Moore. Read by Laural Merlington. (Running Time: 3 hrs.). 2006. 39.25 (978-1-4233-0404-3(7), 9781423304043, BADLE); 24.95 (978-1-4233-0403-6(9), 9781423304036, BAD); 39.25 (978-1-4233-0402-9(0), 9781423304029, Brinc Audio MP3 Lib); audio compact disk 24.95 (978-1-4233-0401-2(2), 9781423304012, Brilliance MP3) Brilliance Audio.

Jesus, the One & Only. unabr. ed. Beth Moore. (Running Time: 11 hrs.). 2009. 39.97 (978-1-4418-2533-9(9), 9781441825339, Brinc Audio MP3 Lib); 39.97 (978-1-4418-2535-3(5), 9781441825353, BADLE); 19.99 (978-1-4418-2534-6(7), 9781441825346, BAD); audio compact disk 97.97 (978-1-4418-2531-5(2), 9781441825315, BriAudCD Unabrid) Brilliance Audio.

Jesus, the One & Only. unabr. ed. Beth Moore. Read by Laural Merlington. (Running Time: 11 hrs.). 2009. 19.99 (978-1-4418-2532-2(0), 9781441825322, Brilliance MP3); audio compact disk 19.99 (978-1-4418-2530-8(4), 9781441825308, Bril Audio CD Unabri) Brilliance Audio.

***Jesus: the Only Way to God: Must You Hear the Gospel to be Saved?** unabr. ed. John Piper. Narrated by Dave Heath. (ENG.). 2010. 5.98 (978-1-59644-885-8(7)); audio compact disk 5.98 (978-1-59644-884-1(9)) christianaud.

Jesus to the World: Roaring Lambs. Perf. by NewSong. 1 cass. 1999. 7.98 (978-0-7601-2880-0(4)) Provident Music.

Jesus to the World: Roaring Lambs. Perf. by NewSong. 1 cass. 1999. 8.98 (978-0-7601-3155-8(4)) Provident Music.

Jesus... up Close & Personal CD Series. 2005. audio compact disk 40.00 (978-1-59834-058-7(1)) Walk Thru the Bible.

Jesus vs. Justice. Leonard Peikorr. 1 cass. (Philosophy: Who Needs It? Ser.). 1997. 12.95 (LPXXC26) Second Renaissance.

Jesus, Wakening to Resurrection. Kenneth Wapnick. 1 CD. (Running Time: 2 hrs. 48 mins. 31 secs). 2006. 13.00 (978-1-59142-259-4(0), 3m126); audio compact disk 17.00 (978-1-59142-253-2(1), CD126) Foun Miracles.

***Jesus Wants to Save Christians: A Manifesto for the Church in Exile.** unabr. ed. Rob Bell & Don Golden. (Running Time: 3 hrs. 25 mins. 0 sec.). (ENG.). 2008. 12.99 (978-0-310-28999-9(8)) Zondervan.

Jesus Was Not a Christian & Buddha Was Not a Buddhist: Separating Spiritual Truth from Institutional Fiction. abr. ed. Scott Morrison. 1 cass. (Running Time: 1 hr.). 1998. 7.50 (978-1-882496-27-3(2)) Twnty Frst Cntry Ren.
Being ruthlessly honest with our most cherished spiritual & religious fantasies.

Jesus Way: A Conversation on the Ways Jesus Is the Way. unabr. ed. Eugene H. Peterson. Read by Grover Gardner. (Running Time: 10 hrs. 30 mins. 0 sec.). (ENG.). 2007. audio compact disk 28.98 (978-1-59644-462-1(2)) christianaud.

Jesus Way: A Conversation on the Ways That Jesus Is the Way. unabr. ed. Eugene H. Peterson. Narrated by Grover Gardner. (Running Time: 10 hrs. 30 mins. 0 sec.). (ENG.). 2007. lp 19.98 (978-1-59644-463-8(0)) christianaud.

***Jesus Way: A Conversation on the Ways that Jesus Is the Way.** unabr. ed. Eugene H. Peterson. Narrated by Grover Gardner. (ENG.). 2007. 16.98 (978-1-59644-464-5(9), Hovel Audio) christianaud.

***Jesus We Need to Know.** Michael Wilcox. 2010. audio compact disk 14.99 (978-1-60641-065-3(2)) Deseret Bk.

Jesus, Who Is He. 1 CD. (Running Time: 36 mins.). (J). 2002. audio compact disk 6.99 (978-1-57583-529-7(0), 3001CD) Twin Sisters.
Jesus, who is He? He's the Son of God, the Prince of Peace. He's the risen Lord and Savior. He's the King of Kings, the Lord of Lords. He's the Light of the World. With these all-new, original praise and worship songs centered on Christ, kids, and adults, will honor the One who gave His life that they might one day live with Him.

Jesus, Yoga, & the Way of Happiness: A Christian Yoga Daily Devotional. Andrea Vidrine. 2006. pap. bk. 21.99 (978-1-59879-293-5(8)) Lifevest Pub.

Jesus You Can't Ignore: What You Must Learn from the Bold Confrontations of Christ. abr. ed. John MacArthur. 2009. audio compact disk 24.99 (978-1-4002-0228-7(0)) Nelson.

Jesus 101. 3 cass. (Running Time: 4 hrs. 30 mins.). 2000. 15.00 (978-1-930761-18-6(X)) TGMinist.

Jesus: 90 Days with the One & Only. unabr. ed. Beth Moore. Narrated by Renee Ertl. (Personal Reflection Ser.). (ENG.). 2007. 17.49 (978-1-60814-262-0(0)) Oasis Audio.

Jet Lag. Barrie Konicov. 1 cass. 11.98 (978-0-87082-342-8(6), 076) Potentials.
A discussion on jet lag, an experience the author says is quite unnecessary.

Jeu de la Vie. 1 CD. (Running Time: 1 hr.).Tr. of Game of Life & How to Play It. 2001. bk. 18.95 (978-2-89558-019-5(7)) Pub: Coffragants CAN. Dist(s): Penton Overseas

Jeu de la vie. Florence Scovel Shinn. Illus. by Marie-Jose Beaudoin. 1 cass., bklet. (Running Time: 90 mins.).Tr. of Game of Life & How to Play It. (FRE.). cass. & audio compact disk 14.95 (978-2-921997-50-8(9)) Pub: Coffragants CAN. Dist(s): Penton Overseas
Recorded completely in international French language by well-known actors or speakers.

Jew Bill. Perf. by Joe Knight et al. 1 cass. 1.00 (HS331) Esstee Audios.
Radio drama.

Jew in the Lotus: A Poet's Rediscovery of Jewish Identity in Buddhist India. abr. ed. Rodger Kamenetz. Read by Michael Tucker. 2 cass. (Running Time: 3 hrs.). 1997. 17.95 (978-1-57453-134-3(4)) Audio Lit.
The story of one man's journey into the mystical heart of Judaism begins with the Dalai Lama's call to a group of Jewish leaders to unravel the mystery of Judaism's spiritual survival.

Jewed 'I-Hoi/Earth Movements. deluxe ed. Ofelia Zepeda. (ENG.). 1997. audio compact disk 20.00 (978-1-888553-06-2(5)) Pub: Kore Pr. Dist(s): Chicago Distribution Ctr

Jewel. Bret Lott. 2004. 13.95 (978-0-7435-4890-8(6)) Pub: S&S Audio. Dist(s): S and S Inc

Jewel. unabr. ed. Bret Lott. Read by Kate Forbes. 10 vols. (Running Time: 15 hrs.). 2001. bk. 84.95 (978-0-7927-2435-3(6), CSL 324, Chivers Sound Lib); audio compact disk 115.95 (978-0-7927-9982-5(8), SLD 033, Chivers Sound Lib) AudioGO.
Set in the backwoods of Mississippi, Jewel & her husband are blessed with five fine children. When Brenda Kay is born in 1943, a fine healthy baby, last-born & most welcome. When their life took a change; how an unforseen event can set us on course without reason.

Jewel in the Crown. unabr. ed. Paul Scott. Read by Sam Dastor. 16 cass. (Running Time: 16 hrs.). (Raj Quartet: No. 1). 1995. 124.95 (978-0-7451-6577-6(X), CAB 1193) Pub: Chivers Audio Bks GBR. Dist(s): AudioGO
It is India, 1942 & two rapes occur simultaneously: that of an English girl in Mayapore & that of an Indian by the British. As physical violence & racial animosity play their part, the spectrum of Anglo-Indian relations is vividly evoked in a brilliant assessment of the emotions, personal clashes & historical reasons that eventually took India, the Jewel in the Imperial Crown, from its setting.

Jewel in the Crown. unabr. collector's ed. Paul Scott. Read by Richard Brown. 8 cass. (Running Time: 12 hrs.). (Raj Quartet: No. 1). 1991. 64.00 (978-0-7366-2063-5(X), 2871-B) Books on Tape.
Part I of the Raj Quartet. Britons & Indians caught at the end of an epoch. Exciting & powerful.

Jewel in the Crown. unabr. collector's ed. Paul Scott. Read by Richard Brown. 8 cass. (Running Time: 12 hrs.). (Raj Quartet: No. 1). 1991. 64.00 (978-0-7366-2062-8(1), 2871-A) Books on Tape.
Britons & Indians caught at the end of an epoch. Exciting & powerful.

***Jewel of Liberation.** Jack Kornfield. (Running Time: 10:00:00). 2011. audio compact disk 99.00 (978-1-60407-083-5(8)) Sounds True.

Jewel of Seven Stars. Bram Stoker. Read by Alfred von Lecteur. 2009. 27.95 (978-1-60112-999-4(8)) Babblebooks.

Jewel of Tharn. abr. ed. Jeffrey Lord. Read by Lloyd James. Abr. by Edward McClure. 2 vols. No. 3. 2003. 18.00 (978-1-58807-358-7(0)); (978-1-58807-776-9(4)) Am Pubng Inc.

Jewel of Tharn. abr. ed. Jeffrey Lord. Read by Carol Eason. Abr. by Ted McClure. 3 CDs. (Running Time: 3 hrs.). (Richard Blade Adventure Ser.: No. 3). 2004. audio compact disk 25.00 (978-1-58807-494-2(3)) Am Pubng Inc.
British secret agent Richard Blade's current mission is to investigate a parallel universe. He must fight to survive in a world of stagnation, brutal oppression, and violent intrigue. Finding himself in a position to overthrow the oppressors and restore a civilization, he must find the strength, skill, wit, and patience to strike at the right place and time while manipulating those who would use him for their own ends.

Jewel of Zandor. unabr. ed. Roger A. Smith. Read by Cameron Beierle. 6 cass. (Running Time: 7 hrs. 30 min.). 2001. 39.95 (978-1-58116-004-8(6)) Books in Motion.
At the end of the world's most recent war in 2502, the earth's population lives under thick acrylic domes due to contamination and pollution. And population is controlled by enforcing a maximum age of 65. Professor Art Champlin decides to escape to an existence beyond the domes.

Jewel Ornament of Liberation. Read by Osel Tendzin. 9 cass. 1977. 92.50 (A055) Vajradhatu.
Eight talks: 1) Shunyata, The Essence of Samsara & Nirvana; 2) The Working Basis; 3) Meeting Spiritual Friends; 4) Karma & the Six Realms; 5) Soft Spot; 6) The Aspiration & Accomplishment of the Bodhisattva Vow; 7) The Attitude & Practice of the Bodhisattva; 8) Buddha Activity.

Jewel That Was Ours. Colin Dexter. 2 cass. (Running Time: 3 hrs.). (ENG., 2001. (978-0-333-90435-0(4)) Macmillan UK GBR.

Jewel That Was Ours. unabr. ed. Colin Dexter. Read by Frederick Davidson. 6 cass. (Running Time: 8 hrs. 30 mins.). 1996. 44.95 (978-0-7861-0980-7(7), 1757) Blckstn Audio.
The case seems so simple, Inspector Morse deems it beneath his notice. A wealthy, elderly American tourist has a heart attack in her room at Oxford's luxurious Randolph Hotel. Missing from the scene is the lady's handbag, which contained the Wolvercote Tongue, a priceless jewel that her late husband had bequeathed to the Ashmolean Museum just across the street.

Jewel That Was Ours. unabr. ed. Colin Dexter. Read by Michael Pennington. 8 cass. (Running Time: 12 hrs.). (Inspector Morse Mystery Ser.: Bk. 9). 2000. 59.95 (978-0-7451-4090-2(4), CAB 778) Pub: Chivers Audio Bks GBR. Dist(s): AudioGO
For Oxford, the arrival of American tourists is not unusual, until one of them is found dead at the Randolph Hotel. Chief Inspector Morse is intrigued by the simultaneous theft of an antique jewel from the victim's handbag. Then a naked and battered corpse is dragged from the River Cherwall.

Jewel That Was Ours. unabr. ed. Colin Dexter. Narrated by Patrick Tull. 7 cass. (Running Time: 9 hrs. 30 mins.). (Inspector Morse Mystery Ser.: Vol. 9). 1992. 60.00 (978-1-55690-683-1(8), 92315E7) Recorded Bks.
Inspector Morse investigates two deaths that appear tied to a missing jewel that was to be donated to the prestigious collection at the Ashmoleon Museum in Oxford.

Jewel Tree of Tibet. Robert Thurman. 12 CDs. (Running Time: 9 hrs 30 min). 2005. audio compact disk 79.95 (978-1-59179-317-5(3), AF00937D) Sounds True.
With The Jewel Tree of Tibet: The Enlightenment Engine of Tibetan Buddhism, Robert Thurman makes available his first complete learning course on audio. According to its lineage holders, Tibetan Buddhism is "a wish-fulfilling gem tree" that offers the gifts of enlightenment and happiness to all who seek it. Now, in twelve detailed sessions, listeners have the opportunity to join this acclaimed scholar and practitioner to learn the core teachings of this vast lineage. Includes many authentic meditations and traditional practices.

Jewelled Path. unabr. ed. Rosalind Laker, pseud. Read by Liz Holliss. 12 CDs. (Running Time: 13 hrs. 23 mins.). (Isis Ser.). (J). 2002. audio compact disk 99.95 (978-0-7531-1481-0(X)) Pub: ISIS Lrg Prnt GBR. Dist(s): Ulverscroft US
Oliver Lindsay is reluctant to permit his daughter, Irene, to study jewelry design. When Irene, caught up in a romance with a married diamond dealer, oversteps the mark, Olive's retribution is unswerving.

Jewelled Path. unabr. ed. Rosalind Laker, pseud & Liz Hollis. 12 cass. (Running Time: 13 hrs. 23 mins.). (Isis Ser.). (J). 2002. 94.95 (978-0-7531-1007-2(5)) Pub: ISIS Lrg Prnt GBR. Dist(s): Ulverscroft US

Jewelry in Argentina: A Strategic Reference 2006. Compiled by Icon Group International, Inc. Staff. 2007. ring bd. 195.00 (978-0-497-35801-3(8)) Icon Grp.

Jewelry in France: A Strategic Reference 2006. Compiled by Icon Group International, Inc. Staff. 2007. ring bd. 195.00 (978-0-497-35952-2(9)) Icon Grp.

Jewelry in Germany: A Strategic Reference 2007. Compiled by Icon Group International, Inc. Staff. 2007. ring bd. 195.00 (978-0-497-35975-1(8)) Icon Grp.

Jewelry in Taiwan: A Strategic Reference 2006. Compiled by Icon Group International, Inc. Staff. 2007. ring bd. 195.00 (978-0-497-82431-0(0)) Icon Grp.

Jewels of Maihar. Perf. by Ali A. Khan. 1 cass. 8.98 (A0052-0) Sound Photosyn.
With Mahapurush Misra on Tabla.

Jewels of Terror, Set. unabr. ed. Janet L. Roberts. 6 cass. 1998. 69.95 (978-1-872672-43-4(4)) Pub: Magna Story GBR. Dist(s): Ulverscroft US

Jewels of Tessa Kent. abr. ed. Judith Krantz. Read by Alison Fraser. 2 cass. 1999. 18.00 (FS9-43297) Highsmith.

Jewels of Tessa Kent. unabr. ed. Judith Krantz. Read by Kate Harper. 12 vols. (Running Time: 18 hrs.). 2000. bk. 96.95 (978-0-7927-2309-7(0), CSL 198, Chivers Sound Lib) AudioGO.
When she is just fourteen, Tessa Kent gives birth to a daughter. her parents, devout Catholics, raise the infant, maggie, as their own child. At sixteen, Tessa is discovered by Hollywood; by nineteen she's an international movie star. Maggie is eighteen when she learns the truth, and mortally wounded, she breaks all ties with Tessa and begins work at a famed Manhattan auction house. When a life-altering crisis makes Tessa determined to end this estrangement, the only way she can find to reach her daughter is through an auction of the valuable jewels that were lavished on her by her late husband.

***Jewels of the Cabots.** abr. ed. John Cheever. Read by Meryl Streep et al. (ENG.). 2009. (978-0-06-125289-1(1), Caedmon) HarperCollins Pubs.

***Jewels of the Cabots.** unabr. ed. John Cheever. Read by Meryl Streep et al. (ENG.). 2009. (978-0-06-196862-4(5), Caedmon) HarperCollins Pubs.

Jewels of the Sun. Nora Roberts. Read by Patricia Daniels. (Irish Trilogy: Vol. 1). 2009. 69.99 (978-1-60775-877-6(6)) Find a World.

***Jewels of the Sun.** abr. ed. Nora Roberts. Read by Patricia Daniels. (Running Time: 3 hrs.). (Irish Trilogy: Vol. 1). 2010. audio compact disk 9.99 (978-1-4418-5092-8(9), 9781441850928, BCD Value Price) Brilliance Audio.

Jewels of the Sun. abr. ed. Nora Roberts. 2 cass. (Irish Trilogy: Vol. 1). 1999. 17.95 (FS9-51090) Highsmith.

Jewels of the Sun. unabr. ed. Nora Roberts. Read by Patricia Daniels. 8 cass. (Running Time: 10 hrs.). (Irish Trilogy: Vol. 1). 1999. 73.25 (978-1-56740-691-7(2), 1567406912, Unabridge Lib Edns) Brilliance Audio.
Determined to re-evaluate her life, Jude Murray flees America to take refuge in Faerie Hill Cottage, where she immerses herself in the study of Irish Folklore, and discovers hope for the future in the magic of the past. Finally back home in Ireland after years of traveling, Aidan Gallagher possesses an uncommon understanding of his country's haunting myths. Although he's devoted to managing the family pub, a hint of wildness still glints in his stormy eyes. In Jude, he sees a woman who can both soothe his heart and stir his blood. And he begins to share the legends of the land with her, while they create a passionate history of their own.

Jewels of the Sun. unabr. ed. Nora Roberts. Read by Patricia Daniels. (Running Time: 10 hrs.). (Irish Trilogy: Vol. 1). 2005. 39.25 (978-1-59600-957-8(8), 9781596009578, BADLE); 24.95 (978-1-59600-956-1(X), 9781596009561, BAD); 32.95 (978-1-59600-951-6(9), 9781596009516, BAU); audio compact disk 39.25 (978-1-59600-955-4(1), 9781596009554, Brinc Audio MP3 Lib); audio compact disk 24.95 (978-1-59600-954-7(3), 9781596009547, Brilliance MP3); audio compact disk 97.25 (978-1-59600-953-0(5), 9781596009530, BriAudCD Unabrid); audio compact disk 36.95 (978-1-59600-952-3(7), 9781596009523, Bril Audio CD Unabri) Brilliance Audio.

Jewels of the Sun. unabr. ed. Nora Roberts. 8 cass. (Irish Trilogy: Vol. 1). 1999. 73.25 (FS9-51034) Highsmith.

Jewish Attitudes Toward Illness & Healing. 1 cass. (Care Cassettes Ser.: Vol. 10, No. 4). 1983. 10.80 Assn Prof Chaplains.

Jewish Cemetery at Newport see Treasury of Henry Wadsworth Longfellow

Jewish Cemetery at Newport see Best Loved Poems of Longfellow

Jewish Folklore. Read by Tim O'Connor. 1 cass. (Running Time: 1 hr. per cass.). 1982. 10.00 (LSS1136) Esstee Audios.
Tales about piety, meekness, survival & morality. In his brief introduction, O'Connor discusses the role of literature in the Jewish culture.

Jewish Holiday Songs for Children. Rachel Buchman. (J). 1997. pap. bk. 24.95 (978-0-7866-1350-2(5), 95623P) Mel Bay.

Jewish Holiday Songs for Children. Rachel Buchman. (J). 1997. pap. bk. 29.95 (978-0-7866-1349-6(1), 95623CDP) Mel Bay.

Jewish Holiday Songs for Children. Rachel Buchman. 1 cass. (Running Time: 59 min.). (Family Ser.). (J). (ps-7). 1993. 9.98 (978-1-886767-20-1(3), 8028) Rounder Records.
Songs for every season of the Jewish calendar. Along with holiday stories, games & dances, these exuberant selections will delight children & parents alike.

Jewish Holiday Songs for Children. Perf. by Rachel Buchman. 1 cass. (Running Time: 59 min.). (Family Ser.). (J). (ps-7). 1993. audio compact disk 14.98 (978-1-886767-21-8(1), 8028) Rounder Records.

Jewish Holiday Stories. Short Stories. As told by Jim Weiss. 1 CD. (Running Time: 1 hr.). (J). (gr. 2). 2001. audio compact disk 14.95 (978-1-882513-75-8(4), 1124-028) Greathall Prods.
Three stories that form the basis for three Jewish holidays: Chanukah, Purim and Passover.

Jewish Idea of God. Read by Nancy Lewman. 1 cass. (Running Time: 32 min. per cass.). 1978. 10.00 (RJ120) Esstee Audios.
Introductory lecture on the dominant concepts of God according to Jewish interpretation.

Jewish Intellectual History. Instructed by David Ruderman. 12 CDs. (Running Time: 12 hrs.). 2002. bk. 69.95 (978-1-56585-521-2(3), 4647) Teaching Co.

Jewish Intellectual History, Parts I-II. Instructed by David Ruderman. 12 cass. (Running Time: 12 hrs.). bk. 54.95 (978-1-56585-520-5(5), 4647) Teaching Co.

Jewish Mysticism. Jane Brown. 2 cass. (Running Time: 2 hrs. 45 min.). (Common Territory, Different Maps: the Archetypal Underpinnings of Religious Practice Ser.). 1994. 18.95 set. (978-0-7822-0490-2(2), 554) C G Jung IL.

Jewish New Testament- MP3. Narrated by Jonathan Settel. (ENG.). 2008. 49.99 (978-1-880226-57-5(X)) Messianic Jewish Pubs.

Jewish New Testament-Audio CD. Tr. by David Stern. 2007. audio compact disk 49.99 (978-1-880226-38-4(3)) Messianic Jewish Pubs.

Jewish Roots of Our Faith. 2003. 23.95 (978-1-888992-43-4(3)); audio compact disk 27.95 (978-1-888992-44-1(1)) Catholic Answers.

Jewish Short Stories from Eastern Europe & Beyond. Short Stories. 10 cds. 2003. audio compact disk 72.00 (978-0-657-14377-0(4)) Ntnl Yiddish Bk Ctr.

Jewish Short Stories from Eastern Europe & Beyond. Read by Alan Alda et al. Hosted by Leonard Nimoy. Music by Hankus Netsky. 9 cass. (Running Time: 13 hrs.). 1997. 80.00 Set. (978-0-9655315-0-4(3)) Ntnl Yiddish Bk Ctr.
Captures the rich & diverse legacy of modern Jewish life through 31 short stories by Sholem Aleichem, Isaac Babel, I. L. Peretz, Grace Paley, Philip Roth & many others.

Jewish Spirituality: The Essential Kabbalah, The Jew in the Lotus & The Legend of the Baal-Shem. abr. ed. Daniel Chanan Matt et al. Read by Edward Asner et al. 6 cass. (Running Time: 9 hrs.). 1998. bk. 49.95 (978-1-57453-277-7(4)) Audio Lit.
Includes "The Essential Kabbalah," & "The Jew in the Lotus," & "The Legend of the Baal-Shem".

Jewish Stories from the Old World to the New. unabr. ed. Short Stories. Isaac Bashevis Singer et al. Read by Richard Dreyfuss et al. Narrated by Leonard Nimoy. Music by Yale Strom. 9 CDs. (Running Time: 18 hrs.). 1998. audio compact disk 100.00 (978-0-9672485-1-6(5)) KCRW.

Jewish Stories from the Old World to the New, Set. unabr. ed. Isaac Bashevis Singer et al. Read by Richard Dreyfuss et al. Narrated by Leonard Nimoy. Music by Yale Strom. 12 cass. (Running Time: 18 hr.). 1998. 100.00 (978-0-9672485-0-9(7)) KCRW.
Narrated by Nimoy/Leonard, with original music by Storm/Yale.

Jewish Traditions: Chanukah, Holidays & Heritage. Perf. by Janice Buckner. 1 cass. (Running Time: 1 hr.). (Learn along Song Ser.). (J). 2001. 10.00; audio compact disk 15.00 Moonlight Rose.
Includes full song lyrics and features a karaoke-style Sing-It-Yourself instrumental version of each tune. The feature is designed for classrooms, children's choirs and budding performers.

Jewish View of Charity. 10.00 (RJ126) Esstee Audios.

Jewish View of God. 10.00 (RJ120) Esstee Audios.

Jews: Story of a People. unabr. ed. Howard Fast. Narrated by Nelson Runger. 9 cass. (Running Time: 12 hrs. 15 mins.). 1988. 78.00 (978-1-55690-265-9(4), 88750E7) Recorded Bks.
Brings the history of the Jewish people into focus, from Genesis to contemporary times.

Jews & Catholics: A New Relationship. John Pawlikowski. 1 cass. (Running Time: 53 mins.). 2001. 9.95 (A8061) St Anthony Mess Pr.
As we reverse anti-Semitism, we open the door to interreligious dialogue and to an even deeper understanding of the mystery of the Church.

Jews & Non-Jews. 10.00 (RJ127) Esstee Audios.

Jews, God & History. unabr. ed. Max I. Dimont. Read by Anna Fields. 13 cass. (Running Time: 19 hrs.). 1999. 85.95 Set. (978-0-7861-1263-0(8), 2187) Blckstn Audio.
The story of a people escaping annihilation & cultural death, fighting, falling back, advancing. Infused wint an almost miraculous life force, they have survived the death civilzations & have triumphantly contributed to man's spiritual & intellectual heritage for some four thousand years.

Jewtopia: The Chosen Book for the Chosen People. abr. ed. Bryan Fogel & Sam Wolfson. (Running Time: 3 hrs.). (ENG.). 2006. 14.98 (978-1-59483-563-6(2)) Pub: Hachet Audio. Dist(s): HachBkGrp

Jewtopia: The Chosen Book for the Chosen People. abr. ed. Bryan Fogel & Sam Wolfson. (Running Time: 3 hrs.). (ENG.). 2009. 39.98 (978-1-60788-150-6(0)) Pub: Hachet Audio. Dist(s): HachBkGrp

Jezebel. Perf. by Bette Davis. 1 cass. (Running Time: 60 min.). 1946. 7.95 (DD-8850) Natl Recrd Co.
"Jezebel" is an 1850 love story of a southern belle from New Orleans. Her behavior stirs up trouble by her stubbornness & spite, but she makes amends when a plague strikes. "Morning Glory" is the story of a young girl struggling to become a great Broadway actress. She falls in love with the wrong man, but hard work to reach stardom is her real passion.

Jezebel: Rev. 2:18-29. Ed Young. 1986. 4.95 (978-0-7417-1553-1(8), 553) Win Walk.

Jezyk Anglielski. Assimil Staff. 1 cass. (Running Time: 1 hr. 30 min.).Tr. of English with Ease. 1999. pap. bk. 75.00 (978-2-7005-1656-2(7)) Pub: Assimil FRA. Dist(s): Distribks Inc

JFK: Reckless Youth. abr. ed. Nigel Hamilton. Read by Nigel Hamilton. 2 cass. (Running Time: 3 hrs.). 2000. 7.95 (978-1-57815-063-2(9), 1034, Media Bks Audio) Media Bks NJ.
Based on a wealth of never previously published letters & documents & more than 2,000 interviews. A portrait of a young John F. Kennedy.

JFK: Reckless Youth. abr. ed. Nigel Hamilton. Read by Nigel Hamilton. 2 cass. (Running Time: 3 hrs.). 1993. 16.95 (978-1-879371-56-9(1), 20280) Pub Mills.
The Kennedy that emerges from this book is, behind his playboy facade, vastly more driven & more serious than historians have ever before portrayed him. Though Joseph Kennedy reluctantly transferred the family's political mantle to his second son in 1944, the presidential dream that the ambassador had reserved for his eldest son was JFK's own secret ambition.

JFK: Reckless Youth. unabr. ed. Nigel Hamilton. Read by Alexander Adams. 12 cass. (Running Time: 18 hrs.). 1994. 96.00 (3369-A); 80.00 (3369-B) Books on Tape.
JFK from birth to first congressional election. It's solid history with lots of spice - including an incident with the FBI that leaves you shaking your head. Kennedy comes off as intelligent, magnetic & loyal - yet with notable defects that time might have cured. He was presidential, all right. The tragedy is the timber was still green.

JFK: Reckless Youth. unabr. ed. Nigel Hamilton. Read by Alexander Adams. 22 cass. (Running Time: 33 hrs.). 1994. 176.00 (978-0-7366-2629-3(8), 3369A/B) Books on Tape.

JFK: The Four Steps to President. 10.00 (HTA506) Esstee Audios.

JFK: The President. 10.00 (HTA507) Esstee Audios.

JFK Vol. 1: The Kennedy Tapes. Ed. by Pent. 1992. cass. & audio compact disk 10.95 (978-1-885959-03-4(6), JRCD 7012) Jerden Recs.
Featuring highlights from 16 speeches given by President John F. Kennedy during his Presidency, 1960-63.

JFK Vol. 2: The Kennedy Tapes. Ed. by Pent. 1 cass. (Running Time: 79 min.). 1995. cass. & audio compact disk 10.98 (978-1-885959-21-8(4), JRCS 7047) Jerden Recs.
More great speeches from the immortal American President. Vol. II includes the Cuban Missile Crisis, the Berlin Crisis, Civil Rights, "Ich Bin Ein Berliner," remarks made at a rally the morning of his assassination, & much more!.

JFK Reads the Declaration of Independence. 8.00 (HTA505) Esstee Audios.

JFK: the Kennedy Tapes, Volumes 1 And 2. John F. Kennedy. Contrib. by John F. Kennedy. (Playaway Young Adult Ser.). 2008. 39.99 (978-1-60640-687-8(6)) Find a World.

Jibberish & Rhyme. abr. ed. Poems. Kevin Berg. Read by Kevin Berg. Read by Susan Skadron. 1 cass. (Running Time: 1 hr.). Dramatization. (J). (gr. k-6). 8.95 (978-0-9636795-1-2(1)) Child Tech Bks.
Selected poems of book Jibberish & Rhyme. Come take a journey on the magical melody of Jibberish & Rhyme.

Jicarilla Apache. unabr. ed. Alan Wilson & Rita V. Martine. 4 cass. (Running Time: 4 hrs.). (APA & ENG.). (gr. 9-12). 1996. pap. bk. 75.00 (978-0-88432-903-9(8), AFAP10) J Norton Pubs.
Provides vocabulary & sentence structures used in everyday conversation. Following a pronunciation section, lesson units include dialogs, textual & grammatical explanations & exercises for review & practice. Cultural notes on Apache humor, taboos & idiomatic usages are interspersed in the 21 lesson units. A special feature is the regular comparison throughout of Jicarilla Apache with western Apache & other Apachean languages.

Jiffy Phrasebook. 1 cass. 6.95 ea. Langenscheidt.

Jig. Campbell Armstrong. 2009. 104.95 (978-1-4079-0432-0(9)); audio compact disk 124.95 (978-1-4079-0433-7(7)) Pub: Soundings Ltd GBR. Dist(s): Ulverscroft US

Jiggleworm. ed. Heather Carr. Des. by Greg Carr. Illus. by Greg Carr. Lyrics by Michael St. James. Score by Michael St. James. Narrated by Sara Hofer. 1 CD. (J). 2005. bk. 21.95 (978-0-9768450-0-3(8), Gigglet) Ke Bk Moderne.
The CD includes a narrarated track of The Jiggleworm story by Sara Hofer with theme music/sound effects/character voicing, a Theme track without narraration used to read the book to a child. It includes orginal songs by Michael St. James. It also includes interactive CD-ROM content for PC/MAC.

Jigsaw. Anthea Fraser. Read by Jacqueline Tong. 5 cass. 49.95 (978-0-7927-3389-8(4), CSL 722); audio compact disk 64.95 (978-0-7927-3390-4(8), SLD 722) AudioGO.

Jigsaw. unabr. ed. Ed McBain, pseud. Read by Jonathan Marosz. 5 cass. (Running Time: 5 hrs.). (87th Precinct Ser.: Bk. 24). 1997. 30.00 (978-0-7366-3641-4(2), 4303) Books on Tape.
A piece of a jigsaw is found in a victim's hand. Detectives of the 87th Precinct must work fast: they're dealing with an expert in the game of murder & the bodies keep piling up.

Jigsaw Jones: Runaway Dog & Stinky Science Project. unabr. ed. James Preller. Read by Oliver Wyman. (J). 2007. 34.99 (978-1-60252-760-7(1)) Find a World.

Jigsaw Jones: The Case of the Snowboarding Superstar & the Case of the Christmas Snowman. unabr. ed. James Preller. Read by Oliver Wyman. (J). 2007. 34.99 (978-1-60252-761-4(X)) Find a World.

Jigsaw Jones Mystery - Mummy Mystery & Glow-in-the-Dark Ghost. unabr. ed. James Preller. Read by Oliver Wyman. (J). 2007. 34.99 (978-1-60252-685-3(0)) Find a World.

***Jigsaw Jones 06: The Case of the Mummy Mystery.** Weston Woods Staff. (YA). audio compact disk 14.95 (978-0-545-05039-5(1)) Weston Woods.

***Jigsaw Jones 7: The Case of the Runaway Dog.** Weston Woods Staff. (YA). audio compact disk 14.95 (978-0-545-05041-8(3)) Weston Woods.

***Jigsaw Jones 9: Case of/Stinky Science Project.** Weston Woods Staff. (YA). audio compact disk 14.95 (978-0-545-05040-1(5)) Weston Woods.

Jihad. abr. ed. Stephen Coonts & Jim DeFelice. Read by J. Charles. (Running Time: 14400 sec.). (Deep Black Ser.: No. 5). 2007. audio compact disk

14.99 (978-1-59737-356-2(7), 9781597373562, BCD Value Price) Brilliance Audio.
Please enter a Synopsis.

Jihad. abr. unabr. ed. Stephen Coonts & Jim DeFelice. Read by J. Charles. (Running Time: 39600 sec.). (Deep Black Ser.: No. 5). 2007. audio compact disk 97.25 (978-1-59600-354-5(5), 9781596003545, BACDLib Ed) Brilliance Audio.

Jihad. unabr. ed. Stephen Coonts & Jim DeFelice. Read by J. Charles. (Running Time: 11 hrs.). (Deep Black Ser.: No. 5). 2007. 39.25 (978-1-59710-843-0(X), 9781597108430, BADLE); 24.95 (978-1-59710-842-3(1), 9781597108423, BAD); audio compact disk 24.95 (978-1-59600-355-2(3), 9781596003552, Brilliance MP3); 82.25 (978-1-59600-351-4(0), 9781596003514, BrilAudUnabridg); audio compact disk 39.25 (978-1-59600-356-9(1), 9781596003569, Brinc Audio MP3 Lib); audio compact disk 36.95 (978-1-4233-0642-9(2), 9781423306429, Bril Audio CD Unabri) Brilliance Audio.

Jihad: The Archetype of Spiritual Warfare. Read by Robert Moore. 1 cass. (Running Time: 90 min.). 1988. 10.95 (978-0-7822-0177-2(6), 304) C G Jung IL.
A study of the archetype of warfare on both a sociopolitical & personal level, & the various manifestations of this archetype in religious traditions.

Jihad Germ. T. N. Rivers. Narrated by Dave Giorgio. (ENG.). 2008. audio compact disk 24.95 (978-1-60031-037-9(0)) Spoken Books.

Jihad Germ: A Novel of National Security. T. N. Rivers. Voice by AudioBrite. (ENG.). 2008. 9.95 (978-0-9799326-2-5(9)) Pirate Island.

Jihad in America: America's New War. Chuck Missler. 2 CDs. (Running Time: 2 hours). (Briefing Packages by Chuck Missler). 2001. audio compact disk 19.95 (978-1-57821-155-5(7)) Koinonia Hse.
Jesus died for Muslims and we must reach out to them in God's love. We must also be aware of the implications of their occultic religion.September 11, 2001On that day, life in America changed. The attack on America's sovereign soil was a wake-up call, and it certainly isn't over. We are, indeed, at war. We are engaged in Islam's "Jihad". Most Americans - and even most Christians - have no real awareness of the nature of Islam: its origin, its agenda and its methods. We each must understand the realities and not be blind-sighted by misleading propaganda. Get up-to-date on what is really happening. There is much to pray about.

Jihad Next Door: The Lackawanna Six & Rough Justice in an Age of Terror. unabr. ed. Dina Temple-Raston. (Running Time: 25200 sec.). 2007. 72.95 (978-1-4332-0304-6(9)); audio compact disk 81.00 (978-1-4332-0305-3(7)) Blckstn Audio.

Jihad Next Door: The Lackawanna Six & Rough Justice in an Age of Terror. unabr. ed. Dina Temple-Raston. Read by Marguerite Gavin. (Running Time: 25200 sec.). 2007. audio compact disk 29.95 (978-1-4332-0203-2(4)) Blckstn Audio.

Jihad Next Door: The Lackawanna Six & Rough Justice in the Age of Terror. unabr. ed. Dina Temple-Raston. Read by Marguerite Gavin. (Running Time: 25200 sec.). 2007. 29.95 (978-1-4332-0201-8(8)); audio compact disk 29.95 (978-1-4332-0202-5(6)) Blckstn Audio.

Jihadi Salafis: Name of the Enemy. Quintan Wiktorowicz. Narrated by Grover Gardner. 1. (Running Time: 1 hr. 30 min.). 2004. audio compact disk 15.95i (978-1-58472-804-7(3), Pocket Univ) Sound Room.
It is extremely important that we, as a nation, learn as much as we can about those who have vowed to kill all Americans. This production explains who they are, how they came to be and what their intentions are.1 CD; 1 hr. 30 mins.

Jill & the Hill. Shaun Gayle & Pat Owsley. 1 cass. (Shaun Gayle's Sports Tales Ser.). (J). (gr. k-4). 1994. 8.99 (3-0006) David C Cook.

Jill Paquette. Contrib. by Jill Paquette. Prod. by Eldon Winter et al. 2003. audio compact disk 9.99 (978-5-552-10446-8(3)) Pt of Grace Ent.

Jill Spiegel Tells Her Story. Jill Spiegel. 1 cass. (Running Time: 40 mins.). 2002. 15.00 (978-0-9643325-5-3(8)) Goal Gtrs MN.
Shares her hilarious adventures and her success fundamentals. Learn how she flirted with Oprah and Katie Couric. She'll show you how to make your dreams come true too.

Jill Spiegel's Best Tips. Jill Spiegel. 1 cass. (Running Time: 40 mins.). 2001. 15.00 (978-0-9643325-3-9(1)) Goal Gtrs MN.
Zaps you into felling empowered, succeed into instinct, build instant rapport, feel guided by life, lue each moment with energy and confidence.

Jill Spiegel's Top Dating Tips. Jill Spiegel. 1 cass. (Running Time: 40 mins.). 2001. 15.00 (978-0-9643325-4-6(X)) Goal Gtrs MN.
Inspires her listeners with concise, hands-on dating tips, master healthy dating, meet people everywhere, draw your soul mate to you, feel great about your life and yourself.

***Jim & Me.** unabr. ed. Dan Gutman. Narrated by Johnny Heller. 4 cass. (Running Time: 4 hrs.). (J). (gr. 4-6). 2009. 33.75 (978-1-4361-6102-2(9)); audio compact disk 46.75 (978-1-4361-6107-7(X)) Recorded Bks.

Jim Baker's Blue-Jay Yarn see Best of Mark Twain

Jim Barnes see Ann Struthers

Jim Barnes. unabr. ed. Read by Jim Barnes. 1 cass. (Running Time: 29 min.). 1985. 10.00 New Letters.
Jim Barnes reads poems that deal with Midwest & Native American themes.

Jim Barnes & Ann Struthers. unabr. ed. Jim Barnes & Ann Struthers. Read by Jim Barnes & Ann Struthers. 1 cass. (Running Time: 29 min.). 1991. 10.00 (011384) New Letters.

Jim Blaine's Ram see Best of Mark Twain

Jim Bowie: Frontier Legend, Alamo Hero. unabr. ed. J. R. Edmondson. Read by Benjamin Becker. 1 MP3-CD. (Running Time: 2 hrs.). (Library of American Lives & Times Ser.). 2009. 19.99 (978-1-4233-9422-8(4), 9781423394228, Brilliance MP3); 39.97 (978-1-4233-9423-5(2), 9781423394235, Brinc Audio MP3 Lib); 39.97 (978-1-4233-9424-2(0), 9781423394242, BADLE); audio compact disk 19.99 (978-1-4233-9420-4(8), 9781423394204, Bril Audio CD Unabri) Brilliance Audio.

Jim Bowie: Frontier Legend, Alamo Hero. unabr. ed. J. R. Edmondson. Read by Benjamin Becker. 2 CDs. (Running Time: 2 hrs.). (Library of American Lives & Times Ser.). (J). (gr. 4-8). 2009. audio compact disk 39.97 (978-1-4233-9421-1(6), 9781423394211, BriAudCD Unabrid) Brilliance Audio.

Jim Cramer's Mad Money: Watch TV, Get Rich. abr. unabr. ed. James J. Cramer. Read by James J. Cramer. Told to Cliff Mason. 2006. 17.95 (978-0-7435-6175-4(9)) Pub: S&S Audio. Dist(s): S and S Inc

Jim Cramer's Real Money: Sane Investing in an Insane World. abr. ed. James J. Cramer. Narrated by James J. Cramer. 5 cass. (Running Time: 6 hrs. 15 mins.). 2007. 41.75 (978-1-4281-5744-6(1)); audio compact disk 56.75 (978-1-4281-5469-8(8)) Recorded Bks.

Jim Cramer's Real Money: Sane Investing in an Insane World. abr. ed. James J. Cramer. Read by James J. Cramer. 2006. 17.95 (978-0-7435-6124-2(4)); audio compact disk 29.95 (978-0-7435-6123-5(6)) Pub: S&S Audio. Dist(s): S and S Inc

Jim Cramer's Stay Mad for Life: Get Rich, Stay Rich (Make Your Kids Even Richer) abr. ed. James J. Cramer. Read by James J. Cramer. Told to Cliff Mason. 5 CDs. (Running Time: 6 hrs. 0 mins. 0 sec.). (ENG.). 2007. audio compact disk 29.95 (978-0-7435-7108-1(8)) Pub: S&S Audio. Dist(s): S and S Inc

Jim Curry's Test. unabr. collector's ed. Max Brand. Read by Jonathan Marosz. 6 cass. (Running Time: 6 hrs.). 1995. 36.00 (978-0-7366-2993-5(9), 3682) Books on Tape.
Outlaw & gambler strike a deal over 20,000 dollar haul. Who'll get stiffed?.

Jim Fay Presents Parenting at It's Best. 2004. audio compact disk (978-1-930429-57-4(6)) Love Logic.

Jim Gill Makes It Noisy in Boise, Idaho. Perf. by Jim Gill. 1 cass. (Running Time: 90 mins.). (J). 1996. 10.00 (978-0-9679038-3-5(1), JGM 200); audio compact disk 15.00 (978-0-9679038-2-8(3), JGM 200) J Gill.
Music play activities & poems for young children.

Jim Gill Sings Do Re Mi on His Toe Leg Knee. Perf. by Jim Gill. 1 cass. (Running Time: 90 mins.). (J). 1999. 10.00 (978-0-9679038-5-9(8), JGM 30D); audio compact disk 15.00 (978-0-9679038-4-2(X), JGM 30D) J Gill.

Jim Gill Sings Moving Rhymes for Modern Times. unabr. ed. Jim Gill. 1 CD. (Running Time: 44 mins.). (J). (ps-2). 2006. audio compact disk 15.00 (978-0-9679038-7-3(4)) J Gill.

Jim Gill Sings the Sneezing Song & Other Contagious Tunes. Perf. by Jim Gill. 1 CD. (Running Time: 90 mins.). (J). 1993. audio compact disk 15.00 (978-0-9679038-0-4(7), JGM 100); 10.00 (978-0-9679038-1-1(5), JGM 100) J Gill.

Jim Gill's Irrational Anthem...and More Salutes to Nonsense. 2001. audio compact disk 15.00 (978-0-9679038-8-0(2)) J Gill.
Music Play activities and poems for young children.

Jim Gills Irrational Anthem...and More Salutes to Nonsense. 2001. 10.00 (978-0-9679038-9-7(0)) J Gill.

Jim Harrison. Interview. Interview with Jim Harrison. 1 cass. (Running Time: 54 min.). 13.95 (978-1-55644-106-6(1), 4082) Am Audio Prose.
Interview covers a variety of Harrison's artistic & thematic concerns, including his response to critics who dismiss him as a "macho" writer.

Jim Kelly's Guitar Workshop. Jim Kelly. 1998. pap. bk. 19.95 (978-0-7935-8572-4(4), 00695230, Berklee Pr) H Leonard.

Jim Metcalf's Journal & Please to Begin. Jim Metcalf. Narrated by Jim Metcalf. 1 cass. (Running Time: 33 hrs. NaN mins.). (ENG.). 2000. 15.95 (978-1-56554-762-9(4)) Pelican.

Jim Ringer: Waitin' for the Hard Times to Go. 1 cass. 9.98 (C-47) Folk-Legacy.
Jim's first, & best, recording, for sure.

Jim Rohn Smoothe Mixx: Lessons of the Seasons. Executive Producer Roy Daley-Smoothe. As told by Jim Rohn. Voice by Jim Rohn. 2007. audio compact disk 29.99 (978-1-4276-2533-5(6)) AardGP.

Jim the Boy: A Novel. Tony Earley. 2001. (978-1-58621-086-1(6)) Hachet Audio.
Portrait of Jim, a boy growing up in the 20th century, with his widowed mother and her three bachelor brothers. A profound act of historical and psychological imagination.

Jim the Boy: A Novel. unabr. ed. Tony Earley. Read by L. J. Ganser. (ENG.). 2005. 14.98 (978-1-59483-460-8(1)) Pub: Hachet Audio. Dist(s): HachBkGrp

Jim Thorpe. 1 cass. (Running Time: 1 hr. 30 mins.). (SmartReader Ser.). (J). 1999. tchr. ed. 19.95 (978-0-7887-0545-8(8), 79331T3) Recorded Bks.
He was the greatest athlete of the 20th century, winning four Olympic gold medals. But adversity made him a hero for all Native Americans.

Jim Thorpe: Athlete of the 20th Century. John Bergez. (Overcoming the Odds Sports Biographies Ser.). 2001. audio compact disk 18.95 (978-1-4105-0169-1(8)) D Johnston Inc.

Jim Thorpe Vol. 6: Althele of the 20th Century. John Bergez. Ed. by Jerry Stemach et al. Illus. by Jeff Ham. Narrated by Bernard Mixon. Contrib. by Ted S. Hasselbring. (Start-to-Finish Books). (J). (gr. 2-3). 2002. 100.00 (978-1-58702-957-8(X)) D Johnston Inc.

Jim Thorpe Vol. 6: Athlete of the 20th Century. John Bergez. Ed. by Jerry Stemach et al. Illus. by Jeff Ham. Narrated by Bernard Mixon. Contrib. by Ted S. Hasselbring. (Start-to-Finish Books). (J). (gr. 2-3). 2001. 35.00 (978-1-58702-543-3(4)) D Johnston Inc.

Jim Thorpe Vol. 6: Athlete of the 20th Century. unabr. ed. John Bergez. Ed. by Jerry Stemach et al. Illus. by Jeff Ham. Narrated by Bernard Mixon. Contrib. by Ted S. Hasselbring. 1 cass. (Running Time: 1 hr.). (Start-to-Finish Books). (J). (gr. 2-3). 2001. (978-1-58702-382-8(2), F42) D Johnston Inc.
This book tells the incredible and touching story of perhaps the most gifted athlete who ever lived. Born in a cabin on a reservation in Indian Territory (Oklahoma), Native American Jim Thorpe rose from obscurity to become the most famous athlete in the world. In the 1912 Olympics, he achieved the unprecedented feat of winning gold medals in the two most grueling tests of all-around athletic excellence: the pentathlon and the decathlon.

Jim Thorpe, Original All-American. unabr. ed. Joseph Bruchac. Read by Joseph Bruchac. 5 CDs. (Running Time: 6 hrs. 26 mins.). (YA). (gr. 6-9). 2007. audio compact disk 50.00 (978-0-7393-6229-7(1), Listening Lib) Pub: Random Audio Pubg. Dist(s): Random
Jim Thorpe was one of the greatest athletes who ever lived. He played professional football, Major League Baseball, and won Olympic gold medals in track and field. He'll forever be remembered by the sports community and by the Native American community, who consider him a hero on par with Crazy Horse. Born on the Sac and Fox Reservation in 1887, Jim was sent as a young boy to various Indian boarding schools - strict, cold places that didn't allow their students to hold on to their Native American traditions. Jim ran away from school many times, until he found his calling at Pennsylvania's Carlisle School. There, coach Pop Warner (who is as famous today as Thorpe himself) recognized Jim's athletic excellence and welcomed him onto the football and track teams. Glory followed, as did surprising disgrace. But through everything, Jim was a person to admire - an engaging, spirited, and impressive young man.

Jim Ugly. unabr. ed. Sid Fleischman. Narrated by Kerin McCue. 2 pieces. (Running Time: 2 hrs. 45 mins.). (gr. 4 up). 1994. 19.00 (978-1-55690-458-5(4), 92322E7) Recorded Bks.
When Jake's dad decides to "die" to escape the bounty-hunter looking to collect the 25,000 dollar price on his head, Jake is left fatherless & companionless except for the big sandy-colored mongrel, Jim Ugly. When Jake realizes that the two of them have something in common - they both want to find Jake's dad - they form a search party of two & take off across the mountains to San Francisco.

Jimi Hendrix: An Audio Biography in His Own Words. unabr. ed. Geoffrey Giuliano. Read by Jimi Hendrix. (YA). 2008. 34.99 (978-1-60514-782-6(6)) Find a World.

Jimmy Durante. 2 cass. (Running Time: 2 hrs.). 10.95 Set in vinyl album. (978-1-57816-058-7(8), JD2401) Audio File.
Good night, Mrs. Calabash, wherever you are! The great Schnozzola himself with fun guest stars & a good comedy cast. Commercials for Rexall Drugs. Includes: "October 8, 1947" Guest Eddie Cantor joins Jimmy as the boys reflect on their days in Show Business. "February 25, 1948" Guest Victor Moore has a free pass to the track, so he & Jimmy go to the races. "April 7, 1948" Jimmy coaxes guest Dorothy Lamour to run for president of the United States. They travel cross-country to get the nation's reaction to a female president. "April 21, 1948" The Schnozzola's former vaudeville partners Lou Clayton & Eddie Jackson recall the good old days at the Dover Club in 1923.

Jimmy Durante & Friends. Hosted by Jimmy Durante. 1952. audio compact disk 12.95 (978-1-57970-504-6(9), Audio-For) J Norton Pubs.

Jimmy Durante & Friends. unabr. ed. Perf. by Jimmy Durante et al. (Running Time: 59 min.). 12.95 (499) J Norton Pubs.
The "Schnozzola" looks back at some of his old shows & sings a few of his hit songs. Side two is a show co-hosted by Garry Moore.

Jimmy Durante & Garry Moore & Bulldog Drummond: Comedy Caravan & The Bookshop. unabr. ed. 1 cass. (Running Time: 60 min.). Dramatization. 7.95 Norelco box. (CM 7249) Natl Recrd Co.
Jimmy Durante: Comedy from "The Nose" & "The Haircut" as Schnozzola Durante & Garry team up for a Music School sketch. As professor Durante explains in his music lecture..."the piano consists of the white notes, the black notes, & the cracks." Included with Jim & Garry is Her Nibs, Miss Georgia Gibbs. Bulldog Drummond: Out of the fog...out of the night...& into his American adventure comes Bulldog Drummond. Captain Hugh Drummond encounters a mysterious young woman during a thunderstorm. She forces him into a bookshop at gun point & then she disappears.

Jimmy Durante Show: Dorothy Lamour & Christmas Show with Rose Marie. Perf. by Dorothy Lamour & Rose Marie. 1 cass. (Running Time: 1 hr.). 2001. 6.98 (2161) Radio Spirits.

Jimmy Durante Show: Lou Clayton, Eddie Jackson & Lucille Ball. Perf. by Louise Clayton et al. 1 cass. (Running Time: 1 hr.). 2001. 6.98 (1756) Radio Spirits.

Jimmy Durante Show: Victor Moore & Lucille Ball. Perf. by Victor Moore & Lucille Ball. 1 cass. (Running Time: 1 hr.). 2001. 6.98 (1548) Radio Spirits.

Jimmy Rose see Great American Short Stories, Vol. III, A Collection

Jimmy Rose. unabr. ed. Herman Melville. Perf. by Walter Covell. 1 cass. (Running Time: 50 min.). Dramatization. 1985. 7.95 (S-66) Jimcin Record.

Jimmy Rose & The Fiddler. Herman Melville. 1 cass. 1989. 7.95 (S-66) Jimcin Record.
Two minor masterpieces.

Jimmy Santiago Baca. unabr. ed. Jimmy Santiago Baca. Read by Jimmy Santiago Baca. Interview with Robert Stewart. Prod. by Rebekah Presson. 1 cass. (Running Time: 29 min.). 1991. 10.00 (041291) New Letters.
Mexican-American poet has published six books of poetry & won several awards for his writing. Here he discusses & reads from his works.

Jimmy Sniffles Dognapped! Scott Nickel. 1 CD. (Jimmy Sniffles Ser.). (J). (gr. 3-5). 2007. audio compact disk 14.60 (978-1-59889-999-3(6)) CapstoneDig.
Tells the story of how Jimmy's nose helps solves the crime of the disappearing dogs. Written in graphic-novel format.

Jimmy Sniffles Dognapped! Scott Nickel. (J). (gr. 3-5). 2007. bk. 21.52 (978-1-4342-0379-3(4)) Ston A Bks.

Jimmy Swaggart Made Me Catholic! 2005. 27.95 (978-1-888992-83-0(2)); audio compact disk 24.95 (978-1-888992-82-3(4)) Catholic Answers.

Jimmy the Kid. unabr. collector's ed. Donald E. Westlake. Read by Michael Kramer. 6 cass. (Running Time: 6 hrs.). (Dortmunder Ser.). 1996. 48.00 (978-0-7366-3517-2(3), 4154) Books on Tape.
Dortmunder should have never listened to his cohort, Andy Kelp, who says he's got a fail-safe plan to pull off the perfect kidnapping. It's all laid out in a crime novel, claims Kelp. Dortmunder has doubts.

Jimmy Zangwow's Out-of-This-World Moon-Pie Adventure. unabr. ed. Tony DiTerlizzi. Narrated by L. J. Ganser. 1 cass. (Running Time: 20 mins.). (J). 2001. pap. bk. & stu. ed. 34.00 Recorded Bks.
Jimmy Zangwow just has to have a chocolaty Moon Pie. His mother tells him to wait for supper & sends him outside to play. He climbs aboard the junk jumbilee jalopy that he has been building.

Jimmy Zangwow's Out-of-This-World Moon-Pie Adventure. unabr. ed. Tony DiTerlizzi. Narrated by L. J. Ganser. 1 cass. (Running Time: 15 mins.). (gr. k up). 2001. 10.00 (978-0-7887-4397-9(X), 96324E7) Recorded Bks.

Jim's Dog Muffins. Miriam Cohen. (Miriam Cohen Ser.). (J). (ps-6). 1988. bk. 13.90 (SAC 6541-A) Spoken Arts.

Jim's Dog Muffins. unabr. ed. Miriam Cohen. 1 cass. (Running Time: 7 min.). (J). (gr. k-3). 1990. pap. bk. 15.95 (6541-A) Spoken Arts.

Jingle Bell Christmas (Medley) - ShowTrax. Arranged by Mac Huff. 1 CD. (Running Time: 6 mins.). 2000. audio compact disk 30.00 (08742383) H Leonard.
This is a medley just for SSA choirs that will almost sing itself! Super easy & a blast to perform. Includes: "Jingle Bell Rock"; "Jingle Bells" & "Jingle, Jingle, Jingle.".

Jingle Bells. Photos by Michael Scott. 1 cd. audio compact disk 10.98 (978-1-57908-397-7(8), 1670) Platinm Enter.

Jingle Bells, Level 3. (Yamaha Clavinova Connection Ser.). 2004. disk 0.82 (978-0-634-09600-6(1)) H Leonard.

Jingle Bells, Batman Smells! (P. S. So Does May.) unabr. ed. Barbara Park. Read by Lana Quintal. (Running Time: 2700 sec.). (Junie B., First Grader Ser.: No. 8). (ENG.). (J). (gr. 1-4). 2005. audio compact disk 14.99 (978-0-307-28256-9(2), ImaginStudio) Pub: Random Audio Pubg. Dist(s): Random

Jingle Bells, Homework Smells. Diane deGroat. Illus. by Diane deGroat. Read by Jason Harris & Peter Pamela Rose. 1 CD. (Running Time: 12 mins.). (J). (ps-3). 2008. pap. bk. 18.95 (978-1-4301-0421-6(X)) Live Oak Media.

Jingle Bells, Rudolph & Other Children's Christmas Songs. 1 cass. 3.98 Clamshell. (978-1-55886-149-7(1), BB/PT 456) Smarty Pants.

Jingle Jolly Christmas Holly. Narrated by Frances Donnell. Text by Frances Donnell. Illus. by Donna Merchant. Arranged by Storch Brothers Studios. Prod. by Storch Brothers Studios. Magaret E. Storch. (ENG.). (J). 2008. bk. 18.95 (978-0-9770893-3-8(9)) 2 Do Bks.

Jingle Spells: 20 Songs to Spell By. (J). 2006. audio compact disk 10.00 (978-1-933945-13-2(3)) Talking Finger.

Jingo. Terry Pratchett. Read by Tony Robinson. (Running Time: 3 hrs. 0 mins. 0 sec.). (Discworld Ser.). (ENG.). 2006. audio compact disk 22.95 (978-0-552-15417-8(2), Corgi RHG) Pub: Transworld GBR. Dist(s): IPG Chicago

Jingo. unabr. ed. Terry Pratchett. Read by Nigel Planer. 8 cass. (Running Time: 12 hrs.). (Discworld Ser.). (J). 2000. 69.95 (978-0-7531-0521-4(7), 000203) Pub: ISIS Lrg Prnt GBR. Dist(s): Ulverscroft US
A weathercock has risen from the sea of Discworld & suddenly you can tell which way the wind is blowing. A new land has surfaced & so have old feuds. Discworld goes to war.

Jingo. unabr. ed. Terry Pratchett. Read by Nigel Planer. 10 CDs. (Running Time: 11 hrs.). (Discworld Ser.). (J). 2001. audio compact disk 89.95 (978-0-7531-0884-0(4), 108844) Pub: ISIS Lrg Prnt GBR. Dist(s): Ulverscroft US

Jingo Django. unabr. ed. Sid Fleischman. Read by William Duris. 3 cass. (Running Time: 3 hrs.). (J). 1997. 24.95 (CCA3362, Chivers Child Audio) AudioGO.

Jinnie. Josephine Cox. Read by Carole Boyd. 8 cass. (Running Time: 12 hrs.). 2002. 69.95 (978-0-7540-0880-4(0), CAB 2302) Pub: Chivers Audio Bks GBR. Dist(s): AudioGO

Jinnie. unabr. ed. Josephine Cox. Read by Carole Boyd. 8 CDs. (Running Time: 12 hrs.). 2002. audio compact disk 79.95 (978-0-7540-5538-9(8), CAC 229) Pub: Chivers Audio Bks GBR. Dist(s): AudioGO

Jinx. Meg Cabot. Read by Amber Sealey. 6 cds. (Running Time: 7 hrs. 15 mins.). 2007. audio compact disk 50.00 (978-0-7393-6095-8(7), Random AudioBks) Pub: Random Audio Pubg. Dist(s): Random

Jinx. unabr. ed. Meg Cabot. Read by Amber Sealey. (Running Time: 26100 sec.). (ENG.). (J). (gr. 9-12). 2007. audio compact disk 34.00 (978-0-7393-3863-6(3), Listening Lib) Pub: Random Audio Pubg. Dist(s): Random

Jinxed. Carol Higgins Clark. (Regan Reilly Mystery Ser.: No. 6). 2004. 15.95 (978-0-7435-4891-5(4)) Pub: S&S Audio. Dist(s): S and S Inc

Jinxed. unabr. ed. Carol Higgins Clark. Read by Deborah Hazlett. 6 vols. (Running Time: 9 hrs.). (Regan Reilly Mystery Ser.: No. 6). 2002. bk. 54.95 (978-0-7927-2701-9(0), CSL 487, Chivers Sound Lib); audio compact disk 64.95 (978-0-7927-2726-2(6), SLD 487, Chivers Sound Lib) AudioGO.
Fresh from tracking down a diamond thief in Manhattan, Regan Reilly returns to her Los Angeles office only to discover her horoscope says now is not really the best time to get started on a new case. Undaunted, she sets out to locate a missing young heiress. But Regan finds herself thwarted by a string of misadventures, inexplicably jinxed as she races up and down the Pacific Coast highway. Just when things seem to be turning from bad to worse, New York cop Jack Reilly steps in with some timely reinforcement.

Jip, His Story. unabr. ed. Katherine Paterson. Narrated by John McDonough. 4 pieces. (Running Time: 6 hrs.). (gr. 4 up). 1997. 35.00 (978-0-7887-1345-3(0), 95194E7) Recorded Bks.
An African-American orphan's perilous search for his heritage.

Jip, His Story. unabr. ed. Katherine Paterson. Read by John McDonough. 4 cass. (J). (gr. 2). 1997. Rental 11.50 Recorded Bks.

Jip, His Story. unabr. ed. Katherine Paterson. Narrated by John McDonough. 6 CDs. (Running Time: 6 hrs.). (gr. 4 up). 2000. audio compact disk 58.00 (978-0-7887-4967-4(6), C1312E7) Recorded Bks.

Jip, His Story, Set. unabr. ed. Katherine Paterson. Read by John McDonough. 4 cass. (J). (gr. 2). 1997. bk. 57.99 (978-0-7887-1711-6(1), 40579) Recorded Bks.

Jirafa - Oso: Spanish Take-Home Parent Pack. 1 cass. (Take-Home Parent Packs Ser.). 1993. pap. bk. 16.95 (978-1-56334-379-7(7)) Hampton-Brown.

J'irai cracher sur vos tombes, Set. Boris Vian. Read by G. Robien & C. Deis. 2 cass. (FRE.). 1991. 26.95 (1297-VSL) Olivia & Hill.
Set in postwar United States, it recounts the story of Lee, the light-skinned son of a black man & a white woman, who becomes part of the white world in order to avenge the humiliations he & his race have endured. Vian was charged with obscenity for writing this bestseller of 1947.

Jitter Joint. Howard Swindle. Narrated by Richard Ferrone. 7 CDs. (Running Time: 7 hrs. 30 mins.). audio compact disk 69.00 (978-0-7887-4636-9(7)) Recorded Bks.

Jitter Joint. unabr. ed. Howard Swindle. Narrated by Richard Ferrone. 6 cass. (Running Time: 7 hrs. 30 mins.). 1999. 56.00 (978-0-7887-3481-6(4), 95875E7) Recorded Bks.
At a residential treatment clinic, a homicide detective's battle against alcoholism is interrupted by a series of murders. Each corpse carries an AA slogan - -and a mysterious link to the detective's past.

Jitter Joint. unabr. ed. Howard Swindle. Narrated by Richard Ferrone. 7 CDs. (Running Time: 7 hrs. 30 min.). 2000. audio compact disk 69.00 (C1211E7) Recorded Bks.

Jitterbug. unabr. ed. Loren D. Estleman. Read by Garrick Hagon. 8 vols. (Running Time: 8 hrs.). (Detroit Ser.). 1999. bk. 69.95 (978-0-7927-2264-9(7), CSL 153, Chivers Sound Lib) AudioGO.
It is Detroit during World War II & workers have been brought in to replace the men fighting in the war. For the first time Southern white & blacks are working together. But with the black market, rationing & the Mafia; Detroit is also a powder-keg. Through this tense world cuts a killer, a self-appointed soldier savaging the defenseless. Lieutenant Zagreb's job is to catch the killer, keep the city from exploding & save his own troubled soul.

Jitterbug. unabr. ed. Loren D. Estleman. Narrated by Peter F. James. 7 cass. (Running Time: 10 hrs.). 1998. 60.00 (978-0-7887-3120-4(3), 95783E7) Recorded Bks.
Recreates the high-powered energy & racial unrest of Detroit during World War II. With a brutal, serial killer targeting ration coupon hoarders, Lieutenant Zagreb relies on illegal, strong-arm tactics to smoke out the killer.

Jitterbug: A Remedy for the Examination Blues. Chana Sharfstein. Illus. by Paul Leung. 1989. 10.95 (978-0-916177-58-4(0)) Am Eng Pubns.

Jnana Yoga. (198) Yoga Res Foun.

Jnana Yoga. Swami Jyotirmayananda. 1 cass. (Running Time: 1 hr.). 1990. 12.99 Yoga Res Foun.

Jo McDougall: The Woman in the Next Booth. unabr. ed. Jo McDougall. Read by Jo McDougall. 1 cass. (Running Time: 29 min.). 1987. 10.00 (111387) New Letters.
Poet reads from her new book "The Woman in the Next Booth" & talks about writing.

Jo of the Chalet School. abr. ed. Elinor Brent-Dyer. 2000. 9.99 (978-0-00-102522-6(8)) Pub: HarpC GBR. Dist(s): Trafalgar

Joan: The Mysterious Life of the Heretic Who Became a Saint. unabr. ed. Donald Spoto. (Running Time: 7 hrs. 30 mins. 0 sec.). (ENG.). 2007. audio compact disk 59.99 (978-1-4001-3400-7(5)) Pub: Tantor Media. Dist(s): IngramPubServ

Joan: The Mysterious Life of the Heretic Who Became a Saint. unabr. ed. Donald Spoto. Read by Dick Hill. (Running Time: 7 hrs. 30 mins. 0 sec.). (ENG.). 2007. audio compact disk 29.99 (978-1-4001-0400-0(9)); audio compact disk 19.99 (978-1-4001-5400-5(6)) Pub: Tantor Media. Dist(s): IngramPubServ

Joan & Peter. unabr. ed. H. G. Wells. Read by Flo Gibson. 14 cass. (Running Time: 19 hrs. 30 min.). (gr. 8 up). 1999. 42.95 (978-1-55685-597-9(4)) Audio Bk Con.
Full of love, tragedy, World War I scenes & perspectives on German, Irish, Russian, British & American issues & values. Joan & Peter, orphaned at five & with four guardians, run the gamut.

Joan Baez: The First Ten Years. Perf. by Joan Baez. 1 cass. (Running Time: 60 min.). (Vanguard Folk Ser.). (J). 10.98 (2251); audio compact disk 16.98 (D2251) MFLP CA.

Joan of Arc. Mary Gordon. Read by Mari Bevon. 4 cass. (Running Time: 6 hrs.). 2000. 24.95 (978-0-7366-4946-9(8)) Books on Tape.

***Joan of Arc.** unabr. ed. Mark Twain. Read by Michael Anthony. (Running Time: 15 hrs. 30 mins.). 2010. 29.95 (978-0-7861-7305-1(X)); audio compact disk 99.00 (978-0-7861-6286-4(4)) Blckstn Audio.

Joan of Arc. unabr. ed. Mark Twain. Read by Michael Anthony. (YA). 2008. 84.99 (978-1-60514-733-8(8)) Find a World.

Joan Sprung: Ballads & Butterflies. 1 cass. 9.98 (C-60) Folk-Legacy.
Debut recording of a fine Connecticut singer & songmaker.

Joan Sprung: Pictures to My Mind. 1 cass. 9.98 (C-73) Folk-Legacy.
Another fine collection of songs from a Connecticut artist.

Joanie Bartels Best of the Magic Series. Read by Joanie Bartels. 1 cass. (Running Time: 24 min.). (Magic Ser.). (J). 1994. 9.98 (978-1-881225-31-7(3)) Discov Music.
Full length audio cassette & complete full color lyric book with words to selected songs from The Magic Series & photos of Joanie.

Joanie Bartels' Simply Magic Stories & Activities. Read by Joanie Bartels. 1 cass. (J). 1994. 6.99 incl. activity bk. with crayons. (978-1-881225-28-7(3)) Discov Music.
Activity book filled with dot-to-dots, mazes, coloring; includes audio cassette featuring the songs "There's a Hippo in My Tub" & "Dinosaur Rock 'n' Roll".

Joanie Bartel's Simply Magic Stories & Activities. Read by Joanie Bartels. 1 cass. (J). 1994. 6.99 incl. activity bk. with crayons. (978-1-881225-29-4(1)) Discov Music.
Activity book filled with dot-to-dots, mazes, coloring; includes audio cassette featuring the songs "On the Road to Where We're Going" & "Sillie Pie".

Joanna Stratton. unabr. ed. Joanna Stratton. Read by Joanna Stratton. 1 cass. (Running Time: 29 min.). 1989. 10.00 New Letters.
Stratton reads from Pioneer Women & is interviewed about compiling these diary excerpts of Kansas pioneer women.

Job. Douglas Kennedy. 2004. 14.95 (978-0-7435-4892-2(2)) Pub: S&S Audio. Dist(s): S and S Inc

Job. unabr. collector's ed. Douglas Kennedy. Read by John Edwardson. 10 cass. (Running Time: 15 hrs.). 1998. 80.00 (978-0-7366-4247-7(1), 4746) Books on Tape.
Life is good for Ned & Lizzie Allen & then his company is sold, he's fired, Lizzie takes an assignment in Los Angeles & Ned is left with nowhere else to look.

Job: A Comedy of Justice. unabr. ed. Robert A. Heinlein. (Running Time: 15 hrs. 50 mins.). (ENG.). 2009. 29.95 (978-1-4332-5157-3(4)); 85.95 (978-1-4332-5154-2(X)); audio compact disk 118.00 (978-1-4332-5155-9(8)) Blckstn Audio.

Job: A Man of Heroic Endurance. 2004. 74.00 (978-1-57972-572-3(4)); audio compact disk 74.00 (978-1-57972-571-6(6)) Insight Living.

Job: Your Biography. Neville Goddard. 1 cass. (Running Time: 62 min.). 1963. 8.00 (4) J & L Pubns.
Neville taught Imagination Creates Reality. He was a powerfully influential teacher of God as Consciousness.

Job & the Mystery of Suffering. Richard Rohr. 10 cass. (Running Time: 9 hrs. 10 min.). 69.95 Set, incl. study guide. (AA2297) Credence Commun.
Rohr gives explanations of what the text meant when written & how it applies to American culture now.

Job Burnout in the Medical Professions: Signs, Symptoms, Causes & Prevention. Arline Zeidler. 1 cass. (Running Time: 50 min.). 1997. bk. 20.00 (978-1-58111-019-7(7)) Contemporary Medical.
Characteristics, personality traits of people likely to suffer; definition, symptoms, factors, prevention of job burnout; relaxation exercises.

Job Coaching Strategies: One-day multimedia training session for job Coaches. Steve Tenpas. 2002. spiral bd. 179.00 (978-1-57861-518-6(6), IEP Res); spiral bd. 179.00 (978-1-57861-522-3(4), IEP Res) Attainment.

Job Commentary. collector's ed. Chuck Missler. 1 MP3 CD-ROM. (Running Time: 8 hours). (Chuck Missler Commentaries). 2002. cd-rom 29.95 (978-1-57821-181-4(6)) Koinonia Hse.
The book of Job pulls away our illusions and presents life as it really is. Nothing is more valuable than a valid perspective. One of the most painful - but essential - blessings is the stripping away of our delusions and erroneous presuppositions! That is why it is so important to let the Spirit of God set us straight by the Word of God, correcting our thinking and 'renewing our minds' (Romans 12:2).

Job for You: Program from the Award Winning Public Radio Series. Interview. Hosted by Fred Goodwin. Comment by John Hockenberry. 1 CD. (Running Time: 1 hr). (Infinite Mind Ser.). 2003. audio compact disk 21.95 (978-1-932479-09-6(0), LCM 253) Lichtenstein Creat.
Looking for a new job? Wish you were? Afraid you will be? This week on The Infinite Mind, we focus on how to find "The Job For You." Dr, Fred Goodwin's guests include Richard Bolles, author of the biggest-selling career book ever (seven million copies), "What Color Is Your Parachute?"; Dr. Ann Marie Ryan, president of the Society for Industrial and Organizational Psychology; Dr. Steffanie Wilk, professor of Management at the Wharton School of the University of Pennsylvania; and career coach Sharon Jordan-Evans. Also featured are a slew of career changers including oboist Blair Tindall, currently in the orchestra pit on Broadway in Man of La Mancha, but whose decision to trade the concert hall for the newsroom had some surprising consequences; management consultant Richard Cuff; teacher turned web designer Robert Boyle; and Elizabeth Betts, formerly homeless and crack-addicted, who at the age of 43 is holding down her very first full-time job... and loving it. The show also features a report on an organization called Career Transition for Dancers and how it's helping some dancers stretch themselves in new ways. John Hockenberry offers thoughts on what constitutes the perfect job: volunteering.

Job-Hunting Program. unabr. ed. Read by Tom Galloway. 8 cass. bk. 49.50 set, incl. 88p. manual. (978-0-88432-463-8(X), S01960) J Norton Pubs.
This program is a self-administered learning system especially designed for executives who know what they want & are qualified for a better paying, more personally rewarding job. Galloway will teach you the techniques & information tools you'll need to be more effective in the job-hunt process. You'll get specific suggestions on how to answer the 50 hardest interview questions.

Job Interviews, Auditions, Presentations, Oh My! Dean A. Montalbano. 2 cds. (Running Time: 2.25 hrs). (Hypnotic Sensory Response Audio Ser.). 2004. audio compact disk 39.95 (978-1-932086-20-1(X)) L Lizards Pub Co.

Job Interviews, Auditions, Presentations, oh my! Set: A Self Hypnotic. 2001. 39.95 (978-0-9708772-9-1(3)) L Lizards Pub Co.

Job of My Life. Michael Popkin. 1 cass. (Running Time: 22 min.). 1992. 5.00 (K1327) Active Parenting.
Original music from the Active Parenting Today video discussion program.

Job Performance Indicator. Sanford G. Kulkin. 8 cass. (Running Time: 4 hrs.). 1994. bk. 95.00 (978-1-58034-007-6(5)) IML Pubns.
Powerful tool for expanding one's consulting business. Measures how an employee views his or her job performance in five different areas. Ideal resource for helping employers & employees see "eye-to-eye" on performance appraisals.

Job Search: The Total System. Ken Dawson & Sheryl Dawson. 6 cass. (Running Time: 9 hrs.). 1989. 89.95 incl. wkbk. & study guide. Dawson & Dawson.
Series provides a complete program of job search with motivational success stories. Covers self-assessment, resume preparation, references, networking, telemarketing, interviewing, & negotiating, with specific practical steps to get a better job, with a better company, for better pay.

Job Search Curriculum: Read, Analyze & Respond to Job Ads. Ellen McPeek Glisan. (gr. 7-12). 2005. audio compact disk 69.00 (978-1-57861-472-1(4), IEP Res) Attainment.

Job Search Solution: The Ultimate System for Finding a Great Job Now! unabr. ed. Tony Beshara. Read by Tony Beshara. (Running Time: 12 hrs.). (ENG.). 2008. 29.98 (978-1-59659-320-6(2), GildAudio) Pub: Gildan Media. Dist(s): HachBkGrp

Job Searching Mastery: How to Win the Job of Your Dreams. Steven Green. 2 cass. (Running Time: 3 hrs.). 1997. 15.95 (978-1-55977-496-3(7)) CareerTrack Pubns.

Job-Seeking Seminar. Speeches. Peggy O. Swager. 1. (Running Time: 1 hour). 2003. audio compact disk 9.95 (978-0-9726526-2-9(0)) Hi Caliber.
Peggy Swager's popular job seeking seminar has key information for people looking for a job, or for those wanting to improve their current job position. Peggy learned how both sides of the hiring process works while working for a job recruiter. She shares behind the scene information as she tell people how to find jobs in this competitive job market. Included on the CD:Why resumes fail. Different kinds of resumes and how to when to use them. The rules for successfully faxing and emailing resumes. Where to find good paying/permanent jobs that are often overlooked. Secrets that Job Recruiter use, that you need to use. Interviewing tips. The myths about online resumes and how to make them work for you.

Jobs Around My Neighborhood/Oficios en Mi Vecindario. abr. ed. Created by Mark Wesley & Gladys Rosa-Mendoza. (English Spanish Foundations Ser.). (J). 2008. audio compact disk 9.95 (978-1-931398-59-6(3)) Me Mi Pubng.

Jobs at School: Early Explorers Emergent Set A Audio CD. Benchmark Education Staff. (J). 2006. audio compact disk 10.00 (978-1-4108-7597-6(0)) Benchmark Educ.

Job's Counsel for Enduring Verbal Assaults. 2004. audio compact disk 14.00 (978-1-57972-584-6(8)) Insight Living.

Jobs in a Community Audio CD. Adapted by Benchmark Education Company Staff. Based on a work by Cynthia Swain. (Early Explorers Set C Ser.). (J). (gr. k-1). 2008. audio compact disk 10.00 (978-1-60437-521-3(3)) Benchmark Educ.

Jobs to Be Proud Of: Profiles of Workers Who Are Blind or Visually Impaired. unabr. ed. Deborah Kendrick. Pref. by Linda Ellerbee. 2 cass. (Running Time: 1 hrs. 75 min.). 1993. 23.95 (978-0-89128-264-8(5)) Am Foun Blind.
Twelve vital & engaging blind & visually impaired people who are working at jobs they love. Offers insights, strategies & creative ideas. No special equipment necessary for playing - commerical okay.

Jocelyn Osgood in Ascent into Asgard. unabr. ed. Geoffrey McSkimming. Read by Geoffrey McSkimming. (Running Time: 5 hrs.). (Jocelyn Osgood Ser.). (YA). 2009. audio compact disk 63.95 (978-1-74093-550-0(0)) Pub: Bolinda Pubng AUS. Dist(s): Bolinda Pub Inc

***Jocelyn Osgood in xylophones above Zarundi.** Geoffrey McSkimming. Read by Geoffrey McSkimming. (Running Time: 5 hrs. 25 mins.). (Jocelyn Osgood Ser.). (J). 2010. 64.99 (978-1-74214-636-2(8), 9781742146362) Pub: Bolinda Pubng AUS. Dist(s): Bolinda Pub Inc

Jocelyn Osgood in xylophones above Zarundi. unabr. ed. Geoffrey McSkimming. Read by Geoffrey McSkimming. (Running Time: 5 hrs. 25 mins.). (Jocelyn Osgood Ser.). (J). 2009. audio compact disk 63.95 (978-1-74093-857-0(7)) Pub: Bolinda Pubng AUS. Dist(s): Bolinda Pub Inc

Jodi Benson & Friends Sing Songs from the Beginners Bible. Illus. by Jodi Benson. 1 cass. (J). 10.98 (978-0-917143-21-2(3)) Sparrow TN.

Joe. unabr. ed. Larry Brown. Narrated by Tom Stechschulte. 6 cass. (Running Time: 7 hrs.). 2000. 51.00 (978-0-7887-0407-9(9), 94599E7) Recorded Bks.
In the Mississippi countryside, a friendship between a middle-aged, alcoholic contractor & an abused teen-aged boy becomes a bizarre rite of passage for both of them.

Joe & Marilyn: A Memory of Love. unabr. ed. Roger Kahn. Read by Dick Hill. 1 MP3-CD. (Running Time: 10 hrs.). 2009. 39.97 (978-1-4233-7777-1(X), 9781423377771, Brinc Audio MP3 Lib); 39.97 (978-1-4233-7779-5(6), 9781423377795, BADLE); 24.99 (978-1-4233-7776-4(1), 9781423377764, Brilliance MP3); 24.99 (978-1-4233-7778-8(8), 9781423377788, BAD); audio compact disk 97.97 (978-1-4233-7775-7(3), 9781423377757, BriAudCD Unabrid); audio compact disk 29.99 (978-1-4233-7774-0(5), 9781423377740, Bril Audio CD Unabri) Brilliance Audio.

Joe & Marilyn: A Memory of Love. unabr. collector's ed. Roger Kahn. Read by Dick Estell. 7 cass. (Running Time: 10 hrs. 30 mins.). 1988. 56.00 (978-0-7366-1400-9(1), 2289) Books on Tape.
They lived in the headlines & on the edge. He was the most famous & probably the finest ballplayer of his generation. She was America's blonde. They were intense, impassioned lovers & long after that, gentle & loving friends. All that didn't work between Joe DiMaggio & Marilyn Monroe was their marriage.

Joe Barbera, President, Hanna Barbera Productions, & Margaret Loesch, Director, Children's Programming, NBC-TV see Scene Behind the Screen: The Business Realities of the TV Industry

***Joe Biden.** unabr. ed. Jules Witcover. (ENG.). 2010. (978-0-06-206275-8(1), Harper Audio); (978-0-06-206162-1(3), Harper Audio) HarperCollins Pubs.

Joe DiMaggio: The Hero's Life. unabr. ed. Richard Ben Cramer. Read by Richard Ben Cramer. 16 vols. (Running Time: 24 hrs.). 2001. bk. 124.95 (978-0-7927-2490-2(9), CSL 379, Chivers Sound Lib) AudioGO.
Joe DiMaggio was a mirror off our best self & he was also the loneliest hero we ever had. A nation of fans would give him anything, but what he wanted most was to hide the life he chose. This is a story that seeps through the twentieth century, bringing to light along the way not just America's national

game, but her movie stars, mobsters, pols, writers the birth (& the price) of modern national celebrity.

Joe DiMaggio: The Hero's Life. unabr. ed. Richard Ben Cramer. Read by Richard Ben Cramer. 2 CDs. (Running Time: 10 hrs.). 2002. audio compact disk 49.95 (978-0-7927-2662-3(6), CMP 379, Chivers Sound Lib) AudioGO.
Joe DiMaggio was a mirror of our best self, and he was also the loneliest hero we ever had. A nation of fans would have given him anything, but what he wanted most was to hide the life he chose. This is the story Joe DiMaggio never wanted to tell, and never wanted anyone else to tell. It is the story of grace and greed. His dignity, pride and hidden shame.

Joe DiMaggio: The Yankee Clipper. Contrib. by Joe DiMaggio. 1 CD. (Running Time: 1 hour). 2000. audio compact disk 15.95 Soundworks Intl.
Compilation of quotes & interviews.

Joe Dimaggio, the Yankee Clipper. unabr. ed. Geoffrey Giuliano. Read by Geoffrey Giuliano. (YA). 2007. 34.99 (978-1-60252-613-6(3)) Find a World.

Joe Diorio Trio Live. Joe Diorio. 2006. audio compact disk 14.95 (09782CD) Mel Bay.

Joe E. Brown: Alibi Ike. unabr. ed. Perf. by William Frawley et al. 1 cass. (Running Time: 60 min.). Dramatization. 1937. 7.95 Norelco box. (CC-5015) Natl Recrd Co.
Lux Radio Theatre's delightful baseball story of a rookie with the Chicago Cubs. Frank Tarrell is a super-star pitcher & a great long-ball hitter who has one terrible habit...he has an alibi for everything that goes wrong. A shy romance blossoms that is both refreshing & entertaining. Crooked gamblers complicate Frank's life by trying to get him to throw a couple of games. Babe Ruth & his wife talk briefly during the show with Cecil B. DeMille. A thoroughly enjoyable show from the 1935 comedy hit, Alibi Ike.

Joe Girard Set, Set. abr. ed. Joe Girard. Read by Joe Girard. (Running Time: 23400 sec.). 2006. audio compact disk 29.95 (978-0-06-087709-5(X)) HarperCollins Pubs.

Joe Gores. Interview with Joe Gores et al. 1 cass. (Running Time: 53 min.). 1985. 13.95 (978-1-55644-145-5(2), 5112) Am Audio Prose.
The author describes his days as a working detective, talks about the mystique of Dashiel Hammet, & discusses the "how to's" on writing mysteries for TV & film.

Joe Hickerson: With a Gathering of Friends. 1 cass. 9.98 (C-39) Folk-Legacy.
Songs from the head of the Folksong Archive.

Joe Hickerson No. 1: Drive Dull Care Away. 1 cass. 9.98 (C-58) Folk-Legacy.
Almost another Golden Ring, great songs & harmonies.

Joe Hickerson No. 2: Drive Dull Care Away. 1 cass. 9.98 (C-59) Folk-Legacy.
Companion volume to "Joe Hickerson: Drive Dull Care Away, One". More fine songs.

Joe Hill Meets Local Government. Contrib. by Claudia Albano. 1 cass. Alliance Innov.

Joe Jones. unabr. ed. Anne Lamott. Read by Barbara Rosenblat. (YA). 2008. 54.99 (978-1-60252-974-8(4)) Find a World.

Joe Magarac see American Tall Tales

Joe Morgan: Offensive Baseball. Read by Joe Morgan. 1 cass. 9.95 (978-0-89811-064-7(5), 7115) Lets Talk Assocs.
Joe Morgan talks about the people & events that influenced his career, & his approach to his speciality.

Joe Pace & The Colorado Mass Choir: So Good. Perf. by Colorado Mass Choir, Staff & Joseph Pace, II. 1 cass., 1 CD. (Running Time: 1 hr. 6 mins.). 1998. 10.98 (978-0-7601-2278-5(4), 01241-43111-4); audio compact disk 15.98 CD. (978-0-7601-2279-2(2), 01241-43111-2) Provident Mus Dist.
Runs the gamut between traditional & contemporary gospel, delivering messages of love, faith & spiritual commitment.

Joe Pasquale Three. abr. ed. Joe Pasquale. Read by Joe Pasquale. 1 cass. (Running Time: 1 hr.). 1999. 9.35 (978-1-86117-184-9(6)) Ulvrscrft Audio.
Joe is an utter nutter who can reduce an audience to fits of hysterical laughter simply by walking on stage.

Joe Pass No. 3: Virtuoso. Contrib. by Alan De Mause. 1985. 10.98 (978-1-56222-620-6(7), 94059C) Mel Bay.

Joe Pass - Off the Record. Tr. by Roland Leone. 1995. bk. 24.95 (978-0-7866-1744-9(6), 94890CDP) Mel Bay.

Joe Pass Live!! Contrib. by Roland Leone. 1996. bk. 29.95 (978-0-7866-1861-3(2), 94380CDP) Mel Bay.

Joe Pass Note by Note. 1993. 10.98 (978-1-56222-848-4(X), 95019C) Mel Bay.

Joe Pass Plays the Blues. Contrib. by Roland Leone. 1993. bk. 19.95 (978-0-7866-0972-7(9), 94109P); 10.98 (978-1-56222-625-1(8), 94109C) Mel Bay.

Joe Rudi: Out Fielding. Read by Joe Rudi. 1 cass. 9.95 (7119) Lets Talk Assocs.
Joe Rudi talks about the people & events which influenced his career, & his own approach to his speciality.

***Joe Sherlock, Kid Detective Audio Collection.** unabr. ed. Dave Keane. Read by Fred Berman. (ENG.). 2007. (978-0-06-126231-9(5)); (978-0-06-126230-2(7)) HarperCollins Pubs.

Joe Sherlock, Kid Detective Audio Collection: The Haunted Toolshed -The Neighborhood Stink -The Missing Monkey-Eye Diamond. unabr. ed. Dave Keane. Read by Fred Berman. 3 CDs. (Running Time: 14400 sec.). (J). (gr. 2-5). 2007. audio compact disk 22.95 (978-0-06-122760-8(9), HarperChildAud) HarperCollins Pubs.

Joe Torre's Ground Rules for Winners: Twelve Keys to Managing Team Players, Tough Bosses, Setbacks, & Success. abr. ed. Joe Torre. 2004. 10.95 (978-0-7435-4893-9(0)) Pub: S&S Audio. Dist(s): S and S Inc

***Joel.** Joel Sonnenberg. Told to Gregg Lewis. (Running Time: 8 hrs. 22 mins. 0 sec.). (ENG.). 2008. 19.99 (978-0-310-30463-0(6)) Zondervan.

Joel & Amos. deluxe ed. Chuck Missler. 8 cass. (Running Time: 12 hrs.). (Heirloom Edition Ser.). 1996. im. lthr. 4.95 (978-1-880532-11-9(5)) Koinonia Hse.
The books of Joel and Amos are referred to as "minor prophets" (based on the number of pages), but they contain some of the most fascinating and provocative prophecies you'll find anywhere in the Scriptures. The Book of Joel is devoted almost entirely to "The Day of the Lord". And the Book of Amos parallels the United States in a most disturbing way. Both studies are very timely for us today.

Joel & Amos Commentary. Chuck Missler. 1 MP3 CD-ROM. (Running Time: 8 hours). (Chuck Missler Commentaries). 2002. cd-rom 29.95 (978-1-57821-183-8(2)) Koinonia Hse.

***Joel & Cat Set the Story Straight.** unabr. ed. Nick Earls & Rebecca Sparrow. (Running Time: 5 hrs. 55 mins.). (YA). 2010. audio compact disk 63.95 (978-1-921415-79-1(7), 9781921415791) Pub: Bolinda Pubng AUS. Dist(s): Bolinda Pub Inc

Joel C. Rosenberg CD Collection: The Last Jihad, the Last Days, & the Ezekiel Option. abr. ed. Joel C. Rosenberg. Read by Dick Hill & Patrick G. Lawlor. (Running Time: 16 hrs.). 2007. audio compact disk 34.95 (978-1-4233-1684-8(3), 9781423316848, BACD) Brilliance Audio.

Joel's Army. Jack Deere. 1 cass. (Running Time: 90 mins.). (Joel's Army Ser.: Vol. 1). 2000. 5.00 (JD06-001) Morning NC.
This overview of the end-time church is powerful encouragement to pursue God's purposes for our times.

Joel's Army Series. Jack Deere. 2 cass. (Running Time: 3 hrs.). 2000. 10.00 (JD06-000) Morning NC.
Includes: "Joel's Army" & "The Last-Day Outpouring of the Spirit." This overview of the end-time church is powerful encouragement to pursue God's purposes for our times.

Joe's Law: America's Toughest Sheriff Takes on Illegal Immigration, Drugs, & Everything Else That Threatens America. unabr. ed. Sheriff Joe Arpaio & Len Sherman. Read by Phil Gigante. (Running Time: 8 hrs.). 2008. 24.95 (978-1-4233-6432-0(5), 9781423364320, BAD); 39.25 (978-1-4233-6433-7(3), 9781423364337, BADLE) Brilliance Audio.

Joe's Law: America's Toughest Sheriff Takes on Illegal Immigration, Drugs, & Everything Else That Threatens America. unabr. ed. Len Sherman & Joe Arpaio. Read by Phil Gigante. (Running Time: 28800 sec.). 2008. audio compact disk 24.95 (978-1-4233-6430-6(9), 9781423364306, Brilliance MP3) Brilliance Audio.

Joe's Law: America's Toughest Sheriff Takes on Illegal Immigration, Drugs, & Everything Else That Threatens America. unabr. ed. Len Sherman & Sheriff Joe Arpaio. Read by Phil Gigante. (Running Time: 8 hrs.). 2008. audio compact disk 39.25 (978-1-4233-6431-3(7), 9781423364313, Brlnc Audio MP3 Lib); audio compact disk 87.25 (978-1-4233-6429-0(5), 9781423364290, BriAudCD Unabrid); audio compact disk 29.95 (978-1-4233-6428-3(7), 9781423364283, Bril Audio CD Unabri) Brilliance Audio.

Joey: A Story Told in Film by Tom Brown Activity Book Written by George Robinson & Barbara Maines. rev. ed. Tom Brown & Barbara Maines. 2000. 46.95 (978-1-873942-28-4(1)) Pub: P Chapman GBR. Dist(s): SAGE

Joey: The True Story of One Boy's Relationship with God. unabr. ed. Joseph F. Girzone. Narrated by Nelson Runger. 3 cass. (Running Time: 3 hrs. 30 mins.). 1997. 26.00 (978-0-7887-1752-9(9), 95230E7) Recorded Bks.
Joey is a boy like any other, eagerly looking forward to a lifetime of adventure. But as he becomes a talented musician, his sunny world splinters into a maze of confusion & trouble.

Joey Goat. Created by Kane Press. (Let's Read Together Ser.). (J). 2005. 2.95 (978-1-57565-030-2(4)) Pub: Kane Pr. Dist(s): Lerner Pub

Joey Goat. Created by Kane Press. (Let's Read Together Ser.). 2005. audio compact disk 4.25 (978-1-57565-178-1(5)) Pub: Kane Pr. Dist(s): Lerner Pub

Joey Pigza Loses Control. unabr. ed. Jack Gantos. 3 cass. (Running Time: 3 hrs. 50 mins.). (Joey Pigza Ser.: Bk. 2). (J). (gr. 5-9). 2004. 30.00 (978-0-8072-8725-5(3), Listening Lib) Random Audio Pubg.
Joey feels prepared to face the most mysterious member of his family, his estranged father, Carter Pigza. He convinces his skeptical mom to let him spend part of his summer vacation getting to know his dad again. The only problem is that Joey's dad is just as wired as Joey used to be. Carter believes that Joey can kick his ADD the way he himself kicked alcoholism, cold turkey. But when Carter flushes his meds, Joey has to decide if being friends with his dad is worth losing his hard-won self-control.

Joey Pigza Loses Control. unabr. ed. Jack Gantos. Read by Jack Gantos. 3 cass. (Running Time: 3 hrs. 30 mins.). (Joey Pigza Ser.: Bk. 2). (J). (gr. 4-7). 2004. 30.00 (978-0-8072-8728-6(8), YA248CX, Listening Lib) Random Audio Pubg.
When Joey Pigza meets his dad for the first time in years, he meets a grown-up version of his old out-of-control self. Carter Pigza is as wired as Joey used to be before his stint in special ed & before he got his new meds.

Joey Pigza Loses Control. unabr. ed. Jack Gantos. Read by Jack Gantos. 3 vols. (Running Time: 3 hrs. 50 mins.). (Joey Pigza Ser.: Bk. 2). (J). (gr. 5-9). 2004. pap. bk. 36.00 (978-0-8072-8726-2(1), LyA 248 SP, Listening Lib); audio compact disk 30.00 (978-1-4000-8616-0(7), Listening Lib) Random Audio Pubg.

Joey Pigza Loses Control. unabr. ed. Jack Gantos. Read by Jack Gantos. (ENG.). (J). (gr. 5). 2009. audio compact disk 30.00 (978-0-7393-8103-8(2), Listening Lib) Pub: Random Audio Pubg. Dist(s): Random

Joey Pigza Swallowed the Key. Jack Gantos. Read by Jack Gantos. 3 CDs. (Running Time: 2 hrs. 58 mins.). (Joey Pigza Ser.: Bk. 1). (J). (gr. 5-9). 2004. audio compact disk 30.00 (978-0-8072-2003-0(5), Listening Lib) Random Audio Pubg.

Joey Pigza Swallowed the Key. collector's ed. Jack Gantos. Read by Jack Gantos. 2 cass. (Running Time: 3 hrs.). (Joey Pigza Ser.: Bk. 1). (J). 2000. 18.00 (978-0-7366-9006-5(9), 5159) Books on Tape.
Joey Pigza has a hard time controlling himself & his "meds" are no match for his intense hyperactivity. To add to his problem, his mom has been warned that if he keeps acting up he could be transferred to the downtown special-ed center.

Joey Pigza Swallowed the Key. unabr. ed. Jack Gantos. Read by Jack Gantos. 2 cass. (Joey Pigza Ser.: Bk. 1). (J). (gr. 1-8). 1999. 23.00 (LL 0150, Chivers Child Audio) AudioGO.

Joey Pigza Swallowed the Key. unabr. ed. Jack Gantos. Read by Jack Gantos. 2 vols. (Running Time: 2 hrs. 58 mins.). (Joey Pigza Ser.: Bk. 1). (J). (gr. 5-9). 2004. pap. bk. 29.00 (978-0-8072-8166-6(2), YA120SP, Listening Lib); 23.00 (978-0-8072-8165-9(4), YA120CX, Listening Lib) Random Audio Pubg.
Joey Pigza is wired, really wired. His prescription "meds" are no match for his mood swings. One minute he's sitting at his desk like any other kid; next he's out of control & taking time-out in the hallway. Joey knows he's a disappointment to people who care about him. To add to his problem, his mom has been warned that if he keeps acting up he could be transferred to the downtown special-ed center.

Joey Pigza Swallowed the Key. unabr. ed. Jack Gantos. Read by Jack Gantos. (Running Time: 3 hrs. 36 mins.). (ENG.). (J). (gr. 5). 2009. audio compact disk 27.00 (978-0-7393-8113-7(X), Listening Lib) Pub: Random Audio Pubg. Dist(s): Random

Joey Runs Away. 2004. bk. 24.95 (978-0-89719-780-9(1)); pap. bk. 14.95 (978-1-56008-058-9(2)); 8.95 (978-1-56008-393-1(X)); cass. & flmstrp 30.00 (978-0-89719-576-8(0)) Weston Woods.

Joey's Case. unabr. ed. K. C. Constantine. Read by Lloyd James. 7 cass. (Running Time: 10 hrs. 30 min.). (Mario Balzic Ser.). 1997. 56.00 (978-0-7366-3783-1(4), 4455) Books on Tape.
Mario Balzic has been dodging Albert Castelucci for months. You can try to console a man whose only son has been shot to death but Castelucci doesn't want Balzic's sympathy.

Johann Sebastian Bach. Read by Jeremy Siepmann & John Shrapnel. 4 CDs. (Running Time: 4 hrs. 35 min.). (Life & Works Ser.). 2003. pap. bk. 35.99 (978-1-84379-022-8(X)) Naxos.

Johanna Lindsey: A Man to Call My Own, a Loving Scoundrel, Captive of My Desires. abr. ed. Johanna Lindsey. Read by Laural Merlington. (Running Time: 18 hrs.). 2007. audio compact disk 34.95 (978-1-4233-2319-8(X), 9781423323198, BACD) Brilliance Audio.

***Johanna Lindsey: All I Need Is You, Joining.** abr. ed. Johanna Lindsey & 2-In-1 Cd Coll. (Running Time: 6 hrs.). 2010. audio compact disk 19.99 (978-1-4418-5049-2(X), 9781441850492) Brilliance Audio.

Johanna Lindsey CD Collection 3: A Loving Scoundrel, Captive of My Desires, No Choice but Seduction. abr. ed. Johanna Lindsey. Read by Laural Merlington. (Running Time: 17 hrs.). 2011. audio compact disk 34.99 (978-1-4418-1194-3(X), 9781441811943, BACD) Brilliance Audio.

***Johanna Lindsey CD Collection 6: The Heir, the Devil Who Tamed Her, A Rogue of My Own.** abr. ed. Johanna Lindsey. (Running Time: 14 hrs.). 2010. audio compact disk 29.99 (978-1-4418-6160-3(2), 9781441861603, BACD) Brilliance Audio.

Johannes Brahms. Read by Jeremy Siepmann & Jasper Britton. 4 CDs. (Running Time: 5 hrs.). (Life & Works Ser.). 2003. pap. bk. 35.99 (978-1-84379-057-0(2)) Naxos.

Johannine Letters. William F. Maestri. Read by William F. Maestri. 2 cass. (Running Time: 2 hrs.). 16.95 set. (TAH216) Alba Hse Comns.

John. Niall Williams. Read by Nicholas Bell. (Running Time: 10 hrs. 20 mins.). 2009. 84.99 (978-1-74214-291-3(5), 9781742142913) Pub: Bolinda Pubng AUS. Dist(s): Bolinda Pub Inc

John. deluxe ed. Chuck Missler. 10 cass. (Running Time: 15 hrs.). (Heirloom Edition Ser.). 1996. 89.95 Incls. notes. (978-1-880532-21-8(2)) Koinonia Hse.
For God so loved the world, that he gave his only begotten Son, that whosoever believeth in him should not perish, but have everlasting life. - John 3:16 Because of its emphasis on "the Love of God" and Jesus' being the incarnation of that Love, many believe this gospel is the most important for new and old Christians alike to take to heart. Written by the "disciple whom Jesus loved", the book of John is organized around seven miracles, seven discourses and seven "I AM" statements. This study is so deep "an elephant can bathe in it, and yet an infant can wade in it.".

John. unabr. ed. Cynthia Lennon. Read by Rosalyn Landor. 10 CDs. (Running Time: 10 hrs.). 2005. audio compact disk 90.00 (978-1-4159-2588-1(7)); 72.00 (978-1-4159-2587-4(9)) Books on Tape.
When she was eighteen years old, a girl named Cynthia Powell met a boy named John Lennon and they fell in love. Their ten-year relationship coincided with the start of the Beatles phenomenon - from Liverpool's dockside clubs to the dizzying worldwide fame that followed. And Cynthia Lennon, John's first wife, was an integral part of the swirl of events that are now an indelible part of the history of rock and roll. In John, Cynthia recalls those times with the loving honesty of an insider, offering new and fascinating insights into the life of John Lennon and the early days of the Beatles. And with the perspective only years can provide she also tells the compelling story of her marriage to a man who was to become a music legend, a cultural hero and a defining figure of the twentieth century. Cynthia has seldom talked in any detail about her marriage and the painful events that followed John's tragic assassination in 1980. Now she candidly reveals the good and the bad, the loving and the cruel sides of John. She tells of the breakdown of their marriage and the beginning of his relationship with Yoko Ono in more detail than has ever been disclosed before and documents the difficulties estrangement from John - and his subsequent death - brought for herself and their son, Julian. In John, Cynthia Lennon has created a vivid portrait of the 1960s, the Beatles and the man she never stopped loving.

John. unabr. ed. Niall Williams & Niall Williams. Read by Nicholas Bell. (Running Time: 37320 sec.). 2008. audio compact disk 93.95 (978-1-921415-24-1(X), 9781921415241) Pub: Bolinda Pubng AUS. Dist(s): Bolinda Pub Inc

John, Pt. 1. (LifeLight Ser.). 2002. audio compact disk 15.00 (978-0-570-07893-7(8), 20-3348) Concordia.

John, Pt. 2. (LifeLight Ser.). 2002. audio compact disk 15.00 (978-0-570-07899-9(7), 20-3354) Concordia.

John, XPt. 1. (LifeLight Bible Studies: Course 7). 13.95 (20-2275) Concordia.

John, XPt. 2. (LifeLight Bible Studies: Course 8). 13.95 Set. (20-2280) Concordia.

John A. Williams: Interview with John A. Williams & Kay Bonetti. 1 cass. 1989. 13.95 (978-1-55644-344-2(7), 9082) Am Audio Prose.

John Adams. 1 cass. 10.00 (HTA503) Esstee Audios.
An analysis of the presidency of the first Adams has a remarkable application to today.

John Adams. David McCullough. Narrated by Nelson Runger. 26 CDs. (Running Time: 30 hrs. 30 mins.). audio compact disk 158.00 (978-1-4025-2069-3(7)) Recorded Bks.

John Adams. movie tie-in abr. ed. David McCullough. Read by Edward Herrmann. 9 CDs. (Running Time: 100 hrs. 0 mins. 0 sec.). (ENG.). 2008. audio compact disk 29.95 (978-0-7435-7242-2(4)) Pub: S&S Audio. Dist(s): S and S Inc

John Adams. movie tie-in unabr. ed. David McCullough. Read by Edward Herrmann & Nelson Runger. (Running Time: 30 hrs. 0 mins. 0 sec.). (ENG.). 2008. audio compact disk 59.95 (978-0-7435-7243-9(2)) Pub: S&S Audio. Dist(s): S and S Inc

John Adams. unabr. ed. David McCullough. Narrated by Nelson Runger. 21 cass. (Running Time: 30 hrs. 30 mins.). 2001. 139.00 (978-0-7887-9472-8(8), 96791) Recorded Bks.
His presidency falling between Washington and Jefferson, John Adams has often been overlooked. But here is a fresh portrait that shows Adams as a brilliant, compassionate man who was absolutely integral to the realization of independence.

John Adams. unabr. ed. David McCullough. 2004. 60.95 (978-0-7435-5086-4(2)) Pub: S&S Audio. Dist(s): S and S Inc

John Adams & the Undeclared War with France. Kenneth Bruce. Dramatization. (Excursions in History Ser.). 12.50 Alpha Tape.

John & Teresa: Voices of a Man & a Woman. Constance FitzGerald. 1 cass. 1987. 7.95 (TAH191) Alba Hse Comns.
Through a series of vibrant Teresian images of Christ, Sr. Constance highlights the prolonged struggle of a 16th century woman for liberation from potentially destructive images of God & self into transformed, full human consciousness.

John & the Inquisition. Kieran Kavanaugh. 1 cass. (Running Time: 53 min.). 1992. 7.95 (TAH284) Alba Hse Comns.
St. John of the Cross & the inquisition.

John Anderson, My Jo see Poetry of Robert Burns & Border Ballads

John Arden: Sergeant Musgrave's Dance. unabr. ed. John Arden. Perf. by Gordon Jackson. Composed by Dudley Moore. 2 cass. 17.95 (SCN 206) J Norton Pubs.
Passionate plea against violence & war but handled in a chilling way, combining prose, poetry & song.

John Arden: The Old Man Sleeps Alone. unabr. ed. John Arden. 1 cass. 12.95 (ECN214) J Norton Pubs.
Conveys the social & political tensions of twelfth century England through the legend surrounding the great Cathedral of Durham & its Lady Chapel.

John Ashbery. unabr. ed. John Ashbery. 1 cass. (Author Speaks Ser.). 1991. 14.95 J Norton Pubs.
Archival recordings of 20th-century authors.

John Ashbery. unabr. ed. Read by John Ashbery. 1 cass. (Running Time: 29 min.). Incl. John Ashbery: Selected Poems; 1987. 10.00 New Letters.
Poet gives recital presentation at the Kansas City Art Institute.

John Ashbery: Selected Poems see John Ashbery

John Balaban. unabr. ed. Read by John Babalan. 1 cass. (Running Time: 29 min.). 1985. 10.00 New Letters.
Drawn from Balaban's experiences backpacking the highways of America: he reads from "Walking Down into Cebolla Canyon" & "Blue Mountain".

John Barrington Cowles see Tales of the Supernatural

John Betjeman: Selected Poems. abr. ed. Read by John Betjeman. 10.95 (978-0-8045-0710-3(4), SAC 710) Spoken Arts.

John Bollinger: The Use of Price Patterns & Oscillators with Trading Bands to Generate Buy & Sell Signals. Read by John Bollinger. 1 cass. 30.00 Dow Jones Telerate.
John will briefly outline the history of trading bands before discussing the construction & implementation of Bollinger Bands. A description of the typical buy & sell patterns generated by price action in relation to the bands will follow. In the second half of his talk he will discuss the use of several oscillators in conjunction with trading bands used to produce buy & sell signals. He will finish with a discussion of forecasting commodity price movements using stock prices, trading bands & oscillators.

John Bradshaw on Surviving Divorce. unabr. ed. John Bradshaw. 1 cass. (Running Time: 1 hrs. 30 min.). 1987. 12.00 (978-1-57388-020-6(5)) J B Media.
For those anticipating, going through, or having completed a divorce.

John Bradshaw Poetry - Music of the Soul. John Bradshaw. 1 CD. (Running Time: 90 mins.). 2000. audio compact disk 17.95 J B Media.
A collection of classic & contemporary poems spanning the gamut of human emotions movingly presented against a background of beautifully crafted & inspiring music.

John Brown. Read by Lary Lewman. 1 cass. 1.00 (HB266) Esstee Audios.
Radio drama.

John Brown, Rose & the Midnight Cat. 2004. 8.95 (978-0-89719-901-8(4)); cass. & flmstrp 30.00 (978-0-89719-501-0(9)) Weston Woods.

John Bunyan. abr. ed. Sam Wellman. 1 cass. (Running Time: 1 hrs. 30 min.). (Heroes of the Faith Ser.). (C). 4.97 (978-1-57748-090-7(2)) Barbour Pub.

John Bunyan: His Life, Times & Work. unabr. ed. John Brown. Read by Nadia May. (Running Time: 8.5 hrs. NaN mins.). 2009. 29.95 (978-1-4332-6686-7(5)); audio compact disk 70.00 (978-1-4332-6683-6(0)) Blckstn Audio.

John Bytheway COLL. John Bytheway. 2008. audio compact disk 39.95 (978-1-59038-993-5(X)) Deseret Bk.

John C Maxwell's Leadership Series. unabr. ed. John Maxwell. (Running Time: 17 hrs. 30 mins. 0 sec.). (ENG.). 2009. audio compact disk 28.98 (978-1-59644-833-9(4), Hovel Audio) christianaud.

John Calvin: The Story of One of Christianity's Most Influential Leaders. unabr. ed. William Lindner. Read by Lloyd James. (Running Time: 19800 sec.). (Men of Faith (Blackstone) Ser.). 2007. 23.95 (978-0-7861-2426-8(1)); audio compact disk 24.00 (978-0-7861-8829-1(4)) Blckstn Audio.

***John Calvin & his passion for the majesty of God.** unabr. ed. John Piper. Narrated by Michael Koontz. (ENG.). 2009. 5.98 (978-1-59644-770-7(2), Hovel Audio) christianaud.

John Calvin & his passion for the majesty of God. unabr. ed. John Piper. Narrated by Michael Koontz. (Running Time: 1 hr. 6 mins. 0 sec.). (ENG.). 2009. audio compact disk 8.98 (978-1-59644-769-1(9), Hovel Audio) christianaud.

John Cardinal O'Connor, Mass & Homily; Most Rev. James C. Timlin, Mass & Homily. 1 cass. (National Meeting of the Institute, 1995 Ser.). 4.00 (95N8) IRL Chicago.

John Case CD Collection: The Syndrome, the Murder Artist, Ghost Dancer. abr. ed. John Case. Read by Dick Hill. (Running Time: 18 hrs.). 2009. audio compact disk 34.99 (978-1-4233-7970-6(5), 9781423379706, BACD) Brilliance Audio.

***John chancellor makes me Cry.** abr. ed. Anne Rivers Siddons. Read by Dana Ivey. (ENG.). 2005. (978-0-06-087916-7(5), Harper Audio); (978-0-06-087917-4(3), Harper Audio) HarperCollins Pubs.

John Cheever. Interview with John Cheever. 1 cass. (Running Time: 25 min.). 1978. 11.95 (L012) TFR.
Cheever talks about his book "Falcon," which departs from his usual urbane subjects to deal with incarceration, fratricide, homosexuality & drug addiction.

John Cheever. unabr. ed. John Cheever. 1 cass. (Author Speaks Ser.). 1991. 14.95 J Norton Pubs.
Archival recordings of 20th-century authors.

***John Cheever Audio Collection.** unabr. ed. John Cheever. Read by Meryl Streep et al. (ENG.). 2004. (978-0-06-079964-9(1), Caedmon); (978-0-06-074402-1(2), Caedmon) HarperCollins Pubs.

John Cheever Audio Collection. unabr. ed. John Cheever. Read by Ben Cheever et al. 6 CDs. (Running Time: 6 hrs. 30 mins.). 2009. audio compact disk & audio compact disk 14.99 (978-0-06-196535-7(9), Caedmon) HarperCollins Pubs.

John Ciardi, Set, Pts. 1 & 11. unabr. ed. Read by John Ciardi. 2 cass. (Running Time: 29 min.). 1985. 10.00 ea. One-sided cass.; 18.00 Two-sided cass. New Letters.
Popular poet, etymologist, & radio commentator John Ciardi reads poems about war, Italy, & aging.

John Ciardi Memorial. unabr. ed. John Ciardi. Read by John Ciardi. 1 cass. (Running Time: 29 min.). 1991. 10.00 (050286) New Letters.

John Coltrane's Giant Steps. Chris Raschka. Illus. by Chris Raschka. 11 vols. (Running Time: 15 mins.). pap. bk. 16.95 (978-0-87499-972-3(3)); pap. bk. (978-0-87499-974-7(X)); pap. bk. 18.95 (978-1-59112-416-0(6)); pap. bk. (978-1-59112-603-4(7)) Live Oak Media.

John Coltrane's Giant Steps. Chris Raschka. Illus. by Chris Raschka. (Running Time: 15 mins.). 2002. 9.95 (978-0-87499-971-6(5)); audio compact disk 12.95 (978-1-59112-415-3(8)) Live Oak Media.

John Coltrane's Giant Steps. abr. ed. Contrib. by John Coltrane. 11 vols. (Running Time: 15 mins.). (Live Oak Readalong Ser.). (J). (ps-4). 2002. bk. 25.95 (978-0-87499-973-0(1)) Pub: Live Oak Media. Dist(s): AudioGO
Jazz great John Coltrane's classic "Giant Steps" serves as the backdrop to this treatment with the printed page as the stage, and sheets of color to match Coltrane's "sheets of sound".

John Commentary. Chuck Missler. 1 MP3 CD-ROM. (Running Time: 8 hours). (Hierloom Edition). 2001. cd-rom 44.95 (978-1-57821-166-1(2)) Koinonia Hse.
Because of its emphasis on "the Love of God" and Jesus' being the incarnation of that Love, many believe this gospel is the most important for new and old Christians alike to take to heart. Written by the "disciple whom Jesus loved", the book of John is organized around seven miracles, seven discourses and seven "I AM" statements. This study is so deep "an elephant can bathe in it, and yet an infant can wade in it.".

John Cowley. unabr. ed. John Cowley. 1 cass. (Author Speaks Ser.). 1991. 14.95 J Norton Pubs.
Archival recordings of 20th-century authors.

John D. Founding Father of Rockefellers. unabr. ed. David F. Hawke. Narrated by Tom West. 5 cass. (Running Time: 7 hrs. 30 mins.). 1982. 44.00 (978-1-55690-266-6(2), 82011E7) Recorded Bks.
The founder of Standard Oil became the richest man in the world.

John Day Fossil Beds in Oregon. Garry De Young. 1 cass. 5.00 De Young Pr.

John Dewey: The United States (1859-1952) abr. ed. Narrated by Charlton Heston. (Running Time: 8004 sec.). (Audio Classics: the Giants of Philosophy Ser.). 2006. audio compact disk 25.95 (978-0-7861-6935-1(4)) Pub: Blckstn Audio. Dist(s): NetLibrary CO

John Dewey: The United States (1859-1952) unabr. ed. John J. Stuhr. Read by Charlton Heston. Ed. by McElroy Smith & Wendy McElroy. 2 cass. (Running Time: 3 hrs.). (Giants of Philosophy Ser.). 1991. 17.95 Set. (978-0-938935-28-5(3), 10312) Knowledge Prod.
Dewey believed that the scientific method, when applied to human affairs, can enhance personal happiness & community cooperation.

John Dewey: The United States (1859-1952), Set. unabr. ed. Read by Charlton Heston. 2 cass. (Giants of Philosophy Ser.). 17.95 (K128) Blckstn Audio.
See how one of the world's most important philosophers created a complete system of thought, including his views on ethics, metaphysics, politics & aesthetics. Learn about his epistemology - how we know what we know.

John Diamond. unabr. ed. Leon Garfield. Narrated by Ron Keith. 5 pieces. (Running Time: 5 hrs. 45 mins.). (YA). 2003. 45.00 (978-1-4025-1715-0(7)) Recorded Bks.
The adventure of 12-year-old William Jones? lifetime begins when he hears his father?s footsteps, pacing back and forth late at night across the floor of the bedroom beneath his own even though his father is dead. To stop the restless pacing of his father?s ghost, William goes to London to find John Diamond, the son of the man his father cheated two decades earlier. In a strange, shadowy world of thieves, swindlers, and cutthroats, William tries to make amends for the sins of his father before someone with a 20-year-old grudge kills him!.

John Doe: Level 1. Antoinette Moses. Contrib. by Philip Prowse. (Running Time: 43 mins.). (Cambridge English Readers Ser.). (ENG.). 1999. 9.45 (978-0-521-65618-4(4)) Cambridge U Pr.

John Donne: Love Poems. unabr. ed. Poems. John Donne. Narrated by Edward Herrmann. 1 cass. (Running Time: 1 hr. 30 mins.). 1990. 10.00 (978-1-55690-267-3(0), 90025E7) Recorded Bks.
Twenty-nine secular & religious poems by the 17th Century poet. Includes: "The Flea"; "To His Mistress Going to Bed"; "Elegy 16" & "A Valediction Forbidding Mourning".

John Donne: Selected Poems. abr. ed. John Donne. 18.99 (978-1-85998-693-6(5), HoddrStoughton) Pub: Hodder General GBR. Dist(s): Trafalgar

John Donne: Selected Poems. unabr. ed. Poems. John Donne. Read by Frederick Davidson. 2 cass. (Running Time: 3 hrs.). 1992. 17.95 (978-0-7861-0357-7(4), 1314) Blckstn Audio.
Donne has been called the greatest English love poet, & this collection includes love poems, songs & elegies as well as religious poems inspired by his renunciation of Catholicism & his struggle for assurance & salvation. (Donne became a celebrated preacher before the courts of James & Charles I). Also included are "Anniversaries," reflecting Donne's interest in Copernican astronomy, & "The Storm" & "The Calm," commemorating voyages he took with the likes of Sir Walter Raleigh.

John Donne: Poems. unabr. ed. John Donne. Read by Ensemble Cast Staff. 2 CDs. (Running Time: 8100 sec.). (ENG.). 2006. audio compact disk 16.95 (978-1-59887-040-4(8), 1598870408, HighBridge Classics) Pub: HighBridge. Dist(s): Workman Pub
The best of this brilliant poet, read by leading actors of the British stage and screen: Stella Gonet, Haydn Gwynne, David Horovitch, Alex Jennings, Jeremy Northam, and Nathaniel Parker.

John Dos Passos. unabr. ed. John Dos Passos. 1 cass. (Author Speaks Ser.). 1991. 14.95 J Norton Pubs.
Archival recordings of 20th-century authors.

John Dos Passos Reads His Poetry. unabr. ed. John Dos Passos. Read by John Dos Passos. 1cass. (Running Time: 1 hr. 16 min.). 1966. 12.95 (23045) J Norton Pubs.

John Edgar Wideman. unabr. ed. John Edgar Wideman. Read by John Edgar Wideman. 1 cass. (Running Time: 29 min.). 1986. 10.00 New Letters.
Award-winning black author, Wideman, reads excerpts from his new novel "Reuben" about a black man in Pennsylvania who becomes a self-taught lawyer.

John Edgar Wideman II: Philadelphia Fire. unabr. ed. John Edgar Wideman. Read by John Edgar Wideman. Interview with Rebekah Presson. 1 cass. (Running Time: 29 min.). 1991. 10.00 (020891) New Letters.
Wideman reads from his new novel, "Philadelphia Fire", which was inspired by the bombing of the Move house in 1987.

John Edgar Wideman Interview with Kay Bonetti. Interview. Interview with John Edgar Wideman & Kay Bonetti. 1 cass. (Running Time: 78 min.). 1985. 13.95 (978-1-55644-137-0(1), 5082) Am Audio Prose.

John F. Kennedy. Prod. by A&E Television Network Staff. 1 cass. 1997. 9.95 (978-0-7670-0438-1(8)) A & E Home.
Presidents.

John F. Kennedy. unabr. ed. (Biography Ser.). (J). (ps). 1988. bk. 27.90 (SAC 6546) Spoken Arts.

John Frame & Cornelius Van Til. Gordon Clark. 1 cass. (Lectures on Apologetics: No. 14). 5.00 Trinity Found.

John Frederick Nims. unabr. ed. John F. Nims. Read by John F. Nims. 1 cass. (Running Time: 29 min.). 1986. 10.00 New Letters.
A reading by the Chicago poet & translator.

John Gardner. Interview with John Gardner. 1 cass. (Running Time: 20 min.). 1979. 10.95 (L027) TFR.
Scores all of literature since Shakespeare & says the failure of modern writing is that it doesn't concern practical things, such as bringing up kids.

John Gardner. unabr. ed. John Gardner. Interview with John Gardner. 1 cass. (Running Time: 29 min.). 1985. 10.00 New Letters.
Gardner discusses his controversial critical work "On Moral Fiction" & reads excerpts from "Grendel".

John Gielgud. Gyles Brandreth. 5 CDs. (Isis (CDs) Ser.). (J). 2005. audio compact disk 59.95 (978-0-7531-2405-5(X)) Pub: ISIS Lrg Prnt GBR. Dist(s): Ulverscroft US

John Gielgud. unabr. ed. Gyles Brandreth. Read by Gyles Brandreth. 4 cass. (Running Time: 5 hrs.). (Isis Ser.). (J). 2002. 44.95 (978-0-7531-1307-3(4)) Pub: ISIS Lrg Prnt GBR. Dist(s): Ulverscroft US
For eight decades Gielgud dominated his profession, as a classical actor playing the definitive Hamlet, Richard II and Lear, and later, in plays by Printer and Alan Bennett. In his twenties he appeared in silent movies and more than half a century later, he became a Hollywood star. Gyles Brandeth pays tribute to this fascinating character, renowned for his witty anecdotes and accidental insults, which he called "Gielgoofs".

John Giorno. unabr. ed. John Giorno. Read by John Giorno. 1 cass. (Running Time: 29 min.). 1988. 10.00 (042288) New Letters.
The founder of Giorno Poetry Systems, Inc. is responsible for some of the most innovative recordings of poets & musicians.

John Glenn Set: A Memoir. abr. ed. Read by John Glenn. Mem. of John Glenn. Contrib. by Nick Taylor. 5 CDs. (Running Time: 6 hrs.). 2000. audio compact disk 29.95 (Random AudioBks) Random Audio Pubg.

John Gray Presents: Men Are from Mars, Women Are from Venus: Live on Broadway. unabr. ed. John Gray. Read by John Gray. 4 cass. (Running Time: 6 hrs.). 1999. 24.95 Set. (978-1-55935-298-7(1)) Soundelux.
Gray recounts witty anecdotes, role plays both genders, & interacts with the audience in a way which informs & delights with the understanding of the humorous differences between men & women.

John Gray's Positive Parenting. unabr. ed. John Gray. 1 cass. (Running Time: 240 min.). 1999. 24.95 (978-1-55935-331-1(7)) Soundelux.
Discusses communication skills that will help you raise cooperative, confident, compassionate children. Live seminar.

John Gregory Dunne. Interview with John Gregory Dunne. 1 cass. (Running Time: 25 min.). 1979. 10.95 (L019) TFR.
Dunne talks about his book "True Confessions" & movie "A Star is Born.".

John Grisham Value Collection: A Time to Kill; The Firm; The Client. abr. ed. John Grisham. Read by Michael Beck et al. 10 CDs. (Running Time: 12 hrs.). (John Grisham Ser.). (ENG.). 2004. audio compact disk 34.95 (978-0-7393-1264-3(2), Random AudioBks) Pub: Random Audio Pubg. Dist(s): Random

John H. Gibbon Jr. Lecture: From Palliation to Prevention: Boons & Boomerangs. 1 cass. (Named Lectures: C85-NL2). 1985. 7.50 (8532) Am Coll Surgeons.

John Halifax, Gentleman. Dinah Maria Mulock Craik. Read by Anais 9000. 2008. 33.95 (978-1-60112-189-9(X)) Babblebooks.

John Hancock: Independent Boy. Kathryn Cleven Sisson. Read by Patrick G. Lawlor. (Running Time: 7200 sec.). (Young Patriots Ser.). (J). 2007. 22.95 (978-1-4332-0159-2(3)) Blckstn Audio.

John Hancock: Independent Boy. unabr. ed. Kathryn Cleven Sisson. Read by Patrick G. Lawlor. (Young Patriots Ser.). (J). 2007. 34.99 (978-1-60252-663-1(X)) Find a World.

John Handcox: Songs, Poems, & Stories of the Southern Tenant Farmers Union. Prod. by Mark Jackson. Contrib. by Joe Glazer & Michael Honey. 1 CD with booklet. (West Virginia University Press Sound Archives Ser.: 5). 2004. bk. 16.00 (978-0-937058-90-9(4)) West Va U Pr.

John Henry see American Tall Tales

John Henry. 2004. pap. bk. 18.95 (978-1-55592-749-3(1)); pap. bk. 38.75 (978-1-55592-688-5(6)); pap. bk. 32.75 (978-1-55592-250-4(3)); pap. bk. 14.95 (978-1-55592-048-7(9)); audio compact disk 12.95 (978-1-55592-735-6(1)) Weston Woods.

John Henry. Julius Lester. Narrated by Samuel L. Jackson. Music by Crystal Taleifero. 1 cass., 5 bks. (Running Time: 18 min.). (J). pap. bk. 32.75 Weston Woods.
Based on an African American folk ballad.

John Henry. Julius Lester. Narrated by Samuel L. Jackson. Music by Crystal Taleifero. 1 cass. (Running Time: 18 min.). (J). (ps-4). pap. bk. 12.95 Weston Woods.
One side with page turn signals, one side without.

John Henry. unabr. ed. Julius Lester. Narrated by Samuel L. Jackson & Crystal Taliefero. 1 cass. (Running Time: 19 min.). (J). (ps-4). 1998. pap. bk. 8.95 (978-0-7882-0086-1(0), RAC377) Weston Woods.
Based on an African American folk ballad, this story tells of the legendary contest to the death between a spirited man with a hammer & a steam drill to build a tunnel through the Allegheny Mountains f West Virginia. It's not how long you live, but how well you do the living, John Henry proclaims, awe inspiring words for all of us.

John Henry. unabr. ed. Julius Lester. Narrated by Samuel L. Jackson. Music by Crystal Taleifero. 1 cass. (Running Time: 18 min.). (J). (ps-4). 1998. bk. 24.95 (978-0-7882-0682-5(6), HRA377) Weston Woods.
Based on an African American folk ballad.

***John Henry / John Henry.** Christianne C. Jones. Tr. by Sol Robledo. Illus. by Ben Peterson. (Read-it! Readers en Español). (SPA.). 2008. audio compact disk 9.27 (978-1-4048-4468-1(6)) CapstoneDig.

John Henry Boogie - ShowTrax. Arranged by Roger Emerson. 1 CD. 2000. audio compact disk 19.95 H Leonard.
His legend & his hammer are brought to a new generation in this boogie woogie arrangement that drives from beginning to end.

John Henry Days: A Novel. Colson Whitehead. Narrated by Peter Jay Fernandez. 12 cass. (Running Time: 18 hrs.). 98.00 (978-1-4025-0613-0(9)); audio compact disk 142.00 (978-1-4025-2941-2(4)) Recorded Bks.

John Henry Newman: His Inner Life. unabr. ed. Zeno Van den Barselaar. Read by Al Covaia. 8 cass. 32.95 set. (310) Ignatius Pr.
This definitive spiritual biography by the Newman scholar draws on letters, diaries, & unpublished sermons to elucidate the convert's path to holiness.

John Huff's Leavetaking (Short Story) see Fantastic Tales of Ray Bradbury

John I, II, & III Commentary. collector's ed. Chuck Missler. 1 MP3 CD-ROM. (Running Time: 8 hours). (Chuck Missler Commentaries). 2001. cd-rom 29.95 (978-1-57821-158-6(1)) Koinonia Hse.
*But whoever has this world's good and sees that his brother has need, and shuts up his bowels of compassion from him, how dwells the love of God in him? My little children, let us not love in word, neither in tongue; but in deed and in truth. - I John 3:17-18The early church in the 1st century was under attack from both the inside and the outside. So what has changed? It should not surprise us that the Holy Spirit has anticipated every conceivable form of attack and diversion, and the three epistles of John are full of insight that is timely for each of us - at the personal level as well as the corporate. This MP3 CD-ROM is self-contained and includes: * Over 20 hours of Verse-by-Verse audio teaching through I,II,& III John as MP3 files. * Extensive searchable study notes as PDF files. * A special message from Chuck Missler. * Listings of other MP3 resources. * Real? Player and Real? Juke Box. This program will play MP3 audio files. * Adobe Acrobat?*

*Reader.This program will read the PDF notes. * Third John - Introduction: John's background. Contrasts between John's various books. Addenda: the Most Painful Sin. * Second John: Gnostic heresies. Who is the "Elect Lady"? What is Truth? * First John 1: Heptadic structure. The importance of fellowship. Christian's "bar of soap." * First John 2:1-14: Test of Attitude, Actions, Affection. Spiritual maturity. * First John 2:15-29: The Love that God hates. The will of God. The Stoics; the Epicureans; more on the Gnostics. * First John 3: God the Father loves us; God the Son died for us; God the Holy Spirit lives in us. * First John 4: God is Love. God's dwelling places. A Christian's confidence.* First John 5: How do we know for sure...? Christians do not practice sin. Review of Christian "birthmarks.".*

***John I II III Commentary.** Chuck Missler. (ENG.). 2010. audio compact disk 44.95 (978-1-57821-471-6(8)) Koinonia Hse.

***John Iron's Ticket to Hell.** Dee Linford. 2009. (978-1-60136-398-5(2)) Audio Holding.

John Irving. Interview with John Irving. 1 cass. (Running Time: 30 min.). 1979. 12.95 (L037) TFR.
Irving talks about the "World According to Garp," how he conceived it, how he wrote it & how he dealt with its success. He explains why one of his characters had to become a leader in the women's movement.

John Irving Reads: Pension Grillparzer. unabr. ed. John Irving. Read by John Irving. 1 cass. (Running Time: 1 hr. 04 min.). 1987. 9.95 (978-0-945353-39-3(1), M10339) Pub: Audio Partners. Dist(s): PerseuPGW
A complete story from "The World According to Garp".

John J. Nance: Medusa's Child - Saving Cascadia - Orbit. abr. ed. John J. Nance. Read by John J. Nance. (Running Time: 18 hrs.). 2007. audio compact disk 34.95 (978-1-4233-2315-0(7), 9781423323150, BACD) Brilliance Audio.

John J. Sweeney: Let Market Graphics Guide Your Trading. Read by John J. Sweeney & Thom Hartle. 1 cass. 30.00 Dow Jones Telerate.
During this session Thomas Hartle & John Sweeney demonstrate trading strategies developed by examining past market behavior. This workshop will introduce you to new graphic depictions of market action which go beyond bar charts to show the trading edge of market behavior. Using graphs & charts as examples, Thom & John will show you how to look at your trading market in a way which few other traders exploit.

John James Audobon see Poetry of Benet

John Johnson: Strange Creek Fiddling 1947. Composed by John Johnson. 1 CD. (West Virginia University Press Sound Archives Ser.: Vol. 3). 2001. audio compact disk 15.95 (978-0-937058-57-2(2)) Pub: West Va U Pr. Dist(s): Chicago Distribution Ctr

John Keats: Selected Poems. unabr. ed. Poems. John Keats. Read by Frederick Davidson. 2 cass. (Running Time: 2 hrs. 30 mins.). 1993. 17.95 (978-0-7861-0367-6(1), 1324) Blckstn Audio.
Keats was not a political poet. His prime passion was for art & beauty. His muse was the goddess of Beauty & Truth. His worship of her found its finest expression in his immortal odes, which stand unique in literature, unexcelled in perfection.

John Keats: Selected Poems. unabr. ed. John Keats & Bernard Mayes. (Running Time: 3 hrs. NaN mins.). 2008. 19.95 (978-1-4332-5428-4(X)); audio compact disk 33.00 (978-1-4332-5427-7(1)) Blckstn Audio.

John Kenneth Galbraith. Interview with John Kenneth Galbraith. 1 cass. (Running Time: 15 min.). 1973. 9.95 (L026) TFR.
Galbraith talks of his career in the diplomatic corps, his Canadian boyhood & his friendship with the Kennedy's, particularly Jacqueline.

John Kenneth Galbraith: Economics & the Press. Narrated by John Kenneth Galbraith. 1 cass. (Running Time: 1 hr.). 9.00 (K0130B090, HarperThor) HarpC GBR.

John Kensella's Lament for Mrs. Mary Moore see Dylan Thomas Reading

John Knoepfle. unabr. ed. Read by John Knoepfle. 1 cass. (Running Time: 29 min.). 1985. 10.00 New Letters.
Poems by the Illinois author of "Rivers Into Islands" & "Whetstone".

John Lennon. abr. ed. Alan Clayson. Read by Mike Read. 3 CDs. (Running Time: 3 hrs. 36 mins.). 2003. audio compact disk (978-1-86074-532-4(6)) Sanctuary Pubng GBR.
Biographers of the late John Lennon have depicted him as being everything from barking mad to sitting at the right hand of God. Alan Clayson's popular biography finds the real Beatle in the myriad of conflicting images. This audio version is packed with all the facts, quotes, and trivia a fan could want, as well as a detailed discography of Lennon's work with the Beatles and beyond.

John Lennon. abr. ed. Philip Norman. Read by Graeme Malcolm. 10 CDs. (Running Time: 12 hrs. 30 mins.). 2008. audio compact disk 39.95 (978-0-06-167256-9(4), Harper Audio) HarperCollins Pubs.

***John Lennon: The Life.** abr. ed. Philip Norman. Read by Graeme Malcolm. (ENG.). 2008. (978-0-06-173824-1(7)); (978-0-06-173825-8(5)) HarperCollins Pubs.

John Lescroart: Dead Irish, the Vig, Hard Evidence. abr. ed. John Lescroart. Read by David Colacci. (Running Time: 18 hrs.). (Dismas Hardy Ser.: Nos. 1-3). 2008. audio compact disk 34.95 (978-1-4233-5249-5(1), 9781423352495, BACD) Brilliance Audio.

John Lescroart: The First Law, the Second Chair, the Motive. abr. ed. John Lescroart. (Running Time: 18 hrs.). (Dismas Hardy Ser.: Nos. 9-11). 2007. audio compact disk 34.95 (978-1-4233-2317-4(3), 9781423323174, BACD) Brilliance Audio.

John Lescroart: The Hearing, the Oath, the Hunt Club. abr. ed. John Lescroart. Read by Robert Lawrence & Guerin Barry. (Running Time: 18 hrs.). 2008. audio compact disk 34.95 (978-1-4233-5156-6(8), 9781423351566, BACD) Brilliance Audio.

John Lescroart: The Hunt Club, the Suspect, Betrayal. abr. ed. John Lescroart. (Running Time: 18 hrs.). 2009. audio compact disk 34.99 (978-1-4233-9731-1(2), 9781423397311, BACD) Brilliance Audio.

***John Lescroart CD Collection 5: The 13th Juror, the Mercy Rule, Nothing but the Truth.** abr. ed. John Lescroart. Read by David Colacci. (Running Time: 18 hrs.). 2010. audio compact disk 29.99 (978-1-4418-6164-1(5), 9781441861641, BACD) Brilliance Audio.

John Lescroart Collection: The Hearing; The Oath; The First Law. abr. ed. John Lescroart. Read by Robert Lawrence. 12 cass. (Running Time: 18 hrs.). (Dismas Hardy Ser.: Nos. 7-9). 2004. 29.95 (978-1-59355-633-4(0), 1593556330) Brilliance Audio.
The Hearing (Laura Grafton, Russell Byers): The call comes at midnight. It looks like a tragic and petty murder - a rising star in San Francisco's legal firmament found shot in a dark alley. But for homicide lieutenant Abe Glitsky, the crime cuts horribly close to home - unknown to anyone, the victim was his daughter. The Oath (Jim Bond, Russell Byers): When the head of San Francisco's largest HMO dies in his own hospital, no one doubts that it is anything but the result of massive injuries inflicted by a random hit-and-run accident. But the autopsy soon tells a different story - an overdose of potassium killed him, and the attending physician, Eric Kensing, becomes the prime suspect. Dismas Hardy goes on the offensive, believing that the murder had little to do with his client, and everything to do with business. The First Law (Laura Grafton, Mike Council): They date back to the wilder days of San Francisco's vigilante past, a private police force that keeps watch for paying clients. Unfortunately, Sam Silverman - an elderly pawnshop owner and a friend of Lt. Abe Glitsky's father - could no longer afford Patrol Special protection, and he may have paid with his life. Dismas Hardy, putting together a high-stakes lawsuit against the security firm, steps cautiously into a world where the only law is survival.

John Lilly Workshop 90. John Lilly & Francis Jeffrey. 2 cass. 18.00 set. (A0699-90) Sound Photosyn.
His most recent.

John Lindsay-Nineteen Sixty-Nine & Nineteen Seventy-Three: Anatomy of a Replay see Campaigning, Innovative: Four Case Studies

John Locke's Political Philosophy. Harry Binswanger. 3 cass. (Running Time: 4 hrs. 30 min.). 1991. 39.95 Set. (978-1-56114-123-4(2), CB05D) Second Renaissance.

John Masefield: Reading Sea Fever & Other Poems. unabr. ed. John Masefield. Perf. by John Masefield. 1 cass. 1984. 12.95 (978-0-694-50108-3(5), SWC 1147) HarperCollins Pubs.

John Maxwell Audio Assortment AMS. Zondervan Publishing Staff. 2006. audio compact disk 203.88 (978-0-8297-0072-5(2)) Pub: Vida Pubs. Dist(s): Zondervan

John McCutcheon's Four Seasons: Autumnsongs. Music by John McCutcheon & Si Kahn. (Running Time: 44 hrs.). (J). (gr. 4-10). 1998. 9.98 (978-1-57940-035-4(3)); audio compact disk 14.98 (978-1-57940-034-7(5)) Rounder Records.
Award-winning family music pioneer John McCutcheon continues his Grammy-nominated "Four Seasons" cycle with "Autumnsongs". Once again John serves up a heaping helping of music, fun & insight. He remembers watching the World Series with his Dad, being the new kid in school, welcoming a noisy new sister into the family & the quiet reflection of a Thanksgiving Day gathering. He honors farmworkers' leader Cesar Chavez, offers up a new Labor Day anthem & even includes a recipe for s'mores. The music is world class, the songs are unforgettable & adults are as welcome as children. Prove to yourself that autumn is more than a brief stop between summer & winter.

John McCutcheon's Four Seasons: Springsongs, Vol. 4. Perf. by John McCutcheon. 1 CD. (J). 1998. audio compact disk 14.98 (978-1-57940-036-1(1)) Rounder Records.
Catchy songs for kids. Includes: "I Hope I Make It," "Spring Fever," "Frog on a Log," "Fishin," "April Fool," "Dog's Life," & "Summer Is A-Coming".

John McCutcheon's Four Seasons: Wintersongs. Perf. by John McCutcheon. 1 cass. (Running Time: 44 min.). (Family Ser.). (J). (gr. 1-9). 1995. 9.98 (978-1-886767-07-2(6), 8038); audio compact disk 14.98 (978-1-886767-06-5(8), 8038) Rounder Records.
McCutcheon reminds us of experiences both personal & universal, from a child's eager anticipation of the first snowfall to memories of the last thaw of winter.

John McCutcheon's Four Seasons Vol. 4: Springsongs. Perf. by John McCutcheon. 1 cass. (Running Time: 42 mins.). (J). 1998. 9.98 (978-1-57940-037-8(X)) Rounder Records.
Catchy songs for kids. Includes: "I Hope I Make It," "Spring Fever," "Frog on a Log," "Fishin," "April Fool," "Dog's Life," & "Summer Is A-Coming".

John McPhee Reader. unabr. ed. John McPhee. Read by Dan Lazar. 12 cass. (Running Time: 18 hrs.). 1987. 96.00 (978-0-7366-1067-4(7), 1994) Books on Tape.
Articles from the New Yorker that range from tennis to oranges & atomic fission to wilderness conservation.

John Milton: Comus. unabr. ed. John Milton. Perf. by Ronald Pickup & Barbara Jefford. Adapted by R. D. Smith. 1 cass. 12.95 (ECN 100) J Norton Pubs.
Milton invented the pagan god Comus, whose evil designs on the Lady are frustrated by Sabrina, the goddess of the Severn, the river flowing by Ludlow, the town in the West of England where the first performance took place.

John Mort. unabr. ed. John Mort. Read by John Mort. 1 cass. (Running Time: 29 min.). 1986. 10.00 New Letters.
John Mort discusses writing about the Vietnam experience & reads a short story "The New Captain" from his book, "Tanks".

***John Mortonson's Funeral: A Tale of Terror.** Ambrose Bierce. 2009. (978-1-60136-519-4(5)) Audio Holding.

John Muir: My Life of Adventure. John Muir. Retold by Garth Gilchrist. 1 cass. (Running Time: 1 hr. 5 mins.). (John Muir: Audio Stories with Garth Gilchrist Ser.). (YA). (gr. k-6). 2004. 9.95 (978-1-58469-019-1(4)); audio compact disk 16.95 (978-1-58469-020-7(8)) Dawn CA.
Ranges from young Johnny's escapades among Scottish castle ruins to the hair-raising adventures of Muir the mountain man.

John Muir's Alaska Adventures: The Glacier That Saved America. Tim Hostiuck. Read by Tim Hostiuck. (Running Time: 45 min.). 1993. 14.00 (978-1-928952-00-8(3)) Misty Peaks.
Muir's lone quest for inspiration on an Alaskan glacier reveals how he touched millions as Father of America's national parks while being torn between family obligations, a public calling & an obsession for wild places, freedom & adventure.

John Murphy: Blending Traditional Technical Indicators with Intermarket Analysis. Read by John A. Murphy. 1 cass. 30.00 Dow Jones Telerate.
John will show how to blend technical analysis utilizing traditional charting with some of his favorite indicators. He will describe how these blend with intermarket analysis which includes the relationships between commodities, bonds, & stocks & also stock market sector analysis.

John Neff on Investing. John Neff. Read by Edward Lewis. Told to S. L. Mintz. (Running Time: 34200 sec.). 2006. audio compact disk 72.00 (978-0-7861-6886-6(2)) Blckstn Audio.

John Neff on Investing. unabr. ed. John Neff. 6 cass. (Running Time: 8 hrs. 30 mins.). 2000. 44.95 (978-0-7861-1864-9(4), 2663) Blckstn Audio.
Jeff Neff has proven time & again over the past three decades that bucking the system can pay off big. Now retired form mutual fund management, he is ready to share the investment strategies that earned him international recognition as the "investor's investor".

John Neff on Investing. unabr. ed. John Neff. Read by Edward Lewis. Told to S. L. Mintz. (Running Time: 34200 sec.). 2006. audio compact disk 29.95 (978-0-7861-7470-6(6)) Blckstn Audio.

John Neff on Investing. unabr. ed. John Neff & S. L. Mintz. Read by Edward Lewis. 7 cass. (Running Time: 10 hrs.). 2006. 49.95 (978-0-7861-1869-4(5), 2668) Blckstn Audio.

John Newton: From Disgrace to Amazing Grace. Jonathan Aitken. Read by Jonathan Aitken. Frwd. by Philip Yancey. (Running Time: 13 hrs. 30 mins.). 2007. audio compact disk 39.99 (978-1-4335-0141-8(4)) CrosswayIL.

John Nichols. Interview. Interview with John Nichols & Kay Bonetti. 1 cass. (Running Time: 55 min.). 13.95 (978-1-55644-050-2(2), 2092) Am Audio Prose.
Focuses on Nichols' transformation into a writer devoted to finding a polemical art.

John of the Cross As Mystic & Poet. Keith J. Egan. 1 cass. 1987. 9.95 (TAH190) Alba Hse Comns.
Human effort on its own is ever so limited. John's life shows both human effort & divine gift. He journeyed into the very depths & center of himself where mystic & poet are one in their experience. We are all called to this same integration.

John Osborne: Luther. unabr. ed. John Osborne. Perf. by Clive Merrison et al. 2 cass. 15.95 (SCN 223) J Norton Pubs.
Biographical play about the 16th century German reformer that concentrates on the inner man.

John Patitucci: Electric Bass. John Patitucci. Ed. by Daniel Thress. Contrib. by Troy Millard et al. 1 cass. (Video Transcription Ser.). bk. 21.95 (BD072) DCI Music Video.
The electric bass book & audio cassette features detailed transcriptions of the exercises in the book as well as compositions performed on the tape. Electric bass focuses on technique, time/groove & ethnic grooves.

John, Paul, George & Ben. Lane Smith. Narrated by James Earl Jones. 1 CD. (Running Time: 10 mins.). (J). (gr. 2-5). 2007. bk. 29.95 (978-0-439-02754-0(3), WHCD807); bk. 24.95 (978-0-439-02753-3(5), WHRA807) Weston Woods.
This humorous and factual history of five lads who grew up to become Founding Fathers brings the early days of American history to life with sass and substance, in Lane Smith's inimitable style.

John Paul II, Never Forgotten see Juan Pablo II Inolvidable

John Paul Jones: A Sailor's Biography. unabr. ed. Samuel Eliot Morison. Read by John MacDonald. 10 cass. (Running Time: 1 hr. 30 min. per cass.). 1958. Rental 17.50 Set. (2398) Books on Tape.
Samuel Eliot Morison captures the complex & fascinating character of John Paul Jones, legendary naval hero of the American Revolution.

John Paul Jones: A Sailor's Biography. unabr. ed. Samuel Eliot Morison. Read by John MacDonald. 10 cass. (Running Time: 15 hrs.). 1989. 80.00 (978-0-7366-1527-3(X), 2398) Books on Tape.

John Paul Jones: Sailor, Hero, Father of the American Navy. unabr. ed. Evan Thomas. Read by Dan Cashman. 12 CDs. (Running Time: 13 hrs. 49 mins. 48 sec.). (ENG.). 2003. audio compact disk 44.99 (978-1-4001-0104-7(2), 130364); audio compact disk 22.99 (978-1-4001-5104-2(X)); audio compact disk 89.99 (978-1-4001-3104-4(9)) Pub: Tantor Media. Dist(s): IngramPubServ

John Paul Jones' Memoir of the American Revolution Presented to King Louis XVI of France. John Paul Jones. 1979. audio compact disk (978-0-8444-0264-2(8)) Bow Hist.

***John Peel Remembered: Margrave of the Marshes & Home Truths Special.** John Peel & Sheila Ravenscroft. Compiled by British Broadcasting Corporation Staff. (Running Time: 2 hrs. 0 mins. 0 sec.). (ENG., 2010. audio compact disk 24.95 (978-1-84607-191-1(7)) Pub: AudioGO. Dist(s): Perseus Dist

John Philip Duck. (J). 2004. bk. 27.95 (978-0-8045-6932-3(0)); bk. 29.95 (978-0-8045-4127-5(2)) Spoken Arts.

John Pugsley: Common Sense Economics. (Running Time: 90 min.). (Remanent Tapes). 1979. 10.00 (R301) Freeland Pr.
A reader, an observer & a graduate of the Free Enterprise Institute, the author talks about territorial history & the folklore that colors the populate's beliefs.

John Pugsley: The Doomsday Factor. (Running Time: 60 min.). (Cal State Univ., Long Beach). 1982. 9.00 (F140) Freeland Pr.
Cites various instances of involvement with foreign governments that have created our present economic situations, & shows the real causes of inflation.

John Quincy Adams: A Public Life, a Private Life. unabr. ed. Paul C. Nagel. Read by Jeff Riggenbach. 14 cass. (Running Time: 19 hrs.). 2000. 89.95 (978-0-7861-1717-8(6), 2521) Blckstn Audio.
Nagel probes deeply into the psyche of this cantankerous, misanthropic, erudite, hardworking son of a former president whose remarkable career spanned many offices: minister to Holland, Russia & England, U.S. senator, secretary of state, president of the United States (1825-29), & finally, U.S. representative (the only ex-president to serve in the House). On the basis of a thorough study of Adams' seventy-ye[illegible]ary.

John Quincy Adams: A Public Life, a P[illegible] Life. unabr. ed. Paul C. Nagel. Read by Jeff Riggenbach. (Running Ti[illegible] hrs. 0 mins.). 2010. 44.95 (978-1-4417-1887-7(7)); audio compact disk 123.00 (978-1-4417-1884-6(2)) Blckstn Audio.

John Ransom's Andersonville Diary. collector's ed. John Ransom. Read by Dick Estell. 9 cass. (Running Time: 9 hrs.). 1988. 54.00 (978-0-7366-1328-6(5), 2232) Books on Tape.
John Ransom, Brigade Quartermaster of the Ninth Michigan Calvary, was only 20 years old when he became a prisoner of war in eastern Tennessee in 1863. He had everything to live for & much to live with. A war was on & he was in it & things were happening that seemed worth putting down from day to day. The result is a straightforward diary, free of the embroideries & purple passages of many an author of the time.

John Ransom's Diary. 7 cds. (Running Time: 7 hrs.). 2004. audio compact disk (978-0-9755663-6-7(9)) Alcazar AudioWorks.
An extraordinary day-to-day documentary of the Civil War's most infamous Confederate prison, Camp Sumter, better known as Andersonville-where 13,000 wretched Union prisoners died within barely 14 months...under conditions which bear witness to man's inhumanity to man...and one man's undaunted spirit to survive to tell the dreadful tale.The Diary seems to mirror Ransom's changing attitudes from the moody early staccato sentences when he is first captured to the resigned and eventually cheerful prose when the war draws to a close.

John Ransom's Diary. John Ransom. Narrated by David Thorn. (Running Time: 8 hrs. 30 mins.). 2004. 27.95 (978-1-59912-518-3(8)) Iofy Corp.

John Ransom's Diary Andersonville. John Ransom. Ed. by David Thorn. 6 cass. (Running Time: 8 hrs. 30 mins.). 2004. 49.95 (978-0-7861-2833-4(X), 3365); audio compact disk 56.00 (978-0-7861-8341-8(1), 3365) Blckstn Audio.

John Robinson: Taking Football. Read by John Robinson. 4 cass. (Running Time: 2 hrs.). (Exceptional Teachers in Sports Ser.). 39.95 Lets Talk Assocs.
Coach Robinson offers many of the what, how & whys of his own teaching.

John Saul CD Collection 2: Punish the Sinners, When the Wind Blows, the Unwanted. abr. ed. John Saul. (Running Time: 18 hrs.). 2006. audio compact disk 34.95 (978-1-59737-714-0(7), 9781597377140) Brilliance Audio.
Punish the Sinners: Something is happening to the young girls of St. Francis Xavier High School - something evil. In bloodlet and terror a suicide contagion has swept the town...while a dark order of its holy men enacts a

secret medieval ritual. Is hysteria manipulating these innocent children into violent self-destruction? Or has a supernatural force, a thirteenth-century madness, returned to...Punish the Sinners. When the Wind Blows: The children were waiting. Waiting for centuries. Waiting for someone to hear their cries. Now nine-year-old Christie Lyons has come to live in the house on the hill - the house where no children have lived for fifty years. Now little Christie will sleep in the old-fashioned nursery on the third floor. Now Christie's terror will begin... The Unwanted: Cassie Winslow is sixteen. She has just lost her mother in a terrible accident. Now, lonely and frightened, she has come to live with the father she barely knows and his new family in tiny False Harbor on Cape Cod. For Cassie, the strange, unsettling dreams that come to her suddenly in the dead of night are merely the beginning. Very soon, Cassie Winslow will come to know the terrifying powers that are her gift. And in the village of False Harbor, nothing will ever be the same.

John Sayles. Interview. Interview with John Sayles & Kay Bonetti. 1 cass. (Running Time: 1 hr. 22 min.). 13.95 (978-1-55644-082-3(0), 3122) Am Audio Prose.
Contains a discussion with this 1983 recipient of a MacArthur Award about his management of his multimedia talents, focusing on craft & vision of his fiction.

John Schlesinger see Movie Makers Speak: Directors

John Schultz. unabr. ed. John Schultz. Read by John Schultz. 1 cass. (Running Time: 29 min.). 1987. 10.00 New Letters.
Author reads a story set during the Korean war.

John Sebastian Teaches Blues Harmonica: A Complete Guide for Beginners. John Sebastian. (Listen & Learn Ser.). 1996. audio compact disk 19.95 (978-0-7935-6047-9(0)) Pub: Homespun Video. Dist(s): H Leonard

John Shea's Christmas Stories: Themes from Matthew & Luke. John Shea. Read by John Shea. 2006. audio compact disk 14.95 (978-0-87946-321-2(X)) ACTA Pubns.

John Shea's Christmas Tapes. John Shea. 2 cass. (Running Time: 90 min. per cass.). 1992. 15.95 Set. (978-0-87946-076-1(8), 320) ACTA Pubns.
Two of John Shea's tapes, "Behold the Vulnerable God" & "The Spiritual Center of Christmas" in a boxed set.

John Sherman - So Inclined. John Sherman. 1998. pap. bk. 19.95 (978-0-7866-3635-8(1), 96841BCD) Mel Bay.

John Standefer's 'Picture-Perfect' TAB Guitar Manuscript Book. John Standefer. 2003. per. 7.95 (978-0-7866-6936-3(5), 20509) Mel Bay.

John Steinbeck: In Search of America. unabr. ed. Joseph Schiffman. 1 cass. (Running Time: 26 min.). (Six American Authors Ser.). 1969. 12.95 (23047) J Norton Pubs.
Life, thought, art & relevance of John Steinbeck.

***John Stott on the Bible & the Christian Life: Six Sessions on the Authority, Interpretation, & use of Scripture.** John R. W. Stott. (Running Time: 7 hrs. 0 mins. 0 sec.). (Zondervan Legacy Ser.). (ENG.). 2006. 12.99 (978-0-310-27299-1(8)) Zondervan.

John Sutter see Twentieth-Century Poetry in English, No. 7, Recordings of Poets Reading Their Own Poetry

John Taylor: Messenger of Salvation. Matthew J. Haslam. 5 cass. 2004. 7.98 (978-1-57734-914-3(8)) Covenant Comms.

John the Baptist Did Not Doubt. Steve Thompson. 1 cass. (Running Time: 90 mins.). (Baptism of Power Ser.: Vol. 1). 2000. 5.00 (ST02-001) Morning NC.
This discussion of the baptism of power that Jesus referred to will help you discover the spiritual power available to every Christian.

John the Baptizer. 4 cass. (Running Time: 6 hrs.). 1998. 20.95 (978-1-57972-297-5(0)) Insight Living.

John, the Rabbit: And other Folk Songs, Singing Games & Play Parties. Jill Trinka. (ENG.). 2005. spiral bd. 34.95 (978-1-57999-619-2(1)) GIA Pubns.

***John the Revelator.** unabr. ed. Peter Murphy. Read by Gerard Doyle. (Running Time: 9 hrs. 30 mins.). 2010. 29.95 (978-1-4417-1699-6(8)); 59.95 (978-1-4417-1695-8(5)); audio compact disk 90.00 (978-1-4417-1696-5(3)) Blckstn Audio.

John Thompson's Modern PNO Method. John Thompson. pap. bk. 16.90 (978-1-4234-1606-7(6)) Pub: Willis Music Co. Dist(s): H Leonard

John Tower: Tough Choices for America's Defense. (Running Time: 60 min.). 1989. 11.95 (K0530B090, HarperThor) HarpC GBR.

John Travolta & the New Angels. Ben Young. 1997. 4.95 (978-0-7417-6027-2(4), B0027) Win Walk.

John Updike. Interview with John Updike. 1 cass. (Running Time: 25 min.). 1978. 13.95 (L076) TFR.
Updike traces his career & makes no apologies for doing tricky things with sentences, saying "a writers job is to write".

John Updike. unabr. ed. John Updike. 1 cass. (Author Speaks Ser.). 1991. 14.95 J Norton Pubs.
Archival recordings of 20th-century authors.

John Updike. unabr. ed. Read by John Updike. 1 cass. (Running Time: 29 min.). Incl. Facing Nature. John Updike. 1987. (17); 1987. 10.00 (17) New Letters.
Updike reads from his latest book of poems.

John Updike, No. 11. John Updike. Read by John Updike. 1 cass. (Running Time: 29 min.). 1987. 10.00 (092587) New Letters.
Updike discusses his craft & reads poems from his book, "Facing Nature." This is the second part of the interview contained in Part 1.

John Updike Audio Collection. unabr. ed. John Updike. Read by John Updike. 5 CDs. (Running Time: 6 hrs.). 2003. audio compact disk 29.95 (978-0-06-057721-6(5)) HarperCollins Pubs.

***John Updike Audio Collection.** unabr. ed. John Updike. Read by John Updike. (ENG.). 2004. (978-0-06-075416-7(8), Harper Audio) HarperCollins Pubs.

***John Updike Audio Collection.** unabr. ed. John Updike. Read by John Updike. (ENG.). 2004. (978-0-06-081334-5(2), Harper Audio) HarperCollins Pubs.

John Vennari Series, Set. Perf. by John Vennari. 15 cass. 98.00 Cath Treas.
Includes: "Catholicism Dissolved: The New Evangelization"; "The Truth about Communion in the Hand"; "Evolution, Secularism & the Attack on the Church"; "Children's Rights"; "The Sacred Heart & the French Revolution"; "Teilhard de Chardin: False Prophet"; "Catholicizing a Nation: The Six Points of Father Denis Fahey"; "Evolution & Geology"; "Is the 'New Catechism' a Source of Hope?"; "The Catholic Teaching on the Coming of AntiChrist"; "The Ecumenical Church of the Third Millennium"; "The Hideous Error of Women Priests" & "Father Pierre de Smet, S.J.: Missionary & Hero 1801-1873." Plus "Akita Warnings " & "The Holy Eucharist" with Fr. John O'Connor.

John Wain Reads Contemporary English Poetry. unabr. ed. Read by John Wain. 1 cass. (Running Time: 27 min.). (YM-YWHA Poetry Center Ser.). 1967. 12.95 (23228) J Norton Pubs.

John Wayne Story. unabr. ed. George Carpozi. Read by Peter Wheeler. 4 cass. (Running Time: 6 hrs.). 2001. 54.95 (60369) Pub: Soundings Ltd GBR. Dist(s): Ulverscroft US

John Wayne's America: The Politics of Celebrity. Garry Wills. 2004. 10.95 (978-0-7435-4894-6(9)) Pub: S&S Audio. Dist(s): S and S Inc

John Weinzweig. John Weinzweig. 2004. audio compact disk 24.95 (978-0-662-33319-7(5)) Pub: Canadian Broadcasting CAN. Dist(s): Georgetown Term

John Wesley. unabr. ed. Basil Miller. Read by Lloyd James. (Running Time: 14400 sec.). (Men of Faith (Blackstone) Ser.). 2007. 23.95 (978-0-7861-2430-5(X)) Blckstn Audio.

John Wesley: The Extraordinary Little Man Who Spearheaded England's Greatest Spiritual Awakening! unabr. ed. Basil Miller. Read by Lloyd James. 4 CDs. (Running Time: 14400 sec.). (Men of Faith (Blackstone) Ser.). 2007. audio compact disk 32.00 (978-0-7861-8826-0(X)) Blckstn Audio.

John Wooden. 1 cass. (Reading With Winners: Ser. 2). 1984. 32.95 incl. wrksht, table, tchr's guide. (978-0-89811-188-0(9), 9901D) Lets Talk Assocs.

John Wooden: Talking Basketball. Read by John Wooden. 4 cass. (Running Time: 2 hrs.). (Exceptional Teachers in Sports Ser.). 39.95 Lets Talk Assocs.
Coach Wooden answers "coaching-type" questions in a direct & informal manner.

John Woods. John Woods. Read by John Woods. 1 cass. (Running Time: 29 min.). Incl. Salt Stone Selected Poems; Valley of Minor Animals; 1987. 10.00 New Letters.
Reads from his works & talks about his writing.

John Wyman Fingerstyle Acoustic Craft. 2003. audio compact disk 14.99 (978-0-9710052-2-8(2)) Winter Harvest.

John Wyndham: The Day of the Triffids. abr. ed. John Wyndham. Read by David Ashford. Contrib. by Doreen Estall. 4 cass. 22.95 (SCN 189) J Norton Pubs.
A chilling tale of walking, flesh-eating plants, with whip-like stings, which overrun Britain after the population has been blinded in a cosmic disaster.

***John Wyndham Collection: Five Full-Cast BBC Radio Dramas.** John Wyndham. Narrated by Full Cast. (Running Time: 12 hrs. 0 mins. 0 sec.). (ENG.). 2010. audio compact disk 99.95 (978-1-4084-6811-1(5)) Pub: AudioGO. Dist(s): Perseus Dist

John Yount. Interview. Interview with John Yount & Kay Bonetti. 1 cass. 1986. 13.95 (978-1-55644-170-7(3), 6122) Am Audio Prose.
The author of "Wolf at the Door," "The Trappers Last Shot," "Hardcastle," & "Toots in Solitude," discusses the art of fiction & craft of writing, & the composition, structure & themes of his four novels.

Johnathan Phillips: CD Maxi Single. Executive Producer Taffi L. Dollar. (ENG.). (YA). 2007. audio compact disk 8.00 (978-1-59944-153-5(5)) Creflo Dollar.

Johndro Birth Charts. H. Douglas Miller. 1 cass. 8.95 (860) Am Fed Astrologers.

John/Jean Poinet by 1739 of Burlington, New Jersey, Pierre Poinset Laine, 1699 of Charles Town, South Carolina & Some of Their Descendants. Doris J. Poinsett. 2002. audio compact disk 8.00 (978-0-7884-2191-4(3)) Heritage Bk.

Johnnie Alone. Elizabeth A. Webster. Read by Christopher Scott. 6 cass. (Running Time: 9 hrs.). 1999. 54.95 (68580) Pub: Soundings Ltd GBR. Dist(s): Ulverscroft US

Johnny & His Rose: A True Story of Eternal Love. abr. ed. Johnny L. Ellis & Abraham Rose. Frwd. by G. Roszettae Foster. 2007. audio compact disk 15.00 (978-0-9789461-5-9(4)) His Rose Inc.

Johnny & the Bomb. Terry Pratchett. 2 cass. (Running Time: 3 hrs.). (ENG.). 2000. 16.99 (978-0-552-14458-2(4), Corgi RHG) Pub: Transworld GBR. Dist(s): Trafalgar

Johnny & the Dead. Terry Pratchett. 2 cass. (Running Time: 3 hrs.). (ENG.). (J). 2003. 16.99 (978-0-552-14033-1(3), Corgi RHG) Pub: Transworld GBR. Dist(s): Trafalgar

Johnny & the Dead. unabr. ed. Terry Pratchett. Read by Richard Mitchley. 4 CDs. (Running Time: 6 hrs.). (J). 2002. audio compact disk 34.95 (978-0-7540-6522-7(7), CHCD 022, Chivers Child Audio) AudioGO.

Johnny Appleseed see American Tall Tales

Johnny Appleseed. 2004. pap. bk. 32.75 (978-1-55592-251-1(1)); pap. bk. 14.95 (978-1-55592-064-7(0)); 8.95 (978-1-55592-990-9(7)) Weston Woods.

Johnny Appleseed. Reeve Lindbergh. Illus. by Kathy Jakobsen. 1 cass., 5 bks. (Running Time: 15 min.). (J). pap. bk. 32.75 Weston Woods.

Johnny Appleseed. Reeve Lindbergh. Illus. by Kathy Jakobsen. 1 cass., . (Running Time: 15 min.). (J). pap. bk. 12.95 Weston Woods.

Johnny Appleseed. Reeve Lindbergh. Illus. by Kathy Jakobsen. Narrated by Mary McDonnell. Music by Randy Scruggs. 1 cass. (Running Time: 15 min.). (J). (gr. k-5). 2000. pap. bk. 12.95 (QPRA399) Weston Woods.
John Chapman was his real name but almost everyone remembers him by his legendary name, Johnny Appleseed, the man who sprinkled apple seeds & planted trees all across the Midwest. His legacy remains strong today, not only for his botanical achievements, but also for the stories that he shared with children.

Johnny Appleseed. Perf. by Kate Smith. 1 cass. (J). 3.98 Clamshell. (978-1-55886-140-4(8), BB/PT 447) Smarty Pants.

***Johnny Appleseed.** Weston Woods Staff. (J). audio compact disk 12.95 (978-0-439-72260-5(8)) Weston Woods.

Johnny Appleseed: Gentle Hero. unabr. ed. Marc J. Levitt. Read by Marc J. Levitt. 1 cass. (Running Time: 45 mins.). (gr. 1-4). 1993. 12.00 (978-0-87483-176-4(8)) Pub: August Hse. Dist(s): Natl Bk Netwk
Marc Joel Levitt uses a beloved piece of American history to teach children respect for nature & humanitarian values.

Johnny Appleseed & Other American Legends. Melody Warnick. Read by Tavia Gilbert & Steven McLaughlin. 1 CD. (Running Time: 0 hr. 48 mins. 0 sec.). (PlainTales Explorers Ser.). (ENG.). (J). (gr. k-2). 2009. audio compact disk 12.95 (978-0-9820282-5-4(3)) Pub: PlainTales. Dist(s): IPG Chicago

Johnny Appleseed & Other Stories about America: Johnny Appleseed; Martin's Big Words; Players in Pigtails; This Land Is Your Land. unabr. ed. Reeve Libdbergh et al. Read by Mary McDonnell et al. (J). 2008. 44.99 (978-1-60514-944-8(6)) Find a World.

Johnny Appleseed & Paul Bunyan, Vol. 4. unabr. ed. Adrien Stoutenburg. Read by Ed Begley. 1 cass. (J). 1984. 9.95 (978-0-89845-524-3(3), CDL5 1321) HarperCollins Pubs.

Johnny Crow's Garden. 2004. 8.95 (978-1-56008-939-1(3)); cass. & flmstrp 30.00 (978-1-56008-696-3(3)) Weston Woods.

Johnny Crow's Garden; Magic Michael; Pancho; White Snow, Bright Snow. 2004. (978-0-89719-805-9(0)) Weston Woods.

Johnny Crow's Garden; Magic Michael; Panchp; White Snow, Bright Snow. 2004. cass. & flmstrp (978-0-89719-714-4(3)) Weston Woods.

Johnny Got His Gun. unabr. ed. Dalton Trumbo. Narrated by William Dufris. Frwd. by Cindy Sheehan. 6 CDs. (Running Time: 7 hrs. 30 mins. 0 sec.). (ENG.). 2008. audio compact disk 29.99 (978-1-4001-0655-4(9)); audio compact disk 19.99 (978-1-4001-5655-9(6)); audio compact disk 59.99 (978-1-4001-3655-1(5)) Pub: Tantor Media. Dist(s): IngramPubServ

Johnny Guitar Watson Songs. Johnny Watson. 2004. bk. 24.95 (978-3-8024-0425-2(4)) Voggenreiter Pubs DEU.

Johnny on a Spot. unabr. ed. Charles MacArthur. Perf. by Brad Hall et al. 1 cass. (Running Time: 1 hr. 30 min.). 1994. 19.95 (978-1-58081-022-7(5), CTA25) L A Theatre.
A 1940's political satire about radio, cynical newsmen, rigged elections, corrupt politicians & sex scandals.

***Johnny Ramsey - I Believe, Therefore I Speak.** Arranged by Polishing the Pulpit. 2010. audio compact disk 25.00 (978-1-60644-106-0(X)) Heart Heart.

***Johnny Ramsey - Overviews of Bible Books.** Arranged by Polishing the Pulpit. 2010. audio compact disk 25.00 (978-1-60644-105-3(1)) Heart Heart.

Johnny Tremain. Esther Forbes. Read by Grace Conlin. 8 CDs. (Running Time: 8 hrs. 30 mins.). 2003. audio compact disk 64.00 (978-0-7861-9830-6(3), 1472) Blckstn Audio.

Johnny Tremain. abr. ed. Esther Forbes. Perf. by E. G. Marshall et al. 2 cass. (J). 1984. 19.95 (978-0-694-50404-6(1), SWC 2049) HarperCollins Pubs.

Johnny Tremain. unabr. ed. Esther Forbes. Read by Grace Conlin. 7 CDs. (Running Time: 10 hrs. 30 mins.). (J). 2000. audio compact disk 56.00 (z1472) Blckstn Audio.
The year is 1773; & the scene is Boston. Johnny Tremain is fouteen & apprenticed to a silversmith. He is cheerful & clever until the tragic day when a crucible of molten silver breaks & Johnny's right hand is burned . After a period of despair Johnny becomes a dispatch rider, that brings him in touch with some of Boston patriots, such as John Hancock & Samuel Adams.

Johnny Tremain. unabr. ed. Esther Forbes. Read by Frances Cassidy. 6 cass. (Running Time: 8 hrs. 30 mins.). 2003. 44.95 (978-0-7861-0687-5(5), 1472) Blckstn Audio.
The year is 1773; the scene is Boston. Johnny Tremain is fourteen & apprenticed to a silversmith. He is gifted & knows it. He is vivacious & clever & lords it over the other apprentices until the tragic day when a crucible of molten silver breaks & Johnny's right hand is so burned as to be useless. After a period of despair & humiliation, Johnny becomes a dispatch rider for the Committee of Public Safety, a job that brings him in touch with Otis, Hancock, John & Samuel Adams, & other Boston patriots, & with all the exciting currents & undercurrents that were to lead to the Tea Party & the Battle of Lexington. There, on the battlefield, he learns from Dr. Warren that his maimed hand can be cured so that he can use a musket & some day return to his trade.

Johnny Tremain, unabr. ed. Esther Forbes. Narrated by George Guidall. 7 pieces. (Running Time: 9 hrs. 30 mins.). (gr. 6 up). 1994. 60.00 (978-0-7887-0017-0(0), 94216E7) Recorded Bks.
Johnny Tremain, a young & talented apprentice silversmith, is swept up in the turbulent events that presage the American Revolution. Associating with Sam Adams, Paul Revere, John Hancock & other courageous Sons of Liberty, Johnny discovers the role he must play in the cause for freedom.

Johnny Tremain. unabr. ed. Esther Forbes. Read by Grace Conlin. 1 CD. (Running Time: 9 hrs.). (J). 2001. audio compact disk 19.95 (zm1472) Blckstn Audio.
Johnny Tremain is fourteen & apprenticed to a silversmith. He is cheerful & clever & lords it over the other apprentices until the tragic day when a crucible of molten silver breaks & Johnny's right hand is so burned as to be useless.

Johnny Tremain. unabr. ed. Esther Forbes. Read by Grace Colin. 6 cass. (Running Time: 8 hrs 30 mins.). 2005. 29.95 (978-0-7861-3450-2(X), E1472) Blckstn Audio.

Johnny Tremain. unabr. ed. Esther Forbes. Read by Grace Conlin. 8 CDs. (Running Time: 30600 sec.). (J). (ps-7). 2005. audio compact disk 29.95 (978-0-7861-8027-1(7), ZE1472) Blckstn Audio.

Johnny Tremain: A Story of Boston in Revolt. unabr. ed. Esther Forbes. Read by Grace Conlin. (Running Time: 30600 sec.). (J). (gr. 4-7). 2008. audio compact disk 19.95 (978-1-4332-1041-9(X)) Blckstn Audio.

Johnny Tremain: A Story of Boston in Revolt. unabr. ed. Esther Forbes & Esther Forbes. Read by Grace Conlin. 13 vols. (Running Time: 32400 sec.). (J). (ps-7). 2005. DVD & audio compact disk 24.95 (978-0-7861-9655-5(6), 1472) Blckstn Audio.

Johnny Voodoo, unabr. ed. Dakota Lane. Narrated by Alyssa Bresnahan. 4 pieces. (Running Time: 5 hrs. 15 mins.). (gr. 8 up). 1997. 35.00 (978-0-7887-0792-6(2), 94942E7) Recorded Bks.
Life is pretty lonely for Deirdre after she moves from Manhattan to a tiny bayou town. She just knows she will never fit in at her new high school. But when she sees Johnny Voodoo, she feels fully alive for the first time.

Johnny Winter: A Step-by-Step Breakdown of the Guitar Styles & Techniques of a Blues Legend. Dave Rubin. Johnny Winter. 2007. pap. bk. 22.99 (978-1-4234-1641-8(4), 1423416414) H Leonard.

John's McCutcheon's Four Seasons: Summersongs. Perf. by John McCutcheon. 1 cass. (Running Time: 44 min.). (Family Ser.). (J). (gr. 1-9). 1995. 9.98 (978-1-886767-03-4(3), 8036); audio compact disk 14.98 (978-1-886767-02-7(5), 8036) Rounder Records.
A series of family albums celebrating each season of the year. Summersongs masterfully evokes children's sentiments of summer, from swimming holes, ice cream men & lawn mowers to backyard camping & meteor showers.

John's Story: The Last Eyewitness. unabr. ed. Tim LaHaye & Jerry B. Jenkins. Read by Robertson Dean. 9 CDs. (Running Time: 11 hrs.). Bk. 1. (ENG.). (gr. 8). 2006. audio compact disk 34.95 (978-0-14-305922-6(X), PengAudBks) Penguin Grp USA.

Johnson Family Singers: We Sang for Our Supper. Kenneth M. Johnson. Intro. by Charles Wolfe. (ENG., 1997. audio compact disk 18.00 (978-1-57806-034-4(6)) U Pr of Miss.

Johnstown Flood. abr. ed. David McCullough. Read by Edward Herrmann. 2005. 21.95 (978-0-7435-5032-1(3)) Pub: S&S Audio. Dist(s): S and S Inc

Johnstown Flood. abr. unabr. ed. David McCullough. Read by Edward Herrmann. 8 CDs. (Running Time: 100 hrs. 0 mins. 0 sec.). (ENG.). 2005. audio compact disk 39.95 (978-0-7435-4086-5(7)) Pub: S&S Audio. Dist(s): S and S Inc

Johnstown Flood. unabr. ed. David McCullough. Read by Grover Gardner. 6 cass. (Running Time: 9 hrs.). 1990. 48.00 Set. (978-0-7366-1690-4(X), 2537) Books on Tape.
At the end of the last century, Johnstown was the center of a booming coal & steel industry. In the mountains above, an earthen dam had been thrown together to make a lake for an exclusive summer resort patronized by the era's millionaires, among them Andrew Carnegie & Andrew Mellon. The symbolism was too good for nature not to cooperate. It did on May 31, 1889. The dam burst, sending a wall of water smashing through Johnstown, killing more than 2000 townspeople. It was a tragedy that became a national scandal. One hundred years later it has become a cautionary tale. As told by the author, it takes on great drama & authenticity. The flood is almost Biblical, & it holds the listener in thrall.

Join In. Günter Gerngross & Herbert Puchta. (SPA.). 2001. 8.00 (978-84-8323-142-5(5)) Cambridge U Pr.

Join In. 2nd ed. Günter Gerngross & Herbert Puchta. (Running Time: 1 hr. 23 mins.). (SPA.). 2001. audio compact disk 10.00 (978-84-8323-160-9(3)) Cambridge U Pr.

Join In. 3rd ed. Günter Gerngross & Herbert Puchta. (Running Time: 1 hr. 16 mins.). (SPA.). 2001. 8.00 (978-84-8323-158-6(1)); audio compact disk 10.00 (978-84-8323-161-6(1)) Cambridge U Pr.

Join In. 4th ed. Günter Gerngross & Herbert Puchta. (Join In Ser.). (SPA.). 2001. (978-84-8323-159-3(X)); audio compact disk (978-84-8323-162-3(X)) Cambridge U Pr.

Join In, No. 2. Günter Gerngross & Herbert Puchta. (ENG.). 2000. audio compact disk 23.00 (978-0-521-77370-6(9)) Cambridge U Pr.

Join In, No. 2. Günter Gerngross & Herbert Puchta. (Join In Ser.). (SPA.). 2001. (978-84-8323-157-9(3)) Cambridge U Pr.

Join In, No. 3. Günter Gerngross & Herbert Puchta. Cass. 3. (Running Time: 1 hr. 10 mins.). (ENG.). 2000. 24.15 (978-0-521-77511-3(6)) Cambridge U Pr.

Join In, Vol. 4. Günter Gerngross & Herbert Puchta. 4 cass. (Running Time: 1 hr. 6 mins.). (ENG.). 2001. 24.15 (978-0-521-00014-7(9)); audio compact disk 24.15 (978-0-521-00015-4(7)) Cambridge U Pr.

Join In: Starter. Günter Gerngross & Herbert Puchta. (Running Time: 1 hr. 2 mins.). 2000. 23.00 (978-0-521-77514-4(0)) Cambridge U Pr.

Join In: Starter. Günter Gerngross & Herbert Puchta. (ENG.). 2000. audio compact disk 24.15 (978-0-521-77372-0(5)) Cambridge U Pr.

Join In Bk. 1: French Edition. Günter Gerngross & Herbert Puchta. (Running Time: 1 hr. 31 mins.). (Join In Ser.). (FRE.). 2000. 15.00 (978-0-521-78843-4(9)) Cambridge U Pr.

Join In Bk. 1: French Edition. Günter Gerngross & Herbert Puchta. (Join In Ser.). 2000. audio compact disk 15.00 (978-0-521-78845-8(5)) Cambridge U Pr.

Join in Starter. Günter Gerngross & Herbert Puchta. (Running Time: 44 mins.). (SPA.). 2001. audio compact disk 10.00 (978-84-8323-130-2(1)) Cambridge U Pr.

Join in Starter. 2nd ed. Günter Gerngross & Herbert Puchta. (Running Time: 1 hr. 6 mins.). (SPA.). 2001. 8.00 (978-84-8323-137-1(9)); audio compact disk 10.00 (978-84-8323-138-8(7)) Cambridge U Pr.

Join in Starter 1. Günter Gerngross & Herbert Puchta. (Running Time: 44 mins.). (SPA.). 2001. 8.00 (978-84-8323-129-6(8)) Cambridge U Pr.

Join in 1. Günter Gerngross & Herbert Puchta. (Running Time: 1 hr. 37 mins.). (SPA.). 2001. audio compact disk 10.00 (978-84-8323-143-2(3)) Cambridge U Pr.

Join In 1. Günter Gerngross & Herbert Puchta. Cass. 1. (Running Time: 1 hr. 34 mins.). (ENG.). 2000. 23.00 (978-0-521-77513-7(2)) Cambridge U Pr.

Join In 1. Günter Gerngross & Herbert Puchta. (ENG.). 2000. audio compact disk 23.00 (978-0-521-77371-3(7)) Cambridge U Pr.

Join In 2. Günter Gerngross & Herbert Puchta. Cass. 2. (Running Time: 1 hr. 14 mins.). (ENG.). 2000. 24.15 (978-0-521-77512-0(4)) Cambridge U Pr.

Join In 2: French Edition. Günter Gerngross & Herbert Puchta. (Running Time: 1 hr. 12 mins.). (Join In Ser.). 2000. 15.00 (978-0-521-78844-1(7)) Cambridge U Pr.

Join In 2: French Edition. Günter Gerngross & Herbert Puchta. (Join In Ser.). 2000. audio compact disk 15.00 (978-0-521-78846-5(3)) Cambridge U Pr.

***Join in 2: Class Audio CDs (2)** Jack C. Richards & Kerry O'Sullivan. 2008. audio compact disk 39.95 (978-0-19-436782-0(7)) Pub: OUP-CN CAN. Dist(s): OUP

Join in 3. Günter Gerngross & Herbert Puchta. (ENG.). 2000. audio compact disk 24.15 (978-0-521-77369-0(5)) Cambridge U Pr.

Join the Club 1. Lisa Naylor. (Join the Club Ser.). (ENG.). (C). 2002. audio compact disk 26.88 (978-0-07-242803-2(1), 0072428031, ESL/ELT) Pub: McGrw-H Hghr Educ. Dist(s): McGraw

Join the Parade! abr. ed. Composed by Rachel Sumner. 1 cass. (Running Time: 48 mins.). (Rachel's Fun Time Ser.). (J). 2002. 9.98 (978-1-886673-10-6(1), RR-06) Rachels Recs.
Memorable songs, fabulous production, too.

Join the Parade! abr. ed. Composed by Rachel Sumner. 1 CD. (Running Time: 51 mins.). (Rachel's Fun Time Ser.). (J). 2002. audio compact disk 14.98 (978-1-886673-11-3(X), RR-CD6) Rachels Recs.

Join the Rhythm Band Wagon. 1 cass. (Running Time: 1 hr.). (J). 2001. pap. bk. 18.95 (KIM 0845C); pap. bk. & pupil's gde. ed. 19.95 (KIM 0845) Kimbo Educ.
Pass out your rhythm instruments because we're ready for some rhythm band fun. Children hear the rhythm instruments on Side A while they read instrument symbols on 13 mini-charts. Children play along with piano accompaniment on Side B. Includes 13 Mini-charts.

Join Us for English Activity Book Starter. Herbert Puchta & Günter Gerngross. (ENG.). 2006. audio compact disk 24.15 (978-0-521-67910-7(9)) Cambridge U Pr.

Join Us for English Pupil's Book Starter. Herbert Puchta & Günter Gerngross. (ENG.). 2006. audio compact disk 23.00 (978-0-521-67908-4(7)) Cambridge U Pr.

Join Us for English Song Starter. Herbert Puchta & Günter Gerngross. (ENG.). 2006. audio compact disk 23.00 (978-0-521-67909-1(5)) Cambridge U Pr.

Join Us for English 1 Activity Book. Herbert Puchta & Günter Gerngross. (ENG.). 2006. audio compact disk 22.00 (978-0-521-67920-6(6)) Cambridge U Pr.

Join Us for English 1 Activity Book Audio CD Polish Edition. Günter Gerngross & Herbert Puchta. 2008. audio compact disk 23.00 (978-0-521-69493-3(0)) Cambridge U Pr.

Join Us for English 1 Pupil's Book. Herbert Puchta & Günter Gerngross. (ENG.). 2006. stu. ed. 23.10 (978-0-521-67918-3(4)) Cambridge U Pr.

Join Us for English 1: Songs. Herbert Puchta & Günter Gerngross. (ENG.). 2006. audio compact disk 23.10 (978-0-521-67919-0(2)) Cambridge U Pr.

Join Us for English 1 Songs Audio CD Polish Edition. Günter Gerngross & Herbert Puchta. 2008. audio compact disk 23.00 (978-0-521-69494-0(9)) Cambridge U Pr.

Join Us for English 2 Pupil's Book. Herbert Puchta & Günter Gerngross. (ENG.). 2006. stu. ed. 24.15 (978-0-521-67928-2(1)) Cambridge U Pr.

Join Us for English 2: Songs. Herbert Puchta & Günter Gerngross. (ENG.). 2006. audio compact disk 24.15 (978-0-521-67929-9(X)) Cambridge U Pr.

Join Us for English 3 Pupil's Book. Herbert Puchta & Günter Gerngross. (ENG.). 2006. stu. ed. 23.00 (978-0-521-67940-4(0)) Cambridge U Pr.

Join Us for English 3 Songs. Herbert Puchta & Günter Gerngross. (ENG.). 2006. audio compact disk 24.15 (978-0-521-67941-1(9)) Cambridge U Pr.

Join Us for English 4: Songs. Herbert Puchta & Günter Gerngross. (ENG.). 2006. audio compact disk 23.00 (978-0-521-67951-0(6)) Cambridge U Pr.

Join Us for English 4 Pupil's Book. Herbert Puchta & Günter Gerngross. (ENG.). 2006. stu. ed. 23.00 (978-0-521-67950-3(8)) Cambridge U Pr.

Joiner King. abr. ed. Troy Denning. Read by Jonathan Davis. 4 CDs. (Running Time: 5 hrs.). (Star Wars: Bk. 1). (ENG.). 2005. audio compact disk 27.50 (978-0-7393-2034-1(3), Random AudioBks) Pub: Random Audio Pubg. Dist(s): Random

Joining. abr. ed. Johanna Lindsey. Read by Sharon Williams. (Running Time: 3 hrs.). 2009. audio compact disk 14.99 (978-1-4233-6625-6(5), 9781423366256) Brilliance Audio.

Joining. unabr. ed. Johanna Lindsey. Read by Sharon Williams. (Running Time: 9 hrs.). 2009. 39.97 (978-1-4233-6624-9(7), 9781423366249, BADLE); 24.99 (978-1-4233-6623-2(9), 9781423366232, BAD); 24.99 (978-1-4233-6621-8(2), 9781423366218, Brilliance MP3); 39.97 (978-1-4233-6622-5(0), 9781423366225, Brinc Audio MP3 Lib); audio compact disk 29.99 (978-1-4233-6619-5(0), 9781423366195, Bril Audio CD Unabri); audio compact disk 92.97 (978-1-4233-6620-1(4), 9781423366201, BriAudCD Unabrid) Brilliance Audio.

Joining. unabr. ed. Johanna Lindsey. Read by Sharon Williams. 6 cass. 1999. 57.25 (FS9-50899) Highsmith.

Joining Hands with Other Lands: Multicultural Songs & Games. 1 LP. (Running Time: 1 hr.). (J). (ps-3). 2001. pap. bk. 11.95 (KIM 9130); pap. bk. 14.95 (KIM 9130CD) Kimbo Educ.
Introduce children to the customs, culture & language of other lands. Songs include Caribbean Mango Song, Sasha & Natasha, Many Ways to Say Hello, Chinese New Year, The Food Song, Uno, Uno, Dos, Dos, Native American Names & more. Guide with lyrics and activities included.

Joining Hands with Other Lands: Multicultural Songs & Games. 1 cass. (Running Time: 1 hr.). (J). (ps-8). 2001. pap. bk. 10.95 (KIM 9130C) Kimbo Educ.

Joining Hearts & Voices: With One Voice. Bach Choir. 2004. audio compact disk 16.98 (978-0-8066-3398-5(0)) Augsburg Fortress.
Selected hymns and songs from With One Voice, sung by the Bach Choir of Holy Trinity Lutheran Church in New York City. Various accompaniments join with the choir to create a wonderful listening experience.

Joint Operations. unabr. ed. Keith Douglass. Read by David Hilder. 5 cass. (Running Time: 7 hrs. 30 mins.). (Carrier Ser.: No. 16). 2001. 30.00 Books on Tape.
Tombstone Magruder leads his men, with the help of SEAL Team Seven, to repel a Chinese attack on Hawaii.

Joint Ventures in Health Care. 1985. bk. 85.00; 50.00 PA Bar Inst.

Joints & Glands Exercises I. unabr. ed. Ed. by R. Ballentine. 1 cass. (Running Time: 1 hr.). 2004. 9.95 (978-0-89389-172-5(X), CS209RVMO) Himalayan Inst.
Exercises & postures to increase circulation & flexibility. Designed especially for people with limited physical ability.

Joints & Glands Exercises II, Vol. 2. unabr. ed. Himalayan Institute Staff. Read by Himalayan Institute Staff. 1 cass. (Running Time: 1 hr.). 1986. 8.95 (978-0-89389-167-1(3), CS210MO) Himalayan Inst.
Ideal for beginning yoga students, these exercises help prepare the student for the traditional hatha yoga exercises.

Jojo's Story, Level 2. Antoinette Moses. Contrib. by Philip Prowse. (Running Time: 1 hr. 15 mins.). (Cambridge English Readers Ser.). (ENG., 2001. 9.00 (978-0-521-79755-9(1)) Cambridge U Pr.

Joke That Made Ed's Fortune see Man That Corrupted Hadleyburg & Other Stories

Joke that Made Ed's Fortune see Favorite Stories by Mark Twain

Joker One: A Marine Platoon's Story of Courage, Leadership, & Brotherhood. unabr. ed. Donovan Campbell. Narrated by David Drummond. 1 MP3-CD. (Running Time: 11 hrs. 30 mins. 0 sec.). (ENG.). 2009. audio compact disk 24.99 (978-1-4001-6074-7(X)); audio compact disk 69.99 (978-1-4001-4074-9(9)) Pub: Tantor Media. Dist(s): IngramPubServ

Joker One: A Marine Platoon's Story of Courage, Leadership, & Brotherhood. unabr. ed. Donovan Campbell. Read by David Drummond. 9 CDs. (Running Time: 11 hrs. 30 mins. 0 sec.). (ENG.). 2009. audio compact disk 34.99 (978-1-4001-1074-2(2)) Pub: Tantor Media. Dist(s): IngramPubServ

Jokers & One-Eyed Jacks. unabr. ed. Bernie Kite. Read by Gene Engene. 2001. 49.95 (978-1-58116-072-7(0)) Books in Motion.
A mysterious letter sends Bear Walker on a journey 30 years into his past, back to his home town. But he and his friends from Eureka Gulch find that old ghosts still linger, and a man's deeds live long after him.

Jokes My Father Never Taught Me: Life, Love, & Loss with Richard Pryor. Rain Pryor. 2006. audio compact disk 29.95 (978-0-06-123085-1(5)) HarperCollins Pubs.

Joke's Over. unabr. ed. Ralph Steadman. Read by James Adams. Frwd. by Kurt Vonnegut. (Running Time: 43200 sec.). 2007. 54.95 (978-1-4332-0419-7(3)); audio compact disk 55.00 (978-1-4332-0420-3(7)) Blckstn Audio.

Joke's Over: Ralph Steadman on Hunter S. Thompson. unabr. ed. Ralph Steadman. Read by James Adams. Frwd. by Kurt Vonnegut. (Running Time: 43200 sec.). 2007. 24.95 (978-1-4332-0421-0(5)); audio compact disk 24.95 (978-1-4332-0422-7(3)) Blckstn Audio.

Joke's Over: Ralph Steadman on Hunter S. Thompson. unabr. ed. Ralph Steadman & James Adams. Frwd. by Kurt Vonnegut. (Running Time: 43200 sec.). 2007. audio compact disk 29.95 (978-1-4332-0423-4(1)) Blckstn Audio.

Jokes, Riddles & Games. abr. ed. Nina Mattikow. Perf. by Purple Balloon Players. 1 cass. (Running Time: 60 min.). (Cassettes for Kids Ser.). (J). 1992. 5.95 (978-1-55569-527-9(2), 20003) Great Am Audio.
Laugh, sing & play with giggly, silly, fun-filled games, jokes, riddles, tongue twisters & sing-alongs.

Jokes to Go. Perf. by Kip Adotta. 2001. audio compact disk 16.98 (978-1-929243-34-1(0)) Uproar Ent.

Jokester see Science Fiction Favorites of Isaac Asimov

Jolie Blonde & the Three Heberts - Les Trois Cochons. Narrated by Sheila Hebert-Collins. 1 cass. (Running Time: 23 hrs. NaN mins.). (ENG.). (J). (gr. k-3). 1999. 9.95 (978-1-56554-728-5(4)) Pelican.
Cajun storyteller & author narrates her "Cajun twists" on the tales of "Goldilocks & the three Bears," & "Three Little Pigs." The child-like voice quality of the narrator with its Cajun accent adds a whimsical touch to the stories.

Jolie Blon's Bounce. James Lee Burke. Narrated by Mark Hammer. 11 cass. (Running Time: 15 hrs.). (Dave Robicheaux Ser.). 102.00 (978-1-4025-2395-3(5)) Recorded Bks.

Jolie Blon's Bounce. abr. ed. James Lee Burke. (Dave Robicheaux Ser.). 2004. 15.95 (978-0-7435-4904-2(X)) Pub: S&S Audio. Dist(s): S and S Inc

Jolie Blon's Bounce. abr. ed. James Lee Burke. Read by Will Patton. 6 CDs. (Running Time: 6 hrs. 30 mins. 0 sec.). (Dave Robicheaux Ser.). 2006. audio compact disk 14.95 (978-0-7435-5206-6(7), S&S Encore) Pub: S&S Audio. Dist(s): S and S Inc

Jolie Blon's Bounce. unabr. ed. James Lee Burke. Narrated by Mark Hammer. 11 cass. (Running Time: 15 hrs.). (Dave Robicheaux Ser.). 2002. 49.95 (978-1-4025-2396-0(3), RG088) Recorded Bks.
Dave Robicheaux, the Louisiana cop who's easily one of the most complex and compelling protagonists in mystery fiction, confronts his own demons as well as a brutal adversary who might be the devil himself in this dark thriller. Robicheaux doesn't believe Tee Bobby Hulin, a drug addicted musical genius, has murdered a prostitute and a teenager. Burke looks to the lower depths to find his villain, and the creature that emerges, as if from some primordial swamp, strikes a new kind of fear in everyone he encounters.

Jolie Blon's Bounce. unabr. ed. James Lee Burke. Read by Mark Hammer. 13 CDs. (Running Time: 15 hrs.). (Dave Robicheaux Ser.). 2002. audio compact disk 124.00 (978-1-4025-2966-5(X), C1855) Recorded Bks.

Jolie Blon's Bounce. unabr. ed. James Lee Burke. (Dave Robicheaux Ser.). 2004. 27.95 (978-0-7435-4905-9(8)) Pub: S&S Audio. Dist(s): S and S Inc

Jolly Corner & the Pupil, Set. unabr. ed. Henry James. Narrated by Flo Gibson. 3 cass. (Running Time: 4 hrs.). 1984. 16.95 (978-1-55685-013-4(1)) Audio Bk Con.
In "The Jolly Corner," the protagonist (perhaps Henry James) returns to the brownstone house he lived in as a young man in the hope of revisiting his past. Something or someone else lurks there & one night he makes a frightening discovery. In "The Pupil," a young tutor befriends his pupil & tries to spare him from the destructive whimsies & extravagant behavior of his family.

Jolly Mon. unabr. ed. Jimmy Buffett & Savannah Jane Buffett. Read by Savannah Jane Buffett. Ed. by Liz Van Doren. 1 cass. (Running Time: 31 min.). (J). (ps). 1990. 8.00 (978-0-15-240533-5(X)) Harcourt CAN CAN.
On this exciting audiocassette, Jimmy Buffett & his daughter, Savannah Jane, recount their story of music, enchantment, & adventure, accompanied by an original score that echoes the joy & simplicity of life on the beautiful islands of the Caribbean.

Jolly Songs (in print letters US) (J). 2005. audio compact disk 17.50 (978-1-84414-079-4(2)) Pub: Jolly Lrning GBR. Dist(s): Am Intl Dist

Jon Anderson. Interview with Elizabeth Gips. 1 cass. 1999. 11.00 (32012) Big Sur Tapes.
Anderson is an inspired composer, stream of consciousness lyricist and singer in the rock band, Yes - 1995 Santa Cruz.

Jon Gibson: The Hits. Perf. by Jon Gibson. 1 CD. 1999. audio compact disk 16.98 (KMGD9241) Provident Mus Dist.

Jon Silkin. unabr. ed. Jon Silkin. 1 cass. (Running Time: 29 min.). (New Letters on the Air Ser.). 1992. 10.00 (101891) New Letters.
Silkin reads his own poems & talks about his interest in war literature.

Jon Vickers Narrates Strauss: Enoch Arden. Perf. by Jon Vickers & Marc-Andre Hamelin. 2 CDs. audio compact disk 16.99 VAI Audio.
Richard Strauss's great setting of the Tennyson poem for narrator & piano. The legendary opera star Jon Vickers makes his recording debut as narrator in this powerful and moving performance.

Jon Wilcox: Stages of My Life. 1 cass. 9.98 (C-45) Folk-Legacy.
A collection of new songs from a California singer & songmaker.

Jonah. (Burl Ives Bible-Time Stories Ser.). (J). (ps-2). 1976. 5.99 (978-0-89191-799-1(3), 97998) David C Cook.

Jonah. James Herbert. Read by Jamie Glover. 3 CDs. (Running Time: 3 hrs. 0 mins. 0 sec.). (ENG.). 2008. audio compact disk 24.95 (978-0-230-70448-0(4)) Pub: Macmillan UK GBR. Dist(s): IPG Chicago

Jonah: The Reluctant Prophet. Chuck Missler. 2 cass. (Running Time: 2.5 hours plus). (Briefing Packages by Chuck Missler). 1994. vinyl bd. 14.95 Incls. notes. (978-1-880532-65-2(4)) Koinonia Hse.
See God's hand at work in the life of one of His prophets to bring repentance to one of the largest cities of the ancient world and discover lessons from Jonah's life that we can apply to ourselves.What does Jesus mean when he speaks of "the sign of the prophet Jonah" in Matthew 12? Study this "whale of a tale," validated by Jesus, with special significance for the New Testament believer.

Jonah Pt. I: Running from God. 1978. 4.94 (978-0-7417-1007-9(2)) Win Walk.

Jonah Pt. II: Running from God. 1978. 4.95 (978-0-7417-1008-6(0)) Win Walk.

Jonah & the Great Fish. 2004. bk. 24.95 (978-1-56008-042-8(6)); 8.95 (978-0-89719-951-3(0)); cass. & flmstrp 30.00 (978-0-89719-563-8(9)) Weston Woods.

Jonah & the Great Fish; Mary Had a Little Lamb; Elves & the Shoemaker, the; Silver Cow. 2004. (978-1-56008-821-9(4)); cass. & flmstrp (978-0-89719-758-8(5)) Weston Woods.

Jonah, Nahum & Obadiah Commentary. Chuck Missler. 1 CD-ROM. (Running Time: 8 hours aprox). (Chuck Missler Commentaries). 2004. cd-rom 29.95 (978-1-57821-265-1(0)) Koinonia Hse.
*Did you realize that there are at least three prophets in the Old Testament that were called specifically to prophesy regarding the Gentiles? Obviously, most of the Bible deals with history - both past and future - through the "lens" of Israel. But here are three short books that focus on Gentile history and each one has a specific application to you and me today.This brand new commentary includes: * 4 sessions on The Book of Jonah Tape 1: The call and flight of Jonah Tape 2: Jonah's prayer from the belly of the fish Tape 3: The mission to Nineveh Tape 4: The vine, the worm, and the east wind * 2 sessions on The Book of Nahum Tape 1: The Burden of Nineveh Tape 2: Woe to the bloody city * 1 session on The Book of Obadiah* As a special bonus we've included our related Briefing Pack The Next Holocaust & The Refuge In Edom.*

***Jonas Brothers CD.** Sarah Tieck. (Big Buddy Biographies CD Ser.). 2010. cd-rom 27.07 (978-1-61613-072-5(5)) ABDO Pub Co.

***Jonas Brothers Site CD.** Sarah Tieck. (Big Buddy Biographies Site CD Ser.). 2010. cd-rom 57.07 (978-1-61613-252-1(3)) ABDO Pub Co.

Jonas Salk & the Polio Vaccine. Katherine Krohn. Illus. by Al Milgrom. (Inventions & Discovery Ser.). (ENG.). (gr. 3-4). 2007. audio compact disk 6.95 (978-1-4296-1116-9(2)) CapstoneDig.

Jonas Salk & the Polio Vaccine (INK Audiocassette) (Inventions & Discovery Ser.). (ENG.). 2007. audio compact disk 5.95 (978-0-7368-7991-0(9)) CapstoneDig.

Jonathan Eberhart: Life's Trolley Ride. 1 cass. 9.98 (C-82) Folk-Legacy.
Old & new songs by a powerful singer & guitarist.

Jonathan Edwards. Barbour Books Staff. 1998. 4.97 (978-1-57748-363-2(4)) Barbour Pub.

Jonathan Edwards. unabr. ed. David J. Vaughan. Read by Lloyd James. (Running Time: 3 mins.). 2007. 23.95 (978-0-7861-2427-5(X)) Blckstn Audio.

Jonathan Edwards: One of America's Greatest Theologians Whose Preaching Sparked the Great Awakenings. unabr. ed. David J. Vaughan. Read by Lloyd James. 4 CDs. (Running Time: 9000 sec.). (Men of Faith (Blackstone) Ser.). 2002. audio compact disk 24.00 (978-0-7861-8827-7(8)) Blckstn Audio.

Jonathan Holden. unabr. ed. Read by Jonathan Holden. 1 cass. (Running Time: 29 min.). 1985. 10.00 New Letters.
Holden's award-winning books include "Design for A House".

Jonathan le Goeland. Richard Bach. 1 cass., bklet. (Running Time: 90 mins.). (French Audiobooks Ser.).Tr. of Jonathan Livingston Seagull. (FRE.). pap. bk. 14.95 (978-2-921997-92-8(4)) Pub: Coffragants CAN. Dist(s): Penton Overseas
Recorded completely in international French language by well-known actors or speakers.

Jonathan Livingston Seagull see Jonathan le Goeland

Jonathan Livingston Seagull. abr. ed. Richard Bach. Read by Richard Bach. 1 cass. 1984. 8.98 (CDL5 1639) HarperCollins Pubs.

Jonathan Park: No Looking Back. Douglas W. Phillips. 2004. 25.00 (978-1-929241-88-0(7)); audio compact disk 29.00 (978-1-929241-87-3(9)) STL Dist NA.
The second album in this exciting audio series. Featuring twelve new episodes.

Jonathan Park: The Hunt for Beowulf. Roy Pat. Dramatization. 2006. audio compact disk 16.99 (978-0-9787559-1-(X)) Vsn Forum.

Jonathan Park - The Adventure Begins: Twenty-Four Exciting Episodes in the Jonathan Park Radio Drama. Contrib. by Vision Forum Staff. 2004. 25.00 (978-1-929241-86-6(0)); audio compact disk 29.00 (978-1-929241-85-9(2)) STL Dist NA.

Jonathan Schwartz Plays Horn. 1 CD. (Running Time: 70 mins.). 2005. audio compact disk 11.00 (978-0-9753828-1-3(0)) Betty B Hedenberg.

Jonathan Strange & Mr. Norrell. Susanna Clarke. Read by Simon Prebble. 2004. 29.95 (978-1-59397-742-9(5)) Pub: Macmill Audio. Dist(s): Macmillan

Jonathan Strange & Mr. Norrell. unabr. ed. Susanna Clarke. Read by Simon Prebble. 18 cass. 2005. 124.95 (978-0-7927-3530-4(7), CSL 779); audio compact disk 139.95 (978-0-7927-3531-1(5), SLD 779) AudioGO.

Jonathan Strange & Mr. Norrell. unabr. rev. ed. Susanna Clarke. Read by Simon Prebble. 26 CDs. (Running Time: 32 hrs. 0 mins. 0 sec.). (ENG.). 2004. audio compact disk 59.95 (978-1-59397-741-2(7)) Pub: Macmill Audio. Dist(s): Macmillan

Jonathan Swift. unabr. ed. A. L. Rowse. Read by Erik Bauersfeld. 8 cass. (Running Time: 8 hrs.). 1979. 48.00 (978-0-7366-0180-1(5), 1182) Books on Tape.
Swift portrayed as a tragic figure - vacillating between instinct & reason, between success & failure.

***Jonathan Thomas & his Christmas on the Moon.** RadioArchives.com. (Running Time: 390). (ENG.). 2006. audio compact disk 17.98 (978-1-61081-053-1(8)) Radio Arch.

Jonathan Wild. Henry Fielding. Read by Jill Masters. 6 cass. (Running Time: 9 hrs.). 1989. 39.00 incl. album. (C-143) Jimcin Record.
By the author of Tom Jones.

Jonathan Wild. unabr. ed. Henry Fielding. Read by Jill Masters. 6 cass. (Running Time: 8 hrs. 30 mins.). 1985. 44.95 (978-0-7861-0529-8(1), 2028) Blckstn Audio.
Jonathan Wild is the most notorious criminal of his generation - a gang leader, receiver, blackmailer & protection-racketeer. Through him, Fielding relays a moral satire on the true nature of greatness when it is not legitimized by political institutions or worldly eminence as he romanticizes the "greatness" of his hero even unto the gallows. This is a masterful satire in which the law & the criminal underworld intermingle.

Jonathon Letters: One Family's Use of Support As They Took in, & Fell in Love with, a Troubled Child. Michael Trout & Lori Thomas. 6 CDs. (Running Time: 9 hrs. 48 mins.). 2005. audio compact disk 29.95 (978-0-9761546-0-0(9)) Infant Parent.
The Jonathon Letters: One Family's Use of Support as They Took in, and Fell in Love With, a Troubled Child gathers together an exchange of letters between a foster/adopt mom and a specialized clinician far away. Their common interest: the struggle between a particularly wounded four-year-old boy who was certain he could not be loved, and the family with whom he had been placed, who were determined to love him. Unbeknownst to the correspondents, they were recording the story of the tortuously slow and unsteady opening up of the soul of a little boy...The family happened to have that rare combination of internal and external resources that seem necessary, if any family is to survive the screaming, the resistance to attachment, the "crazy lying", the aggressiveness, the manipulations, and the rage that are often seen in children with Reactive Attachment Disorder. The reader is privileged to come to know a family with a unique persistence, and a driving energy that allowed them to keep bouncing back after each regression, and - ultimately - to understand Jonathon's defiance and rage as his cry for the very thing he resisted most.

Joni: An Unforgettable Story. unabr. ed. Zondervan Publishing Staff & Joni Eareckson Tada. (Running Time: 6 hrs. 0 mins. 0 sec.). (ENG.). 2003. 15.99 (978-0-310-26158-2(9)) Zondervan.

Jonny Magic & the Card Shark Kids. David Kushner. Read by David Kushner. (Running Time: 8 hrs.). (C). 2005. 19.95 (978-1-59912-917-4(5)) Iofy Corp.

Jonny Magic & the Card Shark Kids: How a Gang of Geeks Beat the Odds & Stormed Las Vegas. David Kushner. Read by David Kushner. 5 CDs. (Running Time: 28800 sec.). 2005. audio compact disk 27.95 (978-1-59316-069-2(0)) Listen & Live.

Joplin: Maple Leaf Rag. Ed. by Peter Pickow. 1 CD. (Running Time: 1 hr.). (Concert Performer Ser.). 2004. audio compact disk 6.95 (978-0-8256-1747-8(2), AM949806) Pub: Music Sales. Dist(s): H Leonard

***Jordan.** abr. ed. J. J. Benitez. (Caballo de Troya (Playaway) Ser.). (SPA.). 2009. 59.99 (978-1-61574-784-9(2)) Find a World.

Jordan County. Shelby Foote. Narrated by Tom Parker. (Running Time: 10 hrs.). 2002. 30.95 (978-1-59912-519-0(6)) Iofy Corp.

Jordan County. unabr. ed. Shelby Foote. Read by Tom Parker. 7 cass. (Running Time: 10 hrs.). 2002. 49.95 (978-0-7861-2309-4(5), 2995) Blckstn Audio.
Before Shelby Foote undertook his epic history of the Civil War, he wrote this fictional chronicle, "a landscape in narrative", of Jordan County, Mississippi, a place where the traumas of slavery, war, and Reconstruction are as tangible as rock formations. The seven stories in Jordan County move backward in time, from 1950 to 1797, and through the lives of characters as diverse as a black horn player doomed by tuberculosis and convulsive jealousy, a tormented and ineffectual fin-de-siecle aristocrat, and a half-wild frontiersman who builds a plantation in Choctaw territory only to watch it burn at the close of the Civil War.

Jordan Maxwell Radio Interviews, Vol. 1. Jordan Maxwell. (Running Time: 296 mins.). 2004. audio compact disk 34.95 (978-0-9749840-0-1(0)) Truthseekers Net.

Jorge, el Monito Ciclista. Tr. of Curious George Rides a Bike. (SPA.). 2004. 8.95 (978-0-7882-0263-6(4)) Weston Woods.

Jorge Morel: Solo Pieces for the Young Guitarist. Jorge Morel. 2009. pap. bk. 14.99 (978-0-7866-7626-2(4)) Mel Bay.

Jorgito. Tr. of Georgie. (SPA.). 2004. 8.95 (978-0-7882-0250-6(2)) Weston Woods.

Jorie Graham: Region of Unlikeness. unabr. ed. Jorie Graham. Read by Jorie Graham. 1 cass. (Running Time: 29 min.). 1990. 10.00 (030990) New Letters.
Graham is a widely published poet who teaches at the prestigious Iowa Writers' Workshop. She reads from her forthcoming book, "Region of Unlikeness".

Jornado. unabr. ed. E. R. Slade. Read by Gene Engene. 4 cass. (Running Time: 5 hrs. 30 min.). 1994. 26.95 (978-1-55686-486-5(8)) Books in Motion.
Clint Evans had been hunting Blake Dixon for five years, ever since Dixon raped & killed Clint's wife. Suddenly, the two enemies were face to face.

Jorobado de Notra Dame: Nuestra Senora de Paris. abr. ed. Victor Hugo. 2. (Running Time: 7200 sec.). (SPA.). 2007. audio compact disk 16.95 (978-1-933499-07-9(9)) Fonolibro Inc.

Jorobado de Nuestra Señora. abr. ed. Victor Hugo. 3 CDs. (SPA.). 2002. audio compact disk 17.00 (978-958-9494-84-4(6)) YoYoMusic.

Jo's Boys. unabr. ed. Louisa May Alcott. Read by Flo Gibson. 6 cass. (Running Time: 9 hrs.). (J). 1996. 24.95 (978-1-55685-437-8(4)) Audio Bk Con.
A shipwreck, an imprisonment for manslaughter, career choices, courtships, weddings, theatricals & larks are viewed as Jo's boys become young men.

Jo's Boys. unabr. ed. Louisa May Alcott. Read by C. M. Herbert. 7 cass. (Running Time: 10 hrs.). 1999. 49.95 (978-0-7861-1288-3(3), 2188) Blckstn Audio.
Set ten years after "Little Men," "Jo's Boys" revisits Plumfield, the New England school still presided over by Jo & her husband, Professor Bhaer. Jo's Boys - including sailor Emil, promising musician Nat, & rebellious Dan - are grown. Jo herself remains at the center of this tale, holding her boys fast through shipwreck & storm, disappointment...& even murder.

Jo's Boys. unabr. ed. Louisa May Alcott. Narrated by Barbara Caruso. 8 cass. (Running Time: 10 hrs. 15 mins.). (YA). 2001. pap. bk. & stu. ed. 87.20 Recorded Bks.
Jo March Bhaer returns as the compassionate mentor to the boys & girls of Plumfield school.

Jo's Boys. unabr. ed. Louisa May Alcott. Narrated by Barbara Caruso. 8 pieces. (Running Time: 10 hrs. 15 mins.). (gr. 6 up). 2001. 70.00 (978-0-7887-4562-1(X), 96333E7) Recorded Bks.

***Jo's Boys.** unabr. ed. Louisa May Alcott. Read by C. M. Hebert. (Running Time: 9 hrs. 30 mins.). 2010. 29.95 (978-1-4417-4565-1(3)); audio compact disk 90.00 (978-1-4417-4562-0(9)) Blckstn Audio.

Jose: El destino de un hombre: Serie Heroes de la fe. 2000. (978-1-57697-841-2(9)) Untd Bible Amrcas Svce.

Jose Hombre de Integridad y Perdon. Charles R. Swindoll.Tr. of Joseph: A Man of Integrity & Hope. 2007. audio compact disk 34.00 (978-1-57972-800-7(6)) Insight Living.

José Martí: Digitalizada: Toda su Poesia. Carlos Ripoll. (SPA.). 2006. pap. bk. 29.99 (978-0-9745229-5-1(3), 0-9745229-5-3) Ediciones.

Josef Gabriel Rheinberger: Motets, Masses & Hymns. Gloriae Dei Cantores. 1 CD. 2000. audio compact disk 16.95 (978-1-55725-251-7(3), GDCD108) Paraclete MA.

Josefina Story Quilt. unabr. abr. ed. Eleanor Coerr. Read by Ann Bobby. Illus. by Bruce Degen. 1 cass. (Running Time: 15 min.). (I Can Read Bks.). (J). (ps-3). 1995. 8.99 (978-0-694-70012-7(6), LauraGeringer) HarperCollins Pubs.

Josefina Story Quilt: An I Can Read Book. unabr. ed. Eleanor Coerr. Narrated by Barbara Caruso. 1 cass. (Running Time: 18 mins.). (I Can Read Bks.). (gr. 2 up). 1997. 10.00 (978-0-7887-0903-6(8), 95041E7) Recorded Bks.
In 1850, young Faith & her pet chicken, Josefina, can't stay out of trouble as the family travels by wagon train to California.

Josef's Journey. Elsie Poorbaugh. Narrated by Allen Hite. (ENG.). 2009. audio compact disk 12.95 (978-1-60031-053-9(2)) Spoken Books.

Joseph. Robert C. Bowden. 1 cass. 9.95 (10001085); audio compact disk 14.95 (2800713) Covenant Comms.
An original Robert Bowden composition commemorating the life of the prophet Joseph Smith.

Joseph. unabr. ed. Sheila P. Moses. (Running Time: 3 hrs.). 2010. 19.99 (978-1-4233-9227-9(2), 9781423392279, BAD); 39.97 (978-1-4233-9228-6(0), 9781423392286, BADLE) Brilliance Audio.

Joseph. unabr. ed. Sheila P. Moses. (Running Time: 3 hrs.). 2011. 19.99 (978-1-4233-9225-5(6), 9781423392255, Brilliance MP3); 39.97 (978-1-4233-9226-2(4), 9781423392262, Brinc Audio MP3 Lib); audio compact disk 19.99 (978-1-4233-9223-1(X), 9781423392231); audio compact disk 49.97 (978-1-4233-9224-8(8), 9781423392248, BriAudCD Unabrid) Brilliance Audio.

Joseph: A Man of Integrity & Forgiveness. Charles R. Swindoll. 2007. audio compact disk 42.00 (978-1-57972-765-9(4)) Insight Living.

Joseph: A Man of Integrity & Forgiveness, Set. Charles R. Swindoll. 6 cass. (Running Time: 10 hrs.). 1998. 30.95 (978-1-57972-076-6(5)) Insight Living.
Bible study on the life of Joseph & how his example will challenge you to have a positive, faith-filled attitude even when facing seemingly impossible circumstances.

Joseph: A Man of Integrity & Hope see Jose Hombre de Integridad y Perdon

Joseph Able Trivett of Butler, TN. 1 cass. 9.98 (C-2) Folk-Legacy.
Unaccompanied ballads & songs from East Tennessee.

Joseph: An Overview: Gen. 50:26. Ed Young. 1988. 4.95 (978-0-7417-1689-7(5), 689) Win Walk.

Joseph & His Brethren: Readings from the Old Testament. unabr. ed. George B. Harrison. 1 cass. (Running Time: 26 min.). 12.95 (23121) J Norton Pubs.
Readings from the Old Testament Series recounts the story of Joseph & his brothers.

Joseph & His Brothers KJV. Perf. by George W. Sarris. 5 CD's. (Running Time: about 1 hour each). (World's Greatest Stories Ser.: Volume 5). (J). 1998. audio compact disk 7.95 (978-0-9767744-9-5(6)) GWSPubs.
Bible stories read dramatically by George W. Sarris. The texts for all the stories are taken directly, word for word, from the King James Version Bible, with the addition of carefully selected music and sound effects. Vol 5 contains the complete story of Joseph from Genesis 37 to 50.

Joseph & His Brothers NIV. Perf. by George W. Sarris. 5 CD's. (Running Time: about 1 hour each). (World's Greatest Stories Ser.: Volume 5). (J). 1998. audio compact disk 7.95 (978-0-9767744-4-0(5)) GWSPubs.
Bible stories read dramatically by George W. Sarris. The texts for all the stories are taken directly, word for word, from the New International Version Bible, with the addition of carefully selected music and sound effects. Vol 5 contains the complete story of Joseph from Genesis 37 to 50.

Joseph & Nyoka. (J). 2008. audio compact disk 24.95 (978-0-9820885-1-7(5)) TBell.

Joseph Andrews. Henry Fielding. Read by Anais 9000. 2008. 27.95 (978-1-60112-185-1(7)) Babblebooks.

Joseph B. Stowell: Short Term Trading, the Bond Futures Contract & Other Markets - a Master Trading Plan. Read by Joseph B. Stowell. 1 cass. 30.00 Dow Jones Telerate.
Participants will be taught several short term trading techniques for the Bond Futures Contract - foreign exchange, energy, & miscellaneous futures - through this use of the daily bar chart. Beginning as well as experienced traders will find a great deal of useful information in the presentation. Joseph will discuss mechanical entry points, protective stops, & profit objectives for short term trades of two to five days. Joseph's presentation will show you the integration of the various short term trading signals & how they form a Master Trading Plan for participating in the Bond Futures market.

Joseph Banks: A Life. unabr. ed. Patrick O'Brian. Read by David Case. 11 cass. (Running Time: 16 hrs. 30 mins.). 1995. 88.00 (3808) Books on Tape.
Most admirers of Patrick O'Brian know him only for his Aubrey/Maturin series about the British Navy during the Napoleonic Wars. For more than 40 years, Banks was the president of Britain's Royal Society. A naturalist & an explorer, he helped establish the Kew Gardens (London) as one of the world's greatest botanical centers; he was also one of Australia's founding fathers.

Joseph Brodsky. unabr. ed. Read by Joseph Brodsky & Rebekah Presson. Ed. by James McKinley. 1 cass. (Running Time: 29 min.). (New Letters on the Air Ser.). 1991. 10.00 (090691); 18.00 2-sided cass. New Letters.
Brodsky is interviewed by Rebekah Presson & reads from his work.

Joseph Brodsky: A Maddening Space. Joseph Brodsky. 1 cass. 1997. 10.95 (978-1-57523-177-8(8)) Unapix Enter.

Joseph Brodsky Reads His Poetry. unabr. ed. Joseph Brodsky. Read by Joseph Brodsky. 1 cass. (Running Time: 60 min.). 1988. 9.95 (978-0-89845-795-7(5), CPN 1836) HarperCollins Pubs.

Joseph Bruchac, Vol. II. unabr. ed. Ed. by Jim McKinley. Prod. by Rebekah Presson. 1 cass. (Running Time: 29 min.). (New Letters on the Air Ser.). 1994. 10.00 (031293) New Letters.
A Native American poet, storyteller & editor, Bruchac says his most important job is that of husband, father & caretaker of his ancestral home, in which he lives. Bruchac reads poems & stories from a new collection that mixes historical fact with Indian myth.

Joseph Bruchac Two. unabr. ed. Poems. Joseph Bruchac. Ed. by James McKinley. Prod. by Rebeah Presson. 1 cass. (Running Time: 29 min.). (On the Air Ser.). 1993. 10.00 (031293) New Letters.
Native American reads his poetry (interview).

Joseph Campbell: This Business of the Gods. unabr. ed. Sam Keen & Donald Sandner. 2 cass. (Running Time: 1 hr. 58 min.). 1988. 18.00 Set. (05704) Big Sur Tapes.
Give a window into Joseph Campbell that compassionately probes his shadow side, given by close friends & colleagues who recognized & forgave him his faults. What emerges is a portrait of a man with strong opinions who maintained a generous spirit even for many with whom he disagreed.

Joseph Campbell, a Modern American Sage. unabr. ed. Stephan Hoeller. 1 cass. (Running Time: 1 hr. 30 min.). 1987. 11.00 (40011) Big Sur Tapes.
Speaks of Campbell's regard for art & artist as prophetic agents, expressing our culture's "myths of eternity & the future," & emphasizing "the incredible importance of that aesthetic revelation, without which the entire mythic reality has no ability to come forth".

Joseph Campbell & C. G. Jung. unabr. ed. Donald Sandner. 1 cass. (Running Time: 45 min.). 1988. 11.00 (10203) Big Sur Tapes.
Campbell & Jung were among the boldest believers in an inner psychic dimension of human life, & were the most far reaching in their views of this inner landscape. Sandner's eloquent talk elucidates key points of their work.

Joseph Campbell & C. G. Jung on Myth & Personality: Mysticism vs. Individuation. Robert Segal. 3 cass. (Running Time: 4 hrs. 30 min.). 1995. 24.95 set. (978-0-7822-0486-5(4), 562) C G Jung IL.
Through lecture & discussion, this workshop assesses as well as compares the outlooks of these two influential thinkers. How each views the origin, the function, & the meaning of myth are examined. Several well-known myths are used to explore the distinctive approach of each.

Joseph Campbell & the Gnostic Challenge of Mythic Imagination. unabr. ed. Stephan Hoeller. 1 cass. (Running Time: 1 hr. 30 min.). 1992. 11.00 (40017) Big Sur Tapes.
As we approach the end of the 20th Century, the need to integrate what Hoeller calls "the Mythic Imagination" into our world-view grows ever more desperate. Without this integration, unconscious forces could promote inconceivable catastrophes. The mythic traditions of Gnosticism & the visionary efforts of Carl Jung & Joseph Campbell can provide us sources for the transformative wisdom we need to survive.

Joseph Campbell & the Power of Myth. abr. ed. Joseph Campbell & Bill Moyers. 6 cass. (Running Time: 5 hrs. 48 min.). 1989. 34.95 (978-0-930407-16-2(4)) Parabola Bks.
In this classic series of conversations with Bill Moyers, Campbell inspires us with his conviction that mythology defines and guides both individual lives and the culture at large. Drawing on resources from ancient history to modern times, Campbell takes us on an journey through the stories and myths of the world's cultures and traditions and challenges us to see the presence of a heroic journey in our own lives.

Joseph Conrad: Heart of Darkness & Other Stories. unabr. ed. Joseph Conrad. Read by Ralph Cosham. 6 cass. (Running Time: 6 hrs.). (Great Authors Ser.). 1997. 34.95 Incl. collector's box set, literary notes, & author's picture & biography. (978-1-883049-75-1(X), Commuters Library) Sound Room.
Also included: "The Secret Sharer," a story of identity & "Amy Foster," a story of a castaway's new life.

Joseph Conrad: The Three Lives. unabr. ed. Read by Heywood Hale Broun & Frederick R. Karl. 1 cass. (Running Time: 56 min.). (Broun Radio Ser.). 12.95 (40369) J Norton Pubs.
Frederick R. Karl and Broun recall Conrad's youth in Poland, his second life as a French seaman, & his third as an important writer in English. They failed to agree on which of his books is the most satisfying.

Joseph Conrad: Youth. unabr. ed. Joseph Conrad. Read by Robert Hardy. 1 cass. 12.95 (ECN 091) J Norton Pubs.
Marlowe regards the sea as a challenge &, by meeting it, discovers in himself great reserves of courage & endurance.

Joseph E. Johnston: A Civil War Biography. unabr. collector's ed. Craig L. Symonds. Read by Dick Estell. 13 cass. (Running Time: 19 hrs. 30 min.). 1993. 104.00 (978-0-7366-2390-2(6), 3161) Books on Tape.
A great Southern field commander, Johnston was seen by Grant & Sherman as the Union's most skillful opponent.

Joseph F. Smith Dramatized History. 1 cass. 9.95 (978-1-57734-588-6(6), 0400548); audio compact disk 14.95 (978-1-57734-589-3(4), 0400556) Covenant Comms.
Includes a rare sample of his actual recorded voice.

Joseph File. unabr. ed. Alf Harris. Read by Rusty Nelson. 8 cass. (Running Time: 8 hrs. 48 min.). 2001. 49.95 (978-1-55686-748-4(4)) Books in Motion.
Why was recent graduate and job seeker David Campbell hired as a Vice President of World Ways Airlines? Suddenly people around him start dying, and he realizes he knows too much.

Joseph Geha: Through & Through - Toledo Stories. unabr. ed. Joseph Geha. Read by Joseph Geha. Interview with Rebekah Presson. 1 cass. (Running Time: 29 min.). 1991. 10.00 (030191) New Letters.
Geha's first book, "Through & Through: Toledo Stories", portrays life in an Arab Christian family through a series of interrelated short stories.

Joseph Gelineau: Psalms of David. Joseph Gelineau. Perf. by Cathedral Singers. 1995. 10.95 (357); audio compact disk 15.95 (357) GIA Pubns.

Joseph Had a Little Overcoat. 2004. bk. 24.95 (978-1-55592-083-8(7)); pap. bk. 18.95 (978-0-7882-0325-1(8)); pap. bk. 32.75 (978-0-7882-0326-8(6)); pap. bk. 14.95 (978-0-7882-0324-4(X)); audio compact disk 12.95 (978-1-55592-949-7(4)) Weston Woods.

Joseph Had a Little Overcoat. Simms Taback. Illus. by Simms Taback. 14 vols. (Running Time: 15 mins.). pap. bk. (978-1-59112-608-9(8)) Live Oak Media.

Joseph Had a Little Overcoat. Simms Taback. Illus. by Simms Taback. (Running Time: 15 mins.). 2001. 9.95 (978-0-87499-781-1(X)); audio compact disk 12.95 (978-1-59112-410-8(7)) Live Oak Media.

Joseph Had a Little Overcoat. Simms Taback. Illus. by Simms Taback. 11 vols. (Running Time: 15 mins.). (Live Oak Readalong Ser.). (J). 2001. bk. 28.95 (978-1-59112-412-2(3)) Pub: Live Oak Media. Dist(s): AudioGO

Joseph Had a Little Overcoat. Simms Taback. Narrated by Rob Reiner. 1 cass. (Running Time: 6 min.). (J). (gr. k-3). 2004. 8.95 (978-1-55592-977-0(X)) Weston Woods.
Joseph the tailor is very resourceful. When his overcoat becomes old and worn, he makes it into a jacket, then his jacket into a vest. And so on until he has nothing left - then he makes something out of that!.

Joseph Had a Little Overcoat. unabr. ed. Simms Taback. Read by Simms Taback. 11 vols. (Running Time: 15 mins.). (Live Oak Readalong Ser.). (J). (ps-2). 2001. bk. 25.95 (978-0-87499-783-5(6)) Pub: Live Oak Media. Dist(s): AudioGO
Joseph makes a jacket from his old, worn coat. When the jacket wears out, Joseph makes a vest, and so on, until he has only enough to cover a button. Cut outs emphasize the use and reuse of the material and add to the general sense of fun.

Joseph Haydn. Read by Jeremy Siepmann. 4 CDs. (Running Time: 4 hrs. 30 min.). (Life & Works Ser.). 2003. pap. bk. 35.99 (978-1-84379-069-3(6)) Naxos.

Joseph Haydn: His Life & Works. unabr. ed. Jeremy Siepmann & David Timson. 4 CDs. (Running Time: 5 hrs.). 2009. audio compact disk 28.98 (978-962-634-951-9(4), Naxos AudioBooks) Naxos.

Joseph Heller. Interview with Joseph Heller. 1 cass. (Running Time: 20 min.). 1978. 11.95 (L035) TFR.
The author of "Catch-22" & "Something Happened" compares these two books & concludes that they are both about fear. He reveals that the original impulse in both cases was a first line that just popped into his head.

Joseph Langland: Any Body's Song. Joseph Langland. Read by Joseph Langland. 1 cass. (Running Time: 29 min.). 1987. 10.00 (100987) New Letters.
Massachusetts poet reads & talks about the influence of music on his poetry.

Joseph Learns Prudence. (Running Time: 60 min.). (Mother Angelica Live Ser.). 1987. 10.00 (978-1-55794-086-5(X), T37) Eternal Wrd TV.

Joseph Nicholson & William E. Taylor. unabr. ed. Read by Joseph Nicholson & William E. Taylor. 1 cass. (Running Time: 29 min.). 1986. 10.00 New Letters.
Taylor reads poems about Poland from his "Krakow Journal." Nicholson reads a sequence of surreal prose poems.

Joseph P. Kennedy Presents: His Hollywood Years. unabr. ed. Cari Beauchamp. (Running Time: 17 hrs. 0 mins.). 2009. 44.95 (978-1-4332-6109-1(X)); audio compact disk 95.95 (978-1-4332-6105-3(7)) Blckstn Audio.

Joseph P. Kennedy Presents: His Hollywood Years. unabr. ed. Cari Beauchamp. Narrated by Pam Ward. 14 CDs. (Running Time: 18 hrs.). 2009. audio compact disk 120.00 (978-1-4332-6106-0(5)) Blckstn Audio.

Joseph P. Kennedy Presents: His Hollywood Years. unabr. ed. Cari Beauchamp. Read by Pam Ward. 14 CDs. (Running Time: 17 hrs.). 2009. audio compact disk 34.95 (978-1-4332-6108-4(1)) Blckstn Audio.

Joseph Restores His Family. 1 cass. (Running Time: 60 min.). (Mother Angelica Live Ser.). 1987. 10.00 (978-1-55794-088-9(6), T39) Eternal Wrd TV.

Joseph Schumpeter & Dynamic Economic Change. unabr. ed. Laurence S. Moss. Ed. by Israel M. Kirzner & Mike Hassell. Narrated by Louis Rukeyser. 2 cass. (Running Time: 80 min. per cass.). Dramatization. (Great Economic Thinkers Ser.). (YA). (gr. 10 up). 1988. 17.95 (978-0-938935-38-4(0), 10208) Knowledge Prod.
Schumpeter saw capitalism as a system of dynamic change - a process of "creative destruction interrupting existing equilibrium conditions." Entrepreneurs continually disrupt the status quo, reorganizing economic resources to produce better goods & services.

Joseph Shumpeter & Dynamic Economic Change: Capitalism as Creative Destruction. Laurence Moss. Read by Louis Rukeyser. (Running Time: 9000 sec.). (Great Economic Thinkers Ser.). 2006. audio compact disk 25.95 (978-0-7861-6929-0(X)) Pub: Blckstn Audio. Dist(s): NetLibrary CO

Joseph Smith. Robert V. Remini. Read by Del Roy. 2002. 40.00 (978-0-7366-8919-9(2)) Books on Tape.

Joseph Smith - A True Prophet of God. unabr. ed. Duane S. Crowther. Read by Duane S. Crowther. 1 cass. (Running Time: 60 min.). 1979. 13.98 (978-0-88290-137-4(0), 1804) Horizon Utah.
Includes prophecies and historical items on the prophet Joseph Smith. Many of Joseph's prophecies are included as well as his major contributions.

Joseph Smith the Prophet. Truman G. Madsen. 4 cass. 1986. 22.95 Set. (978-1-57008-041-8(0), Bkcraft Inc) Deseret Bk.

Joseph Smith Translation: The Precious Truths Restored. W. Jeffrey Marsh. 2004. 9.95 (978-1-59156-132-3(9)) Covenant Comms.

Joseph Spence - The Complete Folkways Recordings 1958, Intermediate-Advanced Level. Joseph Spence. Tr. by Lenny Carlson. 1997. pap. bk. 29.95 (978-0-7866-2926-8(6), 96577CDP) Mel Bay.

Joseph the Tailor: And Other Jewish Tales. Read by Syd Lieberman. 1 cass. (Running Time: 47 min.). (World Storytelling from August House Ser.). (gr. 2-5). 1995. 12.00 (978-0-87483-426-0(0)) Pub: August Hse. Dist(s): Natl Bk Netwk
The wisdom - & wit - of traditional Jewish & biblical stories.

Josephine: A Life of the Empress. Carolly Erickson. Narrated by Davina Porter. 13 CDs. (Running Time: 15 hrs.). 2000. audio compact disk 124.00 (978-0-7887-4764-9(9), C1257E7) Recorded Bks.
A provocative new perspective on Josephine & her marriage to Napoleon. Her story is as turbulent as the revolutionary era in which she lived.

Josephine: A Life of the Empress. unabr. ed. Carolly Erickson. Read by S. Patricia Bailey. 9 cass. (Running Time: 13 hrs.). 2000. 62.95 (978-0-7861-1761-1(3), 2564) Blckstn Audio.
The author brings the complex, charming, ever resilient Josephine to life in this memorable portrait, one that carries the reader from the sensual richness of her childhood in the tropics to her final lonely days at Malmaison.

Josephine: A Life of the Empress. unabr. ed. Carolly Erickson. Read by Anna Fields. (Running Time: 46800 sec.). 2007. audio compact disk 29.95 (978-0-7861-6203-1(1)); audio compact disk & audio compact disk 90.00 (978-0-7861-6202-4(3)) Blckstn Audio.

Josephine: A Life of the Empress. unabr. ed. Carolly Erickson. Narrated by Davina Porter. 11 cass. (Running Time: 15 hrs.). 2000. 93.00 (978-0-7887-4072-5(5), 96008E7) Recorded Bks.

Josephine Clare. unabr. ed. Read by Josephine Clare. 1 cass. (Running Time: 29 min.). 1985. 10.00 New Letters.
Clare reads poems about family & motherhood from her book, "Mammato-Cumulus".

Josephine Humphreys. unabr. ed. Josephine Humphreys. Read by Josephine Humphreys. 1 cass. (Running Time: 29 min.). 1988. 10.00 New Letters.
Humphreys reads from her novel Rich in Love & is interviewed.

Josephine Jacobsen. Interview with Josephine Jacobsen. 1 cass. (Running Time: 25 min.). 1977. 10.95 (L038) TFR.
Jacobsen points to the increasing recognition of poetry by women & reads from her work.

Joseph's Mansions. unabr. ed. Richard Pitman & Joe McNally. Read by Raymond Sawyer. 10 cass. (Running Time: 11 hrs. 45 min.). (978-0-7531-1189-5(6)) ISIS Audio GBR.
In Frankie Houlihan, Richard Pitman introduces a wonderful new hero a man who quit the priesthood for love and then loses his wife in a flying accident. Trying to rebuild his life, Frankie accepts a job with a security team which investigates criminal activity in the world of horse-racing and that is how he comes to be involved in more ways than one in a suspenseful story of kidnap, cloning and family rivalry in London, Lambourn and Dublin. No average thriller, this is a rich, warm novel with wide appeal.

Joseph's Robe. 1 cass. (J). (978-0-944391-71-6(0)) DonWise Prodns.
Narrates biblical story designed especially for children.

Josephus: Thrones of Blood, a History of the Time of Jesus - 37 B.C. to 70 A.D. Barbour Books Staff. 1998. 4.97 (978-1-57748-208-6(5)) Barbour Pub.

Josh McDowell on Knowing God's Will, Josh McDowell. Read by Josh McDowell. 1 cass. (Running Time: 90 min.). 2000. 7.99 (978-1-886463-82-0(4)) Oasis Audio.
Apologist & internationally respected speaker, Josh McDowell is repeatedly asked, "How can I know God's will?" Josh says, "We're talking about your life now. What is God's will in it? This is where the going gets real good, so let's get right down to the nitty gritty".

Joshua. (Burl Ives Bible-Time Stories Ser.). (J). (ps-2). 1979. 5.99 (978-0-89191-610-9(5), 26104) David C Cook.

Joshua. David T. Demola. 13 cass. 52.00 (S-1047) Faith Fellow Min.

Joshua. unabr. ed. Joseph F. Girzone. Narrated by David Laundra. 6 cass. (Running Time: 8 hrs.). 1993. 51.00 (978-1-55690-908-5(X), 93404E7) Recorded Bks.
A woodcarver takes up residence in a small town & his quiet loving ways, inspired by the teachings of Jesus, become a blessing to his neighbors & a threat to the religious establishment.

Joshua: The Homecoming. Joseph F. Girzone. Narrated by Ed Sala. 5 cass. (Running Time: 7 hrs.). 45.00 (978-1-4025-2897-2(3)) Recorded Bks.

Joshua: The Homecoming. Joseph F. Girzone. Narrated by Ed Sala. 6 CDs. (Running Time: 7 hrs.). 1999. audio compact disk 58.00 (978-1-4025-3815-5(4)) Recorded Bks.

Joshua: The Homecoming. unabr. ed. Joseph F. Girzone. Narrated by Raymond Todd. 5 cass. (Running Time: 7 hrs.). 2001. 39.95 (978-0-7861-2112-0(2), 2873); audio compact disk 48.00 (978-0-7861-9641-8(6), 2873) Blckstn Audio.
The countdown to the year 2000 affects people in different ways, some are curious, others anxious, and still others panic. Amid this atmosphere of uncertainty, a quiet solitary man comes again to the tiny town of Auburn. This carpenter, known as Joshua, first arrived nearly two decades earlier and transformed everyone with his words of peace and actions of love. However, in the years since he left, many of his friends have died and a generation has grown up not knowing him. Now, with the new millennium on the horizon, Joshua reassures everyone by reminding them of the lessons he shared with them years before.

Joshua: The Homecoming. unabr. ed. Joseph F. Girzone. Read by Raymond Todd. 5 cass. (Running Time: 8 hrs.). 2001. 39.95 Blckstn Audio.

Joshua: The Homecoming. unabr. ed. Joseph F. Girzone. Narrated by David Laundra. 8 CDs. (Running Time: 7 hrs.). 2000. audio compact disk 63.00 (978-0-7887-3966-8(2), C1121E7) Recorded Bks.
A woodcarver takes up residence in a small town & his quiet loving ways, inspired by the teachings of Jesus, become a blessing to his neighbors & a threat to the religious establishment.

Joshua - Victory Through God: As Told by God's Animals. Joe Loesch. Illus. by Brian T. Cox. (J). 2006. bk. 13.50 (978-1-932332-62-9(6)) Toy Box Prods.

Joshua & Esther, Vol. 4. Read by George W. Sarris. 1 cass. (World's Greatest Stories Ser.). 1996. 10.98 (978-1-57919-099-6(5)) Randolf Prod.
Dramatic word-for-word readings of excerpts from the New International Version of the Bible. Includes Battle of Jerricho & the complete book of Esther.

Joshua & Esther KJV. Perf. by George W. Sarris. 5 CD's. (Running Time: about 1 hour each). (World's Greatest Stories Ser.: Volume 4). (J). 1996. audio compact disk 7.95 (978-0-9767744-8-8(8)) GWSPubs.
Bible stories read dramatically by George W. Sarris. The texts for all the stories are taken directly, word for word, from the King James Version Bible, with the addition of carefully selected music and sound effects. Vol 4 contains Joshua & the Battle of Jericho, and the complete book of Esther.

Joshua & Esther NIV. Perf. by George W. Sarris. 5 CD's. (Running Time: about 1 hour each). (World's Greatest Stories Ser.: Volume 4). (J). 1996. audio compact disk 7.95 (978-0-9767744-3-3(7)) GWSPubs.
Bible stories read dramatically by George W. Sarris. The texts for all the stories are taken directly, word for word, from the New International Version Bible, with the addition of carefully selected music and sound effects. Vol 4 contains Joshua & the Battle of Jericho, and the complete book of Esther.

Joshua Commentary. deluxe ed. Chuck Missler. 16 cass. (Running Time: over 16 hours). (Heirloom Edition Ser.). 1996. im. lthr. 69.95 incls. notes & notebk,. (978-1-880532-24-9(7)) Koinonia Hse.
Under close examination, the Book of Joshua seems to be a precursor to the book of Revelation: another Yehoshua, as Commander-in-Chief, will dispossess the Planet Earth of its usurpers - first sending in two witnesses, then with a series of judgments of sevens, finally defeating the kings with signs in the sun and moon while the kings of the earth all hide in caves. What does the name "Joshua" mean?.

Joshua Commentary: Verse-by-Verse with Chuck Missler. Chuck Missler. 1 MP3 CD-ROM. (Running Time: 16 hrs.). 2000. cd-rom 39.95 (978-1-57821-126-5(3)) Koinonia Hse.
Seems to be a precursor to the book of Revelation: another Yehoshua, as Commander-in-Chief, will dispossess the Planet Earth of its usurpers, first sending in two witnesses, then with a series of judgements of sevens, finally defeating the kings with signs in the sun and moon while the kings of the earth all hide in caves. What does the name "Joshua" mean?.

***Joshua, Rahab, & the Promised Land.** unabr. ed. Zondervan. (Running Time: 0 hr. 15 mins. 18 sec.). (Best-Loved Stories of the Bible, NIrV Ser.). (ENG.). (J). 2010. 1.99 (978-0-310-86503-2(4)) Pub: Zondkidz. Dist(s): Zondervan

Joshua Tree. Rudy Vanderlans. 2004. bk. 35.00 (978-0-9669409-2-3(X)) Pub: Emig. Dist(s): Gingko Press

Joshua's Bible. unabr. ed. Shelly Leanne. Narrated by Dion Graham. 11 cass. Library Ed. (Running Time: 15 hrs.). 2004. 99.75 (978-1-4025-6052-1(4), K1055); 49.95 (978-1-4025-6053-8(2), RG745) Recorded Bks.
Shelly Leanne has spent many years in South Africa and Kenya teaching and studying politics and culture. She brings her expertise to Joshua's Bible, a touching tale of faith and courage. African American reverend Joshua Clay welcomes the chance to minister in South Africa. Once there, however, he is caught between others' expectations and his own beliefs. Turning to God, Joshua must gather the strength to search for answers and bring some peace to a grief-stricken land.

Joshua's Family. unabr. ed. Joseph F. Girzone. Read by Tom Parks. (Running Time: 7 hrs.). 2010. 39.97 (978-1-4233-8405-2(9), 9781423384052, Brlnc Audio MP3 Lib); 24.99 (978-1-4233-8404-5(0), 9781423384045, Brilliance MP3); 39.97 (978-1-4233-8407-6(5), 9781423384076, BADLE); 24.99 (978-1-4233-8406-9(7), 9781423384069, BAD); audio compact disk 24.99 (978-1-4233-8402-1(4), 9781423384021, Bril Audio CD Unabri); audio compact disk 82.97 (978-1-4233-8403-8(2), 9781423384038, BriAudCD Unabrid) Brilliance Audio.

Joshua's Fun Time: A Place to Be, a Time to See. (J). (ps-3). 1996. 9.95 (978-0-9710704-2-4(3)) Bloojay.

Joshua's Fun Time: His Name Was Fala. (J). (ps-5). 1998. 9.95 (978-0-9710704-3-1(1)) Bloojay.

Joshua's Hammer. abr. ed. David Hagberg. Read by Bruce Watson. Abr. by Odin Westgaard. 4 vols. (Kirk McGarvey Ser.). 2003. (978-1-58807-682-3(2)) Am Pubng Inc.

Joshua's Masai Mask. unabr. ed. Dakari Hru. 1 cass. (Running Time: 12 min.). (J). (gr. k-4). 1994. 25.90 (978-0-8045-6811-1(1), 6811) Spoken Arts.
American Bookseller Pick of the Lists.

Josiah, the Mighty Reformer. Dan Comer. 1 cass. 3.00 (50) Evang Outreach.

Josie, Set. unabr. ed. Lynda Page. 12 cass. 1998. 108.95 (978-1-85903-124-7(2)) Pub: Magna Story GBR. Dist(s): Ulverscroft US

Josie & the Snow. 2004. 8.95 (978-1-56008-940-7(7)); cass. & flmstrp 30.00 (978-1-56008-697-0(1)) Weston Woods.

Journal for Jordan: A Story of Love & Honor. abr. ed. Dana Canedy. Read by Dana Canedy. (ENG.). 2008. audio compact disk 29.95 (978-0-7393-5860-3(X), Random AudioBks) Pub: Random Audio Pubg. Dist(s): Random

Journal of a Solitude. 1982. (2121) Am Audio Prose.

***Journal of a UFO Investigator.** unabr. ed. David Halperin. (Running Time: 10 hrs. NaN mins.). (ENG.). 2011. 29.95 (978-1-4417-7518-4(8)); 65.95 (978-1-4417-7515-3(3)); audio compact disk 29.95 (978-1-4417-7517-7(X)); audio compact disk 90.00 (978-1-4417-7516-0(1)) Blckstn Audio.

Journal of Charlotte L. Forten, a Free Negro in the Slave Era see Black Pioneers in American History, Vol. 1, 19th Century

Journal of Mrs Pepys: Portrait of a Marriage. Sara George. Read by Susannah Harker. 8 vols. (Running Time: 12 hrs.). 2003. 69.95 (978-0-7540-8353-5(5)) Pub: Chivers Audio Bks GBR. Dist(s): AudioGO

***Journal of the Gun Years.** unabr. ed. Richard Matheson. Read by Stefan Rudnicki. (Running Time: 7 hrs. 30 mins.). 2011. 29.95 (978-1-4417-3988-9(2)); 54.95 (978-1-4417-3984-1(X)); audio compact disk 24.95 (978-1-4417-3987-2(4)); audio compact disk 69.00 (978-1-4417-3985-8(8)) Blckstn Audio.

Journal of the Gun Years. unabr. collector's ed. Richard Matheson. Read by Larry McKeever. 8 cass. (Running Time: 8 hrs.). 1992. 48.00 (978-0-7366-2285-1(3), 3071) Books on Tape.
Frank Leslie was in Silver Gulch when he spotted gunfighter-lawman Clay Halser, a frontier legend. It was to be Halser's last day.

Journal of the Plague Year. Daniel Defoe. Read by Alfred von Lecteur. 2009. 27.95 (978-1-60112-994-9(7)) Babblebooks.

Journal of the Plague Year. abr. ed. Daniel Defoe. Read by Tim Behrens. 4 cass. (Running Time: 4 hrs. 30 min.). Dramatization. 1992. 26.95 (978-1-55686-437-7(X), 437) Books in Motion.
A "Maynard's English Classic Series" abridgment with interesting notes by & about the author. Detailed account by the author about one of the plagues that swept through London.

Journal of the Plague Year, unabr. ed. Daniel Defoe. Narrated by Nelson Runger. 6 cass. (Running Time: 9 hrs.). 1988. 51.00 (978-1-55690-268-0(9), 88360E7) Recorded Bks.
The plague of 1665 was followed by the Great Fire of London in 1666: great disasters evoking great responses.Those events re-fashioned the London landscape & Defoe re-fashioned English literature.

Journal of the Plague Year. unabr. collector's ed. Daniel Defoe. Read by Dan Lazar. 8 cass. (Running Time: 8 hrs.). 1976. 48.00 (978-0-7366-0019-4(1), 1030) Books on Tape.
Daniel Defoe's classic account of a city under siege by the Black Plague carries the listener across 4 centuries & steeps him in the terror of assault by a relentless & implacable foe.

Journal of Visual Impairment & Blindness. unabr. ed. 74.00 Personal annual subscript.; 104.00 Institutional annual subscript. Am Foun Blind.
Contains major articles from research & practice domains on a wide variety of subjects including rehabilitation, psychology, education, medicine lifestyle & employment, sensory aids, early childhood development, sociology & social welfare, as they relate to visual impairment. An interdisciplinary journal for practitioners & researchers professionally concerned with blind & visually impaired persons.

Journal Search: The Writings of Mary Baker Eddy. 1996. audio compact disk 149.00 (978-1-878641-04-5(2)) Aequus Inst Pubns.

Journal Vol. 1. Contrib. by Tru-Life et al. 2005. audio compact disk 17.98 (978-5-559-01458-6(3)) C Mason Res.

Journaling Tapes: Writing from the Heart. Carolyn D. Wall et al. 2 cass. (Running Time: 2 hrs.). 49.95 incl. script Set. (001) Write Page.
A 6 weeks course includes instruction & 46 daily exercises plus 101 ideas for journaling.

Journaling Tapes Vol. 1: Writing From the Heart. Carolyn D. Wall et al. Read by Carolyn D. Wall. 2 cass. (Running Time: 2 hrs.). 1998. bk. 49.95 Set, incl. wkbk. Write Page.

Journaling to Wholeness: How Writing Can Speed Your Personal Healing, Set. David Grudermeyer & Rebecca Grudermeyer. 2 cass. 18.95 INCL. HANDOUTS. (T-54) Willingness Wrks.

Journalism in Tennessee see Man That Corrupted Hadleyburg & Other Stories

Journalism in Tennessee see Best of Mark Twain

Journalism in Tennessee see Favorite Stories by Mark Twain

Journalist's Song see Osbert Sitwell Reading His Poetry

Journals (My Love for Layne) A. J. Spencer, 1st. (ENG.). 2008. audio compact disk 10.99 (978-0-9755851-5-3(0)) A Eanes.

Journals of Eleanor Druse: My Investigation of the Kingdom Hospital Incident. unabr. ed. Eleanor Druse. Read by Eleanor Druse. 4 cass. (Running Time: 6 hrs.). 2004. 26.98 (978-1-4013-9842-2(1)) Pub: Hyperion. Dist(s): HarperCollins Pubs

Journals of James Boswell: 1762-1795. unabr. collector's ed. John Wain. Read by Ian Whitcomb. 14 cass. (Running Time: 21 hrs.). 1995. 112.00 (978-0-7366-3175-4(5), 3844) Books on Tape.
An account of London's life, high & low, during the mid-18th century. Boswell knew everyone that mattered, it seems, including Edmund Burke, Voltaire, Jean Jacques Rousseau, Captain James Cook, & David Hume. But he wrote the most about Dr. Samual Johnson, a man he worshipped & for whose biography he is best known.

Journals of Lewis & Clark. unabr. ed. Bernard DeVoto. Read by Bob Erickson. 14 cass. (Running Time: 21 hrs.). 1983. 112.00 (978-0-7366-0376-8(X), 1355) Books on Tape.
This is a condensation of the Lewis & Clark journals, edited for the general reader.

Journals of Lewis & Clark: Excerpts from the History of the Lewis & Clark Expedition. unabr. ed. Nicholas Biddle. Narrated by Norman Dietz. 3 cass. (Running Time: 4 hrs. 30 mins.). 1992. 26.00 (978-1-55690-693-0(5), 92355E7) Recorded Bks.
Excerpts from the History of the Lewis & Clark Expedition, compiled in 1814 by Nicholas Biddle from the journals of Meriwether Lewis & William Clark & edited in 1893 by Elliot Coues.

Journals of the Pioneers, Pt. 1. unabr. ed. Frederick Drimmer. Narrated by Jack Hrkach. 5 cass. (Running Time: 7 hrs.). 1981. 44.00 (978-1-55690-269-7(7), 81260E7) Recorded Bks.
Actual accounts by early pioneers held captive by American Indians. An essential & thought-provoking contribution to our understanding of the relationship between settlers & tribespeople.

Journals of the Pioneers, Pt. 2. unabr. ed. Frederick Drimmer. Narrated by Jack Hrkach. 5 cass. (Running Time: 7 hrs. 30 mins.). 1981. 44.00 (978-1-55690-270-3(0), 81261E7) Recorded Bks.

***Journey.** Perf. by Timothy Byler. 2009. audio compact disk (978-0-9822237-3-4(0)) Palm Tree.

Journey. Josephine Cox. Narrated by Carole Boyd. 8 CDs. 2006. audio compact disk 79.95 (978-0-7927-4070-4(X), SLD 977) AudioGO.

Journey. Sarah Stewart. Illus. by David Smalls. 11 vols. (Running Time: 12 mins.). pap. bk. 16.95 (978-0-87499-922-8(7)); pap. bk. (978-0-87499-924-2(3)); pap. bk. 18.95 (978-1-59112-344-6(5)); pap. bk. (978-1-59112-556-3(1)) Live Oak Media.

Journey. Sarah Stewart. Illus. by David Smalls. (Running Time: 12 mins.). 2002. 9.95 (978-0-87499-921-1(9)); audio compact disk 12.95 (978-1-59112-343-9(7)) Live Oak Media.

Journey. Sarah Stewart. Read by Daisy Egan. 11 vols. (Running Time: 12 mins.). (J). 2002. bk. 28.95 (978-1-59112-345-3(3)) Pub: Live Oak Media. Dist(s): AudioGO

Journey. Eddie Thomas & Frank Thomas. 1 cass. 1994. 9.95 (978-1-885154-48-4(8)) Thomasfilms.
Introduction & history of the Natchez Trace Parkway (narration) & Original RoadMusic from the driving tour, Natchez Trace Parkway: A Road Through the Wilderness.

Journey. abr. ed. Jed Selter & Gil Turney. Read by Charlie O'Dowd. 1 cass. (Running Time: 80 mins.). 2000. 18.00 (978-1-58807-062-3(X)) Am Pubng Inc.
Through this thought-provoking allegory, authors Jed Selter and Gil Turney explore the complex issues of relationships and distill the tenets for creating and maintaining authentic, enduring bonds.

Journey. abr. ed. Sarah Stewart. Read by Daisy Egan. 11 vols. (Running Time: 12 mins.). (J). (ps-2). 2002. bk. 25.95 (978-0-87499-923-5(5)) Pub: Live Oak Media. Dist(s): AudioGO
A young Amish girl, her mother, and a friend take a trip from their farm home to Chicago. The experience is recalled through diary entries that contrast the child's reactions to the wonder of the city against related images from home.

***Journey.** unabr. ed. Wanda Brunstetter. Narrated by Jaimee Draper. (Running Time: 11 hrs. 0 mins. 0 sec.). (Kentucky Brothers Ser.). (ENG.). 2011. audio compact disk 34.99 (978-1-59859-858-2(9)) Oasis Audio.

Journey. unabr. ed. Kathryn Lasky. Read by Pamela Garelick. (Running Time: 21600 sec.). (Guardians of Ga'Hoole Ser.: Bk. 2). (J). (gr. 3-7). 2006. 44.95 (978-0-7861-4675-8(3)); audio compact disk 45.00 (978-0-7861-6784-5(X)) Blckstn Audio.

***Journey.** unabr. ed. Kathryn Lasky. Read by Pamela Garelick. (Running Time: 6 hrs.). (Guardians of Ga'Hoole Ser.: Bk. 2). 2010. audio compact disk 24.95 (978-1-4417-5542-1(X)) Blckstn Audio.

Journey. unabr. ed. Kathryn Lasky. Read by Pamela Garelick. (Running Time: 6 hrs.). (Guardians of Ga'Hoole Ser.: Bk. 2). (gr. 3-7). 2010. audio compact disk 29.95 (978-0-7861-7416-4(1)) Blckstn Audio.

Journey. unabr. ed. Kathryn Lasky. Read by Pamela Garelick. (Guardians of Ga'Hoole Ser.: Bk. 2). (J). 2007. 44.99 (978-1-60252-503-0(X)) Find a World.

Journey. unabr. ed. James A. Michener. Read by Larry McKeever. 6 cass. (Running Time: 9 hrs.). 1995. 48.00 (978-0-7366-2976-8(9), 3667) Books on Tape.
Four English aristocrats head for the Klondike. Petty ideas of patriotism nearly do them in.

Journey, Vol. 1. unabr. ed. Tina Michelle. 1 cass. (Running Time: 45 mins.). (Meditation Ser.). 2000. 10.00 (978-0-9678861-1-4(2)) WingedOne.
Four meditations designed to bring one into the Angelic Realm.

Journey: From the Ego Self to the True Self. Kenneth Wapnick. 16 CDs. 2003. audio compact disk 82.00 (978-1-59142-103-0(9), CD86) Foun Miracles.

Journey: How to Live by Faith in an Uncertain World. abr. ed. Billy Graham & Billy Graham. Read by Reathel Bean. (Running Time: 21600 sec.). (ENG.). 2006. audio compact disk 25.00 (978-0-7393-3968-8(0), Random AudioBks) Pub: Random Audio Pubg. Dist(s): Random

Journey: How to Live by Faith in an Uncertain World. unabr. ed. Billy Graham. Read by John H. Mayer. 7 cass. (Running Time: 10 hrs. 30 mins.). 2006. 63.00 (978-1-4159-3176-9(3)); audio compact disk 81.00 (978-1-4159-3177-6(1)) Books on Tape.

***Journey: My Political Life.** abr. ed. Tony Blair. Read by Tony Blair. (ENG.). 2010. audio compact disk 50.00 (978-0-7393-6983-8(0), Random AudioBks) Pub: Random Audio Pubg. Dist(s): Random

Journey along the Inside Passage-CD. Composed by Richard Olsenius. 2007. audio compact disk 9.95 (978-0-9794327-0-5(7)) Amer land gall.

Journey Back. unabr. ed. Johanna Reiss. Narrated by Johanna Reiss. 4 pieces. (Running Time: 5 hrs. 15 mins.). (gr. 7 up). 1989. 54.00 (978-0-7887-9960-0(6), 96850) Recorded Bks.
World War II has finally ended. Thirteen-year-old Annie de Leeuw and her sister have spent almost three years hiding in the upstairs room of a remote farmhouse in Holland. Now they can go home to rejoin their father and older sister. But saying goodbye to the courageous family who hid them is very difficult for Annie. And she finds that being home again isn't easy either. Her older sister has become a devout Christian. Her widowed father marries a wealthy woman who rejects the unsophisticated Annie. Gradually the teenager feels torn between nostalgia for the farm and desire for her new mother's approval.

Journey Back to Self: Reclaiming Your Emotional Energy. (ENG.). 2008. audio compact disk 9.99 (978-0-615-22479-4(2)) Try New Pers.

Journey Back to the Mother: The Pathway Home. unabr. ed. Sheilan. Read by Sheilan. Contrib. by Joanne Shenandoah & Peter Kater. 2 cass. (Running Time: 1 hr. 38 min.). 1998. bk. 17.00 (978-0-9663805-1-4(7)) Sheilan Prodns.
Read with music, the Mother gives us the Big Story, a perspective that takes one out of our own small world & awakens us to our path & helps us move forward with vision.

Journey Back to the Second & Third Century Church: A Dramatic Lecture. Jane M. deVyver. Perf. by Jane M. deVyver. 1 cass. (Running Time: 65 min.). 1992. 4.95 (978-1-881211-04-4(5)) Firebird Videos.
Early Christian church history, thought & practices. Intellecutal history, past & present.

Journey Between. Perf. by Martin Cradick & Baka Beyond Staff. 1 cass., 1 CD. 8.78 (HNBL 1415); audio compact disk 12.78 CD Jewel box. (HNBL 1415) NewSound.

Journey Beyond the Beyond: Magic Lands, Book 1. unabr. ed. Robert Stanek, pseud. Narrated by Karl Fehr. (Running Time: 3 hrs. 30 mins.). (ENG.). (J). 2009. 15.95 (978-1-57545-340-8(1), RP Audio Pubng) Pub: Reagent Press. Dist(s): OverDrive Inc

Journey Beyond Thought: A Return to the Christ State. Raymond Karczewski. 3 cass. (Running Time: 60 min. per cass.). 1994. 30.00 set in album. (978-0-9638391-2-1(8)) Ark Enter.
A psychological, philosophical, spiritual examination of the conditioned mind. It's practical approach touches upon all aspects of societal conditioning from the political & religious to the metaphysical. It serves as a guide to personal freedom & balance.

Journey Beyond Words. unabr. ed. Brent Hoskell. Perf. by Gary Arnold. 1 cass. (Running Time: 1 hr.). 1997. pap. bk. 12.95 (978-1-57867-213-4(9)) Windhorse Corp.
The Joshua-endowed guide to the study & applicatiion of the Ceruse at the level of one's most innermost sanctuary.

***Journey by Peyote Rattle.** Perf. by Alexander Alich. Prod. by Alexander Alich. Kati Meden. (ENG.). 2010. audio compact disk 17.00 (978-0-9710275-5-8(2), FoxTales) FoxFire Institute.

Journey Cake, Ho! 2004. pap. bk. 14.95 (978-0-7882-0613-9(3)); 8.95 (978-1-56008-941-4(5)); cass. & flmstrp 30.00 (978-1-56008-698-7(X)) Weston Woods.

Journey Closer. Perf. by Form. 1 cass. 1999. 10.98 (978-1-58229-103-1(9), Howard Bks); audio compact disk 16.98 (978-1-58229-102-4(0), Howard Bks) Pub: S and S. Dist(s): S and S Inc
Highlighted by strong alternative guitar sounds with genuine praise & worship lyrics. In each song there is a passionate expression of worship & praise to Christ our Lord.

Journey Continues. unabr. ed. Interview with Donna Lander. 1 cass. (Running Time: 55 min.). (ENG & HEB.). 1997. 12.95 (978-1-890161-27-9(6), SWP614C); audio compact disk 15.95 CD. (978-1-890161-28-6(4), SWP614CD) Sounds Write.
Extended play recording of Hebrew & English songs that parallel the Ma'yan Passover Haggadah.

Journey for Healing with Kuan Yin. Nicki Scully. Perf. by Roland Barker & Jerry Garcia. 1 CD. 2004. audio compact disk 16.00 (978-0-9623365-8-4(0)) N Scully.

Journey for Home: Music & Meditation. Deanna Light & Paul Tate. (Running Time: 4047 sec.). 2008. audio compact disk 14.95 (978-1-58459-375-1(X)) Wrld Lib Pubns.

Journey from Frustration to Fulfillment. Gary V. Whetstone. 6 cass. (Running Time: 9 hrs.). (Freedom Ser.). 1994. pap. bk. 50.00 (978-1-58866-218-7(7), VROO6A) Gary Whet Pub.
Are you living in frustration knowing that God has a plan, purpose, & destiny in store for you, but not yet fulfilling it?.

Journey Home. unabr. ed. Micah Sadigh. Read by Micah Sadigh. 1 cass. (Running Time: 45 mins.). (Metamusic Meditation Ser.). 2000. 14.95 (978-1-56102-354-7(X)) Inter Indus.
Music to aide in relaxation & meditation.

Journey Home, Set. Jennie L. Hansen. 2 cass. 11.98 (978-1-57734-167-3(8), 07001533) Covenant Comms.

Journey Home: Some Words in Defense of the American West. unabr. collector's ed. Edward Abbey. Read by Paul Shay. 6 cass. (Running Time: 9 hrs.). 1988. 48.00 (978-0-7366-1357-6(9), 2257) Books on Tape.
The American West & this book is written in its defense.""He offers a portrait of the West that we'll not soon forget. He gives us the observations of a man who left the urban world to think about the natural world & the myths buried therein.".

***Journey in Consciousness.** Barry Long. 2006. 24.95 (978-1-899324-21-7(6)) Pub: B Long Bks. Dist(s): AtlasBooks

Journey in Consciousness: Exploring the Truth Behind Existence. Barry Long. 2 cass. (Running Time: 2 hrs. 32 mins.). (ENG.). 1996. audio compact disk 17.95 (978-1-899324-06-4(2)) Pub: B Long Bks. Dist(s): AtlasBooks
The quest of consciousness is self-knowledge. Includes "The Unbelieveable Truth" & "Who I Am".

Journey in Ladakh. abr. ed. Andrew Harvey. Read by Andrew Harvey. 2 cass. (Running Time: 3 hrs.). 1997. 17.95 (978-1-57453-153-4(0)) Audio Lit.

Journey in Ladakh. unabr. ed. Andrew Harvey. Read by Richard Brown. 7 cass. (Running Time: 10 hrs. 30 mins.). 1990. 56.00 (978-0-7366-1738-3(8), 2578) Books on Tape.
A Journey in Ladakh is not only a pilgrimage of the spirit but also an arduous, physical passage to a remote part of the world - the highest, most barren, least populous region in India. It is Ladakh, where Buddist meditations have taken place since three centuries before the birth of Christ & where the purest form of Tibetan Buddhism is still practiced, to which the author aspired. Andrew Harvey shares his spiritual as well as his physical journey with us. We share his discovery of silence, his carefully tendered question, his inner struggles as the precepts of Tibetan Buddhism are revealed. Harvey ultimately comes to perceive a harmony that does not exclude Western theology but embraces & surpasses it in its understanding of humanity.

Journey in Spoken Word & Music: Acoustic Poets Network. Poems. Zoe Jade Austin et al. Read by Zoe Jade Austin. Perf. by Paula Curci & Tullio J. Vacchio. 1 CD. (Emissary Ser.). 1999. audio compact disk 12.00 P Curci.
Full 14 pieces of spoken word, poetry & music.

Journey into Adaptation with Max Axiom, Super Scientist. Agnieszka Biskup & Barbara Schulz. Illus. by Cynthia Martin. (Graphic Science Ser.). (ENG.). (gr. 3-4). 2007. audio compact disk 6.95 (978-1-4296-1123-7(5)) CapstoneDig.

Journey into Cyprus. unabr. collector's ed. Colin Thubron. Read by Richard Brown. 8 cass. (Running Time: 12 hrs.). 1990. 64.00 (978-0-7366-1739-0(6), 2579) Books on Tape.
It was an unique journey - a 600-mile trek on foot around Cyprus in the last year of the island's peace. Colin Thubron writes about it with great immediacy, intertwining myth, history & personal anecdote. What emerges is a tapestry from which characters & places, architectures & landscape all spring vividly to life. As a guide to the island & its survival through centuries of turmoil, Journey into Cyprus is invaluable. As a fine narrative of travel, it is compelling.

Journey into Darkness. Cathy LeSage. 1 CD. (Running Time: 1 hr. 30 mins.). 2005. audio compact disk 12.95 (978-0-660-18916-1(X)) Pub: Canadian Broadcasting CAN. Dist(s): Georgetown Term

Journey into Darkness: Follow the FBI's Premier Investigative Profiler as He Penetrates the Minds & Motives of the Most Terrifying Serial Criminals. John E. Douglas. Based on a work by Mark Olshaker. 2004. 10.95 (978-0-7435-4906-6(6)) Pub: S&S Audio. Dist(s): S and S Inc

Journey into Healing: Awakening the Wisdom Within You. unabr. ed. Deepak Chopra. 1 cass. 1996. 10.00 (51000) Books on Tape.
Essential ideas from the work of Deepak Chopra, M.D. are arranged to create a transcendent experience for the listener, a journey into healing. Along the path, we discover that what we think & feel can actually change our biology. We learn how to go beyond self-imposed limitations that create disease, & to seek that place inside ourselves that is one with the infinite intelligence of the universe, the source of life.

Journey into Inner Light. Darlana Montague. Read by Darlana Montague. 1 cass. (Running Time: 20 min.). 1987. 9.95 (978-1-889529-01-1(X)) Two Feathers.
Voice guided meditation with music.

Journey into Light-Music. 2007. audio compact disk 19.95 (978-1-56136-409-1(6)) Master Your Mind.

Journey into Peace: A Series of Meditations. Faye M. Kimball. Ed. by Janece J. Robertson. Illus. by Devereaux Chivington. 4 cass. (Running Time: 46 min.). 1989. 17.95 Set. Turning Pointe Pub.
These gently guided meditations set you, the listener, along a path for connecting with your internal teacher, helping you heal wounds from the past, forgiving yourself & others, & setting a positive direction for your life.

Journey into Power: How to Sculpt your Ideal Body, Free your True Self, & Transform your life with Baptiste Power Vinyasa Yoga. abr. ed. Baron Baptiste. 2004. 12.95 (978-0-7435-4907-3(4)) Pub: S&S Audio. Dist(s): S and S Inc

***Journey into Reading: Resource Kit Level C.** ed. Continental Press Staff. 2007. pap. bk. 19.95 (978-0-8454-5317-9(3)) Continental Pr.

***Journey into Reading: Resource Kit Level D.** ed. Continental Press Staff. 2007. pap. bk. 19.95 (978-0-8454-5318-6(1)) Continental Pr.

***Journey into Reading: Resource Kit Level E.** ed. Continental Press Staff. 2007. pap. bk. 19.95 (978-0-8454-5319-3(X)) Continental Pr.

***Journey into Reading: Resource Kit Level F.** ed. Continental Press Staff. 2007. pap. bk. 19.95 (978-0-8454-5320-9(3)) Continental Pr.

***Journey into Reading: Resource Kit Level G.** ed. Continental Press Staff. 2007. pap. bk. 19.95 (978-0-8454-5321-6(1)) Continental Pr.

***Journey into Reading: Resource Kit Level H.** ed. Continental Press Staff. 2007. pap. bk. 19.95 (978-0-8454-5322-3(X)) Continental Pr.

Journey into Sleep: Hypnosis for Power Naps & Deep Rest. Scripts. Sheri Menelli. 2 CDs. 2006. audio compact disk 39.95 (978-0-9747853-3-2(4)) Pub: White Hrt Pub. Dist(s): IPG Chicago

Journey into Space. Jane Murphy. 1 cass. (Running Time: 1 hr.). (J). 1988. pap. bk. 10.95 (KIM 9108C); pap. bk. & pupil's gde. ed. 11.95 (KIM 9108) Kimbo Educ.
Children develop a better understanding of space & our role in it. When they look up into the starry night sky, they will imagine what it must be like to be on a space shuttle. They will know what eating, sleeping, working & even exercising in space is like. They can even experience what it would be like to walk on the moon! Rocket Rock, My space Suit, Gravity, The Planet Song, Footsteps One The Moon, The Weightless Workout, Space is a Place & more. Includes guide.

Journey into the Elemental Kingdom: Meditations for Transformation. Voice by Jeni Miller. Music by Stephen Jacob. 2007. audio compact disk 20.00 (978-0-9798715-0-4(6)) Je Miller.

Journey into the Heart of the Beloved. Dawn Fleming. Music by Harry Henshaw. (ENG.). 2007. audio compact disk 18.00 (978-0-9797795-2-7(9)) Infinite Wisdom.

Journey into the Hush Arbor: Contemporary Music CD. 2006. audio compact disk 8.00 (978-0-687-49727-0(2)) Abingdon.

Journey into the Hush Arbor: Spirituals CD. 2006. audio compact disk 6.00 (978-0-687-49737-9(X)) Abingdon.

Journey into the Minds of Executives. Interview with Herbert Simon. 1 cass. (Running Time: 1 hr.). 9.00 (OP-79-10-12, HarperThor) HarpC GBR.

Journey Inward. Swami Amar Jyoti. 1 cass. 1983. 9.95 (D-8) Truth Consciousness.
Simple faith & devotion opens the way to the journey within. The way is straight, vast, engrossing, easy to discover. The journey's end.

Journey Not My Own. Jan Dravecky & Connie Neal. 2 cass. (Running Time: 60 min. per cass.). 1996. 14.99 (978-0-310-20558-6(1)) Zondervan.

Journey of a Thousand Miles: My Story. unabr. ed. Lang Lang & David Ritz. Narrated by Feodor Chin. 6 CDs. (Running Time: 6 hrs. 45 mins.). 2008.

Journey to the Center of the Earth. unabr. ed. Jules Verne. Read by Stephan Cox. (YA). 2007. 59.99 (978-1-59895-857-7(7)) Find a World.

***Journey to the Center of the Earth.** unabr. ed. Jules Verne. (Running Time: 10 hrs. 0 mins.). 2010. 16.99 (978-1-4001-8605-1(6)) Tantor Media.

***Journey to the Center of the Earth.** unabr. ed. Jules Verne. Narrated by Ed Sala. (Running Time: 10 hrs. 30 mins. 0 sec.). (ENG.). 2010. 22.99 (978-1-4001-6605-3(5)); audio compact disk 65.99 (978-1-4001-4605-5(4)); audio compact disk 32.99 (978-1-4001-1605-8(8)) Pub: Tantor Media. Dist(s): IngramPubServ

Journey to the Center of the Earth. unabr. collector's ed. Jules Verne. Read by Tom Collette. 8 cass. (Running Time: 12 hrs.). (J). (gr. 3-7). 1998. 64.00 (978-0-7366-3849-4(0), 9023) Books on Tape.
The story of Professor Lindenbrock, his nephew Axel & their quest for the secrets contained at the earth's core. Led by Hans, their Icelandic guide, Lidenbrock & Axel explore the mysteries of a never-before-seen subterranean world.

***Journey to the Center of the Earth: Bring the Classics to Life.** adpt. ed. Jules Verne. (Bring the Classics to Life Ser.). 2008. pap. bk. 21.95 (978-1-55576-652-8(8)) EDCON Pubng.

Journey to the Center of the Earth: Classic Collection. unabr. ed. Jules Verne. Read by Simon Prebble. 8 CDs. (Running Time: 10 hrs.). 2008. audio compact disk 29.95 (978-1-4332-4381-3(4)) Blckstn Audio.

Journey to the Center of the Heart. Alan Cohen. Read by Alan Cohen. Music by Raphael. 1 cass. 1995. CD. (978-0-910367-98-1(1)) A Cohen.
Four creative visualizations for mind & spirit.

Journey to the Centre of Earth. Jules Verne. Read by Daniel Philpott. (Running Time: 2 hrs. 30 mins.). 1995. 22.95 (978-1-60083-791-3(3)) Iofy Corp.

Journey to the Cross. Read by Lee Lefebre. 1 cass. (Running Time: 1 hr. 25 min.). (GraceLife Conference Ser.: Vol. 5). 1993. 6.00 (978-1-57838-110-4(X)); 6.00 (978-1-57838-009-1(X)) CrossLife Express.
Christian living.

Journey to the Crystal Palace: An Extra-Ordinary Guided Meditation. Scripts. Jackie Haverty. Read by Jackie Haverty. Perf. by Paul Armitage. Ed. by Francis Mitchell. Composed by Paul Armitage. 1 CD. (Running Time: 60 min.). 2002. audio compact disk 17.95 (978-1-895814-25-5(1), NWP125) NewWorld Pub CAN.

Journey to the Edge & Milestones Toward Recovery. Jeanette Keil. Read by Neva Duyndam. 1 cass. 1989. 9.95 (978-1-878159-01-4(1)) Duvall Media.
A moving & articulate account of the author's experience with schizophrenia & her journey toward recovery.

Journey to the Emerald City. abr. ed. Roger Connors & Tom Smith. (Running Time: 2 hrs. 52 mins. 4 sec.). (Smart Audio Ser.). (ENG.). 2003. 10.00 (978-1-60814-563-8(8), SmartTapes) Oasis Audio.

Journey to the Emerald City. abr. ed. Roger Connors et al. (Running Time: 2 hrs. 52 mins. 4 sec.). (Smart Audio Ser.). (ENG.). 2009. audio compact disk 14.99 (978-1-59859-615-1(2), SmartTapes) Oasis Audio.

Journey to the Emerald City Set: Achieve a Competitive Edge by Creating a Culture of Accountability. abr. ed. Roger Connors & Tom Smith. 2 cass. (Running Time: 180 min.). 2000. 17.95 (978-1-886463-84-4(0)) Oasis Audio.
The transformation of corporate culture has largely eluded the recent wave of performance improvement innovations. Connors and Smith fill this gap by outlining how their processes for culture change work not only in theory but also in practice. This volume provides hands-on, concrete tools for helping organizations fulfill their potential.

Journey to the Fluted Mountain: Stories & Music of the Colorado Trail. Julie Davis. 1 cass. 1997. 10.00 Boxed. (978-0-9659737-0-0(0), 1003) Winter Wind.
Stories & music based on nationally known storyteller Julie Davis's spiritual journey on the Colorado Trail with her dog & park animals in the summer of 1996.

Journey to the Golden Pyramid. Richard Gordon. 1 cass. 1994. pap. bk. 10.00 (978-0-931892-83-7(X)) B Dolphin Pub.

Journey to the Inner Child. Patricia O'Malley. Perf. by Barry Weiss. 1 cass. (Running Time: 50 min.). 1998. (978-1-892450-10-4(0), 152) Promo Music.
Guided imagery.

Journey to the Jade Sea. unabr. ed. John Hillaby. Read by John Hillaby. 6 cass. (Running Time: 9 hrs.). 2001. 54.95 (978-1-85695-434-1(X), 89071) Pub: ISIS Audio GBR. Dist(s): Ulverscroft US
"Few would make the journey & fewer still would describe it half so well." - Financial Times.

Journey to the Moon... & Beyond. (Running Time: 30 min.). (YA). (gr. 9 up). BackPax Int.
Exciting audio journey for kids, parents & even teachers.

Journey to the Mountaintop: The Road to Your Dreams. Short Stories. Steven Edwards. 2 DVDs. (Running Time: 2 hrs 15 min). 2006. audio compact disk 21.95 (978-0-9778654-0-6(1)) Creative Innov.
Unique 2 DVD set that inspires listeners to reach out and go after the Dreams that they have. Narrated by World Renowned Author and Motivational Speaker Steven Edwards. He will move you and help you take the steps needed to fulfill your life's hopes and dreams.

Journey to the New World: The Diary of Remember Patience Whipple, Mayflower 1620. Kathryn Lasky. Read by Barbara Rosenblat & Bonnie Kelley-Young. Directed By Robin Miles. (Dear America Ser.). (J). (gr. 3-7). 2008. bk. 39.95 (978-1-4301-0369-1(8)); audio compact disk 28.95 (978-1-4301-0367-7(1)) Live Oak Media.

Journey to the River Sea. unabr. ed. Eva Ibbotson. Narrated by Patricia Conolly. 6 pieces. (Running Time: 8 hrs.). (gr. 5 up). 2002. 54.00 (978-1-4025-2736-4(5)) Recorded Bks.

Journey to the Tenth Planet: A David Foster Starman Adventure. abr. ed. Michael D. Cooper. Abr. by Michael D. Cooper. Read by Charlie O'Dowd. 2 cass. (Running Time: 180 mins.). (Starman Ser.: No. 3). 2004. 18.00 (978-1-58807-476-8(5)); (978-1-58807-793-6(4)) Am Pubng Inc.
An astronomer, harnessing telescopes located on the far side of the moon, makes an astonishing discovery: There is a planet that lies beyond Pluto! Starlight Enterprise decides to send an expedition to explore the planet Nyx, and the Starman trio are going along. Trouble begins almost at once: The ship jointly built by Nolan Mining Enterprises and Starlight Enterprises experiences near catastrophic failure midway to the planet. What's worse, a spirit of fear begins creeping upon the crew: Rumors abound that the planet Nyx is a planet of doom. When the ship lands, the Starmen take a shuttlecraft down to the surface to explore - and when they return they find their ship is gone! Events soon throw the Starmen into a desperate conflict with an ancient extraterrestrial menace, and the only weapon the Starmen have is their own courage. The Starmen must battle not only alien foes, but desperate human foes as well as they fight for life on the Planet of Darkness.

Journey to the Underworld. Edie Hartshorne & Norma Churchill. 1 cass. 9.00 (A0206-87) Sound Photosyn.
Music & storied slides from ICSS Shamanism 1987.

Journey to the Western Isles of Scotland. unabr. ed. Samuel Johnson & James Boswell. Narrated by Patrick Tull & Alexander Spencer. 3 cass. (Running Time: 4 hrs. 30 mins.). 1988. 26.00 (978-1-55690-273-4(5), 88970E7) Recorded Bks.
In 1773, an unlikely pair, a dominant figure of English literature & a young lawyer, set out on horseback to follow roads & cattle-trails across the Highlands to the Western Islands of Scotland.

Journey to the 5th Dimension Vol. 2: An Extra-Ordinary Guided Meditation. 2nd ed. Scripts. Jackie Haverty. Read by Jackie Haverty. Perf. by Paul Armitage. Ed. by Francis Mitchell. Composed by Paul Armitage. Illus. by Diane Parks. 1 CD. (Running Time: 60 min.). Dramatization. 2004. audio compact disk 17.95 (978-1-895814-30-9(8), NWP130) NewWorld Pub CAN.

***Journey to Victorious Praying: Finding Discipline & Delight in Your Prayer Life.** unabr. ed. Bill Thrasher. (ENG.). 2010. 17.99 (978-0-9830140-5-8(1)) Sozo Media.

Journey to Within. Bartholomew. Read by Mary Margaret Moore. 1 cass. (Running Time: 57 min.). 10.00 High Mesa Pr.
Channeled info using the major arcana of Tarot as doorways to wholeness, to be master of our lives.

Journey with Eagle & Elephant. Nicki Scully & Jerry Garcia. Photos by Roland Barker. 1 CD. 2004. audio compact disk 16.00 (978-0-9623365-7-7(2)) N Scully.

Journey with Jesus (Cassette) Created by Gospel Gospel Vision Staff. (YA). 2003. 7.95 (978-0-910683-96-8(4)) Townsnd-Pr.

Journey with Jesus (CD) Created by Gospel Gospel Vision Staff. (YA). 2003. audio compact disk 13.95 (978-0-910683-97-5(2)) Townsnd-Pr.

Journey with St. Therese of Lisieux: Doctor of the Church. John Russell. 3 cass. (Running Time: 3 hrs. 51 mins.). 1999. 29.95 (TAH410) Alba Hse Comns.
Examines traditional & recent aspects of the Saint's life & works & explores her relevance for today through an enlightened lens of contemporary research & applications.

Journey Without Maps. unabr. ed. Graham Greene. Read by Richard Green. 7 cass. (Running Time: 10 hrs. 30 mins.). 1989. 56.00 (978-0-7366-1664-5(0), 2513) Books on Tape.
"I watched from the other end of the bar; she wept & didn't care a damn ... I thought even then of Africa, not a particular place, but a shape, a strangeness, a wanting to know. The unconscious mind is often sentimental; I have written 'a shape,' & the shape of course is roughly that of the human heart." White men were not particularly welcome in Liberia in 1935 when Graham Greene went there - his first journey outside Europe. Drawn by curiosity about a republic founded for freed slaves &, above all, by the mystery of Africa, he traveled with his young cousin & a chain of porters from the border of Sierra Leone over jungles & deserts & down to the coast at Grand Bassa.

Journeying Moon. unabr. collector's ed. Ernle Bradford. Read by Arthur Addison. 6 cass. (Running Time: 9 hrs.). 1995. 48.00 (978-0-7366-3060-3(0), 3742) Books on Tape.
Times were awful in post-WWII Britain when Ernle Bradford recalled the words of Chekov he had read years earlier: "Life does not come again." Bradford's reflection galvanized him & his wife: they bought a 10-ton Dutch cutter & made the Mediterranean their home.

Journeying with the Children Mystics. Tessa Bielecki. 3 cass. 27.00 (3 CASS.) Sound Horizons AV.

***Journeys: An Anthology of Life.** A. L. Hotchkin. (Running Time: 300). (ENG.). 2010. 14.95 (978-1-934889-62-6(8)) Lbook Pub.

Journeys: Christmas. 1997. 7.99 (978-0-7601-1198-7(7), C50042); 11.99 (CD50042) Brentwood Music.
Captures the emotions of moments of life through comforting hymns & light ambient music perfectly designed to accompany you on your way as you seek communion with the Creator.

Journeys: Listening / Speaking. Setsuko Toyama & Carl Adams. 2002. 43.85 (978-0-13-242090-7(2)) Longman.

Journeys: Listening / Speaking, Level 2. Stacy A. Hagen. 2002. 41.75 (978-0-13-242116-4(X)) Longman.

Journeys: Listening / Speaking, Level 3. David Anderson. 2002. bk. 41.75 (978-0-13-242132-4(1)) Longman.

Journeys: Prayer. (J). 1997. 7.99 (978-0-7601-1194-9(4), C50037); audio compact disk 9.99 CD. (978-0-7601-1195-6(2), CD50037) Brentwood Music.

Journeys: Worship. 1997. 7.99 (978-0-7601-1196-3(0), C50040); audio compact disk 9.99 CD. (978-0-7601-1197-0(9), CD50040) Brentwood Music.

Journeys Beyond the Brain. unabr. ed. Stanislav Grof. 1 cass. (Running Time: 1 hr. 26 min.). 1979. 11.00 (00806) Big Sur Tapes.

Journey's Echo. unabr. collector's ed. Freya Stark. Read by Donada Peters. 7 cass. (Running Time: 7 hrs.). 1991. 42.00 (978-0-7366-2011-6(7), 2827) Books on Tape.
Essays on solo travel in the Middle East.

Journey's End. Swami Amar Jyoti. 1 cass. 1976. 9.95 (C-38) Truth Consciousness.
Real acceptance of Truth & Grace without clutching anything else. All pervadedness of God's Grace.

Journey's End. unabr. ed. Josephine Cox. 7 CDs. (Running Time: 30600 sec.). 2006. audio compact disk 74.95 (978-0-7927-4494-8(2), SLD 1024) AudioGO.

Journey's End. unabr. ed. Josephine Cox. Narrated by Carole Boyd. 4 CDs. (Running Time: 30600 sec.). 2006. audio compact disk 44.95 (978-0-7927-4566-2(3), CMP 1024) AudioGO.

Journey's End: The Memories & Traditions of Daisy Turner & Her Family. Interview. Executive Producer Jane Beck. Prod. by Ev Grimes. Narrated by Barbara Jordan. Voice by Daisy Turner et al. 1 CD. (Running Time: 1 hr., 18 mins.,1 sec.). 2007. audio compact disk 14.95 (978-0-916718-30-5(1)) VT Folklife Ctr.

Journeys for Disciples. Bob Ravenscroft. Read by Bob Ravenscroft. 1 cd. (Running Time: 1 hr. 1 min.). 1998. audio compact disk 9.95 (978-1-889387-10-9(X), Morning Lght Media) Crtve Commns MO.

Journeys in Inner Space. unab. ed. Perf. by Eknath Easwaran. 1 cass. (Running Time: 1 hr.). 1984. 7.95 (978-1-58638-556-9(9)) Nilgiri Pr.

Journeys in Sound & Healing. Kate Marks. 1 cass. 10.00 (978-0-9637489-1-1(2)) Full Circle MA.

Journeys into Meditation & Music. Hal A. Lingerman & Lingerm. Read by Hal A. Lingerman. 2 cass. (Running Time: 2 hrs.). 1994. 10.95 (978-0-8356-2094-9(8), Quest) Pub: Theos Pub Hse. Dist(s): Natl Bk Netwk

Journeys into Past Lives. Read by Denise Linn. 2 cass. (Running Time: 2 hrs.). 2000. 16.95 Hay House.

Journeys into Past Lives. Denise Linn. 2 CDs. 2005. audio compact disk 18.95 (978-1-4019-0661-0(3)) Hay House.

Journeys of Socrates: An Adventure. abr. ed. Dan Millman. Read by Sam Tsoutsouvas. 2005. audio compact disk 29.95 (978-0-06-076335-0(3)) HarperCollins Pubs.

***Journeys of Socrates: An Adventure.** abr. ed. Dan Millman. Read by Sam Tsoutsouvas. (ENG.). 2005. (978-0-06-084304-5(7), Harper Audio); (978-0-06-084303-8(9), Harper Audio) HarperCollins Pubs.

Journeys to Bethlehem. Albert Zabel. 2004. bk. 12.00 (978-0-687-07364-1(2)) Abingdon.

Journeys Worship. 1 cass., 1 CD. 7.99; audio compact disk 9.99 CD. Provident Mus Dist.

Joy. Perf. by Daughters of St. Prod. by Daughters of St. 2004. audio compact disk 16.95 (978-0-8198-3981-7(7), 332-157) Pauline Bks.
Share the Joy of Christmas with the Daughters of St. Paul!For the past ten years, the Daughters of St. Paul have performed a Christmas concert in Staten Island, New York. In 2004, Chaz Palminteri invited them to appear in his new Christmas film: in Noel, the Daughters appear in the opening scene as an outdoor choir singing to passersby in the middle of Manhattan. Joy, combining traditional Christmas music with contemporary carols, is sure to become a holiday classic in every home!1. Joy (to the World)2. Do You Hear What I Hear?3. Hark! The Herald Angels Sing4. The New Twelve Days of Christmas5. Sing to the King6. All Alone on Christmas7. Jingle Bell Rock8. Perfect Christmas Night9. Happy Christmas10. Angels We Have Heard on High.

Joy. Victoria Christopher Murray. Narrated by Susan Spain. 9 cass. (Running Time: 12 hrs.). 81.00 (978-1-4025-0768-7(2)) Recorded Bks.

Joy. Eldon Taylor. Read by Eldon Taylor. Interview with Progress Aware Staff. 1 cass. (Running Time: 62 min.). 16.95 incl. script. (978-1-55978-298-2(6), 020112) Progress Aware Res.
Verbal coaching soundtrack with underlying subliminal affirmations & sound matrix frequencies for brain entrainment.

Joy. unabr. ed. Read by Steven Domienik et al. 2 cass. (Running Time: 1 hrs. 46 min.). 1998. 12.00 Set. (978-0-88028-203-1(7), 1487) Forward Movement.
Reflections on joy by 25 different people Award of Excellence, Audio/Educational in Electronic Media/Agency from Polly Bond Awards, Episcopal Comunicators.

Joy: A Major Spiritual Force. Kenneth Copeland. 4 cass. 1986. 20.00 Set incl. study guide. (978-0-88114-750-6(8)) K Copeland Pubns.
Biblical principles for victorious living.

Joy: Falling in Love with Life. Instructed by Stuart Wilde. 1 cass. (Self-Help Tape Ser.). 11.95 (978-0-930603-46-5(X)) White Dove NM.
SIDE A - Stuart Wilde reminds you to celebrate life no matter what. He gives you practical techniques for re-establishing & sustaining joy & exhilaration in your heart. A nice gift for a friend. SIDE B - A subliminal tape crammed full of positive affirmations to lift your spirits.

Joy: Songs for the Spirit. Contrib. by Dean Diehl & Ed Kee. 1 CD. 2000. audio compact disk 9.99 (978-0-7601-3187-9(2), SO33210) Pub: Brentwood Music. Dist(s): Provident Mus Dist
Songs include: "The Ride of Life," "Happy," "Heavenly," "We Will glorify," "Be Ye Glad" & more.

Joy: The Emotion Everyone Wants. Lois F. Timmins. 1 cass. (Running Time: 55 min.). 1986. 12.95 (978-0-931814-12-9(X)) Comn Studies.
Of all the feelings, joy is the only one which is about 95% positive, yet it is the most elusive, the most paradoxical, & the rarest. Joy cannot be felt by trying or choosing to feel it. Joy cannot be attained by direct effort, but is always a bi-product of other efforts - mostly very taxing ones. Coping with feelings allows joy to be felt more often.

Joy! a Soulful Celebration of the Season. Contrib. by Dave Williamson. 1997. 11.98 (978-0-7601-1342-4(4), 75602096); 85.00 (978-0-7601-1345-5(9), 75606450); 85.00 (978-0-7601-1346-2(7), 75606314); 4.00 (978-0-7601-1348-6(3), 75602097); 4.00 (978-0-7601-1349-3(1), 75602094); 4.00 (978-0-7601-1350-9(5), 75602098); 4.00 (978-0-7601-1351-6(3), 75602095) Pub: Brentwood Music. Dist(s): H Leonard

Joy! a Soulful Celebration of the Season. Contrib. by Dave Williamson. 1997. audio compact disk 85.00 (978-0-7601-1347-9(5), 75606315) Pub: Brentwood Music. Dist(s): H Leonard

Joy after Sorrow. Perf. by Barolk Folk Staff. 1 cass. (Running Time: 40 min.). (J). 9.98 (978-1-877737-26-8(7), 2205); audio compact disk 12.98 (978-1-877737-27-5(5), D2205) MFLP CA.
Western European music, from early Renaissance dances to a Mozart trio, is explored on this gorgeous musical canvas. The title track is just one of many traditional folk tunes from England, Ireland & the Continent.

Joy & Bliss of Surrender. Swami Amar Jyoti. 2 cass. 1977. 12.95 (C-40) Truth Consciousness.
'Start with surrender & end with surrender.' The no man's land between seeking & finding. Knowing true freedom.

Joy & Gladness. Perf. by Gloriae Dei Cantores. 1 CD. (Running Time: 72 mins and 18 secs). 2006. audio compact disk 12.99 (978-1-55725-492-4(3)) Paraclete MA.

Joy & Peace Series, Set. Elbert Willis. 4 cass. 13.00 Set. Fill the Gap.

Joy & Promise: A Spiritual Renewal Seminar. 4 cass. bk. Set, incl. manual. (2008) Family Mtrs.
Topics include: The Gift of Joy, Love & Faith; The Fountain of Joy; Painting Life with Shades of Joy & The Joy & Promise of Family.

Joy & Sorrows of Sobriety. Daniel J. Anderson. 1 cass. 1986. 8.95 incl. bk. (1486) Hazelden.

Joy at Work: A Revolutionary Approach to Fun on the Job. Dennis W. Bakke. Read by Dennis W. Bakke. 6. (Running Time: 6 hrs.). (ENG.). 2005. audio compact disk 30.00 (978-0-9762686-2-8(0)) Pub: PVG. Dist(s): Perseus Dist
Imagine a company where people love coming to work and are highly productive on a daily basis. Imagine a company whose top executives, in a quest to create the most ?fun? workplace ever, obliterate labor-management divisions and push decision-making responsibility down to the plant floor. Could such a company compete in today?s bottom-line corporate world? Could it even turn a profit?Well, imagine no more. In Joy at Work, Dennis W. Bakke tells the true story of this extraordinary company?and how, as its co-founder and longtime CEO, he challenged the business establishment with revolutionary ideas that could remake America?s organizations. It is the story of AES, whose business model and operating ethos ??let?s have fun??were conceived during a 90-minute car ride from Annapolis, Maryland, to Washington, D.C. In the next two decades, it became a worldwide energy giant with 40,000 employees in 31 countries and revenues of $8.6 billion. It?s a remarkable tale told by a remarkable man: Bakke, a farm boy who was shaped by his religious faith, his years at Harvard Business School, and his experience working for the Federal Energy Administration. He rejects workplace drudgery as a noxious remnant of the Industrial Revolution. He believes work should be fun, and at AES he set out to prove it could be. Bakke sought not the empty ?fun? of the Friday beer blast but the joy of a workplace where every person, from custodian to CEO, has the power to use his or her God-given talents free of needless corporate bureaucracy. In Joy at Work, Bakke tells how he helped create a company where every decision made at the top was lamented as a lost chance to delegate

responsibility?and where all employees were encouraged to take the ?game-winning shot, ? even when it wasn?t a slam-dunk.Perhaps Bakke?s most radical stand was his struggle to break the stranglehold of ?creating shareholder value? on the corporate mind-set and replace it with more timeless values: integrity, fairness, social responsibility, and, above all, fun. And Bakke doesn?t shrink from describing the assault on his leadership when AES was sucked into the Enron downdraft and faced a plunging stock price. At this moment of crisis, influential colleagues and directors distanced themselves from the values that had made AES one of the most celebrated companies in the world.Joy at Work offers a model for the 21st-century company that treats its people with respect, gives them unprecedented responsibility, and holds them strictly accountable?because it?s the right thing to do, not just because it makes good business sense. More than any book you?ve ever read, Dennis Bakke?s Joy at Work will force you to question everything you thought you knew about corporate success.

Joy at Work: A Revolutionary Approach to Fun on the Job. unabr. ed. Dennis W. Bakke. Read by Dennis W. Bakke. 6. (Running Time: 6 hrs.). (ENG.). 2005. 26.00 (978-0-9762686-1-1(2)) Pub: PVG. Dist(s): Perseus Dist

Joy Beyond Our Dreams: Music for Lent & Easter. Contrib. by John Angotti. 2008. audio compact disk 17.00 (978-1-58459-379-9(2)) Wrld Lib Pubns.

Joy Comes in the Morning. David Danner. 1981. 75.00 (978-0-7673-1848-8(X)) LifeWay Christian.

Joy Comes in the Morning. David Danner. 1981. 11.98 (978-0-7673-1849-5(8)) LifeWay Christian.

Joy Comes in the Morning: A Novel. Jonathan Rosen. 11 CDs. (Running Time: 13 hrs.). 2004. audio compact disk 88.00 (978-0-7861-8543-6(0), 3301) Blckstn Audio.

Joy Comes in the Morning: A Novel. unabr. ed. Jonathan Rosen. Read by Lorna Raver. 13 pieces. (Running Time: 13 hrs.). 2005. audio compact disk 24.95 (978-0-7861-8518-4(X), 3301); audio compact disk 44.95 (978-0-7861-8583-2(X), ZE3301); reel tape 34.95 (978-0-7861-2732-0(5), E3301) Blckstn Audio.

Deborah Green is a woman of passionate contradictions, a rabbi struggling with her own doubts and desires. Her life changes when she visits the hospital room of Henry Friedman, an older man who has attempted suicide. His parents were murdered in the Holocaust when he was a child, and all his life he has struggled with painful questions. Can happiness come after such loss or does the very wish profane the dead? Can religious promises ever be fulfilled? Deborah's encounter with Henry draws her into his world, which includes his wife Helen, a photographer fiercely devoted to her husband but frightened by him, too; his son, Lev, a science reporter who left his fiancee at the altar; and Lev's best friend from childhood, Neal, whose life fell apart after a psychotic break. As Deborah and Lev fall in love, they strive to bind themselves to something sacred in the midst of modern chaos.

Joy Comes in the Morning Library Ed. A Novel. unabr. ed. Jonathan Rosen. 9 cass. (Running Time: 13 hrs.). 2004. 62.95 (978-0-7861-2779-5(1), 3301) Blckstn Audio.

Deborah Green is a woman of passionate contradictions: a rabbi who craves faith and goodness while wrestling with her own doubts and desires. Her life changes when she visits the hospital room of Henry Friedman, an older man who has attempted suicide. His parents were murdered in the Holocaust when he was a child, and all his life he has struggled with painful questions. Can happiness come after such loss or does the very wish profane the dead? Can religious promises ever be fulfilled?.

Joy Diet: 10 Daily Practices for a Happier Life. unabr. ed. Martha Beck. 6 CDs. (Running Time: 7 hrs.). audio compact disk 40.00 (978-0-7366-9319-6(X)) Books on Tape.

***Joy Fielding CD Collection: Mad River Road, Heartstopper.** abr. ed. Joy Fielding. Read by Judith West. (Running Time: 12 hrs.). 2010. audio compact disk 19.99 (978-1-4418-5039-3(2), 9781441850393, BACD) Brilliance Audio.

***Joy Fielding CD Collection 2: Charley's Web, Still Life.** abr. ed. Joy Fielding. (Running Time: 12 hrs.). 2010. audio compact disk 19.99 (978-1-4418-6161-0(0), 9781441861610, BACD) Brilliance Audio.

Joy Harjo & Barney Bush. unabr. ed. Joy Harjo & Barney Bush. Read by Joy Harjo. 1 cass. (Running Time: 29 min.). 1983. 10.00 (051383) New Letters.

Native American poets Harjo & Bush read from their work.

Joy Harjo II. unabr. ed. Joy Harjo. 1 cass. (Running Time: 29 min.). (New Letters on the Air Ser.). 1992. 10.00 (091391) New Letters.

In addition to reading her poems & talking about them, Harjo plays the saxophone in this program.

***Joy I'd Never Known: When I Gave up Control, I Found .** abr. ed. Jan Dravecky & Connie Neal. (Running Time: 2 hrs. 0 mins. 0 sec.). (ENG.). 2005. 9.99 (978-0-310-26071-4(X)) Zondervan.

Joy in the Morning. 1 cass. 10.98 (978-1-57908-277-2(7), 1370); audio compact disk 15.98 CD. (978-1-57908-276-5(9), 1370) Platinm Enter.

Joy Is Being. Swami Amar Jyoti. 1 dolby cass. 1983. 9.95 (K-60) Truth Consciousness.

What is joy, Ananda? Being near Him. Using the help that is always given. Clear guidelines for change & revival.

Joy Is Coming: Heart Outreach Ministries. Cornell Burton. 1 CD. (Running Time: 1 hr. 30 mins.). 2004. audio compact disk 15.98 (978-5-559-39488-6(2)) Pub: Pt of Grace Ent. Dist(s): STL Dist NA

Joy Is Experienced. Elbert Willis. 1 cass. (Outcome of Abiding in Jesus Ser.). 4.00 Fill the Gap.

Joy Joy Joy. Perf. by Kim Robertson & Steve Kujala. 1 cass. 9.98 (462); audio compact disk 17.98 (D462) MFLP CA.

The crisp sounds of flute & harp filtering like sunlight through traditional French & Irish tunes, as well as seasonal carols, illuminate the spirit of winter festivity.

Joy Killer #1: Circumstances: Philippians 2:1-30. Ed Young. 1995. 4.95 (978-0-7417-2060-3(4), 1060) Win Walk.

Joy Killer #2: People: Philippians 2:1-30. Ed Young. 1995. 4.95 (978-0-7417-2061-0(2), 1061) Win Walk.

Joy Killer #3: Things: Philippians 3:1-30. Ed Young. 1995. Rental 4.95 (978-0-7417-2062-7(0), 1062) Win Walk.

Joy Killer #4:Worry: Philippians 4:1-23. Ed Young. 1995. 4.95 (978-0-7417-2064-1(7), 1064) Win Walk.

Joy Luck Club. abr. ed. Amy Tan. Read by Amy Tan. 2 cass. (Running Time: 3 hrs.). 2001. 18.00 (978-1-59040-034-0(8), Phoenix Audio) Pub: Amer Intl Pub. Dist(s): PerseuPGW

Drawn together by their past, four women meet once a week for forty years to share stories and create joy and luck out of unimaginable catastrophe.

Joy Luck Club. unabr. ed. Amy Tan. Read by Gwendoline Yeo. (YA). 2008. 54.99 (978-1-60514-783-3(4)) Find a World.

Joy of Boredom. William Wait. 1 cass. 1996. 9.98 (978-1-57734-010-2(8), 06005381) Covenant Comms.

How to not become a busybody, tattler & faultfinder.

Joy of Christmas. Read by Mother Basilea Schlink. 1 cass. (Running Time: 30 min.). 1985. (0290) Evang Sisterhood Mary.

Includes: As True Children; His Name Shall Be Mighty God; There Is Room in Our Hearts for You.

Joy of Depression. William Wait. 1 cass. 7.98 (978-1-55503-227-2(3), 060097) Covenant Comms.

Two marvelously funny talks on a very serious topic.

***Joy of Eating Well: A Practical Guide To- Transform Your Relationship with Food- Overcome Emotional Eating- Achieve Lasting Results.** Andrew Weil MD & Carolyn Ross MD, MPH. (Running Time: 2:00:00). 2010. audio compact disk 19.95 (978-1-60407-078-1(1)) Sounds True.

Joy of Enlightenment: An Ascending Pathway of Truth. unabr. ed. Eduardo Mischl. Read by Eduardo Mischl. 3 cass. (Running Time: 2 hrs. 16 min.). 1998. 19.95 Set. (978-0-9665139-0-5(8), ISP001) Inesource Pr.

An overview of the secular pathway to spiritual enlightenment; How one begins a practice of self-development focused on finding the inner truths.

Joy of Exercise. Barrie Konicov. Read by Barrie Konicov. 1 cass. 16.98 (SC-II 077) Potentials.

Joy of Exercise. Barrie Konicov. 1 CD. 2003. audio compact disk 16.98 (978-0-87082-960-4(2)) Potentials.

Even with the best intentions, many people need a push to make exercise a routine part of their lives. This program will give you that push. Play it at bedtime and you will awaken with a desire to exercise. You will find the self-hypnosis on track 1 and the subliminal on track 2. The easy-listening music of the subliminal, together with the self-hypnosis, is the original format which most people love and with which they are most familiar.

Joy of Exercise. Barrie Konicov. 2 CDs. 2003. audio compact disk 27.98 (978-1-56001-980-0(8)) Potentials.

Joy of Exercise, Set. Barrie Konicov. 2 cass. 14.98 (978-1-56001-315-0(X), SCII 077) Potentials.

Even with the best of intentions, many people need a shove to make exercise a routine part of their lives. Play it at bedtime & you can awaken with a desire to exercise.

Joy of Exercise: Babbling Brook. Eldon Taylor. 1 cass. 16.95 (978-1-55978-471-9(7), 5326F) Progress Aware Res.

Joy of Exercise: Hypnotic & Subliminal Learning. David Illig. 2000. 14.99 (978-0-86580-004-5(9)) Success World.

Joy of Exercise: Soundtrack: Leisure Listening. Eldon Taylor. 1 cass. (Running Time: 62 min.). 16.95 (978-0-940699-38-0(9), 5326B) Progress Aware Res.

Musical soundtrack with underlying subliminal affirmations.

Joy of Exercise: Soundtrack: Musical Themes. Eldon Taylor. 1 cass. (Running Time: 62 min.). 16.95 incl. script. (978-0-940699-39-7(7), 5326C) Progress Aware Res.

Joy of Exercise: Soundtrack: Synthesized Moments. Eldon Taylor. 1 cass. (Running Time: 62 min.). 16.95 (978-0-940699-76-2(1), 5326D) Progress Aware Res.

Joy of Exercise: Soundtrack: Tropical Lagoon. Eldon Taylor. 1 cass. (Running Time: 62 min.). 16.95 (978-0-940699-77-9(X), 5326A) Progress Aware Res.

Environmental soundtrack with underlying subliminal affirmations.

Joy of Fearing God: The Fear of the Lord Is a Life-Giving Fountain. Jerry Bridges. 2 cass. (Running Time: 3 hrs.). (ENG.). 1998. 14.95 (978-1-57856-057-8(8), WaterB Pr) Pub: Doubday Relig. Dist(s): Random

Revealing look at what the Bible says about why Christians should fear God. Leads to the startling discovery that the fear of God is the key to joyful, fulfilling, & genuine intimacy with God.

Joy of Humor: Environmental Theme. Eldon Taylor. 1 cass. 16.95 (978-1-55978-483-2(0), 5354F) Progress Aware Res.

Joy of Humor: Soundtrack: Synthesized Moments. Eldon Taylor. 1 cass. (Running Time: 62 min.). 16.95 incl. script. (978-0-940699-60-1(5), 5354D) Progress Aware Res.

Musical soundtrack with underlying subliminal affirmations.

Joy of Living. Richard Prigmore. Read by Martin Zevin. Perf. by Art Holbrook. 2 cass. (Running Time: 2 hrs.). 1997. 14.95 (978-0-9661708-1-8(4)) Bright Angel.

Inspiirational adventure spiritual & humorous for the whole family.

Joy of Living. Read by Mary Richards. (Subliminal Impact Ser.). 12.95 (607) Master Your Mind.

Discusses how to set the imagination free to experience a heightened sense of aliveness & confidence.

Joy of Living: Unlocking the Secret & Science of Happiness. abr. ed. Yongey Mingyur Rinpoche & Eric Swanson. Read by Jason Scott Campbell. (Running Time: 23400 sec.). (ENG.). 2007. audio compact disk 29.95 (978-0-7393-4167-4(7), Random AudioBks) Pub: Random Audio Pubg. Dist(s): Random

Joy of Living - in the Now. enl. ed. Interview with Darleen Wodzenski. Contrib. by Arthur Holbrook. 2 cass. (Running Time: 2 hrs.). Dramatization. (YA). (gr. 11 up). 1998. 14.95 Set. (978-0-9661708-2-5(2)) Bright Angel.

Joy of Living Free from Fear. unabr. ed. Jack Boland. Read by Jack Boland. 2 cass. (Running Time: 2 hrs.). 19.95 set. (978-0-88152-060-6(8), BA30) Master Mind.

Joy of Loneliness. William Wait. 1 cass. 5.98 (978-1-55503-101-5(3), 06003117) Covenant Comms.

Love & loneliness are flip sides of the same coin.

Joy of Loneliness. William Wait. 1 cass. 2004. 3.95 (978-1-57734-407-0(3), 34441492) Covenant Comms.

Joy of Love. William Wait. 1 cass. 3.95 (978-1-57734-408-7(1), 34441506) Covenant Comms.

Joy of Marriage. William Wait. 1 cass. 5.98 (978-1-55503-102-2(1), 0600164) Covenant Comms.

With his wit, marriage yesterday & today are explored.

Joy of Marriage. William Wait. 1 cass. 2004. 3.95 (978-1-57734-409-4(X), 34441514) Covenant Comms.

Joy of Meditating: A Beginner's Guide to the Art of Meditation. abr. ed. Salle Merrill Redfield. Read by Salle Merrill Redfield. 1 CD. (Running Time: 1 hr.). (ENG.). 2002. audio compact disk 16.98 (978-1-58621-410-4(1)) Pub: Hachet Audio. Dist(s): HachBkGrp

Joy of Meditating: A Beginner's Guide to the Art of Meditation. abr. ed. Salle Merrill Redfield. (ENG.). 2005. 14.98 (978-1-59483-352-6(4)) Pub: Hachet Audio. Dist(s): HachBkGrp

Joy of Meditating: A Beginner's Guide to the Art of Meditation. abr. ed. Salle Merrill Redfield. (Running Time: 1 hr.). (ENG.). 2009. 24.98 (978-1-60788-098-1(9)) Pub: Hachet Audio. Dist(s): HachBkGrp

Joy of Meditation - Compassion & the Peaceful Mind. Swami Amar Jyoti. 1 cass. 1995. 10.95 (SAT-101) Truth Consciousness.

Calm as a candle in a windless place; doing nothing, being everything. Compassion removes tension, readies mind for focus & wisdom.

Joy of Overcoming: The Candelabra of the Soul. Jonathan Murro. Read by Jonathan Murro. 1 cass. 7.95 A R Colton Fnd.

Discusses the goal of God-Realization.

Joy of Practices. Swami Amar Jyoti. 1 cass. 1978. 9.95 (P-10) Truth Consciousness.

Patience & steadiness in hard pratices. Stages of practice. The impersonal attitude of the Master. On Realized Souls & cosmic evolution.

Joy of Recovery: Creating a New Life. abr. ed. Nina Mattikow. 3 cass. (Running Time: 3 hrs.). Dramatization. (Personal Achievement Ser.). 1992. 19.95 Set. (978-1-55569-561-3(2), 43002) Great Am Audio.

A personal support system for starting over. This comprehensive, easy to follow program is a blueprint for creating a new life!.

Joy of Repentance. William Wait. 1 cass. 5.98 (978-1-55503-224-1(9), 06004059) Covenant Comms.

Joy of Retirement: Finding Happiness, Freedom, & the Life You've Always Wanted. unabr. ed. David C. Borchard & Patricia A. Donohoe. Read by Sean Pratt. (Running Time: 11 hrs.). (ENG.). 2008. 29.98 (978-1-59659-260-5(5), GildAudio) Pub: Gildan Media. Dist(s): HachBkGrp

Joy of School: Ending Dropout. Eldon Taylor. 1 cass. (Running Time: 62 min.). (Inner Talk Ser.). 1997. 16.95 incl. script. (978-1-55978-528-0(4), 53813F) Progress Aware Res.

Soundtrack - Brook with underlying subliminal affirmations.

Joy of School: Ending Dropout: Contemporary Moments. Eldon Taylor. 1 cass. 16.95 (978-1-55978-610-2(8), 53813N) Progress Aware Res.

Joy of Science, Pt. 2. 6 cass. (Running Time: 6 hrs.). 2001. 299.95 (978-1-56585-001-9(7)) Teaching Co.

Joy of Science, Pt. 3. 6 cass. (Running Time: 6 hrs.). 2001. 299.95 (978-1-56585-002-6(5)) Teaching Co.

Joy of Science, Pt. 4. 6 cass. (Running Time: 6 hrs.). 2001. 299.95 (978-1-56585-003-3(3)) Teaching Co.

Joy of Science, Pt. 5. 6 cass. (Running Time: 6 hrs.). 2001. 299.95 (978-1-56585-004-0(1)) Teaching Co.

Joy of Science, Pts. I-V. Instructed by Robert Hazen. 30 CDs. (Running Time: 30 hrs.). 2001. bk. 169.95 (978-1-56585-275-4(3), 1100) Teaching Co.

Joy of Science, Pts. I-V, Vol. 1. Instructed by Robert Hazen. 30 cass. (Running Time: 30 hrs.). 2001. 119.95 (978-1-56585-000-2(9), 1100) Teaching Co.

Joy of Science, Vol. 2. Instructed by Robert Hazen. 6 CDs. (Running Time: 6 hrs.). 2001. audio compact disk 449.95 (978-1-56585-276-1(1)) Teaching Co.

Joy of Science, Vol. 3. Instructed by Robert Hazen. 6 CDs. (Running Time: 6 hrs.). 2001. audio compact disk 449.95 (978-1-56585-277-8(X)) Teaching Co.

Joy of Science, Vol. 4. Instructed by Robert Hazen. 6 CDs. (Running Time: 6 hrs.). 2001. audio compact disk 449.95 (978-1-56585-278-5(8)) Teaching Co.

Joy of Science, Vol. 5. Instructed by Robert Hazen. 6 CDs. (Running Time: 6 hrs.). 2001. audio compact disk 449.95 (978-1-56585-279-2(6)) Teaching Co.

Joy of Selling. unabr. ed. Steve Chandler. Read by Steve Chandler. (YA). 2007. 49.99 (978-1-60252-646-4(X)) Find a World.

Joy of Selling. unabr. ed. Steve Chandler. Read by Steve Chandler. (Running Time: 5 hrs.). (ENG.). 2003. audio compact disk 24.95 (978-1-56511-833-1(2), 1565118332) Pub: HighBridge. Dist(s): Workman Pub

Joy of Sex. Read by Mary Richards. (Subliminal Impact Ser.). 12.95 (620) Master Your Mind.

Having let go of limitations & negative feelings of the past, one can be empowered with vitality & energy.

Joy of Stress. Peter Hanson. Read by Peter Hanson. (Running Time: 1 hr.). 8.95 (T 87) Listen USA.

Shows how stress can be a joy when you know how to put it to work. The right balance can lead to a longer, more energized life.

Joy of Stress. Loretta LaRoche. Read by Loretta LaRoche. 2 cass. (Running Time: 1 hr. 18 min.). 2001. 14.95 (WG817) WGBH Boston.

Shows you how to prevent "hardening of the attitude" and use humor to break the negative and irrational thought patterns that cause stress and re-frame them into powerful, positive tools for change.

Joy of Training. Michael Pearl. (ENG.). 2006. audio compact disk 26.00 (978-1-892112-23-1(X)) Pub: No Greater Joy. Dist(s): STL Dist NA

Joy of Wine: An Insider's Guide to the Major Varietals. Rob Geddes. 2007. audio compact disk 79.95 (978-0-9795255-3-7(5)) Now You Know.

Joy of Work. Eldon Taylor. 1 cass. (Running Time: 62 min.). (Inner Talk Ser.). 16.95 incl. script, (978-1-55978-574-7(8), 5381L) Progress Aware Res.

Soundtrack - Classics with underlying subliminal affirmations.

***Joy of Work.** abr. ed. Scott Adams. Read by Scott Adams. (ENG.). 2005. (978-0-06-089800-7(3), Harper Audio); (978-0-06-089799-4(6), Harper Audio) HarperCollins Pubs.

Joy of Work: Ocean. Eldon Taylor. Read by Eldon Taylor. Ed. by Leslie Brice. 1 cass. (Running Time: 1 hr.). 1992. 16.95 (978-1-56705-327-2(0)) Gateways Inst.

Self improvement.

Joy of Work: Tropical Lagoon. Eldon Taylor. 1 cass. 16.95 (978-1-55978-351-4(6), 5381A) Progress Aware Res.

Joy of Working. unabr. ed. Denis Waitley & Reni L. Witt. 1 cass. 1987. 9.95 (978-0-07-067834-7(0)) HarperCollins Pubs.

Involves goal-setting, self-reliance, pride & motivation.

Joy of Working: Thirty Ways to Love Your Job, Set. Denis Waitley & Reni L. Witt. 6 cass. 49.95 (705AX) Nightingale-Conant.

Imagine getting 30 proven ideas to make your job more fulfilling & rewarding! That's what this fun & practical program will do for you. Discover how to reap the highest rewards from your job. Learn how to spot new opportunities & go after them with gusto. Find out why happy workers are more successful in life.

Joy of Your Nature. 2006. audio compact disk 15.00 (978-1-890246-36-5(0)) B Katie Int Inc.

Joy of 33 Recital Pieces. Denes Agay. (Piano Ser.). 2004. audio compact disk 19.95 (978-0-8256-8110-3(3), YK21934) Pub: Music Sales. Dist(s): H Leonard

Joy-Prayer Connection. Creflo A. Dollar. 2 cass. (Running Time: 3 hrs.). 2000. 10.00 (978-1-931172-58-5(7), TS235, Kidz Faith) Pub: Creflo Dollar. Dist(s): STL Dist NA

Joy School. unabr. ed. Elizabeth Berg. Read by Jen Taylor. 4 vols. (Running Time: 6 hrs.). 2001. bk. 39.95 (978-0-7927-2466-7(6), CSL 355, Chivers Sound Lib) AudioGO.

Thirteen-year-old Katie is new to her Missouri town, living alone with a stern, inaccessible father following her mother's death. Unable to fit in at school, she forges alliances wherever she can: with her housekeeper, with a pimply fellow misfit named Cynthia & with the gorgeous Taylor, who gets her kicks out of shoplifting. Most frustrating of all is Katie's alliance with a handsome 23-year-old who shares her love for checkers but doesn't return her crush.

Joy School. unabr. ed. Elizabeth Berg. Read by Jen Taylor. 6 CDs. (Running Time: 9 hrs.). 2001. audio compact disk 64.95 (978-0-7927-9942-9(9), SLD 093, Chivers Sound Lib) AudioGO.

Joy to the World. 4 cass. (Running Time: 5 hrs. 3 min.). 1995. 28.95 5 CDs set. Ignatius Pr.
Recorded in stereo Surround Sound by various performers, this feast of Christmas favorites includes "Hymns of Christmas," with 25 popular carols; "Handel: the Messiah," with 24 selections from the Christmas classic; "A Baroque Christmas," with music by Bach, Vivaldi, Pachelbel, Handel, & others; & "A Nutcracker Christmas," with Tchaikovsky's "Nutcracker" Suite & selections by Mozart, Strauss, Beethoven, & more.

Joy to the World. 1 cd. audio compact disk 10.98 (978-1-57908-391-5(9), 1664) Platinm Enter.

Joy to the World. Directed By Dennis Glore. Contrib. by Bill & Gloria Gaither and Their Homecoming Friends & Bill Gaither. Prod. by Patricia Branan Wendell. (Gaither Gospel Ser.). 2005. 19.98 (978-5-558-66427-0(4)) Spring House Music.

Joy to the World. Perf. by Harry Simeone Chorale. 1 cass. 3.98 Clamshell. (978-1-55886-148-0(3), BB/PT 455) Smarty Pants.

Joy to the World. Contrib. by Third Day. (Soundtraks Ser.). 2007. audio compact disk 8.99 (978-5-557-56221-8(4)) Christian Wrld.

Joy to the World. Albin C. Whitworth. 2001. 11.98 (978-0-633-01702-6(7)); audio compact disk 16.98 (978-0-633-01703-3(5)) LifeWay Christian.

***Joy to the World: A Christmas Collection.** Ceoltoiri Caoimhin. (ENG.). 2002. 19.95 (978-1-85607-386-8(6)) Pub: Columba Press IRL. Dist(s): Dufour

***Joy to the World: A Christmas Collection.** Ceoltoiri Caoimhin. (ENG.). 2003. audio compact disk 25.95 (978-1-85607-385-1(8)) Pub: Columba Press IRL. Dist(s): Dufour

Joy/Becoming Your Potential. Marianne Williamson. Read by Marianne Williamson. 1 cass. (Running Time: 90 mins.). (Lectures on a Course in Miracles). 1999. 10.00 (978-1-56170-237-4(4), M740) Hay House.

Joyce Carol Oates. unabr. ed. Joyce Carol Oates. Read by Joyce Carol Oates. 1 cass. (Running Time: 29 min.). 1989. 10.00 New Letters.
Oates reads from her novel American Appetites & is interviewed.

Joyce in the Belly of the Big Truck; A Modern Day Jonah Story audio Book. Joyce A. Cascio. 2007. audio compact disk 19.99 (978-0-9762373-5-8(0)) Nineveh.

Joyce's Ulysses, Pts. I-II. Instructed by James Heffernan. 12 CDs. (Running Time: 12 hrs.). 2001. bk. 69.95 (978-1-56585-288-4(5), 237) Teaching Co.

Joyce's Ulysses, Pts. I-II, Vol. 1. Instructed by James Heffernan. 12 cass. (Running Time: 12 hrs.). 2001. 54.95 (978-1-56585-033-0(5), 237) Teaching Co.

Joyce's Ulysses, Vol. 2. Instructed by James Heffernan. 6 cass. (Running Time: 6 hrs.). 2001. 129.95 (978-1-56585-036-1(X)); audio compact disk 179.95 (978-1-56585-291-4(5)) Teaching Co.

Joyeux Noel - Learning Songs & Traditions in French. Judy Mahoney. Illus. by Barb Bjornson. 1 CD. (Running Time: 1 hr. 10 mins.). (FRE.). (gr. k-4). 2006. lib. bdg. 19.95 (978-1-59972-061-6(2), Tch Me) Teach Me.

Joyful Dedication unto Him. Swami Amar Jyoti. 1 cass. 1979. 9.95 (R-23) Truth Consciousness.
The meaning of love. Expanding our consciousness & breaking the barrier of distinction. Merging into the Source.

Joyful Journey. abr. ed. Patsy Clairmont et al. (Running Time: 2 hrs. 0 mins. 0 sec.). (ENG.). 2003. 10.99 (978-0-310-26072-1(8)) Zondervan.

Joyful Living. Barry Tesar. 1 cass. (Running Time: 1 hr.). 1992. 9.98 (978-1-56470-017-9(8)) Success Cass.
Subliminal program.

Joyful Mysteries / Misterios Gozosos: The Holy Rosary Audio CD / el Santo Rosario Audio CD, Vol. 1. Kenneth L. Davison, Jr.. Kenneth L. Davison, Jr. Prod. by Brian Shields. Music by Eric Genuis.Tr. of Misterios Gozosos. (ENG & SPA.). (J). 2007. audio compact disk 15.00 (978-0-9801121-0-8(9)) Holy Heroes.

Joyful Mysteries of the Rosary. unabr. ed. Perf. by Benedictine Sisters of Erie Staff. 1 cass. (Running Time: 30 min.). 1998. 7.00 (978-1-890890-31-5(6)) Benetvision.
Contemporary & creative presentation of the rosary includes meditations & musical accompaniments.

Joyful Noise. 1 cass., 1 CD. 10.98 (978-1-57908-321-2(8), 1394); audio compact disk 15.98 CD. (978-1-57908-320-5(X)) Platinm Enter.

Joyful Noise: Poems for Two Voices. unabr. ed. Paul Fleischman. Narrated by Barbara Caruso. 1 cass. (Running Time: 3 hrs.). (gr. 2 up). 1997. 10.00 (978-0-7887-1818-2(5), 95282E7) Recorded Bks.
Grasshoppers, fireflies & other busy insects light up the pages of this rib-tickling book of poetry.

Joyful Noise: Poems for Two Voices, Homework. unabr. ed. Poems. Paul Fleischman. 1 cass. (Running Time: 20 min.). (J). 1997. bk. 23.20 (978-0-7887-1835-9(5), 40615) Recorded Bks.
Grasshoppers, fireflies & other busy insects light up the pages of this rib-tickling book of poetry.

Joyful Noise & I Am Phoenix: Poems for Two Voices. unabr. ed. Poems. Paul Fleischman. Perf. by Melissa Hughes & Scott Snively. 1 cass. (Running Time: 35 min.). (J). 2001. 17.95 (978-1-883332-47-1(8)); audio compact disk 17.95 (978-1-883332-70-9(2)) Audio Bkshelf.
Paul Fleischman is a master of sound, incorporating a soaring, energetic musicality into his writing.

***Joyful Noise & I Am Phoenix: Poems for Two Voices.** unabr. ed. Paul Fleischman. Read by John Bedford Lloyd & Anne Twomey. (ENG.). 2008. (978-0-06-176282-6(2)); (978-0-06-176281-9(4)) HarperCollins Pubs.

Joyful Parenting: Tuning into Your Child. Sally O. Walshaw. Read by Sally O. Walshaw. Read by Fred Williams & Laura Mitchell. Perf. by Fred Williams. 1 cass. (Running Time: 73 mins.). 1999. 10.95 (978-0-9670275-8-6(6)); audio compact disk 13.95 (978-0-9670275-9-3(4)) McCloud Pubng.
Simplifies difficult parenting situations for every type of parent of any type of child.

Joyful Path of Good Fortune: The Complete Buddhist Path to Enlightenment. 2nd ed. Geshe Kelsang Gyatso. Narrated by Michael Sington. 20 CDs. (Running Time: 22 hrs. 0 mins. 0 sec.). (ENG.). 2005. audio compact disk 39.95 (978-0-948006-96-8(X)) Pub: Tharpa Pubns GBR. Dist(s): IPG Chicago

Joyful Sing Allelula! Greg Skipper. 1993. 40.00 (978-0-7673-1834-1(X)) LifeWay Christian.

Joyful, Sing, Alleluia! Greg Skipper. 1993. 11.98 (978-0-7673-1833-4(1)) LifeWay Christian.

Joyful, Sing Alleluia Cassette Kit. 1993. 54.95 (978-0-7673-1439-8(5)) LifeWay Christian.

Joyful Wisdom: Embracing Change & Finding Freedom. abr. unabr. ed. Eric Swanson & Yongey Mingyur. Read by Feodor Chin. (ENG.). 2009. audio compact disk 34.95 (978-0-7393-7717-8(5), Random AudioBks) Pub: Random Audio Pubg. Dist(s): Random

Joyous Adventure: The Law of Attraction in Action. Esther Hicks & Jerry Hicks. 2009. audio compact disk 19.95 (978-1-4019-2381-5(X), 625) Hay House.

Joyous Birthing. Read by Mary Richards. 1 cass. (Running Time: 90 min.). (Series Two Thousand). 2007. audio compact disk 19.95 (978-1-56136-105-2(4)) Master Your Mind.

Joyous Day. Eldon Taylor. 1 cass. (Running Time: 62 min.). (Inner Talk Ser.). 16.95 incl. script. (978-1-55978-514-3(4), 53791F) Progress Aware Res.
Soundtrack - Brook with underlying subliminal affirmations.

Joyous Day: Music Theme. Eldon Taylor. 1 cass. 16.95 (978-0-940699-17-5(6), 53791D) Progress Aware Res.

Joyous Sex (Female) 1 cass. (Running Time: 45 min.). (Relationship Ser.). 9.98 (978-1-55909-050-6(2), 48) Randolph Tapes.
Promotes a healthy, loving sexual relationship with communication, acceptance & trust. Subliminal messages are heard 3-5 minutes before becoming ocean sounds or music.

Joyous Sex (Male) 1 cass. (Running Time: 45 min.). (Relationship Ser.). 9.98 (47) Randolph Tapes.

Joyous Way: The Joy of Dedication & Happiness Is. Brenton Yorgason & Blaine Yorgason. 1 cass. 5.98 (978-1-55503-117-6(X), 0600792) Covenant Comms.

***Joy's Life Diet.** unabr. ed. Joy Bauer. Read by Joy Bauer. (ENG.). 2008. (978-0-06-173826-5(3)); (978-0-06-173828-9(X)) HarperCollins Pubs.

Joys of Christmas Past: Thirty-One Timeless Christmas Poems. unabr. ed. Poems. Read by Rosalyn Landor & Tony Jay. Ed. by Kathy Sjogren & Dave Field. 1 cass. (Running Time: 40 min.). (J). (gr. 3 up). 1991. reel tape 14.95 (978-1-883446-00-0(7)) Poet Tree CA.
This collection of heartwarming Christmas poems offers an alternative to the usual Christmas fare. Professional actors read the familiar "A Visit from St. Nicholas" (also known as "The Night before Christmas") & dozens of other turn-of-the-century American & English poems that capture the innocence & simple joys of a time gone by. Delightful holiday music accompanies the readings.

Joys of Love. unabr. ed. Madeleine L'Engle. Read by Maggi-Meg Reed. 6 CDs. (Running Time: 7 hrs. 0 mins. 0 sec.). (ENG.). (YA). (gr. 7). 2008. audio compact disk 29.95 (978-1-4272-0464-6(0)) Pub: Macmill Audio. Dist(s): Macmillan

Joys of Monastic Life. unabr. ed. Jack Kornfield. 4 cass. (Running Time: 5 hrs. 27 min.). 1998. 36.00 Set. (AG009) Big Sur Tapes.
Achaan Sumedho, Sister Sundara, Brother David Stiendl-Rast, Ani Pema Chodron, & Sister Columba reflect on their personal spiritual life & monastic experience.

Joy's Twin. Elbert Willis. 1 cass. (Joy & Peace Ser.). 4.00 Fill the Gap.

JoySongs: Music From Vacation Bible School. Francine M. O'Connor. Perf. by Liguori JoySingers & Kenneth Daust. 1 cass. (Running Time: 21 mins.). (J). (gr. 1-6). 1995. 9.95 (978-0-89243-797-9(9), T8885); audio compact disk 14.95 (978-0-89243-851-8(7)) Liguori Pubns.
A collection of children's music.

Joystick Nation. Ed. by Marco A. V. Bitetto. 1 cass. 2000. (978-1-58578-086-0(3)) Inst of Cybernetics.

Juan en la Ciudad. unabr. ed. Michael Rodriguez. 2000. 7.99 (978-0-8297-2534-6(2)) Pub: Vida Pubs. Dist(s): Zondervan

Juan en la Ciudad. unabr. ed. Michael Rodriguez. 2000. audio compact disk 14.99 (978-0-8297-2535-3(0)) Zondervan.

Juan Felipe Herrera. unabr. ed. Juan F. Herrera. 1 cass. (Running Time: 29 min.). (New Letters on the Air Ser.). 1992. 10.00 (011792) New Letters.
The California Chicano poet reads & talks about his journey from migrant farmworkers' child to university professor.

Juan Pablo II Inolvidable. Mariano de Blas.Tr. of John Paul II, Never Forgotten. (SPA.). 2009. audio compact disk 25.00 (978-1-935405-17-7(9)) Hombre Nuevo.

Juan Rulfo: Voz del Autor. Juan Rulfo. Read by Felipe Garrido. (Entre Voces Ser.). 2008. audio compact disk 14.99 (978-5-557-36833-9(7)) Fondo CA.

Juan Serrano - Flamenco Concert Selections. Juan Serrano. (ENG & SPA.). 1993. 10.98 (978-0-87166-668-0(5), 93698 EN/SP) Mel Bay.

Juan Serrano - Flamenco Concert Selections. Juan Serrano. (ENG & SPA.). 1981. bk. 32.95 (978-0-7866-0921-5(4), 93698CDP) Mel Bay.

Juan Serrano - Flamenco Guitar Solos. Juan Serrano. 1993. bk. 20.95 (978-0-7866-1136-2(7), 94831P); spiral bd. 25.95 (978-0-7866-1135-5(9), 94831CDP); 10.98 (978-1-56222-680-0(0), 94831C) Mel Bay.

Juan Serrano/Flamenco Guitar Solos. Juan Serrano. (ENG.). 2000. spiral bd. 24.95 (978-0-7866-5912-8(2), 94831BCD) Mel Bay.

Juan Tenorio. Jose Zorilla. (SPA.). pap. bk. 20.95 (978-88-7754-594-7(1)) Pub: Cideb ITA. Dist(s): Distribks Inc

Juanita la Langosta Espanola. Johnny Morris. Tr. by Yanitzia Canetti. Composed by David Haslam. Contrib. by Orquesta Filarmonica de Londres. Narrated by Rosi Amador. Conducted by Stephen Simon. (J). (ps-3). 2002. audio compact disk 16.98 (978-1-932684-15-5(8)) Simon Simon.

Juanita Maria Sophia Bug Diva: Lived down South in the West. Carri Blake-Brekke. Lyrics by Carri Blake-Brekke. Illus. by Jo Lynn Melton. (Mrs. B'S Story Time-. . with A Twist! Ser.). (J). 2004. pap. bk. 11.95 (978-0-9720549-3-5(6)) Moms Pride.

Juba Dance. R. Nathaniel Dett. 1995. audio compact disk 2.95 (978-0-87487-661-1(3)) Alfred Pub.

Jubal Sackett. unabr. ed. Louis L'Amour. Read by John Curless. 7 cass. (Running Time: 10 hrs. 30 mins.). (Sacketts Ser.: No. 4). 2000. 34.95 (978-0-7366-4908-7(5), 5214) Books on Tape.
Wilderness explorer Jubal Sackett was the son of Barnabas Sackett, the first of that line to come to the New World. Jubal feared no man, nor did he back away from any challenge. His determination to blaze new trails took him across the vast savage North American continent fighting amount the Indian tribes, Jubal forged a legend as a powerful medicine man that they call "Ni'kwana, master of mysteries." And with Itchakomi, the proud Natchez princess, he set an example of courage that future Sacketts would follow.

Jubal Sackett. unabr. ed. Louis L'Amour. Read by John Curless. 10 CDs. (Running Time: 39600 sec.). (Sacketts Ser.: No. 4). (ENG.). 2005. audio compact disk 30.00 (978-0-7393-1902-4(7)) Pub: Random Audio Pubg. Dist(s): Random

Jubilante: The Joys of Intercession. Michael Lattiboudeaire. 1 CD. (Prophetic Life - The Joys of Intercession Ser.: Vol. 17). 1998. 18.95 CD. (978-1-889448-18-3(4), Great House) Great Hse Pub.

Jubilation Mass: Ritual Music for the Liturgy. James Chepponis. 1 cass. 1999. 10.95 (CS-465); 10.95 (CS-465); audio compact disk 15.95 (CD-465); audio compact disk 15.95 (CD-465) GIA Pubns.

Jubilee. Excerpts. Margaret Walker. Read by Margaret Walker. 2 cass. (Running Time: 2 hrs.). 1991. 13.95 (978-1-55644-368-8(4), 11041) Am Audio Prose.
Virtuoso reading of this classic novel.

Jubilee! - Play-along Spirituals: Bb Instruments - Grade 3 - Book/CD Pack. Composed by Stephen Bulla. 2004. pap. bk. 12.95 (978-90-431-1576-6(2), 9043115762) H Leonard.

Jubilee! - Play-along Spirituals: C Instruments - Grade 3 - Book/CD Pack. Stephen Bulla. 2003. pap. bk. 12.95 (978-90-431-1582-7(7), 9043115827) H Leonard.

Jubilee! - Play-along Spirituals: Eb Instruments - Grade 3 - Book/CD Pack. Composed by Stephen Bulla. 2003. pap. bk. 12.95 (978-90-431-1577-3(0), 9043115770) H Leonard.

Judah P. Benjamin: The Jewish Confederate. unabr. ed. Eli N. Evans. Read by Wolfram Kandinsky. 15 cass. (Running Time: 22 hrs. 30 min.). 1993. 120.00 (978-0-7366-2581-4(X), 3328) Books on Tape.
Biography of powerful Jewish-American Confederate politician. Benjamin was Secretary of State to Jefferson Davis.

Judaism. Norman Solomon. Read by David Horovitch. 3 cds. 2004. audio compact disk 22.98 (978-962-634-322-7(2), Naxos AudioBooks) Naxos.

Judaism. unabr. ed. Geoffrey Wigoder. Read by Ben Kingsley. Ed. by Walter Harrelson & Mike Hassell. Prod. by Pat Childs. (Running Time: 10800 sec.). (Religion, Scriptures, & Spirituality Ser.). 2006. audio compact disk 25.95 (978-0-7861-6483-7(2)) Pub: Blckstn Audio. Dist(s): NetLibrary CO

Judaism. unabr. ed. Geoffrey Wigoder. Read by Ben Kingsley. Ed. by Walter Harrelson & Mike Hassell. 2 cass. (Running Time: 3 hrs.). Dramatization. (Religion, Scriptures & Spirituality Ser.). 1994. 17.95 (978-1-56823-010-8(9), 10453) Pub: Knowledge Prod. Dist(s): APG
Judaism is both a religion & a way of life. It has several major forms of traditions (Orthodox, Conservative, Reform, & Reconstructionist Judaism); it also is the parent religion of both Christianity & Islam. Jewish sacred literature preserves the ancient oral tradition through the Hebrew Bible (which Christians call the Old Testament) & other writings (in particular, the Talmud). Judaism exalts the divine gifts of the Torah, God's teaching or instruction.

Judaism in the Age of Jesus. unabr. ed. Samuel Sandmel. 1 cass. (Running Time: 27 min.). 12.95 (31009) J Norton Pubs.
Focuses on Jews' dissatisfaction with Roman rule & various divisions of Judaism.

Judaism in the Light of Yoga. (184) Yoga Res Foun.

Judaism in the Light of Yoga. Swami Jyotirmayananda. 1 cass. (Running Time: 1 hr.). 1990. 12.99 Yoga Res Foun.

Judas *see* **Twentieth-Century Poetry in English, No. 26, Recordings of Poets Reading Their Own Poetry**

Judas. Steve Jackson. 2009. 69.95 (978-0-7531-4280-6(5)); audio compact disk 89.95 (978-0-7531-4281-3(3)) Pub: Isis Pubng Ltd GBR. Dist(s): Ulverscroft US

Judas: A Biography: John 18:1-5. Ed Young. 1985. 4.95 (978-0-7417-1445-9(0), 445) Win Walk.

Judas Child. unabr. ed. Carol O'Connell. Read by Erika Leigh. (Running Time: 14 hrs.). 2009. 24.99 (978-1-4233-9062-6(8), 9781423390626, Brilliance MP3); 39.97 (978-1-4233-9063-3(6), 9781423390633, Brlnc Audio MP3 Lib); 24.99 (978-1-4233-9064-0(4), 9781423390640, BAD); 39.97 (978-1-4233-9065-7(2), 9781423390657, BADLE) Brilliance Audio.

***Judas Child.** unabr. ed. Carol O'Connell. Read by Erika Leigh. (Running Time: 14 hrs.). 2010. audio compact disk 29.99 (978-1-4418-3996-1(8), 9781441839961, Bril Audio CD Unabri); audio compact disk 89.97 (978-1-4418-3997-8(6), 9781441839978, BriAudCD Unabrid) Brilliance Audio.

Judas Country, Set. unabr. ed. Gavin Lyall. 7 cass. 1998. 76.95 (978-1-85903-212-1(5)) Pub: Magna Story GBR. Dist(s): Ulverscroft US

***Judas Gate.** abr. ed. Jack Higgins. (Running Time: 6 hrs.). 2011. 9.99 (978-1-4418-9627-8(9), 9781441896278, BAD) Brilliance Audio.

***Judas Gate.** abr. ed. Jack Higgins. Read by Simon Vance. (Running Time: 6 hrs.). 2011. audio compact disk 24.99 (978-1-4418-1631-3(3), 9781441816313) Brilliance Audio.

***Judas Gate.** unabr. ed. Jack Higgins. Read by Simon Vance. (Running Time: 9 hrs.). 2011. 24.99 (978-1-4418-1627-6(5), 9781441816276, Brilliance MP3); 39.97 (978-1-4418-1628-3(3), 9781441816283, Brlnc Audio MP3 Lib); audio compact disk 34.99 (978-1-4418-1625-2(9), 9781441816252); audio compact disk 79.97 (978-1-4418-1626-9(7), 9781441816269, BriAudCD Unabrid) Brilliance Audio.

Judas Goat. unabr. collector's ed. Robert B. Parker. Read by Michael Prichard. 6 cass. (Running Time: 6 hrs.). (Spenser Ser.). 1989. 48.00 (978-0-7366-1571-6(7), 2438) Books on Tape.
Spenser has gone to London & not to see the Queen. He's gone to track down a bunch of bombers who've blown away his client's wife & kids. His job is to catch them. Or kill them. His client isn't choosy. But there are nine killers to one Spenser - long odds. Hawk helps balance the equation. The rest depends on a wild plan. Spenser will get one of the terrorists to play Judas Goat - to lead him to the others. Trouble is, he hasn't counted on her being very blond, very beautiful & very dangerous.

Judas Judge. Michael McGarrity. Read by Bruce Greenwood. (Kevin Kerney Ser.: Bk. 5). 2004. 15.95 (978-0-7435-4908-0(2)) Pub: S&S Audio. Dist(s): S and S Inc

***Judas Kiss.** unabr. ed. J. T. Ellison. Read by Joyce Bean. (Running Time: 10 hrs.). (Taylor Jackson Ser.). 2010. 24.99 (978-1-4418-3859-9(7), 9781441838599, Brilliance MP3); 24.99 (978-1-4418-3861-2(9), 9781441838612, BAD); 39.97 (978-1-4418-3860-5(0), 9781441838605, Brlnc Audio MP3 Lib); 39.97 (978-1-4418-3862-9(7), 9781441838629, BADLE); audio compact disk 79.97 (978-1-4418-3858-2(9), 9781441838582, BriAudCD Unabrid); audio compact disk 29.99 (978-1-4418-3857-5(0), 9781441838575, Bril Audio CD Unabri) Brilliance Audio.

Judas Kiss. unabr. ed. Victoria Holt. Read by Eva Haddon. 10 cass. (Running Time: 10 hrs.). 1998. 84.95 (978-0-7540-0154-6(7), CAB 1577) Pub: Chivers Audio Bks GBR. Dist(s): AudioGO
The Bavarian Kingdom seemed like a fairy tale to Pippa Ewell, who left behind Greystone Manor & the memories of Conrad, the handsome stranger who swept her breathlessly into his arms & heart. But Pippa had come to find the truth behind her sister's death. Suddenly the fairy tale kingdom glittered with evil & danger.

Judas Kiss. unabr. collector's ed. Victoria Holt. Read by Donada Peters. 8 cass. (Running Time: 12 hrs.). 1994. 64.00 (978-0-7366-2672-9(7), 3409) Books on Tape.
Mysterious stranger has stolen young Englishwoman's heart; now someone is trying to take her life.

Judas Mandate. Clive Egleton. Read by Gordon Griffin. 8 cass. (Sound Ser.). (J). 2002. 69.95 (978-1-84283-187-8(9)) Pub: ISIS Lrg Prnt GBR. Dist(s): Ulverscroft US

Judas, My Brother. unabr. ed. Frank Yerby. Read by Dan Lazar. 13 cass. (Running Time: 19 hrs. 30 min.). 1980. 104.00 (978-0-7366-0430-7(8), 1402) Books on Tape.
The adventures of Nathan, a young Jew of great vitality. Born in the years preceding Christ, Nathan lives through that watershed era & emerges transformed by the intensity of his experience.

Judas Pair. Jonathan Gash. Narrated by Christopher Kay. 7 CDs. (Running Time: 8 hrs.). 2004. audio compact disk 61.00 (978-1-84197-091-2(3)) Recorded Bks.

Judas Pair. Jonathan Gash. Narrated by Christopher Kay. 6 cass. (Running Time: 8 hrs.). (Lovejoy Mystery Ser.). 1999. 53.00 (978-1-84197-004-2(2), H1004E7) Recorded Bks.
Antiques dealer Lovejoy is commissioned to hunt down what he considers to be a mythical object, the Judas pair, the supposed thirteenth pair of duelling pistols made by the famous maker Durs. After two murders, Lovejoy is certain that the pistols do exist & are now in the hands of the murderer. Will he find them & the murderer before the murderer reaches him?.

Judas Pair. unabr. ed. Jonathan Gash. Narrated by Christopher Kay. 1 CD. (Lovejoy Mystery Ser.). 1999. audio compact disk 61.00 (C1123E7, Clipper Audio) Recorded Bks.

Judas Pair, Set. unabr. ed. Jonathan Gash. Narrated by Christopher Kay. 6 cass. 1999. 53.00 (H1004K4, Clipper Audio) Recorded Bks.

Judas Sheep. Stuart Pawson & Andrew Wincott. 2008. 61.95 (978-1-84652-387-8(7)); audio compact disk 79.95 (978-1-84652-388-5(5)) Pub: Magna Story GBR. Dist(s): Ulverscroft US

Judas Strain. unabr. ed. James Rollins. Read by Peter Jay Fernandez. (Running Time: 57600 sec.). (Sigma Force Ser.: Bk. 4). 2007. audio compact disk 44.95 (978-0-06-125644-8(7), Harper Audio) HarperCollins Pubs.

***Judas Strain.** unabr. ed. James Rollins. Read by Peter Jay Fernandez. (ENG.). 2007. (978-0-06-147588-7(2), Harper Audio); (978-0-06-147590-0(4), Harper Audio) HarperCollins Pubs.

Judas Testament. unabr. ed. Daniel Easterman. 12 cass. (Running Time: 15 hrs.). 2003. 99.00 (978-1-84197-709-6(8)) Recorded Bks.

Judas Today; Jesus Today. Jonathan Murro. Read by Jonathan Murro. 1 cass. 7.95 A R Colton Fnd.
Discusses the goal of God-Realization.

Judas Tree. unabr. ed. Matt Braun. Read by Gene Engene. 6 cass. (Running Time: 6 hrs. 54 min.). (Luke Starbuck Ser.: Bk. 4). 2001. 39.95 (978-1-58116-078-9(X)) Books in Motion.
Unchecked lawlessness in the mining town of Virginia City, Montana, has given way to vigilante mob rule and summary execution. Luke goes undercover to investigate the world of corrupt politicians and a gang of murderous robbers.

Judas Unchained. unabr. ed. Peter F. Hamilton. Read by John Lee. Narrated by John Lee. (Running Time: 39 hrs. 0 mins. 0 sec.). (ENG.). 2008. audio compact disk 79.99 (978-1-4001-0763-6(6)); audio compact disk 49.99 (978-1-4001-5763-1(3)); audio compact disk 159.99 (978-1-4001-3763-3(2)) Pub: Tantor Media. Dist(s): IngramPubServ

Jude, an Emergency Epistle. Dan Corner. 1 cass. 3.00 (111) Evang Outreach.

Jude Commentary. Chuck Missler. 8 CD's. (Running Time: 8 hours aprox). (Chuck Missler Commentaries). 2006. audio compact disk 44.95 (978-1-57821-354-2(1)) Koinonia Hse.
The book of Jude is a tiny book, tragically neglected by students, yet overflowing with fascinating Old Testament references and allusions: lessons from Israel in the wilderness, the angels that sinned, the strange events of Sodom and Gomorrah, and other insights from Cain, Balaam, as well as the mysterious person known as Enoch. This collection of 8 individual audio CDs contains more than 8 hours of verse-by-verse commentary on the book of Jude coupled with extensive study notes. Plus, as an added bonus, this package also includes the fully automated MP3 CD-ROM for a total of 9 CDs! Jude One: Jude 1- 4 - Introduction. Jude Two: Jude 5 - Israel in the wilderness, Numbers 14, I Corinthians 10, and Hebrews 3&4. Jude Three: Jude 6 - The Angels that sinned, Isaiah 14, Ezekiel 28, and Genesis 6. Jude Four: Jude 7&8 - Sodom and Gomorrah, Genesis 18 and 19. Jude Five: Jude 9&10 - Michael, Satan, and the body of Moses, Deuteronomy 34, Revelation 11&12, and Matthew 17. Jude Six: Jude 11&13 - Cain, Balaam, and Korah, Genesis 4, Numbers 16, 22-25, and 31. Jude Seven: Jude 14&15 - Enoch, Genesis 5. Jude Eight: Jude 16- 25 - Lessons and conclusions.

Jude Commentary: Verse by verse with Chuck Missler. Chuck Missler. 1 MP3 CD-ROM. (Running Time: 8 hours aprox). (Chuck Missler Commentaries). 2000. cd-rom 29.95 (978-1-57821-106-7(9)) Koinonia Hse.

Jude Commentary: Verse by Verse with Chuck Missler. deluxe ed. Chuck Missler. 8 cass. (Running Time: 6 hrs.). (Heirloom Edition Ser.). 1996. im. lthr. 34.95 Incls. notes. (978-1-880532-40-9(9)) Koinonia Hse.

Jude im Dorn. Jacob W. Grimm & Wilhelm K. Grimm. 1 cass. (Running Time: 60 min.). (Bruder Grimm Kinder & Hausmarchen Ser.: GR-05). (GER.). 1996. pap. bk. 19.50 (978-1-58085-210-4(6)) Interlingua VA.

***jude thaddeus home program audio Book: The Proven Solution for Addictions.** Mark Scheeren. (ENG., 2010. 34.99 (978-0-9845679-3-5(3)) Baldwin Res.

Jude the Obscure. Thomas Hardy. 2003. audio compact disk 115.95 (978-0-7540-9456-2(1)) Pub: Chivers Audio Bks GBR. Dist(s): AudioGO

Jude the Obscure. abr. ed. Thomas Hardy. Narrated by Michael Pennington. 2 cass. (Running Time: 3 hrs.). 1999. 13.95 (978-1-85998-789-6(3), HoddrStoughton) Pub: Hodder General GBR. Dist(s): Trafalgar
Depicting the lives of individuals who are trapped by forces beyond their control. Jude Fawley, a poor villager, wants to enter the divinity school at Christminster (Oxford University). Sidetracked by Arabella Donn, an earthy country girl who pretends to be pregnant by him, Jude marries her and is then deserted. He earns a living as a stonemason at Christminster; there he falls in love with his independent-minded cousin, Sue Bridehead. Out of a sense of obligation, Sue marries the schoolmaster Phillotson, who has helped her. Unable to bear living with Phillotson, she returns to live with Jude and eventually bears his children out of wedlock. Their poverty and the weight of society's disapproval begin to take a toll on Sue and Jude; the climax occurs when Jude's son by Arabella hangs Sue and Jude's children and himself. In penance, Sue returns to Phillotson and the church. Jude returns to Arabella and eventually dies miserably.

Jude the Obscure. abr. ed. Thomas Hardy. 3 CDs. (Running Time: 4 Hrs. 30 Mins.). 2004. audio compact disk 9.99 (978-1-57050-044-2(4)) Multilingua.

Jude the Obscure. unabr. ed. Thomas Hardy. Read by Frederick Davidson. 11 cass. (Running Time: 16 hrs.). (gr. 9-12). 1997. 76.95 (978-0-7861-1249-4(2), 2158) Blckstn Audio.
"Jude of the Obscure" caused an uproar, involved Hardy's frank treatment of sexual themes, & his unconventional portrayal of the pillars of Victorian society.

Jude the Obscure. unabr. ed. Thomas Hardy. Read by Stephen Thorne. 12 cass. (Running Time: 18 hrs.). 2000. 79.95 (SAB 028) Pub: Chivers Audio Bks GBR. Dist(s): AudioGO
This is the classic story of Jude Fawley, who dreams of love when he meets his spirited and intelligent cousin, Sue Bridehead. Already unhappily married, Jude defies conventional morality, thus risking the chance of making social outcasts of them both.

Jude the Obscure. unabr. ed. Thomas Hardy & Frederick Davidson. (Running Time: 15 hrs. NaN mins.). 2008. 29.95 (978-1-4332-5410-9(7)); audio compact disk 110.00 (978-1-4332-5409-3(3)) Blckstn Audio.

Jude the Obscure. unabr. collector's ed. Thomas Hardy. Read by Jill Masters. 12 cass. (Running Time: 18 hrs.). (YA). 1983. 96.00 (978-0-7366-3978-1(0), 9526) Books on Tape.
"Jude the Obscure," Hardy's last novel, is generally acknowledged to be his finest. Yet its publication met with attacks by the press, abusive letters & a bishop's burning of the book. The cause of the uproar? Hardy treated the sexual theme of his book frankly: less frankly than he had wished, but more than was acceptable.

Jude the Obscure, Set. Thomas Hardy. Read by Flo Gibson. 10 cass. (Running Time: 14 hrs. 30 min.). 1995. 44.95 (978-1-55685-364-7(5)) Audio Bk Con.
Jude's youthful ambitions to be a teacher or theologian lead to his intellectual growth, but his romantic entanglements with Arabella & Sue lead to tragic results.

Jude's Final Written Words. Dan Corner. 1 cass. 3.00 (51) Evang Outreach.

Judge. unabr. ed. Steve Martini. Narrated by George Guidall. 10 cass. (Running Time: 14 hrs. 15 mins.). (Paul Madriani Ser.: No. 4). 85.00 (978-0-7887-0466-6(4), 94659E7) Recorded Bks.
The police department's credibility & a despised judge's career hinge on the verdict of the most celebrated trial of the year. As Paul Madriani & his new partner, Lenore Goya, dig into the evidence, their diligence pays off in an electrifying 11th-hour discovery that casts shadow of doubt into every corner of the Capital City legal system. Available to libraries only.

Judge. unabr. ed. James E. Thierry. Read by Rusty Nelson. 6 cass. (Running Time: 6 hrs.). 2001. 39.95 (978-1-58116-039-0(9)) Books in Motion.
Interim Municipal Court Judge Andy MacTavish finds underworld involvement in the activities of the Prosecuting Attorney. And when his own judgeship becomes the target of those under suspicion, MacTavish realizes his position could be fatal.

Judge, Set. abr. ed. Steve Martini. Read by Stanley Tucci. 4 cass. (Running Time: 4 hrs. 30 mins.). (Paul Madriani Ser.: No. 4). 1998. 12.98 (978-0-671-58209-8(7), 493061, Audioworks) S&S Audio.
Judge Armando Acosta is arrested for soliciting a decoy "prostitute" & then charged with her subsequent murder. The judge is forced to ask for help from a long-time enemy, attorney Paul Madriani, who faces the most daunting case of his career.

Judge & Jury. unabr. ed. James Patterson & Andrew Gross. Read by Joe Mantegna. 7 CDs. (Running Time: 8 hrs.). 2006. audio compact disk 63.00 (978-1-4159-3099-1(6)); 45.00 (978-1-4159-3098-4(8)) Books on Tape.
Andie DeGrasse, an aspiring actress and single mom, is not your typical juror. Hoping to get dismissed from the pool, she tells the judge that most of her legal knowledge comes from a bit part curling around a stripper's pole in The Sopranos. But she still ends up as juror number 11 in a landmark trial against a notorious mob boss. The case quickly becomes the new Trial of the Century. Mafia don Dominic Cavello, known as the Electrician, is linked to hundreds of gruesome, unspeakable crimes. Senior FBI agent Nick Pellisante has been tracking him for years. He knows Cavello's power reaches far beyond the courtroom, but the FBI's evidence against the ruthless killer is ironclad. Conviction is a sure thing. As the jury is about to reach a verdict, the Electrician makes one devastating move that no one could have predicted. The entire nation is reeling, and Andie's world is shattered. For her, the hunt for the Electrician becomes personal, and she and Pellisante come together in an unbreakable bond: they will exact justice - at any cost.

Judge & Jury. unabr. ed. James Patterson & Andrew Gross. Read by Joe Mantegna. (Running Time: 7 hrs.). (ENG.). 2006. 14.98 (978-1-59483-524-7(1)) Pub: Hachet Audio. Dist(s): HachBkGrp

Judge & Jury. unabr. ed. James Patterson & Andrew Gross. Read by Joe Mantegna. (Running Time: 7 hrs.). (ENG.). 2009. 59.98 (978-1-60788-163-6(2)) Pub: Hachet Audio. Dist(s): HachBkGrp

Judge Breaks Silence Pt. 1: Psalm 50. Ed Young. 1989. 4.95 (978-0-7417-1750-4(6), 750) Win Walk.

Judge Breaks Silence Pt. II: Psalm 50. Ed Young. 1989. 4.95 (978-0-7417-1751-1(4), 751) Win Walk.

Judge Dee at Work: Eight Chinese Detective Stories. unabr. ed. Short Stories. Robert H. Van Gulik. Narrated by Frank Muller. 3 cass. (Running Time: 4 hrs.). (Judge Dee Mysteries Ser.). 1986. 26.00 (978-1-55690-274-1(3), 86560E7) Recorded Bks.
Five stories include: "Murder on the Lotus Pond"; "The Two Beggars"; "The Wrong Sword"; "The Coffins of the Emperor" & "Murder on New Year's Eve.".

Judge for a Day: Audiocassette. (Greetings Ser.: Vol. 1). (gr. 3-5). 10.00 (978-0-7635-1796-0(8)) Rigby Educ.

Judge Righteous Judgment, Pt. 2. Derek Prince. 1 cass. (Running Time: 60 min.). (Judging: When? Why? How? Ser.). 5.95 (I-4078) Derek Prince.

Judgement, Forgiveness & Love. Swami Amar Jyoti. 1 cass. 1987. 9.95 (L-13) Truth Consciousness.
Judge ye not. Adopting a spiritual outlook in trying situations. A practical approach without hurting or hatred.

Judgement in Stone. unabr. ed. Ruth Rendell. Read by Carole Hayman. 6 cass. (Running Time: 6 hrs.). 1993. 54.95 (978-0-7451-6231-7(2), CAB 215) AudioGO.

***Judgement Night.** 2010. audio compact disk (978-1-59171-265-7(3)) Falcon Picture.

Judgement of Believers, I. Dan Corner. 1 cass. 3.00 (52) Evang Outreach.

Judgement of Believers, II. Dan Corner. 1 cass. 3.00 (53) Evang Outreach.

Judgement of Strangers. Andrew Taylor. Read by Ric Jerrom. 8 cass. (Running Time: 12 hrs.). 2002. 69.95 (978-0-7540-0873-6(8), CAB 2295) Pub: Chivers Audio Bks GBR. Dist(s): AudioGO

Judgement on Deltchev. unabr. ed. Eric Ambler. Read by Bernard Mayes. 6 cass. (Running Time: 8 hrs. 30 mins.). 1989. 44.95 (978-0-7861-0102-3(4), 1095) Blckstn Audio.
This book is about an English journalist named Foster who is sent to a Balkan city to cover the treason trial of an apparent victim of a Soviet frameup & finds out more than it is safe to know.

Judgement on Deltchev. unabr. collector's ed. Eric Ambler. Read by Richard Brown. 6 cass. (Running Time: 9 hrs.). 1988. 48.00 (978-0-7366-1292-0(0), 2199) Books on Tape.
A young British playwrite, Foster, is asked to cover the trial of Yordan Deltchev, seemingly a victim of a Soviet frameup.

Judgement Ring Books Bk. 1: The Chinook River Princess. unabr. ed. Jack Duckworth. 2000. audio compact disk 29.95 (978-0-9679119-0-8(7)) Expert Sys.

Judgement Seat: 11 Cor. 5:10-11. Ed Young. 1990. 4.95 (978-0-7417-1784-9(0), 784) Win Walk.

Judgement Seat of Christ. Derek Prince. 1 cass. (Running Time: 60 min.). 5.95 (I-4179) Derek Prince.

Judges. David T. Demola. 10 cass. 40.00 (S-1047) Faith Fellow Min.

Judges. unabr. ed. Elie Wiesel. Narrated by George Guidall. 5 cass. (Running Time: 6 hrs. 30 mins.). 2002. 52.00 (978-1-4025-2201-7(0)) Recorded Bks.
Five survivors of a plane crash take shelter in the home of an enigmatic man. He locks them in, informs them he is their judge, and announces the least worthy of them will be sentenced to death.

Judges. unabr. ed. Elie Wiesel. Narrated by George Guidall. 4 cass. (Running Time: 6 hrs. 30 mins.). 2004. 19.99 (978-1-4025-2483-7(8), 01724) Recorded Bks.

Judges Commentary. Chuck Missler. 1 MP3 CD-ROM. (Running Time: 16 hours). (Chuck Missler Commentaries). 2002. cd-rom 39.95 (978-1-57821-190-6(5)) Koinonia Hse.
Explore Judges verse-by-verse with Chuck Missler. This is a 2-volume set with eight audios in each volume, including notes.

Judge's Daughter. Ruth Hamilton. 2007. 84.95 (978-0-7531-3739-0(9)) Pub: ISIS Audio GBR. Dist(s): Ulverscroft US

Judge's Daughter. Ruth Hamilton. Read by Marlene Sidaway. (Running Time: 48600 sec.). 2007. audio compact disk 99.95 (978-0-7531-2705-6(9)) Pub: ISIS Audio GBR. Dist(s): Ulverscroft US

Judge's House see Tales of Terror & the Supernatural: A Collection

Judge's House. 1980. (N-37) Jimcin Record.

Judge's Role in Discovery. James McElhaney et al. 1 cass. (Running Time: 35 min.). (Training the Advocate: The Pretrial Stage Ser.). 1985. 20.00 (FAPTA08) Natl Inst Trial Ad.

Judges Through Kings Bible. Ty Fischer & Emily Fischer. Perf. by Steve Scheffler. 1998. 6.95 (978-1-930710-86-3(0)) Veritas Pr PA.

Judging, Feeling & Not Being Moralistic. Leonard Peikoff. 4 cass. (Running Time: 4 hrs. 30 min.). 1996. 49.95 Set. (978-1-56114-206-4(9), LP41D) Second Renaissance.
An intensive analysis of the process of making evaluative judgments.

Judging Time. Leslie Glass. Read by Jane E. Lawder. 4 cass. (Running Time: 360 min.). No. 4. 2000. 25.00 (978-1-58807-056-2(5)) Am Pubng Inc.

Judging Time. abr. ed. Leslie Glass. Read by M. J. Wilde. 4 vols. No. 4. 2003. (978-1-58807-736-3(5)) Am Pubng Inc.

Judging: When? Why? How? Pt. 1: The Right to Judge. Derek Prince. 1 cass. (I-4077) Derek Prince.

Judgment. abr. ed. D. W. Buffa. Read by Ron McLarty. (ENG.). 2005. 14.98 (978-1-59483-417-2(2)) Pub: Hachet Audio. Dist(s): HachBkGrp

Judgment. abr. ed. William Jeremiah Coughlin. Read by Ken Pogue. 4 cass. (Running Time: 6 hrs.). 2001. 25.00 (978-1-59040-161-3(1), Phoenix Audio) Pub: Amer Intl Pub. Dist(s): PerseuPGW

Judgment. unabr. ed. D. W. Buffa. Read by Dennis Predovic. (ENG.). 2005. 16.98 (978-1-59483-416-5(4)) Pub: Hachet Audio. Dist(s): HachBkGrp

Judgment. unabr. ed. D. W. Buffa. Read by Dennis Predovic. (Running Time: 13 hrs.). (ENG.). 2009. 69.98 (978-1-60788-099-8(7)) Pub: Hachet Audio. Dist(s): HachBkGrp

Judgment: How Winning Leaders Make Great Calls. Noel Tichy & Warren G. Bennis. Narrated by L. J. Ganser. (Running Time: 36900 sec.). 2007. audio compact disk 34.99 (978-1-4281-3738-7(6)) Recorded Bks.

Judgment Calls. Alafair Burke. Read by Betty Bobbitt. (Running Time: 9 hrs. 45 mins.). 2009. 89.99 (978-1-74214-195-4(1), 9781742141954) Pub: Bolinda Pubng AUS. Dist(s): Bolinda Pub Inc

Judgment Calls. unabr. ed. Alafair Burke. Read by Betty Bobbitt. 8 cass. (Running Time: 9 hrs. 45 mins.). 2005. 64.00 (978-1-74093-552-4(7)); audio compact disk 98.95 (978-1-74093-553-1(5)) Pub: Bolinda Pubng AUS. Dist(s): Bolinda Pub Inc

Judgment Day! Islam, Israel & the Nations. Dave Hunt. Read by Gary Carmichael. (Running Time: 15 hrs.). (ENG.). 2007. audio compact disk 25.99 (978-1-928660-56-9(8)) Pub: Berean Call. Dist(s): STL Dist NA

Judgment in Death. abr. ed. J. D. Robb, pseud. (Running Time: 21600 sec.). (In Death Ser.). 2007. audio compact disk 14.99 (978-1-4233-1736-4(X), 9781423317364, BCD Value Price) Brilliance Audio.

Judgment in Death. unabr. ed. J. D. Robb, pseud. (Running Time: 39600 sec.). (In Death Ser.). 2007. audio compact disk 24.95 (978-1-4233-1731-9(9), 9781423317319, Brilliance MP3); audio compact disk 102.25 (978-1-4233-1730-2(0), 9781423317302, BriAudCD Unabrid); audio compact disk 39.25 (978-1-4233-1732-6(7), 9781423317326, Brinc Audio MP3 Lib) Brilliance Audio.

Judgment in Death. unabr. ed. J. D. Robb, pseud. Read by Susan Ericksen. (Running Time: 11 hrs.). (In Death Ser.). 2007. 39.25 (978-1-4233-1734-0(3), 9781423317340, BADLE); 24.95 (978-1-4233-1733-3(5), 9781423317333, BAD); 82.25 (978-1-4233-3721-8(2), 9781423337218, BrilAudUnabridg); audio compact disk 36.95 (978-1-4233-1729-6(7), 9781423317296, Bril Audio CD Unabri) Brilliance Audio.

Judgment of Paris: The Revolutionary Decade That Gave the World Impressionism. Ross King. 2 CDs. 2006. audio compact disk 49.95 (978-0-7927-3966-1(3), CMP 905) AudioGO.

Judgment of Paris: The Revolutionary Decade That Gave the World Impressionism. Ross King. Narrated by Tristan Layton. 9 cass. (Running Time: 53160 sec.). 2006. 79.95 (978-0-7927-3906-7(X), CSL 905); audio compact disk 112.95 (978-0-7927-3907-4(8), SLD 905) AudioGO.

Judgment of Paris: The Revolutionary Decade That Gave the World Impressionism. Ross King. 2006. 29.95 (978-1-59397-875-2(2)) Pub: Macmill Audio. Dist(s): Macmillan

Judgment of Paris: The Revolutionary Decade That Gave the World Impressionism. abr. ed. Ross King. 2006. 17.95 (978-1-59397-876-1(6)) Pub: Macmill Audio. Dist(s): Macmillan

Judgment Seat of Christ. Jack Van Impe. 1977. 7.00 (978-0-934803-23-6(4)) J Van Impe.
Dr. Van Impe presents a Biblical review of the "Bema Seat" judgment.

Judith Minty: Killing the Bear. unabr. ed. Judith Minty. 1 cass. (Running Time: 29 min.). 1986. 10.00 (042586) New Letters.

Judo. Eldon Taylor. 1 cass. (Running Time: 62 min.). (Inner Talk Ser.). 16.95 incl. script. (978-1-55978-194-7(7), 5398C) Progress Aware Res.
Soundtrack - Musical Themes with underlying subliminal affirmations.

Judo: Babbling Brook. Eldon Taylor. 1 cass. 16.95 (978-1-55978-509-9(8), 5398F) Progress Aware Res.

Judo: Rhythm. Eldon Taylor. Read by Eldon Taylor. Ed. by Leslie Brice. 1 cass. (Running Time: 1 hr.). 1992. 16.95 (978-1-56705-328-9(9)) Gateways Inst.
Self improvement.

Judo: Stream. Eldon Taylor. Read by Eldon Taylor. Ed. by Leslie Brice. 1 cass. (Running Time: 1 hr.). 1992. 16.95 (978-1-56705-329-6(7)) Gateways Inst.

Judy Canova: The Queen of the Hillbillies. unabr. ed. Perf. by Judy Canova et al. 2 cass. (Running Time: 2 hrs.). Dramatization. 1997. 10.95 (978-1-57816-150-8(9)) Audio File.

Judy Canova Show: Santa Gets Stuck in the Chimney & Pedro Plays Santa Clause. Perf. by Judy Canova et al. 1 cass. (Running Time: 1 hr.). 2001. 6.98 (2222) Radio Spirits.

Judy Garland. Radio Spirits Publishing Staff & Smithsonian Institution Staff. 3 CDs. (Running Time: 3 hrs.). 2006. bk. 19.98 (978-1-57019-815-1(2), OTR 40132) Pub: Radio Spirits. Dist(s): AudioGO

Judy Litman (audio, text, illustrations, & covers with player included), the boxed set of the Tide of War, Blades of Grass, the Wonder of the World, & People, Places, & Things. Judy Litman. Perf. by Judy Litman. (ENG.). 2009. 4.99 (978-0-9672800-6-6(0)) J Litman Pubn.

Judy Moody. Megan McDonald. Narrated by C. J. Critt. 2 CDs. (Running Time: 1 hr. 45 mins.). (Judy Moody Ser.: No. 1). (gr. 1 up). audio compact disk 22.00 (978-0-7887-6153-9(6)) Recorded Bks.

Judy Moody. unabr. ed. Megan McDonald. Narrated by C. J. Critt. 2 CDs. (Running Time: 1 hrs. 45 min.). (J). (gr. 3-5). 2001. audio compact disk 22.00 (C1377) Recorded Bks.
Judy Moody's in a bad mood. The first day of third grade & all the kids will be wearing bright new T-shirts that say "Disney World" or "Sea World." But all she did was visit Gramma & none of her T-shirts say anything. Mr. Todd asks everyone to make a "Me" collage. Collecting things in her life leads to fun adventures. A toad gives Judy & her best friend an idea for a new secret club. Her parents even let her buy a Venus Flytrap, so she can have the most interesting pet in the whole class. Judy Moody has her trials to contend with - like being the only girl at a birthday party & putting up with her little "bother" Stink. But through it all, her irrepressible wit & resourcefulness shine.

Judy Moody. unabr. ed. Megan McDonald. Narrated by Ed Sala & C. J. Critt. 2 pieces. (Running Time: 1 hr. 45 mins.). (Judy Moody Ser.: No. 1). (gr. 1 up). 2001. 19.00 (978-0-7887-5353-4(3), 96575E7) Recorded Bks.
Judy Moody's in a bad mood. It's the first day of third grade, & all the kids will have bright new t-shirts that say "Disney World" or "Sea World." All she did this summer was visit Gramma. But Judy's mood brightens when she's assigned to make a "Me" collage.

Judy Moody. unabr. ed. Megan McDonald. Narrated by Kate Forbes. 2 cass. (Running Time: 1 hr. 30 mins.). (Judy Moody Ser.: No. 1). 2004. 9.99 (978-1-4025-7451-1(7), 70124) Recorded Bks.
Judy Moody¿s in a bad mood. It¿s the first day of third grade, and all the kids will be wearing bright new T-shirts that say "Disney World"or "Sea World." But all she did was visit Gramma, and none of her T-shirts say anything. Judy¿s mood suddenly improves when Mr. Todd asks everyone to make a "Me" collage. Collecting things to tell the story of her life leads to fun adventures. A toad gives Judy and her best friend an idea for a new secret club. She gets to show off her band-aid collection. Her parents even let her buy a Venus Flytrap, so she can have the most interesting pet in the whole class.

***Judy Moody & Stink: The Holly Joliday.** unabr. ed. Megan McDonald. Read by Barbara Rosenblat. (Running Time: 1 hr.). 2010. audio compact disk 9.99 (978-1-4418-8928-7(0), 9781441889287, Candlewick Bril) Brilliance Audio.

***Judy Moody & Stink: The Mad, Mad, Mad, Mad Treasure Hunt.** unabr. ed. Megan McDonald. Read by Barbara Rosenblat. (Running Time: 1 hr.). 2010. audio compact disk 9.99 (978-1-4418-8934-8(5), 9781441889348, Candlewick Bril) Brilliance Audio.

***Judy Moody & Stink: the Holly Joliday: The Holly Joliday.** unabr. ed. Megan McDonald. Read by Barbara Rosenblat. (Running Time: 1 hr.). 2010. 24.97 (978-1-4418-8933-1(7), 9781441889331, Candlewick Bril); 9.99 (978-1-4418-8932-4(9), 9781441889324, Candlewick Bril); audio compact disk 9.99 (978-1-4418-8930-0(2), 9781441889300, Candlewick Bril); audio compact disk 24.97 (978-1-4418-8931-7(0), 9781441889317, Candlewick Bril); audio compact disk 24.97 (978-1-4418-8929-4(9), 9781441889294, Candlewick Bril) Brilliance Audio.

***Judy Moody & Stink: the Mad, Mad, Mad, Mad Treasure Hunt: The Mad, Mad, Mad, Mad Treasure Hunt.** unabr. ed. Megan McDonald. Read by Barbara Rosenblat. (Running Time: 1 hr.). 2010. 24.97 (978-1-4418-8939-3(6), 9781441889393, Candlewick Bril); 9.99 (978-1-4418-8938-6(8), 9781441889386, Candlewick Bril); audio compact disk 9.99 (978-1-4418-8936-2(1), 9781441889362, Candlewick Bril); audio compact disk 24.97 (978-1-4418-8935-5(3), 9781441889355, Candlewick Bril); audio compact disk 24.97 (978-1-4418-8937-9(X), 9781441889379, Candlewick Bril) Brilliance Audio.

Judy Moody Declares Independence. unabr. ed. Megan McDonald. Narrated by Kate Forbes. 2 cass. (Running Time: 1 hr. 45 mins.). (Judy Moody Ser.: No. 6). 2005. 19.75 (978-1-4193-7197-4(5), 98049) Recorded Bks.
After visiting the Freedom Trail in Boston, Judy Moody declares her independence. Her demands include freedom from brushing her hair, freedom from her little brother Stink, freedom from homework, and freedom for an early bedtime. Will Judy be able to prove to her parents she's responsible enough for her freedoms? Megan McDonald's latest charming addition to the Judy Moody series will have listeners "star spangled bananas" over the young heroine's escapades.

Judy Moody Gets Famous! abr. ed. Megan McDonald. Narrated by Kate Forbes. 1 cass. (Running Time: 1 hr. 30 mins.). (Judy Moody Ser.: No. 2). (gr. 1 up). 2002. 10.00 (978-1-4025-2020-4(4)) Recorded Bks.
Judy wants to be famous after seeing her classmate Jessica in the newspaper for winning the spelling bee. After several hilarious attempts at stardom, Judy is finally contented with the satisfaction of helping others.

Judy Moody Gets Famous! unabr. ed. Megan McDonald. Narrated by Kate Forbes. 2 cass. (Running Time: 1 hr. 30 mins.). (Judy Moody Ser.: No. 2). 2004. 9.99 (978-1-4025-7455-9(X), 70144) Recorded Bks.

Judy Moody Goes to College. unabr. ed. Megan McDonald. Narrated by Kate Forbes. 2 cass. (Running Time: 1 hr. 30 mins.). (J). (gr. 2-4). 2008. 25.75 (978-1-4361-5901-2(6)); audio compact disk 25.75 (978-1-4361-5906-7(7)) Recorded Bks.

Judy Moody Predicts the Future. unabr. ed. Megan McDonald. Narrated by Kate Forbes. 2 cass. (Running Time: 1 hr. 30 mins.). (Judy Moody Ser.: No. 4). 2004. 9.99 (978-1-4025-7684-3(6), 70154) Recorded Bks.
We learn that third grader Judy Moody has a mood for everything, and the mood ring she gets as her mystery prize after eating seven bowls of cereal proves it. Even better, the ring unleashes some awesome predicting powers Judy never even knew she had. Soon, her classmates can't wait to hear the next prediction from Madame M (for Moody, of course) about whether the afternoon spelling test is making them feel amber (nervous), light blue (happy) or green (jealous). But when her friends start to doubt her talents, no one will believe Madame M's biggest prediction of all: that Mr. Todd, their teacher, is in a red mood (meaning L-O-V-E!).

Judy Moody Saves the World! Megan McDonald. Narrated by Kate Forbes. (Running Time: 1 hr. 30 mins.). (Judy Moody Ser.: No. 3). (gr. 1 up). 10.00 (978-1-4025-2023-5(9)) Recorded Bks.

Judy Moody Saves the World! unabr. ed. Megan McDonald. Narrated by Kate Forbes. 2 cass. (Running Time: 1 hr. 30 mins.). (Judy Moody Ser.: No. 3). 2004. 9.99 (978-1-4025-7453-5(3), 70134) Recorded Bks.
Class 3T is studying the environment, and Judy Moody is in the mood to save the planet. The only trouble is, her efforts never work out like she hopes they will. Whether it¿s parents who won¿t recycle, a brother who gets mad at her for freeing his frog, or classmates who don¿t appreciate her efforts to save trees by hiding all their pencils, Judy can¿t seem to get anyone as excited about the importance of the environment as she is. Isn¿t there anything Judy can do to save the world?.

Judy Ray 1 & 11. unabr. ed. Judy Ray. Read by Judy Ray. 2 cass. (Running Time: 29 min.). 1986. 10.00 ea. One-sided cass.; 18.00 Two-sided cass. New Letters.
On the first program Judy Ray reads from "Pebble Rings" recalling travels & her English childhood; the second program was recorded at a public reading at a writers conference in Kansas City.

Juego CD A viva Voz y Nuevo Testamento TLA. (SPA.). (YA). 2004. audio compact disk (978-1-933218-69-4(X)) Untd Bible Amrcas Svce.

Juego de Los Cuentos. Jorge Bucay. 2004. audio compact disk 44.95 (978-84-7871-201-4(1)) Pub: RBA Libros ESP. Dist(s): Santillana

Juegos/Canciones. Mercedes Limona.Tr. of Games & Songs. (SPA.). (J). 2000. bk. 18.95 (978-84-85546-04-6(0)) Pub: Servicios Edits ESP. Dist(s): AIMS Intl

Juez por un Dia. (Saludos Ser.: Vol. 1). (SPA.). (gr. 3-5). 10.00 (978-0-7635-1803-5(4)) Rigby Educ.

Jugador. abr. ed. Fyodor Dostoyevsky. 3 CDs.Tr. of Igrok. (SPA.). 2002. audio compact disk 17.00 (978-958-9494-91-2(9)) YoYoMusic.

Jugalbandi, Vol. 1. Music by Buddhaditya Mukherjee & Bhajan Sopori. 1 cass. 1992. (A92056) Multi-Cultural Bks.

Jugalbandi, Vol. 2. Music by Shahid Parvez & Faiyaz H. Khan. 1 cass. 1992. (A92057) Multi-Cultural Bks.

Jugalbandi, Vol. 3. Music by Arjun Shejwal & Fazel Qureshi. 1 cass. 1992. (A92058) Multi-Cultural Bks.

Jugalbandi, Vol. 4. Music by Vishwamohan Bhatt & Ronu Majumdar. 1 cass. 1992. (A92059); audio compact disk (CD A92059) Multi-Cultural Bks.

***Jugando en el agua Audio CD.** Francisco Blane. Adapted by Benchmark Education Company, LLC. (My First Reader's Theater Ser.). (SPA.). (J). 2009. audio compact disk 10.00 (978-1-935470-77-9(9)) Benchmark Educ.

Jugger. unabr. ed. Richard Stark, pseud. Read by Michael Kramer. 3 cass. (Running Time: 4 hrs. 30 mins.). (Parker Ser.). 2001. 28.00 (978-0-7366-8268-8(6)) Books on Tape.
Parker is an antihero. He is a thief with ruthless and brutal methods, and a basic hatred of mankind. Still, his projection of pure power makes him someone to watch. One person knows his secrets - an old safecracker, or "jugger," named Joe Sheer. Out of his mind with the pressure being exerted on him by Captain Abner Younger to tell all, Sheer calls Parker for help. Parker comes out to Sheer's Nebraska town - to kill Sheer before he cracks and sells Parker down the river. But when he gets there, Sheer is already dead, and something very valuable has gone missing. Now, someone is gunning for Parker. However, that someone may have underestimated how difficult Parker is to kill.

Juggler of Worlds. unabr. ed. Larry Niven & Edward M. Lerner. Read by Tom Weiner. (Running Time: 13 hrs. 0 mins.). (ENG.). 2009. 29.95 (978-1-4332-5332-4(1)); 79.95 (978-1-4332-5329-4(1)); audio compact disk 99.00 (978-1-4332-5330-0(5)) Blckstn Audio.

Juggletime. unabr. ed. Dave Finnigan. Perf. by Joey Kline. 1 cass. (Running Time: 30 min.). (J). (ps-3). 1991. 6.00 (1-20450) Jugglebug.
Parents Choice Award, 1992. 16 instructional songs teaching scarf play & scarf juggling; soundtrack to Juggletime video.

Juggling Babies. Barry Louis Polisar. 1 CD. (ENG.). (J). (gr. k-6). 1988. audio compact disk 14.95 (978-0-938663-46-1(1), 5151 CD) Pub: Rainbow Morn. Dist(s): IPG Chicago
Barry Louis Polisar, described recently as the "bad boy of children's music today," is back! His latest album, Juggling Babies & a Career, takes a musical look at childhood through the eyes of a father of twins.

Juggling Babies. Perf. by Barry Louis Polisar. 1 cass. (J). (gr. 3-6). 1987. 9.95 (978-0-938663-02-7(X), 5151) Rainbow Morn.

Juggling Work, Home & Personal Life Audio CD. 2006. audio compact disk 15.00 (978-0-9717456-2-9(5)) Office Dynamics.

Juicy Truth About Johnny Appleseed. (J). 1993. 6.98 (978-1-884159-00-8(1)) Carousel Classics.

Juin Forty-Four...Ma Normandie, Set. 5 cass. (FRE.). 1995. 46.95 (1734-RF) Olivia & Hill.
The personal experience of Leo Saint Aubin, a 26-year-old Canadian who lands with the Allied Forces on 6 June '44. This production of the Canadian Broadcasting Company gathers many oral documents.

Juju: A Social History & Ethnography of an African Popular Music. Christopher A. Waterman. 1 cass. (Running Time: 90 min.). (Chicago Studies in Ethnomusicology Ser.). 1990. 28.00 (978-0-226-87466-1(4)) Pub: U Ch Pr. Dist(s): Chicago Distribution Ctr

Juke Box Love Song see Poetry of Langston Hughes

Jules & Jim, Set. Henri-Pierre Roche. Read by G. Bejean & C. Deis. 4 cass. (FRE.). 1991. 34.95 (1481-VSL) Olivia & Hill.
The story on which Truffaut's classic film is based. The enduring friendship of two writers, Jules, a German & Jim, a Frenchman & the women they share, including the unpredictable Kate.

Jules Verne: An Exploratory Biography. unabr. collector's ed. Herbert Lottman. Read by Jonathan Reese. 10 cass. (Running Time: 15 hrs.). 1999. 80.00 (978-0-7366-4868-4(2), 5093) Books on Tape.
Pioneer writer of science fiction is revealed as an uncanny forcaster of the 20th Century.

Julia: An Intimate Biography. James Spada. Read by Ellen Archer. 11 vols. 2004. 89.95 (978-0-7927-3140-5(9), CSL 632, Chivers Sound Lib) AudioGO.

Julia: An Intimate Biography. unabr. ed. James Spada. Read by Ellen Archer. 13 CDs. (Running Time: 18 hrs.). 2004. audio compact disk 112.95 (978-0-7927-3141-2(7), SLD 632, Chivers Sound Lib) AudioGO.

Julia Alvarez see Antes de Ser Libre Before We Were Free

***Julia Fairchild.** Louise Gaylord. Perf. by Anna Nicholas. Narrated by Anna Nicholas. (Running Time: 464). (ENG.). 2010. 14.99 (978-0-9827081-8-7(1)) AuthorsDig.

Julia Gillian (and the Art of Knowing) unabr. ed. Alison McGhee. Read by Emily Bauer. (J). 2008. 34.99 (978-1-60514-784-0(2)) Find a World.

Julia Gillian (and the Art of Knowing) unabr. ed. Alison McGhee. Read by Emily Bauer. 3 CDs. (Running Time: 2 hrs. 55 mins.). (J). (gr. 2-5). 2008. audio compact disk 39.95 (978-0-545-07239-7(5)) Scholastic Inc.

Julia Older. unabr. ed. Read by Julia Older. 1 cass. (Running Time: 29 min.). 1985. 10.00 New Letters.
Julia Older reads from "Hermaphrodite in America" & "Donts & Others"; she also plays musical interludes on flute.

Julian Lee Rayford. unabr. ed. Julian L. Rayford. Read by Julian L. Rayford. 2 cass. (Running Time: 1 hr.). 1986. 10.00 ea. One-sided cass.; 18.00 Two-sided cass. New Letters.
The late folklorist & artist from Mobile, Alabama, recreates street cries & chants from the Gulf Coast area & reads some of his poems.

Julia's Last Hope. Janette Oke. Narrated by Alexandra O'Karma. 5 cass. (Running Time: 6 hrs. 30 mins.). 1990. 48.00 (978-0-7887-4952-0(8), K0007E7) Recorded Bks.
When the lumber mill closes in the mountain town of Calder Springs, John Harrigan loses his job. Now, relying on her faith in God more than ever, Julia Harrigan looks for a way to help her husband & her children.

***Julia's Way.** Elizabeth Lord. 2010. 69.95 (978-0-7531-4946-1(X)); audio compact disk 84.95 (978-0-7531-4947-8(8)) Pub: Isis Pubng Ltd GBR. Dist(s): Ulverscroft US

Julie. unabr. ed. Jean Craighead George. Narrated by Christina Moore. 4 pieces. (Running Time: 5 hrs. 15 mins.). (gr. 5 up). 1994. 35.00 (978-0-7887-0136-8(3), 94361E7) Recorded Bks.
This sequel to "Julie of the Wolves," answers the question: What happened to Julie after she left the wolf pack? She returns from a solitary life in the wilderness to confront the changing world of her father's village.

Julie. unabr. ed. Jean Craighead George. Narrated by Christina Moore. 5 CDs. (Running Time: 5 hrs. 15 mins.). (gr. 5 up). 2000. audio compact disk 40.00 (978-0-7887-3734-3(1), C1105E7) Recorded Bks.

***Julie.** unabr. ed. Catherine Marshall. Narrated by Cassandra Campbell. (Running Time: 14 hrs. 43 mins. 35 sec.). (ENG.). 2010. 34.99 (978-1-60814-694-9(4), SpringWater); audio compact disk 49.99 (978-1-59859-746-2(9), SpringWater) Oasis Audio.

***Julie: An American Girl.** unabr. ed. Megan McDonald. Narrated by Ali Ahn. 1 Playaway. (Running Time: 8 hrs. 15 mins.). (J). (gr. 4-6). 2009. 59.75 (978-1-4407-6363-2(1)); 51.75 (978-1-4361-2932-9(X)); audio compact disk 77.75 (978-1-4407-6357-1(7)) Recorded Bks.

***Julie: An American Girl.** unabr. collector's ed. Megan McDonald. Narrated by Ali Ahn. 7 CDs. (Running Time: 8 hrs. 15 mins.). (J). (gr. 4-6). 2009. audio compact disk 44.95 (978-1-4407-6361-8(5)) Recorded Bks.

Julie & Jackie & the Calendar: A Children's Book. Karla Carey. Illus. by Dennis Nolan. 1 cass. (Julie & Jackie Ser.). (J). 1990. pap. bk. 8.00 incl. children's bk. (978-1-55768-025-9(6)) LC Pub.

Julie & Jackie & the Calendar: The Music Book. Karla Carey. Illus. by Dennis Nolan. 1 cass. (Julie & Jackie Ser.). (J). 1990. pap. bk. 6.00 (978-1-55768-175-1(9)) LC Pub.

Julie & Jackie & the Calendar: The Musical Play. Karla Carey. Illus. by Dennis Nolan. 2 cass. (Julie & Jackie Ser.). (J). 1990. pap. bk. 35.00 incl. musical play. (978-1-55768-150-8(3)) LC Pub.

Julie & Jackie at Christmas-Time: A Children's Book. Karla Carey. 1 cass. (J). 1988. bk. 14.00; 8.00 (978-1-55768-026-6(4)) LC Pub.

Julie & Jackie at Christmas-Time: The Music Book. Karla Carey. 1 cass. (J). 1988. 6.00 (978-1-55768-176-8(7)) LC Pub.

Julie & Jackie at Christmas-Time: The Music Book. Karla Carey. Illus. by Dennis Nolan. 1 cass. (Julie & Jackie Ser.). (YA). 1990. bk. 14.00 (978-1-55768-201-7(1)) LC Pub.

Julie & Jackie at Christmas-Time: The Musical Play. Karla Carey. Illus. by Dennis Nolan. 2 cass. (Julie & Jackie Ser.). (J). 1990. pap. bk. 35.00 incl. musical play. (978-1-55768-151-5(1)) LC Pub.

Julie & Jackie at the Circus: A Children's Book. Karla Carey. 1 cass. (J). 1988. bk. 14.00; 8.00 (978-1-55768-027-3(2)) LC Pub.

Julie & Jackie at the Circus: The Music Book. Karla Carey. 1 cass. (J). 1988. bk. 14.00; 6.00 (978-1-55768-177-5(5)) LC Pub.

Julie & Jackie at the Circus: The Musical Play. Karla Carey. Illus. by Dennis Nolan. 2 cass. (Julie & Jackie Ser.). (J). 1990. pap. bk. 35.00 incl. musical play. (978-1-55768-152-2(X)) LC Pub.

Julie & Jackie Go A'Journeying: A Children's Book. Karla Carey. 1 cass. (J). 1988. bk. 14.00 LC Pub.

Julie & Jackie Go A'Journeying: A Children's Book. Karla Carey. Illus. by Dennis Nolan. 1 cass. (Julie & Jackie Ser.). (J). 1990. pap. bk. 8.00 (978-1-55768-028-0(0)) LC Pub.

Julie & Jackie Go A'Journeying: The Music Book. Karla Carey. 1 cass. (J). 1988. bk. 14.00; 6.00 (978-1-55768-178-2(3)) LC Pub.

Julie & Jackie Go A'Journeying: The Musical Play. Karla Carey. Illus. by Dennis Nolan. 2 cass. (Julie & Jackie Ser.). (J). 1990. pap. bk. 35.00 incl. musical play. (978-1-55768-153-9(8)) LC Pub.

Julie & Jackie Go A'Journeying: The Play & Musical Play (with Music Book, Story-and-Song Cassette & Piano Cassette) Karla Carey. Illus. by Dennis Nolan. (Julie & Jackie Ser.). (J). 1990. pap. bk. 8.00 (978-1-55768-003-7(5)) LC Pub.

Julie & Jackie on the Ranch: A Children's Book. Karla Carey. 1 cass. (J). 1988. bk. 14.00; 8.00 (978-1-55768-029-7(9)) LC Pub.

Julie & Jackie on the Ranch: The Music Book. Karla Carey. 1 cass. (J). 1988. bk. 14.00; 6.00 (978-1-55768-179-9(1)) LC Pub.

Julie & Jackie on the Ranch: The Musical Play. Karla Carey. Illus. by Dennis Nolan. 2 cass. (Julie & Jackie Ser.). (J). 1990. pap. bk. 35.00 incl. musical play. (978-1-55768-154-6(6)) LC Pub.

Julie & Jackie on the Ranch: The Play & Musical Play (with Music Book, Story-and-Song Cassette & Piano Cassette) Karla Carey. Illus. by Dennis Nolan. (Julie & Jackie Ser.). (J). 1990. pap. bk. 8.00 (978-1-55768-004-4(3)) LC Pub.

Julie & Julia. abr. ed. Julie Powell. Read by Julie Powell. (Running Time: 6 hrs.). (ENG.). 2009. audio compact disk 16.98 (978-1-60024-532-9(3)) Pub: Hachet Audio. Dist(s): HachBkGrp

Julie & Julia: 365 Days, 524 Recipes, 1 Tiny Apartment Kitchen. abr. ed. Julie Powell. (ENG.). 2005. 14.98 (978-1-59483-251-2(X)) Pub: Hachet Audio. Dist(s): HachBkGrp

Julie & Julia: 365 Days, 524 Recipes, 1 Tiny Apartment Kitchen. abr. ed. Julie Powell. Read by Julie Powell. 5 CDs. (Running Time: 6 hrs.). (ENG.). 2005. audio compact disk 29.98 (978-1-59483-106-5(8)) Pub: Hachet Audio. Dist(s): HachBkGrp

Julie & Julia: 365 Days, 524 Recipes, 1 Tiny Apartment Kitchen. abr. ed. Julie Powell. (Running Time: 6 hrs.). (ENG.). 2009. 44.98 (978-1-60788-062-2(8)) Pub: Hachet Audio. Dist(s): HachBkGrp

Julie & Romeo. abr. ed. Jeanne Ray. 2 cass. 2000. 17.95 (978-1-56740-900-0(8), Nova Audio Bks) Brilliance Audio.
Meet the Cacciamanis & the Rosemans, rival florists & bitter enemies for as long as either family can remember (although no one can recall precisely why) until one fateful day when divorced Julie Roseman & widowed Romeo Cacciamani meet by chance at a small business seminar in the Boston Sheraton. More than flowers bloom as a result & when their respective families, horrified, find out about the budding romance, all hell breaks loose.

Julie & Romeo. unabr. ed. Read by Jeanne Ray. 4 cass. (Running Time: 6 hrs.). 2000. 24.95 (978-1-56740-355-8(7), 1567403557, BAU) Brilliance Audio.
Meet the Cacciamanis and the Rosemans, rival florists and bitter enemies for as long as either family can remember (although no one can recall precisely why) until one fateful day when divorced Julie Roseman and widowed Romeo Cacciamani meet by chance at a small business seminar in the Boston Sheraton. More than flowers bloom as a result and when their respective families - horrified - find out about the budding romance, all hell breaks loose.

Julie & Romeo. unabr. ed. Jeanne Ray. Read by Jeanne Ray. (Running Time: 6 hrs.). 2007. 39.25 (978-1-4233-1441-7(7), 9781423314417, BADLE); 24.95 (978-1-4233-1440-0(9), 9781423314400, BAD); audio compact disk 39.25 (978-1-4233-1439-4(5), 9781423314394, Brlnc Audio MP3 Lib); audio compact disk 74.25 (978-1-4233-1437-0(9), 9781423314370, BriAudCD Unabrid); audio compact disk 26.95 (978-1-4233-1436-3(0), 9781423314363, Bril Audio CD Unabri); audio compact disk 24.95 (978-1-4233-1438-7(7), 9781423314387, Brilliance MP3) Brilliance Audio.

Julie & Romeo Get Lucky. unabr. ed. Jeanne Ray. Read by Jeanne Ray. (Running Time: 7 hrs.). 2005. 39.25 (978-1-59737-453-8(9), 9781597374538, BADLE); 24.95 (978-1-59737-452-1(0), 9781597374521, BAD); 29.95 (978-1-59737-446-0(6), 9781597374460, BAU); audio compact disk 39.25 (978-1-59737-451-4(2), 9781597374514, Brlnc Audio MP3 Lib); audio compact disk 74.25 (978-1-59737-449-1(0), 9781597374491, BriAudCD Unabrid); audio compact disk 24.95 (978-1-59737-450-7(4), 9781597374507, Brilliance MP3); audio compact disk 29.95 (978-1-59737-448-4(2), 9781597374484, Bril Audio CD Unabri) Brilliance Audio.
Busy with aging parents, grown kids, grandchildren, and their two flower shops, all Julie Roseman and Romeo Cacciamani want is to find ten minutes alone together. They find their wish answered in a most unexpected way when a back injury puts Romeo flat on his back in Julie's bedroom for a few weeks. Julie already had her hands full at home with one daughter's family. But when her eldest daughter is put on pregnancy bed rest and joins the household with her husband, Julie must find a way to keep the peace, keep her sanity, and keep their two flower shops running amidst the pandemonium. Beguilingly wise, warm-heartedly funny, and impossible to put down, Jeanne Ray's new story is pure delight.

Julie Andrews' Collection of Poems, Songs, & Lullabies. unabr. ed. Julie Andrews & Emma Walton Hamilton. Read by Julie Andrews & Emma Walton Hamilton. Illus. by James McMullan. (Running Time: 2 hrs. 30 mins.). (ENG.). 2009. 16.98 (978-1-60024-759-0(8)) Pub: Hachet Audio. Dist(s): HachBkGrp

Julie Andrews' Collection of Poems, Songs, & Lullabies. unabr. ed. Julie Andrews & Emma Walton Hamilton. Read by Emma Walton Hamilton. Illus. by James McMullan. 4 CDs. (Running Time: 2 hrs. 30 mins.). (ENG.). 2009. audio compact disk 24.98 (978-1-60024-758-3(X)) Pub: Hachet Audio. Dist(s): HachBkGrp

Julie Garwood CD Collection: Killjoy/Murder List/and Slow Burn. abr. ed. Julie Garwood. Read by Joyce Bean & Laural Merlington. (Running Time: 64800 sec.). 2006. audio compact disk 34.95 (978-1-4233-1678-7(9), 9781423316787, BACD) Brilliance Audio.
Killjoy: Avery Delaney's razor-sharp mind and ability to gather data and decipher evidence has made her an expert crime analyst for the FBI. But soon she will have to use every one of her skills on a case that hits painfully close to home. Avery's workaholic aunt, Carolyn Salvetti, persuades her niece to join her for the two weeks of luxury and decadence. But Carolyn never makes it to Utopia... Murder List: When Chicago detective Alec Buchanan is offered a prime position with the FBI, he takes it as the perfect opportunity to leave the Windy City and follow in his brothers' footsteps to the top echelons of law enforcement. But first he must complete one last assignment: acting as a glorified bodyguard to hotel heiress Regan Hamilton Madison. The gorgeous exec has become entangled in some potentially deadly business: Someone has e-mailed her a graphic crime-scene photo - and the victim is no stranger. Slow Burn: Living a successful life in Charleston, South Carolina, Kate MacKenna has always been able to turn her challenges into triumphs. But now the fates seem to be lining up against her . . . in a lethal fashion. Dylan Buchanan's convinced that she's merely having a spell of bad luck - until he discovers how many people want Kate dead.

Julie of the Wolves. abr. ed. Jean Craighead George. Read by Irene Worth. (Running Time: 3600 sec.). (J). (gr. 4-7). 2006. audio compact disk 14.95 (978-0-06-123518-4(0), HarperChildAud) HarperCollins Pubs.

Julie of the Wolves. unabr. ed. Jean Craighead George. 1 cass. (Running Time: 1 hr. 30 mins.). 2003. 7.99 (978-0-06-058443-6(2)) HarperCollins Pubs.

Julie of the Wolves. unabr. ed. Jean Craighead George. Narrated by Christina Moore. 3 pieces. (Running Time: 4 hrs. 30 mins.). (gr. 7 up). 27.00 (978-1-55690-777-7(X), 93138E7) Recorded Bks.
A young Eskimo girl runs away from home & becomes lost on the tundra, but she is saved when she is adopted by a pack of wolves. Available to libraries only.

Julie of the Wolves. unabr. ed. Jean Craighead George. Narrated by Christina Moore. 4 CDs. (Running Time: 4 hrs. 30 mins.). (gr. 7 up). 2000. audio compact disk 39.00 (978-0-7887-3449-6(0), C1055E7) Recorded Bks.

Julie Roy Jeffrey. unabr. ed. Julie R. Jeffrey. 1 cass. (Running Time: 29 min.). (New Letters on the Air Ser.). 1992. 10.00 (101191) New Letters.
Jeffrey talks about her latest work, "Converting to the West: A Biography of Narcissa Whitman," & tells about how it sheds new light on the relationships between missionaries & Native Americans in the Oregon Territory of the 19th century.

Julie's Wolf Pack. Jean Craighead George. Narrated by Christina Moore. 5 CDs. (Running Time: 4 hrs. 30 mins.). (gr. 5 up). audio compact disk 48.00 (978-0-7887-9526-8(0)) Recorded Bks.

Julie's Wolf Pack. unabr. ed. Jean Craighead George. Narrated by Christina Moore. 4 pieces. (Running Time: 4 hrs. 30 mins.). (gr. 5 up). 1999. 40.00 (978-0-7887-3830-2(5), 96067E7) Recorded Bks.
The adventures of Julie's wolves continue as a new wolf leader takes over the pack. Kapu is strong & wise, but he must lead his pack through many dangers if it is to survive.

Julie's Wolf Pack. unabr. ed. Jean Craighead George. Narrated by Christina Moore. 4 cass. (Running Time: 4 hrs. 30 mins.). (YA). 2000. pap. bk. & stu. ed. 53.20 (978-0-7887-3849-4(6), 41047X4); wbk. ed. 110.30 (978-0-7887-3874-6(7), 47039) Recorded Bks.

Juliet. unabr. ed. Anne Fortier. Read by Cassandra Campbell. 2010. audio compact disk 40.00 (978-0-7393-8495-4(3), Random AudioBks) Pub: Random Audio Pubg. Dist(s): Random

Juliet Dove, Queen of Love. Bruce Coville. 3 cassette. (Running Time: 4 hours). (Magic Shop Bks.). (J). 2003. 24.00 (978-1-932076-49-3(2)) Full Cast Audio.

Juliet, Naked. unabr. ed. Nick Hornby. Read by Jennifer Wiltsie et al. 8 CDs. (Running Time: 9 hrs.). (ENG.). (gr. 12 up). 2009. audio compact disk 29.95 (978-0-14-314490-8(1), PengAudBks) Penguin Grp USA.

***Juliet, Naked.** unabr. ed. Nick Hornby. Narrated by Bill Irwin et al. 8 CDs. (Running Time: 9 hrs.). 2009. 92.75 (978-1-4407-5830-0(1)) Recorded Bks.

Juliette Low: Girl Scout Founder. Helen Boyd Higgins. Read by Lynn Taccogna. (Running Time: 7200 sec.). (Young Patriots Ser.). (J). (gr. 4-7). 2007. 22.95 (978-1-4332-0149-3(6)) Blckstn Audio.

Juliette Low: Girl Scout Founder. unabr. ed. Helen Boyd Higgins. Read by Lynn Taccogna. (Young Patriots Ser.). (J). 2007. 34.99 (978-1-60252-664-8(8)) Find a World.

Julip. unabr. ed. Harrison, Jim Harrison. (Running Time: 1 hr. 0 mins.). (ENG.). 2009. 29.95 (978-1-4332-9102-9(9)); 44.95 (978-1-4332-9098-5(7)); audio compact disk 55.00 (978-1-4332-9099-2(5)) Blckstn Audio.

Julius Caesar. Perf. by Richard Dreyfuss et al. Ed. by William Shakespeare. 2 cass. Dramatization. (YA). (gr. 8 up). 1998. 16.95 (13108FA) Filmic Archives.
Skies over ancient Rome blaze with terrifying portents in this tale of duplicity & murder.

Julius Caesar. Perf. by Dublin Gate Theatre Staff. Ed. by William Shakespeare. 1 cass. (Running Time: 55 min.). Dramatization. 10.95 (978-0-8045-0809-4(7), SAC 7007) Spoken Arts.
The full telling of the play in key scenes with narrative bridges.

Julius Caesar. Perf. by Quicksilver Radio Theatre. 1 cass. (Running Time: 1 hr.). Dramatization. 2001. 12.95 (QUSL003) Lodestone Catalog.

Julius Caesar. William Shakespeare. Ed. by Naxos Audiobooks Staff. (Running Time: 3 hrs. 13 mins.). (New Cambridge Shakespeare Audio Ser.). (ENG.). 2001. 27.99 (978-0-521-79468-8(4)) Cambridge U Pr.

Julius Caesar. William Shakespeare. (Running Time: 3 hrs. 15 mins.). 2004. 24.95 (978-1-60083-763-0(8)) Iofy Corp.

Julius Caesar. William Shakespeare. Narrated by Full Cast Production Staff. (Running Time: 2 hrs.). (C). 2006. 14.95 (978-1-60083-045-7(5)) Iofy Corp.

Julius Caesar. William Shakespeare. 2 CDs. (Running Time: 7200 sec.). 1994. audio compact disk 25.95 (978-1-58081-317-4(8)) Pub: L A Theatre. Dist(s): NetLibrary CO

Julius Caesar. William Shakespeare. Read by Samuel West. 3 CDs. (Running Time: 2 hrs. 30 mins.). Dramatization. (Plays of William Shakespeare Ser.). 2000. audio compact disk 22.98 (978-962-634-205-3(6), NA320512) Naxos.

Julius Caesar. abr. ed. Ed. by William Shakespeare. 3 CDs. (Running Time: 3 hrs.). 2005. audio compact disk 19.95 (978-0-660-18963-5(1)) Pub: Canadian Broadcasting CAN. Dist(s): Georgetown Term

***Julius Caesar.** abr. ed. William Shakespeare. Read by (null) Cast. (ENG.). 2003. (978-0-06-074271-3(2), Caedmon) HarperCollins Pubs.

***Julius Caesar.** abr. ed. William Shakespeare. Read by (null) Cast. (ENG.). 2004. (978-0-06-081332-1(6), Caedmon) HarperCollins Pubs.

Julius Caesar. unabr. ed. Read by Audio Partners Staff. Ed. by William Shakespeare. 2 cass. (Running Time: 2 hrs. 27 mins.). 2004. 17.95 (978-1-932219-56-2(0), Atlntc Mnthly) Pub: Grove-Atltic. Dist(s): PerseuPGW
Julius Caesar is the most powerful man in Rome, but his power threatens the republic's very existence. A conspiracy is hatched, one with terrible consequences for Caesar and the conspirators. At its heart is the noble Brutus, caught in a tragic conflict between friendship and duty. Performed by Michael Feast, Adrian Lester, and the Arkangel cast.

Julius Caesar. unabr. ed. Perf. by Bonnie Bedelia et al. Ed. by William Shakespeare. 2 cass. (Running Time: 2 hrs. 1 min.). 1994. 23.95 (978-1-58081-027-2(6), RDP21) L A Theatre.
The skies over ancient Rome blaze with terrifying portents & soothsayers warn Julius Caesar of approaching doom. As conspiracy swirls around him, Shakespeare explores the deep repercussion of political murder on the human heart. The classic tale of duplicity, betrayal & murder.

Julius Caesar. unabr. ed. J. F. C. Fuller. Read by Frederick Davidson. 10 cass. (Running Time: 14 hrs. 30 mins.). 1995. 69.95 (978-0-7861-0815-2(0), 1638) Blckstn Audio.
Fuller illuminates a century of Roman history as well as Caesar's history, bringing to life Caesar's wars, his armies, his equipment, & his methods. Brilliant in design & impressive in scope, "Julius Caesar" clarifies how the military, political, & economic aspects of the Roman Republic worked together to produce a man whose name has come down to use as a synonym for absolute authority.

Julius Caesar. unabr. ed. Michael Grant. Narrated by Nelson Runger. 6 cass. (Running Time: 9 hrs.). 1996. 51.00 (978-0-7887-0314-0(5), 94506E7) Recorded Bks.
Reveals a strategic genius matched by an equal measure of ruthlessness. During the wars in Gaul, Egypt, Africa & elsewhere, entire populations were wiped out & these genocides were tempered only when seen to be counterproductive to Caesar's ambition, which was boundless. He scorned the Roman Republic, setting himself up as a godlike Imperator.

Julius Caesar. unabr. ed. Gilbert Highet. 1 cass. (Running Time: 23 min.). 1968. 12.95 (23087) J Norton Pubs.
Discussion of whether Julius Caesar was a reformer & hero or a traitor who deserved to die.

Julius Caesar. unabr. ed. Read by LA Theatre Works Staff & L. A. Theatre Works. Ed. by William Shakespeare. 2 cass. (Running Time: 2 hrs.). (YA). (gr. 9 up). 1998. 16.95 (978-0-8072-3568-3(7), CB142CXR, Listening Lib) Random Audio Pubg.
The skies over ancient Rome blaze with terrifying portents in this classic tale of duplicity & murder.

Julius Caesar. unabr. ed. Perf. by Ralph Richardson. Ed. by William Shakespeare. 2 cass. (Running Time: 2 hrs.). Dramatization. 2000. pap. bk. 37.20 (40743E5); 22.00 (21515E5) Recorded Bks.

Julius Caesar. unabr. ed. Perf. by Ralph Richardson & Anthony Quale. Ed. by William Shakespeare. 2 cass. (Running Time: 2 hrs. 13 mins.). Dramatization. 17.95 (H106) Blckstn Audio.
There are no heroes, only heroic words spoken by men of ambition, arrogance & jealousy. This tragedy explores the minds & motives of assassins plotting to murder a public man - & then shows the consequences of their act.

Julius Caesar. unabr. ed. Perf. by Ralph Richardson & Anthony Quayle. Ed. by William Shakespeare. 2 cass. (Running Time: 2 hrs. 13 min.). (J). (gr. 9-12). 1996. 18.00 (978-0-89845-954-8(0), CPN 230) HarperCollins Pubs.

Julius Caesar. unabr. ed. William Shakespeare. Narrated by Flo Gibson. (Running Time: 2 hrs. 38 mins.). 2004. 14.95 (978-1-55685-762-1(4)) Audio Bk Con.

Julius Caesar. unabr. ed. William Shakespeare. Narrated by Arkangel Cast Staff et al. (Running Time: 11280 sec.). (Arkangel Shakespeare Ser.). (ENG.). 2005. audio compact disk 24.95 (978-1-932219-11-1(0)) Pub: AudioGO. Dist(s): Perseus Dist

Julius Caesar. unabr. ed. William Shakespeare. Narrated by Michael Feast et al. (Running Time: 8820 sec.). (Arkangel Shakespeare Ser.). (ENG.). 2005. audio compact disk 24.95 (978-1-932219-16-6(1)) Pub: AudioGO. Dist(s): Perseus Dist

Julius Caesar. unabr. ed. William Shakespeare. Read by Paterson Joseph & David Burke. Narrated by David Troughton et al. (Running Time: 9720 sec.). (Arkangel Shakespeare Ser.). (ENG.). 2006. audio compact disk 24.95 (978-1-932219-34-0(X)) Pub: AudioGO. Dist(s): Perseus Dist
Titus returns victorious to Rome, bringing Tamora, Queen of the Goths, as his captive. When Tamora's son is condemned to die, she vows revenge. Performed by David Troughton, Harriet Walker, and the Arkangel cast.

Julius Caesar. unabr. ed. William Shakespeare. Read by Richard Dreyfuss et al. (YA). 2008. 34.99 (978-1-60514-785-7(0)) Find a World.

Julius Caesar. unabr. ed. William Shakespeare. Read by Audio Partners Staff. 2 cass. (Running Time: 3 hrs. 8 mins.). (Arkangel Shakespeare Ser.). 2004. 17.95 (978-1-932219-51-7(X), Atlntc Mnthly); 17.95 (978-1-932219-49-4(8), Atlntc Mnthly) Pub: Grove-Atltic. Dist(s): PerseuPGW
While England is threatened by rebellion, King Henry's scapegrace son Hal haunts the taverns of London, accompanied by the dissolute Falstaff and his band of rogues. Will Hal own up to his duty as Prince of Wales, or will Falstaff's influence prove too strong? Performed by Julian Glover, Jamie Glover, Richard Griffiths, and the Arkangel cast.

Julius Caesar. unabr. ed. Perf. by Nigel Stock et al. Ed. by William Shakespeare. 3 cass. 22.95 (SCN 102) J Norton Pubs.
The proper limits of political power & the menace of potential dictators, emerges clearly in this recording.

Julius Caesar. unabr. abr. ed. William Shakespeare & William Shakespeare. Perf. by Ralph Richardson & Anthony Quayle. 2 CDs. (Running Time: 2 hrs. 13 min.). Dramatization. (Caedmon Shakespeare Ser.: Vol. 2). (gr. 9-12). 1995. 25.00 (978-0-694-51583-7(3), Harper Audio) HarperCollins Pubs.

Julius Caesar, Pt. 1. William Shakespeare. 1 cass. (Running Time: 1 hr.). (Radiobook Ser.). 1987. 4.98 (978-0-929541-41-9(3)) Radiola Co.

Julius Caesar, Pt. 2. William Shakespeare. Read by Samuel West. 3 cass. (Running Time: 2 hrs. 30 mins.). Dramatization. (Plays of William Shakespeare Ser.). 2000. 17.98 (978-962-634-705-8(8), NA320514, Naxos AudioBooks) Naxos.

Julius Caesar, Pt. 2. abr. ed. William Shakespeare. Perf. by Swan Theatre Players. 1 cass. (Running Time: 52 min.). Dramatization. 10.95 (978-0-8045-0817-9(8), SAC 8015) Spoken Arts.
The complete play in key scenes & acts, with narrative bridges.

Julius Caesar, Pt. 2. unabr. ed. William Shakespeare. Perf. by John Gielgud et al. 3 cass. 21.95 (SCN 089) J Norton Pubs.
Emphasises the play's concern with the exigencies of war & leadership.

Julius Caesar, Set. William Shakespeare. Ed. by Naxos Audiobooks Staff. (Running Time: 3 hrs. 6 mins.). (New Cambridge Shakespeare Audio Ser.). (ENG.). 2001. audio compact disk 29.99 (978-0-521-79469-5(2)) Cambridge U Pr.

Julius Caesar: The Pursuit of Power. unabr. collector's ed. Ernle Bradford. Read by Walter Zimmerman. 8 cass. (Running Time: 12 hrs.). 1988. 64.00 (978-0-7366-1424-5(9), 2310) Books on Tape.
When Julius Caesar was murdered in 44 B.C., he was one of the most powerful men in the world. His overwhelming ambition had made him a military tribune, praetor, consul, dictator, & in the eyes of many, a god. Only one title eluded him: King.

Julius Caesar, a Play by William Shakespeare. As told by Alan Venable. William Shakespeare. (Classic Literature Ser.). 2005. pap. bk. 69.00 (978-1-4105-0713-6(0)); audio compact disk 18.95 (978-1-4105-0711-2(4)) D Johnston Inc.

Julius Caesar & the Story of Rome, Julius Caesar and The Story of Rome. ed. As told by Jim Weiss. Based on a play by William Shakespeare. (Storyteller's Version Ser.: 1124-044). (ENG.). (J). 2009. 14.95 (978-1-882513-61-1(4)) Pub: Greathall Prods. Dist(s): Allegro Dist

Julius, el Rey de la Casa. Kevin Henkes. Read by Susan Rybin.Tr. of Julius, the Baby of the World. (J). (ps-3). 2007. pap. bk. 16.95 (978-1-4301-0118-5(0)); pap. bk. 45.95 (978-1-4301-0119-2(9)); pap. bk. 18.95 (978-1-4301-0120-8(2)); pap. bk. 48.95 (978-1-4301-0121-5(0)) Live Oak Media.

Julius, the Baby of the World see Julius, el Rey de la Casa

Julius, the Baby of the World. Kevin Henkes. Read by Laura Hamilton. 11 vols. (Running Time: 16 mins.). (Live Oak Readalong Ser.). (J). 2003. pap. bk. 16.95 (978-1-59112-249-4(X)) Pub: Live Oak Media. Dist(s): AudioGO

Julius, the Baby of the World. Kevin Henkes. Illus. by Kevin Henkes. (Running Time: 16 mins.). 2003. audio compact disk 12.95 (978-1-59112-491-7(3)) Live Oak Media.

Julius, the Baby of the World. Kevin Henkes. Illus. by Kevin Henkes. 11 vols. (Running Time: 16 mins.). (J). 2003. bk. 25.95 (978-1-59112-250-0(3)); bk. 28.95 (978-1-59112-518-1(9)); pap. bk. 33.95 (978-1-59112-251-7(1)); pap. bk. 35.95 (978-1-59112-523-5(5)) Live Oak Media.

Julius, the Baby of the World/Julius, el Rey de la Casa. Kevin Henkes. Read by Laura Hamilton & Susan Rybin. (J). (ps-3). 2007. pap. bk. 33.95 (978-1-4301-0122-2(9)); pap. bk. 37.95 (978-1-4301-0123-9(7)) Live Oak Media.

July in Washington from "For the Union Dead" see Twentieth-Century Poetry in English, No. 32-33, Recordings of Poets Reading Their Own Poetry

July's People. unabr. ed. Nadine Gordimer. Read by Nadia May. 4 cass. (Running Time: 5 hrs. 30 mins.). 1993. 32.95 (978-0-7861-0412-3(0), 1364) Blckstn Audio.
For years, it has been what is called a "deteriorating situation." Now it is war. All over South Africa, cities are battlegrounds. Bam & Maureen Smales have to drive with their children to July's remote home village. For fifteen years July has been the decently treated black servant, totally dependent on them. Now he becomes their host, their savior - their keeper.

Jump. unabr. ed. Tim Maleeny. (Running Time: 7.5 hrs. 0 mins.). (ENG.). 2009. 29.95 (978-1-4332-9013-8(8)); 54.95 (978-1-4332-9009-1(X)); audio compact disk 69.00 (978-1-4332-9010-7(3)) Blckstn Audio.

Jump! The Adventures of Brer Rabbit. abr. ed. Malcolm Jones. Read by Whoopi Goldberg. Ed. by Liz Van Doren. Contrib. by Van D. Parks. Composed by Van Dyke Parks. 1 cass. (Running Time: 43 min.). (J). (gr. 1-5). 1990. bk. 20.00 (978-0-15-241351-4(0)) Harcourt.
On this engaging audiocassette, Whoopi Goldberg has added wit & humor to Brer Rabbit's sassy & stylish capers in Hominy Grove. Van Dyke Parks dramatic & melodic score enhances the funny & perceptive performance to create a memorable listening experience.

Jump Aerobics: Jump Rope Activities. Instructed by Don Disney. 1 cass. (Running Time: 1 hr.). (J). (gr. 2 up). 2001. pap. bk. 10.95 (KIM 2095C); pap. bk. & stu. ed. 11.95 (KIM 2095) Kimbo Educ.
Exciting routines combine dance, aerobic exercise & rope jumping. Improve balance, strength, coordination, flexibility, etc. Includes 9 to 5, Thank God I'm a Country Boy, The Devil Went down to Georgia, & more. Includes manual.

Jump at the Sun. unabr. ed. Kathleen McGhee-Anderson. Perf. by Tommy Hicks et al. 1 cass. (Running Time: 1 hr. 37 mins.). 1994. 19.95 (978-1-58081-148-4(5), TPT53) L A Theatre.

Jump Children. Perf. by Marcy Marxer. 1 cass. (Running Time: 39 min.). (Family Ser.). (J). (ps-5). 1987. 9.98 (8012); audio compact disk 14.98 (8012) Rounder Records.
Eight years after its release, "Jump Children" still shows up on "Best" lists & reviews because it's chock full of energy, great songs, top-notch musicianship & Marcy's sweet voice.

Jump Down: Songs & Rhymes for the Very Young. Lisa Monet. 1 cass. (J). (ps). 1989. 9.98 Norelco. (978-1-877737-07-7(0), 2162) MFLP CA.
Lullabies for children.

Jump, Frog, Jump! see Salta, Ranita, Salta!, Grades K-3

Jump, Frog, Jump! Robert Kalan. Illus. by Byron Barton. 14 vols. (Running Time: 6 mins.).Tr. of Salta, Ranita, Salta!. 2001. pap. bk. 35.95 (978-1-59112-729-1(7)) Live Oak Media.

Jump, Frog, Jump! Robert Kalan. Illus. by Byron Barton. 11 vols. (Running Time: 6 mins.).Tr. of Salta, Ranita, Salta!. (J). (ps-2). 2001. bk. 25.95 (978-0-87499-787-3(9)); pap. bk. 33.95 (978-0-87499-788-0(7)) Live Oak Media.

Jump, Frog, Jump! Robert Kalan. Read by Peter Fernandez. 11 vols. (Running Time: 6 mins.).Tr. of Salta, Ranita, Salta!. (J). (ps-2). 2001. pap. bk. 16.95 (978-0-87499-786-6(0)) Pub: Live Oak Media. Dist(s): AudioGO
Have fun figuring out how the frog keeps from getting himself caught when he tries to catch a fly in this cumulative tale.

Jump, Frog, Jump! Robert Kalan. Illus. by Byron Barton. (Running Time: 6 mins.).Tr. of Salta, Ranita, Salta!. (J). (ps-1). 2001. 12.95 (978-1-59112-726-0(2)) Live Oak Media.

Jump, Frog, Jump. Robert Kalan. Read by Peter Fernandez. 11 vols. (Running Time: 6 mins.). (J). 2001. pap. bk. 18.95 (978-1-59112-727-7(0)) Pub: Live Oak Media. Dist(s): AudioGO

Jump, Frog, Jump! & the Salta Ranita Salta. Robert Kalan. Illus. by Byron Barton. 22 vols. (Running Time: 10 mins.). 2001. pap. bk. 33.95 (978-0-87499-804-7(2)) Live Oak Media.

Jump Frog Jump cassette LC-611CS. 9.95 (978-1-59112-503-7(0)) Live Oak Media.

***Jump Jump & the Ice Queen.** RadioArchives.com. (Running Time: 375). (ENG.). 2005. audio compact disk 17.98 (978-1-61081-041-8(4)) Radio Arch.

Jump Start Action Songs. abr. ed. 1 CD. (Running Time: 38 mins.). (J). (gr. k-4). 2002. audio compact disk 14.95 (978-1-56346-112-5(9)) Kimbo Educ.
Motivating action songs to jumpstart children's minds and motor development. The songs help strengthen memory retention, comprehension, creativity, social skills, vocabulary development.

Jump Start Your Life: Bust Your Rut. Scripts. James W. Walkenhorst. Prod. by Bust Your Rut. 1. (Running Time: 75 mins,). 2004. audio compact disk 17.95 (978-0-9748655-0-8(8)) Bust Yr Rut.
Self Improvement at it's Finest!You want the best life has to offer, now you can have it!You know you want optimum health, fabulous relationships and abundant wealth, so what is holding you back? Use this information in this program to advance your life to a new level of success.Keep this program at your fingertips 24x7 as your constant source for life changing information. Whether your life needs to change a little or your life needs to change dramatically, you will refer to this program again and again.Jump Start Your Life. After all it's your life!.

Jump Start Your Sales: An Audio Program to Build Sales Skills. Caroline Pfouts. 6 cass. 1998. bk. 149.00 Set. (978-0-9663465-0-3(5)) Jasper Pubns.
Twelve lessons on how to do sales work.

Jump Start Your Sales: An Audio Program to Build Sales Skills. Caroline Pfouts. 6 cass. 1988. pap. bk. 12.00 (978-0-9663465-1-0(3)) Jasper Pubns.

Jump Tales. Read by Jackie Torrence. 1 cass. (Running Time: 44 min.). (Family Ser.). (J). 1991. 9.98 (8020) Rounder Records.
One of America's most beloved & talented storytellers presents five of her favorite jump tales, about pirates, ghosts, & plain everyday people.

Jump the Shark: When Good Things Go Bad. abr. ed. Jon Hein. Narrated by Jon Hein. 2 cass. (Running Time: 3 hrs. 30 mins.). (From Hit Websites Ser.). (YA). 2002. 17.95 (978-1-885408-89-1(7)); audio compact disk 23.95 (978-1-885408-90-7(0)) Listen & Live.
A riotous compendium of those priceless moments when the magic vanishes, the ratings go south, and the mighty become the fallen (who would have guessed a blue Gap dress could send Bill Clinton over the shark?). From the creator of the immensely popular website that has coined a catch phrase comes the book that is bound to be the pop-culture sensation of the season.

Jump to the Beat. 1 CD. (Running Time: 1 hr.). (YA). (gr. k up). 2001. pap. bk. 14.95 (KIM 8097CD) Kimbo Educ.
Fun-filled rope jumping activities that combine aerobics & precision rope jumping skills. Beginner & advanced routines to 7 recent hits including Thriller, Beat Street Strut & Billie Jean. Manual with easy-to-follow steps included.

Jump to the Beat: A Jump Aerobics Thriller for All Ages. Instructed by Don Disney. 1 cass. (Running Time: 1 hr.). (J). (gr. k up). 2001. pap. bk. 10.95 (KIM 8097C); pap. bk. & stu. ed. 11.95 (KIM 8097) Kimbo Educ.

Jumpin' Jack. Jack Grunsky. 1 cass., 1 CD. (J). 8.78 (YR 35); audio compact disk 11.18 CD Jewel box. (YR 35) NewSound.
Includes: "Iko Iko," "Songbirds," "Name Game," "With My Own Two Hands" & many more.

Jumpin' Jack. Perf. by Jack Grunsky. 1 cass. (J). (gr. 4 up). 10.98 (978-0-945267-76-8(2), YM035-CN); audio compact disk 13.98 (978-0-945267-75-1(4), YM035-CD) Youngheart Mus.
Songs include: "Iko Iko"; "Songbird"; "Name Game"; "With My Own Two Hands"; "Cha Cha Cha"; "Mrs. Tuckaway"; "Les Petites Marionnettes"; "Sun Dancer"; "Gift of Wings"; "Something New"; "Jumping Jack"; "Buskers & Clowns"; "Charango Charango" & more.

***Jumpin' Numbers & Shakin' Shapes, Vol. 1.** Created by Heidi Butkus. Lyrics by Heidi Butkus. Arranged by Mike Cravens. (ENG.). (J). 2002. audio compact disk 15.00 (978-0-9845641-0-1(1)) HeidiSongs.

***Jumpin' Numbers 11-30, Vol. 2.** Created by Heidi Butkus. Lyrics by Heidi Butkus. Arranged by Alan DeVries. (ENG.). (J). 2002. audio compact disk 15.00 (978-0-9845641-1-8(X)) HeidiSongs.

Jumping Frog. Mark Twain. (Reading & Training, Beginner Ser.). (J). (gr. 4-7). 2005. pap. bk. 21.95 (978-88-530-0138-2(0)) Cideb ITA.

Jumping Frogs to Cannibalism. unabr. ed. Mark Twain. Read by Thomas Becker. 2 cass. (Running Time: 2 hrs. 12 min.). 1994. lib. bdg. 18.95 Set. (978-1-883049-31-7(8)) Sound Room.
A collection of ten stories including: "The Notorious Jumping Frogs of Calavarous County," "What Stumped the Blue Jays," "The Story of the Old Ram," "Tom Quartz," & "Cannibalism in the Cars.".

Jumping Frogs to Cannibalism, Set. unabr. ed. Mark Twain. Read by Thomas Becker. 2 cass. (Running Time: 2 hrs. 15 mins.). (Mark Twain Ser.). 1994. bk. 16.95 (978-1-883049-17-1(2), 390212, Commuters Library) Sound Room.
A collection of ten stories includes: "The Notorious Jumping Frog of Calaveras County," "What Stumped the Bluejays," "Tom Quartz," "My Watch," "The Story of the Old Ram," "A Speech," "How I Edited an Agricultural Paper," "Journalism in Tennessee," "The Facts in the Great Beef Contract" & "Cannibalism in the Cars.".

Jumping in the House of God. World Wide Message Tribe. 1 cass., 1 CD. 10.98 (46222-4); audio compact disk 15.98 CD. (46222-2) Warner Christian.

Jumping the Cracks. Victoria Blake & Trudy Harris. 2009. 69.95 (978-1-84652-401-1(6)); audio compact disk 89.95 (978-1-84652-372-4(9)) Pub: Magna Story GBR. Dist(s): Ulverscroft US

Jumping the Line: The Adventures & Misadventures of an American Radical. William Herrick. Read by William Herrick. Intro. by Paul Berman. 8 cass. (Running Time: 11 hrs.). 1997. 34.95 Set. (978-0-9668567-0-5(8), 52100); 18.00 Set. (978-0-9668567-1-2(6), 52092) MediaBay Audio.
Herrick chronicles his life of both conviction & disillusionment.

Jumping the Nail. unabr. ed. Eve Bunting. Narrated by Julie Dretzin. 3 cass. (Running Time: 4 hrs.). (YA). 2000. pap. bk. & stu. ed. 43.25 (978-0-7887-3009-2(6), 40891X4) Recorded Bks.
Dru & her friends at La Paloma High School are horrified when Scooter & his girlfriend jump the Nail. Leaping from the top of the steep cliff, they drop 90 feet to the California water below. Although they aren't hurt, Dru worries that their daring feat may set off a dangerous chain reaction.

Jumping the Nail. unabr. ed. Eve Bunting. Narrated by Julie Dretzin. 3 pieces. (Running Time: 4 hrs.). (gr. 9 up). 2000. 29.00 (978-0-7887-2979-9(9), 95752E7) Recorded Bks.

Jumping the Nail, Class set. Eve Bunting. Read by Julie Dretzin. 3 cass. (Running Time: 4 hrs. 1 min.). (YA). 1999. wbk. ed. 109.80 (978-0-7887-3039-9(8), 46856) Recorded Bks.

Jumping the Queue. unabr. ed. Mary Wesley. Read by Anna Massey. 6 cass. (Running Time: 6 hrs. 30 min.). (Audio Bks.). 1991. 54.95 set. (978-0-7451-6350-5(5)) AudioGO.
Matilda Poliport, recently widowed, has decided to end it all. But her meticulously planned bid for graceful oblivion is foiled when she finds herself trying to prevent the suicide of another lost soul, Hugh Warner, on the run from the police & life begins again for both of them.

***Jumping the Scratch.** unabr. ed. Sarah Weeks. Read by Stephen Spinella. (ENG.). 2006. (978-0-06-119060-5(8)); (978-0-06-119062-9(4)) HarperCollins Pubs.

Jumping Through Fires: Escaping Religion for the God of Grace. unabr. ed. David Nasser. (Running Time: 4 hrs. 19 mins. 48 sec.). (ENG.). 2009. audio compact disk 21.98 (978-1-59644-771-4(0), Hovel Audio) christianaud.

***Jumping through Fires: The gripping story of one man's escape from revolution to Redemption.** unabr. ed. David Nasser. Narrated by Lloyd James. (ENG.). 2009. 12.98 (978-1-59644-772-1(9), Hovel Audio) christianaud.

Jumping to Conclusions. unabr. ed. Wanda E. Brunstetter. Read by Ellen Grafton. (Running Time: 3 hrs.). (Rachel Yoder Ser.). 2009. 39.97 (978-1-4418-0685-7(7), 9781441806857, Brinc Audio MP3 Lib); 14.99 (978-1-4418-0684-0(9), 9781441806840, Brilliance MP3); 14.99 (978-1-4418-0686-4(5), 9781441806864, BAD); 39.97 (978-1-4418-0687-1(3), 9781441806871, BADLE); audio compact disk 14.99 (978-1-4418-0682-6(2), 9781441806826, Bril Audio CD Unabri); audio compact disk 44.97 (978-1-4418-0683-3(0), 9781441806833, BriAudCD Unabrid) Brilliance Audio.

Jumpstart the 21-day plan to lose weight get fit & increase your energy And: The 21-Day Plan to Lose Weight, Get Fit, & Increase Your Energy & Enthusiasm for Life. Denise Austin. 2004. 7.95 (978-0-7435-4909-7(0)) Pub: S&S Audio. Dist(s): S and S Inc

Jumpstart Your Publishing Dreams: Insider Secrets to Skyrocket Your Success. Read by W. Terry Whalin. (ENG.). 2009. audio compact disk 39.95 (978-1-935085-51-5(4)) WTW Pr.

June Jordan. unabr. ed. Ed. by Jim McKinley. Prod. by Rebekah Presson. 1 cass. (Running Time: 29 min.). (New Letters on the Air Ser.). 1994. 10.00 (020593) New Letters.
The outspoken poet & black activist talks about using poetry "to save lives." She also reads her own poems which have been praised for "effectively uniting in poetic form the personal everyday struggle & the political oppression of blacks." Jordan says poetry is now more inclusive & that she is fighting for all oppressed people.

Junebug. unabr. ed. Alice Mead. Narrated by Peter Francis James. 2 pieces. (Running Time: 2 hrs.). (gr. 3 up). 1997. 19.00 (978-0-7887-0735-3(3), 94912E7) Recorded Bks.
Alice Mead gently portrays a dangerous world as seen through the eyes of a child who refuses to give up his optimism & hope. In the dingy Auburn Street project where Junebug lives, ten is the age when young boys start joining gangs & working for drug dealers. Junebug's mother tries to keep him safe, but Junebug's time is running out. His tenth birthday is coming up soon.

Junebug & the Reverend. Alice Mead. Narrated by Peter Francis James. 4 CDs. (Running Time: 4 hrs. 30 mins.). (gr. 4 up). audio compact disk 42.00 (978-1-4025-2311-3(4)) Recorded Bks.

Junebug & the Reverend. unabr. ed. Alice Mead. Narrated by Peter Francis James. 3 pieces. (Running Time: 4 hrs. 30 mins.). (gr. 4 up). 2002. 28.00 (978-0-7887-5025-0(9)) Recorded Bks.

Juneteenth: A Novel. Ralph Ellison. Ed. by John F. Callahan. Narrated by Peter Jay Fernandez. 12 CDs. (Running Time: 14 hrs.). 2000. audio compact disk 116.00 (978-0-7887-4898-1(X), C1273E7) Recorded Bks.
When racist Senator Adam Sunraider is downed by an assassin's bullet, he mysteriously summons an elderly black minister to his deathbed. As the two men relive their memories of a shared history, they gradually reveal the secrets of their past. Both hope to find redemption as they converge upon the tragic series of events that first brought them together. Ellison scholar John F. Callahan carefully assembled this rich, passionate composition from thousands of pages of notes.

Juneteenth: A Novel. unabr. ed. Ralph Ellison. Ed. by John F. Callahan. Narrated by Peter Jay Fernandez. 10 cass. (Running Time: 14 hrs.). 2000. 93.00 (978-0-7887-4309-2(0), 96053E7) Recorded Bks.
Ralph Ellison spent 40 years creating this saga. Carefully assembled from thousands of pages of note, it speaks poetically & wisely of the burden of racism that black & white Americans have always shared.

Jung. Anthony Stevens. Read by Tim Pigott-Smith. 3 cds. 2003. audio compact disk 22.98 (978-962-634-298-5(6)) Naxos.

Jung, Alchemy, Astrology & Metaphysics. Sara A. Keller. 1 cass. 8.95 (622) Am Fed Astrologers.
An AFA Convention workshop tape.

Jung & Nietzsche. Read by James Jarrett. 2 cass. (Running Time: 2 hrs.). 1988. 16.95 Set. (978-0-7822-0098-0(2), 318) C G Jung IL.

Jung & Synchronicity. unabr. ed. Stephan Hoeller. 1 cass. (Running Time: 1 hr. 30 min.). 1996. 11.00 (40018) Big Sur Tapes.
Hoeller describes how other cultures make use of their sense of connectedness & how we can develop this sense.

Jung, Astrology & Archetypes of Collective Unconsciousness. John Taimiazzo. 1 cass. 8.95 (337) Am Fed Astrologers.
Impact of 3 outer planets on our transformation.

Jung, Astrology & Rudhyar. unabr. ed. Dane Rudhyar. 2 cass. (Running Time: 2 hrs.57 min.). 1970. 18.00 Set. (10110) Big Sur Tapes.
Correspondences & contrasts between the works & ideas of C. G. Jung & Dane Rudhyar. Personal myths & archetypal consciousness, empirical science & metaphysical speculation, symbols & "the shadow side of God" are among the topics.

Jung, Jungians, & Homosexuality. Robert Hopcke. Read by Robert Hopcke. 2 cass. (Running Time: 2 hrs.). 1991. 16.95 set. (978-0-7822-0383-7(3), 472) C G Jung IL.
This lecture examines the writings of Jung on the issues of homosexuality - his attitudes, his theories, & what post-Jungians have drawn from these writings. Using Jungian insights, Robert Hopcke proposes a new & more affirmative way of thinking about homosexuality which takes into account both contemporary psychological thought on sexual orientation & the sociopolitical critique launched by Gay Liberation.

Jung on Incarnation: "Every Man Has to Carry a God" Read by T. J. Kapacinskas. 1 cass. (Running Time: 2 hrs.). (Patterns of Divinity Ser.: No. 5). 1988. 12.95 (978-0-7822-0110-9(5), 305) C G Jung IL.

Jung, Tarot & Astrology. unabr. ed. Stephan Hoeller. 1 cass. (Running Time: 1 hr. 30 min.). 1981. 11.00 (40014) Big Sur Tapes.

Jungian Analysis: An Overview. Read by Murray Stein. 2 cass. (Running Time: 3 hrs. 30 min.). 1987. 21.95 Set. (978-0-7822-0270-0(5), 266) C G Jung IL.

Jungian Look at the Bible. As told by Richard D. Grant. 1 CD. (Running Time: 72min). 2003. pap. bk. 11.95 (978-1-932226-20-1(6)) Wizard Acdmy.
Abraham, Isaac, Jacob, Joseph and Moses, Matthew, Mark, Luke and John, The Lord's Supper and the Lord's Prayer, The Good Samaritan, the Parable of the Sower, and 12-Step Recovery programs all make an appearance in this amazing scriptural expository of the Myers-Briggs personality types. (And believe it or not, Captain Kirk, Scotty, Bones and Spock pop in to make important points as well!)You'll feel as though you're staring into the mirror of your life.72 mesmerizing minutes on a Sunday morning withRichard D. Grant, PhD.

Jungian Psyche: A Deeper Look at Analytical Psychology. Murray Stein. Read by Murray Stein. 19 cass. (Running Time: 16 hrs. 45 min.). 1991. 99.95 complete set. (978-0-7822-0370-7(1), 458S) C G Jung IL.
This course offers a careful exploration of some of Jung's key theoretical texts. Aimed at giving the advanced student of analytical psychology a greater appreciation of the details of Jung's theoretical model of the psyche, the class proceeds in a systematic fashion through the basic concepts & considers how they interrelate to form a whole. Suggested readings from Jung's Collected Works are announced at the start of each class tape.

Jungian Psychology & Eastern Religions. Read by Diane Martin. 2 cass. (Running Time: 4 hrs.). 1987. 21.95 Set. (978-0-7822-0157-4(1), 274) C G Jung IL.

Jungian Psychology & Higher Education. Read by Charles Taylor & John Dunne. 2 cass. (Running Time: 2 hrs. 30 min.). 1984. 18.95 Set. (978-0-7822-0308-0(6), ND7301) C G Jung IL.

Jungian Psychology & Human Spirituality: Liberation from Tribalism in Religious Life. Read by Robert Moore. 5 cass. (Running Time: 7 hrs.). 1989. 39.95 Set. (978-0-7822-0192-5(X), 386) C G Jung IL.
Although it is important that people find & affirm their common human spiritual roots, it is time to realize that tribalism in human culture, politics, & religion must be transcended. Jungian thought may be a vehicle to assist in facilitating that process.

Jungian Psychology & Kohut's Self Psychology. Read by Lionel Corbett & Cathy Rives. 13 cass. (Running Time: 14 hrs.). 1989. 74.95 Set. (978-0-7822-0045-4(1), 382S) C G Jung IL.

Jungian Psychology & Primitive Religions. Read by Louise Mahdi. 1 cass. (Running Time: 90 min.). 1987. 10.95 (978-0-7822-0151-2(2), 275) C G Jung IL.

Jungian Psychology & Religion. Chester P. Michael. 1985. 24.00 (978-0-940136-11-3(2)) Open Door Inc.

Jungian Psychology & Wisdom of the East & West. unabr. ed. Joseph Henderson. 1 cass. (Running Time: 57 min.). 1971. 11.00 (06603) Big Sur Tapes.
Henderson relates Jung & Eastern philosophy in their mutual emphasis on the unreality of the ego.

Jungian Symbolism in Astrology. Alice Howell. 6 cass. 18.00 (OC97) Sound Horizons AV.

Jungian Theories. Pat Hardin. Read by Patricia Hardin. 1 cass. (Running Time: 90 min.). 1994. 8.95 (1151) Am Fed Astrologers.
Jungian theories & astrology.

Jungian View of Georgia O'Keeffe. Read by Lucille Klein. 1 cass. (Running Time: 90 min.). 1988. 10.95 (978-0-7822-0128-4(8), 320) C G Jung IL.

Jungian Views on Aging. Read by Lionel Corbett. 1 cass. (Running Time: 90 min.). 1984. 10.95 (978-0-7822-0038-6(9), 154) C G Jung IL.

***Jungle.** 2010. audio compact disk (978-1-59171-241-1(6)) Falcon Picture.

***Jungle.** Clive Cussler & Jack Du Brul. (Oregon Files Ser.). (ENG.). 2011. audio compact disk 29.95 (978-0-14-242889-4(2), PengAudBks); audio compact disk 39.95 (978-0-14-242890-0(6), PengAudBks) Penguin Grp USA.

Jungle. Dorling Kindersley Publishing Staff. (Eyewitness Videos Ser.). (ENG.). (J). (gr. 3). 2009. 12.99 (978-0-7566-5825-0(X)) DK Pub Inc.

Jungle. Upton Sinclair. Retold by Eric Metzgar. (Classic Literature Ser.). 2006. pap. bk. 69.00 (978-1-4105-0790-7(4)); audio compact disk 18.95 (978-1-4105-0788-4(2)) D Johnston Inc.

Jungle. Upton Sinclair. Narrated by Flo Gibson. 2007. audio compact disk 36.95 (978-1-55685-891-8(4)) Audio Bk Con.

Jungle. unabr. ed. Upton Sinclair. Read by Robert Morris. 11 cass. (Running Time: 16 hrs.). 1994. 76.95 (978-0-7861-0789-6(8), 1514) Blckstn Audio.
The dramatic expose of the Chicago meat-packing industry at the turn of the century which prompted an investigation by Theodore Roosevelt, culminating in the pure-food legislation of 1906.

Jungle. unabr. ed. Upton Sinclair. Read by Robert Morris. (Running Time: 16 hrs. 30 mins.). (J). 2007. audio compact disk 29.95 (978-0-7861-7321-1(1)) Blckstn Audio.

Jungle. unabr. ed. Upton Sinclair. Read by Robert Morris. (Running Time: 54000 sec.). 2007. 19.95 (978-0-7861-4718-2(0)); audio compact disk 19.95 (978-0-7861-6578-0(2)) Blckstn Audio.

Jungle. unabr. ed. Upton Sinclair. Read by Robert Morris. (J). 2008. 84.99 (978-1-60514-734-5(6)) Find a World.

Jungle, unabr. ed. Upton Sinclair. Narrated by George Guidall. 11 cass. (Running Time: 15 hrs. 45 mins.). 1994. 91.00 (978-1-55690-977-1(2), 94116E7) Recorded Bks.
Few books have so affected radical social change as this one did when it was published serially in 1906. Exposing unsanitary conditions in the meat-packing industry in Chicago, Sinclair's novel gripped Americans by the stomach, contributing to the passage of the first Food & Drug Act. Jurgis Rudkus, a Lithuanian immigrant comes to America in search of a fortune for his family. He accepts the harsh realities of a working-man's lot, laboring with naive vigor - until, his health & family sacrificed, he understands how the heavy wheels of the industrial machine can crush even the strongest spirit.

Jungle. unabr. ed. Upton Sinclair. Narrated by Paul Boehmer. (Running Time: 16 hrs. 0 mins. 0 sec.). (ENG.). 2009. audio compact disk 65.99 (978-1-4001-4040-4(4)); audio compact disk 22.99 (978-1-4001-6040-2(5)); audio compact disk 32.99 (978-1-4001-1040-7(8)) Pub: Tantor Media. Dist(s): IngramPubServ

Jungle, Set. unabr. ed. Upton Sinclair. Read by Flo Gibson. 9 cass. (Running Time: 13 hrs.). 1997. 28.95 (978-1-55685-473-6(0), 473-0) Audio Bk Con.
A Lithuanian family comes to America to seek their living. The ghastly & often brutal descriptions of work in Chicago stockyards & the grim consequences of extreme poverty made this book a kind of landmark that paved the way for many reforms & stirred up the Socialists.

Jungle Boogie. (J). (ps-3). 1999. audio compact disk 16.66 (978-0-7634-0523-6(X)) W Disney Records.

Jungle Book. 1 cass. (Classic Soundtrack Ser.). (J). 11.99 (978-0-7634-0340-9(7)); 11.99 Norelco. (978-0-7634-0339-3(3)); audio compact disk 19.99 (978-0-7634-0342-3(3)) W Disney Records.

Jungle Book. 1 cass. (Read-Along Ser.). (J). (ps-3). 1990. bk. 7.99 (978-1-55723-005-8(6)) W Disney Records.

Jungle Book. 1 CD. (Classic Soundtrack Ser.). (J). (ps-3). 1997. audio compact disk 19.99 (978-0-7634-0341-6(5)) W Disney Records.

Jungle Book. Read by Rebecca C. Burns. Ed. by John Rowe. (Running Time: 16680 sec.). (ENG.). (J). (gr. 4-7). 2004. audio compact disk 19.99 (978-1-4001-5120-2(1)) Pub: Tantor Media. Dist(s): IngramPubServ

Jungle Book. Ed. by John Rowe. Narrated by Flo Gibson. Audio Book Contractors. (ENG.). (J). 2008. audio compact disk 24.95 (978-1-60646-029-0(3)) Audio Bk Con.

Jungle Book. Short Stories. Ed. by John Rowe. As told by Jim Weiss. 1 cass. (Running Time: 1 hr.). Dramatization. (Storyteller's Version Ser.). (J). (gr. 2 up). 1994. 10.95 (978-1-882513-14-7(2), 1124-14); audio compact disk 14.95 (978-1-882513-39-0(8), 1124-014) Greathall Prods.
The vivid characters from Kipling's original stories are brought to life as we follow the remarkable story of a young boy raised among wolves and other wild creatures of the Indian Jungle. Includes: "Mowgli's Brothers," "Tiger! Tiger!," "Red Dog" and "The Spring Running".

Jungle Book. Ed. by John Rowe. Narrated by Tony Roberts. (Running Time: 3 hrs.). (J). 2006. 14.95 (978-1-59912-976-1(0)) Iofy Corp.

Jungle Book. Ed. by John Rowe. (J). 1985. 4.95 (978-0-913675-41-0(5)) McGraw.

Jungle Book. Ed. by John Rowe. 2005. audio compact disk 34.95 (978-1-4193-5992-7(4)) Recorded Bks.

Jungle Book. Read by Madhav Sharma. Ed. by John Rowe. (Running Time: 3 hrs. 45 mins.). (J). 1999. 24.95 (978-1-60083-794-4(8)) Iofy Corp.

Jungle Book. Read by Jim Weiss. 1 cass., 1 CD. (Running Time: 1 hr.). (J). (GHP14) NewSound.

Jungle Book. abr. ed. Nina Mattikow. Perf. by Purple Balloon Players. 4 cass. (Running Time: 4 hrs.). Dramatization. (Wood Cassette Toys Ser.). (J). 1992. 19.95 Set. (978-1-55569-563-7(9), 24001) Great Am Audio.
The Rudyard Kipling classic stories spring to life in this enthralling collection of stories about Mowgli, an orphan boy raised by wolves.

Jungle Book. abr. adpt. ed. Rudyard Kipling. (Bring the Classics to Life: Level 1 Ser.). (ENG.). (gr. 4-7). 2008. audio compact disk 12.95 (978-1-55576-420-3(7)) EDCON Pubng.

Jungle Book. unabr. ed. Read by Rebecca Burns. Ed. by John Rowe. (YA). 2007. 39.99 (978-1-59895-798-3(8)) Find a World.

Jungle Book. unabr. ed. Read by Windsor Davies. Ed. by John Rowe. 2 cass. (Read-Along Ser.). (J). 34.95 Incl. read-along bk., learner's guide & exercises. (S23917) J Norton Pubs.

Jungle Book. unabr. ed. Rudyard Kipling. Narrated by Rebecca C. Burns. (Running Time: 4 hrs. 30 mins. 0 sec.). (ENG.). (J). (gr. 4-7). 2008. audio compact disk 19.99 (978-1-4001-0881-7(0)) Pub: Tantor Media. Dist(s): IngramPubServ

Jungle Book, unabr. ed. Ed. by John Rowe. Narrated by Flo Gibson. 4 cass. (Running Time: 6 hrs.). (J). 1984. 19.95 (978-1-55685-056-1(5)) Audio Bk Con.
Mowgli, lost in the deep jungle as a baby, is brought up by a family of wolves. Through many legendary adventures he is befriended & protected by Bagheera, the black panther & Baloo, the brown bear.

Jungle Book. unabr. ed. Ed. by John Rowe. Narrated by Rebecca C. Burns. (Running Time: 4 hrs. 30 mins. 0 sec.). (ENG.). (J). (gr. 4-7). 2008. 19.99 (978-1-4001-5881-2(8)); audio compact disk 39.99 (978-1-4001-3881-4(7)) Pub: Tantor Media. Dist(s): IngramPubServ

Jungle Book. unabr. ed. Read by Walter Zimmerman et al. Ed. by John Rowe. 4 cass. (Running Time: 6 hrs.). Dramatization. (J). 1980. 28.00 (C-41) Jimcin Record.
Extraordinary adventures of Mowgli & his friends. Consists of: "Mowgli's Brothers," "Kaa's Hunting," "Tiger-Tiger!," "The White Seal," "Rikki-Tikki-Tavi," "Toomai of the Elephants," "Servants of the Queen".

Jungle Book. unabr. collector's ed. Read by Rebecca C. Burns. Ed. by John Rowe. 5 cass. (Running Time: 5 hrs.). (J). (gr. 4-7). 1995. 30.00 (978-0-7366-3218-8(2), 3881) Books on Tape.
When forest animals succor Mowgli, a human, he is little more than a baby. But through his wits & their kindness, he reaches adulthood. Paradox exists in this paradise, but nowhere more forcefully than in Shere Khan, the formidable Bengal tiger. In the contest between Shere Khan & Mowgli that must occur, which will triumph: the human intelligence of Mowgli, or the deep, instinctive cunning of the wily striped cat?.

Jungle Book, Vol. 1. Ed. by John Rowe. 1 cass. Dramatization. (J). 10.95 (978-0-8045-0929-9(8), SAC 929) Spoken Arts.
Includes "Mowgli's Brothers" & "Rikki-Tikki-Tavi".

Jungle Book, Vol. 2. Perf. by Christopher Casson et al. Ed. by John Rowe. 1 cass. (Running Time: 44 min.). (J). (gr. 1-6). 1986. 10.95 (978-0-8045-0933-6(6), SAC 933) Spoken Arts.

Jungle Book, Vol. 2. Ed. by John Rowe. 2005. audio compact disk 34.95 (978-1-4193-5993-4(2)) Recorded Bks.

Jungle Book, Vol. 3. Perf. by Christopher Casson et al. Ed. by John Rowe. 1 cass. (Running Time: 44 min.). (J). (gr. 1-6). 1986. 10.95 (978-0-8045-0951-0(4), SAC 951) Spoken Arts.
Includes "Kaa's Hunting" & "The White Seal".

Jungle Book, Vol. 4. Perf. by Christopher Casson et al. Ed. by John Rowe. 1 cass. (Running Time: 44 min.). (J). (gr. 1-6). 1986. 10.95 (978-0-8045-0952-7(2), SAC 952) Spoken Arts.
Includes "The Miracle of Purun Bhagat" & "Letting in the Jungle".

Jungle Book: A BBC Radio Full-Cast Dramatization. Rudyard Kipling. (Running Time: 2 hrs. 0 mins. 0 sec.). (ENG.). 2009. audio compact disk 24.95 (978-1-60283-756-0(2)) Pub: AudioGO. Dist(s): Perseus Dist

Jungle Books. abr. ed. Rudyard Kipling. Read by Madhav P. Sharma. 3 CDs. (Running Time: 3 hrs. 46 mins.). (J). (gr. 4-7). 1995. audio compact disk 22.98 (978-962-634-035-6(5), NA303512, Naxos AudioBooks) Naxos.
A collection of stories of the boy Mowgli and his jungle companions. A 1995 Naird Award for children's storytelling.

***Jungle Books.** abr. ed. Rudyard Kipling. Read by Wanda McCaddon. (Running Time: 5.5 hrs. NaN mins.). (ENG.). 2011. 29.95 (978-1-4417-8331-8(8)); audio compact disk 55.00 (978-1-4417-8329-5(6)) Blckstn Audio.

Jungle Books. unabr. ed. Rudyard Kipling. Read by Wanda McCaddon. 4 cass. (Running Time: 6 hrs.). (J). 1999. 32.95 (B1002) Blckstn Audio.
Kipling's breathtaking descriptions of the jungles of Central India are all the more amazing when you realize that he had never been there.

Jungle Books. unabr. ed. Rudyard Kipling. Read by Wanda McCaddon. 4 cass. (Running Time: 5 hrs. 30 mins.). 2006. 32.95 (978-0-7861-2205-9(6), 2980) Blckstn Audio.

Jungle Books I, unabr. ed. Rudyard Kipling. Narrated by Flo Gibson. 4 cass. (Running Time: 5 hrs.). (gr. 5 up). 1981. 36.00 (978-1-55690-275-8(1), 81190E7) Recorded Bks.
A collection of fantastic fables that features Mowgli the Wolf Boy, Bagheera the Panther, Baloo the Bear & many more.

Jungle Books II, unabr. ed. Rudyard Kipling. Narrated by Patrick Tull. 6 pieces. (Running Time: 8 hrs.). (gr. 5 up). 1991. 53.00 (978-1-55690-276-5(X), 91325E7) Recorded Bks.
Baloo the bear, Shere Khan the tiger & Mowgli the man cub return in this magical sequel to Kipling's beloved children's classic.

Jungle Bungalow. Kathleen Gibson. 1 cass., 1 CD. (Running Time: 35 min.). (J). (ps-6). 1998. 10.00 (978-1-888862-05-8(X), RR1130); audio compact disk 15.00 CD. (978-1-888862-07-2(6), RR1130) Rompin Records.
Musical celebration of our friends & our earth featuring fun, danceable, singable music that is authentically for the whole family, straight from the heart & the funny bone. Includes original songs in many ethnic styles.

Jungle Dogs. unabr. ed. Graham Salisbury. Narrated by Graham Salisbury. 4 pieces. (Running Time: 4 hrs.). (gr. 5 up). 2000. 37.00 (978-0-7887-4244-6(2), 96212E7) Recorded Bks.
When Boy's teacher asks his class to write about someone they look up to, Boy is stumped. There's nothing remarkable about the people around him. His parents work, his sister dates someone named Slime & his brother belongs to a street gang. When Boy ultimately faces the fear & violence in his life, he writes a paper that leaves his teacher speechless.

Jungle Dogs. unabr. ed. Graham Salisbury. Read by Graham Salisbury. 4 cass. (Running Time: 4 hrs.). (YA). (gr. 5 up). 2000. pap. bk. & stu. ed. 59.95 (978-0-7887-4336-8(8), 41131) Recorded Bks.

Jungle Dogs, Class set. Graham Salisbury. Read by Graham Salisbury. 4 cass. (Running Time: 4 hrs.). (YA). (gr. 5 up). 2000. wbk. ed. 204.80 (978-0-7887-4437-2(2), 47128) Recorded Bks.

Jungle Drums. unabr. ed. Graeme Base. Read by Graeme Base. 1 CD. (Running Time: 20 mins.). (J). (gr. k-2). 2007. audio compact disk 39.95 (978-1-74093-825-9(9)) Pub: Bolinda Pubng AUS. Dist(s): Bolinda Pub Inc

Jungle drums & the peasant Prince. Graeme Base & Li Cunxin. Read by Graeme Base & Paul English. (J). 2009. 39.99 (978-1-74214-162-6(5), 9781742141626) Pub: Bolinda Pubng AUS. Dist(s): Bolinda Pub Inc

***Jungle Effect: Healthiest Diets from Around the World - Why They Work & How to Make Them Work for You.** unabr. ed. Daphne Miller. Narrated by Heather Hathaway. Frwd. by Andrew Weil. Prod. by Brett Barry. (ENG.). 2010. 19.99 (978-0-9829787-0-2(7)) IP LLC.

Jungle Is Neutral. unabr. ed. F. Spencer Chapman. Read by Rupert Keenlyside. 10 cass. (Running Time: 1 hr. 30 min. per cass.). 1986. 80.00 (1782) Books on Tape.
For more than three years, Chapman lived in the Malayan jungle - training Chinese Guerillas, harassing Japanese. Twice he was captured, twice he escaped. He suffered black-water fever, pneumonia & tick-typhus, in addition to almost chronic malaria. Yet the jungle provides food & water, & unlimited cover for friend or foe. It is the attitude of mind that determines whether you go under or survive - the jungle is neutral.

Jungle Law. Victoria Vinton. Narrated by Henry Strozier. (Running Time: 37800 sec.). 2005. audio compact disk 34.99 (978-1-4193-5779-4(4)) Recorded Bks.

Jungle Love: Level 5. Margaret Johnson. Contrib. by Philip Prowse. (Running Time: 3 hrs. 16 mins.). (Cambridge English Readers Ser.). (ENG.). 2002. 15.75 (978-0-521-75085-1(7)) Cambridge U Pr.

Jungle Lovers. unabr. ed. Paul Theroux. Read by Michael Prichard. 7 cass. (Running Time: 10 hrs. 30 min.). 1984. 56.00 (978-0-7366-0921-0(0), 1864) Books on Tape.
A Massachusetts salesman enters a small African country caught up in the throes of revolution. An entrepreneur, he immediately opens an insurance brokerage. He then marries a local businesswoman & together they set up housekeeping in a local brothel. There the couple play host to an antic assortment of callers.

Jungle Quest Intrigue. unabr. ed. Willa Lambert. Read by Laurie Klein. 6 cass. (Running Time: 7 hrs. 30 min.). 1994. 39.95 (978-1-55686-533-6(3)) Books in Motion.
Two men disappear while on an expedition into the Amazon Basin. The daughter of one & son of the other join forces to search for them. The rescue turns into stark survival.

Jungle Safari Sing-along Book soft Back. Created by Music Movement and Magination. Lyrics by Tim Smith. Music by Tim Smith. Illus. by Deborah Gross. (ENG.). (J). 2009. pap. bk. 14.95 (978-1-935572-00-8(8)) MMnM Bks.

Jungle Safari Small Group Reading Pack. Created by Music Movement and Magination. Lyrics by Tim Smith. Music by Tim Smith. Illus. by Deborah Gross. (ENG.). (J). 2009. pap. bk. 39.95 (978-1-935572-01-5(6)) MMnM Bks.

Jungle Tales of Tarzan. Edgar Rice Burroughs. Read by Shelly Frasier. (Running Time: 8 hrs.). 2003. 27.95 (978-1-60083-648-0(8), Audiofy Corp) Iofy Corp.

Jungle Tales of Tarzan. unabr. ed. Edgar Rice Burroughs. Narrated by Shelly Frasier. 7 CDs. (Running Time: 8 hrs. 8 mins.). (Tarzan Ser.). (ENG.). (YA). 2003. audio compact disk 39.00 (978-1-4001-0082-8(8)); audio compact disk 20.00 (978-1-4001-5082-3(5)) Pub: Tantor Media. Dist(s): IngramPubServ
In this collection of 12 short stories, Burroughs returns to Tarzan's early years providing new depth and detail to the Lord of the Jungle, during his time among the great apes. Having learned to read from his father's books, Tarzan seeks to apply his knowledge to the world around him and to learn more about life, death, dreams, God, love, and friendship. Tarzan challenges his best friend Taug, in a fight to the death, but then risks his life to save him; he has nightmares after eating rancid elephant meat only to awake and be faced with a live, man-eating gorilla; twice he sports a lion's skin to play a practical joke, but he doesn't always have the last laugh! The Jungles Tales include: 1)Tarzan's First Love, 2)The Capture of Tarzan, 3)The Fight for the Balu, 4)The God of Tarzan, 5)Tarzan and the Black Boy, 6)The Witch-Doctor Seeks Vengeance, 7)The End of Bukawai, 8)The Lion, 9)The Nightmare, 10)The Battle for Teeka, 11)A Jungle Joke, and 12)Tarzan Rescues the Moon Tarzan #6.

Jungle Tales of Tarzan. unabr. ed. Edgar Rice Burroughs. Read by Shelly Frasier. (Tarzan Ser.). (ENG.). 2003. audio compact disk 78.00 (978-1-4001-3082-5(4)) Pub: Tantor Media. Dist(s): IngramPubServ

Jungle Tales of Tarzan, with EBook. unabr. ed. Edgar Rice Burroughs. Narrated by Shelly Frasier. (Running Time: 8 hrs. 0 mins. 0 sec.). (Tarzan Ser.). (ENG.). 2009. 19.99 (978-1-4001-6119-5(3)); audio compact disk 27.99 (978-1-4001-1119-0(6)) Pub: Tantor Media. Dist(s): IngramPubServ

Jungle Tales of Tarzan, with eBook. unabr. ed. Edgar Rice Burroughs. Narrated by Shelly Frasier. (Running Time: 8 hrs. 0 mins. 0 sec.). (Tarzan Ser.). (ENG.). 2009. audio compact disk 55.99 (978-1-4001-4119-7(2)) Pub: Tantor Media. Dist(s): IngramPubServ

Jungle Two Jungle. 1 cass. (J). 11.99 Norelco. (978-0-7634-0244-0(3)); audio compact disk 19.99 (978-0-7634-0247-1(8)) W Disney Records.

Jungle Two Jungle. 1 cass. (J). (ps-3). 1997. 11.99 (978-0-7634-0245-7(1)); audio compact disk 19.99 CD. (978-0-7634-0246-4(X)) W Disney Records.

Jungle Vampire: An Awfully Beastly Business. unabr. ed. David Sinden et al. Read by Gerard Doyle. 3 CDs. (Running Time: 2 hrs. 30 mins. 0 sec.). (Awfully Beastly Business Ser.). (J). (gr. 3-6). 2009. audio compact disk 19.99 (978-0-7435-9965-8(9)) Pub: S&S Audio. Dist(s): S and S Inc

Jung's Answer to Job. John Giannini. Read by John Giannini. 5 cass. (Running Time: 6 hrs 20 min.). 1993. 39.95 set. (978-0-7822-0434-6(1), 513) C G Jung IL.

Jung's Challenge to Biblical Hermeneutics. Read by Wayne Rollins. 1 cass. (Running Time: 90 min.). 1985. 10.95 (978-0-7822-0230-4(6), 169) C G Jung IL.

Jung's Challenge to Contemporary Religion Conference. 10 cass. (Running Time: 14 hrs.). 1985. 74.95 Set. (978-0-7822-0002-7(8), JCCR) C G Jung IL.

Jung's Commentary on the Spiritual Exercises of Ignatius Loyola. Read by Thomas P. Lavin. 4 cass. (Running Time: 8 hrs.). 1988. 35.95 Set. (978-0-7822-0137-6(7), 339S) C G Jung IL.

Jung's Concept of the Anima. Read by Murray Stein. 2 cass. (Running Time: 2 hrs.). 1989. 16.95 Set. (978-0-7822-0288-5(8), 365) C G Jung IL.

Jung's Concept of the Animus. Read by Lucille Klein. 2 cass. (Running Time: 2 hrs.). 1989. 16.95 Set. (978-0-7822-0129-1(6), 373) C G Jung IL.

Jung's Critique of the Christian Notions of Good & Evil. Read by Carrin Dunne. 1 cass. (Running Time: 90 min.). 1985. 10.95 (978-0-7822-0060-7(5), 164) C G Jung IL.

Jung's Encounter with Buddhism. Read by Diane Martin. 1 cass. (Running Time: 90 min.). 1991. 10.95 (978-0-7822-0162-8(8), 437) C G Jung IL.
In his writings, Jung credits Eastern meditative experience with influencing his development of the concept of the collective unconscious. In this lecture, Martin compares the life of Jung the "spiritual voyage," with the life of Shakyamuni, & examines the assertions of Buddhist theoreticians & practioners that Jung transferred distortions from one culture to another, sometimes confusing Buddhism with Hunduism. Chicago Jung Institute faculty member Martin has studied Buddhism & Zen for 25 years.

Jung's Gnosticism & Contemporary Gnosis. Read by June Singer. 1 cass. (Running Time: 2 hrs.). 1985. 10.95 (978-0-7822-0260-1(8), 167) C G Jung IL.

Jung's Green Christ: A Healing Symbol for Christianity. Read by Murray Stein. 1 cass. (Running Time: 90 min.). 1985. 10.95 (978-0-7822-0266-3(7), 163) C G Jung IL.

Jung's Typology & the Cultural Ideal of the "Civilized Person" Read by Diane Martin. 2 cass. (Running Time: 2 hrs. 30 min.). 1987. 18.95 Set. (978-0-7822-0156-7(3), 251) C G Jung IL.

Junie B., First Grader: Aloha-Ha-Ha! unabr. ed. Barbara Park. Read by Lana Quintal. (Running Time: 4560 sec.). (Junie B., First Grader Ser.: No. 9). (ENG.). (J). (gr. 1-7). 2006. audio compact disk 14.99 (978-0-7393-3553-6(7), ImaginStudio) Pub: Random Audio Pubg. Dist(s): Random

Junie B., First Grader: Aloha-ha-ha/Jingle Bells, Batman Smells! (P. S. So Does May) Barbara Park. Read by Lana Quintal. 2 CDs. (Running Time: 2 hrs. 32 mins.). (Junie B., First Grader Ser.: Bks. 8 & 9). (J). (ps-3). 2006. audio compact disk 20.40 (978-0-7393-3801-8(3)) Pub: Books on Tape. Dist(s): NetLibrary CO

Junie B., First Grader: Aloha-Ha-Ha/Jingle Bells, Batman Smells! (P.S. So Does May) Barbara Park. Read by Lana Quintal. 2 cass. (Running Time: 2 hrs. 32 mins.). (Junie B., First Grader Ser.: Nos. 8 & 9). (J). (ps-3). 2006. 18.40 (978-0-7393-3829-2(3)) Books on Tape.

Junie B., First Grader: Books 21-24. unabr. ed. Barbara Park. Read by Lana Quintal. 2 cass. (Running Time: 3 hrs. 37 mins.). (Junie B., First Grader Ser.). (J). (gr. k-3). 2004. 23.00 (978-1-4000-9475-2(5)); audio compact disk 30.00 (978-1-4000-9504-9(2)) Books on Tape.
Junie B.'s first grade adventures continue with four more stories in one laugh-out-loud collection!.

Junie B., First Grader: Cheater Pants. Barbara Park. (Junie B., First Grader Ser.: No. 4). (J). (gr. k-3). 2004. 17.00 (978-0-8072-2351-2(4), ImaginStudio) Pub: Random Audio Pubg. Dist(s): Random

Junie B., First Grader (at Last!) unabr. ed. Barbara Park. Read by Lana Quintal. (Running Time: 48 mins.). (Junie B., First Grader Ser.: No. 1). (J). (gr. k-3). 2004. pap. bk. 17.00 (978-0-8072-1020-8(X), S FTR 258 SP, Listening Lib) Random Audio Pubg.

Junie B. Jones Bks. 1-8: Stupid Smelly Bus - Monkey Business - Big Fat Mouth - Sneaky Peaky Spying - Yucky Blucky Fruitcake - That Meanie Jim's Birthday - Handsome Warren - Monster under Her Bed. unabr. ed. Barbara Park. Read by Lana Quintal. (Running Time: 6 hrs.). (ENG.). (J). 2003. audio compact disk 30.00 (978-0-8072-1867-9(7), ImaginStudio) Pub: Random Audio Pubg. Dist(s): Random

Junie B. Jones & a Little Monkey Business. Barbara Park. Narrated by Christina Moore. (Running Time: 15 mins.). (Junie B. Jones Ser.: No. 2). (J). (gr. k-3). audio compact disk 19.00 (978-1-4025-2312-0(2)) Recorded Bks.

Junie B. Jones & a Little Monkey Business. unabr. ed. Barbara Park. Narrated by Christina Moore. 1 cass. (Running Time: 15 mins.). (Junie B. Jones Ser.: No. 2). (J). (gr. k-3). 1998. 11.00 (978-0-7887-2617-0(X), 95621E7) Recorded Bks.
Junie has a new baby brother. She hasn't seen him yet but Grandma says he's a cute little monkey. Maybe her parents will let her bring him to school on Pet Day.

Junie B. Jones & a Little Monkey Business, Vol. 2. unabr. ed. Barbara Park. Read by Lana Quintal. 1 cass. (Running Time: 44 mins.). (Junie B. Jones Ser.: Vol. 2). (J). (gr. k-3). 2004. pap. bk. 17.00 (978-0-8072-0779-6(9), LFTR 238 SP, Listening Lib) Random Audio Pubg.
It's pooey on B-A-B-I-E-S until Junie B. finds out that her new dumb baby brother is a big fat deal. Her two bestest friends are giving her everything they own just to see him.

Junie B. Jones & Her Big Fat Mouth. unabr. ed. Barbara Park. Read by Lana Quintal. 1 cass. (Running Time: 37 mins.). (Junie B. Jones Ser.: No. 3). (J). (gr. k-3). 2004. pap. bk. 17.00 (978-0-8072-0780-2(2), LFTR 239 SP, Listening Lib) Random Audio Pubg.
Junie B.'s having a rough week. "Cause Monday is Job Day, and Junie B. told her class that she's got the bestest job of all. Only, what the heck is it.

Junie B. Jones & Her Big Fat Mouth. unabr. ed. Barbara Park. Narrated by Christina Moore. 1 cass. (Running Time: 45 mins.). (Junie B. Jones Ser.: No. 3). (J). (gr. k-3). 1999. 12.00 (978-0-7887-2952-2(7), 95653E7) Recorded Bks.
Why does Junie keep getting that horrible sickish feeling in her tummy? Why does she feel like P.U.? Junie has a Big Problem: she doesn't know what she wants to be when she grows up. And worse yet, she can't seem to keep fibs from coming out of her mouth.

Junie B. Jones & Her Big Fat Mouth. unabr. ed. Barbara Park. Read by Christina Moore. 1 cass. (Running Time: 45 mins.). (Junie B. Jones Ser.: No. 3). (J). (gr. k-3). 1999. pap. bk. & stu. ed. 24.24 (978-0-7887-2982-9(9), 40864) Recorded Bks.

Junie B. Jones & Her Big Fat Mouth, Class set. unabr. ed. Barbara Park. Read by Christina Moore. 1 cass. (Running Time: 45 mins.). (Junie B. Jones Ser.: No. 3). (J). (gr. k-3). 1999. 72.70 (978-0-7887-3012-2(6), 46829) Recorded Bks.

Junie B. Jones & Some Sneaky Peeky Spying. unabr. ed. Barbara Park. Read by Lana Quintal. 1 cass. (Running Time: 39 mins.). (Junie B. Jones Ser.: No. 4). (J). (gr. k-3). 2004. pap. bk. 17.00 (978-0-8072-0781-9(0), LFTR 240 SP, Listening Lib) Random Audio Pubg.
Junie B. is the bestest spier in the whole world. But when she spies on Mrs., she could get into real trouble.

Junie B. Jones & Some Sneaky Peeky Spying. unabr. ed. Barbara Park. Narrated by Christina Moore. 1 cass. (Running Time: 45 mins.). (Junie B. Jones Ser.: No. 4). (J). (gr. k-3). 1999. pap. bk. & stu. ed. 23.24 (978-0-7887-3169-3(6), 40904X4) Recorded Bks.
Junie B. Jones knows she shouldn't spy on people, even though it is lots of fun. So when she spies on Mrs., her kindergarten teacher, Junie B. ends up a big problem. As the world's funniest (& most curious) kindergartner, Junie B. has fans of all ages laughing out loud. Includes study guide.

Junie B. Jones & Some Sneaky Peeky Spying. unabr. ed. Barbara Park. Narrated by Christina Moore. 1 cass. (Running Time: 45 mins.). (Junie B. Jones Ser.: No. 4). (J). (gr. k-3). 2000. 11.00 (978-0-7887-3203-4(X), 95652E7) Recorded Bks.

Junie B. Jones & Some Sneaky Peeky Spying, Class set. Barbara Park. Read by Christina Moore. 1 cass. (Running Time: 45 mins.). (Junie B. Jones Ser.: No. 4). (J). (gr. k-3). 1999. stu. ed. 71.70 (978-0-7887-3215-7(3), 46871) Recorded Bks.

Junie B. Jones & That Meanie Jim's Birthday, Vol. 6. unabr. ed. Barbara Park. Read by Lana Quintal. 1 cass. (Running Time: 57 mins.). (Junie B. Jones Ser.: No. 6). (J). (gr. k-3). 2004. pap. bk. 17.00 (978-0-8072-0642-3(3), Listening Lib) Random Audio Pubg.

Junie B. Jones & the Mushy Gushy Valentine. unabr. ed. Barbara Park. Read by Lana Quintal. 1 cass. (Running Time: 44 mins.). (Junie B. Jones Ser.: No. 14). (J). (gr. k-3). 2004. pap. bk. 17.00 (978-0-8072-0335-4(1), Listening Lib) Random Audio Pubg.

Junie B. Jones & the Stupid Smelly Bus. unabr. ed. Barbara Park. Read by Lana Quintal. 1 cass. (Running Time: 45 mins.). (Junie B. Jones Ser.: Vol. 1). (J). (gr. k-3). 2004. pap. bk. 17.00 (978-0-8072-0778-9(0), LFTR 237 SP, Listening Lib) Random Audio Pubg.
Meet Junie. B. Jones, kindergartner. She's so scared of the school bus and the meanies on it that when it's time to go home, she doesn't.

Junie B. Jones & the Stupid Smelly Bus. unabr. ed. Barbara Park. Narrated by Christina Moore. 1 CD. (Running Time: 45 mins.). (Junie B. Jones Ser.: No. 1). (J). (gr. k-3). audio compact disk 12.00 (978-0-7887-4940-7(4), C1303E7) Recorded Bks.
Junie is afraid to ride the school bus home, so she doesn't. Park tackles a young child's first-day-of-school fears with humor & insight.

Junie B. Jones & the Stupid Smelly Bus. unabr. ed. Barbara Park. Narrated by Christina Moore. 1 cass. (Running Time: 45 mins.). (Junie B. Jones Ser.: No. 1). (J). (gr. k-3). 1998. 10.00 (978-0-7887-2267-7(0), 95529E7) Recorded Bks.

Junie B. Jones & the Yucky Blucky Fruitcake. unabr. ed. Barbara Park. Read by Lana Quintal. 1 cass. (Running Time: 55 mins.). (Junie B. Jones Ser.: No. 5). (J). (gr. k-3). 2004. pap. bk. 17.00 (978-0-8072-0641-6(5), Listening Lib) Random Audio Pubg.

Junie B. Jones Collection. Barbara Park. Read by Lana Quintal. 3 CDs. (Running Time: 2 hrs. 51 mins.). (J). (gr. 2-5). 2004. audio compact disk 25.50 (978-1-4000-8987-1(5), Listening Lib); audio compact disk 25.50 (978-1-4000-8623-8(X), Listening Lib) Pub: Random Audio Pubg. Dist(s): NetLibrary CO

Junie B Jones Collection. Read by Lana Quintal. 3 CDs. (Running Time: 3 hrs. 3 mins.). (Junie B. Jones Ser.). (J). (gr. 2-5). 2004. audio compact disk 30.00 (978-0-8072-2011-5(6), Listening Lib) Random Audio Pubg.

Junie B. Jones Collection. unabr. ed. Barbara Park. Read by Lana Quintal. 2 cass. (Running Time: 7 hrs. 9 mins.). (Junie B. Jones Ser.). (ENG.). (J). (gr. 2-5). 2002. 13.00 (978-0-8072-0617-1(2), S YA 413 CX, Listening Lib) Pub: Random Audio Pubg. Dist(s): Random
"Junie B. Jones Is a Graduation Girl, #17: All the children in Room Nine are excited when they get their bright white graduation gowns. But when an accident happens, can Junie B. find a way to fix things? Or will she have to miss graduation and stay a kind".

Junie B. Jones Collection, Bks. 1-4. unabr. ed. Barbara Park. 2 cass. (Running Time: 2 hrs. 46 mins.). (Junie B. Jones Ser.). (J). (gr. 2-5). 2004. 23.00 (978-0-8072-0683-6(0), Listening Lib); audio compact disk 25.50 (978-0-8072-1167-0(2), S YA 355 CD, Listening Lib) Pub: Random Audio Pubg. Dist(s): NetLibrary CO
Four Junie B. Jones stories in one collection means four times the laughs!.

Junie B. Jones Collection, Bks. 1-8. unabr. gif. ed. Barbara Park. Read by Lana Quintal. 5 CDs. (Junie B. Jones Ser.). (J). (gr. 1-4). 2002. audio compact disk 36.00 (978-0-8072-0738-3(1), Listening Lib) Random Audio Pubg.

Junie B. Jones Collection, Bks. 9-16. unabr. ed. Barbara Park. Read by Lana Quintal. 5 CDs. (Running Time: 19620 sec.). (ENG.). (J). (gr. 1-4). 2005. audio compact disk 30.00 (978-0-307-28258-3(9), ImaginStudio) Pub: Random Audio Pubg. Dist(s): Random

Junie B. Jones Collection, Bks. 13-16. unabr. ed. Barbara Park. Read by Lana Quintal. 2 cass. (Running Time: 2 hrs. 51 mins.). (Junie B. Jones Ser.). (J). (gr. 2-5). 2004. 23.00 (978-0-8072-8840-5(3), LL0221, Listening Lib) Random Audio Pubg.
Includes "Junie B. Jones Is (Almost) a Flower Girl", "Junie B. Jones & the Mushy Gushy Valentine", "Junie B. Jones Has a Peep in Her Pocket" and" Junie B. Jones Is Captain Field Day".

Junie B. Jones Collection, Bks. 17-20. abr. ed. Barbara Park. Read by Lana Quintal. 2 cass. (Running Time: 2 hr. 30 mins.). (J). 2002. pap. bk. 23.00 (978-0-8072-0965-3(1), Listening Lib) Random Audio Pubg.
Junie B. is back and is headed for first grade with four more adventures: Junie B. Jones Is a Graduation Girl, Junie B. Jones, First Grader (at last), Junie B. Jones, First Grader: Boss of Lunch, Junie B. Jones, First Grader: Toothless Wonder.

Junie B. Jones Collection, Bks. 17-24. unabr. ed. Barbara Park. Read by Lana Quintal. (Running Time: 24480 sec.). (Junie B. Jones Ser.). (ENG.). (J). (gr. 1-4). 2007. audio compact disk 34.00 (978-0-7393-5634-0(8), Listening Lib) Pub: Random Audio Pubg. Dist(s): Random

Junie B. Jones Collection Bks. 9-12. unabr. ed. Barbara Park. Read by Lana Quintal. 2 cass. (Running Time: 2 hrs. 37 mins.). (Junie B. Jones Ser.). (J). (gr. 2-5). 2004. 23.00 (978-0-8072-0524-2(9), LL0220, Listening Lib) Random Audio Pubg.
The world's funniest kindergartner is back with four more silly escapades. Includes "Junie B. Jones Is Not a Crook," "Junie B. Jones Is a Party Animal," "Junie B. Jones Is a Beauty Shop Guy," & "Junie B. Jones Smells Something Fishy".

Junie B. Jones Has a Monster under Her Bed. unabr. ed. Barbara Park. Read by Lana Quintal. 1 cass. (Running Time: 41 mins.). (Junie B. Jones Ser.: No. 8). (J). (gr. k-3). 2004. pap. bk. 17.00 (978-0-8072-0644-7(X), Listening Lib) Random Audio Pubg.

Junie B. Jones Has a Peep in Her Pocket. unabr. ed. Barbara Park. Read by Lana Quintal. 1 cass. (Running Time: 43 mins.). (Junie B. Jones Ser.: No. 15). (J). (gr. k-3). 2004. pap. bk 17.00 (978-0-8072-0336-1(X), Listening Lib) Random Audio Pubg.

Junie B. Jones Is a Beauty Shop Guy. unabr. ed. Barbara Park. 1 cass. (Running Time: 40 mins.). (Junie B. Jones Ser.: No. 11). (J). (gr. k-3). 2004. pap. bk. 17.00 (978-0-8072-0532-7(X), Listening Lib) Random Audio Pubg.

Junie B. Jones Is a Graduation Girl. unabr. ed. Barbara Park. Read by Lana Quintal. (Running Time: 47 mins.). (Junie B. Jones Ser.: No. 17). (J). (gr. k-3). 2004. pap. bk. 17.00 (978-0-8072-1019-2(6), S FTR 257 SP, Listening Lib) Random Audio Pubg.

Junie B. Jones Is a Party Animal. unabr. ed. Barbara Park. Read by Lana Quintal. 1 cass. (Running Time: 39 mins.). (Junie B. Jones Ser.: No. 10). (J). (gr. k-3). 2004. pap. bk. 17.00 (978-0-8072-0531-0(1), Listening Lib) Random Audio Pubg.

Junie B. Jones Is (Almost) a Flower Girl. unabr. ed. Barbara Park. Read by Lana Quintal. 1 cass. (Running Time: 49 mins.). (Junie B. Jones Ser.: No. 13). (J). (gr. k-3). 2004. pap. bk. 17.00 (978-0-8072-0334-7(3), Listening Lib) Random Audio Pubg.

Junie B. Jones Is Captain Field Day. unabr. ed. Barbara Park. Read by Lana Quintal. 1 cass. (Running Time: 47 mins.). (Junie B. Jones Ser.: No. 16). (J). (gr. k-3). 2004. pap. bk. 17.00 (978-0-8072-0337-8(8), Listening Lib) Random Audio Pubg.

Junie B. Jones Is Not a Crook. unabr. ed. Barbara Park. Read by Lana Quintal. (Running Time: 39 mins.). (Junie B. Jones Ser.: No. 9). (J). (gr. k-3). 2004. pap. bk. 17.00 (978-0-8072-0530-3(3), Listening Lib) Random Audio Pubg.

Junie B. Jones Loves Handsome Warren. unabr. ed. Barbara Park. Read by Lana Quintal. 1 cass. (Running Time: 42 mins.). (Junie B. Jones Ser.: No. 7). (J). (gr. k-3). 2004. pap. bk. 17.00 (978-0-8072-0643-0(1), Listening Lib) Random Audio Pubg.

Junie B. Jones Smells Something Fishy. unabr. ed. Barbara Park. 1 cass. (Running Time: 40 mins.). (Junie B. Jones Ser.: No. 12). (J). (gr. k-3). 2004. pap. bk. 17.00 (978-0-8072-0533-4(8), Listening Lib) Random Audio Pubg.

Junior Environment on File. Victoria Chapman & Associates. (gr. 4-9). 2001. audio compact disk 149.95 (978-0-8160-4210-4(1)) Facts On File.

Junior Environmental Activities on File. Victoria Chapman & Associates. (gr. 4-9). 2001. audio compact disk 149.95 (978-0-8160-4211-1(X)) Facts On File.

Junior Homer: The Tale of Troy/the Adventures of Odysseus. Benedict Flynn. Read by Benjamin Soames. (Playaway Young Adult Ser.). (ENG.). (YA). (gr. 8-12). 2009. 59.99 (978-1-60775-750-4(8)) Find a World.

Junior Homer Box Set. unabr. ed. Benedict Flynn. Read by Benjamin Soames. 4 CDs. bk. 28.98 (978-962-634-237-4(4), NAX23712) Naxos.

Junior Jedi Training Manual. Rhino Records Staff. 1 cass. (Running Time: 1 hr. 30 mins.). (Star Wars Ser.). (J). 1999. pap. bk. 5.98 (978-0-7379-0002-6(4), R4 75669); pap. bk. 9.98 (978-0-7379-0003-3(2), R2 75669) Rhino Enter.

Junior Jedi Training Manual. ltd. ed. Rhino Records Staff. 1 CD. (Running Time: 1 hr. 30 mins.). (Star Wars Ser.). (J). 2001. bk. 19.98 (R2 75679) Rhino Enter.

Junior Jukebox Totebooks. Prod. by PC Treasures Staff. (J). 2007. (978-1-60072-051-2(X)) PC Treasures.

Junior Science Diagrams on File: For Grades K Through 5. Diagram Group. (gr. 4-9). 2004. audio compact disk 199.95 (978-0-8160-5154-0(2)) Facts On File.

Junior Science Experiments on File#153, Vol. 1. (gr. 4-9). 2004. cd-rom & audio compact disk 149.95 (978-0-8160-5813-6(X)) Facts On File.

Junior Science Experiments on File#153, Vol. 2. (gr. 4-9). 2006. cd-rom & audio compact disk 149.95 (978-0-8160-6292-8(7)) Facts On File.

Junior Science Experiments on File#153, Vol. 3. (gr. 4-9). 2006. cd-rom & audio compact disk 149.95 (978-0-8160-6293-5(5)) Facts On File.

Junior State Maps on File. Facts on File, Inc. Staff. (J). (gr. 4-9). 2003. audio compact disk 149.95 (978-0-8160-4999-8(8)) Facts On File.

Junior Timelines on File. rev. ed. Valerie Tomaselli-Moschovitis. (J). (gr. 4-9). 2005. audio compact disk 149.95 (978-0-8160-5121-2(6)) Facts On File.

Juniper Tree. Prod. by Phil Rosenthal. 1 cass. (Running Time: 45 min.). (J). (gr. k-6). 1994. 9.98 (978-1-879305-17-5(8), AM-C-115) Am Melody.
Folk favorites & delightful new songs performed by a variety of acclaimed folk/bluegrass musicians. Parent's Choice Award.

***Junk: A Griff Carver, Hallway Patrol Novel.** unabr. ed. Jim Krieg. (ENG.). (J). 2011. audio compact disk 28.00 (978-0-307-91541-2(7), Listening Lib) Pub: Random Audio Pubg. Dist(s): Random

Junk Car & Doc Gamble Day. 1 cass. (Running Time: 60 min.). Dramatization. (Fibber McGee & Molly Ser.). 1949. 6.00 Once Upon Rad.
Radio broadcasts - humor.

Junk-Food Files. Steck-Vaughn Staff. 1 cass. (Running Time: 45 min.). 2003. (978-0-7398-8422-5(0)) SteckVau.

Junkyard Dog. unabr. ed. Robert Campbell. Narrated by Peter Waldren. 4 cass. (Running Time: 5 hrs. 15 mins.). (Jimmy Flannery Mystery Ser.: Vol. 1). 1991. 35.00 (978-1-55690-277-2(8), 91231E7) Recorded Bks.
Jimmy Flannery investigates the bombing of an abortion clinic.

Juno & the Paycock: Scenes from Acts One & Three see Sean O'Casey Reading Juno & the Paycock & Other Works

JUNOS as a Second Language - Podcast. 2008. (978-1-935312-58-1(8)) Juniper Net.

Jupiter. Joyce Levine. 1 cass. (Integrating Astrological Cycles Ser.). 1995. 11.95 (978-1-885856-07-4(5)) Vizualizations.
Astrology. Side 1 informational. Side 2 guided meditation.

Jupiter: A Novel. unabr. ed. Ben Bova & Ben Bova. Read by Christian Noble & David Warner. Intro. by Harlan Ellison. 10 CDs. (Running Time: 12 hrs. 0 mins. 0 sec.). (Grand Tour Ser.). (ENG.). 2005. audio compact disk 44.95 (978-1-59397-488-6(4)) Pub: Macmill Audio. Dist(s): Macmillan

Jupiter in Pisces Nineteen Eighty-Six to Nineteen Eighty-Seven. Greg Konrad. 1 cass. 8.95 (549) Am Fed Astrologers.
Esoteric & exoteric - what to expect.

Jupiter-Saturn Opposition. Stephanie Clement. 1 cass. 8.95 (752) Am Fed Astrologers.

Jupiter's Bones. abr. ed. Faye Kellerman. Read by Jordan Lage. (Peter Decker & Rina Lazarus Novel Ser.). 2004. 15.95 (978-0-7435-4910-3(4)) Pub: S&S Audio. Dist(s): S and S Inc

Jupiter's Bones. unabr. ed. Faye Kellerman. Read by Norman Dietz. 12 vols. (Running Time: 18 hrs.). (Peter Decker & Rina Lazarus Novel Ser.). 2000. bk. 96.95 (978-0-7927-2370-7(8), CSL 259, Chivers Sound Lib) AudioGO.
Dr. Emil Euler Ganz was considered as eminent astrophysicist, a world renowned professor with a brilliant reputation. Then, without warning, he vanished. After ten years, he suddenly reappeared as "Father Jupiter," founder of a pseudoscientific cult - the Order of Rings of God. For fifteen years he ruled hundreds of disciples with spiritual words & an iron fist. Now Ganz is found dead, a fifth of vodka & a vial of pills by his bedside.

Jurisprudence. Jeremy M. Miller. 4 cass. (Running Time: 5 hrs. 45 mins.). (Outstanding Professors Ser.). 1996. 63.00 (978-0-940366-78-7(9), 28416) West.
Lecture given by a prominent American law school professor.

Jurisprudence. 2nd ed. Jeremy M. Miller. 1 cass. 1999. 49.95 (978-0-314-24220-4(1)) Sum & Substance.

Juror. George Dawes Green. 1999. (978-1-57042-780-0(1)) Hachet Audio.

Juror. abr. ed. George Dawes Green. Read by Lolita Davidovich & Jonathan Heard. (Running Time: 3 hrs.). (ENG.). 2009. 14.98 (978-1-60024-671-5(0)) Pub: Hachet Audio. Dist(s): HachBkGrp

Juror. abr. ed. George Dawes Green. Read by Lolita Davidovich & John Heard. (Running Time: 3 hrs.). (ENG.). 2009. audio compact disk 16.98 (978-1-60024-670-8(2)) Pub: Hachet Audio. Dist(s): HachBkGrp

Juror. abr. ed. George Dawes Green. Read by Lolita Davidovich & John Heard. (YA). 2001. 7.95 (978-1-57815-218-6(6), Media Bks Audio); audio compact disk 11.99 (978-1-57815-540-8(1), Media Bks Audio) Media Bks NJ.

Juror. unabr. ed. George Dawes Green. Read by William Dufris. 8 cass. 1997. 69.95 Set. (960307) Eye Ear.
Single mother Annie Laird makes a huge mistake when she joins the jury at the murder trial of mob boss Louie Buffano. Immediately, Annie is contacted by the "Teacher", a Buffano lackey, who makes it clear that her life, & that of her son Oliver, depend on her saying two words: "Not Guilty".

Juror. unabr. ed. George Dawes Green. Read by William Dufris. 8 cass. (Running Time: 12 hrs.). (Isis Cassettes Ser.). 1999. 69.95 (978-0-7531-0043-1(6), 960307) Pub: ISIS Audio GBR. Dist(s): Ulverscroft US

Juror, unabr. ed. George Dawes Green. Read by William Dufris. 10 CDs. (Running Time: 11 hrs. 45 min.). 1999. audio compact disk 99.95 (978-0-7531-0709-6(0), 107090) Pub: ISIS Audio GBR. Dist(s): Ulverscroft US

Jury. Fern Michaels. (Sisterhood Ser: No. 4). (978-0-671-31103-2(4), Free Pr) S and S.

Jury. abr. ed Steve Martini. (Paul Madriani Ser.: No. 6). 2006. 18.95 (978-0-7435-6368-0(9), Audioworks) Pub: S&S Audio. Dist(s): S and S Inc

Jury. abr. ed. Fern Michaels. Read by Laural Merlington. (Running Time: 10800 sec.). (Sisterhood Ser.: No. 4). 2007. audio compact disk 14.99 (978-1-59737-569-6(1), 9781597375696, BCD Value Price) Brilliance Audio.
Please enter a Synopsis.

Jury. unabr. ed. Steve Martini. Read by William Dufris. 6 vols. (Running Time: 9 hrs.). (Paul Madriani Ser.: No. 6). 2001. bk. 54.95 (978-0-7927-2485-8(2), CSL 374, Chivers Sound Lib); audio compact disk 79.95 (978-0-7927-9933-7(X), SLD 084, Chivers Sound Lib) AudioGO.
Paul Madriani has ample reason to suspect he's representing a guilty man. Dr. David Crone has been charged with the murder of a young colleague: twenty-six year-old Kalista Jordan. When a key witness for the prosecution ends up dead, leaving an incriminating note behind, Crone's acquittal seems certain. But Madriani is left with nagging doubts about his clients - doubts that are answered with a stunning revelation and a shattering climax.

Jury. unabr. ed. Fern Michaels. Read by Laural Merlington. (Running Time: 7 hrs.). (Sisterhood Ser.: No. 4). 2006. 39.25 (978-1-59737-567-2(5), 9781597375672, BADLE); 24.95 (978-1-59737-566-5(7), 9781597375665, BAD); 69.25 (978-1-59737-561-0(6), 9781597375610, BrilAudUnabridg); audio compact disk 82.25 (978-1-59737-563-4(2), 9781597375634, BriAudCD Unabrid); audio compact disk 39.25 (978-1-59737-565-8(9), 9781597375658, Brlnc Audio MP3 Lib); audio compact disk 24.95 (978-1-59737-564-1(0), 9781597375641, Brilliance MP3); audio compact disk 29.95 (978-1-59737-562-7(4), 9781597375627, Bril Audio CD Unabri) Brilliance Audio.
Please enter a Synopsis.

Jury: The People vs. Juan Corona. unabr. collector's ed. Victor Villaseñor. Read by Michael Prichard. 7 cass. (Running Time: 10 hrs. 30 min.). 1996. 56.00 (978-0-7366-3395-6(2), 4043) Books on Tape.
People move to places like Yuba City, California to avoid what happened there. In 1973, the D.A. indicted Juan Corona, a farm labor contractor, for the murder of 25 victims. The evidence bodies & parts thereof was ghastly & seemingly convincing.

Jury of One. unabr. ed. David Ellis. Read by Sandra Burr. 9 cass. (Running Time: 13 hrs.). 2004. 34.95 (978-1-59086-769-3(6), 1590867696, BAU); 92.25 (978-1-59086-770-9(X), 159086770X, CD Unabrid Lib Ed) Brilliance Audio.
In Jury of One, Shelly Trotter, an able and determined lawyer and a children's rights advocate, is thrust into a world in which she's completely unschooled - the criminal court. Her client is a seventeen-year-old accused of killing a policeman, and she begins to suspect that he may have been involved in an undercover operation to entrap dirty cops, though his role in the scheme remains unclear. Was he the target or the bait-and what does the prosecution really have against him? Then comes the shocker: Shelly fears that she has a connection to this boy, something she has kept secret for years, knowledge that she has hidden from her family and friends for most of her adult life. And as the evidence against the boy mounts, she finds that nothing - not legal ethics, not a statewide political campaign that

could swing in the balance-will stop her from keeping him off death row. For with this client, she is truly a jury of one.

Jury of One. unabr. ed. David Ellis. Read by Sandra Burr. (Running Time: 13 hrs.). 2004. 39.25 (978-1-59335-542-5(4), 1593355424, Brlnc Audio MP3 Lib); 24.95 (978-1-59335-283-7(2), 1593352832, Brilliance MP3) Brilliance Audio.

Jury of One. unabr. ed. David Ellis. Read by Sandra Burr. (Running Time: 13 hrs.). 2004. 39.25 (978-1-59710-407-4(8), 1597104078, BADLE); 24.95 (978-1-59710-406-7(X), 159710406X, BAD) Brilliance Audio.

Jury of Six. unabr. ed. Matt Braun. Narrated by Richard Ferrone. 5 cass. (Running Time: 6 hrs. 30 mins.). 1999. 44.00 (978-0-7887-0397-3(8), 94589E7) Recorded Bks.

When hardened range detective Luke Starbuck joins an uneasy Sheriff Pat Garrett to track down Billy the Kid's dangerous trail, they gallop toward a conclusion no one can predict.

Jury Selection. Irving Younger. Read by Irving Younger. 3 cass. (Running Time: 3 hrs.). 1985. pap. bk. 70.00 Set. (978-0-943380-41-4(3)) PEG MN.

The process of jury selection.

Jury Selection. Speeches. Perf. by Irving Younger. Created by Irving Younger. 2 CDs. (Running Time: 3 hours). 2004. pap. bk. 199.00 (978-1-932831-02-3(9)) PEG MN.

Jury Selection & Opening Techniques. Perry S. Bechtle. 1 cass. (Running Time: 1 hr.). 1985. 20.00 PA Bar Inst.

***Just a Classic Minute, Vol. 7.** Created by Ian Messiter. Narrated by Full Cast. (Running Time: 2 hrs. 0 mins. 0 sec.). (ENG.). 2010. audio compact disk 24.95 (978-1-4084-6736-7(4)) Pub: AudioGO. Dist(s): Perseus Dist

Just a Closer Walk with Thee, Level 2. (Yamaha Clavinova Connection Ser.). 2004. disk 0.82 (978-0-634-09590-0(0)) H Leonard.

Just a Corpse at Twilight. unabr. ed. Janwillem Van de Wetering. Narrated by George Guidall. 5 cass. (Running Time: 6 hrs. 45 mins.). (Grijpstra & DeGier Mystery Ser.). 1998. 44.00 (978-0-7887-2181-6(X), 95477E7) Recorded Bks.

Henk Brijpstra is pulled into a case that threatens to ruin his best friend & colleague, Rinus DeGier.

Just a Few Words, Mr Lincoln. 2004. pap. bk. 18.95 (978-1-55592-437-9(9)); pap. bk. 38.75 (978-1-55592-438-6(7)); 8.95 (978-1-55592-998-5(2)); audio compact disk 12.95 (978-1-55592-915-2(X)) Weston Woods.

Just a Few Words Mr Lincoln. 2004. pap. bk. 32.75 (978-1-55592-352-5(6)); pap. bk. 14.95 (978-1-55592-045-6(4)) Weston Woods.

Just a Few Words, Mr. Lincoln: The Story of the Gettysburg Address. Jean Fritz. Illus. by Charles Robinson. Narrated by Rex Robbins. 1 cass., 5 bks. (Running Time: 1 hr.). pap. bk. 32.75 Weston Woods.

Describes the President's burdens of office, his devotion to his young son & the significance of the brief declamation dedicating the dead of battle to the survival of the union.

Just a Few Words, Mr. Lincoln: The Story of the Gettysburg Address. Jean Fritz. Illus. by Charles Robinson. Narrated by Rex Robbins. 1 cass. (Running Time: 1 hr.). (J). pap. bk. 12.95 Weston Woods.

Just a Guy: Notes from a Blue Collar Life. abr. ed. Bill Engvall. (Running Time: 12600 sec.). (ENG.). 2007. audio compact disk 19.95 (978-1-4272-0114-0(5)) Pub: Macmill Audio. Dist(s): Macmillan

Just a Guy: Notes from a Blue Collar Life. unabr. ed. Bill Engvall. Read by Bill Engvall. (Running Time: 23400 sec.). (ENG.). 2007. audio compact disk 29.95 (978-1-4272-0116-4(1)) Pub: Macmill Audio. Dist(s): Macmillan

Just a Handful: Poems of Rare & Endangered Wildlife. unabr. ed. Poems. Elizabeth Barchas. Illus. by Elizabeth Barchas. 1 cass. (Running Time: 11 min.). (J). (gr. 5-10). 1995. pap. bk. 9.95 (978-0-9632621-5-8(7)) High Haven Mus.

Includes eight original poems & piano music by a talented teenager.

***Just a Horse of Mine.** Alan LeMay. 2009. (978-1-60136-394-7(X)) Audio Holding.

Just a Horse of Mine. Alan LeMay. (Running Time: 0 hr. 30 mins.). 2000. 10.95 (978-1-60083-523-0(6)) Iofy Corp.

Just a Kiss Away. abr. ed. Jill Barnett. Read by Sherilynn Cooke. 1 cass. (Running Time: 90 min.). 1996. 6.99 (978-1-57096-042-0(9), RAZ 943) Romance Alive Audio.

When pampered Southern Belle Eulalie "Lollie" Grace LaRue finds herself caught in the middle of a revolution on a lush Pacific island, only rugged soldier of fortune Sam Forester can protect her. But can he protect himself from the madcap blonde beauty & the growing attraction between them?.

Just a Little Bit More Positive. unabr. ed. Read by Bob Richards. 1 cass. (Running Time: 30 min.). 15.00 B R Motivational.

A recorded live speech by Bob Richards telling stories of great Olympic athletes who had to overcome weaknesses & changed them into their most powerful force in winning.

Just a Little Rainbow. Bodie Wagner. (J). 1989. audio compact disk 14.95 (978-0-939065-70-7(3)) Gentle Wind.

Just a Little Rainbow. Bodie Wagner. 1 cass. (Running Time: 36 min.). (J). (ps-3). 1989. 9.95 (978-0-939065-49-3(5), GW1053) Gentle Wind.

With horns & whistlers & a chuckle in his voice Bodie Wagner's songs invite children to sing & laugh along. Includes a heartwarming short story about the dreamtime friendship between a sleeping child & a very young dragon who flies on a feather.

Just a Nickle. Perf. by Ray Milland. 1954. (MM-5135) Natl Recrd Co.

Just a Saying. Catherine Cookson. Read by Anne Dover. 2 cass. (Running Time: 1 hr. 30 mins.). (Soundings Ser.). (J). 2004. 24.95 (978-1-84283-540-1(8)); audio compact disk 34.95 (978-1-84283-588-3(2)) Pub: ISIS Lrg Prnt GBR. Dist(s): Ulverscroft US

Just a Smack at Auden see Twentieth-Century Poetry in English: Recordings of Poets Reading Their Own Poetry

Just a Tiny Baby - ShowTrax. John Jacobson & John Higgins. 1 CD. 2000. audio compact disk 19.95 (09970204) H Leonard.

A gentle calypso flavors this easily-learned Christmas original. Features simple choreography & is offered.

Just above a Whisper. unabr. ed. Lori Wick. Read by Barbara Rosenblat. (Running Time: 28800 sec.). (Tucker Mills Trilogy). 2006. audio compact disk 63.00 (978-0-7861-6331-1(3)) Blckstn Audio.

Just above a Whisper. unabr. ed. Lori Wick. Narrated by Barbara Rosenblat. (Tucker Mills Trilogy). (ENG.). 2005. 17.49 (978-1-60814-264-4(7)); audio compact disk 25.99 (978-1-59859-080-7(4)) Oasis Audio.

Just above My Head. James Baldwin. Read by James Baldwin. 1 cass. (Running Time: 47 min.). 10.95 (978-1-55644-093-9(6), 4021) Am Audio Prose.

Just after Sunset. unabr. ed. Stephen King. Read by Stephen King. (Running Time: 14 hrs. 45 mins.). 2009. 61.75 (978-1-4361-9249-1(8)); 113.75 (978-1-4361-7828-0(2)); audio compact disk 123.75 (978-1-4361-7829-7(0)) Recorded Bks.

Just after Sunset. unabr. ed. Stephen King. Read by Stephen King. Read by Jill Eikenberry et al. 13 CDs. (Running Time: 15 hrs. 0 mins. 0 sec.). (ENG.). 2008. audio compact disk 49.99 (978-0-7435-7531-7(8)) Pub: S&S Audio. Dist(s): S and S Inc

Just after Sunset. unabr. collector's ed. Stephen King. Read by Stephen King. 13 CDs. (Running Time: 14 hrs. 45 mins.). 2009. audio compact disk 49.95 (978-1-4361-7830-3(4)) Recorded Bks.

Just Americans: How Japanese Americans Won a War at Home & Abroad. unabr. ed. Robert Asahina. Read by Patrick G. Lawlor. (Running Time: 10 hrs. 30 mins. 0 sec.). (ENG.). 2006. audio compact disk 24.99 (978-1-4001-5281-0(X)); audio compact disk 34.99 (978-1-4001-0281-5(2)); audio compact disk 69.99 (978-1-4001-3281-2(9)) Pub: Tantor Media. Dist(s): IngramPubServ

Just Annoying! Andy Griffiths. Read by Stig Wemyss. (Running Time: 2 hrs. 43 mins.). (J). 2009. 54.99 (978-1-74214-391-0(1), 9781742143910) Pub: Bolinda Pubng AUS. Dist(s): Bolinda Pub Inc

Just Annoying! unabr. ed. Andy Griffiths. Read by Stig Wemyss. 2 cass. (Running Time: 2 hrs. 43 mins.). (J). 2000. 24.00 (978-1-74030-206-7(0), 500850) Pub: Bolinda Pubng AUS. Dist(s): Bolinda Pub Inc

Just Annoying! unabr. ed. Andy Griffiths. Read by Stig Wemyss. 3 CDs. (Running Time: 2 hrs. 43 mins.). (J). 2003. audio compact disk 54.95 (978-1-74030-882-3(4)) Pub: Bolinda Pubng AUS. Dist(s): Bolinda Pub Inc

Just Another Angel. unabr. ed. Mike Ripley. Read by Raymond Sawyer. 6 cass. (Running Time: 8 hrs.). (Isis Ser.). (J). 2000. 54.95 (978-0-7531-0660-0(4), 990714) Pub: ISIS Lrg Prnt GBR. Dist(s): Ulverscroft US

Rule of Life No. 477: When a woman admits that it's difficult for her to ask for something, leave immediately. Forgetting his own good advice, trumpet-player Angel (christened Fitzroy Maclean Angel) agrees to help the enigmatic Jo Scamp, a lady of brief but intimate acquaintance. What begins with a simple recovery of stolen jewelry develops into violence involving a deranged London gangster & a policeman with a vendetta. The first of Mike Ripley's Angel books, successfully establishing the sharp & genuinely funny series.

Just as I Am. Contrib. by David Phelps. (Praise Hymn Soundtracks Ser.). 2004. audio compact disk 8.98 (978-5-559-68500-7(3)) Pt of Grace Ent.

Just As I Am. abr. ed. Billy Graham. Read by Cliff Barrows. 2004. audio compact disk 19.95 (978-0-06-058485-6(8)) HarperCollins Pubs.

***Just As I Am.** abr. ed. Billy Graham. Read by Cliff Barrows. (ENG.). 2004. (978-0-06-075418-1(4), Harper Audio); (978-0-06-081789-3(5), Harper Audio) HarperCollins Pubs.

Just As I Am: The Autobiography of Billy Graham. Billy Graham. Read by Jonathan Reese. 20 cass. (Running Time: 30 hrs.). 1997. 160.00 (978-0-7366-3715-2(X), 4399-A/B) Books on Tape.

America's most famous preacher reflects on his career, from its beginnings to his associations with the presidents.

Just As I Am: The Autobiography of Billy Graham. unabr. ed. Billy Graham. Read by Jonathan Reese. 11 cass. (Running Time: 16 hrs. 30 mins.). 1997. 88.00 (4399-A); 72.00 (4399-B) Books on Tape.

Now, at age seventy-eight, Billy Graham looks back on his life in the pulpit, before the cameras, & in the hearts of Americans from coast to coast.

Just Be. Tanya L. Weiker & Heidi M. Weiker. Voice by Linda Miller. (Running Time: 5040 sec.). 2007. audio compact disk 17.99 (978-1-60462-071-9(4)) Tate Pubng.

Just Be Yourself. Michael D. Christensen. 1 cass. 1997. 9.95 (978-1-57008-344-0(4), Bkcraft Inc); audio compact disk 14.95 CD. (978-1-57008-360-0(6), Bkcraft Inc) Deseret Bk.

Just Be Yourself! Ella the Elegant Elephant; Ruby the Copycat; Bad Case of Stripes. unabr. ed. Carmela D'Amico et al. Read by Diana Canova et al. (J). 2007. 34.99 (978-1-60252-910-6(8)) Find a World.

Just Be Yourself: Music for Children. Diana Carter Coates. 1 cass. (J). 1998. 14.99 Edna.

Original educational children's music.

Just Beethoven. MTL Staff. Illus. by Kathleen Francour. (Flitterbyes Classical Masterpieces Ser.). (ENG.). (J). 2003. audio compact disk 6.95 (978-1-59125-406-5(X)) Penton Overseas.

Just Beethoven Classical Masterpieces. Penton. (ENG.). 2004. audio compact disk (978-1-59125-397-6(7)) Penton Overseas.

Just Between Ourselves. unabr. ed. Alan Ayckbourn. Perf. by Alfred Molina et al. 1 cass. (Running Time: 1 hr. 33 mins.). 2000. 20.95 (978-1-58081-166-8(3), TPT142) L A Theatre.

Just Breathe. abr. ed. Susan Wiggs. Read by Sandra Burr. (Running Time: 6 hrs.). 2009. audio compact disk 14.99 (978-1-4233-5193-1(2), 9781423351931) Brilliance Audio.

Just Breathe. unabr. ed. Susan Wiggs. Read by Sandra Burr. 1 MP3-CD. (Running Time: 14 hrs.). 2008. 39.25 (978-1-4233-5189-4(4), 9781423351894, Brlnc Audio MP3 Lib); 39.25 (978-1-4233-5191-7(6), 9781423351917, BADLE); 24.95 (978-1-4233-5190-0(8), 9781423351900, BAD); 24.95 (978-1-4233-5188-7(6), 9781423351887, Brilliance MP3); audio compact disk 107.25 (978-1-4233-5187-0(8), 9781423351870, BriAudCD Unabrid); audio compact disk 31.99 (978-1-4233-5186-3(X), 9781423351863, Bril Audio CD Unabri) Brilliance Audio.

Just Breathe: An Abridged Audio Book with Exercises. Weston Jolly. Read by Weston Jolly. 1 CD. (Running Time: 50 mins.). 2003. audio compact disk 15.95 (978-0-9701207-8-6(8)) Age of Aware.

An awe inspiring dialog from Heaven about the remembrance of breath and your direct connection with the Divine. Weston Jolly shares an intimate conversation with God about the power of breath.

Just by Your Mercy: 25 Ageless Psalms for Life's Journey. Contrib. by Rick Brown & Tom Calvani. Prod. by Eric Wyse & Brenda Boswell. 2006. audio compact disk 15.95 (978-1-59856-266-8(5)); audio compact disk 11.97 (978-1-59856-603-1(2)) Hendrickson MA.

Just Call Me Angel, Set. Dan Yates & Anita Stansfield. 2 cass. 1996. 11.98 Set. (978-1-55503-980-6(4), 07001398) Covenant Comms.

When angels start matchmaking, there's no telling what will happen.

Just Call Me Stupid, unabr. ed. Tom Birdseye. Narrated by Johnny Heller. 3 pieces. (Running Time: 4 hrs.). (gr. 4 up). 1997. 27.00 (978-0-7887-0680-6(2), 94852E7) Recorded Bks.

Heartwarming story of a fifth-grade boy who begins to overcome his reading disability with the help of a wise friend.

Just Cause. John Katzenbach. 2004. 10.95 (978-0-7435-4911-0(2)) Pub: S&S Audio. Dist(s): S and S Inc

Just Courage. unabr. ed. Gary Haugen. (Running Time: 3 hrs. 18 mins. 0 sec.). (ENG.). 2009. audio compact disk 18.98 (978-1-59644-811-7(3)) christianaud.

***Just Courage: God's Great Expedition for the Restless Chrisitan.** unabr. ed. Gary A. Haugen. Narrated by Dave Heath. (ENG.). 2009. 10.98 (978-1-59644-812-4(1), christianSeed) christianaud.

***Just Crazy!** unabr. ed. Andy Griffiths. (Running Time: 3 hrs. 30 mins.). (J). 2003. audio compact disk 28.00 (978-1-74030-889-2(1)) Pub: Bolinda Pubng AUS. Dist(s): Bolinda Pub Inc

***Just Disgusting!** unabr. ed. Andy Griffiths. (Running Time: 3 hrs.). (J). 2003. audio compact disk 54.95 (978-1-74030-890-8(5)) Pub: Bolinda Pubng AUS. Dist(s): Bolinda Pub Inc

***Just Do Something: How to Make a Decision Without Dreams, Visions, Fleeces, Open Doors, Random Bible Verses, Casting Lo.** unabr. ed. Kevin DeYoung. Narrated by Adam Verner. (ENG.). 2010. 9.98 (978-1-59644-869-8(5)) christianaud.

***Just Do Something: How to Make a Decision Without Dreams, Visions, Fleeces, Open Doors, Random Bible Verses, Casting Lots, Liver Shivers, Writing in the Sky, Etc.** unabr. ed. Kevin DeYoung. Narrated by Adam Verner. (Running Time: 2 hrs. 45 mins. 0 sec.). (ENG.). 2010. audio compact disk 15.98 (978-1-59644-868-1(7)) christianaud.

Just Ella. Margaret Peterson Haddix. Read by Alyssa Bresnahan. 4 cass. (Running Time: 5 hrs. 15 mins.). (J). 2000. pap. bk. & stu. ed. 61.00 (978-0-7887-4337-5(6), 41132) Recorded Bks.

Junie B. Jones knows she shouldn't spy on people, even though it is lots of fun. So when she spies on Mrs., her kindergarten teacher, Junie B. ends up a big problem. As the world's funniest (& most curious) kindergartner, Junie B. has fans of all ages laughing out loud.

Just Ella. unabr. ed. Margaret Peterson Haddix. Narrated by Alyssa Bresnahan. 4 pieces. (Running Time: 5 hrs. 15 mins.). (gr. 7 up). 2000. 37.00 (978-0-7887-4248-4(5), 96216E7) Recorded Bks.

Just Ella, Class set. unabr. ed. Margaret Peterson Haddix. Read by Alyssa Bresnahan. 4 cass. (Running Time: 5 hrs. 15 mins.). (YA). (gr. 7 up). 2000. pap. bk. 215.30 (978-0-7887-4438-9(0), 47129) Recorded Bks.

In this continuation of the Cinderella story, Ella has gotten what she wanted by taking control of her own destiny. But now she has serious doubts about what "happily" really means.

Just Enough Light for the Step I'm On: Trusting God in the Tough Times. abr. ed. Stormie Omartian. Read by Stormie Omartian. (Running Time: 12600 sec.). 2008. audio compact disk 18.99 (978-0-7369-2458-0(2)) Harvest Hse.

Just Folks: A Firesign Chat. Perf. by Firesign Theatre. Text by Firesign Theatre. 1 CD. (Running Time: 39 mins). Dramatization. 2005. audio compact disk 15.95 (978-1-59938-025-4(0)) Lode Cat.

It's 1977. James Earl (Jimmy) Carter has been elected, and he will soon be sworn in as the 39th President of the United States. The Firesign Theatre (fresh off their own Surrealist Party campoon) takes on the task of welcoming the new President and introducing him to the residents of his new home, DuCktown, USA, which is inhabited by the usual unusual Firesign characters, from drunkards to truckers, and from TV hosts to rocket scientists. Join Peggy Blisswhips, Peter Protector, Mutt N Smut, Wernor Von Hardhat, Little Guy - Bill Collector, and Ben Bland (and his all day matinee), plus, the occasional Indian, who is passed around for good measure.

Just for Laughs. unabr. ed. Terry Gross. (ENG.). 2010. audio compact disk 24.95 (978-1-59887-897-4(2), 1598878972) Pub: HighBridge. Dist(s): Workman Pub

Just for Newborns. Eldon Taylor. 1 cass. (Running Time: 62 min.). (Inner Talk Ser.). 16.95 incl. script. (978-1-55978-134-3(3), 5349C) Progress Aware Res.

Soundtrack - Musical Themes with underlying subliminal affirmations.

Just for Newborns: Babbling Brook. Eldon Taylor. 1 cass. 16.95 (978-1-55978-480-1(6), 5349F) Progress Aware Res.

Just for the Summer. unabr. ed. Judy Astley. Read by Rachel Atkins. 6 cass. (Running Time: 9 hrs.). 2000. 54.95 (978-0-7531-0842-0(9), 000406) Pub: ISIS Audio GBR. Dist(s): Ulverscroft US

Clare is more than usually ready for her vacation in Cornwall. Her teenage daughter, Miranda, has been behaving strangely; her husband, Jack, is wanting a change in lifestyle; her small children are tiresome; & she herself is contemplating a bit of extra-marital adventure with Eliot, the overweight author in the adjoining holiday property.

Just for the Summer. unabr. ed. Judy Astley. Read by Rachel Atkins. 6 CDs. (Running Time: 25200 sec.). (Isis (CDs) Ser.). 2006. audio compact disk 64.95 (978-0-7531-2508-3(0)) Pub: ISIS Lrg Prnt GBR. Dist(s): Ulverscroft US

Just for Women: Keys to Effective Communication. unabr. ed. Andrea Nierenberg. 4 cass. (Running Time: 4 hrs.). 1999. 22.00 (978-1-879755-10-9(6)) Recorded Pubns.

Presents a strategy for self empowerment, self esteem, motivation, networking, presentation skills & self marketing.

Just for You, Bks. 1-3. Perf. by Dennis Alexander. 1 CD. (ENG.). 1999. audio compact disk 10.95 (978-0-7390-0347-3(X), 16457) Alfred Pub.

Just for You & Me. William Smith. (Running Time: 60 min.). 2002. audio compact disk 16.98 (978-0-9727644-9-0(6)) Pub: Pt of Grace Ent. Dist(s): STL Dist NA

Just for You & Me. William Smith & Renew Voices For Christ. (Running Time: 1 hr.). 2003. audio compact disk 16.98 (978-5-552-54296-3(7)) Pub: Pt of Grace Ent. Dist(s): STL Dist NA

Just Give Up: A Simple Guide to Spiritual Surrender. Scott Morrison. 1 cass. (Running Time: 1 hr.). 1998. 7.50 (978-1-882496-13-6(2)) Twnty Frst Cntry Ren.

A nuts & bolts explanation of what is involved in the process of giving yourself wholeheartedly to the awakened life.

Just Good Friends, Level 3. Penny Hancock. Contrib. by Philip Prowse. (Running Time: 1 hr. 52 mins.). (Cambridge English Readers Ser.). (ENG.). 2000. 15.75 (978-0-521-77532-8(9)) Cambridge U Pr.

Just Having Church: Live. Contrib. by Chicago Mass Choir. 2007. audio compact disk 16.98 (978-5-557-63537-0(8)) Pt of Grace Ent.

Just Heaven Fun. Perf. by Robert G. Lee. Prod. by Randy Ray. 1 cass. (Running Time: 60 min.). 1995. 9.98 (978-1-57919-072-9(3)) Randolf Prod.

Stand up comedy.

Just Hold Me! Embraced by the Savior's Love. Don H. Staheli. 1 CD. 2004. audio compact disk 12.95 (978-1-59038-392-6(3)) Deseret Bk.

What is there about a hug, about being held close by one whose affection we crave, that mans so much to us? An embrace can erase fear, overcome anger, heal hearts, and foster love. And while we generally think of a hug as being a physical gesture of affection, the author points out that a true embrace encoimpasses much more. Just Hold Me! offers a unique look at an age-old custom and discusses some of the ways we experience "hugs" in both a physical and spiritual sense. With wonderful insights and practical appliations, this book on CD reminds us that when times are difficult we cna turn to the Savior's embrace.

Just Imagine. Susan Elizabeth Phillips. Narrated by Cristine McMurdo-Wallis. 10 CDs. (Running Time: 11 hrs. 30 mins.). audio compact disk 97.00 (978-1-4025-2909-2(0)) Recorded Bks.

Just Imagine. unabr. ed. Susan Elizabeth Phillips. Narrated by Cristine McMurdo-Wallis. 8 cass. (Running Time: 11 hrs. 30 mins.). 2002. 79.00 (978-0-7887-9582-4(1), L1022) Recorded Bks.

A spirited young woman, Kit Weston has lost her southern home and family in the war. Baron Cain, a northerner, now owns her beloved plantation Risen Glory. Kit would like to murder him. But since she is an orphan, much to her

horror, he is appointed as her guardian. Both are headstrong and independent, yet there is a powerful attraction between them. The war between their wills - and their hearts - is just beginning.

Just in Case: The Y2K Crisis. Perf. by Will McCracken. Contrib. by Barbara Stahura & Robert Yehling. 1 cass. pap. bk. (978-0-9668938-8-5(3)) Your Hometown.
Straight talk about the problems & potentials in the Y2K computer crisis.

Just in Time. abr. ed. AIO Team Staff. Created by Focus on the Family Staff & Marshal Younger. 4 cass. (Adventures in Odyssey Gold Ser.). (ENG.). (J). (gr. 3-7). 2005. audio compact disk 24.99 (978-1-58997-076-2(4)) Pub: Focus Family. Dist(s): Tyndale Hse

Just in Time (from Bells Are Ringing) - ShowTrax. Music by Jule Styne. Arranged by Steve Zegree. 1 CD. (Running Time: 5 mins.). 2000. audio compact disk 19.95 (08741755) H Leonard.
Styne's great standard in a medium swing with lots of tasty vocal jazz surprises.

Just Jazz: Live at the Blue Note. Perf. by Lionel Hampton. 1 cass., 1 CD. 7.98 (TA 33313); audio compact disk 12.78 CD Jewel box. (TA 83313) NewSound.

Just Joking! unabr. ed. Andy Griffiths. Read by Stig Wemyss. 2 cass. (Running Time: 2 hrs. 20 mins.). (J). 2004. 24.00 (978-1-876584-97-9(1), 591010) Bolinda Pubng AUS.
Andy Griffiths discovered at an early age he had a talent for annoying his parents. Since then he has gone on to annoy many other people - including family, friends, neighbors, teachers and complete strangers - with his silly noises, idiotic questions, stupid comments, bad jokes, pointless stories and inappropriate behavior.

***Just Kate.** unabr. ed. Linda Lael Miller. (Running Time: 8 hrs.). 2011. audio compact disk 19.99 (978-1-4418-7117-6(9), 9781441871176, Bril Audio CD Unabri) Brilliance Audio.

Just Like a Movie, Level 1. Sue Leather. Contrib. by Philip Prowse. 1 cass. (Running Time: 34 mins.). (Cambridge English Readers Ser.). (ENG.). 2000. 9.45 (978-0-521-78814-4(5)) Cambridge U Pr.

Just Like a Tree see Bloodline

Just Like a Woman: Stories by Leslea Newman. Lesleá Newman. Read by Lesleá Newman. 2 cass. (Running Time: 3 hrs.). 2001. 18.00 (978-0-9702152-3-9(1)) Fluid Wds.

Just Like Jesus for Tweens. unabr. ed. Max Lucado. Narrated by Brian Keeler. 4 cass. (Running Time: 6 hrs.). 2001. 42.00 (978-0-7887-5144-8(1), K0032E7) Recorded Bks.
Good news to comfort & challenge you, by revealing how God loves you just the way you are even if you were born with a sour outlook or are consumed with worry.

***Just Like Us: The True Story of Four Mexican Girls Coming of Age in America.** Helen Thorpe. (ENG.). 2010. audio compact disk 39.99 (978-1-61120-014-0(8)) Dreamscap OH.

Just Listen. unabr. ed. Sarah Dessen. Read by Jennifer Ikeda. 10 CDs. (Running Time: 12 hrs.). (YA). 2006. audio compact disk 104.75 (978-1-4193-9440-9(1), C3730); 85.75 (978-1-4193-9435-5(5), 98375) Recorded Bks.
Garnering five ALA Best Book for Young Adult honors with her first five novels, Sara Dessen delivers the bittersweet story of a dissatisfied model and the offbeat guy who teaches her that only truth can set her free. As her beautiful, self-assured image flashes across the TV screen, Annabel Greene is the ideal 17-year-old girl. But the glitter of her commercials is a far cry from Annabel is a social outcast. Can music-obsessed Owen with his commitment to truth convince Annabel to reveal a dark secret and bravely confront reality?.

Just Listen: Live Recordings of the Choir, Orchestra & Ensemble. 1 CD. (YA). (gr. 7). 1999. audio compact disk 10.00 (978-0-88028-215-4(0)) Forward Movement.

Just Listen 'n Learn: Greek. bk. (978-0-318-60134-2(6), Passport Bks) McGraw-Hill Trade.

Just Listen 'n Learn Arabic. Nadira Auty et al. 3 cass. (Running Time: 3 hrs.). 1991. 29.95 Set. (Passport Bks) McGraw-Hill Trade.

Just Listen 'n Learn Business German. Ed. by Brian Hill. 1 cass. (Just Listen N' Learn Ser.). (ENG & GER.). (C). 1995. pap. bk. 32.95 (978-0-8442-9750-7(X), X9750-X, Passport Bks) McGraw-Hill Trade.

Just Listen 'n Learn French Plus. 3 cass. (Running Time: 3 hrs.). 1990. pap. bk. 29.95 (Passport Bks) McGraw-Hill Trade.

Just Listen 'n Learn German. Ed. by Brian Hill. 3 CDs. (Running Time: 3 hrs.). (GER.). 1995. bk. 39.95 (978-0-8442-4659-8(X), Passport Bks) McGraw-Hill Trade.

Just Listen 'n Learn German Plus. 3 cass. (Running Time: 3 hrs.). 1990. 29.95 Set, incl. bklt. (Passport Bks) McGraw-Hill Trade.
This self-study program will increase fluency. Lessons are intensive listening/speaking sessions that stress everyday topics & selections from German radio broadcasts.

Just Listen 'n Learn German Plus. Ed. by Brian Hill. 3 cass. (Running Time: 3 hrs.). 27.00 (Natl Textbk Co) M-H Contemporary.
Second level of practice for intermediate students of German.

Just Listen 'n Learn Spanish Plus. Ed. by Brian Hill. 3 cass. (Running Time: 3 hrs.). 27.00 (Natl Textbk Co) M-H Contemporary.
Focuses on the speaking, listening, & reading skills needed for everyday communication in Spanish.

Just Listen 'n Learn Spanish 2. Brian Hill et al. 1 cass. (Running Time: 30 mins.). 1985. 12.00 (978-0-8442-7512-3(3)) Pub: McGraw-Hill Trade. Dist(s): McGraw

Just Listen to Some of My Poetry 'Fore i Diiie - Jaya Mangelou. Poems. Eric Durchholz. Perf. by Eric Durchholz. 1. (Running Time: 68 mins.). Dramatization. Vol. 1. (C). 2002. audio compact disk 8.95 (978-0-9670297-5-7(9)) Concrete Bks.

Just Live It. Dave Privett. 2002. audio compact disk 15.00 (978-1-58302-210-8(4)) One Way St.

Just Married. unabr. ed. Zoe Barnes. Read by Trudy Harris. 10 cass. (Running Time: 12 hrs. 55 mins.). (Isis Cassettes Ser.). (J). 2004. 84.95 (978-0-7531-1828-3(9)) Pub: ISIS Lrg Prnt GBR. Dist(s): Ulverscroft US

Just Me. 2004. bk. 24.95 (978-0-7882-0555-2(2)); pap. bk. 14.95 (978-0-7882-0620-7(6)); 8.95 (978-1-56008-942-1(3)); cass. & flmstrp 30.00 (978-1-56008-699-4(8)) Weston Woods.

Just Me. unabr. ed. Marie Hall Ets. 1 read-along cass. (Running Time: 9 min.). (J). (ps-4). 9.95 Live Oak Media.
A little boy imitates the movements & actions of the animals on & around his farm home but discovers when he runs to greet his father that, "I ran like nobody else at all. Just me!".

Just Me. unabr. ed. Marie Hall Ets. Illus. by Marie Hall Ets. Read by Linda Terheyden. 11 vols. (Running Time: 9 mins.). (J). (gr. k-3). pap. bk. 15.95 (978-0-941078-73-3(6)) Live Oak Media.

Just Me: What Your Child Wants You to Know about Parenting. Just Jackie. 2006. 16.95 (978-0-9762849-2-5(8)) Pub: One Blue Button. Dist(s): AtlasBooks

***Just Me & the Trees: A Children's Guide to Meditation.** Julia Cohn. Voice by Julia Cohn. Ed. by Geri Hearne. Illus. by Gerarda Connolly. (ENG.). (J). 2010. cd-rom & audio compact disk (978-0-9800954-1-8(7)) Joy Media.

Just Me This Time: John P. Kee. Perf. by John P. Kee. 1 cass., 1 CD. Provident Mus Dist.

Just Men. Randy Smith. 1999. 75.00 (978-0-7673-9726-1(6)); 11.98 (978-0-7673-9715-5(0)); audio compact disk 85.00 (978-0-7673-9725-4(8)); audio compact disk 16.98 (978-0-7673-9706-3(1)); audio compact disk 12.00 (978-0-7673-9657-8(X)) LifeWay Christian.

Just Mozart Classical Masterpieces. Penton. (ENG.). 2003. audio compact disk 6.95 (978-1-59125-398-3(5)) Penton Overseas.

Just One Look. Harlan Coben. Read by Carrington MacDuffie. 2004. audio compact disk 90.00 (978-1-4159-0247-9(X)) Books on Tape.

Just One Step. 1 CD. (Running Time: 45 mins.). 2001. audio compact disk 14.98 Lighthse Recs.

Just One Step. 1 cass. (Running Time: 45 mins.). (J). 2001. 9.98 (978-0-9634024-8-6(X)) Lighthse Recs.

Just One Touch. Perf. by Lori Wilke. 1 cass. (Running Time: 5 min.). 1992. 9.98 Sound track. (978-1-891916-29-8(7)) Spirit To Spirit.

Just One World. Perf. by Mr. AL & Stephen Fite. 1 cass. (J). 10.95 Child Like.

Just Plain Bill see Great Soap Operas: Selected Episodes

Just Plain Folks. abr. ed. Lorraine Johnson-Coleman. (ENG.). 2006. 14.98 (978-1-59483-847-7(X)) Pub: Hachet Audio. Dist(s): HachBkGrp

***Just Plain Foolishness.** unabr. ed. Wanda E. Brunstetter. Read by Ellen Grafton. (Running Time: 3 hrs.). (Rachel Yoder - Always Trouble Somewhere Ser.). 2010. 14.99 (978-1-4418-1192-9(3), 9781441811929, BAD); 39.97 (978-1-4418-1191-2(5), 9781441811912, Brinc Audio MP3 Lib); 39.97 (978-1-4418-1193-6(1), 9781441811936, BADLE); 14.99 (978-1-4418-1190-5(7), 9781441811905, Brilliance MP3); audio compact disk 44.97 (978-1-4418-1189-9(3), 9781441811899, BriAudCD Unabrid); audio compact disk 14.99 (978-1-4418-1188-2(5), 9781441811882, Bril Audio CD Unabri) Brilliance Audio.

Just Relax. Matthew Manning. 1 cass. 11.95 (MM-121) White Dove NM.
Just Relax was recorded after many requests from people who felt that a quick 15 minute relaxation exercise before work would help keep a positive attitude throughout the day. Side One is a relaxation exercise describing a walk through a meadow complete with nature sounds. Side Two is an imaginary walk along the seashore at sunset.

Just Relax: Soothing Deep Relaxation. abr. ed. David Swenson. Perf. by David Swenson. 1 cass. (Running Time: 1 hr.). 10.95 (978-1-891252-07-5(0)) Ashtanga Yoga.

Just Representin' Perf. by Gilbert Esquivel. 2001. audio compact disk 16.98 (978-1-929243-35-8(9)) Uproar Ent.

Just Revenge. abr. ed. Alan M. Dershowitz. 2001. 7.95 (978-1-57815-266-7(6)) Media Bks NJ.

Just Rewards. Barbara Taylor Bradford. Read by Terry Donnelly. 2 CDs. (Emma Harte Ser.: No. 6). 2006. audio compact disk 49.95 (978-0-7927-3955-5(8), CMP 887) AudioGO.

Just Rewards. Barbara Taylor Bradford. Read by Terry Donnelly. 11 CDs. (Running Time: 51000 sec.). (Emma Harte Ser.: No. 6). 2006. audio compact disk 99.95 (978-0-7927-3883-1(7), SLD 887) AudioGO.

Just Rewards. Barbara Taylor Bradford. Read by Terry Donnelly. (Emma Harte Ser.: No. 6). 2006. 23.95 (978-1-59397-880-8(4)) Pub: Macmill Audio. Dist(s): Macmillan

Just Rewards. abr. ed. Barbara Taylor Bradford. Read by Kate Burton. (Running Time: 5 hrs. 0 mins. 0 sec.). (Emma Harte Ser.: No. 6). 2006. 14.95 (978-1-59397-879-2(0)) Pub: Macmill Audio. Dist(s): Macmillan

Just Rewards. unabr. ed. Barbara Taylor Bradford. Read by Terry Donnelly. 11 CDs. (Running Time: 13 hrs. 0 mins. 0 sec.). No. 6. (ENG.). 2006. audio compact disk 39.95 (978-1-55927-802-7(1)) Pub: Macmill Audio. Dist(s): Macmillan

Just Say Meow! Lisa L. Lilly. 1 cass. 9.00 (A0663-90) Sound Photosyn.
Lisa talks with Faustin about everything at once - her body-building days, adopted dad John Lilly, her days with Mapplethorpe, government corruption, global issues, & much more.

Just Say No! A Novel. abr. ed. Omar R. Tyree. 2004. 15.95 (978-0-7435-4914-1(7)) Pub: S&S Audio. Dist(s): S and S Inc

Just Say No! A Novel. unabr. ed. Omar R. Tyree. Read by Bill Quinn. 14 vols. (Running Time: 21 hrs.). 2002. bk. 110.95 (978-0-7927-2522-0(0), CSL 411, Chivers Sound Lib) AudioGO.
Darin Harmon and John Williams have been best friends since they were toddlers. During their sophomore year in college, John showcases his musical genius in a homecoming talent show that changes both their lives forever. As John's R&B career begin, he asks Darin to tag along as his manager. For Darin, dealing with John's rising fame and fortune proves a difficult challenge. The more the two adapt to the dangerous celebrity lifestyle of big money, fast women and recreational drugs, the harder it gets for both of them to "just say no".

Just Say No to Being Cranky: Winning Keys to Emotional Wellness. abr. ed. Perf. by Angela Brown et al. 1 cass. (Running Time: 60 mins.). (Words of Wellness Ser.: Vol. 10). 2000. 14.95 (978-0-9673451-4-7(6), LLP310) Life Long Pubg.
Simple & easy to apply tips anybody can use on how to handle road rage, bad days, disappointments, frustrations & other common lifestyle problems.

Just Say NU: Yiddish for Every Occasion (When English Just Won't Do) abr. unabr. ed. Michael Wex. Read by Michael Wex. (Running Time: 25200 sec.). (ENG.). 2007. audio compact disk 29.95 (978-1-4272-0187-4(0)) Pub: Macmill Audio. Dist(s): Macmillan

Just Say Yes Rap & We're Somebody. Art Fettig. Perf. by Paul Lee Marr. 1 cass. (J). (gr. 4-8). 1992. 5.95 Growth Unltd.
Kids sing along with "Just Say Yes & We're Somebody" tape.

Just Shall Live by Faith. Kenneth Copeland. 11 cass. 1991. 55.00 Set. (978-0-88114-959-3(4)) K Copeland Pubns.
In-depth teaching on faith.

Just Shy of Harmony. Philip Gulley. Narrated by Norman Dietz. 6 CDs. (Running Time: 7 hrs.). 2002. audio compact disk 58.00 (978-1-4025-3814-8(6)) Recorded Bks.

Just Shy of Harmony. unabr. ed. Philip Gulley. Narrated by Norman Dietz. 5 cass. (Running Time: 7 hrs.). 2002. 54.00 (978-1-4025-2723-4(3), RG149) Recorded Bks.
Taking readers into the life of a small midwestern town, Gulley fills this book with quirky and eccentric residents and an extra helping of kindly spirit. Just Shy of Harmony is a beautiful novel of mysteries and miracles. With an entertaining narration by Norman Dietz, both Gulley fans and first-time listeners are in for a real treat.

Just So Stories see Histoires Comme Ca

Just So Stories. Rudyard Kipling. Narrated by Flo Gibson. (ENG.). (J). 2008. audio compact disk 19.95 (978-1-60646-066-5(8)) Audio Bk Con.

Just So Stories. Rudyard Kipling. Contrib. by Shelly Frasier. (ENG.). (J). 2009. 54.99 (978-1-60775-761-0(3)) Find a World.

Just So Stories. Rudyard Kipling. Read by Geoffrey Palmer. (Running Time: 3 hrs. 30 mins.). 2006. 24.95 (978-1-60083-795-1(6)) Iofy Corp.

Just So Stories. Rudyard Kipling. Read by Shelly Frasier. (ENG.). (J). (gr. 4-7). 2003. audio compact disk 52.00 (978-1-4001-3064-1(6)) Pub: Tantor Media. Dist(s): IngramPubServ

Just So Stories. unabr. ed. Rudyard Kipling. Narrated by Shelly Frasier. (Running Time: 3 hrs. 0 mins. 0 sec.). (ENG.). (J). (gr. 4-7). 2008. 17.99 (978-1-4001-5867-6(2)); audio compact disk 17.99 (978-1-4001-0867-1(5)); audio compact disk 35.99 (978-1-4001-3867-8(1)) Pub: Tantor Media. Dist(s): IngramPubServ

Just So Stories. unabr. abr. ed. Rudyard Kipling. Read by Boris Karloff. (J). 2005. audio compact disk 13.95 (978-0-06-078882-7(8), HarperChildAud) HarperCollins Pubs.

Just So Stories: Children's Radio Theatre. Rudyard Kipling. Perf. by Josh Billings et al. Directed By Joan Bellsey. Music by John Ramo & Zenon Slawinski. 1 cass. (Running Time: 51 min.). (J). (gr. 1-6). 1981. 9.95 (978-0-939065-07-3(X), GW 1007) Gentle Wind.
Dramatization of some of Kipling's "Just So Stories" including; "The Crab that Played With the Sea," "How the Rhinoceros Got His Skin," "The Beginning of the Armadillos," "How the Camel Got His Hump".

Just So Stories, Set, For Little Children see Children's Poems & Stories

Just So Stories Set: For Little Children. Rudyard Kipling. Read by Johnny Morris. 3 cass. (Running Time: 3 hrs. 25 min.). (J). (gr. 1 up). 19.95 (CC/005) C to C Cassettes.
Kipling's stories that were written for his three children & were read aloud to them by Kipling.

Just So Stories Set: For Little Children. Rudyard Kipling. Perf. by Children's Radio Theatre Staff. Adapted by Children's Radio Theatre Staff. (Running Time: 52 mins.). (J). 1981. audio compact disk 14.95 (978-0-939065-83-7(5)) Gentle Wind.

Just So Stories Set: For Little Children. Rudyard Kipling. Read by Geoffrey Palmer. 3 cass. (Running Time: 3 hrs. 30 mins.). (J). 2002. 17.98 (978-962-634-750-8(3)) Naxos.
Written in the late 1800s and meant to be read aloud, reveal the author's love of language as an almost musical medium, his deep affection for India, and his refusal to patronize or simplify for the sake of a young audience. This delightful recording presents Kipling's complete collection of enchanting animal tales.

Just So Stories Set: For Little Children. Rudyard Kipling. Read by Geoffrey Palmer. 3 CDs. (Running Time: 3 hrs. 30 mins.). (J). (gr. 3-5). 2002. audio compact disk 22.98 (978-962-634-250-3(1), NA325012) Naxos.

Just So Stories Set: For Little Children. abr. ed. Rudyard Kipling. Narrated by Gene Lockhart. 2 cass. (Running Time: 1 hr. 44 min.). Incl. Cat That Walked by Himself. Rudyard Kipling. (J). (816); Elephant's Child. Rudyard Kipling. (J). (816); How the Camel Got His Hump. Rudyard Kipling. (J). (816); How the Leopard Got His Spots. (J). (816); How the Rhinoceros Got His Skin. Rudyard Kipling. (J). (816); How the Whale Got His Throat. Based on a story by Rudyard Kipling. (J). (816); (J). 12.95 (978-0-89926-128-7(0), 816) Audio Bk.

Just So Stories Set: For Little Children. unabr. ed. Rudyard Kipling. Narrated by Flo Gibson. 3 cass. (Running Time: 4 hrs. 30 min.). (J). 1984. (978-1-55685-058-5(1), 82020) Audio Bk Con.
"How The Whale Got His Throat," "The Elephant's Child," "How The Alphabet Was Made," & "The Butterfly That Stamped" are but a few of these enchanting tales of the dawn of the world.

Just So Stories Set: For Little Children. unabr. ed. Rudyard Kipling. Read by Johnny Morris. 3 cass. (Running Time: 3 hrs.). (J). 1995. 24.95 (978-1-85549-066-6(8), CTC 005, Chivers Child Audio) AudioGO.

Just So Stories Set: For Little Children. unabr. ed. Rudyard Kipling. Read by Johnny Morris. 3 cass. (Running Time: 4 hrs., 30 min.). (J). (gr. 1-8). 1999. 24.95 (CTC 005, Chivers Child Audio) AudioGO.

Just So Stories Set: For Little Children. unabr. ed. Rudyard Kipling. Read by Johanna Ward. 3 cass. (Running Time: 4 hrs.). (J). (gr. 3-5). 1995. 23.95 (978-0-7861-0656-1(5), 1558) Blckstn Audio.
A collection of 12 stories & 12 poems, Kipling wrote "Just So Stories" to be read aloud to children & adults. Its stories involve cats & dogs, kangaroos & tortoises, hedgehogs & jaguars, whales & leopards, & many other beings which are brought to life in an exotic Eastern landscape of "high & far times ago." Drawn from the enchanting tales told to Kipling as a child in India, "Just So Stories" sires the magic of the dawn of the world, when animals could talk & think like people.

Just So Stories Set: For Little Children. unabr. ed. Rudyard Kipling. Read by Laurie Klein. 2 cass. (Running Time: 2 hrs. 30 min.). Dramatization. 1991. 16.95 (978-1-55686-382-0(9), 382) Books in Motion.
Contents include The Elephant's Child, How the Camel Got His Hump, How the Whale Got His Throat, How the Leopard Got His Spots, How the Kangaroo Got His Legs, How the Rhinoceros Got His Skin, The Beginning of the Armadilloes, The Butterfly That Stamped, The Cat That Walked by Himself.

Just So Stories Set: For Little Children. unabr. ed. Rudyard Kipling. Read by Johnny Morris. 1 cass. (Running Time: 1 hr. 30 mins.). (J). 1995. 9.95 (978-1-85549-242-4(3), CTC 107) Pub: Cover To Cover GBR. Dist(s): AudioGO
Some of the stories included here: "How the Camel Got His Hump", "How the Leopard Got His Spots", "The Beginning of the Armadillos", & "The Sing-Song of Old Man Kangaroo".

Just So Stories Set: For Little Children, unabr. ed. Short Stories. Rudyard Kipling. Narrated by Flo Gibson. 3 pieces. (Running Time: 4 hrs. 30 mins.). (gr. 4 up). 1982. 27.00 (978-1-55690-278-9(6), 82020E7) Recorded Bks.
Fantastic fables from the Indian sub-continent including: "How the Elephant Got His Trunk," "The Cat Who Walked by Himself," "The Crab That Played with the Sea" & "How the Camel Got His Hump".

Just So Stories Set: For Little Children. unabr. collector's ed. Rudyard Kipling. Read by Rebecca C. Burns. 3 cass. (Running Time: 3 hrs.). (J). (ps-3). 1997. 28.00 (978-0-7366-3570-7(X), 4220) Books on Tape.
How did the leopard get its spots? These entertaining stories, drawn from the tales Kipling's Indian nurses told to him, answer this question & many more.

Just So Stories Vol. 1: For Little Children. unabr. ed. Rudyard Kipling. Perf. by Christopher Casson et al. (Running Time: 45 min.). Dramatization. (J). 10.95 (978-0-8045-1015-8(6), SAC 1015) Spoken Arts.
Includes "How the Whale Got His Throat," "How the Camel Got His Hump," "How the Rhinoceros Got His Skin" & "The Elephant's Child".

Just So Stories Vol. 2: For Little Children. unabr. ed. Rudyard Kipling. Perf. by Christopher Casson et al. (Running Time: 52 min.). Dramatization. (J). 10.95 (978-0-8045-1016-5(4), SAC 1016) Spoken Arts.
Includes "How the Leopard Got His Spots," "The Sing-Song of Old Man Kangaroo" & "The Beginning of the Armadillos".

Just So Stories Vol. 3: For Little Children. unabr. ed. Rudyard Kipling. Perf. by Christopher Casson et al. (Running Time: 51 min.). Dramatization. (J). 10.95 (978-0-8045-1017-2(2), SAC 1017) Spoken Arts.
The Cat That Walked by Himself, & The Butterfly That Stamped.

Just Stupid! Andy Griffiths. Read by Stig Wemyss. (Running Time: 2 hrs. 45 mins.). (J). 2009. 54.99 (978-1-74214-392-7(X), 9781742143927) Pub: Bolinda Pubng AUS. Dist(s): Bolinda Pub Inc

Just Stupid! unabr. ed. Andy Griffiths. 2 cass. (Running Time: 2 hrs. 45 mins.). (J). 2004. 24.00 (978-1-74030-484-9(5)) Pub: Bolinda Pubng AUS. Dist(s): Bolinda Pub Inc

Just Stupid! unabr. ed. Andy Griffiths. Read by Stig Wemyss. 3 CDs. (Running Time: 2 hrs. 45 mins.). (J). 2004. audio compact disk 54.95 (978-1-74030-888-5(3)) Pub: Bolinda Pubng AUS. Dist(s): Bolinda Pub Inc

Just Take My Heart. abr. ed. Mary Higgins Clark. Read by Jan Maxwell. (Running Time: 5 hrs. 0 mins. 0 sec.). 2009. audio compact disk 29.99 (978-0-7435-7965-0(8)) Pub: S&S Audio. Dist(s): S and S Inc

Just Take My Heart. unabr. ed. Mary Higgins Clark. Read by Jan Maxwell. 7 CDs. (Running Time: 7 hrs. 30 mins. 0 sec.). 2009. audio compact disk 39.99 (978-0-7435-7967-4(4)) Pub: S&S Audio. Dist(s): S and S Inc

***Just Take My Heart: A Novel.** abr. ed. Mary Higgins Clark. Read by Jan Maxwell. (Running Time: 5 hrs. 0 mins. 0 sec.). (ENG.). 2011. audio compact disk 14.99 (978-1-4423-3766-4(4)) Pub: S&S Audio. Dist(s): S and S Inc

Just the Way You Are. unabr. ed. Christina Dodd. Read by Natalie Ross. (Running Time: 9 hrs.). (Lost Texas Hearts Ser.: No. 1). 2009. 24.99 (978-1-4418-0879-0(5), 9781441808790, Brilliance MP3); 24.99 (978-1-4418-0881-3(7), 9781441808813, BAD); 39.97 (978-1-4418-0880-6(9), 9781441808806, Brlnc Audio MP3 Lib); 39.97 (978-1-4418-0882-0(5), 9781441808820, BADLE); audio compact disk 29.99 (978-1-4418-0885-1(X), 9781441808851, Bril Audio CD Unabri); audio compact disk 89.97 (978-1-4418-0878-3(7), 9781441808783, BriAudCD Unabrid) Brilliance Audio.

Just Too Good to Be True. unabr. ed. E. Lynn Harris. Read by Mirron Willis et al. (ENG.). 2008. audio compact disk 29.95 (978-0-7393-6635-6(1), Random AudioBks) Pub: Random Audio Pubg. Dist(s): Random

Just Tricking! Andy Griffiths. Read by Stig Wemyss. (Running Time: 2 hrs. 20 mins.). (J). 2009. 44.99 (978-1-74214-393-4(8), 9781742143934) Pub: Bolinda Pubng AUS. Dist(s): Bolinda Pub Inc

Just Tricking! unabr. ed. Andy Griffiths. Read by Stig Wemyss. 2 CDs. (Running Time: 2 hrs. 20 mins.). (J). 2003. audio compact disk 43.95 (978-1-74030-887-8(5)) Pub: Bolinda Pubng AUS. Dist(s): Bolinda Pub Inc

Just Until. Contrib. by Kierra Kiki Sheard & Brandon Egerton. 2005. audio compact disk 9.98 (978-5-558-92018-5(1)) Pt of Grace Ent.

Just Us: 14 Complete Notation & Tab Transcriptions. Buster B. Jones & Thomas Redmond. (ENG.). 2009. spiral bd. 24.99 (978-0-7866-6060-5(0)) Mel Bay.

Just Voices: A Cappella Anthems for Any Occasion. Compiled by Joseph Martin. 2007. audio compact disk 16.95 (978-5-557-49818-0(4), Glory Snd); audio compact disk 15.98 (978-5-557-49817-3(6), Glory Snd) Shawnee Pr.

Just Wait till You Have Children of Your Own! Erma Bombeck & Bil Keane. Narrated by Barbara Rosenblat. 2 CDs. (Running Time: 2 hrs. 30 mins.). 2000. audio compact disk 22.00 (978-0-7887-4911-7(0), C1292E7) Recorded Bks.
If you're young, old or in the middle, get ready to laugh out loud as the author celebrates both the joys & difficulties of watching children grow into adults. Proves that humor is the best way to keep on keel, even with a teenager in the house.

Just Wait till You Have Children of Your Own! unabr. ed. Erma Bombeck & Bil Keane. Read by Nancy Dannevik. 3 cass. (Running Time: 3 hrs.). 1981. 24.00 (978-0-7366-0311-9(5), 1299) Books on Tape.
A sketch of the teenagers of today. Written primarily from the point of view of parents who see themselves as only slightly older teenagers, the contests between children & their parents are humorous & familiar.

Just Wait till You Have Children of Your Own! unabr. ed. Erma Bombeck & Bil Keane. Narrated by Barbara Rosenblat. 2 cass. (Running Time: 2 hrs. 30 mins.). 2000. 22.00 (978-0-7887-4314-6(7), 96190E7) Recorded Bks.
If you're young, old or in the middle, get ready to laugh out loud as the author celebrates both the joys & difficulties of watching children grow into adults. Proves that humor is the best way to keep on keel, even with a teenager in the house.

Just Walk Across the Room: Simple Steps Pointing People to Faith. Bill Hybels. Read by Don Reed. (Running Time: 8 hrs. 0 mins. 0 sec.). (ENG., 2006. audio compact disk 24.99 (978-0-310-27223-6(8)) Zondervan.

Just Walk Across the Room Audio Download: Four Sessions on Simple Steps Pointing People to Faith. Bill Hybels. (Running Time: 8 hrs. 0 mins. 0 sec.). (ENG.). 2007. 14.99 (978-0-310-27224-3(6)) Zondervan.

Just Wanna Say Thanks. Thomas L. Mitchell. 2004. audio compact disk 12.98 (978-5-559-33138-6(4)) Pub: Pt of Grace Ent. Dist(s): STL Dist NA

Just Watch the Fur Fly. Karen Scott. Read by Karen Scott. 1 cass. (Running Time: 37 min.). (J). 10.66 (978-0-9657252-9-3(4)) Tuxedo Enterpr.

***Just When I Thought I'D Dropped My Last Egg: Life & Other Calamities.** unabr. ed. Kathie Lee Gifford. Read by Kathie Lee Gifford. 4 CDs. (Running Time: 5 hrs.). 2009. audio compact disk 40.00 (978-1-4159-6339-5(8), BksonTape) Pub: Random Audio Pubg. Dist(s): Random

Just When I Thought I'D Dropped My Last Egg: Life & Other Calamities. unabr. ed. Kathie Lee Gifford. Read by Kathie Lee Gifford. 2009. audio compact disk 29.95 (978-0-7393-8335-3(3), Random AudioBks) Pub: Random Audio Pubg. Dist(s): Random

Just Who Will You Be? unabr. ed. Maria Shriver. Read by Maria Shriver. (Running Time: 3600 sec.). 2008. audio compact disk 14.95 (978-1-4013-9136-2(2), Harper Audio) Pub: Hyperion. Dist(s): HarperCollins Pubs

Just William. Richmal Crompton. 6 cass. (J). 1998. 37.45 Box set. (978-0-563-55806-4(7)) BBC WrldWd GBR.
A loveable scamp whose pranks usually end in disaster.

Just William Home for the Holidays. unabr. ed. Richmal Crompton. 2 cass. (Running Time: 3 hrs.). 2002. (978-1-901768-53-4(8)) CSA Telltapes GBR.

Just William Stories. Richmal Crompton. Read by Martin Jarvis. 4 cass. (Running Time: 6 hrs.). (J). 1998. 25.25 Set. (978-1-901768-22-0(8)) Pub: CSA Telltapes GBR. Dist(s): Ulverscroft US

***JustBE Free.** Created by Master Del Pe. (ENG.). 2010. audio compact disk (978-0-9826358-0-3(X)) AquarianLife.

***JustBE Song.** Created by Master Del Pe. (ENG.). 2010. audio compact disk (978-0-9826358-1-0(8)) AquarianLife.

Justice. Dan Mahoney & Christopher Lane. 8 cass. (Running Time: 11 hrs. 30 mins.). 2002. 56.95 (978-0-7861-2539-5(X), 3175) Blckstn Audio.

Justice. Larry Watson. 1996. 10.95 (978-0-7435-4915-8(5)) Pub: S&S Audio. Dist(s): S and S Inc

Justice. abr. ed. Faye Kellerman. Read by Buck Schirner. 2 cass. (Running Time: 3 hrs.). (Peter Decker & Rina Lazarus Novel Ser.). 2000. 7.95 (978-1-57815-172-1(4), 1115, Media Bks Audio) Media Bks NJ.

Justice. abr. ed. Faye Kellerman. Read by Buck Schirner. 3 CDs. (Running Time: 3 hrs.). (Peter Decker & Rina Lazarus Novel Ser.). 2000. audio compact disk 11.99 (978-1-57815-506-4(1), 1115 CD3, Media Bks Audio) Media Bks NJ.
Peter Decker squares off against his toughest opponent yet, as the LAPD's world famous detectice.

***Justice.** abr. ed. Karen Robards. (Running Time: 6 hrs.). (Jessica Ford Ser.). 2011. 9.99 (978-1-61106-130-7(X), 9781611061307, BAD); audio compact disk 24.99 (978-1-61106-128-4(8), 9781611061284, BACD) Brilliance Audio.

Justice! abr. ed. Dana Fuller Ross, pseud. Read by Lloyd James. 4 vols. (Wagons West: Bk. 3). 2003. 25.00 (978-1-58807-394-5(7)); (978-1-58807-647-2(4)) Am Pubng Inc.

Justice! abr. ed. Dana Fuller Ross, pseud. Read by Lloyd James. 5 vols. (Wagons West: Bk. 3). 2004. audio compact disk 30.00 (978-1-58807-397-6(1)); audio compact disk (978-1-58807-635-9(0)) Am Pubng Inc.

Justice. unabr. ed. Faye Kellerman. Read by Bernadette Dunne. 10 cass. (Running Time: 15 hrs.). (Peter Decker & Rina Lazarus Novel Ser.). 1996. 80.00 (978-0-7366-3275-1(1), 3931) Books on Tape.
All parents suffer when someone else's child is killed. Then they move on. Not so Peter Decker, LAPD homicide detective: it's his job to stay focused on the murder of a prom queen.

Justice. unabr. ed. Dan Mahoney. Read by Christopher Lane. 9 CDs. (Running Time: 11 hrs. 30 mins.). 2001. audio compact disk 72.00 (978-0-7861-9038-6(8), 3175) Blckstn Audio.

Justice. unabr. ed. Dan Mahoney. Read by Christopher Lane. (Running Time: 11 hrs. 30 mins.). 2004. audio compact disk 24.95 (978-0-7861-8861-1(8), 3175) Blckstn Audio.

Justice. unabr. ed. Dan Mahoney. Narrated by Christopher Lane. 8 pieces. (Running Time: 11 hrs. 30 mins.). 2004. reel tape 39.95 (978-0-7861-2535-7(7), 100382); audio compact disk 49.95 (978-0-7861-9040-9(X), 110315) Blckstn Audio.
Detective First Grade Brian McKenna and his partner Cisco Sanchez are chasing a killer that all of New York City is rooting for, a vigilante of supreme technical skill, physical power, and intelligence who signs himself "Justice." Justice is executing drug dealers, helping the police close unsolved cases, and providing those in need with stolen drug money-creating a nightmare for the police commissioner, the mayor, and the two detectives. McKenna and Sanchez must work to outsmart the killer, discover his next victim, and find out who is helping Justice in his quest for revenge.

***Justice.** unabr. ed. Karen Robards. (Running Time: 13 hrs.). (Jessica Ford Ser.). 2011. audio compact disk 38.99 (978-1-4418-4307-4(8), 9781441843074, Bril Audio CD Unabri) Brilliance Audio.

Justice: Crimes, Trials, & Punishments. Dominick Dunne. Narrated by Dominick Dunne. 15 CDs. (Running Time: 18 hrs.). audio compact disk 142.00 (978-1-4025-3473-7(6)) Recorded Bks.

Justice: Crimes, Trials, & Punishments. Dominick Dunne. Narrated by Dominick Dunne. 12 cass. (Running Time: 18 hrs.). 2001. 98.00 (978-1-4025-1164-6(7), 96960) Recorded Bks.
A collections of essays that chronicles the crimes of the rich and famous. From O.J. Simpson to Claus von Bulow, here are the murder cases that dominated the news. One particularly poignant chapter covers the flawed trial of a man who murdered the author's daughter, actress Dominique Dunne.

Justice: Crimes, Trials, & Punishments. abr. ed. Dominick Dunne. Read by Dominick Dunne. 6 CDs. (Running Time: 6 hrs.). 2004. audio compact disk 39.95 (978-1-931056-97-7(8), N Millennium Audio) Pub: New Millenn Enter. Dist(s): PerseuPGW
The author's finest & most personal courtroom accounts of the sensational trials of Claus von Bulow & O. J. Simpson. He presents the mystery surrounding the death of Martha Moxley & the recent indictment of Michael Skakel. Also includes his recount of the trial of the man that strangled his daughter Dominique & the outrageous sentence that permitted his release in only two & a half years.

Justice: Crimes, Trials, & Punishments. unabr. ed. Dominick Dunne. Read by Dominick Dunne. 12 cass. (Running Time: 18 hrs.). 2004. 39.95 (978-1-931056-96-0(X), N Millennium Audio) Pub: New Millenn Enter. Dist(s): PerseuPGW

Justice: What's the Right Thing to Do? abr. ed. Michael J. Sandel. (Running Time: 6 hrs. 0 mins. 0 sec.). (ENG.). 2009. audio compact disk 29.99 (978-1-4272-0816-3(6)) Pub: Macmill Audio. Dist(s): Macmillan

Justice & Liberty in a Free Society. Read by John Hospers et al. 2 cass. (Running Time: 2 hrs.). (Cal State Univ., Long Beach Ser.). 1981. 18.00 (F121) Freeland Pr.
Three approaches on a vital issue. Panel discussion.

Justice & Mercy. Linda Eyre & Richard Eyre. 2 cass. (Running Time: 3 hrs.). (Teaching Your Children Values Ser.). (J). (ps-7). 2000. bk. 16.95 (978-1-56015-795-3(X)) Penton Overseas.
Tape 1: a coaching, "how-to" program for parents; Tape 2: "Alexander's Amazing Adventures" program featuring stories, songs, sound effects & background music, that helps children ages 4-12 to develop social skills, communication skills & life skills. Includes activity cards.

Justice, Charity, Community: Our Trinity on Earth. Megan McKenna. 1 cass. (Running Time: 50 min.). 8.95 Credence Commun.
Justice doesn't happen much without a supportive community. And charity without justice just doesn't happen. So McKenna talks about the central role of the community in bringing real justice & charity into the world.

***Justice Denied.** abr. ed. J. A. Jance. Read by J. R. Horne. (ENG.). 2007. (978-0-06-153704-2(7), Harper Audio); (978-0-06-153703-5(9), Harper Audio) HarperCollins Pubs.

Justice Denied. abr. ed. J. A. Jance. Contrib. by J. R. Horne. (Running Time: 21600 sec.). (J. P. Beaumont Mystery Ser.). 2007. audio compact disk 29.95 (978-0-06-125663-9(3), Harper Audio) HarperCollins Pubs.

Justice Denied. unabr. ed. Jerry Ahern. Read by Alan Zimmerman. 3 vols. No. 8. 2003. (978-1-58807-529-1(X)) Am Pubng Inc.

Justice Denied. unabr. ed. Jerry Ahern. Read by Alan Zimmerman. 3 vols. (Running Time: 4 hrs. 30 mins.). (Defender Ser.: No. 8). 2003. 22.00 (978-1-58807-028-9(X)) Am Pubng Inc.
Holden is the only man that can stop the FLNA's master plan to take over America, leaving him to be the most hunted man in America. And, while the U. S. President lies wounded in a secret hideaway, even Holden cant stop the FLNA from putting their puppet in the White House. Now, with the most skilled commandos in the U.S. fighting at his side, Holden must rescue the President before the FLNAs deadly assassins close inor America is doomed.

Justice Denied. unabr. ed. Jerry Ahern. Read by Alan Zimmerman. 4 vols. No. 8. 2004. audio compact disk 28.00 (978-1-58807-270-2(3)); audio compact disk (978-1-58807-701-1(2)) Am Pubng Inc.

Justice Denied. unabr. ed. Robin Bowles. Read by David A. Baldwin. 10 cass. (Running Time: 13 hrs. 41 mins.). 2004. 80.00 (978-1-74030-155-8(2), 500739) Pub: Bolinda Pubng AUS. Dist(s): Lndmrk Audiobks

***Justice Denied.** unabr. ed. J. A. Jance. Read by Alan Nebelthau. (ENG.). 2007. (978-0-06-153706-6(3), Harper Audio); (978-0-06-153705-9(5), Harper Audio) HarperCollins Pubs.

Justice Denied. unabr. ed. J. A. Jance. Read by Alan Nebelthau. (Running Time: 37800 sec.). (J. P. Beaumont Mystery Ser.). 2007. audio compact disk 39.95 (978-0-06-125662-2(5), Harper Audio) HarperCollins Pubs.

Justice Denied. unabr. ed. J. A. Jance. Narrated by Alan Nebelthau. 8 CDs. (Running Time: 10 hrs.). (J. P. Beaumont Mystery Ser.). 2007. audio compact disk 92.75 (978-1-4281-5581-7(3)) Recorded Bks.

Justice Denied. unabr. ed. Robert K. Tanenbaum. Read by Connor O'Brien. 8 cass. (Running Time: 12 hrs.). (Butch Karp Mystery Ser.). 1997. 64.00 (978-0-7366-3688-9(9), 4367) Books on Tape.

Justice for All of Creation. Thomas Merton. 1 cass. 8.95 (AA2457) Credence Commun.

Justice for Freddie. unabr. ed. Gerry W. Gotro. Read by Rusty Nelson. 8 cass. (Running Time: 9 hrs.). 2001. 49.95 (978-1-55686-756-9(5)) Books in Motion.
An American businessman turned psychopathic killer took bush pilot Freddie's life. When Freddie's friends try to find him in the wilderness, more men died before they found "Justice for Freddie".

Justice for None. abr. ed. Gene Hackman & Daniel Lenihan. Read by John Peakes. (Running Time: 6 hrs.). 2004. audio compact disk 74.25 (978-1-59355-664-8(0), 1593556640, BACDLib Ed) Brilliance Audio.
In their second novel, Gene Hackman and Daniel Lenihan bring to life the harsh plains and smouldering courtrooms of the Midwest: the small town of Vermilion, Illinois, on the brink of the Great Depression. Boyd Carter is a troubled World War I veteran on the run from the law, suspected of murdering his estranged wife and her lover. Only a female reporter for the Chicago Tribune and the head of a sanitarium for veterans are not convinced of Boyd's guilt. Boyd joins forces with another wrongly accused man, an African-American, and the two begin to face their shadowed pasts while fighting against the odds of justice.

Justice for None. unabr. ed. Gene Hackman & Daniel Lenihan. Read by John Peakes. 8 CDs. (Running Time: 11 hrs.). 2004. 24.95 (978-1-59335-324-7(3), 1593353243, Brilliance MP3); 39.25 (978-1-59335-486-2(X), 159335486X, Brlnc Audio MP3 Lib); 34.95 (978-1-59355-660-0(8), 1593556608, BAU); 87.25 (978-1-59355-661-7(6), 1593556616, BrilAudUnabridg) Brilliance Audio.

Justice for None. unabr. ed. Gene Hackman & Daniel Lenihan. Read by John Peakes. (Running Time: 11 hrs.). 2004. 39.25 (978-1-59710-408-1(6), 1597104086, BADLE); 24.95 (978-1-59710-409-8(4), 1597104094, BAD) Brilliance Audio.

Justice Hall. Laurie R. King. Narrated by Jenny Sterlin. 12 cass. (Running Time: 16 hrs. 45 mins.). (Mary Russell Mystery Ser.: Vol. 6). 2002. 104.00 (978-1-4025-1794-5(7), 97025) Recorded Bks.
Mary Russell and her husband, Sherlock HOlmes are now on their sixth thrilling outing together.

Justice Holmes Decisions. abr. ed. Oliver W. Holmes, Jr. Perf. by E. G. Marshall. 1 cass. 1984. 12.95 (978-0-694-50343-8(6), SWC 1662) HarperCollins Pubs.

Justice Is a Woman. unabr. ed. Catherine Cookson. Read by Elizabeth Henry. 8 cass. (Running Time: 12 hrs.). (Sound Ser.). 2004. 69.95 (978-1-85496-889-0(0), 68890) Pub: UlverLrgPrint GBR. Dist(s): Ulverscroft US

Justice of Justification: Romans 3:21-31. Ed Young. 1996. 4.95 (978-0-7417-2110-5(4), 1110) Win Walk.

Justice of Justification: Romans 3:25-31. Ed Young. 1984. 4.95 (978-0-7417-1357-5(8), 357) Win Walk.

Justice of the Mountain Man. abr. ed. William W. Johnstone. Read by Doug van Liew. 4 cass. (Running Time: 6 hrs.). (Mountain Man Ser.: No. 26). 2002. 24.95 (978-1-890990-92-3(2), 99092) Otis Audio.
Western with sound effects.

Justice Returned to Love. Kenneth Wapnick. 4 CDs. 2005. audio compact disk 24.00 (978-1-59142-183-2(7), CD81) Foun Miracles.

Justice Riders. Chuck Norris et al. (Running Time: 27000 sec.). 2006. audio compact disk 55.00 (978-0-7861-7195-8(2)) Blckstn Audio.

Justice Riders. unabr. ed. Ken Abraham et al. Narrated by Lee Horsley. 6 CDs. (Justice Riders Ser.). (ENG.). 2005. audio compact disk 27.99 (978-1-59859-100-2(2)) Oasis Audio.

Justice Riders. unabr. ed. Chuck Norris et al. Narrated by Lee Horsley. (Justice Riders Ser.). (ENG.). 2005. 19.59 (978-1-60814-265-1(5)) Oasis Audio.

Justice vs. Mercy. unabr. ed. Nathaniel Branden. 1 cass. (Running Time: 1 hr. 13 min.). (Basic Principles of Objectivism Ser.). 12.95 (571) J Norton Pubs.
Covers the nature of justice; the importance of passing moral judgments; & the virtue of pride.

Justifiable Means. Terri Blackstock. 2 cass. (Running Time: 90 min.). (Sun Coast Chronicles Ser.). 1996. 14.99 (978-0-310-21001-6(1)) Zondervan.

Justifiable Means. abr. ed. Terri Blackstock. (Running Time: 3 hrs. 0 mins. 0 sec.). (Sun Coast Chronicles Ser.). (ENG.). 2003. 10.99 (978-0-310-26073-8(6)) Zondervan.

Justification: Becoming a Child of God. Scott Hahn. 4 cass. 1995. 22.95 Set. (5269-C) Ignatius Pr.
Scott Hahn tackles three of the most controversial doctrines that divide Catholics & Fundamentalists: Justification, Infant Baptism & being "Born Again." But Scott doesn't just answer the Fundamentalist challenge to these doctrines: he actually shows how these three issues are vitally intertwined & together make up one beautiful reality known as Divine Sonship.

Justification & the Roman Doctrine of Salvation. Richard Bennett. 1 cass. (Conference on Christianity & Roman Catholicism Ser.: No. 5). 5.00 Trinity Found.

Justification by Faith: Romans 3:21-22. Ed Young. 1984. 4.95 (978-0-7417-1355-1(1), 355) Win Walk.

Justification by Faith: Romans 3:21-24. Ed Young. 1996. 4.95 (978-0-7417-2109-9(0), 11091109) Win Walk.

Justification by Faith: Romans 3:23-24. Ed Young. 1984. 4.95 (978-0-7417-1356-8(X), 356) Win Walk.

Justin Bayard. Jon Cleary. Read by Christopher Kay. 4 cass. (Running Time: 6 hrs.). 1999. 44.95 (60458) Pub: Soundings Ltd GBR. Dist(s): Ulverscroft US

Justin Morgan Had a Horse. unabr. ed. Marguerite Henry. Read by Patrick G. Lawlor. 3 CDs. (Running Time: 4 hrs.). 2003. audio compact disk 24.00 (978-0-7861-9177-2(5), 3075) Blckstn Audio.

Justin Morgan Had a Horse. unabr. ed. Marguerite Henry. Read by Patrick Lawler. 3 cass. (Running Time: 4 hrs.). 2003. 23.95 (978-0-7861-2405-3(9), 3075) Blckstn Audio.
Joel Goss knows that Little Bub is a special colt, even though he's a runt. And when schoolteacher Justin Morgan asks Joel to break the colt in, Joel is thrilled. Soon word about Little Bub has spread throughout the entire Northeast that this spirited colt can pull heavier loads than a pair of oxen and run faster than thoroughbreds!.

Justin Morgan Had a Horse. unabr. ed. Marguerite Henry. Read by Patrick G. Lawlor. 3 cass. (Running Time: 3 hrs.). 2005. 14.95 (978-0-7861-3451-9(8), E3075); audio compact disk 16.95 (978-0-7861-8028-8(5), ZE3075) Blckstn Audio.

Justin Morgan Had a Horse. unabr. ed. Marguerite Henry. Read by Patrick G. Lawlor. (Running Time: 12600 sec.). (J). (ps-7). 2005. DVD & audio compact disk 29.95 (978-0-7861-8154-4(0), ZM3075) Blckstn Audio.

Justin Morgan Had a Horse, unabr. ed. Marguerite Henry. Narrated by John McDonough. 3 pieces. (Running Time: 4 hrs.). (gr. 3 up). 1997. 27.00 (978-0-7887-0884-8(8), 95022E7) Recorded Bks.
A poor school teacher received a horse & her tiny colt in payment for some work. He wished he had been given money instead. But to everyone's surprise, the small, brown colt soon displays special abilities: "Bub" can pull more than a team of oxen & he can run faster than a racehorse. Traces the history of one of the most famous breeds of American horses.

Justin Stone Speaks: On T'ai Chi Chih. Created by Justin F. Stone. 2005. audio compact disk 11.95 (978-1-882290-07-9(0)) Good Karma.

***Justin Wilson's Cajun Fables CD.** Justin Wilson & Jay Hadley. Narrated by Justin Wilson. (Running Time: 29 hrs. NaN mins.). (ENG.). (J). 2010. audio compact disk 15.95 (978-1-58980-785-3(5)) Pelican.

Justine. abr. ed. Lawrence Durrell. Read by Nigel Anthony. 3 CDs. (Running Time: 4 hrs.). (Alexandria Quartet Ser.: Vol. I). 1995. audio compact disk 22.98 (978-962-634-040-0(1), NA304012, Naxos AudioBooks) Naxos.

Justine. abr. ed. Lawrence Durrell. Read by Nigel Anthony. 3 cass. (Running Time: 4 hrs.). (Alexandria Quartet Ser.: Vol. I). 1996. 17.98 (978-962-634-540-5(3), NA304014, Naxos AudioBooks) Naxos.

Justine. unabr. ed. Lawrence Durrell. Read by Richard Brown. 7 cass. (Running Time: 10 hrs. 30 mins.). (Alexandria Quartet Ser.). 1994. 56.00 (978-0-7366-2712-2(X), 3442) Books on Tape.
Characters play hide & seek in the bedrooms of pre-WW II Alexandria.

Justine Bayard. abr. ed. Jon Cleary. 4 cass. (Running Time: 6 hrs.). (Sound Ser.). 1994. 44.95 (978-1-85496-045-0(8)) Pub: UlverLrgPrint GBR. Dist(s): Ulverscroft US

Justinian's Flea: Plague, Empire, & the Birth of Europe. unabr. ed. William Rosen. Narrated by Barrett Whitener. (Running Time: 12 hrs. 0 mins. 0 sec.). (ENG.). 2007. audio compact disk 75.99 (978-1-4001-3385-7(8)) Pub: Tantor Media. Dist(s): IngramPubServ

Justinian's Flea: Plague, Empire, & the Birth of Europe. unabr. ed. William Rosen. Read by Barrett Whitener. (Running Time: 12 hrs. 0 mins. 0 sec.). (ENG.). 2007. audio compact disk 37.99 (978-1-4001-0385-0(1)); audio compact disk 24.99 (978-1-4001-5385-5(9)) Pub: Tantor Media. Dist(s): IngramPubServ

Juvenilia of Jane Austen. Narrated by Flo Gibson. 6 cass. (Running Time: 1 hr. 30 min. per cass.). 1986. 24.95 (978-1-55685-014-1(X)) Audio Bk Con.
Written between the ages of twelve & fifteen, this delightful "exercise book" is full of violence & hilarity.

Juvenilia of Marc-Antoine Muret. Marc Antoine Muret & Kirk M. Summers. (LAT & ENG.). 2006. audio compact disk 9.95 (978-0-8142-9114-6(7)) Pub: Ohio St U Pr. Dist(s): Chicago Distribution Ctr

Juvie Three. unabr. ed. Gordon Korman. Narrated by Christopher Evan Welch. 5 cass. (Running Time: 5 hrs. 30 mins.). (YA). (gr. 6-10). 2008. 41.75 (978-1-4361-5923-4(7)); audio compact disk 51.75 (978-1-4361-5928-9(8)) Recorded Bks.

Jyubei Ninpucho: Soundtrack. 1 CD. 2003. audio compact disk 14.98 (978-1-57813-402-1(1), CD/005, ADV Music) A D Vision.

***JZ Knight, Mi Vida en el Mas Alla.** Des. by Holo-Graphics. (YA). 2010. 25.00 (978-1-935262-12-1(2)) Bel Shanai.

K

K. unabr. ed. Mary Roberts Rinehart. Read by Laurie Klein. 8 cass. (Running Time: 9 hrs. 42 min.). Dramatization. 1992. 49.95 (978-1-55686-446-9(9), 446) Books in Motion.
Though K. LeMoyne, the unknown outsider, is only a boarder in Sidney Page's house, her interest in him becomes more than casual curiosity. Who is this quiet gray-templed, distinguished man who says nothing about his past.

K Blows Top: A Cold War Comic Interlude, Starring Nikita Khrushchev, America's Most Unlikely Tourist. unabr. ed. Peter Carlson. (Running Time: 7.5 hrs. 0 mins.). 2009. 29.95 (978-1-4332-7969-0(X)); 54.95 (978-1-4332-7965-2(7)); audio compact disk 24.95 (978-1-4332-7968-3(1)); audio compact disk 69.00 (978-1-4332-7966-9(5)) Blckstn Audio.

K. C. Jones: A Nice Guy Who Wins. unabr. ed. K. C. Jones & Joe Johnston. Read by K. C. Jones. 1 cass. (Running Time: 1 hr. 30 min.). 1990. 7.95 (978-0-922067-01-5(5)) Johnston Mus Grp.
One of basketball's legendary stars tells of his rise from the projects of San Francisco to the NBA Hall of Fame. He overcame poverty & oppression to collect championships in high school, college, the Olympics, & even NBA championships as both player & coach.

K. D. Lang: All You Get Is Me. abr. ed. Victoria Starr. Read by Delphine Blue. Ed. by Fran Landt. 2 cass. (Running Time: 3 hrs.). 1998. 16.95 set. (978-1-882071-60-9(3)) B-B Audio.
In k.d. lang all you get is me, Victoria Starr explores the life of the artist who has broken all the rules of pop culture while becoming one of the worlds most beloved singers. k.d. lang: all you get is me traces k.d.s path from college dropout to pop.

K Is for Killer. abr. ed. Sue Grafton. Read by Judy Kaye. 3 CDs. (Running Time: 3 hrs.). (Kinsey Millhone Mystery Ser.). (ENG.). 2004. audio compact disk 14.99 (978-0-7393-1421-0(1), RH Aud Price) Pub: Random Audio Pubg. Dist(s): Random

K Is for Killer. unabr. ed. Sue Grafton. Read by Mary Peiffer. 7 cass. (Running Time: 10 hrs. 30 min.). (Kinsey Millhone Mystery Ser.). 1995. 56.00 (978-0-7366-3043-6(0), 3725) Books on Tape.

K+-Meson Production in Nuclei. Markus Buescher. (Schriften des Forschungszentrums Jülich: 29). 2005. audio compact disk (978-3-89336-398-8(X)) Forschung Julich DEU.

K-Pax. abr. ed. Gene Brewer. Read by Tom Casaletto. 3 CDs. (Running Time: 3 hrs.). 2001. audio compact disk 53.25 (978-1-58788-927-1(7), 1587889277, CD Lib Edit) Brilliance Audio.
Imagine a time and space traveler from another planet. One that looks human and exemplifies the ideal world he comes from, a world free from human nature's greed and cruelty. That creature would be "prot", as he calls himself, the newest patient at the Manhattan Psychiatric Institute. Prot seems to know more than he should about faster-than-the-speed-of-light-travel. And besides drawing constellations as viewed from K-PAX, the name of his home planet, "prot" can describe its orbit around double suns in unpublished detail. Who is "prot" and where did he really come from? Why does he have the ability to cure severe mental cases? And to disappear at will? And to charm everyone he comes into contact with? Bizarre delusion or reality? Listen in as a psychiatrist who specializes in delusional behavior documents his sessions with the man from K-PAX.

K-Pax. unabr. ed. Gene Brewer. Read by Tom Casaletto. 6 cass. (Running Time: 7 hrs.). 2001. 29.95 (978-1-58788-838-0(6), 1587888386, BAU) Brilliance Audio.

K-Pax. unabr. ed. Gene Brewer. Read by Tom Casaletto. (Running Time: 7 hrs.). 2004. 39.25 (978-1-59335-349-0(9), 1593353499, Brlnc Audio MP3 Lib) Brilliance Audio.

K-Pax. unabr. ed. Gene Brewer. Read by Tom Casaletto. (Running Time: 7 hrs.). 2004. 39.25 (978-1-59710-432-6(9), 1597104329, BADLE); 24.95 (978-1-59710-433-3(7), 1597104337, BAD) Brilliance Audio.

K-Pax. unabr. ed. Gene Brewer. Read by Tom Casaletto. (Running Time: 7 hrs.). 2004. 24.95 (978-1-59335-002-4(3), 1593350023) Soulmate Audio Bks.

K-PAX. unabr. ed. Gene Brewer. Read by Tom Casaletto. 3 CDs. (Running Time: 5 hrs.). 2002. audio compact disk 62.25 (978-1-59086-548-4(0)) Brilliance Audio.

Ka 'Ekake Li'ili'i O Mekiko. Lilinoe Andrews. Illus. by Lilinoe Andrews. (J). (gr. 2-3). 1999. pap. bk. 5.95 (978-1-58191-086-5(X)) Aha Punana Leo.

Ka Holo Ka'a Me Tutu. Lilinoe Andrews. Illus. by Brook Parker. 1 cass. (HAW.). (J). 1992. pap. bk. 8.95 (978-1-890270-17-9(2)) Aha Punana Leo.

Ka Nohona Kua'aina. Lilinoe Andrews. Illus. by Lilinoe Andrews. 1 cass. (HAW.). (J). (gr. 2-3). 1999. pap. bk. 5.95 (978-1-58191-053-7(3)) Aha Punana Leo.

Ka 'Omole Kupaianaha O Ka Lua. Laiana Wong. Illus. by Kaipo Morales. 1 cass. (HAW.). (J). (gr. 1-2). 1999. pap. bk. 5.95 (978-1-58191-074-2(6)) Aha Punana Leo.

Ka 'O'o 'A'a O Alaka'i. Laiana Wong. Illus. by 'Oiwi Jones. 1 cass. (HAW.). (J). (gr. 2-3). 1999. pap. bk. 5.95 (978-1-58191-073-5(8)) Aha Punana Leo.

Ka Ua Poko. Laiana Wong. Illus. by Craig Neff. 1 cass. (HAW.). (J). (gr. 3-4). 1999. pap. bk. 5.95 (978-1-58191-075-9(4)) Aha Punana Leo.

Ka Uliuli 'Ana O Ka Maka O Ka Manu'u. Elsie Jimmie. Illus. by Elsie Jimmie. Tr. by Hiapo K. Perreira. (HAW.). (J). (gr. 3-4). 1996. pap. bk. 3.95 (978-1-890270-30-8(X)) Aha Punana Leo.

Kaa's Hunting. unabr. ed. Rudyard Kipling. Read by Cindy Hardin & Walter Zimmerman. Dramatization. (J). 1980. 7.95 (N-42) Jimcin Record.
Kaa, the python, helps rescue Mowgli from the monkey people in this story from "The Jungle Book".

***Kaa's Hunting: A Story from the Jungle Books.** Rudyard Kipling. 2009. (978-1-60136-508-8(X)) Audio Holding.

Kaaterskill Falls. unabr. ed. Allegra Goodman. Narrated by Suzanne Toren. 9 cass. (Running Time: 12 hrs. 30 mins.). 1999. 83.00 (978-0-7887-2919-5(5), 95711E7) Recorded Bks.
A rare look into the closed world of an Orthodox Jewish community. Kaaterskill Falls in the late 1970s is a small town in the Catskills where the followers of a strict rabbi gather each summer.

Kabayashi Maru. Julia Ecklar. (Star Trek Ser.). 2004. 10.95 (978-0-7435-4675-1(X)) Pub: S&S Audio. Dist(s): S and S Inc

Kabbalah. Z'ev B. Halevi. 2 cass. 1992. 18.00 set. (OC284-63) Sound Horizons AV.

Kabbalah: Kabbalah & the Rise of Mysticism. Chuck Missler. 2 CD's. (Running Time: 2 hours). (Briefing Packages by Chuck Missler). 2005. audio compact disk 19.95 (978-1-57821-278-1(2)) Koinonia Hse.
"Whether disillusioned by the self-imposed blinders and myopia of contemporary "science," or frustrated by the moral bankruptcy of unbridled materialism, increasing numbers of desperate people are now seeking "answers" outside the realm of natural phenomena and are pursuing the supernatural. The anguished plea of the disenfranchised now begs the question, "Is there anyone out there?"Beyond the beguiling allure of many contemporary forms of ancient paganism, such as the New Age, Wicca, and others, many people have become attracted to a form of Hebrew mysticism known as Kabbalah. The popular press is speckled with articles of prominent Hollywood personalities who have taken up a popular contemporary version of KabbalahIt is particularly paradoxical to find these occultic practices embedded within Judaism, despite the numerous explicit prohibitions against all forms of the occult recorded throughout the very Torah that is so highly venerated among the Jews. . . . .Anyone with a modicum of Biblical literacy should realize that occult practices are expressly prohibited in the Scriptures. Scripture condemns by name spiritism, mediumism (?channeling?), and necromancy, and various forms of sorcery and divination, including astrology and magic. In ancient Israel, divination was a capital crime; if someone was caught casting a horoscope, or other occultic practice, they were put to death. Why?Because God is jealous of His uniqueness, and He alone knows what the future holds. To intrude on His office is to attempt to intrude on His glory. Occult activity also courts deception and betrayal from the demonic realm, and promotes evil under the guise of legitimate religious practice. Occult involvement will eventually lead to judgment for those who refuse to forsake it."Join Chuck as he delves deeply into the hidden world of Kabbalah and exposes the lies and traps that Satan has laid there for the unwary.

Kabbalah-Doorway to the Mind. Edward Hoffman. 1 cass. 1995. 16.00 (978-0-8356-2098-7(0), Quest) Pub: Theos Pub Hse. Dist(s): Natl Bk Netwk
History, meditations, and dream insight of the Kabbalah. Includes an illustrated Tree of Life diagram.

Kabbalah Kirtan: An Ecstatic New Form of Devotional Singing. Yofiyah. (Running Time: 1 hr. 10 mins.). 2006. audio compact disk 17.98 (978-1-59179-524-7(9), M1078D) Sounds True.

Kabbalah Life 101. unabr. ed. Rav Berg. 5 cass. (Running Time: 250 min.). 2001. reel tape 49.95 (978-1-57189-104-4(8)) Jodere Grp.
Kabbalist Berg's insights into the eternal journey of the human soul exposes the hidden faces of our past spiritual lives.

Kabbalah Meditation. David A. Cooper. 2 CDs. 2004. audio compact disk 19.95 (978-1-59179-271-0(1), AW00268D) Sounds True.
Ancient Jewish mystics sought to become "vessels for God's light" through meditation. Now learn 11 step-by-step meditations based on Judaism's long-hidden tradition, taught by this respected author and rabbi.

Kabbalah One - Basic Course. 8 cass. (Running Time: 12 hrs.). 1999. 89.95 Set. (83-0066) Explorations.
For 4,000 years the mystical wisdom of Kabbalah was a tightly-guarded secret. Only in this century did the ancient vaults to this spiritual system open up, for everyone to learn how to interpret the mysteries created by our five senses.

Kabbalah Works: Secrets for Purposeful Living. unabr. ed. David Aaron. Read by David Aaron. 5 CDs. (Running Time: 4 hrs.). (ENG.). 2005. audio compact disk 19.98 (978-1-59659-024-3(6)) Pub: Gildan Media. Dist(s): HachBkGrp

***Kabbalistic Approach to Fixing the World.** unabr. ed. Shlomo Carlebach. 2010. audio compact disk (978-1-61544-079-5(8)) Better Listen.

Kabbalistic Universe (Lecture) Z'ev B. Halevi. 4 cass. 36.00 set. (OC285-63) Sound Horizons AV.

Kabbalistic Universe (Meditation) Z'ev B. Halevi. 2 cass. 18.00 set. (OC286-63) Sound Horizons AV.

Kabloona. Gontran de Poncins in collaboration with Lewis Galantière. Narrated by Grover Gardner. (Running Time: 9 hrs. 30 mins.). 2004. 30.95 (978-1-59912-520-6(X)) Iofy Corp.

Kabloona. unabr. ed. Gontran De Poncins. Read by Ralph Cosham. 20 cass. (Running Time: 11 hrs. 30 mins.). 2005. reel tape 29.95 (978-0-7861-2913-3(1), E3399) Blckstn Audio.

Kabloona: Among the Inuit. Gontran de Poncins. (Running Time: 11 hrs. 18 mins.). 2005. 65.95 (978-0-7861-2914-0(X)) Blckstn Audio.

Kabloona: Among the Inuit. unabr. ed. Gontran de Poncins. 8 CDs. (Running Time: 9 hrs. 30 mins.). 2005. audio compact disk 81.00 (978-0-7861-8233-6(4)) Blckstn Audio.

Kabloona: Among the Inuit. unabr. ed. Gontran de Poncins. Read by Grover Gardner. Told to Lewis Galantiere. 9 CDs. (Running Time: 34200 sec.). 2005. audio compact disk 32.95 (978-0-7861-8234-3(2), ZE3399) Blckstn Audio.

Kabloona: Among the Inuit. unabr. ed. Gontran de Poncins. Read by Grover Gardner. Contrib. by Lewis Galantiere. 45 CDs. (Running Time: 34200 sec.). 2005. DVD & audio compact disk 29.95 (978-0-7861-8311-1(X), ZM3399) Blckstn Audio.

Kabrit Mawon (Book & Tape) Maude Heurtelou. (CRP.). (J). 2006. 19.00 (978-1-58432-310-5(8)) Educa Vision.

Kabul Beauty School: An American Woman Goes Behind the Veil. unabr. ed. Deborah Rodriguez. Read by Bernadette Dunne. Told to Kristin Ohlson. (Running Time: 32400 sec.). 2007. 29.95 (978-0-7861-4923-0(X)); audio compact disk 29.95 (978-0-7861-5898-0(0)) Blckstn Audio.

Kabul Beauty School: An American Woman Goes Behind the Veil. unabr. ed. Deborah Rodriguez. Read by Bernadette Dunne. (Running Time: 32400 sec.). 2007. 59.95 (978-0-7861-6869-9(2)); audio compact disk 72.00 (978-0-7861-6868-2(4)); audio compact disk 29.95 (978-0-7861-7024-1(7)) Blckstn Audio.

***KaChing: How to Run an Online Business that Pays & Pays.** unabr. ed. Joel Comm. Read by Walter Dixon. (Running Time: 8 hrs.). (ENG.). 2010. 29.98 (978-1-59659-617-7(1), GildAudio) Pub: Gildan Media. Dist(s): HachBkGrp

Kaddish. Leon Wieseltier. 4 cass. (Running Time: 6 hrs.). 1999. 25.95 Audio Lit.

Kaddish, abr. ed. Leon Wieseltier. Read by Theodore Bikel. 4 cass. (Running Time: 6 hrs.). 1999. 24.95 (978-1-57453-292-0(8)) Audio Lit.

Kaffir Boy, abr. ed. Mark Mathabane. Read by Howard Rollins. 2 cass. (Running Time: 3 hrs.). 2000. 7.95 (978-1-57815-149-3(X), 1108, Media Bks Audio) Media Bks NJ.
This is how it felt to grow up under the South African system of legalized racism. We learn about the daily life of families in a world in which beatings, unexplained arrests & murder are commonplace.

Kafka: The Metamorphosis. Franz Kafka. Read by Alan Hewitt. 2 cass. (Running Time: 2 hrs. 15 min.). 15.95 Set. (12156FA) Filmic Archives.
Bleak allegory on the nature of man, wherein Gregor rediscovers life as a large insect.

Kafka: The Metamorphosis, Set. unabr. ed. Franz Kafka. Read by Alan Hewitt. 2 cass. (Running Time: 2 hrs. 15 min.). (Cassette Bookshelf Ser.). 1987. 15.95 (978-0-8072-3533-1(4), CB 117 CXR, Listening Lib) Random Audio Pubg.

Kafka Set: The Metamorphosis. unabr. ed. Franz Kafka. Read by Alan Hewitt. 2 cass. (Running Time: 2 hrs. 15 min.). (Cassette Bookshelf Ser.). 1987. 15.98 Library ed. (978-0-8072-3451-8(6), CB117CX, Listening Lib) Random Audio Pubg.

Kafka in 90 Minutes. unabr. ed. Paul Strathern. Read by Robert Whitfield. 2 cass. (Running Time: 1 hr. 30 mins.). 2005. 16.95 (978-0-7861-3430-4(5)); audio compact disk 16.95 (978-0-7861-7980-0(5)) Blckstn Audio.

Kafka in 90 Minutes. unabr. ed. Paul Strathern. Read by Robert Whitfield. (Running Time: 2 hrs. NaN mins.). 2009. audio compact disk 24.00 (978-0-7861-7938-1(4)); audio compact disk 22.95 (978-0-7861-3034-4(2)) Blckstn Audio.

Kafka on the Shore. Haruki Murakami. Read by Sean Barret. (Running Time: 7 hrs.). 2001. 78.95 (978-1-60083-796-8(4)) Iofy Corp.

Kafka on the Shore. unabr. ed. Haruki Murakami. Read by Sean Barrett & Oliver Le Sueur. (YA). 2007. 109.99 (978-1-59895-858-4(5)) Find a World.

Kafka on the Shore. unabr. ed. Haruki Murakami. Read by Oliver Le Sueur & Sean Barrett. 14 CDs. (Running Time: 68700 sec.). 2006. bk. 89.98 (978-962-634-405-7(9), Naxos AudioBooks) Naxos.

Kahless. Michael Jan Friedman. (Star Trek). 2004. 10.95 (978-0-7435-4628-7(8)) Pub: S&S Audio. Dist(s): S and S Inc

Kahuna Power QuickSurf: One Hour to Seize Your Wave & Revolutionize Your Life! Excerpts. Based on a book by Frank F. Lunn. 1. (Running Time: 1 hr. 12 min.). 2006. audio compact disk 9.95 (978-0-9728300-3-4(0)) Kahuna Empowerment.
This is NOT another ?how to deal with change? message. Brace yourself? this is a ?how to master change survival course!? In this single hour, you will develop the mind-set and secret language of an entrepreneur. The KahunaPower QuickSurf CD will equip you with seven essential surfing skills guaranteed to revolutionize your business and personal life! More than concepts and theories, this is a gift of tools and practical insights you can apply immediately to your life. After experiencing this KahunaPower CD single you will be transformed. You will never look at change with anxiety and fear again!.

Kahuna Tradition. Charlotte Berney. 1 cass. 9.00 (A0379-88) Sound Photosyn.
Orenstein & Saklani appear on this unedited tape, recorded at ICSS '88.

Kai Gets the Point. (J). 2006. audio compact disk (978-1-933835-06-8(0)) Part Dev.

Kai Korero: A Cook Islands Maori Coursebook. Tai Carpentier & Clive Beaumont. 1996. 8.95 (978-0-908597-15-4(0)) Pub: Pasifika Pr NZL. Dist(s): UH Pr

Kajla Didi. A. Mohit. Voice by Sheema Mohit. 1 cass. (Running Time: 90 mins.). 1999. audio compact disk 10.00 (978-0-9647672-5-6(2)) Beacon Hse IN.

Kalachakra - Hindu & Tibetan Astrology. Anders Johansson. 1 cass. 8.95 (176) Am Fed Astrologers.
Researching reincarnation with modern cases.

Kalahari Typing School for Men. Alexander McCall Smith. Narrated by Lisette Lecat. 5 cass. (Running Time: 7 hrs. 15 mins.). (No. 1 Ladies' Detective Agency Ser.: No. 4). 2004. 24.99 (978-1-4025-4178-0(3), 02974) Recorded Bks.

Kalahari Typing School for Men. unabr. ed. Alexander McCall Smith. 5 cass. Library ed. (Running Time: 7 hrs. 15 min.). (No. 1 Ladies' Detective Agency Ser.: No. 4). 2003. 45.00 (978-1-4025-4379-1(4), 97359) Recorded Bks.

Kalahari Typing School for Men. unabr. ed. Alexander McCall Smith. 5 cass. (Running Time: 8.5 hrs.). (No. 1 Ladies' Detective Agency Ser.: No. 4). 2003. 24.99 Recorded Bks.

Kalahari Typing School for Men. unabr. ed. Alexander McCall Smith. 6 CDs. (Running Time: 7 hrs. 15 mins.). (No. 1 Ladies' Detective Agency Ser.: No. 4). 2004. audio compact disk 29.99 (978-1-4025-4706-5(4), 01132) Recorded Bks.
Precious Ramotswe's comfortable existence as the only detective in Botswana is suddenly rattled when the Satisfaction Guaranteed Detective Agency opens, and its brochure proclaims, Don't take any chances! Entrust your enquiries to a MAN! But with wisdom on her side, Mma Ramotswe figures to upstage her competition.

Kaleidoscope. Theresa Gurlacz. 1 cass. 8.95 (412) Am Fed Astrologers.
Review of a variety of charts.

Kaleidoscope: Kultur, Literatur und Grammatik. 5th ed. Jack R. Moeller. (ENG & GER.). (978-0-395-89345-6(3)) CENGAGE Learn.

Kaleidoscope: Sound/Spelling Card Stories CD. SRA/McGraw-Hill. (Kaleidoscope Ser.). (gr. 2-6). 15.90 (978-0-07-584223-1(8)) SRA McGraw.

Kaleidoscope of Cultures. unabr. ed. Julian C. Hollick. 1 cass. (Running Time: 60 min.). (Passages to India Ser.). 1991. 15.00 (978-1-56709-003-1(6), 1003) Indep Broadcast.
Language, race, religion, geography & climate - India is so diverse that by rights it should not really be a country at all; & yet it is this very diversity that contains within it the secret that somehow binds Indians together.

Kaleidoskop: Kultur, Literatur und Grammatik. 2nd ed. Jack R. Moeller et al. (C). 1987. reel tape 135.16 (978-0-395-42433-9(X)) CENGAGE Learn.

Kaleka Hua'olelo Hale. Illus. by Kip Parker & Marie Leilehua McDonald. 1 cass. (ENG & HAW.). (C). 1998. 8.95 (978-1-58191-014-8(2)) Aha Punana Leo.
Hawaiian language including flashcards.

Kaleka 'Olelo Hale'aina. 1 cass. (ENG & HAW.). (C). 1996. 5.95 (978-0-9645646-6-4(1)) Aha Punana Leo.

Kaleka 'Olelo Haleku'ai. 1 cass. (ENG & HAW.). (C). 1996. 5.95 (978-0-9645646-5-7(3)) Aha Punana Leo.

Kaleka 'Olelo Panako. 1 cass. (ENG & HAW.). (C). 1996. 5.95 (978-0-9645646-7-1(X)) Aha Punana Leo.

Kaleka 'Olelo Pokole. 1 cass. (ENG & HAW.). (C). 1995. 8.95 (978-0-9645646-8-8(8)) Aha Punana Leo.

Kalevala: Finnish Mythology. Erkki Pirtola. 2 cass. 1993. 18.00 set. (OC325-70) Sound Horizons AV.

Kalevala: National Epic of Finland, Chapters XXIX-XXX. abr. ed. Read by Ian Richardson. 1 cass. 1984. 12.95 (SWC 1688) HarperCollins Pubs.

Kalikimaka see Legend of Kalikimaka with Christmas Hawaiian-Style CD: Hawaiian Christmas & Music

***Kalilah, the Whispered Promise.** Dexter Griffin. (J). 2009. 6.95 (978-0-9770363-2-5(4)) Fi Si Pub.

Kalimantaan, unabr. collector's ed. C. S. Godshalk. Read by Donada Peters. 11 cass. (Running Time: 16 hrs. 30 mins.). 1999. 88.00 (978-0-7366-4366-5(4), 4819) Books on Tape.
One hundred & sixty years ago, a young Englishman founded a private raj on the coast of Borneo. A tropical version of Victorian society grafted on to one of the most violent cultures on earth, it sprawled over an area the size of England itself. Behind this tale of adventure & conquest, however, lies one even more powerful, one that concerns the realm of the heart & is about love in absurd conditions, the tenacity of it as well as our ability to miss it repeatedly & with perverse genius.

Kalki Avatar, the Coming Prophet. unabr. ed. Swami Amar Jyoti. 1 cass. (Satsangs of Swami Amar Jyoti). 1997. 9.95 (978-0-933572-27-0(1), K-161) Truth Consciousness.
The expected tenth incarnation of Lord Vishnu. Upliftment of Earth into a higher dimension. On Divine Love.

Kalki, Prophet of Our Age. Swami Amar Jyoti. 1 cass. 1990. 9.95 (K-124) Truth Consciousness.
The Avatars come as a last resort. After giving all possible chances, they do what is needed, though it may be painful. What Their coming means to each of us.

Kallet, Epstein & Cicione: Only Human. 1 cass., 1 CD. 9.98 (C-5061); audio compact disk 14.98 CD. (CD-5061) Folk-Legacy.
Another splendid recording by these three artists.

Kallet, Epstein & Cicione: Angels in Daring. 1 cass., 1 CD. 9.98 (C-506); audio compact disk 14.98 CD. (CD-506) Folk-Legacy.
The first recording of the very popular trio.

Kallyope Yell see Poetry of Vachel Lindsay

Kamal CD for Valencia Part 1. rev. ed. Kamal. (ENG.). 2010. 62.50 (978-1-60250-143-0(2)) Kendall-Hunt.

Kana Flashcards Audio Companion (CD) Improve Listening Skills with the Kana Flashcards Audio Companion. Max Hodges & Tomoko Okazaki. Narrated by Arisa Fujii & Fumiya Ito. 2006. audio compact disk 16.00 (978-0-9748694-6-9(5)) White Rabbit FL.

Kandy-Kolored Tangerine-Flake Streamline Baby. unabr. collector's ed. Tom Wolfe. Read by Michael Prichard. 8 cass. (Running Time: 12 hrs.). 1989. 64.00 (978-0-7366-1665-2(9), 2514) Books on Tape.
In this book, his first, Tom Wolfe took a fresh look at the American scene of the early 1960s & zeroed in on the more exotic forms of status-seeking then in vogue from New York to Los Angeles. In the Twist, bouffant hairdos, stock-car racing & rock concerts Wolfe found a unique American energy. In the title piece he eulogizes the flamboyant kustomized kars that California teens constructed with intense artistic dedication.

Kane & Abel. Jeffrey Archer. Narrated by Ken Howard. 2 cass. (Running Time: 3 hrs.). 2000. 14.95 (978-0-00-104759-4(0)) Pub: HarpC GBR. Dist(s): Trafalgar
William Lowell Kane and Abel Rosnovski, one the son of a Boston millionaire, the other a penniless Polish immigrant, two men born on the same day on opposite sides of the world, their paths destined to cross in the ruthless struggle to build a fortune.

Kane & Abel. abr. rev. ed. Jeffrey Archer. Read by Jeff Harding. 3 CDs. (Running Time: 3 hrs. 0 mins. 0 sec.). 2004. audio compact disk 14.95 (978-1-55927-979-6(6)) Pub: Macmill Audio. Dist(s): Macmillan

Kane & Abel, Set. unabr. ed. Jeffrey Archer. Read by Steven Pacey. 14 cass. 1997. 110.95 AudioGO.
William Lowell Kane, son of a Boston millionaire, & Abel Rosnovski, a poor Polish immigrant. Two men born on the same day on opposite sides of the world, their paths destined to cross. Linked by an all-consuming hatred that begins when one issues the other an impossible ultimatum, it seems they were brought together to save & finally destroy each other.

Kanga & Baby Roo Come to the Forest. A. A. Milne. Illus. by Ernest H. Shepard. Narrated by Peter Dennis. (J). 1995. bk. 9.00 (978-1-57375-050-9(6)) Audioscope.

Kangaroo see Gathering of Great Poetry for Children

Kangaroo Island. 1 cass. (Running Time: 35 min.). (J). (gr. k-4). 2001. pap. bk. 19.95 (SP 7007C) Kimbo Educ.
A story of a fire in an Australian Mailee Forest.

Kaniksu. unabr. ed. Thomas Lacy. Read by Jack Sondericker. 3 cass. (Running Time: 3 hrs. 45 min.). 1995. 21.95 (978-1-55686-605-0(4)) Books in Motion.
These memoirs, written with gentle humor & deft insight, capture earlier years of inspiring Idaho & Montana landscapes & colorful personalities.

KanKicks. Natalie R. Manor. 2 cass. (Running Time: 60 min.). (Kicks Ser.). 1990. 14.95 Set. (978-1-881680-00-0(2)) Events Extraord.
Automobile exercise to reduce stress & stay alert.

Kansas: 10th Anniversary. Contrib. by Jennifer Knapp et al. Prod. by Mark Stuart & Mark Lee. 2008. audio compact disk 13.99 (978-5-557-47835-9(3)) Gotee Records.

Kansas City Marshall. Perf. by Henry Fonda. 1 cass. (Running Time: 60 min.). 1947. 7.95 (WW-5155) Natl Recrd Co.
In "Kansas City Marshall" it is May, 1874 & Wyatt Earp rides into Witchita, Kansas. He wants to go into business, but he is made sheriff, to bring law & order into the city. The story "Yellow Sky" is a western drama that takes place in an old mining city that is almost a ghost town. Peck is pitted against four outlaws for a prize of $50,000 in stolen gold.

Kant in 90 Minutes. Paul Strathern. Narrated by Robert Whitfield. (Running Time: 1 hr. 30 mins.). 2003. 17.95 (978-1-59912-521-3(8)) Iofy Corp.

Kant in 90 Minutes. unabr. ed. Paul Strathern. Read by Robert Whitfield. (Running Time: 1 hr. 30 mins.). (Philosophers in 90 Minutes Ser.). 2004. reel tape 14.95 (978-0-7861-2533-3(0)) Blckstn Audio.

Kant in 90 Minutes. unabr. ed. Paul Strathern. Read by Robert Whitfield. 1 CD. (Running Time: 1 hr. 30 mins.). (Philosophers in 90 Minutes Ser.). 2000. audio compact disk 14.95 (978-0-7861-9042-3(6)) Blckstn Audio.
Immanuel Kant taught and wrote prolifically about physical geography yet never traveled further than forty miles from his home in Königsberg. How appropriate it is then that in his philosophy he should deny that all knowledge was derived from experience. Kant's aim was to restore metaphysics. He insisted that all experience must conform to knowledge. According to Kant, space and time are subjective; along with various "categories," they help us to see the phenomena of the world-though never its true reality.

Kant in 90 Minutes. unabr. ed. Paul Strathern. Read by Robert Whitfield. 2 CDs. (Running Time: 1 hr. 30 mins.). 2001. audio compact disk 16.00 (978-0-7861-9090-4(6), 3116) Blckstn Audio.

Kant in 90 Minutes. unabr. ed. Paul Strathern. Read by Robert Whitfield. (Running Time: 1 hr. 30 mins.). 2004. 14.95 (978-0-7861-2437-4(7), 3116) Blckstn Audio.

Kant's Foundations of Ethics: What Is Enlightenment? & the Fundamental Principles of the Metaphysics of Morals. Immanuel Kant. Tr. by Leo Rauch from GER. Voice by Albert A. Anderson. 4 cass. (Running Time: 4 hrs. 30 min.). (World of the Mind Ser.). 1998. audio compact disk 30.00 Set. (978-1-887250-16-0(6)) Agora Pubns.
The two works included in this volume articulate the most fundamental principles of Kant's ethical world view. "What Is Enlightenment?" (1784) & "Fundamental Principles of the Metaphysics of Morals" (1785) were written in the period between the American Revolution & the French Revolution. Taken together they challenge all free people to think about the requirements for self-determination both in our individual lives & in our public & private institutions.

Kanza Collecting. Poems. Repha Buckman. Contrib. by Mike Ferguson & Mike Sanders. 1 cass. 10.00 (978-0-940559-06-6(4)) Tri Crown Pr.

Kapampangan Newspaper Reader. (Philippine Language Ser.). 1992. 13.00 (978-0-931745-85-0(3)) Dunwoody Pr.

Kapampangan Newspaper Reader, Set. Alma M. Davidson & Leonardo A. Pineda. 2 cass. (Running Time: 1 hr. 30 min. per cass.). (MIS.). 1992. 19.00 (3071) Dunwoody Pr.
Forty-five selections provide the student with a wide range of articles & all necessary lexical & grammatical information to make the link between spoken language & various genres of published & broadcast media. Also known as Pampanggo.

Kaplan Word Power: Vocabulary Building for Success. unabr. abr. ed. Kaplan Educational Center Staff. 2 CDs. (Running Time: 13 hrs. 0 mins. 0 sec.). 2003. audio compact disk 19.95 (978-0-7435-2998-3(7), Sound Ideas) Pub: S&S Audio. Dist(s): S and S Inc
You'll Never Be at a Loss for Words Again. The words you use say a lot about who you are and where you're headed. Whether you want to express yourself clearly to impress a prospective employer during a job interview, or just brush up on those pesky words you encounter every so often reading the newspaper, Kaplan Word Power® is the essential tool to help you expand your daily vocabulary. Energize Your Vocabulary with: Must-know everyday words that are the essentials of a good vocabulary Engaging lessons to help you utilize words in context Hot words often found on standardized tests like the SAT and GRE Tips to help you figure out new words, roots, and more.

Kara, the lonely Falcon. Joseph F. Girzone. Narrated by Alexandra O'Karma. (Running Time: 1 hr. 15 mins.). 15.00 (978-1-4025-1756-3(4)); audio compact disk 19.00 (978-1-4025-2079-2(4)) Recorded Bks.

Karain: A Memory see Tales of Unrest

Karaliene. unabr. ed. Egle Zalcic. 1 cass. (Running Time: 26 min.). (LIT.). bk. 19.95 (SLT101) J Norton Pubs.

Karate. Eldon Taylor. 1 cass. (Running Time: 62 min.). (Inner Talk Ser.). 16.95 incl. script. (978-1-55978-248-7(X), 5393C) Progress Aware Res.
Soundtrack - Musical Themes with underlying subliminal affirmations.

Karate Princess & the Last Griffin: And, the Karate Princess in Monsta Trouble. unabr. ed. Read by Jeremy Strong & Judy Bennett. 3 cass. (Running Time: 4 hrs. 30 mins.). (J). 2002. 24.95 (978-0-7540-5246-3(X), CCA3684, Chivers Child Audio) AudioGO.

***Kardashian Konfidential.** unabr. ed. Kourtney Kardashian et al. (Running Time: 6 hrs. 0 mins. 0 sec.). (ENG., 2010. audio compact disk 19.95 (978-1-4272-1126-2(4)) Pub: Macmill Audio. Dist(s): Macmillan

Karen Kingsbury Firstborn CD Collection: Fame, Forgiven, Found, Family, Forever. abr. ed. Karen Kingsbury. Read by Sandra Burr. (Running Time: 20 hrs.). (Firstborn Ser.). 2008. audio compact disk 36.95 (978-1-4233-5244-0(0), 9781423352440, BACD) Brilliance Audio.

Karen Kingsbury Redemption CD Collection: Redemption, Remember, Return, Rejoice, Reunion. abr. ed. Karen Kingsbury & Gary Smalley. Read by Sandra Burr. (Running Time: 20 hrs.). (Redemption Ser.). 2008. audio compact disk 36.95 (978-1-4233-5158-0(4), 9781423351580, BACD) Brilliance Audio.

Karen Kingsbury Sunrise CD Collection: Sunrise, Summer, Someday, Sunset. abr. ed. Karen Kingsbury. Read by Sandra Burr. (Running Time: 28 hrs.). (Sunrise Ser.). 2009. audio compact disk 36.99 (978-1-4233-7968-3(3), 9781423379683, BACD) Brilliance Audio.

Karen Robards: Bait, Superstition, Vanished. abr. ed. Karen Robards. Read by Joyce Bean. (Running Time: 18 hrs.). 2007. audio compact disk 34.95 (978-1-4233-3428-6(0), 9781423334286, BACD) Brilliance Audio.

Karen Swenson. unabr. ed. Read by Karen Swenson. 1 cass. (Running Time: 29 min.). 1985. 10.00 New Letters.
Karen Swenson's books include "An Attic of Ideals" & "East West".

Karen Yamashita. unabr. ed. Karen Yamashita. 1 cass. (Running Time: 29 min.). (New Letters on the Air Ser.). 1992. 10.00 (022892) New Letters.
Yamashita reads from her first novel, "Through the Arc of the Rain Forest," a futuristic fantasy set in Brazil & talks about Japanese immigrants to Brazil.

Karen Yamashita. unabr. ed. Karen Yamashita. Ed. by James McKinley. Prod. by Rebeah Presson. 1 cass. (Running Time: 29 min.). (On the Air Ser.). 1992. 10.00 New Letters.
Author talks about the vanishing rain forest, reads from futuristic novel Through the End of the Rain Forest, set to Brazilian music.

Karenge ya Marenge see Poetry of Countee Cullen

***Karin Slaughter CD Collection: Beyond Reach, Fractured, Undone.** abr. ed. Karin Slaughter. (Running Time: 18 hrs.). 2010. audio compact disk 29.99 (978-1-4418-6166-5(1), 9781441861665, BACD) Brilliance Audio.

Karizma CD: Featuring Vinnie Colaiuta, David Garfield, Neil Stubenhaus, Mike Landau. Vinnie Colaiuta et al. 2001. audio compact disk 15.98 (978-0-634-03089-5(2), 0634030892) Pub: Hudson Music. Dist(s): H Leonard

Karl Hess: Liberty As A Do-It-Yourself Project. (Running Time: 60 min.). (Cypress College). 1980. 9.00 (F109) Freeland Pr.
Talks about "action" taking precedence over "words" on such issues as the economy, politics & so-called ecological solutions; the Libertarians role as the "Marines"; do it now - no time for being "hermits.".

Karl Hess: Survivalism & Liberty. (Running Time: 60 min.). (Long Beach City College). 1983. 9.00 (F148) Freeland Pr.
Through witicisms & anecdotes the author informs us how to survive in this country.

Karl Hess: The Nuts & Bolts of Technology & Freedom. (Running Time: 60 min.). (Cal State Univ., Long Beach). 1981. 9.00 (F120) Freeland Pr.
Suggests that actions on a local - not vocal - level are an effective method for attaining a free society.

Karl Hess: Workshop at CSULB Philosophy Association. (Running Time: 90 min.). (Workshop Speeches). 1983. 10.00 (FW600) Freeland Pr.

Karl Marx: Das Kapital. unabr. ed. David R. Steel. Ed. by Israel M. Kirzner & Mike Hassell. Narrated by Louis Rukeyser. 2 cass. (Running Time: 75 min. per cass.). Dramatization. (Great Economic Thinkers Ser.). 1988. 17.95 (978-0-938935-32-2(1), 10202) Knowledge Prod.
Marx viewed capitalism as the systematic exploitation of workers by owners of capital. Many modern ideas about profits, interest, monopoly & antagonism between workers & employers find their roots in the Marxian view of economics.

Karl Marx: das Kapital: From Capitalist Exploitation to Communist Revolution. David Ramsay Steele. Read by Louis Rukeyser. (Running Time: 10800 sec.). (Great Economic Thinkers Ser.). 2006. audio compact disk 25.95 (978-0-7861-7326-6(2)) Pub: Blckstn Audio. Dist(s): NetLibrary CO

Karma: What It Is & How to Change It. Asha Praver. 1 cass. (Change the World Or Change Yourself Ser.). 9.95 (AT-59) Crystal Clarity.
Includes: The nature of the satanic force; how God uses Satan; karma & reincarnation as proof of a benign God; gaining control of your magnetism.

Karma & Compassion. Swami Amar Jyoti. 1 cass. 1988. 9.95 (F-16) Truth Consciousness.
The infallible law. The meaning of compassion. Spiritual values for the common man.

Karma & Reincarnation. Swami Amar Jyoti. 1 cass. 1987. 9.95 (F-13) Truth Consciousness.
Karma the subconscious mind. How does reincarnation take place? The Journey on the astral plane. What are ghosts? Master guides true disciples in finishing karmas.

Karma & Reincarnation. George King. 2007. audio compact disk (978-0-937249-39-0(4)) Aetherius Soc.

Karma & Reincarnation: Transcending Your Past, Transforming Your Future. unabr. ed. Elizabeth Clare Prophet & Patricia R. Spadaro. 1 cass. (Running Time: 1 hr. 30 mins.). 2002. 18.95 (978-0-922729-72-2(7), 942-057) Pub: Summit Univ. Dist(s): Natl Bk Netwk

Karma & Spiritual Growth. Swami Amar Jyoti. 2 dolby cass. 1984. 12.95 (F-9) Truth Consciousness.
Attending to our karmas & learning how to deal with them, a prerequisite for spiritual growth. How Karma works.

Karma & Your Natal Chart. Claire Abbate. Read by Claire Abbate. 1 cass. (Running Time: 90 min.). 1994. 8.95 (1108) Am Fed Astrologers.
Indicators of Karma in the natal horoscope.

Karma, Grace, & Liberation. Swami Amar Jyoti. 1 cass. 1989. 9.95 (F-17) Truth Consciousness.
Relationship between our karmas & the grace, mercy, & benevolence of Guru or Divine Mother.

Karma in Its Effect on Character - Para-Bhakti or Supreme Devotion. unabr. ed. Vivekananda. Read by Alan Arkin & John Batiste. 1 cass. (Running Time: 40 min.). 1990. 7.95 (978-1-882915-09-5(7)) Vedanta Ctr Atlanta.
How actions & reactions mold character; the nature of devotion to God, how to attain & practice.

Karma, Reincarnation & Christianity. Elizabeth Clare Prophet. 1 cass. (Running Time: 1 hr.). 1996. 18.95 (978-0-922729-65-4(4)) Pub: Summit Univ. Dist(s): Natl Bk Netwk

***Karma Release Meditation.** Diana Cooper. Andrew Brel. (Running Time: 1 hr. 0 mins. 0 sec.). (ENG.). 2010. audio compact disk 14.95 (978-1-84409-526-1(6)) Pub: Findhorn Pr GBR. Dist(s): IPG Chicago

Karma Releasing: Clearing Away Painful Patterns from Your Past. Doreen Virtue. 1 cass. (Running Time: 1 hr.). 1999. 10.95 (978-1-56170-644-0(2), 485) Hay House.
A lecture helping to clear away bad Karma.

Karma Releasing: Clearing Away Painful Patterns from Your Past. Doreen Virtue. 1 CD. 2004. audio compact disk 10.95 (978-1-4019-0399-2(1)) Hay House.

Karma! The Jury Is Still Out. unabr. ed. Tekonsha & Chief Little Summer. Interview with Warm Night Rain. 1 CD. (Karma! The Jury is Still Out!). 1999. audio compact disk 15.95 CD. (978-1-880440-17-9(2)) Piqua Pr.
The effect past life deeds can play on current life.

Karma Yoga. 1 cass. (Running Time: 1 hr.). 12.99 (197); 12.99 (103) Yoga Res Foun.

Karma Yoga, No. 2. Swami Jyotirmayananda. 1 cass. (Running Time: 1 hr.). 1990. 12.99 Yoga Res Foun.

Karma Yoga, No. 3. Swami Jyotirmayananda. 1 cass. (Running Time: 1 hr.). 1990. 12.99 Yoga Res Foun.

Karma Yoga: Balancing Activity & Meditation. Daya Mata. 1984. 6.50 (2122) Self Realization.
Explains how each of us can come to feel, in both activity & meditation, the joyous awareness of God's presence. Topics include: Learning to enjoy life's responsibilities; how to let God flow through our actions; knowing & accepting ourselves; overcoming feelings of guilt; simple ways to strengthen will power & create good habits.

Karma Yoga & Its Deeper Meaning. Swami Amar Jyoti. 1 cass. 1978. 9.95 (G-4) Truth Consciousness.
The path of Karma Yoga - what it is, who should follow it, how to do it, & its results.

Karma Yoga & Liberation. Swami Amar Jyoti. 1 cass. 1989. 9.95 (G-12) Truth Consciousness.
The all-important attitude needed for genuine Karma Yoga. Why Karma Yoga is necessary on the path.

Karma Yoga & True Discipleship. Swami Amar Jyoti. 1 cass. 1976. 9.95 (G-1) Truth Consciousness.
Work as a medium for spiritual evolution. What we are, more important than what we do.

Karmapas: Holders of the Mahamudra Lineage. Vajracarya. Read by Chogyam Trungpa. 5 cass. 1976. 45.00 (A045) Vajradhatu.
Five talks: 1) Basic Sanity & the Lineage; 2) Tusum Khyenpa, the first Karmapa; 3) Karma Pakshi & Rangjung Dorje; 4) The Black Crown; 5) Devotion & Leadership in the Karmapa Principle.

Karmic Capitalism. Bruce Goldberg. (ENG.). 2005. audio compact disk 17.00 (978-1-57968-103-6(4)) Pub: B Goldberg. Dist(s): Baker Taylor

Karmic Capitalism. Bruce Goldberg. Read by Bruce Goldberg. 1 cass. (Running Time: 30 min.). (ENG.). 2007. 13.00 (978-1-885577-98-6(2)) Pub: B Goldberg. Dist(s): Baker Taylor
How to become financially independent while growing spiritually.

Karmic Capitalism CD Album. Bruce Goldberg. (ENG.). 2005. audio compact disk 75.00 (978-1-57968-027-5(5)) Pub: B Goldberg. Dist(s): Baker Taylor

Karmic Capitalism Program Cassette Album. Bruce Goldberg. Read by Bruce Goldberg. 6 cass. (Running Time: 30 min.). (ENG.). 2007. 65.00 (978-1-885577-99-3(0)) Pub: B Goldberg. Dist(s): Baker Taylor
Shows how to become financially independent while growing spiritually.

Karmic Dimensions of Astrology. Elayne J. Manago. 1 cass. 8.95 (695) Am Fed Astrologers.
An AFA Convention workshop tape.

Karmic Relationships. Joan Kellogg. 1 cass. 8.95 (683) Am Fed Astrologers.

Karstens Way. Peter Oosterhuis. (ENG.). 2000. 16.99 (978-1-881273-36-3(9)) Pub: Northfield Pub. Dist(s): Moody
Golf, anyone? Karsten's Way tells the story of an ingenious man who took a long shot to improve his game and the game of millions of golfers around the world. His goal: to help golfers play their best and enjoy the game.Read the dramatic life story of Karsten Solheim, inventor of the PING golf club - the club that revolutionized the game of golf. Solheim's rise from shoemaker to world-recognized golf club designer and manufacturer is one of American industry's greatest success stories.Understand how Karsten Solheim's faith in God propelled him toward success. His passion for quality and belief in himself and his ideas became the hallmarks of his success and that of his business, the Karsten Manufacturing Company. An inspiring read for anyone with ambitious dreams and a love for the exciting game of golf. Audio Cassette.

Kasey & the Dream Forest: Songs of the Dream Forest. Kurt Reetz. 2000. audio compact disk 8.99 (978-1-931179-04-1(2)) Long Hill Prod.

***Kasey to the Rescue: The Remarkable Story of a Monkey & a Miracle.** unabr. ed. Ellen Rogers. (Running Time: 9 hrs. 0 mins.). 2010. 15.99 (978-1-4001-8954-0(3)); 24.99 (978-1-4001-6954-2(2)); audio compact disk 34.99 (978-1-4001-1954-7(5)) Pub: Tantor Media. Dist(s): IngramPubServ

***Kasey to the Rescue (Library Edition) The Remarkable Story of a Monkey & a Miracle.** unabr. ed. Ellen Rogers. (Running Time: 9 hrs. 0 mins.). 2010. 34.99 (978-1-4001-9954-9(9)); audio compact disk 83.99 (978-1-4001-4954-4(1)) Pub: Tantor Media. Dist(s): IngramPubServ

Kashi. Music by Rajan Mishra & Sajan Mishra. 1 cass. (Tirth Ser.: Vol. 1). 1996. (D96001) Multi-Cultural Bks.

Kashmir: Symphonic Led Zeppelin. Perf. by London Philharmonic Orchestra, The. 1 cass., 1 CD. 8.78 (PHI 454145); audio compact disk 14.38 CD Jewel box. (PHI 454145) NewSound.

Kaspar Hauser. Anselm. audio compact disk 12.95 (978-0-8219-3801-0(0)) EMC-Paradigm.

Kassulke's Field, abr. ed. Johnny Quarles. Read by Michael Waugh. 4 cass. (Running Time: 6 hrs.). 1999. 24.95 (978-1-890990-19-0(1)) Otis Audio.
In 1869, in Swisher Texas, Paul Kassulke is beginning a new life with a saloon & big plans to start one of the first baseball teams in the new frontier. Ezra & Hattie Cole are back, along with Sunday Allen & Tess Jackson. Brack & Leah Haynes have returned home from Europe, & Deputy Thad Rollings is stumbling through his new role as sheriff & his first love.

Kata: The Essence & Inner Meaning. Sid Campbell. (Running Time: 3 hrs.). 29.95 (978-0-682-87109-9(5)) Gong Prods.

Katani's Jamaican Holiday. unabr. ed. Annie Bryant. Read by Pamella D'Pella. (Running Time: 17940 sec.). (Beacon Street Girls Special Adventure Ser.: No. 4). (ENG.). (J). (gr. 4). 2008. audio compact disk 19.95 (978-0-7393-7332-3(3), Listening Lib) Pub: Random Audio Pubg. Dist(s): Random

Kate Hannigan. unabr. ed. Catherine Cookson. Read by Juliet Stevenson. 6 cass. (Running Time: 6 hrs.). 1993. 54.95 (978-0-7451-5850-1(1), CAB 063) AudioGO.

Kate Hannigan's Daughter. unabr. ed. Catherine Cookson. Read by Elizabeth Henry. 10 cass. (Running Time: 15 hrs.). 2001. 84.95 (27456) Pub: Soundings Ltd GBR. Dist(s): Ulverscroft US

Kate Hannigan's Girl, Set. unabr. ed. Catherine Cookson. Read by Elizabeth Henry. 10 cass. (Running Time: 13 hrs. 30 mins.). (Sound Ser.). 2000. 84.95 (978-1-86042-745-9(6), 27456) Pub: UlverLrgPrint GBR. Dist(s): Ulverscroft US

Kate Millett. Interview with Kate Millet. 1 cass. (Running Time: 15 min.). 1970. 9.95 (L053) TFR.
The feminist philosopher talks on her book, "Sexual Politics".

Kate Remembered. A. Scott Berg. Read by Tony Goldwyn. 6 cass. 2004. 54.95 (978-0-7927-3087-3(9), CSL 611, Chivers Sound Lib); audio compact disk 79.95 (978-0-7927-3088-0(7), SLD 611, Chivers Sound Lib); audio compact disk 29.95 (978-0-7927-3089-7(5), CMP 611, Chivers Sound Lib) AudioGO.

Kate Shelley & the Midnight Express. Margaret K. Wetterer. Illus. by Karen Ritz. (On My Own History Ser.). (J). (gr. 2-5). 1991. pap. bk. 6.95 (978-0-87614-541-8(1), Carolrho Bks) Lerner Pub.

Kate Shelley & the Midnight Express. Margaret K. Wetterer. Illus. by Karen Ritz. 14 vols. (Running Time: 14 mins.). 1991. pap. bk. 39.95 (978-1-59112-664-5(9)) Live Oak Media.

Kate Shelley & the Midnight Express. Margaret K. Wetterer. Illus. by Karen Ritz. (Running Time: 14 mins.). (J). (gr. k-4). 1991. 12.95 (978-1-59112-662-1(2)) Live Oak Media.

Kate Shelley & the Midnight Express. unabr. ed. Margaret K. Wetterer. Read by Jerry Terheyden. Illus. by Karen Ritz. 1 cass. (Running Time: 14 mins.). (Historical Fiction Ser.). (J). (gr. 1-6). 1991. bk. 24.95 (978-0-87499-243-4(5)); pap. bk. 16.95 (978-0-87499-242-7(7)) Pub: Live Oak Media. Dist(s): AudioGO
A recounting of a true story of 15 year old Kate Shelley, who in 1881 left the safety of her Iowa farm home to brave darkness, torrential downpour & a swollen river to get out word that a nearby railroad bridge had been swept away.

Kate Shelley & the Midnight Express, Grades 1-6. unabr. ed. Margaret K. Wetterer. Read by Jerry Terheyden. Illus. by Karen Ritz. 14 vols. (Running Time: 14 mins.). (Historical Fiction Ser.). (J). 1991. pap. bk. & tchr. ed. 37.95 Reading Chest. (978-0-87499-244-1(3)) Live Oak Media.

Kateri Tekakwitha: Mohawk Maid. Evelyn M. Brown. 5 cass. (J). 22.95 (504) Ignatius Pr.
The dramatic tale of a saintly Mohowk girl.

Kate's Return, Set. Cheri Crane. 2 cass. 1996. 3.47 (978-1-55503-992-9(8), 07001401) Covenant Comms.
A heartwarming sequel to "Kate's Turn".

Kate's Story. Billy Hopkins. Read by Christopher Kay. 12 cass. (Sound Ser.). (J). 2002. 94.95 (978-1-84283-191-5(7)) Pub: ISIS Lrg Prnt GBR. Dist(s): Ulverscroft US

Kate's Turn, Set. abr. ed. Cheri Crane. 2 cass. 11.98 (978-1-55503-746-8(1), 079427) Covenant Comms.
A condensed novel every mother & daughter should hear.

Katharine Hepburn. abr. ed. Barbara Leaming. Read by Sandra Burr. (Running Time: 3 hrs.). 2008. 24.95 (978-1-4233-5427-7(3), 9781423354277, Brilliance MP3); 24.95 (978-1-4233-5429-1(X), 9781423354291, BAD); 39.25 (978-1-4233-5428-4(1), 9781423354284, Brinc Audio MP3 Lib); 39.25 (978-1-4233-5430-7(3), 9781423354307, BADLE) Brilliance Audio.

Katharine, the Virgin Widow. unabr. ed. Jean Plaidy & Anne Flosnik. (Running Time: 12 hrs. 5 mins.). 2008. 29.95 (978-1-4332-5338-6(0)); 72.95 (978-1-4332-5335-5(6)); audio compact disk 90.00 (978-1-4332-5336-2(4)) Blckstn Audio.

Katherine Hepburn, abr. ed. Barbara Leaming. Read by Sandra Burr. 2 cass. (Running Time: 3 hrs.). 2000. 7.95 (978-1-57815-139-4(2), 1098, Media Bks Audio) Media Bks NJ.
Hollywood has produced many stars, but no one compares to Katharine Hepburn. There are documents that finally illuminate the mystery of Hepburn, her friends & her family.

Katherine Mansfield's Best Stories. Katherine Mansfield. Narrated by Flo Gibson. (ENG.). 2008. audio compact disk 29.95 (978-1-60646-018-4(8)) Audio Bk Con.

Katherine Mansfield's Best Stories, Set. unabr. ed. Katherine Mansfield. Read by Flo Gibson. 6 cass. (Running Time: 9 hrs.). 1997. 24.95 (978-1-55685-465-1(X), 465-X) Audio Bk Con.
A collection of nineteen stories such as "Prelude", "The Doll's House" & "At the Bay" will linger long in memory. Death, faithlessness, prejudice, cruelty & love are treated with passion, yet with a rich purity of the language.

Katherine Pyle Book of Fairy Tales, Set unabr. ed. Katherine Pyle. Narrated by Flo Gibson. 4 cass. (Running Time: 6 hrs.). (J). (gr. 1-4). 1998. 19.95 (978-1-55685-636-5(9)) Audio Bk Con.
These old tales are full of mystery, adventure & intriguing characters.

Katherine's Song. Composed by David Lane. 1 CD. 2004. audio compact disk 14.95 (978-0-9746122-1-8(9)) Edit etc Ltd.
Original songs that range from soft rock to new age jazz.

Kathleen Madigan Live! unabr. ed. Kathleen Madigan. 1 cass. 6.95; audio compact disk 10.95 Wildstone Media.
Kathleen was recently voted Female Comedian Of The Year at the prestigious American Comedy Awards & after listening to this live recording you'll know why!.

Kathleen Raine. unabr. ed. Read by Kathleen Raine. 1 cass. (Running Time: 29 min.). 1985. 10.00 New Letters.
Reading by English poet & critic of the generation of Auden & Spender.

Kathryne Pirtle - Works for Unaccompanied Clarinet: The Music of J. S. Bach. Composed by J. S. Bach. Kathryne Pirtle. (ENG.). 2005. audio compact disk 12.95 (978-0-634-08682-3(0), 0634086820) H Leonard.

Kathy Troccoli. Perf. by Kathy Troccoli. 1 cass. 1994. audio compact disk Brentwood Music.
Dove nominee for female vocalist of the year, this self-titled release further establishes Kathy as a core Christian artist, featuring the No. 1 songs My Life is in Your Hands & Mission of Love.

Kathy Troccoli: Corner of Eden. Perf. by Kathy Troccoli. 1 cass., 1 CD. 1998. 10.98 (978-0-7601-2473-4(6)); audio compact disk 16.98 (978-0-7601-2474-1(4)) Provident Music.

Kathy Troccoli: Love & Mercy. 1997. 10.98 (978-0-7601-1360-8(2), C10003); audio compact disk 16.98 CD. (CD10003) Brentwood Music.
Deals with several relevant issues of today. Includes "Love One Another," "How Would I Know," "A Baby's Prayer," & more.

Kathy Troccoli: Love One Another. Perf. by Amy Grant et al. 1997. audio compact disk 3.99 CD. (978-0-7601-1416-2(1), MCDS40160) Pub: Brentwood Music. Dist(s): Provident Mus Dist
Along with the attention this will bring to the HIV/AIDS cause, proceeds from the CD single will go to His Touch Ministries.

Katie Milk Solves Crimes: And So On. unabr. ed. Annie Caulfield. Read by India Fisher. 4 CDs. (Running Time: 17100 sec.). (J). (gr. 2-5). 2007. audio compact disk 34.95 (978-1-4056-5637-5(9), Chivers Child Audio) AudioGO.

Katie Milk Solves Reality-TV Crimes. unabr. ed. Annie Caulfield. Read by India Fisher. 4 CDs. (Running Time: 4 hrs. 25 mins.). (J). (gr. 3-6). 2008. audio compact disk 34.95 (978-1-4056-5951-2(3), Chivers Child Audio) AudioGO.

Katie Mulholland. unabr. ed. Catherine Cookson. Read by Susan Jameson. 14 cass. (Running Time: 14 hrs.). 1996. 110.95 (978-0-7451-6618-6(0), CAB 1234) AudioGO.
Dismissed from the house after her ensuing pregnancy, Katie must raise her child on her own. And although she does eventually come to know both love & power, the fear & hatred engendered by the man who dishonored her return to haunt & threaten her.

***Katie up & down the Hall: The True Story of How One Dog Turned Five Neighbors into a Family.** unabr. ed. Glenn Plaskin. (Running Time: 8 hrs.). (ENG.). 2010. 21.98 (978-1-60941-039-1(4)); audio compact disk 26.98 (978-1-60941-038-4(6)) Pub: Hachet Audio. Dist(s): HachBkGrp

Katie's Kitchen. unabr. ed. Dee Williams. Narrated by Nadia May. 9 CDs. (Running Time: 10 hrs.). 2001. audio compact disk 72.00 (978-0-7861-9633-3(5), 2883) Blckstn Audio.
With little money but full of determination, widowed and impoverished Katherine Carter takes lodgings in Docklands London and begins to rebuild her life. But little does anyone know of the horrors 1914 will unleash.

Katie's Kitchen. unabr. ed. Dee Williams. Narrated by Nadia May. 7 cass. (Running Time: 10 hrs.). 2001. 49.95 (978-0-7861-2123-6(8), 2883) Blckstn Audio.

Katie's Plight. Carla Jackson. Ed. by Cathy Cowan. Illus. by Jane Maciel. 1 cass. (Running Time: 20 min.). (J). (ps-7). 1997. pap. bk. 8.95 (978-0-9669166-0-7(3)) Beajo Pub.

Katie's Plight. Carla Jackson. Read by Carla Jackson. 1 cass. (Running Time: 18 min.). (J). (gr. 2-4). 1999. 8.95 (978-0-9669166-1-4(1)) Beajo Pub.
The story of the friendship between a troublesome spider, Spike, & a sophisticated butterfly, Katie. Informs children about developing self esteem & its impact on relationships & personal success.

Katrina. Interview. Hosted by Peter Kramer. Comment by John Hockenberry. 1 CD. (Running Time: 1 hr). (Infinite Mind Ser.: 392). 2005. 21.95 (978-1-933644-19-6(2), LCM 392) Lichtenstein Creat.
With thousands dead, tens of thousands homeless and a mass exodus from the Gulf Coast, what can we expect the impact will be over the next few months. What will it take for the nation to heal?"The Road to Recovery" features the nation's top psychiatrist, Dr. Thomas Insel, director of the National Institute of Mental Health, who discusses the impact of Hurricane Katrina, and says "let's rebuild the mental health system, and do it better."Also, historian James Gregory takes us back 70 years to a time when hundreds of thousands of Oklahoma residents fled natural disaster and wandered the country in search of a better life. He identifies a growing concern about the sustainability of America's sympathy, based on the history of public sentiment about migrants of all backgrounds in previous times.We hear from sociologist Betty Morrow, who specializes in disaster recovery, about the experiences of those affected by Hurricane Andrew. She says Katrina victims will need lots of help and that the nation is likely to forget about them in a short while.We also speak with the directors of the National Center for Post Traumatic Stress and the National Center for Child Traumatic Stress, Drs. Matthew Friedman and Alan Steinberg, and examine mental health right now and expectations for the coming months. They provide helpful tips for self and family care.And we take a trip to Poccotola, Mississippi where a remarkable camp has been set up to shelter and treat the families with autistic children who survived the hurricane.

Katy Didd Bigg Cassette. Stephen Cosgrove. 2004. 5.00 (978-1-58804-392-4(4)) PCI Educ.

Ka'u Papa Hula. Na'ilima Gaison. Illus. by Maile Ka'ai. 1 cass. (HAW.). (J). 1999. pap. bk. 6.95 (978-1-58191-066-7(5)) Aha Punana Leo.

Kauai Beaches. Lori Stitt. 2004. audio compact disk 4.95 (978-1-57306-176-6(X)) Bess Pr.

Kaufman's Favorite 50 Celtic Jigs & Waltzes for Mandolin. Compiled by Mel Bay Publications. 2008. spiral bd. 22.95 (978-0-7866-7125-0(4)) Mel Bay.

Kay Boyle: Interview with Kay Boyle & Kay Bonetti. Interview. Kay Boyle. Interview with Kay Boyle. Interview with Kay Bonetti. 1 cass. (Running Time: 49 min.). 1985. 13.95 (978-1-55644-123-3(1), 5012) Am Audio Prose.
The author's comparisons of the counter-culture of the 20's in Paris in which she was a central figure, & she addresses the scope of her prolific writing life.

Kay Hooper Fear CD Collection: Hunting Fear, Chill of Fear, Sleeping with Fear. abr. ed. Kay Hooper. Directed By Bill Weideman. Narrated by Dick Hill & Kathy Garver. (Running Time: 16 hrs.). (Fear Trilogy). 2007. audio compact disk 34.95 (978-1-4233-3427-9(2), 9781423334279, BACD) Brilliance Audio.

Kay Kyser's Kollege of Musical Knowledge. 1 cass. (Running Time: 1 hr.). 2001. 6.98 (2082) Radio Spirits.
Comedy game show of special interest to service men and women.

Kaye Gibbons. unabr. ed. Read by Kaye Gibbons & Rebekah Presson. Ed. by James McKinley. 1 cass. (Running Time: 29 min.). (New Letters on the Air Ser.). 1991. 10.00 (062191); 18.00 2-sided cass. New Letters.
Gibbons is interviewed by Rebekah Presson.

Kazakh, Colloquial. unabr. ed. Zhoumagaly Abouv & Kurtulus Oxtopcu. Read by Zhoumagaly Abuov & Sawliye Tajibayeva. 3 cass. (Running Time: 3 hrs. 30 mins.). 1994. pap. bk. 75.00 (978-0-88432-784-4(1), AFKA10) J Norton Pubs.
Includes 64-page text & reference cards.

Kazakh Language Course. 1994. 175.00 (978-0-7605-0489-5(X)) Rector Pr.

Kazan: Wolf-Dog of the North. unabr. ed. James Oliver Curwood. Read by Kevin Foley. 6 cass. (Running Time: 7 hrs. 30 min.). 1996. 39.95 (978-1-55686-739-2(5)) Books in Motion.
Part-wolf, part Husky, he lived his life in the wilderness. He knew starvation, bitter cold, & suffering at the cruel hand of man. He was fearless & a giant among his kind.

Ke Kanaka Mahi'ai Pomaika'i. Lilinoe Andrews. Illus. by Brook Parker. 1 cass. (HAW.). (J). 1999. pap. bk. 6.95 (978-1-58191-076-6(2)) Aha Punana Leo.

Ke Nui A'e Au. Keiki C. Kawai'ae'a. Photos by Arna L. Johnson. (HAW., (J). 1995. bk. 8.95 (978-1-890270-19-3(9)) Aha Punana Leo.

Keats. John Keats. (978-1-85998-224-2(7), HoddrStoughton) Hodder General GBR.

Keats. John Keats. 1989. 18.95 (978-1-85998-205-1(0), HoddrStoughton) Pub: Hodder General GBR. Dist(s): Trafalgar

Keats, John: Odes. unabr. ed. Narrated by Martin Jarvis. 1 cass. 12.95 (ECN 138) J Norton Pubs.
Reflects on the nature of God & how through suffering recongnises grace. Includes Sir Ralph Richardson presenting his favourite of Marvell's verse.

Keen, Fitful Gusts Are Whispering **see Poetry of Keats**

Keen Vision. Eldon Taylor. 1 cass. (Running Time: 62 min.). (Inner Talk Ser.). 16.95 incl. script. (978-1-55978-136-7(X), 5352C) Progress Aware Res.
Soundtrack - Musical Themes with underlying subliminal affirmations.

Keen Vision: Babbling Brook. Eldon Taylor. 1 cass. 16.95 (978-1-55978-482-5(2), 5352F) Progress Aware Res.

Keen Vision: Easy. Eldon Taylor. Read by Eldon Taylor. Ed. by Leslie Brice. 1 cass. (Running Time: 1 hr.). 1992. 16.95 (978-1-56705-237-4(1)) Gateways Inst.
Self improvement.

Keen Vision: Ocean. Eldon Taylor. Read by Eldon Taylor. Ed. by Leslie Brice. 1 cass. (Running Time: 1 hr.). 1992. 16.95 (978-1-56705-238-1(X)) Gateways Inst.

Keen Vision: Stream. Eldon Taylor. Read by Eldon Taylor. Ed. by Leslie Brice. 1 cass. (Running Time: 1 hr.). 1992. 16.95 (978-1-56705-239-8(8)) Gateways Inst.

Keep. unabr. ed. Jennifer Egan. Narrated by Jeff Gurner & Geneva Carr. 7 CDs. (Running Time: 28980 sec.). (Sound Library). 2006. audio compact disk 74.95 (978-0-7927-4261-6(3), SLD 984) AudioGO.

Keep. unabr. ed. F. Paul Wilson. Read by Michael Prichard. 10 cass. (Running Time: 15 hrs.). (Adversary Cycle Ser.: Bk. 1). 1983. 80.00 (978-0-7366-0846-6(X), 1797) Books on Tape.
An eerie fortress castle called "The Keep" stands atop Dinu Pass in the Balkan Alps. A commander of Nazi troops establishes a sentry base within its massive, cross-covered walls. Soon afterward he sends a cryptic message to his headquarters in Warsaw: "Something Is Murdering my Men." An Elite SS extermination squad is dispatched to the scene. But it is no match for what waits.

***Keep: Unabridged Value-Priced Edition.** Jennifer Egan. Narrated by Jeff Gurner & Geneva Carr. (Running Time: 8 hrs. 0 mins. 0 sec.). (ENG.). 2010. audio compact disk 14.95 (978-1-60283-990-8(5)) Pub: AudioGO. Dist(s): Perseus Dist

***Keep a Little Secret.** Dorothy Garlock. (Running Time: 8 hrs. 0 mins. 0 sec.). (ENG.). 2011. audio compact disk 29.95 (978-1-60998-168-6(5)) Pub: AudioGO. Dist(s): Perseus Dist

Keep Awake. 7339th ed. Composed by Rory Cooney & Claire Cooney. 2001. audio compact disk 16.00 (978-1-58459-048-4(3)) Wrld Lib Pubns.

Keep 'em Coming Back: SalonOvations' Guide to Salon Promotion & Client Retention. Joan Hoffman & Salonovations Staff. 1 cass. (SalonOvations Ser.). 1996. pap. bk. 10.95 (978-1-56253-308-3(8), Milady) Pub: Delmar. Dist(s): CENGAGE Learn

Keep Every Last Dime: Leave Your Legacy to Family - Not to the Taxman. Richard W. Duff. 2 cass. (Running Time: 3 hr. 30 min.). (RPL Audio Books Ser.). 1998. 16.95 (978-1-879755-06-2(8), 506) Recorded Pubns.
Identify the pitfalls to avoid costly taxation.

Keep Going: The Art of Perseverance. Joseph M. Marshall, III. Read by Joseph M. Marshall, III. 4 CDs. (Running Time: 13500 sec.). 2006. audio compact disk 29.95 (978-1-59179-469-1(2), AW01051D) Sounds True.

Keep in Mind: Reflections for the Mornings & Evenings of Lent. Lucien Deiss. 1 cass. 2000. 11.00 (978-1-58459-062-0(9)); 16.00 (978-1-58459-050-7(5)) Wrld Lib Pubns.
Collection of daily meditation.

Keep it Simple: Scriptural Wisdom for Teenage Girls. Nancy Wilson. 4 CDs. (ENG.). 2006. audio compact disk 12.00 (978-1-59128-531-1(3)) Canon Pr ID.

Keep it Simple-mp3: Scriptural Wisdom for Teenage Girls. Read by Nancy Wilson. 4 cass. 2006. 12.00 (978-1-59128-532-8(1)) Canon Pr ID.

Keep it Simple-mp3: Scriptural Wisdom for Teenage Girls. Read by Nancy Wilson. 4. (YA). 2006. 9.50 (978-1-59128-530-4(5)) Canon Pr ID.

Keep Lookin Up. Contrib. by Johnathan Crumpton & Russell Mauldin. Prod. by Ed Kee. (ENG.). 2008. audio compact disk 24.99 (978-5-557-46521-2(9), Brentwood-Benson Music) Brentwood Music.

Keep Me All the Way. Perf. by F. C. Barnes. 1 cass. 1997. audio compact disk 15.98 CD. (D2206) Diamante Music Grp.
Pastor of the Redd Budd Holy Church in Rocky Mount, North Carolina, this new release finds Rev. Barnes maintaining his tradition for delivering songs in the grand "take it to church" Gospel style.

Keep Me Close. abr. ed. Francis Clare. 3 cass. (Running Time: 3 hrs.). (ENG.). 2001. audio compact disk (978-0-333-90720-7(5)) Macmillan UK GBR.

Keep Me Close. unabr. ed. Clare Francis. Read by Robert Powell. 10 cass. (Running Time: 47580 sec.). 2000. 84.95 (978-0-7540-0510-0(0), CAB1933) AudioGO.
Catherine has become a victim in her own home. First a string of nuisance calls, then a vicious attack by a mystery intruder. As she struggles to come to terms with her injuries, two men seem anxious to uncover the truth. There is Terry Devlin, the local boy made good from Catherine's almost forgotten past. And Simon Jardine, her husband's business partner. But do either of them really want justice?.

Keep Me Close. unabr. ed. Clare Francis. Read by Robert Powell. 10 CDs. (Running Time: 15 hrs.). 2000. audio compact disk 94.95 (978-0-7540-5384-2(9), CCD 075) Pub: Chivers Audio Bks GBR. Dist(s): AudioGO
Catherine has become a victim in her own home. First, a string of nuisance calls, then a vicious attack by a mysterious intruder. As she struggles to come to terms with her injuries, two men seem anxious to uncover the truth.

Keep Me Close. 2nd abr. rev. ed. Clare Francis & Frances Tomelty. 2 cass. (Running Time: 3 hrs.). 2001. (978-0-333-78003-9(5)) Macmillan UK GBR.

Keep on Dancing. Sally Worboyes. (Soundings (CDs) Ser.). 2007. audio compact disk 84.95 (978-1-84559-434-3(7)) Pub: ISIS Lrg Prnt GBR. Dist(s): Ulverscroft US

Keep on Dancing. unabr. ed. Sally Worboyes. Read by Annie Aldington. 8 cass. (Running Time: 12 hrs.). 2001. 69.95 (978-1-86042-891-3(6), 28916) Pub: Soundings Ltd GBR. Dist(s): Ulverscroft US
Rosie Curtis is devastated when her brother Tommy is viciously murdered after dabbling in the criminal underworld. While she fights to stage her show & put Tommy's killers away for good, her brother's smiling face appears in her thoughts, telling her to keep on dancing.

Keep on Knocking: Luke11:5-8;18:1-8. Ed Young. (J). 1981. 4.95 (978-0-7417-1204-2(0), A0204) Win Walk.

Keep on Making a Way. Perf. by Reed's Temple Choir. 2002. audio compact disk Provident Mus Dist.

Keep on Shakin' Doug Lipman. Perf. by Doug Lipman. (J). 1999. audio compact disk 14.95 (978-0-939065-86-8(X)) Gentle Wind.

Keep on Shaking. Perf. by Doug Lipman. (J). (ps-5). 1982. 9.95 (978-0-939065-13-4(4), GW 1013) Gentle Wind.
Stories for children including; "Stop That Shaking," "The Old Woman & Her Pig," "Good Night Sleep Tight," "Big Dog," "Rabbit & Buzzard," "Old Doc Jones," "Three Sillies," "China Doll".

Keep on Singing & Dancing. Perf. by Jean R. Feldman. 1 cass. (J). 10.95; audio compact disk 14.95 Child Like.

Keep on Trying. Dan Litchford. 1 cass. 9.95 (978-1-57734-484-1(7), 06006027) Covenant Comms.
An upbeat & entertaining talk for youth.

Keep on Trying; Act & Not Be Acted Upon. C. Daniel Litchford, Jr. 1 cass. 6.98 (978-1-55503-272-2(9), 06004113) Covenant Comms.
Teaches youth to succeed.

Keep Some Secret Admirers Secret (an Essay from Things I've Learned from Women Who've Dumped Me) abr. ed. Eric Slovin. Read by Eric Slovin. Ed. by Ben Karlin. (Running Time: 15 mins.). (ENG.). 2008. 1.98 (978-1-60024-337-0(1)) Pub: Hachet Audio. Dist(s): HachBkGrp

Keep Texting from Taking Over. Brad Wilcox & Russell Wilcox. 2009. audio compact disk 14.95 (978-1-60641-061-5(X)) Deseret Bk.

Keep the Aspidistra Flying. unabr. ed. George Orwell. Read by Richard Brown. 6 cass. (Running Time: 10 hrs.). 1993. 49.95 (978-0-7861-0300-3(0), 1264) Blckstn Audio.
This is the story of Gordon Comstock, a poor young man who works by day in a grubby London bookstore & spends his evenings shivering in a rented room, trying to write. Gordon has published a slim volume of verse (entitled Mice); he is determined to keep free of the "money world" of safe, lucrative jobs, marriage, family responsibilities. This world, to Gordon, spells the end of art & aspidistra, the homely, indestructible house plant that stands in every middle-class British window.

Keep the Aspidistra Flying. unabr. ed. George Orwell. Read by Michael Kitchen. 8 cass. (Running Time: 12 hrs.). 2000. 59.95 (978-0-7540-0114-0(8), CAB 1537) Pub: Chivers Audio Bks GBR. Dist(s): AudioGO

Keep the Aspidistra Flying. unabr. ed. George Orwell. Narrated by Patrick Tull. 6 cass. (Running Time: 9 hrs.). 1988. 49.00 (978-1-55690-279-6(4), 88450E7) Recorded Bks.
An impoverished young man struggles to be an author.

Keep the Aspidistra Flying. unabr. collector's ed. George Orwell. Read by Richard Green. 6 cass. (Running Time: 6 hrs.). 1983. 36.00 (978-0-7366-0565-6(7), 1537) Books on Tape.
Writer who rebels against the twin British middle-class preoccupations, money & respectability. Cut off from both, Comstock must fly alone in his great gamble to win respect & admiration in his chosen calling.

Keep the Bowl Empty. Tara Singh. 1 cass. (Running Time: 60 min.). (Exploring a Course in Miracles Ser.). 1990. 9.95 (978-1-55531-251-0(9), A274) Life Action Pr.
When one's life has been simplified by eliminating judgment & reaction, a different world is revealed.

Keep the Bowl Empty. Tara Singh. (Running Time: 1 hr.). 1997. 10.95 (978-1-55531-282-4(9)) Pub: Life Action Pr. Dist(s): APG

Keep the Candle Burning. Contrib. by Point of Grace. (Ultimate Tracks (Word Tracks) Ser.). 2006. audio compact disk 8.99 (978-5-558-26951-2(0), Word Music) Word Enter.

Keep the Candle Burning - ShowTrax. Perf. by Point of Grace Staff. Arranged by Kirby Shaw. 1 CD. (Running Time: 5 mins.). 2000. audio compact disk 19.95 (08595552) H Leonard.
This uplifting song is an exuberant affirmation of the power within us all. Fantastic vocal harmonies & a great hook!.

Keep the Change: A Clueless Tipper's Quest to Become the Guru of the Gratuity. unabr. ed. Steve Dublanica. Read by Dan John Miller. (Running Time: 10 hrs.). 2010. 24.99 (978-1-4233-9605-5(7), 9781423396055, Brilliance MP3); 24.99 (978-1-4233-9607-9(3), 9781423396079, BAD); 39.97 (978-1-4233-9606-2(5), 9781423396062, Brlnc Audio MP3 Lib); 39.97 (978-1-4233-9608-6(1), 9781423396086, BADLE); audio compact disk 29.99 (978-1-4233-9603-1(0), 9781423396031, Bril Audio CD Unabri); audio compact disk 79.97 (978-1-4233-9604-8(9), 9781423396048, BriAudCD Unabrid) Brilliance Audio.

Keep the Flame Alive. 4 cass. (Running Time: 1 hr. per cass.). 1989. 15.00 (090) Key of David.
Features a set of 8 talks based on the book "Keep the Flame Alive," which integrates the Pentecostal Gifts and Catholic Teachings.

Keep the Lights Burning, Abbie. Peter Roop & Connie Roop. Interview with Peter E. Hanson. 1 readalong cass. (Running Time: 10 min.). (J). (ps-4). 1989. 9.95 Live Oak Media.
A retelling of the true tale of young Abbie Burgess who, in 1856, filled in for her absent father & kept a Maine lighthouse in operation during a brutal, four-week-long winter storm.

Keep the Lights Burning, Abbie. Peter Roop & Connie Roop. Illus. by Peter E. Hanson. 14 vols. (Running Time: 10 mins.). 1989. pap. bk. 39.95 (978-1-59112-667-6(3)) Live Oak Media.

Keep the Lights Burning, Abbie. Peter Roop & Connie Roop. Illus. by Peter E. Hanson. (Running Time: 10 mins.). (J). (gr. k-4). 1989. 12.95 (978-1-59112-665-2(7)) Live Oak Media.

Keep the Lights Burning, Abbie. unabr. ed. Peter Roop & Connie Roop. Read by Rick Adamson. Illus. by Peter E. Hanson. Interview with Peter E. Hanson. 14 vols. (Running Time: 10 mins.). (Historical Fiction Ser.). (J). 1989. pap. bk. & tchr. ed. 37.95 Reading Chest. (978-0-87499-136-9(6)) Live Oak Media.

Keep the Lights Burning, Abbie. unabr. ed. Peter Roop & Connie Roop. Read by Rick Adamson. Illus. by Peter E. Hanson. Interview with Peter E. Hanson. 11 vols. (Running Time: 10 mins.). (Historical Fiction Ser.). (J). (gr. 1-6). 1989. bk. 24.95 (978-0-87499-135-2(8)); pap. bk. 16.95 (978-0-87499-134-5(X)) Pub: Live Oak Media. Dist(s): AudioGO
A retelling of the true tale of young Abbie Burgess who, in 1856, kept a Maine lighthouse in operation during a brutal winter storm.

Keep the Spirit. Tickle Tune Typhoon Staff. 1 cass. (Running Time: 39 min.). (J). (gr. k-6). 1989. 9.98 (978-0-945337-07-2(8)) Tickle Tune Typhoon.
Presents a Holiday collection of music celebrating the festive winter season & the spirit of Christmas.

Keep the Spirit. Perf. by Tickle Tune Typhoon. 1 cass. 9.98 (428) MFLP CA.
Gifted musicians & dazzling vocalists add their exuberant arrangements & warmhearted magic to Christmas celebrations. Songs include "Jingle Bells," "Deck the Halls," "Little Drummer Boy," "Hanukah," "Rudolph the Red-Nosed Reindeer.".

Keep Travelin' Rider. unabr. ed. Read by Louis L'Amour. (Running Time: 5400 sec.). 2008. 9.95 (978-1-4332-0985-7(3)); 15.95 (978-1-4332-0983-3(7)); audio compact disk 9.95 (978-1-4332-0986-4(1)); audio compact disk & audio compact disk 19.95 (978-1-4332-0987-1(X)); audio compact disk & audio compact disk 17.00 (978-1-4332-0984-0(5)) Blckstn Audio.

Keep Travelin' Rider; Lit a Shuck for Texas; The Nestor & the Piute. abr. ed. Louis L'Amour. 2 cass. (Running Time: 3 hrs.). (Louis L'Amour Collector Ser.:). 2000. 7.95 (978-1-57815-099-1(X), 1070, Media Bks Audio) Media Bks NJ.
The adventures of the brave men & women who settled the American frontier.

Keep Walking: One Man's Journey to Feed the World One Child at a Time. abr. unabr. ed. Larry Jones. Narrated by Chris Fabry. (Running Time: 7 hrs. 30 mins. 0 sec.). (ENG.). 2007. audio compact disk 25.99 (978-1-59859-335-8(8)) Oasis Audio.

***Keep Walking: One Man's Journey to Feed the World One Child at a Time.** unabr. ed. Larry Jones. Narrated by Chris Fabry. (ENG.). 2007. 18.19 (978-1-60814-664-2(2)) Oasis Audio.

Keep Your Brain Alive: 83 Neurobic Exercises to Help Prevent Memory Loss & Increase Mental Fitness. abr. ed. Lawrence C. Katz & Manning Rubin. Read by Manning Rubin. 2 CDs. (Running Time: 2 hrs.). (ENG., 2008. audio compact disk 14.95 (978-1-59887-824-0(7), 1598878247) Pub: HighBridge. Dist(s): Workman Pub

Keep Your Brain Alive: 83 Neurobic Exercises to Hlep Prevent Memory Loss & Increase Mental Fitness. abr. ed. Lawrence C. Katz & Manning Rubin. Read by Manning Rubin. (Playaway Adult Nonfiction Ser.). (ENG.). 2009. 34.99 (978-1-60812-507-4(6)) Find a World.

Keep Your Feet Moving: Favorite Teaching & Healing Tales CD. Short Stories. Bill O'Hanlon. Narrated by Bill O'Hanlon. 1 CD. (Running Time: 45 mins.). 2009. audio compact disk 16.95 (978-0-9823573-4-7(6), 7347) Crown Hse GBR.

Keep Your Feet Moving: Stories for Inspiration & Change. 1 CD. (Running Time: 1 hr.). 2004. audio compact disk 15.00 (978-0-9764498-2-9(X)) O'H O'H Inc.
After a workshop or talk, participants often ask where they can get a copy of one of the stories Bill O'Hanlon has told. Until now, the answer was "Nowhere." In this new audio collection of his favorite teaching and healing stories, Bill uses humor and emotional engagement to validate, transmit lessons, get you to laugh and to change you deeply in an effortless way. Share these stories with friends, clients or students. It makes a great gift.

Keep Your Mind on Jesus. Perf. by Chicago Mass Choir. 1 cass., 1 CD. 10.98 (978-1-57908-319-9(6), 1381); audio compact disk 15.98 CD. (978-1-57908-318-2(8)) Platinm Enter.

Keep Your Mind on Jesus. Perf. by Chicago Mass Choir. 1 cass. 9.98; audio compact disk 15.98 CD. Platinum Chrst Dist.

Keeper. unabr. ed. Kathi Appelt. Read by Kathi Appelt. 5 CDs. (Running Time: 5 hrs. 30 mins. 0 sec.). (ENG.). (J). 2010. audio compact disk 29.99 (978-0-7435-9953-5(5)) Pub: S&S Audio. Dist(s): S and S Inc

***Keeper.** unabr. ed. Mal Peet. (Running Time: 7 hrs.). 2011. 19.99 (978-1-4558-0070-4(8), 9781455800704, Candlewick Bril); 39.97 (978-1-4558-0071-1(6), 9781455800711, Candlewick Bril); 19.99 (978-1-4558-0067-4(8), 9781455800674, Candlewick Bril); 39.97 (978-1-4558-0068-1(6), 9781455800681, Candlewick Bril); audio compact disk 22.99 (978-1-4558-0065-0(1), 9781455800650, Candlewick Bril); audio compact disk 49.97 (978-1-4558-0066-7(X), 9781455800667, Candlewick Bril) Brilliance Audio.

Keeper: An Atticus Kodiak Novel. unabr. ed. Greg Rucka. Narrated by John Randolph Jones. 7 cass. (Running Time: 10 hrs.). 1998. 60.00 (978-0-7887-1876-2(2), 95298E7) Recorded Bks.
A tantalizing glimpse into the life-&-death world of professional bodyguards. Atticus Kodiak, cunning, resourceful & tough as nails, is trapped in a race against time in this riveting, realistic look at the abortion rights battlefield.

Keeper Martin's Tale. unabr. ed. Robert Stanek, pseud. 9 CDs. (Running Time: 11 hrs. 20 mins.). Dramatization. (Ruin Mist Chronicles: Bk. 1). 2007. audio compact disk 49.95 (978-1-57545-803-8(9), RP Audio Pubng) Reagent Press.
Perfect for the young and the young at heart! Keeper Martin's Tale is a refreshingly unique fantastic adventure where its only limits are the limits of your imagination. Inside, you'll discover the breathtaking world of Ruin Mist where the mystical and the magical abound, and you'll fall in love with three heroes: a boy who would become a mage, a princess who is fleeing a dying kingdom, and a warrior elf who undertakes an epic journey. The adventure begins NOW!.

Keeper Martin's Tale: Ruin Mist Chronicles, Book 1. unabr. ed. Robert Stanek, pseud. Narrated by Karl Fehr. (Running Time: 12 hrs. 20 mins.). (Ruin Mist Chronicles Ser.). 2008. audio compact disk 59.95 (978-1-57545-341-5(X), RP Audio Pubng) Reagent Press.

Keeper of Secrets. Judith Cutler. 2007. 61.95 (978-0-7531-3794-9(1)); audio compact disk 79.95 (978-0-7531-2775-9(X)) Pub: ISIS Audio GBR. Dist(s): Ulverscroft US

Keeper of the Circles: Answering the Call to Wholeness. Toby Sally Evans. Lyrics by Toby Sally Evans. 2005. pap. bk. 22.00 (978-0-9762728-0-9(6)) SageBrush Exchange.

Keeper of the Doves. Betsy Byars. 2 cass. (Running Time: 2 hrs. 33 mins.). (J). (gr. 3-7). 2004. 23.00 (978-0-8072-1660-6(7), Listening Lib) Random Audio Pubg.

Keeper of the Dream. Perf. by Kevin Locke. 1 cass. (Running Time: 49 min.). 1994. 9.98 Norelco. (978-1-56628-038-9(9), EB 2968); audio compact disk 13.98 CD. (978-1-56628-037-2(0), EB D2698) MFLP CA.
Collection of authentic flute solos of the Lakota people of the Northern plains mixed with sounds of the natural world.

Keeper of the Grail. unabr. ed. Michael P. Spradlin. Read by Paul Boehmer. 6 CDs. (Running Time: 7 hrs. 17 mins.). (Youngest Templar Ser.: Bk. 1). (YA). (gr. 5-8). 2008. audio compact disk 50.00 (978-0-7393-6784-1(6), Listening Lib) Pub: Random Audio Pubg. Dist(s): Random
Raised by monks, the orphan Tristan never dreamed that he might see the world or discover the truth about his past. But that changes the day that the Knights Templar ride through the abbey on their way to fight in the Holy Land for Richard the Lionheart's Crusade. Overnight Tristan becomes a squire to Sir Thomas, one of the Templar's most courageous knights. But he also finds himself entrusted with the most sacred relic in all of Christendom, the Holy Grail. With the chaos of war surrounding him, Tristan teams up with a young archer from Sherwood Forest and a deadly Al Hashshashin warrior. But even with their help, can he safely bring the Holy Grail back to England and escape the evil men who follow in its wake?.

Keeper of the Grail. unabr. ed. Michael P. Spradlin. (J). (gr. 7). 2008. audio compact disk 34.00 (978-0-7393-6782-7(X), Listening Lib) Pub: Random Audio Pubg. Dist(s): Random

Keeper of the Keys. abr. ed. Perri O'Shaughnessy. Read by Laural Merlington & Dick Hill. (Running Time: 14400 sec.). 2007. audio compact disk 14.99 (978-1-4233-1772-2(6), 9781423317722, BCD Value Price) Brilliance Audio.

Keeper of the Keys. unabr. ed. Perri O'Shaughnessy. Read by Dick Hill & Laural Merlington. (Running Time: 9 hrs.). 2006. 49.97 (978-1-4233-1770-8(X), 9781423317708, BADLE); 24.95 (978-1-4233-1769-2(6), 9781423317692, BAD); 74.25 (978-1-4233-1764-7(5), 9781423317647, BrilAudUnabridg); audio compact disk 34.95 (978-1-4233-1765-4(3), 9781423317654, Bril Audio CD Unabri); audio compact disk 24.95 (978-1-4233-1767-8(X), 9781423317678, Brilliance MP3) Brilliance Audio.
The New York Times bestselling author of the acclaimed Nina Reilly series returns with a bold and gripping new work, a masterful stand-alone that will delight devoted fans - and gamer legions of new ones. This haunting and original tale of love, obsession, and the secrets that we keep - especially from ourselves - begins with a sudden, inexplicable vanishing. For ambitious, troubled architect Ray Jackson, the questions start one sultry California summer night when his wife, Leigh, disappears. No phone call, no ransom note, no body to reveal whether she has left of her own accord and is alive, or is dead. Although it's clear they had a passionate, close relationship, Ray Jackson is not looking for his wife. Why? Enter Kathleen,

old friend of Leigh's, who shows up demanding answers. Ray wants answers, too, but his questions seem strange and shady to Kat. Suspected by his wife's best friend and the police, Ray launches a desperate, alarming search of his own. Using a collection of keys he has hoarded since he was a boy - keys to homes he once lived in - Ray invades each house, one by one. Will he unlock secrets from his past that will help him make sense of a life that appears to be disintegrating? Or will he expose chilling secrets that may have scarred him past redemption? Kat can't figure him out. Still, hoping to find answers to her own gnawing, emotional questions, she throws in her lot with him, at times terrified he killed her friend, and at other times convinced he's an innocent man. Past and present collide as the deceits and subterfuges are exposed, and Ray Jackson is confronted with the most agonizing decision of his life - to face his own violence-laden past, acting to prevent another murder - or not. His choice will leave nothing and no one the same.

Keeper of the Keys. unabr. ed. Perri O'Shaughnessy. Read by Merlington Laural & Dick Hill. (Running Time: 9 hrs.). 2006. audio compact disk 92.25 (978-1-4233-1766-1(1), 9781423317661, BriAudCD Unabrid) Brilliance Audio.

Keeper of the Keys. unabr. ed. Perri O'Shaughnessy. Read by Dick Hill & Laural Merlington. (Running Time: 32400 sec.). 2006. audio compact disk 39.25 (978-1-4233-1768-5(8), 9781423317685, Brinc Audio MP3 Lib) Brilliance Audio.

Keeper of the King. Nigel Bennett & P. N. Elrod. Abr. by Diane Duane. 2 cass. (Running Time: 3 hrs. 35mins.). 1997. 21.00 (978-0-9657255-1-4(0)) Buzzy Multimed.

***Keeper of the King.** P. N. Elrod & Nigel Bennett. As told by Nigel Bennett. Abr. by Diane Duane. (Running Time: 220). (ENG.). (C). 2010. 14.99 (978-0-9827792-0-0(8)) Buzzy Multimed.

Keeper of the Night. unabr. ed. Kimberly Willis Holt. Read by Vivian McLaughlin. 4 CDs. (Running Time: 4 hrs. 1 min.). (J). (gr. 7 up). 2004. audio compact disk 35.00 (978-0-8072-1618-7(6), S YA 436 CD, Listening Lib) Random Audio Pubg.

Keeper of Time. Dale & Reenie Nattress. Prod. by Dale & Reenie Nattress. Perf. by High Sierra Players Staff. Narrated by Gary Stilwell. Score by David Fabrizio. Directed By David Fabrizio. Illus. by Rickey R. Mallory. 1 CD. (Running Time: 48 mins.). Dramatization. (ENG.). 2004. audio compact disk 12.95 (978-1-58124-682-7(X)) Pub: Fiction Works. Dist(s): Brodart

Keepers 3: The Wizard's Scepter. Jackie French Koller. Narrated by Davina Porter. 3 cass. (Running Time: 4 hrs.). (J). 2004. 29.75 (978-1-4025-8036-9(3)) Recorded Bks.

Keepers Bk. 1: A Wizard Named Nell. unabr. ed. 4 cass. (Running Time: 4 hrs. 30 min.). 2004. 37.00 (978-1-4025-6997-5(1)) Recorded Bks.

Keepers of Life: Native Plant Stories. unabr. ed. Joseph Bruchac et al. Read by Joseph Bruchac. 2 vols. (Running Time: 2 hrs. 13 mins.). (Keepers Ser.). (ENG.). (ps-3). 1991. audio compact disk 16.95 (978-1-55591-214-7(1)) Pub: Fulcrum Pub. Dist(s): Consort Bk Sales

Keepers of the Animals: Native American Animal Stories. unabr. ed. Short Stories. Michael J. Caduto & Joseph Bruchac. 2 vols. (Running Time: 1 hr.47 mins.). (Keepers Ser.). (ps-3). 1992. bk. 16.95 (978-1-55591-128-7(5)) Pub: Fulcrum Pub. Dist(s): Consort Bk Sales

Keepers of the Earth. Michael J. Caduto. Read by Joseph Bruchac. 2 CDs. (Running Time: 2 hrs. 13 min.). (J). (gr. k up). instr.'s gde. ed. 9.98 (695); 16.98 (398) MFLP CA.

Stories that combine Native American vision stories & scientific explorations to help children understand the influence they have on their surroundings.

Keepers of the Earth: Native American Stories & Environmental Activities for Children. unabr. ed. Michael J. Caduto & Joseph Bruchac. 2 cass. (Running Time: 2 hrs. 13 mins.). (Keepers Ser.). 1991. bk. 16.95 (978-1-55591-099-0(8)) Pub: Fulcrum Pub. Dist(s): Consort Bk Sales

Keepers of the House. unabr. ed. Shirley Ann Grau. Read by Anna Fields. 7 cass. (Running Time: 10 hrs.). 1997. 49.95 Set. (978-0-7861-1116-9(X), 1879) Blckstn Audio.

Abigail was the last keeper of the house, the last to know the Howland family's secrets. Now, in the name of all her brothers & sisters, she must take her bitter revenge on the small-minded Southern town that shamed them, persecuted them, but could never destroy them.

Keepin' the Baby Awake. Perf. by Miserable Offenders. 1 cass. 1996. 11.95 (MoreHse Pubng); audio compact disk 15.95 CD. (MoreHse Pubng) Church Pub Inc.

Combines new rhythms & harmonies with unusual instruments to create a refreshing change from the usual holiday renditions.

Keeping a Head in School Set: A Student's Book about Learning Abilities & Learning Disorders. unabr. ed. Melvin D. Levine. 6 cass. (Running Time: 9 hrs.). (J). (gr. 4-10). 44.00 (978-0-8388-2070-4(0), 2070) Ed Pub Serv.

Gain important insights into problems with a program that combines realism with justifiable optimism.

Keeping a Positive Attitude of Faith. Speeches. Joel Osteen. 1 Cass. (Running Time: 30 Mins.). (J). 2000. Rental 6.00 (978-1-59349-056-0(9), JA0056) J Osteen.

Keeping & Throwing Away: 1 Peter 2:1-10. Ed Young. 1983. 4.95 (978-0-7417-1273-8(3), 273) Win Walk.

Keeping Astrology Legal. Elizabeth Gauerke. 1 cass. 8.95 (130) Am Fed Astrologers.

Prevent problems or know what to do when they occur.

Keeping Bad Company. Ann Granger. Read by Kim Hicks. 8 vols. (Running Time: 12 hrs.). (Fran Varady Crime Novel Ser.). 2003. 69.95 (978-0-7540-8380-1(2)) Pub: Chivers Audio Bks GBR. Dist(s): AudioGO

Keeping Balance: Finding Stability in Stressful Times. unabr. ed. 1 cass. (Running Time: 1 hr. 30 mins.). 1999. (978-0-9700349-5-3(4)) Mayfield Present.

Keeping Close to Your Customer. Robert H. Waterman, Jr. 1 cass. (Running Time: 55 min.). 8.95 (978-0-88684-079-2(1)) Listen USA.

***Keeping Company.** unabr. ed. Tami Hoag. 5 CDs. (Running Time: 6 hrs. 0 mins. 0 sec.). (ENG.). 2010. audio compact disk 19.95 (978-1-60283-955-7(7)) Pub: AudioGO. Dist(s): Perseus Dist

Keeping Cool. unabr. ed. Elizabeth Doyle Carey. Read by Stina Nielsen. 6 CDs. (Running Time: 7 hrs. 15 mins.). (Callahan Cousins Ser.: No. 3). (J). (gr. 4-6). 2006. audio compact disk 64.75 (978-1-4281-1038-0(0)); 49.75 (978-1-4281-1033-5(X)) Recorded Bks.

The author continues the wholesome series that features four 12-year-old girls enjoying life on their Grandma Gee's Gull Island estate. When the other cousins tease Kate for her old-lady pastimes of cooking, decorating, and knitting, she decides it's time to become "cool." Kate draws up a list of things to do. But after Grandma Gee discusses the folly of being cool and the need to focus on what really matters, Kate's not so sure. And then something unexpected happens.

Keeping Cool When Parenting Heats Up: Tips for Staying Calm & Collected. Charles Fay & Leah Wells. 2008. audio compact disk 9.95 (978-1-930429-99-4(1)) Love Logic.

Keeping Faith. unabr. ed. Jodi Picoult. Narrated by Eliza Foss & Julia Gibson. 16 cass. (Running Time: 19 hrs. 15 mins.). 2008. 66.95 (978-1-4193-6936-0(9)); 113.75 (978-1-4193-6935-3(0)); audio compact disk 72.95 (978-1-4193-6938-4(5)); audio compact disk 123.75 (978-1-4193-6937-7(7)) Recorded Bks.

Keeping in Touch with Reality. J. O. Smith. 1 cass. 10.00 (SP100052) SMI Intl.

Keeping track of the reality of the physical world is fairly easy, but the world of human relationships can be a completely different manner. J. O. Smith shows you how to deal with life from a mature & adult point of view.

Keeping It off. Shad Helmstetter. 1 cass. (Self-Talk Cassettes Ser.). 10.95 (978-0-937065-44-0(7)) Grindle Pr.

Keeping it Real. Renfroe Anita. 2004. DVD & audio compact disk 19.99 (978-1-894300-85-8(8)) Crown Video Dupl CAN.

***Keeping It Simple: The Most Effective Way to Run Your Organization.** Mac Hammond. 2010. audio compact disk 24.00 (978-1-57399-462-0(6)) Mac Hammond.

Keeping Kids Safe. abr. ed. Richard W. Eaves & Richard L. Bloom. 2 cass. 1997. 15.95 Set. (978-1-55977-738-4(9)) CareerTrack Pubns.

Based on the book by Richard W. Eaves & Richard L. Bloom. Topics: Making your home secure; Choosing a day care center; Building your child's self-esteem; Making your kids aware of the dangers of sexual abuse from strangers; Exercising care with guns in the house; & Listening to your kids.

Keeping Pace: A Guide for the Up-to-Date Litigator. (Running Time: 5 hrs. 30 min.). 1995. 92.00 Incl. 280p. coursebk. (20604) NYS Bar.

Provides updates on recent developments in several major areas of litigation. The presentations offer insights into the art of blending new rules & technologies with classic trial tactics. Both the plaintiff's & defendant's perspectives are discussed.

***Keeping Promise Rock.** Amy Lane. (ENG.). 2010. 14.99 (978-1-61581-980-5(0)) Dreamspinner.

Keeping Quilt. Patricia Polacco. Narrated by Patricia Polacco. 1 cass. (Running Time: 15 min.). (J). (gr. k-3). 2001. bk. 26.95 (978-0-8045-6842-5(1), 6842) Spoken Arts.

Polacco traces the movement of a quilt from generation to generation.

Keeping Score. unabr. ed. Linda Sue Park. Read by Julie Pearl. 4 CDs. (Running Time: 4 hrs. 35 mins.). (J). (gr. 4-6). 2008. audio compact disk 38.00 (978-0-7393-6508-3(8), Listening Lib) Pub: Random Audio Pubg. Dist(s): Random

Most people call her Maggie. Her brother, Joey-Mick, calls her Mags. Mom calls her Margaret Olivia Fortini (when she's angry). Dad always calls her Maggie-o - after Joe DiMaggio, his favorite baseball player. Maggie and Joey-Mick aren't Yankee fans like Dad; their team is the Brooklyn Dodgers. Although Maggie doesn't play baseball herself, she knows the game. She can recite the players' stats, understands complicated plays, cheers when the Dodgers win - and suffers when they lose. Even with Maggie's support and prayers, the Dodgers fail to win the World Series, season after season. Adding to her disappointment, the letters she sends to her friend and baseball mentor, Jim - serving in the army in Korea - aren't answered. No matter what she does, Maggie can't seem to break Jim's long silence. Or help the Dodgers. Will anything she tries ever make a difference?.

***Keeping Secrets.** Gwen Madoc. 2010. 69.95 (978-1-4079-0833-5(2)); audio compact disk 89.95 (978-1-4079-0834-2(0)) Pub: Soundings Ltd GBR. Dist(s): Ulverscroft US

Keeping the Conciousness of God. 1 cass. (Running Time: 90 min.). (Devotion Ser.). 9.95 (SC-8) Crystal Clarity.

Yogananda as an example of one who lived for God; how to live in the world & express the consciousness of God; humble self-offering as an expression of devotion; why loving God makes you joyful.

Keeping the Edge. unabr. ed. Dick Schaaf. Read by Glenn Birney. (Running Time: 11 hrs. 30 mins.). 1998. 56.95 (978-0-7861-1076-6(7)) Blckstn Audio.

Keeping the Edge: Giving Customers the Service They Demand. unabr. ed. Dick Schaaf. Read by Glenn Birney. 8 cass. (Running Time: 12 hrs.). 1997. 56.95 (105169) Blckstn Audio.

By looking at what has worked for corporations such as Home Depot, Merck & McDonald's & what has not for others such as American Express, Disney & Acura, Schaaf provides a renewed sense of service direction for CEOs, corporate managers & small-business owners alike.

Keeping the Faith: African American Sermons of Liberation. Ed. by Jim Haskins. Intro. by Maya Angelou. (Running Time: 56 mins.). 2005. pap. bk. 18.95 (978-0-9755746-6-9(3)) Sensei Pubns.

***Keeping the Feast: One Couple's Story of Love, Food, & Healing in Italy.** unabr. ed. Paula Butturini. Narrated by Renée Raudman. (Running Time: 7 hrs. 0 mins.). 2010. 29.99 (978-1-4001-9622-7(1)); 14.99 (978-1-4001-8622-8(6)) Tantor Media.

***Keeping the Feast: One Couple's Story of Love, Food, & Healing in Italy.** unabr. ed. Paula Butturini. Narrated by Renée Raudman. (Running Time: 7 hrs. 30 mins. 0 sec.). (ENG.). 2010. 19.99 (978-1-4001-6622-0(5)); audio compact disk 59.99 (978-1-4001-4622-2(4)); audio compact disk 29.99 (978-1-4001-1622-5(8)) Pub: Tantor Media. Dist(s): IngramPubServ

Keeping the Fire: From Burnout to Balance. Ruth J. Luban. Read by Ruth J. Luban. 2 cass. (Running Time: 2 hrs.). 1994. 18.95 set. (978-0-9641741-1-5(1)) R Luban Audio & Bks.

A unique approach to professional burnout, emphasizing it's a process borne of chronic stress, & a call from our deepest selves. Includes self-assessement & healing strategies.

Keeping the House. unabr. ed. Ellen Baker. Read by Christine Williams. (Running Time: 59400 sec.). 2007. 32.95 (978-1-4332-0042-7(2)); 85.95 (978-1-4332-0040-3(6)) Blckstn Audio.

Keeping the House. unabr. ed. Ellen Baker. Read by Christline Williams. 13 CDs. (Running Time: 59400 sec.). 2007. audio compact disk 32.95 (978-1-4332-0043-4(0)) Blckstn Audio.

Keeping the House. unabr. ed. Ellen Baker. Read by Christine Williams. (Running Time: 59400 sec.). 2007. audio compact disk 108.00 (978-1-4332-0041-0(4)) Blckstn Audio.

Keeping the House. unabr. ed. Ellen Baker & Christine Williams. (Running Time: 59400 sec.). 2007. audio compact disk 29.95 (978-1-4332-0044-1(9)) Blckstn Audio.

Keeping the Inner Peace. Swami Amar Jyoti. 1 cass. 1988. 9.95 (B-19) Truth Consciousness.

Bringing the mind to be relaxed, balanced attitude. God won't forget about us if we reduce our desires. The way to Wisdom. Seeing the beauty in everything.

Keeping the Mind Active in Advancing Years. Instructed by Manly P. Hall. 8.95 (978-0-89314-157-8(7), C810607) Philos Res.

Keeping the Moon. Sarah Dessen. (Running Time: 7 hrs.). (ENG.). (YA). (gr. 7 up). 2009. audio compact disk 29.95 (978-0-14-314468-7(5), PengAudBks) Penguin Grp USA.

***Keeping the Moon.** unabr. ed. Sarah Dessen. Narrated by Stina Nielsen. 6 cass. (Running Time: 6 hrs. 30 mins.). (YA). (gr. 7 up). 2009. 51.75 (978-1-4407-0469-7(4)); audio compact disk 66.75 (978-1-4407-0473-4(2)) Recorded Bks.

Keeping the Right Focus. Swami Amar Jyoti. 2 dolby cass. 1984. 12.95 (M-48) Truth Consciousness.

Anchoring our consciousness on the Goal, concentration follows. Guidelines for focused living.

Keeping the Right Perspective on Problems. Speeches. Joel Osteen. 1 Cass. (Running Time: 30 Mins.). (J). 2000. 6.00 (978-1-59349-054-6(2), JA0054) J Osteen.

Keeping the Secrets of Jesus CD. Glenn. 2009. audio compact disk 19.99 (978-1-932960-10-5(4)) Kardo Intl Min.

Keeping-up the Good Work: Case Discussions. Leonard J. Haas & John L. Malouf. (Running Time: 50 min.). 1989. 13.95 (978-0-943158-37-2(0), KUGW-TBP, Prof Resc Pr) Pro Resource.

Features authors that illustrate the process for reaching ethically appropriate decisions in a mental health practice.

Keeping Watch. Laurie R. King. Narrated by Richard Ferrone. 11 cass. (Running Time: 16 hrs. 15 mins.). 2003. 108.00 (978-1-4025-3870-4(7)) Recorded Bks.

Keeping Watch. Laurie R. King. 9 cass. (Running Time: 16 hrs. 15 mins.). 2004. 34.99 (978-1-4025-3627-4(5), 02564) Recorded Bks.

Keeping Your Focus on God's Plan. Lynne Hammond. 1 cass. (Running Time: 1 hr.). 2005. 5.00 (978-1-57399-220-6(8)) Mac Hammond.

Keeping Your Health. unabr. ed. Milton Diamond. 1 cass. (Running Time: 1 hr.). (Human Sexuality Ser.). 12.95 (34022) J Norton Pubs.

Keeping Your Heart of Compassion Open. Speeches. Joel Osteen. 1 Cass. (Running Time: 30 Mins.). 2002. 6.00 (978-1-59349-153-6(0), JA0153) J Osteen.

***Keepsake.** abr. ed. Tess Gerritsen. Read by Carolyn McCormick & Alyssa Bresnahan. (ENG.). 2010. audio compact disk 14.99 (978-0-307-75094-5(9), Random AudioBks) Pub: Random Audio Pubg. Dist(s): Random

Keepsake. unabr. ed. Tess Gerritsen. 7 cass. (Jane Rizzoli & Maura Isles Ser.: Bk. 7). 2008. 90.00 (978-1-4159-5804-9(1), BksonTape); audio compact disk 90.00 (978-1-4159-5594-9(8), BksonTape) Pub: Random Audio Pubg. Dist(s): Random

For untold years, the perfectly preserved mummy had lain forgotten in the dusty basement of Boston's Crispin Museum. Now its sudden rediscovery by museum staff is both a major coup and an attention-grabbing mystery. Dubbed "Madam X," the mummy - to all appearances, an ancient Egyptian artifact - seems a ghoulish godsend for the financially struggling institution. But medical examiner Maura Isles soon discovers a macabre message hidden within the corpse - horrifying proof that this "centuries-old" relic is instead a modern-day murder victim. To Maura and Boston homicide detective Jane Rizzoli, the forensic evidence is unmistakable, its implications terrifying. And when the grisly remains of yet another woman are found in the hidden recesses of the museum, it becomes chillingly clear that a maniac is at large - and is now taunting them. Archaeologist Josephine Pulcillo's blood runs cold when the killer's cryptic missives are discovered, and her darkest dread becomes real when the carefully preserved corpse of yet a third victim is left in her car like a gruesome offering - or perhaps a ghastly promise of what's to come. The twisted killer's familiarity with post-mortem rituals suggests to Maura and Jane that he may have scientific expertise in common with Josephine. Only Josephine knows that her stalker shares a knowledge even more personally terrifying: details of a dark secret she had thought forever buried. Now Maura must summon her own dusty knowledge of ancient death traditions to unravel his twisted endgame. And when Josephine vanishes, Maura and Jane have precious little time to derail the Archaeology Killer before he adds another chilling piece to his monstrous collection.

Keepsake. unabr. ed. Tess Gerritsen. Read by Deirdre Lovejoy. (Jane Rizzoli & Maura Isles Ser.: Bk. 7). 2008. audio compact disk 44.95 (978-0-7393-4328-9(9), Random AudioBks) Pub: Random Audio Pubg. Dist(s): Random

Keesha's House. unabr. ed. 2 cassettes. (Running Time: 2:15 hrs). (J). 2004. 19.75 (978-1-4025-9930-9(7)) Recorded Bks.

Keewatin. unabr. ed. Paul Sullivan. Read by Cameron Beierle. 4 cass. (Running Time: 4 hrs. 42 min.). (Legends of the North Ser.). 2001. 26.95 (978-1-58116-083-3(6)) Books in Motion.

In a far north land of ice and snow, a lone figure walks to survive the hardships of climate, loneliness and hunger. He has little chance to survive long, and his odds are going down, now that a great white bear stalks him.

Kegs of Powder: Tales of the New River Gorge. Melody Bragg. Music by Mike Morningstar. (ENG.). 1997. 12.95 (978-0-9795156-1-3(0)) Mtn Whispers Pubng.

Kegs of Powder: Tales of the New River Gorge (Vol. 1) Melody Bragg. Music by Mike Morningstar. Narrated by Ross Ballard. (ENG.). 2005. audio compact disk 12.95 (978-0-9717801-6-3(1)) Mtn Whispers Pubng.

Keiki Calabash: Hawaii Kids Songs. 2001. audio compact disk 8.99 (978-0-89610-936-0(4)) Island Heritage.

Keine Panik!, Set. unabr. ed. Angelika Raths. 2 cass. (Running Time: 1 hr.). (GER.). (YA). 1997. 23.50 (978-3-468-49816-9(0)) Langenscheidt.

Keine Panik!, Set. unabr. ed. Angelika Raths. 2 CDs. (Running Time: 2 hrs.). (GER.). (YA). 2005. audio compact disk 28.00 (978-3-468-49817-6(9)) Langenscheidt.

Keiserens Nye Klaer Vol. 102: The Emperor's New Clothes. 2nd ed. Ed. by Janne Lillestol. Tr. by Janne Lillestol. Prod. by Scott Zins. Illus. by Marta Bohlmark. 1 cass. (Running Time: 18 min.). (Listen & Learn Language Ser.: Vol. LL0399). (ENG & NOR.). 1999. pap. bk. 15.95 (978-1-892623-08-9(0)) Intl Book.

English & Norwegian bilingual text with the Norwegian narration.

Keith Green. Contrib. by Keith Green. Prod. by Bill Maxwell. (Early Years (EMI-Cmg) Ser.). 2006. audio compact disk 7.99 (978-5-558-24617-9(0)) Pt of Grace Ent.

Keith Harrison. unabr. ed. Read by Keith Harrison. 1 cass. (Running Time: 29 min.). 1985. 10.00 New Letters.

Originally from Australia but living in Minnesota, Harrison reads poems about both locations.

Keith Urban. Contrib. by Keith Urban. Prod. by Matt Rollings. 1999. audio compact disk 16.98 (978-5-555-92299-1(X)) Capitol AUS.

Kejsarens Nya Klader Vol. 2: The Emperor's New Clothes. 2nd unabr. ed. Read by Ingrid Bohlmark. Tr. by Marta Bohlmark. Prod. by Scott Zins. Illus. by Marta Bohlmark. 1 cass. (Running Time: 13 min.). (Listen & Learn Language Audio Ser.: Vol. LL0399). (ENG & SWE.). 1999. pap. bk. 15.95 (978-1-892623-02-7(1)) Intl Book.

English & Swedish bilingual text with the Swedish narration.

Kelly Cherry. Interview. Interview with Kelly Cherry & Kay Bonetti. 1 cass. (Running Time: 51 min.). 13.95 (978-1-55644-006-9(5), 1032) Am Audio Prose.

Highlighting Cherry's fiction & its philosophical stance, plus her use of autobiographical elements in the story.

Kelly Cherry. unabr. ed. Kelly Cherry. Read by Kelly Cherry. 1 cass. (Running Time: 29 min.). 1987. 10.00 (15) New Letters.
Cherry reads from her new poetry.

Kellys & the O'Kellys. unabr. ed. Anthony Trollope. Read by Flo Gibson. 11 cass. (Running Time: 16 hrs.). 1997. 34.95 (978-1-55685-440-8(4), 440-4) Audio Bk Con.
Set in Ireland the upper class courtship of Lord Ballantine for Fanny Wyndam & the lower class romance between Martin Kelly & Ann Lynch meet with many obstacles.

Kelly's Chance. unabr. ed. Wanda E. Brunstetter. Narrated by Jaimee Draper. (Running Time: 5 hrs. 14 mins. 36 sec.). (Brides of Lehigh Canal Ser.). (ENG.). 2010. 16.09 (978-1-60814-636-9(7)); audio compact disk 22.99 (978-1-59859-693-9(4)) Oasis Audio.

Kempler in the Netherlands 1987. unabr. ed. Walter Kempler. 3 cass. 33.95 Kempler Inst.
4 lectures providing ready tools for furthering mental health, benefitting personal relationships & improving therapeutic skills.

Ken & the Samurai. Susannah Brin. Narrated by Larry A. McKeever. (Fantasy Ser.). (J). 2001. 10.95 (978-1-58659-067-3(7)); audio compact disk 14.95 (978-1-58659-331-5(5)) Artesian.

Ken Cohen's Guide to Healthy Breathing: A Practical Course in Breathing Techniques to Rejuvenate & Transform Your Life. unabr. abr. ed. Ken Cohen. 1 CD. (Running Time: 4500 sec.). 2006. audio compact disk 15.95 (978-1-59179-441-7(2), AW00329D) Sounds True.

Ken Follett. Interview with Ken Follett. 1 cass. (Running Time: 25 min.). 1980. 11.95 (L025) TFR.
Follett talks about "The Eye of the Needle," "Trifle" & other thrillers. He details his method of plotting a novel & how, as a former newspaperman, he had to train himself to write long.

Ken Houston. 1 cass. (Reading With Winners: Ser. 2). 1984. 32.95 incl. 5 bklets, scorecards, wksheets tablet, & tchr's. guide. (978-0-89811-192-7(7), 9905D) Lets Talk Assocs.

Ken Houston: All-Pro Safety. Read by Ken Houston. 1 cass. 9.95 (978-0-89811-109-5(9), 7160) Lets Talk Assocs.
Ken Houston talks about the people & events which influenced his career, & his own approach to his specialty.

Ken Kesey. unabr. ed. Ken Kesey. Read by Ken Kesey. 1 cass. (Running Time: 29 min.). 1989. 10.00 New Letters.
Kesey reads from Caverns & is interviewed.

Ken Rand's Pretty Good Short Stories, No. 1. Short Stories. Keen Rand. Read by Keen Rand. one CD. (Running Time: 70 minutes). 2005. (978-1-933846-05-7(4)) Med Man.

Kendall Morse: Lights along the Shore. 1 cass. 9.98 (C-57) Folk-Legacy.
A varied collection with a Maine accent.

Kendall Morse: Seagulls & Summer People. 1 cass. 9.98 (C-79) Folk-Legacy.
Maine humor at its authentic best.

Kendrick Girls. unabr. ed. Elizabeth Ann Hill. Read by Tanya Myers. 4 cass. (Running Time: 5 hrs. 15 min.). 1999. 57.95 (978-1-85903-254-1(0)) Pub: Magna Story GBR. Dist(s): Ulverscroft US
After the murder, many were doubtful that a young woman could have committed such an act. She did indeed have a heavy debt to pay, but not quite the way everyone supposed.

Kenilworth, Set. unabr. ed. Walter Scott, Sr. Read by Grover Gardner. 12 cass. (Running Time: 18 hrs.). 1989. 39.95 (978-1-55685-153-7(7)) Audio Bk Con.
Presents the legend of Amy Robsart & her secret marriage to the Earl of Leicester.

Kennedy & Nixon: The Rivalry That Shaped Postwar America. unabr. ed. Christopher Matthews. Narrated by Nelson Runger. 12 CDs. (Running Time: 13 hrs. 45 mins.). 1999. audio compact disk 106.00 (978-0-7887-3416-8(4), C1022E7) Recorded Bks.
Vividly traces the lasting impacts John F. Kennedy & Richard M. Nixon had on each other's political campaigns & their presidencies.

Kennedy & Nixon: The Rivalry That Shaped Postwar America. unabr. ed. Christopher Matthews. Narrated by Nelson Runger. 10 cass. (Running Time: 13 hrs. 45 mins.). 1997. 85.00 (978-0-7887-0811-4(2), 94960E7) Recorded Bks.

Kennedy Assassination. 10.00 Esstee Audios.
Includes the story as it unfolded & excerpts from the broadcasts of the day of the murder.

***Kennedy Detail: JFK's Secret Service Agents Break Their Silence.** unabr. ed. Gerald Blaine & Lisa McCubbin. Narrated by Alan Sklar. (Running Time: 11 hrs. 30 mins.). 2010. 17.99 (978-1-4001-8969-4(1)); 29.99 (978-1-4001-6969-6(0)); audio compact disk 39.99 (978-1-4001-1969-1(3)) Pub: Tantor Media. Dist(s): IngramPubServ

***Kennedy Detail (Library Edition) JFK's Secret Service Agents Break Their Silence.** unabr. ed. Gerald Blaine & Lisa McCubbin. Narrated by Alan Sklar. (Running Time: 11 hrs. 30 mins.). 2010. 39.99 (978-1-4001-9969-3(7)); audio compact disk 95.99 (978-1-4001-4969-8(X)) Pub: Tantor Media. Dist(s): IngramPubServ

Kennedy-Johnson Years. (Presidency Ser.). 10.00 Esstee Audios.
The New Frontier is explored.

***Kennedy Men.** abr. ed. Laurence Leamer. Read by Laurence Leamer. (ENG.). 2005. (978-0-06-085892-6(3), Harper Audio); (978-0-06-085891-9(5), Harper Audio) HarperCollins Pubs.

Kennedy Women. abr. ed. Laurence Leamer. Read by Sandra Burr. 2 cass. (Running Time: 3 hrs.). 2000. 7.95 (978-1-57815-015-1(9), 1064, Media Bks Audio) Media Bks NJ.
They kept the faith, the hope & above all, silence.

Kennedys. unabr. ed. Peter Collier & David Horowitz. Read by Christopher Hurt. 14 cass. (Running Time: 20 hrs. 30 mins.). 1990. 89.95 (978-0-7861-0154-2(7), 1139) Blckstn Audio.
Years in the making, based on hundreds of interviews with family members & associates, extensive research into archives & sources unused until now, this is the nationwide best-seller whose very publication caused an uproar in the press...the first & only book to fully penetrate the Kennedy inner sanctum & reveal the true, all too human saga behind America's most famous family.

Kennedys: America's Emerald Kings. abr. ed. Thomas Maier. Read by Alan Sklar. 6 cass. (Running Time: 9 hrs. 40 mins.). 2003. 29.95 (978-1-57270-369-8(5)); audio compact disk 34.95 (978-1-57270-370-4(9)) Pub: Audio Partners. Dist(s): PerseuPGW
This is a densely detailed, compelling account of the infamous Kennedy dynasty - with a new understanding of how the Irish Catholic immigrant experience shaped every aspect of their lives. Meticulously researched both in the U.S. and abroad, the book examines the Kennedys as exemplars of the Irish Catholic experience. Author Thomas Maier begins with Patrick Kennedy's arrival in Boston in 1848, then delves into the deeper currents of the Kennedy story and the ways in which their immigrant background shaped their values - and, in turn, 20th-century America - for over five generations. As the first and only Roman Catholic ever elected to a high national office in America, John F. Kennedy ran for president in keeping with the family's tradition of navigating the cultural divide that began in Boston's Irish ward and ended in a tragedy from which the country continues to suffer. Reader Alan Sklar brings his seasoned skills to this moving story of America's first dynasty.

Kennedys: An American Drama. unabr. ed. Peter Collier & David Horowitz. Read by Grover Gardner. 15 cass. (Running Time: 22 hrs. 30 mins.). 1984. 120.00 (978-0-7366-1496-2(6), 2372) Books on Tape.
This is the first & only book to fully penetrate the Kennedy inner sanctum & reveal the true, all-too-human saga behind America's most famous family.

Kennedys: The Third Generation. abr. ed. Barbara Gibson & Ted Schwarz. Read by Karen White. 4 cass. (Running Time: 6 hrs.). 1999. 24.95 (978-0-7366-4638-3(8), 5058) Books on Tape.
An insider's look at the scandals, triumphs and unparalleled tragedies that have shaped one of the most influential dynasties in America.

Kennedys: The Third Generation. abr. ed. Barbara Gibson & Ted Schwarz. Read by Karen White. 4 CDs. (Running Time: 6 hrs.). 2001. audio compact disk 32.00 Books on Tape.
Their name is synonymous with power and privilege, sex and scandal. As personal secretary to Rose Kennedy, Barbara Gibson had access to all three generations of the clan and was privy to goings on at Hyannisport and Palm Beach. Gibson gives us an insider's look at the extraordinary triumphs, unparalleled tragedies and terrible disgraces that have created one of the most influential dynasties in America - and defined its next generation. Included in this special edition is a new chapter on John F. Kennedy Jr.'s life, loves, career, marriage to Carolyn Bessette and their tragic untimely death.

Kennedys: The Third Generation. abr. ed. Barbara Gibson & Ted Schwarz. Read by Karen White. 4 CDs. (Running Time: 6 hrs.). 1999. audio compact disk 29.95 (978-0-7366-4678-9(7), 5058-CDR) Books on Tape.
The name is synonymous with power & privilege, sex & scandal. No American family had known the public scrutiny of the Kennedys. As personal secretary to Rose Kennedy, Barbara Gison had access to all three generations of the clan & was privy to goings on at Hyannisport & Palm Beach.

Kennedys: The Third Generation. collector's ed. Barbara Gibson & Ted Schwarz. Read by Karen White. 4 cass. (Running Time: 6 hrs.). 1999. 24.95 (978-0-7366-4676-5(0), 5058) Books on Tape.

Kennedys: The Third Generation. collector's ed. Barbara Gibson & Ted Schwarz. Read by Karen White. 4 cass. (Running Time: 6 hrs.). 2000. 32.00 (978-0-7366-5199-8(3)) Books on Tape.

Kennedys - America's Emerald Kings. unabr. ed. Thomas Maier. Read by Alan Sklar. (YA). 2007. 89.99 (978-1-60252-912-0(4)) Find a World.

Kennedys at War, 1937-1945. unabr. ed. Edward J. Renehan, Jr. 11 cassettes. (Running Time: 14.5 hrs). 2004. 89.75 (978-1-4025-8692-7(2)) Recorded Bks.

Kenneth Koch Reading His Poems. unabr. ed. Kenneth Koch. Read by Kenneth Koch. 1 cass. (Running Time: 50 min.). 10.95 (978-0-8045-1154-4(3), SAC 1154) Spoken Arts.

Kenneth Rexroth. unabr. ed. Kenneth Rexroth. 1 cass. (Running Time: 29 min.). 1981. 10.00 (020981) New Letters.

Kennt Uns Jesus-Kennen wir Inn? see Does Jesus Know Us? Do We Know Him?

Kenntnisse: Advanced German Course. Claire Burke et al. (GER.). 1999. bk. 89.95 (978-0-415-16396-5(X)) Pub: Routledge. Dist(s): Taylor and Fran

Kenny & the Dragon. unabr. ed. Tony DiTerlizzi. Read by Alan Cumming. (Running Time: 2 hrs. 0 mins. 0 sec.). (ENG.). (J). 2008. audio compact disk 17.99 (978-0-7435-7212-5(2)) Pub: S&S Audio. Dist(s): S and S Inc

Kenny's Window see Maurice Sendak

Kent State Pt. 1: What Happened & Why. unabr. ed. James A. Michener. Read by Larry McKeever. 9 cass. (Running Time: 13 hrs. 30 min.). 1995. 72.00 (978-0-7366-2941-6(6), 3637-A) Books on Tape.
This meticulous account of the deadly confrontation between Vietnam-era student protesters & Ohio's national guard offers the tragic before & after details of a heart-breaking episode in America's recent history.

Kent State Pt. 2: What Happened & Why. James A. Michener. Read by Larry McKeever. 8 cass. (Running Time: 12 hrs.). 1995. 64.00 (3637-B) Books on Tape.

Kente Colors, Audiocassette. Debbie Chocolate. (Metro Reading Ser.). (J). (gr. k). 2000. 8.46 (978-1-58120-979-2(7)) Metro Teaching.

Kentucky! Dana Fuller Ross, pseud. Read by Lloyd James. Abr. by Odin Westgaard. 4 vols. (Wagons West Ser.: No. 20). 2004. (978-1-58807-621-2(0)) Am Pubng Inc.

Kentucky! abr. ed. Dana Fuller Ross, pseud. Read by Lloyd James. Abr. by Odin Westgaard. 4 vols. (Wagons West Ser.: No. 20). 2004. 25.00 (978-1-58807-152-1(9)) Am Pubng Inc.

Kentucky Heat. abr. ed. Fern Michaels. Read by Laural Merlington. (Running Time: 4 hrs.). (Kentucky Trilogy). 2009. audio compact disk 9.99 (978-1-4418-0816-5(7), 9781441808165, BCD Value Price) Brilliance Audio.

Kentucky Heat. unabr. ed. Fern Michaels. Read by Laural Merlington. 8 cass. (Running Time: 11 hrs.). (Kentucky Trilogy: No. 2). 2002. 32.95 (978-1-58788-239-5(6), 1587882396, BAU); 87.25 (978-1-58788-240-1(X), 158788240X, Unabridge Lib Edns) Brilliance Audio.
With Nealy, horses come first. So when her two grown children's irresponsible acts nearly cost her Shufly, the foal that carries all of her hopes for the Triple Crown, she throws them both off Blue Diamond Farm, an action that changes their future - and her own. To the world, Nealy looks unbreakable. Inside, her heart has shattered. Estranged from her daughter Emmie and son Nick, she struggles alone to build her racing stables into the best in Kentucky - and Shufly into the horse of the century. When Hatch Littletree, her ex-husband's law partner, pays an unexpected visit, he brings Nealy much-needed comfort. But he also brings turmoil. A tough Native American and a brilliant attorney, Hatch is determined to see Nealy heal the painful rift with her children. He's also a man Nealy cannot resist. Raw with emotion, and yet filled with unstoppable energy, Nealy will stand strong in the face of bitter disappointments and one night of terror that could mean the end of her dreams...and maybe her life.

Kentucky Heat. unabr. ed. Fern Michaels. Read by Laural Merlington. (Running Time: 11 hrs.). (Kentucky Trilogy: No. 2). 2004. 39.25 (978-1-59335-330-8(8), 1593353308, Brinc Audio MP3 Lib) Brilliance Audio.

Kentucky Heat. unabr. ed. Fern Michaels. Read by Laural Merlington. (Running Time: 11 hrs.). (Kentucky Trilogy). 2004. 39.25 (978-1-59710-410-4(8), 1597104108, BADLE); 24.95 (978-1-59710-411-1(6), 1597104116, BAD) Brilliance Audio.

***Kentucky Heat.** unabr. ed. Fern Michaels. Read by Laural Merlington. (Running Time: 12 hrs.). (Kentucky Trilogy). 2010. audio compact disk 29.99 (978-1-4418-4004-2(4), 9781441840042, Bril Audio CD Unabri); audio compact disk 89.97 (978-1-4418-4005-9(2), 9781441840059, BriAudCD Unabrid) Brilliance Audio.

Kentucky Heat. unabr. ed. Fern Michaels. Read by Laural Merlington. (Running Time: 11 hrs.). (Kentucky Trilogy: No. 2). 2004. 24.95 (978-1-59335-020-8(1), 1593350201) Soulmate Audio Bks.

Kentucky Pride. unabr. ed. Larry D. Names. Read by Maynard Villers. 8 cass. (Running Time: 10 hrs.). (Creed Ser.: Bk. 4). 2001. 49.95 (978-1-55686-808-5(1)) Books in Motion.
Hunted by Union troops for a crime he didn't commit, Slate Creed frequents the gambling dens of New Orleans in search of his brother's killers.

Kentucky Rich. Fern Michaels. Read by Laural Merlington. (Playaway Adult Fiction Ser.). (ENG.). 2009. 54.99 (978-1-60775-672-9(2)) Find a World.

Kentucky Rich. abr. ed. Fern Michaels. Read by Laural Merlington. (Running Time: 4 hrs.). (Kentucky Trilogy). 2009. audio compact disk 9.99 (978-1-4418-0815-8(9), 9781441808158, BCD Value Price) Brilliance Audio.

Kentucky Rich. unabr. ed. Fern Michaels. Read by Laural Merlington. 7 cass. (Running Time: 10 hrs.). (Kentucky Trilogy: No. 1). 2001. 32.95 (978-1-58788-236-4(1), 1587882361, BAU); 78.25 (978-1-58788-237-1(X), 158788237X, Unabridge Lib Edns) Brilliance Audio.
Nealy Coleman is no longer the troubled teenager who slipped away from home thirty years ago with her illegitimate child. She's now rich, sophisticated and renowned in the racing world. And she's come back to SunStar, her family's thoroughbred horse farm to confront the secrets of her past. Nealy's shocking return will change everything for her two brothers; for her daughter, Emmie; and for all the Thorntons and Colemans who have connections to SunStar. As the truth about her family is revealed, Nealy will find herself faced with the greatest challenges of her life - challenges that will test her courage in unexpected ways and reveal what is truly important.

Kentucky Rich. unabr. ed. Fern Michaels. Read by Laural Merlington. (Running Time: 10 hrs.). (Kentucky Trilogy: No. 1). 2004. 39.25 (978-1-59335-329-2(4), 1593353294, Brinc Audio MP3 Lib) Brilliance Audio.

Kentucky Rich. unabr. ed. Fern Michaels. Read by Laural Merlington. (Running Time: 10 hrs.). (Kentucky Trilogy). 2004. 39.25 (978-1-59710-412-8(4), 1597104124, BADLE); 24.95 (978-1-59710-413-5(2), 1597104132, BAD) Brilliance Audio.

***Kentucky Rich.** unabr. ed. Fern Michaels. Read by Laural Merlington. (Running Time: 11 hrs.). (Kentucky Trilogy). 2010. audio compact disk 29.99 (978-1-4418-4006-6(0), 9781441840066, Bril Audio CD Unabri); audio compact disk 89.97 (978-1-4418-4007-3(9), 9781441840073, BriAudCD Unabrid) Brilliance Audio.

Kentucky Rich. unabr. ed. Fern Michaels. Read by Laural Merlington. (Running Time: 10 hrs.). (Kentucky Trilogy: No. 1). 2004. 24.95 (978-1-59335-019-2(8), 1593350198) Soulmate Audio Bks.

Kentucky Sunrise. Fern Michaels. Read by Laural Merlington. (Playaway Adult Fiction Ser.). (ENG.). 2009. 59.99 (978-1-60775-864-8(4)) Find a World.

Kentucky Sunrise. abr. ed. Fern Michaels. Read by Laural Merlington. (Running Time: 4 hrs.). (Kentucky Trilogy). 2009. audio compact disk 9.99 (978-1-4418-0817-2(5), 9781441808172, BCD Value Price) Brilliance Audio.

Kentucky Sunrise. unabr. ed. Fern Michaels. Read by Laural Merlington. 7 cass. (Running Time: 10 hrs.). (Kentucky Trilogy: No. 3). 2002. 82.25 (978-1-58788-243-2(4), 1587882434, Unabridge Lib Edns) Brilliance Audio.
Kentucky Sunrise finds Nealy once again hellbent on producing a Derby winner and on showing the world that she's not a quitter. Newly married to lawyer Hatch Littletree, and with her daughter Emmie running the family's famous stables, Blue Diamond Farms, Nealy should finally be content. But returning to Blue Diamond Farms for a family reunion sends Nealy reeling. Emmie has let the farm slide, and she has picked a small, gutsy colt to send to the Derby - a nice horse, but clearly the wrong one. Suddenly Nealy is back in the game, ready to prove she's not too old to back a winner - even if it means taking on another colt as her personal project. Nealy's determined not to let Emmie's poor judgment undermine the reputation of the business she worked so hard to build. But the damage to her relationship with her daughter may be irreparable, until a stranger walks into her life, holding out the promise of hope for the future.

Kentucky Sunrise. unabr. ed. Fern Michaels. Read by Laural Merlington. (Running Time: 10 hrs.). (Kentucky Trilogy: No. 3). 2004. 39.25 (978-1-59335-340-7(5), 1593353405, Brinc Audio MP3 Lib) Brilliance Audio.

Kentucky Sunrise. unabr. ed. Fern Michaels. Read by Laural Merlington. (Running Time: 10 hrs.). (Kentucky Trilogy). 2004. 39.25 (978-1-59710-415-9(9), 1597104159, BADLE); 24.95 (978-1-59710-414-2(0), 1597104140, BAD) Brilliance Audio.

***Kentucky Sunrise.** unabr. ed. Fern Michaels. Read by Laural Merlington. (Running Time: 11 hrs.). (Kentucky Trilogy). 2010. audio compact disk 29.99 (978-1-4418-4008-0(7), 9781441840080, Bril Audio CD Unabri); audio compact disk 89.97 (978-1-4418-4009-7(5), 9781441840097, BriAudCD Unabrid) Brilliance Audio.

Kentucky Sunrise. unabr. ed. Fern Michaels. Read by Laural Merlington. (Running Time: 10 hrs.). (Kentucky Trilogy: No. 3). 2004. 24.95 (978-1-59335-018-5(X), 159335018X) Soulmate Audio Bks.

Kentucky Wildcat Basketball Experience: Go Big Blue. Narrated by Cawood Ledford. Contrib. by A. B. Chandler et al. 1999. audio compact disk 18.95 (978-1-58757-039-1(4)) Pub: Univ of KY. Dist(s): Rich & Rich

Kepler, unabr. collector's ed. John Banville. Read by Grover Gardner. 8 cass. (Running Time: 8 hrs.). 1987. 48.00 (978-0-7366-1219-7(X), 2137) Books on Tape.
Historical novel depicting the life & times of the 16th century mathematician & astronomer Johannes Kelper, forerunner of Newton.

Kept Busy: No. 4 in the River Rqad Poetry Series. Joanne Burns. Read by Joanne Burns. Executive Producer Carol Jenkins. (ENG.). 2008. audio compact disk 18.00 (978-0-9804148-3-7(0)) RivRoad AUS.

Kept in the Dark. unabr. ed. Nina Bawden. Read by Carole Boyd. 3 cass. (Running Time: 3 hrs.). (J). 1997. 23.98 (LL 0059, Chivers Child Audio) AudioGO.

Kept in the Dark. unabr. ed. Anthony Troll[illegible] Read by Walter Zimmerman. 6 cass. (Running Time: 8 hrs. 30 mins.) [illegible] 14.95 (978-0-7861-0596-0(8), 2085) Blckstn Audio.
A probing psychological portrait of the nea[illegible] destruction of a marriage - a novel that combines keen insights with vigorous emotional strength. Jealousy, guilt, excessive pride & compulsion all sweep across its surface.

Kept in the Dark. unabr. ed. Anthony Trollope. Read by Jill Masters. 6 cass. (Running Time: 8 hrs. 30 min.). Dramatization. 1982. 39.00 (C-67) Jimcin Record.
"Kept in the Dark" gives us a psychological portrait of the destructive effect of past secrets on a marriage. The husband is George Western, self-willed & fatally proud. His wife, Cecilia, possesses a complicated mixture of pride & submissiveness that leads her inexorably to deceit.

Kept in the Dark. unabr. collector's ed. Anthony Trollope. Read by Jill Masters. 6 cass. (Running Time: 9 hrs.). 1982. 48.00 (978-0-7366-3861-6(X), 9067) Books on Tape.
George Western is self-willed & fatally proud. His wife, Cecilia, possesses a complicated mixture of pride & submissiveness that leads her inexorably to

deceit. These difficulties are compounded by hypocritical friends & the reappearance of Cecilia's egotistical former suitor, Sir Francis Geraldine.

Kept in the Dark, Set. Anthony Trollope. Read by Flo Gibson. 5 cass. (Running Time: 7 hrs.). 1996. 20.95 (978-1-55685-403-3(X)) Audio Bk Con.
Mr. Western tells of being jilted by his fiance before proposing to Cecilia Holt. Somehow, both before & after their marriage. Cecilia can never find the right moment to say that she jilted Sir Francis Geraldine. When the truth comes out there is an eruption.

Kept in the Dark, Set. unabr. ed. Nina Bawden. Read by Carole Boyd. 3 cass. (J). 1996. 23.98 (978-0-8072-7215-2(9), LL 0059, Listening Lib) Random Audio Pubg.
There's something mysterious about the house Bosie, Clara & Noel have come to stay in. Surrounded by its overgrown garden, it looks lonely. But are the shuttered windows to keep burglars out or prisoners in? To the three children, staying with grandparents they've never met before all seems very strange. Then David arrives on the scene. He seems friendly on the surface, but is he something else altogether?.

Kept in the Dark, Set. unabr. ed. Read by Carole Boyd. Ed. by Nina Bawden. 3 cass. (J). 23.98 (978-0-8072-7217-6(5), YA803CX, Listening Lib) Random Audio Pubg.

Kept Woman. unabr. ed. Louise Bagshawe. Read by Lucy Scott. 10 cass. (Running Time: 14 hrs.). 2001. 84.95 (978-0-7531-1191-8(8)) Pub: ISIS Audio GBR. Dist(s): Ulverscroft US

Kerala Dream: A Shaman's Dream Project. Rara Avis & Craig Kohland. (Running Time: 4260 sec.). 2005. audio compact disk 16.98 (978-1-59179-275-8(4), M922D) Sounds True.
The music of Shaman's Dream has become the soundtrack of L.A.'s exploding yoga scene for almost a decade, heard in studios and homes across the country. Seeking the perfect sound for her new DVD series Yoga Shakti, world-renowned teacher Shiva Rea invited friends Craig Kohland and Rara Avis to accompany her across the globe, to blend the spiritual traditions of India with down-tempo urban beats in a visionary offering of rhythm and sacred sound. Building on the momentum of Shaman's Dream's four previous albums, Kerala Dream infuses Indian antiquity with introspective ambient textures ideal for yoga, dance, meditation, healing arts, and more.

Kermit Unpigged. 1 cass. (J). (gr. 3-9). Norelco. (978-1-884676-10-9(3)); audio compact disk Blister with Norelco. (978-1-884676-11-6(1)); audio compact disk (978-1-884676-13-0(8)); audio compact disk Blister with CD. (978-1-884676-12-3(X)) J Henson Recs.

Kernok le Pirate, Set. Eugene Sue. Read by G. Bejean & C. Deis. 2 cass. (FRE.). 1995. 26.95 (1677-VSL) Olivia & Hill.
This author brings his experience & love of the sea to the story. Join Kernok for an adventure on the high seas.

Kerplunk! Stories. unabr. ed. Patrick F. McManus. Narrated by Dick Hill. (Running Time: 6 hrs. 0 mins. 0 sec.). (ENG.). 2007. audio compact disk 29.99 (978-1-4001-0541-0(2)); audio compact disk 59.99 (978-1-4001-3541-7(9)) Pub: Tantor Media. Dist(s): IngramPubServ

Kerplunk! Stories. unabr. ed. Patrick F. McManus. Read by Dick Hill. (Running Time: 6 hrs. 0 mins. 0 sec.). (ENG.). 2007. audio compact disk 19.99 (978-1-4001-5541-5(X)) Pub: Tantor Media. Dist(s): IngramPubServ

Kerry. abr. ed. Grace Livingston Hill. Read by Aimee Lilly. 2 cass. (Running Time: 1 hr. 30 mins. per cass.). (Grace Livingston Hill Romances Ser.). 2004. 8.99 (978-1-886463-55-4(7)) Oasis Audio.
Pursued by an evil man and surrounded by danger, lovely young Kerry finds courage in the miracle of love.

Kettle of Dreams. 1 Cass. (Running Time: 35:27 mins). (J). (gr. k-3). 2005. 11.00 (978-0-9761468-0-3(0)) Greg n Steve.

Kettle of Dreams. 1 CD. (Running Time: 35:27 mins). (J). (gr. 3-6). 2005. audio compact disk 14.00 (978-0-9761468-1-0(9)) Greg n Steve.

Keturah & Lord Death. unabr. ed. Martine Leavitt. Read by Alyssa Bresnahan. 6 cass. (Running Time: 6 hrs. 30 mins.). (YA). (gr. 7 up). 2007. 56.75 (978-1-4281-4644-0(X)); audio compact disk 66.75 (978-1-4281-4649-5(0)) Recorded Bks.

Keur Moussa: Sacred Chant & African Rhythms from Senegal. unabr. ed. Perf. by Monks of Senegal. 1 CD. (Running Time: 42 min.). 1997. audio compact disk 16.98 (978-1-56455-482-6(1), MM00337D) Sounds True.
Pulsing African rhythms fused with sacred Western chant. With koras, tabala, balafon & more.

Key. Patricia Wentworth. 2008. 61.95 (978-0-7531-3129-9(3)); audio compact disk 79.95 (978-0-7531-3130-5(7)) Pub: Isis Pubng Ltd GBR. Dist(s): Ulverscroft US

Key: The Missing Secret for Attracting Anything You Want. unabr. ed. Joe Vitale, Jr. (Running Time: 5 hrs.). (ENG.). 2007. 24.98 (978-1-59659-174-5(9), GildAudio) Pub: Gildan Media. Dist(s): HachBkGrp

Key: The Missing Secret for Attracting Anything You Want. unabr. ed. Joe Vitale, Jr.. Read by Joe Vitale, Jr. (Running Time: 5 hrs.). (ENG.). 2007. audio compact disk 29.98 (978-1-59659-149-3(8), GildAudio) Pub: Gildan Media. Dist(s): HachBkGrp

Key & Tone Clusters. unabr. ed. Joyce Carol Oates. Perf. by Edward Asner et al. 1 cass. (Running Time: 1 hr. 19 min.). 1991. 19.95 (978-1-58081-065-4(9)) L A Theatre.
Two short plays offers us a glimpse into Oates world of unusual occurrences & chance encounters.

Key Automobile Dealers & Service Companies of Russia. 6th rev. ed. BIA. (J). 2006. audio compact disk 289.00 (978-1-4187-5232-3(0)) Bus Info Agency.

Key Automobile Dealers & Service Companies of Russia. 6th rev. ed. BIA. (J). 2006. audio compact disk 249.00 (978-1-4187-5231-6(2)) Bus Info Agency.

Key Banking, Finance, Insurance, & Real Estate Companies of Russia. 6th rev. ed. BIA. (J). 2006. audio compact disk 289.00 (978-1-4187-5045-9(X)) Bus Info Agency.

Key Banking, Finance, Insurance, & Real Estate Companies of Russia. 6th rev. ed. BIA. (J). 2006. audio compact disk 249.00 (978-1-4187-5044-2(1)) Bus Info Agency.

Key Banking, Financial, & Insurance Companies of Asia. 6th rev. ed. BIA. (J). 2006. audio compact disk 249.00 (978-1-4187-4840-1(4)) Bus Info Agency.

Key Banking, Financial, & Insurance Companies of Asia. 6th rev. ed. BIA. (J). 2006. audio compact disk 219.00 (978-1-4187-4839-5(0)) Bus Info Agency.

Key Banking, Financial, & Insurance Companies of Austria. 6th rev. ed. BIA. (J). 2006. audio compact disk 289.00 (978-1-4187-4716-9(5)) Bus Info Agency.

Key Banking, Financial, & Insurance Companies of Austria. 6th rev. ed. BIA. (J). 2006. audio compact disk 249.00 (978-1-4187-4715-2(7)) Bus Info Agency.

Key Banking, Financial, & Insurance Companies of Belgium. 6th rev. ed. BIA. (J). 2006. audio compact disk 259.00 (978-1-4187-4730-5(0)) Bus Info Agency.

Key Banking, Financial, & Insurance Companies of Belgium. 6th rev. ed. BIA. (J). 2006. audio compact disk 259.00 (978-1-4187-4729-9(7)) Bus Info Agency.

Key Banking, Financial, & Insurance Companies of Denmark. 6th rev. ed. BIA. (J). 2006. audio compact disk 289.00 (978-1-4187-4746-6(7)) Bus Info Agency.

Key Banking, Financial, & Insurance Companies of Denmark. 6th rev. ed. BIA. (J). 2006. audio compact disk 219.00 (978-1-4187-4745-9(9)) Bus Info Agency.

Key Banking, Financial, & Insurance Companies of France. 6th rev. ed. BIA. (J). 2006. audio compact disk 259.00 (978-1-4187-4764-0(5)) Bus Info Agency.

Key Banking, Financial, & Insurance Companies of France. 6th rev. ed. BIA. (J). 2006. audio compact disk 259.00 (978-1-4187-4763-3(7)) Bus Info Agency.

Key Banking, Financial, & Insurance Companies of Germany. 6th rev. ed. BIA. (J). 2006. audio compact disk 289.00 (978-1-4187-4780-0(7)) Bus Info Agency.

Key Banking, Financial, & Insurance Companies of Germany. 6th rev. ed. BIA. (J). 2006. audio compact disk 249.00 (978-1-4187-4779-4(3)) Bus Info Agency.

Key Banking, Financial, & Insurance Companies of Italy. 6th rev. ed. BIA. (J). 2006. audio compact disk 289.00 (978-1-4187-4803-6(X)) Bus Info Agency.

Key Banking, Financial, & Insurance Companies of Portugal. 6th rev. ed. BIA. (J). 2006. audio compact disk 249.00 (978-1-4187-4957-6(5)) Bus Info Agency.

Key Banking, Financial, & Insurance Companies of Portugal. 6th rev. ed. BIA. (J). 2006. audio compact disk 219.00 (978-1-4187-4956-9(7)) Bus Info Agency.

Key Banking, Financial, & Insurance Companies of the United Kingdom. 6th rev. ed. BIA. (J). 2006. audio compact disk 289.00 (978-1-4187-4894-4(3)) Bus Info Agency.

Key Banking, Financial, & Insurance Companies of the United Kingdom. 6th rev. ed. BIA. (J). 2006. audio compact disk 249.00 (978-1-4187-4893-7(5)) Bus Info Agency.

Key Banking, Financial, Insurance, & Real Estate Companies in Switzerland. 6th rev. ed. BIA. (J). 2006. audio compact disk 289.00 (978-1-4187-4911-8(7)) Bus Info Agency.

Key Banking, Financial, Insurance, & Real Estate Companies in Switzerland. 6th rev. ed. BIA. (J). 2006. audio compact disk 249.00 (978-1-4187-4910-1(9)) Bus Info Agency.

Key Banking, Financial, Insurance, & Real Estate Companies of the Netherlands. 6th rev. ed. BIA. (J). 2006. audio compact disk 289.00 (978-1-4187-4825-8(0)) Bus Info Agency.

Key Banking, Financial, Insurance, & Real Estate Companies of the Netherlands. 6th rev. ed. BIA. (J). 2006. audio compact disk 249.00 (978-1-4187-4824-1(2)) Bus Info Agency.

Key Building Material Manufacturers of Russia & the Former Soviet Republics. 6th rev. ed. BIA. (J). 2006. audio compact disk 289.00 (978-1-4187-5033-6(6)) Bus Info Agency.

Key Building Material Manufacturers of Russia & the Former Soviet Republics. 6th rev. ed. BIA. (J). 2006. audio compact disk 249.00 (978-1-4187-5032-9(8)) Bus Info Agency.

Key Chemical Manufacturers of Russia & the Former Soviet Republics. 6th rev. ed. BIA. (J). 2006. audio compact disk 289.00 (978-1-4187-5026-8(3)) Bus Info Agency.

Key Chemical Manufacturers of Russia & the Former Soviet Republics. 6th rev. ed. BIA. (J). 2006. audio compact disk 249.00 (978-1-4187-5025-1(5)) Bus Info Agency.

Key Clothing & Textile Manufacturers in Asia. 6th rev. ed. BIA. (J). 2006. audio compact disk 289.00 (978-1-4187-4834-0(X)) Bus Info Agency.

Key Clothing & Textile Manufacturers in Asia. 6th rev. ed. BIA. (J). 2006. audio compact disk 249.00 (978-1-4187-4833-3(1)) Bus Info Agency.

Key Clothing, Footwear, & Textile Manufacturers of Russia & the Former Soviet Republics. 6th rev. ed. BIA. (J). 2006. audio compact disk 289.00 (978-1-4187-5024-4(7)) Bus Info Agency.

Key Clothing, Footwear, & Textile Manufacturers of Russia & the Former Soviet Republics. 6th rev. ed. BIA. (J). 2006. audio compact disk 249.00 (978-1-4187-5023-7(9)) Bus Info Agency.

Key Construction Companies of Austria. 6th rev. ed. BIA. (J). 2006. audio compact disk 289.00 (978-1-4187-4707-7(6)) Bus Info Agency.

Key Construction Companies of Austria. 6th rev. ed. BIA. (J). 2006. audio compact disk 249.00 (978-1-4187-4706-0(8)) Bus Info Agency.

Key Construction Companies of Belgium. 6th rev. ed. BIA. (J). 2006. audio compact disk 289.00 (978-1-4187-4723-7(8)) Bus Info Agency.

Key Construction Companies of Belgium. 6th rev. ed. BIA. (J). 2006. audio compact disk 249.00 (978-1-4187-4722-0(X)) Bus Info Agency.

Key Construction Companies of Denmark. 6th rev. ed. BIA. (J). 2006. audio compact disk 289.00 (978-1-4187-4739-8(4)) Bus Info Agency.

Key Construction Companies of Denmark. 6th rev. ed. BIA. (J). 2006. audio compact disk 249.00 (978-1-4187-4738-1(6)) Bus Info Agency.

Key Construction Companies of Italy. 6th rev. ed. BIA. (J). 2006. audio compact disk 289.00 (978-1-4187-4795-4(5)) Bus Info Agency.

Key Construction Companies of Italy. 6th rev. ed. BIA. (J). 2006. audio compact disk 249.00 (978-1-4187-4794-7(7)) Bus Info Agency.

Key Construction Companies of Portugal. 6th rev. ed. BIA. (J). 2006. audio compact disk 289.00 (978-1-4187-4950-7(8)) Bus Info Agency.

Key Construction Companies of Portugal. 6th rev. ed. BIA. (J). 2006. audio compact disk 249.00 (978-1-4187-4949-1(4)) Bus Info Agency.

Key Construction Companies of Russia Volume 1. 6th rev. ed. BIA. (J). 2006. audio compact disk 289.00 (978-1-4187-5186-9(3)) Bus Info Agency.

Key Construction Companies of Russia Volume 1. 6th rev. ed. BIA. (J). 2006. audio compact disk 249.00 (978-1-4187-5185-2(5)) Bus Info Agency.

Key Construction Companies of Russia Volume 2. 6th rev. ed. BIA. (J). 2006. audio compact disk 289.00 (978-1-4187-5240-8(1)) Bus Info Agency.

Key Construction Companies of Russia Volume 2. 6th rev. ed. BIA. (J). 2006. audio compact disk 249.00 (978-1-4187-5239-2(8)) Bus Info Agency.

Key Construction Companies of Spain. 6th rev. ed. BIA. (J). 2006. audio compact disk 289.00 (978-1-4187-4934-7(6)) Bus Info Agency.

Key Construction Companies of Spain. 6th rev. ed. BIA. (J). 2006. audio compact disk 249.00 (978-1-4187-4933-0(8)) Bus Info Agency.

Key Construction Companies of Sweden. 6th rev. ed. BIA. (J). 2006. audio compact disk 289.00 (978-1-4187-4919-4(2)) Bus Info Agency.

Key Construction Companies of Sweden. 6th rev. ed. BIA. (J). 2006. audio compact disk 249.00 (978-1-4187-4918-7(4)) Bus Info Agency.

Key Construction Companies of Switzerland. 6th rev. ed. BIA. (J). 2006. audio compact disk 289.00 (978-1-4187-4904-0(4)) Bus Info Agency.

Key Construction Companies of Switzerland. 6th rev. ed. BIA. (J). 2006. audio compact disk 249.00 (978-1-4187-4903-3(6)) Bus Info Agency.

Key Construction Companies of the Netherlands. 6th rev. ed. BIA. (J). 2006. audio compact disk 289.00 (978-1-4187-4816-6(1)) Bus Info Agency.

Key Construction Companies of the Netherlands. 6th rev. ed. BIA. (J). 2006. audio compact disk 249.00 (978-1-4187-4815-9(3)) Bus Info Agency.

Key Construction Companies of the United Kingdom. 6th rev. ed. BIA. (J). 2006. audio compact disk 289.00 (978-1-4187-4885-2(4)) Bus Info Agency.

Key Construction Companies of the United Kingdom. 6th rev. ed. BIA. (J). 2006. audio compact disk 249.00 (978-1-4187-4884-5(6)) Bus Info Agency.

Key Electronics & Electrical Equipment Manufacturers of Russia & the Former Soviet Republics. 6th rev. ed. BIA. (J). 2006. audio compact disk 289.00 (978-1-4187-5028-2(X)) Bus Info Agency.

Key Electronics & Electrical Equipment Manufacturers of Russia & the Former Soviet Republics. 6th rev. ed. BIA. (J). 2006. audio compact disk 249.00 (978-1-4187-5027-5(1)) Bus Info Agency.

***Key Elements to Algebra Success - Digital Version of the Teacher & Student Book.** 2010. audio compact disk (978-1-57290-402-6(X)) Natl Trning.

***Key Elements to Mathematics Success Level F - Digital Version of the Teacher & Student Book.** 2010. audio compact disk (978-1-57290-401-9(1)) Natl Trning.

***Key Elements to Mathematics Success Level G - Digital Version of the Teacher & Student Book.** 2010. audio compact disk (978-1-57290-400-2(3)) Natl Trning.

***Key Elements to Mathematics Success Level H - Digital Version of the Teacher & Student Book.** 2010. audio compact disk (978-1-57290-366-1(X)) Natl Trning.

Key Farms of Spain. 6th rev. ed. BIA. (J). 2006. audio compact disk 249.00 (978-1-4187-4931-6(1)) Bus Info Agency.

Key Farms of Spain. 6th rev. ed. BIA. (J). 2006. audio compact disk 219.00 (978-1-4187-4930-9(3)) Bus Info Agency.

Key Fish Farms & Suppliers of Russia. 6th rev. ed. BIA. (J). 2006. audio compact disk 289.00 (978-1-4187-5266-8(5)) Bus Info Agency.

Key Fish Farms & Suppliers of Russia. 6th rev. ed. BIA. (J). 2006. audio compact disk 249.00 (978-1-4187-5265-1(7)) Bus Info Agency.

Key Food Manufacturers of Russia & the Former Soviet Republics, Volume 1. 6th rev. ed. BIA. (J). 2006. audio compact disk 289.00 (978-1-4187-5051-0(4)) Bus Info Agency.

Key Food Manufacturers of Russia & the Former Soviet Republics, Volume 1. 6th rev. ed. BIA. (J). 2006. audio compact disk 249.00 (978-1-4187-5050-3(6)) Bus Info Agency.

Key Food Manufacturers of Russia & the Former Soviet Republics, Volume 2. 6th rev. ed. BIA. (J). 2006. audio compact disk 289.00 (978-1-4187-5037-4(9)) Bus Info Agency.

Key Food Manufacturers of Russia & the Former Soviet Republics, Volume 2. 6th rev. ed. BIA. (J). 2006. audio compact disk 249.00 (978-1-4187-5036-7(0)) Bus Info Agency.

Key Food Manufacturers of Russia & the Former Soviet Republics, Volume 3. 6th rev. ed. BIA. (J). 2006. audio compact disk 289.00 (978-1-4187-4996-5(6)) Bus Info Agency.

Key Food Manufacturers of Russia & the Former Soviet Republics, Volume 3. 6th rev. ed. BIA. (J). 2006. audio compact disk 249.00 (978-1-4187-4995-8(8)) Bus Info Agency.

Key Food Wholesalers of Russia. 6th rev. ed. BIA. (J). 2006. audio compact disk 289.00 (978-1-4187-5230-9(4)) Bus Info Agency.

Key Food Wholesalers of Russia. 6th rev. ed. BIA. (J). 2006. audio compact disk 249.00 (978-1-4187-5229-3(0)) Bus Info Agency.

Key Household Goods Manufacturers of Russia & the Former Soviet Republics. 6th rev. ed. BIA. (J). 2006. audio compact disk 289.00 (978-1-4187-5295-8(9)) Bus Info Agency.

Key Household Goods Manufacturers of Russia & the Former Soviet Republics. 6th rev. ed. BIA. (J). 2006. audio compact disk 249.00 (978-1-4187-5294-1(0)) Bus Info Agency.

Key Industrial Machinery Manufacturers of Russia & the Former Soviet Republics. 6th rev. ed. BIA. (J). 2006. audio compact disk 289.00 (978-1-4187-5035-0(2)) Bus Info Agency.

Key Industrial Machinery Manufacturers of Russia & the Former Soviet Republics. 6th rev. ed. BIA. (J). 2006. audio compact disk 249.00 (978-1-4187-5034-3(4)) Bus Info Agency.

Key Livestock, Crop, & Service Companies of Russia, Volume 1. 6th rev. ed. BIA. (J). 2006. audio compact disk 289.00 (978-1-4187-5260-6(6)) Bus Info Agency.

Key Livestock, Crop, & Service Companies of Russia, Volume 1. 6th rev. ed. BIA. (J). 2006. audio compact disk 249.00 (978-1-4187-5259-0(2)) Bus Info Agency.

Key Livestock, Crop, & Service Companies of Russia, Volume 2. 6th rev. ed. BIA. (J). 2006. audio compact disk 289.00 (978-1-4187-5262-0(2)) Bus Info Agency.

Key Livestock, Crop, & Service Companies of Russia, Volume 2. 6th rev. ed. BIA. (J). 2006. audio compact disk 249.00 (978-1-4187-5261-3(4)) Bus Info Agency.

Key Lumber & Furniture Manufacturers of Russia & the Former Soviet Republics. 6th rev. ed. BIA. (J). 2006. audio compact disk 289.00 (978-1-4187-5222-4(3)) Bus Info Agency.

Key Lumber & Furniture Manufacturers of Russia & the Former Soviet Republics. 6th rev. ed. BIA. (J). 2006. audio compact disk 249.00 (978-1-4187-5221-7(5)) Bus Info Agency.

Key Manufacturers & Suppliers of Medical Equipment & Drugs of Russia. 6th rev. ed. BIA. (J). 2006. audio compact disk 289.00 (978-1-4187-5302-3(5)) Bus Info Agency.

Key Manufacturers & Suppliers of Medical Equipment & Drugs of Russia. 6th rev. ed. BIA. (J). 2006. audio compact disk 249.00 (978-1-4187-5301-6(7)) Bus Info Agency.

Key Mining Companies of Russia & the Former Soviet Republics. 6th rev. ed. BIA. (J). 2006. audio compact disk 289.00 (978-1-4187-5022-0(0)) Bus Info Agency.

Key Mining Companies of Russia & the Former Soviet Republics. 6th rev. ed. BIA. (J). 2006. audio compact disk 249.00 (978-1-4187-5021-3(2)) Bus Info Agency.

Key Note Recognition: Ear Training Development Contains one CD. Bruce E. Arnold. (ENG., 1999. pap. bk. 23.99 (978-1-890944-30-8(0)) Muse Eek.

Key of Healing. Steven Halpern. 1 cass. (Running Time: 1 hr.). 1996. 9.95 (978-1-55961-377-4(7)) Relaxtn Co.

Key of Knowledge. abr. ed. Nora Roberts. Read by Susan Ericksen. 5 CDs. (Running Time: 4 hrs.). (Key Trilogy: Vol. 2). 2003. audio compact disk 69.25 (978-1-59086-904-8(4), 1590869044, BACDLib Ed) Brilliance Audio.
What happens when the very gods depend on mortals for help? That's what three very different young women find out when they are invited to Warrior's Peak. To Dana Steele books and the knowledge they hold are the key to contentment. But now that search for knowledge must include the second key needed to release three souls held captive by an evil god. She won't be

alone, for she's formed fast frienships with two very different women. She can't allow herself to be distracted by the return of the man who broke her heart so long ago, for a danger beyond anyone's imagination is determined to keep her from completing her quest.

Key of Knowledge. abr. ed. Nora Roberts. Read by Susan Ericksen. (Running Time: 4 hrs.). (Key Trilogy: Vol. 2). 2005. audio compact disk 14.99 (978-1-59600-413-9(4), 9781596004139, BCD Value Price) Brilliance Audio.

Key of Knowledge. unabr. ed. Nora Roberts. Read by Susan Ericksen. 7 cass. (Running Time: 11 hrs.). (Key Trilogy: Vol. 2). 2003. 32.95 (978-1-59086-323-7(2), 1590863232); 82.25 (978-1-59086-324-4(0), 1590863240, Unabridge Lib Edns) Brilliance Audio.

Key of Knowledge. unabr. ed. Nora Roberts. Read by Susan Ericksen. (Running Time: 11 hrs.). (Key Trilogy: Vol. 2). 2004. 39.25 (978-1-59335-631-6(5), 1593356315, Brlnc Audio MP3 Lib) Brilliance Audio.

Key of Knowledge. unabr. ed. Nora Roberts. Read by Susan Ericksen. (Running Time: 10 hrs.). (Key Trilogy: Vol. 2). 2004. 39.25 (978-1-59710-416-6(7), 1597104167, BADLE); 24.95 (978-1-59710-417-3(5), 1597104175, BAD) Brilliance Audio.

Key of Knowledge. unabr. ed. Nora Roberts. Read by Susan Ericksen. (Running Time: 11 hrs.). (Key Trilogy: Vol. 2). 2009. audio compact disk 97.97 (978-1-4233-5674-5(8), 9781423356745, BriAudCD Unabrid); audio compact disk 29.99 (978-1-4233-5673-8(X), 9781423356738, Bril Audio CD Unabri) Brilliance Audio.

Key of Knowledge. unabr. ed. Nora Roberts. Read by Susan Ericksen. (Running Time: 11 hrs.). (Key Trilogy: Vol. 2). 2004. 24.95 (978-1-59335-258-5(1), 1593352581) Soulmate Audio Bks.

Key of Light. abr. ed. Nora Roberts. Read by Susan Ericksen. 5 CDs, Library ed. (Running Time: 4 hrs.). (Key Trilogy: Vol. 1). 2003. audio compact disk 69.25 (978-1-59086-902-4(8), 1590869028, BACDLib Ed) Brilliance Audio.
What happens when the very gods depend on mortals for help? That's what three very different young women find out when they are invited to Warrior's Peak. The Malory Price Life Plan does not include a quixotic quest - but the strangers on Warrior's Peak claim that she must find a key that will release three souls held captive by an evil god. Little does she know that the quest will bring her two new friends, the love of her life, and danger beyond anyone's imagination.

Key of Light. abr. ed. Nora Roberts. Read by Susan Ericksen. (Running Time: 4 hrs.). (Key Trilogy: Vol. 1). 2005. audio compact disk 14.99 (978-1-59600-412-2(6), 9781596004122, BCD Value Price) Brilliance Audio.

Key of Light. abr. ed. Nora Roberts & #1 Key Trilogy. (Key Trilogy: Vol. 1). 2010. audio compact disk 9.99 (978-1-4418-4183-4(0)) Brilliance Audio.

Key of Light. unabr. ed. Nora Roberts. Read by Susan Ericksen. 6 cass. (Running Time: 10 hrs.). (Key Trilogy: Vol. 1). 2003. 82.25 (978-1-59086-320-6(8), 1590863208, Unabridge Lib Edns) Brilliance Audio.

Key of Light. unabr. ed. Nora Roberts. Read by Susan Ericksen. (Running Time: 11 hrs.). (Key Trilogy: Vol. 1). 2004. 39.25 (978-1-59335-516-6(5), 1593355165, Brlnc Audio MP3 Lib) Brilliance Audio.

Key of Light. unabr. ed. Nora Roberts. Read by Susan Ericksen. (Running Time: 10 hrs.). (Key Trilogy: Vol. 1). 2004. 39.25 (978-1-59710-419-7(1), 1597104191, BADLE); 24.95 (978-1-59710-418-0(3), 1597104183, BAD) Brilliance Audio.

Key of Light. unabr. ed. Nora Roberts. Read by Susan Ericksen. (Running Time: 11 hrs.). (Key Trilogy: Vol. 1). 2009. audio compact disk 97.97 (978-1-4233-5672-1(1), 9781423356721, BriAudCD Unabrid); audio compact disk 29.99 (978-1-4233-5671-4(3), 9781423356714, Bril Audio CD Unabri) Brilliance Audio.

Key of Light. unabr. ed. Nora Roberts. Read by Susan Ericksen. (Running Time: 11 hrs.). (Key Trilogy: Vol. 1). 2004. 24.95 (978-1-59335-250-9(6), 1593352506) Soulmate Audio Bks.

Key of the Garden see Secret Garden: A Young Reader's Edition of the Classic Story

***Key of Valor.** Nora Roberts. 2010. audio compact disk 9.99 (978-1-4418-5698-2(6)) Brilliance Audio.

Key of Valor. abr. ed. Nora Roberts. Read by Susan Ericksen. 5 CDs, Library ed. (Running Time: 4 hrs.). (Key Trilogy: Vol. 3). 2003. audio compact disk 69.25 (978-1-59086-906-2(0), 1590869060, BACDLib Ed) Brilliance Audio.
What happens when the very gods depend on mortals for help? That's what three very different young women find out when they are invited to Warrior's Peak. Light and Knowledge have succeeded in their quest, and two of the keys have been found. The final, and last, test goes to Zoe McCourt - Valor. Zoe has the courage to raise her young son alone, and to face all the adversity life has thrown at them. But will she have the courage to face a foe determined to do anything to stop the third key from being found - even destroying everything - and everyone - she loves?.

Key of Valor. abr. ed. Nora Roberts. Read by Susan Ericksen. (Running Time: 4 hrs.). (Key Trilogy: Vol. 3). 2005. audio compact disk 14.99 (978-1-59600-414-6(2), 9781596004146, BCD Value Price) Brilliance Audio.

Key of Valor. unabr. ed. Nora Roberts. Read by Susan Ericksen. 6 cass. (Running Time: 10 hrs.). (Key Trilogy: Vol. 3). 2003. 82.25 (978-1-59086-328-2(3), 1590863283, BAudLibEd) Brilliance Audio.

Key of Valor. unabr. ed. Nora Roberts. Read by Susan Ericksen. (Running Time: 11 hrs.). (Key Trilogy: Vol. 3). 2004. 39.25 (978-1-59335-643-9(9), 1593356439, Brlnc Audio MP3 Lib); 24.95 (978-1-59335-266-0(2), 1593352662, Brilliance MP3) Brilliance Audio.

Key of Valor. unabr. ed. Nora Roberts. Read by Susan Ericksen. (Running Time: 10 hrs.). (Key Trilogy: Vol. 3). 2004. 39.25 (978-1-59710-420-3(5), 1597104205, BADLE); 24.95 (978-1-59710-421-0(3), 1597104213, BAD) Brilliance Audio.

Key of Valor. unabr. ed. Nora Roberts. Read by Susan Ericksen. (Running Time: 11 hrs.). (Key Trilogy: Vol. 3). 2009. audio compact disk 97.97 (978-1-4233-5676-9(4), 9781423356769, BriAudCD Unabrid); audio compact disk 29.99 (978-1-4233-5675-2(6), 9781423356752, Bril Audio CD Unabri) Brilliance Audio.

Key Point Review for Modern Real Estate Practice: A Quick & Easy Review of the #1 Prelicensing Classic! 15th ed. 2 cass. (Running Time: 120 min.). 2000. 26.95 (978-0-7931-3725-1(X)) Kaplan Pubng.

Key Poultry Farms & Suppliers of Russia. 6th rev. ed. BIA. (J). 2006. audio compact disk 289.00 (978-1-4187-5264-4(9)) Bus Info Agency.

Key Poultry Farms & Suppliers of Russia. 6th rev. ed. BIA. (J). 2006. audio compact disk 249.00 (978-1-4187-5263-7(0)) Bus Info Agency.

Key Resources on Community Colleges: A Guide to the Field & Its Literature. Arthur M. Cohen et al. (Higher Education Ser.). 1986. bk. 60.00 (978-1-55542-020-8(6), Jossey-Bass) Wiley US.

Key Resources on Student Services: A Guide to the Field & Its Literature. Albert B. Hodd & Cathann Arceneaux. (Higher & Adult Education Ser.). 1990. bk. 40.95 (978-1-55542-230-1(6), Jossey-Bass) Wiley US.

Key Russian Manufacturers & Suppliers of Automobile & Accessories. 6th rev. ed. BIA. (J). 2006. audio compact disk 289.00 (978-1-4187-5002-2(6)) Bus Info Agency.

Key Russian Manufacturers & Suppliers of Automobile & Accessories. 6th rev. ed. BIA. (J). 2006. audio compact disk 249.00 (978-1-4187-5001-5(8)) Bus Info Agency.

Key Russian Manufacturers & Suppliers of Baby Care & Food. 6th rev. ed. BIA. (J). 2006. audio compact disk 289.00 (978-1-4187-5006-0(9)) Bus Info Agency.

Key Russian Manufacturers & Suppliers of Baby Care & Food. 6th rev. ed. BIA. (J). 2006. audio compact disk 249.00 (978-1-4187-5005-3(0)) Bus Info Agency.

Key Russian Manufacturers & Suppliers of Beverages & Tobacco. 6th rev. ed. BIA. (J). 2006. audio compact disk 289.00 (978-1-4187-5000-8(X)) Bus Info Agency.

Key Russian Manufacturers & Suppliers of Beverages & Tobacco. 6th rev. ed. BIA. (J). 2006. audio compact disk 249.00 (978-1-4187-4999-6(0)) Bus Info Agency.

Key Russian Manufacturers & Suppliers of Books & Publishing Materials. 6th rev. ed. BIA. (J). 2006. audio compact disk 289.00 (978-1-4187-5008-4(5)) Bus Info Agency.

Key Russian Manufacturers & Suppliers of Books & Publishing Materials. 6th rev. ed. BIA. (J). 2006. audio compact disk 249.00 (978-1-4187-5007-7(7)) Bus Info Agency.

Key Russian Manufacturers & Suppliers of Candies, Chocolate, Sugar, Nuts, & Seeds. 6th rev. ed. BIA. (J). 2006. audio compact disk 289.00 (978-1-4187-5010-7(7)) Bus Info Agency.

Key Russian Manufacturers & Suppliers of Candies, Chocolate, Sugar, Nuts, & Seeds. 6th rev. ed. BIA. (J). 2006. audio compact disk 249.00 (978-1-4187-5009-1(3)) Bus Info Agency.

Key Russian Manufacturers & Suppliers of Clothing & Textiles. 6th rev. ed. BIA. (J). 2006. audio compact disk 289.00 (978-1-4187-5049-7(2)) Bus Info Agency.

Key Russian Manufacturers & Suppliers of Clothing & Textiles. 6th rev. ed. BIA. (J). 2006. audio compact disk 249.00 (978-1-4187-5048-0(4)) Bus Info Agency.

Key Russian Manufacturers & Suppliers of Cosmetics & Toiletries. 6th rev. ed. BIA. (J). 2006. audio compact disk 289.00 (978-1-4187-5018-3(2)) Bus Info Agency.

Key Russian Manufacturers & Suppliers of Cosmetics & Toiletries. 6th rev. ed. BIA. (J). 2006. audio compact disk 249.00 (978-1-4187-5017-6(4)) Bus Info Agency.

Key Russian Manufacturers & Suppliers of Dairy Products. 6th rev. ed. BIA. (J). 2006. audio compact disk 289.00 (978-1-4187-5012-1(3)) Bus Info Agency.

Key Russian Manufacturers & Suppliers of Dairy Products. 6th rev. ed. BIA. (J). 2006. audio compact disk 249.00 (978-1-4187-5011-4(5)) Bus Info Agency.

Key Russian Manufacturers & Suppliers of Electronics. 6th rev. ed. BIA. (J). 2006. audio compact disk 289.00 (978-1-4187-5016-9(6)) Bus Info Agency.

Key Russian Manufacturers & Suppliers of Electronics. 6th rev. ed. BIA. (J). 2006. audio compact disk 249.00 (978-1-4187-5015-2(8)) Bus Info Agency.

Key Russian Manufacturers & Suppliers of Fats & Oils. 6th rev. ed. BIA. (J). 2006. audio compact disk 249.00 (978-1-4187-5014-5(X)) Bus Info Agency.

Key Russian Manufacturers & Suppliers of Fats & Oils. 6th rev. ed. BIA. (J). 2006. audio compact disk 219.00 (978-1-4187-5013-8(1)) Bus Info Agency.

Key Russian Manufacturers & Suppliers of Footwear. 6th rev. ed. BIA. (J). 2006. audio compact disk 289.00 (978-1-4187-4998-9(2)) Bus Info Agency.

Key Russian Manufacturers & Suppliers of Footwear. 6th rev. ed. BIA. (J). 2006. audio compact disk 249.00 (978-1-4187-4997-2(4)) Bus Info Agency.

Key Russian Manufacturers & Suppliers of Furniture, Fixtures, & Household Goods. 6th rev. ed. BIA. (J). 2006. audio compact disk 289.00 (978-1-4187-5004-6(2)) Bus Info Agency.

Key Russian Manufacturers & Suppliers of Furniture, Fixtures, & Household Goods. 6th rev. ed. BIA. (J). 2006. audio compact disk 249.00 (978-1-4187-5003-9(4)) Bus Info Agency.

Key Russian Manufacturers & Suppliers of Household Goods. 6th rev. ed. BIA. (J). 2006. audio compact disk 289.00 (978-1-4187-5228-6(2)) Bus Info Agency.

Key Russian Manufacturers & Suppliers of Household Goods. 6th rev. ed. BIA. (J). 2006. audio compact disk 249.00 (978-1-4187-5227-9(4)) Bus Info Agency.

Key Russian Manufacturers & Suppliers of Meat & Meat Products. 6th rev. ed. BIA. (J). 2006. audio compact disk 249.00 (978-1-4187-5020-6(4)) Bus Info Agency.

Key Russian Manufacturers & Suppliers of Meat & Meat Products. 6th rev. ed. BIA. (J). 2006. audio compact disk 219.00 (978-1-4187-5019-0(0)) Bus Info Agency.

Key Russian Manufacturers & Suppliers of Pharmaceuticals. 6th rev. ed. BIA. (J). 2006. audio compact disk 289.00 (978-1-4187-5043-5(3)) Bus Info Agency.

Key Russian Manufacturers & Suppliers of Pharmaceuticals. 6th rev. ed. BIA. (J). 2006. audio compact disk 249.00 (978-1-4187-5042-8(5)) Bus Info Agency.

Key Russian Wholesalers of Consumer & Industrial Goods. 6th rev. ed. BIA. (J). 2006. audio compact disk 289.00 (978-1-4187-5236-1(3)) Bus Info Agency.

Key Russian Wholesalers of Consumer & Industrial Goods. 6th rev. ed. BIA. (J). 2006. audio compact disk 249.00 (978-1-4187-5235-4(5)) Bus Info Agency.

Key Russian Wholesalers of Industrial Machinery, Building Materials, & Electronics. 6th rev. ed. BIA. (J). 2006. audio compact disk 289.00 (978-1-4187-5234-7(7)) Bus Info Agency.

Key Russian Wholesalers of Industrial Machinery, Building Materials, & Electronics. 6th rev. ed. BIA. (J). 2006. audio compact disk 249.00 (978-1-4187-5233-0(9)) Bus Info Agency.

Key Sanitation Service Companies of Russia. 6th rev. ed. BIA. (J). 2006. audio compact disk 289.00 (978-1-4187-5041-1(7)) Bus Info Agency.

Key Sanitation Service Companies of Russia. 6th rev. ed. BIA. (J). 2006. audio compact disk 249.00 (978-1-4187-5040-4(9)) Bus Info Agency.

Key Stage 3 Strategy: Geography. Jackie Arundale et al. 2004. audio compact disk 244.00 (978-0-340-81502-1(7), HodderMurray) Pub: Hodder Edu GBR. Dist(s): Trans-Atl Phila

Key to a Successful Marriage. Derek Prince. 1 cass. 5.95 (001) Derek Prince.
A successful marriage is a covenant entered by the sacrifice of two lives laid down.

***Key to Creation.** unabr. ed. Kevin J. Anderson. Read by Scott Brick. (Running Time: 19 hrs. 30 mins.). (Terra Incognita Ser.). (ENG.). 2011. 29.98 (978-1-61113-812-2(4)) Pub: Hachet Audio. Dist(s): HachBkGrp

Key to Eternal Life. 1985. (0204) Evang Sisterhood Mary.

Key to Everything see May Swenson

Key to Human Temperament. Nancy Edwards. 1 cass. 8.95 (656) Am Fed Astrologers.
An AFA Convention workshop tape.

Key to Jesus' Sufferings. Read by Basilea Schlink. 1 cass. (Running Time: 30 min.). 1985. (0220) Evang Sisterhood Mary.
Discusses a source of blessing & renewal for our lives & the way to Jesus' heart.

Key to Life. Elbert Willis. 1 cass. (Divine Guidance Guidelines Ser.). 4.00 Fill the Gap.

Key to Midnight. unabr. ed. Leigh Nichols, pseud & Dean Koontz. Read by Tanya Eby. (Running Time: 11 hrs.). 2009. 24.99 (978-1-4418-1712-9(3), 9781441817129, Brilliance MP3); 39.97 (978-1-4418-1713-6(1), 9781441817136, Brlnc Audio MP3 Lib); 24.99 (978-1-4418-1714-3(X), 9781441817143, BAD); 39.97 (978-1-4418-1715-0(8), 9781441817150, BADLE); audio compact disk 38.99 (978-1-4418-1710-5(7), 9781441817105, Bril Audio CD Unabri); audio compact disk 97.97 (978-1-4418-1711-2(5), 9781441817112, BriAudCD Unabrid) Brilliance Audio.

Key to Motivation. Bob Conklin. 1 cass. 10.00 (SP100008) SMI Intl.
Everyone talks about motivation, but you can do something about it. Learn where motivation comes from & how to use it. Once you have the key, it's easy to be more effective in your work & to get more done.

Key to Motivation. abr. ed. Bob Conklin. 1 cass. (Running Time: 29 min.). 11.00 (978-0-89811-012-8(2), 5147) Meyer Res Grp.
Learn where motivation comes from & how to use it.

Key to Peace of God: Romans 5:1-2. Ben Young. 1996. 4.95i (978-0-7417-6002-9(9), B0002) Win Walk.

Key to Perfection. Swami Amar Jyoti. 1 cass. 1987. 9.95 (K-148) Truth Consciousness.
There is nothing undivine in God's scheme. True fulfillment, divine vision: seeing the Perfection as it is. Does God Exist? The highest therapy.

Key to Real Unity: Romans 15:1-13. Ben Young. 1997. 4.95 (978-0-7417-6037-1(1), B0037) Win Walk.

Key to Rebecca. unabr. ed. Ken Follett. Read by Gene Eugene. 12 cass. (Running Time: 13 hrs.). Incl. Key to Rebecca. Ken Follett. Read by Gene Eugene. (190); Key to Rebecca. Ken Follett. Read by Gene Eugene. (190); Key to Rebecca. Ken Follett. Read by Gene Eugene. (190); 64.95 (978-1-55686-190-1(7), 112675) Books in Motion.
Alex Wolff, German agent, slips into Cairo during World War II. He attempts to help Rommel take over the city but finds opposition from a British Intelligence officer named William VanDam. Wolff uses a code whose key is secreted in a famous novel entitled "Rebecca.".

Key to Rebecca. unabr. ed. Ken Follett. Read by Richard Green. 8 cass. (Running Time: 12 hrs.). 1981. 64.00 (978-0-7366-0596-0(7), 1563) Books on Tape.
Infiltrated into the kaleidoscopic world of wartime Cairo, a lone German agent, Alex Wolff, using a code whose key is buried in Daphne DuMaurier's famous novel, "Rebecca," works to help Rommel gain the city. He is opposed by a singular British Intelligence officer. Both men have as companions loneliness & danger, each burns with equal commitment & discipline.

Key to Rebecca. unabr. ed. Ken Follett. Narrated by Peter Fernandez. 9 cass. (Running Time: 11 hrs. 30 mins.). 1989. 78.00 (978-1-55690-280-2(8), 89690E7) Recorded Bks.
Cairo, 1942. Rommel & his armies are in striking distance of the city. All he needs is the key to the defenses & "The Sphinx," his agent in place, is there to get it for him. Now, one renegade Englishman & one brave girl are all that can keep him out.

***Key to Rondo.** Emily Rodda. Read by Edwina Wren. (Running Time: 9 hrs. 25 mins.). (J). 2010. 84.99 (978-1-74214-608-9(2), 9781742146089) Pub: Bolinda Pubng AUS. Dist(s): Bolinda Pub Inc

Key to Rondo. unabr. ed. Emily Rodda. Read by Edwina Wren. (Running Time: 9 hrs. 25 mins.). (J). 2009. audio compact disk 87.95 (978-1-921415-54-8(1), 9781921415548) Pub: Bolinda Pubng AUS. Dist(s): Bolinda Pub Inc

***Key to Rondo.** unabr. ed. Emily Rodda. Read by Edwina Wren. (Running Time: 9 hrs. 25 mins.). (J). 2010. 43.95 (978-1-74214-719-2(4), 9781742147192) Pub: Bolinda Pubng AUS. Dist(s): Bolinda Pub Inc

Key to Spiritual & Psychic Development - Table Tipping: An Exciting & Direct Communication Tool for Connecting with Your Spirit Guides & Higher self for Personal & Universal Knowledge. unabr. ed. Angela M. Mattey. Prod. by Angela M. Mattey. 1 cass. (Running Time: 40 min.). 1993. 17.95 (978-1-882836-00-0(6)) Pub: TAM Ent. Dist(s): New Leaf Dist
Meditation tape accompanies book (The Key to Spiritual & Psychic Development) as a supplement to the spiritual process of Table Tipping to communicate with angels, spirit guides, & one's Higher Self.

Key to Spiritual & Psychic Development - Table Tipping: Guided Meditation & Energy Circle Protection Process for Table Tipping. Angela M. Mattey. Read by Angela M. Mattey. 1 cass. (Running Time: 40 min.). 1993. 18.95 (978-1-882836-01-7(4)) TAM Ent.

Key to the Indian. unabr. ed. Lynne Reid Banks. Read by Lynne Reid Banks. 4 cass. (Running Time: 6 hrs.). (Indian in the Cupboard Ser.: No. 5). (J). (gr. 4-7). 1999. 32.00 (LL 0134, Chivers Child Audio) AudioGO.

Key to the Indian. unabr. ed. Lynne Reid Banks. Read by Lynne Reid Banks. 4 vols. (Running Time: 5 hrs. 28 mins.). (Indian in the Cupboard Ser.: No. 5). (J). (gr. 3-7). 1999. pap. bk. 38.00 (978-0-8072-8076-8(3), YA995SP, Listening Lib) Random Audio Pubg.
When Little Bear & the Iroquois tribe are in deep trouble with English settlers, only Omri & his father can help, but first they must find a way to get to that time period & back - not to mention survive a brutal attack on the long house.

Key to the Indian, Set. unabr. ed. Lynne Reid Banks. Read by Lynne Reid Banks. 4 cass. (Indian in the Cupboard Ser.: No. 5). (J). (gr. 4-7). 1999. 29.98 (FS9-43434) Highsmith.

Key to the Keys, Vol. II. Gale Pederson. 1 cass. 1985. 15.95 (978-0-88432-116-3(9), S1550) J Norton Pubs.
Takes you from the very basics, teaching the keys of the piano, signatures, note values, tempo, phrasing & chords, so that you can play short, familiar melodies.

Key to the Keys, Vol. 2. unabr. ed. Gale Pederson. 2 cass. 35.00 Set, incl. bklt. (978-0-88432-141-5(X), S01555) J Norton Pubs.
Basic home-study course provides an easy, enjoyable way to learn how to play the piano. Volume I covers the basics of fingering & chords & the playing of simple melodies. Volume II covers more advanced piano-playing skills.

Key to the Keys, Vols. 1 & 2. unabr. ed. Gale Pederson. 3 cass. bk. 35.00 (S0155X) J Norton Pubs.

Key to the Promise of God: Romans 4:13-25. Ed Young. 1984. 4.95 (978-0-7417-1361-2(6), 361) Win Walk.

Key to the Promises of God: Romans 4:13-25. Ed Young. 1996. 4.95 (978-0-7417-2112-9(0), 1112) Win Walk.

Key to the Supernatural. Kenneth E. Hagin. 4 cass. (How to Be an Overcomer Ser.). 17.00 Faith Lib Pubns.
Learn how unity & harmony in the Body of Christ is one key to supernaturally overcoming the problems of life.

Key to the Treasure. unabr. ed. Peggy Parish. 1 read-along cass. (Running Time: 38 min.). (Middle Grade Cliffhangers Ser.). (J). (gr. 3-5). 1982. 15.98 incl. Bk. & guide. (978-0-8072-1092-5(7), SWR 27 SP, Listening Lib) Random Audio Pubg.
Liza, Bill & Jed love their grandparents' stories about the treasure map over the mantel. They hope to be the ones to solve this century-old family mystery.

Key to the Vaults: Matthew 7:7-12. Ed Young. (J). 1979. 4.95 (978-0-7417-1088-8(9), A0088) Win Walk.

Key to Vital Living: The Biological Rejuvenation Program. Kathleen A. Hartford. 2007. ring bd. (978-0-9749070-3-1(0)) Grelin Pr.

Key to Your Child's Success. Michele Borba. 1 cass. (Running Time: 45 min.). (J). (gr. k-8). 1996. 10.00 (978-1-880396-49-0(1), JP9649-1) Jalmar Pr.
Provides a wealth of proven techniques & ideas about developing your child's self-esteem, improving achievement & behavior.

Key to Zion. Bodie Thoene & Brock Thoene. Narrated by Suzanne Toren. 11 cass. (Running Time: 16 hrs.). (Zion Chronicles: Bk. 5). 1988. 96.00 (978-1-4025-4419-4(7)) Recorded Bks.

Key to Zion. unabr. ed. Bodie Thoene & Brock Thoene. (Zion Chronicles: Bk. 5). 2000. audio compact disk 19.95 (2788) Blckstn Audio.
Haj Amin Husseini and the Arab Palestinians have impatiently waited for the day when the British finalize their military evacuation from Palestine, but their power has gradually eroded. Five Mid-Eastern nations have gathered around the tiny country to divide it up for themselves, totally ignoring the interests of the Palestinians in their greedy conspiracy to destroy the Jews.

Key to Zion. unabr. ed. Bodie Thoene & Brock Thoene. Read by Susan O'Malley. 11 cass. (Running Time: 16 hrs.). (Zion Chronicles: Bk. 5). 2001. 76.95 (978-0-7861-2020-8(7), 2788); audio compact disk 104.00 (978-0-7861-9716-3(1), 2788) Blckstn Audio.

Key Transportation & Communication Companies of Austria. 6th rev. ed. BIA. (J). 2006. audio compact disk 289.00 (978-1-4187-4709-1(2)) Bus Info Agency.

Key Transportation & Communication Companies of Austria. 6th rev. ed. BIA. (J). 2006. audio compact disk 249.00 (978-1-4187-4708-4(4)) Bus Info Agency.

Key Transportation & Communication Companies of Belgium. 6th rev. ed. BIA. (J). 2006. audio compact disk 289.00 (978-1-4187-4725-1(4)) Bus Info Agency.

Key Transportation & Communication Companies of Belgium. 6th rev. ed. BIA. (J). 2006. audio compact disk 289.00 (978-1-4187-4724-4(6)) Bus Info Agency.

Key Transportation & Communication Companies of Denmark. 6th rev. ed. BIA. (J). 2006. audio compact disk 249.00 (978-1-4187-4741-1(6)) Bus Info Agency.

Key Transportation & Communication Companies of Denmark. 6th rev. ed. BIA. (J). 2006. audio compact disk 219.00 (978-1-4187-4740-4(8)) Bus Info Agency.

Key Transportation & Communication Companies of France. 6th rev. ed. BIA. (J). 2006. audio compact disk 289.00 (978-1-4187-4759-6(9)) Bus Info Agency.

Key Transportation & Communication Companies of France. 6th rev. ed. BIA. (J). 2006. audio compact disk 249.00 (978-1-4187-4758-9(0)) Bus Info Agency.

Key Transportation & Communication Companies of Germany. 6th rev. ed. BIA. (J). 2006. audio compact disk 289.00 (978-1-4187-4775-6(0)) Bus Info Agency.

Key Transportation & Communication Companies of Germany. 6th rev. ed. BIA. (J). 2006. audio compact disk 249.00 (978-1-4187-4774-9(2)) Bus Info Agency.

Key Transportation & Communication Companies of Italy. 6th rev. ed. BIA. (J). 2006. audio compact disk 289.00 (978-1-4187-4798-5(X)) Bus Info Agency.

Key Transportation & Communication Companies of Italy. 6th rev. ed. BIA. (J). 2006. audio compact disk 249.00 (978-1-4187-4797-8(1)) Bus Info Agency.

Key Transportation & Communication Companies of Portugal. 6th rev. ed. BIA. (J). 2006. audio compact disk 289.00 (978-1-4187-4952-1(4)) Bus Info Agency.

Key Transportation & Communication Companies of Portugal. 6th rev. ed. BIA. (J). 2006. audio compact disk 249.00 (978-1-4187-4951-4(6)) Bus Info Agency.

Key Transportation & Communication Companies of Spain. 6th rev. ed. BIA. (J). 2006. audio compact disk 289.00 (978-1-4187-4936-1(2)) Bus Info Agency.

Key Transportation & Communication Companies of Spain. 6th rev. ed. BIA. (J). 2006. audio compact disk 249.00 (978-1-4187-4935-4(4)) Bus Info Agency.

Key Transportation & Communication Companies of the Netherlands. 6th rev. ed. BIA. (J). 2006. audio compact disk 289.00 (978-1-4187-4819-7(6)) Bus Info Agency.

Key Transportation & Communication Companies of the Netherlands. 6th rev. ed. BIA. (J). 2006. audio compact disk 249.00 (978-1-4187-4818-0(8)) Bus Info Agency.

Key Transportation & Communication Companies of the United Kingdom. 6th rev. ed. BIA. (J). 2006. audio compact disk 289.00 (978-1-4187-4888-3(9)) Bus Info Agency.

Key Transportation & Communication Companies of the United Kingdom. 6th rev. ed. BIA. (J). 2006. audio compact disk 249.00 (978-1-4187-4887-6(0)) Bus Info Agency.

Key Trilogy CD Collection: Key of Light; Key of Knowledge; Key of Valor. abr. ed. Nora Roberts. Read by Susan Ericksen. (Running Time: 12 hrs.). (Key Trilogy: Vols. 1-3). 2006. audio compact disk 29.95 (978-1-59737-722-5(8), 9781597377225) Brilliance Audio.
Key of Light: The Malory Price Life Plan does not include a quixotic quest - but the strangers on Warrior's Peak claim that she must find a key that will release three souls held captive by an evil god. Little does she know that the quest will bring her two new friends, the love of her life, and danger beyond anyone's imagination. Key of Knowledge: To Dana Steele books and the knowledge they hold are the key to contentment. But now that search for knowledge must include the second key needed to release three souls held captive by an evil god. She won't be alone, for she's formed fast friendships with two very different women. She can't allow herself to be distracted by the return of the man who broke her heart so long ago, for a danger beyond anyone's imagination is determined to keep her from completing her quest. Key of Valor: Light and Knowledge have succeeded in their quest, and two of the keys have been found. The final, and last, test goes to Zoe McCourt - Valor. Zoe has the courage to raise her young son alone, and to face all the adversity life has thrown at them. But will she have the courage to face a foe determined to do anything to stop the third key from being found - even destroying everything - and everyone - she loves?.

Key West see Poetry of Hart Crane

Key Wholesalers & Retailers Database of the United Kingdom. 6th rev. ed. BIA. (J). 2006. audio compact disk 469.00 (978-1-4187-4889-0(7)) Bus Info Agency.

Key Wholesalers & Retailers of Spain. 6th rev. ed. BIA. (J). 2006. audio compact disk 289.00 (978-1-4187-4939-2(7)) Bus Info Agency.

Key Wholesalers & Retailers of Spain. 6th rev. ed. BIA. (J). 2006. audio compact disk 249.00 (978-1-4187-4938-5(9)) Bus Info Agency.

Key Wholesalers & Retailers of the United Kingdom. 6th rev. ed. BIA. (J). 2006. audio compact disk 289.00 (978-1-4187-4891-3(9)) Bus Info Agency.

Key Wholesalers & Retailers of the United Kingdom. 6th rev. ed. BIA. (J). 2006. audio compact disk 249.00 (978-1-4187-4890-6(0)) Bus Info Agency.

Key Words of the Christian Life. Warren W. Wiersbe. Read by Warren W. Wiersbe. 3 cass. 14.95 (978-0-8474-2210-4(0)) Back to Bible.
Help you understand those words that are sometimes hard to understand. Words such as: propitiation, predestination, justification, glorification, sanctification & others.

Keyboard, Vol. 2. Daniel Scott & Sorcha Armstrong. 2004. audio compact disk 12.95 (978-0-7119-8774-6(2), AM969694) Music Sales.

***Keyboard Basics.** Created by Alfred Publishing. (Play (Alfred) Ser.). (ENG.). 2010. (978-0-7390-6586-0(6)) Alfred Pub.

Keyboard Beginnings - Book I: Music for Young Children, Book I. Judy Kagel. (ENG., (J). 1996. spiral bd. 24.95 (978-0-9820682-0-5(4)) JBK Music.

Keyboard by Chords. 1 cass. pap. bk. 19.95 Incl. 2 charts. (V-2) Duane Shinn.
Learn how to play any keyboard - piano, synthesizer, organ, electronic keyboard - by chords! Enables any keyboard player to play songs using a chord system rather than having to be tied to a printed score.

Keyboard Chords. 1 CD. (Running Time: 1 hr.). (Step One Ser.). 1997. audio compact disk 7.95 (978-0-8256-1611-2(5)) Pub: Music Sales. Dist(s): H Leonard

Keyboard Chords. Gary Turner. (Progressive Ser.). 2004. pap. bk. 24.95 (978-1-86469-064-4(X), 256-117) Kolala Music SGP.

Keyboard Conversations with Jeffrey Siegel, Pianist: The Romance of the Piano. unabr. ed. Jeffrey Siegel. (Running Time: 3600 sec.). (ENG.). 2006. audio compact disk 14.95 (978-0-7393-3267-2(8), Random AudioBks) Pub: Random Audio Pubg. Dist(s): Random

Keyboard Conversations with Jeffrey Siegel, Pianist: The Romanticism of the Russian Soul. unabr. ed. Jeffrey Siegel. (Running Time: 3600 sec.). (ENG.). 2006. audio compact disk 14.95 (978-0-7393-3265-8(1), Random AudioBks) Pub: Random Audio Pubg. Dist(s): Random

Keyboard Made Easy. Ed. by Alfred Publishing. (ENG.). 2001. audio compact disk 10.00 (978-1-929395-29-3(9)) Pub: Workshop Arts. Dist(s): Alfred Pub

Keyboard Magic: A Band in a Book. (J). 1992. bk. 19.95 (978-0-938971-89-4(1)) JTG Nashville.

Keyboard Method. Gary Turner. 2004. pap. bk. 16.95 (978-1-959540-46-5(7)) Pub: Kolala Music SGP. Dist(s): Bookworld

Keyboard Method for Young Beginners, Bk. 3. Andrew Scott. 1 CD. (Progressive Ser.). (J). 1997. pap. bk. (978-0-947183-43-1(4)) Kolala Music SGP.

Keyboard Technique: Suitable for All Types of Electronic Keyboard. Peter Gelling. (Progressive Ser.). 1998. pap. bk. 19.95 (978-1-875690-73-2(5), 256-118) Kolala Music SGP.

Keyboard Wisdom: Theory & Technique. Steven Goomas. 2004. pap. bk. 22.95 (978-0-7866-4671-5(3), 99270BCD) Pub: Mel Bay. Dist(s): Koen Levy

Keyboarding CD. Marcia Tisdale. (Expert Systems for Teachers). 2004. tchr. ed. (978-1-931680-93-6(0), Expert Systms Teach) TeachPoint.

Keyboards in Contemporary Praise & Worship. Contrib. by Ed Kerr. (Running Time: 1 hr. 30 mins.). 2006. 29.50 (978-5-558-17940-8(6)) Pt of Grace Ent.

KeyChamp 2.0 Macintosh Site License, Pack. 2nd ed. Walter M. Sharp & Cengage Learning South-Western Staff. (ENG.). (C). 2003. 853.95 (978-0-538-43458-4(9)) Pub: South-West. Dist(s): CENGAGE Learn

Keynesian Revolution. unabr. ed. Fred Glahe. Ed. by Israel M. Kirzner. Narrated by Louis Rukeyser. 2 cass. (Running Time: 75 min. per cass.). Dramatization. (Great Economic Thinkers Ser.). (YA). (gr. 10 up). 1988. 17.95 (978-0-938935-41-4(0), 10211) Knowledge Prod.
In 1936, John Maynard Keynes introduced his view that capitalism is capable of remarkable efficiency, yet prone to instability caused by weak consumer demand. Keynes' analysis led directly to active government policies for stimulating demand, including deficit spending.

Keynesian Revolution: Capitalism as a Flawed System, & Ideas for a New Order. Fred Glahe & Frank Vorhies. Read by Louis Rukeyser. (Running Time: 9000 sec.). (Great Economic Thinkers Ser.). 2006. audio compact disk 25.95 (978-0-7861-6946-7(X)) Pub: Blckstn Audio. Dist(s): NetLibrary CO

Keynesian Revolution: Capitalism as a Flawed System, & Ideas for a New Order. unabr. ed. Fred Glahe & Frank Vorhies. Read by Louis Rukeyser. Ed. by Israel Kirzner & Mike Hassell. Prod. by Pat Childs. 2 CDs. (Running Time: 9000 sec.). (Audio Classics Ser.). 2007. audio compact disk 19.95 (978-1-4332-0018-2(X)) Blckstn Audio.

Keynesianism & the Philosophical Overthrow of Gold. John Ridpath. 1 cass. (Running Time: 90 min.). 1990. 12.95 (978-1-56114-127-2(5), CR04C) Second Renaissance.

Keynote AIDS: The Growing Dimensions of National Threat. Michael Gottlieb. (AIDS: The National Conference for Practitioners). 1986. 9.00 (978-0-932491-43-5(X)) Res Appl Inc.

Keynote Plus: A Book for Teachers. Tim Cain. (Running Time: 2 hrs. 3 mins.). (ENG., 1989. 88.00 (978-0-521-35457-8(9)) Cambridge U Pr.

Keynote Presentation: Health Care Challenges & Priorities in 1986 & Beyond. Richard A. Gephardt. 1 cass. 9.00 (TAPE 1) Recorded Res.

Keys of Hell. unabr. ed. Jack Higgins. Read by Christian Rodska. 4 cass. (Running Time: 10 hrs.). 2004. 24.95 (978-1-59007-304-9(5)) Pub: New Millenn Enter. Dist(s): PerseuPGW

Keys of Hell. unabr. ed. Jack Higgins. Read by Christina Rodska. 4 CDs. (Running Time: 10 hrs.). 2004. audio compact disk 29.95 (978-1-59007-305-6(3)) Pub: New Millenn Enter. Dist(s): PerseuPGW

***Keys of Hell.** unabr. ed. Jack Higgins. Read by Michael Page. (Running Time: 5 hrs.). 2011. 24.99 (978-1-4418-4540-5(2), 9781441845405, Brilliance MP3); 39.97 (978-1-4418-4541-2(0), 9781441845412, Brlnc Audio MP3 Lib); audio compact disk 29.99 (978-1-4418-4538-2(0), 9781441845382, Bril Audio CD Unabri); audio compact disk 87.97 (978-1-4418-4539-9(9), 9781441845399, BriAudCD Unabrid) Brilliance Audio.

Keys of Hell. unabr. collector's ed. Jack Higgins. Read by Larry McKeever. 4 cass. (Running Time: 4 hrs.). 1985. 24.00 (978-0-7366-0504-5(5), 1478) Books on Tape.
Super spy Paul Chavasse is given a job: get into Albania & put a dangerous agent out of commission - permanently. What Chavasse doesn't know is that someone has set a trap for him - someone who has waited a long time for revenge - someone who has planned his destruction - someone who holds the keys to hell.

Keys of Life. 2005. audio compact disk (978-0-9772969-0-3(3)) PFC Inc.

Keys of Power. Zondervan Publishing Staff. 2006. audio compact disk 14.99 (978-0-8297-4889-5(X)) Pub: Vida Pubs. Dist(s): Zondervan

Keys of the Kingdom. Kenneth Copeland. 3 cass. 1986. 15.00 Set. (978-0-88114-779-7(6)) K Copeland Pubns.
Biblical teaching on Kingdom living.

Keys of the Kingdom. A. J. Cronin. Read by Gregory Peck. (DD8845) Natl Recrd Co.

Keys of the Palace: Selections from Peter Pelham's Repertoire Played on Period Instruments in the Governor's Palace. 1 CD. 2002. audio compact disk (978-0-87935-223-3(X)) Colonial Williamsburg.
Colonial Williamsburg Foundation harpsichordist Michael Monaco plays 18th-century musical selections on the organ, harpsichord, and pianoforte. Recorded in Colonial Williamsburg?s Governor's Palace, the music includes selections that Monaco?s 18th-century counterpart, Peter Pelham?a teacher, civil servant, and the foremost musician in colonial Williamsburg?would have played. The selections are played on period keyboard instruments in the Governor's Palace. These include a Jacob Kirchman harpsichord, an Abraham Adcock and Peter Pether chamber organ, and a James Ball square pianoforte.

Keys to a Successful Marriage Series, Set. Elbert Willis. 4 cass. 13.00 Fill the Gap.

Keys to Building Self-Esteem. James D. MacArthur. 1 cass. 5.98 (978-1-55503-211-1(7), 06003878) Covenant Comms.
The basic elements of self-esteem & how to make them work.

Keys to Compatibility: Opening the Door to a Marvelous Marriage, Vol. 2. Mac Hammond & Lynne Hammond. (ENG.). 2007. audio compact disk 30.00 (978-1-57399-336-4(0)) Mac Hammond.

Keys to Compatibility Set: Opening the Door to a Marvelous Marriage. Mac Hammond. 6 cass. (Running Time: 6 hrs). (Happily Ever after Ser.: Vol. 2). 1995. Mac Hammond.
Opposites attract, or so they say. But differences in temperament & outlook often result in conflict between husbands & wives.

Keys to Courageous Living: 2007 CCEF Annual Conference. Featuring Edward T. Welch. 2007. audio compact disk 29.99 (978-1-934885-22-2(3)) New Growth Pr.

Keys to Effective Evangelsim. John MacArthur, Jr. 4 cass. (John MacArthur's Bible Studies). 16.25 (HarperThor) HarpC GBR.

Keys to Effective Presentations: Capitol Learning Audio Course. Jill Kamp Melton. Prod. by TheCapitol.Net. (ENG.). 2008. 47.00 (978-1-58733-081-0(4)) TheCapitol.

Keys to Entrepreneurial Success: Take the First Step Toward the American Dream! unabr. ed. Center for Entrepreneurial Leadership, Inc. Staff. Ed. by Jeffry A. Timmons. 3 cass. (Running Time: 4 hrs.). 1996. 29.95 Set. Kauffman Ctr.
Get practical, down to earth advice from ten successful entrepreneurs about starting your own business.

Keys to God's Abundance. Derek Prince. 3 cass. 14.95 (I-GA1) Derek Prince.

Keys to God's Abundance. Gary V. Whetstone. (Practical Ministry Ser.: Vol. PM 202). (C). 1997. 180.00 (978-1-58866-039-8(7)) Gary Whet Pub.

Keys to Good Government. unabr. ed. David Barton. Read by David Barton. 1 cass. 1994. 4.95 (978-0-925279-40-8(4)) Wallbuilders.
A survey of the Founders' views on how to establish good govemments, & an examination of their specific instructions on how to preserve good government. Learn how to reapply their principles today.

Keys to Handling Pressure. Creflo A. Dollar. 2008. audio compact disk 14.00 (978-1-59944-695-0(2)) Creflo Dollar.

Keys to Hearing from God. Speeches. Creflo A. Dollar. 3 cass. (Running Time: 4 hrs.). 2002. 15.00 (978-1-59089-491-0(X)) Creflo Dollar.

Keys to Higher Awareness. Wayne W. Dyer. Read by Wayne W. Dyer. 1 cass. (Running Time: 90 min.). 1994. 10.95 (978-1-56170-072-1(X), 236) Hay House.

Keys to Higher Awareness. abr. ed. Wayne W. Dyer. 1 CD. 2005. audio compact disk 10.95 (978-1-4019-0442-5(4)) Hay House.

Keys to Kingdom. Aliso Armstrong & Robert Rohm. 2005. audio compact disk 44.95 (978-0-9741435-1-4(0)) Pax Pr Inc.

Keys to Opportunity. Ronald A. Moore. 1 cass. (Running Time: 46 min.). (Think Plaid Ser.: No. 1). 1995. (978-0-9655823-1-5(0)) Keys to Opptnity.
Motivational materials to help people live better lives, one day at a time.

Keys to Option Mentoring. Created by Barry Neil Kaufman. 3 CDs. (Running Time: 49 mins., 44 mins., 37 mins.). 2006. audio compact disk 49.00 (978-1-887254-21-2(8)) Epic Century.
A "must" CD series for those wanting insight into the guidelines, training process and intention of The Option Process Dialogue. This series is an invaluable resource for anyone in the helping and/or counseling professions, as well as for anyone searching for a more effective, loveing and accepting way to deal with themselves and those around them. What is shared here can be applied personally and/or professionally. The gift of a question is the most fundamental resource and tool for sharing The Option Process. The mentor (facilitator) provides an accepting environment in which those exploring are encouraged to find their own answers. The role of The Option Process mentor is presented by Barry Neil Kaufman. He shares the uplifting notion of the mentor as "happy detective", then itemizes attributes which are simply stated and easily understood. The presentation then expands on these ideas through a revealing question-and-answer session on mentoring with an advanced mentor training group.

Keys to Power - Key 1 see Llaves Del Poder: Desprendimiento - Tesoro Espiritual - Material

Keys to Power - Key 1: Detachment - Spiritual Treasure - Material Treasure: Detachment - Spiritual Treasure - Material Treasure. Dario Silva-Silva. Read by Dario Silva-Silva. (Running Time: 1 hr.). (C). 2003. 14.95 (978-1-60083-308-3(X), Audiofy Corp) Iofy Corp.

Keys to Power - Key 11 & 12: the Agreement - the Generosity: The Agreement - the Generosity. Dario Silva-Silva. Read by Dario Silva-Silva. (Running Time: 1 hr.). (C). 2006. 14.95 (978-1-60083-315-1(2), Audiofy Corp) Iofy Corp.

Keys to Power - Key 13: the Prayer: The Prayer. Dario Silva-Silva. Read by Dario Silva-Silva. (Running Time: 1 hr.). (C). 2006. 14.95 (978-1-60083-316-8(0), Audiofy Corp) Iofy Corp.

Keys to Power - Key 2 see Llaves Del Poder Pautas para Una Vida Plena

Keys to Power - Key 2: Productivity - Sowing & Harvest - Reduction or Production: Productivity - Sowing & Harvest - Reduction or Production. Dario Silva-Silva. Read by Dario Silva-Silva. (Running Time: 1 hr.). (C). 2003. 14.95 (978-1-60083-309-0(8), Audiofy Corp) lofy Corp.

Keys to Power - Key 3 see Llaves del Poder: Causalidad - Accion y Reaccion - Causa y Efecto

Keys to Power - Key 3: Causality - Action & Reaction - Cause & Effect: Causality - Action & Reaction - Cause & Effect. Dario Silva-Silva. Read by Dario Silva-Silva. (Running Time: 1 hr.). (C). 2003. 14.95 (978-1-60083-310-6(1), Audiofy Corp) lofy Corp.

Keys to Power - Key 4 see Llaves Del Poder: Palabra - Bendecir O Maldecir - Crear O Destruir

Keys to Power - Key 4: to Bless or to Curse - to Crerate or to Destroy: To Bless or to Curse - to Crerate or to Destroy. Dario Silva-Silva. Read by Dario Silva-Silva. (Running Time: 1 hr.). (C). 2003. 14.95 (978-1-60083-311-3(X), Audiofy Corp) lofy Corp.

Keys to Power - Key 5 & 6: the Faith - the Praise: The Faith - the Praise. Dario Silva-Silva. Read by Dario Silva-Silva. (Running Time: 1 hr.). (C). 2006. 14.95 (978-1-60083-312-0(8), Audiofy Corp) lofy Corp.

Keys to Power - Key 7 & 8: the Rest - the Restitution: The Rest - the Restitution. Dario Silva-Silva. Read by Dario Silva-Silva. (Running Time: 1 hr.). (C). 2006. 14.95 (978-1-60083-313-7(6), Audiofy Corp) lofy Corp.

Keys to Power - Key 9 & 10: the Silence - the Obedience: The Silence - the Obedience. Dario Silva-Silva. Read by Dario Silva-Silva. (Running Time: 1 hr.). (C). 2006. 14.95 (978-1-60083-314-4(4), Audiofy Corp) lofy Corp.

Keys to Real Faith. Featuring Bill Winston. 4. 2004. 20.00 (978-1-59544-018-1(6)); audio compact disk 32.00 (978-1-59544-019-8(4)) Pub: B Winston Min. Dist(s): Anchor Distributors
In this four-tape series, you will discover the answers you need to avoid the pitfalls of life. God wants us to use our faithto avoid the traps of the enemy and take dominion over the challenges of life.

Keys to Riches in Estate Planning. Ted Delong. Read by Ted Delong. 6 cass. (Running Time: 5 hrs. 20 min.). 1994. 69.00 Set. (978-1-885661-01-2(0)) Estate Protection.
No. 1 All about trusts; No. 2 How to fill out a trust application - with application enclosed; No. 3 Selling secrets; No. 4 Recruiting archetype; No. 5 Leadership with achievement; No. 6 a winning lifestyle.

Keys to Riches in Estate Planning. Ted Delong. Read by Ted Delong. 6 cass. (Running Time: 5 hrs. 20 min.). 1996. pap. bk. 59.90 (978-1-885661-00-5(2)) Estate Protection.

Keys to Self-Control. Mac Hammond. 4 cass. (Running Time: 3 hrs). 2005. 20.00 (978-1-57399-226-8(7)) Mac Hammond.
Would you like to be a more disciplined person? This series will show you how to strengthen your resolve in everything from losing weight, to acquiring a new skill, to spening more time with God.

Keys To Spiritual Growth: Logos December 21, 1997. Ben Young. 1997. 4.95 (978-0-7417-6061-6(4), B0061) Win Walk.

Keys to Successful Advent Preaching. 1 cass. (Running Time: 12 min.). (Advent Celebration 98 Ser.). 1998. 5.00 (978-1-57849-096-7(0)) Mainstay Church.

Keys to Successful Adventure Preaching: You're Invited to a Wedding. Read by David Mains & Greg A. Koupoulas. 1 cass. (Running Time: 12 min.). (Fifty Day Spiritual Adventure 1999 Ser.). 1998. 5.00 (978-1-57849-139-1(8)) Mainstay Church.

Keys to Successful Christian Living. Kenneth E. Hagin. 6 cass. 24.00 (34H) Faith Lib Pubns.

***Keys to the Demon Prison.** Brandon Mull. (Fablehaven Ser.: Bk. 5). 2010. audio compact disk 49.99 (978-1-60641-261-9(2), Shadow Mount) Deseret Bk.

Keys to the Garden. unabr. ed. Susan Sallis. Read by Ann Dover & Anne Dover. 10 cass. (Running Time: 11 hrs. 15 mins.). (Soundings Ser.). (J). 2004. 84.95 (978-1-86042-608-7(5)) Pub: ISIS Lrg Prnt GBR. Dist(s): Ulverscroft US

Keys to the Kingdom. 2001. (978-1-59024-029-8(4)); audio compact disk (978-1-59024-030-4(8)) B Hinn Min.

Keys to the Kingdom Series. unabr. ed. Dudley Hall. 3 cass. (Running Time: 4 hrs. 30 mins.). 2000. 15.00 (DH01-000) Morning NC.
Includes "The Essential Question," "Stewardship: Key to Maturity" & "Following is a Good Word." These messages outline three essentials for successful Christian living.

Keys to the Kingdom #1: Mister Monday: The Keys to the Kingdom #1. unabr. ed. Garth Nix. Read by Allan Corduner. (Keys to the Kingdom Ser.). (ENG.). (J). (gr. 4). 2010. audio compact disk 45.00 (978-0-307-70607-2(9), Listening Lib) Pub: Random Audio Pubg. Dist(s): Random

Keys to the Kingdom #2: Grim Tuesday: The Keys to the Kingdom #2. unabr. ed. Garth Nix. Read by Allan Corduner. (Keys to the Kingdom Ser.). (ENG.). (J). (gr. 4). 2010. audio compact disk 39.00 (978-0-307-70608-9(7), Listening Lib) Pub: Random Audio Pubg. Dist(s): Random

Keys to the Kingdom #3: Drowned Wednesday: The Keys to the Kingdom #3. unabr. ed. Garth Nix. Read by Allan Corduner. (Keys to the Kingdom Ser.). (ENG.). (J). (gr. 4). 2010. audio compact disk 45.00 (978-0-307-70609-6(5), Listening Lib) Pub: Random Audio Pubg. Dist(s): Random

Keys to the Kingdom #7: Lord Sunday: The Keys to the Kingdom #7. unabr. ed. Garth Nix. Read by Allan Corduner. (ENG.). (J). (gr. 4). 2010. audio compact disk 34.00 (978-0-7393-7367-5(6), Listening Lib) Pub: Random Audio Pubg. Dist(s): Random

Keys to the Street. abr. ed. Ruth Rendell. Read by Sharon Williams. 2 cass. (Running Time: 3 hrs.). 2000. 7.95 (978-1-57815-173-8(2), 1116, Media Bks Audio) Media Bks NJ.
A tale of Londons homeless puts Marys life in danger.

Keys to the Street. abr. ed. Ruth Rendell. Read by Sharon Williams. 3 CDs. (Running Time: 3 hrs.). 2000. audio compact disk 11.99 (978-1-57815-507-1(X), 1116 CD3, Media Bks Audio) Media Bks NJ.

Keys to the Street. unabr. ed. Ruth Rendell. Read by Simon Russell Beale. 10 CDs. (Running Time: 15 hrs.). 2003. audio compact disk 94.95 (978-0-7540-5569-3(8), CCD 260) AudioGO.

Keys to the Street. unabr. ed. Ruth Rendell. Read by Donada Peters. 8 cass. (Running Time: 12 hrs.). 1996. 64.00 (978-0-913369-30-2(6), 4183) Books on Tape.
When Mary Jago donates her bone marrow to help a complete stranger, the act bonds her with the young man who lives from her transfusion. He will change Mary's life in ways she could never imagine.

Keys to the Street. unabr. ed. Ruth Rendell. Read by Simon Russell Beale. 8 cass. (Running Time: 12 hrs.). 2000. 59.95 (978-0-7540-0011-2(7), CAB 1434) Pub: Chivers Audio Bks GBR. Dist(s): AudioGO
Margo Jago donated her bone marrow to save the life of someone she didn't know. However, this generous act led to the bitter break-up with Alistair. For him, it was as though her beauty had been plundered. But the man whose life she saved would change Mary's life in a way she never imagined.

Keys to the Word. Arthur T. Pierson. 2009. audio compact disk 13.95 (978-0-578-00779-3(7)) Sapphire Dig.

Keys to Understanding the Book of Revelation. Richard D. Draper. 4 cass. 2004. 19.95 (978-1-57734-863-4(X)); audio compact disk 21.95 (978-1-57734-864-1(8)) Covenant Comms.

Keys to Understanding Your Bible. (Running Time: 1 hr). 2005. (978-0-9762892-9-6(6)) Bible Facts.

Keys to Unlocking the Harvest. Marc Estes. 3 cass. (Running Time: 4 hrs. 30 mins.). 2000. (978-1-886849-19-8(6)) CityChristian.

Keys to Victory: Joshua 8. Ed Young. 1985. 4.95 (978-0-7417-1452-7(3), 452) Win Walk.

Keys to Winning for the Equestrian Series. Created by Laura Boynton King. 5 CD's. 2002. audio compact disk 89.95 (978-0-9748885-6-9(7)) Summit Dynamics.
A 5 volume series designed to help the horseback rider be more relaxed, fearless, confident and successful.

Kf2: The Take Over. Executive Producer Taffi L. Dollar. (ENG.). (J). 2007. audio compact disk 14.99 (978-1-59944-152-8(7)) Creflo Dollar.

Khansahib Talking. Ali A. Khan. 1 cass. 9.00 (A0319-88) Sound Photosyn.
The Maestro talking with Brian, with Faustin, & with classes at the Ali Akbar College of Music.

Khevrisa - European Klezmer Music. Perf. by Zev Feldman et al. 1 CD. (Running Time: 70 mins.). (AFR.). 2000. audio compact disk 15.00 (SFW 40486) Smithsonian Folkways.
The history of Klezmer.

Khmer Basic Course Vol. 1 (FSI) CDs & Text. 19 CDs. (Running Time: 13 hrs.). (Foreign Service Institute Basic Course Ser.). (KHM.). 2005. audio compact disk 255.00 (978-1-57970-191-8(4), AFKH01D) J Norton Pubs.

Khmer Basic Course Vol. 2 (FSI) CDs & Text. 29 CDs. (Running Time: 21 hrs.). (Foreign Service Institute Basic Course Ser.). (KHM.). 2005. audio compact disk 295.00 (978-1-57970-192-5(2), AFKH50D) J Norton Pubs.

Kiahawk: Blood Arrows. unabr. ed. Craig Fraley. Read by Kevin Foley. 6 cass. (Running Time: 6 hrs. 6 min.). (Kiahawk Ser.: Bk. 6). 2001. 39.95 (978-1-55686-844-3(8)) Books in Motion.
When police find a string of murder victims, all evidence points to Josh. But Detective Wallace knows the killings are the work of the evil spirit Chawkaterro.

Kiahawk: Forgotten Arrows. unabr. ed. Craig Fraley. Read by Kevin Foley. 6 cass. (Running Time: 7 hrs. 48 min.). (Kiahawk Ser.: Bk. 2). 1995. 39.95 (978-1-55686-590-9(2)) Books in Motion.
The deadly feud between modern reservation Indians & white men of Lake Shanoha continue. Framed for murders committed by unscrupulous residents of modern Lake Shanoha the Kiahawks use mystical powers to conjure up a great warrior from the past to defend them.

Kiahawk - Burning Arrows. unabr. ed. Craig Fraley. Read by Kevin Foley. 4 cass. (Running Time: 5 hrs. 12 min.). (Kiahawk Ser.: Bk. 1). 1994. 26.95 (978-1-55686-545-9(7)) Books in Motion.
Here is a deadly feud between modern reservation Indians & white men played out in a small desert community called Lake Shanoha, Nevada.

Kibbles Rockin' Clubhouse: Vol. 1 Expressing Yourself, Vol. 1. Ed. by Eugene Scott Productions. Prod. by NoteAbilities. Executive Producer Scott Leslie et al. Characters created by Scott Leslie. Executive Producer Ann Leslie et al. Music by Angela Neve. (ENG.). (J). 2007. DVD & audio compact disk 34.99 (978-0-9800436-0-0(3)) Note Inc.

***Kick.** unabr. ed. Walter Dean Myers. Illus. by Ross Workman. 2011. (978-0-06-203651-3(3)) HarperCollins Pubs.

Kick Ass in College: A Guerrilla Guide to College Success. Gunnar Fox. Read by Gunnar Fox. 2005. audio compact disk (978-0-9762928-4-5(X)) KICK ASS Med.

Kick Butt, Take Names. 1 cass. (Running Time: 1 hr.). 2000. 15.95 Prof Pride.
Record call info side 1, questions side 2. Not for beginners. Fast paced.

***Kick the Can.** 2010. audio compact disk (978-1-59171-281-7(5)) Falcon Picture.

Kicking His Mother. unabr. ed. Gilbert Highet. Read by Gilbert Highet. 1 cass. (Running Time: 30 min.). 9.95 (23298-A) J Norton Pubs.

Kicks & Giggles- Out of Production: Flannery O'Connor. 18.2. 2006. 12.00 (978-1-59128-593-9(3)); 12.00 (978-1-59128-595-3(X)) Canon Pr ID.

Kid. unabr. ed. Kevin Lewis. Narrated by Glen McCready. 7 cass. (Running Time: 7 hrs. 30 mins.). 2004. 69.75 (978-1-84505-061-0(4), H1659MC, Clipper Audio) Recorded Bks.

Kid & the Big Hunt. Elmore Leonard. 2004. 5.95 (978-0-7435-4672-0(5)) Pub: S&S Audio. Dist(s): S and S Inc

***Kid Appeal: A Story from Guys Read: Funny Business.** unabr. ed. David Lubar. (ENG.). 2010. (978-0-06-202770-2(0)); (978-0-06-206248-2(4)) HarperCollins Pubs.

Kid Breckenridge. unabr. ed. Bernard Palmer. Read by Rusty Nelson. 6 cass. (Running Time: 8 hrs. 30 min.). 2001. 39.95 (978-1-55686-802-3(2)) Books in Motion.
Young Breck changes his name and his gunslinging past to start his own spread, only to be faced with former "friends" bent on taking all they can out of John's new life.

Kid in King Arthur's Court. 1 cass. (J). 1995. 12.98 (978-1-55723-872-6(3)); 19.98 (978-1-55723-873-3(1)) W Disney Records.

Kid Next Door. unabr. ed. Janice Lee Smith. Narrated by Johnny Heller. 1 cass. (Running Time: 1 hr.). (Adam Joshua Capers Ser.). (gr. 2 up). 1998. 10.00 (978-0-7887-2274-5(3), 95502E7) Recorded Bks.
Adam Joshua & his best friend next door share everything. But when they run out of space for their things in the tree house, they run out of time for each other. A fun-filled tale of a young boy learning about true friendship.

Kid Skills Interpersonal Skill Series: A Lasting Friend: Friendship: Making Friends. unabr. ed. J. Thomas Morse. 1 cass. (Running Time: 30 min.). Dramatization. (J). (gr. 1-3). 1985. 13.95 incl. bk., check-up chart, parent guide, activity guide, lyric sheet & audio cassette with story & 2 original songs. (978-0-934275-20-0(3)) Fam Skills.
In this tale a child leams the skills for making friends from a very unique new acquaintance.

Kid Skills Interpersonal Skill Series: An Island Adventure: Self-Esteem: Being A Friend to Myself. unabr. ed. J. Thomas Morse et al. 1 cass. (Running Time: 30 min.). Dramatization. (KidSkills Interpersonal Skill Ser.). (J). (gr. 1-3). 1985. bk. 13.95 incl. bk., check-up chart, parent guide, activity guide, lyric sheet & audio cassette with story & 2 original songs. (978-0-934275-14-9(9)) Fam Skills.
This story is an adventure in leaming to be a friend with oneself & it features some surprises.

Kid Skills Interpersonal Skill Series: Choices! Choices! Choices!: Responsibility: Making & Living with Choices. unabr. ed. Betty Gouge. 1 cass. (Running Time: 20 min.). Dramatization. (J). (ps-1). 1986. 11.95 incl. bk., parent guide with activity lyric sheets with 2 original songs. (978-0-934275-23-1(8)) Fam Skills.
Even young children must make choices & live with consequences. This story develops decision-making & coping skills in a no-pressure way. Simplified for pre-school audiences.

Kid Skills Interpersonal Skill Series: Feeling Fun House: Feelings: Dealing With Feelings. unabr. ed. J. Thomas Morse. 1 cass. (Running Time: 30 min.). Dramatization. (KidSkills Interpersonal Skills Ser.). (J). 1985. 13.95 incl. bk., check-up chart, parent guide activity guide, lyric sheet & 2 original songs. (978-0-934275-17-0(3)) Fam Skills.
Children leam what meaningful things feelings tell us & that they are a matter of choice. They develop skills for dealing with their own feelings successfully.

Kid Skills Interpersonal Skill Series: Land of Listening: Listening: Getting & Giving Attention. unabr. ed. J. Thomas Morse. 1 cass. (Running Time: 30 min.). Dramatization. (Kidskills Interpersonal Skill Ser.). (J). (gr. 1-3). 1985. 13.95 incl. bk., check-up chart, parent guide, activity guide, lyric & 2 original songs. (978-0-934275-15-6(7)) Fam Skills.
Heada, Heartly & Doofer lead children to the magical Land of Listening where they leam how to be good listeners from a very unusual teacher.

Kid Skills Interpersonal Skill Series: Let's Share: Friendship: Sharing. unabr. ed. Betty Gouge. 1 cass. (Running Time: 20 min.). Dramatization. (J). (ps-1). 1986. 11.95 incl. bk., parent guide with activities, lyric sheet & 2 original songs. (978-0-934275-27-9(0)) Fam Skills.
Sharing is a fundamental skill for young children to master before entering school. This story shows how in fun, rewarding ways.

Kid Skills Interpersonal Skill Series: My Feelings & Me: Feelings: Dealing with Feelings. unabr. ed. Betty Gouge. 1 cass. (Running Time: 20 min.). Dramatization. (J). (ps-1). 1986. 11.95 incl. bk., parent guide with activities, lyric sheet & 2 original songs. (978-0-934275-24-8(6)) Fam Skills.
Pre-school youngsters have many moods & feelings they don't understand. This story teaches the importance of feelings & how to express them appropriately. Simplified for pre-school audiences.

Kid Skills Interpersonal Skill Series: Wonderful You: Self-Awareness: Accepting & Knowing Myself. unabr. ed. Betty Gouge. 1 cass. (Running Time: 20 min.). Dramatization. (J). (ps-1). 1986. 11.95 incl. bk., parent guide with activities, lyric sheet & 2 original songs. (978-0-934275-26-2(2)) Fam Skills.
A story of self-awareness & self-affirmation. In addition to body image, special consideration is given to thoughts, feelings & actions.

Kid Stays in the Picture. Robert Evans. Read by Robert Evans. (Playaway Adult Nonfiction Ser.). (ENG.). 2009. 59.99 (978-1-60812-586-9(6)) Find a World.

Kid Stays in the Picture. abr. ed. Robert Evans. Read by Robert Evans. 4 cass. (Running Time: 6 hrs.). 2001. 25.00 (978-1-59040-077-7(1), Phoenix Audio) Pub: Amer Intl Pub. Dist(s): PerseuPGW
Robert Evans' fascinating account of his rise, fall and rise again in show business. Hear revealing tales of movie legends, including Errol Flynn, Ava Gardner, Jack Nicholson, Warren Beatty and Sharon Stone. Laced throughout are stories of his liaisons with some of the world's most beautiful women. His candor is shocking as he recounts the lurid, dark years of the '80s, chronicling his cocaine bust, his implication in "The Cotton Club Murders," and his self-committal and escape from a mental hospital. And lastly, being back in the cat-bird seat of power, once again sending shock waves through Hollywood and the world.

Kid Stays in the Picture. abr. ed. Robert Evans. As told by Robert Evans. 6 CDs. (Running Time: 6 hrs.). 2004. audio compact disk 39.95 (978-1-59007-225-7(1)) Pub: New Millenn Enter. Dist(s): PerseuPGW
The fascinating rise, fall and rise again of legendary producer Robert Evans. This is one life story you'll never forget: a kid actor in New york on radio plays, popularizing "women in pants" at Evan-Picone, being discovered poolside at the Beverly Hills Hotel by Norma Shearer, becoming the first actor to ever run a motion picture studio, reviving the moribund Paramount Pictures, overseeing production of Love Story, The Godfather, Chinatown, Rosemary's Baby, The Odd Couple, marriage to golden girl Ali McGraw and birth of son Joshua, long friendships with Nicholson, Beatty, and Hoffman, disgrace and drugs...the Cotton Club scandal...self-commitment and escape from a mental institution...and an eventual triumphant retum to the catbird seat. An extraordinary raconteur, Evans spares no one least of all himself, on this legendary no-holds-barred Hollywood journey.

Kid Stays in the Picture. abr. ed. Robert Evans. Read by Robert Evans. 4 cass. (Running Time: 6 hrs.). 2004. 28.00 (978-1-59007-182-3(4)) New Millenn Enter.

Kid Who Became President. Dan Gutman. Narrated by Scott Shina. 4 CDs. (Running Time: 4 hrs.). (gr. 4 up). audio compact disk 39.00 (978-1-4025-1960-4(5)) Recorded Bks.

Kid Who Became President. Dan Gutman. Narrated by Scott Shina. 3 pieces. (Running Time: 4 hrs.). (gr. 4 up). 2001. 28.00 (978-0-7887-5351-0(7)) Recorded Bks.
The sequel to "The Kid Who Ran for President," in which Judson accepts his new job as President. A typical seventh grader, Judson roller blades, loves gory movies and plays video games. He brings an innocence and honesty to the office of President that no one has ever seen before.

Kid Who Only Hit Homers see Muchacho Que Bateaba Solo Jonrones

***Kid Who Only Hit Homers.** unabr. ed. Matt Christopher. (ENG.). (J). 2010. audio compact disk 22.00 (978-0-307-71073-4(4), Listening Lib) Pub: Random Audio Pubg. Dist(s): Random

Kid Who Ran for President. Dan Gutman. Narrated by Scott Shina. 3 CDs. (Running Time: 2 hrs. 45 mins.). (gr. 5 up). audio compact disk 29.00 (978-0-7887-9514-5(7)) Recorded Bks.

Kid Who Ran for President. Dan Gutman. Narrated by Scott Shina. 2 pieces. (Running Time: 2 hrs. 45 mins.). (gr. 5 up). 2001. 19.00 (978-0-7887-5039-7(9), 96469E7) Recorded Bks.
Some kids want to be President when they grow up. Twelve-year-old Judson Moon wants to be President right now! "Grown-ups have a thousand years to mess up the world," Judson explains, "Now it's our turn".

Kid You Sing My Songs. unabr. ed. Lois Wyse. Read by Lois Wyse. 2 cass. (Running Time: 2 hrs. 5 min.). 1994. 15.95 Set. (978-0-9627187-7-9(7), 20060) Pub Mills.
This is a little book about being in tune with love, about having it & holding it & how we live when one partner leaves, & there's nobody there to sing your songs.

Kiddies Favorites. 1 cass. (Running Time: 90 mins.). (Baby's First Ser.). (J). (ps-k). 2000. audio compact disk 8.95 (978-1-56015-741-0(0)) Penton Overseas.
Includes "Baa Baa Blacksheep," "Itsy Bitsy Spider," "Little Boy Blue" & "Three Blind Mice.".

Kiddies Favourties. Jennifer Young. 1 CD. (Running Time: 90 mins.). (Baby's First Ser.). (J). (ps-k). 2000. audio compact disk 12.95 (978-1-56015-740-3(2)) Penton Overseas.

Kiddieworks: Aerobic Activities for Kids. unabr. ed. Judith Scott. Read by Judith Scott. (J). 1985. 9.95 (978-0-89845-408-6(5), CPN 1743) HarperCollins Pubs.
Judith Scott leads games & describes new ways for kids to twist & turn & jump. Gets kids moving & teaches them about fitness in an active way.

Kiddin' Around. 1 cass. (J). (ps-4). 1988. 9.98 Norelco. (978-1-877737-15-2(1), MLP #247) MFLP CA.

Kidding Around. 1998. 14.99 (978-1-60689-166-7(9)) Pub: Youngheart Mus. Dist(s): Creat Teach Pr

Kidding Around with Greg & Steve. Music by Greg Scelsa & Steve Millang. 1 cass. (J). stu. ed. 10.95 (YM7C) Kimbo Educ.
Musical magic makes children feel good about learning, living, working & playing. Say Hello, Copy Cat, Safety Break, The Body Rock, Believe in Yourself, Rhyme Time, Hokey Pokey, The Hugging Song & more. includes lyric guide.

Kidding Around with Greg & Steve. Music by Greg Scelsa & Steve Millang. 1 cass . (Running Time: 1 hr.). (J). 2001. pap. bk. 10.95 (YM7C); pap. bk. 14.95 (YM7CD) Kimbo Educ.

Kidding Around with Greg & Steve. Music by Greg Scelsa & Steve Millang. 1 cass. (J). (ps-3). 1985. 10.98 (978-0-945267-01-0(0), YM 007-CN); audio compact disk 13.98 (YM-007-CD) Youngheart Mus.
Singing & movement activities.

Kiddush Ha-Shem: An Epic of 1648. Sholem Asch. Narrated by George Guidall. 5 CDs. (Running Time: 6 hrs). 2002. audio compact disk 44.95 (978-1-893079-16-8(3), JCCAUDIOBOOKS) Jewish Contempry Classics.
The gripping tale of one Jewish family's fate during the terrible Cossack pogroms in 1648.

Kiddush Ha-Shem: An Epic of 1648. unabr. ed. Sholem Asch. Read by George Guidall. 3 cass. (Running Time: 4 hrs.). 2001. pap. bk. 29.95 Jewish Contempry Classics.

Kiddush Ha-Shem: An Epic of 1648. unabr. ed. Sholem Asch. 4 cass. (Running Time: 6 hrs.). 2001. 34.95 (978-1-893079-09-0(0), JCCAUDIOBOOKS) Jewish Contempry Classics.
Translated into English from the original Yiddish, Kiddush HaShem (literally meaning, Santification of the Name) is a gripping tale of one Jewish family's fate during the infamous Cossack pogroms in the Ukraine in 1648. AudioFile Earphones Award Winner.

Kidfiddle. Jerry Silverman. 1990. pap. bk. 15.95 (978-0-7866-1023-5(9), 94386P); 9.98 (978-0-87166-979-7(X), 94386C) Mel Bay.

Kidnap! John Escott. (Dominoes Ser.). 2006. 14.25 (978-0-19-424415-2(6)) OUP.

Kidnap at the Catfish Cafe. Patricia Reilly Giff. Illus. by Lynne Avril Cravath. 1999. 9.95 (978-0-87499-611-1(2)); 9.95 (978-0-87499-612-8(0)) Live Oak Media.

Kidnap at the Catfish Cafe. Patricia Reilly Giff. Read by Dana Lubotsky. Illus. by Lynne Avril Cravath. (Running Time: 5640 sec.). (Live Oak Mysteries Ser.). (J). (gr. 4-7). 2006. audio compact disk 22.95 (978-1-59519-842-6(3)) Live Oak Media.

Kidnap at the Catfish Cafe. Patricia Reilly Giff. Read by Dana Lubotsky. Illus. by Lynne Avril Cravath. (Live Oak Mysteries Ser.). (J). 2006. pap. bk. 27.95 (978-1-59519-843-3(1)) Live Oak Media.

Kidnap at the Catfish Cafe. unabr. ed. Patricia Reilly Giff. Read by Dana Lubotsky. 2 cass. (Running Time: 1 hr. 34 mins.). (Adventures of Minnie & Max Ser.). (J). (gr. 4-7). 1999. 16.95 (978-0-87499-556-5(6), OAK002) Pub: Live Oak Media. Dist(s): AudioGO
Dana Lubotsky portrays Minnie & other characters with style. Minnie has decided to open a detective agency. Her brother/guardian Orlando is not so sure she has the necessary skills, but she has two friends who are willing to help her solve her first mystery.

Kidnap at the Catfish Cafe. unabr. ed. Patricia Reilly Giff. Read by Dana Lubotsky. Illus. by Lynne W. Cravath. 2 vols. (Running Time: 1 hr. 34 mins.). (Adventures of Minnie & Max Ser.). (J). (gr. 4-7). 1999. bk. 30.95 (978-0-87499-554-1(X)); pap. bk. 23.95 (978-0-87499-553-4(1)) Live Oak Media.
This unabridged recording, is pure delight, the humor & subject matter are a perfect fit. Dana Lubotsky portrays Minnie & other characters with style. Minnie has decided to open a detective agency. Her brother/guardian Orlando is not so sure she has the necessary skills, but she has two friends who are willing to help her solve her first mystery.

Kidnap at the Catfish Cafe. unabr. ed. Patricia Reilly Giff. Read by Dana Lubotsky. Illus. by Lynne W. Cravath. (Adventures of Minnie & Max Ser.). (J). (gr. 4-7). 2000. pap. bk. & tchr. ed. 32.95 Reading Chest. (978-0-87499-555-8(8)) Live Oak Media.

Kidnapped. 2 cass. (Running Time: 2 hrs.). (Adventure Theatre Ser.). (YA). (gr. 5-8). 2002. 16.95 (978-1-56994-536-0(5)) Monterey Media Inc.
Hoodwinked by a villainous Uncle and swept into slavery aboard a ship bound for the Americas, a young man embarks on a great adventures.

Kidnapped. Robert Louis Stevenson. Read by Jim Weiss. 2002. 40.00 (978-0-7366-8810-9(2)); audio compact disk 48.00 (978-0-7366-9120-8(0)) Books on Tape.

Kidnapped. Robert Louis Stevenson. Ed. by Jerry Stemach et al. Retold by Alan Venable. Contrib. by Ted S. Hasselbring. (Start-to-Finish Books). (J). (gr. 2-3). 2002. (978-1-58702-806-9(9)) D Johnston Inc.

Kidnapped. Robert Louis Stevenson. Ed. by Jerry Stemach et al. Retold by Alan Venable. Contrib. by Ted S. Hasselbring. (Start-to-Finish Books). (J). (gr. 2-3). 2002. 100.00 (978-1-58702-945-5(6)) D Johnston Inc.

Kidnapped. Robert Louis Stevenson. Narrated by Frederick Davidson. (Running Time: 7 hrs. 30 mins.). 1989. 27.95 (978-1-59912-522-0(6)) Iofy Corp.

Kidnapped. Robert Louis Stevenson. Read by John Sessions. (Running Time: 2 hrs. 30 mins.). 2001. 20.95 (978-1-60083-797-5(2)) Iofy Corp.

Kidnapped. Robert Louis Stevenson. Read by John Chatty. 7 cass. (Running Time: 8 hrs.). 1989. 42.00 incl. album. (C-14) Jimcin Record.
Adventure on the high seas.

Kidnapped. Robert Louis Stevenson. (J). 1985. 4.95 (978-0-87188-166-3(7)) McGraw.

Kidnapped. Robert Louis Stevenson. Read by John Sessions. 2 cass. (Running Time: 2 hrs. 38 mins.). (YA). 1997. 13.98 (978-962-634-617-4(5), NA211714, Naxos AudioBooks) Naxos.

Kidnapped. Robert Louis Stevenson. Narrated by Ralph Cosham. (Running Time: 23940 sec.). (Unabridged Classics in MP3 Ser.). (ENG.). 2008. audio compact disk 14.95 (978-1-58472-523-7(0), In Aud) Sound Room.

Kidnapped. Robert Louis Stevenson. Read by Ralph Cosham. (Running Time: 23940 sec.). (Unabridged Classics in MP3 Ser.). (ENG.). 2008. audio compact disk 24.00 (978-1-58472-524-4(9), In Aud) Sound Room.

Kidnapped. Robert Louis Stevenson. Narrated by Flo Gibson. (ENG.). 2008. audio compact disk 29.95 (978-1-55685-999-1(6)) Audio Bk Con.

Kidnapped. Robert Louis Stevenson. Read by Alfred von Lecteur. 2009. 27.95 (978-1-60112-993-2(9)) Babblebooks.

Kidnapped. Retold by Alan Venable. Robert Louis Stevenson. (Classic Adventures Ser.). 2002. audio compact disk 18.95 (978-1-4105-0188-2(4)) D Johnston Inc.

Kidnapped. abr. ed. St. Charles Players & Robert Louis Stevenson. 1 cass. (Running Time: 1 hr. 30 min.). Dramatization. 2002. 16.95 (Monterey SoundWorks) Monterey Media Inc.

Kidnapped. abr. ed. Robert Louis Stevenson. Read by John Sessions. 2 CDs. (Running Time: 2 hrs. 38 mins.). (J). (gr. 6-8). 1997. audio compact disk 17.98 (978-962-634-117-9(3), NA211712) Naxos.

Kidnapped. abr. ed. Robert Louis Stevenson. 1 cass. (Running Time: 43 min.). (J). 10.95 (978-0-8045-1058-5(X), SAC1058) Spoken Arts.

Kidnapped. abr. adpt. ed. Robert Louis Stevenson. (Bring the Classics to Life: Level 3 Ser.). (ENG.). 2008. audio compact disk 12.95 (978-1-55576-448-7(7)) EDCON Pubng.

Kidnapped. unabr. ed. Robert Louis Stevenson. Narrated by Flo Gibson. 6 cass. (Running Time: 7 hrs. 37 min.). (gr. 6 up). 2002. 24.95 (978-1-55685-675-4(X),) Audio Bk Con.
A fiendish uncle plots the shanghai-ing of his Scotch nephew, David Balfour. A Highland Jacobite, Alan Breck, comes to his rescue, and their wild flight from the King's forces is part of this classic adventure.

Kidnapped. unabr. ed. Robert Louis Stevenson. Read by Frederick Davidson. 5 cass. (Running Time: 7 hrs.). (J). (gr. 6-12). 1989. 39.95 (978-0-7861-0064-4(8), 1061) Blckstn Audio.
In this spirited & romantic saga, a young heir named David Balfour meets his miserly uncle Ebenezer who has illegally taken control of the Balfour estate.

Kidnapped. unabr. ed. Robert Louis Stevenson. Read by Michael Page. 7 CDs. (Running Time: 8 hrs.). (Classic Collection). 2001. audio compact disk 37.95 (978-1-58788-608-9(1), 1587886081, CD Unabridged); audio compact disk 96.25 (978-1-58788-609-6(X), 158788609X, CD Unabrid Lib Ed) Brilliance Audio.
Set in the aftermath of the Jacobite Rebellion of 1745, Kidnapped (1886) sustains a gripping narrative. It is told by David Balfour, a young Whig and Lowlander, who is tracked by his miserly uncle, survives attempted murder, kidnap and shipwreck and, in the company of Alan Breck, a Jacobite, escapes through the Highlands. Kidnapped is an adventure story in which the tensions run deep, not only between pursuer and pursued, but in ancient misunderstandings between the two heroes themselves: Whig and Jacobite, Lowland rationalist and romantic Highlander.

Kidnapped. unabr. ed. Robert Louis Stevenson. Read by Michael Page. (Running Time: 8 hrs.). 2005. 39.25 (978-1-59737-036-3(3), 9781597370363, BADLE); 24.95 (978-1-59737-035-6(5), 9781597370356, BAD); audio compact disk 39.25 (978-1-59737-034-9(7), 9781597370349, Brlnc Audio MP3 Lib); audio compact disk 24.95 (978-1-59737-033-2(9), 9781597370332, Brilliance MP3) Brilliance Audio.

Kidnapped. unabr. ed. Robert Louis Stevenson. Ed. by Jerry Stemach et al. Retold by Alan Venable. Contrib. by Ted S. Hasselbring. 1 cass. (Running Time: 1 hr.). (Start-to-Finish Books). (J). (gr. 2-3). 2002. (978-1-58702-791-8(7)) D Johnston Inc.
The story of kidnapped takes place in 1751, six years after a fierce Scottish rebellion against King George. When modest 17-year-old David Balfour discovers that he may be the rightful heir to a rich estate, his greedy lowland Scottish uncle has him kidnapped to be sent to America as a slave. Accidentally joining forces with Alan Breck, a fiercely unrepentant Scottish rebel and soldier of fortune, David escapes his fate as a slave, but finds himself instead fleeing desperately across the Scottish highlands as a fugitive from unjust charges.

Kidnapped. unabr. ed. Robert Louis Stevenson. Read by Ralph Cosham. (YA). 2007. 59.99 (978-1-59895-859-1(3)) Find a World.

Kidnapped. unabr. ed. Robert Louis Stevenson. Narrated by Carlos Cardona. 5 cass. (Running Time: 6 hrs. 30 mins.). 1999. 44.00 (978-1-55690-281-9(6), 79030E7) Recorded Bks.
Kidnapped Scottish boy & friend - one of Bonnie Prince Charlie's supporters - have adventures & escapes against a background of Scottish landscape & history.

Kidnapped. unabr. ed. Robert Louis Stevenson. Read by Ralph Cosham. 5 cds. (Running Time: 6 hrs 38 mins). (YA). 2002. audio compact disk 29.95 (978-1-58472-273-1(8), 075, In Aud) Pub: Sound Room. Dist(s): Baker Taylor
Young David Balfour is the rightful heir, but his uncle has other plans. The story recounts Master Balfour's escape on the high seas and his adventures making his way back across the Scottish Highlands.

Kidnapped. unabr. ed. Robert Louis Stevenson. 5 cass. 1996. 49.95 (978-1-86015-437-9(9)) Pub: UlverLrgPrint GBR. Dist(s): Ulverscroft US
An account of David Balfour's trials & tribulations as he falls afoul of his miserly uncle who has him abducted while on board ship in order to steal his inheritance. After rescuing Alan Breck on the high seas, they are shipwrecked, witness a murder & are themselves suspected, effect a hazardous escape & exact revenge on the wicked Ebenezer thereby regaining David's rightful legacy.

***Kidnapped.** unabr. ed. Robert Louis Stevenson. Narrated by Steven Crossley. (Running Time: 8 hrs. 30 mins.). 2010. 15.99 (978-1-4001-8583-2(1)) Tantor Media.

***Kidnapped.** unabr. ed. Robert Louis Stevenson. Narrated by Steven Crossley. (Running Time: 8 hrs. 30 mins. 0 sec.). (ENG.). 2010. 22.99 (978-1-4001-6583-4(0)); audio compact disk 65.99 (978-1-4001-4583-6(X)); audio compact disk 32.99 (978-1-4001-1583-9(3)) Pub: Tantor Media. Dist(s): IngramPubServ

Kidnapped. unabr. collector's ed. Robert Louis Stevenson. Read by Angela Cheyne. 7 cass. (Running Time: 7 hrs.). (YA). 1977. 42.00 (978-0-7366-0059-0(0), 1071) Books on Tape.
A young man is cheated of his inheritance, then shanghaied to the Carolinas.

***Kidnapped: Bring the Classics to Life.** adpt. ed. Robert Louis Stevenson. (Bring the Classics to Life Ser.). 2008. pap. bk. 21.95 (978-1-55576-503-3(3)) EDCON Pubng.

Kidnapped & Treasure Island. unabr. ed. Robert Louis Stevenson. Read by Ralph Cosham. 1 cd. (Running Time: 12 hrs 31 mins). (YA). 2002. audio compact disk 18.95 (978-1-58472-389-9(0), In Aud) Pub: Sound Room. Dist(s): Baker Taylor
MP3 format.

Kidnapping of Aaron Greene. unabr. ed. Terry Kay. Narrated by George Guidall. 9 cass. (Running Time: 13 hrs.). 1999. 81.00 (978-0-7887-4368-9(6), 95895E7) Recorded Bks.
Shy mail clerk Aaron Greene is kidnapped & his abductors demand 10 million dollars. But the money must come from the bank where Aaron works. This gripping thriller probes deep into Americans moral fabric, asking: What is the value of a human life?.

Kidnapping of Christina Lattimore. unabr. ed. Joan Lowery Nixon. Narrated by Julie Dretzin. 6 pieces. (Running Time: 6 hrs. 45 mins.). (gr. 9 up). 1979. 54.00 (978-0-7887-5026-7(7), 96361) Recorded Bks.
Christina Lattimore's family is wealthy and powerful. She attends the best private high school. Yet Christina feels trapped by her family's expectations. Frustrated and angry at her situation, she pays little attention when a strange car follows her home one night. Its headlights are the last thing she remembers until she wakes up in captivity. Christina is terrified when she realizes kidnappers are holding her for ransom. But after her rescue, she faces an even greater shock. Her family thinks she was an accomplice in her own kidnapping!.

***Kidnapping of Roseta Uvaldo.** Zane Grey. 2009. (978-1-60136-547-7(0)) Audio Holding.

Kids & Cash. unabr. collector's ed. Ken Davis & Tom Taylor. Read by John MacDonald. 7 cass. (Running Time: 10 hrs. 30 min.). 1984. 56.00 (978-0-7366-0681-3(5), 1641) Books on Tape.
A book that helps parents relate to their kids on the controversial & often delicate subject of money!.

***Kids Are Americans Too.** unabr. ed. Bill O'Reilly. Read by Rick Adamson. (ENG.). 2007. (978-0-06-155470-4(7)); (978-0-06-155471-1(5)) HarperCollins Pubs.

Kids Are Americans Too. unabr. ed. Bill O'Reilly. Read by Rick Adamson. (Running Time: 9000 sec.). (gr. 4-7). 2007. audio compact disk 24.95 (978-0-06-136349-8(9), Harper Audio) HarperCollins Pubs.

Kids Are Americans Too. unabr. ed. Bill O'Reilly. Read by Rick Adamson. 2008. audio compact disk 14.95 (978-0-06-171863-2(7), Harper Audio) HarperCollins Pubs.

Kids Around the World Audio Cassette. Prod. by Caleb Project. (ENG.). (J). 2000. 6.25 (978-1-932329-98-8(6), CalebProj) Caleb Res.

Kid's Box. Caroline Nixon & Michael Tomlinson. 3 CDs. (ENG.). 2008. audio compact disk 42.00 (978-0-521-68805-5(1)); audio compact disk 42.00 (978-0-521-68811-6(6)) Cambridge U Pr.

Kid's Box: Teacher's Book 4. Caroline Nixon et al. (ENG., 2009. audio compact disk 40.00 (978-0-521-68822-2(1)) Cambridge U Pr.

Kid's Box 3 Audio CDs (3) Caroline Nixon & Michael Tomlinson. (ENG., 2008. audio compact disk 58.80 (978-0-521-68817-8(5)) Cambridge U Pr.

Kid's Box 5 Audio CDs (3) Caroline Nixon & Michael Tomlinson. (Running Time: 3 hrs. 6 mins.). (ENG.). 2009. audio compact disk 42.00 (978-0-521-68827-7(2)) Cambridge U Pr.

Kid's Box 6 Audio CDs (3) Caroline Nixon & Michael Tomlinson. (Running Time: 3 hrs. 39 mins.). (ENG.). 2009. audio compact disk 41.00 (978-0-521-68832-1(9)) Cambridge U Pr.

Kids Can Clean Too! (J). 2005. audio compact disk (978-1-933796-08-6(1)) PC Treasures.

Kids Can Have Jobs: Early Explorers Emergent Set A Audio CD. Benchmark Education Staff. (J). 2006. audio compact disk 10.00 (978-1-4108-7599-0(7)) Benchmark Educ.

Kids' Classic Stories: Cinderella; Sleeping Beauty; Beauty & the Beast; Rapunzel; Goldilocks & the Three Bears; Little Red Riding Hood; the Frog Price; the Princess & the Pea. unabr. ed. Twin Sisters Productions. Read by Twin Sisters. (J). 2008. 44.99 (978-1-60514-648-5(X)) Find a World.

Kids' Classic Stories: Jack & the Beanstalk; Hansel & Gretel; Three Little Pigs; the Town & Country Mouse; the Hare & the Tortoise; the Little Gingerbread Man; Rumplestiltskin; the Ugly Duckling. unabr. ed. Twin Sisters Productions. Read by Twin Sisters. (J). 2008. 44.99 (978-1-60514-589-1(0)) Find a World.

Kids Collection of Greatest Classics, Vol. 3. 1 CD. (Running Time: 48 mins.). 2002. audio compact disk 14.98 (978-1-893851-05-4(2)) Kids Coll.

Kids Coping with War: Confidence & Relaxation for Children. Michael S. Prokop. 1 cass. (Running Time: 43 min.). (J). (gr. k-7). 9.95 (978-0-933879-39-3(3)) Alegra Hse Pubs.
This tape is designed to complement the text as it helps improve children's self-concepts as they learn about stress, war, & themselves. Warmly teaches stress reduction & relaxation techniques that can be practiced daily. A helpful guide for children ages 5-12.

Kids' Favorite Songs. 1 cass. (J). 1997. 9.98 (Sony Wonder); audio compact disk 13.98 CD. (Sony Wonder) Sony Music Ent.
Includes classic tunes from everyone's childhood that have a special Sesame Street twist to them. Elmo, Snuffleupagus, Big Bird, Elmo, the Count, Oscar the Grouch, The Oinker Sisters & the kids sing songs such as: Row, Row, Row Your Boat, Old MacDonald, This Little Pig Went to Market, Home on the Range & more.

Kid's Favorites: 6 Cassette Dramatized Audio Stories. 2006. 22.50 (978-1-60079-020-1(8)) YourStory.

Kid's Favorites: 6 CD Dramatized Audio Stories. 2006. 22.50 (978-1-60079-044-7(5)) YourStory.

Kids Favorites: 6 Great Character-Building Stories. 3 CDs. (Running Time: 3 hrs.). (Your Story Hour Ser.). 2006. audio compact disk 24.99 (978-0-8127-0401-3(0)) Review & Herald.

Kids for the Earth. Sundance/Newbridge, LLC Staff. (Early Science Ser.). (gr. k-3). 2007. audio compact disk 12.00 (978-1-4007-6191-3(3)); audio compact disk 12.00 (978-1-4007-6190-6(5)); audio compact disk 12.00 (978-1-4007-6192-0(1)) Sund Newbridge.

Kids Go Crazy. Crazy Curt and the Fireballs. 1 CD. (Running Time: 31 min.). (J). (ps-1). 1995. audio compact disk 14.98 (978-1-893967-06-9(9), EKCD5008) Emphasis Ent.
Collection of songs that teach & entertain, in a context that is musically diverse - rock, blues, folk, country & a smattering of jazz.

Kids Go Crazy. Perf. by Crazy Curt and the Fireballs. 1 cass. (Running Time: 31 min.). (J). (ps-1). 1999. 9.98 (978-1-893967-07-6(7), EKC5008) Emphasis Ent.
Collection of songs that teach & entertain, in a context that is musically diverse - rock, blues, folk, country & a smattering of jazz.

Kids Hits: 10 Radio Hits for Kids. Prod. by Matt Huesmann. (J). (ps-3). 2006. audio compact disk 7.99 (978-5-558-21021-7(4)) Pt of Grace Ent.

Kids Hymnal: 80 Songs & Hymns. Contrib. by John DeVries. Created by Stephen Elkins. 2008. audio compact disk 14.95 (978-1-59856-259-0(2)) Hendrickson MA.

Kids in Action. Greg Scelsa. 1 CD. (Running Time: 1 hr.). (J). 2001. pap. bk. 14.95 (YM 017CD) Kimbo Educ.
Beanie Bag Dance, Goin' on a Bear Hunt, Can't Sit Still, Can You Leap Like a Frog?, Get Set, Let's Dance, New Beginning & more.

Kids in Action. Greg Scelsa. 1 cass. (Running Time: 1 hr.). (J). (ps-4). 2001. pap. bk. 10.95 (YM 017C) Kimbo Educ.

Kids in Destiny. 2002. audio compact disk 14.99 (978-1-59185-160-8(2)) CharismaLife Pub.

Kids in Grief. 1 cass. (Care Cassettes Ser.: Vol. 20, No. 3). 1993. 10.80 Assn Prof Chaplains.

Kids in J. O. Y. Land. (Power Tool Box Ser.: Vol. 3). (J). (gr. 1-6). 1998. ring bd. 164.99 (978-1-57405-045-5(1)) CharismaLife Pub.

Kids in Leadership Enhanced. 2002. audio compact disk 19.99 (978-1-59185-149-3(1)) CharismaLife Pub.

Kids in Motion. 1988. 9.95 Creat Teach Pr.

Kids in Motion. 1998. 14.99 (978-1-60689-169-8(3)) Pub: Youngheart Mus. Dist(s): Creat Teach Pr

Kids in Motion. Greg Scelsa. 1 cass. (Running Time: 1 hr.). (J). 2001. pap. bk. 10.95 (YM 8C); pap. bk. 14.95 (YM 8CD) Kimbo Educ.
Creative movement activities with Greg & Steve, The Temptations & others. Titles: Body Rock, Animal Action, The Freeze, Count Bounce, Shadow Dancing, Tummy Tango & more. Includes guide.

Kids in Motion. Music by Greg Scelsa. Intro. by Scott Baio. Music by Steve Millang. 1 CD. (J). (ps-3). 1987. audio compact disk 13.98 (YM-008-CD) Youngheart Mus.
Creative movement activities with music & printed lyrics & activity suggestions.

Kids in Motion. Music by Greg Scelsa & Steve Millang. Intro. by Scott Baio. 1 cass. (J). (ps-3). 1987. 10.98 (978-0-945267-02-7(9), YM-008-CN) Youngheart Mus.

Kids in Service Enhanced. 2002. audio compact disk 19.99 (978-1-59185-146-2(7)) CharismaLife Pub.

Kids in the Word Enhanced. 2002. audio compact disk 19.99 (978-1-59185-152-3(1)) CharismaLife Pub.

Kids Kalliope. 1 CD. (Running Time: 1 hr.). 2000. audio compact disk 15.00 (978-1-58302-156-9(6)) One Way St.
Contains 30 caliope tunes which offer great instrumental music for clowns, magicians, puppeteers, mimes, jugglers and other kinds of performances.

Kids' Kreations, Bk. 2. Anna L. Page et al. 1 cass. 1998. pap. bk. 49.95 (978-0-88284-929-4(8), 18038) Alfred Pub.

Kids Learn Spanish. unabr. ed. Twin Sisters Productions. Read by Twin Sisters. (J). 2007. 59.99 (978-1-60252-658-7(3)) Find a World.

Kids Love Counting. Acorn Staff. 9.95 (978-1-56938-029-1(5)) Acorn Inc.

Kids Love Lullabies. Acorn Staff. 9.95 (978-1-56938-030-7(9)) Acorn Inc.

Kids Love the Circus. Acorn Staff. 9.95 (978-1-56938-027-7(9)) Acorn Inc.

Kids Love Trains. 1 cass. (J). 7.98 (AMP 538) NewSound.
Includes: "Kids Love Trains," "John Henry," "Where Do You Work" & more.

Kids Make Music. 1 cass. (Running Time: 30 min.). (J). (ps-5). 1994. 7.95 (978-1-880947-09-8(9)) Bogner Ent.
(A) side has the songs from the video, (B) side has the instrumentals from the video.

Kids Make Music, Babies Make Music, Too! 1 cass. (Music Rhapsody Ser.). (ps). 1999. audio compact disk 14.95 (978-0-9653636-5-5(1), 6001) Music Rhapsody.
Contains the music of all three videos - "Babies Make Music," "Kids Make Music ." & "Kids Make Music Too!" Songs & rhymes for movement, dance, singing & small percussion instruments.

Kids Make Music, Babies Make Music Too! Lynn Kleiner. 1 cass. 1998. audio compact disk 14.95 CD. Music Rhapsody.

Kids-n-Gangs Don't Mix: A Parent's Survival Guide for Raising Kids Today. unabr. ed. Joseph Davis et al. Read by Joseph Davis et al. 4 cass. (Running Time: 3 hrs. 20 min.). 1997. pap. bk. 29.95 Set. (978-1-889315-02-7(8)) Dvis & Assocs.
Guide to identifying gang behaviors & activities. How to intervene. How to prevent school violence.

Kid's New Testament-CEV. Created by Casscom Media. (J). (ps-k). 2003. 21.99 (978-1-930034-14-3(8)); audio compact disk 24.99 (978-1-930034-15-0(6)) Casscomm.

Kid's New Testament-CEV. Created by Casscom Media. (J). (ps). 2004. audio compact disk 39.99 (978-1-930034-66-2(0)) Casscomm.

Kids New Testament-Dramatized. 12 cass. (J). 2004. 21.99 (978-0-88368-825-0(5)) Whitaker Hse.

Kids NT-Dramatized: Red Disc Case. 15 CDs. (J). 2004. audio compact disk 39.95 (978-0-88368-823-6(9)) Whitaker Hse.

Kids of the Polk Street School. unabr. ed. Patricia Reilly Giff. 12 read-along cass. (Follow the Reader Ser.). (J). (gr. 1-2). 1987. 175.98 (978-0-8072-0156-5(1), FTR 975, Listening Lib) Random Audio Pubg.
Join the kids in Ms. Rooney's second grade class as they learn & grow through an entire school year filled with fun & surprises.

Kids of the Twenty-First Century Sing New Holiday Songs. (J). (gr. k-6). 10.00; 12.00 Teaching & Activity Guide. Kids Twnty-Frst Cent.

Kids on the Mountain: Old Time Appalachian Music for Kids & Adults. Arranged by Tom Draughon. 1 CD. (Running Time: 41 mins). (J). 2001. audio compact disk 16.00 (978-0-9768082-0-6(X)) Heartistry Music.
Kids on the Mountain is Appalachian Old Time music packaged for kids and adults as well. Emma and Micah are kids growing up on a mountain in the Great Smokies in the 1800s. The talk about facets of their lives and this sets the stage for the next song or fiddle tune. Kids on the Mountain is a wonderful introduction to the history and music of pioneer families in the Appalachian Mountains.

Kids on the Move! (16 Get up & Go Songs for Young Singers) Composed by Sally K. Albrecht & Jay Althouse. (ENG.). 2006. audio compact disk 34.95 (978-0-7390-3870-3(2)) Alfred Pub.

Kids on the Rock, 1. 1999th ed. 1 cass. (J). 1999. 9.99 SPLIT-TRACK, REP.. Gospel Lght.
Twelve fresh & clever songs about God & the Bible that speak to today's children & helps them t build their lives on the solid rock of Gods Word.

Kids on the Rock, I. 1999th ed. 1 CD. (J). 1999. audio compact disk SPLIT-TRACK, REP. Gospel Lght.

Kids on the Rock, II. 1999th ed. 1 cass. (J). 1999. 9.99; audio compact disk Split-track, Rep. Gospel Lght.
Twelve songs.

Kids on the Rock: More Songs. 1999th ed. 1 CD. (J). 1999. audio compact disk Gospel Lght.
Thirty-three songs.

***Kids, Parents, & Power Struggles.** abr. ed. Mary Sheedy Kurcinka. Read by Mary Sheedy Kurcinka. (ENG.). 2005. (978-0-06-088898-5(5), Harper Audio); (978-0-06-088897-8(0), Harper Audio) HarperCollins Pubs.

Kids' Party Songs! Prod. by Twin Sisters Productions Staff. 1 CD. (Running Time: 30 mins). (J). 2005. audio compact disk 4.99 (978-1-57583-800-7(1)) Twin Sisters.
Play and sing along with musical games and party songs! Over 30 minutes of music and games add up tons of fun to kids' parties. Perfect for birthday parties, sleepovers, classroom celebrations, afternoon fun, and family gatherings. BONUS! Includes 50 fun things to do with kids!.

***Kid's Piano Course 2: The Easiest Piano Method Ever!** Christine H. Barden et al. (ENG., 2010. pap. bk. 16.99 (978-0-7390-6247-0(6)) Alfred Pub.

Kids Play Piano by Ear: Piano "By Ear" unabr. ed. David W. Lawrence. Perf. by Martha Peebles. 2 cass. (Running Time: 1 hr. 15 min.). (Rapid Music Development Ser.: Vol. 201). (J). (gr. 2-10). 1994. 59.95 Set. (978-1-890122-05-8(X)) Kingdom Ent.
Teaching children & adults how to understand the piano, create chords, & play songs with rhythm.

Kids Radio Hits: The Best of Christian Music... for Kids! Created by Ed Kee & Brian Green. (Running Time: 2700 sec.). (ENG.). (J). 2008. audio compact disk 16.99 (978-5-557-45085-0(8), Brentwood-Benson Music) Brentwood Music.

Kids Rhyme for Story Time. unabr. ed. Alfreda C. Doyle. Read by Alfreda C. Doyle. 1 cass. (Running Time: 30 min.). (YA). (gr. 7-12). 1994. 14.95 (978-1-56820-113-9(3)) Story Time.
A collection of stories for kids of all ages that educate as well as entertain.

Kids Sing Christmas. 1 cass. (J). (978-0-7601-0777-5(7), V25068) Brentwood Music.
Over 30 of the most-loved Christmas melodies for children, featuring: Angels We Have Heard on High, Silent Night, Go Tell it on the Mountain, & more.

***Kids Sing Christmas: Joyful Christmas Music for Children.** Compiled by Barbour Publishing, Inc. 2010. audio compact disk 9.99 (978-1-61626-060-6(2), Barbour Bks) Barbour Pub.

Kids Sing Praise, Vol. 2. 1 cass. (J). (978-1-55897-862-1(3), V5071R); (BK3030R) Brentwood Music.
Features: Zacchaeus Was a Wee Little Man, Climb, Climb up Sunshine Mountain, Standin' in the Need of Prayer, He is Lord & over 20 more.

Kids Sing Praise, Vol. 3. 1 cass. (J). (978-1-55897-221-6(8), V5066R) Brentwood Music.
Features: I am a "C", Fill in the Blanks, How Did Moses Cross the Red Sea?, Abundawonderful Life & over 20 more.

Kid's Songs with a Holler-Along Handbook. unabr. ed. Nancy Cassidy & John Cassidy. 1 cass. (J). 14.95 incl. hdbk. (S23940) J Norton Pubs.

Kids Spooky Songs & Stories. (J). 1995. 5.50 (978-1-57375-081-3(6)) Audioscope.

Kids Spooky Sounds & Stories. 1 cass. (J). 1995. 8.00 (978-1-57375-082-0(4)) Audioscope.

Kids' Stories & Songs. Karen Mitzo Hilderbrand & Kim Mitzo Thompson. (J). 2007. 44.99 (978-1-60252-762-1(8)) Find a World.

Kids Stuff. Mary Miche. 1 cass. (J). (gr. 2-7). 1986. 11.50 (978-1-883505-01-1(1)) Song Trek Music.
Selection of 14 educational songs on a variety of topics for children.

Kids Talk: Discussion Starter. 1 cass. (Running Time: 1 hr.). (J). (gr. 5-6). 6.99 Gospel Lght.
Real talk with real kids on vital topics.

Kids World. 1998. 9.95 (978-0-9656156-1-7(8)) Dream Flight Prods.
Original songs which build character and raise self-esteem.

Kids World. (J). 1998. 14.95 (978-0-9656156-6-2(9)); audio compact disk 12.95 (978-0-9656156-9-3(3)) Dream Flight Prods.
Original kid's songs that build character and raise self esteem.

KidSing! Campfire Songs! 30 All-Time Best Camp Songs. Thomas Nelson. (J). 2010. audio compact disk 10.99 (978-1-4003-1585-7(9)) Nelson.

Kidsing! Christmas: 17 Carols & Hymns. Contrib. by Don Lynch. Prod. by Mark Stitts et al. (J). (ps-5). 2007. audio compact disk 5.99 (978-1-4003-1088-3(1)) Nelson.

KidSing! Everlasting God! Thomas Nelson. (J). 2010. audio compact disk 10.99 (978-1-4003-1557-4(3)) Nelson.

KidSing! God of Wonders! Thomas Nelson. (J). 2010. audio compact disk 10.99 (978-1-4003-1556-7(5)) Nelson.

KidSing! How Great Is Our God! Thomas Nelson. (J). 2010. audio compact disk 10.99 (978-1-4003-1555-0(7)) Nelson.

Kidsing! Volume 1: 60 Hymns, Choruses & Silly Songs. Contrib. by Dan Lynch. Prod. by Mike Stitts et al. (J). (ps-5). 2007. audio compact disk 9.99 (978-1-4003-1086-9(5)) Nelson.

Kidsing! Volume 2: 60 More Hymns, Choruses, & Silly Songs. Contrib. by Dan Lynch et al. Prod. by Mark Stitts & Mike Stitts. Contrib. by Kim Sipus. (J). (ps-5). 2007. audio compact disk 9.99 (978-1-4003-1087-6(3)) Nelson.

Kidsongs. 1990. 9.98 (978-0-87166-977-3(3), 94382C) Mel Bay.

Kidsongs. Jerry Silverman. 1990. bk. 16.95 (978-0-7866-1021-1(2), 94382P) Mel Bay.

Kidsongs: Cars, Boats, Trains, Planes & Other Things That Go. Prod. by Bruce Gowers et al. 1 cass. (Running Time: 26 min.). (J). 1992. 7.98 (978-1-880528-07-5(X), 4-26987) Warner Bros.
Cassette with lyric book.

Kidsongs: Old MacDonald Had a Farm & Other Favorite Songs about Animals. Prod. by Bruce Gowers et al. 1 cass. (Running Time: 28 min.). (J). 1992. 7.98 (978-1-880528-05-1(3), 4-26985) Warner Bros.
Cassette with lyric book.

Kidsongs: Sing along Songs. Prod. by Bruce Gowers et al. 1 cass. (Running Time: 28 min.). (J). 1992. pap. bk. 7.98 (978-1-880528-06-8(1), 4-26986) Warner Bros.

Kidsongs: What I Want to Be When I Grow Up. Prod. by Bruce Gowers et al. 1 cass. (Running Time: 26 min.). (J). 1992. 7.98 (978-1-880528-08-2(8), 4-26988) Warner Bros.

***Kidtunes Songbook & Activity Guide Combo Pack.** Ed. by Elizabeth C. Axford. Compiled by Elizabeth C. Axford. (ENG.). (J). 2008. audio compact disk 24.95 (978-1-931844-16-1(X)) Pub: Piano Pr. Dist(s): BkWhole

Kidz Bop Christmas. Created by Razor & Tie. (J). (ps-3). 2006. audio compact disk 11.99 (978-5-558-16953-9(2)) Pt of Grace Ent.

Kidz Bop to Go 1. unabr. ed. Collection of 20 Hit Songs. Read by Sung By Kids For Kids. (J). 2006. 34.99 (978-1-59895-558-3(6)) Find a World.

Kidz Bop to Go 2. unabr. ed. Collection of 20 Hit Songs. Read by Sung By Kids For Kids. (J). 2006. 34.99 (978-1-59895-559-0(4)) Find a World.

Kidz Faith Songs. Speeches. Creflo A. Dollar. 1 CD. (Running Time: 1 hr. 20 mins.). 1999. audio compact disk 13.00 (978-1-59089-128-5(7)) Creflo Dollar.

Kidz Faith Songs. Speeches. Creflo A. Dollar. 1 cass. (Running Time: 1 hr. 20 mins.). (ENG.). 2002. audio compact disk 9.00 (978-1-59089-127-8(9)) Pub: Creflo Dollar. Dist(s): STL Dist NA

Kidz of the Neighborhood. Joseph Linn. 1 CD. (Running Time: 1 hr.). (J). (gr. 3-6). 1992. audio compact disk 80.00 (MU-9148T) Lillenas.
What better way than music to teach children about living in the world - God's neighborhood! As they sing & listen to the 18 arrangements they will begin to understand creation, cultural differences, relationships, the church & sharing your faith. Fun & faith go together with all the songs. The songs from this collection may be performed individually or add the 3 sketches to create short thematic presentations. Created for kids ages 8 to 11. Unison with optional 2-part, split channel.

Kidz of the Neighborhood: Songs to Change the World. Arranged by Joseph Linn. 1 cass. (Running Time: 1 hr.). (J). 1992. 12.99 (TA-9148C) Lillenas.

Kidz of the Neighborhood: Songs to Change the World - Arranged for Young Voices. Joseph Linn. 1 cass. (Running Time: 1 hr.). (J). (gr. 3-6). 1992. 80.00 (MU-9148C) Lillenas.

Kierkegaard in 90 Minutes. Paul Strathern. 1 Cass. (Running Time: 1 hr. 30 mins.). 2004. 14.95 (978-0-7861-2436-7(9), 3115) Blckstn Audio.

Kierkegaard in 90 Minutes. Paul Strathern. Narrated by Robert Whitfield. (Running Time: 1 hr. 30 mins.). 2003. 17.95 (978-1-59912-523-7(4)) Iofy Corp.

Kierkegaard in 90 Minutes. unabr. ed. Paul Strathern. Read by Robert Whitfield. 1 cass. (Running Time: 1 hr. 30 mins.). (Philosophers in 90 Minutes Ser.). 2000. reel tape 14.95 (978-0-7861-2532-6(2)) Blckstn Audio.

Kierkegaard in 90 Minutes. unabr. ed. Paul Strathern. Read by Robert Whitfield. 2 CDs. (Running Time: 1 hr. 30 mins.). (Philosophers in 90 Minutes Ser.). 2004. audio compact disk 14.95 (978-0-7861-9043-0(4)) Blckstn Audio.

Kierkegaard in 90 Minutes. unabr. ed. Paul Strathern. Read by Robert Whitfield. 2 CDs. (Running Time: 1 hr. 30 mins.). 2006. audio compact disk 16.00 (978-0-7861-9089-8(2), 3115) Blckstn Audio.

Kieth Erickson: TV Viewing Tips. Read by Kieth Erickson. 1 cass. 9.95 (978-0-89811-103-3(X), 7154) Lets Talk Assocs.
Kieth Erickson talks about the people & events which influenced his career, & his approach to his specialty.

Kikaider Anime Legends Collection. (YA). 2006. DVD 39.98 (978-1-59409-743-0(7)) Bandai Ent.

***Kill.** unabr. ed. L. J. Smith. Read by Khristine Hvam. (Running Time: 6 hrs.). (Forbidden Game Ser.: Bk. 3). 2010. audio compact disk 19.99 (978-1-4418-7543-3(3), 9781441875433, Bril Audio CD Unabri) Brilliance Audio.

***Kill: How to Close Every Sale-Every Time.** unabr. ed. Mark Stevens. (Running Time: 2 hrs.). (ENG.). 2009. 10.98 (978-1-59659-487-6(X), GildAudio) Pub: Gildan Media. Dist(s): HachBkGrp

Kill All the Lawyers, Set. 4 cass. 1998. 25.99 (978-1-894144-01-8(5)) JD Prodns CAN.

Kill All the Lawyers: A Solomon vs. Lord Novel. unabr. ed. Paul Levine. Read by William Dufris. (Running Time: 1 hr. 0 mins.). (ENG.). 2009. 29.95 (978-1-4332-2729-5(0)); 59.95 (978-1-4332-2725-7(8)); audio compact disk 76.00 (978-1-4332-2726-4(6)) Blckstn Audio.

Kill & Tell. abr. ed. Linda Howard. Read by Natalie Ross. (Running Time: 6 hrs.). 2010. audio compact disk 14.99 (978-1-4418-2541-4(X), 9781441825414, BACD) Brilliance Audio.

Kill & Tell. collector's ed. William X. Kienzle. Read by Edward Holland. 6 cass. (Running Time: 9 hrs.). (Father Koesler Mystery Ser.: No. 6). 2000. 48.00 (978-0-7366-4991-9(3)) Books on Tape.

Kill & Tell. unabr. ed. Linda Howard. Read by Natalie Ross. (Running Time: 9 hrs.). 2010. 39.97 (978-1-4233-6337-8(X), 9781423363378, Brinc Audio MP3 Lib); 24.99 (978-1-4233-6336-1(1), 9781423363361, Brilliance MP3); 24.99 (978-1-4233-6338-5(8), 9781423363385, BAD); 39.97 (978-1-4418-5028-7(7), 9781441850287, BADLE); audio compact disk 92.97 (978-1-4233-6335-4(3), 9781423363354, BriAudCD Unabrid); audio compact disk 29.99 (978-1-4233-6334-7(5), 9781423363347, Bril Audio CD Unabri) Brilliance Audio.

Kill Artist. Daniel Silva. 4 cass. (Running Time: 6 hrs.). (Gabriel Allon Ser.: No. 1). 2000. 25.95 (Random AudioBks) Random Audio Pubg.
Gabriel Allon was a key operative in secret Israeli intelligence missions. When his wife & daughter fell victim to the danger that accompanied him everywhere, Gabriel quit & devoted himself to the work of art restoration previously a cover for his secret missions but now Ari Shamron, the head of Israeli intelligence, needs Gabriel's particular kind of experience to thwart a Palestinian plot to destroy the peace negotiations in the Middle East. The architect of this plot, a Palestinian zealot named Tariqu, is a lethal part of Gabriel's past & so as the two begin an intercontinental game of hide & seek, with life & death as the prizes, the motives are as personal as they are political.

Kill Artist. Daniel Silva. Narrated by George Guidall. 11 CDs. (Running Time: 11 hrs. 45 mins.). (Gabriel Allon Ser.: No. 1). 2001. audio compact disk 111.00 (978-1-4025-0501-0(9), C1557) Recorded Bks.
After the assassination of his wife and son, Gabriel Allon retires from his brutal anti-terrorist career and loses himself in his previous cover job: art restoration. But when the Palestinian terrorist responsible for the death of Gabriel's family begins a killing spree designed to destroy Middle East peace talks, Gabriel once again slips into the shadowy world of international intrigue.

Kill Artist. abr. ed. Daniel Silva. 5 CDs. (Running Time: 360 min.). (Gabriel Allon Ser.: No. 1). 2001. audio compact disk 29.95 (978-0-375-41668-2(4), Random AudioBks) Random Audio Pubg.

Kill Artist. unabr. ed. Daniel Silva. Narrated by George Guidall. 8 cass. (Running Time: 11 hrs. 45 mins.). (Gabriel Allon Ser.: No. 1). 2001. 71.00 (978-0-7887-5983-3(3), 96357K8) Recorded Bks.
After the assassination of his wife & son, Gabriel Allon retires from his anti-terrorist career & loses himself in his previous cover job: art restoration. But when the Palestinian terrorist responsible for the death of Gabriel's family begins a killing spree designed to destroy Middle East peace talks, Gabriel once again slips into the shadowy world of international intrigue.

Kill Bill. abr. rev. ed. Quentin Tarantino. 4 cass. (Running Time: 6 hrs.). 2003. 25.98 (978-1-4013-9739-5(5)); audio compact disk 31.98 (978-1-4013-9743-2(3)) Pub: Hyperion. Dist(s): HarperCollins Pubs

Kill Bin Laden: A Delta Force Commander's Account of the Hunt for the World's Most Wanted Man. unabr. ed. Dalton Fury. Read by David Drummond. 11 CDs. (Running Time: 11 hrs. 30 mins. 0 sec.). (ENG.). 2008. audio compact disk 37.99 (978-1-4001-0969-2(8)); audio compact disk 24.99 (978-1-4001-5969-7(5)); audio compact disk 75.99 (978-1-4001-3969-9(4)) Pub: Tantor Media. Dist(s): IngramPubServ

Kill Chain. unabr. ed. Meg Gardiner. Read by Tanya Eby Sirois. (Running Time: 11 hrs.). (Evan Delaney Ser.). 2008. 39.25 (978-1-4233-6148-0(2), 9781423361480, Brinc Audio MP3 Lib); 39.25 (978-1-4233-6150-3(4), 9781423361503, BADLE); 24.95 (978-1-4233-6147-3(4), 9781423361473, Brilliance MP3); 24.95 (978-1-4233-6149-7(0), 9781423361497, BAD); audio compact disk 97.25 (978-1-4233-6146-6(6), 9781423361466, BriAudCD Unabrid); audio compact disk 32.99 (978-1-4233-6145-9(8), 9781423361459, Bril Audio CD Unabri) Brilliance Audio.

Kill Clause. abr. ed. Gregg Hurwitz. Read by Peter Friedman. 4 cass. (Running Time: 6 hrs.). 2003. 25.95 (978-0-06-055948-9(9), Harper Audio) HarperCollins Pubs.

***Kill Clause: A Novel.** abr. ed. Gregg Hurwitz. Read by Peter Friedman. (ENG.). 2004. (978-0-06-078640-3(X), Harper Audio) HarperCollins Pubs.

***Kill Clause: A Novel.** abr. ed. Gregg Hurwitz. Read by Peter Friedman. (ENG.). 2004. (978-0-06-081429-8(2), Harper Audio) HarperCollins Pubs.

Kill for Me. unabr. ed. Karen Rose. Read by Tavia Gilbert. (Running Time: 16 hrs. 0 mins.). 2009. 44.95 (978-1-4332-6073-5(5)); audio compact disk 29.95 (978-1-4332-6072-8(7)); audio compact disk 110.00

An Asterisk (*) at the beginning of an entry indicates that the title is appearing for the first time.

(978-1-4332-6070-4(0)); audio compact disk 89.95 (978-1-4332-6069-8(7)) Blckstn Audio.

Kill Hawk. unabr. ed. Will C. Knott. Read by Maynard Villers. 4 cass. (Running Time: 4 hrs. 6 min.). (Golden Hawk Ser.: Bk. 5). 1996. 26.95 (978-1-55686-686-9(0)) Books in Motion.
Hawk learns of a cache of hidden gold coins & sets out to find the treasure. But others learn of his secret & set out to kill Hawk & steal the gold.

Kill Me. Stephen White. Read by Dick Hill. (Dr. Alan Gregory Ser.). 2009. 75.00 (978-1-60775-536-4(X)) Find a World.

Kill Me. abr. ed. Stephen White. Read by Dick Hill. 5. (Running Time: 21600 sec.). (Dr. Alan Gregory Ser.). 2007. audio compact disk 14.99 (978-1-59737-668-6(X), 9781597376686, BCD Value Price) Brilliance Audio.

Kill Me. unabr. ed. Stephen White. Read by Dick Hill. (Running Time: 43200 sec.). (Dr. Alan Gregory Ser.). 2005. audio compact disk 24.95 (978-1-59335-740-5(0), 9781593357405, Brilliance MP3); audio compact disk 39.25 (978-1-59335-874-7(1), 9781593358747, Brinc Audio MP3 Lib); audio compact disk 36.95 (978-1-4233-0174-5(9), 9781423301745, Bril Audio CD Unabri) Brilliance Audio.
His plan was simple: pay someone to kill him if his life ever turned into a half-life - if he ever were to be kept alive by machines. He makes a deal with an organization called The Death Angels to end his life if he were ever in a situation where he would be a burden on his family. Except one day he gets a call that he has an incurable disease. If it passes a certain threshold The Death Angels will find him and kill him, because that's what he paid them to do. However, due to another life-changing event, he decides he doesn't want to die after all. He must tie up some loose ends. He must find a way out of this arrangement. He must escape The Death Angels before it's too late.

Kill Me. unabr. ed. Stephen White. Read by Dick Hill. (Running Time: 12 hrs.). (Dr. Alan Gregory Ser.). 2006. 39.25 (978-1-59710-941-3(X), 9781597109413, BADLE); 24.95 (978-1-59710-940-6(1), 9781597109406, BAD); 87.25 (978-1-59355-568-9(7), 9781593555689, BrilAudUnabridg); audio compact disk 102.25 (978-1-59355-571-9(7), 9781593555719, BACDLib Ed) Brilliance Audio.

Kill Me Again. unabr. ed. Paul Bishop. Read by Stephanie Brush. 8 cass. (Running Time: 10 hrs. 24 min.). (Fey Croaker Mystery Ser.: Bk. 1). 1996. 49.95 (978-1-55686-614-2(3)) Books in Motion.
Introducing Fey Croaker, homocide detective. She's a tough L.A. cop with savvy. This is the baffling case of a currently murdered person who was listed as murdered years ago.

***Kill Me If You Can.** unabr. ed. James Patterson & Marshall Karp. (Running Time: 8 hrs.). (ENG.). 2011. 26.98 (978-1-60941-188-6(9)); audio compact disk & audio compact disk 34.98 (978-1-60788-467-5(4)) Pub: Hachet Audio. Dist(s): HachBkGrp

Kill the Competition. unabr. ed. Stephanie Bond. 9 cass. (Running Time: 12 hrs. 45 min.). 2004. 79.75 (978-1-4025-7677-5(3)) Recorded Bks.

***Kill the Dead.** unabr. ed. Richard Kadrey. Read by MacLeod Andrews. (Running Time: 12 hrs.). (Sandman Slim Ser.). 2010. 24.99 (978-1-4418-0668-0(7), 9781441806680, BAD); 39.97 (978-1-4418-0669-7(5), 9781441806697, BADLE); 24.99 (978-1-4418-0666-6(0), 9781441806666, Brilliance MP3); 39.97 (978-1-4418-0667-3(9), 9781441806673, Brinc Audio MP3 Lib); audio compact disk 29.99 (978-1-4418-0664-2(4), 9781441806642, Bril Audio CD Unabri); audio compact disk 79.97 (978-1-4418-0665-9(2), 9781441806659, BriAudCD Unabrid) Brilliance Audio.

Kill the Messenger. abr. ed. Tami Hoag. Read by Erik Davies. 5 CDs. (Running Time: 18900 sec.). (ENG.). 2005. audio compact disk 14.99 (978-0-7393-2147-8(1), RH Aud Price) Pub: Random Audio Pubg. Dist(s): Random

Kill the Messenger. unabr. ed. Tami Hoag. 9 cass. (Running Time: 13 hrs. 30 min.). 2004. 90.00 (978-0-7366-9756-9(X)); audio compact disk 96.00 (978-0-7366-9758-3(6)) Books on Tape.
One grueling day in L.A., Jace Damon - a bike messenger working for a sleazy LA lawyer - is attacked when trying to deliver a package. The attacker pursues him attempting to take the package, but Jace escapes. When he returns to the office, he finds the lawyer dead, and the police suspecting him of the murder. In order for him to clear his name and save both his life and the life of his young brother, Jace takes off - on the run from both the law and the killer himself.

Kill the Shogun. collector's ed. Dale Furutani. Read by Jonathan Marosz. 5 cass. (Running Time: 7 hrs. 30 min.). 2000. 40.00 (978-0-7366-5645-0(6)) Books on Tape.
Matsuyama Kaze, the masterless seventeenth-century Japanese warrior, continues his search for his dead lord's kidnapped daughter.

Kill Zone. David Hagberg. Read by Bruce Watson. Abr. by Odin Westgaard. 4 vols. (Kirk McGarvey Ser.). 2004. (978-1-58807-683-0(0)) Am Pubng Inc.

Kill Zone. abr. ed. Jack Coughlin. Read by Scott Sowers. (Running Time: 6 hrs. 0 mins. 0 sec.). (ENG.). 2007. audio compact disk 29.95 (978-1-4272-0200-0(1)) Pub: Macmill Audio. Dist(s): Macmillan

Killed by a Woman: Judges 9:54. Ed Young. 1982. 4.95 (978-0-7417-1231-8(8), 231) Win Walk.

Killer Alone. unabr. ed. Vic J. Hanson. Read by John Chancer. 3 cass. (Running Time: 4 hrs. 30 min.). (Audio Books Ser.). 1992. 34.95 (978-1-85496-713-8(4)) Pub: UlverLrgPrint GBR. Dist(s): Ulverscroft US
Lawman turned bounty hunter, Lockhamer was a killer alone. This time the bounty did not matter, because the Hanray brothers were scum, & he was the man to exterminate them. The first brother was easy, but someone got to the second brother before Lockhamer could. Then the third brother, a deadly gunfighter, waited in a beleaguered town with Lockhamer's woman & her boy held captive.

Killer Angels. Michael Shaara. Narrated by George Guidall. 8 cas. (Running Time: 14 hrs.). 34.95 (978-1-4025-2365-6(3)) Recorded Bks.

Killer Angels. unabr. ed. Michael Shaara. Read by George Hearn. 9 cass. (Running Time: 13 hrs. 30 mins.). 1994. 62.95 (978-1-886175-00-6(4), C137) Blckstn Audio.
A Pulitzer-Prize-winner & one of the most moving novels about war to be published in our time, "The Killer Angels" re-enacts the four bloody & courageous days during which two armies fought for their conflicting dreams on the battlefield at Gettysburg. Michael Shaara reconstructs the thoughts & conversations of men who come to personify the complex historical, tactical, & personal motives that defined Gettysburg. "When the 20th Maine countercharges at Little Round Top, when Pickett's men breach the Union line at Cemetery Ridge, Shaara has a sentient observer there to register the terror & the bravery, the precarious balance of machine & man that made Gettysburg one of the last human battles. His achievement is combining these passages of apocalyptic immediacy with smaller scenes that dramatize the historian's cultural understandings.

Killer Angels. unabr. ed. Michael Shaara. Read by George Hearn & Ronald Maxwell. 9 cass. (Running Time: 12 hrs. 41 min.). 1994. 49.95 Set. (978-1-886175-01-3(2)) Cathedral Audio.
Library bound edition of full length, unabridged, recording of "The Killer Angels" historical novel.

Killer Angels. unabr. ed. Michael Shaara. Read by Stephen Hoye. Intro. by Jeff Shaara. (Running Time: 13 hrs. 30 mins.). (ENG.). 2004. audio compact disk 40.00 (978-0-7393-0905-6(6)) Pub: Random Audio Pubg. Dist(s): Random

Killer Angels. unabr. ed. Michael Shaara. Narrated by George Guidall. 10 cass. (Running Time: 14 hrs. 15 mins.). 1991. 85.00 (978-1-55690-282-6(4), 91118E7) Recorded Bks.
An accurate recreation in novel form of the Battle of Gettysburg.

Killer Angels. unabr. ed. Michael Shaara. Narrated by George Guidall. 12 CDs. (Running Time: 14 hrs. 15 mins.). 2000. audio compact disk 109.00 (978-0-7887-3980-4(8), C1099) Recorded Bks.
Provides an accurate fictional re-enactment of the battle of Gettysburg & fills in the psychological gaps with provocative portraits of the men who fought there.

***Killer Angels.** unabr. ed. Michael Shaara. Read by Stephen Hoye. Intro. by Jeff Shaara. (Running Time: 13 hrs. 30 mins.). (ENG.). 2011. audio compact disk 19.99 (978-0-307-93288-4(5), Random AudioBks) Pub: Random Audio Pubg. Dist(s): Random

Killer Angels. unabr. collector's ed. Michael Shaara. Read by Ken Ohst. 9 cass. (Running Time: 13 hrs. 30 min.). 1986. 72.00 (978-0-7366-1031-5(6), 1961) Books on Tape.
In four bloody & courageous days, two armies fought for their conflicting dreams at Gettysburg. As men died on those Pennsylvania fields so did our national innocence. The battle forged America's destiny in a cruel panorama of valor, blood & heartbreak.

Killer Angels, Set. unabr. ed. Michael Shaara. Read by George Hearn & Ronald F. Maxwell. 9 cass. (Running Time: 12 hrs. 40 min.). 1994. bk. 49.95 Cathedral Audio.

Killer Boots. unabr. ed. Wendy Jenkins. Read by Peter Hardy. 2 cass. (Running Time: 2 hrs. 45 mins.). 2002. (978-1-74030-253-1(2), 500957) Bolinda Pubng AUS.

Killer Carlin. Perf. by George Carlin. 2000. audio compact disk 16.98 (978-1-929243-10-5(3)) Uproar Ent.

Killer Diller. unabr. ed. Clyde Edgerton. Narrated by Norman Dietz. 6 cass. (Running Time: 8 hrs. 15 mins.). 51.00 (978-1-55690-682-4(X), 92112E7) Recorded Bks.
Shuttled among orphanages & foster homes since he was 11, Wesley Benfield is trying to turn over a new leaf. But two things are keeping him from a straight & narrow kind of existence: lust for Phoebe & a National Steel Dobro bottleneck guitar. Available to libraries only.

Killer Dreams. abr. ed. Iris Johansen. Read by Jennifer Van Dyck. (Running Time: 21600 sec.). (ENG.). 2007. audio compact disk 14.99 (978-0-7393-6576-2(2), Random AudioBks) Pub: Random Audio Pubg. Dist(s): Random

Killer Dreams. unabr. ed. Iris Johansen. 9 cass. (Running Time: 13 hrs.). 2006. 81.00 (978-1-4159-3045-8(7)); audio compact disk 99.00 (978-1-4159-3046-5(5)) Books on Tape.

Killer from the Pecos. Louis L'Amour. 1 cass. (Running Time: 1 hr.). 2001. 10.95 (BMDD007) Lodestone Catalog.

***Killer from the Pecos - Lit a Shuck for Texas - Turkeyfeather Riders.** unabr. ed. Louis L'Amour. (ENG.). 2010. 14.99 (978-0-307-74877-5(4), Random AudioBks) Pub: Random Audio Pubg. Dist(s): Random

Killer Genesis. abr. ed. Axel Kilgore. Read by Charlton Griffin. 2 vols. No. 1. 2003. (978-1-58807-648-9(2)) Am Pubng Inc.

Killer Genesis. abr. rev. ed. Axel Kilgore. Read by Charlton Griffin. 2 cass. (Running Time: 3 hrs.). (Mercenary Ser.: No. 1). 2004. 18.00 (978-1-58807-189-7(8)) Am Pubng Inc.
Hank Frost, mercenary, tracks a rogue who killed his men. The hunt explodes in Central Africa where Communists, a CIA-trained army, and a dictator vie for Frost's attention and to be the instrument of his death. Frost is hard-pressed to find any allies in this melee, so he must rely on his own instincts and survival skills as he lays his own trap.

Killer Genesis. abr. rev. ed. Axel Kilgore. Read by Carol Eason. 4 CDs. (Running Time: 4 hrs.). (Mercenary Ser.: No. 1). 2004. audio compact disk 25.00 (978-1-58807-325-9(4)) Am Pubng Inc.

Killer Hand. Radio Spirits Publishing Staff. Read by William Conrad. 2005. audio compact disk 9.98 (978-1-57019-810-6(1)) Radio Spirits.

***Killer Heat.** abr. ed. Linda Fairstein. Read by Blair Brown. (Alexandra Cooper Mysteries Ser.). (ENG.). 2010. audio compact disk 14.99 (978-0-307-75091-4(4), Random AudioBks) Pub: Random Audio Pubg. Dist(s): Random

Killer Heat. unabr. ed. Linda Fairstein. Read by Bernadette Dunne. 7 cass. (Alexandra Cooper Mysteries Ser.). 2008. 110.00 (978-1-4159-5020-3(2), BksonTape); audio compact disk 110.00 (978-1-4159-4438-7(5), BksonTape) Pub: Random Audio Pubg. Dist(s): Random
It's August in New York, and the only thing that's hotter than the pavement is Manhattan D.A. Alex Cooper's professional and personal life. Just as she's claiming an especially gratifying victory in a rape case, she gets the call: The body of a young woman has been found in an abandoned building. The brutality of the murder is disturbing enough, but when a second body, beaten and disposed of in exactly the same manner, is found off the Belt Parkway, the city's top brass want the killer found fast, before the tabloids can start churning out ghoulish serial killer headlines. Between dodging the bullets of the gang members who are infuriated by Alex's most recent courtroom victory and keeping a rendezvous with a charming restaurateur, a serial killer on the loose is the last thing she needs on her plate right now. Then a third victim is found, and it becomes clear to Alex and her team that time is not on their side. Through Alex's peerless interrogation skills - and one big break - the search becomes focused on someone who has a twisted obsession with the military. Once again Linda Fairstein brilliantly orchestrates a gripping mix of cutting-edge legal issues and forensics, New York City history, and spine-tingling suspense.

Killer in the Rain & Other Stories. abr. ed. Raymond Chandler. Perf. by Elliott Gould. 4 cass. (Running Time: 6 hrs.). 2004. 25.00 (978-1-59007-062-8(3)) Pub: New Millenn Enter. Dist(s): PerseuPGW
In his early works, "Killer in the Rain" and "The Curtain," Chandler laid the groundwork for his signature character, the legendary Philip Marlowe. Marlowe, the hero of such novels as The Big Sleep and Farewell, My Lovely, takes center stage in the gripping "Goldfish" and "Finger Man".

Killer in the Trap. E. A. Olsen. Illus. by L. Le Blanc. (Oceanography Ser.). (J). (gr. 3 up). 1970. pap. bk. 10.60 (978-0-87783-190-7(4)) Oddo.

Killer Instinct. Joseph Finder. Narrated by Scott Brick. 7 cass. (Running Time: 44400 sec.). (Sound Library). 2006. 59.95 (978-0-7927-4004-9(1), CSL 931); audio compact disk & audio compact disk 29.95 (978-0-7927-4222-7(2), CMP 931) AudioGO.

Killer Instinct. Joseph Finder. 2006. 25.95 (978-1-59397-908-9(8)) Pub: Macmill Audio. Dist(s): Macmillan

Killer Instinct. abr. ed. Joseph Finder. 2006. 17.95 (978-1-59397-907-2(X)) Pub: Macmill Audio. Dist(s): Macmillan

Killer Instinct. abr. ed. Joseph Finder. Read by Scott Brick. 5 CDs. (Running Time: 21600 sec.). (ENG.). 2006. audio compact disk 24.95 (978-1-59397-895-2(2)) Pub: Macmill Audio. Dist(s): Macmillan

Killer Instinct. abr. ed. Joseph Finder. Read by Scott Brick. (Running Time: 6 hrs. 0 mins. 0 sec.). (ENG.). 2009. audio compact disk 14.99 (978-1-4272-0809-5(3)) Pub: Macmill Audio. Dist(s): Macmillan

Killer Instinct. unabr. ed. Joseph Finder. Narrated by Scott Brick. 10 CDs. (Running Time: 44400 sec.). (Sound Library). 2006. audio compact disk 94.95 (978-0-7927-4005-6(X), SLD 931) AudioGO.

Killer Instinct. unabr. ed. Joseph Finder. Read by Scott Brick. 10 CDs. (Running Time: 41400 sec.). (ENG.). 2006. audio compact disk 39.95 (978-1-59397-896-9(0)) Pub: Macmill Audio. Dist(s): Macmillan

Killer Market. unabr. ed. Margaret Maron. Narrated by C. J. Critt. 6 cass. (Running Time: 8 hrs. 15 mins.). (Deborah Knott Mystery Ser.: No. 5). 2000. 51.00 (978-0-7887-2944-7(6), 95724E7) Recorded Bks.
Story takes Judge Knott to the hub of the furniture industry where she soon finds herself suspected of murder.

Killer of Eagles. unabr. ed. Vickie Britton & Loretta Jackson. Read by Stephanie Brush. 6 cass. (Running Time: 8 hrs. 12 min.). (Ardis Cole Ser.: Bk. 6). 2001. 39.95 (978-1-58116-031-4(3)) Books in Motion.
Ardis is called to the Pine Ridge Reservation to help a friend find her missing niece. Medicine man Jim-Walks-Alone shares his disturbing vision about a "killer of eagles" responsible for the woman's disappearance.

Killer Pancake. abr. ed. Diane Mott Davidson. Read by Barbara Rosenblat. 2 cass. (Goldy Schulz Culinary Mysteries Ser.: No. 5). 2001. 7.95 (978-1-57815-193-6(7), Media Bks Audio) Media Bks NJ.

Killer Pancake. unabr. ed. Diane Mott Davidson. Read by Barbara Rosenblat. 8 cass. (Running Time: 12 hrs.). (Goldy Schulz Culinary Mysteries Ser.: No. 5). 2004. 34.95 (978-1-59007-347-6(9)); audio compact disk 59.95 (978-1-59007-439-8(4)) Pub: New Millenn Enter. Dist(s): PerseuPGW

Killer Pancake. unabr. ed. Diane Mott Davidson. Narrated by Barbara Rosenblat. 8 cass. (Running Time: 11 hrs. 15 mins.). (Goldy Schulz Culinary Mysteries Ser.: No. 5). 1997. 70.00 (978-0-7887-0837-4(6), 94982E7) Recorded Bks.
While catering a cosmetics company luncheon, the intrepid caterer, Goldy, witnesses the hit & run death of a rising young sales associate. Could the death have anything to do with the animal rights picket line in the parking lot...or with the exotic blue rose found near the victim's body.

Killer Pancake, Set. abr. ed. Diane Mott Davidson. Read by Barbara Rosenblat. 2 cass. (Running Time: 3 hrs.). (Goldy Schulz Culinary Mysteries Ser.: No. 5). 1995. 16.95 (978-1-57511-005-9(9), 393521) Pub Mills.

Killer Pentatonics for Guitar. Composed by Dave Celentano. 2001. pap. bk. 19.95 (978-1-57424-113-6(3), 1574241133) Pub: Centerstream Pub. Dist(s): H Leonard

***Killer Smile.** abr. ed. Lisa Scottoline. Read by Kate Burton. (ENG.). 2004. (978-0-06-081380-2(6), Harper Audio); (978-0-06-077904-7(5), Harper Audio) HarperCollins Pubs.

***Killer Smile.** unabr. ed. Lisa Scottoline. (ENG.). 2004. (978-0-06-081379-6(2), Harper Audio) HarperCollins Pubs.

Killer Smile. unabr. ed. Lisa Scottoline. Read by Barbara Rosenblat. 5 CDs. (Running Time: 7 hrs.). 2004. audio compact disk 39.95 (978-0-06-075823-3(6)) HarperCollins Pubs.

***Killer Smile.** unabr. ed. Lisa Scottoline. Read by Barbara Rosenblat. (ENG.). 2004. (978-0-06-077903-0(9), Harper Audio) HarperCollins Pubs.

Killer Summer. abr. ed. Ridley Pearson. Read by Phil Gigante. (Running Time: 6 hrs.). (Sun Valley Ser.). 2009. audio compact disk 24.99 (978-1-4418-0717-5(9), 9781441807175, BACD) Brilliance Audio.

Killer Summer. abr. ed. Ridley Pearson. Read by Phil Gigante. (Running Time: 6 hrs.). (Sun Valley Ser.). 2010. audio compact disk 14.99 (978-1-4418-2603-9(3), 9781441826039, BCD Value Price) Brilliance Audio.

Killer Summer. unabr. ed. Ridley Pearson. Read by Phil Gigante. (Running Time: 9 hrs.). (Sun Valley Ser.). 2009. 39.97 (978-1-4233-8352-9(4), 9781423383529, Brinc Audio MP3 Lib); 39.97 (978-1-4233-8354-3(0), 9781423383543, BADLE); 24.99 (978-1-4233-8351-2(6), 9781423383512, Brilliance MP3); 24.99 (978-1-4233-8353-6(2), 9781423383536, BAD); audio compact disk 89.97 (978-1-4233-8350-5(8), 9781423383505, BriAudCD Unabrid); audio compact disk 29.99 (978-1-4233-8349-9(4), 9781423383499, Bril Audio CD Unabri) Brilliance Audio.

Killer View. abr. ed. Ridley Pearson. (Running Time: 6 hrs.). 2009. audio compact disk 14.99 (978-1-4233-2142-2(1), 9781423321422, BCD Value Price) Brilliance Audio.

Killer View. unabr. ed. Ridley Pearson. Read by Christopher Lane. 1 MP3-CD. (Running Time: 9 hrs.). (Sun Valley Ser.). 2008. 24.95 (978-1-4233-2137-8(5), 9781423321378, Brilliance MP3); 39.25 (978-1-4233-2140-8(5), 9781423321408, BADLE); 39.25 (978-1-4233-2138-5(3), 9781423321385, Brinc Audio MP3 Lib); 24.95 (978-1-4233-2139-2(1), 9781423321392, BAD); audio compact disk 34.95 (978-1-4233-2135-4(9), 9781423321354, Bril Audio CD Unabri); audio compact disk 92.25 (978-1-4233-2136-1(7), 9781423321361, BriAudCD Unabrid) Brilliance Audio.

Killer Weekend. Ridley Pearson. Read by Christopher Lane. (Playaway Adult Fiction Ser.). 2008. 79.99 (978-1-60640-898-8(4)) Find a World.

Killer Weekend. unabr. ed. Ridley Pearson. Read by Christopher Lane. (Running Time: 7 hrs.). (Sun Valley Ser.). 2007. 39.25 (978-1-4233-2130-9(8), 9781423321309, BADLE); 24.95 (978-1-4233-2129-3(4), 9781423321293, BAD); 69.25 (978-1-4233-2124-8(3), 9781423321248, BrilAudUnabridg); audio compact disk 29.95 (978-1-4233-2125-5(1), 9781423321255, Bril Audio CD Unabri); audio compact disk 24.95 (978-1-4233-2127-9(8), 9781423321279, Brilliance MP3); audio compact disk 87.25 (978-1-4233-2126-2(X), 9781423321262, BriAudCD Unabrid); audio compact disk 39.25 (978-1-4233-2128-6(6), 9781423321286, Brinc Audio MP3 Lib) Brilliance Audio.

Killer Weekend. unabr. ed. Ridley Pearson. (Running Time: 7 hrs.). 2009. audio compact disk 14.99 (978-1-4233-2132-3(4), 9781423321323, BCD Value Price) Brilliance Audio.

Killer Whales & Dolphins, The Singing Whales. unabr. ed. David Attenborough. 1 cass. (Running Time: 54 min.). (Animal Language Ser.). 12.95 J Norton Pubs.

Killer Whales & Randall Eaton's Orca Project in the State of Washington. Hosted by Nancy Pearlman. 1 cass. (Running Time: 28 min.). 10.00 (1209) Educ Comm CA.

***Killer Within: In the Company of Monsters.** unabr. ed. Philip Carlo. Read by Kent Bateman. (Running Time: 8.5 hrs. NaN mins.). (ENG.). 2011. 29.95 (978-1-4417-7858-1(6)); 54.95 (978-1-4417-7855-0(1)); audio compact disk 29.95 (978-1-4417-7857-4(8)) Blckstn Audio.

***Killer Within (Library Edition) In the Company of Monsters.** unabr. ed. Philip Carlo. Read by Kent Bateman. (Running Time: 8.5 hrs. NaN mins.). (ENG.). 2011. audio compact disk 76.00 (978-1-4417-7856-7(X)) Blckstn Audio.

Killers see Stories of Ernest Hemingway

Killer's Choice. unabr. ed. Ed McBain, pseud. Read by Paul Shay. 6 cass. (Running Time: 6 hrs.). (87th Precinct Ser.: Bk. 5). 1991. 36.00 (978-0-7366-2064-2(8), 2872) Books on Tape.
Two headline-grabbing murders add up to big trouble.

Killer's Cousin. unabr. ed. Nancy Werlin. Read by Nick Podehl. (Running Time: 6 hrs.). 2009. 39.97 (978-1-4233-8103-7(3), 9781423381037, BADLE); 24.99 (978-1-4233-8080-1(0), 9781423380801, Brilliance MP3); 24.99 (978-1-4233-8084-9(3), 9781423380849, BAD); audio compact disk 54.97 (978-1-4233-8078-8(9), 9781423380788, BriAudCD Unabrid); audio compact disk 26.99 (978-1-4233-8076-4(2), 9781423380764, Bril Audio CD Unabri) Brilliance Audio.

Killer's Cousin. unabr. ed. Nancy Werlin. Read by Nick Podehl et al. 1 MP3-CD. (Running Time: 6 hrs.). 2009. 39.97 (978-1-4233-8082-5(7), 9781423380825, Brlnc Audio MP3 Lib) Brilliance Audio.

Killer's Payoff. unabr. ed. Ed McBain, pseud. Read by Paul Shay. 6 cass. (Running Time: 6 hrs.). (87th Precinct Ser.: Bk. 6). 1991. 36.00 (978-0-7366-2065-9(6), 2873) Books on Tape.
Politician's wife has a deadly secret.

Killer's Wake. unabr. ed. Bernard Cornwell. Read by David Case. 8 cass. (Running Time: 12 hrs.). 2001. 64.00 (978-0-7366-8385-2(2)) Books on Tape.
John Rossendale's home is the sea; in his 38-foot cutter, he is far away from his disagreeable, contentious family and his role as black sheep and heir to an impoverished earldom. Still, mystery and danger have a way of finding him even when he is far from any coast. He is obliged to return home to England on account of a mysterious painting which disappeared from the family's house years ago and which everyone suspects him of possessing. Blackmail and violence follow, and in the end Rossendale must contend with a deadly enemy at sea in the Channel Islands - an enemy he may not be able to survive.

Killer's Wedge. unabr. ed. Ed McBain, pseud. Read by Paul Shay. 6 cass. (Running Time: 6 hrs.). (87th Precinct Ser.: Bk. 7). 1992. 36.00 (978-0-7366-2105-2(9), 2909) Books on Tape.
A woman with a bomb & a short fuse has a score to settle with Det. Steve Carella of the 87th.

Killer's Wife. unabr. ed. Bill Floyd. Read by Isabel Keating. 6 CDs. (Running Time: 7 hrs. 30 mins.). 2008. audio compact disk 64.95 (978-0-7927-5252-3(X)) AudioGO.

Killigrew Clay, Set. unabr. ed. Rowena Summers. 10 cass. (Storysound Ser.). (J). 1997. 89.95 (978-1-85903-133-9(1)) Pub: Mgna Lrg Print GBR. Dist(s): Ulverscroft US

***Killing: A Selection from the John Updike Audio Collection.** unabr. ed. John Updike. Read by John Updike. (ENG.). 2009. (978-0-06-196242-4(2), Caedmon); (978-0-06-196241-7(4), Caedmon) HarperCollins Pubs.

Killing Aurora. unabr. ed. Helen Barnes. Read by Suzi Dougherty. 5 cass. (Running Time: 6 hrs.). (YA). 2000. 40.00 (978-1-74030-228-9(1)) Pub: Bolinda Pubng AUS. Dist(s): Bolinda Pub Inc

Killing Cassidy. Jeanne M. Dams. 5 cass. (Running Time: 7 hrs. 30 mins.). (Dorothy Martin Mystery Ser.: Bk. 6). 2001. 40.00 (978-0-7366-6368-7(1)) Books on Tape.
Dorothy Martin & her husband, Alan Nesbitt, recently retired from Scotland Yard, get word that she has received a small inheritance. But she must travel from her home in England to her native Indiana to claim it. The deceased has also left a letter suggesting that he's been murdered.

Killing Che. unabr. ed. Chuck Pfarrer. (Running Time: 18 hrs. 30 mins. 0 sec.). (ENG.). 2007. audio compact disk 34.99 (978-1-4001-5336-7(0)) Pub: Tantor Media. Dist(s): IngramPubServ

Killing Che. unabr. ed. Chuck Pfarrer. Read by William Dufris. (Running Time: 18 hrs. 30 mins. 0 sec.). (ENG.). 2007. audio compact disk 99.99 (978-1-4001-3336-9(X)); audio compact disk 49.99 (978-1-4001-0336-2(3)) Pub: Tantor Media. Dist(s): IngramPubServ
A rich, complex historical novel in the spirit of Graham Greene and John Le Carre, Killing Ché is a personal and political thriller that pits history's most infamous insurgent against a conflicted and world-weary CIA officer. The year is 1967; Vietnam is in flames and half a world away few realize that a firefight on a jungle road in Latin America is the beginning of a new and secret war. In the Ñancahuazú Valley of Bolivia international revolutionary Ché Guevara leads a band of guerillas determined to liberate a continent. Paul Hoyle, a CIA paramilitary officer, joins a team of operatives sent to crush the Bolivian insurgency. When a recovered backpack reveals that Che Guevara is in command of the rebels, the stage is set for a duel between world ideologies.

***Killing Critics.** unabr. ed. O' et al. Read by Laural Merlington. (Running Time: 12 hrs.). 2010. audio compact disk 89.97 (978-1-4418-4025-7(7), 9781441840257, BriAudCD Unabrid) Brilliance Audio.

Killing Critics. unabr. ed. Carol O'Connell. Read by Laural Merlington. (Running Time: 11 hrs.). 2009. 24.99 (978-1-4233-9058-9(X), 9781423390589, Brilliance MP3); 39.97 (978-1-4233-9059-6(8), 9781423390596, Brlnc Audio MP3 Lib); 24.99 (978-1-4233-9060-2(1), 9781423390602, BAD); 39.97 (978-1-4233-9061-9(X), 9781423390619, BADLE) Brilliance Audio.

***Killing Critics.** unabr. ed. Carol O'Connell. Read by Laural Merlington. (Running Time: 12 hrs.). 2010. audio compact disk 29.99 (978-1-4418-4026-4(5), 9781441840264) Brilliance Audio.

Killing Dance. abr. ed. Laurell K. Hamilton. (Running Time: 8 hrs.). (Anita Blake, Vampire Hunter Ser.: No. 6). (ENG.). 2010. audio compact disk 29.95 (978-0-14-314428-1(6), PenAudBks) Pub: Pnguin Bks Ltd GBR. Dist(s): Penguin Grp USA

Killing Dance. unabr. ed. Laurell K. Hamilton. (Running Time: 14 hrs.). (Anita Blake, Vampire Hunter Ser.: No. 6). (ENG.). 2010. audio compact disk 39.95 (978-0-14-314406-9(5), PenAudBks) Pub: Pnguin Bks Ltd GBR. Dist(s): Penguin Grp USA

***Killing Edge.** Heather Graham. Contrib. by Julia Whelan. (Playaway Adult Fiction Ser.). (ENG.). 2010. 74.99 (978-1-4418-5623-4(4)) Find a World.

***Killing Edge.** abr. ed. Heather Graham. Read by Julia Whelan. (Running Time: 5 hrs.). 2010. audio compact disk 24.99 (978-1-4418-2553-7(3), 9781441825537) Brilliance Audio.

***Killing Edge.** abr. ed. Heather Graham. Read by Julia Whelan. (Running Time: 5 hrs.). 2010. 9.99 (978-1-4418-9351-2(2), 9781441893512, BAD) Brilliance Audio.

***Killing Edge.** unabr. ed. Heather Graham. Read by Julia Whelan. (Running Time: 10 hrs.). 2010. 24.99 (978-1-4233-9875-2(0), 9781423398752, BAD); 39.97 (978-1-4233-9874-5(2), 9781423398745, Brlnc Audio MP3 Lib); 39.97 (978-1-4233-9876-9(9), 9781423398769, BADLE); 24.99 (978-1-4233-9873-8(4), 9781423398738, Brilliance MP3); audio compact disk 92.97 (978-1-4233-9872-1(6), 9781423398721, BriAudCD Unabrid); audio compact disk 34.99 (978-1-4233-9871-4(8), 9781423398714) Brilliance Audio.

Killing Floor. abr. ed. Lee Child. Read by Dick Hill. 3 CDs. (Running Time: 3 hrs.). (Jack Reacher Ser.). 2004. audio compact disk 14.99 (978-1-59355-558-0(X), 159355558X, BCD Value Price) Brilliance Audio.
All is not well in Margrave, Georgia. The sleepy, forgotten town hasn't seen a crime in decades, but within the span of three days it witnesses events that leave everyone stunned. An unidentified man is found beaten and shot to death on a lonely country road. The police chief and his wife are butchered on a quiet Sunday morning. Then a bank executive disappears from his home, leaving his keys on the table and his wife frozen with fear. The easiest suspect is Jack Reacher - an outsider, a man just passing through. But Reacher is not just any drifter. He is a tough ex-military policeman, trained to think fast and act faster. He has lived with and hunted the worst: the hard men of the American military gone bad.

Killing Floor. abr. ed. Lee Child. Read by Dick Hill. (Running Time: 3 hrs.). (Jack Reacher Ser.). 2009. audio compact disk 9.99 (978-1-4418-0826-4(4), 9781441808264, BCD Value Price) Brilliance Audio.

Killing Floor, unabr. ed. Lee Child. Read by Lee Child. Read by Dick Hill. 12 cass. (Running Time: 15 hrs.). (Jack Reacher Ser.). 1997. 105.25 (978-1-56100-806-3(0), 1561008060, Unabridge Lib Edns) Brilliance Audio.
A terrifying thriller that's unforgettable. "I was eating eggs and drinking coffee. I was in a booth, at a window, reading somebody's abandoned newspaper. Outside, the rain had stopped but the glass was still pebbled with bright drops. I saw the police cruisers pull into the gravel lot. They were moving fast and crunched to a stop. Light bars flashing and popping. Doors burst open, policemen jumped out. Two from each car, weapons ready. Two revolvers, two shotguns. This was heavy stuff. One revolver and one shotgun ran to the back. One of each rushed the door. I just sat and watched them. I knew who was in the diner. A cook in back. Two waitresses. Two old men. And me. This operation was for me. I had been in town less than half an hour." - from the opening of this searing tale of honor and revenge where Jack Reacher, a former military cop, hunts down his brother's killers. In the bestselling tradition of John Sandford and Stephen Hunter, the listener will be entertained non-stop until the end.

Killing Floor. unabr. ed. Lee Child. Read by Dick Hill. 12 cass. (Running Time: 15 hrs.). (Jack Reacher Ser.). 2004. 29.95 (978-1-59355-557-3(1), 1593555571, BAU) Brilliance Audio.
All is not well in Margrave, Georgia. The sleepy, forgotten town hasn't seen a crime in decades, but within the span of three days it witnesses events that leave everyone stunned. An unidentified man is found beaten and shot to death on a lonely country road. The police chief and his wife are butchered on a quiet Sunday morning. Then a bank executive disappears from his home, leaving his keys on the table and his wife frozen with fear. The easiest suspect is Jack Reacher - an outsider, a man just passing through. But Reacher is not just any drifter. He is a tough ex-military policeman, trained to think fast and act faster. He has lived with and hunted the worst: the hard men of the American military gone bad.

Killing Floor. unabr. ed. Lee Child. Read by Dick Hill. (Running Time: 15 hrs.). (Jack Reacher Ser.). 2004. 39.25 (978-1-59335-648-4(X), 159335648X, Brlnc Audio MP3 Lib); 24.95 (978-1-59335-296-7(4), 1593352964, Brilliance MP3) Brilliance Audio.

Killing Floor. unabr. ed. Lee Child. Read by Dick Hill. (Running Time: 15 hrs.). (Jack Reacher Ser.). 2004. 39.25 (978-1-59710-423-4(X), 159710423X, BADLE); 24.95 (978-1-59710-422-7(1), 1597104221, BAD) Brilliance Audio.

Killing Floor. unabr. ed. Lee Child. Read by Dick Hill. (Running Time: 54000 sec.). (Jack Reacher Ser.). 2007. audio compact disk 112.25 (978-1-4233-3986-1(X), 9781423339861, BriAudCD Unabrid); audio compact disk 38.95 (978-1-4233-3985-4(1), 9781423339854, Bril Audio CD Unabri) Brilliance Audio.

Killing Floor. unabr. ed. Lee Child. Read by Dick Hill. (Jack Reacher Ser.). (YA). 2008. 99.99 (978-1-60514-816-8(4)) Find a World.

Killing for Sport: Inside the Minds of Serial Killers. unabr. ed. Scripts. Pat Brown. 5 CDs. (Running Time: 6 hrs.). 2003. audio compact disk 34.95 (978-1-59007-372-8(X), N Millennium Audio) Pub: New Millenn Enter. Dist(s): PerseuPGW

Killing for Sport: Inside the Minds of Serial Killers. unabr. ed. Scripts. Pat Brown. 4 cass. (Running Time: 6 hrs.). 2004. 24.95 (978-1-59007-371-1(1)) Pub: New Millenn Enter. Dist(s): PerseuPGW

Killing for the Hawks. Frederick E. Smith. 8 cass. (Running Time: 10 hrs. 35 mins.). (Story Sound Ser.). (J). 2004. 69.95 (978-1-85903-753-9(4)) Pub: Mgna Lrg Print GBR. Dist(s): Ulverscroft US

Killing Frost. R. D. Wingfield. (Jack Frost Ser.: Bk. 6). 2008. 89.95 (978-0-7531-2982-1(5)); audio compact disk 99.95 (978-0-7531-2983-8(3)) Pub: Isis Pubng Ltd GBR. Dist(s): Ulverscroft US

Killing Game. abr. ed. Iris Johansen. Read by Becky Ann Baker. 3 cass. (Eve Duncan Ser.). 1999. 25.00 (FS9-50993) Highsmith.

Killing Game, unabr. ed. Iris Johansen. Read by Laurel Lefkow. 8 vols. (Running Time: 10 hrs.20 mins.). (Eve Duncan Ser.). 2000. bk. 69.95 (978-0-7927-2338-7(4), CSL 227, Chivers Sound Lib) AudioGO.
The killer knew the pain Eve Duncan felt for her murdered daughter, Bonnie, whose body was never found. He knew that as one of the nation's top forensic sculptors, she would insist on identifying nine skeletons unearthed on a bluff near Georgia's Talladega falls. And he knew that she wouldn't resist the temptation of believing that one of those skeletons might be Bonnie's. But this is only the beginning of the killer's sadistic game, for he won't stop until he has the prize he wants the most, Eve's life.

Killing Game. unabr. ed. Iris Johansen. Read by Laurel Lefkow. 10 CDs. (Running Time: 15 hrs.). (Eve Duncan Ser.). 2001. audio compact disk 94.95 (978-0-7927-9962-7(3), SLD 013, Chivers Sound Lib) AudioGO.

Killing Giants: 1 Samuel 17. Ben Young. (YA). 2000. 4.95 (978-0-7417-6226-9(9), B0226) Win Walk.

***Killing Giants: 10 Strategies to Topple the Goliath in Your Industry.** unabr. ed. Stephen Denny. Read by Don Hagen. (Running Time: 6 hrs.). (ENG.). 2011. 27.00 (978-1-59659-642-9(2), GildAudio); audio compact disk 29.98 (978-1-59659-631-3(7), GildAudio) Pub: Gildan Media. Dist(s): HachBkGrp

Killing Ground. Jack Higgins. Read by Christopher Lane. (Sean Dillon Ser.). 2009. 69.99 (978-1-60812-670-5(6)) Find a World.

Killing Ground. abr. ed. Jack Higgins. Read by Christopher Lane. (Running Time: 6 hrs.). (Sean Dillon Ser.). 2008. audio compact disk 14.99 (978-1-4233-5749-0(3), 9781423357490, BCD Value Price) Brilliance Audio.

Killing Ground. unabr. ed. Jack Higgins. Read by Christopher Lane. (Running Time: 8 hrs.). (Sean Dillon Ser.). 2008. 39.25 (978-1-4233-1502-5(2), 9781423315025, BADLE); 24.95 (978-1-4233-1501-8(4), 9781423315018, BAD); 92.25 (978-1-4233-1496-7(4), 9781423314967, BrilAudUnabridg); audio compact disk 39.25 (978-1-4233-1500-1(6), 9781423315001, Brlnc Audio MP3 Lib); audio compact disk 97.25 (978-1-4233-1498-1(0), 9781423314981, BriAudCD Unabrid); audio compact disk 24.95 (978-1-4233-1499-8(9), 9781423314998, Brilliance MP3); audio compact disk 34.95 (978-1-4233-1497-4(2), 9781423314974, Bril Audio CD Unabri) Brilliance Audio.
Please enter a Synopsis.

Killing Ground. unabr. ed. Douglas Reeman. Read by David Rintoul. 8 cass. (Running Time: 12 hrs.). 2000. 59.95 (978-0-7451-4093-3(9), CAB 781) Pub: Chivers Audio Bks GBR. Dist(s): AudioGO
The Battle of the Atlantic was a full-scale war with no rules and no mercy. This is the story, seen through British and German eyes, of an ordinary destroyer, HMS Gladiator, struggling to protect the embattled Merchant Navy convoys on the unpredictable and often violent Western Ocean, bitterly known as the "Killing Ground".

Killing Ground. unabr. ed. Gerald Seymour. Read by Jonathon Oliver. 14 cass. (Running Time: 17 hr. 30 min.). (Isis Ser.). (J). 1997. 99.95 (978-0-7531-0208-4(0), 970910) Pub: ISIS Lrg Prnt GBR. Dist(s): Ulverscroft US
A young English schoolteacher is invited to return to her job as nanny to the family of a well-to-do Sicilian family. But this time she is the central figure in a desperate plot by the U.S. Drug Enforcement Agency to trap Mario Rugerrio, putative head of the Sicilian Mafia.

Killing-Ground. unabr. collector's ed. Elleston Trevor. Read by Christopher Hurt. 8 cass. (Running Time: 8 hrs.). 1986. 48.00 (978-0-7366-0571-7(1), 1543) Books on Tape.
Trevor depicts the men of a tank squadron as they cross the silent, darkened Channel, storm the "invincible" coast & sweep into Falaise.

Killing Grounds. collector's ed. Dana Stabenow. Read by Marguerite Gavin. 6 cass. (Running Time: 9 hrs.). (Kate Shugak Ser.). 2000. 48.00 (978-0-7366-5464-7(X)) Books on Tape.
While deck-handing on a fishing boat, Kate Shugak hauls in the dead body of the most disliked fisherman around. Kate's search for the killer isn't making her too popular in town - especially since he's being hailed as the catch of the day.

Killing Illness - Killing Fear. Jason Winters. Read by Jason Winters. Read by Steven R. Bell. 1 cass. (C). 1986. pap. bk. 7.95 (978-0-9621388-1-2(9)) Vinton.
Natural Health Info.

Killing Jar. David Docherty. Narrated by Gordon Griffin. 9 cass. (Running Time: 12 hrs. 45 mins.). 82.00 (978-1-84197-393-7(9)) Recorded Bks.

Killing Jar. unabr. ed. David Docherry. Narrated by Gordon Griffin. 9 cass. (Running Time: 12 hrs. 45 mins.). 2002. 42.95 (978-1-4025-2488-2(9), RG121) Recorded Bks.

Killing Karma. Geraldine Evans. 2009. 54.95 (978-1-4079-0501-3(5)); audio compact disk 64.95 (978-1-4079-0502-0(3)) Pub: Soundings Ltd GBR. Dist(s): Ulverscroft US

Killing Kindness. unabr. ed. Reginald Hill. Read by Colin Buchanan. 6 CDs. (Running Time: 9 hrs.). (Dalziel & Pascoe Ser.). 2002. audio compact disk 79.90 (978-0-7540-5446-7(2), CCD 137) AudioGO.

Killing Kindness, Set. unabr. ed. Reginald Hill. Read by Colin Buchanan. 8 cass. (Running Time: 12 hr.). (Dalziel & Pascoe Ser.). 1999. 69.95 (978-0-7540-0382-3(5), CAB1805) AudioGO.
When Mary Dinwoodie is found murdered, a mysterious caller phones the local paper with a quotation from Hamlet. Detective Dalziel is unimpressed by the call, & furious when Sergeant Wield calls in a clairvoyant. Meanwhile, the killer strikes again & again.

Killing Man. abr. ed. Mickey Spillane. 2006. 8.95 (978-0-7435-6249-2(6)) Pub: S&S Audio. Dist(s): S and S Inc

Killing Man. unabr. ed. Mickey Spillane. Read by Larry McKeever. 8 cass. (Running Time: 8 hrs.). (Mike Hammer Ser.). 1992. 48.00 (978-0-7366-2227-1(6), 3017) Books on Tape.
A dead man is in Mike Hammer's chair. His loyal secretary lies on the floor, beaten. The only clues are a strange note & ten chopped-off fingers. Mike is determined to put a bullet where it will do the most good.

Killing Me Softly. unabr. ed. Nicci French. Read by Julian Franklyn. 8 cass. (Running Time: 11 hrs.). (Isis Ser.). (J). 2000. 69.95 (978-0-7531-0751-5(1), 000211) Pub: ISIS Lrg Prnt GBR. Dist(s): Ulverscroft US
Alice London is a young woman who seems to have it all. Then one day she meets a stranger & impulsively gives up her safe life for a passionate affair.

Killing Me Softly. unabr. ed. Nicci French. Read by Julia Franklin. 10 CDs. (Running Time: 11 hrs. 21 mins.). (Isis Ser.). (J). 2002. audio compact disk 89.95 (978-0-7531-1485-8(2)) Pub: ISIS Lrg Prnt GBR. Dist(s): Ulverscroft US

Killing Me Softly, Set. unabr. ed. Marjorie Eccles. Read by Marie McCarthy. 6 cass. (Running Time: 8 hrs.). 1999. 69.95 (978-1-85903-270-1(2)) Pub: Magna Story GBR. Dist(s): Ulverscroft US
In the fight against drugs, Detective Sergeant Gil Mayo finds that even Lavenstock isn't immune. His team seems to be getting nowhere, but when a member of a well-known & respected family is killed, inquiries takes another direction. As Mayo & his assistant Abigail Moon investigate the death, more & more unsavory details of the victim's private life are revealed, & it becomes clear that many people, including his own family, had a motive for killing him. When Mayo & Abigail finally uncover the truth it becomes clear the murder is the first link in a chain of further death & destruction.

Killing Mister Watson. Peter Matthiessen. Read by Norman Dietz et al. 10 Cass. (Running Time: 17 Hrs.). 39.95 (978-1-4025-5844-3(9)) Recorded Bks.

Killing Mister Watson. unabr. ed. Peter Matthiessen. Narrated by Norman Dietz et al. 12 cass. (Running Time: 17 hrs.). 1991. 97.00 (978-1-55690-283-3(2), 91320E7) Recorded Bks.
When Matthiessen was 17, he was told the story of Edgar J. Watson, a popular & successful planter who had been murdered by his neighbors in 1910. This is his attempt to piece together the life of a mysterious man who became a legend & the dangerous legend that destroyed him.

Killing Moon. abr. ed. Chuck Hogan. 2007. 17.95 (978-0-7435-6411-3(1), Audioworks) Pub: S&S Audio. Dist(s): S and S Inc

***Killing Mr. Griffin.** unabr. ed. Lois Duncan. Read by Dennis Butkis & Dennis Holland. (Running Time: 7 hrs. 30 mins.). (ENG.). (YA). 2010. 17.98 (978-1-60788-911-3(0)) Pub: Hachet Audio. Dist(s): HachBkGrp

Killing Mr. Griffin. unabr. ed. Lois Duncan. 1 cass. (Running Time: 1 hr. 28 min.). (Young Adult Cliffhangers Ser.). (YA). (gr. 7 up). 1987. pap. bk. 15.98 (978-0-8072-1854-9(5), JRH 119SP, Listening Lib) Random Audio Pubg.

Killing Mr. Griffin, unabr. ed. Lois Duncan. Narrated by Ed Sala. 5 pieces. (Running Time: 6 hrs. 15 mins.). (gr. 7 up). 1998. 44.00 (978-0-7887-1802-1(9), 95274E7) Recorded Bks.
Mr. Griffin is the least-liked teacher at Del Norre High School. When a group of classmates decide to kidnap him, the plan is only to scare their English teacher. Sometimes plans go horribly wrong.

Killing Mr. Griffin. unabr. ed. Lois Duncan. Read by Ed Sala. 5 cass. (Running Time: 6 hrs. 15 min.). (YA). (gr. 7 up). 1998. 13.00 CD. Recorded Bks.
About a youthful prank that goes bad, as the participants try to hide the results & the effect it has on the lives of those involved.

Killing Mr. Griffin, Class Set. unabr. ed. Lois Duncan. Read by Ed Sala. 5 cass., 10 bks. (Running Time: 6 hrs. 15 min.). (J). 1997. bk. 109.80 (978-0-7887-2712-2(5), 46300) Recorded Bks.
Mr. Griffin is the least-liked teacher at Del Norre High School. When a group of classmates decide to kidnap him, the plan is only to scare their English teacher. Sometimes plans go horribly wrong.

Killing Mr. Griffin, Homework Set. unabr. ed. Lois Duncan. Read by Ed Sala. 5 cass. (Running Time: 6 hrs. 15 min.). (J). 1997. bk. 56.75 (978-0-7887-1898-4(3), 40634) Recorded Bks.

Killing My Own Snakes: A Memoir. Ann Leslie. Read by Ann Leslie. 3 CDs. (Running Time: 7 hrs. 0 mins. 0 sec.). (ENG.). 2008. audio compact disk 26.95 (978-0-230-70432-9(8)) Pub: Macmillan UK GBR. Dist(s): IPG Chicago

Killing Night. unabr. ed. Jonathon King. Read by David Colacci. (Running Time: 9 hrs.). (Max Freeman Ser.). 2005. 39.25 (978-1-59710-424-1(8), 9781597104241, BADLE); 24.95 (978-1-59710-425-8(6), 9781597104258, BAD) Brilliance Audio.

Killing Night. unabr. ed. Jonathon King. Read by David Colacci. (Running Time: 9 hrs.). (Max Freeman Ser.: No. 4). 2005. 24.95 (978-1-59335-711-5(7), 9781593357115, Brilliance MP3); 39.25 (978-1-59335-845-7(8), 9781593358457, Brlnc Audio MP3 Lib); 29.95 (978-1-59355-310-4(2), 9781593553104, BAU); 82.25 (978-1-59355-311-1(0), 9781593553111, BrilAudUnabridg); audio compact disk 34.95 (978-1-59355-312-8(9), 9781593553128, Bril Audio CD Unabri); audio compact disk 92.25 (978-1-59355-313-5(7), 9781593553135, BriAudCD Unabrid) Brilliance Audio.
Please enter a Synopsis.

***Killing of Crazy Horse.** unabr. ed. Thomas Powers. (Running Time: 22 hrs. 0 mins.). 2010. 24.99 (978-1-4001-8874-1(1)); 54.99 (978-1-4001-9874-0(7)); 39.99 (978-1-4001-6874-3(0)); audio compact disk 131.99 (978-1-4001-4874-5(X)); audio compact disk 54.99 (978-1-4001-1874-8(3)) Pub: Tantor Media. Dist(s): IngramPubServ

Killing of Monday Brown. unabr. ed. Sandra West Prowell. Read by Susie Breck. (Running Time: 8 hrs.). 2009. 39.97 (978-1-4233-8497-7(0), 9781423384977, Brlnc Audio MP3 Lib); 39.97 (978-1-4233-8499-1(7), 9781423384991, BADLE); 24.99 (978-1-4233-8496-0(2), 9781423384960, Brilliance MP3); 24.99 (978-1-4233-8498-4(9), 9781423384984, BAD) Brilliance Audio.

***Killing of the Tinkers.** Ken Bruen. 2010. 44.95 (978-0-7531-4481-7(6)); audio compact disk 51.95 (978-0-7531-4482-4(4)) Pub: Isis Pubng Ltd GBR. Dist(s): Ulverscroft US

***Killing Orders.** Sara Paretsky. Narrated by Kathleen Turner. 3 CDs. (Running Time: 3 hrs. 0 mins. 0 sec.). (ENG.). 2010. audio compact disk 29.95 (978-1-4084-6695-7(3)) Pub: AudioGO. Dist(s): Perseus Dist

Killing Orders. Sara Paretsky. Read by Donada Peters. (V. I. Warshawski Novel Ser.). 1993. audio compact disk 56.00 (978-0-7366-7066-1(1)) Books on Tape.

Killing Orders. unabr. ed. Sara Paretsky. Read by Donada Peters. 7 CDs. (Running Time: 10 hrs. 30 mins.). (V. I. Warshawski Novel Ser.). 2001. audio compact disk 56.00 Books on Tape.
V. I. Warshawski faces unholy trinity of corporate conspirators, Chicago's underworld bosses & the Church itself.

Killing Orders. unabr. ed. Sara Paretsky. Read by Susan Ericksen. (Running Time: 10 hrs.). (V. I. Warshawski Ser.). 2010. 24.99 (978-1-4418-3550-5(4), 9781441835505, Brilliance MP3); 24.99 (978-1-4418-3552-9(0), 9781441835529, BAD); 39.97 (978-1-4418-3551-2(2), 9781441835512, Brlnc Audio MP3 Lib); 39.97 (978-1-4418-3553-6(9), 9781441835536, BADLE); audio compact disk 29.99 (978-1-4418-3548-2(2), 9781441835482, Bril Audio CD Unabri); audio compact disk 89.97 (978-1-4418-3549-9(0), 9781441835499, BriAudCD Unabrid) Brilliance Audio.

Killing Orders. unabr. collector's ed. Sara Paretsky. Read by Donada Peters. 8 cass. (Running Time: 8 hrs.). (V. I. Warshawski Novel Ser.). 1993. 64.00 (978-0-7366-2391-9(4), 3162) Books on Tape.

Killing Pablo. Mark Bowden. 2004. 15.95 (978-0-7435-1881-9(0)) Pub: S&S Audio. Dist(s): S and S Inc

Killing Pablo: The Hunt for the World's Greatest Outlaw. Mark Bowden. Narrated by Pete Bradbury. 9 CDs. (Running Time: 10 hrs. 30 mins.). audio compact disk 89.00 (978-1-4025-3493-5(0)) Recorded Bks.

Killing Pablo: The Hunt for the World's Greatest Outlaw. collector's ed. Mark Bowden. Narrated by Pete Bradbury. 8 cass. (Running Time: 10 hrs. 30 mins.). 2002. 37.95 (978-1-4025-1341-1(0), 96631) Recorded Bks.
The drugs, the sex, the excess, the violence - this is the true story of Pablo Escobar, the most successful drug-dealer in history.

Killing Pablo: The Hunt for the World's Greatest Outlaw. unabr. ed. Mark Bowden. Narrated by Pete Bradbury. 7 cass. (Running Time: 10 hrs. 30 mins.). 2002. 71.00 (978-1-4025-1340-4(2)) Recorded Bks.

Killing Rain. Barry Eisler. Read by Michael McConnohie. (Running Time: 36000 sec.). (John Rain Ser.: Bk. 4). 2005. audio compact disk 34.95 (978-1-59316-068-5(2)) Listen & Live.

Killing Rain. unabr. ed. Barry Eisler. Read by Michael McConnohie. (YA). 2006. 49.99 (978-1-59895-194-3(7)) Find a World.

Killing Raven. unabr. ed. Margaret Coel. 6 cass. (Running Time: 8 hrs.). (Wind River Ser.). 2004. 39.95 (978-1-58116-987-4(6)); audio compact disk 43.95 (978-1-58116-988-1(4)) Books in Motion.
When the body of a white man is recovered from a shallow grave in one of the most troubled corners of the Wind River Reservation, Father John O'Malley knows that if the murderer isn't caught quickly, this tragedy will only be the beginning.

Killing Romance: 11 Timothy 3:1-2. Ed Young. 1986. 4.95 (978-0-7417-1533-3(3), 533) Win Walk.

Killing Rommel. unabr. ed. Steven Pressfield. Narrated by Alfred Molina. (Running Time: 10 hrs. 30 mins.). 2008. 56.75 (978-1-4361-3258-9(4)) Recorded Bks.

Killing Rommel. unabr. ed. Steven Pressfield. Narrated by Alfred Molina. 9 cass. (Running Time: 10 hrs. 30 mins.). 2008. 46.95 (978-1-4281-8079-6(6)); 72.75 (978-1-4281-8078-9(8)); audio compact disk 39.99 (978-1-4281-8077-2(X)); audio compact disk 102.75 (978-1-4281-8080-2(X)) Recorded Bks.

Killing Sacred Cows: Cd Album. Created by Awmi. (ENG.). 2009. audio compact disk 35.00 (978-1-59548-181-8(8)) A Wommack.

Killing Season. abr. ed. Ralph Compton. Narrated by Jim Gough. 4 cass. (Running Time: 6 hrs.). (Gun Ser.). 2000. 24.95 (978-1-890990-47-3(7)) Otis Audio.
Gunfighter Nathan Stone finds no peace or safety after avenging the murders of his parents as he is forced to defend his reputation against some of the most feared & famous gunfighters of the 1870s Wild West.

Killing Sky. Andy Straka. Read by Charlie O'Dowd. 4 vols. No. 2. 2003. (978-1-58807-601-4(6)) Am Pubng Inc.

Killing Sky. unabr. ed. Andy Straka. Read by Charlie O'Dowd. 4 cass. (Running Time: 6 hrs.). (Frank Pavlicek Mysteries: No. 2). 2003. 25.00 (978-1-58807-140-8(5)) Am Pubng Inc.
Years ago, homicide detective Frank Pavlicek left the NYPD under less than ideal circumstances. Now the divorced father of a teenage daughter, he works as a private investigator in Charlottesville, Virginia, where he indulges his passion for falconry and savors the thrill of the hunt. When her twin sister, Cartwright, disappears, Cassidy Drummond can't help wondering if her father, a congressman known as much for his philandering as for his politics, has something to do with it. Desperate and deeply frightened, she turns to Frank Pavlicek for help. But, despite a long list of possible culprits and the fact that Cartwright's car has been found with blood on the seats Frank isn't convinced it's foul play. Soon the falconer is following a treacherous trail of family secrets and sinister scandals to the most dangerous discovery of all: the truth.

Killing the Fatted Calf. Susan Kelly. Read by Gordon Griffin. 8 cass. (Sound Ser.). (J). 2002. 69.95 (978-1-84283-225-7(5)) Pub: ISIS Lrg Prnt GBR. Dist(s): Ulverscroft US

Killing the Lawyers. unabr. ed. Reginald Hill. Read by Simon J. Williamson. 8 cass. (Running Time: 10 hrs. 35 min.). (Joe Sixsmith Ser.). 1998. 83.95 (978-1-85903-235-0(4)) Pub: Magna Story GBR. Dist(s): Ulverscroft US
When Joe Sixsmith turns to Luton's top firm for assistance in an insurance dispute, he gets assaulted verbally by one partner and physically by another. When someone tries to kill Joe, he gets a little upset.

Killing the Sale. unabr. ed. Todd Duncan. Narrated by Todd Duncan. (Smart Tapes Ser.). (ENG.). 2004. 18.19 (978-1-60814-266-8(3), SmartTapes) Oasis Audio.

Killing the Sale: The 10 Fatal Mistakes Salespeople Make & How to Avoid Them. abr. ed. Todd Duncan. Read by Todd Duncan. 4 cass. (Running Time: 4 hrs.). (Smart Audio Ser.). 25.99 (978-1-58926-660-5(9)) Oasis Audio.

Killing the Sale: The 10 Fatal Mistakes Salespeople Make & How to Avoid Them. abr. unabr. ed. Todd Duncan. Narrated by Todd Duncan. 4 CDs. (Running Time: 4 hrs.). (Smart Audio Ser.). (ENG.). 2004. audio compact disk 25.99 (978-1-58926-661-2(7)) Oasis Audio.

Killing the Shadows. unabr. ed. Val McDermid. Read by Vari Sylvester. 10 cass. (Running Time: 14 hrs.). 2001. 34.95 (978-1-58788-624-9(3), 1587886243, BAU); 107.25 (978-1-58788-625-6(1), 1587886251, Unabridge Lib Edns) Brilliance Audio.
A killer is on the loose, blurring the line between fact and fiction. His prey - the writers of crime novels who have turned psychological profilers into the heroes of the nineties. But this killer is like no other. His bloodlust shatters all the conventional wisdom surrounding the motives and mechanics of how serial killers operate. And for one woman, the desperate hunt to uncover his identity becomes a matter of life and death. Professor Fiona Cameron is an academic psychologist who uses computer technology to help police forces track serial offenders. She used to help the Met, but vowed never to work for them again when they went against her advice and badly screwed up an investigation as a consequence. Still smarting from the experience, she's working a case in Toledo when her lover, thriller writer Kit Martin, tells her a fellow crime novelist has been murdered. It's not her case, but Fiona can't help taking an interest. Which is just as well, because before too long the killer strikes again. And again. And Fiona is caught up in a race against time, not only to save a life, but to bring herself redemption, both personal and professional. Rich in atmosphere, Killing the Shadows uses the backdrops of city and country to create an air of threatening menace, culminating in a tense confrontation between hunter and hunted, a confrontation that can have only one outcome.

Killing the Shadows. unabr. ed. Val McDermid. Read by Vari Sylvester. (Running Time: 14 hrs.). 2005. 39.25 (978-1-59600-717-8(6), 9781596007178, Brlnc Audio MP3 Lib); 49.97 (978-1-59600-719-2(2), 9781596007192, BADLE); 24.95 (978-1-59600-718-5(4), 9781596007185, BAD); 24.95 (978-1-59600-716-1(8), 9781596007161, Brilliance MP3) Brilliance Audio.

***Killing the Shadows.** unabr. ed. Val McDermid. Read by Vari Sylvester. (Running Time: 17 hrs.). 2010. audio compact disk 29.99 (978-1-4418-4000-4(1), 9781441840004, Bril Audio CD Unabri); audio compact disk 89.97 (978-1-4418-4001-1(X), 9781441840011, BriAudCD Unabrid) Brilliance Audio.

Killing the Shadows. unabr. ed. Val McDermid. Read by Vari Sylvester. 12 cass. (Running Time: 18 hrs,). 2001. 94.95 (978-0-7531-1068-3(7), 010202) Pub: ISIS Audio GBR. Dist(s): Ulverscroft US
A killer is on the loose, blurring the lines between fact & fiction. His prey - the writers of crime novels. His bloodlust shatters all the conventional wisdom surrounding the motives & mechanics of how serial killers operate. For Fiona Cameron, an academic psychologist, the desperate hunt to uncover his identity becomes a matter of life & death. She soon finds herself caught in a race against time to save a life & find personal redemption.

Killing the Shadows. unabr. ed. Val McDermid. Read by Vari Sylvester. 14 CDs. (Running Time: 17 hrs. 2 mins.). (Isis (CDs) Ser.). (J). 2004. audio compact disk 104.95 (978-0-7531-2286-0(3)) Pub: ISIS Lrg Prnt GBR. Dist(s): Ulverscroft US

Killing the Spirit: Higher Education in America. unabr. ed. Page Smith. Read by Michael Wells. 8 cass. (Running Time: 11 hrs. 30 mins.). 1990. 56.95 (978-0-7861-0196-2(2), 1172) Blckstn Audio.
A fascinating narrative history of higher education, from its origins in Europe through its numerous stages of development, by the distinguished historian who gave us "A People's History of the United States.".

Killing Time. Caleb Carr. Read by Caleb Carr. 2004. 23.95 (978-0-7435-2012-6(2)) Pub: S&S Audio. Dist(s): S and S Inc

Killing Time. abr. ed. Linda Howard. Read by Joyce Bean. (Running Time: 6 hrs.). 2006. audio compact disk 16.99 (978-1-59600-857-1(1), 9781596008571, BCD Value Price) Brilliance Audio.
Please enter a Synopsis.

Killing Time. unabr. ed. Robert J. Conley. Narrated by Herb Duncan. 5 cass. (Running Time: 6 hrs. 30 mins.). 1991. 44.00 (978-1-55690-284-0(0), 91323E7) Recorded Bks.
A man seeks vengeance, but a killer hired by his intended victims is out to stop him. Marshal Bluff Luton is out for one thing & one thing only, vengeance. Toad & Jasper Jessup were spotted in Wichita County & Luton aims to make sure they never show their faces anywhere again. But the Jessup boys have hired a professional gunslinger who is no ordinary hired gun. A talkative, congenial man, he sits in a corner of the train, his steely grey eyes boring into the back of Luton's head, waiting for just the right killing time.

Killing Time. unabr. ed. Robert J. Conley. Read by Ronald Wilcox. 4 cass. (Running Time: 6 hrs.). 1995. 25.00 (978-1-883268-16-9(8), 694298) Spellbinders.
Oliver Colfax, a hired gun who admits he's out to kill Sheriff Bluff Luton yet goes so far as to save his life until he can find the right "Killing Time".

Killing Time. unabr. ed. Cynthia Harrod-Eagles. Read by Nigel Graham. 8 cass. (Running Time: 12 hrs.). (Bill Slider Mystery Ser.: No. 6). (J). 2004. 69.95 (978-0-7531-0136-0(X), 970305) Pub: ISIS Lrg Prnt GBR. Dist(s): Ulverscroft US

Killing Time. unabr. ed. Linda Howard. Read by Joyce Bean. (Running Time: 10 hrs.). 2005. 39.25 (978-1-59710-905-5(3), 9781597109055, BADLE); 24.95 (978-1-59710-904-8(5), 9781597109048, BAD); 39.25 (978-1-59335-808-2(3), 9781593358082, Brlnc Audio MP3 Lib); 32.95 (978-1-59086-178-3(7), 9781590861783, BAU); 82.25 (978-1-59086-179-0(5), 9781590861790, BrilAudUnabridg); audio compact disk 97.25 (978-1-59086-182-0(5), 9781590861820, BriAudCD Unabrid); audio compact disk 36.95 (978-1-59086-181-3(7), 9781590861813, Bril Audio CD Unabri); audio compact disk 24.95 (978-1-59335-674-3(9), 9781593356743, Brilliance MP3) Brilliance Audio.
In 1985, a time capsule was buried in the front lawn of a small town courthouse, to be reopened in 2085. But just twenty years later, in the middle of the night, the capsule is dug up and its contents stolen. And that same night, one of the contributors to the capsule is brutally slain in his home - with no sign of forced entry or indication of a struggle. One by one, the other time capsule contributors are murdered. Other than the sudden, mysterious appearance of the intriguing Nikita Stover, the local police have absolutely no leads. And while Nikita's no murderer, it's true she has plenty of secrets. With more at stake than anyone else realizes, the smart-talking Nikita is determined to catch this cunning killer...while at the same time battling her own deepening feelings for a man and a world in which she doesn't belong.

Killing Time, unabr. collector's ed. Thomas Berger. Read by Ron Shoop. 8 cass. (Running Time: 12 hrs.). 1987. 64.00 (978-0-7366-1230-2(0), 2148) Books on Tape.
The hero, Joseph Detweller, is the world's most courteous, sensitive, sincere & likable killer. He is even innocent of the fact that a crime has been committed. This tough & bizarre story breaks all the rules. it is not a whodunit, because the killer is already known. It is not a detective story or a sociological treatise on crime because it is told from the point of view of the criminal.

Killing Time: A Novel of the Future. unabr. ed. Caleb Carr. Read by Philip Goodwin. 8 vols. (Running Time: 12 hrs.). 2000. bk. 69.95 (978-0-7927-2444-5(5), CSL 333, Chivers Sound Lib) AudioGO.
Much of the world enjoys the great wealth generated by the triumph of information technology. In the year of 2023, poverty grips many countries, wars rage over natural resources & the failure of international regulatory agencies has resulted in an expanding black market in all forms of weapons including nuclear devices.

Killing Time: A Novel of the Future. unabr. ed. Caleb Carr. Read by Philip Goodwin. 10 CDs. (Running Time: 15 hrs.). 2001. audio compact disk 94.95 (978-0-7927-9999-3(2), SLD 050, Chivers Sound Lib) AudioGO.
Much of the world enjoys the great wealth generated by the triumph of information technology, in the year of 2023. Poverty grips many countries, wars rage over natural resources & the failure of international regulatory agencies has resulted in an expanding black market in all forms of weapons including nuclear devices.

Killing Touch. unabr. ed. Matt Braun. Read by Ron Varela. 4 cass. (Running Time: 6 hrs.). 2001. 26.95 (978-1-58116-070-3(4)) Books in Motion.
Joan Fallon has the power. A select few know that she can heal the sick with her hands. But only she knows that she can also bring sweet peace to the dying. Eric Hall has a mission. Someone is using their psychic powers to kill and it's his job to find out who.

Killing Wedge. unabr. ed. Jerry Ahern. Read by Alan Zimmerman. 2 vols. No. 2. 2002. (978-1-58807-505-5(2)) Am Pubng Inc.

Killing Wedge. unabr. ed. Jerry Ahern. Read by Alan Zimmerman. 3 vols. (Running Time: 4 hrs. 30 mins.). (Defender Ser.: No. 2). 2002. 22.00 (978-1-58807-022-7(0)) Am Pubng Inc.
On every street and in every major city, the battle for America is raging, and one man is caught in the killing crossfire. To the FLNA terrorists, he is the deadliest of enemies. To a gutless government, he is a dangerous fanatic. Only one thing is certain: all that stands between America and total chaos is David Holden and The Patriots. Now the ex-SEAL commando is leading his special team of freedom fighters on a blood-soaked mission to stop a sinister conspiracy, for a master assassin has Americas last hope in his lethal cross hairs. Standing between victory and death is a pull of the trigger and THE DEFENDER.

Killing Wedge. unabr. ed. Jerry Ahern. Read by Alan Zimmerman. 4 vols. No. 2. 2003. audio compact disk 28.00 (978-1-58807-264-1(9)); audio compact disk (978-1-58807-695-3(4)) Am Pubng Inc.

Killing Yourself to Live: 85% of a True Story. unabr. ed. Chuck Klosterman. Read by Patrick G. Lawlor. (Running Time: 8 hrs. 0 mins. 0 sec.). (ENG.). 2005. audio compact disk 29.99 (978-1-4001-0170-2(0)); audio compact disk 19.99 (978-1-4001-5170-7(8)); audio compact disk 59.99 (978-1-4001-3170-9(7)) Pub: Tantor Media. Dist(s): IngramPubServ

Killing Zone. abr. ed. Rex Burns. Read by Charlton Griffin. Abr. by Mary Bevoni. 2 vols. No. 7. 2003. (978-1-58807-671-7(7)) Am Pubng Inc.

Killings. unabr. collector's ed. Calvin Trillin. Read by Barrett Whitener. 6 cass. (Running Time: 6 hrs.). 1998. 36.00 (978-0-7366-4027-5(4), 4526) Books on Tape.
A renowned journalist travels to America to report on various murders.

Killings at Badger's Drift. unabr. ed. Caroline Graham. Read by Hugh Ross. 8 CDs. (Running Time: 12 hrs.). (Chief Inspector Barnaby Ser.: Bk. 1). 2002. audio compact disk 79.95 (978-0-7540-5501-3(9), CCD 192) AudioGO.

Killings at Badger's Drift. unabr. ed. Caroline Graham. Read by Hugh Ross. 8 cass. (Running Time: 12 hrs.). (Chief Inspector Barnaby Ser.: Bk. 1). 1996. 59.95 (978-0-7451-6621-6(0), CAB 1237) Pub: Chivers Audio Bks GBR. Dist(s): AudioGO
In the village of Badger's Drift, a stroll in the woods for Emily Simpson brings an abrupt end to her life. Emily sees something that she was never meant to see & someone makes sure she will never reveal it.

Killings Tale. W. A. Frankonis. 2. (Running Time: 2 hours). Dramatization. 2004. audio compact disk 16.95 (978-1-892613-12-7(3)) NYS Theatre Inst.
Serial murder stalks Shakespeare's Globe Theatre during rehearsals for MACBETH, with Shakespeare himself becoming both suspect and potential victim.WINNER OF 2004 AUDIE AWARD.

Killjoy. Ann Cleeves. Read by Gordon Griffin. 6 cass. (Running Time: 27000 sec.). (Sound Ser.). 2002. 54.95 (978-1-84283-185-4(2)) Pub: ISIS Lrg Prnt GBR. Dist(s): Ulverscroft US

Killjoy. abr. ed. Julie Garwood. Read by Joyce Bean. (Running Time: 21600 sec.). 2006. audio compact disk 16.99 (978-1-4233-1939-9(7), 9781423319399) Brilliance Audio.
Avery Delaney has tried to put the past far behind her. Abandoned by her rapacious, conniving mother when she was only three days old, Avery was raised by her grandmother and beloved aunt Carolyn. Then, when she was ten, she saw her grandmother murdered in cold blood, before Avery herself was shot and left for dead. Miraculously, she survived. The killer was soon

caught, convicted, and is currently serving a life sentence in Florida. This traumatic experience propels Avery into a life of law and order. Her razor-sharp mind and ability to gather data and decipher evidence has made Avery an expert crime analyst for the FBI. But soon she will have to use every one of her skills on a case that hits painfully close to home. Avery's workaholic aunt, Carolyn Salvetti, is certain her (hopefully soon-to-be ex-)husband sent her the gold embossed reservation to the posh Utopia Spa in the mountains of Colorado. At first she is resistant, but then she figures it will be a welcome respite from the cutthroat advertising business, not to mention a networking extravaganza. Plus she persuades her niece to join her for the two weeks of luxury and decadence. But Carolyn never makes it to Utopia. Under false pretenses, she is taken to an isolated retreat by a handsome stranger with a dazzling smile, suave demeanor, and the darkest of motives. His name is Monk, a hired assassin. Now, with scant clues and fewer resources, Avery must track down and save Carolyn - and outmaneuver a brilliant killer who is part of an elaborate plot of madness and lethal vengeance.

Killjoy. unabr. ed. Julie Garwood. Read by Joyce Bean. 8 cass. (Running Time: 12 hrs.). 2002. 34.95 (978-1-59086-239-1(2), 1590862392, BAU); audio compact disk 102.25 (978-1-59086-243-8(0), 1590862430, CD Unabrid Lib Ed); 87.25 (978-1-59086-240-7(6), 1590862406, Unabridge Lib Edns); audio compact disk 40.95 (978-1-59086-242-1(2), 1590862422, CD Unabridged) Brilliance Audio.

Killjoy. unabr. ed. Julie Garwood. Read by Joyce Bean. (Running Time: 12 hrs.). 2004. 39.25 (978-1-59335-339-1(1), 1593353391, Brinc Audio MP3 Lib) Brilliance Audio.

Killjoy. unabr. ed. Julie Garwood. Read by Joyce Bean. (Running Time: 12 hrs.). 2004. 39.25 (978-1-59710-426-5(4), 1597104264, BADLE); 24.95 (978-1-59710-427-2(2), 1597104272, BAD) Brilliance Audio.

Killjoy. unabr. ed. Julie Garwood. Read by Joyce Bean. (Running Time: 12 hrs.). 2004. 24.95 (978-1-59335-017-8(1), 1593350171) Soulmate Audio Bks.

***Killjoy-ABR.** Julie Garwood & Suspense. 2010. audio compact disk 9.99 (978-1-4418-5652-4(8)) Brilliance Audio.

Kills. Linda Fairstein. Read by Blair Brown. (Alexandra Cooper Mysteries Ser.). 2004. 15.95 (978-0-7435-3923-4(0)) Pub: S&S Audio. Dist(s): S and S Inc

Kills. unabr. ed. Linda Fairstein. 8 cass. (Running Time: 11 hrs.). (Alexandra Cooper Mysteries Ser.). 2004. 79.75 (978-1-4025-8654-5(X)) Recorded Bks.

Killshot. Elmore Leonard. Read by Bruce Boxleitner. 2 cass. (Running Time: 3 hrs.). 2001. 18.00 (978-1-59040-131-6(X), Phoenix Audio) Pub: Amer Intl Pub. Dist(s): PerseuPGW

Killshot. Elmore Leonard. Contrib. by Rider Strong. (Playaway Adult Fiction Ser.). (ENG.). 2009. 64.99 (978-1-60640-667-0(1)) Find a World.

***Killshot.** unabr. ed. Elmore Leonard. Read by Ron Mclarty. (ENG.). 2010. (978-0-06-206270-3(0), Harper Audio); (978-0-06-199380-0(8), Harper Audio) HarperCollins Pubs.

Kilmeny of the Orchard. unabr. ed. L. M. Montgomery. Read by Grace Conlin. 3 cass. (Running Time: 4 hrs. 30 min.). (YA). 1999. 23.95 (1811) Blckstn Audio.
When twenty-four-year-old Eric Marshall arrives on Prince Edward Island to become a substitute schoolmaster, he has a bright future in his wealthy family's business. Fate throws in his path a beautiful, mysterious girl named Kilmeny Gordon. She immediately captures Eric's heart. But she is mute. For the first time in his life Eric must work hard for something he wants badly...for Kilmeny to return his love.

Kilmeny of the Orchard. unabr. ed. L. M. Montgomery. Read by Grace Conlin. 3 cass. (Running Time: 4 hrs.). 2001. 23.95 (978-0-7861-1039-1(2), 1811) Blckstn Audio.

***Kilo Class.** abr. ed. Patrick Robinson. Read by Stephen Lang. (ENG.). 2004. (978-0-06-081833-3(6), Harper Audio); (978-0-06-081836-4(0), Harper Audio) HarperCollins Pubs.

Kilo Class, unabr. ed. Patrick Robinson. Narrated by George Guidall. 11 cass. (Running Time: 16 hrs.). 1998. 96.00 (978-0-7887-1974-5(2), 95361E7) Recorded Bks.
China is purchasing Kilo class submarines in an attempt to close nearby international waters. Determined to keep the seas open, the U.S. Navy sends out secret Black Op squads on missions so dangerous, one mistake could set off World War III.

Kilo Class. unabr. ed. Patrick Robinson. Narrated by George Guidall. 14 CDs. (Running Time: 16 hrs.). 2000. audio compact disk 134.00 (978-0-7887-4467-9(4), C1164E7) Recorded Bks.

Kilu Mammo see Silly Mammo: An Ethiopian Tale

Kim. Rudyard Kipling. 2007. 27.95 (978-1-60112-014-4(1)) Babblebooks.

Kim. Rudyard Kipling. Narrated by Walter Covell. (Running Time: 12 hrs.). 1982. 54.95 (978-1-59912-859-7(4)) Iofy Corp.

Kim. Rudyard Kipling. Read by Madhav Sharma. (Running Time: 3 hrs.). 1998. 20.95 (978-1-60083-798-2(0)) Iofy Corp.

Kim. Rudyard Kipling. Read by Walter Covell. 8 cass. (Running Time: 12 hrs.). 1989. 48.00 incl. album. (C-107) Jimcin Record.
High adventure in far-off India.

Kim. Rudyard Kipling. Read by Madhav P. Sharma. 2 cass. (Running Time: 3 hrs.). 1994. 28.98 (978-962-634-518-4(7), NA201814, Naxos AudioBooks) Naxos.
Set in the days of the British Raj, this is a tale of an Irish orphan-boy who has lived free in the streets of Lahore before setting out, with a Tibetan Lama, on a double quest.

Kim. Rudyard Kipling. 1 cass. (Running Time: 53 min.). Dramatization. 10.95 (978-0-8045-1065-3(2), SAC 1065) Spoken Arts.

Kim. abr. ed. Rudyard Kipling. Read by Madhav P. Sharma. 2 CDs. (Running Time: 3 hrs.). (J). 1994. audio compact disk 17.98 (978-962-634-018-9(5), NA201812, Naxos AudioBooks) Naxos.

Kim. adpt. ed. Rudyard Kipling. (Bring the Classics to Life Ser.). (ENG.). 2008. audio compact disk 12.95 (978-1-55576-580-4(7)) EDCON Pubng.

Kim. unabr. ed. Rudyard Kipling. Read by Sam Dastor. 8 cass. (Running Time: 12 hrs.). (gr. 3-5). 1999. 34.95 (978-1-57270-112-0(9), F81112u) Pub: Audio Partners. Dist(s): PerseuPGW
An Irish ophan becomes a disciple of a Tibetan Lama & is later enlisted into the Great Game, the dangerous world of British espionage.

Kim. unabr. ed. Rudyard Kipling. (Running Time: 10 hrs. 50 mins.). (ENG.). 2009. 29.95 (978-1-4332-8974-6(6)); 65.95 (978-1-4332-8973-6(3)); audio compact disk 100.00 (978-1-4332-8974-3(1)); audio compact disk 19.95 (978-1-4332-8976-7(8)) Blckstn Audio.

Kim. unabr. ed. Rudyard Kipling. Read by Ben Cross. 2 cass. (Read-Along Ser.). (J). 34.95 Incl. read-along bk., learner's guide & exercises. (S23923) J Norton Pubs.

Kim, unabr. ed. Rudyard Kipling. Narrated by Margaret Hilton. 10 pieces. (Running Time: 13 hrs. 30 mins.). (gr. 4 up). 1988. 85.00 (978-1-55690-285-7(9), 88720E7) Recorded Bks.
Story of the orphan son of an Irish soldier in 19th-century India & his adventures as a British secret agent among the bazaars, princesses, soldiers & mysterious holy men.

***Kim.** unabr. ed. Rudyard Kipling. Narrated by Simon Vance. (Running Time: 10 hrs. 30 mins.). 2010. 16.99 (978-1-4001-8567-2(X)) Tantor Media.

***Kim.** unabr. ed. Rudyard Kipling. Narrated by Simon Vance. (Running Time: 10 hrs. 30 mins. 0 sec.). (ENG.). 2010. 22.99 (978-1-4001-6567-4(9)); audio compact disk 65.99 (978-1-4001-4567-6(8)); audio compact disk 32.99 (978-1-4001-1567-9(1)) Pub: Tantor Media. Dist(s): IngramPubServ

Kim. unabr. collector's ed. Rudyard Kipling. Read by Stuart Langton. 8 cass. (Running Time: 12 hrs.). (J). 1998. 64.00 (978-0-7366-4153-1(X), 4656) Books on Tape.
A boy is orphaned in India & his life on the streets involves him in espionage.

Kim, Set. Rudyard Kipling. Read by Flo Gibson. 7 cass. (Running Time: 10 hrs. 30 min.). 1995. 25.95 (978-1-55685-371-5(8)) Audio Bk Con.
Kimball O'Hara, an Irish orphan, is raised in Lahore by an Indian woman. When his parentage is discovered he is, to his regret, sent to a British school, but returns to his wanderings with an old llama & to heroic adventures.

***Kim: Bring the Classics to Life.** adpt. ed. Rudyard Kipling. (Bring the Classics to Life Ser.). 2008. pap. bk. 21.95 (978-1-55576-650-4(1)) EDCON Pubng.

Kim - Kimi, unabr. ed. Hadley Irwin. Narrated by Christina Moore. 4 pieces. (Running Time: 5 hrs. 30 mins.). (gr. 4 up). 1997. 35.00 (978-0-7887-0685-1(3), 94859E7) Recorded Bks.
Kim Andrews' mother is American; her father who died before she was born, was Japanese. Unless she can locate her father's family, she will be isolated from a part of who she is.

Kim Hill. Perf. by Kim Hill. 1 cass. 1988. audio compact disk Brentwood Music.
The best selling Christian debut of that era, this self-titled debut release features the classics, Psalm One, Refuge & Faithful.

Kim, Kari & Kevin Storybook. Kay Kuzma. 1 cass. (Running Time: 60 min.). (J). 5.95 (978-0-910529-08-2(6)) Family Mtrs.
Features non-fiction for children.

Kim, Kari & Kevin's Winning Ways. Kay Kuzma. Read by Kay Kuzma. 1 cass. (Running Time: 1 hr.). (J). 5.95 (978-0-910529-09-9(4)) Family Mtrs.

Kim Robertson - Treasures of the Celtic Harp. Kim Robertson. 1999. pap. bk. 27.95 (978-0-7866-4039-3(1), 97226CDP) Mel Bay.

Kim Robertson - Treasures of the Celtic Harp. Kim Robertson. 2002. bk. 27.95 (978-0-7866-6622-5(6), 97226BCD) Mel Bay.

Kim Williams: A Missoula Sampler. Comment by Kim Williams. 1 cass. (Running Time: 60 min.). 11.95 (G0100B090, HarperThor) HarpC GBR.

Kimberley Sun. Di Morrissey. Read by Kate Hood. (Running Time: 14 hrs. 40 mins.). 2009. 104.99 (978-1-74214-262-3(1), 9781742142623) Pub: Bolinda Pubng AUS. Dist(s): Bolinda Pub Inc

Kimberly Sun. unabr. ed. Di Morrissey. Read by Kate Hood. (Running Time: 53100 sec.). 2006. audio compact disk 113.95 (978-1-74093-794-8(5)) Pub: Bolinda Pubng AUS. Dist(s): Bolinda Pub Inc

Kimera: Soundtrack. 1 CD. 2003. audio compact disk 14.98 (978-1-57813-342-0(4), CKM/001) ADV.

Kimidori Character CD. Perf. by Yuri Shimatori. (YA). 2007. 9.98 (978-1-59409-851-2(4)) Bandai Ent.

Kinch. Matt Braun. Narrated by Jack Garrett. 6 CDs. (Running Time: 6 hrs. 30 mins.). 2000. audio compact disk 58.00 (978-0-7887-4763-2(0), C1256E7) Recorded Bks.
In the summer of 1871, gunfire erupted in Newton, Kansas. In just 90 seconds, six men were dead. The man responsible for most of them was a consumptive 17-year-old named Kinch Riley. Although Riley disappeared after this battle, his name lives on in Western lore.

Kinch. unabr. ed. Matt Braun. Narrated by Jack Garrett. 5 cass. (Running Time: 6 hrs. 30 mins.). 2000. 46.00 (978-0-7887-4070-1(9), 95766E7) Recorded Bks.

***Kind of Acquaintance.** David Armstrong. 2010. 61.95 (978-1-4079-0977-6(0)); audio compact disk 71.95 (978-1-4079-0978-3(9)) Pub: Soundings Ltd GBR. Dist(s): Ulverscroft US

Kind of Blue. Perf. by Miles Davis. 1 cass., 1 CD. 6.38 (CBS 64935); audio compact disk 9.58 CD Jewel box. (CBS 64935) NewSound.

***Kind of Friends We Used to Be.** unabr. ed. Frances O'Roark Dowell. Narrated by Jessica Almasy. 4 cass. (Running Time: 4 hrs. 45 mins.). (J). (gr. 5-7). 2009. 51.75 (978-1-4361-7200-4(4)); audio compact disk 66.75 (978-1-4361-7204-2(7)) Recorded Bks.

Kind of Grace: The Autobiography of the World's Greatest Female Athlete. abr. ed. Jackie Joyner-Kersee & Sonja Steptoe. (Running Time: 1 hr. 30 mins.). (ENG.). 2006. 14.98 (978-1-59483-658-9(2)) Pub: Hachet Audio. Dist(s): HachBkGrp

Kind of Immortality. unabr. ed. Margaret Thomson Davis. Narrated by Jean Simmons. 10 cass. (Running Time: 13 hrs. 30 mins.). 1999. 89.00 (978-1-84197-025-7(5), H1024E7) Recorded Bks.
Bessie is stuck in a misfit, loveless marriage to her father's accountant, due to a mistake made many years ago. Her husband & strict Quaker family object vehemently to her only joy, her painting, but local art dealer Gregory Seymour has a different view - of Bessie & her work. Jennifer is also unhappy at home, due to the latest of her mother's long stream of lovers. When violence erupts, she runs away to London, yet she finds herself drawn back to Bessie, of all people & her connection to the older woman.

Kind of People that God Uses. Jack Deere. 1 cass. (Running Time: 90 mins.). (Receiving Spiritual Gifts Ser.: Vol. 4). 2000. 5.00 (JD03-004) Morning NC.
This is a powerful debunking of arguments against the use of spiritual gifts & reveals major hindrances to believers walking in the power of God.

Kind of Silence, Program 12. Read by Juan Rulfo. (F007FB090) Natl Public Radio.

***Kind of Stopwatch.** (ENG.). 2010. audio compact disk (978-1-59171-150-6(9)) Falcon Picture.

Kind One. unabr. ed. Tom Epperson. (Running Time: 11 hrs. 5 mins.). 2009. 29.95 (978-1-4332-5986-9(9)); audio compact disk 29.95 (978-1-4332-5985-2(0)); audio compact disk 90.00 (978-1-4332-5983-8(4)); audio compact disk 72.95 (978-1-4332-5982-1(6)) Blckstn Audio.

Kinda. Read by Peter Davison. 2001. 9.99 (978-0-563-38831-9(5)) London Brdge.

Kinder lernen Deutsch Lieder aus der Loseblattsammlung CD. Perf. by Brigitte Jonen-Dittmar & Laureen Sherman.Tr. of Children learn German - Songs from the Collection CD. (GER.). (J). 2004. audio compact disk 20.00 (978-1-932737-01-1(4)) Amer Assn Teach German.

Kinder Lernen Deutsch Liederheft. Brigitte Jonen-Dittmar & Laureen Sherman. 1 cass. 1994. pap. bk. 15.00 (978-0-942017-18-2(8)) Amer Assn Teach German.

Kindergarten Book: If Only You Knew How Your Mommy Missed You When You Left for Kindergarten. S. A. Blackman. Illus. by Judith Kneen Petz. (J). (ps-1). 2002. 29.99 (978-1-929409-12-9(5), 500) Blade Pubg.
The first day of kindergarten has finally arrived but mommy is having trouble letting go. Should she wait in the car. Hide behind a tree to catch a glimpse of her little one at lunch. A touching, humorous, vividly illustrated tale of a mother learning to let go.

Kindling the Flame of Enlightenment. Read by Osel Tendzin. 3 cass. 1977. 31.50 (A063) Vajradhatu.
Four talks: 1) Mahayana, Training to be Genuine; 2) Discovery of Buddha-Nature; 3) Making Friends with Self & Other; 4) Skillful Means.

Kindly Ones. unabr. ed. Jonathan Littell. Read by Grover Gardner. Tr. by Charlotte Mandell. 31 CDs. (Running Time: 39 hrs.). Orig. Title: Les Bienveillantes. 2009. audio compact disk 159.00 (978-1-4332-7916-4(9)) Blckstn Audio.

Kindly Ones. unabr. ed. Jonathan Littell. Tr. by Charlotte Mandell. (Running Time: 32 hrs. 0 mins.). Orig. Title: Les Bienveillantes. 2009. 44.95 (978-1-4332-7919-5(3)) Blckstn Audio.

***Kindly Ones.** unabr. ed. Jonathan Littell. Read by Grover Gardner. Orig. Title: Les Bienveillantes. (ENG.). 2009. (978-0-06-189092-5(8), Harper Audio); (978-0-06-189651-4(9), Harper Audio) HarperCollins Pubs.

Kindly Ones, Part A. unabr. ed. Jonathan Littell. Tr. by Charlotte Mandell. (Running Time: 32 hrs. 0 mins.). Orig. Title: Les Bienveillantes. 2009. 95.95 (978-1-4332-7915-7(0)) Blckstn Audio.

Kindly Ones, Part B. unabr. ed. Jonathan Littell. Tr. by Charlotte Mandell. (Running Time: 32 hrs. 0 mins.). Orig. Title: Les Bienveillantes. 2009. 79.95 (978-1-4332-8767-1(6)) Blckstn Audio.

Kindly Ones- Audio CD: No. 7 in the River Road Poetry Series. Susan Hampton. Read by Susan Hampton. Executive Producer Carol Jenkins. (ENG.). 2008. audio compact disk 18.00 (978-0-9804148-6-8(5)) RivRoad AUS.

Kindness & Friendliness. Linda Eyre & Richard Eyre. 2 cass. (Running Time: 3 hrs.). (Teaching Your Children Values Ser.). (J). (ps-7). 2000. pap. bk. 16.95 (978-1-56015-794-6(1)) Penton Overseas.
Tape 1: a coaching, "how-to" program for parents; Tape 2: "Alexander's Amazing Adventures" program featuring stories, songs, sound effects & background music, that helps children ages 4-12 to develop social skills, communication skills & life skills. Includes activity cards.

Kindness & Joy: Expressing the Gentle Love. Harold G. Koenig. (Running Time: 4740 sec.). 2006. audio compact disk 19.95 (978-1-59947-108-2(6)) Pub: Templeton Pr. Dist(s): Chicago Distribution Ctr

Kindness of Healing. Kenneth Wapnick. 2 CDs. 2003. audio compact disk 10.00 (978-1-59142-115-3(2), CD54) Foun Miracles.
The Course's teaching that both sickness and healing are in the mind is often misunderstood, leading students to deny their own pain and illness, bypass treatment, and to deal harshly with others, thus negating Jesus' gentle approach throughout the Course. In this class, the principles of sickness and healing and their common misapplications are discussed. Students are therefore helped to learn that being faithful to the Course's principles means at the same time being faithful to the love that is the source of Jesus' kind of message.

***Kindness of Mrs. Radcliffe.** abr. ed. Noel Coward. Read by Simon Jones. (ENG.). 2006. (978-0-06-125291-4(3), Harper Audio) HarperCollins Pubs.

Kindness of Women, unabr. collector's ed. J. G. Ballard. Read by David Case. 8 cass. (Running Time: 12 hrs.). 1996. 64.00 (978-0-7366-3518-9(1), 4155) Books on Tape.
Begins in Shanghai toward the close of the war. Young James goes from the prison camp to England, a wrenching change. It takes years - through prep school, medical school & the Royal Air Force - for him to find his balance. He finally settles into a happy period of family life.But a sudden tragedy shatters his idyllic world & James falls headlong into the craze of the 1960s. It's through the kindness of women in his life that he's led to confront the traumas of his childhood.

Kindness/Living Your Capacity. Marianne Williamson. Read by Marianne Williamson. 1 cass. (Running Time: 90 mins.). (Lectures on a Course in Miracles). 1999. 10.00 (978-1-56170-238-1(2), M741) Hay House.

Kindred. unabr. ed. Octavia E. Butler. Narrated by Kim Staunton. 8 cass. (Running Time: 11 hrs.). 1998. 72.00 (978-0-7887-2180-9(1), 95476E7) Recorded Bks.
As a young African-American woman is repeatedly wrenched through time from her modern California home to antebellum Maryland, she realizes that she has been given a mission - one that could affect her very existence.

Kindred in Death. abr. ed. J. D. Robb, pseud. Read by Susan Ericksen. 5 CDs. (Running Time: 6 hrs.). (In Death Ser.). 2010. audio compact disk 9.99 (978-1-4233-8383-3(4), 9781423383833, BCD Value Price) Brilliance Audio.

Kindred in Death. unabr. ed. J. D. Robb, pseud. Read by Susan Ericksen. 1 MP3-CD. (Running Time: 13 hrs.). (In Death Ser.). 2009. 39.97 (978-1-4233-8379-6(6), 9781423383796, Brinc Audio MP3 Lib); 24.99 (978-1-4233-8378-9(8), 9781423383789, Brilliance MP3); 24.99 (978-1-4233-8380-2(X), 9781423383802, BAD); 39.97 (978-1-4233-8381-9(8), 9781423383819, BADLE); audio compact disk 38.99 (978-1-4233-8376-5(1), 9781423383765, Bril Audio CD Unabri); audio compact disk 99.97 (978-1-4233-8377-2(X), 9781423383772, BriAudCD Unabrid) Brilliance Audio.

Kindred Souls. Edna P. Gurewitsch. Narrated by Bernadette Dunne. (Running Time: 10 hrs. 30 mins.). 2003. 34.95 (978-1-59912-524-4(2)) Iofy Corp.

Kindred Souls. unabr. ed. Edna P. Gurewitsch. Read by Bernadette Dunne. 8 cass. (Running Time: 11 hrs. 30 mins.). 2003. 56.95 (978-0-7861-2556-2(X), 3163); audio compact disk 72.00 (978-0-7861-9097-3(3), 3163) Blckstn Audio.

Kindred Spirits. Bonnie Rideout. 2002. bk. 24.95 (978-0-7866-6632-4(3), 98278BCD) Mel Bay.

Kindred Spirits: A Musical Portrait of Scotland's Women. 2000. audio compact disk 15.98 (978-0-7866-4683-8(7), 98278CD) Mel Bay.

Kinemage Supplement to Introduction to Protein Structure. 2nd rev. ed. Jane S. Richardson & David C. Richardson. 1999. cd-rom 44.00 (978-0-8153-3326-5(9)) Taylor and Fran.

Kinesen see Man from Beijing

Kinetic City Super Crew. 1 CD. (Running Time: 1 hr.). 2001. audio compact disk 15.95 (KCSC001); audio compact disk 15.95 (KCSC002); audio compact disk 15.95 (KCSC023) Lodestone Catalog.

King & Priest. Featuring Bill Winston. 2. 2002. audio compact disk 16.00 (978-1-59544-059-4(3)) Pub: B Winston Min. Dist(s): Anchor Distributors
Where there is no vision (Revelation Knowledge), the people perish! Pastor Bill Winston shares a prophetic word in this powerful teaching on Kings & Priests. These two royalties work together to manifest the Kingdom of God in the earth.One gets the vision, the other gathers the porvision. Do you know which one you are? Find out today by ordering Kings & Priests.

King & the Cowboy: Theodore Roosevelt & Edward the Seventh, Secret Partners. unabr. ed. David Fromkin. (Running Time: 6 hrs. 0 mins. 0 sec.). (ENG.). 2008. audio compact disk 59.99 (978-1-4001-3966-8(X)); audio compact disk 19.99 (978-1-4001-5966-6(0)) Pub: Tantor Media. Dist(s): IngramPubServ

King & the Cowboy: Theodore Roosevelt & Edward the Seventh, Secret Partners. unabr. ed. David Fromkin. (Running Time: 6 hrs. 0 mins. 0 sec.). (ENG.). 2008. audio compact disk 29.99 (978-1-4001-0966-1(3)) Pub: Tantor Media. Dist(s): IngramPubServ

***King & the Thrush: Tales of Goodness & Greed.** unabr. ed. As told by Tim Jennings & Leanne Ponder. 1 CD. (Running Time: 49 mins.). (J). (gr. 1 up). 2010. audio compact disk 12.00 (978-0-9793554-4-8(3)) Eastern Coyote.

King Arthur. unabr. ed. Marc Brown. Read by Mark Linn-Baker. Text by Stephen Krensky. 1 cass. (Running Time: 41 mins.). (Arthur Chapter Bks.: Bk. 13). (J). (gr. 2-4). 2004. pap. bk. 17.00 (978-0-8072-0344-6(0), Listening Lib) Random Audio Pubg.

King Arthur. unabr. ed. Sbc118 Cae. 4 cass. Incl. Excalibur. (J). (SBC 118); Story of Sir Galahad. (J). (SBC 118); Story of Sir Lancelot. (J). (SBC 118); Sword in the Anvil. (J). (SBC 118); (J). 1985. 29.95 (978-0-89845-020-0(9), SBC 118) HarperCollins Pubs.

King Arthur, Set. unabr. ed. 4 cass. (J). 1985. HarperCollins Pubs.

King Arthur & Chivalry, Pts. I-II. Instructed by Bonnie Wheeler. 12 CDs. (Running Time: 12 hrs.). 2000. audio compact disk 179.95 (978-1-56585-294-5(X)) Teaching Co.

King Arthur & Chivalry, Pts. I-II, Vol. 1. Instructed by Elizabeth Vandiver. 12 cass. (Running Time: 12 hrs.). 2000. 129.95 (978-1-56585-039-2(4)) Teaching Co.

King Arthur & Chivalry, Vol. 2. Instructed by Elizabeth Vandiver. 6 cass. (Running Time: 6 hrs.). 2000. 129.95 (978-1-56585-040-8(8)) Teaching Co.

King Arthur & Chivalry, Vol. 2. Instructed by Bonnie Wheeler. 6 CDs. (Running Time: 6 hrs.). 2000. audio compact disk 179.95 (978-1-56585-295-2(8)) Teaching Co.

King Arthur & His Knights. Read by Jim Weiss. 1 cass. (J). (gr. 2-8). 1999. 9.95 (1124-06); audio compact disk 14.95 (1124-006) Greathall Prods.

King Arthur & His Knights. Short Stories. As told by Jim Weiss. 1 cass. (Running Time: 1 hour). Dramatization. (Storyteller's Version Ser.). (J). (gr. k up). 1990. 10.95 (978-1-882513-06-2(1), 1124-06); audio compact disk 14.95 (978-1-882513-31-4(2), 1124-006) Greathall Prods.
Brings King Arthur and His Knights to life with action and grandeur, at a level which children can really grasp. Includes: "The Sword in the Stone," "King Arthur, Guinevere," "Sir Percival Meets a Lady," "The Round Table," "Sir Lancelot's Journey," "A Queen," "Sir Bedivere" and "Merlin's Magic".

King Arthur & His Knights. Read by Jim Weiss. 1 cass., CD. (Running Time: 1 hr.). (J). (GHP6) NewSound.

King Arthur & His Knights. unabr. ed. Read by Jim Weiss. 1 cass. (Running Time: 60 mins.). (J). 2000. 9.86 Books on Tape.
Once there was a spot known as Camelot and now young listeners can hear some of it's magical and enchanting stories.

King Arthur & Knights at the Round Table. Benedict Flynn. Read by Sean Bean. (Running Time: 2 hrs. 30 mins.). 2001. 20.95 (978-1-60083-799-9(9)) Iofy Corp.

King Arthur & Other Kings see Roi Arthur et Autres Rois

King Arthur & the Knights of the Round Table. unabr. ed. Benedict Flynn. Read by Sean Bean. (J). 2007. 39.99 (978-1-60252-505-4(6)) Find a World.

King Arthur & the Knights of the Round Table. unabr. ed. Benedict Flynn. Read by Sean Bean. 2 cass. (Running Time: 2 hrs. 29 mins.). (J). 1997. 13.98 (978-962-634-638-9(8), NA213814, Naxos AudioBooks) Naxos.
The heroic King Arthur, the wizard, Merlin, the brave Sir Lancelot, the beautiful Guinevere and the evil Morgana le Fey - and its exciting, magical plot will enchant the younger listener in this version especially for children.

King Arthur & the Knights of the Round Table. unabr. ed. Benedict Flynn. Read by Sean Bean. 2 CDs. (Running Time: 2 hrs. 29 mins.). (Junior Classics Ser.). (J). (gr. 3-8). 1997. audio compact disk 17.98 (978-962-634-138-4(6), NA213812) Naxos.
The heroic King Arthur, the wizard Merlin, the brave Sir Lancelot, the beautiful Guinevere and evil Morgana le Fey - and its exciting, magical plot will enchant the younger listener in this version especially for children.

King Arthur Collection. unabr. abr. ed. Howard Pyle. Read by Ian Richardson. 2004. audio compact disk 25.95 (978-0-06-073934-8(7)) HarperCollins Pubs.

***King Balak Curse Maker, King Jesus Curse Breaker.** Katie Souza. (ENG.). 2011. audio compact disk 10.00 (978-0-7684-0261-2(1)) Pub: Expected End. Dist(s): Destiny Image Pubs

King Bidgood's in the Bathtub. Audrey Wood & Distribution Media Staff. (J). 1986. pap. bk. 21.26 (978-0-676-31644-5(1)) RandomHse Pub.

King Charlie. unabr. collector's ed. Max Brand. Read by Jonathan Marosz. 7 cass. (Running Time: 7 hrs.). 1995. 42.00 (978-0-7366-2991-1(2), 3680) Books on Tape.
A young, gunslinging thrill-seeker joins a gang of train tramps who adopt an orphaned girl.

King Cohn: The Life & Times of Hollywood Mogul Harry Cohn. abr. ed. Bob Thomas. Read by John Landis. 4 cass. (Running Time: 6 hrs.). 2004. 25.00 (978-1-931056-00-7(5), N Millennium Audio) New Millenn Enter.
Harry Cohn was a self-invented tyrant who ran Columbia Studios as his personal fiefdom. Extensive reviews & research fuel the author's portrayal of a Broadway song plugger turned powerful player.

King Cohn: The Life & Times of Hollywood Mogul Harry Cohn. unabr. ed. Bob Thomas. Read by John Landis. 8 cass. (Running Time: 12 hrs.). (Hollywood Classics Ser.). 2004. 35.00 (978-1-59007-013-0(5)) Pub: New Millenn Enter. Dist(s): PerseuPGW
Details the mogul's rise from New York City song plugger - to Poverty Row impresario - to one of the most powerful men in Hollywood during the studio's golden era.

King Con. unabr. ed. Stephen J. Cannell. Read by Stephen J. Cannell. 4 cass. (Running Time: 6 hrs.). 2002. 12.99 (978-1-57815-291-9(7), 4437, Media Bks Audio); audio compact disk 14.99 (978-1-57815-548-4(7), 4437CD5, Media Bks Audio) Media Bks NJ.
Beano Bates is King Con to his fellow grifters. con-artist extraordinaire with a taste for the fast life. When he runs afoul of mob boss Joe "Dancer" Rina, he wants not only to save his skin but also to pursue his own unique brand of justice.

King David. Jonathan Kirsch. Read by Jonathan Kirsch. 2000. audio compact disk 80.00 (978-0-7366-6867-5(5)) Books on Tape.

King David. unabr. ed. Jonathan Kirsch. 10 CDs. (Running Time: 15 hrs.). 2001. audio compact disk 80.00 Books on Tape.
The real story of David, King of the Jews, his greatness & his weaknesses, a hero of flesh & blood.

King David. unabr. collector's ed. Jonathan Kirsch. Read by Jonathan Kirsch. 8 cass. (Running Time: 12 hrs.). 2000. 64.00 (978-0-7366-5596-5(4)) Books on Tape.

King Dork. unabr. ed. Frank Portman. Read by Lincoln Hoppe. 8 cass. (Running Time: 11 hrs. 57 mins.). (J). (gr. 4-7). 2006. 55.00 (978-0-7393-3125-5(6), Listening Lib); audio compact disk 70.00 (978-0-7393-3123-1(X), Listening Lib) Pub: Random Audio Pubg. Dist(s): Random

King Dork. unabr. ed. Frank Portman. Read by Lincoln Hoppe. 10 CDs. (Running Time: 43800 sec.). (ENG.). (J). (gr. 5-12). 2006. audio compact disk 48.00 (978-0-7393-3113-2(2), Listening Lib) Pub: Random Audio Pubg. Dist(s): Random

King Fisher's Road. unabr. ed. Shepard Rifkin. Narrated by John Randolph Jones. 5 cass. (Running Time: 6 hrs. 15 mins.). 1992. 44.00 (978-1-55690-684-8(6), 92108E7) Recorded Bks.
Kirby Fisher survived an Apache attack to become the most respected & feared man in the territory. Beating all the odds, there was no one left to oppose him. Then a man named Carson is dropped, more dead than alive, into King's life. Tough & intelligent, Carson is the first man King has come across in years who can offer him any kind of a fight. But Carson isn't ready, not yet. King will nurse him along until the greenhorn is ripe to turn his wits & his gun against the very man who created him.

King for Brass Cobweb. 1 cass. (Running Time: 052 mins.). (J). (ps-3). 2001. 9.95 (978-0-89084-903-3(X), 080119) BJUPr.

King for Brass Cobweb, Set. Dawn L. Watkins. (J). (ps-3). 2000. pap. bk. 14.98 (978-0-89084-904-0(8), 100073) BJUPr.

King for Kids: School & Family Edition. abr. ed. Ed. by Clayborne Carson. Contrib. by Martin Luther King, Jr. 2 CDs. (Running Time: 3 hrs.). (ENG.). 2008. audio compact disk 19.98 (978-1-60024-098-0(4)) Pub: Hachet Audio. Dist(s): HachBkGrp

King for Kids: School & Family Edition. unabr. abr. ed. Ed. by Clayborne Carson. (Running Time: 3 hrs.). (ENG.). 2008. 14.98 (978-1-60024-099-7(2)) Pub: Hachet Audio. Dist(s): HachBkGrp

King Henry IV: The Shadow of Succesion. William Shakespeare. Contrib. by Harry Althaus et al. (Playaway Young Adult Ser.). (YA). (gr. 8-12). 2008. 39.99 (978-1-60640-632-8(9)) Find a World.

King Henry IV: The Shadow of Succession. William Shakespeare. Contrib. by Harry Althaus et al. Adapted by David Bevington & Charles Newell. (Running Time: 7140 sec.). 2008. audio compact disk 25.95 (978-1-58081-378-5(X)) Pub: L A Theatre. Dist(s): NetLibrary CO

King Henry IV: The Shadow of Succession. unabr. ed. William Shakespeare. Perf. by Nicholas Rudall et al. 1 cass. (Running Time: 2 hrs.). 1997. 22.95 (978-1-58081-028-9(4), CTA58) L A Theatre.
Drama of a young man who can only come into his own with his father's death, & the father who longs to live on in the immortal mirror of his son. The deeply personal story of Prince Hal's coming of age & explores his relationships with his own two father figures, the mistrusting King Henry IV & the irrepressible Falstaff.

King Hit: Words & Music. Stephen Oliver. Illus. by Matt Ottley. Composed by Matt Ottley. 2007. audio compact disk 16.00 (978-1-876819-70-5(7), IP Digital AUS) Pub: Interactive Pubns AUS. Dist(s): CD Baby

King is Coming: Best of Bill Gaither. Bill Gaither Trio Staff. 2002. audio compact disk Provident Mus Dist.

King James Bible. Narrated by James Earl Jones. 12 cass. (Proven Wisdom Ser.). (ENG.). 2003. 29.99 (978-1-58926-359-8(6)) Oasis Audio.

King James Bible. unabr. ed. 2005. 47.99 (978-1-58926-862-3(8), 6862); audio compact disk 47.99 (978-1-58926-863-0(6), 6863) Pub: Oasis Audio. Dist(s): TNT Media Grp

King James Bible. unabr. ed. Narrated by James Earl Jones. 16 CDs. (Running Time: 19 hrs.). (Proven Wisdom Ser.). (ENG.). 2003. audio compact disk 34.99 (978-1-58926-360-4(X)) Oasis Audio.

King James Bible. unabr. ed. Read by Alexander Scourby. 15 CDs. (Running Time: 22 hrs. 30 mins.). 2001. audio compact disk 74.95 Books on Tape.
It is, by all accounts, one of his greatest lifelong achievements. Alexander Scourby's dramatic and moving narration of the Bible has touched and inspired millions. It is for that reason he is known as "the voice of the Word".

King James Bible New Testament. unabr. ed. 2005. 29.99 (978-1-58926-860-9(1), 6860); audio compact disk 29.99 (978-1-58926-861-6(X), 6861) Pub: Oasis Audio. Dist(s): TNT Media Grp

King James Version Bible. Narrated by Paul Mims. 48 cass. - 4 albums. 1996. vinyl bd. 99.99 (978-1-58968-002-9(2), 1025A); 84.97 (978-1-58968-006-7(5), 1015S) Chrstn Dup Intl.

King James Version Bible. Narrated by Paul Mims. 48 cass. (Running Time: 48 hrs.). 1995. vinyl bd. 99.99 incl. carrying case with handle. (978-1-58968-003-6(0), 1013H) Chrstn Dup Intl.
The complete authorized King James Version of the Bible.

King James Version Bible: The New Testament. Braun Media LLC. (ENG.). 2008. 1.00 (978-1-59987-646-7(9)) Braun Media.

King James Version Bible: The Old Testament First Chronicles to Malachi. Braun Media LLC. (ENG.). 2008. 1.00 (978-1-59987-645-0(0)) Braun Media.

King James Version Bible: The Old Testament Genesis to Second Kings. Braun Media Staff. 2008. 1.00 (978-1-59987-644-3(2)) Braun Media.

King James Version Bible Psalms. Narrated by Paul Mims. 4 cass. - sleeve. 1996. 9.97 (978-1-58968-007-4(3), 1102S) Chrstn Dup Intl.

King James Version Complete Bible. deluxe ed. Read by Paul Mims. 61 CDs - 4 albums. 1997. vinyl bd. 189.99 (978-1-58968-015-9(4)) Chrstn Dup Intl.

King James Version Complete Bible (Spoken Word) deluxe ed. Read by Paul Mims. 64 cass. - albums. 1997. vinyl bd. 129.97 (978-1-58968-012-8(X)) Chrstn Dup Intl.

King James Version Holy Bible - the New Testament: New Testament. unabr. ed. King James Version. Read by George Vafiadis. (YA). 2006. 59.99 (978-1-59895-666-5(3)) Find a World.

King James Version Holy Bible - the Old Testament: Old Testament. unabr. ed. King James Version. Read by George Vafiadis. (YA). 2006. 79.99 (978-1-59895-667-2(1)) Find a World.

King James Version New Testament. deluxe ed. Read by Paul Mims. 1997. audio compact disk 59.99 (978-1-58968-014-2(6)) Chrstn Dup Intl.

King James Version New Testament & Psalms Bible. Narrated by Paul Mims. 16 cass. - sleeve. (Running Time: 16 hrs.). 1996. 29.97 twin-pak with full-color sleeves. (978-1-58968-008-1(1), 1018S) Chrstn Dup Intl.
The King James Version of the New Testament & Psalms.

King James Version New Testament Bible. Narrated by Paul Mims. 12 cass. - album. 1996. vinyl bd. 29.99 (978-1-58968-001-2(4), 1006A); 24.97 (978-1-58968-005-0(7), 1016S) Chrstn Dup Intl.

King James Version New Testament Bible(Spoken Word) deluxe ed. Narrated by Paul Mims. 16 cass. - album. 1996. vinyl bd. 39.97 (978-1-58968-010-4(3), 1004A) Chrstn Dup Intl.

King James Version of the Bible: Ecclesiastes see Cambridge Treasy Malory

King James Version Old Testament. deluxe ed. Read by Paul Mims. 45 CDs - 2 albums. 1997. vinyl bd. 159.99 (978-1-58968-013-5(8)) Chrstn Dup Intl.

King James Version Old Testament Bible. Narrated by Paul Mims. 36 cass. - 3 albums. 1996. vinyl bd. 79.99 (978-1-58968-000-5(6), 1005A); 69.97 (978-1-58968-004-3(9), 1016S) Chrstn Dup Intl.

King James Version Old Testament Bible (Spoken Word) deluxe ed. Narrated by Paul Mims. 48 cass. 1996. vinyl bd. 99.97 (978-1-58968-009-8(X), 1003A) Chrstn Dup Intl.

King James Version Psalms & Proverbs. deluxe ed. Read by Paul Mims. 1 CD. 1998. audio compact disk 19.99 (978-1-58968-016-6(2)) Chrstn Dup Intl.

King James Version Psalms & Proverbs Bible (Spoken Word) deluxe ed. Narrated by Paul Mims. 6 cass. - album. 1996. vinyl bd. 14.97 (978-1-58968-011-1(1), 1100A) Chrstn Dup Intl.

King Jesus, Pt. A. unabr. collector's ed. Robert Graves. Read by Peter MacDonald. 7 cass. (Running Time: 10 hrs. 30 min.). 1988. 56.00 (978-0-7366-1271-5(8), 2181-A) Books on Tape.
Graves recounts the life of Jesus from the perspective of those living at the time.

King Jesus, Pt. B. collector's unabr. ed. Robert Graves. Read by Peter MacDonald. 6 cass. (Running Time: 9 hrs.). 1988. 48.00 (978-0-7366-1272-2(6), 2181-B) Books on Tape.

***King John.** abr. ed. William Shakespeare. (ENG.). 2006. (978-0-06-112639-0(X), Caedmon); (978-0-06-112640-6(3), Caedmon) HarperCollins Pubs.

King John. unabr. ed. William Shakespeare. Read by Michael Feast & Michael Maloney. (Running Time: 8880 sec.). (Arkangel Shakespeare Ser.). (ENG.). 2006. audio compact disk 19.95 (978-1-932219-17-3(X)) Pub: AudioGO. Dist(s): Perseus Dist

King John. unabr. ed. William Shakespeare. Read by Audio Partners Staff. 2 cass. (Running Time: 2 hrs. 28 mins.). (Arkangel Shakespeare Ser.). 2004. 17.95 (978-1-932219-57-9(9), Atlntc Mnthly) Pub: Grove-Atltic. Dist(s): PerseuPGW

King John's Christmas. Victoria Ebel-Sabo. 1994. 5.95 (978-0-318-65056-2(8), C8812CT) Kjos.

King Kong. Violet Crown Radio Players. Based on a book by Merian C. Cooper. (ENG.). 2007. audio compact disk 12.99 (978-1-934814-04-8(0)) Red Planet Au.

King Kong. Edgar Wallace & Merian C. Cooper. Read by Stefan Rudnicki. (Running Time: 19800 sec.). (King Kong Ser.). 2005. 34.95 (978-0-7861-4350-4(9)); audio compact disk 45.00 (978-0-7861-7536-9(2)) Blckstn Audio.

King Kong. unabr. ed. Edgar Wallace & Merian C. Cooper. Read by Stefan Rudnicki. Comment by Ray Bradbury et al. 5 CDs. (Running Time: 25200 sec.). 2005. audio compact disk 19.95 (978-0-7861-7630-4(X), ZE3555) Blckstn Audio.

King Kong. unabr. ed. Edgar Wallace & Merian C. Cooper. Read by Stefan Rudnicki. Comment by Ray Harryhausen et al. Contrib. by Delos W. Lovelace. 5 cass. (Running Time: 6 hrs.). 2005. 19.95 (978-0-7861-3761-9(4), E3555) Blckstn Audio.
King Kong... Taller than a five-story building, capable of crushing airplanes with his bare hands, ruler of a lost empire of prehistoric monsters. Now in audio, the world-famous story of beauty and the beast which has thrilled and amazed countless millions all over the world.

King Kong. unabr. ed. Edgar Wallace & Merian C. Cooper. Read by Stefan Rudnicki. Comment by Ray Harryhausen et al. Contrib. by Delos W. Lovelace. 1 MP3. (Running Time: 6 hrs.). 2005. 29.95 (978-0-7861-7873-5(6), ZM3555) Blckstn Audio.

King Lear see Shakespeare

King Lear see Evil, Exploration Of

King Lear. (Audio BookNotes Guide). (C). 2002. audio compact disk 9.95 (978-1-929011-04-9(0)) Scholarly Audio.

King Lear. William Shakespeare. Ed. by Jerry Stemach et al. Retold by Richard Ganci. Illus. by Bob Stotts. Narrated by Nick Sandys. Contrib. by Ted S. Hasselbring. 1 cass. (Running Time: 1 hr.). (J). (gr. 2-3). 2000. (978-1-58702-323-1(7)) D Johnston Inc.
An old English King, tired of his kingly duties, plans to divide his kingdom between his three daughters and to entrust himself to their care. To decide how to divide up the kingdom, King Lear asks each of his three daughters to tell him how much they love him. His two eldest daughters, Regan and Goneril, shower him with false praise and words of love. But his youngest daughter, Cordelia, who truly loves her father, cannot speak falsely. She looks down at the floor and save nothing.

King Lear. William Shakespeare. Ed. by Jerry Stemach. Retold by Jerry Stemach & Richard Ganci. Narrated by Nick Sandys. 2000. audio compact disk 200.00 (978-1-58702-485-6(3)) D Johnston Inc.

King Lear. William Shakespeare. Ed. by Jerry Stemach et al. Retold by Richard Ganci. Illus. by Bob Stotts. Narrated by Nick Sandys. Contrib. by Ted S. Hasselbring. (Start-to-Finish Books). (J). (gr. 2-3). 2002. 100.00 (978-1-58702-965-3(0)) D Johnston Inc.

King Lear. William Shakespeare. Read by Paul Scofield et al. (Running Time: 3 hrs. 30 mins.). 2006. 24.95 (978-1-60083-800-2(6)) Iofy Corp.

King Lear. William Shakespeare. Narrated by Full Cast Production Staff. (Running Time: 3 hrs.). (C). 2006. 14.95 (978-1-60083-046-4(3)) Iofy Corp.

King Lear. William Shakespeare. Perf. by Paul Scofield et al. 3 cass. (Running Time: 3 hrs. 30 mins.). Dramatization. 2002. 17.98 (978-962-634-744-7(9), nA324414); audio compact disk 22.98 (978-962-634-244-2(7), NA324412) Naxos.
Perhaps Shakespear's most profoundly searching and disturbing tragedy, the story of a foolish and self-indulgent king who learns, late in life and after terrible suffering, the value of self-knowledge. The play asks the ancient questions about God and the meaning of pain with uncompromising directness, but provides no reassuring answers.

King Lear. William Shakespeare. Perf. by Dublin Gate Theatre Staff. 1 cass. Dramatization. 10.95 (978-0-8045-0784-4(8), SAC 7110) Spoken Arts.

King Lear. William Shakespeare. Read by Paul Scofield. Told to Alec McCowen & Kenneth Branagh. (Playaway Young Adult Ser.). (ENG.). 2009. 59.99 (978-1-60812-516-6(5)) Find a World.

King Lear. Jerry Stemach. William Shakespeare. (Classic Literature Ser.). 2000. audio compact disk 18.95 (978-1-4105-0153-0(1)) D Johnston Inc.

King Lear. abr. ed. William Shakespeare. 3 CDs. (Running Time: 3 hrs.). 2005. audio compact disk 24.95 (978-0-660-19003-7(6)) Pub: Canadian Broadcasting CAN. Dist(s): Georgetown Term

***King Lear.** abr. ed. William Shakespeare. Read by Paul Scofield & (null) Cast. (ENG.). 2003. (978-0-06-074328-4(X), Caedmon) HarperCollins Pubs.

***King Lear.** abr. ed. William Shakespeare. Read by Paul Scofield & (null) Cast. (ENG.). 2004. (978-0-06-081470-0(5), Caedmon) HarperCollins Pubs.

King Lear. unabr. ed. William Shakespeare. Contrib. by Clive Merrison et al. (Running Time: 10980 sec.). (Arkangel Shakespeare Ser.). (ENG.). 2005. audio compact disk 24.95 (978-1-932219-18-0(8)) Pub: AudioGO. Dist(s): Perseus Dist
King Lear divides his kingdom between his three daughters, basing the portions, so he believes, on the depth of their love for him. This profoundly moving, nihilistic drama is one of Shakespeare's mightiest achievements and one of the greatest tragedies in world literature. Performed by Trevor Peacock, Julia Ford, and the Arkangel Cast.

King Lear. unabr. ed. William Shakespeare. Read by Paul Scofield et al. 3 cass. (Running Time: 2 hrs. 30 mins.). Dramatization. 20.00 (H104) Blckstn Audio.
A tragic tale of vanity, lust & betrayal. The story of a proud king whose monumental blindness to the realities of his world empower the very evil that destroys him in the end.

King Lear. unabr. ed. William Shakespeare. Read by Paul Scofield et al. 3 cass. (Running Time: 1 hr. per cass.). 1995. 36.00 (A104) Blckstn Audio.
A tragic tale of vanity, lust & betrayal, "King Lear" is as great a work as has ever been written in any language. "King Lear", the crowning achievement of Shakespeare's brilliant & prolific career, is the story of a proud king whose monumental blindness to the realities of his world empower the very evil that destroys him in the end. An unforgettable exploration of what it means to be human.

King Lear. unabr. ed. William Shakespeare. Read by John Gielgud. 3 CDs. (Running Time: 4 hrs. 30 mins.). 2001. audio compact disk 33.00 Books on Tape.
A king foolishly divides his kingdom between his scheming two oldest daughters and estranges himself from the daughter who loves him. So begins this profoundly moving and disturbing tragedy that, perhaps more than any other work in literature, challenges the notion of a coherent and just universe. The king and others pay dearly for their shortcomings–as madness, murder, and the anguish of insight and forgiveness that arrive too late combine to make this an all-embracing tragedy of evil and suffering. Each Edition Includes: • Comprehensive explanatory notes • Vivid introductions and the most up-to-date scholarship • Clear, modernized spelling and punctuation, enabling contemporary readers to understand the Elizabethan English • Completely updated, detailed bibliographies and performance histories • An interpretive essay on film adaptations of the play, along with an extensive filmography From the Paperback edition.

King Lear. unabr. ed. William Shakespeare. Read by Audio Partners Staff. 2 cass. (Running Time: 3 hrs. 3 mins.). (Arkangel Shakespeare Ser.). 2004. 17.95 (978-1-932219-58-6(7), Atlntc Mnthly) Pub: Grove-Atltic. Dist(s): PerseuPGW
King Lear divides his kingdom between his three daughters, basing the portions, so he believes, on the depth of their love for him. This profoundly moving, nihilistic drama is one of Shakespeare's mightiest achievements and one of the greatest tragedies in world literature. Performed by Trevor Peacock, Julia Ford, and the Arkangel Cast.

King Lear. unabr. ed. William Shakespeare. 3 cass. 1999. 20.00 (FS9-51071) Highsmith.

King Lear. unabr. ed. William Shakespeare. 2 cass. (Running Time: 3 hrs.). (Arkangel Complete Shakespeare Ser.). 2001. 17.95 (PengAudBks) Penguin Grp USA.

King Lear. unabr. ed. William Shakespeare. 3 cass. (Running Time: 3 hrs.). Dramatization. 2000. pap. bk. 38.20 (40745E5); 26.00 (21513E5) Recorded Bks.

King Lear. unabr. ed. William Shakespeare. Read by Grover Gardner. 3 cass. (Running Time: 4 hrs. 30 min.). 1995. 16.95 (978-1-55685-234-3(7)) Audio Bk Con.
King Lear divides his kingdom between his two duplicitous daughters, banishing the loving Cordelia & the steadfast Kent. Another father, Gloucester, utterly mistakes the integrity of one son, Edgar, & the ruthless greed of the bastard, Edmund. These acts of folly launch a hugely moving search for dignity, self-knowledge & wisdom of the grandest of scales.

King Lear. unabr. ed. William Shakespeare & Naxos Audiobooks Staff. 3 cass. (Running Time: 3 hrs. 7 mins.). (New Cambridge Shakespeare Audio Ser.). (ENG.). 2002. 27.99 (978-0-521-01236-2(8)) Cambridge U Pr.

King Lear. unabr. ed. William Shakespeare et al. Perf. by Paul Scofield & Rachel Roberts. 4 cass. Dramatization. HarperCollins Pubs.
Cast includes: Pamela Brown, Cyril Cusack, Robert Stephens, John Stride, Wallas Eaton, John Rigers, Trevor Martin, Michael Aldridge, Andrew Keir, Arthur Hewlett, Willoughby Goddard, Ronald Ibbs, Ann Bell.

King Lear. unabr. ed. William Shakespeare et al. Perf. by Paul Scofield & Rachel Roberts. 4 cass. (Running Time: 6 hrs.). Dramatization. 1984. 35.92 (978-0-89845-155-9(8), CP 233) HarperCollins Pubs.

King Lear, Set. William Shakespeare. Contrib. by Naxos Audiobooks Staff. (Running Time: 3 hrs. 6 mins.). (New Cambridge Shakespeare Audio Ser.). (ENG.). 2002. audio compact disk 30.99 (978-0-521-01235-5(X)) Cambridge U Pr.

King Lear, Vol. 1. William Shakespeare. Ed. by Jerry Stemach et al. Retold by Richard Ganci. Illus. by Bob Stotts. Narrated by Nick Sandys. Contrib. by Ted S. Hasselbring. (Start-to-Finish Books). (J). (gr. 2-3). 2000. 35.00 (978-1-58702-486-3(1)) D Johnston Inc.

King Lear: An A+ Audio Study Guide. unabr. ed. Roger Rees. (Running Time: 1 hr.). (ENG.). 2006. 5.98 (978-1-59483-712-8(0)) Pub: Hachet Audio. Dist(s): HachBkGrp

King Leopold's Ghost: A Story of Greed, Terror, & Heroism in Colonial Africa. unabr. ed. Adam Hochschild. Read by Geoffrey Howard. 9 cass. (Running Time: 13 hrs. 30 mins.). 2000. 72.00 (978-0-7366-4917-9(4), 5225) Books on Tape.
In the 1880s, as the European powers were carving up Africa, King Leopold II of Belgium seized for himself the vast unexplored territory surrounding the Congo River. Carrying out a genocidal plundering of the Congo, he looted its rubber, brutalized its people, and ultimately slashed its population by ten million, while shrewdly cultivating his reputation as a great humanitarian. Heroic efforts to expose these crimes eventually led to the first great human rights movement of the twentieth century.

King Leopold's Soliloquy. Mark Twain. Read by Joe Knight. 1 cass. (Running Time: 25 min. per cass.). 1979. 10.00 (HW110) Esstee Audios.
Mark Twain was particularly disturbed by the 1890 atrocities of King Leopold in the Belgian Congo, in which a people were brutally subdued & 10 million blacks lost their lives. He gave vent to his feelings in this soliloquy, published as a pamphlet, in which Twain indicated that as absolute monarch, Leopold could have stopped these atrocities easily but chose not to.

King Lion's Gifts: A Story from Nelson Mandela's Favorite African Folktales. Read by Ricardo Chavira. Compiled by Nelson Mandela. (Running Time: 10 mins.). (ENG.). 2009. 1.99 (978-1-60024-818-4(7)) Pub: Hachet Audio. Dist(s): HachBkGrp

King Me: What Every Son Wants & Needs from His Father. abr. ed. Steve Farrar. Read by Chris Fabry. 2 pieces. 19.99 (978-1-58926-908-8(X)) Oasis Audio.

King Me: What Every Son Wants & Needs from His Father. abr. ed. Steve Farrar. Narrated by Chris Fabry. (ENG.). 2005. audio compact disk 17.99 (978-1-58926-909-5(8)) Oasis Audio.

King Me: What Every Son wants & Needs from His Father. abr. ed. Steve Farrar. Narrated by Chris Fabry. (ENG.). 2005. 12.59 (978-1-60814-267-5(1)) Oasis Audio.

King Must Die. unabr. ed. Mary Renault. Read by Peter MacDonald. 9 cass. (Running Time: 13 hrs. 30 min.). 1986. 72.00 (978-0-7366-0870-1(2), 1820) Books on Tape.
A young hero is sent to reclaim the dynasty from a stiffling matriarch.

King Must Die. unabr. ed. Mary Renault. Narrated by Walt MacPherson. 9 cass. (Running Time: 13 hrs.). 1982. 78.00 (978-1-55690-286-4(7), 82053E7) Recorded Bks.
The triumph of Theseus, Prince of Athens, over the half-man - half-bull that haunts the labyrinth beneath the palace of Knossos becomes reality.

King of Attolia. Megan Whalen Turner. Read by Jeff Woodman. 9. (Running Time: 10 hrs. 50 mins.). 2006. 65.75 (978-1-4281-1714-3(8)); audio compact disk 97.75 (978-1-4281-1719-8(9)) Recorded Bks.

***King of Capital: The Remarkable Rise, Fall, & Rise Again of Steve Schwarzman & Blackstone.** unabr. ed. David Carey & John E. Morris. Narrated by George K. Wilson. (Running Time: 12 hrs. 0 mins. 0 sec.). 2010. 29.99 (978-1-4526-5000-5(4)); 39.99 (978-1-4526-2000-8(8)); 17.99 (978-1-4526-7000-3(5)); audio compact disk 39.99 (978-1-4526-0000-0(7)); audio compact disk 95.99 (978-1-4526-3000-7(3)) Pub: Tantor Media. Dist(s): IngramPubServ

King of Comedy: The Life & Art of Jerry Lewis. abr. ed. Shawn Levy. Read by Marty Ingeles. 2 cass. (Running Time: 3 hr.). 1997. 17.95 (978-1-57453-126-8(3)) Audio Lit.
Jerry Lewis has influenced comedians from Lenny Bruce to Jim Carrey and has been named a Chevalier of the French Legion of Honor. A funny, dark and very American success story.

King of Dragons. collector's ed. Carol Fenner. Read by Allan Ruck. 3 cass. (Running Time: 5 hrs.). (J). 2000. 32.00 (978-0-7366-9020-1(4)) Books on Tape.
A touching story of a homeless boy & his father. Eleven-year-old Ian & his father have been homeless for several years. When his father fails to return one night, Ian must follow the precautions his father has taught him in order to continue his survival.

King of Dragons. unabr. ed. Carol Fenner. Read by Allan Ruck. 3 cass. (Running Time: 5 hrs.). (J). (gr. 4-7). 2000. 30.00 (978-0-8072-8218-2(9), LL0171, Listening Lib) Random Audio Pubg.
Eleven-year-old Ian & his father have been homeless for several years. When his father fails to return one night, Ian must follow the precautions his father has taught him in order to continue his survival.

King of Hearts. unabr. ed. G. Wayne Miller. Read by Patrick Cullen. 6 cass. (Running Time: 8 hrs. 30 mins.). 2000. 44.95 (978-0-7861-1897-7(0), 2690); audio compact disk 56.00 (978-0-7861-9797-2(8), 2690) Blckstn Audio.
Amazing story of how a group of renegade Minnesota surgeons, led by Dr. Walt Lillehei, made medical history by becoming the first doctors to operate deep inside the human heart. He did what experts considered to be an impossible feat: opened the heart, repaired fatal defects & made the miraculous routine. Miller draws on archival research & exclusive interview with Lillehei & legendary pioneers such as Christian Barnard, taking listeners into the lives of these doctors & their patients as they progress toward their landmark achievement.

King of Hearts: A Cassandra Swann Bridge Mystery. unabr. ed. Susan Moody. Read by Julia Franklin. 7 cass. (Running Time: 9 hrs. 15 min.). 1998. 76.95 (978-1-85903-230-5(3)) Pub: Magna Story GBR. Dist(s): Ulverscroft US
Cassie Swann decides to look further into the murder, twenty years ago, of her father.

***King of Kings: Warrior of Rome, Book II.** unabr. ed. Harry Sidebottom. Read by Stefan Rudnicki. (Running Time: 13 hrs.). 2010. 29.95 (978-1-4417-5881-1(X)); 79.95 (978-1-4417-5877-4(1)); audio compact disk 109.00 (978-1-4417-5878-1(X)) Blckstn Audio.

King of Lies. unabr. ed. John Hart. 11 CDs. (Running Time: 46800 sec.). 2006. audio compact disk 39.99 (978-1-4193-9612-0(9)) Recorded Bks.

King of Little Things. Bil Lepp. 2008. 12.95 (978-1-891852-61-9(2)) Pub: Quarrier Pr. Dist(s): WV Book Co

King of Ragtime. unabr. ed. Larry Karp. (Running Time: 8.5 hrs. NaN mins.). 2008. 29.95 (978-1-4332-5201-3(5)); 54.95 (978-1-4332-5199-3(X)); audio compact disk 70.00 (978-1-4332-5200-6(7)) Blckstn Audio.

King of Shadows. Susan Cooper. Read by Jim Dale. 3 cass. (Running Time: 5 hrs.). (J). 2001. 15.95 (978-0-7540-5213-5(3)) AudioGO.
The author traces the journey of boy actor Nat Field, who travels from the states to perform as puck at the globe theatre. As the story unfolds Nat comes face to face with Shakespeare who passes a helping hand through time to help Nat.

King of Shadows. unabr. ed. Susan Cooper. Read by Jim Dale. 3 vols. (Running Time: 4 hrs. 49 mins.). (J). (gr. 5-9). 2004. pap. bk. 36.00 (978-0-8072-8388-2(6), Listening Lib); 30.00 (978-0-8072-8387-5(8), YA186CX, Listening Lib) Random Audio Pubg.
Nat Field has had his share of loss & horror. His escape is his talent for acting & he's been picked to perform at the new Globe Theater in London, a reproduction of Shakespeare's own playhouse. As rehearsal begins, strange, eerie echoes of the past begin creeping in. Nat falls ill & wakes to find he has traveled back in time to 1599 where he is to act at the original Glove. His costar is William Shakespeare himself.

King of Slippery Falls. Sid Hite. Read by Patrick G. Lawlor. (Running Time: 4 hrs.). (gr. k-12). 2005. reel tape 24.95 (978-0-7861-3523-3(9)); audio compact disk 27.00 (978-0-7861-7828-5(0)) Blckstn Audio.

King of Slippery Falls. Sid Hite. Read by Patrick G. Lawlor. (Running Time: 12600 sec.). (J). (gr. k-12). 2005. audio compact disk 29.95 (978-0-7861-8019-6(6)) Blckstn Audio.

King of Slippery Falls. unabr. ed. Sid Hite. Read by Patrick G. Lawlor. (YA). 2007. 34.99 (978-1-59895-877-5(1)) Find a World.

King of the Barbareens. unabr. ed. Janet Hitchman. Read by Ann Beach. 8 cass. (Running Time: 12 hrs.). 2000. 54.95 (978-0-7531-0677-8(9), 991217) Pub: ISIS Audio GBR. Dist(s): Ulverscroft US
In 1919, at age 2 1/2, the author heard the person she called Gran say sharply, "She's no relative of mine. None whatever." And that was how she discovered that orphans were fed & clothed but did not belong to anyone.

King of the Cats. 2004. bk. 24.95 (978-0-7882-0648-1(6)); pap. bk. 14.95 (978-0-7882-0647-4(8)); 8.95 (978-1-56008-943-8(1)); 8.95 (978-0-7882-0305-3(3)); cass. & flmstrp 30.00 (978-1-56008-700-7(5)) Weston Woods.

King of the Cats. unabr. ed. Retold by Paul Galdone. 1 cass. (Running Time: 15 min.). (J). (gr. k-4). 2001. pap. bk. 16.90 (978-0-8045-6517-2(1), 6517) Spoken Arts.
One dark night, the gravedigger sees nine black cats carrying a coffin into the cemetery. Does his cat know something?.

King of the Cats: The Life & Times of Adam Clayton Powell, Jr. unabr. ed. Wil Haygood. Read by Duncan Morgan. 14 cass. (Running Time: 21 hrs.). 1996. 112.00 (978-0-7366-3351-2(0), 4002); Rental 14.95 (4002) Books on Tape.
Perhaps knowing that his grandfather was a slave made Adam Clayton Powell, Jr. such a crusader for racial equality. This certainly gave him a focal point, but it was Powell's own drive that made him succeed. He was Harlem's first black congressman, a seat he held for more than 30 years. As a senior member of the house, Powell also spearheaded Lyndon Johnson's War on Poverty. But Powell's success contained the seeds of his downfall. Flamboyant & reckless, without care for his reputation, he let hubris ruin him. Out of office, without friends or influence, rejected by followers, friends & former associates, he died virtually alone in 1972.

King of the Corner. unabr. ed. Loren D. Estleman. Narrated by Richard Ferrone. 7 cass. (Running Time: 10 hrs.). (Detroit Ser.: Vol. 3). 1992. 60.00 (978-1-55690-663-3(3), 92405E7) Recorded Bks.
Former big league pitcher Doc Miller gets out of prison to find that his hometown of Detroit has changed beyond his recognition.

King of the Golden River see Favorite Children's Stories: A Collection

King of the Golden River see Childhood Legends

King of the Golden River. abr. ed. John Ruskin. Narrated by Elinor G. Hoffman. 2 cass. (Running Time: 50 min.). (J). 12.95 (978-0-89926-135-5(3), 823) Audio Bk.

King of the Golden River. unabr. ed. John Ruskin. Read by John Chatty. 1 cass. (Running Time: 82 min.). Dramatization. 1980. 8.95 (N-41) Jimcin Record.
Two stories of faith & the power of magic.

King of the Jews. unabr. ed. Leslie Epstein. Read by Noah Waterman. 8 cass. (Running Time: 11 hrs. 30 mins.). 1997. 56.95 (978-0-7861-1178-7(X), 1924) Blckstn Audio.
This masterpiece is a brilliant work of black humor that has taken its place as a classic novel about the Holocaust. Set in Poland, it is the story of I. C. Trumpleman, the indiscreet director of an orphanage. When the Germans invade & the Jewish community is forced into a ghetto, he becomes the leading figure caught in making choices about who will live & who will starve.

***King of the Jews: A Novel.** unabr. ed. Leslie Epstein. Read by Noah Waterman. (Running Time: 10 hrs. 30 mins.). 2010. 29.95 (978-1-4417-5130-0(0)); audio compact disk 100.00 (978-1-4417-5128-7(9)) Blckstn Audio.

King of the Middle March. unabr. ed. 6 cass. (Running Time: 9:12 hrs.). 2004. 40.00 (978-0-8072-0550-1(8), Listening Lib) Random Audio Pubg.

King of the Mild Frontier. unabr. ed. Chris Crutcher. Read by Chris Crutcher. (Running Time: 17640 sec.). (ENG.). (J). (gr. 5). 2005. audio compact disk 30.00 (978-0-307-28254-5(6), Listening Lib) Pub: Random Audio Pubg. Dist(s): Random

King of the Mild Frontier: An Ill-Advised Autobiography. unabr. ed. 3 cass. (Running Time: 4:54 hrs.). 2004. 30.00 (978-1-4000-9477-6(1), Listening Lib); audio compact disk 35.00 (978-1-4000-9500-1(X), Listening Lib) Random Audio Pubg.

***King of the Mountains.** Anonymous. 2009. (978-1-60136-532-3(2)) Audio Holding.

King of the Pond. Short Stories. Carl Sommer. Narrated by Carl Sommer. 1 cass. Dramatization. (Another Sommer-Time Story Ser.). (J). (gr. 1-4). 2003. bk. 16.95 (978-1-57537-565-6(6)) Advance Pub.

King of the Pond. Carl Sommer. Narrated by Carl Sommer. 1 cass. Dramatization. (Another Sommer-Time Story Ser.). (J). (gr. k-4). 2003. lib. bdg. 23.95 (978-1-57537-766-7(7)) Advance Pub.
Character Education story narrated by the author Carl Sommer with a character song by Karacter Kidz.

***King of the Pond / el Rey del Estanque.** ed. Carl Sommer. Illus. by Greg Budwine. (Another Sommer-Time Story Bilingual Ser.). (ENG & SPA.). (J). 2009. bk. 26.95 (978-1-57537-181-8(2)) Advance Pub.

King of the Romans. unabr. ed. John Gorman. Read by Stuart Langston. 5 cass. (Running Time: 7 hrs.). 2002. 39.95 (978-0-7861-2314-8(1), 3000); audio compact disk 48.00 (978-0-7861-9434-6(0), 3000) Blckstn Audio.
When Clovis moves to conquer Gaul in a.d. 486, only Syagrius, King of the Romans, has the courage to stand in his way and pays a fearful price for his defiance. Shattered by a defeat that costs him his wife, his son, his city, and his army, Syagrius wanders through the collapsing world of a dying empire to find refuge with a procurator broken by his past, a centurion haunted by betrayal, and a priestess desperate for love, all too proud and too honorable to compromise with the corruption that threatens to destroy them. And there, on a beach in Crete, they make their final stand together.

***King of the Romans.** unabr. ed. John Gorman. Read by Stuart Langton. (Running Time: 7 hrs. 0 mins.). 2010. 29.95 (978-1-4417-5088-4(6)) Blckstn Audio.

King of the Streets. unabr. ed. John Baker. Read by Cornelius Garrett. 7 cass. (Running Time: 9 hrs.). (Isis Ser.). (J). 2003. 61.95 (978-0-7531-1617-3(0)); audio compact disk 71.95 (978-0-7531-2224-2(3)) Pub: ISIS Lrg Prnt GBR. Dist(s): Ulverscroft US
Sam Turner is helping the woman from Scottish Widows track the murderer of her husband and is investigating the death of a teenage runaway.

King of the Wind: The Story of the Godolphin Arabian. Marguerite Henry. Read by David McCallum. 4 cass. (Running Time: 5 hrs. 10 mins.). (J). 2000. 30.00 (978-0-7366-9038-6(7)) Books on Tape.
Dramatic story about a stallion & a stable boy as they travel around the globe to secure the horse's place among champions.

King of the Wind: The Story of the Godolphin Arabian. unabr. ed. Marguerite Henry. Read by David McCallum. 4 vols. (Running Time: 3 hrs. 18 mins.). (J). (gr. 4-7). 2004. pap. bk. 38.00 (978-0-8072-8697-5(4), YA239SP, Listening Lib); 32.00 (978-0-8072-8696-8(6), YA239CX, Listening Lib) Random Audio Pubg.

King of the Wind: The Story of the Godolphin Arabian, unabr. ed. Marguerite Henry. Narrated by Davina Porter. 3 pieces. (Running Time: 4 hrs.). (gr. 4 up). 1993. 27.00 (978-1-55690-959-7(4), 93445E7) Recorded Bks.
The story of the Godolphin Arabian, one of the three founding sires of the thoroughbred breed, born in the stables of a Sultan, sold as a cart horse on the streets of Paris & saved from obscurity by an English lord.

King of the World: Muhammad Ali & the Rise of an American Hero. abr. ed. David Remnick. Read by Dick Hill. (Running Time: 6 hrs.). 2005. audio compact disk 16.99 (978-1-59600-107-7(0), 9781596001077, BCD Value Price); audio compact disk 74.25 (978-1-59600-108-4(9), 9781596001084, BACDLib Ed) Brilliance Audio.
There had been mythic sports figures before Cassius Clay, but when he burst upon the sports scene in the 1950s, he broke the mold. Those were the years when boxing and boxers were at the mercy of the mob and the whim of the sportswriters. If you wanted a shot at a title, you did it their way. Young Clay did it his way - with little more than an Olympic gold medal to his credit, he danced into Sonny Liston's b[illegible] view and provoked the terrifying champ into accepting him as [illegible]xt challenger. The rest is history. Muhammad Ali has become a [illegible] hero, an American icon, a self-invented legend. As both a mirror and a molder of his times, Ali became the most recognizable face on the planet, a key figure in the cultural battles of the times. This is the story of his self-creation, and his rise to glory, told by a master storyteller.

King of the World: Muhammad Ali & the Rise of an American Hero. abr. ed. David Remnick. Read by Dick Hill. (Running Time: 6 hrs.). 2006. 39.25 (978-1-4233-0116-5(1), 9781423301165, BADLE); 24.95 (978-1-4233-0115-8(3), 9781423301158, BAD); 39.25 (978-1-4233-0114-1(5), 9781423301141, Brlnc Audio MP3 Lib); audio compact disk 24.95 (978-1-4233-0113-4(7), 9781423301134, Brilliance MP3) Brilliance Audio.

King of the World: Muhammad Ali & the Rise of an American Hero. abr. ed. David Remnick. Read by Dick Hill. 4 cass. 1999. 24.95 (FS9-43339) Highsmith.

King of Torts see Rey de los Pleitos

King of Torts. Read by Michael Beck. 8 cass. (Running Time: 12 hrs.). 2003. 64.00 (978-0-7366-8988-5(5)) Books on Tape.

King of Torts. John Grisham. 2003. audio compact disk 80.00 (978-0-7366-8989-2(3)) Books on Tape.

King of Torts. abr. ed. John Grisham. Read by Dennis Boutsikaris. 5 CDs. (Running Time: 6 hrs.). (John Grisham Ser.). (ENG.). 2005. audio compact disk 14.99 (978-0-7393-2358-8(X), Random AudioBks) Pub: Random Audio Pubg. Dist(s): Random

King of Torts. unabr. ed. John Grisham. Read by Michael Beck. (YA). 2007. 64.99 (978-0-7393-7501-3(6)) Find a World.

King of Torts; The Last Juror. abr. ed. John Grisham. Read by Dennis Boutsikaris & Terrence Mann. (Running Time: 43200 sec.). (ENG.). 2007. audio compact disk 29.95 (978-0-7393-5778-1(6), Random AudioBks) Pub: Random Audio Pubg. Dist(s): Random

King of Zunga. Jeffrey Lord. Read by Lloyd James. 2 vols. No. 12. 2004. 18.00 (978-1-58807-367-9(X)); (978-1-58807-785-1(3)) Am Pubng Inc.

King o'the Cats see Three Little Pigs & Other Fairy Tales

King Prthu: The Divine King. 1 cass. (Spiritual Stories Ser.). 5.00 Bhaktivedanta.

***King, Queen, Knave.** unabr. ed. Vladimir Nabokov. (Running Time: 9 hrs.). 2010. 24.99 (978-1-4418-7269-2(8), 9781441872692, BAD); 39.97 (978-1-4418-7270-8(1), 9781441872708, BADLE) Brilliance Audio.

***King, Queen, Knave.** unabr. ed. Vladimir Nabokov. Read by Christopher Lane. (Running Time: 10 hrs.). 2010. 24.99 (978-1-4418-7267-8(1), 9781441872678, Brilliance MP3); 39.97 (978-1-4418-7268-5(X), 9781441872685, Brlnc Audio MP3 Lib); audio compact disk 29.99 (978-1-4418-7265-4(5), 9781441872654, Bril Audio CD Unabri); audio compact disk 74.97 (978-1-4418-7266-1(3), 9781441872661, BriAudCD Unabrid) Brilliance Audio.

King Rat. abr. ed. James Clavell. Read by David Case. 4 cass. (Running Time: 6 hrs.). 1999. 24.95 (978-0-7366-4600-0(0)) Books on Tape.
The time is World War II. The place is a brutal prison camp deep in Japanese-occupied territory. An American corporal seeks dominance over both captives & captors alike. His weapons are human courage, unblinking understanding of human weaknesses & total willingness to exploit every opportunity to enlarge his power & corrupt or destroy anyone who stands in his path.

King Rat, unabr. collector's ed. James Clavell. Read by David Case. 11 cass. (Running Time: 16 hrs. 30 min.). 1999. 88.00 (978-0-7366-4558-4(6), 4965-R) Books on Tape.

King Richard II. William Shakespeare. Narrated by Full Cast Production Staff. (Running Time: 2 hrs.). 2006. 14.95 (978-1-59912-988-4(4)) Iofy Corp.

King Richard II. unabr. ed. William Shakespeare. Read by Arkangel Cast. Narrated by Rupert Graves et al. (Arkangel Shakespeare Ser.). (ENG.). 2005. audio compact disk 24.95 (978-1-932219-28-9(5)) Pub: AudioGO. Dist(s): Perseus Dist
The sensitive and poetic Richard II is undoubtedly the rightful king of England, but he is unscrupulous and weak. When his cousin Henry Bolingbroke returns from banishment to usurp the crown, Richard's right to the throne proves of little help to him. Richard is forced to abdicate, but as his power is stripped away, he gains dignity and self-awareness, and he meets his death heroically. Performed by Rupert Graves, Julian Glover, and the Arkangel cast.

King Richard II. unabr. ed. William Shakespeare. Read by Audio Partners Staff. 2 cass. (Running Time: 2 hrs. 52 mins.). (Arkangel Shakespeare Ser.). 2004. 17.95 (978-1-932219-68-5(4), Atlntc Mnthly) Pub: Grove-Atltic. Dist(s): PerseuPGW
The banished Henry Bolingbroke returns to usurp the crown of his cousin, the weak and unscrupulous Richard II. Richard gains dignity as his duties are stripped away, but Bolingbroke's power grab throws Britain into turmoil. Performed by Rupert Graves, Julian Glover, and the Arkangel cast.

King Richard II, Vol. 3. abr. ed. William Shakespeare. 3 CDs. (Running Time: 3 hrs.). 2005. audio compact disk 12.95 (978-0-660-18967-3(4)) Pub: Canadian Broadcasting CAN. Dist(s): Georgetown Term

King Richard III. William Shakespeare. Read by Kenneth Branagh. (Running Time: 3 hrs. 30 mins.). 2005. 24.95 (978-1-60083-802-6(2)) Iofy Corp.

King Richard III. William Shakespeare. Perf. by Kenneth Branagh et al. Prod. by Nicolas Soames. 3 cass. (Running Time: 3 hrs. 30 min.). Dramatization. (Plays of William Shakespeare Ser.: Vol. 8). 2001. 17.98 (978-962-634-717-1(1), NA321714, Naxos AudioBooks); audio compact disk 22.98 (978-962-634-217-6(X), NA321712, Naxos AudioBooks) Naxos.
One of Shakespeare's most popular and frequently performed plays. Richard of Gloucester will stop at nothing to gain control of the throne occupied by his brother, Edward IV.

King Richard III. William Shakespeare. Contrib. by Kenneth Branagh et al. (Playaway Young Adult Ser.). (ENG.). (YA). 2009. 59.99 (978-1-60812-517-3(3)) Find a World.

***King Richard III.** abr. ed. William Shakespeare. Read by Robert Stephens & (null) Cast. (ENG.). 2003. (978-0-06-079961-8(7), Caedmon); (978-0-06-074323-9(9), Caedmon) HarperCollins Pubs.

King Richard III. unabr. ed. William Shakespeare. Read by Robert Stephens et al. 3 cass. (Running Time: 3 hrs.). Dramatization. 20.00 (H173) Blckstn Audio.
A tragedy, a comedy & a history all rolled into one, it is Shakespeare at his most colorful, witty & devilishly entertaining best.

King Richard III. unabr. ed. William Shakespeare & Naxos Audiobooks Staff. Contrib. by Kenneth Branagh & Nicholas Farrell. 3 cass. (Running Time: 3 hrs. 19 mins.). Dramatization. (New Cambridge Shakespeare Audio Ser.). (ENG., (C). 2001. 26.99 (978-0-521-00634-7(1)) Cambridge U Pr.

King Richard III. unabr. abr. ed. William Shakespeare. Read by Robert Stephens. 3 cass. (Running Time: 3 hrs.). (gr. 9-12). 1996. 20.00 (978-0-694-51704-6(6), CPN 223) HarperCollins Pubs.

King Richard III, Set. unabr. ed. William Shakespeare. Contrib. by Naxos Audiobooks Staff et al. 3 CDs. (Running Time: 3 hrs. 20 mins.). Dramatization. (New Cambridge Shakespeare Audio Ser.). (ENG., (C). 2001. audio compact disk 29.99 (978-0-521-00639-2(2)) Cambridge U Pr.

***King Richard the Second.** abr. ed. William Shakespeare. Read by Sir John Gielgud & (null) Cast. (ENG.). 2006. (978-0-06-112479-2(6), Caedmon); (978-0-06-112610-9(1), Caedmon) HarperCollins Pubs.

King Solomon's Carpet. unabr. ed. Barbara Vine, pseud. Read by Michael Pennington. 8 cass. (Running Time: 8 hrs.). 1993. 69.95 (978-0-7451-4108-4(0), CAB 791) AudioGO.
Jarvis loves the London Underground with its hidden tunnels, spectacular incidents & awful accidents. His house overlooks the Jubilee Line, where people gather from the tube. He observes Tom, the lost peddler & Alice, who wants to forget the baby she deserted. The Underground harbors strange characters.

King Solomon's Carpet. unabr. ed. Barbara Vine, pseud. Narrated by Davina Porter. 9 cass. (Running Time: 13 hrs.). 1992. 78.00 (978-1-55690-628-2(5), 92102E7) Recorded Bks.
Jarvis lets out rooms in the rambling old house he owns in London. When Axel - the enigma who hates London's underground tube, yet spends his time riding it - moves in, Jarvis' diverse tenants are joined together in a disturbing nightmare.

King Solomon's Mines. H. Rider Haggard. Read by John Richmond. 6 cass. (Running Time: 8 hrs. 30 mins.). 2000. 44.95 (978-0-7861-1772-7(9), 2575) Blckstn Audio.
This great novel of African adventure continues to be a favorite among those who love a thrilling tale. Perhaps the reason for its enduring appeal is that it is a story filled with qualities close to the human heart: adventure, discovery, desire for immortality, terror, search for the primitive.

King Solomon's Mines. H. Rider Haggard. (ENG.). 2008. audio compact disk 19.95 (978-1-60245-176-6(1)) GDL Multimedia.

King Solomon's Mines. H. Rider Haggard. Read by Bill Homewood. (Running Time: 4 hrs.). 1999. 24.95 (978-1-60083-803-3(0)) Iofy Corp.

King Solomon's Mines. H. Rider Haggard. Read by Walter Covell. 7 cass. (Running Time: 10 hrs.). 1989. 35.00 incl. album. (C-47) Jimcin Record.
Adventure in darkest Africa.

King Solomon's Mines. abr. ed. H. Rider Haggard. Read by Stan Winiarski. Ed. by Marilyn Kay. 2 cass. (Running Time: 2 hrs. 30 min.). 1987. pap. bk. 12.95 (978-1-882071-12-8(3), 014) B-B Audio.
An adventure of Allan Quatermain, hunter & trader.

King Solomon's Mines. abr. ed. H. Rider Haggard. 2000. 16.95 (978-0-929071-12-1(3)) B-B Audio.

King Solomon's Mines. abr. ed. H. Rider Haggard. Narrated by Stan Winiarski. 2 cass. (Running Time: 3 hrs.). 2001. 16.95 (978-0-929071-72-5(7)) B-B Audio.
Join Allan Quatermain, hunter and trader, in the most exciting African adventure ever. An ancient map, a lost man, and countless egg-sized diamonds lead to action-filled confrontations with a lost tribe, a hidden country, and the deadly centuries-old sec.

King Solomon's Mines. abr. ed. H. Rider Haggard. 3 CDs. (Junior Classics Ser.). (J). (ps-7). 2005. audio compact disk 22.98 (978-962-634-354-8(0)) Naxos UK GBR.

King Solomon's Mines. unabr. ed. H. Rider Haggard. Narrated by Flo Gibson. 5 cass. (Running Time: 7 hrs.). (gr. 10 up). 2000. 20.95 (978-1-55685-641-9(5)) Audio Bk Con.
Three men on a perilous journey to an unknown land in Africa in search of a friend & diamond mines encounter many adventures.

King Solomon's Mines. unabr. ed. H. Rider Haggard. Read by Jack Sondericker. 8 cass. (Running Time: 8 hrs. 36 min.). 2001. 49.95 (978-1-58116-082-6(8)); audio compact disk 52.00 (978-1-58116-121-2(2)) Books in Motion.
African explorer Allan Quatermain and his two companions search for the fabled diamond mine of the Biblical King Solomon, deep in the heart of Africa. The trio braves parching deserts and icy mountains, survives wicked witchcraft and fierce tribes, only to be lured into an eerie stalactite cave of skeletons, and narrowly escape being buried alive in a tomb of diamonds.

King Solomon's Mines, unabr. ed. H. Rider Haggard. Narrated by Patrick Tull. 7 cass. (Running Time: 9 hrs. 45 mins.). 2001. 60.00 (978-1-55690-845-3(8), 93212E7) Recorded Bks.
Set in the late 1880's, a group of English explorers penetrate deep into the African wilderness in search of the fabled diamond mines of King Solomon.

***King Solomon's Mines.** unabr. ed. H. Rider Haggard. Read by Stefan Rudnicki. (Running Time: 10 hrs.). 2010. 29.95 (978-1-4417-0777-2(8)); 65.95 (978-1-4417-0773-4(5)); audio compact disk 90.00 (978-1-4417-0774-1(3)) Blckstn Audio.

***King Solomon's Mines.** unabr. ed. Henry Rider Haggard. Narrated by Simon Prebble. (Running Time: 9 hrs. 0 mins.). 2010. 78.99 (978-1-4526-3062-5(3)); 22.99 (978-1-4526-5062-3(4)); 32.99 (978-1-4526-0062-8(7)); 15.99 (978-1-4526-7062-1(5)) Tantor Media.

King Solomon's Mines. unabr. collector's ed. H. Rider Haggard. Read by Ian Whitcomb. 6 cass. (Running Time: 9 hrs.). (J). 1984. 48.00 (978-0-7366-0928-9(8), 1872) Books on Tape.

***King Solomon's Mines (Library Edition)** unabr. ed. Henry Rider Haggard. Narrated by Simon Prebble. (Running Time: 9 hrs. 0 mins.). 2010. 32.99 (978-1-4526-2062-6(8)) Tantor Media.

King Suckerman: A Novel. abr. ed. George P. Pelecanos. Read by Richard J. Brewer. 4 cass. (Running Time: 6 hrs.). 2001. 24.95 (978-1-57511-095-0(4)) Pub Mills.
In the wrong place at the wrong time, Vietnam vet & record store owner Marcus Clay & his friend, small-time dealer Dimitri Karras, find themselves in possession of a fortune belonging to a movie-loving, psychotic ex-con & a shotgun-toting, Afro-wearing "white-boy-wanna-be-black-boy cracker." Marcus & Dimitri try to elude the inevitable confrontation, which comes as the Fourth of July fireworks erupt on the Mall.

King Tut: Tales from the Tomb. Diana Briscoe. (High Five Reading - Green Ser.). (ENG.). (gr. 3-4). 2007. audio compact disk 5.95 (978-1-4296-1422-1(6)) CapstoneDig.

King Tut's Tomb. Ed. by Jerry Stemach et al. Contrib. by Ted S. Hasselbring. (Start-to-Finish Books). (J). (gr. 2-3). 2002. (978-1-58702-832-8(8)) D Johnston Inc.

King Tut's Tomb. Ed. by Jerry Stemach et al. Contrib. by Ted S. Hasselbring. (Start-to-Finish Books). (J). (gr. 2-3). 2002. 100.00 (978-1-58702-079-7(3)) D Johnston Inc.

King Tut's Tomb. Alan Venable. (Ancient History Ser.). 2002. audio compact disk 18.95 (978-1-4105-0177-6(9)) D Johnston Inc.

King Tut's Tomb. unabr. ed. Ed. by Jerry Stemach et al. Contrib. by Ted S. Hasselbring. 1 cass. (Running Time: 1 hr.). (Start-to-Finish Books). (J). (gr. 2-3). 2002. (978-1-58702-817-5(4)) D Johnston Inc.
In 1922, an archeologist named Howard Carter discovered the tomb of the pharaoh Tutankhamun. The result was a worldwide frenzy over "King Tut," and later an endless stream of excitement about supposed curses of the mummies. Eighty years later, still very little is known about Tutankhamun, but a lot is known about the exciting story that led to his exhumation. The discovery of King Tuts Tomb was an amazing and dramatic event in the history of archeology. This book tells the story of Howard Carter's career.

King Within: A Study in Masculine Psychology. Read by Robert Moore. 7 cass. (Running Time: 7 hrs.). 1989. 44.95 Set. (978-0-7822-0194-9(6), 400S) C G Jung IL.
The archetype of the King is the central archetype in the masculine psyche. Without dis-identification from this archetype - & without a dynamic connection to it - a man will be immobilized by grandiosity, lost in depression, & bereft of a sense of meaning, just order, & connection with the creative springs of the psyche.

***King 9 Will Not Return.** 2010. audio compact disk (978-1-59171-183-4(5)) Falcon Picture.

Kingdom. Contrib. by Sound of the New Breed & Don Moen. Prod. by Israel Houghton & Arthur Strong. 2007. audio compact disk 16.98 (978-5-557-57367-2(4)) Integrity Music.

Kingdom: Arabia & the House of Sa'ud. unabr. ed. Robert Lacey. Read by Frederick Davidson. 16 cass. (Running Time: 23 hrs. 30 mins.). 1994. 99.95 (978-0-7861-0643-1(3), 1458) Blckstn Audio.
The story of a country - a country of astonishing contrasts: where routine computer printouts open with the words "In the name of God," where men who grew up in goat-hair tents now dominate the money markets of the world, & where murderers & adulterers are publicly executed in the street. The story of a family - a family that has fought its way from poverty & obscurity to wealth & power the like of which the world has never known, a family characterized by fierce loyalty among its members, ruthlessness toward its enemies, & dedication to one of the world's most severe & demanding creeds. The Kingdom is Sa'udi Arabia - the only country in the world to bear the name of the family that rules it.

Kingdom: How to Press into the Kingdom of God: Experiencing Heaven on Earth. Steve Krotoski. 4. 2007. bk. 19.99 (978-0-9779550-1-5(X), TK1AB) PWL.
Live Experiencing the Kingdom of GodDo you want to see the Kingdom of God every day? Do you want to strengthen your relationship with God? This new book by author, teacher, and evangelist Steve Krotoski will show you how. Recommended by pastors and as seen on TV, The Kingdom will help you strengthen your faith, understand the Kingdom of God, know God's goodness, experience miracles and more...Leam how you can see the Kingdom of God right now! Includes access to Study Guide for individuals, groups, and churchesIn The Kingdom you will:Understand the Kingdom of GodKnow the Goodness of GodExperience MiraclesDo the Father's WillLive in Peace, Wisdom, and PowerHave All Your Needs MetBe Healed by JesusRecommended by pastors144 PagesISBN 0-9779550-0-1.

Kingdom Alliance. unabr. ed. Robert Stanek, pseud. 9 CDs. (Running Time: 11 hrs. 20 mins.). Dramatization. (Ruin Mist Chronicles: Bk. 3). 2007. audio compact disk 49.95 (978-1-57545-806-9(3), RP Audio Pubng) Reagent Press.
The dramatic continuation of Keeper Martin's Tale.

Kingdom Alliance: Ruin Mist Chronicles, Book 2. unabr. ed. Robert Stanek, pseud. Narrated by Karl Fehr. (Running Time: 11 hrs. 20 mins.). (Ruin Mist Chronicles Ser.). 2008. audio compact disk 59.95 (978-1-57545-342-2(8), RP Audio Pubng) Reagent Press.

Kingdom & the Crown Vol. 1: Fishers of Men. unabr. ed. Gerald N. Lund. 17 cass. (Running Time: 17 hrs.). 2001. 39.95 (978-1-57345-950-1(X), Shadow Mount) Deseret Bk.
In an ancient land in a time foretold by prophets, a babe was bom beneath a shining star. Thirty years later, Jesus of Nazareth began teaching a message of hope, peace, and love. He claimed to be the Son of God, and his words - and his life - would change the world.

Kingdom & the Crown Vol. 2: Come unto Me. unabr. ed. Read by Larry A. McKeever. 16 cass. (Running Time: 16 hrs.). 2001. 39.95 (978-1-57008-716-5(4), Shadow Mount) Deseret Bk.

Kingdom by the Sea. unabr. ed. Robert Westall. Narrated by Ron Keith. 4 pieces. (Running Time: 6 hrs.). (gr. 6 up). 1995. 35.00 (978-0-7887-0183-2(5), 94408E7) Recorded Bks.
Help young adults understand the painful psychological effects of warfare, & the history of World War II England, with this riveting story of a boy struggling to survive the Nazi air raids over London.

Kingdom by the Sea, Set. unabr. ed. Robert Westall. Read by Ron Keith. 4 cass. (Running Time: 6 hrs. 00 min.). (J). 1995. Rental 11.50 (94408) Recorded Bks.

Kingdom by the Sea: A Journey Around Great Britain. unabr. ed. Paul Theroux. Narrated by Ron Keith. 10 cass. (Running Time: 14 hrs. 30 mins.). 1990. 85.00 (978-1-55690-287-1(5), 90059E7) Recorded Bks.
American-bom Paul Theroux had lived in England for 11 years when he realized he'd explored dozens of exotic locations without discovering anything about his adopted home. So, with a knapsack on his back, he set out to explore by walking & by short train trips.

Kingdom by the Sea: His Candid & Compulsive Account of a Journey Round the Coast of Great Britian. unabr. ed. Paul Theroux. Read by Michael Prichard. 10 cass. (Running Time: 15 hrs.). 1984. 80.00 (978-0-7366-1010-0(3), 1943) Books on Tape.
Paul Theroux's latest journey rolls along the coast of England. He decided such a tour would offer the truest picture of the state of the kingdom.

Kingdom Come. Elliot S. Maggin. 1999. (978-1-57042-741-1(0)) Hachet Audio.

Kingdom Come. abr. ed. Tim Green. Read by Scott Brick. (Running Time: 6 hrs.). (ENG.). 2006. 14.98 (978-1-59483-503-2(9)) Pub: Hachet Audio. Dist(s): HachBkGrp

Kingdom Come: The Final Victory. Tim LaHaye & Jerry B. Jenkins. Read by Steve Sever. (Running Time: 10800 sec.). (Left Behind Ser.). (ENG.). 2007. audio compact disk 19.99 (978-0-8423-6192-7(8), Tyndale Audio) Tyndale Hse.

***Kingdom for the Brave.** Tamara Mckinley. 2010. 89.95 (978-1-4079-0663-8(1)); audio compact disk 99.95 (978-1-4079-0664-5(X)) Pub: Soundings Ltd GBR. Dist(s): Ulverscroft US

Kingdom in a Horse. unabr. ed. Maria Wojciechowska. 1 cass. (Running Time: 47 min.). (J). 1991. 15.98 incl. pap. bk. & guide. (978-0-8072-1076-5(5), SWR 17 SP, Listening Lib) Random Audio Pubg.

Kingdom is Here - Dwell in It. Rick Joyner. 1 cass. (Running Time: 90 mins.). (Heart of David Ser.: Vol. 3). 2000. 5.00 (RJ13-003) Morning NC.
"Restoring the Tabernacle of David," "Restoration is Hard Work" & "the Kingdom is Here - Dwell in it." These tapes not only address the need for a foundation of truth; they impart the essential devotion of having a love for the truth.

Kingdom Keepers. unabr. ed. Ridley Pearson. Read by Gary Littman. (Running Time: 6 hrs.). (Kingdom Keepers Ser.: No. 1). 2005. 24.95 (978-1-4233-0691-7(0), 9781423306917, Brilliance MP3); 69.25 (978-1-4233-0688-7(0), 9781423306887, BriAudUnabridg); 26.95 (978-1-4233-0687-0(2), 9781423306870, BAU); audio compact disk 39.25 (978-1-4233-0692-4(9), 9781423306924, Brlnc Audio MP3 Lib); audio compact disk 82.25 (978-1-4233-0690-0(2), 9781423306900, BriAudCD

Unabrid); audio compact disk 29.95 (978-1-4233-0689-4(9), 9781423306894, Bril Audio CD Unabri) Brilliance Audio.
Using a cutting-edge technology called DHI - which stands for both Disney Host Interactive and Daylight Hologram Imaging - Finn Whitman, an Orlando teen, and four other kids are transformed into hologram projections that guide guests through the park. The new technology turns out, however, to have unexpected effects that are both thrilling and scary. Soon Finn finds himself transported in his DHI form into the Magic Kingdom at night. Is it real? Is he dreaming? Finn's confusion only increases when he encounters Wayne, an elderly Imagineer who tells him that the park is in grave danger. Led by the scheming witch, Maleficent, a mysterious group of characters called the Overtakers is plotting to destroy Disney's beloved realm, and maybe more. This gripping high-tech tale will thrill every kid who has ever dreamed of sneaking into Walt Disney World after hours and wondered what happens at night, when the park is closed.

***Kingdom Keepers IV.** unabr. ed. Ridley Pearson. (Running Time: 7 hrs.). (Kingdom Keepers Ser.). 2011. 39.97 (978-1-61106-973-0(4), 9781611069730, BADLE); 24.99 (978-1-61106-970-9(X), 9781611069709, Brilliance MP3); 39.97 (978-1-61106-971-6(8), 9781611069716, Brlnc Audio MP3 Lib); audio compact disk 29.99 (978-1-61106-968-6(8), 9781611069686, Bril Audio CD Unabri); audio compact disk 60.97 (978-1-61106-969-3(6), 9781611069693, BriAudCD Unabrid) Brilliance Audio.

Kingdom Life. 12 cass. 35.95 (2057, HarperThor) HarpC GBR.

***Kingdom of Blood.** Chuck Missler & Dave Hunt. (ENG.). 2009. audio compact disk 19.95 (978-1-57821-450-1(5)) Koinonia Hse.

Kingdom of Blood: The History of the Church. Chuck Missler & Dave Hunt. 2 cass. (Running Time: 3 hours). (Briefing Packages by Chuck Missler). 1996. vinyl bd. 14.95 Incls. notes . (978-1-880532-49-2(2)) Koinonia Hse.

Kingdom of Comfort. Contrib. by Delirious. 2008. audio compact disk 13.99 (978-5-557-47121-3(9)) Pt of Grace Ent.

Kingdom of Darkness. Vincent M. Walsh. 1 cass. 1986. 4.00 Key of David.
Personal stories & examples told to promote a full understanding of the basic powers of the Renewal.

Kingdom of Faith Treasure Principles: Examining Yourself Whether Ye Be in the Faith. 2006. audio compact disk 12.00 (978-0-9742312-3-5(1)) Treasure The Monemt.

Kingdom of God. 2004. 15.00 (978-1-59544-005-1(4)) Pub: B Winston Min. Dist(s): Anchor Distributors

Kingdom of God. Megan McKenna. Read by Megan McKenna. 1 cass. (Running Time: 1 hr. 05 min.). 1993. 9.95 (978-7-900784-97-1(7), AA2665) Credence Commun.
Begin with a parable. Layer on a story. Start asking questions: tough questions, illuminating questions. Add a little background, make some parallels with today. All of a sudden you understand the Kingdom of God wiht revelatory clarity.

Kingdom of God. Featuring Bill Winston. 3. 2004. audio compact disk 24.00 (978-1-59544-006-8(2)) Pub: B Winston Min. Dist(s): Anchor Distributors
The kingdom of God is a new and powerful reality, a mysterywhich is only revealed to those who have accepted Jesus Christ as Lord. When you operate in this earth using the principles of the kingdom of God, you will manifest miracles and your life will be a sign and a wonder.

Kingdom of God: Days of Heaven on Earth. Gloria Copeland. (ENG.). 2006. audio compact disk 20.00 (978-1-57562-904-9(6)) K Copeland Pubns.

Kingdom of God Days of Heaven on Earth. Gloria Copeland. Perf. by Gloria Copeland. 5 cass. (Running Time: 5 hrs.). 1996. cass. & video 25.00 Set. (978-1-57562-139-5(8)) K Copeland Pubns.
Biblical teaching on the kingdom of God.

Kingdom of God Process. Creflo A. Dollar. 20.00 (978-1-59089-112-4(0)) Pub: Creflo Dollar. Dist(s): STL Dist NA

Kingdom of God System: Living Life as God Intended. Speeches. Creflo A. Dollar. 3 Cass. (Running Time: 3 hrs. 30 mins.). 2006. 15.00 (978-1-59944-048-4(2)); audio compact disk 21.00 (978-1-59944-049-1(0)) Creflo Dollar.

***Kingdom of Heaven: The Nondual Teachings of Jesus Christ, Vol. 3.** Featuring Adyashanti. (ENG.). 2010. audio compact disk 29.00 (978-1-933986-83-8(2)) Open Gate Pub.

Kingdom of Heaven is Like. Guy Finley. 7 CDs. (Running Time: 10 hrs. 30 mins.). 2002. audio compact disk 18.95 (978-1-929320-10-3(8)) Life of Learn.
Modern parables that touch the timeless in us. Six stories that help us fall in love all over again with the he living light that awaits within.

Kingdom of Kush. Compiled by Benchmark Education Staff. 2005. audio compact disk 10.00 (978-1-4108-5483-4(3)) Benchmark Educ.

Kingdom of Lies: An Inspector Keen Dunliffe Mystery. Lee Wood. Read by Ralph Cosham. (Running Time: 57600 sec.). 2005. audio compact disk 108.00 (978-0-7861-7543-7(5)) Blckstn Audio.

Kingdom of Lies: An Inspector Keen Dunliffe Mystery. N. Lee Wood. Read by Ralph Cosham. (Running Time: 57600 sec.). 2005. 89.95 (978-0-7861-3784-8(3)) Blckstn Audio.

Kingdom of Lies: An Inspector Keen Dunliffe Mystery. unabr. ed. N. Lee Wood. Read by Ralph Cosham. 12 CDs. (Running Time: 57600 sec.). 2005. audio compact disk 32.95 (978-0-7861-7786-8(1), ZE3510) Blckstn Audio.

Kingdom of Lies: An Inspector Keen Dunliffe Mystery. unabr. ed. N. Lee Wood. 13 vols. (Running Time: 57600 sec.). 2005. audio compact disk 29.95 (978-0-7861-8007-3(2), ZM3510) Blckstn Audio.

Kingdom of Ohio. unabr. ed. Matthew Flaming. Narrated by Todd McLaren. (Running Time: 11 hrs. 30 mins.). 2009. 17.99 (978-1-4001-8500-9(9)); 34.99 (978-1-4001-9500-8(4)) Tantor Media.

Kingdom of Ohio. unabr. ed. Matthew Flaming. Narrated by Todd McLaren. (Running Time: 11 hrs. 30 mins. 0 sec.). (ENG.). 2010. 24.99 (978-1-4001-6500-1(8)); audio compact disk 69.99 (978-1-4001-4500-3(7)); audio compact disk 34.99 (978-1-4001-1500-6(0)) Pub: Tantor Media. Dist(s): IngramPubServ

Kingdom of Royth. Jeffrey Lord. Read by Lloyd James. 2 vols. 2004. 18.00 (978-1-58807-364-8(5)) Am Pubng Inc.

Kingdom of Royth. Jeffrey Lord. Read by Lloyd James. 2 vols. No. 9. 2004. (978-1-58807-782-0(9)) Am Pubng Inc.

Kingdom of Shadows. unabr. ed. Barbara Erskine. Read by Lesley Mackie. 24 cass. (Running Time: 30 hrs. 44 mins.). (Isis Ser.). (J). 2002. 127.95 (978-0-7531-1460-5(7)) Pub: ISIS Lrg Prnt GBR. Dist(s): Ulverscroft US
Clare Roland is rich, beautiful and unhappy. The childless wife of a City banker, she is obsessed by her ancestry and a strange, inexplicable dream. In 1306: Isobel, Countess of Buchan, is persecuted for her part in crowning Robert the Bruce, her lover. Duncairn Castle, Isobel's home, Clare's heritage, becomes the battle-ground for passions spanning the centuries.

Kingdom of Shadows. unabr. ed. Alan Furst. Read by Stephen Thorne. 8 cass. (Running Time: 12 hrs.). (Isis Cassettes Ser.). (J). 2001. 69.95 (978-0-7531-1079-9(2), 010108) Pub: ISIS Lrg Prnt GBR. Dist(s): Ulverscroft US
Set in March 1938, Austrian fascists run wild in the streets of Vienna. In Paris, Nicholas Morath, former Hungarian cavalry officer, returns home to his young mistress. He has been in Slovakia performing a quiet favor for his uncle Polanyi, a diplomat. Desperate to stop his country's drift into alliance with Nazi Germany, Polanyi trades in conspiracy but it is Morath who does his work for him. Drawn deeper & deeper into danger, quiet favors become secret missions & Paris moves closer towards war.

Kingdom of Shadows. unabr. ed. Alan Furst. Read by Stephen Thorne. 8 CDs. (Running Time: 12 hrs.). (Isis Ser.). (J). 2001. audio compact disk 79.95 (978-0-7531-1241-0(8), 1241-8) Pub: ISIS Lrg Prnt GBR. Dist(s): Ulverscroft US

Kingdom of Silence: An Inspector Keen Dunliffe Mystery. unabr. ed. Lee Wood. Read by Ralph Cosham. (Running Time: 10 hrs. 5 mins.). 2009. 29.95 (978-1-4332-1865-1(8)); audio compact disk 29.95 (978-1-4332-1864-4(X)); audio compact disk 65.95 (978-1-4332-1861-3(5)); audio compact disk 90.00 (978-1-4332-1862-0(3)) Blckstn Audio.

Kingdom of the Golden Dragon. unabr. ed. Isabel Allende. Read by Blair Brown.Tr. of Reino del Dragón de Oro. (YA). 2004. 29.95 (978-0-06-059759-7(3)) HarperCollins Pubs.

Kingdom on the Waves. unabr. ed. M. T. Anderson. Read by Peter Francis James. (Astonishing Life of Octavian Nothing, Traitor to the Nation Ser.: Vol. 2). (ENG.). (J). (gr. 9). 2008. audio compact disk 50.00 (978-0-7393-6786-5(2), Listening Lib) Pub: Random Audio Pubg. Dist(s): Random

Kingdom on the Waves. unabr. ed. M. T. Anderson. Read by Peter Francis James. 11 CDs. (Running Time: 13 hrs. 15 mins.). (Astonishing Life of Octavian Nothing, Traitor to the Nation Ser.: Vol. 2). (YA). (gr. 9 up). 2008. audio compact disk 75.00 (978-0-7393-6788-9(9), Listening Lib) Pub: Random Audio Pubg. Dist(s): Random

***Kingdom People.** Rick McKinley. (ENG.). 2011. 14.99 (978-0-310-77314-6(8)) Zondervan.

Kingdom, Power & Glory Audio Series. (ENG.). 2008. audio compact disk 34.95 (978-0-9795136-7-1(7)) Kings High Way.

Kingdom, Power & Glory MP3 Series. (ENG.). 2008. 19.95 (978-0-9795136-9-5(3)) Kings High Way.

Kingdom Principles. Kenneth Copeland & Bill Winston. 3 cass. (BVOV Ser.). 2006. 15.00 (978-1-57562-881-3(3)); 30.00 (978-1-57562-883-7(X)); audio compact disk 15.00 (978-1-57562-882-0(1)) K Copeland Pubns.

Kingdom Principles. Myles Munroe. 2007. 24.99 (978-1-4245-0723-8(5)) Tre Med Inc.

Kingdom Principles: Preparing for Kingdom Experience & Expansion. Myles Munroe. (Running Time: 21840 sec.). (Understanding the Kingdom Ser.). 2008. audio compact disk 34.99 (978-0-7684-2605-2(7)) Destiny Image Pubs.

***Kingdom Triangle: Recover the Christian Mind, Renovate the Soul, Restore the Spirit's Power.** unabr. ed. J. P. Moreland. (Running Time: 8 hrs. 59 mins. 0 sec.). (ENG.). 2009. 19.99 (978-0-310-77199-9(4)) Zondervan.

Kingdom Where Nobody Dies: A John Mcintire Mystery. unabr. ed. Kathleen Hills. Read by William Dufris. (Running Time: 37800 sec.). 2007. 65.95 (978-1-4332-1279-6(X)); audio compact disk 29.95 (978-1-4332-1281-9(1)); audio compact disk & audio compact disk 81.00 (978-1-4332-1280-2(3)) Blckstn Audio.

Kingdoms & the Elves of the Reaches. unabr. ed. Robert Stanek, pseud. Narrated by John Goodman. 5 CDs. (Running Time: 5 hrs. 40 minutes). (YA). 2005. audio compact disk 29.95 (978-1-57545-801-4(2), RP Audio Pubng) Reagent Press.
Unleash the power of your imagination and enter a world you've never dreamed existed! Best-selling author Robert Stanek delivers an epic fantasy adventure that will open your mind and your heart. Perfect for the young and the young at heart! The Kingdoms & The Elves Of The Reaches is a refreshingly unique fantastic adventure where its only limits are the limits of your imagination. Inside, you'll discover the breathtaking world of Ruin Mist where the mystical and the magical abound, and you'll fall in love with three heroes: a boy who would become a mage, a princess who is fleeing a dying kingdom, and a warrior elf who undertakes an epic journey. The adventure begins with Book 1.

Kingdoms & the Elves of the Reaches: Keeper Martin's Tales, Book 1. unabr. ed. Robert Stanek, pseud. Narrated by Karl Fehr. (Running Time: 6 hrs. 30 mins.). (ENG.). (J). 2008. 16.95 (978-1-57545-343-9(6), RP Audio Pubng) Pub: Reagent Press. Dist(s): OverDrive Inc

Kingdoms & the Elves of the Reaches Book 1. unabr. ed. Robert Stanek, pseud. Read by Karl Fehr. (J). 2008. 54.99 (978-1-60514-590-7(4)) Find a World.

Kingdoms & the Elves of the Reaches II. unabr. ed. Robert Stanek, pseud. Narrated by John Goodman. 5 CDs. (Running Time: 5 hrs. 40 min.). (ENG.). (J). 2005. audio compact disk 29.95 (978-1-57545-802-1(0), RP Audio Pubng) Reagent Press.
The adventure continues! Unleash the power of your imagination and enter a world you've never dreamed existed! Best-selling author Robert Stanek delivers an epic fantasy adventure that will open your mind and your heart. Perfect for the young and the young at heart! The Kingdoms & The Elves Of The Reaches is a refreshingly unique fantastic adventure where its only limits are the limits of your imagination. Inside, you'll discover the breathtaking world of Ruin Mist where the mystical and the magical abound, and you'll fall in love with three heroes: a boy who would become a mage, a princess who is fleeing a dying kingdom, and a warrior elf who undertakes an epic journey.

Kingdoms & the Elves of the Reaches II: Keeper Martin's Tales, Book 2. unabr. ed. Robert Stanek, pseud. Narrated by Karl Fehr. (Running Time: 5 hrs. 50 mins.). (ENG.). (J). 2008. 19.95 (978-1-57545-344-6(4), RP Audio Pubng) Pub: Reagent Press. Dist(s): OverDrive Inc

Kingdoms & the Elves of the Reaches III. unabr. ed. Robert Stanek, pseud. 4 CDs. (Running Time: 5 hrs. 1 mins.). Dramatization. (ENG.). (J). 2005. audio compact disk 29.95 (978-1-57545-804-5(7), RP Audio Pubng) Reagent Press.
Best-selling author Robert Stanek delivers a story that is perfect for the young and the young at heart! The Kingdoms and The Elves of the Reaches is a refreshingly unique fantastic adventure where its only limits are the limits of your imagination. Inside you'll discover the breathtaking world of Ruin Mist where the mystical and the magical abound, and you'll fall in love with three heroes: a boy who would become a mage, a princess who is just now seeing the world around her, and a warrior elf who undertakes an epic journey. In Book 2, Adrina, Vilmos, and Seth turned the tide in the greatest challenge Great Kingdom had faced in hundreds of years: the dissolution of the Kingdom Alliance and the battle to save Quashan'. Now they must solve an even greater challenge as they work to save the Elves of the Reaches.

Kingdoms & the Elves of the Reaches III: Keeper Martin's Tales, Book 3. unabr. ed. Robert Stanek, pseud. Narrated by Karl Fehr. (Running Time: 5 hrs. 30 mins.). (ENG.). (J). 2008. 19.95 (978-1-57545-345-3(2), RP Audio Pubng) Pub: Reagent Press. Dist(s): OverDrive Inc

Kingdoms & the Elves of the Reaches III: Keeper Martin's Tales, Book 3. unabr. ed. Robert Stanek, pseud. Read by Karl Fehr. (YA). 2008. 54.99 (978-1-60514-683-6(8)) Find a World.

Kingdoms & the Elves of the Reaches IV. unabr. ed. Robert Stanek, pseud. 4 CDs. (Running Time: 5 hrs. 1 mins.). Dramatization. (YA). 2005. audio compact disk 29.95 (978-1-57545-805-2(5), RP Audio Pubng) Reagent Press.
Here is the fourth volume in Robert Stanek's magnificent Keeper Martin's Tales - the series fans have called "The Star Wars" of fantasy. Filled with mystery, intrigue, adventure, and magic the books transport us to a world unlike any other. Praised as an "instant" classic, Robert Stanek's outstanding series has quickly become a favorite. The Kingdoms and the Elves of the Reaches IV To turn back the tides of war, Queen Mother sent her most trusted warriors on a perilous journey across the Great Sea. But the elves were betrayed by one of their own. Only a handful survived the ambush that followed, only two reached the far shores. But they did not find quick allies. They found a kingdom under siege and a shattered alliance. The elves proved themselves to the men that defended Quashan'. They along with the mysterious Xith, the would-be mage Vilmos, Princess Adrina and their friends helped turn the battle in Great Kingdom's favor. For their support, the elves were granted an audience with the king. Yet great deeds could not undo the past, or change the prejudice of men. Elves and men are enemies, as it has been through time. The Alder King had his own concerns. The kingdom alliance was shattered. An ally, and a great king was dead. War between the kingdoms seemed inevitable. If there was any hope of restoring the alliance, he must rid the kingdom of the enemy's spies. But was such a thing possible without the backing of those he needed the most?.

Kingdoms & the Elves of the Reaches IV: Keeper Martin's Tales, Book 4. unabr. ed. Robert Stanek, pseud. Narrated by Karl Fehr. (Running Time: 5 hrs. 50 mins.). (ENG.). (J). 2008. 19.95 (978-1-57545-346-0(0), RP Audio Pubng) Pub: Reagent Press. Dist(s): OverDrive Inc

Kingdoms & the Elves of the Reaches IV: Keeper Martin's Tales, Book 4. unabr. ed. Robert Stanek, pseud. Read by Karl Fehr. (YA). 2008. 54.99 (978-1-60514-894-6(6)) Find a World.

Kingdom's Call. unabr. ed. Chuck Black. Narrated by Andy Turvey. (Kingdom Ser.). (ENG.). (J). 2008. 10.49 (978-1-60814-271-2(X)); audio compact disk 14.99 (978-1-59859-403-4(6)) Oasis Audio.

Kingdom's Call Audio Book Drama, Book 4. Chuck Black. Executive Producer Chuck Black. Prod. by Matt Hall. Voice by Andy Turvey. Music by Emily Elizabeth Black. (Kingdom Ser.: Book 4). (ENG.). (YA). 2007. audio compact disk 19.95 (978-0-9679240-7-6(3)) Perfect Praise.

Kingdom's Dawn. unabr. ed. Chuck Black. Narrated by Andy Turvey. (Kingdom Ser.). (ENG.). (J). 2008. 10.49 (978-1-60814-268-2(X)) Oasis Audio.

Kingdom's Dawn. unabr. ed. Chuck Black. Read by Dawn Marshall. Narrated by Andy Turvey. (Running Time: 3 hrs. 46 mins. 11 sec.). (Kingdom Ser.). (ENG.). (J). (gr. 7-12). 2008. audio compact disk 14.99 (978-1-59859-383-9(8)) Oasis Audio.

Kingdom's Dawn Audio Book Drama, Book 1. Chuck Black. Executive Producer Chuck Black. Voice by Andy Turvey. Composed by Emily Elizabeth Black. (Kingdom Ser.: Book 1). (ENG.). (YA). 2005. audio compact disk 19.95 (978-0-9679240-4-5(9)) Perfect Praise.

Kingdom's Dream. unabr. ed. Iris Gower. Read by Di Langford. 8 cass. 2001. (978-0-7531-1161-1(6)) ISIS Audio GBR.
When the line engineered by Isambard Kingdom Brunel creates a silver track into Swansea, the women of the town little realize what effect the coming of the railway will have on their lives. The peaceful outskirts of Swansea are changed for ever as the navvies build a shantytown alongside the railway track and roam the streets looking for trouble. Katie Cullen, an innocent Irish girl, is confronted by some of the men and rescued by Bull Beynon, the foreman. She finds herself falling in love with Bull but he already has a woman living in his track-side hut, the dark-eyed Nia Jones. As the new line into Swansea is forged, Katie and Nia find they are caught in a network of lies and deceit. Their lives become involved with the women at the Mainwaring Pottery, in the town now dominated by the monster they call the Great Western Railway.

Kingdom's Edge. unabr. ed. Chuck Black. Narrated by Andy Turvey. (Kingdom Ser.). (ENG.). (J). 2008. 10.49 (978-1-60814-270-5(1)) Oasis Audio.

Kingdom's Edge. unabr. ed. Chuck Black. Read by Dawn Marshall. Narrated by Andy Turvey. (Running Time: 2 hrs. 51 mins. 15 sec.). (Kingdom Ser.). (ENG.). (J). (gr. 7-12). 2008. audio compact disk 14.99 (978-1-59859-385-3(4)) Oasis Audio.

Kingdom's Edge Audio Book Drama, Book 3. Chuck Black. Executive Producer Chuck Black. Voice by Andy Turvey. Music by Emily Elizabeth Black. (Kingdom Ser.: Book 3). (ENG.). (YA). 2006. audio compact disk 19.95 (978-0-9679240-6-9(5)) Perfect Praise.

Kingdom's Hope. unabr. ed. Chuck Black. Narrated by Andy Turvey. (Kingdom Ser.). (ENG.). (J). 2008. 10.49 (978-1-60814-269-9(8)) Oasis Audio.

Kingdom's Hope. unabr. ed. Chuck Black. Read by Dawn Marshall. Narrated by Andy Turvey. (Running Time: 3 hrs. 33 mins. 51 sec.). (Kingdom Ser.). (ENG.). (J). (gr. 7-12). 2008. audio compact disk 14.99 (978-1-59859-384-6(6)) Oasis Audio.

Kingdom's Hope Audio Book Drama, Book 2. Chuck Black. Executive Producer Chuck Black. Voice by Andy Turvey. Music by Emily Elizabeth Black. (Kingdom Ser.: Book 2). (ENG.). (YA). 2005. audio compact disk 19.95 (978-0-9679240-5-2(7)) Perfect Praise.

Kingdom's Quest. unabr. ed. Chuck Black. Narrated by Andy Turvey. (Kingdom Ser.). (ENG.). (J). 2008. 10.49 (978-1-60814-272-9(8)) Oasis Audio.

Kingdom's Quest. unabr. ed. Chuck Black. Read by Dawn Marshall. Narrated by Andy Turvey. (Running Time: 4 hrs. 33 mins. 10 sec.). (Kingdom Ser.). (ENG.). (J). (gr. 8-12). 2008. audio compact disk 14.99 (978-1-59859-404-1(4)) Oasis Audio.

Kingdom's Quest Audio Book Drama, Book 5. Chuck Black. Executive Producer Chuck Black. Prod. by Matt Hall. Voice by Andy Turvey. Music by Emily Elizabeth Black. (Kingdom Ser.: Book 5). (ENG.). (YA). 2007. audio compact disk 19.95 (978-0-9679240-8-3(1)) Perfect Praise.

Kingdom's Reign. unabr. ed. Chuck Black. Narrated by Andy Turvey. (Kingdom Ser.). (ENG.). (J). 2008. 10.49 (978-1-60814-273-6(6)); audio compact disk 14.99 (978-1-59859-405-8(2)) Oasis Audio.

Kingdom's Reign Audio Book Drama, Book 6. Chuck Black. Executive Producer Chuck Black. Prod. by Matt Hall. Voice by Andy Turvey. Music by Emily Elizabeth Black. (Kingdom Ser.: Book 6). (ENG.). (YA). 2007. audio compact disk 19.95 (978-0-9679240-9-0(X)) Perfect Praise.

Kingfish: The Reign of Huey P. Long. unabr. ed. Richard D. White & Richard D. White, Jr. Read by Patrick Cullen. (Running Time: 41400 sec.). 2006.

65.95 (978-0-7861-4672-7(9)); audio compact disk 81.00 (978-0-7861-6734-0(3)); audio compact disk 29.95 (978-0-7861-7400-3(5)) Blckstn Audio.

Kingfisher. unabr. ed. Gerald Seymour. Read by Nigel Graham. 12 cass. (Running Time: 15 hr. 30 min.). (Isis Ser.). (J). 2001. 94.95 (978-0-7531-0326-5(5), 980403) Pub: ISIS Lrg Prnt GBR. Dist(s): Ulverscroft US
The student's arrest was witnessed by only a small minority. It took place without siren, without flashing light & more ominously, it was not mentioned in the Kiev news. The nature of this arrest did however, prompt the other three students (all Ukranian Jews) to try for freedom-their aim being to escape to Israel via Europe. Hijacking a plane & making for the West, they are refused help by one country after another. Unable to bargain with hijackers as a matter of moral principle, many of the Western countries face a dilemma; not only are the hijackers Jewish, but also have hijacked an enemy plane. This provokes divided sympathies so that when the plane inevitably runs out of fuel & is forced to land in England, the authorities have to decide whether these men should be treated as political refugees or as murderous criminals.

Kingfisher. unabr. ed. Gerald Seymour. 14 CDs. (Isis Ser.). (J). 2003. audio compact disk 104.95 (978-0-7531-1723-1(1)) Pub: ISIS Lrg Prnt GBR. Dist(s): Ulverscroft US

Kingfishers Catch Fire. unabr. ed. Rumer Godden. Narrated by Sheri Blair. 6 cass. (Running Time: 8 hrs.). 1981. 51.00 (978-1-55690-288-8(3), 81080E7) Recorded Bks.
A young widow & her two children set up home in rural Kashmir with some surprising results.

Kingless Land. unabr. ed. Ed Greenwood. Read by Nadia May. 9 cass. (Running Time: 12 hrs. 30 mins.). 2001. 62.95 (978-0-7861-2043-7(6), P2803); audio compact disk 88.00 (978-0-7861-9707-1(2), ZP2803); audio compact disk 19.95 (978-0-7861-9520-6(7), PZM2803) Blckstn Audio.
Aglirta is known as the Kingless Land, a once-prosperous and peaceful river valley under the protection of a noble sovereign, now fallen into lawlessness and tyranny. The only hope for peace lies in the restoration of the Sleeping King, but he has been ensorcelled.

Kingmaker. Brian Haig & Scott Brick. 2 cass. (Running Time: 2 hrs. 20 mins.). 2000. 18.00 (978-0-7366-9083-6(2)) Books on Tape.

Kingmaker. abr. ed. Brian Haig. Read by John Rubinstein. (ENG.). 2005. 14.98 (978-1-59483-351-9(6)) Pub: Hachet Audio. Dist(s): HachBkGrp

Kingpins of the Pimps: The william perry Story. Tr. of English. (ENG., (YA). 2002. audio compact disk 12.00 (978-0-9747451-0-7(3)) High Des Pub Co.

Kings. (Dovetales Ser.: Tape 6). pap. bk. 6.95 (978-0-944391-41-9(9)); 4.95 (978-0-944391-21-1(4)) DonWise Prodns.

King's Acre. unabr. ed. Christine Marion Fraser. Read by Vivien Heilbron. 10 cass. (Running Time: 15 hrs.). 2000. 84.95 (978-0-7540-0551-3(8), CAB 1974) Pub: Chivers Audio Bks GBR. Dist(s): AudioGO

Kings & Priests. Featuring Bill Winston. 2. 2002. 10.00 (978-1-59544-058-7(5)) Pub: B Winston Min. Dist(s): Anchor Distributors
Where there is no vision (Revelation Knowledge), the people perish! Pastor Bill Winston shares a prophetic word in this powerful teaching on Kings & Priests. These two royalties work together to manifest the Kingdom of God in the earth. One gets the vision, the other gathers the provision. Do you know which one you are? Find out today by ordering Kings & Priests.

Kings & Priests. Featuring Bill Winston. 2005. audio compact disk 16.00 (978-1-59544-152-2(2)) Pub: B Winston Min. Dist(s): Anchor Distributors

Kings & Priests: Understanding Our Priestly Ministry. Fern Halverson. 1 cass. 1997. 54.00 (978-1-57399-041-7(8)) Mac Hammond.
Teaching about the old testament priesthood.

Kings & Queens of England. Richard Hampton & David Weston. Read by Derek Jacobi. (Running Time: 2 hrs. 30 mins.). 2004. 21.95 (978-1-59912-963-1(9)) Iofy Corp.

King's Bishop: An Owen Archer Mystery. unabr. ed. Candace Robb. Read by Stephen Thorne. 8 cass. (Running Time: 10 hrs. 15 min.). (Isis Ser.). (J). 1997. 69.95 (978-0-7531-0084-4(3), 970704) Pub: ISIS Lrg Prnt GBR. Dist(s): Ulverscroft US
A snowy March, 1367, & King Edward is impatient to have his privy councilor, William of Wykeham, confirmed as Bishop of Winchester, but Pope Urban V is stalling, deterred by the man's wealth & political ambition. Thus Owen Archer finds himself heading a deputation from York to Fountains Abbey, to win support for Wykeham from the powerful Cistercian Abbots. He places his old comrade Ned Townley in charge of the fellow company to Rievaulx, hoping to dispel rumors of Ned's involvement in a mysterious death. But just days out of York, trouble erupts; first a friar disappears, then Ned vanishes, following news of murder at Windsor.

King's Book. Louise Vernon. Narrated by Fern Ebersole. (ENG.). (J). 2008. audio compact disk 15.95 (978-0-9801244-3-9(3)) IG Publish.

King's Cake. (Sails Literacy Ser.). (gr. k up). 10.00 (978-0-7578-2650-4(4)) Rigby Educ.

King's Coat. Dewey Lambdin. Read by John Lee. (Alan Lewrie Naval Adventures Ser.). 2001. 72.00 (978-0-7366-7033-3(5)); audio compact disk 88.00 (978-0-7366-7614-4(7)) Books on Tape.

King's Coat. unabr. collector's ed. Dewey Lambdin. Read by John Lee. 11 CDs. (Running Time: 13 hrs. 12 min.). 2001. audio compact disk 88.00 Books on Tape.

King's Coat. unabr. collector's ed. Dewey Lambdin. Read by John Lee. 9 cass. (Running Time: 13 hrs. 30 min.). (Alan Lewrie Naval Adventures Ser.: Bk. 1). 2001. 72.00 Books on Tape.
A young libertarian in the British Navy finds, as he heads for the war-torn American colonies, that he is a born sailor.

King's Commission. Dewey Lambdin. Read by John Lee. (Alan Lewrie Naval Adventures Ser.). 2001. audio compact disk 104.00 (978-0-7366-8517-7(0)) Books on Tape.

King's Commission. unabr. ed. Dewey Lambdin. Read by John Lee. 11 cass. (Running Time: 16 hrs. 30 mins.). (Alan Lewrie Naval Adventures Ser.: Vol. 3). 2001. 88.00 (978-0-7366-8265-7(1)) Books on Tape.
Alan Lewrie, midshipman aboard the DESPERATE, has helped defeat the French CAPRICIEUSE off St. Kitts, but has an even greater cause for celebration: His commission as lieutenant and posting to the brig o' war SHRIKE, which he joins as first officer. Lewrie takes up patrolling the North American coast, and attempts to induce the Seminole and Muskogee tribes to ally themselves with the British against the rebellious colonists. In negotiation with the Indians, Lewrie finds a willing Indian maiden, but must leave her to return to the Caribbean, and to fight alongside Captain Horatio Nelson in the battle of Turks Island.

King's Croft, Set unabr. ed. Christine M. Fraser. Read by Vivien Heilbron. 10 cass. 1999. 84.95 (CAB 1716) AudioGO.

***King's Cross: The History of the World in the Story of Jesus.** Timothy Keller. (ENG.). 2011. audio compact disk 29.95 (978-0-14-242876-4(0), PengAudBks) Penguin Grp USA.

Kings Dreams & Schemes Choral. Jimmy Travis Getzen. 2000. audio compact disk 16.98 (978-0-633-01366-0(8)) LifeWay Christian.

Kings Dreams Schemes Cd Promo Pak. Jimmy Travis Getzen. 2000. audio compact disk 12.00 (978-0-633-01372-1(2)) LifeWay Christian.

King's English: A Guide to Modern Usage. unabr. collector's ed. Kingsley Amis. Read by Richard Green. 7 cass. (Running Time: 10 hrs. 30 min.). 2001. 56.00 (978-0-7366-7164-4(1)) Books on Tape.
An idiosyncratic and delightful romp through the craft of writing English well.

King's Equal. Katherine Paterson. Narrated by Davina Porter. (Running Time: 45 mins.). (gr. 2 up). audio compact disk 12.00 (978-0-7887-6158-4(7)) Recorded Bks.

King's Equal. Katherine Paterson. Narrated by Davina Porter. 1 cass. (Running Time: 45 mins.). (gr. 2 up). 2001. 10.00 (978-0-7887-5279-7(0), 96552E7) Recorded Bks.
In a faraway country, a dying king reluctantly makes the vain Prince Raphael his heir - on one condition. In order to be crowned, Raphael must first marry a woman who is his equal in beauty, intelligence & wealth. Meanwhile, in a far corner of the kingdom, Rosamund - a kind, cheerful farmer's daughter - tends the goats on a mountain. When she visits the palace, even Raphael concedes she is his equal. But what does Rosamund think of Raphael?.

King's Equal. unabr. ed. Katherine Paterson. Narrated by Davina Porter. 1 CD. (Running Time: 15 min.). (YA). (gr. 5-8). 2001. audio compact disk 12.00 (C1382) Recorded Bks.
In a faraway country, a dying king reluctantly makes the vain Prince Raphael his heir - on one condition. In order to be crowned, Raphael must first marry a woman who is his equal in beauty, intelligence & wealth. Meanwhile, in a far corner of the kingdom, Rosamund - a kind, cheerful farmer's daughter - tends the goats on a mountain. When she visits the palace, even Raphael concedes she is his equal. But what does Rosamund think of Raphael?.

King's Farewell. unabr. ed. Christine Marion Fraser. Read by Vivien Heilbron. 8 cass. (Running Time: 12 hrs.). 2002. 69.95 (978-0-7540-0749-4(9), CAB 2171) AudioGO.
It is winter, 1930. Evie Grant is mourning the death of her beloved husband, Davie, and trying to keep the family together in a Glasgow gripped by poverty and unemployment. Her sadness lifts dramatically when John Simpson comes into her life. Evie feels powerless to resist this charming man's advances and is relieved at the financial security he seems to offer. She marries him despite her family's opposition, blind to the consequences they fear.

***King's Fifth.** unabr. ed. Scott O'Dell. Read by Jonathan Davis. (Running Time: 8 hrs.). 2010. 24.99 (978-1-4418-5954-9(3), 9781441859549, Brilliance MP3); 39.97 (978-1-4418-5955-6(1), 9781441859556, Brlnc Audio MP3 Lib); 39.97 (978-1-4418-5956-3(X), 9781441859563, BADLE); audio compact disk 24.99 (978-1-4418-5952-5(7), 9781441859525, Bril Audio CD Unabri); audio compact disk 69.97 (978-1-4418-5953-2(5), 9781441859532, BriAudCD Unabrid) Brilliance Audio.

King's General. unabr. ed. Daphne Du Maurier. Read by Donada Peters. 10 cass. (Running Time: 15 hrs.). 80.00 (978-0-7366-0939-5(3), 1882) Books on Tape.

King's General. unabr. ed. Daphne Du Maurier. Read by Juliet Stevenson. 10 cass. (Running Time: 15 min.). 2000. 69.95 (978-0-7451-4373-6(3), CAB 1056) Pub: Chivers Audio Bks GBR. Dist(s): AudioGO
Sir Richard Grenvile had been blessed with the brilliant skills of leadership, and was in love with Honor Harris of Lanrest. As the Civil War raged on, the shadow of the Royalists closed in on Richard and Honor, and a secret from Grenvile's past lay in waiting for Honor.

Kings I & II Commentary: Verse-by-Verse with Chuck Missler. Chuck Missler. 1 MP3 CD-ROM. (Running Time: 16 hours). (Chuck Missler Commentaries). 2003. audio compact disk 39.95 (978-1-57821-223-1(5)) Koinonia Hse.
I and II Kings provide a record of Israel's history from the beginning of the movement to place Solomon on David's throne through the end of the reign of Zedekiah, Judah's last king. There are great lessons to be learned from Israel's desire to be "like those around us" and its consequences.Explore I and II Kings verse-by-verse with Chuck Missler. This is a 2 volume set with eight audios including notes.

Kings in Grass Castles. unabr. ed. Mary Durack. Read by Jenny Seedsman. 12 cass. (Running Time: 18 hrs.). 1998. 96.00 (978-1-86340-658-1(1), 560713) Pub: Bolinda Pubng AUS. Dist(s): Lndmrk Audiobks
When Patrick Durack left Ireland for Australia in 1853, he was to found a dynasty of pioneers, & build an empire of cattle-land. His grand-daughter, Mary, has rebuilt the saga of the Duracks, that is the story of Australia itself.

Kings in grass castles - Re-release. unabr. ed. Mary Durack. Read by Jenny Seedsman. (Running Time: 17 hrs. 30 mins.). 2009. audio compact disk 123.95 (978-1-74214-108-4(0), 9781742141084) Pub: Bolinda Pubng AUS. Dist(s): Bolinda Pub Inc

King's Legacy: A Story of Wisdom for the Ages. unabr. ed. Jim Stovall. Narrated by Bill Myers. (Running Time: 2 hrs. 31 mins. 32 sec.). (ENG.). 2009. 11.19 (978-1-60814-521-8(2)); audio compact disk 15.99 (978-1-59859-582-6(2)) Oasis Audio.

King's Mapmaker: Early Explorers Fluent Set A Audio CD. Benchmark Education Staff. (J). 2006. audio compact disk 10.00 (978-1-4108-7640-9(3)) Benchmark Educ.

***King's Oak.** abr. ed. Anne Rivers Siddons. Read by Hume Cronyn & Jessica Tandy. (ENG.). 2005. (978-0-06-087900-6(9), Harper Audio); (978-0-06-087901-3(7), Harper Audio) HarperCollins Pubs.

***Kings of Clonmel.** abr. ed. John Flanagan. (Running Time: 11 hrs.). Bk. 8. (J). 2010. audio compact disk 39.95 (978-0-14-242850-4(7), PengAudBks) Penguin Grp USA.

Kings of Comedy. 8 cass. (Running Time: 12 hrs.). 2003. 39.98 (978-1-57019-605-8(2), 4494) Radio Spirits.

Kings of Comedy. Radio Spirits Staff. Read by Bob Hope. 12 CDs. (Running Time: 12 hrs.). 2005. audio compact disk 39.98 (978-1-57019-606-5(0), 4495) Radio Spirits.

Kings of Comedy. ltd. ed. 5 vols. (Running Time: 5 hrs.). (Limited Edition Chronical Ser.). 2003. bk. 39.95 (978-1-55569-951-2(0), OTR49502) Pub: Great Am Audio. Dist(s): AudioGO

Kings of Comedy. ltd. ed. 5 vols. (Running Time: 5 hrs.). (Limited Edition Chronical Ser.). 2002. bk. (978-1-55569-949-9(9), OTR43502) Radio Spirits.

Kings of Swing. 1 cass. or 1 CD. (Running Time: 1 hrs. 1 min.). 5.98; 4.20 demo CD.; audio compact disk 8.98 CD. Lifedance.
Popular big bands play "American Patrol," "Let's Jump," "Limehouse Blues," "On the Sunny Side of the Street," "One O'Clock Jump," "Perdido," "Rhapsody in Blue," "Sing, Sing, Sing," "Tea for Two," "Tuxedo Junction," "Woodchoppers Ball," & more. Includes some vocals. Demo CD or cassette available.

Kings of the East. Chuck Missler. 2 CDs. (Running Time: 120 min. aprox.). (Briefing Packages by Chuck Missler). 2006. audio compact disk 19.95 (978-1-57821-338-2(X)) Koinonia Hse.
The original birth of civilization began in the Middle East and migrated westward - to Greece, to Rome, and then to the nations of northern Europe. As Henry Luce so aptly quipped in 1941, "The twentieth century was the American Century." And indeed it was. But the centroid of power continues to migrate westward: it is widely anticipated that the 21st century will be the "Asian Century."With recent shifts in the economic centers of the world, most notably the decline of the U.S., the Far East is quickly rising to fill the void.As both an international corporate executive and as a recognized Biblical authority, Chuck Missler explores the Kings of the East as an overlooked element of the prophetic scenario. --To monitor how this prophetic area is developing in light of current events, visit our Strategic Trends Area on the Khouse Web-site.(will open a new browser window) ---------------------------------Each Audio CD Briefing Pack contains two Compact Discs, with extensive supporting study notes, all packaged in a standard CD jewel case.

Kings of the Nile: Gods & Pharaohs of Ancient Egypt. Alan Venable. (Ancient History Ser.). 2002. audio compact disk 18.95 (978-1-4105-0178-3(7)) D Johnston Inc.

Kings of the Nile: Gods & Pharaohs of Ancient Egypt. Ed. by Jerry Stemach et al. Contrib. by Ted S. Hasselbring. (Start-to-Finish Books). (J). (gr. 2-3). 2002. (978-1-58702-833-5(6)) D Johnston Inc.

Kings of the Nile: Gods & Pharaohs of Ancient Egypt. unabr. ed. Ed. by Jerry Stemach et al. Contrib. by Ted S. Hasselbring. 1 cass. (Running Time: 1 hr.). (Start-to-Finish Books). (J). (gr. 2-3). 2002. (978-1-58702-818-2(2), F51) D Johnston Inc.
This book provides a background on 3.000 years of ancient Egypt and its rulers, including such topics as the dependence of ancient Egypt on the yearly Nile flood and the growth of the power of the pharaohs. It describes the origins of such famous aspects of Egyptian culture as the mummies and the pyramids. The book also explains hieroglyphics and how their meaning was uncovered.

***Kings of the Vagabonds.** unabr. ed. Neal Stephenson. Read by Simon Prebble. (Running Time: 11 hrs.). (Baroque Cycle Ser.). 2010. audio compact disk 79.97 (978-1-4418-7652-2(9), 9781441876522, BriAudCD Unabrid) Brilliance Audio.

***Kings of Vagabonds.** unabr. ed. Neal Stephenson. Read by Simon Prebble. (Running Time: 11 hrs.). (Baroque Cycle Ser.). 2010. 24.99 (978-1-4418-7653-9(7), 9781441876539, Brilliance MP3); 39.97 (978-1-4418-7655-3(3), 9781441876553, BADLE); 39.97 (978-1-4418-7654-6(5), 9781441876546, Brlnc Audio MP3 Lib); audio compact disk 29.99 (978-1-4418-7651-5(0), 9781441876515, Bril Audio CD Unabri) Brilliance Audio.

King's Privateer. unabr. ed. Dewey Lambdin. Read by John Lee. 9 cass. (Running Time: 13 hrs. 30 mins.). (Alan Lewrie Naval Adventures Ser.). 2001. 72.00 (978-0-7366-8307-4(0)) Books on Tape.
Alan Lewrie teams up with his dastardly father to plunder the Far East as a privateer.

King's Ransom. James Grippando. Narrated by George Guidall. 11 CDs. (Running Time: 12 hrs. 30 mins.). audio compact disk 111.00 (978-1-4025-1532-3(4)) Recorded Bks.

King's Ransom. James Grippando. Narrated by George Guidall. 9 cass. (Running Time: 12 hrs. 30 mins.). 2001. 81.00 (978-0-7887-5348-0(7), 96572) Recorded Bks.
Attorney Nick Rey's enviable life changes forever when guerrilla captors demand three million dollars for the return of his father, kidnapped while on business in Colombia.

King's Ransom. abr. ed. James Grippando. Read by John Bedford Lloyd. 4 cass. (Running Time: 6 hrs.). 2001. 25.95 (978-0-694-52460-0(3), Harper Audio) HarperCollins Pubs.
Janes Grippando, the bestselling author of five novels including Under Cover of Darkness and The Pardon, demonstrates his trademark gifts once again in a taut new tale of intrigue that will keep you guessing to the final, breathtaking scene. Nick Rey is on the career fast track at a hot Miami law firm when he is suddenly plunged headfirst into a dangerous bid to save his father. Matthew Rey has been kidnapped while on business in Columbia's exotic port city of Cartagena. The ransom demand of three million dollars is far more than the Rey family can ever hope to raise.Fortunately, Matthew had purchased an insurance policy to protect against just such a threat. Unfortunately, the kidnappers seem to know all about the policy, and the insurance company, suspecting fraud, is refusing to pay out. With nowhere to turn, Nick links up with Alex, a beautiful, street-smart woman who may be the only person capable of negotiating with Matthew's abductors. But Nick soon discovers that the gravest dangers to him and his family are not the kidnappers and their guns, but the men in suits: lawyers, to be exact, at a powerful firm with something to hide, and they will stop at nothing to keep Nick from unleashing the truth. Performed by John Bedford Lloyd.

King's Ransom. unabr. ed. James Grippando. Narrated by George Guidall. 11 CDs. (Running Time: 12 hrs. 30 mins.). 2002. audio compact disk 111.00 (C1628) Recorded Bks.

King's Ransom. unabr. ed. Ed McBain, pseud. Read by Paul Shay. 7 cass. (Running Time: 7 hrs.). (87th Precinct Ser.: Bk. 10). 1991. 42.00 (978-0-7366-1894-6(5), 2721) Books on Tape.
A boy is kidnapped & you're trapped for ransom. But what if the boy isn't your son? And what if paying the ransom will queer the biggest deal of your life? What do you do then? Throw away your future or sacrifice a kid? That's the question Douglas King has to answer. And if you're Detective Steve Carella or any of the boys at the 87th Precinct, you can only keep trying to find the kidnappers & hope that King will give them the payoff. Because if he doesn't, in a day or two you know you'll have a case of murder on your hands.

***King's Ransom Low Price.** abr. ed. James Grippando. Read by John Bedford Lloyd. (ENG.). 2004. (978-0-06-082419-8(0), Harper Audio); (978-0-06-082420-4(4), Harper Audio) HarperCollins Pubs.

King's Secret Matter. unabr. ed. Jean Plaidy & Anne Flosnik. (Running Time: 14 hrs. 5 mins.). 2008. 29.95 (978-1-4332-5290-7(2)); 85.95 (978-1-4332-5288-4(0)); audio compact disk 110.00 (978-1-4332-5289-1(9)) Blckstn Audio.

King's Shadow. unabr. ed. Elizabeth Alder. Narrated by Ron Keith. 7 pieces. (Running Time: 9 hrs. 15 mins.). (gr. 6 up). 2001. 60.00 (978-0-7887-1782-6(0), 95256E7) Recorded Bks.
This story of a young scribe is a fascinating glimpse of life in the Dark Age.

King's Swift Rider: A Novel on Robert the Bruce. unabr. ed. Mollie Hunter. Narrated by Steven Crossley. 5 cass. (Running Time: 7 hrs. 30 mins.). (YA). 1999. pap. bk. & stu. ed. 67.95 (978-0-7887-3010-8(X), 40892X4) Recorded Bks.
Pays homage to one of Scotland's greatest kings with this action-packed novel of 14th-century Scottish rebellion, in which the bravery & honor of a proud people come alive.

King's Swift Rider: A Novel on Robert the Bruce, unabr. ed. Mollie Hunter. Narrated by Steven Crossley. 5 pieces. (Running Time: 7 hrs. 30 mins.). (gr. 7 up). 1999. 44.00 (978-0-7887-2980-5(2), 95662E7) Recorded Bks.

King's Swift Rider: A Novel on Robert the Bruce, Class set. unabr. ed. Mollie Hunter. Read by Steven Crossley. 5 cass. (Running Time: 7 hrs. 30 mins.). (YA). 1999. 221.80 (978-0-7887-3040-5(1), 46857) Recorded Bks.

***King's Taster.** unabr. ed. Kenneth Oppel. Read by Fred Berman. (ENG.). 2009. (978-0-06-178457-6(5)); (978-0-06-190200-0(4)) HarperCollins Pubs.

Kings Will Bow. Perf. by Walter Hallam et al. 1 cass. 2000. bk. 10.00 (978-1-930663-00-8(5)) W Hallam Minist.

The new "sound" of God. The music department, along with our church family, joined together for an awesome night of praise & worship.

Kingship of Self-Control. William George Jordan. Read by Charlie Tremendous Jones. (Laws of Leadership Ser.). (ENG.). 2009. audio compact disk 19.95 (978-1-933715-53-7(7)) Executive Bks.

Kingslayer. L. Ron Hubbard. 2 cass. 2003. 25.00 (978-1-59212-169-4(1)) Gala Pr LLC.

Kingslayer. L. Ron Hubbard. Perf. by R. F. Daley et al. Directed By Jim Meskimen. Composed by David Campbell. 3 CDs. (Running Time: 2 hrs. 45 mins.). 2003. audio compact disk 29.95 (978-1-59212-168-7(3)) Gala Pr LLC.

Kingsley Amis: A Biography. collector's ed. Eric Jacobs. Read by Stuart Langton. 10 cass. (Running Time: 15 hrs.). 2000. 80.00 (978-0-7366-5620-7(0)) Books on Tape.

Kingsley Amis arrived on the English literary scene with the publication of his classic novel Lucky Jim in 1954 & few writers since have provoked such wildly disparate degrees of laughter, admiration & dismay in the reading public. For better or worse, Amis was known almost as much for his personality as for his work as a novelist.

Kingston Kate. unabr. ed. Elizabeth Waite. Read by Annie Aldington. 12 cass. (Running Time: 16 hrs.). 1999. 94.95 (978-1-86042-576-9(3), 25763) Pub: Soundings Ltd GBR. Dist(s): Ulverscroft US

To catch a glimpse of her red hair, sparkling eyes & shapely figure was to think Kate Kearsley a very lucky young woman indeed. The eighteen-year-old daughter of a successful boatyard owner in Littleton Green, a charming hamlet near Kinston-upon-Thames, she saw good in everyone & loved where she lived. But Kate was anything but lucky. She was too young to remember the day in 1905, when her brother David drowned in the Thames, but time had not healed the wounds of her grieving parents, nor lessened the violence meted out by her guilt-ridden & drunken father to his log-suffering wife. When Kate herself becomes a victim, Hilda Kearsley can take no more. Kate, so suddenly an orphan, is devasted. How does she recover from such terrible loss? With the love & sympathy of friends & relatives like Mary Kennedy, Charles Collier & her Aunt Dolly & a motherless child called Joshua, she somehow finds a way.

Kinks - Jam with Guitar. Professional Guitar Workshop Staff. audio compact disk 26.95 (978-1-85909-588-1(7), Warner Bro) Alfred Pub.

Kinship. Trudy B. Krisher. Narrated by Julia Gibson. 6 cass. (Running Time: 8 hrs. 30 mins.). (YA). 1997. 54.00 (978-0-7887-9025-6(0)) Recorded Bks.

Kinvara. unabr. ed. Christine M. Fraser. Read by Christopher Kay. 10 cass. (Running Time: 810 min.). 2000. 84.95 (978-1-86042-464-9(3), 24643) Pub: Soundings Ltd GBR. Dist(s): Ulverscroft US

Kinvara Affairs. Christine Marion Fraser. Read by Lesley Mackie. 10 CDs. (Sound Ser.). (J). 2002. audio compact disk 89.95 (978-1-84283-237-0(9)) Pub: ISIS Lrg Prnt GBR. Dist(s): Ulverscroft US

Kinvara Wives. unabr. ed. Christine M. Fraser. Read by Lesley Mackie. 9 cass. (Running Time: 12 hrs.). 2000. 79.95 (978-1-86042-647-6(6), 26476) Pub: Soundings Ltd GBR. Dist(s): Ulverscroft US

Kinvara Wives. unabr. ed. Christine Marion Fraser. Read by Rose Heilbron. 9 CDs. (Running Time: 5 hrs. 4 mins.). (Sound Ser.). 2002. audio compact disk 84.95 (978-1-86042-938-5(6)) Pub: UlverLrgPrint GBR. Dist(s): Ulverscroft US

Kiowa, Myths & Legends. unabr. ed. Perf. by Jill Momaday. 2 cass. (Running Time: 3 hrs.). 22.95 (S11310) J Norton Pubs.

Traditional Native American tales accompanied by authentic tribal music.

Kiowa, Storyteller. unabr. ed. Narrated by Gerald Hausman. 1 cass. (Running Time: 1 hr.). 12.95 (C11317) J Norton Pubs.

Anthology of myths & stories based on Native American symbols & culture.

Kiowa Trail. unabr. ed. Louis L'Amour. Read by Ron McLarty. (Running Time: 16200 sec.). (ENG.). 2006. audio compact disk 21.00 (978-0-7393-3340-2(2), Random AudioBks) Pub: Random Audio Pubg. Dist(s): Random

Kiowa Verdict. Cynthia Haseloff. 2009. (978-1-60136-285-8(4)) Audio Holding.

Kipling Short Stories & Poems. Rudyard Kipling. Narrated by Flo Gibson. 2009. audio compact disk 16.95 (978-1-60646-118-1(4)) Audio Bk Con.

Kipling Short Stories & Poems, Set. unabr. ed. Poems. Rudyard Kipling. Read by Flo Gibson. 2 cass. (Running Time: 3 hrs.). 1994. 14.95 (978-1-55685-319-7(X)) Audio Bk Con.

Kipling's versatility is readily demonstrated in such stories as "Wee Willie Winkie", "A Bank Fraud", "A Second Rate Woman", & "An Habitation Enforced" & by such poems as "Gunga Din", "Danny Deever", "If", & "The Last of the Light Brigade".

Kipling's Jungle Books & Just So Stories. unabr. ed. Rudyard Kipling. Read by Christopher Casson & Eve Watkinson. 6 cass. (Running Time: 4 hrs. 30 min.). (J). 1987. 55.00 (978-0-8045-0063-0(0), PCC 63) Spoken Arts.

Includes: Mowgli's Brothers, Rikki-Tikki-Tavi, Tiger! Tiger!, Toomai of the Elephants, Kaa's Hunting, the White Seal, the Miracle of Purun Bhagat, Letting in the Jungle, How the Whale Got His Throat, How the Camel Got His Hump, How the Rhinoceros Got His Skin, the Elephant's Child, How the Leopard Got His Spots, the Sing-Song of Old Man Kangaroo & the Beginning of the Armadillos.

Kiptips. (gr. 3-8). 2003. spiral bd. 29.00 (978-1-57861-489-9(9), IEP Res) Attainment.

Kira-Kira. unabr. ed. Cynthia Kadohata. 4 cass. (J). 2005. 35.00 (978-0-307-28188-3(4)) Random.

Kira-Kira. unabr. ed. Cynthia Kadohata. 4 CDs. (YA). 2005. audio compact disk 32.30 (978-0-307-28189-0(2)) Pub: Random Audio Pubg. Dist(s): NetLibrary CO

Kira-Kira. unabr. ed. Cynthia Kadohata. Read by Elaina Erika Davis. 5 CDs. (Running Time: 4 hrs. 30 mins.). (ENG.). (J). (gr. 3). 2005. audio compact disk 28.00 (978-0-307-28186-9(8), Listening Lib) Pub: Random Audio Pubg. Dist(s): Random

Kiriakos, Set. Don Turner. Read by Christopher Kay. 4 cass. 1999. 44.95 (62035) Pub: Soundings Ltd GBR. Dist(s): ISIS Pub

Kirinyaga. unabr. ed. Mike Resnick. Read by Paul Garcia. (Running Time: 36000 sec.). 2006. 65.95 (978-0-7861-4647-5(8)) Blckstn Audio.

Kirinyaga. unabr. ed. Mike Resnick. Read by Paul Michael Garcia. (Running Time: 36000 sec.). 2006. audio compact disk 81.00 (978-0-7861-6790-6(4)); audio compact disk 29.95 (978-0-7861-7421-8(8)) Blckstn Audio.

Kirk Kilgour. 1 cass. (Reading With Winners: Ser. 2). 1984. 32.95 incl. 5 bklets., scorecards, wksht. tablet & tchr's guide. (978-0-89811-190-3(0), 9903D) Lets Talk Assocs.

Kirk Kilgour: Volleyball Great with Guts. Read by Kirk Kilgour. 1 cass. 9.95 (978-0-89811-084-5(X), 7135) Lets Talk Assocs.

Kirk Kilgour talks about the people & events which influenced his career, & his own approach to his speciality.

Kirkpatrick Sale. unabr. ed. Read by Kirkpatrick Sale & Conger Beasly. Ed. by James McKinley. 1 cass. (Running Time: 29 min.). (New Letters on the Air Ser.). 1992. 10.00 (100292); 18.00 2-sided cass. New Letters.

Sale is interviewed by Conger Beasly & reads from The Conquest of Paradise: Christopher Columbus & the Columbus Legacy.

Kirsty's Surprise. Sara Hunter. Read by Tom Chapin. Illus. by Kerry Maguire. Narrated by Tom Chapin. 1 cass. (Running Time: 10 min.). (Humane Society of the United States Animal Tales Ser.). (J). (gr. k-3). 1998. pap. bk. 19.95 (978-1-58021-011-9(2)) Benefactory.

Some cows & bulls had played too rough & Kirsty wasn't tough enough. Brought to Farm Sanctuary, Kirsty recovers from her broken leg. Several months later, she delivers a big surprise.

Kirsty's Surprise. Sara Hunter. Read by Tom Chapin. Illus. by Kerry Maguire. Narrated by Tom Chapin. 1 cass. (Running Time: 10 min.). (Humane Society of the United States Animal Tales Ser.). (J). (gr. 1-5). 1998. pap. bk. 9.95 (978-1-58021-013-3(9)) Benefactory.

Kirsty's Vineyard. Anna Jacobs. 2008. 69.95 (978-1-4079-0301-9(2)); audio compact disk 84.95 (978-1-4079-0302-6(0)) Pub: Soundings Ltd GBR. Dist(s): Ulverscroft US

Kirtan! The Art & Practice of Ecstatic Chant. Jai Uttal. 2 CDs. (Running Time: 2 hrs. 30 mins.). 2006. audio compact disk 24.95 (978-1-59179-106-5(5), W740D) Sounds True.

Kirtana. Robert Gass. 2006. audio compact disk (978-1-891319-81-5(7)) Spring Hill CO.

Kirundi. Foreign Service Institute Staff. 14 cass. (Running Time: 14 hrs.). 2001. pap. bk. 245.00 (AFKR10) J Norton Pubs.

A member of the Bantu language family, Kirundi is the principal language of Burundi. The course provides basic dialogs, grammatical notes & exercises.

Kirundi Basic Course. unabr. ed. Foreign Service Institute Staff. 9 cass. (Running Time: 6 hrs.). (J). (gr. 10-12). 1946. pap. bk. 295.00 (978-0-88432-376-1(5), AFKR10) J Norton Pubs.

Includes 240-page text.

Kiss see Great French & Russian Stories, Vol. 1, A Collection

Kiss. Ted Dekker & Erin Healy. Read by Pam Turlow. (Playaway Adult Fiction Ser.). 2009. 59.99 (978-1-60812-766-5(4)) Find a World.

Kiss. Jill Mansell. 2009. 89.95 (978-0-7531-3228-9(1)); audio compact disk 99.95 (978-0-7531-3229-6(X)) Pub: Isis Pubng Ltd GBR. Dist(s): Ulverscroft US

Kiss. Perf. by Trin-I-Tee 5:7. 2002. audio compact disk Provident Mus Dist.

Kiss. abr. ed. Ed McBain, pseud. Read by Len Cariou. 2 cass. (Running Time: 3 hrs.). (87th Precinct Ser.: Bk. 44). 2000. 7.95 (978-1-57815-052-6(3), 1013, Media Bks Audio) Media Bks NJ.

The 87th Precinct continues with a hard look at what passes for love in a city grown used to crimes of passion.

Kiss. unabr. ed. Anton Chekhov. Read by Jim Killavey. 1 cass. (Running Time: 56 min.). Dramatization. 1981. 7.95 (N-82) Jimcin Record.

Penetrating studies of human nature.

Kiss. unabr. ed. Anton Chekhov. Read by Richard Setlok. 2 cass. (Running Time: 2 hrs. 20 min.). 1993. lib. bdg. 18.95 Set. (978-1-883049-24-9(5)) Sound Room.

A collection of short fiction: "The Kiss", "Not Wanted", "The Helpmate", "A Misfortune", "The Head of the Family", "Expensive Lessons", "The Trousseau", & "Anyuta".

Kiss. unabr. ed. Ted Dekker & Erin Healy. Narrated by Pam Turlow. (Running Time: 11 hrs. 4 mins. 53 sec.). (ENG.). 2009. 24.49 (978-1-60814-492-1(5)) Oasis Audio.

Kiss. unabr. ed. Ted Dekker & Erin Healy. Read by Adam Verner. Narrated by Pam Turlow. (Running Time: 11 hrs. 4 mins. 53 sec.). (ENG.). 2009. audio compact disk 34.99 (978-1-59859-513-0(X)) Oasis Audio.

Kiss. unabr. ed. John Lutz. Read by Multivoice Production Staff. (Running Time: 8 hrs.). 2008. 24.95 (978-1-4233-5957-9(7), 9781423359579, BAD); 24.95 (978-1-4233-5955-5(0), 9781423359555, Brilliance MP3); 39.25 (978-1-4233-5956-2(9), 9781423359562, Brinc Audio MP3 Lib); 39.25 (978-1-4233-5958-6(5), 9781423359586, BADLE) Brilliance Audio.

Kiss. unabr. ed. Ed McBain, pseud. Read by Paul Shay. 8 cass. (Running Time: 12 hrs.). (87th Precinct Ser.: Bk. 44). 1992. 64.00 (978-0-7366-2286-8(1), 3072) Books on Tape.

A contract killer is playing bodyguard to the wife of an investment broker. Finally two near-fatal accidents send her to police detective Steve Carella. But Steve's mind is on his father's murderers' trial, not on the case.

Kiss, Set. Kathryn Harrison. Read by Kathryn Harrison. 4 cass. (Running Time: 4 hrs. 45 mins.). 1997. 21.95 (978-1-55935-261-1(2), 495289) Soundelux.

In this extraordinary memoir, one of the best young writers in America today transforms into a work of art the darkest passage imaginable in a young woman's life: an obsessive love affair between father & daughter.

Kiss, Set. unabr. ed. Short Stories. Anton Chekhov. Read by Richard Setlok. 2 cass. (Running Time: 2 hrs.). (Anton Chekhov Ser.). 1993. bk. 16.95 (978-1-883049-05-8(9), 390213, Commuters Library) Sound Room.

A collection of short fiction: "The Kiss", "Not Wanted", "The Helpmate", "A Misfortune", "The Head of the Family", "Expensive Lessons", "The Trousseau" & "Anyuta".

Kiss: A Novel of the 87th Precinct. unabr. ed. Ed McBain, pseud. Read by David Colacci. (Running Time: 9 hrs.). (87th Precinct Ser.). 2009. 39.97 (978-1-4233-8583-7(7), 9781423385837, Brinc Audio MP3 Lib); 24.99 (978-1-4233-8582-0(9), 9781423385820, Brilliance MP3); 39.97 (978-1-4233-8585-1(3), 9781423385851, BADLE); 24.99 (978-1-4233-8584-4(5), 9781423385844, BAD) Brilliance Audio.

Kiss: The Unauthorized Biography of Kiss. Scott Gigney. (Maximum Ser.). (ENG.). 2001. audio compact disk 14.95 (978-1-84240-071-5(1)) Pub: Chrome Dreams GBR. Dist(s): IPG Chicago

K.I.S.S. - Selling Techniques That Really Work. Fred Herman. Read by Earl Nightingale. 6 cass. 45.00 Set. (517A) Nightingale-Conant.

Kiss- the Classic Interviews. Interview. 1. (Running Time: 60 mins). (Classic Interview Ser.). 2005. audio compact disk (978-1-84240-311-2(7)) Chrome Dreams GBR.

Kiss are without doubt the most theatrical and distinctive Rock band of ourtime. Selling hundreds of millions of albums worldwide, the Kiss brand isimmediately identifiable. Having played sold out arenas across the globeduring the 80's and 90's, these outrageously flamboyant performers remain agreat inspiration to many of today's artists from Marilyn Manson to QueensOf The Stone Age.Guitar Player journalist Steven Rosen interviewed the 3 keymembers of Kiss in 1979, at a time when the band were trying to be takenmore seriously as musicians, and not just seen as cartoon gimmicks. On theday of the interviews, as they never had before, Kiss showed up in publicwithout the high heels and the make up. Over the course of more than twohours, Rosen discovered precisely what it was that made these Gods Of Glamtick, what their hopes were for the future and how the Kiss masterplan,devised by bass player Gene Simmons, was holding up.The fascinating resultscan now be heard for the first time on this very disc, which contains thebulk of those interviews, during which, both metaphorically and in realityKiss weren't hiding behind the greasepaint.

Kiss an Angel. unabr. collector's ed. Susan Elizabeth Phillips. Read by Anna Fields. 8 cass. (Running Time: 12 hrs.). 1996. 64.00 (978-0-7366-3450-2(9), 4094) Books on Tape.

Daisy Devreaux hates her father's ultimatum; marry Alex Markov or go to jail. Alex puts Daisy to work in his traveling circus, expecting the harsh realities will break her. Instead, he finds she's got heart enough for both of them.

Kiss & Make-Up. unabr. ed. Scripts. Gene Simmons. Read by Gene Simmons. 8 CDs. (Running Time: 9 hrs.). 2004. 49.95 (978-1-59007-299-8(5)); 29.95 (978-1-59007-298-1(7)) Pub: New Millenn Enter. Dist(s): PerseuPGW

Kiss & Tell. Shannon Tweed & Julie McCarron. 2004. 27.95 (978-1-59007-584-5(6)) Pub: New Millenn Enter. Dist(s): PerseuPGW

Kiss & Tell. unabr. ed. Shannon Tweed & Julie McCarron. 6 CDs. (Running Time: 6 hrs.). 2004. audio compact disk 34.95 (978-1-59007-585-2(4)) Pub: New Millenn Enter. Dist(s): PerseuPGW

Kiss & the Duel. unabr. ed. Anton Chekhov. Read by Fred Williams. 6 cass. (Running Time: 9 hrs.). 2000. 44.95 (978-0-7861-1788-8(5), 2587) Blckstn Audio.

In "The Kiss" a lonely, love-starved soldier keeps a secret rendezvous for another man & becomes enamoured with a woman he is never to see again. "The Duel" describes the collisions between men & women in hopeless relationships & how two men are driven to settle the score that results by meeting clandestinely on a bridge with their pistols in hand.

***Kiss & the Duel & Other Stories.** unabr. ed. Anton Chekhov. Read by Fred Williams. (Running Time: 8.5 hrs. NaN mins.). (ENG.). 2011. 29.95 (978-1-4417-8524-4(8)); audio compact disk 76.00 (978-1-4417-8522-0(1)) Blckstn Audio.

***Kiss at Midnight.** Eloisa James. Read by Susan Duerden. (ENG.). 2010. (978-0-06-206052-5(X), Harper Audio) HarperCollins Pubs.

***Kiss at Midnight.** unabr. ed. Eloisa James. Read by Susan Duerden. (ENG.). 2010. (978-0-06-201962-2(7), Harper Audio) HarperCollins Pubs.

Kiss Before the Apocalypse. unabr. ed. Thomas E. Sniegoski. Read by Luke Daniels. (Running Time: 8 hrs.). (Remy Chandler Ser.). 2010. 24.99 (978-1-4418-1754-9(9), 9781441817549, Brilliance MP3); 24.99 (978-1-4418-1756-3(5), 9781441817563, BAD); 39.97 (978-1-4418-1755-6(7), 9781441817556, Brinc Audio MP3 Lib); 39.97 (978-1-4418-1757-0(3), 9781441817570, BADLE); audio compact disk 29.99 (978-1-4418-1752-5(2), 9781441817525, Bril Audio CD Unabri); audio compact disk 97.97 (978-1-4418-1753-2(0), 9781441817532, BriAudCD Unabrid) Brilliance Audio.

Kiss for Little Bear. (J). 2004. bk. 24.95 (978-0-89719-885-1(9)); pap. bk. 32.75 (978-1-55592-252-8(X)); pap. bk. 32.75 (978-1-55592-253-5(8)); pap. bk. 14.95 (978-1-56008-059-6(0)); 8.95 (978-1-56008-944-5(X)); 8.95 (978-1-56008-143-2(0)); cass. & flmstrp 30.00 (978-1-56008-701-4(3)) Weston Woods.

Kiss for Little Bear. Else Holmelund Minarik. 1 cass. (Running Time: 4 min.). (I Can Read Bks.). (J). (ps-1). pap. bk. 12.95 (RAC141) Weston Woods.

Little Bear's drawing for Grandmother inspires a kiss from her to hen to cat to skunk to little skunk & back again until it finally reaches Little Bear.

Kiss for Little Bear. Else Holmelund Minarik. Illus. by Maurice Sendak. 1 cass., 5 bks. (Running Time: 3 min.). (J). pap. bk. 32.75 Weston Woods.

From the book by Elsa Holmelund Minarik.

Kiss for Little Bear. Else Holmelund Minarik. Illus. by Maurice Sendak. 1 cass. (Running Time: 3 min.). (J). bk. 24.95; pap. bk. 12.95 (PRA141) Weston Woods.

Kiss for Little Bear. abr. ed. Maurice Sendak & Else Holmelund Minarik. Illus. by Maurice Sendak. 1 cass. (I Can Read Bks.). (J). (ps-2). 1991. 8.95 (978-1-55994-263-8(0), TBC 2630) HarperCollins Pubs.

Kiss Gone Bad. Jeff Abbott. Narrated by L. J. Ganser. 8 cass. (Running Time: 10 hrs. 45 mins.). 74.00 (978-1-4025-1896-6(X)) Recorded Bks.

Kiss Gone Bad. unabr. ed. Jeff Abbott. Narrated by L. J. Ganser. 8 cass. (Running Time: 10 hrs. 45 mins.). 2002. 39.95 (978-1-4025-1897-3(8), RF947) Recorded Bks.

Death has come to the sleepy town of Port Leo-but is it suicide or murder? The son of a Senator is found on a friend's yacht, shot in the face. Judge Whit Mosley defies political pressure by conducting an inquest, and his investigation takes him places better left alone.

Kiss Goodbye. unabr. ed. Jane Adams. Read by Glen McCready. 6 cass. (Running Time: 8 hrs.). (Story Sound Ser.). 2007. 54.95 (978-1-85903-977-9(4)) Pub: Magna Story GBR. Dist(s): Ulverscroft US

Kiss Goodbye. unabr. ed. Jane Adams. Read by Glen McCready. 7 CDs. (Running Time: 8 hrs.). (Story Sound CD Ser.). 2007. audio compact disk 71.95 (978-1-84652-090-7(8)) Pub: Mgna Lrg Print GBR. Dist(s): Ulverscroft US

Kiss in the Hotel, Joseph Conrad & Other Stories. Howard Norman. (Running Time: 30 min.). 8.95 (AMF-227) Am Audio Prose.

Talks about the native peoples & the isolation of the Canadian north.

***Kiss in Time.** unabr. ed. Alex Flinn. (Running Time: 8 hrs.). 2010. 24.99 (978-1-4418-4976-2(9), 9781441849762, BAD); 39.97 (978-1-4418-4977-9(7), 9781441849779, BADLE) Brilliance Audio.

***Kiss in Time.** unabr. ed. Alex Flinn. Read by Nick Podehl & Angela Dawe. (Running Time: 8 hrs.). 2010. 24.99 (978-1-4418-4974-8(2), 9781441849748, Brilliance MP3) Brilliance Audio.

***Kiss in Time.** unabr. ed. Alex Flinn. Read by Angela Dawe & Nick Podehl. (Running Time: 8 hrs.). 2010. 39.97 (978-1-4418-4975-5(0), 9781441849755, Brinc Audio MP3 Lib) Brilliance Audio.

***Kiss in Time.** unabr. ed. Alex Flinn. Read by Nick Podehl & Angela Dawe Podehl. (Running Time: 8 hrs.). 2010. audio compact disk 69.97 (978-1-4418-4973-1(4), 9781441849731, BriAudCD Unabrid) Brilliance Audio.

***Kiss in Time.** unabr. ed. Alex Flinn. Read by Angela Dawe Podehl & Nick Podehl. (Running Time: 8 hrs.). (YA). 2010. audio compact disk 24.99 (978-1-4418-4972-4(6), 9781441849724, Bril Audio CD Unabri) Brilliance Audio.

***Kiss It Good-Bye: The Mystery, the Mormon, & the Moral of the 1960 Pittsburgh Pirates.** John Moody. 2010. audio compact disk 29.99 (978-1-60641-258-9(2), Shadow Mount) Deseret Bk.

***Kiss Low Price.** abr. ed. Ed Mcbain. Read by Len Cariou. (ENG.). 2006. (978-0-06-114069-3(4), Harper Audio); (978-0-06-114068-6(6), Harper Audio) HarperCollins Pubs.

Kiss Me, Deadly. unabr. ed. Mickey Spillane. Read by Larry McKeever. 8 cass. (Running Time: 8 hrs.). (Mike Hammer Ser.). 1992. 48.00 (978-0-7366-2180-9(6), 2977) Books on Tape.

Friends & enemies warn Mike Hammer to drop his feud with the Mafia, but Mike is sore & thirsty for revenge. Defying the police & the FBI, he pits himself against the Mob.

***Kiss Me Deadly: 13 Tales of Paranormal Love.** unabr. ed. Trish Telep Editors. (Running Time: 16 hrs.). 2010. audio compact disk 79.97

(978-1-4418-7214-2(0), 9781441872142, BriAudCD Unabrid) Brilliance Audio.

***Kiss Me Deadly: 13 Tales of Paranormal Love.** unabr. ed. Compiled by Trish Telep Editors. (Running Time: 12 hrs.). 2010. 39.97 (978-1-4418-7217-3(5), 9781441872173, BADLE); 24.99 (978-1-4418-7215-9(9), 9781441872159, Brilliance MP3); 39.97 (978-1-4418-7216-6(7), 9781441872166, Brlnc Audio MP3 Lib) Brilliance Audio.

***Kiss Me Deadly: 13 Tales of Paranormal Love.** unabr. ed. Compiled by Trish Telep Editors. (Running Time: 16 hrs.). (YA). 2010. audio compact disk 29.99 (978-1-4418-7213-5(2), 9781441872135, Bril Audio CD Unabri) Brilliance Audio.

***Kiss Me If You Can.** unabr. ed. Carly Phillips. (Running Time: 8 hrs.). 2010. 24.99 (978-1-4233-5217-4(3), 9781423352174, BAD); 39.97 (978-1-4233-5218-1(1), 9781423352181, BADLE) Brilliance Audio.

***Kiss Me If You Can.** unabr. ed. Carly Phillips. Read by Sherri Slater. (Running Time: 9 hrs.). 2010. 24.99 (978-1-4233-5215-0(7), 9781423352150, Brilliance MP3); 39.97 (978-1-4233-5216-7(5), 9781423352167, Brlnc Audio MP3 Lib); audio compact disk 34.99 (978-1-4233-5213-6(0), 9781423352136, Bril Audio CD Unabri); audio compact disk 87.97 (978-1-4233-5214-3(9), 9781423352143, BriAudCD Unabrid) Brilliance Audio.

Kiss Me, Kill Me: And Other True Cases. unabr. ed. Ann Rule. Read by Staci Snell. 8 cass. (Running Time: 12 hrs.). 2004. 99.00 (978-1-4159-1604-9(7)); audio compact disk 88.40 (978-1-4159-1605-6(5)) Pub: Books on Tape. Dist(s): NetLibrary CO

In this absorbing portrayal of lovers who kill and the men and women who are their victims, Ann Rule expertly analyzes shocking, headline-making cases, unmasking the motives that transform sex and passion into deadly crimes. The first case is that of an ex-Marine judo instructor who seduced women and then destroyed their lives. A deadly blind date, a blood red rose left behind by a killer, a mystery finally solved by a brilliant cold case pair of detectives, a marriage based on false and murderous promises, the fatal manipulations of a faithless wife.

Kiss Me Like A Stranger: My Search for Love & Art. Gene Wilder. 2005. 19.95 (978-1-59397-660-6(7)) Pub: Macmill Audio. Dist(s): Macmillan

Kiss Me While I Sleep. abr. ed. Linda Howard. Read by Joyce Bean & Dick Hill. (Running Time: 6 hrs.). 2007. audio compact disk 14.99 (978-1-4233-3358-6(6), 9781423333586, BCD Value Price) Brilliance Audio.

Kiss Me While I Sleep. unabr. ed. Linda Howard. Read by Joyce Bean & Dick Hill. (Running Time: 11 hrs.). 2004. 39.25 (978-1-59335-807-5(5), 1593358075, Brlnc Audio MP3 Lib); 24.95 (978-1-59335-673-6(0), 1593356730, Brilliance MP3); 82.25 (978-1-59086-173-8(6), 1590861736, BrilAudUnabridg) Brilliance Audio.

It's a job that makes a killing. Efficient, professional, and without apology, Lily Mansfield is a hired assassin, working as a contract agent for the CIA. Her targets are the powerful and corrupt, those who can't be touched by the law. Now, after 18 years of service, Lily has been drawn into a dangerous game that hasn't been sanctioned, seeking vengeance for her own reasons. Each move bolder than the next, she is compromising her superiors, drawing unwanted attention and endangering her very life. Though stress and shock have made her feel somewhat invincible and a little cocky, Lily knows that she too can be taken out in an instant. And if it's her time, so be it. She intends to go down fighting. A CIA agent himself, Lucas Swain recognizes the signs of trauma in the line of fire. His orders are to either bring her in or bring her down. Yet he too is drawn into the game with Lily Mansfield, dancing on a tightrope as he tries to avoid a major international incident while still battling a tenacious foe who is dogging their every step. Keeping laser focus on her task at hand while vigilantly watching her back, Mansfield never sees the lethal peril that lies directly in her path . . . and how loyalty has a price.

Kiss Me While I Sleep. unabr. ed. Linda Howard. Read by Dick Hill & Joyce Bean. 7 cass. (Running Time: 11 hrs.). 2004. 32.95 (978-1-59086-172-1(8), 1590861728, BAU) Brilliance Audio.

It's a job that makes a killing. Efficient, professional, and without apology, Lily Mansfield is a hired assassin, working as a contract agent for the CIA. Her targets are the powerful and corrupt, those who can't be touched by the law. Now, after 18 years of service, Lily has been drawn into a dangerous game that hasn't been sanctioned, seeking vengeance for her own reasons. Each move bolder than the next, she is compromising her superiors, drawing unwanted attention and endangering her very life. Though stress and shock have made her feel somewhat invincible and a little cocky, Lily knows that she too can be taken out in an instant. And if it's her time, so be it. She intends to go down fighting. A CIA agent himself, Lucas Swain recognizes the signs of trauma in the line of fire. His orders are to either bring her in or bring her down. Yet he too is drawn into the game with Lily Mansfield, dancing on a tightrope as he tries to avoid a major international incident while still battling a tenacious foe who is dogging their every step. Keeping laser focus on her task at hand while vigilantly watching her back, Mansfield never sees the lethal peril that lies directly in her path . . . and how loyalty has a price.

Kiss Me While I Sleep. unabr. ed. Linda Howard. Read by Joyce Bean & Hill Dick. 9 CDs. (Running Time: 11 hrs.). 2004. audio compact disk 36.95 (978-1-59086-175-2(2), 1590861752, Bril Audio CD Unabri) Brilliance Audio.

Kiss Me While I Sleep. unabr. ed. Linda Howard. Read by Joyce Bean & Dick Hill. 6 CDs. (Running Time: 11 hrs.). 2004. audio compact disk 92.25 (978-1-59086-176-9(0), 1590861760, BriAudCD Unabrid) Brilliance Audio.

It's a job that makes a killing. Efficient, professional, and without apology, Lily Mansfield is a hired assassin, working as a contract agent for the CIA. Her targets are the powerful and corrupt, those who can't be touched by the law. Now, after 18 years of service, Lily has been drawn into a dangerous game that hasn't been sanctioned, seeking vengeance for her own reasons. Each move bolder than the next, she is compromising her superiors, drawing unwanted attention and endangering her very life. Though stress and shock have made her feel somewhat invincible and a little cocky, Lily knows that she too can be taken out in an instant. And if it's her time, so be it. She intends to go down fighting. A CIA agent himself, Lucas Swain recognizes the signs of trauma in the line of fire. His orders are to either bring her in or bring her down. Yet he too is drawn into the game with Lily Mansfield, dancing on a tightrope as he tries to avoid a major international incident while still battling a tenacious foe who is dogging their every step. Keeping laser focus on her task at hand while vigilantly watching her back, Mansfield never sees the lethal peril that lies directly in her path . . . and how loyalty has a price.

Kiss Me While I Sleep. unabr. ed. Linda Howard. Read by Joyce Bean & Dick Hill. (Running Time: 11 hrs.). 2004. 39.25 (978-1-59710-428-9(0), 1597104280, BADLE); 24.95 (978-1-59710-429-6(9), 1597104299, BAD) Brilliance Audio.

***Kiss of Crimson.** unabr. ed. Lara Adrian. Narrated by Hillary Huber. (Running Time: 11 hrs. 0 mins.). (Midnight Breed Ser.). 2010. 17.99 (978-1-4001-8458-3(4)); 24.99 (978-1-4001-6458-5(3)); audio compact disk 69.99 (978-1-4001-4458-7(2)); audio compact disk 34.99 (978-1-4001-1458-0(6)) Pub: Tantor Media. Dist(s): IngramPubServ

Kiss of Death. Jamie Rix. Read by Robert Llewelyn. 3 CDs. (J). 2005. audio compact disk 29.95 (978-0-7540-6670-5(3), Chivers Child Audio) AudioGO.

***Kiss of Death.** unabr. ed. Rachel Caine. Narrated by Cynthia Holloway. (Running Time: 8 hrs. 0 mins. 0 sec.). (Morganville Vampires Ser.). (ENG.). 2010. 19.99 (978-1-4001-6534-6(2)); 15.99 (978-1-4001-8534-4(3)); audio compact disk 29.99 (978-1-4001-1534-1(5)); audio compact disk 71.99 (978-1-4001-4534-8(1)) Pub: Tantor Media. Dist(s): IngramPubServ

Kiss of Death. unabr. ed. Linda Palmer. Read by Celeste Lawson. (Running Time: 30600 sec.). (Daytime Mysteries Ser.). 2007. 54.95 (978-1-4332-0583-5(1)); audio compact disk 29.95 (978-1-4332-0585-9(8)); audio compact disk 63.00 (978-1-4332-0584-2(X)) Blckstn Audio.

***Kiss of Death (Library Edition)** unabr. ed. Rachel Caine. Narrated by Cynthia Holloway. (Running Time: 8 hrs. 0 mins.). (Morganville Vampires Ser.). 2010. 29.99 (978-1-4001-9534-3(9)) Tantor Media.

Kiss of Hot Sun, Set. Nancy Buckingham. Read by Katherine Hunt. 4 cass. 1999. 44.95 (72574) Pub: Soundings Ltd GBR. Dist(s): ISIS Pub

***Kiss of Midnight.** unabr. ed. Lara Adrian. Narrated by Hillary Huber. (Running Time: 11 hrs. 30 mins.). (Midnight Breed Ser.: No. 1). 2010. 17.99 (978-1-4001-8457-6(6)) Tantor Media.

***Kiss of Midnight.** unabr. ed. Lara Adrian. Narrated by Hillary Huber. (Running Time: 11 hrs. 30 mins. 0 sec.). (Midnight Breed Ser.: No. 1). (ENG.). 2010. 24.99 (978-1-4001-6457-8(5)); audio compact disk 34.99 (978-1-4001-1457-3(8)); audio compact disk 69.99 (978-1-4001-4457-0(4)) Pub: Tantor Media. Dist(s): IngramPubServ

Kiss of Shadows. abr. ed. Laurell K. Hamilton. Read by Laural Merlington. (Running Time: 6 hrs.). (Meredith Gentry Ser.: No. 1). 2008. audio compact disk 14.99 (978-1-4233-6234-0(9), 9781423362340, BCD Value Price) Brilliance Audio.

Kiss of Shadows. unabr. ed. Laurell K. Hamilton. Read by Laural Merlington. 11 cass. (Running Time: 15 hrs.). (Meredith Gentry Ser.: No. 1). 2000. 34.95 (978-1-58788-124-4(1), 1587881241, BAU) Brilliance Audio.

"All it would take was my true name being mentioned after dark, and it would float back to my aunt. She was the Queen of Air and Darkness, and that meant that anything said in the dark was hers to hear, eventually. The fact that spotting the missing Elven American Princess had become more popular than spotting Elvis helped. Her magic was always chasing blind leads. Princess Meredith skiing in Utah. Princess Meredith dancing in Paris. Princess Meredith gambling in Vegas. After three years I was still a front-page story for the tabloids, though the latest headlines had been speculating that I was as dead as the King of Rock and Roll . . ." In fact, Meredith has been posing as a human in Los Angeles, living as a private investigator specializing in supernatural crime. But now Doyle, the Queen's chief bodyguard and assassin, has been dispatched to fetch her back - whether she likes it or not. And suddenly Meredith finds herself a pawn in her dreaded aunt's plans . . . plans that affect the future of the entire UnSeelie Court. The requirements of the job: to enjoy the constant company of the most beautiful - and immortal - men in the world. The reward: the crown - and the opportunity to continue to live. The penalty; death.

Kiss of Shadows. unabr. ed. Laurell K. Hamilton. Read by Laural Merlington. (Running Time: 15 hrs.). (Meredith Gentry Ser.: No. 1). 2004. 24.95 (978-1-59335-311-7(1), 1593353111, Brilliance MP3); 39.25 (978-1-59335-472-5(X), 159335472X, Brlnc Audio MP3 Lib) Brilliance Audio.

Kiss of Shadows. unabr. ed. Laurell K. Hamilton. Read by Laural Merlington. (Running Time: 15 hrs.). (Meredith Gentry Ser.: No. 1). 2004. 39.25 (978-1-59710-431-9(0), 1597104310, BADLE); 24.95 (978-1-59710-430-2(2), 1597104302, BAD) Brilliance Audio.

Kiss of Shadows. unabr. ed. Laurell K. Hamilton. Read by Laural Merlington. (Running Time: 15 hrs.). (Meredith Gentry Ser.: No. 1). 2007. audio compact disk 122.25 (978-1-4233-3384-5(5), 9781423333845, BriAudCD Unabrid); audio compact disk 38.95 (978-1-4233-3383-8(7), 9781423333838, Bril Audio CD Unabri) Brilliance Audio.

Kiss of the Bees. unabr. ed. J. A. Jance. Read by Gene Engene. 12 cass. (Running Time: 16 hrs. 30 min.). (Brandon Walker Ser.: Bk. 2). 2001. 64.95 (978-1-55686-961-7(4)) Books in Motion.

For Diana Ladd's family, the death of Andrew Carlisle in prison meant their long nightmare was finally over. But when Diana's daughter is kidnapped, clues point to a diabolical killer who could be a disciple of the famous killer.

Kiss of the Highlander. unabr. ed. Karen Marie Moning. (Running Time: 11 hrs.). (Highlander Ser.). 2008. 39.25 (978-1-4233-4152-9(X), 9781423341529, BADLE); 24.95 (978-1-4233-4151-2(1), 9781423341512, BAD) Brilliance Audio.

Kiss of the Highlander. unabr. ed. Karen Marie Moning. Read by Phil Gigante. 10 cass. (Running Time: 39600 sec.). (Highlander Ser.). 2008. 97.25 (978-1-4233-4146-8(5), 9781423341468, BrilAudUnabridg); audio compact disk 39.25 (978-1-4233-4150-5(3), 9781423341505, Brlnc Audio MP3 Lib); audio compact disk 102.25 (978-1-4233-4148-2(1), 9781423341482, BriAudCD Unabrid); audio compact disk 29.95 (978-1-4233-4147-5(3), 9781423341475, Bril Audio CD Unabri); audio compact disk 24.95 (978-1-4233-4149-9(X), 9781423341499, Brilliance MP3) Brilliance Audio.

Kiss Remembered. Erin St. Claire, pseud. Narrated by Barbara McCulloh. 4 cass. (Running Time: 5 hrs. 30 mins.). 47.00 (978-1-4025-1609-2(6)) Recorded Bks.

Kiss Remembered. unabr. ed. Erin St. Claire, pseud. Narrated by Barbara McCulloh. 4 cass. (Running Time: 5 hrs. 30 mins.). 2002. 29.95 (978-1-4025-1695-5(9), RF833) Recorded Bks.

Heading back to college at the age of 26, Shelley Browning didn't expect the searing memory of Professor Grant Chapman's kiss to come flooding back. Certain he wouldn't remember, Shelley keeps her distance until he asks her to have an innocent cup of coffee with him. Time had changed little between them she realizes, but would their careers, their dreams and their hearts, be worth risking for them to be together.

Kiss Remembered. unabr. ed. Erin St. Claire, pseud. Read by Karen Ziemba. 4 CDs. (Running Time: 5 hrs. 0 mins. 0 sec.). 2006. audio compact disk 14.95 (978-0-7435-5204-2(0), S&S Encore) Pub: S&S Audio. Dist(s): S and S Inc

Kiss the Girls. abr. ed. James Patterson. Read by Robert Guillaume & Chris Noth. (Alex Cross Ser.: No. 2). (ENG.). 2005. 14.98 (978-1-59483-324-3(9)) Pub: Hachet Audio. Dist(s): HachBkGrp

Kiss the Girls. abr. ed. James Patterson. Read by Robert Guillaume & Chris Noth. (Running Time: 3 hrs.). (Alex Cross Ser.: No. 2). (ENG.). 2009. 24.98 (978-1-60788-083-7(0)) Pub: Hachet Audio. Dist(s): HachBkGrp

Kiss the Girls. abr. ed. James Patterson. Read by Chris Noth & Robert Guillaume. 3 CDs. (Running Time: 3 hrs.). (Alex Cross Ser.: No. 2). (ENG.). 2005. audio compact disk 17.98 (978-1-59483-119-5(X)) Pub: Hachet Audio. Dist(s): HachBkGrp

Kiss the Girls, unabr. ed. James Patterson. Read by Michael Kramer. 8 cass. (Running Time: 12 hrs.). (Alex Cross Ser.: No. 2). 1995. 64.00 (978-0-7366-3082-5(1), 3762) Books on Tape.

Kiss the Girls. unabr. ed. James Patterson. Narrated by Ferrone Guidall. 9 cass. (Running Time: 12 hrs. 50 min.). (Alex Cross Ser.: No. 2). Rental 17.50 Set. (94532) Recorded Bks.

Someone has kidnapped Detective Alex Cross' niece, & Cross must find her before she becomes another grisly statistic.

Kiss the Girls, unabr. ed. James Patterson. Narrated by Richard Ferrone & George Guidall. 9 cass. (Running Time: 12 hrs. 30 mins.). (Alex Cross Ser.: No. 2). 78.00 (978-0-7887-0340-9(4), 94532E7) Recorded Bks.

Two twisted & clever killers are at work. One calls himself Casanova & collects beautiful women off college campuses from the Carolinas to Florida, building an exotic collection of sexual slaves. The other, the Gentleman Caller, is terrorizing Los Angeles with unspeakable murders. Black detective Alex Cross' latest case may involve both of them & this time it's personal. Someone has kidnapped his niece & Cross must find her before she becomes another grisly statistic. Available to libraries only.

Kiss Tomorrow Hello: Notes from the Midlife Underground by Twenty-Five Women over Forty. unabr. ed. (Running Time: 50400 sec.). 2007. 79.95 (978-0-7861-6904-7(4)); audio compact disk 29.95 (978-0-7861-7055-5(7)); audio compact disk 99.00 (978-0-7861-6903-0(6)) Blckstn Audio.

Kiss Tomorrow Hello: Notes from the Midlife Underground by Twenty-Five Women over Forty. unabr. ed. Ed. by Claire Davis. (Running Time: 50400 sec.). 2007. 29.95 (978-0-7861-4917-9(5)); audio compact disk 29.95 (978-0-7861-5929-1(4)) Blckstn Audio.

Kiss Yesterday Goodbye, Set. Allan Stella. Read by Jill Shilling. 2 cass. 1999. 21.95 (MRC1037) AudioGO.

Kiss Yo-Yo Diets & Fat Goodbye-Forever! Created by Leslie Van Romer. 2006. audio compact disk 299.00 (978-1-934123-17-1(X)) Appleten.

Kiss Your Ear: Spice Series. Short Stories. 1 CD. (Running Time: 71:54). Dramatization. 2004. mass mkt. 15.95 (978-0-9759671-0-2(X)) Sounds Pubng Inc.

SoundsErotic original short erotic, audio stories are sensual stories for lovers. Stories are written by award winning writers and read by professional voice talent.

Kisscut. Karin Slaughter. Read by Clarinda Ross. (Grant County Ser.: Bk. 2). 2002. 72.00 (978-0-7366-8786-7(6)); audio compact disk 88.00 (978-0-7366-8800-0(5)) Books on Tape.

***Kisscut.** abr. ed. Karin Slaughter. Read by Patricia Kalember. (ENG.). 2004. (978-0-06-078294-8(3), Harper Audio) HarperCollins Pubs.

***Kisscut.** abr. ed. Karin Slaughter. Read by Patricia Kalember. (ENG.). 2004. (978-0-06-081444-1(6), Harper Audio) HarperCollins Pubs.

Kissed a Sad Goodbye. unabr. ed. Deborah Crombie. Narrated by Jenny Sterlin. 10 cass. (Running Time: 14 hrs. 30 mins.). (Duncan Kincaid/Gemma James Novel Ser.). 1999. 87.00 (978-0-7887-3751-0(1), 95869E7) Recorded Bks.

When Kincaid & Gemma investigate the murder of a beautiful young head of a tea company, they discover not only were the details of her death strange, but her life was a mystery to those who knew her best.

Kisser. unabr. ed. Stuart Woods. Contrib. by Tony Roberts. 6 CDs. (Running Time: 8 hrs.). (Stone Barrington Ser.: No. 17). (ENG.). (gr. 12 up). 2010. audio compact disk 29.95 (978-0-14-314538-7(X), PengAudBks) Penguin Grp USA.

***Kisser.** unabr. ed. Stuart Woods. Narrated by Tony Roberts. 6 CDs. (Running Time: 8 hrs.). 2010. audio compact disk 80.00 (978-0-307-71415-2(2), BksonTape) Pub: Random Audio Pubg. Dist(s): Random

Kisses from the Sea: A 30-Minute Romance Series. Suzette Barclay. 1. (Running Time: 50 mins.). 2005. audio compact disk 7.95 (978-0-9746860-8-0(5)) City Life Bks.

Kissing Games of the World. Sandi Kahn Shelton. Read by Myra Platt. (Running Time: 46800 sec.). 2008. audio compact disk 29.95 (978-1-59316-168-2(9)) Listen & Live.

Kissing Garden. unabr. ed. Charlotte Bingham. Read by Judy Bennett. 12 cass. (Running Time: 18 hrs.). 2000. 96.95 (978-0-7540-0461-5(9), CAB 1884) Pub: Chivers Audio Bks GBR. Dist(s): AudioGO

As children, George & Amella were friends who loved to roam the Sussex Downs. One day, caught in a thunderstorm, the now mature George realizes that the way he feels about Amella has changed. But World War I has begun & George is sent off to the front line. But when he returns after four years, Amella finds that the boy she loved has gone.

***Kissing Hand.** Audrey Penn. Illus. by Ruth E. Harper & Nancy M. Leak. (ENG.). (J). 2010. bk. (978-0-7569-9299-6(0)) Perfect Learn.

***Kissing Sin.** unabr. ed. Keri Arthur. Narrated by Angela Dawe. (Running Time: 10 hrs. 30 mins.). (Riley Jenson Guardian Ser.). 2010. 16.99 (978-1-4526-7002-7(1)); 34.99 (978-1-4526-0002-4(3)); 24.99 (978-1-4526-5002-9(0)) Tantor Media.

***Kissing Sin (Library Edition)** unabr. ed. Keri Arthur. Narrated by Angela Dawe. (Running Time: 10 hrs. 30 mins.). (Riley Jenson Guardian Ser.). 2010. 34.99 (978-1-4526-2002-2(4)); 83.99 (978-1-4526-3002-1(X)) Tantor Media.

Kissing the Bee. Kathe Koja. Read by Sarah Gorman. (Playaway Young Adult Ser.). (ENG.). (YA). (gr. 9-12). 2009. 34.99 (978-1-60812-709-2(5)) Find a World.

Kissing the Bee. unabr. ed. Kathe Koja. Narrated by Chelsea Mixon. 3 CDs. (Running Time: 2 hrs. 45 mins.). (YA). (gr. 7 up). 2008. audio compact disk 34.00 (978-1-934180-39-6(4)) Full Cast Audio.

Kissing the Gunner's Daughter, unabr. ed. Ruth Rendell. Narrated by Davina Porter. 10 cass. (Running Time: 14 hrs. 30 mins.). (Inspector Wexford Mystery Ser.: Bk. 15). 1992. 85.00 (978-1-55690-790-6(7), 92424K8) Recorded Bks.

Inspector Wexford is horrified by the carnage he encounters at Tancred Manor, home of a famous anthropologist, but he is determined to do all that he can for 17-year-old Daisy, the only survivor of the mass murders that obliterated her family.

Kissing the Gunner's Daughter. unabr. collector's ed. Ruth Rendell. Read by Donada Peters. 9 cass. (Running Time: 13 hrs. 30 min.). (Inspector Wexford Mystery Ser.: Bk. 15). 1993. 72.00 (978-0-7366-2337-7(X), 3116) Books on Tape.

Chief Inspector Wexford investigates murder & the lethal consequences of kissing the gunner's daughter.

Kissing the Rain. Kevin Brooks. Narrated by Dave John. 8 cass. (Running Time: 10 hrs. 45 mins.). (YA). 2004. 84.75 (978-1-4193-0390-6(2)) Recorded Bks.

Kissing Toads. Nancy Hastings. 1 cass. 8.95 (145) Am Fed Astrologers.

Synastry, natal and progressed, shows growth in relationships.

Kissing Worldly Dating Goodbye. Taffi L. Dollar. 2 cass. (Running Time: 3 hrs.). 2000. 10.00 (978-1-931172-01-1(3), TS296, Kidz Faith) Pub: Creflo Dollar. Dist(s): STL Dist NA

The teachings on Christian dating.

Kissinger Pt. 1: A Biography. unabr. collector's ed. Walter Isaacson. Read by Jonathan Reese. 13 cass. (Running Time: 19 hrs. 30 min.). 1994. 104.00 (978-0-7366-2685-9(9), 3421A) Books on Tape.
Critical though sympathetic study of relationship between Henry Kissinger's personality & foreign policy he pursued.

Kissinger Pt. 2: A Biography. unabr. collector's ed. Walter Isaacson. Read by Jonathan Reese. 13 cass. (Running Time: 19 hrs. 30 min.). 1994. 104.00 (978-0-7366-2686-6(7), 3421-B) Books on Tape.

Kitchen Chemistry. Compiled by Benchmark Education Staff. 2006. audio compact disk 10.00 (978-1-4108-6690-5(4)) Benchmark Educ.

Kitchen Confidential: Adventures in the Culinary Underbelly. unabr. ed. Anthony Bourdain. Read by Anthony Bourdain. 7 CDs. (Running Time: 9 hrs.). (ENG.). 2005. audio compact disk 20.00 (978-0-7393-3235-1(X), Random AudioBks) Pub: Random Audio Pubg. Dist(s): Random

Kitchen Doctor: Taste & the Elements. Ingrid Naiman. 4 cass. (Running Time: 6 hrs.). 40.00 (978-1-882834-99-0(2)) Seventh Ray.
The pharmacology of food based on ayurveda. Describes symptoms of excess consumption of each type of food & how to correct symptoms with food & herbs.

Kitchen God's Wife. Amy Tan. Read by Gwendoline Yeo. (Playaway Adult Fiction Ser.). 2008. 69.99 (978-1-60640-668-7(X)) Find a World.

Kitchen God's Wife. unabr. ed. Amy Tan. Read by Amy Tan. 12 cass. (Running Time: 18 hrs.). 2001. 53.00 (978-1-59040-035-7(6), Phoenix Audio) Pub: Amer Intl Pub. Dist(s): PerseuPGW
A moving story of two women who have kept each other's secrets for forty years.

***Kitchen House: A Novel.** unabr. ed. Kathleen Grissom. Read by Bahni, Orlagh and Turpin Cassidy. (Running Time: 12 hrs. 30 mins.). 2010. 29.95 (978-1-4417-6127-9(6)); 72.95 (978-1-4417-6123-1(3)); audio compact disk 29.95 (978-1-4417-6126-2(8)); audio compact disk 105.00 (978-1-4417-6124-8(1)) Blckstn Audio.

Kitchen Notes, Set. Melinda Lee & Chris Lane. 2 cass. (Running Time: 2 hrs.). (Discovery Ser.). 1992. pap. bk. 15.95 (978-1-56015-209-5(5)) Penton Overseas.
Answers, anecdotes & amazing ideas about food & cooking.

Kitchen Privileges: A Memoir. unabr. ed. Mary Higgins Clark. 2004. 15.95 (978-0-7435-4513-6(3)) Pub: S&S Audio. Dist(s): S and S Inc

***Kitchen Recordings.** Larry Egan. Sean O'Driscoll. (ENG.). 2004. audio compact disk 22.95 (978-0-8023-8155-2(3)) Pub: Clo Iar-Chonnachta IRL. Dist(s): Dufour

Kitchen Table Wisdom: Stories That Heal. abr. ed. Rachel Naomi Remen. Read by Rachel Naomi Remen. 2 cass. (Running Time: 3 hrs.). 1996. 17.95 (978-1-57453-063-6(1), 394448) Audio Lit.
Through real-life stories drawn from her career as a physician and her extensive experience as a patient, Dr. Remen offers us the hope that any of our experiences, no matter how hard, it can be used to grow in wisdom and teach us to love.

***Kitchener's Last Volunteer.** Henry Allingham. 2010. 61.95 (978-1-4079-0913-4(4)); audio compact disk 79.95 (978-1-4079-0914-1(2)) Pub: Soundings Ltd GBR. Dist(s): Ulverscroft US

Kite. Alma Flor Ada. (Stories for the Year 'Round Ser.). (J). (gr. k-3). 4.95 (978-1-58105-310-4(X)) Santillana.

Kite. abr. ed. W. O. Mitchell. 3 CDs. (Running Time: 10800 sec.). (ENG.). 2005. audio compact disk 24.95 (978-0-86492-399-8(6)) Pub: BTC Audiobks CAN. Dist(s): U Toronto Pr

Kite Fighters. unabr. ed. Linda Sue Park. Narrated by Norm Lee. 2 pieces. (Running Time: 2 hrs. 45 mins.). 2000. 19.00 (978-1-4025-4121-6(X)) Recorded Bks.

Kite Flyer & Other Stories: Reading Level 2. 1993. 16.00 (978-0-88336-562-5(6)) New Readers.

Kite Race. Michele Sobel Spirn. (J). (ps-1). 1988. 9.95 (978-0-685-25199-7(3)) Jan Prods.

Kite Race. unabr. ed. Michele Sobel Spirn. 1 cass. (Running Time: 5 min.). (Happy Endings! Ser.). (J). (gr. k-2). 1988. bk. 16.99 (978-0-87386-055-0(1)) Jan Prods.
Don is looking forward to entering his dragon kite, which he & his father made, in the upcoming kite race; however, he would be happier if his friend, Tim, also had a kite to enter.

Kite Race. unabr. ed. Michele Sobel Spirn. 1 cass. (Running Time: 5 min.). (Happy Endings! Ser.). (J). (ps-1). 1988. pap. bk. 9.95 (978-0-87386-051-2(9)) Jan Prods.

Kite Runner. Khaled Hosseini. 2005. 39.99 (978-1-59895-029-8(0)) Find a World.

Kite Runner. Khaled Hosseini. 2006. cd-rom 39.99 (978-1-59895-478-4(4)) Find a World.

Kite Runner. abr. ed. Khaled Hosseini. Read by Khaled Hosseini. 5 CDs. (Running Time: 60 hrs. 0 mins. 0 sec.). (ENG.). 2003. audio compact disk 30.00 (978-0-7435-3024-8(1), Audioworks) Pub: S&S Audio. Dist(s): S and S Inc

Kite Runner. unabr. ed. Khaled Hosseini. Read by Khaled Hosseini. 11 CDs. (Running Time: 120 hrs. 0 mins. 0 sec.). (ENG.). 2005. audio compact disk 39.95 (978-0-7435-4523-5(0)) Pub: S&S Audio. Dist(s): S and S Inc
A Stunning Novel of Hope and Redemption Taking us from Afghanistan in the final days of the monarchy to the present, The Kite Runner is the unforgettable and beautifully told story of the friendship between two boys growing up in Kabul. Raised in the same household and sharing the same wet nurse, Amir and Hassan grow up in different worlds: Amir is the son of a prominent and wealthy man, while Hassan, the son of Amir's father's servant, is a Hazara - a shunned ethnic minority. Their intertwined lives, and their fates, reflect the eventual tragedy of the world around them. When Amir and his father flee the country for a new life in California, Amir thinks that he has escaped his past. And yet he cannot leave the memory of Hassan behind him. The Kite Runner is a novel about friendship and betrayal, and about the price of loyalty. It is about the bonds between fathers and sons, and the power of fathers over sons - their love, their sacrifices, and their lies. Written against a backdrop of history that has not been told in fiction before, The Kite Runner describes the rich culture and beauty of a land in the process of being destroyed. But through the devastation, Khaled Hosseini offers hope: through the novel's faith in the power of reading and storytelling, and in the possibilities he shows us for redemption.

Kite Runner. unabr. ed. Khaled Hosseini. Read by Khaled Hosseini. 2006. 23.95 (978-0-7435-6449-6(9)) Pub: S&S Audio. Dist(s): S and S Inc

Kites Sail High. unabr. ed. Ruth Heller. 1 cass. (Running Time: 11 min.). (J). (gr. k-5). 1989. pap. bk. 17.95 (978-0-8045-6562-2(7), 6562) Spoken Arts.
Romp through an explanation of verbs with humorous text & lively graphics. Reading Rainbow Review title. American Bookseller Pick of the Lists.

Kit's Law. abr. ed. Donna Morrissey. Narrated by Mary Walsh. 4 cass. (Running Time: 5 hrs.). (ENG.). 2001. 24.95 (978-0-86492-283-0(3)) Pub: BTC Audiobks CAN. Dist(s): U Toronto Pr

Kit's Wilderness. David Almond. 3 cass. (Running Time: 4 hrs. 30 mins.). (J). 2000. 24.00 (978-0-7366-9017-1(4)) Books on Tape.
The Watson family moves to Stoneygate, an old coal mining town, to care for Kit's grandfather. There Kit meets John Askew, another boy whose family has worked in the mines. As Kit's grandfather tells him stories of the mine's past, Askew takes Kit into the mines, where the boys look for the childhood ghosts of their long-gone ancestors.

Kit's Wilderness. unabr. ed. David Almond. Read by Charles Keating. 3 vols. (Running Time: 5 hrs. 4 mins.). (J). (gr. 7 up). 2004. pap. bk. 36.00 (978-0-8072-8216-8(2), Listening Lib); 30.00 (978-0-8072-8215-1(4), LL0166, Listening Lib) Random Audio Pubg.
The Watson family moves to Stoneygate, an old coal-mining town, to care for Kit's grandfather. When Kit meets John Askew, another boy whose family has worked in the mines. As Kit's grandfather tells him stories of the mine's past, Askew takes Kit into the mines, where the boys look for the childhood ghosts of their long gone ancestors.

Kitty & Her Boys. June Francis. 10 cass. (Running Time: 13 hrs. 15 mins.). (Story Sound Ser.). (J). 2004. 84.95 (978-1-85903-685-3(6)) Pub: Mgna Lrg Print GBR. Dist(s): Ulverscroft US

Kitty & the Dead Man's Hand. unabr. ed. Carrie Vaughn. Narrated by Marguerite Gavin. (Running Time: 7 hrs. 30 mins. 0 sec.). (Kitty Norville Ser.). (ENG.). 2010. 24.99 (978-1-4001-6262-8(9)); 14.99 (978-1-4001-8262-6(X)); audio compact disk 69.99 (978-1-4001-4262-0(8)); audio compact disk 34.99 (978-1-4001-1262-3(1)) Pub: Tantor Media. Dist(s): IngramPubServ

Kitty & the Midnight Hour. unabr. ed. Carrie Vaughn. Narrated by Marguerite Gavin. (Running Time: 7 hrs. 0 mins. 0 sec.). (Kitty Norville Ser.). (ENG.). 2009. 24.99 (978-1-4001-6258-1(0)); audio compact disk 34.99 (978-1-4001-1258-6(3)); audio compact disk 69.99 (978-1-4001-4258-3(X)) Pub: Tantor Media. Dist(s): IngramPubServ

Kitty & the Silver Bullet. unabr. ed. Carrie Vaughn. Narrated by Marguerite Gavin. (Running Time: 9 hrs. 0 mins. 0 sec.). (Kitty Norville Ser.). (ENG.). 2009. 24.99 (978-1-4001-6261-1(0)); audio compact disk 69.99 (978-1-4001-4261-3(X)); audio compact disk 34.99 (978-1-4001-1261-6(3)) Pub: Tantor Media. Dist(s): IngramPubServ

***Kitty & the Silver Bullet.** unabr. ed. Carrie Vaughn. Narrated by Marguerite Gavin. (Running Time: 9 hrs. 0 mins.). (Kitty Norville Ser.). 2009. 15.99 (978-1-4001-8261-9(1)); 34.99 (978-1-4001-9261-8(7)) Tantor Media.

Kitty Foyle. Perf. by Ginger Rogers. 1 cass. (Running Time: 1 hr.). 7.95 (DD8835) Natl Recrd Co.

***Kitty Goes to War.** unabr. ed. Carrie Vaughn. (Running Time: 9 hrs. 0 mins.). (Kitty Norville Ser.). 2010. 15.99 (978-1-4001-8801-7(6)); 34.99 (978-1-4001-9801-6(1)) Tantor Media.

***Kitty Goes to War.** unabr. ed. Carrie Vaughn. Narrated by Marguerite Gavin. 1 MP3-CD. (Running Time: 7 hrs. 30 mins. 0 sec.). (Kitty Norville Ser.). 2010. 24.99 (978-1-4001-6801-9(5)); audio compact disk 34.99 (978-1-4001-1801-4(8)); audio compact disk 83.99 (978-1-4001-4801-1(4)) Pub: Tantor Media. Dist(s): IngramPubServ

Kitty Goes to Washington. unabr. ed. Carrie Vaughn. Narrated by Marguerite Gavin. (Running Time: 9 hrs. 0 mins. 0 sec.). (Kitty Norville Ser.). (ENG.). 2009. 24.99 (978-1-4001-6259-8(9)); audio compact disk 34.99 (978-1-4001-1259-3(1)); audio compact disk 69.99 (978-1-4001-4259-0(8)) Pub: Tantor Media. Dist(s): IngramPubServ

Kitty Rainbow. Wendy Robertson. Read by Trudy Harris. 10 cass. (Storysound Ser.). (J). 1999. 84.95 (978-1-85903-295-4(8)) Pub: Mgna Lrg Print GBR. Dist(s): Ulverscroft US

***Kitty Raises Hell.** unabr. ed. Carrie Vaughn. Narrated by Marguerite Gavin. (Running Time: 9 hrs. 30 mins.). (Kitty Norville Ser.). 2010. 16.99 (978-1-4001-8263-3(8)); 24.99 (978-1-4001-6263-5(7)); 34.99 (978-1-4001-9263-2(3)); audio compact disk 69.99 (978-1-4001-4263-7(6)); audio compact disk 34.99 (978-1-4001-1263-0(X)) Pub: Tantor Media. Dist(s): IngramPubServ

Kitty Takes a Holiday. unabr. ed. Carrie Vaughn. Narrated by Marguerite Gavin. (Running Time: 8 hrs. 30 mins. 0 sec.). (Kitty Norville Ser.). (ENG.). 2009. 24.99 (978-1-4001-6260-4(2)); audio compact disk 34.99 (978-1-4001-1260-9(5)); audio compact disk 69.99 (978-1-4001-4260-6(1)) Pub: Tantor Media. Dist(s): IngramPubServ

***Kitty Takes a Holiday.** unabr. ed. Carrie Vaughn. Narrated by Marguerite Gavin. (Running Time: 8 hrs. 30 mins.). (Kitty Norville Ser.). 2009. 15.99 (978-1-4001-8260-2(3)) Tantor Media.

***Kitty's House of Horrors.** unabr. ed. Carrie Vaughn. Narrated by Marguerite Gavin. 1 MP3-CD. (Running Time: 8 hrs. 0 mins. 0 sec.). (Kitty Norville Ser.). 2010. 19.99 (978-1-4001-6542-1(3)); 15.99 (978-1-4001-8542-9(4)); 29.99 (978-1-4001-9542-8(X)); audio compact disk 59.99 (978-1-4001-4542-3(2)); audio compact disk 29.99 (978-1-4001-1542-6(6)) Pub: Tantor Media. Dist(s): IngramPubServ

***Kiwi Wars.** Garry Douglas Kilworth. 2010. 69.95 (978-1-4079-0847-2(2)); audio compact disk 79.95 (978-1-4079-0848-9(0)) Pub: Soundings Ltd GBR. Dist(s): Ulverscroft US

KJB & His Family Tree. Paul Sandberg. Perf. by Todd Liebenow & Dave Privett. 1 cass. (Running Time: 29 min.). Dramatization. 1996. 15.00 incl. script. (978-1-58302-040-1(3), STP-21) One Way St.
Twelve three to five minute puppet programs featuring Kid James - a Bible character, & his bookmark sidekick Mark De Page. They present the history of our Bible.

KJB & His Family Tree. Paul Sandberg. Voice by Todd Liebenow & Dave Privett. Prod. by Dale Liz VonSeggen. 2001. audio compact disk 15.00 (978-1-58302-188-0(4)) One Way St.

KJV Set: Black Case. unabr. ed. Perf. by Alexander Scourby. 48 cass. (Running Time: 50 hrs.). 1991. 74.95 (978-1-56563-421-3(7)) Hendrickson MA.
The world's best-loved translation of the Bible is brought to life in this powerful, word-for-word narration by renowned British dramatist Alexander Scourby. A convenient way to hear God's word at any time of the day. The nylon carrying case helps keep the cassettes protected and organized at home or on the go. And the limited lifetime warranty ensures years of listening pleasure.

KJV Set: Burgundy Case. unabr. ed. Perf. by Alexander Scourby. 48 cass. (Running Time: 50 hr.). 1991. 74.95 (978-1-56563-422-0(5)) Hendrickson MA.

KJV Bible. Steve Johnson. 2005. 29.95 (978-1-56563-950-8(2)) Hendrickson MA.

KJV Bible, Set. Read by Stephen Johnston. 44 cass. 1999. 64.95 full color cardboard package. (978-1-56563-316-2(4)) Hendrickson MA.

KJV Bible, Set. Read by Stephen Johnston. 44 cass. 1997. 64.95 Black nylon package. (978-1-56563-319-3(9)); 64.95 Set, burgundy nylon package. (978-1-56563-321-6(0)) Hendrickson MA.
Be refreshed and encouraged by God's Word at any time of the day when you listen to the beloved King James Version of the Bible, read word-for-word over a soft musical background by narrator Stephen Johnston.• Available in New Testament and Complete Bible versions. • Cassettes are offered in black, burgundy or navy blue portable nylon cases with full-color descriptive wraps. • Enjoy hearing the Bible while on the go, at home, or in personal or group Bible study. • The limited lifetime warranty ensures years of listening pleasure.

KJV Bible, Set. Narrated by Alexander Scourby. 48 cass. 1991. 79.95 (978-1-56563-387-2(3)) Hendrickson MA.
The world's best-loved translation of the Bible is brought to life in this powerful word-for-word narration by renowned British dramatist Alexander Scourby. This dramatized edition features the voices of dozens of actors and actresses, sound effects and background music. A convenient way to hear God's word at any time of the day. The limited lifetime warranty ensures years of listening pleasure.

KJV Bible, Set. Narrated by Alexander Scourby. 48 cass. 1998. 69.95 (978-1-56563-386-5(5)) Hendrickson MA.

KJV Bible, Set. unabr. ed. Perf. by Alexander Scourby. 62 CDs. (Running Time: 50 hr.). 1999. 189.95 (978-1-56563-479-4(9)) Hendrickson MA.
King James.

KJV Bible Set: Blue Case. unabr. ed. Read by Stephen Johnston. 44 cass. (Running Time: 50 hrs.). 1997. 64.95 Incl. blue nylon case with handle. (978-1-56563-446-6(2)) Hendrickson MA.
Be refreshed and encouraged by God's Word at any time of the day when you listen to the beloved King James Version of the Bible, read word-for-word over a soft musical background by narrator Stephen Johnston.• Available in New Testament and Complete Bible versions. • Cassettes are offered in black, burgundy or navy blue portable nylon cases with full-color descriptive wraps. • Enjoy hearing the Bible while on the go, at home, or in personal or group Bible study. • The limited lifetime warranty ensures years of listening pleasure.

KJV Bible New Testament, Set. unabr. ed. Perf. by Alexander Scourby. 15 CDs. (Running Time: 18 hrs.). 1999. bk. 54.95 INCL. HARDCOVER CASE. (978-1-56563-482-4(9)) Hendrickson MA.
King James.

KJV Bible New Testament: Burgundy Case, Set. unabr. ed. Perf. by Alexander Scourby. 12 cass. (Running Time: 18 hr.). 1991. 19.95 (978-1-56563-420-6(9)) Hendrickson MA.
The world's best-loved translation of the Bible is brought to life in this powerful, word-for-word narration by renowned British dramatist Alexander Scourby. A convenient way to hear God's word at any time of the day. The nylon carrying case helps keep the cassettes protected and organized at home or on the go. And the limited lifetime warranty ensures years of listening pleasure.

KJV Complete Bible. Narrated by Alexander Scourby. 48 cass. 2004. 79.99 (978-0-88368-828-1(X), 77828X) Pub: Whitaker Hse. Dist(s): Anchor Distributors

KJV Complete Bible. Created by Zondervan Publishing Staff. (Running Time: 75 hrs. 0 mins. 0 sec.). (ENG.). 2007. audio compact disk 79.99 (978-0-310-93609-1(8)) Zondervan.

KJV Complete Bible, Set. Narrated by Alexander Scourby. 62 CDs. 1998. 199.95 (978-1-56563-390-2(3)) Hendrickson MA.

KJV Complete Bible MP3 CDs. Andrew Zorsky. 5. (Running Time: 70 hrs. 20 mins.). 2005. (978-0-89957-423-3(8)) AMG Pubs.

KJV Complete Bible Supersaver. Narrated by Alexander Scourby. 2004. bk. 89.88 (978-0-529-11343-6(0)) Nelson.

KJV Dramatized Bible Audio Download. Zondervan Publishing Staff. (Running Time: 75 hrs. 0 mins. 0 sec.). (ENG.). 2007. 49.99 (978-0-310-92500-2(2)) Zondervan.

KJV Dramatized Complete Bible Supersaver. Narrated by Alexander Scourby. 2004. bk. 36.88 (978-0-529-11780-9(0)) Nelson.

KJV New Testament, Set. Read by Stephen Johnston. 14 CDs. 1999. 49.95 (978-1-56563-322-3(9)); 16.95 Set, full-color cardboard package. (978-1-56563-312-4(1)) Hendrickson MA.

KJV New Testament, Set. Read by Stephen Johnston. 11 cass. 1997. bk. 19.95 (978-1-56563-315-5(6)); 19.95 Black nylon package. (978-1-56563-313-1(X)) Hendrickson MA.
Be refreshed and encouraged by God's Word at any time of the day when you listen to the beloved King James Version of the Bible, read word-for-word over a soft musical background by narrator Stephen Johnston.• Available in New Testament and Complete Bible versions. • Cassettes are offered in black, burgundy or navy blue portable nylon cases with full-color descriptive wraps. • Enjoy hearing the Bible while on the go, at home, or in personal or group Bible study. • The limited lifetime warranty ensures years of listening pleasure.

KJV New Testament, Set. Narrated by Alexander Scourby. 12 cass. 1991. 19.95 (978-1-56563-385-8(7)) Hendrickson MA.
The world's best-loved translation of the Bible is brought to life in this powerful, word-for-word narration by renowned British dramatist Alexander Scourby. This dramatized edition features the voices of dozens of actors and actresses, sound effects and background music. A convenient way to hear God's word at any time of the day. The limited lifetime warranty ensures years of listening pleasure.

KJV New Testament, Set. Alexander Scourby. 15 CDs. 1998. audio compact disk 57.95 (978-1-56563-389-6(X)) Hendrickson MA.

KJV New Testament, Set. Narrated by Alexander Scourby. 12 cass. 1998. 17.95 (978-1-56563-384-1(9)) Hendrickson MA.

KJV New Testament: Dramatized. Created by Zondervan Publishing Staff. (Running Time: 18 hrs. 0 mins. 0 sec.). (ENG.). 2006. audio compact disk 24.99 (978-0-310-93610-7(1)) Zondervan.

KJV New Testament Set: Blue Case. unabr. ed. Perf. by Alexander Scourby. 12 cass. (Running Time: 18 hr.). 1991. 19.95 (978-1-56563-449-7(7)) Hendrickson MA.
The world's best-loved translation of the New Testament is brought to life in this powerful, word-to-word, voice-only narration by reowned British dramatist Alexander Scourby. There are 12 high quality audio cassettes, which are each digitally mastered in stereo for enhanced listening enjoyment.

KJV New Testament Bible: Premium Edition. unabr. ed. Narrated by Steven Stevens. 1996. 24.99 (978-0-8499-6161-8(0)) Nelson.

KJV New Testament Dramatized Audio Download. Zondervan Publishing Staff. (Running Time: 18 hrs. 0 mins. 0 sec.). (ENG.). 2006. 16.24 (978-0-310-92499-9(5)) Zondervan.

KJV New Testament on Audio. Stephen Johnston. 2006. audio compact disk 39.95 (978-1-56563-973-7(1)) Hendrickson MA.

KJV New Testament on Audio: Dramatized New Edition. Stephen Johnston. Dramatization. 2006. audio compact disk 39.95 (978-1-56563-976-8(6)) Hendrickson MA.

KJV New Testament: Promise Edition. Read by Roscoe L. Browne. 12 cass. 9.99 (978-0-529-07089-0(8), WBC-15) Nelson.
God's promises are emphasized & highlighted.

KJV NT on CD: Voice Only Johnston Complete Voice. abr. ed. 2006. bk. 24.97 (978-1-59856-071-8(9)) Hendrickson MA.

KJV on Mp3. Hendrickson Publishers, Inc. Staff. 2004. 29.95 (978-1-56563-776-4(3)) Hendrickson MA.

KKK. 10.00 Esstee Audios.
A recording of a KKK meeting at Rising Sun, Md. after the Martin Luther King riots.

Klassentreffen: Kassetten. Paul Webster. 1 cass. (Cambridge Express German Ser.). (GER.). 1996. 144.00 (978-0-521-42700-5(2)) Cambridge U Pr.

Kleber's Convoy. unabr. ed. Antony Trew. Read by Peter Wickham. 6 cass. (Running Time: 7.5 hrs.). (Sound Ser.). (J). 2002. 54.95 (978-1-84283-333-9(2)) Pub: ISIS Lrg Prnt GBR. Dist(s): Ulverscroft US

Klecka Plays Broege & Karlins. Paul Rey Klecka. Timothy Broege & William Karlins. 1998. audio compact disk 18.00 (978-0-8101-3707-3(0)) Pub: Northwestern U Pr. Dist(s): Chicago Distribution Ctr

Klezmer: A Marriage of Heaven & Earth. 1 CD. (Running Time: 1 hr.). (Musical Expeditions Ser.). 1996. pap. bk. 19.95 (978-1-55961-383-5(1), Ellipsis Arts) Relaxtn Co.

Klezmer Katz. Lesley H. Choy. 1 cass. 1993. pap. bk. 24.95 (978-0-9637580-0-2(4)) Fox-Haycroft.

Klinefelter Syndrome - A Bibliography & Dictionary for Physicians, Patients, & Genome Researchers. Compiled by Icon Group International, Inc. Staff. 2007. ring bd. 28.95 (978-0-497-11246-2(9)) Icon Grp.

Klingon. Hillary Bader. (Star Trek Ser.). 2004. 10.95 (978-0-7435-4643-0(1)); 7.95 (978-0-7435-4270-8(3)) Pub: S&S Audio. Dist(s): S and S Inc

Klingon Way: A Warrior's Guide. Marc Okrand. 2004. 7.95 (978-0-7435-4274-6(6)) Pub: S&S Audio. Dist(s): S and S Inc

Klone & I. unabr. ed. Danielle Steel. Read by Babo Harrison. 4 cass. 1999. 25.95 (FS9-43221) Highsmith.

Kluge: The Haphazard Construction of the Human Mind. Gary Marcus. Read by Stephen Hoye. (Playaway Adult Nonfiction Ser.). (ENG.). 2009. 60.00 (978-1-60775-633-0(1)) Find a World.

Kluge: The Haphazard Construction of the Human Mind. unabr. ed. Gary Marcus. Narrated by Stephen Hoye. (Running Time: 6 hrs. 30 mins. 0 sec.). (ENG.). 2008. audio compact disk 59.99 (978-1-4001-3751-0(9)) Pub: Tantor Media. Dist(s): IngramPubServ

Kluge: The Haphazard Construction of the Human Mind. unabr. ed. Gary Marcus. Read by Stephen Hoye. 6 CDs. (Running Time: 6 hrs. 30 mins. 0 sec.). (ENG.). 2008. audio compact disk 29.99 (978-1-4001-0751-3(2)); audio compact disk 19.99 (978-1-4001-5751-8(X)) Pub: Tantor Media. Dist(s): IngramPubServ

Kluge Bauerntochter. Jacob W. Grimm & Wilhelm K. Grimm. 1 cass. (Running Time: 60 min.). (Bruder Grimm Kinder & Hausmarchen Ser.). (GER.). 1996. pap. bk. 19.50 (978-1-58085-212-8(2), GR-07) Interlingua VA.
Includes German transcription. Includes title story, Die Rabe, Die kluge Bauerntochter, Das Ratsel, Der liebste Roland. The combination of written text & clarity & pace of diction will open the door for intermediate & advanced students to genuine comprehension & the use of literary texts for advancement in rapid understanding of written & oral language materials. The audio text plus written text concept makes foreign languages accessible to a much wider range of students than books alone.

Knack: How Street-Smart Entrepreneurs Learn to Handle Whatever Comes Up. unabr. ed. Bo Burlingham & Norm Brodsky. Read by Sean Pratt. (Running Time: 10 hrs.). (ENG.). 2009. audio compact disk 39.98 (978-1-59659-273-5(7)) Pub: Gildan Media. Dist(s): HachBkGrp

Knave of Hearts. unabr. ed. Philippa Carr. Read by Anita Wright. 10 cass. (Running Time: 15 hrs.). 2001. 84.95 (978-0-7531-0993-9(X), 001007) Pub: ISIS Audio GBR. Dist(s): Ulverscroft Co.

Knee Deep in Paradise. abr. ed. Brett Butler. Read by Brett Butler. (Running Time: 4 hrs.). 2008. 39.25 (978-1-4233-5834-3(1), 9781423358343, BADLE); 39.25 (978-1-4233-5832-9(5), 9781423358329, Brinc Audio MP3 Lib); 24.95 (978-1-4233-5833-6(3), 9781423358336, BAD); 24.95 (978-1-4233-5831-2(7), 9781423358312, Brilliance MP3) Brilliance Audio.

***Knee Deep in Plums.** Sheila Newberry. Read by Julia Franklin. 2010. 34.95 (978-1-84652-607-7(8)); audio compact disk 38.95 (978-1-84652-608-4(6)) Pub: Magna Story GBR. Dist(s): Ulverscroft US

Knee-High to a Fiddler. 2002. audio compact disk 14.95 (978-0-911205-04-6(7)) N Dak Coun Arts.

Knee to the Groin. Pablo Francisco. Read by Pablo Francisco. 2000. audio compact disk 16.98 (978-1-929243-14-3(6)) Uproar Ent.

Kneeknock Rise. Natalie Babbitt. Read by Suzanne Toren. 2 cass. (Running Time: 2 hrs. 18 mins.). (J). 2000. 18.00 (978-0-7366-9171-0(5)) Books on Tape.
Fable.

Kneeknock Rise. unabr. ed. Natalie Babbitt. Read by Suzanne Toren. 2 cass. (Running Time: 2 hrs.). (J). (gr. 1-8). 1997. 23.00 (LL 0073) AudioGO.

Kneeknock Rise. unabr. ed. Natalie Babbitt. Read by Suzanne Toren. 2 cass. (Running Time: 1 hr. 42 mins.). (J). (gr. 3-7). 1996. 23.00 (978-0-8072-7617-4(0), YA902CX, Listening Lib) Random Audio Pubg.
From the moment young Egan arrives in Instep for the annual fair, he is entranced by the fable surrounding the peak of Knee-Knock Rise. The story is that of stormy nights, when the rain drives harsh & cold.

Kneeknock Rise. unabr. ed. Natalie Babbitt. Read by Suzanne Toren. 2 vols. (Running Time: 1 hr. 42 mins.). (J). (gr. 3-7). 1996. pap. bk. 29.00 (978-0-8072-7618-1(9), YA902SP, Listening Lib) Random Audio Pubg.

Kneel & Fight: Solo Track. Randy Kettereing. Perf. by Christine Wyrtzen. 1 cass. (50-Day Spiritual Adventure Ser.). 1993. 9.99 (978-1-879050-30-3(7)) Chapel of Air.
Accompaniment track for solo singer.

Kneeling Christian. Unknown Christian, The et al. (Pure Gold Classics Ser.). (ENG., 2007. pap. bk. 14.99 (978-0-88270-397-8(8)) Bridge-Logos.

Kneeling in Bethlehem. Ann Weems. Read by Ann Weems. 1 cass. 1996. 16.95 (978-0-664-25682-1(1)) Westminster John Knox.

Knick Knack Paddy Whack: Mother Goose on the Loose & Other Teeny Tiny Tales. Short Stories. 1 CD. (Running Time: 51 Minutes). (J). 1997. audio compact disk 15.00 (978-0-9760432-2-5(X)) D Ferlatte.

Knick Knack Paddy Whack 2: Mother Goose Still on the Loose & a Few Animal Tales Too. Short Stories. 1 CD. (Running Time: 64 Minutes). (J). 2003. audio compact disk 15.00 (978-0-9760432-5-6(4)) D Ferlatte.

Kniest Dysplasia - A Bibliography & Dictionary for Physicians, Patients, & Genome Researchers. Compiled by Icon Group International, Inc. Staff. 2007. ring bd. 28.95 (978-0-497-11247-9(7)) Icon Grp.

Knife Edge. Paul Adam. 2009. 89.95 (978-0-7531-4342-1(9)); audio compact disk 99.95 (978-0-7531-4343-8(7)) Pub: Isis Pubng Ltd GBR. Dist(s): Ulverscroft US

Knife Edge. unabr. ed. David Rollins. Read by Mel Foster. (Running Time: 14 hrs.). (Vin Cooper Ser.). 2009. 39.97 (978-1-4233-3256-5(3), 9781423332565, Brinc Audio MP3 Lib); 39.97 (978-1-4233-3258-9(X), 9781423332589, BADLE); 24.99 (978-1-4233-3257-2(1), 9781423332572, BAD); audio compact disk 89.97 (978-1-4233-3254-1(7), 9781423332541, BriAudCD Unabrid) Brilliance Audio.

Knife Edge. unabr. ed. David A. Rollins. Read by Mel Foster. (Running Time: 14 hrs.). (Vin Cooper Ser.). 2009. 24.99 (978-1-4233-3255-8(5), 9781423332558, Brilliance MP3); audio compact disk 38.99 (978-1-4233-3253-4(9), 9781423332534, Bril Audio CD Unabri) Brilliance Audio.

Knife in the Back. Bill Crider. Narrated by Cristine McMurdo-Wallis. 5 cass. (Running Time: 7 hrs. 15 mins.). 2004. 49.75 (978-1-4025-7292-0(1)); audio compact disk 55.80 (978-1-4025-8775-7(9)) Recorded Bks.

***Knife Music.** unabr. ed. David Carnoy. (Running Time: 12 hrs. 30 mins.). 2010. audio compact disk 32.95 (978-1-4417-6245-0(0)) Blckstn Audio.

***Knife Music.** unabr. ed. David Carnoy. Read by Kristoffer Tabori. (Running Time: 12 hrs. 30 mins.). 2010. 29.95 (978-1-4417-6246-7(9)); 72.95 (978-1-4417-6243-6(4)); audio compact disk 105.00 (978-1-4417-6244-3(2)) Blckstn Audio.

Knife of Dreams. Robert Jordan. Read by Kate Reading & Michael Kramer. (Wheel of Time Ser.: Bk. 11). 2005. 41.95 (978-1-59397-766-5(2)) Pub: Macmill Audio. Dist(s): Macmillan

Knife of Dreams. unabr. ed. Robert Jordan. Read by Kate Reading & Michael Kramer. 25 cass. (Wheel of Time Ser.: Bk. 11). 2005. 129.00 (978-1-4159-2239-2(X)); audio compact disk 159.00 (978-1-4159-2240-8(3)) Books on Tape.

Knife of Dreams. unabr. ed. Robert Jordan. Read by Kate Reading & Michael Kramer. 21 CDs. (Running Time: 32 hrs. 0 mins. 0 sec.). (Wheel of Time Ser.: Bk. 11). (ENG.). 2005. audio compact disk 69.95 (978-1-59397-765-8(4)) Pub: Macmill Audio. Dist(s): Macmillan

***Knife of Never Letting Go.** unabr. ed. Patrick Ness. Read by Nick Podehl. (Running Time: 12 hrs.). (Chaos Walking Ser.). 2010. 14.99 (978-1-4418-8903-4(5), 9781441889034, Candlewick Bril); 39.97 (978-1-4418-8904-1(3), 9781441889041, Candlewick Bril); audio compact disk 14.99 (978-1-4418-8901-0(9), 9781441889010, Candlewick Bril); audio compact disk 19.99 (978-1-4418-5267-0(0), 9781441852670, Candlewick Bril); audio compact disk 39.97 (978-1-4418-8902-7(7), 9781441889027, Candlewick Bril); audio compact disk 69.97 (978-1-4418-8900-3(0), 9781441889003, Candlewick Bril) Brilliance Audio.

Knife Thrower, Set. abr. ed. Boyd C. Richardson. 2 cass. 11.98 (978-1-55503-696-6(1), 0700983) Covenant Comms.

Knight at Dawn. unabr. ed. Mary Pope Osborne. 1 cass. (Running Time: 40 mins.). (Magic Tree House Ser.: No. 2). (J). (gr. k-3). 2004. pap. bk. 17.00 (978-0-8072-0331-6(9), Listening Lib) Random Audio Pubg.

Knight for a Day. Perf. by Joel Pierson & Juliet Youngren. 1 cass. 1998. 29.95 (978-1-57677-111-2(3), CURT001) Lodestone Catalog.

Knight in Shining Armor. Jude Deveraux & Stephanie Zimbalist. 2004. 10.95 (978-0-7435-4916-5(3)) Pub: S&S Audio. Dist(s): S and S Inc

Knight of Shadows. Roger Zelazny. Read by Roger Zelazny. 2 vols. (Chronicles of Amber: Bk. 9). 2003. (978-1-58807-534-5(6)) Am Pubng Inc.

Knight of Shadows. Roger Zelazny. Read by Roger Zelazny. 2 vols. (Chronicles of Amber: Bk. 9). 2004. audio compact disk 25.00 (978-1-58807-261-0(4)); audio compact disk (978-1-58807-692-2(X)) Am Pubng Inc.

Knight of Shadows. abr. ed. Roger Zelazny. 2 cass. (Running Time: 3 hrs.). (Chronicles of Amber: Bk. 9). 2003. 18.00 (978-1-58807-134-7(0)) Am Pubng Inc.
Merlin pursues the mysterious disappearances of the two people dearest to him: Julia, once murdered and now reincarnated as his enemy; and his father, Corwin, who, never visible, leaves behind tantalizing signs of life. But, the powers of Order and Chaos intervene, attempting to force Merlin to choose once and for all where his allegiance lies: the Courts of Chaos, Amber, the Lorgus, or the Unicorn. Deftly woven of suspense, intrigue, and imagery, Knight of Shadows is another colorful piece of the Amber puzzle, as well as a work of sophisticated fantasy by one of our leading word magicians.

Knight of the Word. unabr. ed. Terry Brooks. Narrated by George Wilson. 8 cass. (Running Time: 11 hrs. 45 mins.). (Word & the Void Ser.: Bk. 2). 2000. 75.00 (978-0-7887-2516-6(5), 95589E7) Recorded Bks.
Every night, John Ross, a Knight of the Word, dreams of a nightmarish world & every day he stalks the demons who could make these dreams come true. Now, having failed to prevent an unspeakable act of horror, he has become the tempting prey for these voracious fiends.

Knight Templar. unabr. ed. Leslie Charteris. Read by David Case. 7 cass. (Running Time: 7 hrs.). (Saint Ser.). 1991. 42.00 (978-0-7366-1923-3(2), 2747) Books on Tape.
Simon Templar, aka The Saint, is back, this time with a vengeance! His dearest friend has been murdered & The Saint is out for revenge! The Saint rescues an heiress from a fate too horrifying to contemplate, squares off against arch-villain Dr. Marius & thwarts a plot that could plunge the world into a great war. Happily for The Saint & for his legion of followers, victory marches with virtue & The Saint is to be found on the side of the angels.

Knightmare. abr. ed. Engle & Barnes. Read by Full Cast Production Staff. (Running Time: 7200 sec.). (Strange Matter Ser.). (J). (gr. 4-7). 2006. audio compact disk 25.25 (978-1-4233-0867-6(0), 9781423308676, BACDLib Ed) Brilliance Audio.
Mitchell Garrison has made a terrible mistake. While on a class field trip to the museum, Mitchell's friend, Howard, dares him to snatch a small, unguarded artifact from around the neck of an old, emerald suit of armor. Cracking under the pressure of his pal calling him "chicken," Mitchell reluctantly agrees, but soon comes to regret it. That night, with the stolen piece of history tucked safely under his bed, Mitchell finds it difficult to sleep. It isn't very long after he closes his eyes that he has his first nightmare. Terrible visions of monsters, beasts, and wild men attack him in his sleep, trying to stop him from reaching his final opponent, an ominous, emerald suit of armor... just like the one at the museum! The dream always ends the same way; the knight strikes Mitchell down. When things from the dreamworld start happening in real life, Mitchell pleads with Howard and their other friend, Keri, for help. He knows in his gut that he must return the artifact to where it belongs... before the Knightmare comes true.

Knightmare. abr. ed. Engle & Barnes. (Running Time: 2 hrs.). (Strange Matter Ser.). 2006. 9.95 (978-1-4233-0868-3(9), 9781423308683, BAD) Brilliance Audio.

Knightmare. abr. ed. Engle & Julian Barnes. Read by Multivoice Production Staff. (Running Time: 2 hrs.). (Strange Matter Ser.). 2006. 25.25 (978-1-4233-0869-0(7), 9781423308690, BADLE) Brilliance Audio.

Knightmare. abr. ed. Marion Engle & Johnny Ray Barnes, Jr. (Running Time: 7200 sec.). (Strange Matter Ser.). (J). (gr. 4-7). 2006. audio compact disk 9.95 (978-1-4233-0866-9(2), 9781423308669, BACD) Brilliance Audio.

Knights & Mongols. Lance Auburn Everette. 3 CDs. (Running Time: 3 hrs.). (Michael Ser.: No. 6). 2005. audio compact disk 9.99 (978-1-58943-487-5(0)) Am Pubng Inc.
This is the sixth book in a truly unique series of historical action-adventure novels: Michael. Sometimes, in history, things worked out for the best against all odds. Maybe Somebody intervened on the side of the correct path - even when we didn't know what that path was. But to intervene in the affairs of human beings without disrupting civilization completely is to wield human tools - and human weapons. So when the Archangels arrive to Change Things, watch out! Published for the first time ever by Americana Publishing. Michael: Spirituality - with an edge.

Knight's Cross. unabr. collector's ed. E. M. Nathanson & Aaron Bank. Read by John MacDonald. 10 cass. (Running Time: 10 hrs.). 1995. 60.00 (978-0-7366-2943-0(2), 3638) Books on Tape.
Captain Aaron Bank offers a chilling World War II scenario of what might have happened had his undercover troops captured Hitler. Vivid action, great history.

Knights of Bushido. unabr. ed. Lord Russell of Liverpool. Read by Richard Brown. 8 cass. (Running Time: 12 hrs.). 1988. 64.00 (978-0-7366-1305-7(6), 2212) Books on Tape.
A record of Japanese war crimes & atrocities as told by eye-witnesses in their statements to post-war Allied commissions of investigation.

Knights of Dark Renown. unabr. ed. David Gemmell. Narrated by Christopher Kay. 12 cass. (Running Time: 14 hrs. 15 mins.). 1999. 89.00 (978-1-84197-055-4(7), H1044E7) Recorded Bks.
Features an unlikely set of heroes battling impossible odds. The King of The Nine Duchies has become a tyrant, championed by the unstoppable Red Knights. The Knights of the Gabala, legendary defenders of truth & right, could defeat them, but they went on a quest to combat evil six years ago & have never returned. So it is left to the ordinary people - including a runaway slave, a saga poet & a disgraced knight - to fight as best as they may.

Knights of Dark Renown. unabr. ed. David Gemmell. Narrated by Christopher Kay. 13 CDs. (Running Time: 14 hrs. 15 mins.). 2000. audio compact disk 120.00 (978-1-84197-137-7(5), C1247E7) Recorded Bks.

Knights of the Cross. unabr. ed. Piers Paul Read. Read by Ric Jerrom. 10 cass. (Running Time: 10 hrs.). 1998. 84.95 (978-0-7540-0129-4(6), CAB1552, Chivers Child Audio) AudioGO.
Michael Latham, leading expert in Soviet affairs, finds himself at the age of 37. Sourly, he contemplates the success of his two friends from Cambridge days: Gordon Taylor, Sunday Gazette editor & George Harding at the Ministry of Defense. Then Harding is found murdered & Latham must infiltrate a religious group known as the Knights of the Cross, Harding's suspected murderers.

Knights of the Kitchen Table. unabr. ed. Jon Scieszka. Read by William Dufris. 1 cass. (Running Time: 47 mins.). (Time Warp Trio Ser.: No. 1). (J). (gr. 2-5). 1998. pap. bk. 17.00 (978-0-8072-0391-0(2), FTR193SP, Listening Lib) Random Audio Pubg.
Joe & his friends travel to King Arthur's time.

Knit the Season. unabr. ed. Kate Jacobs. (Running Time: 10 hrs. 0 mins.). (Friday Night Knitting Club Ser.). 2009. 29.95 (978-1-4417-0122-0(2)); 59.95 (978-1-4417-0118-3(4)); audio compact disk 90.00 (978-1-4417-0119-0(2)) Blckstn Audio.

Knit the Season. unabr. ed. Kate Jacobs. (Running Time: 8 hrs.). (ENG.). (gr. 12 up). 2009. audio compact disk 39.95 (978-0-14-314535-6(5)) Penguin Grp USA.

Knit Together: Discover God's Pattern for Your Life. abr. ed. Debbie Macomber. Read by Sonja Lanzener. Told to Sara Horn. (Running Time: 3 hrs.). (ENG.). 2007. 19.98 (978-1-59483-946-7(8)) Pub: Hachet Audio. Dist(s): HachBkGrp

Knit Two. unabr. ed. Kate Jacobs. Read by Carrington MacDuffie. (Running Time: 10 hrs. 5 mins.). (Friday Night Knitting Club Ser.). 2008. 29.95 (978-1-4332-6602-7(4)); audio compact disk 79.95 (978-1-4332-6598-3(2)); audio compact disk 99.00 (978-1-4332-6599-0(0)) Blckstn Audio.

Knit Two. unabr. ed. Kate Jacobs. Read by Carrington MacDuffie & Ron McLarty. 9 CDs. (Running Time: 11 hrs.). (ENG.). (gr. 12 up). 2008. audio compact disk 39.95 (978-0-14-314447-2(2)) Penguin Grp USA.

Knit with Courage, Live with Hope. Annie Modesitt. (ENG.). 2009. audio compact disk 24.95 (978-0-9817491-8-1(6)) Holton Hse.

KnitKnit: Profiles Projects from Knitting?s New Wave. Sabrina Gschwandtner. Narrated by Sabrina Gschwandtner. (ENG.). 2008. audio compact disk 29.95 (978-0-9796073-7-0(X)) Knitting Out.

Knitting. Anne Bartlett. Read by Beverley Dunn. (Running Time: 8 hrs. 10 mins.). 2009. 74.99 (978-1-74214-191-6(9), 9781742141916) Pub: Bolinda Pubng AUS. Dist(s): Bolinda Pub Inc

Knitting. unabr. ed. Anne Bartlett. Read by Beverley Dunn. (Running Time: 29400 sec.). 2006. audio compact disk 83.95 (978-1-74093-783-2(X)) Pub: Bolinda Pubng AUS. Dist(s): Bolinda Pub Inc

Knitting Circle. Ann Hood. Read by Hillary Huber. (Running Time: 36000 sec.). 2007. 59.95 (978-0-7861-6917-7(6)); audio compact disk 72.00 (978-0-7861-6916-0(8)) Blckstn Audio.

Knitting Circle. unabr. ed. Ann Hood. Read by Hillary Huber. (Running Time: 36000 sec.). 2007. 29.95 (978-0-7861-4910-0(8)); audio compact disk 29.95 (978-0-7861-5936-9(7)) Blckstn Audio.

Knitting Circle. unabr. ed. Ann Hood. Read by Hillary Huber. (Running Time: 36000 sec.). 2007. audio compact disk 29.95 (978-0-7861-7062-3(X)) Blckstn Audio.

Knitting Lessons: Tales from the Knitting Path. Lela Nargi. Narrated by Julia Olson. (ENG.). 2008. audio compact disk 29.95 (978-0-9796073-6-3(1)) Knitting Out.

Knitting Memories: Reflections on the Knitter's Life. Ed. by Lela Nargi. 2007. audio compact disk 29.95 (978-0-9796073-0-1(2)) Knitting Out.

Knitting Memories: Reflections on the Knitter's Life. abr. ed. Lela Nargi et al. Read by Kymberly Dakin. (YA). 2008. 54.99 (978-1-60514-895-3(4)) Find a World.

Knitting Yarns & Spinning Tales: A Knitter's Stash of Wit & Wisdom. Ed. by Kari Cornell. Narrated by Greta Cunningham & Meg Swansen. (ENG.). 2009. audio compact disk 29.95 (978-0-9825470-0-7(5)) Knitting Out.

Knives at Dawn: America's Quest for Culinary Glory at the Legendary Bocuse d'or Competition. unabr. ed. Andrew Friedman. Narrated by Sean Runnette. (Running Time: 11 hrs. 30 mins.). 2009. 17.99 (978-1-4001-8509-2(2)) Tantor Media.

Knives at Dawn: America's Quest for Culinary Glory at the Legendary Bocuse d'or Competition. unabr. ed. Andrew Friedman. Narrated by Sean Runnette. (Running Time: 11 hrs. 30 mins. 0 sec.). (ENG.). 2010. 24.99 (978-1-4001-6509-4(1)); audio compact disk 34.99 (978-1-4001-1509-9(4)) Pub: Tantor Media. Dist(s): IngramPubServ

Knives at Dawn: America's Quest for Culinary Glory at the Legendary Bocuse d'Or Competition. unabr. ed. Andrew Friedman. Narrated by Sean Runnette. (Running Time: 11 hrs. 30 mins. 0 sec.). (ENG.). 2010. audio compact disk 69.99 (978-1-4001-4509-6(0)) Pub: Tantor Media. Dist(s): IngramPubServ

Knock at Midnight. unabr. ed. Clayborne Carson. Read by Keith David & Jay Gregory. (ENG.). 2005. 14.98 (978-1-59483-326-7(5)) Pub: Hachet Audio. Dist(s): HachBkGrp

Knock at Midnight: Inspiration from the Great Sermons of Reverend Martin Luther King, Jr. unabr. ed. Clayborne Carson & Peter Holloran. Read by Martin Luther King et al. (Running Time: 8 hrs.). (ENG.). 2009. 59.98 (978-1-60788-106-3(3)) Pub: Hachet Audio. Dist(s): HachBkGrp

Knock at Midnight: Inspiration from the Great Sermons of Reverend Martin Luther King, Jr. unabr. ed. Read by Jay Gregory et al. 8 CDs. (Running Time: 8 hrs.). (ENG., 2005. audio compact disk 39.98 (978-1-59483-100-3(9)) Pub: Hachet Audio. Dist(s): HachBkGrp

Knock Down. abr. ed. Dick Francis. Read by Tim Pigott-Smith. 2008. audio compact disk 14.95 (978-0-06-149223-5(X), Harper Audio) HarperCollins Pubs.

Knock Down. unabr. ed. Dick Francis. Read by Tony Britton. 6 cass. (Running Time: 6 hrs.). 1995. 54.95 (978-0-7451-6830-2(2), CAB 613) AudioGO.
A vicious gang of horse dealers threaten bloodstock agent Jonah Dereham's reputation & life when his honesty endangers their crooked motives. But the criminal-minded men have underestimated Dereham. They threaten him, burn his home & even attempt to kill him. But they will soon wish they had never met Jonah Dereham.

Knock Down. unabr. ed. Dick Francis. Read by David Case. 6 cass. (Running Time: 6 hrs.). 1994. 48.00 (978-0-7366-2780-1(4), 3499) Books on Tape.
Ex-jockey Jonah Dereham bids for a young steeplechaser, but gets knocked on his head for his trouble.

Knock Down. unabr. ed. Dick Francis. Read by Tony Britton. 6 cass. (Running Time: 9 hrs.). 2000. 49.95 (CAB 613) Pub: Chivers Audio Bks GBR. Dist(s): AudioGO
A vicious gang of horse dealers threaten bloodstock agent Jonah Dereham's life when his honesty endangers their crooked motives. They threaten him, burn his home, and attempt to kill him. But they will soon wish they had never met Jonah Dereham!.

Knock Down. unabr. ed. Dick Francis. Narrated by Neil Hunt. 5 cass. (Running Time: 6 hrs. 45 mins.). 1994. 44.00 (978-0-7887-0106-1(1), 94347E7) Recorded Bks.
Dirty deeds among thoroughbred bloodstock agents put ex-jockey Jonah Dereham in harm's way.

Knock, Knock, Knockin' at Heaven's Door. abr. ed. Mary B. Good. Perf. by Mimi G. Good & Kristofer Simmons. 2 cass. (Running Time: 3 hrs. 20 min.). (J). (gr. 9 up). 1997. 18.95 Set. (978-0-9627976-1-3(8)) M B Good.

Knock on Every Door: A Motivational & Inspirational True Life Story. deluxe ed. Edward D. Carry. Ed. by Karen Sones & Paul La Pinn. (Running Time: 35 mins.). 2004. audio compact disk 16.95 (978-0-9633590-7-0(X)) Target Mktg-Mgmt.

Knock on Every Door Sold As Package: A Motivational & Inspirational True Life Story. Edward D. Curry. Ed. by Karey. Contrib. by Todd Washburon. 2004. pap. bk. 24.95 (978-0-9633590-5-6(3)) Target Mktg-Mgmt.

***Knock Out.** Catherine Coulter. 2010. audio compact disk 14.99 (978-1-4233-6528-0(3)) Brilliance Audio.

Knock Out. abr. ed. Catherine Coulter. (Running Time: 6 hrs.). (FBI Thriller Ser.: No. 13). 2009. audio compact disk 26.99 (978-1-4233-6527-3(5), 9781423365273, BACD) Brilliance Audio.

Knock Out. unabr. ed. Catherine Coulter. (Running Time: 12 hrs.). (FBI Thriller Ser.: No. 13). 2009. 24.99 (978-1-4233-6523-5(2), 9781423365235, Brilliance MP3) Brilliance Audio.

Knock Out. unabr. ed. Catherine Coulter. Read by Renée Raudman & Paul Costanzo. (Running Time: 12 hrs.). (FBI Thriller Ser.: No. 13). 2009. 39.97 (978-1-4233-6524-2(0), 9781423365242, Brlnc Audio MP3 Lib) Brilliance Audio.

Knock Out. unabr. ed. Catherine Coulter. Read by Renée Raudman. (Running Time: 12 hrs.). (FBI Thriller Ser.: No. 13). 2009. 39.97 (978-1-4233-6526-6(7), 9781423365266, BADLE) Brilliance Audio.

Knock Out. unabr. ed. Catherine Coulter. Read by Renée Raudman & Paul Costanza. (Running Time: 12 hrs.). (FBI Thriller Ser.: No. 13). 2009. 24.99 (978-1-4233-6525-9(9), 9781423365259, BAD) Brilliance Audio.

Knock Out. unabr. ed. Catherine Coulter. Read by Paulo Costanzo & Renée Raudman. 10 CDs. (Running Time: 12 hrs.). (FBI Thriller Ser.: No. 13). 2009. audio compact disk 36.99 (978-1-4233-6521-1(6), 9781423365211, Bril Audio CD Unabri) Brilliance Audio.

Knock Out. unabr. ed. Catherine Coulter. Read by Renée Raudman & Paul Costanza. (Running Time: 12 hrs.). (FBI Thriller Ser.: No. 13). 2009. audio compact disk 97.97 (978-1-4233-6522-8(4), 9781423365228, BriAudCD Unabrid) Brilliance Audio.

***Knock Out.** unabr. ed. Catherine Coulter. Narrated by Paul Costanzo & Renée Raudman. 1 Playaway. (Running Time: 12 hrs.). 2009. 69.99 (978-1-60847-818-7(1)) Find a World.

Knock Your Socks Off Service on the Phone, Set. Ron Zemke. 2 cass. 1999. 89.95 incl. wkbk. multiple choice tests . (80248CHDG) AMACOM.
The legendary customer service guru provides winning tips & techniques. 0.5 CEUs. Course level: Fundamentals.

Knocked Out by My Nunga-Nungas: Further, Further Confessions of Georgia Nicolson. Louise Rennison. Narrated by Stina Nielsen. 4 CDs. (Running Time: 4 hrs. 15 mins.). (Confessions of Georgia Nicolson Ser.: No. 3). (gr. 9 up). 2004. audio compact disk 39.00 (978-1-4025-3316-7(0)) Recorded Bks.
Life should be all yummy scrumbos for 14-year-old Georgia Nicolson. With Robbie the Sex God (!) as her new boyfriend, her biggest worry should be about exactly where "ear nibbling" fits on the emergency snogging scale. These further, further adventures of the irrepressible star of Angus, Thongs, and Full Frontal Snogging will have listeners everywhere laughing like loons on loon tablets.

Knocked Out by My Nunga-Nungas: Further, Further Confessions of Georgia Nicolson. unabr. ed. Louise Rennison. Narrated by Stina Nielsen. 3 pieces. (Running Time: 4 hrs. 15 mins.). (Confessions of Georgia Nicolson Ser.: No. 3). (gr. 9 up). 2002. 28.00 (978-1-4025-2748-7(9)) Recorded Bks.

Knocked Out by My Nunga-Nungas: Further, Further Confessions of Georgia Nicolson. unabr. ed. Louise Rennison & Louise Rennison. 3 cass. (Running Time: 4 hrs.). (Confessions of Georgia Nicolson Ser.: No. 3). 2004. 14.99 (978-1-4025-3683-0(6), 70034) Recorded Bks.

Knocker on Death's Door, unabr. ed. Ellis Peters, pseud. Narrated by Simon Prebble. 5 cass. (Running Time: 7 hrs. 15 mins.). (Inspector George Felse Mystery Ser.: Vol. 10). 1994. 44.00 (978-1-55690-991-7(8), 94130E7) Recorded Bks.
The day after a Gothic door is returned to its original place in the Mottisham village church, two men are found dead in its shadow. The Welsh villagers, closed & suspicious of outsiders, believe their deaths were not accidental, but part of an ancient legend that told of an unrepentant monk who tried to gain entrance to the church by grasping the door's iron knocker.

Knocker; The Winning Ball. Zane Grey. 1 cass. (Running Time: 1 hr. 4 mins.). 2000. (978-0-7588-0023-7(1), Acme Record); audio compact disk (978-0-7588-0024-4(X), Acme Record) Goss Commns.
A collection of two baseball stories.

Knocking on Heaven's Door. Mark Chironna. 4 cass. 1992. 25.00 Set. (978-1-56043-921-9(1)) Destiny Image Pubs.

Knocking on the Door: Shorter Writings. unabr. collector's ed. Alan Paton. Read by Stuart Courtney. 10 cass. (Running Time: 15 hrs.). 1983. 80.00 (978-0-7366-0348-5(4), 1334) Books on Tape.
A collection of 70 poems, short stories, articles & speeches.

Knopf National Poetry Month Collection. unabr. ed. Sarah Arvio et al. (Running Time: 3600 sec.). (ENG.). 2007. audio compact disk 19.95 (978-0-7393-4331-9(9), Random AudioBks) Pub: Random Audio Pubg. Dist(s): Random

Knothole in the Closet: A Story about Belle Boyd, a Confederate Spy. 1 CD. (Running Time: 24 mins.). 2003. audio compact disk 24.00 (978-1-58472-276-2(2), In Aud) Sound Room.

Knothole in the Closet: A Story about Belle Boyd, a Confederate Spy. Marilyn Weymouth Seguin. 1 cd. (Running Time: 45 mins). (J). 2002. pap. bk. 35.00 (978-1-58472-277-9(0), In Aud) Pub: Sound Room. Dist(s): Baker Taylor

Knothole in the Closet: A Story about Belle Boyd, a Confederate Spy. unabr. ed. Marilyn Weymouth Seguin. 1 cd. (Running Time: 45 mins). (J). 2002. audio compact disk 16.95 (978-1-58472-275-5(4), In Aud) Pub: Sound Room. Dist(s): Baker Taylor

Knothole in the Closet - A Story about Belle Boyd, A Confederate Spy. unabr. ed. Marilyn Weymouth Seguin. Read by Kate Fleming. (J). 2007. 34.99 (978-1-60252-565-8(X)) Find a World.

Knotholes Are for "Seeing" Therapy Through Poetry, Prose & Other Writings. unabr. ed. 3 cass. (Running Time: 3 hrs.). 1996. pap. bk. 17.95 Set. (978-1-879518-09-4(0)) Busn Living Pubns.

Knots on a Counting Rope. unabr. ed. Bill Martin, Jr. & John Archambault. 1 cass. (Running Time: 13 min.). (J). (gr. k-5). 1992. pap. bk. 17.90 (978-0-8045-6559-2(7), 6559) Spoken Arts.
An Indian boy sits with his grandfather and listens to stories. The boy ties knots on his "counting rope", a metaphor for the passage of time. This is a powerful story about blindness, love and courage.

Knotted Strings. abr. ed. Jake Page. Read by Buck Schirner. 2 cass. (Running Time: 3 hrs.). 2000. 7.95 (978-1-57815-016-8(7), 1040, Media Bks Audio) Media Bks NJ.
The author shows his knowledge of the history, landscape & culture of the Desert Southwest, in a story of murder & sabotage on tribal Indian land.

Know Can Do! How to Put Learning into Action. unabr. ed. Ken Blanchard et al. Read by Mark Barbolak. 2 CDs. (Running Time: 2 hrs. 0 mins. 0 sec.). (ENG.). 2007. audio compact disk 19.95 (978-1-4272-0251-2(6)) Pub: Macmill Audio. Dist(s): Macmillan

Know-How: The 8 Skills That Separate People Who Perform from Those Who Don't. unabr. ed. Ram Charan. Read by Arthur Morey. (Running Time: 32400 sec.). (ENG.). 2007. audio compact disk 34.95 (978-0-7393-4122-3(7), Random AudioBks) Pub: Random Audio Pubg. Dist(s): Random

Know-It-All: One Man's Humble Quest to Become the Smartest Person in the World. abr. ed. A. J. Jacobs & G. N. Cantor. Read by Geoffrey Cantor. 6 CDs. (Running Time: 7 hrs. 45 mins.). (ENG.). 2004. audio compact disk 29.95 (978-1-56511-908-6(8), 1565119088) Pub: HighBridge. Dist(s): Workman Pub

Know-It-All: One Man's Humble Quest to Become the Smartest Person in the World. unabr. ed. A. J. Jacobs. Read by Geoffrey Cantor. 12 CDs. (Running Time: 15 hrs.). (ENG.). 2004. audio compact disk 39.95 (978-1-56511-905-5(3), 1565119053) Pub: HighBridge. Dist(s): Workman Pub

Know-Nothings. unabr. ed. Michele Sobel Spirn. Narrated by John McDonough. 1 cass. (Running Time: 15 mins.). (gr. 1 up). 1999. 10.00 (978-0-7887-2618-7(8), 95622E7) Recorded Bks.

Know The Real You. Gary V. Whetstone. 4 cass. (Running Time: 6 hrs.). (Empowerment Ser.). 1994. pap. bk. 35.00 (978-1-58866-191-3(1), VEO13A) Gary Whet Pub.
One of the most critical, but least understood areas we learn about in this life is who we are.

Know the Score. Ed. by Marco A. V. Bitetto. 1 cass. 1999. (978-1-58578-101-0(0)) Inst of Cybernetics.

Know the Truth. Kenneth Copeland. Perf. by Kenneth Copeland. 1 cass. (Take Hold of Your Victory! Ser.: Tape 1). 1995. cass. & video 5.00 (978-1-57562-000-8(6)) K Copeland Pubns.
Biblical teaching on victory.

***Know What Makes Them Tick.** unabr. ed. Max Siegel & G. F. Lichtenberg. Read by Clifton Duncan. (ENG.). 2010. (978-0-06-200770-4(X), Harper Audio) HarperCollins Pubs.

***Know What Makes Them Tick: How to Successfully Negotiate Almost Any Situation.** unabr. ed. Max Siegel & G. F. Lichtenberg. Read by Clifton Duncan. (ENG.). 2010. (978-0-06-200418-5(2), Harper Audio) HarperCollins Pubs.

Know What You Believe. unabr. ed. Paul E. Little. Read by Larry A. McKeever. 5 CDs. (Running Time: 5 hrs. 30 mins.). 2000. audio compact disk 40.00 (978-0-7861-9904-4(0), 2543) Blckstn Audio.

Know What You Believe, unabr. ed. Paul E. Little. Read by Larry A. McKeever. 4 cass. (Running Time: 5 hrs. 30 mins.). 2000. 32.95 (978-0-7861-1738-3(9), 2543) Blckstn Audio.
Helps believers understand the basic truths of their Christian faith. Clearly explains what the Bible teaches with regard to: the Holy Trinity, Christ's death & resurrection, the angelic & demonic realms, sin & salvation & coming events.

Know What You Believe. unabr. ed. Paul E. Little. Read by Larry A. McKeever. 1 CD. (Running Time: 6 hrs.). 2001. audio compact disk 19.95 (zm2543) Blckstn Audio.

Know What You Believe: Connecting Faith & Truth. unabr. ed. Paul Little. 5 CDs. (Running Time: 6 hrs. 0 mins. 0 sec.). (ENG.). 2006. audio compact disk 23.98 (978-1-59644-391-4(X), Hovel Audio) christianaud.

***Know What You Believe: Connecting Faith & Truth.** unabr. ed. Paul E. Little. Narrated by Lloyd James. (ENG.). 2006. 14.98 (978-1-59644-392-1(8), Hovel Audio) christianaud.

Know When to Fold Them: John 19:24, 623. Ed Young. 1987. 4.95 (978-0-7417-1623-1(2), 623) Win Walk.

Know Who You Are. Contrib. by Rose Leibundguth. 2001. 8.00 (978-1-931262-06-4(3)) Rose Leibund.

Know Who You Believe: The Magnificent Connection. unabr. ed. Paul Little. 3 CDs. (Running Time: 3 hrs. 45 mins. 0 sec.). (ENG.). 2006. audio compact disk 21.98 (978-1-59644-395-2(2), Hovel Audio) christianaud.

***Know Who You Believe: The Magnificent Connection.** unabr. ed. Paul E. Little. Narrated by Lloyd James. (ENG.). 2006. 12.98 (978-1-59644-396-9(0), Hovel Audio) christianaud.

Know Why You Believe, unabr. ed. Paul E. Little. Read by Larry McKeever. 4 cass. (Running Time: 5 hrs. 30 mins.). 2000. 32.95 (978-0-7861-1648-5(X), 2476) Blckstn Audio.
A thinking person's book designed to help you carefully examine the claims of the Christian faith.

Know Why You Believe. unabr. ed. Paul E. Little. Read by Larry McKeever. 5 CDs. (Running Time: 5 hrs. 30 mins.). 2000. audio compact disk 40.00 (978-0-7861-9912-9(1), 2476) Blckstn Audio.

Know Why You Believe: Connecting Faith & Reason. unabr. ed. Paul Little. 5 CDs. (Running Time: 5 hrs. 30 mins. 0 sec.). (ENG.). 2006. audio compact disk 23.98 (978-1-59644-393-8(6), Hovel Audio) christianaud.

***Know Why You Believe: Connecting Faith & Reason.** unabr. ed. Paul E. Little. Narrated by Lloyd James. (ENG.). 2006. 14.98 (978-1-59644-394-5(4), Hovel Audio) christianaud.

Know You Love Jesus. Contrib. by Rose Leibundguth. 2001. 8.00 (978-1-931262-07-1(1)) Rose Leibund.

Know Your Bird Sounds Vol. 1: Yard, Garden, & City Birds. Lang Elliott. 1 cass. (Running Time: 65 min.). 1994. audio compact disk 16.95 CD. (2649, Creativ Pub) Quayside.
A complete audio guide to the songs & calls of 35 common birds of residential settings, city parks, & urban areas of eastern & central North America. Includes 48-page booklet.

Know Your Bird Sounds Vol. 1: Yard, Garden, & City Birds. Lang Elliott. 1 cass. (Running Time: 65 min.). 1994. 12.95 (2648, NrthWrd Bks) TandN Child.

Know Your Bird Sounds Vol. 2: Birds of the Countryside. Lang Elliott. 1 cass. (Running Time: 65 min.). 1994. 12.95 (2650, NrthWrd Bks) TandN Child.
A complete audio guide to the songs & calls of 35 common birds of meadow, woodland, marsh, & seashore habitats of eastern & central North America. Includes 48-page booklet.

Know Your Bird Sounds, Vol. 2: Birds of the Countryside. Lang Elliott. 1 cass. (Running Time: 65 min.). 1994. audio compact disk 16.95 CD. (2651, Creativ Pub) Quayside.

Know Your Body Spanish Activities/Blacklines K-3. 3rd rev. ed. Kendall/Hunt. 2007. audio compact disk 249.95 (978-0-7575-3448-5(1)) Kendall-Hunt.

Know Your Body Spanish Activities/Blacklines 4-6. 3rd rev. ed. Kendall/Hunt. 2007. audio compact disk 249.95 (978-0-7575-4129-2(1)) Kendall-Hunt.

Know Your Enemy. David T. Demola. 1 cass. 4.00 (S-1084-4) Faith Fellow Min.

Know Your Narcissists Set: Tips on Coping with Self-Centered People. David Grudermeyer & Rebecca Grudermeyer. 2 cass. 18.95 INCL. HANDOUTS. (T19) Willingness Wrks.

Know Your Own Heart. unabr. ed. Dianthus. 1 cass. (Running Time: 1 hr. 21 min.). (ENG.). 1996. 11.00 (978-1-890372-00-2(5)) Dianthus.
Power of the heart & its connection to the soul.

Know Your Pig: A Playful Relationship Guide for Understanding Your Man. Micheal Coogan & William Burton. Narrated by Courtney Custer. 2007. audio compact disk 16.95 (978-1-60031-020-1(6)) Spoken Books.

Know Your Power: A Message to America's Daughters. unabr. ed. Nancy Pelosi & Amy Hill Hearth. Read by Nancy Pelosi. 3 CDs. (Running Time: 3 hrs.). (ENG.). 2008. audio compact disk 22.00 (978-0-7393-7709-3(4), Random AudioBks) Pub: Random Audio Pubg. Dist(s): Random

Know Your Vitamins: For a Healthier Life. Donald Myren et al. 1 cass. 1988. 6.95 SCE Prod & List & Lrn.
Information for the general public & students of vitamins on the ways in which vitamins affect the human body.

KnowBrainer iMusic Accelerated Innovation & Creativity Soundtrack: Accelerated Innovation & Creativity Soundtrack. Music by Gerald Haman. 2005. 99.97 (978-0-929607-16-0(3)) SolnsPeople.

Knowing Christ Today: Why We Can Trust Spiritual Knowledge. unabr. ed. Dallas Willard. (Running Time: 7 hrs. 0 mins. 0 sec.). (ENG.). 2009. audio compact disk 26.98 (978-1-59644-579-6(3), Hovel Audio) christianaud.

***Knowing Christ Today: Why We Can Trust Spiritual Knowledge.** unabr. ed. Dallas Willard. Narrated by David Cochran Heath. (ENG.). 2009. 16.98 (978-1-59644-580-2(7), Hovel Audio) christianaud.

Knowing God. Created by Awmi. (ENG.). 2008. audio compact disk 30.00 (978-1-59548-105-4(2)) A Wommack.

Knowing God. Charles R. Swindoll. 1 cass. 1990. bk. 10.99 (978-0-8499-1257-3(1)) Nelson.

Knowing God: From Genesis to Revelation - Walking Through the Book of Books. 2005. 15.00 (978-1-933561-07-3(6)) BFM Books.

Knowing God as Father. Derek Prince. 3 cass. 14.95 (I-GF1) Derek Prince.

Knowing God Intimately: Being as Close to Him as You Want to Be. abr. ed. Joyce Meyer. (ENG.). 2005. 14.98 (978-1-59483-236-9(6)) Pub: Hachet Audio. Dist(s): HachBkGrp

Knowing God Intimately: Being as Close to Him as You Want to Be. abr. ed. Joyce Meyer. (Running Time: 6 hrs.). (ENG.). 2009. 44.98 (978-1-60024-959-4(0)) Pub: Hachet Audio. Dist(s): HachBkGrp

Knowing God's Will. unabr. ed. Elisabeth Elliot. Read by Elisabeth Elliot. 2 cass. (Running Time: 2 hrs. 25 min.). 1989. 14.95 (978-0-8474-2011-7(6)) Back to Bible.
An encouragement to trust in an all-knowing God for direction in the pathway of life.

Knowing God's Will: Knowing God's Will Series, August. Ben Young. 2000. 4.95 (978-0-7417-6195-8(5), B0195) Win Walk.

Knowing God's Will: Speaking God's Language. Speeches. Creflo A. Dollar. 3 cass. (Running Time: 3 hrs 15 mins.). 2006. 15.00 (978-1-59944-039-2(3)); audio compact disk 21.00 (978-1-59944-040-8(7)) Creflo Dollar.

Knowing God's Will: Speaking God's Language. Speeches. Creflo A. Dollar. 3 CDs. (Running Time: 3 hrs. 15 mins.). 2006. DVD 36.00 (978-1-59944-041-5(5)) Creflo Dollar.

***Knowing Jesse: A Mother's Story of Grief, Grace, & Everyday Bliss.** Marianne Leone. Perf. by Marianne Leone. (ENG.). 2010. audio compact disk 39.99 (978-1-61120-010-2(5)) Dreamscap OH.

Knowing Our Emotions, Improving Our World. Contrib. by Daniel Goleman. 2007. audio compact disk 14.95 (978-1-934441-01-5(5)) More Than Snd.

Knowing Ourselves. Swami Amar Jyoti. 1 cass. 1979. 9.95 (J-24) Truth Consciousness.
Awakening to our True Identity. Answers ultimately come from relaxation, not thinking.

Knowing Scripture. unabr. ed. R. C. Sproul. (Running Time: 4 hrs. 30 mins. 0 sec.). (ENG.). 2009. audio compact disk 18.98 (978-1-59644-664-9(1), christianSeed) christianaud.

***Knowing Scripture.** unabr. ed. R. C. Sproul. Narrated by Rob Dean. (ENG.). 2009. 10.98 (978-1-59644-665-6(X), christianSeed) christianaud.

***Knowing the Economy of God: How to apply God's financial principles to your normal & everyday Life.** unabr. ed. Tom Meaglia. Read by Tom Meaglia. Read by Reba Toney. Ed. by Heidi Hancock Davison. Fred Smith. Executive Producer Kappa Studios. (Running Time: 315 minutes). (ENG.). 2010. audio compact disk 12.95 (978-0-615-40976-4(8)) Meaglia Finan.

***Knowing the Enemy: Jihadist Ideology & the War on Terror.** unabr. ed. Mary Habeck. Narrated by Jo Anna Perrin. (Running Time: 5 hrs. 30 mins. 0 sec.). 2010. 19.99 (978-1-4001-6909-2(7)); 13.99 (978-1-4001-8909-0(8)); audio compact disk 24.99 (978-1-4001-1909-7(X)) Pub: Tantor Media. Dist(s): IngramPubServ

***Knowing the Enemy (Library Edition) Jihadist Ideology & the War on Terror.** unabr. ed. Mary Habeck. Narrated by Jo Anna Perrin. (Running Time: 5 hrs. 30 mins. 0 sec.). 2010. audio compact disk 59.99 (978-1-4001-4909-4(6)) Pub: Tantor Media. Dist(s): IngramPubServ

Knowing the Secret to your Inner Self (audio) Will Knowing the secret make you a better You? Talitha Barnett. 2008. audio compact disk 14.99 (978-1-60604-456-8(7)) Tate Pubng.

Knowing the Totality. Swami Amar Jyoti. 1 dolby cass. 1984. 9.95 (R-55) Truth Consciousness.
Going beyond intellect & theology, rejecting nothing, to see the full Vision. The dilemma of free choice. How we perpetuate our beliefs in ignorance.

Knowing the Triune God. Mary A. Fatula. 5 cass. 1988. 39.95 (TAH199) Alba Hse Comns.
Sr. Mary Ann employs insights of past theologians & mystics to reflect on the mystery of the triune God.

Knowing the Will of God. Theodore H. Epp. Read by Theodore H. Epp. 1 cass. (Running Time: 45 min.). 1984. 4.95 (978-0-8474-2244-9(5)) Back to Bible.
Conditions necessary for the believer who wants to know the will of God are discussed in these messages from Proverbs 3:5, 6.

Knowing the Will of God. Lee Lefebre. Read by Lee Lefebre. 1 cass. (Running Time: 1 hr. 20 min.). 1987. 6.00 (978-1-57838-019-0(7)) CrossLife Express.
Christian living.

Knowing Who We Are in Christ, Set. Bobby Hilton. 4 cass. (Running Time: 6 hrs.). 1999. 18.00 (978-1-930766-00-6(9)) Bishop Bobby.

Knowing Your Motivational Gift. Nathaniel Holcomb. 9 cass. (Running Time: 13 hrs. 30 mins.). 1999. (978-1-930918-30-6(5)) Its All About Him.

Knowing Your Real Father: Creed: a Faith Worth Dying for Series. Ben Young. 2000. 4.95 (978-0-7417-6216-0(1), B0216) Win Walk.

Knowing Your Self: 100 Self Awareness Exercises. Executive Producer Wexler Jack. (ENG.). 2008. audio compact disk 29.95 (978-0-9774495-1-4(3)) J Wexler PhD.

Knowledge & Human Relationships. J. Krishnamurti. 1 cass. (Running Time: 1 hr.). (Krishnamurti with Dr. Allan W. Anderson Ser.: No. 2). 8.50 (APA742) Krishnamurti.
These 1974 dialogues cover the entire spectrum of Krishnamurti's teaching in a series highly regarded for its depth of inquiry into each particular subject.

Knowledge & Persons. Gordon Clark. 1 cass. (Lectures on the Holy Spirit: No. 2). 5.00 Trinity Found.

Knowledge & Spirit. Douglas Sloan. 2 cass. 1992. 18.00 set. (OC317-69) Sound Horizons AV.

Knowledge & Transformation. J. Krishnamurti. 1 cass. (Running Time: 1 hr.). (Krishnamurti with Dr. Allan W. Anderson Ser.: No. 1). 8.50 (APA741) Krishnamurti.

Knowledge & Understanding: A lecture by aldous Huxley. Speeches. Aldous Huxley. (Running Time: 50 MINS). 2006. audio compact disk 9.95 (978-0-87481-957-1(1)) Vedanta Pr.

Knowledge, Foreknowledge, & the Gospel AudioBook. Douglas Wilson. Read by Aaron Wells. (ENG.). 2007. audio compact disk 10.00 (978-1-59128-210-5(1)) Canon Pr ID.

Knowledge in a Nutshell. Charles Reichblum. Read by Dan Cashman. 2 cass. (Running Time: 3 hrs.). 2000. 17.95 (978-0-7366-5045-8(8)) Books on Tape.
Trivia about history, sports and much more will educate and entertain you.

Knowledge in a Nutshell. collector's ed. Charles Reichblum. Read by Dan Cashman. 8 cass. (Running Time: 12 hrs.). 2000. 64.00 (978-0-7366-5088-5(1)) Books on Tape.
You'll find out about the U.S. state that no longer exists, why hamburgers are called hamburgers, even though there's no ham in them, who was the youngest U.S. President (it wasn't John F. Kennedy), what were the biggest animals who ever lived (it wasn't the dinosaurs) & much more.

Knowledge in a Nutshell on Sports. Charles Reichblum. Read by Dan Cashman. 1 cass. (Running Time: 1 hr. 30 min.). 2000. 9.95 (978-0-7366-5046-5(6)) Books on Tape.
Trivia about sports will educate and entertain you.

Knowledge Leaders for the New Millennium: Creators of the Information Future. 1 cass. 1999. 40.00 (978-0-87111-504-1(2)) SLA.

Knowledge of the Holy. unabr. ed. A. W. Tozer. Read by Scott Brick. (Running Time: 4 hrs. 30 min. 0 sec.). (ENG.). 2007. audio compact disk 18.98 (978-1-59644-431-7(2)) christianaud.

***Knowledge of the Holy.** unabr. ed. A. w. Tozer. Narrated by Scott Brick. (ENG.). 2007. 10.98 (978-1-59644-432-4(0), Hovel Audio) christianaud.

***Known & Unknown: A Memoir.** Donald Rumsfeld. (Running Time: 32 hrs.). (ENG.). 2011. audio compact disk 49.95 (978-0-14-242838-2(8), PengAudBks); audio compact disk 39.95 (978-1-61176-000-2(3), PengAudBks) Penguin Grp USA.

Known Dead. Donald Harstad. Narrated by Ron McLarty. 10 CDs. (Running Time: 12 hrs.). 2001. audio compact disk 97.00 (978-0-7887-5201-8(4), C1358E7) Recorded Bks.
It started as a simple raid on a marijuana patch, but erupted into high power gunfire & bloody deaths. Now Deputy Sheriff Carl Houseman must find out who was firing & what else they were protecting.

Known Dead. unabr. ed. Donald Harstad. Narrated by Ron McLarty. 9 cass. (Running Time: 12 hrs.). 2000. 80.00 (978-0-7887-4064-0(4), 96054E7) Recorded Bks.

Known to Evil. unabr. ed. Walter Mosley. Contrib. by Mirron Willis. (Running Time: 10 hrs.). (Leonid McGill Mystery Ser.). (gr. 12 up). 2010. audio compact disk 29.95 (978-0-14-314537-0(1), PengAudBks) Penguin Grp USA.

Known World. unabr. ed. Edward P. Jones. Read by Kevin Free. 2004. audio compact disk 39.95 (978-0-06-076273-5(X)) HarperCollins Pubs.

***Known World.** unabr. ed. Edward P. Jones. Read by Kevin Free. (ENG.). 2004. (978-0-06-077411-0(8), Harper Audio) HarperCollins Pubs.

***Known World.** unabr. ed. Edward P. Jones. Read by Kevin Free. (ENG.). 2004. (978-0-06-081392-5(X), Harper Audio) HarperCollins Pubs.

Knucklehead. Skip Press & Skip Press Staff. Narrated by Larry A. McKeever. (Sport Ser.). (J). 2000. 10.95 (978-1-58659-038-3(3)) Artesian.

Knucklehead. Skip Press Staff. Narrated by Larry A. McKeever. (Sport Ser.). (J). 2000. audio compact disk 14.95 (978-1-58659-292-9(0)) Artesian.

Knucklehead. abr. ed. 1 cass. (Running Time: 40 min.). 1999. 10.95 (54118) Artesian.

Knucklehead: Tall Tales & Almost True Stories about Growing up Scieszka. unabr. ed. Jon Scieszka. Read by Jon Scieszka. (Running Time: 2 hrs.). 2009. 19.99 (978-1-4233-9976-6(5), 9781423399766, Brilliance MP3); 39.97 (978-1-4233-9977-3(3), 9781423399773, Brlnc Audio MP3 Lib); 39.97 (978-1-4233-9978-0(1), 9781423399780, BADLE); audio compact disk 19.99 (978-1-4233-9974-2(9), 9781423399742) Brilliance Audio.

Knucklehead: Tall Tales & Almost True Stories about Growing up Scieszka. unabr. ed. Jon Scieszka. Read by Jon Scieszka. 2 CDs. (Running Time: 2 hrs.). (J). (gr. 3-6). 2009. audio compact disk 42.97 (978-1-4233-9975-9(7), 9781423399759, BriAudCD Unabrid) Brilliance Audio.

Knuffle Bunny: A Cautionary Tale. unabr. ed. Mo Willems. Illus. by Mo Willems. 1 CD. (Running Time: 10 mins.). (J). (ps-1). 2006. bk. 29.95 (978-0-439-90583-1(4)); bk. 24.95 (978-0-439-90577-0(X)) Weston Woods.
Trixie, Daddy and Knuffle Bunny take a trip to the neighborhood laundromat, but their exciting adventure takes an unexpected turn when Trixie realizes something is missing.

Knuffle Bunny & Other Stories about Families: Knuffle Bunny; That New Animal; Three Cheers for Catherine the Great; I Love You Like Crazy Cakes; Elizabeti's Doll. unabr. ed. Mo Willems et al. Read by Mo Willems et al. (J). 2008. 44.99 (978-1-60514-945-5(4)) Find a World.

Knuffle Bunny Too: A Case of Mistaken Identity. Narrated by Mo Willems & Trixie Willems. Music by Scotty Huff & Robert Reynolds. Animated by Karen Villarreal. 1 CD. (Running Time: 10 mins.). (J). (ps-2). 2009. bk. 29.95 (978-0-545-13456-9(0)); audio compact disk 12.95 (978-0-545-13446-0(3)) Weston Woods.

Knute Rockne. unabr. ed. Guernsey Van Riper, Jr. Read by Lloyd James. 4 cass. (Running Time: 5 hrs. 30 mins.). (Childhood of Famous Americans Ser.). (gr. 1-3). 2001. pap. bk. 35.95 (978-0-7861-2068-0(1), K2829) Blckstn Audio.
This biography focuses on the childhood of the legendary football coach at Notre Dame, who won fame for his insistence on good sportsmanship & his football strategy.

Knyghtes Tale: In Middle English. Geoffrey Chaucer. Read by Richard Bebb. (Running Time: 9352 sec.). (Complete Classics Ser.). 2006. audio compact disk 17.98 (978-962-634-415-6(6), Naxos AudioBooks) Naxos.

Knyghtmare! Steve Barlow & Steve Skidmore. (Running Time: 25800 sec.). (Tales of the Dark Forest Ser.). (J). (gr. 3-6). 2006. audio compact disk 59.95 (978-1-4056-5560-6(7)) AudioGo GBR.

Ko Sepa Paikikala. Lilinoe Andrews. Illus. by Lilinoe Andrews. (HAW.). (J). 1994. pap. bk. 6.95 (978-1-890270-21-6(0)) Aha Punana Leo.

***Koala of Death: A Gunn Zoo Mystery.** unabr. ed. Betty Webb. (Running Time: 8 hrs. 30 mins.). 2010. 29.95 (978-1-4417-5427-1(X)); 54.95 (978-1-4417-5423-3(7)); audio compact disk 76.00 (978-1-4417-5424-0(5)) Blckstn Audio.

Kobra Manifesto. unabr. collector's ed. Adam Hall. Read by Michael Prichard. 6 cass. (Running Time: 9 hrs.). (Quiller Ser.). 1984. 48.00 (978-0-7366-0604-2(1), 1570) Books on Tape.
Following leads that have left a trail of agents missing or dead, Quiller uncovers an international terrorist group known as Kobra. His global pursuit culminates in a high-tension drama involving a bomb-rigged jetliner & an American hostage.

Koda's New Neighborhood. Joy Frost. 1 CD. (Running Time: 20 Minutes). (J). 2005. audio compact disk 14.00 (978-0-9764828-0-2(0)) Joy Stories.

Koda's New Neighborhood CD with Finger Puppet. Joy Frost. 1 CD. (Running Time: 20 Minutes). (J). 2005. audio compact disk 20.00 (978-0-9764828-1-9(9)) Joy Stories.
Discouraged and disappointed by a family move to a new neighborhood, Koda, a white cat, learns that he can make friends and become comfortable as he learns to accept the differences in his new neighborhood. A child can learn to accept change (a move, a newteacher, new friends) as a natural part of life and that he/she has a role in how the change is accepted. Suggested age 4-9 years old.Through ?Koda?s New Neighborhood?a child learns: ?That change is a fact of life.?That it is okay to feel sad about having to make a change.?That making friends is a process that helps to make change acceptable.?That over time changes can be positive.?That one can comfort oneself.?Factual information about cats.

Koine Greek New Testament: Learning the Basics of NT Greek. unabr. ed. Spiros Zodhiates & George Hadjiantoniou. Rev. by James H. Gee. 22 cass. (Greek Studies). (GRE.). 2005. 109.99 (978-0-89957-149-2(2)) Pub: AMG Pubs. Dist(s): STL Dist NA

Koinonia: A Recipe for Authentic Fellowship. 1998. 20.95 (978-1-57972-287-6(3)) Insight Living.

Koinonia: Receta para una Comunion Autentica. Charles R. Swindoll.Tr. of Koinonia: A Recipe for Authentic Fellowship. 2008. audio compact disk 27.00 (978-1-57972-815-1(4)) Insight Living.

Koinonia: A Recipe for Authentic Fellowship see Koinonia: Receta para una Comunion Autentica

Koizumi Itsuki Character CD. Perf. by Daisuke Ono. (YA). 2007. 9.98 (978-1-59409-852-9(2)) Bandai Ent.

***Kokoda.** unabr. ed. Paul Ham. Read by Peter Byrne. (Running Time: 21 hrs. 30 mins.). 2010. 54.95 (978-1-74214-829-8(8), 9781742148298); audio compact disk 123.95 (978-1-74214-828-1(X), 9781742148281) Pub: Bolinda Pubng AUS. Dist(s): Bolinda Pub Inc

Kokopelli's Flute. unabr. ed. William Hobbs. Narrated by Johnny Heller. 3 pieces. (Running Time: 4 hrs.). (gr. 5 up). 1997. 27.00 (978-0-7887-0599-1(7), 94777E7) Recorded Bks.
Tepary Jones leads a life of constant adventure. But he gets more excitement than even he can handle when he plays an ancient flute grave robbers left behind. Magic from the Distant Time, when people & animals could trade places, ensnares Tepary in a world of danger & suspense.

Kolaimni Healing. Patricia A. Garza. Read by Patricia A. Garza. Ed. by Patricia H. Keeler. 1 cass. (Running Time: 70 min.). 1991. 8.00 (978-1-879559-03-5(X)) Galaxy OH.

Kolymsky Heights. unabr. ed. Lionel Davidson. Read by Geoffrey Howard. 9 cass. (Running Time: 13 hrs. 30 min.). 1995. 54.00 (978-0-7366-3061-0(9), 3743) Books on Tape.
Johnny Porter, adventurer & scholar, treks over the steppes of Asia to snag a package vital to humankind. Sucks you in from page one.

Komarr. unabr. ed. Lois McMaster Bujold. Read by Grover Gardner. (Running Time: 45000 sec.). (Vorkosigan Ser.). 2007. 65.95 (978-1-4332-0257-5(3)); audio compact disk 81.00 (978-1-4332-0258-2(1)); audio compact disk 29.95 (978-1-4332-0259-9(X)) Blckstn Audio.

***Komedy Kingdom.** RadioArchives.com. (Running Time: 585). (ENG.). 2007. audio compact disk 29.98 (978-1-61081-068-5(6)) Radio Arch.

Komm Mit!, Level 1. 3rd ed. Holt, Rinehart and Winston Staff. 12 CDs. 2002. audio compact disk 367.80 (978-0-03-065874-7(8)) Holt McDoug.
12 discs filled with dialogues, songs, readings, and other selections, as well as assessment activities.

Komm Mit!, Level 3. 3rd ed. Holt, Rinehart and Winston Staff. 2002. audio compact disk 367.80 (978-0-03-065877-8(2)) Holt McDoug.

Komm Mit! Level 2. 3rd ed. Holt, Rinehart and Winston Staff. 2002. audio compact disk 367.80 (978-0-03-065876-1(4)) Holt McDoug.

Komm Mit! Level 2: Holt German. Holt, Rinehart and Winston Staff. (YA). 1995. 305.80 (978-0-03-095063-6(5)) Holt McDoug.

Komm Mit! Level 3: Holt German. Holt, Rinehart and Winston Staff. 1995. 305.80 (978-0-03-095077-3(5)) Holt McDoug.

Komm Mit! Level 1. Holt, Rinehart and Winston Staff. 1995. 321.13 (978-0-03-032528-1(5)) Holt McDoug.

Komuso: The Healing Art of Zen Shakuhachi. Ronnie Nyogetsu Seldin. 1 CD. (Running Time: 1 hr.). 2000. audio compact disk 15.95 (978-1-55961-610-2(5)) Sounds True.

Konaya Armiya. Isaac Babel. 1 cass. (Running Time: 1 hrs.).Tr. of Red Calvary. (RUS.). 1997. pap. bk. 19.50 (978-1-58085-582-2(2)) Interlingua VA.

Konpe Kabrit ak Konpe Kodenn. Maude Heurtelou. Illus. by Louis Louissaint. 1 cass. (Running Time: 1 hr.).Tr. of Turkey & Goat. (CRP.). (J). (gr. 3-5). 1999. pap. bk. 19.00 (978-1-881839-94-1(X)) Educa Vision.

Kontakt Deutsch: Deutsch fuer Berufliche Situationen. Udo Miebs & Leena Vehovirta. 1 cass. (Running Time: 1 hr. 30 min.). (GER.). 2005. 23.95 (978-3-468-90525-4(4)) Langenscheidt.

Kontakte. 3rd unabr. ed. Tracy D. Terrell. 10 cass. (Running Time: 15 hrs.). 1996. 55.10 (978-0-07-912239-1(6), Mc-H Human Soc) McGrw-H Hghr Educ.

Kontakte: A Communicative Approach. 2nd ed. Tracy D. Terrell et al. 1992. (978-0-07-063792-4(X)) McGraw.

Kontakte: A Communicative Approach. 2nd ed. Tracy D. Terrell et al. 1992. 19.25 (978-0-07-063791-7(1)) McGraw.

Kontakte: A Communicative Approach. 4th ed. Terrell. 1 cass. (Running Time: 1 hr.). (C). 2000. stu. ed. 13.43 (978-0-07-230910-2(5), Mc-H Human Soc) Pub: McGrw-H Hghr Educ. Dist(s): McGraw

Kontakte: A Communicative Approach. 4th ed. Tracy D. Terrell. 1 CD. (Running Time: 1 hr.). (C). 2000. audio compact disk 13.43 (978-0-07-230909-6(1), Mc-H Human Soc) Pub: McGrw-H Hghr Educ. Dist(s): McGraw

Kontakte: A Communicative Approach (Student Edition + Listening Comprehension Audio Cassette) 4th ed. Tracy D. Terrell et al. (C). 2000. bk. & stu. ed. 60.25 (978-0-07-234219-2(6), Mc-H Human Soc) McGrw-H Hghr Educ.

Kontakte Knupfen. Rainer Wicke. 1 cass. (Running Time: 1 hr. 20 mins.). 1996. 11.95 (978-3-468-49667-7(2)) Langenscheidt.

Kontakte Laboratory Audio Program: A Communicative Approach. 5th ed. Terrell et al. 2006. audio compact disk 62.19 (978-0-07-327922-0(6), Mc-H Human Soc) Pub: McGrw-H Hghr Educ. Dist(s): McGraw

Konusulan Ingilizce see English for Turks

Kookaburra & Other Stories. unabr. ed. 1 CD. (Running Time: 1 hr. 7 mins.). 2002. audio compact disk 14.95 (978-0-9709865-1-1(3)) Gifts Art.

Kooks. M. D. Baer. Read by Jamie Cohen. (Running Time: 21600 sec.). 2006. 44.95 (978-0-7861-4565-2(X)); audio compact disk 45.00 (978-0-7861-7049-4(2)) Blckstn Audio.

Kooks. unabr. ed. M. D. Baer. Read by Jamie Cohen. (Running Time: 21600 sec.). 2006. audio compact disk 29.95 (978-0-7861-7561-1(3)) Blckstn Audio.

Kooky Kountry. (Silly-Wackly-Goofy-Flaky Ser.). (J). 1997. 7.00 (978-1-57375-066-0(2)) Audioscope.

Kool Karaoke. 1999. audio compact disk 24.95 (978-1-894302-08-1(7)) Pub: Vorton Tech CAN. Dist(s): H Leonard

Kool Songs. Perf. by Kazoo the Roo. 1 cass.; 1 CD. 1998. 7.98 (978-1-56628-119-5(9), 72551); audio compact disk 11.98 CD. (978-1-56628-118-8(0), 72551D) MFLP CA.

Koop: The Memoirs of America's Family Doctor. unabr. ed. C. Everett Koop. Read by Christopher Hurt. 9 cass. (Running Time: 13 hrs.). 1991. 62.95 (978-0-7861-0322-5(1), 1283) Blckstn Audio.
When the Reagan administration named C. Everett Koop, M. D., Surgeon General of the United States, many greeted the appointment with derision. "Dr. Unqualified," "The New York Times" called him, primarily because of his highly publicized opposition to abortion. It was almost a year before the Senate would confirm his hotly contested nomination. Dr. Koop confounded critics & allies alike with his nonideological approach to health issues, his refreshingly forthright public pronouncements, & his vigorous campaign to mobilize America against the scourge of AIDS. By the time he resigned eight years later, he was universally hailed as the most effective & outspoken Surgeon General in American history.

Korea Pt. 1: The Untold Story of the War. unabr. collector's ed. Joseph C. Goulden. Read by Wolfram Kandinsky. 14 cass. (Running Time: 21 hrs.). 1991. 112.00 (978-0-7366-1924-0(0), 2748-A) Books on Tape.
Korea: The Untold Story of the War is the definitive account of one of the two great tragedies in modern U.S. history. It was America's first no-win, limited objective, undeclared war - a police action. It cost 52,246 American lives, many of them veterans of WW II who were recalled to active service in the emergency. Korea covers every aspect of the war, political as well as military, including the peace negotiations & settlement, the consequences of which reverberate to this day.

Korea Pt. 2: The Untold Story of the War. collector's ed. Joseph C. Goulden. Read by Wolfram Kandinsky. 15 cass. (Running Time: 22 hrs. 30 min.). 1991. 120.00 (978-0-7366-1925-7(9), 2748-B) Books on Tape.
The definitive account of one of the two great tragedies in modern U. S. history. It was America's first no-win, limited objective, undeclared war - a police action. It cost 52,246 American lives, many of them veterans of WW II who were recalled to active service in the emergency. Korea covers every aspect of the war, political as well as military, including the peace negotiations & settlement, the consequences of which reverberate to this day.

Korean. Berlitz Editors & Berlitz Publishing Staff. 1 CD. (Running Time: 1 hr. 10 mins.). (Berlitz Travel Pack Ser.). (ENG & KOR., 2003. audio compact disk 21.95 (978-981-246-200-8(7), 462007) Pub: Berlitz Pubng. Dist(s): Langenscheidt

Korean. Ed. by Berlitz Publishing. (PHRASE BOOK & CD Ser.). (KOR & ENG., 2008. audio compact disk 12.95 (978-981-268-479-0(4)) Pub: APA Pubns Serv SGP. Dist(s): Langenscheidt

Korean. Penton Overseas, Inc. Staff. 2 cass. (Running Time: 80 min.). (Language - Thirty Library). bk. 16.95 set in vinyl album. Moonbeam Pubns.
Using the proven method based on the famous U.S. Military accelerated language learning program, Language/30 courses stress conversationally useful words & phrases.

Krsna: The Supreme Personality of Godhead. Srila Prabhupada. 32 cass. 60.00 Album. Bhaktivedanta.

Krsna Blesses Sudama (A); Krsna Liberates Vidyadhara (B) 1 cass. (Spiritual Stories Ser.). 5.00 Bhaktivedanta.

Krsna Consiousness at Home. 1 cass. 5.00 Bhaktivedanta.
Instructional guide to home worship.

Krsna Kidnaps & Marries Rukmini. 1 cass. (Spiritual Stories Ser.). 5.00 Bhaktivedanta.

Krsna Lifts Govardhana Hill (A); Baby Krsna Outwits Trnavarta (B) 1 cass. (Spiritual Stories Ser.). 5.00 Bhaktivedanta.

Krsna Subdues Kaliya (A); Mother Yasoda Binds Krsna (B) 1 cass. (Spiritual Stories Ser.). 5.00 Bhaktivedanta.

Krueger's Men: The Secret Nazi Counterfeit Plot & the Prisoners of Block 19. unabr. ed. Lawrence Malkin. Narrated by Michael Prichard. (Running Time: 8 hrs. 0 mins. 0 sec.). (ENG.). 2006. audio compact disk 29.99 (978-1-4001-0292-1(8)); audio compact disk 59.99 (978-1-4001-3292-8(4)) Pub: Tantor Media. Dist(s): IngramPubServ

Krueger's Men: The Secret Nazi Counterfeit Plot & the Prisoners of Block 19. unabr. ed. Lawrence Malkin. Read by Michael Prichard. (Running Time: 8 hrs. 0 mins. 0 sec.). (ENG.). 2006. audio compact disk 19.99 (978-1-4001-5292-6(5)) Pub: Tantor Media. Dist(s): IngramPubServ

Kryon Bk. 1: The End Times. abr. ed. Lee Carroll. Read by Lee Carroll. 2 cass. (Running Time: 3 hrs.). 1997. 17.95 (978-1-57453-168-8(9)) Audio Lit.
Introduces channeled information from the entity known as Kryon. Kryon explains his work on Earth: to remind us to remember that the universe never abandons us.

Kryon Bk. 2: Don't Think Like a Human! abr. ed. Lee Carroll. Read by Lee Carroll. 2 cass. (Running Time: 3 hrs.). 1997. 17.95 (978-1-57453-169-5(7)) Audio Lit.
Kryon answers questions about Earth changes, live essence medicines, past life relationships, Atlantean technology & the nature of extraterrestrials.

Kryon Bk. 3: Alchemy of the Human Spirit. abr. ed. Lee Carroll. Read by Lee Carroll. 2 cass. (Running Time: 3 hrs.). 1997. 17.95 (978-1-57453-170-1(0)) Audio Lit.

Krystal Meyers. Contrib. by Krystal Meyers. Prod. by Ian Eskelin & Wizardz of Oz. Contrib. by Jordyn Conner & Robert Beeson. 2005. audio compact disk 11.99 (978-5-559-01492-0(3)) Essential Recs.

K'tonton in Israel: A Visit with Ki'onton & K'tonton on Kibbutz, Vol. 1. unabr. ed. Sadie Rose Weilerstein. Read by Judy Chernak. Perf. by Judy Chernak. 4 cass. (Running Time: 44 min.). Dramatization. (K'tonton in Israel Ser.). (J). (ps-4). 1986. pap. bk. 10.95 (978-0-944633-11-3(0), KB101) J Chernak.
Jewish Tom Thumb travels to Israel to explore his heritage - in story & song - through exciting escapades in the Land of the Bible today.

K'tonton in Israel Vol. 1: A Visit with Ki'onton & K'tonton on Kibbutz. unabr. ed. Sadie Rose Weilerstein. Read by Judy Chernak. Perf. by Judy Chernak. 4 cass. (Running Time: 44 min.). Dramatization. (K'tonton in Israel Ser.). (J). (ps-4). 1986. 8.95 (978-0-944633-01-4(3), K1001) J Chernak.

K'tonton in Israel Series, Sadie Rose Weilerstein. Read by Judy Chernak. Perf. by Judy Chernak. 3 cass. 3 bks. (Running Time: 1 hr. 19 min.). Dramatization. (Read-Along Book & Cassette Ser.). (J). (ps-4). 1986. pap. bk. 29.95 (978-0-944633-33-5(1), KBS1-2-3) J Chernak.
Jewish Tom Thumb travels to Israel to explore his heritage - in story & song - through exciting escapades in the Land of the Bible.

K'tonton in Jerusalem: Adventure in the Old City. Sadie Rose Weilerstein. Read by Judy Chernak. Perf. by Judy Chernak. 1 cass. (Running Time: 40 min.). Dramatization. (K'tonton in Israel Ser.: Vol. 3). (J). (ps-4). 1986. pap. bk. 10.95 (978-0-944633-13-7(7), KB103); 8.95 (978-0-944633-03-8(X), K1003) J Chernak.
America's favorite thumb-size hero learns about the War for Independence & reaches Rachel's Tomb on his way to Jerusalem.

K'tonton in Jerusalem: Adventure on Yom Ha'atzma'ut Israel's Independence Day. unabr. ed. Sadie Rose Weilerstein. Read by Judy Chernak. Perf. by Judy Chernak. 1 cass. (Running Time: 35 min.). Dramatization. (K'tontin in Israel Ser.: Vol. 2). (J). (ps-4). 1986. pap. bk. 10.95 (978-0-944633-12-0(9), KB102); 8.95 (978-0-944633-02-1(1), K1002) J Chernak.
Jewish Tom Thumb travels to Israel to explore his heritage - in story & song - through exciting escapades in the Land of the bible.

Ku-Klux-Klan see Poetry & Reflections

Kubla Khan see Poetry of Coleridge

Kubla Khan see Rime of the Ancient Mariner

Kubla Khan see Famous Story Poems

***Kudos Healthy Lifestyles Advantage TM: Stress Reduction Techniques.** Ife Ojugbeli. 2010. (978-1-4507-0177-8(9)) Indep Pub IL.

***Kull: Exile of Atlantis.** unabr. ed. Robert E. Howard. Narrated by Todd McLaren. (Running Time: 12 hrs. 0 mins.). 2009. 17.99 (978-1-4001-8227-5(1)); 34.99 (978-1-4001-9227-4(7)) Tantor Media.

Kull: Exile of Atlantis. unabr. ed. Robert E. Howard. Narrated by Todd McLaren. (Running Time: 12 hrs. 0 mins. 0 sec.). (ENG.). 2010. 24.99 (978-1-4001-6227-7(0)); audio compact disk 69.99 (978-1-4001-4227-9(X)); audio compact disk 34.99 (978-1-4001-1227-2(3)) Pub: Tantor Media. Dist(s): IngramPubServ

Kumar Gandharva. Music by Kumar Gandharva. 1 cass. (Baithak Ser.: Vol. 3). 1993. (A93013) Multi-Cultural Bks.

Kumar Gandharva. Music by Kumar Gandharva. 1 cass. (Baithak Ser.: Vol. 4). 1993. (A93014) Multi-Cultural Bks.

Kumar Gandharva, Vol. 1. Music by Kumar Gandharva. 1 cass. (Baithak Ser.). 1993. (A93011) Multi-Cultural Bks.

Kumar Gandharva, Vol. 2. Music by Kumar Gandharva. 1 cass. (Baithak Ser.). 1993. (A93012) Multi-Cultural Bks.

Kundalini & the Chakra System. Joseph Campbell. 1 cass. 1981. 10.95 Dolphin Tapes.

Kundalini Meditation: Guided Chakra Practices to Activate the Energy of Awakening. Harijiwan Khalsa. (Running Time: 2:21:02). 2010. audio compact disk 19.95 (978-1-59179-749-4(7)) Sounds True.

Kundalini Upasana, No. 1. Swami Jyotirmayananda. Read by Swami Jyotirmayananda. 1 cass. (Running Time: 60 min.). 12.99 (719) Yoga Res Foun.

Kundalini Upasana, No. 2. Swami Jyotirmayananda. 1 cass. (Running Time: 1 hr.). 1990. 12.99 Yoga Res Foun.

Kundalini Upasana, No. 3. Swami Jyotirmayananda. 1 cass. (Running Time: 1 hr.). 1990. 12.99 Yoga Res Foun.

Kundalini Upasana, No. 4. Swami Jyotirmayananda. 1 cass. (Running Time: 1 hr.). 1990. 12.99 Yoga Res Foun.

Kundalini Upasana, No. 5. Swami Jyotirmayananda. Read by Swami Jyotirmayananda. 1 cass. (Running Time: 60 min.). 12.99 (720) Yoga Res Foun.

Kundalini Upasana, No. 9. Swami Jyotirmayananda. Read by Swami Jyotirmayananda. 1 cass. (Running Time: 60 min.). 12.99 (721) Yoga Res Foun.

Kundalini Upasana No. 6: Swadhishthana. Swami Jyotirmayananda. 1 cass. (Running Time: 1 hr.). 1990. 12.99 Yoga Res Foun.

Kundalini Upasana No. 7: Manipura. Swami Jyotirmayananda. 1 cass. (Running Time: 1 hr.). 1990. 12.99 Yoga Res Foun.

Kundalini Upasana No. 8: Anahata. Swami Jyotirmayananda. 1 cass. (Running Time: 1 hr.). 1990. 12.99 Yoga Res Foun.

Kundalini Upasana No. 10: Ajna. Swami Jyotirmayananda. 1 cass. (Running Time: 1 hr.). 1990. 12.99 Yoga Res Foun.

Kundalini Upasana No. 11: Sahasrara. Swami Jyotirmayananda. 1 cass. (Running Time: 1 hr.). 1990. 12.99 Yoga Res Foun.

Kundu. unabr. ed. Morris West. 5 cass. (Running Time: 6 hrs. 25 mins.). 2004. 40.00 (978-1-74030-746-8(1)) Pub: Bolinda Pubng AUS. Dist(s): Lndmrk Audiobks

Kuperman's Fire. unabr. ed. John J. Clayton. Read by Anthony Heald. (Running Time: 43200 sec.). 2007. audio compact disk 72.00 (978-1-4332-1109-6(2)); audio compact disk 29.95 (978-1-4332-1110-2(6)) Blckstn Audio.

Kuperman's Fire. unabr. ed. John J. Clayton & Anthony Heald. (Running Time: 43200 sec.). 2007. 59.95 (978-1-4332-1108-9(4)) Blckstn Audio.

Kurdish Basic Course. Abdulla & Ernest N. McCarus. 7 cass. 1967. 64.16 Set. U MI Lang Res.

Kurellian Dawn. unabr. ed. Rene Smeraglia. Read by Maynard Villers. 8 cass. (Running Time: 9 hrs. 12 min.). 1996. 49.95 (978-1-55686-644-9(5)) Books in Motion.
One hundred years into the future, a space ship from Earth encounters an alien battle force heading toward the planet Kurell, a protectorate of the Earth/Terran Federation.

Kurgan Rising. Cavan Scott. 2009. audio compact disk 15.95 (978-1-84435-361-3(3)) Pub: Big Finish GBR. Dist(s): Natl Bk Netwk

Kurs Govornog Engleskog Jezika see English for Jugo-Slavs

Kurt Vonnegut Jr. Interview with Kurt Vonnegut. 1 cass. (Running Time: 25 min.). 1978. 12.95 (L077) TFR.
Vonnegut talks about the excitement he has engendered among youthful readers, perhaps because he himself is fascinated by such questions as, Is there a God? Who are we? & Where are we going?.

***Kurt Vonnegut Jr. Audio Collection.** abr. ed. Kurt Vonnegut. Read by Kurt Vonnegut. (ENG.). 2005. (978-0-06-084593-3(7), Caedmon); (978-0-06-084592-6(9), Caedmon) HarperCollins Pubs.

Kushiel's Avatar. unabr. ed. Jacqueline Carey. Narrated by Anne Flosnik. (Running Time: 32 hrs. 30 mins. 0 sec.). (Kushiel's Legacy Ser.). (ENG.). 2009. audio compact disk 39.99 (978-1-4001-5951-2(2)); audio compact disk 59.99 (978-1-4001-0951-7(5)) Pub: Tantor Media. Dist(s): IngramPubServ

Kushiel's Avatar. unabr. ed. Jacqueline Carey. Read by Anne Flosnik. Narrated by Anne Flosnik. (Running Time: 32 hrs. 30 mins. 0 sec.). (Kushiel's Legacy Ser.). (ENG.). 2009. audio compact disk 119.99 (978-1-4001-3951-4(1)) Pub: Tantor Media. Dist(s): IngramPubServ

Kushiel's Chosen. unabr. ed. Jacqueline Carey. Narrated by Anne Flosnik. (Running Time: 28 hrs. 30 mins. 0 sec.). (Kushiel's Legacy Ser.). (ENG.). 2009. audio compact disk 59.99 (978-1-4001-0950-0(7)); audio compact disk 39.99 (978-1-4001-5950-5(4)); audio compact disk 119.99 (978-1-4001-3950-7(3)) Pub: Tantor Media. Dist(s): IngramPubServ

Kushiel's Dart. Jacqueline Carey. Read by Anne Flosnik. (Playaway Adult Fiction Ser.). (ENG.). 2009. 109.99 (978-1-60847-923-8(4)) Find a World.

Kushiel's Dart. unabr. ed. Jacqueline Carey. Narrated by Anne Flosnik. (Running Time: 32 hrs. 30 mins. 0 sec.). (Kushiel's Legacy Ser.). (ENG.). 2009. audio compact disk 64.99 (978-1-4001-0949-4(3)); audio compact disk 129.99 (978-1-4001-3949-1(X)); audio compact disk 44.99 (978-1-4001-5949-9(0)) Pub: Tantor Media. Dist(s): IngramPubServ

Kushiel's Justice. unabr. ed. Jacqueline Carey. Narrated by Simon Vance. (Running Time: 26 hrs. 0 mins. 0 sec.). (Kushiel's Legacy Ser.). (ENG.). 2009. audio compact disk 39.99 (978-1-4001-5953-6(9)); audio compact disk 59.99 (978-1-4001-0953-1(1)); audio compact disk 119.99 (978-1-4001-3953-8(8)) Pub: Tantor Media. Dist(s): IngramPubServ

Kushiel's Mercy. unabr. ed. Jacqueline Carey. Narrated by Simon Vance. (Running Time: 24 hrs. 30 mins. 0 sec.). (Kushiel's Legacy Ser.). (ENG.). 2008. audio compact disk 59.99 (978-1-4001-0954-8(X)); audio compact disk 119.99 (978-1-4001-3954-5(6)); audio compact disk 39.99 (978-1-4001-5954-3(7)) Pub: Tantor Media. Dist(s): IngramPubServ

Kushiel's Scion. unabr. ed. Jacqueline Carey. Narrated by Simon Vance. (Running Time: 28 hrs. 30 mins. 0 sec.). (Kushiel's Legacy Ser.). (ENG.). 2008. audio compact disk 119.99 (978-1-4001-3952-1(X)); audio compact disk 59.99 (978-1-4001-0952-4(3)); audio compact disk 39.99 (978-1-4001-5952-9(0)) Pub: Tantor Media. Dist(s): IngramPubServ

Kuwaiti Oil Fires. Skip Press & Skip Press Staff. Narrated by Larry A. McKeever. (Disaster Ser.). (J). 2003. audio compact disk 14.95 (978-1-58659-288-2(2)) Artesian.

Kuwaiti Oil Fires. unabr. ed. Skip Press & Skip Press Staff. Narrated by Larry A. McKeever. 1 cass. (Running Time: 40 min.). (Take Ten Ser.). (J). (gr. 3-12). 2003. 10.95 (978-1-58659-029-1(4), 54114) Artesian.

KVMR Sacred Dance Interview. Justyn Vallori & E. J. Gold. Read by Menlo Macfarlane. 1 cass. (Running Time: 1 hr. 30 min.). 1985. 9.98 (TP156) Union Label.
A radio interview on the history of objective theater, neolithic dance traditions & modern dance, previewing "The Oracle & the Garden" dance performance.

Kwaidan. unabr. collector's ed. Lafcadio Hearn. Read by Walter Covell. 3 cass. (Running Time: 3 hrs.). 1987. 18.00 (978-0-7366-3933-0(0), 9171) Books on Tape.
Contains 17 stories including Loichi, the blind biwa player who was called to perform for the dead; of Muso, the journeying priest who encountered a man-eating goblin; of the samurai who outwitted the ghost of a dead man, more.

Kwanzaa. unabr. ed. A. P. Porter. Read by Renee Jean Simon. Illus. by Janice Lee Porter. 1 cass. (Running Time: 12 mins.). (J). (gr. 1-6). 1993. bk. 24.95 (978-0-87499-250-2(8)); pap. bk. 15.95 (978-0-87499-249-6(4)) Live Oak Media.
An introduction to the week-long African-American holiday that traces its history, explores its meaning, & explains its celebration.

Kwanzaa. unabr. ed. A. P. Porter. 1 cass. (Running Time: 12 min.). (J). (gr. 2-6). 1993. 9.95 Live Oak Media.

Kwanzaa Fable. unabr. ed. Eric V. Copage. Read by Gregory T. Daniel. 1 cass. (Running Time: 1 hr. 30 min.). 1997. 11.95 (978-1-57453-138-1(7)) Audio Lit.

Kwanzaa Folktales. 1 cass. (Running Time: 1 hr.). 1999. 9.98 Hachet Audio.
Includes traditional & original tales.

Kwanzaa Folktales. Lewis Gordon. 1998. (978-1-57042-697-1(X)) Hachet Audio.

Kwanzaa Folktales. abr. ed. Gordon Lewis. Read by Jonelle Allen et al. (Running Time: 30 mins.). (ENG.). 2009. 14.98 (978-1-60788-069-1(5)) Pub: Hachet Audio. Dist(s): HachBkGrp

Kwanzaa for Young People (and Everybody Else) 1 CD. (Running Time: 30 min.). 2001. pap. bk. & tchr. ed. 12.99 Charphelia Pubns.
Children and adults present a musical feast while teaching the holiday's seven principles.

Kwanzaa for Young People (And Everyone Else!) Activities & Music Inspired by the Kwanzaa Holiday. Geanora Bonner et al. 1 CD. (Running Time: 30 min.). 2002. pap. bk. 19.95 (978-0-9713831-1-1(1), CH70003) Charphelia Pubns.

Kwanzaa, Grades 1-6. unabr. ed. A. P. Porter. Read by Renee Jean Simon. Illus. by Janice Lee Porter. 14 vols. (Running Time: 12 mins.). (J). 1993. pap. bk. & tchr. ed. 33.95 Reading Chest. (978-0-87499-251-9(6)) Live Oak Media.
An introduction to the week-long African-American holiday that traces its history, explores its meaning, & explains its celebration.

Kwanzaa Suite: A Musical Celebration. Composed by Stan Spottswood. 1 bk, 1 CD. (Running Time: 1 hr). 2002. ring bd. 39.95 (978-0-937203-96-5(3), 96-3) World Music Pr.
Companion audio CD includes demonstration performances by members of the Appalachian Children's Choir and the Stan Spottswood Combo plus full accompaniment tracks by the Stan Spottswood Combo. (Not available separately, only in kit with book and musical scores.).

Kwidan. Lafcadio Hearn. Read by Walter Covell. 3 cass. (Running Time: 3 hrs.). 1989. 21.00 incl. album. (C-171) Jimcin Record.
Supernatural stories from Japan.

Kydd. Julian Stockwin. Read by John Lee. 2001. 56.00 (978-0-7366-7034-0(3)) Books on Tape.

Kyle Rote: Soccer. Read by Kyle Rote. 1 cass. 9.95 (978-0-89811-073-9(4), 7124) Lets Talk Assocs.
Kyle Rote talks about the people & events which influenced his career, & his own approach to his speciality.

Kyon Character CD. Perf. by Tomokazu Sugita. (YA). 2007. 9.98 (978-1-59409-849-9(2)) Bandai Ent.

Kyon's Sister Character CD. Perf. by Sayaka Aoki. (YA). 2007. 9.98 (978-1-59409-848-2(4)) Bandai Ent.

Kyrgyz Musical Instruments. Vladimir Gusev. Tr. by Elena Mironova & Taalaibek Abdiev. (ENG & RUS., 2002. bk. 91.50 (978-9967-11-126-4(7)) Pub: Soros-Kyrgyzstan KGZ. Dist(s): Coronet Bks

Kyros Live: The Global Church Sings. Perf. by Gary Gillete. Ed. by Abe Caceres & Bob Foley. Intro. by David P. Foley. 1 CD. 1999. audio compact disk 12.95 (978-1-930099-00-5(2)) World House.

Kyros Live: The Global Church Sings. Perf. by Gary Gillette. Ed. by Abe Caceres & Bob Foley. Intro. by David P. Foley. 1 cass. 1999. 8.95 (978-1-930099-01-2(0)) World House.

K2: Life & Death on the World's Most Dangerous Mountain. abr. unabr. ed. Ed Viesturs & David Roberts. Read by Fred Sanders. (ENG.). 2009. audio compact disk 40.00 (978-0-7393-8470-1(8), Random AudioBks) Pub: Random Audio Pubg. Dist(s): Random

L

L. A. Business. Mark Paul Sebar. Voice by Mark Paul Sebar. 1 CD. (Running Time: 74 mins.). 2003. audio compact disk 9.99 (978-1-930246-05-8(6), 1930246056) Sebar Pubng.
A wealthy business woman is defrauded out of her company & estate & left for dead on the mean streets of L.A. She has to survive her amnesia, a hitman & street gangs.

L. A. Candy. Lauren Conrad. Contrib. by Lauren Conrad. (L. A. Candy Ser.: Bk. 1). 2009. 59.99 (978-1-61587-742-3(8)) Find a World.

***L. A. Candy.** unabr. ed. Lauren Conrad. Read by Lauren Conrad. (L. A. Candy Ser.: Bk. 1). 2009. (978-0-06-190201-7(2)) HarperCollins Pubs.

***L. A. Candy.** unabr. ed. Lauren Conrad. Read by Lauren Conrad. (L. A. Candy Ser.: Bk. 1). 2009. (978-0-06-180359-8(6)) HarperCollins Pubs.

L. A. Confidential. unabr. collector's ed. James Ellroy. Read by John MacDonald. 10 cass. (Running Time: 15 hrs.). (L. A. Quartet). 1991. 80.00 (978-0-7366-2012-3(5), 116014) Books on Tape.
Los Angeles, 1953: six innocent people gunned down at an all-night diner. Three policemen arrive to investigate: Ed Exley, goaded by his father's success on the force, burning to eclipse him; Bud White, witness to his mother's murder, a time bomb with a badge; & Jack Vincennes, former addict, a shake-down artist who works celebrities.

L. A. Connections: Power, Obsession, Murder, Revenge. Jackie Collins. 2004. 15.95 (978-0-7435-4054-4(9)) Pub: S&S Audio. Dist(s): S and S Inc

L. A. Dead. unabr. ed. Stuart Woods. Read by Robert Lawrence. 6 cass. (Running Time: 9 hrs.). (Stone Barrington Ser.: No. 6). 2000. 29.95 (978-1-58788-073-5(3), 1587880733, BAU); 57.25 (978-1-58788-074-2(1), 1587880741, Unabridge Lib Edns); audio compact disk 35.95 (978-1-58788-169-5(1), 1587881691, CD Unabridged); audio compact disk 73.25 (978-1-58788-180-0(2), 1587881802, Unabridge Lib Edns) Brilliance Audio.
Stone Barrington, the always surprising attorney and investigator, finds himself caught between two alluring women - one who has been left at the altar and another who is suspected of murder. Stone is in the midst of plans to marry Dolce, the daughter of a New York mafioso, when he is suddenly called to the side of Arrington Calder, a woman he has loved and lost, but never forgotten. To her horror, Arrington believes she is about to be indicted for the murder of her husband; one of America's most beloved film stars. With both enemies and friends swarming around her, Stone is the only person she can trust to gather her defense. But how much does Arrington actually remember about the night of the murder? And can Stone really trust her? The evidence against her mounts, the trial date looms, and Stone's feelings for her return. But even he doesn't know what danger the truth will bring.

L. A. Dead. unabr. ed. Stuart Woods. Read by Robert Lawrence. 7 CDs . (Running Time: 9 hrs.). (Stone Barrington Ser.: No. 6). 2004. 24.95 (978-1-59335-316-2(2), 1593353162, Brilliance MP3); 39.25 (978-1-59335-475-6(4), 1593354754, Brinc Audio MP3 Lib) Brilliance Audio.

L. A. Dead. unabr. ed. Stuart Woods. Read by Robert Lawrence. (Running Time: 9 hrs.). (Stone Barrington Ser.: No. 6). 2004. 39.25 (978-1-59710-435-7(3), 1597104353, BADLE); 24.95 (978-1-59710-434-0(5), 1597104345, BAD) Brilliance Audio.

L. A. Noir, Pt. 1. collector's ed. James Ellroy. Read by Michael Prichard. 14 cass. (Running Time: 21 hrs.). 1999. 112.00 (978-0-7366-4319-1(2), 4792-A) Books on Tape.
Dectective Lloyd Hopkins takes on three mesmerizing cases as he prowls Los Angeles's dark streets.

L. A. Noir, Pt. 2. unabr. collector's ed. James Ellroy. Read by Michael Prichard. 8 cass. (Running Time: 12 hrs.). 1999. 64.00 (978-0-7366-4320-7(6), 4792-B) Books on Tape.

L. A. Outlaws. abr. ed. T. Jefferson Parker. Read by David Colacci & Susan Ericksen. (Running Time: 6 hrs.). (Charlie Hood Novel Ser.: Bk. 1). 2009. audio compact disk 14.99 (978-1-4233-0604-7(X), 9781423306047, BCD Value Price) Brilliance Audio.

L. A. Outlaws. unabr. ed. T. Jefferson Parker. Read by David Colacci & Susan Ericksen. (Running Time: 11 hrs.). (Charlie Hood Novel Ser.: Bk. 1). 2008. 39.25 (978-1-4233-0602-3(3), 9781423306023, BADLE) Brilliance Audio.

L. A. Outlaws. unabr. ed. T. Jefferson Parker. Read by Susan Ericksen & David Colacci. (Running Time: 11 hrs.). (Charlie Hood Novel Ser.: Bk. 1). 2008. 24.95 (978-1-4233-0601-6(5), 9781423306016, BAD); 97.25 (978-1-4233-0596-5(5), 9781423305965, BrilAudUnabridg) Brilliance Audio.

L. A. Outlaws. unabr. ed. T. Jefferson Parker. Read by David Colacci & Susan Ericksen. 10 CDs. (Running Time: 11 hrs.). (Charlie Hood Novel Ser.: Bk. 1). 2008. audio compact disk 36.95 (978-1-4233-0597-2(3), 9781423305972, Bril Audio CD Unabri); audio compact disk 24.95 (978-1-4233-0599-6(X), 9781423305996, Brilliance MP3) Brilliance Audio.

L. A. Outlaws. unabr. ed. T. Jefferson Parker. Read by Susan Ericksen & David Colacci. 10 CDs. (Running Time: 11 hrs.). (Charlie Hood Novel Ser.: Bk. 1). 2008. audio compact disk 97.25 (978-1-4233-0598-9(1), 9781423305989, BriAudCD Unabrid) Brilliance Audio.

L. A. Outlaws. unabr. ed. T. Jefferson Parker. Read by David Colacci & Susan Ericksen. 1 MP3-CD. (Running Time: 11 hrs.). (Charlie Hood Novel Ser.: Bk. 1). 2008. audio compact disk 39.25 (978-1-4233-0600-9(7), 9781423305989, BriAudCD Unabrid) Brilliance Audio.

L. A. Requiem. Robert Crais. Narrated by Ron McLarty & Jenny Sterlin. 12 CDs. (Running Time: 13 hrs. 45 mins.). (Elvis Cole Ser.). 2000. audio compact disk 116.00 (978-0-7887-4896-7(3), C1271E7) Recorded Bks.
A gritty, harrowing look into the minds of a serial killer & the men determined to stop him. Elvis Cole & former cop Frank Pike have been partners in a detective agency for 12 years. After an ex-girlfriend of Pike's disappears, the girl's father asks them to help the police with the search. Soon Cole & Pike find themselves battling both a hostile police department & a madman.

L. A. Requiem. unabr. ed. Robert Crais. Narrated by Jenny Sterlin. 10 cass. (Running Time: 13 hrs. 45 mins.). (Elvis Cole Ser.). 2000. 93.00 (978-0-7887-4037-4(7), 96108E7) Recorded Bks.

L. A. Requiem, Set. abr. ed. Robert Crais. Read by John Bedford Lloyd. 4 cass. (Elvis Cole Ser.). 1999. 25.00 (FS9-50942) Highsmith.

***L. A. Times.** abr. ed. Stuart Woods. Read by Tony Roberts. (ENG.). 2006. (978-0-06-084207-9(5), Harper Audio); (978-0-06-084206-2(7), Harper Audio) HarperCollins Pubs.

L. A. Times, unabr. ed. Stuart Woods. Narrated by Richard Ferrone. 7 cass. (Running Time: 10 hrs. 15 mins.). 1993. 60.00 (978-1-55690-905-4(5), 93401E7) Recorded Bks.
Vinnie Callabrese, a New York mafia hood makes it big as a Hollywood producer, until his buddies from the old neighborhood decide to help themselves to a piece of his pie.

L' Assommoir see Treasury of French Prose

L' Esprit Manouche: A Comprehensive Study of Gypsy Jazz Guitar. Derek Sebastian & Romane Sebastian. 2004. per. 29.95 (978-0-7866-6894-6(6), 20014BCD) Mel Bay.

L. Francis Herreshoff Reader. unabr. collector's ed. L. Francis Herreshoff. Read by Grover Gardner. 7 cass. (Running Time: 10 hrs. 30 mins.). 1984. 56.00 (978-0-7366-0523-6(1), 1497) Books on Tape.
Master maritime designer talks about boats & the sea.

L Is for Lawless. unabr. ed. Sue Grafton. Read by Mary Peiffer. 7 cass. (Running Time: 10 hrs. 30 min.). (Kinsey Millhone Mystery Ser.). 1996. 56.00 (978-0-7366-3305-5(7), 3959) Books on Tape.
Sleuthing for a friend, Kinsey Millhone, P.I., uncovers a decades-old robbery. Can she retrieve the stashed look & stay alive? An "Our Gang" comedy that will take her halfway across the country & leave her with a major headache.

L. M. Rosenberg. unabr. ed. Read by L. M. Rosenberg. 1 cass. (Running Time: 29 min.). 1985. 10.00 New Letters.
One of a weekly half-hour radio program with authors talking & presenting their own works.

***L. O. V. E. Putting Your Love Styles to Work for You.** . Les and Leslie Parrott. (Running Time: 4 hrs. 18 mins. 55 sec.). (ENG.). 2009. 21.99 (978-0-310-77289-7(3)) Zondervan.

L-Shaped Room. unabr. ed. Lynne Reid Banks. Read by Harriet Walter. 8 cass. (Running Time: 8 hrs.). 1993. 69.95 (978-0-7451-4152-7(8), CAB 835) AudioGO.
Jane Graham is unmarried & pregnant when she is turned out of the house by her irate father. She finds an insect-ridden apartment to rent & feels as though her life has become worthless. Fortunately, her kind neighbors teach her to have a positive disposition & faith in herself.

L Tiny Tea Cassette. Stephen Cosgrove. 2004. 5.00 (978-1-58804-426-6(2)) PCI Educ.

***La Bete.** unabr. ed. David Hirson. Perf. by Michael Cumpsty et al. 2 CDs. (Running Time: 2 hrs.). 2009. audio compact disk 25.95 (978-1-58081-577-2(4)) L A Theatre.

La cueva del descubrimiento see Discovery Cove

La-Li-Luo Dance Songs. unabr. ed. Alan R. Thrasher. 1 cass. (Running Time: 29 mins.). (CHI., bk. 24.50 (SCH115) J Norton Pubs.
These dances are vigorously aerobic & much favored by young people at local festivals in the high plateaus & mountains of central Yunnan Background information on the setting & culture of this dance-song tradition are given in the book as well as musical notation.

***la Recherche de Mariana.** Dominique Renaud. (Collection Decouverte). (FRE.). (YA). 2009. audio compact disk (978-2-09-032622-2(0)) Cle Intl FRA.

La Une. Alphonse Allais. Read by G. Faraoun. 1 cass. (FRE.). 1991. 21.95 (1003-VSL) Olivia & Hill.
"Je ne lis pas les journaux, mais quand je lis je ne m'embete pas," said Alphonse Allais, author & humorist of the late 1890's. Allais offers us solutions, each wackier than the last, to our daily "problems.".

Lab Audio Program Cassettes to accompany Dicho y Hecho Beginning Spanish, 7th Edition. 7th ed. Laila M. Dawson et al. (ENG.). (C). 2004. 44.95 (978-0-471-59355-3(9)) Wiley US.

Lab Management 2002. 2002. audio compact disk 65.00 (978-1-58464-034-9(0)) Natl Conf Stds Labs.

Lab Mnl Cd-Agricultural Mechan. 5th ed. Ray V. Herren. (C). 2005. audio compact disk 199.95 (978-1-4018-7227-4(1)) Pub: Delmar. Dist(s): CENGAGE Learn

Lab Mnl Cd-Agriscience 4e. 4th ed. (C). 2005. audio compact disk 199.95 (978-1-4018-7766-8(4)) Pub: Delmar. Dist(s): CENGAGE Learn

***Lab on CD C.** 2nd ed. (C). 2004. audio compact disk 26.95 (978-0-619-21636-8(0)) Pub: Course Tech. Dist(s): CENGAGE Learn

Labels, Movements, & Other Hazards. SERCON Panel. 1 cass. 9.00 (A0115-87) Sound Photosyn.
At the Science Fiction writers convention with Watson, Kessel, Bratman, Kadrey, & Soukup.

Laberintos see Labyrinths

Labor. unabr. ed. Murray Newton Rothbard. 1 cass. (Running Time: 1 hr. 6 min.). (Introduction to Free Market Economics Ser.). 12.95 (309) J Norton Pubs.
The minimum wage; population.

Labor & Unions. unabr. ed. Murray Newton Rothbard. 1 cass. (Running Time: 1 hr. 24 min.). (Introduction to Free Market Economics Ser.). 12.95 (308) J Norton Pubs.
Covers discrimination; child labor laws; immigration quotas; history of American unionism; business-union collusion; "right-to-work" laws.

Labor Arbitration: The 1988 National Conference. 1988. 185.00 (978-1-55917-384-1(X)) Natl Prac Inst.

Labor Arbitration: The 1989 San Francisco Conference. unabr. ed. 5 cass. 1989. 125.00 Set. (978-1-55917-403-9(X), 9110) Natl Prac Inst.
How advocates can change the outcome of an arbitration case.

***Labor Day.** unabr. ed. Joyce Maynard. Read by Wilson Bethel. (ENG.). 2009. (978-0-06-195640-9(6), Harper Audio); (978-0-06-196159-5(0), Harper Audio) HarperCollins Pubs.

***Labor Day Murder.** Wayne Zurl. Read by Christopher Graybill. (ENG.). 2009. audio compact disk 2.99 (978-0-9825278-2-5(9)) Mind Wings Aud.

***Labor Day Murder: A Sam Jenkins Mystery.** Wayne Zurl. Read by Christopher Graybill. (Running Time: 52). (ENG.). 2009. 2.99 (978-1-61114-013-2(7)) Mind Wings Aud.

Laboratory & Scientific Equipment in Romania: A Strategic Reference 2007. Compiled by Icon Group International, Inc. Staff. 2007. ring bd. 195.00 (978-0-497-82397-9(7)) Icon Grp.

Laboratory Course for Programming with Java - CD-ROM Version. 2nd rev. ed. Nell Dale. 2008. audio compact disk 55.95 (978-0-7637-5889-9(2)) Jones Bartlett.

Laboratory Course in C++ 5th rev. ed. Nell Dale. 2009. audio compact disk 50.95 (978-0-7637-7883-5(4)) Jones Bartlett.

Laboratory Electronics for Scientists: Hands On. Instructed by Howard V. Malmstadt et al. 6 cass. (Running Time: 6 hrs.). 680.00 incl. 165pp. manual, 82pp. experiment manual & experimenter's kit. (74) Am Chemical.
Designed to help users increase their efficiency & effectiveness in the modern scientific laboratory.

Laboratory Equipment in Czech Republic: A Strategic Reference 2007. Compiled by Icon Group International, Inc. Staff. 2007. ring bd. 195.00 (978-0-497-35906-5(5)) Icon Grp.

Laboratory Equipment in United Kingdom: A Strategic Reference 2006. Compiled by Icon Group International, Inc. Staff. 2007. ring bd. 195.00 (978-0-497-82454-9(X)) Icon Grp.

***Laboratory Manual for Elementary Chemistry Cd.** rev. ed. Aniliker. (ENG.). 2010. audio compact disk 26.15 (978-0-7575-5610-4(8)) Kendall-Hunt.

Labours of Hercules. unabr. ed. Agatha Christie. Read by Hugh Fraser. (Audio Editions Mystery Masters Ser.). 2005. 29.95 (978-1-57270-456-5(X)) Pub: Audio Partners. Dist(s): PerseuPGW
First published in book form in 1947, The Labours of Hercules comprises an even dozen mysteries starring Christie's most popular sleuth, the ever-dignified Hercule Poirot. The introductory chapter of the collection sets up the rest of the book. At a dinner party, another guest compares the labors of Poirot to those of Hercules, and the little Belgian is not amused. He has already decided to retire, but makes up his mind to take on 12 great cases - each somehow reflecting the labors accomplished by Hercules - as a farewell to crime solving. All of the cases are quite different from each other, from searching for a lost poet to hunting down a particularly ferocious murderer, from solving mysterious deaths of religious cult members to saving a young would-be politician from potential blackmailers. Frequent Christie interpreter Hugh Fraser brings stories like "The Cretan Bull" and "The Apples of the Hesperides" to dazzling life.

Labours of Hercules: 12 Hercule Poirot Mysteries. unabr. ed. Agatha Christie. Narrated by Hugh Fraser. (Running Time: 31500 sec.). (Hercule Poirot Mystery Ser.). (ENG.). 2005. audio compact disk 31.95 (978-1-57270-457-2(8)) Pub: AudioGO. Dist(s): Perseus Dist

Labrador Pact. unabr. ed. Matt Haig. Read by Simon Jones. 6 CDs. (Running Time: 6 hrs. 45 mins.). (ENG.). 2008. audio compact disk 29.95 (978-1-59887-102-9(1), 1598871021) Pub: HighBridge. Dist(s): Workman Pub

Labyrinth of Evil. abr. ed. James Luceno. Read by Jonathan Davis. (Running Time: 5 hrs.). (AU Star Wars Ser.). (ENG.). 2005. audio compact disk 27.50 (978-0-7393-1735-8(0)) Pub: Random Audio Pubg. Dist(s): Random

Labyrinth of Uncle Mark. Jay O'Callahan. Perf. by Jay O'Callahan. CD. (Running Time: 59 mins, 51 secs). Dramatization. (YA). 2007. audio compact disk 15.00 (978-1-877954-54-2(3)) Pub: Artana Prodns. Dist(s): High Windy Audio
Could an Irish Catholic man, a brilliant lawyer from Cambridge, Massachusetts and a Japanese Canadian dress designer become Romeo and Juliet writ large? What happens when the woman you marry is treated like the enemy?.

Labyrinths. unabr. ed. Short Stories. Jorge Luis Borges. Narrated by Henry Strozier. 2 cass. (Running Time: 3 hrs.).Tr. of Laberintos. 1983. 18.00 (978-1-55690-289-5(1), 83061E7) Recorded Bks.
Short stories of the fantastic & surreal by one of South America's most prominent literary figures.

Lace Knitting to Go: 25 Lovely Laces to Use for Edgings, Embellishments, & More. Andrea Tung & Chronicle Books Staff. (ENG., 2008. audio compact disk 16.95 (978-0-8118-6423-7(5)) Pub: Chronicle Bks. Dist(s): HachBkGrp

***Lace Reader.** unabr. ed. Brunonia Barry. Read by Alyssa Bresnahan. (ENG.). 2008. (978-0-06-170243-3(9)); (978-0-06-170244-0(7)) HarperCollins Pubs.

Lace Reader. unabr. ed. Brunonia Barry. Read by Alyssa Bresnahan. 10 CDs. (Running Time: 11 hrs. 30 mins.). 2008. audio compact disk 39.95 (978-0-06-166155-6(4), Harper Audio) HarperCollins Pubs.

Lace Reader. unabr. ed. Brunonia Barry. Read by Alyssa Bresnahan. 10 CDs. (Running Time: 11 hrs. 45 mins.). 2008. audio compact disk 123.75 (978-1-4361-4096-6(X)) Recorded Bks.

Laced. abr. ed. Carol Higgins Clark. (Regan Reilly Mystery Ser.: No. 10). 2007. 17.95 (978-0-7435-6409-0(X)) Pub: S&S Audio. Dist(s): S and S Inc

Laced. abr. ed. Carol Higgins Clark. Read by Carol Higgins Clark. (Running Time: 4 hrs. 30 mins. 0 sec.). No. 10. (ENG.). 2009. audio compact disk 14.99 (978-0-7435-8041-0(9)) Pub: S&S Audio. Dist(s): S and S Inc

Lacey's Day. Jack Eadon. Read by Phoebe Greene & Jose Villarreal. Prod. by Red Planet Audiobooks. (ENG.). 2008. audio compact disk 18.99 (978-1-934814-05-5(9)) Red Planet Au.

Laceys of Liverpool. unabr. ed. Maureen Lee. Read by Clare Higgins. 12 cass. (Running Time: 18 hrs.). 2002. 96.95 (978-0-7540-0800-2(2), CAB2222) AudioGO.

Laches see Phaedrus

Lachesis Passage, Set. June Fisher et al. Perf. by John N. Peters et al. 3 CDs. audio compact disk 24.95 (WIRE001) Lodestone Catalog.

Lack of Evidence. Dan Yates. 3 cass. 2004. 14.95 (978-1-59156-226-9(0)) Covenant Comms.

Lacquer Screen. unabr. ed. Robert H. Van Gulik. Narrated by Frank Muller. 4 cass. (Running Time: 4 hrs. 30 mins.). (Judge Dee Mysteries Ser.). 1988. 35.00 (978-1-55690-290-1(5), 88080E7) Recorded Bks.
Judge Dee, a 7th Century Chinese magistrate & his assistant go undercover among gangsters & rogues to solve a case involving suicide, blackmail & a secret hidden in the panels of an ornamental screen.

Lacuna. unabr. ed. Barbara Kingsolver. Read by Barbara Kingsolver. 2009. audio compact disk 44.99 (978-0-06-085356-3(5), Harper Audio) HarperCollins Pubs.

***Lacuna.** unabr. ed. Barbara Kingsolver. Read by Barbara Kingsolver. (ENG.). 2009. (978-0-06-196713-9(0), Harper Audio); (978-0-06-196714-6(9), Harper Audio) HarperCollins Pubs.

***Lacuna.** unabr. ed. Barbara Kingsolver. Read by Barbara Kingsolver. 1 Playaway. (Running Time: 19 hrs. 30 mins.). 2009. 64.75 (978-1-4407-5856-0(5)); 113.75 (978-1-4407-5853-9(0)); audio compact disk 123.75 (978-1-4407-5854-6(9)) Recorded Bks.

***Lacuna.** unabr. collector's ed. Barbara Kingsolver. Read by Barbara Kingsolver. 16 CDs. (Running Time: 19 hrs. 30 mins.). 2009. audio compact disk 72.95 (978-1-4407-5855-3(7)) Recorded Bks.

Lad, a Dog, unabr. ed. Albert Payson Terhune. Narrated by John McDonough. 8 pieces. (Running Time: 10 hrs. 45 mins.). (gr. 5 up). 1997. 69.00 (978-0-7887-1104-6(0), 95097E7) Recorded Bks.
Lad, a champion collie, bravely defends The Place from intruders. Through the years, he makes friends with the neighboring animals & raises his own family.

Lad of Evesham Vale. unabr. ed. Fred Archer. Read by Vincent Brimble. 5 cass. (Running Time: 5 hrs.). 2000. 34.95 (978-0-7531-0559-7(4), 990615) Pub: ISIS Audio GBR. Dist(s): Ulverscroft US
Fred Archer, the master of the rural tale has gathered together a fine collection of Worcestershire country folk. From the alluring barmaid Amy Lights, "a rural Venus" to the Reverend Vernon, who rides a tricycle "religiously" & excels at funerals, all the characters embody earthy, warm & ruddy humor. Central to the tale is Sacco, a builder's apprentice, who seduces the local girls & startles older folk with his much prized motorbike. With a witty remark & a quick answer to all of life's perplexing questions, Sacco is a likable scoundrel. He is indeed a true "lad" of Evesham Vale.

Ladder of Life. 4 cass. (J). 1997. 30.00 Set, incl. 8 story bks., activity & songbk. (2014) Family Mtrs.
Character building stories for preschoolers & early school age children.

Ladder of Years. Anne Tyler. Read by C.J. Critt. 34.95 (978-1-4025-4527-6(4)) Recorded Bks.

Ladder of Years. unabr. ed. Anne Tyler. Read by Mary Peiffer. 9 cass. (Running Time: 13 hrs. 30 min.). 1995. 72.00 (978-0-7366-3176-1(3), 3845) Books on Tape.
A forty-year-old woman, mother of three grown children, walks away from her marriage on a sudden impulse. In Tyler's magical tale, Delia Grinstead is propelled to leave her physician husband, hitch a ride to a small quaint town & settle in.

Ladder of Years. unabr. ed. Anne Tyler. Narrated by C. J. Critt. 11 cass. (Running Time: 15 hrs. 45 mins.). 1999. 91.00 (978-0-7887-0451-2(6), 94641E7) Recorded Bks.
The timid doctor's wife walks away from her family, detaching herself from all that is familiar & embarking on a quixotic journey.

Ladders & Ventilation DVD. International Association of Fire Chiefs Staff & National Fire Protection Association. 2005. 473.95 (978-0-7637-3609-5(0)) Jones Bartlett.

Laddie: A True Blue Story. unabr. ed. Gene Stratton-Porter. Read by Laurie Klein. 12 cass. (Running Time: 14 hrs. 30 min.). Dramatization. 1990. 64.95 (978-1-55686-346-2(2), 346) Books in Motion.
A captivating, good-humored look at family life in a small farming community in Indiana in the early 1900's.

Ladies see Chamber Music

Ladies & Gentlemen: There's a World out There. unabr. ed. Nathaniel Branden. 1 cass. (Running Time: 49 min.). 12.95 (588) J Norton Pubs.

Ladies Farm. Viqui Litman. Narrated by Cynthia Darlow. 6 cass. (Running Time: 8 hrs. 15 mins.). 58.00 (978-1-4025-1619-1(3)) Recorded Bks.

Ladies' Farm. unabr. ed. Viqui Litman. Narrated by Cynthia Darlow. 6 cass. (Running Time: 8 hrs. 15 mins.). 2002. 34.95 (978-1-4025-1623-8(1), RF864) Recorded Bks.
When four divorced and widowed friends, Pauline, Della, Kat and Rita, decide to open a retreat especially for women who just need to get away from it all, The Ladies Farm is born. Situated beside a lazy river in the idyllic location of Sydonia, Texas, The Ladies Farm seems poised for great success. Then one day Barbara Morrison, the rich widow of Della's secret lover, arrives in her bright red T bird - and she's brought a whole load of trouble with her.

Ladies' Man. unabr. ed. Elinor Lipman. Read by Beth Fowler. 7 CDs. (Running Time: 10 hrs.). 2004. audio compact disk 74.95 (978-0-7927-3168-9(9), SLD 221, Chivers Sound Lib) AudioGO.
Thirty unmarried years have passed since Harvey Nash failed to show up at his own engagement party. Today, the near-bride and her two sisters, Lois and Kathleen, blame Harvey for their spinsterhood until Harvey returns to the scene of his first romantic crime one cold April night. Now older, filled with regrets (sort of) and more charming than ever, he's reinvented himself as Nash Harvey, jingle composer and chronic bachelor. Despite the sisters' scars and grudges and his platinum tongue and roving eye, this old flame soon becomes an improbable catalyst for the untried and the long overdue.

Ladies' Man, unabr. ed. Elinor Lipman. Read by Beth Fowler. 6 vols. (Running Time: 9 hrs.). (Chivers Sound Library American Collections). 2004. 54.95 (978-0-7927-2332-5(5), CSL 221, Chivers Sound Lib) AudioGO.

Ladies of Grace Adieu: And Other Stories. unabr. ed. Susanna Clarke. Read by Simon Prebble & Davina Porter. 6 CDs. (Running Time: 25680 sec.). 2006. audio compact disk 64.95 (978-0-7927-4514-3(0), SLD 1044) AudioGO.

Ladies of Letters... & More. abr. ed. Lou Wakefield & Carole Hayman. 4 CDs. (Running Time: 5 hrs.). 2003. audio compact disk 39.95 (978-0-563-52384-0(0)) AudioGO.

Ladies of Letters Collection: Radio Dramatization. abr. ed. Lou Wakefield & Carole Hayman. 3 CDs. (Running Time: 4 hrs. 30 mins.). 2003. audio compact disk 39.95 (978-0-563-49606-9(1)) BBC Worldwide.

***Ladies of Liberty.** abr. ed. Cokie Roberts. Read by Cokie Roberts. (ENG.). 2008. (978-0-06-126264-7(1), Harper Audio); (978-0-06-126263-0(3), Harper Audio) HarperCollins Pubs.

Ladies of Liberty: The Women Who Shaped Our Nation. unabr. abr. ed. Cokie Roberts. Read by Cokie Roberts. (Running Time: 36000 sec.). 2008. audio compact disk 39.95 (978-0-06-122725-7(0)) HarperCollins Pubs.

Ladies of Missalonghi. unabr. ed. Colleen McCullough. Read by Mary Woods. 5 cass. (Running Time: 5 hrs.). 1989. 30.00 (978-0-7366-1498-6(2), 2374) Books on Tape.
Members of the Hurlingford clan fear John Smith is stealing their valley out from under them, but what Smith is really stealing is a heart - specifically the heart of a gentle & romantically untutored young woman, Missy Wright.

Ladies of Missalonghi. unabr. ed. Colleen McCullough. Narrated by Davina Porter. 4 cass. (Running Time: 5 hrs. 30 mins.). 1988. 35.00 (978-1-55690-291-8(3), 88010E7) Recorded Bks.
A young, unattached woman in Byron, Australia invites romance into her life.

Ladies of the Court. abr. ed. Michael Mewshaw. Read by Luca Bercovici. 2 cass. (Running Time: 3 hrs.). Dramatization. bk. 16.95 set. (978-1-56703-023-5(8)) High-Top Sports.

Ladies of the Lake. abr. ed. Haywood Smith. Read by Cynthia Darlow. (Running Time: 5 hrs. 0 mins. 0 sec.). (ENG.). 2009. audio compact disk 24.99 (978-1-4272-0795-1(X)) Pub: Macmill Audio. Dist(s): Macmillan

***Ladies of the Lake.** unabr. ed. Haywood Smith. Narrated by Cynthia Darlow. 11 CDs. (Running Time: 14 hrs.). 2009. audio compact disk 99.95 (978-0-7927-6665-0(2)) AudioGO.

***Ladies Sing Christmas: Contemporary & Traditional Favorites.** Contrib. by Tom Fettke. (ENG.). 2003. audio compact disk 90.00 (978-5-557-69308-0(4)) Lillenas.

Ladies Who Launch: Embracing Entrepreneurship & Creativity as a Lifestyle. unabr. ed. Victoria Colligan. Read by Joyce Bean. Told to Amy Swift. (Running Time: 8 hrs. 0 mins. 0 sec.). (ENG.). 2007. audio compact disk 29.99 (978-1-4001-0456-7(4)) Pub: Tantor Media. Dist(s): IngramPubServ

Ladies Who Launch: Embracing Entrepreneurship & Creativity as a Lifestyle. unabr. ed. Victoria Colligan & Beth Schoenfeldt. Read by Joyce Bean. Told to Amy Swift. (Running Time: 8 hrs. 0 mins. 0 sec.). (ENG.). 2007. audio compact disk 59.99 (978-1-4001-3456-4(0)); audio compact disk 19.99 (978-1-4001-5456-2(1)) Pub: Tantor Media. Dist(s): IngramPubServ

Ladies Who Launch: Embracing Entrepreneurship & Creativity as a Lifestyle. unabr. ed. Victoria Colligan et al. Read by Joyce Bean. (YA). 2008. 54.99 (978-1-60252-975-5(2)) Find a World.

Ladies Wild see Fourteen American Masterpieces

Ladies with Options. unabr. ed. Cynthia Hartwick. Narrated by Barbara McCulloh. 8 cass. (Running Time: 10 hrs. 45 mins.). 2004. 62.00 (978-1-4025-0941-4(3)) Recorded Bks.
The Larksdale ladies meet over coffee cake and crafts every Saturday morning. But one day, when they take a long, hard look at their finances, they realize they will be very poor in their old age. So they decide to become an investment club and earn enough for a more comfortable retirement. Their rise from modest investors to millionaires is an adventure that exceeds their wildest expectations.

Lado English Series, Level 1. 3rd ed. Robert Lado. 2002. 111.65 (978-0-13-522251-5(6)) Longman.

Lado English Series, Level 2. 3rd ed. Robert Lado. 2002. bk. 111.65 (978-0-13-522277-5(X)) Longman.

Lado English Series, Level 3. 3rd ed. Robert Lado. 2002. 111.65 (978-0-13-522293-5(1)) Longman.

Lado English Series, Level 4. 3rd ed. Robert Lado. 2002. 111.65 (978-0-13-522319-2(9)) Longman.

Lado English Series, Level 5. 3rd ed. Robert Lado. 2002. 111.65 (978-0-13-522335-2(0)) Longman.

Lado English Series, Level 6. 3rd ed. Robert Lado. 2002. 111.65 (978-0-13-522350-5(4)) Longman.

Lado Positivo del Fracaso: Como Convertir los Errores en Puentes Hacia el Exito abr. ed. John C. Maxwell. (Running Time: 2 hrs. 50 mins.). (SPA.). 2008. audio compact disk 24.99 (978-1-60255-117-6(0)) Pub: Grupo Nelson. Dist(s): Nelson

Lady. unabr. collector's ed. Thomas Tryon. Read by Dan Lazar. 8 cass. (Running Time: 12 hrs.). 1978. 64.00 (978-0-7366-0095-8(7), 1103) Books on Tape.
Seen through the eyes of an 8-year-old boy, Woody, we meet Lady, a charming widow, owner of an imposing home on the Green. As does Woody, we come to care for & love his "special friend." But there is more to Lady than meets the eye, & we share Woody's fear as he closes in on Lady's terrible secret.

Lady & the Monk: Four Seasons in Kyoto. unabr. ed. Pico Iyer. Read by Geoffrey Howard. 8 cass. (Running Time: 11 hrs. 30 mins.). 2000. 56.95 (978-0-7861-1787-1(7), 2586) Blckstn Audio.
When Pico Iyer decides to go to Kyoto & live in a monastery, he does so to learn about Zen Buddhism from the inside, to get to know Kyoto, one of the loveliest old cities in the world & to find out something about Japanese culture today. Then he meets Sachiko, a vivacious, attractive, thoroughly educated, eccentrically speaking English wife of a Japanese "salaryman".

***Lady & the Monk: Four Seasons in Kyoto.** unabr. ed. Pico Iyer. Read by Geoffrey Howard. (Running Time: 11 hrs. 5 mins.). (ENG.). 2011. 29.95 (978-1-4417-8530-5(2)); audio compact disk 100.00 (978-1-4417-8528-2(0)) Blckstn Audio.

Lady & the Panda: The True Adventures of the First American Explorer to Bring Back China's Most Exotic Animal. unabr. ed. Vicki Croke. Read by Lorna Raver. 11 CDs. (Running Time: 11 hrs.). 2005. audio compact disk 99.00 (978-1-4159-2166-1(0)); 81.00 (978-1-4159-2118-0(0)) Books on Tape.
Here is the astonishing true story of Ruth Harkness, the Manhattan bohemian socialite who, against all but impossible odds, trekked to Tibet in 1936 to capture the most mysterious animal of the day: a bear that had for countless centuries lived in secret in the labyrinth of lonely cold mountains. In The Lady and the Panda, Vicki Constantine Croke gives us the remarkable account of Ruth Harkness and her extraordinary journey, and restores Harkness to her rightful place along with Sacajawea, Nellie Bly, and Amelia Earhart as one of the great woman adventurers of all time.

Lady & the Poet. (23286-A) J Norton Pubs.

Lady & the Tramp. 1 cass. (Classic Soundtrack Ser.). (J). 11.99 Norelco. (978-0-7634-0335-5(0)); audio compact disk 19.99 (978-0-7634-0338-6(5)) W Disney Records.

Lady & the Tramp. 1 cass. (Read-Along Ser.). (J). 2000. bk. 7.99 (978-1-55723-016-4(1)) W Disney Records.

Lady & the Tramp. 1 cass. (Classic Soundtrack Ser.). (J). (ps-3). 1997. 11.99 (978-0-7634-0336-2(9)); audio compact disk 19.99 CD. (978-0-7634-0337-9(7)) W Disney Records.

Lady & the Unicorn. unabr. ed. Tracy Chevalier. Read by Terry Donnelly & Robert Blumenfeld. 5 vols. 2004. 54.95 (978-0-7927-3112-2(3), CSL 621, Chivers Sound Lib); audio compact disk 74.95 (978-0-7927-3113-9(1), SLD 621, Chivers Sound Lib) AudioGO.

Lady & the Unicorn. unabr. ed. Isolde Martyn. Read by Rebecca Macauley. 13 cass. (Running Time: 19 hrs. 30 mins.). 2004. 104.00 (978-1-876584-32-0(7), 590893) Pub: Bolinda Pubng AUS. Dist(s): Lndmrk Audiobks
In 1470 the Wars of the Roses threatens to tear England apart. Overnight a man can find himself set against his brother or unable to trust the woman in his arms. For the beautiful & spirited ward of Warwick the Kingmaker, Margery, freedom is the only prize worth fighting for. Disgraced & banished to a nunnery after the philandering Edward IV seduced her, she is determined that no man will ever decide her fate again. Torn between her loyalty to her cause & a dangerous attraction to a man she should despise, Margery's mission becomes a race against time to outwit her enemies & her husband.

Lady Anna. Anthony Trollope. 1 CD. (Running Time: 12.6 hours). 2007. 16.95 (978-1-60112-010-6(9)) Babblebooks.

Lady Anna. unabr. ed. Anthony Trollope. Narrated by Flo Gibson. (Running Time: 13 hrs.). 2004. 28.95 (978-1-55685-768-3(3)) Audio Bk Con.

***Lady Audley's Secret.** M. E. Braddon. Narrated by Flo Gibson. (ENG.). 2010. audio compact disk 39.95 (978-1-60646-176-1(1)) Audio Bk Con.

Lady Audley's Secret. Mary Elizabeth Braddon. Read by Anais 9000. 2009. 33.95 (978-1-60112-225-4(X)) Babblebooks.

Lady Audley's Secret. abr. ed. Mary Elizabeth Braddon. Narrated by Juliet Stevenson. 4 CDs. (Running Time: 5 hrs.). (ENG.). 2010. audio compact disk 26.95 (978-1-934997-55-0(2)) Pub: CSAWord. Dist(s): PerseuPGW

Lady Audley's Secret, Set. unabr. ed. Mary Elizabeth Braddon. Read by Flo Gibson. 10 cass. (Running Time: 15 hrs.). (Classic Books on Cassette Ser.). 1988. 44.95 (978-1-55685-117-9(0)) Audio Bk Con.
The mystery of a modern thriller pervades the twists of plot in this remarkable Victorian novel about a lady haunted by more than one terrible secret.

Lady Bates see Twentieth-Century Poetry in English, No. 7, Recordings of Poets Reading Their Own Poetry

Lady Be Good. collector's ed. Susan Elizabeth Phillips. Read by Anna Fields. 8 cass. (Running Time: 12 hrs.). 1999. 64.00 (978-0-7366-4610-9(8), 4996) Books on Tape.
Lady Emma Wells-Finch, the oh-so-proper headmistress of England's St. Gertrude School for Girls, comes to Texas on a mission, she has two weeks to ruin her reputation. The only thing that will save her from losing everything she holds dear is complete & utter disgrace. World famous playboy-athlete Kenny Traveler has been blackmailed into chauffeuring Lady Emma around. Suspended from the sport he loves, he needs to prove himself completely respectable to get back into the game & when a gorgeous man who can't afford another scandal meets a hardheaded woman who's determined to cause one, anything can happen, even love.

Lady Bird. abr. ed. Jan Jarboe Russell. Read by Shauna Zurbrugg. 4 cass. (Running Time: 6 hrs.). 2001. 25.00 (978-1-59040-110-1(7), Phoenix Audio) Pub: Amer Intl Pub. Dist(s): PerseuPGW

***Lady Blue Eyes: My Life with Frank Sinatra.** unabr. ed. Barbara Sinatra. (ENG.). 2011. audio compact disk 32.00 (978-0-307-74732-7(8), Random AudioBks) Pub: Random Audio Pubg. Dist(s): Random

Lady Boss. Judy Collins. 2004. 10.95 (978-0-7435-4917-2(1)) Pub: S&S Audio. Dist(s): S and S Inc

Lady Bought with Rifles. unabr. ed. Jeanne Williams. Read by Stephanie Brush. 12 cass. (Running Time: 13 hrs. 30 min.). 1995. 64.95 (978-1-55686-610-4(0)) Books in Motion.
Educated at a prim English boarding school, Miranda Greenleaf was ripped from the only life she'd ever known & thrown headlong into a harsh, violent, pre-revolutionary Mexico.

Lady Carliss & the Waters of Moorue. unabr. ed. Chuck Black. Narrated by Andy Turvey & Dawn Marshall. (Running Time: 5 hrs. 17 mins. 25 sec.). (Knights of Arrethtrae Ser.). (ENG.). 2010. 13.99 (978-1-60814-618-5(9)); audio compact disk 19.99 (978-1-59859-672-4(1)) Oasis Audio.

Lady Chapel. unabr. ed. Candace Robb. Read by Stephen Thorne. 10 cass. (Running Time: 10 hrs. 45 min.). 1997. 84.95 (978-0-7531-0086-8(X), 970107) Pub: ISIS Audio GBR. Dist(s): Ulverscroft US
High summer in 1365, & Owen Archer finds himself once again called upon by Archbishop Thorseby to exercise his skills as detective. A man is murdered in the shadow of the Minster, his right hand severed & the evidence points to a wool merchant last seen quarreling with him. But a complex web of rivalries surrounds the wool traders, & Owen is unsure where to turn first. His only witness is a young boy, his only suspect a mysterious hooded woman - & neither can be found.

Lady Chatterley's Lover. Michael Squires. Read by Fabio Camero. (Running Time: 3 hrs.). 2002. 16.95 (978-1-60083-189-8(3), Audiofy Corp) Iofy Corp.

Lady Chatterley's Lover. Michael Squires. Read by Emilia Fox. (Running Time: 5 hrs. 30 mins.). 2003. 27.95 (978-1-59912-964-8(7)) Iofy Corp.

Lady Chatterley's Lover. Michael Squires & Judi Dench. 2 CDs. (Running Time: 3 Hours). 2004. audio compact disk 11.99 (978-1-57050-032-9(0)) Multilingua.

Lady Chatterley's Lover. abr. ed. D. H. Lawrence. Read by Emilia Fox. (Running Time: 5 hrs. 0 mins. 0 sec.). (ENG.). 2008. audio compact disk 26.95 (978-1-934997-08-6(0)) Pub: CSAWord. Dist(s): PerseuPGW

Lady Chatterley's Lover. abr. ed. Michael Squires. Narrated by Elizabeth Coulter. 2 cass. (Running Time: 3 hrs. 4 min.). 12.95 (978-0-89926-156-0(6), 844) Audio Bk.

Lady Chatterley's Lover, abr. ed. Michael Squires. Read by Jill Daly. Ed. by Marilyn Kay. 2 cass. (Running Time: 3 hrs.). 1986. 12.95 (978-1-882071-10-4(7), 012) B-B Audio.
A sensitive woman attempts to cope with her husband's physical & emotional paralysis but finds that she must fulfill her own needs at a very basic level.

Lady Chatterley's Lover. abr. ed. Michael Squires. 2000. 16.95 (978-0-929071-68-8(9)) B-B Audio.

Lady Chatterley's Lover. abr. ed. Michael Squires. Read by Judi Dench. 3 vols. (Classics Collection). 1987. audio compact disk 11.99 (978-1-57815-524-8(X), Media Bks Audio) Media Bks NJ.

Lady Chatterley's Lover. abr. ed. Michael Squires. Read by Judi Dench. 2 cass. (Running Time: 3 hrs.). 2000. 7.95 (978-1-57815-121-9(X), 1083, Media Bks Audio) Media Bks NJ.
A relationship between Constance Chatterley, her husband & other characters, deal with themes of inhumanity & love.

Lady Chatterley's Lover, unabr. ed. Michael Squires. Narrated by Margaret Hilton. 9 cass. (Running Time: 12 hrs. 45 mins.). 1988. 78.00 (978-1-55690-292-5(1), 88100E7) Recorded Bks.
Constance Chatterley finds new meaning in her life through a relationship with the gamekeeper on her husband's estate.

Lady Chatterley's Lover. unabr. collector's ed. Michael Squires. Read by Richard Brown. 9 cass. (Running Time: 13 hrs. 30 mins.). 1987. 72.00 (978-0-7366-1127-5(4), 2050) Books on Tape.
The story of Constance Chatterley, a lovely young woman whose parts are all in good working order. Not so her husband, Clifford. He wears repression like a suit of armor. So when Constance is thrown into contact with Oliver Mellors, her husband's gamekeeper, the results are explosive. He restores not only her sexuality but her zest in life & living.

Lady Daisy. unabr. ed. Dick King-Smith. Read by Nigel Lambert. 2 cass. (Running Time: 3 hrs.). (J). (gr. 1-8). 1999. 23.00 (LL 0062, Chivers Child Audio) AudioGO.

Lady Daisy. unabr. ed. Dick King-Smith. Read by Nigel Lambert. 2 cass. (YA). 1999. 16.98 (FS9-31424) Highsmith.

Lady Daisy, Set. unabr. ed. Dick King-Smith. Read by Nigel Lambert. 2 cass. (J). 1996. 16.98 (978-0-8072-7550-4(6), YA872CX, Listening Lib) Random Audio Pubg.
Ned has to endure relentless ridicule when he starts playing with a doll! His father would rather he play with his new football. But this is no ordinary doll, because Lady Daisy can talk to Ned! Soon many people are interested in Lady Daisy, & when she is stolen, suspects abound. Ned's courage & ingenuity play a big part in rescuing Lady Daisy, & bringing her back to the family.

Lady Death: Motion Picture Soundtrack. 1 CD. 2004. audio compact disk 14.98 (978-1-57813-915-6(5), CLD/001) ADV.

Lady Elizabeth. unabr. ed. Alison Weir. Read by Rosalyn Landor. 16 CDs. (Running Time: 20 hrs. 30 mins.). (ENG.). 2008. audio compact disk 39.95 (978-0-7393-6850-3(8), Random AudioBks) Pub: Random Audio Pubg. Dist(s): Random

Lady, First: My Life in the Kennedy White House & the American Embassies of Paris & Rome. unabr. ed. Letitia Baldrige. Read by Anna Fields. 10 cass. (Running Time: 15 hrs.). 2001. 80.00 (978-0-7366-8327-2(5)) Books on Tape.
Letitia Baldrige is most famous as the social secretary of the Kennedy White House, who brought grace and formality to Camelot. She is also well known as one of the definitive authors on etiquette. It is therefore no surprise that this autobiography touches only lightly on controversy or scandal. What it has to offer instead is the course of a remarkable life, in which Baldridge did more work in more demanding positions than can be believed. She served as social secretary to both the wife of the ambassador to France and Clare Booth Luce, the ambassador to Rome. She worked for three trying years for the Kennedys, then opened her own PR firm and authored a welter of books. Her gentility and work ethic shine through this memoir.

Lady Friday. unabr. ed. Garth Nix. Narrated by Allan Corduner. 6 CDs. (Running Time: 7 hrs. 10 mins.). (Keys to the Kingdom Ser.: No. 5). (YA). (gr. 6-9). 2007. audio compact disk 55.00 (978-0-7393-5096-6(X)) Pub: Random Audio Pubg. Dist(s): Random

Lady Friday. unabr. ed. Garth Nix. Read by Allan Corduner. (Running Time: 25800 sec.). (Keys to the Kingdom Ser.: No. 5). (ENG.). (J). (gr. 4-7). 2007. audio compact disk 39.00 (978-0-7393-4909-0(0), Listening Lib) Pub: Random Audio Pubg. Dist(s): Random

Lady in Question. unabr. ed. Victoria Alexander. Narrated by Jill Tanner. 9 cass. (Running Time: 13 hrs.). 2003. 79.75 (978-1-4193-1185-7(9), L1130MC) Recorded Bks.

Lady in Satin. Perf. by Billie Holiday. 1 cass., 1 CD. 4.78 (CBS 65144); audio compact disk 9.58 CD Jewel box. (CBS 65144) NewSound.

Lady in the Dark see Sound of Modern Drama: The Crucible

Lady in the Dark. (SAC 7146) Spoken Arts.

Lady in the Lake. abr. ed. Raymond Chandler. Read by Elliott Gould. 2 cass. (Running Time: 2 hrs 30 min). 2004. 18.00 (978-1-59007-093-2(3)); audio compact disk 25.00 (978-1-59007-094-9(1)) Pub: New Millenn Enter. Dist(s): PerseuPGW
A couple of missing wives'one a rich man's and one a poor man's become the objects of Marlowe's investigation. One of them may have gotten a Mexican divorce and married a gigolo and the other may be dead. Marlowe's not sure he cares about either one, but he's not paid to care.

Lady in the Locker Room. abr. ed. Susan Fornoff. Read by Lani Minella. 2 cass. (Running Time: 3 hrs.). Dramatization. bk. 16.95 set. (978-1-56703-015-0(7)) High-Top Sports.

Lady in the Painting. Retold by Fred Fang-Yu Wang. 2 cass. (Running Time: 2 hrs.). (CHI.). pap. bk. 49.50 (CHOF01) J Norton Pubs.
This well-known Chinese folktale can be used following completion of "Read Chinese," Vol. I or a similar beginning text in written Chinese, which introduces at least 300 characters. The characters are printed in full & simplified forms & pronunciation is given in both Yale & pinyin romanization without English translation. Audio cassettes can also be used as listening comprehension for beginners or as a "brush up" for those who know "a little" Chinese.

Lady in the Painting. rev. ed. Fred Wang. 2 cass. 1983. 8.95 ea. incl. suppl. materials. (978-0-88710-044-4(9)) Yale Far Eastern Pubns.

Lady in the Palazzo: At Home in Umbria. unabr. ed. Marlena De Blasi. (Running Time: 10 hrs. 0 mins. 0 sec.). (ENG.). 2007. audio compact disk 69.99 (978-1-4001-3343-7(2)) Pub: Tantor Media. Dist(s): IngramPubServ

Lady in the Palazzo: At Home in Umbria. unabr. ed. Marlena Deblasi. Read by Laural Merlington. 8 CDs. (Running Time: 10 hrs. 0 mins. 0 sec.). (ENG.). 2007. audio compact disk 34.99 (978-1-4001-0343-0(6)); audio compact disk 24.99 (978-1-4001-5343-5(3)) Pub: Tantor Media. Dist(s): IngramPubServ

Lady in the Tower. unabr. ed. Jean Plaidy. Read by Anne Flosnik. (Running Time: 14 hrs. 50 mins.). 2008. 29.95 (978-1-4332-4806-1(9)); 85.95 (978-1-4332-4804-7(2)); audio compact disk 99.00 (978-1-4332-4805-4(0)) Blckstn Audio.

Lady in the Tower. unabr. ed. Jean Plaidy. Read by Frances Jeater. 14 cass. (Running Time: 17 hrs.). 1997. 99.95 (978-1-85695-217-0(7), 961212) Pub: ISIS Audio GBR. Dist(s): Ulverscroft US
This is the love story which rocked the foundations of the Church & changed the course of English history, the story of an obsessive love which turned into a murderous hate.

Lady in the Van: A BBC Radio Full-Cast Dramatization. Alan Bennett. (Running Time: 2 hrs. 0 mins. 0 sec.). (ENG.). 2009. audio compact disk 24.95 (978-1-60283-736-2(8)) Pub: AudioGO. Dist(s): Perseus Dist

Lady in Waiting: Developing Your Love Relationships. Jackie Kendall & Debby Jones. Read by Cath Lalgee. (ENG.). 2008. 24.99 (978-1-4245-0856-3(8)) Tre Med Inc.

Lady in White, Level 4. Colin B. Campbell. Contrib. by Philip Prowse. (Running Time: 2 hrs. 21 mins.). (Cambridge English Readers Ser.). (ENG.). 2000. 15.75 (978-0-521-66495-0(0)) Cambridge U Pr.

Lady into Fox, unabr. ed. David Garnett. Read by Flo Gibson. 2 cass. (Running Time: 2 hrs. 30 min.). 1999. 14.95 (978-1-55685-566-5(4)) Audio Bk Con.
Fable of a man's wife turning into a fox & the consequently sometimes horrific results.

Lady Killer. abr. ed. Lisa Scottoline. Read by Kate Burton. 5 CDs. (Running Time: 6 hrs.). 2008. audio compact disk 29.95 (978-0-06-145920-7(8), Harper Audio) HarperCollins Pubs.

***Lady Killer.** abr. ed. Lisa Scottoline. Read by Kate Burton. (ENG.). 2008. (978-0-06-162965-5(0)); (978-0-06-162966-2(9)) HarperCollins Pubs.

Lady Killer. unabr. ed. Ed McBain, pseud. Read by Steve Dunn. 4 cass. (Running Time: 4 hrs.). (87th Precinct Ser.: Bk. 8). 1995. 39.95 (CAB 320) AudioGO.
The letter read, "I will kill the lady tonight at eight. What can you do about it?" But who was the lady, the new hooker in town, singer Lady Jane Astor, or socialite mother Mrs. Barrister? The boys at the 87th precinct have only twelve hours to find a crank or stop a killer.

Lady Killer. unabr. ed. Ed McBain, pseud. Read by Jonathan Marosz. 5 cass. (Running Time: 5 hrs.). (87th Precinct Ser.: Bk. 8). 1996. 30.00 (978-0-7366-3219-5(0), 3882) Books on Tape.
As the mercury rises, so do the tensions. It's broiling midsummer & the city grows ever hotter. It's steam heat with a vengeance. Is it vengeance that drives a killer? The cops know he's out there. He had told them: "I will kill the lady tonight at 8:00. What can you do about it?" The trouble is, no one knows the killer - or whom he plans to kill. Can the boys at the 87th precinct meet the killer's challenge?.

Lady Killer. unabr. ed. Lisa Scottoline. Read by Barbara Rosenblat. 9 CDs. (Running Time: 10 hrs. 30 mins.). 2008. audio compact disk 39.95 (978-0-06-145299-4(8), Harper Audio) HarperCollins Pubs.

***Lady Killer.** unabr. ed. Lisa Scottoline. Read by Barbara Rosenblat. (ENG.). 2008. (978-0-06-162963-1(4)); (978-0-06-162964-8(2)) HarperCollins Pubs.

Lady Killer. unabr. ed. Lisa Scottoline. Narrated by Barbara Rosenblat. 9 cass. (Running Time: 10 hrs. 30 mins.). 2007. 46.95 (978-1-4281-8053-6(2)); 72.75 (978-1-4281-8052-9(4)); audio compact disk 51.95 (978-1-4281-8055-0(9)); audio compact disk 102.75 (978-1-4281-8054-3(0)) Recorded Bks.

Lady Knight. unabr. ed. Tamora Pierce. Read by Bernadette Dunne. 9 CDs. (Running Time: 11 hrs. 11 mins.). (Protector of the Small Quartet Ser.: Bk. 4). (YA). (gr. 6-9). 2009. audio compact disk 65.00 (978-0-7393-7974-5(7), Listening Lib) Pub: Random Audio Pubg. Dist(s): Random

Lady Knight. unabr. ed. Tamora Pierce. Read by Bernadette Dunne. (Protector of the Small Ser.: No. 4). (ENG.). (J). (gr. 5). 2009. audio compact disk 44.00 (978-0-7393-7972-1(0), Listening Lib) Pub: Random Audio Pubg. Dist(s): Random

Lady, Lady, I Did It! An 87th Precinct Mystery. unabr. ed. Ed McBain, pseud. Read by Jonathan Marosz. 5 cass. (Running Time: 5 hrs.). (87th Precinct Ser.: Bk. 14). 1996. 30.00 (978-0-7366-3495-3(9), 4135) Books on Tape.
Detectives Carella & Kling see in the bookstore murder scene four bodies lying in pools of blood. Then Kling realizes one of the victims is his fiancee, Claire! Now all of the cops in the 87th Precinct work the case & they have one question.

Lady Luck's Map of Vegas. unabr. collector's ed. Barbara Samuel. Read by Bernadette Dunne. 9 CDs. (Running Time: 10 hrs.). 2005. audio compact disk 81.00 (978-1-4159-0813-6(3)); 63.00 (978-1-4159-0812-9(5)) Books on Tape.
A successful web designer, forty-year-old India has a fabulously hip life in Denver. When her father passes away, India's flamboyant mother, Eldora, has no plans to mourn peacefully. She insists they hit the road on an unpredictable journey to the city that changed her life forever, so many years ago - Las Vegas. Along the way, they'll look for India's twin, Gypsy, a brilliant artist who lives a nomadic life in the remote mountain towns of New Mexico. Eldora and India set sail down Route 66, each carrying a heavy secret that keeps her from moving forward. Along the way, Eldora will finally reveal to her daughter the truth about her past - and India will be forced to face her own truths about the future.

Lady Macbeth. unabr. ed. Susan Fraser King. Narrated by Wanda McCaddon. (Running Time: 11 hrs. 30 mins. 0 sec.). (ENG.). 2008. audio compact disk 37.99 (978-1-4001-0615-8(X)); audio compact disk 75.99 (978-1-4001-3615-5(6)) Pub: Tantor Media. Dist(s): IngramPubServ

Lady Macbeth. unabr. ed. Susan Fraser King. Read by Wanda McCaddon. (Running Time: 11 hrs. 30 mins. 0 sec.). (ENG.). 2008. audio compact disk 24.99 (978-1-4001-5615-3(7)) Pub: Tantor Media. Dist(s): IngramPubServ

Lady Macbeth: A Novel. unabr. ed. Susan Fraser King. Read by Wanda Mccaddon. (YA). 2008. 59.99 (978-1-60514-963-9(2)) Find a World.

Lady Molly of Scotland Yard. unabr. ed. Emmuska Orczy. Narrated by Flo Gibson. 5 cass. (Running Time: 7 hrs. 30 mins.). (gr. 10 up). 2000. 20.95 (978-1-55685-649-5(0)) Audio Bk Con.
The beautiful, charming Lady Molly solves many grisly crimes with remarkable intuition & gusto.

***Lady Most Likely... A Novel in Three Parts.** unabr. ed. Julia Quinn et al. (ENG.). 2010. (978-0-06-204940-7(2), Harper Audio) HarperCollins Pubs.

Lady of Abu Simbel. unabr. ed. Christian Jacq. Read by Stephen Thorne. 8 cass. (Running Time: 12 hrs.). 2001. 69.95 (000107) Pub: ISIS Audio GBR. Dist(s): Ulverscroft US

Lady of Abu Simbel. unabr. ed. Christian Jacq. Read by Stephen Thorne. 10 CDs. (Running Time: 39600 sec.). (Isis Ser.). 2000. audio compact disk 89.95 (978-0-7531-1135-2(7), 111357) Pub: ISIS Lrg Prnt GBR. Dist(s): Ulverscroft US

Lady of Abu Simbel Vol. 4. Christian Jacq. Read by Martin Shaw. 2 cass. (Running Time: 3 hrs.). 1999. 16.85 (978-0-671-03362-0(X)) S and S Inc.
After the epic battle of Kadesh, Ramses returns to his beloved Royal Consort, Nefertari, but Ramses' trials are not over, & soon he must confront Moses, his childhood friend who has returned to Egypt to demand the exodus of the Hebrew people.

Lady of Abu Simbel Vol. 4. unabr. ed. Christian Jacq. Read by Stephen Thorne. 8 cass. (Running Time: 12 hrs.). (Ramses Ser.: Vol. 4). (J). 2000. 69.95 (978-0-7531-0592-4(6), 000107) Pub: ISIS Lrg Prnt GBR. Dist(s): Ulverscroft US
Will the vigilance of the Pharaoh's loyal servants & the magic of the Lady of Abu Simbel be sufficient to protect the Son of the Light?.

Lady of Avalon. unabr. ed. Marion Zimmer Bradley. Narrated by Davina Porter. 12 cass. (Running Time: 18 hrs.). 1998. 97.00 (978-0-7887-2039-0(2), 95403E7) Recorded Bks.
Enchanting romance, lush historical detail & daring exploits are skillfully blended in this prequel to "The Mist of Avalon".

***Lady of Avalon.** unabr. ed. Marion Zimmer Bradley. Narrated by Rosalyn Landor. (Running Time: 17 hrs. 30 mins.). (Avalon Ser.). 2010. 21.99 (978-1-4001-8778-2(8)); 34.99 (978-1-4001-6778-4(7)); 49.99 (978-1-4001-1778-9(X)) Tantor Media.

***Lady of Avalon (Library Edition)** unabr. ed. Marion Zimmer Bradley. Narrated by Rosalyn Landor. (Running Time: 17 hrs. 30 mins.). (Avalon Ser.). 2010. 49.99 (978-1-4001-9778-1(3)); 119.99 (978-1-4001-4778-6(6)) Tantor Media.

Lady of Hay. unabr. ed. Barbara Erskine. Narrated by Judith Boyd. 20 cass. (Running Time: 28 hrs.). 1999. 162.00 (978-1-84197-027-1(1), H1026E7) Recorded Bks.
Is reliving past existance really possible? Jo Clifford didn't think so. To prove it, she underwent hypnosis - only to relive the tragic misery of Matilda, Lady of Hay. Matilda's life, her hopeless marriage, her passion for the breathtaking Richard de Clare, all lead Jo to a chilling conclusion. Her past & present are eerily similar. To relive experiences in a trance is one thing, having them return to haunt her after eight hundred years is something else entirely.

Lady of Hidden Intent. abr. ed. Tracie Peterson. Narrated by Aimee Lilly. (Ladies of Liberty, Book 1 Ser.). (ENG.). 2008. 16.09 (978-1-60814-016-9(4)) Oasis Audio.

Lady of Hidden Intent. abr. ed. Tracie Peterson. Narrated by Aimee Lilly. (Running Time: 21600 sec.). (Ladies of Liberty Ser.: Vol. 2). (ENG.). 2008. audio compact disk 22.99 (978-1-59859-341-9(2)) Oasis Audio.

Lady of Hidden Intent. unabr. ed. Tracie Peterson. Narrated by Barbara Caruso. 8 CDs. (Running Time: 9 hrs. 45 mins.). (Ladies of Liberty Ser.: Vol. 2). 2008. audio compact disk 92.75 (978-1-4361-0794-5(6)) Recorded Bks.
Award-winning author Tracie Peterson is acclaimed for authentic historical romances that enthrall and inspire. In this compelling sequel to A Lady of High Regard, an 1850s British nobleman sends his daughter to Philadelphia to conceal her past and start a new life as a seamstress. But she soon fears a young lawyer may remember who she really is and jeopardize her father's only chance for freedom.

Lady of High Regard. abr. ed. Tracie Peterson. Narrated by Judith West. (Ladies of Liberty, Book 1 Ser.). (ENG.). 2007. 13.99 (978-1-60814-017-6(2)) Oasis Audio.

Lady of High Regard. abr. ed. Tracie Peterson. Narrated by Judith West. (Running Time: 21600 sec.). (Ladies of Liberty Ser.: Vol. 1). (ENG.). 2007. audio compact disk 19.99 (978-1-59859-245-0(9)) Oasis Audio.

Lady of High Regard. unabr. ed. Tracie Peterson. Read by Barbara Caruso. 8 cass. (Running Time: 9 hrs.). (Ladies of Liberty Ser.: Vol. 1). 2007. 67.75 (978-1-4281-7402-3(8)) Recorded Bks.

Lady of Launay. Anthony Trollope. Read by Diane Burrows. 3 cass. (Running Time: 3 hrs.). 1989. 21.00 (C-181) Jimcin Record.
Victorian romance.

***Lady of Light & Shadows.** C. L. Wilson. (Running Time: 16 mins.). (Tairen Soul Ser.). 2009. 19.95 (978-1-897331-35-4(5), AudioRealms) Dorch Pub Co.

Lady of Lincoln. Ann Barker. 2008. 61.95 (978-1-4079-0293-7(8)); audio compact disk 71.95 (978-1-4079-0294-4(6)) Pub: Soundings Ltd GBR. Dist(s): Ulverscroft US

Lady of No Man's Land. unabr. ed. Jeanne Williams. Read by Stephanie Brush. 12 cass. (Running Time: 15 hrs.). 2001. 64.95 (978-1-55686-784-2(0)) Books in Motion.
Leaving Sweden for the American Frontier, seventeen-year-old Kirsten Mordal is determined to pursue her dream of claiming and farming her own homestead.

Lady of Quality. unabr. ed. Frances Hodgson Burnett. Read by Laurie Klein. 6 cass. (Running Time: 8 hrs. 54 min.). Dramatization. (J). 1992. 39.95 (978-1-55686-445-2(0), 445) Books in Motion.
Set in 17th century England, this is a tale of a tempestuous stable brat who overcomes all to become a lady of quality.

Lady of Quality. unabr. ed. Georgette Heyer. Read by Eve Matheson. 8 cass. (Running Time: 35400 sec.). 1997. 59.95 (978-0-7451-6730-5(6), CAB 1346) Pub: Chivers Audio Bks GBR. Dist(s): AudioGO
When spirited and independent Miss Annis Wynchwood embroils herself in the affairs of a runaway heiress, she is destined to see a good deal of Mr. Carleton, Lucilla's uncivil and high-handed guardian. But amid the chafing restrictions of bath society, Annis has to admit that at least Mr. Oliver Carleton is never boring.

Lady of Secret Devotion. abr. ed. Tracie Peterson. Narrated by Aimee Lilly. (Ladies of Liberty, Book 1 Ser.). (ENG.). 2008. 16.09 (978-1-60814-018-3(0)) Oasis Audio.

Lady of Secret Devotion. abr. ed. Tracie Peterson. Narrated by Aimee Lilly. (Ladies of Liberty Ser.: Vol. 3). (ENG.). 2008. audio compact disk 22.99 (978-1-59859-387-7(0)) Oasis Audio.

Lady of Stonewycke. Michael R. Phillips & Judith Pella. Narrated by Davina Porter. 8 cass. (Running Time: 10 hrs. 45 mins.). (Stonewycke Trilogy: Bk. 3). 71.00 (978-0-7887-5274-2(X)) Recorded Bks.

Lady of the Barge. unabr. ed. W. W. Jacobs. Read by Walter Covell. 3 cass. (Running Time: 4 hrs. 30 min.). Dramatization. 1982. 18.00 (C-68) Jimcin Record.
Consists of: "The Lady of the Barge," "The Monkey's Paw," "The Well," "Bill's Paper Chase," "Cupboard Love," "In the Library," "Captain Rogers," "A Tiger's Skin," "A Mixed Proposal," "An Adulteration Act," "A Golden Venture," "Three at Table".

***Lady of the Butterflies: A Novel.** unabr. ed. Fiona Mountain. (Running Time: 21 hrs. 30 mins.). 2010. 24.99 (978-1-4001-8752-2(4)); 49.99 (978-1-4001-9752-1(X)) Tantor Media.

***Lady of the Butterflies: A Novel.** unabr. ed. Fiona Mountain. Narrated by Josephine Bailey. (Running Time: 21 hrs. 30 mins. 0 sec.). (ENG.). 2010. 34.99 (978-1-4001-6752-4(3)); audio compact disk 119.99 (978-1-4001-4752-6(2)); audio compact disk 49.99 (978-1-4001-1752-9(6)) Pub: Tantor Media. Dist(s): IngramPubServ

Lady of the Camelias. Alexandre Dumas. Read by Laura García. (Running Time: 3 hrs.). 2001. 16.95 (978-1-60083-172-0(9), Audiofy Corp) Iofy Corp.

Lady of the Camellias. Alexandre Dumas. Read by Laura Paton. (Running Time: 2 hrs. 30 mins.). 1999. 20.95 (978-1-60083-804-0(9)) Iofy Corp.

Lady of the Camellias. abr. ed. Alexandre Dumas. Read by Laura Paton et al. 2 cass. (Running Time: 2 hr. 15 mins.). (Works of Alexandre Dumas). 1996. 13.98 (978-962-634-528-3(4), NA202814, Naxos AudioBooks) Naxos.
The tragic but doomed love of Marguerite and Armand, recounted in La Dame aux Camelias, became one of the great love stories from its first publication in 1848.

Lady of the Camellias: La Dame Aux Camelias. abr. ed. Alexandre Dumas. Contrib. by Daniel Philpott et al. 2 CDs. (Running Time: 7790 sec.). (Classic Fiction Ser.). 2006. audio compact disk 17.98 (978-962-634-369-2(9), Naxos AudioBooks) Naxos.

Lady of the Light & Shadows. C. Wilson. (Running Time: 16 mins.). (Tairen Soul Ser.). 2009. audio compact disk 39.95 (978-1-897304-58-7(7)) Dorch Pub Co.

***Lady of the Line.** Philip Mccutchan. 2010. 54.95 (978-1-4079-0674-4(7)); audio compact disk 71.95 (978-1-4079-0675-1(5)) Pub: Soundings Ltd GBR. Dist(s): Ulverscroft US

Lady of the West. unabr. ed. Linda Howard. Read by Natalie Ross. (Running Time: 13 hrs.). 2008. 39.25 (978-1-4233-6297-5(7), 9781423362975, Brinc Audio MP3 Lib); 24.95 (978-1-4233-6298-2(5), 9781423362982, BAD) Brilliance Audio.

Lady of the West. unabr. ed. Linda Howard. Read by Natalie Ross-Turski. (Running Time: 13 hrs.). 2008. 24.95 (978-1-4233-6296-8(9), 9781423362968, Brilliance MP3) Brilliance Audio.

Lady of the West. unabr. ed. Linda Howard. Read by Natalie Ross. (Running Time: 13 hrs.). 2008. audio compact disk 92.25 (978-1-4233-6295-1(0), 9781423362951, BriAudCD Unabrid) Brilliance Audio.

Lady of the West. unabr. ed. Linda Howard. Read by Natalie Ross-Turski. (Running Time: 13 hrs.). 2008. audio compact disk 29.95 (978-1-4233-6294-4(2), 9781423362944, Bril Audio CD Unabri) Brilliance Audio.

Lady of the West. unabr. ed. Linda Howard. Read by Natalie Ross. (Running Time: 13 hrs.). 2009. 39.97 (978-1-4418-5029-4(5), 9781441850294, BADLE) Brilliance Audio.

Lady on My Left. unabr. ed. Catherine Cookson. Read by Patricia Gallimore. 6 cass. (Running Time: 9 hrs.). 2000. 54.95 (978-1-86042-373-4(6), 23736) Pub: Soundings Ltd GBR. Dist(s): Ulverscroft US
Alison Read had for some years lived & worked with Paul Aylmer, her appointed guardian. Paul, an experienced antique dealer, had come to rely on Alison, until a chain of events was set off that led to the exposure of a secret he had for years managed to conceal.

Lady on the Landing. Dianne Forsyth. 1 cass. 6.75 (KGOC117) Ken Mills Found.
Contains such favorites as: "Send in the Clowns," "One Note Samba".

Lady on the Move for the Lord. Deborah Thornton. Illus. by Deborah Thornton. 1 cass. 1995. pap. bk. 9.98 (978-0-9636638-3-2(6)) Inspirat Prayer.
Lecture tape.

Lady or the Tiger see Great American Short Stories

Lady or the Tiger see Tales of Adventure & Suspense

Lady or the Tiger. Frank Richard Stockton. 10.00 (LSS1118) Esstee Audios.

Lady or the Tiger. unabr. ed. Frank Richard Stockton. 1 cass. 7.95 (N-21) Jimcin Record.

Lady or the Tiger. unabr. ed. Frank Richard Stockton. 1 cass. (Running Time: 26 min.). (Creative Short Story Audio Library Ser.). (YA). (gr. 7-12). 1995. 11.00 (978-0-8072-6106-4(8), CS902CX, Listening Lib) Random Audio Pubg.

Lady or the Tiger & Other Stories. unabr. ed. Frank Richard Stockton. Read by Walter Zimmerman et al. 4 cass. (Running Time: 6 hrs.). Dramatization. 1982. 28.00 (C-72) Jimcin Record.
Includes "The Discourager of Hesitancy," "Mr. Tolman," "Our Archery Club," "The Griffon & the Minor Canon," "His Wife's Deceased Sister," "The Transferred Ghost," "Our Story," "Old Pypes & the Dryad".

Lady or the Tiger & Other Stories. unabr. collector's ed. Frank Richard Stockton. Read by Walter Zimmerman et al. 5 cass. (Running Time: 5 hrs.). (Jimcin Recording Ser.). (J). 1982. 30.00 (978-0-7366-3865-4(2), 9072) Books on Tape.
Other stories include: "Our Archery Club," "The Griffon & the Miner Canon," "His Wife's Deceased Sister," "The Transferred Ghost," "Our Story" & "Old Pypes & the Dryad".

Lady or the Tiger & the Voyages of Sinbad. 1 cass. (Running Time: 1 hr.). (Radiobook Ser.). 1987. 4.98 (978-0-929541-08-2(1)) Radiola Co.
Two complete stories.

Lady Queen: The Notorious Reign of Joanna I, Queen of Naples, Jerusalem, & Sicily. unabr. ed. Nancy Goldstone. Narrated by Josephine Bailey. (Running Time: 13 hrs. 0 mins. 0 sec.). (ENG.). 2009. 24.99 (978-1-4001-6412-7(5)); audio compact disk 75.99 (978-1-4001-4412-9(4)); audio compact disk 37.99 (978-1-4001-1412-2(8)) Pub: Tantor Media. Dist(s): IngramPubServ

***Lady Queen: The Notorious Reign of Joanna I, Queen of Naples, Jerusalem, & Sicily.** unabr. ed. Nancy Goldstone. Narrated by Josephine Bailey. (Running Time: 13 hrs. 0 mins.). 2009. 18.99 (978-1-4001-8412-5(6)) Tantor Media.

Lady Sackville, Set. Susan M. Alsop. Read by Flo Gibson. 6 cass. (Running Time: 9 hrs.). 1990. 24.95 (978-1-55685-167-4(7)) Audio Bk Con.
The beautiful Victoria Sackville was the toast of Washington & British society. She fascinated President Arthur, the Prince of Wales, William Waldorf Astor, J. P. Morgan & Rudyard Kipling, & left a trail of ardent suitors in her always interesting & sometimes shocking past. Her life was indeed a romantic novel.

Lady Sa's Imagine This Portfolio Vol. I: A Touch of Motivation: Motivational Messages, gif. ed. Speeches. Created by Lady SA. 1. (Running Time: 55 minutes and 17 sec). Dramatization. 2005. audio compact disk 19.95 (978-0-9763193-0-6(6)) Speaking Engage.
Lady SA's Motivational Messages offers a glimpse of Hope: A glimpse of Reality to all Classes of people: regardless of Ethnicity, Social and Economic class. A glimpse of Love... A glimpse of Prosperity... A glimpse of Despair... A glimpse of Peace... A glimpse of Happiness... A glimpse of the use of Imagining...A glimpse of the necessity to use Logic...and ultimately; these motivational messages are intended to offer A glimpse of Faith, Encouragement, Entertainment and Motivation. These dramatizations will depict Everyday, Ordinary Events, Circumstances, and Issues -that touches the lives and spirits of all people.

Lady Susan. Jane Austen. 3 CDs. (Running Time: 3 hrs.). Dramatization. 2003. audio compact disk (978-0-9746806-1-3(3)) Alcazar AudioWorks.
The beautiful widow, Lady Susan, has an eye toward re-marrying well, and marrying off her teenage daughter. To achieve her objectives, she spins a tale of Victorian humor and manipulation. In the end, she outsmarts even herself.The story is told through the means of letters written by various members of the family and one old friend which clearly tells whose side they are on in the struggle to get the ladies married.

Lady Susan. Jane Austen. Read by Kerri Harris. 3 cass. (Running Time: 2 hrs. 30 mins.). 2001. 14.95 (978-0-9729683-0-0(X), bws166U) Bkworm Audio.
Unabridged AudioLady Susan is a unique novel written entirely in the form of correspondence. The action moves swiftly as Lady Susan, a beautiful coquette who is irresistible to men and cruel to her daughter, manipulates events in a manner that is fascinating even in it's deviousness.

Lady Susan. Jane Austen. Read by Jane Austen. 2 cass. (Running Time: 27.00 hrs.). 2005. 24.95 (978-0-7861-3017-7(2), 3426); audio compact disk 27.00 (978-0-7861-8084-4(6), 3426) Blckstn Audio.

Lady Susan. Jane Austen. Narrated by Laurelle Westaway. (Running Time: 3 hrs.). 2005. 20.95 (978-1-59912-525-1(0)) Iofy Corp.

Lady Susan. Jane Austen. Narrated by Cindy Hardin Killavey. (Running Time: 2 hrs. 30 mins.). 2006. 16.95 (978-1-59912-809-2(8)) Iofy Corp.

Lady Susan. Jane Austen. Read by Cindy Hardin. 3 cass. (Running Time: 3 hrs.). 1989. 21.00 incl. album. (C-144) Jimcin Record.
Early example of Austen's genius.

Lady Susan. Jane Austen. Read by Harriet Walter et al. 2 cass. (Running Time: 2 hrs. 30 min.). 2001. 13.98 (978-962-634-728-7(7), NA222814,

Naxos AudioBooks); audio compact disk 17.98 (978-962-634-228-2(5), NA222812, Naxos AudioBooks) Naxos.
Tells the story of the recently widowed Lady Susan Vernon, intelligent but highly manipulative, who is intent on gaining financially secure relationships for both herself and her wayward but shy teenage daughter Frederica.

Lady Susan. unabr. collector's ed. Jane Austen. Read by Cindy Hardin. 3 cass. (Running Time: 3 hrs.). 1985. 18.00 (978-0-7366-3908-8(X), 9144) Books on Tape.
Lady Susan, a clever & ruthless widow, determines that her daughter is going to marry a man whom both detest. Lady Susan sets her own sights on her sister-in-law's brother, all the while keeping an old affair simmering on the back burner. But people refuse to play the roles they are assigned.

Lady Susan & the Watsons, Set. unabr. ed. Jane Austen. Narrated by Flo Gibson. 3 cass. (Running Time: 4 hrs. 30 min.). 1984. 16.95 (978-1-55685-015-8(8)) Audio Bk Con.
"Lady Susan" is written in letters & each correspondent comes vividly to life, as do the family members in the fragment, "The Watsons.".

Lady Susan; the Watsons; Sanditon. unabr. ed. Jane Austen. Read by Norma West. 6 cass. (Running Time: 7 hrs.). (Isis Ser.). (J). 2002. 54.95 (978-0-7531-1527-5(1)) Pub: ISIS Lrg Prnt GBR. Dist(s): Ulverscroft US
LADY SUSAN, with its wicked, beautiful, intelligent and energetic heroine, is a sparkling melodrama that takes its tone from the outspoken and robust 18th century. Written later, and probably abandoned after her father's death, THE WATSONS is a tantalising and highly delightful story whose vitality and optimism centres on the marital prospects of the Watson sisters in a small provincial town. SANDITON, Jane Austen's last fiction, is set in a seaside town; its themes concern the new speculative consumer society and foreshadow the great social upheavals of the Industrial Revolution.

Lady Susan/the Watsons/Sanditon. unabr. ed. Jane Austen. Read by Norma West. 6 CDs. (Running Time: 6 hrs. 30 min.). (Isis Ser.). (J). 2003. audio compact disk 64.95 (978-0-7531-2239-6(1)) Pub: ISIS Lrg Prnt GBR. Dist(s): Ulverscroft US

Lady Was a Printer. Perf. by Lynn Fontane. 1 cass. 10.00 (MC1025) Esstee Audios.
Radio drama.

Lady Winchester. unabr. ed. Kirby Jonas. Read by James Drury. 8 cass. (Running Time: 11 hrs. 48 min.). 2001. 64.95 (978-1-58116-102-1(6)) Books in Motion.
When her husband is mysteriously shot down in their home, Kathryn Winchester must turn from her Quaker ways, and save her husband with a gun. As her children and a motley group of allies stand beside her, Kate prepares to fight the most desperate battle of her life.

Lady Windermere's Fan. Oscar Wilde. (Running Time: 1 hr. 45 mins.). 2001. 20.95 (978-1-60083-806-4(5)) Iofy Corp.

Lady Windermere's Fan. Oscar Wilde. Perf. by Juliet Stevenson et al. 2 cass. (Running Time: 1 hr. 43 mins.). Dramatization. (Classic Drama Ser.). 1997. 13.98 (978-962-634-611-2(6), NA211114, Naxos AudioBooks) Naxos.

Lady Windermere's Fan, unabr. ed. Oscar Wilde. Read by Flo Gibson. 2 cass. (Running Time: 2 hrs.). 1999. 14.95 (978-1-55685-572-6(9)) Audio Bk Con.
In this comedy of manners Mrs. Erlynne is suspected of having an affair with Lady Windemere's husband. A misplaced fan causes further complications.

Lady Windermere's Fan. unabr. ed. Oscar Wilde. Read by A. Full Cast. (YA). 2008. 34.99 (978-1-60514-984-4(5)) Find a World.

Lady Windermere's Fan. unabr. ed. Oscar Wilde. Perf. by Eric Stoltz et al. 1 cass. (Running Time: 1 hr. 23 mins.). 2001. 20.95 (978-1-58081-136-1(1), TPT130) L A Theatre.
A lord, his wife, her admirer & an infamous blackmailer converge in the irreverent satire that launched Wilde's succession of classic social comedies.

Lady Windermere's Fan. unabr. ed. Oscar Wilde. Perf. by Roger Rees et al. 2 CDs. (Running Time: 1 hr. 23 mins.). 2001. audio compact disk 25.95 (978-1-58081-195-8(7), CDTPT130) Pub: L A Theatre. Dist(s): NetLibrary CO
Lady Windermere is jealous of her husband's interest in an older woman. The fact that the older woman just happens to be Lady Windermere's long-presumed-dead mother is just the beginning of this divinely funny comedy.

Lady Windermere's Fan. unabr. ed. Oscar Wilde. Perf. by Juliet Stevenson et al. 2 CDs. (Running Time: 1 hr. 43 mins.). Dramatization. (Classic Drama Ser.). 1997. audio compact disk 17.98 (978-962-634-111-7(4), NA211112, Naxos AudioBooks) Naxos.

Lady Windermere's Fan. unabr. ed. Oscar Wilde. Read by Stephanie Beacham & Nicky Henson. 2 cass. (Running Time: 3 hrs.). (Oscar Wilde Drama Ser.). 1997. 16.95 (PengAudBks) Penguin Grp USA.

Lady with Carnations. unabr. ed. A. J. Cronin. Read by Judy Geeson. 4 cass. 23.80 (D-128) Audio Bk.
Lady with Carnations is the name of a famous Holbein miniature. Katherine Lorimer, by hard work, flair & courage, has worked her way to the top of a trade that traditionally belongs to men. Having acquired the Holbein despite fierce competition, she feels no triumph but a terrible anxiety.

Ladybird & Love among the Haystacks, unabr. ed. D. H. Lawrence. Narrated by Margaret Hilton & Victoria Morgan. 3 cass. (Running Time: 3 hrs. 30 mins.). 1987. 26.00 (978-1-55690-293-2(X), 87830E7) Recorded Bks.
Two novellas concerning the passion of men for women. In the first, an injured German prisoner-of-war awakens a grieving woman's passion; in the second, Maurice & Geoffrey are brothers, farmers & virgins until a rainy night when Paula & Lydia chance along.

Ladybug at Orchard Avenue. Kathleen Weidner Zoehfeld. 1 cass. (Running Time: 35 min.). (J). (gr. k-4). 2001. pap. bk. 19.95 (SP 5009C) Kimbo Educ.
As winter approaches, ladybug searches for food. Includes read along book.

Ladybug at Orchard Avenue. Kathleen Weidner Zoehfeld. Narrated by Alexi Komisar. Illus. by Thomas Buchs. 1 cass. (Smithsonian's Backyard Ser.). (J). (ps-2). 1996. 5.00 (978-1-56899-262-4(9), C5009) Soundprints.
As the autumn chill warns of winter, obstacles in the rose garden hinder ladybug's search for the food she needs for hibernation. An ant strikes out with its powerful jaws, but ladybug's forewings protect her. Undaunted, she plods on with her favorite delicacy, aphids, just beyond reach. But time is running out. Will she have enough to eat when winter arrives?.

Lady's Life in the Rocky Mountains, Set. unabr. ed. Isabella Lucy Bird. Read by Flo Gibson. 5 cass. (Running Time: 7 hrs. 30 min.). (gr. 8 up). 1989. 20.95 (978-1-55685-141-4(3)) Audio Bk Con.
Descriptive letters written in 1873 by a courageous & spirited Englishwoman telling her sister of her adventures on horseback over 800 miles of wilderness.

Lady's Maid's Bell see Great Ghost Stories - Volume 1

Ladystinger, unabr. ed. Craig Smith. Narrated by George Guidall. 6 cass. (Running Time: 8 hrs. 15 mins.). 1994. 51.00 (978-0-7887-0035-4(9), 94234E7) Recorded Bks.
A beautiful scam artist is enlisted by a cop to pull a sting on an international ring of criminals. For Maggie It's a scam that posed minimal risk, until she meets a man with a better confidence game. As the action heats up & the scene shifts to Jamaica, Maggie discovers there are more than two players. Now she'll need all her wits & a lion's share of luck to escape with her life.

Laer at Tale Dansk see Learn to Speak Danish

Laetrile: Where Do We Go from Here? unabr. ed. Wynn Westover. 1 cass. (Running Time: 28 min.). 12.95 (939) J Norton Pubs.

Laetrile Court Cases. unabr. ed. George Kell. 1 cass. (Running Time: 27 min.). 12.95 (936) J Norton Pubs.

L'Affaire. unabr. ed. Diane Johnson. 9 cass. (Running Time: 13 hrs. 30 min.). 2003. 72.00 (978-0-7366-9502-2(8)) Books on Tape.

Lagoon see Tales of Unrest

Lagoon see Heart of Darkness & Other Stories

Lagoon. Joseph Conrad. 1 cass. (Running Time: 41 mins.). 1999. (978-0-7588-0001-5(0), Acme Record); audio compact disk (978-0-7588-0002-2(9), Acme Record) Goss Commns.

Lagoon. unabr. ed. Joseph Conrad. 1 cass. Dramatization. 8.95 (S-22) Jimcin Record.

Lagoon & an Outpost of Progress. Joseph Conrad. 1 cass. 1989. 7.95 (S-22) Jimcin Record.
Two of Conrad's early works.

Laguna Heat. unabr. ed. T. Jefferson Parker. Read by Christopher Lane. (Running Time: 10 hrs.). 2008. 24.95 (978-1-4233-5536-6(9), 9781423355366, BAD); 39.25 (978-1-4233-5537-3(7), 9781423355373, BADLE); audio compact disk 24.95 (978-1-4233-5534-2(2), 9781423355342, Brilliance MP3); audio compact disk 29.95 (978-1-4233-5532-8(6), 9781423355328, Bril Audio CD Unabri); audio compact disk 92.25 (978-1-4233-5533-5(4), 9781423355335, BriAudCD Unabrid); audio compact disk 39.25 (978-1-4233-5535-9(0), 9781423355359, Brlnc Audio MP3 Lib) Brilliance Audio.

Laguna Heat, unabr. ed. T. Jefferson Parker. Narrated by Peter Jay Fernandez. 7 cass. (Running Time: 10 hrs. 15 mins.). 1989. 60.00 (978-1-55690-294-9(8), 89800E7) Recorded Bks.
Sergeant Tom Shephard, of the Laguna Police, investigates a brutal & bizarre murder, unraveling a 40-year-old mystery wrapped in sleazy sex, blackmail & suicide. In Laguna Beach, the heat is on.

Laguna Laurel Park & Bolsa Chica Preserve, Orange County, California. Hosted by Nancy Pearlman. 1 cass. (Running Time: 27 min.). 10.00 (1121) Educ Comm CA.

Lahti File, Level 3. Richard MacAndrew. As told by Jonathan Keeble. Contrib. by Philip Prowse. (Running Time: 1 hr. 40 mins.). (Cambridge English Readers Ser.). (ENG.). 2003. 15.75 (978-0-521-75083-7(0)) Cambridge U Pr.

Lair. unabr. ed. James Herbert. Read by Gareth Armstrong. 7 CDs. (Running Time: 8 hrs.). (Isis (CDs) Ser.). (J). 2006. audio compact disk 71.95 (978-0-7531-2459-8(9)) Pub: ISIS Lrg Prnt GBR. Dist(s): Ulverscroft US

Lair. unabr. ed. James Herbert & James Herbert. Read by Gareth Armstrong. 6 cass. (Running Time: 26400 sec.). (Isis Cassettes Ser.). 2006. 54.95 (978-0-7531-3445-0(4)) Pub: ISIS Lrg Prnt GBR. Dist(s): Ulverscroft US

***Lair of Bones: The Runelords, Book 4.** unabr. ed. David Farland. Read by Ray Porter. (Running Time: 17 hrs.). (Runelords Ser.). 2010. 44.95 (978-1-4417-5315-1(X)); 89.95 (978-1-4417-5311-3(7)); audio compact disk 123.00 (978-1-4417-5312-0(5)) Blckstn Audio.

Lair of the Jade Tiger. unabr. ed. J. Thomas Morse. 1 cass. (Running Time: 30 min.). Dramatization. (KidSkills Interpersonal Skill Ser.). (J). (gr. 1-3). 1986. 13.95 (978-0-934275-21-7(1)); Fam Skills.
Keeping friends & developing strong, lasting relationships requires specific skills. This story brings the subject of friendship to life in a new & intriguing way.

Lair of the Lizard. collector's ed. E. C. Ayres. Read by Barrett Whitener. 6 cass. (Running Time: 9 hrs.). 1999. 48.00 (978-0-7366-4551-5(9), 4960) Books on Tape.
In the fourth outing for Ayres's Florida P. I. Tony Lowell, a good friend of his daughter Ariel, a Hispanic woman from Santa Fe, has disappeared & all indications point to four play. Tony reluctantly agrees to go to Santa Fe to track down the missing woman. Assisted by his old acquaintance, P. I. Joshua Croft & at Ariel's insistence, a New Age mystic, Lowell soon finds himself in over his head in a situation involving deeply divided cultures, traditions & a general western mistrust of outsiders. Stubbornly pressing forward, Lowell discovers that the missing woman, Alicia Sandoval, was once married to a violent felon who has continued to stalk her. He then discovers something even more chilling, the felon, a locally popular man, was previously married to a woman who also disappeared & whose remains have just been found in a high mountain cave.

Laity & Pastors: Building Trust Relationships: Proceedings of the 45th Annual Convention Association of Evangelicals, Buffalo, New York. Read by Al Taylor. 1 cass. (Running Time: 60 min.). 1987. 4.00 (334) Nat Assn Evan.

Lake see Fantastic Tales of Ray Bradbury

Lake Effect: Two Sisters & a Town's Toxic Legacy. Nancy A. Nichols. 2008. audio compact disk 24.95 (978-1-59726-520-1(9), Shearwater Bks) Pub: Island Pr. Dist(s): Chicago Distribution Ctr

Lake Frome Monster, Set. unabr. ed. Arthur W. Upfield. Read by Nigel Graham. 4 cass. (Running Time: 5 hrs.). (Inspector Napoleon Bonaparte Mystery Ser.). 1994. 34.00 (978-1-85695-505-8(2), 94370) Recorded Bks.
In the Australian outback of the 1930's, Inspector Bonaparte investigates a murder that local aborigines claim was committed by a legendary monster dwelling in Lake Frome. After poking around the dead man's campsite, though, Bony knows this story is not native superstition, but a hurried attempt at a cover-up.

***lake has no Saint.** stacey waite. (ENG.). 2010. audio compact disk 12.00 (978-1-932195-99-6(8)) Tupelo Pr Inc.

Lake House. unabr. ed. James Patterson. Read by Hope Davis & Stephen Lang. (ENG.). 2005. 14.98 (978-1-59483-283-3(8)) Pub: Hachet Audio. Dist(s): HachBkGrp

Lake House. unabr. ed. James Patterson. Read by Hope Davis & Stephen Lang. (Running Time: 7 hrs. 30 mins.). (ENG.). 2009. 59.98 (978-1-60024-971-6(X)) Pub: Hachet Audio. Dist(s): HachBkGrp

Lake in the Clouds. unabr. ed. Sara Donati. 10 cass. (Running Time: 25 hrs. 30 mins.). (Wilderness Ser.: No. 3). 2002. 56.00 (978-0-7366-8805-5(6)) Books on Tape.
Nathaniel Bonner is a white man who has been accepted into the Mohawk tribe, and who has won the heart of English immigrant Elizabeth. Nathaniel's half-Mohawk daughter, Hannah, is the focus of this book. She must tend a feverish, pregnant runaway slave, Selah Voyager, whom the Bonners hide while she recovers. However, Hannah's childhood friend Liam returns as a bounty hunter intent on recapturing Selah, who is wanted for murder. These two arrivals set into motion the gripping events that follow in the New York settlement of Paradise, sending the Bonners on a desperate journey to Canada to save Selah and her unborn child.

Lake in the Clouds, Pt. A. unabr. ed. Sara Donati. 10 cass. (Running Time: 13 hrs.). (Wilderness Ser.: No. 3). 2002. 96.00 (978-0-7366-8684-6(3)) Books on Tape.

Lake Isle of Innisfree see Gathering of Great Poetry for Children

Lake Isle of Innisfree see Poetry of William Butler Yeats

Lake Lady see Childe Rowland & Other British Fairy Tales

Lake Mead Mystery Matter & The Jimmy Carter Matter. 1 cass. (Running Time: 60 min.). Dramatization. (Yours Truly, Johnny Dollar Ser.). 1959. 6.00 Once Upon Rad.
Radio broadcasts - mystery & suspense.

Lake News. Melissa Leo. Read by Jen Taylor. 12 CDs. (Running Time: 18 hrs.). 2000. audio compact disk 110.95 (978-0-7927-9960-3(7), SLD 011, Chivers Sound Lib) AudioGO.
Lily Blake, wrongly accused of having an affair with a newly appointed Cardinal, forms an uneasy alliance with John Kipling, publisher of her hometown newspaper & a man with scores to settle.

Lake News, unabr. ed. Melissa Leo. Read by Jen Taylor. 10 vols. (Running Time: 13 hrs.). 2000. bk. 84.95 (978-0-7927-2350-9(3), CSL 239, Chivers Sound Lib) AudioGO.
When a reporter wrongly accuses Lily Blake of having an affair with a newly appointed Cardinal, she becomes an instant Pariah. She returns to her hometown of Lake Henry, New Hampshire. Driven to exact justice against the media that has damaged her reputation, she forms an uneasy alliance with the publisher of the newspaper & a man who has his own scores to settle.

Lake of Darkness. unabr. ed. Ruth Rendell. Read by David Suchet. 6 cass. (Running Time: 9 hrs.). 2000. 49.95 (978-0-7451-6238-6(X), CAB 250) Pub: Chivers Audio Bks GBR. Dist(s): AudioGO
Martin Urban has led a comfortable life, until he wins the lottery and decides to help the poor. Finn lives a dangerous life and also comes into money. But his came in cash, wrapped in newspaper. Finn is also interested in helping people, as long as the price is right. And so the good intentions of one become fatally entangled with the madness of another.

***Lake of Dreams: A Novel.** Kim Edwards. (Running Time: 17 hrs.). (ENG.). 2011. audio compact disk 39.95 (978-0-14-242839-9(6), PengAudBks) Penguin Grp USA.

Lake Shore Limited. unabr. ed. Sue Miller. Read by Sue Miller. (ENG.). 2010. audio compact disk 35.00 (978-0-307-71511-1(6), Random AudioBks) Pub: Random Audio Pubg. Dist(s): Random

Lake Superior Visions. 1 cass. (Running Time: 60 min.). 1994. audio compact disk 15.95 CD. (2635, Creativ Pub) Quayside.
Native American flute music accompanied by earthy percussion, bells, & rain sticks. Authentic nature sounds complement this primitive music performed by Anakwad.

Lake Superior Visions. 1 cass. (Running Time: 60 min.). 1994. 9.95 (2634, NrthWrd Bks) TandN Child.

Lake Tahoe Voices: Writing about Lake Tahoe on Audio. 1 CD. (Running Time: 73:28). (ENG.). 2006. audio compact disk (978-0-9778825-0-2(0)) Faultline Audio.
Lake Tahoe Voices is a collection of stories about Lake Tahoe on audio, ranging from a traditional Washo creation tale to 1914. Authors include, a pair of Washo storytellers, Thomas Starr King, Mark Twain, Isabella Bird, John Vance Cheney and Hazel King. The collection affords a unique glimpse into Lake Tahoe's long lost past.

Lake Tyndal. Max Brand. (Running Time: 0 hr. 18 mins.). 1999. 10.95 (978-1-60083-487-5(6)) Iofy Corp.

***Lake Tyndal.** Max Brand. 2009. (978-1-60136-414-2(8)) Audio Holding.

Lake Wobegon Days. abr. ed. Garrison Keillor. 4 CDs. (Running Time: 4 hrs. 45 mins.). (ENG.). 1999. audio compact disk 36.95 (978-1-56511-314-5(4), 1565113144) Pub: HighBridge. Dist(s): Workman Pub

Lake Wobegon Loyalty Days: A Recital for Mixed Baritone & Orchestra. abr. unabr. ed. Garrison Keillor & Minnesota Orchestra Staff. Conducted by Philip Brunelle. 1 CD. (Running Time: 1 hr.). (ENG.). 1990. audio compact disk 13.95 (978-0-942110-34-0(X), 094211034X) Pub: HighBridge. Dist(s): Workman Pub

Lake Wobegon Sampler. Garrison Keillor. 1 cass. 1986. 5.95 (978-0-440-85047-2(9), Random AudioBks) Random Audio Pubg.

Lake Wobegon Summer 1956. abr. ed. Garrison Keillor. Read by Garrison Keillor. 6 CDs. (Running Time: 6 hrs. 30 mins.). (ENG.). 2001. audio compact disk 36.95 (978-1-56511-501-9(5), 1565115015) Pub: HighBridge. Dist(s): Workman Pub

Lake Wobegon Summer 1956. abr. ed. Garrison Keillor. Read by Garrison Keillor. 4 cass. (Running Time: 6 hrs. 30 min.). 2001. 29.95; audio compact disk 34.95 HighBridge.

Lake Wobegon U. S. A. unabr. abr. ed. Garrison Keillor. Contrib. by Garrison Keillor. 4 CDs. (Running Time: 5 hrs.). (ENG.). 1993. audio compact disk 36.95 (978-1-56511-008-3(0), 1565110080) Pub: HighBridge. Dist(s): Workman Pub

Lakes & Streams. Perf. by W. A. Mathieu. 1 cass. 1991. 9.95 (978-1-55961-106-0(5)); 9.95 Incl. bk. pack. (978-1-55961-090-2(5)); audio compact disk 13.95 CD. (978-1-55961-158-9(8)) Relaxtn Co.

Lakes of the Sangre de Cristo Mountains: Indexed Atlas with over 200 Photographs. Wojtek Rychlik. (ENG., 2009. audio compact disk 19.00 (978-0-9842554-0-5(0)) PikesPeak.

Lakeshore Christmas. Susan Wiggs. Contrib. by Joyce Bean. (Lakeshore Chronicles: Bk. 6). 2009. 59.99 (978-1-4418-1029-8(3)) Find a World.

Lakeshore Christmas. abr. ed. Susan Wiggs. Read by Joyce Bean. (Running Time: 5 hrs.). (Lakeshore Chronicles: Bk. 6). 2009. audio compact disk 24.99 (978-1-4233-5201-3(7), 9781423352013, BACD) Brilliance Audio.

Lakeshore Christmas. abr. ed. Susan Wiggs. Read by Joyce Bean. (Running Time: 5 hrs.). (Lakeshore Chronicles: Bk. 6). 2010. audio compact disk 14.99 (978-1-4233-5202-0(5), 9781423352020, BCD Value Price) Brilliance Audio.

Lakeshore Christmas. unabr. ed. Susan Wiggs. Read by Joyce Bean. (Running Time: 10 hrs.). (Lakeshore Chronicles: Bk. 6). 2009. 39.97 (978-1-4233-5198-6(3), 9781423351986, Brlnc Audio MP3 Lib); 39.97 (978-1-4233-5200-6(9), 9781423352006, BADLE); 24.99 (978-1-4233-5199-3(1), 9781423351993, BAD); 24.99 (978-1-4233-5197-9(5), 9781423351979, Brilliance MP3); audio compact disk 79.97 (978-1-4233-5196-2(7), 9781423351962, BriAudCD Unabrid); audio compact disk 34.99 (978-1-4233-5195-5(9), 9781423351955, Bril Audio CD Unabri) Brilliance Audio.

Lakhótiya Wóglaka Po! - Speak Lakota! Level 1 Audio CD. Prod. by Jan Ullrich & Wilhelm Meya. Featuring Kayo Bad Heart Bull et al. 1 CD. (Running Time: 80 Mins.). (DAK, ENG & SIO.). 2004. audio compact disk 14.95 (978-0-9761082-1-4(6)) Lakota Con.
Lakhótiya Wóglaka Po! - Speak Lakota! Level 1 Audio CD is the audio component of the the Level 1 textbook. Designed as a companion product to the textbook, it provides an important aural dimension to the textbook, especially in areas of word pronunciation and phrase inflection. Narrated by trained Lakota educators, the CD provides exceptionally clear and

appropriately-paced narration both from male and female speakers and among different age speakers. The Audio CD covers vocabulary and dialogue in all Units from 1 to 24. Particularly useful for students as well as teachers, the CD assists in forming good language speaking habits and helps reinforce Lakota orthography.

Lakhótiya Wóglaka Po! - Speak Lakota! Level 2 Audio CD. Excerpts. Prod. by Jan F. Ullrich. Lakota Language Consortium. 1 CD. (Running Time: 80 mins). (DAK, ENG & SIO.). 2006. audio compact disk 14.95 (978-0-9761082-6-9(7)) Lakota Con.

Lakhotiya Woglaka Po! - Speak Lakota! Level 2 Audio CD is the audio component of the the Level 2 textbook. Designed as a companion product to the textbook, it provides an important aural dimension to the textbook, especially in areas of word pronunciation and phrase inflection. Narrated by trained Lakota educators, the CD provides exceptionally clear and appropriately-paced narration both from male and female speakers and among different age speakers. The Audio CD covers vocabulary and dialogue in all Units from 1 to 12. Particularly useful for students as well as teachers, the CD assists in forming good language speaking habits and helps reinforce Lakota orthography.

Lakota Sundance Songs, Taku Wakan. unabr. ed. 1 cass. 12.95 (C11151) J Norton Pubs.

Lakota Way. 2005. 59.95 (978-0-7861-4370-2(3)); audio compact disk 72.00 (978-0-7861-7534-5(6)) Blckstn Audio.

Lakota Way. Short Stories. Joseph M. Marshall, III. Prod. by CD Sound. 1 CD. (Running Time: 1 hr. 11 mins. 34 secs.). 2002. audio compact disk 14.98 (978-0-9650872-9-2(8)) Scoria.

Lakota Way: Mp3. unabr. ed. Joseph M. Marshall, III. Read by Joseph M. Marshall, III. (Running Time: 10 hrs.). (J). 2007. audio compact disk 29.95 (978-0-7861-7819-3(1)) Blckstn Audio.

Lakota Way: Native American Wisdom on Ethics & Character. unabr. ed. Joseph M. Marshall, III. Read by Joseph M. Marshall, III. (Running Time: 1 hr. 30 mins.). 2004. audio compact disk 15.00 (978-0-7861-8487-3(6)) Blckstn Audio.

Lakota Way: Stories & Lessons for Living. unabr. ed. Joseph M. Marshall, III. Read by Joseph M. Marshall, III. (Running Time: 32400 sec.). 2007. audio compact disk 25.95 (978-0-7861-6146-1(9)) Blckstn Audio.

Lakota Winds. unabr. ed. Janelle Taylor. Read by Denica Fairman. 10 vols. (Running Time: 10 hrs.). 1999. bk. 84.95 (978-0-7927-2282-3(5), CSL 171, Chivers Sound Lib) AudioGO.

When Wind Dancer's wife & son are slaughtered by the Crow tribe, he becomes embittered & lonely. Then he meets Chumani, who has also lost her husband & child to the Crow. A respected Lakota medicine man sees their union in a sacred vision. But can they overcome the past in order to succumb to a love that would ultimately save their people?.

Lamb. Bernard Mac Laverty. Read by Conor Mullen. (Running Time: 16260 sec.). (Chivers Audio Bks.). 2003. 39.95 (978-0-7540-8417-4(5)) Pub: Chivers Audio Bks GBR. Dist(s): AudioGO

***Lamb.** unabr. ed. Christopher Moore. Read by Fisher Stevens. (ENG.). 2007. (978-0-06-126265-4(X), Harper Audio); (978-0-06-126266-1(8), Harper Audio) HarperCollins Pubs.

Lamb: AudioBook, CD. (J). 2004. audio compact disk (978-1-890082-41-3(4)) GS Intl CAN.

Lamb: The Gospel According to Biff, Christ's Childhood Pal. unabr. ed. Christopher Moore. Read by Fisher Stevens. (Running Time: 54000 sec.). 2007. audio compact disk 44.95 (978-0-06-123878-9(3)) HarperCollins Pubs.

Lamb: VBS Audio Cassette. (J). 2003. (978-1-890082-40-6(6)) GS Intl CAN.

Lamb - Audio Edition w/ Booklet. (J). 2001. (978-1-890082-20-8(1)) GS Intl CAN.

Lamb & the Dove. Elbert Willis. 1 cass. (Resurrection Living Ser.). 4.00 Fill the Gap.

Lamb & the Fuhrer: Jesus Talks with Hitler. unabr. ed. Ravi Zacharias. (Running Time: 2 hrs. 4 mins. 9 sec.). (Great Conversations Ser.). (ENG.). 2005. audio compact disk 16.99 (978-1-59859-020-3(0)) Oasis Audio.

Lamb & the Fuhrer: Jesus Talks with Hitler. unabr. ed. Ravi K. Zacharias. (Great Conversations Ser.). (ENG.). 2005. 11.89 (978-1-60814-274-3(4)) Oasis Audio.

Lamb Chop's Sing-Along, Play-Along. abr. ed. Shari Lewis. 1 cass. (Running Time: 35 min.). (J). (gr. k-3). 1988. 7.95 (978-0-89845-773-5(4), CPN1826) HarperCollins Pubs.

Lamb in Love. unabr. ed. Carrie Brown. Read by David Rintoul. 8 vols. (Running Time: 12 hrs.). (Chivers Sound Library American Collections). 1999. bk. 69.95 (978-0-7927-2318-9(X), CSL 207, Chivers Sound Lib) AudioGO.

Set in a rural English village the year of the Apollo moon landing, tells of two unlikely people, Norris Lamb & Vida Stephen, who have known each other for over twenty years. After knowing her all this time, Norris has fallen in love & he's not sure what to.

Lamb of Glory. Contrib. by Camp Kirkland. (ENG.). 1995. 12.00 (978-0-00-511567-1(1)) Lillenas.

Lamb of God. Perf. by Donna Summer. 1 cass. 1999. Provident Music.

Lamb or Lion. John Kilpatrick. 1 cass. 7.00 (978-0-7684-0023-6(6)) Destiny Image Pubs.

Lambs of God. unabr. ed. Marele Day. Read by Penelope Shelton. 7 cass. (Running Time: 10 hrs. 30 min.). 1998. (978-1-86442-229-0(7), 580437) Bolinda Pubng AUS.

For Iphigenia, Margarita & Carla the rhythm of nature & the rituals of the church have joined to make an encompassing whole, a garment as fitting for their lives as their homespun clothes. The three nuns have forgotten the world outside. Until a worldly priest forges his way in.

Lambs of London. Peter Ackroyd. Narrated by Alex Jennings. 5 CDs. (Running Time: 22440 sec.). (Sound Library). 2006. audio compact disk 59.95 (978-0-7927-4009-4(2), SLD 933) AudioGO.

Lamb's Supper: The Mass as Heaven on Earth. Scott Hahn. 3 cass. (Running Time: 4 hrs.). 2004. 19.99 (978-1-4025-2485-1(4), 01744) Recorded Bks.

Lamb's Supper: The Mass as Heaven on Earth. Scott Hahn. 2001. audio compact disk 30.95 (978-1-57058-386-5(2)) Pub: St Joseph Communs. Dist(s): STL Dist NA

Lamb's Supper: The Mass as Heaven on Earth. unabr. ed. Scott Hahn. Read by Gus Lloyd. 3 cass. (Running Time: 4 hrs.). 2002. 19.99 (978-1-4025-1163-9(9)) Recorded Bks.

Theologian Scott Hahn, a convert to the Catholic Church, this insightful book examines the universal appeal of the Mass.

Lamb's Tale: A Christmas Musical for Kids. Martha Bolton & Dennis Allen. 1 cass. (Running Time: 35 min.). (J). 2001. 80.00 (MU-9239C); 12.99 (TA-9239C); 54.99 (TA-9239PK); audio compact disk 80.00 (MU-9239T) Lillenas.

Meet Zeke - a young Bethlehem boy trying to decide what he wants to be when he grows up. He seems sadly destined to be a shepherd just like his father & his father's father &... But what a change occurs when Zeke's special little lamb, Snowflake, gets lost. In his search, Zeke discovers a newborn King & the joy of fitting into God's plan for his life. Here's a creative concept, from a gifted team, that's certain to delight your children & your church family. An imaginative script weaves together some charming new songs featuring a taste of jazz, Broadway show tunes & a little '50s rock & roll. Most of all, it's fun & promises to deliver a lasting impression. Unison, optional 2-part. Accompaniment compact disc includes stereo trax & split-channel trax.

Lament see Dylan Thomas Reading: And Death Shall Have No Dominion and Other Poems

Lament see Dylan Thomas Reading His Poetry

Lament see Bet

Lament for a Lost Lover. unabr. ed. Philippa Carr. Read by Marie McCarthy. 10 cass. (Running Time: 11 hrs.). (Isis Ser.). (J). 2001. 84.95 (978-1-85695-283-5(5), 960803) Pub: ISIS Lrg Prnt GBR. Dist(s): Ulverscroft US

Lament for Raymond Carver. Raymond Carver. 1 CD. (Running Time: 1 hr.). 2001. audio compact disk 14.95 (FCLC594) Lodestone Catalog.

Reflective stories & poems of jump to life in a musical landscape that expertly fuses blues, jazz, rock & classical inputs.

Lament of the Border Widow see Poetry of Robert Burns & Border Ballads

***Lamentaciones de Jeremias: The Lamentations of Jeremiah.** Charles R. Swindoll. 2009. audio compact disk 27.00 (978-1-57972-857-1(X)) Insight Living.

Lamentation. unabr. ed. Ken Scholes. Read by Orson Scott Card et al. 11 CDs. (Running Time: 15 hrs. 0 mins. 0 sec.). (Psalms of Isaak Ser.). (ENG.). 2009. audio compact disk 44.95 (978-1-4272-0625-1(2)) Pub: Macmill Audio. Dist(s): Macmillan

Lamentations of Jeremiah. 4 cass. (Running Time: 6 hrs.). 1998. 20.95 (978-1-57972-306-4(3)) Insight Living.

Lamorna Wink. Martha Grimes. Read by Donada Peters. (Richard Jury Novel Ser.). 1999. audio compact disk 72.00 (978-0-7366-5207-0(8)) Books on Tape.

Lamorna Wink. Martha Grimes. Read by Michael Tudor Barnes. 10 CDs. (Richard Jury Novel Ser.). (J). 2002. audio compact disk 89.95 (978-1-84283-238-7(7)) Pub: ISIS Lrg Prnt GBR. Dist(s): Ulverscroft US

Lamorna Wink. unabr. ed. Martha Grimes. Read by Donada Peters. 7 cass. (Running Time: 10 hrs. 30 mins.). (Richard Jury Novel Ser.). 1999. 56.00 (978-0-7366-4796-0(1), 5144) Books on Tape.

With Richard Jury on a chase to Northern Ireland. Melrose Plant heads for Cornwall and a seaside respite. His sojourn ends when he takes up the plight of a young waiter, Johnny Wells, whose aunt has disappeared. Plant turns to Macalvie, a commander in the Devon and Cornwall police for help. Macalvie is conducting his own investigation into the murder of a woman near the hamlet of Lamorna Cove. Macalvie and Melrose repair to Lamorna's only pub, The Wink, but have barely sampled the local ale before another murder occurs, this one at the hospice.

Lamorna Wink. unabr. ed. Martha Grimes. Read by Donada Peters. 9 CDs. (Running Time: 13 hrs. 30 mins.). (Richard Jury Novel Ser.). 2001. audio compact disk 72.00 Books on Tape.

The tragic past of the Bletchley family consumes Melrose Plant until Richard Jury comes to set things right.

L'Amour Round-Up. unabr. ed. Louis L'Amour. Read by John Malloy & Stan Winiarski. 4 cass. (Running Time: 5 hrs.). 1998. 19.95 (978-1-882071-39-5(5)) B-B Audio.

The Old West may have been a mighty big place, but Louis LAmour takes it to you story by story. Four of our favorite Western tapes give you almost five hours of wide-open adventure. A bargain round-up that includes Desert Death Song, His Brothers D.

Lamp from the Warlock's Tomb. unabr. ed. John Bellairs. Narrated by Betty Low. 3 cass. (Running Time: 4 hrs. 30 mins.). (Anthony Monday Mystery Ser.: No. 3). (gr. 5 up). 1992. 27.00 (978-1-55690-607-7(2), 92212E7) Recorded Bks.

In this classic children's thriller, Anthony Monday lights an antique oil lamp & unleashes a terrible monster that wants to destroy the world.

Lamp of the Wicked. Phil Rickman. (Merrily Watkins Ser.). 2007. audio compact disk 109.95 (978-0-7531-2625-7(7)) Pub: ISIS Lrg Prnt GBR. Dist(s): Ulverscroft US

Lamp of the Wicked. Phil Rickman. Read by Emma Powell. 15 cass. (Running Time: 19 hrs. 20 mins.). (Merrily Watkins Ser.). 2007. 104.95 (978-0-7531-3593-8(0)) Pub: ISIS Lrg Prnt GBR. Dist(s): Ulverscroft US

Lamplight on the Thames. Pamela Evans. Read by Annie Aldington. 10 cass. (Running Time: 13 hrs. 35 min.). (Sound Ser.). 2001. 84.95 (978-1-86042-954-5(8)) Pub: UlverLrgPrint GBR. Dist(s): Ulverscroft US

Bella had always been drawn to the river, and the house in the promenade where she had first met Dezi Bennett. The child and the young airman had become unlikely friends, though both families had disapproved. Years later, their love blossomed, and it seemed that nothing, not even the feud between their fathers, could prevent their marriage. Until Bob's tragic death and his dying request to Bella.

Lamps in the House. unabr. ed. Catherine C. Clark. 6 cass. 1998. 69.95 Set. (978-1-872672-46-5(9)) Pub: Magna Story GBR. Dist(s): Ulverscroft US

***Lampshade: A Holocaust Detective Story from Buchenwald to New Orleans.** unabr. ed. Mark Jacobson. (Running Time: 9 hrs. 30 mins.). 2010. 16.99 (978-1-4001-8881-9(4)); 24.99 (978-1-4001-6881-1(3)); audio compact disk 34.99 (978-1-4001-1881-6(6)); audio compact disk 83.99 (978-1-4001-4881-3(2)) Pub: Tantor Media. Dist(s): IngramPubServ

Làn Gàidhlig: Full of Gaelic. Jamie MacDonald. (GAE & ENG.). 2006. spiral bd. 19.95 (978-1-55932-302-4(7)) ScotPr.

Lancaster Penn Dutch Country Circle Tour. 1 cass. (Running Time: 90 min.). 12.95 (CCI-204) Comp Comms Inc.

Features a tour through the heart of Lancaster County, to a much simpler way of life that is reflective of the strong religious beliefs of the Amish & Mennonites.

Lancaster Pennsylvania Dutch Country: Circle Tour. 1 cass. (Running Time: 90 min.). (Guided Auto Tape Tour). 12.95 (E1); Comp Comms Inc.

***Lancaster Target.** Jack Currie. 2010. 54.95 (978-1-4079-0785-7(9)); audio compact disk 64.95 (978-1-4079-0786-4(7)) Pub: Soundings Ltd GBR. Dist(s): Ulverscroft US

Lance & the Shield. unabr. ed. Robert Marshall Utley. Read by Grover Gardner. 9 cass. (Running Time: 13 hrs. 30 min.). 1994. 72.00 Set. (978-0-7366-2825-9(8), 3534) Books on Tape.

A solid biography of Sitting Bull, the Sioux warrior who held off the Feds for 25 years. Where is he now that we need him?.

Lance Armstrong: Champion for Life! Ian Young. (High Five Reading Ser.). (ENG.). (gr. 4 up). 2004. audio compact disk 5.95 (978-0-7368-3855-9(4)) CapstoneDig.

Lance Armstrong: Champion for Life! Ian Young. (High Five Reading - Purple Ser.). (ENG.). (gr. 4-5). 2007. audio compact disk 5.95 (978-1-4296-1446-7(3)) CapstoneDig.

Lancelot. Chrétien de Troyes. pap. bk. 21.95 (978-88-7754-785-9(5)) Pub: Cideb ITA. Dist(s): Distribks Inc

Lancelot. unabr. ed. Walker Percy. Read by Tom Parker. 5 cass. (Running Time: 7 hrs.). 1995. 39.95 (978-0-7861-0669-1(7), 1571) Blckstn Audio.

Lancelot Andrewes Lamar, a disenchanted liberal lawyer, finds himself confined in a "nuthouse" with memories that don't seem worth remembering. Yet a visit from an old friend & classmate, now a psychiatrist-priest, gives Lance the perfect opportunity to recount his journey of dark violence. Through recollection, Lance returns to the day his world began to unravel - the day he accidentally discovered that he is not the father of his youngest daughter. That discovery touched off Lance's obsession to: reverse the degeneration of modern America & begin a new age of chivalry & romance.

Lancelot: Level 1. Chrétien de Troyes. bk. 14.95 (978-2-09-032981-0(5), CL9815E) Pub: Cle Intl FRA. Dist(s): Continental Bk

Lancelot & Elaine & the Passing of Arthur, Set. abr. ed. Alfred Lord Tennyson. Perf. by Basil Rathbone. 2 cass. 1984. 19.95 (978-0-694-50382-7(7), SWC 2022) HarperCollins Pubs.

Land. Mildred D. Taylor. Read by Ruben Santiago-Hudson. 7 vols. (Running Time: 10 hrs. 56 mins.). (J). (gr. 5-9). 2004. 58.00 (978-0-8072-2035-1(3), Listening Lib); audio compact disk 55.25 (978-0-8072-1768-9(9), Listening Lib) Pub: Random Audio Pubg. Dist(s): NetLibrary CO

Land. unabr. ed. Mildred D. Taylor. Read by Ruben Santiago-Hudson. 7 cass. (Running Time: 10 hrs. 56 mins.). (J). (gr. 5-9). 2004. 50.00 (978-0-8072-0619-5(9), Listening Lib) Random Audio Pubg.

Paul-Edward Logan, grandfather of Cassie, is born during the Civil War, the son of a white plantation owner father and a former slave mother. His father sees to it that he and his sister enjoy many of the same privileges as their white half-brothers. But at the age of 14, Paul-Edward runs away to fulfill his dream - to own land as good as his father's plantation.

Land & the Throne. Kelley Varner. 4 cass. 1992. 25.00 Set. (978-0-938612-81-0(5)) Destiny Image Pubs.

Land As Symbol: The American Indian. Interview with Peter Nabokov. 1 cass. (Running Time: 1 hr.). 10.95 (G0440B090, HarperThor) HarpC GBR.

***Land Between: Finding God in Difficult Transitions.** unabr. ed. Zondervan Publishing Staff & Jeff Manion. (Running Time: 4 hrs. 27 mins. 17 sec.). (ENG.). 2010. 19.99 (978-0-310-41053-9(3)) Zondervan.

Land Development Versus Open Space - MonteVideo & Circle X. Hosted by Nancy Pearlman. 1 cass. (Running Time: 30 min.). 10.00 (408) Educ Comm CA.

Land Girls. unabr. ed. Angela Huth. Read by Carole Boyd. 8 cass. 1997. 69.95 Set. (950301) Eye Ear.

Land Girls. unabr. ed. Angela Huth. Read by Carole Boyd. 8 cass. (Running Time: 12 hrs.). (Isis Ser.). (J). 1997. 69.95 (978-1-85695-910-0(4), 950301) Pub: ISIS Lrg Prnt GBR. Dist(s): Ulverscroft US

Land Girls. unabr. ed. Angela Huth. Read by Carole Boyd. 12 CDs. (Running Time: 12 hrs.). (Isis Ser.). (J). 2000. audio compact disk 99.95 (978-0-7531-0699-0(X), 10699X) Pub: ISIS Lrg Prnt GBR. Dist(s): Ulverscroft US

The year is 1941 & John & Faith Lawrence's farmhands have been called away to serve their country. Desperate for help, the Lawrences take advantage of England's new Land Army plan, which brings young women out of the house & into the fields. But the three "land girls" that John & Faith receive may be more trouble than they bargained for.

Land God Gave to Cain. unabr. ed. Hammond Innes. Narrated by Michael Sinclair. 7 cass. (Running Time: 10 hrs. 15 mins.). 1989. 60.00 (978-1-55690-296-3(4), 89500E7) Recorded Bks.

Adventure of railroads, iron ore prospecting & frontier survival in Canadian Northeast.

Land God Gave to Cain. unabr. collector's ed. Hammond Innes. Read by Jon Voight. 7 cass. (Running Time: 10 hrs. 30 min.). 1984. 56.00 (978-0-7366-0854-1(0), 1805) Books on Tape.

Ian Ferguson sets out across Canada's desolate north on a quest to unravel the mystery surrounding the bizarre connection with his grandfather's murder some 50 years before.

Land I Lost. Quang Nhuong Huynh. Read by Bob Thompsom. (5121); 12.95 (978-1-55644-140-0(1), 5121) Am Audio Prose.

For juvenile & adult audiences.

Land Is Bright. Alistair Horne. 6 cass. (Running Time: 9 hrs.). 2001. 48.00 (978-0-7366-6354-0(1)) Books on Tape.

British historian Alistair Horne takes us on a tour of the United States in the middle of the twentieth century. With many famous upper crust friends from his prep school days in the States, Horne investigates virtually every aspect of American life as he travels from New York to Gettysburg to Detroit, Chicago, St. Louis & San Francisco.

Land of a Thousand Hills: My Life in Rwanda. unabr. ed. Rosamond Halsey Carr & Ann Howard Halsey. Read by C. M. Herbert. 7 cass. (Running Time: 10 hrs.). 2000. 49.95 (978-0-7861-1805-2(9), 2604); audio compact disk 72.00 (978-0-7861-9859-7(1), 2604) Blckstn Audio.

Marriage to a hunter explorer took Rosamond Halsey Carr to what was then the Belgian Congo & divorce left her determined to stay on, in Rwanda, as the manager of a flower plantation. In the ensuing half century she witnessed the fall of colonialism, the wars for independence, the loss of her friend Diane Fossey & the relentless clashes of the Hutus & Tutsis. And finally, 1994's horrific genocide of which she provides a personal, first hand account that is unparalleled & underscores her continued devotion to the country by her decision to care for more than one hundred of its orphaned children.

Land of Counterpane see Child's Garden of Verses

Land of Echoes. Daniel Hecht. Read by Anna Fields. (Running Time: 16 hrs.). 2004. 44.95 (978-1-59912-526-8(9)) Iofy Corp.

Land of Echoes. unabr. ed. Daniel Hecht. Read by Anna Fields. 11 cass. (Running Time: 16 hrs.). (Cree Black Thriller Ser.: No. 2). 2004. 76.95 (978-0-7861-2689-7(2), 3220) Blckstn Audio.

Nothing in Cree's training as a Harvard-trained clinical psychologist or her experience as a paranormal investigator has prepared her for Tommy Keeday's case. A talented young Navajo, Tommy has recently been exhibiting bizarre symptoms that his family believes are signs of possession by a chindi, a hostile spirit. As Cree struggles to find answers, she becomes increasingly aware that Tommy and the people who surround him have some deep and disturbing secrets.

Land of Echoes. unabr. ed. Daniel Hecht. Read by Anna Fields. 13 CDs. (Running Time: 16 hrs.). (Cree Black Thriller Ser.: No. 2). 2000. audio compact disk 104.00 (978-0-7861-8687-7(9), 3220) Blckstn Audio.

Land of Echoes. unabr. ed. Daniel Hecht. Read by Anna Fields. 10 pieces. (Cree Black Thriller Ser.: No. 2). 2004. reel tape 39.95 (978-0-7861-2659-0(0)); audio compact disk 49.95 (978-0-7861-8877-2(4)) Blckstn Audio.

Land of Echoes. unabr. ed. Daniel Hecht. Read by Anna Fields. (Running Time: 16 hrs.). (Cree Black Thriller Ser.: No. 2). 2006. audio compact disk 24.95 (978-0-7861-8612-9(7), 3220) Blckstn Audio.

Land of Enchantment. Meatball Fulton & Jamie Sams. 2 cass. (Running Time: 2 hrs.). 2001. 18.00 (ZBSF015); audio compact disk 22.50 (ZBSF016) Lodestone Catalog.
Mojo Sam encounters some amazing physical & psychic twists & turns in New Mexico. You can follow Mojo the VooDoo man into his discovery of Native American spirituality.

Land of Enchantment, Vol. 1. unabr. ed. Thomas M. Lopez. 2 CDs. (Running Time: 2 hr. 30 min.). (Movin' on with Mojo Ser.). 1997. audio compact disk 22.50 (978-1-881137-81-8(3), ZBSF016) ZBS Found.
Mojo is challenged by southwestern-Native American philosophy when he visits New Mexico.

Land of Enchantment, Vol. 1, Set. unabr. ed. Thomas M. Lopez. 2 cass. (Running Time: 2 hr. 30 min.). (Movin' on with Mojo Ser.). 1997. 18.00 (978-1-881137-80-1(5), ZBSF015) ZBS Found.

Land of Fire. Chris Ryan. Narrated by Gordon Griffin. 9 cass. (Running Time: 12 hrs. 15 mins.). 2002. 87.00 (978-1-84197-471-2(4)) Recorded Bks.

Land of Green Ginger. unabr. ed. Winifred Holtby. Read by Elizabeth Proud. 8 cass. (Running Time: 10 hrs. 30 min.). (Isis Ser.). (J). 1992. 69.95 (978-1-85695-470-9(6), 92076) Pub: ISIS Lrg Prnt GBR. Dist(s): Ulverscroft US

Land of Lincoln: Adventures in Abe's America. unabr. ed. Andrew Ferguson. Read by Simon Vance. 9 CDs. (Running Time: 11 hrs. 0 mins. 0 sec.). (ENG.). 2007. audio compact disk 34.99 (978-1-4001-0432-1(7)) Pub: Tantor Media. Dist(s): IngramPubServ

Land of Lincoln: Adventures in Abe's America. unabr. ed. Andrew Ferguson. Read by Patrick G. Lawlor. (Running Time: 11 hrs. 0 mins. 0 sec.). (ENG.). 2007. audio compact disk 24.99 (978-1-4001-5432-6(4)); audio compact disk 69.99 (978-1-4001-3432-8(3)) Pub: Tantor Media. Dist(s): IngramPubServ

Land of Little Rain. Mary H. Austin. Read by Terry Tempest Williams. 2 cass. (Running Time: 3 hrs.). 1992. 16.95 (978-0-939643-39-4(1), NrthWrd Bks) TandN Child.
Classic account of the desert country of southeastern California from Owen's Valley to the Mojave Desert. First published in 1903, The Land of Little Rain chronicles a harsh landscape, richly endowed with plant and animal life and peopled by a colorful cast of prospectors, miners, ranchers, herders and the Shoshone and Paiute Indians who preceded them.

***Land of Mango Sunsets.** abr. ed. Dorothea Benton Frank. Read by Nanette Savard. (ENG.). 2007. (978-0-06-128739-8(3), Harper Audio); (978-0-06-128740-4(7), Harper Audio) HarperCollins Pubs.

Land of Mango Sunsets. abr. ed. Dorothea Benton Frank. Read by Nanette Savard. 2009. audio compact disk 14.99 (978-0-06-178025-7(1), Harper Audio) HarperCollins Pubs.

Land of Nod see Child's Garden of Verses

Land of Nod - Musical Verses, Vol. 1. (J). 2004. audio compact disk 16.99 (978-0-9764109-1-1(5)) Pillar Rock.

Land of Oz see Oz

Land of Oz. L. Frank Baum. Narrated by Anna Fields. (Running Time: 5 hrs. 30 mins.). 2002. 24.95 (978-1-59912-678-4(8)) Iofy Corp.

Land of Oz. L. Frank Baum. Read by Jim Killavey. 3 cass. (Running Time: 4 hrs. 30 min.). (Oz Ser.). (YA). (gr. 5-8). 1989. 18.00 incl. album. (C-58) Jimcin Record.
Further adventures in fantasy.

Land of Oz. unabr. ed. L. Frank Baum. Read by Anna Fields. 4 cass. (Running Time: 5 hrs. 30 mins.). 2002. 32.95 (978-0-7861-2240-0(4), 2964); audio compact disk 40.00 (978-0-7861-9496-4(0), 2964) Blckstn Audio.
Young Tip runs away from his guardian, the witch Mombi, taking with him Jack Pumpkinhead and the wooden Saw-Horse, and flees to the Emerald City where he learns the incredible secret of his past.

Land of Oz, unabr. ed. L. Frank Baum. Narrated by Flo Gibson. 3 pieces. (Running Time: 4 hrs.). (Oz Ser.). (gr. 4 up). 1980. 27.00 (978-1-55690-295-6(6), 80121E7) Recorded Bks.
A new hero, Tip, escapes from his guardian witch & flees with friends to the Emerald City in Oz.

***Land of Painted Caves.** unabr. ed. Jean M. Auel. Read by Sandra Burr. (Running Time: 29 hrs.). (Earth's Children Ser.). 2011. 29.99 (978-1-4418-8825-9(X), 9781441888259, BAD); 29.99 (978-1-4418-8823-5(3), 9781441888235, Brilliance MP3); 44.97 (978-1-4418-8824-2(1), 9781441888242, Brinc Audio MP3 Lib); audio compact disk 42.99 (978-1-4418-8821-1(7), 9781441888211, Bril Audio CD Unabri); audio compact disk 99.97 (978-1-4418-8822-8(5), 9781441888228, BriAudCD Unabrid) Brilliance Audio.

Land of Sleepytime. Composed by David Kowaleski et al. (J). (gr. k-6). 1997. 9.98 (978-0-9656196-0-8(5)); audio compact disk 14.98 CD. (978-0-9656196-1-5(3)) Junie Moon Mus.
Positive & nurturing stories set to soothing music.

***Land of the Burning Sands.** unabr. ed. Rachel Neumeier. Narrated by Paul Michael Garcia. (Running Time: 13 hrs. 0 mins.). (Griffin Mage Ser.). 2010. 18.99 (978-1-4001-8972-4(1)); 24.99 (978-1-4001-6972-6(0)); audio compact disk 37.99 (978-1-4001-1972-1(3)) Pub: Tantor Media. Dist(s): IngramPubServ

***Land of the Burning Sands (Library Edition)** unabr. ed. Rachel Neumeier. Narrated by Paul Michael Garcia. (Running Time: 13 hrs. 0 mins.). (Griffin Mage Ser.). 2010. 37.99 (978-1-4001-9972-3(7)); audio compact disk 90.99 (978-1-4001-4972-8(X)) Pub: Tantor Media. Dist(s): IngramPubServ

Land of the Golden Apple. Eve Makis. 2008. 61.95 (978-0-7531-3181-7(1)); audio compact disk 84.95 (978-0-7531-3182-4(X)) Pub: Isis Pubng Ltd GBR. Dist(s): Ulverscroft US

Land of the Living. unabr. ed. Nicci French. Read by Anne Flosnik. 7 cass. (Running Time: 10 hrs.). 2003. 32.95 (978-1-59086-184-4(1), 1590861841, BAU); 82.25 (978-1-59086-185-1(X), 159086185X, CD Unabrid Lib Ed) Brilliance Audio.
Abbie Devereaux lies flat on her back, her arms and legs tied down, her head covered with a hood. She senses, but can't see, the eyes that watch her. She feels the unknown hands that touch her in the dark. She knows she has been kidnapped, even though she has little memory of her most recent past. And she knows that all she has to do is stay alive, even though everything she is experiencing tells her she won't. Miraculously, she escapes. One nightmare is over...but another is about to begin. No one believes her story. Not the police who find her beaten and bruised on the outskirts of London, not the psychologists who interview her at the hospital. Desperate to piece together the fragments of her life and prove she is telling the truth, she returns to a strangely familiar existence. She discovers, but cannot remember why, she moved out of her boyfriend's apartment, left her job as an office planner, and moved in with a roommate who herself has mysteriously disappeared. Now trying to reclaim both her mind and her life -and stop a monstrous psycho-killer - she must dare to retrace her steps to the place where the horror began.

Land of the Living. unabr. ed. Nicci French. Read by Anne Flosnik. (Running Time: 10 hrs.). 2004. 39.25 (978-1-59335-378-0(2), 1593353782, Brinc Audio MP3 Lib) Brilliance Audio.

Land of the Living. unabr. ed. Nicci French. Read by Anne Flosnik. (Running Time: 10 hrs.). 2004. 39.25 (978-1-59710-437-1(X), 159710437X, BADLE); 24.95 (978-1-59710-436-4(1), 1597104361, BAD) Brilliance Audio.

Land of the Living. unabr. ed. Nicci French. Read by Anne Flosnik. (Running Time: 10 hrs.). 2004. 24.95 (978-1-59335-095-6(3), 1593350953) Soulmate Audio Bks.

Land of the Living Dead. 6 episodes on 3 cas. (Running Time: 60 min. per cass.). (Adventures by Morse Collection). 1998. 19.98 Boxed set. (4305) Radio Spirits.
South America is the setting for werewolves, voodoo practicioners & an ominous prophecy for the end of the world.

Land of the Nightingales. unabr. ed. Sally Stewart. Read by Jacqueline King. 12 cass. (Running Time: 14 hrs. 20 min.). (Sound Ser.). 2001. 94.95 (978-1-86042-119-8(9), 21199) Pub: UlverLrgPrint GBR. Dist(s): Ulverscroft US
Phoebe, and her sister, Lydia, had never understood why the 'land of nightingales' was such an emotive subject within the family, but when their father died it suddenly became clear. His will revealed that Phoebe and Lydia had a Spanish half-brother - Juan Rodriquez. As Phoebe and Lydia finally found a happiness of their own in England, the past continually intruded on their tranquil lives.

Land of the Nightingales, Set. unabr. ed. Sally Stewart. Read by Jacqueline King. 12 cass. 1999. 94.95 (21199) Pub: Soundings Ltd GBR. Dist(s): Ulverscroft US

Land of the Polar Bear - Arctic Life. Steck-Vaughn Staff. 1 cass. (Running Time: 90 min.). (J). 1999. (978-0-7398-2443-6(0)) SteckVau.

Land of the Shadow. unabr. ed. Gilbert Morris. Read by Maynard Villers. 8 cass. (Running Time: 11 hrs. 30 min.). (Appomattox Ser.: Bk. 4). 1998. 49.95 (978-1-55686-836-8(7)) Books in Motion.
Photographer Paul Bristol is requested at the battlefront of the Civil War to capture the bravery of the Confederates on film. With Frankie Aimes, an independent young woman as his assistant, they face danger on the battlefield. However, another danger is looming over them, Frankie is hiding a secret that could get them both killed.

Land of the Silver Apples. unabr. ed. Nancy Farmer. Read by Gerard Doyle. 11 cass. (Running Time: 13 hrs. 50 mins.). (Sea of Trolls Trilogy: No. 2). (YA). (gr. 5-9). 2007. 88.75 (978-1-4281-6646-2(7)); audio compact disk 108.75 (978-1-4281-7103-9(7)) Recorded Bks.

Land of the Silver Apples. unabr. ed. Nancy Farmer. Read by Gerard Doyle. (Running Time: 13 hrs. 30 mins. 0 sec.). No. 2. (ENG.). (J). (gr. 4-7). 2007. audio compact disk 39.95 (978-0-7435-6912-5(1)) Pub: S&S Audio. Dist(s): S and S Inc

Land of the Three Elves. (ENG.). (J). 2008. audio compact disk 15.95 (978-0-9820885-0-0(7)) TBell.

Land of Yahoe: Children's Entertainments from the Days Before Television. (J). 1999. (978-1-886767-17-1(3)); audio compact disk (978-1-886767-16-4(5)) Rounder Records.
Designed for children of grade school age or older, features some of the folk songs & stories that have given pleasure to so many generations of American children. Unlike most folk music records for children, these selections are not re-creations by urban performers; instead, some of our most skilled traditional musicians have been asked to perform their favorite childhood songs & stories. The result is a collection of folklore that is not only highly musical, but, through its wide spectrum of native voices, directly speaks of America's farms, ranches & mountain cabins.

Land Speaks! unabr. ed. Dean Marshall & Marie Kirkendoll. 3 cass. (Running Time: 3 hrs.). 1986. 29.95 incl. bklet. (978-1-55585-079-1(0)) Quest NW Pub.
Train your mind to pick up messages from plants, trees, flowers, Nature Spirits & even from the Angelic Beings who work each day in the Nature Kingdom.

Land That Time Forgot. Edgar Rice Burroughs. Read by Raymond Todd. 3 CDs. (Running Time: 4 hrs. 30 min.). 2001. audio compact disk 24.00 (978-0-7861-9725-5(0), z2776) Blckstn Audio.
Adventurer Bowen Tyler & the crew of the U-33 discover the mysterious forgotten continent of Caspak, where the savage denizens of a thousand lost ages roam vast primeval jungles.

Land That Time Forgot. Edgar Rice Burroughs. Read by Brian Holsopple. 3 CDs. (Running Time: 4 mins.). 2009. audio compact disk 25.95 (978-1-897304-33-4(1)) Dorch Pub Co.

Land That Time Forgot. Edgar Rice Burroughs. Narrated by Raymond Todd. (Running Time: 4 hrs.). 2000. 22.95 (978-1-59912-679-1(6)) Iofy Corp.

Land that Time Forgot. Edgar Rice Burroughs. 2007. audio compact disk 25.95 (978-0-8095-7198-7(6)) Diamond Book Dists.

***Land That Time Forgot.** Edgar Rice Burroughs. Read by Brian Holsopple. 3 CDs. (Running Time: 4 mins.). 2009. 19.95 (978-1-897331-20-0(7), AudioRealms) Dorch Pub Co.

Land That Time Forgot. unabr. ed. Edgar Rice Burroughs. Read by Raymond Todd. 1 CD. (Running Time: 4 hrs.). 1998. audio compact disk 19.95 (2451) Blckstn Audio.

Land That Time Forgot. unabr. ed. Edgar Rice Burroughs. Read by Raymond Todd. 3 cass. (Running Time: 4 hrs. 30 min.). 2001. 23.95 (978-0-7861-2006-2(1), 2776) Blckstn Audio.

Land That Time Forgot. unabr. ed. Edgar Rice Burroughs. Read by Raymond Todd. (Running Time: 4 hrs.). 2001. 24.95 (978-0-7861-9264-9(X)) Blckstn Audio.

Land That Time Forgot. unabr. ed. Edgar Rice Burroughs. Read by David Sharp. 8 cass. (Running Time: 10 hrs. 42 min.). 1994. 49.95 (978-1-55686-499-5(X)) Books in Motion.
Bowen Tyler, his reluctant crew & a blonde heroine, find themselves marrooned in a nightmare world of mighty dinosaurs & bestial apemen who kill on sight.

Land That Time Forgot, Set. unabr. ed. Edgar Rice Burroughs. Read by Michael Russotto. 3 cass. (Running Time: 4 hrs.). 1994. 16.95 (978-1-55685-342-5(4)) Audio Bk Con.
Trapped aboard an enemy submarine during World War I, Bowen Tyler, the lady he loves, & an assortment of comrades & German enemies are borne to the uncharted continet of Caspak. There they come face-to-face with monstrous creatures long thought to be extinct, including the earliest ancestors of the human race.

Land Use Institute: Planning, Regulation, Litigation, Eminent Domain, & Compensation. 13 cass. (Running Time: 18 hrs. 30 min.). 1995. 200.00 Set; incl. study guide. (MA34) Am Law Inst.

Land Use Practice. 1988. bk. 105.00; 50.00 PA Bar Inst.

***Land Without Mercy.** Wayne D. Overholser. 2009. (978-1-60136-444-9(X)) Audio Holding.

Land Without Mercy. Wayne D. Overholser. (Running Time: 0 hr. 12 mins.). 1998. 10.95 (978-1-60083-454-7(X)) Iofy Corp.

Landed Gentry: Inside America's Propertied Class. unabr. ed. Sophy Burnham. 1 cass. (Running Time: 56 min.). 12.95 (40345) J Norton Pubs.
Burnham is indignant that rich & privileged Americans fail to fulfill their potential in public service as the British do. She claims they consider success to be in bad taste, that they are racist & involved with silly social rituals.

Landfall. unabr. ed. Nevil Shute. Read by Alex Jennings. 6 cass. (Running Time: 9 hrs.). 2000. 49.95 (978-0-7451-4159-6(5), CAB 842) Pub: Chivers Audio Bks GBR. Dist(s): AudioGO
A Coastal Command Anson strikes at a U-boat in the channel, while a British submarine in the same waters is reported missing. A young pilot stands accused of a ghastly error that sent his own countrymen to their deaths. Only fate can offer the last chance to redeem his good name.

Landforms. Steck-Vaughn Staff. (J). 2002. (978-0-7398-6215-5(4)) SteckVau.

Landing. unabr. ed. Emma Donoghue. Narrated by Laura Hicks. 9 CDs. (Running Time: 11 hrs. 24 mins.). 2007. audio compact disk 89.95 (978-0-7927-4841-0(7), Chivers Sound Lib) AudioGO.
Sile is a stylish citizen of the new Dublin, a veteran flight attendant who's traveled the world. Jude is a twenty-five-year-old archivist, stubbornly attached to the tiny town of Ireland, Ontario, in which she was born and raised. On her first plane trip, Jude's and Sile's worlds touch and snag at Heathrow Airport. In the course of the next year, their lives, and those of their friends and families, will be drawn into a new, shaky orbit.

Landing It: My Life on & off the Ice. abr. ed. Scott Hamilton & Lorenzo Benet. Read by Doug Ordunio. 2 CDs. (Running Time: 3 hrs.). 2001. audio compact disk 24.00 Books on Tape.
Now for the first time ever, Scott Hamilton tells the full story of his remarkable life, on and off the ice.

Landing It: My Life on & off the Ice. abr. ed. Scott Hamilton & Lorenzo Benet. Read by Doug Ordunio. 2 cass. (Running Time: 3 hrs.). 1999. 17.95 (978-0-7366-4681-9(7), 5069-R); audio compact disk 19.95 (978-0-7366-4682-6(5), 5069-CDR) Books on Tape.
Scott Hamilton talks candidly about the early hurdles thrown in his path. A childhood disease that stunted his growth, the wrenching decision to leave home at age thirteen to train with other Olympic hopefuls, the death of his mother from breast cancer, yet nothing could stop him from achieving his goal. Scott Hamilton came to dominate the sport in the late 1970s & skated away with Olympic gold in 1984. Thirteen years later Scott was still skating professionally, performing on TV specials & commentating for CBS Sports. In 1997, however, Scott found himself in the toughest competition of his life, battling testicular cancer & win he did, performing on prime-time television just seven months later.

Landing It: My Life on & off the Ice. collector's ed. Scott Hamilton & Lorenzo Benet. Read by Doug Ordunio. 10 cass. (Running Time: 15 hrs.). 1999. 80.00 (978-0-7366-4755-7(4), 5069) Books on Tape.

Landing It: My Life on & off the Ice. collector's ed. Scott Hamilton & Lorenzo Benet. Read by Doug Ordunio. 2 cass. (Running Time: 2 hrs.). 2000. 12.95 (978-0-7366-5200-1(0), 5069) Books on Tape.
Scott Hamilton talks candidly about the early hurdles thrown in his path. A childhood disease that stunted his growth, the wrnching decision to leave home at age thirteen to train with other Olympic hopefuls, the death of his mother from breast cancer, yet nothing could stop him from achieving his goal. Scott Hamilton came to dominate the sport in the late 1970s & skated away with Olympic gold in 1984. Thirteen years later Scott was still skating professionally, performing on TV specials & commentating for CBS Sports. In 1997, however, Scott found himself in the toughest competition of his life, battling testicular cancer & win he did, performing on prime-time television just seven months later.

Landlady see Poetry & Voice of Margaret Atwood

Landlord's Tale: Paul Revere's Ride see Best Loved Poems of Longfellow

***Landmark: The Inside Story of America's New Health Care Law & What It Means for Us All.** unabr. ed. Washington Post Staff. Read by Pam Ward. 1 Playaway. (Running Time: 10 hrs. 30 mins.). 2010. 59.99 (978-1-4417-6122-4(5)) Blckstn Audio.

***Landmark: The Inside Story of America's New Health Care Law & What It Means for Us All.** unabr. ed. Washington Post Staff. Read by Pam Ward. 1 MP3-CD. (Running Time: 10 hrs.). 2010. 29.95 (978-1-4417-6119-4(5)); 29.98 (978-1-4417-6115-6(2)); audio compact disk 24.95 (978-1-4417-6118-7(7)) Blckstn Audio.

Landmark Speeches & Sermons of Martin Luther King, Jr, Set. unabr. ed. Clayborne Carson et al. Read by Keith David et al. 15 CDs. (Running Time: 16 hrs.). (ENG.). 2009. audio compact disk 49.98 (978-1-60024-850-4(0)) Pub: Hachet Audio. Dist(s): HachBkGrp

Landmarks. Perf. by Ciaran Brennan. 1 cass., 1 CD. 8.78 (ALT 83083); audio compact disk 13.58 CD Jewel box. (ALT 83083) NewSound.

Landmarks in Music: The Rochester Jazz Collection. 1998. audio compact disk 15.98 (978-0-9641706-5-0(5)) Landmark Soc.

Landmarks of Esoteric Literature. Manly P. Hall. 5 cass. (Running Time: 150 min.). 1999. 40.00 set incl. album. (978-0-89314-158-5(5), S800171) Philos Res.

Lando. unabr. ed. Read by Josh Hamilton. 4 CDs. (Running Time: 16200 sec.). (Louis L'Amour Ser.). (ENG.). 2006. audio compact disk 29.95 (978-0-7393-2114-0(5), Random AudioBks) Pub: Random Audio Pubg. Dist(s): Random
One of the great sagas of our time, the chronicle of the Sackett family is perhaps the crowning achievement of one of our greatest storytellers. In Lando, Louis L'Amour has created an unforgettable portrait of a unique hero. A man never to count out.... For six long years Orlando Sackett survived the horrors of a brutal Mexican prison. He survived by using his skills as a boxer and by making three vows. The first was to exact revenge on the hired killers who framed him. The second was to return to his father. And the third was to find Gin Locklear. But the world has changed a lot since Lando left it. His father is missing. The woman he loves is married. And the killers want him dead. Hardened physically and emotionally, Lando must begin an epic journey to resolve his past, even if it costs him his life. From the Paperback edition.

Landower Legacy. unabr. collector's ed. Victoria Holt. Read by Donada Peters. 10 cass. (Running Time: 15 hrs.). 1993. 80.00 (978-0-7366-2582-1(8), 3329) Books on Tape.
In her serach for truth Caroline Tressidor ends up in the arms of a man with a legacy of murder.

Landry News. unabr. ed. Andrew Clements. Read by Andrew McCarthy. 2 cass. (Running Time: 2 hrs. 33 mins.). (J). (gr. 3-7). 2004. 23.00 (978-0-8072-8781-1(4), YA266CX, Listening Lib) Random Audio Pubg.
Cara Landry is a budding journalist. When she posts a scathing editorial about her burned-out teacher on the bulletin board one afternoon, everything changes. Prodded into action for the first time in years, Mr. Larson challenges his fifth-grade students to create a real newspaper.

Landry News. unabr. ed. Andrew Clements. Read by Andrew McCarthy. 2 cass. (Running Time: 2 hrs. 33 mins.). (Middle Grade Cassette Librariestm

Ser.). (gr. 3-7). 2004. pap. bk. 29.00 (978-0-8072-8782-8(2), S YA 266 SP, Listening Lib) Random Audio Pubg.
"Cara Landry is a budding journalist. When she posts a scathing editorial about her burned-out teacher on the bulletin board, everything changes. Prodded into action for the first time in years, Mr. Larson challenges his fifth-grade students to create a real newspaper. Soon The Landry News gets more attention than either Cara or her teacher bargained.".

Landry News. unabr. ed. Andrew Clements. Read by Zoe Kazan. (Running Time: 3 hrs. 0 mins. 0 sec.). (ENG.). (J). 2009. audio compact disk 14.99 (978-0-7435-8172-1(5)) Pub: S&S Audio. Dist(s): S and S Inc

***Lands Beyond the Sea.** Tamara Mckinley. 2010. 94.95 (978-1-4079-0660-7(7)); audio compact disk 99.95 (978-1-4079-0661-4(5)) Pub: Soundings Ltd GBR. Dist(s): Ulverscroft US

Landscape. Julia E. Wade. 1 cass. 1999. 12.95 (978-1-891987-01-4(1)) Wade Music.

Landscape Near an Aerodrome see Twentieth-Century Poetry in English, No. 9, Recordings of Poets Reading Their Own Poetry

Landscape of the Inner Planes. Tricia McCannon. 2 cass. 1996. 20.00 (978-1-886932-05-0(0)) Hrzns Unltd.
Self help, self actualization, or spirituality, especially death, out of body, reincarnation. Egyptian & Tibetan book of the dead, the holographic universe & a meditation.

Landscape Restoration Handbook. Donald Harker et al. 1999. audio compact disk 199.95 (978-0-8493-2235-8(9), 2235) Pub: CRC Pr. Dist(s): Taylor and Fran

Landscape Turned Red. unabr. ed. Stephen W. Sears. Read by Michael Wells. 9 cass. (Running Time: 90 min. per cass.). 1991. audio compact disk 29.95 set. (978-0-7861-0223-5(3), 1196) Blckstn Audio.
In "Landscape Turned Red" Stephen Sears recreates the vivid drama of Antietam - & drama it is, pitting highstakes military gambler Robert E. Lee against George B. McClellan, the general with every soldierly quality but one, the will to fight. Stephen Sear's subject is not just generals & their tactics, however; it is the emotions & experiences of the men in the ranks, too, & their stories emerge here with powerful authenticity.

Landscape Turned Red. unabr. ed. Stephen W. Sears. Narrated by Peter Johnson. 9 cass. (Running Time: 13 hrs. 30 mins.). 1986. 78.00 (978-1-55690-297-0(2), 86670E7) Recorded Bks.
An account of the Battle of Antietam in 1862. Draws upon a survey made after the war by two of the me who fought in this battle.

Landscape Turned Red. unabr. collector's ed. Stephen W. Sears. Read by Dick Estell. 10 cass. (Running Time: 15 hrs.). (Christopher Enterprises Recording Ser.). 1987. 80.00 (978-0-7366-1095-7(2), 2021) Books on Tape.
September 17, 1862: Antietam. It was the bloodiest day in American history, & with the possible exception of Gettysburg, the most pivotal battle of the Civil War.

Landscape Turned Red: The Battle of Antietam. Stephen W. Sears. Read by Barrett Whitener. (Running Time: 52200 sec.). 2006. 79.95 (978-0-7861-4361-0(4)); audio compact disk 99.00 (978-0-7861-7525-3(7)) Blckstn Audio.

Landscape Turned Red: The Battle of Antietam. unabr. ed. Stephen W. Sears. Read by Barrett Whitener. 10 cass. (Running Time: 52200 sec.). 2005. 29.95 (978-0-7861-3656-8(1), E3524); audio compact disk 29.95 (978-0-7861-7745-5(4), ZE3524) Blckstn Audio.

Landscape Turned Red: The Battle of Antietam. unabr. ed. Stephen W. Sears. Read by Barrett Whitener. 13 vols. (Running Time: 52200 sec.). 2005. audio compact disk 29.95 (978-0-7861-7971-8(6), ZM3524) Blckstn Audio.

Landscape with Tractor. unabr. ed. Poems. Henry Taylor. Read by Henry Taylor. 1 cass. (Running Time: 55 min.). 1985. 12.95 (23660) J Norton Pubs.
Taylor reads from all his books & works in manuscript.

***Landscaper's Secret: True Stories that will challenge you to discern the voice of God.** unabr. ed. John Gordon. Narrated by Ray Porter. (ENG.). 2010. 10.98 (978-1-59644-943-5(8)); audio compact disk 16.98 (978-1-59644-942-8(X)) christianaud.

Landscapes: I. New Hampshire; II. Virginia Sweeney among the Nightingales see Twentieth-Century Poetry in English, No. 3, Recordings of Poets Reading Their Own Poetry

Landscapes of a Magic Valley. John Nichols. Read by John Nichols. 1 cass. (Running Time: 90 min.). 1988. 12.95 (978-0-939643-15-8(4)) Audio Pr.
Features essays originally included in On The Mesa & The Last Beautiful Days of Autumn.

Landscaping Spanish. (SPA.). 2003. cd-rom (978-0-9747887-5-3(9)) Spanish Acad Cu Inst.

Landslides & Avalanches: Proceedings of the 11th International Conference & Field Trip on Landslides, Norway, September 2005. Senneset/Kare. 2005. audio compact disk (978-0-415-38683-8(7)) Taylor and Fran.

Landsman. unabr. ed. Peter Charles Melman. Read by Daniel Oreskes. (YA). 2008. 74.99 (978-1-60252-976-2(0)) Find a World.

***Landsman: Unabridged Value-Priced Edition.** Peter Charles Melman. Narrated by Daniel Oreskes. (Running Time: 11 hrs. 0 mins. 0 sec.). (ENG.). 2010. audio compact disk 14.95 (978-1-60283-992-2(1)) Pub: AudioGO. Dist(s): Perseus Dist

Lang Lang: Playing with Flying Keys. unabr. ed. Lang Lang. Adapted by Michael French. (Running Time: 4 hrs. 58 mins.). (ENG.). (J). 2008. 14.00 (978-0-7393-6423-9(5)) Pub: Random Audio Pubg. Dist(s): Random

Lang Lang: Playing with Flying Keys. unabr. ed. Lang Lang. Read by Andrew Pang. Adapted by Michael French. (ENG.). (J). (gr. 4). 2008. audio compact disk 28.00 (978-0-7393-6422-2(7), Listening Lib) Pub: Random Audio Pubg. Dist(s): Random

Lang Lang: Playing with Flying Keys. unabr. ed. Lang Lang. Read by Andrew Pang. Adapted by Michael French. 4 CDs. (Running Time: 4 hrs. 58 mins.). (J). (gr. 4-8). 2008. audio compact disk 38.00 (978-0-7393-6424-6(3), Listening Lib) Pub: Random Audio Pubg. Dist(s): Random

Lang Tuteng see Wolf Totem

l'Anglais des Sciences. 1 cass. (Running Time: 1 hr., 30 min.). (ENG & FRE., 1997. pap. bk. 75.00 (978-2-7005-1338-7(X)) Pub: Assimil FRA. Dist(s): Distribks Inc

Langoliers. unabr. ed. Stephen King. Read by Willem Dafoe. 7 CDs. (Running Time: 9 hrs.). (ENG., 2008. audio compact disk 36.95 (978-1-59887-747-2(X), 159887747X) Pub: HighBridge. Dist(s): Workman Pub

Langston Hughes. Contrib. by Unapix Inner Dimension Staff. 1 cass. 1997. 10.95 (978-1-57523-171-6(9)) Unapix Enter.

Langston Hughes. unabr. abr. ed. Langston Hughes. Read by Langston Hughes. Ed. by J. D. McClatchy. 1 CD. (Running Time: 1 hr. 2 mins.). (Voice of the Poet Ser.). (ENG.). 2002. audio compact disk 19.95 (978-0-553-71491-3(0)) Pub: Random Audio Pubg. Dist(s): Random

Langston Hughes: The Making of a Poet. Langston Hughes. Read by Langston Hughes. 1 cass. (Running Time: 30 min.). 10.95 (F0020B090, HarperThor) HarpC GBR.

Langston Hughes: The Poetic Rebirth of Self-Identity. Gwendolyn J. Crenshaw & Aesop Enterprise Inc. Staff. 1 cass. (Heroes & Sheroes Ser.). (J). (gr. 3-12). 1991. (978-1-880771-05-1(5)) AESOP Enter.

Langston Hughes Reads. Langston Hughes. Read by Langston Hughes. 1 cass. (Running Time: 60 mins.). (YA). (gr. 4 up). 1999. 12.95 (CDL-5710) African Am Imag.

Langston Hughes Reads. Langston Hughes. Read by Langston Hughes. 1 cass. (Running Time: 50 min.). 15.95 (8123Q) Filmic Archives.
An unforgettable program as Langston Hughes reads some of his most memorable poems, including "One Way Ticket", "The Negro Speaks of Rivers", "Puzzled", "Trumpet Player", "Ballad of the Gypsy", "Southern Mammy Sings", "Dinner Guest: Me", "The Merry-Go-Round", "Ku Klux Klan", "The South", & many others.

Langston Hughes Reads. unabr. ed. Poems. Langston Hughes. Read by Langston Hughes. 1 cass. (Running Time: 50 mins.). 11.95 (H169) Blckstn Audio.
Includes: "One Way Ticket," "The Negro Speaks of Rivers," "Puzzled," "Ballad of the Gypsy," "Migrant," "Intern at Provident Hospital," "Ku Klux Klan," "The South," "Mulatto" & "Out of Work.".

Langston Hughes Reads. unabr. ed. Narrated by Langston Hughes. 1 cass. 1999. 16.00 (21523) Recorded Bks.

Langston Hughes Reads, Set. abr. ed. Poems. Langston Hughes. Read by Langston Hughes. 1 cass. (Running Time: 50 min.). 1992. 12.00 (978-1-55994-571-4(0), DCN 1640) HarperCollins Pubs.
Includes: "One Way Ticket", "The Negro Speaks of Rivers", "Puzzled", "Trumpt Players, 52nd Street", "Ballad of the Gypsy", "Reads Kid Sleepy", "Southern Mammy Sings", "Migrant", "Dinner Guest: Me", "Cultural Exchange", "Mama & Daughter", "Sylvester's Dying Bed", "Intern at Provident Hospital", "Merry-go-Round", "Ku Klux Klan", "The South", "Mulatto", "Out of Work", "In Explanation of Our Times".

Langston Hughes Reads & Talks About His Poems. unabr. ed. Langston Hughes. Read by Langston Hughes. 10.95 (978-0-8405-1064-8(0), SAC 7140) Spoken Arts.

Langston Hughes Reads His Poetry. abr. ed. Poems. Langston Hughes. Read by Langston Hughes. 1 cass. (Running Time: 60 mins.). 2000. 12.00 (978-0-694-52273-6(2)) HarperCollins Pubs.

Language. (High Point Ser.). (gr. 6-12). audio compact disk 16.25 (978-0-7362-0916-8(6)); audio compact disk 16.25 (978-0-7362-0948-9(4)); audio compact disk 16.25 (978-0-7362-0980-9(8)) Hampton-Brown.

Language. unabr. ed. Aldous Huxley. 1 cass. (Running Time: 56 min.). (Human Situation Ser.). 1959. 11.00 (01117) Big Sur Tapes.

Language: Key to Human Understanding. unabr. ed. Samuel I. Hayakawa. 1 cass. 12.95 (978-0-88432-228-3(9), C23002) J Norton Pubs.
Hayakawa, former U. S. Senator and famed linguist, discusses words & the way we use them & blocks to the communication process & how to overcome them.

Language: The Use, Misuse, & Abuse of Words. Manly P. Hall. 8.95 (978-0-89314-159-2(3), C880925) Philos Res.
Deals with psychology & self-help.

Language - Thirty Brief Courses. unabr. ed. Charles Berlitz. 2 cass. (FRE.). 18.95 Set; phrase guide bk. (N1022); 18.95 Set; phrase guide bk. (N1027); 18.95 Set; phrase guide bk. (N1030) Books on Tape.
A quick, highly condensed introduction to the words & phrases you'll need to communicate effectively.

Language - Thirty Library. 33 cass. bk. 559.35 set. Moonbeam Pubns.
Using the proven method based on the famous U.S. Military accelerated language learning program, Language/30 courses stress conversationally useful words & phrases.

Language & Definitions. unabr. ed. Barbara Branden. 1 cass. (Running Time: 1 hr. 36 min.). (Principles of Efficient Thinking Ser.). 12.95 (707) J Norton Pubs.
Language as the tool of thought; the substitution of images & emotions for language; non-verbal & subverbal thought; basic principles of definitions.

Language & Life of Symbols. 8 cass. (Running Time: 11 hrs. 30 min.). 1995. 56.95 set. (978-0-7822-0499-5(6), SYMBOL) C G Jung IL.
This course elucidates the nature of this central feature of psychological life by exploring the structure & dynamics of the ego/self axis & the mechanics of symbol formation & by providing a guided tour of several realms within the language of the symbol from an archetypal perspective.

Language & Problems of Knowledge. Noam Chomsky. Read by Grover Gardner. 2 cass. (Running Time: 2 hrs. 30 mins.). 1996. 17.95 (978-1-879557-36-9(3)) Pub: Audio Scholar. Dist(s): Penton Overseas

Language & Travel Guide to Indonesia. 2nd ed. Gary Chandler. (ENG., 2006. 21.95 (978-0-7818-1152-1(X)) Hippocrene Bks.

***Language Boosters, Gr. 1 Ebook: 100 Practice Pages for Strengthening Language Proficiency.** Roseanne Greenfield-Thong. (J). 2009. 15.99 (978-1-60689-924-3(4)) Creat Teach Pr.

***Language Boosters, Gr. 2 Ebook: 100 Practice Pages for Strengthening Language Proficiency.** Colleen Dobelmann & Amy Stern. (J). 2009. 15.99 (978-1-60689-943-4(0)) Creat Teach Pr.

***Language Boosters, Gr. 3 Ebook: 100 Practice Pages for Strengthening Language Proficiency.** Colleen Dobelmann & Amy Stern. (J). 2009. 15.99 (978-1-60689-944-1(9)) Creat Teach Pr.

Language Development & Reading Comprehension. Holt, Rinehart and Winston Staff. 1998. 21.00 (978-0-03-051749-5(4)) Holt McDoug.

Language Development & Reading Comprehension. Holt, Rinehart and Winston Staff. 1998. audio compact disk 458.26 (978-0-03-050618-5(2)) Holt McDoug.

Language, Dreams & Psyche. Leland Roloff. Read by Leland Roloff. 5 cass. (Running Time: 7 hrs. 20 min.). 1992. 39.95 set. (978-0-7822-0388-2(4), 485) C G Jung IL.
The dream is a visual-linguistic event of considerable complexity. Of particular interest, in addition to the amplification of images, is to understand how the language conter of the brain functions in dreams. This functioning is experienced by encountering signs, hearing linguistic events, & listening to the language in which the dream is encoded & reported. Jungian analyst Lee Roloff leads a course exploring the depth linguistic elements of the unconscious experience.

Language Dynamics Spanish: Answer Keys & English Translations. Mark Frobose. (SPA., 2002. per. 21.99 (978-1-893564-81-7(9)) Macmill Audio.

Language Dynamics Spanish: Answer Keys & Tapescript. Mark Frobose. (SPA.). 2002. per. 67.99 (978-1-893564-80-0(0)) Macmill Audio.

Language for Everyday Life. Ingrid Wisniewska. Contrib. by Jayme Adelson-Goldstein. (Step Forward Ser.). 2006. audio compact disk 54.95 (978-0-19-439241-9(4)) OUP.

Language for Everyday Life Class. Jayme Adelson-Goldstein. (Step Forward Ser.). 2007. audio compact disk 54.95 (978-0-19-439874-9(9)) OUP.

Language for the Care of Souls. Read by John Van Eenwyk. 2 cass. (Running Time: 3 hrs.). 1986. 18.95 (978-0-7822-0313-4(2), 213) C G Jung IL.

Language God Talks: On Science & Religion. unabr. ed. Herman Wouk. Read by Bob Walter. (Running Time: 5 hrs.). (ENG.). 2010. 18.98 (978-1-60788-182-7(9)); audio compact disk 26.98 (978-1-60788-181-0(0)) Pub: Hachet Audio. Dist(s): HachBkGrp

Language in Pop Culture: Program from the Award Winning Public Radio Series. Interview. Hosted by Fred Goodwin. Comment by John Hockenberry. 1CD. (Running Time: 1 hr.). (Infinite Mind Ser.). 2000. audio compact disk 21.95 (978-1-932479-60-7(0), LCM 136) Lichtenstein Creat.
anguage is our most powerful tool... we use it to communicate our thoughts, our fears, our emotions and our ideas. This hour of The Infinite Mind explores the art and science of language in contemporary culture. We hear slang from the streets of New York City and from researchers who study slang among college students. A spoken word artist and a team of slam poets talk about how they use and manipulate language to explore their own lives. And a report on how and why minority communities take derogatory words aimed at them and embrace them for their own use. Guests include: Spalding Gray, spoken word artist; Dr. Connie Eble, an English professor and Linguist at University of North Carolina - Chapel Hill; The Urbana Slam Poetry Team, the current National Slam Poetry Team Champions; and Dr. Ronald Butters, a professor of English and Cultural Anthropology at Duke University. Commentary by John Hockenberry.

Language in Use, Set. Adrian Doff & Christopher Jones. (Running Time: 1 hr. 38 mins.). 1999. 42.00 (978-0-521-62703-0(6)) Cambridge U Pr.

Language in Use: Beginner Self-Study. Adrian Doff & Christopher Jones. (Running Time: hrs. mins.). (ENG.). 1999. 15.75 (978-0-521-62702-3(8)) Cambridge U Pr.

***Language in Use Beginner Class Audio CDs (2)** Adrian Doff & Christopher Jones. (Running Time: 1 hr. 33 mins.). (ENG.). 2010. audio compact disk 41.00 (978-0-521-13910-6(4)) Cambridge U Pr.

***Language in Use Intermediate Class Audio CDs (2)** Adrian Doff & Christopher Jones. (Running Time: 1 hr. 38 mins.). (ENG.). 2010. audio compact disk 41.00 (978-0-521-15537-3(1)) Cambridge U Pr.

Language in Use Intermediate Self-Study, Set. Adrian Doff & Christopher Jones. 2 cass. (Running Time: 3 hrs.). (ENG.). 1994. 24.15 (978-0-521-43561-1(7)) Cambridge U Pr.

Language in Use Intermediate Tests. Patricia Aspinall & George Bethell. (Running Time: hrs. mins.). (ENG.). 1998. 24.15 (978-0-521-55599-9(X)) Cambridge U Pr.

***Language in Use Pre-Intermediate Class Audio CDs (2)** 2nd ed. Adrian Doff & Christopher Jones. (Running Time: 1 hr. 24 mins.). (ENG.). 2010. audio compact disk 41.00 (978-0-521-16841-0(4)) Cambridge U Pr.

Language in Use Pre-Intermediate New Edition, Set. 2nd rev. ed. Adrian Doff & Christopher Jones. (Running Time: 1 hr. 23 mins.). 2000. 40.00 (978-0-521-77403-1(9)) Cambridge U Pr.

Language in Use Pre-Intermediate Self-Study. 2nd rev. ed. Adrian Doff & Christopher Jones. (Running Time: 34 mins.). (ENG.). 2000. 15.75 (978-0-521-77402-4(0)) Cambridge U Pr.

Language in Use Split Edition Intermediate Self-Study. Adrian Doff & Christopher Jones. Cass. A. (Running Time: hrs. mins.). (ENG.). 1994. 15.75 (978-0-521-43562-8(5)) Cambridge U Pr.

Language in Use Upper-Intermediate: Self-Study. Adrian Doff & Christopher Jones. (Running Time: hrs. mins.). (ENG.). 1997. 15.75 (978-0-521-55545-6(0)) Cambridge U Pr.

***Language in Use Upper Intermediate Class Audio CDs (2)** Adrian Doff & Christopher Jones. (Running Time: 1 hr. 50 mins.). (ENG.). 2009. audio compact disk 41.00 (978-0-521-13077-6(8)) Cambridge U Pr.

Language of Adam, Pt. A. unabr. ed. Gilbert Highet. 1 cass. (Running Time: 30 min). (Gilbert Highet Ser.). 9.95 (23323) J Norton Pubs.
What language did Adam speak to Eve? Explanation of the meanings some names have & how they go back into history.

Language of Adam & Lifetime Labels (audio CD) Gilbert Highet. (ENG.). 2006. audio compact disk 9.95 (978-1-57970-441-4(7), Audio-For) J Norton Pubs.

Language of Archetypes: Discover the Forces That Shape Your Destiny. Caroline Myss. 10 CDs. (Running Time: 44100 sec.). 2006. audio compact disk 99.00 (978-1-59179-353-3(X), F958D) Sounds True.

Language of Business. unabr. ed. 4 cass. (English As a Second Language Course Ser.). bk. & pap. bk. 59.50 (978-0-88432-189-7(4), S32524) J Norton Pubs.
Deals with correspondence, cables, & other business practices.

Language of Business: Vocabulary for Business Professionals. Jim Stanley & Peg L. Pickering. 6 cass. 69.95 Set, incl. 90p. wkbk. (135-C47) Natl Seminars.
You know it's true...you can master every aspect of your job...you can lead others to on-the-job excellence...you can be directly responsible for new organizational productivity & profitability...but if your vocabulary harms or limits your credibility, it will do the same thing to your career! This program contains more than 1,000 words & an extensive, fun-to-use workbook. Enhance your ability to communicate effectively & with confidence to boost your career...immediately!.

***Language of Emotions: What Your Feelings Are Trying to Tell You.** Karla McLaren. (Running Time: 6:00:00). 2010. audio compact disk 69.95 (978-1-59179-773-9(X)) Sounds True.

Language of Feelings. David S. Viscott. 1 cass. 10.00 (SP100028) SMI Intl.
Do you try to bury your feelings?...deny them?...or learn from them? Your feelings have an important message for you. Listen & learn to interpret what your feelings want to say to you. You'll be more of a winner.

Language of God: A Scientist Presents Evidence for Belief. abr. unabr. ed. Francis S. Collins. Read by Francis S. Collins. 5 CDs. (Running Time: 7 hrs. 0 mins. 0 sec.). (ENG.). 2006. audio compact disk 29.95 (978-0-7435-5431-2(0), Audioworks) Pub: S&S Audio. Dist(s): S and S Inc

Language of God: A Scientist Presents Evidence for Belief. unabr. ed. Francis S. Collins. Read by Francis S. Collins. 2006. 17.95 (978-0-7435-6590-5(8), Audioworks) Pub: S&S Audio. Dist(s): S and S Inc

Language of Happiness. unabr. ed. Robert Muller. 1 cass. (Running Time: 56 min.). 1983. 11.00 (04101) Big Sur Tapes.

Language of Letting Go. abr. ed. Melody Beattie. Read by Melody Beattie. 2 cass. (Running Time: 3 hrs.). 1998. 11.95 (978-1-57453-267-8(7)) Audio Lit.
Meditations are based on allowing oneself to feel one's emotions & accepting our powerlessness in order to discover our real power. Reflections & insights provide a guide to realizing each day as an opportunity for growth.

Language of Letting Go. unabr. ed. Melody Beattie. Read by Gabrielle De Cuir. 8 cass. (Running Time: 12 hrs.). (Western Life Ser.). 2000. 35.00 (978-1-57453-374-3(6)) Audio Lit.
This modern classic of recovery & self-help offers strength, inspiration, guidance & wisdom based on the Twelve Step philosophy. Whether listeners relax with a single imagery exercise or recharge with an hour's journey to a

quiet place within, they will find help with core issues such as denial, acceptance, self-esteem, powerlessness & spirituality.

***Language of Life.** unabr. ed. Francis S. Collins. Read by Greg Itzin. (ENG.). 2010. (978-0-06-196758-0(0), Harper Audio) HarperCollins Pubs.

Language of Life: A Festival of Poets. unabr. ed. Bill Moyers. 8 cass. 1996. 26.95 set. (47427) Books on Tape.
Fascinating conversations with 18 American poets celebrates the power of the word to create a world of thought & emotion. Based on PBS series.

***Language of Life: DNA & the Revolution in Personalized Medicine.** unabr. ed. Francis S. Collins. Read by Greg Itzin. (ENG.). 2010. (978-0-06-196757-3(2), Harper Audio) HarperCollins Pubs.

Language of Literature. (gr. 10 up). 2002. (978-0-395-97160-4(8), 2-80696); audio compact disk (978-0-395-97137-6(3), 2-80684); audio compact disk (978-0-618-28971-4(2), 2-04275); audio compact disk (978-0-618-28991-2(7), 2-04283) Holt McDoug.

Language of Literature. (gr. 6 up). 2002. (978-0-618-03257-0(6), 2-70923); audio compact disk (978-0-618-03248-8(7), 2-70914); audio compact disk (978-0-618-28959-2(3), 2-04263); audio compact disk (978-0-618-28967-7(4), 2-04271); audio compact disk (978-0-618-28984-4(4), 2-04279) Holt McDoug.

Language of Literature. (gr. 7 up). 2002. (978-0-618-03260-0(6), 2-70926); audio compact disk (978-0-618-14678-9(4), 2-04090); audio compact disk (978-0-618-28960-8(7), 2-04264); audio compact disk (978-0-618-28968-4(2), 2-04272) Holt McDoug.

Language of Literature. (gr. 8 up). 2002. (978-0-618-03263-1(0), 2-70929); audio compact disk (978-0-618-14706-9(3), 2-04118); audio compact disk (978-0-618-28961-5(5), 2-04265); audio compact disk (978-0-618-28969-1(0), 2-04373); audio compact disk (978-0-618-28988-2(7), 2-04281) Holt McDoug.

Language of Literature. (gr. 9 up). 2002. (978-0-395-97157-4(8), 2-80693); audio compact disk (978-0-395-97134-5(9), 2-80681); audio compact disk (978-0-618-28989-9(5), 2-04282) Holt McDoug.

Language of Literature: Audio Library Package. (gr. 6 up). 2001. (978-0-618-03258-7(4), 2-70924) Holt McDoug.

Language of Literature: Audio Library Package. (gr. 7 up). 2001. audio compact disk (978-0-618-03251-8(7), 2-70917) Holt McDoug.

Language of Literature: Audio Library Package. (gr. 8 up). 2001. audio compact disk (978-0-618-03254-9(1), 2-70920) Holt McDoug.

Language of Literature: English Learners/SAE English Grammar Survival Kit (Copymasters) (gr. 8 up). 2001. audio compact disk (978-0-618-15828-7(6), 2-80942) Holt McDoug.

Language of Literature: Selection Summaries. (gr. 9 up). 2002. audio compact disk (978-0-618-28962-2(3), 2-04266) Holt McDoug.

Language of Literature: Selection Summaries (Haitian Creole) (CRP.). (gr. 9 up). 2002. audio compact disk (978-0-618-28970-7(4), 2-04274) Holt McDoug.

Language of Love. Michael Ballam & Deanna Edwards. 2 cass. 12.98 (1100408) Covenant Comms.
Teaches compassion through word & song.

Language of Love in Marriage. Lucile Johnson. 1 cass. 9.95 (978-1-57734-482-7(0), 06006000) Covenant Comms.
Keys to finding joy in marriage.

Language of Meekness. Elbert Willis. 1 cass. (Might of Meekness Ser.). 4.00 Fill the Gap.

Language of Men. unabr. ed. Norman Mailer. Read by Tom Carlin. 1 cass. (Running Time: 50 min.). 10.95 (978-0-8045-1158-2(6), SAC 1158) Spoken Arts.
An army cook discovers the crucial rituals for acceptance & respect.

Language of Real Estate. 1 cass. (Running Time: 1 hr. 30 mins.). 2001. 27.95 (978-0-7931-4366-5(7), Dearbrn Real Est Ed) Kaplan Pubng.

Language of Real Estate. 2nd abr. ed. Contrib. by Dearborn Financial Publishing Staff. 1 cass. 1997. 27.95 (978-0-7931-1229-6(X), Dearbrn Real Est Ed) Kaplan Pubng.

Language of Secrets. unabr. ed. Dianne Dixon. Read by Rebecca Lowman. (ENG.). 2010. audio compact disk 30.00 (978-0-307-70437-5(8), Random AudioBks) Pub: Random Audio Pubg. Dist(s): Random

Language of Sex: Experiencing the Beauty of Sexual Intimacy. unabr. ed. Gary Smalley & Ted Cunningham. Read by Paul Michael. (Running Time: 6 hrs. 48 mins. 0 sec.). (ENG.). 2008. audio compact disk 21.98 (978-1-59644-598-7(X), christianSeed) christianaud.

***Language of Sex: Experiencing the Beauty of Sexual Intimacy.** unabr. ed. Greg Smalley & Ted Cunningham. Narrated by Paul Michael. (ENG.). 2008. 12.98 (978-1-59644-599-4(8), christianSeed) christianaud.

Language of the Millennium. Perf. by Kevin Davidson. 1 CD. 2000. audio compact disk 16.98 (978-0-7601-3452-8(9), SO33210) Pub: Brentwood Music. Dist(s): Provident Mus Dist
Includes: "War Zone," "Since He Changed Me," "Born to Win," "Look Up" & more.

***Language of Trust: Selling Ideas in a World of Skeptics.** unabr. ed. Michael Maslansky. Narrated by Michael Maslansky. (Running Time: 7 hrs. 26 mins. 43 sec.). (ENG.). 2010. 18.19 (978-1-60814-721-2(5), SpringWater); audio compact disk 25.99 (978-1-59859-766-0(3), SpringWater) Oasis Audio.

Language of Values: A Forgotten Tongue. 2001. Rental 21.95 (978-0-7583-4364-2(7)); audio compact disk Rental 24.95 (978-0-7583-4365-9(5)) Huge Print.

Language Pack. 12th ed. Hodges. 1995. audio compact disk 35.50 (978-0-15-502176-1(1)) Harcourt.

Language Pragmatics & NLD: It's As Plain As the Nose on Your Face. Sue Diamond. 1 cass. (Running Time: 1 hr. 15 min.). 1998. bk. 20.00 (978-1-58111-058-6(8)) Contemporary Medical.
Describes pragmatic language, problem solving & language processing in NLD. Explains role-playing, & exercises to improve speech.

Language Study in Education. unabr. ed. D. Scarborough. 1 cass. 1986. 12.95 (E7590) J Norton Pubs.
Examines the aims of language study, including language varieties & classroom interaction. Discusses social & conventional attitudes compared with the principles of linguistics.

Language Success in Spanish. Peter Leimbigler. 6 CDs. (Running Time: 5 hrs. 44 min.). (SPA.). 2003. bk. 195.00 (978-1-57970-093-5(4), AFS501) J Norton Pubs.
beginning-level Latin American Spanish course.

Language Tape. (High Point Ser.). (gr. 6-12). reel tape 13.61 (978-0-7362-0914-4(X)); reel tape 13.61 (978-0-7362-0946-5(8)); reel tape 13.61 (978-0-7362-0978-6(6)) Hampton-Brown.

Language to Infinity: A Selection from Cornell University Press. Michel Foucault. 2 cass. (Running Time: 2 hrs. 30 min.). 1996. 17.95 Set. (978-1-879557-38-3(X)) Audio Scholar.
Writing so as not to die is a task undoubtedly as old as the word. So opens the title essay of "Language to Infinity," a collection of four of his most important essays. The range, brilliance, & singularity of philosopher - critic - historian Michel Foucault's ideas have gained great currency throughout the Western intellectual community.

Language, Truth & Revelation, Pt. 1. Gordon Clark. 1 cass. (Lectures on Apologetics: No. 11). 5.00 Trinity Found.

Language, Truth & Revelation, Pt. 2. Gordon Clark. 1 cass. (Lectures on Apologetics: No. 12). 5.00 Trinity Found.

Language, Truth & Revelation, Pt. 3. Gordon Clark. 1 cass. (Lectures on Apologetics: No. 13). 5.00 Trinity Found.

Languages of Africa: Igbo. 12 cass. (Running Time: 12 hrs. 30 mins.). pap. bk. 225.00 J Norton Pubs.

Languages of Africa: Kirundi. 14 cass. (Running Time: 14 hrs.). pap. bk. 245.00 (AFKR10) J Norton Pubs.

Languages of Africa: Swahili. Foreign Service Institute Staff. 20 cass. (Running Time: 21 hrs.). (SWA.). (J). (gr. 10-12). pap. bk. 275.00 incl. text. (978-0-88432-041-8(3), AFW426) J Norton Pubs.
A mixture of Bantu & Arabic languages, is used in both government & in trade in the region of the Congo & in a large part of East Africa.

Language/30 Afrikaans CDs & Booklet. 2 CDs. (Running Time: 90). (AFR.). 2005. audio compact disk 26.95 (978-1-57970-105-5(1), AF1048D) J Norton Pubs.

Language/30 Xhosa CDs & Booklet. 2 CDs. (Running Time: 1 hr. 30 mins.). (Language/30 Brief Course Ser.). (XHO.). 2005. audio compact disk 26.95 (978-1-57970-159-8(0), AF1056D) J Norton Pubs.

Language/30 Zulu CDs & Booklet. 2 CDs. (Running Time: 1 hr. 30 mins.). (Language/30 Brief Course Ser.). (ZUL.). 2005. audio compact disk 26.95 (978-1-57970-160-4(4), AF1049D) J Norton Pubs.

Lani Goose Sings...for Hawaii's Children. Elithe A. Kahn. Illus. by Allison Ruble. 1 cass. (J). (ps up). 1988. 14.95 (978-0-944264-03-4(4)) Pacfic Printng & Pubng.

Lani People. J. F. Bone. Read by Anais 9000. 2009. 27.95 (978-1-60112-218-6(7)) Babblebooks.

Lanigan's Woods. unabr. ed. Robert Clark. Read by Kevin Foley. 6 cass. (Running Time: 7 hrs. 20 min.). 1996. 39.95 (978-1-55686-714-9(X)) Books in Motion.
When the Lanigan's purchased a wooded acreage with an old but well-maintained house they were told it was haunted. It was, but the spirit became their protector when most needed.

L'Animalerie en Comptines. Kidzup Productions Staff. 1 cass. (Running Time: 90 mins.). (Kidzup Foreign Language Ser.). (FRE.). (J). 1999. 8.99 (978-1-894281-35-5(7)) Pub: Kidzup CAN. Dist(s): Penton Overseas
A classic repertoire of international favorites.

Lanna Language. Kobkan Thangpijaigul & Scribner Messenger. 1 cass. (Running Time: 1 hr. 30 min.). (THA & MIS.). 1995. 12.00 (3118) Dunwoody Pr.
Intended for native speakers of Thai & for non-Thais fluent in, or very familiar with, Thai. Materials were selected from available tapes of conversations & monologues. Comprised of four dialogs, each consisting of conversation between two native speakers, & seven readings.

Lanny Cordola Salvation Medicine Show. 1 CD. 1999. audio compact disk 16.98 (KMGD8643) Provident Mus Dist.

Lanny Watkin: Fast Game. Read by Lanny Watkin. 1 cass. 9.95 (978-0-89811-098-2(X), 7149) Lets Talk Assocs.
Lanny Watkin talks about the people & events which influenced his career, & his own approach to his specialities.

Lantern. Gabriel Marcel. (Running Time: 69 min). 2003. audio compact disk 15.00 (978-0-9715192-3-7(4)) Marcel Srud.

Lantern Bearers. unabr. ed. Rosemary Sutcliff. Read by Johanna Ward. 8 CDs. (Running Time: 8 hrs. 30 mins.). 2001. audio compact disk 64.00 (978-0-7861-9733-0(1), 2761) Blckstn Audio.
Brings to life the turbulent time when the last of the Romans in Britain were struggling to carry foward what light they could into the Dark Ages that were to follow.

Lantern Bearers. unabr. ed. Rosemary Sutcliff. Read by Johanna Ward. 6 cass. (Running Time: 8 hrs. 30 mins.). (gr. 4). 2001. 44.95 (978-0-7861-1991-2(8), 2761) Blckstn Audio.

Lanterna. Perf. by Henry Frayne & Kevin Salemme. 1 cass., 1 CD. 8.78 (RYKO 10388); audio compact disk 12.78 CD Jewel box. (RYKO 10388) NewSound.

Lao Complete Set. unabr. ed. University of Iowa, CEEDE Staff. 1 cass. (You & Others Ser.). (LAO.). 1989. 17.00 Incl. tchr's. guide & student text. (978-0-7836-0731-3(8), 8927) Triumph Learn.
Lao readings of fictional episodes which address common situations. An awareness program for interpersonal relationships & situations.

Lao Teaching Set. unabr. ed. University of Iowa, CEEDE Staff. 5 cass. (Tales of Marvel & Wonder Ser.). (LAO.). 1988. 99.00 Set, incl. tchr's. guide, activity masters, ESL grammar activity masters & the ESL grammar activity masters tchr's. guide. (978-0-7836-1092-4(0), 9992) Triumph Learn.
Twenty-three Indochinese fables.

Laparoscopy - Uses & Abuses. 2 cass. (Gynecology & Obstetrics Ser.: C84-GO5). 1984. 15.00 (8436) Am Coll Surgeons.

Lapham's Rules of Influence: A Careerist's Guide to Success, Status, & Self-Congratulation. Lewis Lapham. Narrated by Lewis Lapham. 2 cass. (Running Time: 2 hrs.). 22.00 (978-0-7887-4888-2(2)) Recorded Bks.

Lapis Lazuli see Evening with Dylan Thomas

Lapis Lazuli see Poetry of William Butler Yeats

Lardners: My Family Remembered. unabr. ed. Ring Lardner, Jr. Read by Daniel Grace. 8 cass. (Running Time: 12 hrs.). 1977. 64.00 (978-0-7366-0045-3(0), 1056) Books on Tape.
Ring Lardner Jr. examines the source of his father's talent & gives us a picture of life with a celebrity in the 1920's & 1930's.

Laredo. unabr. ed. Hank Mitchum. Read by Charlie O'Dowd. 4 vols. (Running Time: 6 hrs.). (Stagecoach Ser.: No. 2). 2003. 25.00 (978-1-58807-185-9(5)) Am Pubng Inc.
At high noon, the dusty, border pueblo of Laredo will be charged with excitement. The wily wolf of an outlaw, Bart Campion-a legend along the Rio Grande-is finally caught and is about to be hung for murder. Spectators from all over the rugged spine of Texas and beyond fill the Laredo-bound stages, including vulnerable eighteen-year-old Molly Bishop, who is desperate to have Bart reveal the answer to the question that has shadowed her entire life. For help, she turns to the strong young rancher, Owen Pryor, who has his own dark score from the past to settle with Bart and his gang. And he will get his chance, because Bart's longriders are also headed for Laredo - sworn to spring Bart free and turn the streets of Laredo to blood.

Large Print Song Book (Blue) Singing for Pleasure. l.t. ed. Ulverscroft Staff. 1964. bk. 9.99 (978-0-85456-288-6(5)) Pub: UlverLrgPrint GBR. Dist(s): Ulverscroft US

***Large Story for Men.** John Eldredge. (ENG.). 2011. audio compact disk 22.99 (978-1-933207-42-1(6)) Ransomed Heart.

Larger Venture. Neville Goddard. 1 cass. (Running Time: 62 min.). 1964. 8.00 (103) J & L Pubns.
Neville taught Imagination Creates Reality. He was a powerfully influential teacher of God as Consciousness.

Largest Contract in History: Mark 14:32-42. Ed Young. 1999. 4.95 (978-0-7417-2204-1(6), 1204) Win Walk.

Largo. 1 cass., 1 CD. 8.78 (MERC 536877); audio compact disk 13.58 CD Jewel box. (MERC 536877) NewSound.

***Lark in the Morning.** Coilin O. Confhaola. (ENG.). 1990. 11.95 (978-0-8023-7043-3(8)) Pub: Clo Iar-Chonnachta IRL. Dist(s): Dufour

Lark Rise. unabr. ed. Flora Thompson. Read by Mollie Harris. 7 cass. (Running Time: 8 hrs. 45 min.). (Isis Ser.). (J). 1994. 61.95 (978-1-85695-760-1(8), 931003) Pub: ISIS Lrg Prnt GBR. Dist(s): Ulverscroft US

Lark Rise to Candleford. unabr. ed. Flora Thompson. Read by Mollie Harris. 19 CDs. (Running Time: 28 hrs. 30 min.). 2001. audio compact disk 124.95 (978-0-7531-0968-7(9), 0968-9) Pub: ISIS Audio GBR. Dist(s): Ulverscroft US
Lark Rise is the distillation of Flora Thompson's childhood memories of a remote north Oxfordshire village, the people who lived & worked in it & a way of life that has totally disappeared. As she & her brother grow up, they often go on visits over to Candleford, to see their cousins & to absorb the pleasures of a larger community. At 14 Laura has "grown up" & takes a job at the Post Office in Candleford Green. Her father lovingly makes her a polished wooden trunk on which her initials are picked out in brass nails & her mother sets to work to provide her with "three of everything," neatly finished with crocheted edges.

Lark Rise to Candleford. unabr. collector's ed. Flora Thompson. Read by Jill Masters. 15 cass. (Running Time: 22 hrs. 30 min.). 1993. 120.00 (978-0-7366-2477-0(5), 3239) Books on Tape.
Endearing & precise autobiographical memoir of English country life at the end of the last century.

***Lark Rise to Candleford.** Flora Thompson. Narrated by Olivia Hallinan. 4 CDs. (Running Time: 5 hrs. 0 mins. 0 sec.). (ENG.). 2010. audio compact disk 34.95 (978-1-4084-0956-5(9)) Pub: AudioGO. Dist(s): Perseus Dist

Larklight: A Rousing Tale of Dauntless Pluck in the Farthest Reaches of Space. Philip Reeve. Read by Greg Steinbruner. 8. (Running Time: 8 hrs. 75 mins.). (Larklight Ser.: No. 1). 2007. 61.75 (978-1-4281-3447-8(6)); audio compact disk 87.75 (978-1-4281-3452-2(2)) Recorded Bks.

Larkrigg Fell. unabr. ed. Freda Lightfoot. Read by Marie McCarthy. 12 cass. (Running Time: 15 hrs. 40 mins.). (Sound Ser.). 2002. 94.95 (978-1-86042-681-0(6)) Pub: UlverLrgPrint GBR. Dist(s): Ulverscroft US
The Brandon twins are dissimilar in every way except in their love of their home, Larkrigg Hall. Beth, the romantic, dreams of an idyllic rural life, Sarah is ambitious and ready to take risks with the family business. But jealousy and greed mar their uncertain relationship, so that when tragedy strikes, both sisters are forced to come to terms with a very different situation. Sarah goes off to Italy, while Beth suffers the loss of the one she loves. Having to face emotional suffering or financial ruin, Beth learns to fight for, or lose, the things that matter most to her.

Larky Mavis. Brock Cole. Narrated by Jenny Sterlin. (Running Time: 15 mins.). (gr. k up). 10.00 (978-1-4025-1725-9(4)) Recorded Bks.

Larky Mavis. Brock Cole. Narrated by Jenny Sterlin. (Running Time: 15 mins.). (J). 2001. audio compact disk 12.75 (978-1-4193-1741-5(5)) Recorded Bks.

Larnelle: First Love. Perf. by Larnelle Harris. 1 cass., 1 CD. 1998. 10.98 (978-0-7601-1507-7(9)); audio compact disk 16.98 CD. (978-0-7601-1508-4(7)) Provident Mus Dist.
Encouraging songs that will cause you to praise, cry, laugh, worship & most importantly get back to your "first love"...the love of God.

Larnelle Collector's Series. Perf. by Larnelle Harris. 2 cass., 2 CDs. 1998. 16.99 Set. (978-0-7601-1790-3(X)); audio compact disk 19.99 CD. (978-0-7601-1791-0(8)) Provident Mus Dist.

Larousse dict Illustre. bk. 35.95 (978-2-03-540171-7(2)) Pub: Librairi Larousse FRA. Dist(s): Distribks Inc

Larry & the Meaning of Life. unabr. ed. Janet Tashjian. Read by Matt Green. 4 CDs. (Running Time: 4 hrs. 31 mins.). (YA). (gr. 8 up). 2008. audio compact disk 38.00 (978-0-7393-7276-0(9), Listening Lib) Pub: Random Audio Pubg. Dist(s): Random

Larry Bond's First Team. unabr. ed. Larry Bond & Jim De Felice. Read by Scott Brick. 2004. audio compact disk 90.00 (978-1-4159-0243-1(7)) Books on Tape.
A group of four specialists from military and intelligence backgrounds who have been given free rein and unlimited funds to strike like lightning on global terror. They have a tough job ahead of them. A shipment of radioactive waste headed across the former Soviet Union has gone missing. It could easily be used to make a "dirty bomb" which could render an American city uninhabitable for centuries. With time running out the Team must identify and liquidate the threat. They are unaware that their shadowy enemy has already decided on its first target: Honolulu.

Larry Bond's First Team: Angels of Wrath. abr. ed. Larry Bond & Jim DeFelice. 2006. 14.95 (978-1-59397-728-3(X)) Pub: Macmill Audio. Dist(s): Macmillan

***Larry Bond's Red Dragon Rising: Shadows of War.** unabr. ed. Larry Bond and Jim DeFelice. Read by Luke Daniels. (Running Time: 15 hrs.). (Red Dragon Ser.). 2010. audio compact disk 19.99 (978-1-61106-208-3(X), 9781611062083, Bril Audio CD Unabri) Brilliance Audio.

***Larry Bond's Red Dragon Rising: Edge of War: Edge of War.** unabr. ed. Larry Bond & Jim DeFelice. Read by Luke Daniels. (Running Time: 13 hrs.). (Red Dragon Ser.). 2010. 39.97 (978-1-4233-7023-9(6), 9781423370239, BADLE); 24.99 (978-1-4233-7022-2(8), 9781423370222, BAD); 39.97 (978-1-4233-7021-5(X), 9781423370215, Brlnc Audio MP3 Lib); 24.99 (978-1-4233-7020-8(1), 9781423370208, Brilliance MP3) Brilliance Audio.

Larry Boy & the Fib from Outer Space. Veggie Tales Ser.). (ps-3). 1999. pap. bk. 6.95 (978-1-57064-625-6(2)) Lyrick Pub.

Larry Heinemann. unabr. ed. Larry Heinemann. Read by Larry Heinemann. 1 cass. (Running Time: 29 min.). 1989. 10.00 New Letters.
Heinemann talks about his novel Paco's Story & reads an essays on Post-Vietnam Stress.

Larry Kaplan: Worth All the Telling. 1 cass., 1 CD. 9.98 (C-122); audio compact disk 14.98 CD. (CD-122) Folk-Legacy.
All new songs by an unusually talented songmaker.

Larry King's Favorite Classic Radio Shows. Created by Radio Spirits. (Running Time: 10800 sec.). (Legends of Radio Ser.). 2004. 9.98 (978-1-57019-735-2(0)) Radio Spirits.

Larry King's Favorite Classic Radio Shows. Created by Radio Spirits. 10 CDs. (Running Time: 36000 sec.). (Legends of Radio Ser.). 2005. audio compact disk 39.98 (978-1-57019-732-1(6), OTR 48152) Pub: Radio Spirits. Dist(s): AudioGO

Larry Levis. unabr. ed. Read by Larry Levis. 1 cass. (Running Time: 29 min.). 1985. 10.00 New Letters.
One of a weekly half-hour radio program with authors talking & presenting their own works.

Larry Littlebird. unabr. ed. Larry Littlebird. Read by Larry Littlebird. 1 cass. (Running Time: 29 min.). 1990. 10.00 (042090) New Letters.
A plains Indian who is an actor, filmmaker & storyteller, talks about the importance of stories in Indian life & tells a story about the hunting ritual followed in his tribe.

Larry Long: Well May the World Go. Perf. by Larry Long. 1 CD. (Running Time: 55 mins.). (YA). (gr. 9 up). 2000. audio compact disk 15.00 Smithsonian Folkways.

Larry Long - Here I Stand - Elders' Wisdom, Children's Song: Larry Long with the Youth & Elders of Rural Alabama. Perf. by Larry Long. Contrib. by Pacers Small School Cooperative, University of Alabama Staff. 1 CD. (Running Time: 1 hr. 10 mins.). 1996. audio compact disk Smithsonian Folkways.
Alabama elders talk about their lives, & children from rural schools sing compositions based on the elders' words.

Larry Long - Well May the World Go: Songs of Work, Love, Community & Hope. Anno. by Larry Long. Prod. by Larry Long. Prod. by Billy Peterson & Steve McKinstry. 1 CD. (Running Time: 56 min.). 2000. audio compact disk Smithsonian Folkways.
Telling the stories of hard-working people in a way that highlights the courage, deep personal experiences, & heroism found in their lives is a tradition for which Woody Guthrie is famous & which Larry Long carries on in this new release. Eclectic & richly orchestrated, this CD reflects the complexity of the human experience in the world today. Annotation includes description of the events & interviews with song subjects.

Larry Woiwode. Interview. Interview with Larry Woiwode & Kay Bonetti. 1 cass. (Running Time: 1 hr.). 13.95 (978-1-55644-118-9(5), 4142) Am Audio Prose.
This contains an interview which includes an excellent discussion of the structure & history of composition of "Beyond the Bedroom Wall," plus a variety of other issues related to Woiwode's craft & thematic concerns.

Larryboy: the Soundtrack. Contrib. by VeggieTales. (J). (ps-3). 2006. audio compact disk 10.99 (978-5-558-33014-4(7)) Big Idea.

***Larry's Kidney: Being the True Story of How I Found Myself in China with my Black Sheep Cousin & His Mail Order Bride, Skirting the Law to Get him a Transplant & Save His Life.** Daniel Asa Rose. Narrated by Daniel Asa Rose. (ENG.). 2010. 18.99 (978-0-9827081-7-0(3)) AuthorsDig.

Larry's Party. abr. ed. Carol Shields. Read by R. H. Thomson. 4 CDs. (Running Time: 18000 sec.). (ENG.). 2006. audio compact disk 29.95 (978-0-86492-467-4(4)) Pub: BTC Audiobks CAN. Dist(s): U Toronto Pr

Larry's Party. abr. ed. Carol Shields. Narrated by R. H. Thomson. 4 Tapes. (Running Time: 18000 sec.). (Between the Covers Collection). (ENG.). 1998. 24.95 (978-0-86492-191-8(8)) Pub: Goose Ln Eds CAN. Dist(s): U Toronto Pr
Novel about an ordinary guy made extraordinary by his creator's perception, irony, & wit.

Larry's Party. unabr. ed. Carol Shields. Read by Bernadette Dunne. 8 cass. (Running Time: 12 hrs.). 1998. 64.00 (978-0-7366-4112-8(2), 4617) Books on Tape.
Charming story of a floral designer from the 70s through the 90s.

Larry's Party. unabr. ed. Carol Shields. Read by Carol Shields. 4 cass. (Running Time: 6 hrs.). 1997. 24.95 (PengAudBks) Penguin Grp USA.

Larry's Party. unabr. ed. Carol Shields. Narrated by Alyssa Bresnahan. 9 cass. (Running Time: 13 hrs.). 1998. 78.00 (978-0-7887-1873-1(8), 95295E7) Recorded Bks.
The dramatic twist of a maze designer, follows false trails until he emerges victoriously. He celebrates by hosting his birthday party.

LaRue. 1 cass. 1999. 10.98 (978-0-7601-2845-9(6)); audio compact disk 16.98 (978-0-7601-2844-2(8)) Provident Music.

Las Almas Muertas. abr. ed. Nicolai Gogol. Read by Santiago Munevar. 3 CDs.Tr. of Dead Souls. (SPA.). 2002. audio compact disk 17.00 (978-958-8161-08-2(8)) YoYoMusic.

***Las Aventuras de un Violonchelo: Historias y Memorias.** Carlos Prieto. Prologue by Alvaro Mutis. (Tezontle Ser.). (SPA., 1998. pap. bk. 31.99 (978-968-16-7100-6(7)) Pub: Fondo MEX. Dist(s): Fondo CA

Las Bellas Hijas De Mufaro see Mufaro's Beautiful Daughters

Las Bellas Hijas de Mufaro. John L. Steptoe. Illus. by John L. Steptoe. 14 vols. (Running Time: 20 mins.). 1998. pap. bk. 43.95 (978-1-59519-139-7(9)); 9.95 (978-0-87499-464-3(0)); audio compact disk 12.95 (978-1-59519-137-3(2)) Live Oak Media.

Las Bellas Hijas de Mufaro. John L. Steptoe. Illus. by John L. Steptoe. 11 vols. (Running Time: 20 mins.). (SPA.). (J). 1998. pap. bk. 18.95 (978-1-59519-138-0(0)) Pub: Live Oak Media. Dist(s): AudioGO

Las Canciones del Tio Sombrero. Penton Overseas, Inc. Staff. 1 CD. (Running Time: 1 hr.). (SPA.). (J). 2002. audio compact disk 4.99 (978-1-59125-158-3(3)) Penton Overseas.
Each CD contains a collection of 12 popular Spanish songs. Words and phrases are taught by using simple rhythms. A great way to learn Spanish.

Las cuatro Estaciones. Mariano de Blas.Tr. of Four Seasons. (SPA.). 2009. audio compact disk 35.00 (978-1-935405-11-5(X)) Hombre Nuevo.

Las Estaciones de Esteban. Steck-Vaughn Staff. (SPA.). 1999. (978-0-7398-0745-3(5)) SteckVau.

Las familias tienen reglas Audio CD: Emergent Set A. Benchmark Education Staff. Ed. by Cynthia Swain. (Early Explorers Ser.). (J). 2008. audio compact disk 10.00 (978-1-60437-242-7(7)) Benchmark Educ.

Las flores del cumpleaños Audio CD: Emergent Set A. Benchmark Education Staff. Ed. by Cynthia Swain. (Early Explorers Ser.). (J). 2008. audio compact disk 10.00 (978-1-60437-239-7(7)) Benchmark Educ.

***Las Leyes de la Productividad.** Tr. of Laws of Productivity. (SPA.). 2007. audio compact disk 24.00 (978-0-944129-25-8(0)) High Praise.

Las Llaves Del Poder Pautas para Una Vida Plena. unabr. ed. Dario Silva-Silva. Read by Dario Silva-Silva. (SPA.). 2006. audio compact disk 13.00 (978-958-8218-71-7(3)) Pub: Yoyo Music COL. Dist(s): YoYoMusic

Las Mujeres y el Dinero. Suze Orman. 2008. audio compact disk 24.95 (978-1-933499-78-9(8)) Fonolibro Inc.

***Las Necesidades Ayer Y Hoy Audio Cd.** Matthew Frank. Adapted by Benchmark Education Company, LLC. (Content Connections Ser.). (SPA.). (J). 2009. audio compact disk 10.00 (978-1-935472-62-9(3)) Benchmark Educ.

La's Orchestra Saves the World. Alexander McCall Smith. 2009. 39.99 (978-1-4407-6284-0(8)) Recorded Bks.

***Las Partes de una Planta Audio Cd.** Debra Castor. Adapted by Benchmark Education Company, LLC. (Content Connections Ser.). (SPA.). (J). 2009. audio compact disk 10.00 (978-1-935472-63-6(1)) Benchmark Educ.

***Las Plantas Y Las Estaciones Audio Cd.** Margaret Mcnamara. Adapted by Benchmark Education Company, LLC. (Content Connections Ser.). (SPA.). (J). 2009. audio compact disk 10.00 (978-1-935472-64-3(X)) Benchmark Educ.

Las profecias de los últimos Tiempos. P. Juan Rivas. (SPA.). (YA). 2000. audio compact disk 18.95 (978-1-935405-91-7(8)) Hombre Nuevo.

***Las profecias de San Malaquias.** Padre Juan Rivas. (SPA.). (YA). 2010. audio compact disk 22.95 (978-0-9825744-0-9(1)) Hombre Nuevo.

Las Promesas de Dios: Programa de Navidad. Maria Ester H. de Sturtz et al. 2005. pap. bk. 19.99 (978-0-7586-0943-4(4)) Concordia.

***Las rayas de los animales Audio CD.** Francisco Blane. Adapted by Benchmark Education Company, LLC. (My First Reader's Theater Ser.). (SPA.). (J). 2009. audio compact disk 10.00 (978-1-935470-72-4(8)) Benchmark Educ.

***Las Reglas en Casa Audio Cd.** Margaret Mcnamara. Adapted by Benchmark Education Company, LLC. (Content Connections Ser.). (SPA.). (J). 2009. audio compact disk 10.00 (978-1-935472-66-7(6)) Benchmark Educ.

***Las Reglas en la Escuela Audio Cd.** Margaret Mcnamara. Adapted by Benchmark Education Company, LLC. (Content Connections Ser.). (SPA.). (J). 2009. audio compact disk 10.00 (978-1-935472-67-4(4)) Benchmark Educ.

Las reglas en la Escuela Audio CD: Emergent Set A. Benchmark Education Staff. Ed. by Katherine Scraper. (Early Explorers Ser.). (J). 2008. audio compact disk 10.00 (978-1-60437-244-1(3)) Benchmark Educ.

Las Relaciones Peligrosas. abr. ed. Choderlos De Laclos. 3 CDs.Tr. of Dangerous Connections. (SPA.). 2002. audio compact disk 17.00 (978-958-43-0185-7(3)) YoYoMusic.

Las Sabias Mujeres de la Habana. Jose Raul Bernardo. Narrated by Jose Raul Bernardo. 9 cass. (Running Time: 12 hrs.). 82.00 (978-1-4025-2468-4(4)) Recorded Bks.

Las siete columnas de la Fe. P. Juan Rivas. (SPA.). 2002. audio compact disk 18.95 (978-1-935405-94-8(2)) Hombre Nuevo.

Las Siete "D" para Triunfar. Rafael Ayala. 2 cass. (Running Time: 2 hrs.). (SPA.). 2003. 20.00 (978-1-931059-12-1(8)) Taller del Exito.
Filled with practical tips to help you reach your goals and develop a new attitude towards life. It includes vital information to increase our personal effectiveness and quality of life.

Las siete Palabras. Juan Rivas Pozas. (SPA.). 2009. audio compact disk 18.95 (978-1-935405-09-2(8)) Hombre Nuevo.

Las tablas de multiplicar, Canciones, Vol. 4. (Sabio Y Prudente Ser.).Tr. of Multiplication Tables, Songs. (SPA.). 2004. 7.99 (978-0-8254-0954-7(3), Edit Portavoz) Kregel.

Las tablas de multiplicar, canciones y Pistas, Vol. 4. (Sabio Y Prudente Ser.).Tr. of Multiplication Tables, Songs & Music. (SPA.). 2004. audio compact disk 12.99 (978-0-8254-0955-4(1), Edit Portavoz) Kregel.

Las Tinieblas y el Amanecer. 2004. audio compact disk 60.00 (978-1-57972-574-7(0)) Insight Living.

Las Tres Cabras Gruff. Tr. of Billy Goats Gruff. (SPA.). 2004. 8.95 (978-0-7882-0268-1(5)) Weston Woods.

Las Vegas to Red Rock Canyon: A Journey Westward via Blue Diamond & Spring Mountain Ranch. unabr. ed. Ed. by Bill McCoy. 1 CD. (Running Time: 1 hr.). (Travelog Recorded Driving Tours Ser.). 2002. audio compact disk 19.95 (978-1-931739-10-8(2)) Travelog Corp.
Recorded car tour of Las Vegas to Red Rock Canyon. Every travelog tour includes a detailed map, turn-by-turn directions and a tour and save card for discounts along the route. A companion website, wee.travelog.com provides tour updates, local events, games and trip planning resources. All tours are written by leading travel writers.

Las Vegas/Hoover Dam: Including Boulder City, Lake Mead & Valley of Fire State Park. unabr. ed. Bill McCoy. 1 CD. (Running Time: 1 hr.). (Travelog Recorded Driving Tours Ser.). 2002. audio compact disk 19.95 (978-1-931739-09-2(9)) Travelog Corp.
Recorded car tour of Las Vegas/Hoover Dam. Every travelog tour includes a detailed map, turn-by-turn directions and a tour and save card for discounts along the route. A companion website, www.travelog.com provides tour updates, local events, games and trip planning resources. All tours are written by leading travel writers.

Las 21 Cualidades Indispensables de un Lider: Conviertase en una Persona Que los Demas Quieren Seguir. unabr. ed. John C. Maxwell & Charles F. Stanley. (Running Time: 13200 sec.). (SPA.). 2006. audio compact disk 22.99 (978-0-88113-990-7(4)) Pub: Grupo Nelson. Dist(s): Nelson

Las 21 Leyes Irrefutables del Liderazgo: Siga Estas Leyes, y la Gente lo Seguira A Usted. abr. ed. John C. Maxwell. (Running Time: 15000 sec.). (SPA.). 2007. audio compact disk 24.99 (978-1-60255-068-1(9)) Pub: Grupo Nelson. Dist(s): Nelson

Las 70 Semanas de Daniel. Chuck Missler. 2 cass. (Running Time: 3 hrs.). (Briefing Packages by Chuck Missler).Tr. of Daniel's 70 Weeks. 2000. vinyl bd. 19.95 (978-1-57821-114-2(X)) Koinonia Hse.
This briefing package is a perfect tool for foundational encouragement and an excellent witnessing tool. We are looking forward to breaking down the barriers of language and reaching out to a new and hungry group of people with our unique style of teaching. For Spanish-speaking patrons, we will also be taking orders at (877) 274-3346.

Laser Use in Thoracic Surgery. Moderated by Joseph I. Miller. 2 cass. (Thoracic Surgery Ser.: TH-2). 1986. 19.00 (8666) Am Coll Surgeons.

Lasers & Photonics in Germany: A Strategic Reference 2007. Compiled by Icon Group International, Inc. Staff. 2007. ring bd. 195.00 (978-0-497-35976-8(6)) Icon Grp.

Lassie Come Home. abr. ed. Eric M. Knight. Read by David McCallum. 1 cass. (J). 1991. 9.95 (978-0-89845-801-5(3), CPN 1389) HarperCollins Pubs.

Lassie (OST) 1 cass., 1 CD. (J). 6.38 (SME 66414); audio compact disk 9.58 CD Jewel box. (SME 66414) NewSound.

Last Act in Palmyra. unabr. ed. Lindsey Davis. Narrated by Donal Donnelly. 13 cass. (Running Time: 18 hrs. 45 mins.). (Marcus Didius Falco Ser.). 1997. 104.00 (978-0-7887-1306-4(X), 95144E7) Recorded Bks.
To perform a little espionage for the government, Falco heads to the eastern edges of the empire with his patrician girlfriend, Helena, in tow.

Last Action Hero, Set. unabr. ed. Robert Tine. Read by Tom Noonan. 4 cass. (Running Time: 5 hrs.). 1993. 22.95 (978-1-56876-011-7(6)) Soundlines Ent.
Sergeant Jack Slater has never lost a battle in the war against crime. He is also the greatest fictional hero on the big screen. Slater's movie world gets shaken up when a magical ticket blasts 11 year-old Danny Madigan out of his movie seat & into the movie. Teamed with his favorite hero, Danny gets to live a fantasy, as he crashes cars & takes on the bad guys.

Last American Man. unabr. ed. Elizabeth Gilbert. (Running Time: 7 hrs.). (ENG.). 2009. audio compact disk 29.95 (978-0-14-242824-5(8), PengAudBks) Penguin Grp USA.

***Last Apprentice: Night of the Soul Stealer.** unabr. ed. Joseph Delaney. Read by Christopher Evan Welch. (ENG.). 2007. (978-0-06-155431-5(6)); (978-0-06-155432-2(4)) HarperCollins Pubs.

***Last Apprentice: Attack of the Fiend.** unabr. ed. Joseph Delaney. Read by Christopher Evan Welch. Illus. by Patrick Arrasmith. (ENG.). 2009. (978-0-06-193908-2(0), GreenwillowBks); (978-0-06-196160-1(4), GreenwillowBks) HarperCollins Pubs.

***Last Apprentice: Clash of the Demons.** unabr. ed. Joseph Delaney. Read by Christopher Evan Welch. (ENG.). 2009. (978-0-06-187025-5(0), GreenwillowBks); (978-0-06-190272-7(1), GreenwillowBks) HarperCollins Pubs.

***Last Apprentice: Curse of the Bane.** unabr. ed. Joseph Delaney. Read by Christopher Evan Welch. (ENG.). 2006. (978-0-06-122939-8(3), GreenwillowBks); (978-0-06-122938-1(5), GreenwillowBks) HarperCollins Pubs.

***Last Apprentice: Revenge of the Witch.** unabr. ed. Joseph Delaney. Read by Christopher Evan Welch. (ENG.). 2005. (978-0-06-088786-5(9), GreenwillowBks); (978-0-06-088785-8(0), GreenwillowBks) HarperCollins Pubs.

***Last Apprentice: Rise of the Huntress.** unabr. ed. Joseph Delaney. Read by Christopher Evan Welch. (ENG.). 2010. (978-0-06-206207-9(7), GreenwillowBks); (978-0-06-199677-1(7), GreenwillowBks) HarperCollins Pubs.

***Last Apprentice: the Spook's Tale.** unabr. ed. Joseph Delaney. Read by Christopher Evan Welch. (ENG.). 2009. (978-0-06-182985-7(4), GreenwillowBks); (978-0-06-189652-1(7), GreenwillowBks) HarperCollins Pubs.

***Last Apprentice: Wrath of the Bloodeye.** unabr. ed. Joseph Delaney. Read by Christopher Evan Welch. (ENG.). 2009. (978-0-06-189653-8(5), GreenwillowBks); (978-0-06-182982-6(X), GreenwillowBks) HarperCollins Pubs.

Last Assassin. Barry Eisler. (John Rain Ser.: Bk. 5). 2007. 69.95 (978-0-7531-3845-8(X)); audio compact disk 84.95 (978-0-7531-2833-6(0)) Pub: ISIS Audio GBR. Dist(s): Ulverscroft US

Last Assassin. Barry Eisler. Read by Michael Mcconnohie. (Running Time: 10 hrs.). (John Rain Ser.: Bk. 5). 2006. 23.95 (978-1-60083-340-3(3)) Iofy Corp.

Last Assassin. unabr. ed. Barry Eisler. Read by Michael McConnohie. 8 CDs. (Running Time: 36000 sec.). (John Rain Ser.: Bk. 5). 2006. audio compact disk 34.95 (978-1-59316-080-7(1), LL172) Listen & Live.

Last Asset. Based on a story by Edith Wharton. 2007. 5.00 (978-1-60339-091-0(X)); audio compact disk 5.00 (978-1-60339-092-7(8)) Listenr Digest.

Last Barrier. Swami Amar Jyoti. 1 cass. 1987. 9.95 (M-72) Truth Consciousness.
When the ego blinds, we don't see further. Working to lighten ego. The role of Grace. Pitfalls on the seeker's way. Using God's treasure judiciously, moderation in living.

Last Battle see Complete Chronicles of Narnia

Last Battle see Chronicles of Narnia Super-Soundbook

Last Battle. C. S. Lewis. 2 cass. (Running Time: 3 hrs.). (Chronicles of Narnia Ser.). (J). 2001. 16.99 (BMDD019) Lodestone Catalog.

Last Battle. unabr. ed. C. S. Lewis. Read by Patrick Stewart. Contrib. by Patrick Stewart. (Running Time: 018000 sec.). (Chronicles of Narnia Ser.). 2005. audio compact disk 29.95 (978-0-06-079332-6(5)) HarperCollins Pubs.

Last Battle. adpt. ed. Read by Paul Scofield et al. C. S. Lewis. 3 CDs. (Running Time: 240 hrs. 0 mins.). (Radio Theatre: Chronicles of Narnia Ser.). (ENG.). (J). (gr. 3). 2007. audio compact disk 14.97 (978-1-58997-518-7(9)) Tyndale Hse.

Last Battle. unabr. ed. C. S. Lewis. 2 cass. (Running Time: 3 hrs.). (Chronicles of Narnia Ser.). (J). (gr. 4-8). 16.99 (D106) Blckstn Audio.
Years after they helped Prince Caspian become King, Eustace & Jill return to help their friend when Narnia faces its darkest hour.

***Last Battle.** unabr. ed. C. S. Lewis. Read by Patrick Stewart. 2005. (978-0-06-085447-8(2)); (978-0-06-085448-5(0)) HarperCollins Pubs.

Last Battle. unabr. abr. ed. C. S. Lewis. Read by Patrick Stewart. (Chronicles of Narnia Ser.). (J). 2004. audio compact disk 27.50 (978-0-06-059782-5(8)) HarperCollins Pubs.

Last Battle. unabr. collector's ed. Cornelius Ryan. Read by Bill Kelsey. 12 cass. (Running Time: 18 hrs.). 1991. 96.00 (978-0-7366-1984-4(4), 2801) Books on Tape.
The battle for Berlin, the last offensive against Hitler's Third Reich, began at 4 a.m., Monday, April 16, 1945. At that moment, flares burst in the skies above the Oder River, triggering an artillery barrage that opened the Russian assault. Before it ended, 250,000 people would be killed. As the attack began, Berliners waited, numb & terrified, clinging to the only politics that mattered - the politics of survival. For them, to endure had become more important than to win.

Last Battle, Set. C. S. Lewis. 2 cass. (Chronicles of Narnia Ser.). (J). (gr. 4-8). 1999. 16.99 (BMDD019, Random AudioBks) Random Audio Pubg.

Last Best Hope. abr. ed. Read by Ed McBain, pseud. 4 cass. (Running Time: 6 hrs.). (Matthew Hope Mystery Ser.: No. 13). 2000. 12.99 (978-1-57815-181-3(3), 4419, Media Bks Audio) Media Bks NJ.
Jill Lawton wants Matthew Hope to her husband, Jack. Her tale is commonplace: a middle-aged husband goes north to look for work, finds another woman, doesn't come back. But a corpse turns up on a Calusa beach with Jack Lawton's ID in his pocket.

Last Best Hope. abr. ed. Ed McBain, pseud. Read by Ed McBain, pseud. 5 cass. (Running Time: 7 hrs. 30 mins.). (Matthew Hope Mystery Ser.: No. 13). (YA). 2001. audio compact disk 11.99 (978-1-57815-535-4(5), Media Bks Audio) Media Bks NJ.
For Matthew Hope, the Lawton case signals a change in his life, an ending of relationships, a shift in values and a look into the dark night of his own soul.

Last Best Hope. unabr. ed. Ed McBain, pseud. Read by Jonathan Marosz. 5 cass. (Running Time: 7 hrs. 30 min.). (Matthew Hope Mystery Ser.: No. 13). 1998. 40.00 (978-0-7366-4215-6(3), 4713) Books on Tape.

Last Best Hope. unabr. collector's ed. Ed McBain, pseud. Read by Jonathan Marosz. 6 CDs. (Running Time: 9 hrs.). (Matthew Hope Mystery Ser.: No. 13). 2001. audio compact disk 48.00 Books on Tape.
The Florida-based attorney meets a Jill in search of her Jack. Seems that her husband went north to look for work, found another woman, and didn't come back. Now Jill Lawton wants a divorce. No sweat for Mr. Hope - until a corpse turns up with Jack Lawton's ID in his pocket. Hope is about to discover that the Lawtons have carried on a kinky sex life that leads to some seedy places and even seedier people.

Last Best Hope: Restoring Conservatism & America's Promise. abr. unabr. ed. Joe Scarborough. Read by Joe Scarborough. (ENG.). 2009. audio compact disk 35.00 (978-0-7393-8502-9(X), Random AudioBks) Pub: Random Audio Pubg. Dist(s): Random

Last Boat to Cadiz. Barnaby Conrad. Read by Grover Gardner. (Running Time: 5 hrs. 30 mins.). 2003. 24.95 (978-1-59912-527-5(7)) Iofy Corp.

Last Boat to Cadiz. unabr. ed. Conrad Barnaby. Read by Gardner Grover. 4 cass. (Running Time: 5 hrs. 30 mins.). 2004. 32.95 (978-0-7861-2715-3(5), 3275); audio compact disk 40.00 (978-0-7861-8639-6(9), 3275) Blckstn Audio.

Last Book in the Universe. unabr. ed. Rodman Philbrick. Read by Jeremy Davies. 3 cass. (Running Time: 4 hrs. 25 mins.). (J). (gr. 5-9). 2004. 30.00

An Asterisk (*) at the beginning of an entry indicates that the title is appearing for the first time.

(978-0-8072-8843-6(8), Listening Lib); pap. bk. 36.00 (978-0-8072-8844-3(6), LYA 272 SP, Listening Lib) Random Audio Pubg.
Spaz, as he is called, has escaped the mind probes that are rotting everyone else's minds. He still has a memory, something rare in the frightening world in which he lives. In this world, nobody remembers books anymore, yet one old man named Ryter is writing one, even though he knows the possible terrible result of his actions.

***Last Boy: Mickey Mantle & the End of America's Childhood.** unabr. ed. Jane Leavy. 2010. (978-0-06-198807-3(3), Harper Audio); (978-0-06-198808-0(1), Harper Audio) HarperCollins Pubs.

Last Boy: Mickey Mantle & the End of America's Childhood. unabr. ed. Jane Leavy. 2010. audio compact disk 49.99 (978-0-06-176768-5(9), Harper Audio) HarperCollins Pubs.

***Last Breath.** unabr. ed. Joe Hill. (ENG.). 2007. (978-0-06-155228-1(3)); (978-0-06-155231-1(3)) HarperCollins Pubs.

Last Breath: A Novel of Suspense. abr. ed. Mariah Stewart. Read by Laural Merlington. (Running Time: 21600 sec.). 2008. audio compact disk 14.99 (978-1-4233-1919-1(2), 9781423319191, BCD Value Price) Brilliance Audio.

Last Breath: A Novel of Suspense. unabr. ed. Mariah Stewart. Read by Laural Merlington. (Running Time: 9 hrs.). 2007. 39.25 (978-1-4233-1917-7(6), 9781423319177, BADLE); 24.95 (978-1-4233-1916-0(8), 9781423319160, BAD); 82.25 (978-1-4233-1911-5(7), 9781423319115, BrilAudUnabridg); audio compact disk 24.95 (978-1-4233-1914-6(1), 9781423319146, Brilliance MP3); audio compact disk 34.95 (978-1-4233-1912-2(5), 9781423319122, Bril Audio CD Unabri); audio compact disk 39.25 (978-1-4233-1915-3(X), 9781423319153, Brinc Audio MP3 Lib); audio compact disk 92.25 (978-1-4233-1913-9(3), 9781423319139, BriAudCD Unabrid) Brilliance Audio.

Last Buffalo Hunt. unabr. ed. Gary McCarthy. Read by Maynard Villers. 4 cass. (Running Time: 5 hrs. 42 min.). 1996. 26.95 (978-1-55686-720-0(4)) Books in Motion.
Thomas Atherton & Sally, a con woman, set out to find the last surviving herd of the near extinct buffalo & collect a $5000 reward.

Last Bus to Woodstock. Colin Dexter. 2 cass. (Running Time: 3 hrs.). (ENG., 2001. (978-0-333-90663-7(2)) Macmillan UK GBR.

Last Bus to Woodstock. unabr. ed. Colin Dexter. Read by Terrence Hardiman. 8 cass. (Running Time: 12 hrs.). (Inspector Morse Mystery Ser.: Bk. 1). 2000. 59.95 (978-0-7451-4296-8(6), CAB 979) Pub: Chivers Audio Bks GBR. Dist(s): AudioGO
The death of Sylvia Kaye figured dramatically into Thursday afternoon's paper. Inspector Morse knew that the events on Wednesday evening had been actions motivated by love, hate and jealousy. While the rest of the police force was looking for a dangerous man wanted for murder and rape, Morse was convinced the murderer was someone close to Sylvia, someone very close.

***Last Call.** unabr. ed. James Grippando. Read by Jonathan Davis. (ENG.). 2007. (978-0-06-157295-1(0)); (978-0-06-157298-2(5)) HarperCollins Pubs.

Last Call. unabr. ed. James Grippando. Read by Jonathan Davis. (Running Time: 37800 sec.). 2008. audio compact disk 39.95 (978-0-06-145270-3(X), Harper Audio) HarperCollins Pubs.

Last Call. unabr. ed. James Grippando. Read by Jonathan Davis. 9 cass. (Running Time: 10 hrs. 30 mins.). (Jack Swyteck Ser.). 2007. 72.75 (978-1-4281-9819-7(9)) Recorded Bks.

Last Call. unabr. ed. James Grippando. Read by Jonathan Davis. 9 CDs. (Running Time: 10 hrs. 30 mins.). (Jack Swyteck Ser.: Bk. 7). 2007. audio compact disk 102.75 (978-1-4281-9821-0(0)) Recorded Bks.

***Last Call.** unabr. ed. Tim Powers. Read by Bronson Pinchot. (Running Time: 17 hrs.). 2010. 44.95 (978-1-4417-5737-1(6)); 89.95 (978-1-4417-5733-3(3)); audio compact disk 123.00 (978-1-4417-5734-0(1)); audio compact disk 34.95 (978-1-4417-5736-4(8)) Blckstn Audio.

Last Call: The Rise & Fall of Prohibition. abr. ed. Daniel Okrent. Read by Daniel Okrent. 8 CDs. (Running Time: 10 hrs.). 2010. audio compact disk 39.99 (978-0-7435-9921-4(7)) Pub: S&S Audio. Dist(s): S and S Inc

Last Call at the Blue Note. Perf. by Oscar Peterson & Bobby Durham. 1 cass., 1 CD. 7.98 (TA 33314); audio compact disk 12.78 CD Jewel box. (TA 83314) NewSound.

Last Camel Died at Noon. unabr. ed. Elizabeth Peters, pseud. Read by Susan O'Malley. 9 cass. (Running Time: 13 hrs.). (Amelia Peabody Ser.: No. 6). 2001. 62.95 (978-0-7861-1990-5(X), 2760); audio compact disk 88.00 (978-0-7861-9734-7(X), 2760) Blckstn Audio.
Neither Amelia nor Emerson believe the message is authentic, but the treasure map proves an irresistible temptation. Survival depends on Amelia's solving a mystery as old as ancient Egypt & as timeless as greed & revenge.

Last Camel Died at Noon. unabr. ed. Elizabeth Peters, pseud. Narrated by Barbara Rosenblat. 11 cass. (Running Time: 15 hrs. 45 mins.). (Amelia Peabody Ser.: No. 6). 1991. 91.00 (978-1-55690-300-7(6), 91318E7) Recorded Bks.
Amelia Peabody, a Victorian archaeologist, goes looking for a missing man in the Sudan.

Last Campaign. abr. ed. Tim Champlin. Read by Robert Smith. (Running Time: 3 hrs.). (Five Star Westerns Ser.). 2007. 39.25 (978-1-4233-3570-2(8), 9781423335702, BADLE); 24.95 (978-1-4233-3569-6(4), 9781423335696, BAD); audio compact disk 24.95 (978-1-4233-3567-2(8), 9781423335672, Brilliance MP3); audio compact disk 39.25 (978-1-4233-3568-9(6), 9781423335689, Brinc Audio MP3 Lib) Brilliance Audio.

Last Campaign. unabr. ed. Tim Champlin. Read by Richard Choate. 6 cass. (Running Time: 9 hrs.). 1997. 48.00 (978-0-7366-3813-5(X), 4481) Books on Tape.
It's 1886 in Canon de los Embudos, Mexico & general George Crook is holding a peace conference with the last wild band of Apache renegades & their chief Geronimo.

Last Campaign: Robert F. Kennedy & 82 Days That Inspired America. Thurston Clarke. Read by Pete Larkin. (Playaway Adult Nonfiction Ser.). 2008. 54.99 (978-1-60640-516-1(0)) Find a World.

Last Campaign: Robert F. Kennedy & 82 Days That Inspired America. unabr. ed. Thurston Clarke. Read by Pete Larkin. 9 CDs. (Running Time: 10 hrs. 45 mins.). (ENG., 2008. audio compact disk 34.95 (978-1-59887-668-0(6), 1598876686) Pub: HighBridge. Dist(s): Workman Pub

Last Car to Elysian Fields. abr. ed. James Lee Burke. Read by Will Patton. (Dave Robicheaux Ser.). 2004. 15.95 (978-0-7435-4918-9(X)) Pub: S&S Audio. Dist(s): S and S Inc

Last Car to Elysian Fields. abr. ed. James Lee Burke. Read by Will Patton. (Running Time: 7 hrs. 0 mins. 0 sec.). (Dave Robicheaux Ser.). 2007. audio compact disk 14.95 (978-0-7435-6106-8(6)) Pub: S&S Audio. Dist(s): S and S Inc

Last Car to Elysian Fields. unabr. ed. James Lee Burke. Read by Will Patton. (Dave Robicheaux Ser.). 2004. 29.95 (978-0-7435-5093-2(5)) Pub: S&S Audio. Dist(s): S and S Inc

Last Cataclysm see Classical Russian Poetry

Last Catholic in America. unabr. ed. John Powers. Narrated by John MacDonald. 5 cass. (Running Time: 6 hrs. 30 mins.). 1982. 44.00 (978-1-55690-301-4(4), 82044E7) Recorded Bks.
The story of growing up in Chicago in the 50s under the tutelage of vengeful nuns. Get ready for Garbage Annie, Filthy Felix & more in a hilarious swing through Catholic education.

Last Cavalier: Being the Adventures of Count Sainte-Hermine in the Age of Napoleon. unabr. ed. Alexandre Dumas. (Running Time: 18 hrs. 0 mins.). (ENG.). 2009. 95.95 (978-1-4417-0223-4(7)); 79.95 (978-1-4417-0326-2(8)); audio compact disk 160.00 (978-1-4417-0224-1(5)) Blckstn Audio.

Last Cavalier: Being the Adventures of Count Sainte-Hermine in the Age of Napoleon. unabr. ed. Alexandre Dumas. (Running Time: 31 hrs. 30 mins.). (ENG.). 2010. 59.95 (978-1-4417-0227-2(X)); audio compact disk 54.95 (978-1-4417-0226-5(1)) Blckstn Audio.

Last Centurion. unabr. ed. John Ringo. Read by Dan John Miller. (Running Time: 16 hrs.). 2008. 24.95 (978-1-4233-7094-9(5), 9781423370949, Brilliance MP3); 39.25 (978-1-4233-7097-0(X), 9781423370970, BADLE); 39.25 (978-1-4233-7095-6(3), 9781423370956, Brinc Audio MP3 Lib); 24.95 (978-1-4233-7096-3(1), 9781423370963, BAD); audio compact disk 112.25 (978-1-4233-7093-2(7), 9781423370932, BriAudCD Unabrid); audio compact disk 32.99 (978-1-4233-7092-5(9), 9781423370925, Bril Audio CD Unabri) Brilliance Audio.

Last Chance. Hank Mitchum. Read by Charlie O'Dowd. 4 vols. No. 19. 2004. 25.00 (978-1-58807-202-3(9)); (978-1-58807-962-6(7)) Am Pubng Inc.

Last Chance. Scripts. Hank Mitchum. 5 CDs. (Running Time: 6 hrs.). (Stagecoach Ser.: No. 19). 2005. 14.99 (978-1-58807-771-4(3)) Am Pubng Inc.
For Kelly O'Brian, Denver meant a new life. For Dan Sullivan, a blind Civil War veteran, Denver meant reunion with his fiance. Against angry Kiowa and ravenous wolves, Dan proves his courage knows no handicap. But when the driver and shotgunner are shot at Last Chance, the fate of the stagecoach is left to Dan and Kelly who must make the most important decision of her life.

Last Chance Cafe. abr. ed. Linda Lael Miller. 2004. 15.95 (978-0-7435-4919-6(8)) Pub: S&S Audio. Dist(s): S and S Inc

Last Chance Cafe. unabr. ed. Linda Lael Miller. Read by Christine Marshall. 10 CDs. (Running Time: 15 hrs.). 2002. audio compact disk 94.95 (978-0-7927-2732-3(0), SLD 438, Chivers Sound Lib) AudioGO.
Rancher Chance Qualtrough has deep roots in Primrose Creek. Now, at the local diner, he is about to encounter his future: Hallie O'Rourke and her two young daughters, taking refuge from a storm. But Chance doesn't know that Hallie is fleeing a danger so threatening she dares not ask anyone for help. Slowly, as Chance and Hallie break down barriers of fear and doubt, trust takes hold. Hope replaces despair. And a fragile attraction grows into an undeniable passion . .

Last Chance for Animals' Chris DeRose Exposes Fur Farms, Elephant Poaching, & Vivisection. Hosted by Nancy Pearlman. 1 cass. (Running Time: 29 min.). 10.00 (1020) Educ Comm CA.

Last Chance Millionaire: It's Not Too Late to Become Wealthy. abr. ed. Douglas R. Andrew. (Running Time: 3 hrs.). (ENG.). 2007. 14.98 (978-1-59483-921-4(2)) Pub: Hachet Audio. Dist(s): HachBkGrp

Last Chance Millionaire: It's Not Too Late to Become Wealthy. unabr. ed. Douglas R. Andrew. (Running Time: 13 hrs. 30 mins.). (ENG.). 2007. 16.98 (978-1-60024-018-8(6)) Pub: Hachet Audio. Dist(s): HachBkGrp

Last Chance Saloon. unabr. ed. Marian Keyes. Narrated by Juanita McMahon. 13 cass. (Running Time: 18 hrs.). 2000. 111.00 (978-1-84197-122-3(7), H1119E7) Recorded Bks.
Tara, Katherine & Finian, friends since adolescence, are full proof that eccentricity is the spice of life. Strikingly different, yet worryingly similar, they all moved from rural Ireland to London to "seize the day" or something like that.

Last Child. unabr. ed. John Hart. Read by Scott Sowers. (Running Time: 14 hrs. 36 mins.). 2009. 69.95 (978-0-7927-6419-9(6), Chivers Sound Lib) AudioGO.

***Last Child.** unabr. ed. John Hart. Read by Scott Sowers. 1 Playaway. (Running Time: 15 hrs.). 2009. 110.95 (978-0-7927-6492-2(7)); audio compact disk 110.95 (978-0-7927-6378-9(5)) AudioGO.

Last Child. unabr. ed. John Hart. Read by Scott Sowers. (Running Time: 15 hrs. 0 mins. 0 sec.). (ENG.). 2009. audio compact disk 39.95 (978-1-4272-0666-4(X)) Pub: Macmill Audio. Dist(s): Macmillan

Last Christian: A Novel. unabr. ed. David Gregory. Read by Lincoln Hoppe. (ENG.). 2010. audio compact disk 30.00 (978-0-307-71519-7(1), Random AudioBks) Pub: Random Audio Pubg. Dist(s): Random

***Last Christmas: The Private Prequel.** unabr. ed. Kate Brian, pseud. Narrated by Justine Eyre. (Running Time: 7 hrs. 0 mins.). 2010. 14.99 (978-1-4001-8240-4(9)) Tantor Media.

Last Christmas: The Private Prequel. unabr. ed. Kate Brian, pseud. Narrated by Justine Eyre. (Running Time: 6 hrs. 30 mins. 0 sec.). (Private Ser.). (ENG.). (gr. 9-12). 2010. 19.99 (978-1-4001-6240-6(8)); audio compact disk 29.99 (978-1-4001-1240-1(0)); audio compact disk 59.99 (978-1-4001-4240-8(7)) Pub: Tantor Media. Dist(s): IngramPubServ

***Last Christmas (Library Edition) The Private Prequel.** unabr. ed. Kate Brian, pseud. Narrated by Justine Eyre. (Running Time: 7 hrs. 0 mins.). 2010. 29.99 (978-1-4001-9240-3(4)) Tantor Media.

Last Chronicle of Barset. unabr. ed. Anthony Trollope. Read by Simon Vance. (Running Time: 109800 sec.). 2007. audio compact disk 44.95 (978-1-4332-1116-4(5)) Blckstn Audio.

Last Chronicle of Barset, Pt. 1. unabr. collector's ed. Anthony Trollope. Read by David Case. 11 cass. (Running Time: 16 hrs. 30 min.). 1993. 88.00 (978-0-7366-2583-8(6), 3330-A) Books on Tape.
Trollope satirizes the complacent life of vicarages in this final installment of the Barsetshire Chronicles.

Last Chronicle of Barset, Pt. 2. collector's ed. Anthony Trollope. Read by David Case. 12 cass. (Running Time: 18 hrs.). 1993. 96.00 (978-0-7366-2584-5(4), 3330-B) Books on Tape.

Last Chronicle of Barset, Pt. 2. unabr. ed. Anthony Trollope. 9 cass. (Running Time: 13 hrs. 30 mins.). 1992. 59.95 Audio Bk Con.

Last Chronicle of Barset, Pt. 2, set. Anthony Trollope. 9 cass. (Running Time: 13 hrs. 30 min.). 59.95 Audio Bk Con.
In the grand finale to the Barchster novels, the proud curate Mr. Crawley is accused of theft & many familiar characters take sides. Bishop & Mrs. Proudie, Archdeacon & Mrs. Grantly, Reverend Harding, the Thomes, the Greshams, Lady Lufton, Johnny Eames & Lily Dale are among those involved in this tale of pathos, intrigue & love, which frequently leads to laughter.

Last Chronicle of Barset: Part One. unabr. ed. Anthony Trollope. Read by Simon Vance. (Running Time: 57600 sec.). 2007. 79.95 (978-1-4332-1114-0(9)); audio compact disk 99.00 (978-1-4332-1115-7(7)) Blckstn Audio.

Last Chronicle of Barset: Part Two. unabr. ed. Anthony Trollope. Read by Simon Vance. (Running Time: 52200 sec.). 2007. 85.95 (978-1-4332-1096-9(7)); audio compact disk 99.00 (978-1-4332-1097-6(5)) Blckstn Audio.

Last Chronicle of Barset (Part 1), Vol. 11. unabr. ed. Anthony Trollope. Read by Flo Gibson. 12 cass. (Running Time: 18 hrs.). 1992. 39.95 (978-1-55685-259-6(2)) Audio Bk Con.
In the grand finale to the Barchester novels, the proud curate Mr. Crawley is accused of theft & many familiar characters take sides. Bishop & Mrs. Proudie, Archdeacon & Mrs. Grantly, Reverend Harding, the Thomes, the Greshams, Lady Lufton, Johnny Eames & Lily Dale are among those involved in this tale of pathos, intrigue & love, which frequently leads to laughter.

Last Chronicle of Barset (Part 2), Vol. 2. unabr. ed. Anthony Trollope. Narrated by Flo Gibson. (Running Time: 13 hrs. 1 min.). 1992. 28.95 (978-1-55685-814-7(0)) Audio Bk Con.

Last Chronicle of Barset (Parts 1 And 2) unabr. ed. Anthony Trollope. Narrated by Flo Gibson. (Running Time: 30 hrs. 58 mins.). 1992. 59.95 (978-1-55685-815-4(9)) Audio Bk Con.

Last Citadel: A Novel of the Battle of Kursk. unabr. ed. David L. Robbins. Read by George Guidall. 15 CDs. (Running Time: 17 hrs. 25 mins.). 2004. audio compact disk 109.75 (978-1-4025-8658-3(2)); 99.75 (978-1-4025-6953-1(X)) Recorded Bks.
David L. Robbins brings to life the largest battle the world has ever seen in this dramatic novel. In 1943, Hitler attempts one final offensive to conquer Russia. With their fearsome new Tiger tanks, the Germans throw everything against the Red Army. But the Russians are determined to defend the motherland no matter what the cost. As two million soldiers clash, the fate of the world is on the line.

Last Command. unabr. ed. Lucasfilm Ltd. Staff. Read by Larry McKeever. 13 cass. (Running Time: 1 hr. 30 min. per cass.). (Star Wars: Bk. 3). 1996. 104.00 Set. (3815); Rental 19.50 (3815) Books on Tape.
When Grand Admiral Thrawn attacks the fragile New Republic, he commands a devastating new technology: cloned soldiers. Thrawn's final siege leaves the Republic only one hope: Luke Skywalker, who, with his commando group, may be able to destroy Thrawn's deadly cloning machines. But that's just what C'baoth, a Dark Jedi on Thrawn's side, expects - & wants. Luke will fall into his lap, where C'baoth can crush him once & for all.

Last Confession see Poetry of William Butler Yeats

***Last Confession.** unabr. ed. Solomon Jones. (Running Time: 10 hrs. 30 mins.). 2010. 29.95 (978-1-4417-6431-7(3)); 65.95 (978-1-4417-6428-7(3)); audio compact disk 90.00 (978-1-4417-6429-4(1)); audio compact disk 29.95 (978-1-4417-6430-0(5)) Blckstn Audio.

Last Confession. unabr. ed. Morris West. Read by James Condon. 4 cass. (Running Time: 7 hrs. 45 mins.). 2001. 32.00 (978-1-74030-453-5(5)) Pub: Bolinda Pubng AUS. Dist(s): Bolinda Pub Inc

Last Confession. unabr. ed. Morris West. Read by James Condon. 7 CDs. (Running Time: 7 hrs. 45 mins.). 2002. audio compact disk 83.95 (978-1-74030-690-4(2)) Pub: Bolinda Pubng AUS. Dist(s): Bolinda Pub Inc

Last Continent. unabr. ed. Terry Pratchett. Read by Nigel Planer. 8 cass. (Running Time: 12 hrs.). (Discworld Ser.). (J). 2001. 69.95 (978-0-7531-0522-1(5), 990203); audio compact disk 89.95 (978-0-7531-0742-3(2), 107422) Pub: ISIS Lrg Prnt GBR. Dist(s): Ulverscroft US
This is a lighthearted tour of the fantasy land of Fourecks, a very Australian sort of place, with brief courses in theoretical physics & evolution thrown in for good measure. The inept & cowardly wizard Rincewind, habitually runs into trouble as fast as he flees. Rincewind's arrival in Fourecks has distorted the space-time continuum & he has to sort it out before the whole place dries up & blows away.

Last Coyote. abr. ed. Michael Connelly. Read by Dick Hill. 3 CDs. (Running Time: 3 hrs.). (Harry Bosch Ser.: No. 4). 2003. audio compact disk 14.99 (978-1-59086-526-2(X), 159086526X, BAU); audio compact disk 62.25 (978-1-59086-572-9(3), 1590865723, BAU) Brilliance Audio.
Harry attacked his commanding officer and is suspended indefinitely, pending a psychiatric evaluation. At first he resists the LAPD shrink, but finally recognizes that something is troubling him and has for a long time. In 1961, when Harry was twelve, his mother, a prostitute, was brutally murdered with no one ever accused of the crime. With the spare time a suspension brings, Harry opens up the thirty-year-old file on the case and is irresistibly drawn into a past he has always avoided. It's clear that the case was fumbled and the smell of a cover-up is unmistakable. Someone powerful was able to divert justice and Harry vows to uncover the truth. As he relentlessly follows the broken pieces of the case, the stirred interest causes new murders and pushes Harry to the edge of his job... and his life.

Last Coyote. unabr. ed. Michael Connelly. Read by Dick Hill. (Running Time: 13 hrs.). (Harry Bosch Ser.: No. 4). 2005. 39.25 (978-1-59600-932-5(2), 9781596009325, BADLE); 24.95 (978-1-59600-931-8(4), 9781596009318, BAD); 29.95 (978-1-59600-926-4(8), 9781596009264, BAU); audio compact disk 39.25 (978-1-59600-930-1(6), 9781596009301, Brinc Audio MP3 Lib); audio compact disk 24.95 (978-1-59600-929-5(2), 9781596009295, Brilliance MP3); audio compact disk 112.25 (978-1-59600-928-8(4), 9781596009288, BriAudCD Unabrid); audio compact disk 38.95 (978-1-59600-927-1(6), 9781596009271, Bril Audio CD Unabri) Brilliance Audio.

***Last Coyote-ABR.** Michael Connelly & #4 Harry Bosch Series. 2010. audio compact disk 9.99 (978-1-4418-5661-6(7)) Brilliance Audio.

Last Crossing. abr. ed. Guy Vanderhaeghe. Read by John Henry Cox et al. (Playaway Adult Fiction Ser.). (ENG.). 2009. 59.99 (978-1-60812-737-5(0)) Find a World.

Last Dance see Paddington for Christmas

Last Dance. Ed McBain, pseud. (87th Precinct Ser.: Bk. 50). 2004. 15.95 (978-0-7435-1964-9(7)) Pub: S&S Audio. Dist(s): S and S Inc

Last Dance. abr. ed. Ed McBain, pseud & Ed McBain. Read by Ed McBain & Ed McBain. (Running Time: 4 hrs. 30 mins. 0 sec.). Bk. 50. (ENG.). 2007. audio compact disk 14.95 (978-0-7435-6098-6(1)) Pub: S&S Audio. Dist(s): S and S Inc

Last Dance. unabr. ed. Ed McBain, pseud. Read by Garrick Hagon. 8 CDs. (Running Time: 12 hrs.). (87th Precinct Ser.: Bk. 50). 2001. audio compact disk 79.95 (978-0-7927-9985-6(2), SLD 036, Chivers Sound Lib) AudioGO.
The hanging death of an old man in a shabby apartment in a meager section of the 87th Precinct, takes detectives Carella, Meyer, Brown & Weeks on a search through Isola's seedy strip clubs & to the bright lights of the Theatre district.

An Asterisk (*) at the beginning of an entry indicates that the title is appearing for the first time.

these changes & the physical limitations that come with age, is a true & distinctly individual story, the story of an American hero.

Last Fish Tale: The Fate of the Atlantic & Survival in Gloucester, America's Oldest Fishing Port & Most Original Town. unabr. ed. Mark Kurlansky. Read by Grover Gardner. (Running Time: 23400 sec.). 2008. 29.95 (978-1-4332-1478-3(4)); 54.95 (978-1-4332-1476-9(8)); audio compact disk 29.95 (978-1-4332-1480-6(6)); audio compact disk 90.00 (978-1-4332-1477-6(6)); audio compact disk & audio compact disk 29.95 (978-1-4332-1479-0(2)) Blckstn Audio.

***Last Flight.** (ENG.). 2010. audio compact disk (978-1-59171-260-2(2)) Falcon Picture.

Last Flight of the Dragon Lady. Contrib. by Bob Vernon & John Fornof. Prod. by Focus on the Family Staff. 2 CDs. (Last Chance Detectives Ser.). (ENG.). (YA). 2004. audio compact disk 14.97 (978-1-58997-271-1(6)) Pub: Focus Family. Dist(s): Tyndale Hse

Last Flight Of 007. Frank Woodson. Narrated by Larry A. McKeever. (Disaster Ser.). (J). 2002. audio compact disk 14.95 (978-1-58659-289-9(0)) Artesian.

Last Flight of 007. unabr. ed. Frank Woodson. Narrated by Larry A. McKeever. 1 cass. (Running Time: 40 min.). (Disaster Ser.). (J). 2002. 10.95 (978-1-58659-030-7(8), 54115) Artesian.

Last Four of Revelation's Seven Churches. Derek Prince. 1 cass. 5.95 (4369) Derek Prince.

The close of this age confronts us with a choice between two kinds of church: Philadelphia or Laodicea. Which will you choose?.

Last Free Bird. 2004. 8.95 (978-1-56008-945-2(8)); cass. & flmstrp 30.00 (978-1-56008-702-1(1)) Weston Woods.

Last Full Measure. abr. ed. Read by Stephen Lang. Ed. by Jeff Shaara. 4 cass. 1999. 25.95 (FS9-34649) Highsmith.

Last Full Measure, Pt. 1. unabr. collector's ed. Read by Dick Estell. Ed. by Jeff Shaara. 8 cass. (Running Time: 12 hrs.). 1998. 64.00 (978-0-7366-4209-5(9), 4708-A) Books on Tape.

Last Full Measure, Pt. 2. unabr. collector's ed. Read by Dick Estell. Ed. by Jeff Shaara. 8 cass. (Running Time: 12 hrs.). 1998. 64.00 (978-0-7366-4210-1(2), 4708-B) Books on Tape.

The final book in a Civil War trilogy follows Lee & Grant from the aftermath of Gettysburg to Appomattox. A magnificent historical novel.

Last Gentleman: A Novel. unabr. ed. Walker Percy. Read by Wolfram Kandinsky. 11 cass. (Running Time: 16 hrs.). 1994. 76.95 (978-0-7861-0420-8(1), 1372) Blckstn Audio.

The main narrative of the novel deals with Bill Barrett's adventures as he becomes involved in the complex troubles, loves, & fortunes of a Southern family, the Vaughts, who are living in the shadow of their youngest son's illness. The settings are New York & Livittown; a university town in Alabama; Shut Off, Louisiana; & finally Santa Fe, New Mexico. "The Last Gentleman" is an ambitious, eventful, funny, & compulsively readable novel about the dilemmas of modern man. It is sure to be acclaimed as the major work of one of the most original of all American writers.

Last Girls. Lee Smith. Narrated by Linda Stephens. 10 cass. (Running Time: 14 hrs. 45 mins.). 93.00 (978-1-4025-2512-4(5)) Recorded Bks.

Last Girls. abr. ed. Lee Smith. Read by Lee Smith. 10 CDs. (Running Time: 12 hrs. 30 mins.). 2002. audio compact disk 36.95 (978-1-56511-702-0(6), 1565117026) Pub: HighBridge. Dist(s): Workman Pub

Last Girls. unabr. ed. Lee Smith. Read by Lee Smith. (YA). 2006. 49.99 (978-1-59895-567-5(5)) Find a World.

Last Good Kiss. James Crumley. Read by James Crumley. 1 cass. (Running Time: 69 min.). 1992. 13.95 (978-1-55644-375-6(7), 12021) Am Audio Prose.

Crumley reads chapters one & eight from his much admired detective novel.

Last Good Kiss. James Crumley. Read by Rob McQuay. 6 cass. (Running Time: 9 hrs.). 1997. 48.00 (978-0-7366-3818-0(0), 4486) Books on Tape.

A Montana investigator traces a missing girl to the demimonde of Haight Ashbury.

***Last Goodbye.** abr. ed. Reed Arvin. Read by Dylan Baker. (ENG.). 2005. (978-0-06-082391-7(7), Harper Audio); (978-0-06-082390-0(9), Harper Audio) HarperCollins Pubs.

Last Gospel: A Multi-voiced Production Bringing 14 Characters to Life. unabr. ed. David Howard. 6 cass. (Running Time: 8 hrs. 30 min). 2000. 54.95 (978-1-58444-116-8(X)) DiscUs Bks.

Last Grain Race. unabr. ed. Eric Newby. Narrated by Michael Sinclair. 7 cass. (Running Time: 10 hrs.). 1989. 60.00 (978-1-55690-303-8(0), 89620E7) Recorded Bks.

A young man ships out on the "Moshulu," one of the last square riggers running grain to Australia. As the majestic tall ship sailed over history's horizon racing to be first into oblivion, the sky over Europe turned black.

Last Grain Race. unabr. collector's ed. Eric Newby. Read by Ken Scott. 7 cass. (Running Time: 10 hrs. 30 mins.). 1992. 56.00 (978-0-7366-2106-9(7), 2910) Books on Tape.

Sail on one of the last wind-driven sailing ships with the author as a young man.

Last Great Victory Pt. 1: The End of WW II. collector's ed. Stanley Weintraub. Read by Jonathan Reese. 11 cass. (Running Time: 16 hrs. 30 min.). 1997. 88.00 (978-0-7366-3810-4(5), 4479-A) Books on Tape.

For all parties, the last month of WW II was filled with tension & fear. A renowned historian brings this climate of anxiety to life.

Last Great Victory Pt. 2: The End of WW II. unabr. collector's ed. Stanley Weintraub. Read by Jonathan Reese. 11 cass. (Running Time: 16 hrs. 30 min.). 1997. 88.00 (978-0-7366-3811-1(3), 4479-B) Books on Tape.

Brings life to the tensions & fears of the last thirty days of World War II.

Last Gunfighter 1: The Drifter. Based on a novel by William W. Johnstone. (Last Gunfighter Ser.: No. 1). 2008. audio compact disk 19.99 (978-1-59950-462-9(6)) GraphicAudio.

Last Gunfighter 10: Manhunt. William W. Johnstone. (Last Gunfighter Ser.: No. 10). 2009. audio compact disk 19.99 (978-1-59950-559-6(2)) GraphicAudio.

Last Gunfighter 11: Violent Sunday. William W. Johnstone. (Last Gunfighter Ser.: No. 11). 2009. audio compact disk 19.99 (978-1-59950-575-6(4)) GraphicAudio.

Last Gunfighter 12: Renegades. William W. Johnstone. (Last Gunfighter Ser.: No. 12). 2009. audio compact disk 19.99 (978-1-59950-590-9(8)) GraphicAudio.

Last Gunfighter 13: Savage County. Based on a novel by William W. Johnstone. (Last Gunfighter Ser.: No. 13). 2009. audio compact disk 19.99 (978-1-59950-603-6(3)) GraphicAudio.

Last Gunfighter 14: The Devil's Legion. Based on a novel by William W. Johnstone & J. A. Johnstone. (Last Gunfighter Ser.: No. 14). 2009. audio compact disk 19.99 (978-1-59950-610-4(6)) GraphicAudio.

Last Gunfighter 15: Avenger. Based on a novel by William W. Johnstone. (Last Gunfighter Ser.: No. 15). 2010. audio compact disk 19.99 (978-1-59950-626-5(2)) GraphicAudio.

Last Gunfighter 16: Hell Town. Based on a novel by William W. Johnstone. (Last Gunfighter Ser.: No. 16). 2010. audio compact disk 19.99 (978-1-59950-633-3(5)) GraphicAudio.

***Last Gunfighter 17: Ambush Valley.** William W. Johnstone. (Last Gunfighter Ser.: No. 17). 2010. audio compact disk 19.99 (978-1-59950-651-7(3)) GraphicAudio.

***Last Gunfighter 18: Killing Ground.** William W. Johnstone. (Last Gunfighter Ser.: No. 18). 2010. audio compact disk 19.99 (978-1-59950-668-5(8)) GraphicAudio.

***Last Gunfighter 19: Slaughter.** William W. Johnstone. 2010. audio compact disk 19.99 (978-1-59950-685-2(8)) GraphicAudio.

Last Gunfighter 2: Reprisal. Based on a novel by William W. Johnstone. (Last Gunfighter Ser.: No. 2). 2008. audio compact disk 19.99 (978-1-59950-470-4(7)) GraphicAudio.

***Last Gunfighter 20: Sudden Fury.** William W. Johnstone. 2011. audio compact disk 19.99 (978-1-59950-732-3(3)) GraphicAudio.

Last Gunfighter 3: Ghost Valley. Based on a novel by William W. Johnstone. (Last Gunfighter Ser.: No. 4). 2008. audio compact disk 19.99 (978-1-59950-478-0(2)) GraphicAudio.

Last Gunfighter 4: The Forbidden. William W. Johnstone. (Last Gunfighter Ser.: No. 3). 2008. audio compact disk 19.99 (978-1-59950-494-0(4)) GraphicAudio.

Last Gunfighter 5: Showdown. William W. Johnstone. (Last Gunfighter Ser.: No. 6). 2008. audio compact disk Rental 19.99 (978-1-59950-501-5(0)) GraphicAudio.

Last Gunfighter 6: Imposter. William W. Johnstone. (Last Gunfighter Ser.: No. 5). 2008. audio compact disk 19.99 (978-1-59950-511-4(8)) GraphicAudio.

Last Gunfighter 7: Rescue. William W. Johnstone. (Last Gunfighter Ser.: No. 7). 2009. audio compact disk 19.99 (978-1-59950-517-6(7)) GraphicAudio.

Last Gunfighter 8: The Burning. William W. Johnstone. (Last Gunfighter Ser.: No. 8). 2009. audio compact disk 19.99 (978-1-59950-526-8(6)) GraphicAudio.

Last Gunfighter 9: No Man's Land. William W. Johnstone. (Last Gunfighter Ser.: No. 9). 2009. audio compact disk 19.99 (978-1-59950-556-5(8)) GraphicAudio.

Last Happy Hour. unabr. ed. Charles Hackett. Read by Jonathan Reese. 8 cass. (Running Time: 8 hrs.). 1979. 48.00 (978-0-7366-0172-6(4), 1174) Books on Tape.

Tells of three brilliant but incompetent officers who are removed from combat during World War II. Stationed on a French tugboat permanently moored in an English port, the three ride it out for the duration in circumstances of manic comedy. After 30 years the men find themselves reunited, a circumstance which provides the framework for this tale.

Last Harbinger. Roger Gregg. (Running Time: 2 hrs.). 2005. 21.95 (978-1-59912-940-2(X)) Iofy Corp.

Last Hawk. unabr. ed. Catherine Asaro. Read by Anna Fields. 10 cass. (Running Time: 15 hrs.). 2001. 69.95 (978-0-7861-2021-5(5), P2789) Blckstn Audio.

When Kelric, a scion of the imperial family of Skolia, crash-lands his fighter on the off-limits planet of Coba, he figures it will be only a short time before he makes his way home. But he fails to account for the powerful matriarchy of Coba, the mistresses of the great estates who do not want the Empire to know about their recent cultural advances. First they take him prisoner. Then, one by one, the most powerful women on the planet fall in love with him.

Last Hawk: A New Novel of the Skolian Empire. unabr. ed. Catherine Asaro. Read by Anna Fields. (Running Time: 50400 sec.). 2006. audio compact disk 99.00 (978-0-7861-6634-3(7)); audio compact disk 29.95 (978-0-7861-7351-8(3)) Blckstn Audio.

Last Hero. unabr. ed. Leslie Charteris. Read by David Case. 7 cass. (Running Time: 7 hrs.). (Saint Ser.). 1991. 42.00 (978-0-7366-1895-3(3), 2722) Books on Tape.

The Saint returns in another adventure of adversarial confrontation. This time we learn how the Saint first met Rayt Marius, an evil genius who finds in the Saint a superior intelligence & a stronger moral purpose. Dr. Marius is out to destroy the world & it's up to the Saint to stop him. He must beat Marius at his own game, neutralize a powerful death ray & rescue the world from catastrophe & war.

Last Hero, Pt. I. unabr. ed. Peter Forbath. Read by Robert Whitfield. 11 cass. (Running Time: 16 hrs.). 1999. 76.95 (978-0-7861-1674-4(9), 2502A,B) Blckstn Audio.

A famous explorer's heroic relief expedition to a beleaguered British outpost deep in the heart of Africa. The British Empire, at its zenith, is shocked by the fall of Khartoum & the murder of General Gordon. But word reaches London that all is not lost.

Last Hero, Pt. II. unabr. ed. Peter Forbath. Read by Robert Whitfield. 8 cass. (Running Time: 16 hrs.). 1999. 56.95 (978-0-7861-1713-0(3), 2502A,B) Blckstn Audio.

Last Hero: A Life of Henry Aaron. abr. ed. Howard Bryant. Read by Dominic M. Hoffman. (ENG.). 2010. audio compact disk 35.00 (978-0-307-73688-8(1), Random AudioBks) Pub: Random Audio Pubg. Dist(s): Random

Last Hero: The Life of Mickey Mantle. David Falkner. Read by Jonathan Marosz. 2000. 48.00 (978-0-7366-5907-9(2)) Books on Tape.

Last Hero: The Life of Mickey Mantle. unabr. ed. David Falkner. Read by Jonathan Morosz. 6 cass. (Running Time: 7 hrs. 30 min.). 2000. 48.00 Books on Tape.

Mickey Mantle was one of the greatest baseball players ever at a time when baseball was the only sport that mattered.

Last Heroes, unabr. ed. W. E. B. Griffin. Read by Michael Mitchell. 8 cass. (Running Time: 12 hrs.). (Men at War Ser.: No. 1). 1998. 64.00 (978-0-7366-4907-0(5), 4602) Books on Tape.

June 1941. In preparation for war, President Roosevelt assembles the most complex espionage organization in history, the Office of Strategic Services. Young & daring, the officers of the OSS disperse throughout the world to conduct operations on which may hinge the outcome of the war.

Last Hill in a Vista **see Twentieth-Century Poetry in English, No. 2, Recordings of Poets Reading Their Own Poetry**

Last Holiday Concert. Andrew Clements. Read by Fred Berman. 2 cass. (J). 2004. 23.00 (978-1-4000-9470-7(4), Listening Lib); audio compact disk 25.50 (978-1-4000-9493-6(3), Listening Lib) Pub: Random Audio Pubg. Dist(s): NetLibrary CO

Last Honest Woman. unabr. ed. Nora Roberts. Read by Marie Caliendo. (Running Time: 7 hrs.). (O'Hurleys Ser.). 2009. 14.99 (978-1-4418-3001-2(4), 9781441830012, Brilliance MP3); 39.97 (978-1-4418-2999-3(7), 9781441829993, Brlnc Audio MP3 Lib); 39.97 (978-1-4418-3000-5(6), 9781441830005, BADLE); audio compact disk 24.99 (978-1-4418-2996-2(2), 9781441829962, Bril Audio CD Unabri); audio compact disk 79.97 (978-1-4418-2997-9(0), 9781441829979, BriAudCD Unabrid) Brilliance Audio.

***Last Honest Woman.** unabr. ed. Nora Roberts. Read by Marie Caliendo. (Running Time: 7 hrs.). (O'Hurleys Ser.). 2010. audio compact disk 14.99 (978-1-61106-123-9(7), 9781611061239, BCD Value Price) Brilliance Audio.

Last Hostage. abr. ed. John J. Nance. Read by John J. Nance. 4 cass. Library ed. (Running Time: 6 hrs.). 2003. 62.25 (978-1-59086-669-6(X), 159086669X, CD Lib Edit); audio compact disk 74.25 (978-1-59086-865-2(X), 159086865X, BACDLib Ed) Brilliance Audio.

High above the Rocky Mountains, a routine airline flight becomes a midair standoff as 130 passengers listen to their captain relate the unprecedented demands of an unseen hijacker. Federal and state officials must hunt down, arrest, and indict the murderer of a young girl, and do it all in eight hours - or the airplane will be blown out of the sky. With the airline in confusion, the media pursuing, and the hijacker forcing the aircraft into wild maneuvers as they head toward Salt Lake City, the FBI reluctantly fields its closest hostage negotiator, a rookie female agent and psychologist named Katherine Bronsky. Immediately, Bronsky finds herself sucked into the vortex of an impossible war of wills between a volatile, unstable hijacker holding the trigger to a bomb and stonewalling Justice Department officials who have no real intention of meeting the lone gunman's demands. When the hijacker suddenly refuses to land at Salt Lake City, Kat commandeers a business jet and races after the low-flying 737. As the jetliner runs low on fuel, she's stunned to discover that the man with the gun is none other than the murdered girl's father, and that one of his hostages is a front-runner to become the new Attorney General of the United States. Successful at last in getting him to land in a remote Colorado airport, Bronsky's brave and desperate attempts to reason with the hijacker backfire, and she becomes a hostage herself. Now discounted and ignored by her superiors in Washington for losing control, Bronsky's only hope to save the passengers and crew of AirBridge Flight 90 is to solve the wrenching mystery of who killed an eleven-year-old girl in a dark Connecticut forest two years before. And for that, all she has is an airborne phone and precious few hours before the bomb detonates. Nance ratchets up the tension with expertly crafted twists and turns that converge into an unforgettably wrenching dilemma. But one thing finally becomes clear. The only person who can safely land AirBridge Flight 90 and save its 130 passengers is dangerously close to death. And if the clock runs out, The Last Hostage will never see the light of day.

Last Hostage. abr. ed. John J. Nance. Read by John J. Nance. (Running Time: 6 hrs.). 2006. 39.25 (978-1-4233-0120-2(X), 9781423301202, BADLE); 39.25 (978-1-4233-0118-9(8), 9781423301189, Brlnc Audio MP3 Lib); audio compact disk 24.95 (978-1-4233-0117-2(X), 9781423301172, Brilliance MP3) Brilliance Audio.

Last Hostage. abr. ed. John J. Nance. Read by John J. Nance. (Running Time: 6 hrs.). 2006. 24.95 (978-1-4233-0119-6(6), 9781423301196, BAD) Brilliance Audio.

***Last Hunt.** Bruce Coville. (ENG.). (YA). 2010. audio compact disk 85.00 (978-1-936223-18-3(X)) Full Cast Audio.

Last Hymn: Rev. 22:13-21. Ed Young. 1987. 4.95 (978-0-7417-1588-3(0), 588) Win Walk.

Last in Convoy. unabr. ed. James Pattinson. 8 CDs. 2007. audio compact disk 79.95 (978-1-84559-511-1(4)) Pub: Soundings Ltd GBR. Dist(s): Ulverscroft US

Last in Convoy. unabr. ed. James Pattinson. Read by Terry Wale. 8 cass. 2007. 69.95 (978-1-84559-467-1(3)) Pub: Soundings Ltd GBR. Dist(s): Ulverscroft US

Last Innocent Man. Read by Michael Russotto. Ed. by Phillip Margolin. 6 cass. (Running Time: 9 hrs.). 1996. 48.00 (978-0-7366-3290-4(3), 3945) Books on Tape.

A lawyer & family man is accused of killing a cop. The Ice Man, David Nash defends him despite doubts.

***Last Innocent Man.** unabr. ed. Phillip Margolin. (Running Time: 8 hrs.). 2010. 39.97 (978-1-61106-224-3(1), 9781611062243, BADLE); 14.99 (978-1-61106-223-6(3), 9781611062236, BAD) Brilliance Audio.

***Last Innocent Man.** unabr. ed. Phillip Margolin. Read by Christopher Lane. (Running Time: 8 hrs.). 2010. 39.97 (978-1-61106-222-9(5), 9781611062229, Brlnc Audio MP3 Lib); 14.99 (978-1-61106-221-2(7), 9781611062212, Brilliance MP3); audio compact disk 69.97 (978-1-61106-220-5(9), 9781611062205, BriAudCD Unabrid); audio compact disk 19.99 (978-1-61106-219-9(5), 9781611062199, Bril Audio CD Unabri) Brilliance Audio.

Last Innocent Man. unabr. ed. Read by Michael Russotto. Ed. by Phillip Margolin. 6 cass. (Running Time: 9 hrs.). 1996. 48.00 Set. (3945) Books on Tape.

The papers call him the Ice Man. David Nash, a defense attorney, is cool & unruffled - almost unbeatable in the courtroom. Most of his clients are guilty, a few of them monsters. Suddenly, Nash is tortured by questions: what is the cost of each rapist & killer set free to society - & to his soul?.

Last Jihad. Joel C. Rosenberg. 2009. audio compact disk 9.99 (978-1-4418-2662-6(9)) Brilliance Audio.

Last Jihad. unabr. ed. Joel C. Rosenberg. Read by Dick Hill. (Running Time: 10 hrs.). 2004. 24.95 (978-1-59710-443-2(4), 1597104434, BAD) Brilliance Audio.

***Last Jihad.** unabr. ed. Joel C. Rosenberg. Read by Dick Hill. (Running Time: 10 hrs.). 2010. audio compact disk 89.97 (978-1-4418-4020-2(6), 9781441840202, BriAudCD Unabrid) Brilliance Audio.

***Last Jihad.** unabr. ed. Joel C. Rosenberg & Thriller. Read by Dick Hill. 8 CDs. (Running Time: 10 hrs.). 2010. audio compact disk 29.99 (978-1-4418-3989-3(5), 9781441839893) Brilliance Audio.

Last Jihad: A Novel. abr. ed. Joel C. Rosenberg. Read by Dick Hill. (Running Time: 4 hrs.). 2004. audio compact disk 69.25 (978-1-59355-856-7(2), 1593558562, BACDLib Ed); audio compact disk 14.99 (978-1-59355-855-0(4), 1593558554, BCD Value Price) Brilliance Audio.

Jon Bennett is a top Wall Street strategist turned senior White House advisor. But nothing has prepared him for the terror that he will face. Saddam Hussein dispatches his top hit men to assassinate the President of the United States. Iraqi terrorists spread carnage throughout London, Paris, and Riyadh...and the Butcher of Baghdad has a nuclear ace in his hand that he has not yet played. Only a solid Arab-Israeli coalition against Iraq can keep the U.S. and other Western nations from certain devastation. And only Bennett and his beautiful partner, Erin McCoy, can make that happen. Their secret project - a billion dollar oil deal off the coast of Gaza - could be the basis for an historic peace treaty and enormous wealth for every Israeli and Palestinian. But just before the treaty can be signed, Israeli commandos foil an Iraqi scud missile launch, recovering a nuclear warhead and evidence that the next attack will level Washington, New York, and Tel Aviv. Now, the Israeli prime minister gives the American President an ultimatum: melt down Baghdad within one hour...or Israel will do it herself. From Jerusalem, Bennett and McCoy must summon all of their stealth and savvy to save themselves - and the world - from absolute destruction.

Last Jihad: A Novel. unabr. ed. Joel C. Rosenberg. Read by Dick Hill. 6 cass. (Running Time: 10 hrs.). 2002. 29.95 (978-1-59086-636-8(3), 1590866363,

Last Man on the Moon. abr. ed. Eugene Cernan. Read by Eugene Cernan. (Running Time: 6 hrs.). 2009. 39.97 (978-1-4233-8647-6(7), 9781423386476, Brinc Audio MP3 Lib); 39.97 (978-1-4233-8649-0(3), 9781423386490, BADLE); 24.99 (978-1-4233-8646-9(9), 9781423386469, Brilliance MP3); 24.99 (978-1-4233-8648-3(5), 9781423386483, BAD) Brilliance Audio.

Last Man Out: The Story of the Springhill Mine Disaster. Melissa Fay Greene. Narrated by Henry Strozier. 8 cass. (Running Time: 10 hrs.). 2002. 70.00 (978-1-4025-3868-1(5)) Recorded Bks.

Last Man Out: The Story of the Springhill Mine Disaster. Melissa Fay Greene. 6 cass. (Running Time: 9 hrs. 45 mins.). 2004. 29.99 (978-1-4025-3626-7(7), 02554) Recorded Bks.

Last Man Standing. David Baldacci. Narrated by Jason Culp. 19 CDs. (Running Time: 22 hrs.). audio compact disk 174.00 (978-1-4025-1769-3(6)) Recorded Bks.

Last Man Standing. David Baldacci. Narrated by Jason Culp. 15 CDs. (Running Time: 21 hrs.). 2002. audio compact disk 20.50 (96857) Recorded Bks.
Web London, a member of the FBI's elite Hostage Rescue Team, roars into a darkened alley one night with his team members, only to be ambushed seconds later. He's the sole survivor, and the cloud of suspicion is upon him. He seeks the help of psychiatrist Claire Daniels, as he searches to discover what really happened that deadly night.

Last Man Standing. abr. ed. David Baldacci. Read by Ron McLarty. (ENG.). 2005. 14.98 (978-1-59483-264-2(1)); audio compact disk 14.98 (978-1-59483-080-8(0)) Pub: Hachet Audio. Dist(s): HachBkGrp

Last Man Standing. unabr. ed. David Baldacci. Read by Jason Culp. 15 cass. (Running Time: 22 hrs. 30 mins.). 2001. 44.98 Books on Tape.
An FBI agent's Hostage Rescue Team is massacred; he is both the sole survivor and the prime suspect.

Last Man Standing. unabr. ed. David Baldacci. Read by Jason Culp. (ENG.). 2005. 16.98 (978-1-59483-396-0(6)) Pub: Hachet Audio. Dist(s): HachBkGrp

Last Man Standing. unabr. ed. David Baldacci. Read by Jason Culp. (Running Time: 22 hrs. 30 mins.). (ENG.). 2009. 74.98 (978-1-60788-070-7(9)) Pub: Hachet Audio. Dist(s): HachBkGrp

Last Man Standing. unabr. ed. David Baldacci. Narrated by Jason Culp. 15 cass. (Running Time: 22 hrs.). 2002. 122.00 (978-0-7887-9925-9(8), 96857) Recorded Bks.
A boobytrap destroys an entire FBI Hostage Rescue Team on a drug raid in a Washington, D.C. alley. The only man to survive the blazing steel from the .50 calibers is Special Agent Web London, the team's leader who mysteriously freezes up at a crucial moment. Now everyone in the Bureau is wondering how - or why - Web was the only man left alive. Soon, Web is on a mission to find out who's responsible for the ambush. But first he needs to find a missing undercover operative and a small boy.

Last Man Standing: The Landen Legacy. Cory D. Carpenter. 2007. audio compact disk 19.99 (978-1-60247-683-7(7)) Tate Pubng.

Last Marlin: A Father-Son Story. unabr. ed. Fred Waitzkin. Read by Lloyd James. 7 cass. (Running Time: 10 hrs. 30 mins.). 2001. 49.95 (2707) Blckstn Audio.
Young Fred is a Jewish boy that grows up in the fifties stretched between the divergent values of parents who cannot tolerate one another.

***Last Marlin: The Story of a Father & Son.** unabr. ed. Fred Waitzkin. Read by Lloyd James. (Running Time: 10 hrs. NaN mins.). (ENG.). 2011. 29.95 (978-1-4417-8484-1(5)); audio compact disk 90.00 (978-1-4417-8482-7(9)) Blckstn Audio.

Last Mile Home. Read by Bruce Kerr. Perf. by Di Morrissey. 4 cass. (Running Time: 6 hrs.). 2001. (500431) Bolinda Pubng AUS.

last mile Home. Di Morrissey. Read by Bruce Kerr. (Running Time: 5 hrs. 55 mins.). 2009. 69.99 (978-1-74214-266-1(4), 9781742142661) Pub: Bolinda Pubng AUS. Dist(s): Bolinda Pub Inc

Last Mile Home. unabr. ed. Di Morrissey. Read by Bruce Kerr. 6 CDs. (Running Time: 5 hrs. 55 mins.). 2005. audio compact disk 77.95 (978-1-74030-956-1(1)) Pub: Bolinda Pubng AUS. Dist(s): Bolinda Pub Inc

Last Mission. unabr. ed. Harry Mazer. 1 cass. (Running Time: 1 hr. 14 min.). (Young Adult Cliffhangers Ser.). (YA). (gr. 7 up). 1985. 15.98 incl. bk. & guide. (978-0-8072-1822-8(7), JRH111SP, Listening Lib) Random Audio Pubg.
The story of a 15 year-old American Jewish boy who lies his way into military service in World War II.

Last Mission. unabr. ed. Harry Mazer. Narrated by George Guidall. 4 cass. (Running Time: 5 hrs. 15 mins.). (gr. 8). 1992. 35.00 (978-1-55690-596-4(3), 92201E7) Recorded Bks.
Jack Raab joins a bomber crew in 1944 to fly missions over Germany. Jack, a 15-year-old, uses a false I.D. & lies his way into the U.S. Air Force. Shot down behind enemy lines he is sent to a German POW camp. It is a dangerous situation for any Allied pilot, but it is especially dangerous for Jack, who is now a Jew on Nazi soil.

***Last Narco: Inside the Hunt for el Chapo, the World's Most-Wanted Drug Lord.** unabr. ed. Malcolm Beith. (Running Time: 8 hrs. 0 mins. 0 sec.). (ENG.). 2010. 24.99 (978-1-4001-6895-8(3)); 16.99 (978-1-4001-8895-6(4)); audio compact disk 34.99 (978-1-4001-1895-3(6)) Pub: Tantor Media. Dist(s): IngramPubServ

***Last Narco (Library Edition) Inside the Hunt for el Chapo, the World's Most-Wanted Drug Lord.** unabr. ed. Malcolm Beith. (Running Time: 8 hrs. 0 mins. 0 sec.). (ENG.). 2010. audio compact disk 83.99 (978-1-4001-4895-0(2)) Pub: Tantor Media. Dist(s): IngramPubServ

Last Night. Contrib. by Karen Peck & New River. (Soundtraks Ser.). 2007. audio compact disk 8.99 (978-5-557-56223-2(0)) Christian Wrld.

Last Night at Chateau Marmont. abr. ed. Lauren Weisberger. (Running Time: 6 hrs. 0 mins. 0 sec.). 2010. audio compact disk 29.99 (978-0-7435-8380-0(9)) Pub: S&S Audio. Dist(s): S and S Inc

Last Night at Chateau Marmont. unabr. ed. Lauren Weisberger. (Running Time: 13 hrs. 30 mins. 0 sec.). 2010. audio compact disk 39.99 (978-1-4423-0448-2(0)) Pub: S&S Audio. Dist(s): S and S Inc

Last Night at the Lobster. unabr. ed. Stewart O'Nan. Read by Jonathan Davis. 3 CDs. (Running Time: 5 hrs.). 2007. audio compact disk 39.95 (978-0-7927-5045-1(4)) AudioGO.
Perched in the far corner of a run-down New England mall, the Red Lobster hasn't been making its numbers and headquarters has pulled the plug. But manager Manny DeLeon still needs to navigate a tricky last shift. With only four shopping days left until Christmas, Manny must convince his near-mutinous staff to hunker down and serve the final onslaught of hungry retirees, lunatics, and holiday office parties. All the while, he's wondering how to handle the waitress he's still in love with, his pregnant girlfriend at home, and where to find the present that will make everything better.. Last Night at the Lobster is a poignant yet redemptive look at what a man does when he discovers that his best might not be good enough.

Last Night at the Lobster. unabr. ed. Stewart O'Nan. Read by Jonathan Davis. (YA). 2008. 39.99 (978-1-60514-591-4(2)) Find a World.

Last Night at the Lobster. unabr. ed. Stewart O'Nan. Narrated by Jonathan Davis. (Running Time: 13800 sec.). (ENG.). 2007. audio compact disk 19.95 (978-1-60283-304-3(4)) Pub: AudioGO. Dist(s): Perseus Dist

***Last Night in Twisted River.** unabr. ed. John Irving. Read by Arthur Morey. 20 CDs. (Running Time: 24 hrs. 30 mins.). 2009. audio compact disk 100.00 (978-1-4159-6576-4(5), BksonTape) Pub: Random Audio Pubg. Dist(s): Random

Last Night in Twisted River. unabr. ed. John Irving. Read by Arthur Morey. (ENG.). 2009. audio compact disk 60.00 (978-0-7393-2032-7(7), Random AudioBks) Pub: Random Audio Pubg. Dist(s): Random

***Last Night of a Jockey.** 2010. audio compact disk (978-1-59171-193-3(2)) Falcon Picture.

Last Noel. Heather Graham. Read by Christopher Lane. (Playaway Adult Fiction Ser.). (ENG.). 2009. 59.99 (978-1-60775-674-3(9)) Find a World.

Last Noel. unabr. ed. Heather Graham. Read by Christopher Lane. (Running Time: 6 hrs.). 2007. 39.25 (978-1-4233-4394-3(8), 9781423343943, BADLE); 24.95 (978-1-4233-4393-6(X), 9781423343936, BAD); 74.25 (978-1-4233-4388-2(3), 9781423343882, BrilAudUnabridg); audio compact disk 39.25 (978-1-4233-4392-9(1), 9781423343929, Brinc Audio MP3 Lib); audio compact disk 82.25 (978-1-4233-4390-5(5), 9781423343905, BriAudCD Unabrid); audio compact disk 29.95 (978-1-4233-4389-9(1), 9781423343899, Bril Audio CD Unabri); audio compact disk 24.95 (978-1-4233-4391-2(3), 9781423343912, Brilliance MP3) Brilliance Audio.

Last Noel: A Christmas Musical for Children. Composed by Ruth Schram & Scott Schram. Contrib. by Tim Hayden. (ENG.). 2007. audio compact disk 14.95 (978-0-7390-4484-1(2)); audio compact disk 59.95 (978-0-7390-4485-8(0)) Alfred Pub.

Last of Squire Ennismore see Weird Stories

Last of the Amazons. Steven Pressfield. 10 cass. (Running Time: 14 hrs. 30 mins.). 106.00 (978-1-4025-1900-0(1)) Recorded Bks.

***Last of the Breed.** unabr. ed. Louis L'Amour. Read by David Strathairn. (ENG.). 2010. audio compact disk 30.00 (978-0-307-73754-0(3), Random AudioBks) Pub: Random Audio Pubg. Dist(s): Random

Last of the Dixie Heroes. unabr. ed. Peter Abrahams. Read by Buck Schirner. 6 cass. (Running Time: 9 hrs.). 2001. 29.95 (978-1-58788-271-5(X), 158788271X, BAU); 57.25 (978-1-58788-272-2(8), 1587882728, Unabridge Lib Edns) Brilliance Audio.
Roy Hill married the girl of his dreams, dotes on his eleven-year-old son, and is next in line for a big promotion in the Atlanta office of a global corporation. Then, almost imperceptibly it all starts to unravel. He is losing control of his life. When his best friend joins a Civil War reenactment group, spending his weekends in camps where the year is forever 1863, Roy finds the idea laughable . . . even though he is the descendent and namesake of a Confederate Civil War hero. But when he visits the regiment just to be polite, something unexpected happens, gradually opening Roy's eyes to the secret of a distant conflict that never ended - and leading him down a path that grows more menacing at every turn. With his job disappearing in a way he could never have foreseen, his whole life slipping out of control, Roy falls deeper and deeper into the Rebel past. A strange and powerful idea takes hold: that his life went wrong long before he was born, in the fateful campaigns that preceded the burning of Atlanta. Among the men, a hard-core splinter group is formed - with Roy at its center. On an ancient battlefield, the once-clear lines between reenactment and reality begin to disappear. When his son is taken hostage is it real? When the old muskets fire will they still fire blanks? Or will a bloody history come stunningly to life? An extraordinary novel about the fate of men and women no longer in step with the rhythms of the modern world, marching back into Southern history to make things right, Last of the Dixie Heroes is Peter Abrahams's most dazzlingly original work yet.

Last of the Dixie Heroes. unabr. ed. Peter Abrahams. Read by Buck Schirner. (Running Time: 9 hrs.). 2005. 39.25 (978-1-59600-723-9(0), 9781596007239, BADLE); 24.95 (978-1-59600-722-2(2), 9781596007222, BAD); 39.25 (978-1-59600-721-5(4), 9781596007215, Brinc Audio MP3 Lib); 24.95 (978-1-59600-720-8(6), 9781596007208, Brilliance MP3) Brilliance Audio.

Last of the Mohicans see Último de los Mohicanos

Last of the Mohicans. Abr. by Marvin Alts. Based on a book by James Fenimore Cooper. (ENG.). 2007. 5.00 (978-1-60339-097-2(9)); audio compact disk 5.00 (978-1-60339-098-9(7)) Listenr Digest.

Last of the Mohicans. James Fenimore Cooper. Narrated by Jim Killavey. (Running Time: 14 hrs. 30 mins.). 1993. 35.95 (978-1-59912-823-8(3)) Iofy Corp.

Last of the Mohicans. James Fenimore Cooper. Read by Hope, William Hope. (Running Time: 4 hrs.). 2000. 24.95 (978-1-60083-807-1(3)) Iofy Corp.

Last of the Mohicans. James Fenimore Cooper. Read by Fabio Camero. (Running Time: 3 hrs.). 2002. 16.95 (978-1-60083-186-7(9), Audiofy Corp) Iofy Corp.

Last of the Mohicans. James Fenimore Cooper. Narrated by Theodore Bikel. (Running Time: 2 hrs. 30 mins.). (J). 2006. 14.95 (978-1-59912-984-6(1)) Iofy Corp.

Last of the Mohicans. James Fenimore Cooper. Read by William Hope. 3 cass. (Running Time: 4 hrs.). 1996. 17.98 (978-962-634-587-0(X), NA308714, Naxos AudioBooks) Naxos.
The story of the intrepid frontiersman & scout, Natty Bumppo, known as Hawkeye & his closest companion, Mohican Chief Chingachgook & Chingachgook's son, Uncas, the last surviving member of the Mohican tribe.

Last of the Mohicans. James Fenimore Cooper & Bill Bowler. (Dominoes Ser.). 2003. 19.50 (978-0-19-424387-2(7)) OUP.

Last of the Mohicans. abr. ed. James Fenimore Cooper. Read by William Hope. 3 CDs. (Running Time: 4 hrs.). 1996. audio compact disk 22.98 (978-962-634-087-5(8), NA308712, Naxos AudioBooks) Naxos.

Last of the Mohicans. abr. ed. James Fenimore Cooper. Read by Lou Diamond Phillips. 2 cass. (Running Time: 3 hrs.). 2004. 18.00 (978-1-59007-122-9(0)) Pub: New Millenn Enter. Dist(s): PerseuPGW
It is 1757. The English and French are engaged in a savage, bloody war for control of the North American continent. Making tenuous, shifting alliances with various Indian tribes, the two European powers struggle to gain the upper hand on unfamiliar, forested battlegrounds. Caught in the middle is Hawkeye, a white scout who was raised among the Indians. Not fully belonging to either world, Hawkeye has learned to respect the best of both civilizations. But with war swirling around him, Hawkeye must finally struggle to save his own life and those of a small band of colonists.

Last of the Mohicans. unabr. ed. James Fenimore Cooper. Read by Wolfram Kandinsky. 13 cass. (Running Time: 19 hrs. 30 min.). 1993. 85.95 (978-0-7861-0453-6(8), 1405) Blckstn Audio.
The setting for this historical romance is the French & Indian War, a war which pitted England & its American colonists against the French & their Indian allies. While the French & Indians besiege Fort William Henry on Lake George, Cora & Alice Munro, daughters of the English commander, are on their way to join their father, accompanied by Major Duncan Heyward (Alice's fiance), the singing teacher David Gamut, & the treacherous Indian Magua, who secretly serves the French. Magua's plan to betray the party to the Iroquois is foiled by the scout Hawkeye (Natty Bumppo) & his companions, old chief Chingachgook & his son Uncas, the "last of the Mohicans." This trio of loyal & stalwart friends - who embody a code of manly purity, honor, & heroics - are involved in a series of attacks, captures, fights, & rescues, in their quest to protect the virtuous sisters from the evil Magua & his band of Iroquois thugs.

***Last of the Mohicans.** unabr. ed. James Fenimore Cooper. Read by Stefan Rudnicki. (Running Time: 15 hrs. 0 mins.). 2010. 85.95 (978-1-4332-9203-3(3)); audio compact disk 32.95 (978-1-4332-9206-4(8)); audio compact disk 123.00 (978-1-4332-9204-0(1)) Blckstn Audio.

Last of the Mohicans. unabr. ed. James Fenimore Cooper. Read by Bill Weideman. (Running Time: 15 hrs.). 2004. 39.25 (978-1-59335-372-8(3), 1593353723, Brinc Audio MP3 Lib) Brilliance Audio.
The Last of the Mohicans is a story of romance and adventure on the American frontier. It is a story of love and loyalty, and of America's coming of age. While the French and Indians besiege Fort William Henry, Cora and Alice Munro, daughters of the English commander, are on their way to join him. They are accompanied by Major Duncan Heyward, Alice's fiance, and by the treacherous Indian Magua, who secretly serves the French. Magua plans to betray the party to the Iroquois, and to claim Cora as his squaw, but he is foiled by the scout Hawkeye and his companions, Chingachgook and his son Uncas, who deliver the girls to their father. After the fall of the fort, the girls are given safe passage by the French, but Magua captures them and they become prisoners of the Indians. To rescue Alice and Cora, Hawkeye and Uncas lead the Mohicans against the Hurons, an action filled with unforeseen consequences for all of them.

Last of the Mohicans. unabr. ed. James Fenimore Cooper. Read by Bill Weideman. (Running Time: 15 hrs.). 2004. 39.25 (978-1-59710-447-0(7), 1597104477, BADLE); 24.95 (978-1-59710-446-3(9), 1597104469, BAD) Brilliance Audio.

Last of the Mohicans. unabr. ed. James Fenimore Cooper. Read by Bill Weideman. (Running Time: 54000 sec.). (Classic Collection (Brilliance Audio) Ser.). 2005. audio compact disk 112.25 (978-1-59737-136-0(X), 9781597371360, BriAudCD Unabrid); audio compact disk 44.95 (978-1-59737-135-3(1), 9781597371353, Bril Audio CD Unabri) Brilliance Audio.

Last of the Mohicans. unabr. ed. James Fenimore Cooper. Read by William Costello. (YA). 2006. 64.99 (978-1-59895-681-8(7)) Find a World.

Last of the Mohicans. unabr. ed. James Fenimore Cooper. Read by Jim Killavey. 11 cass. (Running Time: 15 hrs. 15 min.). 1984. 69.00 (C-112) Jimcin Record.
Famous tale of the last "noble savage".

Last of the Mohicans, unabr. ed. James Fenimore Cooper. Narrated by Larry McKeever. 11 cass. (Running Time: 15 hrs. 30 mins.). 2001. 91.00 (978-1-55690-298-7(0), 89630E7) Recorded Bks.
Hawkeye & Chingachgook are caught up in the French & Indian War in 1757.

Last of the Mohicans. unabr. ed. James Fenimore Cooper. Read by Bill Weideman. (Running Time: 15 hrs.). 2004. 24.95 (978-1-59335-097-0(X), 159335097X) Soulmate Audio Bks.
The Last of the Mohicans is a story of romance and adventure on the American frontier. It is a story of love and loyalty, and of America's coming of age. While the French and Indians besiege Fort William Henry, Cora and Alice Munro, daughters of the English commander, are on their way to join him. They are accompanied by Major Duncan Heyward, Alice's fiance, and by the treacherous Indian Magua, who secretly serves the French. Magua plans to betray the party to the Iroquois, and to claim Cora as his squaw, but he is foiled by the scout Hawkeye and his companions, Chingachgook and his son Uncas, who deliver the girls to their father. After the fall of the fort, the girls are given safe passage by the French, but Magua captures them and they become prisoners of the Indians. To rescue Alice and Cora, Hawkeye and Uncas lead the Mohicans against the Hurons, an action filled with unforeseen consequences for all of them.

Last of the Mohicans. unabr. ed. James Fenimore Cooper. Narrated by William Costello. (Running Time: 15 hrs. 0 mins. 0 sec.). (ENG.). 2009. audio compact disk 72.99 (978-1-4001-4080-0(3)); audio compact disk 35.99 (978-1-4001-1080-3(7)) Pub: Tantor Media. Dist(s): IngramPubServ

Last of the Mohicans. unabr. ed. James Fenimore Cooper. Read by William Costello. (Running Time: 15 hrs. 0 mins. 0 sec.). (Tantor Unabridged Classics Ser.). (ENG.). 2009. 27.99 (978-1-4001-6080-8(4)) Pub: Tantor Media. Dist(s): IngramPubServ

***Last of the Mohicans.** unabr. ed. James Fenimore Cooper. Read by Stefan Rudnicki. (Running Time: 15 hrs. 0 mins.). 2010. 29.95 (978-1-4332-9207-1(6)) Blckstn Audio.

Last of the Mohicans. unabr. abr. ed. James Fenimore Cooper. Read by Lou Diamond Philips. (Running Time: 9000 sec.). 2007. audio compact disk 24.00 (978-1-4332-0547-7(5)) Blckstn Audio.

Last of the Mohicans. unabr. abr. ed. James Fenimore Cooper. Read by Lou Diamond Phillips. (Running Time: 9000 sec.). 2007. audio compact disk 19.95 (978-1-4332-0548-4(3)) Blckstn Audio.

Last of the Mohicans. unabr. collector's ed. James Fenimore Cooper. Read by William Costello & Jim Killavey. 11 cass. (Running Time: 16 hrs. 30 mins.). (YA). 1994. 88.00 (978-0-7366-2687-3(5), 3422) Books on Tape.
The white frontiersman Hawkeye is nobly matched with Uncas, the Indian of the title.

Last of the Mohicans, Set. James Fenimore Cooper. Read by Flo Gibson. 10 cass. (Running Time: 14 hrs.). 44.95 (978-1-55685-399-9(8)) Audio Bk Con.
Pursuit, escape, capture & death in the forest near Fort Henry during the French & Indian wars are part of this sweeping tale of gallantry, treachery & friendship in the wilderness of 18th century upstate New York.

Last of the Mohicans, Set. unabr. ed. James Fenimore Cooper. Read by Wolfram Kandinsky. 13 cass. 1999. 85.95 (FS9-34207) Highsmith.

***Last of the Mohicans Audio Book CD: Bring the Classics to Life.** adpt. ed. James Fenimore Cooper. (Bring the Classics to Life Ser.). (J). 2008. audio compact disk 12.95 (978-1-55576-584-2(X)) EDCON Pubng.

***Last of the Mohicans: Bring the Classics to Life.** adpt. ed. James Fenimore Cooper. (Bring the Classics to Life Ser.). 2008. pap. bk. 21.95 (978-1-55576-654-2(4)) EDCON Pubng.

Last of the Nephilim. unabr. ed. Bryan Davis. Narrated by Peter Sandon. (Oracles of Fire Ser.). (ENG.). (J). 2008. 10.49 (978-1-60814-275-0(2)) Oasis Audio.

Last of the Nephilim. unabr. ed. Bryan Davis. Read by Peter Sandon. (Running Time: 13 hrs. 25 mins. 29 sec.). (Oracles of Fire Ser.). (ENG.). (J). 2009. audio compact disk 39.99 (978-1-59859-632-8(2)) Oasis Audio.

Last of the Plainsmen. Zane Grey. Narrated by Adams Morgan. (Running Time: 8 hrs. 30 mins.). 1999. 27.95 (978-1-59912-680-7(X)) Iofy Corp.

Last of the Plainsmen. unabr. ed. Zane Grey. Read by Adams Morgan. 6 cass. (Running Time: 8 hrs. 30 mins.). 2000. 44.95 (978-0-7861-1804-5(0),

2603); audio compact disk 56.00 (978-0-7861-9863-4(X), 2603) Blckstn Audio.
Speaks firsthand of the great man's courage & prowess; how Buffalo Jones roped the ferocious cougar & took it, clawing & spitting, back to camp; how he nearly captured White King, the glorious leader of a herd of wild mustangs; & how the whole party made camp under the Aurora Borealis & hunted polar wolves.

***Last of the Summer Wine, Vol. 1.** Created by Roy Clarke. Narrated by Full Cast Production Staff. 2 CDs. (Running Time: 2 hrs. 0 mins. 0 sec.). (ENG.). 2010. audio compact disk 24.95 (978-0-563-49509-3(X)) Pub: AudioGO. Dist(s): Perseus Dist

Last of the Wine. unabr. ed. Mary Renault. Read by Peter MacDonald. 11 cass. (Running Time: 16 hrs. 30 min.). 1982. 88.00 (978-0-7366-0521-2(5), 1495) Books on Tape.
Written as an autobiography, it is the story of Alexias, son of an aristocratic officer during the Third Peloponnesian War. At the heart of Alexias' story is his love for Lysis, another of Socrates' noble proteges, with whom he lives out the romantic ideal of those times. It is their lot to see Athens drained by war & manipulated by oligarches who subvert democracy & impose a reign of terror. In restoring freedom to the city, Alexias & his friend risk their lives & treasures.

Last of the Wine. unabr. ed. Mary Renault. Narrated by George Wilson. 11 cass. (Running Time: 16 hrs. 15 mins.). 1990. 91.00 (978-1-55690-299-4(9), 90061E7) Recorded Bks.
Set in Greece during the Peloponnesian War, this sweeping historical novel portrays Alexias, a lad of good family who becomes a soldier during an era rich with history & portent. Major characters include Socrates, Plato, the playwrights Euripides & Aristophanes & many more who participate in the great athletic games, expeditions & sieges of the Greek Civil War.

Last One In. abr. ed. Engle & Barnes. (Running Time: 2 hrs.). (Strange Matter Ser.). 2006. 9.95 (978-1-4233-0864-5(6), 9781423308645, BAD) Brilliance Audio.

Last One In. abr. ed. Engle & Julian Barnes. Read by Multivoice Production Staff. (Running Time: 2 hrs.). (Strange Matter Ser.). 2006. 25.25 (978-1-4233-0865-2(4), 9781423308652, BADLE) Brilliance Audio.

Last One In. abr. ed. Engle & Engle. (Running Time: 7200 sec.). (Strange Matter Ser.). (J). (gr. 4-7). 2006. audio compact disk 25.25 (978-1-4233-0863-8(8), 9781423308638, BACDLib Ed); audio compact disk 9.95 (978-1-4233-0862-1(X), 9781423308621, BACD) Brilliance Audio.
Michelle Boyd enjoyed her first time water-skiing on beautiful Lake Wataga. She floated peacefully, waiting for the boat to rocket off, pulling her into another thrilling ride. Then her sister saw the dark shape gliding through the water, relentless, large and powerful. It broke the surface with a tremendous splash, a large brown hump as wrinkled as an elephant... and as fast as a ski boat. Watched through the sinister eyes of the oldest living resident of the lake, Michelle and Erin learn a dark and terrible secret. A secret submerged in the murky depths of Lake Wataga for forty years has returned to watch, to wait... and to feed.

Last One in Is a Rotten Egg. abr. ed. Leonard Kessler. Illus. by Leonard Kessler. 1 cass. (I Can Read Bks.). (J). (ps-3). 1969. 8.99 (978-1-55994-356-7(4), 285382) HarperCollins Pubs.

***Last One in Is a Rotten Egg.** unabr. ed. Leonard Kessler. (ENG.). 2007. (978-0-06-143473-0(6)) HarperCollins Pubs.

***Last Oracle.** unabr. ed. James Rollins. Read by Peter Jay Fernandez. (ENG.). 2008. (978-0-06-168822-5(3)); (978-0-06-168823-2(1)) HarperCollins Pubs.

Last Oracle. unabr. ed. James Rollins. Read by Peter Jay Fernandez. (Sigma Force Ser.: Bk. 5). 2009. audio compact disk 19.99 (978-0-06-172760-3(1), Harper Audio) HarperCollins Pubs.

Last Orders. unabr. ed. Graham Swift. Read by Ensemble Cast. (YA). 2007. 49.99 (978-1-60252-842-0(X)) Find a World.

Last Orders. unabr. ed. Graham Swift et al. Read by Simon Prebble. 7 CDs. (Running Time: 8 hrs. 30 mins.). (ENG.). 2003. audio compact disk 34.95 (978-1-56511-765-5(4), 1565117654) Pub: HighBridge. Dist(s): Workman Pub

Last orders at Harrods. Michael Holman. Read by Jerome Pride. (Running Time: 9 hrs. 45 mins.). 2009. 79.99 (978-1-74214-451-1(9), 9781742144511) Pub: Bolinda Pubng AUS. Dist(s): Bolinda Pub Inc

Last Orders at Harrods: An African Tale. unabr. ed. Michael Holman. Read by Jerome Pride. (Running Time: 35100 sec.). 2008. audio compact disk 87.95 (978-1-921334-92-4(4), 9781921334924) Pub: Bolinda Pubng AUS. Dist(s): Bolinda Pub Inc

Last Parallel. unabr. collector's ed. Martin Russ. Read by Dan Lazar. 8 cass. (Running Time: 12 hrs.). 1978. 64.00 (978-0-7366-0151-1(1), 1151) Books on Tape.
Martin Russ was one of those unusual young men who wanted to serve in Korea as a marine. He recounts his experiences - as a boot, on the line & even R&R's.

Last Patriot. abr. ed. Brad Thor. Read by Armand Schultz. (Running Time: 6 hrs. 0 mins. 0 sec.). (ENG.). 2010. audio compact disk 14.99 (978-1-4423-0470-3(7)) Pub: S&S Audio. Dist(s): S and S Inc

Last Picture Show: A Novel. unabr. ed. Larry McMurtry. Narrated by John Randolph Jones. 6 cass. (Running Time: 8 hrs. 45 mins.). (Last Picture Show Trilogy: No. 1). 1989. 51.00 (978-1-55690-304-5(9), 89810E7) Recorded Bks.
An almost-true story about a small town in Texas that ought to exist if it doesn't, with characters like Sam the Lion, the delectable Jacy & Ruth Popper, the coach's wife.

Last Picture Show: A Novel. unabr. collector's ed. Larry McMurtry. Read by Wolfram Kandinsky. 6 cass. (Running Time: 9 hrs.). (Last Picture Show Trilogy: No. 1). 1984. 48.00 (978-0-7366-0764-3(1), 1721) Books on Tape.
In the face of imminent responsibility, fitful boredom, all night drinking bouts & the mystery & allure of blossoming sexuality, the simple town's young continually return to the flickering promises & radiant ideals of the nightly picture show. At least until the evening of the last picture show.

Last Place. unabr. ed. Laura Lippman. Read by Laurence Bouvard. 10 cass. (Running Time: 12 hrs. 15 min.). (Tess Monaghan Ser.: No. 7). (J). 2003. 84.95 (978-0-7531-1694-4(4)); audio compact disk 99.95 (978-0-7531-1715-6(0)) Pub: ISIS Lrg Prnt GBR. Dist(s): Ulverscroft US
When private investigator Tess Monaghan starts to investigate a series of unsolved homicides she is convinced that the culprit. who the police say is dead, is alive. He is alive and has found another victim to stalk: Tess.

Last Place Gets the Blue Ribbon: Matt. 20:1-16. Ed Young. 1993. 4.95 (978-0-7417-1955-3(X), 955) Win Walk.

Last Plantagenets. unabr. collector's ed. Thomas B. Costain. Read by David Case. 12 cass. (Running Time: 18 hrs.). (History of the Plantaganets Ser.). 1993. 96.00 (978-0-7366-2550-0(X), 3301) Books on Tape.
Final volume in A History of the Plantagenets covers the century from 1377 to 1485 when civil war ravaged England.

Last Precinct. Patricia Cornwell. Read by Kate Reading. 8 cass. (Running Time: 12 hrs.). (Kay Scarpetta Ser.: No. 11). 2000. 39.95 (H369) Blckstn Audio.
Virginia's Chief Medical Examiner Kay Scarpetta is an object of suspicion & criminal investigation. The nightmare perpetrated on Scarpetta's doorstep continues as she discovers that the so-called Werewolf murders have extended to New York City & into the darkest corners of her past.

Last Precinct. Patricia Cornwell. Read by Kate Reading. (Kay Scarpetta Ser.: No. 11). 2000. audio compact disk 112.00 (978-0-7366-6177-5(8)) Books on Tape.

Last Precinct. unabr. ed. Patricia Cornwell. Read by Kate Reading. 12 cass. (Running Time: 18 hrs.). (Kay Scarpetta Ser.: No. 11). 2000. 96.00 (978-0-7366-5646-7(4), 5445) Books on Tape.
Kay Scarpetta's mandate to investigate the four-hundred-year-old violent death of one of America's first settlers at Jamestown, attracts headlines, and more, their of a person or persons unknown. Kay and those closest to her soon find themselves the targets of hate crimes that are clearly inspired by her connection to the archaeological excavation. At first more nuisance than assault, the nature of the attacks quickly escalates to violence. Worse still, those sworn to protect prove to be the enemy, forcing Scarpetta, her niece Lucy, and Detective peter Marino to take matters into their own hands.

Last Precinct. unabr. collector's ed. Patricia Cornwell. Read by Kate Reading. 14 CDs. (Running Time: 21 hrs.). (Kay Scarpetta Ser.: No. 11). 2001. audio compact disk 112.00 Books on Tape.
Virginia's Chief Medical Examiner finds herself under criminal investigation. The nightmare perpetrated on Scarpetta's doorstep continues as she discovers that the so-called Werewolf murders may have extended to New York City. When a formidable female assistant district attorney is brought into the case, Scarpetta struggles to make the truth prevail against unnerving evidence to the contrary. Tested interminably, she turns inward to ask, Where do you go when there is nowhere left?.

Last Promise. unabr. ed. Richard Paul Evans. 6 vols. (Running Time: 9 hrs.). 2002. bk. 54.95 (978-0-7927-2716-3(9), CSL 502, Chivers Sound Lib); audio compact disk 79.95 (978-0-7927-2745-3(2), SLD 502, Chivers Sound Lib) AudioGO.
When Eliana moved to Italy to follow hwer heart, the future was bright with promise. But once she settled into the small rustic village, she found her husband to be a very different man. Over time he distanced himself from her, leaving Eliana to care for their young son. When fellow American Ross Story, a deeply thoughtful man with a mysterious passion for art, arrives at the same villa, a chance encounter causes Eliana and Ross to look at their lives anew.

Last Queen. unabr. ed. C. W. Gortner. (Running Time: 11 hrs. 0 mins.). 2008. 29.95 (978-1-4332-1576-6(4)); 29.95 (978-1-4332-1574-2(8)); 65.95 (978-1-4332-1572-8(1)); audio compact disk 29.95 (978-1-4332-1575-9(6)); audio compact disk 90.00 (978-1-4332-1573-5(X)) Blckstn Audio.

Last Question see Science Fiction Favorites of Isaac Asimov

Last Question see Best of Isaac Asimov

Last Question see Isaac Asimov Library

Last Raider. Douglas Reeman. Read by David Rintoul. 9 cass. 79.95 (978-0-7927-3822-0(5), CSL 877); audio compact disk 110.95 (978-0-7927-3823-7(3), SLD 877) AudioGO.

Last Rail: The Building of the Transcontinental Railroad. Darice Bailer. Illus. by Bill Farnsworth. 1 cass. Dramatization. (Smithsonian Odyssey Ser.). (ENG.). (J). (gr. 2-5). 1996. 7.95 (978-1-56899-369-0(2), C6003) Soundprints.
Lucy has been trying all day to take a picture of her friends at the Smithsonian's National Museum of American History. But they just can't stand still. Her most recent attempt is in Railroad Hall. When Lucy drops her camera, she's afraid she'll never get any pictures taken. As she picks it up, she looks through the camera lens. To her surprise, her friends are gone. She now sees a large group of workers & business men wearing clothes like the ones in an old western movie. Lucy has become Andrew Russell, the man who took the famous photograph of the driving of the golden spike into the last rail.

Last Raven. abr. ed. Craig Thomas. Read by Craig Thomas. 2 cass. (Running Time: 3 hrs.). 2000. 7.95 (978-1-57815-046-5(9), 1041, Media Bks Audio) Media Bks NJ.
At the height of the Cold War, the CIA & KGB are in on a conspiracy to assassinate a high-rank Soviet reforming politician.

Last Refuge: A Tale of Money & Murder in the Hamptons. unabr. ed. Chris Knopf. Read by Stefan Rudnicki. (Running Time: 39600 sec.). 2006. 65.95 (978-0-7861-4753-3(9)); audio compact disk 81.00 (978-0-7861-6337-3(2)); audio compact disk 29.95 (978-0-7861-7256-6(8)) Blckstn Audio.

Last Refuge of Scoundrels: A Revolutionary Novel. unabr. ed. Paul Lussier. Narrated by George Guidall. 9 CDs. (Running Time: 10 hrs. 45 mins.). 2001. audio compact disk 97.00 (978-1-4025-0500-3(0), C1556) Recorded Bks.
Intelligent, entertaining, and raucous, Last Refuge of Scoundrels reveals the humanity behind those staid countenances of the founding fathers. Few historians will admit that the driving force behind the American Revolution was a patriotic prostitute who lived for "the Cause." She and her lover, an aide to the brilliant General George Washington, were strategic players in the fight for independence. Together with an unsung army of cooks, jack tars, and washerwomen, they sparked a brilliant and successful guerrilla war.

Last Refuge of Scoundrels: A Revolutionary Novel. unabr. ed. Paul Lussier. Narrated by George Guidall. 9 cass. (Running Time: 10 hrs. 45 mins.). 2001. 82.00 (978-0-7887-5449-4(1)) Recorded Bks.
The driving force behind the American Revolution is a prostitute who lives for "the Cause." Aided by her compatriot lover, she helps the brilliant George Washington achieve victory despite the bumbling old men we know as the founding fathers.

Last Reminder. Stuart Pawson & Andrew Wincott. 2009. 61.95 (978-1-84652-373-1(7)); audio compact disk 79.95 (978-1-84652-374-8(5)) Pub: Magna Story GBR. Dist(s): Ulverscroft US

***Last Report on the Miracles at Little No Horse.** unabr. ed. Louise Erdrich. Read by Anna Fields. (ENG.). 2005. (978-0-06-082444-0(1), Harper Audio); (978-0-06-079796-6(7), Harper Audio) HarperCollins Pubs.

Last Report on the Miracles at Little No Horse: A Novel. Louise Erdrich. 9 cass. (Running Time: 13 hrs. 30 mins.). 2001. 72.00 (978-0-7366-6351-9(7)) Books on Tape.
For more than a half century, Father Damien Modeste has served the Ojibwe on a remote reservation. Now, nearing the end of his life, Damien dreads the discovery of his physical identity, for he is a woman who has lived as a man. A troubled colleague comes to the reservation to investigate the life of the possibly false saint, Sister Leopolda.

Last Report on the Miracles at Little No Horse: A Novel. abr. unabr. ed. Louise Erdrich. Read by Anna Fields. 10 cass. (Running Time: 14 hrs. 30 min.). 2001. 39.95 (978-0-694-52408-2(5)) HarperCollins Pubs.

Last Rights. Philip Shelby. 2004. 10.95 (978-0-7435-4920-2(1)) Pub: S&S Audio. Dist(s): S and S Inc

Last Rights. unabr. ed. Marya Mannes & David Hendin. 1 cass. (Running Time: 56 min.). 12.95 (40055) J Norton Pubs.
The authors in an interview with Heywood Hale Broun discuss the old-fashioned belief in dignity at the end of life, & answer many troubling questions about the definition of death, care of terminal medical patients, & euthanasia.

Last Rights. unabr. ed. Tim Sebastian. Read by Alex Jennings. 8 cass. (Running Time: 8 hrs.). 1995. 69.95 (978-0-7451-6495-3(1), CAB 1111) AudioGO.
Edward Bell's mother had left the Soviet Union 30 years ago, a political troublemaker. Now, with the Cold War over, a Russian businessman is found dead in London. Suddenly, his family's tainted past collides with Edward's present. Now Edward must choose between the death of a principle & the life of a human being.

Last Rites. David Wishart. Read by Michael Tudor Barnes. 8 cass. (Sound Ser.). (J). 2002. 69.95 (978-1-84283-211-0(5)) Pub: ISIS Lrg Prnt GBR. Dist(s): Ulverscroft US

Last Rites. unabr. ed. John Harvey. Narrated by Ron Keith. 8 cass. (Running Time: 10 hrs. 45 mins.). 2000. 71.00 (978-1-84197-042-4(5), H1056E7) Recorded Bks.
Charlie Resnick fascinates crime novel fans with his love for hot jazz & his cool eye for discovering the truth. In his years as a police inspector, Charlie has seen all manner of crimes & has worked with the best & worst in law enforcement. But now he's feeling tired & jaded. Nottingham is consumed by drug wars & gang feuds & when a brutal prisoner escapes his police guards, the search for him uncovers appalling layers of corruption within the police ranks. As the rumpled detective nears a crossroads in his career, he wonders what will happen in his personal life, too.

***Last Rites of Jeff Myrtlebank.** (ENG.). 2010. audio compact disk (978-1-59171-252-7(1)) Falcon Picture.

***Last Rock & Roll Show.** Daniel White. 2009. (978-1-61584-021-2(4)) Indep Pub IL.

Last Rose of Summer. unabr. ed. Di Morrissey. Read by Stephanie Daniel. 9 cass. (Running Time: 16 hrs. 30 mins.). 2001. (978-1-74030-165-7(X), 500953) Bolinda Pubng AUS.

Last Run. Hilary Norman. 2009. 69.95 (978-1-4079-0323-1(3)); audio compact disk 84.95 (978-1-4079-0324-8(1)) Pub: Soundings Ltd GBR. Dist(s): Ulverscroft US

***Last Sacrifice.** unabr. ed. Richelle Mead. Contrib. by Emily Shaffer. (Running Time: 13 hrs.). (Vampire Academy Ser.: Bk. 6). (ENG.). 2010. audio compact disk 39.95 (978-0-14-242817-7(5), PengAudBks) Penguin Grp USA.

Last Sanctuary, unabr. ed. Craig Holden. Narrated by Richard Ferrone. 10 cass. (Running Time: 14 hrs.). 85.00 (978-0-7887-0525-0(3), 94720E7) Recorded Bks.
A harrowing portrayal of an innocent man trapped by events beyond his control. Holden, author of "The River Sorrow," infuses a spellbinding story with brilliant insights into tortured & lonely souls. Available to libraries only.

Last Scout. unabr. ed. Will Cook. Read by William Dufris. 4 cass. (Running Time: 5 hrs.). (Sagebrush Western Ser.). (J). 1999. 44.95 (978-1-57490-228-0(8)) Pub: ISIS Lrg Prnt GBR. Dist(s): Ulverscroft US

Last Season: A Team in Search of Its Soul. unabr. ed. Phil Jackson. Read by Stephen Hoye. 7 CDs. (Running Time: 8 hrs.). 2004. audio compact disk 63.00 (978-1-4159-0835-8(4)); 54.00 (978-1-4159-0834-1(6)) Books on Tape.
The nine-time NBA Champion coach Phil Jackson offers his personal account of the Lakers' extraordinary 2003-2004 season.

Last Secret. unabr. ed. Mary McGarry Morris. Narrated by Renée Raudman. 10 CDs. (Running Time: 12 hrs. 0 mins. 0 sec.). (ENG.). 2009. audio compact disk 69.99 (978-1-4001-4215-6(6)); audio compact disk 24.99 (978-1-4001-6215-4(7)); audio compact disk 34.99 (978-1-4001-1215-9(X)) Pub: Tantor Media. Dist(s): IngramPubServ

Last Secret of Fatima: My Conversations with Sister Lucia. Tarcisio Bertone. Read by Frank Montenegro et al. 2009. 39.95 (978-0-86716-908-9(7)) St Anthony Mess Pr.

Last Seen. abr. ed. Matt Cohen. Narrated by R. H. Thomson. 2 cass. (Running Time: 2 hrs. 30 mins.). (ENG.). 2005. 16.95 (978-0-86492-301-1(5)) Pub: BTC Audiobks CAN. Dist(s): U Toronto Pr

Last Seen Breathing. unabr. ed. David Williams. Read by Robin Welch. 7 cass. (Running Time: 9 hrs. 15 mins.). 1999. 76.95 (978-1-85903-273-2(7)) Pub: Magna Story GBR. Dist(s): Ulverscroft US
The market town of Tawrbrach is shocked by the accidental death of Rhonwen Spencer Griffith, rich widow & leading light of the Operatic Society. Her son Elwyn dies soon after, apparently from natural causes. Chief Inspector Merlin Parry thinks differently when he receives a copy of a memo Elwyn sent demanding money from three members of the Operatic Society for his mother's secret, explicit diaries. What really happened at "Madam" Rhonwen's parties? Why is the rector so concerned about the diaries & why didn't Elwyn's wife know they existed?.

Last seen Leaving. Kelly Braffet. Read by Kevagne Kalisch. (Running Time: 9 hrs. 15 mins.). 2009. 79.99 (978-1-74214-192-3(7), 9781742141923) Pub: Bolinda Pubng AUS. Dist(s): Bolinda Pub Inc

Last seen Leaving. unabr. ed. Kelly Braffet. Read by Kevagne Kalisch. (Running Time: 9 hrs. 15 mins.). 2007. audio compact disk 87.95 (978-1-74093-960-7(3), 9781740939607) Pub: Bolinda Pubng AUS. Dist(s): Bolinda Pub Inc

Last Seen Wearing. unabr. ed. Veronica Black, pseud. 4 cass. (Storysound Ser.). (J). 1998. 44.95 (978-1-85903-210-7(9)) Pub: Mgna Lrg Print GBR. Dist(s): Ulverscroft US

Last Seen Wearing: An Inspector Morse Mystery. unabr. ed. Colin Dexter. Read by Michael Pennington. 6 cass. (Running Time: 8 hrs.). (Inspector Morse Mystery Ser.). 2000. 29.95 (978-1-57270-145-8(5), N61145u) Pub: Audio Partners. Dist(s): PerseuPGW
Valerie Taylor was last seen two years ago at the age of seventeen. She was presumed dead. But if Valerie is dead, who wrote a mysterious letter to her parents? Now, a body has turned up, forcing Inspector Morse to reopen the case. Morse soon finds himself in the challenge of his career.

Last Seen Wearing: An Inspector Morse Mystery. unabr. ed. Colin Dexter. Read by Michael Pennington. 8 cass. (Running Time: 12 hrs.). (Inspector Morse Mystery Ser.: Bk. 2). 2000. 59.95 (978-0-7451-4122-0(6), CAB 805) Pub: Chivers Audio Bks GBR. Dist(s): AudioGO
Valerie Taylor is missing, and the case has landed on Inspector Morse's desk. His clues are a pot-smoking boyfriend, strip clubs and abortion clinics. But, they all lead nowhere. The missing girl has spread her sexual favors far and wide, and Morse is soon the victim of temptation.

Last Seminar. Steve Warren. 1 cass. (Running Time: 47 min.). 1988. 7.95 (978-0-938117-03-2(3)) Altair Pub UT.
A spoof of America's seminar business. It focuses on the winner-millionaire-success type programs.

Last September. unabr. ed. Elizabeth Bowen. Read by Fiona Shaw. 8 cass. 1999. 69.95 (978-0-7540-0280-2(2), CAB1703) AudioGO.

An Asterisk (*) at the beginning of an entry indicates that the title is appearing for the first time.

Last Seven Days of the Prophet Joseph Smith. Ivan J. Barrett. 2 cass. 11.98 (978-1-55503-121-3(8), 070033) Covenant Comms.
New insights, little known historical facts.

***Last Sherlock Holmes Story.** Michael Dibdin. Narrated by Robert Glenister. (Running Time: 7 hrs. 0 mins. 0 sec.). (ENG.). 2011. audio compact disk 39.95 (978-1-4084-6824-1(7)) Pub: AudioGO. Dist(s): Perseus Dist

Last Shot: A Final Four Mystery. unabr. ed. John Feinstein. Read by John Feinstein. 5 CDs. (Running Time: 5 hrs. 36 mins.). (YA). 2005. audio compact disk 38.25 (978-0-307-20671-8(8)) Pub: Books on Tape. Dist(s): NetLibrary CO

Last Shot: A Final Four Mystery. unabr. ed. John Feinstein. Read by John Feinstein. 4 cass. (Running Time: 5 hrs. 36 mins.). (YA). 2005. 35.00 (978-1-4000-9935-1(8), Listening Lib) Random Audio Pubg.
Danny and Bridge-Ann Robison have just 48 hours to figure out who is blackmailing one of the star Basketball players and why.

Last Shot: A Final Four Mystery. unabr. ed. John Feinstein. Read by John Feinstein. 5 CDs. (Running Time: 5 hrs. 36 mins.). (ENG.). (YA). (gr. 7). 2005. audio compact disk 30.00 (978-0-307-20644-2(0), Listening Lib) Pub: Random Audio Pubg. Dist(s): Random
Steven Thomas is one of two lucky winners of the U.S. Basketball Writer’s Association’s contest for aspiring journalists. His prize? A trip to New Orleans and a coveted press pass for the Final Four. It’s a basketball junkie’s dream come true! But the games going on behind the scenes between the coaches, the players, the media, the money-men, and the fans turn out to be even more fiercely competitive than those on the court. Steven and his fellow winner, Susan Carol Anderson, are nosing around the Superdome and overhear what sounds like a threat to throw the championship game. Now they have just 48 hours to figure out who is blackmailing one of MSU’s star players . . . and why. Praise for John Feinstein: “The best writer of sports books in America today.”—The Boston Globe “Feinstein’s beat, it turns out, isn’t sports; it’s human nature.”—People on A March to Madness “A basketball junkie’s nirvana.”—Sports Illustrated on A March to Madness “One of the best sportswriters alive!”—Larry King, USA Today on A Good Walk Spoiled From the Hardcover edition.

Last Shot: City Streets, Basketball Dreams, unabr. ed. Darcy Frey. Narrated by Tom Stechschulte. 6 cass. (Running Time: 8 hrs. 30 mins.). 51.00 (978-0-7887-0270-9(X), 94479E7) Recorded Bks.
This electrifying true story takes us into the tangled lives of four African American hoop stars from the Coney Island ghetto. Frey follows the teenagers from weekend pick-up games to recruiting sessions, from high school classrooms to high profile basketball camps. Available to libraries only.

Last Siege. unabr. ed. Jonathan Stroud. Read by David Thorn. (Running Time: 24360 sec.). (ENG.). (J). (gr. 7). 2006. audio compact disk 39.00 (978-0-7393-3660-1(6), Listening Lib) Pub: Random Audio Pubg. Dist(s): Random

Last Sin Eater. abr. ed. Francine Rivers. Read by Anita Lustrea. 2 cass. (Running Time: 3 hrs.). 1995. 17.99 (978-1-886463-20-2(4)) Oasis Audio.
Cadi Forbes knows it's forbidden, that doing so will bring curses down on her, but something deep & instinctive moves her, against all dire warnings, to find the "sin eater.".

Last Sin Eater. abr. ed. Francine Rivers. Narrated by Anita Lustrea. (ENG.). 2007. 10.49 (978-1-60814-276-7(0)); audio compact disk 14.99 (978-1-59859-230-6(0)) Oasis Audio.

Last Six Million Seconds, unabr. ed. John Burdett. Narrated by Simon Prebble. 10 cass. (Running Time: 13 hrs. 45 mins.). 1997. 85.00 (978-0-7887-0914-2(3), 95054E7) Recorded Bks.
A timely tale of Hong Kong's final days under British rule. Royal Hong Kong Police Chief Inspector Chan Siu-kai, known as Charlie, stumbles on a grisly triple homicide involving three headless bodies. As he races to solve the case before China takes over, friends & foes oppose his investigation.

Last Six Million Seconds. unabr. collector's ed. John Burdett. Read by Stuart Langton. 9 cass. (Running Time: 13 hrs. 30 min.). 1997. 72.00 (978-0-913369-88-3(8), 4384) Books on Tape.

Last Snow. abr. ed. Eric Lustbader. Read by Richard Ferrone. (Running Time: 7 hrs. 0 mins. 0 sec.). (ENG.). 2010. audio compact disk 29.99 (978-1-4272-0880-4(8)) Pub: Macmill Audio. Dist(s): Macmillan

Last Snow. unabr. ed. Eric Lustbader. Read by Richard Ferrone. (Running Time: 13 hrs. 0 mins. 0 sec.). (ENG.). 2010. audio compact disk 39.99 (978-1-4272-0878-1(6)) Pub: Macmill Audio. Dist(s): Macmillan

Last Song. abr. ed. Nicholas Sparks. Read by Pepper Binkley & Scott Sowers. (Running Time: 7 hrs.). (ENG.). 2009. 14.98 (978-1-60024-639-5(7)) Pub: Hachet Audio. Dist(s): HachBkGrp

Last Song. abr. ed. Nicholas Sparks. Read by Pepper Binkley & Scott Sowers. (Running Time: 7 hrs.). (ENG.). 2010. audio compact disk 14.98 (978-1-60788-253-4(1)) Pub: Hachet Audio. Dist(s): HachBkGrp

***Last Song.** unabr. ed. Nicholas Sparks. Narrated by Pepper Binkley & Scott Sowers. 1 MP3-CD. (Running Time: 12 hrs. 30 mins.). 2009. 59.99 (978-1-60024-960-0(4)); audio compact disk 99.99 (978-1-60024-956-3(6)) Pub: Hachet Audio. Dist(s): HachBkGrp

Last Song. unabr. ed. Nicholas Sparks. Read by Pepper Binkley & Scott Sowers. (Running Time: 12 hrs. 30 mins.). (ENG.). 2009. 26.98 (978-1-60024-642-5(7)) Pub: Hachet Audio. Dist(s): HachBkGrp

Last Song. unabr. ed. Nicholas Sparks. Read by William F. Pepper et al. 11 CDs. (Running Time: 12 hrs. 30 mins.). (ENG.). 2009. audio compact disk 39.98 (978-1-60024-640-1(0)) Pub: Hachet Audio. Dist(s): HachBkGrp

Last Sons: DC Universe. Based on a novel by Alan Grant. 2010. audio compact disk 19.99 (978-1-59950-648-7(3)) GraphicAudio.

Last Spymaster. abr. ed. Gayle Lynds. Read by David Colacci. (Running Time: 21600 sec.). 2007. audio compact disk 14.99 (978-1-59737-614-3(0), 9781597376143, BCD Value Price) Brilliance Audio.

Last Spymaster. unabr. ed. Gayle Lynds. Read by David Colacci. (Running Time: 14 hrs.). 2006. 39.25 (978-1-59737-611-2(6), 9781597376112, BADLE); 24.95 (978-1-59737-610-5(8), 9781597376105, BAD); 92.25 (978-1-59737-607-5(8), 9781597376075, BrilAudUnabridg); audio compact disk 39.25 (978-1-59737-609-9(4), 9781597376099, Brinc Audio MP3 Lib); audio compact disk 107.25 (978-1-59737-613-6(2), 9781597376136, BriAudCD Unabrid); audio compact disk 24.95 (978-1-59737-608-2(6), 9781597376082, Brilliance MP3); audio compact disk 36.95 (978-1-4233-0092-2(0), 9781423300922) Brilliance Audio.
Charles Jay Tice was a spy's spy. As the CIA's Berlin station chief towards the end of the Cold War, he was famous and revered for his many successful operations and for often outwitting the legendary Stasi head, Marcus Wolf. Whe he was revealed a traitor - having sold sensitive secrets to the Russians for years - it sent a chill through the entire Western intelligence apparatus. Incarcerated for life in the toughest of maximum security prisons, under near constant surveillance, Tice has been left to slowly rot. Then Tice disappears from his cell, leaving no evidence as to how he managed his escape and no sensible clues as to where he's going. CIA recovery specialist Elaine Cunningham is quietly assigned the case - she has to find Tice quickly, and bring him back quietly, before the world finds out that the CIA has lost track of the most dangerous spy. But what at first seems a challenging assignment becomes something more as she slowly uncovers evidence that there is a much bigger, deeper conspiracy going on and Tice's escape may involve much more than one old spook's last run for freedom.

Last Stand. abr. ed. Matt Braun. Read by Jim Gough. 4 cass. (Running Time: 6 hrs.). 2002. 24.95 (978-1-890990-82-4(5), 99082) Otis Audio.
Western with sound effects.

***Last Stand: Custer, Sitting Bull, & the Battle of the Little Big Horn.** unabr. ed. Nathaniel Philbrick. Read by George Guidall. 10 CDs. (Running Time: 12 hrs.). (ENG.). 2010. audio compact disk 39.95 (978-0-14-242769-9(1), PengAudBks) Penguin Grp USA.

Last Stand of Fox Company: A True Story of U. S. Marines in Combat. Bob Drury. Read by Michael Prichard. (Playaway Adult Nonfiction Ser.). (ENG.). 2009. 64.99 (978-1-60847-896-5(3)) Find a World.

Last Stand of Fox Company: A True Story of U. S. Marines in Combat. unabr. ed. Bob Drury & Tom Clavin. Narrated by Michael Prichard. (Running Time: 12 hrs. 0 mins. 0 sec.). (ENG.). 2009. audio compact disk 34.99 (978-1-4001-1016-2(5)); audio compact disk 69.99 (978-1-4001-4016-9(1)) Pub: Tantor Media. Dist(s): IngramPubServ

Last Stand of Fox Company: A True Story of U. S. Marines in Combat. unabr. ed. Bob Drury & Tom Clavin. Read by Michael Prichard. (Running Time: 12 hrs. 0 mins. 0 sec.). (ENG.). 2009. audio compact disk 24.99 (978-1-4001-6016-7(2)) Pub: Tantor Media. Dist(s): IngramPubServ

Last Stand of the Tin Can Sailors: The Extraordinary World War II Story of the U. S. Navy's Finest Hour. unabr. ed. James D. Hornfischer. 12 cass. (Running Time: 18 hrs.). 2004. 96.00 (978-0-7366-9747-7(0)) Books on Tape.

Last Star, abr. ed. Kitty Kelley. Read by Susan Strasberg. 2 cass. (Running Time: 3 hrs.). 2000. 7.95 (978-1-57815-140-0(6), 1099, Media Bks Audio) Media Bks NJ.
She's America's most popular, most highly publicized actress. Her life has been as extravagant & dramatic as the roles she has played.

Last Station. unabr. ed. Jay Parini. Read by Jay Parini. Interview with Rebekah Presson. 1 cass. (Running Time: 29 min.). 1990. 10.00 (092190) New Letters.
Parini's novel, "The Last Station", is about the last year of Leo Tolstoy's life. Parini reads from the fictional diaries of three characters close to Tolstoy & talks about the development of the novel & its difference of opinion with much of the biographical data previously published about Tolstoy.

Last Stories of the Old Duck Hunters, Vol. 3. abr. ed. Gordon MacQuarrie. Read by Karl Schmidt. 2 cass. (Running Time: 2 hrs. 30 min.). (Gordon MacQuarrie Trilogy). 1994. 16.95 set. (978-1-57223-016-3(9), 169) Willow Creek Pr.
Entertaining stories from the pages of the Gordon MacQuarrie trilogy. Classic hunting & fishing yarns from a master storyteller. Winner of the 1995 Ben Franklin award - Best Audio.

***Last Straw.** unabr. ed. Jeff Kinney. Narrated by Ramon de Ocampo. 1 Playaway. (Running Time: 2 hrs. 15 mins.). (Diary of a Wimpy Kid Ser.). (J). (gr. 4-8). 2009. 54.75 (978-1-4407-2985-0(9)); 25.75 (978-1-4407-2975-1(1)); audio compact disk 25.75 (978-1-4407-2979-9(4)) Recorded Bks.

***Last Straw.** unabr. ed. Jeff Kinney. Narrated by Ramon de Ocampo. 2 CDs. (Running Time: 2 hrs. 15 mins.). (Diary of a Wimpy Kid Ser.). (J). (gr. 4-8). 2010. audio compact disk 14.99 (978-1-4407-7818-6(3)) Recorded Bks.

Last Street Novel. unabr. ed. Omar R. Tyree. Read by Richard Allen. (YA). 2008. 64.99 (978-1-60252-977-9(9)) Find a World.

Last Street Novel. unabr. ed. Omar R. Tyree. Read by Richard Allen. 11 CDs. (Running Time: 14 hrs. 0 mins. 0 sec.). (ENG.). 2007. audio compact disk 39.99 (978-1-4001-0492-5(0)); audio compact disk 79.99 (978-1-4001-3492-2(7)); audio compact disk 29.99 (978-1-4001-5492-0(8)) Pub: Tantor Media. Dist(s): IngramPubServ

Last Summer of the Death Warriors. unabr. ed. Francisco X. Stork. Read by Ryan Gesell. (J). (gr. 9). 2010. 37.00 (978-0-307-70699-7(0), Listening Lib) Pub: Random Audio Pubg. Dist(s): Random

Last Summer (of You & Me) unabr. ed. Ann Brashares. (Running Time: 9 hrs.). (ENG.). (gr. k-8). 2007. audio compact disk 34.95 (978-0-14-305766-6(9), PengAudBks) Penguin Grp USA.

Last Supper see Twentieth-Century Poetry in English, No. 26, Recordings of Poets Reading Their Own Poetry

Last Supper. Charles McCarry. Read by Stefan Rudnicki. (Running Time: 54000 sec.). 2006. 85.95 (978-0-7861-4564-5(1)); audio compact disk 99.00 (978-0-7861-7075-3(1)) Blckstn Audio.

Last Supper. unabr. ed. Read by Gayle D. Erwin. 1 cass. (Running Time: 1 hr.). 1992. 4.95 (978-1-56599-506-2(6), C-6) Yahshua Pub.
John 13: 1-17.

Last Supper. unabr. ed. Charles McCarry. 10 cass. (Running Time: 54000 sec.). 2006. 29.95 (978-0-7861-4400-6(9)) Blckstn Audio.

Last Supper. unabr. ed. Charles McCarry. Read by Stefan Rudnicki. 12 CDs. (Running Time: 54000 sec.). 2006. audio compact disk 32.95 (978-0-7861-7438-6(2)); audio compact disk 29.95 (978-0-7861-7769-1(1)) Blckstn Audio.

***Last Supper - Judas Hands Jesus over - Peter's Denial - Jesus & Pilate.** unabr. ed. Zondervan. (Running Time: 0 hr. 18 mins. 22 sec.). (Best-Loved Stories of the Bible, NIrV Ser.). (ENG.). (J). 2010. 1.99 (978-0-310-86533-9(6)) Pub: Zondkidz. Dist(s): Zondervan

Last Suppers. abr. ed. Diane Mott Davidson. Read by Barbara Rosenblat. 3 CDs. (Running Time: 3 hrs.). (Goldy Schulz Culinary Mysteries Ser.: No. 4). 2000. audio compact disk 11.99 (978-1-57815-515-6(0), 1133 CD3, Media Bks Audio) Media Bks NJ.
Colorado caterer Goldy Bear is about to marry homicide detective Tom Schulz, when she gets a phone call from Tom saying that he's found Father Olsen at the rectory shot & dying. When the police arrive Tom has disappeared. It's up to Goldy to decipher Tom's cryptic message.

Last Suppers. abr. ed. Diane Mott Davidson. Read by Barbara Rosenblat. 2 cass. (Goldy Schulz Culinary Mysteries Ser.: No. 4). 2001. 7.95 (978-1-57815-194-3(5), Media Bks Audio) Media Bks NJ.

Last Suppers. abr. ed. Diane Mott Davidson. Read by Barbara Rosenblat. 2 cass. (Running Time: 3 hrs.). (Goldy Schulz Culinary Mysteries Ser.: No. 4). 1994. 16.95 (978-1-879371-75-0(8), 40290) Pub Mills.
It should be the happiest day of Goldy's life...After years of struggling to put the disaster of her first marriage behind her, she has finally found the courage to love again & soon she'll be walking down the aisle. But, moments after Goldy's put the finishing touches on the scrumptious reception feast & just before the ceremony is to begin, she receives an urgent call from the groom himself. The wedding is off & the reason is murder.

Last Suppers. unabr. ed. Diane Mott Davidson. Perf. by Mandy Norwood. 7 cass. (Running Time: 10. hrs. 30 min.). (Goldy Schulz Culinary Mysteries Ser.: No. 4). 2004. 32.95 (978-1-59007-345-2(2)) Pub: New Millenn Enter. Dist(s): PerseuPGW

Last Suppers. unabr. ed. Diane Mott Davidson. Read by Barbara Rosenblat. 8 CDs. (Running Time: 9 hrs. 30 min.). (Goldy Schulz Culinary Mysteries Ser.: No. 4). 2004. audio compact disk 49.95 (978-1-59007-440-4(8)) Pub: New Millenn Enter. Dist(s): PerseuPGW

Last Suppers. unabr. ed. Diane Mott Davidson. Narrated by Barbara Rosenblat. 7 cass. (Running Time: 9 hrs. 30 mins.). (Goldy Schulz Culinary Mysteries Ser.: No. 4). 1997. 60.00 (978-0-7887-0666-0(7), 94843E7) Recorded Bks.
Caterer Goldy Bear's wedding day becomes a nightmare when her groom calls her from the scene of a murder & then disappears.

Last Surgeon. unabr. ed. Michael Palmer. Read by John Bedford Lloyd. (Running Time: 11 hrs. 0 mins. 0 sec.). (ENG.). 2010. audio compact disk 39.99 (978-1-4272-0874-3(3)) Pub: Macmill Audio. Dist(s): Macmillan

Last Tales. unabr. collector's ed. Isak Dinesen. Read by Wanda McCaddon. 10 cass. (Running Time: 15 hrs.). 1984. 80.00 (978-0-7366-0917-3(2), 1860) Books on Tape.
The 12 tales in this volume represent the last things that Miss Dinesen wrote prior to her death in 1962.

Last Tales of Uncle Remus. unabr. ed. 3 cass. (Running Time: 4 hrs.). 2003. 37.00 (978-0-7887-9048-5(X)) Recorded Bks.

Last Templar. unabr. ed. Raymond Khoury. Read by Richard Ferrone. (Running Time: 14 hrs.). (ENG.). (gr. 8 up). 2006. audio compact disk 39.95 (978-0-14-305933-2(5), PengAudBks) Penguin Grp USA.

Last Temptation. unabr. ed. Val McDermid. Narrated by Gerard Doyle. 12 cass. (Running Time: 16 hrs. 30 mins.). 2002. 98.00 (978-1-4025-3333-4(0)) Recorded Bks.

Last Ten Years of Life Can Be the Most Important. Instructed by Manly P. Hall. 8.95 (978-0-89314-160-8(7), C840617) Philos Res.

Last Thing This World Needs Is Another Weight Loss Program: A Complete, Holistic Approach that Makes it Easier to Succeed in Health, Nutrition, & Weight Loss. Sandy Jost. 3 CDs. 2006. audio compact disk (978-1-932153-26-2(8)) ONE Health Pubng.
This holistic program provides one CD called "Food for Your BODY," with information about what foods to eat and how they communicate with the body; a second CD called "Food for Your MIND," which helps a person to envision success; and a third CD called "Food for Your SOUL," which addresses the deeper issues of why one eats so that the listener can find new ways to satisfy that internal hunger.

Last Things. unabr. ed. C. P. Snow. Read by John MacDonald. 9 cass. (Running Time: 13 hrs. 30 min.). (Strangers & Brothers Ser.). 1985. 72.00 (978-0-7366-0446-8(4), 1420) Books on Tape.
This encounter with death leads Sir Lewis to re-evaluate his own life & achievements & to adopt a fresh slant on the achievements of others.

Last Three Planets. 1 cass. (Running Time: 29 min.). 14.95 (23330) MMI Corp.
Discusses Uranus, Neptune, Pluto. History of discovery, to present day knowledge.

***Last Time I Saw You: A Novel.** unabr. ed. Elizabeth Berg. Read by Elizabeth Berg. 7 CDs. 2010. audio compact disk 80.00 (978-0-307-71374-2(1), BksonTape) Pub: Random Audio Pubg. Dist(s): Random

Last Time I Saw You: A Novel. unabr. ed. Elizabeth Berg. Read by Elizabeth Berg. (ENG.). 2010. audio compact disk 35.00 (978-0-307-71372-8(5), Random AudioBks) Pub: Random Audio Pubg. Dist(s): Random

Last Time They Met. abr. ed. Anita Shreve. Read by Lainie Cooke. 4 cass. (Running Time: 6 hrs.). 2001. 29.98 Books on Tape.
A man and woman sustain a life-long passionate relationship even though they've been together only three times.

Last Time They Met. abr. ed. Anita Shreve. Read by Blair Brown. (ENG.). 2005. 14.98 (978-1-59483-422-6(9)) Pub: Hachet Audio. Dist(s): HachBkGrp

Last Time They Met. abr. ed. Anita Shreve. Read by Blair Brown. 5 CDs. (Running Time: 6 hrs.). (ENG.). 2008. audio compact disk 17.98 (978-1-60024-100-0(X)) Pub: Hachet Audio. Dist(s): HachBkGrp

Last Time They Met. unabr. ed. Anita Shreve. Read by Lainie Cooke. (ENG.). 2005. 16.98 (978-1-59483-421-9(0)) Pub: Hachet Audio. Dist(s): HachBkGrp

Last Time They Met. unabr. collector's ed. Anita Shreve. Read by Lainie Cooke. 8 cass. (Running Time: 9 hrs. 36 min.). 2001. 44.98 Books on Tape.

Last Time We Were Children. Penny J. Johnson. (Running Time: 2700 sec.). (ENG.). 2008. audio compact disk 14.99 (978-1-60604-449-0(4)) Tate Pubng.

Last to Be Chosen. Perf. by Ray Boltz. 1 cass. 1999. Provident Music.

***Last to Die.** abr. ed. James Grippando. Read by Ken Howard. (ENG.). 2004. (978-0-06-082405-1(0), Harper Audio); (978-0-06-082406-8(9), Harper Audio) HarperCollins Pubs.

Last Town on Earth. Thomas Mullen. Narrated by Henry Strozier. (Running Time: 56700 sec.). 2006. audio compact disk 39.99 (978-1-4193-9802-5(4)) Recorded Bks.

Last Trail. Zane Grey. Read by Michael Prichard. (Playaway Adult Fiction Ser.). 2009. 59.99 (978-1-60775-766-5(4)) Find a World.

Last Trail. Zane Grey. Narrated by Michael Prichard. (Ohio River Trilogy). (ENG.). 2005. audio compact disk 59.99 (978-1-4001-3134-1(0)) Pub: Tantor Media. Dist(s): IngramPubServ

Last Trail. unabr. ed. Zane Grey. Read by Robert Morris. 6 cass. (Running Time: 8 hrs. 30 mins.). 1996. 44.95 (978-0-7861-0935-7(1), 1689) Blckstn Audio.
After the American Revolution, Jonathan Zane became a celebrated scout on the frontier. His adventurous spirit & love of the wild led him to Fort Henry, scene of countless Indian attacks. Farmers had been murdered, women abducted & cabins burned. Zane teamed with legendary scout Lewis Wetzel to mete out justice to Indians & inciting outlaws & settlers began to enjoy the lush Ohio Valley in peace. Then one day while on the trail of outlaws, Wetzel gave Zane an admonition & shared a startling secret.

Last Trail. unabr. ed. Zane Grey. Read by Robert Morris. (Running Time: 28800 sec.). 2007. audio compact disk 55.00 (978-0-7861-6120-1(5)); audio compact disk 29.95 (978-0-7861-6121-8(3)) Blckstn Audio.

Last Trail. unabr. ed. Zane Grey. Read by Gene Engene. 6 cass. (Running Time: 8 hrs.). 1989. 39.95 (978-1-55686-308-0(X), 308) Books in Motion.
A group of travelers are saved from a band of Indians by a legendary hero.

Last Trail. unabr. ed. Zane Grey. Narrated by Michael Prichard. (Running Time: 8 hrs. 30 mins. 0 sec.). (Ohio River Ser.). (ENG.). 2009. lab manual ed. 55.99 (978-1-4001-3928-6(7)); audio compact disk 19.99 (978-1-4001-5928-4(8)); audio compact disk 27.99 (978-1-4001-0928-9(0)) Pub: Tantor Media. Dist(s): IngramPubServ

***Last Train from Hiroshima: The Survivors Look Back.** unabr. ed. Charles R. Pellegrino. Narrated by Arthur Morey. (Running Time: 13 hrs. 0 mins.).

2010. 18.99 (978-1-4001-8563-4(7)); 37.99 (978-1-4001-9563-3(2)); 24.99 (978-1-4001-6563-6(6)); audio compact disk 75.99 (978-1-4001-4563-8(5)); audio compact disk 37.99 (978-1-4001-1563-1(9)) Pub: Tantor Media. Dist(s): IngramPubServ

Last Train North. unabr. ed. Clifton L. Taulbert. Narrated by Peter Francis James. 4 cass. (Running Time: 5 hrs.). 1994. 35.00 (978-1-55690-990-0(X), 94129E7) Recorded Bks.
He offers an interesting complement to traditional books about growing up black in the South in the 60s. His story is upbeat & brimming with an untried young man's enthusiasm as he prepares to embark upon a thrilling, sometimes painful, odyssey. With a backdrop of racial tension, the Vietnam war, & a presidential assassination, Taulbert's autobiographical account is warm, dignified & uplifting.

Last Train of Christmas. Kaye Jacobs Volk. 1 cass. 1.77 (978-1-57734-184-0(8), 06005675) Covenant Comms.

Last Train to Memphis: The Rise of Elvis Presley. abr. ed. Peter Guralnick. Read by J. Charles. 2 cass. (Running Time: 3 hrs.). 2000. 7.95 (978-1-57815-017-5(5), 1050, Media Bks Audio) Media Bks NJ.
A fresh, realistic look at the early years in the life of Elvis Presley.

Last Train to Paradise. Les Standiford. Read by Del Roy. 2002. 48.00 (978-0-7366-8784-3(X)); audio compact disk 56.00 (978-0-7366-8785-0(8)) Books on Tape.

Last True Story I'll Ever Tell. unabr. ed. John Crawford. Read by Patrick G. Lawlor. (Running Time: 6 hrs. 0 mins. 0 sec.). (ENG.). 2005. audio compact disk 24.99 (978-1-4001-0174-0(3)) Pub: Tantor Media. Dist(s): IngramPubServ

Last True Story I'll Ever Tell: An Accidental Soldier's Account of the War in Iraq. John Crawford. Read by Patrick G. Lawlor. (Playaway Adult Nonfiction Ser.). 2008. 49.99 (978-1-60640-972-5(7)) Find a World.

Last True Story I'll Ever Tell: An Accidental Soldier's Account of the War in Iraq. unabr. ed. John R. Crawford. Read by Patrick G. Lawlor. (Running Time: 6 hrs. 0 mins. 0 sec.). (ENG.). 2005. audio compact disk 49.99 (978-1-4001-3174-7(X)) Pub: Tantor Media. Dist(s): IngramPubServ

Last True Story I'll Ever Tell: An Accidental Soldier's Account of the War in Iraq. unabr. ed. John R. Crawford & Patrick G. Lawlor. (Running Time: 6 hrs. 0 mins. 0 sec.). (ENG.). 2005. audio compact disk 19.99 (978-1-4001-5174-5(0)) Pub: Tantor Media. Dist(s): IngramPubServ

Last Tsar: The Life & Death of Nicholas II. unabr. ed. Edvard Radzinsky. Read by Wolfram Kandinsky. 15 cass. (Running Time: 22 hrs. 30 min.). 1993. 120.00 (3117) Books on Tape.
A fascinating portrait of the monarch & a convincing account of the final days of the royal family.

Last Tycoon. abr. ed. F. Scott Fitzgerald. (Classic Stage Ser.). 2003. audio compact disk 14.99 (978-1-894003-35-3(7)) Pub: Scenario Prods CAN. Dist(s): Baker Taylor

Last Tycoon. unabr. ed. F. Scott Fitzgerald. Read by William Roberts. 4 cass. (Running Time: 6 hrs.). 2000. 39.95 (978-0-7540-0523-0(2), CAB 1946) AudioGO.
Fitzgerald's last work & died without completing it. The tycoon hero is Stahr & caught in the crossfire of his own effortless cynicism & his silent secret vulnerability, he inhabits a world dominated by business, alcohol & promiscuity.

Last Tycoon; Vanity Fair. unabr. ed. F. Scott Fitzgerald & William Makepeace Thackeray. Contrib. by Lucio Agostini. 2 cass. (Running Time: 120 min.). 2000. (978-1-894003-14-8(4)) Scenario Prods CAN.
The tragic story of Munroe Stahr, a brilliant young studio executive and his relationships with the actors, writers and directors who move within the world of 1930s Hollywood. He has the power to make anyone's dreams come true... except his own.

Last Tycoons: The Secret History of Lazard Frères & Co. abr. ed. William D. Cohan. Read by David Aaron Baker. (Running Time: 32400 sec.). (ENG.). 2007. audio compact disk 34.95 (978-0-7393-4197-1(9), Random AudioBks) Pub: Random Audio Pubg. Dist(s): Random

***Last Unicorn.** Peter S. Beagle. Read by Peter S. Beagle. Music by Jeff Slingluff. Prod. by Connor Cochran & Lively Jim. Engineer Lively Jim. (ENG.). 2005. 30.00 (978-0-9706801-0-5(4)) Conlan Pr.

Last Voice You Hear. Mick Herron. 8 cass. (Isis Cassettes Ser.). (J). 2005. 69.95 (978-0-7531-2107-8(7)); audio compact disk 84.95 (978-0-7531-2385-0(1)) Pub: ISIS Lrg Prnt GBR. Dist(s): Ulverscroft US

Last Voyage, unabr. ed. Hammond Innes. Narrated by Nelson Runger. 5 cass. (Running Time: 7 hrs.). 1988. 44.00 (978-1-55690-305-2(7), 88995E7) Recorded Bks.
A fictional re-creation of Captain James Cook's journals & the events leading to February 14, 1779, on a beach in Hawaii where Cook met his death.

Last Voyage. unabr. collector's ed. Hammond Innes. Read by Paul Shay. 8 cass. (Running Time: 8 hrs.). 1984. 48.00 (978-0-7366-0861-9(3), 1812) Books on Tape.
Innes imagines the private journal that Captain James Cook might have kept on the voyage that ended in his death in 1779.

Last Voyage of Columbus: Being the Epic Tale of the Great Captain's Fourth Expedition, Including Accounts of Mutiny, Shipwreck, & Discovery. abr. ed. Martin Dugard. Read by Simon Jones. (YA). 2007. 49.99 (978-1-60252-614-3(1)) Find a World.

Last Voyage of Columbus: Being the Epic Tale of the Great Captain's Fourth Expedition Including Accounts of Swordfight, Mutiny, Shipwreck, Gold, War, Hurrican, & Discovery. abr. ed. Martin Dugard. Read by Simon Jones. (ENG.). 2005. 14.98 (978-1-59483-169-0(6)) Pub: Hachet Audio. Dist(s): HachBkGrp

Last Voyage of Columbus: Being the Epic Tale of the Great Captain's Fourth Expedition, Including Accounts of Swordfight, Mutiny, Shipwreck, Gold, War, Hurricane, & Discovery. abr. ed. Martin Dugard. Read by Simon Jones. (Running Time: 6 hrs.). (ENG.). 2009. 44.98 (978-1-60788-047-9(4)) Pub: Hachet Audio. Dist(s): HachBkGrp

Last Voyage of Sinbad Singh. unabr. ed. Toni Sweeney. Read by Jerry Sciarrio. 6 cass. (Running Time: 7 hrs. 30 min.). 2001. 39.95 (978-1-58116-071-0(2)) Books in Motion.
Sinbad Singh is known throughout the galaxy as an adventurer and smuggler. When Andrea Talltrees hires Sinbad to find her husband's lost spaceship, the two uncover a plot by the Serapian Army to secretly infiltrate the Earth.

Last Voyage of the Karluk. Robert A. Bartlett. Read by Frank Holden. 1 mp3. (Running Time: 25200 sec.). 2005. audio compact disk 24.95 (978-0-9734223-5-1(1)) Pub: Rattling Bks CAN. Dist(s): Hse Anansi

Last Voyage of the Lusitania. Kenneth Bruce. 1 cass. (Running Time: 1 hr.). (Excursions in History Ser.). 12.50 Alpha Tape.

Last Voyage of the "Resolute" see Man Without a Country

***Last Watcher.** D. B. Clifton. Read by Simon Prebble. (Running Time: 70). (ENG.). 2009. 2.99 (978-1-61114-014-9(5)); audio compact disk 2.66 (978-0-9825278-5-6(3)) Mind Wings Aud.

Last Week. unabr. ed. Marcus J. Borg & John Dominic Crossan. Read by Alan Sklar. 7 CDs. (Running Time: 30600 sec.). (ENG.). 2006. audio compact disk 32.95 (978-1-59887-037-4(8), 1598870378) Pub: HighBridge. Dist(s): Workman Pub

Last Week in December. unabr. ed. Ursula Dubosarsky. 2 cass. (Running Time: 3 hrs. 45 mins.). (J). 2004. 24.00 (978-1-74030-737-6(2)) Pub: Bolinda Pubng AUS. Dist(s): Bolinda Pub Inc

Last Week in December. unabr. ed. Ursula Dubosarsky. 4 CDs. (Running Time: 3 hrs. 45 mins.). (J). 2004. audio compact disk 57.95 (978-1-74093-131-5(1)) Pub: Bolinda Pubng AUS. Dist(s): Bolinda Pub Inc

Last Week of Jesus. unabr. ed. Keith A. Butler. 3 cass. (Running Time: 4 hrs. 30 mins.). 2001. 15.00 (A135) Word Faith Pubng.

***Last Werewolf.** unabr. ed. Glen Duncan. (ENG.). 2011. audio compact disk 40.00 (978-0-307-91733-1(9), Random AudioBks) Pub: Random Audio Pubg. Dist(s): Random

Last Wife of Henry VIII. unabr. ed. Carolly Erickson. Narrated by Terry Donnelly. 9 CDs. (Running Time: 44040 sec.). 2006. audio compact disk 89.95 (978-0-7927-4616-4(3), SLD 1059); audio compact disk 54.95 (978-0-7927-4617-1(1), CMP 1059) AudioGO.

Last Wife of Henry VIII. unabr. ed. Carolly Erickson. Read by Terry Donnelly. 4 CDs. (Running Time: 12 hrs. 0 mins. 0 sec.). (ENG.). 2006. audio compact disk 39.95 (978-1-59397-962-1(2)) Pub: Macmill Audio. Dist(s): Macmillan

Last Will & Testament. unabr. ed. E. X. Ferrars. Read by Diana Bishop. 4 cass. (Running Time: 6 hrs.). (Sound Ser.). 2004. 44.95 (978-1-85496-692-6(8), 980704) Pub: UlverLrgPrint GBR. Dist(s): Ulverscroft US
The death of Virginia's friend, Mrs. Arliss, was causing problems. Mrs. Arliss had had a penchant for changing her will, but the bequests in her last one were surprising, to say the least. Was it actually her last? Then Virginia learned that the money bequeathed was non-existent. When the most valuable remaining legacy vanished & three people died violently, the relationships of those connected with the testator were complicated ... their motives equally so.

Last Will Be First. 6 cass. 19.95 (20141, HarperThor) HarpC GBR.

Last Wolf of Ireland, unabr. ed. Elona Malterre. Narrated by Donal Donnelly. 3 pieces. (Running Time: 3 hrs. 30 mins.). (gr. 6 up). 1992. 27.00 (978-1-55690-598-8(X), 92203E7) Recorded Bks.
The last wolf in Ireland was killed in a place called Barne's Gap in 1786. This is the story of that wolf & of the boy & girl who tried to save him.

Last Word. unabr. ed. Kathy Herman. Narrated by Tim Lundeen. (Running Time: 10 hrs. 10 mins. 2 sec.). (Sophie Trace Ser.). (ENG.). 2009. 20.99 (978-1-60814-533-1(6)); audio compact disk 29.99 (978-1-59859-593-2(8)) Oasis Audio.

Last Word on the Middle East Pt. 1: God's Predetermined Purpose. Derek Prince. 1 cass. (I-7009) Derek Prince.

Last Word on the Middle East Pt. 2: Our Response to God's Purpose. Derek Prince. 1 cass. (I-7010) Derek Prince.

Last Words. Lorraine Taylor. 3 cass. (Running Time: 4 hrs.). 2004. 14.95 (978-1-59156-222-1(8)) Covenant Comms.

Last Words: A Memoir. abr. ed. George Carlin. Read by Patrick Carlin. Told to Tony Hendra. 5 CDs. (Running Time: 6 hrs. 0 mins. 0 sec.). (ENG.). 2009. audio compact disk 29.99 (978-1-4423-0318-8(2)) Pub: S&S Audio. Dist(s): S and S Inc

Last Words for the Last Days. Warren W. Wiersbe. Read by Warren W. Wiersbe. 1 cass. 14.95 (978-0-8474-2231-9(3)) Back to Bible.
In these four messages for the New Year, he warns Christians to be mindful of the Scriptures, not to be ignorant, to be diligent & to beware of false prophets.

Last 100 Days, Pt. 1. collector's ed. John Toland. Read by John MacDonald. 10 cass. (Running Time: 15 hrs.). 1988. 80.00 (978-0-7366-1375-0(7), 2270-A) Books on Tape.
Germany was so badly beaten that hardly anyone was left to organize the surrender.

Last 100 Days, Pt. 2. collector's ed. John Toland. Read by John MacDonald. 8 cass. (Running Time: 12 hrs.). 1988. 64.00 (978-0-7366-1376-7(5), 2270-B) Books on Tape.

Lasting Impressions. Leta N. Childers. Read by Leta N. Childers. 1 cass. (Running Time: 1 hr. 50 min.). 1999. bk. 6.50 (978-1-58495-002-8(1)) DiskUs Publishing.
Romantic comedy.

Lasting Intimacy & Fulfillment, John Gray. Read by John Gray. 2 cass. (Running Time: 2 hrs. 45 min.). (Secrets of Successful Relationships Ser.). 1994. 17.95 (978-1-886095-04-5(3)) Genesis Media Grp.
A seminar series helping people understand the opposite sex.

Lasting Love: How to Avoid Marital Failure. Alistair Begg. Read by Alistair Begg. 2 cass. (Running Time: 3 hrs.). (ENG.). 1997. 14.99 (978-0-8024-3402-9(9)) Moody.
If you fail to plan, you plan to fail. Months, even years, before the wedding, couples start planning their special day. She finds the perfect dress; he refines the details of their honeymoon get-away. They test the caterer's delicacies and listen to endless music choices. This will be the first day of the rest of their beautiful life together. Yet even with all that planning, statistics say their marriage has only a 50% chance of surviving. While no one takes that blissful walk down the isle with a mapped-out plan to destroy their marriage, most of us will never take the time and effort required to preserve our marriages before they hit rock-bottom. In Lasting Love, Alistair Begg urges all married couples and those contemplating marriage to take to heart what God has told His people about creating and preserving a fulfilling marriage. Realize that marital failure can happen to anyone - even you Listen to your spouse Don't take your mate for granted Be daring and imaginative in displaying your affection Work hard to make your marriage a success Let Alistair Begg teach you how to guard your marriage and stand firm against anything or anyone that would draw your attention away from your spouse. God created marriages to last. Will yours? Audio Cassette.

Lasting Love Relationships. Sondra Ray. 2 cass. 1995. pap. bk. 16.95 (978-1-879323-23-0(0)) Sound Horizons AV.
The best-selling author of "Loving Relationships" & "The Only Diet There Is" on spoken word for the first time! Here Sondra Ray, founder of The Loving Relationships Training, speaks directly to the problems & challenges of relationships. Communicating universal truths about all aspects of life, Sondra identifies "The Five Biggies" (basic patterns) that unconsciously affect us most frequently & more.

Lastness see Poetry & Voice of Galway Kinnell

Late Antiquity: Crisis & Transformation. Instructed by Thomas F. X. Noble. 2008. 199.95 (978-1-59803-489-9(8)); audio compact disk 99.95 (978-1-59803-490-5(1)) Teaching Co.

Late August see Poetry & Voice of Margaret Atwood

Late Bloomer. abr. ed. Fern Michaels. Read by Michele Pawk. 2004. 15.95 (978-0-7435-4921-9(X)) Pub: S&S Audio. Dist(s): S and S Inc

Late Bloomers. unabr. collector's ed. Brendan Gill. Read by Barrett Whitener. 2 cass. (Running Time: 3 hrs.). 1998. 17.95 (978-0-7366-3990-3(X), 4269) Books on Tape.
An inspirational proof that great life achievements don't necessarily happen only to younger people. A profile of 75 extraordinary people.

Late Eight. Ken Bleile. 2006. pap. bk. 79.95 (978-1-59756-082-5(0)) Plural Pub Inc.

Late for the Wedding. unabr. ed. Amanda Quick, pseud. 8 cass. (Running Time: 12 hrs.). 2003. 64.00 (978-0-7366-9137-6(5)) Books on Tape.

Late Great Planet Earth. unabr. ed. Hal Lindsey. Told to C. C. Carlson. (Running Time: 23400 sec.). 2007. 44.95 (978-1-4332-0711-2(7)); audio compact disk 29.95 (978-1-4332-0713-6(3)); audio compact disk 45.00 (978-1-4332-0712-9(5)) Blckstn Audio.

Late Great United States. unabr. ed. Mark Hitchcock. Narrated by Lloyd James. (Running Time: 6 hrs. 15 mins. 0 sec.). (ENG.). 2009. audio compact disk 21.98 (978-1-59644-694-6(3), Hovel Audio) christianaud.

***Late Great United States.** unabr. ed. Mark Hitchcock. Narrated by Lloyd James. (ENG.). 2009. 12.98 (978-1-59644-695-3(1), Hovel Audio) christianaud.

Late, Lamented Molly Marx. unabr. ed. Sally Koslow. Read by Tanya Eby. (Running Time: 12 hrs.). 2009. 24.99 (978-1-4233-8546-2(2), 9781423385462, BAD); 39.97 (978-1-4233-8545-5(4), 9781423385455, Brlnc Audio MP3 Lib) Brilliance Audio.

Late, Lamented Molly Marx. unabr. ed. Sally Koslow. Read by Tanya Eby Sirois & Tanya Eby. 1 MP3-CD. (Running Time: 12 hrs.). 2009. 24.99 (978-1-4233-8544-8(6), 9781423385448, Brilliance MP3) Brilliance Audio.

Late, Lamented Molly Marx. unabr. ed. Sally Koslow. Read by Tanya Eby Sirois. (Running Time: 12 hrs.). 2009. 39.97 (978-1-4233-8547-9(0), 9781423385479, BADLE) Brilliance Audio.

Late, Lamented Molly Marx. unabr. ed. Sally Koslow. Read by Tanya Eby. 10 CDs. (Running Time: 12 hrs.). 2009. audio compact disk 97.97 (978-1-4233-8543-1(8), 9781423385431, BriAudCD Unabrid) Brilliance Audio.

Late, Lamented Molly Marx. unabr. ed. Sally Koslow. Read by Tanya Eby Sirois & Tanya Eby. 10 CDs. (Running Time: 12 hrs.). 2009. audio compact disk 29.99 (978-1-4233-8542-4(X), 9781423385424, Bril Audio CD Unabri) Brilliance Audio.

Late Lark Singing. Sybil Marshall. Read by Norma West. 16 cass. (Running Time: 21 hrs.). (Delightful Swithinford Ser.). (J). 2004. 104.95 (978-1-84283-354-4(5)) Pub: ISIS Lrg Prnt GBR. Dist(s): Ulverscroft US

Late Last Night. Joe Scruggs. 1 cass. (Running Time: 35 min.). (J). (ps-2). 1984. 9.95 (978-0-916123-05-5(7), CLS-421) Ed Graphics Pr.
Features 11 songs for children as well as their parents & teachers.

Late Last Night. Joe Scruggs. 1 cass. (J). 7.98 (LY 9422); audio compact disk 11.98 CD. (LY 9423) NewSound.

***Late, Late at Night.** unabr. ed. Rick Springfield. Read by Rick Springfield. (Running Time: 14 hrs. 0 mins. 0 sec.). (ENG.). 2010. audio compact disk 39.99 (978-1-4423-3751-0(6)) Pub: S&S Audio. Dist(s): S and S Inc

Late Man, unabr. collector's ed. James P. Girard. Read by John Edwardson. 7 cass. (Running Time: 10 hrs. 30 min.). 1995. 56.00 (978-0-7366-3177-8(1), 3846) Books on Tape.
A serial murder binds a cop & two reporters in a relentless search for a strangler. Sexual obsession is the glue.

Late Middle Ages. Instructed by Philip Daileader. 2007. 129.95 (978-1-59803-342-7(5)); audio compact disk 69.95 (978-1-59803-343-4(3)) Teaching Co.

Late Night Thoughts on Listening to Mahler's Ninth Symphony, unabr. ed. Lewis Thomas. Narrated by George Guidall. 4 cass. (Running Time: 5 hrs. 15 mins.). 1992. 35.00 (978-1-55690-715-9(X), 92420E7) Recorded Bks.
A collection of essays ranging from the riddle of smelling to nuclear proliferation. We are introduced to Thomas' concerns: the natural altruism of organisms; the inter-relatedness of all creatures; the fragility of the human species; the uneasiness of life on a threatened planet.

Late Phoenix. unabr. ed. Catherine Aird. Read by Robin Bailey. 4 cass. (Running Time: 4 hrs. 47 mins.). (C. D. Sloan Mystery Ser.). 2001. 24.95 (978-1-57270-160-1(9), N41160u, Audio Edits Mystry) Pub: Audio Partners. Dist(s): PerseuPGW
The skeleton of a mother & her unborn baby are found in the rubble of German bombs during redevelopment decades after the war.

Late Romantic Music for Cello & Piano. 2007. audio compact disk 25.00 (978-1-931569-07-1(X)) Pub: U of Wis Pr. Dist(s): Chicago Distribution Ctr

Late Spring. unabr. ed. R. F. Delderfield. Read by Christian Rodska. 8 cass. (Running Time: 12 hrs.). (To Serve Them All My Days Ser.: Bk. 1). 2000. 59.95 (CAB 712) Pub: Chivers Audio Bks GBR. Dist(s): AudioGO

Late Wasp see Twentieth-Century Poetry in English, No. 23, Recordings of Poets Reading Their Own Poetry

***Lateness of the Hour.** 2010. audio compact disk (978-1-59171-151-3(7)) Falcon Picture.

Latent Human Potentialities. unabr. ed. Aldous Huxley. 1 cass. (Running Time: 1 hr. 14 min.). (Human Situation Ser.). 1959. 11.00 (01120) Big Sur Tapes.

Later Years. Tom Dolgoff. Read by Tom Dolgoff. 1 cass. (Running Time: 1 hr. 06 min.). (Executive Seminar Ser.). 1987. 10.00 (978-1-56948-009-0(5)) Menninger Clinic.
Thomas Dolgoff discusses the impact of the later years from a developmental perspective. He challenges us to examine our stereotypes about aging, & shows how the understanding of our own aging & mortality is crucial for the realization of our full potential at earlier life stages.

Latest Period in Yiddish Literature. unabr. ed. Maurice Samuel. Read by Poetry Center Staff. 1 cass. (Running Time: 48 min.). (On Yiddish Ser.). 1967. 12.95 (23238) J Norton Pubs.
Reviews modern Yiddish poetry & relays their inherent charm through translation & comprehensive explanation.

Lathe of Heaven. unabr. ed. Ursula K. Le Guin. Read by Susan O'Malley. 5 cass. (Running Time: 7 hrs. 30 mins.). 1999. 39.95 (756010) Blckstn Audio.
George Orr's dreams do change the world. He is the only one who knows it, he & the power-mad psychiatrist who forces George to dream a better world into existence, a world that is free from war, disease, overpopulation & all human misery. But for every man-made dream of utopia, there is a terrifying, unforeseeable consequence; so George must dream & dream again, forever seeking a perfect future until the very essence of cosmic reality begins to disintegrate.

Lathe of Heaven. unabr. ed. Ursula K. Le Guin. Read by Susan O'Malley. 5 cass. (Running Time: 7 hr. 30 min.). 2003. 39.95 (978-0-7861-1303-3(0), DH71D) Blckstn Audio.
George Orr's dreams do change the world. He is the only one who knows it...he & the power-mad psychiatrist who is forcing George to dream a new reality. But for every man-made dream of utopia, there is a terrifying, unforeseeable consequence; so George must dream & dream again,

forever seeking a perfect future-until the very essence of cosmic reality begins to disintegrate.

Latices & Hamentashens. Fran Avni. Read by Fran Avni. 1 cass. (J). (ps-4). 1992. 9.98 (978-1-877737-87-9(9), MLP 429) MFLP CA.
Songs of Chanukah & Purim, joyous & festive.

Latin. 2 cass. (Running Time: 80 min.). (Language - Thirty Library). bk. 16.95 set in vinyl album. Moonbeam Pubns.
Using the proven method based on the famous U.S. Military accelerated language leaming program, Language/30 courses stress conversationally useful words & phrases.

Latin. unabr. ed. Ed. by Charles Berlitz. 2 cass. (Running Time: 1 hr. 30 mins.). (Language/30 Brief Course Ser.). pap. bk. 21.95 (AF1058) J Norton Pubs.
Quick, highly condensed introduction to the words & phrases you'll need to communicate effectively in the country you're visiting. Cassettes & phrase guide book are in a vinyl album.

Latin: A Structural Approach. Sweet et al. 6 cass. 1966. 57.43 U MI Lang Res.

Latin: Language 30. Educational Services Corporation Staff. 2004. audio compact disk 21.95 (978-1-931850-13-1(5)) Educ Svcs DC.

Latin: Language/30. rev. ed. Educational Services Corporation Staff. Intro. by Charles Berlitz. 2 cass. (LAT.). 1995. pap. bk. 21.95 (978-0-910542-89-0(9)) Educ Svcs DC.
Latin self-teaching language course.

Latin America & the Caribbean: An Annotated History. Barbara Brodman. Illus. by Tedy M. Pacheco. 2 CDs. (Running Time: 3 hrs.). (C). 2001. audio compact disk 65.00 (978-1-879857-88-9(X)) SFEAA.
A history of Latin America through the 19th Century, with original text, videotaped lectures and study guides.

Latin America & the Caribbean Demographic Observatory: Mortality - Year II (Includes CD-ROM). United Nations. (ENG & FRE.). 2008. pap. bk. 25.00 (978-92-1-021065-2(4)) Untd Nat Pubns.

Latin American Spanish Speed Cassette. Mark Frobose. 3 cass. (Running Time: 3 hrs.). (SPA.). 2000. 24.00 (978-1-893564-83-1(5)) Macmill Audio.

Latin American Trumpet Music. Gabriel Rosati. 1996. spiral bd. 15.00 (978-0-7866-0726-6(2), 95601BCD) Mel Bay.

Latin Bass Book. Oscar Stagnaro & Chuck Sher. 2005. pap. bk. 34.00 (978-1-883217-11-2(3), 00242133) Pub: Sher Music. Dist(s): H Leonard

Latin Fiesta: Instrumental. Prod. by One Voice Records Staff. 2002. audio compact disk Provident Mus Dist.

Latin Music Through the Ages. unabr. ed. Lafayette C. Singers. 1 cass. (Running Time: 45 mins.). pap. bk. 29.50 (SLT150) J Norton Pubs.

***Latin Music U. S. A. - DVD & CD Set.** Prod. by Wgbh. (ENG.). (C). 2009. DVD & audio compact disk 44.99 (978-1-60883-129-6(9)) PublicMedia.

Latin Percussion in Perspective. Dominick Moio. 1997. pap. bk. 19.95 (978-0-7866-2870-4(7), 96682BCD) Mel Bay.

Latin Playground. abr. ed. Putumayo. 1 CD. (Running Time: 40 mins.). (World Playground Ser.). (SPA.). (J). 2002. audio compact disk 15.98 (978-1-58759-055-9(7)) Putumayo Wrld.
Nine Latin American cultures are represented, from Flaco Jiminez' Tex-Mex style to the rhythmic songs presented by artists from Cuba, Ecuador, Venezuela and other countries.

Latin Primer I Computer Flash Cards. Featuring Julie Garfield. (LAT.). (J). 2008. audio compact disk 20.00 (978-1-935000-14-3(4)) LogosPr.

Latin Primer II: Pronunciation Aid. Read by Julie Garfield. (YA). 1994. cd-rom 10.00 (978-1-59128-019-4(2)) Canon Pr ID.

Latin Primer II Computer Flash Cards. Featuring Julie Garfield. (J). 2008. audio compact disk 20.00 (978-1-935000-15-0(2)) LogosPr.

Latin Primer III Computer Flash Cards. Featuring Julie Garfield. (J). 2008. audio compact disk 20.00 (978-1-935000-16-7(0)) LogosPr.

Latin Primer 1 - Audio Guide. Mackenzie Miller. Voice by Chelsea Jones. (ENG & LAT.). (J). 2009. suppl. ed. 10.00 (978-1-59128-378-2(7)) Canon Pr ID.

Latin Pronunciation Aid: For Primer I. Featuring Julie Garfield. (Mars Hill Textbook Ser.). (YA). 1992. 10.00 (978-1-885767-76-9(5)) Canon Pr ID.

Latin sans Peine. 1 cass. (Running Time: 1 hr., 30 min.). (FRE & LAT.). 2000. bk. 75.00 (978-2-7005-1343-1(6)) Pub: Assimil FRA. Dist(s): Distribks Inc

Latin Siesta: Instrumental. Executive Producer Jose Pepe Garces. Prod. by Gloria Garces. 2002. audio compact disk 13.98 Provident Mus Dist.

Latin Teacher Pronunciation Guide. 12.00 (978-1-59166-135-1(8)) BJUPr.

Latin Themes for Alto Sax. Max Charles Davies. 2008. pap. bk. 19.95 (978-1-84761-126-0(5), 1847611265) Pub: Schott Music Corp. Dist(s): H Leonard

Latin Themes for Cello. Max Charles Davies. 2008. pap. bk. 19.95 (978-1-84761-122-2(2), 1847611222) Pub: Schott Music Corp. Dist(s): H Leonard

Latin Themes for Clarinet. Max Charles Davies. 2008. pap. bk. 19.95 (978-1-84761-125-3(7), 1847611257) Pub: Schott Music Corp. Dist(s): H Leonard

Latin Themes for Flute. Max Charles Davies. 2008. pap. bk. 19.95 (978-1-84761-123-9(0), 1847611230) Pub: Schott Music Corp. Dist(s): H Leonard

Latin Themes for Oboe. Max Charles Davies. 2008. pap. bk. 19.95 (978-1-84761-124-6(9), 1847611249) Pub: Schott Music Corp. Dist(s): H Leonard

Latin Themes for Tenor Saxophone. Max Charles Davies. 2008. pap. bk. 19.95 (978-1-84761-129-1(X), 184761129X) Pub: Schott Music Corp. Dist(s): H Leonard

Latin Themes for Trombone. Max Charles Davies. 2008. pap. bk. 19.95 (978-1-84761-128-4(1), 1847611281) Pub: Schott Music Corp. Dist(s): H Leonard

Latin Themes for Trumpet. Max Charles Davies. 2008. pap. bk. 19.95 (978-1-84761-127-7(3), 1847611273) Pub: Schott Music Corp. Dist(s): H Leonard

Latin Themes for Viola. Max Charles Davies. 2008. pap. bk. 19.95 (978-1-84761-121-5(4), 1847611214) Pub: Schott Music Corp. Dist(s): H Leonard

Latin Themes for Violin. Max Charles Davies. 2008. pap. bk. 19.95 (978-1-84761-120-8(6), 1847611206) Pub: Schott Music Corp. Dist(s): H Leonard

Latin Via Ovid: Audio Materials. Norma Goldman & Jacob E. Nyenhuis. 2002. audio compact disk 255.00 (978-0-8143-3146-0(7), Great Lks Bks); 255.00 (978-0-8143-3144-6(0), Great Lks Bks) Wayne St U Pr.
Both instructors and students benefit from these audio materials that provide an interactive way to learn while reinforcing what is gained from the lessons within the textbook. They enable students to read Latin aloud with pleasure and confidence, allow for better vocabulary understanding, and help students to appreciate and duplicate the rhythms of spoken Latin.

Latina Christiana I Pronunciation Tape: Introduction to Christian Latin. 2nd rev. ed. Cheryl Lowe. 1 cass. (Running Time: 70 mins.). (J). 2001. 4.95 (978-1-930953-03-1(8), 104T) Memoria.

Latina Christiana II Pronunciation Tape: Introduction to Christian Latin. 2nd ed. Based on a book by Cheryl Lowe. 1 cass. (Running Time: 70 mins.). (J). 2001. 4.95 (978-1-930953-08-6(9)) Memoria.

Latina Christiana 1, Set. 2004. pap. bk. 39.95 (978-1-930953-00-0(3)) Memoria.

Latina Christiana 1 Pronou. 2004. bk. 4.95 (978-1-930953-04-8(6)) Memoria.

Latina Christiana 2, Set. 2004. pap. bk. 39.95 (978-1-930953-05-5(4)) Memoria.

Latina Christiana 2 Pronou. 2004. bk. 4.95 (978-1-930953-09-3(7)) Memoria.

Latinitas for Solo Guitar. Alfonso Montes. 2008. pap. bk. 14.95 (978-0-7866-0849-2(8)) Mel Bay.

Latino. (Running Time: 60 mins.). 2002. audio compact disk 15.99 (978-1-904972-45-7(4)) Global Jrny GBR GBR.

Latino Legends: Hispanics in Major League Baseball. (High Five Reading - Green Ser.). (ENG.). (gr. 3-4). 2007. audio compact disk 5.95 (978-1-4296-1442-9(0)) CapstoneDig.

Latino Legends: Hispanics in Major League Baseball. Michael Silverstone. (High Five Reading - Green Ser.). (ENG.). (gr. 4 up). 2003. audio compact disk 5.95 (978-0-7368-2852-9(4)) CapstoneDig.

***Latino Wave.** abr. ed. Jorge Ramos. Read by Jonathan Davis. (ENG.). 2004. (978-0-06-081785-5(2), Harper Audio); (978-0-06-081784-8(4), Harper Audio) HarperCollins Pubs.

Latin's Not So Tough! - Pronunciation Cassette Tape for Levels 1-3: A Classical Latin Pronunciation Tape. Read by Karen Mohs & Amy Mohs. Text by Karen Mohs. 1 cass. (Running Time: 51 mins.). (J). 1999. suppl. ed. 8.00 (978-1-931842-77-8(9), LA-TP-123) Greek n Stuff.
This pronunciation cassette tape is designed to be used with the Latin's Not So Tough! Level 1, Level 2, and Level 3 workbooks. It features the classical pronunciation of the letters, diphthongs, special consonant sounds, words, and paradigms taught in the first three levels.

Latin's Not So Tough! - Pronunciation Cassette Tape for Levels 4-5: A Classical Latin Pronunciation Tape. Read by Karen Mohs & Amy Mohs. Text by Karen Mohs. 1 cass. (Running Time: 71 mins.). (YA). 1999. suppl. ed. 8.00 (978-1-931842-78-5(7), LA-TP-45) Greek n Stuff.
This pronunciation cassette tape is designed to be used with the Latin's Not So Tough! Level 4 and Level 5 workbooks. It features the classical pronunciation of the letters, diphthongs, special consonant sounds, words, and paradigms taught in the fourth and fifth levels.

Latin's Not So Tough! - Pronunciation CD for Levels 1-3: A Classical Latin Pronunciation CD. Read by Karen Mohs & Amy Mohs. Text by Karen Mohs. 1 CD. (Running Time: 17 mins.). (J). 1999. suppl. ed. 10.00 (978-1-931842-75-4(2), LA-CD-123) Greek n Stuff.
This pronunciation CD is designed to be used with the Latin's Not So Tough! Level 1, Level 2, and Level 3 workbooks. It features the classical pronunciation of the letters, diphthongs, special consonant sounds, words, and paradigms taught in the first three levels.

Latin's Not So Tough! - Pronunciation CD for Levels 4-5: A Classical Latin Pronunciation CD. Read by Karen Mohs & Amy Mohs. Text by Karen Mohs. 1 CD. (Running Time: 41 mins.). (J). 1999. suppl. ed. 10.00 (978-1-931842-76-1(0), LA-CD-45) Greek n Stuff.
This pronunciation CD is designed to be used with the Latin's Not So Tough! Level 4 and Level 5 workbooks. It features the classical pronunciation of the letters, diphthongs, special consonant sounds, words, and paradigms taught in the fourth and fifth levels.

Latkes & Hamentashen. Fran Avni. 1 LP. (Running Time: 1 hr.). (J). 2001. 14.95 (LS1002CD); 10.95 (LS 1002C) Kimbo Educ.
Chanukah & Purim in song & story. Walking to Jerusalem, Cleaning the Temple, I'm a Dreydle, A silly King, Sas People, Oy, Oy, Uncle Mordecai, The Meanest Man, Purim's Here & more.

Latkes & Hamentashen: Holidays in Song & Story. Fran Avni. 1 cass. (J). (ps-4). 9.98 (429) MFLP CA.
Fran brings to life the people who symbolize the Jewish holidays of Hanukah & Purim. With warm imaginative arrangements, families are musically introduced & invited to celebrate these joyous, festive times.

Latter-Day History of the Church of Jesus Christ of Latter-Day Saints. Brian Kelley & Petrea Kelley. 23 CDs. 2004. bk. 49.95 (978-1-57734-761-3(7)) Covenant Comms.

Latter-Day History of the Church of Jesus Christ of Latter-Day Saints. Compiled by Brian Kelley & Petrea Kelley. 20 cass. 2004. 49.95 (978-1-57734-738-5(2)) Covenant Comms.

Latter-day Insights: The Middle East. Victor L. Ludlow. 2 cass. 2004. 14.95 (978-1-59156-239-9(2)); audio compact disk 14.95 (978-1-59156-240-5(6)) Covenant Comms.

Latter-Day Laughs. 2004. 9.95 (978-1-57734-696-8(3)); audio compact disk 10.95 (978-1-57734-697-5(1)) Covenant Comms.

Latter-Day Prophets. Emerson West. 2 cass. 2004. 11.95 (978-1-57734-318-9(2), 07001886) Covenant Comms.

Latter-Day Saint View of Christ & the Trinity. unabr. ed. Duane S. Crowther. Read by Duane S. Crowther. 1 cass. (Running Time: 90 min.). 1985. 13.98 (978-0-88290-402-3(7), 1815) Horizon Utah.
Documents the roles of Jesus Christ, God the Father and the Holy Ghost and that each member is a separate entity, united with the others in purpose.

Latter End. Patricia Wentworth. 2007. 61.95 (978-0-7531-3804-5(2)); audio compact disk 79.95 (978-0-7531-2785-8(7)) Pub: ISIS Audio GBR. Dist(s): Ulverscroft US

Latter Rain. Perf. by Sonya Barry. 1 cass., 1 CD. 1999. 10.98 (978-1-57908-510-0(5), 1022); audio compact disk 16.98 (978-1-57908-509-4(1), 1022) Platinm Enter.

Laudate: Music of Taize. 1 cass. (Running Time: 87 min.). 10.95; audio compact disk 14.95 CD. Credence Commun.
Three times a day, hundreds of people from all over Europe gather to pray with the ecumenical community of Taize founded in the 1940's for reconciliation of the horrors of the Second World War. When these pilgrims & searchers come to pray with the community near the ancient monastery of Cluny, this is the music they sing. It is recorded live, in prayer, not in concert.

Laugh a Lot! Outrageous Original Activity Songs. Pamela Ott. 1 CD. (Teaching Tunes Ser.). 2000. audio compact disk 14.95 (978-0-8039-6871-4(X), 85087) Corwin Pr.

Laugh a Lot! Outrageous Original Activity Songs. Pamela Ott. 1 cass. (Running Time: 1 hr. 30 mins.). 2000. 14.95 (978-0-7619-7715-5(5), 86649) Corwin Pr.

Laugh Again: Experience Outrageous Joy. Charles R. Swindoll. 7 cass. (Running Time: 12 hrs.). 1998. 34.95 (978-1-57972-027-8(7)) Insight Living.
Bible study focusing on the joy of the Lord with encouraging words from the book of Philippians.

Laugh Again: Experience Outrageous Joy. Charles R. Swindoll. (ENG.). 2008. audio compact disk 46.00 (978-1-57972-795-6(6)) Insight Living.

Laugh & Learn Pharmaceutical Sales Code: Pharmaceutical & Medical Device Ethics & Compliance Training Based on the PHRMA Sales & Marketing Code for Sales Representatives & Marketers. Daniel Farb. 2004. audio compact disk 49.95 (978-1-932634-55-6(X)) Pub: UnivofHealth. Dist(s): AtlasBooks

Laugh & Learn Sales Letters 1: Sales Letter Writing & Psychology Using the Story of a Bumbling Pharmaceutical Sales Representative. Daniel Farb. 2004. audio compact disk 49.95 (978-1-932634-46-4(0)) Pub: UnivofHealth. Dist(s): AtlasBooks

Laugh & Learn Sales Territory Management: Sales Territory Management & Sales Software Overview Using the Story of a Bumbling Pharmaceutical Sales Representative. Daniel Farb & Bruce Gordon. 2004. audio compact disk 49.95 (978-1-932634-48-8(7)) Pub: UnivofHealth. Dist(s): AtlasBooks

Laugh & Learn Sales Time Management: Sales Time Management & Organization Skills Using the Story of a Bumbling Pharmaceutical Sales Representative. Daniel Farb & Bruce Gordon. 2004. audio compact disk 49.95 (978-1-932634-47-1(9)) Pub: UnivofHealth. Dist(s): AtlasBooks

Laugh & Live. Douglas Fairbanks. Narrated by Walter Costello. (Running Time: 2 hrs. 30 mins.). 2005. 17.95 (978-1-59912-529-9(3)) Iofy Corp.

Laugh & Live. unabr. ed. Douglas Fairbanks. Narrated by William Costello. (Running Time: 2 hrs. 30 mins. 0 sec.). (ENG.). 2008. audio compact disk 17.99 (978-1-4001-5803-4(6)) Pub: Tantor Media. Dist(s): IngramPubServ

Laugh & Live. unabr. ed. Douglas Fairbanks. Narrated by William Costello & Walter A. Costello. (Running Time: 2 hrs. 30 mins. 0 sec.). (ENG.). 2008. audio compact disk 35.99 (978-1-4001-3803-6(5)) Pub: Tantor Media. Dist(s): IngramPubServ

Laugh & Live. unabr. ed. Douglas Fairbanks. Read by William Costello. (Running Time: 2 hrs. 30 mins. 0 sec.). (ENG.). 2008. audio compact disk 17.99 (978-1-4001-0803-9(9)) Pub: Tantor Media. Dist(s): IngramPubServ

Laugh & Live. unabr. collector's ed. Douglas Fairbanks, Jr. Read by Walter A. Costello. 3 cass. (Running Time: 3 hrs.). 1993. 24.95 (978-0-7366-2585-2(2), 3331) Books on Tape.
An early Power of Positive Thinking, this autobiography stayed on bestseller lists for years.

Laugh Pac. Perf. by Henny Youngman et al. 6 cass. 1986. 21.95 (978-0-88142-553-6(2)) Soundelux.
A collection of some of the most memorable & hilarious examples of radio humor from the Golden Age of Radio.

Laughing Allegra: The Inspiring Story of a Mother's Struggle & Triumph Raising a Daughter with Learning Disabilities. abr. ed. Anne Ford. 4 cass. (Running Time: 6 hrs.). 2003. 25.99 (978-1-58926-236-2(0), N66L-0120) Oasis Audio.
Touching memoir of a family' struggle with a special needs child from the great-granddaughter of Henry Ford.

Laughing Allegra: The Inspiring Story of a Mother's Struggle & Triumph Raising a Daughter with Learning Disabilities. abr. ed. Anne Ford. Read by Anne Ford. 6 CDs. (Running Time: 6 hrs.). 2003. audio compact disk 29.99 (978-1-58926-237-9(9), N66L-012D) Oasis Audio.
The remarkable honest and inspiring story about the struggle and triumph of raising a child with learning disabilities will be an encouragement to any parent in this situation, and instructional for those who seek to understand how to better help both these children and their families.

Laughing Boy. Stuart Pawson. (Story Sound Ser.). (J). 2005. 69.95 (978-1-85903-736-2(4)); audio compact disk 84.95 (978-1-85903-791-1(7)) Pub: Mgna Lrg Print GBR. Dist(s): Ulverscroft US

Laughing Corpse. abr. ed. Laurell K. Hamilton. Read by Kimberly Alexis. (Running Time: 6 hrs.). (Anita Blake, Vampire Hunter Ser.: No. 2). (ENG.). (gr. 12 up). 2009. audio compact disk 29.95 (978-0-14-314512-7(6), PengAudBks) Penguin Grp USA.

Laughing Corpse. unabr. ed. Laurell K. Hamilton. Read by Kimberly Alexis. (Running Time: 13 hrs.). (Anita Blake, Vampire Hunter Ser.: No. 2). (ENG.). (gr. 12 up). 2009. audio compact disk 39.95 (978-0-14-314402-1(2), PengAudBks) Penguin Grp USA.

Laughing Day. unabr. ed. Dr. Hope. Perf. by Russ T. Nailz. Illus. by Curt Werner. 1 cass. (Running Time: 20 min.). (Life Lessons Ser.: Vol. 1). (J). (gr. k-3). 1998. 12.95 (978-1-885624-51-2(4)) Alpine Pubng.
A young lad who learns a valuable lesson & in turn teaches it to others.

***Laughing Day; El Día para Reir.** Tim 'hope' Anders. (J). 2010. audio compact disk 12.95 (978-1-885624-71-0(9)) Alpine Pubng.

Laughing Gas. unabr. ed. P. G. Wodehouse. Narrated by Simon Prebble. 6 cass. (Running Time: 8 hrs.). 51.00 (978-0-7887-0305-8(6), 94498E7) Recorded Bks.
A proper British earl falls asleep in a dentist's chair & wake sup in the body of America's favorite child star. Available to libraries only.

Laughing in Chinese. unabr. ed. 3 cass. (CHI.). pap. bk. 78.00 (SCH110) J Norton Pubs.
Intermediate/advanced level to strengthen listening, speaking, reading & writing skills.

Laughing, Loving & Living Your Way to the Good Life. unabr. ed. Ed Foreman & Successful Life Team Staff. 8 cass. (Running Time: 12 hrs.). 1983. 80.00 incl. Success Guide. Exec Dev Syst.
Highlights from the 3-day "Succesful Life Course"...including the "Daily Menu" on: how to have a good, happy, enjoyable day every day, how to replace worry with happiness & success, how to better sell your ideas, improve your communications, relax & re-energize, keep the monkey off your back, & others.

Laughing Meditation: Great for Everyone & All Ages. Michele Blood. Ed. by Michele Blood. Illus. by Musivation International Staff. 1 tape. 2002. 12.95 (978-1-890679-45-3(3)) Micheles.
This audio program will lift you up immediately into a world of laughter and abundance. Laughter helps build up your immune system, creates a high vibration, and literally take you from depression and negative thinking into instant positive feeling. Michele created this tape, filled with wonderful laughter and affirmations, to create instant good feelings and healing. After listening to this program you will be happy!!.

Laughing Policeman. unabr. ed. Maj Sjöwall & Per Wahlöö. Read by Tom Weiner. (Running Time: 7 hrs. 0 mins.). 2009. audio compact disk 19.95 (978-1-4332-6353-8(X)) Blckstn Audio.

Laughing Policeman. unabr. ed. Maj Sjöwall & Per Wahlöö. Read by Tom Weiner. (Running Time: 7 hrs. NaN mins.). 2009. 29.95 (978-1-4332-6354-5(8)); audio compact disk 44.95 (978-1-4332-6350-7(5)); audio compact disk 60.00 (978-1-4332-6351-4(3)) Blckstn Audio.

Laughing River: A Folktale for Peace. Elizabeth H. Vage. 1 cass. (Running Time: 30 min.). (J). (gr. 1-5). 1995. 9.95 (978-1-877810-36-7(3)) Rayve Prodns.
A modern folk tale for peace with roots in West African history. Elizabeth Haze Vega tells this story of the fanciful Funga & Alafia tribes with two widely used West African Songs as background. When the Funga tribe becomes upset with the loud singing of the Alafia across the river & decide to attack, their intentions are diverted by the water of the "laughing river" &

the welcome song of the Alafia. The preface includes good factual background information on Orff music & instruments, on African culture, & on a lesson in conflict resolution. The cassette has the story & music on one side & additional music on the other.

Laughing Whitefish. unabr. collector's ed. Robert Traver. Read by Wolfram Kandinsky. 7 cass. (Running Time: 10 hrs. 30 min.). 1982. 56.00 (978-0-7366-0386-7(7), 1363) Books on Tape.
Willy Poe is a young lawyer who is looking for the right girl. He finds her when an Indian woman, Laughing Whitefish, presents him with an almost hopeless case.

Laughs Are on Me. Perf. by Robert G. Lee. Prod. by Randy Ray. 1 cass. (Running Time: 40 min.). 1994. 9.98 (978-1-57919-075-0(8)) Randolf Prod.
Stand up comedy.

Laughs, Luck... & Lucy: How I Came to Create the Most Popular Sitcom of All Time. collector's ed. Mem. of Jess Oppenheimer & Gregg Oppenheimer. 1 CD. (Running Time: 1 hr. 12 min.). 2000. pap. bk. 14.98 (4385) Radio Spirits.
An insider's view of radio and TV history as it was being made. Filled with hilarious stories, behind-the-scenes photos and previously unpublished radio & TV scripts (including the only "I Love Lucy" scripts Lucy & Desi refused to perform). Also included is rare unreleased Lucy comedy performances and outtakes (including recently discovered, never-rerun scenes). Includes a Limited Edition 5X7 photo of Lucy and Desi and Vitameatavegamin bookmar.

Laughs, Luck... & Lucy: How I Came to Create the Most Popular Sitcom of All Time (with I Love Lucy's Lost Scenes Audio CD) Jess Oppenheimer et al. (Television Ser.). 1999. pap. bk. 19.95 (978-0-8156-0584-3(6)) Syracuse U Pr.

Laughs, Luck... & Lucy: How I Came to Create the Most Popular Sitcom of All Time (with Lucy Audio CD) Jess Oppenheimer & Gregg Oppenheimer. (Television Ser.). 1996. bk. 39.95 (978-0-8156-0406-8(8), OPLL) Syracuse U Pr.

Laughter: Chuck's Prescription for Joy. 2003. audio compact disk 14.00 (978-1-57972-556-3(2)) Insight Living.

Laughter: Job 8:21. Ed Young. 1983. 4.95 (978-0-7417-1318-6(7), 318) Win Walk.

Laughter: Program from the Award Winning Public Radio Series. Interview. Hosted by Fred Goodwin. Comment by John Hockenberry. 1 CD. (Running Time: 1 hr.). (Infinite Mind Ser.). 2002. audio compact disk 21.95 (978-1-888064-68-1(4), LCM 230) Lichtenstein Creat.
We all do it. It's fun. It feels good. And many scientists say there's evidence it's good for you. This week on The Infinite Mind we look at laughter, comedy, laugh tracks, and laughter as therapy. Guests include stand-up comedian Eddie Izzard; Dr. Jo-Anne Bachorowski, assistant professor of psychology, Vanderbilt University; and Dr. Robert R. Provine, professor of psychology and neuroscience, University of Maryland, Baltimore County. We examine the pros and cons of recent research looking at laughter as therapy and hear from scientists, therapists, and patients. Plus, why does Hollywood still love the laugh track in a special report featuring writer/producer Larry Gelbart and Bill Lawrence and professional laugh-track sweetener David Maitland. Concluding the show, commentator John Hockenberry answers the age-old riddle "Why did the caterpillar cross the roadway?".

Laughter & Smiles see Risas y Sonrisas: Cognate Folder

Laughter & the Immune System: A Serious Approach. unabr. ed. Interview with Barry Bittman. Contrib. by Stanley Tan & Lee Berk. 1 cass. (Running Time: 46 min.). 1996. 18.95 incl. script. (978-0-9650240-3-7(2), TSA-1001) TouchStar.
Presents a wealth of scientific evidence that supports the wisdom of the ancients & their intuitive understanding of the intricate links between mind & body. Through exceptional research focused on mirthful laughter, the biblical statement, "A merry heart doeth good like a medicine," is scientifically validated.

***Laughter of Dead Kings.** unabr. ed. Elizabeth Peters, pseud. Read by Barbara Rosenblat. (ENG.). 2008. (978-0-06-170251-8(X)); (978-0-06-170253-2(6)) HarperCollins Pubs.

Laughter of Dead Kings. unabr. ed. Elizabeth Peters, pseud. Read by Barbara Rosenblat. 8 CDs. (Running Time: 10 hrs.). (Vicky Bliss Mystery Ser.). 2008. audio compact disk 39.95 (978-0-06-166240-9(2), Harper Audio) HarperCollins Pubs.

Laughter of the Universe, Program 2. Read by Jorge Luis Borges. (F007AB090) Natl Public Radio.

Laughter, the Navajo Way. Alan Wilson. 1 CD. (Running Time: 80 mins.). (NAV.). 2005. audio compact disk 39.00 (978-1-57970-241-0(4), AFNV30D) J Norton Pubs.

Laughter Volume 2: The Essential Ingredient for a Great Attitude. 2008. audio compact disk 15.00 (978-1-57972-819-9(7)) Insight Living.

Launch into Space. Matt Oppenheimer. 1 cass. (Running Time: 1 hr.). (Wonder Tales Ser.). (J). (ps-5). 2000. 11.98 (978-1-930037-03-8(1), WT000C) Inter Media Grp.
The listener pilots the Space Shuttle on a rescue mission.

Launch into the Deep. 2001. 14.99 (978-1-58602-090-3(0)); audio compact disk 29.99 (978-1-58602-092-7(7)) E L Long.

Launching an Orphans Ministry in Your Church. Jason Weber. Told to Paul Pennington. Frwd. by Dennis Rainey. 2007. pap. bk. 9.99 (978-1-57229-989-4(4)) FamilyLife.

Launching the Arrow of Aspiration. unabr. ed. Swami Amar Jyoti. 1 cass. (Running Time: 1 hr.). (Satsangs of Swami Amar Jyoti Ser.). 1999. 9.95 (978-0-933572-61-4(1), M-111) Truth Consciousness.
Aspiration gives us the strength to fly upward. Realism in relationships. Our real goal in life.

Launching Your Day. 1 cassette. (Running Time: 64:19 mins.). 1989. 12.95 (978-1-55841-035-0(X)) Emmett E Miller.
A remarkable achievement - an eyes-open, while-you-work or play meditation. Attune to your deepest values, then gradually energize yourself as you enjoy words of wisdom and self-affirmations. Extend the peace of the sleep state congruently into the activities of everyday life.

Launching Your Day. 1 CD. 1989. audio compact disk 16.95 (978-1-55841-119-7(4)) Emmett E Miller.
A remarkable achievment - an eyes-open, while-you-work or play meditation. Attune to your deepest values, then gradually energize yourself as you enjoy words of wisdom and self-affirmations. Extend the peace of the sleep state congruently into the activities of everyday life.

Launching Your Day: Energizing Affirmations for Peak Performance. Emmett E. Miller. 1 cass. (Running Time: 60 min.). (Emmett Miller, M.D. Cassettes Ser.). 1989. 9.95 Publisher Group.

Laura: America's First Lady, First Mother. abr. ed. Antonia Felix. Read by Antonia Felix. 2 cass. (Running Time: 2 hrs. 30 mins.). 2002. 17.99 (978-1-58926-075-7(9), A54L-0100); audio compact disk 19.99 (978-1-58926-076-4(7), A54L-010D) Oasis Audio.
America has never had a First Lady quite like Laura Bush. A dedicated librarian and devoted mother who hailed from the windswept Texas plains, she fell into the nation's spotlight when her husband, George W. Bush, became the 43rd president of the United States. Though she was shy and reserved at first, everything changed on September 11, 2001, when the World Trade Center and the Pentagon were crushed by terrorist attacks. In the aftermath, Laura rose to the occasion, providing comfort and reassurance amidst what is perhaps the worst crisis we've ever faced - and has since become a beacon of hope and strenght to the nation.

Laura Bush: An Intimate Portrait of the First Lady. unabr. ed. Ronald Kessler. Read by Susan Denaker. 9 CDs. (Running Time: 10 hrs.). 2006. audio compact disk 81.00 (978-1-4159-2898-1(3)); 63.00 (978-1-4159-2897-4(5)) Books on Tape.
In this unprecedented account, Kessler reveals: How Laura's opinions have brought budget changes to a range of federal agencies and have affected her husband's policies, appointments, and worldview. Why Laura told her press secretary in May 2001 she did not want to do any more media interviews. What President Bush said to Laura at the dinner table after giving the "go" for the invasion of Iraq, and what his father, former President George H. W. Bush, wrote him the next day about the war. What Laura's own political opinions are and what her relationship with twin daughters Jenna and Barbara is really like. What Laura says in private about Hillary Clinton, media attacks on her husband, and his victory in the 2004 election. And why Laura, at the age of seventeen, missed a stop sign and caused a fatal accident that tragically left one of her best friends dead. LAURA BUSH offers a remarkable look at the private world of this famously reserved woman, as well as the beliefs and attitudes that shape it. The book will surprise readers whose knowledge of the first lady comes from cautious media interviews and speeches. Laura Bush's approval rating stands at 85 percent. Since opinion polls first began asking about them, no first lady has received a higher rating. This moving biography is the first to penetrate the secret world of the president's stealth counselor who is one of our most admired public figures.

Laura Hendrie. Laura Hendrie. 1-2 cass. (Author & Interview Ser.). 1995. 13.95 (978-1-55644-440-1(0)) Am Audio Prose.

Laura Hendrie Reading & Interview. Laura Hendrie. Read by Laura Hendrie. Interview with Kay Bonetti-Callison. 3 cass. (Running Time: 3 hrs.). 1996. 25.00 Set. (978-1-55644-441-8(9)) Am Audio Prose.

Laura Hendrie Reads from Stygo. unabr. ed. Laura Hendrie. Read by Laura Hendrie. Interview with Kay Bonetti-Callison. 2 cass. (Running Time: 3 hrs.). 1996. 13.95 (978-1-55644-439-5(7)) Am Audio Prose.

Laura Rider's Masterpiece. unabr. ed. Jane Hamilton. Read by Stefan Rudnicki. (Running Time: 7 hrs. 0 mins.). 2009. 29.95 (978-1-4332-7801-3(4)); 44.95 (978-1-4332-7799-3(9)); audio compact disk 60.00 (978-1-4332-7800-6(6)) Blckstn Audio.

Laura Rider's Masterpiece. unabr. ed. Jane Hamilton. Read by Alyssa Bresnahan. 2009. audio compact disk 29.99 (978-0-06-174882-0(X), Harper Audio) HarperCollins Pubs.

***Laura Rider's Masterpiece.** unabr. ed. Jane Hamilton. Read by Alyssa Bresnahan. (ENG.). 2009. (978-0-06-180579-0(3), Harper Audio); (978-0-06-180566-0(1), Harper Audio) HarperCollins Pubs.

Laura Simms Tells Stories Just Right for Kids. Read by Laura Simms. 1 cass. (Running Time: 49 min.). (J). 8.95 (WW732C) Weston Woods.

Laura Simms Tells Stories Just Right for Kids. Short Stories. Laura Simms. 1 cass. (Running Time: 45 mins.). (J). 1999. 9.95 (978-0-938756-53-8(2)) Yellow Moon.
1985 American Library Association Notable Children's Recording.In the stories on this award-winning tape, the listener will be introduced to characters who use their inner strengths to conquer the obstacles set before them. Each of the stories includes a powerful message made memorable by Laura's entertaining storytelling. Told simply, all of the stories on this tape can be understood by children but contain a depth of meaning that will delight every listener.

Laura Simms Tells Stories Just Right for Kids-the Five Mean & Ugly Men; Nasruddin's Donkey; Moon & Otter; Harry Digby the Dancing Man; the King of Togo Togo; the Flower of Life. 2004. 8.95 (978-1-56008-442-6(1)) Weston Woods.

Laurel Canyon: The Inside Story of Rock & Roll's Legendary Neighborhood. Michael Walker. Read by Lloyd James. (Running Time: 30600 sec.). 2006. 54.95 (978-0-7861-4556-0(0)); audio compact disk 63.00 (978-0-7861-7085-2(9)) Blckstn Audio.

Laurel Canyon: The Inside Story of Rock & Roll's Legendary Neighborhood. unabr. ed. Michael Walker. Read by Lloyd James. 6 cass. (Running Time: 30600 sec.). 2006. 29.95 (978-0-7861-4403-7(3)); audio compact disk 29.95 (978-0-7861-7435-5(8)); audio compact disk 29.95 (978-0-7861-7766-0(7)) Blckstn Audio.

Lauren Bacall By Myself. abr. ed. Lauren Bacall. 2 cass. 12.95 (978-0-89926-197-3(3), 867) Audio Bk.

Laurence Gonzales. unabr. ed. Laurence Gonzales. Read by Laurence Gonzales. 1 cass. (Running Time: 29 min.). Incl. Vago. 1987. (25); 1987. 10.00 (25) New Letters.
Gonzales talks about the treatment of writers & reads from his novel.

Laurence Olivier: A Biography. Donald Spoto. Read by Frederick Davidson. 12 cass. (Running Time: 17 hrs. 30 mins.). 2000. 83.95 (978-0-7861-1735-2(4), 2540) Blckstn Audio.
The most famous actor of the 20th century, perhaps the greatest of all time. From his stage roles as Hamlet & Archie Rice to his screen roles as Heathcliff & henry V, his range was unparalled. This book brings life to the private man behind the public persona.

***Laurence Olivier: A Biography.** unabr. ed. Donald Spoto. Read by Frederick Davidson. (Running Time: 17 hrs. 30 mins.). 2010. 44.95 (978-1-4417-5171-3(8)); audio compact disk 123.00 (978-1-4417-5169-0(6)) Blckstn Audio.

Laurence Olivier: A Biography. unabr. ed. Donald Spoto. Read by David Case. 12 cass. (Running Time: 18 hrs.). 1993. 96.00 (978-0-7366-2478-7(3), 3240) Books on Tape.
Beneath the image of the first lord of the theater was a lonely & confused man plagued by self-doubt.

Lauris Edmond. unabr. ed. Lauris Edmond. Read by Lauris Edmond. 1 cass. (Running Time: 29 min.). 1987. 10.00 (12) New Letters.
Edmond reads poems about her native land & talks about what it's like to be a woman of letters in New Zealand.

Laurra Fitzgerald: Fall in the Arms of Jesus. ColdWater Media. (ENG.). (YA). 2009. audio compact disk 14.95 (978-0-9822283-3-3(3)) ColdWater Media.

L'Avare. Molière. audio compact disk 12.95 (978-0-8219-3757-0(X)) EMC-Paradigm.

Lavender Evening Dress see Graveyard of Ghost Tales

Lavender Morning. abr. ed. Jude Deveraux. Read by Gabra Zackman. 5 CDs. (Running Time: 6 hrs. 0 mins. 0 sec.). Bk. 1. (ENG.). 2009. audio compact disk 29.99 (978-0-7435-7971-1(2)) Pub: S&S Audio. Dist(s): S and S Inc

Lavender Morning. abr. ed. Jude Deveraux. Read by Gabra Zackman. (Running Time: 6 hrs. 0 mins. 0 sec.). Bk. 1. (ENG.). 2010. audio compact disk 14.99 (978-1-4423-0474-1(X)) Pub: S&S Audio. Dist(s): S and S Inc

Lavender's Blue see Gathering of Great Poetry for Children

Lavender's Blue Dilly Dilly. Mary Thienes-Schunemann. (J). 2004. spiral bd. 21.95 (978-0-9708397-7-0(4)) Pub: Naturally You. Dist(s): SteinerBooks Inc

Lavinia. unabr. ed. Ursula K. Le Guin. Narrated by Alyssa Bresnahan. (Running Time: 11 hrs. 45 mins.). 2008. 56.75 (978-1-4361-6529-7(6)); 67.75 (978-1-4361-5701-8(3)); audio compact disk 92.75 (978-1-4361-5702-5(1)) Recorded Bks.

Lavinia. unabr. collector's ed. Ursula K. Le Guin. Narrated by Alyssa Bresnahan. 10 CDs. (Running Time: 11 hrs. 45 mins.). 2008. audio compact disk 44.95 (978-1-4361-3855-0(8)) Recorded Bks.

Law. abr. ed. Frederic Bastiat. Read by G Edward Griffin. 1 cass. (Running Time: 1 hr. 30 min.). 1989. 10.00 (978-0-912986-27-2(1)) Am Media.
A classic treatise on the futility of socialism.

Law. unabr. ed. Frederic Bastiat. Read by Bernard Mayes. 2 cass. (Running Time: 2 hrs. 30 mins.). 1990. 17.95 (978-0-7861-0190-0(3), 1167) Blckstn Audio.
The same socialist-communist plans & ideas that were adopted in France in 1848 are now sweeping America, notwithstanding the collapse of communism in Eastern Europe. The explanation & arguments then advanced against socialism by Mr. Bastiat are - word for word - equally valid today.

Law: The Positron. Neville Goddard. 1 cass. (Running Time: 62 min.). 1965. 8.00 (42) J & L Pubns.
Neville taught Imagination Creates Reality. He was a powerfully influential teacher of God as Consciousness.

Law: Use of Imagination. Neville Goddard. 1 cass. (Running Time: 62 min.). 1965. 8.00 (62) J & L Pubns.

Law & Compassion of the Prophets. Swami Amar Jyoti. 1 cass. 1997. 9.95 (K-157) Truth Consciousness.
Sri Rama & all the prophets came to uphold Dharma, to save mankind & Earth itself.

Law & Ethics: The Case of the American Negro. unabr. ed. Eugene V. Rostow. 1 cass. (Running Time: 52 min.). 12.95 (19002) J Norton Pubs.
A chronological account, from 17th century to 1968, of the legal & social status of the Negro.

Law & Grace: Logos June 28, 1998. Ben Young. 1998. 4.95 (978-0-7417-6088-3(6), B0088) Win Walk.

Law & Grace: Logos 03/28/99, B0126. Ben Young. 1999. 4.95 (978-0-7417-6126-2(2), B0126) Win Walk.

Law & the Profits. (1150) Books on Tape.

Law Firm for Sale: The Complete Audio Guide to Selling Your Law Practice. (ENG.). 2009. audio compact disk 247.00 (978-0-9797610-1-0(8)) E Poll & Assocs.

Law Firm Marketing in the Nineties. 1 cass. (Running Time: 50 min.). (CLE TV: The Lawyers' Video Magazine Ser.). 95.00 incl. study guide. (Y701) Am Law Inst.
Covers realistic ways for law practices of all sizes to obtain more business from new & existing clients.

Law for the Layman: Anatomy of a Criminal Trial. Legovac Law Group Staff. Narrated by Robert Sigman. 1 cass. (Law for the Layman Audio-Cassette Ser.). (C). 1992. 16.95 (978-1-878135-25-4(2)) Legovac.
What you need to know before you see a lawyer.

Law for the Layman: Bankruptcy. Legovac Law Group Staff. Narrated by Robert Sigman. 1 cass. (Law for the Layman Audio-Cassette Ser.). (C). 1991. 16.95 (978-1-878135-09-4(0)) Legovac.

Law for the Layman: Contracts. Legovac Law Group Staff. Narrated by Robert Sigman. 1 cass. (Law for the Layman Audio-Cassette Ser.). (C). 1991. 16.95 (978-1-878135-20-9(1)) Legovac.
What you need to know before you see an attorney.

Law for the Layman: Corporations. Legovac Law Group Staff. Narrated by Robert Sigman. 1 cass. (Law for the Layman Audio-Cassette Ser.). (C). 1993. 16.95 (978-1-878135-28-5(7)) Legovac.
What you need to know before you see a lawyer.

Law for the Layman: Driving under the Influence. Legovac Law Group Staff. Narrated by Robert Sigman. 1 cass. (Law for the Layman Audio-Cassette Ser.). (C). 1992. 16.95 (978-1-878135-24-7(4)) Legovac.

Law for the Layman: Family Violence & the Law. Legovac Law Group Staff. Narrated by Robert Sigman. 1 cass. (Law for the Layman Audio-Cassette Ser.). (C). 1992. 16.95 (978-1-878135-22-3(8)) Legovac.

Law for the Layman: Landlord & Tenant. Legovac Law Group Staff. Narrated by Robert Sigman. 1 cass. (Law for the Layman Audio-Cassette Ser.). (C). 1992. 16.95 (978-1-878135-21-6(X)) Legovac.

Law for the Layman: Property, Real & Personal. Legovac Law Group Staff. Narrated by Robert Sigman. 1 cass. (Law for the Layman Audio-Cassette Ser.). (C). 1992. 16.95 (978-1-878135-18-6(X)) Legovac.

Law for the Layman: Small Claims Court. Legovac Law Group Staff. Narrated by Robert Sigman. 1 cass. (Law for the Layman Audio-Cassette Ser.). (C). 1992. 16.95 (978-1-878135-23-0(6)) Legovac.

Law for the Layman: Waging Custody Battles. Robert S. Sigman. Read by Robert S. Sigman. 1 cass. (Law for the Layman Audio-Cassette Ser.). (C). 1991. 16.95 (978-1-878135-16-2(3)) Legovac.

Law for the Layman: Wills, Trusts & Estate Planning. Legovac Law Group Staff. Narrated by Robert Sigman. 1 cass. (Law for the Layman Audio-Cassette Ser.). (C). 1991. 16.95 (978-1-878135-12-4(0)) Legovac.
Information you need to know before you see a lawyer.

Law for the Layman: Worker's Compensation. Legovac Law Group Staff. Narrated by Robert Sigman. 1 cass. (Law for the Layman Audio-Cassette Ser.). (C). 1992. 16.95 (978-1-878135-26-1(0)) Legovac.
What you need to know before you see a lawyer.

Law, Legislation & Rights. unabr. ed. Robert LeFevre. 1 cass. (Running Time: 1 hr. 28 min.). 12.95 (405) J Norton Pubs.
LeFevre discusses the difference between law & legislation, & how the first leads to order & the second to chaos. He then discusses his theory of human rights in a speech he delivered at the Countercon II Conference.

Law Men Die Sudden. Will Cook. Read by Terrence Hazlefort. (Running Time: 1 hr. 12 mins.). 1999. 10.95 (978-1-60083-498-1(1)) Iofy Corp.

Law of Attraction, Pt. 1. unabr. ed. Esther Hicks & Jerry Hicks. 4 CDs. (Running Time: 4 hrs.). 2005. audio compact disk 23.95 (978-1-4019-0734-1(2)) Hay House.

Law of Attraction, Set. unabr. ed. Esther Hicks & Jerry Hicks. 13 CDs. (Running Time: 15 hrs.). 2007. audio compact disk 39.95 (978-1-4019-1972-6(3)) Hay House.

***Law of Attraction: A Novel.** unabr. ed. Allison Leotta. (Running Time: 10 hrs. 0 mins. 0 sec.). (ENG.). 2010. 24.99 (978-1-4001-6880-4(5)); 34.99 (978-1-4001-9880-1(1)); 17.99 (978-1-4001-8880-2(6)); audio compact disk 83.99 (978-1-4001-4880-6(4)); audio compact disk 34.99 (978-1-4001-1880-9(8)) Pub: Tantor Media. Dist(s): IngramPubServ

Law of Attraction: The Basics of the Teachings of Abraham. abr. ed. Esther Hicks & Jerry Hicks. Read by Esther Hicks & Jerry Hicks. (YA). 2007. 34.99 (978-1-60252-687-7(7)) Find a World.

Law of Attraction: The Basics of the Teachings of Abraham. abr. ed. Esther Hicks & Jerry Hicks. 5 CDs. (Running Time: 5 hrs.). 2006. audio compact disk 23.95 (978-1-4019-1235-2(4)) Hay House.

Law of Attraction: The Science of Attracting More of What You Want & Less of What You Don't. unabr. ed. Michael J. Losier. Read by Michael J. Losier. (Running Time: 2 hrs. 30 mins.). (ENG.). 2010. 14.98 (978-1-60024-583-1(8)); audio compact disk 17.98 (978-1-60024-582-4(X)) Pub: Hachet Audio. Dist(s): HachBkGrp

Law of Attraction & How to Use It. Stephen Hawley Martin. 2008. 2.95 (978-1-892538-27-7(X)) Pub: Oaklea Pr. Dist(s): Midpt Trade

Law of Attraction & Other Universal Laws Explained: A Practical Guide to Utilizing these Natural Laws. Christine Sherborne. (ENG.). 2009. audio compact disk 19.95 (978-0-9804386-3-5(2)) Pub: Colourstory AUS. Dist(s): APG

Law of Attraction Directly from Source: Leading Edge Music Leading Edge Thought. Esther Hicks et al. 2008. audio compact disk 15.00 (978-1-4019-2341-9(0)) Hay House.

Law of Attraction Handbook: Revealing the Secrets to Manifest Your Desires Instantly to Success. Prod. by Red Planet Audiobooks. (ENG.). 2008. audio compact disk 12.99 (978-1-934814-06-2(7)) Red Planet Au.

Law of Attraction in the Thought World / Thought Vibration Or see Ley de Atraccion en el Mundo del Pensamiento - Digital Version: Vibracion del Pensamiento

***Law of Attraction Plain & Simple: Create the Extraordinary Life That You Deserve.** unabr. ed. Ricotti Sonia. (Running Time: 1 hr.). (ENG.). 2011. audio compact disk 14.98 (978-1-59659-275-9(3), GildAudio) Pub: Gildan Media. Dist(s): HachBkGrp

Law of Circumcision. Neville Goddard. 1 cass. (Running Time: 62 min.). 1965. 8.00 (80) J & L Pubns.
Neville taught Imagination Creates Reality. He was a powerfully influential teacher of God as Consciousness.

Law of Computer Related Technology Institute. 1984. 60.00 (978-0-317-01248-4(7)) Am IPLA.

Law of Connection: The Science of Using NLP to Create Ideal Personal & Professional Relationships. unabr. ed. Michael J. Losier. Read by Michael J. Losier. (Running Time: 3 hrs.). (ENG.). 2009. 15.98 (978-1-60024-608-1(7)); audio compact disk 22.98 (978-1-60024-606-7(0)) Pub: Hachet Audio. Dist(s): HachBkGrp

Law of Consciousness: Technique for Using the Law of Consciousness. unabr. ed. Lilburn S. Barksdale. Read by Mark Denis. 1 cass. (Running Time: 47 min.). 1979. 9.95 (978-0-918588-39-5(1), 160) NCADD.
Consciousness is the creative power of the universe. We do or become that which we have a consciousness of doing or being. This tape outlines how L.S. Barksdale applied this law to first achieve material success, & subsequently, stress-free living. Learn how to apply this creative power to accomplish your own life objectives.

Law of Evidence. Read by Irving Younger. 225.00 incl. study guide. (NO. 840) Natl Prac Inst.
Nine programs covering all areas of evidence: judicial notice; types of evidence; competence, relevance & materiality; witnesses; hearsay & exceptions; special problems of relevance; privileges; burdens of proof; presumptions.

Law of Evidence. Irving Younger. 1979. 195.00 (978-1-55917-387-2(4)) Natl Prac Inst.

Law of Gravity. unabr. ed. Stephen Horn. 9 cass. (Running Time: 13 hrs. 30 mins.). 2002. 64.00 (978-0-7366-8677-8(0)); audio compact disk 88.00 (978-0-7366-8678-5(9)) Books on Tape.
A former White House lawyer must recover his reputation by unearthing the truth in the disappearance of a Senate Intelligence Committee staf.

Law of Happiness: How Ancient Wisdom & Modern Science Can Change Your Life. unabr. ed. Henry Cloud. Read by Henry Cloud. (Running Time: 4 hrs. 0 mins. 0 sec.). (Secret Things of God Ser.). (ENG.). 2011. audio compact disk 24.99 (978-1-4423-0450-5(2)) Pub: S&S Audio. Dist(s): S and S Inc

Law of Higher Evolution. Swami Amar Jyoti. 1 dolby cass. 1983. 9.95 (R-53) Truth Consciousness.
Evolution beyond freedom of thought & expression. Leaving rajas, progressing through sattwa, can change the world. Freedom of Consciousness, the victory where no one is defeated.

Law of Increase. Kenneth Copeland. 2 cass. 1987. 10.00 (978-0-88114-764-3(8)) K Copeland Pubns.
Biblical teaching on principles of prosperity.

Law of Karma. Swami Jyotirmayananda. 1 cass. (Running Time: 45 min.). 1990. 10.00 Yoga Res Foun.

Law of Liberty. Neville Goddard. 1 cass. (Running Time: 62 min.). 1964. 8.00 (108) J & L Pubns.
Neville taught Imagination Creates Reality. He was a powerfully influential teacher of God as Consciousness.

Law of Life see Great American Short Stories

Law of Life see Love of Life

Law of Nines. unabr. ed. Terry Goodkind. Read by Mark Deakins. 12 CDs. (Running Time: 14 hrs.). (ENG.). (gr. 12 up). 2009. audio compact disk 39.95 (978-0-14-314523-3(1), PengAudBks) Penguin Grp USA.

***Law of Nines.** unabr. ed. Terry Goodkind. Read by Mark Deakins. 12 CDs. 2009. audio compact disk 100.00 (978-0-307-70173-2(5), BksonTape) Pub: Random Audio Pubg. Dist(s): Random

Law of Respect: A Wisdom Principle for Teens & Adults. Alfred D. Harvey, Jr. 2 cass in album. (Running Time: 1 hr. 50 mins.). 2003. 10.00 (978-1-932508-20-8(1)) Doers Pub.
Understand respect and respect in action by seeing how respect, or a lack thereof, affects every area of our lives.

Law of Rewards: Giving What You Can't Keep to Gain What You Can't Lose. unabr. ed. Randy C. Alcorn. Narrated by Randy C. Alcorn. (Running Time: 3 hrs. 32 mins. 33 sec.). (ENG.). 2008. audio compact disk 15.99 (978-1-59859-473-7(7)) Oasis Audio.

Law of Rewards: Giving What You Can't Keep to Gain What You Can't Lose. unabr. ed. Randy C. Alcorn. Narrated by Randy C. Alcorn. (Running Time: 3 hrs. 32 mins. 33 sec.). (ENG.). 2009. 11.19 (978-1-60814-487-7(9)) Oasis Audio.

Law of Second Chances. unabr. ed. James Sheehan. Narrated by Dick Hill. (Running Time: 13 hrs. 0 mins. 0 sec.). (ENG.). 2008. audio compact disk 29.99 (978-1-4001-5662-7(9)); audio compact disk 79.99 (978-1-4001-3662-9(8)) Pub: Tantor Media. Dist(s): IngramPubServ

Law of Second Chances. unabr. ed. James Sheehan. Read by Dick Hill. (Running Time: 13 hrs. 0 mins. 0 sec.). (ENG.). 2008. audio compact disk 39.99 (978-1-4001-0662-2(1)) Pub: Tantor Media. Dist(s): IngramPubServ

Law of Similars. unabr. ed. Chris Bohjalian. Read by Tim Jerome. 8 vols. (Running Time: 12 hrs.). 2000. bk. 69.95 (978-0-7927-2345-5(7), CSL 234, Chivers Sound Lib) AudioGO.
Two years after his wife's accidental death, a Vermont deputy state prosecutor, finds that the stress of raising their daughter alone has left him with a chronic sore throat. Desperate to rid himself of this malady that has eluded conventional medicine, he turns to homeopath Carissa Lake, who cures both his sore throat & his aching loneliness. Just days after Leland realizes he has fallen in love, one of her patients falls into an allergy-induced coma. When Carissa comes under investigation, Leland is faced with a moral & ethical dilemma of enormous proportions.

Law of Similars. unabr. ed. Chris Bohjalian. Read by Tim Jerome. 10 CDs. (Running Time: 15 hrs.). 2002. audio compact disk 94.95 (978-0-7927-2639-5(1), SLD 234, Chivers Sound Lib) AudioGO.

Law of Success. Napoleon Hill. (Running Time: 6 hrs.). (ENG.). (gr. 12 up). 2008. audio compact disk 29.95 (978-0-14-314419-9(7), PengAudBks) Penguin Grp USA.

Law of Success. abr. ed. Napoleon Hill. (ENG.). 2009. audio compact disk 49.99 (978-1-932429-58-9(1)) Pub: Highroads Media. Dist(s): Macmillan

Law of Success: From the Master Mind to the Golden Rule (in Sixteen Lessons) unabr. ed. Napoleon Hill. Read by Grover Gardner. (Running Time: 24 hrs.). (ENG.). 2008. 19.98 (978-1-59659-307-7(5), GildAudio) Pub: Gildan Media. Dist(s): HachBkGrp

Law of Success Vol. 1: Principles of Self-Mastery. unabr. ed. Napoleon Hill. Read by Arthur Morey. (Running Time: 8 hrs. 0 mins. 0 sec.). (ENG.). 2004. audio compact disk 44.95 (978-1-932429-06-0(9)) Pub: Highroads Media. Dist(s): Macmillan

Law of Success Vol. 2: The Principles of Personal Power. unabr. ed. Napoleon Hill. Read by Mario Rosales. (Running Time: 8 hrs. 0 mins. 0 sec.). (ENG.). 2003. audio compact disk 44.95 (978-1-932429-08-4(5)) Pub: Highroads Media. Dist(s): Macmillan

Law of Success Vol. IV: Principles of Personal Integrity. 75th anniv. unabr. ed. Napoleon Hill. Read by Mario Rosales. (Running Time: 8 hrs. 0 mins. 0 sec.). (ENG.). 2003. audio compact disk 44.95 (978-1-932429-12-1(3)) Pub: Highroads Media. Dist(s): Macmillan

Law of Success Complete on 24 CD's: Original, Unabridged Edition. Napoleon Hill. Narrated by R. C. Ossenbach. (ENG.). 2008. audio compact disk 99.95 (978-0-9741925-3-6(8)) Audio Echo.

Law of Supply; The Law of Demand. John Robbins. 1 cass. (Introduction to Economics Ser.: No. 7). 5.00 Trinity Found.

Law of the Anointed One & His Anointing. Creflo A. Dollar. 20.00 (978-1-59089-076-9(0)) Pub: Creflo Dollar. Dist(s): STL Dist NA

***Law of the Broken Earth.** unabr. ed. Rachel Neumeier. (Running Time: 11 hrs. 30 mins. 0 sec.). (Griffin Mage Ser.). 2010. 24.99 (978-1-4001-6973-3(9)); 17.99 (978-1-4001-8973-1(X)); audio compact disk 34.99 (978-1-4001-1973-8(1)) Pub: Tantor Media. Dist(s): IngramPubServ

***Law of the Broken Earth (Library Edition)** unabr. ed. Rachel Neumeier. (Running Time: 11 hrs. 30 mins.). (Griffin Mage Ser.). 2010. 34.99 (978-1-4001-9973-0(5)); audio compact disk 83.99 (978-1-4001-4973-5(8)) Pub: Tantor Media. Dist(s): IngramPubServ

Law of the Desert Born. abr. ed. Louis L'Amour. 2 cass. 10.95 (978-0-89926-216-1(3)) Audio Bk.
Includes westerns: "Law of the Desert Born" & "You Tonto Raiders".

Law of the Desert Born; That Triggernometry Tenderfoot; Horse Heaven. unabr. ed. Louis L'Amour. (ENG.). 2009. audio compact disk 14.99 (978-0-7393-8382-7(5), Random AudioBks) Pub: Random Audio Pubg. Dist(s): Random

***Law of the Garbage Truck: How to Respond to People Who Dump on You, & How to Stop Dumping on Others.** unabr. ed. David J. Pollay. (Running Time: 5 hrs. 30 mins.). (ENG.). 2010. 24.98 (978-1-59659-602-3(3), GildAudio) Pub: Gildan Media. Dist(s): HachBkGrp

***Law of the Garbage Truck: How to Respond to People Who Dump on You, & How to Stop Dumping on Others.** unabr. ed. David J. Pollay. (Running Time: 6 hrs. 30 mins.). 2010. audio compact disk 29.98 (978-1-59659-601-6(5), GildAudio) Pub: Gildan Media. Dist(s): HachBkGrp

Law of the Genes (Side One); The Glory of the Senses (Side Two) Jonathan Murro. 1 cass. 1990. 7.95 A R Colton Fnd.
Lectures by Jonathan Murro, a Teacher of the Higher Life for nearly 40 years.

Law of the Identical Harvest. Neville Goddard. 1 cass. (Running Time: 62 min.). 1970. 8.00 (23) J & L Pubns.
Neville taught Imagination Creates Reality. He was a powerfully influential teacher of God as Consciousness.

Law of the Jungle see Classics of English Poetry for the Elementary Curriculum

Law of the Land (VHS) Directed By Doug Phillips. 2003. 12.00 (978-1-929241-82-8(8)) STL Dist NA.

Law of the Mountain Man. William W. Johnstone. Read by Doug van Liew. 4. (Running Time: 6). (Mountain Man Ser.: No. 5). (978-1-59183-006-1(0), 690513) Otis Audio.

Law of the Yukon see Poetry of Robert W. Service

Law of Vibration: Dream Your Life into Being. Melissa Zollo. (ENG.). 2005. audio compact disk 39.00 (978-0-9741449-5-5(9)) Present Mem.

Law of Victory. Francis Frangipane. 1 cass. (Running Time: 90 mins.). (Strategies for our Cities Ser.: Vol. 4). 2000. 5.00 (FF06-004) Morning NC.
This series provides practical, biblical solutions that have been tested & have born fruit for those with a vision for their cities.

Law Office Management for Small-to-Medium Size Firms. 1981. bk. 40.00; 30.00 PA Bar Inst.

Law or Justice: An Emerging Concept of Citizenship. unabr. ed. Christian Bay. 1 cass. (Running Time: 39 min.). 12.95 (21003) J Norton Pubs.
The "thou shalt obey the law" type of good citizenship is contrasted with Dr. Bay's choice of "Thou shall be just to thy fellow man" argument.

Law Practice Management. 1 cass. 1989. 35.00 (AC-511) PA Bar Inst.

Law School Exam Writing, 2005 ed. (Law School Legends Audio Series) 2005th rev. ed. Charles H. Whitebread, II. (Law School Legends Audio Ser.). 2005. 30.00 (978-0-314-16104-8(X), gilbert); 27.95 (978-0-314-16103-1(1), gilbert) West.

Law School for Experts. Instructed by James Mangraviti, Jr. 2000. 124.99 (978-1-892904-15-7(2)) SEAK.

Law School Legends Audio on Future Interests. 3rd rev. ed. Catherine L. Carpenter. (Law School Legends Audio Ser.). 2008. 40.00 (978-0-314-18087-2(7), gilbert) West.

Law School Legends Audio on Immigration Law. Michael Scaperlanda. 2008. 44.00 (978-0-314-18103-9(2), gilbert) West.

***Laweesh Rock & Other Songs.** Owen Mcbride. (ENG.). 1992. 11.95 (978-0-8023-7072-3(1)) Pub: Clo Iar-Chonnachta IRL. Dist(s): Dufour

Lawless. abr. ed. John Jakes. Read by Bruce Watson. 4 cass. (Running Time: 6 hrs.). (Kent Family Chronicles: No. 7). 1978. 12.99 (978-1-57815-166-0(X), 4415, Media Bks Audio) Media Bks NJ.

Lawless. unabr. collector's ed. John Jakes. Read by Michael Kramer. 15 cass. (Running Time: 22 hrs. 30 min.). (Kent Family Chronicles: No. 7). 1993. 120.00 (978-0-7366-2499-2(6), 3257) Books on Tape.
Post-Civil War prosperity has transformed the nation as well as the Kents.

Lawmaker. Rick Ward. 2009. 28.95 (978-0-9823564-2-5(0)) Spring Morning.

Lawman. unabr. ed. Diana Palmer. Narrated by Todd McLaren. (Running Time: 8 hrs. 30 mins. 0 sec.). (ENG.). 2007. audio compact disk 34.99 (978-1-4001-0495-6(5)); audio compact disk 24.99 (978-1-4001-5495-1(2)); audio compact disk 69.99 (978-1-4001-3495-3(1)) Pub: Tantor Media. Dist(s): IngramPubServ

***Lawman's Debt.** Alan LeMay. 2009. (978-1-60136-445-6(8)) Audio Holding.

***Lawmen Die Sudden!** Will Cook. 2009. (978-1-60136-399-2(0)) Audio Holding.

Lawn Boy. unabr. ed. Gary Paulsen. Read by Tom Parks. 1 MP3-CD. (Running Time: 1 hr.). 2009. 39.97 (978-1-4233-9591-1(3), 9781423395911, Brlnc Audio MP3 Lib); 12.99 (978-1-4233-9590-4(5), 9781423395904, Brilliance MP3); 12.99 (978-1-4233-9592-8(1), 9781423395928, BAD); 39.97 (978-1-4233-9593-5(X), 9781423395935, BADLE); audio compact disk 39.97 (978-1-4233-9589-8(1), 9781423395898, BriAudCD Unabrid); audio compact disk 12.99 (978-1-4233-9588-1(3), 9781423395881, Bril Audio CD Unabri) Brilliance Audio.

***Lawn Boy Returns.** unabr. ed. Gary Paulsen. Read by Tom Parks. (Running Time: 2 hrs.). (YA). 2010. audio compact disk 12.99 (978-1-4418-8329-2(0), 9781441883292, Bril Audio CD Unabri); audio compact disk 39.97 (978-1-4418-8330-8(4), 9781441883308, BriAudCD Unabrid) Brilliance Audio.

***Lawn Boy Returns.** unabr. ed. Gary Paulsen. Read by Tom Parks. (Running Time: 2 hrs.). (YA). 2010. 12.99 (978-1-4418-8331-5(2), 9781441883315, Brilliance MP3); 39.97 (978-1-4418-8332-2(0), 9781441883322, Brlnc Audio MP3 Lib); 12.99 (978-1-4418-8333-9(9), 9781441883339, BAD); 39.97 (978-1-4418-8334-6(7), 9781441883346, BADLE) Brilliance Audio.

Lawrence & the Arabs. unabr. ed. Robert Graves. Read by Joseph Porter. 10 cass. (Running Time: 14 hrs. 30 mins.). 1994. 69.95 (978-0-7861-0781-0(2), 1509) Blckstn Audio.
T.E. Lawrence - Lawrence of Arabia - made his first journey to the region, a four-month walking tour of Syria studying the Crusaders' castles, while still a student at Oxford. He later returned to the area as an archaeologist & at the outbreak of World War I was attached to British army intelligence in Egypt. His brilliance as a desert war strategist made him a hero among the Arabs & a legendary figure throughout the world.

Lawrence & the Arabs. unabr. ed. Robert Graves. Read by Joseph Porter. (Running Time: 13 hrs. 50 mins.). 2008. audio compact disk 99.00 (978-1-4332-5001-9(2)) Blckstn Audio.

Lawrence & the Arabs. unabr. ed. Robert Graves. Read by Joseph Porter. (Running Time: 13 hrs. 50 mins.). 2010. 29.95 (978-1-4332-5002-6(0)) Blckstn Audio.

Lawrence & the Arabs. unabr. ed. Robert Graves. Read by Joseph Porter. (Running Time: 13 hrs. 30 mins.). 2010. audio compact disk 39.95 (978-1-4417-2142-6(8)) Blckstn Audio.

Lawrence & the Arabs. unabr. collector's ed. Robert Graves. Read by Bill Kelsey. 9 cass. (Running Time: 13 hrs. 30 mins.). 1989. 72.00 (978-0-7366-1544-0(X), 2413) Books on Tape.
Robert Graves biography of T. E. Lawrence, "Lawrence of Arabia," whose sucessful exploits in Arabia during WWI made him a legend.

Lawrence Ferlinghetti. Interview with Lawrence Ferlinghetti. 1 cass. (Running Time: 30 min.). 1978. 12.95 (L023) TFR.
Ferlinghetti denies he was ever a member of the "Beat Poets" & reveals some startling facts about his past, including his heroism during W.W.II.

Lawrence Ferlinghetti: The Canticle of Jack Kerouac. unabr. ed. Lawrence Ferlinghetti. Read by Lawrence Ferlinghetti. 1 cass. (Running Time: 29 min.). 1988. 10.00 (042988) New Letters.
Here he talks about his new novel, "Lore in the Days of Rage," & reads a long poem called "The Canticle of Jack Kerouac".

Lawrence Ferlinghetti Live at the Poetry Center. Poems. Perf. by Lawrence Ferlinghetti. Executive Producer Poetry Center Staff. 1 CD. (Running Time: 41:01). 2003. audio compact disk 15.00 (978-0-9720751-3-8(5)) Poetry Ctr.

Lawrence Fraiberg, President, Metromedia TV, & Dennis Swanson, News Director, KABC-TV see Scene Behind the Screen: The Business Realities of the TV Industry

Lawrence Homer: Selected Poems. unabr. ed. Lawrence Homer. Read by Lawrence Homer. Ed. by Harvey Lentchner. 1 cass. pap. bk. 14.90; 7.95 (978-0-9615306-2-4(6)) Poets Playwrights.
The poet reads his own poetry in Poetry Archives of Harvard University & is Poet Laureate, Boston.

Lawrence of Arabia. unabr. ed. Jeremy Wilson. Read by Richard Derrington. 2 cass. (Running Time: 2 hrs. 20 min.). (Isis Ser.). (J). 1999. 24.95 (978-0-7531-0601-3(9), 990517) Pub: ISIS Lrg Prnt GBR. Dist(s): Ulverscroft US
The exploits of T.E. Lawrence as British liaison officer in the Arab Revolt, recounted in his literary masterpiece Seven Pillars of Wisdom, made him one of the most famous Englishmen of his generation.

Lawrence Older of Middle Grove, NY. 1 cass. 9.98 (C-15) Folk-Legacy.
Traditional songs & ballads from the Adirondacks.

Laws of Chaos. Kenneth Wapnick. 2008. 77.00 (978-1-59142-371-3(6)); audio compact disk 86.00 (978-1-59142-370-6(8)) Foun Miracles.

Laws of Harmony. Swami Amar Jyoti. 1 cass. 1985. 9.95 (K-80) Truth Consciousness.
The levels of law; the higher we go, less the rules. Meeting the forces of darkness. Living in harmony with the cosmos.

Laws of Inner Wealth: Principles for Spiritual & Material Abundance. John Templeton. 4 cass. (Running Time: 4 hrs.). 1997. (978-1-55525-052-2(1), 16660A) Nightingale-Conant.
Grow rich in spirit.

Laws of Lifetime Growth: Always Make Your Future Bigger Than Your Past. unabr. ed. Dan Sullivan & Catherine Nomura. Read by Jonathan Marosz. (Running Time: 2 hrs. 30 mins.). (ENG.). 2008. 19.98 (978-1-59659-244-5(3), GildAudio) Pub: Gildan Media. Dist(s): HachBkGrp

Laws of Our Fathers. abr. ed. Scott Turow. 2 cass. (Running Time: 4 hrs.). 1996. 20.80 (978-0-671-57741-4(7), 908770, Audioworks) S&S Audio.

Laws of Our Fathers. abr. ed. Scott Turow. 2004. 15.95 (978-0-7435-4922-6(8)) Pub: S&S Audio. Dist(s): S and S Inc

Laws of Our Fathers. unabr. ed. Scott Turow. Read by Orlagh Cassidy et al. (Running Time: 24 hrs. 30 mins.). (ENG.). 2010. 24.98 (978-1-60788-375-3(9)) Pub: Hachet Audio. Dist(s): HachBkGrp

Laws of Our Fathers. unabr. ed. Scott Turow. Read by Orlagh Cassidy et al. (Running Time: 24 hrs. 30 mins.). (ENG.). 2010. audio compact disk 29.98 (978-1-60788-374-6(0)) Pub: Hachet Audio. Dist(s): HachBkGrp

Laws of Our Fathers, Pt. 1. unabr. ed. Scott Turow. Read by Alexander Adams. 8 cass. (Running Time: 12 hrs.). 1997. 64.00 (978-0-7366-3642-1(0), 4304-A) Books on Tape.
When a middle-aged woman, liberal & activist, visits the ghetto, someone shoots her for her trouble. Then her son is charged with ordering the hit.

Laws of Our Fathers, Pt. 2. unabr. ed. Scott Turow. 8 cass. (Running Time: 12 hrs.). 1997. 64.00 (978-0-7366-3643-8(9), 4304-B) Books on Tape.

Laws of Persuasion for Trial Attorneys. Prod. by Advantage Legal Seminars. (ENG.). 2008. 177.00 (978-0-9795737-0-5(X)) Anzman Publg.

Laws of Productivity see Las Leyes de la Productividad

Laws of Prosperity. Kenneth Copeland. 6 cass. 1982. bk. 0.30 (978-0-938458-38-8(8)) K Copeland Pubns.
Explanation of biblical prosperity.

***Laws of Spiritual Developent.** (ENG.). 2010. 19.95 (978-1-934162-48-4(5)) New Life.

Laws of Spiritual Development (Tape Album) 1989. 19.95 (978-0-911203-38-7(9)) New Life.

Laws of the Heavens. unabr. ed. David Barton. Read by David Barton. 1 cass. (Running Time: 1 hr.). 1990. 4.95 (978-0-925279-09-5(9), A03) Wallbuilders.
In this presentation you'll learn the meaning of "the Laws of Nature & of Nature's God" - the eight words form the Declaration of Independence which explain how Great Britain's violations of God's laws led to the initiation of the American Revolution.

Laws of the Kingdom Vol. I: As Presented by the Spirit World, Through the Automatic Writings of Frances Bird. unabr. ed. Frances Bird. Read by Kenneth Carey. 5 cass. (Running Time: 6 hrs. 40 min.). (Automatic Writings Ser.: Vol. I). 1988. pap. bk. 44.95 (978-1-55768-701-2(3)) LC Pub.
Gives insight into the nature of life awaiting one in the spirit world, with explanations of what it takes following the transition called death.

Laws of the Kingdom Vol. II: As Presented by the Spirit World, Through the Automatic Writings of Frances Bird. unabr. ed. Frances Bird. Read by Kenneth Carey. 8 cass. (Running Time: 11 hrs. 20 min.). (Automatic Writings Ser.). 1989. 62.95 LC Pub.
Gives insight into the nature of life awaiting one in the spirit world, with explanations of what takes place following the transition, called death.

Laws of the Spirit. Kenneth Copeland. 4 cass. 1982. bk. & stu. ed. 20.00 (978-0-938458-31-9(0)) K Copeland Pubns.
Understanding God's spiritual laws.

Laws of Thinking: 20 Secrets to Using the Divine Power of Your Mind to Manifest Prosperity. abr. ed. E. Bernard Jordan. Read by E. Bernard Jordan. 4 CDs. (ENG.). 2007. audio compact disk 23.95 (978-1-4019-1825-5(5)) Hay House.

Laws That Govern Life. Creflo A. Dollar. 25.00 (978-1-59089-089-9(2)) Pub: Creflo Dollar. Dist(s): STL Dist NA

Laws That Govern the Christian Family. unabr. ed. Creflo A. Dollar. 2001. 35.00 (978-1-931172-87-5(0), Kidz Faith) Pub: Creflo Dollar. Dist(s): STL Dist NA

Lawyer-Client Communication in Estate Planning. Read by Edith M. Doyle & K. Bruce Friedman. (Running Time: 3 hrs.). 1992. 89.00 Incl. Ethics: 30 min., Law Practice Management: 2.30 hrs., & 217p. tape materials. (ES-55248) Cont Ed Bar-CA.
Assists you in communicating with your client before, during, & after drafting, & in managing an estate planning practice. The panel covers interviewing the client, anticipating the client's questions, using computers & graphics, identifying ethical problems, educating & counseling the client, drafting readable instruments, explaining the instruments by "plain English" letters, implementing the plan, following up & maintaining client contact, post-death administration, & counseling individual fiduciaries.

Lawyer Investigator. Edmund J. Pankau. 4 cass. (Running Time: 6 hrs.). 1997. 59.95 (978-0-9679281-0-4(9)) Cloak & Data.

Lawyer Trust Accounts: Audio CD & CD-ROM with Forms. Jay Foonberg. 2007. cd-rom & audio compact disk 79.95 (978-0-9795671-4-8(9)) Ntl Academy Law.

Lawyering Skills: Depositions & Trials. Peter B. Knapp & Ann Juergens. Ed. by Roger S. Haydock. (American Casebook Ser.). 1996. 44.00 (978-0-314-08912-0(8)) West Pub.

Lawyering Skills: Interviewing, Counseling & Negotiation. Peter B. Knapp et al. (American Casebook Ser.). 1996. 44.00 (978-0-314-08913-7(6)) West Pub.

Lawyering Skills: Mediation & Arbitration. Peter B. Knapp et al. (American Casebook Ser.). 1996. 44.00 (978-0-314-08914-4(4)) West Pub.

Lawyering Skills: Practice & Planning. Roger S. Haydock. (American Casebook Ser.). 1996. 1517.00 (978-0-314-09438-4(5), West Lglwrks) West.

Lawyers' Liability for Vexatious Acts. Read by G. Thomas Miller. 1 cass. 1989. 20.00 (AL-63) PA Bar Inst.

Lawyer's Management Principles: A Course for Assistants: Student Syllabus. Harold W. Adams & Ray Stringham. (YA). (gr. 11-12). 1975. 86.90 (978-0-89420-200-1(6), 101000) Natl Book.

Lay Aside the Weights. Speeches. Joel Osteen. 1 Cass. (Running Time: 30 Mins.). 2001. 6.00 (978-1-59349-089-8(5), JA0089) J Osteen.

Lay down My Sword & Shield. unabr. ed. James Lee Burke. Read by Will Patton. 8 CDs. (Running Time: 9 hrs. 30 mins. 0 sec.). 2010. audio compact disk 39.99 (978-1-4423-0370-6(0)) Pub: S&S Audio. Dist(s): S and S Inc

Lay it Down. 2004. DVD & audio compact disk 19.99 (978-0-01-222984-2(9)) D Christiano Films.

Lay It Down. Contrib. by Jaci Velasquez. (Ultimate Tracks (Word Tracks) Ser.). 2006. audio compact disk 8.98 (978-5-558-26980-2(4), Word Music) Word Enter.

Lay It on the Line. unabr. ed. Catherine Dain. Read by Stephanie Brush. 6 CDs. (Running Time: 7 hrs. 6 min.). 2001. audio compact disk 39.00 (978-1-58116-206-6(5)) Books in Motion.
An ex-chorus girl asks Freddie O'Neal to help her father who is being conned. The case gets complicated when a murder and a mess of family secrets come to light.

Lay It on the Line. unabr. ed. Catherine Dain. Read by Stephanie Brush. 6 cass. (Running Time: 7 hrs. 6 min.). (Freddie O'Neal Mystery Ser.: Bk. 3). 2001. 39.95 (978-1-58116-105-2(0)) Books in Motion.

Lay of the Last Minstrel. unabr. ed. Walter Scott, Sr. Read by Robert L. Halvorson. 3 cass. (Running Time: 270 min.). 21.95 (40) Halvorson Assocs.

Lay of the Last Minstrel - Breathes There a Man see Classics of English Poetry for the Elementary Curriculum

Lay Participation in a Congregation's Pastoral Ministry. Ron Sunderland. 1986. 10.80 (0605) Assn Prof Chaplains.

Lay Women's Retreat of Faith. Fr. Hardon. 12 cass. 48.00 Set. (92F) IRL Chicago.

Lay Women's Ten Commandments Retreat. Fr. Hardon. 11 cass. 44.00 (93U) IRL Chicago.

Laying down the Rails: A Live Workshop with Sonya Shafer. Sonya Shafer. (ENG.). 2008. audio compact disk 7.95 (978-1-61634-048-3(7)) Simply Char.

Laying down the Rails: A Live Workshop with Sonya Shafer. Sonya Shafer. (ENG.). 2008. 5.95 (978-1-61634-054-4(1)) Simply Char.

Laying Hold of Your Inheritance. Creflo A. Dollar. 20.00 (978-1-59089-039-4(6)) Pub: Creflo Dollar. Dist(s): STL Dist NA

Laying on of Hands. Nathaniel Holcomb. 4 cass. (Running Time: 6 hrs.). 1999. (978-1-930918-25-2(9)) Its All About Him.

Laying the Atlantic Cable. Kenneth Bruce. 1 cass. (Running Time: 1 hr.). Dramatization. (Excursions in History Ser.). 12.50 Alpha Tape.

Laying the Foundation, Album 1. Derek Prince. 5 cass. 24.95 (B-LTF1) Derek Prince.

Laying the Foundation, Album 2. Derek Prince. 5 cass. 24.95 (B-LTF2) Derek Prince.

Laying the Ghost. Judy Astley. 2008. 61.95 (978-0-7531-3827-4(1)); audio compact disk 79.95 (978-0-7531-2811-4(X)) Pub: ISIS Audio GBR. Dist(s): Ulverscroft US

Layman Called & Gifted: National Association of Evangelicals, 47th Annual Convention, Columbus, Ohio, March 7-9, 1989. James Garlow. 1 cass. (Workshops Ser.: No. 8-Wednesda). 1989. 4.25 ea. 1-8 tapes.; 4.00 ea. 9 tapes or more. Nat Assn Evan.

Laymen Trained & Sent: National Association of Evangelicals, 47th Annual Convention, Columbus, Ohio, March 7-9, 1989. James Garlow. 1 cass. (Workshops Ser.: No. 17-Wednesd). 1989. 4.25 ea. 1-8 tapes.; 4.00 ea. 9 tapes or more. Nat Assn Evan.

Layoff. Tana Reiff. (That's Life Ser.: Bk. 3). 1994. 10.95 (978-0-7854-1097-3(X), 40713) Am Guidance.

***Layover in Dubai.** unabr. ed. Dan Fesperman. (Running Time: 11 hrs.). 2010. 24.99 (978-1-4233-4678-4(5), 9781423346784, BAD); 39.97 (978-1-4233-4679-1(3), 9781423346791, BADLE) Brilliance Audio.

***Layover in Dubai.** unabr. ed. Dan Fesperman. Read by Christopher Lane. (Running Time: 11 hrs.). 2010. 24.99 (978-1-4233-4676-0(9), 9781423346760, Brilliance MP3); 39.97 (978-1-4233-4677-7(7), 9781423346777, Brinc Audio MP3 Lib); audio compact disk 29.99 (978-1-4233-4674-6(2), 9781423346746, Bril Audio CD Unabri); audio compact disk 82.97 (978-1-4233-4675-3(0), 9781423346753, BriAudCD Unabrid) Brilliance Audio.

Lazarillo de Tormes. Read by Juan Camacho. 2 cass. (Running Time: 2 hrs.). (SPA.). 1996. pap. bk. 29.50 set. (978-1-58085-250-0(5)) Interlingua VA.
Includes dual Spanish-English transcript. The combination of written text & clarity & pace of diction will open the door for intermediate & advanced students to genuine comprehension & the use of literary texts for advancement in rapid understanding of written & oral language materials. The audio text plus written text concept makes foreign languages accessible to a much wider range of students than books alone.

Lazarillo De Tormes. Mendoza. audio compact disk 12.95 (978-0-8219-3812-6(6)) EMC-Paradigm.

Lazarillo de Tormes. Ed. by William T. Tardy. 1 cass. (Dos Novelas Picarescas Ser.). 15.00 (Natl Textbk Co) M-H Contemporary.
Introduces intermediate students of Spanish to view of Spanish history, customs & traditions of the 1500's.

Lazarillo de Tormes. unabr. ed. Read by Fabio Camero. 3 CDs. (SPA.). 2001. audio compact disk 17.00 (978-958-9494-34-9(X)) YoYoMusic.

Lazarillo of Tormes. Read by Fabio Camero. (Running Time: 3 hrs.). 2001. 16.95 (978-1-60083-158-4(3), Audiofy Corp) Iofy Corp.

Lazarus. unabr. ed. Morris West. 7 cass. (Running Time: 14 hrs.). (Vatican Trilogy). 2004. 56.00 (978-1-74030-686-7(4)) Pub: Bolinda Pubng AUS. Dist(s): Lndmrk Audiobks

***Lazarus Awakening: Finding Your Place in the Heart of God.** unabr. ed. Joanna Weaver. Narrated by Anna-Lisa Horton. (Running Time: 7 hrs. 0 mins. 0 sec.). (ENG.). 2011. audio compact disk 25.99 (978-1-59859-851-3(1)) Oasis Audio.

Lazarus Child. unabr. ed. Robert Mawson. Read by David Case. 8 cass. (Running Time: 12 hrs.). 1998. 64.00 (978-0-7366-4237-8(4), 4735) Books on Tape.
A search for a miracle & a testament to the power of family love.

Lazarus Incident. unabr. ed. Gerry W. Gotro. Read by Rusty Nelson. 8 cass. (Running Time: 9 hrs. 24 min.). 2001. 49.95 (978-1-58116-033-8(X)) Books in Motion.
Amy Danson's search for her long-missing father turns to discovery, as Carla McKenzie and the crew from North Wind find the downed Tiger Moth aircraft, and the remains of the two pilots. But one corpse has a bullet hole in the back of his head.

Lazarus Strain. Ken McClure. 2007. 61.95 (978-0-7531-2850-3(0)); audio compact disk 79.95 (978-0-7531-2851-0(9)) Pub: ISIS Audio GBR. Dist(s): Ulverscroft US

Lazarus Vendetta. abr. ed. Robert Ludlum & Patrick Larkin. Read by Scott Brick. 5 CDs. (Running Time: 6 hrs. 0 mins. 0 sec.). (Covert-One Ser.). (ENG.). 2007. audio compact disk 14.95 (978-1-4272-0312-0(1)) Pub: Macmill Audio. Dist(s): Macmillan

Lazarus Vendetta. abr. rev. ed. Robert Ludlum & Patrick Larkin. 5 CDs. (Running Time: 6 hrs. 0 mins. 0 sec.). (Covert-One Ser.). (ENG., 2004. audio compact disk 29.95 (978-1-59397-416-9(7)) Pub: Macmill Audio. Dist(s): Macmillan

Lazarus Vendetta. unabr. ed. Robert Ludlum & Patrick Larkin. 8 cass. (Covert-One Ser.). 2005. 69.95 (978-0-7927-3322-5(3), CSL 695); audio compact disk 99.95 (978-0-7927-3323-2(1), SLD 695); audio compact disk 49.95 (978-0-7927-3324-9(X), CMP 695) AudioGO.

Lazarus Vendetta. unabr. rev. ed. Robert Ludlum & Patrick Larkin. Read by Scott Brick & Scott Sowers. 11 CDs. (Running Time: 13 hrs. 0 mins. 0 sec.). (Covert-One Ser.). (ENG.). 2004. audio compact disk 44.95 (978-1-59397-434-3(5)) Pub: Macmill Audio. Dist(s): Macmillan

Lazy Daughter. unabr. ed. 1 cass. (Running Time: 20 min.). Dramatization. (Magic Looking Glass Ser.). (J). (gr. 2-6). 1989. 9.95 (978-0-7810-0018-5(1), NIM-CW-126-4-C) NIMCO.
A story of Irish descent.

Lazy Duck: Audiocassette. Jo Windsor. Illus. by Philip Webb. (Sails Literacy Ser.). (gr. k up). 10.00 (978-0-7578-2651-1(2)) Rigby Educ.

Lazy Eye. unabr. ed. Jacqueline Jacques. Read by Stephen Thorne. 12 cass. (Running Time: 18 hrs.). 2001. 94.95 (978-1-86042-832-6(0), 28320) Pub: Soundings Ltd GBR. Dist(s): Ulverscroft US

lazy girl's guide to losing weight & getting Fit. A. J. Rochester. Read by A. J. Rochester. (Running Time: 10 hrs. 10 mins.). 2009. 84.99 (978-1-74214-447-4(0), 9781742144474) Pub: Bolinda Pubng AUS. Dist(s): Bolinda Pub Inc

Lazy Girl's Guide to Losing Weight & Getting Fit. unabr. ed. (Running Time: 36720 sec.). 2007. audio compact disk 93.95 (978-1-74093-965-2(4), 9781740939652) Pub: Bolinda Pubng AUS. Dist(s): Bolinda Pub Inc

Lazy Lions, Lucky Lambs. unabr. ed. Patricia Reilly Giff. Read by Suzanne Toren. 1 cass. (Running Time: 1 hr. 7 mins.). (Follow the Reader Ser.). (J). (gr. 1-2). 1985. pap. bk. 17.00 incl. bk. & guide. (978-0-8072-0102-2(2), FTR106SP, Listening Lib) Random Audio Pubg.
Follow the kids in Ms. Rooney's second-grade class as they learn & grow through an entire school year filled with fun & surprises. Corresponding Month: March.

Lazy Man's Guide to Death & Dying. E. J. Gold. 1 cass. (Running Time: 1 hr.). 15.00 (MT010) Union Label.
Author reads excerpts with his own original music.

Lazy Mary. 1 read-along cass. (J). 1986. pap. bk. 5.95 Wright Group.
Story about Lazy Mary; her mother tries & tries but nothing will get her out of bed.

Lazy Person's Guide to Investing. Paul B. Farrell. Read by Nick Summers. (Running Time: 3 hrs. 30 mins.). (C). 2006. 21.95 (978-1-60083-331-1(4)) Iofy Corp.

Lazy Person's Guide to Investing. abr. ed. Paul B. Farrell. Read by Nick Summers. 3 CDs. (Running Time: 13800 sec.). 2006. audio compact disk 19.95 (978-1-59316-078-4(X), LL170) Listen & Live.

Lazy Way to Lose Weight: Achieve Your Ideal Weight. 2001. 17.95 (978-0-9709302-3-1(2)) Growth Enrich.

Lazy Way to Lose Weight: Achieving Your Ideal Weight. (978-0-9709302-2-4(4)) Growth Enrich.

Lazy Way to Lose Weight: Hypnosis Weight Control Program. Mark E. Wilkins. 2006. audio compact disk 17.95 (978-0-9709302-5-5(9)) Growth Enrich.

Le Petit Prince see Little Prince

Lead Belly's Last Sessions. Perf. by Lead Belly. Anno. by Sean Killeen et al. 4 cass. 1994. audio compact disk (0-9307-40068-2-5) Smithsonian Folkways.
Recordings from 1948, contains 96 songs & includes two unissued tracks plus songs such as "Midnight Special," "Goodnight Irene," "Rock Island Line" & "Easy Rider".

Lead Belly's Last Sessions. Perf. by Lead Belly. Anno. by Sean Killeen et al. 4 cass. 1994. Set, incl. 24p bklet. (0-9307-400680-9307-40068-2-5) Smithsonian Folkways.

Lead Generation for the Complex Sale: Boost the Quality & Quantity of Leads to Increase Your ROI. Brian J. Carroll. 2008. audio compact disk 28.00 (978-1-933309-60-6(1)) Pub: A Media Intl. Dist(s): Natl Bk Netwk

Lead Guitar Licks. Brett Duncan. (Progressive Ser.). 1997. pap. bk. 19.95 (978-1-875726-00-4(4), 256-120) Kolala Music SGP.

***Lead Like Ike: Ten Business Strategies from the CEO of D-Day.** unabr. ed. Geoff Loftus. Narrated by Mort Crim. (Running Time: 9 hrs. 23 mins. 42 sec.). (ENG.). 2010. 20.99 (978-1-60814-685-7(5), SpringWater); audio compact disk 29.99 (978-1-59859-734-9(5), SpringWater) Oasis Audio.

Lead Like Jesus. unabr. ed. Ken Blanchard et al. (ENG.). 2004. 12.59 (978-1-60814-277-4(9)) Oasis Audio.

Lead Like Jesus: Lessons from the Greatest Leadership Role Model of All Time. unabr. ed. Ken Blanchard. 4 cass. (Running Time: 6 hrs.). 2004. 27.99 (978-1-58926-727-5(3), 6727) Oasis Audio.

Lead Like Jesus: Lessons from the Greatest Leadership Role Model of All Time. unabr. ed. Ken Blanchard et al. 5 CDs. (Running Time: 5 hrs. 0 mins. 4 sec.). (ENG.). 2004. audio compact disk 17.99 (978-1-58926-728-2(1), 6728) Oasis Audio.

Lead Like Jesus: Lessons from the Greatest Leadership Role Model of All Time. unabr. ed. Rick Warren & Bill Hybels. Read by Rick Warren & Bill Hybels. Frwd. by Ken Blanchard. 5 CDs. (Running Time: 6 hrs.). 2004. audio compact disk 40.00 (978-0-7861-8446-0(9), 3371) Blckstn Audio.

Lead Me On: Digitally Remastered. Contrib. by Amy Grant. Prod. by Brown Bannister. 2007. audio compact disk 13.99 (978-5-557-62604-0(2)) Pt of Grace Ent.

***Lead Sell or Get Out of the Way: The 7 Traits of Great Sellers.** unabr. ed. Ron Karr. (Running Time: 7 hrs.). (ENG.). 2010. 27.98 (978-1-59659-568-2(X), GildAudio) Pub: Gildan Media. Dist(s): HachBkGrp

Lead Singer: Vocal Techniques Pop to Rock: Level 2. Contrib. by Breck Alan. 2007. DVD 19.95 (978-5-557-87742-8(8)) MVD Ent.

Lead the Field. abr. ed. Earl Nightingale. 6 cass. (Running Time: 40 hrs. 0 mins. 0 sec.). (ENG.). 2002. audio compact disk 29.95 (978-0-7435-2081-2(5), Nightgale) Pub: S&S Audio. Dist(s): S and S Inc
The magic word in life is ATTITUDE. It determines your actions, as well as the actions of others. It tells the world what you expect from it. When you accept responsibility for your attitude, you accept responsibility for your entire life.

Lead the Field. unabr. ed. Earl Nightingale. Read by Earl Nightingale. 6 cass. (Running Time: 6 hrs.). 1991. 59.95 (978-1-55525-000-3(9), 116-2A) Nightingale-Conant.
At 29, Earl Nightingale stumbled onto the secret of success. Within a week he had doubled his income. A week later he doubled it again. Soon, he was one of the highest paid people in his field. At 35, wealthy beyond his dreams.

Lead the Field. unabr. ed. Earl Nightingale. 6 cass. (Running Time: 6 hrs.). 2000. wbk. ed. 69.95 (978-1-55525-019-5(X), 116-2CD) Nightingale-Conant.

Lead the Way. Arranged by Steven V. Taylor. 1 cass. (Running Time: 1 hr.). (YA). 2001. 90.00 (MU-9151C); audio compact disk 90.00 (MU-9151T) Lillenas.
Here are 50 great songs for group or solo performances with your teens. You can get it in accompaniment double compact disc, full stereo. This sequel to the Dare to Run book promises to be just as popular.

Leadbelly Sings Folk Songs. Perf. by Lead Belly et al. Contrib. by Moses Asch. 1 cass. 1989. (0-9307-400100-9307-40010-2-8); audio compact disk (0-9307-40010-2-8) Smithsonian Folkways.
1940s recordings of 15 songs including "Stewball," "Linin Track" & "On a Monday".

Leaden Echo & the Golden Echo see Dylan Thomas Reading

Leaden Skies. unabr. ed. Anna Parker. (Running Time: 9 hrs. 0 mins.). (ENG.). 2009. 29.95 (978-1-4332-9064-0(2)); 59.95 (978-1-4332-9060-2(X)); audio compact disk 90.00 (978-1-4332-9061-9(8)) Blckstn Audio.

Leader Arts Sailing New Seas. abr. ed. Leonard Sweet. 1 cass. (Running Time: 90 min.). 2002. 17.99 (978-0-310-23479-1(4)) Zondervan.

Leader in Me: How Schools & Parents Around the World Are Inspiring Greatness, One Child at a Time. abr. ed. Stephen R. Covey. Read by Stephen R. Covey. (Running Time: 1 hr. 0 mins. 0 sec.). (ENG.). 2008. audio compact disk 15.00 (978-0-7435-8079-3(6)) Pub: S&S Audio. Dist(s): S and S Inc

Leader in Me: How Schools & Parents Around the World Are Inspiring Greatness, One Child at a Time. unabr. ed. Stephen R. Covey. Read by Stephen R. Covey. (Running Time: 10 hrs. 0 mins. 0 sec.). (ENG.). 2008. audio compact disk 34.95 (978-1-933976-75-4(6)) Pub: Franklin Covey. Dist(s): S and S Inc

Leader in You. abr. ed. Dale Carnegie. Read by Stuart Levine & Ross Klavan. 2004. 7.95 (978-0-7435-4924-0(4)) Pub: S&S Audio. Dist(s): S and S Inc

Leader in You: How to Win Friends, Influence People & Succeed in a Changing World. Dale Carnegie. Narrated by Jack Garrett. 6 cass. (Running Time: 8 hrs.). 64.00 (978-0-7887-5318-3(5)) Recorded Bks.

Leader in You: How to Win Friends, Influence People, & Succeed in a Completely Changed World. abr. ed. Dale Carnegie et al. Read by Stuart Levine et al. 2 CDs. (Running Time: 13 hrs. 0 mins. 0 sec.). (ENG.). 2001. audio compact disk 19.95 (978-0-7435-0412-6(7), Sound Ideas) Pub: S&S Audio. Dist(s): S and S Inc

Leader-Manager Profile Facilitator Guide. James P. Eicher. 1999. wbk. ed. 62.30 (978-0-925652-99-7(7)) Orgn Design & Dev.

***Leader Who Had No Title: A Modern Fable on Real Success in Business & in Life.** unabr. ed. Robin Sharma. Read by Holter Graham. 6 CDs. (Running Time: 7 hrs.). 2010. audio compact disk 29.99 (978-1-4423-3431-1(2)) Pub: S&S Audio. Dist(s): S and S Inc

Leaders: The Strategies of Taking Charge. Warren Bennis & Burt Nanus. 1986. 39.95 (3012) SyberVision.

Shows how to become the kind of person others look to for inspiration & guidance. How to develop the knowledge, the skills, & the understanding to become an excellent manager, a better parent, a more successful businessperson & a more highly respected member of the community. Topics include - The Essence of Leadership: Your Key to Personal Power; Unveiling the Mystery: The 10 Dominant Characteristics of an Effective Leader; The Visionary Leader: How to Create a Vision of the Future; The Management of Self: How to Lead Others Through Self-Mastery & Example.

Leaders at All Levels: Deepening Your Talent Pool to Solve the Succession Crisis. unabr. ed. Ram Charan. Read by Sean Pratt. (Running Time: 5 hrs. 50 mins.). (ENG.). 2007. 24.95 (978-1-59659-185-1(4), GildAudio) Pub: Gildan Media. Dist(s): HachBkGrp

Leaders at All Levels: Deepening Your Talent Pool to Solve the Succession Crisis. unabr. rev. ed. Ram Charan. Read by Sean Pratt. (Running Time: 6 hrs.). (ENG.). 2008. audio compact disk 29.98 (978-1-59659-125-7(0), GildAudio) Pub: Gildan Media. Dist(s): HachBkGrp

Leaders Can Help Audio CD. Adapted by Benchmark Education Company Staff. Based on a work by Cynthia Swain. (Early Explorers Set C Ser.). (J). (gr. k-1). 2008. audio compact disk 10.00 (978-1-60437-518-3(3)) Benchmark Educ.

Leaders in the Animal Movement, Pt. 1. Hosted by Nancy Pearlman. 1 cass. (Running Time: 31 min.). 10.00 (528) Educ Comm CA.

Leaders in the Animal Movement, Pt. 2. Hosted by Nancy Pearlman. 1 cass. (Running Time: 31 min.). 10.00 (529) Educ Comm CA.

Leader's Number One Enemy - Pride. Speeches. Joel Osteen. 1 Cass. (Running Time: 30 Mins.). 2001. 6.00 (978-1-59349-094-2(1), JA0094) J Osteen.

Leaders of the New Century. ed. Mark Thompson & Richard Wilson. 1 CD. (Running Time: 51 mins. 20 secs.). (Leaders of the New Century Ser.). 2001. audio compact disk 17.99 (978-0-9719341-1-5(8)) NPBI.

In depth leadership interviews with Michael Dell (Dell Computer), Jack Greenberg (McDonald's Corporation), and Klaus Schwab (World Economic Forum). Also included are short insights from Jack Welch (General Electric) and Quincy Jones (Musician, Composer and Producer).

Leaders of the New Century. unabr. ed. Mark Thompson & Richard Wilson. 8 CDs. (Running Time: 8 hrs.). (Leaders of the New Century Ser.). 2002. audio compact disk 17.99 (978-0-9719341-0-8(X)) NPBI.

In depth leadership interviews with some of the pivotal leaders of our day. The project has been interviewing many of the top leaders in the sports, entertainment and business community. 38 leaders include Jack Welch, Donna Dubinsky, Michael Dell, Kim Polese, Herb Kelleher, david Stern, Candice Carpenter, Quincy JOnes and Charles Schwab.

Leaders of the New Century. 2nd unabr. ed. Mark Thompson & Richard Wilson. 1 CD. (Running Time: 1 hr. 1 min.). (Leaders of the New Century Ser.). 2001. 17.99 (978-0-9719341-2-2(6)) NPBI.

In depth leadership interviews with Charles Schwab (The Charles Schwab Corporation), Ed Miller (AXA Financial), Wick Simmons (The Nasdaq Stock Market), and Dick Grasso (The New York Stock Exchange). Also included is a short insight from Lance Armstrong (Tour de France Champion).

Leaders of the New Century. 3rd unabr. ed. Mark Thompson & Richard Wilson. 1 CD. (Running Time: 55 mins.). (Leaders of the New Century Ser.). 2001. audio compact disk 17.99 (978-0-9719341-3-9(4)) NPBI.

In depth leadership interviews with Jack Welch (General Electric), Brad Anderson (Best Buy), and Herb Kelleher (Southwest Airlines). Also included are short insights from Benjamin Zander (Boston Philharmonic) and Steve Young (Found Inc./San Francisco 49ers).

Leaders of the New Century. 4th unabr. ed. Mark Thompson & Richard Wilson. 1 CD. (Running Time: 50 mins.). (Leaders of the New Century Ser.). 2001. audio compact disk 17.99 (978-0-9719341-4-6(2)) NPBI.

In depth leadership interviews with David Stern (National Basketball Association), Candice Carpenter (I Village), and Hatim Tyabji (ByteMobile/Veriphone). Also included are short insights from Larry Ellison (Oracle Corporation) and Carl Lewis (Olympic Athlete of the Century).

Leaders of the New Century. 5th ed. Mark Thompson & Richard Wilson. 1 CD. (Running Time: 52 mins.). (Leaders of the New Century Ser.). 2001. audio compact disk 17.99 (978-0-9719341-5-3(0)) NPBI.

In depth leadership interviews with Robert Galvin (Motorola Inc.), James Kouzes (The Leadership Challenge), and Herb Kelleher (Southwest Airlines). Also included are short insights from Carly Fiorina (Hewlett-Packard Company) and Donna Dubinsky (Handspring).

Leaders of the New Century. 6th ed. Mark Thompson & Richard Wilson. 1 CD. (Running Time: 46 mins.). (Leaders of the New Century Ser.). 2001. audio compact disk 17.99 (978-0-9719341-6-0(9)) NPBI.

in depth leadership interviews with Quincy Jones (Musician, composer, producer), Greg Foster (IMAX Corporation), and President Jimmy Carter (Carter Center). Also included are short insights from Sally Field (Actress, director) and Tenzin Gyatso (His Hollines The 14th Dalai Lama).

Leaders of the New Century. 7th ed. Mark Thompson & Richard Wilson. 1 CD. (Running Time: 1 hr. 4 mins.). (Leaders of the New Century Ser.). 2001. audio compact disk 17.99 (978-0-9719341-7-7(7)) NPBI.

In depth leadership interviews with Jack Welch (General Electric), Douglas Daft (The Coca-Cola Company), Terry Pearce (Leadership Communications), and Dr. Rachel Remen (Physician, teacher, author). Also included is a short insight from Bruce Katz (Entrepreneur. The Well, Business for Social Responsibility, Rockport Shoes).

Leaders of the New Century. 8th ed. Mark Thompson & Richard Wilson. 1 CD. (Running Time: 1 hr. 1 min.). (Leaders of the New Century Ser.). 2001. audio compact disk 17.99 (978-0-9719341-8-4(5)) NPBI.

In depth leadership interviews with Steve Forbes (Forbes, Inc), Kim Polese (Marimba, Inc.) Eric Benhamou (SCom Corporation/Palm, Inc.), and James Wetherbe (Professor, speaker, author). Also included is a short insight from John Chambers (Cisco Systems, Inc.).

Leaders of the Third Millenium see Lideres del Tercer Milenio

***Leader's Way: The Art of Making the Right Decisions in Our Careers, Our Companies, & the World at Large.** unabr. ed. Dalai Lama XIV & Laurens van den Muyzenberg. 5 CDs. (Running Time: 6 hrs.). 2009. audio compact disk 80.00 (978-1-4159-6401-9(7), BksonTape) Pub: Random Audio Pubg. Dist(s): Random

Leader's Way: The Art of Making the Right Decisions in Our Careers, Our Companies, & the World at Large. unabr. ed. Dalai Lama XIV & Lauren Van den Muyzenberg. Read by Feodor Chin & Marc Cashman. (ENG.). 2009. audio compact disk 29.95 (978-0-7393-8383-4(3), Random AudioBks) Pub: Random Audio Pubg. Dist(s): Random

***Leaders Who Last.** unabr. ed. Dave Kraft. Narrated by Raymond Todd. (ENG.). 2010. 10.98 (978-1-59644-222-1(0)); audio compact disk 15.98 (978-1-59644-221-4(2)) christianaud.

***Leadership.** L. Ron Hubbard. (ENG.). 2002. audio compact disk 15.00 (978-1-4031-1464-8(1)) Bridge Pubns Inc.

Leadership. Betty L. Randolph. (Success Ser.). 1989. 9.98 (978-1-55909-101-5(0), 84S) Randolph Tapes.

Imbues the qualities needed to be a good leader, the ability to take charge & make good decisions.

Leadership: A Collection of Favorite Quotations. abr. ed. Rudolph W. Giuliani & Ken Kurson. Read by Rudolph W. Giuliani & Tony Roberts. 5 CDs. (Running Time: 6 hrs.). 2003. audio compact disk 31.98 (978-1-4013-9823-1(5), Hyperion Audio) Pub: Hyperion. Dist(s): HarperCollins Pubs

Leadership: Creativity, Character, & the Courage to Succeed. abr. ed. James M. Kouzes et al. 1 cass. (Running Time: 1 hrs. 50 min.). (Career Development Ser.: Vol. 1). 1999. 19.95 (978-1-892655-00-4(4)) Powerplay Audio.

Powerful program that will stimulate & inspire the listener to become a better leader in all areas of life.

Leadership: The Critical Difference. Brian S. Tracy. Read by Brian S. Tracy. 2 cass. (Effective Manager Seminar Ser.: No. 3). stu. ed. & wbk. ed. 95.00 (745VD) Nightingale-Conant.

To be effective, a manager must also be a leader. Step-by-step guidance.

Leadership: Three Essential Questions for Executives. 2007. audio compact disk 14.95 (978-0-9712007-0-8(X)) Shadowbrook.

Leadership Set: Effective Spiritual Keys for Today's Leaders. Tom Marshall & Tom Muccio. 1993. 40.00 (978-0-935779-16-5(7)) Crown Min.

Leadership - A Spiritual Journey. Kriyananda, pseud. (Running Time: 2hrs.). 14.95 (ST-18) Crystal Clarity.

Explains: how becoming a good leader will help you progress spiritually; centeredness, magnetism & humility as keys to successful leadership; yoga techniques vs. psychology as a way of overcoming negative qualities.

Leadership - Great Leaders, Great Teams, Great Results: The 4 Imperatives of Great Leaders. unabr. ed. Stephen R. Covey. Read by Stephen R. Covey. (YA). 2008. 34.99 (978-1-60514-651-5(X)) Find a World.

***Leadership & Crisis.** unabr. ed. Bobby Jindal et al. Read by Sean Runnette. (Running Time: 8.5 hrs. NaN mins.). (ENG.). 2010. 29.95 (978-1-4417-8097-3(1)); 54.95 (978-1-4417-8094-2(7)); audio compact disk 29.95 (978-1-4417-8096-6(3)); audio compact disk 76.00 (978-1-4417-8095-9(5)) Blckstn Audio.

Leadership & Organizational Change. Glenn Swogger. Read by Glenn Swogger. 1 cass. (Running Time: 23 min.). (Executive Seminar Ser.). 1987. 10.00 (978-1-56948-010-6(9)) Menninger Clinic.

Glenn Swogger, Jr. MD, discusses the emotional aspects of change in organizations, with special emphasis on the role of the leader responsible for the management of the change process.

Leadership & Self-Deception: Getting out of the Box. unabr. ed. Arbinger Institute Staff. Narrated by William Dufris. (ENG.). 2004. audio compact disk 24.95 (978-1-57270-444-2(6)) Pub: AudioGO. Dist(s): Perseus Dist

When Tom Callum, a troubled executive struggling with his new job, is asked to spend two days meeting with the executive vice president at the Zagrum Company, he unexpectedly learns about self-deception. Self-deception results when someone acts contrary to what they know is right. By ignoring that altruistic, internal voice, one triggers a chain of events that ultimately result in destructive behavior.The "disease" of self-deception underlies all leadership problems in today's organizations. However well intentioned they may be, leaders who deceive themselves always end up undermining their own performance. This straightforward audio uses Tom Callum's story to demonstrate that while knowing how to avoid this problem is central to business relationships and success, awareness is equally important in one's personal relationships.

Leadership & Spirituality. unabr. ed. Instructed by Larry Willard. 5 cass. (Running Time: 7 hrs. 30 mins.). 2000. 39.75 (978-1-57383-510-7(2), RG3002S) Regent College CAN.

Leadership for Jesus Christ, both among his people & in the world at large, requires us to possess a significant measure of the character of Christ & the power of Christ.

Leadership & Supervisory Skills for Women. Susan Carnahan. 6 cass. 4.95 addtl. wkbk. (125-C47) Natl Seminars.

Risk-taking. Assertiveness. Power. All are characteristics vital for success in today's business world. This program shows you how to refocus your energies, face your special challenges, gain visibility & recognition & go for the rewards you deserve.

Leadership & the New Science: Discovering Order in a Chaotic World, 2nd unabr. ed. Margaret J. Wheatley. Read by Margaret J. Wheatley. 4 cass. (Running Time: 6 hrs.). 1999. 24.95 (978-1-57453-340-8(1)) Audio Lit.

Updated & expanded, this program cuts to the heart of the real problems & real solutions of anyone wishing for more meaning, potential & creativity in his or her workplace & life.

Leadership & the One Minute Manager: Increasing Effectiveness Through Situational Leadership. Ken Blanchard et al. 2 cass. 27.95 (221A); Nightingale-Conant.

Helps you learn which leadership style suits each of your people & teaches you how to become a flexible & successful leader.

Leadership & the Sexes: Using Gender Science to Create Success in Business. unabr. ed. Barbara Michael & Annis Gurian. Read by Jonathan Marosz. (Running Time: 7 hrs. 30 mins.). (ENG.). 2008. 24.98 (978-1-59659-321-3(0), GildAudio) Pub: Gildan Media. Dist(s): HachBkGrp

Leadership & Vision. Ramon J. Aldag & Buck Joseph. Narrated by Jeff Woodman. 3 CDs. (Running Time: 3 hrs.). 2005. audio compact disk 19.95 (978-1-59316-043-2(7)) Listen & Live.

Leadership & Vision is part of The New York Times Pocket MBA Series, a reference series easily accessible to all businesspersons, from first-level managers to the executive suite. The 12-volume series is written by Ph.D.s who teach in the finest graduate business programs in the country, and edited by business editors from The New York Times. The structure of each volume presents an unparalleled synopsis of crucial principles of specific areas of business expertise.Learn the 25 keys to supervising and motivating management staff to realize your company vision, to ensure HR departments fulfill their crucial role in recruitment and employee retention and satisfaction.

Leadership & Vision: 25 Keys to Motivation. unabr. ed. Ramon J. Aldag & Buck Joseph. Read by Jeff Woodman. 2 cass. (Running Time: 3 hrs.). (New York Times Pocket MBA Ser.). 2000. pap. bk. 27.95 Listen & Live.

Learn the 25 keys to supervising & motivating management staff to realize your company vision, to ensure HR departments fulfill their crucial role in recruitment & employee retention & satisfaction.

Leadership & Vision: 25 Keys to Motivation. unabr. ed. Ramon J. Aldag & Buck Joseph. Read by Jeff Woodman. 2 cass. (Running Time: 2 hrs. 30 mins.). (New York Times Pocket MBA Ser.). 2000. 16.95 (978-1-885408-48-8(X), LL041) Listen & Live.

Leadership & Wise Choices. Eldon Taylor. Read by Eldon Taylor. Interview with XProgress Aware Staff. 1 cass. (Running Time: 62 min.). (Child Guidance Ser.). 16.95 incl. script. (978-1-55978-667-6(1), 3002) Progress Aware Res.

Story & soundtrack with underlying subliminal affirmations.

***Leadership Beyond Reason: How Great Leaders Succeed by Harnessing the Power of Their Values, Feelings, & Intuition.** unabr. ed. John Townsend. (Running Time: 7 hrs. 0 mins. 0 sec.). (ENG.). 2011. audio compact disk 25.99 (978-1-59859-874-2(0)) Oasis Audio.

Leadership by Design (for Dentists) Marsha Freeman. 2 cass. (Running Time: 90 min.). 1997. (978-0-910167-41-3(9)) Freemn Assoc.

Shows how the dentist leads the creation of an ideal office - by design.

Leadership by the Book: Tools to Transform Your Workplace. Ken Blanchard et al. 1999. 12.00 (978-1-57856-313-5(5)) Doubday Relig.

Leadership by the Book: Tools to Transform Your Workplace. abr. ed. Ken Blanchard et al. Read by Sam Freed. (ENG.). 2007. audio compact disk 15.00 (978-0-7393-4333-3(5), Random AudioBks) Pub: Random Audio Pubg. Dist(s): Random

Leadership Challenge: Skills for Taking Charge. Warren Bennis. 1 cass. (Running Time: 42 min.). 8.95 (978-0-88684-049-5(X)) Listen USA.

Leadership Challenge: The Most Trusted Source on Becoming a Better Leader. 4th unabr. rev. ed. James M. Kouzes. Read by James M. Kouzes. (Running Time: 12 hrs.). (ENG.). 2007. audio compact disk 29.98 (978-1-59659-122-6(6), GildAudio) Pub: Gildan Media. Dist(s): HachBkGrp

Leadership Code: Five Rules to Lead By. unabr. ed. Dave Ulrich et al. Read by Sean Pratt. (Running Time: 3 hrs. 30 mins.). (ENG.). 2009. 24.98 (978-1-59659-323-7(7), GildAudio) Pub: Gildan Media. Dist(s): HachBkGrp

Leadership Development. Bruce Goldberg. (ENG.). 2005. audio compact disk 17.00 (978-1-57968-102-9(6)) Pub: B Goldberg. Dist(s): Baker Taylor

Leadership Development. Bruce Goldberg. Read by Bruce Goldberg. 1 cass. (Running Time: 25 min.). (ENG.). 2006. 13.00 (978-1-885577-72-6(9)) Pub: B Goldberg. Dist(s): Baker Taylor

Through self-hypnosis learn how to acquire & maximize the ability to lead others in professional pursuits.

Leadership Development: Keys to Advancement. Rick Joyner. 2005. audio compact disk 24.99 (978-1-929371-63-1(2)) Pub: Morning NC. Dist(s): Destiny Image Pubs

Leadership During Adversity: How You Can Become a Proven Leader. Mac Hammond. 2009. audio compact disk 30.00 (978-1-57399-423-1(5)) Mac Hammond.

Leadership During Hard Times. Mac Hammond. 2009. audio compact disk 6.00 (978-1-57399-411-8(1)) Mac Hammond.

***Leadership Ellipse: Shaping How We Lead by Who We Are.** unabr. ed. Robert Fryling. Narrated by Arthur Morey. (ENG.). 2010. 12.98 (978-1-59644-883-4(0), Hovel Audio) christianaud.

***Leadership Ellipse: Shaping How We Lead by Who We Are.** unabr. ed. Robert A. Fryling & Robert Fryling. Narrated by Arthur Morey. (Running Time: 6 hrs. 30 mins. 0 sec.). (ENG.). 2010. audio compact disk 21.98 (978-1-59644-882-7(2), Hovel Audio) christianaud.

***Leadership Engine.** abr. ed. Noel M. Tichy. Read by Noel M. Tichy. (ENG.). 2006. (978-0-06-114198-0(4), Harper Audio); (978-0-06-114199-7(2), Harper Audio) HarperCollins Pubs.

Leadership Enrichment. 3 cass. (Running Time: 1 hr.). 1989. 10.00 (089) Key of David.

Contains 6 talks for leaders on enrichment in growth of the Holy Spirit.

Leadership for Literacy: The Agenda for the 1990s. Chisman, Forrest P., and Associates. (Higher Education Ser.). 1990. bk. 47.00 (978-1-55542-247-9(0), Jossey-Bass) Wiley US.

Leadership for Saints. Duncan & Pinegar. 5 cass. 2004. 19.95 (978-1-59156-063-0(2)); audio compact disk 19.95 (978-1-59156-064-7(0)) Covenant Comms.

Leadership from the Inside Out: Becoming a Leader for Life. 2nd unabr. ed. Kevin Cashman. Narrated by Alan Sklar. 7 CDs. (Running Time: 7 hrs.). 2009. audio compact disk 74.95 (978-0-7927-5778-8(5)) AudioGO.

Leadership from the Inside Out: Becoming a Leader for Life. 2nd unabr. ed. Kevin Cashman. Narrated by Alan Sklar. 6 CDs. (ENG.). 2008. audio compact disk 29.95 (978-1-60283-535-1(7)) Pub: AudioGO. Dist(s): Perseus Dist

***Leadership from the Inside Out: Examining the Inner Life of a Healthy Church Leader.** unabr. ed. Kevin G. Harney. (Running Time: 5 hrs. 43 mins. 0 sec.). (Leadership Network Innovation Ser.). (ENG.). 2009. 16.99 (978-0-310-77156-2(0)) Zondervan.

Leadership from the Inside Out: Seven Pathways to Mastery. abr. ed. Kevin Cashman. Read by Kevin Cashman. 2 cass. (Running Time: 3 hrs.). 1999. 14.95 (978-1-890009-30-4(X)) Exec Excell.

A reflective journey of leadership & self-awareness.

Leadership (from the Reference Person's Workshop) Harvey Jackins. 1 cass. 10.00 (978-1-893165-49-6(3)) Rational Isl.

A talk about leadership, to a meeting of Re-evaluation Counseling leaders.

Leadership Gold: Lessons I've Learned from a Lifetime of Leading. abr. ed. John C. Maxwell. (Running Time: 3 hrs. 30 mins.). 2008. audio compact disk 24.99 (978-0-7852-2357-3(6)) Nelson.

Leadership Implications & Contemporary Christianity. 4 cass. (Running Time: 6 hrs.). 2001. 15.00 (978-0-9717393-1-4(5)) OJU Min Assn.

Leadership in a Changing Environment. Somers H. White. 4 cass. (Running Time: 4 hrs.). 100.00 S White.

Leadership in Administration: A Sociological Interpretation. unabr. ed. Philip Selznick. Read by Tom Evens. 5 cass. (Running Time: 1 hr. per cass.). 1989. 50.00 (978-0-942563-01-6(8)); Rental 15.00 (978-0-942563-13-9(1)) CareerTapes.

This management classic focuses on the executive's role in shaping corporate values.

Leadership in Building. Rick Joyner. 1 cass. (Running Time: 90 mins.). (Foundation Ser.: Vol. 5). 2000. 5.00 (RJ05-005) Morning NC.

As an overview of God's plan for His church, this series contains essential truths for everyone who wants to see the church become all that she is called to be.

Leadership in Union-Management Relations. unabr. ed. Ross Stagner. 1 cass. (Running Time: 24 min.). 12.95 (13032) J Norton Pubs.

Leadership Is an Art. abr. ed. Max De Pree. Read by Joseph Campanella. 2 cass. (Running Time: 3 hrs.). 2000. 7.95 (978-0-57815-137-0(6), 1096, Media Bks Audio) Media Bks NJ.
The successful CEO of Herman Miller, Inc., explores how executives & managers can learn the leadership skills that build a better, more profitable organization.

Leadership Is an Art. unabr. ed. Max Depree. Read by Joseph Campanella. (YA). 2008. 34.99 (978-1-60514-841-0(5)) Find a World.

Leadership-Learning Connection: Cultivating, Recognizing, & Applying Organizational Wisdom. Douglas B. Reeves. 2003. video & audio compact disk 14.00 (978-0-9709455-3-2(1)) LeadplusLrn.
Rather than implement another new program or the latest jargon-laden initiative, educational leaders must identify the organizational wisdom that is immediate;y available to them.

Leadership-Learning Connection: Cultivating, Recognizing, & Applying Organizational Wisdom. Douglas B. Reeves. 2002. audio compact disk 15.00 (978-0-9709455-8-7(2)) LeadplusLrn.

Leadership Lessons of Jesus. unabr. ed. Bob Briner & Ray Pritchard. Narrated by Mark Warner. (ENG.). 2008. audio compact disk 22.99 (978-1-59859-398-3(6)) Oasis Audio.

Leadership Lessons of Jesus. unabr. ed. Bob Briner & Ray Pritchard. Narrated by Mark Warner. (ENG.). 2008. 16.09 (978-1-60814-278-1(7)) Oasis Audio.

Leadership Lessons of Jesus: A Timeless Model for Today's Leaders. unabr. ed. Bob Briner & Ray Pritchard. Read by Bob Briner. 2 cass. (Running Time: 2 hrs.). 1997. 15.99 (978-0-8054-2815-5(1)) BH Pubng Grp.
Explores the individual techniques that made Jesus' leadership so powerful, & looking at ways every leader can adapt them.

Leadership Lessons of the Navy Seals: Battle-Tested Strategies for Creating Successful Organizations & Inspiring Extraordinary Results. Joe Cannon. 3 CDs. (Running Time: 4 hrs. 30 min.). 2003. audio compact disk 28.00 (978-1-932378-00-9(6)) Pub: A Media Intl. Dist(s): Natl Bk Netwk
Leadership and teamwork techniques of the military elite, where partnering is mandatory, and failure is never an option.

Leadership Lessons of the Navy Seals: Battle-Tested Strategies for Creating Successful Organizations & Inspiring Extraordinary Results. Joe Cannon & Jeff Cannon. 3 Cass. (Running Time: 4 hrs. 30 min.). 2003. 24.00 (978-0-9724889-7-6(9)) Pub: A Media Intl. Dist(s): Natl Bk Netwk

Leadership Pill: The Missing Ingredient in Motivating People Today. unabr. ed. Ken Blanchard & Marc Muchnick. Read by Walter Bobbie. 2004. 7.95 (978-0-7435-4938-7(4)) Pub: S&S Audio. Dist(s): S and S Inc

Leadership Pill: The Missing Ingredient in Motivating People Today. unabr. ed. Ken Blanchard et al. Read by Walter Bobbie. 1 CD. (Running Time: 11 hrs. 50 mins. 0 sec.). (ENG.). 2003. audio compact disk 14.00 (978-0-7435-3039-2(X), Sound Ideas) Pub: S&S Audio. Dist(s): S and S Inc

Leadership Problems in Communication. unabr. ed. Franklin S. Haiman. 1 cass. (Running Time: 25 min.). 1954. 12.95 (13005) J Norton Pubs.
A discussion of the nature & importance of communications in industrial & business organizations.

Leadership Secrets. unabr. ed. Roger Burgraff. 8 cass. 99.50 incl. booklet. (SO3060) J Norton Pubs.

Leadership Secrets of Attila the Hun. unabr. ed. Wess Roberts. Read by Wess Roberts. Read by James Lurie. (Running Time: 3 hrs.). (ENG.). 2009. 14.98 (978-1-60024-894-8(2)); audio compact disk 19.98 (978-1-60024-893-1(4)) Pub: Hachet Audio. Dist(s): HachBkGrp

Leadership Secrets of Billy Graham. unabr. ed. Harold Myra & Marshall Shelley. Read by Larry Black. (Running Time: 37020 sec.). (ENG.). 2005. audio compact disk 29.99 (978-0-310-25579-6(1)) Zondervan.

Leadership Secrets of Billy Graham. unabr. ed. Harold Myra & Marshall Shelley. (Running Time: 10 hrs. 16 mins. 0 sec.). (ENG.). 2005. 19.49 (978-0-310-26134-6(1)) Zondervan.

Leadership Secrets of Colin Powell. abr. ed. Oren Harari. 3 cass. (Running Time: 4 hrs. 30 mins.). (McGraw Hill Audiobks.). 2003. 24.00 (978-0-9724462-0-4(6)); audio compact disk 28.00 (978-0-9724462-8-0(1)) Pub: A Media Intl. Dist(s): Natl Bk Netwk
Short, snappy, and packed with Powell's depth and spirit, it will help people inspire anyone including themselve to extraordinary performance.

Leadership Series. 2004. audio compact disk (978-1-931713-90-0(1)) Word For Today.

Leadership Series for Successful Living, Vol. 15. Richard Gorham & Orison Swett Marden. Narrated by Richard Gorham. (ENG.). 2006. audio compact disk 49.95 (978-0-9791934-5-3(1)) LshipTools.

Leadership Skills for Managers. 6 cass. pap. bk. & wbk. ed. 165.00 incl. 2 multiple choice tests. (978-0-7612-0795-5(3), 80174NQ1) AMACOM.
Focuses on the practical skills & techniques you need to make the transition from manager to leader. You'll learn how to tap your innate leadership potential so you can: Empower people; Get results; Prepare for the future.

Leadership Skills for Managers, Set. 6 cass. pap. bk. & wbk. ed. 30.00 (978-0-7612-0798-6(8), 80175NQ1) AMACOM.

Leadership, Success, Christianity, & the Future. 1 cass. (Running Time: 1 hr.). 2003. 6.95 (978-1-932631-66-1(6)); audio compact disk 6.95 (978-1-932631-67-8(4)) Ascensn Pr.

Leadership Summit, Vol. 5. unabr. ed. 2000. 60.95 (978-0-310-23546-0(4)) Zondervan.

Leadership Training Course. Frank Hamrick. 2002. 29.95 (978-1-59557-083-3(7)) Psitive Action.

Leadership Training Course on CD. Frank Hamrick. 12 cassettes. (Running Time: 18 hours). (ENG.). (YA). 2002. 29.95 (978-1-929784-89-9(9), ProTeens) Psitive Action.
Frank Hamrick shares the biblical philosophy of youth ministry that has impacted hundreds of churches and thousands of teenagers over the past 30 years.

Leadership Two- Step. 2006. pap. bk. 14.95 (978-0-9759477-5-3(3)) R Nadler.

Leadership: What Is It? 11 Timothy 2:1-26. Ed Young. 1987. 4.95 (978-0-7417-1589-0(9), 589) Win Walk.

Leadership, What Research Tells Us About. unabr. ed. C. R. Ingils. 1 cass. (Running Time: 24 min.). 12.95 (13037) J Norton Pubs.
This stresses the importance of two factors in leadership & administration: (1)Sensitivity to changing environments both internal & external (2) Flexibility in adapting behavior to new organizational requirements.

Leadership 101. Mark Crow. 6 cass. (Running Time: 9 hrs.). 2001. (978-1-931537-26-1(7)) Vision Comm Creat.

Leadership 101. unabr. ed. John Maxwell. (Running Time: 2 hrs. 18 mins. 0 sec.). (ENG.). 2009. audio compact disk 5.98 (978-1-59644-831-5(8), Hovel Audio) christianaud.

Leading a Local Church into Apostolic Ministry. Derek Prince. 1 cass. (Running Time: 60 min.). 5.95 (I-4178) Derek Prince.

Leading a Local Church into Intercession. Derek Prince. 1 cass. (Running Time: 60 min.). 5.95 (I-4177) Derek Prince.

Leading an Entrepreneurial Business: Valuable Insights on How to Create & Grow Successful Businesses. unabr. ed. Center for Entrepreneurial Leadership, Inc. Staff. Contrib. by Jeffry A. Timmons. 3 cass. (Running Time: 5 hrs.). 1997. 29.95 (978-1-891616-05-1(6)) Kauffman Ctr.
The keys to effective leadership presented by ten dynamic entrepreneurs in case studies & interviews.

Leading & Loving Audio Album. Instructed by Bruce Wilkinson. 1999. 19.95 (978-1-885447-97-5(3)) Walk Thru the Bible.
Where should a man go to learn how to lead his family? To his father and mother? To his friends? His TV? In six 26-minute sessions packed with insight, you'll learn why there's only one reliable source of wisdom about the husband's role: God's Word. When you discover how the husband's leadership abilities affect every other aspect of marriage and family, you'll be able to better impact your own marriage as you lead with love, confidence and success.

Leading at Mach 2. unabr. ed. Steve Sullivan. Read by Steve Sullivan. 4 cass. (Running Time: 3 hrs. 11 min.). 1995. 19.95 (978-1-890522-01-8(5)) Motivat Resources.
Redefines the nature of what is needed to lead others effectively & gives the listener the seven components for leadership success.

Leading Business Schools & Business Libraries: North America, Europe, & Asia. 6th rev. ed. BIA. (J). 2006. audio compact disk 289.00 (978-1-4187-5220-0(7)) Bus Info Agency.

Leading Business Schools & Business Libraries: North America, Europe, & Asia. 6th rev. ed. BIA. (J). 2006. audio compact disk 249.00 (978-1-4187-5219-4(3)) Bus Info Agency.

Leading Business Schools & Business Libraries of the USA. 6th rev. ed. BIA. (J). 2006. audio compact disk 289.00 (978-1-4187-5286-6(X)) Bus Info Agency.

Leading Business Schools & Business Libraries of the USA. 6th rev. ed. BIA. (J). 2006. audio compact disk 249.00 (978-1-4187-5285-9(1)) Bus Info Agency.

Leading Change: An Action Plan from the World's Foremost Expert on Business Leadership. unabr. ed. John Kotter. Read by Oliver Wyman. (Running Time: 5 hrs. 30 mins. 0 sec.). (ENG.). 2007. audio compact disk 29.95 (978-1-4272-0232-1(X)) Pub: Macmill Audio. Dist(s): Macmillan

***Leading Change! Leadership Skills to Master Rapid Change.** unabr. ed. Made for Success. Read by Mark; Ziglar, Zig, Sheila Murray; Sanborn Bethel. (Running Time: 8 hrs.). (Made for Success Ser.). 2010. audio compact disk 39.95 (978-1-4417-6763-9(0)) Blckstn Audio.

Leading Change in Difficult Times. Enlightened Leadership Solutions. Moderated by Ed Oakley & Carol Bergmann. (ENG.). 2009. DVD & cd-rom 1497.00 (978-0-9628255-3-8(0)) Enl Leadr Pub.

***Leading Change! (Library Edition) Leadership Skills to Master Rapid Change.** unabr. ed. Made for Success. Read by Mark; Ziglar Bethel. (Running Time: 8 hrs.). (Made for Success Ser.). 2010. audio compact disk 123.00 (978-1-4417-6762-2(2)) Blckstn Audio.

***Leading Character.** unabr. ed. Dan B., Dan B Allender, PLLC. (Running Time: 1 hr. 55 mins. 0 sec.). (Leadership Library). (ENG.). 2008. 14.99 (978-0-310-30251-3(X)) Zondervan.

Leading Chemical Manufacturers of the USA. 6th rev. ed. BIA. (J). 2006. audio compact disk 289.00 (978-1-4187-5204-0(5)) Bus Info Agency.

Leading Chemical Manufacturers of the USA. 6th rev. ed. BIA. (J). 2006. audio compact disk 249.00 (978-1-4187-5203-3(7)) Bus Info Agency.

Leading Children to God. unabr. ed. Gwen Costello. Read by Andrea Star. 2 cass. (Running Time: 1 hr. 23 min.). 1993. 16.95 (978-0-89622-800-9(2)) Twenty-Third.
Teaches prayer techniques for religion teachers to apply for their students in lower elementary grades.

Leading Clothing, Footwear, & Textile Manufacturers of the USA. 6th rev. ed. BIA. (J). 2006. audio compact disk 289.00 (978-1-4187-5212-5(6)) Bus Info Agency.

Leading Clothing, Footwear, & Textile Manufacturers of the USA. 6th rev. ed. BIA. (J). 2006. audio compact disk 249.00 (978-1-4187-5211-8(8)) Bus Info Agency.

Leading Companies in Kazan City, Russia. 6th rev. ed. BIA. (J). 2006. audio compact disk 99.00 (978-1-4187-4976-7(1)) Bus Info Agency.

Leading Companies in Kazan City, Russia. 6th rev. ed. BIA. (J). 2006. audio compact disk 219.00 (978-1-4187-4975-0(3)) Bus Info Agency.

Leading Companies in Krasnodar City, Russia. 6th rev. ed. BIA. (J). 2006. audio compact disk 99.00 (978-1-4187-4979-8(6)) Bus Info Agency.

Leading Companies in Krasnodar City, Russia. 6th rev. ed. BIA. (J). 2006. audio compact disk 219.00 (978-1-4187-4978-1(8)) Bus Info Agency.

Leading Companies in Nizhniy Novgorod City, Russia. 6th rev. ed. BIA. (J). 2006. audio compact disk 289.00 (978-1-4187-4982-8(6)) Bus Info Agency.

Leading Companies in Nizhniy Novgorod City, Russia. 6th rev. ed. BIA. (J). 2006. audio compact disk 249.00 (978-1-4187-4981-1(8)) Bus Info Agency.

Leading Companies in Novosibirsk City, Russia. 6th rev. ed. BIA. (J). 2006. audio compact disk 289.00 (978-1-4187-4985-9(0)) Bus Info Agency.

Leading Companies in Novosibirsk City, Russia. 6th rev. ed. BIA. (J). 2006. audio compact disk 249.00 (978-1-4187-4984-2(2)) Bus Info Agency.

Leading Companies in Rostov City, Russia. 6th rev. ed. BIA. (J). 2006. audio compact disk 99.00 (978-1-4187-4988-0(5)) Bus Info Agency.

Leading Companies in Rostov City, Russia. 6th rev. ed. BIA. (J). 2006. audio compact disk 219.00 (978-1-4187-4987-3(7)) Bus Info Agency.

Leading Companies in St. Petersburg, Russia. 6th rev. ed. BIA. (J). 2006. audio compact disk 289.00 (978-1-4187-4991-0(5)) Bus Info Agency.

Leading Companies in St. Petersburg, Russia. 6th rev. ed. BIA. (J). 2006. audio compact disk 249.00 (978-1-4187-4990-3(7)) Bus Info Agency.

Leading Companies in Volgograd City, Russia. 6th rev. ed. BIA. (J). 2006. audio compact disk 99.00 (978-1-4187-4994-1(X)) Bus Info Agency.

Leading Companies in Volgograd City, Russia. 6th rev. ed. BIA. (J). 2006. audio compact disk 219.00 (978-1-4187-4993-4(1)) Bus Info Agency.

Leading Companies of the Chelyabinsk Region of Russia. 6th rev. ed. BIA. (J). 2006. audio compact disk 289.00 (978-1-4187-5055-8(7)) Bus Info Agency.

Leading Companies of the Chelyabinsk Region of Russia. 6th rev. ed. BIA. (J). 2006. audio compact disk 249.00 (978-1-4187-5054-1(9)) Bus Info Agency.

Leading Companies of the Krasnodar Region of Russia. 6th rev. ed. BIA. (J). 2006. audio compact disk 289.00 (978-1-4187-5065-7(4)) Bus Info Agency.

Leading Companies of the Krasnodar Region of Russia. 6th rev. ed. BIA. (J). 2006. audio compact disk 249.00 (978-1-4187-5064-0(6)) Bus Info Agency.

Leading Companies of the Krasnoyarsk Region of Russia. 6th rev. ed. BIA. (J). 2006. audio compact disk 289.00 (978-1-4187-5057-2(3)) Bus Info Agency.

Leading Companies of the Krasnoyarsk Region of Russia. 6th rev. ed. BIA. (J). 2006. audio compact disk 249.00 (978-1-4187-5056-5(5)) Bus Info Agency.

Leading Companies of the Moscow Region of Russia. 6th rev. ed. BIA. (J). 2006. audio compact disk 289.00 (978-1-4187-5069-5(7)) Bus Info Agency.

Leading Companies of the Moscow Region of Russia. 6th rev. ed. BIA. (J). 2006. audio compact disk 249.00 (978-1-4187-5068-8(9)) Bus Info Agency.

Leading Companies of the Novosibirsk Region of Russia. 6th rev. ed. BIA. (J). 2006. audio compact disk 249.00 (978-1-4187-5053-4(0)) Bus Info Agency.

Leading Companies of the Novosibirsk Region of Russia. 6th rev. ed. BIA. (J). 2006. audio compact disk 249.00 (978-1-4187-5052-7(2)) Bus Info Agency.

Leading Companies of the Omsk Region of Russia. 6th rev. ed. BIA. (J). 2006. audio compact disk 289.00 (978-1-4187-5059-6(X)) Bus Info Agency.

Leading Companies of the Omsk Region of Russia. 6th rev. ed. BIA. (J). 2006. audio compact disk 249.00 (978-1-4187-5058-9(1)) Bus Info Agency.

Leading Companies of the Sverdlovsk Region of Russia. 6th rev. ed. BIA. (J). 2006. audio compact disk 289.00 (978-1-4187-5061-9(1)) Bus Info Agency.

Leading Companies of the Sverdlovsk Region of Russia. 6th rev. ed. BIA. (J). 2006. audio compact disk 249.00 (978-1-4187-5060-2(3)) Bus Info Agency.

Leading Companies of the Tatarstan Region of Russia. 6th rev. ed. BIA. (J). 2006. audio compact disk 289.00 (978-1-4187-5067-1(0)) Bus Info Agency.

Leading Companies of the Tatarstan Region of Russia. 6th rev. ed. BIA. (J). 2006. audio compact disk 249.00 (978-1-4187-5066-4(2)) Bus Info Agency.

Leading Companies of the Tyumen Region of Russia. 6th rev. ed. BIA. (J). 2006. audio compact disk 289.00 (978-1-4187-5063-3(8)) Bus Info Agency.

Leading Companies of the Tyumen Region of Russia. 6th rev. ed. BIA. (J). 2006. audio compact disk 249.00 (978-1-4187-5062-6(X)) Bus Info Agency.

Leading Companies of the Voronezh Region of Russia. 6th rev. ed. BIA. (J). 2006. audio compact disk 289.00 (978-1-4187-5071-8(9)) Bus Info Agency.

Leading Companies of the Voronezh Region of Russia. 6th rev. ed. BIA. (J). 2006. audio compact disk 249.00 (978-1-4187-5070-1(0)) Bus Info Agency.

Leading Electronics & Electrical Equipment Manufacturers of the USA. 6th rev. ed. BIA. (J). 2006. audio compact disk 259.00 (978-1-4187-5206-4(1)) Bus Info Agency.

Leading Electronics & Electrical Equipment Manufacturers of the USA. 6th rev. ed. BIA. (J). 2006. audio compact disk 259.00 (978-1-4187-5205-7(3)) Bus Info Agency.

Leading Food Manufacturers of the USA. 6th rev. ed. BIA. (J). 2006. audio compact disk 259.00 (978-1-4187-5208-8(8)) Bus Info Agency.

Leading Food Manufacturers of the USA. 6th rev. ed. BIA. (J). 2006. audio compact disk 249.00 (978-1-4187-5207-1(X)) Bus Info Agency.

Leading for an Effective Implementation (Tape 2) Gwendolyn D. Galsworth. 1999. 15.00 (978-1-932516-17-3(4)) Quality Method.

Leading for Diversity Video: Promoting Positive Interethnic Relations. Rosemary Henze. 2003. 99.95 (978-1-4129-0517-6(6)) Pub: Corwin Pr. Dist(s): SAGE

Leading for Superior Results. Michael LeBoeuf. 1 cass. (Running Time: 40 min.). 8.95 (978-0-88684-080-8(5)) Listen USA.

Leading from the Front: No Excuse Leadership Tactics for Women. abr. ed. Courtney Lynch & Angie Morgan. Frwd. by Paula Zahn. 2008. audio compact disk 28.00 (978-1-933309-40-8(7)) Pub: A Media Intl. Dist(s): Natl Bk Netwk

Leading Furniture & Fixture Manufacturers of the USA. 6th rev. ed. BIA. (J). 2006. audio compact disk 289.00 (978-1-4187-5200-2(2)) Bus Info Agency.

Leading Furniture & Fixture Manufacturers of the USA. 6th rev. ed. BIA. (J). 2006. audio compact disk 249.00 (978-1-4187-5199-9(5)) Bus Info Agency.

Leading Industrial Machinery & Computer Equipment Manufacturers of the USA. 6th rev. ed. BIA. (J). 2006. audio compact disk 289.00 (978-1-4187-5202-6(9)) Bus Info Agency.

Leading Industrial Machinery & Computer Equipment Manufacturers of the USA. 6th rev. ed. BIA. (J). 2006. audio compact disk 249.00 (978-1-4187-5201-9(0)) Bus Info Agency.

***Leading Kids to Jesus: How to Have One-on-One Conversations about Faith.** David Staal. (Running Time: 4 hrs. 33 mins. 0 sec.). (ENG.). 2009. 14.99 (978-0-310-30473-9(3)) Zondervan.

***Leading Ladies.** abr. ed. Kay Bailey Hutchison. Read by Kay Bailey Hutchison. (ENG.). 2007. (978-0-06-123038-7(3), Harper Audio); (978-0-06-123037-0(5), Harper Audio) HarperCollins Pubs.

Leading Ladies: American Trailblazers. abr. ed. Kay Bailey Hutchison. Read by Kay Bailey Hutchison. 2007. audio compact disk 29.95 (978-0-06-114269-7(7)) HarperCollins Pubs.

Leading Ladies: Radio's Legendary Actresses. Created by Radio Spirits. (Running Time: 10800 sec.). 2004. 9.98 (978-1-57019-742-0(3)); audio compact disk 19.98 (978-1-57019-741-3(5), OTR 30192) Pub: Radio Spirits. Dist(s): AudioGO

Leading Optics, Watches, & Medical Equipment Manufacturers of the USA. 6th rev. ed. BIA. (J). 2006. audio compact disk 289.00 (978-1-4187-5210-1(X)) Bus Info Agency.

Leading Optics, Watches, & Medical Equipment Manufacturers of the USA. 6th rev. ed. BIA. (J). 2006. audio compact disk 249.00 (978-1-4187-5209-5(6)) Bus Info Agency.

Leading the Charge: Leadership Lessons from the Battlefield to the Boardroom. unabr. ed. Tony Zinni & Tony Koltz. Narrated by George K. Wilson. (Running Time: 9 hrs. 30 mins. 0 sec.). (ENG.). 2009. 24.99 (978-1-4001-6405-9(2)); audio compact disk 34.99 (978-1-4001-1405-4(5)); audio compact disk 69.99 (978-1-4001-4405-1(1)) Pub: Tantor Media. Dist(s): IngramPubServ

***Leading the Charge: Leadership Lessons from the Battlefield to the Boardroom.** unabr. ed. Tony Zinni & Tony Koltz. Narrated by George K. Wilson. (Running Time: 9 hrs. 30 mins.). 2009. 16.99 (978-1-4001-8405-7(3)) Tantor Media.

Leading the New Smith-Kline Beecham into New Decade: Computer-Assisted New Drug Applications. 1 cass. 1990. 8.50 Recorded Res.

Leading the Revolution. abr. ed. Gary Hamel. Read by Gary Hamel. 2 CDs. (Running Time: 2 hrs. 30 mins.). (ENG.). 2000. audio compact disk 24.95 (978-1-56511-414-2(0), 1565114140) Pub: HighBridge. Dist(s): Workman Pub
According to Gary Hamel, the professor-turned-strategy-guru , complacent establishment giants & one-strategy start-ups are on the same side of the fence, the wrong side. Corporate complacency & single-strategy business plans leave no room for what Hamel describes as the key to thriving in today's world of business: a deeply embedded capability for continual, radical innovation.

Leading the Team. Jim Pancero. Read by Jim Pancero. 6 cass. (Running Time: 6 hrs.). 1993. 79.95 incl. action guide. (2024) Dartnell Corp.
A breakthrough approach to eliminating sales management mistakes. A chance to "cut the fat" from your daily workload & concentrate on becoming a more effective leader.

Leading Transportation Equipment Manufacturers of the USA. 6th rev. ed. BIA. (J). 2006. audio compact disk 289.00 (978-1-4187-5214-9(2)) Bus Info Agency.

Leading Transportation Equipment Manufacturers of the USA. 6th rev. ed. BIA. (J). 2006. audio compact disk 249.00 (978-1-4187-5213-2(4)) Bus Info Agency.

Leading Travel Agencies in Russia. 6th rev. ed. BIA. (J). 2006. audio compact disk 289.00 (978-1-4187-5047-3(6)) Bus Info Agency.

Leading Travel Agencies in Russia. 6th rev. ed. BIA. (J). 2006. audio compact disk 249.00 (978-1-4187-5046-6(8)) Bus Info Agency.

Leading under Pressure: Strategies to Maximize Peak Performance & Productivity while Maximizing Health & Wellbeing. Gabriela Cora.Tr. of Lideres bajo Presion. (ENG.). 2007. 47.00 (978-1-933437-07-1(3)); bk. 127.00 (978-1-933437-08-8(1)); audio compact disk 47.00 (978-1-933437-06-4(5)) Exe H & W Inc.

Leading under Pressure: Strategies to Maximize Peak Performance, Productivity & Wellbeing. Gabriela Cora-Locatelli.Tr. of Lideres bajo Presion. 2005. 27.00 (978-1-933437-04-0(9)) Exe H & W Inc.
Audio download from live presentation on Leading under Pressure.

Leading Universities, Business Schools, & Business Libraries of Russia. 6th rev. ed. BIA. (J). 2006. audio compact disk 289.00 (978-1-4187-5238-5(X)) Bus Info Agency.

Leading Universities, Business Schools, & Business Libraries of Russia. 6th rev. ed. BIA. (J). 2006. audio compact disk 249.00 (978-1-4187-5237-8(1)) Bus Info Agency.

Leading Wholesalers of Durable Goods of the USA. 6th rev. ed. BIA. (J). 2006. audio compact disk 289.00 (978-1-4187-5216-3(9)) Bus Info Agency.

Leading Wholesalers of Durable Goods of the USA. 6th rev. ed. BIA. (J). 2006. audio compact disk 249.00 (978-1-4187-5215-6(0)) Bus Info Agency.

Leading Wholesalers of Non-Durable Goods of the USA. 6th rev. ed. BIA. (J). 2006. audio compact disk 289.00 (978-1-4187-5218-7(5)) Bus Info Agency.

Leading Wholesalers of Non-Durable Goods of the USA. 6th rev. ed. BIA. (J). 2006. audio compact disk 249.00 (978-1-4187-5217-0(7)) Bus Info Agency.

Leading with a Limp: Take Full Advantage of Your Most Powerful Weakness. abr. ed. Dan B. Allender. Read by Dan B. Allender. (Running Time: 21600 sec.). (ENG.). 2006. audio compact disk 25.99 (978-1-59859-143-9(6)) Oasis Audio.

Leading with a Limp: Take Full Advantage of Your Most Powerful Weakness. abr. ed. Ph.D., Dan B Allender. Narrated by Ph.D., Dan B Allender. (ENG.). 2006. 18.19 (978-1-60814-279-8(5)) Oasis Audio.

Leading with Heart. Marianne Williamson. Read by Marianne Williamson. 1 cass. (Running Time: 90 mins.). (Lectures on a Course in Miracles). 1999. 10.00 (978-1-56170-476-7(8), M846) Hay House.

Leading with Kindness: How Good People Consistently Get Superior Results. unabr. ed. William F. Baker & Michael O'Malley. Read by Jim Bond. (Running Time: 7 hrs.). 2008. 39.25 (978-1-4233-6468-9(6), 9781423364689, BADLE); 24.95 (978-1-4233-6465-8(1), 9781423364658, Brilliance MP3); 39.25 (978-1-4233-6466-5(X), 9781423364665, Brinc Audio MP3 Lib); 24.95 (978-1-4233-6467-2(8), 9781423364672, BAD); audio compact disk 29.95 (978-1-4233-6463-4(5), 9781423364634, Bril Audio CD Unabri); audio compact disk 82.25 (978-1-4233-6464-1(3), 9781423364641, BriAudCD Unabrid) Brilliance Audio.

Leading with Laughter, Vols. 1-6. unabr. ed. Malcolm Kushner. 6 cass. (Running Time: 5 hrs. 30 min.). 2001. 49.95 (978-0-9704598-0-0(7)) M K Assoc.

Leading with Laughter: How U. S. Presidents Use Humor to Relate, Motivate & Communicate. Speeches. Created by Malcolm Kushner. 6CDs. (Running Time: 5hrs, 30 mins). 2004. 59.95 (978-0-9704598-7-9(4)) M K Assoc.
Humorous excerpts of speeches by Presidents Kennedy, Johnson, Ford, Carter, Reagan and Bush.Narration by Malcolm Kushner, America's Favorite Humor Consultant.

Leading with Laughter Vol. 1: President George Bush. Malcolm Kushner. Perf. by George W. Bush. 1 cass. (Running Time: 53 mins.). 2000. 9.95 (978-0-9704598-1-7(5)) M K Assoc.

Leading with My Chin. abr. ed. Jay Leno. Read by Jay Leno. 2 cass., 3 CDs. 1996. audio compact disk 25.00 (978-0-694-51770-1(4)) HarperCollins Pubs.
Against the odds Jay Leno has emerged as the undisputed king of late night television as host of the # 1 -rated The Tonight Show. His twenty-year stand-up career; working alongside the likes of Jerry Seinfeld, Gary Shandling, and David Letterman, was a long, hard, and laugh-filled battle to the top. In this entertaining, anecdote-filled book, Leno delivers the monologue of his life, leaving readers admiring his unstoppable wit and tenacity.

Leading with NLP: Neuro Linguistic Programming: Essential Leadership Skills for Influencing & Managing People. Joseph O'Connor. 1 cass. 1998. (978-0-7225-9912-9(9), HarperThor) HarpC GBR.

Leading with the Heart: Coach K's Successful Strategies for Basketball, Business, & Life. Mike Krzyzewski & Donald T. Phillips. Narrated by Richard M. Davidson. 7 CDs. (Running Time: 7 hrs. 45 mins.). audio compact disk 71.00 (978-0-7887-9862-7(6)) Recorded Bks.

Leading with the Heart: Coach K's Successful Strategies for Basketball, Business & Life. abr. ed. Mike Krzyzewski & Donald T. Phillips. 2 cass. (Running Time: 3 hrs.). 2001. (978-1-58621-015-1(7)) Hachet Audio.
Reveals personal principles for leadership, from dealing with adversity in life or on the basketball court, to taking responsibility for your actions, to learning how to trust your heartfelt instincts in times of trouble. The result is a book that shows how you can be successful in any leadership challenges you face.

Leading with the Heart: Coach K's Successful Strategies for Basketball Business, & Life. abr. ed. Mike Krzyzewski & Donald T. Phillips. (ENG.). 2005. 14.98 (978-1-59483-473-8(3)) Pub: Hachet Audio. Dist(s): HachBkGrp

Leading with the Heart: Coach K's Successful Strategies for Basketball, Business, & Life. unabr. ed. Mike Krzyzewski & Donald T. Phillips. Narrated by Richard M. Davidson. 6 cass. (Running Time: 7 hrs. 45 mins.). 2001. 58.00 (978-0-7887-4861-5(0), 96412E7) Recorded Bks.
Explaining the techniques that have made his program so successful & offers advice on using those same strategies to excel in both your business & personal lives.

Leading Wood & Lumber Manufacturers of the USA. 6th rev. ed. BIA. (J). 2006. audio compact disk 289.00 (978-1-4187-5198-2(7)) Bus Info Agency.

Leading Wood & Lumber Manufacturers of the USA. 6th rev. ed. BIA. (J). 2006. audio compact disk 249.00 (978-1-4187-5197-5(9)) Bus Info Agency.

***Leading Your Child to Jesus: How Parents Can Talk with Their Kids about Faith.** Zondervan. (Running Time: 3 hrs. 2 mins. 23 sec.). (ENG.). 2010. 9.99 (978-0-310-86915-3(3)) Zondervan.

Leading Your Children from Wayward to Wise. Charles R. Swindoll. (ENG.). 2007. audio compact disk 24.00 (978-1-57972-781-9(6)) Insight Living.

Leadville. Hank Mitchum. Read by Charlie O'Dowd. 4 vols. No. 20. 2004. 25.00 (978-1-58807-203-0(7)); (978-1-58807-963-3(5)) Am Pubng Inc.

Leadville. Scripts. Hank Mitchum. 5 CDs. (Running Time: 6 hrs.). (Stagecoach Ser.: No. 20). 2005. 14.99 (978-1-58807-772-1(1)) Am Pubng Inc.
Leadville is a minging town ready to explode. Strikers and strike breakers are facing off. Framed for robbery and murder, Griff Connors, has tracked the real killers to Leadville. Caught between the miners and the owners' thugs, Griff must stand and fight.

Leaf see Robert Penn Warren Reads Selected Poems

League of Frightened Men. Rex Stout. Read by Michael Prichard. (Running Time: 9 hrs.). (Nero Wolfe Ser.). 2005. 27.95 (978-1-59912-385-1(1)) Iofy Corp.

League of Frightened Men. unabr. ed. Rex Stout. Read by Michael Prichard. 6 cass. (Running Time: 9 hrs. 15 mins.). (Nero Wolfe Ser.). 2004. 29.95 (978-1-57270-037-6(8), N61037u) Pub: Audio Partners. Dist(s): PerseuPGW
A group of Harvard alumni asks for Wolfe's help when one of their former classmates appears likely to murder them all. Will Nero & Archie outwit him before he becomes a killer?.

League of Frightened Men. unabr. ed. Rex Stout. Narrated by Michael Prichard. 8 CDs. (Running Time: 9 hrs. 15 mins.). (Nero Wolfe Ser.). (ENG.). 2004. audio compact disk 34.95 (978-1-57270-404-6(7)) Pub: AudioGO. Dist(s): Perseus Dist

League of Frightened Men. unabr. collector's ed. Rex Stout. Read by Michael Prichard. 7 cass. (Running Time: 10 hrs. 30 min.). (Nero Wolfe Ser.). 1994. 56.00 (978-0-7366-2631-6(X), 3370) Books on Tape.
Paul Chapin's college cronies never forgave themselves for the prank that crippled their friend. Yet with Harvard days behind them, they thought they were forgiven - until a class reunion ends in a fatal fall. This league of frightened men seeks Nero Wolfe's help. But are Wolfe's brilliance & Archie's tenacity enough to outwit a most cunning killer?.

League of Night & Fog. unabr. ed. David Morrell. Read by George Ralph. (Running Time: 11 hrs.). 2006. 39.25 (978-1-59737-766-9(X), 9781597377669, BADLE); 24.95 (978-1-59737-765-2(1), 9781597377652, BAD); audio compact disk 102.25 (978-1-59737-762-1(7), 9781597377621, BriAudCD Unabrid); audio compact disk 39.25 (978-1-59737-764-5(3), 9781597377645, Brinc Audio MP3 Lib); audio compact disk 24.95 (978-1-59737-763-8(5), 9781597377638, Brilliance MP3); audio compact disk 29.95 (978-1-59737-761-4(9), 9781597377614) Brilliance Audio.
David Morrell's international thrillers have no equal. Among his classic novels, this story stands as one of his most exciting and brilliant works - a globe-spanning tale that brings together two generations of men and women bound by one murderous legacy. From the Vatican to the Swiss Alps, from Australia to the heartland of America, the two masterful operatives known as Saul and Drew are being drawn together to solve a violent riddle: Why have ten old men been abducted from around the world? When the agents, weary of their own covert wars, begin to investigate, they are pulled into a terrifying cycle of revenge that began in the heart of World War II - and is now forcing sons to pay for their fathers' darkest sins.

Leah Chase: Listen, I Say Like This. Carol Allen. Narrated by Leah Chase. (Running Time: 447 hrs. NaN mins.). (ENG.). 2009. 29.95 (978-1-58980-775-4(8)) Pelican.

Leah Chase: Listen, I Say Like This CD. Carol Allen. Narrated by Leah Chase. (Running Time: 447 hrs. NaN mins.). (ENG.). 2009. audio compact disk 29.95 (978-1-58980-761-7(8)) Pelican.

***Leah's Choice.** Marta Perry. Contrib. by Tanya Eby. (Pleasant Valley Ser.: Bk. 1). 2009. 59.99 (978-1-4418-2732-6(3)) Find a World.

Leah's Choice. abr. ed. Marta Perry. Read by Tanya Eby. (Running Time: 3 hrs.). (Pleasant Valley Ser.: Bk. 1). 2009. audio compact disk 19.99 (978-1-4418-0860-8(4), 9781441808608, BACD) Brilliance Audio.

Leah's Choice. abr. ed. Marta Perry. Read by Tanya Eby. (Running Time: 4 hrs.). (Pleasant Valley Ser.: Bk. 1). 2010. audio compact disk 9.99 (978-1-4418-0861-5(2), 9781441808615, BCD Value Price) Brilliance Audio.

Leah's Choice. unabr. ed. Marta Perry. Read by Tanya Eby. (Running Time: 8 hrs.). (Pleasant Valley Ser.: Bk. 1). 2009. 24.99 (978-1-4418-0856-1(6), 9781441808561, Brilliance MP3); 24.99 (978-1-4418-0858-5(2), 9781441808585, BAD); 39.97 (978-1-4418-0857-8(4), 9781441808578, Brinc Audio MP3 Lib); 39.97 (978-1-4418-0859-2(0), 9781441808592, BADLE); audio compact disk 29.99 (978-1-4418-0854-7(X), 9781441808547, Bril Audio CD Unabri); audio compact disk 79.97 (978-1-4418-0855-4(8), 9781441808554, BriAudCD Unabrid) Brilliance Audio.

Leamos un Cuento. Elda Friedman et al. 2 cass. (J). 45.00 (Natl Textbk Co) M-H Contemporary.
14 original stories about topics that interest children & are told from their perspective.

Lean Back. Perf. by Lori Wilke. 1 cass. (Running Time: 4 min.). 1998. 9.98 Sound track. (978-1-891916-39-7(4)) Spirit To Spirit.

***Lean Body Promise.** abr. ed. Lee Labrada. Read by Lee Labrada. (ENG.). 2005. (978-0-06-085308-2(5), Harper Audio); (978-0-06-085307-5(7), Harper Audio) HarperCollins Pubs.

Lean Mean Thirteen. abr. ed. Janet Evanovich. Read by Lorelei King. (Running Time: 4 hrs. 0 mins. 0 sec.). (Stephanie Plum Ser.: No. 13). (ENG.). 2007. audio compact disk 19.95 (978-1-4272-0120-1(X)) Pub: Macmill Audio. Dist(s): Macmillan

Lean Mean Thirteen. unabr. ed. Janet Evanovich. Read by Lorelei King. 5 cass. (Running Time: 7 hrs. 30 mins.). (Stephanie Plum Ser.: No. 13). 2007. 54.95 (978-0-7927-4927-1(8)) AudioGO.

Lean Mean Thirteen. unabr. ed. Janet Evanovich. Read by Stephanie King. 7 CDs. (Running Time: 7 hrs. 30 mins.). (Stephanie Plum Ser.: No. 13). 2007. audio compact disk 74.95 (978-0-7927-4867-0(0)) AudioGO.

Lean Mean Thirteen. unabr. ed. Janet Evanovich. Read by Lorelei King. 7 CDs. (Running Time: 7 hrs. 30 mins. 0 sec.). (Stephanie Plum Ser.: No. 13). (ENG.). 2007. audio compact disk 34.95 (978-1-4272-0118-8(8)) Pub: Macmill Audio. Dist(s): Macmillan

Lean Mean Thirteen. unabr. ed. Janet Evanovich & Stephanie King. 1 MP3-CD. (Running Time: 7 hrs. 30 mns.). (Stephanie Plum Ser.: No. 13). 2007. 44.95 (978-0-7927-4905-9(7)) AudioGO.

Lean Six Sigma for Service: How to Use Lean Speed & Six Sigma Quality to Improve Services & Transcations. Michael L. George. 2009. audio compact disk 28.00 (978-1-933309-67-5(9)) Pub: A Media Intl. Dist(s): Natl Bk Netwk

Lean Solutions: How Companies & Customers Can Create Value & Wealth Together. abr. ed. Daniel T. Jones & James P. Womack. Read by James P. Womack. 5 CDs. (Running Time: 4 hrs. 30 mins. 0 sec.). (ENG.). 2005. audio compact disk 29.95 (978-0-7435-5011-6(0), Sound Ideas) Pub: S&S Audio. Dist(s): S and S Inc

Lean Solutions: How Companies & Customers Can Create Value & Wealth Together. abr. ed. James P. Womack & Daniel T. Jones. Read by James P. Womack. 2005. 17.95 (978-0-7435-5220-2(2)) Pub: S&S Audio. Dist(s): S and S Inc

Lean Thinking: Banish Waste & Create Wealth in Your Corporation. 2nd abr. ed. James P. Womack & Daniel T. Jones. Read by James P. Womack & Daniel T. Jones. 4 CDs. (Running Time: 43 hrs. 0 mins. 0 sec.). (ENG.). 2003. audio compact disk 30.00 (978-0-7435-3048-4(9), Audioworks) Pub: S&S Audio. Dist(s): S and S Inc

Lean Thinking: Banish Waste & Create Wealth in Your Corporation, 2nd Ed. abr. ed. James P. Womack & Daniel T. Jones. 2004. 15.95 (978-0-7435-4940-0(6)) Pub: S&S Audio. Dist(s): S and S Inc

Leanin' Dog. unabr. ed. K. A. Nuzum. Narrated by Liz Morton. (Running Time: 5 hrs. 30 mins.). (J). (gr. 4-7). 2008. 56.75; 41.75 (978-1-4281-0443-3(7)); audio compact disk 51.75 (978-1-4281-0448-8(8)) Recorded Bks.

Leanin' Dog. unabr. collector's ed. K. A. Nuzum. Narrated by Liz Morton. 5 CDs. (Running Time: 5 hrs. 30 mins.). (J). (gr. 4-7). 2008. audio compact disk 39.95 Recorded Bks.

Leaning into the Wind: Act 5:12-42. Ed Young. 1997. 4.95 (978-0-7417-2156-3(2), A1156) Win Walk.

Leap. unabr. ed. Jane Breskin Zalben. Read by Jonathan Ross & Jennifer Ikeda. 8 cass. (Running Time: 9 hrs.). (YA). (gr. 5-8). 2007. 61.75 (978-1-4281-7196-1(7)); audio compact disk 87.75 (978-1-4281-7201-2(7)) Recorded Bks.

Leap! What Will We Do with the Rest of Our Lives? unabr. ed. Sara Davidson. Narrated by Renée Raudman. (Running Time: 10 hrs. 30 mins. 0 sec.). 2007. audio compact disk 24.99 (978-1-4001-5419-7(7)) Pub: Tantor Media. Dist(s): IngramPubServ

Leap! What Will We Do with the Rest of Our Lives? unabr. ed. Sara Davidson. Read by Renée Raudman. (Running Time: 10 hrs. 30 mins. 0 sec.). (ENG.). 2007. audio compact disk 34.99 (978-1-4001-0419-2(X)); audio compact disk 69.99 (978-1-4001-3419-9(6)) Pub: Tantor Media. Dist(s): IngramPubServ

Leap Before You Look: Shortcuts for Getting Out of Your Mind & into the Moment. unabr. abr. ed. Arjuna Ardagh. 2 CDs. (Running Time: 9000 sec.). 2008. audio compact disk 19.95 (978-1-59179-635-0(0), AW01204D) Sounds True.

Leap Day. 5 cass. (Running Time: 7 hrs). (YA). (gr. 8 up). 2005. 37.75 (978-1-4193-0431-6(3)) Recorded Bks.

Leap of Faith. Patricia Shih. 1 cass. (Running Time: 48 min.). 1988. 9.00 (FF90485) Shih Ents.
Original songs of love, struggle & humor, written by award-winning singer-songwriter. Described as folk fusion or adult acoustic style.

Leap of Faith. unabr. ed. Danielle Steel. 2001. 32.00 (978-0-7366-7045-6(9)) Books on Tape.
Marie-Ange returns to the beloved French chateau of her childhood only to find that life isn't as magical as she thought it would be.

Leap of Faith: Memoirs of an Unexpected Life. abr. ed. Queen Noor. Read by Queen Noor. 4 cass. (Running Time: 6 hrs.). 2002. 25.98 (978-1-4013-9666-4(6)) Hyperion.
A memoir of Queen Noor, covering her childhood in America and education at Princeton, to her years as queen of Jordan and Wife of the late King Hussein.

Leap of Faith: Memoirs of an Unexpected Life. unabr. ed. Queen Noor. Read by Queen Noor. Read by Suzanne Toren. 11 cass. (Running Time: 16 hrs. 6 min.). 2003. 39.95 (978-1-57270-351-3(2)) Pub: Audio Partners. Dist(s): PerseuPGW

***Leap of Faith: Unabridged Value-Priced Edition.** Queen Noor. Narrated by Suzanne Toren. (Running Time: 16 hrs. 6 mins. 0 sec.). (ENG.). 2010. audio compact disk 14.95 (978-1-60998-003-0(4)) Pub: AudioGO. Dist(s): Perseus Dist

Leap of Faith/Atonement of a Nation. Marianne Williamson. Read by Marianne Williamson. 1 cass. (Running Time: 90 mins.). (Lectures on a Course in Miracles). (ENG.). 1999. 10.00 (978-1-56170-662-4(0), M870) Hay House.

Leap of Grace: The Hanuman Chalisa. Perf. by David Newman. Composed by David Newman. 2005. audio compact disk 16.95 (978-0-9763836-6-6(7)) Pranamaya.

Leaphorn & Chee Novels: Includes Skinwalkers - A Thief of Time; Coyote Waits. abr. ed. Tony Hillerman. Read by Tony Hillerman. 2005. audio compact disk 29.95 (978-0-06-079281-7(7)) HarperCollins Pubs.

Leaping Beauty. unabr. ed. Gregory Maguire. Read by Gregory Maguire. (J). 2008. 34.99 (978-1-60514-592-1(0)) Find a World.

***Leaping Beauty.** unabr. ed. Gregory Maguire. Read by Gregory Maguire. (ENG.). 2004. (978-0-06-081840-1(9), Harper Audio); (978-0-06-081841-8(7), Harper Audio) HarperCollins Pubs.

Leaping Frogs. Sundance/Newbridge, LLC Staff. (Early Science Ser.). (gr. k-3). 2007. audio compact disk 12.00 (978-1-4007-6309-2(6)); audio compact disk 12.00 (978-1-4007-6307-8(X)); audio compact disk 12.00 (978-1-4007-6308-5(8)) Sund Newbrdge.

LEAPS Strategies. Instructed by Jon Najarian. 2005. audio compact disk 19.95 (978-1-59280-233-3(8)) Marketplace Bks.

Learn along Songs: Chanukah, Holidays & Heritage. 1 cass. (Running Time: 1 hr.). 2001. 10.00 (978-1-56479-312-6(5)); audio compact disk 15.00 Moonlight Rose.

Learn Along Songs: Everybody's Special. (Running Time: 60 mins.). 2001. audio compact disk 10.00 (978-1-56479-302-7(8)) Moonlight Rose.

Learn along Songs: Songs of the Differently Abled. 1 cass. (Running Time: 1 hr. 5 mins.). (J). 2001. 10.00 (978-1-56479-305-8(2)) Moonlight Rose.

Learn along Songs: There Are Many Ways to Tell a Story. 1 CD. (Running Time: 1 hr. 19 mins.). 2001. audio compact disk 15.00 Moonlight Rose.

Learn along Songs: There Are Many Ways to Tell a Story. 1 cass. (Running Time: 1 hr. 19 mins.). (J). 2001. 10.00 (978-1-56479-310-2(9)) Moonlight Rose.

Learn Along Songs: Yuletide Favorites. 1 CD. (Running Time: 57 min.). 2001. audio compact disk 15.00 Moonlight Rose.

Learn Along Songs: Yuletide Favorites. 1 cass. (Running Time: 57 min.). (J). (gr. k-6). 2001. 10.00 (978-1-56479-311-9(7)) Moonlight Rose.

Learn Anywhere! Eastern Arabic. unabr. ed. Penton Overseas. Read by Penton Overseas. (YA). 2007. 54.99 (978-1-59895-730-3(9)) Find a World.

Learn Anywhere! French. unabr. ed. Henry N. Raymond. Read by Penton Overseas. (YA). 2005. 54.99 (978-1-59895-127-1(0)) Find a World.

Learn Anywhere! German. unabr. ed. Henry N. Raymond. Read by Penton Overseas. (YA). 2005. 54.99 (978-1-59895-129-5(7)) Find a World.

Learn Anywhere! Italian. unabr. ed. Henry N. Raymond. Read by Penton Overseas. (YA). 2005. 54.99 (978-1-59895-128-8(9)) Find a World.

Learn Anywhere! Mandarin. unabr. ed. Henry N. Raymond. Read by Penton Overseas. (YA). 2005. 54.99 (978-1-59895-298-8(6)) Find a World.

Learn Anywhere! Spanish. unabr. ed. Henry N. Raymond. Read by Penton Overseas. (YA). 2005. 54.99 (978-1-59895-126-4(2)) Find a World.

Learn Boogie Woogie Piano: The Artistry of Albert Ammons, Pete Johnson & Meade Lux Lewis. 2nd ed. Colin Davey & Frank Poloney. (Running Time: 77 mins.). Orig. Title: Boogie Woogie Piano, Learn. 2003. spiral bd. 34.95 (978-0-9716129-0-7(0)) Boogie Woogie.

Learn by Series Access 2000 Introductory Concepts & Techniques. Gary B. Shelly et al. 2001. audio compact disk 27.95 (978-0-7895-6020-9(8)) Course Tech.

Learn By Series Office 2000 Brief Concepts & Techniques. Gary B. Shelly & Thomas J. Cashman. 2001. audio compact disk 41.95 (978-0-7895-6033-9(X)) Course Tech.

Learn By Series Office 2000 Introductory Concepts & Techniques. Gary B. Shelly & Thomas J. Cashman. 2001. audio compact disk 70.95 (978-0-7895-6034-6(8)) Course Tech.

Learn by Series PowerPoint 2000 Introductory Concepts & Techniques. Gary B. Shelly et al. 2001. audio compact disk 26.95 (978-0-7895-6027-8(5)) Course Tech.

Learn by Series Word 2000 Introductory Concepts & Techniques. Gary B. Shelly & Thomas J. Cashman. 2000. audio compact disk 27.95 (978-0-7895-6006-3(2)) Course Tech.

Learn Computer Game Programming with CDX & DirectX 7.0. Bil Simser. (Learn Ser.). 2000. pap. bk. 54.95 (978-1-55622-756-1(6)) Wordware Pub.

Learn Easily. Eldon Taylor. Read by Eldon Taylor. Interview with XProgress Aware Staff. Music by Steven Halpern. Interview with XProgress Aware. 1 cass. (Running Time: 62 min.). (EchoTech Ser.). 16.95 incl. script. (978-1-55978-340-8(0), 9904) Progress Aware Res.
Gentle coaching & soundtrack with underlying subliminal affirmations with tones & frequencies to alter brain wave activity.

Learn from the Best Tennis Players in the World: How to Develop More Effective Weapons. Excerpts. Hassan Refay. 4 cass. (Running Time: 60 mins). 2002. Rental 49.95 (978-0-9715787-4-6(5), 0444) H Refay.

Learn from the Best Tennis Players in the World: How to Finish off Opponents & Close Out Matches with Less Effort. Excerpts. Hassan Refay. 4 cass. (Running Time: 60 mins). Dramatization. 2002. 49.95 (978-0-9715787-0-8(2), 0888) H Refay.

Learn from the Best Tennis Players in the World: How to Use Your Emotions to Your Advantage. Excerpts. Hassan Refay. 4 cass. (Running Time: 60 mins). Dramatization. 2002. 49.95 (978-0-9715787-5-3(3), 0555) H Refay.

Learn from the Best Tennis Players in the World: How to Win Key Games. Excerpts. Hassan Refay. 4 cass. (Running Time: 60 mins). Dramatization. 2002. 49.95 (978-0-9715787-2-2(9), 0222) H Refay.

Learn from the Best Tennis Players in the World: How to Win the Big Points. Excerpts. Hassan Refay. 4 cass. (Running Time: 60 mins). 2002. Rental 45.95 (978-0-9715787-3-9(7), 0333) H Refay.

Learn from the Legends: Blues Keyboard. Karen Ann Krieger. (ENG.). 2000. audio compact disk 10.00 (978-0-7390-0962-8(1)) Alfred Pub.

Learn German. Nicole Irving. 1 cass. (Learn Languages Ser.). (YA). (gr. 6-12). 1993. bk. 19.95 (978-0-7460-1440-0(6)) EDC Pubng.

Learn Hawaiian at Home. Kahikahealani Wight. Illus. by Wren. 2 pieces. Orig. Title: Learn Hawaiian at Home Package. (ENG & HAW.). 1992. reel tape 34.95 (978-1-880188-21-7(X)) Bess Pr.
Text & music to accompany exercises in accompanying book.

Learn Hawaiian at Home Package see Learn Hawaiian at Home

Learn How to Relax! unabr. ed. Arnold A. Lazarus. 3 cass. (Running Time: 3 hrs.). 34.50 (S05006) J Norton Pubs.
Teaches all the basic techniques necessary to achieve relaxation in a step-by-step sequence of stress-reducing exercises, both physical & mental. The series of progressive exercises provides a direct method for overcoming tensions & anxieties.

Learn How to Relax CD Set: Relaxation Exercises. Arnold Lazarus. 2 CDs. (Running Time: 180). 2005. audio compact disk 34.50 (978-1-57970-333-2(X), S05006D, Audio-For) J Norton Pubs.
The ability to relax is not something we're born with; instead, it's a skill that mus be learned. This program, by noted psychologist Arnold Lazarus, will teach you all the basic techniques necessary to achieve relaxation in a step-by-step sequence of stress-reducing exercises, both physical and mental. The series of progressive exercises provides a direct method for overcoming tensions and anxieties. (Reissue on CD of original cassette program.).

Learn How to Speak English. Compiled by Maryhelen H. Hoffman. 1 CD-ROM.Tr. of Aprende Como Hablar Ingles. (J). 2002. audio compact disk 19.95 (978-1-928592-26-6(0)) MHP Commns.

Learn How to Think Positively. Glenn Harrold. 2 CDs. (Running Time: 3 hrs.). 2002. audio compact disk 17.95 (978-1-901923-23-0(1)); 11.95 (978-1-901923-03-2(7)) Pub: Divinit Pubing GBR. Dist(s): Bookworld
Combining powerful hypnotherapy techniques with state of the art digital recording technology. Includes: A pleasant voice guiding the listener into a completely relaxed state of mind & body.

Learn How to Use Self Hypnosis with Music to Play Better Golf. Scripts. Ann Schiola & Michael Robinson. Read by Michael Robinson. Composed by Ann Schiola. 1 cd. (Running Time: 34 minutes). 2005. audio compact disk 24.00 (978-0-9745230-3-3(8)) Loxias Audio Pub.

Learn in Your Car: English see Aprenda en Su Auto Ingles Nivel Tres

Learn in Your Car for Kids Spanish 3-Level Set. Henry N. Raymond. 9 CDs. (Running Time: 9 hrs.). (Learn in Your Car Ser.). (SPA & ENG.). 2000. audio compact disk 49.95 (978-1-56015-173-9(0)) Penton Overseas.

Learn in Your Car French. Henry N. Raymond. 3 CDs. (Running Time: 3 hrs.). (Learn in Your Car Ser.). (FRE & ENG.). (gr. 7 up). 2000. pap. bk. 19.95 (978-1-56015-163-0(3)) Penton Overseas.
Learn in your car CD, a foreign language audio series now available in all three levels.

Learn in Your Car French. unabr. ed. Henry N. Raymond. 3 CDs. (Running Time: 3 hrs.). (Learn in Your Car Ser.). (FRE & ENG.). (YA). (gr. 7 up). 1997. audio compact disk 19.95 (978-1-56015-122-7(6)) Penton Overseas.
You learn words & phrases without a textbook. Includes a Listening Guide with entire recorded text.

Learn in Your Car French. unabr. ed. Henry N. Raymond. 3 CDs. (Running Time: 3 hrs.). (Learn in Your Car Ser.). (FRE & ENG.). (YA). (gr. 7 up). 1998. audio compact disk 19.95 (978-1-56015-119-7(6)) Penton Overseas.

Learn in Your Car French 3-Level Set. Henry N. Raymond. 9 CDs. (Running Time: 9 hrs.). (Learn in Your Car Ser.). (FRE & ENG.). 2000. pap. bk. 49.95 (978-1-56015-170-8(6)) Penton Overseas.
Learn in your car, foreign language audio series in three levels of French.

Learn in Your Car German. Henry N. Raymond. 3 CDs. (Running Time: 3 hrs.). (Learn in Your Car Ser.). (GER & ENG.). 2000. pap. bk. 19.95 (978-1-56015-165-4(X)) Penton Overseas.
Learn a foreign language while driving, working out, or anywhere! Level 3 contains expanded vocabulary, advanced grammar & complex sentences to expand your conversational skills.

Learn in Your Car German. Henry N. Raymond. 3 CDs. (Running Time: 3 hrs.). (Learn in Your Car Ser.). (GER & ENG.). (gr. 7 up). 2000. audio compact disk 29.95 (978-1-56015-164-7(1)) Penton Overseas.
A more challenging vocabulary, grammar & more complex sentences to generate confidence in your ability to comprehend & converse.

Learn in Your Car German: Level 1. Henry N. Raymond. 3 CDs. (Running Time: 3 hrs.). (Learn in Your Car Ser.). (GER & ENG.). (gr. 7 up). 1999. pap. bk. 19.95 (978-1-56015-117-3(X)) Penton Overseas.
You learn words & phrases without a textbook. Includes a Listening Guide with entire recorded text.

Learn in Your Car German 3-Level Set. 3rd rev. ed. Henry N. Raymond. 9 CDs. (Running Time: 9 hrs.). (Learn in Your Car Ser.). (GER & ENG.). 2000. audio compact disk 49.95 (978-1-56015-171-5(4)) Penton Overseas.

Learn in Your Car Italian. unabr. ed. Henry N. Raymond. 3 CDs. (Running Time: 3 hrs.). (Learn in Your Car Ser.). (ITA & ENG.). (gr. 7 up). 2000. pap. bk. 29.95 (978-1-56015-166-1(8)) Penton Overseas.
Learn a foreign language while driving, working out, or anywhere! Level 2 contains more challenging vocabulary, more grammar, more complex sentences to generate confidence in your ability to comprehend & converse.

Learn in Your Car Italian. 3rd ed. Henry N. Raymond. 3 CDs. (Running Time: 3 hrs.). (Learn in Your Car Ser.). (ITA & ENG.). (gr. 7 up). 2000. pap. bk. 19.95 (978-1-56015-169-2(2)) Penton Overseas.
Learn a foreign language while driving, working out, or anywhere! Level 3 contains expanded vocabulary, advanced grammar & complex sentences to expand your conversational skills.

Learn in Your Car Italian 3-Level Set. Henry N. Raymond. 9 CDs. (Running Time: 9 hrs.). (Learn in Your Car Ser.). (ITA & ENG.). 2000. pap. bk. 49.95 (978-1-56015-172-2(2)) Penton Overseas.

Learn in Your Car Spanish. Henry N. Raymond. 3 CDs. (Running Time: 4 hrs. 30 mins.). (Learn in Your Car Ser.). (SPA & ENG.). (YA). 1998. lib. bdg. 19.95 (978-1-56015-124-1(2)) Penton Overseas.
You learn words & phrases without a textbook. Includes a Listening Guide with entire recorded text.

Learn in Your Car Spanish. unabr. ed. Henry N. Raymond. 3 CDs. (Running Time: 3 hrs.). (Learn in Your Car Ser.). (SPA & ENG.). (gr. 7 up). 1995. lib. bdg. 29.95 (978-1-56015-149-4(8)) Penton Overseas.

Learn in Your Car Spanish. unabr. ed. Henry N. Raymond. 3 CDs. (Running Time: 3 hrs.). (Learn in Your Car Ser.). (SPA & ENG.). (YA). (gr. 7 up). 1997. lib. bdg. 19.95 (978-1-56015-123-4(4)) Penton Overseas.

Learn Italian with a Native. audio compact disk (978-0-9765160-0-2(4)) Bella Italia.

Learn Japanese: New College Text. John Young & Kimiko Nakajima-Okano. 1984. audio compact disk 102.00 (978-0-8248-2986-5(7)); audio compact disk 102.00 (978-0-8248-2987-2(5)) UH Pr.

Learn Japanese: New College Text. John Young & Kimiko Nakajima-Okano. 1985. audio compact disk 102.00 (978-0-8248-2988-9(3)); audio compact disk 102.00 (978-0-8248-2989-6(1)) UH Pr.

Learn Japanese the Fast & Fun Way. 2nd ed. N. Akiyama & C. Akiyama. 4 cass. (Running Time: 90 min. per cass.). pap. bk. 39.95 Barron.
The basics of reading, writing & speaking.

Learn Log 4.0 Cd-Conc Log 9e. 9th ed. Hurley & Demarco. (C). 2005. audio compact disk 49.95 (978-0-495-00973-3(3)) Pub: Wadsworth Pub. Dist(s): CENGAGE Learn

Learn Mandarin Chinese through Children's Songs from Around the World. Emma / Fung-Ing Lee / Sinonexus. (CHI & ENG., (J). 2007. bk. 49.95 (978-0-9787664-2-9(3)) Sinonexus.

Learn Mandarin Chinese through Chinese Children's Songs. Emma/ Fung-Ing Lee/ Sinonexus. (CHI & ENG., (J). 2007. bk. 49.95 (978-0-9787664-1-2(5)) Sinonexus.

Learn Mandarin through Chinese Proverbs. Compiled by Emma /Fung-Ing Lee/Sinonexus. Emma /Fung-Ing Lee/Sinonexus. (ENG.). (YA). 2007. bk. 49.95 (978-0-9787664-0-5(7)) Sinonexus.

Learn of Me. Read by Wayne Monbleau. 6 cass. (Running Time: 7 hrs.). 1994. 20.00 (978-0-944648-29-2(0), LGT-1224) Loving Grace Pubns.
Religious.

Learn on the Go. unabr. ed. Jonathan T. Pennington. 2 CDs. (Running Time: 3 hrs.). (ENG.). 2001. audio compact disk 22.99 (978-0-310-24382-3(3)) Zondervan.

Learn One Hundred Forty-Four Basic Chords in One Hour. Duane Shinn. 1 cass. 19.95 (CP-9) Duane Shinn.
There are only 12 major chords, 12 minor chords, 12 augmented chords, & 12 diminshed chords. That makes 48. Then each one can be turned upside down (inverted) 3 times. Three times 48 is 144. This one hour course teaches how to form & play all 144 chords.

Learn Quickly. unabr. ed. Dick Sutphen. Read by Dick Sutphen. 1 cass. (Running Time: 1 hr.). (Spirit Guide Meditations). 1999. 14.98 (978-0-87554-633-9(1), SG106) Valley Sun.
With a spirit guide's assistance, accelerate learning speed, assimilate complicated information, think faster & more precisely.

Learn Self Hypnosis: With Hypno-DRUGS Bonus section. Dean A. Montalbano. (Hypnotic Sensory Response Audio Ser.). 2000. 39.95 (978-0-9708772-0-8(X)) L Lizards Pub Co.

Learn Self hypnosis on CD. Dean Montalbano. 3 cd. 2005. audio compact disk (978-1-932086-21-8(8)) L Lizards Pub Co.

Learn Series. Created by Laura Boynton King. 6 CD's. 2002. audio compact disk 109.95 (978-0-9748885-4-5(0)) Summit Dynamics.
A 6 volume series of Self-Hypnosis CD's utilizing specific relaxation techniques and mental imagery. Focus points are maximizing study habits and learning abilities, enhancing creativity and expanding interest.

Learn Spanish. 1 cass. (YA). (gr. 7 up). 1992. bk. 21.95 (978-0-7460-2815-5(6)) EDC Pubng.

Learn Spanish Live. Hosted by Bill Harvey. 6 cass. (Running Time: 4 hrs. 30 min.). (ENG & SPA.). suppl. ed. 29.95 Penton Overseas.
Attend Harvey's nationally recognized language training seminars where you can shout, laugh, & applaud along with a live audience. Receive the basics to understanding & speaking "real-life" Spanish. Teaches over 250 new words & phrases by means of shortcuts, tips, & secrets to successful communication.

Learn Spanish Live! Production Associates, Inc. Staff. Perf. by Bill Harvey. 4 CDs. (Running Time: 4 hrs. 30 mins.). (SPA.). 2003. audio compact disk 32.95 (978-1-887120-63-0(7)) Pub: Prodn Assocs. Dist(s): Penton Overseas
Bill Harvey's nationally recognized teaching approach has been receiving rave reviews for nearly twenty years. His fun-filled seminars have helped thousands learn Spanish, and his best-selling guidebooks continue to attract students of all ages. Bill's tips, shortcuts, and insights come alive in this new and exciting audio cassette program. Includes vocabulary cards. Front-row experience at a live Spanish seminar! Over 4 1/2 hours of practical Spanish instruction One-on-one review included with 6 easy lessons Hundreds of Spanish words and phrases BONUS Easy-to-use Vocabulary Cards.

Learn Spanish Verbs Fast! Stacey Tipton. 2 CDs. (Running Time: 2 hrs 15 min). 2003. audio compact disk 19.99 (978-0-9706829-6-3(4)) Musical Ling.
*Take it with you! While you drive....while you jog.... Are you bored with trying to memorize Spanish verbs? Can't quite get those different tenses down? We have the perfect solution for you. Believe it or not, you don't need to know 501 verbs in order to speak Spanish fluently. By learning the 50 most important verbs, you can begin speaking Spanish immediately!New audio verb learning program from the Musical Linguist. 2 CD set contains 2 hours of verb instruction. Includes:*50 most important Spanish verbs*key verb patterns*6 conjugations for each verb*easy, simple grammar explanations*12 pg. transcript of verb instructionFrom the same company that brought you the Musical Spanish line of products - whose motto is that learning Spanish should be both fun and easy.*

Learn Tagalog Now: English to Tagalog Language Learning CD's. Prod. by Theodore Wiersma, III. 4 CDs. (Running Time: 6 hrs. 10 mins). (TAG & ENG.). 2005. audio compact disk 34.95 (978-0-9771586-0-7(8)) Thirsty Rck.
Learn Tagalog Now consists of 3 Audio Cd's and 1 MP3 Cd. There are 40 lessons which provide basic words, short sentences and partial sentences. A 33 page Lesson Plan Booklet is provided on Cd in both PDF/Doc file format. This course is optimized for those who wish to also use for sleep learning. Best for quickly learning basic words and sentences.

Learn the Bible in 24 Hours. Chuck Missler. 24 audio CDs. (Running Time: 24 hrs). 2002. audio compact disk 99.95 (978-1-57821-182-1(4)) Koinonia Hse.
** What messages replay repeatedly throughout the Scriptures? * Did God somehow change between the Old and New Testaments?* What is the fabric that holds all 66 books together?The intrusions of a hectic world often deprive us of the opportunities to really dig in and explore the Word of God as we would really like to. This series might prove to be an end-run on those frustrated good intentions.This comprehensive series of 24 one-hour studies will take you from the beginning of all things in Genesis to the final culmination in the Book of Revelation.**Obviously, the Bible is truly a lifetime study, but 24 intensive sessions can provide you the strategic grasp that often eludes a detailed study of selected passages. This comprehensive review will provide a perspective from which you can navigate the Scriptures to explore specific studies. One of the astonishing discoveries will be the integrity of the overall design which is visible only through such a comprehensive undertaking.A must for anyone's Bible Study library! This series makes a great gift, so order your copy today!**Learn the Bible in 24 Hours qualifies for course credit through Louisiana Baptist University. Paperwork is included with product.This pack comes with 24 audio CDs as well as one self-contained CD-ROM (compatible with both Windows and Macintosh operating systems), which contains all 24 hours of audio study as MP3 files, as well as over 1,400 PowerPoint slides!.*

Learn the Bible in 24 Hours. ed. Chuck Missler. 2 CD - ROMs. (Running Time: 24 hours). 2002. cd-rom 44.95 (978-1-57821-200-2(6)) Koinonia Hse.
*This comprehensive series of 24 one-hour studies will take you from the beginning of all things in Genesis to the final culmination in the Book of Revelation.** Obviously, the Bible is truly a lifetime study, but 24 intensive sessions can provide you the strategic grasp that often eludes a detailed study of selected passages. This comprehensive review will provide a perspective from which you can navigate the Scriptures to explore specific studies. One of the astonishing discoveries will be the integrity of the overall design which is visible only through such a comprehensive undertaking.*

Learn the Kazakh Language in Seventy Steps: Using 200 Sentence Models. (C). 1993. 19.00 (978-1-881265-14-6(5)) Dunwoody Pr.

Learn the Kazakh Language in Seventy Steps Using Two Hundred Sentence Models. Tangat Tangirberdi kyzy Ayapova. 2 cass. (Running Time: 1 hr. 30 min. per cass.). (KAZ.). 1991. 19.00 (3050) Dunwoody Pr.
The first section is a series of steps to practice phonetics, conversation, grammar, & vocabulary. The second section is designed to reinforce the grammatical material through everyday conversations.

Learn to Control Stress: Before it Controls You. Brian Alman & Peter T. Lambrou. 1992. audio compact disk 22.50 (978-0-87630-662-8(8)) Taylor and Fran.

Learn to Create a Healthy Home! Lisa Beres & Ron Beres. (ENG.). 2006. audio compact disk 19.95 (978-0-9772392-1-4(7)) Green Nest.

Learn to Earn. abr. ed. Peter Lynch & John Rothchild. 1 cass. 9.99 (56764) Books on Tape.
The average high school student knows Nike, The Gap & McDonald's, but few understand how to buy stock in them. At a time students should save for college, understanding the basics about the stock market is vital. The authors offer what schools don't teach: how to read a stock table in a newspaper, how to understand an annual report & how to think like an investor.

Learn to Earn: A Beginner's Guide to the Basics of Investing & Business. abr. ed. Peter Lynch. Read by Peter Lynch. 2 CDs. (Running Time: 1 hr. 30 mins. 0 sec.). (ENG.). 2006. audio compact disk 20.00 (978-0-7435-5594-4(5), Sound Ideas) Pub: S&S Audio. Dist(s): S and S Inc

Learn to Estimate: Early Explorers Fluent Set A Audio CD. Benchmark Education Staff. (J). 2006. audio compact disk 10.00 (978-1-4108-7643-0(8)) Benchmark Educ.

Learn to Fly a Helicopter (Principle #4 - Accept Ambiguity & Uncertainty: Psalm 139:14-15. Ed Young. 1996. 4.95 (978-0-7417-2124-2(4), 1124) Win Walk.

Learn to Listen, Listen to Learn Set: Academic Listening & Note-Taking. 2nd ed. Roni S. Lebauer. 6 cass. 2000. 78.75 (978-0-13-919457-3(6)) Longman.

Learn to Meditate. unabr. ed. Rolf Sovik. Read by Rolf Sovik. 1 cass. (Running Time: 37 mins.). 1998. 7.95 (978-0-89389-164-0(9), CS223MO) Himalayan Inst.
Easy-to-follow, effective instruction is given in deep relaxation & meditation.

Learn to Meditate Kit: The Complete Course in Modern Meditation. Contrib. by Patricia Carrington. 4 cass. (Running Time: 4 hrs.). 1999. pap. bk. & tchr. ed. 39.95 (71-0025) Explorations.
Clinically Standardized Meditation (CSM) is a safe, practical & easy-to-learn method which can be mastered at home in just a few hours. Creates an individual meditation practice to reduce stress, enhance creativity, increase effectiveness at work & improve relationships.

Learn to Play Bach's "Jesus, Joy of Man's Desiring" Duane Shinn. 1 cass. 19.95 incl. sheet music. (T-5) Duane Shinn.
This a tune heard in churches, concerts & even at the Organ Grinder.

Learn to Play Bass. Ed. by Alfred Publishing. (ENG.). 2003. audio compact disk 9.95 (978-0-7390-3346-3(8)) Alfred Pub.

Learn to Play Beethoven's "Moonlight Sonata" Duane Shinn. 1 cass. 19.95 incl. sheet music. (T-3) Duane Shinn.
Analyzes the entire piece in terms of key, chords, dynamics, & rhythm, then explains it slowly, section by section.

Learn to Play Blues Harmonica: Fully Diagrammed for Complete Beginners. Don Baker. 2008. pap. bk. 21.95 (978-1-85720-137-6(X)) Waltons Manu IRL.

Learn to Play Chopin's "Prelude in C Minor" Duane Shinn. 1 cass. 19.95 incl. sheet music. (T-4) Duane Shinn.
This is the tune that Barry Manilow borrowed to create his "Could It Be Magic?" hit.

Learn to Play Classical Guitar Manual: Progressive Complete. Jason Waldron. 2003. pap. bk. 29.95 (978-1-86469-239-6(1), 256-225) Kolala Music SGP.

Learn to Play Drums. Ed. by Alfred Publishing. (Learn to Play Ser.). (ENG.). 2003. audio compact disk 9.95 (978-0-7390-3345-6(X)) Alfred Pub.

Learn to Play Guitar. Ed. by Alfred Publishing. (ENG.). 2003. audio compact disk 9.95 (978-0-7390-3348-7(4)) Alfred Pub.

Learn to Play Irish Fiddle. Phil Berthoud. (ENG.). 2008. per. 19.95 (978-0-7866-0778-5(5)) Mel Bay.

Learn to Play Jazz Guitar Manual: Progressive Complete. Peter Gelling. 2008. bk. 29.95 (978-1-86469-385-0(1)) Kolala Music SGP.

Learn to Play Keyboard. Ed. by Alfred Publishing. (ENG.). 2003. audio compact disk 9.95 (978-0-7390-3347-0(6)) Alfred Pub.

Learn to Play Mountain Dulcimer. Created by Mel Bay Publications Inc. (Running Time: 1 hr. 30 mins.). 2006. 19.95 (978-5-558-09033-8(2)) Mel Bay.

Learn to Play Power Blues Guitar Solos. Alan Warner. 1997. audio compact disk 24.95 (978-0-7119-3386-6(3), AM91062) Music Sales.

Learn to Play Saxophone Manual: Progressive Complete. Peter Gelling. 2003. audio compact disk 29.95 (978-1-86469-259-4(6)) Kolala Music SGP.

Learn to Play "Sing-Along-Songs" 1 cass. bk. 19.95 (T-2) Duane Shinn.

Learn to Play "Social Songs" Such As "Auld Lang Syne," Etc. Duane Shinn. 1 cass. bk. 19.95 (T-2) Duane Shinn.
Presents a book of 19 "social songs" with this cassette course.

Learn to Play the American Penny Whistle: For Complete Beginners. Created by Walton Manufacturing Ltd. 2002. audio compact disk 23.95 (978-0-7866-6449-8(5)) Waltons Manu IRL.

Learn to Play the B & C Button Accordion. Created by Mel Bay Publications Inc. (Running Time: 1 hr. 30 mins.). 2006. 29.95 (978-5-558-08921-9(0)) Mel Bay.

Learn to Play the English Penny Whistle for Complete Beginners. Created by Walton Manufacturing Ltd. 2001. pap. bk. 23.95 (978-0-7866-6147-3(X)) Waltons Manu IRL.

Learn to Play the Guitar. unabr. ed. 2 cass. bk. 19.95 (S23942) J Norton Pubs.
Consists of an instructional 112-p. book attached to a tearproof net bag with one Hohner harmonica & one instructional cassette inside.

Learn to Play the Harmonica. unabr. ed. 1 cass. (Running Time: 75 min. per cass.). bk. 19.95 incl. harmonica. (S23941) J Norton Pubs.

Learn to Play the Irish Mandolin. Contrib. by Anthony Warde. (Running Time: 1 hr.). (ENG.). 2006. 32.95 (978-5-558-08919-6(9)) Waltons Manu IRL.

Learn to Play the Scottish Whistle for Complete Beginners. Created by Walton Manufacturing Ltd. 2001. pap. bk. 23.95 (978-0-7866-6146-6(1)) Waltons Manu IRL.

Learn to Play the Tin Whistle. Contrib. by Vinnie Kilduff. (Running Time: 50 mins.). (ENG.). 2006. 32.95 (978-5-558-08922-6(9)) Waltons Manu IRL.

Learn to Play Two Wedding Songs: The Processional & the Recessional. Duane Shinn. 1 cass. 19.95 (T-6) Duane Shinn.
Explains how to play the two most common wedding songs, the Processional ("Here Comes the Bride"), & the Recessional.

Learn to Read Arabic. Raja T. Nasr. (ARA & ENG.). pap. bk. 14.95 (978-0-86685-194-7(1), LDL62027) Intl Bk Ctr.

Learn to Read Chinese. Paul Unschuld. 2 cass. (Running Time: 2 hrs.). (CHI.). 1994. 30.00 (978-0-912111-50-6(X)) Paradigm Publns.

Learn to Relax see Aprende a Relajarte

Learn to Relax. Lee Pulos. 2 cass. (Running Time: 60 min. per cass.). (Self Hypnosis & Subliminal Reinforcement Ser.). 14.95 (978-1-55569-233-9(8), SUB-8009) Great Am Audio.
Presents tools for positive self-change.

Learn to Relax. Lee Pulos. Read by Lee Pulos. 1 cass. (Running Time: 60 min.). 9.95 (978-1-55569-431-9(4), 4017) Great Am Audio.
Subliminal self-help.

Learn to Relax. unabr. ed. James Richard. 1 cass. (Running Time: 50 mins.). 1982. 9.95 Newtown Psychological Ctr.
Teaches relaxing progressive muscle relaxation & relaxing through autogenic phrases.

Learn to Relax & Let Go. Barry Tesar. 2 cass. 1998. 14.95 (978-1-889800-14-1(7)) TNT Media Grp.
Stress management.

Learn to Relax & Meditate: The Facts to Know & the Easy Exercises to Do to Master Meditation. unabr. ed. Angela M. Mattey. Read by Angela M. Mattey. Perf. by Brian Epp. 1 cass. (Running Time: 1 hr. 10 min.). (How to Be an Awakened Human Ser.: Vol. 1). 1998. 9.95 (978-1-882836-02-4(2)) TAM Ent.
Side A is about the teachings of how to easily & quickly meditate effectively. Side B is three simple guided meditations.

Learn to Sing a Ballad in Mandarin Chinese Teresa Teng, I Wish We Would Last Forever: Expand Your Vocabulary by Learning a Popular Mandarin Chinese Song. Read by Qian Bai & Patrick Scully. Perf. by Teresa Teng. Prod. by George Maverick. Edward Britz. Engineer Chuck Duncan. Prod. by Bai Ma Sing Song Learn. (CHI & ENG., 2009. audio compact disk 16.95 (978-0-9822845-4-4(3)) Bai Ma Sing.

Learn to Sing a HIP HOP Song in Mandarin Chinese: Expand Your Vocabulary by Learning a Popular Mandarin Chinese Song, Wang Rong, Baba Mama. Read by Qian Bai & Patrick Scully. Perf. by Rong Wang. Prod. by George Maverick & Bai Ma Sing Song Learn. Arranged by Chuck Duncan. (ENG & CHI.). 2009. audio compact disk 16.95 (978-0-9822845-6-8(X)) Bai Ma Sing.

Learn to Sing a POP Song in Mandarin Chinese: Expand Your Vocabulary by Learning a Popular Mandarin Chinese Song, Jocie Guo Mei Mei, Don't Panic! Perf. by Jocie Guo. (ENG & CHI.). 2009. audio compact disk 16.95 (978-0-9822845-2-0(7)) Bai Ma Sing.

Learn to Sing a POP Song in Mandarin Chinese: Expand Your Vocabulary by Learning a Popular Mandarin Chinese Song, Jocie Guo Mei Mei, Love Goddess. Perf. by Jocie Guo. (ENG & CHI.). 2009. audio compact disk 16.95 (978-0-9822845-3-7(5)) Bai Ma Sing.

Learn to Sing a POP Song in Mandarin Chinese: Expand Your Vocabulary by Learning a Popular Mandarin Chinese Song, Liu RuoYing, Travel Separately. Perf. by Rene Liu. (ENG & CHI.). 2009. audio compact disk 16.95 (978-0-9822845-1-3(9)) Bai Ma Sing.

Learn to Sing a ROCK Song in Mandarin Chinese: Expand Your Vocabulary by Learning a Popular Mandarin Chinese Song, Second Hand Rose, Late at Night. #20108;#25163;#29611;#29808; Second Hand Rose. (ENG & CHI.). 2009. audio compact disk 16.95 (978-0-9822845-5-1(1)) Bai Ma Sing.

Learn to Sing & Play Guitar. Susan Mazer. (ENG.). 1999. audio compact disk 10.00 (978-0-7390-2597-0(X)) Alfred Pub.

Learn to Sing Like a Pop Star. Shyla Nibbe. 2 CDs. 2003. audio compact disk 49.95 (978-1-59481-000-8(1)) Songbird Ent.

Learn to Speak Danish. unabr. ed. Aage Salling. 6 cass. (Running Time: 7 hrs.). (Self-Instructional Language Courses Ser.). Orig. Title: Laer at Tale Dansk. (DAN.). 1978. pap. bk. 175.00 (978-0-88432-149-1(5), AFDA40) J Norton Pubs.
Introductory course in which you will learn a vocabulary of 1100 of the most commonly used Danish words. Dialogs have been planned to reflect various aspects of everyday life in Denmark. Although grammar instruction is minimized, a concise grammar section is included at the end of the text. There is also a complete vocabulary list in English, German & Spanish. Guide provides translation for the Danish words introduced in each lesson.

Learn to Speak Danish CDs, Text & Learner's Guide. Åge Salling. 6 CDs. (Running Time: 7 hrs.). Orig. Title: Lær at Tale Dansk. (DAN.). 2005. audio compact disk 175.00 (978-1-57970-171-0(X), AFDA40D) J Norton Pubs.

Learn to Speak English, Program Two: Farsi. Read by Barbara Sullivan. 4 cass. (Running Time: 2 hrs. 30 mins.). 49.95 (978-0-929208-39-8(0), 2LBF45) CLL Cupertino.
Provides practice in 90% of our most commonly used words. All directions and practice sentences are spoken in one of 27 languages as well as English. The content is the same in all languages.

Learn to Speak English, Program Two: French. Read by Barbara Sullivan. 4 cass. (Running Time: 2 hrs. 30 mins.). (FRE.). 49.95 (978-0-929208-36-7(6), 2LBFA49) CLL Cupertino.

Learn to Speak English, Program Two: Hindi. Read by Barbara Sullivan. 4 cass. (Running Time: 2 hrs. 30 mins.). (HIN.). 49.95 (978-0-929208-35-0(8), 2LBH46) CLL Cupertino.

Learn to Speak English, Program Two: Portuguese. Read by Barbara Sullivan. 4 cass. (Running Time: 2 hrs. 30 mins.). (POR.). 49.95 (978-0-929208-40-4(4), 2LBPO50) CLL Cupertino.

Learn to Speak English, Program Two: Tagalog. Read by Barbara Sullivan. 4 cass. (Running Time: 2 hrs. 30 mins.). (TAG.). 49.95 (978-0-929208-37-4(4), 2LBT47) CLL Cupertino.

Learn to Speak English, Program Two: Thai. Read by Barbara Sullivan. 4 cass. (Running Time: 2 hrs. 30 mins.). (THA.). 49.95 (978-0-929208-38-1(2), 2LBTH48) CLL Cupertino.

Learn to Study see Aprender a Estudiar

Learn to Touch Type in Only Four Hours: Designed for Users of Computer Terminals, Word Processors, or Typewriters. John B. Morgan. 3 cass. 10.95 incl. script incl. box. (978-0-917551-00-0(1)) Incentive Learn.
Includes six 40-minute exercises with drills on worksheets.

***Learn to Write Read-along Cd.** Ed. by Gillian Snoddy. (J). 2009. audio compact disk 24.99 (978-1-60689-130-8(8)) Creat Teach Pr.

Learn Vocabulary. Margaret M. Bynum. 5 cass. (Running Time: 4 hrs. 22 min.). (YA). (gr. 10-12). 1986. wbk. ed. 59.95 (978-0-913286-91-3(5), 2000, Lrn Inc) Oasis Audio.

Learn with Music Technique Tape. Ivan Barzakov & Pamela Rand. 1 cass. 1998. 9.95 (OLT101) OptimaLearning.
Demonstrate & discuss the famous memory technique, Reading with Music (concert reading) & Opitma Learning psychological preparation for studying & performance.

Learn with Rap Geography. unabr. ed. Patricia B. Murphy. Illus. by Michigan State University, Cartography Center Staff. Music by Alan Bratschi. 1 cass. (Running Time: 27 min.). (Learn with Rap Ser.). (J). (gr. 2-9). 1995. pap. bk. 19.95 (978-0-9648725-0-9(1)) People Are People.
Consists of three educational rap songs that cover three instructional levels, as presented in book: Level I (Grades 2-3) - World Geo-Rap with lyrics & music; World Geo-Rap with missing (fill in the) word & music; World Geo-Rap with music only. Level II (Grades 4-6) - World Geo-Rap with lyrics & music; World Geo-Rap with missing (fill in the) word & music; World Geo-Rap with music only. Level III (Grades 7-9) - The Five Themes of Geography Rap Song with music only.

Learn Your FACTS: Addition & Subtraction. unabr. ed. Twin Sisters Productions. Read by Twin Sisters. (J). 2007. 44.99 (978-1-60252-615-0(X)) Find a World.

Learn Your FACTS: Multiplication & Division. unabr. ed. Twin Sisters Productions. Read by Twin Sisters. 2007. 44.99 (978-1-60252-647-1(8)) Find a World.

Learnables, Bk. 5. Harris Winitz. Illus. by Sydney M. Baker. 1999. pap. bk. 45.00 (978-1-887371-49-0(4)) Intl Linguistics.

Learnables Basic Structures. 2004. audio compact disk 69.00 (978-1-887371-58-2(3)); audio compact disk 49.00 (978-1-887371-62-9(1)) Intl Linguistics.

Learned Hand Pt. 1: The Man & the Judge. unabr. collector's ed. Gerald Gunther. Read by Michael Kramer. 11 cass. (Running Time: 16 hrs. 30 min.). 1995. 88.00 (978-0-7366-3220-1(4), 3883-A) Books on Tape.
The greatest judge never to be appointed to the Supreme Court, Learned Hand embodied the notion of human liberty. A questioning man, Hand was a liberal skeptic, "never too sure he was right." An advocate of judicial restraint, Hand nevertheless ruled for free speech in his obscenity decisions & spoke out against McCarthy. His rulings came to be a rich part of America's story.

Learned Hand Pt. 2: The Man & the Judge. unabr. collector's ed. Gerald Gunther. Read by Michael Kramer. 11 cass. (Running Time: 16 hrs. 30 mins.). 1995. 88.00 (978-0-7366-3221-8(2), 3883-B) Books on Tape.

***Learned Optimism.** abr. ed. Martin Seligman. Read by Martin Seligman. (Running Time: 13 hrs. 0 mins. 0 sec.). (ENG.). 2011. audio compact disk 14.99 (978-1-4423-4113-5(0)) Pub: S&S Audio. Dist(s): S and S Inc

Learned Optimism. abr. ed. Martin E. P. Seligman. Read by Martin E. P. Seligman. 2 CD. (Running Time: 13 hrs. 0 mins. 0 sec.). (ENG.). 2001. audio compact disk 20.00 (978-0-7435-1802-4(0), Sound Ideas) Pub: S&S Audio. Dist(s): S and S Inc
In this bestselling classic one of the pioneers in cognitive psychology helps listeners identify self-defeating thought patterns & how to break through those vicious cycles.

Learner English: A Teacher's Guide to Interference & Other Problems. 2nd ed. Ed. by Michael Swan & Bernard Smith. Contrib. by Penny Ur. (Running Time: 1 hr. 24 mins.). (Cambridge Handbooks for Language Teachers Ser.). (ENG., 2001. tchr. ed. 25.00 (978-0-521-77497-0(7)) Cambridge U Pr.

Learner English: A Teacher's Guide to Interference & Other Problems. 2nd rev. ed. Michael Swan & Bernard Smith. Contrib. by Penny Ur. (Running Time: hrs. mins.). (Cambridge Handbooks for Language Teachers Ser.). (ENG., 2001. audio compact disk 25.00 (978-0-521-00024-6(6)) Cambridge U Pr.

Learners. unabr. ed. Chip Kidd. Read by Bronson Pinchot. (Running Time: 23400 sec.). 2008. 59.95 (978-1-4332-3360-9(6)); audio compact disk & audio compact disk 29.95 (978-1-4332-3364-7(9)); audio compact disk & audio compact disk 80.00 (978-1-4332-3361-6(4)) Blckstn Audio.

Learning - Life in the Castle: An Allegory of the Christian Walk. unabr. ed. Jean Nava. Read by Jean Nava. 6 cass. (Running Time: 10 hrs.). (More Than Conquerors Ser.: Vol. 1). 1999. bk. 15.95 (978-0-9659952-2-1(4)) Kingdom Pr.

Learning about God & Jesus: An Overview of the Gospel in Simple English. Beverly J. Doswald. 2 cass. (Running Time: 1 hr. 45 mins.). 1986. 6.50 (978-0-938783-01-5(7)) Helpful Beginnings.
An overview of the Gospel in very simple English for teenagers & adults with limited English skills & little or no biblical background.

Learning about Gregorian Chant: Gregorian Chant - Its History, Its Musical Form. Perf. by Monks of Solesmes Staff. 2001. audio compact disk 16.95 (978-1-55725-292-0(0)) Paraclete MA.

Learning about Liberty: The Cato University Home Study Course. unabr. ed. Created by Cato University. (Running Time: 12600 sec.). 2007. audio compact disk 59.95 (978-1-4332-0971-0(3)) Blckstn Audio.

Learning about Liberty, Part A: The Cato University Home Study Course. unabr. ed. Cato University. (Running Time: 63000 sec.). 2007. audio compact disk 120.00 (978-1-4332-0969-7(1)) Blckstn Audio.

Learning about Liberty, Part B: The Cato University Home Study Course. unabr. ed. Cato University. (Running Time: 50400 sec.). 2007. audio compact disk 120.00 (978-1-4332-0970-3(5)) Blckstn Audio.

Learning Acceleration. 1 cass. 12.98 (978-0-87554-513-4(0), 1111) Valley Sun.
Powerful suggestions to learn faster & remember what you learn. Also: Your mind has no limits. You easily assimilate complicated information. You are quick to learn & understand. With minimum study, you maximize learning ability. You now unleash your unlimited potential to learn rapidly. You triple your learning speed. You focus your energy & concentration to accelerate learning. Much more.

Learning Acoustic Guitar. Told to Charles Sedlak & Greg Douglass. (Icons of Rock (Smart Way) Ser.). 2007. pap. bk. 24.95 (978-0-9796928-1-9(4)) Pub: Too Smart Pubns. Dist(s): MBBI

Learning Basic Skills Through Music. Hap Palmer. (J). 1989. 11.95; audio compact disk 14.95 Ed Activities.

Learning Basic Skills Through Music, Vol. 1. Perf. by Hap Palmer. 1 LP. (J). lp 11.95 (EA 514) Kimbo Educ.
Colors - Marching Around the Alphabet - The Number March - Put Your Hands up in the Air & more. Black jacket.

Learning Basic Skills Through Music, Vol. 1. Perf. by Hap Palmer. 1 LP. (Running Time: 1 hr.). (J). 2001. pap. bk. 11.95 (EA 514C); pap. bk. 14.95 (EA514CD) Kimbo Educ.
Colors - Marching Around the Alphabet - The Number March - Put Your Hands up in the Air & more. Includes guide.

Learning Basic Skills Through Music, Vol. 2. Perf. by Hap Palmer. 1 LP. (J). lp 11.95 (EA 522) Kimbo Educ.
Parade of Colors - Paper Clocks - Triangle, Circle or Square - One Shape, Three Shapes & more. Red Jacket.

Learning Basic Skills Through Music, Vol. 2. Perf. by Hap Palmer. 1 cass. (Running Time: 1 hr.). (J). 2001. pap. bk. 11.95 (EA 522C) Kimbo Educ.
Parade of Colors - Paper Clocks - Triangle, Circle or Square - One Shape, Three Shapes & more. Includes guide.

Learning Basic Skills Through Music, Vol. 3. Perf. by Hap Palmer. 1 cass. (J). 11.95 blue jacket. (EA 526C); lp 11.95 (EA 526) Kimbo Educ.
Alice's Restaurant - Stop, Look & Listen - Take a Bath - Buckle Your Seat Belt & more. Blue jacket.

Learning Basic Skills Through Music, Vol. 4. Perf. by Hap Palmer. 1 LP. (J). stu. ed. 11.95 (EA 521); 11.95 green jacket. (EA 521C) Kimbo Educ.
Safety Sign - Listen & Do - Under the Stick - Show Me - Hello & more.

Learning Basic Skills Through Music, Vol. 5. Perf. by Hap Palmer. 1 cass. (J). 11.95 beige jacket. (EA 594C); lp 11.95 (EA 594) Kimbo Educ.
Ricky Sticky Man - Tap Out the Answer - Pocket Full of Bs - What I Did Today & more. Beige jacket.

Learning Basic Skills Through Music Vol. 2: Blue. 1 CD. (Running Time: 1 hr.). (J). 2001. pap. bk. 14.95 (EA 526CD) Kimbo Educ.
Colors, Marching Around the Alphabet, Growing, The Elephant & more. Includes guide.

Learning Basic Skills Through Music Vol. 2: Green. 1 CD. (Running Time: 1 hr.). (J). 2001. pap. bk. 14.95 (EA 521CD) Kimbo Educ.

Learning Basic Skills Through Music Vol. 2: Red. 1 CD. (Running Time: 1 hr.). (J). 2001. pap. bk. 14.95 (EA 522CD) Kimbo Educ.

Learning Basque, Set. unabr. ed. Xabier Gereno. 2 cass. (Running Time: 2 hrs.15 mins.). (BAQ & ENG.). 1995. pap. bk. 55.00 (978-0-88432-874-2(0), SBA001) J Norton Pubs.
Introductory course in Basque in the dialect of Bilbao. Part I contains 40 lessons that provide vocabulary, basic sentences & grammar; Part II is devoted to complete charts of verb conjugations & declensions introduced in the preceding lessons. The greatest difficulty for the learner of Basque resides in the verbs, which express in their structures certain relationships not found or implied in English verbs.

Learning Basque CDs & Text. Xabier Gereño. 4 CDs. (Running Time: 2 hrs. 15 mins.). (BAQ.). 2005. audio compact disk 55.00 (978-1-57970-166-6(3), SBA001D) J Norton Pubs.

Learning Bass The Smart Way! Told to Tony Saunders & Rudy Sarzo. (Icons of Rock (Smart Way) Ser.). 2007. pap. bk. 24.95 (978-0-9796928-2-6(2)) Pub: Too Smart Pubns. Dist(s): MBBI

Learning Brain. Eric Jensen. 2 cass. bk. 31.95 (B432-A); pap. bk. 21.95 bk. (B432) Learning Forum.
Discover how to affect how the brain learns, which foods may impair learning & how male & female brains differ.

Learning by Listening, Vol. 1. Ed. by B. Warren & Susan Baker Godoy. Compiled by B. Warren & Susan Baker Godoy. (Music Listening Course Ser.). (J). (gr. k-12). 1998. spiral bd. 25.00 Wiscasset Music.

Learning by Living, Pt. 1. Derek Prince. 1 cass. (Running Time: 60 min.). (B-129) Derek Prince.

Learning by Living, Pt. 2. Derek Prince. 1 cass. (Running Time: 60 min.). (B-130) Derek Prince.

Learning by the Rules: Early Explorers Early Set B Audio CD. Clare O'Brien. Adapted by Benchmark Education Staff. (J). 2007. audio compact disk 10.00 (978-1-4108-8227-1(6)) Benchmark Educ.

Learning-centered Communication. David Nunan. 2 cass. (Running Time: 3 hrs.). pap. bk. & wbk. ed. 47.95 (978-0-8384-9753-1(5)); pap. bk. & wbk. ed. 47.95 (978-0-8384-9725-8(X)) Heinle.

Learning Centers in the Judaic Studies Classroom. Malka Gurkow. 1 cass. (Running Time: 90 mins.). 1999. 6.00 (W60FL) Torah Umesorah.

Learning Chinese the Natural Way for Business. Chin-ning Chu. 1 cass. 1989. 85.00 (978-0-929638-18-8(2)) AMC Pub CA.

Learning Disabilities. 2 cass. (Running Time: 1 hr. per cass). (HarperThor); (I051AB090, HarperThor) HarpC GBR.

Learning Divine Healing Series. Elbert Willis. 4 cass. 13.00 Fill the Gap.

Learning Electric Guitar The Smart Way! Told to Patrick McCormick & Greg Douglass. (Icons of Rock (Smart Way) Ser.). 2007. pap. bk. 24.95 (978-0-9796928-0-2(6)) Pub: Too Smart Pubns. Dist(s): MBBI

Learning English: Cantonese. D. E. Traynor. 4 cass. (Running Time: 2 hrs.). 21.50 Alpha Tape.
Presents a study to aid the student in learning the English language. Each sentence is translated into Cantonese.

Learning English: Mandarin. D. E. Traynor. 4 cass. (Running Time: 2 hrs.). 21.50 Alpha Tape.
Presents a study to aid the student in learning the English language. Each sentence is translated into Mandarin.

Learning English: Tagolog. D. E. Traynor. 4 cass. (Running Time: 2 hrs.). 21.50 Alpha Tape.
Presents a study to aid the student in learning the English language. Each sentence is translated into Tagolog.

Learning English: Vietnamese. D. E. Traynor. 4 cass. (Running Time: 2 hrs.). 21.50 Alpha Tape.
Presents a study to aid the students in learning the English language. Each sentence is translated into Vietnamese.

Learning for Earning. John A. Wanat et al. (gr. 6-9). tchr. ed. 200.00 (978-1-56637-944-1(X)) Goodheart.

***Learning from Data.** 3rd rev. ed. Arthur M. Glenberg & Matthew Andrzejewski. 2009. audio compact disk (978-0-8058-6371-0(0)) L Erlbaum Assocs.

Learning from Dolphins. John Lilly. 1 cass. 10.00 (A0069-79) Sound Photosyn.
From Dr. Lilly's personal collection.

Learning from Stories. unabr. ed. Idries Shah. Read by Idries Shah. Read by London College of Storytellers Staff. 2 vols. (Running Time: 3 hrs.). (Idries Shah Live on Tape Ser.). 1996. bk. 17.00 (978-1-883536-03-9(0), LEST1, Hoopoe Books) ISHK.
A lecture by Idries Shah, plus teaching stories & narratives selected from "Caravan of Dreams" & "The Adventures of Mulla Nasrudin," jokes & tales from the Nasrudin Corpus.

Learning from the Holy Spirit. Kenneth Wapnick. 2 CDs. 2007. audio compact disk 13.00 (978-1-59142-301-0(5), CD52) Foun Miracles.

Learning from the Holy Spirit. Kenneth Wapnick. 1 CD. (Running Time: 2 hrs. 13 mins. 28 secs.). 2007. 11.00 (978-1-59142-311-9(2), 3m52) Foun Miracles.

Learning from the World's Worst Salesmen. unabr. ed. Josef Sanders. 12.95 (978-0-88432-229-0(7), AF1904) J Norton Pubs.
Real sales experiences are presented that provide insight & understanding as to why so many sales people fail to succeed.

Learning from Your Parent's Mistakes (Does Father Really Know Best?) Selected Passages. Ed Young. 1994. 4.95 (978-0-7417-2020-7(5), 1020) Win Walk.

Learning How to & Why to Accept Yourself. Read by Wayne Monbleau. 2 cass. (Running Time: 2 hrs. 30 min.). 1993. 10.00 (978-0-944648-16-2(9), LGT-1191) Loving Grace Pubns.
Religious.

Learning How to Hear God's Voice. Rick Joyner. 1 cass. (Running Time: 90 mins.). (Hearing God Ser.: Vol. 2). 2000. 5.00 (RJ10-002) Morning NC.
"Principles of Spiritual Warfare" & "Putting on the Full Armor of God." These tapes highlight practical truths that lead to certain victory in spiritual warfare.

Learning How to Learn. abr. ed. Read by Learning Forum Staff. 1 cass. (Running Time: 60 min.). (Success Ser.). (YA). (gr. 9-12). 9.95 Learning Forum.
Techniques on life long learning skills.

Learning How to Learn. unabr. ed. Read by Learning Forum Staff. 1 cass. (Running Time: 1 hr.). (Success Ser.). Learning Forum.

Learning Human Biology. 3rd ed. Daniel D. Chiras & Jones and Bartlett Publishers Staff. (C). 2000. stu. ed. 25.95 (978-0-7637-1445-1(3), 1445-3) Jones Bartlett.

Learning Inventor 8 a Process-Based Approach: Teaching Package. Thomas Short & Anthony Dudek. tchr. ed. 34.00 (978-1-59070-332-8(4)) Goodheart.

Learning Irish. unabr. ed. Michael O. Siadhail. 4 cass. (Running Time: 4 hrs.). (Self-Instructional Language Courses). (IRI & ENG.). (YA). (gr. 10-12). pap. bk. 89.95 (978-0-88432-205-4(X), AFIR10) J Norton Pubs.
Beginning-level course of 36 lessons features the Irish used by native speakers of County Galway. Spelling in text is that of official Standard Irish.English translations of text, key vocabulary & exercise instructions are given for each lesson. Appendix includes answer keys & Irish-English/English-Irish vocabularies.

Learning Japanese from Songs. Michiko Sasaki & Hiroko Terauchi. 2001. pap. bk. 37.70 (978-4-7574-0520-2(0)) Pub: ALC JPN. Dist(s): Cheng Tsui

Learning Like Crazy Spoken Spanish, Vol. 2: Spoken Spanish Volume 2. Learning Like Crazy. (ENG.). 2007. 247.00 (978-0-9786090-8-5(5)) Learn Craz Inc.

Learning Logic Resource CD-ROM Tutorial, Version 1. 5 for Concise Introduction to Logic. 7th ed. (C). 2001. audio compact disk 47.95 (978-0-534-52037-3(5)) Pub: Wadsworth Pub. Dist(s): CENGAGE Learn

Learning Lordship Series. Elbert Willis. 4 cass. 13.00 Fill the Gap.

Learning Mechanical Desktop 2004 a Process-Based Approach: Teaching Package. Thomas Short & Anthony Dudek. (gr. 9-13). tchr. ed. 34.00 (978-1-59070-309-0(X)) Goodheart.

***Learning My Name.** Pete Gall. (Running Time: 4 hrs. 11 mins. 0 sec.). (ENG.). 2009. 14.99 (978-0-310-30281-0(1)) Zondervan.

Learning Our Past Life Lessons. Bettye B. Binder. Contrib. by Mary Lynn Cullen. 6 cass. (Running Time: 6 hrs.). 1996. 19.95 (978-1-879005-13-6(1)) Reincarnation Bks.
Lecture, questions & answers on multi-dimensionality.

Learning Potential. rev. ed. Sydney Banks. 2006. (978-1-55105-509-1(0)) Lone Pine Publ CAN.

Learning Power. Eldon Taylor. 2 cass. 29.95 (978-1-55978-745-1(7), 4410) Progress Aware Res.

Learning Practical Tibetan. Andrew Bloomfield & Yanki Tshering. 2 cass. (Running Time: 3 hrs.). Orig. Title: The Tibetan Phrasebook. (TIB.). (gr. 10-12). 1991. pap. bk. 55.00 (978-0-88432-738-7(8), AFTB10) J Norton Pubs.
Easy & clear phonetic system & a simple yet complete grammar. Each chapter begins with a vocabulary list & general information about Tibetan customs & etiquette. The phrases & dialogs of each chapter are recorded by native speakers.

Learning Programming Using Visual Basic.NET with Student CD. William E. Burrows. 2002. bk. 78.50 (978-0-07-285619-4(X)) McGraw-Hill Osborne.

Learning Revolution Audiocassette: How to Learn Anything at Least Five Times Faster, Better, Easier. Gordon Dryden & Jeannette Vos. Read by Gordon Dryden & Jeanette Vos. 8 cass. (Running Time: 12 hrs.). 1996. 89.95 (978-1-880396-46-9(7), SP9646-7) Jalmar Pr.
A life-long learning program for the world's finest computer: your amazing brain.

Learning Skills. unabr. ed. Marianne L. McManus. 3 cass. 1985. 35.00 J Norton Pubs.
Learning skills for successful study.

Learning Solitary Prayer. Jose Hobday. 1 cass. (Running Time: 34 min.). 1988. 7.95 (AA0170) Credence Commun.
Emphasizes the need for stillness, solitude & self-discovery & offers five ways to improve your prayer.

Learning Songs. Created by Publications International Staff. (Take-along Songs Ser.). (J). (ps). 2007. bds. 9.98 (978-1-4127-7437-6(3)) Pubns Intl Ltd.

Learning Spanish Like Crazy Light. Learning Like Crazy. (ENG.). 2007. 41.95 (978-0-9786090-2-3(6)) Learn Craz Inc.

Learning Spanish Like Crazy Super Light. Learning Like Crazy. (ENG.). 2007. 13.97 (978-0-9786090-3-0(4)) Learn Craz Inc.

Learning Spanish Like Crazy, Vol. 1 Vol. 1: Spoken Spanish Volume 1. Scripts. Learning Like Crazy. 15 CDs. 2007. 197.00 (978-0-9766661-0-3(3)) Learn Craz Inc.

Learning Styles, Teaching Styles. 1 cass. (Running Time: 30 min.). 9.95 (D0330B090, HarperThor) HarpC GBR.

Learning System PN 4.0, Vol. 4. Patricia A. Hoefler. 2004. spiral bd. (978-1-56533-330-7(6)) MEDS Pubng.

Learning Tabla with Alla Rakha. Jeffrey M. Feldman & Alla Rakha. 1 cass. 1984. spiral bd. (978-0-9643694-0-5(0)) Digitala.

Learning Tabla with Alla Rakha. Contrib. by Alla Rakha. 1 cass. 1984. 5.95 (978-0-9643694-4-3(3)) Digitala.

Learning the Alphabet Can Be Easy A-Z. Michael Vassar. 1 cass. (Running Time: 26 min.). 2003. 10.95 (978-0-9741043-7-9(X), 02) Mike Mike dist.

Learning the Art of Relaxation. Norman J. Caldwell. Read by Norman J. Caldwell. Ed. by Achieve Now Institute Staff. 1 cass. (Running Time: 20 min.). (Better Health Ser.). 1988. 9.97 (978-1-56273-048-2(7)) My Mothers Pub.
Yes, you can relax at will - faster & easier than ever before! You learn how to control your mind - your body follows!.

Learning the Art of Relaxation: Relax at Will - Faster & Easier Than Ever Before. 1988. 14.95 (978-1-56273-003-1(7)) My Mothers Pub.

Learning the Basics of NT Greek: Greek Vocabulary Cassettes with Syllabus, Set. Spiros Zodhiates. 8 vols. (Greek Study Courses Ser.). 2004. ring bd. 39.99 (978-0-89957-400-4(9)) AMG Pubs.

Learning the Human Game. Alan Watts. 3 CDs. 2004. audio compact disk 24.95 (978-1-59179-266-6(5), AB00130D) Sounds True.

Learning the Language of Birds. Jon Young. Read by Jon Young. 1 cass. (Running Time: 90 min.). (Seeing Through Native Eyes Ser.: Vol. 6). (ENG.). 1997. 12.95 (978-1-57994-003-4(X), A1106) Owlink.
How to hear birds, what they mean, how they can raise our spirits, how to disarm the forest alarm system & enter nature as a welcomed guest.

***Learning the R. O. P. E. S. for Improved Executive Function: Companion CD.** Patricia Schetter. (ENG.). 2008. audio compact disk 10.00 (978-0-9761517-7-7(4)) ABTA Pubns.

Learning the Sitar. David Courtney & Srinivas Koumounduri. (ENG.). 2009. lib. bdg. 24.99 (978-0-7866-7061-1(4)) Mel Bay.

Learning the Tabla, Volume 2. David Courtney. (ENG.). 2009. lib. bdg. 22.99 (978-0-7866-7367-4(2)) Mel Bay.

Learning the Ways of Prayer. Fern Halverson. 1 cass. 1997. 24.00 (978-1-57399-038-7(8)) Mac Hammond.
Teaching on prayer.

Learning the 17 Indisputable Laws of Teamwork. John C. Maxwell. 2001. bk. (978-0-9713226-0-8(0)) Giant Impact.

Learning Through Literature. 2004. pap. bk. 32.75 (978-1-55592-528-4(6)) Weston Woods.

Learning Through Literature: Amazing Grace. (Learning Through Literature Ser.). 2004. pap. bk. 32.75 (978-1-55592-527-7(8)) Weston Woods.

Learning Through Literature: Mufaro's Beautiful Daughters. (Learning Through Literature Ser.). 2004. pap. bk. 32.75 (978-1-55592-525-3(1)) Weston Woods.

Learning Through Literature: Officier Buckle & Gloria. (Learning Through Literature Ser.). 2004. pap. bk. 32.75 (978-1-55592-526-0(X)) Weston Woods.

Learning Through Literature: Paperboy. (Learning Through Literature Ser.). 2004. pap. bk. 32.75 (978-1-55592-524-6(3)) Weston Woods.

Learning to Accept His Verdict. Swami Amar Jyoti. 2 cass. 1982. 12.95 (C-36) Truth Consciousness.
Life, death & lamentation, accepting His verdict in total resignation. The key to meditation. Guru's promise.

Learning to Avoid Unintended Consequences. Leonard A. Renier. Narrated by Stanton Davis. (ENG.). 2007. audio compact disk 24.95 (978-1-60031-014-0(1)) Spoken Books.

Learning to Be You: It's an Inside Job. abr. ed. Brenda Ehrler. 2 vols. (Running Time: 180 min.). 1999. 15.95 (978-0-9668219-1-8(2)) Just Be Pubg.

Learning to Cope with Sight Loss (Audio CD Edition) Six Weeks at a VA Blind Rehabilitation Center. McGee William L. (ENG.). 2010. 12.95 (978-0-9701678-3-5(0)) BMC CA.

***Learning to Die in Miami: Confessions of a Refugee Boy.** unabr. ed. Carlos Eire. (Running Time: 9 hrs. 0 mins. 0 sec.). 2010. 24.99 (978-1-4001-6951-1(8)); 15.99 (978-1-4001-8951-9(9)) Tantor Media.

***Learning to Die in Miami: Confessions of a Refugee Boy.** unabr. ed. Carlos Eire. Narrated by Robert Fass. (Running Time: 9 hrs. 0 mins. 0 sec.). 2010. audio compact disk 34.99 (978-1-4001-1951-6(0)) Pub: Tantor Media. Dist(s): IngramPubServ

***Learning to Die in Miami (Library Edition) Confessions of a Refugee Boy.** unabr. ed. Carlos Eire. (Running Time: 9 hrs. 0 mins.). 2010. 34.99 (978-1-4001-9951-8(4)); audio compact disk 83.99 (978-1-4001-4951-3(7)) Pub: Tantor Media. Dist(s): IngramPubServ

Learning to Do What Jesus Did: How to Pray for Physical, Emotional & Spiritual Healing. Wholeness Ministries Staff. 1999. bk. 39.99 (978-1-57472-232-1(8)) Archer Ellison.

Learning to Fall, Desire, Snow & Skeletons. Short Stories. Ann Beattie. Read by Ann Beattie. 1 cass. (Running Time: 58 min.). 1987. 13.95 (978-1-55644-177-6(0), 7021) Am Audio Prose.
Beattie reads short stories from her collections The Burning House & Where You'll Find Me.

Learning to Heal: Healing as a Way of Life. Gary Arnold. (ENG.). 2003. audio compact disk 24.99 (978-1-57867 005-5(5)) Pub: Windhorse Corp. Dist(s): New Leaf Dist

Learning to Know the Dweller in the Fl[illegible] [illegible]structed by Manly P. Hall. 8.95 (978-0-89314-161-5(5), C831023) Philos [illegible]es.

***Learning to Lead: A Workbook on Becoming a Leader.** unabr. ed. Warren Bennis & Joan Goldsmith. Read by Walter Dixon. (Running Time: 5 hrs.). (ENG.). 2010. 27.98 (978-1-59659-679-5(1), GildAudio) Pub: Gildan Media. Dist(s): HachBkGrp

Learning to Learn: Maximizing Your Performance Potential. D. Trinidad Hunt. Read by D. Trinidad Hunt. 2 cass. (Running Time: 1 hr. 40 min.). (Learning Enhancement Cassette Ser.). 1992. 12.95 set. (978-1-881904-01-4(6)) Elan Ent HI.
Centering & Present Field Awareness techniques. Music (original) designed to enhance learning. For use when studying - reading - writing.

Learning to Learn English: A Course in Learner Training. Gail Ellis & Barbara Sinclair. 1 cass. (Running Time: hrs. mins.). (ENG., 1989. 24.00 (978-0-521-32876-0(4)) Cambridge U Pr.

***Learning to Learn English Audio CD: A Course in Learner Training.** Gail Ellis & Barbara Sinclair. (Running Time: 52 mins.). (ENG.). 2010. audio compact disk 23.00 (978-0-521-18688-9(9)) Cambridge U Pr.

Learning to Like Myself. Charles Beckert. 1 cass. 2004. 3.95 (978-1-57734-371-4(9), 34441093) Covenant Comms.

Learning to Listen in English. Virgina Nelson. 4 cass. tchr. ed., suppl. ed., wbk. ed. 44.95 Midwest European Pubns.
Takes beginning students through the intermediate level without need for supplement.

Learning to Live from the Psalms. Warren W. Wiersbe. Read by Warren W. Wiersbe. 11 cass. (Running Time: 16 hrs. 30 min.). 1988. 42.95 (978-0-8474-2325-5(5)) Back to Bible.
Focuses on Psalms 1-33.

Learning to Live in Tune with Jesus. Read by Mother Basilea Schlink. 1 cass. (Running Time: 30 min.). 1985. (0267) Evang Sisterhood Mary.

Learning to Live Without Violence: A Worktape for Men. abr. ed. Daniel J. Sonkin & Michael Durphy. Read by Adam Gottstein. 2 cass. (Running Time: 1 hr. 55 min.). 1992. 15.95 (978-0-912078-92-2(8)) Volcano Pr.
An adaptation of the book "Learning to Live Without Violence," which may be used alone or in conjunction with the book, to help batterers change their behavior.

Learning to Love. Eknath Easwaran. 1 cass. (Running Time: 57 min.). 1990. 7.95 (978-1-58638-557-6(7), LTL) Nilgiri Pr.
How to enlarge the circle of our love. Includes stories: Buddha & the Tigress; William Tell; St. Teresa of Avila.

***Learning to Love.** unabr. ed. Stephanie Perry Moore. Narrated by Robin Miles. (Running Time: 4 hrs. 30 mins. 0 sec.). (Yasmin Peace Ser.). (ENG.). 2010. audio compact disk 18.98 (978-1-61045-080-5(9), christaudio) christianaud.

Learning to Love Again. unabr. collector's ed. Mel Krantzler. Read by Paul Shay. 8 cass. (Running Time: 8 hrs.). 1986. 48.00 (978-0-7366-0585-4(1), 1553) Books on Tape.
This gives clear guidelines & challenging steps that lead from loneliness to love. The Remembered Pain Stage, absorbing a blow from the past; The Questing Experimental Stage, surveying the possibilities; The Selective-Distancing Stage, a cautious step forward; & The Creative-Commitment Stage, where enduring love begins.

Learning to Operate in the Kingdom of God System. Creflo A. Dollar. 2006. 8.00 (978-1-59944-063-7(6)); audio compact disk 11.00 (978-1-59944-064-4(4)) Creflo Dollar.

Learning to Read Music. unabr. ed. Incentive Learning Systems Staff. 1 cass. pap. bk. 14.95 (978-0-88432-239-9(4), S17065) J Norton Pubs.
Covers all the basics of reading notes, staff, time-signatures, sharps & flats, repeat signs, etc.

Learning to Read Through Music, Games & Reading. Ursula O. Ronnholm. Ed. by Paul F. Ronnholm. Tr. by Miguel Montero. 1985. bk. (978-0-318-61899-9(0)) Two Way Bilingual.

Learning to Relax. Arnold A. Lazarus. 1 cass. (Running Time: 37 min.). 9.95 (C015) A Ellis Institute.
Useful for people who wish to reduce anxiety & tension, as well as for the professional.

Learning to Relax. Arnold A. Lazarus. 1 cass. (Running Time: 37 min.). 9.95 (C015) Inst Rational-Emotive.
Shows you how to relax quickly & easily. Useful for people who wish to reduce anxiety & tension, as well as for the professional.

Learning to Say No. Shad Helmstetter. 1 cass. (Self-Talk Cassettes Ser.). 10.95 (978-0-937065-28-0(5)) Grindle Pr.

Learning to Speak English: Punjabi-Program. (PAN.). 2004. audio compact disk 44.00 (978-1-57451-026-3(6)) CLL Cupertino.

Learning to Speak English 1: Punjabi-Program. (PAN.). 49.95 (978-1-57451-023-2(1)) CLL Cupertino.

Learning to Speak English 1: Urdu-Program. (URD.). 49.95 (978-1-57451-076-8(2)); audio compact disk 44.00 (978-1-57451-078-2(9)) CLL Cupertino.

Learning to Speak English 2: Punjabi-Program. (PAN.). 49.95 (978-1-57451-025-6(8)) CLL Cupertino.

Learning to Speak English 2: Urdu-Program. (URD.). 49.95 (978-1-57451-077-5(0)); audio compact disk 44.00 (978-1-57451-079-9(7)) CLL Cupertino.

Learning to Speak English No. 2: Punjabi-Program. (PAN.). audio compact disk 44.00 (978-1-57451-027-0(4)) CLL Cupertino.

Learning to Speak English Program One: Armenian. 4 cass. (Running Time: 2 hrs. 30 mins.). (ARM.). 49.95 (978-0-929208-20-6(X)) CLL Cupertino.
Provides practice in 90% of our most commonly used words. All directions and practice sentences are spoken in one of 27 languages as well as English. The content is the same in all languages.

Learning to Speak English Program One: Armenian. (AMH.). 2002. audio compact disk 44.00 (978-1-57451-151-2(3)) CLL Cupertino.
Provides practice in 90% of our most community used words. All directions and practice sentences are spoken in one of 27 languages as well as English. The content is the same in all languages.

Learning to Speak English Program One: Portuguese. Read by Barbara Sullivan. 4 cass. (Running Time: 2 hrs. 30 mins.). (POR.). 49.95 (978-0-929208-16-9(1), LBPO28) CLL Cupertino.
Provides practice in 90% of our most commonly used words. All directions and practice sentences are spoken in one of 27 languages as well as English. The content is the same in all languages.

Learning to Speak English Program One: Portuguese. Barbara Sullivan. 2 CDs. (Running Time: 1 hr. 45 mins.). (POR.). 2002. audio compact disk 44.00 (978-1-57451-066-9(5)) CLL Cupertino.

Learning to Speak English Program One: Smoali. Barbara Sullivan. 2 CDs. (Running Time: 1 hr. 45 mins.). (SOM.). 2002. audio compact disk 44.00 (978-1-57451-069-0(X)) CLL Cupertino.

Learning to Speak English Program One: Somali. Barbara Sullivan. 4 cass. (Running Time: 2 hrs. 30 mins.). (SOM.). 2002. 49.95 (978-1-57451-019-5(3)) CLL Cupertino.

Learning to Speak English Program Two: Hmong. Barbara Sullivan. 2 CDs. (Running Time: 1 hr. 45 mins.). 2002. audio compact disk 44.00 (978-1-57451-108-6(4)) CLL Cupertino.

Learning to Speak English Program Two: Indonesian. Barbara Sullivan. 2 CDs. (Running Time: 1 hr. 45 mins.). (IND.). 2002. audio compact disk 44.00 (978-1-57451-109-3(2)) CLL Cupertino.

Learning to Speak English Program Two: Spanish. Read by Barbara Sullivan. 4 cass. (Running Time: 2 hrs. 45 mins.). (SPA.). bk. 49.95 (978-0-929208-25-1(0), 2LBS35) CLL Cupertino.
Features spoken translations by native speakers. The translated sentence is spoken in English, followed by a pause so the learner may practice.

Learning to Speak English Program Two: Spanish. Barbara Sullivan. 2 CDs. (Running Time: 1 hr. 45 mins.). (SPA.). 2002. audio compact disk 44.00 (978-1-57451-119-2(X)) CLL Cupertino.
Provides practice in 90% of our most commonly used words. All directions and practice sentences are spoken in one of 27 languages as well as English. The content is the same in all languages.

Learning to Speak English from Russian, Prog. 1. unabr. ed. Barbara Sullivan. Read by Barbara Sullivan. 4 cass. (Running Time: 2 hrs. 30 min.). (ENG & RUS.). 1990. pap. bk. 49.95 libr. ed. CLL Cupertino.
Provides independent practice of sentences in English for learners ages 8-adult. Library Edition includes paper back. Classroom Edition includes flashcards, worksheets & tests as well as book. Each sentence is preceded by a spoken translation in Russian.

Learning to Speak English from Russian, Prog. 2. unabr. ed. Barbara Sullivan. Read by Barbara Sullivan. 4 cass. (Running Time: 2 hrs. 30 min.). (ENG & RUS.). 1990. pap. bk. 49.95 libr. ed. CLL Cupertino.
Provides independent practice of sentences in English for learners ages 11-adult. Library Edition includes paper back. Classroom Edition includes flashcards, worksheets & tests as well as book. Each sentence is preceded by a spoken translation in Russian.

Learning to Speak English I - Arabic, Class edition. Barbara Sullivan. Read by Barbara Sullivan. 4 cass. (Running Time: 2 hrs. 30 min.). (J). (gr. 3 up). 1986. pap. bk. 49.95 (A22) CLL Cupertino.
Provides independent practice of sentences in english for ages 8-adult. Each sentence is preceded by a translation in Arabic.

Learning to Speak English I - Cambodian (Khmer) Barbara Sullivan. Read by Barbara Sullivan. 4 cass. (Running Time: 2 hrs. 30 min.). (J). (gr. 3 up). 1986. pap. bk. 49.95 classroom ed., incl. flashcards, wksheets & tests. (CM19) CLL Cupertino.
Provides independent practice of sentences in English for ages 8-adult. Each sentence is preceded by a translation in Cambodian.

Learning to Speak English I - Mandarin. Barbara Sullivan. Read by Barbara Sullivan. 4 cass. (Running Time: 2 hrs. 30 min.). (J). (gr. 3 up). 1986. pap. bk. 49.95 classroom ed., incl. flashcards, wksheets & tests. (M13) CLL Cupertino.
Provides independent practice of sentences in English for ages 8-adult. Each sentence is preceded by a translation in Mandarin.

Learning to Speak English I - Spanish. Barbara Sullivan. Read by Barbara Sullivan. 4 cass. (Running Time: 2 hrs. 30 min.). (J). (gr. 3 up). 1986. pap. bk. 49.95 classroom ed. incl. flashcards, wksheets& tests. (S16) CLL Cupertino.
Provides independent practice of sentences in English for age 8-adult. Each sentence is preceded by a translation in Spanish.

Learning to Speak English I - Tagalog (Filipino) Barbara Sullivan. Read by Barbara Sullivan. 4 cass. (Running Time: 2 hrs. 30 min.). (J). (gr. 3 up). pap. bk. 49.95 classroom ed., incl. flashcards, wksheets & tests. (T15) CLL Cupertino.
Provides independent practice of sentences in English for ages 8-adult. Each sentence is preceded by a translation in Tagalog.

Learning to Speak English I - Thai. Barbara Sullivan. Read by Barbara Sullivan. 4 cass. (Running Time: 2 hrs. 30 min.). (J). (gr. 3 up). 1986. pap. bk. 49.95 classroom ed., incl. flashcards, wksheets & tests. (TH23) CLL Cupertino.
Provides independent practice of sentences in English for ages 8-adult. Each sentence is preceded by a translation in Thai.

Learning to Speak English I - Vietnamese. Barbara Sullivan. Read by Barbara Sullivan. 4 cass. (Running Time: 2 hrs. 30 min.). (J). (gr. 3 up). 1986. pap. bk. 49.95 classroom ed., incl. flashcards, wksheets & tests. (V12) CLL Cupertino.
Provides independent practice of sentences in English for ages 8-adult. Each sentence is preceded by a translation in Vietnamese.

Learning to Speak English Korean, Program 1. Barbara Sullivan. Read by Barbara Sullivan. 4 cass. (Running Time: 2 hrs. 30 min.). (J). (gr. 3 up). 1986. pap. bk. 49.95 classrooom ed., incl. flashcards, wksheets & tests. (K11) CLL Cupertino.
Provides independent practice for sentences in English for ages 8-adult. Each sentence is preceded by a translation in Korean.

Learning to Speak English, Program One: Amharic. Barbara Sullivan. 4 cass. (Running Time: 2 hrs. 30 mins.). (AMH.). 2002. 49.95 (978-1-57451-021-8(5)) CLL Cupertino.
Provides practice in 90% of our most commonly used words. All directions and practice sentences are spoken in one of 27 languages as well as English. The content is the same in all languages.

Learning to Speak English, Program One: Arabic. 10 CDs. (Running Time: 15 hrs.). (ARA.). 2002. audio compact disk 44.00 (978-1-57451-074-4(6)) CLL Cupertino.
Provides practice in 90% of our most community used words. All directions and practice sentences are spoken in one of 27 languages as well as English. The content is the same in all languages.

Learning to Speak English, Program One: Arabic. Barbara Sullivan. Read by Barbara Sullivan. 4 cass. (Running Time: 2 hrs. 30 min.). (ARA.). (gr. 3-12). 1986. pap. bk. 49.95 (978-0-929208-06-0(4), LBA22) CLL Cupertino.
Provides independent practice of sentences in english for ages 8-adult. Each sentence is preceded by a translation in Arabic.

Learning to Speak English, Program One: Armenian. Barbara Sullivan. 10 CDs. (Running Time: 15 hrs.). (ARM.). 2002. audio compact disk 44.00 (978-1-57451-024-9(X)) CLL Cupertino.
Provides practice in 90% of our most community used words. All directions and practice sentences are spoken in one of 27 languages as well as English. The content is the same in all languages.

Learning to Speak English, Program One: Cambodian. Barbara Sullivan. Read by Barbara Sullivan. 4 cass., Library ed. (Running Time: 2 hrs. 30 min.). (CAM.). (gr. 3 up). 1986. pap. bk. 49.95 (978-0-929208-05-3(6), LBCM19) CLL Cupertino.
Provides independent practice of sentences in English for ages 8-adult. Each sentence is preceded by a translation in Cambodian.

Learning to Speak English, Program One: Cambodian. Barbara Sullivan. 10 CDs. (Running Time: 15 hrs.). (CAM.). 2002. audio compact disk 44.00 (978-1-57451-050-8(9)) CLL Cupertino.
Provides practice in 90% of our most community used words. All directions and practice sentences are spoken in one of 27 languages as well as English. The content is the same in all languages.

Learning to Speak English, Program One: Cantonese. Barbara Sullivan. Read by Barbara Sullivan. 4 cass. (Running Time: 2 hrs. 30 min.). (J). (gr. 3 up). 1986. pap. bk. 49.95 classroom ed., incl. flashcards, wksheets & tests. (C14) CLL Cupertino.
Provides independent practice of sentence in English for ages 8-adult. Each sentence is preceded by a translation in Cantonese.

Learning to Speak English, Program One: Cantonese. Barbara Sullivan. Read by Barbara Sullivan. 4 cass., Library ed. (Running Time: 2 hrs. 30 min.). (gr. 3 up). 1986. pap. bk. 49.95 (978-0-929208-04-6(8), LBC14) CLL Cupertino.

Learning to Speak English, Program One: Cantonese. Barbara Sullivan. 10 CDs. (Running Time: 15 hrs.). 2002. audio compact disk 44.00 (978-1-57451-051-5(7)) CLL Cupertino.

Learning to Speak English, Program One: Farsi. Read by Barbara Sullivan. 4 cass. (Running Time: 2 hrs. 30 mins.). 49.95 (978-0-929208-15-2(3), LBFA27) CLL Cupertino.
Provides practice in 90% of our most commonly used words. All directions and practice sentences are spoken in one of 27 languages as well as English. The content is the same in all languages.

Learning to Speak English, Program One: Farsi. Barbara Sullivan. 10 CDs. (Running Time: 15 hrs.). 2002. audio compact disk 44.00 (978-1-57451-052-2(5)) CLL Cupertino.
Provides practice in 90% of our most community used words. All directions and practice sentences are spoken in one of 27 languages as well as English. The content is the same in all languages.

Learning to Speak English, Program One: French. Barbara Sullivan. Read by Barbara Sullivan. 4 cass. (Running Time: 2 hrs. 30 min.). (J). (gr. 3 up). 1986. pap. bk. 49.95 classroom ed., incl. flashcards, wksheets & tests. (F24) CLL Cupertino.
Provides independent practice of sentences in English for ages 8-adult. Each sentence is preceded by a translation in French.

Learning to Speak English, Program One: French. Barbara Sullivan. Read by Barbara Sullivan. 4 cass., Library ed. (Running Time: 2 hrs. 30 min.). (FRE.). (gr. 3 up). 1986. pap. bk. 49.95 (978-0-929208-14-5(5), LBF24) CLL Cupertino.

Learning to Speak English, Program One: French. Barbara Sullivan. (FRE.). 2002. audio compact disk 44.00 (978-1-57451-053-9(3)) CLL Cupertino.
Provides practice in 90% of our most commonly used words. All directions and practice sentences are spoken in one of 27 languages as well as English. The content is the same in all languages.

Learning to Speak English, Program One: Hebrew. Barbara Sullivan. 2 CDs. (Running Time: 1 hr. 45 mins.). (HEB.). 2002. audio compact disk 44.00 (978-1-57451-055-3(X)) CLL Cupertino.

Learning to Speak English, Program One: Hindi. Barbara Sullivan. Read by Barbara Sullivan. 4 cass. (Running Time: 2 hrs. 30 min.). (J). (gr. 3 up). 1986. pap. bk. 49.95 classroom ed., incl. flashcards, wksheets & tests. (H21) CLL Cupertino.
Provides independent practice of sentences in English for ages 8-adult. Each sentence is preceded by a translation in Hindi.

Learning to Speak English, Program One: Hindi. Barbara Sullivan. Read by Barbara Sullivan. 4 cass., Library ed. (Running Time: 2 hrs. 30 min.). (HIN.). (gr. 3 up). 1986. pap. bk. 49.95 (978-0-929208-12-1(9), LBH21) CLL Cupertino.

Learning to Speak English, Program One: Hindi. Barbara Sullivan. 2 CDs. (Running Time: 1 hr. 45 mins.). (HIN.). 2002. audio compact disk 44.00 (978-1-57451-056-0(8)) CLL Cupertino.

Learning to Speak English, Program One: Hmong. 4 cass. (Running Time: 2 hrs. 30 mins.). vinyl bd. 49.95 (978-0-929208-21-3(8), HM33) CLL Cupertino.
Provides practice in 90% of our most commonly used words. All directions and practice sentences are spoken in one of 27 languages as well as English. The content is the same in all languages.

Learning to Speak English, Program One: Ilocano. Read by Barbara Sullivan. 4 cass. (Running Time: 2 hrs. 30 mins.). (ILO.). bk. 49.95 (978-0-929208-11-4(0), LBI18) CLL Cupertino.

Learning to Speak English, Program One: Ilocano. Barbara Sullivan. 2 CDs. (Running Time: 1 hr. 45 mins.). (ILO.). 2002. audio compact disk 44.00 (978-1-57451-058-4(4)) CLL Cupertino.

Learning to Speak English, Program One: Indonesian. 4 cass. (Running Time: 2 hrs. 30 mins.). (IND.). 1996. 49.95 (978-1-57451-003-4(7), IN36) CLL Cupertino.

Learning to Speak English, Program One: Indonesian. 2 cass. (Running Time: 80 min.). (Language - Thirty Library). bk. 16.95 set in vinyl album. Moonbeam Pubns.
Using the proven method based on the famous U.S. Military accelerated language learning program, Language/30 courses stress conversationally useful words & phrases.

Learning to Speak English, Program One: Indonesian. Barbara Sullivan. 2 CDs. (Running Time: 1 hr. 45 mins.). (IND.). 2002. audio compact disk 44.00 (978-1-57451-059-1(2)) CLL Cupertino.
Provides practice in 90% of our most commonly used words. All directions and practice sentences are spoken in one of 27 languages as well as English. The content is the same in all languages.

Learning to Speak English, Program One: Italian. Barbara Sullivan. 2 CDs. (Running Time: 1 hr. 45 mins.). (ITA.). 2002. audio compact disk 44.00 (978-1-57451-060-7(6)) CLL Cupertino.

Learning to Speak English, Program One: Italian. unabr. ed. Barbara Sullivan. Read by Barbara Sullivan. 4 cass. (Running Time: 2 hrs. 30 min.). (ENG & ITA.). 1990. bk. & stu. ed. 49.95 (978-0-929208-19-0(6)) CLL Cupertino.
Provides independent practice of sentences in English for learners ages 8-adult. Library Edition includes paper back. Classroom Edition includes flashcards, worksheets & tests as well as book. Each sentence is preceded by a spoken translation in Italian.

Learning to Speak English, Program One: Italian, Prog. 1. unabr. ed. Barbara Sullivan. Read by Barbara Sullivan. 4 cass. (Running Time: 2 hrs. 30 min.). (ENG & ITA.). 1990. pap. bk. 49.95 libr. ed. CLL Cupertino.

Learning to Speak English, Program One: Italian, Prog. 2. unabr. ed. Barbara Sullivan. Read by Barbara Sullivan. 4 cass. (Running Time: 2 hrs. 30 min.). (ENG & ITA.). 1990. pap. bk. 49.95 CLL Cupertino.
Provides independent practice of sentences in English for learners ages 11-adult. Library Edition includes paper back. Classroom Edition includes flashcards, worksheets & tests as well as book. Each sentence is preceded by a spoken translation in Italian.

Learning to Speak English, Program One: Japanese. Barbara Sullivan. Read by Barbara Sullivan. 4 cass. (Running Time: 2 hrs. 30 min.). (J). (gr. 3 up). 1986. pap. bk. 49.95 classroom ed., incl. flashcards, wksheets & tests. (J20) CLL Cupertino.
Provides independent practice of sentences in english for ages 8-adult. Each sentence is preceded by a translation in Japanese.

Learning to Speak English, Program One: Japanese. Barbara Sullivan. Read by Barbara Sullivan. 4 cass., Library ed. (Running Time: 2 hrs. 30 min.). (JPN.). (gr. 3 up). 1986. pap. bk. 49.95 (978-0-929208-08-4(0), LBJ20) CLL Cupertino.

Learning to Speak English, Program One: Japanese. Barbara Sullivan. 2 CDs1 . (Running Time: hr. 45 mins.). (JPN.). 2002. audio compact disk 44.00 (978-1-57451-061-4(4)) CLL Cupertino.
Provides practice in 90% of our most commonly used words. All directions and practice sentences are spoken in one of 27 languages as well as English. The content is the same in all languages.

Learning to Speak English, Program One: Korean. Barbara Sullivan. Read by Barbara Sullivan. 4 cass. (Running Time: 2 hrs. 30 min.). (KOR.). (gr. 3 up). 1986. vinyl bd. 49.95 library ed. (978-0-929208-01-5(3), LBK11) CLL Cupertino.
Provides independent practice for sentences in English for ages 8-adult. Each sentence is preceded by a translation in Korean.

Learning to Speak English, Program One: Korean. Barbara Sullivan. 2 CDs. (Running Time: 1 hr. 45 mins.). (KOR.). 2002. audio compact disk 44.00 (978-1-57451-062-1(2)) CLL Cupertino.
Provides practice in 90% of our most commonly used words. All directions and practice sentences are spoken in one of 27 languages as well as English. The content is the same in all languages.

Learning to Speak English, Program One: Laotian. Barbara Sullivan. Read by Barbara Sullivan. 4 cass. (Running Time: 2 hrs. 30 min.). (J). (gr. 3 up). 1986. pap. bk. 49.95 classroom ed. incl. flashcards, wksheets & tests. (B17) CLL Cupertino.
Provides independent practice of sentences in English for ages 8-adult. Each sentence is preceded by a translation in Laotian.

Learning to Speak English, Program One: Laotian. Barbara Sullivan. Read by Barbara Sullivan. 4 cass., Library ed. (Running Time: 2 hrs. 30 min.). (LAO.). (gr. 3 up). 1986. pap. bk. 49.95 (978-0-929208-07-7(2), LBL17) CLL Cupertino.

Learning to Speak English, Program One: Laotian. Barbara Sullivan. 2 CDs. (Running Time: 1 hr. 45 mins.). (LAO.). 2002. audio compact disk 44.00 (978-1-57451-063-8(0)) CLL Cupertino.
Provides practice in 90% of our most commonly used words. All directions and practice sentences are spoken in one of 27 languages as well as English. The content is the same in all languages.

Learning to Speak English, Program One: Mandarin. Barbara Sullivan. Read by Barbara Sullivan. 4 cass., Library ed. (Running Time: 2 hrs. 30 min.). (gr. 3 up). 1986. pap. bk. 49.95 (978-0-929208-03-9(X), LBM13) CLL Cupertino.
Provides independent practice of sentences in English for ages 8-adult. Each sentence is preceded by a translation in Mandarin.

Learning to Speak English, Program One: Mandarin. Barbara Sullivan. 2 CDs. (Running Time: 1 hr. 45 mins.). 2002. audio compact disk 44.00 (978-1-57451-064-5(9)) CLL Cupertino.
Provides practice in 90% of our most commonly used words. All directions and practice sentences are spoken in one of 27 languages as well as English. The content is the same in all languages.

Learning to Speak English, Program One: Polish. Barbara Sullivan. Read by Barbara Sullivan. 4 cass. (Running Time: 2 hrs. 30 min.). (J). (gr. 3 up). 1986. pap. bk. 49.95 classroom ed., incl. flashcards, wksheets & tests. (P25) CLL Cupertino.
Provides independent practice of sentences in English for ages 8-adult. Each sentence is preceded by a translation in Polish.

Learning to Speak English, Program One: Polish. Barbara Sullivan. Read by Barbara Sullivan. 4 cass., Library ed. (Running Time: 2 hrs. 30 min.). (POL.). (gr. 3 up). 1986. pap. bk. 49.95 (978-0-929208-09-1(9), LBP25) CLL Cupertino.

Learning to Speak English, Program One: Polish. Barbara Sullivan. 2 CDs. (Running Time: 1 hr. 45 mins.). (POL.). 2002. audio compact disk 44.00 (978-1-57451-065-2(7)) CLL Cupertino.
Provides practice in 90% of our most commonly used words. All directions and practice sentences are spoken in one of 27 languages as well as English. The content is the same in all languages.

Learning to Speak English, Program One: Russian. Barbara Sullivan. 2 CDs. (Running Time: 1 hr. 45 mins.). (RUS.). 2002. audio compact disk 44.00 (978-1-57451-067-6(3)) CLL Cupertino.

Learning to Speak English, Program One: Russian. unabr. ed. Barbara Sullivan. Read by Barbara Sullivan. 4 cass. (Running Time: 2 hrs. 30 min.). (ENG & RUS.). 1990. bk. & stu. ed. 49.95 (978-0-929208-18-3(8)) CLL Cupertino.
Provides independent practice of sentences in English for learners ages 8-adult. Library Edition includes paper back. Classroom Edition includes flashcards, worksheets & tests as well as book. Each sentence is preceded by a spoken translation in Russian.

Learning to Speak English, Program One: Serbo-Croatian. Barbara Sullivan. 4 cass. (Running Time: 2 hrs. 30 mins.). (SBC.). 49.95 (978-0-929208-22-0(6)) CLL Cupertino.
Provides practice in 90% of our most commonly used words. All directions and practice sentences are spoken in one of 27 languages as well as English. The content is the same in all languages.

Learning to Speak English, Program One: Serbo-Croatian. Barbara Sullivan. 2 CDs. (Running Time: 1 hr. 45 mins.). (SBC.). 2002. audio compact disk 44.00 (978-1-57451-068-3(1)) CLL Cupertino.

Learning to Speak English, Program One: Spanish. Barbara Sullivan. Read by Barbara Sullivan. 4 cass., Library ed. (Running Time: 2 hrs. 30 min.). (SPA.). (gr. 3 up). 1986. pap. bk. 49.95 (978-0-929208-00-8(5), LBS16) CLL Cupertino.
Provides independent practice of sentences in English for age 8-adult. Each sentence is preceded by a translation in Spanish.

Learning to Speak English, Program One: Spanish. Barbara Sullivan. 2 CDs. (Running Time: 1 hr. 45 mins.). (SPA.). 2002. audio compact disk 44.00 (978-1-57451-070-6(3)) CLL Cupertino.
Provides practice in 90% of our most commonly used words. All directions and practice sentences are spoken in one of 27 languages as well as English. The content is the same in all languages.

Learning to Speak English, Program One: Tagalog. Barbara Sullivan. Read by Barbara Sullivan. 4 cass., Library ed. (Running Time: 2 hrs. 30 min.). (TAG.). (gr. 3 up). pap. bk. 49.95 (978-0-929208-10-7(2), LBT15) CLL Cupertino.
Provides independent practice of sentences in English for ages 8-adult. Each sentence is preceded by a translation in Tagalog.

Learning to Speak English, Program One: Tagalog. Barbara Sullivan. 2 CDs. (Running Time: 1 hr. 45 mins.). (TAG.). 2002. audio compact disk 44.00 (978-1-57451-071-3(1)) CLL Cupertino.
Provides practice in 90% of our most commonly used words. All directions and practice sentences are spoken in one of 27 languages as well as English. The content is the same in all languages.

Learning to Speak English, Program One: Thai. Barbara Sullivan. Read by Barbara Sullivan. 4 cass., Library ed. (Running Time: 2 hrs. 30 min.). (THA.). (gr. 3 up). 1986. pap. bk. 49.95 (978-0-929208-13-8(7), LBTH23) CLL Cupertino.
Provides independent practice of sentences in English for ages 8-adult. Each sentence is preceded by a translation in Thai.

Learning to Speak English, Program One: Vietnamese. Barbara Sullivan. Read by Barbara Sullivan. 4 cass., Library ed. (Running Time: 2 hrs. 30 min.). (VIE.). (gr. 3 up). 1986. pap. bk. 49.95 (978-0-929208-02-2(1), LBV12) CLL Cupertino.
Provides independent practice of sentences in English for ages 8-adult. Each sentence is preceded by a translation in Vietnamese.

Learning to Speak English, Program One: Vietnamese. Barbara Sullivan. 2 CDs. (Running Time: 1 hr. 45 mins.). (VIE.). 2002. audio compact disk 44.00 (978-1-57451-073-7(8)) CLL Cupertino.
Provides practice in 90% of our most commonly used words. All directions and practice sentences are spoken in one of 27 languages as well as English. The content is the same in all languages.

Learning to Speak English, Program Two: Amharic. Barbara Sullivan. 4 cass. (Running Time: 2 hrs. 30 mins.). (AMH.). 2002. 49.95 (978-1-57451-022-5(3)) CLL Cupertino.

Learning to Speak English, Program Two: Arabic, Read by Barbara Sullivan. 4 cass. (Running Time: 4 hrs.). (ARA.). (gr. 5-12). bk. 49.95 (978-0-929208-31-2(5), 2LBA44) CLL Cupertino.
Features spoken translations by native speakers. The translated sentence is spoken in English, followed by a pause so the learner may practice.

Learning to Speak English, Program Two: Armenian. 4 cass. (Running Time: 2 hrs. 30 mins.). (ARM.). 49.95 (978-0-929208-44-2(7)) CLL Cupertino.
Provides practice in 90% of our most commonly used words. All directions and practice sentences are spoken in one of 27 languages as well as English. The content is the same in all languages.

Learning to Speak English, Program Two: Armenian. (AMH.). 2002. audio compact disk 44.00 (978-1-57451-152-9(1)); audio compact disk 44.00 (978-1-57451-100-0(9)) CLL Cupertino.
Provides practice in 90% of our most community used words. All directions and practice sentences are spoken in one of 27 languages as well as English. The content is the same in all languages.

Learning to Speak English, Program Two: Cambodian. Read by Barbara Sullivan. 4 cass., Library ed. (Running Time: 2 hrs. 30 mins.). (CAM.). bk. 49.95 (978-0-929208-30-5(7), 2LBCM41) CLL Cupertino.
Features spoken translations by native speakers. The translated sentence is spoken in English, followed by a pause fo the learner may practice.

Learning to Speak English, Program Two: Cambodian. Barbara Sullivan. 10 cass. (Running Time: 15 hrs.). (CAM.). 2002. audio compact disk 44.00 (978-1-57451-101-7(7)) CLL Cupertino.

Learning to Speak English, Program Two: Cantonese. Read by Barbara Sullivan. 4 cass. (Running Time: 2 hrs. 30 mins.). bk. 49.95 (978-0-929208-29-9(3), 2LBC38) CLL Cupertino.
Features spoken translations by native speakers. The translated sentence is then spoken in English, followed by a pause so the learner may practice.

Learning to Speak English, Program Two: Cantonese. Barbara Sullivan. 10 CDs. (Running Time: 15 hrs.). 2002. audio compact disk 44.00 (978-1-57451-102-4(5)) CLL Cupertino.
Provides practice in 90% of our most community used words. All directions and practice sentences are spoken in one of 27 languages as well as English. The content is the same in all languages.

Learning to Speak English, Program Two: Farsi. Barbara Sullivan. 10 CDs. (Running Time: 15 hrs.). 2002. audio compact disk 44.00 (978-1-57451-103-1(3)) CLL Cupertino.

Learning to Speak English, Program Two: French. Barbara Sullivan. 2 CDs. (Running Time: 1 hr. 45 mins.). (FRE.). 2002. audio compact disk 44.00 (978-1-57451-104-8(1)) CLL Cupertino.
Provides practice in 90% of our most commonly used words. All directions and practice sentences are spoken in one of 27 languages as well as English. The content is the same in all languages.

Learning to Speak English, Program Two: German. Barbara Sullivan. 2 CDs. (Running Time: 1 hr. 45 mins.). (GER.). 2002. audio compact disk 44.00 (978-1-57451-054-6(1)); audio compact disk 44.00 (978-1-57451-105-5(X)) CLL Cupertino.

Learning to Speak English, Program Two: German. unabr. ed. Barbara Sullivan. Read by Barbara Sullivan. 4 cass. (Running Time: 2 hrs. 30 min.). (ENG & GER.). 1990. bk. & stu. ed. 49.95 (978-0-929208-17-6(X)); bk. & stu. ed. 49.95 (978-0-929208-41-1(2)) CLL Cupertino.
Provides independent practice of sentences in English for learners ages 11-adult. Library Edition includes paper back. Classroom Edition includes flashcards, worksheets & tests as well as book. Each sentence is preceded by a spoken translation in German.

Learning to Speak English, Program Two: German, Prog. 1. unabr. ed. Barbara Sullivan. Read by Barbara Sullivan. 4 cass. (Running Time: 2 hrs. 30 min.). (ENG & GER.). 1990. pap. bk. 49.95 libr. ed. CLL Cupertino.
Provides independent practice of sentences in English for learners ages 8-adult. Library Edition includes paper back. Classroom Edition includes flashcards, worksheets & tests as well as book. Each sentence is preceded by a spoken translation in German.

Learning to Speak English, Program Two: German, Prog. 2. unabr. ed. Barbara Sullivan. Read by Barbara Sullivan. 4 cass. (Running Time: 2 hrs. 30 min.). (ENG & GER.). 1990. pap. bk. 49.95 libr. ed. CLL Cupertino.
Provides independent practice of sentences in English for learners ages 11-adult. Library Edition includes paper back. Classroom Edition includes flashcards, worksheets & tests as well as book. Each sentence is preceded by a spoken translation in German.

Learning to Speak English, Program Two: Hebrew. Barbara Sullivan. 2 CDs. (Running Time: 1 hr. 45 mins.). (HEB.). 2002. audio compact disk 44.00 (978-1-57451-106-2(8)) CLL Cupertino.
Provides practice in 90% of our most commonly used words. All directions and practice sentences are spoken in one of 27 languages as well as English. The content is the same in all languages.

Learning to Speak English, Program Two: Hindi. Barbara Sullivan. 2 CDs. (Running Time: 1 hr. 45 mins.). (HIN.). 2002. audio compact disk 44.00 (978-1-57451-107-9(6)) CLL Cupertino.

Learning to Speak English, Program Two: Hmong. 1 cass. 49.95 (978-0-929208-45-9(5)) CLL Cupertino.

Learning to Speak English, Program Two: Indonesian. 4 cass. (Running Time: 2 hrs. 30 mins.). (IND.). 1996. 49.95 (978-1-57451-004-1(5), IN58) CLL Cupertino.

Learning to Speak English, Program Two: Italian. Barbara Sullivan. 2 CDs. (Running Time: 1 hr. 45 mins.). (ITA.). 2002. audio compact disk 44.00 (978-1-57451-110-9(6)) CLL Cupertino.

Learning to Speak English, Program Two: Italian. unabr. ed. Barbara Sullivan. Read by Barbara Sullivan. 4 cass. (Running Time: 2 hrs. 30 min.). (ENG & ITA.). 1990. bk. & stu. ed. 49.95 (978-0-929208-43-5(9)) CLL Cupertino.
Provides independent practice of sentences in English for learners ages 11-adult. Library Edition includes paper back. Classroom Edition includes flashcards, worksheets & tests as well as book. Each sentence is preceded by a spoken translation in Italian.

Learning to Speak English, Program Two: Japanese. Read by Barbara Sullivan. 4 cass. (Running Time: 2 hrs. 30 mins.). (JPN.). bk. 49.95 (978-0-929208-33-6(1), 2LBJ43) CLL Cupertino.
Features spoken translations by native speakers. the translated sentence is spoken in English, followed by a pause so the learner may practice.

Learning to Speak English, Program Two: Japanese. Barbara Sullivan. 2 CDs. (Running Time: 1 hr. 45 mins.). (JPN.). 2002. audio compact disk 44.00 (978-1-57451-111-6(4)) CLL Cupertino.
Provides practice in 90% of our most commonly used words. All directions and practice sentences are spoken in one of 27 languages as well as English. The content is the same in all languages.

Learning to Speak English, Program Two: Korean. Read by Barbara Sullivan. 4 cass. (Running Time: 2 hrs. 30 mins.). (KOR.). bk. 49.95 (978-0-929208-26-8(9), 2LBK37) CLL Cupertino.
Features spoken translations by the native speakers. The translated sentence is spoken in English, followed by a pause so the learner may practice.

Learning to Speak English, Program Two: Korean. Barbara Sullivan. 2 CDs. (Running Time: 1 hr. 45 mins.). (KOR.). 2002. audio compact disk 44.00 (978-1-57451-112-3(2)) CLL Cupertino.
Provides practice in 90% of our most commonly used words. All directions and practice sentences are spoken in one of 27 languages as well as English. The content is the same in all languages.

Learning to Speak English, Program Two: Laotian. Read by Barbara Sullivan. 4 cass. (Running Time: 2 hrs. 30 mins.). (LAO.). bk. 49.95 (978-0-929208-32-9(3), 2LBL42) CLL Cupertino.
Features spoken by native speakers. The translated sentence is spoken in English, followed by a pause so the learner may practice.

Learning to Speak English, Program Two: Laotian. Barbara Sullivan. 2 CDs. (Running Time: 1 hr. 45 mins.). (LAO.). 2002. audio compact disk 44.00 (978-1-57451-113-0(0)) CLL Cupertino.
Provides practice in 90% of our most commonly used words. All directions and practice sentences are spoken in one of 27 languages as well as English. The content is the same in all languages.

Learning to Speak English, Program Two: Mandarin. Read by Barbara Sullivan. 4 cass. (Running Time: 2 hrs. 30 mins.). bk. 49.95 (978-0-929208-28-2(5), 2LBM39) CLL Cupertino.
Features spoken translations by native speakers. The translated sentence is spoken in English, followed by a pause so the learner may practice.

Learning to Speak English, Program Two: Mandarin. Barbara Sullivan. 2 CDs. (Running Time: 1 hr. 45 mins.). 2002. audio compact disk 44.00 (978-1-57451-114-7(9)) CLL Cupertino.
Provides practice in 90% of our most commonly used words. All directions and practice sentences are spoken in one of 27 languages as well as English. The content is the same in all languages.

Learning to Speak English, Program Two: Polish. Barbara Sullivan. 2 CDs. (Running Time: 1 hr. 45 mins.). 2002. audio compact disk 44.00 (978-1-57451-115-4(7)) CLL Cupertino.

Learning to Speak English, Program Two: Portuguese. Read by Barbara Sullivan. 4 cass. (Running Time: 2 hrs. 30 mins.). (POL.). bk. 49.95 (978-0-929208-34-3(X), 2LBP40) CLL Cupertino.
Features spoken translations by native speakers. The translated sentence is spoken in English, followed by a pause so the learner may prawctice.

Learning to Speak English, Program Two: Portuguese. Barbara Sullivan. 2 CDs. (Running Time: 1 hr. 45 mins.). (POR.). 2002. audio compact disk 44.00 (978-1-57451-116-1(5)) CLL Cupertino.
Provides practice in 90% of our most commonly used words. All directions and practice sentences are spoken in one of 27 languages as well as English. The content is the same in all languages.

Learning to Speak English. Program Two: Russian. Barbara Sullivan. 2 CDs. (Running Time: 1 hr. 45 mins.). (RUS.). 2002. audio compact disk 44.00 (978-1-57451-117-8(3)) CLL Cupertino.

Learning to Speak English. Program Two: Russian. unabr. ed. Barbara Sullivan. Read by Barbara Sullivan. 4 cass. (Running Time: 2 hrs. 30 min.). (ENG & RUS.). 1990. bk. & stu. ed. 49.95 (978-0-929208-42-8(0)) CLL Cupertino.
Provides independent practice of sentences in English for learners ages 11-adult. Library Edition includes paper back. Classroom Edition includes flashcards, worksheets & tests as well as book. Each sentence is preceded by a spoken translation in Russian.

Learning to Speak English, Program Two: Serbo-Croatian. 4 cass. (Running Time: 2 hrs. 30 mins.). (SBC.). 49.95 (978-0-929208-46-6(3)) CLL Cupertino.
Provides practice in 90% of our most commonly used words. All directions and practice sentences are spoken in one of 27 languages as well as English. The content is the same in all languages.

Learning to Speak English, Program Two: Serbo-Croatian. Barbara Sullivan. 2 CDs. (Running Time: 1 hr. 45 mins.). (SBC.). 2002. audio compact disk 44.00 (978-1-57451-118-5(1)) CLL Cupertino.

Learning to Speak English, Program Two: Somali. Barbara Sullivan. 4 cass. (Running Time: 2 hrs. 30 mins.). (SOM.). 2002. 49.95 (978-1-57451-020-1(7)); audio compact disk 44.00 (978-1-57451-123-9(8)) CLL Cupertino.

Learning to Speak English, Program Two: Tagalog. Barbara Sullivan. 2 CDs. (Running Time: 1 hr. 45 mins.). (TAG.). 2002. audio compact disk 44.00 (978-1-57451-120-8(3)); audio compact disk 44.00 (978-1-57451-072-0(X)) CLL Cupertino.

Learning to Speak English, Program Two: Thai. Barbara Sullivan. 2 CDs. (Running Time: 1 hr. 45 mins.). (THA.). 2002. audio compact disk 44.00 (978-1-57451-121-5(1)) CLL Cupertino.

Learning to Speak English, Program Two: Vietnamese. Read by Barbara Sullivan. 4 cass. (Running Time: 2 hrs. 30 mins.). (VIE.). bk. 49.95 (978-0-929208-27-5(7), 2LBV36) CLL Cupertino.
Features spoken translations by native speakers. The translated sentence is spoken in English, followed by a pause so the learner may practice.

Learning to Speak English, Program Two: Vietnamese. Barbara Sullivan. 2 CDs. (Running Time: 1 hr. 45 mins.). (VIE.). 2002. audio compact disk 44.00 (978-1-57451-122-2(X)) CLL Cupertino.
Provides practice in 90% of our most commonly used words. All directions and practice sentences are spoken in one of 27 languages as well as English. The content is the same in all languages.

Learning to Speak, Program One: Hmong. Barbara Sullivan. 2 CDs. (Running Time: 1 hr. 45 mins.). 2002. audio compact disk 44.00 (978-1-57451-057-7(6)) CLL Cupertino.

Learning to Trust God. 1 cass. (Running Time: 30 min.). 1985. (0266) Evang Sisterhood Mary.
Covers: The Right Perspective; Dangerous Busyness; What Should I Do When People Have Disappointed Me? "I Shall not Want".

Learning to Trust God: The Law of Miracles. Kriyananda, pseud. 1 cass. 9.95 (ST-61) Crystal Clarity.
Explains: Why miracles are not "miraculous"; what attitudes are important when asking God for help; specific ways to cultivate these attitudes; how God tests us.

Learning to Walk by Grace: A Study of Romans 6-11. 1998. 39.95 (978-1-57972-259-3(8)) Insight Living.

Learning to Walk with God: A Testimony of Faith & Joy. Dwight Hall. 1 cass. 1997. bk. 29.95 (978-1-883012-69-4(4), RP-3100) Remnant Pubns.

Learning to Write Fiction. unabr. ed. Eudora Welty. Read by Eudora Welty. 1 cass. (Running Time: 53 min.). 1961. 12.95 (23065) J Norton Pubs.
The famous writer discusses the ingredients necessary to creative & successful writing, such as a devotion to reading, self-reliance, & daring.

Learning with Circles & Sticks. Perf. by Hap Palmer. 1 cass. (J). 11.95 (EA 585C); lp 10.95 (EA 585) Kimbo Educ.
Stick Band - Magic Stick - Jump & Land - Tap Your Sticks - Makin' Letters & more.

Learning Without Accumulation. abr. ed. Jiddu Krishnamurti. 1 CD. (Running Time: 1 hr.). 2008. audio compact disk 16.95 (978-1-888004-59-5(2)) Pub: K Publications GBR. Dist(s): SCB Distributors
Life is relationship, without relationship there is no life, living. And, in one's relationship, there is a great deal of accumulated memory in that relationship between two people - the hurts, the nagging, the pleasures, the annoyances, the dominations and so on - you know what happens in a relationship.

Learning Your Way Through Chaos. Speeches. Perf. by Paula Underwood. 1 cass. (Running Time: 50 mins.). 2002. 14.00 (978-1-879678-18-7(7)) Tribe Two Pr.
Presented by Paula Underwood at The International Conference on Business and Consciousness, 1998.

Lease or Buy? How to Decide Your Next Car or Truck Deal. unabr. ed. Len Maylis. Read by Len Maylis. 1 cass. (Running Time: 52 min.). 1994. 12.95 Incl. folder. (978-0-9643610-9-6(4)) DriveTime Pub.
Talk radio format with questions from "callers" answered by host/author, who has an extensive background in writing lease programs for auto manufacturers & dealership personnel. Content is consumer oriented with tips on how to avoid leasing pitfalls & make a decision on leasing or purchasing a vehicle.

Least Likely Bride. Jane Feather. Narrated by Jenny Sterlin. 12 CDs. (Running Time: 14 hrs. 30 mins.). audio compact disk 116.00 (978-0-7887-9879-5(0)) Recorded Bks.

Least Likely Bride. unabr. ed. Jane Feather. Narrated by Jenny Sterlin. 10 cass. (Running Time: 14 hrs. 30 mins.). 2001. 88.00 (978-0-7887-4988-9(9), 96410E7) Recorded Bks.
Lady Olivia Granville is a lovely, headstrong scholar. Anthony Caxton is a pirate. When they meet on the high seas, their sparks of passion are as powerful as the wind.

Least of All (gideon) (Paws & Tales Ser.: No. 40). 2002. 3.99 (978-1-57972-498-6(1)); audio compact disk 5.99 (978-1-57972-499-3(X)) Insight Living.

Leather Funnel see Tales of the Supernatural

Leave a Candle Burning. unabr. ed. Lori Wick. Narrated by Barbara Rosenblat. (Tucker Mills Trilogy). (ENG.). (YA). 2006. 24.49 (978-1-60814-280-4(9)); audio compact disk 25.99 (978-1-59859-102-6(9)) Oasis Audio.

***Leave a Footprint - Change the Whole World.** Zondervan. (Running Time: 4 hrs. 46 mins. 29 sec.). (ENG.). (YA). 2010. 9.99 (978-0-310-86967-2(6)) Zondervan.

Leave a Little Bit Undone. unabr. ed. Perf. by Joe Black. Interview with Donna Lander. 1 cass., 1 CD. (Running Time: 43 min.). (ENG & HEB.). 1999. 9.95 (978-1-890161-36-1(5), SWP203C); audio compact disk 15.95 (978-1-890161-37-8(3), SWP203CD) Sounds Write.
Rabbi Black's first adult recording of 12 thought provoking original songs in English & Hebrew with lyrics based on biblical & liturgical texts.

Leave a Message for Willie. unabr. ed. Marcia Muller. Read by Bernadette Dunne. 7 cass. (Running Time: 7 hrs.). (Sharon McCone Mystery Ser.: No. 5). 1997. 56.00 (978-0-7366-3779-4(6), 4452) Books on Tape.
Sharon McCone is contracted to tail one Jerry Levin & her client is no angel. Willie Whelan, flea-market vendor & small time fence. It doesn't take her long to find her man. But his condition & location have her worried, he's got a bullet in the back of his head & he's lying in willie's garage. Sharon's client knows a bad thing when he sees it & goes on the lam. Still, McCone believes that Willie had nothing to do with this. So the race against time begins. She's got to stay one step ahead of the police if she's going to tag a ruthless killer & fee Willie.

Leave it to Beaver: Acts 18:1-3. Ed Young. (J). 1991. 4.95 (978-0-7417-1868-6(5), 868) Win Walk.

Leave It to Psmith. unabr. ed. Read by Frederick Davidson. (Running Time: 30600 sec.). 2008. audio compact disk & audio compact disk 70.00 (978-1-4332-3424-8(6)); audio compact disk & audio compact disk 29.95 (978-1-4332-3425-5(4)) Blckstn Audio.

Leave It to Psmith. unabr. ed. P. G. Wodehouse. Read by Frederick Davidson. 6 cass. (Running Time: 8 hrs. 30 mins.). 1999. 44.95 (978-0-7861-1524-2(6), 2374) Blckstn Audio.
In the guise of a well-known Canadian poet, Psmith is invited to Blandings Castle, & finds that being a convincing poet offers some special problems. The castle is overrun with odd characters & when a couple of real jewel

thieves appears on the scene, the situation becomes more complicated, till it explodes in a hilarious riot of flying flower pots.

Leave It to Psmith. unabr. ed. P. G. Wodehouse. Read by Frederick Davidson. 6 cass. 1999. 44.95 (FS9-50931) Highsmith.

Leave Me Alone, I'm Reading: Finding & Losing Myself in Books. unabr. ed. Maureen Corrigan. Read by Maureen Corrigan. 6 cass. (Running Time: 8 hrs.). 2006. 59.75 (978-1-4193-6260-6(7), 98199) Recorded Bks.
A book reviewer for The Washington Post and NPR's Fresh Air, Maureen Corrigan is obsessed with books - so much so that they caused her to delay marriage. This audiobook explores her obsession with all things literary. Corrigan expertly weaves together her own life story with the stories from the books she loves.

Leave the Grave Green. Deborah Crombie. Narrated by Christopher Kay. 7 cass. (Running Time: 9 hrs. 30 mins.). (Duncan Kincaid/Gemma James Novel Ser.). 63.00 (978-1-84197-252-7(5)); audio compact disk 82.00 (978-1-4025-1545-3(6)) Recorded Bks.

Leave the Grave Green. unabr. ed. Deborah Crombie. Read by Michael Deehy. 6 cass. (Running Time: 32880 sec.). (Duncan Kincaid/Gemma James Novel Ser.). 2005. 54.95 (978-0-7927-3555-7(2), CSL 792); audio compact disk 74.95 (978-0-7927-3556-4(0), SLD 792) AudioGO.

Leave Us Alone: Getting the Government's Hands off Our Money, Our Guns, Our Lives. abr. ed. Grover G. Norquist. 2006. audio compact disk 29.95 (978-0-06-136355-9(3), Harper Audio) HarperCollins Pubs.

Leave Your Pain Behind. Brian Alman. 1992. 21.95 (978-0-87630-665-9(2)) Taylor and Fran.

Leaven of Malice. abr. ed. Robertson Davies & Robertson Davies. Narrated by Earl Pennington. Prod. by CBC Radio Staff. 3 cass. (Running Time: 3 hrs. 30 mins.). (Between the Covers Classics Ser.). (ENG.). 2005. 19.95 (978-0-86492-284-7(1)) Pub: BTC Audiobks CAN. Dist(s): U Toronto Pr

Leaven of Malice. unabr. ed. Robertson Davies. Read by Frederick Davidson. 7 cass. (Running Time: 10 hrs. 30 min.). (Salterton Trilogy). 1997. 49.95 (1946) Blckstn Audio.
The malice behind a false engagement notice is aimed at three people only; but before the leaven of malice has ceased its work, the lives of many Salterton citizens are permanently altered.

Leaven of Malice. unabr. ed. Robertson Davies. Read by Frederick Davidson. 7 cass. (Running Time: 10 hrs.). (Salterton Trilogy: Vol. 2). 2006. 49.95 (978-0-7861-1186-2(0), 1946) Blckstn Audio.

Leaven of Malice: The Salterton Trilogy, Book 3. unabr. ed. Robertson Davies. Read by Frederick Davidson. (Running Time: 9 hrs. 0 mins.). 2010. 29.95 (978-1-4417-2607-0(1)); audio compact disk 76.00 (978-1-4417-2604-9(7)) Blckstn Audio.

Leavenworth Case. Anna Katharine Green. Read by Rebecca Burns. (Playaway Adult Fiction Ser.). (ENG.). 2009. 64.99 (978-1-60775-775-7(3)) Find a World.

Leavenworth Case. Anna Katharine Green. Read by Rebecca C. Burns. (ENG.). 2005. audio compact disk 22.99 (978-1-4001-5126-4(0)); audio compact disk 69.99 (978-1-4001-3126-6(X)); audio compact disk 34.99 (978-1-4001-0126-9(3)) Pub: Tantor Media. Dist(s): IngramPubServ

Leavenworth Case. unabr. ed. Anna Katharine Green. Narrated by Rebecca Burns. (Running Time: 11 hrs. 30 mins. 0 sec.). (ENG.). 2009. audio compact disk 65.99 (978-1-4001-4128-9(1)) Pub: Tantor Media. Dist(s): IngramPubServ

Leavenworth Case: A Lawyer's Story. Anna Katharine Green. Read by Jim Killavey. 9 cass. (Running Time: 12 hrs.). 1989. 59.00 incl. album. (C-148) Jimcin Record.
First detective story by a woman.

Leavenworth Case: A Lawyer's Story. unabr. collector's ed. Anna Katharine Green. Read by Rebecca C. Burns. 8 cass. (Running Time: 12 hrs.). 1985. 64.00 (978-0-7366-4439-6(3), 4730) Books on Tape.
Horatio Leavenworth is a New York merchant whose material wealth is matched by his eminence in the community & reputation for good works. He is also the guardian of two striking nieces who share his Fifth Avenue mansion. Mary, her uncle's favorite, is to inherit his fortune at his death. When Leavenworth is shot to death circumstances point to one of his young wards.

Leavenworth Case, with EBook. unabr. ed. Anna Katharine Green. Narrated by Rebecca Burns. (Running Time: 11 hrs. 30 mins. 0 sec.). (ENG.). 2009. 22.99 (978-1-4001-6128-7(2)); audio compact disk 32.99 (978-1-4001-1128-2(5)) Pub: Tantor Media. Dist(s): IngramPubServ

***Leavenworth Case, with EBook.** unabr. ed. Anna Katharine Green. Narrated by Rebecca Burns. (Running Time: 11 hrs. 30 mins.). 2009. 17.99 (978-1-4001-8128-5(3)) Tantor Media.

***Leavenworth Case, with eBook.** unabr. ed. Anna Katharine Green. Narrated by Rebecca Burns. (Running Time: 11 hrs. 30 mins.). 2009. 32.99 (978-1-4001-9128-4(9)) Tantor Media.

Leaves Must When the Devil Drives. unabr. ed. Fred Secombe. Read by Fred Secombe. 6 cass. (Running Time: 7.5 hrs.). (Sound Ser.). 2002. 54.95 (978-1-84283-165-6(8)) Pub: UlverLrgPrint GBR. Dist(s): Ulverscroft US
Fred Secome sings an old music-hall song at the election of a new bishop. Also appointed is a new curate, John Burton, whose wife is keen to establish relations with the community on the council estate. The Archdeacon, the Venerable Titus Philips, continues his vendetta against the vicar, to the annoyance of his wife. As Rural Dean, it is his responsibility to deal with the death of a priest involved with drugs.John Burton does stirling work on the council estate. This prompts the vicar to begin more visiting in the parish. There he attracts first the attention of a young wife, and then the attention of her husband, who falsely accuses him of an affair.

Leaves of Grass. Poems. Walt Whitman. Narrated by Flo Gibson. 3 CDs. (Running Time: 3 hrs. 46 mins.). 2007. audio compact disk 19.95 (978-1-55685-890-1(6)) Audio Bk Con.

Leaves of Grass, unabr. ed. Poems. Walt Whitman. Read by Flo Gibson. 3 cass. (Running Time: 4 hrs.). 1998. 16.95 (978-1-55685-528-3(1)) Audio Bk Con.
The themes of equality for all people, fertility, sacredness of self, beauty in death, love of comrades & the immortality of the soul prevail.

Leaves of Grass. unabr. ed. Walt Whitman. Read by Robin Field. (Running Time: 11 hrs. 50 mins.). (ENG.). 2009. 72.95 (978-1-4332-7811-2(1)); audio compact disk 90.00 (978-1-4332-7812-9(X)) Blckstn Audio.

***Leaves of Grass.** unabr. ed. Walt Whitman. Read by Mel Foster. (Running Time: 14 hrs. 0 mins.). 2010. 19.99 (978-1-4001-8805-5(9)) Tantor Media.

***Leaves of Grass.** unabr. ed. Walt Whitman. Narrated by Mel Foster. (Running Time: 15 hrs. 30 mins. 0 sec.). (ENG.). 2010. 29.99 (978-1-4001-6805-7(8)); audio compact disk 39.99 (978-1-4001-1805-2(0)); audio compact disk 95.99 (978-1-4001-4805-9(7)) Pub: Tantor Media. Dist(s): IngramPubServ

Leaves of Grass: Classic Collection. unabr. ed. Walt Whitman. Read by Robin Field. (Running Time: 11 hrs. 50 mins.). (ENG.). 2009. 29.95 (978-1-4332-7813-6(8)); audio compact disk 24.95 (978-1-4332-7742-9(5)) Blckstn Audio.

Leaves of Grass: I Hear America Singing. abr. ed. Walt Whitman. Read by Ed Begley. 1 cass. 1984. 12.95 (978-0-694-50030-7(5), SWC 1037) HarperCollins Pubs.

Leaves of Grass Vol. I-III: A Textual Variorum of the Printed Poems, 1855-1856. abr. ed. Walt Whitman. Narrated by Dan O'Herlihy. 2 cass. (Running Time: 1 hr. 44 min.). 12.95 (978-0-89926-160-7(4), 848) Audio Bk.

Leaves of Grass Vol. I-III: A Textual Variorum of the Printed Poems, 1855-1856. unabr. ed. Walt Whitman. Read by Dan O'Herlihy. 6 cass. 35.70 (C-602) Audio Bk.
A collection of 64 poems by the famous American author.

Leaves of Grass Vol. I-III: A Textual Variorum of the Printed Poems, 1855-1856. unabr. ed. Walt Whitman. Read by Noah Waterman. 13 cass. (Running Time: 19 hrs.). 1996. 85.95 (978-0-7861-0919-7(X), 1718) Blckstn Audio.
G. K. Chesterton argued that Walt Whitman was the greatest American. Whitman succeeded in his ambition: to create something uniquely American. His poems have been woven into the very fabric of the American character. From his solemn dirges "When Lilacs Last in the Dooryard Bloom'd" & "O Captain! My Captain!" to the joyous freedom of "Song of Myself," "I Sing the Body Electric," & "Song of the Open Road," "Leaves of Grass" lives on providing inspiration to the people & poets of generations to come.

***Leaving.** Karen Kingsbury. (Bailey Flanigan Ser.). (ENG.). 2011. audio compact disk 19.99 (978-0-310-33149-0(8)) Zondervan.

***Leaving.** Zondervan. (Bailey Flanigan Ser.). (ENG.). 2011. 14.99 (978-0-310-41199-4(8)) Zondervan.

Leaving Atlanta. Tayari Jones. 5 cass. (Running Time: 7 hrs. 30 mins.). 2002. 47.00 (978-1-4025-4402-6(2)) Recorded Bks.

Leaving Cecil Street: A Novel. unabr. ed. Diane McKinney-Whetstone. Narrated by Saidah Arrika Ekulona. 7 cass. (Running Time: 9 hrs. 15 mins.). 2004. 69.75 (978-1-4025-8237-0(4), F0014MC, Griot Aud) Recorded Bks.

Leaving Cheyenne. unabr. ed. Larry McMurtry. Narrated by John Randolph Jones et al. 8 cass. (Running Time: 11 hrs.). 1993. 70.00 (978-1-55690-847-7(4), 93214E7) Recorded Bks.
The story of the love of a woman for two men, one a free-spirited cowhand, the other a rich & successful rancher, is told over the course of 60 years on the West Texas prairie.

Leaving Cheyenne. unabr. collector's ed. Larry McMurtry. Read by Wolfram Kandinsky. 6 cass. (Running Time: 9 hrs.). 1983. 48.00 (978-0-7366-0763-6(3), 1720) Books on Tape.
The story traces a bittersweet three-sided affair.

Leaving Cold Sassy: The Unfinished Sequel to Cold Sassy Tree. unabr. ed. Olive Ann Burns. Read by Frances Cassidy. 6 cass. (Running Time: 9 hrs.). 1992. 48.00 (978-0-7366-3156-3(9), 3828) Books on Tape.
In this sequel to "Cold Sassy Tree," we get to see a grown-up Will Tweedy & the feisty schoolteacher who steals his heart, along with all of the wonderful characters who live in Cold Sassy, Georgia.

Leaving Cold Sassy: The Unfinished Sequel to Cold Sassy Tree. unabr. ed. Olive Ann Burns. Narrated by Jeff Woodman & Barbara Caruso. 6 cass. (Running Time: 9 hrs.). 1996. 51.00 (978-0-7887-0349-2(8), 94541E7) Recorded Bks.
This sequel is a final, loving good-bye to Cold Sassy, Georgia & to one of America's most beloved writers.

Leaving Eden. unabr. ed. Anne D. LeClaire. Read by Pamela Steele. 6 vols. (Running Time: 9 hrs.). 2002. bk. 54.95 (978-0-7927-2706-4(1), CSL 492, Chivers Sound Lib); audio compact disk 79.95 (978-0-7927-2731-6(2), SLD 492, Chivers Sound Lib) AudioGO.
When Glamour Day (and the promise of a complete professional makeover) comes to the Klip-N-Kurl beauty parlor in tiny Lovettsville, Virginia, Tallie Brock sees her ticket to Hollywood and stardom. Yet as the day approaches, Tallie finds herself changing in unexpected ways - while she reaches for the sky like she has never done before.

Leaving Everything Behind: The Songs & Memories of a Cheyenne Woman. Bertha Little Coyote & Virginia Giglio. 1998. audio compact disk 14.95 (978-0-8061-2986-0(7)) U of Okla Pr.

Leaving Fishers. unabr. ed. Margaret Peterson Haddix. 3 cass. (J). (gr. 1-8). 1999. 23.98 (LL 0156, Chivers Child Audio) AudioGO.

Leaving Fishers. unabr. ed. Margaret Peterson Haddix. 3 cass. (YA). 1999. 23.98 (FS9-50967) Highsmith.

Leaving Fishers. unabr. ed. Margaret Peterson Haddix. Read by Vivian Bayubay. 4 cass. (Running Time: 5 hrs. 38 mins.). (YA). (gr. 5 up). 1999. pap. bk. 37.00 (978-0-8072-8122-2(0), YA109SP, Listening Lib); 32.00 (978-0-8072-8121-5(2), YA109CX, Listening Lib) Random Audio Pubg.
The new girl in high school is happy to be befriended by a seemingly wonderful group of students. She soon discovers that the group is a religious cult, & their ever-increasing demands on her lead to a startling conclusion.

Leaving Home. Anita Brookner. Read by Joanna David. 4 cass. (Running Time: 20100 sec.). 2006. 39.95 (978-0-7927-3872-5(1), CSL 894); audio compact disk 59.95 (978-0-7927-3873-2(X), SLD 894) AudioGO.

Leaving Home. unabr. ed. Gail Taylor. Read by Gail Taylor. Ed. by James B. Kirgan. 1 cass. (Running Time: 1 hr. 30 min.). (Essence of Nature Ser.: Vol. 1). (J). 1989. 12.99 stereo. (978-1-878362-01-8(1)) Emerald Ent.
On this tape Thumper, the Samoyed, leaves the pack of sled dogs to begin his adventures. This tape includes the actual sounds one hears in Alaska & while traveling south through Canada.

Leaving Kansas, Bk. 1. unabr. ed. Frank Roderus. Read by Kevin Foley. 4 cass. (Running Time: 5 hrs. 18 min.). 1995. 26.95 (978-1-55686-619-7(4)) Books in Motion.
Tenderfoot Harrison Wilke is disgusted with Redbluff Kansas. His uncle, from whom he stands to inherit a large ranch, can't stand him & Harrison's other "investments" are going awry.

Leaving the Bellweathers. unabr. ed. Kristin Clark Venuti. Read by Michael Page. (Running Time: 4 hrs.). 2009. 24.99 (978-1-4418-0178-4(2), 9781441801784, Brilliance MP3); 39.97 (978-1-4418-0179-1(0), 9781441801791, Brlnc Audio MP3 Lib); 24.99 (978-1-4418-0180-7(4), 9781441801807, BAD); 39.97 (978-1-4418-0181-4(2), 9781441801814, BADLE); audio compact disk 24.99 (978-1-4418-0176-0(6), 9781441801760, Bril Audio CD Unabri) Brilliance Audio.

Leaving the Bellweathers. unabr. ed. Kristin Clark Venuti. Read by Michael Page. 4 CDs. (Running Time: 4 hrs.). (J). (gr. 3-5). 2009. audio compact disk 54.97 (978-1-4418-0177-7(4), 9781441801777, BriAudCD Unabrid) Brilliance Audio.

Leaving the Office Behind. unabr. ed. Barbara Mackoff. Read by Donada Peters. 7 cass. (Running Time: 7 hrs.). 1985. 42.00 (978-0-7366-0842-8(7), 1793) Books on Tape.
Most of us have a lot of trouble making the switch from the job to home & the unfinished business we bring home shortchanges those we love, damages our relationships, & prevents us from enjoying our personal lives. Mackoff examines the problems of people who spend all day being "professional".

Leaving the Rest Unsaid see Robert Graves Reads from His Poetry & the White Goddess

Leaving the Saints: How I Lost the Mormons & Found My Faith. unabr. ed. Martha Beck. Read by Bernadette Dunne. 10 CDs. (Running Time: 13 hrs.). 2005. audio compact disk 90.00 (978-1-4159-1662-9(4)); 72.00 (978-1-4159-1576-9(8)) Books on Tape.
This beautifully written, inspiring memoir explores the powerful yearning toward faith. It offers a rare glimpse inside one of the world's most secretive religions while telling a profoundly moving story of personal courage, survival, and the transformative power of spirituality.

Leaving the Third Chakra. Swami Amar Jyoti. 1 cass. 1980. 9.95 (B-10) Truth Consciousness.
Raising your level of consciousness is light, natural - why does it seem an uphill task? Devoting one year to a changed outlook & seeing the results.

Leaving Vietnam Class set: The True Story of Tuan Ngo. Sarah S. Kilbourne. Read by Jeff Woodman. 1 cass. (Running Time: 45 mins.). (J). (gr. 2 up). 1999. pap. bk. & stu. ed. 22.24 (978-0-7887-3176-1(9), 40911) Recorded Bks.
Tuan Ngo & his father want to escape to freedom in America. But, before they can get there, they will have to endure many days in a cramped fishing boat & many months in a refugee camp.

Leaving Vietnam Class set: The True Story of Tuan Ngo. unabr. ed. Sarah S. Kilbourne. Narrated by Jeff Woodman. 1 cass. (Running Time: 30 mins.). (gr. 2 up). 1999. stu. ed. 10.00 (978-0-7887-3157-0(2), 9583E7) Recorded Bks.

Leaving Vietnam Class set: The True Story of Tuan Ngo. unabr. ed. Sarah S. Kilbourne. Read by Jeff Woodman. 1 cass. (Running Time: 45 mins.). (J). (gr. 2 up). 1999. 70.70 (978-0-7887-3222-5(6), 46878) Recorded Bks.

Leavings. Short Stories. P. D Cacek. Read by P. D Cacek. 2 cass. (Running Time: 3 hrs.). 1999. 17.95 (978-0-9648539-0-4(6)) Wyrmhole.
Includes: "Leavings," "Mime Games," "The Princess," "Here There Be Dragons," "Letting Go," "Tomb with a View," & "Just a Little Bug".

Lebaron Secret. unabr. ed. Stephen Birmingham. Read by multivoice. (Running Time: 12 hrs.). 2009. 24.99 (978-1-4418-0797-7(7), 9781441807977, Brilliance MP3); 24.99 (978-1-4418-0799-1(3), 9781441807991, BAD); 39.97 (978-1-4418-0798-4(5), 9781441807984, Brlnc Audio MP3 Lib); 39.97 (978-1-4418-0800-4(0), 9781441808004, BADLE) Brilliance Audio.

Leber Hereditary Optic Neuropathy - A Bibliography & Dictionary for Physicians, Patients, & Genome Researchers. Compiled by Icon Group International, Inc. Staff. 2007. ring bd. 28.95 (978-0-497-11249-3(3)) Icon Grp.

LeBron James: King of the Court. (High Five Reading - Blue Ser.). (ENG.). (gr. 1-2). 2007. audio compact disk 5.95 (978-1-4296-1430-6(7)) CapstoneDig.

LeBron James: King of the Court. Tom Sibila. (High Five Reading Ser.). (ENG., (gr. 4-5). 2005. audio compact disk 5.95 (978-0-7368-5757-4(5)) CapstoneDig.

***Lecciones de Vida SÃ³lo para Hombres.** Charles R. Swindoll.Tr. of Life Lessons Just for Men. 2009. audio compact disk 19.00 (978-1-57972-851-9(0)) Insight Living.

***Lecciones de Vida SÃ³lo para Mujeres.** Charles R. Swindoll.Tr. of Life Lessons Just for Women. 2009. audio compact disk 19.00 (978-1-57972-847-2(2)) Insight Living.

Lecon Inaugurale au College de France. Roland Barthes. 1 cass. (Running Time: 60 mins.). (College de France Lectures). (FRE.). 1996. 21.95 (1852-LQP) Olivia & Hill.

l'Ecoute de publicites Radio France. 1 cass. (Running Time: 60 mins.). (FRE.). 1991. bk. & wbk. ed. 12.95 (U1) Olivia & Hill.
Collection of French radio commercials.

Lectionary Preaching Planner: 225 Complete Worship Experiences on CD-ROM. Abingdon. 2004. audio compact disk 89.00 (978-0-687-00607-6(4)) Abingdon.

Lecture see Isaac Bashevis Singer Reader

Lecture Lab: Image & Text Management Made Easy. Picture Primal. 1998. cd-rom 115.00 (978-0-7484-0855-9(X)) Taylor and Fran.

Lecture on Conscious Dying. Bruce Goldberg. Read by Bruce Goldberg. 1 cass. (Running Time: 25 min.). (ENG.). 2006. 13.00 (978-1-885577-32-0(X)) Pub: B Goldberg. Dist(s): Baker Taylor
A live presentation of the process of conscious dying, ascension & overcoming bereavement, along with questions & answers.

Lecture on Past Life Regression & Future Life Progression. Bruce Goldberg. 1 cass. (Running Time: 1 hr.). (ENG.). 2005. 13.00 (978-1-885577-18-4(4)) Pub: B Goldberg. Dist(s): Baker Taylor
Side 1 explains the clinical basis & benefits of past life regression & future life progression hypnotherapy. The reverse side describes global assessment techniques for business & personal use.

Lecture Ready, No. 2. Peg Sarosy & Kathy Sherak. (Lecture Ready Ser.). 2006. 39.95 (978-0-19-441714-3(X)) OUP.

Lecture Ready 3: Cassettes (2) Ed. by Oxford Staff. 2006. 39.95 (978-0-19-441722-8(0)) OUP.

Lectures of Dr. Royal Lee, Vol. II. Speeches. Ed. by Mark R. Anderson & Stephanie S. Anderson. Compiled by Mark R. Anderson & Stephanie S. Anderson. 32. 2003. audio compact disk 300.00 (978-0-9645709-3-1(9)) Selene River Pr.

Lectures on Apologetics. Gordon Clark. 16 cass. 80.00 Set. Trinity Found.

Lectures on Faith. 3 cass. 2004. 14.95 (978-1-57734-628-9(9)); audio compact disk 19.95 (978-1-57734-636-4(X)) Covenant Comms.

Lectures on Satire. Ian Arion. 2007. (978-0-9794429-1-9(5)) Dio Delphi Pr.

Lectures on the Holy Spirit. Gordon Clark. 5 cass. 25.00 Trinity Found.

Lectures on the Russian Language. unabr. ed. 3 cass. 14.95 ea. J Norton Pubs.

Lectures Pour Tous: With Test Preparation. Created by McDougal Littell. (McDougal Littell Discovering French: Rouge 3 Ser.). 2006. pap. bk. 14.48 (978-0-618-66114-5(X)) Holt McDoug.

Lecturing Birds on Flying: Can Mathematical Theories Destroy the Financial Markets. unabr. ed. Pablo Triana. Read by Erik Synnestvedt. (Running Time: 15 hrs. 30 mins.). (ENG.). 2009. 39.98 (978-1-59659-429-6(2), GildAudio) Pub: Gildan Media. Dist(s): HachBkGrp

Led Astray. abr. ed. Erin St. Claire, pseud. Read by Karen Ziemba. (Running Time: 7 hrs. 0 mins. 0 sec.). 2008. audio compact disk 14.99 (978-0-7435-6956-9(3)) Pub: S&S Audio. Dist(s): S and S Inc

Led Astray. unabr. ed. Erin St. Claire, pseud. Read by James R. Jenner. 6 cass. (Running Time: 9 hrs.). 2005. 49.75 (978-1-4193-2717-9(8)); audio compact disk 69.75 (978-1-4193-2719-3(4)) Recorded Bks.
In this romance Brown published under the pseudonym Erin St.Clair 20 years ago, the listener must agree to Coleridge's "willing suspension of disbelief." Bob and Sarah Hendren have two sons, Cage and Hal, and have raised Jenny Fletcher since her parents' deaths when she was 14. Malleable and eager to please, Jenny has accepted the Hendrens' plans for

her life. She is engaged to Hal, the favored younger son, who is leaving on a religious mission to Central America. Jenny, terrified for Hal's safety, tries to seduce him into staying. But afire with eagerness for his trip and unwilling to sin before leaving on God's business, Hal gives her a sleeping pill and leaves her alone in the night. Cage hears Jenny's heartbroken sobs and opens her door to check on her. Seeing him silhouetted in the door, Jenny thinks Hal has changed his mind.

Led by Faith: Rising from the Ashes of the Rwandan Genocide. Immaculée Ilibagiza. Told to Steve Erwin. 4 CDs. 2008. audio compact disk 23.95 (978-1-4019-1889-7(1)) Hay House.

Led Zeppelin: The Unauthorized Biography of Led Zeppelin. Alan Clayson. 1 CD. (Maximum Ser.). (ENG., 2001. audio compact disk 14.95 (978-1-84240-170-5(X)) Pub: Chrome Dreams GBR. Dist(s): IPG Chicago

Leda & the Swan see Dylan Thomas Reads the Poetry of W. B. Yeats & Others

Leda & the Swan see Poetry of William Butler Yeats

Ledge Between the Streams. Ved Mehta. Read by David Case. 9 cass. (Running Time: 13 hrs. 30 mins.). 72.00 (978-0-7366-1640-9(3)) Books on Tape.
Fourth volume in the author's autobiography. He leaves India for education in the U.S. at a school for the blind.

Ledge Between the Streams. unabr. ed. Ved Mehta. Read by David Case. 9 cass. (Running Time: 13 hrs. 30 mins.). 1989. 72.00 (2495) Books on Tape.
It's the 1940s, a crucial time in the author's life & in the life of his native India. He recounts the day-to-day joys & sorrows of a large, well-to-do Hindu family in the Punjab. But always in the background is the distant thunder of WW II & the approaching end of the British raj. India's great problem was antagonism between Hindus & Muslims. Independence flared into partition, which in the Punjab left ten million homeless & a million dead. This was not a secure time for a blind boy.

Ledge Between the Streams. unabr. ed. Ved Mehta. Read by Garard Green. 12 cass. (Running Time: 13 hrs. 30 min.). (Isis Ser.). (J). 1991. 94.95 (978-1-85089-718-7(2), 10891) Pub: ISIS Lrg Prnt GBR. Dist(s): Ulverscroft US

Ledger Lines: Learn to Read Those Super-High & Super-Low Notes. Duane Shinn. 1 cass. 19.95 (HAR-11) Duane Shinn.
Explains how to recognize those notes high above the treble staff, or low below the bass clef.

Lee, Pt. A. unabr. collector's ed. Douglas S. Freeman. Read by Jonathan Reese. 10 cass. (Running Time: 15 hrs.). 1993. 80.00 (978-0-7366-2392-6(2), 3163A) Books on Tape.
The son of a Revolutionary War hero, Lee was a product of young America's elite. And he embodied all the conflicts of his time.

Lee, Pt. B. unabr. collector's ed. Douglas S. Freeman. Read by Jonathan Reese. 9 cass. (Running Time: 13 hrs. 30 min.). 1993. 72.00 (978-0-7366-2393-3(0), 3163B) Books on Tape.
The son of a Revolutionary War hero, Lee was a product of young America's elite. And he embodied all the conflicts of his time.

***Lee: A Life of Virtue.** unabr. ed. John Perry. Narrated by William DuFruis. (Running Time: 6 hrs. 24 mins. 17 sec.). (Generals Ser.). (ENG.). 2010. 16.09 (978-1-60814-684-0(7), SpringWater); audio compact disk 22.99 (978-1-59859-733-2(7), SpringWater) Oasis Audio.

Lee: The Last Years. unabr. ed. Read by Michael Anthony. Ed. by Charles Bracelen Flood. 7 cass. (Running Time: 10 hrs.). 1992. 49.95 (978-0-7861-0246-4(2), 1215) Blckstn Audio.
Robert E. Lee, one of the most statuesque figures in American history, vanishes after his dramatic surrender at Appomattox. In fact, he lived only another five years, during which time he did more than any other American to heal the wounds between North & South during the tempestuous postwar period. This is a moving & intimate account of those years, filled with the warmth of family ties & enduring friendships set against the harsh realities of Reconstruction. Though Lee is best remembered for his military campaigns, this was his finest hour, the great forgotten chapter of an extraordinary life.

Lee: The Last Years. unabr. collector's ed. Read by Lawrence M. Vanella. Ed. by Charles Bracelen Flood. 7 cass. (Running Time: 10 hrs. 30 mins.). 1986. 56.00 (978-0-7366-0684-4(X), 1644) Books on Tape.
Robert E. Lee vanished from the stage of history after his dramatic surrender at Appomattox. In fact, although he lived only five more years, he did more than any other American to heal the wounds left from the War between the States. Lee created a model university & showed a still-divided nation how compassion, generosity & conciliation could heal.

Lee & Grant: A Dual Biography. unabr. ed. Gene Smith. Narrated by Peter Johnson. 8 cass. (Running Time: 12 hrs.). 1984. 70.00 (978-1-55690-306-9(5), 84170E7) Recorded Bks.
A dual account of the lives of the two great antagonists, revealing many differences & some surprising similarities.

Lee & Joyce Schulman: Adventure in Freedom. (Running Time: 60 min.). (Long Beach City College). 1983. 9.00 (F146) Freeland Pr.
Offers methods for achieving personal freedom. A therapy session to illustrate the title of this program.

Lee & Joyce Schulman: Self-Liberation: Freedom from Within. (Running Time: 60 min.). (Cal State Univ., Long Beach). 1981. 9.00 (F124) Freeland Pr.
An approach to self-knowledge; with demonstrative interaction with the audience.

Lee Child: Killing Floor, Die Trying, Tripwire. abr. ed. Lee Child. Read by Dick Hill. 6 cass. (Running Time: 9 hrs.). (Jack Reacher Ser.). 2002. bk. 19.95 (978-1-59086-119-6(1), 1590861191, Nova Audio Bks) Brilliance Audio.
In a Chicago suburb, a dentist is met in his office parking lot by three men and ordered into the trunk of his Lexus. On a downtown sidewalk, Jack Reacher and an unknown woman are abducted in broad daylight by two men - practiced and confident - who stop them at gunpoint and hustle them into the same sedan. Then Reacher and the woman are switched into a second vehicle and hauled away, leaving the dentist bound and gagged inside his car with the woman's abandoned possessions, two gallons of gasoline. . . and a burning match. The FBI is desperate to rescue the woman, a Special Agent from the Chicago office, because the FBI always - always - takes care of its own, and because this woman is not just another agent. Reacher and the woman join forces, against seemingly hopeless odds, to outwit their captors and escape. But the FBI thinks Jack is one of the kidnappers - and when they close in, the Bureau snipers will be shooting to kill.

Lee Child: Killing Floor, Die Trying, Tripwire. abr. ed. Lee Child. Read by Dick Hill. (Running Time: 9 hrs.). (Jack Reacher Ser.). 2005. audio compact disk 29.95 (978-1-59737-704-1(X), 9781597377041, BACD) Brilliance Audio.
KILLING FLOOR - "I was eating eggs and drinking coffee. I was in a booth, at a window, reading somebody's abandoned newspaper. Outside, the rain had stopped but the glass was still pebbled with bright drops. I saw the police cruisers pull into the gravel lot. They were moving fast and crunched to a stop. Light bars flashing and popping. Doors burst open, policemen jumped out. Two from each car, weapons ready. Two revolvers, two shotguns. This was heavy stuff. One revolver and one shotgun ran to the back. One of each rushed the door. I just sat and watched them. I knew who was in the diner. A cook in back. Two waitresses. Two old men. And me. This operation was for me. I had been in town less than half an hour." - From the opening of this searing tale of honor and revenge where Jack Reacher, a former military cop, hunts down his brother's killers. DIE TRYING - In a Chicago suburb, a dentist is met in his office parking lot by three men and ordered into the trunk of his Lexus. On a downtown sidewalk, Jack Reacher and an unknown woman are abducted in broad daylight by two men - practiced and confident - who stop them at gunpoint and hustle them into the same sedan. Then Reacher and the woman are switched into a second vehicle and hauled away, leaving the dentist bound and gagged inside his car with the woman's abandoned possessions, two gallons of gasoline...and a burning match. TRIPWIRE - Jack Reacher is settling into lazy Key West when his life is interrupted by a stranger who comes looking for him. When the stranger turns up beaten to death in the Old Town cemetery - fingertips removed - Reacher knows whomever the man was working for is not a friend. Reacher follows the trail to New York.

Lee Child: Persuader, the Enemy, One Shot. abr. ed. Lee Child. Read by Dick Hill. (Running Time: 18 hrs.). (Jack Reacher Ser.). 2007. audio compact disk 34.95 (978-1-4233-2322-8(X), 9781423323228, BACD) Brilliance Audio.

Lee Child: Running Blind, Echo Burning, Without Fail. abr. ed. Lee Child. Read by Dick Hill. (Running Time: 18 hrs.). (Jack Reacher Ser.). 2007. audio compact disk 34.95 (978-1-4233-2318-1(1), 9781423323181, BACD) Brilliance Audio.

Lee Garrison's Quest. unabr. collector's ed. Max Brand. Read by Jonathan Marosz. 7 cass. (Running Time: 7 hrs.). 1995. 42.00 (978-0-7366-3023-8(6), 3706) Books on Tape.
A dying Indian's last words send Jim Garrison after an elusive gray stallion. The chase gets obsessive - with startling results.

Lee in Virginia. unabr. ed. G A Henty. Narrated by John Bolen. (Running Time: 11 hrs. 30 mins. 0 sec.). (ENG.). (J). (gr. 4-7). 2008. audio compact disk 65.99 (978-1-4001-3865-4(5)) Pub: Tantor Media. Dist(s): IngramPubServ

Lee Stetson Performs As John Muir. Hosted by Nancy Pearlman. 1 cass. (Running Time: 29 min.). 10.00 (714) Educ Comm CA.

Lee's Gamble - The South Invades. 1 cass. Dramatization. (Voices of Gettysburg Ser.). 1991. 12.95 Heritage.
Dramatized reconstructions of Civil War-era voices.

Lee's Lieutenants Vol. 1, Pt. 2: A Study in Command. collector's ed. Douglas S. Freeman. Read by Jonathan Reese. 9 cass. (Running Time: 13 hrs. 30 min.). 1994. 72.00 (978-0-7366-2782-5(0), 3500-B) Books on Tape.
Biographer of Robert E. Lee examines the lives of officers in the high command of the Confederate general's Army of Northern Virginia.

Lee's Lieutenants Vol. 2, Pt. 2: A Study in Command. collector's ed. Douglas S. Freeman. Read by Jonathan Reese. 9 cass. (Running Time: 13 hrs. 30 min.). 1994. 72.00 (978-0-7366-2826-6(6), 3535-B) Books on Tape.
Between August 1862 & May 1863, Lee won great victories. He gave the credit to Stonewall Jackson.

Lee's Lieutenants Vol. 3, Pt. 2: A Study in Command. collector's ed. Douglas S. Freeman. Read by Jonathan Reese. 10 cass. (Running Time: 15 hrs.). 1995. 80.00 (978-0-7366-2945-4(9), 3639-B) Books on Tape.
As the critical summer battles of 1863 approached, General Lee counted on two new field commanders to fill the shoes of the fallen Stonewall Jackson.

Lee's Lieutenants Vol. 3, Pt. 2: A Study in Command. unabr. collector's ed. Douglas S. Freeman. Read by Jonathan Reese. 9 cass. (Running Time: 13 hrs. 30 min.). 1994. 72.00 (978-0-7366-2781-8(2), 3500-A) Books on Tape.
Biographer of Robert E. Lee examines the lives of officers in the high command of the Confederate general's Army of Northern Virginia.

Lee's Lieutenants Vol. 3, Pt. 2: A Study in Command. unabr. collector's ed. Douglas S. Freeman. Read by Jonathan Reese. 9 cass. (Running Time: 13 hrs. 30 min.). 1994. 72.00 (978-0-7366-2827-3(4), 3535-A) Books on Tape.
Between August 1862 & May 1863, Lee won great victories. He gave the credit to Stonewall Jackson.

Lee's Lieutenants Vol. 3, Pt. 2: A Study in Command. unabr. collector's ed. Douglas S. Freeman. Read by Jonathan Reese. 10 cass. (Running Time: 15 hrs.). 1995. 80.00 (978-0-7366-2944-7(0), 3639-A) Books on Tape.
As the critical summer battles of 1863 approached, General Lee counted on two new field commanders to fill the shoes of the fallen Stonewall Jackson.

Lees of Virginia: Seven Generations of an American Family. unabr. ed. Paul C. Nagel. Read by Edward Lewis. 11 cass. (Running Time: 16 hrs.). 1999. 76.95 (978-0-7861-1585-3(8), 2414) Blckstn Audio.
The descendants of Richard & Anne Lee have occupied a preeminent place in American history & were among the first families of Virginia. Two were signers of the Declaration of Independence & several others distinguished themselves during the Revolutionary War. Light-Horse Harry Lee was a controversial cavalry officer, whose wild real estate speculation led to imprisonment for debt & finally self-exile in the caribbean. One of Harry's sons, Henry Lee, disgraced the family by seducing his sister-in-law & frittering away Stratford, the Lee's ancestral home. Another son, however, became the family's redeeming figure - Robert E Lee, a brilliant tactician whose ruling motto was self-denial. He remains widely admired for his lofty character & military success.

Lees of Virginia: Seven Generations of an American Family. unabr. ed. Paul C. Nagel. Read by Edward Lewis. (Running Time: 52200 sec.). 2008. audio compact disk & audio compact disk 110.00 (978-1-4332-3434-7(3)); audio compact disk & audio compact disk 29.95 (978-1-4332-3435-4(1)) Blckstn Audio.

Lee's Terrible Swift Sword. unabr. ed. Richard Wheeler. Read by Dick Estell. 10 cass. (Running Time: 15 hrs.). 1995. 80.00 (978-0-7366-3062-7(7), 3744) Books on Tape.
After Lee's zealous troops cleaned up at Fredericksburg & Chancellorsville, their confidence soared. Colorful & dramatic.

***Leeway Cottage.** abr. ed. Beth Gutcheon. Read by Elizabeth Marvel. (ENG.). 2005. (978-0-06-084584-1(8), Harper Audio); (978-0-06-084583-4(X), Harper Audio) HarperCollins Pubs.

Leeway Cottage. unabr. ed. Beth Gutcheon. Read by Susan Ericksen. 9 cass. (Running Time: 53700 sec.). 2005. 79.95 (978-0-7927-3635-6(4), CSL 801); audio compact disk 110.95 (978-0-7927-3636-3(2), SLD 801) AudioGO.

Left Alone for Now. 2003. audio compact disk 10.00 (978-1-58602-139-9(7)) E L Long.

Left alone for Now. 2003. 6.00 (978-1-58602-163-4(X)); audio compact disk 10.00 (978-1-58602-164-1(8)) E L Long.

Left Behind: A Novel of the Earth's Last Days. Tim LaHaye & Jerry B. Jenkins. Read by Richard Ferrone. 10 CDs. (Running Time: 11 hrs. 45 mins.). (Left Behind Ser.: Bk. 1). 2004. audio compact disk 39.95 (978-0-7887-4973-5(0), 00002) Recorded Bks.

Left Behind: A Novel of the Earth's Last Days. abr. ed. Tim LaHaye & Jerry B. Jenkins. Read by Frank Muller. 3 CDs. (Running Time: 180 min.). (Left Behind Ser.: Bk. 1). (ENG.). 2000. audio compact disk 19.99 (978-0-8423-4323-7(7)) Tyndale Hse.

Left Behind: A Novel of the Earth's Last Days. unabr. ed. Tim LaHaye & Jerry B. Jenkins. Read by Jack Sondericker. 12 cass. (Running Time: 12 hrs.). (Left Behind Ser.: Bk. 1). 1998. 64.95 (978-1-55686-868-9(5)) Books in Motion.
Pilot Rayford Steele is flying his 747 to London & contemplating whether or not to commit adultery when a flight attendant gives him some frightening news. Some of their passengers have disappeared into thin air, leaving their clothing as a sign that they ever existed.

Left Behind: A Novel of the Earth's Last Days. unabr. ed. Tim LaHaye & Jerry B. Jenkins. Read by Jack Sondericker. 11 CDs. (Running Time: 12 hrs.). (Left Behind Ser.: Bk. 1). 2001. audio compact disk 71.50 (978-1-58116-125-0(5)) Books in Motion.
When people mysteriously disappear from Capt. Rayford Steele's airplane, the world soon learns of the coming apocalyptic battle between good and evil.

Left Behind: A Novel of the Earth's Last Days. unabr. ed. Tim LaHaye & Jerry B. Jenkins. Narrated by Richard Ferrone. 10 CDs. (Running Time: 11 hrs. 45 mins.). (Left Behind Ser.: Bk. 1). 1999. audio compact disk 91.00 (978-0-7887-3438-0(5), C1044E7) Recorded Bks.
What would happen if millions of people around the world suddenly disappeared? Pilot Rayford Steele is flying his 747 to London & contemplating whether or not to commit adultery when a flight attendant gives him some frightening news. Some of their passengers have disappeared into thin air, leaving their clothing as a sign that they ever existed.

Left Behind: A Novel of the Earth's Last Days. unabr. ed. Tim LaHaye & Jerry B. Jenkins. Narrated by Richard Ferrone. 8 cass. (Running Time: 11 hrs. 45 mins.). (Left Behind Ser.: Bk. 1). 1998. 70.00 (978-0-7887-2494-7(0), 95569E7) Recorded Bks.
What would happen if millions of people around the world suddenly disappeared? Pilot Rayford Steele is flying his 747 to London & contemplating whether or not to commit adultery when a flight attendant gives him some frightening news. Some of their passengers have disappeared into thin air, leaving their clothing as a sign that they ever existed.

Left Behind: A Novel of the Earth's Last Days. unabr. ed. Tim LaHaye & Jerry B. Jenkins. Read by Richard Ferrone. 7 cass. (Running Time: 11 hrs. 45 mins.). (Left Behind Ser.: Bk. 1). 2004. 34.95 (978-0-7887-4972-8(2), 00004) Recorded Bks.
Pilot Rayford Steele is contemplating adultery with a young flight attendant when over 100 of his passengers simply vanish, leaving vacated clothes and bewildered companions. Rayford and the others left behind must deal with mass chaos on top of personal loss. Among the passengers still left is star reporter Cameron "Buck" Williams, who just got the assignment of a lifetime: find out what happened and why. Theories abound, from Christian Rapture to alien abduction. Buck suspects secret meetings between international power brokers are somehow connected. And rising political icon Nicolae Carpathia seems to be at the center of it all.

Left Behind: The Kids. Jerry B. Jenkins & Tim LaHaye. (Left Behind Ser.). 2004. 16.99 (978-0-8423-8421-6(9)) Tyndale Hse.

Left Behind: The Kids. Jerry B. Jenkins & Tim LaHaye. 2004. 16.99 (978-0-8423-8422-3(7)) Tyndale Hse.

Left for Dead: My Journey Home from Everest. unabr. ed. Beck Weathers & Stephen G. Michaud. Read by Buck Schirner. 5 cass. (Running Time: 7 hrs.). 2000. 27.95 (978-1-56740-384-8(0), 1567403840, BAU) Brilliance Audio.

Left for Dead: My Journey Home from Everest. unabr. ed. Beck Weathers & Stephen G. Michaud. Read by Buck Schirner. (Running Time: 7 hrs.). 2005. 24.95 (978-1-59600-607-2(2), 9781596006072, Brilliance MP3); 39.25 (978-1-59600-608-9(0), 9781596006089, Brlnc Audio MP3 Lib) Brilliance Audio.
On May 10, 1996, nine climbers perished in a blizzard high on Mount Everest, the single deadliest day ever on the peak. The following day, one of these victims was given a second chance. His name is Beck Weathers. The tale of Dr. Weathers's miraculous awakening from a deep hypothermic coma was widely reported. But the hidden story of what led the pathologist to Everest in the first place, and his painful recovery after his dramatic rescue, has not been told until now. Brilliant and gregarious, Weathers discovered in his thirties that mountain climbing helped him cope with the black dog of depression. But his self-prescribed therapy came at a steep cost: estrangement from his wife, Peach, and their two children. By the time he left for Everest, his home life had all but disintegrated. Yet when he was reported dead after lying exposed on the mountain for eighteen hours in subzero weather, it was Peach who orchestrated the daring rescue that brought her husband home. Only then, facing months of surgery and the loss of his hands, did Beck Weathers also begin to face himself, his family, his past, and his uncertain future. Candid and uncompromising, Left for Dead is a deeply compelling saga of crisis and change, and of the abiding power of love and family.

Left for Dead: My Journey Home from Everest. unabr. ed. Seaborn Beck Weathers & Stephen G. Michaud. Read by Buck Schirner. (Running Time: 7 hrs.). 2005. 39.25 (978-1-59600-610-2(2), 9781596006102, BADLE); 24.95 (978-1-59600-609-6(9), 9781596006096, BAD) Brilliance Audio.

Left for Dead - Remedies from Help Yourself to Health. Kelly Quinn & Dick Quinn. Read by Kelly Quinn & Dick Quinn. 1 cass. (Running Time: 91 min.). 1994. 12.95 Incl. bklet. (978-0-9632839-1-7(X)); 10.95 Quinn Pubng.
Side 1: "Left for Dead" story of heart attack, failed bypass & health with heart herbs. Side 2: Remedies: herbs for 82 common ailments.

Left Hand Bass Styles for Pop Piano. Duane Shinn. 1 cass. 19.95 (CP-7) Duane Shinn.
Here is a course which shows a dozen different styles you can adapt to your left hand (bass part) while playing various types of "pop" music. Each style is shown in the key of C,F, & G, but can be used in any key.

Left Hand of Darkness. unabr. collector's ed. Ursula K. Le Guin. Read by Ruth Stokesberry. 8 cass. (Running Time: 12 hrs.). (Hainish Ser.). 1987. 64.00 (978-0-7366-1129-9(0), 2052) Books on Tape.
The Terrans have sent a landing party to Gethan & what they find are a people outside their realm of understanding.

Left Hand of God. unabr. ed. Paul Hoffman. Read by Steve West. 10 CDs. (Running Time: 13 hrs.). (ENG.). 2010. audio compact disk 39.95 (978-0-14-242823-8(X), PengAudBks) Penguin Grp USA.

Left Handed Fiddling for Beginners: A Teach Yourself Method. Ryan J. Thomson. 2004. 22.95 (978-0-931877-44-5(X)) Captain Fiddle Pubns.

***Left Neglected.** unabr. ed. Lisa Genova. (Running Time: 11 hrs. 0 mins. 0 sec.). (ENG.). 2011. audio compact disk 39.99 (978-1-4423-3539-4(4)) Pub: S&S Audio. Dist(s): S and S Inc

Left over Fruit: Galatians 5:16-25. Ed Young. 1983. 4.95 (978-0-7417-1306-3(3), 306) Win Walk.

Left shoe & the Foundling. Annie O'Dowd. Read by Annie O'Dowd. (Running Time: 1 hr. 15 mins.). (seadog Adventure: Ser.). (J). 2009. 39.99 (978-1-74214-423-8(3), 9781742144238) Pub: Bolinda Pubng AUS. Dist(s): Bolinda Pub Inc

Left Shoe & the Foundling. unabr. ed. Annie O'Dowd. Read by Annie O'Dowd. 1 CD. (Running Time: 1 hr. 15 mins.). (seadog Adventure: Ser.). (J). (gr. 1-4). 2008. audio compact disk 39.95 (978-1-74093-989-8(1), 9781740939898) Pub: Bolinda Pubng AUS. Dist(s): Bolinda Pub Inc

Left to Tell: Discovering God Amidst the Rwandan Holocaust. abr. ed. Immaculée Ilibagiza. Read by Lisa Reneé Pitts. Told to Steve Erwin. Frwd. by Wayne W. Dyer. 2006. audio compact disk 23.95 (978-1-4019-1149-2(8)) Hay House.

Lefty Kreh's Ultimate Guide to Fly Fishing: Everything Anglers Need to Know by the World's Foremost Fly-Fishing Expert. abr. ed. Lefty Kreh. Narrated by Jeff Riggenbach. (Running Time: 16200 sec.). 2005. audio compact disk 28.00 (978-1-932378-75-7(8)) Pub: A Media Intl. Dist(s): Natl Bk Netwk

Leg in the Subway see Twentieth-Century Poetry in English, No. 26, Recordings of Poets Reading Their Own Poetry

Leg of Gold see Graveyard of Ghost Tales

Legacie see Love Poems of John Donne

Legacies: A Chinese Mosaic. abr. ed. Bette Bao Lord. Read by Bette Bao Lord. 2 cass. (Running Time: 3 hrs.). 1991. 15.95 (978-1-879371-01-9(4)) Pub Mills.
This is a book by the wife of the former ambassador to China. Bette Bao Lord was born in China & came to the U.S. at age 8. This book tells the stories of the harsh treatment of some of her friends & relatives during & after the Cultural Revolution, including during the spring 1989 student uprising.

Legacies: A Chinese Mosaic. unabr. collector's ed. Bette Bao Lord. Read by Penelope Dellaporta. 8 cass. (Running Time: 12 hrs.). 1991. 64.00 (978-0-7366-2013-0(3), 2829) Books on Tape.
"Legacies" is both a record of the author's stay during the uprising at Tiananmen Square & the oral histories of Chinese men & women who lived through the Cultural Revolution.

Legacies of Great Economists. Timothy Taylor. 5 cass. (Running Time: 7 hrs. 30 mins.). bk. 29.95 (978-1-56585-152-8(8), 528) Teaching Co.

Legacy. 1 cass. 10.98 (978-1-57908-315-1(3), 1392); audio compact disk 15.98 (978-1-57908-314-4(5), 1392) Platinm Enter.

Legacy. Terry Franklin & Barbi Franklin. (Running Time: 30 min.). 2002. 9.95 (978-7-901440-01-2(5)) Pub: Tylis Music. Dist(s): STL Dist NA

Legacy. Terry Franklin & Barbi Franklin. (Running Time: 1 hr.). (ENG.). 2004. audio compact disk 14.95 (978-7-901440-08-1(2)) Pub: Tylis Pubng. Dist(s): STL Dist NA

Legacy. Music by Ali Akbar Khan & Asha Bhosele. 1 cass. 1996. (L96014); audio compact disk (CD L96014) Multi-Cultural Bks.

Legacy. Contrib. by Nichole Nordeman. (Running Time: 23 mins.). 2003. 6.99 (978-5-550-31041-0(4)) Pt of Grace Ent.

Legacy. Doc Watson & David Holt. Read by Doc Watson & David Holt. 3 CDs. (Running Time: 3 hrs. 30 min). 2002. audio compact disk 24.95 High Windy Audio.

Legacy. abr. ed. D. W. Buffa. Read by Mark Feuerstein. (ENG.). 2005. 14.98 (978-1-59483-366-3(4)) Pub: Hachet Audio. Dist(s): HachBkGrp

Legacy. abr. ed. Danielle Steel. Read by Arthur Morey. 5 CDs. (Running Time: 5 hrs.). 2010. audio compact disk 24.99 (978-1-4233-8814-2(3), 9781423388142, BACD) Brilliance Audio.

Legacy. abr. ed. Danielle Steel. (Running Time: 6 hrs.). 2011. audio compact disk 14.99 (978-1-4233-8815-9(1), 9781423388159, BCD Value Price) Brilliance Audio.

***Legacy.** abr. ed. Danielle Steel. Read by Arthur Morey. (Running Time: 6 hrs.). 2010. 9.99 (978-1-4418-9395-6(4), 9781441893956, BAD) Brilliance Audio.

Legacy. unabr. ed. Evelyn Anthony. Read by Bill Wallis. 8 cass. (Running Time: 8 hrs.). 1998. 69.95 (978-0-7540-0121-8(0), CAB1544) AudioGO.
After his wife's suicide, Richard Farrington leaves his children & goes on a cruise to Scandinavia where he falls in love & marries Christina Nordohl. His death 12 years later leaves Christina & her daughter with the legacy of a great house, acres of land & a priceless manuscript. But her stepson vows to break the will that has disinherited him. In doing so, Christina & her daughter's lives are now in great danger.

***Legacy.** unabr. ed. Kate Brian, pseud. Narrated by Cassandra Campbell. (Running Time: 6 hrs. 30 mins. 0 sec.). (Private Ser.). (ENG.). 2010. 19.99 (978-1-4001-6236-9(X)); 14.99 (978-1-4001-8236-7(0)); audio compact disk 29.99 (978-1-4001-1236-4(2)) Pub: Tantor Media. Dist(s): IngramPubServ

Legacy. unabr. ed. Howard Fast. Read by Sandra Burr. (Running Time: 12 hrs.). 2008. 24.95 (978-1-4233-7223-3(9), 9781423372233, Brilliance MP3); 24.95 (978-1-4233-7225-7(5), 9781423372257, BAD); 39.95 (978-1-4233-7224-0(7), 9781423372240, Brlnc Audio MP3 Lib); 49.97 (978-1-4233-7226-4(3), 9781423372264, BADLE) Brilliance Audio.

Legacy. unabr. ed. Stephen Frey. Read by George Guidall. 7 cass. (Running Time: 10 hrs.). 66.00 (978-0-7887-2495-4(9), 95570E7) Recorded Bks.
After Wall Street trader Cole Egan receives his father's legacy - a key to a safety deposit box, he suddenly finds himself targeted by unnamed foes in Washington & the Mafia. Available to libraries only.

Legacy. unabr. ed. Nancy Holder & Debbie Viguié. Read by Cassandra Morris. (Running Time: 7 hrs.). (Wicked Ser.). 2010. audio compact disk 24.99 (978-1-4418-3538-3(5), 9781441835383, Bril Audio CD Unabri) Brilliance Audio.

***Legacy.** unabr. ed. Nancy Holder & Debbie Viguié. Read by Cassandra Morris. (Running Time: 7 hrs.). (Wicked Ser.). 2010. 24.99 (978-1-4418-3540-6(7), 9781441835406, Brilliance MP3); 39.97 (978-1-4418-3541-3(5), 9781441835413, Brlnc Audio MP3 Lib); audio compact disk 54.97 (978-1-4418-3539-0(3), 9781441835390, BriAudCD Unabrid) Brilliance Audio.

Legacy. unabr. ed. Cayla Kluver. Read by Anna Chlumsky. (Running Time: 14 hrs.). 2009. 24.99 (978-1-4418-3435-5(4), 9781441834355, BAD); 39.97 (978-1-4418-3436-2(2), 9781441834362, BADLE) Brilliance Audio.

Legacy. unabr. ed. Cayla Kluver. Read by Anna Chlumsky. (Running Time: 14 hrs.). 2009. 24.99 (978-1-4418-3433-1(8), 9781441834331, Brilliance MP3); 39.97 (978-1-4418-3434-8(6), 9781441834348, Brlnc Audio MP3 Lib); audio compact disk 29.99 (978-1-4418-3431-7(1), 9781441834317, Bril Audio CD Unabri); audio compact disk 99.97 (978-1-4418-3432-4(X), 9781441834324, BriAudCD Unabrid) Brilliance Audio.

Legacy. unabr. ed. Danielle Steel. (Running Time: 10 hrs.). 2010. 39.97 (978-1-4233-8813-5(5), 9781423388135, BADLE); 24.99 (978-1-4233-8812-8(7), 9781423388128, BAD) Brilliance Audio.

Legacy. unabr. ed. Danielle Steel. Read by Arthur Morey. 1 MP3-CD. (Running Time: 10 hrs.). 2010. 39.97 (978-1-4233-8811-1(9), 9781423388111, Brlnc Audio MP3 Lib); 24.99 (978-1-4233-8810-4(0), 9781423388104, Brilliance MP3); audio compact disk 92.97 (978-1-4233-8809-8(7), 9781423388098, BriAudCD Unabrid); audio compact disk 38.99 (978-1-4233-8808-1(9), 9781423388081, Bril Audio CD Unabri) Brilliance Audio.

Legacy: A Father's Handbook for Raising Godly Children. Scripts. As told by Stephen Wood. 5 CDs. (Running Time: 6 hrs. 20 mins.). 2006. audio compact disk 29.95 (978-0-9727571-4-0(7)) Family Life Ctr.

Legacy: Doc Watson & David Holt. Perf. by Doc Watson & David Holt. 3 CDs. (Running Time: 4 hrs. 30 mins.). 2002. pap. bk. 24.95 (978-0-942303-35-3(0)) Pub: August Hse. Dist(s): Natl Bk Netwk
Doc Watson's inspiring life story and musical genius come alive. Legacy features a concert with Doc Watson and Davit Hold and conversation looking back over Doc's 79 years in a revealing and entertaining portrait. Includes a 72 page companion booklet filled with historic family photos, additional interviews and stories.

Legacy: John 15:18-16:4. Ed Young. 1992. 4.95 (978-0-7417-1928-7(2), 928) Win Walk.

Legacy: The 10 Greatest Achievements of Pope John Paul II. abr. ed. George Weigel. (Running Time: 3780 sec.). 2005. DVD, audio compact disk, audio compact disk 9.95 (978-1-932927-50-4(6)) Ascensn Pr.

***Legacy (Library Edition)** unabr. ed. Kate Brian, pseud. Narrated by Cassandra Campbell. (Running Time: 6 hrs. 30 mins. 0 sec.). (Private Ser.). (ENG.). 2010. audio compact disk 59.99 (978-1-4001-4236-1(9)) Pub: Tantor Media. Dist(s): IngramPubServ

Legacy of Ashes: The History of the CIA. unabr. ed. Tim Weiner. Read by Stefan Rudnicki. (Running Time: 77400 sec.). 2007. 34.95 (978-1-4332-0198-1(4)) Blckstn Audio.

Legacy of Ashes: The History of the CIA. unabr. ed. Tim Weiner. Read by Stefan Rudnicki. 17 CDs. (Running Time: 77400 sec.). 2007. audio compact disk 34.95 (978-1-4332-0199-8(2)) Blckstn Audio.

Legacy of Ashes: The History of the CIA. unabr. ed. Tim Weiner. (Running Time: 77400 sec.). 2007. 89.95 (978-1-4332-0302-2(2)); audio compact disk 120.00 (978-1-4332-0303-9(0)) Blckstn Audio.

Legacy of Ashes: The History of the CIA. unabr. ed. Tim Weiner. Read by Stefan Rudnicki. (Running Time: 77400 sec.). 2007. audio compact disk 44.95 (978-1-4332-0200-1(X)) Blckstn Audio.

Legacy of Friedrich von Hayek. Friedrich A. Hayek. 2000. 30.00 (978-0-86597-960-4(X)) Pub: Liberty Fund. Dist(s): Chicago Distribution Ctr
In celebration of the one hundredth anniversary of Friedrich von Hayek's birth, this is a series of lectures featuring outstanding scholars of Hayek's work. Speakers include Gary Becker, James Buchanan, Richard Epstein, Ralph Harris, Kurt Leube, Kenneth Minogue, Michael Novak, and Sherwin Rosen. Filmed at the University of Chicago and hosted by Robert Pippin, Chairman of the Committee on Social Thought.

Legacy of Hate: The Long War Against Israel. collector's ed. Chuck Missler & Avi Lipkin. 2 CD's. (Running Time: 2 hours). (Briefing Packages by Chuck Missler). 2001. audio compact disk 19.95 (978-1-57821-151-7(4)) Koinonia Hse.
" Is fanatic Islam a global threat?" How does Islam hope to convert the world? The Middle East conflict is one with deep roots, tracing its history back to the birth of Isaac and Ishmael. Throughout the history of Islam, the primary enemy of Allah has been the Jews and, in modern-day history, the nation of Israel. What is unknown to most is that Christians are next. Avi Lipkin, a former Israeli Defense Intelligence specialist, details many of the causes of tension.Avi Lipkin has spoken to numerous churches, synagogues and civic groups (including radio and TV appearances). He offers compelling proof that fanatic Islam is the number one threat to world peace today.

Legacy of Jesus. 2 cass. 7.95 (22-5, HarperThor) HarpC GBR.

Legacy of Ladysmith. unabr. ed. John Kenny Crane. Narrated by Eric Conger. 11 cass. (Running Time: 16 hrs.). 1989. 91.00 (978-1-55690-307-6(3), 89190E7) Recorded Bks.
A Scottish family hires a young American biographer to research the life story of a shadowy relative rumored to have been a great war hero. Soon the biographer uncovers a bizarre tale of intrigue, passion & tragedy.

Legacy of Love. Gregory Morgan. 2004. audio compact disk 29.95 (978-1-4276-0593-1(9)) AardGP.

Legacy of Silence. unabr. ed. Belva Plain. Read by Kate Harper. 10 cass. (Running Time: 39180 sec.). 2000. 84.95 (978-0-7540-0329-8(9), CAB 1752) Pub: Chivers Audio Bks GBR. Dist(s): AudioGO
It is 1939 & Caroline & Lore are young women living in Berlin amidst the madness engulfing Europe. With the death of their parents at the hands of the Nazis, the two flee to Switzerland. When Caroline's young beau fails to join them there, Lore provides an explanation for his absence that will follow them & those around them, as they grasp for new hope & happiness in America.

Legacy of Sins. Anne Baker. Read by Julia Franklin. 14 CDs. (Running Time: 18 hrs. 40 mins.). (Soundings (CDs) Ser.). (J). 2004. audio compact disk 104.95 (978-1-84283-781-8(9)) Pub: ISIS Lrg Prnt GBR. Dist(s): Ulverscroft US

Legacy of Sins. unabr. ed. Anne Baker. Read by Julia Franklin. 14 cass. (Running Time: 19 hrs.). (Sound Ser.). (J). 2002. 99.95 (978-1-84283-193-9(3)) Pub: ISIS Lrg Prnt GBR. Dist(s): Ulverscroft US

Legacy of the Blue Heron: Living with Learning Disabilities. Harry Sylvester. 2003. 19.95 (978-1-881929-33-8(7)) Oxton Hse Pubs.

Legacy of the Crook'd Staff: An Irish-American Family's Discovery. Characters created by Peter E. Roller. 2008. audio compact disk 40.00 (978-0-9785035-9-8(7)) Tiyospaye Pub.

Legacy of the Dead. unabr. ed. Charles Todd. Narrated by Samuel Gillies. 8 cass. (Running Time: 11 hrs. 15 mins.). (Inspector Ian Rutledge Mystery Ser.: Bk. 4). 2002. 72.00 (978-1-84197-376-0(9)) Recorded Bks.

Legacy of the Dead. unabr. ed. Charles Todd. Read by Samuel Gillies. (Inspector Ian Rutledge Mystery Ser.: Bk. 4). 2001. (978-0-7887-9036-2(6)) Recorded Bks.
Inspector Rutledge, a man haunted by his nightmares from World War I, is in the mountains of Scotland identifying some weathered remains. His search will lead him to old, but still deadly, secrets.

Legacy of the Scottish Harpers. Robin Williamson. Transcribed by Jay Ansill. 1999. spiral bd. 24.95 (978-0-7866-4453-7(2), 98142BCD) Mel Bay.

Legacy of Vengeance: A Sheriff Bramlett Mystery. unabr. ed. John Armistead. Narrated by Mark Hammer. 7 cass. (Running Time: 10 hrs. 30 mins.). (Sheriff Bramlett Mystery Ser.). 1994. 60.00 (978-0-7887-3489-2(X), 95896E7) Recorded Bks.
When a series of execution-style murders rocks a small Mississippi county, the local sheriff looks for something that links the victims. But finding that connection will take him back to 1996 and a chapter of his past he has concealed from everyone.

Legacy of Yalta. 1 cass. (Running Time: 1 hr. 30 min.). 11.95 (K0810B090, HarperThor) HarpC GBR.

Legacy West: Songs from the Mormon Trail. Lisa Arrington. 1 cass. 9.95 (10001352); audio compact disk 14.95 (2800977) Covenant Comms.
Thirteen lost hymns & original melodies from the pioneer era.

Legal & E-Commerce Environment Today: Business in the Ethical, Regulatory, & International Setting Interactive Cd-rom. 3rd ed. Roger LeRoy Miller & Frank B. Cross. 2001. audio compact disk 124.95 (978-0-324-11992-3(5)) South-West.

Legal & Economic Pressures on the Management of Trauma: Trauma Symposium. Moderated by William R. Drucker. 3 cass. (Spring Sessions Ser.: SP-8). 1986. 28.50 (8679) Am Coll Surgeons.

Legal & Practical Aspects of DUI/DWI. John Stephen. 5 cass. (Running Time: 5 hrs.). 1999. 100.00 (37585-10, Lexis Law PR) LEXIS Pub.
Provides a comprehensive resource of practical advice for police officers & investigators on all aspects of DUI DWI. A training tool that contains current & pertinent cases. Technical support & customer support available.

Legal & Practical Aspects of DUI/DWI. 5th rev. ed. John A. Stephen. 1999. reel tape 100.00 (978-0-327-07767-1(0)) LEXIS Pub.

Legal & Vital Aspects of Redemption. Kenneth Copeland. 1 cass. (Revelation of Redemption Ser.: No. 3). 1982. 5.00 (978-0-88114-047-7(3)) K Copeland Pubns.
Indepth biblical study on redemption.

Legal Aspects of Executive Compensation. Contrib. by Kenneth S. Apfel. (Running Time: 4 hrs.). 1984. 70.00 incl. program handbook. NJ Inst CLE.
Highlights of this recording include: compensation in a closely held corporation, nonqualified deferred compensation, restricted property agreements, stock plans.

Legal Aspects of Trade & Investment in the Soviet Union & Eastern Europe. Contrib. by Eugene Theroux. 9 cass. (Running Time: 11 hrs. 30 min.). 1990. 125.00 (T7-9292) PLI.

Legal Career Management: Legal Job Interviewing & Effective Networking. Richard L. Hermann. (Running Time: 10800 sec.). (Sum & Substance Ser.). 2007. 53.00 (978-0-314-18947-9(5), West Lglwrks) West.

Legal Career Management: Preparing for a Job Search & Career Transition. Richard L. Hermann. (Running Time: 16200 sec.). (Sum & Substance Ser.). 2007. 53.00 (978-0-314-18946-2(7), West Lglwrks) West.

Legal Career Management: the Hidden Legal Job Market; Major Employer Complaints; Solo Practice Success. Richard L. Hermann. (Running Time: 16200 sec.). (Sum & Substance Ser.). 2007. 53.00 (978-0-314-18945-5(9), West Lglwrks) West.

Legal Dictation at Eighty - One Hundred Twenty WPM. unabr. ed. Conversa-Phone Institute Staff. 1 cass. (Running Time: 55 min.). (Secretarial Courses Ser.). 1992. 9.95 (978-1-56752-106-1(1)) Conversa-phone.
Dictation of letters given at different speeds. Manual for correcting work. These letters & briefs are using legal terminology.

Legal Ethics: What Every Lawyer Needs to Know. 7 cass. (Running Time: 9 hrs. 30 min.). bk. 95.00 incl. 980-page course handbook. (T6-9141) PLI.

Legal Ethics in an Unethical World. Thomas V. Morris. 2 cass. (Running Time: 1 hr. 28 min.). 1992. 49.95 Set. (FAZ110S) Natl Inst Trial Ad.
A thought-provoking & engaging discussion of a dilemma all practitioners face: the problem of how to make ethical decisions.

Legal Fiction. unabr. ed. E. X. Ferrars. Read by Cameron Stewart. 5 CDs. (Running Time: 5 hrs. 4 mins.). (Isis Ser.). (J). 2002. audio compact disk 59.95 (978-0-7531-1486-5(0)) Pub: ISIS Lrg Prnt GBR. Dist(s): Ulverscroft US
The Decayed Gentlewoman, they had called her as children, an unregarded painting badly in need of cleaning. Later it vanished. But before that, Ginny and her mother had stopped coming to stay in Ardachoil. Colin never knew why. Now suddenly both the Decayed Gentlewoman and Ginny had re-entered his life. After an urgent station announcement at King's Cross and an oddly frantic phone call, Dr. Colin Locke, with his childhood emotions vividly re-awakened, found himself drawn into a maze of suspicions, theft, legal coplexities and finally murder.

Legal Fiction. unabr. ed. Elizabeth Ferrars. Read by Cameron Stewart. 4 cass. (Running Time: 11 hrs.). (Isis Ser.). (J). 2004. 44.95 (978-1-85695-987-2(2), 960212) Pub: ISIS Lrg Prnt GBR. Dist(s): Ulverscroft US

Legal Heat: 50 State Guide to Firearm Laws & Regulations. 2009th ed. Ed. by Jason Nelsen et al. (ENG.). 2009. lib. bdg. (978-0-9841566-0-3(7)) UT Legal Heat.

Legal Issues, Pt. 4. (D035BB090) Natl Public Radio.

Legal Issues: The Long Term Answers. 2007. audio compact disk 17.99 (978-1-934570-02-9(8)) Lanphier Pr.

Legal Issues in Academic Advising: NACADA Webinar Series 07. Featuring Steve Robinson. (ENG.). 2007. audio compact disk 140.00 (978-1-935140-49-8(3)) Nat Acad Adv.

Legal Limit. unabr. ed. Martin Clark. Read by Ed Sala. (Running Time: 16 hrs.). 2008. 61.75 (978-1-4361-6513-6(X)); audio compact disk 123.75 (978-1-4361-2365-5(8)) Recorded Bks.
Martin Clark has been praised as "part John Grisham, part Hunter S. Thompson, and part sheer grit" (Denver Post). Mason Hunt returns to his small Virginia hometown as the county's commonwealth attorney. Mason's brother Gates, who's currently serving a 20-year prison term, thinks Mason should have enough pull to set him free. And when Mason refuses, Gates hatches a plan to destroy his brother's life with a secret they both swore they'd take to the grave.

Legal Malpractice. Robert S. Sigman. Read by Robert S. Sigman. 1 cass. (Running Time: 60 min.). (Law for the Layman Ser.). 1990. 16.95 (978-1-878135-04-9(X)) Legovac.
What you need to know before you see an attorney!.

Legal Open Forum: January Nineteen Eighty-Six. Contrib. by Steve Groome et al. 2 cass. (Running Time: 2 hrs.). 10.00 (#35) CAR LA.
Topics include: How to comply with the new Easton laws; New Smoke Detector laws in California effective January 1986; How to properly market & advertise property for sale & more.

Legal Open Forum: July Nineteen Eighty-Six. Contrib. by Steve Groome et al. 2 cass. (Running Time: 2 hrs.). 10.00 (#35J) CAR LA.
Topics include: Multiple Counter Offers...or how to avoid selling the house; What do you do when the appraisal comes in lower than the sale price; New statutes relating to repayment penalties & more.

Legal Opinion Letters. 1991. 55.00 (AC-600) PA Bar Inst.

Legal Problems of Museum Administration. 12 cass. 1998. 235.00 Incl. course materials. (MC40) Am Law Inst.

Legal Representation of Victims of Domestic Violence. Martha Aleo & Michael M. Greenburg. 1 cass. (Running Time: 1 hr.). 1986. bk. 20.00 PA Bar Inst.

Legal Research for the 21st Century. Berring. 2001. 442.00 (978-0-314-26082-6(X), West Lglwrks); 226.00 (978-0-314-26080-2(3), West Lglwrks); 112.00 (978-0-314-26081-9(1), West Lglwrks); 112.00 (978-0-314-26079-6(X), West Lglwrks) West.

Legal Secretarial - Typewriting & Dictation: Syllabus. Virginia B. Schoepfer. (J). 1974. 102.55 (978-0-89420-159-2(X), 290000) Natl Book.

Legal Strategies for Companies Being Acquired. ReedLogic Staff. 2006. audio compact disk 199.95 (978-1-59701-088-7(X)) Aspatore Bks.

Legal Tender. unabr. ed. Lisa Scottoline. Read by Kathleen O'Malley. 6 cass. (Running Time: 9 hrs.). 1997. 48.00 (978-0-913369-42-5(X), 4221) Books on Tape.
Benedetta "Bennie" Rosato, an attorney who fights police brutality, is beautiful, nearly six feet, blonde & loves playing poker. When police accuse her of murder, it looks bad: Bennie has no alibi & the murder weapon turns up at her place. Bennie will get at the truth, or die trying.

***Legal Tender Low Price: Low Price.** abr. ed. Lisa Scottoline. Read by Kate Burton. (ENG.). 2005. (978-0-06-088653-0(6), Harper Audio); (978-0-06-088654-7(4), Harper Audio) HarperCollins Pubs.

Legal Transcription. Linda Lyle & Howard Doty. 1 cass. 1994. bk. 150.00 (978-1-56118-673-0(2), 56162) Paradigm MN.

Legal Transcription: Student Courseware. Linda R. Lyle & G. Howard Doty. 7 vols. bk. 84.95 (978-0-7638-2194-4(2)); bk. 89.95 (978-0-7638-2196-8(9)) EMC-Paradigm.

Legalizing Hard Drugs. unabr. ed. Roy Childs. 1 cass. (Running Time: 40 min.). 12.95 (336) J Norton Pubs.

Legally Correct Fairy Tales: Bedtime Classics Translated into the Legalese. abr. ed. David Fisher. (ENG.). 2006. 5.98 (978-1-59483-740-1(6)) Pub: Hachet Audio. Dist(s): HachBkGrp

Legally Dead. unabr. ed. Edna Buchanan. Read by Mark Deakins. 9 CDs. (Running Time: 10 hrs. 45 mins.). 2008. audio compact disk 110.00 (978-1-4159-5601-4(4), BksonTape) Pub: Random Audio Pubg. Dist(s): Random

Legally Terminate Employees. PUEI. audio compact disk 199.00 (978-1-934147-97-9(4), CareerTrack) P Univ E Inc.

Legend. Tim Winton. Read by Stig Wemyss. (Running Time: 3 hrs. 30 mins.). (Lockie Leonard Ser.). (YA). 2009. 54.99 (978-1-74214-357-6(1), 9781742143576) Pub: Bolinda Pubng AUS. Dist(s): Bolinda Pub Inc

Legend. abr. ed. Jude Deveraux. 2004. 10.95 (978-0-7435-4941-7(4)) Pub: S&S Audio. Dist(s): S and S Inc

Legend. unabr. ed. Jude Deveraux. Narrated by C. J. Critt. 10 cass. (Running Time: 14 hrs. 30 mins.). 1997. 90.00 (978-0-7887-0840-4(6), 94986E7) Recorded Bks.
Beautiful Kady Long discovers an antique bridal gown in a second-hand shop while shopping for her wedding. When she tries it on, she begins a bewitching journey into the past.

Legend at Gaither's Pond. Directed By Benjy Gaither. Contrib. by Benjy Gaither. Prod. by Benjy Gaither & Jeff Silvey. (Running Time: 35 mins.). (Gaither's Pond Ser.). (J). (ps-3). 2003. 9.98 (978-5-550-25476-9(X)) Spring House Music.

Legend in Green Velvet. Elizabeth Peters, pseud. Read by Grace Conlin. 7 CDs. (Running Time: 7 mins.). (ENG.). 2005. audio compact disk 48.00 (978-0-7861-8777-5(8), 2301) Blckstn Audio.

Legend in Green Velvet. Elizabeth Peters, pseud. Read by Grace Colin. 6. (Running Time: 8). 2008. audio compact disk 48.00 (978-0-7861-8945-8(2)) Blckstn Audio.

Legend in Green Velvet. Elizabeth Peters, pseud. Narrated by Grace Conlin. (Running Time: 7 hrs.). 1997. 27.95 (978-1-59912-531-2(5)) Iofy Corp.

Legend in Green Velvet. unabr. ed. Elizabeth Peters, pseud. Read by Grace Conlin. 5 cass. (Running Time: 7 hrs.). 1998. 39.95 (978-0-7861-1425-2(8), 2301) Blckstn Audio.
Susan loved all things Scottish. So, when the opportunity presented itself, there was no question in her mind but that she would go on the archaeological dig in the Highlands. A cryptic message slipped to Susan by a sinister soap box orator was the first puzzle. Why did he choose her? Why are she & Jamie Erskine suddenly being pursued by the police who wanted to talk to them about...murder?.

Legend in Green Velvet. unabr. ed. Elizabeth Peters, pseud. Read by Grace Conlin. (Running Time: 7 mins.). 2005. 29.95 (978-0-7861-7902-2(3)) Blckstn Audio.

Legend Makers. Catherine Lanigan. Read by Anna Fields. 7 cass. (Running Time: 10 hrs. 30 min.). 1999. 39.95 (978-0-7366-4698-7(1)) Books on Tape.
As part of a three person survey team in search of oil deep in the Amazon jungles, J. J. Callahan finds herself seduced by the exotic beauty of the land & the heady sensuality of two very different men. But the jungle's green walls have a dangerous secret of their own, of a past expedition clouded in mystery, in which there were no survivors. As they approach the heart of the jungle, truths are revealed, betrayals uncovered & M.J. is forced to confront her own demons before history repeats itself.

Legend Makers. collector's ed. Catherine Lanigan. Read by Anna Fields. 7 cass. (Running Time: 10 hrs. 30 min.). 1999. 56.00 (978-0-7366-4655-0(8)) Books on Tape.
As part of a three person survey team in search of oil deep in the Amazon jungles, J.J. Callahan finds herself seduced by the exotic beauty of the land & the heady sensuality of two very different men. But the jungle's green walls have a dangerous secret of their own, of a past expedition clouded in mystery, in which there were no survivors. As they approach the heart of the jungle, truths are revealed, betrayals uncovered & M.J. is forced to confront her own demons before history repeats itself.

Legend of Bagger Vance. movie tie-in ed. Steven Pressfield. Read by Ronny Cox. 2004. 15.95 (978-0-7435-1965-6(5)) Pub: S&S Audio. Dist(s): S and S Inc

Legend of Bagger Vance. unabr. ed. Steven Pressfield. Read by Barrett Whitener. 6 vols. (Running Time: 7 hrs.). 2001. bk. 54.95 (978-0-7927-2452-0(6), CSL 341, Chivers Sound Lib); audio compact disk 79.95 (978-0-7927-9995-5(X), SLD 046, Chivers Sound Lib) AudioGO.
During the Depression year of 1931, the golf links at Krewe Island off Savannah's windswept shore, two legends of the game, meet for a mesmerizing thirty-six hole showdown. One other golfer will also compete, a troubled local war hero, once a champion.

***Legend of Bass Reeves.** unabr. ed. Gary Paulsen. (Running Time: 3 hrs.). 2011. 12.99 (978-1-4558-0162-6(3), 9781455801626, BAD); 39.97 (978-1-4558-0163-3(1), 9781455801633, BADLE); 12.99 (978-1-4558-0160-2(7), 9781455801602, Brilliance MP3); 39.97 (978-1-4558-0161-9(5), 9781455801619, Brinc Audio MP3 Lib); audio compact disk 12.99 (978-1-4558-0158-9(5), 9781455801589, Bril Audio CD Unabri); audio compact disk 39.97 (978-1-4558-0159-6(3), 9781455801596, BriAudCD Unabrid) Brilliance Audio.

Legend of Ben Tree. abr. ed. Paul A. Hawkins. Read by Gary Owens. 4 cass. (Running Time: 6 hrs.). (Ben Tree Saga Ser.). 1999. Rental 24.95 (978-1-890990-20-6(5)) Otis Audio.
The story of the last of the mountain men & the first of the gunslingers. Caught between the white man & the Indian, Ben Tree chooses sides & becomes judge, jury & executioner to those who betray his people & kill his love.

Legend of Buddy Bush. unabr. ed. Shelia P. Moses. Narrated by Cherise Booth. 3 cass. (Running Time: 4 hrs.). (J). (gr. 3-7). 2005. bk. 55.70 (978-1-4193-3575-4(8), 42043); audio compact disk 39.75 (978-1-4193-3864-9(1), C3281); 32.75 (978-1-4193-3573-0(1), 98014) Recorded Bks.
Square, North Carolina. When her uncle, Buddy Bush moves back home from Harlem, it seems like a breath of northern freedom has come with him. But since Buddy doesn't bow to white folks any more, soon he is jail, with the Klan at the cell door. Through Pattie Mae's innocent eyes, life in the deeply segregated South unfolds as she tells of the birth of a legend.

Legend of Catfish & Little Bream. Ronnie Wells. Narrated by Julie Brunet. Composed by Julie Brunet. (Running Time: 050 min.). (J). (ps-3). 2000. 9.95 (978-0-925417-31-2(9)) Acadian Hse Pub.
This 50-minute audiocassette tape has a dramatic reading of the book on one side and a beautiful musical rendition of the story on the other.

Legend of Don Juan. unabr. ed. Armand E. Singer. 1 cass. (Running Time: 25 min.). 12.95 (23138) J Norton Pubs.

Legend of Hiawatha. (Running Time: 1 hr.). 2005. 19.95 (978-1-60083-332-8(2)) Iofy Corp.

Legend of Hiawatha. 1 cass. (Running Time: 1 hr.). (Full - Cast Productions Ser.). (J). (gr. 2-6). 2003. 12.95 (978-1-931953-48-1(1)) Listen & Live.
From his birth, the tribe knew he would be the one to save them. Now, Hiawatha, son of the West Wind, is all grown up and about to take on the most dangerous mission of his life. Listen as a full-cast relives as Hiawatha battles Pearl Feather - the evil one who brings pain, famine and disease to his fellow tribe members.

Legend of Kalikimaka with Christmas Hawaiian-Style CD: Hawaiian Christmas & Music. Robert/Rowen Westerman. Perf. by Robert/Rowen Westerman. Illus. by Eleykaa Tahleh. Music by Robert/Rowen Westerman. Contrib. by Prudencia Westerman.Tr. of Kalikimaka. (J). 2008. bk. 17.95 (978-0-9761992-4-3(6)) Pub: Gold Boy Mus. Dist(s): Booklines Hawaii

Legend of Lao Tse: Thirteen Scenarios for Voice & Piano. Paul Humhreys. Perf. by Paul Humhreys. Tr. by John Wilet. Lyrics by Bertolt Brecht. (ENG.). 2009. audio compact disk 9.99i (978-0-9801378-5-9(3)) Hope Media.

Legend of LeJube Rogue. unabr. ed. P. F. White. Read by Rusty Nelson. 4 cass. (Running Time: 5 hrs. 48 min.). 2001. 26.95 (978-1-55686-795-8(6)) Books in Motion.
Area settlers told stories about the white-eyed stranger roaming the hills seeking vengeance. But what was the real story behind this man schooled in weapons and how to use them?.

Legend of LoneStar Bear Bk. 1: How Lonestar Got His Name. Remi Kramer. Perf. by Bill Darrow. 1 cass. (J). 1988. 9.95 (978-0-945887-05-8(1)) Northwind Pr.
This is the story of Willy, the fishing bear from Idaho, who solves the mystery of the "Green Critters" from outer space & comes to be known as Lonestar Bear.

Legend of LoneStar Bear Bk. 2: Soaring with Eagles. Remi Kramer. Perf. by Bill Darrow. 1 cass. (Running Time: 30 min.). (J). 1990. 9.95 (978-0-945887-06-5(X)) Northwind Pr.
Lonestar Bear is urgently called to Canada to help the Royal Canadian Northwest Mounted Bears solve the mystery in the old ghost town.

Legend of Red Horse Cavern. unabr. ed. Gary Paulsen. Narrated by Jeff Woodman. 1 cass. (Running Time: 1 hr.). (Gary Paulsen's World of Adventure Ser.: Bk. 1). (gr. 4 up). 1997. 10.00 (978-0-7887-0795-7(7), 94945E7) Recorded Bks.
Filled with suspense, action & colorful settings. Two children find the secret of an ancient Apache legend deep in a cave in the mountains. Now they must find their way out before a headless ghost or flesh-&-blood bandits catch up with them.

Legend of Sigurd & Gudrún. unabr. ed. J. R. R. Tolkien. Read by Brian Cox. Ed. by Christopher Tolkien. Intro. by Christopher Tolkien. (ENG.). 2010. audio compact disk (978-0-00-731882-7(0)) HarpC Audio GBR.

Legend of Skull Cliff. unabr. ed. Kristiana Gregory. (Running Time: 1 hr. 45 mins. 0 sec.). (Cabin Creek Mysteries Ser.). (ENG.). (J). 2008. 10.49 (978-1-60814-105-0(5), SpringWater) Oasis Audio.

Legend of Skull Cliff. unabr. ed. Kristiana Gregory. 2 CDs. (Running Time: 1 hr. 21 mins. 19 sec.). (Cabin Creek Mysteries Ser.: Bk. 3). (ENG.). (J). (gr. 3-5). 2008. audio compact disk 14.99 (978-1-59859-388-4(9)) Oasis Audio.

Legend of Sleepy Hollow see Childhood Legends

Legend of Sleepy Hollow. (J). (819) Audio Bk.

Legend of Sleepy Hollow. (J). Audio Bk Con.

Legend of Sleepy Hollow. (J). 2003. audio compact disk 7.99 (978-0-9740847-2-5(7)) GiGi Bks.
Was there really a Headless Horseman? This dramatic story will draw you into the life of Ichabod Crane as you ponder the question. The Washington Irving classic has been rewritten as an "edge of your seat" audio production with updated language for today?s audience.A thrilling story any time of the year. Not intended for the faint of heart.

***Legend of Sleepy Hollow.** Washington Irving & Dave Gutierrez. Illus. by Tod G. Smith. Retold by Blake A. Hoena. (Classic Fiction Ser.). (ENG.). 2010. audio compact disk 14.60 (978-1-4342-2570-2(4)) CapstoneDig.

Legend of Sleepy Hollow. Ed. by Tod Smith. (J). 1993. 6.98 (978-1-884159-02-2(8)) Carousel Classics.

Legend of Sleepy Hollow. Ed. by Tod Smith. 10.00 (LSS1101) Esstee Audios.

Legend of Sleepy Hollow. abr. ed. Perf. by St. Charles Players. 2 cass . (Running Time: 1 hr. 48 mins.). (Mystery Theatre Ser.). 1999. 16.95 (978-1-56994-522-3(5), 328134, Monterey SoundWorks) Monterey Media Inc.
There's a legend in this valley about a ghostly horseman that rides by night. There are many such legends & for school teacher Ichabod Crane the darkness of night holds a special fascination... & fear. For often there is truth in stories, especially ghost stories. And one fated night, Ichabod Crane will discover that the horseman of legend is indeed...headless!.

Legend of Sleepy Hollow. unabr. ed. Read by Ed Begley. Ed. by Tod Smith. 1 cass. Incl. Headless Horseman. (SWC 1242); Ichabod Crane. (SWC 1242); (J). 1984. 12.95 (978-0-694-50174-8(3), SWC 1242) HarperCollins Pubs.

Legend of Sleepy Hollow. unabr. ed. Read by Cindy Hardin & Ivov Hugh. Ed. by Tod Smith. 1 cass. (Running Time: 58 min.). Dramatization. (J). 1977. 7.95 (N-16) Jimcin Record.
Story of Ichabod Crane & the headless horseman.

Legend of Sleepy Hollow. unabr. ed. Read by Hurd Hatfield. Ed. by Tod Smith. 1 cass. (Running Time: 50 min.). 10.95 (978-0-8045-0991-6(3), 7022) Spoken Arts.

***Legend of Sleepy Hollow.** unabr. ed. Washington Irving. Read by Anthony Heald. (Running Time: 1.5 hr. NaN mins.). (ENG.). 2010. 19.95 (978-1-4417-8090-4(4)); 15.95 (978-1-4417-8087-4(4)); audio compact disk 14.95 (978-1-4417-8089-8(0)); audio compact disk 28.00 (978-1-4417-8088-1(2)) Blckstn Audio.

Legend of Sleepy Hollow. unabr. ed. Ed. by Tod Smith. 1 cass. (Running Time: 60 min.). 1994. 14.95 (978-0-88432-673-1(X), SEN280) J Norton Pubs.
Listening/comprehension story including transcript.

Legend of Sleepy Hollow: Abridged. (ENG.). 2007. (978-1-60339-023-1(5)); cd-rom & audio compact disk (978-1-60339-024-8(3)) Listenr Digest.

Legend of Sleepy Hollow: Minibook Edition. Washington Irving. Illus. by Robert Van Nutt. 1 cass. (J). 1993. 9.95 (978-0-88708-321-1(8), SSChildren) SandS Childrens.

Legend of Sleepy Hollow & Rip Van Winkle. Washington Irving. Narrated by George Vafiadis. (Running Time: 7980 sec.). (Unabridged Classics in MP3 Ser.). (YA). 2008. audio compact disk 24.00 (978-1-58472-633-3(4), In Aud) Sound Room.

Legend of Sleepy Hollow & Rip Van Winkle. Washington Irving. Read by George Vafiadis. (Running Time: 2 hrs.). 2002. 19.95 (978-1-59912-087-4(9), Audiofy Corp) Iofy Corp.

Legend of Sleepy Hollow & Rip Van Winkle. unabr. ed. 2 CDs. (Running Time: 2 hrs. 15 min.). (YA). (gr. 7 up). 2002. audio compact disk 25.00 (978-1-58472-100-0(6), Commuters Library) Sound Room.
Takes place in Tarrytown, tells the story of Schoolmaster, Ichabod Crane, a connecticut native, who comes to teach in a oneroom schoolhouse, becomes the neighborhood song master. He reads Cotton Mather, steeps himself in local folklore and competes with Brom Bones for the affections of Katrina.

Legend of Sleepy Hollow & Rip Van Winkle. unabr. ed. Washington Irving. Read by George Vafiadis. 2 cds. (Running Time: 2 hrs 13 mins). (YA). 2002. audio compact disk (978-1-58472-280-9(0), In Aud) Sound Room.
Ichabod Crane's encounters with the Headless Horseman and Rip's long nap.

Legend of Sleepy Hollow & Rip Van Winkle. unabr. ed. Washington Irving. Read by George Vafiadis. 2 CDs. (Running Time: 2 hrs. 30 mins.). 2000. audio compact disk 18.95 (Commuters Library) Sound Room.

Legend of Sleepy Hollow & Rip Van Winkle. unabr. ed. Washington Irving. Read by George Vafiadis. 2 cds. (Running Time: 2 hrs 13 mins). (YA). 2002. audio compact disk 18.95 (978-1-58472-278-6(9), 013, In Aud) Pub: Sound Room. Dist(s): Baker Taylor
Two American classics which tell of the earliest days in Dutch New York. Ichabod Crane's encounter with the Headless Horseman and Rip's long nap reign with the richest of folklore and are truly worth hearing.

Legend of Sleepy Hollow & Rip Van Winkle. unabr. ed. Washington Irving. Read by George Vafiadis. (J). 2007. 34.99 (978-1-59895-860-7(7)) Find a World.

Legend of Sleepy Hollow & Rip Van Winkle: Short Stories by Washington Irving. Noe Venable. Washington Irving. (Classic Literature Ser.). 2005. pap. bk. 69.00 (978-1-4105-0073-1(X)); audio compact disk 18.95 (978-1-4105-0074-8(8)) D Johnston Inc.

Legend of Sleepy Hollow audio CD. Washington Irving. (ENG.). 2006. audio compact disk 9.95 (978-1-57970-431-5(X), Audio-For) J Norton Pubs.

Legend of Spinoza: The Bear Who Speaks from the Heart. unabr. ed. Robert Talltree. Read by David Simmons. Perf. by David Simmons. 1 cass. (Running Time: 32 min.). Dramatization. (J). 1998. 24.95 (978-1-58452-001-6(9)) Spinoza Co.

Legend of Squanto: An Unknown Hero Who Changed the Course of American History. adpt. ed. Read by Peter Brooke et al. Prod. by Focus on the Family Staff. Adapted by Paul McCusker. (Running Time: 240 hrs. 0 mins.). (Radio Theatre Ser.). (ENG.). (J). (gr. 3). 2007. audio compact disk 14.97 (978-1-58997-500-2(6)) Pub: Focus Family. Dist(s): Tyndale Hse

Legend of Squanto: Promo Edition. Focus on the Family Staff. 2 CDs. (Running Time: 1 hr. 40 mins.). (Radio Theatre Ser.). 2005. audio compact disk (978-1-58997-034-2(9)) Focus Family.

Legend of St. Dismas. unabr. ed. Joycelynne Calavano. 3 cass. 14.95 set. (324) Ignatius Pr.
Fr. Peter Gallwey asked a pious lady to "provide gospel truths & high thoughts with a graceful dress" resulting in these charmingly sentimental Victorian poems.

***Legend of St. Nicholas: A Story of Christmas Giving.** Dandi Daley Mackall. (Running Time: 0 hr. 9 mins. 0 sec.). (ENG.). (J). 2009. 15.99 (978-0-310-77249-1(4)) Pub: Zondkidz. Dist(s): Zondervan

Legend of the Baal-Shem. abr. ed. Martin Buber. Read by Theodore Bikel. 2 cass. (Running Time: 3 hrs.). 1995. 16.95 (978-0-944993-40-8(0)) Audio Lit.

Legend of the Bermuda Triangle see Leyenda del Triangulo de las Bermudas

Legend of the Bermuda Triangle, Level 1. 2 cass. (Running Time: 1 hr. 30 mins.). (SmartReader Ser.). (J). 1999. pap. bk. & tchr. ed. 19.95 (978-0-7887-0758-2(2), 79346T3) Recorded Bks.
Why have so many ships & planes disappeared from this perilous area? Are there real explanations, or is the Bermuda Triangle still a mystery?.

Legend of the Bermuda Triangle, Level 2. 2 cass. (Running Time: 1 hr. 30 mins.). (SmartReader Ser.). (J). 1999. pap. bk. & tchr. ed. 19.95 (978-0-7887-0113-9(4), 79301T3) Recorded Bks.

Legend of the Bluebonnet: The Ego-Self Relationship. Read by Louise Bode. 1 cass. (Running Time: 2 hrs.). (Fairytales Ser.: No. 6). 1987. 12.95 (978-0-7822-0019-5(2), 236) C G Jung IL.

***Legend of the Guardians.** unabr. ed. Kathryn Lasky. Read by Pamela Garelick. (Running Time: 16 hrs. 30 mins.). (Guardians of Ga'Hoole Ser.: Bk. 1-3). 2010. 95.95 (978-1-4417-6987-9(0)) Blckstn Audio.

***Legend of the Guardians.** unabr. ed. Kathryn Lasky. Read by Pamela Garelick. (Running Time: 16 hrs. 30 mins.). (Guardians of Ga'Hoole Ser.: Bks. 1-3). 2010. 44.95 (978-1-4417-6990-9(0)); audio compact disk 39.95 (978-1-4417-6989-3(7)); audio compact disk 123.00 (978-1-4417-6988-6(9)) Blckstn Audio.

Legend of the Hummingbird: A Tale from Puerto Rico. Retold by Michael Rose Ramirez. 1 cass. (Running Time: 30 mins.). (Folktales Ser.). (J). (gr. k-4). 1999. 7.95 (978-1-57255-655-3(2)) Mondo Pubng.
In stories, people may be changed into plants or animals for protection or punishment. Meet Alida & Taroo & find out why a beautiful flower & a tiny bird were created.

Legend of the Rose of the Alhambra see Great American Short Stories, Vol. II, A Collection

Legend of the Tumbleweed. unabr. ed. Kirby Jonas. Read by James Drury. 12 cass. (Running Time: 12 hrs. 6 min.). 2001. 64.95 (978-1-58116-000-0(3)) Books in Motion.
Robbing a bank in the wrong town made Tom McLean a notorius man, and put him on the run. But the posse was close behind to see he never made the border. Was the woman the ticket to freedom... or his ride to shallow a grave?.

Legend of the Wandering King. unabr. ed. Laura Gallego Garcia. 5 cass. (Running Time: 7 hrs.). 2005. 24.95 (978-0-7861-3439-7(9)) Blckstn Audio.

Legend of the Wandering King. unabr. ed. Laura Gallego Garcia. Read by Patrick Fraley. 6 CDs. (Running Time: 16200 sec.). (J). (gr. 3-7). 2005. audio compact disk 24.95 (978-0-7861-7989-3(9)) Blckstn Audio.

Legend of the Wandering King. unabr. ed. Laura Gallego Garcia. Read by Patrick Fraley. 13 vols. (Running Time: 16200 sec.). (J). (gr. 4-10). 2005. audio compact disk 24.95 (978-0-7861-8113-1(3)) Blckstn Audio.

Legend of the Wandering King. unabr. ed. Laura Gallego García. Read by Pat Fraley. (Running Time: 4 hrs. 30 mins.). (J). 2005. audio compact disk 36.00 (978-0-7861-7947-3(3)) Blckstn Audio.

Legend of the Wandering King. unabr. ed. Laura Gallego García. Read by Pat Fraley. (J). 2007. 34.99 (978-1-59895-928-4(X)) Find a World.

Legendary Country Singers. Perf. by Hank Williams. 1 cass. 1999. 9.99 (SGC961); audio compact disk 9.99 (SHC960) Time-Life.

Legendary Jazz. 3 cass. 1998. 35.94 (978-1-56826-973-3(0)) Rhino Enter.

Legendary Leadership. Andrew Wood. 1 CD. 2000. audio compact disk 179.95; 149.95 Personal Quest.

Everyone has the potential to be a great leader. By recognizing the key traits of great leaders, you can either improve on the position you already have or begin to develop your talents & position yourself for the future.

Legendary Service. Ken Blanchard et al. Read by Ken Blanchard et al. 6 cass. 1989. 69.95 (LS0007) K Blanchard.

Learn the ten fundamentals of Legendary Service, understand the financial rewards of exceptional service, & hear how service role models like Nordstrom & American Honda rose to the top.

Legendary Service. Ken Blanchard et al. 6 cass. 59.95 (1061PAD) Nightingale-Conant.

A completely new way of responding to customer needs. You receive a step-by-step presentation of the ten fundamentals that will lead your company to truly legendary service levels.

Legendary Singing Cowboys. Friedman-Fairfax and Sony Music Staff. 1 cass. (CD Ser.). 1995. pap. bk. 16.98 (978-1-56799-230-4(7), Friedman-Fairfax) M Friedman Pub Grp Inc.

Legendary West Virginia Fiddler from 1947 Field Recordings, Vol. 1. Intro. by John A. Cuthbert. Prod. by Danny Williams. 1 CD. (West Virginia University Press Sound Archives Ser.: Vol. 1). 2001. audio compact disk 16.00 (978-0-937058-51-0(3)) Pub: West Va U Pr. Dist(s): Chicago Distribution Ctr

Legende de Saint Julien l'Hospitalier. Gustave Flaubert. 1 cass. (Running Time: 90 min.). (FRE.). bk. 22.50 Interlingua VA.

Includes dual language French-English transcription. The combination of written text & clarity & pace of diction will open the door for intermediate & advanced students to genuine comprehension & the use of literary texts for advancement in rapid understanding of written & oral language materials. The audio text plus written text concept makes foreign languages accessible to a much wider range of students than books alone.

Legends. 1 cass. (Running Time: 30 min.). 9.95 (F0260B090, HarperThor) HarpC GBR.

Legends, Vol. 4. abr. ed. Anne McCaffrey & Robert A. Silverberg. Read by Sam Tsoutsouvas et al. 4 cass. (Running Time: 360 min.). (Stories by the Masters of Fantasy Ser.: Vol. 4). 1999. 34.95 (978-0-694-52113-5(2)) HarperCollins Pubs.

Legends: A Novel of Dissimulation. Robert Littell. (ENG.). 2005. 25.95 (978-1-58567-696-5(9)) Pub: Overlook Pr. Dist(s): Penguin Grp USA

Legends: A Novel of Dissimulation. unabr. ed. Robert Littell. Read by Grover Gardner. 10 cds. (Running Time: 13 hrs). 2005. audio compact disk 39.95 (978-1-57270-485-5(3)) Pub: Audio Partners. Dist(s): PerseuPGW

For Martin Odum, both remembering and forgetting his past are dangerous options. A CIA agent turned private detective, Odum is struggling through a labyrinth of memories of past identities - or "legends" in CIA parlance. Is he really Martin Odum? Or is he Dante Pippen, IRA explosives maven? Or Lincoln Dittmann, Civil War expert? Or yet another legend? Is he suffering from multiple personality disorder, brainwashing, or simply exhaustion? Can he trust the CIA psychiatrist, or the Deputy Director of Operations? What about Stella Kastner, the young Russian woman who hires him to find her brother-in-law? As Odum redeploys his dormant skills to solve Stella's case, he travels the globe battling danger and disorientation. Part Three Faces of Eve, part The Spy Who Came in from the Cold, and always pure Robert Littell, Legends again proves his unparalleled prowess as a seductive storyteller, exploring the clandestine but always very human world of secret agents.

Legends: Graded Readings from American History, 52 People Who Made A Difference. Michael Ryall. 2 CDs. (Graded Readings From American History Ser.). (gr. 4-12). 2006. pap. bk. & stu. ed. 28.00 (978-0-86647-239-5(8)) Pro Lingua.

Legends: 52 People Who Made A Difference. Michael Ryall. 2 CDs. 2006. audio compact disk 20.00 (978-0-86647-225-8(8)) Pro Lingua.

Legends & Songwriters. Perf. by Judy Garland et al. 2 CDs. (Running Time: 2 hrs.). 1999. audio compact disk 19.98 (4207) Radio Spirits.

***Legends from the Trove: Famous Treasure Found & Lost.** Helen McCormick. Voice by Ephraim L. McCormick. Prod. by TBT Publisher Staff. (YA). 2010. audio compact disk (978-0-9818619-9-9(7)) TBT Pub.

Legends, Lies & Myths of World History. unabr. ed. Richard Sherman. Read by Arte Johnson. 4 cass. (Running Time: 6 hrs.). 2001. 25.00 (978-1-59040-092-0(5), Phoenix Audio) Pub: Amer Intl Pub. Dist(s): PerseuPGW

Legends of Comedy. unabr. ed. Perf. by Jack Benny et al. 10 vols. (Running Time: 10 hrs.). (10-Hour Collections). 2002. bk. 34.98 (978-1-57019-360-6(6), OTR4463) Pub: Radio Spirits. Dist(s): AudioGO

Legends of Country Blues Guitar. Stefan Grossman. 1997. bk. 22.95 (978-0-7866-2856-8(1), MB95269BCD) Mel Bay.

Legends of Dracula. Thomas Streissguth. Read by Scott Brick. 1 CD. (Running Time: 1 hr. 30 mins.). (Biography Ser.). (YA). 2000. audio compact disk 18.00 (5223-CD) Books on Tape.

He weaves the chilling tale of the real-life Prince Dracula, explains vampire legends & shows how these stories as well as Bella Lugosi's definitive film portrayal of Dracula have evolved into one of the most terrifying figures of popular culture.

Legends of Dracula. collector's ed. Thomas Streissguth. Read by Scott Brick. 1 cass. (Running Time: 90 mins.). (Biography Ser.). (YA). (gr. 5-12). 2000. 9.95 (978-0-7366-5036-6(9), 5223) Books on Tape.

Legends of Dracula. collector's unabr. ed. Thomas Streissguth. Read by Scott Brick. 2 CDs. (Running Time: 3 hrs.). 2000. audio compact disk 24.00 (978-0-7366-5220-9(5)) Books on Tape.

Legends of Dracula. unabr. ed. Thomas Streissguth. Read by Scott Brick. 1 cass. (Running Time: 1 hrs. 30 min.). 2000. 9.95 (978-0-7366-4709-0(0)) Books on Tape.

Legends of Fianna. 1 CD. (Running Time: 58 mins.). (Abbey Theatre Reads Ser.).Tr. of Filíocht, Fiannaíocht agus sleachta as Leabhair. (IRI.). 2006. audio compact disk 15.95 (978-1-57970-375-2(5), ABB005D, Audio-For) J Norton Pubs.

Poetry and prose readings, including the reading of a chapter from the ancient saga of Diarmuid and Gráinne.

Legends of Maui As Told by Lani Goose. Elithe A. Kahn. Illus. by Tom Shiu. 1 cass. (J). (ps-6). 1989. 8.95 (978-0-944264-04-1(2)) Pacfic Printng & Pubng.

Legends of Oahu As Told by Lani Goose. Elithe A. Kahn. Illus. by Tom Shiu. 1 cass. (J). 1987. pap. bk. 8.95 (978-0-944264-01-0(8)) Pacfic Printng & Pubng.

Legends of Radio: Abbott & Costello. unabr. ed. Perf. by Bud Abbott et al. 10 vols. (Running Time: 10 hrs.). (10-Hour Collections). 2002. bk. 34.98 (978-1-57019-502-0(1), OTR40014) Pub: Radio Spirits. Dist(s): AudioGO

Bud Abbott and Lou Costello preserved the rich oral traditions of vaudeville and burlesque-and became two of radio's biggest stars in the process. Each week 20 million listeners tuned in to hear Bud and Lou's legendary verbal antics, which inspired countless comedians who followed. The duo's radio popularity paved the way for their success as the top box-office team of the 1940s. Relive the Golden Age of Radio with 20 hilarious episodes of The Abbott & Costello Show, featuring such guest stars as Jane Wyman, Marlene Dietrich and the Andrews Sisters. This one-of-a-kind collection also includes the duo's signature "Who's on First?" routine-the most famous sketch of all time.

Legends of Radio: Abbott & Costello. unabr. ed. Perf. by Lou Costello et al. 10 vols. (Running Time: 10 hrs.). (10-Hour Collections). 2002. bk. 39.98 (978-1-57019-503-7(X), OTR40012) Pub: Radio Spirits. Dist(s): AudioGO

Legends of Radio: Best of Suspense. Featuring Orson Welles et al. 20 vols. (Running Time: 20 hrs.). (20 Hour Collections). bk. 69.98 (978-1-57019-625-6(7), OTR40682) Pub: Radio Spirits. Dist(s): AudioGO

Legends of Radio: Best of Suspense. Featuring Orson Welles et al. 20 vols. (Running Time: 20 hrs.). (20 Hour Collections). 2003. bk. 59.98 (978-1-57019-626-3(5), OTR40684) Pub: Radio Spirits. Dist(s): AudioGO

Legends of Radio: Detectives & Crime Fighters. 10 vols. (Running Time: 10 hrs.). (10-Hour Collections). bk. 39.98 (978-1-57019-615-7(X), OTR47092) Pub: Radio Spirits. Dist(s): AudioGO

Legends of Radio: Famous Finales. 10 CDs. (Running Time: 10 hrs.). 2005. audio compact disk 39.98 (978-1-57019-716-1(4), OTR 48102) Pub: Radio Spirits. Dist(s): AudioGO

Legends of Radio: Good Versus Evil. 20 CDs. (Running Time: 20 hrs.). 2005. audio compact disk 69.98 (978-1-57019-712-3(1), OTR43422) Pub: Radio Spirits. Dist(s): AudioGO

Legends of Radio: Masked Marvels. 10 CDs. (Running Time: 10 hrs.). 2004. 39.98 (978-1-57019-714-7(8), OTR 48092) Pub: Radio Spirits. Dist(s): AudioGO

Legends of Radio: The Best of Fibber Mcgee & Molly. 20 vols. (Running Time: 20 hrs.). (20 Hour Collections). bk. 69.98 (978-1-57019-688-1(5), OTR43412) Pub: Radio Spirits. Dist(s): AudioGO

Legends of Radio: The Best of Fibber Mcgee & Molly. 20 vols. (Running Time: 20 hrs.). (20 Hour Collections). 2004. bk. 59.98 (978-1-57019-689-8(3), OTR43414) Pub: Radio Spirits. Dist(s): AudioGO

Legends of Radio: The Shadow. 10 cass. (Running Time: 10 hrs.). (10-Hour Collections). bk. 39.98 (978-1-57019-594-5(3), OTR47052) Pub: Radio Spirits. Dist(s): AudioGO

Legends of Radio: The Shadow. Read by The Shadow Staff. 10 vols. (Running Time: 10 hrs.). (10-Hour Collections). 2002. bk. 34.98 (978-1-57019-593-8(5), OTR47054) Pub: Radio Spirits. Dist(s): AudioGO

Legends of Radio: The Ultimate Gunsmoke Collection. 20 vols. (Running Time: 20 hrs.). (20 Hour Collections). bk. 69.98 (978-1-57019-666-9(4), OTR40722) Pub: Radio Spirits. Dist(s): AudioGO

Legends of Radio: The Ultimate Gunsmoke Collection. 20 vols. (Running Time: 20 hrs.). (20 Hour Collections). 2003. bk. 59.98 (978-1-57019-667-6(2), OTR40724) Pub: Radio Spirits. Dist(s): AudioGO

Legends of Radio: The Ultimate Jack Benny Collection. 20 vols. (Running Time: 20 hrs.). (20 Hour Collections). bk. 69.98 (978-1-57019-664-5(8), OTR40702) Pub: Radio Spirits. Dist(s): AudioGO

Legends of Radio: The Ultimate Jack Benny Collection. Read by Jack Benny. 20 vols. (Running Time: 20 hrs.). (20 Hour Collections). 2003. bk. 59.98 (978-1-57019-665-2(6), OTR40704) Pub: Radio Spirits. Dist(s): AudioGO

Legends of Radio: The Ultimate Sherlock Holmes Collection. 20 vols. (Running Time: 20 hrs.). (20-Hour Collections). bk. 69.98 (978-1-57019-598-3(6), OTR40652) Pub: Radio Spirits. Dist(s): AudioGO

Legends of Radio: The Ultimate Sherlock Holmes Collection. 20 vols. (Running Time: 20 hrs.). (20-Hour Collections). 2002. bk. 59.98 (978-1-57019-597-6(8), OTR40654) Pub: Radio Spirits. Dist(s): AudioGO

Legends of Radio: The Whistler. 20 CDs. (Running Time: 20 hrs.). 2002. audio compact disk 69.98 (42272); 59.98 (42274) Radio Spirits.

The biggest appeal of one of radio's most popular mystery programs wasn't whodunit and why, but how the killer would eventually be trapped by a sinister twist, the strange ending to tonight's story. What does it take to turn ordinary people into killers, to make everyday life turn upside down? The answers are all here.

Legends of Radio Greatest Radio Adventures: The Shadow. unabr. ed. Perf. by Orson Welles et al. 20 vols. (Running Time: 20 hrs.). (20 Hour Collections). 2002. bk. 59.98 (978-1-57019-500-6(5), OTR40034) Pub: Radio Spirits. Dist(s): AudioGO

"Who knows what evil lurks in the hearts of men? The Shadow knows..."TM The Shadow's sinister laugh thrilled radio listeners for a quarter of a century and helped the show become the longest-running mystery series ever. Drawn from the pages of a pulp magazine, The ShadowTM set the style for mystery drama and today is synonymous with the best of the Golden Age of Radio. Relive the greatest adventures of Lamont Cranston, the master crime fighter who is "never seen, only heard," in 40 spine-tingling episodes starring Orson Welles, Bill Johnstone and Bret Morrison.

Legends of Radio Road Trip: Humorous Travel Tales. 10 CDs. (Running Time: 10 hrs.). 2006. audio compact disk 39.98 (978-1-57019-817-5(9), OTR 43642) Pub: Radio Spirits. Dist(s): AudioGO

Legends of Radio Science Fiction Classics. Contrib. by Robert A. Heinlein et al. 10 vols. (Running Time: 10 hrs.). 2004. bk. 34.98 (978-1-57019-697-3(4), OTR40074) Pub: Radio Spirits. Dist(s): AudioGO

Legends of the Fall see Wolf: A False Memoir

Legends of the Great Lakes. Perf. by Carl Behrend. 1998. audio compact disk 14.99 (978-0-9728212-2-3(8)) Old Country Bks.

Legends of the Mushuau Innu: People from the Barrens. abr. ed. Barbara Worthy. Prod. by Barbara Worthy. 2 CDs. (Running Time: 7200 sec.). (Legends Ser.). 2005. audio compact disk 19.95 (978-0-660-19379-3(5)) Canadian Broadcasting CAN.

Legends of the Old Massett Haida: Gaaw Xaadee Gyaahlaangaay, 5. abr. ed. Barbara Worthy. 2 CDs. (Running Time: 7200 sec.). (Legends Ser.). 2007. audio compact disk 19.95 (978-0-660-19616-9(6), CBC Audio) Pub: Canadian Broadcasting CAN. Dist(s): Georgetown Term

In July 2005 the people of Old Massett retold the ancient stories of creation, lessons and values. These stories were told in their original form with the people of Old Massett reading the parts of the ancient mythical characters. The recordings of these tales were mixed with the actual sounds - ravens, eagles, frogs, ocean, wind and rain - found on Haida Gwaii, also known as the Queen Charlotte Islands.This bilingual CD is a preservation project by CBC Radio and the Haida Heritage and Repatriation Society. The team worked closely with the fluent speakers of Xaad kil to record these legends in their original oral form.This enthralling two-CD project is the fifth volume of the CBC Audio Legends series.

Legends of the Shuswap Volume 4: The Secwepemc People of British Columbia, Vol. 4. Short Stories. Canadian Broadcasting Corporation Staff. 2 CDs. (Running Time: 7200 sec.). (Legends Ser.). (NAI.). 2006. audio compact disk 19.95 (978-0-660-19472-1(4), CBC Audio) Pub: Canadian Broadcasting CAN. Dist(s): Georgetown Term

***Legends Vol. 1.** abr. ed. Robert Silverberg. Read by Frank Muller & Sam Tsoutsouvas. (ENG.). 2006. (978-0-06-112119-7(3), Harper Audio); (978-0-06-112118-0(5), Harper Audio) HarperCollins Pubs.

***Legends Vol. 2.** abr. ed. Robert Silverberg. Read by Sam Tsoutsouvas et al. (ENG.). 2006. (978-0-06-112117-3(7), Harper Audio); (978-0-06-112116-6(9), Harper Audio) HarperCollins Pubs.

***Legends Vol. 3.** abr. ed. Robert Silverberg. Read by Sam Tsoutsouvas et al. (ENG.). 2006. (978-0-06-112115-9(0), Harper Audio); (978-0-06-112114-2(2), Harper Audio) HarperCollins Pubs.

***Legends Vol. 4.** abr. ed. Robert Silverberg. Read by Sam Tsoutsouvas et al. (ENG.). 2006. (978-0-06-112112-8(6), Harper Audio); (978-0-06-112113-5(4), Harper Audio) HarperCollins Pubs.

***Legends Volume 1 CD Set.** Narrated by Todd McCartney. (ENG.). 2009. audio compact disk 39.95 (978-0-911647-87-7(2)) Pub: Western Horseman. Dist(s): Globe Pequot

Legion of Marketing Heroes. Willie Davis. 2008. audio compact disk 12.95 (978-1-932226-65-2(6)) Wizard Acdmy.

Legionnaire. abr. ed. Barry Sadler. Read by Charlton Griffin. 2 vols. (Casca Ser.: No. 11). 2003. 18.00 (978-1-58807-111-8(1)); (978-1-58807-541-3(9)) Am Pubng Inc.

Legionnaire. abr. ed. Barry Sadler. Read by Charlton Griffin. 2 vols. (Casca Ser.: No. 11). 2004. audio compact disk 25.00 (978-1-58807-285-6(1)); audio compact disk (978-1-58807-716-5(0)) Am Pubng Inc.

Legionnaire. unabr. ed. Seymour Ragland. Read by Stephanie Brush. 6 cass. (Running Time: 6 hrs.). 39.95 (978-1-55686-701-9(8)) Books in Motion.

An unruly young Frenchman from a wealthy family is sent to the disciplinary unit of the Foreign Legion, tempered by the loss at Dien Bien Phu & loved by a young American woman.

Legislating in the U. S. Senate: Capitol Learning Audio Course. Martin Gold. Prod. by TheCapitol.Net. (ENG.). 2008. 47.00 (978-1-58733-077-3(6)) TheCapitol.

Legislation & Regulations Affecting Managed Accounts Series. Incl. Legislation & Regulations Affecting Managed Accounts Series: CFTC's Exclusive Jurisdiction. C. Duncan.; Legislation & Regulations Affecting Managed Accounts Series: How Much Regulation of Commodity Markets Is Necessary? R. Gray.; Legislation & Regulations Affecting Managed Accounts Series: How to Structure a Public Fund in 1984. R. Amedeo & R. J. Horowitz.; Legislation & Regulations Affecting Managed Accounts Series: Legal Restriction Covering Marketing Managed Accounts. M. Mitchell.; Legislation & Regulations Affecting Managed Accounts Series: New Approaches to Regulatory Obstacles. D. Matteson & R. Goldstein.; Legislation & Regulations Affecting Managed Accounts Series: New Legal Developments (1985) in Money Management. J. Rosen & R. Nathan.; Legislation & Regulations Affecting Managed Accounts Series: Protecting the Investor, Advisor & Broker in a Fund. L. Poulson.; Legislation & Regulations Affecting Managed Accounts Series: Regulatory Aspects of Ag Options. D. Kass & A. Gialnella.; Legislation & Regulations Affecting Managed Accounts Series: Structure of International Funds; Legislation & Regulation of Foreign Trading. D. G. Bean & E. Schroder.; 90.00 Set. (Mngd Acct Reprts); 15.00 ea. Futures Pub.

Legislation & Regulations Affecting Managed Accounts Series: CFTC's Exclusive Jurisdiction see Legislation & Regulations Affecting Managed Accounts Series

Legislation & Regulations Affecting Managed Accounts Series: How Much Regulation of Commodity Markets Is Necessary? see Legislation & Regulations Affecting Managed Accounts Series

Legislation & Regulations Affecting Managed Accounts Series: How to Structure a Public Fund in 1984 see Legislation & Regulations Affecting Managed Accounts Series

Legislation & Regulations Affecting Managed Accounts Series: Legal Restriction Covering Marketing Managed Accounts see Legislation & Regulations Affecting Managed Accounts Series

Legislation & Regulations Affecting Managed Accounts Series: New Approaches to Regulatory Obstacles see Legislation & Regulations Affecting Managed Accounts Series

Legislation & Regulations Affecting Managed Accounts Series: New Legal Developments (1985) in Money Management see Legislation & Regulations Affecting Managed Accounts Series

Legislation & Regulations Affecting Managed Accounts Series: Protecting the Investor, Advisor & Broker in a Fund see Legislation & Regulations Affecting Managed Accounts Series

Legislation & Regulations Affecting Managed Accounts Series: Regulatory Aspects of Ag Options see Legislation & Regulations Affecting Managed Accounts Series

Legislation & Regulations Affecting Managed Accounts Series: Structure of International Funds; Legislation & Regulation of Foreign Trading see Legislation & Regulations Affecting Managed Accounts Series

Legislative Roundup 1989. unabr. ed. Ed. by James P. Klein. 1 cass. (Running Time: 25 min.). (Quarterly Employee Benefits Audio Reports). 1990. 55.00 series of 4. (T7-9286) PLI.

The Employee Benefits Reports, a quarterly Series of audiocassettes, is designed to keep practitioners & their clients informed of key litigation, legislation & regulatory actions. This audio series annually provides four twenty to thirty minute reports by experts on the most recent developments affecting employee benefits.

Legs see Gathering of Great Poetry for Children

Legs see Ink Truck

Legs. abr. ed. William Kennedy. Read by Jason Robards. 2 cass. (Running Time: 3 hrs.). (Albany Cycle Ser.). 2000. 7.95 (978-1-57815-188-2(0), 1128, Media Bks Audio); audio compact disk 11.99 (978-1-57815-514-9(2), 1128 CD3, Media Bks Audio) Media Bks NJ.

True to both life & myth LEGS evokes the flamboyant career of the legendary gangster Jack "Legs" Diamond, who was finally murdered in Albany.

Legs. unabr. collector's ed. William Kennedy. Read by Wolfram Kandinsky. 8 cass. (Running Time: 12 hrs.). (Albany Cycle Ser.). 1986. 64.00 (978-0-7366-1100-8(2), 2026) Books on Tape.

Evokes the career of the legendary gangster Jack "Legs" Diamond, who was finally murdered in Albany.

***Legs Are the Last to Go.** unabr. ed. Diahann Carroll. Read by Diahann Carroll. (ENG.). 2008. (978-0-06-170613-4(2)); (978-0-06-170614-1(0)) HarperCollins Pubs.

Legs Are the Last to Go: Aging, Acting, Marrying, Mothering, & Everything Else I Learned along the Way. unabr. ed. Diahann Carroll & Bob Morris. Read by Diahann Carroll. 7 CDs. (Running Time: 8 hrs.). 2008. audio compact disk 34.95 (978-0-06-166459-5(6), Harper Audio) HarperCollins Pubs.

Legs the Caterpillar. Ben Rosenbaum. Read by Ben Rosenbaum. Contrib. by Beth Schapira. 1 cass. (Running Time: 21 min.). (J). (ps-3). 1997. pap. bk. 14.95 (978-0-9650244-6-4(6)); 9.95 (978-0-9650244-5-7(8)) Inter Contntl Pubs.
A story about a slow moving, unhappy caterpillar who wants to fly like his insect friends Buzzy the bumble-bee, Skippy the grasshopper, Pesty the fly, etc. who look down on him & feel sorry for him for he can't fly.

Legs the Caterpillar. abr. l.t. ed. Ben Rosenbaum. Read by Ben Rosenbaum. Ed. by Inter Continental Publishers Staff. Illus. by Eric Somers. Contrib. by Beth Schapira. 1 cass. (Running Time: 21 min.). (J). (ps-3). 1995. lib. bdg. 14.95 (978-0-9650244-1-9(5), 125) Inter Contntl Pubs.

Legs the Caterpillar. l.t. ed. Ben Rosenbaum. Read by Ben Rosenbaum. Ed. by Inter Continental Publishers Staff. Illus. by Eric Somers. Contrib. by Beth Schapira. 1 cass. (Running Time: 21 min.). (J). (gr. k-3). 1995. bk. 19.95 (978-0-9650244-0-2(7), 125) Inter Contntl Pubs.

Lehman Engel Musical Theater Workshop. unabr. ed. Instructed by Lehman Engel. 24 cass. (Running Time: 30 hrs.). 195.00 Incl. "Listener's Guide". (S11500) J Norton Pubs.
Edited version of recordings made at actual workshop sessions. Learn the essential elements that go into the making of a hit musical, how to choose materials for a libretto, place songs in a scene, compose ballads, charm songs & much more - from the master.

Leif the Lucky. unabr. ed. Ingri Parin D'Aulaire & Edgar Parin D'Aulaire. 1 cass. (Running Time: 6 min.). (J). (gr. 3-5). 1993. pap. bk. 15.00 (6512-I) Spoken Arts.

Leigh. unabr. ed. Lyn Cote. Read by Anna Fields. (Running Time: 28800 sec.). (Women of Ivy Manor Ser.). 2006. 54.95 (978-0-7861-4653-6(2)); audio compact disk 63.00 (978-0-7861-6780-7(7)); audio compact disk 29.95 (978-0-7861-7413-3(7)) Blckstn Audio.

Leisure Parks in Germany: A Strategic Reference 2007. Compiled by Icon Group International, Inc. Staff. 2007. ring bd. 195.00 (978-0-497-35977-5(4)) Icon Grp.

L'élégance du Hérisson see Elegance of the Hedgehog

Lemay. unabr. ed. Barrett Tillman. Read by Tom Weiner. (Running Time: 21600 sec.). (Great Generals Ser.). 2007. audio compact disk 55.00 (978-0-7861-6235-2(X)) Blckstn Audio.

Lemay. unabr. ed. Barrett Tillman. Read by Tom Weiner. Frwd. by Wesley K. Clark. (Running Time: 21600 sec.). (Great Generals Ser.). 2007. 25.95 (978-0-7861-4798-4(9)); 44.95 (978-0-7861-4802-8(0)); audio compact disk 25.95 (978-0-7861-6239-0(2)); audio compact disk 29.95 (978-0-7861-7202-3(9)) Blckstn Audio.

Lemming Condition. abr. ed. Alan Arkin. Read by Alan Arkin. 1 cass. (Running Time: 55 min.). 1995. 9.95 (978-0-944993-16-3(8)) Audio Lit.
The story of a young lemming who calls into question the blind urge of his fellows to drown themselves in the sea.

Lemon Swamp & Other Places: A Carolina Memoir. unabr. collector's ed. Mamie G. Fields. Read by Mary Woods. 8 cass. (Running Time: 12 hrs.). 1987. 64.00 (978-0-7366-1168-8(1), 2091) Books on Tape.
Autobiographical account of a gifted black family in South Carolina at the turn of the century.

Lemon Table. unabr. ed. Julian Barnes. 4 cass. (Running Time: 6 hrs.). 2004. 39.95 (978-0-7927-3407-9(6)); audio compact disk 64.95 (978-0-7927-3408-6(4)) AudioGO.

Lemon Tree: An Arab, a Jew, & the Heart of the Middle East. Sandy Tolan. Read by Sandy Tolan. (Playaway Adult Nonfiction Ser.). 2008. 49.99 (978-1-60640-519-2(5)) Find a World.

Lemon Tree: An Arab, a Jew, & the Heart of the Middle East. unabr. ed. Sandy Tolan. Read by Sandy Tolan. 9 CDs. (Running Time: 11 hrs.). (ENG.). 2006. audio compact disk 36.95 (978-1-56511-988-8(6), 1565119886) Pub: HighBridge. Dist(s): Workman Pub

Lemonade Diet: A Master Cleanse Audio CD. Interview. Featuring Peter Glickman. Prod. by John Sipos. Engineer Chris Kastner. Des. by Maggy Graham. 1. (Running Time: 66 Mins.). 2004. audio compact disk 15.95 (978-0-9755722-1-4(0)) Pub: P Glickman. Dist(s): Midpt Trade
A study published in Business Week magazine in 2003 revealed that two out of three Americans were overweight and nearly half of them were so overweight their health was badly affected. According to the US Dept. of Health and Human Services, obesity was the number two cause of preventable death in the United States in 2001 and was expected to pass the number one cause, smoking, in 2005!Since 1976, when Stanley Burroughs published his book, The Master Cleanser, hundreds of thousands of people have discovered just how easy it is to lose weight, have amazingly more energy and feel really good by just drinking lemonade made with maple syrup and cayenne pepper!Most people don't realize it's not only how much you eat, but what you eat. This is particularly true if you're concerned about keeping weight off after losing it. In addition, most people are unaware their lack of energy and lack of interest in life can be part of their weight problem.This audio CD by Peter Glickman, author of Lose Weight, Have More Energy & Be Happier in 10 Days, covers the widespread nature of obesity, the body's method of handling toxins by creating fat cells and storing the toxins in them, three inspiring live testimonials, and half an hour on how to do the cleanse, what pitfalls to avoid and makes a great companion to either of the books above.Track 1: Introduction 25:10Track 2: Testimonials 9:31Track 3: The "Nitty Gritty" 31:30(details of how to do the cleanse)Total running time: 66:11.

Lemur. unabr. ed. Benjamin Black. Read by John Keating. (Running Time: 4 hrs. 30 mins.). 2008. 29.96 (978-0-7927-5585-2(5), Chivers Sound Lib); audio compact disk 49.95 (978-0-7927-5468-8(9), Chivers Sound Lib) AudioGO.

Lemur. unabr. ed. Benjamin Black. Read by John Keating. 4 CDs. (Running Time: 4 hrs. 30 mins. 0 sec.). 2008. audio compact disk 24.95 (978-1-4272-0478-3(0)) Pub: Macmill Audio. Dist(s): Macmillan

Lemur Landing: A Story of a Madagascan Tropical Dry Forest. Deborah Dennard. Illus. by Kristin Kest. (Soundprints' Wild Habitats Ser.). (ENG.). (J). (gr. 1-4). 2005. 8.95 (978-1-59249-107-0(3), SC7019) Soundprints.

Lemurian Atlantean Vision Wheel. David Jungclaus. Read by David Jungclaus. 1 cass. (Running Time: 1 hr. 30 min.). 1991. 10.00 (978-1-883682-02-6(9)) Lost Wrld Pub.
A voice & tone meditation to move you into deep healing & vision.

Lemurian Viewpoint. 2007. audio compact disk 30.00 (978-0-9760127-1-9(5)) Lemurian Fellow.

Lemurian Viewpoint Volume 1. 2007. audio compact disk 10.00 (978-0-9760127-2-6(3)) Lemurian Fellow.

Lemurian Viewpoint Volume 2. 2007. audio compact disk 10.00 (978-0-9760127-3-3(1)) Lemurian Fellow.

Lemurian Viewpoint Volume 3. 2007. audio compact disk 10.00 (978-0-9760127-4-0(X)) Lemurian Fellow.

Lemurian Viewpoint Volume 4. 2007. audio compact disk 10.00 (978-0-9760127-5-7(8)) Lemurian Fellow.

Lemurs. John M. Bennett & Jake Berry. 1 cass. (Running Time: 60 min.). 1993. pap. bk. 5.00 (978-0-935350-40-1(3)) Luna Bisonte.

Lena, unabr. ed. Jacqueline Woodson. Narrated by Kate Forbes. 2 cass. (Running Time: 3 hrs.). (YA). 1999. pap. bk. & stu. ed. 42.95 (978-0-7887-3646-9(9), 41012X4) Recorded Bks.

Lena, unabr. ed. Jacqueline Woodson. Narrated by Kate Forbes. 2 pieces. (Running Time: 3 hrs.). (gr. 7 up). 1999. 20.00 (978-0-7887-3528-8(4), 95675E7) Recorded Bks.
Lena & her younger sister Dion feel they have no choice but to leave their home & take to the open road. Their mother is dead & their father has done terrible things to the girls. This completes the poignant odyssey begun in "I Hadn't Meant to Tell You This." Addresses issues of racism & child abuse.

Lena, Class set. Jacqueline Woodson. Read by Kate Forbes. 2 cass. (Running Time: 3 hrs.). (YA). (gr. 7 up). 1999. stu. ed. 187.80 (978-0-7887-3676-6(0), 46979) Recorded Bks.

Lenape, Set. unabr. ed. Nora T. Dean. 2 cass. (Running Time: 71 mins.). 1979. pap. bk. 49.95 (978-0-88432-285-6(8), AFLE10) J Norton Pubs.
Introductory-level course in four lessons, with illustrated booklet & glossary, covering greetings, weather expressions, useful phrases, prayer words, food terms, names of birds & kinship terms.

Lender Liability: Theories & Practice. 1988. 95.00 (AC-467) PA Bar Inst.

Lender Liability & Other Complex Litigation Involving Financial Institutions. 8 cass. (Running Time: 10 hrs. 30 min.). 1994. stu. ed. 155.00 (MD117) Am Law Inst.
Advanced course analyzes in detail a variety of topics pertaining to lender liability & other complex commercial litigation involving financial institutions.

Lender Liability Litigation: Recent Developments. unabr. ed. Contrib. by Mason C. Brown. 7 cass. (Running Time: 10 hrs.). 1989. 50.00 course handbk. (T7-9229) PLI.
This recording of PLI's September 1989 program emphasizes current developments in lender liability & is designed to provide both substantive & practical information to all practitioners who represent either lenders or borrowers. The program's panel of experienced lawyers from both inside & outside of financial institutions addresses the legal theories & issues currently being asserted against lenders. Borrower & lender lawyers provide practical insight into the problems they have actually faced in courtrooms & conference rooms throughout the United States.

Lengthen Your Shuffle. Ed Pinegar & George Durrant. 2004. 9.95 (978-1-57734-981-5(4)) Covenant Comms.

Lenin: A New Biography. unabr. collector's ed. Dmitri Volkogonov. Read by Geoffrey Howard. 15 cass. (Running Time: 22 hrs. 30 min.). 1999. 120.00 (978-0-7366-4727-4(9), 5065) Books on Tape.
The author portrays Lenin as a cruel & totalitarian leader responsible for some of the worst excesses of the Soviet state.

Lenine. Henri Guillemin. 1 cass. (FRE.). 1991. 22.95 (1211-VSL) Olivia & Hill.

Leningen & the Ants. 10.00 (MC1003) Esstee Audios.

Leninism: 19th Century Origins & 20th Century Impact. John Ridpath. Read by John Ridpath. 2 cass. (Running Time: 3 hrs.). 1987. 24.95 (978-1-56114-039-8(2), HR02D) Second Renaissance.
A broad examination of how Lenin came to power in 1917. How the centuries-long tradition of statism in Russia made it a seedbed for communism. The connection between the "messianism" of Russia's Eastern Orthodox Church & the spirit of revolutionary totalitarianism inculcated by Leninism. The theoretical changes Lenin brought to Marxism. How the ideas of Marxism-Leninism exert a major influence upon today's world.

Lenin's Tomb: The Last Days of the Soviet Empire, Vol. 1. David Remnick. 11 cass. (Running Time: 16.5 hrs.). 2001. 88.00 (978-0-7366-6725-8(3)) Books on Tape.

Lenin's Tomb: The Last Days of the Soviet Empire, Vol. 2. David Remnick. 11 cass. (Running Time: 16.5 hrs.). 2001. 80.00 (978-0-7366-6726-5(1)) Books on Tape.

***Lennie Niehaus Plays the Blues - Companion CD Only.** Lennie Niehaus. 1999. audio compact disk 9.95 (978-1-56224-077-6(3)) Jamey Aebersold.

Lenny Bruce: The Making of a Prophet. (ENG., 2008. audio compact disk 24.95 (978-0-9799477-1-1(5)) Media mbd.

Lenny Kravitz: The Unauthorized Biography of Lenny Kravitz. Martin Harper. (Maximum Ser.). (ENG.). 2001. audio compact disk 14.95 (978-1-84240-033-3(9)) Pub: Chrome Dreams GBR. Dist(s): IPG Chicago

Lens of Life & Other Poems. Garry De Young. 1 cass. 5.00 De Young Pr.

Lent see Evening with Dylan Thomas

Lenten Devotions: The Stations of the Cross & Seven Last Words. Created by ACTA Publications. (Running Time: 6300 sec.). 2008. audio compact disk 14.95 (978-0-87946-354-0(6)) ACTA Pubns.

Lenten Journey with Jesus. Isaias Powers. Read by Isaias Powers. Read by Andrea Star. 2 cass. (Running Time: 1 hr. 40 min.). 1993. vinyl bd. 16.95 (978-0-89622-801-6(0)) Twenty-Third.
Daily reflections & prayers during 40 days of Lent, scriptural based, uplifting, challenging.

Lenten Meditation. Jerry Kolb. 1986. 10.80 (0903) Assn Prof Chaplains.

Lentil see Periquin

Lentil. 2004. bk. 24.95 (978-1-56008-229-3(1)); pap. bk. 14.95 (978-0-7882-0596-5(X)); 8.95 (978-1-56008-946-9(6)); cass. & flmstrp 30.00 (978-0-89719-534-8(5)) Weston Woods.

Lentil. unabr. ed. Robert McCloskey. Narrated by Johnny Heller. 1 cass. (Running Time: 15 mins.). (ps up). 2001. 10.00 (978-0-7887-5028-1(3), 96485E7) Recorded Bks.
Lentil wants to make music, but has a terrible singing voice. So he saves up his pennies & buys a harmonica. Only Old Sneep, the town grouch, doesn't like Lentil's harmonica playing. Old Sneep doesn't like much of anything. He plans to ruin the upcoming town parade, but Lentil has plans of his own.

Lenton Croft Robberies see Classic Detective Stories, Vol. I, A Collection

Lenton Croft Robberies see Martin Hewitt, Investigator

Lenton Croft Robberies. unabr. ed. Arthur Morrison. Read by Walter Covell. (Running Time: 52 min.). Dramatization. 1981. 7.95 (N-77) Jimcin Record.
Martin Hewitt tracks an invisible thief.

Leo. Narrated by Patricia G. Finlayson. Music by Mike Cantwell. Contrib. by Marie De Seta & TMY Communications Staff. 1 cass. (Running Time: 30 min.). (Astrologer's Guide to the Personality Ser.: Vol. 5). 1994. 7.99 (978-1-878535-16-0(1)) De Seta-Finlayson.
Astrological description of the sign of Leo; individually customized, covering love, money, career, relationships & more.

Leo: July Twenty-Three - August Twenty-Two. Barrie Konicov. 1 cass. 11.98 (978-0-87082-094-6(X), 078) Potentials.
The author, Barrie Konicov, explains how each sign of the Zodiac has its positive & negative aspects & that as individuals, in order to master our own destiny, we must enhance our positive traits.

Leo: July Twenty-Three-August Twenty-Two. Barrie Konicov. 1 cass. 2000. 16.98 (978-1-56001-562-8(4)) Potentials.

Leo: Unleash the Power of Your True Self. 1 cass. (Running Time: 1 hr.). 1999. 9.99 (978-1-928996-04-0(3)) MonAge.

Leo: Your Relationship with the Energy of the Universe. Loy Young. 1993. 9.95 (978-1-882888-17-7(0)) Aquarius Hse.

Leo Cherne: McCarthyism see Buckley's Firing Line

Leo, el Retono Tardio. Robert Kraus. Illus. by Jose Aruego. 1 cass. (Running Time: 10 min.).Tr. of Leo the Late Bloomer. (SPA.). (J). bk. 24.95 Weston Woods.
"What's the matter with Leo?" his father asks, when Leo can't read, write, draw, eat neatly or speak. "He's just a late bloomer," explains his mother - & sure enough, one day, in his own good time, Leo shows everyone how glorious it is to finally bloom.

Leo, el Retono Tardio. Robert Kraus. Tr. by Teresa Mlawer.Tr. of Leo the Late Bloomer. (SPA.). (J). (gr. k-1). 2004. 8.95 (978-0-7882-0136-3(0), WW6045) Weston Woods.

Leo Sowerby: American Master of Sacred Song. Gloriae Dei Cantores. 2 CDs. 1994. audio compact disk 33.95 (978-1-55725-043-8(X), GDCD 016) Paraclete MA.

Leo the Late Bloomer see Leo, el Retono Tardio

Leo the Late Bloomer. (SPA.). 2004. bk. 24.95 (978-0-7882-0135-6(2)); bk. 24.95 (978-1-56008-033-6(7)); pap. bk. 18.95 (978-1-55592-806-3(4)); pap. bk. 18.95 (978-1-55592-774-5(2)); pap. bk. 38.75 (978-1-55592-756-1(4)); pap. bk. 38.75 (978-1-55592-789-9(0)); pap. bk. 32.75 (978-1-55592-254-2(6)); pap. bk. 32.75 (978-1-55592-255-9(4)); pap. bk. 14.95 (978-1-55592-661-8(4)); pap. bk. 14.95 (978-1-55592-165-1(5)); 8.95 (978-0-89719-923-0(5)); cass. & flmstrp 30.00 (978-0-89719-523-2(X)); audio compact disk 12.95 (978-1-55592-874-2(9)) Weston Woods.

Leo the Late Bloomer. Robert Kraus. Narrated by Mary Beth Hurt. 1 cass., 5 bks. (Running Time: 4 min.). (J). pap. bk. 32.75 Weston Woods.
Leo learns to read, write & speak all in his own good time.

Leo the Late Bloomer. Robert Kraus. Illus. by Jose Aruego. Narrated by Mary Beth Hurt. 1 cass. (Running Time: 4 min.). (J). (ps-4). bk. 24.95 Weston Woods.

Leo the Late Bloomer. Robert Kraus. Narrated by Mary Beth Hurt. Music by Ernest V. Troost. 1 cass. (Running Time: 4 min.). (J). (ps-3). 2004. pap. bk. 8.95 (978-1-56008-112-8(0), PRAC287) Weston Woods.
Leo learns to read, write & speak all in his own good time.

Leo the Late Bloomer Spanish. 2004. pap. bk. 32.75 (978-1-55592-651-9(7)) Weston Woods.

Leo Tolstoi: Fables, Tales, Stories. unabr. ed. 2 cass., bklet. (Running Time: 2 hrs.). (RUS.). pap. bk. 39.50 (978-1-57970-011-9(X), SRU1115) J Norton Pubs.
Includes the famous short story "Prisoner in the Caucasus," which relates the capture & escape of a Russian officer held for ransom by Tartar tribesmen in the early 19th century.

Leo Tolstoy: Fables, Tales, Stories. unabr. ed. 2 cass. (RUS.). bk. 29.50 (SRU1215) J Norton Pubs.

Leocadia. unabr. ed. Jean Anouilh. Perf. by Ian Abercrombie et al. 1 cass. (Running Time: 1 hr. 26 min.). 1993. 19.95 (978-1-58081-070-8(5)) L A Theatre.
Amanda, a charming & practical hatmaker is hired by an eccentric Duchess to save her lovelorn son. Distracting the Prince from his memories seems like an impossible task, but the route away from romance proves to be surprisingly romantic.

Leon & the Champion Chip. unabr. ed. Allen Kurzweil. Read by Matt Labyorteaux. (J). 2008. 39.99 (978-1-60252-978-6(7)) Find a World.

Leon & the Champion Chip. unabr. ed. Allen Kurzweil. Read by Matt Labyorteaux. (J). 2005. audio compact disk 25.95 (978-0-06-082056-5(X), HarperChildAud) HarperCollins Pubs.

***Leon & the Champion Chip.** unabr. ed. Allen Kurzweil. Read by Matt Labyorteaux. (ENG.). 2005. (978-0-06-088974-6(8), GreenwillowBks); (978-0-06-088971-5(3), GreenwillowBks) HarperCollins Pubs.

Leon & the Spitting Image. unabr. ed. Allen Kurzweil. Read by Mark Linn-Baker. (J). 2008. 44.99 (978-1-60252-979-3(5)) Find a World.

***Leon & the Spitting Image.** unabr. ed. Allen Kurzweil. Read by Mark Linn-baker. (ENG.). 2005. (978-0-06-084588-9(0), GreenwillowBks); (978-0-06-084589-6(9), GreenwillowBks) HarperCollins Pubs.

***Leon, Bruja y Ropero.** C. S. Lewis. 2010. audio compact disk 17.95 (978-1-933499-93-2(1)) Fonolibro Inc.

Leon Edel. Leon Edel. Read by Leon Edel. Prod. by New Letters on the Air Staff. 1 cass. (Running Time: 30 min.). 8.00 (NL 37) Am Audio Prose.
Leon Edel discusses using psychoanalytical techniques to tell the story of an author & reads from a biography of Henry David Thoreau that debunks many of the previously held notions about the writer & naturalist.

Leon Edel. unabr. ed. Read by Heywood Hale Broun & Leon Edel. 1 cass. (Running Time: 56 min.). (Broun Radio Ser.). 12.95 (40179) J Norton Pubs.
The author of "Bloomsbury" talks about the highly creative, eccentric set.

Leon Edel. unabr. ed. Leon Edel. Read by Leon Edel. 1 cass. (Running Time: 29 min.). 1989. 10.00 New Letters.
Biographer Leon Edels reads from a biography of Henry David Thoreau & is interviewed.

Leon Edel on Thoreau. unabr. ed. Leon Edel. Read by Leon Edel. Interview with James McKinley. 1 cass. (Running Time: 29 min.). 1991. 10.00 (010689) New Letters.

Leon Hale Reads from His Work. Leon Hale. Read by Leon Hale. 1 cass. (ENG.). 1989. 11.00 (978-0-940672-51-2(0)) Pub: Winedale Pub. Dist(s): Tex AM Univ Pr

Leon Kolankiewicz, a Naturalist in Alaska's Rainforest & His Salmon Research & Bear Encounters; Texas' Peregrine Falcons & Bats. Hosted by Nancy Pearlman. 1 cass. (Running Time: 29 min.). 10.00 (1215) Educ Comm CA.

Leon, la Bruja y el Ropero. C. S. Lewis. Narrated by Karl Hoffmann. 5 CDs. (Running Time: 21600 sec.). (Cronicas de Narnia Ser.). (SPA.). 2007. audio compact disk 24.95 (978-1-933499-64-2(8)) Fonolibro Inc.

Leon Panetta: What Congress Would Do with Bush's Budget. (Running Time: 60 min.). 1989. 10.95 (K0730B090, HarperThor) HarpC GBR.

Leon Ruge, EDL Level 12. (Fonolibros Ser.: Vol. 28). (SPA.). 2003. 11.50 (978-0-7652-1017-3(7)) Modern Curr.

Leon Valiente, Leon Miedoso. Joan Stimson.Tr. of Brave Lion, Scared Lion. (SPA.). (J). (gr. k-1). 4.95 (978-0-590-91079-8(5), SO1230) Scholastic Inc.

Leonard Bernstein: A Life. unabr. collector's ed. Meryle Secrest. Read by Kimberly Schraf. 12 cass. (Running Time: 18 hrs.). 1996. 96.00 (978-0-7366-3291-1(3), 3946) Books on Tape.
To describe Leonard Bernstein as larger than life misses the mark. Composer, charismatic personality, teacher, lover of beautiful women & handsome young men, folk hero - Bernstein did it all.

Leonard Michaels. unabr. ed. Leonard Michaels. Read by Leonard Michaels. Interview with James McKinley. 1 cass. (Running Time: 29 min.). 1991. 10.00 (031089) New Letters.

Leonard Peikoff Show. 12th ed. 1 cass. 49.95 (LPXXD12) Second Renaissance.
Incls. Regulatory Agencies-FDA, Best of Everything (Mars Rock), Dole's Acceptance Speech, & Richard Salsman Interview (Regulatory Agencies-SEC).

Leonard Peikoff Show. 13th ed. 1 cass. 49.95 (LPXXD13) Second Renaissance.
Incls. Ken Iverson Interview by Gary Hull, Who Creates Wealth?, Air Strike Against Iraq, Who Won the Wrong War?.

Leonard Peikoff Show. 14th ed. 1 cass. 49.95 (LPXXD14) Second Renaissance.
Best of Everthing (Dirty Words), News Jog (Addition, Plus), Mary Ann Sures Interview (What Is Art?), Proposition 211-Lawyers vs Doctors.

Leonard Peikoff Show. 15th ed. 1 cass. 49.95 (LPXXD15) Second Renaissance.
Clinton-Dole-Second Debate, & How to Vote, Steve Allen & Jayne Meadows Interview, Election Results, Equal Opportunity.

Leonard Peikoff Show. 16th ed. 1 cass. 49.95 (LPXXD16) Second Renaissance.
Managed Care: Dr. Art Astorino Interview, John Allison Interview, A Picture is Not an Argument, Martin Anderson Interview.

Leonard Peikoff Show: Introductory Sampler Tape. 1 cass. (Running Time: 35 min.). 7.95 (LP41X) Second Renaissance.
Listen to excerpts, taken from several shows (from different Editions) on various issues.

Leonard Randolph. unabr. ed. Read by Leonard Randolph. 1 cass. (Running Time: 29 min.). 1985. 10.00 New Letters.
One of a weekly half-hour radio program with authors talking & presenting their own works. Randolph reads from "Scar Tissue".

Leonardo: The First Scientist. unabr. ed. Michael White. Narrated by Christopher Kay. 9 cass. (Running Time: 12 hrs. 30 mins.). 2002. 82.00 (978-1-84197-340-1(8)) Recorded Bks.

Leonardo da Vinci see Leonardo da Vinci

Leonardo da Vinci. Hugh Griffith. 1 CD. (Running Time: 1 hr. 30 min.). (Art & Music Ser.). 2003. audio compact disk (Naxos AudioBooks) Naxos.

Leonardo Da Vinci. Sherwin B. Nuland. Read by Scott Brick. 2000. audio compact disk 32.00 (978-0-7366-7070-8(X)) Books on Tape.

Leonardo da Vinci. collector's ed. Sherwin B. Nuland. Read by Scott Brick. 3 cass. (Running Time: 4 hrs. 30 min.). Orig. Title: Leonardo da Vinci. 2000. 28.00 (978-0-7366-5621-4(9)) Books on Tape.
Takes us deep into the first truly modern, empirical mind, one that was centuries ahead of its time.

Leonardo da Vinci. collector's unabr. ed. Sherwin B. Nuland. Read by Scott Brick. 4 CDs. (Running Time: 6 hrs.). Orig. Title: Leonardo da Vinci. 2001. audio compact disk 32.00 Books on Tape.
A succinct yet complete biography of one of the greatest artists, scientists and thinkers of all times.

Leonardo the First Scientist. Michael White. Narrated by Christopher Kay. 11 CDs. (Running Time: 12 hrs. 30 mins.). audio compact disk 115.00 (978-1-4025-3289-4(X)) Recorded Bks.

Leonardo, the Terrible Monster. Narrated by Mo Willems. 1 CD. (Running Time: 8 mins.). (J). (ps-3). 2007. bk. 29.95 (978-0-439-02766-3(7), WHCD801); bk. 24.95 (978-0-439-02765-6(9), WHRA801) Weston Woods.
Leonardo is terrible at being a monster. He can't seem to frighten anyone. Then he comes up with a plan to find the perfect nervous little boy and scare the tuna salad out of him. Will his plan succeed, or will he come up with a better idea?.

Leon's Story. unabr. ed. Leon Walter Tillage. Narrated by Graham Brown. 1 cass. (Running Time: 1 hr. 15 mins.). (gr. 5 up). 1997. 10.00 (978-0-7887-1819-9(3), 95281E7) Recorded Bks.
Young Leon wonders why the white children ride the school bus & he walks, but in 1940s North Carolina, that's just the way things are. The author retells his fascinating life story, an acclaimed presentation he has given countless times for Baltimore middle school students.

Leon's Story. unabr. ed. Leon Walter Tillage. Read by Graham Brown. 1 cass. (Running Time: 1 hr. 15 min.). (J). (gr. 5). 1997. 10.00 (95281) Recorded Bks.
Young Leon asks why the white children ride the school bus & he walks. In 1940s North Carolina, everyone tells him, "that's just the way things are.".

Leon's Story, Homework. unabr. ed. Leon Walter Tillage. Read by Graham Brown. 1 cass. (Running Time: 1 hr. 15 min.). (J). 1997. bk. 30.70 (978-0-7887-1833-5(9), 40613) Recorded Bks.

Leopard Hunts in Darkness. Wilbur Smith. Read by Martin Jarvis. 2 cass. (Running Time: 3 hrs.). (ENG., 2001. 16.99 (978-0-333-78243-9(7)) Pub: Macmillan UK GBR. Dist(s): Trafalgar
He is the son of Ballantynes, the powerful dynasty that had conquered a continent. Today, amid the violent conflicts of emerging Africa, Craig Mellow confronts a bloody colonial past and a perilously uncertain future.

Leopard Hunts in Darkness. unabr. ed. Wilbur Smith. Read by Stephen Thorne. 14 cass. (Running Time: 65640 sec.). (Ballantyne Novels Ser.). 2000. 110.95 (978-0-7540-0500-1(3), CAB1923) AudioGO.
Sole survivor of the Ballantyne family, bestselling author Craig Mellow fled Africa when the Bush War ended. Now, disillusioned & empty of inspiration in New York, he is asked to return to his roots in Africa on a secret mission funded by the World Bank. His tasks is to send back information on ivory poaching & signs of Soviet interference in the country. He finds himself caught up in a bloody tribal war & pitted against a power-crazed fanatic who would plunge his country into a new Dark Age.

Leopard Hunts in Darkness, Pt. 1. unabr. collector's ed. Wilbur Smith. Read by Richard Brown. 7 cass. (Running Time: 10 hrs. 30 min.). (Ballantyne Novels Ser.). 1989. 56.00 (978-0-7366-1528-0(8), 2399-A) Books on Tape.
An author stranded in New York feels compelled to return to his African home. What he finds is not just change, but mortal danger.

Leopard Hunts in Darkness, Pt. 2. collector's ed. Wilbur Smith. Read by Richard Brown. 8 cass. (Running Time: 12 hrs.). (Ballantyne Novels Ser.). 1989. 64.00 (978-0-7366-1529-7(6), 2399-B) Books on Tape.

Leopard Sword. unabr. ed. 4 cass. (Running Time: 5 hrs. 15 min.). (J). 2003. 37.00 (978-1-4025-5577-0(6)) Recorded Bks.
On a perilous journey that takes them through beautiful Greek islands and treacherous Roman streets, Hubert and Edmund find the adventures of their lives are just beginning. Set upon by pirates, betrayed by allies, challenged to a deadly joust, and trapped between warring political factions, the squires learn there is only one real test of honor: remaining true to friends.

Leopards Kill. abr. ed. Jim DeFelice. Read by William Dufris. (Running Time: 6 hrs.). 2008. audio compact disk 14.99 (978-1-4233-3156-8(7), 9781423331568, BCD Value Price) Brilliance Audio.

Leopards Kill. unabr. ed. Jim DeFelice. Read by William Dufris. (Running Time: 10 hrs.). 2007. 39.25 (978-1-4233-3154-4(0), 9781423331544, BADLE); 24.95 (978-1-4233-3153-7(2), 9781423331537, BAD); 82.25 (978-1-4233-3148-3(6), 9781423331483, BrilAudUnabridg); audio compact disk 24.95 (978-1-4233-3151-3(6), 9781423331513, Brilliance MP3); audio compact disk 36.95 (978-1-4233-3149-0(4), 9781423331490, Bril Audio CD Unabri); audio compact disk 97.25 (978-1-4233-3150-6(8), 9781423331506, BriAudCD Unabrid) Brilliance Audio.

Leopards Kill. unabr. ed. Jim DeFelice. Read by William Dufris. (Running Time: 36000 sec.). 2007. audio compact disk 39.25 (978-1-4233-3152-0(4), 9781423331520, Brlnc Audio MP3 Lib) Brilliance Audio.

Leopold & the Congo. 10.00 (HE825) Esstee Audios.
Mark Twain talks about imperialism.

Leopold the See-Through Crumbpicker. 2004. 8.95 (978-1-56008-947-6(4)); cass. & flmstrp 30.00 (978-1-56008-703-8(X)) Weston Woods.

Leota's Garden. abr. ed. Francine Rivers. Narrated by Flo Schmidt. (ENG.). 2004. 10.49 (978-1-60814-281-1(7)); audio compact disk 14.99 (978-1-58926-671-1(4)) Oasis Audio.

Leper of Saint Giles. Ellis Peters, pseud. Perf. by Derek Jacobi & Sean Pertwee. 1 cass. (Running Time: 1 hr. 20 min.). Dramatization. (Chronicles of Brother Cadfael Ser.: Vol. 5). 1999. 9.95 (978-1-56938-267-7(0), AMP-2670) Acorn Inc.
On the eve of a great wedding at the abbey, the groom - powerful Baron - mysteriously rides off alone into the night & is never seen alive again. Cadfael must track down the killer.

Leper of Saint Giles. unabr. ed. Ellis Peters. Read by Johanna Ward. 5 cass. (Running Time: 7 hrs.). (Chronicles of Brother Cadfael Ser.: Vol. 5). 1999. 39.95 (978-0-7861-1260-9(3), 2181) Blckstn Audio.
Setting out for the Saint Giles colony outside Shrewsbury, Brother Cadfael has more pressing matters on his mind than the grand wedding coming to his abbey. Yet as fate would have it, Cadfael arrives at Saint Giles just as the nuptial party passes the colony's gates. What lies ahead? Murder.

Leper of Saint Giles. unabr. ed. Ellis Peters, pseud. Narrated by Patrick Tull. 7 cass. (Running Time: 9 hrs. 15 mins.). (Chronicles of Brother Cadfael Ser.: Vol. 5). 1992. 60.00 (978-1-55690-686-2(2), 92339E7) Recorded Bks.
Brother Cadfael, medieval monk & herbologist, is called upon to clear a young man wrongly accused of murder & hiding in a leper colony.

***Leper of Saint Giles: The Fifth Chronicle of Brother Cadfael.** unabr. ed. Ellis Peters. Read by Johanna Ward. (Running Time: 7 hrs. 30 mins.). (Chronicles of Brother Cadfael Ser.). 2010. 29.95 (978-1-4417-5121-8(1)); audio compact disk 69.00 (978-1-4417-5119-5(X)) Blckstn Audio.

Leprechaun in Late Winter. unabr. ed. Mary Pope Osborne. Read by Mary Pope Osborne. (Magic Tree House Ser.: Bk. 43). (ENG.). (J). (gr. 1). 2010. 15.00 (978-0-7393-7296-8(3), Listening Lib) Pub: Random Audio Pubg. Dist(s): Random

Leprechaun's St. Patrick's Day. Read by Sarah K. Blazek. 1 cass. (Running Time: 23 hrs. NaN mins.). (Night Before Christm Ser.). (ENG.). (J). (ps-3). 1996. 9.95 (978-1-56554-387-4(4)) Pelican.

Lernen mit Allen Sinnen. Contrib. by Brigitte Jonen-Dittman. (GER.). 2000. (978-0-942017-77-9(3), 4-6486) Amer Assn Teach German.

Lernen Sie Spanish Lesen, Impara a leggere in Spagnolo, Aprenda a ler Espanhol, Apprenez à lire L'espagnol see Aprendiendo a Leer con Mili y Molo: Learn How to Read in Spanish

Leroy, the Lizzard. Claudia Cherness. Read by May Davenport. 1 cass. (Running Time: 15 min.). (Read & Color Tales Ser.: Vol. 5). (J). (ps-3). 1996. pap. bk. 6.95 (978-0-943864-86-0(0)) Davenport.
Lizzard wants to be like the boy with two feet to walk tall, & does so, until he discovers it is better to be himself with four feet.

Les Aspin, Maverick Congressman: Defending America. (Running Time: 60 min.). 1989. 11.95 (K0750B090, HarperThor) HarpC GBR.

Lesch-Nyhan Syndrome - A Bibliography & Dictionary for Physicians, Patients, & Genome Researchers. Compiled by Icon Group International, Inc. Staff. 2007. ring bd. 28.95 (978-0-497-11250-9(7)) Icon Grp.

Leslie. abr. ed. Omar R. Tyree. Read by Heather Alicia Sims. 2004. 15.95 (978-0-7435-4942-4(2)) Pub: S&S Audio. Dist(s): S and S Inc

Leslie Marmon Silko. unabr. ed. Leslie Marmon Silko. 1 cass. (Running Time: 29 min.). (New Letters on the Air Ser.). 1992. 10.00 (121391) New Letters.
Silko reads from her epic novel, "The Almanac of the Dead," & talks about a return to tribal values in the Americas.

Leslie Sansone's Eat Smart, Walk Strong: The Secrets to Effortless Weight Loss. abr. ed. Leslie Sansone. (Running Time: 4 hrs.). (ENG.). 2006. 14.98 (978-1-59483-494-3(6)) Pub: Hachet Audio. Dist(s): HachBkGrp

Leslie Sansone's Eat Smart, Walk Strong: The Secrets to Effortless Weight Loss. abr. ed. Leslie Sansone. (Running Time: 4 hrs.). (ENG.). 2009. 39.98 (978-1-60788-111-7(X)) Pub: Hachet Audio. Dist(s): HachBkGrp

***Leslie Sbrocco Talks about Wine 1.** abr. ed. Leslie Sbrocco. (ENG.). 2006. (978-0-06-135554-7(2), Harper Audio) HarperCollins Pubs.

***Leslie Sbrocco Talks about Wine 2.** abr. ed. Leslie Sbrocco. (ENG.). 2006. (978-0-06-135555-4(0), Harper Audio) HarperCollins Pubs.

Leslie Ullman. unabr. ed. Read by Leslie Ullman. 1 cass. (Running Time: 29 min.). 1985. 10.00 New Letters.
Ullman reads from "Natural Histories," winner of the 1978 Yale Series of Younger Poets.

Less Is More: How Great Companies Use Productivity As a Competitive Tool in Business. unabr. ed. Jason Jennings. Read by Jason Jennings. 6 cass. (Running Time: 8 hrs.). 2004. 29.95 (978-1-59007-267-7(7)); audio compact disk 34.95 (978-1-59007-268-4(5)) Pub: New Millenn Enter. Dist(s): PerseuPGW
The companies profiled here, which range from finance, manufacturing and industry, share one secret: they operate at peak productivity. The author studied their methods and operations and lays out the secrets to success in clear, easy-to-follow steps. An invaluable resource for everyone in business.

Less Rock, More Talk: A Spoken Word Compilation. Contrib. by Mykel Board et al. 1 CD. (Running Time: 1 hr.). (AK Press Audio Ser.). (ENG.). 2001. audio compact disk 13.98 (978-1-873176-84-9(8)) Pub: AK Pr GBR. Dist(s): Consort Bk Sales

Less Stress. Joseph Currier. Intro. by A. E. Whyte. 1 cass. (Running Time: 49 min.). (Listen & Learn USA! Ser.). 8.95 (978-0-88684-023-5(6)) Listen USA.
Explains how understanding stress can work for you.

Less Stress CD Series. 2005. audio compact disk 17.00 (978-1-59834-052-5(2)) Walk Thru the Bible.

Less Stress Surgery: A Guided Imagery Relaxation Tape, Vol. 1. unabr. ed. Neil F. Neimark. 1 cass. (Running Time: 1 hr.). 1998. 14.95 (978-1-893557-00-0(6)) R E P Tech.
Help for a healthy & speedy recovery. Includes sygle plastic box.

Less Than Kind. David Armstrong. Read by Michael Tudor Barnes. 5 cass. (Running Time: 21600 sec.). (Soundings Ser.). 2005. 49.95 (978-1-84283-516-6(5)) Pub: ISIS Lrg Prnt GBR. Dist(s): Ulverscroft US

Less Than Zero. unabr. ed. Bret Easton Ellis. Read by Christian Rummel. (Running Time: 5 hrs.). 2009. 39.97 (978-1-4418-0627-7(X), 9781441806277, Brlnc Audio MP3 Lib); 24.99 (978-1-4418-0626-0(1), 9781441806260, Brilliance MP3); 39.97 (978-1-4418-0628-4(8), 9781441806284, BADLE); audio compact disk 24.99 (978-1-4418-0624-6(5), 9781441806246, Bril Audio CD Unabri); audio compact disk 69.97 (978-1-4418-0625-3(3), 9781441806253, BriAudCD Unabrid) Brilliance Audio.

Lesser Creatures. Amy Pirnie. 2008. 61.95 (978-1-84559-922-5(5)); audio compact disk 71.95 (978-1-84559-923-2(3)) Pub: Soundings Ltd GBR. Dist(s): Ulverscroft US

Lesson before Dying. Romulus Linney. Perf. by Keith Glover et al. Based on a book by Ernest J. Gaines. 2 cass. (Running Time: 1 hr. 25 mins.). 2002. 20.95 (978-1-58081-238-2(4), WTA16) L A Theatre.
Set in a small Louisiana Cajun community in the late 1940s. Jefferson, a young illiterate black man is falsely convicted of murder. A schoolteacher, Grant Wiggins, agrees to talk with the condemned man. The two men forge a bond as they come to understand what it means to resist and defy one's fate.

Lesson before Dying. abr. ed. Ernest J. Gaines. Read by Lionel Mark Smith. 2001. 7.95 (978-1-57815-214-8(3), Media Bks Audio) Media Bks NJ.

Lesson Before Dying. abr. ed. Ernest J. Gaines. (ENG.). 2006. 14.98 (978-1-59483-764-7(3)) Pub: Hachet Audio. Dist(s): HachBkGrp

Lesson before Dying. unabr. ed. Ernest J. Gaines. Read by Jay Long. 7 CDs. (Running Time: 8 hrs.). (ENG.). 2005. audio compact disk 30.00 (978-0-7393-2367-0(9), Random AudioBks) Pub: Random Audio Pubg. Dist(s): Random

Lesson before Dying. unabr. ed. Romulus Linney. Perf. by Keith Glover et al. Based on a book by Ernest J. Gaines. 2 CDs. (Running Time: 1 hr. 25 mins.). 2002. audio compact disk 25.95 (978-1-58081-228-3(7), CDWTA16) Pub: L A Theatre. Dist(s): NetLibrary CO

Lesson before Dying. unabr. collector's ed. Ernest J. Gaines. Read by Jay Long. 6 cass. (Running Time: 9 hrs.). 1994. 48.00 (978-0-7366-2688-0(3), 3423) Books on Tape.
Jefferson, a young black man in Louisiana in the 1940s is convicted of the murder of a white liquor store owner & is condemned to death. Grant Wiggins, a black teacher, is compelled to impart something of his own learning & pride to the condemned man & the two form a surprising bond.

***Lesson Booster: Got Empathy?** Cerebellum Academic Team. (Running Time: 13 mins.). (Lesson Booster Ser.). 2010. cd-rom 79.95 (978-1-59443-698-7(3)) Cerebellum.

***Lesson Booster Elementary Series.** Cerebellum Academic Team. (Running Time: 25 mins.). (Lesson Booster Ser.). 2008. cd-rom 149.95 (978-1-58565-364-5(0)) Cerebellum.

***Lesson Booster Middle School Series.** Cerebellum Academic Team. (Running Time: 1 hr. 27 mins.). (Lesson Booster Ser.). 2010. cd-rom 454.95 (978-1-58565-365-2(9)) Cerebellum.

***Lesson Booster 8 Series Set.** Cerebellum Academic Team. (Running Time: 1 hr. 52 mins.). (Lesson Booster Ser.). 2010. cd-rom 574.98 (978-1-58565-363-8(2)) Cerebellum.

Lesson for Humanity. Swami Amar Jyoti. 2 cass. 1987. 12.95 (K-96) Truth Consciousness.
Many stages & dimensions of reality: we are occupied with our dreams. The blindness of ego; inviting the way of pain. Examples from epics & scriptures. Liberation from self-delusion.

Lesson from Austria. Kitty Werthman. 1 cass. (Running Time: 1 hr. 30 min.). 10.00 (978-0-912986-29-6(8), AC24) Am Media.
The author, who lived through Hitler's rise to power in Austria, tells of free benefits & promises of reform which eventually destroyed freedom for women & all people as well.

Lesson in Dying. Ann Cleeves. 6 CDs. (Sound Ser.). (J). 2003. audio compact disk 64.95 (978-1-84283-520-3(3)) Pub: ISIS Lrg Prnt GBR. Dist(s): Ulverscroft US

Lesson in Dying. Ann Cleeves. Read by Gordon Griffin. 6 cass. (Sound Ser.). (J). 2003. 54.95 (978-1-84283-300-1(6)) Pub: ISIS Lrg Prnt GBR. Dist(s): Ulverscroft US

Lesson in Ecology: Psalm 104. Ed Young. 1989. 4.95 (978-0-7417-1764-1(6), 764) Win Walk.

Lesson in Nutrition: Romans 14:13-23. Ed Young. 1984. 4.95 (978-0-7417-1402-2(7), 402) Win Walk.

Lesson in Nutrition: Romans 14:13-23. Ed Young. 1997. 4.95 (978-0-7417-2141-9(4), 1141) Win Walk.

Lesson, Level 1A, Amanda V. Lethco et al. 1 CD. (Running Time: 1 hr.). (Alfred's Basic Piano Library Ser.). (ENG.). 1996. audio compact disk 8.95 (978-0-7390-1886-6(8), 14541) Alfred Pub.

Lesson of Love. Perf. by Ashley Cleveland. Prod. by Kenny Greenberg. 1 CD. (Running Time: 1 hrs. 30 mins.). 1995. audio compact disk Brentwood Music.
Critically acclaimed Nashville singer/songwriter, Ashley's sophomore effort was produced by husband Kenny Greenberg & features the No. 1 CHR hit, He Is.

Lesson of the Hour: Why the Negro Is Lynched. abr. ed. Frederick Douglass. Perf. by Fred Morsell. 1 cass. (Running Time: 76 min.). (Frederick Douglass's Greatest Speeches). (C). 1993. 11.99 (978-1-883210-02-1(X)); audio compact disk 13.99 (978-1-883210-03-8(8)) TBM Records.
Frederick Douglass's last great speech "The Lesson of the Hour" traces how racial attitudes & patterns of behavior developed during reconstruction. Electrifying & somber, it is as timely as if written today & suggests a solution to justice.

***Lessons at the Halfway Point: Wisdom for Midlife.** unabr. ed. Michael Levine. Read by Michael Levine. (Running Time: 2.5 hrs. NaN mins.). (ENG.). 2011. 19.95 (978-1-4417-8494-0(2)); audio compact disk 28.00 (978-1-4417-8492-6(6)) Blckstn Audio.

Lessons at the Halfway Point: Wisdom for Midlife. unabr. ed. Michael K. Levine. Read by Michael K. Levine. 1 cass. (Running Time: 2 hrs. 30 mins.). 2000. 14.95 (978-0-7861-1887-8(3), 2686) Blckstn Audio.
A deeply though-provoking look at one man's courageous journey to understanding life from the perspective of having just turned forty. A reflection on the past as well as an optimistic look to a challenging future.

Lessons de la Sobriete. 1 cass. (FRE.). 1986. 6.50 (978-0-933685-10-9(6), TP-50) A A Grapevine.
Brief descriptions of recovery from alcoholism through the program of Alcoholics Anonymous.

Lessons from a Father to His Son. abr. ed. John Ashcroft. Read by John Ashcroft. 2 cass. (Running Time: 2 hrs.). 1998. 15.99 (978-0-7852-7092-8(2), 70922) Nelson.
John Ashcroft received a rich legacy of lessons from his father. Robert Ashcroft knew the importance of character, honesty, integrity & faith.

Lessons from a Seasoned Veteran: Ecc. 12:2-8. Ed Young. 1994. 4.95 (978-0-7417-2011-5(6), 1011) Win Walk.

Lessons from David. 2003. 20.00 (978-1-881541-85-1(1)) A Wommack.

Lessons from David. Created by AWMI. 4 CDs. (ENG.). 2004. audio compact disk (978-1-59548-039-2(0)) A Wommack.

Lessons from Elijah. Created by AWMI. (ENG.). 2007. 30.00 (978-1-59548-100-9(1)); audio compact disk 30.00 (978-1-59548-098-9(6)) A Wommack.

Lessons from Elijah. Created by Andrew Wommack. 3. (Running Time: 3 cass.). 2003. audio compact disk 21.00 (978-1-881541-94-3(0)) A Wommack.

***Lessons from History.** Featuring Ravi Zacharias. 1999. audio compact disk 9.00 (978-1-61256-035-9(0)) Ravi Zach.

Lessons from History: Jude 5-9. Ed Young. 1989. 4.95 (978-0-7417-1741-2(7), 741) Win Walk.

Lessons from Joseph. 5 Cassette Tapes. 2005. (978-1-59548-056-9(0)); audio compact disk (978-1-59548-055-2(2)) A Wommack.

Lessons from Leacock. abr. ed. Stephen Leacock & Christopher Newton. Perf. by Shaw Festival Cast Staff. Prod. by CBC Radio Staff. 1 cass. (Running Time: 1 hr.). (Between the Covers Classics). (ENG.). 2000. 14.95 (978-0-86492-279-3(5)) Pub: BTC Audiobks CAN. Dist(s): U Toronto Pr

***Lessons from Royalty.** Featuring Ravi Zacharias. 1990. audio compact disk 9.00 (978-1-61256-042-7(3)) Ravi Zach.

***Lessons from San Quentin: Everything I needed to know about life I learned in Prison.** unabr. ed. Bill Dallas & George Barna. (ENG.). 2009. 14.98 (978-1-59644-732-5(X), Hovel Audio) christianaud.

Lessons from San Quentin: Everything I needed to know about life I learned in Prison. unabr. ed. Bill Dallas & George Barna. Read by Bill Dallas. (Running Time: 5 hrs. 25 mins. 48 sec.). (ENG.). 2009. audio compact disk 24.98 (978-1-59644-731-8(1), Hovel Audio) christianaud.

Lessons from the Animal People. Short Stories. Dovie Thomason. Music by Ulali. 1 cass. (Running Time: 1 hr. 30 min.). (J). 1996. 9.95 (978-0-938756-50-7(8), 037); audio compact disk 14.95 (978-0-938756-51-4(6), 037D) Yellow Moon.
Collection of nine stories from different Native American tribes. Stories invoke a self-examination by describing mistakes, bad choices & sometimes unruly antics of the animal people.

Lessons from the Christmas Story. Andrew Wommack. 4 cass. (Running Time: 4 hrs.). 2004. audio compact disk 28.00 (978-1-881541-89-9(4)) A Wommack.

Lessons from the Christmas Story: (for Every Season) 4 cass. 2002. 20.00 (978-1-881541-80-6(0)) A Wommack.

Lessons from the Forests. Ben Mathes. 2 cass. (Running Time: 60 min.). 1995. 12.95 (978-1-886463-21-9(2)) Oasis Audio.
Explorer, adventurer Ben Mathes has been traveling the forests & remote rivers of the world since 1978. "Lessons from the Forest" is a collection of his wild & fascinating personal experiences.

Lessons from the Heavenly Council. R. G. Hilson. 2008. audio compact disk 9.95 (978-1-60031-044-7(3)) Spoken Books.

Lessons from the Road. unabr. ed. Nigel James. Narrated by Nigel James. (Running Time: 4 hrs. 3 mins. 54 sec.). (ENG.). 2008. 13.99 (978-1-60814-466-2(6)); audio compact disk 19.99 (978-1-59859-507-9(5)) Oasis Audio.

Lessons from the Trading Trenches: Tips, Techniques & War Stories. Instructed by Lewis Borselino. 2005. audio compact disk 19.95 (978-1-59280-235-7(4)) Marketplace Bks.

Lessons from the Trading Trenches: Tips, Techniques & War Stories. Instructed by Louis Borsellino. (Trade Secrets Audio Ser.). 2000. 19.95 (978-1-883272-81-4(5)) Marketplace Bks.

***Lessons from War in a Battle of Ideas.** Featuring Ravi Zacharias. 2000. audio compact disk 9.00 (978-1-61256-060-1(1)) Ravi Zach.

***Lessons from Wendell Winkler Volume 5.** Arranged by Polishing the Pulpit. 2010. audio compact disk 25.00 (978-1-60644-103-9(5)) Heart Heart.

***Lessons from Wendell Winkler Volume 6.** Arranged by Polishing the Pulpit. 2010. audio compact disk 25.00 (978-1-60644-104-6(3)) Heart Heart.

Lessons in Air Conditioning & Refrigeration. Jerry Killinger & LaDonna Killinger. (gr. 9-13). 2002. audio compact disk 133.28 (978-1-56637-742-3(0)) Goodheart.

Lessons in Chinese Commerce for the New Millennium. 2nd rev. ed. Jane C. M. Kuo. 3 CDs. (C). 2002. audio compact disk 45.95 (978-0-88727-411-4(0)) Cheng Tsui.

Lessons in Chinese Commerce for the New Millennium, Vol. 2. Jane C. M. Kuo. 3 CDs. (C). 2001. audio compact disk 45.95 (978-0-88727-410-7(2)) Cheng Tsui.

Lessons in Electricity. Jerry Killinger & LaDonna Killinger. (gr. 9-13). 1999. audio compact disk 133.28 (978-1-56637-523-8(1)) Goodheart.

Lessons in Electricity for Air Conditioning. Jerry Killinger & LaDonna Killinger. (gr. 9-13). 2002. audio compact disk 133.28 (978-1-56637-849-9(4)) Goodheart.

Lessons in Embodiment. Rosie Spiegel. Read by Rosie Spiegel. 4 cass. 1995. SRG Pubng.
Guided lessons in yoga & movement. Discussion of self-empowered approach to health & wellness.

Lessons in Intimacy... the Lover's Touch. Diana Daffner. 1 CD. (Running Time: 65 min.). 2004. audio compact disk 19.95 (978-0-9672900-1-0(5)) Dynamic.
Couples are guided to look into each other's eyes, touch one another's hearts, and deepen their experience of emotional and physical intimacy.

Lessons in Leadership Vol. 1: Mac Hammond Speaks to Business Professionals, Narrated by Mac Hammond. 6 cass. (Best of the Winner's Luncheons Ser.: Vol. 1). 1998. 36.00 (978-1-57399-073-8(6)) Mac Hammond.
Teaching on scriptural business principles of effective leadership.

Lessons in Leadership Vol 1: The Best of the Winner's Luncheons. Mac Hammond. 6 CDs. (Running Time: 5 hours). 2002. audio compact disk 30.00 (978-1-57399-147-6(3)) Mac Hammond.
Mac Hammond Speaks to Business Professionals About Growing in Influence.

Lessons in Life's Valleys. Iyanla Vanzant. Interview with Iyanla Vanzant. Interview with Justine W. Toms. 2 cass. (Running Time: 2 hrs.). 1999. 16.95 (978-1-56170-696-9(5), 4010) Hay House.

Lessons in Living. unabr. ed. Jack Boland. Read by Jack Boland. 2 cass. (Running Time: 2 hrs.). 19.95 (978-0-88152-057-6(8), BA26) Master Mind.

***Lessons in Loss & Living: Hope & Guidance for Confronting Serious Illness & Grief.** unabr. ed. Michele A. Reiss. Narrated by Renée Raudman. (Running Time: 6 hrs. 30 mins.). 2010. 14.99 (978-1-4526-7040-9(4)); 29.99 (978-1-4526-2040-4(7)); 19.99 (978-1-4526-5040-1(3)); audio compact disk 71.99 (978-1-4526-3040-3(2)); audio compact disk 29.99 (978-1-4526-0040-6(6)) Pub: Tantor Media. Dist(s): IngramPubServ

***Lessons in Loving: A Journey into the Heart.** David Robert Ord. (ENG.). 2006. audio compact disk 26.95 (978-1-897238-31-8(2)) Pub: Namaste Pub CAN. Dist(s): PerseuPGW

Lessons in Mastery: How to Use Your Personal Power to Create an Extraordinary Life! Anthony Robbins. 6 cass. (Running Time: 6 hrs.). 1998. 59.95 (978-1-55525-053-9(X), 17650A); audio compact disk (978-1-55525-054-6(8), 17650CD) Nightingale-Conant.
Master your power.

Lessons in Mastery: How to Use Your Personal Power to Create an Extraordinary Life! unabr. abr. ed. Anthony Robbins. (Running Time: 60 hrs. 0 mins. 0 sec.). (ENG.). 2002. audio compact disk 39.95 (978-0-7435-2515-2(9), Nightgale) Pub: S&S Audio. Dist(s): S and S Inc
With Lessons in Mastery, you will learn how to: Experience true happiness; Harness your decision-making power; Decode the language of emotion; Anticipate and prepare for major life changes; Commit yourself to daily improvement; Replace dormant resources with new assets that will improve the quality of your life; Empower Yourself to take the right moves at the right time.

Lessons in Modern Hebrew, Level 1. Edna A. Coffin. 9 cass. 77.40 U MI Lang Res.

Lessons in Modern Hebrew, Level 2. Edna A. Coffin. 15 cass. 110.95 U MI Lang Res.

Lessons in Modern Hebrew, Levels 1 & 2. Edna A. Coffin. 24 cass. 151.09 U MI Lang Res.

Lessons in Science Safety with Max Axiom, Super Scientist. Donald B. Lemke et al. Illus. by Tod Smith. (Graphic Science Ser.). (ENG.). (gr. 3-4). 2007. audio compact disk 6.95 (978-1-4296-1126-8(X)) CapstoneDig.

Lessons in Yoga, Fourteen Steps to Higher Awareness. 2nd rev. ed. Kriyananda, pseud. 16 cass. (Running Time: 20 hrs.). Incl. Lessons in Yoga, Fourteen Steps to Higher Awareness: Esoterica of the Spiritual Path; Lessons in Yoga, Fourteen Steps to Higher Awareness: First Steps in Yoga & Meditation; Lessons in Yoga, Fourteen Steps to Higher Awareness: How & Why to Develop Your Magnetism; Lessons in Yoga, Fourteen Steps to Higher Awareness: How to Become a Dynamo of Energy; Lessons in Yoga, Fourteen Steps to Higher Awareness: How to Control Your Subconscious Mind; Lessons in Yoga, Fourteen Steps to Higher Awareness: How to Develop Good Habits; Lessons in Yoga, Fourteen Steps to Higher Awareness: How to Focus Your Mental Powers; Lessons in Yoga, Fourteen Steps to Higher Awareness: How to Test Your Spiritual Progress; Lessons in Yoga, Fourteen Steps to Higher Awareness: Pathways to God: Heart, Head, Hands; Lessons in Yoga, Fourteen Steps to Higher Awareness: Secret Teachings in the Bible; Lessons in Yoga, Fourteen Steps to Higher Awareness: The Eight Steps to Self-Realization; Lessons in Yoga, Fourteen Steps to Higher Awareness: Watering the Flowers of Self-Realization; Lessons in Yoga, Fourteen Steps to Higher Awareness: Weeding Your Garden of Self-Realization; Lessons in Yoga, Fourteen Steps to Higher Awareness: What is a Guru?; Set pap. bk. 124.00 complete course. (978-0-916124-16-8(9)) Crystal Clarity.
This tape course was compiled from over 500 hours of lectures & classes by Swami Kriyananda. The tapes stand alone as a comprehensive course in "practical spiritual living".

Lessons in Yoga, Fourteen Steps to Higher Awareness: Esoterica of the Spiritual Path see Lessons in Yoga, Fourteen Steps to Higher Awareness

Lessons in Yoga, Fourteen Steps to Higher Awareness: First Steps in Yoga & Meditation see Lessons in Yoga, Fourteen Steps to Higher Awareness

Lessons in Yoga, Fourteen Steps to Higher Awareness: How & Why to Develop Your Magnetism see Lessons in Yoga, Fourteen Steps to Higher Awareness

Lessons in Yoga, Fourteen Steps to Higher Awareness: How to Become a Dynamo of Energy see Lessons in Yoga, Fourteen Steps to Higher Awareness

Lessons in Yoga, Fourteen Steps to Higher Awareness: How to Control Your Subconscious Mind see Lessons in Yoga, Fourteen Steps to Higher Awareness

Lessons in Yoga, Fourteen Steps to Higher Awareness: How to Develop Good Habits see Lessons in Yoga, Fourteen Steps to Higher Awareness

Lessons in Yoga, Fourteen Steps to Higher Awareness: How to Focus Your Mental Powers see Lessons in Yoga, Fourteen Steps to Higher Awareness

Lessons in Yoga, Fourteen Steps to Higher Awareness: How to Test Your Spiritual Progress see Lessons in Yoga, Fourteen Steps to Higher Awareness

Lessons in Yoga, Fourteen Steps to Higher Awareness: Pathways to God: Heart, Head, Hands see Lessons in Yoga, Fourteen Steps to Higher Awareness

Lessons in Yoga, Fourteen Steps to Higher Awareness: Secret Teachings in the Bible see Lessons in Yoga, Fourteen Steps to Higher Awareness

Lessons in Yoga, Fourteen Steps to Higher Awareness: The Eight Steps to Self-Realization see Lessons in Yoga, Fourteen Steps to Higher Awareness

Lessons in Yoga, Fourteen Steps to Higher Awareness: Watering the Flowers of Self-Realization see Lessons in Yoga, Fourteen Steps to Higher Awareness

Lessons in Yoga, Fourteen Steps to Higher Awareness: Weeding Your Garden of Self-Realization see Lessons in Yoga, Fourteen Steps to Higher Awareness

Lessons in Yoga, Fourteen Steps to Higher Awareness: What is a Guru? see Lessons in Yoga, Fourteen Steps to Higher Awareness

Lessons Learned. unabr. ed. Nora Roberts. Read by Nellie Chalfont. (Running Time: 7 hrs.). (Great Chefs Ser.). 2009. 24.99 (978-1-4418-3007-4(3), 9781441830074, Brilliance MP3); 39.97 (978-1-4418-3005-0(7), 9781441830050, Brlnc Audio MP3 Lib); 39.97 (978-1-4418-3006-7(5), 9781441830067, BADLE) Brilliance Audio.

Lessons Learned. unabr. ed. Nora Roberts. Read by Nellie Chalfant. (Running Time: 7 hrs.). (Great Chefs Ser.). 2009. audio compact disk 24.99 (978-1-4418-3002-9(2), 9781441830029, Bril Audio CD Unabri); audio compact disk 79.97 (978-1-4418-3003-6(0), 9781441830036, BriAudCD Unabrid) Brilliance Audio.

Lessons Learned Collection: I Love You Because You're You; Miss Spider's Tea Party; Pigsty. unabr. ed. Liza Baker et al. Read by Kirsten Krohn & Skip Hinnant. (J). 2007. 34.99 (978-1-60252-843-7(8)) Find a World.

***Lessons of History.** exp. unabr. ed. Will Durant & Ariel Durant. Narrated by Grover Gardner. 1 MP3-CD. (Running Time: 5 hrs. 30 mins.). 2010. 39.95 (978-0-7927-6992-7(9)); audio compact disk 59.95 (978-0-7927-6991-0(0)) AudioGO.

Lessons of History. 2nd unabr. rev. exp. ed. Will Durant & Ariel Durant. Read by Grover Gardner. 4 cass. 2004. 25.95 (978-1-57270-395-7(4)) Pub: Audio Partners. Dist(s): PerseuPGW

Lessons of History. 2nd unabr. rev. exp. ed. Will Durant & Ariel Durant. Narrated by Grover Gardner & John Little. 4 CDs. (Running Time: 5 hrs.). (ENG.). 2004. audio compact disk 27.95 (978-1-57270-396-4(2)) Pub: AudioGO. Dist(s): Perseus Dist

Lessons of History: Neh. 9:1-38. Ed Young. 1990. 4.95 (978-0-7417-1818-1(9), 818) Win Walk.

Lessons of the Holy Spirit. Kenneth Wapnick. 4 CDs. 2005. audio compact disk 24.00 (978-1-59142-197-9(7), CD112) Foun Miracles.

***Lessons of the Holy Spirit.** Kenneth Wapnick. 2009. 19.00 (978-1-59142-471-0(2)) Foun Miracles.

Lessons That Man Must Learn. unabr. ed. Robert A. Monroe. Read by Robert A. Monroe. (Running Time: 45 min.). (Explorer Ser.). 1983. 12.95 (978-1-56113-021-4(4), 22) Monroe Institute.
Comments from the Council of Love about the dawning Aquarian Age.

Lessons to Learn/Allowing Your Changes. Marianne Williamson. Read by Marianne Williamson. 1 cass. (Running Time: 90 mins.). (Lectures on a Course in Miracles). 1999. 10.00 (978-1-56170-239-8(0), M742) Hay House.

Lester Sumrall - Man of Faith & Destiny. Lester Sumrall. 5 cass,. (Running Time: 7 hrs. 30 mins.). 1999. 20.00 (978-1-58568-079-5(6)) Sumrall Pubng.

***Lestrade & the Sawdust Ring.** M. J. Trow. 2010. 69.95 (978-1-4079-0755-0(7)); audio compact disk 84.95 (978-1-4079-0756-7(5)) Pub: Soundings Ltd GBR. Dist(s): Ulverscroft US

***Lestrade & the Sign of Nine.** M. J. Trow. 2010. 61.95 (978-1-4079-0758-1(1)); audio compact disk 79.95 (978-1-4079-0759-8(X)) Pub: Soundings Ltd GBR. Dist(s): Ulverscroft US

Let All Creation Sing. Paul Tate. 1 cass. 1998. 11.00 (978-0-937690-56-7(2), 7468-7470); audio compact disk 16.00 CD. (978-0-937690-55-0(4)) Wrld Lib Pubns.
Contemporary religious music.

Let All Together Praise Vol. 5: Ars Antiqua Choralis, Perf. by Cathedral Singers. 1997. 10.95 (335); audio compact disk 15.95 (335) GIA Pubns.

Let Earth Receive Her King. E. D. Kee. 2001. 54.95 (978-0-633-01680-7(2)); 40.00 (978-0-633-01678-4(0)); 11.98 (978-0-633-01676-0(4)); audio compact disk 59.95 (978-0-633-01681-4(0)); audio compact disk 45.00 (978-0-633-01679-1(9)); audio compact disk 16.98 (978-0-633-01677-7(2)) LifeWay Christian.

Let Every Day Be Christmas. Daya Mata. 1984. 6.50 (2114) Self Realization.
Discusses the universal message of love & truth exemplified in the life of Jesus. Topics include: the inner purpose of Christmas; parallels in the lives & teachings of Christ & Krishna; bringing God into your life through meditation; the eternal message of divine love & how it applies to the problems of today's world.

Let Every Instrument be Tuned for Praise: Insturmental Music by Bob Moore. Bob Moore. 2000. 10.95 (CS-491) GIA Pubns.

Let Every Insturment be Tuned for Praise: Instrumental By Bob Moore. Bob Moore. 2000. audio compact disk 15.95 (CD-491) GIA Pubns.

Let Every Nation Know. Robert Dallek & Terry Golway. 2007. pap. bk. 19.95 (978-1-4022-0922-2(3), MediaFusion) Sourcebks.

Let Every Voice Sing Christmas: Contemporary Praise for Youth or Young Adults. Beverly Darnall. Arranged by John Darnall. 1 cass. (Running Time: 25 min.). (YA). 1996. 80.00 (MU-9201C); audio compact disk 80.00 (MU-9201T) Lillenas.
Christmas musical using contemporary arrangements of familiar carols intertwined with expressive new songs. Using a variety of dramatic techniques including mime & rhymed recitation, along with three narrators to tell the story of our Savior's birth. Perfect for youth choirs & young adult choirs. Also excellent for those churches that offer programs outside the church setting, such as shopping malls, schools or similar outreach-type ministries. An offering of praise & worship to the birth of Christ. An experience your congregation will not soon forget. An accompaniment cassette with Side 1, stereo trax & side 2, split-channel form.

Let Everything That Has Breath. Contrib. by Great Worship Songs Praise Band. Prod. by Luke Gambill. (Great Worship Songs Ser.). 2008. audio compact disk 12.99 (978-5-557-42742-5(2), Brentwood-Benson Music) Brentwood Music.

Let Freedom Ring. Contrib. by Bill & Gloria Gaither and Their Homecoming Friends et al. Prod. by Bill Gaither & Luke Renner. (Gaither Gospel Ser.). 2002. 19.98 (978-5-550-14842-6(0)) Spring House Music.

Let Freedom Ring. Perf. by Timothy Wright. 1 cass. 1997. audio compact disk 15.99 (D5211) Diamante Music Grp.
Rev. Wright teams up with his concert choir from New York City & the Voices of Ebenezer AME Church & delivers a gospel music offering that will take the listener to another level.

***Let Freedom Ring.** abr. ed. Sean Hannity. Read by Sean Hannity. (ENG.). 2004. (978-0-06-081355-0(5), Harper Audio); (978-0-06-076412-8(0), Harper Audio) HarperCollins Pubs.

Let Freedom Ring: Winning the War of Liberty over Liberalism. abr. ed. Sean Hannity. Read by Sean Hannity. 4 cass. (Running Time: 6 hrs.). 2002. 25.95 (978-0-06-051812-7(X)) HarperCollins Pubs.

***Let Freedom Ring: Winning the War of Liberty over Liberalism.** abr. ed. Sean Hannity. Read by Sean Hannity. 2010. audio compact disk 14.99 (978-0-06-202043-7(9), Harper Audio) HarperCollins Pubs.

***Let George Do It.** Perf. by Bob Bailey & Francis Robinson. 2010. audio compact disk 39.98 (978-1-57019-949-3(3)) Radio Spirits.

Let George Do It: Bookworm Turns & Opportunity Knocks Twice. Perf. by Bob Bailey. 1 cass. (Running Time: 1 hr.). 2001. 6.98 (2263) Radio Spirits.

Let George Do It: Cousin Jeff & Brookdale Orphanage. Perf. by Bob Bailey. 1 cass. (Running Time: 1 hr.). 2001. 6.98 (2461) Radio Spirits.

Let George Do It: Father Who Had Nothing & Death Wears a Gray Sports Coat. Perf. by Bob Bailey. 1 cass. (Running Time: 1 hr.). 2001. 6.98 (1680) Radio Spirits.

Let George Do It: Santa Clause in Glass & Christmas in January. Perf. by Bob Bailey. 1 cass. (Running Time: 1 hr.). 2001. 6.98 (2223) Radio Spirits.

Let George Do It: Stranger than Fiction & A Matter of Doubt. Perf. by Bob Bailey. 1 cass. (Running Time: 1 hr.). 2001. 6.98 (1509) Radio Spirits.

Let George Do It: The Roundabout Murder & The Motif is Murder. Perf. by Bob Bailey. 1 cass. (Running Time: 1 hr.). 2001. 6.98 (1681) Radio Spirits.

***Let George Do It, Volume 1.** RadioArchives.com. (Running Time: 600). (ENG.). 2005. audio compact disk 29.98 (978-1-61081-032-6(5)) Radio Arch.

Let Go. abr. ed. Robert A. Monroe. Read by Robert A. Monroe. (Running Time: 30 min.). (Human Plus Ser.). 1989. 14.95 (978-1-56102-016-4(8)) Inter Indus.
Break free. Reduce or release emotional reactions.

Let Go & Let God. Barry Tesar. 1 cass. (Running Time: 1 hr.). (Subliminal Inspiration Ser.). 1992. 9.98 (978-1-56470-005-6(4)) Success Cass.
Subliminal program.

Let Go, Let God. Wally Amos. 1999. 10.95 (978-0-87159-842-4(6)) Unity Schl Christ.

Let Go, Let God: 31 Inspirational Messages from Daily Word Magazine. Read by Wally Amos. (Running Time: 216000 sec.). 2008. audio compact disk 15.95 (978-0-87159-892-9(2), Unity Hse) Unity Schl Christ.

***Let Go of the Guilt.** Mason Betha & Twyla Betha. (ENG.). (YA). 2007. 36.00 (978-1-60989-004-9(3)) Born To Succee.

Let Go of the Struggle. Joan Fericy. 1 cass. (Running Time: 60 min.). 1989. 8.95 (978-0-9622371-2-6(4)) J Ferícy.
Self-help.

Let God Choose Your Mate Pt. 1: A Prudent Wife is From the Lord, Derek Prince. 1 cass. (B-4079) Derek Prince.

Let God Choose Your Mate Pt. 2: How to Find the Right Mate. Derek Prince. 1 cass. (B-4080) Derek Prince.

Let Heaven & Nature Swing. Genevox Music Staff. 2003. audio compact disk 16.98 (978-0-633-09326-6(2)) LifeWay Christian.

Let Heaven & Nature Swing. Don Marsh. 2001. 75.00 (978-0-633-01671-5(3)); 11.98 (978-0-633-01669-2(1)); audio compact disk 85.00 (978-0-633-01672-2(1)); audio compact disk 16.98 (978-0-633-01670-8(5)) LifeWay Christian.

Let Heaven & Nature Swing instrumental Listening Cassette. Don Marsh. 2003. 11.98 (978-0-633-09327-3(0)) LifeWay Christian.

Let It Be Easy: Simple Actions to Create an Extraordinary Life. Tolly Burkan. 2006. audio compact disk 14.95 (978-1-57178-204-5(4)) Coun Oak Bks.

Let it Bleed. unabr. ed. Ian Rankin. Narrated by Samuel Gillies. 8 cass. (Running Time: 10 hrs. 30 mins.). 2001. 72.00 (978-1-84197-246-6(0)) Recorded Bks.
Lucky is the writer who develops a loyal following. These fans can hardly wait for the next book to appear on the shelves. This series is about Scottish detective John Rebus, and what gives the series a special edge is the skillful weaving of Edinburgh into the action so that it becomes an integral part of the plot. Rankin also presents us with a "tarnished hero"; Rebus is a troubled, sometimes violent cop who thinks nothing of ignoring the rules in order to track down a killer. In this particular book, listeners come to know more of Rebus's personal life and why his mood is as gloomy and dour as the Scottish weather.

Let It Go. Read by Paul Fair. 1 cass. (Running Time: 45 min.). (Relaxation Ser.). 1996. 12.95 (978-1-889896-04-5(7), S4056) Strs Les Inc.
Stress reduction.

Let It Shine. Jim Rule. Perf. by Tim Horrigan. Prod. by Tim Horrigan. 1 cass. (Running Time: 36 min.). (J). (ps-4). 1996. 10.00 (978-1-886037-04-5(3), 2702); audio compact disk 15.00 (2702) PNO Tuna.
Collection of 12 original songs intended for children & parents based on the Golden Rule.

Let It Shine! Perf. by Jim Rule & Tim Horrigan. 1 cass. (Running Time: 36 min.). 1996. audio compact disk 15.00 CD. PNO Tuna.
Twelve original songs intended for children & parents.

Let It Snow, Baby... Let It Reindeer. Contrib. by Relient K. Prod. by Mark Lee Townsend & Matthew Thiessen. 2007. audio compact disk 13.99 (978-5-557-59286-4(5)) Gotee Records.

Let Loose the Tigers. unabr. ed. Josephine Cox. Read by Maggie Ollerenshaw. 8 cass. (Running Time: 8 hrs.). 1997. 69.95 (978-0-7540-0051-8(6), CAB 1474) AudioGO.
Queenie Bedford left Blackburn & Rick Marsden, the man she loved but could never marry. In 1965, she returned to stand by her friend Sheila Thorogood, imprisoned for running a brothel. Sheila's Edwardian house was sadly neglected, but Queenie transformed it into a respectable guesthouse. While in Blackburn, Queenie runs into Rick. Their meeting unlocks crucial secrets from the past that threaten to tear their lives apart.

Let Love Be Victorious. 1985. (0223) Evang Sisterhood Mary.

Let Me Be a Woman, Elisabeth Elliot. 4 cass. (Running Time: 6 hrs.). 1992. 14.99 (978-0-8474-2048-3(5)) Loizeaux.
Spirituality for women.

Let Me Be the Boss: Poems for Kids to Perform. Brod Bagert & Boyds Mills Press Staff. (ENG., (YA). (gr. 2-4). 1996. reel tape 9.95 (978-1-56397-540-0(8)) Boyds Mills Pr.

Let Me Be the Boss: Poems for Kids to Perform. unabr. ed. Poems. Brod Bagert. Read by Brod Bagert. 1 cass. (Running Time: 41 min.). (J). (gr. k-5). 1995. bk. 9.00 (978-1-887746-05-2(6)) Juliahouse Pubs.
Brod Bagert reads & performs poems from his popular book of children's poetry.

Let me be the One. Jo Goodman. Narrated by Virginia Leishman. 11 cass. (Running Time: 15 hrs. 15 mins.). 95.00 (978-1-4025-3619-9(4)) Recorded Bks.

Let Me Call You Sweetheart. abr. ed. Mary Higgins Clark. Read by Bess Armstrong. (Running Time: 30 hrs. 0 mins. 0 sec.). (ENG.). 2009. audio compact disk 9.99 (978-0-7435-8349-7(3)) Pub: S&S Audio. Dist(s): S and S Inc

Let Me Call You Sweetheart. unabr. ed. Mary Higgins Clark. Read by Mary Peiffer. 6 cass. (Running Time: 9 hrs.). 1995. 48.00 (978-0-7366-3197-6(6), 3861) Books on Tape.
Why does a district attorney re-open a 10-year-old murder case? Maybe she's spooked when she sees two women with the victim's face.

Let Me Enjoy see Poetry of Thomas Hardy

Let Me Entertain You. abr. unabr. ed. David Brown. Frwd. by Peter Bart. 8 cass. (Running Time: 12 hrs.). (Hollywood Classics Ser.). 2004. 34.95 (978-1-931056-45-8(5), N Millennium Audio) New Millenn Enter.
A self-portrait, in selective memory of a man who has led many lives, all of them full of risk, accomplishment & above all humanity. Astonishing stories about encounters with the famous and notorious and the all-powerful, including Mafia chieftains, Presidents, the reclusive Howard Hughes, the super-rich J. paul Getty, William Randolph Hearst and the super-famous Marilyn Monroe, Robert kennedy, irving Berlin, paul Newman, Orson Welles, Steven Spielberg, Robert Redford, and many more.

Let Me Go: My Mother & the Ss. Helga Schneider. 4 CDs. (Running Time: 4 hrs. 30 mins.). 2004. audio compact disk 32.00 (978-0-7861-8380-7(2), 3306) Blckstn Audio.

Let Me Go: My Mother & the Ss. unabr. ed. Helga Schneider. Ed. by Barbara Rosenblat. 4 cass. (Running Time: 4 hrs. 30 mins.). 2004. 32.95 (978-0-7861-2831-0(3), 3306) Blckstn Audio.

Let Me Go: My Mother & the Ss. unabr. ed. Helga Schneider. Read by Barbara Rosenblat. 4 CDs. 2004. audio compact disk 25.95 (978-0-7861-8578-8(3)) Blckstn Audio.

Let Me Go: My Mother & the Ss. unabr. ed. Helga Schneider. Read by Barbara Rosenblat. 4 cass. (Running Time: 4 hrs. 30 mins.). 2005. reel tape 24.95 (978-0-7861-2737-5(6), E3306); audio compact disk 24.95 (978-0-7861-8513-9(9), 3306) Blckstn Audio.

Let Me Tell You a Story: A Lifetime in the Game. abr. ed. Red Auerbach & John Feinstein. Read by Arnie Mazer. (Running Time: 3 hrs. 30 mins.). (ENG.). 2009. 39.98 (978-1-60024-654-8(0)) Pub: Hachet Audio. Dist(s): HachBkGrp

Let Me Tell You a Story: A Lifetime in the Game. abr. ed. John Feinstein. Read by Arnie Mazer. (ENG.). 2005. 14.98 (978-1-59483-143-0(2)) Pub: Hachet Audio. Dist(s): HachBkGrp

Let Me Whisper in Your Ear. unabr. ed. Mary Jane Clark. Read by Laura Hicks. 8 vols. (Running Time: 15 hrs.). (KEY News Ser.: Bk. 3). 2001. bk. 69.95 (978-0-7927-2426-1(7), CSL 315, Chivers Sound Lib) AudioGO.
When the remains of a twelve-year-old boy, missing for thirty years, are discovered buried where Palisades Amusement Park once stood, reporter Laura Walsh sees her chance to move beyond the obits to Hourglass, KEY New's answer to Sixty Minutes.But when Hourglass host Gwenyth Gilpatric meets a devastating end, Laura's ready-to-air obit raises not only the suspicions of her co-workers, but of the police.

Let Me Whisper in Your Ear. unabr. ed. Mary Jane Clark. Read by Laura Hicks. 6 CDs. (Running Time: 9 hrs.). (KEY News Ser.: Bk. 3). 2002. audio compact disk 64.95 (978-0-7927-2733-0(9), SLD 315, Chivers Sound Lib) AudioGO.
Reporter Laura Walsh has an uncanny ability to have celebrities' obituaries ready to roll. When the remains of a 12-year-old boy, missing for 30 years, are discovered where Palisades Amusement Park once stood, Laura sees her chance to move to KEY News' answer to Sixty Minutes. But when the glamorous host meets a devasting end, Laura's ready-to-air obit raises not only the suspicions of her co-workers, but those of the police.

Let My People Go see Classic American Poetry

Let My People Go. Winans, The. 1 cass., 1 CD. 7.98 (25344-4); audio compact disk 11.98 (25344-2) Warner Christian.

Let My People Think CD Series. 2004. audio compact disk 40.00 (978-1-59834-056-3(5)) Walk Thru the Bible.

Let Not Your Heart Be Troubled. Kenneth Copeland. 2 cass. 1991. 10.00 Set. (978-0-88114-834-3(2)) K Copeland Pubns.
Biblical teaching on facing difficulties.

Let Not Your Heart Be Troubled. Kenneth Copeland. (ENG.). 2009. audio compact disk 10.00 (978-1-57562-983-4(6)) K Copeland Pubns.

Let Robots Melt. Perf. by Kenneth G. Mills. 1 CD. (Running Time: 1 hrs. 8 min.). 1997. audio compact disk 14.98 Ken Mills Found.
Nine keyboard soliloquies, spontaneously composed & recorded live on 4 MIDI keyboards, each representing different orchestral sounds. Includes "Romance," Keepre," & "The Curtain Rises".

Let Sleeping Dogs Lie. John R. Erickson. 2 cass. (Running Time: 2 hrs.). (Hank the Cowdog Ser.: No. 6). (J). (gr. 2-5). 1989. 16.95 (978-0-87719-140-7(9)) Lone Star Bks.

Let Sleeping Dogs Lie. unabr. ed. John R. Erickson. Read by John R. Erickson. 2 cass. (Running Time: 3 hrs.). (Hank the Cowdog Ser.: No. 6). (J). (gr. 2-5). 2001. 16.95 (978-0-7366-6895-8(0)) Books on Tape.
A chicken killer is loose on the ranch & Hank must interrogate every possible suspect. Could Drover, his longtime sidekick, be guilty of chickicide?.

Let Sleeping Dogs Lie. unabr. ed. John R. Erickson. Read by John R. Erickson. Illus. by Gerald L. Holmes. 2 cass. (Hank the Cowdog Ser.: No. 6). (J). (gr. 2-5). 1986. bk. 13.95 (978-0-916941-16-1(7)) Maverick Bks.

Let Sleeping Dogs Lie. unabr. ed. John R. Erickson. Read by John R. Erickson. 2 cassettes. (Running Time: approx 3 hours). (Hank the Cowdog Ser.: No. 6). (J). 2002. 17.99 (978-1-59188-306-7(7)) Maverick Bks.

Let Sleeping Dogs Lie. unabr. ed. John R. Erickson. Read by John R. Erickson. 3 CDs. (Running Time: Approx 3 hours). (Hank the Cowdog Ser.: No. 6). (J). 2002. audio compact disk 19.99 (978-1-59188-606-8(6)) Maverick Bks.
Who?or what?has been killing chickens on the ranch? And what is Hank the Cowdog, Head of Ranch Security, going to do about it? Using his top-notch law enforcement skills, Hank launches one of the hardest-hitting investigations of his career. No one is to be trusted, and everyone is a suspect?even Hank! With no clues and no evidence, the case seems uncrackable. Can Hank solve the crime?and prove his own innocence?before he?s relieved of his command?Includes two original songs, ?Bark at the Mailman Battle Hymn? and ?I?m Locked in the Jailhouse with Buzzards on the Roof.?.

Let Sleeping Dogs Lie. unabr. ed. John R. Erickson. 2 cass. (Running Time: 3 hrs.). (Hank the Cowdog Ser.: No. 6). (J). (gr. 2-5). 1998. 17.00 (21648B3) Recorded Bks.

Let Sleeping Dogs Lie. unabr. collector's ed. John R. Erickson. 3 CDs. (Running Time: 4 hrs. 30 mins.). (Hank the Cowdog Ser.: No. 6). (J). (gr. 2-5). 2001. audio compact disk 28.00 Books on Tape.
Who's killing the ranch's chickens? What's Ranch Security going to do about it? These are the critical questions in Hank's adventure. A fiendish murderer is loose on the ranch. Never has Hank followed so many clues or interrogated more suspects. Everyone turns out to be a suspect - including Drover... and even Hank himself.

***Let Sleeping Rogues Lie.** unabr. ed. Sabrina Jeffries. Read by Justine Eyre. (Running Time: 10 hrs.). (School for Heiresses Ser.). 2010. 19.99 (978-1-4418-4722-5(7), 9781441847225, Brilliance MP3); 39.97 (978-1-4418-4723-2(5), 9781441847232, Brinc Audio MP3 Lib); 19.99 (978-1-4418-4724-9(3), 9781441847249, BAD); 39.97 (978-1-4418-4725-6(1), 9781441847256, BADLE); audio compact disk 19.99 (978-1-4418-4720-1(0), 9781441847201, Bril Audio CD Unabri); audio compact disk 79.97 (978-1-4418-4721-8(9), 9781441847218, BriAudCD Unabrid) Brilliance Audio.

Let Sleeping Vets Lie. unabr. ed. James Herriot. Read by Christopher Timothy. 8 cass. (Running Time: 12 hrs.). (Vet Ser.: Bk. 3). 2000. 59.95 (978-0-7451-4322-4(9), CAB 1005) Pub: Chivers Audio Bks GBR. Dist(s): AudioGO
With two years' experience behind him, James Herriot still feels privileged working as an assistant vet at the Darrowby practice.

Let Story Guide You: Why Some Lives Make Sense an Others Don't. abr. unabr. ed. Donald Miller. (Running Time: 5 hrs.). 2009. audio compact disk 24.99 (978-0-7852-2339-9(8)) Nelson.

Let That Dog Ride. (J). 2005. audio compact disk (978-1-933796-11-6(1)) PC Treasures.

Let the Circle Be Unbroken, unabr. ed. Mildred D. Taylor. Narrated by Lynne Thigpen. 10 pieces. (Running Time: 13 hrs. 30 mins.). (Logan Family Saga Ser.: Pt. 2). (gr. 6 up). 1997. 87.00 (978-0-7887-0186-3(X), 94411E7) Recorded Bks.
This sequel to "Roll of Thunder, Hear My Cry" reveals what happens to the Logan family after T.J. is arrested. Explores the racism, prejudice & justice in 1930's Mississippi.

Let the Drum Speak. unabr. collector's ed. Linda L. Shuler. Read by Frances Cassidy. 12 cass. (Running Time: 18 hrs.). (Time Circle Quartet Ser.: Vol. 3). 1996. 96.00 (978-0-7366-3537-0(8), 4184) Books on Tape.
Tells the story of Antelope, daughter of Kwani, revered Anazasi teacher. Antelope & her infant daughter journey with Antelope's mate, Chomoc, to a large, sophisticated trading village ruled by Great Sun.

Let the Fire Fall: Acts 10:23-48. Ed Young. 1998. 4.95 (978-0-7417-2167-9(8), A1167) Win Walk.

Let the Holy Spirit Guide. Rex C. Reeve. 2004. 9.95 (978-1-59156-219-1(8)); audio compact disk 11.95 (978-1-59156-220-7(1)) Covenant Comms.

Let the Light Shine Everywhere. Swami Amar Jyoti. 1 cass. 1982. 9.95 (M-24) Truth Consciousness.
Human birth, the crossroads of evolution; deciding which way to go. Looking forward & upward to the Lord to give us light.

Let the Lord Arise. Perf. by Lori Wilke. 1 cass. (Running Time: 6 min.). 1992. 9.98 Sound track. (978-1-891916-21-2(1)) Spirit To Spirit.

Let the Men Sing! 10 Reproducible Chorals for Tenor & Baritone Vocals. Created by Greg Gilpin. 2009. pap. bk. 49.95 (978-1-59235-252-4(9)) Shawnee Pr.

***Let the Nations Be Glad.** unabr. ed. John Piper. Narrated by Raymond Todd. (ENG.). 2008. 16.98 (978-1-59644-615-1(3), Hovel Audio) christianaud.

Let the Nations Be Glad. unabr. ed. John Piper. Narrated by Raymond Todd. (Running Time: 9 hrs. 0 mins. 0 sec.). (ENG.). 2008. lp 19.98 (978-1-59644-622-9(6), Hovel Audio); audio compact disk 26.98 (978-1-59644-614-4(5), Hovel Audio) christianaud.

Let the Ocean Worry: Ocean Waves & Melodies Wash Tensions Away. Fred Weinberg & Joe Beck. 1 cass. (Running Time: 1 hr.). 1993. 9.95 (978-1-55961-243-2(6)) Relaxtn Co.

Let the Praises Ring. Contrib. by Lincoln Brewster & Don Moen. 2006. audio compact disk 16.98 (978-5-558-11369-3(3)) Integrity Music.

Let the Reason be Love: A Song of Faith. Merrill Osmond. 2003. audio compact disk 24.95 (978-0-9724770-1-7(2)) Pub: Tidal Wave Bks. Dist(s): STL Dist NA

Let the Reedeemed of the Lord Say So. bk. 6.00 (978-0-687-76226-2(X)) Abingdon.

Let the Rivers Flow. Created by Allegis Publications. 2007. audio compact disk 24.99 (978-5-557-69949-5(X)) Allegis.

Let Them Eat Fruitcake. unabr. ed. Melody Carlson. Narrated by Pam Turlow. (Running Time: 7 hrs. 49 mins. 35 sec.). (86 Bloomberg Place Ser.). (ENG.). 2008. 18.19 (978-1-60814-282-8(5)); audio compact disk 25.99 (978-1-59859-422-5(2)) Oasis Audio.

Let There Be a Temple, Vol. 5. Srila Prabhupada. 10 cass. (Lilamrta Ser.). 39.00 Bhaktivedanta.
Gives a detailed account of Srila Prabhupada's determination to build the temples in Bombay, Vrndavana & Mayapur.

Let There Be Light. Perf. by Michael O'Brien. 1 cass. 1999. (751-321-3690) Brentwood Music.

Let There Be Peace on Earth. Perf. by Robert Kochis & Robin Kochis. 1 cass. (Running Time: 41 mins.). 1999. 10.95 (T8529); audio compact disk 15.95 (K6250) Liguori Pubns.
Songs include: "Let There Be Peace on Earth," "In the Garden," "Were You There," "You Are Near" & more.

***Let There Be Peace on Earth & Other Uplifting Piano Pieces.** Created by Hal Leonard Corp. (ENG.). 2010. pap. bk. 12.99 (978-1-4234-9761-5(9), 1423497619) H Leonard.

Let There Be Praise. Contrib. by Sandi Patty. 2008. audio compact disk 9.99 (978-5-557-42747-0(3), Word Records) Word Enter.

Let Thy Will Be Done: Seeing God in You. Speeches. Creflo A. Dollar. 2 cass. (Running Time: 3 hrs.). 2001. (978-1-59089-146-9(5)) Creflo Dollar.

Let Us Alone! - Structure of Government. Ayn Rand. 1 cass. (Running Time: 1 hr.). 1993. 12.95 (978-1-56114-256-9(5), AR43C) Second Renaissance.

Let Us Be Thankful. Daya Mata. 1984. 6.50 (2108) Self Realization.
Discusses the value of appreciating all of life's blessings & principles vital to success in meditation & daily living, including how to develop concentration; the power of meditation techniques; loyalty, devotion, humility, cheerfulness & positive thinking.

Let Us Break Bread Together - ShowTrax. Arranged by Kirby Shaw. 1 CD. (Running Time: 5 mins.). 2000. audio compact disk 19.95 (08595534) H Leonard.
Complete with Dixieland instrumentation, this deliciously soulful setting of one of the great old gospel songs develops into a full-out final verse.

Let Us Rejoice. Katherine M. Duke. 1 cass. 3.99 Marimae Publ.
A taste of the anointed worship & praise ministry of Katherine is experienced. Also included is the bonus track "It's Good to Know" which reminds & reassures the believer of God's undying promise to love us through all that we experience in life. Performance - instrumental track of each song is also included.

Let Wisdom Sing: Stories of Profound Insight & the Songs They Inspired. Azra Simonetti. Tr. by Chris Marietta Rhyne. Prod. by Randy Emata. Illus. by Zolina Zeravica Lydon. 2000. pap. bk. 19.99 (978-0-9701062-7-8(0)) N S P Pubng.

***Let Your Goddess Grow! 7 Spiritual Lessons on Female Power & Positive Thinking.** Charlene M. Proctor. (Running Time: 480). (C). 2009. 24.99 (978-0-9766012-4-1(9)) Goddess Netwk.

Let Your Heart Sing. Gurumayi Chidvilasananda. 1 cass. (Running Time: 1 hr. 4 mins.). 2001. 10.95 (107213, Siddha Yoga Pubs); audio compact disk 15.95 (108213, Siddha Yoga Pubs) SYDA Found.
Gurumayi explains why chanting is such a valuable spiritual practice and how it infuses a seeker with fresh energy and enthusiasm. This talk offers inspiration to incorporate chanting into your schedule and immediately experience its benefits.

Let Your Holy Rain Fall Down. Composed by David M. Edwards & Regi Stone. Contrib. by Robert Sterling. 2007. audio compact disk 24.98 (978-5-557-49186-0(4), Word Music) Word Enter.

Let Your Imagination Fly. (J). 2005. audio compact disk (978-1-933796-10-9(3)) PC Treasures.

Let Your Kingdom Come. Composed by Bob Kauflin. Contrib. by Robert Sterling. 2007. audio compact disk 24.98 (978-5-557-49185-3(6), Word Music) Word Enter.

Let Your Life Speak: Listening for the Voice of Vocation. unabr. ed. Parker J. Palmer. (Running Time: 3 hrs. 0 mins.). (ENG.). 2009. 24.95 (978-1-4332-2197-2(7)); audio compact disk 30.00 (978-1-4332-2198-9(5)) Blckstn Audio.

Let Your Life Speak: Listening for the Voice of Vocation. unabr. ed. Parker J. Palmer. Read by Stefan Rudnicki. (Running Time: 3 hrs.). (ENG.). 2009. 19.95 (978-1-4332-2201-6(9)); audio compact disk 19.95 (978-1-4332-2200-9(0)) Blckstn Audio.

Let Your Mind Alone see Thurber Carnival

Let Your Music Soar: The Emotional Connection. Corky Siegel & Peter Krammer. Illus. by Holly Siegel. 2007. pap. bk. 19.95 (978-90-77256-26-8(1)) Pub: Nova Vista Publ BEL. Dist(s): AtlasBooks

Let Your Soul be Your Pilot: An Audio Program to Help You Find Your Direction. 1 CD. (Running Time: 45 mins.). 2004. audio compact disk 15.00 (978-0-9764498-3-6(8)) O'H O'H Inc.
Feeling soul sick, lost or off course? This CD audio program, filled with engaging stories and clear guidelines, will help you reconnect with your soul's passion and energy and navigate your way through this world. You'll learn to recognize and use four deep signals that can tell you what to do and where to go that has integrity and leads you to the life you are meant to

lead. Popular speaker Bill O'Hanlon and your own soul are your guides for this trip.

Let Your Soul Be Your Pilot: Finding Your Direction in Life. Short Stories. Bill O'Hanlon. Narrated by Bill O'Hanlon. 1 CD. (Running Time: 60 mins). 2009. audio compact disk 16.95 (978-0-9823573-1-6(1), 7316) Crown Hse GBR.

Let Your Voice Be Heard! Songs from Ghana & Zimbabwe: Multipart & Game Songs Arranged & Annotated for Grades K-12. 2nd rev. ed. Abraham Kobena Adzenyah et al. 1997. pap. bk. 29.95 (978-0-937203-75-0(0)) World Music Pr.

Let Yourself Go: The Freedom & Power of Life Beyond Belief. Arjuna Ardagh. 6 CDs. (Running Time: 24300 sec.). 2006. audio compact disk 69.95 (978-1-59179-521-6(4), AF01075D) Sounds True.

L'éternel Mari. unabr. ed. Fyodor Dostoyevsky. Read by Yves Belluardo. (YA). 2007. 79.99 (978-2-35569-037-2(5)) Find a World.

Lethal Gorilla. unabr. ed. Paul Zindel. 3 cass. (Running Time: 3 hrs. 15 min.). (P. C. Hawke Mysteries Ser.: No. 4). (978-1-4025-1810-2(2)) Recorded Bks.
People say New York City is a jungle. Still, P.C. Hawke is a little surprised when his best friend, Mackenzie, invites him to tag along with her police coroner mother to examine a scientist who has been mauled by jaguars at the Bronx Wildlife Conservation Park. But when the two teenage sleuths learn that the scientist actually died because he was given a lethal dose of gorilla blood after the attack, they quickly realize that the most vicious predator imaginable is loose in the park?a human killer!.

Lethal Guardian. abr. ed. M. William Phelps. Read by J. Charles. (Running Time: 6 hrs.). 2009. audio compact disk 14.99 (978-1-4233-4940-2(7), 9781423349402, BCD Value Price) Brilliance Audio.

Lethal Guardian. unabr. ed. M. William Phelps. Read by J. Charles. (Running Time: 13 hrs.). 2008. 39.25 (978-1-4233-4938-9(5), 9781423349389, BADLE); 24.95 (978-1-4233-4937-2(7), 9781423349372, BAD); audio compact disk 39.25 (978-1-4233-4936-5(9), 9781423349365, Brlnc Audio MP3 Lib); audio compact disk 117.25 (978-1-4233-4934-1(2), 9781423349341, BriAudCD Unabrid); audio compact disk 38.95 (978-1-4233-4933-4(4), 9781423349334, Bril Audio CD Unabri); audio compact disk 24.95 (978-1-4233-4935-8(0), 9781423349358, Brilliance MP3) Brilliance Audio.

Lethal Heritage Bk. 1: Blood of Kerensky Trilogy. abr. ed. Michael A. Stackpole. 2 cass. (Running Time: 3 hrs.). (Battletech: Vol. 1). 2002. 9.95 (978-1-931953-30-6(9)) Listen & Live.

Lethal Intent. Quintin Jardine. Read by James Bryce. 10 cass. (Running Time: 13 hrs. 35 mins.). (Isis Cassettes Ser.). (J). 2005. 84.95 (978-0-7531-2149-8(2)) Pub: ISIS Lrg Prnt GBR. Dist(s): Ulverscroft US

Lethal Intent. unabr. ed. Quintin Jardine. Read by James Bryce. 12 CDs. (Running Time: 13 hrs. 34 mins.). (Isis (CDs) Ser.). (J). 2005. audio compact disk 99.95 (978-0-7531-2453-6(X)) Pub: ISIS Lrg Prnt GBR. Dist(s): Ulverscroft US

Lethal Justice. abr. ed. Fern Michaels. Read by Laural Merlington. (Running Time: 10800 sec.). (Sisterhood Ser.: Bk. 6). 2007. audio compact disk 14.99 (978-1-59737-589-4(6), 9781597375894, BCD Value Price) Brilliance Audio.
Please enter a Synopsis.

Lethal Justice. unabr. ed. Fern Michaels. Read by Laural Merlington. 7 CDs. (Running Time: 28800 sec.). (Sisterhood Ser.: Bk. 6). 2006. audio compact disk 87.25 (978-1-59737-583-2(7), 9781597375832, BriAudCD Unabrid); 69.25 (978-1-59737-581-8(0), 9781597375818, BrilAudUnabridg); audio compact disk 24.95 (978-1-59737-584-9(5), 9781597375849, Brilliance MP3); audio compact disk 29.95 (978-1-59737-582-5(9), 9781597375825, Bril Audio CD Unabri) Brilliance Audio.

Lethal Justice. unabr. ed. Fern Michaels. Read by Laural Merlington. (Running Time: 8 hrs.). (Sisterhood Ser.: No. 6). 2006. 39.25 (978-1-59737-587-0(X), 9781597375870, BADLE); 24.95 (978-1-59737-586-3(1), 9781597375863, BAD); audio compact disk 39.25 (978-1-59737-585-6(3), 9781597375856, Brlnc Audio MP3 Lib) Brilliance Audio.

Lethal Legacy. abr. ed. Linda Fairstein. Read by Blair Brown. (Alexandra Cooper Mysteries Ser.). (ENG.). 2009. audio compact disk 29.95 (978-0-7393-5864-1(2), Random AudioBks) Pub: Random Audio Pubg. Dist(s): Random

***Lethal Lineage.** unabr. ed. Charlotte Hinger. Read by To be Announced. (Running Time: 8 hrs. NaN mins.). (ENG.). 2011. 29.95 (978-1-4417-7773-7(3)); 54.95 (978-1-4417-7770-6(9)); audio compact disk 76.00 (978-1-4417-7771-3(7)) Blckstn Audio.

Lethal Partner. unabr. ed. Jake Page. Read by Jonathan Marosz. 6 cass. (Running Time: 9 hrs.). 1997. 48.00 (978-0-913369-64-7(0), 4305) Books on Tape.
In this atmospheric mystery, Mo Bowdre, a blind sculptor, & his Hopi girlfriend are caught up in the Santa Fe art scene - & a sensational murder. Elijah Potts, gallery owner, knows that a cache of previously unreported Georgia O'Keefes will make his fortune.

Lethal Seduction. unabr. ed. Jackie Collins. Read by Carrington MacDuffie. 12 vols. (Running Time: 18 hrs.). 2001. bk. 96.95 (978-0-7927-2443-8(7), CSL 332, Chivers Sound Lib) AudioGO.
Madison Castelli is having problems, her ex-live-in lover who walked out on her is trying to walk back in & her new lover is giving her a hard time.

Lethal Seduction. unabr. ed. Jackie Collins. Read by Carrington MacDuffie. 12 CDs. (Running Time: 18 hrs.). 2001. audio compact disk 110.95 (978-0-7927-9925-2(9), SLD 076, Chivers Sound Lib) AudioGO.
Madison Castelli is having problems - her ex-live-in lover who walked out on her is trying to walk back in. Her new lover is giving her a hard time. And her father turns out to be a man with deadly secrets.

Lethally Blond. Kate White. Read by Renée Raudman. (Playaway Adult Fiction Ser.). 2008. 84.99 (978-1-60640-597-0(7)) Find a World.

Lethally Blond. abr. ed. Kate White. Read by Renée Raudman. 5 CDs. (Running Time: 6 hrs.). (Bailey Weggins Ser.). 2008. audio compact disk 14.99 (978-1-4233-3456-9(6), 9781423334569, BCD Value Price) Brilliance Audio.

Lethally Blond. unabr. ed. Kate White. Read by Renée Raudman. (Running Time: 10 hrs.). (Bailey Weggins Ser.). 2007. 39.25 (978-1-4233-3454-5(X), 9781423334545, BADLE); 24.95 (978-1-4233-3453-8(1), 9781423334538, BAD); 82.25 (978-1-4233-3448-4(5), 9781423334484, BrilAudUnabridg); audio compact disk 34.95 (978-1-4233-3449-1(3), 9781423334491, Bril Audio CD Unabri); audio compact disk 24.95 (978-1-4233-3451-4(5), 9781423334514, Brilliance MP3); audio compact disk 97.25 (978-1-4233-3450-7(7), 9781423334507, BriAudCD Unabrid); audio compact disk 39.25 (978-1-4233-3452-1(3), 9781423334521, Brlnc Audio MP3 Lib) Brilliance Audio.

L'étoile de Laura. unabr. ed. Klaus Baumgart. Read by Vincent Byrd Le Sage. (J). 2007. 84.99 (978-2-35569-003-7(0)) Find a World.

Letra Escarlata. abr. ed. Nathaniel Hawthorne. 3 CDs.Tr. of Scarlet Letter. (SPA.). 2002. audio compact disk 17.00 (978-958-9494-93-6(5)) YoYoMusic.

Letreros en la Carretera de la Vida. 2004. audio compact disk 17.00 (978-1-57972-664-5(X)) Insight Living.

Let's Be Enemies. 2004. 8.95 (978-1-56008-948-3(2)); cass. & flmstrp 30.00 (978-1-56008-704-5(8)) Weston Woods.

Let's be Heard. Grant. 2004. 9.95 (978-0-7435-4964-6(3)) Pub: S&S Audio. Dist(s): S and S Inc

Let's Begin. 3rd ed. Ritsuko Nakata et al. (Let's Go Third Edition Ser.). 2007. audio compact disk 39.95 (978-0-19-439417-8(4)) OUP.

Let's Chant, Let's Sing. Carolyn Graham. 1995. 24.50 (978-0-19-434649-8(8)); audio compact disk 24.50 (978-0-19-434688-7(9)) OUP.

Let's Chant, Let's Sing. Carolyn Graham. 1995. 24.50 (978-0-19-434653-5(6)) OUP.

Let's Chant, Let's Sing. Carolyn Graham. 1996. audio compact disk 24.50 (978-0-19-434689-4(7)) OUP.

Let's Chant, Let's Sing. Carolyn Graham. 1996. audio compact disk 24.50 (978-0-19-434896-6(2)) OUP.

Let's Chant, Let's Sing. Carolyn Graham. 1997. 24.50 (978-0-19-434895-9(4)) OUP.

Let's Chant, Let's Sing. Carolyn Graham. 1999. 24.50 (978-0-19-435888-0(7)); audio compact disk 24.50 (978-0-19-435893-4(3)) OUP.

Let's Chant, Let's Sing. Carolyn Graham. 1999. audio compact disk 24.50 (978-0-19-435894-1(1)) OUP.

Let's Chant, Let's Sing. Carolyn Graham. 1999. 24.50 (978-0-19-435890-3(9)) OUP.

Let's Chant, Let's Sing, Bk. 3. Carolyn Graham. 1996. 24.50 (978-0-19-434754-9(0)) OUP.

Let's Chant, Let's Sing, No. 3. Carolyn Graham. 1996. audio compact disk 24.50 (978-0-19-434755-6(9)) OUP.

Let's Clean up Our Act: Songs for the Earth. Perf. by Tom Callinan & Ann Shapiro. 1 cass. (Running Time: 40 min.). (J). (gr. 1-6). 1990. 9.98 (978-1-879305-05-2(4), AM-C-106) Am Melody.
Contemporary folk songs on environmental issues. Accompanying booklet includes song lyrics, suggested educational activities, a glossary & a resource list.

Let's Dance. 1 cass. (Running Time: 20 min.). (J). (ps-1). 1995. 3.99 (978-1-57341-034-2(9), MG028AC) Am Port Films.

Let's Dance. unabr. ed. Frances Fyfield & Frances Hegarty. Read by Di Langford. 6 cass. (Running Time: 7 hrs. 45 min.). (Isis Cassettes Ser.). 1997. 54.95 (978-0-7531-0181-0(5), 970605) Pub: ISIS Audio GBR. Dist(s): Ulverscroft US
Isabel Burley returns to her childhood home to look after her mother, who is suffering from Alzheimer's disease. She is looking for the love she lacked as a child. Isolated by her mother's growing dementia, the two women become locked in a relationship of hatred & simmering violence, with roots that go deep into the past.

Let's Do the Pharaoh! Jeremy Strong & Jeremy Strong. Read by Sylvester McCoy. 2 CDs. (Running Time: 5820 sec.). (J). 2005. audio compact disk 21.95 (978-0-7540-6647-7(9)) AudioGo GBR.

Let's Exercise. 1 cass. (Running Time: 60 min.). 10.95 (SP8) Psych Res Inst.
Motivation to design & follow individual exercise programs.

Let's Face It: 90 Years of Living, Loving, & Learning. Kirk Douglas. Read by Jason Alexander. (Playaway Adult Nonfiction Ser.). 2008. 44.99 (978-1-60640-762-2(7)) Find a World.

Let's Face It: 90 Years of Living, Loving, & Learning. unabr. ed. Kirk Douglas. (Running Time: 6 hrs. 30 mins.). 2008. 19.95 (978-1-4332-0990-1(X)) Blckstn Audio.

Let's Face It: 90 Years of Living, Loving, & Learning. unabr. ed. Kirk Douglas. Read by Jason Alexander. (Running Time: 21600 sec.). 2008. 44.95 (978-1-4332-0988-8(8)); audio compact disk 19.95 (978-1-4332-0991-8(8)); audio compact disk & audio compact disk 29.95 (978-1-4332-0992-5(6)); audio compact disk & audio compact disk 45.00 (978-1-4332-0989-5(6)) Blckstn Audio.

Let's Fill up the House with Stories & Songs. unabr. ed. Rives Collins & Julie Shannon. Read by Rives Collins. 1 cass. (Running Time: 1 hr. 01 min.). (J). (gr. k-6). 1999. 10.00 (978-1-888019-03-2(4)); audio compact disk 15.00 (978-1-888019-02-5(6)) L M Alleycat Mus.

Let's Fix the Kids! Complete Parenting Program: LDS Version. 6th unabr. ed. James J. Jones. 1997. pap. bk. 199.00 (978-0-9666984-4-2(4)) Familyhood Inc.

Let's Fix the Kids! Complete Parenting Program: Standard Version. 6th unabr. ed. James J. Jones. 1997. pap. bk. 199.00 (978-0-9666984-3-5(6)) Familyhood Inc.

Let's Fly with Mary Poppins. Prod. by Walt Disney Productions Staff. 1 cass. (Archive Collections). (J). (ps-3). 1998. 22.50 (978-0-7634-0397-3(0)) W Disney Records.

***Let's Get Creative.** Perf. by Monty Harper & Mister Billy. 1 CD. (Running Time: 43 mins.). (J). (ps-3). 2009. audio compact disk 14.95 (978-0-9701081-8-0(4)) Monty Harper.

Let's Get Organized. 1 cass. (Running Time: 60 min.). 10.95 (017) Psych Res Inst.
Spend less valuable time by getting organized & efficent through mental programming.

Let's Get Organized: The Effective Management of Activity, Time & Space. 2004. audio compact disk 19.95 (978-0-9759720-0-7(6)) A B and C Pub.

Let's Get Organized - the Audio Book: The Effective Management of Activity, Time & Space. Scripts. D. L. Chiacchia. Narrated by Robert Hope Larder. 1 CD. (Running Time: 53 mins., 49 secs). 2004. audio compact disk 14.95 (978-0-9759720-1-4(4)) A B and C Pub.

Let's Get Physical. unabr. ed. Sherry Ashworth. 8 cass. (Isis Cassettes Ser.). (J). 2005. 69.95 (978-0-7531-1991-4(9)) Pub: ISIS Lrg Prnt GBR. Dist(s): Ulverscroft US

Let's Get Quiet: The Smooth Jazz Experience. Contrib. by Ben Tankard. 2007. audio compact disk 17.98 (978-5-557-92864-9(2), Verity) Brentwood Music.

Lets Get Real or Lets Not Play. abr. ed. Mahan Khalsa. 2006. 35.95 (978-1-933976-24-2(1)) Pub: Franklin Covey. Dist(s): S and S Inc

Let's Get Real or Let's Not Play: The Demise of Dysfunctional Selling & the Advent of Helping Clients Succeed. unabr. ed. Mahan Khalsa & Randy Illig. Read by Randy Illig. Frwd. by Stephen R. Covey. (Running Time: 7 hrs.). (ENG.). 2008. 29.98 (978-1-59659-299-5(0), GildAudio) Pub: Gildan Media. Dist(s): HachBkGrp

Let's Get Real or Let's Not Play: The Demise of Dysfunctional Selling & the Advent of Helping Clients Succeed. unabr. ed. Mahan Khalsa & Randy Illig. Read by Randy Illig. Frwd. by Stephen R. Covey. (Running Time: 7 hrs.). (ENG.). 2008. audio compact disk 29.98 (978-1-59659-206-3(0), GildAudio) Pub: Gildan Media. Dist(s): HachBkGrp

Let's Get the Rhythm of the Band. Cheryl Mattox & Cheryl W. Mattox. (J). 1997. pap. bk. 19.95 (978-0-938971-96-2(4)) JTG Nashville.
Illus. history in word, art & song of African-American music (3 centuries).

Let's Go. 2nd rev. ed. K. Frazier. 2000. 17.50 (978-0-19-436478-2(X)) OUP.

Let's Go. 3rd ed. Ritsuko Nakata et al. (Let's Go Third Edition Ser.). 2007. audio compact disk 39.95 (978-0-19-439422-2(0)) OUP.

Let's Go, No. 2. 3rd ed. R. Nakata et al. (Let's Go Third Edition Ser.). 2007. audio compact disk 39.95 (978-0-19-439419-2(0)) OUP.

Let's Go, No. 5. 2nd rev. ed. Ritsuko Nakata et al. (Let's Go Second Edition Ser.). 2000. 22.75 (978-0-19-436488-1(7)) OUP.

Let's Go, No. 6. 2nd rev. ed. Ristuku Nakata et al. (Let's Go Second Edition Ser.). 2000. 22.75 (978-0-19-436498-0(4)) OUP.

Let's Go, Vol. 3. 2nd rev. ed. K. Frazier et al. (Let's Go Second Edition Ser.). 2000. 22.75 (978-0-19-436468-3(2)) OUP.

Let's Go Level 5. Ritsuko Nakata. (Let's Go Second Edition Ser.). 1998. 22.75 (978-0-19-435293-2(5)) OUP.

Let's Go Back. Dan Corner. 1 cass. 3.00 (55) Evang Outreach.

Let's Go Fishing! How Lifestyle Evangelism Can Make a Soul Winner Out of Even You. Mac Hammond. 4 cass. (Running Time: 50 min. per cass.). 1997. 24.00 (978-1-57399-059-2(0)) Mac Hammond.
How to win souls.

Let's Go, Froggy! unabr. ed. Jonathan Lo[illegible]n. Narrated by John McDonough. 1 cass. (Running Time: 15 mins.). (J). [illegible]). 1999. pap. bk. & stu. ed. 24.24 (978-0-7887-3647-6(7), 41013X[illegible]corded Bks.

Let's Go, Froggy! unabr. ed. Jonathan London. Narrated by John McDonough. 1 cass. (Running Time: 15 mins.). (ps up). 1999. 10.00 (978-0-7887-3509-7(8), 95903E7) Recorded Bks.
Froggy & his father are going for a bike ride today. But before they can go, Froggy must find his helmet. Then he can't remember where he put his butterfly net. And he's hungry. Will he & his father ever go riding?.

Let's Go, Froggy!, Class set. Jonathan London. Read by John McDonough. 1 cass. (Running Time: 15 mins.). (J). (ps up). 1999. stu. ed. 90.70 (978-0-7887-3677-3(9), 46980) Recorded Bks.

Let's Go Math, Level 2. Ann Edson & Allan A. Schwartz. 8 cass. 89.95 incl. 8 activity bks., guide. (978-0-89525-031-5(4), AKC 61) Ed Activities.
Counting by two's & five's, using place value, counting to 999, pints & quarts, making change, using fractions, introducing multiplication, inches, feet, centimeters & meters.

Let's Go Picture Dictionary. R. Nakata et al. 1999. 39.95 (978-0-19-435978-8(6)) OUP.

Let's Go Readers. Barbara Hoskins. 2004. 13.25 (978-0-19-436987-9(0)) OUP.

Let's Go Third Edition 1. 3rd ed. R. Nakata et al. (Let's Go Third Edition Ser.). 2007. audio compact disk & audio compact disk 39.95 (978-0-19-439418-5(2)) OUP.

Let's Go to the Beach: A History of Sun & Fun by the Sea. unabr. ed. Elizabeth Van Steenwyk. Read by Anna Fields. 3 cass. (Running Time: 4 hrs.). 2002. 23.95 (978-0-7861-2193-9(9), 2940) Blckstn Audio.
From the bathhouses of the ancient Greeks to Venice Beach and Coney Island, take a multifaceted and well researched look at beaches and their attendant customs. The text explores such historical transformations as the evolution of the waterways from places of commerce to venues of health and recreation, as well as the bathing suit's revealing journey from full-body cover-up to string bikini. Information about environmental concerns (including beach safety and preservation) along with quirky facts and trivia round out this intriguing volume.

***Let's Go to the Beach: A History of Sun & Fun by the Sea.** unabr. ed. Elizabeth Van Steenwyk. Read by Anna Fields. (Running Time: 3 hrs.). 2010. 19.95 (978-1-4417-6752-3(5)); audio compact disk 30.00 (978-1-4417-6750-9(9)) Blckstn Audio.

Let's Go 3, Third Edition: Audio CD: Audio CD. 3rd ed. Ed. by Oxford Staff. (Let's Go Third Edition Ser.). 2007. audio compact disk 39.95 (978-0-19-439420-8(4)) OUP.

Let's Go 4. 3rd rev. ed. Ed. by Oxford Staff. (Let's Go Third Edition Ser.). 2007. audio compact disk 39.95 (978-0-19-439421-5(2)) OUP.

Let's Go 6. 3rd ed. Ritsuko Nakata et al. (Let's Go Third Edition Ser.). 2007. audio compact disk 39.95 (978-0-19-439423-9(9)) OUP.

Let's Have a Musical Rhythm Band. Phoebe Diller. (ENG.). 2002. audio compact disk 19.95 (978-0-7390-2354-9(3)) Alfred Pub.

Let's Have a Party with Lewis Grizzard. Read by Lewis Grizzard. 1 cass. 1987. 9.98 (978-5-552-07121-0(2)) Sthrn Tracks.

Let's Have a Party with Lewis Grizzard. unabr. ed. Lewis Grizzard. Read by Lewis Grizzard. 1 cass. (Running Time: 1 hr.). 1989. 9.98 (978-0-945258-02-5(X), STC-009); audio compact disk 9.98 (978-0-945258-06-3(2), STCD-009) Sthrn Tracks.
Southern humor.

Let's Hear It for the Boy (from Footloose) - ShowTrax. Arranged by Alan Billingsley. 1 CD. (Running Time: 5 mins.). 2000. audio compact disk 19.95 (08201158) H Leonard.
The 1948 #1 hit by Deniece Williams finds new life in the new hit Broadway production.

Let's Hear It for the Deaf Man. unabr. ed. Ed McBain, pseud. Read by Jonathan Marosz. 6 cass. (Running Time: 6 hrs.). (87th Precinct Ser.: Bk. 27). 1998. 36.00 (978-0-7366-3776-3(1), 4449) Books on Tape.
"With your assistance I'm going to steal $500,000 on the last day of April." That's what the phone call said & then the bizarre series of photos began arriving.

Let's Help This Planet. Kim Brodey & Jerry Brodey. 1994. 10.98 (978-0-9695319-1-3(5)) Consort Bk Sales.

Let's Jam. audio compact disk 9.95 (978-1-893907-18-8(X), 256-542) Watch & Learn.

Let's Jam! Country & Bluegrass. 2 CDs. (Watch & Learn Ser.). 2001. audio compact disk 9.95 (978-1-893907-19-5(8), 256-543) Watch & Learn.

Let's Jam! Jazz & Blues. Peter Vogl. 3 CDs. (Running Time: 74 minutes). (Watch & Learn Ser.). 2002. audio compact disk 9.95 (978-1-893907-20-1(1), 256-545) Watch & Learn.

Let's Jam 4. 4 CDs. audio compact disk 9.95 (978-1-893907-45-4(7), 256-546) Watch & Learn.

Let's Just Praise The Lord: 11 Samuel 24. Ed Young. 1982. Rental 4.95 (978-0-7417-1246-2(6), 246) Win Walk.

Let's Keep Talking. Stanley Thornes. 1 cass. (C). 1983. 85.00 (978-0-7175-1184-6(7)) St Mut.

Let's Learn French Coloring Book with Crayons. Contrib. by Anne-Francoise Hazzan. 1 cass. (Let's Learn Ser.). (FRE.). (J). 1992. pap. bk. 9.95 (978-0-8442-9183-3(8)) M-H Contemporary.

Let's Learn Korean. 2nd rev. ed. B. J. Jones. 1 cass. 1998. pap. bk. 19.50 (978-0-930878-41-2(8)) Hollym Intl.

Let's Learn Spanish Coloring Book with Crayons. Contrib. by Anne-Francoise Hazzan. 1 cass. (Let's Learn Ser.). (SPA.). (J). 1993. pap. bk. 9.95 (978-0-8442-9172-7(2)) M-H Contemporary.
Foreign language study.

Let's Learn the Hawaiian Alphabet. Patricia A. Murray. Illus. by Cliff Tanaka. (J). (ps). 1988. 13.95 (978-0-89610-079-4(0)) Island Heritage.

Let's Learn to Count in Hawaiian. Keiki C. Kawai'ae'a. Illus. by Cliff Tanaka. (J). (ps). 1988. 13.95 (978-0-89610-080-0(4)) Island Heritage.

Let's Learn Tuvan: Tuvan Language Course. Kaadyr-ool A. Bicheldei et al. Ed. by J. Eric Slone. 2000. pap. bk. 40.00 (978-1-58490-029-0(6)) Scientific Consulting.

Let's Look at Nineteen Eighty-Seven. Joyce Balbontin. 1 cass. 8.95 (491) Am Fed Astrologers.
An AFA Convention workshop tape.

Let's Make an Assertive Deal. Arynne Simon. 1 cass. 1995. 14.95 (978-1-882389-19-3(0)) Wilarvi Communs.
Working with another to build a better relationship.

Let's Make Friends & Not Lose Customers. Janet S. Rush & George Barker. Read by Janet S. Rush. 6 cass. 1987. 69.95 (978-1-56207-213-1(7)) Zig Ziglar Corp.
Janet Sue Rush will help you handle irate customers, improve your listening skills & build your company's image.

***Let's Measure CD.** (Let's Measure CD Ser.). 2010. cd-rom 119.58 (978-1-61613-076-3(8)) ABDO Pub Co.

Lets Measure It!/Lets Skip-Count. Steck-Vaughn Staff. 2002. (978-0-7398-5996-4(X)) SteckVau.

***Let's Measure Site CD.** (Let's Measure Site CD Ser.). 2010. cd-rom 256.74 (978-1-61613-256-9(6)) ABDO Pub Co.

Let's Multiply. 1 CD or 1 cass. (Running Time: 1 hr.). (J). (gr. 1-2). 2000. pap. bk. & act. bk. ed. 12.99 (978-1-894281-82-9(9), ABCD090043) Pub: Kidzup CAN. Dist(s): Penton Overseas
Promotes learning of key multiplication concepts through 12 using music and math activities.

Let's Play. Perf. by Raffi. 1 cass. (J). 2002. 11.98; audio compact disk 17.98 Rounder Kids Mus Dist.

Let's Play. abr. ed. 1 CD. (Running Time: 49 mins. 29 sec.). (J). (ps). 2002. audio compact disk 17.98 (978-1-57940-079-8(5)) Rounder Records.
Raffi sings 16 songs about magic rain and sunshine, spiders and baby trees, peacocks and chimps and play.

Let's Play a Game Everyone Wins. (J). (ps-4). 1985. bk. (978-0-318-59511-5(7)) Listen USA.

Let's Play a Game Everyone Wins. Joseph Currier. 1 read-along cass. (WellinWorld Ser.: 2-9). (J). (ps-4). 1985. bk. 8.95 incl. bk. (978-0-88684-178-2(X), TC:114604) Listen USA.
A Wellin story about cooperative play; from a series developed to promote more cooperative personal relationships in children.

***Let's Play Doctor.** abr. ed. Mark Leyner & Billy Goldberg. Read by Mark Leyner. (ENG.). 2008. (978-0-06-123017-2(0), Harper Audio); (978-0-06-123018-9(9), Harper Audio) HarperCollins Pubs.

Let's Play the Recorder: Beginning Children's Method. Created by Hal Leonard Corporation Staff. 2006. pap. bk. 24.98 (978-1-59615-314-1(8), 1596153148) Pub: Music Minus. Dist(s): H Leonard

***Let's Play Ukulele.** Created by Ukulele Puapua. 2009. pap. bk. 7.95 (978-0-9774083-5-1(3)) Uketree Records.

Let's Practice Faith: Music. Celia Whitler. (Firelight Ser.). (gr. 7-9). 2004. audio compact disk 5.99 (978-0-8066-6517-7(3)) Augsburg Fortress.

Let's Pretend. 2 cass. (Running Time: 2 hrs.). (J). 10.95 (978-1-57816-065-5(0), LP2401) Audio File.
Radio's outstanding children's theatre presents four classic stories featuring "Uncle" Bill Adams, the "Chief Pretender" & such young "Pretenders" as Gwen Davies, Jack Grimes, Bob Readick, Sybil Trent & Arthur Anderson. Includes: "Hansel & Gretel," "Robin Hood," "Night Before Christmas," & "Bluebeard".

Let's Pretend. 2 CDs. (Running Time: 2 hrs.). 2004. audio compact disk 10.95 (978-1-57816-223-9(8)) Audio File.

Let's Pretend. collector's ed. 6 cass. (Running Time: 9 hrs.). Dramatization. 1998. bk. 34.98 (4017) Radio Spirits.
Welcome to the land of make-believe where gallant kings and queens walk through emerald halls and drink from golden goblets. Where characters donned in purple robes travel in coaches driven by talking horses. (18 episodes).

Let's Read a Horoscope. Doris C. Doane. 1 cass. 1992. 8.95 (1027) Am Fed Astrologers.

Let's Read Together. Incl. Foxy Fox. 1 cass. Illus. by Eva V. Cockrille. (Let's Read Together Ser.). (J). (ps-2). 1996. pap. bk. 8.95 (978-1-57565-008-1(8)); Patty Cat. 1 cass. Illus. by Benton Mahan. (Let's Read Together Ser.). (J). (ps-2). 1996. pap. bk. 8.95 (978-1-57565-005-0(3)); Penny Hen. 1 cass. Illus. by Eva V. Cockrille. (Let's Read Together Ser.). (J). (ps-2). 1996. pap. bk. 8.95 (978-1-57565-006-7(1)); Perky Otter. 1 cass. Illus. by Eva V. Cockrille. (Let's Read Together Ser.). (J). (ps-3). 1998. pap. bk. 8.95 (978-1-57565-050-0(9)); Rooney 'Roo. 1 cass. Illus. by Eva V. Cockrille. (Let's Read Together Ser.). (J). (ps-3). 1998. pap. bk. 8.95 (978-1-57565-049-4(5)); Suzy Mule. 1 cass. Illus. by Eva V. Cockrille. (Let's Read Together Ser.). (J). (ps-2). 1997. pap. bk. 8.95 (978-1-57565-036-4(3)); Tiny Tiger. 1 cass. Illus. by Eva V. Cockrille. (Let's Read Together Ser.). (J). (ps-2). 1997. pap. bk. 8.95 (978-1-57565-034-0(7)); Wally Walrus. 1 cass. Illus. by Jan Pyk. (Let's Read Together Ser.). (J). (ps-3). 1998. pap. bk. 8.95 (978-1-57565-051-7(7)); (J). (ps-3). 1996. Set pap. bk. 8.95 ea. Kane Pr.

Let's Read Together. Barbara deRubertis. (J). (ps-3). 1998. pap. bk. 134.25 (978-1-57565-087-6(8)) Kane Pr.
These book cassette packages introduce phonics through simple rhyming stories.

Let's Reign. Darrell Yancey & True Convenant. (Running Time: 30 min.). 2002. 11.98 (978-0-9727644-8-3(8)) Pub: Pt of Grace Ent. Dist(s): STL Dist NA

Let's Review: Spanish with Compact Disk. José M. Díaz & Maria F. Nadel. (Let's Review Ser.). (SPA.). 2003. pap. bk. 16.95 (978-0-7641-7216-8(6)) Barron.

Let's Rock & Read: Learn Reading Skills Through Fun Songs. James Bryer. 1 cass. (J). 1992. 8.95 (978-0-9622499-3-8(9)) Soundbox Pubns.

Let's Scare the Teacher to Death! unabr. ed. Tom B. Stone. Narrated by Jeff Woodman. 2 cass. (Running Time: 2 hrs. 30 mins.). (Graveyard School Ser.: No. 8). (gr. 3-7). 2001. 19.00 (978-0-7887-0709-4(4), 94885E7) Recorded Bks.
An adventure of spooky danger & grisly humor centers around a school so weird that its students are dying to go to class.

Lets Show Our Gratitude. Derek Prince. 1 cass. (Running Time: 60 min.). (B-091) Derek Prince.

***Let's Sing a Book.** Music by Patricia A. Stevens, Sr.. Patricia A. Stevens, Sr. (ENG.). (J). 2009. audio compact disk 20.00 (978-0-9843994-0-6(2)) P A Stevens.

Let's Sing about Math. 1 cass. (J). (ps-3). 1998. 8.95 (978-1-881641-88-9(0)) Pencil Point.

Let's Sing & Learn. Contemporary Books Staff. 1 cass. (J). 1996. 47.70 (978-0-8092-3026-6(7)) M-H Contemporary.

Let's Sing & Learn: Family Favorites Songs & Games. 1 cass. 1999. 4.99 (978-0-7601-2437-6(X)) Provident Music.

Let's Sing & Learn: 24 Fun Time Favorites. 1 CD. 1999. audio compact disk 4.99 (978-0-00-513329-3(7)) Provident Music.

Let's Sing & Learn Bible Songs. 1 cass. 1999. wbk. ed. 4.99 (978-0-00-513081-0(6)) Provident Music.

Let's Sing & Learn in French. Neraida Smith. 1 cass. (Running Time: 1 hr.). 9.95 (Natl Textbk Co) M-H Contemporary.

Let's Sing & Learn in French. Neraida Smith et al. (Let's Sing & Learn Ser.). (FRE., (J). 1994. pap. bk. 9.95 (978-0-8442-1454-2(X), 1454X, Passport Bks) McGraw-Hill Trade.

Let's Sing & Learn Silly Songs. 1 cass. 1999. wbk. ed. 4.99 (978-0-00-513093-3(X)) Provident Music.

Let's Sing & Learn Sunday School. 1 cass. 1999. wbk. ed. 4.99 (978-0-00-513087-2(5)) Provident Music.

Let's Sing & Play to Grow. Karen Jorgenson & Marty Richardson. 1 cass. 1987. pap. bk. 15.00 (978-0-9618222-0-0(1)) Sing Grow Pr.

Let's Sing It! Perf. by Mark Vineis. Lyrics by Mark Vineis. Music by Billy Cobin. 1 cass. (Running Time: 15 min.). (J). 2002. 10.95 (978-1-879531-53-6(4)) Mondo Pubng.

Let's Speak Creole. unabr. ed. Albert Valdman. 12 cass. (Running Time: 12 hrs.). (CRP.). 1988. pap. bk. 245.00 (978-0-88432-720-2(5), SCR100) J Norton Pubs.
Teaches beginning & intermediate learners phonology, grammar & vocabulary. Designed especially for persons who need a working command of the language to communicate with monolingual speakers. Includes extensive glossary.

Let's Speak Creole (Ann Pale Kreyol) CDs & Text. Albert Valdman. 12 CDs. (Running Time: 12 hrs.). (CRP.). 2005. audio compact disk 245.00 (978-1-57970-111-6(6), SCR100D) J Norton Pubs.

Let's Speak Hawaiian. unabr. ed. D. M. Kahananui & A. P. Anthony. 8 cass. (Running Time: 8 hrs. 30 mins.). (HAW.). (gr. 10-12). 1974. pap. bk. 225.00 (978-0-88432-446-1(X), AFHW10) J Norton Pubs.
A beginning-level course emphasizing the development of conversational skills through dialogs & drills. The text includes directed responses, questions & answers, short narratives & pattern practice.

Let's Speak Hawaiian CDs & Text. 8 CDs. (Running Time: 8 hrs. 30 mins.). (HAW.). 2005. audio compact disk 225.00 (978-1-57970-238-0(4), AFHW10D) J Norton Pubs.

Let's Speak Mohawk. unabr. ed. David K. Maracle. 3 cass. (Running Time: 3 hrs.). (J). (gr. 10-12). 1993. pap. bk. 65.00 (978-0-88432-706-6(X), AFMH10) J Norton Pubs.
Deals with the acquisition of sounds of the language & necessary grammatical tools. Provides accurate pronunciation & intonation.

Let's Speak Mohawk CDs & Text. David Kanatawakhon-Maracle. 3 CDs. (NAI.). 2005. audio compact disk 65.00 (978-1-57970-239-7(2), AFMH10D) J Norton Pubs.

Let's start smart alphabet & letter sounds Cd&dvd. Prod. by TLC for Kids. (ENG.). (J). 2007. DVD & audio compact disk 19.99 (978-1-934557-00-6(5)) TLC Music.

Let's start smart blends & digraphs Cd&dvd. Prod. by TLC for Kids. (ENG.). (J). 2007. DVD & audio compact disk 19.99 (978-1-934557-03-7(X)) TLC Music.

Let's start smart long vowel word families Cd&dvd. Prod. by TLC for Kids. (ENG.). (J). 2007. DVD & audio compact disk 19.99 (978-1-934557-02-0(1)) TLC Music.

Let's start smart multiple sounds & spellings Cd&dvd. Prod. by TLC for Kids. (ENG.). (J). 2007. DVD & audio compact disk 19.99 (978-1-934557-04-4(8)) TLC Music.

Let's start smart multiplications Cd&dvd. (ENG.). (J). 2008. DVD & audio compact disk 19.99 (978-1-934557-05-1(6)) TLC Music.

Let's start smart short vowel word families Cd&dvd. Prod. by TLC for Kids. (ENG.). (J). 2007. DVD & audio compact disk 19.99 (978-1-934557-01-3(3)) TLC Music.

***Let's Take the Long Way Home: A Memoir of Friendship.** unabr. ed. Gail Caldwell. (Running Time: 5 hrs. 0 mins. 0 sec.). 2010. 19.99 (978-1-4001-6560-5(1)); 14.99 (978-1-4001-8560-3(2)); 29.99 (978-1-4001-9560-2(8)); audio compact disk 29.99 (978-1-4001-1560-0(4)); audio compact disk 59.99 (978-1-4001-4560-7(0)) Pub: Tantor Media. Dist(s): IngramPubServ

Let's Talk! Jim Boulden. (J). (gr. 1-5). 1999. pap. bk. 79.95 (978-1-892421-30-2(5), 051CDK) Boulden Pubng.

Let's Talk. Koop & Steve Johnson. 1 cass. 1992. 14.99 (978-0-310-59788-9(9)) Zondervan.

Let's Talk. 2nd rev. ed. Leo Jones. 2 cass. (Running Time: 2 hrs.). (Let's Talk Ser.). 2001. 43.00 (978-0-521-75076-9(8)) Cambridge U Pr.

Let's Talk. 2nd rev. ed. Leo Jones. (Running Time: 3 hrs.). (ENG.). 2007. audio compact disk 59.00 (978-0-521-69286-1(5)) Cambridge U Pr.

Let's Talk. 2nd rev. ed. Leo Jones. (Running Time: 3 hrs.). (ENG., 2007. audio compact disk 59.00 (978-0-521-69283-0(0)) Cambridge U Pr.

Let's Talk Advanced American English. Victoria Liu & Joseph B. Durra. Prod. by Victoria Liu. (Let's Talk Ser.). 1992. bk. 108.00 (978-1-881906-02-5(7)) JBD Pub.

Let's Talk Audio Sampler 1-3. Leo Jones. 2 cass. (Running Time: 3 hrs.). 2000. (978-0-521-92589-1(4)) Cambridge U Pr.
The engaging task-based listening activities focus student listening and are recorded in natural, conversational American English. Features interviews, conversations, news reports, and other interesting listening texts.

Let's Talk Business. Weiss Kelly. 1 cass. 8.95 (685) Am Fed Astrologers.
An AFA Convention workshop tape.

Let's Talk Cantonese. Victoria Liu & Joseph B. Durra. 4 cass. (CHI & ENG., 2003. 49.95 (978-1-881906-04-9(3), LETABT) Pub: JBD Pub. Dist(s): China Bks

Let's Talk Cheyenne. Cheyenne Translation Project Staff. Narrated by Ted Risingsun. 2 cass. (Running Time: 2 hrs.). 2001. pap. bk. 15.95 (AFCN10) J Norton Pubs.
Mini-course centers around basic themes of everyday living: greetings, weather, eating & drinking, people & relatives. Also included are numbers, common verbs, animate & inanimate objects, commands, questions & answers & simple conversation.

Let's Talk Cheyenne. Ted Risingsun & Wayne Leman. 2 cass. (Running Time: 2 hrs). (CHY.). 1999. pap. bk. 35.00 (978-1-57970-091-1(8), AFCN01) J Norton Pubs.
self-instructional program for basic Cheyenne.

Let's Talk Cheyenne CDs & Text. Ted Risingsun. 2 CDs. (Running Time: 2 hrs.). (CHY.). 2005. audio compact disk 35.00 (978-1-57970-170-3(1), AFCN01D) J Norton Pubs.

Let's Talk Metric. 9.00 (CM11) Esstee Audios.

Let's Talk Music. Perf. by Kidzup Productions Staff. 1 cass. (J). 1997. 8.99 (K7 019601); audio compact disk 12.99 (KCD 019601) Kidzup Prodns.
About the environment, computers, believing in one's self.

Let's Talk 1. Leo Jones. 1 cass. (Running Time: 1 hr. 30 mins.). (Let's Talk Ser.). 2001. 43.00 (978-0-521-77693-6(7)) Cambridge U Pr.

Let's Talk 3. Leo Jones. 3 cass. (Running Time: 1 hr. 30 mins.). (Let's Talk Ser.). 2001. 43.00 (978-0-521-77690-5(2)) Cambridge U Pr.
1. GETTING ACQUAINTED 1A First impressions 1B Working together 2. COMMUNICATION 2A Announcements and signs 2B Feelings and gestures 3. BREAKING THE LAW 3A Crime and punishment 3B Solving crimes 4. MYSTERIES AND SURPRISES 4A That's strange! 4B It's hard to believe, but . . . 5. EDUCATION 5A Happy days? 5B Brain power 6. FAME AND FORTUNE 6A Famous people 6B Can money buy happiness? 7. AROUND THE WORLD 7A People and languages 7B When in Rome . . . 8. TECHNOLOGY 8A Can you explain it? 8B User-friendly? 9. HEALTH AND FITNESS 9A Staying healthy 9B Coping with stress? 10. NATURAL FORCES 10A What awful weather! 10B The ring of fire 11. NEWS AND CURRENT EVENTS 11A Today's news 11B People and the news 12. RELATIONSHIPS 12A Friendship 12B .Looking for love 13. ADVENTURE 13A Please be careful! 13B Exciting - or dangerous? 14. SELF-IMPROVEMENT 14A How to be popular 14B Managing your life 15. TRAVEL AND TOURISM 15A Travelers or tourists? 15B Fantastic journeys 16. THE REAL WORLD 16A Using the phone 16B The ideal job.

Let's Talk 3. 2nd rev. ed. Leo Jones. (Running Time: 3 hrs.). (ENG., 2007. audio compact disk 59.00 (978-0-521-69289-2(X)) Cambridge U Pr.

Let's Visit Lullaby Land. 1 cass. (Running Time: 1 hr.). (J). 2001. 10.95 (KIM 2065C) Kimbo Educ.
A delightful collection of restful music for quiet times. Famous traditional lullabies from around the world plus unforgettable popular tunes sung in a gentle, soothing style. The Children's Prayer, Edelweiss, Goodnight My Someone, Yesterday & more.

Let's Write a Mystery. Ralph McInerny. Read by Ralph McInerny. 12 cass. (Running Time: 12 hrs.). 1993. 89.00 (978-1-883222-00-0(1)) Quodlibetal.
24 half hour lessons on 12 audio tapes accompanied by McInerny's mystery novel "Death of a Donor" & a workbook.

Let's Write a Novel. Ralph McInerny. Read by Ralph McInerny. 12 cass. (Running Time: 12 hrs.). 1993. wbk. ed. 89.00 (978-1-883222-01-7(X)) Pub: Quodlibetal. Dist(s): Vandamere
24 half hour lessons on 12 audio tapes accompanied by McInerny's demonstration novel "Prudence of the Flesh" & a workbook.

Let's Write Short Stories. Ralph McInerny. Read by Ralph McInerny. 6 cass. (Running Time: 6 hrs.). 1993. 49.00 (978-1-883222-02-4(8)) Quodlibetal.
12 half hour lessons on 6 audio tapes accompanied by six McInerny demonstration short stories & a workbook.

Letter. Richard Paul Evans. Read by Richard Thomas. (Christmas Box Ser.: Bk. 3). 1997. 9.95 (978-0-7435-4965-3(1)) Pub: S&S Audio. Dist(s): S and S Inc

Letter. unabr. ed. Michele Sobel Spirn. 1 cass. (Running Time: 5 min.). (Read Along ... For Fun Ser.). (J). (ps-2). 1984. bk. 16.99 (978-0-934898-70-6(7)); pap. bk. 9.95 (978-0-934898-82-9(0)) Jan Prods.
It is Bob's first day at school; some of the children can read & some of the children can't. When the day is over, Sally gives Bob a Letter. "Read it at home," she says. Bob cannot read. What will he do?.

Letter from America. Alistair Cooke. 13 CDs. (Running Time: 13 hrs.). 2005. audio compact disk 112.95 (978-0-7927-3735-3(0), BBCD 127) AudioGO.

Letter from Home. unabr. ed. Carolyn G. Hart. 6 cass. (Running Time: 9 hrs.). 2003. 54.00 (978-0-7366-9564-0(8)) Books on Tape.
Young reporter, Gretchen Gilman, who investigates the puzzling murder of an acquaintance. Gretchen's assignments at the local newspaper weren't very exciting, but the job was a good opportunity for a young woman with talent and ambition. That summer everyone was talking about Faye Tatum, who was found dead in her living room. Gretchen knew that the circumstances of Faye's life and death were much different than people imagined, and she was determined to uncover the truth once and for all - even if it meant writing a story that would haunt her for the rest of her life.

Letter from Li Po see Conrad Aiken Reading

Letter of Intent, Comfort Letters & Gentleman's Agreements. Read by Harris Ominsky. 1 cass. 1990. 20.00 (AL-101) PA Bar Inst.

Letter of Marque. Patrick O'Brian. Read by Simon Vance. (Running Time: 34200 sec.). (Aubrey-Maturin Ser.). 2006. 59.95 (978-0-7861-4520-1(X)); audio compact disk 72.00 (978-0-7861-7184-2(7)) Blckstn Audio.

Letter of Marque. Patrick O'Brian. 10 CDs. (Running Time: 11.5 Hrs). (Aubrey-Maturin Ser.). 2004. audio compact disk 29.95 (978-1-4025-9426-7(7)) Recorded Bks.

Letter of Marque. Patrick O'Brian. Read by Robert Hardy. 2 cass. (Running Time: 3 hrs.). (Aubrey-Maturin Ser.). 1999. 16.85 (978-0-00-105547-6(X)) Ulvrscrft Audio.
Jack Aubrey is a naval officer, a post captain of experience & capacity. When the story opens he has been struck off the Navy list for a crime he has not committed.

Letter of Marque. unabr. ed. Patrick O'Brian. Read by Simon Vance. (Running Time: 34200 sec.). (Aubrey-Maturin Ser.). 2006. 29.95 (978-0-7861-4688-8(5)); audio compact disk 29.95 (978-0-7861-6649-7(5)) Blckstn Audio.

Letter of Marque. unabr. ed. Patrick O'Brian. Read by Richard Brown. 8 cass. (Running Time: 12 hrs.). (Aubrey-Maturin Ser.). 1993. 64.00 (978-0-7366-2434-3(1), 3199) Books on Tape.
Jack Aubrey & Stephen Maturin sail against the French to redeem Aubrey's tarnished name. Twelfth in Aubrey-Maturin series.

Letter of Marque. unabr. ed. Patrick O'Brian. Narrated by Patrick Tull. 8 cass. (Running Time: 11 hrs. 30 mins.). (Aubrey-Maturin Ser.). 1995. 70.00 (978-0-7887-0165-8(7), 94390E7) Recorded Bks.
The Surprise, sold by the Royal Navy & purchased by Stephen Maturin, with the disgraced Jack Aubrey in command, sets sail on its first mission as a Letter of Marque, carrying official permission to engage in piracy.

Letter of Marque. unabr. ed. Patrick O'Brian. Read by Patrick Tull. 7 Cass. (Running Time: 11.5 Hrs). (Aubrey-Maturin Ser.). 2004. 29.95 (978-1-4025-9425-0(9)) Recorded Bks.

Letter of Marque. unabr. ed. Read by Simon Vance. (Running Time: 34200 sec.). (Aubrey-Maturin Ser.). 2006. audio compact disk 29.95 (978-0-7861-7618-2(0)) Blckstn Audio.

Letter of Mary. unabr. ed. Laurie R. King. Narrated by Jenny Sterlin. 8 cass. (Running Time: 10 hrs. 45 mins.). (Mary Russell Mystery Ser.: Vol. 3). 1997. 70.00 (978-0-7887-0649-3(7), 94826E7) Recorded Bks.
An old friend is murdered, the Holmes' cottage is ransacked, & Mary, the young wife of Sherlock Holmes, is faced with a particularly dangerous & painful case.

Letter of the Day - Home Version. (Running Time: 45 mins.). (J). 2005. audio compact disk 15.95 (978-0-9706094-1-0(8)) Effective Lit Meth.
The Letter Of The Day - Home Version is a program that teaches the foundations of literacy through song. Each letter of the alphabet has a respective song which is beautifully orchestrated and song. There is a School Version of Letter Of The Day that is formatted into individual lessons (see ISBN090609442).

Letter of the Day - School Version. Ricki Korey Birnbaumi. 1 CD. (Running Time: 1 hr. 15 mins.). (J). 2005. audio compact disk 15.95 (978-0-9706094-4-1(2)) Effective Lit Meth.
The Letter Of The Day - School Version is a program geared for children at the beginning and early stages of learning to read (ages 3-8 years) which teaches the foundational skills necessary to learn to read and spell through music. Each letter has a corresponding song which is beautifully orchestrated and sung. Children will love to learn each song and sing them over and over again. The Letter Of The Day - School Version is formatted into individual lessons that the teacher can utilize in his/her literacy program and is also perfect for home schooling. The is also a Home Version of Letter Of The Day (see ISBN 0970609418) which is a review of the individual songs. There are individual alphabet cards which can be purchased separately from the publisher who can be contacted at www.earlyphonics.com.

Letter of the Law. abr. ed. Tim Green. Read by Keith Szarabajka. (Casey Jordan Ser.: Bk. 1). (ENG.). 2005. 14.98 (978-1-59483-456-1(3)) Pub: Hachet Audio. Dist(s): HachBkGrp

Letter of the Law. unabr. ed. Tim Green. Narrated by Richard Poe. 7 cass. (Running Time: 9 hrs.). (Casey Jordan Ser.: Bk. 1). 2001. 59.00 (978-0-7887-4981-0(1), 96478E7) Recorded Bks.
An open & shut case when law professor Eric Lipton is seen driving away from the home of a mutilated student & is later caught fleeing the country with woman's bloody underwear. But Casey Jordan injected reasonable doubt into the minds of the jurors. She then finds her own doubts rise to the surface & puts her own life in jeopardy.

Letter Sounds. 1 cass. (Running Time: 1 hr.). (J). (ps-k). 2001. pap. bk. 13.95 (RL 911CD) Kimbo Educ.
Kids learn the alphabet & the most common sounds each letter makes. Fun songs & games. Activity book included.

Letter Sounds - Phonics for Beginners. rev. ed. Brad Caudle & Richard Caudle. Perf. by Brad Caudle et al. 1 cass. (Running Time: 55 min.). (J). (ps-2). 1997. 12.95 (978-1-878489-63-0(1), RL963) Rock N Learn.
Catchy songs with educational lyrics teach phonetic basics for learning to read. Covers the alphabet & sounds letters make, as well as blends. Includes full-color illustrated book.

Letter Sounds - Phonics for Beginners. rev. ed. Brad Caudle & Richard Caudle. Perf. by Brad Caudle et al. Illus. by Anthony Guerra. 1 cass. (Running Time: 55 min.). (Rock 'N Learn Ser.). (J). (gr. k-2). 1997. pap. bk. 12.99 (978-1-878489-11-1(9), RL911) Rock N Learn.

Letter to Amy see Carta a Amy

Letter to Amy. (J). 2004. bk. 24.95 (978-0-89719-887-5(5)); pap. bk. 14.95 (978-1-56008-060-2(4)); 8.95 (978-1-56008-949-0(0)); 8.95 (978-1-56008-144-9(9)); cass. & flmstrp 30.00 (978-1-56008-705-2(6)) Weston Woods.

Letter to Amy. Ezra Jack Keats. 1 cass. (Running Time: 6 min.). (J). (ps-3). 8.95 (RAC114) Weston Woods.
Peter wants to invite a girl to his birthday party but extraordinary circumstances conspire to threaten his plan.

Letter to Amy. Ezra Jack Keats. 1 cass. (Running Time: 6 min.). (J). (ps-3). 2000. pap. bk. 12.95 (PRA114) Weston Woods.

Letter to Dr. & Mrs. J. G. Holland, Summer 1862 see Poems & Letters of Emily Dickinson

Letter to Ishmael in the Grave. Short Stories. Rosellen Brown. Read by Rosellen Brown. 1 cass. (Running Time: 1 hr.). 1982. 12.95 (978-1-55644-038-0(3), 2031) Am Audio Prose.

Letter to John L. Graves, April 1856 see Poems & Letters of Emily Dickinson

Letter to Louise & Frances Norcross, July 1879 see Poems & Letters of Emily Dickinson

Letter to Maria Whitney, Summer 1883 see Poems & Letters of Emily Dickinson

Letter to Mrs. J. G. Holland, June 1884 see Poems & Letters of Emily Dickinson

Letter to My Daughter. unabr. ed. Maya Angelou. Read by Maya Angelou. (ENG.). 2008. audio compact disk 25.00 (978-0-7393-7038-4(3), Random AudioBks) Pub: Random Audio Pubg. Dist(s): Random

***Letter to My Daughter: A Novel.** unabr. ed. George Bishop. Narrated by Tavia Gilbert. (Running Time: 5 hrs. 0 mins.). 2010. 13.99 (978-1-4001-8694-5(3)); 19.99 (978-1-4001-6694-7(2)); audio compact disk 49.99 (978-1-4001-4694-9(1)); audio compact disk 24.99 (978-1-4001-1694-2(5)) Pub: Tantor Media. Dist(s): IngramPubServ

Letter to My Wife. Prod. by John Wing, Jr.. Hosted by John Wing, Jr. (Running Time: 1 hr.). 2005. audio compact disk 15.95 (978-0-660-18653-5(5)) Pub: Canadian Broadcasting CAN. Dist(s): Georgetown Term

Letter to Otis P. Lord, December 3, 1882 see Poems & Letters of Emily Dickinson

Letter to Richard Woodhouse see Cambridge Treasury of English Prose: Austen to Bronte

Letter to Sally Jenkins, December 1880 see Poems & Letters of Emily Dickinson

Letter to Susan Gilbert Dickinson, October 1883 see Poems & Letters of Emily Dickinson

Letter to T. W. Higginson, April 15, 1862 see Poems & Letters of Emily Dickinson

Letter to T. W. Higginson, April 25, 1862 see Poems & Letters of Emily Dickinson

Letter to the Romans. Gil Bailie. 6 cass. (Running Time: 8 hrs. 30 min.). 39.95 Credence Commun.
The Letter to the Romans changed Christianity. It is matched in power by few religious documents. In it Paul wrestles with the questions facing all Christians. What makes a person holy? And why? And where is Christ in the process? Bailie keeps the power intact while making it clear with small words & big ideas. He makes it clear just how Christianity is the new aeon, & why the crucifixion changed the world. And you.

Letter Writing for the Office: Syllabus. 2nd ed. Carl W. Salser. (J). 1975. 194.90 (978-0-89420-160-8(3), 110800) Natl Book.

Lettere Famigliari. Giuseppe Baretti. Read by Elsa Proverbio. 4 cass. (Running Time: 4 hrs.). (Letterati, Memorialisti E Viaggiatori Del 700 Ser.). (ITA.). 1996. pap. bk. 49.50 (978-1-58085-460-3(5)) Interlingua VA.

Letters: Abridged. (ENG.). 2007. (978-1-60339-051-4(0)); cd-rom & audio compact disk (978-1-60339-052-1(9)) Listenr Digest.

Letters & Forms. (Timesaving Software Tools for Teachers Ser.). 2004. audio compact disk 19.99 (978-1-57690-696-5(5)) Tchr Create Ma.

Letters & Life of Henry Adams. unabr. ed. Louis Kronenberger. 1 cass. (Running Time: 46 min.). 1968. 12.95 (23039) J Norton Pubs.
A report on the life & times of Henry Adams as revealed in his letters.

Letters & Numbers. 1 cass. (Early Learning Ser.). (J). bk. (TWIN 407) NewSound.
Learn letter names, beginning sounds, counting to twenty & a whole lot more.

Letters & Numbers. 2004. bk. 12.99 (978-1-57583-300-2(X)) Twin Sisters.

Letters & Numbers Music. Kim Mitzo Thompson & Karen Mitzo Hilderbrand. Arranged by Hal Wright. (J). 1997. pap. bk. & act. bk. ed. 13.99 (978-1-57583-297-5(6), Twin 407) Twin Sisters.

Letters & Poems of Thomas Hardy. unabr. ed. Thomas Hardy. 2 cass. (Running Time: 2 hr. 30 min.). 2000. 13.98 (NA219314) Naxos.
Poetry & letters that reflect aspects of the author's personality.

Letters for Emily. Camron Wright. 2004. 15.95 (978-0-7435-4966-0(X)) Pub: S&S Audio. Dist(s): S and S Inc

Letters for the Last Generation: Understanding the End-Times, Learning from the Seven Churches. Mac Hammond. 10 cass. (Running Time: 10 hrs.). (Last Millennium Ser.: Vol. 1). 1999. (978-1-57399-086-8(8)) Mac Hammond.
As the sixth millennium of human history comes to a close, there's no shortage of interest in, or teaching about, the biblical book of Revelation.

Letters from a Skeptic: A Son Wrestles with His Father's Questions about Christianity. unabr. ed. Greg Boyd. Narrated by Greg Boyd. (Running Time: 6 hrs. 0 mins. 0 sec.). (ENG.). 2008. 13.99 (978-1-60814-283-5(3)) Oasis Audio.

Letters from a Skeptic: A Son Wrestles with His Father's Questions about Christianity. unabr. ed. Greg Boyd & Edward K. Boyd. Narrated by Greg Boyd. (Running Time: 6 hrs. 0 mins. 0 sec.). (ENG.). 2008. audio compact disk 19.99 (978-1-59859-402-7(8)) Oasis Audio.

Letters from America: the Elections: Presented by Alistair Cooke. Read by Alistair Cooke. (Running Time: 1 hr. 0 mins. 0 sec.). (ENG.). 2009. audio compact disk 24.95 (978-1-60283-770-6(8)) Pub: AudioGO. Dist(s): Perseus Dist

Letters from an Age of Reason, Pt. 1. unabr. ed. Nora Hague. Read by Mary Peiffer. 12 cass. (Running Time: 18 hrs.). 2001. 96.00 (978-0-7366-8081-3(0)) Books on Tape.
A romantic adventure full of passion and sophistication, Nora Hague's book, set in the 1860s, explores the shifting moral environments of Civil War-era America and Victorian England. Arabella Leeds, the young and eligible daughter of New York society parents, has fallen in love with Aubrey Paxton, a mulatto slave from a New Orleans household. Both of them must overcome obstacles to find each other and fulfill their love. Arabella must critically examine the social and sexual roles which she was brought up to fulfill, while Aubrey must confront his presence in a society which will turn him away no matter how well he can pass for white. Together, they encounter the racy demimonde of their society, and together they come to a passionate sexual awakening.

Letters from an Age of Reason, Pt. 2. unabr. ed. Nora Hague. Read by Mary Peiffer. 10 cass. (Running Time: 15 hrs.). 2001. 80.00 (978-0-7366-8301-2(1)) Books on Tape.
Arabella Leeds, the young and eligible daughter of New York society parents, has fallen in love with Aubrey Paxton, a mulatto slave from a New Orleans household. Both of them must overcome obstacles to find each other and fulfill their love. Arabella must critically examine the social and sexual roles which she was brought up to fulfill, while Aubrey must confront his presence in a society which will turn him away no matter how well he can pass for white. Together, they encounter the racy demimonde of their society, and together they come to a passionate sexual awakening.

Letters from an Age of Reason, Pt. A. unabr. ed. Nora Hague. Read by Mary Peiffer. 12 cass. (Running Time: 18 hrs.). 2001. 72.00 Books on Tape.
During the Civil War and after, a New York Society girl and a New Orleans mulatto slave struggle to fulfill their love for one another.

Letters from an Age of Reason, Pt. B. unabr. ed. Nora Hague. Read by Mary Peiffer. 10 cass. (Running Time: 15 hrs.). 2001. 60.00 Books on Tape.

Letters from an Understanding Friend. Isaias Powers & Andrea Star. Read by Isaias Powers. 3 cass. (Running Time: 3 hrs. 30 min.). (YA). (gr. 9 up). 1986. 24.95 (978-0-89622-339-4(6)) Twenty-Third.
Reflections & meditations as though written by Jesus while on his way to Jerusalem before his last days on Calvary.

Letters from Atlantis. abr. ed. Robert A. Silverberg. Read by Tom Parker. 3 cass. (Running Time: 4 hrs.). 1999. 23.95 (978-0-7861-1582-2(3), 2411) Blckstn Audio.
It was a legendary island, a fantastic island, Atlantis. Or as its prince called it, Athilan. Roy had traveled through time with his partner, Lora, to find it & now he was tantalizingly close to its shore.

Letters from Atlantis. unabr. ed. Robert A. Silverberg & Lloyd James. 3 CDs. (Running Time: 4 hrs.). 2000. audio compact disk 24.00 (978-0-7861-9947-1(4), 2411) Blckstn Audio.
Roy has traveled through time with his partner, Lora, to find a fantastic island, Atlantis.

Letters from Jitvapur, Letters 1-4. unabr. ed. Julian C. Hollick. 1 cass. (Running Time: 60 min.). 1991. 15.00 (978-1-56709-066-6(4), 1049) Indep Broadcast.
"The Rhythm of the Days" examines the rhythm of Indian village life. "Should Girls Go to School?" Villagers are torn between the weight of tradition & their consciences in deciding whether to send their girls to school & whether to marry them off before puberty or let them choose as adults at the risk of becoming social outcasts. "Pa'an Wallahs & Chai Wallahs." This program explores the two great social institutions in all of India - pa'an chewing & drinking innumerable cups of chai. "Binda Devi & Rodi Paswan." The village of Jitvapur is made up of a multitude of castes, which live in self-contained clusters around ponds & rarely meet socially.

Letters from Jitvapur, Letters 5-8. unabr. ed. Julian C. Hollick. 1 cass. (Running Time: 60 min.). 1991. 15.00 (978-1-56709-067-3(2), 1051) Indep Broadcast.
"Tilling the Soil" examines how the landless laborers from the backward castes, or the Untouchables, work the land owned by the upper caste Brahmins. "Going to the Movies" features an outing to the local cinema in Madhubani. "Abdul Malik & the Muslim Weavers" examines the fear some villagers have of progress because it means change, & change can also mean risk. "Trying to Go Straight in Rayhyam" follows the efforts of the local development officer who is trying to transform a bunch of petty thieves into model capitalists.

Letters from My Windmill see Lettres de Mon Moulin

Letters from Nuremberg: My Father's Narrative of a Quest for Justice. unabr. ed. Christopher J. Dodd. 11 CDs. (Running Time: 14 hrs. 0 mins. 0 sec.). (ENG.). 2007. audio compact disk 37.99 (978-1-4001-0539-7(0)) Pub: Tantor Media. Dist(s): IngramPubServ

Letters from Nuremberg: My Father's Narrative of a Quest for Justice. unabr. ed. Christopher J. Dodd & Lary Bloom. Narrated by Michael Prichard. (Running Time: 14 hrs. 0 mins. 0 sec.). (ENG.). 2007. audio compact disk 24.99 (978-1-4001-5539-2(8)); audio compact disk 75.99 (978-1-4001-3539-4(7)) Pub: Tantor Media. Dist(s): IngramPubServ

***Letters from Obedience School - Audio.** Mark Teague. (Dear Mrs. Larue Ser.). (ENG.). 2011. audio compact disk 9.99 (978-0-545-31520-3(4)) Scholastic Inc.

***Letters from Obedience School, Audio Library Edition.** Mark Teague. (Dear Mrs. Larue Ser.). (ENG.). 2011. audio compact disk 18.99 (978-0-545-31537-1(9)) Scholastic Inc.

***Letters from Rifka.** unabr. ed. Karen Hesse. (Running Time: 3 hrs.). 2010. 39.97 (978-1-4418-1816-4(2), 9781441818164, BADLE); 24.99 (978-1-4418-1815-7(4), 9781441818157, BAD) Brilliance Audio.

***Letters from Rifka.** unabr. ed. Karen Hesse. Read by Angela Dawe. (Running Time: 3 hrs.). 2010. 24.99 (978-1-4418-1813-3(8), 9781441818133, Brilliance MP3); 39.97 (978-1-4418-1814-0(6), 9781441818140, Brinc Audio MP3 Lib); audio compact disk 62.97 (978-1-4418-1812-6(X), 9781441818126, BriAudCD Unabrid) Brilliance Audio.

***Letters from Rifka.** unabr. ed. Karen Hesse. Read by Angela Dawe. (Running Time: 3 hrs.). (YA). 2010. audio compact disk 24.99 (978-1-4418-1811-9(1), 9781441818119, Bril Audio CD Unabri) Brilliance Audio.

Letters from Syria. unabr. collector's ed. Freya Stark. Read by Donada Peters. 8 cass. (Running Time: 8 hrs.). 1990. 48.00 (978-0-7366-1861-8(9), 2692) Books on Tape.
These letters, written early in Freya Stark's career, describe her discovery of the Near East. Since then, that part of the world has become central in Stark's life. Readers of her later works will find a special fascination in these accounts of her first impressions. Traveling to Brumana by way of Brindisi & Rhodes, she became a part of the local community. There she learned to think, & speak, in colloquial Arabic. Her efforts opened doors long closed to outsiders, particularly women.

Letters from the Earth: Uncensored Writings. abr. ed. Mark Twain. Read by Carl Reiner. 4 cass. (Running Time: 6 hrs.). (Ultimate Classics Ser.). 2004. 25.00 (978-1-931056-02-1(1), N Millennium Audio); audio compact disk 39.95 (978-1-59007-014-7(3)) Pub: New Millenn Enter. Dist(s): PerseuPGW
Raised in a raucous family of beggars and thieves, Tom dreams and reads of princely life to escape his miserable 16th-century London existence. After wandering to Westminster and meeting benevolent Prince Edward Tudor (who bears an uncanny resemblance to the ragamuffin Tom), the pair exchange clothes and unwittingly identities.

Letters from the Earth: Uncensored Writings. unabr. ed. Mark Twain. Read by Carl Reiner. 6 cass. (Running Time: 9 hrs.). (Ultimate Classics Ser.). 2004. 34.95 (978-1-931056-29-8(3), N Millennium Audio) New Millenn Enter.
These essays, stories & sketches present Twain at his most vitriolic. "The Damned Human Race" proves that a snake is a higher form than an English earl & "Papers of the Adam Family" is a sardonic look at the Bible's first couple.

***Letters from the Land of Cancer.** unabr. ed. Walter Wangerin Jr. (Running Time: 5 hrs. 28 mins. 4 sec.). (ENG.). 2010. 16.99 (978-0-310-77353-5(9)) Zondervan.

Letters from the Light: An Afterlife Journal. abr. ed. Elsa Barker. Read by Mitchell Ryan. 2 cass. (Running Time: 3 hrs.). 1996. 17.95 (978-1-57453-028-5(3), 330097) Audio Lit.

Letters I Never Wrote, Conversations I Never Had. Ben Bissell. 2 cass. (Running Time: 2 hrs.). 20.00 C Bissell.
This audio book provides a model for completing unfinished grief & anger in our lives toward those now deceased. In this moving reading of his popular book published by Macmillan, which is now out of print, Ben shares his personal insights.

Letters of a Woman Homesteader. 4 CDs. (Running Time: 4 hrs. 19 min.). (Our American Heritage Ser.). (J). 2003. pap. bk. 62.00 (978-1-58472-527-5(3), In Aud); audio compact disk 43.00 (978-1-58472-472-8(2), In Aud) Sound Room.

Letters of a Woman Homesteader. Elinore Pruitt Steward. Narrated by Rebecca Burns. (Running Time: 5 hrs. 30 mins.). 2004. 24.95 (978-1-59912-532-9(3)) Iofy Corp.

Letters of a Woman Homesteader. Elinore Pruitt Stewart. Read by Kate Fleming. (Running Time: 19200 sec.). (Unabridged Classics in MP3 Ser.). (ENG.). (YA). (gr. 7-12). 2008. audio compact disk 14.95 (978-1-58472-679-1(2), In Aud) Sound Room.

Letters of a Woman Homesteader. Elinore Pruitt Stewart. Read by Kate Fleming. (Running Time: 5 hrs 19 mins.). 2003. 23.95 (978-1-59912-088-1(7), Audiofy Corp) Iofy Corp.

Letters of a Woman Homesteader. unabr. ed. Elinore P. Stewart. Read by Flo Gibson. 3 cass. (Running Time: 4 hrs. 30 min.). (gr. 8 up). 1989. 16.95 (978-1-55685-146-9(4)) Audio Bk Con.
These letters reveal the isolation, beauty, & joy of working on the prairie.

Letters of a Woman Homesteader. unabr. ed. Elinore Pruitt Stewart. Read by Kate Fleming. (YA). 2007. 44.99 (978-1-59895-861-4(5)) Find a World.

Letters of a Woman Homesteader. unabr. ed. Elinore Pruitt Stewart. Narrated by Rebecca C. Burns. (Running Time: 4 hrs. 30 mins. 0 sec.). (ENG.). 2008. audio compact disk 19.99 (978-1-4001-0801-5(2)); audio compact disk 19.99 (978-1-4001-5801-0(X)); audio compact disk 39.99 (978-1-4001-3801-2(9)) Pub: Tantor Media. Dist(s): IngramPubServ

Letters of a Woman Homesteader. unabr. collector's ed. Elinore P. Stewart. Read by Rebecca C. Burns. 5 cass. (Running Time: 5 hrs.). 1997. 30.00 (978-0-913369-83-8(7), 4377) Books on Tape.

Letters of Elizabeth Barrett & Robert Browning. unabr. ed. Elizabeth Barrett Browning & Robert Browning. Read by Flo Gibson. 12 cass. (Running Time: 17 hrs. 30 mins.). 1994. 39.95 (978-1-55685-323-4(8)) Audio Bk Con.
These lyrical love letters trace Elizabeth Barrett & Robert Browning's romance as it progresses to their elopement. The threatening presence of her possessive father haunts their relationship. There are many references to contemporary writers.

Letters of Evelyn Waugh. unabr. ed. Read by Ken Scott. Ed. by Mark Amory. 23 cass. (Running Time: 34 hrs. 30 mins.). 1989. 184.00 (978-0-7366-1595-2(4), 2457-A/B) Books on Tape.
Evelyn Waugh was one of the great literary practitioners of the 20th century. The same is true of his letters. Though not intended for publication, Waugh's correspondence was by turns witty, profound & impeccable. He was an indefatigable writer & exchanged letters with some of the most noteworthy people of the century - on literary style with Graham Greene, religion with Thomas Merton. His interests ranged from society to politics to fashion. He was irreverent & acid-tongued, famous for his dislike of Americans.

Letters of Evelyn Waugh, Pt. 1. unabr. ed. Mark Amory. Read by Ken Scott. 11 cass. (Running Time: 16 hrs. 30 mins.). 1989. 88.00 (2457-A) Books on Tape.

Letters of Evelyn Waugh, Pt. 2. unabr. ed. Mark Amory. Read by Ken Scott. 12 cass. (Running Time: 18 hrs.). 1989. 96.00 (2457-B) Books on Tape.

Letters of Jefferson & A Neglected American (audio CD) Gilbert Highet. (ENG.). 2006. audio compact disk 9.95 (978-1-57970-437-7(9), Audio-For) J Norton Pubs.

Letters of John & Abigail Adams: 1774-1777. unabr. ed. Abigail S. Adams & John Adams. Perf. by George Grizzard & Kathryn Walker. 2 cass. 1984. 19.95 (978-0-694-50437-4(8), SWC 2083) HarperCollins Pubs.
Their description of the battle of Bunker Hill, the signing of the Declaration of Independence & the grim war year of 1777 which ended with the battle of Saratoga.

Letters of Love & Sensibility. Jane Austen. Narrated by Flo Gibson. (ENG.). 2008. audio compact disk 16.95 (978-1-60646-036-8(6)) Audio Bk Con.

Letters of Love & Sensibility. unabr. ed. Jane Austen. Narrated by Flo Gibson. (Running Time: 1 hr. 54 mins.). 2007. 14.95 (978-1-55685-765-2(9)) Audio Bk Con.

***Letters of St. Thérèse of Lisieux.** St. Thérèse of Lisieux. Read by Anne Breiling. (ENG.). 2009. audio compact disk 15.95 (978-1-936231-08-9(5)) Cath Audio.

Letters of the Romantic Poets. unabr. ed. 10.95 (978-0-8045-1069-1(5), SAC 7125) Spoken Arts.

Letters of Thomas Jefferson. unabr. ed. Thomas Jefferson. 1 cass. (Running Time: 30 min.). (Gilbert Highet Ser.). 9.95 (23302) J Norton Pubs.
President Jefferson's character is revealed through his letters & the poetry of Ralph Waldo Emerson is discussed & compared with Whitman's.

Letters of Virginia Woolf. unabr. ed. Read by Heywood Hale Broun & Nigel Nicolson. 1 cass. (Running Time: 56 min.). (Broun Radio Ser.). 12.95 (40219) J Norton Pubs.
A conversation with the editor of the first of 6 volumes of letters from 1888 to 1912.

Letters on Literature & Politics. unabr. ed. Edward Wilson. 1 cass. (Running Time: 56 min.). 12.95 (40305) J Norton Pubs.

Letters to a Young Artist: Straight-up Advice on Making a Life in the Arts - for Actors, Performers, Writers, & Artists of Every Kind. Anna Deavere Smith. Read by Anna Deavere Smith. (Running Time: 16200 sec.). 2006. 34.95 (978-0-7861-4498-3(X)) Blckstn Audio.

Letters to a Young Artist: Straight-up Advice on Making a Life in the Arts - for Actors, Performers, Writers, & Artists of Every Kind. unabr. ed. Anna Deavere Smith. Read by Anna Deavere Smith. 4 CDs. (Running Time: 16200 sec.). 2006. audio compact disk 36.00 (978-0-7861-7231-3(2)) Blckstn Audio.
From "the most exciting individual in American theater" (Newsweek), here is Anna Deavere Smith's brass-tacks advice to aspiring artists of all stripes. In the manner of Rilke's Letters to a Young Poet, Deavere Smith mentors her young artist over a period of five years, sharing her hard won wisdom about the challenges and rewards of the artistic life. Drawing on her own life experiences as an actor, teacher, and playwright, Deavere Smith provides a motivating example for how to pursue one's art without compromise, while offering tips on everything from how to stay healthy to building a diverse network of friends and professional alliances. Honest, passionate, and inspiring, this audiobook has life-changing potential.

Letters to a Young Artist: Straight-up Advice on Making a Life in the Arts-for Actors, Performers, Writers, & Artists of Every Kind. unabr. ed. Anna Deavere Smith. 4 CDs. (Running Time: 16200 sec.). 2006. audio compact disk 29.95 (978-0-7861-7475-1(7)) Blckstn Audio.

Letters to a Young Artist: Straight-Up Advice on Making a Life in the Arts-For Actors, Performers, Writers, & Artists of Every Kind. unabr. ed. Anna Deavere Smith. 4 cass. (Running Time: 6 hrs.). (YA). 2006. 29.95 (978-0-7861-4386-3(X)) Blckstn Audio.

Letters to a Young Poet. unabr. ed. Read by Stephen Mitchell. Tr. by Stephen Mitchell. Ed. by Rainer Maria Rilke. 1 cass. (Running Time: 1 hr. 15 min.). (Spiritual Classics Ser.). 1995. 10.95 (978-0-944993-11-8(7)) Audio Lit.
Seen through Rilke's eyes, everyday difficulties love, sex, solitude, sadness & doubt become the archetypal elements of the human drama we are all called to live. He challenges us "...to live everything. Live the questions now. Perhaps then, someday far in the future, you will gradually, without even noticing it, live your way into the answers".

Letters to a Young Teacher. unabr. ed. Jonathan Kozol. Read by David Drummond. (YA). 2008. 54.99 (978-1-60514-787-1(7)) Find a World.

Letters to a Young Teacher. unabr. ed. Jonathan Kozol. Read by David Drummond. 5 CDs. (Running Time: 5 hrs. 30 mins. 0 sec.). (ENG.). 2007. audio compact disk 29.99 (978-1-4001-0546-5(3)); audio compact disk 59.99 (978-1-4001-3546-2(X)); audio compact disk 19.99 (978-1-4001-5546-0(0)) Pub: Tantor Media. Dist(s): IngramPubServ

Letters to an Endangered Species I. Raymond Karczewski. 1 cass. (Running Time: 45 min.). 1994. 10.00 incl. dustcover. (978-0-9638391-1-4(X)) Ark Enter.
An insightful examination into the deterioration of modern day man through psychological pressure. Subjects: power, freedom, intelligence, government & religion.

Letters to an Endangered Species II. Raymond Karczewski. 1 cass. (Running Time: 45 min.). 1994. 10.00 incl. dustcover. (978-0-9638391-3-8(6)) Ark Enter.
Powerful & incisive in its penetration into the collective mind. Subjects: Children of God, reality, mind control, & balance.

Letters to an Endangered Species III. Raymond Karczewski. 1 cass. (Running Time: 45 min.). 1994. 10.00 (978-0-9638391-4-5(4)) Ark Enter.
A powerful & insightful examination into the deterioration of modern day man through psychological pressure. Subjects: The Emperor Is Naked, Communication, The Civilized Mind, Wimpy's Dilemma.

Letters to an Endangered Species IV. Raymond Karczewski. 1 cass. (Running Time: 45 min.). 1994. 10.00 (978-0-9638391-5-2(2)) Ark Enter.
A powerful & insightful examination into the deterioration of modern day man through psychological pressure.

Letters to Churches: Timeless Lessons for the Body of Christ. 1998. 25.95 (978-1-57972-240-1(7)) Insight Living.

Letters to Ebay: Hilarious Emails, Crazy Auctions, & Bongos for Grandma. abr. ed. Art Farkas. 2007. 4.98 (978-1-60024-197-0(2)) Pub: Hachet Audio. Dist(s): HachBkGrp

Letters to Gabriel: The True Story of Gabriel Michael Santorum. Karen Garver Santorum. 1 cass. 1998. bk. 14.99 (978-1-56814-528-0(4)) CCC of America.
Gabriel Michael's short, but meaningful time on earth & a tribute to the sanctity of life, the deep faith of the Santorums, & the power of love & family.

Letters to Gabriel: The True Story of Gabriel Michael Santorum. Karen Garver Santorum. Frwd. by Mother Teresa of Calcutta. Intro. by Laura Schlessinger. Illus. by Leah Campos. 1 cass. 1998. 19.99 (978-1-56814-530-3(6)) CCC of America.

***Letters to God.** Patrick Doughtie & John Perry. (Running Time: 6 hrs. 20 mins. 11 sec.). (Letters to God Ser.). (ENG.). 2010. 14.99 (978-0-310-59737-7(4)) Zondervan.

Letters to His Son. unabr. ed. Lord Chesterfield. Read by Robert L. Halvorson. 5 cass. (Running Time: 7 hrs. 30 mins). 35.95 (44) Halvorson Assocs.

***Letters to His Son-1746-1747: On the Fine Art of becoming a MAN of the WORLD & a GENTLEMAN.** Lord Chesterfield. Narrated by David Thorn. Engineer Bobbie Frohman. (ENG.). 2006. audio compact disk 17.95 (978-0-9843490-3-6(0)) Alcazar AudioWorks.

***Letters to Malcolm: Chiefly on Prayer.** unabr. ed. C. S. Lewis. Read by Ralph Cosham. (Running Time: 4 hrs. 30 mins.). 2010. 19.95 (978-1-4417-6295-5(7)); 34.95 (978-1-4417-6292-4(2)); audio compact disk 49.00 (978-1-4417-6293-1(0)); audio compact disk 24.95 (978-1-4417-6294-8(9)) Blckstn Audio.

Letters to My Daughters. abr. ed. Mary Matalin. 2004. 15.95 (978-0-7435-4319-4(X)) Pub: S&S Audio. Dist(s): S and S Inc

***Letters to Sam: A Grandfather's Lessons on Love, Loss, & the Gifts of Life.** unabr. ed. Daniel Gottlieb. (Running Time: 3 hrs. 48 mins.). (ENG.). 2010. 24.98 (978-1-59659-596-5(5), GildAudio) Pub: Gildan Media. Dist(s): HachBkGrp

Letters to Seven Churches. Chuck Missler. 2 cass. (Running Time: 3 hrs.). 1999. 14.95 Koinonia Hse.
The Book of Acts covers about 30 years; Chapters 2 & 3 of the Book of Revelations cover the next 2,000. This study explores the seven letters by Jesus Christ to actual historical churches & the church age they represent. Also includes many insightful personal applications as we apply each letter to ourselves.

Letters to the Churches see Cartas a las Iglesias

Letters to the President. Ed. by Trevor McNevan. Contrib. by Hawk Nelson. Prod. by Aaron Sprinkle. 2005. audio compact disk 13.98 (978-5-558-78000-0(2)) Tooth & Nail.

Letters to the Seven Churches. Chuck Missler. 2 CD's. (Running Time: 120 mins.). (Briefing Packages by Chuck Missler). 1993. audio compact disk 19.95 (978-1-57821-299-6(5)) Koinonia Hse.
The Book of Acts covers about 30 years; Chapters 2 and 3 of the Book of Revelation cover the next 2,000.This study will explore the seven letters by Jesus Christ to actual historical churches and the church ages they represent. These letters describe, with amazing precision, the unfolding of all church history in advance. This chronicle fills the gap between the 69th and 70th Week of Daniel.We will also find many insightful personal applications as we apply each letter to ourselves.Four Levels of Application:1: Local: actual, historic churches with validated needs, and so on. Archeological discoveries have confirmed this.2: Admonitory: "Hear what the Spirit says to the churches." Applies to all churches throughout history. Any church can be "mapped" in terms of these seven characteristics.3: Homiletic: personal. "He that hath an ear let him hear..." each letter applies to each of us. There is some element of each of the "churches" in everyone of us; perhaps the most important application of the entire book.4: Prophetic: These letters describe, with amazing precision, the unfolding of all church history. In any other order, this would not be true. (This chronicle fills the "gap" between the 69th and 70th Week of Daniel. The Book of Acts covers about 30 years, chapters 2&3 of the Book of Revelation covers the next 2,000.).

Letters to the Seven Churches. Chuck Missler. 2 cass., set. (Running Time: 1 hr. 30 min.). 1993. vinyl bd. 14.95 (978-1-880532-87-4(5)) Koinonia Hse.
In this study Chuck Missler explores the seven letters by Jesus Christ to actual historical churches.

Letters to Young Black Men. Danie Whyte. (ENG.). 2008. audio compact disk 13.99 (978-0-9785333-6-6(4)) Pub: Torch Legacy. Dist(s): STL Dist NA

Letters to Your Unconscious. Contrib. by Nick Kemp. (Running Time: 37 mins.). audio compact disk 24.95 (978-0-9545993-1-7(4)) Pub: Human Alchemy GBR. Dist(s): Crown Hse

Letting Go! 1 cass. (Running Time: 45 min.). (Relationship Ser.). 9.98 (978-1-55909-053-7(7), 50); 9.98 90 min. extended length stereo music. (978-1-55909-054-4(5), 50X) Randolph Tapes.
Teaches how to 'let-go' of unhealthy attachments. Subliminal messages are heard 3-5 minutes before becoming ocean sounds or music.

Letting Go. Swami Amar Jyoti. 1 cass. Orig. Title: Spirituality is Scientific. 1977. 9.95 (B-14) Truth Consciousness.
The real meaning of letting go. Detachment on the spiritual path. Mastery of nature by good & evil forces.

Letting Go. Pam Rhodes. Read by Julia Franklin. 10 cass. (Sound Ser.). (J). 2002. 84.95 (978-1-84283-222-6(0)) Pub: ISIS Lrg Prnt GBR. Dist(s): Ulverscroft US

Letting Go. Perf. by Lori Wilke. 1 cass. (Running Time: 4 min.). 1998. 9.98 Music sound track. (978-1-891916-36-6(X)) Spirit To Spirit.

Letting Go. unabr. ed. Philip Roth. Read by Luke Daniels. (Running Time: 26 hrs.). 2009. 44.97 (978-1-4418-0114-2(6), 9781441801142, Brlnc Audio MP3 Lib); 44.97 (978-1-4418-0116-6(2), 9781441801166, BADLE); 29.99 (978-1-4418-0115-9(4), 9781441801159, BAD); 29.99 (978-1-4418-0113-5(8), 9781441801135, Brilliance MP3); audio compact disk 99.97 (978-1-4418-0112-8(X), 9781441801128, BriAudCD Unabrid); audio compact disk 39.99 (978-1-4418-0111-1(1), 9781441801111, Bril Audio CD Unabri) Brilliance Audio.

Letting Go: A Spirituality of Subtraction. Richard Rohr. 8 cass. (Running Time: 8 hrs.). 2001. 64.95 (A4200) St Anthony Mess Pr.
In our culture, "the good life" means getting more. This series challenges listeners to subtract - that is, to release whatever hinders us from siding with the cosmic Christ, whether that be in our inner world or outer world.

Letting Go & Becoming. Marianne Williamson. 4 CDs. 2004. audio compact disk 23.95 (978-1-4019-0407-4(6)) Hay House.

Letting Go & Becoming. Marianne Williamson. 4 cass. (Running Time: 4 hrs.). 1998. 25.00 (978-1-56170-581-8(0), M862) Hay House.
Lectures on letting go, spirituality, forgiveness & more.

Letting Go & Becoming. Marianne Williamson. 4 CDs. 2004. audio compact disk 23.95 (978-1-4019-0456-2(4)) Hay House.

Letting Go, Moving On: Comforting Meditations to Help Heal Grief, Divorce & Separation. Lucinda Drayton. (Simple Truths Ser.). 2007. audio compact disk 17.95 (978-1-905835-05-8(1)) Divinit Pubing GBR.

Letting Go of Anger - Living Peacefully. Scott Sulak. 2 cass. (Running Time: 2 hrs.). 1998. 15.00 (978-1-932659-00-9(5)) Change For Gd.

Letting Go of Anxiety. 2007. audio compact disk 19.95 (978-1-56136-122-9(4)) Master Your Mind.

Letting Go of Chocolate. Read by Mary Richards. (Subliminal Impact Ser.). 12.95 (629) Master Your Mind.
Discusses how to rid your life of chocolate.

Letting Go of Judgment: Entering the Stately Calm Within. Kenneth Wapnick. 3 CDs. 2004. audio compact disk 20.00 (978-1-59142-127-6(6), CD92) Foun Miracles.
These classes were part of a two-day Academy program entitled "Letting Go of Judgment," held at the Foundation in November 2003. A major focus of these classes was on turning to the "stately calm within" whenever tempted to judge others. We learn from Jesus that choosing to attack and condemn others leads to our pain-the cost of the belief in victimization-while letting go of judgment brings us peace. Judgment is seen as a "cosmic setup," wherein we seek to justify our thoughts of separation and differences, serving the ego's hidden agenda of proving that its separation from God is real. Bringing this agenda to Jesus' gentle forgiveness lets the pain of our judgments go, to be replaced by the peace and love of the stately calm within.

***Letting Go of Judgment: Entering the Stately Calm Within.** Kenneth Wapnick. 2010. 16.00 (978-1-59142-474-1(7)) Foun Miracles.

Letting Go of Relationships: Cutting the Cord. Patricia O'Malley. Perf. by Barry Weiss. 1 cass. (Running Time: 50 min.). 1998. 11.95 (978-1-892450-17-3(8), 140) Pub: Promo Music. Dist(s): Penton Overseas
It's time to move on & to rid & release yourself of relationships that cause you stress, pain & distress. Freedom is the goal.

Letting Go of Self-Protection: 2007 CCEF Annual Conference. Featuring Jayne Clara. 2007. audio compact disk 11.99 (978-1-934885-09-3(6)) New Growth Pr.

Letting Go of Stress. 1 cassette. (Running Time: 79:47 mins.). 1980. 12.95 (978-1-55841-023-7(6)) Emmett E Miller.
Four guided imagery and deep relaxation experiences teach powerful techniques for melting away stress and its symptoms. Learn to use progressive relaxation, autogenic self-suggestion, creative visualization and treat yourself to everyone's favorite, "A Trip to the Beach". Dr. Miller's incredibly relaxing voice, at its best here, is enhanced by a beautiful,, specially composed score performed by famed musician, Steven Halpern. No healing library is complete without this one!.

Letting Go of Stress. Michael P. Kelly. 1 cass. 1992. 14.95 (978-1-883700-04-1(3)) ThoughtForms.
Self help.

Letting Go of Stress. Emmett E. Miller & Steven Halpern. 1 cass. (YA). (gr. 9 up). 1989. 5.60 Brown & Benchmark.
To accompany "Comprehensive Stress Management," 3rd Edition by Jerrold S. Greenberg. A well-known collection of effective stress reduction techniques, widely used in stress management programs. This program is free to adoptors of Greenberg: Comprehensive Stress Management.

Letting Go of Stress: Four Effective Techniques for Relaxation & Stress Reduction. Emmett E. Miller. Read by Emmett E. Miller. 1 cass. (Running Time: 1 hr.). 1996. 10.00 (978-1-56170-368-5(0), 393) Hay House.
Release stress through 4 amazingly effective techniques.

Letting Go of Stuff. unabr. ed. Darren Johnson. 1 cass. (Running Time: 45 min.). 1995. 6.95 (978-0-9652307-0-4(8)) InsideOut Learning.
Teaches how to manage "self" as challenges/changes in life create obstacles to reaching goals & fulfilling dreams.

Letting Go of Tension. Layne A. Longfellow. Read by Layne A. Longfellow. 1 cass. 1986. 12.00 Lect Theatre.
Teaches muscle relaxation & basic meditation.

Letting Go of the Conditioned Mind. Swami Amar Jyoti. 1 dolby cass. 1984. 9.95 (J-47) Truth Consciousness.
Wisdom awakens in the relaxed mind; stopping the struggle & applying the solutions. The need for real change in ourselves, which comes only from within.

Letting Go of the Past. Speeches. Joel Osteen. 1 Cass. (Running Time: 30 Mins.). 2002. 6.00 (978-1-59349-146-8(8), JA0146) J Osteen.

Letting Go of the Past. Speeches. Joel Osteen. 3 audio cass. (J). 2002. 12.00 (978-1-931877-19-0(X), JAS015) J Osteen.

Letting Go of the Past - Up from Depression. Robert E. Griswold. Read by Robert E. Griswold. 1 cass. (Super Strength Ser.). 1992. 10.95 (978-1-55848-304-0(7)) EffectiveMN.
Two non-subliminal programs that help overcome past negative events & get a fresh start.

***Letting Go of the Past + Up from Depression: Overcome Past Negative Events & Get a Fresh Start With the Help of These Powerful & Enjoyable Audio Programs.** Robert E. Griswold. 2003. audio compact disk 14.95 (978-1-55848-104-6(4)) EffectiveMN.

Letting Go of Your Bananas. unabr. ed. Daniel Drubin. Read by Alan Sklar. (Running Time: 3 hrs. 0 mins. 0 sec.). (ENG.). 2006. audio compact disk 19.99 (978-1-4001-0322-5(3)) Pub: Tantor Media. Dist(s): IngramPubServ

Letting Go of Your Bananas: How to Become More Successful by Getting Rid of Everything in Your Life. unabr. ed. Daniel T. Drubin. Read by Alan Sklar. (Running Time: 3 hrs. 0 mins. 0 sec.). (ENG.). 2006. audio compact disk 19.99 (978-1-4001-5322-0(0)); audio compact disk 39.99 (978-1-4001-3322-2(X)) Pub: Tantor Media. Dist(s): IngramPubServ

Letting Go of Your Ended Love Relationship. Michael Broder. 1 cass. 14.95 (C053) A Ellis Institute.
This interactive tape program takes you through the important steps you'll need to help you pick up the pieces of an ended love relationship. Includes many helpful exercises.

Letting Go of Your Ended Love Relationship. Michael Broder. 1 cass. 14.95 (C053) Inst Rational-Emotive.

Letting Go with Love: The Grieving Process. 2007. audio compact disk (978-0-9613714-9-4(8)) La Mariposa.

Letting Go with Love: The Grieving Process. abr. ed. Nancy D. O'Connor. Read by Nancy D. O'Connor. 2 cass. (Running Time: 2 hrs.).Tr. of Dejalos Ir con Amor. 1984. vinyl bd. 15.95 (978-0-9613714-3-2(9)) La Mariposa.
A self-help guidebook that explains the grieving process in everyday terms, & looks at the challenges of recovering from every type of loss through death, including: death of a spouse, parents, children, siblings, friends, suicide, abortion, miscarriage, one's own death, etc. It also covers the depersonalization of dying, the stages & feelings of grief, individual coping style, & techniques for handling loss.

Letting Go/Commitment to Joy. Marianne Williamson. Read by Marianne Williamson. 1 cass. (Running Time: 90 mins.). (Lectures on a Course in Miracles). 1999. 10.00 (978-1-56170-240-4(4), M743) Hay House.

Letting Happiness In: The Fine Art of Stretching Your Comfort Zone. David Grudermeyer & Rebecca Grudermeyer. 2 cass. suppl. ed. 18.95 (T-21) Willingness Wrks.

***Letting in the Jungle: A Story from the Jungle Books.** Rudyard Kipling. 2009. (978-1-60136-509-5(8)) Audio Holding.

Lettre a Francois Rollinat see Treasury of French Prose

Lettre à une Mère. unabr. ed. René Frydman. Read by Dominique Vovk. (YA). 2007. 69.99 (978-2-35569-091-4(X)) Find a World.

Lettres see Treasury of French Prose

Lettres a Sa Fille. Madame de Sevigne. Read by Juliette Greco. 1 cass. (FRE.). 1991. 24.95 (1136-EF) Olivia & Hill.
Mme de Sevigne's lively letters reporting daily life & gossip at the court of Louis XIV to her daughter, Madame de Grigan, have set standards for the epistolary style.

Lettres de la Religieuse Portugaise. Read by Elisabeth De Berts. 1 cass. (FRE.). 1991. 17.95 (1466-DI) Olivia & Hill.
Five letters written by a Portuguese nun to her lover, a French officer, who has deserted her.

Lettres de Mon Moulin see Treasury of French Prose

Lettres de Mon Moulin. Alphonse Daudet. 3 cass. (Running Time: 3 hrs.).Tr. of Letters from My Windmill. (FRE.). 1996. 39.50 (978-1-58085-357-6(9)) Interlingua VA.

Lettres de Mon Moulin. Short Stories. Alphonse Daudet. Read by Henri Tisot et al. 2 cass.Tr. of Letters from My Windmill. (FRE.). 1991. 26.95 (1041-H) Olivia & Hill.
Famous collection of tales set in Provence.

lettres de mon Moulin. unabr. ed. Alphonse Daudet. Read by Yves Belluardo. (J). 2007. 69.99 (978-2-35569-047-1(2)) Find a World.

Lettres de Mon Moulin, Vol. 1. unabr. ed. Alphonse Daudet. Read by Georges Riquier. 1 cass.Tr. of Letters from My Windmill. (FRE.). 11.95 (978-0-8045-0931-2(X), SAC 7176) Spoken Arts.
The Stories of "La Chevre de M. Seguin" & "Le Secret de Maitre Cornille.".

Lettres de Mon Moulin, Vol. 11. unabr. ed. Alphonse Daudet. Read by Georges Riquier. 1 cass.Tr. of Letters from My Windmill. (FRE.). 11.95 (978-0-8045-0932-9(8), SAC 7177) Spoken Arts.
"La Mule du Pape.".

Lettres Persanes see Treasury of French Prose

Lettres persanes. Charles de Secondat Montesquieu. 4 cass. (FRE.). 1992. 36.95 (1590-LV) Olivia & Hill.
This collection of imaginary letters written & received by two Persians who visit Paris in the 1720s provided the author with a vehicle to criticize a great variety of social problems of his time. Selected letters read by a group of actors.

Lettuce Delights Cookbook: A Collection of Lettuce Recipes. Karen Jean Matsko Hood. 2005. audio compact disk 13.95 (978-1-59649-973-7(7)) Whspmg Pine.

Lettuce Delights Journal: A Daily Journal. Karen Jean Matsko Hood. 2005. audio compact disk Rental 13.95 (978-1-59649-978-2(8)) Whsprng Pine.

Lettuce Delights Menu Cookbook: A Collection of Lettuce-themed Menus. Karen Jean Matsko Hood. 2005. audio compact disk 13.95 (978-1-59649-981-2(8)) Whsprng Pine.

Levántate y Resplandece. unabr. ed. Torre Fuerte & Heriberto Hermosillo. (SPA.). 1999. 7.99 (978-0-8297-2530-8(X)) Pub: Vida Pubs. Dist(s): Zondervan

Levántate y Resplandece. unabr. ed. Heriberto Hermosillo. 1999. audio compact disk 11.99 (978-0-8297-2531-5(8)) Zondervan.

Levantine Arabic. Ernest N. McCarus et al. 10 cass. 1978. 81.98 Set. U MI Lang Res.

Levantine Arabic Pronunciation. unabr. ed. Foreign Service Institute Staff. 10 cass. (Running Time: 9 hrs. 30 mins.). (ARA.). (YA). (gr. 10-12). 1972. pap. bk. 225.00 (978-0-88432-038-8(3), AFA244) J Norton Pubs.
This course is intended only as an introduction to pronunciation for the urban dialects of Lebanon, Syria & Jordan.

Levantine Arabic Pronunciation CDs & Text. 10 CDs. (Running Time: 9 hrs. 30 mins.). (Foreign Service Institute Basic Course Ser.). (ARA.). 2005. audio compact disk 225.00 (978-1-57970-164-2(7), AFA244D) J Norton Pubs.

Level II Trading Warfare: The Underground Trader's Powerful Weapons for Winning. Instructed by Jea Yu. 1 cass. (Running Time: 90 mins.). (Trade Secrets Audio Ser.). 2002. 19.95 (978-1-931611-73-2(4)) Marketplace Bks.
This exciting new video shares the tools accomplished trader, Jea Yu, uses to determine the trend, find precise entry points and his preferred method for placing orders in Level II trading. It also explains what noodles, cranks and cross locks are - and why they're so important for Level II traders. If you're looking to find out why day traders fail - and how to avoid falling into the same trap - this is a must see video!.

Level of Human Consciousness. unabr. ed. Robert A. Monroe. Read by Robert A. Monroe. (Running Time: 45 min.). (Explorer Ser.). 1983. 12.95 (978-1-56113-011-5(7), 12) Monroe Institute.
Explorer reports on travels & communications with other entities.

Level One: Accordion see Primer Nivel: Acordeon

Level One: Bass see Primer Nivel: Bajo

Level One: Chorus/Singing see Primer Nivel: Canto

Level One: Drums see Primer Nivel: Bateria

Level One: Harmony see Primer Nivel: Armonia

Level One: Reading/Writing Music see Primer Nivel: Solfeo

Level One: Saxophone see Primer Nivel: Saxofon

Level One: Six String Bass see Primer Nivel: Bajo Sexto

Level One: Trumpet see Primer Nivel: Trompeta

Level One: Violin see Primer Nivel: Violin

Level 1 Introductory CD. 2001. audio compact disk 15.00 (978-1-58561-050-1(X)) Shurley Inst Mats.

Level 2 Introductory CD. 2001. audio compact disk 15.00 (978-1-58561-046-4(1)) Shurley Inst Mats.

Level 3 Introductory CD. 2001. audio compact disk 15.00 (978-1-58561-042-6(9)) Shurley Inst Mats.

Level 3 Practice CDs. 2001. audio compact disk 25.00 (978-1-58561-043-3(7)) Shurley Inst Mats.

Level 4: Virus Hunters of the CDC. Joseph B. McCormick et al. 1999. audio compact disk (978-0-7607-1211-5(5)) Barnes & Noble Inc.

Level 4 Introductory CD. 2001. audio compact disk 15.00 (978-1-58561-038-9(0)) Shurley Inst Mats.

Level 4 Practice CDs. 2001. audio compact disk 25.00 (978-1-58561-039-6(9)) Shurley Inst Mats.

Level 5 Introductory CD. 2001. audio compact disk 15.00 (978-1-58561-034-1(8)) Shurley Inst Mats.

Level 5 Practice CDs. 2001. audio compact disk 25.00 (978-1-58561-035-8(6)) Shurley Inst Mats.

Level 6 Introductory CD. 2001. audio compact disk 15.00 (978-1-58561-030-3(5)) Shurley Inst Mats.

Level 6 Practice CDs. 2001. audio compact disk 25.00 (978-1-58561-031-0(3)) Shurley Inst Mats.

Level 7 Introductory CD. 1995. audio compact disk 12.00 (978-1-58561-014-3(3)) Shurley Inst Mats.

***Leveled Readers, Grade 1 Level Red.** Created by Harcourt School Publishers. (Leveled Readers Ser.). (ENG.). 2006. audio compact disk (978-0-15-358683-5(4)) Harcourt Schl Pubs.

Levels of Conciousness: Realms of the Masters. George King. 2006. audio compact disk (978-0-937249-31-4(9)) Aetherius Soc.

Levels of Consciousnessâ€"the Spirit Worlds. 2006. audio compact disk (978-0-937249-30-7(0)) Aetherius Soc.

Levels of Human Development. Andrew Cusack. 1 cass. (Running Time: 1 hr. 01 min.). 1995. 8.95 (TAH342) Alba Hse Comns.
Realizing the uniqueness in individuals will allow the priest to relate with them in a truly human way. The priest must look at others from the perspective that they are not problems to be solved, but rather that each individual is a mystery to be discovered - an expression of the love of God.

Levels of Love. Swami Amar Jyoti. 1 cass. 1979. 9.95 (K-23) Truth Consciousness.
The stages of love. What is soul & soulmate? Love between Guru & disciple. Paying the price on all levels.

Levels of the Game. unabr. ed. John McPhee. Read by Walter Zimmerman. 5 cass. (Running Time: 5 hrs.). 1989. 30.00 (978-0-7366-1572-3(5), 2439) Books on Tape.
Levels of the Game is a narrative of a tennis match played by Arthur Ashe & Clark Graebner at Forest Hills. The book begins with the ball rising into the air for the initial serve, & ends with the final point. McPhee provides a stroke-by-stroke description. Also, he examines each player's background & shows how it has molded his game. Ashe thinks that Graebner, being a middle-class dentist's son from Cleveland, plays stiff & compact Republican tennis. Graebner will acknowledge that this is true, & for his part thinks that Ashe, being black & from Richmond, will have a game that is bold, loose, liberal, flat-out Democratic. When physical assets are about equal, psychology is paramount to any game.

Leven Thumps & the Eyes of the Want. Obert Skye. (Leven Thumps Ser.: Bk. 3). (J). 2007. audio compact disk 39.95 (978-1-59038-822-8(4)) Deseret Bk.

Leven Thumps & the Gateway to Foo. Obert Skye. (Leven Thumps Ser.: Bk. 1). (J). 2005. audio compact disk 29.95 (978-1-59038-408-4(3), Shadow Mount) Deseret Bk.

Leven Thumps & the Gateway to Foo. unabr. ed. Obert Skye. Read by E. B. Stevens. (Leven Thumps Ser.: Bk. 1). (J). 2006. 20.95 (978-0-7435-6201-0(1)) Pub: S&S Audio. Dist(s): S and S Inc

Leven Thumps & the Gateway to Foo. unabr. abr. ed. Obert Skye. Read by E. B. Stevens. (Running Time: 10 hrs. 30 mins. 0 sec.). Bk. 1. (J). (gr. 4-7). 2006. audio compact disk 34.95 (978-0-7435-6200-3(3)) Pub: S&S Audio. Dist(s): S and S Inc

Leven Thumps & the Ruins of Alder. Obert Skye. (Leven Thumps Ser.: Bk. 5). 2009. audio compact disk 39.95 (978-1-60641-158-2(6), Shadow Mount) Deseret Bk.

Leven Thumps & the Whispered Secret. Obert Skye. (Leven Thumps Ser.: Bk. 2). (J). 2006. audio compact disk 39.95 (978-1-59038-514-2(4), Shadow Mount) Deseret Bk.

Leven Thumps & the Whispered Secret. unabr. ed. Obert Skye. Read by E. B. Stevens. (Leven Thumps Ser.: Bk. 2). (J). 2006. 23.95 (978-0-7435-6203-4(8)) Pub: S&S Audio. Dist(s): S and S Inc

Leven Thumps & the Whispered Secret. unabr. abr. ed. Obert Skye. Read by E. B. Stevens. (Running Time: 11 hrs. 30 mins. 0 sec.). Bk. 2. (J). (gr. 4-7). 2006. audio compact disk 39.95 (978-0-7435-6202-7(X)) Pub: S&S Audio. Dist(s): S and S Inc

Leven Thumps & the Wrath of Ezra. Obert Skye. (Leven Thumps Ser.: Bk. 4). 2008. audio compact disk 39.95 (978-1-59038-979-9(4), Shadow Mount) Deseret Bk.

***Leverage.** unabr. ed. Joshua C. Cohen. (Running Time: 9.5 hrs. NaN mins.). (ENG.). 2011. 29.95 (978-1-4417-7532-0(3)); 59.95 (978-1-4417-7529-0(3)); audio compact disk 29.95 (978-1-4417-7531-3(5)) Blckstn Audio.

***Leverage (Library Edition)** unabr. ed. Joshua C. Cohen. (Running Time: 9.5 hrs. NaN mins.). 2011. audio compact disk 90.00 (978-1-4417-7530-6(7)) Blckstn Audio.

Leveraging Technology for Your Legislative Campaigns: Effectively Using E-Newsletters, Email Alerts, Podcasts, & Your Website. Ed. by TheCapitol.Net. 2006. 107.00 (978-1-58733-035-3(0)) TheCapitol.

Leveraging Technology in Your Office: The in's & Out's of Blogs & Blogging. Ed. by TheCapitol.Net. 2005. audio compact disk 107.00 (978-1-58733-028-5(8)) TheCapitol.

Leveraging the Universe & Engaging the Magic. unabr. abr. ed. Mike Dooley. Read by Mike Dooley. 4 CDs. (Running Time: 5 hrs. 0 mins. 0 sec.). (ENG.). 2008. audio compact disk 29.95 (978-0-7435-7139-5(8)) Pub: S&S Audio. Dist(s): S and S Inc

Leviathan. George H. Smith. Read by Craig Deitschman. (Running Time: 9000 sec.). (Giants of Political Thought Ser.). 2006. audio compact disk 25.95 (978-0-7861-6981-8(8)) Pub: Blckstn Audio. Dist(s): NetLibrary CO

Leviathan. abr. ed. Thomas Hobbes. Read by Craig Deitschmann. 2 cass. (Running Time: 2 hrs.). Dramatization. (Giants of Political Thought Ser.: Vol. 10). 1986. 17.95 (978-0-938935-10-0(0), 390278) Knowledge Prod.
This work contains one of the most compelling arguments ever set forth in favor of a strong, centralized government. Although condemned by many political theorists, this powerful book continues to fascinate. The presentation includes ideas of this classic work, with a narrative explanation of the author's character, his times, the controversies he faced & the opinions of critics & supporters.

Leviathan. unabr. ed. Thomas Hobbes. Read by Robert L. Halvorson. 2 cass. (Running Time: 2 hrs. 30 mins). 14.95 (34) Halvorson Assocs.

Leviathan. unabr. ed. Scott Westerfeld. Read by Alan Cumming. 7 CDs. (Running Time: 8 hrs.). (Leviathan Trilogy: Bk. 1). (YA). 2009. audio compact disk 29.99 (978-0-7435-8388-6(4)) Pub: S&S Audio. Dist(s): S and S Inc

Leviathan: The History of Whaling in America. Eric Jay Dolin. Read by James Boles. (Playaway Adult Nonfiction Ser.). (ENG.). 2008. 69.99 (978-1-60640-705-9(8)) Find a World.

Leviathan: The History of Whaling in America. unabr. ed. Eric Jay Dolin. Read by James Boles. 13 CDs. (Running Time: 16 hrs. 0 mins. 0 sec.). (ENG.). 2007. audio compact disk 39.99 (978-1-4001-0484-0(X)); audio compact disk 79.99 (978-1-4001-3484-7(6)); audio compact disk 29.99 (978-1-4001-5484-5(7)) Pub: Tantor Media. Dist(s): IngramPubServ

Leviathan: Thomas Hobbes. abr. ed. Wendy McElroy. Narrated by Craig Deitschman. 2 cass. (Running Time: 2 hrs.). Dramatization. (Audio Classics Ser.: Vol. 10). 1986. 17.95 (978-0-938935-11-7(9), 390291) Knowledge Prod.

***Leviathans of Jupiter.** unabr. ed. Ben Bova. Read by To be announced. (Running Time: 15 hrs. NaN mins.). (Grand Tour Ser.). (ENG.). 2011. 29.95 (978-1-4417-8124-6(2)) Blckstn Audio.

***Leviathans of Jupiter.** unabr. ed. Ben Bova. Read by To be Announced. (Running Time: 15 hrs. NaN mins.). (Grand Tour Ser.). (ENG.). 2011. 85.95 (978-1-4417-8121-5(8)) Blckstn Audio.

***Leviathans of Jupiter.** unabr. ed. Ben Bova. Read by To be announced. (Running Time: 15 hrs. NaN mins.). (Grand Tour Ser.). 2011. audio compact disk 34.95 (978-1-4417-8123-9(4)) Blckstn Audio.

***Leviathans of Jupiter.** unabr. ed. Ben Bova. Read by To be Announced. (Running Time: 15 hrs. NaN mins.). (Grand Tour Ser.). (ENG.). 2011. audio compact disk 118.00 (978-1-4417-8122-2(6)) Blckstn Audio.

Levite Genes. Kathie Hill. 1997. 75.00 (978-0-7673-9013-2(X)) LifeWay Christian.

Levite Genes Cassette Promo Pak. Kathie Hill. 1997. 8.00 (978-0-7673-9052-1(0)) LifeWay Christian.

Levite Genes Choir Cassette. Kathie Hill. 1997. 11.98 (978-0-7673-9007-1(5)) LifeWay Christian.

Levite Genes Stereo/Split Acc Cd. Kathie Hill. 1997. audio compact disk 85.00 (978-0-7673-9027-9(X)) LifeWay Christian.

Leviticus Commentary. Chuck Missler. 1 MP3 CD-ROM. (Running Time: 16 hours). (Chuck Missler Commentaries). 2002. cd-rom 39.95 (978-1-57821-191-3(3)) Koinonia Hse.
It may come as a surprise to discover that there are a number of Biblical experts who regard the Book of Leviticus as the most important book of the Bible! The Book of Leviticus cannot be "read;" it has to be studied. But fasten your seat belts! It's going to be an exciting and highly privileged excursion!.

Levity Effect: Why It Pays to Lighten Up. unabr. ed. Scott Christopher & Adrian Gostick. Read by Scott Christopher. (Running Time: 19800 sec.). 2008. 34.95 (978-1-4332-1229-1(3)); audio compact disk 29.95 (978-1-4332-1233-8(1)); audio compact disk & audio compact disk 50.00 (978-1-4332-1230-7(7)) Blckstn Audio.

Levity Effect: Why It Pays to Lighten Up. unabr. ed. Adrian Gostick. (Running Time: 7 hrs. 0 mins.). (ENG.). 2008. audio compact disk 24.95 (978-1-4332-1232-1(3)) Blckstn Audio.

Levity Effect: Why It Pays to Lighten Up. unabr. ed. Adrian Gostick & Scott Christopher. Read by Scott Christopher. (Running Time: 19800 sec.). (ENG.). 2008. 24.95 (978-1-4332-1231-4(5)) Blckstn Audio.

Lew Wallace: Boy Writer. Martha E. Schaaf. Read by Patrick G. Lawlor. (Running Time: 7200 sec.). (Young Patriots Ser.). (J). (gr. 4-7). 2007. 22.95 (978-1-4332-0147-9(X)); audio compact disk 24.00 (978-1-4332-0148-6(8)) Blckstn Audio.

Lew Wallace: Boy Writer. unabr. ed. Martha E. Schaaf. Read by Patrick G. Lawlor. (Young Patriots Ser.). (J). 2007. 34.99 (978-1-60252-665-5(6)) Find a World.

Lewis & Clark: Songs of the Journey. Perf. by Bobby Horton. Arranged by Bobby Horton. Composed by Kindra Ankney. Lyrics by Kindra Ankney. 2001. audio compact disk 15.00 (978-0-9708434-0-1(2)) Edge-Of-Woods.

Lewis & Clark: Sounds of Discovery. Contrib. by Lisa Dowhaniuk. 1 cass. (Running Time: 61 mins.). 1998. 9.98 (978-0-9650872-4-7(7), MM0150C); audio compact disk 14.98 (978-0-9650872-3-0(9), MM0150D) Scoria.
A journey recreating songs & sounds as they may have been heard by the members of the Corps of Discovery. The journey begins in Washington D.C. in 1802 & follows the route of the expedition to the west coast & back.

Lewis & Clark: The Final Steps. Ed. by Laura Reeves. Narrated by Peter B. Lewis. Prod. by Peter B. Lewis. 1 cass. (Running Time: 30 min.). Vol. #10. 2001. 15.95 (978-1-930827-21-9(0), Car Tours) Audisee Sound.
Take your family and friends on a driving tour of Lewis and Clark's final steps to the Pacific Coast.

Lewis & Clark: The Great American Expedition. unabr. ed. Joe Loesch. Read by Ron Jordan. (YA). 2008. 54.99 (978-1-60252-980-9(9)) Find a World.

Lewis & Clark Vol. 10: The Final Steps. Laura Reeves. Narrated by Peter B. Lewis. Prod. by Peter B. Lewis. 2001. audio compact disk 19.95 (978-1-930827-11-0(3), Car Tours) Audisee Sound.

Lewis & Clark Expedition. Kenneth Bruce. 1 cass. (Running Time: 1 hr.). Dramatization. (Excursions in History Ser.). 12.50 Alpha Tape.
Exploring the west.

Lewis & Clark Expedition. Cerebellum Academic Team. (Running Time: 30 mins.). (Just the Facts Ser.). 2010. 24.95 (978-1-59163-390-7(7)) Cerebellum.

Lewis & Clark Journals. Gary E. Moulton & Patrick Cullen. 14 cass. (Running Time: 19 hrs. 30 mins.). 2002. 89.95 (978-0-7861-2818-1(6), 3342) Blckstn Audio.

Lewis & Clark Trail of Discovery: Final Steps. Laura Reeves. Read by Peter B. Lewis et al. 1 cass. (Running Time: 1 hr.). 2001. 15.95; audio compact disk 19.95 Lone Pine.

Lewis Carroll: A Biography. unabr. collector's ed. Morton N. Cohen. Read by David Case. 8 cass. (Running Time: 12 hrs.). 1997. 64.00 (978-0-7366-4000-8(2), 4500-A); 64.00 (978-0-7366-4001-5(0), 4500-B) Books on Tape.
A scholar studies the strange but accomplished mathematician, photographer, & writer of "Alice in Wonderland".

Lewis Carroll: Alice Adventures in Wonderland & Through the Looking-Glass Including the Short Film the Delivery. unabr. ed. Lewis Carroll, pseud. Read by Michael York & Harlan Ellison. (Running Time: 6.5 hrs. 0 mins.). 2008. audio compact disk 24.95 (978-1-4332-5569-4(3)) Blckstn Audio.

Lewis Carroll Set: Alice Adventures in Wonderland & Through the Looking Glass Including the Short Film the Delivery. unabr. ed. Lewis Carroll, pseud. Read by Michael York & Harlan Ellison. (Running Time: 6.5 hrs. 0 mins.). 2008. 29.95 (978-1-4332-5570-0(7)) Blckstn Audio.

Lewis Grizzard - "One Last Time" Lewis Grizzard. Read by Lewis Grizzard. Ed. by Bill Anderson. 1 cass. (Running Time: 43 min.). 1994. 9.98 (978-0-945258-26-1(7), STC-0050); audio compact disk 9.98 (978-0-945258-27-8(5), STCD-0050) Sthrn Tracks.
Southern humor comedy cassette.

Lewis Grizzard Live. Read by Lewis Grizzard. 1 cass. 1986. 9.98 (978-5-551-52287-4(3)) Sthrn Tracks.

Lewis Percy. unabr. ed. Anita Brookner. Read by Judith Whale. 8 cass. (Running Time: 11 hrs. 13 min.). (Isis Cassettes Ser.). 1997. 69.95 (978-1-85089-572-5(4), 92034) Pub: ISIS Audio GBR. Dist(s): Ulverscroft US

Lewis the Lemur Adventures, The Belly of the Beast - Audio Book, Vol. 1. P. J. Nickels. Narrated by Paul Mackenzie. Music by Maynard Williams. Voice by Ashleah Hughes. Music by Ashleah Hughes. Prod. by R. E. Hughes. (Running Time: 54). (ENG.). 2009. audio compact disk 9.95 (978-0-9824960-1-5(X)) Pennie Rich.

Lex Luger. unabr. ed. Donald V. Allen. Read by Lex Luger. 1 cass. (Running Time: 30 min.). Dramatization. (Official Audio Biography Series of the World Wrestling Federation). 5.99 (978-1-56703-040-2(8)) High-Top Sports.

Lexipedia Hispanica. 2006. cd-rom (978-1-56409-085-0(X)) EBP Latin Am.

LexisNexis - Illinois Primary Law. 3rd rev. ed. Publisher's Editorial Staff. audio compact disk 1107.00 (978-0-327-10725-5(1)) Pub: LexisNexis. Dist(s): LEXIS Pub

LexisNexis - Massachusetts Primary Law. 3rd rev. ed. audio compact disk 1362.00 (978-0-327-10733-0(2)) Pub: LexisNexis. Dist(s): LEXIS Pub

LexisNexis Advanced Trademark Strategies Conference Audiotape. 3rd rev. ed. Speeches. 2002. reel tape 299.00 (978-1-930146-63-1(9)) Pub: LexisNexis Mealey. Dist(s): LEXIS Pub
A compilation of select speaker presentations from LexisNexis Advanced Trademark Strategies Conference, April 2002.

LexisNexis Advanced Trademark Strategies Conference Audiotape. 3rd rev. ed. Compiled by LexisNexis Staff. 2003. reel tape 399.00 (978-1-59579-130-6(2)) Pub: LexisNexis Mealey. Dist(s): LEXIS Pub

LexisNexis & Variety Digital Rights Management Conference Audio CD (April 2007) 2007. 750.00 (978-1-59579-684-4(3)) Pub: LexisNexis Mealey. Dist(s): LEXIS Pub

LexisNexis CD - Veterans Benefits Manual & Related Laws & Regulations on CD-ROM, 2007 Edition. 1905. audio compact disk 192.00 (978-1-4224-4058-2(3)) Pub: LexisNexis. Dist(s): LEXIS Pub

LexisNexis Ethics Teleconference Series: Attorney Advertising Audio CD (November 2007) 2007. 149.00 (978-1-59579-782-7(3)) Pub: LexisNexis Mealey. Dist(s): LEXIS Pub

LexisNexis Ethics Teleconference Series: Contingency Fee Relationships in Light of Santa Clara V. Atlantic Richfield Company Case Audio CD (July 2007) 2007. 149.00 (978-1-59579-720-9(3)) Pub: LexisNexis Mealey. Dist(s): LEXIS Pub

LexisNexis Ethics Teleconference Series: Ethical Witness Preparation & Deposition Conduct Audio CD (December 2007) 2007. 149.00 (978-1-59579-794-0(7)) Pub: LexisNexis Mealey. Dist(s): LEXIS Pub

LexisNexis Ethics Teleconference Series: Life in the Fast Lane ... or the Road to Disbarment? Audio CD (September 2007) 2007. 149.00 (978-1-59579-729-2(7)) Pub: LexisNexis Mealey. Dist(s): LEXIS Pub

LexisNexis Ethics Teleconference Series: Weathering Mass Tort & Class Action Settlements & Negotiations Audio CD (February 2008) 2008. 149.00 (978-1-59579-838-1(2)) Pub: LexisNexis Mealey. Dist(s): LEXIS Pub

LexisNexis Intellectual Property 101 Teleconference Series: Content Licensing & Open Source Audio CD (January 2008) 2008. 149.00 (978-1-59579-816-9(1)) Pub: LexisNexis Mealey. Dist(s): LEXIS Pub

LexisNexis Intellectual Property 101 Teleconference Series: Domain Name Audio CD (February 2008) 2008. 149.00 (978-1-59579-773-5(4)) Pub: LexisNexis Mealey. Dist(s): LEXIS Pub

LexisNexis Intellectual Property 101 Teleconference Series: Trademark Audio CD (October 2007) 2007. 149.00 (978-1-59579-745-2(9)) Pub: LexisNexis Mealey. Dist(s): LEXIS Pub

LexisNexis Med School for Lawyers: Toxicology & Exposure Determination for Causal Assessment Audio CD (July 2007) 2007. 149.00 (978-1-59579-702-5(5)) Pub: LexisNexis Mealey. Dist(s): LEXIS Pub

LexisNexis Presents: Punitive Damages Teleconference: the Impact of the Williams V. Phillip Morris Decision Audio CD (May 2007) 2007. audio compact disk 249.00 (978-1-59579-700-1(9)) Pub: LexisNexis Mealey. Dist(s): LEXIS Pub

LexisNexis Presents: the Wall Street Forum: Asbestos Conference Audiotape. 3rd rev. ed. Compiled by LexisNexis Staff. 2003. reel tape 225.00 (978-1-59579-132-0(9)) Pub: LexisNexis Mealey. Dist(s): LEXIS Pub

LexisNexis Presents: Trademark Law: Beyond the Basics Conference Audiotape. 3rd rev. ed. Compiled by LexisNexis Staff. 2003. reel tape 225.00 (978-1-59579-160-3(4)) Pub: LexisNexis Mealey. Dist(s): LEXIS Pub

LexisNexis Presents Wall Street Forum: Asbestos. Compiled by LexisNexis Staff. 2006. audio compact disk 225.00 (978-1-59579-062-0(4)) Pub: LexisNexis Mealey. Dist(s): LEXIS Pub

LexisNexis Presents: Wall Street Forum: Asbestos Audiotape. Compiled by LexisNexis Staff. 2004. reel tape 399.00 (978-1-59579-454-3(9)) Pub: LexisNexis Mealey. Dist(s): LEXIS Pub

LexisNexis Presents Wall Street Forum: Asbestos Conference Audiotape. Compiled by LexisNexis Staff. 2005. reel tape 225.00 (978-1-59579-343-0(7)) Pub: LexisNexis Mealey. Dist(s): LEXIS Pub

LexisNexis Professional Development Teleconference Series: Negotiating Skills that Will Improve Any Legal Practice Audio CD (September 2007) 2007. 149.00 (978-1-59579-740-7(8)) Pub: LexisNexis Mealey. Dist(s): LEXIS Pub

LexisNexis Teleconference: Emerging Trends in Digital Rights Management Audio CD (October 2007) 2007. 149.00 (978-1-59579-758-2(0)) Pub: LexisNexis Mealey. Dist(s): LEXIS Pub

LexisNexis Teleconference: Finding the Skeleton in the Closet - How to Conduct Superior Expert Research Audio CD (September 2007) 2007. 149.00 (978-1-59579-737-7(8)) Pub: LexisNexis Mealey. Dist(s): LEXIS Pub

LexisNexis Teleconference: Managing Outside Counsel Costs Audio CD (September 2007) 2007. 149.00 (978-1-59579-732-2(7)) Pub: LexisNexis Mealey. Dist(s): LEXIS Pub

LexisNexis Teleconference Series: DRM & Filtering - the Hard Questions Audio CD (December 2007) 2007. 149.00 (978-1-59579-795-7(5)) Pub: LexisNexis Mealey. Dist(s): LEXIS Pub

LexisNexis Teleconference Series: Litigating Your Client's Copyright Case - How to Avoid It & How to Win Audio CD (March 2007) 2007. 249.00 (978-1-59579-638-7(X)) Pub: LexisNexis Mealey. Dist(s): LEXIS Pub

LexisNexis Wall Street Forum: Asbestos Conference Audiotape. 5th rev. ed. Speeches. 2002. reel tape 299.00 (978-1-930146-89-1(2)) Pub: LexisNexis Mealey. Dist(s): LEXIS Pub
A compilation of select speaker presentations from LexisNexis Wall Street Forum: Asbestos Conference, July 2002.

LexisNexis Women in the Law Summit Audio CD (September 2007) 2007. 199.00 (978-1-59579-736-0(X)) Pub: LexisNexis Mealey. Dist(s): LEXIS Pub

LexisNexis Women in the Law Teleconference Series: From Associate to Partner - Advancing in Your Firm Audio CD (July 2007) 2007. audio compact disk 149.00 (978-1-59579-718-6(1)) Pub: LexisNexis Mealey. Dist(s): LEXIS Pub

LexisNexis Women in the Law Teleconference Series: The Advantages & Disadvantages of Going in-House Audio CD (October 2007) 2007. 149.00 (978-1-59579-756-8(4)) Pub: LexisNexis Mealey. Dist(s): LEXIS Pub

LexisNexis Women in the Legal Profession Summit: Rainmaking, Negotiating & Collaborative Development Audio CD (April 2008) 2008. 325.00 (978-1-59579-853-4(6)) Pub: LexisNexis Mealey. Dist(s): LEXIS Pub

LexisNexis Women in the Legal Profession Summit: Rainmaking, Negotiating & Collaborative Development Audio CD (January 2008) 2008. 325.00 (978-1-59579-815-2(3)) Pub: LexisNexis Mealey. Dist(s): LEXIS Pub

Lexus: Navajo Two-Step & Skip Dance Songs. Perf. by Southwestern Singers. 1 cass. 7.98 (CANR 7169) NewSound.

Lexus & the Olive Tree: Understanding Globalization. Thomas L. Friedman. Narrated by George Wilson. 16 cass. (Running Time: 23 hrs. 15 mins.). 135.00 (978-1-4025-1727-3(0)) Recorded Bks.

Lexus & the Olive Tree: Understanding Globalization. abr. ed. Thomas L. Friedman. Read by Thomas L. Friedman. 3 CDs. (Running Time: 30 hrs. 0 mins. 0 sec.). (ENG.). 2001. audio compact disk 25.00 (978-0-7435-0411-9(9), Sound Ideas) Pub: S&S Audio. Dist(s): S and S Inc

***Ley de Atraccion en el Mundo del Pensamiento - Digital Version: Vibracion del Pensamiento.** William Walker Atkitson. Prod. by FonoLibro Inc. (Running Time: 168).Tr. of Law of Attraction in the Thought World / Thought Vibration Or. (SPA.). 2010. 12.95 (978-1-61154-012-3(7)) Fonolibro Inc.

Ley de la Atraccion. Norberto Garcia. 2008. audio compact disk 11.95 (978-968-15-2343-5(1)) Pub: Ed Mex MEX. Dist(s): Giron Bks

***Ley de la Atraccion en el Mundo.** William Walker Atkinson. 2010. audio compact disk 17.95 (978-1-933499-95-6(8)) Fonolibro Inc.

***Leyenda del Jinete sin Cabeza.** Washington Irving & Dave Gutierrez. Tr. by Sara Tobon. Illus. by Tod G. Smith. Retold by Blake A. Hoena. (Classic Fiction Ser.). (SPA.). 2010. audio compact disk 14.60 (978-1-4342-2575-7(5)) CapstoneDig.

Leyenda del Triangulo de las Bermudas. 1 cass. (Running Time: 1 hr. 30 mins.). (SmartReader Ser.).Tr. of Legend of the Bermuda Triangle. (SPA & ENG.). (J). 1999. pap. bk. & tchr. ed. 19.95 (978-0-7887-0284-6(X), 79324T3) Recorded Bks.

Leyendas con Canciones. 1997. spiral bd. 31.95 (978-0-9650980-2-1(8)) Dolo Publns.

Leyendas Del Mundo Hispano. Susan Bacon & Nancy Humbach. (SPA.). (YA). (gr. 9-12). 2000. audio compact disk 10.97 (978-0-13-016535-0(2), Prentice Hall) P-H.

Li Bai & du Fu CD. Zu-yan Chen & Hong Zhang. 2007. 13.95 (978-0-88727-622-4(9)) Cheng Tsui.

Li-Fraumeni Syndrome - A Bibliography & Dictionary for Physicians, Patients, & Genome Researchers. Compiled by Icon Group International, Inc. Staff. 2007. ring bd. 28.95 (978-0-497-11251-6(5)) Icon Grp.

Li-Young Lee: The City in Which I Love You. unabr. ed. Li-Young Lee. Read by Li-Young Lee. Interview with Rebekah Presson. 1 cass. (Running Time: 29 min.). 1990. 10.00 (120790) New Letters.
Lee reads from his second book, "The City in Which I Love You", which was this year's Lamont Poetry Selection.

Liability Crisis in America: Doctors vs. Lawyers vs. Insurers. 1 cass. (Running Time: 90 min.). 11.95 (G0340B090, HarperThor) HarpC GBR.

Liaisons Dangereuses see Treasury of French Prose

Liaisons Dangereuses. Choderlos de Laclos. Read by Cecile Brune & Francois Berland. 8 cass. (FRE.). 1991. 64.95 (1576-77) Olivia & Hill.
The Comte de Valmont & his former mistress, Madame de Merteuil, conspire to seduce two innocent women.

Liaisons Dangereuses, Pt. 1. Choderlos de Laclos. Read by Cecile Brune & Francois Berland. 4 cass. (FRE.). 1992. 36.95 (1576-LV) Olivia & Hill.
The Comte de Valmont & his former mistress, Madame de Merteuill, conspire to seduce two innocent women. This 18th-century epistolary masterpiece (filmed as "Dangerous Liaisons") now enjoys an outstanding reading by Cecile Brune, Francois Berland & 12 actors.

Liaisons Dangereuses, Pt. 2. Choderlos de Laclos. Read by Cecile Brune & Francois Berland. 4 cass. (FRE.). 1991. 36.95 (1577-LV) Olivia & Hill.

***Liam Gillick: An Idea Just Out of Reach.** Ed. by Robert Eikmeyer. Liam Gillick. (ENG.). 2010. audio compact disk 35.00 (978-3-941185-46-3(2)) Pub: Verlag fur Moderne DEU. Dist(s): Dist Art Pubs

Lian: The Collection of the Articles from Internet Experience Sharing Conference for Practitioners in China, Pt. 2. (CHI.). 2006. bk. 1950.00 (978-1-60181-001-4(6)) Minghui.

Lian: The Collection of the Articles from Internet Experience Sharing Conference for Practitioners in China, Pt. 3. 2006. bk. 1950.00 (978-1-60181-002-1(4)) Minghui.

Liar. unabr. ed. Justine Larbalestier. Read by Channie Waites. (Running Time: 8 hrs.). 2009. 39.97 (978-1-4418-0203-3(7), 9781441802033, Brlnc Audio MP3 Lib); 24.99 (978-1-4418-0202-6(9), 9781441802026, Brilliance MP3); 24.99 (978-1-4418-0204-0(5), 9781441802040, BAD); 39.97 (978-1-4418-0205-7(3), 9781441802057, BADLE); audio compact disk 29.99 (978-1-4418-0200-2(2), 9781441802002, Bril Audio CD Unabri) Brilliance Audio.

Liar. unabr. ed. Justine Larbalestier. Read by Channie Waites. 8 CDs. (Running Time: 9 hrs.). (YA). (gr. 9 up). 2009. audio compact disk 69.97 (978-1-4418-0201-9(0), 9781441802019, BriAudCD Unabrid) Brilliance Audio.

Liar. unabr. ed. Winifred Morris. Narrated by Scott Shina. 3 pieces. (Running Time: 4 hrs.). (gr. 7 up). 2001. 28.00 (978-0-7887-5525-5(0)) Recorded Bks.
14-year-old Alex has head lies all his life. Confused and on probation, Alex has just moved into his grandparents' home in Oregon. If he can't stay out of trouble here, he will be sent to a "training camp" for delinquents. When a girl is unexpectedly kind to him, Alex wonders if he could trust someone.

Liar in Your Life: The Way to Truthful Relationships. unabr. ed. Robert Feldman. Read by Bob Walter. (Running Time: 9 hrs.). (ENG.). 2009. 24.98 (978-1-60024-655-5(9)) Pub: Hachet Audio. Dist(s): HachBkGrp

Liar in Your Life: The Way to Truthful Relationships. unabr. ed. Robert Feldman. Read by Robert Feldman. Read by Bob Walter. (Running Time: 9 hrs.). (ENG.). 2009. audio compact disk 34.98 (978-1-60024-653-1(2)) Pub: Hachet Audio. Dist(s): HachBkGrp

***Liar, Liar.** unabr. ed. Gary Paulsen. (Running Time: 3 hrs.). (YA). 2011. 14.99 (978-1-4558-0149-7(6), 9781455801497, BAD); 39.97 (978-1-4558-0150-3(X), 9781455801503, BADLE); 14.99 (978-1-4558-0147-3(X), 9781455801473, Brilliance MP3); 39.97 (978-1-4558-0148-0(8), 9781455801480, Brlnc Audio MP3 Lib); audio compact disk 14.99 (978-1-4558-0145-9(3), 9781455801459, Bril Audio CD Unabri); audio compact disk 39.97 (978-1-4558-0146-6(1), 9781455801466, BriAudCD Unabrid) Brilliance Audio.

***Liar, Liar: A Cat Deluca Mystery.** unabr. ed. K. J. Larsen. (Running Time: 8 hrs.). 2010. 29.95 (978-1-4417-4238-4(7)); 54.95 (978-1-4417-4235-3(2)); audio compact disk 76.00 (978-1-4417-4236-0(0)) Blckstn Audio.

Liar, Liar, Pants on Fire! unabr. ed. Miriam Cohen. (Miriam Cohen Ser.). (J). (ps-6). 1988. bk. 13.90 (978-0-8045-6649-0(6), SAC 6515-C) Spoken Arts.

***Liars & Saints.** unabr. ed. Maile Meloy. Read by Kirsten Potter. (Running Time: 9 hrs.). 2010. 29.95 (978-1-4417-5681-7(7)); 59.95 (978-1-4417-5677-0(9)); audio compact disk 29.95 (978-1-4417-5680-0(9)); audio compact disk 90.00 (978-1-4417-5678-7(7)) Blckstn Audio.

Liars & Thieves. abr. ed. Stephen Coonts. Read by Guerin Barry. (Running Time: 6 hrs.). (Tommy Carmellini Ser.: No. 4). 2007. audio compact disk 14.99 (978-1-4233-3421-7(3), 9781423334217, BCD Value Price) Brilliance Audio.

Liars & Thieves. abr. ed. Stephen Coonts. Read by Eric G. Dove. (Running Time: 6 hrs.). (Tommy Carmellini Ser.: No. 4). 2009. audio compact disk 26.99 (978-1-4233-3464-4(7), 9781423334644, BACD) Brilliance Audio.

Liars & Thieves. abr. ed. Stephen Coonts. Read by Eric G. Dove. (Running Time: 6 hrs.). (Tommy Carmellini Ser.: No. 4). 2010. audio compact disk 14.99 (978-1-4233-3465-1(5), 9781423334651, BCD Value Price) Brilliance Audio.

Liars & Thieves. unabr. ed. Stephen Coonts. Read by Guerin Barry. 8 CDs. (Running Time: 11 hrs.). (Tommy Carmellini Ser.: No. 4). 2004. 24.95 (978-1-59335-306-3(5), 1593353065, Brilliance MP3); 39.25 (978-1-59335-464-0(9), 1593354649, Brlnc Audio MP3 Lib) Brilliance Audio.
Tommy Carmellini - who dazzled thriller fans in Stephen Coonts's CUBA and LIBERTY - is the CIA's top man for jobs that require extreme stealth, breaking-and-entering skills, and split-second, sometimes lethal, decisions. In LIARS & THIEVES, he's sent to post guard duty at a farmhouse in Virginia's remote Blue Ridge Mountains, where top government operatives are debriefing a star defector: the ultimate KGB insider, a man with records on every operation and every dirty trick the shadowy intelligence agency has ever run, from Lenin to Putin. Carmellini arrives to find the guards shot dead, and a ruthless team of commandos - American commandos - slaughtering everyone in sight, then setting the house on fire. He escapes a hail of bullets and a deadly mountain car chase with what seems to be the sole survivor, a beautiful and mysterious translator who steals his car and leaves him for dead at the first chance. What secrets did the defector know? Who would have killed to prevent him from talking? And how could a hit team act so fast, so efficiently, and so murderously without intimate, inside knowledge of the debriefing? Smart money says someone in the U.S. government is behind the massacre and is now after Carmellini. And that begs the biggest question of all: in a world where nothing is as it seems and no one is who he pretends to be, who can Carmellini trust? Finding out will be terrifying. The answer may be deadly.

Liars & Thieves. unabr. ed. Stephen Coonts. Read by Guerin Barry. (Running Time: 11 hrs.). (Tommy Carmellini Ser.: No. 4). 2004. 39.25 (978-1-59710-448-7(5), 1597104485, BADLE); 24.95 (978-1-59710-449-4(3), 1597104493, BAD) Brilliance Audio.

Liars & Thieves. unabr. ed. Stephen Coonts. Read by Eric G. Dove. (Running Time: 15 hrs.). (Tommy Carmellini Ser.: No. 4). 2009. 24.99 (978-1-4233-3460-6(4), 9781423334606, Brilliance MP3); 39.97 (978-1-4233-3463-7(9), 9781423334637, BADLE); 39.97 (978-1-4233-3461-3(2), 9781423334613, Brlnc Audio MP3 Lib); 24.99 (978-1-4233-3462-0(0), 9781423334620, BAD); audio compact disk 36.99 (978-1-4233-3458-3(2), 9781423334583, Bril Audio CD Unabri); audio compact disk 97.97 (978-1-4233-3459-0(0), 9781423334590, BriAudCD Unabrid) Brilliance Audio.

Liars & Thieves: A Novel. Stephen Coonts. Read by Guerin Barry. (Tommy Carmellini Ser.: No. 1). 2009. 69.99 (978-1-60775-870-9(9)) Find a World.

Liars & Thieves: A Novel. unabr. ed. Stephen Coonts. Read by Guerin Barry. 9 CDs. (Running Time: 11 hrs.). (Tommy Carmellini Ser.: No. 1). 2004. audio compact disk 33.95 (978-1-58788-568-6(9), 1587885689, Bril Audio CD Unabri); audio compact disk 97.25 (978-1-58788-569-3(7), 1587885697, BriAudCD Unabrid) Brilliance Audio.

Liars Anonymous: Creating a Safe Place to Begin Telling the Truth. Scott Morrison. 1 cass. (Running Time: 1 hr.). 1999. 7.50 (978-1-882496-17-4(5)) Twnty Frst Cntry Ren.
Lying keeps one separte & distrustful. The art of intimate friendship requires that one drop all agendas & vested interest in the other, & create a safe environment in which both can be completely open.

Liars' Club: A Memoir. Mary Karr. Read by Bernadette Dunne. 1998. audio compact disk 88.00 (978-0-7366-8285-5(6)) Books on Tape.

Liars' Club: A Memoir. unabr. ed. Mary Karr. Read by Bernadette Dunne. 9 cass. (Running Time: 13 hrs. 30 min.). 1998. 72.00 (978-0-7366-4179-1(3), 4677) Books on Tape.
This splendidly crafted memoir recounts growing-up poor in Texas, a place where tall-tales & dark secrets hold sway.

Liar's Diary. abr. ed. Patry Francis. Read by Marie Caliendo. (Running Time: 21600 sec.). 2008. audio compact disk 14.99 (978-1-4233-2719-6(5), 9781423327196, BCD Value Price) Brilliance Audio.

Liar's Diary. unabr. ed. Patry Francis. Read by Marie Caliendo. (Running Time: 11 hrs.). 2007. 39.25 (978-1-4233-2717-2(9), 9781423327172, BADLE); 24.95 (978-1-4233-2716-5(0), 9781423327165, BAD); 82.25 (978-1-4233-2711-0(X), 9781423327110, BrilAudUnabridg); audio compact disk 97.25 (978-1-4233-2713-4(6), 9781423327134, BriAudCD Unabrid); audio compact disk 39.25 (978-1-4233-2715-8(2), 9781423327158, Brlnc Audio MP3 Lib); audio compact disk 24.95 (978-1-4233-2714-1(4), 9781423327141, Brilliance MP3); audio compact disk 36.95 (978-1-4233-2712-7(8), 9781423327127, Bril Audio CD Unabri) Brilliance Audio.

Liar's Game. unabr. ed. Eric Jerome Dickey. Narrated by Peter Jay Fernandez & Patricia R. Floyd. 9 cass. (Running Time: 12 hrs. 45 mins.). 2000. 83.00 (978-0-7887-4360-3(0), 96312E7) Recorded Bks.
Follows two young professionals in their search to understand each other & their pasts. The fast-paced world of Los Angeles provides the perfect backdrop for this hot, very modern love story.

Liar's Lullaby. unabr. ed. Meg Gardiner. Read by Susan Ericksen. (Running Time: 12 hrs.). (Jo Beckett Ser.). 2010. audio compact disk 36.99 (978-1-4418-2001-3(9), 9781441820013, Bril Audio CD Unabri) Brilliance Audio.

***Liar's Lullaby.** unabr. ed. Meg Gardiner. Read by Susan Ericksen. (Running Time: 11 hrs.). (Jo Beckett Ser.). 2010. 24.99 (978-1-4418-2005-1(1), 9781441820051, BAD); 39.97 (978-1-4418-2004-4(3), 9781441820044, Brlnc Audio MP3 Lib); 39.97 (978-1-4418-2006-8(X), 9781441820068, BADLE); 24.99 (978-1-4418-2003-7(5), 9781441820037, Brilliance MP3); audio compact disk 89.97 (978-1-4418-2002-0(7), 9781441820020, BriAudCD Unabrid) Brilliance Audio.

Liar's Lullaby. unabr. ed. Meg Gardiner. (Running Time: 12 hrs.). (Jo Beckett Ser.). 2011. audio compact disk 36.99 (978-1-4418-2007-5(8), 9781441820075, Bril Audio CD Unabri) Brilliance Audio.

Liar's Poker: Rising Through the Wreckage on Wall Street. abr. ed. Michael Lewis. Read by Michael Lewis. (Running Time: 10800 sec.). (ENG.). 2007. audio compact disk 14.99 (978-0-7393-5730-9(1), Random AudioBks) Pub: Random Audio Pubg. Dist(s): Random

Liar's Poker: Rising Through the Wreckage on Wall Street. unabr. ed. Michael Lewis. Read by Jonathan Reese. 7 cass. (Running Time: 10 hrs. 30 min.). 1991. Rental 11.95 (2773) Books on Tape.
When Michael Lewis joined Salomon Brothers in 1985, the firm was already a Wall Street legend. It turned profits in underwriting & syndicate, but its heart was in trading, particularly bonds. Trading takes brio. Salomon rewarded its traders in their daily gambles with huge bonuses. Traders approached million-dollar deals like a game.

Libation for Our Ancestors Vol. 1: A Family & Communal Activity at Kwanzaa, Tarik Karenga. Read by Tarik Karenga. Music by Chike K. Omo. Contrib. by Norbert Bein-Kozakewycz. 2 cass. (Running Time: 60 min.). 1998. pap. bk. 14.95 (978-0-9669742-0-1(4)) Synergy.
To teach cultural practice & enjoy Kwanzaa music.

Libel Litigation, 1992. (Patents, Copyrights, Trademarks, & Literary Property Ser.). 1992. pap. bk. 175.00 (978-0-685-69459-6(3)) PLI.

Liberal Crack-Up. unabr. ed. R. Emmett Tyrell, Jr. Read by Thomas Andrews. 6 cass. (Running Time: 8 hrs. 30 mins.). 1990. 44.95 (978-0-7861-0161-0(X), 1144) Blckstn Audio.
The author exposes the cheap thought & affronts to common sense that have caused American liberalism to disintegrate into a riot of outlandish enthusiasms during the past two decades.

Liberal Education & Education for Citizenship see Transmitting the Western Heritage Through Education

Liberal Fascism: The Secret History of the American Left, from Mussolini to the Politics of Meaning. Jonah Goldberg. Read by Johnny Heller. (Playaway Adult Nonfiction Ser.). 2008. 69.99 (978-1-60640-870-4(4)) Find a World.

Liberal Fascism: The Secret History of the American Left, from Mussolini to the Politics of Meaning. unabr. ed. Jonah Goldberg. (Running Time: 16 hrs. 0 mins. 0 sec.). (ENG.). 2008. audio compact disk 29.99 (978-1-4001-5704-4(8)) Pub: Tantor Media. Dist(s): IngramPubServ

Liberal Fascism: The Secret History of the American Left, from Mussolini to the Politics of Meaning. unabr. ed. Jonah Goldberg. Read by Johnny Heller. (Running Time: 16 hrs. 0 mins. 0 sec.). (ENG.). 2008. audio compact disk 39.99 (978-1-4001-0704-9(0)); audio compact disk 79.99 (978-1-4001-3704-6(7)) Pub: Tantor Media. Dist(s): IngramPubServ

Liberalism. unabr. ed. Ludwig von Mises. Read by Nadia May. 6 cass. (Running Time: 8 hrs. 30 mins.). 1991. 44.95 (978-0-7861-0240-2(3), 1210) Blckstn Audio.
Mises was a careful & logical theoretician who believed that ideas rule the world. "The ultimate outcome of the struggle," between liberalism & totalitarianism, says Mises, "will not be decided by arms, but by ideas.

Liberalism Is a Mental Disorder. Michael Savage. 2005. audio compact disk 27.99 (978-1-58926-937-8(3)) Oasis Audio.

Liberalism Is a Mental Disorder. abr. ed. Michael Savage. Read by Mark Warner. 4 pieces. 25.99 (978-1-58926-938-5(1)) Oasis Audio.

Liberalism Is a Mental Disorder: An Oasis Recording. abr. ed. Michael Savage. Read by Mark Warner. (Running Time: 6 hrs.). 2005. audio compact disk 45.00 (978-0-7861-7827-8(2)) Blckstn Audio.

Liberalism Is a Mental Disorder: Savage Solutions. abr. ed. Michael Savage. Narrated by Mark Warner. (ENG.). 2005. 19.59 (978-1-60814-284-2(1)) Oasis Audio.

***Liberando Tu Gloria Verdadera.** Tr. of Releasing Your True Glory. (SPA.). 2009. audio compact disk 18.00 (978-0-944129-33-3(1)) High Praise.

***Liberate Your Self: The Courage to Let Go & Live Fearlessly.** Guy Finley. 2009. 24.95 (978-1-929320-66-0(3)); audio compact disk 34.95 (978-1-929320-65-3(5)) Life of Learn.

Liberated from the World. Reuven Doron. 1 cass. (Running Time: 90 mins.). (Back to the Garden Ser.: Vol. 3). 2000. 5.00 (RD05-003) Morning NC.
The message presented in this series will woo you back to the intimacy & innocence of the Garden.

Liberated Soul. Swami Amar Jyoti. 1 cass. 1991. 9.95 (K-129) Truth Consciousness.
Examples from the lives of great Avadhuts, Shukadeva & other Mahatmas, illustrate the height of spirituality.

Liberated Woman: Proverbs 31:10-31. Ed Young. 1992. 0.95 (978-0-7417-1899-0(5), 899) Win Walk.

Liberating Atlantis: A Novel of Alternate History. unabr. ed. Harry Turtledove. Narrated by Todd McLaren. 2 MP3-CDs. (Running Time: 17 hrs. 30 mins. 0 sec.). (Atlantis Ser.). (ENG.). 2009. 29.99 (978-1-4001-6253-6(X)); audio compact disk 79.99 (978-1-4001-4253-8(9)); audio compact disk 39.99 (978-1-4001-1253-1(2)) Pub: Tantor Media. Dist(s): IngramPubServ

***Liberating Atlantis: A Novel of Alternate History.** unabr. ed. Harry Turtledove. Narrated by Todd McLaren. (Running Time: 17 hrs. 30 mins.). (Atlantis Ser.). 2009. 21.99 (978-1-4001-8253-4(0)) Tantor Media.

Liberating Paris. Linda Bloodworth Thomason. 2005. audio compact disk 29.99 (978-1-4193-3924-0(9)) Recorded Bks.

Liberating Paris. unabr. ed. Linda Bloodworth-Thomason. 4 cass. (Running Time: 6 hr.). 2000. 24.98 (978-1-57042-805-0(0)) Hachet Audio.

Liberating Spirit: The Gospel Alternative. Rosemary Haughton. Read by Rosemary Haughton. 1 cass. (Running Time: 45 min.). 7.95 (TAH184) Alba Hse Comns.

Liberating the adult within moving from childish Responsibility. Peter D. Kramer. 2004. 7.95 (978-0-7435-4973-8(2)) Pub: S&S Audio. Dist(s): S and S Inc

Liberating Truth for Israel & the Church, Pt. 1. Derek Prince. 1 cass. (Running Time: 60 min.). 5.95 (A-4248) Derek Prince.

Liberating Truth for Israel & the Church, Pt. 2. Derek Prince. 1 cass. (Running Time: 60 min.). 5.95 (A-4249) Derek Prince.

Liberation. Swami Amar Jyoti. 1 cass. 1987. 9.95 (M-74) Truth Consciousness.
Liberation, our natural state & birthright: why is it so elusive? Understanding ourselves, the gateway to learning. Freedom from our own conditioning & self-delusion.

Liberation. unabr. ed. Robert A. Monroe. Read by Roland Simon. 1 cass. (Running Time: 30 min.). (Human Plus Ser.). (FRE.). 1992. 14.95 (978-1-56102-058-4(3)) Inter Indus.
Break free. Reduce or release emotional reactions.

Liberation: The Open Door. Sivananda Radha. 1 cass. (Running Time: 90 min.). 1974. 7.95 (978-0-931454-55-4(7)) Timeless Bks.
Introduction to the nature of Yoga as the path of liberation.

Liberation & Death. Sogyal Rinpoche. 2 cass. 18.00 (OC20L) Sound Horizons AV.

Liberation de Paris. Henri Amouroux. 2 cass. (Francais sous l'occupation Ser.). (FRE.). 1991. 26.95 (1242-RF) Olivia & Hill.

Liberation from Poverty. Elbert Willis. 1 cass. (Prosperity Insights Ser.). 4.00 Fill the Gap.

Liberation in Southern Africa: An Overview: Liberation in Southern Africa see Liberation in Southern Africa: The Search for a Compassionate Solution

Liberation in Southern Africa: Apartheid in South Africa & Race Relations in the United States see Liberation in Southern Africa: The Search for a Compassionate Solution

Liberation in Southern Africa: Friends, Nonviolence & Liberation in Southern Africa see Liberation in Southern Africa: The Search for a Compassionate Solution

Liberation in Southern Africa: Namibia: The Hidden Test of South Africa's Intensions see Liberation in Southern Africa: The Search for a Compassionate Solution

Liberation in Southern Africa: The Search for a Compassionate Solution. 7 cass. Incl. Liberation in Southern Africa: An Overview: Liberation in Southern Africa. Vincent Harding. 1981.; Liberation in Southern Africa: Apartheid in South Africa & Race Relations in the United States. Zoharah Simmons. 1981.; Liberation in Southern Africa: Friends, Nonviolence & Liberation in Southern Africa. Louis Forrest. 1981.; Liberation in Southern Africa: Namibia: The Hidden Test of South Africa's Intensions. Ken Martin. 1981.; Liberation in Southern Africa: The Struggle for Liberation in South Africa & Around the World. Alfred Moleah. 1981.; Liberation in Southern Africa: Toward a Compassionate Response. Adam Curle. 1981.; Liberation in Southern Africa: What Are the Lessons of Zimbabwe for South Africa - If Any? Lyle Tatum. 1981.; 1981. 24.50 Set.; 4.50 ea. Pendle Hill.

Liberation in Southern Africa: The Struggle for Liberation in South Africa & Around the World see Liberation in Southern Africa: The Search for a Compassionate Solution

Liberation in Southern Africa: Toward a Compassionate Response see Liberation in Southern Africa: The Search for a Compassionate Solution

Liberation in Southern Africa: What Are the Lessons of Zimbabwe for South Africa - If Any? see Liberation in Southern Africa: The Search for a Compassionate Solution

Liberation Movements. unabr. ed. Olen Steinhauer. Read by Bo Foxworth & Lorna Raver. 6 CDs. (Running Time: 23400 sec.). 2006. audio compact disk 81.00 (978-0-7861-5985-7(5)); audio compact disk 29.95 (978-0-7861-7105-7(7)) Blckstn Audio.

Liberation Movements. unabr. ed. Olen Steinhauer. Read by Bo Foxworth et al. (Running Time: 23400 sec.). 2006. 65.95 (978-0-7861-4895-0(0)) Blckstn Audio.

Liberation of Consciousness. Guy Finley. (ENG.). 2004. 24.95 (978-1-929320-40-0(X)) Life of Learn.

Liberation of Consciousness. Guy Finley. 2004. reel tape 27.95 (978-1-929320-17-2(5)); audio compact disk 39.95 (978-1-929320-18-9(3)) Life of Learn.

Liberation of Europe. abr. ed. Rick Atkinson. (ENG.). 2005. 26.00 (978-0-7435-2796-5(8)) Pub: S&S Audio. Dist(s): S and S Inc

Liberation of Gabriel King. unabr. ed. K. L. Going. Read by Robert Keefe. 2 cass. (Running Time: 3 hrs.). (YA). 2005. 23.00 (978-0-307-24615-8(9), Listening Lib); audio compact disk 30.00 (978-0-307-24616-5(7), Listening Lib) Pub: Random Audio Pubg. Dist(s): Random

Liberation Road: A Novel of World War II & the Red Ball Express. unabr. ed. David L. Robbins. Narrated by George Guidall. 12 cass. (Running Time: 17 hrs.). 2005. 109.75 (978-1-4193-4875-4(2), 98086) Recorded Bks.
New York Times best-selling author David L. Robbins has thrilled and moved readers with his masterful historical fiction. Liberation Road is a riveting tale of combat, race relations and fate set after the Normandy invasion of World War II. As the Allies march toward German-occupied Paris, the trucks of the Red Ball Express race to keep the troops supplied. Driving one truck is Joe Amos, a soldier who wants to fight on the front lines, but is denied by the color of his skin.

Liberation Through Right Action. Swami Amar Jyoti. 1 cass. 1987. 9.95 (G-13) Truth Consciousness.
The genesis of Karma Yoga. Spontaneous creativity vs. thinking & planning. Selflessness & freedom; efforts & Grace. Natural unfoldment, the very hallmark of spirituality.

Liberation upon Hearing in the Between: Living with the Tibetan Book of the Dead. Robert Thurman. 4 CDs. (Running Time: 18000 sec.). 2005. audio compact disk 29.95 (978-1-59179-354-0(8), W959D) Sounds True.

Liberator. Miguel Cassina. 1998. 4.99 (978-0-8297-2653-4(5)) Pub: Vida Pubs. Dist(s): Zondervan

Liberator. Paul Dengelegi. Read by Charlton Griffin. Characters created by Barry Sadler. 2 vols. (Casca Ser.: No. 23). 2004. 18.00 (978-1-58807-123-1(5)); (978-1-58807-569-7(9)) Am Pubng Inc.

Liberator of Jedd. abr. ed. Jeffrey Lord. Read by Lloyd James. Abr. by Odin Westgaard. 2 vols. No. 5. 2003. 18.00 (978-1-58807-360-0(2)); (978-1-58807-778-3(0)) Am Pubng Inc.

Liberator of Jedd. abr. ed. Jeffrey Lord. Read by Carol Eason. Abr. by Odin Westgaard. 3 CDs. (Running Time: 3 hrs.). (Richard Blade Adventure Ser.: No. 5). 2004. audio compact disk 25.00 (978-1-58807-496-6(X)) Am Pubng Inc.
A World of Death. The dying Empress has two last commands for Blade: Marry the Child-Princess, and lead the Jedds into the North country. The first is no hardship, but the second pits him against a maniacal floating brain that wants him to perform the most bizarre of all his feats in Dimension X. Armed with only his naked passion, he battles all his enemies, but is helpless against one - the dreaded Yellow Plague.

Liberators. James Pattinson. (Soundings Ser.). (J). 2005. 61.95 (978-1-84559-037-6(6)); audio compact disk 79.95 (978-1-84559-082-6(1)) Pub: ISIS Lrg Prnt GBR. Dist(s): Ulverscroft US

Liberia. unabr. ed. Loren Robinson. Read by Cameron Beierle. 8 cass. (Running Time: 10 hrs.). 2001. 49.95 (978-1-58116-028-4(3)) Books in Motion.
Captain Todd Brandon fought with valor in the War of 1812 against the British invasion. And when the war was over, President Madison had a new role for Brandon - as special agent to the President, he is assigned the task of escorting free negroes to a new colony in Africa.

Liberia Our African Promise Land. 2nd rev. ed. Selena Gennehma Horace. 2 CDs. (Running Time: 3 hrs.). 2003. audio compact disk 20.00 (978-0-9727007-1-9(4)) Horasel Prod.
Information about the great migration of African tribes during the decline of the empires of Mali and Ghana to present day Liberia.

Liberta. Cinza Medaglia. pap. bk. 19.95 (978-88-7754-368-4(X)) Pub: Cideb ITA. Dist(s): Distribks Inc

Libertad. unabr. ed. Dominion & Zondervan Publishing Staff. 2003. 9.99 (978-0-8297-3354-9(X)) Pub: Zondervan. Dist(s): Vida Pubs

Libertad Emocional: Emotional Freedom Technique in Spanish. Barbara Stone. 1 cass. (Running Time: 15 mins.). 2001. 8.95 (978-1-893129-05-4(5), 006) Stonepower.
Spanish version of a powerful energy psychology intervention to rapidly relieve trauma, stress and other emotional disturbances with self-help exercises from Thought Field Therapy Health and Fitness.

Libertarian Class Analysis. unabr. ed. John Hagel & Walter E. Grinder. 1 cass. (Running Time: 1 hr. 11 min.). 12.95 (386) J Norton Pubs.

Libertarian Foundations for Personal Conduct & Happiness. unabr. ed. Peter Breggin. 1 cass. (Running Time: 1 hr. 12 min.). 12.95 (267) J Norton Pubs.

Libertarian Morality. unabr. ed. John Hospers. 1 cass. (Running Time: 1 hr. 4 min.). 12.95 (743) J Norton Pubs.

Libertarian Party Principles. unabr. ed. Edward H. Crane. 1 cass. (Running Time: 26 min.). 12.95 (339) J Norton Pubs.

Libertarian Temperament. unabr. ed. John Hospers. 1 cass. (Running Time: 50 min.). 12.95 (200) J Norton Pubs.

Libertarian View of the American Revolution. unabr. ed. William Marina. 1 cass. (Running Time: 48 min.). 1976. 12.95 (748) J Norton Pubs.

Libertarianism: A Primer. unabr. ed. David Boaz. Read by Jeff Riggenbach. 8 cass. (Running Time: 12 hrs.). 1998. 56.95 (2251) Blckstn Audio.
Presents the essential guidebook to the libertarian perspective, detailing its roots, central tenets, solutions to contemporary policy dilemmas & future in American politics.

Libertarianism: A Primer. unabr. ed. David Boaz. Read by Jeff Riggenbach. 8 cass. (Running Time: 11 hrs. 30 mins.). 1998. 56.95 (978-0-7861-1348-4(0), 2251) Blckstn Audio.
Presents the essential guidebook to the libertarianism perspective, detailing its roots, central tenets, solutions to contemporary policy dilemmas, & future in American politics. Must reading for understanding one of the most exciting & hopeful movements of our time.

Libertarianism: A Primer. unabr. ed. David Boaz. Read by Jeff Riggenbach. (Running Time: 41400 sec.). 2007. audio compact disk 29.95 (978-0-7861-7222-1(3)); audio compact disk 81.00 (978-0-7861-5812-6(3)) Blckstn Audio.

Libertarianism: Questions & Answers. Peter Schwartz. Read by Peter Schwartz. 1 cass. (Running Time: 50 min.). 1985. 7.95 (978-1-56114-088-6(0), HS03C) Second Renaissance.
Further Elaboration on Mr. Schwartz's essay on Libertarianism.

Libertarianism & Feminism. unabr. ed. Sharon Presley et al. 1 cass. (Running Time: 58 min.). 12.95 (741) J Norton Pubs.

Libertarianism & Freedom. unabr. ed. Phillip A. Luce. 1 cass. (Running Time: 1 hr. 28 min.). 12.95 (170) J Norton Pubs.

Libertarianism & Social Philosophy. unabr. ed. Tibor R. Machan. 1 cass. (Running Time: 37 min.). 12.95 (742) J Norton Pubs.

Libertarianism in American History. unabr. ed. Murray Newton Rothbard & Joseph R. Peden. 1 cass. (Running Time: 1 hr. 28 min.). 12.95 (387) J Norton Pubs.

Liberte: Poemes choisis. Poems. Paul Éluard. Read by Sarah Boreo. 1 cass. (FRE.). 1991. 22.95 (1449-LQP) Olivia & Hill.
A poem, or rather a hymn to liberty, was written in 1942, the worst year of the war. Copies were parachuted to the French Underground by the British Air Force. The poem has become a symbol of the Resistance.

Liberte, Egalite, Fraternite - an Anthology of French Political Thought. Read by Charles Boyer. 1 cass. (Running Time: 1 hr.). (FRE.). 1997. pap. bk. 19.50 (978-1-58085-369-9(2)) Interlingua VA.
Includes French transcription. The combination of written text & clarity & pace of diction will open the door for intermediate & advanced students to genuine comprehension & the use of literary texts for advancement in rapid understanding of written & oral language materials. The audio text plus written text concept makes foreign languages accessible to a much wider range of students than books alone.

Libertine see Dylan Thomas Reads the Poetry of W. B. Yeats & Others

Liberty. abr. ed. Stephen Coonts. Read by Guerin Barry. (Running Time: 6 hrs.). (Jake Grafton Novel Ser.: Vol. 10). 2010. audio compact disk 9.99 (978-1-4418-0837-0(X), 9781441808370, BCD Value Price) Brilliance Audio.

Liberty. unabr. ed. Stephen Coonts. Read by Guerin Barry. 10 cass. (Running Time: 15 hrs.). (Jake Grafton Novel Ser.: Vol. 10). 2003. 36.95 (978-1-58788-559-4(X), 158788559X, BAU); 97.25 (978-1-58788-560-0(3), 1587885603, Unabridge Lib Edns); audio compact disk 112.25 (978-1-58788-563-1(8), 1587885638, CD Unabrid Lib Ed); audio compact disk 40.95 (978-1-58788-562-4(X), 158788562X, CD Unabridged) Brilliance Audio.
On a quiet park bench in Manhattan - just miles from the ruins of the World Trade Center - a spymaster delivers a chilling secret message to Jake Grafton: A rogue Russian general has sold four nuclear warheads to a radical Islamic terrorist group, the Sword of Islam. The group intends to detonate them in America in the ultimate terror strike, the apocalypse that will trigger a holy war between Western civilization and the Muslim world. After passing the message on to his peers, Grafton is charged by the president with assembling a secret team to find the warheads before America's population centers are consumed by a nuclear holocaust. As he hunts for terrorists, Grafton soon finds himself up to his neck in power politics, techno-billionaires, money-grubbing traitors, anarchists, and spies. He also discovers that the terrorists don't all come from the Middle East. They come from places close to home. They masquerade as patriots. Some may even have the president's ear. With the survival of Western civilization at stake, Grafton pulls out all the stops. Calling on the assistance of the indomitable Toad Tarkington, and CIA burglar Tommy Carmellini, he raids the prisons to assemble his team while the clock ticks toward Armageddon.

Liberty. unabr. ed. Stephen Coonts. Read by Guerin Barry. (Running Time: 15 hrs.). (Jake Grafton Novel Ser.: Vol. 10). 2004. 39.25 (978-1-59335-451-0(7), 1593354517, Brlnc Audio MP3 Lib) Brilliance Audio.

Liberty. unabr. ed. Stephen Coonts. Read by Guerin Barry. (Running Time: 15 hrs.). (Jake Grafton Novel Ser.: Vol. 10). 2004. 39.25 (978-1-59710-451-7(5), 1597104515, BADLE); 24.95 (978-1-59710-450-0(7), 1597104507, BAD) Brilliance Audio.

Liberty. unabr. ed. Stephen Coonts. Read by Guerin Barry. (Running Time: 15 hrs.). (Jake Grafton Novel Ser.: Vol. 10). 2004. 24.95 (978-1-59335-101-4(1), 1593351011) Soulmate Audio Bks.

Liberty. unabr. ed. Garrison Keillor. Read by Garrison Keillor. (ENG.). 2009. audio compact disk 19.99 (978-1-59887-935-3(9), 1598879359) Pub: HighBridge. Dist(s): Workman Pub

Liberty & Property. Ludwig von Mises. 1 CD. (Running Time: 43 mins.). 2006. audio compact disk 12.95 (978-1-57970-378-3(X), AF0400D, Audio-For) J Norton Pubs.
With a forceful style and superb use of language, Mises outlines the nature, function and effects of capitalism. He demolishes many of the myths surrounding the Industrial Revolution, shows why political freedom is impossible without economic freedom, points out the differences between government and the market, and demonstrates how socialism destroys freedom.

Liberty & Property. unabr. ed. Ludwig von Mises. 1 cass. (Running Time: 43 min.). 12.95 (400) J Norton Pubs.
Mises outlines the nature, function & effects of capitalism. He demolishes many of the myths surrounding the Industrial Revolution, shows why political freedom is impossible without economic freedom, points out the difference between government & the market, & demonstrates how socialism destroys freedom.

Liberty & Tyranny: A Conservative Manifesto. unabr. ed. Mark R. Levin. Read by Mark R. Levin. Read by Adam Grupper. 6 CDs. (Running Time: 7 hrs.). 2009. audio compact disk 29.99 (978-0-7435-7220-0(3)) Pub: S&S Audio. Dist(s): S and S Inc

Liberty Comes Alive. Maureen Mulvaney. 1 cass. (J). (gr. 3-12). 9.95 (978-0-9616923-0-8(8)) MGM & Assocs.

***Liberty Defined: The 50 Urgent Issues That Affect Our Freedom.** unabr. ed. Ron Paul. (Running Time: 6 hrs. 30 mins.). (ENG.). 2011. 19.98 (978-1-60941-910-3(3)); audio compact disk & audio compact disk 24.98 (978-1-60941-907-3(3)) Pub: Hachet Audio. Dist(s): HachBkGrp

Liberty DeVito: Off the Record. Interview with Dan Thress. Contrib. by John Riley et al. 1 cass. pap. bk. 26.95 (BD074) DCI Music Video.
Incredible book & audio package featuring eleven songs from the original Billy Joel Studio Masters. Drum tracks have been removed so you can recreate the session with you as the drummer.

Liberty Falling. unabr. ed. Nevada Barr. Narrated by Barbara Rosenblat. 9 cass. (Running Time: 12 hrs.). (Anna Pigeon Ser.: No. 7). 1999. 83.00 (978-0-7887-3465-6(2), 95649E7) Recorded Bks.
When park ranger Anna Pigeon isn't sitting at her gravely ill sister's bedside, she is hiking the ruins of Ellis Island. But suddenly the Island & the Statue of Liberty are the scenes of unusual deaths. The park service claims they are accidents, but Anna wonders if there is a common purpose behind them.

Liberty for All. unabr. ed. Michele Sobel Spirn. 1 cass. (Running Time: 20 min.). (Time Traveler Ser.). (J). (gr. 3-6). 1984. bk. 16.99 (978-0-934898-63-8(4)); pap. bk. 9.95 (978-0-934898-75-1(8)) Jan Prods.
Traveling back in time, Diana & Tom land in the middle of a Revolutionary War Battle. The American rebels are trapped. Diana & Tom volunteer their help.

Liberty, Love & Responsibility. unabr. ed. Peter Breggin. 1 cass. (Running Time: 1 hr. 20 min.). 12.95 (29346) J Norton Pubs.
A discussion of the nature of love & its importance in our lives. In a warm & personal analysis, Breggin begins with first principles & then applies them to everyday problems in love relationships.

Liberty of Obedience. unabr. ed. Elisabeth Elliot. Read by Elisabeth Elliot. 1 cass. (Running Time: 45 min.). 1989. 4.95 (978-0-8474-2135-0(X)) Back to Bible.
A challenge to examine one's obedience to God, through the eyes of God's freedom, grace & love.

Liberty vs. Power. unabr. ed. Jarret B. Wollstein. 1 cass. (Running Time: 29 min.). 12.95 (987) J Norton Pubs.

Libido Breakthrough. abr. ed. Brenda D. Adderly. Read by Brenda D. Adderly. 2 cass. (Running Time: 3 hrs.). 2001. 18.00 (978-1-59040-116-3(6)) Pub: Amer Intl Pub. Dist(s): PerseuPGW

Libido's Best: Erotic Audio Sex & Sensibility. Prod. by Molly Kenefick. (Running Time: 74 mins.). 2001. 11.95 (978-1-886238-36-7(7)); audio compact disk 11.95 (978-1-886238-35-0(9)) Passion Press.

Libra. Don DeLillo. Read by Michael Prichard. 2000. audio compact disk 128.00 (978-0-7366-8288-6(0)) Books on Tape.

Libra. Narrated by Patricia G. Finlayson. Music by Mike Cantwell. Contrib. by Marie De Seta & TMY Communications Staff. 1 cass. (Running Time: 30 min.). (Astrologer's Guide to the Personality Ser.: Vol. 7). 1994. 7.99 (978-1-878535-18-8(0)) De Seta-Finlayson.
Astrological description of the sign of Libra; individually customized, covering love, money, career, relationships & more.

Libra. collector's ed. Don DeLillo. Read by Michael Prichard. 13 cass. (Running Time: 19 hrs. 30 min.). 2000. 104.00 (978-0-7366-4925-4(5)) Books on Tape.
A fictional speculation on one of modern history's central events: the assassination of John F. Kennedy.

Libra: September Twenty-Three - October-Twenty-Two. Barrie Konicov. 1 cass. (Hypno-Astrology Ser.). 11.98 (978-0-87082-095-3(8), 079) Potentials.
The author, Barrie Konicov, explains how each sign of the Zodiac has its positive & negative aspects, & that as individuals, in order to master our own destiny, we must enhance our positive traits.

Libra: September Twenty-Three - October Twenty-Two. Barrie Konicov. 4 cass. 16.98 (978-1-56001-567-3(5), SC-II HA079) Potentials.

Libra: The Cat Who Saved Silicon Valley. Lincoln Taiz. Illus. by Lee Taiz. (J). 2002. pap. bk. 14.95 (978-0-9723044-0-5(1), AGP-1) Amsea Group.

Libra: Unleash the Power of Your True Self. 1 cass. (Running Time: 1 hr.). 1999. 9.99 (978-1-928996-06-4(X)) MonAge.

Libra: Your Relationship with the Energy of the Universe. Loy Young. 1993. 9.95 (978-1-882888-19-1(7)) Aquarius Hse.

Librarian from the Black Lagoon. Mike Thaler. Read by Alexander Gould. (Running Time: 9 hrs. 35 mins.). 2007. 8.95 (978-0-439-02770-0(5)); audio compact disk 12.95 (978-0-439-02769-4(1)) Scholastic Inc.

Librarian from the Black Lagoon. unabr. ed. Mike Thaler. Read by Alexander Gould. Illus. by Jared D. Lee. 1 CD. (Running Time: 9 mins.). (J). (gr. k-2). 2007. pap. bk. 18.95 (978-0-439-02774-8(8)); pap. bk. 14.95 (978-0-439-02773-1(X)) Scholastic Inc.

Librarian of Congress, James Billington: To Honor the Intellect. (Running Time: 60 min.). 1989. 11.95 (K0460B090, HarperThor) HarpC GBR.

Librarians Speaking: A. G. Mackenzie. Interview with A. G. Mackenzie. Prod. by David Gerard. 50.00 St Mut.
The librarian discusses experience of the profession & its evolution during the past fifty years as well as own individual contributions to scholarship or library development.

Librarians Speaking: A. W. McClellan. Interview with A. W. McClellan. Prod. by David Gerard. 80.00 St Mut.

Librarians Speaking: Dr. Robert Shackleton. Interview with Robert Shackleton. Prod. by David Gerard. 80.00 St Mut.

Librarians Speaking: Evelyn Evans. Interview with Evelyn Evans. Prod. by David Gerard. 50.00 St Mut.
The librarian discusses experiences of the profession & its evolution during the past fifty years as well as own individual contributions to scholarship or library development.

Librarians Speaking: F. G. B. Hutchings. Interview with F. G. Hutchings. Prod. by David Gerard. 80.00 St Mut.
The librarian discusses experience of the profession & its evolution during the past fifty years as well as own individual contributions to scholarship or library development.

Librarians Speaking: Frank Gardner. Interview with Frank Gardner. Prod. by David Gerard. 50.00 St Mut.

Librarians Speaking: Harold Lancour. Interview with Harold Lancour. Prod. by David Gerard. 50.00 St Mut.

Librarians Speaking: Howard Nixon. Interview with Howard Nixon. Prod. by David Gerard. 50.00 St Mut.

Librarians Speaking: J. N. L. Myers. Interview with J. N. Myers. Prod. by David Gerard. 50.00 St Mut.

Librarians Speaking: Kenneth Humphreys. Interview with Kenneth Humphreys. Prod. by David Gerard. 50.00 St Mut.

Librarians Speaking: Lorna Paulin. Interview with Lorna Paulin. Prod. by David Gerard. 50.00 St Mut.

Librarians Speaking: Sir Frank Francis. Interview with Frank Francis. Prod. by David Gerard. 50.00 St Mut.

Librarians Speaking: Sir Frederick Dainton. Interview with Frederick Dainton. Prod. by David Gerard. 50.00 St Mut.
The librarian discusses experiences of the profession & its evolution during the past fifty years as well as own individual contributions to scholarship or library development.

Librarians Speaking: The Making of a Bibliography. Prod. by David Gerard. 50.00 St Mut.

Librarians Speaking: Thomas Kelly. Interview with Thomas Kelly. Prod. by David Gerard. 50.00 St Mut.
The librarian discusses experience of the profession & its evolution during the past fifty years as well as own individual contributions to scholarship or library development.

Librarians Speaking: W. A. Munford. Interview with W. A. Munford. Prod. by David Gerard. 50.00 St Mut.

Library. 1 cass. (Running Time: 35 min.). (J). (gr. k-3). 2001. bk. 24.95 (VX-54C) Kimbo Educ.
Elizabeth doesn't like dolls & she doesn't like to skate. She likes to read books. Lots of books. Includes read along book.

Library. Sarah Stewart. Read by Randye Kaye. Illus. by David Small. 1 cass. (J). 2000. pap. bk. 19.97 (978-0-7366-9189-5(8)) Books on Tape.
Gentle humorous verse.

Library. Sarah Stewart. Illus. by David Small. 14 vols. (Running Time: 6 mins.). pap. bk. 35.95 (978-1-59519-010-9(4)) Live Oak Media.

Library. Sarah Stewart. Illus. by David Small. (Running Time: 6 mins.). 1996. 9.95 (978-1-59112-075-9(6)); audio compact disk 12.95 (978-1-59519-008-6(2)) Live Oak Media.

Library. Sarah Stewart. Read by Randye Kaye. Illus. by David Small. 11 vols. (Running Time: 6 mins.). (J). (gr. 1-6). 1996. bk. 25.95 (978-0-87499-359-2(8)) Live Oak Media.
Elizabeth Brown doesn't like to play with dolls & she doesn't like to skate. What she does like to do is read books. Lots of books. The only problem is that her library has gotten so big she can't even use her front door anymore. What should Elizabeth Brown do? Start her own public library, of course.

Library. unabr. ed. Sarah Stewart. Read by Randye Kaye. Illus. by David Small. 11 vols. (Running Time: 6 mins.). (Live Oak Readalong Ser.). (J). (gr. 1-6). 1996. pap. bk. 16.95 (978-0-87499-608-1(2)) AudioGO.

Library: An Unquiet History. unabr. ed. Matthew Battles. 5 cass. (Running Time: 7 hrs. 30 min.). 2003. 63.00 (978-0-7366-9672-2(5)) Books on Tape.
For rare-books librarian Matthew Battles, libraries represent a compelling paradox. On the one hand, they exist to collect and preserve knowledge. On the other hand, they have been used to control, restrict, and sometimes obliterate knowledge. Battles takes us on a spirited foray from classical scriptoria to medieval monasteries, from the Vatican to the British Library, from socialist reading rooms and rural home libraries to the Information Age. At the same time, he gives due attention to both what has been found and what has been lost - from the clay tablets of ancient Mesopotamia to the storied Alexandrian libraries in Egypt, from the burned scrolls of China's Q'ing Dynasty to the book pyres of the Hitler Youth.

Library, Build Your Own, Pt. 1. unabr. ed. Gilbert Highet. 1 cass. (Running Time: 30 min). (Gilbert Highet Ser.). 9.95 (23335) J Norton Pubs.
Advice on building a personal library: the delights & rewards found only in reading.

Library Collection. Abr. by iSummaries Staff. 2007. audio compact disk 299.95 (978-1-934488-26-3(7)) L England.

Library Lion. Michelle Knudsen. Illus. by Kevin Hawkes. Narrated by Christine Marshall. 1 CD. (Running Time: 15 mins.). (J). (ps-2). 2008. bk. 28.95 (978-1-4301-0292-2(6)) Live Oak Media.

Library Lion. Michelle Knudsen. Illus. by Kevin Hawkes. Narrated by Christine Marshall. 1 cass. (Running Time: 15 mins.). (J). (ps-2). 2008. bk. 25.95 (978-1-4301-0289-2(6)) Live Oak Media.
Although Miss Merriweather is a stickler for rules, there doesn't seem to be any about lions in the library. And, this lion is very good about following the rules - until something scary happens to Miss Merriweather, and the only way the lion can help is by breaking the rules.

Library Macintosh. 2 cass. 1990. 16.00 set. Recorded Res.

Library of Doom, Part I: Poison Pages/Eyein the Graveyard/Teh Book That Dripped Blood. abr. ed. Michael Dahl. Read by Full Cast Production Staff. (Playaway Children Ser.). (J). 2008. 34.99 (978-1-60640-966-4(2)) Find a World.

Library of Doom, Part II: Attack of the Paper Bats/the Beast Beneath the Stairs/the Smashing Scroll. abr. ed. Michael Dahl. Read by Full Cast Production Staff. (Playaway Children Ser.). (J). 2008. 39.99 (978-1-60640-968-8(9)) Find a World.

Library Orientation: Syllabus. 2nd ed. Janet Bohlool. (J). 1975. 101.70 (978-0-89420-161-5(1), 140800) Natl Book.

Library Paradox. Catherine Shaw. 2008. 84.95 (978-1-4079-0175-6(3)); audio compact disk 89.95 (978-1-4079-0176-3(1)) Pub: Soundings Ltd GBR. Dist(s): Ulverscroft US

Library Policeman: Three Past Midnight. unabr. ed. Stephen King. Read by Ken Howard. (ENG., 2008. audio compact disk 36.95 (978-1-59887-749-6(6), 1598877496) Pub: HighBridge. Dist(s): Workman Pub

Libre Soy. 2001. 7.99 (978-0-8297-3454-6(6)) Pub: Vida Pubs. Dist(s): Zondervan

Libro de las Tierras Virgenes. unabr. ed. Rudyard Kipling. (SPA.). 2005. audio compact disk 59.99 (978-958-8218-77-9(2)) Pub: Yoyo Music COL. Dist(s): YoYoMusic

Libro dei Mori. Ed. by Cristiana Grocometti. Narrated by Maurizio Falyhera. (Visions of the World Ser.). (ITA.). 1999. bk. 29.95 (978-1-58214-128-2(2)) Language Assocs.

Libro dei Mori, Vol. 2. Ed. by Cristiana Grocometti. Narrated by Maurizio Falyhera. (Visions of the World Ser.). (ITA.). 1999. bk. 19.95 (978-1-58214-127-5(4)) Language Assocs.

Libro Ilustrado Sobre Cristobal Colon. unabr. ed. David A. Adler. 1 cass. (Running Time: 12 mins.).Tr. of Picture Book of Christopher Columbus. (SPA.). (J). (gr. 2-3). 1993. 14.95 (978-0-87499-313-4(X), LK5315) Live Oak Media.
Readalong of the Spanish translation of A Picture Book of Christopher Columbus.

Libro Ilustrado Sobre Martin Luther King, Hijo. David A. Adler. Illus. by Robert Casilla. 11 vols. (Running Time: 14 mins.).Tr. of Picture Book of Martin Luther King, Jr.. 1993. bk. 28.95 (978-1-59519-175-5(5)); pap. bk. 39.95 (978-1-59519-174-8(7)); 9.95 (978-1-59112-076-6(4)); audio compact disk 12.95 (978-1-59519-172-4(0)) Live Oak Media.

Libro Ilustrado Sobre Martin Luther King, Hijo. unabr. ed. David A. Adler. Read by Angel Pineda. Illus. by Robert Casilla. 11 vols. (Running Time: 14 mins.).Tr. of Picture Book of Martin Luther King, Jr.. (SPA.). (J). (gr. 1-6). 1993. bk. 25.95 (978-0-87499-297-7(4)); pap. bk. & tchr. ed. 37.95 Reading Chest. (978-0-87499-298-4(2)) Live Oak Media.
Readalong of the translation of A Picture Book of Martin Luther King, Jr.

Libros para Contar. abr. ed. Alma Flor Ada. (Libros para Contar / Stories for the Telling Ser.). (SPA.). (J). (ps-3). 2008. audio compact disk 15.95 (978-1-60396-346-6(4), Alfaguara) Santillana.

License to Steal. unabr. ed. Walter Shaw. Read by Joe Barrett. (Running Time: 7 hrs. 0 mins.). 2009. audio compact disk 24.95 (978-1-4332-3574-0(9)) Blckstn Audio.

License to Steal. unabr. ed. Walter T. Shaw & Mary Jane Robinson. Read by Joe Barrett. (Running Time: 7 hrs. NaN mins.). 2009. audio compact disk 60.00 (978-1-4332-3572-6(2)); audio compact disk 54.95 (978-1-4332-3571-9(4)) Blckstn Audio.

License to Steal. unabr. ed. Walter T. Shaw & Mary Jane Robinson. Read by Joe Barrett. (Running Time: 7 hrs. 0 mins.). 2009. 29.95 (978-1-4332-3575-7(7)) Blckstn Audio.

Licensed to Kill see Ship That Died of Shame

Lick & a Promise: Spank! Series. 2005. audio compact disk 15.95 (978-0-9759671-5-7(0)) Sounds Pubng Inc.

Lick of Frost. Laurell K. Hamilton. Read by Laural Merlington. (Meredith Gentry Ser.: No. 6). 2008. 69.99 (978-1-60640-790-5(2)) Find a World.

Lick of Frost. abr. ed. Laurell K. Hamilton. Read by Laural Merlington. (Running Time: 6 hrs.). (Meredith Gentry Ser.: No. 6). 2008. audio compact disk 14.99 (978-1-4233-4046-1(9), 9781423340461, BCD Value Price) Brilliance Audio.

Lick of Frost. unabr. ed. Laurell K. Hamilton. (Running Time: 9 hrs.). (Meredith Gentry Ser.: No. 6). 2007. 39.25 (978-1-4233-4044-7(2), 9781423340447, BADLE); 24.95 (978-1-4233-4043-0(4), 9781423340430, BAD) Brilliance Audio.

Lick of Frost. unabr. ed. Laurell K. Hamilton. Read by Laural Merlington. 9 cass. (Running Time: 9 hrs.). (Meredith Gentry Ser.: No. 6). 2007. 92.25 (978-1-4233-4038-6(8), 9781423340386, BrilAudUnabridg); audio compact disk 97.25 (978-1-4233-4040-9(X), 9781423340409, BriAudCD Unabrid); audio compact disk 39.25 (978-1-4233-4042-3(6), 9781423340423, Brinc Audio MP3 Lib); audio compact disk 24.95 (978-1-4233-4041-6(8), 9781423340416, Brilliance MP3); audio compact disk 36.95 (978-1-4233-4039-3(6), 9781423340393, Bril Audio CD Unabri) Brilliance Audio.

Licks of Love: Short Stories & a Sequel, Rabbit Remembered. John Updike. Read by Michael Prichard. 2001. audio compact disk 88.00 (978-0-7366-6220-8(0)) Books on Tape.

Licks of Love: Short Stories & a Sequel, Rabbit Remembered. unabr. ed. John Updike. Read by Michael Prichard. 9 cass. (Running Time: 13 hrs. 30 mins.). 2001. 72.00 (978-0-7366-6038-9(0)) Books on Tape.
A story in which an American banjo virtuoso demonstrates his licks to an enthralled Soviet audience in the heart of the Cold War.

Licks of Love: Short Stories & a Sequel, Rabbit Remembered. unabr. ed. John Updike. Read by Jonathan Marosz. 9 cass. (Running Time: 12 hrs.). 2001. 34.95 (978-0-7366-5985-7(4)) Books on Tape.
A dozen short stories & a novella from one of America's greatest men of letters.

Licks of Love: Short Stories & a Sequel, Rabbit Remembered. unabr. collector's ed. Short Stories. John Updike. Read by Jonathan Marosz. Narrated by Michael Prichard. 11 CDs. (Running Time: 12 hrs.). 2001. audio compact disk 39.95 (978-0-7366-5986-4(2)) Books on Tape.

Liddy & the Volcanoes. Godwin Chu. (Natural Disasters Ser.). 2001. audio compact disk 18.95 (978-1-4105-0164-6(7)) D Johnston Inc.

Liddy & the Volcanoes. Godwin Chu. Ed. by Jerry Stemach. Illus. by Jeff Ham. Narrated by Denise Jordan Walker. 2001. audio compact disk 200.00 (978-1-58702-527-3(2)) D Johnston Inc.

Liddy & the Volcanoes, Vol. 3. Godwin Chu. Ed. by Jerry Stemach et al. Illus. by Jeff Ham & Susan Baptist. Narrated by Denise Jordan Walker. Contrib. by Ted S. Hasselbring. (Start-to-Finish Books). (J). (gr. 2-3). 2001. 35.00 (978-1-58702-528-0(0)) D Johnston Inc.

Liddy & the Volcanoes, Vol. 3. Godwin Chu. Ed. by Jerry Stemach et al. Illus. by Jeff Ham & Susan Baptist. Narrated by Denise Jordan Walker. Contrib. by Ted S. Hasselbring. (Start-to-Finish Books). (J). (gr. 2-3). 2002. 100.00 (978-1-58702-952-3(9)) D Johnston Inc.

Liddy & the Volcanoes, Vol. 3. unabr. ed. Godwin Chu. Ed. by Jerry Stemach et al. Illus. by Jeff Ham & Susan Baptist. Narrated by Denise Jordan Walker. Contrib. by Ted S. Hasselbring. 1 cass. (Running Time: 1 hr.). (Start-to-Finish Books). 2001. (978-1-58702-377-4(6), F37K2) D Johnston Inc.
Young Liddy Miller's father, a geologist, is always talking about volcanoes. Then, when Liddy is 14, she witnesses a volcanic eruption firsthand. Liddy is camping with her parents near Mount St. Helens when the sleeping giant erupts. This experience serves to peak Liddy's curiosity about volcanos. Through kitchen sink lessons and science project experiments, Liddy learns about volcanos. But Liddy's volcano education intensifies when she and her father pack their bags to visit volcanos.

Lider Conforme Al Corazon de Dics. Palemon Camu. (SPA.). 2004. 25.00 (978-0-89985-432-8(X)) Christ for the Nations.

lider de la próxima generación audio Libro: Cinco elementos esenciales para los forjadores del Futuro. unabr. ed. (SPA.). 2007. audio compact disk 16.99 (978-987-557-140-2(7)) Zondervan.

Lider De 360: Como Desarrollar Su Influencia Desde Cualquier Posicion en Su Organizacion. abr. ed. John C. Maxwell. (Running Time: 3 hrs. 30 mins.). (SPA.). 2006. audio compact disk 24.99 (978-0-88113-946-4(7)) Pub: Grupo Nelson. Dist(s): Nelson

Liderazgo Centrado en Principios. Stephen R. Covey. 4 cass. (Running Time: 4 hrs.).Tr. of Principle-Centered Leadership. (SPA.). 2002. 24.95 (978-970-05-1014-9(X)) Taller del Exito.
Shows us how to avoid the pitfalls of ineffective people. In order to harness your drive to succeed in all areas, we must learn to center our lives according to a set of certain basic principles.

Liderazgo con Proposito: Volume 1: Lecciones de Liderazgo Basadas en Nehemias. Rick Warren. (SPA.). (gr. 8-11). 2006. audio compact disk 19.99 (978-0-8297-4895-6(4)) Pub: Vida Pubs. Dist(s): Zondervan

Liderazgo en tiempo de Crisis. Prod. by HLM. (SPA.). 2004. 11.99 (978-1-885630-83-4(2)) Jayah Producc.

Liderazgo en tiempos de Crisis. Prod. by HLM. (SPA.). 2004. audio compact disk 14.99 (978-1-885630-84-1(0)) Jayah Producc.

Liderazgo, principios de Oro: Las Lecciones que he Aprendido de una Vida de Liderazgo. abr. ed. John C. Maxwell. (Running Time: 4 hrs. 25 mins.). (SPA.). 2008. audio compact disk 24.99 (978-1-60255-034-6(4)) Pub: Grupo Nelson. Dist(s): Nelson

***Liderazgo Progresivo.** Juan G. Ruelas. (SPA.). 2010. audio compact disk 20.00 (978-0-9825883-3-8(X)) Editorial Equipov.

Liderazgo Real. abr. ed. John C. Maxwell. (Running Time: 4 hrs. 40 mins.). (SPA.). 2006. audio compact disk 24.99 (978-0-88113-991-4(2)) Pub: Grupo Nelson. Dist(s): Nelson

Lideres bajo Presion see Leading under Pressure: Strategies to Maximize Peak Performance & Productivity while Maximizing Health & Wellbeing

Lideres bajo Presion see Leading under Pressure: Strategies to Maximize Peak Performance, Productivity & Wellbeing

Lideres bajo Presion see Leading under Pressure: Strategies to Maximize Peak Performance & Productivity while Maximizing Health & Wellbeing

Lideres del Tercer Milenio. Miguel Angel Cornejo. 2 cass. (Running Time: 2 hrs.).Tr. of Leaders of the Third Millenium. (SPA.). 2002. 20.00 (978-968-6210-45-3(8)) Taller del Exito.
A compendium of the keys to succeed in life contributed by today's leaders and visionaries.

Lideres y Dirigentes. P. Juan Rivas. (SPA.). (YA). 2003. audio compact disk 18.95 (978-1-935405-95-5(0)) Hombre Nuevo.

Lie. Michael Weaver. 1998. (978-1-57042-182-2(X)) Hachet Audio.

Lie. abr. ed. Michael Weaver. Read by Edward Herrmann. (ENG.). 2006. 9.99 (978-1-59483-832-3(1)) Pub: Hachet Audio. Dist(s): HachBkGrp

Lie. unabr. ed. Michael Weaver. Read by Brian Emerson & Patrick Cullens. 8 cass. (Running Time: 11 hrs. 30 mins.). 1998. 56.95 (978-0-7861-1318-7(9), 2243) Blckstn Audio.
The eyes of the world are locked on the International Conference on Human Rights being held in Germany. What cannot be seen are the powerful intrigues underlying the conference. A web is tightening around the President of the United States. As an even greater threat is about to cast a terrifying global shadow, unless two young lovers can reveal that the entire conference is a lie.

Lie: A Novel by the Author of Impulse. abr. ed. Michael Weaver. Read by Edward Herrmann. 2 cass. 2001. 7.95 (978-1-57815-203-2(8), Media Bks Audio) Media Bks NJ.

Lie: Evolution. 1 cass. (Running Time: 1 hr.). 12.99 (978-0-89051-287-6(6)) Master Bks.

Lie: Evolution - Audio. Narrated by Tom Dooley. 2005. audio compact disk 15.99 (978-0-89051-446-7(1)) Master Bks.
This is the most powerful message for Christians witnessing to this generation. Completely debunks the myth of evolution.

Lie by Moonlight. abr. ed. Amanda Quick, pseud. Read by Anne Flosnik. (Running Time: 6 hrs.). 2006. audio compact disk 16.99 (978-1-59600-847-2(4), 9781596008472) Brilliance Audio.
Please enter a Synopsis.

Lie by Moonlight. unabr. ed. Amanda Quick, pseud. Read by Anne Flosnik. (Running Time: 9 hrs.). 2005. 39.25 (978-1-59710-827-0(8), 9781597108270, BADLE); 24.95 (978-1-59710-826-3(X), 9781597108263, BAD); 29.95 (978-1-59355-466-8(4), 9781593554668, BAU); cass., cass., DVD 74.25 (978-1-59355-467-5(2), 9781593554675, BrilAudUnabridg); DVD & audio compact disk 39.25 (978-1-59335-859-4(8), 9781593358594, Brlnc Audio MP3 Lib); DVD, audio compact disk, audio compact disk 92.25 (978-1-59355-469-9(9), 9781593554699, BriAudCD Unabrid); audio compact disk 34.95 (978-1-59355-468-2(0), 9781593554682, Bril Audio CD Unabri); audio compact disk 24.95 (978-1-59335-725-2(7), 9781593357252, Brilliance MP3) Brilliance Audio.

Lie down in Darkness. unabr. collector's ed. William Styron. Read by Wolfram Kandinsky. 14 cass. (Running Time: 21 hrs.). 1984. 112.00 (978-0-7366-0929-6(6), 1873) Books on Tape.
The South looms dark & ominous in the background of Styron's first novel. The author focuses on the region's biblical rhetoric, racial conflicts & headlong industrialization.

Lie down with Lions. abr. ed. Ken Follett. 2 cass. (Running Time: 3 hrs.). (ENG., 2001. (978-0-333-73529-9(3)) Macmillan UK GBR.

Lie down with Lions. unabr. ed. Ken Follett. Read by Richard Green. 9 cass. (Running Time: 13 hrs. 30 mins.). 1986. 72.00 (978-0-7366-0591-5(6), 1558) Books on Tape.
In Afghanistan there is a remote valley called the Valley of Five Lions. A young Englishwoman, a French physician & a roving American have their own reasons for journeying to this place where mountain-bred rebels wage a guerilla war against the invading Russians. A Russian commander plots to use his own secret weapon & a brave woman uncovers a plot that forces her to make a terrifying decision.

Lie down with Lions. unabr. ed. Ken Follett. Read by Multivoice Production Staff. (Running Time: 10 hrs.). 2004. 24.95 (978-1-59335-748-1(6), 1593357486, Brilliance MP3); 39.25 (978-1-59335-882-2(2), 1593358822, Brlnc Audio MP3 Lib); 29.95 (978-1-59355-652-5(7), 1593556527, BAU) Brilliance Audio.
Ellis, the American. Jean-Pierre, the Frenchman. They were two men on opposite sides of the cold war, with a woman torn between them. Together, they formed a triangle of passion and deception, racing from terrorist bombs in Paris to the violence and intrigue of Afghanistan - to the moment of truth and deadly decision for all of them... "A deadly romantic triangle, a clandestine mission with global stakes, an exotic location, a plot as gripping and ingenious as Eye of the Needle ... engineered to perfection with breathless acceleration. I couldn't put it down!" - Los Angeles Times "Masterful... plot and counterplot, treachery, cunning and killing ... keep you on edge every moment" - Associated Press.

Lie down with Lions. unabr. ed. Ken Follett. (Running Time: 10 hrs.). 2004. 24.95 (978-1-59710-452-4(3), 1597104523, BAD) Brilliance Audio.

Lie down with Lions. unabr. ed. Ken Follett. Read by Multivoice Production Staff. (Running Time: 10 hrs.). 2004. 39.25 (978-1-59710-453-1(1), 1597104531, BADLE) Brilliance Audio.

Lie down with Lions. unabr. ed. Ken Follett. Read by Multivoice Production Staff. (Running Time: 10 hrs.). 2007. audio compact disk 38.95 (978-1-4233-2863-6(9), 9781423328636, Bril Audio CD Unabri); audio compact disk 97.25 (978-1-4233-2864-3(7), 9781423328643, BriAudCD Unabrid) Brilliance Audio.

Lie down with Lions; Eye of the Needle; Triple. unabr. ed. Ken Follett. (Running Time: 31 hrs.). 2009. audio compact disk 39.99 (978-1-4233-8652-0(3), 9781423386520) Brilliance Audio.

Lieberman's Day. unabr. ed. Stuart M. Kaminsky. Narrated by George Guidall. 6 cass. (Running Time: 7 hrs. 30 mins.). (Abe Lieberman Mystery Ser.: Vol. 3). 2000. 51.00 (978-0-7887-0418-5(4), 94610E7) Recorded Bks.
One December day, Lieberman's family is suddenly crippled by a violent crime. Veteran Chicago cop, Abe Liberman searches relentlessly for the criminals involved.

Lieberman's Law. unabr. ed. Stuart M. Kaminsky. Read by Scott Harrison. 7 cass. (Running Time: 10 hrs. 30 mins.). (Abe Lieberman Mystery Ser.: Vol. 5). 1999. 49.95 (1840) Blckstn Audio.
A Chicago police detective, he is reminded just how deep the roots of hate & revenge can go when the local temple to which he & his wife belong is vandalized. Suspicion quickly falls on both militant Jewish & Muslim groups who oppose the temple's moderate stance on Palestine. But it's also clear that local skinheads are involved & that the rampage that led to the deaths of three young Muslims has only just begun.

Lieberman's Law. unabr. ed. Stuart M. Kaminsky. Read by Scott Harrison. 7 cass. (Running Time: 10 hrs.). (Abe Lieberman Mystery Ser.: Vol. 5). 1997. 49.95 (978-0-7861-1070-4(8), 1840) Blckstn Audio.
Chicago police detective Abe Lieberman is reminded just how deep the roots of hate & revenge can go when the local temple to which he & his wife belong is vandalized. Suspicion quickly falls on both militant Jewish & Muslim groups who oppose the temple's moderate stance on Palestine. But it's also clear that local skinheads are involved, & that the rampage that led to the deaths of three young Muslims has only just begun.

Lieberman's Law. unabr. ed. Stuart M. Kaminsky. Narrated by George Guidall. 7 cass. (Running Time: 10 hrs.). (Abe Lieberman Mystery Ser.: Vol. 5). 1996. 60.00 (978-0-7887-0586-1(5), 94705E7) Recorded Bks.
When his synagogue is desecrated and its priceless Torah is stolen, veteran police detective Abe Lieberman embarks on an investigation that links two unlikely allies.

Lieberman's Thief. unabr. ed. Stuart M. Kaminsky. Read by David Colacci. (Running Time: 7 hrs.). 2008. 24.95 (978-1-4233-5933-3(X), 9781423359333, BAD); 24.95 (978-1-4233-5931-9(3), 9781423359319, Brilliance MP3); 39.25 (978-1-4233-5932-6(1), 9781423359326, Brlnc Audio MP3 Lib); 39.25 (978-1-4233-5934-0(8), 9781423359340, BADLE) Brilliance Audio.

Liebestod. Short Stories. James McKinley. Read by James McKinley. 1 cass. (Running Time: 23 min.). 12.95 (978-1-55644-074-8(X), 3081) Am Audio Prose.
McKinley reads his short stories including "Meridians".

Lieder. 2 CDs. (GER.). audio compact disk 69.95 (978-0-8219-2623-9(3)) EMC-Paradigm.

Lieder, 1. 2 CDs. (GER.). audio compact disk 64.95 (978-0-8219-2515-7(6)) EMC-Paradigm.

Liens on Personal Injury Recoveries. Read by James R. Chiosso et al. (Running Time: 3 hrs.). 1989. 65.00 Incl. 182p. tape materials. (TO-53110) Cont Ed Bar-CA.
Learn how to determine the validity of liens, understand the basis for negotiating compromise, & accurately account for liens in calculating plaintiff's recovery.

Lies & the Lying Liars Who Tell Them: A Fair & Balanced Look at the Right. unabr. ed. Al Franken. Read by Al Franken. 6 CDs. (Running Time: 10 hrs.). (ENG.). 2003. audio compact disk 34.95 (978-1-56511-797-6(2), 1565117972) Pub: HighBridge. Dist(s): Workman Pub

Lies, Lies, Lies: Program from the Award Winning Public Radio Series. Interview. Hosted by Fred Goodwin. Comment by John Hockenberry. 1 CD. (Running Time: 1 hr). 2001. audio compact disk 21.95 (978-1-932479-61-4(9), LCM 161) Lichtenstein Creat.
The show starts off with a look at a character from the children's animated show "Rugrats," and follows up with a look at real children, with child psychiatrist Dr. Elizabeth Berger. Dr. Paul Ekman, University of California, San Francisco, clues us into what he's found in over thirty years of researching why and how people lie. J.J. Newberry, of the Institute of Analytic Interviewing, tells us how he puts Dr. Ekman's findings into action in training police. And is lying in therapy necessarily bad? According to some psychiatrists, lies, fantasy, dreams, and the truth itself are all grist for the mill. We also hear from filmmaker Pola Rapaport, about her recent documentary, "Family Secrets." Plus, John Hockenberry recalls the Rodney King case, in which the adage "the camera never lies" was turned on its head.

Lies My Father Told Me/Never Had It So Good. Ted Allan & Charles Israel. Contrib. by Lucio Agostini. 2 cass. (Running Time: 2 hrs.). (Stage Ser.). 2004. 18.99 (978-1-894003-15-5(2)) Pub: Scenario Prods CAN. Dist(s): PerseuPGW
A story of Jewish family battling the pressures between three generations in this comedy-drama set in 1920s Montreal. Together with this story is Charles Israel's "Never Had It So Good." After World War II, an American Army Colonel stationed in occupied Germany has orders to set up a school on lands recently developed into a Kibbutz by Jewish concentration camp survivors. As the two groups are at odds, Dorothy, the Colonel's daughter arrives to visit her father. She meets Peter, the Kibbutz leader and to the Colonel's dismay the two begin a relationship.

Lies My Teacher Told Me: Everything Your American History Textbook Got Wrong. James W. Loewen. Narrated by Brian Keeler. 10 cass. (Running Time: 14 hrs. 45 mins.). 93.00 (978-1-4025-2879-8(5)) Recorded Bks.

Lies My Teacher Told Me: Everything Your American History Textbook Got Wrong. unabr. ed. James W. Loewen. Narrated by Brian Keeler. 12 CDs. (Running Time: 14 hrs. 45 mins.). 2004. audio compact disk 29.99 (978-1-4025-7937-0(3), 01562) Recorded Bks.
James W. Loewen, a sociology professor and distinguished critic of history education, puts 12 popular textbooks under the microscope-and what he discovers will surprise you. In his opinion, every one of these texts fails to make its subject interesting or memorable. Worse still is the proliferation of blind patriotism, mindless optimism and misinformation filling the pages. From the truth about Christopher Columbus to the harsh reality of the Vietnam War, Loewen picks apart the lies we've been told. This is a book that will forever change your view of the past.

Lies of Locke Lamora. unabr. ed. Scott Lynch. (Running Time: 23 hrs. 0 mins. 0 sec.). (Gentlemen Bastards Ser.). (ENG.). 2009. audio compact disk 109.99 (978-1-4001-4051-0(X)); audio compact disk 54.99 (978-1-4001-1051-3(3)) Pub: Tantor Media. Dist(s): IngramPubServ

Lies of Locke Lamora. unabr. ed. Scott Lynch. Read by Michael Page. (Running Time: 23 hrs. 0 mins. 0 sec.). (Gentlemen Bastards Ser.). (ENG.). 2009. audio compact disk 39.99 (978-1-4001-6051-8(0)) Pub: Tantor Media. Dist(s): IngramPubServ

Lies of Silence. unabr. ed. Brian Moore. Narrated by Steven Crossley. 5 cass. (Running Time: 7 hrs.). 1997. 44.00 (978-0-7887-1304-0(3), 95141E7) Recorded Bks.
Michael Dillon is climbing the ladder of success. He is manager of a luxury hotel in Belfast, his wife is gorgeous, his girlfriend adores him. The IRA has a deadly plan, however, that will put Michael in an impossible position, caught between bombs & conflicting loyalties.

Lies That Bind. unabr. ed. Edward De Angelo. Read by Bruce Reizen. 7 cass. (Running Time: 10 hrs.). 2000. 32.95 (978-1-58788-093-3(8), 1587880938, BAU) Brilliance Audio.
Executive VP Peter Morrison, divorced father of 13-year-old Sam, has always suspected - deep down inside - that Sam is not his biological child. This doubt gnaws at him until he seizes an opportunity to have their blood tested and his horrible fears confirmed. Furious, confused, and hurt, he lashes out at his ex-wife. She retaliates by refusing to let him see Sam, and by telling the boy that his beloved father is really no such thing. In an effort to regain visitation rights, Peter sues for the return of years of generous child support payments. In the ensuing courtroom battle, he is forced to confront whether he can still be a father to a boy who has no biological or legal connection to him. This is a finely wrought, gripping page-turner that addresses the very definition of fatherhood - is it blood, money, or love?.

Lies That Bind. unabr. ed. Edward De Angelo. Read by Bruce Reizen. (Running Time: 10 hrs.). 2005. 39.25 (978-1-59600-614-0(5), 9781596006140, BADLE); 24.95 (978-1-59600-613-3(7), 9781596006133, BAD) Brilliance Audio.

Lies That Bind. unabr. ed. Edward DeAngelo. Read by Bruce Reizen. (Running Time: 10 hrs.). 2005. 24.95 (978-1-59600-611-9(0), 9781596006119, Brilliance MP3); 39.25 (978-1-59600-612-6(9), 9781596006126, Brlnc Audio MP3 Lib) Brilliance Audio.

Lies the Government Told You: Myth, Power, & Deception in American History. unabr. ed. Andrew P. Napolitano. Narrated by Andrew P. Napolitano. (Running Time: 11 hrs. 56 mins. 54 sec.). (ENG.). 2010. 24.49 (978-1-60814-654-3(5), SpringWater); audio compact disk 34.99 (978-1-59859-711-0(6), SpringWater) Oasis Audio.

Lies Women Believe: And the Truth That Sets Them Free. abr. ed. Nancy Leigh DeMoss. 4 cass. (Running Time: 5 hrs.). 2003. 24.99 (978-1-58926-108-2(9), M64L-0120) Oasis Audio.
Exposes areas of deception common to many Christian women - lies about God, sin, priorities, marriage and family, emotions, and more. Deals honestly with women¿s delusions and illusions and then gently leads them to the truth of God¿s word that leads to true freedom.

Lies Women Believe: And the Truth That Sets Them Free. abr. ed. Nancy Leigh DeMoss. Narrated by Lisa Helm. (ENG.). 2003. 19.59 (978-1-60814-285-9(X)) Oasis Audio.

Lies Women Believe: And the Truth That Sets Them Free. unabr. ed. Nancy Leigh DeMoss. Narrated by Lisa Helm. 4 CDs. (Running Time: 5 hrs.). (ENG.). 2003. audio compact disk 27.99 (978-1-58926-109-9(7), M64L-012D) Oasis Audio.

Lies Women Believe, & The Truth That Sets Them Free! 2000. (978-0-940110-07-6(5)) Life Action Publishing.

Lies Women Believe Conf Audio. Nancy Leigh DeMoss. (ENG.). 2007. audio compact disk 19.99 (978-0-940110-76-2(8)) Life Action Publishing.

Lies You Believe about Sex: Logos Feb. 13, 2000. Ben Young. 2000. 4.95 (978-0-7417-6169-9(6), B0169) Win Walk.

Lies Young Women Believe: And the Truth That Sets Them Free. unabr. ed. Nancy Leigh DeMoss & Dannah Gresh. Narrated by Christie O. King. (ENG.). (YA). 2008. 11.89 (978-1-60814-286-6(8)) Oasis Audio.

Lies Young Women Believe: And the Truth That Sets Them Free. unabr. ed. Nancy Leigh DeMoss & Dannah Gresh. Read by Christie King. (Running Time: 5 hrs. 9 mins. 51 sec.). (YA). 2008. audio compact disk 16.99 (978-1-59859-326-6(9)) Oasis Audio.

***Lieutenant.** unabr. ed. Kate Grenville. Read by Nicholas Bell. (Running Time: 7 hrs. 5 mins.). 2010. audio compact disk 77.95 (978-1-74214-058-2(0), 9781742140582) Pub: Bolinda Pubng AUS. Dist(s): Bolinda Pub Inc

Lieutenant Cameron RNVR. unabr. ed. Philip McCutchan. 5 cass. 1998. 63.95 (978-1-85903-068-4(8)) Pub: Magna Story GBR. Dist(s): Ulverscroft US

Lieutenant Fury. G. S. Beard. 2008. 84.95 (978-1-4079-0279-1(2)); audio compact disk 99.95 (978-1-4079-0280-7(6)) Pub: Soundings Ltd GBR. Dist(s): Ulverscroft US

Lieutenant Hornblower. C. S. Forester. Read by Geoffrey Howard. 2002. 48.00 (978-0-7366-8901-4(X)); audio compact disk 56.00 (978-0-7366-9126-0(X)) Books on Tape.

Lieutenant Hornblower. unabr. ed. C. S. Forester. Read by Bill Kelsey. 8 cass. (Running Time: 12 hrs.). (Hornblower Ser.). 2001. 29.95 (978-0-7366-6759-3(8)) Books on Tape.
Hornblower assumes first independent command.

Lieutenant Hornblower. unabr. collector's ed. C. S. Forester. Read by Bill Kelsey. 8 cass. (Running Time: 8 hrs.). (Hornblower Ser.: No. 2). 1984. 48.00 (978-0-7366-0651-6(3), 1612) Books on Tape.
This is the seventh novel in the Horatio Hornblower saga. Hornblower emerges from his apprenticeship as midshipman to assume the responsibilites that await him as a lieutenant.

Lieutenants. unabr. collector's ed. W. E. B. Griffin. Read by Michael Russotto. 11 cass. (Running Time: 16 hrs. 30 min.). (Brotherhood of War Ser.: No. 1). 1995. 88.00 (978-0-7366-2916-4(5), 3613) Books on Tape.
WWII through the eyes of the men forged in the heat of battle.

Life. 1 cass. (First Steps in Science Ser.). (J). 12.00 (6366-0, Natl Textbk Co) M-H Contemporary.
Helps children in grades 1-4 discover the process of scientific investigation. Part of the First Steps in Science Program.

Life. Emmet Fox. 1 cass. (Running Time: 60 min.). (Sermon on the Mount Ser.). 9.95 HarperCollins Pubs.
Includes "Choosing the Life I Live".

***Life.** unabr. ed. Keith Richards & James Fox. Read by Keith Richards et al. (Running Time: 22 hrs. 30 mins.). 2010. 24.98 (978-1-60788-645-7(6)) Pub: Hachet Audio. Dist(s): HachBkGrp

***Life.** unabr. ed. Keith Richards & James Fox. Read by Keith Richards et al. 20 CDs. (Running Time: 22 hrs. 30 mins.). (ENG., 2010. audio compact disk 34.98 (978-1-60024-240-3(5)) Pub: Hachet Audio. Dist(s): HachBkGrp

Life: A Required Course. Kenneth Wapnick. 2008. 17.00 (978-1-59142-373-7(2)); audio compact disk 22.00 (978-1-59142-372-0(4)) Foun Miracles.

Life! Reflections on Your Journey. Louise L. Hay. 1 cass. 10.00 164T. (364) Hay House.
Deals with growing up, relatonships, work, spirituality, our elder years, death...& many of the problems, fears, & challenges that these passages bring.

Life! Reflections on Your Journey. abr. ed. Louise L. Hay. Read by Louise L. Hay. 2 cass. (Running Time: 2 hrs.). 1998. 15.95 (978-1-56170-216-9(1), 364) Hay House.
Louise reads the text of her book, which covers aspects of life including health, happiness being an elder of excellence.

***Life Actually (MP3)** Contrib. by Di Warren et al. 2005. 12.00 (978-1-921068-14-0(0)) Matthias MediaAUS AUS.

Life after Death. S. D. Gordon & Dan Harmon. 1998. 4.97 (978-1-57748-209-3(3)) Barbour Pub.

Life after Death: The Burden of Proof. abr. ed. Deepak Chopra. Read by Deepak Chopra. (YA). 2007. 44.99 (978-0-7393-7507-5(5)) Find a World.

Life after Death: The Burden of Proof. abr. ed. Deepak Chopra. Read by Deepak Chopra. (Running Time: 5 hrs.). (ENG.). 2006. audio compact disk 27.95 (978-0-7393-3439-3(5), Random AudioBks) Pub: Random Audio Pubg. Dist(s): Random

Life after Death: The Burden of Proof. unabr. ed. Deepak Chopra. 8 CDs. (Running Time: 9 hrs. 30 mins.). 2006. audio compact disk 68.85 (978-1-4159-3292-6(1)) Pub: Books on Tape. Dist(s): NetLibrary CO

Life after Death: The Evidence. unabr. ed. Dinesh D'Souza. (Running Time: 9 hrs. 0 mins.). (ENG.). 2009. 29.95 (978-1-4417-0633-1(X)); 59.95 (978-1-4417-0629-4(1)); audio compact disk 76.00 (978-1-4417-0630-0(5)); audio compact disk & audio compact disk 29.95 (978-1-4417-0632-4(1)) Blckstn Audio.

Life after death a renowned psychic reveals what happens to us when we Die. Mary T. Brown. 2004. 7.95 (978-0-7435-4974-5(0)) Pub: S&S Audio. Dist(s): S and S Inc

Life after Loss: A Practical Guide to Renewing Your Life after Experiencing Major Loss. 4th unabr. ed. Bob Deits. Read by Steve Blane. (Running Time: 8 hrs.). (ENG.). 2008. 24.98 (978-1-59659-250-6(8), GildAudio) Pub: Gildan Media. Dist(s): HachBkGrp

Life after Lunch. unabr. ed. Sarah Harrison. Read by Sarah Harrison. 10 cass. (Running Time: 10 hrs.). 1997. 84.95 (978-0-7540-0029-7(X), CAB 1452) AudioGO.
Laura & Susan have had a love/hate relationship since their schooldays. Laura presides hopefully over a large family while Susan is exuberantly independent. At their regular lunches they view each other with a mixture of deep affection & suspicion. But when the balance suddenly alters, the two friends are surprised to discover something new & potentially wonderful about life after lunch.

Life after Marriage: Divorce As a New Beginning. unabr. ed. Mary Ann Singleton. Read by Nancy Dannevik. 7 cass. (Running Time: 7 hrs.). 1979. 42.00 (978-0-7366-0124-5(4), 1131) Books on Tape.
Designed as a self-help guide for divorced women. The author gives counsel on topics ranging from establishing credit to housekeeping while working full-time, as she explores the personal & psychological consequences of divorce.

Life after Mississippi. unabr. ed. James A. Autry. Read by James A. Autry. 1 cass. (Running Time: 90 min.). 1990. 9.95 (978-0-916242-63-3(3)) Yoknapatawpha.

Life after Television. unabr. ed. George Gilder. Read by Jeff Riggenbach. 2 cass. (Running Time: 2 hrs. 30 mins.). 2000. 17.95 (978-0-7861-0491-8(0), 1442) Blckstn Audio.

Life after Television. unabr. ed. George Gilder. Read by Jeff Riggenbach. 2 cass. (Running Time: 3 hrs.). 2000. 17.95 (1442) Blckstn Audio.
Why doesn't our technology better inform & uplift us? Because, writes Gilder, U.S. culture is mired in the increasingly outmoded, centralized, "spud-farm" technology of TV.

***Life after the pmp Exam.** Prod. by Praizion Media. 2010. audio compact disk 14.99 (978-1-934579-16-9(5)) Praizion Medis.

Life All Around Me by Ellen Foster. unabr. ed. Kaye Gibbons. Read by Kaye Gibbons. 3 cass. (Running Time: 5 hrs.). 2006. 36.00 (978-1-4159-2451-8(1)) Books on Tape.

Life among the Apaches. unabr. ed. John C. Cremony. Read by Gene Engene. 8 cass. (Running Time: 10 hrs. 30 mins.). Dramatization. 1990. 49.95 (978-1-55686-339-4(X), 102590) Books in Motion.
An exciting day by day account of the way it was in "Apacheria," as the Indian fighters called the Southwestern desert & mountains of California, Arizona & New Mexico. A down-in-the-dirt, action-filled account of each skirmish fought by Major C. Cremony.

Life & Achievements of Thomas Edison. Edwin Locke. 4 cass. (Running Time: 4 hrs. 30 min.). 1997. 39.95 (978-1-56114-387-0(1), EL45C) Second Renaissance.
An examination of the vast accomplishments of "the greatest inventor in history".

Life & Adventures of Nat Love, Better Known in the Cattle Country as "Deadwood Dick" see Black Pioneers in American History, Vol. 1, 19th Century

***Life & Adventures of Nicholas Nickleby.** unabr. ed. Charles Dickens. Narrated by Simon Vance. (Running Time: 37 hrs. 0 mins.). 2010. 35.99 (978-1-4526-7024-9(2)); 44.99 (978-1-4526-5024-1(1)); audio compact disk 64.99 (978-1-4526-0024-6(4)) Pub: Tantor Media. Dist(s): IngramPubServ

***Life & Adventures of Nicholas Nickleby (Library Edition)** unabr. ed. Charles Dickens. Narrated by Simon Vance. (Running Time: 37 hrs. 0 mins.). 2010. 64.99 (978-1-4526-2024-4(5)); audio compact disk 155.99 (978-1-4526-3024-3(0)) Pub: Tantor Media. Dist(s): IngramPubServ

Life & Adventures of Santa Claus. unabr. ed. Julie Lane. 2 cass. (J). 1995. 16.95 (978-0-9615664-2-5(6)) Parkhurst Brook Pubs.

Life & Afterlife. unabr. ed. Thomas Merton. Read by Thomas Merton. 2 cass. (Running Time: 1 hr. 22 min.). (Life & Prayer Ser.: No. 2). 1982. 19.95 Elec Paperback.
Tells why Christians must be active participants in God's plans for this world & how they will share in His glory in the world to come.

Life & Celebration. unabr. ed. Thomas Merton. Read by Thomas Merton. 1 cass. (Running Time: 52 min.). (Life & Prayer Ser.: No. 1). 1972. 10.95 Elec Paperback.
Commentary by the author on the Holy Week liturgy as an eschatological event & his faith in the "Church Jubilant" celebrating the world.

Life & Community. unabr. ed. Thomas Merton. Read by Thomas Merton. 1 cass. (Running Time: 56 min.). (Life & Prayer Ser.: No. 1). 1972. 10.95 Elec Paperback.
Views on the essence of community life & on the relationship between youth, the mass media & community.

Life & Contemplation. unabr. ed. Thomas Merton. Read by Thomas Merton. 1 cass. (Running Time: 59 min.). (Life & Prayer Ser.: No. 1). 1972. 10.95 Elec Paperback.
The relationship of contemplation to everyday life: the conscience of a Christian monk & his reflections on a Buddhist monk.

Life & Death Cycle. unabr. ed. Keith A. Butler. 4 cass. (Running Time: 6 hrs.). 2001. 20.00 (A17) Word Faith Pubng.

Life & Death in Shanghai. Nien Cheng. Read by Allison Green. 13 cass. (Running Time: 20 hrs. 30 min.). 1993. 84.60 (978-1-56544-023-4(4), 150001); Rental 12.00 30 day rental Set. (150001) Literate Ear.
Nien Cheng, fifty-one year old widow of a former Koumintang diplomat, was held in solitary confinement in Shanghai Detention House No. 1 for nearly seven years. A victim of the Cultural Revolution, she was charged with espionage & interrogated & tortured. She was never brought to trial. This is her story.

Life & Death in Shanghai. unabr. ed. Nien Cheng. Read by Penelope Dellaporta. 8 cass. (Running Time: 12 hrs.). 1987. 64.00 (2109-A); 64.00 (2109-B) Books on Tape.
Survived seven years as a prisoner of the Red Guards.

Life & Death in Shanghai, Pts. A & B. unabr. ed. Nien Cheng. Read by Penelope Dellaporta. 16 cass. (Running Time: 24 hrs.). 1987. 128.00 (978-0-7366-1189-3(4), 2109-A/B) Books on Tape.
The widow of a former Chinese diplomat tells of the seven years she spent in solitary confinement during the 1960's Cultural Revolution in China. Part 1 of 2.

Life & Death of an Ancient Forest - Stopping Clearcutting in Oregon's Siskiyou Mountains. Hosted by Nancy Pearlman. 1 cass. (Running Time: 29 min.). 10.00 (719) Educ Comm CA.

Life & Death of Harriett Frean. May Sinclair. Read by Anais 9000. 2008. 27.95 (978-1-60112-169-1(5)) Babblebooks.

Life & Death of New York City. unabr. ed. John Hospers. 1 cass. (Running Time: 56 min.). 12.95 (225) J Norton Pubs.
Hospers talks about his experiences in New York; how government taxation & regulation are destroying the city, how free enterprise could solve current city problems, & about the problems of libertarians in politics.

Life & Death of NY City. John Hospers. (ENG.). 1972. audio compact disk 12.95 (978-1-57970-497-1(2), Audio-For) J Norton Pubs.

Life & Death of Peter Kelly. Abdul Aziz Said. 1 cass. 1993. 9.00 (OC345-72) Sound Horizons AV.

Life & God's Love. unabr. ed. Thomas Merton. Read by Thomas Merton. 1 cass. (Running Time: 54 min.). (Life & Prayer Ser.: No. 1). 1972. 10.95 Elec Paperback.
Discusses the dynamism of God's love at work in our lives & the obstacles to a personal relationship with God.

Life & Hazardous Times of Charles Bukowski: Neither Bought for Gold nor to the Devil Sold. Keith Rodway et al. (Enlightenment Ser.). (ENG., 2000. audio compact disk 15.95 (978-1-84240-002-9(9)) Pub: Chrome Dreams GBR. Dist(s): IPG Chicago

Life & Health Audio Review. 2nd ed. Ed. by Kaplan Publishing Staff. 2005. 29.00 (978-1-4195-3744-8(X)) Dearborn Financial.

Life & Legacy of the Roman Empire, Course No. 847. Ori Soltes. 2 pts., 16 lectures. 84.91 Teaching Co.
These are history lectures the way you always dreamed they would be done: the events of political & military history are recounted with flair, but alongside them & undiminished in stature are the developments in philosophy, the visual & literary arts & what they tell us about the interior lives of the Romans & the development of the mind & sensibility of the west.

Life & Liberty. abr. ed. Adam Rutledge. Read by Charlie O'Dowd. 6 vols. (Running Time: 6 hrs.). (Patriots Ser.: No. 4). 2003. 30.00 (978-1-58807-088-3(3)) Am Pubng Inc.
In the British colonies of North America, there arose a band of brave men and women who forged a free and independent nation. Their names live on today, as does their legacy, and we proudly call them the Patriots. In British-ruled Boston, 1776, a dangerous ring of false Patriots threatens the lives of true freedom fighters such as Daniel Reed, who is thrown into the lot with General George Washington's Continental Army, but is soon divided from his cause and the woman he loves by murderous Redcoats. It is a treacherous time as well for fiery rebel spy Roxanne Darragh, who is captured by the British, and for young, hotheaded Quincy Reed, who is on a perilous expedition through the untamed western frontier. Risking exposure and death threats, undercover Patriot and daring, double agent Elliot Markham will fight a deadly battle against a lawless legion of ruthless criminals who could extinguish the shining flame of independence forever.

Life & Liberty. unabr. ed. Adam Rutledge. Read by Charlie O'Dowd. 6 vols. No. 4. 2003. (978-1-58807-566-6(4)) Am Pubng Inc.

Life & Loves of a She-Devil. unabr. ed. Fay Weldon. Narrated by Davina Porter. 5 cass. (Running Time: 7 hrs. 15 mins.). 1988. 44.00 (978-1-55690-308-3(1), 88180E7) Recorded Bks.
A woman seeks revenge on her adulterous husbands. Ruth, humble & lumpish, good wife & mother, is doing her best in spite of the daily humiliations, dutifully attending to the needs & oh-so-many wants of her handsome husband, Bobbo, looking after her not-quite-nice kids & feeding all the pets.

Life & Music of Bach, Beethoven & Mozart. Rachel S. Siegel. Read by Robert M. Mitchell. 3 cass. (Running Time: 3 hrs.). 26.50 N Star Recs.
Sides A: narration of the composers' lives.

Life & Music of Edward MacDowell. Gail Smith. 1997. pap. bk. 27.95 (978-0-7866-2514-7(7), 96192P) Mel Bay.

Life & Music of Johann Sebastian Bach. Rachel S. Siegel. Read by Robert M. Mitchell. 1 cass. (Running Time: 1 hr.). 9.95 (NS0019) N Star Recs.
Side A: a narration of the real-life drama that inspired his music. Side B: fully-orchestrated selections from his works.

Life & Music of Ludwig Van Beethoven. Rachel S. Siegel. Read by Robert M. Mitchell. 1 cass. (Running Time: 1 hr.). 9.95 (NS0020) N Star Recs.

Life & Music of Wolfgang Amadeus Mozart. Rachel S. Siegel. Read by Robert M. Mitchell. 1 cass. (Running Time: 1 hr.). 9.95 (NS0021) N Star Recs.
Side A: the events that shaped Mozart's life & influenced his musical compositions. Side B: fully-orchestrated selections from his works.

Life & Operas of Verdi, Parts I-IV. Instructed by Robert Greenberg. 32 CDs. (Running Time: 24 hrs.). 2003. bk. 129.95 (978-1-56585-746-9(1), 790) Teaching Co.

Life & Operas of Verdi, Pts. I-IV. Instructed by Robert Greenberg. 16 cass. (Running Time: 24 hrs.). 2003. bk. 99.95 (978-1-56585-745-2(3), 790) Teaching Co.

Life & Prayer: Journey in Christ. unabr. ed. Thomas Merton. Read by Thomas Merton. 1 cass. (Running Time: 53 min.). (Life & Prayer Ser.: No. 1). 1972. 10.95 Elec Paperback.
Life is a journey & Christ is the way, says the author, speaking on prayer & spirituality.

Life & Prayer: The Desert Source. unabr. ed. Thomas Merton. 1 cass. (Running Time: 46 min.). (Life & Prayer Ser.: No. I). 1982. 10.95 Elec Paperback.
Talks about the prayer & spirituality of the early Desert Fathers.

Life & Prayer: The Jesus Prayer. unabr. ed. Thomas Merton. Read by Thomas Merton. 1 cass. (Running Time: 58 min.). (Life & Prayer Ser.: No. 1). 1972. 10.95 Elec Paperback.
Discusses the person of Christ in prayer, & the theology & practice of "the Jesus prayer" of the Eastern Church.

Life & Prophecy. unabr. ed. Thomas Merton. Read by Thomas Merton. 1 cass. (Running Time: 57 min.). (Life & Prayer Ser.: No. 1). 1972. 10.95 Elec Paperback.
Explains the scriptural roots of the prophetic vocation & the role of the monk as prophet to modern man.

Life & Rebirth. Yeshi Donden. 2 cass. 18.00 (OC10L) Sound Horizons AV.

Life & Solitude. unabr. ed. Thomas Merton. Read by Thomas Merton. 1 cass. (Running Time: 56 min.). (Life & Prayer Ser.: No. 1). 1972. 10.95 Elec Paperback.
The author talks about the 11th-century hermits who inspired him to become one, together with his famous farewell talk before entering the hermitage, "A Life Without Care".

Life & Spiritual Teaching of St. Therese of Lisieux. Frederick L. Miller. Read by Frederick L. Miller. 4 cass. (Running Time: 4 hrs.). 17.00 (978-0-911988-84-0(X), 361910) AMI Pr.
A brief biographical sketch interspersed with the Marion aspects of her spiritual teaching.

Life & Teaching of Guru Nanak. 1 cass. (Running Time: 1 hr.). 12.99 (609) Yoga Res Foun.

Life & Teaching of the Masters of the Far East. abr. ed. Baird T. Spalding. 3 CDs. (Running Time: 10200 sec.). 2007. audio compact disk 21.95 (978-0-87516-818-0(3), Devorss Pubns) DeVorss.

Life & Teaching of the Masters of the Far East, Vols. 1-3. Baird T. Spalding. Music by William Ackerman. 2 cass. (Running Time: 2 hrs. 49 min.). 2003. 17.95 (978-0-87516-571-4(0)) DeVorss.
Descriptions of Far East travels in 1894, unfolds a doctrine that sheds newlight on the Christian faith & the Wisdom religion of the world.

Life & Teachings of Naropa. Read by Osel Tendzin. 4 cass. 1977. 45.00 (A053) Vajradhatu.
Four talks: 1) Expectation as the Working Basis; 2) Pain & Freedom; 3) Shock & Prajna; 4) Hallucination & the Search for the Guru.

Life & the Holy Spirit. unabr. ed. Thomas Merton. Read by Norman Merton. 1 cass. (Running Time: 55 min.). (Life & Prayer Ser.: No. 1). 1972. 10.95 Elec Paperback.
Observations on the Holy Spirit as the source of & life for Christians.

Life & the Path. Swami Amar Jyoti. 1 dolby cass. 1984. 9.95 (K-63) Truth Consciousness.
The flame of Light within forges the path on which we evolve. Distracted from this path, we lose life itself.

Life & Times of Christmas Calvert . . . Assassin. unabr. ed. John William Wainwright. Narrated by Christopher Kay. 5 cass. (Running Time: 7 hrs.). 2000. 47.00 (978-1-84197-126-1(X), H1124E7) Recorded Bks.
As an old man, Christmas Calvert looks back on his exhilarating past. In the army, he was classed "remarkable amoral." This & his deadly accuracy with a gun, make Calvert unique. So he joins The Squad, the elite assassins answerable only to Colonel Dansey & Sergeant Pollard.

Life & Times of Churchill. 2 cass. (Running Time: 90 min.). (Heroes of History Ser.). 1987. 13.95 (978-1-55569-173-8(0), HOH-1400) Great Am Audio.
The compelling life story of the impish, cigar-chomping leader of Britain who galvanized the entire Western world through its darkest, yet "finest hour." Narrated with the actual voice of this unique leader & orator.

Life & Times of Elijah see Vida y los Tiempos de Elias

Life & Times of F.D.R. 2 cass. (Running Time: 90 min.). (Heroes of History Ser.). 1987. 13.95 (978-1-55569-171-4(4), HOH-1200) Great Am Audio.
The actual voice & compelling life story of America's only four-term President, who led the U. S. during the depression & World War II.

Life & Times of Frederick Douglass: His Early Life as a Slave, His Escape from Bondage, & His Complete History to the Present Time see Black Pioneers in American History, Vol. 1, 19th Century

Life & Times of JFK. 2 cass. (Running Time: 90 min.). (Heroes of History Ser.). 1987. 13.95 (978-1-55569-170-7(6), HOH-1100) Great Am Audio.
A narrated tour including the actual voice, turbulent events & compelling life story of America's youngest President who was youth, humor, optimism & vigor personified.

Life & Times of Mark Twain: A Light & Enlightening Lecture for Middle School, Featuring Elliot Engel. (YA). 2001. bk. 15.00 (978-1-890123-40-6(4)) Media Cnslts.

Life & Times of Martin Luther. unabr. ed. J. H. D'Aubigne. Read by Nadia May. 15 cass. (Running Time: 22 hrs. 30 mins.). 1993. 95.95 (1386) Blckstn Audio.
To understand the Protestant Reformation, the best place to begin is with a study of Martin Luther's path from Catholic friar to founder of the Lutheran faith.

Life & Times of Martin Luther. unabr. ed. J. H. D'Aubigne. Read by Nadia May. 15 cass. (Running Time: 22 hrs.). 2006. 95.95 (978-0-7861-0434-5(1), 1386) Blckstn Audio.

Life & Times of Queen Elizabeth I & II. Elizabeth Jenkins & Pearson Philips. Read by Karen Archer & Nanette Newman. (Running Time: 6 hrs. 15 mins.). 2006. 38.95 (978-1-60083-809-5(X)) Iofy Corp.

Life & Times of Queen Elizabeth I & II. Elizabeth Jenkins & Pearson Phillips. Read by Karen Archer & Nanette Newman. 6 cass. (Running Time: 8 hrs..). 2002. 32.98 (978-962-634-745-4(7), NA624514); audio compact disk 38.98 (978-962-634-245-9(5), NA624512) Naxos.
Throughout her vivid life, Elizabeth I was the center of a complicated web of political intrigue. Elizabeth Jenkins' classic biography reveals the woman behind the skillful politician, showing her belief in personal sacrifice to secure peace for the country she loved more than any man. Through changes in the lifestyle and expectations of peoples and nations, Elizabeth II has proved to be the constitutional monarch par excellence. And even when her family has been rocked by scandals, she has maintained a quiet dignity.

Life & Times of the Thunderbolt Kid: A Memoir. unabr. ed. Bill Bryson. Read by Bill Bryson. 6 CDs. (Running Time: 7 hrs. 30 mins.). 2006. audio compact disk 53.55 (978-1-4159-3295-7(6)) Pub: Books on Tape. Dist(s): NetLibrary CO

Life & Times of the Thunderbolt Kid: A Memoir. unabr. ed. Bill Bryson. Read by Bill Bryson. (YA). 2006. 44.99 (978-0-7393-7505-1(9)) Find a World.

Life & Times of the Thunderbolt Kid: A Memoir. unabr. ed. Bill Bryson. Read by Bill Bryson. 6 CDs. (Running Time: 7 hrs. 30 mins.). (ENG.). 2006. audio compact disk 29.95 (978-0-7393-1523-1(4)) Pub: Random Audio Pubg. Dist(s): Random

Life & Times of Truman. 2 cass. (Running Time: 90 min.). (Heroes of History Ser.). 1987. 13.95 (978-1-55569-172-1(2), HOH-1300) Great Am Audio.
A narrated tour including the actual voice, turbulent events & compelling life story of "Give 'em Hell Harry" the colorful, feisty Missourian who faced the most agonizing decision in world history.

Life & Times of William Shakespeare. unabr. ed. Peter Levi. Read by Nadia May. 13 cass. (Running Time: 19 hrs.). 1995. 85.95 (978-0-7861-0866-4(5), 1664) Blckstn Audio.
One of the most important books on William Shakespeare, this superb biography is both authoritative & extremely readable. It is the first modern biography of Shakespeare since the Victorian Age to pay full attention to his life & times, to his works, & to the numerous & subtle connections among them. Peter Levi emphasizes the background of Shakespeare's life - the local & national events that shaped his experiences, his family & friends, & the Elizabethan people with whom he shared his life & populated his plays. Bringing together new work & new discoveries & reexamining the famous legends about Shakespeare, Levi uses the writings of modern historians to shed light on the poet's life. This valuable work will be the definitive life of Shakespeare for many years to come.

Life & Times of William Shakespeare. unabr. ed. Peter Levi & Nadia May. (Running Time: 18 hrs. NaN mins.). 2008. 44.95 (978-1-4332-5420-8(4)); audio compact disk 120.00 (978-1-4332-5419-2(0)) Blckstn Audio.

Life & Truth. unabr. ed. Thomas Merton. Read by Norman Merton. 1 cass. (Running Time: 53 min.). (Life & Prayer Ser.: No. 1). 1972. 10.95 Elec Paperback.
Reflections on the love of Truth as the source of life & happiness, based on the meditations of the medieval monk & mystic, Guigo the Carthusian.

Life & Work. unabr. ed. Thomas Merton. Read by Thomas Merton. 1 cass. (Running Time: 51 min.). (Life & Prayer Ser.: No. 1). 1972. 10.95 Elec Paperback.
A commentary on work - from the Shakers' philosophy of "work as worship" to the problems facing Christians in a technological world.

Life & Work of D. H. Lawrence - 1953. Stephen Spender. 1 cass. (Running Time: 58 Min.). 1999. 11.00 (JN012) Big Sur Tapes.

Life & Work of Marcel Proust. Neville Jason. Read by Neville Jason. 3 cass. (Running Time: 3 hrs. 30 mins.). 2002. 17.98 (978-962-634-752-2(X), NA325214); audio compact disk 22.98 (978-962-634-252-7(8), NA325212) Naxos.
The first audio-biography of Marcel Proust tells the story of one of the world's most original and admired literary geniuses. From his youth in the salons of Belle Epoque Paris, we follow his progress through to his later years when, as a near recluse, he writes through the nights in his cork-lined bedroom.

Life & Work of Mark Twain, Pts. I-II. Instructed by Stephen Railton. 12 cass. (Running Time: 12 hrs.). 2002. bk. 54.95 (978-1-56585-511-3(6), 2567); bk. 69.95 (978-1-56585-512-0(4), 2567) Teaching Co.

Life & Works - Frederic Chopin. unabr. ed. Jeremy Siepmann. Read by Jeremy Siepmann. Read by Anton Lesser et al. (YA). 2008. 54.99 (978-1-60514-897-7(0)) Find a World.

Life & Works - Wolfgang Amadeus Mozart. unabr. ed. Jeremy Siepmann. Read by Jeremy Siepmann. Read by Nichola Boulton. (YA). 2008. 54.99 (978-1-60514-898-4(9)) Find a World.

Life & Works: Dvorak. Jeremy Siepmann. 4 CDs. audio compact disk 35.99 (978-1-84379-070-9(X), 8.558101-04) NaxMulti GBR.

Life & Works of Bach. Jeremy Siepmann. Read by Jeremy Siepmann. Read by John Sapnel. (Running Time: 3 hrs. 30 mins.). (C). 2005. 33.95 (978-1-60083-810-1(3)) Iofy Corp.

Life & Works of Beethoven. Jeremy Siepmann. Read by Jeremy Siepmann. Read by Bob Peck. (Running Time: 5 hrs.). (C). 2005. 28.95 (978-1-60083-812-5(X)) Iofy Corp.

Life & Works of Beethoven. Jeremy Siepmann. Read by Jeremy Siepmann. 4 cass. (Running Time: 5 hrs.). (Histories of Music Ser.). 2001. 22.98 (978-962-634-715-7(5), NA421514, Naxos AudioBooks); audio compact disk 28.98 (978-962-634-215-2(3), NA421512, Naxos AudioBooks) Naxos.
Ludwig Van Beethoven (1770-1827) is considered by many to be the greatest composer who ever lived. His music helped define the classical style.

Life & Works of Beethoven. unabr. ed. Jeremy Siepmann. Read by Jeremy Siepmann. Read by Bob Peck et al. (YA). 2008. 54.99 (978-1-60514-896-0(2)) Find a World.

Life & Works of Brahms. Jeremy Siepmann. Read by Jeremy Siepmann. Read by Jasper Britton. (Running Time: 3 hrs. 45 mins.). (C). 2005. 33.95 (978-1-60083-811-8(1)) Iofy Corp.

Life & Works of Chopin. Jeremy Siepmann. Read by Jeremy Siepmann. Read by Anton Lesser. (Running Time: 5 hrs.). (C). 2005. 28.95 (978-1-60083-813-2(8)) Iofy Corp.

Life & Works of Chopin. Jeremy Siepmann. Read by Jeremy Siepmann. 4 cass. (Running Time: 5 hrs.). (Histories of Music Ser.). 2001. 22.98 (978-962-634-719-5(8), NA421914, Naxos AudioBooks); audio compact disk 28.98 (978-962-634-219-0(6), NA421912, Naxos AudioBooks) Naxos.
Frederic Francois Chopin (1810-1849) brought romantic music to unprecedented heights of expressiveness.

Life & Works of Dvorak. Jeremy Siepmann. Read by Jeremy Siepmann. Read by Sean Barrett. (Running Time: 3 hrs. 15 mins.). (C). 2005. 33.95 (978-1-60083-814-9(6)) Iofy Corp.

Life & Works of Haydn. Jeremy Siepmann. Read by Jeremy Siepmann. Read by Dave Timson. (Running Time: 3 hrs. 30 mins.). (C). 2005. 33.95 (978-1-60083-815-6(4)) Iofy Corp.

Life & Works of Liszt. Jeremy Siepmann. Read by Jeremy Siepmann. Read by Neville Jason. (Running Time: 2 hrs. 30 mins.). (C). 2005. 20.95 (978-1-60083-816-3(2)) Iofy Corp.

Life & Works of Marcel Proust. Neville Jason. Read by Neville Jason. (Running Time: 3 hrs. 30 mins.). (C). 2006. 24.95 (978-1-60083-817-0(0)) Iofy Corp.

Life & Works of Mozart. Jeremy Siepmann. Read by Jeremy Siepmann. Read by Nicholas Boulton. (Running Time: 3 hrs. 45 mins.). (C). 2006. 33.95 (978-1-60083-818-7(9)) Iofy Corp.

Life & Works of Schubert. Jeremy Siepmann. Read by Jeremy Siepmann. Read by Tom George. (Running Time: 3 hrs. 30 mins.). (C). 2005. 33.95 (978-1-60083-820-0(0)) Iofy Corp.

Life & Works of Tchaikovsky. Jeremy Siepmann. Read by Jeremy Siepmann. Read by Malcolm Sinclair. (Running Time: 3 hrs.). (C). 2006. 33.95 (978-1-60083-821-7(9)) Iofy Corp.

Life & Works of Verdi. Jeremy Siepmann. Read by Jeremy Siepmann. Read by Freddie Jones. (Running Time: 3 hrs. 15 mins.). (C). 2005. 33.95 (978-1-60083-822-4(7)) Iofy Corp.

Life & Works of William Butler Yeats. Read by Jim Norton et al. Compiled by John Kavanagh. 2 cass. (Running Time: 2 hrs. 30 mins.). 2002. 13.98 (978-962-634-764-5(3), NA226414); audio compact disk 17.98 (978-962-634-264-0(1), NA226412) Naxos.
The life of William Butler Yeats is a remarkable one, poet, playwright, essayist,politician, oculist, astroloqer, founder of a national theater, voluminous correspondent, lover, husband and father. it was a life that extended to a packed, sometimes frantic 73 years, and left us with what many consider to be one of the finest collections of poetry from one voice.

Life & Writings of C. S. Lewis. Instructed by Louis Markos. 6 pieces. (Running Time: 6 hrs.). (C). bk. 29.95 (978-1-56585-065-1(3), 297); bk. 39.95 (978-1-56585-316-4(4), 297) Teaching Co.

Life & Writings of Geoffrey Chaucer. Instructed by Seth Lerer. 6 CDs. (Running Time: 6 hrs.). 1998. audio compact disk 54.95 (978-1-59803-210-9(0)) Teaching Co.

Life & Writings of Geoffrey Chaucer. Instructed by Seth Lerer. 6 cass. (Running Time: 6 hrs.). 1999. 39.95 (978-1-56585-069-9(6)); audio compact disk 134.95 (978-1-56585-713-1(5)) Teaching Co.

Life & Writings of John Milton. Instructed by Seth Lerer. 6 cass. (Running Time: 6 hrs.). 1999. 39.95 (978-1-56585-070-5(X)); audio compact disk 134.95 (978-1-56585-714-8(3)) Teaching Co.

Life & Writings of John Milton. Instructed by Seth Lerer. 6 CDs. (Running Time: 6 hrs.). 2006. 54.95 (978-1-59803-245-1(3)) Teaching Co.

***Life As A Grownup Audio CD.** Susan Diane Matz. Read by Susan Diane Matz. (ENG.). 2010. 15.95 (978-0-9841054-5-8(X)) Abriev Ent.

Life as a Novelist. Pat Conroy. 1 cass. (Running Time: 1 hr. 16 mins.). 2001. 12.95 Smithson Assocs.

Life as a Phenomenal Thing, Program 8. Read by Luis Rafael Sánchez. (F007DB090) Natl Public Radio.

Life As a Waking Dream. Interview with Arleen Lorrance & Diane K. Pike. 1 cass. (Running Time: 60 min.). 9.95 Teleos Inst.

Life As Art. unabr. ed. Perf. by Eknath Easwaran. 1 cass. (Running Time: 1 hr.). 1990. 7.95 (978-1-58638-558-3(5)) Nilgiri Pr.

Life As Physics: A New Electromagnetic Paradigm. Dwight Bulkley. 1 cass. 9.00 (A0298-88) Sound Photosyn.

Life As We Knew It. unabr. ed. Susan Beth Pfeffer. Read by Emily Bauer. 7 CDs. (J). (gr. 4-7). 2006. audio compact disk 46.75 (978-0-7393-3789-9(0)) Pub: Random Audio Pubg. Dist(s): NetLibrary CO

Life As We Knew It. unabr. ed. Susan Beth Pfeffer. Read by Emily Bauer. 7 CDs. (Running Time: 9 hrs.). (ENG.). (J). (gr. 5). 2006. audio compact disk 45.00 (978-0-7393-3683-0(5), Listening Lib) Pub: Random Audio Pubg. Dist(s): Random

Life at Risk: A Closer Look at Assisted Suicide. 12 cass. (Running Time: 12 hrs.). (YA). (gr. 9 up). 1997. 50.00 (978-0-9663691-1-3(4)) Donehey VA.
Featuring twenty speakers at the March 1997 "Life at Risk" conference exploring the legal, medical, ethical & policy concerns about physician-assisted suicide.

Life at the Beach: Early Explorers Emergent Set A Audio CD. Benchmark Education Staff. (J). 2006. audio compact disk 10.00 (978-1-4108-7585-3(7)) Benchmark Educ.

Life at the Frontier: Leadership Through Courageous Conversation. Featuring David Whyte. 2 CD's. 2004. audio compact disk 20.00 (978-1-932887-15-0(6)) Many Rivers Pr.
Presentation given by David Whyte in early 2004. This is a 2-CD set.

Life at Work: The Joy of Discovering What You Were Born to Do. Thomas Moore. Read by Lloyd James. (Playaway Adult Nonfiction Ser.). 2008. 54.99 (978-1-60640-763-9(5)) Find a World.

Life at Work: The Joy of Discovering What You Were Born to Do. unabr. ed. Thomas Moore. Read by Lloyd James. (Running Time: 23400 sec.). (ENG.). 2008. audio compact disk 24.95 (978-1-4332-0534-7(3)); audio compact disk 29.95 (978-1-4332-0535-4(1)) Blckstn Audio.

Life at Work: The Joy of Discovering What You Were Born to Do. unabr. ed. Thomas Moore. Read by Lloyd James. (Running Time: 23400 sec.). (ENG.). 2008. 29.95 (978-1-4332-0533-0(5)); 44.95 (978-1-4332-0531-6(9)); audio compact disk & audio compact disk 55.00 (978-1-4332-0532-3(7)) Blckstn Audio.

Life Audio Review. 2nd ed. Ed. by Kaplan Publishing Staff. 2005. 19.00 (978-1-4195-3745-5(8)) Dearborn Financial.

Life Basic Training. 1995. 29.95 (978-1-880828-69-4(3)) Touch Pubns.

Life Before Birth & a Time to Be Born. unabr. ed. Peter W. Nathanielsz. Read by Peter W. Nathanielsz. 6 cass. (Running Time: 8 hrs. 30 mins.). 1995. 44.95 (978-0-7861-0893-0(2), 1679) Blckstn Audio.
Describes the fascinating wonders of our prenatal origins as we prepare to take on the challenges of independent life. It is "must listen" for every parent with or awaiting a new baby.

Life Before Her Eyes. unabr. ed. Laura Kasischke. Read by Carrington MacDuffie. (Running Time: 25200 sec.). 2007. 19.95 (978-1-4332-0027-4(9)); 54.95 (978-1-4332-0025-0(2)); audio compact disk 19.95 (978-1-4332-0028-1(7)); audio compact disk 63.00 (978-1-4332-0026-7(0)) Blckstn Audio.

Life Before Her Eyes. unabr. ed. Laura Kasischke & Blackstone Audio. (Running Time: 8 mins.). (J). 2007. audio compact disk 29.95 (978-1-4332-0029-8(5)) Blckstn Audio.

Life Before Man. unabr. ed. Margaret Atwood. Read by Lorelei King. 10 cass. (Running Time: 15 hrs.). 2003. 84.95 (978-0-7540-0938-2(6), CAB 2360) AudioGO.

Life Begins: An Amazing Multimedia Journey: Conception to Birth. (gr. 7-13). 2002. tchr. ed. 93.28 (978-1-56637-796-6(X)) Goodheart.

Life Begins at Retirement. Eldon Taylor. Read by Eldon Taylor. Ed. by Leslie Brice. 6 cass. (Running Time: 6 hrs.). 1992. 69.95 (978-1-56705-370-8(X)) Gateways Inst.
Self improvement.

Life Begins Conception to Birth. 2004. audio compact disk 69.95 (978-0-9672777-0-7(1)) Quality Multi.

Life Beyond Earth. abr. ed. Timothy Ferris. Read by Timothy Ferris. 2 cass. (Running Time: 3 hrs.). 2004. 15.00 (978-1-931056-13-7(7), N Millennium Audio); audio compact disk 15.00 (978-1-931056-14-4(5), N Millennium Audio) New Millenn Enter.
Discoveries about the origins of life as known on earth with recent revelations about the sun's planets & their moons in order to suggest possible abodes for life in this solar system & beyond. He explains why many scientists are convinced that life is abundant throughout the universe & considers how, one day we may contact alien civilizations.

***Life Beyond Measure.** abr. ed. Sidney Poitier. Read by Sidney Poitier. (ENG.). 2008. (978-0-06-163257-0(0)); (978-0-06-163258-7(9)) HarperCollins Pubs.

Life Beyond Measure: Letters to My Great-Granddaughter. abr. ed. Sidney Poitier. Read by Sidney Poitier. 2008. audio compact disk 29.95 (978-0-06-157114-5(8), Harper Audio); audio compact disk 34.95 (978-0-06-156849-7(X), Harper Audio) HarperCollins Pubs.

Life Beyond Measure: Letters to My Great-Granddaughter. unabr. ed. Sidney Poitier. 6 cass. (Running Time: 10 hrs.). 2008. 90.00 (978-1-4159-5617-5(0), BksonTape); audio compact disk 90.00 (978-1-4159-5618-2(9), BksonTape) Pub: Random Audio Pubg. Dist(s): Random

Life Beyond the Earth, Pt. I. 1 cass. (Running Time: 28 min.). 14.95 (23242) MMI Corp.
Astronomers debate possibilities of extraterrestrial life, great "Moon Hoax," conditions necessary to support life.

Life Beyond the Earth, Pt. II. 1 cass. (Running Time: 28 min.). 14.95 (23349) MMI Corp.

Life Board: Creating & Using the Life Board. unabr. ed. Melody Ivory. 1 cass. (Running Time: 1 hr.). 1999. 8.00 (978-0-9655918-5-0(9)) Human Perform.

Life-Books: Autobiography the Easy Way. Gordon Yaswen. Read by Gordon Yaswen. 2 cass. (Running Time: 2 hrs.). 1992. 18.60 (978-0-9620747-3-8(X)) Yascom Endeavors.

Life by Design. PUEI. 2006. audio compact disk 49.95 (978-1-933328-78-2(9), CareerTrack) P Univ E Inc.

Life by Design: Life by Choice... Not by Chance. abr. ed. Rick Brinkman. 2 cass. (Running Time: 3 hrs.). 2000. 17.95 (978-1-55977-962-3(4)) CareerTrack Pubns.

Life by Stereo. Contrib. by J R et al. 2007. audio compact disk 14.98 (978-5-557-60936-4(9)) C Mason Res.

Life Challenges. David Freudberg. Perf. by Elisabeth Kubler-Ross et al. 6 cass. (Running Time: 6 hrs.). (Kindred Spirits Ser.: Vol. 3). 1984. 24.95 (978-0-9640914-6-7(1)) Human Media.
A listening library of spiritual wisdom from the world's great traditions. Words from Elisabeth Kubler-Ross, MD, Rabbi Harold Kushner, Editor Norman Cousins & others in subjects ranging from laughter as good medicine, suffering, aging process, dying, & bereavement.

Life Changes. unabr. ed. Milton Diamond. 1 cass. (Running Time: 1 hr.). (Human Sexuality Ser.). 12.95 (34006) J Norton Pubs.

Life Changing Revelations in the Lord's Prayer. 2003. (978-1-59024-159-2(2)); audio compact disk (978-1-59024-158-5(4)) B Hinn Min.

Life Changing Revelations in the Lord's Prayer. 2001. (978-1-59024-020-5(0)); audio compact disk (978-1-59024-022-9(7)) B Hinn Min.

Life-Changing Walk: Luke 24:1-49. Ed Young. 1996. 4.95 (978-0-7417-2094-8(9), 1094) Win Walk.

Life Class. unabr. ed. Pat Barker. Narrated by Russell Boulter. 1 MP3-CD. (Running Time: 7 hrs. 55 mins.). 2008. 39.95 (978-0-7927-5324-7(0)); audio compact disk 64.95 (978-0-7927-5239-4(2)) AudioGO.
In the spring of 1914, a group of young students gather in an art studio for a life-drawing class. Paul Tarrant and Elinor Brooke are two components of a love triangle, and at the outset of the war, they turn to each other. After volunteering for the Red Cross, Paul must confront the fact that life, love, and art will never be the same for him. Pat Barker is unrivaled in her ability to convey simple, moving human truths. Her skill in relaying the harrowing experience of modern warfare is matched by the depth of insight she brings to the experience of love and the morality of art in a time of war. Life Class is one of her genuine masterpieces.

Life Class. unabr. ed. Pat Barker. Read by Russell Boulter. (YA). 2008. 59.99 (978-1-60514-899-1(7)) Find a World.

***Life Class: Unabridged Value-Priced Edition.** Pat Barker. Narrated by Russell Boulter. (Running Time: 7 hrs. 55 mins. 0 sec.). (ENG.). 2010. audio compact disk 14.95 (978-1-60283-993-9(X)) Pub: AudioGO. Dist(s): Perseus Dist

Life Comes to the Archbishop. George Eppley. Read by David Pfaff. (ENG.). 2006. audio compact disk 22.00 (978-0-9662805-3-1(9)) E & D Prodns.

Life, Crime & Capture of John Wilkes Booth: With a Full Sketch of the Conspiracy of which he was the Leader, & the Pursuit, Trial & Execution of his Accomplices. George Alfred Townsend. Narrated by Erik Sellin. 4 CDs. 2007. audio compact disk 16.99 (978-0-9764805-3-2(0)) C CD Bks.

Life, Crime & Capture of John Wilkes Booth: With a Full Sketch of the Conspiracy of which he was the Leader, & the Pursuit, Trial & Execution of his Accomplices. abr. ed. George Alfred Townsend. (ENG.). 2009. audio compact disk (978-1-935513-00-1(1)) C CD Bks.

Life Cycle & the Death Cycle. Kenneth Copeland. 4 cass. 1992. 20.00 (978-0-88114-847-3(4)) K Copeland Pubns.
Teaching on practical Christian living.

Life Cycle fo a Butterfly. Bobbie Kalman. (Life Cycle Ser.). (ENG.). (J). 2005. audio compact disk 10.00 (978-0-7787-7688-8(3)) CrabtreePubCo CAN.

Life Cycle of a Butterfly Audio CD. Adapted by Benchmark Education Company Staff. Based on a work by Margaret McNamara. (Content Connections Ser.). (J). (gr. k-2). 2008. audio compact disk 10.00 (978-1-60634-890-1(6)) Benchmark Educ.

Life Cycle of a Frog. Bobbie Kalman. (Life Cycle Ser.). (ENG.). (J). 2005. audio compact disk 10.00 (978-0-7787-7692-5(1)) CrabtreePubCo CAN.

Life Cycle of a Frog Audio CD. Adapted by Benchmark Education Company Staff. Based on a work by Margaret McNamara. (Content Connections Ser.). (J). (gr. k-2). 2008. audio compact disk 10.00 (978-1-60634-889-5(2)) Benchmark Educ.

Life Cycle of a Honeybee. Bobbie Kalman. (Life Cycle Ser.). (ENG.). (J). 2005. audio compact disk 10.00 (978-0-7787-7690-1(5)) CrabtreePubCo CAN.

Life Cycle of a Lion. Bobbie Kalman. (Life Cycle Ser.). (ENG.). (J). 2005. audio compact disk 10.00 (978-0-7787-7694-9(8)) CrabtreePubCo CAN.

Life Cycle of Bees. Compiled by Benchmark Education Staff. 2006. audio compact disk 10.00 (978-1-4108-6660-8(2)) Benchmark Educ.

Life Cycle of Oak Trees. Compiled by Benchmark Education Staff. 2006. audio compact disk 10.00 (978-1-4108-6661-5(0)) Benchmark Educ.

Life Cycle of Pine Trees. Compiled by Benchmark Education Staff. 2006. audio compact disk 10.00 (978-1-4108-6662-2(9)) Benchmark Educ.

Life Cycles - Personality Profiles. Frank L. Natter. 1 cass. (Running Time: 90 min.). (Improving Your Personal Problem-Solving Ser.). 1989. 10.00 (978-1-878287-65-6(6), ATA-9) Type & Temperament.
Basics of Psychological Type as related to Problem-Solving; Focus on effects of Life Cycles & Personality Profiles.

Life Cycles Audio CD Theme Set: Set of 6 Set B. Adapted by Benchmark Education Staff. (English Explorers Ser.). (J). (gr. 3-6). 2007. audio compact disk 60.00 (978-1-4108-9823-4(7)) Benchmark Educ.

Life Cycles Large & Small. John Townley. 1 cass. (Running Time: 90 min.). 1984. 8.95 (350) Am Fed Astrologers.

Life, Death, & Dying. Chogyam Trungpa. 1 cass. 1974. 10.00 Vajradhatu.
A discussion on death experiences & the "Tibetan Book of the Dead.".

Life, Death & Miracles. Joy Mills. 1 CD. (Running Time: 1 hr. 30 mins.). 2001. audio compact disk 19.95 (978-0-9671280-4-7(8)) J Mills & Assocs.

Life Decoded: My Genome - My Life. unabr. ed. J. Craig Venter. Narrated by Dick Hill. 14 CDs. (Running Time: 17 hrs. 0 mins. 0 sec.). (ENG.). 2007. audio compact disk 39.99 (978-1-4001-0571-7(4)) Pub: Tantor Media. Dist(s): IngramPubServ

Life Decoded: My Genome - My Life. unabr. ed. J. Craig Venter. Read by Dick Hill. (Running Time: 17 hrs. 0 mins. 0 sec.). (ENG.). 2007. audio compact disk 29.99 (978-1-4001-5571-2(1)); audio compact disk 79.99 (978-1-4001-3571-4(0)) Pub: Tantor Media. Dist(s): IngramPubServ

Life Decoded: My Genome - My Life. unabr. ed. J. Craig Venter. Read by Dick Hill. (YA). 2008. 64.99 (978-1-60514-652-2(8)) Find a World.

Life Delightful & Noble. Swami Amar Jyoti. 1 cass. 1982. 9.95 (A-22) Truth Consciousness.
Crystal clear directions for a delightful & noble life for all. Taking a vow to work on it.

Life Diet: Four Steps to Thin Forever. abr. unabr. ed. Joy Bauer. Read by Joy Bauer. 2009. audio compact disk 22.99 (978-0-06-173128-0(5), Harper Audio) HarperCollins Pubs.

Life Direction Exploration: Discover & Clarify Your Full Potential in Life. Mark Bancroft. Read by Mark Bancroft. 1 cass., bklet. (Running Time: 60 min.). (Spirituality & Consciousness Ser.). 1998. 12.95 (978-0-9665539-0-1(X), EnSpire Aud) EnSpire Pr.
Two complete sessions plus printed instructionmanual/guidebook. With healing music soundtrack.

Life Direction Exploration: Discover & Clarify Your Full Potential in Life. Mark Bancroft. Read by Mark Bancroft. 1 CD, 1 bklet. (Running Time: 60 min.). (Spirituality & Consciousness Ser.). 2006. audio compact disk 20.00 bklet. (978-0-9665539-1-8(8)) EnSpire Pr.

Life Divine on Earth. Swami Amar Jyoti. 2 cass. 1978. 12.95 (O-12) Truth Consciousness.
Life Divine, a total transformation of human life. On ages & cycles, earthquakes & holocausts. Control of Prana & opening the third eye.

Life Everlasting. abr. ed. Whitlow Robert. 6 cass. (Running Time: 10 hrs.). 2004. 29.99 (978-1-58926-694-0(3), 6694); audio compact disk 34.99 (978-1-58926-695-7(1), 6695) Oasis Audio.

Life Everlasting. abr. ed. Robert Whitlow. Narrated by Rob Lamont. (Santee Ser.). (ENG.). 2004. 24.49 (978-1-60814-287-3(6)) Oasis Audio.

Life Expectancy. unabr. ed. Dean Koontz. Read by John Bedford Lloyd. 10 CDs. (Running Time: 11 hrs. 30 mins.). (Dean Koontz Ser.). (ENG.). 2004. audio compact disk 44.95 (978-0-7393-1553-8(6)) Pub: Random Audio Pubg. Dist(s): Random

Life Extension. Read by Jack Schwarz. 2 cass. 25.00 (#301) Aletheia Psycho.

Life-Extension, Purposeful Relaxation, Differential (Multiple) "Feeling" (Psychophysiological) Awareness & Communication. Russell E. Mason. 1975. bk. 70.00 (978-0-89533-018-5(0)) F I Comm.

Life for a Life see Tales from a Troubled Land

Life Force. unabr. ed. Fay Weldon. Read by Jacqueline King. 6 cass. (Running Time: 8 hrs. 30 min.). 1994. 54.95 (978-1-85695-719-9(5), 940408) Pub: ISIS Audio GBR. Dist(s): Ulverscroft US
Into the lives of four female friends erupts Leslie Beck, an old (but not yet extinguished) flame. Recently widowed & somewhat weepy, Leslie is still a man with the Life Force - a force which he is more than willing to share with old & new friends. Provided of course, that they are women. As the friends are catapulted back into their murky pasts, old secrets stir & old rivalries are resurrected.

Life Force: Access the Energy Field Around You. Denise Linn. 2 cass. (Running Time: 1 hrs. 30 min.). 1998. 16.95 (978-1-56170-541-2(1), 446) Hay House.
Make life however you want it to be by accessing the positive energy around you.

Life Force: The Psycho-Historical Recovery of the Self. abr. ed. Jean Houston. Read by Jean Houston. 2 cass. (Running Time: 3 hrs.). 1993. 10.95 (978-0-8356-2100-7(6), Quest) Pub: Theos Pub Hse. Dist(s): Natl Bk Netwk

Life-Giver. Derek Prince. 1 cass. (I-4142) Derek Prince.

Life-Giving Waters & the Thirst for God. Margaret Dorgan. 4 cass. (Running Time: 3 hrs. 30 min.). 1991. 33.95 (TAH251) Alba Hse Comns.
This set focuses on four deep currents in Carmelite spirituality, longing, inwardness, suffering & celebration.

Life God Blesses. unabr. ed. Jim Cymbala & Sorenson. 2002. 19.99 (978-0-310-24799-9(3)) Zondervan.

Life God Blesses: The Secret of Enjoying God's Favor. unabr. ed. Zondervan Publishing Staff & Jim Cymbala. (Running Time: 3 hrs. 0 mins. 0 sec.). (ENG.). 2004. 20.99 (978-0-310-26159-9(7)) Zondervan.

Life God Rewards. Global Vision Staff. (ENG.). 2003. 19.99 (978-1-932131-12-3(4)); 19.99 (978-1-932131-13-0(2)) Pub: Glob Vision. Dist(s): STL Dist NA

Life, Hope & Healing: Prescriptions from the Heart. Bernie S. Siegel. Read by Bernie S. Siegel. 6 cass. 49.95 Set. (519AD) Nightingale-Conant.
How you can live a richer, fuller life.

Life in a Medieval Carmelite Monastery. Keith J. Egan. 1 cass. (Running Time: 1 hr. 06 min.). 1992. 7.95 (TAH283) Alba Hse Comns.
Carmelite life in medieval times.

Life in a Pond. Sundance/Newbridge, LLC Staff. (Early Science Ser.). (gr. k-3). 2007. audio compact disk 12.00 (978-1-4007-6380-1(0)); audio compact disk 12.00 (978-1-4007-6381-8(9)); audio compact disk 12.00 (978-1-4007-6379-5(7)) Sund Newbrdge.

Life in a Retirement Community: Residents Perspective in Pursuit of Well-Being. Jerry Griffin. 1986. 10.80 (0804) Assn Prof Chaplains.

Life in a Rural Community Audio CD. Adapted by Benchmark Education Company Staff. Based on a work by Margaret McNamara. (Content Connections Ser.). (J). (gr. k-2). 2008. audio compact disk 10.00 (978-1-60634-901-4(5)) Benchmark Educ.

Life in a Suburban Community Audio CD. Adapted by Benchmark Education Company Staff. Based on a work by Margaret McNamara. (Content Connections Ser.). (J). (gr. k-2). 2008. audio compact disk 10.00 (978-1-60634-902-1(3)) Benchmark Educ.

Life in a Tree. Sundance/Newbridge, LLC Staff. (Early Science Ser.). (gr. k-3). 2007. audio compact disk 12.00 (978-1-4007-6463-1(7)); audio compact disk 12.00 (978-1-4007-6462-4(9)); audio compact disk 12.00 (978-1-4007-6461-7(0)) Sund Newbrdge.

Life in America Complete Kindergarten Kit. 2000. audio compact disk 21.95 (978-0-9713911-9-2(X)) Life in America.

Life in America New World CD Set (7-12), Vol. 2. 2000. audio compact disk 75.00 (978-0-9713911-1-6(4)) Life in America.

Life in an Indian Village. unabr. ed. Julian C. Hollick. 4 cass. (Running Time: 4 hrs.). 1990. 50.00 (978-1-56709-060-4(5), 1039) Indep Broadcast.
A record of ten days in the lives of the villagers of Jitvapur in the northern Indian state of Bihar.

Life in an Urban Community Audio CD. Adapted by Benchmark Education Company Staff. Based on a work by Margaret McNamara. (Content Connections Ser.). (J). (gr. k-2). 2008. audio compact disk 10.00 (978-1-60634-903-8(1)) Benchmark Educ.

***Life in Comedy: An Evening of Favorites from a Writer's Life.** unabr. ed. Garrison Keillor. Contrib. by Garrison Keillor. (ENG.). 2010. audio compact disk 19.95 (978-1-61573-079-7(6), 1615730796) Pub: HighBridge. Dist(s): Workman Pub

Life in Darwin's Universe. unabr. collector's ed. Gene Bylinsky. Read by Justin Hecht. 6 cass. (Running Time: 9 hrs.). 1987. 48.00 (978-0-7366-0559-5(2), 1531) Books on Tape.
The unique premise of this story is that just as the laws of physics & chemistry apply throughout the cosmos, so must Darwin's principles of evolution.

***Life in Defiance: A Novel.** Zondervan Publishing Staff & Mary E. DeMuth. (Running Time: 11 hrs. 31 mins. 34 sec.). (Defiance Texas Ser.). (ENG.). 2010. 14.99 (978-0-310-33019-6(X)) Zondervan.

Life in General. Perf. by MxPx. 1 CD. 1996. audio compact disk 15.99 (TND1060) Diamante Music Grp.
"Life in General" will be a more mature record, again dealing with life's relationships, whether it be with God, with your parents, or with girlfriends.

Life in Mr. Lincoln's Navy. Dennis J. Ringle. Read by Butch Hoover. (ENG.). 2009. 74.99 (978-1-61574-621-7(8)) Find a World.

Life in Occupied America. abr. ed. Ward Churchill. 2 CDs. (Running Time: 3 hrs.). (ENG.). 2003. audio compact disk 14.98 (978-1-902593-72-2(3)) Pub: AK Pr GBR. Dist(s): Consort Bk Sales

Life in Shakespeare's London. unabr. ed. 10.95 (978-0-8045-1037-0(7), SAC 1037) Spoken Arts.

Life in the Damn Tropics see Vivir en el Maldito Tropico

Life in the Fat Lane. Cherie Bennett. Read by Christina Moore. 5 cass. (Running Time: 7 hrs. 15 mins.). (YA). (gr. 7 up). 1999. pap. bk. & stu. ed. 57.24 (978-0-7887-2665-1(X), 40825) Recorded Bks.
Lara Ardeche is a homecoming queen & beauty pageant winner, the "perfect" girl, until she finds, to her horror, that her weight is out of control. A sensitive treatment of body image issues.

Life in the Fat Lane. unabr. ed. Cherie Bennett. Narrated by Christina Moore. 5 pieces. (Running Time: 7 hrs. 15 mins.). (gr. 7 up). 1999. 44.00 (978-0-7887-2635-4(8), 95493E7) Recorded Bks.
Lara Ardeche is a homecoming queen & beauty pageant winner - the "perfect" girl - until she finds, to her horror, that her weight is out of control. A sensitive treatment of body image issues.

Life in the Fat Lane, Class set. Cherie Bennett. Read by Christina Moore. 5 cass. (Running Time: 7 hrs. 15 mins.). (YA). (gr. 7 up). 1999. stu. ed. 114.70 (978-0-7887-3131-0(9), 46867) Recorded Bks.
Lara Ardeche is a homecoming queen & beauty pageant winner, the "perfect" girl until she finds, to her horror, that her weight is out of control. A sensitive treatment of body image issues.

Life in the Nazi Ghetto. 10.00 (HE829) Esstee Audios.
How the Nazis operated their system & how the oppressed managed to keep a sense of sanity in the midst of madness.

Life in the Real World: Ecc. 7:1-14. Ed Young. 1993. 4.95 (978-0-7417-1988-1(6), 988) Win Walk.

Life in the Sea. Sundance/Newbridge, LLC Staff. (Early Science Ser.). (gr. k-3). 2007. audio compact disk 12.00 (978-1-4007-6389-4(4)); audio compact disk 12.00 (978-1-4007-6388-7(6)); audio compact disk 12.00 (978-1-4007-6390-0(8)) Sund Newbrdge.

Life in the Trinity: Elizabeth in Dijon & the Trinitarian Dimension of Christian Mysticism. unabr. ed. Margaret Dorgan. 1 cass. (Running Time: 51 min.). 1992. 7.95 (TAH281) Alba Hse Comns.
This cassette combines theology & mysticism to reflect upon the mystery of a God Who is Three-in-One. It focuses upon a Carmelite, Blessed Elizabeth of the Trinity, who reveals the radiance of a profound Christian spirituality, to nourish & enlighten us today in our longing for God.

Life in the Twentieth Century: Innocent Beginnings, 1917-1950. collector's ed. Arthur M. Schlesinger, Jr. Narrated by Nelson Runger. 20 cass. (Running Time: 28 hrs.). 2002. 74.95 (978-1-4025-1518-7(9), 96725) Recorded Bks.
One of the finest historians of our age. For years he has helped Americans understand who they are and where they've come from. In this first volume of memoirs he turns a keen eye on his own remarkable life, from his Midwestern upbringing and his days at Harvard, to his involvement with World War Ii.

Life in the Twentieth Century: Innocent Beginnings, 1917-1950. unabr. ed. Arthur M. Schlesinger, Jr. Narrated by Nelson Runger. 20 cass. (Running Time: 28 hrs.). 2002. 159.00 (978-0-7887-9099-7(4)) Recorded Bks.

Life in the Twenty-First Century. Manly P. Hall. 6 cass. (Running Time: 180 min.). 1999. 40.00 set incl. album. (978-0-89314-162-2(3), S881009) Philos Res.

Life in the U. S. A. R. Jordania. 1985. 20.00 (978-0-07-033063-4(8)) McGraw.

Life in Their Hands. (J). 2002. (978-0-7398-5120-3(9)) SteckVau.

Life in Their Hands Level 2. (J). 2002. audio compact disk (978-0-7398-5330-6(9)) SteckVau.

Life in Western America. Pace International Research, Inc. Staff. 1984. 3.25 (978-0-89209-081-5(2)) Pace Grp Intl.

***Life in Year One: What the World Was Like in First-Century Palestine.** unabr. ed. Scott Korb. Narrated by Sean Runnette. (Running Time: 6 hrs. 30 mins.). 2010. 29.99 (978-1-4001-9588-6(8)); 14.99 (978-1-4001-8588-7(2)) Tantor Media.

***Life in Year One: What the World Was Like in First-Century Palestine.** unabr. ed. Scott Korb. Narrated by Sean Runnette & Arthur Morey. (Running Time: 6 hrs. 30 mins. 0 sec.). 2010. 19.99 (978-1-4001-6588-9(1)); audio compact disk 29.99 (978-1-4001-1588-4(4)); audio compact disk 59.99 (978-1-4001-4588-1(0)) Pub: Tantor Media. Dist(s): IngramPubServ

Life Insurance Company Products: Thursday-Friday, October 22-23, 1997, Grand Hyatt, Washington, D.C. 8 cass. 275.00 Incl. course materials. (MC26) Am Law Inst.
Course of study on federal & state securities & insurance laws, banking regulations, & ERISA matters. Examines significant recent developments under the federal securities laws, state insurance laws, banking laws, & ERISA as they relate to fixed & separate accounts of life insurance companies.

Life Insurance in China: A Strategic Reference 2006. Compiled by Icon Group International, Inc. Staff. 2007. ring bd. 195.00 (978-0-497-35884-6(0)) Icon Grp.

Life Insurance Planning after TRA '86. William B. Lynch. (Running Time: 30 min.). 25.00 Am Soc Chart.
Examines the demise of the deduction of loan interest & alternative ways of funding life insurance.

Life Insurance Policy: 11 Peter 1:1-11. Ed Young. 1983. 4.95 (978-0-7417-1308-7(X), 308) Win Walk.

Life Insurance Services in Ecuador: A Strategic Reference 2007. Compiled by Icon Group International, Inc. Staff. 2007. ring bd. 195.00 (978-0-497-35924-9(3)) Icon Grp.

Life Interrupted: It's Not All about Me (audio) Chris M. Tatevosian. 2008. audio compact disk 17.99 (978-1-60696-724-9(X)) Tate Pubng.

Life Interrupted: The Unfinished Monologue. Spalding Gray. Read by Sam Shepard. Intro. by Francine Prose. 2005. 8.95 (978-1-59397-844-0(8)) Pub: Macmill Audio. Dist(s): Macmillan

Life Interrupted: The Unfinished Monologue. unabr. ed. Spalding Gray. Read by Sam Shepard. Intro. by Francine Prose. 2 CDs. (Running Time: 2 hrs. 0 mins. 0 sec.). (ENG.). 2006. audio compact disk 14.95 (978-1-59397-792-4(1)) Pub: Macmill Audio. Dist(s): Macmillan

Life Is A. B. L. T. About Balance, Love & Trust. Joanne Leone. 1 CD. (Running Time: 1 hr.). 2001. audio compact disk 10.95 (978-1-931355-01-8(0)) Insight Out CA.
Tools to rid yourself of the shadows & darkness of life when you're feeling sandwiched into a corner. Learn how to reconnect with what you value most, how to exercise your personal power & how to experience meaningful relationships. Stretch old growth patterns to experience more peace & joy.

Life Is a Choice. Mac Hammond. 1 CD. (Running Time: 1 hr.). 2005. audio compact disk 5.00 (978-1-57399-257-2(7)) Mac Hammond.

Life Is a Football Game. Troy Dunn. 1 cass. 2004. 9.95 (978-1-55503-362-0(8), 061974); audio compact disk 10.95 (978-1-55503-964-6(2), 2500701) Covenant Comms.
A powerful message on the plan of salvation.

Life Is a Quest for Joy. J. Donald Walters. 2001. audio compact disk 9.95 (978-1-56589-760-1(9)) Pub: Crystal Clarity. Dist(s): Natl Bk Netwk

Life Is a Quest for Joy. J. Donald Walters. 2005. audio compact disk 15.95 (978-1-56589-761-8(7)) Pub: Crystal Clarity. Dist(s): Natl Bk Netwk

Life Is a Series of Presentations: 8 Ways to Punch up Your People Skills at Work, at Home, Anytime, Anywhere. abr. ed. Tony Jeary. Told to Kim Dower. Based on a work by J. E. Fishman. 2004. 15.95 (978-0-7435-3926-5(5)) Pub: S&S Audio. Dist(s): S and S Inc

Life Is a Test: How to Meet Life's Challenges Successfully. unabr. ed. Esther Jungreis. Read by Mare Winningham. (Running Time: 9 hrs.). (ENG.). 2008. 24.98 (978-1-60024-457-5(2)); audio compact disk 34.98 (978-1-60024-456-8(4)) Pub: Hachet Audio. Dist(s): HachBkGrp

Life Is a Trust. unabr. ed. Perf. by Eknath Easwaran. 1 cass. (Running Time: 1 hr.). 1986. 7.95 (978-1-58638-559-0(3)) Nilgiri Pr.

***Life Is a Verb Audiobook: 37 Days to Wake up, Be Mindful, & Live Intentionally.** Patti Digh. Read by Patti Digh. (Running Time: 400). (ENG.). 2010. 34.95 (978-0-9827657-0-8(3)) Pattl Digh.

Life Is but a Dream: Wise Techniques for an Inspirational Journey. unabr. ed. Marcia Wieder. Read by Marcia Wieder. (Running Time: 6 hrs.). (ENG.). 2009. 24.98 (978-1-59659-382-4(2), GildAudio) Pub: Gildan Media. Dist(s): HachBkGrp

Life Is Choices, Hope Is a Decision. R. Lee Muehlberg. Read by R. Lee Muehlberg. 1 cass. (Running Time: 1 hr. 22 min.). 11.95 (978-0-9653342-2-8(8)) Muehlberg Pr.
Collection of thoughts offering practical help to listeners who are struggling to reach a goal or beyond a goal or help listeners who are finding it hard to know where they stand or what to live by anymore.

Life Is Fine see Poetry of Langston Hughes

Life Is Friends: A Complete Guide to the Lost Art of Connecting in Person. unabr. ed. Jeanne Martinet. Read by Jeanne Martinet. 6 CDs. (ENG.). 2009. audio compact disk 24.95 (978-1-60283-581-8(0)) Pub: AudioGO. Dist(s): Perseus Dist

Life is Hard: An Audio Guide to Healing Emotional Pain. John Preston. 1 cass. (Running Time: 060 min.). 1996. 11.95 (978-0-915166-99-2(2)) Impact Christian.

Life Is Hard: An Audio Guide to Healing Emotional Pain. John Preston. (ENG.). 2008. audio compact disk 15.95 (978-1-886230-75-0(7)) Impact Pubs CA.

Life Is Not a Destination - Audio Version. Short Stories. Narrated by Ben Mukkala. Intro. by Dorothy Mukkala. 5 CDs. (Running Time: 5 hrs. 35 mins.). 2005. audio compact disk 29.95 (978-0-9709971-5-9(9)) Stl Wtr.
Unabridged audio version of of original book, "Life is Not a Destination" read by the author, Ben Mukkala.

Life Is Short, Wear Your Party Pants. Loretta LaRoche. 2 CDs. 2003. audio compact disk 18.95 (978-1-4019-0254-4(5), 2545) Hay House.

Life Is the Destiny. Alex Stuart. Read by Margaret Marsh. 4 cass. 1999. 44.95 (61942) Pub: Soundings Ltd GBR. Dist(s): ISIS Pub

Life Is Unfoldment. Swami Amar Jyoti. 1 dolby cass. 1984. 9.95 (A-29) Truth Consciousness.
By a process of unfoldment, not by achievement or accomplishment, life blooms & inner consciousness unfolds effortlessly.

Life Is What You Make It: Find Your Own Path to Fulfillment. abr. unabr. ed. Peter Buffett. Read by Peter Buffett. (ENG.). 2010. audio compact disk 30.00 (978-0-307-73573-7(7), Random AudioBks) Pub: Random Audio Pubg. Dist(s): Random

***Life Is What You Make It: So Make It the Best You Can.** unabr. ed. Bob Merritt. (ENG.). 2010. 14.98 (978-1-61045-026-3(4)) christianaud.

***Life Is What You Make It: So Make It the Best You Can.** unabr. ed. Bob Merritt. (Running Time: 6 hrs. 0 mins. 0 sec.). (ENG.). 2011. audio compact disk 24.98 (978-1-61045-027-0(2)) christianaud.

Life Is Worth Living. Fulton J. Sheen. 6 cass. 1995. 39.95 Set. (1000-C) Ignatius Pr.
Sheen's messages are full of practical advice & spiritual insight that will give you inspiration, guidance & peace of mind in facing the many challenges of daily life.

Life Is Worth Living: Archbishop Fulton Sheen. Narrated by Fulton Sheen. (ENG.). 2008. audio compact disk 99.99 (978-1-930034-00-6(8)) Casscomm.

Life Lessons. Elisabeth Kubler-Ross & David Kessler. Read by David Kessler. 2000. audio compact disk 56.00 (978-0-7366-7076-0(9)) Books on Tape.

Life Lessons. collector's unabr. ed. Elisabeth Kubler-Ross & David Kessler. 5 cass. (Running Time: 7 hrs. 30 min.). 2000. 40.00 (978-0-7366-5936-9(6)) Books on Tape.
Is this really how I want to live my life? Each one of us at some point asks this question. The tragedy is not that life is short but that we often see only in hindsight what really matters. Elizabeth Kubler-Ross joins with David Kessler to guide readers through the practical & spiritual lessons we need to learn so that we can live life to its fullest in every moment. Many years of working with the dying have shown the authors that certain lessons come up over & over again. Some of these lessons can be difficult to master, but even the attempts to understand them are deeply rewarding.

Life Lessons. unabr. collector's ed. Elisabeth Kubler-Ross & David Kessler. Read by David Kessler. 7 CDs. (Running Time: 10 hrs. 30 mins.). 2001. audio compact disk 56.00 Books on Tape.
Following a near fatal stroke, famed author Elisabeth Kubler-Ross writes not about death and dying but about life and living.

Life Lessons: Experts on Death & Dying Teach Us about the Mysteries of Life & Living. unabr. ed. Elisabeth Kubler-Ross. Read by David Kessler. 5 cass. (Running Time: 7 hrs.). 2001. 20.00 (978-0-7366-5696-2(0)) Books on Tape.
Is this really how I want to live my life? Each one of us at some point asks the question. The tragedy is not that life is short but that we often see only in hindsight what really matters. This is the first book on life & living. Guiding readers through the practical & spiritual lessons we need to learn so that we can live life to its fullest in every moment. Many years of working with the dying have shown the authors that certain lessons come up over & over again. Some of these lessons can be difficult to master, but even the attemps to understand them are deeply rewarding.

Life Lessons & Reflections. abr. ed. Montel Williams. Read by Montel Williams. 1 cass. (Running Time: 90 mins.). 2000. 10.95 Hay House.

Life Lessons from James. Frank Damazio. 6 cass. (Running Time: 9 hrs.). 2000. (978-1-886849-70-9(6)) CityChristian.

Life Lessons from the Great Books. Instructed by J. Rufus Fears. 2009. 199.95 (978-1-59803-515-5(0)); audio compact disk 269.95 (978-1-59803-516-2(9)) Teaching Co.

Life Lessons Just for Men see Lecciones de Vida SÃ³lo para Hombres

Life Lessons Just for Men. 2007. audio compact disk 24.00 (978-1-57972-748-2(4)) Insight Living.

Life Lessons Just for Women see Lecciones de Vida SÃ³lo para Mujeres

Life Lessons Just for Women. Charles R. Swindoll. 2008. audio compact disk 24.00 (978-1-57972-812-0(X)) Insight Living.

Life Lessons of T'ai Chi: The Ancient Wisdom of the Moving Meditation that Is T'ai Chi. 2005. 19.95 (978-0-9656103-9-1(X)) Easy St Enterp.

Life, Liberty, & the Pursuit of Healthiness: Dr. Dean's Commonsense Guide for Anything That Ails You. abr. ed. Dean Edell. Read by Dean Edell. 2 CDs. (Running Time: 3 hrs.). 2004. audio compact disk 22.00 (978-0-06-058574-7(9)) HarperCollins Pubs.

***Life, Liberty, & the Pursuit of Healthiness: Real Questions & Real Answers to Help.** abr. ed. Dean Edell. Read by Dean Edell. (ENG.). 2004. (978-0-06-075234-7(3), Harper Audio) HarperCollins Pubs.

***Life, Liberty, & the Pursuit of Healthiness: Real Questions & Real Answers to Help.** abr. ed. Dean Edell. Read by Dean Edell. (ENG.). 2004. (978-0-06-081339-0(3), Harper Audio) HarperCollins Pubs.

Life, Love & the Pursuit of Happiness, This Sacred Mystery. Christopher Love. Read by Christopher Love. 1 cass. (Running Time: 90 min.). 1997. 10.95 (978-1-891820-01-4(X)) World Sangha Pubg.
Self-hypnosis meditation for healing, self-improvement & realizing our full & powerful potential as spiritual beings.

Life Management for Busy Women: Living Out God's Plan with Passion & Purpose. abr. ed. Elizabeth George. 4 cass. (Running Time: 5 hrs.). 2002. 25.99 (978-1-58926-099-3(6), H61L-0100) Oasis Audio.
Sourcebook will strike a chord with women hungering to live orderly lives that are a testimony to their faith.

Life Management for Busy Women: Living Out God's Plan with Passion & Purpose. unabr. ed. Elizabeth George. Narrated by Aimee Lilly. (ENG.). 2003. 20.99 (978-1-60814-288-0(4)) Oasis Audio.

Life Matters: Creating a Dynamic Balance of Work, Family, Time & Money. A. Roger Merrill & Rebecca R. Merrill. 2003. 19.95 (978-1-933976-29-7(2)) Pub: Franklin Covey. Dist(s): S and S Inc

Life Matters: Creating a Dynamic Balance of Work, Family, Time & Money. abr. ed. A. Roger Merrill & Rebecca R. Merrill. 2006. 11.95 (978-1-933976-26-6(8)) Pub: Franklin Covey. Dist(s): S and S Inc

Life Mini CD: 5 Pack. (ENG.). 2002. audio compact disk 14.99 (978-1-56399-198-1(5)) CampCrus.

Life near 310 Kelvin. Greg Keith. Prod. by Steven Gulie. 1 CD. (Running Time: 1 hr. 30 mins.). 1998. audio compact disk 9.95 (978-0-943389-31-8(3)) Snow Lion-SLG Bks.

Life of an American Slave. Frederick Douglass. Read by Jonathan Reese. (Running Time: 14400 sec.). (Unabridged Classics in Audio Ser.). (ENG.). 2005. audio compact disk 49.99 (978-1-4001-3047-4(6)); audio compact disk 24.99 (978-1-4001-0047-7(X)) Pub: Tantor Media. Dist(s): IngramPubServ

Life of Buddha. Eknath Easwaran. 1 cass. (Running Time: 55 mins.). (Easwaran on Tape Ser.). 1989. 7.95 (978-1-58638-560-6(7)) Nilgiri Pr.

Life of Charles Dickens. John Forster. Narrated by Flo Gibson. 27 cass. (Running Time: 40 hrs. 20 mins). 2006. 67.95 (978-1-55685-859-8(0)) Audio Bk Con.

Life of Charlotte Brontë. unabr. ed. Elizabeth Gaskell. Read by Flo Gibson. 12 cass. (Running Time: 17 hrs. 30 min.). (Classic Books on Cassettes Ser.). 1988. 39.95 (978-1-55685-115-5(4)) Audio Bk Con.
A deeply sympathetic & definitive biography related by her close friend mostly by the method of using Charlotte's letters.

Life of Christ. Fulton J. Sheen. 15 cass. 59.95 (928) Ignatius Pr.
A deep look into the person of Christ by the illustrious Bishop of our age.

Life of Christ, Vol. 2. Read by George W. Sarris. 1 cass. (World's Greatest Stories Ser.). 1995. 10.98 (978-1-57919-100-9(2)); audio compact disk 10.98 (978-1-57919-095-8(2)) Randolf Prod.
Dramatic word-for-word readings of excerpts from the New International Version of the Bible. Includes passages on the Real Story of Christmas, Jesus' baptism/temptation, Real Story of Easter, Healing of the Blind Man, & things Jesus said & did.

Life of Christ: Dramatized Scenes from His Life & Ministry. 4 cass. 2004. 19.95 (978-1-59156-147-7(7)); audio compact disk 19.95 (978-1-59156-148-4(5)) Covenant Comms.

Life of Christ: The Birth, the Death & Resurrection of Jesus Christ, in Music. Contrib. by Richard Martin. Prod. by Eric Wyse. 2007. audio compact disk 12.98 (978-5-557-57597-3(9)) Vital BGR.

Life of Christ: The the Gospel of Luke. unabr. rev. ed. 2002. audio compact disk 14.99 (978-0-310-94489-8(9)) Zondervan.

Life of Christ KJV. Perf. by George W. Sarris. 5 CD's. (Running Time: about 1 hour). (World's Greatest Stories Ser.: Volume 2). (J). 1989. audio compact disk 7.95 (978-0-9767744-6-4(1)) GWSPubs.
Bible stories read dramatically by George W. Sarris. The texts for all the stories are taken directly, word for word, from the King James Version Bible, with the addition of carefully selected music and sound effects. Vol 2 contains The Birth of Christ, The Baptism & Temptation of Jesus, The Healing of the Blind Man, Things Jesus Said & Did, The Crucifixion & Resurrection.

Life of Christ NIV. Perf. by George W. Sarris. 5 CD's. (Running Time: about 1 hour each). (World's Greatest Stories Ser.: Volume 2). (J). 1989. audio compact disk 7.95 (978-0-9767744-1-9(0)) GWSPubs.
Bible stories read dramatically by George W. Sarris. The texts for all the stories are taken directly, word for word, from the New International Version Bible, with the addition of carefully selected music and sound effects. Vol. 2 contains The Birth of Christ, The Baptism & Temptation of Jesus, The Healing of the Blind Man, Things Jesus Said & Did, and The Crucifixion & Resurrection.

Life of Christ: the Gospel of Luke: The Gospel of Luke. unabr. ed. Zondervan Publishing Staff. (Running Time: 2 hrs. 49 mins. 0 sec.). (NIV Audio Bible Ser.). (ENG.). 2003. 8.99 (978-0-310-26160-5(0)) Zondervan.

Life of Dante. Benedict Flynn. Read by John Sapnel. (Running Time: 1 hr.). 2005. 16.95 (978-1-60083-824-8(3)) Iofy Corp.

Life of Dante. Read by John Shrapnel. Ed. by Benedict Flynn. 1 cass. (Running Time: 1 hr. 20 min.). 2001. 9.98 (978-962-634-723-2(6), NA122314, Naxos AudioBooks); audio compact disk 14.98 (978-962-634-223-7(4), NA122312, Naxos AudioBooks) Naxos.

***Life of David Brainerd.** unabr. ed. Jonathan Edwards. Narrated by Nick Cordileone. (Running Time: 10 hrs. 0 mins. 0 sec.). (ENG.). 2004. 16.98 (978-1-59644-019-7(8), Hovel Audio) christianaud.

Life of David Brainerd: Chiefly Extracted from His Diary. unabr. ed. Jonathan Edwards. Ed. by Scott P. Chaplin. Narrated by Nick Cordileone. 1 MP3 CD. (Running Time: 10 hrs. 0 mins. 0 sec.). (ENG.). 2004. lp 19.98 (978-1-59644-018-0(X), Hovel Audio) christianaud.
Though he was orphaned at age fourteen, repeatedly struck with debilitating illnesses, and unfairly expelled from college, Brainerd allowed nothing to deter him from serving God wholeheartedly. He traveled thousands of miles by horseback across treacherous terrain to preach the gospel to remote Indians. Their benefit ultimately brought about his early death at the age of 29. This book not only offers a captivating story, but an uplifting buoy for those who are weary, distant, or discouraged.

Life of David Brainerd: Chiefly Extracted from His Diary. unabr. abr. ed. Jonathan Edwards. 9 CDs. (Running Time: 10 hrs. 0 mins. 0 sec.). (Classic Biographies Ser.). (ENG.). 2004. audio compact disk 28.98 (978-1-59644-017-3(1), Hovel Audio) christianaud.

Life of Edith Stein. Alice Von Hildebrand. 1 cass. 1990. 2.50 (978-1-56036-064-3(X)) AMI Pr.

Life of Emily Dickinson. unabr. ed. Read by Heywood Hale Broun & Richard B. Sewall. 1 cass. (Running Time: 56 min.). (Broun Radio Ser.). 12.95 (40098) J Norton Pubs.
Richard Sewall discusses the biography of the New England poet.

Life of Faith & the Future of the Planet. David Steindl-Rast. 1 cass. (Running Time: 1 hr. 15 min.). 1990. 7.95 (TAH234) Alba Hse Comns.
This program clarifies the relationship between our own, personal, inner spiritual life & the external landscape of our physical environment; increasing our sense of belonging & in the process reveals the ultimate, unchanging meaning of life.

Life of Fear see Great American Essays: A Collection

Life of Galileo. unabr. abr. ed. Bertolt Brecht. Tr. by David Hare & David Hare. 2 CDs. (Running Time: 6900 sec.). (L. A. Theatre Works Audio Theatre Collections). 2008. audio compact disk 25.95 (978-1-58081-379-2(8)) Pub: L A Theatre. Dist(s): NetLibrary CO

Life of General Jeb Stuart. unabr. ed. Mary L. Williamson. Read by Lloyd James. 4 cass. (Running Time: 4 hrs. 30 mins.). 2006. 32.95 (978-0-7861-2465-7(2), 3100); audio compact disk 32.00 (978-0-7861-8790-4(5), 3100) Blckstn Audio.

Life of Greece, Pt. 2. collector's ed. Will Durant & Ariel Durant. Read by Alexander Adams. 10 cass. (Running Time: 15 hrs.). (Story of Civilization Ser.). 1994. 80.00 (978-0-7366-2738-2(3), 3464-B) Books on Tape.
Re-creates Greek civilization from the prehistoric culture of Crete to the Roman conquest.

Life of Horatio Lord Nelson, unabr. ed. Robert Southey. Read by Frederick Davidson. 7 cass. (Running Time: 10 hrs.). 1995. 49.95 (978-0-7861-0853-4(3), 1651) Blckstn Audio.
Having entered the British Navy at the age of twelve, Horatio Lord Nelson achieved the rank of captain at the age of twenty. As captain, he was quickly recognized as a magnetic & controversial figure. He triumphed at Cape St. Vincent & the Nile, but failed at Tenerife & Boulogne. With the glories of Copenhagen & Trafalgar yet ahead of him, his ardent passion for Emma Hamilton, the wife of a British Ambassador, cast a heavy shadow over his career.

Life of Jesus. Featuring John Eldredge. (ENG.). 2009. audio compact disk Rental 12.99 (978-1-933207-35-3(3)) Ransomed Heart.

Life of Jesus. Francois Mauriac. Tr. by Julie Kerman. 7 cass. 28.95 (301) Ignatius Pr.
Life of Jesus by one of the century's great French writers.

Life of Jesus: Dramatic Eyewitness Accounts from the Luke Reports. adpt. ed. Prod. by Focus on the Family Staff. Adapted by Dave Arnold & Paul McCusker. (Running Time: 8 hrs. 30 mins.). (Radio Theatre Ser.). (ENG.). 2006. audio compact disk 49.97 (978-1-58997-368-8(2)) Pub: Focus Family. Dist(s): Tyndale Hse

Life of Jesus: 13 Cassette Dramatized Audio Stories. 2006. 48.75 (978-1-60079-018-8(6)) YourStory.

Life of Jesus: 13 CD Dramatized Audio Stories. 2006. 48.75 (978-1-60079-041-6(0)) YourStory.

Life of Jesus Christ. James Stalker. 1 MP3-CD. (Running Time: 4 hrs. 3 mins.). (ENG.). 2006. 7.00 (978-0-9772747-2-7(1)) Tree City.
Born in 1848, James A Stalker was educated at the University of Edinburgh, and was both a pastor and theologian in the free Church of Scotland. Stalker also became professor of Church History and Christian Ethics at Free Church College. Little is known about his life, although he was a prolific author. In 1879, Stalker published his best known work, The Life of Jesus Christ, as a ?Handbook for Bible Classes.? In it, the reader is provided with a beautiful and memorable portrait, with the main features of Christ?s life, death, and resurrection described clearly and concisely. James Stalker died in 1929. His book, The Life of Jesus Christ, has been reprinted many times and in many languages, a testament to its enduring quality.

Life of Jesus, the Christ: A Chronicle in Scripture & Song. Karla Carey. 1 cass. (Running Time: 90 min.). (Inspiration in Words & Music Ser.). 12.95 (978-1-55768-534-6(7)) LC Pub.

Life of Johnson. James Boswell. Read by Billy Hartman. (Running Time: 2 hrs. 30 mins.). 1998. 20.95 (978-1-60083-825-5(1)) Iofy Corp.

Life of Johnson. James Boswell. Read by Billy Hartman. 2 cass. (Running Time: 2 hrs. 36 mins.). 1994. 22.98 (978-962-634-520-7(9), NA202014, Naxos AudioBooks) Naxos.
Boswell's biography of his friend and hero Samuel Johnson is an acknowledged classic full of humorous anecdote and rich characterization. Johnson's complex humanity is set within a vivid picture of 18th Century London.

Life of Johnson. abr. ed. James Boswell. Read by Billy Hartman. 2 CDs. (Running Time: 2 hrs. 36 mins.). 1994. audio compact disk 15.98 (978-962-634-020-2(7), NA202012, Naxos AudioBooks) Naxos.
Boswell's biography of his friend and hero Samuel Johnson is an acknowledged classic, full of humorous anecdote and rich characterization. Johnson's complex humanity is set within a vivid picture of 18th century London.

Life of Johnson. abr. ed. James Boswell. Read by Billy Hartman. 2 CDs. (Running Time: 9360 sec.). 2006. audio compact disk 17.98 (978-962-634-370-8(2), Naxos AudioBooks) Naxos.

Life of Joy, Peace & Fulfillment: Hypnosis. Created by Laura Rubinstein. 1. (Running Time: 50 mins). (LBR Relaxation Ser.: No. 2). 1999. audio compact disk (978-0-9749845-0-6(7)) L Rubinstein.
Hypnosis CD with two tracks. 20-25 minutes each. One track is a power nap that will instruct you to wake up at the end. The second track can be used to fall asleep to.

Life of Knute Rockne. Perf. by Ronald Reagan & Pat O'Brien. 1 cass. (Running Time: 60 min.). 1940. 7.95 (DD-8810) Natl Recrd Co.
Rockne was a good deal more than just a coach to his players, so there is more to this story than just football. It's the story of hard driving fighter who always made life exciting, of the woman he loved, & the adventures they shared.

Life of Lincoln. Narrated by Andrew L. Barnes. Prod. by Legacy Audio Books. Illus. by JoAnn M. Mirlenbrink. (ENG.). 2009. cd-rom 29.95 (978-0-9816561-0-6(2)) Pub: Legacy Audio Bks. Dist(s): Bk Clearing Hse

Life of Lord Krishna. 16 cass. 60.00 Set, incl. 1 vinyl album. Bhaktivedanta.
From the complete 10th Canto & Chapters 30 & 31 of the 11th Canto of Srimad-Bhagavatam.

Life of Mary: A Poem-Novella. unabr. ed. Charlotte Mandel. Read by Charlotte Mandel. Frwd. by Sandra M. Gilbert. 1 cass. (Running Time: 45 mins.). (Listen to the Poet Ser.). 1988. pap. bk. 7.00 (978-0-938158-10-3(4)) Saturday Pr.
A dramatic reading of the entire poem-novella by the author, with musical interweave composed & performed by guitarist David Hauer. The original paperback has an introduction by Sandra M. Gilbert. The work re-visions the biblical Mary & Michelangelo's Pieta through the feminist consciousness of a contemporary young mother.

Life of Mary: A Poem-Novella. unabr. ed. Charlotte Mandel. Read by Charlotte Mandel. Contrib. by David Hauer. Music by David Hauer. 1 cass. (Running Time: 45 min.). (Listen to the Poet Ser.). 1993. 9.00 (978-0-938158-14-1(7)) Saturday Pr.

Life of Mozart. Edward Holmes. Read by David Case. (Tantor Unabridged Classics Ser.). (ENG.). 2009. 69.99 (978-1-60775-787-0(7)) Find a World.

Life of Mozart. Edward Holmes. Read by David Case. (Running Time: 11 hrs. 45 mins.). (C). 2003. 29.95 (978-1-60083-663-3(1), Audiofy Corp) Iofy Corp.

Life of Mozart. Edward Holmes. Read by David Case. (Running Time: 42300 sec.). (ENG.). 2004. audio compact disk 39.99 (978-1-4001-0098-9(4)) Pub: Tantor Media. Dist(s): IngramPubServ

Life of Mozart. Edward Holmes. Read by David Case. (ENG.). 2005. audio compact disk 79.99 (978-1-4001-3098-6(0)) Pub: Tantor Media. Dist(s): IngramPubServ

Life of Mozart. Edward Holmes. Read by David Case. (Running Time: 42300 sec.). (ENG.). 2004. audio compact disk 22.99 (978-1-4001-5098-4(1)) Pub: Tantor Media. Dist(s): IngramPubServ

Life of Mozart. unabr. collector's ed. Edward Holmes. Read by David Case. 8 cass. (Running Time: 12 hrs.). 1991. 64.00 (978-0-7366-1985-1(2), 2802) Books on Tape.
Mozart, glorious & tragic, lived a short 35 years. He died in poverty (but not in despair), & left a priceless legacy in his music, also in the intensity with which he pursued his artistic vision. His music was controversial, too complex for most concert goers, yet it heralded a new musical era. Except for Edward Holmes, the shards of Mozart's life might never have been so richly assembled. Holmes was born in 1797, six years after Mozart died. But many of Mozart's contemporaries were still living when Holmes began his work. His meetings with them add richness & immediacy to this story, keeping it as fresh & readable today as it was when first published more than 100 years ago.

Life of Mozart, with EBook. unabr. ed. Edward Holmes. Narrated by David Case. (Running Time: 12 hrs. 0 mins. 0 sec.). (ENG.). 2009. 22.99 (978-1-4001-6121-8(5)); audio compact disk 32.99 (978-1-4001-1121-3(8)) Pub: Tantor Media. Dist(s): IngramPubServ

Life of Mozart, with eBook. unabr. ed. Edward Holmes. Narrated by David Case. (Running Time: 12 hrs. 0 mins. 0 sec.). (ENG.). 2009. audio compact disk 65.99 (978-1-4001-4121-0(4)) Pub: Tantor Media. Dist(s): IngramPubServ

Life of Napoleon. unabr. collector's ed. Arthur Griffiths. Read by Bill Kelsey. 5 cass. (Running Time: 7 hrs. 30 min.). 1995. 40.00 (978-0-7366-3063-4(5), 3745) Books on Tape.
Many hailed Napoleon as another Alexander the Great. That's why his demise was so wretched. A no-nonsense account.

Life of Oscar Wilde. Hesketh Pearson. Read by Simon Russell Beale. (Running Time: 3 hrs. 30 mins.). (C). 1999. 24.95 (978-1-60083-826-2(X)) Iofy Corp.

Life of Oscar Wilde. abr. ed. Hesketh Pearson. Read by Simon Russell Beale. 3 CDs. (Running Time: 3 hrs. 36 mins.). 1995. audio compact disk 22.98 (978-962-634-068-4(1), NA306812, Naxos AudioBooks) Naxos.

Life of Oswald Chambers: Abandoned to God. David McCasland. Read by Tedd Seelye. 2 cass. (Running Time: 3 hrs.). 1995. 19.95 (978-1-886463-09-7(3)) Oasis Audio.
Learn of his life, his sense of humor, his love for children & of his commitment to God.

***Life of Our Lord: Written for His Children During the Years 1846 To 1849.** unabr. ed. Charles Dickens. Narrated by David Aikman. (Running Time: 1 hr. 31 mins. 1 sec.). (ENG.). 2010. 9.09 (978-1-60814-763-2(0)); audio compact disk 12.99 (978-1-59859-781-3(7)) Oasis Audio.

Life of Pi. unabr. ed. Yann Martel. Read by Jeff Woodman & Alexander Marshall. (YA). 2006. 49.99 (978-1-59895-647-4(7)) Find a World.

Life of Pi. unabr. ed. Yann Martel. Read by Jeff Woodman. Told to Alexander Marshall. 9 CDs. (Running Time: 11 hrs.). (ENG.). 2003. audio compact disk 36.95 (978-1-56511-780-8(8), 1565117808) Pub: HighBridge. Dist(s): Workman Pub

Life of Riley. Ed. by William Bendix. (CC-2939) Natl Recrd Co.

Life of Riley. Perf. by William Bendix et al. (ENG.). 2008. audio compact disk 31.95 (978-1-57019-871-7(3)) Radio Spirits.

Life of Riley. Contrib. by William Bendix. (Running Time: 10800 sec.). 2004. 9.98 (978-1-57019-557-0(9)) Radio Spirits.

***Life of Riley.** Perf. by William Bendix & Paula Winslowe. 2010. audio compact disk 31.95 (978-1-57019-936-3(1)) Radio Spirits.

Life of Riley. abr. ed. 2 cass. Dramatization. bk. 16.95 set. (978-1-56703-019-8(X)) High-Top Sports.

Life of Riley, Vol. 1. collector's ed. Perf. by Chester A. Riley et al. 6 cass. (Running Time: 9 hrs.). 1998. bk. 34.98 (4009) Radio Spirits.
18 classic episodes that chronicle the misadventures of Chester A. Riley, a riveter & family man along with his co-worker, Gillis & Digby O'Dell " the friendly undertaker".

Life of Riley, Vol. 2. Created by Irving Brecher. (Running Time: 10800 sec.). 2004. 9.98 (978-1-57019-746-8(6)); audio compact disk 9.98 (978-1-57019-745-1(8)) Radio Spirits.

Life of Riley, Vol. 2. collector's ed. Perf. by Chester A. Riley et al. 6 cass. (Running Time: 9 hrs.). 1998. bk. 34.98 (4152) Radio Spirits.

Life of Riley, Vol. 3. collector's ed. Perf. by Chester A. Riley. 6 cass. (Running Time: 9 hrs.). 2000. bk. 34.98 (4550) Radio Spirits.
Riveter Chester A. Riley, a "typical" family man, managed to change any anthill of a problem into a disaster. Riley's mishaps include his wife, their two children, co-worker Gillis and Digby "Digger" O'Dell, the friendly undertaker.18 episodes.

Life of Riley: A Love Letter to Peg & Where Does All the Money Go? Perf. by William Bendix. 1 cass. (Running Time: 1 hr.). 2001. 6.98 (1567) Radio Spirits.

Life of Riley: Anniversary Misunderstandings & Riley Refuses to Help Peg. Perf. by William Bendix. 1 cass. (Running Time: 1 hr.). 2001. 6.98 (1812) Radio Spirits.

Life of Riley: Bab's Elderly Boyfriend & Thanksgiving Flashback. Perf. by William Bendix. 1 cass. (Running Time: 1 hr.). 2001. 6.98 (1761) Radio Spirits.

Life of Riley: Basketball Game - Bribe? & Riley the Rent Collector. Perf. by William Bendix. 1 cass. (Running Time: 1 hr.). 2001. 6.98 (2604) Radio Spirits.

Life of Riley: Case of Nerves. 6 cass. (Running Time: 6 hrs.). 1999. 19.98 (AB271) Radio Spirits.

Life of Riley: Christmas Bonuses & Nortre Dame Football Tickets. Perf. by William Bendix. 1 cass. (Running Time: 1 hr.). 2001. 6.98 (1763) Radio Spirits.

Life of Riley: Christmas Club & New Year's Eve is for Kids. Perf. by William Bendix. 1 cass. (Running Time: 1 hr.). 2001. 6.98 (1511) Radio Spirits.

Life of Riley: Christmas in Store Window & Hawkins Story. Perf. by William Bendix. 1 cass. (Running Time: 1 hr.). 2001. 6.98 (1759) Radio Spirits.

Life of Riley: Doing Housework & The Perfect Mate for Babs. Perf. by William Bendix. 1 cass. (Running Time: 1 hr.). 2001. 6.98 (2421) Radio Spirits.

Life of Riley: Driver's License & The Collection Agent. Perf. by William Bendix. 1 cass. (Running Time: 1 hr.). 2001. 6.98 (1932) Radio Spirits.

Life of Riley: Election Flashback - Riley Campaigns & The Problem Child. Perf. by William Bendix. 1 cass. (Running Time: 1 hr.). 2001. 6.98 (1760) Radio Spirits.

Life of Riley: Gillis Moves in Next Door & Junior Drops Out of School. Perf. by William Bendix. 1 cass. (Running Time: 1 hr.). 2001. 6.98 (1757) Radio Spirits.

Life of Riley: Junior Wants to Become a Fireman. Perf. by William Bendix. 1 cass. (Running Time: 1 hr.). 2001. 6.98 (1873) Radio Spirits.

Life of Riley: Junior's Basketball Team & Babs's Wedding - Baby-Sitting. Perf. by William Bendix. 1 cass. (Running Time: 1 hr.). 2001. 6.98 (1764) Radio Spirits.

Life of Riley: Meeting Chester & Summer Job in San Francisco. Perf. by William Bendix. 1 cass. (Running Time: 1 hr.). 2001. 6.98 (1758) Radio Spirits.

Life of Riley: Old Man Riley & Babs Wants Privacy. Perf. by William Bendix. 1 cass. (Running Time: 1 hr.). 2001. 6.98 (2618) Radio Spirits.

Life of Riley: Riley & Mrs. Morris & Riley's Sister Visits after Being Jilted. Perf. by William Bendix. 1 cass. (Running Time: 1 hr.). 2001. 6.98 (1762) Radio Spirits.

Life of Riley: Riley & the Aardvark & Comic Books. Perf. by William Bendix. 1 cass. (Running Time: 1 hr.). 2001. 6.98 (2039) Radio Spirits.

Life of Riley: Riley Buys a Hamburger Stand & Riley's Big Surprise. Perf. by William Bendix. 1 cass. (Running Time: 1 hr.). 2001. 6.98 (1894) Radio Spirits.

Life of Riley: Riley Invites 200 Service Men to His Party & Riley is Arrested. Perf. by William Bendix. 1 cass. (Running Time: 1 hr.). 2001. 6.98 (2224) Radio Spirits.

Life of Riley: Riley is Best-Dressed Man & Uncle Baxter Goes to New York. Perf. by William Bendix. (Running Time: 1 hr.). 2001. 6.98 (2462) Radio Spirits.

Life of Riley: Riley is Going to Arabia! & Riley's Old Flame Creates Problems. Perf. by William Bendix. 1 cass. (Running Time: 1 hr.). 2001. 6.98 (1765) Radio Spirits.

Life of Riley: Riley Rents a House & Telephone Story. Perf. by William Bendix. 1 cass. (Running Time: 1 hr.). 2001. 6.98 (2181) Radio Spirits.

Life of Riley: Riley Scares Boys from Babs & Chester Thrown off a Bus. Perf. by William Bendix. 1 cass. (Running Time: 1 hr.). 2001. 6.98 (2018) Radio Spirits.

Life of Riley: Riley the Civil Servant & Riley & the Kiss in the Dark. Perf. by William Bendix. 1 cass. (Running Time: 1 hr.). 2001. 6.98 (2481) Radio Spirits.

Life of Riley: Riley the Gambler & Riley Thinks He's Promoted. Perf. by William Bendix. 1 cass. (Running Time: 1 hr.). 2001. 6.98 (2399) Radio Spirits.

Life of Riley: Riley Tries to Impress Junior & Riley Gets Medical Advice. Perf. by William Bendix. 1 cass. (Running Time: 1 hr.). 2001. 6.98 (1983) Radio Spirits.

Life of Riley: Riley's Double Wedding & Riley's Dancing Lessons. Perf. by William Bendix. 2001. 6.98 (1549) Radio Spirits.

Life of Riley: Riley's Pay is Missing & The Soap Box Derby Race. Perf. by William Bendix. 1 cass. (Running Time: 1 hr.). 2001. 6.98 (1906) Radio Spirits.

Life of Riley: Riley's Second Honeymoon & Riley's Tonsillitis Operation. Perf. by William Bendix. 1 cass. (Running Time: 1 hr.). 2001. 6.98 (2200) Radio Spirits.

Life of Riley: Riley's Wedding & Riley Invites Self to Boss's Party. Perf. by William Bendix. 1 cass. (Running Time: 1 hr.). 2001. 6.98 (1766) Radio Spirits.

Life of Riley: Surprise. 6 cass. (Running Time: 6 hrs.). 1999. 19.98 (AB270) Radio Spirits.

Life of Riley: The Barber Chair & Riley's Birthday. Perf. by William Bendix. 1 cass. (Running Time: 1 hr.). 2001. 6.98 (2245) Radio Spirits.

Life of Riley: The Expectant Father & A Date for New Year's. Perf. by William Bendix. 1 cass. (Running Time: 1 hr.). 2001. 6.98 (1947) Radio Spirits.

Life of Riley: The Initiation & Junior Wants a Dog. Perf. by William Bendix. 1 cass. (Running Time: 1 hr.). 2001. 6.98 (1963) Radio Spirits.

Life of Riley: "The Other Woman" & "The Dinner Party" unabr. ed. Perf. by William Bendix. 1 cass. (Running Time: 60 min.). Dramatization. 1947. 7.95 Norelco box. (CC-8785) Natl Recrd Co.
The Other Woman: Riley gets involved, by mistake of course, with another woman. It gets complicated as Riley, even though innocent, tries to cover-up his dinner appointment with her. This mix-up is full of laughs ala the bumbling Bendix-Riley. Drell. The Dinner Party: Riley puts on a fancy dinner for his daughter Babs. He rents a large mahogony dinner table, only it is a combination dinner-casino table. The fun starts when they sit down to eat. Dreft.

Life of Riley: Wedding Anniversary & Five Dollars is Missing. Perf. by William Bendix. 1 cass. (Running Time: 1 hr.). 2001. 6.98 (2581) Radio Spirits.

Life of Riley: Win a Buick Contest & Thanksgiving with the Gillises. Perf. by William Bendix. 1 cass. (Running Time: 1 hr.). 2001. 6.98 (2439) Radio Spirits.

Life of Riley: Women & Men Equal? & Busy Signal. Perf. by William Bendix. 1 cass. (Running Time: 1 hr.). 2001. 6.98 (2084) Radio Spirits.

Life of Riley: Women in the Workplace & Riley the Househusband. Perf. by William Bendix. 1 cass. (Running Time: 1 hr.). 2001. 6.98 (1510) Radio Spirits.

Life of Robert E. Lee. Mary L. Williamson. Narrated by Lloyd James. (Running Time: 3 hrs.). (C). 2003. 20.95 (978-1-59912-681-4(8)) Iofy Corp.

Life of Robert E. Lee. unabr. ed. Mary L. Williamson. Read by Lloyd James. 2 CDs. (Running Time: 2 hrs. 30 mins.). 2003. audio compact disk 16.95 (978-0-7861-9297-7(6), 3059) Blckstn Audio.

Life of Robert E. Lee. unabr. ed. Mary L. Williamson. Read by Lloyd James. 2 cass. (Running Time: 2 hrs. 30 mins.). 2003. 17.95 (978-0-7861-2382-7(6), 3059) Blckstn Audio.
While teaching pupils to read, why not fix in their minds the names and deeds of our great men, thereby laying the foundation of historical knowledge and instilling true patriotism into their youthful souls.

Life of Robert E. Lee. unabr. ed. Mary L. Williamson. Read by Lloyd James. (YA). 2007. 39.99 (978-1-59895-930-7(1)) Find a World.

Life of Samuel Johnson. abr. ed. James Boswell. Read by Jim Killavey. 24 cass. (Running Time: 35 hrs.). 1989. 109.00 (C-196) Jimcin Record.
The most famous biography ever written.

Life of Samuel Johnson, Pt. 1. collector's ed. James Boswell. Read by Jim Killavey. 12 cass. (Running Time: 18 hrs.). 1989. 96.00 (978-0-7366-3950-7(0), 9196A) Books on Tape.
Johnson was the leading literary scholar of his age, but Boswell made him immortal.

Life of Samuel Johnson, Pt. 2. unabr. ed. James Boswell. Read by Bernard Mayes. 14 cass. (Running Time: 57 hrs.). 1998. 89.95 (978-0-7861-1344-6(8), 2242A,B,C) Blckstn Audio.
A perceptive, lifelike portrait of Dr. Johnson.

Life of Samuel Johnson, Pt. 2. unabr. collector's ed. James Boswell. Read by Jim Killavey. 12 cass. (Running Time: 18 hrs.). 1989. 96.00 (978-0-7366-3951-4(9), 9196-B) Books on Tape.
Johnson was the leading literary scholar of his age, but Boswell made him immortal.

Life of Samuel Johnson, Pt. 3. unabr. ed. James Boswell. Read by Bernard Mayes. 16 cass. (Running Time: 57 hrs.). 1998. 99.95 (978-0-7861-1343-9(X), 2242A,B,C); 49.95 (978-0-7861-1345-3(6), 2242A,B,C) Blckstn Audio.
A perceptive, lifelike portrait of Dr. Johnson.

Life of Shakespeare. Hesketh Pearson. Read by Simon Russell Beale. (Running Time: 2 hrs. 30 mins.). 2005. 20.95 (978-1-60083-827-9(8)) Iofy Corp.

Life of Shakespeare. Hesketh Pearson. Read by Simon Russell Beale. 2 cass. (Running Time: 2 hrs. 30 min.). 2001. 13.98 (978-962-634-716-4(3), NA221614, Naxos AudioBooks); audio compact disk 17.98 (978-962-634-216-9(1), NA221612, Naxos AudioBooks) Naxos.
Considered the greatest playwright the world has ever known, William Shakespeare (1564-1616) wrote thirty-seven plays. His widely studied works continue to be performed and enjoyed by audiences the world over.

Life of St. Augustine. unabr. ed. F. W. Farrar. Read by Frederick Davidson. 5 cass. (Running Time: 7 hrs.). 1997. 39.95 (978-0-7861-1197-8(6), 1960) Blckstn Audio.
The greatest Western philosopher for 1,000 years & a dominant influence on the history of Christian theology, St. Augustine's beliefs about guilt, sin & redemption color Christian theology even today.

Life of St. Catherine of Siena. Raymond of Capua. 11 cass. 43.95 (758) Ignatius Pr.
The official life of St. Catherine written by her spiritual director.

Life of St. Mary of Egypt by St. Sophronius, Pt. 2. unabr. ed. Perf. by Jane M. deVyver. 1 cass. (Running Time: 55 min.). (Treasury of Orthodox Christian Prayers Ser.: Vol. 2). 1998. 6.95 (978-1-881211-46-4(0)) Firebird Videos.
Read liturgically during Great Lent, this "Life" is an example of the power of repentance & God's forgiveness. St. Mary lived in the Trans-Jordan desert for 47 years, after renouncing her former debauched life. St. Zosimas encountered her & learned of her life story, which was written down by St. Sophronius.

Life of Stonewall Jackson. unabr. ed. Mary L. Williamson. Read by Lloyd James. 3 cass. (Running Time: 4 hrs.). 2002. 23.95 (978-0-7861-2199-1(8), 2947); audio compact disk 24.00 (978-0-7861-9480-3(4), 2947) Blckstn Audio.
In this brief sketch of our great Southern hero, I have endeavored to portray, amid the blaze of his matchless military genius, the unchanging rectitude of his conduct, the stern will power by which he conquered all difficulties, his firm belief in an overruling Providence, and his entire submission to the Divine Will. These traits of character were the corner-stones upon which he reared the edifice of his greatness and upon which the young people of our day will do well to build.

Life of Stonewall Jackson. unabr. ed. Mary L. Williamson. Read by Lloyd James. (YA). 2007. 39.99 (978-1-59895-931-4(X)) Find a World.

Life of the Believer Series: 42 Bible Studies & Workbooks. Chuck Smith. (ENG.). 2007. 25.99 (978-1-932941-16-6(9)) Word For Today.

Life of the Beloved: Spiritual Living in a Secular World. Henri J. M. Nouwen. 1 cass. 1996. 18.00 (978-0-8245-3014-3(4), Crossroad Classic) Pub: Crossroad NY. Dist(s): IPG Chicago
This personal witness to a God who calls us the beloved is the fruit of a long friendship between journalist-writer Fred Bratman & Henri Nouwen. Henri is trying to respond to Fred's questions about living a spiritual life in the midst of a secular world.

Life of the Beloved: Spiritual Living in a Secular World. abr. ed. Henri J. M. Nouwen. Read by Henri J. M. Nouwen. (Running Time: 9000 sec.). 2006. audio compact disk 19.95 (978-0-86716-797-9(1)) St Anthony Mess Pr.
How does one live a spiritual life in a secular world? Henri Nouwen responds from the depths of his heart to this dilemma posed by his friend Fred Bratman. Newly available on CD for the first time, this audiobook is recorded by Nouwen himself. His own interpretive reading of the text lends a sense of immediacy to the production.

Life of the Buddha. Dharmachari Shantigarbha & Michael Venditozzi. 14.95 (978-1-899507-06-1(X), Weathill) Shambhala Pubns.

Life of the Initiate. Swami Amar Jyoti. 1 cass. 1982. 9.95 (E-22) Truth Consciousness.
Going to higher evolution. When to ask for Guru's help & when is help given? The initiated life.

Life of the Party: The Biography of Pamela Digby Churchill Hayward Harriman. unabr. ed. Christopher Ogden. Read by Kate Reading. 13 cass. (Running Time: 19 hrs. 30 min.). 1996. 104.00 (978-0-913369-31-9(4), 4185) Books on Tape.
Long before Bill Clinton picked her as a U. S. diplomat to France, Pamela Harriman had an international reputation.

Life of Thomas More. unabr. ed. Peter Ackroyd. Read by Frederick Davidson. 4 cass. (Running Time: 6 hrs.). (ENG.). 1991. 44.95 (978-0-7861-0268-6(3), 1234) Blckstn Audio.
About calls for environmentalist to regain a sense of perspective, stop hating humanity & deal with facts instead of letting their ardor carry them into the realm of "noble lies.".

Life of Thomas More. unabr. ed. Peter Ackroyd. Read by Frederick Davidson. 13 cass. (Running Time: 19 hrs.). 1999. 85.95 (978-0-7861-1521-1(1), 2371) Blckstn Audio.
Story of a great man of the church & arguably the most brilliant lawyer the English-speaking world has ever known.

Life of Thomas More. unabr. ed. Peter Ackroyd. Narrated by Patrick Tull. 14 cass. (Running Time: 18 hrs. 45 mins.). 1999. 112.00 (978-0-7887-3117-4(3), 95663E7) Recorded Bks.
Let's you see Thomas More as a human being, albeit one of formidable intellect & indisputable moral courage.

Life of Tulasi Devi: From Brahma-Vaivarta Purana. 3 cass. 15.00 Set, incl. 1 vinyl album. Bhaktivedanta.
Every devotee will want to find out why: Tulasi Devi is considered one of the Lord's greatest devotees; she descended from the spiritual world to this realm; she performed thousands of years of austerity to obtain Lord Visnu as her husband; she became both the sacred Tulasi plant as well as the holy Gandake River; all worship of Lord Visnu must contain an offering of Tulasi leaves; the Lord allowed Tulasi to curse Him to become a stone - a stone in which He manifests Himself as the Salagrama-sila.

Life of Wolfgang Amadeus Mozart. Perry Keenlyside. Read by Nigel Anthony et al. 3 cass. (Running Time: 3 hrs. 30 mins.). 1997. 17.98 (978-962-634-644-0(2), NA314414, Naxos AudioBooks) Naxos.
The story of today's most often performed classical composer's accomplishments during his short life of just 35 years. Specially written for Naxos.

Life of Wolfgang Amadeus Mozart. unabr. ed. Perry Keenlyside. Read by Nigel Anthony. 3 cass. (Running Time: 4 hrs. 30 mins.). 2001. 21.98 Books on Tape.
A musical biography of perhaps the most naturally gifted musical genius of all time. Includes 70 excerpts of his music.

Life of Wolfgang Amadeus Mozart. unabr. ed. Perry Keenlyside. Read by Nigel Anthony et al. 3 CDs. (Running Time: 3 hrs. 39 mins.). 1997. audio compact disk 22.98 (978-962-634-144-5(0), NA314412, Naxos AudioBooks) Naxos.
The story of today's most often performed classical composer's accomplishments during his short life of just 35 years. Specially written for Naxos.

Life on a Little Known Planet: A Biologist's View of Insects & Their World. abr. unabr. ed. Howard Ensign Evans. Read by Scott Brick. 10 cass. (Running Time: 6 hrs.). 2004. 39.95 (978-1-931056-34-2(X), N Millennium Audio) New Millenn Enter.
This classic audiobook is natural history at its best. The world of insects is a "little-known planet," the realm of the cockroach and the cricket, the wasp and the bedbug. With the precision and authority of a distinguished biologist and the wit and the grace of an accomplished writer muses on the uniqueness of dragonflies, the romantic impulses of butterflies, the musicianship of crickets and the mysteries of the firefly.

***Life on Air.** rev. ed. Read by David Attenborough. (Running Time: 20 hrs. 0 mins. 0 sec.). (ENG.). 2010. audio compact disk 49.95 (978-1-4084-6750-3(X)) Pub: AudioGO. Dist(s): Perseus Dist

Life on Earth. unabr. ed. David Attenborough. Read by Malcolm Ruthven. 8 cass. (Running Time: 10 hrs. 30 min.). (Isis Ser.). (J). 1993. 69.95 (978-1-85695-502-7(8), 93076) Pub: ISIS Lrg Prnt GBR. Dist(s): Ulverscroft US

Life on the Go: The Key to Weight Loss & Healthy Eating. Jack Goldberg & Karen O'Mara. 1 cass. 1999. 9.95 (978-0-9670846-1-9(X)) Go Corp.
Companion to the book "Go Diet".

Life on the Halfshell: Native Songs of a Cape Cod Son. Poems. Ron Buck. Narrated by Ron Buck. 1. (Running Time: 1 hr. 20 mins). 2005. 14.95 (978-0-9759314-4-8(X)) TJMF Pub.

***Life on the Mississippi.** unabr. ed. Mark Twain. Read by Grover Gardner. (Running Time: 9 hrs.). 2010. 29.95 (978-1-4417-6474-4(7)); 59.95 (978-1-4417-6471-3(2)); audio compact disk 76.00 (978-1-4417-6472-0(0)); audio compact disk 24.95 (978-1-4417-6473-7(9)) Blckstn Audio.

***Life on the Mississippi.** unabr. ed. Mark Twain. Narrated by Michael Prichard. (Running Time: 16 hrs. 0 mins. 0 sec.). 2010. 27.99 (978-1-4526-5047-0(0)); 20.99 (978-1-4526-7047-8(1)); audio compact disk 35.99 (978-1-4526-0047-5(3)) Pub: Tantor Media. Dist(s): IngramPubServ

***Life on the Mississippi (Library Edition)** unabr. ed. Mark Twain. Narrated by Michael Prichard. (Running Time: 16 hrs. 0 mins.). 2010. 35.99 (978-1-4526-2047-3(4)); audio compact disk 85.99 (978-1-4526-3047-2(X)) Pub: Tantor Media. Dist(s): IngramPubServ

Life on the Mississippi 1983. abr. ed. Mark Twain. Read by Ed Begley. 1 cass. 1984. 12.95 (978-0-694-50171-7(9), SWC 1234) HarperCollins Pubs.

Life on the Mississippi 1983. unabr. ed. Mark Twain. Narrated by Norman Dietz. 12 cass. (Running Time: 14 hrs. 30 mins.). 1986. 97.00 (978-1-55690-309-0(X), 86930E7) Recorded Bks.
Mark Twain's semi-biographical account of life & trade on the river: a floodstream of poker games, river lore, cockfights & Mardi Gras.

Life on the Mississippi 1983. unabr. collector's ed. Mark Twain. Read by Michael Prichard. 8 cass. (Running Time: 12 hrs.). 1977. 64.00 (978-0-7366-0057-6(4), 1069) Books on Tape.
Mark Twain wrote it originally as a series of articles titled "Old Times on the Mississippi." It abounds with enthusiasm for his early life on the river.

Life on the Other Side: A Psychic's Tour of the Afterlife. abr. ed. Read by Sylvia Browne. Sylvia Browne. 3 CDs. (Running Time: 3 hrs.). (ENG.). 2005. audio compact disk 22.95 (978-1-56511-999-4(1), 1565119991) Pub: HighBridge. Dist(s): Workman Pub

***Life on the Refrigerator Door.** unabr. ed. Alice Kuipers. Read by Dana Delany & Amanda Seyfried. (ENG.). 2007. (978-0-06-155429-2(4)); (978-0-06-155430-8(8)) HarperCollins Pubs.

Life Passages. Blaine Yorgason. 1 cass. 5.98 (978-1-55503-025-4(4), 06003362) Covenant Comms.
Personal story of his mother & father's unique courtship & marriage.

Life Planning. Robb E. Dalton. Read by Robb E. Dalton. 2 cass. (Running Time: 3 hrs.). (National Seminars Ser.). 1998. 17.95 (978-1-886463-47-9(6)) Oasis Audio.
Hear how you can establish a life plan that will help you find balance between your work, recreation & personal life.

***Life Preservers.** abr. ed. Harriet Lerner. Read by Harriet Lerner. (ENG.). 2005. (978-0-06-089419-1(9), Harper Audio); (978-0-06-089418-4(0), Harper Audio) HarperCollins Pubs.

***Life Principles: Feeling Good by Doing Good - the Audiobook in CD Format.** Bruce Weinstein. Read by Bruce Weinstein. (Running Time: 165 MINUTES). (ENG.). 2006. audio compact disk 19.95 (978-0-615-35541-2(2)) Ethics Guy.

Life Sciences on File#153;, New Edition, CD-ROM. Diagram Group. (gr. 6-12). 2004. audio compact disk 149.95 (978-0-8160-5811-2(3)) Facts On File.

Life Sentence. Judith Cutler. (Isis (CDs) Ser.). (J). 2006. audio compact disk 79.95 (978-0-7531-2529-8(3)) Pub: ISIS Lrg Prnt GBR. Dist(s): Ulverscroft US

Life Sentence. unabr. ed. Judith Cutler. Read by Diana Bishop. 7 cass. (Running Time: 9 hrs. 30 mins.). (Isis Cassettes Ser.). (J). 2006. 61.95 (978-0-7531-3578-5(7)) Pub: ISIS Lrg Prnt GBR. Dist(s): Ulverscroft US

Life Sentence. unabr. ed. David Ellis. Read by Dick Hill. 8 cass. (Running Time: 11 hrs.). 2003. 34.95 (978-1-59086-361-9(5), 1590863615, BAU); 87.25 (978-1-59086-362-6(3), 1590863623, CD Unabrid Lib Ed) Brilliance Audio.
Jon Soliday is legal counsel to a powerful politician - also his childhood best friend - who is running for governor. The two have shared political success and undying loyalty. They also share a dark secret from the summer of 1979: a party that resulted in the death of a teenage girl. Soliday was implicated, but through his friend's political connections, escaped legal trouble. Soliday remembers little from that night, but carries an uncertain guilt he can't shake. Now, as the players from 1979 fall prey to an unknown killer, Soliday himself is accused of murder. And as the puzzle unfolds, the people he most suspects are those he has entrusted with his defense - his ambitious defense attorney and his oldest friend. A man's past, both what he

remembers and what he fears, has never felt so crushing - and may well leave him without a future.

Life Sentence. unabr. ed. David Ellis. Read by Dick Hill. (Running Time: 11 hrs.). 2004. 39.25 (978-1-59335-596-8(3), 1593355963, Brlnc Audio MP3 Lib) Brilliance Audio.

Life Sentence. unabr. ed. David Ellis. Read by Dick Hill. (Running Time: 11 hrs.). 2004. 39.25 (978-1-59710-454-8(X), 159710454X, BADLE); 24.95 (978-1-59710-455-5(8), 1597104558, BAD) Brilliance Audio.

Life Sentence. unabr. ed. David Ellis. Read by Dick Hill. (Running Time: 11 hrs.). 2004. 24.95 (978-1-59335-136-6(4), 1593351364) Soulmate Audio Bks.

Life Sentences. unabr. ed. Laura Lippman. Read by Linda Emond. 2009. audio compact disk 39.99 (978-0-06-171471-9(2), Harper Audio) HarperCollins Pubs.

***Life Sentences.** unabr. ed. Laura Lippman. Read by Linda Emond. (ENG.). 2009. (978-0-06-180534-9(3), Harper Audio); (978-0-06-180535-6(1), Harper Audio) HarperCollins Pubs.

***Life Sentences.** unabr. ed. Laura Lippman. Narrated by Linda Emond. 1 Playaway. (Running Time: 10 hrs.). 2009. 64.75 (978-1-4361-9247-7(1)); 113.75 (978-1-4361-7825-9(8)); audio compact disk 123.75 (978-1-4361-7826-6(6)) Recorded Bks.

***Life Sentences.** unabr. collector's ed. Laura Lippman. Narrated by Linda Emond. 9 CDs. (Running Time: 10 hrs.). 2009. audio compact disk 49.95 (978-1-4361-7827-3(4)) Recorded Bks.

Life Series. Contrib. by Bill Gillham & Anabel Gillham. Directed By Fred Carpenter. Prod. by Mars Hill Productions Staff. 6 cass. 1996. cass. & video 35.00 audio cass. (978-0-9624056-7-9(1)) Mars Hill TX.

Life Skill Academics: Reading Skills in Everyday Life: Literacy. Ellen McPeek Glisan. 2003. spiral bd. 29.00 (978-1-57861-496-7(1), IEP Res) Attainment.

Life Skills. unabr. ed. Katie Fforde. Narrated by Davina Porter. 8 cass. (Running Time: 11 hrs. 30 mins.). 2000. 71.00 (978-0-7887-3996-5(4)) Recorded Bks.
Suddenly released from her engagement & out of work, Julia Fairfax is looking for a new direction in her life. When a classified ad catches her eye, she embarks on a hilarious trip through the English canals in a rickety hotel boat. Along the way, she encounters hard-to-please guests, an unsettling ex-boyfriend & the challenges of cooking in a tiny galley with rattling crockery.

Life Skills: Teaching Attitudes & Behaviors for Success in Life. James Cisek & Anthea George. 1985. pap. bk. & tchr. ed. 59.95 (978-0-9604510-9-8(9)) Life Skills.

Life Skills Academics Series: Academics meet life skills in the real World. Ellen McPeek Glisan. 2003. spiral bd. 79.00 (978-1-57861-519-3(4), IEP Res) Attainment.

Life Skills & Test Prep 3 Audio CD. 2008. (978-0-13-515809-8(5)) Pearson Educ.

Life Stages. Nolan Brohaugh et al. Read by Nolan Brohaugh et al. Ed. by Ellen Harkins & Patricia Magerkurth. 4 cass. (Running Time: 1 hr. 55 min.). 1991. 35.00 (978-1-56948-014-4(1)) Menninger Clinic.

Life Stories: Profiles from the New Yorker. Read by Amy Irving et al. Ed. by David Remnick. 3 CDs. (Running Time: 5 hrs.). 2000. audio compact disk 36.95 (Random AudioBks) Random Audio Pubg.
Compilation includes telling, subtle & often funny portraits of figures that come from every field of human endeavor & accomplishment.

Life Story. Joyce Balbontin. 1 cass. 8.95 (381) Am Fed Astrologers.

Life Story of a Kahuna Healer. Tanice Foltz. 1 cass. 9.00 (A0211-87) Sound Photosyn.
This video from ICSS, also contains Thomas Pinkson: Huichol Pilgrimage Revisited; Ralph Metzner; Hallucinogens & Contemporary North American Shamanic Practices; Ruth-Inge Heinze: reads Charles Muses' "The Shamanic Way in Ancient Egypt;" beginning of Stanley Krippner: Concept of Energy Medicine in Indigenous Healing.

Life Story of Orison Swett Marden: The Father of the American Success Movement. Narrated by Richard Gorham. Richard Gorham. (ENG.). 2008. 34.95 (978-0-9798305-1-8(6)) LshipTools.

Life Strategies: Doing What Works Doing What Matters. abr. ed. Phil McGraw. Read by Phil McGraw. 5 CDs. (Running Time: 50 hrs. 0 mins. 0 sec.). 2000. audio compact disk 32.00 (978-0-7435-0059-3(8), Sound Ideas) Pub: S&S Audio. Dist(s): S and S Inc
*If you are: * capable of more than you are accomplishing * frustrated that you are not making more money * stuck in a rut and not getting what you want * bored with yourself * silently enduring an emotionally barren life or marriage * trudging, zombie-like, through an unchallenging career * just "going through the motions" of your life * living in a comfort zone that yields too little challenge * living a lonely existence with little hope for change then hold on as Dr. Phillip McGraw takes you on a guided tour of your life to honestly label the problems and causes that control your destiny. Life Strategies will give you the most honest explanation of your life and how you got where you are that has ever been published. Dr. McGraw is results-based and measures success in terms of changed lives, not rhetoric. This audiobook is a plain-talk, entertaining way to learn to take control of your life, right now. In this audiobook, the author describes the ten Laws of Life that every person needs to know. Learn them, use them, and improve virtually every aspect of your life, from work to home to spiritual to physical. Ignore them and you'll continue to pay the price. With Life Strategies, Dr. McGraw tells you how to strategically control your life, rather than continue as a frustrated passenger.*

Life Strategies: Doing What Works Doing What Matters. abr. ed. Phil McGraw. Read by Phil McGraw. 2006. 18.95 (978-0-7435-6168-6(6)) Pub: S&S Audio. Dist(s): S and S Inc

Life Strategies for Dealing with Bullies. unabr. ed. Jay McGraw. Read by Jay McGraw. (Running Time: 3 hrs. 0 mins. 0 sec.). (ENG.). (J). 2008. audio compact disk 19.99 (978-0-7435-7961-2(5)) Pub: S&S Audio. Dist(s): S and S Inc

Life Strategies for Teens. Jay McGraw. Read by Jay McGraw. Read by Joan Collins. 3 CD. (Running Time: 20 hrs. 0 mins. 0 sec.). (ENG.). (gr. 7-12). 2000. wbk. ed. 20.00 (978-0-7435-0434-8(8), Sound Ideas) Pub: S&S Audio. Dist(s): S and S Inc
Whether you are a teen looking for a little help or a parent or grandparent wanting to provide guidance, this book tackles the challenges of adolescence like no other, combining proven techniques for dealing with life's obstacles & the youth & wit of the writer.

Life Success Manuscripts. unabr. ed. Thomas D. Willhite. Read by Jim McMahan. 6 cass. (Running Time: 7 hrs.). 1997. pap. bk. & wbk. ed. 145.00 (978-0-9659994-1-0(6)) PSI Pub.
Details the principles of life success & their applications.

Life Support. abr. ed. Robert Whitlow. Read by Rob Lamont. (Santee Ser.). (ENG.). 2003. 24.49 (978-1-60814-289-7(2)) Oasis Audio.

Life Support. abr. ed. Robert Whitlow. Read by Rob Lamont. 6 cass. (Running Time: 10 hrs.). 2004. 29.99 (978-1-58926-262-1(X)); audio compact disk 34.99 (978-1-58926-263-8(8)) Oasis Audio.

Life Support. unabr. ed. Tess Gerritsen. Narrated by George Guidall. 8 cass. (Running Time: 11 hrs.). 1997. 75.00 (978-0-7887-1753-6(7), 95231E7) Recorded Bks.
From the overnight mayhem of an emergency room to the cutting-edge technology of fetal tissue research, this story will leave the listener gasping.

Life That Lives on Man. unabr. collector's ed. Michael Andrews. Read by Paul Shay. 6 cass. (Running Time: 6 hrs.). 1988. 36.00 (978-0-7366-1306-4(4), 2213) Books on Tape.
A look at the parasitic bugs & organisms that live in, on & around humans.

***Life That Lost Its Focus.** Featuring Ravi Zacharias. 2005. audio compact disk 9.00 (978-1-61256-023-6(7)) Ravi Zach.

Life That Matters: The Legacy of Terri Schiavo - A Lesson for Us All. abr. ed. Suzanne Schindler Vitadamo et al. Read by Don Leslie & Kate McIntyre. (Running Time: 3 hrs.). (ENG.). 2006. 14.98 (978-1-59483-502-5(0)) Pub: Hachet Audio. Dist(s): HachBkGrp

Life That Prays. Elbert Willis. 1 cass. (Secret to Believing Prayer Ser.). 4.00 Fill the Gap.

Life, the Universe & Everything. Douglas Adams. 5 CD. (Running Time: 5 hrs. 20 min.). 2001. audio compact disk (978-0-7531-1272-4(8)) ISIS Audio GBR.
The unhappy inhabitants of planet Krikkit are sick of looking at the night sky above their heads - so they plan to destroy it. The universe, that is. Now only five individuals stand between the killer robots of Krikkit and their goals of annihilation. They are Arthur Dent, a mild- mannered space and time traveller, who tries to learn how to fly by throwing himself at the ground and missing; Ford Prefect, his best friend who decides to go insane to see if he likes it; Slartibartfast, the indomitable Vice-President of the Campaign for Real Time, who travels in a ship powered by irrational behavior; Zaphod Beeblebrox, the two-headed, three-armed, ex-head honcho of the universe; and Trillian, the sexy space cadet who is torn between the persistent Thunder God and a very depressed Beeblebrox.

Life, the Universe & Everything. unabr. ed. Douglas Adams. Read by Martin Freeman. (Running Time: 20700 sec.). (ENG.). 2006. audio compact disk 29.95 (978-0-7393-3209-2(0), Random AudioBks) Pub: Random Audio Pubg. Dist(s): Random

Life, the Universe & Everything, Vol. 4. unabr. ed. Douglas Adams. Read by Douglas Adams. 4 cass. (Running Time: 6 hrs.). 2004. 25.00 (978-1-59007-264-6(2)) Pub: New Millenn Enter. Dist(s): PerseuPGW

Life, the Universe & Everything, Vol. 5. unabr. ed. Douglas Adams. Read by Douglas Adams. 5 CDs. (Running Time: 6 hrs.). 2004. audio compact disk 39.95 (978-1-59007-265-3(0)) Pub: New Millenn Enter. Dist(s): PerseuPGW

Life These Days: Stories from Lake Wobegon. abr. unabr. ed. Garrison Keillor. Contrib. by Garrison Keillor. 3 CDs. (Running Time: 3 hrs.). (ENG.). 1998. audio compact disk 30.00 (978-1-56511-307-7(1), 1565113071) Pub: HighBridge. Dist(s): Workman Pub

Life-Threatening Acid-Based Disturbances. Read by Jerome P. Kassirer. 1 cass. (Running Time: 9 min.). 1985. 12.00 (C8560) Amer Coll Phys.

Life-Threatening Sepsis. Moderated by Lloyd D. MacLean. 2 cass. (General Sessions Ser.: GS-5). 1986. 19.00 (8633) Am Coll Surgeons.

Life Through Death. Neville Goddard. 1 cass. (Running Time: 62 min.). 1964. 8.00 (32) J & L Pubns.
Neville taught Imagination Creates Reality. He was a powerfully influential teacher of God as Consciousness.

***Life Together: The Classic Exploration of Faith in Community.** unabr. ed. Dietrich Bonhoeffer. Narrated by Paul Michael. (ENG.). 2007. 10.98 (978-1-59644-434-8(7), Hovel Audio) christianaud.

Life Together: The Classic Exploration of Faith in Community. unabr. ed. Dietrich Bonhoeffer. Read by Paul Michael. (Running Time: 3 hrs. 30 mins. 0 sec.). (ENG.). 2007. audio compact disk 18.98 (978-1-59644-433-1(9)) christianaud.

Life under the Stars: A Novel of Lies, Truths & Half-Truths. unabr. ed. Anthony Pellicano. 6 cass. 2004. 29.95 (978-1-59007-594-4(3), N Millennium Audio); audio compact disk 34.95 (978-1-59007-595-1(1), N Millennium Audio) New Millenn Enter.

Life Visioning: A Four-Stage Evolutionary Journey to Live as Divine Love. Michael Bernard Beckwith. (Running Time: 20700 sec.). 2008. audio compact disk 69.95 (978-1-59179-617-6(2)) Sounds True.

Life Visioning Process: An Evolutionary Journey to Live as Divine Love. abr. ed. Michael Bernard Beckwith. (Running Time: 9000 sec.). 2008. audio compact disk 19.95 (978-1-59179-616-9(4)) Sounds True.

Life Was Never Meant to Be a Struggle. Stuart Wilde. Read by Stuart Wilde. 1 CD. 2005. audio compact disk 10.95 (978-1-4019-0452-4(1)) Hay House.

Life We Take for Granted. 1985. (0210) Evang Sisterhood Mary.

Life Well Lived. Charles R. Swindoll. (ENG.). 2007. audio compact disk 24.00 (978-1-57972-791-8(3)) Insight Living.

Life Well Lived CD: An in Depth Study of Ecclesiastes. Perf. by Tommy Nelson. (ENG.). 2009. audio compact disk 59.95 (978-1-928828-20-4(5)) Hudson Prods.

Life Wild & Perilous: Mountain Men & the Paths to the Pacific. unabr. ed. Robert Marshall Utley. Narrated by Richard M. Davidson. 10 cass. (Running Time: 15 hrs.). 1998. 85.00 (978-0-7887-2040-6(6), 95404E7) Recorded Bks.
Compelling true saga of how the West was won. Puts you on the trail with legendary trappers & mountain men like Jim Bridger, Kit Carson, Tom Fitzpatrick & Jeddediah Smith.

Life with a Master. Kriyananda, pseud. 4 cass. (Running Time: 4 hrs.). 28.00 (LS-2) Crystal Clarity.
A compilation of Swami Kriyananda's best talks about the life of Yogananda.

Life with Eb & Flo. Karen McDaniel. Perf. by Dave Privett & Liz Von Seggen. 1 cass. (Running Time: 46 min.). Dramatization. 1995. 15.00 incl. script. (978-1-58302-041-8(1), STP-12) One Way St.
Eight two-character puppet programs ranging from four to seven minutes.

Life with Eb & Flo. Karen McDaniel. Perf. by Dave Privett & Liz VonSeggen. 2001. audio compact disk 15.00 (978-1-58302-183-5(3)) One Way St.
Pre-recording of eight Christian puppet scripts.

Life with Father/Life with Mother. unabr. collector's ed. Clarence Day, Jr. Read by Dan Lazar. 7 cass. (Running Time: 10 hrs. 30 mins.). 1979. 56.00 (978-0-7366-0137-5(6), 1141) Books on Tape.
480 Madison Avenue, New York, was the home of the Clarence Day family in the 1880's. Here in the leisured ambience of that time & place, Clarence Jr., John, Whitney, Harlan & their mother Vinnie & various domestics enjoy the singular experience of life with father.

Life with Karol: My Forty-Year Friendship with the Man Who Became Pope. Stanislaw Dziwisz. Read by Norman Dietz. (Playaway Adult Nonfiction Ser.). (ENG.). 2009. 59.99 (978-1-60775-767-2(2)) Find a World.

Life with Karol: My Forty-Year Friendship with the Man Who Became Pope. unabr. ed. Cardinal Stanislaw Dziwisz. Read by Norman Dietz. 7 CDs. (Running Time: 8 hrs. 0 mins. 0 sec.). (ENG.). 2008. audio compact disk 29.99 (978-1-4001-0619-6(2)); audio compact disk 59.99 (978-1-4001-3619-3(9)) Pub: Tantor Media. Dist(s): IngramPubServ

Life with Karol: My Forty-Year Friendship with the Man Who Became Pope. unabr. ed. Stanislaw Dziwisz. Read by Norman Dietz. 1 MP3-CD. (Running Time: 8 hrs. 0 mins. 0 sec.). (ENG.). 2008. audio compact disk 19.99 (978-1-4001-5619-1(X)) Pub: Tantor Media. Dist(s): IngramPubServ

Life with Luigi. Perf. by J. Carrol Naish & Alan Reed. 2 cass. (Running Time: 2 hrs.). 10.95 (978-1-57816-063-1(4), LL2401) Audio File.
Includes: "March 11, 1952" The Internal Revenue Services wants to talk to Luigi about his 1951 income taxes. "January 9, 1949" On a bet with Pasquale, Luigi has a blind date with a telephone operator. "April 15, 1952" When Luigi complains of having trouble sleeping at night, Pasquale tries to convince him that not being married to Rosa is the cause. "June 5, 1949" When Luigi's night school class collects money for a gift for Miss Spaulding, Pasquale steers Luigi to the race track. Commercials for Wrigley's Gum.

Life with Luigi. collector's ed. Perf. by J. Carrol Naish & Alan Reed. 6 cass. (Running Time: 9 hrs.). 2000. bk. 34.98 (4554) Radio Spirits.
The lovable immigrant Luigi Basco runs an antique store in Chicago. Next door is the Spaghetti Palace, run by his countryman and sponsor Pasquale, who sees Luigi as a prospective son-in-law for his 300 pound daughter, Rosa.18 heart-warming tales.

Life with Luigi: Car Accident & Ukulele. Perf. by J. Carrol Naish. 1 cass. (Running Time: 1 hr.). 2001. 6.98 (2373) Radio Spirits.

Life with Luigi: July 4th Parade & Fire in the Store. Perf. by J. Carrol Naish. 1 cass. (Running Time: 1 hr.). 2001. 6.98 (2083) Radio Spirits.

Life with Luigi: Luigi Can't Sleep at Night & Antique Dealers Dinner. Perf. by J. Carrol Naish. 1 cass. (Running Time: 1 hr.). 2001. 6.98 (1579) Radio Spirits.

Life with Luigi: Luigi Throws a Party at the Store & Columbus Day. Perf. by J. Carrol Naish. 1 cass. (Running Time: 1 hr.). 2001. 6.98 (2463) Radio Spirits.

Life with Luigi: Pasquale Plays a Prank on Luigi. Perf. by J. Carrol Naish. 1 cass. (Running Time: 1 hr.). 2001. 6.98 (2422) Radio Spirits.

Life with Luigi: The Car & Electric Bill. Perf. by J. Carrol Naish. 1 cass. (Running Time: 1 hr.). 2001. 6.98 (2374) Radio Spirits.

Life with Luigi: The IRS Makes a Visit & Luigi is Homesick. Perf. by William Bendix. 1 cass. (Running Time: 1 hr.). 2001. 6.98 (1512) Radio Spirits.

Life with Luigi: The Traffic Light & The Boys Club. Perf. by J. Carrol Naish. 1 cass. (Running Time: 1 hr.). 2001. 6.98 (2540) Radio Spirits.

Life with Luigi: The Wedding. Perf. by J. Carrol Naish. 6 cass. (Running Time: 6 hrs.). 1999. 19.98 (AB254) Radio Spirits.

Life with Luigi: Train to Buffalo & Luigi Sells Ice Cream. Perf. by J. Carrol Naish. 1 cass. (Running Time: 1 hr.). 2001. 6.98 (2375) Radio Spirits.

Life with Luigi & Casey, Crime Photographer. unabr. ed. Perf. by J. Carol Nash et al. 1 cass. (Running Time: 60 min.). Dramatization. 7.95 Norelco box. (CM-7745) Natl Recrd Co.
Life with Luigi: Luigi's night school Americanization class decides to have a picnic at the beach. His classmates get him a date with Shirley Smith. Friend "Pasquale" would rather have Luigi date his daughter & so fixes him up with an old fashioned swimsuit. Sponsored by Wrigley's Spearmint Chewing Gum. Casey, Crime Photographer: Bad Little Babe. Ace Cameraman who covers the crime news of a great city. Casey gets a phone call from a woman warning him that his life is in danger. She is soon found very dead! Captain Logan, of homicide, has a plan...but if it fails our ace cameraman will be the late Casey.

Life with Max, Audiocassette. Judy Carlson. (Metro Reading Ser.). (J). (gr. k). 2000. 8.46 (978-1-58120-996-9(7)) Metro Teaching.

Life with My Sister Madonna. abr. ed. Christopher Ciccone. Read by Christopher Ciccone. 2008. 17.95 (978-0-7435-8005-2(2)) Pub: S&S Audio. Dist(s): S and S Inc

Life Without a Center. Featuring Adyashanti. (ENG.). 2009. audio compact disk 40.00 (978-1-933986-59-3(X)) Open Gate Pub.

Life Without a Crutch. 2 cass. (Running Time: 3 hrs.). 1995. 17.95 (978-1-878436-17-7(1)) OPEN TX.
Provides compelling reasons to confront dependency & break the cycle. An ideal introduction to any recovery program, no matter what the addiction or treatment method.

Life Without Ed: How One Woman Declared Independence from Her Eating Disorder & How You Can Too. Jenni Schaefer & Thom Rutledge. 2009. audio compact disk 28.00 (978-1-933309-86-6(5)) Pub: A Media Intl. Dist(s): Natl Bk Netwk

Life Without God: Romans 1:24-32. Ed Young. 1996. 4.95 (978-0-7417-2107-5(4), 1107) Win Walk.

Life Without Limits. Mark Crow. 7 cass. (Running Time: 10 hrs. 30 mins.). 2002. (978-1-931537-32-2(1)) Vision Comm Creat.

Life Without Limits: Clarify What You Want, Redefine Your Dreams, Become the Person You Want to Be. abr. ed. Lucinda Bassett. 2 cass. (Running Time: 180 min.). 2001. 18.00 (978-0-694-52484-6(0)) HarperCollins Pubs.

Life Without Summer: A Novel. unabr. ed. Lynne Griffin. Read by Tanya Eby Sirois. (Running Time: 9 hrs.). 2009. 39.97 (978-1-4233-9057-2(1), 9781423390572, BADLE); 24.99 (978-1-4233-9056-5(3), 9781423390565, BAD); 24.99 (978-1-4233-9054-1(7), 9781423390541, Brilliance MP3); 39.97 (978-1-4233-9055-8(5), 9781423390558, Brlnc Audio MP3 Lib); audio compact disk 28.99 (978-1-4233-9052-7(0), 9781423390527); audio compact disk 92.97 (978-1-4233-9053-4(9), 9781423390534, BriAudCD Unabrid) Brilliance Audio.

Life You Save May Be Your Own. Paul Elie & Lloyd James. 16 cass. (Running Time: 22 hrs. 30 mins.). 2002. 99.95 (978-0-7861-2853-2(4), 3344) Blckstn Audio.

Life You've Always Wanted. unabr. ed. John Ortberg. 2002. 29.99 (978-0-310-24806-4(X)) Zondervan.

Life You've Always Wanted: Spiritual Disciplines for Ordinary People. unabr. ed. Zondervan Publishing Staff & John Ortberg. (Running Time: 8 hrs. 0 mins. 0 sec.). (ENG.). 2003. 10.99 (978-0-310-26161-2(9)) Zondervan.

Life 101: Everything We Wish We Had Learned about Life in School - But Didn't. Peter McWilliams. Read by Peter McWilliams. 1991. 22.95 (978-0-931580-95-6(1)) Mary Bks.

Lifeblood. unabr. ed. P. N. Elrod. Read by Barrett Whitener. (Running Time: 7.5 hrs. 0 mins.). (ENG.). 2009. 29.95 (978-1-4417-0267-8(9)); 54.95 (978-1-4417-0263-0(6)); audio compact disk 69.00 (978-1-4417-0264-7(4)) Blckstn Audio.

Lifeboat VC. 1986. (1717) Books on Tape.

***Lifecycle Investing: A New, Safe, & Audacious Way to Improve the Performance of Your Retirement Portfolio.** unabr. ed. Ian Ayres & Barry Nalebuff. (Running Time: 7 hrs. 0 mins.). 2010. 14.99 (978-1-4001-8690-7(0)) Tantor Media.

An Asterisk (*) at the beginning of an entry indicates that the title is appearing for the first time.

***Lifecycle Investing: A New, Safe, & Audacious Way to Improve the Performance of Your Retirement Portfolio.** unabr. ed. Ian Ayres & Barry Nalebuff. Narrated by Gerry Gartenberg. (Running Time: 6 hrs. 30 mins. 0 sec.). (ENG.). 2010. 19.99 (978-1-4001-6690-9(X)); audio compact disk 29.99 (978-1-4001-1690-4(2)); audio compact disk 59.99 (978-1-4001-4690-1(9)) Pub: Tantor Media. Dist(s): IngramPubServ

Lifecycles. Ed. by Robert A. Monroe. 1 cass. (Running Time: 30 min.). (Meta Music Artist Ser.). 1992. 14.95 (978-1-56102-247-2(0)) Inter Indus.
Textured synthesizers & the changing sound of an evolving human heartbeat to poignantly portray the course of a lifetime, from birth to death.

LifeForce Yoga(r) Bhavana - Say Yes to Yourself Guided Visualization. Amy Weintruab. 2008. audio compact disk 20.00 (978-0-9747380-4-8(2), LifeForce Yoga) Amy Wein.

***LifeForce Yoga Chakra Clearing Meditation to Manage Your.** Amy Weintraub. 2009. audio compact disk 20.00 (978-0-9747380-5-5(0)) Amy Wein.

LifeForce Yoga(r) Yoga Nidra to Manage Your Mood & Relaxation for Sleep. Amy Weintraub. 2008. audio compact disk 20.00 (978-0-9747380-3-1(4), LifeForce Yoga) Amy Wein.

Lifeguard. James Patterson & Andrew Gross. 2005. 90.00 (978-1-4159-2324-5(8)); audio compact disk 96.00 (978-1-4159-2325-2(6)) Books on Tape.

Lifeguard. unabr. ed. Short Stories. Mary Morris. Narrated by Alyssa Bresnahan et al. 5 cass. (Running Time: 6 hrs.). 1997. 49.00 (978-0-7887-1754-3(5), 95232E7) Recorded Bks.
In this collection of stories about a young lifeguard facing the traumas of incipient adulthood, a young wife doubts her husband's loyalty & a mural takes on a life of its own.

Lifeguard. unabr. ed. James Patterson & Andrew Gross. Read by Billy Campbell. (ENG.). 2005. 14.98 (978-1-59483-243-7(9)) Pub: Hachet Audio. Dist(s): HachBkGrp

Lifeguard. unabr. ed. James Patterson & Andrew Gross. Read by Billy Campbell. (Running Time: 7 hrs.). (ENG.). 2007. audio compact disk 14.98 (978-1-60024-253-3(7)) Pub: Hachet Audio. Dist(s): HachBkGrp

Lifeguard. unabr. ed. James Patterson & Andrew Gross. Read by Billy Campbell. (Running Time: 7 hrs.). (ENG.). 2009. 59.98 (978-1-60788-051-6(2)) Pub: Hachet Audio. Dist(s): HachBkGrp

***Lifeguard: A Selection from the John Updike Audio Collection.** unabr. ed. John Updike. Read by John Updike. (ENG.). 2009. (978-0-06-196243-1(0), Caedmon); (978-0-06-196244-8(9), Caedmon) HarperCollins Pubs.

Lifeline. unabr. ed. V. C. Andrews & John Francome. Read by Martyn Read. 11 CDs. (Running Time: 11 hrs. 50 mins.). (Isis Ser.). (J). 2002. audio compact disk 99.95 (978-0-7531-1102-4(0)) Pub: ISIS Lrg Prnt GBR. Dist(s): Ulverscroft US
Unlike some of his fellow jockeys, Tony Byrne has never taken a bung & never ridden a dishonest race. Star rider Freddy Montague, however, has never stuck to the rules. For both men, the guarantees run out once Freddy's gravy train comes off the rails, turning the gravy into blood.

Lifeline. unabr. ed. John Francome. Read by Martyn Read. 10 cass. (Running Time: 15 hrs.). 2001. 84.95 (978-0-7531-1020-1(2), 010301) Pub: ISIS Audio GBR. Dist(s): ISIS Pub

Lifelines. Christina Baldwin. 6 CDs. (Running Time: 7 hrs. 30 mins.). 2005. audio compact disk 69.95 (978-1-59179-229-1(0), F876D) Sounds True.

Lifelines. unabr. ed. Helen Cannam. 6 cass. (Running Time: 7 hrs. 30 mins.). (Soundings Ser.). (J). 2005. 54.95 (978-1-84559-096-3(1)) Pub: ISIS Lrg Prnt GBR. Dist(s): Ulverscroft US

***Lifelong Health: Achieving Optimum Well-Being at Any Age.** Instructed by Anthony A. Goodman. 2010. audio compact disk 269.95 (978-1-59803-661-9(0)) Teaching Co.

Lifeplan for High-Level Wellness. Elaine L. Willis. 1 cass. 1991. 10.00 (978-0-926454-01-9(3)) Found Wellness.
Health & wellness.

Lifeprints. 2003. 17.00 (978-1-56420-320-5(4)); 17.00 (978-1-56420-347-2(6)); audio compact disk 18.00 (978-1-56420-321-2(2)); audio compact disk 17.00 (978-1-56420-322-9(0)) New Readers.

LifePrints, Level 1. 1993. 12.00 (978-0-88336-047-7(0)) New Readers.

LifePrints, Level 2. 1993. 12.00 (978-0-88336-049-1(7)) New Readers.

LifePrints, Level 3. 1993. 12.00 (978-0-88336-050-7(0)) New Readers.

Lifeprints, Vol. 2. 2003. 17.00 (978-1-56420-348-9(4)); audio compact disk 17.00 (978-1-56420-323-6(9)) New Readers.

Lifeprints, Vol. 3. 2003. 18.00 (978-1-56420-349-6(2)) New Readers.

***Life's a Beach.** unabr. ed. Claire Cook. Narrated by Kymberly Dakin. (Running Time: 7 hrs. 0 mins. 0 sec.). (ENG.). 2010. audio compact disk 14.95 (978-1-60283-991-5(3)) Pub: AudioGO. Dist(s): Perseus Dist

Life's a Beach. unabr. ed. Claire Cook. Read by Kymberly Dakin. (YA). 2007. 59.99 (978-1-60252-913-7(2)) Find a World.

Life's a Campaign: What Politics Has Taught Me about Friendship, Rivalry, Reputation, & Success. unabr. ed. Chris Matthews. Read by Chris Matthews. (Running Time: 16200 sec.). (ENG.). 2007. audio compact disk 29.95 (978-0-7393-5754-5(9), Random AudioBks) Pub: Random Audio Pubg. Dist(s): Random

Life's a Funny Proposition, Horatio. unabr. ed. Barbara Garland Polikoff. Narrated by Ramon de Ocampo. 2 pieces. (Running Time: 2 hrs. 30 mins.). (gr. 4 up). 1992. 19.00 (978-0-7887-9377-6(2), 96740) Recorded Bks.
Feeling cheated by the hand he has been dealt, 12-year-old Horatio Tuckerman is having a tough time. Two years ago, his dad died of lung cancer. Embittered and anguished, Horatio's life has been a whirlwind of change since losing his best friend. A one-time city kid, Horatio now lives in a small Wisconsin town. His grandfather O.P. (the Old Professor) has moved in and taken over his bedroom. Even worse, his mother Evie, a dentist, is dating a guy nicknamed "Pink Gums Paul." Remarkably, with the help of O.P. and others, Horatio begins to see that he can get through rough times by accepting life on life's terms - realizing that life's a funny proposition, after all.

Life's Answers/God's Covenant. Gary Whetstone. 4. Whitaker Hse.

Life's Big Decisions: Hebrews 11:23-29. Ed Young. 1992. 4.95 (978-0-7417-1925-6(8), 925) Win Walk.

Life's Bitter Pool. Derek Prince. 1 cass. 5.95 (084) Derek Prince.
Often, man's disappointments are God's appointments - but we can only discover His purposes in them as we respond in faith.

Life's Breath: Easy Breathing & Full Yogic Breathing. unabr. ed. Rama Berch. 1 cass. (Running Time: 50 min.). (Relaxations Ser.: Vol. 2). 1992. (978-1-930559-02-8(X)); audio compact disk (978-1-930559-03-5(8)) STC Inc.
A guided breathing to relax, refresh & improve health.

Life's Challenges, Your Opportunities. unabr. ed. John Hagee. Read by John Hagee. Narrated by Jon Gauger. (Running Time: 8 hrs. 13 mins. 37 sec.). (ENG.). 2008. audio compact disk 29.99 (978-1-59859-425-6(7)) Oasis Audio.

Life's Challenges, Your Opportunities. unabr. ed. John Hagee. Narrated by Jon Gauger. (Running Time: 8 hrs. 13 mins. 37 sec.). (ENG.). 2009. 20.99 (978-1-60814-467-9(4)) Oasis Audio.

Life's Cycles: Karma & Rebirth. 1 cass. (Running Time: 1 hr.). 1989. 8.95 (978-0-8356-1907-3(9)) Theos Pub Hse.
Examines death & reincarnation.

***Life's Golden Ticket.** unabr. ed. Brendon Burchard. Read by Richard Rohan. (ENG.). 2007. (978-0-06-144996-3(2), Harper Audio); (978-0-06-144995-6(4), Harper Audio) HarperCollins Pubs.

Life's Golden Ticket CD: An Inspirational Novel. abr. unabr. ed. Brendon Burchard. 2007. audio compact disk 29.95 (978-0-06-128524-0(2), Harper Audio) HarperCollins Pubs.

Life's Greatest Lessons: 20 Things That Matter. abr. ed. Hal Urban. 2004. 11.95 (978-0-7435-3921-0(4)) Pub: S&S Audio. Dist(s): S and S Inc

Lifes Greatest Mystery: Logos November 7, 1999. Ben Young. 1999. 4.95 (978-0-7417-6155-2(6), B0155) Win Walk.

Life's Healing Choices: Freedom from Your Hurts, Hang-Ups, & Habits. abr. ed. John Baker. Read by John Baker. Frwd. by Rick Warren. (Running Time: 6 hrs. 0 mins. 0 sec.). (ENG.). 2007. audio compact disk 29.95 (978-0-7435-7095-4(2)) Pub: S&S Audio. Dist(s): S and S Inc

Life's Higher Goals. unabr. ed. Read by Bob Richards. 1 cass. (Running Time: 30 min.). 15.00 B R Motivational.
A recorded live speech by Bob Richards on this classic & timeless theme - set a goal for yourself & follow through with everything you've got.

Life's Ideals. unabr. ed. William James. Read by Robert L. Halvorson. 5 cass. (Running Time: 450 min.). 35.95 (56) Halvorson Assocs.

Life's Journeys According to Mister Rogers: Things to Remember along the Way. unabr. ed. Fred Rogers & Fred Rogers. Read by Lily Tomlin et al. 1 CD. (Running Time: 1 hr.). 2005. audio compact disk 16.98 (978-1-4013-8232-2(0)) Pub: Hyperion. Dist(s): HarperCollins Pubs

Life's Little Annoyances: True Tales of People Who Just Can't Take It Anymore. abr. ed. Ian Urbina. 2005. 8.95 (978-1-59397-840-2(5)) Pub: Macmill Audio. Dist(s): Macmillan

Life's Missing Instruction Manual: The Guidebook You Should Have Been Given at Birth. unabr. ed. Joe Vitale, Jr.. Read by Joe Vitale, Jr. (Running Time: 5 hrs.). (ENG.). 2007. audio compact disk 29.98 (978-1-59659-096-0(3), GildAudio) Pub: Gildan Media. Dist(s): HachBkGrp

Life's Purpose. Neville Goddard. 1 cass. (Running Time: 62 min.). 1969. 8.00 (19) J & L Pubns.
Neville taught Imagination Creates Reality. He was a powerfully influential teacher of God as Consciousness.

Life's Survival Kit III. 2001. 30.00 (978-1-58602-102-3(8)) E L Long.

Life's Three Essential Tools. 2005. audio compact disk (978-0-9762037-9-7(0)) Ctr Soulful.

Life's Too Short... To Play It Safe, to Work All the Time, to Hold Grudges. unabr. ed. John Ortberg. 2004. 17.99 (978-1-58926-101-3(1)); audio compact disk 19.99 (978-1-58926-102-0(X)) Oasis Audio.

Life's Too Short to Waste: Ecc. 11:7-12:1. Ed Young. 1994. 4.95 (978-0-7417-2008-5(6), 1008) Win Walk.

Life's Up's & Down's: Poetic & Inspirational Poems & Readings Inspired by Life! Priscilla McGhee. 1 CD. (Running Time: 1 hr. 30 min.). 2003. pap. bk. 18.95 (978-0-9724795-3-0(8)) Prestigious P Pubng.
Encourages a positive life style and encourages others to live a Christian life, a positive life and to embrace Christ.

Life's Wake-up Calls. Tanny M. Mann. Narrated by Brent D. Mann. 1 cass. (Running Time: 1 hr.). 1997. 9.95 (978-0-9656667-1-8(9)) Sales Networks.

Life's Work: On Becoming a Mother. Rachel Cusk. Narrated by Gerri Halligan. 4 cass. (Running Time: 5 hrs. 45 mins.). 40.00 (978-1-84197-483-5(8)) Recorded Bks.

Life's 3 Most Important Questions. 3 CDs. 2005. audio compact disk (978-1-59548-046-0(3)) A Wommack.

Life's 3 Most Important Questions. 3 Cassette Tapes. 2005. (978-1-59548-047-7(1)) A Wommack.

Lifesaver Kit. 6 CD Set. (Running Time: 6 hrs.). 2002. audio compact disk (978-1-930429-23-9(1)) Love Logic.

Lifesigns: Intimacy, Fecundity, & Ecstasy in Christian Perspective. Henri J. M. Nouwen. Read by Dan Anderson. (Running Time: 10800 sec.). (ENG.). 2007. audio compact disk 25.95 (978-0-86716-827-3(7)) St Anthony Mess Pr.

Lifeskills Program, Set. Faison Covington et al. 12 cass. 1990. 12.50 CHAANGE.
Ten session psycho-educational process for anxious children 6 to 15 years old. Includes workbook with a parent-professional manual.

LifeSkills Training Relaxation CD. Gibert J. Botvin. (ENG.). (J). 2007. audio compact disk (978-0-933665-59-0(8)) Princeton Hlth.

Lifesong. Contrib. by Casting Crowns. Prod. by Mark A. Miller. Contrib. by Terry Hemmings. 2005. audio compact disk 13.99 (978-5-558-86680-3(2)) Beach St.

Lifesong. Contrib. by Johnathan Crumpton & B. J. Davis. Prod. by Ed Kee. (ENG.). 2008. audio compact disk 24.99 (978-5-557-48380-3(2), Brentwood-Benson Music) Brentwood Music.

LifeSongs, Vol. 1. 1 CD. (Running Time: 1 hr.). (ps up). 2004. audio compact disk 16.98 (978-0-8066-4272-7(6)) Augsburg Fortress.
For use with children's choirs and in Sunday School. A compilation of new and familiar music.

LifeSongs, Vol. 2. 1 CD. (Running Time: 1 hr.). (gr. 2 up). 2004. audio compact disk 16.98 (978-0-8066-4273-4(4)) Augsburg Fortress.

***Lifestyle & Career Advice.** unabr. ed. Various Authors. (Running Time: 1 hr. 30 mins.). (GetAbstract Ser.). 2009. 78.00 (978-1-4417-3378-8(7)); audio compact disk 80.00 (978-1-4417-3375-7(2)) Blckstn Audio.

Lifestyle Freedom Pack: Stop Getting Rejected! Randy Gage. (ENG.). 2002. audio compact disk 16.00 (978-0-9762299-6-4(X)) Prime Concepts Grp.

Lifestyle of Love. Kenneth Copeland. 3 cass. 2006. (978-1-57562-868-4(6)) K Copeland Pubns.

Lifestyle of Love: 3 Messages. Kenneth Copeland. 4 CDs. 2006. audio compact disk (978-1-57562-869-1(4)) K Copeland Pubns.

Lifestyle Thin. Trenna Daniells & Trenna Sutphen. 4 cass. (Running Time: 4 hrs.). 1986. 29.95 (978-0-918519-13-9(6)) Trenna Prods.
Provides a self-help method to losing weight & keeping it off. Includes: "Understanding Why You Can't Lose Weight"; "The Reasons Behind Your Overeating Habits"; "Why You Sabotage Your Own Weight-Loss Efforts"; "How to Overcome Your Desire for Immediate Gratification"; "Understanding Your Own Eating Patterns"; "Habits & Viewpoints"; "What You Need to Know to Achieve Your Ideal Weight & Maintain It Forever".

Lifetime Astrology. A. T. Mann. 1 cass. 8.95 (222) Am Fed Astrologers.
Logarithmic time scale used for dating & interpreting chart.

Lifetime Labels, Pt. B. (23323) J Norton Pubs.

Lifetime of Health: Guided Reading. 5th ed. Holt, Rinehart and Winston Staff. (SPA.). 2005. audio compact disk 235.66 (978-0-03-039418-8(X)) Holt McDoug.

Lifetime of Health: Guided Reading Program. 4th ed. Holt, Rinehart and Winston Staff. (SPA.). Date not set. audio compact disk 228.80 (978-0-03-068364-0(5)) Holt McDoug.

Lifetime of Health: Guided Reading Program. 4th ed. Holt, Rinehart and Winston Staff. 2004. audio compact disk 235.66 (978-0-03-065208-0(1)) Holt McDoug.

Lifetime of Health: Sexual Responsibility: Guided Reading Program. 4th ed. Holt, Rinehart and Winston Staff. (SPA.). 2004. audio compact disk 61.60 (978-0-03-069027-3(7)) Holt McDoug.

Lifetime of Riches: The Biography of Napoleon Hill. abr. ed. Michael J. Ritt, Jr. & Kirk Landers. Read by Michael McConnohie. (Running Time: 3 hrs. 0 mins. 0 sec.). (ENG.). 2003. audio compact disk 26.95 (978-1-932429-19-0(9)) Pub: Highroads Media. Dist(s): Macmillan

Lifetime of Success: Parents, Kids & Reading. unabr. ed. Linda Crafton & Penny Silvers. 4 cass. (Running Time: 2 hrs. 40 min.). 1993. instr.'s hndbk. ed. (978-0-9652639-0-0(8)) Ctr for Lrng & Litrcy.
The set describes early reading development, the role of the parent, choosing & reading books, & making the home a literate environment.

Lifetime of Wisdom. unabr. ed. Read by Joni Eareckson Tada. (Running Time: 6 hrs. 45 mins. 0 sec.). (ENG.). 2009. audio compact disk 32.99 (978-0-310-28953-1(X)) Zondervan.

***Lifetime of Wisdom: Embracing the Way God Heals You.** unabr. ed. Joni Eareckson Tada. (Running Time: 6 hrs. 45 mins. 0 sec.). (ENG.). 2009. 21.99 (978-0-310-28954-8(8)) Zondervan.

Lifetime Prediction. A. T. Mann. 1 cass. (Running Time: 90 min.). 1994. 8.95 (223) Am Fed Astrologers.

Lifetime Reporting the News. Walter Cronkite. 1 cass. (Running Time: 1 hr. 26 mins.). 2001. 12.95 Smithson Assocs.

Lifetime Strategies for Personal Effectiveness. Garrison Krause. 6 cass. (Running Time: 6 hrs.). 1993. 59.95 set. (374A) Nightingale-Conant.

Lifprints, Vol. 3. 2003. audio compact disk 17.00 (978-1-56420-324-3(7)) New Readers.

Lift. Contrib. by Audio Adrenaline. (Collectors Ser.). 2002. 6.99 (978-5-552-49531-3(4)) FF Rcds.

Lift. unabr. ed. Kelly Corrigan. Read by Kelly Corrigan. (ENG.). 2010. audio compact disk 17.00 (978-0-307-73675-8(X), Random AudioBks) Pub: Random Audio Pubg. Dist(s): Random

Lift Every Voice: Expecting the Most & Getting the Best from All of God's Children. abr. ed. Walter Turnbull et al. Read by Gregory T. Daniel. 2 cass. (Running Time: 3 hrs.). 1997. 17.95 (978-1-57453-116-9(6)) Audio Lit.
Dr. Walter Turnbull dreamed of creating opportunities & better lives for the children of Harlem. This is the story of how he realized his dream.

Lift High the Lord: Songs & Sketches for Contemporary Praise. Des. by Joseph Linn. 1993. audio compact disk 75.00 (978-0-685-72858-1(7), MU-9164T) Lillenas.

Lift Him High: Church of the Redeemer Choir. Conducted by Kareem Riley. 1 CD. 2005. 15.98 (978-0-9766566-3-0(9)) GraphicVisions MD.

Lift Him up, Vol. 1. Contrib. by Don Marsh. 1980. 16.98 (978-0-00-254219-7(6), 75609256) Pub: Brentwood Music. Dist(s): H Leonard

Lift Him up, Vol. 2. Contrib. by Don Marsh. 1987. 16.98 (978-0-00-519328-0(1), 75609261) Pub: Brentwood Music. Dist(s): H Leonard

Lift Him up, Vol. 3. Contrib. by Don Marsh. 1986. 16.98 (978-0-00-154238-9(9), 75609266) Pub: Brentwood Music. Dist(s): H Leonard

Lift Him up, Vol. 4. Contrib. by Don Marsh. 1988. 16.98 (978-0-00-693223-9(1), 75609235) Pub: Brentwood Music. Dist(s): H Leonard

Lift Him up, Vol. 5. Contrib. by Don Marsh. 1995. 30.00 (978-0-00-508464-9(4), 75608260) Pub: Brentwood Music. Dist(s): H Leonard

Lift Him up - the Best Of. Contrib. by Elmo Mercer & Don Marsh. 1994. 16.98 (978-0-00-501182-9(5), 75608063) Pub: Brentwood Music. Dist(s): H Leonard

Lift Him up/Glorify Thy Name. (Running Time: 4800 sec.). (Songs 4 Worship Ser.). 2002. 14.95 (978-5-552-60244-5(7)) Integrity Music.

Lift Little Voices: Songs & Musical Games for Young Children. Carol Greene & Deborah Carter. (J). (ps-2). 10.99 (978-0-570-00783-8(6), 22-2896); audio compact disk 15.99 (978-0-570-00784-5(4), 22-2897) Concordia.

Lift Off. unabr. ed. Robert A. Monroe. Read by Robert A. Monroe. (Running Time: 45 min.). (Gateway Experience - Freedom Ser.). 1983. 14.95 (978-1-56113-262-1(4)) Monroe Institute.
Become comfortable in a perspective away from the body.

Lift off in English see Despegue en Ingles

Lift off to Courage. 1996. 12.50 (978-1-893027-28-2(7)) Path of Light.

Lift Thine Eyes. 1 cass. 8.98 (120049) Covenant Comms.
Includes "Come, Come Ye Saints" & "Climb Every Mountain.".

Lift up the Cross. Angel Christ. 2005. audio compact disk 15.95 (978-0-9713534-4-2(1)) Pub: C R M. Dist(s): STL Dist NA

Lift up Your Hearts. unabr. ed. Perf. by Denise Morency Gannon. 1 CD. (Running Time: 43 min.). (ENG.). 1997. cass. & cd-rom 12.95 (978-0-9656982-1-4(1), C0197) Morgan Music.
Traditional & contemporary vocal music for troubled times, bereavement, meditation. Includes "On Eagle's Wings," "Amazing Grace," "Shall we Gather at the River," "Ave Maria" (Norbet) & more.

Lifted Up. Guy Galli. 6 cass. 2004. 19.95 (978-1-59156-180-4(9)); audio compact disk 19.95 (978-1-59156-199-6(X)) Covenant Comms.

Lifted up by Angels. unabr. ed. Lurlene McDaniel. Narrated by Kate Forbes. 4 pieces. (Running Time: 4 hrs. 45 mins.). (Angels Trilogy: No. 2). (gr. 7 up). 2001. 39.00 (978-0-7887-4567-6(0), 96039E7) Recorded Bks.
Leah would rather work in a bed & breakfast inn all summer than sail to Fiji with her family. She wants to be near Ethan, whose kind Amish family befriended her while she was in the hospital.

Lifted up by Angels. unabr. ed. Lurlene McDaniel. Narrated by Kate Forbes. 4 cass. (Running Time: 4 hrs. 45 mins.). (Angels Trilogy: No. 2). (YA). 2001. pap. bk. & stu. ed. 53.24 Recorded Bks.

Lifted Veil & Castle Rackrent. unabr. ed. George Eliot & Maria Edgeworth. Read by Flo Gibson. 3 cass. (Running Time: 4 hrs.). (gr. 10 up). 1999. 16.95 (978-1-55685-625-9(3)) Audio Bk Con.
In "The Lifted Veil", despite Latimer's horrifying visions of the "pale fatal-eyed" Bertha Grant, he falls under her spell in this chilling tale. In "Castle Rackrent", Thady, an Irish manservant, tells of his trials & tribulations with his various masters with humor & occasional acerbity.

An Asterisk (*) at the beginning of an entry indicates that the title is appearing for the first time.

Light in the Window. unabr. ed. Jan Karon. Narrated by John McDonough. 12 cass. (Running Time: 16 hrs. 30 mins.). (Mitford Ser.: Bk. 2). 1999. 97.00 (978-0-7887-0646-2(2), 94823K8) Recorded Bks.
Father Tim finds his heart drawn to his lovely neighbor, Cynthia while a wealthy widow pursues him with seductive casseroles.

Light in Zion. Bodie Thoene & Brock Thoene. 1 CD. (Running Time: 15 hrs.). (Zion Chronicles: Bk. 4). 2001. audio compact disk 19.95 (2759) Blckstn Audio.
The British have almost totally withdrawn from any interference between the battles of the Jews and the Arab soldiers of Haj Amin Husseini. The eve of Passover finds the Jews of Jerusalem being starved by an Arab siege. While Moshe and his Jewish troops risk opening the Arab-held pass of Bab el Wad for a food convoy to save their people, David and Ellie search the Mediterranean for a freighter loaded with weapons for the Muslim Jihad and the bands of Arab soldiers who still vow to drive the Jews into the sea. And Rachel?s mother-heart agonizes over her fever-ravaged infant.

Light in Zion. unabr. ed. Bodie Thoene & Brock Thoene. Read by Susan O'Malley. 10 cass. (Running Time: 14 hrs. 30 mins.). (Zion Chronicles: Bk. 4). 2001. 69.95 (978-0-7861-1989-9(6), 2759); audio compact disk 96.00 (978-0-7861-9735-4(8), 2759) Blckstn Audio.
Opens in April 1948, only six weeks before the final evacuation of the British from Israel. The dream for the rebirth of the Jewish nation now appears doomed to extinction. The British have almost totally withdrawn from any interference between the battles of the nearly unarmed Jews and the Arab soldiers of Haj Amin Husseini. The eve of Passover finds the Jewish sector of Jerusalem being starved into submission by an Arab siege. While Moshe and his Jewish troops risk their lives to open the Arab-held pass of Bab el Wad for a food convoy to save their people, David and Ellie search the Mediterranean for a freighter loaded with weapons for the Muslim Jihad and the bands of Arab soldiers who still vow to drive the Jews into the sea. And Rachel's mother-heart agonizes over her fever-ravaged infant.

Light Inside. Perf. by Gary Chapman. Prod. by Michael Omartian. 1 CD. 1994. audio compact disk Brentwood Music.
Gary wrote & recorded the Grammy & Dove nominate The Light Inside with producer Michael Omartian. Features: Sweet Glow of Mercy & Sweet Jesus.

Light Is Born. Swami Amar Jyoti. 2 cass. 1987. 12.95 (K-97) Truth Consciousness.
Given on Janmashtami, the birthday of Krishna, & the harmonic convergence. The great play of the Prophets, their Divine Vision. Our conscious participation; the clearing process; the changing age.

***Light Man.** Henry James. Henry James. Narrated by William Coon. (Running Time: 87). (ENG.). 2010. 6.95 (978-0-9844138-0-5(4)) Pub: Eloq Voice. Dist(s): OverDrive Inc

Light of Burning Shadows. unabr. ed. Chris Evans. Narrated by Michael Kramer. (Running Time: 10 hrs. 30 mins. 0 sec.). (Iron Elves Ser.: Bk. 2). (ENG.). 2010. audio compact disk 69.99 (978-1-4001-4321-4(7)) Pub: Tantor Media. Dist(s): IngramPubServ

Light of Burning Shadows: Book Two of the Iron Elves. unabr. ed. Chris Evans. Narrated by Michael Kramer. (Running Time: 10 hrs. 30 mins. 0 sec.). (Iron Elves Ser.). (ENG.). 2010. 24.99 (978-1-4001-6321-2(8)); audio compact disk 34.99 (978-1-4001-1321-7(0)) Pub: Tantor Media. Dist(s): IngramPubServ

***Light of Burning Shadows: Book Two of the Iron Elves.** unabr. ed. Chris Evans. Narrated by Michael Kramer. (Running Time: 10 hrs. 30 mins.). (Iron Elves Ser.). 2010. 16.99 (978-1-4001-8321-0(9)) Tantor Media.

Light of Day. unabr. ed. Eric Ambler. Read by Frederick Davidson. 5 cass. (Running Time: 7 hrs.). 1988. 39.95 (978-0-7861-0037-8(0), 1036) Blckstn Audio.
Arthur Simpson, a somewhat ordinary Englishman, gets caught in a web of international intrigue. His choice is either to become part of an international jewel heist or spend the rest of his life confined to a Turkish jail.

Light of Day. unabr. ed. Graham Swift. Read by Graeme Malcolm. (YA). 2007. 44.99 (978-1-60252-844-4(6)) Find a World.

Light of Day. unabr. collector's ed. Eric Ambler. Read by Richard Brown. 8 cass. (Running Time: 8 hrs.). 1987. 48.00 (978-0-7366-1220-3(3), 2138) Books on Tape.
Crime thriller in which a small-time crook gets caught up in a major jewel robbery.

Light of Evening. unabr. ed. 7 cass. (Running Time: 32700 sec.). 2006. 64.95 (978-0-7927-4546-4(9), CSL 1015); audio compact disk 79.95 (978-0-7927-4485-6(3), SLD 1015) AudioGO.

Light of Home. Perf. by Joanna Carlson. Prod. by Brent Bourgeois. 1 CD. 1995. audio compact disk Brentwood Music.
Joanna's debut project for Reunion features the top 10 song Miracle & Belong to Me.

Light of Laughing Flowers: An Advanced Teacher of God. Kenneth Wapnick. 1 CD. (Running Time: 2 hrs. 26 mins. 44 secs.). 2006. 12.00 (978-1-59142-305-8(8), 3m138); audio compact disk 15.00 (978-1-59142-304-1(X), CD138) Foun Miracles.

Light of Other Days. unabr. ed. Arthur C. Clarke & Stephen Baxter. Read by Dick Hill. (Running Time: 10 hrs.). 2007. 39.25 (978-1-4233-3076-9(5), 9781423330769, BADLE); 24.95 (978-1-4233-3075-2(7), 9781423330752, BAD) Brilliance Audio.

Light of Other Days. unabr. ed. Arthur C. Clarke & Stephen Baxter. Read by Dick Hill. (Running Time: 10 hrs.). 2007. 39.25 (978-1-4233-3074-5(9), 9781423330745, Brinc Audio MP3 Lib); 24.95 (978-1-4233-3073-8(0), 9781423330738, Brilliance MP3) Brilliance Audio.

Light of the Anointing. Kenneth Copeland. Perf. by Kenneth Copeland. 1 cass. (Anointed & His Anointing Ser.: Tape 8). 1995. cass. & video 5.00 (978-1-57562-035-0(9)) K Copeland Pubns.
Biblical teaching on the anointing.

Light of the Guru. Swami Amar Jyoti. 1 dolby cass. 1984. 9.95 (E-27) Truth Consciousness.
God shines in the Guru. The meaning & great message of Guru Purnima. On worship, faith & trust.

Light of the Moon. abr. ed. Luanne Rice. Read by Blair Brown. (Running Time: 21600 sec.). (ENG.). 2008. audio compact disk 29.95 (978-0-7393-4360-9(2), Random AudioBks) Pub: Random Audio Pubg. Dist(s): Random

Light of the World. 1 cass. (Max Lucado's God Came Near). 1998. 8.98 Mastertrax. (978-1-58229-055-3(5)) Brentwood Music.

***Light of the World.** Featuring Adyashanti. (ENG.). 2009. audio compact disk 29.00 (978-1-933986-66-1(2)) Open Gate Pub.

Light of the World. Perf. by Max Lucado. 1 cass. 1999. 8.99 (Howard Bks) S and S.
Song of praise & words of inspiration for the Christmas season.

Light of the World. Stan Pethel. 1992. 75.00 (978-0-7673-1370-4(4)) LifeWay Christian.

Light of the World. Perf. by Point of Grace Staff. 1 cass. 1999. Provident Music.

Light of the World. Solas. Perf. by Siobhan Mullin et al. 1994. 10.95 (351); audio compact disk 15.95 (351) GIA Pubns.

Light of Western Stars. unabr. ed. Zane Grey. Read by Robert Morris. 10 cass. (Running Time: 14 hrs. 30 mins.). 1996. 69.95 (978-0-7861-0975-3(0), 1752) Blckstn Audio.
When proud, young New York debutante Madeline Hammond goes west in search of her brother, she encounters much more than cultural shock: revolutionary Mexicans, outlaw cowboys, a corrupt sheriff, & the tough fearless Gene Stewart - the only man who can save her life & capture her heart. After she buys a cattle ranch close to the Mexican border, her new life becomes one long ride on the bronco of danger & adventure during which she develops the strength & integrity of a mature woman.

Light of Western Stars. unabr. ed. Zane Grey. Read by Gene Engene. 12 cass. (Running Time: 13 hrs.). Incl. Light of Western Stars. Zane Grey. Read by Gene Engene. (175); Light of Western Stars. Zane Grey. Read by Gene Engene. (175); Light of Western Stars. Zane Grey. Read by Gene Engene. (175); 64.95 (978-1-55686-175-8(3), 175) Books in Motion.
When Madeline Hammond, a New York society beauty, bought a ranch near the turbulent Mexican Frontier, she got more than she's ever bargained for-a bloody revolution, the ravages of a bandit raid, abduction by Mexican guerillas & rescue by the daring Gene Stewart, the legendary El Capitan. Then one day the tables were turned. The bandits sentenced Stewart to death & Madeline rode into the lawless wilds of Mexico in a desperate bid for the life of her newfound love.

Light on Life: The Yoga Way to Wholeness, Inner Peace, & Ultimate Freedom. abr. ed. B. K. S. Iyengar et al. Read by Patricia Walden. 2005. 14.95 (978-1-59397-843-3(X)); audio compact disk 24.95 (978-1-59397-787-0(5)) Pub: Macmill Audio. Dist(s): Macmillan

Light on Snow. unabr. ed. Anita Shreve. Read by Alyson Silverman. (ENG.). 2005. 14.98 (978-1-59483-144-7(0)) Pub: Hachet Audio. Dist(s): HachBkGrp

Light on Snow. unabr. ed. Anita Shreve. Read by Alyson Silverman. (Running Time: 7 hrs.). (Replay Edition Ser.). (ENG.). 2008. audio compact disk 14.98 (978-1-60024-102-4(6)) Pub: Hachet Audio. Dist(s): HachBkGrp

Light on Snow. unabr. ed. Anita Shreve. Read by Alyson Silverman. (Running Time: 7 hrs.). (ENG.). 2009. 59.98 (978-1-60024-875-7(6)) Pub: Hachet Audio. Dist(s): HachBkGrp

Light on the Path. Mabel Collins. 1 cass. (Running Time: 1 hr.). 2000. 5.95 (978-0-8356-2006-2(9), Quest) Pub: Theos Pub Hse. Dist(s): Natl Bk Netwk

Light on the Path. unabr. ed. Mabel Collins. 2 cass. (Running Time: 2 hrs.). (ENG.). 1990. 17.00 (978-0-911500-22-6(7)) Theos U Pr.
A theosophic classic comprising rules & precepts of the spiritual path, with notes & commentary by the author.

Light Princess. abr. ed. George MacDonald. Perf. by Glynis Johns. 1 cass. (J). 1985. 8.98 (978-0-89845-065-1(9), CP 1676) HarperCollins Pubs.
Lack of gravity causes the frivolous princess & her perplexed royal parents much chagrin. When the handsome prince touches her levitating heart, Victorian decorum abounds.

Light Princess. unabr. ed. George MacDonald. 1 cass. (Running Time: 34 min.). (Middle Grade Cliffhangers Ser.). (J). (gr. 4-5). 1981. 15.98 incl. bk. & guide. (978-0-8072-1088-8(9), SWR 25 SP, Listening Lib) Random Audio Pubg.
A young princess cursed with weightlessness floats along until a prince offers to trade his life for hers. Love & compassion break the evil spell.

Light Princess. unabr. ed. George MacDonald. 2 CDs. (Running Time: 1 hr. 36 mins. 0 sec.). (Classic Fairy Tale Collection). (ENG.). (J). (gr. 4-7). 2004. audio compact disk 15.98 (978-1-59644-043-2(0), Hovel Audio) christianaud.
The Light Princess is a short story that is warm and humorous, with a surprisingly poignant conclusion. A princess doomed by a witch to lose her a??gravitya?? results in a silly heroine that has neither physical nor spiritual weight. George MacDonalda??s masterful teaching on the subject of sacrificial love is delivered eloquently in the events and characters of this engaging story.

Light Princess. unabr. ed. George MacDonald. Read by Full Cast Production Staff. (J). 2007. 34.99 (978-1-59895-932-1(8)) Find a World.

***Light Princess.** unabr. ed. George MacDonald. Narrated by Veronica Murphy. (Running Time: 1 hr. 36 mins. 0 sec.). (ENG.). 2004. 9.98 (978-1-59644-041-8(4), Hovel Audio) christianaud.

Light Princess & Other Stories. unabr. ed. George MacDonald. Read by Frederick Davidson. 6 cass. (Running Time: 9 hrs.). 1988. 44.95 (978-0-7861-0144-3(X), 1129) Blckstn Audio.

***Light Speed Algebra: Essential Quadratics.** Cerebellum Academic Team. (Running Time: 1 hr.). (Light Speed Ser.). 2010. cd-rom 14.98 (978-1-58565-439-0(6)) Cerebellum.

***Light Speed Algebra: Linear Equations & Polynomials.** Cerebellum Academic Team. (Running Time: 1 hr.). (Light Speed Ser.). 2010. cd-rom 14.98 (978-1-58565-438-3(8)) Cerebellum.

***Light Speed Algebra: Solving, Simplifying, & Slope.** Cerebellum Academic Team. (Running Time: 1 hr.). (Light Speed Ser.). 2010. cd-rom 14.98 (978-1-58565-437-6(X)) Cerebellum.

***Light Speed Algebra: The Powers & Functions.** Cerebellum Academic Team. (Running Time: 1 hr.). (Light Speed Ser.). 2010. cd-rom 14.98 (978-1-58565-436-9(1)) Cerebellum.

Light Speed AP English Language & Comp. Exam Prep. Cerebellum Academic Team. (Running Time: 52 mins.). (Teaching Systems Ser.). 2010. cd-rom 14.98 (978-1-59443-119-7(1)) Cerebellum.

Light Speed Chemistry AP Exam Prep. Cerebellum Academic Team. (Running Time: 55 mins.). (Teaching Systems Ser.). 2010. cd-rom 14.98 (978-1-59443-121-0(3)) Cerebellum.

Light Speed History of the U. S. AP Exam Prep. Cerebellum Academic Team. (Running Time: 1 hr. 12 mins.). (Teaching Systems Ser.). 2010. cd-rom 14.98 (978-1-59443-120-3(5)) Cerebellum.

***Light Speed Super Pack.** Cerebellum Academic Team. (Running Time: 4 hrs.). (Light Speed Ser.). 2010. cd-rom 49.98 (978-1-58565-440-6(X)) Cerebellum.

***Light Speed U. S. Gov & Politics AP Exam Prep.** Cerebellum Academic Team. (Running Time: 58 mins.). 2010. cd-rom 14.98 (978-1-59443-122-7(1)) Cerebellum.

Light That Failed. Rudyard Kipling. Read by Flo Gibson. 5 cass. (Running Time: 7 hrs. 30 min.). 1990. 20.95 (978-1-55685-163-6(4)) Audio Bk Con.
With war correspondents in the Sudan, Dick Heldar, a gifted printer, learned to perfect his art depicting battle scenes. Years later an old spear wound causes blindness & he struggles to regain control of his life & his love for Maisie.

Light That Failed. Rudyard Kipling. Read by David Thorn & Stuart Bennett. (Running Time: 30600 sec.). 2005. audio compact disk 63.00 (978-0-7861-7581-9(8)) Blckstn Audio.

Light That Failed. Rudyard Kipling. Read by David Thorn et al. (Running Time: 30600 sec.). 2005. 54.95 (978-0-7861-3797-8(5)) Blckstn Audio.

Light That Failed. Rudyard Kipling. Narrated by Donna Barkman. (Running Time: 7 hrs.). 1982. 46.95 (978-1-59912-869-6(1)) Iofy Corp.

Light That Failed. unabr. ed. Rudyard Kipling. Read by David Thorn & Stuart Bennett. (Running Time: 30600 sec.). 2005. audio compact disk 29.95 (978-0-7861-7856-8(6)) Blckstn Audio.

Light That Failed. unabr. ed. Rudyard Kipling. Read by Donna Barkman. 6 cass. (Running Time: 8 hrs. 30 min.). Dramatization. 1982. 34.00 (C-65) Jimcin Record.
Strongly autobiographical in content, this is the story of artist Dick Heldar who faced many battles in life - the final one being blindness.

Light the Fire Within You. Ida Greene. 6 cass. (Running Time: 4 hrs.). 1991. cass. & cd-rom 49.95 (978-1-881165-16-3(7)) People Skills.

Light These Lights: Debbie Friedman Sings Chanukah Songs for the Whole Family. Perf. by Debbie Friedman. Prod. by David Bravo. Arranged by David Bravo. (Running Time: 37 min.). (ENG & HEB.). (YA). 2003. audio compact disk 15.95 (978-1-890161-51-4(9)) Sounds Write.

Light Thickens. Ngaio Marsh. Read by James Saxon. 8 CDs. (Running Time: 12 hrs.). 2002. audio compact disk 79.95 (978-0-7540-5528-0(0), CCD 219) Pub: Chivers Audio Bks GBR. Dist(s): AudioGO

Light to My Path. unabr. ed. Lynn Austin. Narrated by Christina Moore. 13 CDs. (Running Time: 15 hrs. 30 mins.). (Refiner's Fire Ser.: No. 3). 2005. audio compact disk 119.75 (978-1-4193-2795-7(X), CK129); 109.75 (978-1-4193-2793-3(3), K1134) Recorded Bks.
Renowned author Lynn Austin has received three Christy Awards for Historical Fiction - two for the first books in this Refiner's Fire series. Raised on a South Carolina plantation as the house pet of her white master's daughter, Kitty never made a decision for herself. Now as a young adult, she must preserve her faith while making the biggest decision ever: stay with her master and go south to avoid the Yankees or run away tonight for the North with Grady, the field slave she has come to love.

Light Touch. Kushner. 2004. 7.95 (978-0-7435-4549-5(4)) Pub: S&S Audio. Dist(s): S and S Inc

Light up your Life **see Enciende tu Vida**

Light Wins. Scott Huckabay. 2007. audio compact disk 19.25 (978-0-923550-03-5(8)) Tetrahedron Pub.

Light Within Illusion. Swami Amar Jyoti. 1 cass. 1991. 9.95 (K-135) Truth Consciousness.
Starting with the correct premise: all is Divine. Then what is illusion?.

Light Years. Elizabeth Jane Howard. 2001. pap. bk. (978-0-333-90800-6(7)) Macmillan UK GBR.

Light Years. rev. ed. Elizabeth Jane Howard. 4 cass. (Running Time: 6 hrs.). (ENG., 2001. (978-0-333-67558-8(4)) Macmillan UK GBR.

Light Years. unabr. ed. Elizabeth Jane Howard. Read by Jill Balcon. 12 cass. (Cazalet Chronicles: Vol. 1). 1999. 96.95 (SAB 052) AudioGO.

Light Years. unabr. ed. Elizabeth Jane Howard. Read by Jill Balcon. 14 CDs. (Running Time: 21 hrs.). 2002. audio compact disk 115.95 (978-0-7540-5488-7(8), CCD 179) Pub: Chivers Pr GBR. Dist(s): AudioGO

Light Years. unabr. collector's ed. Elizabeth Jane Howard. Read by Donada Peters. 11 cass. (Running Time: 16 hrs. 30 min.). (Cazalet Chronicles: Vol. 1). 1997. 88.00 (978-0-7366-4020-6(7), 4518) Books on Tape.
First book, it is 1937 & the WWII is only a distant cloud on the horizon. As the various Cazalet households prepare for their summer pilgrimage to the family estate in Sussex, we meet the entire cast. There's bluff, hearty Edward, in love with but by no means faithful to his wife, Villy, Hugh, wounded in the Great War, but devoted to pregnant Sybil, Rupert, who worships the body if not the mind of his child-bride, Zoe, & Rachel, the spinster sister, conducting a desperate clandestine love affair under the family roof.

Light Your Candle. Short Stories. Carl Sommer. Narrated by Carl Sommer. 1 cass. Dramatization. (Another Sommer-Time Story Ser.). (J). 2003. bk. 16.95 (978-1-57537-567-0(2)) Advance Pub.

Light Your Candle. Carl Sommer. Narrated by Carl Sommer. 1 cass. Dramatization. (Another Sommer-Time Story Ser.). (J). (gr. k-4). 2003. lib. bdg. 23.95 (978-1-57537-768-1(3)) Advance Pub.
Character Education story with character song by Karacter Kidz.

***Light Your Candle / Enciende Tu Vela.** ed. Carl Sommer. Illus. by Kennon James. (Another Sommer-Time Story Bilingual Ser.). (ENG & SPA.). (J). 2009. bk. 26.95 (978-1-57537-182-5(0)) Advance Pub.

***Lightbringer Trilogy Bk. 1: The Black Prism, 3 of 3.** Brent Weeks. 2011. audio compact disk 19.99 (978-1-59950-743-9(9)) GraphicAudio.

***Lightbringer Trilogy (Book 1) The Black Prism (1 Of 3)** Brent Weeks. 2011. audio compact disk 19.99 (978-1-59950-724-8(2)) GraphicAudio.

***Lightbringer Trilogy (Book 1) The Black Prism (2 Of 3)** Brent Weeks. 2011. audio compact disk 19.99 (978-1-59950-733-0(1)) GraphicAudio.

Lighten Up! unabr. ed. Ken Davis. 2000. 17.99 (978-0-310-22974-2(X)) Zondervan.

***Lighten Up! Great Stories from One of America's Favorite Storytellers.** abr. ed. Ken Davis. (Running Time: 1 hr. 55 mins. 0 sec.). (ENG.). 2003. 10.99 (978-0-310-26074-5(4)) Zondervan.

***Lighten Up: Love What You Have, Have What You Need, Be Happier with Less.** unabr. ed. Peter Walsh. (Running Time: 8 hrs. 30 mins.). 2010. 29.99 (978-1-4526-0012-3(0)); 71.99 (978-1-4526-3012-0(7)); 19.99 (978-1-4526-5012-8(8)); 15.99 (978-1-4526-7012-6(9)) Tantor Media.

Lighten Up! The Amazing Power of Grace under Pressure. C. W. Metcalf. 5 cass. 49.95 (15030-C47) Natl Seminars.
The single greatest predicator of good physical health is good mental health. Tap into the remarkably liberating power of humor.

Lighten Up! The Amazing Power of Grace under Pressure. C. W. Metcalf. 4 cass. 1994. 49.95 (15030AX) Nightingale-Conant.
Filled with warm stories & amusing anecdotes that will elevate, comfort, inspire & humor you when you need it most, Lighten Up! offers a healthy new outlook on life. It can help you reduce the pressure & frustration of reaching a quota, balancing the budget or just standing in a long checkout line. Includes bonus cassette with fun-filled humor visualizations you can use & enjoy.

Lighten Up! The Power of Grace under Pressure. C. W. Metcalf. 4 cass. 49.95 (15030AS) Pryor Resources.
Here's a healthy new outlook on life that leaves a lasting impact on your work, productivity, & creativity. Prepare to laugh more, be happier, & live longer.

Lighten Up & Live. unabr. ed. Jeanne E. Sexson. Read by Jeanne E. Sexson. 1 cass. (Running Time: 60 min.). 1992. 10.00 (978-0-9613817-1-4(X)) J E Sexson.
A tongue-in-cheek yet practical motivational tape. A woman's view of living, loving & laughing with an emphasis on laughter & its importance to health & quality of life.

***Lighten up (Library Edition) Love What You Have, Have What You Need, Be Happier with Less.** unabr. ed. Peter Walsh. (Running Time: 8 hrs. 30 mins.). 2010. 29.99 (978-1-4526-2012-1(1)) Tantor Media.

Lighten Up! The Power of Humor in Management. Matt Weinstein. 1 cass. (Running Time: 52 min.). 8.95 (978-0-88684-091-4(0)) Listen USA.
Learn how to use humor in business & why it is healthy.

Lighthawk - An Environmental Air Force. Hosted by Nancy Pearlman. 1 cass. (Running Time: 29 min.). 10.00 (704) Educ Comm CA.

Lighthearted Gourmet: Recipes for Lighter, Healthier Dinners, Romantic Solo Piano Music. Sharon O'Connor. (Sharon O'Connor's Menus & Music Ser.). 1995. bk. 24.95 (978-1-883914-09-7(4)) Menus & Music.

Lighthearted William see Gathering of Great Poetry for Children

Lighthouse. (Paws & Tales Ser.: Vol. 10). (J). 2001. 3.99 (978-1-57972-404-7(3)); audio compact disk 5.99 (978-1-57972-405-4(1)) Insight Living.

Lighthouse. Perf. by Cathedrals, The et al. 2002. audio compact disk Provident Mus Dist.

Lighthouse. collector's unabr. ed. P. D. James. 11 CDs. (Running Time: 13 hrs.). (Adam Dalgliesh Mystery Ser.). 2005. audio compact disk 81.60 (978-1-4159-2496-9(1)) Pub: Books on Tape. Dist(s): NetLibrary CO

Lighthouse. unabr. collector's ed. P. D. James. 9 cass. (Running Time: 13 hrs.). (Adam Dalgliesh Mystery Ser.). 2005. 81.00 (978-1-4159-2495-2(3)) Books on Tape.

Lighthouse Cass. Hopkins Mary. 2004. 10.95 (978-1-929617-03-6(8)) L I M Prodns.

Lighthouse Keeper. unabr. ed. James Michael Pratt. Read by James Daniels. (Running Time: 6 hrs.). 2010. 39.97 (978-1-4418-3596-3(2), 9781441835963, Brlnc Audio MP3 Lib); 24.99 (978-1-4418-3595-6(4), 9781441835956, Brilliance MP3); 39.97 (978-1-4418-3598-7(9), 9781441835987, BADLE); 24.99 (978-1-4418-3597-0(0), 9781441835970, BAD) Brilliance Audio.

***Lighthouse Keepers.** unabr. ed. Adrian McKinty. Read by Gerard Doyle. (Running Time: 12 hrs. 5 mins.). (Lighthouse Ser.). (ENG.). 2011. 29.95 (978-1-4417-7942-7(6)); 72.95 (978-1-4417-7939-7(6)); audio compact disk 32.95 (978-1-4417-7941-0(8)); audio compact disk 105.00 (978-1-4417-7940-3(X)) Blckstn Audio.

***Lighthouse Land.** unabr. ed. Adrian McKinty. (Running Time: 14 hrs.). (Lighthouse Trilogy). 2011. 29.95 (978-1-4417-7151-3(4)); 79.95 (978-1-4417-7148-3(4)); audio compact disk 32.95 (978-1-4417-7150-6(6)); audio compact disk 109.00 (978-1-4417-7149-0(2)) Blckstn Audio.

Lighthouse Mystery. Gertrude Chandler Warner. Read by Phyllis Newman. 2 cass. (Running Time: 2 hrs. 15 mins.). (Boxcar Children Ser.: No. 8). (J). (gr. 2-5). 2000. 18.00 (978-0-7366-9177-2(4)) Books on Tape.

Lighthouse Mystery. unabr. ed. Gertrude Chandler Warner. Read by Phyllis Newman. 2 cass. (Running Time: 2 hrs. 14 mins.). (Boxcar Children Ser.: No. 8). (J). (gr. 2-4). 1995. pap. bk. 28.00 (978-0-8072-7541-2(7), YA877SP, Listening Lib); 23.00 (978-0-8072-7540-5(9), YA877CX, Listening Lib) Random Audio Pubg.
The Alden children once again use their wit & ingenuity to solve a puzzling mystery.

***Lighthouse War.** unabr. ed. Adrian McKinty. (Running Time: 14 hrs. 5 mins.). (Lighthouse Trilogy). (ENG.). 2011. 29.95 (978-1-4417-7441-5(6)); 85.95 (978-1-4417-7438-5(6)); audio compact disk 32.95 (978-1-4417-7440-8(8)); audio compact disk 118.00 (978-1-4417-7439-2(4)) Blckstn Audio.

Lighting Fires in Snow see Twentieth-Century Poetry in English, No. 26, Recordings of Poets Reading Their Own Poetry

Lightkeeper's Daughter. Iain Lawrence. Narrated by Ed Sala. 5 pieces. (Running Time: 7 hrs. 15 mins.). (YA). 2002. 48.00 (978-1-4025-4126-1(0)) Recorded Bks.

Lightnin Hopkins. Perf. by Sam Hopkins. Anno. by Sam Charters. 1 CD. (Running Time: 31 min.). 1990. audio compact disk (0-9307-40019-2-9) Smithsonian Folkways.
Recording of Hopkins' first acoustic sessions, with updated notes & remastered sound.

Lightnin' Hopkins. Perf. by Sam Hopkins. Anno. by Sam Charters. 1 cass. (Running Time: 31 min.). 1990. Remastered. (0-9307-400190-9307-40019-2-9) Smithsonian Folkways.

Lightning see May Swenson

Lightning see Twentieth-Century Poetry in English, No. 8, Recordings of Poets Reading Their Own Poetry

Lightning. Ed McBain, pseud. Read by Jonathan Marosz. 7 cass. (Running Time: 10 hrs. 30 min.). (87th Precinct Ser.: Bk. 37). 1999. 56.00 (978-0-7366-4624-6(8), 5009) Books on Tape.
A hangman murderer & serial rapist unleash terror on the streets of New York City.

Lightning. abr. ed. Dean Koontz. Read by Peter Marinker. 2 cass. (Running Time: 3 hrs. 0 mins. 0 sec.). (ENG.). 1988. 17.00 (978-0-671-65237-1(0), 391071, Audioworks) Pub: S&S Audio. Dist(s): S and S Inc
Laura Shane has a guardian angel, a stranger, who has protected her over the years from misfortunes. As an adult, Laura must deal with certain dangers by herself, the stranger helpless to protect her. Then Laura must help the stranger fight against a growing evil empire.

Lightning. abr. ed. Dean Koontz. Read by Peter Marinker. 2004. 10.95 (978-0-7435-4975-2(9)) Pub: S&S Audio. Dist(s): S and S Inc

Lightning. unabr. ed. Dean Koontz. Read by Christopher Lane. (Running Time: 14 hrs.). 2007. 39.25 (978-1-4233-3901-4(0), 9781423339014, BADLE); 24.95 (978-1-4233-3900-7(2), 9781423339007, BAD); 92.25 (978-1-4233-3895-6(2), 9781423338956, BrilAudUnabridg); audio compact disk 112.25 (978-1-4233-3897-0(9), 9781423338970, BriAudCD Unabrid); audio compact disk 39.25 (978-1-4233-3899-4(5), 9781423338994, Brlnc Audio MP3 Lib); audio compact disk 24.95 (978-1-4233-3898-7(7), 9781423338987, Brilliance MP3); audio compact disk 40.95 (978-1-4233-3896-3(0), 9781423338963, Bril Audio CD Unabri) Brilliance Audio.

Lightning: A Fred Carver Mystery. unabr. ed. John Lutz. Read by Edward Lewis. 8 cass. (Running Time: 8 hrs.). (P. I. Fred Carver Mystery Ser.). 1996. 48.00 (978-0-7366-3519-6(X), 4156) Books on Tape.
Parked near an abortion clinic, Fred Carver, Florida P.I., watches his girlfriend Beth with admiration as she walks toward the building to cancel her appointment. They've agreed to keep their unborn child, even though it presents unique struggles. Suddenly, the clinic explodes, hurling Beth backwards. A doctor & a patient die, several are injured. Beth loses the baby. The police arrest a religious zealot, but Carver has doubts. His search for the truth leads him down a deadly path.

***Lightning Keeper.** abr. ed. Starling Lawrence. Read by Terence Aselford. (ENG.). 2006. (978-0-06-087838-2(X), Harper Audio); (978-0-06-087837-5(1), Harper Audio) HarperCollins Pubs.

Lightning Keeper. unabr. abr. ed. Starling Lawrence. Read by Terence Aselford. (Running Time: 28800 sec.). 2006. audio compact disk 39.95 (978-0-06-087255-7(1)) HarperCollins Pubs.

Lightning Song. unabr. ed. Lewis Nordan. Read by Nick Sullivan. 8 vols. (Running Time: 12 hrs.). 2000. bk. 69.95 (978-0-7927-2283-0(3), CSL 172, Chivers Sound Lib) AudioGO.
Leroy Dearman is twelve, and he lives on a llama farm in Mississippi when Uncle Harris arrives in a sports car, full of new ideas. He sets up a pretty grand bachelor pad in the attic, complete with a telephone, a TV set, and a stack of Playboy magazines. He is, you might say, romance itself. Life on the llama farm takes on an entirely different flavor. Electricity fills the house, equilibrium tilts, lightning strikes, and Leroy finds himself kissing his innocence good-bye.

***Lightning Speed Memory.** Igor Lacerda. 2009. audio compact disk (978-1-61623-789-9(9)) Indep Pub IL.

Lightning Strikes. unabr. ed. V. C. Andrews. Read by Liza Ross. 8 cass. (Running Time: 9 hrs. 54 mins.). (Hudson Ser.: Vol. 2). (J). 2002. 69.95 (978-0-7531-1121-5(7)); audio compact disk 84.95 (978-0-7531-1263-2(9)) Pub: ISIS Lrg Prnt GBR. Dist(s): Ulverscroft US
Enrolled in one of England's most prestigious drama schools, Rain Arnold is sent to live with her Great Aunt Lenora, of the renowned Endfield family. But something is not right. rain hears footsteps at night and the high-pitched laughter of a little girl. And everything about the place, the air, the silence, even the somber household staff, is as cold and soulless as a museum. She senses that behind the icy sheen of wealth and privilege lies something unspeakable. Something that could turn Rain's most precious dreams into a inescapable nightmare.

Lightning Thief. collector's unabr. ed. Rick Riordan. Read by Jesse Bernstein. 8 CDs. (Running Time: 10 hrs.). (Percy Jackson & the Olympians Ser.: Bk. 1). (J). (gr. 4-7). 2005. audio compact disk 51.00 (978-0-307-24531-1(4), BksonTape); 45.00 (978-0-307-24529-8(2), BksonTape) Random Audio Pubg.
The gods of Olympus are alive in the 21st century. They still fall in love with mortals and have children who might become great heroes, but most of these children meet horrible fates at the hands of monsters by the age of 12. Only a few leam the truth of their identity and make it to Half Blood Hill.

Lightning Thief. unabr. ed. Rick Riordan. Read by Jesse Bernstein. 7 CDs. (Running Time: 36720 sec.). (Percy Jackson & the Olympians Ser.: Bk. 1). (ENG.). (J). (gr. 5). 2005. audio compact disk 19.99 (978-0-307-24530-4(6), Listening Lib) Pub: Random Audio Pubg. Dist(s): Random

Lightposts for Living: The Art of Choosing a Joyful Life. Thomas Kinkade. 2000. (978-1-58621-032-8(7)) Hachet Audio.

Lightposts for Living: The Art of Choosing a Joyful Life. abr. ed. Thomas Kinkade. (ENG.). 2006. 14.98 (978-1-59483-679-4(5)) Pub: Hachet Audio. Dist(s): HachBkGrp

Lights & Laughter: Joel Ben Izzy Spins Hanukkah Tales. Joel Ben Izzy. 1 cass. (Running Time: 70 min.). 2002. 12.00 (978-0-9712976-1-6(4)); audio compact disk 17.00 (978-0-9712976-0-9(6)) J B Izzy.

Lights in the Hallway see Poetry & Voice of James Wright

Lights of London. unabr. ed. Gilda O'Neill. Read by Carole Boyd. 8 cass. (Running Time: 12 hrs.). 1999. 69.95 (978-0-7540-0289-5(6), CAB 1712) AudioGO.

Lights of London. unabr. ed. Gilda O'Neill. Read by Carole Boyd. 8 cass. (Running Time: 12 hrs.). 1999. 69.95 (CAB 1712) AudioGO.

Lights Out. 2 CDs. (Running Time: 2 hrs.). 2004. audio compact disk 10.95 (978-1-57816-225-3(4)) Audio File.

Lights Out. 1 CD. (Running Time: 1 hr.). Dramatization. (Old-Time Radio Blockbusters Ser.). 2002. audio compact disk 4.98 (978-1-57019-396-5(7), OTR7707) Pub: Radio Spirits. Dist(s): AudioGO
Incl.: "Knock on the Door," "Murder in the Script Department.".

Lights Out. Perf. by Frank Lovejoy. 1 cass. (Running Time: 60 min.). (Old Time Radio Classic Singles Ser.). 4.95 (978-1-57816-112-6(6), LO112) Audio File.
Includes: 1) "Until Dead" (2/2/43). 2) "Meteor Man" (12/22/42).

Lights Out. Perf. by Frank Lovejoy. 1 cass. (Running Time: 60 min.). 1943. 7.95 (MM-7040) Natl Recrd Co.
In the story "Until Dead," a man found guilty of murdering his wife believes that his friend did it. He swears that he will break out of jail & kill him. In "The Meteor Man," when one of a multiple of shooting stars lands near Professor Adams' house, it cracks open & he finds flesh inside..flesh that keeps growing & starts talking.

Lights Out. Arch Oboler. 2 cass. (Running Time: 2 hrs.). bk. & vinyl bd. 10.95 (978-1-57816-064-8(2), LO2401) Audio File.
Includes: "The Archer" (4-13-43) A young woman, about to be killed by thugs, is rescued by a ghost with a bow & arrow! "Murder Castle" (4-3-43) Women who answer help wanted ads enter a mysterious castle & are never heard from again. "Lord Marley's Guest" (9-7-43) An American movie starlet, staying in the home of an English Lord, takes a boat ride that ends in danger. "Sakhalin" (8-10-43) The story of a murderous Russian prison official during the time of the Czars.

Lights Out. Created by Radio Spirits. (Running Time: 32400 sec.). 2004. audio compact disk 39.98 (978-1-57019-610-2(9)) Radio Spirits.

Lights Out. Created by Radio Spirits. Contrib. by Wyllis Cooper & Arch Oboler. (Running Time: 32400 sec.). 2004. audio compact disk 39.98 (978-1-57019-612-6(5)) Radio Spirits.

Lights Out. collector's ed. Arch Oboler. 6 cass. (Running Time: 9 hrs.). 2001. bk. 34.98 (4425) Radio Spirits.
18 horrific stories.

Lights Out, Vol. 2. Created by Radio Spirits. (Running Time: 32400 sec.). 2004. 39.98 (978-1-57019-611-9(7)) Radio Spirits.

Lights Out: A Study in Horror. Perf. by Peter Lorre. (MM-2437) Natl Recrd Co.

Lights Out! Christmas Story & Darrell Hall's Thoughts. Hosted by Arch Oboler. 1 cass. (Running Time: 1 hr.). 2001. 6.98 (1853) Radio Spirits.

Lights Out: Knock on the Door & Murder in the Script Department. 1 CD. (Running Time: 1 hr.). (Old-Time Radio Blockbusters Ser.). 2001. audio compact disk 4.98 (7707) Radio Spirits.

Lights Out! Man in the Middle & Haunted Cell. Perf. by Arch Oboler. 1 cass. (Running Time: 1 hr.). 2001. 6.98 (2464) Radio Spirits.

Lights Out! Money, Money, Money & Super Feature. Hosted by Arch Oboler. 1 cass. (Running Time: 1 hr.). 2001. 6.98 (2182) Radio Spirits.

Lights Out: The Coffin in Studio B. 1 cass. (Running Time: 1 hr.). Dramatization. 1930. 7.95 (MM8425) Natl Recrd Co.
In "Lights Out" two men are rehearsing a "Lights Out" show that is about to go on the air in a few minutes. They are interrupted by a coffin salesman who shows one of them a catalog of coffins. Thinking it's a gag & in order to get rid of him, he makes a choice... a fatal one. In "The Shadow" episode, Lamont Cranston & Margo Lane are at a opera listening to a tenor sing "Pagliacci" when all of a sudden he loses his voice. A few weeks later another tenor is killed while singing "Pagliacci." The Shadow is called upon to solve these unusual happenings.

Lights Out - The Shadow. 1 cass. (Running Time: 60 min.). (Old Time Radio Classic Singles Ser.). 4.95 (978-1-57816-113-3(4), LS134) Audio File.
Includes: 1) "Coffin in Studio B" Actors find a coffin salesman in the studio (1930). 2) "Tenor with the Broken Voice" Opera singers die when singing a certain song (12/5/37).

Lights Out & The Aldrich Family: Sub-Basement & Homer "Becomes Engaged" unabr. ed. 1 cass. (Running Time: 60 min.). Dramatization. 7.95 Norelco box. (MM9284) Natl Recrd Co.
Arch Oboler, the master of mystery, narrates this exciting Lights Out drama about a department store employee who persuades his wife to explore the tunnels beneath the store. He has a special reason for taking her to the sub-basement, but they both encounter horror. A real chiller! Sponsored by Ironized Yeast. The Aldrich Family: The troubles of Henry Aldrich...starring Ezra Stone as Henry & Jackie Kelk as Homer. Homer observes the first anniversary of his date with Agnes, who expects a gift for the occasion...an engagement ring! With those wonderful commercials from J-E-L-L-O.

Lights Out Liverpool. unabr. ed. Maureen Lee. Read by Maggie Ollerenshaw. 10 cass. (Running Time: 10 hrs.). 1998. 84.95 (978-0-7540-0142-3(3), CAB1565) AudioGO.
It is 1939 & England is on the verge of war. For Annie, the outbreak of war means constant worry for her twin boys. For Sheila, the birth of her sixth child is eclipsed by fear for her husband's safety, while her sister Eileen finds work in a factory. And when Freda & Dicky, the least cared for children in the neighborhood are evacuated, their lives change from beyond recognition.

Lights Out Tonight. Mary Jane Clark. (KEY News Ser.: Bk. 9). 2006. 17.95 (978-1-59397-916-4(9)) Pub: Macmill Audio. Dist(s): Macmillan

Lights Out Tonight. unabr. ed. Mary Jane Clark. Narrated by Isabel Keating. 4 cass. (Running Time: 25440 sec.). (KEY News Ser.: Bk. 9). 2006. 39.95 (978-0-7927-4026-1(2), CSL 942); audio compact disk 64.95 (978-0-7927-4027-8(0), SLD 942); audio compact disk & audio compact disk 29.95 (978-0-7927-4246-3(X), CMP 942) AudioGO.

Lightship. Brian Floca. 1 cass. (Running Time: 9 mins.). (J). (gr. k-3). 2007. bk. 27.95 (978-0-8045-6962-0(2)); bk. 29.95 (978-0-8045-4185-5(X)) Spoken Arts.

LightWave 8 Project Handbook. Patrik Beck. 2004. bk. 49.95 (978-1-58450-339-2(4)) Chrles River Media.

Lightwood Duo Christmas. Lightwood Duo Staff. 1 cass. (Running Time: 1 hr.). 9.95 (10001417); audio compact disk 14.95 (28001060) Covenant Comms.
Christmas favorites on the "light" side.

Like a Charm: A Novel in Voices. John Connolly et al. Read by Susan Eriksen. Ed. by Karin Slaughter. 9 vols. 2004. bk. 44.95 (978-0-7927-3238-9(3), SLD 662, Chivers Sound Lib); bk. 27.95 (978-0-7927-3239-6(1), CMP 662, Chivers Sound Lib) AudioGO.

Like a Donkey Between Two Bales of Hay: Puer & Senex in Midlife. Read by Thomas P. Lavin. 2 cass. (Running Time: 1 hr. 45 min.). 1991. 16.95 Set. (978-0-7822-0144-4(X), 431) C G Jung IL.

Like a Rose: A Celebration of Football. Rick Telander. 1 DVD. 2004. bk. 19.95 (978-1-58261-891-3(7)) Pub: Sports Pub. Dist(s): IngramPubServ

Like a Star. Jim Rule. Perf. by Tim Horrigan. Prod. by Tim Horrigan. 1 cass. (Running Time: 40 min.). (J). (ps-4). 1999. 10.00 (978-1-886037-10-6(8), 2705); audio compact disk 15.00 PNO Tuna.
Collection of 14 original songs intended for children & parents based on the Golden Rule.

Like Christmas All Year 'Round. Perf. by Dennis Jernigan. 1 CD. (Running Time: 1 hr.). 1999. audio compact disk (978-1-58229-092-8(X)) Brentwood Music.
Originally recorded live at Bethesda Community Church & Body of Christ, Fort Worth, Texas, Dennis leads the congregation into an evening of Celebration & worship during the Christmas season. Songs Include: "Starry Night"; "Joy to the World (He Is King)"; "Jesus Is King of Kings"; "Like the Snow"; "Little Child (In the Manger Lay)"; "Glory to God in the Highest"; "Like Christmas All Year "Round"; "Joy! Joy to the World"; "Emmanuel (God with Us)"; "Hallelujah! Christ Jesus Is Born"; "Light of the World"; "The Blessing Song"; "Jesus Will Reign" plus 2 new songs. Digitally remixed & mastered.

Like Christmas All Year 'Round. Perf. by Dennis Jernigan. 1 cass. (Running Time: 1 hr.). 1999. 9.99 (978-1-58229-093-5(8), Howard Bks) Pub: S and S. Dist(s): S and S Inc

Like Father, Like Daughter. unabr. ed. Anne Baker. Read by Julia Franklin. 17 CDs. (Running Time: 17.5 hrs.). (Soundings (CDs) Ser.). (J). 2002. audio compact disk 109.95 (978-1-84283-312-4(X)) Pub: ISIS Lrg Prnt GBR. Dist(s): Ulverscroft US

Like Father, Like Daughter. unabr. ed. Anne Baker. Read by Julia Franklin. 14 cass. (Running Time: 17 hrs. 30 min.). (Sound Ser.). 2001. 99.95 (978-1-84283-076-5(7)) Pub: UlverLrgPrint GBR. Dist(s): Ulverscroft US
Rebelling against the domineering man she believes to be her father, Elin Jones flees her Welsh home and takes a job as housemaid to the wealthy Oxley family. Seduced and left pregnant by Mr. Laurence, the handsome heir, Elin agrees to marry the family butler, to find herself condemned to a life of poverty and abuse. Only her love for her daughter Laura keeps her going.

Like Father, Like Son: 1 John 3:1-10. Ed Young. 1984. 4.95 (978-0-7417-1385-8(3), 385) Win Walk.

Like Gold Refined. unabr. ed. Janette Oke. Read by Marguerite Gavin. 6 CDs. (Running Time: 8 hrs. 30 mins.). (Prairie Legacy Ser.: Bk. 4). 2002. audio compact disk 48.00 (978-0-7861-9387-5(5), 3024); 44.95 (978-0-7861-2365-0(6), 3024) Blckstn Audio.
Virginia loves her life, living on the farm with her beloved Jonathan and their children, not far from her parents and her grandparents. But what troubles her is the gradual physical decline in Grandma Marty and Grandpa Clark. She cannot imagine life without their welcoming smiles and words of wisdom that arise from their life experiences and solid faith in God. And their daughter Mindy, who has blessed their home ever since her mother left the tiny child with them, has been encouraged to pray for that mother all these years. Is God answering that prayer, or is the worst nightmare any family could face now upon them?.

Like Gold Refined. unabr. ed. Janette Oke. Narrated by Alexandra O'Karma. 6 cass. (Running Time: 8 hrs. 45 mins.). (Prairie Legacy Ser.: Bk. 4). 2000. 57.00 (978-0-7887-4839-4(4), K0001E7) Recorded Bks.
Virginia Lewis is perfectly content with her peaceful existence, but change looms on the horizon. Grandma Marty & Grandpa Clark are aging & their health is suffering & Virginia's adopted daughter may be torn from the family when her absentee birth mother resurfaces.

Like Hidden Fire: The Plot to Bring down the British Empire. unabr. collector's ed. Peter Hopkirk. Read by David Case. 11 cass. (Running Time: 16 hrs. 30 min.). 1996. 88.00 (978-0-7366-3256-0(5), 3913) Books on Tape.
Under the banner of a Holy War, masterminded in Berlin & unleashed from Constantinople, the Germans & the Turks set out in 1914 to foment violent revolutionary uprisings against the British in India & the Russians in Central Asia. It was a new & more sinister version of the old Great Game, with world domination as its ultimate aim. The Shadowy - & often bloody - struggle was

fought out between intelligence services. Pieced together from the secret intelligence reports of the day & the long-forgotten memoirs of the participants, Peter Hopkirk's latest narrative is an enthralling sequel to the acclaimed "The Great Game," & his three earlier works in Central Asia.

Like Judgement Day: The Ruin & Redemption of a Town Called Rosewood. unabr. ed. Michael D'Orso. Narrated by Richard M. Davidson. 10 cass. (Running Time: 14 hrs. 15 mins.). 1996. 85.00 (978-0-7887-0561-8(X), 94740E7) Recorded Bks.
On New Year's Day 1923, Rosewood, Florida, a town of hard-working, middle class African Americans, was burned to the ground by an angry white mob.

Like Judgment Day. unabr. ed. Mike D'Orso. Narrated by Richard Davidson. 10 cass. (Running Time: 14 hrs. 25 min.). 1996. 85.00 Set. (94740) Recorded Bks.

Like Love. unabr. ed. Ed McBain, pseud. Read by Jonathan Marosz. 6 cass. (Running Time: 6 hrs.). (87th Precinct Ser.: Bk. 16). 1996. 36.00 (978-0-7366-3496-0(7), 4136) Books on Tape.
It's obviously a lover's pact, a double suicide: the note, the naked bodies, empty booze bottles, shut windows & gas pouring out of the stove.

Like Minded, Like Hearted - Out of Eden & NewSong (From Bridges) 1 cass. (Running Time: 1 hr.). 1999. 8.98 (978-0-7601-3150-3(3)) Provident Music.

Like Mother, Like Daughter. abr. ed. Debra Waterhouse. Read by Debra Waterhouse. (Running Time: 3 hrs.). 2008. 39.25 (978-1-4233-7178-6(X), 9781423371786, BADLE); 24.95 (978-1-4233-7177-9(1), 9781423371779, BAD); 24.95 (978-1-4233-7175-5(5), 9781423371755, Brilliance MP3); 39.25 (978-1-4233-7176-2(3), 9781423371762, Brinc Audio MP3 Lib) Brilliance Audio.

Like Snow see Robert Graves Reads from His Poetry & the White Goddess

***Like the Willow Tree - Audio.** Lois Lowry. (Dear America Ser.). (ENG.). 2011. audio compact disk 19.99 (978-0-545-27371-8(4)) Scholastic Inc.

***Like the Willow Tree - Audio Library Edition.** Lois Lowry. (Dear America Ser.). (ENG.). 2011. audio compact disk 29.99 (978-0-545-27372-5(2)) Scholastic Inc.

***Like the Wind: Ar Nos Na Gaoithe.** John Wynne. (ENG.). 2009. audio compact disk 25.95 (978-0-8023-8178-1(2)) Pub: Clo Iar-Chonnachta IRL. Dist(s): Dufour

Like Water for Chocolate: A Novel in Monthly Installments, with Recipes, Romances & Home Remedies. abr. ed. Laura Esquivel. Read by Yareli Arizmendi. (Running Time: 16200 sec.).Tr. of Como Agua para Chocolate. (ENG.). 2006. audio compact disk 14.99 (978-0-7393-3419-5(0), Random AudioBks) Pub: Random Audio Pubg. Dist(s): Random

Like Water for Chocolate: A Novel in Monthly Installments, with Recipes, Romances & Home Remedies. unabr. ed. Laura Esquivel. Read by Kate Reading. 7 cass. (Running Time: 7 hrs.).Tr. of Como Agua para Chocolate. 1994. 56.00 (978-0-7366-2606-4(9), 3349) Books on Tape.
A bestseller in Mexico, a box office hit worldwide, Like Water for Chocolate brings to life a family in turn-of-the-century Mexico. As youngest daughter, Tita's role is celibacy & domestic drudgery, i.e., to remain single & stay at home with her mother. So when Tita falls in love, Mama Elena arranges for Tita's older sister to marry Tita's young man. The story asks: "Whose side are you on".

Likely to Die. Linda Fairstein. (Alexandra Cooper Mysteries Ser.). 2004. 10.95 (978-0-7435-4976-9(7)) Pub: S&S Audio. Dist(s): S and S Inc

Likely to Die. unabr. ed. Linda Fairstein. Read by Bernadette Dunne. 8 cass. (Running Time: 12 hrs.). (Alexandra Cooper Mysteries Ser.). 1999. 64.00 (978-0-7366-4888-2(7), 5110) Books on Tape.
A behind-the-scene view of murder at a major Manhattan hospital.

Li'l Mama's Rules. Sheneska Jackson. Narrated by Patricia R. Floyd. 9 cass. (Running Time: 12 hrs. 15 mins.). 85.00 (978-1-4025-0274-3(5)) Recorded Bks.

Li'l Red Riding Hood - ShowTrax. Perf. by Sam the Sham and the Pharaohs. Arranged by Alan Billingsley. 1 CD. (Running Time: 5 mins.). 2000. audio compact disk 19.95 (08201219) H Leonard.
Sam the Sham's novelty hit of 1966 is a natural for guys' groups with campy comedy that will bring down the house!.

Lila: An Inquiry into Morals. unabr. ed. Robert M. Pirsig. Read by Michael Prichard. 10 cass. (Running Time: 15 hrs.). 1992. 80.00 (978-0-7366-2107-6(5), 2911) Books on Tape.
Thoughtful reflections on the human condition as revealed by Phaedrus & the people he meets, while traveling down the Hudson River.

Lilacs see Richard Wilbur Readings

Lilias Yoga Complete: A Comprehensive Course for Students of Any Level. unabr. rev. ed. Lilias Folan. Read by Lilias Folan. 3 CDs. (Running Time: 3 hrs. 0 mins. 0 sec.). (ENG.). 2004. audio compact disk 19.95 (978-1-59397-527-2(9)) Pub: Macmill Audio. Dist(s): Macmillan

Lilith. unabr. ed. George MacDonald. Read by Michael Zebulon. 7 cass. (Running Time: 10 hrs. 30 min.). 1989. 49.95 (978-0-7861-0206-8(3), 1181) Blckstn Audio.
This intriguing tale delights readers, as it is an excellent example of George MacDonald's allegorical style.

Lilith: Blight or Blessing. Lois Daton. 1 cass. (Running Time: 90 min.). 1984. 8.95 (078) Am Fed Astrologers.

Lilith: L-Book. Fran Heckrotte. Sheri. 2008. 14.95 (978-1-934889-05-3(9)) Lbook Pub.

Lillian Hellman. unabr. ed. Lillian Hellman. 1 cass. (Running Time: 1 hr.). (Author Speaks Ser.). 1991. 14.95 J Norton Pubs.
Archival recordings of 20th-century authors.

***Lilly & the Sockeyes.** Sara Paretsky. 2009. (978-1-60136-541-5(1)) Audio Holding.

Lilly in Phily. John Lilly. 1 cass. (Running Time: 1 hr.). 9.00 (A0246-87) Sound Photosyn.

Lilly on Dolphins. unabr. ed. John Lilly. 1 cass. (Running Time: 1 hr.). 1987. 10.00 (978-1-56964-772-1(0), A0296-78) Sound Photosyn.
From Dr. Lilly's personal collection.

Lilly's Big Day. Kevin Henkes. Read by Laura Hamilton. 1 CD. (Running Time: 29 mins.). (J). (ps-2). 2007. bk. 28.95 (978-1-4301-0030-0(3)) Live Oak Media.

Lilly's Big Day. Kevin Henkes. Read by Laura Hamilton. 1 cass. (Running Time: 29 mins.). (J). (ps-2). 2007. bk. 28.95 (978-1-4301-0027-0(3)) Live Oak Media.

Lilly's Big Day & Other Stories. unabr. ed. Kevin Henkes. Read by Richard Thomas & Christine Ebersole. 1 CD. (Running Time: 3600 sec.). (J). (ps-3). 2006. 14.95 (978-0-06-113044-1(3), HarperChildAud) HarperCollins Pubs.

Lilly's Pond Vol. 1: The Adventure of Silly Willy Caterpillie. Linda L. Lumpkin. 1 CD. (Running Time: 23 mins.). (J). 2000. audio compact disk 13.95 (978-1-891543-01-2(6), Wide-Eyed Pub) MicroNova.

Lilly's Pond Vol. 1: The Adventure of Willy Willy Caterpillie. Linda L. Lumpkin. Read by Linda L. Lumpkin. 1 cass. (Running Time: 23 mins.). (J). (ps-6). 2000. 9.95 (978-1-891543-02-9(4), Wide-Eyed Pub) MicroNova.
A fully scored musical version of the book. Contains 6 original songs.

Lilly's Purple Plastic Purse see Lily y Su Bolso de Plastico Morado

Lilly's Purple Plastic Purse. Kevin Henkes. Read by Laura Hamilton. 11 vols. (Running Time: 16 mins.). (J). (gr. k-3). 2000. pap. bk. 25.95 (978-0-87499-687-6(2)) AudioGO.
Lilly the mouse idolizes her teacher Mr. Slinger, but when she comes to school flaunting three jingly quarters, movie-star glasses & a purple plastic purse, she interrupts Mr. Slinger's lessons. After one too many disruptions, he confiscates the purse until the day's end. Lilly, humiliated, takes revenge by slipping a mean drawing into Mr. Slinger's book bag, only to open her purse & find a conciliatory note from her hero.

Lilly's Purple Plastic Purse. Kevin Henkes. Illus. by Kevin Henkes. 11 vols. (Running Time: 16 mins.). pap. bk. 16.95 (978-0-87499-686-9(4)); pap. bk. (978-0-87499-688-3(0)); pap. bk. 18.95 (978-1-59112-347-7(X)); pap. bk. (978-1-59112-557-0(X)) Live Oak Media.

Lilly's Purple Plastic Purse. Kevin Henkes. Read by Laura Hamilton. 1 cass. (Running Time: 16 mins.). (J). 2000. 9.95 (978-0-87499-685-2(6)) Pub: Live Oak Media. Dist(s): Lectorum Pubns
Lily takes her new purse, movie star sunglasses & three shiny quarters to school to share with her classmates. When things unexpectedly go wrong, Lily learns about patience & forgiveness.

Lilly's Purple Plastic Purse. Kevin Henkes. Illus. by Kevin Henkes. (Running Time: 16 mins.). 2000. audio compact disk 12.95 (978-1-59112-346-0(1)) Live Oak Media.

***Lilly's Wedding Quilt.** unabr. ed. Kelly Long. Read by To be Announced. (Running Time: 10 hrs. 5 mins.). (Patch of Heaven Novels Ser.). (ENG.). 2011. 29.95 (978-1-4417-7717-1(2)); 65.95 (978-1-4417-7714-0(8)); audio compact disk 100.00 (978-1-4417-7715-7(6)) Blckstn Audio.

Lily B. on the Brink of Paris. Elizabeth Cody Kimmel. 3 cass. (Running Time: 4 hrs. 45 mins.). (J). (gr. 4-8). 2004. 25.50 (978-0-8072-2088-7(4), Listening Lib) Pub: Random Audio Pubg. Dist(s): NetLibrary CO
Lily's Likes: Recording daily events in her notebook, alphabetizing books on her shelves, writing top-ten lists.Lily's Dislikes: Family outings, people who make their own beds in hotels (like her mother), and most of the items in her closet. Favorite Meal: Tacos and root beer. Favorite Daydream: Winning the Congressional Medal of Honor by saving the President from attack dogs using only a raincoat and a hanger. Lily is having the most boring summer EVER. Her best friend has abandoned her for Young Executives Camp, and there is nothing to do but go on family outings with her parents. Then Lily meets the coolest girl, Kama, and her incredibly cool parents. And guess what? They're her relatives! This summer is looking up, and Lily things she just might be on the brink of cool.

Lily Golightly. unabr. ed. Pamela Oldfield. Read by Margaret Holt. 14 cass. (Running Time: 21 hrs.). 2000. 99.95 (978-1-86042-740-4(5), 27405) Pub: Soundings Ltd GBR. Dist(s): Ulverscroft US
Newly married Lily Golightly's husband, Patrick, sets sail for New York but soon succumbs to gold fever & plans to go west to California. Lily, Patrick & their young housemaid are joined by an assortment of fellow travelers & together they experience hardship & deprivation, the pain of love & loss & the bitterness of betrayal.

Lily Hand & Other Stories. unabr. ed. Short Stories. Edith Pargeter. Read by Shirley Dixon. 6 cass. (Running Time: 9 hrs.). (Isis Ser.). (J). 2004. 54.95 (978-0-7531-0475-0(X), 981002) Pub: ISIS Lrg Prnt GBR. Dist(s): Ulverscroft US
Pargeter also writes as Ellis Peters. From the creator of "The Brother Cadfael Chronicles" this classic collection of stories ranges geographically across the world, from India to Europe to the old eastern Bloc. The stories are: A Grain of Mustard Seed, Light-Boy' Grim Fairy Tale; Trump of Doom; The Man Who Met Himself; The linnett in the Garden; How Beautiful is Youth; All Souls' Day; The Cradle; My Friend the Enemy; The Lily Hand; A Question of Faith; The Purple Children' I am a Seagull; Carnival Night; & The Ultimate Romeo & Juliet.

Lily in the Valley: Victory in Praise Music & Arts Seminar Mass Choir. Perf. by John P. Kee & Victory in Praise Music and Arts Seminar Mass Choir. 1 cass., 1 CD. (Running Time: 1 hr.). Provident Mus Dist.

Lily-Josephine. unabr. ed. Kate Saunders. Read by Sian Phillips. 12 cass. (Running Time: 12 hrs.). 1999. 96.95 (978-0-7540-0290-1(X), CAB 1713) AudioGO.

***Lily of Love Lane.** Carol Rivers & Annie Aldington. 2010. 99.95 (978-1-84652-519-3(5)); 84.95 (978-1-84652-518-6(7)) Pub: Magna Story GBR. Dist(s): Ulverscroft US

Lily White. Susan Isaacs & Grace Conlin. 14 cass. (Running Time: 20 hrs. 30 mins.). 2002. 89.95 (978-0-7861-1028-5(7), 1803) Blckstn Audio.

Lily White. unabr. ed. Susan Isaacs. 14 cass. (Running Time: 21 hrs.). 1996. 89.95 SET. (1803) Blckstn Audio.
The Jewish American experience interwoven with a mystery. A fiftyish criminal defense attorney saddled with a career con man accused of murdering his latest mark.

Lily White. unabr. ed. Susan Isaacs. Read by Grace Conlin. (Running Time: 20 hrs. 0 mins.). 2010. 44.95 (978-1-4417-1744-3(7)); audio compact disk 123.00 (978-1-4417-1741-2(2)) Blckstn Audio.

Lily y Su Bolso de Plastico Morado. Kevin Henkes. Read by Susan Rybin. 11 vols. (Running Time: 20 mins.).Tr. of Lilly's Purple Plastic Purse. (SPA., (J). (ps-4). 2001. pap. bk. 16.95 (978-0-87499-811-5(5)) Pub: Live Oak Media. Dist(s): AudioGO

Lily y Su Bolso de Plastico Morado. Kevin Henkes. Illus. by Kevin Henkes. 11 vols. (Running Time: 20 mins.).Tr. of Lilly's Purple Plastic Purse. 2001. bk. 25.95 (978-0-87499-812-2(3)); bk. 28.95 (978-1-59519-179-3(8)); pap. bk. 41.95 (978-0-87499-813-9(1)); pap. bk. 43.95 (978-1-59519-178-6(X)); 9.95 (978-0-87499-810-8(7)); audio compact disk 12.95 (978-1-59519-176-2(3)) Live Oak Media.

Lily y Su Bolso de Plastico Morado. Kevin Henkes. Illus. by Kevin Henkes. 11 vols. (Running Time: 20 mins.).Tr. of Lilly's Purple Plastic Purse. (SPA.). (J). 2005. pap. bk. 18.95 (978-1-59519-177-9(1)) Pub: Live Oak Media. Dist(s): AudioGO

Lily's Crossing. Patricia Reilly Giff. Read by Mia Dillon. 3 cass. (Running Time: 4 hrs.). (J). 2000. 24.00 (978-0-7366-9035-5(2)) Books on Tape.
It's the summer of 1944 & Lily is angry that her father has volunteered to go overseas to war. When she befriends the only person at Rockaway Beach near her age, a refugee from Hungary named Albert, she discovers the comforting power of friendship & love.

Lily's Crossing. Patricia Reilly Giff. (YA). 2002. 17.99 (978-0-8072-0878-6(7), Listening Lib) Random Audio Pubg.

Lily's Crossing. unabr. ed. Patricia Reilly Giff. Read by Mia Dillon. 3 vols. (Running Time: 3 hrs. 59 mins.). (J). (gr. 3-7). 2004. pap. bk. 36.00 (978-0-8072-0454-2(4), Listening Lib); 30.00 (978-0-8072-0453-5(6), Listening Lib) Random Audio Pubg.

Lily's Crossing, unabr. ed. Patricia Reilly Giff. Narrated by Christina Moore. 3 pieces. (Running Time: 4 hrs. 15 mins.). (gr. 3 up). 1997. 27.00 (978-0-7887-1106-0(7), 95099E7) Recorded Bks.
Young Lily is looking forward to her 1944 summer vacation at the family beach home. Suddenly her father must go to Europe where the war is raging. No one seems to understand how terrible she feels, until she meets a young refugee with a terrible secret.

Lily's Crossing. unabr. ed. Patricia Reilly Giff. Read by Mia Dillon. 4 CDs. (Running Time: 3 hrs. 45 mins.). (ENG.). (J). (gr. 3). 2005. audio compact disk 19.95 (978-0-307-24322-5(2), Listening Lib) Pub: Random Audio Pubg. Dist(s): Random

***Lily's Journey.** Tania Crosse. Read by Tanya Myers. 2010. 84.95 (978-1-84652-595-7(0)); audio compact disk 99.95 (978-1-84652-596-4(9)) Pub: Magna Story GBR. Dist(s): Ulverscroft US

Limbic. Ed. by Robert A. Monroe. 1 cass. (Running Time: 30 min.). (Meta Music Ser.). 1985. 12.95 (978-1-56102-214-4(4)) Inter Indus.
Permits the contemplative listener an opportunity for deep exploration of areas in the brain/mind system other than the neo-cortex, to experience self at genetic & instinctual levels.

Limbo Rock - ShowTrax. Arranged by Alan Billingsley. 1 CD. (Running Time: 30 min.). 2000. audio compact disk 19.95 (08551446) H Leonard.
How low can you go! This calypso-flavored 1962 pop hit by Chubby Checker is great fun for middle school & elementary groups & makes a super choreography feature.

Lime Street Blues. Maureen Lee. Read by Maggie Ollerenshaw. 10 vols. (Running Time: 15 hrs.). 2003. 84.95 (978-0-7540-8371-9(3)) Pub: Chivers Audio Bks GBR. Dist(s): AudioGO

Limestone Cowboy. Stuart Pawson & Andrew Wincott. 2009. 54.95 (978-1-84652-383-0(4)); audio compact disk 71.95 (978-1-84652-384-7(2)) Pub: Magna Story GBR. Dist(s): Ulverscroft US

Liminoid & the Liminal. Read by Robert Moore. 1 cass. (Running Time: 90 min.). 1984. 9.95 (978-0-7822-0171-0(7), 151) C G Jung IL.

***Limit.** unabr. ed. Kristen Landon. (Running Time: 9 hrs. 30 mins. 0 sec.). (ENG.). (J). 2010. audio compact disk 34.99 (978-1-4423-3416-8(9)) Pub: S&S Audio. Dist(s): S and S Inc

Limitations. unabr. ed. Scott Turow. Read by Stephen Lang. (Running Time: 21600 sec.). (ENG.). 2006. audio compact disk 29.95 (978-0-7393-4155-1(3), Random AudioBks) Pub: Random Audio Pubg. Dist(s): Random

Limited Government & Peace. John Robbins. 1 cass. (Running Time: 1 hr.). (Introduction to Economics Ser.: No. 12). 5.00 Trinity Found.

Limited Liability Entities: Emerging Issues in Drafting Agreements for LLCs & Partnerships. 3 cass. (Running Time: 3 hrs. 30 min.). 1999. 165.00 (D287) Am Law Inst.
Intermediate-level update examines important issues confronting practitioners as they draft operating agreements for limited liability companies (LLCs).

Limited Options. Palma Harcourt. Read by Robert Forster. 6 cass. (Running Time: 9 hrs.). 1989. 54.95 (978-1-85496-292-8(2), 62922) Pub: UlverLrgPrint GBR. Dist(s): Ulverscroft US

Limiting Liberty Pt. 11: 1 Cor. 8:1-13. Ed Young. 1986. 4.95 (978-0-7417-1499-2(X), 499) Win Walk.

Limiting Liberty vol. 498, Part 1: 1 Cor. 8:1-13. Ed Young. 1986. 4.95 (978-0-7417-1498-5(1)) Win Walk.

Limitless Learning: Making Powerful Learning an Everyday Event. Douglas M. McPhee. Frwd. by Arthur L. Costa. 2 cass. (Running Time: 1 hr.). 1996. wbk. ed. 15.00 (1605-F3, ZephPr) Chicago Review.
Teach your students about higher-order thinking, learning styles, & multiple intelligences. Orchestrate learning so the brain will choose to remember, consolidate, integrate, & process information. You'll find powerful instructional ideas to - Create an effective environment; Engage learners; Set the stage with expectancy preparation; & Promote active participation with congruent activities.

Limitless Learning: Making Powerful Learning an Everyday Event. Douglas M. McPhee. 2 cass. (Running Time: 1 hr.). pap. bk. 39.00 OptimaLearning.
New strategies to bring success to all learners. Teaches about higher-order thinking, learning styles, & multiple intelligences. Orchestrates learning so the brain will choose to remember, consolidate, integrate, & process information.

Limitless Play of Perfection. Swami Amar Jyoti. 1 cass. (Running Time: 1 hr.). 1995. 9.95 (K-146) Truth Consciousness.
Perfection includes everything, excludes nothing, because all Perfection is One. Understanding darkness as an ingredient of God's creation.

Limitless Resources for Total Outreach. Derek Prince. 1 cass. (Running Time: 1 hr.). (B-4099) Derek Prince.

Limits of Art & Edges of Science. Terence McKenna. 1 cass. (Running Time: 1 hr.). 1992. 9.00 (OC287-63) Sound Horizons AV.

Limits of Intelligence. 1 cass. (Running Time: 1 hr.). (Opening Up to Superconciousness Ser.). 9.95 (84W) Crystal Clarity.
Includes: How exessive reasoning affects the flow of intuition; the importance of offering intelligence up to a higher reality; ways to draw energy into the higher chakras; learning to talk with your eyes.

Limits of Perception. Swami Amar Jyoti. 1 cass. (Running Time: 1 hr.). 1989. 9.95 (K-112) Truth Consciousness.
God, guru, always give the totality; we see only up to our limit. Yoga science.

Limits of Power: The End of American Exceptionalism. unabr. ed. Andrew J. Bacevich. Read by Eric Conger. 5 CDs. (Running Time: 6 hrs. 0 mins. 0 sec.). (ENG.). 2008. audio compact disk 29.95 (978-1-4272-0688-6(0)) Pub: Macmill Audio. Dist(s): Macmillan

Limits of Science. unabr. ed. Gregory Bateson. 1 cass. (Running Time: 1 hr. 28 min.). 1978. 11.00 (02803) Big Sur Tapes.
Discussion on many topics including human interaction with animals & the difficulties in scientific inquiry any time the human mind enters the picture.

Limits with Love: Effective Discipline Strategies. John F. Taylor. 1 cass. (Running Time: 51 min.). (Answers to ADD Ser.). 1993. 9.95 (978-1-883963-08-8(7)) ADD Plus.
Lecture tape.

Limp Bizkit X-Posed. Chrome Dreams. (ENG., 2002. audio compact disk 14.95 (978-1-84240-162-0(9)) Pub: Chrome Dreams GBR. Dist(s): IPG Chicago

LIMS System for Analytical Chemistry for Technicians. 3rd rev. ed. Laurie Kelly et al. 2004. audio compact disk (978-1-56670-632-2(7)) CRC Pr.

Lin McLean. unabr. ed. Owen Wister. Read by Jack Sondericker. 6 cass. (Running Time: 8 hrs.). 1986. 39.95 (978-1-55686-236-6(9), 236) Books in Motion.
Sequel to Owen Wister's better known book, The Virginian. True to life story of what it was like to be a cow-puncher in the Wyoming Territory before the land was fenced in.

Linchpin: Are You Indispensable? abr. ed. Seth Godin. Read by Seth Godin. (ENG.). 2010. audio compact disk 15.00 (978-0-307-70407-8(6), Random AudioBks) Pub: Random Audio Pubg. Dist(s): Random

***Linchpin: Are You Indispensable?** unabr. ed. Seth Godin. Read by Seth Godin. 7 CDs. (Running Time: 8 hrs. 30 mins.). 2010. audio compact disk 80.00 (978-0-307-70550-1(1), BksonTape) Pub: Random Audio Pubg. Dist(s): Random

Lincoln. Gore Vidal. Read by Grover Gardner. 1993. 72.00 (978-0-7366-2413-8(9)) Books on Tape.

Lincoln. unabr. ed. Lord Charnwood. Read by Robert Whitfield. 11 cass. (Running Time: 16 hrs. 30 min.). 1999. 76.95 (2347) Blckstn Audio.
For eighty years the standard life of the great Emancipator & one of the great classics of modem biography.

Lincoln. unabr. ed. Lord Charnwood. Read by Robert Whitfield. 11 cass. (Running Time: 16 hrs.). 2004. 76.95 (978-0-7861-1496-2(7), 2347) Blckstn Audio.

Lincoln. unabr. ed. Lord Charnwood. Read by Robert Whitfield. (Running Time: 55800 sec.). 2008. audio compact disk 29.95 (978-1-4332-4509-1(4)); audio compact disk & audio compact disk 95.95 (978-1-4332-4508-4(6)) Blckstn Audio.

Lincoln. unabr. ed. David Herbert Donald. Read by Dick Estell. 21 cass. (Running Time: 31 hrs. 30 min.). 1996. 168.00 (978-0-7366-3538-7(6), 4186 A/B) Books on Tape.
So lucid & richly researched, so careful & compelling, it is hard to imagine a more satisfying life of our most admired & least understood president.

Lincoln. unabr. ed. David Herbert Donald. Read by Norman Dietz. 28 cass. (Running Time: 39 hrs. 75 mns.). 2006. 113.75 (978-1-4025-5673-9(X)) Recorded Bks.

Lincoln, Pt. 1. unabr. ed. David Herbert Donald. Read by Dick Estell. 10 cass. (Running Time: 15 hrs.). 1996. 80.00 (4186-A) Books on Tape.
Lincoln was principled but politically ambitious & offers fresh insights on his family life.

Lincoln, Pt. 2. unabr. ed. David Herbert Donald. Read by Dick Estell. 11 cass. (Running Time: 16 hrs. 30 mins.). 1996. 88.00 (4186-B) Books on Tape.
Lincoln was a principled but politically ambitious & offers new insights on his family life.

Lincoln: A Biography. abr. ed. Philip B. Kunhardt & Peter W. Kunhardt. Read by Frank Langella. (ENG.). 2008. audio compact disk 19.99 (978-0-7393-8380-3(9), Random AudioBks) Pub: Random Audio Pubg. Dist(s): Random

Lincoln: A Life of Purpose & Power. Richard J. Carwardine. Read by Dick Hill. (Running Time: 55800 sec.). 2006. audio compact disk 99.00 (978-0-7861-7149-1(9)) Blckstn Audio.

Lincoln: A Life of Purpose & Power. Richard J. Carwardine. Read by Dick Hill. Created by Blackstone Audiobooks. (Running Time: 55800 sec.). 2006. 85.95 (978-0-7861-4499-0(8)) Blckstn Audio.

Lincoln: A Life of Purpose & Power. unabr. ed. Richard Carwardine. 11 cass. (Running Time: 13 hrs. 30 mins.). (YA). 2006. 29.95 (978-0-7861-4388-7(6)) Blckstn Audio.

Lincoln: A Life of Purpose & Power. unabr. ed. Richard Carwardine. Read by Stefan Rudnicki. (Running Time: 15 hrs. 5 mins.). 2009. 29.95 (978-1-4332-6459-7(5)); audio compact disk 89.95 (978-1-4332-6455-9(2)); audio compact disk 110.00 (978-1-4332-6456-6(0)) Blckstn Audio.

Lincoln: A Life of Purpose & Power. unabr. ed. Richard J. Carwardine. Read by Dick Hill. 12 CDs. (Running Time: 55800 sec.). 2006. audio compact disk 32.95 (978-0-7861-7475-5(3)) Blckstn Audio.

Lincoln: A Photobiography. unabr. ed. Russell Freedman. Read by Robert Petkoff. 2 CDs. (Running Time: 2 hrs. 29 mins.). (YA). (gr. 5 up). 2008. audio compact disk 24.00 (978-0-7393-7257-9(2), Listening Lib) Pub: Random Audio Pubg. Dist(s): Random

Lincoln: A Photobiography. unabr. ed. Russell Freedman. Read by Robert Petkoff. (ENG.). (J). (gr. 3). 2008. audio compact disk 19.95 (978-0-7393-7255-5(6), Listening Lib) Pub: Random Audio Pubg. Dist(s): Random

Lincoln: The Biography of a Writer. unabr. ed. Fred Kaplan. Read by Dan John Miller. (Running Time: 15 hrs.). 2008. 39.25 (978-1-4233-7104-5(6), 9781423371045, BADLE); 39.25 (978-1-4233-7102-1(X), 9781423371021, Brlnc Audio MP3 Lib); 24.95 (978-1-4233-7101-4(1), 9781423371014, Brilliance MP3) Brilliance Audio.

Lincoln: The Biography of a Writer. unabr. ed. Fred Kaplan. Read by Dan john Miller. (Running Time: 15 hrs.). 2008. 24.95 (978-1-4233-7103-8(8), 9781423371038, BAD) Brilliance Audio.

Lincoln: The Biography of a Writer. unabr. ed. Fred Kaplan. Read by Dan John Miller. 13 CDs. (Running Time: 15 hrs.). 2008. audio compact disk 107.25 (978-1-4233-7100-7(3), 9781423371007, BriAudCD Unabrid); audio compact disk 34.99 (978-1-4233-7099-4(6), 9781423370994, Bril Audio CD Unabri) Brilliance Audio.

Lincoln: The Prairie Years. Carl Sandburg. Read by Gregory Peck. 1 cass. (Running Time: 60 min.). Incl. Goodbye, Mr. Chips. Perf. by Ronald Colman. (J). 1949. (DD-8040); 1949. 7.95 (DD-8040) Natl Recrd Co.
Carl Sandburg's Lincoln gives you the chance to learn about a great man through this Hallmark Playhouse adaptation.

Lincoln Pt. 1: A Novel. Gore Vidal. Read by Grover Gardner. 9 cass. (Running Time: 13 hrs. 30 min.). (American Chronicles Ser.). 1993. 72.00 (978-0-7366-2412-1(0), 3180-A) Books on Tape.
Fictional portrait of Lincoln as seen through the eyes of those around him.

Lincoln Pt. 2: A Novel. unabr. ed. Gore Vidal. Read by Grover Gardner. 9 cass. (Running Time: 13 hrs. 30 min.). (American Chronicles Ser.: Vol. 1). 1993. 80.00 (3180-B) Books on Tape.
Fictional portrait of Lincoln as seen through the eyes of those around him.

Lincoln & Chief Justice Taney: Slavery, Seccession & the President's War Powers. unabr. ed. James F. Simon. Read by Richard Allen. (Running Time: 11 hrs. 30 mins. 0 sec.). (ENG.). 2006. audio compact disk 69.99 (978-1-4001-3331-4(9)) Pub: Tantor Media. Dist(s): IngramPubServ

Lincoln & Chief Justice Taney: Slavery, Seccession, & the President's War Powers. unabr. ed. James F. Simon. Read by Richard Allen. 8 CDs. (Running Time: 11 hrs. 30 mins. 0 sec.). (ENG.). 2006. audio compact disk 34.99 (978-1-4001-0331-7(2)); audio compact disk 24.99 (978-1-4001-5331-2(X)) Pub: Tantor Media. Dist(s): IngramPubServ

Lincoln & Douglass: An American Friendship. Nikki Giovanni. Illus. by Bryan Collier. Narrated by Danny Glover. Music by Ernest V. Troost. 1 CD. (Running Time: 16 mins.). (J). (ps-3). 2009. bk. 29.95 (978-0-545-13457-6(9)); audio compact disk 12.95 (978-0-545-13447-7(1)) Weston Woods.

Lincoln & His Generals. unabr. collector's ed. T. Harry Williams. Read by Dick Estell. 8 cass. (Running Time: 12 hrs.). 1989. 64.00 (978-0-7366-1484-9(2), 2360) Books on Tape.
Looks at the account of Lincoln's search for a winning general in the war between the states & of Lincoln's emergence as a master strategist & great commander-in-chief.

Lincoln & the Decision for War: The Northern Response to Secession. Russell A. McClintock. (ENG.). 2008. 36.95 (978-0-8078-8635-9(1)); audio compact disk 36.95 (978-0-8078-8637-3(8)) U of NC Pr.

Lincoln & the Negro. unabr. collector's ed. Benjamin Quarles. Read by Jonathan Reese. 7 cass. (Running Time: 10 hrs. 30 min.). 1996. 56.00 (978-0-7366-3292-8(1), 3947) Books on Tape.
In his youth, Lincoln was ambivalent in his attitude toward blacks, but came to believe in their emancipation & equal rights. In a sense, he gave his life for his beliefs. But what did blacks think of him? Not much, at first. But their attitudes evolved with his, & slowly he eamed their respect by opening the Union Army to them, inviting blacks to the White House &, ultimately, issuing the famous proclamation. Lincoln's assassination enshrined him in the black pantheon.

Lincoln Assassination. (Presidency Ser.). 10.00 Esstee Audios.

Lincoln-Douglas Debates. unabr. ed. Abraham Lincoln & Stephen Douglas. Narrated by Richard Dreyfuss & David Strathairn. 2 MP3-CDs. (Running Time: 16 hrs.). 2009. 69.95 (978-0-7927-6173-0(1), Chivers Sound Lib); audio compact disk 115.95 (978-0-7927-6031-3(X), Chivers Sound Lib) AudioGO.

Lincoln-Douglas Debates. unabr. ed. Abraham Lincoln & Stephen Douglas. Narrated by David Strathairn. Richard Dreyfuss. Intro. by Allen C. Guelzo. Narrated by Richard Dreyfuss. 14 CDs. (ENG.). 2008. audio compact disk 39.95 (978-1-60283-402-6(4)) Pub: AudioGO. Dist(s): Perseus Dist

***Lincoln Lawyer.** Michael Connelly. Read by Adam Grupper. (Running Time: 11 hrs.). (Mickey Haller Ser.). 2011. audio compact disk & audio compact disk 17.98 (978-1-60941-786-4(0)) Pub: Hachet Audio. Dist(s): HachBkGrp

Lincoln Lawyer. unabr. ed. Michael Connelly. Read by Adam Grupper. 7 cass. (Running Time: 10 hrs. 30 mins.). (Mickey Haller Ser.). 2005. 90.00 (978-1-4159-2328-3(0)); audio compact disk 90.00 (978-1-4159-2329-0(9)) Books on Tape.

Lincoln Lawyer. unabr. ed. Michael Connelly. Read by Adam Grupper. (Mickey Haller Ser.). (YA). 2007. 69.99 (978-1-60252-688-4(5)) Find a World.

Lincoln Lawyer. unabr. ed. Michael Connelly. Read by Adam Grupper. (Mickey Haller Ser.). 2005. 14.98 (978-1-59483-258-1(7)) Pub: Hachet Audio. Dist(s): HachBkGrp

Lincoln Lawyer. unabr. ed. Michael Connelly. Read by Adam Grupper. (Running Time: 11 hrs.). (ENG.). 2007. audio compact disk 14.98 (978-1-60024-247-2(2)) Pub: Hachet Audio. Dist(s): HachBkGrp

Lincoln Lawyer. unabr. ed. Michael Connelly. Read by Adam Grupper. (Running Time: 11 hrs.). (Mickey Haller Ser.). 2009. 70.98 (978-1-60788-100-1(4)) Pub: Hachet Audio. Dist(s): HachBkGrp

Lincoln on Leadership: Executive Strategies for Tough Times. unabr. ed. Donald T. Phillips. Narrated by Nelson Runger. 5 cass. (Running Time: 6 hrs. 30 mins.). 1992. 44.00 (978-0-7887-3573-8(X), 95938E7) Recorded Bks.
Donald T. Phillips explores Lincoln's effective leadership style. He shares how you can apply successful strategies: seize the initiative, wage only one war at a time, encourage risk-taking, and more.

Lincoln on Leadership: Executive Strategies for Tough Times. unabr. ed. Donald T. Phillips. Narrated by Nelson Runger. 6 CDs. (Running Time: 6 hrs. 30 mins.). 2000. audio compact disk 54.00 (978-0-7887-3979-8(4), C1098E7) Recorded Bks.

Lincoln Poems Audio Book. Dan Guillory. (ENG.). 2009. audio compact disk 19.95 (978-1-932278-54-5(0)) Pub: Mayhaven Pub. Dist(s): Baker Taylor

Lincoln Secret. 2009. 20.00 (978-0-9814822-1-7(X)) Martin Pearl.

Lincoln Theatre see Poetry of Langston Hughes

Lincolns: Portrait of a Marriage. unabr. ed. Daniel Mark Epstein. Narrated by Adam Grupper. (Running Time: 21 hrs. 30 mins.). 2008. 74.95 (978-0-7927-5567-8(7)) AudioGO.

Lincolns: Portrait of a Marriage. unabr. ed. Daniel Mark Epstein. Narrated by Adam Grupper. (Running Time: 78720 sec.). (ENG.). 2008. audio compact disk 39.95 (978-1-60283-414-9(8)) Pub: AudioGO. Dist(s): Perseus Dist

Lincolns: Portrait of a Marriage. unabr. ed. Daniel Mark Epstein. Narrated by Adam Grupper. 16 CDs. (Running Time: 19 hrs.). 2008. audio compact disk 119.95 (978-0-7927-5461-9(1)) AudioGO.
She was witty, tempestuous, a Kentucky blueblood; he was brilliant, moody, a farmer's son born in a log-cabin. They got married on a few hours notice in 1842, when he was thirty-three and she was nearly twenty-four. Spanning their mysterious and troubled courtship in 1840 through his assassination in Ford's Theatre in 1865, Daniel Mark Epstein has produced an incisive and balanced portrait of the Lincolns. The only book-length treatment of the marriage was published in 1953, when scholars lacked today's resources, and were still struggling with deep-seated prejudices about Mary Todd and Abraham Lincoln. For the first time, in The Lincolns: Portrait of a Marriage we can feel the full force of the tragedy that was the slow crumbling of their marriage, knowing it intimately from the first act to the last.

Lincoln's Bloomington & Normal Illinois: A Tour Narrated by Abraham Lincoln. Scripts. Perf. by James Keeran. 1. Dramatization. 2006. 19.95 (978-0-943788-32-6(3)) McLean County.
Abraham Lincoln gives you a tour of Bloomington and Normal sites that he visted, before he became president.

Lincoln's Greatest Speech: The Second Inaugural. unabr. ed. Ronald C. White, Jr. Read by Raymond Todd. 5 cass. (Running Time: 7 hrs.). 2003. 39.95 (978-0-7861-2383-4(4), 3060) Blckstn Audio.
White's analysis of Lincoln's second inaugural speech, given after four years of the unspeakable horror of the Civil War, offers new insight into Lincoln's own victory over doubt and his promise of authority and passion.

Lincoln's Greatest Speech: The Second Inaugural. unabr. ed. Ronald C. White, Jr. Read by Raymond Todd. 6 CDs. (Running Time: 7 hrs.). 2003. audio compact disk 48.00 (978-0-7861-9292-2(5), 3060) Blckstn Audio.

Lincoln's Letters. unabr. ed. Abraham Lincoln. Read by George Vafiadis. 3 cds. (Running Time: 2 hrs 42 mins). 2002. audio compact disk 24.95 (978-1-58472-281-6(9), 025, In Aud) Pub: Sound Room. Dist(s): Baker Taylor

Lincoln's Letters: The Private Man & the Warrior. unabr. ed. Abraham Lincoln. Read by George Vafiadis. 3 cds. (Running Time: 2 hrs 42 mins). 2002. pap. bk. (978-1-58472-283-0(5), In Aud) Sound Room.

Lincoln's Letters: The Private Man & the Warrior. unabr. ed. Abraham Lincoln. Read by George Vail. 2 cass. (Running Time: 2 hrs. 45 mins.). 1995. bk. 16.95 (978-1-883049-50-8(4), Commuters Library); lib. bdg. 18.95 (978-1-883049-51-5(2)) Sound Room.
With humor & humility, Lincoln tells his own story. His ambition, self-doubt, heartbreak, & frustration come across the years with clarity in this wonderful reading. The letters begin when Lincoln was a young man & tell of his courtship & early political life, & continue into the presidency where Lincoln learned to wage war. This audio book provides a unique insight into the man, the times & the making of this country.

Lincoln's Letters & Lincoln's Prose: The Private Man & the Warrior & Major Works by a Great American Writer. unabr. ed. Abraham Lincoln. Read by George Vail. (YA). 2007. 49.99 (978-1-59895-933-8(6)) Find a World.

Lincoln's Letters, Essays & Speeches. Abraham Lincoln. Narrated by George Vafiadis. (Unabridged Classics in MP3 Ser.). (ENG.). 2008. audio compact disk 24.00 (978-1-58472-621-0(0), In Aud); audio compact disk 14.95 (978-1-58472-622-7(9), In Aud) Sound Room.

Lincoln's Letters: the Private Man & the Warrior: The Private Man & the Warrior. Abraham Lincoln. Read by George Vafiadis. (Running Time: 3 hrs.). 2002. 19.95 (978-1-59912-089-8(5), Audiofy Corp) Iofy Corp.

Lincoln's Melancholy: How Depression Challenged a President & Fueled His Greatness. unabr. ed. Joshua Wolf Shenk. Read by Richardson Davidson. (YA). 2007. 44.99 (978-1-60252-507-8(2)) Find a World.

Lincoln's Melancholy: How Depression Challenged a President & Fueled His Greatness. unabr. ed. Joshua Wolf Shenk. Read by Richard M. Davidson & Richard Davidson. 9 CDs. (Running Time: 42300 sec.). (ENG.). 2005. audio compact disk 36.95 (978-1-59887-004-6(1), 1598870041) Pub: HighBridge. Dist(s): Workman Pub

Lincoln's Prose. Abraham Lincoln. Narrated by George Vafiadis. (Our American Heritage Ser.). (ENG.). 2008. audio compact disk 24.00 (978-1-58472-658-6(X), In Aud) Sound Room.

Lincoln's Prose. unabr. ed. Speeches. Abraham Lincoln. Read by George Vafiadis. 3 cds. (Running Time: 2 hrs 43 mins). 2002. audio compact disk 24.95 (978-1-58472-284-7(3), 026, In Aud) Pub: Sound Room. Dist(s): Baker Taylor
A selection of Lincoln's best writings (speeches and essays). It includes the Gettysburg Address.

Lincoln's Prose: Major Works of a Great American Writer. unabr. ed. Abraham Lincoln. Read by George Vafiadis. 3 cds. (Running Time: 2 hrs 43 mins). 2002. pap. bk. (978-1-58472-286-1(X), In Aud) Sound Room.
Includes the Gettysburg Address and other essays.

Lincoln's Prose: Major Works of a Great American Writer. unabr. ed. Abraham Lincoln. Read by George Vail. 2 cass. (Running Time: 2 hrs. 45 mins.). 1995. bk. 16.95 (978-1-883049-52-2(0), Commuters Library); lib. bdg. 18.95 (978-1-883049-53-9(9)) Sound Room.
Abraham Lincoln was an eloquent & articulate author, the best of any of our presidents. The works superbly narrated in this audio book include "The Gettysburg Address," "The Second Inaugural Address," speeches & essays on slavery, law, progress & the philosophy of time. Each is an extraordinary piece of literature in its own right & together they show the depth of thought & feeling of our sixteenth president.

Lincoln's Prose Major Works by a Great American Writer. Abraham Lincoln. Read by George Vafiadis. (Running Time: 3 hrs.). 2002. 19.95 (978-1-59912-090-4(9), Audiofy Corp) Iofy Corp.

Lincoln's Speeches & Letters: With Carl Sandburg. unabr. ed. Abraham Lincoln. Read by Carl Sandburg & Roy P. Basler. 1 cass. (Running Time: 1 hr.). 10.95 (SAC 7033-C) Spoken Arts.
Sandburg explains Lincoln's duality & Basler reads Lincoln's most famous speeches & letters.

Lincoln's Spy Master: Thomas Haines Dudley & the Liverpool Network. unabr. ed. David Hepburn Milton. Read by William Hughes. (Running Time: 21600 sec.). 2007. audio compact disk 19.95 (978-1-4332-0759-4(1)) Blckstn Audio.

Lincoln's Spymaster: Thomas Haines Dudley & the Liverpool Network. unabr. ed. David Hepburn Milton. Read by William Hughes. (Running Time: 21600 sec.). 2007. 22.95 (978-1-4332-0757-0(5)); audio compact disk 24.00 (978-1-4332-0758-7(3)) Blckstn Audio.

Lincoln's Travels on the River Queen Audio Book. Wayne C. Temple. (ENG.). 2007. 23.95 (978-1-932278-66-8(4)) Pub: Mayhaven Pub. Dist(s): Baker Taylor

Lind Talks about Himself. unabr. ed. Jakov Lind. 1 cass. (Running Time: 38 min.). 1966. 12.95 (23186) J Norton Pubs.
Lind reminisces about his background & early years in Vienna, & discusses his realistic style of writing, his philosophy of life, & his political point of view.

Linda Arnold's World of Make Believe. Perf. by Linda Arnold & Ariel Thiermann. Composed by Linda Arnold. Directed By C. D. Taylor. Contrib. by P. J. Swift. 1 cass. (Running Time: 48 min.). (J). 1992. cass. & video 12.95 Hi-Fi, NTSC. (978-1-889212-11-1(3)) Ariel Recs.
Original children's songs composed & performed by Linda Arnold & a children's chorus.

Linda Bradford Raschke: Swing Trading & Short Term Price Patterns. Read by Linda B. Raschke. 1 cass. (Running Time: 1 hr.). 30.00 Dow Jones Telerate.
Linda will present the results of LBR Moore's research efforts of the past year, including a unique technical tool based on Chaos Theory. In addition, she will explain how certain concepts borrowed from Chaos Theory, including positive feedback, noise, & critical points, illustrate important principles of market behavior. Linda will demonstrate specific trading techniques which utilize these concepts & will discuss appropriate moneymanagement skills. She will introduce attendees to many of the specific tools she uses when trading futures for herself as well as those she has successfully taught to other traders.

Linda Goodman's Sun, Star & Love Signs Secrets. abr. ed. Linda Goodman. 36 cass. (Running Time: 53 hrs.). 2001. 286.20 (978-1-57453-239-5(1)) Audio Lit.

Linda Gregg. unabr. ed. Linda Gregg. Read by Linda Gregg. 1 cass. (Running Time: 29 min.). 1989. 10.00 New Letters.
Greggs reads her poetry & is interviewed.

Linda Hogan. unabr. ed. Linda Hogan. Read by Linda Hogan. 1 cass. (Running Time: 29 min.). 1990. 10.00 (040690) New Letters.
Poet Linda Hogan reads her works. Interview was recorded at a literary conference in Aspen, Colorado.

Linda Howard CD Collection: Dying to Please; To Die for; Killing Time. abr. ed. Linda Howard. Narrated by Susan Ericksen et al. (Running Time: 57600 sec.). 2006. audio compact disk 34.95 (978-1-4233-1679-4(7), 9781423316794, BACD) Brilliance Audio.
Dying to Please: First and foremost a butler par excellence, skilled at running large households smoothly and efficiently, Sarah Stevens she is also a trained bodyguard and expert marksman - indispensable to her elderly employer. Then one night she thwarts a burglary in progress. The exposure is enough to catch the attention of a tortured soul who, unbeknownst to Sarah, will stop at nothing to have her for himself. To Die For: Blair Mallory lives the good life. She's pretty, confident, and the owner of a thriving upscale fitness center. But in the shadow of success, a troubled member of the club develops a strange fixation on her, imitating her style and dress. Matters take a darker turn when the look-alike is shot dead. Was this murder a lethal case of mistaken identity - and was Blair the intended victim? Killing Time: In 1985 a time capsule was buried under the front lawn of a small-town county courthouse. Twenty years later, in the dead of night, the capsule is dug up, its contents stolen. One by one, those who had placed items in the time capsule are murdered. Besides his suspicions about the sudden, mysterious appearance of Nikita Stover, the chief investigator, Knox Davis, has absolutely no leads. And while Nikita's no murderer, she seems to be hiding plenty of secrets.

Linda Howard CD Collection 3: To Die for; Drop Dead Gorgeous; Up Close & Dangerous. abr. ed. Linda Howard. (Running Time: 15 hrs.). 2009. audio compact disk 34.99 (978-1-4233-8053-5(3), 9781423380535, BACD) Brilliance Audio.

Linda McCarriston. unabr. ed. Linda McCarriston. Read by Linda McCarriston. 1 cass. (Running Time: 29 min.). Incl. Talking Soft Dutch. 1987. (23); 1987. 10.00 (23) New Letters.
The New England poet reads from her award-winning book.

Linda McCartney: A Portrait. unabr. ed. Danny Fields. Narrated by Allan Smithee. 9 CDs. (Running Time: 10 hrs.). 2001. audio compact disk 89.00 (978-1-84197-250-3(9), C1411) Recorded Bks.
When Linda Eastman married Paul McCartney, many said that it would not last & was doomed from the start. Linda & Paul have had the opportunity to tell Danny Fields how it lasted for nearly 30 years, correcting the distorted portrayal of their relationship painted by the press. What made their relationship so strong? How were she & close ones affected by her cancer? Danny Fields uses his thirty years as an intimate friend & interviews with Linda, Paul, friends, family & stars that circulated in their world, to provide an inspiring, informative & often astonishing biography.

Linda McCartney: A Portrait. unabr. ed. Danny Fields. Narrated by Allan Smithee. 7 cass. (Running Time: 10 hrs.). 2001. 63.00 (978-1-84197-177-3(4), H1161E7) Recorded Bks.
When Linda Eastman married Paul McCartney, many said that it was doomed from the start, but it lasted for nearly 30 years. What made their relationship so strong? Was it as idyllic as shown by the press? How were Linda & close ones affected by her cancer?.

Linda Pastan. unabr. ed. Read by Linda Pastan. 1 cass. (Running Time: 29 min.). 1985. 10.00 New Letters.
Maryland author Linda Pastan's books include "Aspects of Eve" & "Five Stages of Grief".

Linda Tressel. unabr. ed. Anthony Trollope. Read by Flo Gibson. 5 cass. (Running Time: 6 hrs. 30 mins). 1998. 20.95 (978-1-55685-551-1(6)) Audio Bk Con.
Set in Nuremberg, this psychological novel explores the crushing of a young girl's spirit through her aunt's Calvinist fanaticism & insistence on her marriage to an old man against her wishes.

Lindamood (LiPS Clinical Version) Phoneme Sequencing Program for Reading, Spelling & Speech. Patricia Lindamood & Phyllis Lindamood. 1 cass. (Running Time: 90 mins.). (J). (gr. k-12). 2001. tchr. ed., spiral bd., suppl. ed. 249.00 (8620-A1) LinguiSystems.
Meets the needs of those who don't develop phonemic awareness through traditional methods. To aid you in this development, you'll get: manipulatives, step-by-step proven procedures that promote & self-correction scripted examples of dialogues which help students "discover" phonemic concepts.

Lindbergh. A. Scott Berg. Read by Lloyd James. 1999. 72.00 (978-0-7366-4371-9(0)); 104.00 (978-0-7366-4370-2(2), 4806A&B) Books on Tape.
The definitive life of Charles A. Lindbergh - one of the most legendary, controversial & enigmatic figures in American history.

Lindbergh. unabr. ed. Leonard Mosley. Read by James Cunningham. 11 cass. (Running Time: 16 hrs. 30 mins.). 1978. 88.00 (978-0-7366-0121-4(X), 1128) Books on Tape.
This is a provocative narrative of a man who is a genius with machines & the elements, uncomfortable in his dealings with his fellow men & an intimate figure with his close friends & family.

Lindbergh, Pt. 1. unabr. ed. A. Scott Berg. Read by Lloyd James. 13 cass. (Running Time: 19 hrs. 30 mins.). 1999. 104.00 (4806-A) Books on Tape.
The definitive life of Charles A. Lindbergh - one of the most legendary, controversial & enigmatic figures in American history.

Lindbergh, Pt. 2. unabr. ed. A. Scott Berg. Read by Lloyd James. 9 cass. (Running Time: 13 hrs. 30 mins.). 1999. 72.00 (4806-B) Books on Tape.

Lindbergh Alone. unabr. collector's ed. Brenda N. Gill. Read by John MacDonald. 5 cass. (Running Time: 5 hrs.). 1985. 30.00 (978-0-7366-0556-4(8), 1529) Books on Tape.
The story of the extraordinary feat of a great man. The author's intention is not to write Lindbergh's biography but to observe an unknown young man at one moment in history, & to examine the forces that led him to act as he did.

***Lindbergh vs. Roosevelt: The Rivalry That Divided America.** unabr. ed. James P. Duffy. (Running Time: 13 hrs. 30 mins.). 2010. 29.95 (978-1-4417-6386-0(4)) Blckstn Audio.

***Lindbergh vs. Roosevelt: The Rivalry That Divided America.** unabr. ed. James P. Duffy. Read by Tom Weiner. (Running Time: 13 hrs. 30 mins.). 2010. audio compact disk 24.95 (978-1-4417-6385-3(6)) Blckstn Audio.

***Lindbergh vs. Roosevelt (Library Edition) The Rivalry That Divided America.** unabr. ed. James Duffy. Read by Tom Weiner. (Running Time: 13 hrs. 30 mins.). 2010. 54.95 (978-1-4417-6383-9(X)); audio compact disk 69.00 (978-1-4417-6384-6(8)) Blckstn Audio.

Linden Method: The Anxiety & Panic Attacks Elimination Solution. Charles Linden. 61 vols. 1997. bk. 177.00 (978-0-9549803-0-6(1)) LifeWise Pub GBR.

Linden Tree. unabr. ed. Ellie Mathews & Marguerite Gavin. (Running Time: 7 hrs. NaN mins.). 2008. 29.95 (978-1-4332-2881-0(5)); 44.95 (978-1-4332-2877-3(7)); audio compact disk 60.00 (978-1-4332-2878-0(5)) Blckstn Audio.

Lindsay Grant - Consumption Patterns Versus Number of People on the Planet: Voluntary Control of Global Population. Hosted by Nancy Pearlman. 1 cass. (Running Time: 28 min.). 10.00 (1409) Educ Comm CA.

Line & Strength. unabr. ed. Glenn McGrath & Daniel Lane. Read by Shane McNamara. (Running Time: 12 hrs. 35 mins.). 2008. audio compact disk 103.95 (978-1-74214-046-9(7), 9781742140469) Pub: Bolinda Pubng AUS. Dist(s): Bolinda Pub Inc

Line Between the Two. Contrib. by Mark Harris. Prod. by Peter Kipley. 2005. audio compact disk 13.99 (978-5-559-01493-7(1)) INO Rec.

Line by Line: Beginning Typing, Set. 2nd ed. Steven J. Molinsky & Bill Bliss. 1990. 66.15 (978-0-13-536897-8(9)) Longman.

Line in the Sand. unabr. ed. Gerald Seymour. Read by Anthony Head. 12 cass. (Running Time: 12 hrs.). 1999. 96.95 (978-0-7540-0356-4(6), CAB1779) AudioGO.
In a village on the Suffolk coast, Frank Perry waits for his past to arrive. A decade before, he had spied for the government on the Iranian chemical & biological weapons installations. He had privileged access & his information damaged their killing capacity for years. Now, Iran has dispatched its most deadly assassin to claim revenge.

Line in the Sand. unabr. ed. Gerald Seymour. Read by Anthony Head. 12 CDs. (Running Time: 12 hrs.). 1999. audio compact disk 110.95 (978-0-7540-5318-7(0), CCD009) Pub: Chivers Audio Bks GBR. Dist(s): AudioGO
In a village on the Suffolk coast, Frank Perry waits for his past to arrive. A decade before, he had spied for the government on the Iranian chemical & biological weapons installations. He had privileged access & his information damaged their killing capacity for years. Now, Iran will have its revenge & has dispatched its most deadly assassin to fulfil the task.

Line in the Sand. unabr. ed. Gerald Seymour. Narrated by Simon Prebble. 11 cass. (Running Time: 15 hrs. 30 mins.). 2000. 94.00 (978-0-7887-4948-3(X), 96354E7) Recorded Bks.
When sources reveal that Iran's top assassin has targeted Frank Perry for his next kill, the British Security Service wants Frank to move from the quiet English seacoast village where he's been hiding for five years. But having left behind his life & family once before, Frank decides he's through running. As he & the government take protective measures, Frank discovers an unsuspected enemy, the fears & suspicions of his friends & neighbors.

Line in the Sand: Gal. 6:7-8. Ed Young. 1991. 4.95 (978-0-7417-1839-6(1), 839) Win Walk.

Line in the Sand Pledge Sunday: Matthew 6:20-21. Ed Young. 2000. 4.95 (978-0-7417-2245-4(3), 1245) Win Walk.

Line of Beauty. Alan Hollinghurst. Read by Alex Jennings. 11 cass. 2005. 89.95 (978-0-7927-3760-5(1), CSL 846, Chivers Sound Lib); audio compact disk 115.95 (978-0-7927-3761-2(X), SLD 846, Chivers Sound Lib) AudioGO.

Line of Control. Don Pendleton. (Mack Bolan Ser.: No. 91). 2006. 14.99 (978-1-59950-154-3(6)) GraphicAudio.

***Line of Duty.** Terri Blackstock. (Running Time: 10 hrs. 31 mins. 0 sec.). (Newpointe 911 Ser.). (ENG.). 2008. 14.99 (978-0-310-30489-0(X)) Zondervan.

Line of Fire. unabr. ed. W. E. B. Griffin. Read by Michael Russotto. 12 cass. (Running Time: 18 hrs.). (Corps Ser.: Bk. 5). 1992. 96.00 (978-0-7366-2255-4(1), 3044) Books on Tape.
Two marines are trapped at a Buka Island coastwatcher station. A special team gets the rescue assignment.

Line of the Trungpas. Vajracarya. Read by Chogyam Trungpa. 7 cass. (Running Time: 7 hrs.). 1975. 65.50 (A048) Vajradhatu.
Seven talks: 1) The Practicing Lineage; 2) The Kagyu Tradition; 3) Trungmase; 4) Tent Culture; 5) The Fourth Trungpa; 6) The Fifth through the Tenth Trungpa; 7) The Eleventh Trungpa.

Line of Vision. unabr. ed. David Ellis. Read by Dick Hill. (Running Time: 14 hrs.). 2008. 39.25 (978-1-4233-5254-9(8), 9781423352549, BADLE); 24.95 (978-1-4233-5253-2(X), 9781423352532, BAD); audio compact disk 39.25 (978-1-4233-5252-5(1), 9781423352525, Brinc Audio MP3 Lib); audio compact disk 24.95 (978-1-4233-5251-8(3), 9781423352518, Brilliance MP3) Brilliance Audio.

Line Out for a Walk: Familiar Essays. unabr. ed. Joseph Epstein. Read by Michael Russotto. 9 cass. (Running Time: 13 hrs. 30 min.). 1995. 72.00 (978-0-7366-3064-1(3), 3746) Books on Tape.
Epstein eyes the mirror in a series of essays that are more than humorous. You can also trust & identify with them.

Line Up. Perf. by Bill Johnstone & Wally Maher. (ENG.). 2009. audio compact disk 31.95 (978-1-57019-888-5(8)) Radio Spirits.

Line-Up: A Hit-and-Run Accident & An Unexplainable Murder. Perf. by Bill Johnstone. 1 cass. (Running Time: 1 hr.). 2001. 6.98 (1513) Radio Spirits.

Line-Up: The Drinkler Kidnapping & The Stan Farmer Killing. Perf. by Bill Johnstone. 1 cass. (Running Time: 1 hr.). 2001. 6.98 (1767) Radio Spirits.

Lineage & Other Stories. unabr. ed. Bo Lozoff. Read by Bo Lozoff. 2 cass. (Running Time: 2 hrs.). 1990. 15.00 (978-0-9614444-4-0(4)) Human Kind Found.
Four short stories of spiritual awakening.

Lineage of Grace Omnibus. abr. ed. Francine Rivers & Anita Lustrea. 10 CDs. (Running Time: 15 Hours). (Lineage of Grace Ser.: Bks. 1-5). 2004. 39.99 (978-1-58926-644-5(7)) Oasis Audio.

Lineas de Tiempo: El Poder de cCambiar Nuestro Destino. Ramtha. (SPA.). 2008. audio compact disk 25.00 (978-0-9798783-8-1(1)) Voxrames.

Lines on the Mermaid Tavern see Poetry of Keats

Lines on the Road: Diary of a Motorcycle Poet. H. Scott Hackney. Read by H. Scott Hackney. Read by Jennifer E. Quinlan. Ed. by Terry K. Hackney. (ENG., 2008. 19.95 (978-0-9818886-2-0(3)) S Hackney.

Lineup: The World's Greatest Crime Writers Tell the Inside Story of Their Greatest Detectives. unabr. ed. Otto Penzler. Narrated by Justine Eyre et al. 1 MP3-CD. (Running Time: 12 hrs. 0 mins. 0 sec.). 2010. 29.99 (978-1-4001-6360-1(9)) Pub: Tantor Media. Dist(s): IngramPubServ

Lineup: The World's Greatest Crime Writers Tell the Inside Story of Their Greatest Detectives. unabr. ed. Otto Penzler. Narrated by John Lee et al. 10 CDs. (Running Time: 12 hrs. 0 mins. 0 sec.). 2010. audio compact disk 79.99 (978-1-4001-4360-3(8)) Pub: Tantor Media. Dist(s): IngramPubServ

Lineup: The World's Greatest Crime Writers Tell the Inside Story of Their Greatest Detectives. unabr. ed. Otto Penzler. Narrated by Justine Eyre et al. 10 CDs. (Running Time: 12 hrs. 0 mins. 0 sec.). 2010. audio compact disk 39.99 (978-1-4001-1360-6(1)) Pub: Tantor Media. Dist(s): IngramPubServ

***Lineup: The World's Greatest Crime Writers Tell the Inside Story of Their Greatest Detectives.** unabr. ed. Otto Penzler. Narrated by John Allen Nelson et al. (Running Time: 12 hrs. 0 mins.). 2010. 17.99 (978-1-4001-8360-9(X)) Tantor Media.

***Linger.** Maggie Stiefvater. (ENG.). 2010. audio compact disk 79.99 (978-0-545-22614-1(7)) Scholastic Inc.

***Linger.** unabr. ed. Maggie Stiefvater. Narrated by Jenna Lamia & David LeDoux. (Running Time: 10 hrs. 30 mins.). (YA). 2010. audio compact disk 39.99 (978-0-545-20707-2(X)) Scholastic Inc.

Lingerie Queen of Politics. Kat Gallant. (ENG.). 2000. audio compact disk 24.95 (978-0-9842757-3-1(8)) Fallen Tree.

Lingering Shadows: Jungians, Freudians & Anti-Semitism. 6 cass. (Running Time: 6 hrs.). 1989. 100.00 Incl. handouts. Sound Horizons AV.

Lingering Summer. unabr. ed. W Richards. 4 cass. (Running Time: 4 hrs.). 1998. 57.95 (978-1-872672-61-8(2)) Pub: Magna Story GBR. Dist(s): Ulverscroft US

Lingua Latina: Roma Aeterna, Set 11. Hans Orberg. 1990. 26.95 (978-87-997016-8-1(5)) Pub: Domus Latina DNK. Dist(s): Focus Pub-R Pullins

Linguistic Inquiry & Word Count. 2nd rev. ed. James W. Pennebaker et al. 2001. audio compact disk 99.95 (978-1-56321-208-6(0)) Pub: L Erlbaum Assocs. Dist(s): Taylor and Fran

Link. Walt Becker. Read by Dick Hill. 2 cass. (Running Time: 2 hrs.). 1999. 17.95 (FS9-43287) Highsmith.

Link: Uncovering Our Earliest Ancestor. unabr. ed. Colin Tudge. Read by Robert Petkoff. Told to Josh Young. (Running Time: 8 hrs.). (ENG.). 2009. 24.98 (978-1-60024-864-1(0)) Pub: Hachet Audio. Dist(s): HachBkGrp

Link Between Foods & Illness. 2003. audio compact disk 14.95 (978-0-9743448-7-4(7)) NMA Media Pr.

Linking Astrology with Psychology. Judith Cooper. 1 cass. (Running Time: 1 hr.). 8.95 (500) Am Fed Astrologers.
New approach combines with astrological symbolism.

Linking Suburban Churches with Urban Needs: National Association of Evangelicals, 47th Annual Convention, Columbus, Ohio, March 7-9, 1989. Harv Oostdyk. 1 cass. (Running Time: 1 hr.). (Workshops Ser.: No. 23-Wednesd). 1989. 4.25 ea. 1-8 tapes.; 4.00 ea. 9 tapes or more. Nat Assn Evan.

Linnea in Monet's Garden. unabr. ed. Christina Bjork & Lena Anderson. Narrated by Christina Moore. 1 cass. (Running Time: 1 hr.). (gr. 3 up). 1997. 10.00 (978-0-7887-1119-0(9), 95113E7) Recorded Bks.
Linnea is going to France! The little girl will travel with her neighbor, old Mr. Bloom, to see the house & garden where the great artist Monet lived. She can't wait to see the waterlily pond - the scene of her favorite painting. A joyous introduction to Impressionism & the life of one of the most influential artists of this century.

Linthead Stomp: The Creation of Country Music in the Piedmont South. Patrick Huber. (ENG., 2008. 15.00 (978-0-8078-8682-3(3)); audio compact disk 15.00 (978-0-8078-8684-7(X)) U of NC Pr.

Linux Universe: Installation & Configuration. 2nd rev. ed. Thomas Uhl & Stefan Strobel. (C). 1996. pap. bk. 38.95 (978-0-387-94600-9(4), 0387946004) Spri.

Lion see Poetry of Vachel Lindsay

***Lion.** Nelson DeMille. Read by Scott Brick. (Running Time: 9 hrs.). (ENG.). 2011. audio compact disk & audio compact disk 14.98 (978-1-60941-275-3(3)) Pub: Hachet Audio. Dist(s): HachBkGrp

Lion. Joseph Kessel. Read by Antoine Gaubet. 2 cass. (Running Time: 2 hrs.). (FRE.). 1991. bk. 35.95 (1GA055) Olivia & Hill.
The well-known story of Patricia, a lonely little girl in Kenya & King, the lion with whom she has been brought up.

Lion. abr. ed. Nelson DeMille. Read by Scott Brick. (Running Time: 9 hrs.). (ENG.). 2010. 19.98 (978-1-60788-219-0(1)); audio compact disk 29.98 (978-1-60788-218-3(3)) Pub: Hachet Audio. Dist(s): HachBkGrp

***Lion.** unabr. ed. Nelson DeMille. Narrated by Scott Brick. 2 MP3-CDs. (Running Time: 15 hrs. 43 mins.). 2010. 79.99 (978-1-60788-542-9(5)); audio compact disk 124.99 (978-1-60788-541-2(7)) Pub: Hachet Audio. Dist(s): HachBkGrp

Lion. unabr. ed. Nelson DeMille. Read by Scott Brick. (Running Time: 15 hrs. 30 mins.). (ENG.). 2010. 26.98 (978-1-60788-221-3(3)); audio compact disk 39.98 (978-1-60788-220-6(5)) Pub: Hachet Audio. Dist(s): HachBkGrp

Lion Among Men. unabr. ed. Gregory Maguire. Read by John McDonough. (Running Time: 11 hrs. 45 mins.). (Wicked Years Ser.: No. 3). (ENG.). 2008. (978-0-06-171346-0(5), Harper Audio) HarperCollins Pubs.

Lion Among Men. unabr. ed. Gregory Maguire. Read by John Mcdonough. (Wicked Years Ser.: No. 3). 2009. audio compact disk 19.99 (978-0-06-190620-6(4), Harper Audio) HarperCollins Pubs.

***Lion among Men: Volume Three in the Wicked Years.** unabr. ed. Gregory Maguire. Read by John Mcdonough. (ENG.). 2008. (978-0-06-171344-6(9)) HarperCollins Pubs.

Lion & the Mouse. Ed. by Dorothy S. Bishop. 1 cass. (Bilingual Fables). 12.00 (978-0-8442-7579-6(4), Natl Textbk Co) M-H Contemporary.
Features stories in English & French.

Lion & the Mouse & Other Super-Dee-Duper Stories. 1 cass. (Barney Ser.). (J). bk. 6.38 Blisterpack. (LY 9575) NewSound.
Includes: "The King's Minstrel," "The Walnut Tree," "The Little Porridge Pot," "The Turtle & the Beaver," & "The Big Cheese" - all told by Barney & friends.

Lion & the Mouse/Lions. Steck-Vaughn Staff. 1997. (978-0-8172-7372-9(7)) SteckVau.

Lion & the Rat. 2004. bk. 24.95 (978-0-7882-0552-1(8)); pap. bk. 14.95 (978-0-7882-0617-7(6)) Weston Woods.

Lion & the Rat; Hare & the Tortoise. 2004. cass. & flmstrp 30.00 (978-0-89719-614-7(7)) Weston Woods.

Lion & the Unicorn. Richard Harding Davis. Read by Flo Gibson. 3 cass. (Running Time: 4 hrs.). (J). 1990. 16.95 (978-1-55685-178-0(2)) Audio Bk Con.
These stories of war & peace include: "On a Fever Ship," The Man with One Talent," "The Vagrant," & "The Last Ride Together," as well as the romantic title story.

Lion & the Unicorn & Dickens, Dali & Others. collector's ed. George Orwell. Read by Donald Monat. 7 cass. (Running Time: 10 hrs. 30 min.). (J). 1987. 56.00 (978-0-7366-1221-0(1), 2139) Books on Tape.
As I write, highly civilized human beings are flying overhead, trying to kill me. So starts this 1941 study of the English national character, so beautifully displayed during a war that tested it to the limit.

Lion at School & Other Stories. unabr. ed. Philippa Pearce. Read by Jan Francis. 2 cass. (Running Time: 3 hrs.). (J). (gr. 1-8). 1999. 18.95 (CCA 3145, Chivers Child Audio) AudioGO.

Lion Becomes a Lamb: Rev. 5:1-14. Ed Young. 1986. 4.95 (978-0-7417-1560-9(0), 560) Win Walk.

Lion Called Christian: The True Story of the Remarkable Bond Between Two Friends & a Lion. unabr. ed. Anthony Bourke & John Rendall. Narrated by John Lee. 3 CDs. (Running Time: 3 hrs. 30 mins.). 2009. audio compact disk 40.00 (978-1-4159-6455-2(6), BksonTape) Pub: Random Audio Pubg. Dist(s): Random

Lion Called Christian: The True Story of the Remarkable Bond Between Two Friends & a Lion. unabr. ed. Anthony Bourke & John Rendall. Frwd. by George Adamson. (ENG.). 2009. audio compact disk 24.95 (978-0-7393-8458-9(9), Random AudioBks) Pub: Random Audio Pubg. Dist(s): Random

Lion Eyes. unabr. ed. Claire Berlinski. Read by Susan Ericksen. (Running Time: 7 hrs.). 2007. 39.25 (978-1-59710-459-3(0), 9781597104593, BADLE); 24.95 (978-1-59710-458-6(2), 9781597104586, BAD); 69.25 (978-1-59600-248-7(4), 9781596002487, BrilAudUnabridg); audio compact disk 82.25 (978-1-59600-250-0(6), 9781596002500, BriAudCD Unabrid); audio compact disk 29.95 (978-1-59600-249-4(2), 9781596002494, Bril Audio CD Unabri); audio compact disk 39.25 (978-1-59335-972-0(1), 9781593359720, Brinc Audio MP3 Lib); audio compact disk 24.95 (978-1-59335-971-3(3), 9781593359713, Brilliance MP3) Brilliance Audio.
Please enter a Synopsis.

Lion in the Market Place (Principle #2 - Commit Fully to Your Job) Proverbs 26:13-14. Ed Young. 1996. 4.95 (978-0-7417-2122-8(8), 1122) Win Walk.

Lion in the Morning. Perf. by Julian Marley & Damian Marley. Prod. by Stephen Marley. 1 cass. 1996. 9.98 (978-1-56896-155-2(3), 54178-4); audio compact disk 15.98 CD. (978-1-56896-154-5(5), 54178-2) Lightyear Entrtnmnt.
Born in London, Julian began studying music professionally & became a proficient drummer, bassist, guitarist & keyboardist.

Lion in the Valley. unabr. ed. Elizabeth Peters, pseud. Read by Susan O'Malley. 8 cass. (Running Time: 11 hrs. 30 mins.). (Amelia Peabody Ser.:

hrs. 30 mins.). 2000. audio compact disk 89.00 (978-0-7887-4912-4(9), C1293E7) Recorded Bks.
Theodore Roosevelt taught his sons that wealth & influence were inextricably bound with a sense of duty to defend democracy to the death. Using previously unpublished material, the author presents a poignant look at the man whose heroic idealism inspired a nation & ultimately, cost him the life of a war hero son. Includes an interview with the author.

Lion's Pride: Theodore Roosevelt & His Family in Peace & War. unabr. ed. Edward J. Renehan, Jr. Narrated by John McDonough. 9 cass. (Running Time: 10 hrs. 30 mins.). 2000. 72.00 (978-0-7887-4408-2(9), 95876E7) Recorded Bks.
Theodore Roosevelt taught his sons that wealth & influence were inextricable bound with a sense of duty to defend democracy to the death. Using previously unpublished material, the author presents a poignant look at the man whose heroic idealism inspired a nation & ultimately, cost him the life of a war hero son.

Lion's Roar: The Buddhist Path of Non-Aggression. Read by Jangon Kongtrul. 1 cass. 1984. 12.50 (A172) Vajradhatu.

Lion's Roar: The Buddhist Path of Non-Aggression. Vajracarya. 1976. 10.00 Vajradhatu.
A seminar by the scholar & meditation master trained in the philosophical & meditative traditions of Buddhism in Tibet.

Lip Reading. Maureen Lipman. Read by Maureen Lipman. 1 cass. (Running Time: 1 hr. 30 min.). (ENG., 2000. (978-0-14-180260-2(X), PengAudBks) Penguin Grp USA.
Maureen Lipman, the woman who has had both a rose and a sewage system named after her, has a gift for making anything seem funny. Whether it is hot flushes (Wanna make love when I'm not too tired, wanna wear a bra that ain't underwired), trying to make sense of the cricket commentary, (They've dismissed the night-watchman bishop?) or giving the perfect dinner party (place the frozen fish in the freezer and the wine in the microwave), her individual slant on the subject is either refreshing, outrageous or downright priceless (or all of the above).

Lip Reading. unabr. ed. Joyce Storey & Maureen Lipman. Read by Diana Bishop. 8 cass. (Running Time: 6 hrs. 24 min.). (Isis Audio Reminiscence Ser.). 2001. 54.95 (978-0-7531-1021-8(0)) Pub: ISIS Audio GBR. Dist(s): Ulverscroft US
With an RAF husband rarely on leave, Joyce, mother of two, fights her own battles on the home-front - with air raids, in-laws, machine work and poverty - searching always for her dream house and a life to call her own. Joyce Storey, born near Bristol in 1917, began her autobiography at the age of 66. This is a vivid account of an extraordinary working-class woman's life.

***Lip Service.** unabr. ed. Susan Mallery. Read by Julie E. Francis. (Running Time: 10 hrs.). (Lone Star Sisters Ser.). 2010. 19.99 (978-1-4418-7084-1(9), 9781441870841, Brilliance MP3); 39.97 (978-1-4418-7086-5(5), 9781441870865, BADLE); 39.97 (978-1-4418-7085-8(7), 9781441870858, Brlnc Audio MP3 Lib); audio compact disk 19.99 (978-1-4418-7082-7(2), 9781441870827, Bril Audio CD Unabri); audio compact disk 79.97 (978-1-4418-7083-4(0), 9781441870834, BriAudCD Unabrid) Brilliance Audio.

Lippincott Williams & Wilkins Atlas of Anatomy Faculty Resources -Network Version. Patric Tank & Thomas R. Gest. (ENG.). 2008. 795.00 (978-1-60547-127-3(5)) Lppncott W W.

Lippincott's Maternity Nursing Video Series. Lippincott Williams and Wilkins Staff. 2005. (978-0-7817-8511-2(1)) Lppncott W W.

Lippincott's Maternity Nursing Video Series Plus Lippincott's Pediatric Nursing Video Series. Lippincott Williams and Wilkins Staff. 2005. (978-0-7817-9127-4(8)) Lppncott W W.

Lippincott's Pediatric Nursing Video Series. Lippincott Williams and Wilkins Staff. 2005. (978-0-7817-8661-4(4)) Lppncott W W.

Lippincott's Textbook for Nursing Assistants: A Humanistic Approach to Caregiving. Pamela J. Carter. (Point (Lippincott Williams & Wilkins) Ser.). 2008. pap. bk. 89.95 (978-0-7817-8967-7(2)) Lppncott W W.

***Lips Touch: Three Times.** unabr. ed. Laini Taylor. Read by Cassandra Campbell. (Running Time: 7 hrs.). (YA). 2010. audio compact disk 19.99 (978-1-4418-5668-5(4), 9781441856685, Bril Audio CD Unabri) Brilliance Audio.

***Lips Touch: Three Times: Three Times.** unabr. ed. Laini Taylor. (Running Time: 7 hrs.). 2010. 19.99 (978-1-4418-5781-1(8), 9781441857811, BAD); 39.97 (978-1-4418-5782-8(6), 9781441857828, BADLE) Brilliance Audio.

***Lips Touch: Three Times: Three Times.** unabr. ed. Laini Taylor. Read by Cassandra Campbell. (Running Time: 7 hrs.). (YA). 2010. 19.99 (978-1-4418-5779-8(6), 9781441857798, Brilliance MP3); 39.97 (978-1-4418-5780-4(X), 9781441857804, Brlnc Audio MP3 Lib); audio compact disk 59.97 (978-1-4418-5778-1(8), 9781441857781, BriAudCD Unabrid) Brilliance Audio.

Lips Unsealed: A Memoir. abr. ed. Belinda Carlisle. 2010. audio compact disk 30.00 (978-0-307-70467-2(X), Random AudioBks) Pub: Random Audio Pubg. Dist(s): Random

Lipstick & Powder. Sally Worboyes. 2008. 69.95 (978-1-84559-973-7(X)); audio compact disk 79.95 (978-1-84559-974-4(8)) Pub: Soundings Ltd GBR. Dist(s): Ulverscroft US

Lipstick Jungle. abr. ed. Candace Bushnell. Read by Cynthia Nixon. (Running Time: 21600 sec.). 2007. 14.98 (978-1-4013-8733-4(0)); audio compact disk 14.98 (978-1-4013-8734-1(9)) Pub: Hyperion. Dist(s): HarperCollins Pubs

Liquid Geometry. Voice by Renske Skills. (Running Time: 4020 sec.). 2007. audio compact disk 17.98 (978-1-59179-581-0(8)) Sounds True.

Liquid Gospel, Edible Words-mp3. 2002. 32.00 (978-1-59128-383-6(3)) Canon Pr ID.

Liquid Gospel, Edible Words-tape. 12 cass. 2002. 40.00 (978-1-59128-385-0(X)) Canon Pr ID.

Liquid Gospel, Edible Words (2002) 10 cass. 2003. 35.00 (978-1-59128-388-1(4)) Canon Pr ID.

Liquid Mind III: Balance. Music by Liquid Mind. Composed by Chuck Wild. 1 CD. (Running Time: 56 mins.). 1999. audio compact disk 15.98 (978-0-9742661-2-1(4)) Chuck Wild Recs.

Liquid Mind IV: Unity. Music by Liquid Mind. Composed by Chuck Wild. 1 CD. (Running Time: 57 mins). 2000. audio compact disk 15.98 (978-0-9742661-3-8(2)) Chuck Wild Recs.

Liquid Mind V: Serenity. Music by Liquid Mind. Composed by Chuck Wild. 1 CD. (Running Time: 57 mins.). 2001. audio compact disk 15.98 (978-0-9742661-4-5(0)) Chuck Wild Recs.

Liquid Mind VI: Spirit. Music by Liquid Mind. Composed by Chuck Wild. 1 CD. (Running Time: 57 mins.). 2003. audio compact disk 15.98 (978-0-9742661-5-2(9)) Chuck Wild Recs.

Liquidator. John E. Gardner. 5 cass. (Running Time: 6 hrs. 35 mins.). (Story Sound Ser.). (J). 2005. 49.95 (978-1-85903-826-0(3)); audio compact disk 59.95 (978-1-85903-842-0(5)) Pub: Mgna Lrg Print GBR. Dist(s): Ulverscroft US

Lirael, Daughter of the Clayr. Garth Nix. Read by Tim Curry. 13 CDs. (Running Time: 14 hrs. 44 mins.). (Old Kingdom Ser.: No. 2). (J). (gr. 7 up). 2004. audio compact disk 80.00 (978-0-8072-2008-5(6), Listening Lib) Random Audio Pubg.

Lirael, Daughter of the Clayr. unabr. ed. Garth Nix. 9 vols. (Running Time: 14 hrs. 44 mins.). (Old Kingdom Ser.: No. 2). (J). (gr. 7 up). 2004. pap. bk. 61.00 (978-0-8072-0858-8(2), LYA 374 SP, Listening Lib); pap. bk. & tchr.'s planning gde. ed. 53.00 (978-0-8072-0564-8(8), S YA 374 CX, Listening Lib) Pub: Random Audio Pubg. Dist(s): Random
"When a dangerous necromancer threatens to unleash a long-buried evil, Lirael and Prince Sameth are drawn into a battle to save the Old Kingdom and reveal their true destinies.".

Lirica Infantil con Jose-Luis Orozco. Contrib. by Jose-Luis Orozco.Tr. of Hispanic Children's Folklore with Jose-Luis Orozco. (SPA.). (J). (gr. k-2). 12.00 (978-1-57417-012-2(0), AC3681); audio compact disk 16.00 (978-1-57417-001-6(5), AC1653) Pub: Arcoiris Recs. Dist(s): Lectorum Pubns

Lirica Infantil con Jose-Luis Orozco, Vol. 2. Contrib. by Jose-Luis Orozco.Tr. of Hispanic Children's Folklore with Jose-Luis Orozco. (SPA.). (J). (gr. k-2). 12.00 (978-1-57417-013-9(9), AC3682); audio compact disk 16.00 (978-1-57417-002-3(3), AC1655) Pub: Arcoiris Recs. Dist(s): Lectorum Pubns

Lirica Infantil con Jose-Luis Orozco, Vol. 3. Contrib. by Jose-Luis Orozco.Tr. of Hispanic Children's Folklore with Jose-Luis Orozco. (SPA.). (J). (gr. k-2). 12.00 (978-1-57417-014-6(7), AC3253); audio compact disk 16.00 (978-1-57417-003-0(1), AC1657) Pub: Arcoiris Recs. Dist(s): Lectorum Pubns

Lisa Jackson CD Collection: Shiver, Absolute Fear, Lost Souls. abr. ed. Lisa Jackson. Read by Joyce Bean. (Running Time: 18 hrs.). 2009. audio compact disk 34.99 (978-1-4233-9734-2(7), 9781423397342, BACD) Brilliance Audio.

***Lisa Kleypas CD Collection: Sugar Daddy; Blue-Eyed Devil; Smooth Talking Stranger.** abr. ed. Lisa Kleypas. (Running Time: 18 hrs.). 2010. audio compact disk 29.99 (978-1-4418-5997-6(7), 9781441859976, BACD) Brilliance Audio.

Lisbeth Keefe: How to Extrapolate Critical Information from Foreign Exchange & Cash Markets. Read by Lisbeth Keefe. 1 cass. 30.00 Dow Jones Telerate.
Foreign exchange analysis demands an ever evolving set of techniques for dealing with high volatility in one spot currency & low volatility in another. It provides a reliable approach for a market that spends long periods of time reacting only to fundamentals, then suddenly switches to technical trading without warning. Using foreign exchange analysis to follow major related markets allows you to receive early signals of breakouts without long hours of analysis. This discussion will also focus on how future traders extrapolate critical information from cash Forex & its major related markets.

Lisel Mueller. unabr. ed. Read by Lisel Mueller. 1 cass. (Running Time: 29 min.). 1985. 10.00 New Letters.
Mueller's poetry book, "The Need to Stand Still," won the 1981 American Book Award.

Lisey's Story. unabr. ed. Stephen King. Read by Mare Winningham. 2006. 29.95 (978-0-7435-6194-5(5)); 49.95 (978-0-7435-5599-9(6)); audio compact disk 49.95 (978-0-7435-5600-2(3)) Pub: S&S Audio. Dist(s): S and S Inc

Lisey's Story. unabr. ed. Stephen King. Read by Mare Winningham. (Running Time: 20 hrs. 0 mins. 0 sec.). (ENG.). 2008. audio compact disk 21.99 (978-0-7435-8158-5(X)) Pub: S&S Audio. Dist(s): S and S Inc

List see Ship That Died of Shame

List. Steve Martini. 1 cass. 1998. 12.98 (978-0-671-58210-4(0), Audioworks) S&S Audio.

List. abr. ed. Robert Whitlow. Read by Rob Lamont. 6 cass. (Running Time: 10 hrs.). 2003. 29.99; audio compact disk 34.99 Oasis Audio.

List. abr. ed. Robert Whitlow. 6 cass. (Running Time: 9 hrs.). 2004. 30.00 (978-1-58926-260-7(3), 890591) Oasis Audio.
As a struggling young attorney fresh out of law school, Renny Jacobson was pining for the day he could afford the fast cars and sprawling homes of the partners in his Charlotte firm. And with news of his father's death and an ancient, secret inheritance, Renny's life was sure to change forever.

List, unabr. ed. Steve Martini. Narrated by George Guidall. 10 cass. (Running Time: 14 hrs.). 1997. 90.00 (978-0-7887-1755-0(3), 95233E7) Recorded Bks.
Will attorney-turned-novelist Abby Chandlis' scheme to outwit the biggest players in publishing & film pay off, or will she become the victim of her own creation?.

***List.** unabr. ed. Robert Whitlow. Narrated by Rob Lamont. (ENG.). 2003. 24.49 (978-1-60814-739-7(8)) Oasis Audio.

List. unabr. ed. Robert Whitlow. Narrated by Rob Lamont. 8 CDs. (Running Time: 9 hrs.). (ENG.). 2003. audio compact disk 34.99 (978-1-58926-261-4(1), 100408) Oasis Audio.

List & Sell Real Estate Like Crazy! Scripts. Bernice L. Ross. 11. (Running Time: 11 hrs.). 2003. spiral bd. 299.00 (978-0-9725081-1-7(2)) RossdalePress.

List & Sell Real Estate Like Crazy Audio Scripts. Bernice Ross. 2006. audio compact disk 149.00 (978-0-9725081-4-8(7)) RossdalePress.

Listen. Contrib. by Trin-I-Tee 5-7. (Soundtraks Ser.). 2007. audio compact disk 8.99 (978-5-557-52832-0(6)) Christian Wrld.

Listen & Be Listened To. 4 cass. pap. bk. 155.00 incl. 2 multiple choice tests. (978-0-7612-0797-9(X), 80204); pap. bk. & wbk. ed. 30.00 (978-0-7612-0796-2(1), 80205) AMACOM.
You'll learn how to: Reduce costly mistakes & losses caused by miscommunication with both customers & co-workers; Listen with all your senses - & pick up the feelings & messages behind the words; Discriminate between the various nonverbal cues you receive - & send - in every face-to-face communication; Overcome the barriers to good listening; focus on the content of the messages you hear, not the delivery; Improve your memory; Become a more intelligent & discerning listener.

Listen & Enjoy Italian Poetry. Perf. by Listen and Enjoy Staff. 1 cass. (Listen & Enjoy Ser.). 1991. 9.95 Dover.

Listen & Improve Your Italian: Intermediate Level. unabr. ed. 4 cass. (Running Time: 4 hrs.). (ITA.). pap. bk. 59.95 (SIT135) J Norton Pubs.
Features authentic Italian spoken at natural pace & rhythm by native speakers. In continuing episodes you'll hear about Giorgio Ferrante & his adventures. Each scene is interspersed with music & short practice sessions highlight useful language points. Listening guide contains a complete transcript of the recorded material & a handbook to help you review the vocabulary & grammar.

Listen & Improve Your Italian, Plus: Advanced Level. unabr. ed. 4 cass. (ITA.). stu. ed. 11.95 (BIT235); pap. bk. 59.95 (SIT235) J Norton Pubs.

Listen & Learn: An Introduction to Spoken Cornish. Rod Lyon. 1985. 20.00 Pub: Dyllansow Truran GBR. Dist(s): St Mut
A compact introductory course to traditionally spoken Cornish. Provides all that the learner requires to understand what is most important to join in topical, everyday conversations.

Listen & Learn a Language: French. unabr. ed. 3 cass. (Running Time: 60 min.). 1988. 30.50 (20211) Recorded Bks.
Complete mini-courses that teach you to speak, read & understand each language.

Listen & Learn French. 1 cass. (Running Time: 1 hr. 30 min.). Dover.
A Program of recorded speech by native speakers & practical instruction for virtually every travel situation including customs, hotels, illness, currency exchange, sightseeing & more.

Listen & Learn Portuguese. Listen and Learn Staff. 1 cass. (Running Time: 1 hr. 30 min.). 1986. bk. 8.95 (978-0-486-99919-7(X)) Dover.
A program of recorded speech by native speakers & practical instruction for virtually every travel situation, including customs, hotels, illness, currency exchange, sightseeing & more.

Listen & Learn the Esoteric Arts Vol. 1: The Tarot. Tori Hartman. 1 cass. 2000. 10.95 (978-0-9679544-0-0(1)) Pub: Jupiter CA. Dist(s): DeVorss
This new system of learning includes everything you need to know in order to read Tarot cards.

Listen & Learn the Esoteric Arts Vol. 2: Twelve Step Tarot. Tori Hartman. 1 cass. 2000. 10.95 (978-0-9679544-1-7(X)) Pub: Jupiter CA. Dist(s): DeVorss
Teaches how to read the tarot cards based on the 12 Steps of Recovery. Promotes deeper self-awareness of self & recovery.

Listen & Lose. Robert Parrish. 1 cass. (Running Time: 35 min.). 11.00 (978-0-89811-000-5(9), 4561) Meyer Res Grp.
The psychological reasons behind the failure of diets. Also available in Spanish.

Listen & Lose. Robert Parrish. 1 cass. 10.00 (SP100009) SMI Intl.
If you have "tried everything" to lose those extra pounds, explore the psychological reasons behind the failure of diets. Reprogram your subconscious mind to eliminate the desire to overeat. Alter your self-image & you can become slim & stay that way - without dieting.

Listen & Perform. Stephen M. Silvers. 1985. 12.95 (978-0-940296-56-5(X)) Sky Oaks Prodns.
Students follow each command in the TPR student workbook, "Listen & Perform," they will hear a native English speaker.

Listen & Perform - French. Stephen M. Silvers. Read by Eric O. DuFour. Tr. by William Denevan. 2 cass. (Running Time: 1 hr. 30 min.). 1998. 15.95 wkbk. (978-1-56018-453-9(1)) Sky Oaks Prodns.
Follow each command in the TPR workbook, "Listen & Perform" taught in English & French.

Listen & Perform (Spanish) Stephen M. Silvers & Francisco L. Cabello. Read by Francisco L. Cabello. Ed. by James T. Asher. 1 cass. (Running Time: 1 hr. 30 min.). (SPA.). 1991. bk. 15.95 (978-1-56018-475-1(2)); 12.95 (978-1-56018-452-2(3)) Sky Oaks Prodns.

Listen & Say It Right in English. Nina Weinstein. 1 cass. (SPA.). 1994. pap. bk. 29.95 (978-0-8442-0436-9(6), 0436X) M-H Contemporary.

Listen & Say It Right in English. unabr. ed. 3 cass. (Running Time: 1 hr. 30 min. per cass.). bk. 44.50 incl. 96-page text, teacher's manual. (SEN110); 9.95 student text only. (BEN110); 5.95 tchr's manual only. (BEN111) J Norton Pubs.
Students who are interested in communicating effectively outside the classroom.

Listen & Sing. David A. (Associate Professor of Music Theory Damschroder. (ENG.). (C). 1995. 107.95 (978-0-02-870666-5(8)) Pub: Wadsworth Pub. Dist(s): CENGAGE Learn

Listen & Stop Smoking. Robert Parrish. 1 cass. (Running Time: 51 min.). 14.95 (978-0-89811-060-9(2), 7111) Meyer Res Grp.
Quit smoking by listening your way to new habits. Let your cassette player do the work; All you do is enjoy the benefits.

Listen & Stop Smoking. Robert Parrish. 1 cass. 10.00 (SP100024) SMI Intl.
Have you been saying, "I can quit whenever I want to"? Now you really can. Without expensive seminars, fancy filters, or nervous jitters you can listen your way to new habits. Let your cassette player do the work. All you do is enjoy the benefits.

Listen & Win: Communicate for a Competitive Edge. 1 cass. (Running Time: 30 mins.). pap. bk. 99.95 (1034AV); pap. bk. 99.95 (1034AV) J Wilson & Assocs.

Listen Around. Geoffrey Winters & Jim Northfield. (Running Time: 1 hr. 31 mins.). (ENG.). 1990. 42.00 (978-0-521-56919-4(2)) Cambridge U Pr.

Listen First: Focused Listening Tasks for Beginners. Jayme Adelson-Goldstein. 1991. 54.95 (978-0-19-434424-1(X)) OUP.

Listen for It: A Task-Based Listening Course. 2nd rev. ed. Jack C. Richards et al. 1996. audio compact disk 54.95 (978-0-19-434668-9(4)) OUP.

***Listen Here! Intermediate Listening Activities CDs.** Clare West. (Running Time: 2 hrs. 34 mins.). (Georgian Press Ser.). (ENG.). 2010. audio compact disk 27.00 (978-0-521-14042-3(0)) Cambridge U Pr.

Listen In, Bk. 1. 2nd ed. David Nunan. 2002. stu. ed. (978-0-8384-0417-1(0)) Heinle.

Listen In, Bk. 2. 2nd ed. David Nunan. 2002. stu. ed. (978-0-8384-0437-9(5)) Heinle.

Listen In Bk. 1: Assessment. 2nd ed. David Nunan. 2002. audio compact disk (978-0-8384-0430-0(8)) Heinle.

Listen In Bk. 2: Assessment. 2nd ed. David Nunan. 2002. audio compact disk (978-0-8384-0454-6(5)) Heinle.

Listen In Bk. 2: Exam. 2nd ed. David Nunan. 2002. audio compact disk (978-0-8384-0449-2(9)) Heinle.

Listen In Bk. 3: Assessment. 2nd ed. David Nunan. 1 cass. 2002. audio compact disk (978-0-8384-0485-0(5)) Heinle.

Listen Learn & Grow: Around the World. (J). 2002. audio compact disk 7.99 (978-1-930838-27-7(1)) Naxos.

Listen, Learn & Grow: Music to Stimulate & Inspire Young Minds. 1 cass. (Running Time: 30 mins.). (J). 2001. 4.99 (978-1-930838-03-1(4)); audio compact disk 7.99 (978-1-930838-04-8(2)) Naxos.

Listen, Learn & Grow Lullabies: Music to Stimulate & Inspire Young Minds. 1 cass. (Running Time: 30 mins.). (J). 2001. 4.99 (978-1-930838-05-5(0)); audio compact disk 7.99 (978-1-930838-06-2(9), Naxos AudioBooks) Naxos.

Listen Learn & Grow Playtime: Arts & Crafts. (J). 2002. audio compact disk 7.99 (978-1-930838-24-6(7)) Naxos.

Listen Learn & Grow Playtime: Fun & Games. (J). 2002. audio compact disk 7.99 (978-1-930838-25-3(5)) Naxos.

Listen Learn & Grow Playtime: Imagination. (J). 2002. audio compact disk 7.99 (978-1-930838-26-0(3)) Naxos.

Listen My Children. 1 cass. 10.00 Esstee Audios.
Paul Revere's ride & the start of the Revolution.

Listen, Read & Learn Spanish. 1996. bk. 12.95 (978-0-935540-08-6(3)) Plymouth Pr.

Listen, Read & Learn Spanish. 12th ed. Carol L. Flatto & Edwin Flatto. (ENG & SPA.). 1997. bk. 12.95 (978-0-935540-16-1(4)) Plymouth Pr.

Listen to Life with Dr. Joey Faucette: The First Book. Short Stories. 1 CD. (Running Time: 1 hr. 19 mins.). 2003. audio compact disk (978-0-9715074-0-1(6)) Listen to Life.
This CD is the audio book of the book in print by the same title, LISTEN TO LIFE WITH DR. JOEY FAUCETTE: THE FIRST BOOK. It features Dr. Faucette personally sharing these stories.

Listen to Me. abr. ed. Da Avabhasa. 1 cass. 1993. 11.95 (978-0-918801-87-6(7), AT-LM) Dawn Horse Pr.

Listen to Me Stories. unabr. ed. Short Stories. Alicia Aspenwall. Read by Laurie Klein. 2 cass. (Running Time: 1 hr. 30 min.). Dramatization. (J). 1992. 16.95 (978-1-55686-395-0(0), 395) Books in Motion.
Excellent stories of unlikely heroes, strange creatures, evil wizards & good fairies. The stories are: The Light on Burning Mountain, The Box Eating Antarilla, & A Discontented Rooster.

Listen to My Love. Ed. by Micheal D. Rose. 1 cass. (Running Time: 30 min.). (Sounds of Poetry). 1989. pap. bk. 14.95 (978-1-877985-02-7(3)); 9.95 (978-1-877985-01-0(5)) Sound Lrng Systems.
Features a collection of English & American lyric poetry 16th to 20th Century.

Listen to the Drummer Meditations: From Soul-Esteem: the Power of Spiritual Confidence. Scripts. Based on a book by Phylis Clay Sparks. 1 CD. (Running Time: 59 mins.). 2001. audio compact disk 14.95 (978-0-9665284-1-1(7)) Soul-Esteem.

Listen to the Loons. unabr. ed. 1 cass. (Solitudes Ser.). 9.95 (C11212) J Norton Pubs.
This tape tunes in the sounds & experiences of the natural environment.

Listen to the Silence. abr. ed. Marcia Muller. Narrated by Joyce Bean. 2 cass. (Running Time: 3 hrs.). (Sharon McCone Mystery Ser.: No. 20). 2000. 17.95 (978-1-56740-883-6(4), Nova Audio Bks) Brilliance Audio.
After Sharon McCone's father dies of a sudden heart attack, she immediately sets out to scatter his ashes & clear out his house. In a box of legal papers, she finds that she was adopted. No one is Sharon's family will discuss the adoption, so she begins her own search for the truth. her quest takes her deep into Indian country, to the Flathead Reservation in Montana. when her birth mother is critically injured in a hit & run accident, Sharon begins to understand that her search has caused a resurgence of old hatred & fueled present day violence.

Listen to the Silence. unabr. ed. Marcia Muller. Read by Kathy Garver. (Running Time: 6 hrs.). (Sharon McCone Mystery Ser.: No. 20). 2007. 39.25 (978-1-4233-3606-8(2), 9781423336068, BADLE); 24.95 (978-1-4233-3605-1(4), 9781423336051, BAD) Brilliance Audio.

Listen to the Silence. unabr. ed. Marcia Muller. Read by Kathy Garver. (Running Time: 21600 sec.). (Sharon McCone Mystery Ser.: No. 20). 2007. audio compact disk 24.95 (978-1-4233-3603-7(8), 9781423336037, Brilliance MP3); audio compact disk 39.25 (978-1-4233-3604-4(6), 9781423336044, Brlnc Audio MP3 Lib) Brilliance Audio.

Listen to the Storyteller. Perf. by Wynton Marsalis et al. Narrated by Kate Winslet & Graham Greene. Conducted by Robert Sadin & Steven Mercurio. Composed by Patrick J. Doyle. 1 cass. (J). 1999. bk. (SK60283) Sony Music Ent.
New musical tales for children include "The Fiddler & the Dancin' Witch," "The Lesson of the Land" & "The Face in the Lake".

Listen to Your Heart. unabr. ed. Fern Michaels. Read by Joyce Bean. 4 cass. (Running Time: 6 hrs.). 2000. 24.95 (978-1-56740-366-4(2), 1567403662, BAU) Brilliance Audio.
With her parents gone, her twin sister, Kitty, about to be married, and no hint of Mr. Right on the horizon, Josie Dupre is lonesome. Luckily, she has her booming New Orleans catering business, and her fluffy white dog, Rosie, to keep her company. Then, with all the subtlety of Bourbon Street at Mardi Gras, a jumbo-sized Boxer destroys Josie's flowering windowboxes, and in the process, brazenly captures petite Rosie's undying devotion. Now that Rosie and the aptly named Zip are an item, Josie finds herself an unwilling chaperone - and doing her best to avoid Zip's owner, the irritatingly appealing Paul Brouillette. Anyone can see that the wealthy, sexy Paul is little more than a love 'em and leave 'em Cajun playboy. He's all for l'amour, but Josie has no intention of falling for him. Still, ever since Paul came into her life, strange things have been happening. She hears music that isn't there. Then she smells her mother's favorite cologne in an empty room. Maybe her mom's trying to send her a message. Something about finding love where you least expect it . . . And listening to your heart.

Listen to Your Heart. unabr. ed. Fern Michaels. Read by Joyce Bean. (Running Time: 6 hrs.). 2005. 39.25 (978-1-59600-650-8(1), 9781596006508, BADLE); 24.95 (978-1-59600-649-2(8), 9781596006492, BAD); audio compact disk 39.25 (978-1-59600-648-5(X), 9781596006485, Brlnc Audio MP3 Lib); audio compact disk 24.95 (978-1-59600-647-8(1), 9781596006478, Brilliance MP3) Brilliance Audio.

Listen to Your Heart. unabr. ed. Fern Michaels. Read by Joyce Bean. (Running Time: 21600 sec.). 2006. audio compact disk 74.25 (978-1-4233-1453-0(0), 9781423314530, BriAudCD Unabrid); audio compact disk 26.95 (978-1-4233-1452-3(2), 9781423314523, Bril Audio CD Unabri) Brilliance Audio.

Listen to Your Heart Series. Kenneth W. Hagin, Jr. 3 cass. 1991. 12.00 Set. (25J) Faith Lib Pubns.

Listen to Your Hormones: An Unabridged MP3 Audio Book: A Doctor's Guide to Sex, Love & Long Life. 1 MP3 CD. (C). 2005. (978-0-9748634-1-2(6)) Wellness MD Pubns.

Listen Up. unabr. ed. Robert L. Montgomery & Robert Montgomery. Read by Robert L. Montgomery. 2 cass. (Running Time: 1 hr. 10 min.). (Smart Tapes Ser.). (J). (gr. 10-12). 1994. pap. bk. 19.95 Set. (978-1-55678-053-0(2), 3225, Lrn Inc) Oasis Audio.
These peak performance tips for work or school will also help you create lasting friendships & business relationships. Everyone likes a good listener, & with these skills you'll increase your knowledge & understanding in any situation.

Listen with Your Ears. William Janiak. 1 cass. (J). 10.95 incl. guide. (KIM70201C) Kimbo Educ.
Includes We Wash Our Face, We All Are Marching, I Have a Cold, My Name Is, Circle Dance, I Like to Wash, I Like to Jump & more.

Listen with Your Heart!, No. 3. Melea J. Brock. Illus. by Melea J. Brock. 1. (Running Time: 1 hr. 5 mins.). Dramatization. 1994. 10.00 (978-0-9667455-3-5(1)) Right-Side-Up.

Listen with Your Heart: Spiritual Living with the Rule of Saint Benedict. M. Basil Pennington. Ed. by Chaminade Crabtree. 2007. audio compact disk 18.95 (978-1-55725-555-6(5)) Paraclete MA.

Listen Your Way to Success. unabr. ed. Robert L. Montgomery. 3 cass. 59.95 incl. wkbk. (S1815) J Norton Pubs.
Explains how to listen your way to success & increase your ability to motivate, manage & sell. The power of active listening will help you - when participating in meetings, facing conflict, giving & getting instructions, making agreements.

Listen Your Way to Success. unabr. ed. Robert L. Montgomery. Read by Robert L. Montgomery. 3 cass. (Running Time: 60 min. per cass.). (J). (gr. 10-12). 1983. 39.95 incl. guide bk. (978-1-55678-009-7(5), 1522, Lrn Inc) Oasis Audio.
Learn the techniques that keep you focused on the message & avoiding listening traps.

Listener's Bible. Narrated by Max E. McLean. 2001. im. lthr. 199.95 (978-1-931047-17-3(0)); 129.95 (978-1-931047-18-0(9)) Fellow Perform Arts.

Listener's Bible Book of Acts. 2 CDs. 2004. audio compact disk 9.95 (978-1-931047-49-4(9)) Fellow Perform Arts.

Listener's Bible KJV. 4 MP3. 2006. 119.95 (978-1-931047-54-8(5)) Fellow Perform Arts.

Listener's Bible-KJV. Narrated by Max McLean. (Running Time: 288000 sec.). 2006. audio compact disk 119.95 (978-1-931047-53-1(7)); audio compact disk 34.95 (978-1-931047-52-4(9)) Fellow Perform Arts.

Listener's Book of Mark. 2 CDs. (Running Time: 91 mins). 2004. audio compact disk 10.95 (978-1-931047-48-7(0)) Fellow Perform Arts.

Listener's Book of Revelation. Narrated by Max E. McLean. Music by Michael Stanton. 1 CD. (Running Time: 73 mins.). Dramatization. 2002. audio compact disk 7.95 (978-1-931047-29-6(4)) Fellow Perform Arts.

Listener's Book of Romans. Narrated by Max E. McLean. 2002. audio compact disk 7.95 (978-1-931047-28-9(6)) Fellow Perform Arts.

Listener's Book of Ruth. Narrated by Max E. McLean. 1 CD. (Running Time: 15 mins). 2002. audio compact disk 9.95 (978-1-931047-32-6(4)) Fellow Perform Arts.

Listeners Choice. Created by Radio Spirits. (Running Time: 10800 sec.). 2004. 9.98 (978-1-57019-744-4(X)); audio compact disk 9.98 (978-1-57019-743-7(1)) Radio Spirits.

Listener's Complete ESV Bible. 2004. audio compact disk 149.95 (978-1-931047-43-2(X)); audio compact disk 49.95 (978-1-931047-45-6(6)) Fellow Perform Arts.

Listener's Complete MP3 Bible. Narrated by Max E. McLean. 6 CDs. (Running Time: 77 Hours). Dramatization. 2002. audio compact disk 39.95 (978-1-931047-30-2(8)) Pub: Fellow Perform Arts. Dist(s): Spring Arbor Dist
The complete text of the New International Version of the Bible in MP3 audio format.

Listeners Digest 404: They Say in U. S. A., Current Topics & Songs As Heard in American Daily Life. Dee G. Davis. 1 cass. (Running Time: 1 hr.). (YA). 1989. 5.00 bk. (978-0-929350-68-4(5)) Am Spoken English.
Exact sounds shown phonetically with a parallel column in usual spelling & extensive explanations of items not found in smaller dictionaries.

Listeners Digest 405: They Say in U. S. A., Current Topics & Songs As Heard in American Daily Life. unabr. ed. Dee G. Davis. 1 cass. (Running Time: 60 min.). (YA). 1989. 5.00 bk. (978-0-929350-69-1(3)) Am Spoken English.
A collection of excerpts of spontaneous American speech & song.

Listeners Digest 406: They Say in U. S. A., Current Topics & Songs As Heard in American Daily Life. unabr. ed. Dee G. Davis. 1 cass. (Running Time: 60 min.). (YA). 1989. 5.00 bk. (978-0-929350-70-7(7)) Am Spoken English.

Listeners Digest 407: They Say in U. S. A., Current Topics & Songs As Heard in American Daily Life. unabr. ed. Dee G. Davis. 1 cass. (Running Time: 60 min.). (YA). 1989. 5.00 bk. (978-0-929350-71-4(5)) Am Spoken English.

Listeners Digest 408: They Say in U. S. A., Current Topics & Songs As Heard in American Daily Life. unabr. ed. Dee G. Davis. 1 cass. (Running Time: 60 min.). (YA). 1989. 5.00 bk. (978-0-929350-72-1(3)) Am Spoken English.
A collection of excerpts of spontaneous American speech & songs.

Listeners Digest 409: They Say in U. S. A., Current Topics & Songs As Heard in American Daily Life. unabr. ed. Dee G. Davis. 1 cass. (Running Time: 60 min.). (YA). 1989. 5.00 bk. (978-0-929350-73-8(1)) Am Spoken English.
A collection of excerpts of spontaneous American speech & song.

Listeners Digest 410: They Say in U. S. A., Current Topics & Songs As Heard in American Daily Life. unabr. ed. Dee G. Davis. 1 cass. (Running Time: 60 min.). (YA). 1989. 5.00 bk. (978-0-929350-74-5(X)) Am Spoken English.

Listeners Digest 411: They Say in U. S. A., Current Topics & Songs As Heard in American Daily Life. unabr. ed. Dee G. Davis. 1 cass. (Running Time: 60 min.). (YA). 1989. 5.00 bk. (978-0-929350-75-2(8)) Am Spoken English.

Listeners Digest 412: They Say in U. S. A., Current Topics & Songs As Heard in American Daily Life. unabr. ed. Dee G. Davis. 1 cass. (Running Time: 60 min.). (YA). 1989. 5.00 bk. (978-0-929350-76-9(6)) Am Spoken English.

Listeners Digest 413: They Say in U. S. A., Current Topics & Songs As Heard in American Daily Life. unabr. ed. Dee G. Davis. 1 cass. (Running Time: 60 min.). (YA). 1989. 5.00 bk. (978-0-929350-77-6(4)) Am Spoken English.

Listeners Digest 414: They Say in U. S. A., Current Topics & Songs As Heard in American Daily Life. unabr. ed. Dee G. Davis. 1 cass. (Running Time: 60 min.). (YA). 1989. 5.00 bk. (978-0-929350-78-3(2)) Am Spoken English.
A collection of excerpts of spontaneous American speech & songs.

Listeners Digest 415: They Say in U. S. A., Current Topics & Songs As Heard in American Daily Life. Dee G. Davis. 1 cass. (Running Time: 60 min.). 5.00 bk. (978-0-929350-79-0(0)) Am Spoken English.
Contains excerpts from the Bickersons, Giants Eat, Pet Cloud Bob, Marihuana & Today' Youth, & also some songs.

Listeners Digest 416: They Say in U. S. A., Current Topics & Songs As Heard in American Daily Life. unabr. ed. Dee G. Davis. 1 cass. (Running Time: 60 min.). (YA). 1989. 5.00 bk. (978-0-929350-80-6(4)) Am Spoken English.
A collection of excerpts of spontaneous American speech & song.

Listener's Guide to Musical Understanding. 8th ed. Leon Dallin. 4 cass. (Running Time: 4 hrs.). (C). 1993. 87.81 (978-0-697-12512-5(2), Mc-H Human Soc) Pub: McGrw-H Hghr Educ. Dist(s): McGraw

Listener's Guide to the Blues Pt. 1: Son Seals. Hosted by B. B. King. Music by Son Seals. 1 cass. (Running Time: 30 min.). 9.95 (HO-87-02-04, HarperThor) HarpC GBR.

Listener's Guide to the Blues Pt. 2: Koko Taylor. Hosted by B. B. King. Comment by Koko Taylor. 1 cass. (Running Time: 30 min.). 9.95 (C068BB090, HarperThor) HarpC GBR.

Listener's Guide to the Blues Pt. 3: Johnny Copeland. Hosted by B. B. King. Comment by Johnny Copeland. 1 cass. (Running Time: 30 min.). 9.95 (HO-87-02-18, HarperThor) HarpC GBR.

Listener's Guide to the Blues Pt. 4: Lowell Fulson. Hosted by B. B. King. Comment by Lowell Fulson. 1 cass. (Running Time: 30 min.). 9.95 (C068DB090, HarperThor) HarpC GBR.

Listener's John's Gospel. 2 CDs. (Running Time: 116 mins). 2003. audio compact disk 10.95 (978-1-931047-36-4(7)) Fellow Perform Arts.

Listener's MP3 New Testament. 1 MP3. 2004. audio compact disk 19.95 (978-1-931047-47-0(2)) Fellow Perform Arts.

Listener's New Testament. Narrated by Max E. McLean. 2001. im. lthr. 69.95 (978-1-931047-19-7(7)); 39.95 (978-1-931047-20-3(0)) Fellow Perform Arts.

Listener's New Testament, ESV. Narrated by Max E. McLean. 16 CDs. Dramatization. 2003. audio compact disk 39.95 (978-1-931047-34-0(0)) Fellow Perform Arts.

Listener's New Testament, ESV. Narrated by Max E. McLean. 12 cass. 2003. 39.95 (978-1-931047-35-7(9)) Fellow Perform Arts.

Listener's New Testament with Psalms & Proverbs. 22 CDs. Dramatization. 2003. audio compact disk 49.95 (978-1-931047-33-3(2)) Fellow Perform Arts.

Listener's Playhouse: Christmas Eve at Crumps & Sire De Moletroit's Door. 1 cass. (Running Time: 1 hr.). 2001. 6.98 (2225) Radio Spirits.

Listener's Psalms & Proverbs. Narrated by Max E. McLean. 2001. 19.95 (978-1-931047-22-7(7)); audio compact disk 24.95 (978-1-931047-21-0(9)) Fellow Perform Arts.

Listening. 1 cass. (Running Time: 1 hr.). 12.99 (704) Yoga Res Foun.

Listening: Advanced. 4th ed. Adrian Doff & Christopher Jones. Contrib. by Adrian Doff. 2 cass. (Running Time: 2 hrs. 44 mins.). (Cambridge Skills for Fluency Ser.). (ENG.). 1996. 45.15 (978-0-521-36547-5(3)) Cambridge U Pr.

Listening: Intermediate. 2nd ed. Adrian Doff & Carolyn Becket. Contrib. by Adrian Doff. 2 cass. (Running Time: 2 hrs. 11 mins.). (Cambridge Skills for Fluency Ser.). (ENG.). 1991. 45.15 (978-0-521-36545-1(7)) Cambridge U Pr.

Listening: One of the Keys to Success. 1 cass. 7.95 (1687, Lrn Inc) Oasis Audio.

Listening: The Other Half of Communication. Miriam Rheinstein. 1986. 9.75 (978-0-932491-41-1(3)) Res Appl Inc.
Learn the skills it takes to retain what you listen to. Listening training is the key to better concentration training is the key to better concentration, retention, efficiency & work habits & relationships.

Listening Set: A Resource Book of Multi-Level Skills Activities. Miles Craven. (Cambridge Copy Collection). (ENG.). 2004. audio compact disk 45.00 (978-0-521-75462-0(3)) Cambridge U Pr.

Listening - A 90 Minute Workshop: How [illegible]ncrease Awareness of Your Inner Guide. Lee Coit. 1 cass. 1989. [illegible] 978-0-936475-02-8(1)) Las Brisas.
Discusses how to listen to one's inner spiritual voice.

Listening - Transactional Analysis & Rational Living. Frank L. Natter. 1 cass. (Running Time: 90 min.). (Improving Your Personal Problem-Solving Ser.: Pt. II: Relati). 1989. 10.00 (978-1-878287-69-4(9), ATA-12) Type & Temperament.
Anyone in a relationship about which they care deeply (good-shape relationships/difficult relationships) learn of new insights & ways to appreciate & improve those relationships. Natter's comments on the work of Albert Ellis, Thomas Harris & others.

Listening Activities. Holt, Rinehart and Winston Staff. (Ven Conmigo! Ser.). (SPA.). 1998. 22.73 (978-0-03-052283-3(8)) Holt McDoug.

Listening & Speaking. Jayme Adelson-Goldstein et al. (New Oxford Picture Dictionary (1988 Ed.) Ser.). 1993. act. bk. ed. 24.50 (978-0-19-434363-3(4)) OUP.

Listening & Speaking. Angela Blackwell & Therese Naber. (Open Forum Ser.). 2006. 54.95 (978-0-19-441777-8(8)) OUP.

Listening Comprehension Audiocassette to Accompany Dos Mundos. 5th ed. Created by McGraw-Hill Higher Education Staff. 2001. 24.00 (978-0-07-248613-1(9)) McGraw.

Listening Comprehension Audiocassette to Accompany Fokus Deutsch: Beginning German 2. Created by McGraw Hill Humanities. 1 cass. (Running Time: 90 min.). (GER & ENG.). (C). 1999. 16.88 (978-0-07-233461-6(4), 0072334614, Mc-H Human Soc) Pub: McGrw-H Hghr Educ. Dist(s): McGraw

Listening Comprehension CD to Accompany DOS Mundos. Trevor J. Terrell & J. Egasse. 2001. audio compact disk 24.00 (978-0-07-248606-3(6)) McGrw-H Hghr Educ.

Listening Comprehension Skills for Intermediate & Advanced Students: Audio CDs. Diaz. 2 CDs. audio compact disk 28.47 (978-0-13-116414-7(7)) PH School.

Listening Cycles. John R. Boyd & Mary Ann Boyd. 1985. 19.95 (978-0-933759-03-9(7)) Abaca Bks.

Listening Dictation: Understanding English Sentence Structure. Joan Morley. (C). 1984. pap. bk. 85.00 (978-0-472-00203-0(1)) U of Mich Pr.

Listening Focus. Ellen Kisslinger & Michael A. Rost. Illus. by Masaaki Nishiyama & Pam Olsen. (Lingual House Listening Skills Ser.). (J). 1980. 55.00 (978-0-940264-07-6(2), 78393) Longman.

Listening for Cactus. unabr. ed. Mary McGinnis. Read by Mary McGinnis. 1 cass. (Running Time: 60 min.). 1996. 5.95 (978-0-9644196-8-1(8)) Sherman Asher Pub.
Poetry celebrating the seen & unseen, the disability experience & the New Mexico landscape.

Listening for Lions. unabr. ed. Gloria Whelan. Read by Bianca Amato. 5 CDs. (Running Time: 4 hrs. 45 mins.). (J). 2006. audio compact disk 49.75 (978-1-4193-9410-2(X), C3727); 39.75 (978-1-4193-9405-8(3), 98372) Recorded Bks.
National Book Award winner Gloria Whelan introduces Rachel Sheridan, raised by missionary parents in East Africa. When her parents die in the Influenza epidemic of 1919, greedy neighbors the Pritchards force her to act as their daughter in a visit to Grandfather Pritchard in England. They hope to convince Grandfather not to cut them off from a substantial inheritance. But when Rachel and Grandfather become close, she wonders if she can continue the lie.

Listening for the Crack of Dawn. unabr. ed. Donald Davis. Read by Donald Davis. 2 cass. (Running Time: 1 hr. 57 mins.). (American Storytelling Ser.). (J). 1991. 18.00 (978-0-87483-147-4(4)) August Hse.
True stories of growing up in Appalachia in the 1950s & 60s, from first grade through the loss of a friend in Vietnam.

Listening for the Crack of Dawn: A Master Storyteller Recalls the Appalachia of This Youth. Donald Davis. 2 CDs. (Running Time: 1 hr. 57 mins.). (American Storytelling Ser.). 2000. audio compact disk 20.00 (978-0-87483-608-0(5)) Pub: August Hse. Dist(s): Natl Bk Netwk

Listening Heart: On Death, Dying, Illness, & Grief. Ram Dass. 2 cass. 18.00 Set. (A0666-89) Sound Photosyn.

Listening Heart: On Relationships. Ram Dass. 1 cass. 9.00 (A0664-89) Sound Photosyn.

Listening Heart: On Work, Money, & Burnout. Ram Dass. 1 cass. 9.00 (A0665-89) Sound Photosyn.

Listening Heart Vol. 1: Create Your Own Space, Lose the Weight of Your Past. Mary Butler & Richard Ernest. Read by Mary Butler. 1 cass. (Running Time: 30 min.). 1997. mass mkt. 12.50 (978-1-929990-01-6(4)) Listening Heart.
Two guided visual meditations,.

Listening Heart Vol. 2: Winter's Message, The Gift of Giving & Receiving. unabr. ed. Mary Butler & Richard Ernest. Read by Mary Butler & Richard Ernest. 1 cass. (Running Time: 30 min.). 1997. mass mkt. 12.50 (978-1-929990-02-3(2)) Listening Heart.
Two guided visual meditations beginning with a breathing exercise.

Listening Heart Vol. 3: Relax on the Great Salt Lake, Step into the Spotlight. Mary Butler & Richard Ernest. Read by Mary Butler & Richard Ernest. 1 cass. (Running Time: 30 min.). 1998. mass mkt. 12.50 (978-1-929990-03-0(0)) Listening Heart.
Two guided visual meditations.

Listening in the Real World: Clues to English Conversation. Michael A. Rost & Robert K. Stratton. 1978. pap. bk. 88.00 (978-0-685-03057-8(1), 78391) Longman.

Listening into Silence: Beyond Images. Harry Wilmer. 2 cass. (Running Time: 3 hrs.). 1995. 18.95 (978-0-7822-0481-0(3), 557) C G Jung IL.
A workshop which attempts to add to an understanding of eros & of that aspect of humanity & the cosmos out of which language, images, dreams, & communication arise. These tapes include a discussion of the use of silence in films as well as recorded excerpts of a real dream analysis from Dr. Wilmer's analytic practice.

Listening Is an Act of Love: A Celebration of American Life from the StoryCorps Project. abr. ed. Dave Isay. Narrated by Dave Isay. Contrib. by Storycorps Participants. (Running Time: 1 hr.). (ENG.). (gr. 12 up). 2007. audio compact disk 14.95 (978-0-14-314261-4(5), PengAudBks) Penguin Grp USA.

Listening Is the Foundation of Practice. Da Avabhasa. 1 cass. 1992. 11.95 (978-0-918801-59-3(1)) Dawn Horse Pr.

Listening Kit Listening Book: A Program to Build Listening Skills. Susan R. Simms et al. 1992. bk. 109.95 (978-1-55999-235-0(2)) LinguiSystems.

Listening Library. Petera Reynolds. audio compact disk (978-0-553-55423-6(9)) Random Audio Pubg.

Listening Tape for HIGCSE English As a Second Language (Trial Edition) University of Cambridge Local Examinations Syndication Staff. 1 cass. (Running Time: 1 hr. 30 mins.). (Cambridge Open Learning Project in South Africa Ser.). 1997. 8.99 (978-0-521-62533-3(5)) Cambridge U Pr.

Listening Tape for HIGCSE First Language English (Trial Edition) University of Cambridge Local Examinations Syndication Staff. 1 cass. (Running Time: 1 hr. 30 mins.). (Cambridge Open Learning Project in South Africa Ser.). 1997. 8.99 (978-0-521-62532-6(7)) Cambridge U Pr.

Listening Tape for IGCSE English As a Second Language (Trial Edition) University of Cambridge Local Examinations Syndication Staff. 1 cass. (Running Time: 43 mins.). (Cambridge Open Learning Project in South Africa Ser.). 1998. 8.99 (978-0-521-62520-3(3)) Cambridge U Pr.

Listening Tasks: For Intermediate Students of American English. Sandra R. Schecter. Cambridge U Pr.
Designed for students who need to understand authentic English spoken at normal speed in everyday situations. Practical topics, such as calling about an apartment, catching a plane, and finding out what's going on in town, make the material interesting and motivating. Contains improvised dialogs, telephone exchanges, public address announcements, and other short recordings of spontaneous, natural speech.

Listening Tasks: For Intermediate Students of American English. Sandra R. Schecter. 1 cass. (Running Time: 54 mins.). (ENG.). 1984. 24.00 (978-0-521-26258-3(5)) Cambridge U Pr.
A supplement to a listening course for ESL students who need to understand authentic American English spoken at normal speed in everyday situations. Practical topics, such as calling about an apartment, catching a plane, make the material interesting.

Listening Tasks: For Intermediate Students of American English. Sandra R. Schecter. 1 cass. 19.95 Midwest European Pubns.
For students who need to understand English spoken at normal speed in everyday situtations.

Listening Tasks for 40 Topics. Sachie Miyagi. 2003. pap. bk. 29.00 (978-4-89358-539-4(8)) Pub: Bonjinsha JPN. Dist(s): Cheng Tsui

Listening Tasks for 40 Topics, Vol. 2. Sachie Miyagi. 2003. pap. bk. 29.00 (978-4-89358-540-0(1)) Pub: Bonjinsha JPN. Dist(s): Cheng Tsui

Listening Tasks in the Economic Language Exam: Intermediate, Advanced. Istvan Zsigmond Bajko & Marta Pinter. (GER.). 2002. pap. bk. 25.00 (978-963-05-7800-4(X)) Akade Kiado HUN.

Listening: the Forgotten Skill: A Self-Teaching Guide. unabr. rev. ed. Madelyn Burley-Allen. Read by Madelyn Burley-Allen. (Running Time: 6 hrs.). (ENG.). 2007. audio compact disk 29.98 (978-1-59659-079-3(3), GildAudio) Pub: Gildan Media. Dist(s): HachBkGrp

Listening to Body & Soul: Messages of Healing. Galexis. 2 cass. (Running Time: 3 hrs.). 1994. 17.95 Set. (978-1-56089-035-5(5)) Visionary FL.
Integrate, balance, & heal the physical, emotional, mental, & spiritual bodies together. Includes meditation on Side 4.

Listening to Children Audiotapes. unabr. ed. Patricia Wipfler. Read by Patricia Wipfler. Read by Robert Mauldin. 3 cass. (Running Time: 2 hrs. 30 min.). (Listening to Children Ser.). 1993. 15.00 (978-1-891670-24-4(7)) Parents Ldshp.
Written for parents & anyone interested in caring well for children. They explain what children need & want from the people who love them.

Listening to Communicate in English. Virginia Nelson. 4 cass. 44.95 Set, incl. wkbk., tchr's. guide & answer key. Midwest European Pubns.
For intermediate students. Ideal for students who have completed the beginner's program.

Listening to Music. 3rd ed. Ed. by Prentice-Hall Staff. (C). 1999. 37.80 (978-0-13-040238-7(9), Prentice Hall) P-H.

Listening to Music. 3rd ed. Ed. by Jay D. Zorn. (C). 1999. 39.80 (978-0-13-040244-8(3), Prentice Hall) P-H.

Listening to Music: Music from Around the World, Platinum Level. (YA). (gr. 10). 2000. audio compact disk 15.47 (978-0-13-437143-6(7)) P-H.

Listening to Prozac. Peter D. Kramer. 2004. 10.95 (978-0-7435-4978-3(3)) Pub: S&S Audio. Dist(s): S and S Inc

Listening to the Awakener. Swami Amar Jyoti. 1 dolby cass. 1984. 9.95 (K-61) Truth Consciousness.
The Awakener guides us to the Truth existent (Asti) within us, shining (Bhati) & dear (Priya). Real listening to the Truth in every situation means losing a part of ourselves.

***Listening to the Beliefs of Emerging Churches: Five Perspectives.** Ed. by Robert E. Webber. (Running Time: 7 hrs. 11 mins. 0 sec.). (ENG.). 2009. 16.99 (978-0-310-30475-3(X)) Zondervan.

Listening to the Bible-NRSV. abr. ed. Michael Scherer. 16 CDs. 2003. audio compact disk 49.95 (978-0-8198-4507-8(8), 332-183) Pauline Bks.

Listening to Win. unabr. ed. Steve Hays. Read by Charles Harrington Elster. 5 cass. (Running Time: 5 hrs.). 2000. (978-1-931187-18-3(5), LW) Word Success.

Listening to Your Inner Voices. Emmet L. Robinson. Read by Emmet L. Robinson. 2 cass. (Running Time: 1 hr. 23 min.). 1990. 19.95 King Street.
How to find meaningful employment.

Listening Transitions: From Listening to Speaking. Robert Stratton & Michael A. Rost. (YA). 1982. 39.00 (978-0-940264-28-1(5), 78387) Pearson ESL.

Listening Woman. Tony Hillerman. Read by Nelson Runger. 5 cass. (Running Time: 6 hrs.). (Joe Leaphorn & Jim Chee Novel Ser.). 1993. 44.20 (978-1-56544-036-4(6), 250022); Rental 7.80 30 day rental Set. (250022) Literate Ear.
When blind prophets speak of those who cannot be seen, such as ghosts & witches, Lieutenant Joe Leaphorn of the Navajo Tribal Police knows better than to discount them. He does not like to deal with such matters, but he knows his people too well to overlook them.

Listening Woman. Tony Hillerman. Narrated by George Guidall. 4 cass. (Running Time: 6.75 hrs.). (Joe Leaphorn & Jim Chee Novel Ser.). 19.95 (978-1-4025-2541-4(9)) Recorded Bks.

Listening Woman. unabr. ed. Tony Hillerman. Read by Jonathan Marosz. 6 cass. (Running Time: 6 hrs.). (Joe Leaphorn & Jim Chee Novel Ser.). 1994. 48.00 (978-0-7366-2671-2(9), 3408) Books on Tape.
The brutal murders of an old man & a teenage girl leave authorities without a clue. The blind Navajo Listening Woman speaks of ghosts & witches, but Lt. Leaphorn of the tribal police investigates & discovers secrets as well as a 100-year-old conspiracy leading him to the most violent confrontation of his career.

Listening Woman. unabr. ed. Tony Hillerman. Read by George Guidall. 1 CD. (Running Time: 1 hr. 30 min.). (Joe Leaphorn & Jim Chee Novel Ser.). 2005. audio compact disk 14.95 (978-0-06-081510-3(8)) HarperCollins Pubs.

Listening Woman. unabr. ed. Tony Hillerman. Narrated by George Guidall. 6 CDs. (Running Time: 6.5 hrs.). (Joe Leaphorn & Jim Chee Novel Ser.). audio compact disk 29.95 (978-1-4025-2542-1(7)) Recorded Bks.

Listening Woman. unabr. ed. Tony Hillerman. Narrated by George Guidall. 5 cass. (Running Time: 6 hrs. 30 mins.). (Joe Leaphorn & Jim Chee Novel Ser.). 1990. 44.00 (978-1-55690-310-6(3), 90073E7) Recorded Bks.
Lieutenant Joe Leaphorn seeks to head off an American Indian terrorist group. A fistful of investigations have Leaphorn working against the clock: a hit & run attempt; two people bludgeoned to death during a Navajo medicine ceremony; a bank robbery & a militant American Indian terrorist group called the Buffalo Society.

Listening 1: Pre-intermediate. Adrian Doff & Carolyn Becket. (Running Time: 1 hr. 24 mins.). (Cambridge Skills for Fluency Ser.). (ENG., 1991. 25.20 (978-0-521-36544-4(9)) Cambridge U Pr.

Listerdale Mystery: And Eleven Other Stories. unabr. ed. Agatha Christie. Read by Hugh Fraser. (Running Time: 25020 sec.). (Audio Editions Mystery Masters Ser.). 2006. 29.95 (978-1-57270-496-1(9)) Pub: Audio Partners. Dist(s): PerseuPGW

Listerdale Mystery: And Eleven Other Stories. unabr. ed. Agatha Christie. Narrated by Hugh Fraser. (Running Time: 25020 sec.). (Audio Editions Mystery Masters Ser.). (ENG.). 2006. audio compact disk 29.95 (978-1-57270-497-8(7)) Pub: AudioGO. Dist(s): Perseus Dist

Liszt Concerto No. 2 in A Major, S125; Hungarian Fantasia, S123. Composed by Franz Liszt. 2006. pap. bk. 34.98 (978-1-59615-016-4(5), 1596150165) Pub: Music Minus. Dist(s): H Leonard

Liszt's Rhapsody. Composed by Franz Liszt. (Composer's Specials Ser.). 1998. audio compact disk 12.95 (978-0-634-00888-7(9), 0634008889) H Leonard.

Liszt's Rhapsody - ShowTrax. 1 CD. (Running Time: 1 hr.). 2000. audio compact disk 12.95 (00841337) H Leonard.

***Lit.** unabr. ed. Mary Karr. Read by Mary Karr. (ENG.). 2010. (978-0-06-196715-3(7), Harper Audio) HarperCollins Pubs.

***Lit: A Memoir.** unabr. ed. Mary Karr. Read by Mary Karr. (ENG.). 2010. (978-0-06-190158-4(X), Harper Audio) HarperCollins Pubs.

Lit: A Memoir. unabr. ed. Mary Karr. Read by Mary Karr. Read by Renée Raudman. 11 CDs. (Running Time: 13 hrs.). 2010. audio compact disk 39.99 (978-0-06-193900-6(5), Harper Audio) HarperCollins Pubs.

Lit Life. unabr. ed. Kurt Wenzel. Read by Dick Hill. (Running Time: 11 hrs.). 2005. 39.25 (978-1-59600-727-7(3), 9781596007277, BADLE); 24.95 (978-1-59600-726-0(5), 9781596007260, BAD); 39.25 (978-1-59600-725-3(7), 9781596007253, Brlnc Audio MP3 Lib); audio compact disk 24.95 (978-1-59600-724-6(9), 9781596007246, Brilliance MP3) Brilliance Audio.
Set in Manhattan and the Hamptons, LIT LIFE takes us on a romp through the world of two writers. Kyle Clayton, a once-hot-now-not young author/provocateur moves through the New York nightlife in an inebriated haze until he meets his literary hero, the dyspeptic and obscure novelist Richard Whitehurst, who tries to set him right. Whitehurst is suffering his own form of breakdown, due to years of public ambivalence to his work and his own neglect of his much younger wife. As the two spirits collide, they find in the other the crutch they've both been seeking. The question of which is worth more, celebrity or credibility, is one we all grapple with in the publishing industry, and Kyle and Richard do their best to answer it for us.

Litanies with Music. Music by Sheldon Cohen. 1 cass. (Running Time: 30 min.). (Devotional Tape Ser.). 8.95 (978-0-914070-47-4(9), 311) ACTA Pubns.
The only tape to put five litanies approved by the Catholic Church for public prayer to original music.

Litany for Dictatorships see Poetry of Benet

Litany for Dictatorships see Twentieth-Century Poetry in English, No. 23, Recordings of Poets Reading Their Own Poetry

Litany of Loreto. Perf. by William Biersach & Charles A. Coulombe. 12 cass. (Running Time: 1 hr. per cass.). 49.00 (20215); 49.00 (20215) Cath Treas.
Six talks that explore the history of the Litany of the Blessed Virgin Mary, focusing on the origin & explanation of each of Our Lady's royal appellations while drawing on the insights of great Marian Saints. Includes an in-depth discussion of Our Lady's "metaphoric titles".

Literacy, Set. (J). (gr. k-8). 2001. audio compact disk 189.00 (CZW11545) Am Guidance.

Literacy & the Ballot Box: I Want to Vote, but I Can't Read. Audrey Coleman. Read by Audrey Coleman. 1 cass. (Running Time: 30 min.). 9.95 (K0790B090, HarperThor) HarpC GBR.

Literacy & Youth: Getting the Job Done. 1 cass. (Running Time: 30 min.). 9.95 (D0280B090, HarperThor) HarpC GBR.

Literary Britain. unabr. ed. Ronald Hutton. Read by Ronald Hutton. Ed. by Craig Mayes. 3 cass. (Running Time: 3 hrs. 8 min.). (Personal Courier Ser.). 1992. 24.95 Set. (978-1-878877-08-6(9)) Educ Excursions.
An audio tour through Britain, exploring the lives & works of sixteen of Britain's most famous literary figures. Includes Tennyson, Shakespeare, Wordsworth, Byron, Burns, Dickens, Austen, Keats & more.

Literary Circles of Washington. unabr. ed. Edith N. Schafer. Read by Flo Gibson. 2 cass. (Running Time: 2 hrs.). 1994. 14.95 (978-1-55685-333-3(5)) Audio Bk Con.
A walking tour through Georgetown, & the Massachusetts Avenue Corridor & a visit to various historical sites where great writers lived, wrote & entertained. Full of anecdotes & surprising revelations, this is a charming guide for the literary traveler in the nation's capitol.

Literary Criticism of Stephen Spender. unabr. ed. Stephen Spender. 7 cass. 55.00 Set. (S102) J Norton Pubs.

Literary Fiction Collection, Set. Anita Brookner et al. 72 cass. 475.88 AudioGO.

Literary Ladies - the Brontes, Emily Dickinson, Margaret Mitchell Vol. 1: Three Literary Lectures. Featuring Elliot Engel. Directed By Gilfillan Carl. 3 cass. (Running Time: 3 hrs.). 1998. bk. 30.00 (978-1-890123-13-0(7), GS1) Media Cnslts.

Literary Legends. Created by Radio Spirits. 6 CDs. (Running Time: 21600 sec.). (Smithsonian Legendary Performers Ser.). 2004. pap. bk. 34.98 (978-1-57019-802-1(0), OTR 50472) Pub: Radio Spirits. Dist(s): AudioGO

Literary life in Tokyo, 1885-1915: Tayama Katai's memoirs 'Thirty years in Tokyo' Katai Tayama & Kenneth G. Henshall. 1987. reel tape (978-90-04-08119-2(4)) Brill Acad Pub.

Literary London: Bloomsbury & Chelsea. unabr. ed. Andrew Flack. Read by Barbara Duff & Denis J. Sullivan. 1 cass. (Running Time: 1 hr.). Dramatization. (Day Ranger Walking Adventures on Audio Cassette Ser.). 1989. 19.95 (978-1-877894-01-5(X)) Day Ranger.
Scripted dialogue & music to accompany an original walking route of Bloomsbury & Chelsea. Uses first hand accounts, eyewitness stories & brief excerpts of identified literature. Detailed maps included.

Literary Modernism: The Struggle for Modern History. Instructed by Jeffrey Perl. 4 cass. (Running Time: 6 hrs.). 1991. 39.95 (978-1-56585-061-3(0)) Teaching Co.

Literary Modernism: The Struggle for Modern History. Instructed by Jeffrey Perl. 8 CDs. (Running Time: 6 hrs.). 2006. audio compact disk 54.95 (978-1-59803-160-7(0)) Teaching Co.

Literary Mosaic see Tales of the Supernatural

Literary Potpourri. 10.00 (HT404) Esstee Audios.

Literary Style. unabr. ed. Elizabeth R. Bills. 1 cass. (Running Time: 25 min.). (Secrets of Successful Writers Ser.). 1963. 12.95 (23020) J Norton Pubs.
The writer is advised to write about life as he knows it & to do so in a language that is economic, concrete, particular & definite.

Literature: Amaryllis. unabr. ed. 3 cass. (Running Time: 4:05 hrs.). 2004. 30.00 (978-1-4000-9462-2(3), Listening Lib); audio compact disk 35.00 (978-1-4000-9501-8(8), Listening Lib) Random Audio Pubg.

Literature: Reading, Reacting, Writing. Laurie G. Kirszner. 2002. audio compact disk 55.95 (978-0-8384-7268-2(0)) Heinle.

Literature: Reading, Reacting, Writing. 4th ed. Laurie G. Kirszner. audio compact disk 55.95 (978-0-8384-7257-6(5)); audio compact disk 55.95 (978-0-8384-7259-0(1)); audio compact disk 55.95 (978-0-8384-7264-4(8)); audio compact disk 55.95 (978-0-8384-7272-9(9)); audio compact disk 55.95 (978-0-8384-7273-6(7)); audio compact disk 63.95 (978-0-8384-7318-4(0)); audio compact disk 60.95 (978-0-8384-7590-4(6)); audio compact disk 89.95 (978-0-8384-9919-1(8)); audio compact disk 55.95 (978-0-8384-7263-7(X)) Heinle.

Literature: Reading, Reacting, Writing. 4th ed. Laurie G. Kirszner. 2002. audio compact disk 55.95 (978-0-8384-7254-5(0)); audio compact disk 55.95 (978-0-8384-7255-2(9)); audio compact disk 55.95 (978-0-8384-7271-2(0)) Heinle.
The goal of the compact fourth edition is to expand the personal literary canons of both students and instructors - to include works that represent a varied assortment of cultures and view-points - to weave together old and new, past and present, classic and nontraditional, familiar and unfamiliar.

Literature: Timeless Voices, Timeless Themes. (YA). (gr. 11). 2000. stu. ed. 183.47 (978-0-13-434873-5(7)); audio compact disk 39.97 (978-0-13-051113-3(7)); audio compact disk 69.97 (978-0-13-051183-6(8)); audio compact disk 69.97 (978-0-13-051184-3(6)) P-H.

Literature: Timeless Voices, Timeless Themes. (YA). (gr. 12). 2000. audio compact disk 15.47 (978-0-13-435692-1(6)); audio compact disk 39.97 (978-0-13-051114-0(5)) P-H.

Literature: Timeless Voices, Timeless Themes. (YA). (gr. 10). 2001. stu. ed. 183.97 (978-0-13-050839-3(X)) P-H.

Literature: Timeless Voices, Timeless Themes. (YA). (gr. 12). 2000. stu. ed. 183.47 (978-0-13-434874-2(5)) P-H.

Literature: Timeless Voices, Timeless Themes, Bronze Level. (YA). (gr. 7). 2001. audio compact disk 15.47 (978-0-13-051885-9(9)); audio compact disk 69.97 (978-0-13-051195-9(1)) P-H.

Literature: Timeless Voices, Timeless Themes, Copper Level. (J). (gr. 6). 2001. audio compact disk 15.47 (978-0-13-051884-2(0)) P-H.

Literature: Timeless Voices, Timeless Themes, Copper Level (SPA.). (J). (gr. 6). 2001. audio compact disk 69.97 (978-0-13-051193-5(5)) P-H.

Literature: Timeless Voices, Timeless Themes, Gold Level. Joyce Armstrong Carroll et al. (YA). (gr. 9). 2001. audio compact disk 29.97 (978-0-13-437180-1(1)) P-H.

Literature: Timeless Voices, Timeless Themes, Gold Level (SPA.). (YA). (gr. 10). 2000. audio compact disk 69.97 (978-0-13-051181-2(1)) P-H.

Literature: Timeless Voices, Timeless Themes, Gold Level (YA). (gr. 6-12). 2000. audio compact disk 39.97 (978-0-13-051100-3(5)) P-H.

Literature: Timeless Voices, Timeless Themes, Gold Level (YA). (gr. 9). 2000. stu. ed. 183.47 (978-0-13-434871-1(0)); audio compact disk 15.47 (978-0-13-050818-8(7)) P-H.

Literature: Timeless Voices, Timeless Themes, Platinum Level. (YA). (gr. 10). 2000. stu. ed. 183.47 (978-0-13-434872-8(9)) P-H.

Literature: Timeless Voices, Timeless Themes, Platinum Level (YA). (gr. 10). 2000. audio compact disk 39.97 (978-0-13-051112-6(9)); audio compact disk 69.97 (978-0-13-051182-9(X)) P-H.

Literature: Timeless Voices, Timeless Themes, Silver Level. 1 cass. (Running Time: 1 hr. 30 mins.). (YA). (gr. 8). 2001. stu. ed. 183.47 (978-0-13-436398-1(1)); audio compact disk 15.47 (978-0-13-051886-6(7)) P-H.

Literature: Timeless Voices, Timeless Themes, Silver Level (SPA.). (YA). (gr. 8). 2001. audio compact disk 69.97 (978-0-13-051196-6(X)) P-H.

Literature & the American College. unabr. ed. Irving Babbitt. Read by Lois Betterton. 5 cass. (Running Time: 7 hrs.). 1989. 39.95 (978-0-7861-0098-9(2), 1091) Blckstn Audio.
In this classic work originally published in 1908, Babbitt defines & defends the classical discipline of "humanitas" as an answer to the erosion of ethical & cultural standards brought on by scientific naturalism & sentimental humanitarianism.

Literature for English. Goodman. 19.00 (978-0-07-285820-4(6)) M-H Contemporary.

Literature for English, Advanced One. Goodman. 19.00 (978-0-07-285823-5(0)) M-H Contemporary.

Literature for English, Advanced Two. Goodman. 19.00 (978-0-07-285824-2(9)) M-H Contemporary.

Literature for English, Intermediate One. Goodman. 19.00 (978-0-07-285821-1(4)) M-H Contemporary.

Literature for English, Intermediate Two Audiocassettes. Goodman. 19.00 (978-0-07-285822-8(2)) M-H Contemporary.

Literature for Life & Work Book 2. Created by Southwestern Educational Publishing. 1997. 94.50 (978-0-538-66718-0(4)) South-West.

***Literature for Life & Work, Book 2 Teacher's Resource Kit.** Elaine Bowe Johnson & Christine Bideganeta LaRocco. (ENG.). 1997. bk. 813.00 (978-0-538-66724-1(9)) South-West.

Literature of C S Lewis. Timothy B. Shutt. 2004. 87.75 (978-1-4025-8165-6(3)); audio compact disk 87.75 (978-1-4025-8166-3(1)) Recorded Bks.

Literature, The Epic In. unabr. ed. Ralph Bates. Read by Poetry Center Staff. 1 cass. (Running Time: 56 min). 12.95 (23110) J Norton Pubs.
A discussion of the excitement & trend created by Homer, his attributes as an artist & writer along with cultural life influence.

Literatures en Contexte le Monde Francophone. Luce. 1 cass. 1994. bk. 50.95 (978-0-15-501561-6(3)) Heinle.

Litetrax Accompaniment, Vol 69. Created by Hal Leonard Corporation Staff. (ENG.). 2009. audio compact disk 44.99 (978-1-4234-8852-1(0), 1423488520) Pub: Shawnee Pr. Dist(s): H Leonard

Lithuanian: Learn to Speak & Understand Lithuanian with Pimsleur Language Programs. Pimsleur Staff. (Running Time: 500 hrs. 0 mins. NaN sec.). (Compact Ser.). (ENG.). 2004. audio compact disk 115.00 (978-0-7435-3689-9(4), Pimsleur) Pub: S&S Audio. Dist(s): S and S Inc

Lithuanian: Learn to Speak & Understand Lithuanian with Pimsleur Language Programs. unabr. ed. Pimsleur Staff. 5 CDs. (Running Time: 50 hrs. 0 mins. 0 sec.). (Compact Ser.). (LIT & ENG.). 2006. audio compact disk 49.95 (978-0-7435-5064-2(1), Pimsleur) Pub: S&S Audio. Dist(s): S and S Inc

Lithuanian::Learn to Speak & Understand Lithuanian with Pimsleur Language Programs. unabr. ed. Pimsleur Staff & Pimsleur. 5 cass. (Running Time: 500 hrs. 0 mins. NaN sec.). (Pimsleur Language Program Ser.). (LIT & ENG.). 1997. 95.00 (978-0-671-57940-1(1), Pimsleur) Pub: S&S Audio. Dist(s): S and S Inc
SPEAK LITHUANIAN TO LEARN LITHUANIAN The Pimsleur Method will have you speaking Lithuanian in just a few short, easy-to-use lessons. Learn at your own pace, comfortably and conveniently. No books to study. No memorization drills. LEARN LITHUANIAN AS YOU LEARNED ENGLISH You learned English by listening. With Pimsleur, you listen to learn Lithuanian. This Language Program was developed by renowned memory expert, Dr. Paul Pimsleur. His research led him to the realization that the most important use of memory is in language learning. Based on this, Dr. Pimsleur designed a learning program that works for any language. The Pimsleur Language Program is an integrated system which immerses you in the language, encouraging you to hear, understand and use the language all at the same time. Now you can take advantage of Dr. Pimsleur's research. At the completion of these eight lessons you will comfortably understand and speak at a beginner level.

Lithuanian: Short Course, Set. Paul Pimsleur. 5 cass. (Pimsleur Language Learning Ser.). 1996. 149.95 Set, incl. study guide. (0671-57940-1) SyberVision.

***Lithuanian: The Complete Course for Beginners.** 2nd rev. ed. Meilute Ramoniene & Ian Press. (Colloquial Ser.). (LIT & ENG.). 2010. audio compact disk 44.95 (978-0-415-56093-1(4)) Pub: Routledge. Dist(s): Taylor and Fran

Lithuanian for Speakers of English, Compact. unabr. ed. 5 cass. (Running Time: 5 hrs.). (Pimsleur Tapes Ser.). (LIT.). 1996. 129.00 (18560, Pimsleur) S&S Audio.
A ten-lesson-unit program based upon the Pimsleur Spoken Language Programmed Instructional Method, providing basic beginning language training to the ACTFL Novice Level.

Lithuanian Medley. 1 cass., bklet. (Running Time: 1 hr.). (LIT.). pap. bk. 24.95 (978-1-57970-007-2(1), SLT100) J Norton Pubs.

Litigating For & Against the FDIC & the RTC. 8 cass. (Running Time: 10 hrs. 30 min.). 1990. bk. 75.00 incl. course handbook. (T6-9146) PLI.

Litigating in Orphans' Court. 1997. bk. 99.00 (ACS-1364) PA Bar Inst.
If you ever venture into Orphan's Court, you will want to have this in your library.

Litigating Limited Partners' Securities Actions. 6 cass. (Running Time: 7 hrs. 30 min.). bk. 75.00 incl. 505-page course handbook. (T6-9147) PLI.

Litigating Medical Malpractice Claims. 10 cass. (Running Time: 14 hrs. 30 min.). 1996. pap. bk. & stu. ed. 275.00 (MB19) Am Law Inst.
Basic course designed for litigators with limited trial experience.

Litigating the Complex Motor Vehicle "Crashworthiness" Case. unabr. ed. Contrib. by Neil A. Goldberg. 7 cass. (Running Time: 9 hrs. 30 min.). 1989. 50.00 course handbk. (T7-9244) PLI.
In this recording of the October 1989 program, a panel of nationally prominent trial attorneys & experts examine thee complex issues, strategies & state of the art technologies associated with accident reconstruction in the context of motor vehicle litigation in which catastrophic injuries are involved. The program covers prosecution & defense of complex motor vehicle cases involving passenger vehicles, over-the-road & industrial trucks, motorcycles, ATV's & other recreational vehicles.

Litigating the Legal Malpractice Case. 1986. bk. 80.00 incl. book.; 45.00 cass. only.; 35.00 book only. PA Bar Inst.

Litigating the Legal Malpractice Case. 1997. bk. 99.00 (ACS-1299) PA Bar Inst.
Attorney malpractice claims seem to be growing daily. With the expected action by the American Law Institute on liability issues in the Restatement of the Law Governing Lawyers, interest in the field is likely to grow. This serves as an overview of every element of a legal malpractice case, with emphasis on the current cases & cutting edge issues. The expert authors of plaintiff & defense attorneys share their insights on proving damages for lost opportunities to settle, vicarious liability, & the potential liability for failure to maintain an effective system to detect conflicts.

Litigating the Legal Malpractice Case. 1986. 45.00 (AC-335) PA Bar Inst.

Litigating Under Nineteen Hundred & Eighty-Three. 1996. bk. 99.00 (ACS-1129) PA Bar Inst.
This produces more litigation than almost any other federal statute. Keeping up with the latest developments in the field is critical. Focuses on the most important emerging theories & topics relating to 11983 liability. Plantiffs attorneys will learn creative ways for converting their clients concerns into legitimate causes of action. Defense attorneys will find out how to prepare & deliver a strong defense when faced with an innovative claim under the statute.

Litigating with the FDIC & RTC: Asset-Based Claims - A Satellite Program. 1 cass. (Running Time: 3 hrs. 30 min.). 85.00 three audiocass. (T7-9319) PLI.

Litigation As Lobbying: Reproductive Hazards & Interest Aggregation. Julianna S. Gonen. 2003. audio compact disk 9.95 (978-0-8142-9018-7(3)) Pub: Ohio St U Pr. Dist(s): Chicago Distribution Ctr

Litigation Management & Organization: The Winning Edge. Read by Mark A. Dombroff. 125.00 incl. 161-page desk reference. (5314) Natl Prac Inst.
Discussion of a series of organization & management techniques, proven in practice.

Litigation Management & Organization: The Winning Edge. Mark A. Dombroff. 1985. 125.00 (978-1-55917-390-2(4)) Natl Prac Inst.

Litigator & the Personal Computer. 1 cass. 1989. bk. 45.00 (AC-513) PA Bar Inst.

Litigators under Fire: When Litigation Strategy Confronts Ethical Professional Responsibility, April 1998. 2 cass. (Running Time: 3 hrs.). 1998. stu. ed. 175.00 (D275) Am Law Inst.
Nationally recognized experts in the professional responsibility field offer fast-paced, hypothetical-driven discussion of ethical dilemmas & strategic decisions that every litigator & house counsel must make.

Litteratures de la France Medievale. Michel Zink. 1 cass. (Running Time: 60 mins.). (College de France Lectures). (FRE.). 1996. 21.95 (1851-LQP) Olivia & Hill.

Litteratures en Contexte. Luce. (C). bk. 69.95 (978-0-8384-6559-2(5)) Heinle.

***Little Altars Everywhere.** abr. ed. Rebecca Wells. Read by Rebecca Wells. (ENG.). 2009. (978-0-06-196245-5(7), Harper Audio); (978-0-06-196246-2(5), Harper Audio) HarperCollins Pubs.

Little Altars Everywhere. unabr. ed. Rebecca Wells. 7 cass. (Running Time: 10 hrs. 30 mins.). (Ya-Ya Ser.: Bk. 1). 2002. 56.00 (978-0-7366-8727-0(0)); audio compact disk 64.00 (978-0-7366-8799-7(8)) Books on Tape.
A book that stuns - aesthetically, emotionally, psychologically. At its core is Siddalee's dysfunctional Southern family. Now thirty-eight, Siddalee lives in New York and tries to understand a childhood dominated by her beautiful, dramatic mother, Viviane, who drank and then beat and sexually abused her children. Then there's her father, Big Shep, an alcoholic as well, a sensitive Louisiana farmer who can never quite say what he wants, unless it's to yell at his wife. And of course all of them tell their stories, packing full lives into anecdotes and scenes told as adults or remembered as children.

***Little Altars Everywhere.** unabr. ed. Rebecca Wells. Read by Judith Ivey. (ENG.). 2009. (978-0-06-196162-5(0), Harper Audio); (978-0-06-196161-8(2), Harper Audio) HarperCollins Pubs.

Little Angel Comes Home to Stay & Little Angel, Bonjour! unabr. ed. Rachel Anderson. Read by Rachel Anderson. 2 cass. (Running Time: 2 hrs.). (J). 1994. 18.95 (978-0-7451-2455-1(0), CCA 3297) AudioGO.
When Gabrielle finds herself very lonely, she goes to stay with the Potters. But their family is total chaos! There's Mrs. Potter, the twins, Benjy, Don, Matt & the baby. So Gabrielle decides to travel to France, where she finds herself at the mercy of the Potter family again & some invisible biting dogs!.

Little Angel Comes to Stay. unabr. ed. Rachel Anderson. Read by Rachel Anderson. 2 cass. (Running Time: 2 hrs.). (J). 1997. 18.95 (CCA 3297, Chivers Child Audio) AudioGO.

Little Ant. unabr. ed. David Novak. 1 cass. (Running Time: 11 min.). (J). (gr. k-4). 1994. pap. bk. 10.95 (978-0-8045-6828-9(6), 6828) Spoken Arts.

Little Badness. unabr. ed. Josephine Cox. Read by Maggie Ollerenshaw. 10 cass. (Running Time: 10 hrs.). 1995. 84.95 (978-0-7451-6546-2(X), CAB 1162) AudioGO.
Young Cathy Blackthorn had never received much love from her mother. Rather, it was her beloved Aunt Margaret who had been more of a mother than her own could ever be. And when Cathy's father brings home a young orphan & announces that he will be the son they have never had, Cathy despairs of ever winning their love.

Little Bear. abr. ed. Else Holmelund Minarik. Illus. by Maurice Sendak. (I Can Read Bks.). (J). (gr. k-3). 2005. 9.95 (978-0-06-074107-5(4), HarperFestival) HarperCollins Pubs.

Little Bear. unabr. abr. ed. Else Holmelund Minarik. Illus. by Maurice Sendak. 1 cass. (I Can Read Bks.). (J). (gr. k-3). 1990. 8.99 (978-1-55994-234-8(7)) HarperCollins Pubs.

Little Bear: Father Bear Comes Home - Little Bear's Friend - Little Bear's Visit - A Kiss for Little Bear. unabr. ed. Else Holmelund Minarik. Read by Sigourney Weaver. (J). (ps-3). 2007. audio compact disk 14.95 (978-0-06-122743-1(9), HarperChildAud) HarperCollins Pubs.

Little Bear Audio Collection. unabr. anniv. ed. Else Holmelund Minarik & Maurice Sendak. 1 cass. (Running Time: 60 mins.). (J). 1999. 11.98 (Listening Lib) Random Audio Pubg.
Includes: "Little Bear," "Father Bear Comes Home," "Little Bear's Friend," "Little Bear's Visit" & "A Kiss for Little Bear".

Little Bear's Friend. abr. ed. Else Holmelund Minarik. Illus. by Maurice Sendak. (I Can Read Bks.). (J). (ps-ps). 2005. cass., cass. 9.95 (978-0-06-078689-2(2), HarperFestival) HarperCollins Pubs.

Little Bear's Friend. unabr. abr. ed. Else Holmelund Minarik. Illus. by Maurice Sendak. 1 cass. (I Can Read Bks.). (J). (gr. k-3). 1990. 8.95 (978-1-55994-235-5(5)) HarperCollins Pubs.

Little Bear's Visit. 2004. bk. 24.95 (978-1-56008-249-1(6)); pap. bk. 14.95 (978-0-7882-0614-6(1)); pap. bk. 32.75 (978-1-55592-256-6(2)); pap. bk. 32.75 (978-1-55592-257-3(0)); 8.95 (978-1-56008-950-6(4)); cass. & flmstrp 30.00 (978-0-89719-535-5(3)) Weston Woods.

Little Bears Visit. 2004. pap. bk. 14.95 (978-1-55592-717-2(3)) Weston Woods.

Little Bear's Visit. Else Holmelund Minarik. Illus. by Maurice Sendak. 1 read-along cass. (Running Time: 15 min.). (I Can Read Bks.). (J). (ps-1). 1985. bk. 5.98 (978-0-694-00032-6(9), JC-023, HarperTrophy) HarperCollins Pubs.

Little Bear's Visit. Else Holmelund Minarik. Illus. by Maurice Sendak. 1 cass. (Running Time: 15 min.). (J). bk. 24.95; pap. bk. 32.75 Weston Woods.

Little Bear's Visit. Else Holmelund Minarik. Illus. by Maurice Sendak. 1 cass. (Running Time: 14 min.). (J). pap. bk. 12.95 Weston Woods.
A visit to Grandmother & Granfather's house means a perfect day of fun for Little Bear.

Little Bear's Visit. Else Holmelund Minarik. Illus. by Maurice Sendak. (J). (gr. k-3). 2004. 8.95 (978-0-7882-0089-2(5)) Weston Woods.

Little Bear's Visit. unabr. abr. ed. Else Holmelund Minarik. Illus. by Maurice Sendak. 1 cass. (I Can Read Bks.). (J). (gr. k-3). 1990. 8.95 (978-1-55994-236-2(3)) HarperCollins Pubs.

Little Beaver & the Echo CD. unabr. ed. Amy MacDonald. Illus. by Sarah Fox-Davies. (Running Time: 1 hr. 4 mins.). (ENG.). (J). (ps-2). 2004. audio compact disk 7.99 (978-0-7636-2427-9(6)) Pub: Candlewick Pr. Dist(s): Random

Little Bee. unabr. ed. Chris Cleave. Read by Anne Flosnik. 9 CDs. (Running Time: 11 hrs. 0 mins. 0 sec.). (ENG.). 2009. audio compact disk 34.99 (978-1-4001-1171-8(4)); audio compact disk 24.99 (978-1-4001-6171-3(1)); audio compact disk 69.99 (978-1-4001-4171-5(0)) Pub: Tantor Media. Dist(s): IngramPubServ

Little Big Horn. abr. ed. Jerry Robbins. Music by Jeffrey Gage. Prod. by Mark Vander Berg. 2 cass. (Running Time: 2 hrs. 3 mins.). 2001. 18.99 (978-1-929244-09-6(6)) Pub: Colonial Radio. Dist(s): Penton Overseas
Nobody questions General George Armstrong Custer's bravery but everyone wonders what really happened in the Valley of the Little Big Horn. Ride with the Custer brothers & the Seventh Calvary as they advance towards Sitting Bull's braves and their date with destiny.

Little Big Horn/The Bozeman Trail. Perf. by Colonial Radio Theatre Staff. 2 cass. (Running Time: 2 hrs.). 2001. 19.95 (COLR008) Lodestone Catalog.
Custer leads his 7th cavalry in the valley of the Little Big Horn,where his command lost their lives & the Plains Indians lost their way of life. When the treaties were signed, the forts along the trail had to be abandoned & Red Cloud became the only Chief to win a war with the United States.

Little Big Man. unabr. ed. Thomas Berger. Read by Stuart Milligan. 14 cass. (Running Time: 21 hrs.). (Isis Ser.). (J). 2001. 99.95 (978-0-7531-0863-5(1), 000609) Pub: ISIS Lrg Prnt GBR. Dist(s): Ulverscroft US
I am a white man and never forget it, but I was brought up by the Cheyenne Indians from the age of ten. So starts the story of Jack Crabb who won the name Little Big Man. He dressed in skins, feasted on dog, loved four wives and saw his people butchered but eh horse soldiers of General Custer, the man he had sworn to kill. As a white man, Crabb hunted buffalo, tangled with Wyatt Earp, cheated Wild Bill Hickok and survived the Battle of the Little Bighorn.

Little Big Man. unabr. ed. Thomas Berger. Read by Stuart Milligan. 18 CDs. (Running Time: 19 hrs. 4 mins.). (Isis Ser.). (J). 2002. audio compact disk 116.95 (978-0-7531-1395-0(3)) Pub: ISIS Lrg Prnt GBR. Dist(s): Ulverscroft US

Little Big Man, unabr. collector's ed. Thomas Berger. Read by Grover Gardner. 12 cass. (Running Time: 18 hrs.). 1988. 96.00 (978-0-7366-2706-1(5), 3439) Books on Tape.
Jack Crabb is 111 years old. He is the son of two fathers, one white, the other a Cheyenne Indian chief who gave him the name Little Big Man. As a Cheyenne, Crabb feasted on dog, loved four wives & saw his people butchered by horse-soldiers commanded by Custer. As a white man, he helped hunt the buffalo into extinction, tangled with Wyatt Earp, cheated Wild Bill Hickok & lived through the showdown that followed. He also survived the Battle of Little Bighorn, where he fought side by side with Custer himself - even though he'd sworn to kill him.

***Little Big Things.** unabr. ed. Thomas J. Peters. Read by Thomas J. Peters. (ENG.). 2010. (978-0-06-200999-9(0), Harper Audio) HarperCollins Pubs.

***Little Big Things: 163 Ways to Pursue EXCELLENCE.** unabr. ed. Thomas J. Peters. Read by Thomas J. Peters. (ENG.). 2010. (978-0-06-200419-2(0), Harper Audio) HarperCollins Pubs.

Little Bird. unabr. ed. Barbara Sobel. Illus. by Karen Neulinger. 1 cass. (Running Time: 7 min.). (Friends & Neighbors Ser.). (J). (gr. k-2). 1986. lib. bdg. 16.99 incl. hardcover. (978-0-87386-018-5(7)) Jan Prods.
Amy has good intentions when she brings home an injured bird; but her cat, Jack, does not.

Little Bird Audiobook Classics: William Shakespeare, Stories from Twenty Plays. Edith Nesbit. As told by Tony LoVerde. 2007. pap. bk. 29.95 (978-1-933900-08-7(3)) Pub: Open Texture. Dist(s): Natl Bk Netwk

Little Bit Clumsy. Lou Del Bianco. 1 cass. (Running Time: 54 min.). (J). (gr. k-6). 1996. 10.00 (978-0-9642659-4-3(X), CL3385); audio compact disk 15.00 (978-0-9642659-3-6(1)) Story Maker.
Collection of songs & stories from the author's childhood.

Little Bit of Maya. 1 cass., bklet. (Running Time: 60 mins.). pap. bk. 24.95 (AFMY10) J Norton Pubs.
Basic vocabulary conversations & songs in a language that flourished over a thousand years ago are particulary useful for travelers to Mexico's Yucatan peninsula.

Little Bit Wicked: Life, Love, & Faith in Stages. unabr. ed. Kristin Chenoweth & Joni Rodgers. Narrated by Kristin Chenoweth. (Running Time: 6 hrs. 51 mins. 45 sec.). (ENG.). 2009. 23.09 (978-1-60814-483-9(6), SpringWater); audio compact disk 32.99 (978-1-59859-564-2(4), SpringWater) Oasis Audio.

Little Bitty Lies. abr. ed. Mary Kay Andrews. Read by Debra Monk. 6 CDs. (Running Time: 9 hrs.). 2004. audio compact disk 29.95 (978-0-06-074510-3(X)) HarperCollins Pubs.

***Little Bitty Lies.** abr. ed. Mary Kay Andrews. Read by Debra Monk. (ENG.). 2004. (978-0-06-082429-7(8), Harper Audio); (978-0-06-082428-0(X), Harper Audio) HarperCollins Pubs.

Little BK of Atheist Spirituality. Andre Comte-Sponville. 2008. reel tape 19.95 (978-1-4332-0844-7(X)); audio compact disk 19.95 (978-1-4332-0845-4(8)) Blckstn Audio.

Little Black Book of Connections: 6. 5 Assets for Networking Your Way to Rich Relationships. unabr. ed. Jeffrey Gitomer. Read by Jeffrey Gitomer. (Running Time: 4 hrs. 0 mins. 0 sec.). (ENG.). 2009. 49.99 (978-0-7435-7534-8(2)); audio compact disk 29.99 (978-0-7435-7258-3(0)) Pub: S&S Audio. Dist(s): S and S Inc

Little Blue Book of Courage: Timeless Thoughts of Bravery to Shield You in a Changing World. unabr. ed. Ed. by Clinton Galloway. 2003. audio compact disk 29.95 (978-0-9708860-3-3(9)) Phoenix Pubng Corp.

Little Book. unabr. ed. Selden Edwards. Narrated by Jeff Woodman. 13 CDs. (Running Time: 15 hrs.). (ENG.). (gr. 8 up). 2008. audio compact disk 39.95 (978-0-14-314351-2(4), PengAudBks) Penguin Grp USA.

***Little Book of Behavioral Investing: How not to be your own worst enemy (Little Book, Big Profits)** unabr. ed. James Montier. Read by Sean Pratt. (Running Time: 4 hrs.). (ENG.). 2010. 24.98 (978-1-59659-555-2(8), GildAudio) Pub: Gildan Media. Dist(s): HachBkGrp

***Little Book of Big Dividends: A Safe Formula for Guaranteed Returns.** unabr. ed. Charles B. Carlson & Terry Savage. Read by Sean Pratt. (Running Time: 4 hrs.). (ENG.). 2010. 24.98 (978-1-59659-556-9(6), GildAudio) Pub: Gildan Media. Dist(s): HachBkGrp

***Little Book of Bull Moves (Updated & Expanded) How to Keep Your Portfolio up When the Market Is up, down, or Sideways.** unabr. ed. Peter D. Schiff. Read by Sean Pratt. (Running Time: 7 hrs.). (ENG.). 2010. 29.98 (978-1-59659-630-6(9), GildAudio) Pub: Gildan Media. Dist(s): HachBkGrp

***Little Book of Bulletproof Investing: Do's & Don'ts to Protect Your Financial Life.** unabr. ed. Ben Stein & Phil DeMuth. Read by Don Hagen. (Running Time: 4 hrs. 30 mins.). (ENG.). 2010. 27.98 (978-1-59659-570-5(1), GildAudio) Pub: Gildan Media. Dist(s): HachBkGrp

Little Book of Common Sense Investing: The Only Way to Guarantee Your Fair Share of Stock Market Returns. unabr. ed. John C. Bogle. Read by Thom Pinto. 4 CDs. (Running Time: 5 hrs.). 2007. audio compact disk 49.95 (978-0-7927-4731-4(3)) AudioGO.

Little Book of Common Sense Investing: The Only Way to Guarantee Your Fair Share of Stock Market Returns. unabr. ed. John C. Bogle. Read by Thom Pinto. (Running Time: 4 hrs. 30 mins. 0 sec.). (ENG.). 2007. audio compact disk 24.95 (978-1-4272-0145-4(5)) Pub: Macmill Audio. Dist(s): Macmillan

***Little Book of Economics.** unabr. ed. Greg Ip. Read by Sean Pratt. (Running Time: 5 hrs.). (ENG.). 2010. audio compact disk 29.98 (978-1-59659-524-8(8), GildAudio) Pub: Gildan Media. Dist(s): HachBkGrp

Little Book of Forgiveness: Challenges & Meditations for Anyone with Something to Forgive. D. Patrick Miller. 2004. bk. 15.00 (978-0-9656809-8-1(3)) Fearless Bks.

Little Book of MAIN STREET MONEY: 21 Simple Truths That Help Real People Make Real Money. unabr. ed. Jonathan Clements. Read by Sean Pratt. (Running Time: 4 hrs. 30 mins.). (ENG.). 2009. 24.98 (978-1-59659-411-1(X), GildAudio) Pub: Gildan Media. Dist(s): HachBkGrp

***Little Book of Safe Money.** unabr. ed. Jason Zweig. Read by Sean Pratt. (Running Time: 5 hrs. 30 mins.). (ENG.). 2009. 27.98 (978-1-59659-503-3(5), GildAudio) Pub: Gildan Media. Dist(s): HachBkGrp

Little Book of Safe Money. unabr. ed. Jason Zweig. Read by Sean Pratt. (Running Time: 5 hrs. 30 mins.). (ENG.). 2010. audio compact disk 29.98 (978-1-59659-354-1(7), GildAudio) Pub: Gildan Media. Dist(s): HachBkGrp

Little Book of Stress Relief. David Posen. (Running Time: 3 hrs. 30 mins. 0 sec.). (ENG.). 2009. audio compact disk 17.95 (978-1-55263-858-3(8)) Pub: Key Porter CAN. Dist(s): PerseuPGW

Little Book of Train Stories. Heather Amery. (Farmyard Tales Readers Ser.). (J). (ps-3). 2005. bk. 10.95 (978-0-7945-1182-1(1), UsborneU) EDC Pubng.

Little Book of Value Investing. unabr. ed. Christopher H. Browne. Read by John Bedford Lloyd. Frwd. by Roger Lowenstein. (Running Time: 4 hrs. 30 mins. 0 sec.). (ENG.). 2006. audio compact disk 24.95 (978-1-4272-0083-9(1)) Pub: Macmill Audio. Dist(s): Macmillan

Little Book That Beats the Market. unabr. ed. Joel Greenblatt. Read by Adam Grupper. 3 CDs. (Running Time: 3 hrs. 0 mins. 0 sec.). (ENG.). 2006. audio compact disk 19.95 (978-0-7435-5585-2(6), Sound Ideas) Pub: S&S Audio. Dist(s): S and S Inc

Little Book That Beats the Market. unabr. ed. Joel Greenblatt. Read by Adam Grupper. 2006. 11.95 (978-0-7435-6485-4(5)) Pub: S&S Audio. Dist(s): S and S Inc

Little Book That Builds Wealth: Morningstar's Knock-out Formula. unabr. ed. Pat Dorsey. Read by Steve Blane. (Running Time: 5 hrs.). (ENG.). 2008. 24.98 (978-1-59659-233-9(8), GildAudio) Pub: Gildan Media. Dist(s): HachBkGrp

Little Book That Makes You Rich: A Proven Market-Beating Formula for Growth Investing. unabr. ed. Louis Navellier. Read by Mark Barbolak. (Running Time: 4 hrs. 30 mins. 0 sec.). (ENG.). 2007. audio compact disk 24.95 (978-1-4272-0262-8(1)) Pub: Macmill Audio. Dist(s): Macmillan

Little Book That Saves Your Assets: What the Rich Do to Stay Wealthy in up & down Markets. unabr. ed. David M. Darst. Read by Sean Pratt. (Running Time: 5 hrs.). (ENG.). 2008. 14.98 (978-1-59659-266-7(4), GildAudio) Pub: Gildan Media. Dist(s): HachBkGrp

Little Book That Saves Your Assets: What the Rich Do to Stay Wealthy in up & down Markets. unabr. ed. David M. Darst. Read by Sean Pratt. 4 CDs. (Running Time: 5 hrs.). (ENG.). 2008. audio compact disk 19.98 (978-1-59659-208-7(7), GildAudio) Pub: Gildan Media. Dist(s): HachBkGrp

Little Boy & Lost Shoe see Robert Penn Warren Reads Selected Poems

Little Boy Blue. abr. ed. Ed Dee. (ENG.). 2006. 14.98 (978-1-59483-680-0(9)) Pub: Hachet Audio. Dist(s): HachBkGrp

Little Boy Blue. abr. ed. Edward Dee. Read by Len Cariou. 2001. 7.95 (978-1-57815-217-9(8), Media Bks Audio) Media Bks NJ.

Little Boy Blue, Where are You? Audio CD. Adapted by Benchmark Education Company Staff. Based on a work by Brooke Harris. (Reader's Theater Nursery Rhymes & Songs Ser.). (J). (gr. k-1). 2008. audio compact disk 10.00 (978-1-60634-000-4(X)) Benchmark Educ.

Little Boy in Me. George Bloomer. Whitaker Hse.

Little Boy in Me: Songs from the Illustrated Sermon. Perf. by George G. Bloomer. 2001. 9.99 (978-1-892352-34-7(6), Blooming Hse Pubs) Blooming Bks.

Little Boy Lost. unabr. ed. W.H. Hudson. Read by Flo Gibson. 3 cass. (Running Time: 4 hrs. 30 min.). (J). 1995. 16.95 (978-1-55685-378-4(5)) Audio Bk Con.

A mystical story about the thrills of nature as seen by a little boy who wanders through the plains, the high Sierras & along the seashore, where animals & mirages take human shape & the spirits of the Rockies & the ocean lure him on.

Little Boy with the Long Name see Pony Engine & Other Stories for Children

Little Boy's Lullaby: A Songbook. collector's ed. Kurt Strauss & Kim Strauss. (J). 2005. DVD & audio compact disk 35.00 (978-0-9760929-3-3(X)) Blanket Street.

Little Boy's Lullaby Song: A Songbook. Kurt Strauss & Kim Strauss. (J). 2005. audio compact disk (978-0-9760929-2-6(1)) Blanket Street.

Little Boy's Lullaby - A Songbook originated as a beautiful song that was written, produced, performed, recorded and copyrighted by Kurt Strauss and Kim Strauss. It is a unique and heart-warming gift of adoration and dedication from a father to his child...a precious keepsake, with an inspiring melody that will withstand the test of time, accompanied by bold and fantastic illustrations of a child's adventures in dreamland...a small glimpse into the heart and soul of a father as he proudly and protectively watches his child growing older, until "the circle of life has completed itself."This special collection including the book, song CD, and animated storybook DVD provides many wonderful opportunities for parents to create invaluable memories with their children that will last a lifetime. Read, sing, listen, watch and bond with your children over this precious keepsake. Give this special gift to the people in your life who value husbands, fathers, children, love, family and the eternal circle of life.

Little Britches. Cameron Beierle. 7 CDs. (Running Time: 12 hrs.). 2001. audio compact disk 49.95 (978-1-58116-184-7(0)) Books in Motion.

Little Britches: Father & I Were Ranchers. unabr. ed. Ralph Moody. Read by Cameron Beierle. 7 CDs. (Running Time: 8 hrs. 12 min.). (Little Britches Ser.). 2001. audio compact disk 45.50; 39.95 (978-1-58116-159-5(X)) Books in Motion.

The Moody family moves from New Hampshire to a Colorado ranch. Experience the pleasures and perils of ranching in 20th century America, through the eyes of a youngster.

Little Brother. unabr. ed. Cory Doctorow. Read by Kirby Heyborne. 10 CDs. (Running Time: 11 hrs. 54 mins.). (YA). (gr. 9 up). 2008. audio compact disk 70.00 (978-0-7393-7287-6(4), Listening Lib) Pub: Random Audio Pubg. Dist(s): Random

Little Brother. unabr. ed. Cory Doctorow. Read by Kirby Heyborne. (ENG.). (J). 2010. 48.00 (978-0-307-71154-0(4), Listening Lib) Pub: Random Audio Pubg. Dist(s): Random

Little Brown Jay: A Tale from India. Read by Elizabeth Claire. 1 cass. (Running Time: 30 mins.). (Folktales Ser.). (J). (gr. k-4). 1999. 7.95 (978-1-57255-182-4(8)) Mondo Pubng.

A Pourquoi tale of how a magical brown jay helps the beautiful Princess Maya & is rewarded in a wonderful, unexpected way.

Little Brown Jay: A Tale from India. Elizabeth Claire. Illus. by Miriam Katin. (J). 1995. 7.95 (978-1-879531-19-2(4)) Mondo Pubng.

Little Brown Monkey. (Choices & Decisions Ser.). (J). (gr. k-1). 1990. 7.92 (978-0-8123-6494-1(5)) Holt McDoug.

Little Buds ABC's: Sing-along CD. Created by Lemon Vision Productions. (ENG.). (ps-1). 2007. audio compact disk 9.99 (978-5-557-46407-9(7)) Pub: Lemon Vision. Dist(s): STL Dist NA

***Little Buds ABCs DVD.** (ENG.). 2007. audio compact disk 14.99 Pub: Lemon Vision. Dist(s): STL Dist NA

***Little Buds Brotecitos Cd.** (SPA.). 2008. audio compact disk 9.99 Pub: Lemon Vision. Dist(s): STL Dist NA

***Little Buds Brotecitos 123 Dvd.** (SPA.). 2008. audio compact disk 14.99 Pub: Lemon Vision. Dist(s): STL Dist NA

***Little Buds 123s DVD.** (ENG.). 2007. audio compact disk 14.99 Pub: Lemon Vision. Dist(s): STL Dist NA

***Little Buds 123s Sing CD.** (ENG.). 2007. audio compact disk 9.99 Pub: Lemon Vision. Dist(s): STL Dist NA

Little Candle see Carl Sandburg's Poems for Children

Little Child in Us That Never Grows Up. Instructed by Manly P. Hall. 8.95 (978-0-89314-163-9(1), C840415) Philos Res.

Little Children. unabr. ed. Tom Perrotta. Narrated by George Wilson. 10 CDs. (Running Time: 11 hrs. 30 mins.). 2004. audio compact disk 29.99 (978-1-4025-9322-2(8), 01712) Recorded Bks.

Unhappily married Sarah passes her days at the local playground with her three-year-old daughter. When happily unemployed Todd (also married) and Sarah meet, their attraction is immediate. They begin a passionate affair just as their suburban utopia is rattled by the arrival of registered sex offender Ronald James McGorvey. With McGorvey in town, disgusted parents wonder if any of their little children will be safe.

Little Chill. T. C. Boyle. 1 cass. (Running Time: 1 hr.). 1989. 13.95 (A0025B090, HarperThor) HarpC GBR.

Little Christmas. Marylee Sunseri. 1 cass. (J). (ps-6). 1993. 9.95 (978-1-887795-01-2(4)) Piper Grove Mus.

Songs for the Christmas Holiday for children.

Little Christmas Storybook. Read by Arthur Silber, Jr. 2 CDs . (Running Time: 1 hr. 54 mins.). (YA). (gr. 3 up). 1997. audio compact disk 15.00 (978-0-9655675-2-7(4)) Samart.

Christmas stories from Around the World.

Little Christmas Treasures. 1985. (0274) Evang Sisterhood Mary.

Little Class on Murder. unabr. collector's ed. Carolyn G. Hart. Read by Kate Reading. 6 cass. (Running Time: 9 hrs.). (Death on Demand Mystery Ser.: No. 5). 1996. 48.00 (978-0-7366-3419-9(3), 894409) Books on Tape.

Suicide, murder, embezzlement, conspiracy & faculty love affairs face Annie Lawrence, bookstore owner, after she agrees to teach a class on mystery fiction at the college in her quiet South Carolina town. It's more than she bargained for.

Little Colonel. 2006. 22.95 (978-0-7861-4438-9(6)); audio compact disk 24.00 (978-0-7861-7347-1(5)) Blckstn Audio.

Little Colonel. unabr. ed. Annie Fellows Johnston. Read by Anna Fields. 2006. 19.95 (978-0-7861-7722-6(5)) Blckstn Audio.

Little Course in Dreams. Robert Bosnak. Read by Tony Kahn. 2 cass. (Running Time: 2 hrs.). 2001. 16.95 (AZ00006, Shmbhala Lion) Pub: Shambhala Pubns. Dist(s): Sounds True

Little Dancer: Pre-Ballet (Ages 5-8) 1 cass. (J). (gr. k-3). 15.00 incl. guide. (KIM 1017C); lp 15.00 (KIM 1017) Kimbo Educ.

Simple barre exercises, adagio & allegro. Children move creatively while developing coordination & poise.

Little Dinosaurs. unabr. ed. Bernard Most & Don Freeman. (J). (gr. k-1). 1993. bk. 22.95 (978-0-87499-192-5(7)) Live Oak Media.

Little Disturbances of Man & Enormous Changes at the Last Minute. unabr. ed. Read by Grace Paley. 10.95 (978-0-8045-1144-5(6), SAC 1144) Spoken Arts.

Little Ditties for Itty Bitties: Songs for Infants & Toddlers. Created by Michele Valeri. (Running Time: 41). (ENG.). 2009. audio compact disk 12.95 (978-0-9651036-2-6(5)) Cmmnty Music.

Little Dorrit. Charles Dickens. Ian McKellen. (ENG.). 2009. audio compact disk 29.95 (978-1-60283-561-0(6)) Pub: AudioGO. Dist(s): Perseus Dist

Little Dorrit. Charles Dickens. Read by Anton Lesser. (Playaway Young Adult Ser.). (ENG.). (YA). 2008. 189.99 (978-1-60640-652-6(3)) Find a World.

Little Dorrit. unabr. ed. Charles Dickens. Read by Robert Whitfield. 9 cass. (Running Time: 27 hrs.). 2000. 62.95 (978-0-7861-1675-1(7), 2434A,B) Blckstn Audio.

Little Dorrit. unabr. ed. Charles Dickens. Read by Robert Whitfield. 3 pieces. (Running Time: 115200 sec.). 2007. audio compact disk 40.00 (978-0-7861-8259-6(8), 2434A,B) Blckstn Audio.

***Little Dorrit.** unabr. ed. Charles Dickens. Narrated by Antony Ferguson. (Running Time: 37 hrs. 30 mins. 0 sec.). 2010. 44.99 (978-1-4526-5032-6(2)); 35.99 (978-1-4526-7032-4(3)); audio compact disk 64.99 (978-1-4526-0032-1(5)) Pub: Tantor Media. Dist(s): IngramPubServ

Little Dorrit, Bk. II. Charles Dickens. 12 cass. (Running Time: 16 hrs. 30 min.). 1999. 77.95 Audio Bk Con.

Book II, "Riches", follows the Dorrits' introduction to society through fashionable Europe, Arthur's economic decline & Little Dorrit's return to England.

Little Dorrit, Pt. 1. Charles Dickens. 14 cass. (Running Time: 27 hrs.). 1999. 89.95 (978-0-7861-1606-5(4), 2434A,B) Blckstn Audio.

Little Dorrit, Pt. 2. unabr. ed. Charles Dickens. Read by Robert Whitfield. 9 cass. (Running Time: 13 hrs. 30 min.). 1999. 62.95 (2434B) Blckstn Audio.

Little Dorrit, Pt. A. unabr. collector's ed. Charles Dickens. Read by Donada Peters. 12 cass. (Running Time: 18 hrs.). 1993. 96.00 (978-0-7366-2587-6(9), 3333A) Books on Tape.

Glitter of wealth, darkness of debtor's prison form the boundaries of Dicken's mature masterpiece.

Little Dorrit, Pt. B. collector's unabr. ed. Charles Dickens. Read by Donada Peters. 12 cass. (Running Time: 18 hrs.). 1993. 96.00 (978-0-7366-2588-3(7), 3333-B) Books on Tape.

The glitter of wealth & darkness of debtor's prison form the boundaries of Dicken's mature masterpiece.

Little Dorrit: Part 2. unabr. ed. Charles Dickens. Read by Robert Whitfield. (Running Time: 46800 sec.). 2007. audio compact disk 90.00 (978-0-7861-8096-7(X)) Blckstn Audio.

***Little Dorrit (Library Edition)** unabr. ed. Charles Dickens. Narrated by Antony Ferguson. (Running Time: 37 hrs. 30 mins.). 2010. 64.99 (978-1-4526-2032-9(6)); audio compact disk 155.99 (978-1-4526-3032-8(1)) Pub: Tantor Media. Dist(s): IngramPubServ

Little Dorrit: Part 1. unabr. ed. Charles Dickens. Read by Robert Whitfield. (Running Time: 68400 sec.). 2007. audio compact disk 120.00 (978-0-7861-8097-4(8)) Blckstn Audio.

Little Dorrit (Part 1), Bk. I. unabr. ed. Charles Dickens. Read by Flo Gibson. 12 cass. (Running Time: 17 hrs. 30 min.). (gr. 8 up). 1989. 39.95 (978-1-55685-135-3(9)) Audio Bk Con.

Book I, "Poverty," introduces the valiant Little Dorrit, raised in a debtor's prison & working outside its walls to support her father. Befriended by the kind & melancholy Arthur Clennam & due to a surprising twist in fortune, her luck begins to change.

Little Dorrit (Part 2), Vol. 2. unabr. ed. Charles Dickens. Narrated by Flo Gibson. (Running Time: 16 hrs. 13 mins.). 1989. 39.95 (978-1-55685-816-1(7)) Audio Bk Con.

Little Dorrit (Parts 1 And 2) unabr. ed. Charles Dickens. Narrated by Flo Gibson. (Running Time: 33 hrs. 28 mins.). 1989. 64.95 (978-1-55685-817-8(5)) Audio Bk Con.

Little Dragon - Orange Cheeks. Jay O'Callahan. Perf. by Jay O'Callahan. 1 cass. (Running Time: 56 min.). Dramatization. (J). (gr. k up). 1982. 10.00 (978-1-877954-20-7(9), A-4C) Pub: Artana Prodns. Dist(s): Yellow Moon

A new recording of the story of one small dragon who saves the world, plus Orange Cheeks the story of a grandmother who deals warmly & wisely with young Willie's mishaps. Recommended by the National Council of Teachers of English.

Little Dragon & Orange Cheeks. Jay O'Callahan. Photos by Jay O'Callahan. 1 CD. (Running Time: 50 mins.). (YA). (ps up). 2003. audio compact disk 15.00 (978-1-877954-38-2(1)) Artana Prodns.

How can one small dragon save Artana and the world? Elizabeth knows. Also the warm and funny Orange Cheeks.

Little Dragon & Other Stories. Perf. by Jay O'Callahan. 1 cass. (Running Time: 49 min.). (J). (gr. k-8). 1982. 8.95 (978-0-89719-942-1(1), WW718C) Weston Woods.

Includes "Orange Cheeks," "Woe Is Me Bones," & "Tulips".

Little Drivers. (J). 2005. audio compact disk (978-1-933796-16-1(2)) PC Treasures.

Little Drops of Blood. unabr. ed. Bill Knox. Read by James Bryce. 6 cass. (Running Time: 9 hrs.). (Isis Ser.). (J). 2000. 54.95 (978-0-7531-0879-6(8)) Pub: ISIS Lrg Prnt GBR. Dist(s): Ulverscroft US

Little Drummer Boy. 2004. pap. bk. 14.95 (978-1-56008-156-2(2)); 8.95 (978-1-56008-636-9(X)); cass. & flmstrp 30.00 (978-1-56008-706-9(4)) Weston Woods.

Little Drummer Boy. Perf. by Harry Simeone Chorale. 1 cass. (J). 3.98 Clamshell. (978-1-55886-147-3(5), BB/PT 454) Smarty Pants.

Little Drummer Boy, the see Nino Del Tambor

Little Drummer Girl. John le Carré. Read by Michael Jayston. 16 cass. (Running Time: 20 hrs. 10 min.). 2001. 50.95 (978-0-7540-0613-8(1)) AudioGO.

Lured by Israeli Intelligence into the world of espionage, Charlie, a young actress, is plunged into a deceptive & delicate trap to ensnare an elusive Palestinian terrorist.

Little Drummer Girl. unabr. ed. John le Carré. Read by Richard Green. 13 cass. (Running Time: 19 hrs. 30 min.). (George Smiley Novels Ser.). 1983. 104.00 (978-0-7366-0968-5(7), 1910) Books on Tape.

The setting is the tortured Middle East in 1977. Seeking revenge for a series of PLO attacks on Jews throughout Europe, Israeli intelligence agents stalk a lethal & elusive terrorist. A young English actress baits the deadly trap.

Little Drummer Girl, unabr. ed. John le Carré. Narrated by Frank Muller. 12 cass. (Running Time: 18 hrs.). (George Smiley Novels Ser.). 1983. 97.00 (978-1-55690-311-3(1), 83072E7) Recorded Bks.

The quarry is a lethally dangerous terrorist; his hunter, Kurtz. Charlie, a young, bright actress is the bait to catch him.

Little Duke. Charlotte M. Yonge. Narrated by David Thom. Music by Hans Bisner. Engineer Bobbie Frohman. B. J. Bedford. 4 CDs. (Running Time: 4 Hrs. 30 Min.). (J). 2005. audio compact disk (978-0-9793777-7-8(3)) Alcazar AudioWorks.

Little Eagle (Kiowa) unabr. ed. 1 cass. (Running Time: 30 mins.). 12.95 (C19200) J Norton Pubs.

Authentic Indian legends.

Little Earthquakes. abr. ed. Jennifer Weiner. 2004. 15.95 (978-0-7435-4305-7(X)) Pub: S&S Audio. Dist(s): S and S Inc

Little Earthquakes. abr. ed. Jennifer Weiner. Read by Jennifer Weiner. (Running Time: 5 hrs. 0 mins. 0 sec.). (ENG.). 2007. audio compact disk 14.99 (978-0-7435-6680-3(7)) Pub: S&S Audio. Dist(s): S and S Inc

Little Einsteins Musical Missions. Created by Walt Disney Records Staff. Prod. by Ed Mitchell & Ted Kryczko. (J). (ps-1). 2006. audio compact disk 13.98 (978-5-558-54720-7(0)) W Disney Records.

Little Engine That Could. Perf. by Dick Van Patten. 1 cass. (J). 3.98 Clamshell. (978-1-55886-136-7(X), BB/PT 443) Smarty Pants.

Little Engine That Could. unabr. ed. Watty Piper. Read by Suzanne Toren. 1 cass. (Running Time: 13 mins.). (Follow the Reader Ser.). (J). (ps-3). 1986. bk. 17.00 (978-0-8072-0112-1(X), FTR113SH, Listening Lib) Random Audio Pubg.

The well-loved tale of how a train reaches its destination with the help of a friend.

Little Evil Things, Vol. 1. Short Stories. Frank Macchia & Tracy London. 1 cass. (Running Time: 56 mins.). (YA). (gr. 7 up). 1997. 12.95 (978-1-891007-00-2(9), LITT001); audio compact disk 15.95 (978-1-891007-01-9(7), LITT002) Little Evil.

Five tales of terror include: "Transformation," "Little Evil Thing," "The Quiet Child," "It's after Me" & "Parasites".

Little Evil Things, Vol. I. Created by Frank Macchia & Tracy London. 1 cass. (Running Time: 1 hr.). 2001. 12.95 (LITT001); audio compact disk 15.95 (LITT002) Lodestone Catalog.

Dim the lights & settle in for these bite-sized tales of terror.

Little Evil Things, Vol. 2. Short Stories. Frank Macchia & Tracy London. 1 CD. (Running Time: 70 mins.). (J). 1998. audio compact disk 15.95 (978-1-891007-03-3(3), LITT004) Little Evil.

Four new tales of terror include: "The Thing in the Jar," "Sisters," "It's in the Water" & "Blubb".

Little Evil Things, Vol. 2. Short Stories. Frank Macchia & Tracy London. 1 cass. (Running Time: 70 mins.). (YA). (gr. 7 up). 1998. 12.95 (978-1-891007-02-6(5), LITT03) Little Evil.

Four new tales of terror include: "The Thing in the Jar," "Sisters," "It's in the Water" & "Blubb".

Little Evil Things, Vol. II. Created by Frank Macchia & Tracy London. 1 cass. (Running Time: 1 hr.). 2001. 12.95 (LITT003); audio compact disk 15.95 (LITT004) Lodestone Catalog.

Dim the lights & settle in for these bite-sized tales of terror.

Little Evil Things, Vol. III. Created by Frank Macchia & Tracy London. 1 cass. (Running Time: 1 hr.). 2001. 12.95 (LITT005); 12.95 (LITT007); audio compact disk 15.95 (LITT006) Lodestone Catalog.

Little Evil Things, Vol. 3. unabr. ed. Short Stories. Frank Macchia & Tracy London. 1 cass. (Running Time: 1 hr. 8 mins.). Dramatization. (YA). (gr. 7 up). 1999. 12.98 (978-1-891007-04-0(1), LITT005); audio compact disk 15.95 (978-1-891007-05-7(X), LITT006) Little Evil.
Horror stories with continuous music accompaniment include: "Buried Alive," "It's a Boy," "Freaked Out," "The Dolls" & "The Potion".

Little Evil Things, Vol. 4. Short Stories. Frank Macchia & Tracy London. 1 cass. (Running Time: 1 hr. 5 mins.). (YA). (gr. 9 up). 2000. 12.98 (978-1-891007-06-4(8)) Little Evil.
Horror stories with music accompaniment.

Little Evil Things, Vol. IV. Created by Frank Macchia & Tracy London. 1 CD. (Running Time: 1 hr.). 2001. audio compact disk 15.95 (LITT008) Lodestone Catalog.
Dim the lights & settle in for these bite-sized tales of terror.

Little Evil Things, Vol. 4. unabr. ed. Short Stories. Frank Macchia & Tracy London. 1 CD. (Running Time: 1 hr. 5 mins.). (YA). (gr. 9 up). 2000. audio compact disk 15.98 (978-1-891007-07-1(6)) Little Evil.
Horror stories with musical accompaniment.

Little Evil Things, Vol. 5. Frank Macchia & Tracy London. Read by Jim McDonnell. 1 cass. (Running Time: 1 hr.). (YA). 2001. 12.98 (978-1-891007-08-8(4)); audio compact disk 15.95 (978-1-891007-09-5(2)) Little Evil.
Horror stories with modern music and sound design; includes Whispers in the Attic, The Happy Wanderer, O.S. 666, Dreamgirl and The Impaler.

Little Flower: Daniel Chowning. Daniel Chowning. Perf. by Daniel Chowning. 1 cass. (Running Time: 1 hrs.). 1996. pap. bk. (AA2975) Credence Commun.
Distills the teaching of Therese of Lisieux with special emphasis on the mercy of God.

Little Flower: The Life & Times of Fiorello LaGuardia. unabr. collector's ed. Lawrence Elliott. Read by Dick Estell. 6 cass. (Running Time: 9 hrs.). 1987. 48.00 (978-0-7366-1096-4(0), 2022) Books on Tape.
Biography of Fiorello LaGuardia who for 12 years as mayor of New York City, provided what may have been the best reform government in American municipal history.

Little Flowers. unabr. ed. Nicola Thorne. 6 cass. (Running Time: 7 hrs. 14 mins.). (Isis Cassettes Ser.). (J). 2006. 54.95 (978-0-7531-2186-3(7)) Pub: ISIS Lrg Prnt GBR. Dist(s): Ulverscroft US

Little Flowers of St. Francis. Brother Ugolino. 6 cass. 24.95 (922) Ignatius Pr.
Written a century after St. Francis to rekindle the spirituality of the order.

Little Flowers of St. Francis. abr. ed. Raphael Brown & Greg Friedman. 4 CDs. (Running Time: 5 Hours). 2004. audio compact disk 28.95 (978-0-86716-639-2(8)) St Anthony Mess Pr.

Little Flowers of St. Francis. abr. ed. Perf. by Cyril Cusack. 1 cass. (J). 1984. 12.95 (978-0-694-50086-4(0), SWC 1112) HarperCollins Pubs.

Little Foxes. Michael Morpurgo. Read by Bill Wallis. (Running Time: 9960 sec.). (J). (gr. 3-7). 2007. audio compact disk 29.95 (978-1-4056-5573-6(9)) AudioGo GBR.

Little Foxes: 11 Peter 2:10-22. Ed Young. 1983. 4.95 (978-0-7417-1329-2(2), 329) Win Walk.

Little Friend. unabr. ed. Donna Tartt. Read by Karen White. 11 cass. (Running Time: 27 hrs.). 2002. audio compact disk 128.00 (978-0-7366-8837-6(4)) Books on Tape.
A young girl with a brother murdered years ago decides to find and punish his killer.

Little Friends for Little Folks. Janice Buckner. 1 cass. (Running Time: 36 min.). (J). (ps-1). 1986. 9.95 (978-0-939065-32-5(0), GW 1036) Gentle Wind.
Features childrens song including puppet please dance, strange friends, old man on the mountain, orangatango, the planting song & Others.

Little Friends for Little Folks. Janice Buckner. Perf. by Janice Buckner. (J). 1986. audio compact disk 14.95 (978-1-58467-002-5(9)) Gentle Wind.

Little Friends for Little Folks. unabr. ed. Janice Buckner. Perf. by Janice Buckner. Illus. by Susan Gaber. 1 cass. (Running Time: 35 min.). (Janice Buckner Educational Entertainment Ser.). (J). (ps-2). 1988. pap. bk. 15.99 (978-1-56479-000-2(2), MR 101SB) Moonlight Rose.
A colorful fantasy journey through song that stimulates the imagination while reinforcing basic learning skills.

Little Frog Learns to Sing. L. Le Blanc. Illus. by L. Le Blanc. (J). (ps-2). 1967. pap. bk. 7.94 (978-0-87783-191-4(2)) Oddo.

Little Fur. Isobelle Carmody. Read by Isobelle Carmody. (Running Time: 2 hrs. 50 mins.). (Legend of Little Fur Ser.). (J). 2009. 54.99 (978-1-74214-368-2(7), 9781742143682) Pub: Bolinda Pubng AUS. Dist(s): Bolinda Pub Inc

Little Fur: The Legend of Little Fur. unabr. ed. Isobelle Carmody. Read by Isobelle Carmody. (Running Time: 10200 sec.). (Legend of Little Fur Ser.). (J). (gr. 1-11). 2006. audio compact disk 54.95 (978-1-74093-707-8(4)) Pub: Bolinda Pubng AUS. Dist(s): Bolinda Pub Inc

Little Fuzzy. H. Beam Piper. (Running Time: 6 mins.). 2009. audio compact disk 29.95 (978-1-897304-61-7(7)) Dorch Pub Co.

***Little Fuzzy.** H. Beam Piper. (Running Time: 6 mins.). 2009. 19.95 (978-1-897331-11-8(8), AudioRealms) Dorch Pub Co.

Little Fuzzy. H. Beam Piper. 2006. audio compact disk 19.95 (978-0-8095-6271-8(5)) Pub: Wildside. Dist(s): Diamond Book Dists

Little Fuzzy. unabr. abr. ed. H. Beam Piper. Read by Brian Holsopple. Prod. by Fred Godsmark. 5 CDs. (Running Time: 21180 sec.). 2006. audio compact disk 29.95 (978-0-8095-6272-5(3)) Pub: Wildside. Dist(s): Diamond Book Dists

Little Gentleman. unabr. ed. Philippa Pearce. 3 cass. (Running Time: 3 hrs. 45 mins.). (J). 2005. bk. 56.64 (978-1-4193-3601-0(0), 42047) Recorded Bks.

Little Gentleman. unabr. ed. Philippa Pearce. Narrated by Gerard Doyle. 3 cass. (Running Time: 3 hrs. 45 mins.). (J). 2005. 32.75 (978-1-4193-3599-0(5), 98018) Recorded Bks.
Winner of the Whitbread Award and both the Carnegie and Kate Greenaway Medals, Philippa Pearce's books are classics. In this charming tale, young Bet befriends a talking mole while reading aloud in a field. Bet learns that, despite the Little Gentleman's amazing powers, his deepest wish is to be "wholly mole." Only Bet can help him - but the cost may prove too great.

Little Giant of Aberdeen County. unabr. ed. Tiffany Baker. (Running Time: 11 hrs. 0 mins.). 2009. 29.95 (978-1-4332-4696-8(1)); audio compact disk 65.95 (978-1-4332-4693-7(7)); audio compact disk 90.00 (978-1-4332-4694-4(5)) Blckstn Audio.

Little Giant of Aberdeen County. unabr. ed. Tiffany Baker. Read by Carrington MacDuffie. 10 CDs. (Running Time: 12 hrs. 30 mins.). 2009. audio compact disk 29.95 (978-1-4332-4695-1(3)) Blckstn Audio.

Little Girl, Be Careful What You Say see Carl Sandburg's Poems for Children

***Little Girl Lost.** (ENG.). 2010. audio compact disk (978-1-59171-274-9(2)) Falcon Picture.

Little Girl Lost. Katie Flynn. (Soundings (CDs) Ser.). 2007. audio compact disk 99.95 (978-1-84559-578-4(5)) Pub: ISIS Lrg Prnt GBR. Dist(s): Ulverscroft US

Little Girl Lost. Katie Flynn. Read by Anne Dover. 12 cass. (Soundings Ser.). 2007. 94.95 (978-1-84559-281-3(6)) Pub: ISIS Lrg Prnt GBR. Dist(s): Ulverscroft US

Little Girl Who Looked for Happiness. Trenna Daniells. Read by Trenna Daniells. 1 cass. (Running Time: 30 min.). (One to Grow On! Ser.). (J). (gr. 4 up). 6.95 (12008) Trenna Prods.

Little Goat's Coat. (Sails Literacy Ser.). (gr. k up). 10.00 (978-0-7578-5420-0(6)) Rigby Educ.

Little Gold Book of YES! Attitude: How to Find, Build & Keep a YES! Attitude for a Lifetime of Success. unabr. ed. Jeffrey Gitomer. Read by Jeffrey Gitomer. (Running Time: 3 hrs. 0 mins. 0 sec.). (ENG.). 2009. 49.99 (978-0-7435-7377-1(3)) Pub: S&S Audio. Dist(s): S and S Inc

Little Gold Book of Yes! Attitude: How to Find, Build & Keep a Yes! Attitude for a Lifetime of Success. unabr. ed. Jeffrey Gitomer. Read by Jeffrey Gitomer. 4 Cds. (Running Time: 3 hrs. 0 mins. 0 sec.). (ENG.). 2009. audio compact disk 19.99 (978-0-7435-7260-6(2)) Pub: S&S Audio. Dist(s): S and S Inc

Little Golden Treasury: Scuffy the Tugboat, the Poky Little Puppy, Tawny Scrawny Lion, the Saggy Baggy Elephant. unabr. ed. Janette Sebring Lowrey et al. Read by Susan Gregory & Skip Hinnant. (Running Time: 1 hr. 30 mins.). (ENG.). (J). (ps). 2006. audio compact disk 11.95 (978-0-7393-3731-8(9), ImaginStudio) Pub: Random Audio Pubg. Dist(s): Random

Little Gray Mouse in the Carpenter's House. Louie Swift. Perf. by Barry McAlister. 1 cass. (Running Time: 30 min.). Dramatization. (Froggie's Tales: Vol. 3). (J). (ps-3). 2001. 9.95 (978-0-9675577-5-5(5)) Puddleduck Pubg.
Six new original songs, stories & poems for children, with character voices, music & sound effects.

Little Green Book Getting Your Way: How to Speak, Write, Present, Persuade, Influence, & Sell Your Point of View to Others. unabr. ed. Jeffrey Gitomer. Read by Jeffrey Gitomer. (Running Time: 4 hrs. 0 mins. 0 sec.). (ENG.). 2009. 49.99 (978-0-7435-7536-2(9)) Pub: S&S Audio. Dist(s): S and S Inc

Little Green Book of Getting Your Way: How to Speak, Write, Present, Persuade, Influence, & Sell Your Point of View to Others. unabr. ed. Jeffrey Gitomer. Read by Jeffrey Gitomer. (Running Time: 4 hrs. 0 mins. 0 sec.). (ENG.). 2009. audio compact disk 19.99 (978-0-7435-7262-0(9)) Pub: S&S Audio. Dist(s): S and S Inc

Little Grey Rabbit & the Circus. unabr. ed. Alison Uttley. Read by Tammy Grimes. 1 cass. (J). 1984. 9.95 (978-0-694-50825-9(X), CDL5 1507) HarperCollins Pubs.

Little Grey Rabbit Goes to Sea. (J). (CDL5 1510) HarperCollins Pubs.

Little Grey Rabbit's Christmas. abr. ed. Alison Uttley. Read by Tammy Grimes. 1 cass. (J). 1984. 9.95 (978-0-694-50835-8(7), CDL5 1510) HarperCollins Pubs.

Little Grey Rabbit's Valentine. (J). (CDL5 1507) HarperCollins Pubs.

Little Grunt & the Big Egg: A Prehistoric Fairy Tale. Tomie dePaola. 2007. bk. 27.95 (978-0-8045-6944-6(4)); bk. 29.95 (978-0-8045-4158-9(2)) Spoken Arts.

Little Guide to Your Well-Read Life: How to Get More Books in Your Life & More Life from Your Books. Steve Leveen. (Running Time: 13500 sec.). (Little Guides). 2005. audio compact disk 24.50 (978-1-929154-19-7(4)) Pub: Levenger Pr. Dist(s): Consort Bk Sales

Little Hands: Songs for & about Children. Perf. by Jonathan Edwards. Prod. by Phil Rosenthal. 1 cass. (Running Time: 30 min.). (J). (gr. 1-6). 1987. 9.98 (978-1-879305-01-4(1), AM-C-102); audio compact disk 14.98 (978-1-879305-21-2(6), AM-CD-5102) Am Melody.
Sensitive blend of traditional & original songs. 1988 ALA Notable Children's Recording.

Little Hansworst. unabr. ed. 1 cass. (Running Time: 20 min.). Dramatization. (Magic Looking Glass Ser.). (J). (gr. 2-7). 1989. 9.95 (978-0-7810-0039-0(4), NIM-CW-129-4-C) NIMCO.
A Dutch folk tale.

Little Hen Eagle see Zulu & Other African Folktales from Behind the Back of the Mountain

Little Heroes. Jay O'Callahan. Perf. by Jay O'Callahan. 1 cass. (Running Time: 58 min.). (J). (gr. k up). 1985. 10.00 (978-1-877954-07-8(1)) Pub: Artana Prodns. Dist(s): Yellow Moon
Set off on a daring adventure with MICHAEL THE GRASSHOPPER and five other little heroes in these wonderful stories about friendship, imagination and delight.

Little Heroes. Jay O'Callahan. Perf. by Jay O'Callahan. 1 CD. (Running Time: 57 mins. 50 sec.). Dramatization. (J). 2003. audio compact disk 15.00 (978-1-877954-43-6(8)) Pub: Artana Prodns. Dist(s): Yellow Moon
Set off on a daring adventure with "Michael the Grasshopper" and five other little heroes in these wonderful stories about friendship, imagination and delight.

Little Heroes. Jay O'Callahan. 1 cass. (Running Time: 57 min.). (Time for a Tale Storytelling Ser.). (gr. k up). 1987. 9.98 (978-0-942303-03-2(2), HW 1205C) Pub: High Windy Audio. Dist(s): August Hse
Adventure-filled, original stories whose endearing heroes come in all shapes & sizes.

Little History of the World. abr. unabr. ed. Read by Ralph Cosham. 8 cass. (Running Time: 32400 sec.). 2006. 19.95 (978-0-7861-4466-2(1)); audio compact disk 29.95 (978-0-7861-7708-0(X)) Blckstn Audio.

Little History of the World. abr. unabr. ed. E. H. Gombrich. Read by Ralph Cosham. 9 CDs. (Running Time: 32400 sec.). 2006. audio compact disk 19.95 (978-0-7861-7286-3(X)) Blckstn Audio.

Little History of the World. unabr. ed. Read by Ralph Cosham. (Running Time: 32400 sec.). 2006. 59.95 (978-0-7861-4633-8(8)); audio compact disk 72.00 (978-0-7861-6829-3(3)) Blckstn Audio.

Little House. 2004. bk. 24.95 (978-0-89719-888-2(3)); pap. bk. 32.75 (978-1-55592-258-0(9)); pap. bk. 14.95 (978-1-56008-061-9(2)); 8.95 (978-1-56008-952-0(0)); 8.95 (978-1-56008-145-6(7)); cass. & flmstrp 30.00 (978-0-89719-560-7(4)) Weston Woods.

Little House. Virginia Lee Burton. 1 cass., 5 bks. (Running Time: 13 min.). (J). pap. bk. 32.75 Weston Woods.
A little house, used to living in the country, finds out what it is like to live in the city.

Little House. Virginia Lee Burton. 1 cass. (Running Time: 13 min.). (J). (ps-3). bk. 24.95; pap. bk. 12.95 (PRA142); 8.95 (RAC142) Weston Woods.
A little house, used to living in the country, finds out what it is like to live in the city. Caldecott Medal Book.

Little House. unabr. ed. Philippa Gregory. Read by Lindsay Sandison. 8 cass. (Running Time: 9 hrs. 15 min.). (Isis Ser.). (J). 1997. 69.95 (978-0-7531-0288-6(9), 971102) Pub: ISIS Lrg Prnt GBR. Dist(s): Ulverscroft US
It was easy for Elizabeth. She married the man she loved, bore him two children & made a home for him that was the envy of their friends. It was harder for Ruth. She married Elizabeth's son & then found that, somehow, she could never quite measure up. Isolation, deceit & betrayal fill the gaps between the two women & between their two worlds. This complex thriller shows insight into what women want & what women fear, as Ruth confronts the shifting borders of her own sanity.

Little House. unabr. ed. Philippa Gregory. Read by Lindsay Sandison. 9 CDs. (Running Time: 36000 sec.). (Isis Ser.). 2004. audio compact disk 84.95 (978-0-7531-1242-7(6), 1242-6) Pub: ISIS Lrg Prnt GBR. Dist(s): Ulverscroft US

Little House in the Big Woods. Mary Engelbreit. (J). 2003. audio compact disk 41.94 (978-0-06-054363-1(9)) HarperCollins Pubs.

Little House in the Big Woods. unabr. ed. Laura Ingalls Wilder. Read by Cherry Jones. Contrib. by Paul Woodiel. (Running Time: 12600 sec.). (Little House the Laura Years Ser.). (J). (gr. 3-7). 2007. audio compact disk 14.95 (978-0-06-136534-8(3), HarperChildAud) HarperCollins Pubs.

Little House in the Big Woods. unabr. abr. ed. Laura Ingalls Wilder. Read by Cherry Jones. 3 cass. (Running Time: 3 hrs. 30 mins.). (Little House Ser.). (J). (gr. 3-6). 2003. 22.00 (978-0-06-001241-0(2)) HarperCollins Pubs.

Little House on the Freeway: Help for the Hurried Home. Tim Kimmel. (ENG.). 2010. 26.99 (978-1-934384-26-8(7)) Pub: Treasure Pub. Dist(s): STL Dist NA

Little House on the Prairie. unabr. ed. Laura Ingalls Wilder. Read by Cherry Jones. 4 cass. (Running Time: 5 hrs.). (J). 2003. 22.00 (978-0-06-001242-7(0)) HarperCollins Pubs.

Little House on the Prairie. unabr. ed. Laura Ingalls Wilder. Read by Cherry Jones. Contrib. by Paul Woodiel. (Running Time: 19800 sec.). (J). 2008. audio compact disk 14.95 (978-0-06-156305-8(6), HarperChildAud) HarperCollins Pubs.

Little House Sampler: A Collection of Early Stories & Reminiscences. abr. ed. Laura Ingalls Wilder & Rose W. Lane. Read by Judy Collins. 2 cass. (Running Time: 3 hrs.). (J). (gr. 4-7). 1990. 16.00 (978-0-89845-973-9(7), CPN 2125) HarperCollins Pubs.

Little Is Much: 1 Kings 17::8-16. Ed Young. 1987. 4.95 (978-0-7417-1593-7(7), 593) Win Walk.

Little Island. 2004. 8.95 (978-1-56008-953-7(9)); cass. & flmstrp 30.00 (978-1-56008-707-6(2)) Weston Woods.

Little Italies. Short Stories. Created by Canadian Broadcasting Corporation. 6 Cds. (Running Time: 21600 sec.). Dramatization. 2006. audio compact disk 39.95 (978-0-660-19584-1(4), CBC Audio) Canadian Broadcasting CAN.

Little Johnny Brown. Perf. by Ella Jenkins. 1 cass. (J). (ps-4). 1990. (0-9307-45026-4-8) Smithsonian Folkways.
Heartwarming folk songs including "What's Your Name?" "He's Got the Whole World in his Hands," "The Children's Librarian," "Freedom Train," "Mexican Hand Clapping Chant" & more.

Little Johnny's Confession see Brian Patten Reading His Poetry

Little Johnny's Final Letter see Brian Patten Reading His Poetry

Little Juggler. unabr. ed. Barbara Cooney. Read by Joycelynne Calavano. 1 cass. (J). 5.95 (516) Ignatius Pr.
An adaptation with music of the old French legend about Barnaby, the young boy whose talent so delighted Our Lady.

Little Kittens. Lilian Obligado. (J). 1980. 26.61 (978-0-676-31141-9(5)) SRA McGraw.

Little Knell. unabr. ed. Catherine Aird. Read by Bruce Montague. 4 cass. (Running Time: 6 hrs.). 2001. 39.95 (978-0-7540-0574-2(7), CAB1997) Pub: Chivers Audio Bks GBR. Dist(s): AudioGO
It had seemed such a simple job for Whetherspoon & Whetherspoon, Furniture Removers, to clear Whimbrel House of its contents following the death of Colonel Caversham. Only one item proved difficult to maneuver, the heavy coffin containing an egyptian mummy. This job was to be straightforward, for a body, however ancient, has been moved without his consent.

Little Known Evidences of the Book of Mormon. Brenton Yorgason. 1 cass. 7.98 (978-1-55503-027-8(0), 06003435) Covenant Comms.
Fascinating experiences with the Book of Mormon.

Little-known Evidences of the Book of Mormon. Brenton Yorgason. 2004. audio compact disk 11.95 (978-1-59156-375-4(5)) Covenant Comms.

Little Known Eyewitness Accounts of the Coming Forth of the Book of Mormon. Paul Thomas Smith. 2004. 9.95 (978-1-57734-614-2(9)) Covenant Comms.

Little Known Heroes of LDS Church History. Ivan J. Barrett. 2 cass. 11.98 (978-1-55503-122-0(6), 070041) Covenant Comms.
Stories about four early church personalities.

Little Lame Prince. abr. ed. Dinah Maria Mulock Craik. Perf. by Cathleen Nesbitt. 1 cass. (J). 1984. 9.95 (978-0-694-50693-4(1), CDL5 1293) HarperCollins Pubs.
The story tells of a little prince who escaped from the prison tower of his paralysis & on the way conquered the hearts of his countrymen.

Little Language for Little Ones Book & Little Language Songs for Little Ones. Laura C. Dyer. 2001. mass mkt. 24.95 (978-0-9718409-0-4(3)) Lnguage Ltle One.

Little Language for Little Ones Book & Little Language Songs for Little Ones. Laura C. Dyer. 1 Cass. (Running Time: 40 minutes). 2002. mass mkt. 19.95 (978-0-9718409-1-1(1)) Lnguage Ltle One.
The audio cassette contains 40 minutes of original children's songs, each specifically designed with a goal to enhance speech and language skills.

Little Latin Lyric. unabr. ed. Gilbert Highet. Read by Gilbert Highet. 1 cass. (Running Time: 30 min.). 9.95 (23312-A) J Norton Pubs.

Little Learning. unabr. ed. Jane Tesh. (Running Time: 7.5 hrs. 0 mins.). (ENG.). 2009. 29.95 (978-1-4332-9022-0(7)); 54.95 (978-1-4332-9018-3(9)); audio compact disk 69.00 (978-1-4332-9019-0(7)) Blckstn Audio.

Little Learning. unabr. ed. Evelyn Waugh. Read by Ken Scott. 7 cass. (Running Time: 10 hrs. 30 min.). 1987. 56.00 (978-0-7366-1135-0(5), 2058) Books on Tape.
The first & only volume of an autobiography that Evelyn Waugh never completed. It covers his life from infancy to early manhood, thus we know him at Oxford & as a schoolmaster in North Wales.

Little Lefty. unabr. ed. Matt Christopher. Narrated by John Randolph Jones. 2 cass. (Running Time: 1 hr. 45 mins.). (gr. 2 up). 1995. 19.00 (978-0-7887-0179-5(7), 94404E7) Recorded Bks.
The smallest kid on the baseball team gets inspiration from a neighbor who tells him stories of "Little Lefty," a successful pitcher.

Little Light on the Spiritual Laws. Diana Cooper. (Running Time: 2 hrs.). 17.99 (978-1-84032-406-8(6), HoddrStoughton) Pub: Hodder General GBR. Dist(s): Trafalgar

Little Local Murder. unabr. ed. Robert Barnard. Read by Christopher Scott. 6 cass. (Running Time: 23400 sec.). (Soundings Ser.). 2006. 54.95

(978-1-84559-345-2(6)); audio compact disk 64.95 (978-1-84559-367-4(7)) Pub: ISIS Lrg Prnt GBR. Dist(s): Ulverscroft US

Little Lord Fauntleroy. Frances Hodgson Burnett. Narrated by Flo Gibson. 4 cass. (Running Time: 6 hrs. 28 min.). (J). 1985. 19.95 (978-1-55685-059-2(X)) Audio Bk Con.
A little American boy is sent to live in England with his stern grandfather, a British lord, after his father dies. In training to become the heir to a master of vast holdings the little lord brings such joy & kindness that he gradually melts the old lord's heart.

Little Lord Fauntleroy. Frances Hodgson Burnett. Read by Donada Peters. (Running Time: 19680 sec.). (ENG.). (J). (ps-7). 2005. audio compact disk 49.99 (978-1-4001-3128-0(6)) Pub: Tantor Media. Dist(s): IngramPubServ

Little Lord Fauntleroy. abr. ed. Frances Hodgson Burnett. 2002. 7.95 (978-1-57815-270-4(4)) Media Bks NJ.

Little Lord Fauntleroy. abr. ed. Frances Hodgson Burnett. Read by Teresa Gallagher. (Running Time: 8199 sec.). (YA). 2007. bk. 17.98 (978-962-634-460-6(1)) Naxos.

Little Lord Fauntleroy, unabr. ed. Frances Hodgson Burnett. Read by Johanna Ward. 4 cass. (Running Time: 5 hrs. 30 mins.). (gr. 3-5). 1993. 32.95 (978-0-7861-0390-4(6), 1342) Blckstn Audio.
This is a charming story of a seven-year-old American boy, Ceddie Errol, who lived on the edge of poverty in New York. One day he was visited by a gruff lawyer at the tiny house he shared with "Dearest," his widowed mother, & after this visit, his life was never to be the same. For, waiting in England for Ceddie was Dorincourt Castle, where he was to reside as the sole living heir to the irascible, proud, & selfish Earl of Dorincourt. It will be up to this virtuous boy to capture & warm the Earl's heart, & transform him into doting grandfather & responsible landlord.

Little Lord Fauntleroy. unabr. ed. Frances Hodgson Burnett. Read by Johanna Ward. (Running Time: 5.5 hrs. 0 mins.). (ENG.). 2009. 29.95 (978-1-4332-9968-1(2)); audio compact disk 55.00 (978-1-4332-9965-0(8)) Blckstn Audio.

Little Lord Fauntleroy. unabr. ed. Frances Hodgson Burnett. Read by Marilyn Langbehn. 6 cass. (Running Time: 6 hrs.). Dramatization. (J). 1992. 39.95 (978-1-55686-417-9(5), 417) Books in Motion.
A gruff English Earl, feared & loathed by all who know him, is softened & transformed by his common American grandson who is apparent heir to the title.

Little Lord Fauntleroy. unabr. ed. Frances Hodgson Burnett. Read by Wanda McCaddon. 4 cass. (Running Time: 6 hrs.). (J). 1997. 29.95 Set. (42801X) Eye Ear.
A young boy living in a poor area of America is not aware that he is heir to a vast fortune. When his grandfather brings the boy & his mother to England, the boy is separated from his mother by his rich, overbearing & cruel grandfather. Over time, Little Lord Fauntleroy makes his grandfather realize that there is much more to life than money.

Little Lord Fauntleroy. unabr. ed. Frances Hodgson Burnett. Read by Donada Peters. (J). 2008. 44.99 (978-1-60514-653-9(6)) Find a World.

Little Lord Fauntleroy. unabr. ed. Frances Hodgson Burnett. Narrated by Virginia Leishman. 5 pieces. (Running Time: 6 hrs. 15 mins.). (gr. 4 up). 1997. 44.00 (978-0-7887-1797-0(9), 95269E7) Recorded Bks.
An orphaned boy's journey from rags to riches is a story full of surprises.

Little Lord Fauntleroy. unabr. ed. Frances Hodgson Burnett. Narrated by Donada Peters. (Running Time: 5 hrs. 30 mins. 0 sec.). (ENG.). (J). (gr. 4-7). 2008. 19.99 (978-1-4001-5912-3(1)); audio compact disk 22.99 (978-1-4001-0912-8(4)); audio compact disk 45.99 (978-1-4001-3912-5(0)) Pub: Tantor Media. Dist(s): IngramPubServ

Little Lord Fauntleroy. unabr. ed. Frances Hodgson Burnett. Narrated by Donada Peters. 5 CDs. (Running Time: 5:30 hrs.). (ENG.). (J). 2004. audio compact disk 24.99 (978-1-4001-0128-3(X)) Pub: Tantor Media. Dist(s): IngramPubServ

Little Lord Fauntleroy. unabr. collector's ed. Frances Hodgson Burnett. Read by Donada Peters. 6 cass. (Running Time: 6 hrs.). (J). 1994. 36.00 (978-0-7366-2690-3(5), 3425) Books on Tape.
Classic story of a boy's goodness & innocence overcoming an old man's hardness of heart.

Little Lord Fauntleroy, Homework Set. unabr. ed. Frances Hodgson Burnett. Read by Virginia Leishman. 5 cass. (Running Time: 6 hrs. 15 min.). (J). (gr. 5). 1997. bk. 56.24 (978-0-7887-1840-3(1), 40620) Recorded Bks.
An orphaned boy's journey from rags to riches is a story full of surprises.

Little Lost Shoe. Angie Aduddell. (J). 2007. audio compact disk 9.99 (978-1-60247-202-0(5)) Tate Pubng.

Little Love. Jerry Barnes. 1994. audio compact disk 14.95 (978-0-8198-4473-6(X), 332-166) Pauline Bks.

Little Love, a Little Learning. unabr. ed. Nina Bawden. Read by Julia Sands. 8 cass. (Running Time: 9 hrs. 20 min.). (Isis Ser.). (J). 2001. 69.95 (978-0-7531-1047-8(4)) Pub: ISIS Lrg Prnt GBR. Dist(s): Ulverscroft US
The year of the Queen's Coronation and Joanna, Kate and Poll are living in a London suburb with their mother and stepfather, the local doctor. Accepting unquestioningly his unstinting love, they are incurious about their vanished natural father - but the safety of their lives is tenuous. The past arrives to upset the present.

Little Love, a Little Learning. unabr. ed. Nina Bawden. Read by Julia Sands. 8 CDs. (Isis Ser.). (J). 2003. audio compact disk 79.95 (978-0-7531-2241-9(3)) Pub: ISIS Lrg Prnt GBR. Dist(s): Ulverscroft US

Little Match Girl see Hans Christian Andersen's Best Known Stories

Little Match Girl see Petite Fille Aux Allumettes

Little Match Girl see Petite Marchande d'Allumettes

Little Match Girl. Based on a story by Hans Christian Andersen. (J). 2002. pap. bk. 12.95 (978-2-89558-082-9(0)) Pub: Al Stanke CAN. Dist(s): Penton Overseas

Little Match Girl. Read by Marina Orsini. Based on a story by Hans Christian Andersen. Illus. by Annabel Malak. 1 cass. (Running Time: 15 mins.). (Classic Stories Ser.). (J). (ps-2). 2000. cass. & audio compact disk 9.95 (978-2-921997-88-1(6)) Coffragants CAN.
Encourages children to share & makes them aware of the poverty of others without making them feel guilty about receiving presents & being happy during the holidays.

Little Match Girl. unabr. ed. Hans Christian Andersen. Read by Julie Harris. 1 cass. (Running Time: 15 min.). (World of Words Ser.). (J). (gr. k-3). pap. bk. 10.00 (SAC 6500B) Spoken Arts.

Little Match Girl. unabr. ed. Narrated by Julie Harris. 1 cass., 10 bks. (Running Time: 15 min.). (World of Words Ser.). (J). (gr. k-3). 2001. pap. bk. 22.00 (978-0-8045-6702-2(6), 6500-B/10) Spoken Arts.

Little Match Girl & Other Tales. unabr. ed. Hans Christian Andersen. Perf. by Boris Karloff. 1 cass. Incl. Red Shoes. Based on a story by Hans Christian Andersen. (J). (CDL5 1117); Swineherd. Based on a story by Hans Christian Andersen. (J). (CDL5 1117); Thumbelina. Illus. by Hans Christian Andersen. (J). (CDL5 1117); Top & the Ball. Based on a story by Hans Christian Andersen. (J). (CDL5 1117); (J). 1984. 9.95 (978-0-694-50659-0(1), CDL5 1117) HarperCollins Pubs.

Little Memphis Blues Orchestra - Live at the Workplay Theatre: Birmingham, AL - August 7 2006. 2 CD. (Running Time: 2 hrs. 13 mins.). 2006. audio compact disk 14.99 (978-0-9791472-0-3(4)) LMBO Prod.
The Little Memphis Blues Orchestra - Live at the Workplay Theatre, Birmingham, AL - August 7, 2006Over two hours of Blues on this 2 CD audio set. Special Guests Include American Idol Winner Taylor Hicks.

Little Men. Louisa May Alcott. Narrated by Flo Gibson. (ENG.). 2009. audio compact disk 34.95 (978-1-60646-099-3(4)) Audio Bk Con.

***Little Men.** unabr. ed. Louisa May Alcott. Read by C. M. Hébert. (Running Time: 10 hrs. 30 mins.). 2010. 29.95 (978-1-4417-4153-0(4)); audio compact disk 100.00 (978-1-4417-4150-9(X)) Blckstn Audio.

***Little Men.** unabr. ed. Louisa May Alcott. Narrated by Justine Eyre. (Running Time: 10 hrs. 0 mins.). 2010. 16.99 (978-1-4001-8581-8(5)) Tantor Media.

***Little Men.** unabr. ed. Louisa May Alcott. Narrated by Justine Eyre. (Running Time: 10 hrs. 0 mins. 0 sec.). (ENG.). 2010. 22.99 (978-1-4001-6581-0(4)); audio compact disk 32.99 (978-1-4001-1581-5(7)); audio compact disk 65.99 (978-1-4001-4581-2(3)) Pub: Tantor Media. Dist(s): IngramPubServ

Little Men: Life at Plumfield with Jo's Boys. unabr. ed. Louisa May Alcott. Read by Flo Gibson. 8 cass. (Running Time: 10 hrs. 30 min.). (YA). (gr. 4-7). 1991. 26.95 (978-1-55685-200-8(2)) Audio Bk Con.
"Little Men" continues the story of the March family of "Little Women." Jo & her husband, the kindly Professor Bhaer, open a school for boys at Plumfield. As Jo says, "A good, happy, homelike school with me to take care of them & Fritz to teach them.".

Little Men: Life at Plumfield with Jo's Boys. unabr. ed. Louisa May Alcott. Read by C. M. Herbert. 7 cass. (Running Time: 10 hrs.). 1996. 49.95 (978-0-7861-0956-2(4), 1733) Blckstn Audio.
The lovable Jo March - introduced to us in "Little Women" - is now married with two sons of her own & an adopted family of twelve boys. And she couldn't be happier. Since starting an informal school at Plumfield, Jo & Professor Bhaer provide a haven for poor orphaned boys who thrive on warmth, goodness, & the affectionate interest of the March & Bhaer families. Sometimes it's difficult to tame the wild manners & spirits of wild boys who have had no nurturing.

Little Men: Life at Plumfield with Jo's Boys, unabr. ed. Louisa May Alcott. Narrated by Barbara Caruso. 8 pieces. (Running Time: 11 hrs.). (gr. 6 up). 1998. 69.00 (978-0-7887-2640-8(4), 95641E7) Recorded Bks.
In this sequel to "Little Women," Jo March, the irrepressible tomboy, is now married to her professor. But her days continue to be filled with troubles & plenty of adventure - she is raising two sons & 12 orphan boys.

Little Men: Novellas & Stories. Gerald Shapiro. (Sandstone price short Fiction Ser.). 2004. audio compact disk 9.95 (978-0-8142-9039-2(6)) Pub: Ohio St U Pr. Dist(s): Chicago Distribution Ctr

Little Menorah Who Forgot Chanukah. Jerry Sperling. Illus. by Giora Carmi. 1 cass. (gr. k-3). 1993. pap. bk. 10.95 (978-0-8074-0508-6(6), 101971) URJ Pr.

Little Mermaid see Petite Sirene

Little Mermaid. Hans Christian Andersen. (ENG.). 2007. 5.99 (978-1-60339-165-8(7)); audio compact disk 5.99 (978-1-60339-166-5(5)) Listenr Digest.

Little Mermaid. Based on a story by Hans Christian Andersen. 1 cass. (Sing-Along Ser.). (J). bk. 11.99 (978-0-7634-0305-8(9)); bk. 14.99 (978-0-7634-0943-2(X)); 13.99 Norelco. (978-0-7634-0290-7(7)); audio compact disk 19.99 (978-0-7634-0292-1(3)); audio compact disk 19.99 (978-0-7634-0293-8(1)) W Disney Records.

Little Mermaid. Based on a story by Hans Christian Andersen. 1 cass. (J). (ps-3). 1997. 13.99 (978-0-7634-0291-4(5)) W Disney Records.

Little Mermaid. Hans Christian Andersen. 1 cass. (Disney Read-Alongs Ser.). (J). (ps-3). 1997. bk. 7.99 (978-0-7634-0286-0(9)) Walt Disney.

Little Mermaid. Adapted by Claudie Stanke. Illus. by Andre Pijet. 1 cass., bk. (Running Time: 15 mins.). (Classic Stories Ser.). (J). (ps-3). audio compact disk 9.95 (978-2-89517-048-8(7)) Pub: Coffragants CAN. Dist(s): Penton Overseas
Shows children that they cannot have everything their hearts desire. They must learn to make decisions about their choices.

Little Mermaid. unabr. ed. Hans Christian Andersen. Narrated by Aurora Wetzel. 1 cass. (J). (ps up). 1993. 9.95 (978-1-887393-03-4(X)) Aurora Audio.
Extremely moving fairy tale. Mermaid wishes to gain a soul.

Little Mermaid. unabr. ed. Hans Christian Andersen. Perf. by Cathleen Nesbitt. Tr. by R. P. Keigwin. 1 cass. (J). 1984. 9.95 (978-0-694-50672-9(9), CDL5 1230) HarperCollins Pubs.

Little Mermaid: Original Broadway Cast Recording. Composed by Alan Menken. Directed By Francesca Zambello. Contrib. by Howard Ashman & Glenn Slater. (J). (ps-3). 2008. audio compact disk 16.99 (978-5-557-51719-5(7)) W Disney Records.

Little Mermaid: Read Along. Narrated by Roy Dotrice. 1 CD. (Running Time: 1 hr. 30 mins.). (J). 2001. pap. bk. 9.98 (978-0-7634-0799-5(2)) W Disney Records.

Little Mermaid Classic Read along Audio Book. Prod. by PC Treasures Staff. (J). 2007. (978-1-60072-058-1(7)) PC Treasures.

Little Mermaid Read-Along Collection. Based on a story by Hans Christian Andersen. 2 cass. (J). bk. 14.98 incl. Little Mermaid wristwatch. Disney Prod.

Little Mermaid Soundtrack. Based on a story by Hans Christian Andersen. 1 cass. (J). 1992. 12.98 (978-1-55723-292-2(X)) W Disney Records.

Little Minister: Abridged. 2007. (978-1-60339-047-7(2)); cd-rom & audio compact disk (978-1-60339-048-4(0)) Listenr Digest.

Little Money Bible. unabr. ed. Stuart Wilde. 2 cass. (Running Time: 2 hrs.). (ENG.). 1997. 16.95 (978-1-56170-426-2(1), 350) Hay House.
Deals with the E.S.P. of easy money & the art of being in the right place at the right time, with the right idea & the right attitude.

Little Money Bible. unabr. ed. Stuart Wilde. Read by Stuart Wilde. 2 CDs. (Running Time: 2 hrs.). 2006. audio compact disk 18.95 (978-1-4019-0671-9(0)) Hay House.

Little More. Music by Christa Haberstock. 1 CD. (Running Time: 22 mins). 1999. audio compact disk 10.00 (978-0-9760556-5-5(1)) Grnlf Bk Grp.
A Little More, Christa's third releasesince 1997, has been called a "fantastic eclectic blend of instrumentation, combined with beautiful vocals and very stronglywritten songs". CCM magazine portrays A Little More as "a refreshing musical adventure".

Little More about Me. unabr. collector's ed. Pam Houston. Read by Anna Fields. 6 cass. (Running Time: 9 hrs.). 2000. 48.00 (978-0-7366-4842-4(9), 5193) Books on Tape.
Globe-trotting adventures spanning five continents with candor & humor in an emotional journey that hits home. Searching for a place not too safe but not too threatening either, from which to negotiate the insecurities of life. We meet some good dogs, a few good men, a horse named Roany with the presence of a Zen master & a Buddhist named Karma, proving what Houston has always suspected.

Little Mouse see Gathering of Great Poetry for Children

Little Nugget. unabr. ed. P. G. Wodehouse. Read by Frederick Davidson. 5 cass. (Running Time: 7 hrs.). 1997. 39.95 (978-0-7861-1184-8(4), 1942) Blckstn Audio.
Mr. Peter Bums, a none too dedicated schoolmaster, engaged by snobbish Mr. Abney to educate his handpicked pupils, soon finds himself & his enraptured class at the mercy of an American gunman & at the beginning of a series of truly mind boggling adventures in a delicious Wodehouse tale of suspense, excitement & romance.

Little Nuggets of Wisdom: Big Advice from the Small Star of Chelsea Lately. unabr. ed. Chuy Bravo. Read by Brad Wollack. Told to Tom Brunelle. (Running Time: 1 hr.). (ENG.). 2010. 16.98 (978-1-60788-172-8(1)) Pub: Hachet Audio. Dist(s): HachBkGrp

Little of What You Fancy. unabr. ed. H. E. Bates. Read by Bruce Montague. 6 cass. (Running Time: 6 hrs.). 1994. 54.95 (978-0-7451-4221-0(4), CAB 904) AudioGO.
Things may be going well for Primrose Larkin, but they are far less perfect for Pop. In another delightful chapter in the history of the Larkin family, Pop unfortunately suffers a mild heart attack & Ma's solution is to send a succession of women up to his bedroom to tempt him back to health!.

Little Old Lady Who Was Not Afraid of Anything. abr. ed. Linda Williams. Illus. by Megan Lloyd. (Share a Story Ser.). (J). (ps-1). 2006. 9.99 (978-0-06-123217-6(3), HarperFestival) HarperCollins Pubs.

***Little Old Lady Who Was Not Afraid of Anything.** abr. ed. Linda Williams. Read by Linda Dewolf. (ENG.). 2006. (978-0-06-134831-0(7)) HarperCollins Pubs.

Little Old Letter see Poetry of Langston Hughes

Little Old Man of Batignolles see Classic Detective Stories, Vol. III, A Collection

Little One Eye, Little Two Eyes & Little Three Eyes see Goldilocks & the Three Bears & Other Stories

Little One... Good Night: A Lullaby from Vermont. Kathryn Mademann Vaughan. Illus. by Anharad Edson. Music by Joseph R. Rodarte. (J). 2004. per. 19.95 (978-0-9747447-0-4(0)) Chaser Media.

Little Orphan Annie see Great Kid's Shows

***Little Orphan Annie.** RadioArchives.com. (Running Time: 345). (ENG.). 2003. audio compact disk 17.98 (978-1-61081-005-0(8)) Radio Arch.

Little Oxford Dictionary. 6th l.t. ed. L. Little. 1987. bk. 32.50 (978-0-7089-1679-7(1)) Pub: UlverLrgPrint GBR. Dist(s): Ulverscroft US

Little Oz Stories see Oz

Little Peace & Quiet. Rick Charette. Read by Rick Charette. 1 CD. (Running Time: 1 hr.). (J). (gr. k-4). 1993. audio compact disk 12.98 (978-1-884210-07-5(4)) Pine Pt Record.
A collection of songs for children created for resting & relaxing. Soothing musical arrangements combined with delicate imagery. Includes: "It's a Quiet Night", "I'm Not Afraid of the Dark", "Mr. Man in the Moon" & more.

Little Peace & Quiet. Rick Charette & Laurie Bean. Read by Rick Charette. 1 cass. (J). (gr. k-4). 1994. pap. bk. 9.98 (978-1-884210-06-8(6), PPC-006) Energeia Pub.

***Little People.** 2010. audio compact disk (978-1-59171-187-2(8)) Falcon Picture.

Little Pim French Bop. Created by Little Pim Co. (ENG & FRE.). (J). 2009. audio compact disk 14.95 (978-1-935515-38-8(1)) Little Pim.

Little Pim Spanish Bop. Created by Little Pim Co. (ENG & SPA.). (J). 2009. audio compact disk 14.95 (978-1-935515-37-1(3)) Little Pim.

Little Pink Fish: Musical Adventures with Elizabeth Falconer Volume V. 1 CD. (Running Time: 58:23). (J). 2005. audio compact disk 15.00 (978-0-9770499-1-2(4)) Koto World.
Sing the aqua-alphabet with Little Pink Fish, the story of a very determined fish that learns to read! Then meet a mischievous monkey, a hero who sucks his thumb, and a naughty froggy. They are all here, waiting to tell their stories! Award-winning storyteller and musician Elizabeth Falconer brings to life two Japanese folktales, an Okinawan tale, and her own original story of a very special fish.

Little Pink House: A True Story of Defiance & Courage. abr. ed. Jeff Benedict. Read by Maggi-Meg Reed. (Running Time: 8 hrs. 30 mins.). (ENG.). 2009. 24.98 (978-1-60024-482-7(3)); audio compact disk 29.98 (978-1-60024-481-0(5)) Pub: Hachet Audio. Dist(s): HachBkGrp

Little Pink Slips. unabr. ed. Sally Kaslow. (Running Time: 14 hrs. 0 mins. 0 sec.). (ENG.). 2007. audio compact disk 39.99 (978-1-4001-0430-7(0)) Pub: Tantor Media. Dist(s): IngramPubServ

Little Pink Slips. unabr. ed. Sally Koslow. (Running Time: 14 hrs. 0 mins. 0 sec.). (ENG.). 2007. audio compact disk 79.99 (978-1-4001-3430-4(7)); audio compact disk 29.99 (978-1-4001-5430-2(8)) Pub: Tantor Media. Dist(s): IngramPubServ

Little Plastic Castle. Perf. by Ani DiFranco. 1 cass., 1 CD. 7.98 (RBR 12); audio compact disk 12.78 (RBR 12) NewSound.

Little Platinum Book of Cha-Ching: 32. 5 Strategies to Ring Your Own (Cash) Register in Business & Personal Success. unabr. ed. Jeffrey Gitomer. Read by Jeffrey Gitomer. (Running Time: 4 hrs. 0 mins. 0 sec.). (ENG.). 2009. 49.99 (978-0-7435-7537-9(7)); audio compact disk 29.99 (978-0-7435-7264-4(5)) Pub: S&S Audio. Dist(s): S and S Inc

Little Power: Rev. 3:7-13. Ed Young. 1986. 4.95 (978-0-7417-1555-5(4), 555) Win Walk.

Little Prankster Girl Audio CD. Martha Blue. Illus. by Keith Smith. Narrated by Peter A. Thomas & Jessie Ruffenach. (Running Time: 45 mins.). (NAV & ENG.). (J). 2005. audio compact disk 10.95 (978-1-893354-53-1(9)) Pub: Salina Bkshelf. Dist(s): Natl Bk Netwk
No one but Grandmother believes that Little Prankster Girl is mature enough to be taught to weave. Mother thinks she plays too many tricks, Younger Sister says she isn?t smart enough, and Baby is too young to give her any support. Determined to learn anyway, Little Prankster Girl ?borrows? some of her mother?s weaving supplies and practices weaving while she is out herding her family?s flock. This warmhearted story follows Little Prankster Girl through an exasperating but funny trial of her childhood. Readers will identify with Little Prankster Girl?s struggle to win recognition from her family, and will gain courage to make their own bids for greater independence.

Little Prince see Piccolo Principe

Little Prince. Read by Richard Burton. 1 cass. (Running Time: 59 min.). (J). 1993. 9.98 (978-1-56628-006-8(0), MLP3154/WB42532-4) MFLP CA.
The classic story by Antoine de Saint Exupery narrated by Richard Burton & friends.

Little Prince. Antoine de Saint-Exupéry. Read by Humphrey Bower. (Running Time: 2 hrs.).Tr. of Le Petit Prince. (J). 2009. 44.99 (978-1-74214-425-2(X), 9781742144252) Pub: Bolinda Pubng AUS. Dist(s): Bolinda Pub Inc

Little Prince. abr. ed. Antoine de Saint-Exupéry. Perf. by Louis Jourdan. Tr. by Katherine Woods. 1 cass. (Running Time: 1 hr. 10 min.).Tr. of Le Petit

Prince. (J). (gr. 4-6). 1989. 11.00 (978-0-89845-866-4(8), CPN 1695) HarperCollins Pubs.
An innocent exile, the little prince learns the true secret of the heart.

Little Prince. abr. ed. Antoine de Saint-Exupéry. Read by Santiago Munevar. (Running Time: 1 hr.).Tr. of Le Petit Prince. (J). 2002. 14.95 (978-1-60083-136-2(2), Audiofy Corp) Iofy Corp.

Little Prince. unabr. ed. Antoine de Saint-Exupéry. Read by Humphrey Bower. (Running Time: 7200 sec.).Tr. of Le Petit Prince. (J). 2008. audio compact disk 43.95 (978-1-921415-01-2(0), 9781921415012) Pub: Bolinda Pubng AUS. Dist(s): Bolinda Pub Inc

Little Prince. unabr. ed. Antoine de Saint-Exupéry. Read by Santiago Munevar. (Running Time: 3 hrs.).Tr. of Le Petit Prince. (J). 2002. 16.95 (978-1-60083-320-5(9), Audiofy Corp) Iofy Corp.

***Little Princes: One Man's Promise to Bring Home the Lost Children of Nepal.** unabr. ed. Conor Grennan. (ENG.). 2011. (978-0-06-202726-9(3), Harper Audio) HarperCollins Pubs.

Little Princess. Frances Hodgson Burnett. Read by Vanessa Maroney. (Playaway Children Ser.). (J). 2008. 74.99 (978-1-60640-840-7(2)) Find a World.

Little Princess. Frances Hodgson Burnett. Read by Vanessa Maroney. (Running Time: 27900 sec.). (Unabridged Classics in MP3 Ser.). (J). 2008. audio compact disk 24.00 (978-1-58472-528-2(1), In Aud) Sound Room.

Little Princess. Frances Hodgson Burnett. Read by Rebecca C. Burns. (Running Time: 60 sec.). (ENG.). (J). (gr. 4-7). 2004. audio compact disk 19.99 (978-1-4001-5110-3(4)) Pub: Tantor Media. Dist(s): IngramPubServ

Little Princess. Frances Hodgson Burnett. Read by Rebecca C. Burns. (ENG.). (J). (gr. 4-7). 2005. audio compact disk 59.99 (978-1-4001-3110-5(3)) Pub: Tantor Media. Dist(s): IngramPubServ

Little Princess. Frances Burnett. Narrated by Julie Harris. (Running Time: 3 hrs.). (J). 2006. 14.95 (978-1-60083-000-6(5)) Iofy Corp.

Little Princess. unabr. ed. Frances Hodgson Burnett. Narrated by Flo Gibson. 4 cass. (Running Time: 6 hrs.). (J). 1985. 19.95 (978-1-55685-060-8(3)) Audio Bk Con.
The changing fortunes of little Sarah Crewe, from riches to rags to riches, are embellished by her vivid imagination.

Little Princess. unabr. ed. Frances Hodgson Burnett. Read by Justine Eyre. (Running Time: 7 hrs.). 2010. 19.99 (978-1-4418-3103-3(7), 9781441831033, Brilliance MP3); 19.99 (978-1-4418-3111-8(8), 9781441831118, BAD); 39.97 (978-1-4418-3104-0(5), 9781441831040, Brlnc Audio MP3 Lib); 39.97 (978-1-4418-3112-5(6), 9781441831125, BADLE); audio compact disk 49.97 (978-1-4418-3102-6(9), 9781441831026, BriAudCD Unabrid) Brilliance Audio.

Little Princess. unabr. ed. Frances Hodgson Burnett. Read by Rebecca Burns. (J). 2007. 44.99 (978-1-59895-799-0(6)) Find a World.

Little Princess. unabr. ed. Frances Hodgson Burnett & Young Adult. Read by Justine Eyre. (Running Time: 7 hrs.). 2010. audio compact disk 19.99 (978-1-4418-3101-9(0), 9781441831019) Brilliance Audio.

Little Princess: The Story of Sara Crewe. Frances Hodgson Burnett. 4 cass. (Running Time: 6 hrs. 40 min.). (J). 26.95 (978-1-885546-01-2(7)) Big Ben Audio.

Little Princess: The Story of Sara Crewe. Frances Hodgson Burnett. Read by Vanessa Maroney. (Running Time: 7 hrs. 45 mins.). 2002. 22.95 (978-1-59912-091-1(7), Audiofy Corp) Iofy Corp.

Little Princess: The Story of Sara Crewe. Frances Hodgson Burnett. Read by Lucy Whybrow. (Running Time: 2 hrs. 30 mins.). 2006. 20.95 (978-1-60083-829-3(4)) Iofy Corp.

Little Princess: The Story of Sara Crewe. Frances Hodgson Burnett. Read by Lucy Whybrow. 2 cass. (Running Time: 2 hrs. 30 mins.). (J). 2002. 13.98 (978-962-634-754-6(6), NA225414) Naxos.
Sara Crewe is one of the most vivid figures in children's fiction. Born in India and sent to school in England, she is, at first, treated like a princess by her teacher, Miss Minchin. But when it becomes evident that Sara is not the possessor of a princess' fortune, she is dispatched to live in the attic and become a servant. It is the remarkable way in which Sara copes, imagining things are not as bad as they seem, which has made her role model for many young girls, who also hope to experience her happy ending.

Little Princess: The Story of Sara Crewe. abr. ed. Frances Hodgson Burnett. Read by Lucy Whybrow. 2 cass. (Running Time: 2 hrs. 30 mins.). (J). 2002. 17.98 (978-962-634-254-1(4), NA225412, Naxos AudioBooks) Naxos.

Little Princess: The Story of Sara Crewe. unabr. ed. Frances Hodgson Burnett. Read by Wanda McCaddon. 4 cass. (Running Time: 6 hrs. 30 min.). (J). (gr. 3 up). 2004. 24.95 (978-0-945353-94-2(4), H90394u) Pub: Audio Partners. Dist(s): PerseuPGW
Beloved children's classic about good will, depth of character, & imagination rewarded in a riches-to-rags tale of young Sara Crewe. Motion picture tie-in.

Little Princess: The Story of Sara Crewe. unabr. ed. Frances Hodgson Burnett. Read by Johanna Ward. 5 cass. (Running Time: 7 hrs.). (gr. 3-5). 1993. 39.95 (978-0-7861-0398-0(1), 1350) Blckstn Audio.
This touching classic has been a favorite with generations of children & adults. They have delighted in Sara's happiness, wept over her sorrows, & perhaps shared her need: to be recognized as someone unique & special - as a little princess.

Little Princess: The Story of Sara Crewe. unabr. ed. Frances Hodgson Burnett. Read by Laurie Klein. 6 cass. (Running Time: 7 hrs.). Dramatization. (J). 1991. 39.95 (978-1-55686-370-7(5), 370) Books in Motion.
Beautifully crafted & nurturing tale about Sara Crewe's journey from riches to rags to riches.

Little Princess: The Story of Sara Crewe. unabr. ed. Frances Hodgson Burnett. Narrated by Virginia Leishman. 6 pieces. (Running Time: 8 hrs.). (gr. 6 up). 1997. 53.00 . (978-0-7887-0589-2(X), 94766E7) Recorded Bks.
Sarah & the other unforgettable characters of this delightful riches-to-rags tale speak to new generations.

Little Princess: The Story of Sara Crewe. unabr. ed. Frances Hodgson Burnett. Read by Vanessa Maroney. 6 cds. (Running Time: 7 hrs 38 mins). (J). 2002. audio compact disk 33.95 (978-1-58472-287-8(8), 066, In Aud) Pub: Sound Room. Dist(s): Baker Taylor
Living off crumbs in a dreary attic, Sara Crew comforts herself with wondrous stories of adventure and fortune.

Little Princess: The Story of Sara Crewe. unabr. ed. Frances Hodgson Burnett. Read by Vanessa Maroney. 1 cd. (Running Time: 7 hrs 44 mins). (J). 2002. audio compact disk 18.95 (978-1-58472-390-5(4), In Aud) Pub: Sound Room. Dist(s): Baker Taylor
MP3 format.

Little Princess: The Story of Sara Crewe. unabr. collector's ed. Frances Hodgson Burnett. Read by Rebecca C. Burns. 6 cass. (Running Time: 6 hrs.). (J). 1996. 36.00 (978-0-7366-3293-5(X), 3948) Books on Tape.
Sara's father taught her that every girl is a princess, rich or poor. That gift - along with grace, spirit & imagination - gives her serenity & puts the fall from riches to rags in perspective.

Little Princess, with EBook. unabr. ed. Frances Hodgson Burnett. Narrated by Rebecca C. Burns. (Running Time: 6 hrs. 30 mins. 0 sec.). (ENG.). (J). (gr. 4-7). 2008. 19.99 (978-1-4001-5889-8(3)); audio compact disk 22.99 (978-1-4001-0889-3(6)) Pub: Tantor Media. Dist(s): IngramPubServ

Little Princess, with eBook. unabr. ed. Frances Hodgson Burnett. Narrated by Rebecca C. Burns. (Running Time: 6 hrs. 30 mins. 0 sec.). (ENG.). (J). (gr. 4-7). 2008. audio compact disk 45.99 (978-1-4001-3889-0(2)) Pub: Tantor Media. Dist(s): IngramPubServ

Little Princess's Musical Adventure: I-String, II-Woodwind, III-Brass, IV-Percussion. Vera Sharp. Illus. by M. J. Armstrong. Contrib. by Mehli Mehta. 2 cass. (Running Time: 1 hr. 45 min.). Orig. Title: Little Princess's Symphony. (J). (ps-1). 1993. bk. & vinyl bd. 69.00 (978-0-9616987-0-6(5)) V Sharp.
A complete Audio-Visual Music Appreciation Course on The Symphony Orchestra-World-wide Famous Mehli Mehta's Music. Ingenious conception. Four Books (1) String Family, (2) Woodwind Family (3) Brass Family (4) Percussion Family: Text: Rhythm-Rhyme-All synchronized on two-cassettes.

Little Princess's Symphony see Little Princess's Musical Adventure: I-String, II-Woodwind, III-Brass, IV-Percussion

Little Pronto & the Volcano's Fire: A Musical Story. Odds Bodkin. Read by Odds Bodkin. 1 CD. (Running Time: 1 hr. 12 min.). (J). (ps-7). 2001. audio compact disk 14.95 (978-1-882412-35-8(4), Odds Bodkin) Pub: Rivertree. Dist(s): Penton Overseas
Features the adventures of Proto, a young dinosaur.

Little Pronto & the Volcano's Fire: A Musical Story. Odds Bodkin. Read by Odds Bodkin. 1 cass. (Running Time: 1 hr. 12 min.). (Storytelling Audio Ser.). (ps-7). 2001. audio compact disk 14.95 (978-1-882412-34-1(6)) Pub: Rivertree. Dist(s): Penton Overseas

Little Proto & the Volcano's Fire: A Musical Story. rev. ed. Odds Bodkin. Read by Odds Bodkin. 1 cass. (Running Time: 1 hr.). (Storytelling Audio Ser.). 2001. 9.95 (978-1-882412-33-4(8)) Pub: Rivertree. Dist(s): Penton Overseas
Sometimes, friendship is all you need. Another exciting adventure for Little Proto.

Little Proto's T-Rex Adventure: A Musical Dinosaur. Odds Bodkin. 1 CD. (Running Time: 74 min.). Dramatization. (Odds Bodkin Musical Story Collection). (J). (ps-3). audio compact disk 14.95 (978-1-882412-28-0(1)) Rivertree.
Sequel to the original "Adventures of Little Proto." Meet King Geoffrey, the One Eye - the fiercest T-Rex ever to walk the Sea of Grass - & Bump, the lonely Pachycephalosurus who bumps everything in sight. Four original songs complete this Late Cretaceous adventure as Proto learns how Old Wrinkles lost his hom. Is Old Wrinkles the Vanished One Horned King.

Little Proto's T-Rex Adventure: A Musical Dinosaur. Odds Bodkin. 1 cass. (Running Time: 72 min.). Dramatization. (Odds Bodkin Musical Story Collection). 1999. 9.95 Norelco Box. (978-1-882412-29-7(X)) Pub: Rivertree. Dist(s): Penton Overseas

Little Proto's T-Rex Adventure: A Musical Dinosaur Story. Odds Bodkin. Read by Odds Bodkin. 1 cass. (Running Time: 1 hr. 13 mins.). Dramatization. (Odds Bodkin Musical Story Collection). (J). bk. 9.95 (978-1-882412-27-3(3), Odds Bodkin) Pub: Rivertree. Dist(s): Penton Overseas
Sequel to the original "Adventures of Little Proto." Meet King Geoffrey, the One Eye, the fiercest T-Rex ever to walk the Sea of Grass & Bump, the lonely Pachycephalosurus who bumps everything in sight. Four original songs complete this Late Cretaceous adventure as Proto learns how Old Wrinkles lost his hom. Is Old Wrinkles the Vanished One Horned King?.

Little Proto's T-Rex Adventure: A Musical Dinosaur Story. Odds Bodkin. Read by Odds Bodkin. 1 CD. (Running Time: 1 hr. 13 mins.). Dramatization. (Odds Bodkin Musical Story Collection). (J). 1999. bk. 14.95 (978-1-882412-30-3(3)) Pub: Rivertree. Dist(s): Penton Overseas

Little Proto's Trilogy. Odds Bodkin. 2003. audio compact disk 39.95 (978-1-882412-36-5(2)) Pub: Rivertree. Dist(s): Penton Overseas

Little Proto's Trilogy. rev. ed. Odds Bodkin. (Storytelling Audio Ser.). 2003. 26.95 (978-1-882412-37-2(0)) Pub: Rivertree. Dist(s): Penton Overseas

Little Quarterback. Shaun Gayle & Pat Owsley. 1 cass. (Shaun Gayle's Sports Tales Ser.). (J). (gr. k-4). 1994. 8.99 (3-0008) David C Cook.

Little Rap. Mary Blakely. 1 cass. (Rap Pack Ser.). (978-1-882995-09-7(0)) Azuray Learn.
Multi-sensory education. Colors, Numbers, Body Rap - Booklet incl. Early Elementary & up.

Little Red & the Wolf. Steck-Vaughn Staff. 1996. (978-0-8172-6469-7(8)) SteckVau.

***Little Red Book of Sales Answers.** unabr. ed. Jeffrey Gitomer. 1 Playaway. (Running Time: 4 hrs. 45 mins.). 2009. 54.75 (978-1-4407-1119-0(4)); audio compact disk 56.75 (978-1-4407-1117-6(8)) Recorded Bks.

***Little Red Book of Sales Answers.** unabr. collector's ed. Jeffrey Gitomer. 5 CDs. (Running Time: 4 hrs. 45 mins.). 2009. audio compact disk 39.95 (978-1-4407-1118-3(6)) Recorded Bks.

Little Red Book of Sales Answers: 99.5 Real Life Answers That Make Sense, Make Sales, & Make Money. unabr. ed. Jeffrey Gitomer. Read by Jeffrey Gitomer. (Running Time: 5 hrs. 0 mins. 0 sec.). (ENG.). 2009. 49.99 (978-0-7435-7533-1(4)); audio compact disk 29.99 (978-0-7435-7256-9(4)) Pub: S&S Audio. Dist(s): S and S Inc

Little Red Book of Selling: 12.5 Principles of Sales Greatness. unabr. ed. Jeffrey Gitomer. Read by Jeffrey Gitomer. (Running Time: 4 hrs. 30 mins. 0 sec.). (ENG.). 2008. 49.95 (978-0-7435-7376-4(5)) Pub: S&S Audio. Dist(s): S and S Inc

Little Red Buckets. unabr. ed. Lynda M. Nelson. 2 cass. (Running Time: 2 hrs. 30 min.). Dramatization. 1996. 14.95 Set. (978-0-9652802-2-8(5)) Timeless Prods.
Includes music, sound effects, & actors. The story of a little girl who carried "little red buckets" up to an elderly couple & through her acts of kindness discovered a guardian angel.

Little Red Caboose. Perf. by Dick Van Patten. 1 cass. (J). 3.98 Clamshell. (978-1-55886-139-8(4), BB/PT 446) Smarty Pants.

Little Red Cap. unabr. ed. Jacob W. Grimm & Wilhelm K. Grimm. 1 cass. (Follow the Reader Ser.). (J). (gr. k-2). 1995. pap. bk. 15.98 (978-0-8072-0232-6(0), FTR174SP, Listening Lib) Random Audio Pubg.
A new version of a well-loved story featuring a winsome, but naughty, little girl, a more beguiling wolf, & a stouter, braver huntsman.

Little Red Hen see Gallinita Roja

Little Red Hen. 1 cass. (J). 1986. 9.95 (978-0-934323-22-2(4)) Alchemy Comms.

Little Red Hen. (Ladybird Bks.). (ARA., (J). (gr. 1-3). 1987. bk. 12.95 (978-0-86685-632-4(3)) Intl Bk Ctr.

Little Red Hen. (gr. k-1). 10.00 (978-0-7635-5068-4(X)) Rigby Educ.

Little Red Hen. 1 cass. (Easy-to-Read Folktales Ser.). (J). (ps-2). 1985. Scholastic Inc.

Little Red Hen. 2004. bk. 24.95 (978-0-89719-889-9(1)); pap. bk. 18.95 (978-1-55592-807-0(2)); pap. bk. 38.75 (978-1-55592-757-8(2)); pap. bk. 32.75 (978-1-55592-259-7(7)); pap. bk. 14.95 (978-1-56008-062-6(0)); 8.95 (978-1-56008-954-4(7)); 8.95 (978-1-56008-146-3(5)); cass. & flmstrp 30.00 (978-0-89719-552-2(3)); audio compact disk 12.95 (978-1-55592-875-9(7)) Weston Woods.

Little Red Hen. Arlene Capriola & Rigmor Swenson. Ed. by Cherisse Mastry. Illus. by Kathy Burns. 1 cass. (Once upon a Time Ser.). (J). (gr. k-2). 1998. 6.95 (978-1-57022-164-4(2), ECS1642) ECS Lrn Systs.

Little Red Hen. Arlene Capriola & Rigmor Swenson. Ed. by Cherisse Mastry. Illus. by Kathy Burns. 1 cass. (Once upon a Time Ser.). (J). (gr. k-2). 1998. pap. bk. & wbk. ed. 12.95 (978-1-57022-175-0(8)) ECS Lrn Systs.

Little Red Hen. Paul Galdone. 1 read-along cass. (Running Time: 8 min.). (J). pap. bk. 12.95 (PRA155) Weston Woods.
One side with page tum signals, one side without.

Little Red Hen. Paul Galdone. Illus. by Paul Galdone. 1 cass. (Running Time: 11 min.). (J). (ps-k). pap. bk. 12.95 (RAC155) Weston Woods.
An industrious, hardworking hen teaches her friends a thing or two about helping out in the classic story.

Little Red Hen. Retold by Paul Galdone. 1 cass. (Running Time: 8 min.). (J). bk. 24.95; pap. bk. 32.75 Weston Woods.
One side with page tum signals, one side without.

Little Red Hen. Read by Valerie Stephens. (J). (gr. k-3). 2005. audio compact disk 6.00 (978-0-618-70904-5(5), Clarion Bks) HM Harcourt.

Little Red Hen. unabr. ed. Brad Caudle & Melissa Caudle. Read by Brad Caudle. Illus. by Anthony Guerra. 1 cass. (Running Time: 22 min.). (Rock 'N Read Ser.). (J). (gr. 1 up). 1996. pap. bk. 7.95 (978-1-878489-69-2(0), RL969) Rock N Learn.
Educator-developed approach teaches reading skills by using familiar stories & a cassette that presents both a slow version & a faster version for kids to follow along. Stories have a happy ending & teach an important lesson about life.

Little Red Hen. unabr. ed. Paul Galdone. 1 cass. (Running Time: 8 min.). (J). (gr. k-3). 1989. pap. bk. 16.90 (978-0-8045-6519-6(8), 6519) Spoken Arts.
This is an all-time favorite about lazy critters who refuse to help the industrious little hen.

Little Red Hen & Rumplestiltskin Cassette. Sue Arengo. (Classic Tales Ser.). 2004. 14.75 (978-0-19-422091-0(5)) OUP.

Little Red Hen Audio CD. Benchmark Education Company. Based on a work by Brenda Parkes. (Shared Reading Classics Ser.). (J). (gr. k-2). 2009. audio compact disk 10.00 (978-1-60634-766-9(7)) Benchmark Educ.

Little Red Hen Musical. Sara Ridgley & Gavin Mole. (Class Act Productions Ser.). (ENG.). 2000. audio compact disk 24.95 (978-1-85909-657-4(3), Warner Bro) Alfred Pub.

Little Red Lighthouse. 2004. bk. 24.95 (978-1-56008-230-9(5)); pap. bk. 14.95 (978-0-7882-0597-2(8)); 8.95 (978-1-56008-955-1(5)); cass. & flmstrp 30.00 (978-0-89719-536-2(1)) Weston Woods.

Little Red Lighthouse & the Great Gray Bridge. Hildegarde H. Swift. Illus. by Lynd Ward. (Running Time: 14 mins.). 1992. 9.95 (978-1-59112-077-3(2)); audio compact disk 12.95 (978-1-59519-054-3(6)) Live Oak Media.

Little Red Lighthouse & the Great Gray Bridge. unabr. ed. Hildegarde H. Swift. 1 cass. (Running Time: 14 min.). (J). (gr. k-3). 1992. 9.95 Live Oak Media.
The classic story of the proud lighthouse that doubted its worth as a sentinel of safety on the river when a great bridge was erected next to it.

Little Red Lighthouse & the Great Gray Bridge. unabr. ed. Hildegarde H. Swift. Read by Jerry Terheyden. Illus. by Lynd Ward. 11 vols. (Running Time: 14 mins.). (J). (gr. k-3). 1992. bk. 25.95 (978-0-87499-260-1(5)); pap. bk. 16.95 (978-0-87499-259-5(1)) Live Oak Media.

Little Red Lighthouse & the Great Gray Bridge, Grades K-3. unabr. ed. Hildegarde H. Swift. Read by Jerry Terheyden. Illus. by Lynd Ward. 14 vols. (Running Time: 14 mins.). (J). 1992. pap. bk. & tchr. ed. 41.95 Reading Chest. (978-0-87499-261-8(3)) Live Oak Media.

Little Red Lighthouse, the see Pequeno Faro Rojo Y el Gran Puente Gris

Little Red Riding Cap: Yesterday's Fairytales Retold. unabr. ed. Shelia Monique. Read by Shelia Monique. 1 cass., 1 CD. (Running Time: 40 min.). Dramatization. (J). 2001. 17.99 (978-1-928687-00-9(8)) Pub: May Co II Enterp. Dist(s): IPG Chicago
Bases on the book "Little Red Riding Hood.".

Little Red Riding Hood see Storytime Favorites

Little Red Riding Hood see Sleeping Beauty & Other Stories

Little Red Riding Hood see Petit Chaperon Rouge

Little Red Riding Hood see Caperucita Roja

Little Red Riding Hood see Petit Chaperon Rouge

Little Red Riding Hood. 1 cass. (Running Time: 12 min.). (Talking Bear Tapes Ser.). (J). 1986. 4.95 (978-0-89926-206-2(6), 919D) Audio Bk.

Little Red Riding Hood. Scripts. 1 cass. or 1 CD. (Running Time: 25 mins.). (J). (gr. 3-6). 2000. pap. bk. & tchr. ed. 29.59 Bad Wolf Pr.
Little Red's Mom is unusually proud of the Riding Hood family tree, the Woodsman has some spectacularly untalented apprentices, the Wolf needs some ketchup, Granny is a math whiz & Little Red leams how to do the Acorn Dance with an odd band of Squirrels. Sheet music available.

Little Red Riding Hood. Perf. by Jane Altman et al. (Running Time: 7 min.). (J). 5.95 incl. bk. Scholastic Inc.

Little Red Riding Hood. Audio. 1 cass. (Running Time: 15 mins.). (Classic Stories Ser.). (J). (ps-2). 2000. cass. & audio compact disk 9.95 (978-2-921997-83-6(5)) Coffragants CAN.

Little Red Riding Hood. Arlene Capriola & Rigmor Swenson. Ed. by Cherisse Mastry. Illus. by Kathy Burns. 1 cass. (Once upon a Time Ser.). (J). (gr. k-2). 1998. 6.95 (978-1-57022-165-1(0), ECS1650) ECS Lrn Systs.

Little Red Riding Hood. Arlene Capriola & Rigmor Swenson. Ed. by Cherisse Mastry. Illus. by Kathy Burns. 1 cass. (Once upon a Time Ser.). (J). (gr. k-2). 1998. pap. bk. & wbk. ed. 12.95 (978-1-57022-176-7(6)) ECS Lrn Systs.

Little Red Riding Hood. Read by Linda Sorgini. Illus. by Annabel Malak. 1 cass. (Running Time: 15 mins. per cass.). (Classic Stories Ser.). (J). bk. 9.95 Pub: Coffragants CAN. Dist(s): Penton Overseas
The wolf is mean to disobedient children, but Little Red Riding Hood is a very clever, resourceful little girl.

Little Red Riding Hood. l.t. ed. Short Stories. Illus. by Graham Percy. 1 cass. (Running Time: 10 mins.). Dramatization. (J). (ps-3). 2001. bk. 8.49 (978-84-86154-90-5(1)) Pub: Peralt Mont ESP. Dist(s): imaJen

Little Red Riding Hood. unabr. ed. Naomi Fox. Illus. by Neal Fox. Narrated by Robert Guillaume. 1 cass. (Running Time: 15 min.). (J). (ps-1). 1993. bk. 9.95 (978-1-882179-14-5(5)) Confetti Ent.
The Confetti Company, a cast of multi-ethnic children, reenact the classic fairytale told in a modem, updated tempo.

Little Red Riding Hood. unabr. ed. Read by Julie Harris. 1 read-along cass. (World of Words Ser.). (J). (gr. k-3). bk. 15.00 (SAC 6500A) Spoken Arts.

Little Red Riding Hood & Other Children's Favorites. (J). 2005. audio compact disk (978-1-933796-29-1(4)) PC Treasures.

Little Red Riding Hood Classic Read along Audio Book. Prod. by PC Treasures Staff. (J). 2007. (978-1-60072-054-3(4)) PC Treasures.

Little Red Train. Short Stories. Carl Sommer. Narrated by Carl Sommer. 1 CD. Dramatization. (Another Sommer-Time Story Ser.). (J). (gr. 1-4). 2003. bk. 16.95 (978-1-57537-514-4(1)); bk. 16.95 (978-1-57537-563-2(X)) Advance Pub.

Little Red Train. Carl Sommer. Narrated by Carl Sommer. 1 cass. Dramatization. (Another Sommer-Time Story Ser.). (J). (gr. k-4). 2003. lib. bdg. 23.95 (978-1-57537-764-3(0)) Advance Pub.
Character Education story with character song by Karacter Kidz.

***Little Red Train / el Trenecito Rojo.** ed. Carl Sommer. Illus. by Kennon James. (Another Sommer-Time Story Bilingual Ser.). (ENG & SPA.). (J). 2009. bk. 26.95 (978-1-57537-183-2(9)) Advance Pub.

Little Regiment & Other Great Civil War Stories. unabr. ed. Perf. by William Windom & William J. Sanderson. Ed. by Marty Greenberg. 4 cass. (Running Time: 6 hrs.). 2001. 25.00 (978-1-59040-039-5(9), Phoenix Audio) Pub: Amer Intl Pub. Dist(s): PerseuPGW
The War between the States comes alive in this outstanding collection of Civil War stories by some of America's most respected authors, including, Ambrose Bierce, Kate Chopin, Stephen Crane, Louisa May Alcott and Edith Wharton.

Little Richard; Shake It All About. 1 cass. (J). 1996. 5.98 (978-1-55723-379-0(9)); 11.98 (978-1-55723-570-1(8)) W Disney Records.

Little Rock Sound, 1965-69. Bill Jones. audio compact disk 10.00 (978-0-9800897-2-1(7)) Pub: Butler Ctr. Dist(s): U of Ark Pr

***Little Roy Wiggins - Memory Time Book/CD Set.** Dewitt Scott. 2010. pap. bk. 17.99 (978-0-7866-8214-0(0)) Mel Bay.

Little Saigon. unabr. ed. T. Jefferson Parker. Read by David Colacci. (Running Time: 14 hrs.). 2008. 39.25 (978-1-4233-5542-7(3), 9781423355427, Brlnc Audio MP3 Lib); 24.95 (978-1-4233-5541-0(5), 9781423355410, Brilliance MP3); 39.25 (978-1-4233-5544-1(X), 9781423355441, BADLE); 24.95 (978-1-4233-5543-4(1), 9781423355434, BAD); audio compact disk 29.95 (978-1-4233-5539-7(3), 9781423355397, Bril Audio CD Unabri); audio compact disk 97.25 (978-1-4233-5540-3(7), 9781423355403, BriAudCD Unabrid) Brilliance Audio.

Little Saigon, unabr. ed. T. Jefferson Parker. Narrated by George Guidall. 10 cass. (Running Time: 13 hrs. 45 mins.). 1990. 85.00 (978-1-55690-312-0(X), 90013E7) Recorded Bks.
When Chuck Frye's sister-in-law Li is kidnapped in front of hundreds of witnesses, he is catapulted into terror & intrigue stretching from Little Saigon to the CIA & FBI & all the way to Hanoi, where the fate of a group of MIAs is used as bait in a world of betrayal within betrayal, revenge compounded by more revenge & deals within deals.

Little Saint. unabr. collector's ed. Georges Simenon. Read by Michael Prichard. 6 cass. (Running Time: 6 hrs.). 1984. 36.00 (978-0-7366-0541-0(X), 1515) Books on Tape.
Louis Cuchas does not have an easy life, but what he lacks in material blessings he more than makes up with his sunny & cheerful nature. His nickname is the Little Saint. He transforms his gifts of character into artistic expression as a successful painter.

Little Scarlet. unabr. ed. Walter Mosley. Read by Michael Boatman. 5 cass. (Running Time: 7 hrs.). (Easy Rawlins Mystery Ser.). 2004. 45.00 (978-1-4159-0222-6(4)) Books on Tape.
In 1965, during the Watts riots, a white man seeking refuge from a mob hides in a building and is soon after accused of murder.

Little Scarlet. unabr. ed. Walter Mosley. Read by Michael Boatman. (Easy Rawlins Mystery Ser.). (ENG.). 2005. 16.98 (978-1-59483-155-3(6)) Pub: Hachet Audio. Dist(s): HachBkGrp

Little Scarlet. unabr. ed. Walter Mosley. Read by Michael Boatman. (Running Time: 7 hrs. 30 mins.). (ENG.). 2009. 54.98 (978-1-60024-620-3(6)) Pub: Hachet Audio. Dist(s): HachBkGrp

Little Secrets, Playing with Fire. unabr. ed. Emily Blake. Read by Kirsten Kairos. (J). 2007. 34.99 (978-1-60252-845-1(4)) Find a World.

Little Shepherd. Don J. Black. 1 cass. 4.98 (978-1-55503-578-5(7), 06001165); 4.98 (06001165) Covenant Comms.
A Christmas story set at the time of Christ.

Little Shepherd of Kingdom Come. unabr. ed. John Fox, Jr. Read by Maynard Villers. 8 cass. (Running Time: 10 hrs. 30 min.). 1994. 49.95 (978-1-55686-544-2(9)) Books in Motion.
Orphaned as a child, Chad Buford makes his way in life on his own. His Kentucky journey leads him through a world of snobbery, feuds, education & honor in battle in the Civil War.

Little Shepherd of Provence. unabr. ed. Evaleen Stein. Read by Flo Gibson. 2 cass. (Running Time: 2 hrs. 30 min.). (J). (gr. 1 up). 1994. 14.95 (978-1-55685-325-8(4)) Audio Bk Con.
This appealing story about a poor lame shepherd boy, whose kind heart reaps unexpected rewards, is set in the beautiful countryside of southern France.

Little Shiver. Short Stories. As told by Donna L. Washington. 1 CD. (Running Time: 71 min.). (J). 2004. audio compact disk 15.00 (978-0-9769396-2-7(2)) DLW Storyteller.
In this collection of spooky tales, storyteller Donna Washington capably jumps from sweetly lyrical if somewhat creepy vernacular to that which is viscerally slurping and highly animated. These ghost stories will have children glued to their seats as they ponder severed limbs or wonder whether a Cinderella-like heroine will be eaten or if her good-heartedness and some magical intervention will save her. â€œA Big Spooky Houseâ€ is Washingtonâ€(tm)s retelling of a picture-book (Hyperion, 2000) story. The engaging storyteller does a good job humanizing innocent kids and foolish adults and making witches and other nightmarish creatures wonderfully wicked. Just in time for Halloween.- ALA Booklist Review October 2004.

Little Shopping. Cynthia Rylant. Narrated by Suzanne Toren. (Running Time: 30 mins.). (gr. 2 up). 10.00 (978-0-7887-9370-7(5)) Recorded Bks.

Little Sister. abr. ed. Raymond Chandler. Read by Elliott Gould. 2 cass. (Running Time: 3 hrs.). 2004. 18.00 (978-1-59007-099-4(2)); audio compact disk 21.95 (978-1-59007-100-7(X)) Pub: New Millenn Enter. Dist(s): PerseuPGW
Philip Marlowe goes to Hollywood to explore the underworld of glitter capital, trying to find a sweet young thing's missing brother. In deep with a rising movie star, her blackmailing brother, agents, prostitutes, and studio heads, Marlowe sardonically takes on the interlocking levels of Hollywood society.

Little Sister, unabr. ed. Raymond Chandler. Read by Ed Bishop. 6 cass. (Running Time: 6 hrs.). 1993. 54.95 (978-0-7451-5823-5(4), CAB 057) AudioGO.

Little Sleep's-Head Sprouting Hair in the Moonlight see Poetry & Voice of Galway Kinnell

Little Sleepy Eyes. Ed. by J. Aaron Brown. Illus. by Morgan Inc. Staff. 1 cass. (Running Time: 45 min.). (J). (ps). 1994. bk. 12.95 Incl. lyric bk. (978-0-927945-08-0(8)) Someday Baby.
A collection of 8 lullabies with soothing melodies, meaningful lyrics & beautifully orchestrated arrangements. Includes titles "Little Jackie Rabbit", "Things That I Love" & " Little Sleepy Eyes".

Little Sleepy Eyes. Ed. by J. Aaron Brown. Illus. by Morgan Inc. Staff. 1 cass. (Running Time: 45 min.). (J). (ps). 1995. bk. 15.95 (978-0-927945-12-7(6)) Someday Baby.

Little Sleepy Eyes. Created by Hal Leonard Corporation Staff. 1 cass. 2004. pap. bk. 15.95 CD. (978-0-7935-6423-1(9), 0793564239) H Leonard.
Soothing melodies, meaningful lyrics, beautifully orchestrated.

Little Songs for Little Me. Nancy Stewart. 1 cass. (Running Time: 40 min.). (J). (ps). 1992. bk. 24.95 Incl. 3-ring binder. (978-1-885430-06-9(X), FS103); 9.95 (978-1-885430-07-6(8)) Frnds St Music.
Songs for 0-5 year olds includes activity book with song lyrics, chords, activities, felt board, & felt cut-outs.

Little Soul & the Sun. unabr. ed. Neale Donald Walsch. Read by Neale Donald Walsch. Music by Timothy R. Jessup. 1 cass. (Running Time: 30 min.). 1999. 10.95 (978-1-57453-300-2(2)); audio compact disk 15.95 (978-1-57453-301-9(0)) Audio Lit.

Little Soul & the Sun - The Soundtrack. Neale Donald Walsch. Narrated by Neale Donald Walsch. Prod. by Timothy R. Jessup. Illus. by Frank Riccio. 1 CD. (J). 1999. audio compact disk 16.99 (978-0-9675908-0-6(9)) Sound Design.
A dramatization of the book " The Little Soul & Sun" with orchestrated underscore & special effect.

Little Soup's Birthday. unabr. ed. Robert Newton Peck. Narrated by Norman Dietz. 1 cass. (Running Time: 45 mins.). (gr. 4 up). 1997. 10.00 (978-0-7887-0800-8(7), 94949E7) Recorded Bks.
For his tenth birthday party, Soup has planned the food & the games. But he hasn't planned on a huge snowfall that may make it impossible for his friends to get to his house. Join Soup & his best friend as they try to salvage the party in this wholesome tale set in rural Vermont.

Little Soup's Bunny. unabr. ed. Robert Newton Peck. Narrated by Norman Dietz. 1 cass. (Running Time: 45 mins.). (gr. 1 up). 1997. 10.00 (978-0-7887-0896-1(1), 95034E7) Recorded Bks.
Based on the author's own childhood. A tale of friendship, a bunny & a hidden trove of brightly colored, uncooked Easter eggs.

Little Soup's Hayride. unabr. ed. Robert Newton Peck. Narrated by Norman Dietz. 1 cass. (Running Time: 1 hr.). (gr. 1 up). 1997. 10.00 (978-0-7887-1085-8(0), 95089E7) Recorded Bks.
What could be more fun than taking a ride on a horse-drawn hay wagon? Flying down a hill on a hay wagon you make yourself.

Little Soup's Turkey. unabr. ed. Robert Newton Peck. Narrated by Norman Dietz. 1 cass. (Running Time: 45 mins.). (gr. 1 up). 1997. 10.00 (978-0-7887-1339-2(6), 95188E7) Recorded Bks.
Thanksgiving is coming & Soup & Rob can't wait to perform in the school's holiday play. But mix together a live 50-pound turkey, seven sacks of mystery corn, a hot stove & two stagestruck boys & what do you get? A whole peck of trouble.

Little Squeegy Bug. unabr. ed. Bill Martin, Jr. & Michael Sampson. Narrated by John McDonough. 1 cass. (Running Time: 15 mins.). (ps up). 2001. 10.00 (978-1-4025-0921-6(9), 96947) Recorded Bks.
The little squeegy bug doesn't know where he comes from or what he is. He isn't an ant or a cricket, and he definitely isn't a flea. He thinks it might be fun to be a bumblebee, because then he'd have silver wings and a stinger. Buzzer the Bumblebee tells the squeegy bug to climb to the sky and find his own silver wings. When the squeegy bug tries, he doesn't find wings. But he does find two new friends. With help from Creepy the Caterpillar and Haunchy the Spider, the squeegy bug gets more than he ever dreamed of.

Little Stalker. Jennifer Belle. Read by Renée Raudman. (Playaway Adult Fiction Ser.). 2008. 69.99 (978-1-60640-706-6(6)) Find a World.

Little Stalker. unabr. ed. Jennifer Belle. Read by Renée Raudman. 2 MP3-CDs. (Running Time: 11 hrs. 30 mins. 0 sec.). (ENG.). 2007. 29.99 (978-1-4001-5442-5(1)); audio compact disk 39.99 (978-1-4001-0442-0(4)); audio compact disk 79.99 (978-1-4001-3442-7(0)) Pub: Tantor Media. Dist(s): IngramPubServ

Little Stranger. Sarah Waters. (Running Time: 16 hrs.). (ENG.). (gr. 8 up). 2009. audio compact disk 39.95 (978-0-14-314480-9(4), PengAudBks) Penguin Grp USA.

Little Stranger. unabr. ed. Candia McWilliam. Read by Di Langford. 4 cass. (Running Time: 4 hrs.). 1994. 44.95 (978-1-85089-723-1(9), 90014) Pub: ISIS Audio GBR. Dist(s): Ulverscroft US
When Margaret, the new nanny, moved into the lives of Daisy & Solomon, they wondered how they had ever managed without her. Margaret insists that John is brought up in the traditional way, & to Daisy's dismay her son places his love for his nanny first. But she has more control over his life than her own.

Little Swineherd see Widow's Children

Little Things see Gathering of Great Poetry for Children

Little Things of Christmas: Luke 2:1-14. Ed Young. 1993. 4.95 (978-0-7417-1991-1(6), 991) Win Walk.

Little Thumb & Other Classic Tales see Pulgarcita y Otros Cuentos Clasicos

Little Thumb & Other Classic Tales. (Running Time: 1 hr.). 2002. 14.95 (978-1-60083-147-8(8), Audiofy Corp) Iofy Corp.

Little Tiger. unabr. ed. Chung Sook Pierce & Maureen K. Pierce. Read by Christine Clayburg. 12 cass. (Running Time: 12 hrs. 36 min.). 2001. 64.95 (978-1-58116-101-4(8)) Books in Motion.
The true story of capture, peril and escape by a young girl and her brother during the tumultuous 1940's and 50's in North and South Korea.

Little Tim & the Brave Sea Captain. 2004. pap. bk. 14.95 (978-0-7882-0605-4(2)); 8.95 (978-1-56008-956-8(3)); cass. & flmstrp 30.00 (978-1-56008-708-3(0)) Weston Woods.

Little Toot. 2004. bk. 24.95 (978-1-56008-231-6(3)); pap. bk. 14.95 (978-0-7882-0598-9(6)); 8.95 (978-1-56008-957-5(1)); cass. & flmstrp 30.00 (978-1-56008-709-0(9)) Weston Woods.

Little Toot. Perf. by Dick Van Patten. 1 cass. (J). 3.98 Clamshell. (978-1-55886-138-1(6), BB/PT 445) Smarty Pants.

Little Toot - The Story of White Satin - Five Peas in a Pod - Rumplestiltskin - The Little Magic Pot. EDCON Publishing Group Staff. (ENG.). 2008. audio compact disk 12.95 (978-0-8481-0424-5(2)) EDCON Pubng.

Little Town on the Prairie. unabr. ed. Laura Ingalls Wilder. Read by Cherry Jones. (J). 2005. 22.00 (978-0-06-056504-6(7), HarperChildAud); audio compact disk 25.95 (978-0-06-056505-3(5), HarperChildAud) HarperCollins Pubs.

Little Triggers. unabr. ed. Martyn Waites. 6 cass. (Running Time: 8 hrs.). (Story Sound Ser.). (J). 2005. 54.95 (978-1-85903-805-5(0)) Pub: Mgna Lrg Print GBR. Dist(s): Ulverscroft US

Little Turtle see Gathering of Great Poetry for Children

***Little Vampire Women.** unabr. ed. Louisa May Alcott. Read by Caitlin Davies. Illus. by Lynn Messina. (ENG.). 2010. (978-0-06-199757-0(9)); (978-0-06-199530-9(4)) HarperCollins Pubs.

Little Walrus Warning. Carol Young. (J). (ps-2). 2001. bk. 19.95 (SP 4009C) Kimbo Educ.
Little Walrus & his mother join the herd as they start their annual migration north to the Chukchi Sea. Includes book.

Little Walrus Warning. Carol Young. Narrated by Peter Thomas. Illus. by Walter Stuart. 1 cass. (Smithsonian Oceanic Collection). (J). (ps-2). 1996. 5.00 (978-1-56899-276-1(9), C4009) Soundprints.
With spring approaching the icy Alaskan coast, Little Walrus & his mother join the herd as they start their annual migration north to the Chukchi Sea. On the way, Little Walrus learns how to forage for food & climb out of hidden ice crevices. But his true test comes when he is confronted by a hungry polar bear.

Little Website That Could: How to Turn Your Little Caboose into a Cash-Hauling Freight Train! 2 cass. (Running Time: 3 hrs.). 2001. audio compact disk 24.95 (978-0-9708061-0-9(8)) Lttle Web.

Little White Horse. unabr. collector's ed. Elizabeth Goudge. Read by Penelope Dellaporta. 7 cass. (Running Time: 10 hrs. 30 mins.). (J). 1988. 56.00 (978-0-7366-1401-6(X), 2290) Books on Tape.
It is 1842. Maria Merryweather is 13 years old, newly orphaned. Her father's debts have taken away the London home she loved so much. Now there is only enough money to send Maria, her dog Wiggins & her governess Miss Heliotrope to the West Country. There, in a part of the world they have never before seen, they are to live with Sir Benjamin Merryweather, a distant cousin.

Little Women. Retold by Noe Venable. Louisa May Alcott. (Classic Adventures Ser.). 2000. audio compact disk 18.95 (978-1-4105-0150-9(7)) D Johnston Inc.

Little Women. abr. adpt. ed. Louisa May Alcott. (Bring the Classics to Life: Level 1 Ser.). (ENG.). (gr. 3-7). 2008. audio compact disk 12.95 (978-1-55576-414-2(2)) EDCON Pubng.

Little Women. adpt. ed. Philip Glassborrow et al. Adapted by Paul McCusker. Louisa May Alcott. 4 CDs. (Radio Theatre Ser.). (ENG.). 2004. audio compact disk 28.97 (978-1-58997-124-0(8)) Pub: Focus Family. Dist(s): Tyndale Hse

***Little Women.** unabr. ed. Louisa May Alcott. Read by Kate Reading. (ENG.). (J). 2011. audio compact disk 25.00 (978-0-307-74788-4(3), Listening Lib) Pub: Random Audio Pubg. Dist(s): Random

***Little Women.** unabr. ed. Louisa May Alcott. Narrated by Justine Eyre. (Running Time: 17 hrs. 30 mins. 0 sec.). (ENG.). 2010. 29.99 (978-1-4001-6922-1(4)); audio compact disk 39.99 (978-1-4001-1922-6(7)); audio compact disk 95.99 (978-1-4001-4922-3(3)) Pub: Tantor Media. Dist(s): IngramPubServ

***Little Women.** unabr. ed. Louisa May Alcott. Narrated by Justine Eyre. (Running Time: 20 hrs. 0 mins.). 2010. 23.99 (978-1-4001-8922-9(5)) Tantor Media.

Little Women: With Good Wives. Louisa May Alcott. Narrated by Laural Merlington. (ENG.). 2007. 12.95 (978-0-9801087-1-2(3)) Alpha DVD.

Little Women: With Good Wives. Louisa May Alcott. Narrated by Flo Gibson. (J). 2008. audio compact disk 44.95 (978-1-55685-915-1(5)) Audio Bk Con.

Little Women: With Good Wives. Louisa May Alcott. Contrib. by Jemma Redgrave & Gayle Hunnicutt. 3 CDs. (Running Time: 2 hrs. 45 mins.). (J). 2006. audio compact disk 39.95 (978-0-7927-4337-8(7), BBCD 164) AudioGO.

Little Women: With Good Wives. Louisa May Alcott. 1 cass. 18.95 (CART004) CA Artists.

Little Women: With Good Wives. Louisa May Alcott. Narrated by Jean Smart. (Running Time: 2.5 hrs. NaN mins.). 2006. 25.95 (978-1-59912-975-4(2)) Iofy Corp.

Little Women: With Good Wives. Louisa May Alcott. (Read-Along Ser.). (YA). 1994. pap. bk. & stu. ed. 34.95 (978-0-88432-965-7(8), S23935) J Norton Pubs.

Little Women: With Good Wives. Louisa May Alcott. 3 CDs. (Running Time: 3 hrs. 30 mins.). (J). 2003. audio compact disk 21.99 (978-1-58926-180-8(1), C05M-0040, Oasis Kids) Oasis Audio.

Little Women: With Good Wives. Louisa May Alcott. 2 cass. Dramatization. (Children's Classics Ser.). (J). (gr. 4-7). 1998. 13.95 (978-1-55935-188-1(8)) Soundelux.
Story of family life in a 19th century setting.

Little Women: With Good Wives. Louisa May Alcott. Narrated by Rebecca Burns. (Running Time: 63000 sec.). (ENG.). (J). (gr. 4-7). 2005. audio compact disk 89.99 (978-1-4001-3125-9(1)) Pub: Tantor Media. Dist(s): IngramPubServ

Little Women: With Good Wives. John Escott. Louisa May Alcott. Contrib. by Jennifer Basset & Tricia Hedge. (Oxford Bookworms Ser.). 1998. 13.75 (978-0-19-422786-5(3)) OUP.

Little Women: With Good Wives. Perf. by Shelley Long et al. Louisa May Alcott. 1 cass. (Running Time: 1 hr. 30 mins.). 2001. 18.95 (CART004) Lodestone Catalog.

Little Women: With Good Wives. Read by Liza Ross. Louisa May Alcott. (Running Time: 3 hrs. 30 mins.). 2004. 24.95 (978-1-60083-830-9(8)) Iofy Corp.

Little Women: With Good Wives. Read by Liza Ross. Louisa May Alcott. 3 cass. (Running Time: 3 hrs. 30 mins.). (J). (gr. 6-8). 2000. 17.98 (978-962-634-694-5(9), NA319414); audio compact disk 22.98 (978-962-634-194-0(7), NA319412) Naxos.
About the four March sisters, Meg, Jo, Beth and Amy.

Little Women: With Good Wives. Perf. by St. Charles Players. Louisa May Alcott. 2 cass. 1998. 16.95 (978-1-56994-509-4(8), 329314, Monterey SoundWorks) Monterey Media Inc.
The heartwarming classics of the March sisters, Jo, Meg, Beth & Amy. Takes place during & after the Civil War period. Recommended for all ages.

Little Women: With Good Wives. abr. ed. Read by Jamie Lee Curtis. Louisa May Alcott. (Running Time: 12600 sec.). 2007. audio compact disk 19.95 (978-1-4332-0700-6(1)); audio compact disk & audio compact disk 27.00 (978-1-4332-1348-9(6)) Blckstn Audio.

Little Women: With Good Wives. abr. ed. Read by Jamie Lee Curtis. Louisa May Alcott. 4 cass. (Running Time: 6 hrs.). 2004. 25.00 (978-1-59007-125-0(5)) Pub: New Millenn Enter. Dist(s): PerseuPGW
Meet the March sisters: the talented and tomboyish Jo, the beautiful Meg, the frail Beth, and the spoiled Amy, as they pass through the years between girlhood and womanhood. A lively portrait of growing up in the 19th century with lasting vitality and enduring charm.

Little Women: With Good Wives. abr. ed. Read by Julie Harris. Louisa May Alcott. 1 cass. (Running Time: 1 hr.). Incl. First Wedding. (J). (gr. 4-6). 1991. (CPN 1470); Gossip. (J). (gr. 4-6). 1991. (CPN 1470); Merry Christmas. (J).

(gr. 4-6). 1991. (CPN 1470); (J). (gr. 4-6). 1991. 11.00 (978-1-55994-371-0(8), CPN 1470) HarperCollins Pubs.

Little Women: With Good Wives. abr. ed. Perf. by St. Charles Players. Louisa May Alcott. 2 cass. Dramatization. 1999. 16.95 (FS9-43406) Highsmith.

Little Women: With Good Wives. abr. ed. Ed. by Jerry Stemach. Louisa May Alcott. Retold by Noe Venable. Illus. by Jeff Ham. Narrated by Wendy Morgan. 2000. audio compact disk 200.00 (978-1-58702-503-7(5)) D Johnston Inc.

Little Women: With Good Wives. unabr. ed. Louisa May Alcott. Narrated by Flo Gibson. 12 cass. (Running Time: 18 hrs.). (J). 1985. 39.95 (978-1-55685-061-5(1)) Audio Bk Con.
The four March girls learn the lesson of poverty & of growing up in New England during the Civil War. Their dreams, prayers, illnesses & courtships form a lively family portrait.

Little Women: With Good Wives. unabr. ed. Louisa May Alcott. 2 cass. (Read-along Ser.). bk. & pupil's gde. ed. 34.95 (S23935) J Norton Pubs.

Little Women: With Good Wives, unabr. ed. Louisa May Alcott. Narrated by Barbara Caruso. 14 pieces. (Running Time: 20 hrs.). (gr. 7 up). 1997. 112.00 (978-0-7887-0327-0(7), 94519E7) Recorded Bks.
A charming portrait of the joys & hardships of the four sisters in Civil War New England. Separated by the war from their beloved parents, they struggle to find their place in the world.

Little Women: With Good Wives. unabr. ed. Louisa May Alcott. Narrated by Rebecca C. Burns. (Running Time: 17 hrs. 30 mins. 0 sec.). (ENG.). (J). (gr. 4-7). 2008. 27.99 (978-1-4001-5860-7(5)); audio compact disk 35.99 (978-1-4001-0860-2(8)); audio compact disk 72.99 (978-1-4001-3860-9(4)) Pub: Tantor Media. Dist(s): IngramPubServ

Little Women: With Good Wives. unabr. ed. Read by Rebecca Burns. Louisa May Alcott. (YA). 2006. 79.99 (978-1-59895-678-8(7)) Find a World.

Little Women: With Good Wives. unabr. ed. Read by Sandra Burr. Louisa May Alcott. 12 cass. (Running Time: 18 hrs.). (Bookcassette Classic Collection). 1998. 66.25 (978-1-56740-619-1(X), 156740619X, Unabridge Lib Edns) Brilliance Audio.
Meg, Jo, Beth and Amy manage to lead interesting lives despite Father's absence at war and the family's lack of money. Whether they're putting on a play or forming a secret society, their gaiety is infectious. Written from Louisa May Alcott's own experiences, this remarkable novel has been treasured for generations.

Little Women: With Good Wives. unabr. ed. Read by Sandra Burr. Louisa May Alcott. 12 cass. (Running Time: 18 hrs.). 2002. 34.95 (978-1-59086-293-3(7), 1590862937, BAU) Brilliance Audio.

Little Women: With Good Wives. unabr. ed. Read by Sandra Burr. Louisa May Alcott. (Running Time: 18 hrs.). 2004. 44.25 (978-1-59335-335-3(9), 1593353359, Brinc Audio MP3 Lib) Brilliance Audio.

Little Women: With Good Wives. unabr. ed. Read by Sandra Burr. Louisa May Alcott. (Running Time: 18 hrs.). 2004. 44.25 (978-1-59710-460-9(4), 1597104604, BADLE); 29.95 (978-1-59710-461-6(2), 1597104612, BAD) Brilliance Audio.

Little Women: With Good Wives. unabr. ed. Read by Sandra Burr. Louisa May Alcott. (Running Time: 18 hrs.). (Classic Collection (Brilliance Audio) Ser.). 2005. audio compact disk 44.95 (978-1-59737-137-7(8), 9781597371377, Bril Audio CD Unabri); audio compact disk 112.25 (978-1-59737-138-4(6), 9781597371384, BriAudCD Unabrid) Brilliance Audio.

Little Women: With Good Wives. unabr. ed. Read by Sandra Burr. Louisa May Alcott. (Running Time: 18 hrs.). 2004. 29.95 (978-1-59335-015-4(5), 1593350155) Soulmate Audio Bks.

***Little Women: With Good Wives.** unabr. ed. Read by C. M. Hebert. Louisa May Alcott. (Running Time: 19 hrs. 0 mins.). 2010. 44.95 (978-1-4417-4418-0(5)); audio compact disk 123.00 (978-1-4417-4415-9(0)) Blckstn Audio.

Little Women: With Good Wives. unabr. ed. Read by C. M. Herbert. Louisa May Alcott. 13 cass. (Running Time: 19 hrs.). (gr. 9-12). 2001. 85.95 (978-0-7861-1880-9(6), 2679) Blckstn Audio.
The story of the March family, specifically the four daughters: Meg, Jo, Beth, & Amy.

Little Women: With Good Wives. unabr. ed. Read by Kate Reading. Louisa May Alcott. 13 cass. (Running Time: 19 hrs.). 2002. 104.00 (978-0-7366-8608-2(8)) Books on Tape.
The story of beloved matriarch Marmee March and her four daughters, domestic Meg, headstrong Jo, sensitive Beth, and artistic Amy, was first published in 1868, and has never lost favor since. Marmee raises the March girls to womanhood while their father is serving as a chaplain in the Union Army during the Civil War. The caring family, mired in poverty but genteel and refined nonetheless, lives in New England and survives through snow and sisterly squabbles, love and laughter, pranks and plays, illnesses and courtships.

Little Women: With Good Wives. unabr. ed. Read by Kate Reading. Louisa May Alcott. 16 CDs. (Running Time: 19 hrs. 30 mins.). (J). 2002. audio compact disk 128.00 (978-0-7366-8609-9(6)) Books on Tape.

Little Women: With Good Wives. unabr. ed. Read by Mary Starkey. Louisa May Alcott. 12 cass. (Running Time: 15 hrs. 30 min.). (J). 64.95 (978-1-55686-149-9(4), 149) Books in Motion.
The heartwarming story about the March sisters, Jo, Meg, Beth, & Amy. Takes place during & after the Civil War period. A story for all ages.

Little Women: With Good Wives. unabr. collector's ed. Read by Rebecca C. Burns. Louisa May Alcott. 12 cass. (Running Time: 18 hrs.). (YA). (gr. 8 up). 1998. 96.00 (978-0-7366-4123-4(8), 136011) Books on Tape.
Matriarch Marmee March raises her four daughters; domestic Meg, headstrong Jo, sensitive Beth & artistic Amy, to womanhood while their father is serving as a chaplain in the Union Army during the Civil War. The family, poor, but genteel & refined, survives snow, sisterly squabbles, love & laughter, pranks & plays, illnesses & courtships.

Little Women: With Good Wives, Bks. 1 and 2. abr. ed. Louisa May Alcott. 3 CDs. (California Artists Radio Theatre Ser.). 2003. audio compact disk 17.99 (978-1-58926-181-5(X)) Oasis Audio.

Little Women: With Good Wives, Vol. 5. Ed. by Jerry Stemach et al. Louisa May Alcott. Retold by Noe Venable. Illus. by Jeff Ham. Narrated by Wendy Morgan. Contrib. by Ted S. Hasselbring. (Start-to-Finish Books). (J). (gr. 2-3). 2000. 35.00 (978-1-58702-504-4(3)) D Johnston Inc.

Little Women: With Good Wives, Vol. 5. Ed. by Jerry Stemach et al. Louisa May Alcott. Retold by Noe Venable. Illus. by Jeff Ham. Narrated by Wendy Morgan. Contrib. by Ted S. Hasselbring. (Start-to-Finish Books). (J). (gr. 2-3). 2002. 100.00 (978-1-58702-968-4(5)) D Johnston Inc.

Little Women: With Good Wives, Vol. 5. abr. ed. Ed. by Jerry Stemach et al. Louisa May Alcott. Retold by Noe Venable. Illus. by Jeff Ham. Narrated by Wendy Morgan. Contrib. by Ted S. Hasselbring. 1 cass. (Running Time: 1 hr.). (Start-to-Finish Books). (J). (gr. 2-3). 2000. (978-1-58702-301-9(6), F23K2) D Johnston Inc.
Meet the March sisters: good-natured Meg is the eldest. Then there 's Jo whose tomboyish foibles and wild stories cause the family no end of amusement. Next is Beth, who is gentle and kind to everybody. And last is Amy, the spirited baby of the family. With Mr. March away at war, the girls try their best to act like little women. But they can never keep out of mischief for long. The March girls charm Laurie, the rich boy next door, who becomes like a brother to them. The book follows the five of them.

Little Women Soundtrack-on Cd. Prod. by Myattic Studio. (YA). 2000. audio compact disk 89.95 (978-0-7365-3273-0(0)) Films Media Grp.

Little Yellow Dog: Featuring an Original Easy Rawlins Short Story Gray-Eyed Death. unabr. ed. Walter Mosley. Read by Howard Weinberger. 6 cass. (Running Time: 9 hrs.). (Easy Rawlins Mystery Ser.). 1997. 48.00 (978-0-7366-3732-9(X), 4410) Books on Tape.
It's 1963 & Easy has given up the street life & all it's headaches. Now he's a janitor at a high school in Watts & he's seduced by a teacher who has a little yellow dog. She claims her husband's gone mad, but pretty soon she's just plain gone, leaving Easy with the dog & a corpse.

Little Yellow Learning Bus. 4 cass. (Running Time: 4 hrs.). (Wood Cassette Toys Ser.). (J). (gr. k-3). 1991. 19.95 (978-1-55569-485-2(3), 8310) Great Am Audio.
Original songs & stories covering the alphabet, important health & safety rules, how the world began, how people around the world have different beliefs & customs.

Littlejohn. abr. ed. Howard Owen. Read by Howard Owen. 2 cass. (Running Time: 3 hrs.). 1994. 16.95 (978-1-879371-79-8(0), 391080) Pub Mills.
Littlejohn McCain, an 82 year-old North Carolina farmer reflects on his life: a life filled with tragic secrets & unexpected redemption.

Littlest Angel. unabr. ed. Charles Tazwell. Perf. by Judith Anderson. 1 cass. (J). 1984. 9.95 (978-0-89845-172-6(8), CP 1384) HarperCollins Pubs.

Littlest Christmas Tree. 2005. audio compact disk 10.95 (978-0-916773-77-9(9)) Pub: Book Peddlers. Dist(s): PerseuPGW

Littlest Christmas Tree: A Tale of Growing & Becoming. Janie Jasin. Read by Janie Jasin. Perf. by Mary B. Carlson. 1 cass. (Running Time: 30 min.). (J). 1998. 8.95 (978-0-916773-84-7(1)) Pub: Book Peddlers. Dist(s): PerseuPGW
A tiny seedling in a field of pines impatiently waits to grow tall enough to be chosen as a Christmas Tree. Jasin also sings "The Littlest Christmas Tree".

Littlest Christmas Tree: A Tale of Growing & Becoming. Janie Jasin. Illus. by Pam Kurtz. (J). (ps-3). 1998. bk. 19.95 (978-0-916773-82-3(5)) Book Peddlers.

Littlest Dinosaurs. 9.95 (978-1-59112-298-2(8)) Live Oak Media.

Littlest Dinosaurs. Bernard Most. Illus. by Bernard Most. (Running Time: 12 mins.). (J). (gr. k-3). 1993. 9.95 (978-1-59112-078-0(0)) Live Oak Media.

Littlest Dinosaurs. Bernard Most. Read by Jerry Terheyden. (J). (ps-3). 2006. pap. bk. 39.95 (978-1-59519-326-1(X)) Live Oak Media.

Littlest Dinosaurs. unabr. ed. Bernard Most. Read by Jerry Terheyden. 11 vols. (Running Time: 12 mins.). (J). (gr. 1-6). 1993. pap. bk. 16.95 (978-0-87499-191-8(9)) Live Oak Media.

Littlest Dinosaurs, Grades 1-6. Bernard Most. Read by Jerry Terheyden. 14 vols. (Running Time: 12 mins.). (J). 1993. pap. bk. & tchr. ed. 37.95 Reading Chest. (978-0-87499-193-2(5)) Live Oak Media.
While the word usually associated with dinosaurs is big, this book departs from the norm & offers a humorous but factual look at the many smaller members of the dinosaur family.

Littlest Dragon Stories. Margaret Ryan. Read by Sophie Aldred. (Running Time: 3600 sec.). (J). 2001. audio compact disk 9.95 (978-0-7540-6777-1(7)) AudioGo GBR.

Littlest Piggy. Tony Jerris. Read by Tony Jerris. Perf. by Sarah Reynolds & Tom Vazzana. Illus. by Katy Lyness. Narrated by Corinne Aquilina. Composed by Corinne Aquilina. 1 cass. (Running Time: 12 min.). Dramatization. (J). (ps up). 1992. pap. bk. 9.95 (978-0-9630107-2-8(7)) Little Spruce.
"The Littlest Piggy" is the second in a series of children's books/tapes. Piggy leaves the farm to become a rock star. After a wild adventure meeting other talented piggies, "rappers" included, he returns to the others on the farm, a hero & a star. Meet Hokey, Pokey, Sidney & Gilbert, Ralphie the Dog, Tina the Cow.

Littlest Spruce. Tony Jerris. Perf. by Corinne Aquilina et al. Illus. by Tanya Weinberger. 1 cass. (Running Time: 13 hrs. 20 min.). Dramatization. (J). (ps up). 1991. pap. bk. 9.95 (978-0-9630107-1-1(9)) Little Spruce.
An audio narration of the written story with character voices helping to re-create the storybook.

Littlewood Farm 5AM. Created by Edward Schiebel. 1 CD. (Running Time: 74 mins.). 2005. audio compact disk 10.00 (978-1-880977-06-4(0)) Pub: XOXOX Pr. Dist(s): SPD-Small Pr Dist
A digitally recorded ambient sound CD of morning sounds on a farm in central Ohio.

Liturgical Bedlam-mp3. 1999. 22.00 (978-1-59128-311-9(6)) Canon Pr ID.

Liturgical Bedlam (1997) 11 cass. 1997. Rental 30.00 (978-1-59128-313-3(2)) Canon Pr ID.

Liturgical Customs & the Tridentine Mass. Fr. Phillips. 9 cass. (Running Time: 90 min. per cass.). 36.00 Set. (96B) IRL Chicago.

Liturgical Hymns of Praise. Greek Orthodox Archdiocese of North and South Americ. 1 cass. 9.95 (978-1-58438-008-5(X)); audio compact disk 14.95 (978-1-58438-007-8(1)) Greek Orth.

Liturgical Music: St. Francis Mass & St. Alban Benediction. 1 CD. (Running Time: 1 hr. 5 mins.). 2005. audio compact disk 8.00 (978-0-935461-06-0(X)) St Alban Pr CA.
The complete music for a Celebration of the Holy Eucharist in the Full Form Liberal Catholic Rite, as performed at St. Francis Cathedral Chapel in San Diego, California in 1991. Priest, Bishop, Organ, choir, and congregation. Also congregational music from a Celebration of the Benediction of the Most Blessed Sacrament in the Liberal Catholic Rite, as performed at St. Alban Cathedral in Hollywood, California c. 1960. Bishop, Organ, and choir.

Liturgical Year: The Rhythm of the Church. Jeff Cavins. (ENG.). 2007. audio compact disk 9.95 (978-1-934567-09-8(4)) Excorde Inc.

Liturgy: Becoming the Word of God. Megan McKenna. 1 cass. (Running Time: 1 hr.). 2001. 8.95 (A6771) St Anthony Mess Pr.
We become the word of God as we go out and bring the Good News of the Kingdom to the world.

Liturgy, Legacy, & a Ragamuffin Band: Rich Mullins. Perf. by Rich Mullins. 1 cass., 1 CD. 1998. 10.98; audio compact disk 16.98 CD. Provident Mus Dist.

Liturgy of the Presanctified Gifts. Ed. by Choirs of St Vladimir's Seminary. 1972. audio compact disk 18.00 (978-0-88141-172-0(8)) St Vladimirs.

Liturgy of the Word with Children. Voice by Jack Miffleton. 1 cass. (J). 1994. 7.95 (9914) OR Catholic.
Learning about God vs. experiencing God, the importance of story, liturgy of the Word as prayer, etc.

Liturgy of Word with Children. Jack Miffleton. 1 cass. 1994. 7.95 (978-0-00-502516-1(8)) OR Catholic.

Liuxue Shiyong Kouyu see Studying in China

Live. Perf. by Brian Regan. 2000. audio compact disk 16.98 (978-1-929243-15-0(4)) Uproar Ent.

Live a Praying Life Leaders Kit. Jennifer K. Dean. 2006. bk. 59.99 (978-1-59669-020-2(8)) BH Pubng Grp.

Live Action English. Elizabeth Romijn & Contee Seely. Contrib. by John Seely & Robert Dawson. 2 cass., . 1985. 23.25 (978-0-929724-17-1(8), CP178) Pub: Command Performance. Dist(s): Continental Bk

Live Action English. Elizabeth Romijn & Contee Seely. Read by Elizabeth Romjin & Contee Seely. 1 cass. 19.95 Midwest European Pubns.

Live Action English. Seely & Elizabeth Romijn. 1979. bk. 19.00 (978-0-88084-221-1(0)) Alemany Pr.

Live & Learn. Read by Donald Davis. 1 cass. (Running Time: 54 min.). (J). (gr. 4-8). 1984. 8.95 (978-0-89719-978-0(2), WW728C) Weston Woods.
Donald Davis relates true experiences of his childhood. He tells of his fear of a boy, Terrell, who when he meets face to face just wants to be friends.

Live & Learn: The Exploding Frog & other Stories. Short Stories. As told by Donna L. Washington. 1 CD. (Running Time: 56 min 24 sec). (J). 1993. audio compact disk 15.00 (978-0-9769396-0-3(6)) DLW Storyteller.
â€œWashington lends her smooth style and honey voice to this selection of nine tales from around the world. In a cheery, mischievous tone she presents a west African trickster tale, wherein greedy Anansi gets his comeuppance from a wise turtle, and a hilarious rendition of the traditional English tale, â€œThe Three Wishes,â€• wherein the ubiquitous sausage is replaced by a sugar coated doughnut. Washingtonâ€(tm)s retellings have an inherent humor that gives a modern twist to her characters and deliveries: the fairy in â€œThe Three Wishesâ€• is a scowling exasperated sprite; the froggies in â€œThe Frog Kingâ€• have the tone of wheedling toddlers; the spoiled prince in â€œThe Boy Who Wanted the Moonâ€• has a temper tantrum parents (and kids) will recognize, and the three observant little froggies in â€œThe Exploding Frogâ€• are a slapstick comic chorus. Washingtonâ€(tm)s timing is impeccable and her vocal characterizations memorable; her retellings are concise and her selections havea wide range of appeal. Younger listeners will giggle gleefully at the funny surface level, and more sophisticated listeners will be impressed by the layers of meaning Washington so capably communicates.â€• â€" Review from The Bulletin of the Center for Childrenâ€(tm)s Books.

Live & Let Die. Ian Fleming. Read by Robert Whitfield. 6 CDs. (Running Time: 7 hrs.). (James Bond Ser.). 2000. audio compact disk 48.00 (978-0-7861-9805-4(2), 2672) Blckstn Audio.
When 007 goes to Harlem, it's not just for the jazz. Harlem is the kingdom of Mr. Big, black master of crime, voodoo baron, senior partner in S.M.E.R.S.H.'s grim company of death. Those Mr. Big cannot possess he crushes, those who cross him meet painful ends. Like his beautiful prisoner, Solitaire. And her lover, James Bond.

Live & Let Die. Ian Fleming. 5 cass. (Running Time: 7 hrs.). (James Bond Ser.). 2001. 39.95 (978-0-7861-1873-1(3), 2672) Blckstn Audio.

Live & Let Die. unabr. ed. Ian Fleming. Read by Robert Whitfield. 5 cass. (Running Time: 7 hrs. 30 min.). (James Bond Ser.). 2001. 27.95 (978-0-7861-1918-9(7)) Pub: Blckstn Audio. Dist(s): Penton Overseas
James Bond vows to crush Mr. Big, the master criminal whose network of terror is reaping rich profits for the Kremlin.

Live & Let Die. unabr. ed. Ian Fleming. Read by Robert Whitfield. (Running Time: 7 hrs.). (James Bond Ser.). 2006. 24.95 (978-0-7861-9316-5(6), 2672) Blckstn Audio.

Live & Let Die. unabr. ed. Ian Fleming. Read by Simon Vance. (Running Time: 7 hrs. 0 mins.). 2009. audio compact disk 19.95 (978-1-4332-5853-4(6)) Blckstn Audio.

Live & Let Die. unabr. ed. Ian Fleming. Read by David Rintoul. 6 cass. (Running Time: 9 hrs.). (James Bond Ser.: Bk. 2). 2000. 49.95 (CAB 475) Pub: Chivers Audio Bks GBR. Dist(s): AudioGO
007 goes to Harlem, right into the heart of Mr. Big's kingdom: a master of crime, voodoo baron and senior partner of S.M.E.R.S.H.'s grim company of death. Those Mr. Big cannot possess, he crushes! Like his beautiful prisoner, Solitaire, and her lover, James Bond; both are marked victims on a trail of treachery and terror.

Live & Lively, Accompanied by Don Was. Allen Ginsberg. 1 cass. 9.00 (A0601-90) Sound Photosyn.
We caught this modern master with the spirit willing, the audience enthusiastic, & Allen in top form, singing & chanting his poetry - portions of it with electric bass accompaniment.

Live & Thriving at the 30th National Storytelling Festival. Short Stories. Prod. by Susan Klein. 2 CDs. (Running Time: 140 min). (YA). 2003. audio compact disk 24.95 (978-1-879991-31-6(4)) Natl Storytlng Network.
Collection of stories told live at the 30th National Storytelling Festival in Jonesborough, TN.

Live & up Close. Perf. by BeBe Winans. audio compact disk 18.98 Provident Music.

Live Art. Perf. by Bela Fleck et al. 2 cass., 2 CDs. 11.98 Double. (WB 46247); audio compact disk 15.98 (WB 46247) NewSound.

Live at Carnegie Hall. Ray Romano. 2001. audio compact disk 18.97 (Clumbia Music Vid) Sony Music Ent.

Live at Carnegie Hall. Perf. by Sweet Honey in the Rock. 1 cass. (J). (gr. 2 up). 14.98 (2554); audio compact disk 18.98 compact disc. (D2554) MFLP CA.
Album by incomparable a capella singers who received the 1988 N.A.I.R.D. Indie Award for "Best Women's Recording of the Year." Includes new arrangements of some of their best-loved original & traditional songs & is full of the soulful grace, social consciousness & gospel harmonies that have made the group famous.

Live at Carnegie Hall. abr. unabr. ed. David Sedaris. Read by David Sedaris. 1 CD. (Running Time: 1 hr. 10 mins.). (ENG.). (YA). 2003. audio compact disk 17.98 (978-1-58621-564-4(7)) Pub: Hachet Audio. Dist(s): HachBkGrp

Live at Carnegie Hall. unabr. ed. David Sedaris. (ENG.). 2005. 14.98 (978-1-59483-175-1(0)) Pub: Hachet Audio. Dist(s): HachBkGrp

Live at El Morocco. Perf. by Count Basie Orchestra. 1 cass., 1 CD. 7.98 (TA 33312); audio compact disk 12.78 (TA 83312) NewSound.

Live at Joe Segal's Jazz Showcase. Perf. by Ahmad Jamal. 1 cass., 1 CD. 7.98 (TA 33327); audio compact disk 12.78 (TA 83327) NewSound.

Live! at Lipinsky Hall. Boatrockers, The & Thomas Rain Crowe. 2006. audio compact disk 12.50 (978-1-883197-24-7(4)) Pub: New Native Pr. Dist(s): SPD-Small Pr Dist

Live at Michael's Pub with His Big Band. Perf. by Mel Torme. 1 cass., 1 CD. 7.98 (TA 33328); audio compact disk 12.78 CD Jewel box. (TA 83328) NewSound.

Live at the Apollo: The Proclamation. Contrib. by Byron Cage et al. Prod. by Pajam. 2007. audio compact disk 17.98 (978-5-557-60308-9(5)) GospoCen.

Live at the Black Oak Bookstore. Alan Badiner & Catherine Ingram. Read by Alan Badiner & Catherine Ingram. 1 cass. 9.00 (A0731-90) Sound Photosyn.
Speaking of & reading from their respective respectable books.

Live at the Blue Note. Perf. by Oscar Peterson. 1 cass., 1 CD. 7.98 (TA 33304); audio compact disk 12.78 CD Jewel box. (TA 83304) NewSound.

Live at the Blue Note with the Golden Men of Jazz. 1 cass., 1 CD. 7.98 (TA 33308); audio compact disk 12.78 (TA 83308) NewSound.

Live at the Ear. Ed. by Charles Bernstein. Prod. by Richard Dillon. (Running Time: 72 min.). (C). 1994. bk. 15.95 (978-1-885905-36-9(X), 5-7777-2) Dillon Elemenope.
Audio-textual anthology of 13 poets' original recitations at world famous Ear Inn with 32 page booklet including photos & bibliographies. Readers include: Howe, Silliman, Scalapino, Greenwald, Waldrop, Davies, Watten, Hunt, Andrews, Weiner, McCaffery, & Lauterbach.

Live at the Fellowship. Contrib. by VIP Mass Choir et al. Prod. by John P. Kee. 2005. audio compact disk 17.98 (978-5-559-07895-3(6), Verity) Brentwood Music.

***Live at the Galway Shawl.** (ENG.). 11.95 (978-0-8023-7065-5(9)) Pub: Clo Iar-Chonnachta IRL. Dist(s): Dufour

Live! at the Guitar Show: A Collector's Audio Guidebook for American Vintage Guitars. Interview. Hosted by Larry Meiners. 1 CD. (Running Time: 1 hr. 18 mins.). 2003. audio compact disk 15.99 (978-0-9708273-5-7(0)) Flying Vintage.
Live! At The Guitar Show - A Collector's Audio Guidebook For American Vintage Guitars (CD). As a guitar collector, player or enthusiast, did you ever wonder what the most respected instrument dealers in the world think about the vintage guitar phenomenon? Recorded live in Dallas with leading vintage guitar experts discussing the phenomenal vintage guitar market and these significant topics: Gibson 's Les Paul Burst (Flame-top Sunburst), Martin and Gibson Pre-war Flat-tops, and Gibson Mandolins, Fender 's Pre-CBS Stratocaster,Vintage vs. Reissue - Gibson,Fender and Martin Guitars, What 's Hot and What 's Undervalued, Vintage Guitars vs. Wall Street 's Stocks, What Happens As Baby Boomers Sell Their Collections, How Fake Reproduction Guitars Affect the Market, How the Internet has Radically Changed the Guitar Business.Foreword by Rick Nielsen of Cheap Trick and hosted by Larry Meiners. "I pay more right now (for vintage guitars) than I sold guitars for two months ago and that 's how fast this is going up." - Mike Jones, Michael Jones Vintage Guitars"I see a Sunburst (Gibson Les Paul Burst) being $500,000 in a few years." - Timm Kummer, Kummer 's Vintage Instruments "We are starting to see some very serious investors taking money out of 401K (accounts) and other investment avenues and putting them in vintage guitars." - Gary Dick, Gary 's Classic Guitars Vintage experts interviewed: David Davidson, Sam Ash Music (NY) Gary Dick, Gary's Classic Guitars (OH) Norm Harris, Norman 's Rare Guitars (CA) Mike Jones, Michael Jones Vintage Guitars (CO) Timm Kummer, Kummer 's Vintage Instruments (FL) Fred Oster, Vintage Instruments (PA) Dave Rogers, Dave 's Guitar Shop (WI) Tom Van Hoose, Van Hoose Vintage Instruments (TX) Larry Wexer, Laurence Wexer, Ltd. (NY).

Live! At the Stone in San Francisco. Timothy Leary. 1 cass. 9.00 (A0062-87) Sound Photosyn.

Live at the Strand, Vol. 1. Perf. by Kenny Hutson et al. 1 cass. 1997. audio compact disk 13.99 (D3005) Diamante Music Grp.
Also includes: L. S. Underground, Squad Five-O, Spud Gun & many others performing live songs at the Strand Theatre just north of Atlanta.

Live at Tom Fest. Perf. by Puller. 1 CD. 1999. audio compact disk 16.98 (978-1-57908-484-4(2), 5357) Platinm Enter.

Live B. I. G. Elementary Music CD 2006-2007. 2006. audio compact disk 10.00 (978-0-687-64411-7(9)) Abingdon.

Live B. I. G. Elementary Music Compact Disc 2007-2008. 2006. audio compact disk 10.00 (978-0-687-64587-9(5)) Abingdon.

Live B. I. G. Preschool Music CD 2006-2007. 2006. audio compact disk 10.00 (978-0-687-64401-8(1)) Abingdon.

Live B. I. G. Preschool Music CD 2007-2008. 2007. audio compact disk 10.00 (978-0-687-64637-1(5)) Abingdon.

Live Bait. unabr. ed. P. J. Tracy. Read by Buck Schirner. 6 cass. (Running Time: 10 hrs.). (Monkeewrench Ser.). 2004. 32.95 (978-1-59086-630-6(4), 1590866304, BAU) Brilliance Audio.
Minneapolis detectives Leo Magozzi and Gino Rolseth are bored - ever since they solved the Monkeewrench case, the Twin Cities have been in a murder-free dry spell, as people no longer seem interested in killing one another. But when elderly Morey Gilbert is found dead in the plant nursery he runs with his wife, Lily, the crime drought ends - not with a trickle, but with a torrent. Who would kill Morey, a man without an enemy, a man who might as well have been a saint? His tiny, cranky little wife is no help, and may even be a suspect; his estranged son, Jack, an infamous ambulance-chasing lawyer, has his own enemies; and his son-in-law, former cop Marty Pullman, is so depressed over his wife's death a year earlier he's ready to kill himself, but not Morey. The number of victims - all elderly - grows, and the city is fearful once again. Can Grace McBride's cold case-solving software program somehow find the missing link?.

Live Bait. unabr. ed. P. J. Tracy. Read by Buck Schirner. (Running Time: 10 hrs.). (Monkeewrench Ser.). 2004. 39.25 (978-1-59335-647-7(1), 1593356471, Brinc Audio MP3 Lib); 24.95 (978-1-59335-295-0(6), 1593352956, Brilliance MP3) Brilliance Audio.

Live Bait. unabr. ed. P. J. Tracy. Read by Buck Schirner. (Running Time: 10 hrs.). (Monkeewrench Ser.). 2004. 39.25 (978-1-59710-463-0(9), 1597104639, BADLE); 24.95 (978-1-59710-462-3(0), 1597104620, BAD) Brilliance Audio.

Live Before You Die. abr. ed. Mark M. Hood. Read by Mark M. Hood. 2 CDs. (Running Time: 3 hrs.). 2002. audio compact disk 24.95 (978-0-9722600-0-8(5)) M Hood.
Chronicling the most important aspects of mental and physical health.Filled with wit, wisdom and insight into the many ways we can become "move human".

Live BIG Elementary Annual Music CD 2008-09. 2008. audio compact disk 10.00 (978-0-687-65254-9(5)) Abingdon.

Live BIG Preschool Annual Music CD 2008-09. 2008. audio compact disk 10.00 (978-0-687-65274-7(X)) Abingdon.

Live Chains. Poems. John M. Bennett. Read by John M. Bennett. 1 cass. (Running Time: 1 hr. 30 min.). 1990. 5.00 (978-0-935350-22-7(5)) Luna Bisonte.
Live avant-garde poetry performances.

Live Collection, Vol. 1. 1 cass., 1 CD. 1998. 10.98 (978-0-7601-2849-7(9)); audio compact disk 16.98 (978-0-7601-2848-0(0)) Provident Mus Dist.
The experience of a live concert in the home, car or office.

Live Comic Strip: Alexei Sayle. abr. ed. Alexei Sayle. Read by Alexei Sayle. 1 cass. 1998. 9.35 (978-1-86117-174-0(9)) Ulvrscrft Audio.
His approach to comedy is completely different. His act loud, brash & violent, aggressively proud of his working-class origins.

Live Comic Strip: Arnold Brown. abr. ed. Arnold Brown. Read by Arnold Brown. 1 cass. 1998. 9.35 (978-1-86117-166-5(8)) Ulvrscrft Audio.
His catch phrase 'and why not' developed in tandem with his stage career as he progressed from accountant to comic.

Live Comic Strip: French & Saunders. abr. ed. Dawn French & Jennifer Saunders. 1 cass. 1998. 9.35 (978-1-86117-175-7(7)) Ulvrscrft Audio.
Developing their own interpretation of the traditional comic formula, they formed a comedy double act for a laugh. Their strength lay in sharp characterisations of modern-day female sterotypes.

Live Comic Strip: N. Planer P. Richardson. abr. ed. N. Planer & P. Richardson. 1998. 9.35 (978-1-86117-176-4(5)) Ulvrscrft Audio.

Live Comic Strip: R. Mayall & A. Edmonson. abr. ed. Rik Mayall & A. Edmonson. Read by Rik Mayall & A. Edmonson. 1 cass. 1998. 9.35 (978-1-86117-177-1(3)) Ulvrscrft Audio.
Pioneering comedy collective which launched the 'alternative comedy' boom of the 80's.

Live Commentary on Something's Happening! Dave Emory. 1 cass. (Roy Tuckman Interview Ser.). 9.00 (A0565-89) Sound Photosyn.

Live conference with Dr. Ihaleakala & Mabel Katz see Camino Mas Facil: Conferencia en vivo con Dr. Ihaleakala y Mabel Katz

Live Duet Recordings 1963-1980 Vol. 2: Off the Record. Perf. by Bill Monroe & Doc Watson. Anno. by Ralph Rinzler. Contrib. by Ralph Rinzler & Matt Walters. 1 cass. (Running Time: 44 min.). 1993. (0-9307-400640-9307-40064-2-9); audio compact disk (0-9307-40064-2-9) Smithsonian Folkways.

Live Experience. Contrib. by Keith Green et al. 2008. audio compact disk 18.99 (978-5-557-44101-8(8)); audio compact disk 13.99 (978-5-557-44625-9(7)) Pt of Grace Ent.

Live Fire. Stephen Leather. 2009. 84.95 (978-0-7531-4124-3(8)); audio compact disk 99.95 (978-0-7531-4125-0(6)) Pub: Isis Pubng Ltd GBR. Dist(s): Ulverscroft US

Live First Work Second. 2006. 24.95 (978-0-9778746-4-4(8)); audio compact disk 29.95 (978-0-9778746-2-0(1)) Next Gen WI.

Live Flesh. unabr. ed. Ruth Rendell. Narrated by Ron Keith. 8 cass. (Running Time: 11 hrs. 15 mins.). 1991. 70.00 (978-1-55690-313-7(8), 91110E7) Recorded Bks.
Victor Jenner has served his time for his breach of the law. But time has not expunged the memory that he must confront in the flesh.

Live Forever. Elizabeth Peyton. audio compact disk 39.95 (978-4-915877-65-0(5)) Pub: Synergy Inc JPN. Dist(s): Dist Art Pubs

***Live Free or Die.** unabr. ed. John Ringo. Read by Mark Boyett. 1 MP3-CD. (Running Time: 17 hrs.). (Troy Rising Ser.). 2010. 14.99 (978-1-4418-5134-5(8), 9781441851345, Brilliance MP3) Brilliance Audio.

***Live Free or Die.** unabr. ed. John Ringo. Read by Dan John Miller & Mark Boyett. 1 MP3-CD. (Running Time: 14 hrs.). (Troy Rising Ser.). 2010. 39.97 (978-1-4418-5135-2(6), 9781441851352, Brinc Audio MP3 Lib); 39.97 (978-1-4418-5136-9(4), 9781441851369, BADLE) Brilliance Audio.

***Live Free or Die.** unabr. ed. John Ringo. Read by Mark Boyett. 14 CDs. (Running Time: 17 hrs.). (Troy Rising Ser.). 2010. audio compact disk 99.97 (978-1-4418-5133-8(X), 9781441851338, BriAudCD Unabrid); audio compact disk 29.99 (978-1-4418-5132-1(1), 9781441851321, Bril Audio CD Unabri) Brilliance Audio.

Live from Bethlehem. Cindy S. Hansen & Bob Latchaw. 1 cass. (Instant Christmas Pageant Ser.). (J). (gr. k-6). 1992. pap. bk. 24.99 (978-1-55945-095-9(9)) Group Pub.

Live from Death Row. Mumia Abu-Jamal. Read by Mumia Abu-Jamal. 1 CD. (Running Time: 1 hr.). audio compact disk 20.00 (978-1-55940-691-8(7), Voyager CD-ROM) Criterion.
Includes the entire text of "Live from Death Row," almost fifty radio commentaries, taped in prison for radio broadcast & other writings by Jamal. An introduction to his life, from his early membership of the Black Panther Party to his career as an award-winning Philadelphia journalist & supporter of the MOVE organisation.

Live from Delhi. Perf. by Ali A. Khan. 1 cass. 9.98 (A0051-83) Sound Photosyn.
With Shankar Gosh on tabla. Ragas: Mian-Ka Malhar, Desh Malhar.

Live from Hawaii: the Farewell Concert. Contrib. by Audio Adrenaline et al. 2007. 17.99 (978-5-557-62812-9(6)) FF Rcds.

Live from Houston: the Rose of Gospel. Contrib. by Dorinda Clark. Prod. by Asaph Ward. Contrib. by Vicki Mack Lataillade & Claude Lataillade. 2005. audio compact disk 17.98 (978-5-558-93106-8(X)) GospoCen.

Live from New Orleans. Contrib. by Ginny Owens. 2005. audio compact disk 11.99 (978-5-559-08097-0(7)) Rocket.

Live from New York: An Uncensored History of Saturday Night Live. abr. ed. Tom Shales & James Andrew Miller. (YA). 2006. 44.99 (978-1-59895-534-7(9)) Find a World.

Live from New York: An Uncensored History of Saturday Night Live. unabr. ed. Tom Shales & James Andrew Miller. 15 cass. (Running Time: 22 hrs. 30 mins.). 2002. 104.00 (978-0-7366-8862-8(5)) Books on Tape.
Two top terrorism experts explain 9/11 - its past, and what it means for the future.

Live from New York with His Big Band. Louis Bellson. 1 cass., 1 CD. 7.98 (TA 33334); audio compact disk 12.78 (TA 83334) NewSound.

Live from Santa Barbara. unabr. ed. Kenneth Rexroth. Perf. by Kenneth Rexroth. 1 cass. (Running Time: 1 hr.). (Watershed Tapes of Contemporary Poetry). (JPN & ENG.). 1979. 12.95 (23634) J Norton Pubs.
Performs poems from five books to music accompaniment.

Live from the Armed Madhouse. Ak Press Staff & Greg Palast. (AK Press Audio Ser.). (ENG., 2007. audio compact disk 13.98 (978-1-904859-64-2(X)) Pub: AK Pr GBR. Dist(s): Consort Bk Sales

Live from the Beachland Ballroom, Volume 1. Prod. by Michael Salinger. 2002. audio compact disk 12.99 (978-1-881786-59-7(5)) CollinwoodMedia.

Live from Your Center: Teresa & the Momentum of Prayer. unabr. ed. Vilma Seelaus. 4 cass. (Running Time: 3 hrs. 30 min.). 1992. 33.95 (TAH275) Alba Hse Comns.
These talks deal with the dynamic of prayer as God awakening each of us to love. This inner awakening is seen in continuity with the evolution of the universe toward its & our ultimate fulfillment in Christ.

Live in Alaska. Voice by John Yotko. Music by John Yotko & Janet Kuypers. 2002. audio compact disk 6.22 (978-1-891470-63-9(9)) Scars Pubns.
From two live concerts in Fairbanks Alaska, The Second Axing (singer Janet Kuypers and guitarist John Yotko) did covers as well as original pieces of music.

Live in Antigua. 1 cass. 10.98 (978-1-57908-291-8(2), 1374); audio compact disk 15.98 CD. (978-1-57908-290-1(4), 1374) Platinm Enter.

Live in Atlanta: At Morehouse College. Contrib. by Hezekiah Walker & Tara Griggs-Magee. Prod. by Dan Cleary. 1997. audio compact disk 13.99 (978-0-7601-1655-5(5), Verity) Brentwood Music.

Live in Calcutta at Dover Lane, Pt. 1. Perf. by Ali A. Khan. 1 cass. 9.98 (A0049-83) Sound Photosyn.
With Swapan Chaudhuri on Tabla. Raga: Nat Bhairo. Recorded in India by Sound Photosynthesis.

Live in Calcutta at Dover Lane, Pt. 2. Perf. by Ali A. Khan. 1 cass. 8.98 (A0050-83) Sound Photosyn.
With Swapan Chaudhuri on Tabla. Raga: Bhairavi. Recorded in India by Sound Photosynthesis.

Live in Charlotte. Perf. by Twinkie Clark. 2002. audio compact disk Provident Mus Dist.

Live in Detroit II. Perf. by Vickie Winans. 1 cass. 10.98 (978-1-57908-436-3(2), 5325); (978-1-57908-440-0(0)); audio compact disk 16.98 (978-1-57908-435-6(4)) Platinm Enter.

Live in London & More. Ed. by Kevin Bond. Contrib. by Donnie McClurkin et al. 2000. audio compact disk 17.98 (978-0-7601-3529-7(0), Verity) Brentwood Music.

Live in London at Wembley. Directed By Don Moore. Contrib. by Hezekiah Walker & the Love Fellowship Crusade Choir & Paul Wright, III. Prod. by Paul Wright, III & Hezekiah Walker. (Running Time: 1 hr. 10 mins.). 2007. 14.98 (978-5-557-92772-7(7), Verity) Brentwood Music.

Live in Los Angeles. Perf. by GMWA Men's Chorus. 1 CD. 2000. audio compact disk 15.98 (978-0-7601-3442-9(1), SO33210) Pub: Brentwood Music. Dist(s): Provident Mus Dist
Songs include: "Oh Zion," "Have Your Way Lord," "Hope of Glory," "Trust in the Lord" & more.

Live in Mississippi. Perf. by Harvey Watkins, Jr. et al. Prod. by Dottie Peoples. 1 cass. 1997. audio compact disk 15.98 (D2207) Diamante Music Grp.

Live in Nashville. Perf. by Chicago Mass Choir. Prod. by New Haven Records Staff. 2002. audio compact disk Provident Mus Dist.

Live in San Francisco. Perf. by Ali A. Khan. 1 cass. 8.98 (A0056-0) Sound Photosyn.
With Zakir Hussain on tabla. Ragas: Pahari Jhinjoti, Dugeshwari.

Live in Seattle. Contrib. by Shawn McDonald. 2005. audio compact disk 11.99 (978-5-559-10045-6(5)) Pt of Grace Ent.

Live in the End. Neville Goddard. 1 cass. (Running Time: 62 min.). 1968. 8.00 (92) J & L Pubns.
Neville taught Imagination Creates Reality. He was a powerfully influential teacher of God as Consciousness.

Live in Us: Why? Elbert Willis. 1 cass. (Purpose of the Holy Spirit Ser.). 4.00 Fill the Gap.

***Live It, Love It, Earn It: A Woman's Guide to Financial Freedom.** unabr. ed. Marianna Olszewski. (Running Time: 9 hrs.). (ENG.). 2010. 27.98 (978-1-59659-519-4(1), GildAudio) Pub: Gildan Media. Dist(s): HachBkGrp

Live It, Love It, Earn It: A Woman's Guide to Financial Freedom. unabr. ed. Marianna Olszewski. (Running Time: 9 hrs.). (ENG.). 2010. audio compact disk 29.98 (978-1-59659-443-2(8)) Pub: Gildan Media. Dist(s): HachBkGrp

Live Life Like You Mean It: There Is No Better Time Than Now. Paul Vitale. 2006. audio compact disk 15.00 (978-0-9666174-1-2(X)) Vital Comm.

Live Like You Mean It! Seven Celebrations to Rejuvenate Your Soul. Kathy Troccoli. Read by Kathy Troccoli. (Running Time: 10800 sec.). 2006. audio compact disk 27.00 (978-0-7861-7194-1(4)) Blckstn Audio.

Live Like You Mean It! 7 Daily Celebrations to Rejuvenate a Woman's Soul. unabr. ed. Kathy Troccoli. Narrated by Kathy Troccoli. (ENG.). 2005. 13.99 (978-1-60814-290-3(6)) Oasis Audio.

Live Long & Feel Good. Andrew Weil & Michael Toms. 1 cass. (Running Time: 1 hr.). (New Dimensions Ser.). 1998. 10.95 (978-1-56170-507-8(1), 375) Hay House.
Presents better choices for a healthier life. Learn new ways to keep your inherent healing system in peak working order while developing a lifestyle that is sound in mind, body, & spirit.

Live Long & Love It. Elbert Willis. 1 cass. (Angel Protection Guidelines Ser.). 4.00 Fill the Gap.

Live Long, Finish Strong: The Divine Secret to Living Healthy, Happy, & Healed. unabr. ed. Gloria Copeland. Read by Kate McIntyre. (Running Time: 10 hrs.). (ENG.). 2010. 16.98 (978-1-60788-210-7(8)); audio compact disk 24.98 (978-1-60788-209-1(4)) Pub: Hachet Audio. Dist(s): HachBkGrp

Live Longer, Relax. Narrated by Dick Lutz. 1 cass. (Running Time: 9 min.). 1981. 7.95 (978-0-931625-01-5(7), 1) DIMI Pr.
Listen to the voice & relax your muscles as instructed. Use daily to lower your stress level. Same narration in on both sides.

Live Longer, Relax: Female Voice. Narrated by Mary Lutz. 1 cass. (Running Time: 9 min.). 1984. 7.95 (978-0-931625-11-4(4), 11) DIMI Pr.
The female voice is more pleasant than the male voice for many people.

Live Love In 528. Scott Huckabay. Prod. by Leonard G. Horowitz. 1. (Running Time: 60). 2007. audio compact disk 19.25 (978-0-923550-07-3(0)) Tetrahedron Pub.

Live Mindfulness with Marsha M. Linehan, Ph. D. , ABPP, Seattle Intensive, 2004-2005, complete Set. Executive Producer Shree A. Vigil. Prologue by Behavioral Tech. 4 CD's. 2005. audio compact disk 50.00 (978-1-933464-05-3(4)) Behavioral Tech.

Live Monsters. Contrib. by Jars of Clay. 2007. audio compact disk 7.99 (978-5-557-60941-8(5)) Essential Recs.

Live Now, Age Later: Proven Ways to Slow down the Clock. abr. ed. Isadore Rosenfeld. Read by Robert Deyan. 4 cass. (Running Time: 6 hrs.). 1999. 24.95 Set. (978-1-55935-306-9(6)) Soundelux.
Dr. Rosenfeld spells out the details of how to prevent, treat, &/or slow down virtually every disorder & complication of aging, & to live healthier lives.

Live-Oak Growing see Treasury of Walt Whitman

Live Oak Media Cassette Only Collection Set. 50 cass. 1997. 398.00 (978-0-87499-715-6(1)) Live Oak Media.

Live Oak Media Cassette Only Collection Set, Vol. 2. 48 cass. 1997. 382.00 (978-0-87499-815-3(8)) Live Oak Media.

Live Oak Media Cassette Only Collection Set, Vol. 3. 45 cass. 2004. 358.00 (978-1-59519-005-5(8)) Live Oak Media.

Live Oak Media PB/CD Readalong Collection. 5050 vols. pap. bk. 758.00 (978-1-59519-235-6(2)) Live Oak Media.

Live Oak Media PB/CD Readalong Collection, Vol. 3. 4545 vols. pap. bk. 728.00 (978-1-59519-239-4(5)) Live Oak Media.

Live Oak Media Readalong Collection Set. 50 CDs. audio compact disk 518.00 (978-1-59519-234-9(4)) Live Oak Media.

Live Oak Media Readalong Collection Set. 5050 vols. 1997. pap. bk. 678.00 (978-0-87499-714-9(3)) Live Oak Media.

Live Oak Media Readalong Collection Set, Vol. 2. 4848 vols. 1997. pap. bk. 650.00 (978-0-87499-818-4(2)) Live Oak Media.

Live Oak Media Readalong Collection Set, Vol. 2. 4545 vols. 2004. pap. bk. 610.00 (978-1-59519-004-8(X)) Live Oak Media.

Live Oak Media Readalong Collection Set, Vol. 3. 45 CDs. audio compact disk 466.00 (978-1-59519-238-7(7)) Live Oak Media.

Live Oak Music Maker Collection. W. Nikola-Lisa et al. Illus. by W. Nikola-Lisa et al. 77 vols. (Running Time: 1 hr. 6 mins.). 2001. pap. bk. 106.95 (978-0-87499-992-1(8)) Live Oak Media.

Live! On Something's Happening! Sara Nelson & Bill Davis. 1 cass. 9.00 (A0239-90) Sound Photosyn.
Nelson, the Executive Director of the Christic Institute, gives an informative update on the Institute's battles against government corruption.

Live! On Something's Happening! World Research Federation Staff. 1 cass. (Roy Tuckman Interview Ser.). 9.00 (A0226-90) Sound Photosyn.

Live-One Last Time. Contrib. by Clark Sisters et al. Prod. by Donald Lawrence. 2007. audio compact disk 18.99 (978-5-557-59280-2(6)) Pt of Grace Ent.

Live Only Love. 1 cass. 12.98 (978-0-87554-514-1(9), 1112) Valley Sun.
Affirmations direct you to let go & let God, & to awaken to greater consciousness. Also: You respond to others with unconditional love. You are a channel for the light. You remain centered at all times: physically relaxed, emotionally calm, mentally focused & spiritually aware. You deserve love, happiness & prosperity. You manifest love. Love flows through you to one & all. Much more.

Live Performance, Vol. 1. William S. Burroughs. Ed. by Kathelin Hoffman. Illus. by Zelmer Phillips. Contrib. by Robert Palmer. 1 cass. (Running Time: 60 min.). (C). bk. 12.95 (978-0-929856-00-1(7)) Caravan Dreams Prodns.
Features recent extemporaneous live performance by the beat-generation author of naked lunch.

Live Recordings 1956-1969 Vol. 1: Off the Record. Perf. by Bill Monroe et al. Anno. by Ralph Rinzler. 1 cass. (Running Time: 75 min.). 1993. Incl. rare photos & notes. (0-9307-400630-9307-40063-2-0); audio compact disk (0-9307-40063-2-0) Smithsonian Folkways.
Previously unreleased recordings from the 1950s & '60s Monroe concert performances, jam sessions & festival workshops.

Live Right 4 Your Type: The Individualized Prescription for Maximizing Health, Well-Being, & Vitality in Every Stage of Your Life. abr. ed. Peter J. D'Adamo & Catherine Whitney. Read by Robb Webb. 2 cass. (Running Time: 180 min.). 2001. 18.95 (978-0-694-52428-0(X)) HarperCollins Pubs.

Live Set. Perf. by Michael W. Smith. 1 cass. 1987. audio compact disk Brentwood Music.
A great live recording of Michael's early works, featuring Friends, Rocketown & Nothin' But the Blood.

Live Smoke Free Without Gaining Weight! Scott Sulak. 1998. 15.00 (978-1-932659-09-2(9)) Change For Gd.

Live Strong: Inspirational Stories from Cancer Survivors - From Diagnosis to Treatment & Beyond. unabr. ed. Lance Armstrong Foundation Staff. 7 CDs. (Running Time: 9 hrs.). 2005. audio compact disk 54.00 (978-1-4159-2460-0(0)); 45.00 (978-1-4159-2459-4(7)) Books on Tape.
My work with the LAF shows me daily that sharing our stories and learning from one another's experiences helps us cancer survivors continue to survive. Some people think the cancer experience is only about the diagnosis and treatment of cancer, as if after the disease goes into remission, it no longer exists. But survivorship goes beyond remission. Survivorship is an evolution. Survivors from all walks of life talk about what "living strong" in the face of cancer means to them. Since the now ubiquitous LIVESTRONG wristbands became available in May 2004, the Lance Armstrong Foundation has raised more than $50 million for cancer survivorship programs, and the signature phrase has become a battle cry for those who fight the disease every day. Now, the Lance Armstrong Foundation has compiled, from hours of videotaped interviews, poignant and dramatic personal accounts from cancer survivors. Covering a wide range of subjects, from grief to spousal relationships, employment discrimination to coping with medical bills, infertility to fear of recurrence, survivors share their experiences and speak candidly about how cancer has impacted their lives. For twenty-four-year-old Amy it's how her illness changed her relationship with her parents. Mike, a male survivor of breast cancer, talks about gender stereotypes and genetic testing. And Eric, the father of a five-year-old survivor of a brain tumor, recalls how friends and strangers helped his family with financial issues and how the experience brought him and his wife closer together. While heartbreaking at times, these powerfully honest stories are ultimately uplifting and extremely reassuring to patients and their families. They offer the wisdom and hope that only survivors can give. LiveStrong is a remarkable testament to the resilience of the human spirit.

Live the Dream. Josephine Cox. Read by Carole Boyd. 9 CDs. audio compact disk 89.95 (978-0-7927-3819-0(5), SLD 875) AudioGO.

Live the Dream. Josephine Cox. Read by Carole Boyd. 7 cass. (Running Time: 39960 sec.). (J). (gr. 4-7). 2005. 59.95 (978-0-7927-3818-3(7), CSL 875) AudioGO.

Live the Life. Perf. by Michael W. Smith. Prod. by Mark Heimermann. 1 cass., 1 CD. 1998. 10.98 (978-0-7601-1435-3(8)); audio compact disk 16.98 (978-0-7601-1436-0(6)) Provident Music.

Live the Presence of God. unabr. ed. 1 cass. (Running Time: 44 min.). 1992. 7.95 (TAH278) Alba Hse Comns.
This presentation invites us back into our first experience of God's awakening within.

Live Through This: A Mother's Memoir of Runaway Daughters & Reclaimed Love. unabr. ed. Debra Gwartney. Read by Joyce Bean. (Running Time: 9 hrs. 30 mins. 0 sec.). (ENG.). 2009. audio compact disk 19.99 (978-1-4001-6068-6(5)); audio compact disk 59.99 (978-1-4001-4068-8(4)); audio compact disk 29.99 (978-1-4001-1068-1(8)) Pub: Tantor Media. Dist(s): IngramPubServ

Live to Tell. unabr. ed. Lisa Gardner. Read by Ann Marie Lee et al. 11 CDs. (Running Time: 13 hrs. 30 mins.). (ENG.). 2010. audio compact disk 40.00 (978-0-7393-6666-0(1), Random AudioBks) Pub: Random Audio Pubg. Dist(s): Random

Live While You're Still Alive. Jay A. Block. 2005. audio compact disk 29.95 (978-0-9770328-7-7(6)) AardGP.

***Live Wire.** abr. ed. Harlan Coben. (Running Time: 5 hrs.). (Myron Bolitar Ser.). 2011. 9.99 (978-1-4418-9534-9(5), 9781441895349, BAD); audio compact disk 24.99 (978-1-4418-9533-2(7), 9781441895332, BACD) Brilliance Audio.

***Live Wire.** unabr. ed. Harlan Coben. (Running Time: 10 hrs.). (Myron Bolitar Ser.). 2011. 24.99 (978-1-4418-9531-8(0), 9781441895318, BAD); 24.99 (978-1-4418-9529-5(9), 9781441895295, Brilliance MP3); 39.97 (978-1-4418-9530-1(2), 9781441895301, Brinc Audio MP3 Lib); 39.97 (978-1-4418-9532-5(9), 9781441895325, BADLE); audio compact disk 36.99 (978-1-4418-9527-1(2), 9781441895271, Bril Audio CD Unabri); audio compact disk 97.97 (978-1-4418-9528-8(0), 9781441895288, BriAudCD Unabrid) Brilliance Audio.

Live with Passion! Create a Compelling Future with America's Top Business & Life Strategist. unabr. abr. ed. Anthony Robbins. 5 CDs. (Running Time: 60 hrs. 0 mins. 0 sec.). (ENG.). 2002. audio compact disk 39.95 (978-0-7435-2521-3(3), Nightgale) Pub: S&S Audio. Dist(s): S and S Inc
Learn how to: Use 'Quality Quantifiers' to increase your desire for living; Use the power of paradox to launch your plans with confidence and certainty; Replace dormant resources with new assets that will improve the quality of your life.

Live Your Joy. unabr. ed. Bonnie St. John. Read by Bonnie St. John. (Running Time: 4 hrs.). (ENG.). 2009. 24.98 (978-1-59659-410-4(1), GildAudio) Pub: Gildan Media. Dist(s): HachBkGrp

Live Your Joy. unabr. ed. Bonnie St. John. Read by Bonnie St. John. (Running Time: 4 hrs. 30 mins.). (ENG.). 2009. audio compact disk 29.98 (978-1-59659-343-5(1), GildAudio) Pub: Gildan Media. Dist(s): HachBkGrp

Live Your Life (the Ultimate Healer Subliminal Series, 5 Of 6) Tap into your inner wisdom to experience synchronicity, joy, & right Choice. Kyrah Malan. 1 CD. (Running Time: 27 mins). 2006. audio compact disk 39.95 (978-0-9787324-5-5(6), SPS5) K Malan.
The ultimate in subliminal affirmations. Music, messages and binaural beats are specifically designed to work together to help you eliminate struggle. Move in synchronicity, and flow easily with the current of life..What you hear is beautiful music that has been proven in university studies or harmonize and organize your energy field, putting you in a calm, receptive state quickly and easily.What your subconscious hears are specially designed affirmations and suggestions, designed to rewrite subconscious beliefs and change behavior faster and more effectively than any subliminal program available today.The Foundation set is designed to be used in order, each CD building on the effects of the previous CDs, and includes Love Your Life, Release & Relax, Energy & Power, Manifest & Magnetize, Live Your Life, and Spirit & Soul. Can be used independently. Unlike typical subliminal programs which recommend you listen to them for at least 30 days, Ultimate healer CDs help create positive results in only 17 days; some people report results in as little as 2 or 3 days!You can play them during everyday activities, while driving, reading, or at work, or listen to them with headphones. You have freedom and flexibility with The Ultimate Healer Subliminal Series.

Live your Marriage see Vive tu Matrimonio

Lively Music for Rhythm Stick Fun. 1 CD. (Running Time: 1 hr.). (J). 2001. pap. bk. 14.95 (KIM 2000CD) Kimbo Educ.
Exciting tunes that promote rhythm awareness. Children tap out easy rhythm stick routines. Can be used individually or in groups. 12th Street Rag, LeRoy Brown, Alley Cat & more. Includes manual.

Lively Music for Rhythm Stick Fun. 1 cass. (Running Time: 1 hr.). (J). (gr. 4-6). 2001. pap. bk. 10.95 (KIM 2000C); pap. bk. & stu. ed. 11.95 (KIM 2000) Kimbo Educ.

Live...on Something's Happening! Tony Russo. 1 cass. (Roy Tuckman Interview Ser.). 9.00 (A0706-90) Sound Photosyn.
Tony Russo, who with Daniel Ellsberg revealed the Pentagon Papers, which helped end the Vietnam War in the '60s, discusses the Middle East.

Liver Transplantation. Moderated by Harold J. Fallon & Seymour M. Sabesin. Contrib. by Rolland Dickson et al. 1 cass. (Running Time: 90 min.). 1985. 12.00 (D8564) Amer Coll Phys.
This topic is discussed by a moderator & experts who offer differing opinions.

Liverpool Mystery see Classic Detective Stories, Vol. III, A Collection

Liverpool Rose. Katie Flynn. Read by Anne Dover. 12 CDs. (Running Time: 16 hrs. 47 mins.). (Soundings (CDs) Ser.). (J). 2004. audio compact disk 99.95 (978-1-84283-786-3(9)) Pub: ISIS Lrg Prnt GBR. Dist(s): Ulverscroft US

Liverpool Rose. unabr. ed. Katie Flynn. Read by Anne Dover. 12 cass. (Running Time: 16 hrs. 47 mins.). (Sound Ser.). 2002. 94.95 (978-1-84283-216-5(6)) Pub: UlverLrgPrint GBR. Dist(s): Ulverscroft US
Orphaned, Lizzie lives with her Aunt Annie, Uncle Perce and two cousins in Liverpool. Lizzie loves her aunt but is hated by her uncle and escapes when she can. She makes friends with Geoff Gardiner, another orphan, and is teaching him to swim in the Scaldy when Clem Gilligan rescues the pair of them from drowning. As Lizzie's uncle grows more violent, she is forced to flee. Her first instinct is to make for the canal, but finding Clem is not so easy.

Lives & Works of the English Romantic Poets, Pts. I-II. Instructed by Willard Spiegelman. 12 CDs. (Running Time: 12 hrs.). bk. 69.95 (978-1-56585-296-9(6)) Teaching Co.

Lives & Works of the English Romantic Poets, Pts. I-II, Vol. 1. Instructed by Willard Spiegelman. 12 cass. (Running Time: 12 hrs.). bk. 54.95 (978-1-56585-041-5(6)) Teaching Co.

Lives & Works of the English Romantic Poets, Vol. 2. Instructed by Willard Spiegelman. 6 CDs. (Running Time: 6 hrs.). 2002. audio compact disk 179.95 (978-1-56585-297-6(4)) Teaching Co.

***Lives Like Loaded Guns: Emily Dickinson & Her Family's Feuds.** unabr. ed. Lyndall Gordon. Narrated by Wanda McCaddon. (Running Time: 15 hrs. 30 mins.). 2010. 39.99 (978-1-4001-9776-7(7)); 29.99 (978-1-4001-6776-0(0)); 20.99 (978-1-4001-8776-8(1)); audio compact disk 39.99 (978-1-4001-1776-5(3)); audio compact disk 95.99 (978-1-4001-4776-2(X)) Pub: Tantor Media. Dist(s): IngramPubServ

Lives, Lycurgus & Numa. unabr. ed. Plutarch. Read by Robert L. Halvorson. 2 cass. (Running Time: 180 min.). 14.95 (16) Halvorson Assocs.

Lives of a Cell: Notes of a Biology Watcher. unabr. ed. Lewis Thomas. Read by Tom Parker. 3 cass. (Running Time: 4 hrs.). 1995. 23.95 (978-0-7861-0862-6(2), 1660) Blckstn Audio.
Dr. Thomas opens up to the listener a universe of knowledge & perception that is perhaps not wholly unfamiliar to the research scientist, but the world he explores is one of men & women too, a world of complex interrelationships, old ironies, peculiar powers, & intricate languages that give identity to the alienated, direction to the dependent. "The Lives of a Cell" offers a subtle, bold vision of humankind & the world around us - a sense of what gives life - from a writer who seems to draw grace & strength from the very substance of his subject, a man of wit & imagination who takes pleasure in & gives meaning to nearly everything he beholds.

Lives of a Cell: Notes of a Biology Watcher. unabr. ed. Lewis Thomas. Read by Edward Lewis. 3 cass. (Running Time: 4 hrs. 30 mins.). 1998. 14.95 Books on Tape.
A brilliant science writer sets out a series of essays which will make you marvel at the interconnectedness of life.

Lives of a Cell: Notes of a Biology Watcher. unabr. ed. Lewis Thomas. Read by John Steven Linn. 5 cass. (Running Time: 5 hrs.). 1989. Shelf Pub Inc.
"The Lives of a Cell" is a collection essays originally appearing in the "New England Journal of Medicine." Topics include medicine, music, insects & language. Winner of the national book award.

Lives of a Cell: Notes of a Biology Watcher, Set. unabr. ed. Lewis Thomas. Read by Tom Parker. 3 cass. (Running Time: 4 hrs. 30 min.). 1999. 23.95 Blckstn Audio.
Dr. Thomas opens up to the listener a universe of knowledge & perception that is perhaps not wholly unfamiliar to the research scientist, but the world he explores is one of men & women too, a world of complex interrelationships, old ironies, peculiar powers, & intricate languages that give identity to the alienated, direction to the dependent. "The Lives of a Cell" offers a subtle, bold vision of humankind & the world around us - a sense of what gives life - from a writer who seems to draw grace & strength from the very substance of his subject, a man of wit & imagination who takes pleasure in & gives meaning to nearly everything he beholds.

Lives of Christopher Chant. unabr. ed. Diana Wynne Jones. 7 cass. (Running Time: 9 hrs. 15 min.). (Chrestomanci Ser.). 2004. 61.75 (978-1-4025-8462-6(8)) Recorded Bks.

Lives of Extraordinary Women: Rulers, Rebels (And What the Neighbors Thought) unabr. ed. Kathleen Krull. Read by Melissa Hughes. 2 CDs. (Running Time: 2 hrs.). (Lives of Ser.). (YA). (gr. 5 up). 2001. audio compact disk 24.95 (978-1-883332-73-0(7)); 15.95 (978-1-883332-46-4(X)) Audio Bkshelf.
Twenty women who changed history from queens to renegades.

Lives of Girls & Women. abr. ed. Alice Munro. Narrated by Judy Mahbey. 3 cass. (Running Time: 3 hrs.). (Between the Covers Collection). (ENG.). 1998. 19.95 (978-0-86492-260-1(4)) Pub: BTC Audiobks CAN. Dist(s): U Toronto Pr
Alice Munro's first collection of linked stories traces Del Jordan's uneasy passage through adolescence.

Lives of Girls & Women. abr. ed. Alice Munro. 3 CDs. (Running Time: 10800 sec.). (ENG.). 2005. audio compact disk 24.95 (978-0-86492-398-1(8)) Pub: BTC Audiobks CAN. Dist(s): U Toronto Pr

Lives of Girls & Women. unabr. collector's ed. Alice Munro. Read by Jeanne Hopson. 7 cass. (Running Time: 10 hrs. 30 min.). (J). 1983. 56.00 (978-0-7366-0511-3(8), 1485) Books on Tape.
This narrative by Del Jordan tells of her passage through the many phases of growing up in the 1940's & 1950's.

Lives of Great Christians. Instructed by William R. Cook. (ENG.). 2007. 129.95 (978-1-59803-329-8(8)); audio compact disk 69.95 (978-1-59803-330-4(1)) Teaching Co.

***Lives of Harry Lime, Volume 1.** RadioArchives.com. (Running Time: 600). (ENG.). 2010. audio compact disk 29.98 (978-1-61081-173-6(9)) Radio Arch.

***Lives of Harry Lime, Volume 2.** RadioArchives.com. (Running Time: 360). (ENG.). 2010. audio compact disk 17.98 (978-1-61081-184-2(4)) Radio Arch.

Lives of Saints. Hugo Hoever. 10 cass. (Running Time: 10 hrs. 30 min.). 1997. 19.95 (978-0-89942-873-4(8), 873/00) Cathlic Bk Pub.

Lives of the Artists, Vol. 1. unabr. ed. Giorgio Vasari. Read by Nadia May. 13 cass. (Running Time: 19 hrs.). 2000. 85.95 (978-0-7861-1800-7(8), 2599) Blckstn Audio.
His original vision of the arts, in which he sees the artist as divinely inspired, permeates this second volume as much as the first. The lives have a striking immediacy conveyed in the character sketches, anecdotes & detailed recordings of conversations.

Lives of the Artists, Vol. 2. unabr. ed. Giorgio Vasari. Read by Nadia May. 11 cass. (Running Time: 16 hrs.). 2000. 76.95 (978-0-7861-1808-3(3), 2607) Blckstn Audio.

Lives of the Artists: Masterpieces, Messes. unabr. ed. Kathleen Krull. Read by John C. Brown & Melissa Hughes. 2 cass. (Running Time: 2 hrs.). (YA). (gr. 5-9). 1996. 15.95 (978-1-883332-25-9(7), 394113) Audio Bkshelf.
Twenty irreverent portraits of famous people that make listeners want to hear more!.

Lives of the Artists: Masterpieces, Messes (And What the Neighbors Thought) Kathleen Krull. Read by John C. Brown. 1 CD. (Running Time: 2 hrs.). (YA). 1996. audio compact disk 24.95 (978-1-883332-63-1(X)) Audio Bkshelf.

Lives of the Artists: Masterpieces, Messes (& What the Neighbors Thought) unabr. ed. Kathleen Krull. Read by John C. Brown & Melissa Hughes. 2 CDs. (Running Time: 2 hrs.). 2001. audio compact disk 24.95 Audio Bkshelf.

Lives of the Artists: Vol 2. unabr. ed. Vasari Giorgio. Read by Nadia May. 2006. audio compact disk 29.95 (978-0-7861-7354-9(8)) Blckstn Audio.

Lives of the Artists: Vol. 2. unabr. ed. Vasari Giorgio. Read by Nadia May. 2006. audio compact disk 99.00 (978-0-7861-6638-1(X)) Blckstn Audio.

Lives of the Artists: Vol. 3. unabr. ed. Vasari Giorgio. Read by Nadia May. 2006. audio compact disk 29.95 (978-0-7861-7355-6(6)) Blckstn Audio.

Lives of the Artists: Volume 1. unabr. ed. Giorgio Vasari. Read by Nadia May. (Running Time: 66600 sec.). (Lives of the Artists Ser.). 2006. audio compact disk 120.00 (978-0-7861-6637-4(1)) Blckstn Audio.

Lives of the Cat. Perf. by Claudia Christian & Patricia Tallman. 2 cass. (Running Time: 2 hrs.). 2001. 19.95 (RRCA006); audio compact disk 24.95 (RRCA007) Lodestone Catalog.
Annie & her boss are marked for death, as they stand between Richmond & a police takover of the entire sector. But somehow, astoundingly - when Annie gets killed, she doesn't die.

Lives of the Cat. unabr. ed. Perf. by Claudia Christian. 2 CDs. (Running Time: 2 hrs.). Dramatization. 2000. audio compact disk 24.95 (978-0-9660392-5-2(4)) Pub: Radio Repertory. Dist(s): Timberwolf Pr
Full cast science fiction audio adventure.

Lives of the Cat. unabr. ed. Larry Weiner. 2 cass. (Running Time: 2 hrs.). 2000. 19.95 Penton Overseas.

Lives of the Cat. unabr. ed. Larry Weiner. 2 cass. (Running Time: 2 hrs.). (J). 2000. 19.95 (978-0-9660392-4-5(6), RRCA006) Pub: Radio Repertory. Dist(s): Penton Overseas
Detective Annie Manx and her boss are marked for death as they stand between Lieutenant Richmond and a police takeover of the entire sector. But somehow, astoundingly - when Annie gets killed, she doesn't die. Just how many lives does this cat have?.

Lives of the Great Artists. unabr. ed. Giorgio Vasari. Read by Neville Jason. 6 cass. (Running Time: 8 hrs.). (YA). 2002. 32.98 (978-962-634-755-3(4), NA625514, Naxos AudioBooks); audio compact disk 41.98 (978-962-634-255-8(2), NA625512, Naxos AudioBooks) Naxos.
Five hundred years after they were written, this remains the principal source book on that remarkable flowering of Italian painting in the 15th century. Here are biographies of over 35 artists, including Giotto, Cimabue, Cimabue, Ucello, Piero della Francesca, Donatello, Brunelleschi, Fra Angelico, Fra Filippo Lippi, Botticelli, Mantegna, Leonardo da Vinci, Michelangelo Titian and even Vasari himself.

Lives of the Great Composers, Pt. 1. unabr. collector's ed. Harold C. Schonberg. Read by John Edwardson. 11 cass. (Running Time: 16 hrs. 30 min.). 1997. 88.00 (978-0-7366-3803-6(2), 4474-A) Books on Tape.
The author traces a lineage of composers from Claudio Monteverdi in the 1600s to the tonalists of the 1990s.

Lives of the Great Composers, Pt. 2. unabr. collector's ed. Harold C. Schonberg. Read by John Edwardson. 11 cass. (Running Time: 16 hrs. 30 mins.). 1997. 88.00 (978-0-7366-3804-3(0), 4474-B) Books on Tape.
Traces a lineage of composers from Claudio Monteverdi in the 1600's to the tonalists of the 1990's.

Lives of the Kings & Queens of England. rev. unabr. ed. Read by Wanda McCaddon. Ed. by Antonia Fraser. 8 cass. (Running Time: 12 hrs.).

(Self-Help Law Kit Ser.). 1999. 34.95 (978-1-57270-101-4(3), E81101u) Pub: Audio Partners. Dist(s): PerseuPGW
Updating The House of Windsor, a classic chronicle of England's monarchs spanning ten dynasties. Captures the pageantry of royal power in all its grandeur.

Lives of the Kings & Queens of England. unabr. ed. Ed. by Antonia Fraser. Narrated by Wanda McCaddon. (ENG.). 2004. audio compact disk 39.95 (978-1-57270-433-6(0)) Pub: AudioGO. Dist(s): Perseus Dist

Lives of the Kings & Queens of England. unabr. ed. Antonia Fraser. Read by Donada Peters. 8 cass. (Running Time: 12 hrs.). 1997. 64.00 (978-0-913369-54-8(3), 105173) Books on Tape.
With the assistance of eight specialist contributors, noted biographer & historian Fraser explores the political & personal lives of the most despised & most revered, monarchs of England.

Lives of the Kings & Queens of England. unabr. ed. Mary Gordon. Read by Mari Devon. 4 cass. (Running Time: 6 hrs.). 2000. 32.00 (978-0-7366-4977-3(8), 5235) Books on Tape.
For more than five hundred years, the story of Joan of Arc has been an inspiration and a mystery. The least likely of heroines, a peasant girl with no education and no prospects, Joan turned herself into the legendary Maid of Orleans, knight, martyr, and saint. Following a voice she knew was God's, she led an army to victory in battle and crowned the king of France, only to be captured by her English enemies and burned at the stake as a heretic, all by the age of nineteen.

Lives of the Monster Dogs. abr. ed. Kirsten Bakis et al. Read by George DelHoyo & Mary Jo Smith. 2 cass. (Running Time: 3 hrs.). 1999. 17.95 (978-1-57453-112-1(3), 395330) Audio Lit.
The year is 2008. A Malamute arrives in New York City, dressed in an antique jacket & wearing spectacles. He is followed by dogs, all dressed in grand old Prussian style. Results of a mysterious experiment, they become the toast of Manhattan the Monster Dogs.

Lives of the Musicians: Good Times, Bad Times (And What the Neighbors Thought) unabr. ed. Kathleen Krull. Read by John C. Brown & Melissa Hughes. 2 CDs. (Running Time: 2 hrs.). (YA). (gr. 5 up). 1996. audio compact disk 24.95 (978-1-883332-60-0(5)) Audio Bkshelf.

***Lives of the Pirates.** unabr. ed. Kathleen Krull & Kathryn Hewitt. Narrated by Ray Childs & Kimberly Dakin. 2 CDs. (Running Time: 2 hrs.). (YA). (gr. 2 up). 2010. audio compact disk 29.95 (978-1-935430-43-8(2)) Audio Bkshelf.

Lives of the Poets see Cambridge Treasy Burton

Lives of the Presidents: Fame, Shame (And What the Neighbors Thought) unabr. ed. Kathleen Krull. Read by John C. Brown & Melissa Hughes. 3 CDs. (Running Time: 3 hrs.). (YA). (gr. 5 up). 1998. audio compact disk 29.95 (978-1-883332-62-4(1)) Audio Bkshelf.

Lives of the Presidents: Fame, Shame (and What the Neighbors Thought) unabr. ed. Kathleen Krull. Read by John C. Brown & Melissa Hughes. 2 cass. (Running Time: 3 hrs.). (Lives of Ser.). (YA). 1998. 17.95 (978-1-883332-34-1(6)) Audio Bkshelf.
Brief "fly-on-the-wall" biographies of our country's 41 presidents, profiling them, using the kind of fun facts that many listeners will find both memorable & irresistible. Also notes political, academic, business & military achievements as well as favorable personality traits.

Lives of the Prophets, Vols. 1 and 2. abr. ed. Anwar Al-Awlaki. 10 cass. (Running Time: 10 hrs. 30 mins.). 2001. 25.00 (978-1-891540-12-7(2)); audio compact disk 35.00 (978-1-891540-13-4(0)) Al-Basheer Co.

Lives of the Prophets, Vols. 3 and 4. abr. ed. Anwar Al-Awlaki. 8 cass. (Running Time: 8 hrs. 25 mins.). 2001. 35.00 (978-1-891540-14-1(9)); audio compact disk 45.00 (978-1-891540-15-8(7)) Al-Basheer Co.

Lives of the Twelve Caesars. Suetonius. Read by Derek Jacobi. (Running Time: 7 hrs.). 2009. 38.95 (978-1-60083-832-3(4)) Iofy Corp.

Lives of the Twelve Caesars. abr. ed. Gaius Suetonius. Read by Derek Jacobi. 6 CDs. audio compact disk 41.98 (978-962-634-339-5(7), NA633912) Naxos.

Lives of the Vaisnava Saints. Srinivasa Acarya & Narottama D. Thakura. 3 cass. vinyl bd. 15.00 Bhaktivedanta.
Srinivasa & Narottama, two of 16th century India's greatest bhakti mystics, were responsible for disseminating the esoteric message of Lord Caitanya Mahaprabhu to all parts of India. Recounts their transcendental development & experiences, extensive travels through India, highly mystical journeys to the spiritual world, & their converting of thousands of persons into devotees of Lord Krsna. They emanated pure love of God & taught all whom they met how to achieve this blissful state. They organized the very first transcendental book distribution party & the first Gaura Purnima Festival. The ultimate philosophical conceptions of Gaudiya Vaisnavism are to be found in the songs of Narottama Dasa Thakura.

Lives of the Writers: Comedies, Tragedies. unabr. ed. Kathleen Krull. Read by John C. Brown & Melissa Hughes. 2 cass. (Running Time: 2 hrs.). (YA). (gr. 5 up). 1996. 15.95 (978-1-883332-24-2(9), 394112) Audio Bkshelf.
Twenty irreverent portraits of famous people that make listeners want to hear more!.

Live2Shine. Riverview Staff. 1 CD. (Running Time: 45 min.). 2004. audio compact disk 14.95 (978-5-550-64478-2(9)) STL Dist NA.

Livin' in the Rain. Contrib. by Jeff & Sheri Easter. (Christian World Soundtraks Ser.). 2007. audio compact disk 8.99 (978-5-557-60860-2(5)) Christian Wrld.

***Living.** abr. ed. Annie Dillard. Read by Laurence Luckinbill. (ENG.). 2007. (978-0-06-155532-9(0)) HarperCollins Pubs.

Living. unabr. ed. Annie Dillard. Read by Grace Cassidy. 12 cass. (Running Time: 17 hrs. 30 mins.). 1993. 83.95 (978-0-7861-0639-4(5), 1453) Blckstn Audio.
Here is the intimate, murderous tale of three men. Clare Fishburn believes that greatness lies in store for him. John Ireland Sharp, an educated orphan, abandons hope when he sees socialists expel the Chinese workers from the region. Beal Obenchain, who lives in a cedar stump, threatens Clare Fisburn's life. Lummi & Nooksack Indian people fish & farm; explorers climb into the Cascade Mountains to survey. Men struggle to clear the forests; hermits pay their debts in sockeye salmon; miners track gold-bearing streams. Settlers launch a boat & sing by a beach fire. Settlers pour into Whatcom, the harbor town, to catch the boom the railroads bring. All this takes place a hundred years ago, when these vital, ruddy men & women were "the living".

***Living.** unabr. ed. Annie Dillard. Read by Laurence Luckinbill. (ENG.). 2007. (978-0-06-147393-7(6), Harper Audio) HarperCollins Pubs.

Living: Mary Lavin Reads Her Short Story. unabr. ed. Mary Lavin. Read by Mary Lavin. 1 cass. (Running Time: 37 min.). (YM-YWHA Poetry Center Ser.). 1967. 12.95 (23181) J Norton Pubs.

Living @ the Next Level: Transforming Your Life's Frustrations into Fulfillment. unabr. ed. B. Courtney McBath. Narrated by B. Courtney McBath. (Running Time: 5 hrs. 44 mins. 56 sec.). (ENG.). 2008. 16.09 (978-1-60814-291-0(4)) Oasis Audio.

Living a Balanced Life in an Unbalanced World. unabr. ed. David Essel. Read by David Essel. 1 cass. (Running Time: 1 hr. 30 mins.). (David Essel's Dynamic Living Ser.: Vol. 8). 2000. 9.95 (978-1-893074-10-1(2)) D Essel Inc.

Living a Championship Life: A Game Plan for Success. Rick Goodman. (ENG.). 2008. 47.00 (978-0-9795737-8-1(5)) Anzman Publg.

Living A Course in Miracles. Kenneth Wapnick. 4 CDs. 2006. audio compact disk 24.00 (978-1-59142-252-5(3), CD67) Foun Miracles.

Living A Course in Miracles. Kenneth Wapnick. 1 CD. (Running Time: 3 hrs. 58 mins. 42 secs.). 2006. 19.00 (978-1-59142-262-4(0), 3m67) Foun Miracles.

Living a God-Centered Life. Daya Mata. 1986. 8.50 (2126) Self Realization.
Explains how one may actually achieve a God-centered life. Topics include: Personal stories about Paramahansa Yogananda's training; finding joy in our daily work; how to overcome moods & spiritual dryness; the value of longer meditations & how to make them deeper; sustaining a dynamic awareness of God in activity as well as meditation.

Living a Healthy Life with Chronic Conditions: Self-Management of Heart Disease, Arthritis, Diabetes, Asthma, Bronchitis, Emphysema & Others. Kate Lorig et al. (Running Time: 14 hrs. 18 mins. 0 sec.). (ENG.). 2009. audio compact disk 32.95 (978-1-933503-16-5(5)) Pub: Bull Pub. Dist(s): IPG Chicago

Living a Lie. unabr. ed. Josephine Cox. Read by Maggie Ollerenshaw. 10 cass. 1996. 84.95 (978-0-7451-6654-4(7), CAB 1270) AudioGO.
When Lucinda Marsh throws herself in front of a speeding train, she leaves her 12-year-old daughter, Kitty, & her violent husband alone. Aside from her father, all that Kitty has is her childhood sweetheart, Harry. And when her father dies, Kitty is sent to an orphanage where she befriends Georgie, a lively cockney girl. She turns her back on Harry, afraid that her feelings for him will ruin his future. But when fate brings them back together, Kitty wonders if true love can ever die.

Living a Life of Excellence. Speeches. Joel Osteen. 1 Cass. (Running Time: 30 Mins.). (J). 2000. 6.00 (978-1-59349-055-3(0), JA0055) J Osteen.

Living a Life of Faith. Speeches. Joel Osteen. 7 audio cass. (J). 2001. 28.00 (978-1-931877-11-4(4)); audio compact disk 28.00 (978-1-931877-28-2(9), JCS007) J Osteen.

Living a Life of Forgiveness. Speeches. Joel Osteen. 1 Cass. (Running Time: 30 Mins.). (J). 2000. 6.00 (978-1-59349-051-5(8), JA0051) J Osteen.

Living a Life of Inner Peace. unabr. ed. Eckhart Tolle. 2 CDs. (Running Time: 2 hrs. 16 mins. 0 sec.). (ENG.). 2004. audio compact disk 18.95 (978-1-57731-486-8(7)) Pub: New Wrld Lib. Dist(s): PerseuPGW
A Recording Of one of Eckhart Tolle's most moving, transformative lectures, Living a Life of Inner Peace makes the experience of hearing this world-renowned teacher available to those who have not yet been privileged to hear him speak in person. Far less formal than his writing, Tolle's talks are relaxed and funny, conveying his message through story and insightful observation. Tolle makes people laugh at themselves, with the result being powerfully effective therapy. For Tolle and the millions whose lives he's touched, words that are spoken from a state of presence can carry seekers into that same state, the basis for all true spiritual teachings. Beyond the information that is being conveyed, something deeper happens. Where before there was mental noise, a field of alert stillness arises for the listener, signaling the entry to a state of presence that precedes transformation. For those new to Tolle's teachings, this is an ideal introduction. Those familiar with his work should be prepared for something extraordinary.

Living a Life of Love. Speeches. Joel Osteen. 4 audio cass. (J). 2001. 16.00 (978-1-931877-10-7(6)); audio compact disk 16.00 (978-1-931877-26-8(2), JCS006) J Osteen.

Living a Life of Love, Pt. 1. Speeches. Joel Osteen. 1 Cass. (Running Time: 30 Mins.). (J). 2000. 6.00 (978-1-59349-073-7(9), JA0073) J Osteen.

Living a Life of Love, Pt. 2. Short Stories. Joel Osteen. 1 Cass. (Running Time: 30 Mins.). (J). 2000. 6.00 (978-1-59349-074-4(7), JA0074) J Osteen.

Living a Life of Love, Pt. 3. Speeches. Joel Osteen. 1 Cass. (J). 2000. 6.00 (978-1-59349-075-1(5), JA0075) J Osteen.

Living a Life of Love, Pt. 4. Speeches. Joel Osteen. 1 Cass. (Running Time: 30 Mins.). 2000. Rental 6.00 (978-1-59349-076-8(3), JA0076) J Osteen.

Living a Life of Obedience. Speeches. Joel Osteen. 4 audio cass. (J). 2001. 16.00 (978-1-931877-09-1(2)); audio compact disk 16.00 (978-1-931877-27-5(0), JCS005) J Osteen.

Living a Life of Obedience, Pt. 1. Speeches. Joel Osteen. 1 Cass. (Running Time: 30 Mins). (J). 1999. 6.00 (978-1-59349-038-6(0), JA0038) J Osteen.

Living a Life of Obedience, Pt. 2. Speeches. Joel Osteen. 1 Cass. (Running Time: 30 Mins.). (J). 1999. 6.00 (978-1-59349-039-3(9), JA0039) J Osteen.

Living a Life of Obedience, Pt. 3. Speeches. Joel Osteen. 1 Cass. (Running Time: 30 Mins.). (J). 1999. 6.00 (978-1-59349-041-6(0), JA0041) J Osteen.

Living a Life of Obedience, Pt. 4. Speeches. Joel Osteen. 1 Cass. (Running Time: 30 Mins.). (J). 1999. 6.00 (978-1-59349-042-3(9), JA0042) J Osteen.

Living a Life of Unconditional Love. Speeches. Joel Osteen. 1 Cass. (Running Time: 30 mins.). (J). 2000. 6.00 (978-1-59349-052-2(6), JA0052) J Osteen.

Living a Lifestyle of Giving. Speeches. Joel Osteen. 4 audio cass. (J). 2002. 16.00 (978-1-931877-20-6(3), JAS016); audio compact disk 12.00 (978-1-931877-37-4(8), JCS016) J Osteen.

Living a Lifestyle of Giving. Speeches. Based on a book by Joel Osteen. 1 Cass. (Running Time: 30 Mins). 2002. 6.00 (978-1-59349-151-2(4), JA0151) J Osteen.

Living above the Level of Mediocrity. 2002. 48.95 (978-1-57972-453-5(1)); audio compact disk 64.00 (978-1-57972-454-2(X)) Insight Living.

Living above the Level of Mediocrity. Charles R. Swindoll. Read by Charles R. Swindoll. 2 cass. (BookTrax Ser.). 1990. 15.99 (978-0-8499-1284-9(9)) Nelson.
Focuses on the potential within each of us to reach a level of excellence in our lives.

Living Adventures from American History, No. 1. unabr. ed. Allan Kelley. Read by Frances Kelley. 1 cass. (Running Time: 60 min.). Dramatization. (Little People Ser.). (J). (gr. 1-7). 1993. 11.95 (978-1-884428-06-7(1), 428061) Eye Ear.
History comes alive as children's imaginations fill with exciting, educational pictures, while they thrill to the heroic stories & dramatic events that helped America win its independence. Album No. 1 contains the following stories: Paul Revere; Valley Forge; Molly Pitcher; & Nathan Hale.

Living Adventures from American History, No. 2. unabr. ed. Allan Kelley. Read by Frances Kelley. 1 cass. (Running Time: 60 min.). Dramatization. (Living Adventures from American History Ser.: Vol. 2). (J). (gr. 1-4). 1993. 9.95 (978-1-884428-07-4(X), 42807X) Eye Ear.

Living Adventures from the Bible, No. 1. unabr. ed. Allan Kelley. Read by Frances Kelley. 1 cass. (Running Time: 60 min.). Dramatization. (Living Adventures from the Bible Ser.: Vol. 1). (J). (ps up). 1993. 11.95 (978-1-884428-03-6(7), 428037) Eye Ear.

Living Adventures from the Bible, No. 2. unabr. ed. Allan Kelley. Read by Frances Kelley. 1 cass. (Running Time: 60 min.). Dramatization. (Little People Ser.). (J). (gr. 1-7). 1993. 11.95 (978-1-884428-04-3(5), 428045) Eye Ear.

Living Adventures from the Bible, No. 3. unabr. ed. Allan Kelley. Read by Frances Kelley. 1 cass. (Running Time: 60 min.). Dramatization. (Living Adventures from the Bible Ser.: Vol. 3). (J). (ps-3). 1993. 11.95 (978-1-884428-05-0(3), 428053) Eye Ear.

Living Adventures from the Bible: The Talents; Ruth & Naomi; Joseph & His Brothers. Allan Kelley & Frances Kelley. 1 cass. (Running Time: 1 hr.). Dramatization. (J). (gr. k-6). 1985. 9.95 Eye-In-The-Ear.
Our approach to revitalizing & retelling the Bible classics for today's children is non-denominational & truly ecumenical. As such, we appeal to the nation's three major Bible-based religions, even to the non-religious. Our aim - amid the many negative influences in present-day society - is to reach & invigorate the child's imagination in a positive & uplifting way. In preparing these timeless stories for dramatic audio presentation, we bring the Bible to life in young minds by making the stories exciting, inspirational & memorable...all of which can be shared by children with their parents & grandparents.

Living Adventures from the Bible Vol. 1: David & Goliath; The Good Samaritan; The Prodigal Son; Jonah & the Whale. 1 cass. (Running Time: 1 hr.). Dramatization. (J). (gr. k-6). 11.95 (978-0-944168-00-4(0)) Eye-In-The-Ear.

Living Adventures from the Bible Vol. 1: David & Goliath; The Good Samaritan; The Prodigal Son; Jonah & the Whale. 1 cass. (Running Time: 1 hr). 2003. audio compact disk 14.95 (978-0-944168-08-0(6)) Eye-In-The-Ear.
Featuring: David and Goliath; The Good Samaritan; The Prodigal Son, and Jonah and the Whale.

Living Adventures from the Bible Vol. 2: The Lost Sheep; Easther the Heroic Queen; Daniel in the Lion's Den; The Fiery Furnace. 1 CD. (Running Time: 1 hr.). audio compact disk 14.95 (978-0-944168-09-7(4)) Eye-In-The-Ear.

Living Adventures from the Bible Vol. 2: The Lost Sheep; Easther the Heroic Queen; Daniel in the Lion's Den; The Fiery Furnace. 1 cass. (Running Time: 1 hr.). Dramatization. (J). (gr. k-6). 11.95 (978-0-944168-01-1(9)) Eye-In-The-Ear.
Our approach to revitalizing & retelling the Bible classics for today's children is non-denominational & truly ecumenical. As such, we appeal to the nation's three major Bible-based religions, even to the non-religious. Our aim - amid the many negative influences in present-day society - is to reach & invigorate the child's imagination in a positive & uplifting way. In preparing these timeless stories for dramatic audio presentation, we bring the Bible to life in young minds by making the stories exciting, inspirational & memorable...all of which can be shared by children with their parents & grandparents.

Living Adventures from the Bible Vol. 3: The Talents; Ruth & Naomi; Joseph & His Brothers. Allan Kelley. 1 CD. (Running Time: 1 hr.). 1995. audio compact disk 14.95 (978-0-944168-10-3(8)) Eye-In-The-Ear.

Living Adventures from the Bible Vol. 3: The Talents; Ruth & Naomi; Joseph & His Brothers. Allan Kelley & Frances Kelley. 1 cass. (Running Time: 0 hr. 60 min.). 1985. 11.95 (978-0-944168-02-8(7)) Eye-In-The-Ear.

Living an Empowered Life! Techniques for Creating Clarity, Confidence, Optimism, & Wealth! unabr. ed. Denise Lynch. Read by Denise Lynch. (Running Time: 8 hrs.). (ENG.). 2007. audio compact disk 29.98 (978-1-59659-080-9(7), GildAudio) Pub: Gildan Media. Dist(s): HachBkGrp

Living & Dying. Sogyal Rinpoche. 3 cass. 1992. 27.00 set. (OC300-66) Sound Horizons AV.

Living & Dying Today. Sogyal Rinpoche. 4 cass. 1997. 26.00 Set. (978-0-9624884-6-7(1)) Rigpa Pubns.

Living & Laughing Together - Parenting for Fun & Profit. 1 cass. 2000. 7.95 (978-1-886463-97-4(2)) Oasis Audio.

Living & Laughing with Cancer: A Comedian's Journey. Perf. by Dave Fitzgerald & John Docimo. Interview with Darren LaCroix. 1 cass. (Running Time: 40 min.). (YA). (gr. 10 up). 1998. 14.95 (978-0-9669309-1-7(6)) Humor Inst.
Documentary of a survivor from diagnosis to recovery. Interview format along with comedy performance about his health situation. Designed to educate, inspire & give a new perspective to patients & families.

Living & the Dead: Robert McNamara & Five Lives of a Lost War. unabr. ed. Paul Hendrickson. Read by Barrett Whitener. 13 cass. (Running Time: 19 hrs. 30 min.). 1998. 104.00 (978-0-7366-4257-6(9), 4757) Books on Tape.
Reveals the Vietnam War as never-seen before, through the prism of Robert McNamara's flawed logic.

Living As If: Belief Systems in Mental Health Practice. Sarah R. Taggart. (Social & Behavioral Science Ser.). 1994. bk. 33.00 (978-1-55542-652-1(2), Jossey-Bass) Wiley US.

Living As the Light: Meditations & Music. June McIntyre. Read by June McIntyre. 1 cass. (Running Time: 61 min.). 1996. 11.98 (978-1-889045-02-3(0)); audio compact disk 14.98 (978-1-889045-03-0(9)) J McIntyre.
Two fifteen minute meditations with celestial music, leading the listener into the galactical world of sound & imagery followed by instrumental music of the orchestra.

Living at the Horizon. Steve Amerson. 1996. 10.98 (978-7-83491-699-8(8)) Pub: Amerson Mus Min. Dist(s): STL Dist NA

Living at the Horizon. Steve Amerson. (Running Time: 30 min.). (ENG.). 2000. audio compact disk 15.98 (978-7-83491-702-5(1)) Pub: Amerson Mus Min. Dist(s): STL Dist NA

Living at the Horizons Tracks. Steve Amerson. 2005. audio compact disk 29.95 (978-0-00-511426-1(8)) Pub: Amerson Mus Min. Dist(s): STL Dist NA

Living at the Next Level: Transforming Your Life's Frustrations into Fulfillment. unabr. ed. B. Courtney McBath. Narrated by B. Courtney McBath. (Running Time: 5 hrs. 44 mins. 56 sec.). (ENG.). 2008. audio compact disk 22.99 (978-1-59859-358-7(7)) Oasis Audio.

Living Atlanta: KKK. 1 cass. (Running Time: 30 min.). 9.95 (HO-79-11-14, HarperThor) HarpC GBR.

Living Beyond Belief. Gary N. Arnold. (ENG.). 2009. audio compact disk 24.95 (978-1-57867-025-3(X)) Windhorse Corp.

Living Beyond Fear. Jeanne Segal. 7.95 (978-0-87877-074-8(7), New Page Bks) Career Pr Inc.

Living Beyond Miracles. Deepak Chopra & Wayne W. Dyer. 3 CDs. (Running Time: 3 hrs.). (ENG.). 2005. audio compact disk 19.95 (978-1-878424-79-2(3)) Amber-Allen Pub.

Living Beyond Miracles. Wayne W. Dyer & Deepak Chopra. Read by Wayne W. Dyer & Deepak Chopra. 4 cass. (Running Time: 3 hrs. 58 min.). 1993. 24.95 (978-1-882971-04-6(3)) Infinite Poss.
Individual presentations & interactive conversation with Dr. Dyer & Dr. Chopra.

Living Beyond the Limits: A Life in Sync with God. Franklin Graham. 1 cass. 1998. 15.99 (978-0-7852-7074-4(4)) Nelson.
Christian Life.

Living Beyond Your Expectations: Instead of Inside Others' Scripts. Melissa Worthington. Narrated by Melissa Worthington. 1 CD. (Running Time: 40 mins). 2004. audio compact disk 19.95 (978-0-9761093-0-3(1), Prevail Bks) Prevail Pubns.

At some point in our lives, we realized that we've been living under and within someone else's expectations. We begin to hear that little voice inside our head telling us there is more to us than what we're doing and what we've become. In Living Beyond Your Expectations: Instead of Inside Others', Melissa will teach you how to create a new path for your life, in which you will determine your goals and successes.

Living Beyond Yourself: Exploring the Fruit / Spirit. Beth Moore. (YA). 2004. audio compact disk 39.95 (978-0-633-19375-1(5)) LifeWay Christian.

Living Biographies of Famous Novelists. unabr. ed. Henry Thomas & Dana Lee Thomas. Read by Pat Bottino. 8 cass. (Running Time: 11 hrs. 30 mins.). 2006. 56.95 (978-0-7861-1172-5(0), 1959) Blckstn Audio.

Living Biographies of Famous Novelists. unabr. ed. Henry Thomas & Dana L. Thomas. Read by Pat Bottino. 8 cass. (Running Time: 12 hrs.). 1997. 56.95 (1959) Blckstn Audio.

Takes you on a magic carpet to the homes of 20 titans of literature, & you not only become their intimate friend but you acquire an even greater appreciation of their masterpieces.

Living Biographies of Famous Rulers. unabr. ed. Henry Thomas & Dana L. Thomas. Read by Nadia May. 6 cass. (Running Time: 8 hrs. 30 mins.). 1996. 44.95 (978-0-7861-0979-1(3), 1756) Blckstn Audio.

In the indulgence of their egotistical ambitions & reckless whims, the kings, conquerors & dictators have frequently presented a spectacle of dazzling fascination. It is this spectacle, sometimes comic but more often tragic in its results, that the authors have tried to bring back to life in this book. Here are living biographies of these twenty famous rulers: King Solomon; Asoka; Caesar; Augustus; Constantine; Charlemagne; Kublai Khan; Henry VIII; Queen Elizabeth; Montezuma; Ivan the Terrible; Catherine the Great; Louis XIV; Frederick the Great; Napoleon; Queen Victoria; Kaiser Wilhelm; Stalin; Mussolini; & Hitler.

Living Biographies of Famous Women. unabr. ed. Henry Thomas & Dana L. Thomas. Read by S. Patricia Bailey. 7 cass. (Running Time: 10 hrs.). 1999. 49.95 (978-0-7861-1651-5(X), 2479) Blckstn Audio.

Presents a group of human personages who can with dignity & without apology take their place side by side with their masculine peers.

Living Biographies of Famous Women. unabr. ed. Henry Thomas & Dana Lee Thomas. Read by S. Patricia Bailey. (Running Time: 36000 sec.). 2008. audio compact disk & audio compact disk 29.95 (978-1-4332-3439-2(4)); audio compact disk & audio compact disk 80.00 (978-1-4332-3438-5(6)) Blckstn Audio.

Living Biographies of Great Composers. unabr. ed. Henry Thomas & Dana Lee Thomas. Read by Nadia May. 7 cass. (Running Time: 10 hrs.). 2001. 49.95 (978-0-7861-1111-4(9), 1876) Blckstn Audio.

Living Biographies of Great Composers. unabr. ed. Henry Thomas & Dana Lee Thomas. Read by Pat Bottino. 7 cass. (Running Time: 10 hrs. 30 min.). 1997. 49.95 (1876) Blckstn Audio.

Here are vivid stories of men who dreamed, struggled & suffered so that they might give expression to their divine gifts: Bach, Handel, Haydn, Mozart, Beethoven, Schubert, Chopin, Schumann, Liszt, Wagner, Brahms, Tchaikovsky, Debussy & Puccini.

Living Biographies of Great Painters. unabr. ed. Henry Thomas & Dana Lee Thomas. Read by Pat Bottino. 8 cass. (Running Time: 11 hrs. 30 mins.). 1997. 56.95 (978-0-7861-1121-3(6), 1887) Blckstn Audio.

Vivid stories of twenty painters who dreamed, struggled & suffered so that they might give expression to their divine gifts: Giotto, Michelangelo, Raphael, da Vinci, Titian, Rubens, Rembrandt, El Greco, Diego Valasquez, William Hogarth, Joseph Turner, Goya, Jean Baptiste Corot, Jean Francois Millet, van Gogh, Whistler, Renoir, Cezanne & Winslow Homer.

Living Biographies of Great Philosophers. unabr. ed. Henry Thomas & Dana Lee Thomas. 9 CDs. (Running Time: 10 hrs.). 2001. audio compact disk 72.00 (978-0-7861-9690-6(4), 2839) Blckstn Audio.

Included are these great thinkers: Plato and Socrates, Aristotle, Epicurus, Marcus Aurelius, Thomas Aquinas, Francis Bacon, Descartes, Spinoza, Locke, Hume, Voltaire, Kant, Hegel, Schopenhauer, Emerson, Spencer, Nietzsche, William James, Henri-Louis Bergson, and Santayana.

Living Biographies of Great Philosophers. unabr. ed. Henry Thomas & Donna Lee Thomas. Read by Edward Lewis. 7 cass. (Running Time: 10 hrs.). 2001. 49.95 (978-0-7861-2078-9(9), 2839) Blckstn Audio.

Living Biographies of Great Scientists. unabr. ed. Henry Thomas & Dana L. Thomas. Read by Nadia May. 7 cass. (Running Time: 10 hrs.). 1996. 49.95 (978-0-7861-0958-6(0), 1735) Blckstn Audio.

Inspiring story of the great adventurers of the mind. It is an absorbing & intimate account of the lives of twenty eminent scientists who reached the heights of human achievement: Archimedes, Roger Bacon, Copernicus, Galileo, Newton, Lavoisier, Dalton, Humboldt, Huxley, Agassiz, Kelvin, Haeckel, Steinmetz, Faraday, Pasteur, Marie Curie, Mendel, Darwin, Banting & Einstein.

Living Biographies of Religious Leaders. unabr. ed. Henry Thomas & Dana Lee Thomas. Read by Nadia May. 6 cass. (Running Time: 8 hrs. 30 mins.). 2002. 44.95 (978-0-7861-2140-3(8), 2891); audio compact disk 56.00 (978-0-7861-9485-8(5), 2891) Blckstn Audio.

Presents the lives of twenty great founders and leading advocates of the world's foremost religions.

Living Buddha, Living Christ. Thich Nhat Hanh. Read by Ben Kingsley. 2 cass. (Running Time: 120 min.). 2003. 16.00 (62568) Parallax Pr.

Depicts the joyful, contemplative heart at the center of the Gospels and their Christian tradition.

Living Buddha, Living Christ. abr. ed. Thich Nhat Hanh. Read by Ben Kingsley. 2 CDs. (Running Time: 20 hrs. 0 mins. 0 sec.). (ENG.). 2003. audio compact disk 20.00 (978-0-7435-3332-4(1), Sound Ideas) Pub: S&S Audio. Dist(s): S and S Inc

Living by Spiritual Laws. Swami Amar Jyoti. 1 cass. 1986. 9.95 (A-51) Truth Consciousness.

True applicability of Spiritual Law on the material plane, including: right use of matter; simplicity & complexity; self-image; war, peace & openness; love; vegetarianism; needs & wants.

Living by the Universal Truth. Swami Amar Jyoti. 1 cass. 1983. 9.95 (A-25) Truth Consciousness.

Applying the universal laws of truth & harmlessness to solve problems. Our beautiful cosmic connection.

Living Christ: The Lamb of God. Ann Ree Colton & Jonathan Murro. Read by Ann Ree Colton & Jonathan Murro. 1 cass. 7.95 A R Colton Fnd.

Discusses the goal of God-Realization.

Living Confidently in God's Love see God of All Comfort

Living Consciously for Him. Swami Amar Jyoti. 2 dolby cass. 1984. 12.95 (A-28) Truth Consciousness.

In real conscious being, as man should be, spiritual laws govern all aspects of life.

Living Contact. Gloria Copeland. Perf. by Gloria Copeland. 3 cass. 1995. cass. & video 20.00 (978-0-88114-981-4(0)) K Copeland Pubns.

Biblical teaching on walking with Jesus.

***Living Dangerously: The Adventures of Merian C. Cooper, Creator of King Kong.** unabr. ed. Mark Cotta Vaz. Read by Patrick Cullen. (Running Time: 16 hrs. 30 mins.). 2010. 29.95 (978-1-4332-2009-8(1)); 89.95 (978-1-4332-2005-0(9)); audio compact disk 118.00 (978-1-4332-2006-7(7)) Blckstn Audio.

Living Dead: The Beginning. unabr. ed. George Romero. (Running Time: 9 hrs.). (ENG.). 2010. 24.98 (978-1-60788-243-5(4)); audio compact disk 29.98 (978-1-60788-242-8(6)) Pub: Hachet Audio. Dist(s): HachBkGrp

Living Dead Girl. unabr. ed. Elizabeth Scott. Read by Kate Reinders. (Running Time: 3 hrs.). 2009. 39.97 (978-1-4233-9753-3(3), 9781423397533, Brlnc Audio MP3 Lib); 19.99 (978-1-4233-9752-6(5), 9781423397526, Brilliance MP3); 39.97 (978-1-4233-9755-7(X), 9781423397557, BADLE); 19.99 (978-1-4233-9754-0(1), 9781423397540, BAD); audio compact disk 19.99 (978-1-4233-9750-2(9), 9781423397502, Bril Audio CD Unabri) Brilliance Audio.

Living Dead Girl. unabr. ed. Elizabeth Scott. Read by Kate Reinders. 3 CDs. (Running Time: 3 hrs.). (YA). (gr. 9 up). 2009. audio compact disk 49.97 (978-1-4233-9751-9(7), 9781423397519, BriAudCD Unabrid) Brilliance Audio.

***Living Doll.** 2010. audio compact disk (978-1-59171-190-2(8)) Falcon Picture.

Living End. Stanley Elkin. Read by Stanley Elkin. 1 cass. (Running Time: 1 hr. 13 min.). 13.95 (978-1-55644-010-6(3), 1061) Am Audio Prose.

Contains a performance of the entire "Conventional Wisdom" section & Elkin updates Milton, Dante & the earlier prophets.

Living End. unabr. ed. Stanley Elkin. Narrated by George Guidall. 3 cass. (Running Time: 4 hrs.). 1997. 26.00 (978-0-7887-1228-9(4), 95153E7) Recorded Bks.

Irreverent tale of the afterlife. Ellerbee, killed in a holdup, is ushered into a wondrous heaven. But St. Peter has more infernal plans for this baffled hero.

Living Enlightenment: Spiritual Life in the 21st Century. abr. ed. Andrew Cohen. 1 cass. 2003. audio compact disk 10.95 (978-1-883929-40-4(7)) Moksha Pr.

Living Everyday Zen. Charlotte Joko Beck. (Running Time: 11700 sec.). 2008. audio compact disk 24.95 (978-1-59179-805-7(1)) Sounds True.

Living Faith. Swami Amar Jyoti. 1 cass. 1987. 9.95 (D-17) Truth Consciousness.

Right focus means seeing no division between God & the world. With faith, following God's plan, there are no failures. Keeping the mind in peace.

Living Faith: One Day At a Time. Richard Sparks. 2 cass. (Running Time: 2 hrs.). 2001. 16.95 (A8000) St Anthony Mess Pr.

A personal invitation to rediscover a living faith, sustained by God's love, the challenge of life and the virtue of fidelity.

Living Freely. Swami Amar Jyoti. 1 cass. 1981. 9.95 (A-12) Truth Consciousness.

Which boons would we ask of God? Looking forward & upward, not backward & downward. The myth of insecurity.

***Living from the Heart.** Puran Bair & Susanna Bair. Read by Asatar Bair. (ENG., 2010. 13.95 (978-0-9795269-7-8(3)) Lvng Hrt Med.

Living from the Overflow: A Practical Guide to a Life of Plenitude. Michael Bernard Beckwith. (Running Time: 6:44:41). 2010. audio compact disk 69.95 (978-1-59179-754-8(3)) Sounds True.

Living from Your Center. Iyanla Vanzant. 1 CD. (Running Time: 1 hr.). 2006. audio compact disk 15.95 (978-1-59179-193-5(6), W828D) Sounds True.

Living Fully & in Balance: It's Not a Dress Rehearsal - This Is It! Albert Ellis. 1 cass. (Running Time: 67 min.). 9.95 (C048) A Ellis Institute.

Learn to achieve, a well balanced & self actualized life. Techniques for learning to accept ambiguity & uncertainty while achieving maximal satisfaction are outlined.

Living Fully & in Balance: It's Not a Dress Rehearsal - This Is It! Albert Ellis. 1 cass. (Running Time: 67 min.). 9.95 (C048) Inst Rational-Emotive.

Learn to achieve a well balanced & self actualized life. Techniques for learning to accept ambiguity & uncertainty while achieving maximal satisfaction are outlined.

***Living Galaxy.** Sir Charles Shults. (ENG.). 2010. audio compact disk 19.95 (978-1-4507-3083-9(3)) Indep Pub IL.

Living God. unabr. ed. Amar Jyoti. 1 cass. (Running Time: 1 hr. 30 min.). (Satsangs of Swami Amar Jyoti Ser.). 1998. 9.95 (978-0-933572-34-8(4), A57) Truth Consciousness.

Allowing God to live through one's life, show the way, guide, nourish. Spiritual knowledge. Living consciously. Education for Perfection.

Living Health. Anthony Robbins. 6 cass. 195.00 Set incl. 113p. wkbk. (468PAB) Nightingale-Conant.

Discover the proven secrets of lifelong vitality...the benefits of maximum oxygen...how to get the most energy from the foods you eat...how to live at peak levels...how to exercise for maximum results...& more.

Living Heart Diet. Michael E. DeBakey & Antonio Gotto. 1 cass. (Running Time: 56 min.). 8.95 (978-0-88684-094-5(5)) Listen USA.

Provides a healthy diet plan.

Living Hebrew. 2 cass. (Running Time: 1 hr. 20 min.). (LivingLang) Random Info Grp.

Living History. Hillary Rodham Clinton. Read by Kathe Mazur. 2003. audio compact disk 67.46 (978-0-7366-9639-5(3)) Books on Tape.

Living History. unabr. ed. Hillary Rodham Clinton. Read by Kathe Mazur. 16 cass. (Running Time: 24 hrs.). 2003. 58.46 (978-0-7366-9638-8(5)) Books on Tape.

Hillary Clinton, one of the most intelligent and influential women in America, reflects on her 8 years as first lady of the United States.

Living History. unabr. ed. Hillary Rodham Clinton & Hillary Rodham Clinton. Read by Hillary Rodham Clinton & Hillary Rodham Clinton. 6 CDs. (Running Time: 70 hrs. 0 mins. 0 sec.). (ENG.). 2003. audio compact disk 30.00 (978-0-7435-2834-4(4), Audioworks) Pub: S&S Audio. Dist(s): S and S Inc

Living History Stories of the Oregon Trail, Vol. 2. Short Stories. Mary Inman. 1 CD. (Running Time: 76 min.). (J). (gr. 3-8). 1999. audio compact disk 12.00 (978-0-9676981-0-6(3)) M Inman.

Two living history stories told by "Gramma Maudie Miller" & introduced by Mary Inman: Oregon Bound 1843 & Trailblazers of the Oregon Trail.

Living Hope for the End of Days: 365 Days of Devotions from the Book of the Revelation: the Safest Spot in the Universe. 2006. 15.00 (978-1-933561-21-9(1)) BFM Books.

Living in a Box. 1 CD. (Running Time: 53 mins.). 2001. audio compact disk 15.95 (LYNS001) Lodestone Catalog.

Living in a Community. Compiled by Benchmark Education Staff. 2005. audio compact disk 10.00 (978-1-4108-5494-0(9)) Benchmark Educ.

Living in a Green Dream. Julia Jewett. Read by Julia Jewett. 2 cass. (Running Time: 2 hrs. 35 min.). 1997. 18.95 (978-0-7822-0541-1(0), 607) C G Jung IL.

Jung proposes that human psyche is a phenomenon not unlike that of animals & that viewing the psyche in this way will change how a relationship with nature can aid in healing. Jewett's own personal reflection on her move from the city to the Indiana Dunes offers an intimate example of how nature can prompt & mediate crucial aspectss of a person's life.

Living in a Shakespearean World, Perf. by Laurence Olivier et al. 6 CDs. (Running Time: 8 hrs.). 1999. audio compact disk 59.98 (978-0-7379-0029-3(6), RHIN006) Rhino Enter.

Collection of excerpts from the Bard's plays & poems. Includes aspects of humanity, experiences of love, violent passions & the supernatural, dreams & morality - along with a complete reading of "Romeo & Juliet".

Living in a Tent-Looking for a City: Hebrews 1:8-10. Ed Young. 1980. 4.95 (978-0-7417-1144-1(3), A1044) Win Walk.

Living in Community. Stephen Gaskin. 1 cass. 9.00 (A0612-90) Sound Photosyn.

Alison Whitiker asks questions of the one who knows about the particulars of establishing responsibly sharing communities.

Living in English: Basic Skills for the Adult Learner, Set. Betsy J. Blosser. 2 cass. (Running Time: 3 hrs.). (SPA & ENG.). 1992. 43.95 (978-0-8442-7378-5(3), 73783, Natl Textbk Co) Pub: M-H Contemporary. Dist(s): Continental Bk

Living in Excellence. Pat Wilson. 6 cass. 59.95 (144-C47) Natl Seminars.

It's time to take charge & take control of your life. Stop waiting for someone else to answer your questions. Stop wishing for something else to happen. You can make it happen - with the advice & guidance in this breakthrough program. Includes the tips & techniques you need to live in excellence.

Living in Excellence. abr. ed. Pat Wilson. 2 cass. (Running Time: 150 mins.). 2002. 17.99 (978-1-55678-077-6(X), Lrn Inc) Oasis Audio.

Living in Favor, Abundance & Joy: Recorded Live at Lakewood Church. unabr. ed. Joel Osteen. Read by Joel Osteen. (Running Time: 5 hrs. 0 mins. 0 sec.). (ENG.). 2010. audio compact disk 29.99 (978-1-4423-0506-9(1)) Pub: S&S Audio. Dist(s): S and S Inc

Living in God's Glory. Mark Crow. 3 cass. (Running Time: 3 hrs.). 2001. (978-1-931537-12-4(7)) Vision Comm Creat.

Living in God's Love. 3rd rev. ed. 13.00 (978-1-59166-139-9(0)) BJUPr.

Living in God's Love: New York Crusade. unabr. ed. Billy Graham. (ENG.). (gr. 8). 2005. audio compact disk 14.95 (978-0-14-305855-7(X), PengAudBks) Penguin Grp USA.

Living in Harmony: Improving Sibling Relationships. John F. Taylor. 1 cass. (Running Time: 45 min.). (Answers to ADD Ser.). 1993. 9.95 (978-1-883963-09-5(5)) ADD Plus.

Lecture tape.

Living in Harmony: The Art of Understanding Thoughts & Behaviors. Zara D. Wilson. Read by Zara D. Wilson. 1 cass. (Running Time: 40 mins.). 2001. 19.95 (978-0-9709024-0-5(9)) Fitlyland.

Recipe for living in harmony: Expect others to differ, recognize differences, embrace differences and respect differences because they are purposeful.

Living in Hell. unabr. ed. Ghazal Omid. Read by Ghazal Omid. (Running Time: 17 hrs. 53 mins.). (J). 2007. 32.95 (978-0-7861-4920-9(5)); audio compact disk 44.95 (978-0-7861-7052-4(2)); audio compact disk 32.95 (978-0-7861-5926-0(X)) Blckstn Audio.

Living in Hope: Viola Desmond's Story. Marcia Johnson. Contrib. by Klea Scott & Andrew Moodie. Prod. by Gregory J. Sinclair. (Running Time: 3600 sec.). (ENG.). 2007. audio compact disk 15.95 (978-0-660-19737-1(5)) Canadian Broadcasting CAN.

Living in Joy. Eldon Taylor. 2 cass. (Running Time: 62 min. per cass.). (Omniphonics Ser.). 29.95 incl. script Set. (978-1-55978-806-9(2), 4007) Progress Aware Res.

3-D soundtrack with underlying subliminal affirmations, night & day versions.

***Living in Love: Co-hosts of TV's LIFE Today, James & Betty Share Keys to an Exciting & Fulfilling Marriage.** unabr. ed. James Robison & Betty Robison. Narrated by Dean Gallagher & Rebecca Gallagher. (Running Time: 5 hrs. 56 mins. 4 sec.). (ENG.). 2010. 18.19 (978-1-60814-747-2(9)) Oasis Audio.

***Living in Love: James & Betty Share Keys to an Exciting & Fulfilling Marriage.** unabr. ed. James Robison & Betty Robison. Narrated by Dean Gallagher & Rebecca Gallagher. (Running Time: 5 hrs. 56 mins. 4 sec.). (ENG.). 2010. audio compact disk 25.99 (978-1-59859-812-4(0)) Oasis Audio.

Living in Mystery. Ragini E. Michaels. Read by Ragini E. Michaels. Music by Divyam Ambodha. 1 cass. (Running Time: 30 min.). (Facticity Ser.). 1995. 14.95 (978-1-887367-00-4(4), FTAT-204) Facticity Tr.

Supports your unconsciousness mind to recognize & remember the awe, wonder & mystery which lives & breathes us alive each day.

Living in Oneness. Swami Amar Jyoti. 1 cass. 1989. 9.95 (A-44) Truth Consciousness.

Life with an enduring sense of the fundamental truth of Oneness. Love & joy, the Creator/creation relationship. Without exception, whatever we experience is a part of ourselves.

Living in Partnership. Riane Eisler & David Loye. 1 cass. 9.00 (A0404-89) Sound Photosyn.

A visit to the home of the couple that coined the expression "Partnership," & its opposite, "Dominator Society," to see how it works.

Living in Perpetual Peace. unabr. ed. Philip K. Burley. Read by Philip K. Burley. Contrib. by Hilary Stagg. 1 cass. (Running Time: 22 min.). (Stress Management Meditation Ser.). (YA). (gr. 4 up). 1988. 10.00 (978-1-883389-10-9(0)) Adv In Mastery.

A spoken, guided visualization exercise for complete mental, emotional & physical relaxation & stress management.

Living in Prosperity. Kenneth Copeland. 8 cass. 1983. bk. & stu. ed. 40.00 (978-0-938458-21-0(3)) K Copeland Pubns.

How to live in prosperity.

Living in the Balance of Grace & Faith: Cd Album. Created by Awmi. (ENG.). 2009. audio compact disk 35.00 (978-1-59548-187-0(7)) A Wommack.

Living in the Last Days. Gloria Copeland & Billye Brim. (BVOV Ser.). 2006. audio compact disk 15.00 (978-1-57562-855-4(4)) K Copeland Pubns.

Living in the Light. rev. ed. Shakti Gawain. Read by Shakti Gawain. 2 cass. (Running Time: 3 hr.). 1995. 15.95 set. (978-1-882591-03-9(8), 956) Nataraj Pub.

Shakti tells you how to become attuned with the creature power of the universe.

Living in the Light: A Guide to Personal & Planetary Transformation. 2nd abr. rev. ed. Shakti Gawain. Read by Shakti Gawain. 2 cass. (Running Time:

3 hrs.). 1998. 17.95 (978-1-57731-048-8(9)) Pub: New Wrld Lib. Dist(s): PerseuPGW
How to follow one's own intuition & rely on it as a guiding force in life. In addition to balancing feminine & masculine energy, she examines other polarities that we all have.

Living in the Light: On Mastering Creative Visualization. unabr. ed. Shakti Gawain. (Running Time: 1 hr.). (Quest Ser.). 2009. audio compact disk 14.99 (978-1-4233-7828-0(8), 9781423378280, Bril Audio CD Unabri) Brilliance Audio.

Living in the Light: On Mastering Creative Visualization. unabr. ed. Shakti Gawain. Read by Shakti Gawain. (Running Time: 1 hr.). (Quest Ser.). 2009. 39.97 (978-1-4233-8026-9(6), 9781423380269, Brinc Audio MP3 Lib); 14.99 (978-1-4233-8025-2(8), 9781423380252, Brilliance MP3); audio compact disk 39.97 (978-1-4233-8024-5(X), 9781423380245, BriAudCD Unabrid) Brilliance Audio.

Living in the Light of Eternity: Your Life Can Make a Difference. K. P. Yohannan. 4 cass. (Running Time: 6 hrs.). 1999. 15.99 (978-1-56599-989-3(4)) Yahshua Pub.

Living in the Lion's Den... & Surviving. Bruce A. Baldwin. 2 cass. (Running Time: 90 min. per cass.). 1991. 49.95 video, 90 mins. (978-0-933583-16-0(8), VCR 101) Direction Dynamics.
In this acclaimed seminar on lifestyle management, Dr. Baldwin presents specific symptoms of personal burnout as they develop in the home along with effective strategies to reverse this pattern so destructive to marriage, family life, & personal well being.

Living in the Lion's Den...& Surviving. Bruce A. Baldwin. 2 cass. (Running Time: 90 min. per cass.). 1991. 18.95 set, vinyl case. (978-0-933583-18-4(4), PDC 201) Direction Dynamics.

Living in the Moment. Tek Young Lin & Galek Rinpoche. 2 cass. 16.95 (978-1-879323-06-3(0), OC279-62) Sound Horizons AV.

Living in the Now. unabr. ed. David Steindl-Rast. 4 cass. (Running Time: 3 hr. 50 min.). 1988. 36.00 Set. (05109) Big Sur Tapes.
Explores the question, "How do we find the child in us," & looks at practical ways of freeing & feeding the child. "Life-serious is far more serious than dead-serious, & that is playfulness".

Living in the Power of Redemption. Speeches. Creflo A. Dollar. 3 cass. (Running Time: 4 hrs.). 2002. 15.00 (978-1-59089-478-1(2)) Creflo Dollar.

Living in the Presence of God. Swami Amar Jyoti. 1 cass. 1990. 9.95 (A-45) Truth Consciousness.
In presence of mind, perspective changes. Life is transformed into Life Divine, alive & conscious in the present moment.

Living in the Present. 1 cass. (Running Time: 1 hr.). 1979. 7.95 (978-1-58638-561-3(5)) Nilgiri Pr.
Getting over "hurrying sickness" & resentments to live each day fully.

Living in the Spectrum: Autism & Asperger's, Vol. 1. Excerpts. Ed. by Jeff LaDuke. Narrated by Lecia Macryn. (Running Time: 55 mins.). 2004. audio compact disk 16.95 (978-0-9765760-0-6(7)) Mindscape Prods.
Educational audio CD about Autism and Asperger Syndrome containing interviews with people who have Autism & Asperger's, parents and specialists.

Living in the Spirit. 7 cass. 24.95 (2072, HarperThor) HarpC GBR.

Living in the World: Prison or Classroom. Kenneth Wapnick. 8 CDs. 2003. audio compact disk 50.00 (978-1-59142-105-4(5), CD87) Foun Miracles.

***Living in the World: Prison or Classroom.** Kenneth Wapnick. 2010. 40.00 (978-1-59142-389-8(9)) Foun Miracles.

Living Intuitively. abr. ed. Bruce Way. Read by Bruce Way. 2 cass. (Running Time: 2 hrs. 30 min.). 1997. 17.95 (978-1-57453-177-0(8)) Audio Lit.
Will help release your creativity & introduce you to a world of total possibility. Guided workshops & practical exercises show how to open to a fuller, more complete life.

Living Is Forever. 2nd unabr. ed. J. Edwin Carter. Read by Cliff Korradi & Kelly Joyce Neff. Ed. by Robert S. Friedman. 12 cass. (Running Time: 18 hrs.). Dramatization. 1994. pap. bk. 49.95 Set. (978-1-57174-016-8(3)) Hampton RdsPub.
A novel about the disastrous - but ultimately beneficial - changes caused by earthquakes worldwide.

Living Is Now in Session: Proceedings of the 45th Annual Convention National Association of Evangelicals Buffalo, New York. Read by Pamela Heim. 1 cass. (Running Time: 60 min.). 1987. 4.00 (313) Nat Assn Evan.

Living Issues with Dying Patients. Lynwood Swanson & Beverly Kirayoglu. 1986. 10.80 (0206A) Assn Prof Chaplains.

Living It Up. Nan Allen & Dennis Allen. 10 cass. (Running Time: 10 hrs.). (YA). 2001. bk. 54.99 (TA-9246PK); 12.99 (TA-9246C) Lillenas.
A new collection of music & drama from the youth choir's best friends. A powerful package for teens incorporating original songs, contemporary favorites & popular worship choruses. A bible study based on the message & music helping teens internalize the concepts they sing about.

Living Italian. 2 cass. (Running Time: 1 hr. 20 min.). (LivingLang) Random Info Grp.

Living Italian. 2 cass. (Running Time: 1 hr. per cass.). (Living Language Ser.). (ITA.). 1991. bk. 20.00 incl. manual & dictionary. (LivingLang) Random Info Grp.

Living Japanese. 2 cass. (Running Time: 1 hr. 30 min.). (LivingLang) Random Info Grp.

Living Joyfully. Swami Amar Jyoti. 1 cass. 1989. 9.95 (A-43) Truth Consciousness.
Paying attention without getting stuck in misplaced seriousness. Releasing consciousness for a refreshed, free-flowing life.

Living Language Courses. unabr. ed. 2 cass. bk. 29.95 J Norton Pubs.

Living Language English for German Speakers. 2 CDs. (Living Language Ser.). 2005. audio compact disk 39.95 (978-1-57970-176-5(0), AFE610D) J Norton Pubs.

Living Language English for Italian Speakers. 2 CDs. (Running Time: 2 hrs.). (Living Language Ser.). 2005. audio compact disk 39.95 (978-1-57970-178-9(7), AFE615D) J Norton Pubs.

Living Language French: Basic-Intermediate. unabr. ed. 8 CDs. (Running Time: 8 hrs.). (Ultimate Courses Ser.). (FRE & ENG.). 2000. pap. bk. 75.00 (LivingLang) Random Info Grp.

Living Language French: Basic-Intermediate. unabr. ed. 8 cass. (Running Time: 8 hrs.). (Ultimate Courses Ser.). (FRE & ENG.). (C). 2000. pap. bk. 75.00 (LivingLang) Random Info Grp.

Living Language German: Basic-Intermediate. unabr. ed. 8 cass. (Running Time: 8 hrs.). (Ultimate Courses Ser.). (GER & ENG.). (C). 2000. pap. bk. 75.00 (LivingLang); pap. bk. 75.00 (LivingLang) Random Info Grp.

Living Language Italian: Basic-Intermediate. unabr. ed. 8 cass. (Running Time: 8 hrs.). (Ultimate Courses Ser.). (ITA & ENG.). (C). 2000. pap. bk. 75.00 (LivingLang); pap. bk. 75.00 (LivingLang) Random Info Grp.

Living Language Japanese: Basic-Intermediate. unabr. ed. 8 cass. (Running Time: 8 hrs.). (Ultimate Courses Ser.). (JPN & ENG.). (C). 2000. pap. bk. 75.00 (LivingLang); pap. bk. 75.00 (LivingLang) Random Info Grp.

Living Language Spanish: Basic-Intermediate. unabr. ed. 8 cass. (Running Time: 8 hrs.). (Ultimate Courses Ser.). (SPA & ENG.). (C). 2000. pap. bk. 75.00 (LivingLang); pap. bk. 75.00 (LivingLang) Random Info Grp.

Living Latin: A Contemporary Approach. C. W. Ashley. 6 cass. (YA). (gr. 7-12). 1984. 175.00 Set. (978-0-8442-8615-0(X), Natl Textbk Co) M-H Contemporary.

Living Life see Vivir la Vida

Living Life! Anxiety & Stress Free: Reduce Stress through Hypnosis. Trevor H. Scott. 2003. audio compact disk 19.95 (978-0-9763138-7-8(1)) Beverly Hills CA.

Living Life by God's Standards: Measuring up to God's Ways. Short Stories. Taffi L. Dollar. 5 cass. (Running Time: 5 hrs.). 2005. 25.00 (978-1-59089-943-4(1)); audio compact disk 34.00 (978-1-59089-944-1(X)) Creflo Dollar.

Living Life Intentionally. Richard W. Luecke. 1 cass. 1996. 12.00 (978-1-889774-01-5(4)) Lucky Lrning.
Eighty plus messages of inspiration designed primarily for sales people.

Living Life with a Purpose. As told by Frank Damazio. 7 cass. 1998. 35.00 (978-1-886849-39-6(0)) CityChristian.

Living Liturgy: Spirituality, Celebration & Catechesis for Sundays & Solemnities: Year C. 2001. Joyce Ann Zimmerman et al. 2003. audio compact disk 15.95 (978-0-8146-2741-9(2)) Liturgical Pr.

Living Long, Living Strong: Discovering the Requirements for Long Life. Creflo A. Dollar. (ENG.). 2006. audio compact disk 14.00 (978-1-59944-144-3(6)) Creflo Dollar.

Living Longer, Living Better. Barbara Miklos. 6 cass. (Running Time: 5 hrs.). 1999. pap. bk. 49.95 (978-1-930496-00-2(1)) W J Commn Inc.

Living Meditation; A Ministry Anointing. Ann Ree Colton & Jonathan Murro. 1 cass. 7.95 A R Colton Fnd.

Living Memories of the Coulee City Area. Interview. 17 CDs. (Running Time: 20 hrs.). 2007. ring bd. 89.95 (978-0-9673527-2-5(X)) Wallace Bk Co.

Living Myths & Rituals Through Dance. Anna Halprin. 2 cass. 18.00 set. (A0299-88) Sound Photosyn.

Living Now: Secrets of the Extraordinary Life. Guy Finley. (ENG.). 2005. 24.95 (978-1-929320-41-7(8)) Life of Learn.

Living Now: Secrets of the Extraordinary Life. Guy Finley. 2005. reel tape 39.95 (978-1-929320-19-6(1)); audio compact disk 49.95 (978-1-929320-20-2(5)) Life of Learn.

Living on Baby Time. unabr. ed. Susan Besze Wallace & Monica Reed. Narrated by Christian Taylor. (Running Time: 1 hr. 36 mins. 47 sec.). (New Moms' Guides). (ENG.). 2009. 9.09 (978-1-60814-490-7(9)) Oasis Audio.

Living on Baby Time. unabr. ed. Susan Wallace & Monica Reed. Narrated by Christian Taylor. (Running Time: 1 hr. 36 mins. 47 sec.). (New Moms' Guides). (ENG.). 2008. audio compact disk 12.99 (978-1-59859-486-7(9)) Oasis Audio.

***Living on Our Heads: Righting an Upside-down Culture.** unabr. ed. Rod Parsley. (Running Time: 7 hrs. 0 mins. 0 sec.). (ENG.). 2011. audio compact disk 25.99 (978-1-59859-875-9(9)) Oasis Audio.

Living on the Black: Two Pitchers, Two Teams, One Season to Remember. unabr. ed. John Feinstein. Narrated by Mel Foster. (Running Time: 18 hrs. 30 mins. 0 sec.). (ENG.). 2008. audio compact disk 39.99 (978-1-4001-0749-0(0)); audio compact disk 29.99 (978-1-4001-5749-5(8)); audio compact disk 79.99 (978-1-4001-3749-7(7)) Pub: Tantor Media. Dist(s): IngramPubServ

Living on the Edge: Hebrews 11:30-31. Ed Young. 1992. 4.95 (978-0-7417-1926-3(6), 926) Win Walk.

Living on the Faultline: Managing for Shareholder Value in the Age of the Internet. Geoffrey A. Moore. 4 cass. (Running Time: 6 hrs.). 2000. 25.95 HarperCollins Pubs.

Living on the Ragged Edge. 2005. 79.00 (978-1-57972-679-9(8)); audio compact disk 79.00 (978-1-57972-678-2(X)) Insight Living.

Living Oprah: My One-Year Experiment to Walk the Walk of the Queen of Talk. unabr. ed. Robyn Okrant. Read by Robyn Okrant. (Running Time: 8 hrs. 30 mins.). (ENG.). 2010. 24.98 (978-1-60788-359-3(7)) Pub: Center St. Dist(s): HachBkGrp

Living Out the Gospel of Life. John A. Hardon. 9 cass. (Running Time: 90 min. per cass.). 36.00 Set. (95J) IRL Chicago.

Living Outloud, Vol. 1. Perf. by Greg Batton & Yvonne Greer. Interview with John Williams. 2 cass. (Running Time: 2 hr.). 1999. 14.95 (978-0-9675049-0-2(2), Living Out) Power Zone.

Living Outloud, Vol. 2. unabr. ed. Interview with Greg Batton et al. 2 cass. (Running Time: 2 hr.). 1999. 14.95 (978-0-9675049-1-9(0), Living Out) Power Zone.

Living Outside Life's Struggle. Emmet Fox. 1 cass. (Running Time: 60 min.). (Sermon on the Mount Ser.). 9.95 HarperCollins Pubs.

Living Outside the Fortress. unabr. ed. Galexis. 2 cass. (Running Time: 3 hrs.). (Fortress Ser.: Vol. 3). 1997. 19.95 Set. (978-1-56089-049-2(5), G130) Visionary FL.
Emerging from the Fortress, here's what you can do to orient yourself in your new, free but vulnerable life. Meditation included.

Living Outside the Fortress, Pt. 2. unabr. ed. Galexis. 2 cass. (Running Time: 3 hrs.). (Fortress Ser.: Vol. 4). 1997. 19.95 (978-1-56089-052-2(5), G133) Visionary FL.
How to keep your psychic/emotional/physical energy "flowing" in your new life outside the Fortress.

Living Peace & Joy: 15-Minute Guided Relaxations. abr. ed. Gael Chiarella. (Running Time: 2 hrs. 0 mins. 0 sec.). 2007. audio compact disk 19.98 (978-1-55961-842-7(6)) Pub: Relaxtn Co. Dist(s): S and S Inc

Living Portraits of the Church. 2 cass. (Running Time: 4 hrs.). 1998. 11.95 (978-1-57972-288-3(1)) Insight Living.

Living Proof. Genevox Music Staff. 2000. audio compact disk 16.98 (978-0-633-00604-4(1)) LifeWay Christian.

Living Proof. unabr. ed. John Harvey. Narrated by Ron Keith. 6 cass. (Running Time: 8 hrs. 30 mins.). (Charlie Resnick Mystery Ser.: Vol. 7). 1996. 51.00 (978-0-7887-0507-6(5), 94700E7) Recorded Bks.
Nottingham detective Charlie Resnick has returned in a gritty romp through the seamy side of publishing rivalries & British high society.

Living Proof Live. Travis Cottrell. 1998. 11.98 (978-0-7673-9419-2(4)); audio compact disk 16.98 (978-0-7673-9420-8(8)) LifeWay Christian.

Living Proof Live. Travis Cottrell. 1999. audio compact disk 45.00 (978-0-633-03884-7(9)) LifeWay Christian.

Living Proof Live. Travis Cottrell. 2000. 11.98 (978-0-633-00605-1(X)); audio compact disk 45.00 (978-0-633-00602-0(5)) LifeWay Christian.

Living Proof Live, Vol. 2. Travis Cottrell. 2000. 40.00 (978-0-633-00603-7(3)) LifeWay Christian.

***Living Reality: Authentic Awakening in Action.** Featuring Adyashanti. (ENG.). 2009. audio compact disk 42.00 (978-1-933986-65-4(4)) Open Gate Pub.

Living Rich for Less: Create the Lifestyle You Want by Giving, Saving, & Spending Smart. abr. ed. Ellie Kay. Read by Ellie Kay. 3 CDs. (Running Time: 3 hrs. 30 mins.). (ENG.). 2008. audio compact disk 19.95 (978-0-7393-8313-1(2), Random AudioBks) Pub: Random Audio Pubg. Dist(s): Random

***Living Right in a Wrong World.** Charles R. Swindoll. 2009. audio compact disk 50.00 (978-1-57972-866-3(9)) Insight Living.

Living Room. Graham Greene. Contrib. by Julian Sands et al. (Running Time: 5880 sec.). 2006. audio compact disk 25.95 (978-1-58081-348-8(8)) L A Theatre.

Living Russian. 2 cass. (Running Time: 1 hr. 20 min.). (LivingLang) Random Info Grp.

Living Sacrifice. John MacArthur, Jr. 4 cass. 15.95 (20159, HarperThor) HarpC GBR.

Living Sacrifice. John Stevenson. 1 cass. 10.98; audio compact disk 14.98 (978-7-900606-27-3(0)) Destiny Image Pubs.

Living Sacrifice: At the Table of Our Lord: Romans 12:1-2. Ed Young. 1984. 4.95 (978-0-7417-1395-7(0), 395) Win Walk.

Living Sober II. Dennis C. Daley & Gerald T. Rogers. 1996. pap. bk. & wbk. ed. 3.95 (978-1-56215-078-5(2), Jossey-Bass) Wiley US.

Living Sober II Series. Directed By Gerald T. Rogers. Contrib. by Dennis C. Daley. 1996. pap. bk. 395.00 Set, NTSC. (978-1-56215-080-8(4), Jossey-Bass) Wiley US.

Living Sober I. Dennis C. Daley & Gerald T. Rogers. 1994. pap. bk. & tchr. ed. 8.95 (978-1-56215-073-0(1), Jossey-Bass); pap. bk. & wbk. ed. 3.95 (978-1-56215-074-7(X), Jossey-Bass) Wiley US.

Living Sober I, Pt. A. Directed By Gerald T. Rogers. Contrib. by Dennis C. Daley. (Living Sober Ser.: Segment A). 1994. pap. bk. 89.00 NTSC. (978-1-56215-050-1(2), Jossey-Bass) Wiley US.

Living Sober Series. Directed By Gerald T. Rogers. Contrib. by Dennis C. Daley. 1994. pap. bk. 495.00 NTSC. (978-1-56215-079-2(0), Jossey-Bass) Wiley US.

Living Solutions. Excerpts. Thomas Junior Strawser. 2 CDs. (Running Time: 2 hrs.,17 mins). (ENG.). 2002. audio compact disk (978-0-9755695-1-1(1)) My Lvng Solutions.
THE LIVING SOLUTIONS: 2 full length CD's and a 64-page self-acceptance workbook introduce this innovative system and guide readers through fundamental concepts. The Solutions teach a scientific approach to spirituality that offers specific guidelines to improve self-esteem and find the absolute best relationships in life. Sadness, grief, disappointment and other painful feelings are inevitable. However, this CD introduces techniques to live through this pain without experiencing the emotional misery of anger, guilt, remorse, fear, worry, jealousy, and many other self-destructive emotions.

Living Space see Science Fiction Favorites of Isaac Asimov

Living Spanish: Advanced Course. 2 cass. (Running Time: 1 hr. 20 min.). (LivingLang) Random Info Grp.

Living Spirituality. Swami Amar Jyoti. Read by Swami Amar Jyoti. 1 cass. 1982. 9.95 (A-17) Truth Consciousness.
Our first fallacy, separating Creator & creation. Applying spiritual truths to all the problems of the world.

Living Strong Living Long: Discovering the Requirements for Long Life. Creflo A. Dollar. (ENG.). 2006. 10.00 (978-1-59944-143-6(8)) Creflo Dollar.

***Living Successfully with Screwed-up People.** unabr. ed. Elizabeth Brown. Narrated by Pam Ward. (ENG.). 2009. 12.98 (978-1-59644-828-5(8), Hovel Audio) christianaud.

***Living Successfully with Screwed-up People.** unabr. ed. Elizabeth B. Brown & Elizabeth Brown. Narrated by Pam Ward. (Running Time: 7 hrs. 21 mins. 0 sec.). (ENG.). 2009. audio compact disk 21.98 (978-1-59644-827-8(X), Hovel Audio) christianaud.

Living Temple of Witch V01. Christopher Penczak. (Penczak Temple Ser.). 2008. audio compact disk 26.95 (978-0-7387-1430-1(5)) Llewellyn Pubns.

Living Temple of Witchcraft, Vol. 2. Christopher Penczak. (Penczak Temple Ser.). (ENG.). 2009. audio compact disk 27.95 (978-0-7387-1481-3(X)) Llewellyn Pubns.

Living the Beatitudes. Adrian Van Kaam & Susan Muto. 4 cass. (Running Time: 6 hrs. 55 min.). 1994. 34.95 (TAH320) Alba Hse Comns.
Exceptional material, filled with modern examples for personal & group reflection. Excellent for monthly day of recollection. Primarily presented for lay people but good for religious & priests as well. Suitable for a parish course in spirituality.

Living the Blues: Blues Legends. 1 cass. 1999. 9.99 (TRA698); audio compact disk 9.99 (GSCM11) Time-Life.

***Living the Cross Centered Life: Keeping the Gospel the Main Thing.** unabr. ed. C. J. Mahaney. Narrated by Lloyd James. (ENG.). 2007. 14.98 (978-1-59644-514-7(9), Hovel Audio) christianaud.

Living the Cross Centered Life: Keeping the Gospel the Same Thing. unabr. ed. Frwd. by Albert R. Mohler. (Running Time: 3 hrs. 42 mins. 0 sec.). (ENG.). 2007. audio compact disk 23.98 (978-1-59644-513-0(0), Hovel Audio) christianaud.

Living the Diamond Way. Ole Nydahl. 2 cass. 18.00 Set. (A0468-89) Sound Photosyn.

Living the Divine Purpose. Amar Jyoti. 1 cass. (Satsangs of Swami Amar Jyoti Ser.). (C). 1997. 9.95 (A-54) Truth Consciousness.
Recognizing Absolute Truth in every aspect of our lives; making life a yoga. A new covenant with the Lord.

Living the Dream: A Powerful 7 Step Guide to Achieving Your Dreams! Jennifer Yessler & Hug Audio. Read by Diane Burket. Ed. by Dave Bolick et al. Kristen Dewulf & Lisa Pavlock. (ENG.). 2008. audio compact disk 9.99 (978-0-9820704-0-6(3)) HUG.

Living the Dream: A Tribute to Martin Luther King Jr. 1 cass., 1 CD. 8.78 (HIPO 40101); audio compact disk 13.58 NewSound.

Living the Dream Audio Journal: Insights Audio Journal. Jennifer Yessler. Read by Diane Burket. Ed. by Valerie Walker & Tracy Dodson. (ENG.). 2009. spiral bd. 24.99 (978-0-9820704-5-1(4)) HUG.

Living the Dream Audio Workbook: Progress Audio Workbook-A Powerful 7 Step Guide to Achieving Your Dream. Jennifer Yessler. Read by Diane Burket. Ed. by Valerie Walker & Tracy Dodson. (ENG.). 2009. spiral bd. 29.99 (978-0-9820704-4-4(6)) HUG.

Living the Exchanged Life. Read by Lee Lefebre. 1 cass. (GraceLife Conference Ser.: Vol. 8). 6.00 (978-1-57838-120-3(7)) CrossLife Express.
Christian living.

Living the Exchanged Life. Read by Lee Lefebre. 1 cass. (Running Time: 1 hr. 17 min.). (Exchanged Life Conference Ser.: Vol. 8). 1993. 6.00 (978-1-57838-012-1(X)) CrossLife Express.

Living the Fatima Message. John A. Hardon. 1 cass. 1991. 2.50 (978-1-56036-049-0(6)) AMI Pr.

Living the Field: Tapping into the Secret Force of the Universe. Lynne McTaggart. Read by Lynne McTaggart. 6 CDs. (Running Time: 21600 sec.). 2007. audio compact disk 69.95 (978-1-59179-571-1(0), AF01146D) Sounds True.

Living the Good Life: How to Live Sanely in a Troubled World. unabr. collector's ed. Helen Nearing & Scott Nearing. Read by Jill Masters. 6 cass. (Running Time: 9 hrs.). 1986. 48.00 (978-0-7366-1054-4(5), 1981) Books on Tape.
In 1932, they were moved from New York City to a farm in the Green Mountains of Vermont. Their purpose was to seek a simple, satisfying life on the land, away from the stresses of depression & city life. "Living the Good Life" first published in 1954, presents a technical, economic, sociological & psychological report of how they fared.

Living the High Life. Jeremy Pearsons. (ENG.). (YA). 2006. audio compact disk 15.00 (978-1-57562-917-9(8)) K Copeland Pubns.

Living the Kingdom of God Lifestyle. Featuring Bill Winston. 2 cass. 2006. 10.00 (978-1-59544-179-9(4)); audio compact disk 16.00 (978-1-59544-180-5(8)) Pub: B Winston Min. Dist(s): Anchor Distributors

Living the Liberated Life & Dealing with the Pain Body. unabr. ed. Eckhart Tolle. Read by Eckhart Tolle. 3 CDs. (Running Time: 3 hrs.). (Power of Now Teaching Ser.). 2001. audio compact disk 27.95 (978-1-56455-945-6(9)) Sounds True.
Somewhere between the past and the future lies a dimension that is free of problems, free of suffering, free of conflict. This is the essence of all the world?s spiritual teachings. And it is available to you now, in the moment you read this. In Living the Liberated Life and Dealing with the Pain-Body, Eckhart Tolle points a way out of the conditioned mind that keeps us trapped, helpless, and unhappy.

Living the Platinum Rule: How to Get What You Want by Giving Others What They Want. Tony Alessandra. 6 cass. (Running Time: 6 hrs.). 1996. 59.95 (14320A) Nightingale-Conant.

Living the Prosperity Consciousness. Emmet Fox. 1 cass. (Running Time: 60 min.). (Sermon on the Mount Ser.). 9.95 HarperCollins Pubs.

Living the Real Religion. Swami Amar Jyoti. 2 dolby cass. 1985. 12.95 (Q-20) Truth Consciousness.
In the clear blue sky of consciousness, life as it should be. Living according to the basic principles that really matter.

***Living the Skinny Life: The Real Skinny on Fit, Slim, & Healthy.** Made for Success. Read by Crystal Dwyer. (Running Time: 3.5 hrs. NaN mins.). (Made for Success Ser.). (ENG.). 2011. audio compact disk 24.95 (978-1-4417-7262-6(6)); audio compact disk 90.00 (978-1-4417-7261-9(8)) Blckstn Audio.

Living the Trinity. Douglas Jones. (ENG.). 2008. audio compact disk 16.00 (978-1-59128-477-2(5)) Canon Pr ID.

Living the Truth: Transform Your Life Through the Power of Insight & Honesty. abr. ed. Keith Ablow. (Running Time: 3 hrs.). (ENG.). 2007. 14.98 (978-1-59483-900-9(X)) Pub: Hachet Audio. Dist(s): HachBkGrp

Living the Word Filled Life of New Beginnings - by Walking & Praying in the Spirit. 2005. 15.00 (978-1-933561-14-1(9)) BFM Books.

Living the 7 Habits. Stephen R. Covey. 5 cass. 59.95 (10080PAX) Nightingale-Conant.
Expanding on The 7 Habits of Highly Effective People, Covey shows you how the seven habits provide an "anchor" for coping with a rapidly changing world, how to apply these habits to the personal, private & spiritual aspects of your life & how these habits will enable you to live with a sense of constancy amid change. You'll learn to...Deepen your mission statement; Develop an abundance mentality in accordance with natural law; Empower yourself & those around you. Includes workbook & laminated chart.

Living the 7 Habits. abr. ed. Stephen R. Covey. 1 cass. 1996. 9.95 (51994) Books on Tape.
Stephen Covey expands on the principles set forth in his bestseller, "The 7 Habits of Highly Effective People," providing deep insights to help us make the habits part of our daily lives.

Living the 7 Habits: Stories of Courage & Inspiration. Stephen R. Covey. 5 cass. 59.95 Set, incl. wkbk. (267-C47) Natl Seminars.
This program shows how the Seven Habits provide an "anchor" for coping with a rapidly changing world. Change may inspire some to rethink the way they live. Dealing with change is the focus of Covey's newest program.

Living the 7 Habits: Stories of Courage & Inspiration. abr. ed. Stephen R. Covey. Read by Stephen R. Covey. 1 cass. (Running Time: 1 hr. 30 min.). 1995. 12.00 (978-0-671-51994-0(8), 390132, Sound Ideas) S&S Audio.
Expands on the principles set forth in "The 7 Habits of Highly Effective People." Here are valuable insights that will deepen our understanding of the habits & allow us to make them part of our daily lives.

Living the 7 Habits: Understanding Using Succeeding. abr. ed. Stephen R. Covey. Featuring Stephen R. Covey. 1 CD. (Running Time: 11 hrs. 20 mins. 0 sec.). (ENG.). 1999. audio compact disk 14.00 (978-0-671-04650-7(0), Sound Ideas) Pub: S&S Audio. Dist(s): S and S Inc

Living Through Breast Cancer. abr. ed. Carolyn M. Kaelin. Narrated by Bernadette Dunne. Told to Francesca Coltrera. (Running Time: 10800 sec.). 2005. audio compact disk 22.95 (978-1-933310-00-8(6)) STI Certified.

Living Through Grief. Matthew Manning. Read by Matthew Manning. Music by Enid. 2 cass. 21.95 (MM-102) White Dove NM.
This intensive tape took over two years to research & produce. Death arouses many deep emotions. The tape explains these emotions as well as physical symptoms & the five stages of grief. It also examines do's & don'ts for helping the bereaved. Matthew's reassurance & supportive voice in a visualization help you to live through grief & adjust to a new life. Music by the Enid.

Living to Serve. Speeches. Joel Osteen. 1 Cass. (Running Time: 30 Mins.). 2001. 6.00 (978-1-59349-092-8(5), JA0092) J Osteen.

Living Together. unabr. ed. Alan Ayckbourn. Perf. by Alan Ayckbourn. Perf. by Martin Jarvis & Jane Leeves. 1 cass. (Running Time: 1 hr. 23 mins.). 2001. 20.95 (978-1-58081-157-6(4), TPT101) L A Theatre.
The Norman Conquests revolves around a lascivious librarian with designs on three different women. In the second "Battle," events unfold in the living room, where Norman's overindulgence wreaks havoc on his already clumsy approaches to the opposite sex.

Living Trust Alternative: End Probate Worries for Your Family. Louis Austin. 2 cass. (Running Time: 2 hrs.). pap. bk. 18.95 (978-0-9625528-3-0(6)) Hudspeth Pub.
A live seminar featuring living trust attorney, Louis Austin. He explains, in everyday langauge, how a living trust will provide security for you & your family by avoiding probate, saving taxes & much, much more.

Living Trusts. 1991. 60.00 (AC-604) PA Bar Inst.

Living Truth of the Prophets. Swami Amar Jyoti. 1 dolby cass. 1984. 9.95 (Q-19) Truth Consciousness.
The Prophets, our living, guiding beacon lights. Direct Truth vs. priestly authority. "Rebellion" & "independence"; these terms & others are perverted in ego's name.

Living under God's Commanded Blessings. Creflo A. Dollar. 15.00 (978-1-59089-042-4(6)) Pub: Creflo Dollar. Dist(s): STL Dist NA

***Living under the Blessing.** Featuring Mason Betha. (ENG.). 2009. 20.00 (978-1-60989-003-2(5)) Born To Succee.

***Living Unity.** Featuring Adyashanti. (ENG.). 2010. audio compact disk Rental 65.00 (978-1-933986-72-2(7)) Open Gate Pub.

Living up the Street. unabr. ed. Gary Soto. Narrated by Robert Ramirez. 4 pieces. (Running Time: 5 hrs. 30 mins.). (gr. 6 up). 2000. 35.00 (978-0-7887-0429-1(X), 94621E7) Recorded Bks.
Growing up Mexican-American in Fresno, California in the 1950s & 60s might not have been easy, but it was certainly never boring for young Gary Soto, his brother Rick & sister Debra. Gary, author of "The Skirt," teaches creative writing at the University of California, Berkeley. He often writes about what it is like growing up Mexican-American & passes along humorous & compelling life lessons & tales of coming of age.

***Living up There.** Jane Wodening. Narrated by Jane Wodening. (ENG.). 2010. audio compact disk 24.00 (978-0-9790171-2-4(2)) Boneworthy.

Living up to Death. Sogyal Rinpoche. 2 cass. 1992. 18.00 set. (OC299-66) Sound Horizons AV.

Living Versus Existing & Hope. 1 cass. (Recovery Is Forever Ser.). 1981. 8.95 (1537G) Hazelden.

Living Water. Neville Goddard. 1 cass. (Running Time: 62 min.). 1964. 8.00 (97) J & L Pubns.
Neville taught Imagination Creates Reality. He was a powerfully influential teacher of God as Consciousness.

***Living Water: Powerful Teachings from the International Bestselling Author of the Heavenly Man.** Brother Yun. Ed. by Paul Hattaway. (Running Time: 8 hrs. 24 mins. 0 sec.). (ENG.). 2008. 14.99 (978-0-310-30253-7(6)) Zondervan.

Living Water: Powerful Teachings from the International Bestselling Author of the Heavenly Man. unabr. ed. Brother Yun. Ed. by Paul Hattaway. (Running Time: 8 hrs. 24 mins. 0 sec.). (ENG.). 2008. audio compact disk 19.99 (978-0-310-29312-5(X)) Zondervan.

Living Water 50th. Contrib. by John Michael Talbot & Billy Ray Hearn. Prod. by Phil Perkins. 2007. audio compact disk 16.99 (978-5-557-67131-6(5)) TroubadorPub GBR.

Living Well, Dying Well: Tibetan Wisdom Teachings. Sogyal Rinpoche. 1 CD. (Running Time: 4500 sec.). 2006. audio compact disk 14.95 (978-1-59179-511-7(7), AW00218D) Sounds True.
Tibetan Buddhism's essential teachings distilled into one lucid session, with the author of the international bestseller The Tibetan Book of Living and Dying.

***Living Well in a down Economy for Dummies.** abr. ed. Tracy Barr. Read by Brett Barry. (ENG.). 2008. (978-0-06-176387-8(X), Harper Audio); (978-0-06-176388-5(8), Harper Audio) HarperCollins Pubs.

Living Well in a down Economy for Dummies. abr. ed. Tracy L. Barr. Read by Brett Barry. (Playaway Adult Nonfiction Ser.). (ENG.). 2009. 39.99 (978-1-60812-577-7(7)) Find a World.

Living Wills & Medical Powers of Attorney: An Interdisciplinary Approach. 1998. bk. 59.00 (ACS-2109) PA Bar Inst.
When counseling a client regarding an advance health care directive or a medical power of attorney & when drafting these documents, you must be cognizant of the clinical practice setting in which these documents will be used. This manual provides the perspective a major metropolitan teaching hospital & a prominent bioethical center.

Living Wills in Pennsylvania. Read by David L. Hosteter. 1 cass. 1991. 20.00 (AL-107) PA Bar Inst.

Living Wisdom, Loving Life. Louise L. Hay. 4 cass. (Running Time: 4 hrs.). 1996. 49.95 (14090A) Nightingale-Conant.

Living with AIDS. Matthew Manning. 1 cass. 11.95 (MM-107) White Dove NM.
"AIDS has become more than a word, it's a sentence - a death sentence. We need to move beyond superstition & beliefs of inevitable death & realise that we can change these fear based reactions. I hope that this tape will help you transmute such fears so that you can start living more dynamically & more fully in the now. It is not intended to replace orthodox treatments, but I hope that my approach will help you to find a greater quality of life.".

Living with AIDS: One Man's Story. Archie Harrison. Read by Archie Harrison. 1 cass. (Running Time: 2 hrs.). 14.95 (I0190B090, HarperThor) HarpC GBR.

Living with Chronic Pain: The Complete Health Guide to the Causes & Treatment of Chronic Pain. abr. ed. Jennifer P. Schneider. Read by Bernadette Dunne. (Running Time: 10800 sec.). 2006. audio compact disk 22.95 (978-1-933310-12-1(X)) STI Certified.

Living with Confidence in a Chaotic World: What on Earth Should We Do Now? unabr. ed. David Jeremiah. Narrated by Wayne Shepherd. (Running Time: 7 hrs. 29 mins. 25 sec.). (ENG.). 2009. 19.59 (978-1-60814-599-7(9)); audio compact disk 27.99 (978-1-59859-647-2(0)) Oasis Audio.

Living with Coronary Disease. Robert Stromberg. 1986. 10.80 (0406) Assn Prof Chaplains.

Living with God's Kids. Kay Kuzma. 4 cass. (Running Time: 2 hrs.). 1992. bk. 30.00 (2003) Family Mtrs.
Insightful & innovative counsel to parents.

Living with Grace. Created by Bill Bauman. 2006. audio compact disk 15.00 (978-0-9765138-6-5(2)) Ctr Soulful.

Living with Intention: The Science of Using Thoughts to Change Your Life & the World. Lynne McTaggart. (Running Time: 18900 sec.). 2008. audio compact disk 69.95 (978-1-59179-947-4(3)) Sounds True.

Living with Jazz: An Appreciation. Frank P. Tirro. 3 CDs. (C). 1996. pap. bk. (978-0-15-503165-4(1)) Harcourt Coll Pubs.

Living with Joy: How You Can Stay Healthier. unabr. ed. Carl A. Hammerschlag. Read by Carl A. Hammerschlag. 3 cass. (Running Time: 2 hrs. 10 min.). (YA). 1993. 39.95 (978-1-889166-13-1(8)) Turtle Isl Pr.
Staying healthy, how to deal with cancer, guided imagery, stories for children, psychoneuroimmunology.

Living with Joy No. 1: The Science of Psychoneuroimmunology. unabr. ed. Carl A. Hammerschlag. Read by Carl A. Hammerschlag. 1 cass. (Running Time: 46 min.). (YA). 1993. 39.95 (978-1-889166-14-8(6)) Turtle Isl Pr.
This new medical science tells us that how you come to the stressful events in your life are more important than the events themselves. Your spirit can influence your destiny.

Living with Joy No. 2: Dealing with Cancer. Carl A. Hammerschlag. Read by Carl A. Hammerschlag. 1 cass. (Running Time: 44 min.). (YA). 1993. 39.95 (978-1-889166-15-5(4)) Turtle Isl Pr.
Practical ways about how to deal with cancer more effectively.

Living with Joy No. 3: Healing Stories for Children. unabr. ed. Carl A. Hammerschlag. Read by Carl A. Hammerschlag. 1 cass. (Running Time: 36 min.). (YA). 1993. 39.95 (978-1-889166-16-2(2)) Turtle Isl Pr.
Questions children ask about dealing with ordinary ups & downs.

Living with Leanne. unabr. ed. Margaret Clark. Read by Kate Hosking. 3 cass. (Running Time: 3 hrs. 35 mins.). 2002. (978-1-74030-251-7(6), 500851) Bolinda Pubng AUS.

Living with Love. J. Krishnamurti. (Running Time: 1 hr. 8 mins.). 2008. audio compact disk 16.95 (978-1-888004-54-0(1)) Pub: K Publications GBR. Dist(s): SCB Distributors

Living with Mindfulness & Purpose: Using Thoughts to Discover True Meaning & Happiness. Diane L. Tusek. Read by Diane L. Tusek. (ENG.). 2009. 39.99 (978-1-61574-705-4(2)) Find a World.

Living with Money-mp3. Read by Douglas Wilson. 1992. 12.00 (978-1-59128-221-1(7)) Canon Pr ID.

***Living with Questions.** unabr. ed. Dale Fincher. (Running Time: 6 hrs. 47 mins. 0 sec.). (ENG.). (YA). 2009. 9.99 (978-0-310-67005-6(5)) Zondervan.

Living with Sophia. Joan Chamberlain Engelsman. Read by Joan Chamberlain Engelsman. 1 cass. (Running Time: 1 hrs. 30 min.). 10.95 (978-0-7822-0527-5(5), 593) C G Jung IL.
Acknowledging the feminine dimension of the divine involves reconnecting the social, physical, political & psychological elements of our selves into a dynamic spirituality that is both prayerful & prophetic. Presentation discusses some of the theological images & issues that have begun to illuminate this process.

Living with the Dead: The Grateful Dead Story. abr. ed. Rock Scully & David Dalton. Read by Rock Scully. 2 cass. (Running Time: 3 hrs.). 1995. bk. 20.00 CD. (978-1-57042-379-6(2)); 17.00 Set. (978-1-57042-371-0(7)) Hachet Audio.
A memoir from 20-year Dead manager. Rock Scully tells about life with the wildest touring band of all time.

Living with the Himalayan Masters. unabr. ed. Swami Rama. Read by D. C. Rao. Intro. by Pandit R. Tigunait. 7 cass. (Running Time: 10 hrs. 30 mins.). 1998. audio compact disk 39.95 (978-0-89389-168-8(1), AB601MO) Pub: Himalayan Inst. Dist(s): Natl Bk Netwk

Living with the Lord. Read by Mother Basilea Schlink. 1 cass. (Running Time: 30 min.). 1985. (0208) Evang Sisterhood Mary.
Includes: At One with the Will of God; Daring Faith; Lay Down Your Life!; God, a Father of Comfort; Heavenly Home.

Living With the Past, the Present, & the Future. Instructed by Manly P. Hall. 8.95 (978-0-89314-164-6(X), C830925) Philos Res.

Living with Yogananda. Kriyananda, pseud. 1 cass. (Running Time: 85 min.). 9.95 (79-FS) Crystal Clarity.
Stories about Paramhansa Yogananda from Kriyananda's personal notebook.

Living with Your Choice: Healing the Emotional Wounds of Abortion. unabr. ed. Eric A. Braun & Laura Lee Gaudio. Read by Eric A. Braun & Laura Lee Gaudio. 2 cass. (Running Time: 40 min. per cass.). 1990. pap. bk. 19.95 (978-0-9625268-0-0(0)) Applied Wisdom.

Living Without Hipocrisy CD Series. 2003. audio compact disk 22.00 (978-1-59834-009-9(3)) Walk Thru the Bible.

Living Without Limits. abr. ed. Deepak Chopra & Wayne W. Dyer. 1 cass. (Running Time: 48 mins.). (ENG.). 1996. reel tape 11.95 (978-1-878424-23-5(8)) Amber-Allen Pub.

Living Without Limits. abr. ed. Deepak Chopra & Wayne W. Dyer. 1 CD. (Running Time: 2880 sec.). (ENG.). 2005. audio compact disk 12.95 (978-1-878424-96-9(3)) Amber-Allen Pub.

Living Without Limits: 10 Keys to Unlocking the Champion in You. Judy Siegle & Cindy Fahy. 2005. audio compact disk 14.95 (978-0-9766206-1-7(8)) Life V Pub Co.

Living Without Rules: Luke 6:20-45. Ed Young. 1996. 4.95 (978-0-7417-2090-0(6), 1090) Win Walk.

Living Without Stress or Fear: Essential Teachings on the True Source of Happiness. unabr. ed. Thich Nhat Hanh. (Running Time: 6:26:28). 2009. audio compact disk 69.95 (978-1-59179-725-8(X)) Sounds True.

Living Yesterday Today: Job 29:2. Ed Young. 1983. 4.95 (978-0-7417-1324-7(1), 324) Win Walk.

Living Your Dream. John Gray & John Selby. 2004. 11.95 (978-0-7435-4868-7(X)) Pub: S&S Audio. Dist(s): S and S Inc

Living Your Hearts Desire: How to Discover & Distinguish God's Personal Plan for You. 2. (Running Time: 2 hrs.). 2002. 10.00 (978-1-57399-104-9(X)) Mac Hammond.
In this two-tape series, Mac Hammond reveals the surest way to know God's will is as easy as idengifying the desires of your heart.

Livingstone & His African Journeys. unabr. collector's ed. Elspeth Huxley. Read by Walter Zimmerman. 6 cass. (Running Time: 6 hrs.). 1989. 36.00 (978-0-7366-1573-0(3), 2440) Books on Tape.
David Livingstone's journeys in Central Africa put more on the map of the dark continent than any other explorer's. He was the first European to cross Africa. He traced the Zambesi to its source & discovered one of the wonders of the world - the Victoria Falls. He was not only an explorer & geographer, but an anthropologist, botanist, ethnologist &, above all, a medical missionary. As a poor boy from Glasgow, he taught himself Greek, Latin & mathematics, so in 1840 when he arrived in Cape Town at age 27, it was with an unshakable purpose. It was severely tested over the next 30 years. Elspeth Huxley, herself an expert on Africa, portrays Livingstone as selfless. His own harsh judgment on himself was that he had failed to make sufficient discoveries or to convert Africans to Christianity in the numbers he had hoped.

Livre Blanc du Gouvernement de Transition. Gérard Latortue. (FRE.). 2007. cd-rom & audio compact disk 20.00 (978-1-58432-404-1(X)) Educa Vision.

Liz: An Intimate Biography of Elizabeth Taylor. unabr. ed. C. David Heymann. Read by Frances Cassidy. 13 cass. (Running Time: 19 hrs. 30 mins.). 1996. 104.00 (978-0-7366-3222-5(0), 3884) Books on Tape.
This intimate biography of a screen legend tells the many stories of Elizabeth Taylor...or the story of the many Elizabeth Taylors, take your pick. Rich with anecdotes & insights from more than a thousand interviews, Heymann presents Liz - the child star, the Oscar-winning actress, the eight-time wife, the fund-raiser for AIDS research & the person behind the persona. Liz is Hollywood's last great star. Though troubled by illnesses & injuries, drugs & alcohol, sex & scandal, she remains firmly fixed as a modern icon. Her lilac eyes dance with the joy of celebrity & cloud with the pain of it.

Liz Rosenberg. unabr. ed. Read by Liz Rosenberg & Rebekah Presson. Ed. by James McKinley. 1 cass. (Running Time: 29 min.). (New Letters on the Air Ser.). 1983. 10.00 (061083); 18.00 2-sided cass. New Letters.
Rosenberg is interviewed by Rebekah Presson & reads from her work.

Liza of Lambeth, unabr. ed. W. Somerset Maugham. Narrated by Davina Porter. 3 cass. (Running Time: 3 hrs. 30 mins.). 1987. 26.00 (978-1-55690-314-4(6), 87820E7) Recorded Bks.
A poor working-girl in the East End of London struggles to survive.

Liza of Lambeth. unabr. collector's ed. W. Somerset Maugham. Read by Wanda McCaddon. 5 cass. (Running Time: 5 hrs.). 1980. 30.00 (978-0-7366-0244-0(5), 1240) Books on Tape.
Tells of a warm-hearted young girl, smothered by the drab & sordid environment of London's tenement district. Externally, Liza fits this scene, but underneath stirs an unspoiled nature & warmth & a heart craving love & affection.

Lizard in the Fire. Short Stories. Read by Michael Meade. 1 cass. (Running Time: 60 min.). 1990. 9.95 (978-0-938756-28-6(1)); 10.95 Boxed. (978-0-938756-48-4(6)) Yellow Moon.
Two African stories with discussion of their relevance to the male psyche. Here are two stories in which the son encounters the great feminine in the world. In each story, when the youth leaves home, the separation evokes an initiation.

Lizard's Song see Cancion del Lagarto

Lizzie. Louise Brindley. Read by Julia Sands. 6 cass. (Storysound Ser.). (J). 1999. 54.95 (978-1-85903-292-3(3)) Pub: Mgna Lrg Print GBR. Dist(s): Ulverscroft US

Lizzie Borden. Elizabeth Engstrom. Read by Denise S. Utter. 8 cass. (Running Time: 10 hrs.). 1994. 44.95 (978-1-55686-522-0(8)) Books in Motion.
Did she do It? Did Lizzie Borden really kill her father & stepmother with an axe? Only Lizzie knows for certain. Here is a fictionalized version of what could have occurred.

Lizzie Bright & the Buckminster Boy. unabr. ed. Gary D. Schmidt. 5 cass. (Running Time: 6 hrs. 49 mins.). (YA). (gr. 6-9). 2005. 40.00 (978-0-307-20725-8(0), Listening Lib) Random Audio Pubg.
From the sad and shameful actual destruction of an island community in 1912, Schmidt weaves an evocative novel. When Turner Buckminster arrives in Phippsburg, ME, it takes him only a few hours to start hating his new home. Friendless and feeling the burden of being the new preacher's son, the 13-year-old is miserable until he meets Lizzie Bright Griffin, the first African American he has ever met and a resident of Malaga Island, an impoverished community settled by freed or possibly escaped slaves. Despite his father's and the town's stern disapproval, Turner spends time with Lizzie, learning the wonders of the Maine coast. For some minor infraction, Turner's father makes the boy visit elderly Mrs. Cobb, reading to her and playing the organ. Lizzie joins him, and this unlikely threesome takes comfort in the music. The racist town elders, trying to attract a lucrative tourist trade, decide to destroy the shacks on Malaga and to remove the community, including 60 graves in their cemetery. The residents are sent to the Home for the Feeble-Minded in Pownal. When Mrs. Cobb dies and leaves her house to Turner, he sets off to bring Lizzie home, only to find that she died shortly after arriving at the institution. Turner stands up to the racism of the town. His father, finally proud of him, stands with him-a position that results in the reverend's death. Although the story is hauntingly sad, there is much humor, too. Schmidt's writing is infused with feeling and rich in imagery.

Lizzie Bright & the Buckminster Boy. unabr. ed. Gary D. Schmidt. Read by Sam Freed. 6 CDs. (Running Time: 6 hrs. 49 mins.). (YA). (gr. 6-9). 2005. audio compact disk 42.50 (978-0-307-28185-2(X), Listening Lib) Pub: Random Audio Pubg. Dist(s): NetLibrary CO

Lizzie Bright & the Buckminster Boy. unabr. ed. Gary D. Schmidt. Read by Sam Freed. (Running Time: 6 hrs. 30 mins.). (ENG.). (J). (gr. 4-7). 2005. audio compact disk 34.00 (978-0-307-28183-8(3), Listening Lib) Pub: Random Audio Pubg. Dist(s): Random

Lizzie Dripping. Helen Cresswell. Read by Tina Heath. 2 cass. (Running Time: 2 hrs. 25 min.). (J). (gr. 2-5). 16.50 (978-0-14-088141-7(7), CC/044) C to C Cassettes.
Lizzie Dripping always tries to make life more exciting than it is if you leave it to itself. The results are unpredictable!.

Lizzie Nonsense Book & DVD Pack. Jan Ormerod. 2008. audio compact disk (978-1-921272-46-2(5)) Little Hare Bks AUS.

Lizzie of Langley Street. Carol Rivers. Read by Tanya Myers. 9 cass. (Running Time: 12 hrs.). (Story Sound Ser.). (J). 2005. 76.95 (978-1-85903-828-4(X)); audio compact disk 99.95 (978-1-85903-882-6(4)) Pub: Mgna Lrg Print GBR. Dist(s): Ulverscroft US

Llamado de la Selva. unabr. ed. Jack London. Read by Carlos J. Vega. 3 CDs.Tr. of Call of the Wild. (SPA.). 2002. audio compact disk 17.00 (978-958-9494-70-7(6)) YoYoMusic.

Llaman a la Puerta. Tr. of Doorbell Rang. 1991. 9.95 (978-1-59112-154-1(X)) Live Oak Media.

Llaman a la Puerta. Pat Hutchins. 1 cass. (Running Time: 35 min.). (SPA.). (J). 2001. 15.95 (VXS-41C) Kimbo Educ.

Llaman a la Puerta. Pat Hutchins. Illus. by Pat Hutchins. 14 vols. (Running Time: 6 mins.). 1996. pap. bk. 39.95 (978-1-59519-182-3(8)); 9.95 (978-1-59112-079-7(9)); audio compact disk 12.95 (978-1-59519-180-9(1)) Live Oak Media.

Llaman a la Puerta. Pat Hutchins. Illus. by Pat Hutchins. 11 vols. (Running Time: 6 mins.). (SPA.). (J). 1996. pap. bk. 18.95 (978-1-59519-181-6(X)) Pub: Live Oak Media. Dist(s): AudioGO

Llaman a la Puerta. unabr. ed. Pat Hutchins. Illus. by Pat Hutchins. Read by Susan Rybin. 14 vols. (Running Time: 6 mins.). (SPA.). 1996. pap. bk. & tchr. ed. 37.95 Reading Chest. (978-0-87499-372-1(5)) Live Oak Media.
Hutchins' mouthwatering story about Mama's freshly baked cookies will certainly appeal to Spanish speakers. The spirited illustrations, filled with cookies, interracial children, toys, & a cat, add a buoyant tone to this picture book that also teaches a thing or two about addition & subtraction in an appetizing manner.

Llaman a la Puerta. unabr. ed. Pat Hutchins. Illus. by Pat Hutchins. Read by Susan Rybin. 1 cass. (Running Time: 6 mins.). (SPA.). (J). (gr. k-3). 1996. bk. 24.95 (978-0-87499-371-4(7)); pap. bk. 16.95 (978-0-87499-370-7(9), LK1625) Pub: Live Oak Media. Dist(s): AudioGO

Llaves del Poder: Causalidad - Accion y Reaccion - Causa y Efecto. unabr. ed. Dario Silva.Tr. of Keys to Power - Key 3. (SPA.). 2003. audio compact disk 13.00 (978-958-8218-11-3(X)) YoYoMusic.

Llaves Del Poder: Desprendimiento - Tesoro Espiritual - Material. unabr. ed. Dario Silva.Tr. of Keys to Power - Key 1. (SPA.). 2003. audio compact disk 13.00 (978-958-8218-10-6(1)) YoYoMusic.

Llaves Del Poder: Palabra - Bendecir O Maldecir - Crear O Destruir. unabr. ed. Dario Silva.Tr. of Keys to Power - Key 4. (SPA.). 2003. audio compact disk 13.00 (978-958-8218-12-0(8)) YoYoMusic.

Llaves Del Poder Pautas para Una Vida Plena. unabr. ed. Silva-Silva Dario. (SPA.). 2006. audio compact disk 13.00 (978-958-8218-74-8(8)) Pub: Yoyo Music COL. Dist(s): YoYoMusic

Llaves Del Poder Pautas para Una Vida Plena. unabr. ed. Dario Silva.Tr. of Keys to Power - Key 2. (SPA.). 2003. audio compact disk 13.00 (978-958-8218-09-0(8)) YoYoMusic.

Llaves Del Poder Pautas para Una Vida Plena. unabr. ed. Dario Silva-Silva. (SPA.). 2006. audio compact disk 13.00 (978-958-8218-75-5(6)) Pub: Yoyo Music COL. Dist(s): YoYoMusic

Llaves del Poder 9 y 10: El Silencio - La Obediencia. unabr. ed. Dario Silva-Silva. Read by Dario Silva-Silva. (SPA.). 2006. audio compact disk 13.00 (978-958-8218-73-1(X)) YoYoMusic.

Llaves 7 Y 8: El Reposo - La Restitucion. unabr. ed. Dario Silva-Silva. Read by Dario Silva-Silva. (SPA.). 2006. audio compact disk 13.00 (978-958-8218-72-4(1)) Pub: Yoyo Music COL. Dist(s): YoYoMusic

LLC Picture Book Companion Audio CD- Vol. 1. Speeches. Narrated by Marilyn Circle Eagle. Prod. by Lakota Language Consortium. 1. (Running Time: 12 min.). (DAK.). (J). 2008. audio compact disk 14.95 (978-0-9821107-0-6(7)) Lakota Con.

Llegó el Amor. unabr. ed. Maria del Sol. 2002. audio compact disk 9.99 (978-0-8297-3702-8(2)) Zondervan.

Lleuad yn Olau. T. Llew Jones & Tympan. 2005. audio compact disk 13.99 (978-0-9546025-1-2(X)) Tympan GBR.

Lloyd Van Brunt. unabr. ed. Lloyd Van Brunt. Read by Lloyd Van Brunt. 1 cass. (Running Time: 29 min.). 1989. 10.00 New Letters.
Van Brunt reads his poetry & is interviewed.

Lo Mejor de Danilo Montero en Vivo. unabr. ed. Danilo Montero. 2 cass. (Running Time: 3 hrs.). 2004. 9.99 (978-0-8297-4564-1(5)) Pub: Vida Pubs. Dist(s): Zondervan

Lo Mejor de Marcos. unabr. ed. Marcos Witt.Tr. of Best of Marcos. (SPA.). 2003. 9.99 (978-0-8297-4384-5(7)); 9.99 (978-0-8297-4454-5(1)) Pub: Vida Pubs. Dist(s): Zondervan

***Lo mejor de Marcos Witt.** (SPA.). 2009. audio compact disk 19.99 (978-0-8297-6155-9(1)) Pub: CanZion. Dist(s): Zondervan

Lo Mejor de Marcos Witt. Marcos Witt. (SPA.). 2004. audio compact disk 14.99 (978-0-8297-4572-6(6)) Pub: Vida Pubs. Dist(s): Zondervan
No doubt Marcos Witt has been one of the most important promoters of Spanish praise and worship music. Rejoice together with Marcos by listening to the songs that brought a revival to church worship in Latin America, in this selection of the best of his albums «Sana nuestra tierra», «Vivencias», «Dios al mundo amó», «Enciende una luz», «Homenaje a Jesús» and «Él volverá».Songs:- Enciende una luz- Amaré al Señor mi Dios- Me asombra Tu amor- Yo no podría vivir- Mi primer amor- ¿Quién como Tú?- Tengo la palabra- Padre nuestro- Dios ha sido fiel- Jesús, eres mi buen pastor- Danzaré, cantaré- Dios al mundo amó.

Lo Mejor de Marcos Witt,Lo 3. unabr. ed. Marcos Witt. 2004. 9.99 (978-0-8297-4574-0(2)) Pub: Vida Pubs. Dist(s): Zondervan

Lo Mejor de Og Mandino. Og Mandino. 1 cass. (Running Time: 1 hr. 30 mins.).Tr. of Best of Og Mandino. (SPA.). 2001. Astran.

Lo mejor de ti: 7 Pasos para Mejorar Tu Vida Diaria. abr. ed. Joel Osteen. (Running Time: 6 hrs. 0 mins. 0 sec.). (SPA & ENG.). 2008. audio compact disk 29.95 (978-0-7435-7281-1(5)) Pub: S&S Audio. Dist(s): S and S Inc

Lo Que Ella Dice... lo Que el Entiende. Frances Soldi.Tr. of What She Says, What He Understands. (SPA.). 2003. (978-1-931059-30-5(6)) Taller del Exito.
Takes you by the hand through innovative concepts and illustrative metaphors related to the communication between couples from the man's and the woman's perspective.

Lo Que Esta en Mi Corazón. unabr. ed. Marcela Serrano. (SPA.). 2007. 67.75 (978-1-4281-6857-2(5)) Recorded Bks.

Lo Que Ha Hecho por Mi. unabr. ed. Ruth Rios. (SPA.). 2001. 9.99 (978-0-8297-3159-0(8)) Pub: Vida Pubs. Dist(s): Zondervan

Lo Que Los Esposos Desean see What Husbands Wish Their Wives Knew about Men

Lo Que Roba Nuestra Fe. Palemon Camu. 6 cass. (SPA.). 2003. 29.99 (978-0-89985-400-7(1)); audio compact disk 35.00 (978-0-89985-422-9(2)) Christ for the Nations.

Lo Que Todo Padre Desea Para Sus Hijos: Lo Que Todo Hijo Necesita de Sus Padres. Wayne W. Dyer. 2003. (978-1-931059-38-1(1)) Taller del Exito.

Load of Trouble. Barbara Davoll & Dennis Hockerman. Illus. by David Hockerman. 1 cass. (Christopher Churchmouse Ser.). (J). (gr. 4-7). 1988. bk. 11.99 (978-0-89693-618-8(X), 3-1618) David C Cook.

Loamhedge. Brian Jacques. Narrated by Brian Jacques. 12 CDs. (Running Time: 13 hrs. 30 mins.). (Redwall Ser.). 2004. audio compact disk 29.99 (978-1-4025-8739-9(2), 02492) Recorded Bks.

Loamhedge. unabr. ed. Brian Jacques. Narrated by Brian Jacques. 10 cass. (Running Time: 13 hrs. 30 mins.). (Redwall Ser.). 2003. 88.75 (978-1-4025-8228-8(5), 97702MC, Griot Aud) Recorded Bks.
New York Times best-selling author Brian Jacques has millions of copies in print of his tales starring the remarkable creatures of Mossflower country. In Loamhedge, Braggon the otter and Sarobando the squirrel embark on a special quest to a forgotten Abbey. But as soon as they are gone, Redwall Abbey is attacked by the ruthless searat Raga Bol and his villainous cronies.

Loan Documentation for Lawyers & Lenders: Practice under Revised Article 9 of the U. C. C. William H. Henning. 6 cass. (Running Time: 6 hrs.). 2001. pap. bk. 185.00 (978-0-943380-61-2(8)) PEG MN.

Lobbying for Foreign Agents & Foreign Principals: Capitol Learning Audio Course. Cleta Mitchell & Alan Rutenberg. Prod. by TheCapitol.Net. (ENG.). 2007. 47.00 (978-1-58733-070-4(9)) TheCapitol.

Lobbying for Libertarianism. unabr. ed. 1 cass. (Running Time: 32 min.). 12.95 (744) J Norton Pubs.
Explains how to influence government through lobbying.

Lobbying under the New Disclosure & Gift Ban Requirements: New ALI-ABA Course of Study - Friday-Saturday, February 21-22, 1997, Washington, D. C. ALI-ABA Committee on Continuing Professional Education. 7 cass. (Running Time: 9 hrs.). 1997. 295.00 (MB49) Am Law Inst.
Examines all aspects of the legislative process. Discusses the process & the various means to affect the outcome of the legislation under consideration. A faculty of Congressional staff members (both past & present) & practitioners describe what can happen in the legislative process, & why certain things happen.

Lobiaurs: Get Discovered. Lyrics by Daniel Gellasch & Sunshine Williams. 1. (Running Time: 41hrs.57mins). Orig. Title: The Lobiaurs Get Discovered. 2005. audio compact disk 10.00 (978-1-59971-287-1(3)) AardGP.

Lobiaurs Get Discovered see Lobiaurs: Get Discovered

Lobo: Songs & Games of Latin America. (Running Time: 1 hr.). (J). 1999. (978-1-57940-029-3(9)); audio compact disk Rounder Records.
Recorded on location in Mexico, Puerto Rico & Ecuador, these songs & singing games reveal the inner world of children, a realm of fantasy & reality co-existing in peaceful harmony. The collection consists of both songs from Spain brought by colonists centuries ago (& their variants in the New World) & songs created in the Americas with native roots & borrowings from Africa & the United States. Regardless of origins, these songs are an invitation to group activity: Form a circle & follow directions - clap hands or tap out a rhythm, play-act, dance & sing. Everyone can do it.

Lobo Estepario. abr. ed. Hermann Hesse. Read by Daniel Quintero.Tr. of Steppenwolf. (SPA.). 2006. audio compact disk 17.00 (978-958-8218-69-4(1)) Pub: Yoyo Music COL. Dist(s): YoYoMusic

Lobo y las Siete Cabritas. l.t. ed. Short Stories. Illus. by Graham Percy. 1 cass. (Running Time: 10 mins). Dramatization. (SPA.). (J). (ps-3). 2001. bk. 9.95 (978-84-86154-88-2(X)) Peralt Mont ESP.

Lobster Chronicles: Life on a Very Small Island. unabr. ed. Linda Greenlaw. Read by Linda Greenlaw. 5 cass. Library ed. (Running Time: 7 hrs.). 2002. 69.25 (978-1-59086-099-1(3), 1590860993, Unabridge Lib Edns); 27.95 (978-1-59086-098-4(5), 1590860985, BAU) Brilliance Audio.
After seventeen years at sea, Linda Greenlaw figured it was time to take a break from her career as a swordboat captain. She felt she needed to return to Isle au Haut - a tiny island seven miles from the Maine coast with a population of 70 year-round residents, 30 of whom were her relatives. She would pursue a simpler life; move back in with her parents and get to know them again; become a professional lobsterman; and find a guy, build a house, have kids, and settle down. But all doesn't go as planned. The lobsters resolutely refuse to crawl out from under their rocks and into the traps she and her stern man (AKA, her father) have painstakingly set. Her fellow Islanders, an extraordinary collection of characters, draw her into their bizarre Island intrigues. Guys prove even more elusive than lobsters. And as mainlanders increasingly fish waters that are supposed to be reserved for Islanders, she realizes that the Island might be heading for a "gear war," a series of attacks that had in the past escalated from sabotage of equipment to extreme violence. Then, just when she thinks things couldn't get much worse, something happens that forces her to reevaluate everything she thought she knew about life, luck, and lobsters.

Lobster Chronicles: Life on a Very Small Island. unabr. ed. Linda Greenlaw. Read by Linda Greenlaw. (Running Time: 7 hrs.). 2004. 39.25 (978-1-59335-452-7(5), 1593354525, Brlnc Audio MP3 Lib) Brilliance Audio.

Lobster Chronicles: Life on a Very Small Island. unabr. ed. Linda Greenlaw. Read by Linda Greenlaw. (Running Time: 7 hrs.). 2004. 39.25 (978-1-59710-464-7(7), 1597104647, BADLE); 24.95 (978-1-59710-465-4(5), 1597104655, BAD) Brilliance Audio.

Lobster Chronicles: Life on a Very Small Island. unabr. ed. Linda Greenlaw. Read by Linda Greenlaw. (Running Time: 7 hrs.). 2004. 24.95 (978-1-59335-100-7(3), 1593351003) Soulmate Audio Bks.

Lobster King. E. A. Olsen. (Oceanography Ser.). (J). (gr. 3 up). 1970. pap. bk. 10.60 (978-0-87783-192-1(0)) Oddo.

Lobsterpot Labyrinths see Twentieth-Century Poetry in English, No. 28, Recordings of Poets Reading Their Own Poetry

Lobsters. Short Stories. Charles Stross. Narrated by Jared Doreck & Shondra Marie. 1 CD. (Running Time: 70 min.). (Great Science Fiction Stories Ser.). 2005. audio compact disk 10.99 (978-1-884612-46-6(6)) AudioText.

Lobsters of the World. L. B. Holthuis. 1995. audio compact disk 114.00 (978-3-540-14198-3(7)) Spri.

Lobsters of the World. L. B. Holthuis. 1996. audio compact disk 96.00 (978-3-540-14197-6(9)) Spri.

Lobster's Secret. Kathleen M. Hollenbeck. 1 cass. (Running Time: 35 min.). (J). (ps-2). 2001. bk. 19.95 (SP 4010C) Kimbo Educ.
Lobster slips in & out of sheltering rocks & plants in search of food. Includes book.

Lobster's Secret. Kathleen M. Hollenbeck. Narrated by Peter Thomas. Illus. by Jon Weiman. 1 cass. (Smithsonian Oceanic Collection). (J). (ps-2). 1996. 5.00 (978-1-56899-283-9(1), C4010) Soundprints.
Beneath the nighttime waters of the Maine coast, a creature of the night crawls out of hiding in search of food. Slipping in & out of sheltering rocks & plants, Lobster conceals his secret from his predators. Although his shell appears to be strong & hard, Lobster has little protection from attack.

Lobster's Secret, Incl. Sm. & Lg. Plush Toy. Kathleen M. Hollenbeck. Illus. by Jon Weiman. Narrated by Peter Thomas. (Smithsonian Oceanic Collection). (J). (ps-2). 1996. bk. 38.95 (978-1-56899-652-3(7)) Soundprints.

Local Allusions in Joyce's Ulysses. unabr. ed. Joseph Prescott. 1 cass. (Running Time: 14 min.). 1970. 12.95 (23072) J Norton Pubs.
Deals with an aspect of James Joyce's "Ulysses", on which readers often need help: the Irish background.

Local & State GOVT. Compiled by Benchmark Education Staff. 2005. audio compact disk 10.00 (978-1-4108-5468-1(X)) Benchmark Educ.

Local Area Networks: Selection, Implementation, Expansion. 2 cass. 1990. 16.00 set. Recorded Res.

Local Area Networks: Text with Encore CD. Orin Thomas & Gary Govanus. (Netability Ser.). 2006. audio compact disk 54.95 (978-0-7638-2202-6(7)) Paradigm MN.

Local Business Taxes. 1986. bk. 80.00; 35.00 PA Bar Inst.

Local Custom. unabr. ed. Sharon Lee & Steve Miller. Narrated by Michael Shanks. 8. (Running Time: 10 hrs). Dramatization. (ENG.). 2006. audio compact disk 47.95 (978-0-9657255-7-6(X), Buzzy Audio) Buzzy Multimed.

Local Girls. abr. ed. Alice Hoffman. Read by Laural Merlington & Aasne Vigesaa. (Running Time: 3 hrs.). 2009. audio compact disk 9.99 (978-1-4418-1261-2(X), 9781441812612, BCD Value Price) Brilliance Audio.

Local Girls. abr. ed. Alice Hoffman. 2 cass. 1999. 17.95 (FS9-50885) Highsmith.

Local Girls. unabr. ed. Alice Hoffman. Read by Laural Merlington & Aasne Vigesaa. (Running Time: 4 hrs.). 2009. 24.99 (978-1-4418-1257-5(1), 9781441812575, Brilliance MP3); 24.99 (978-1-4418-1259-9(8), 9781441812599, BAD); 39.97 (978-1-4418-1258-2(X), 9781441812582, Brlnc Audio MP3 Lib); 39.97 (978-1-4418-1260-5(1), 9781441812605, BADLE); audio compact disk 24.99 (978-1-4418-1255-1(5), 9781441812551, Bril Audio CD Unabri); audio compact disk 69.97 (978-1-4418-1256-8(3), 9781441812568, BriAudCD Unabrid) Brilliance Audio.

Local Girls. unabr. ed. Alice Hoffman. 3 cass. 1999. 23.95 (FS9-43906) Highsmith.

***Local Habitation: An October Daye Novel.** unabr. ed. Seanan McGuire. Read by Mary Robinette Kowal. 1 MP3-CD. (Running Time: 12 hrs.). (October Daye Ser.). 2010. 14.99 (978-1-4418-5935-8(7), 9781441859358, Brilliance MP3); 24.99 (978-1-4418-5937-2(3), 9781441859372, BAD); 39.97 (978-1-4418-5936-5(5), 9781441859365, Brlnc Audio MP3 Lib); 39.97 (978-1-4418-5938-9(1), 9781441859389, BADLE); audio compact disk 29.99 (978-1-4418-5933-4(0), 9781441859334, Bril Audio CD Unabri); audio compact disk 89.97 (978-1-4418-5934-1(9), 9781441859341, BriAudCD Unabrid) Brilliance Audio.

Local Man Moves to the City: Loose Talk from American Radio Company. unabr. ed. Garrison Keillor. Contrib. by Garrison Keillor. (Running Time: 4500 sec.). (ENG.). 2005. audio compact disk 13.95 (978-1-59887-002-2(5), 1598870025) Pub: HighBridge. Dist(s): Workman Pub

Local Opportunities in the Decade of the '90s' National Association of Evangelicals, Columbus Ohio March 7-9, 1989. Jay Kesler. (Leadership Sessions Ser.: No. 6-Tuesday). 1989. 4.25 1-8 tapes.; 4.00 9 tapes or more. Nat Assn Evan.

Local Press see Osbert Sitwell Reading His Poetry

Local Scores. Terrance Cox. 1 CD. (Running Time: 1 hr. 2 mins.). 2004. audio compact disk 12.95 (978-1-894177-09-2(6)) Pub: Cyclops Pr CAN. Dist(s): Literary Pr Gp
One of the most exciting collaborations of poetry and music ever produced, and debuts here in oral form accompanied by a musical tour de force.

Local Space Astrology. Steve Cozzi. 1 cass. 8.95 (066) Am Fed Astrologers.
Practical use of individual planetary lines - -compass directions.

Local, State & Federal Taxes Affecting Real Estate Transactions. 1995. bk. 99.00 (ACS-969); bk. 99.00 (ACS-969) PA Bar Inst.
Geared for the general real estate practitioner, this will help you prepare for the often unforeseen tax consequences of the decisions you make in handling everyday transactions.

Local Wonders: Seasons in the Bohemian Alps. unabr. ed. Ted Kooser. Read by Ted Kooser. (Running Time: 5 hrs. 0 mins.). (ENG.). 2009. 19.95 (978-1-4332-2433-1(X)); 34.95 (978-1-4332-2429-4(1)); audio compact disk 49.00 (978-1-4332-2430-0(5)) Blckstn Audio.

Locally Unpopular Land Uses (LULUs) 1996. bk. 99.00 (ACS-1058) PA Bar Inst.
Focuses on locally unpopular land uses which include group homes, homeless shelters, AIDS hospices, "adult" uses, communications towers & "big box retailers." These controversial uses of land are generating hotly-contested disputes before governing bodies & zoning hearing boards in municipalities throughout the Commonwealth.

Locational Astrology & Myers-Briggs. Mary Beim. 1 cass. 1992. 8.95 (1008) Am Fed Astrologers.

Loch. unabr. ed. Paul Zindel. Narrated by George Guidall. 3 pieces. (Running Time: 4 hrs.). (gr. 5 up). 1997. 27.00 (978-0-7887-0394-2(3), 94586E7) Recorded Bks.
Tale of a fifteen-year-old boy's encounter with a Loch Ness-like monster trapped in a chilly New England lake. Will the boy befriend it or join those bent on destroying it?.

***Lochan.** John Beag. (ENG.). 1992. 11.95 (978-0-8023-7084-6(5)) Pub: Clo Iar-Chonnachta IRL. Dist(s): Dufour

Lochinvar see Classics of English Poetry for the Elementary Curriculum

Lock & Key. unabr. ed. Sarah Dessen. Contrib. by Rebecca Soler. 10 CDs. (Running Time: 11 hrs.). (ENG.). (gr. 7 up). 2008. audio compact disk 39.95 (978-0-14-314305-5(0), PengAudBks) Penguin Grp USA.

***Lock Artist.** Steve Hamilton. Contrib. by MacLeod Andrews. (Playaway Adult Fiction Ser.). 2010. 64.99 (978-1-4418-3792-9(2)) Find a World.

Lock Artist. unabr. ed. Steve Hamilton. Read by MacLeod Andrews. (Running Time: 13 hrs.). 2010. 24.99 (978-1-4418-1546-0(5), 9781441815460, Brilliance MP3); 24.99 (978-1-4418-1548-4(1), 9781441815484, BAD); 39.97 (978-1-4418-1547-7(3), 9781441815477, Brlnc Audio MP3 Lib); 39.97 (978-1-4418-1549-1(X), 9781441815491, BADLE); audio compact disk 29.99 (978-1-4418-1544-6(9), 9781441815446, Bril Audio CD Unabri); audio compact disk 89.97 (978-1-4418-1545-3(7), 9781441815453, BriAudCD Unabrid) Brilliance Audio.

Lockdown: scape from Furnace 1. unabr. ed. Alexander Gordon Smith. Read by Alex Kalajzic. (Running Time: 8 hrs.). (Escape from the Furnace Ser.). 2009. 24.99 (978-1-4418-3033-3(2), 9781441830333, Brilliance MP3); 24.99 (978-1-4418-3035-7(9), 9781441830357, BAD); 39.97 (978-1-4418-3034-0(0), 9781441830340, Brlnc Audio MP3 Lib); 39.97 (978-1-4418-3036-4(7), 9781441830364, BADLE); audio compact disk 24.99 (978-1-4418-3031-9(6), 9781441830319, Bril Audio CD Unabri) Brilliance Audio.

Lockdown: scape from Furnace 1. unabr. ed. Alexander Gordon Smith. Read by Alex Kalajzic. 7 CDs. (Running Time: 8 hrs.). (Escape from the Furnace Ser.: Bk. 1). (YA). (gr. 9 up). 2009. audio compact disk 60.97 (978-1-4418-3032-6(4), 9781441830326, BriAudCD Unabrid) Brilliance Audio.

Locke: The Last Rural Chinese Town in America. 1 cass. (Running Time: 30 min.). 9.95 (B0290B090, HarperThor) HarpC GBR.

Locked In A Room With All The Doors Open: 1 John 1:5-10. Ed Young. (J). 1980. 4.95 (978-0-7417-1132-8(X), A0132) Win Walk.

Locked in the Library! unabr. ed. Stephen Krensky. Read by Mark Linn-Baker. Characters created by Marc Brown. 1 cass. (Running Time: 40 mins.). (Arthur Chapter Bks.: Bk. 6). (J). (gr. 2-4). 1998. pap. bk. 17.00 (978-0-8072-0388-0(2), FTR192SP, Listening Lib) Random Audio Pubg.
Francine & Arthur get locked in the library together.

Locked Inside. unabr. ed. Nancy Werlin. Read by Emily Durante. 1 MP3-CD. (Running Time: 6 hrs.). 2009. 39.97 (978-1-4233-8070-2(3), 9781423380702, Brlnc Audio MP3 Lib); 39.97 (978-1-4233-8074-0(6), 9781423380740, BADLE); 24.99 (978-1-4233-8068-9(1), 9781423380689, Brilliance MP3); 24.99 (978-1-4233-8072-6(X), 9781423380726, BAD); audio compact disk 54.97 (978-1-4233-8066-5(5), 9781423380665, BriAudCD Unabrid); audio compact disk 26.99 (978-1-4233-8064-1(9), 9781423380641, Bril Audio CD Unabri) Brilliance Audio.

Locked Room. unabr. ed. Maj Sjöwall & Per Wahlöö. (Running Time: 1 hr. 0 mins.). 2009. 29.95 (978-1-4332-6363-7(7)); 59.95 (978-1-4332-6359-0(9)); audio compact disk 76.00 (978-1-4332-6360-6(2)) Blckstn Audio.

Locked Rooms. Laurie R. King. Narrated by Jenny Sterlin. (Mary Russell Mystery Ser.: Vol. 8). 2005. audio compact disk 39.99 (978-1-4193-3515-0(4)) Recorded Bks.

Locked Rooms. unabr. ed. Laurie R. King. Narrated by Jenny Sterlin. 12 CDs. (Running Time: 14 hrs.). (Mary Russell Mystery Ser.: Vol. 8). 2005. audio compact disk 119.75 (978-1-4193-4064-2(6), C3301); 94.75 (978-1-4193-4062-8(X), 98036) Recorded Bks.
Although other writers have tried, no one has matched King's ability to capture the allure of Sir Arthur Conan Doyle's legendary sleuth, Sherlock Holmes. Locked Rooms finds Holmes and wife Mary Russell arriving in San Francisco in 1924. They quickly learn there may be a great deal more to Mary's childhood in this city than either of them ever knew.

Locket. Richard Paul Evans. Read by Richard Thomas. 2004. 9.95 (978-0-7435-4972-1(4)) Pub: S&S Audio. Dist(s): S and S Inc

Locket. unabr. ed. Richard Paul Evans. Read by William Dufris. 8 vols. (Running Time: 12 hrs.). 2001. bk. 69.95 (978-0-7927-2451-3(8), CSL 340, Chivers Sound Lib) AudioGO.
After the death of his mother, Michael Keddington finds employment at the Arcadia nursing home where he befriends Esther, a reclusive but beautiful elderly woman who lives in mourning for her youth & lost love.

Locket. unabr. ed. Richard Paul Evans. Read by William Dufris. 8 CDs. (Running Time: 12 hrs.). 2001. audio compact disk 79.95 (978-0-7927-9943-6(7), SLD 094, Chivers Sound Lib) AudioGO.

Lockie Leonard, Human Torpedo. unabr. ed. Tim Winton. Read by Stig Wemyss. 3 cass. (Running Time: 3 hrs.). (Lockie Leonard Ser.: Bk. 1). (YA). 2004. 28.00 (978-1-86442-317-4(X), 581261) Bolinda Pubng AUS.
Lockie, hot surf-rat is in love. The human torpedo is barely settled into his new school, & already he's got a girl on his mind. And not just any girl: it has to be Vicki Streeton, the smartest, prettiest, richest girl in class. What chance have you got when your dad's a cop, your mum's a frighteningly understanding parent, your brother wets the bed & the teachers take an instant dislike to you? It can only mean trouble, worry, mega-embarrassment & some wild, wild times.

***Lockie Leonard, Legend.** unabr. ed. Tim Winton. Read by Stig Wemyss. (Running Time: 3 hrs. 30 mins.). (Lockie Leonard Ser.). (YA). 2004. audio compact disk 28.00 (978-1-74093-399-5(0)) Pub: Bolinda Pubng AUS. Dist(s): Bolinda Pub Inc

Lockie Leonard, Legend. unabr. ed. Tim Winton. Read by Stig Weymess. 3 cass. (Running Time: 3 hrs. 30 mins.). (Lockie Leonard Ser.: Bk. 3). (YA). (gr. 5-8). 2004. 28.00 (978-1-86442-316-7(1), BAB981262) Bolinda Pubng AUS.
Lockie has survived the worst year on record. His first year of high school, settling into a new town, his mad love affair - it's all behind him. He's about to turn fourteen & things are looking up. But his little brother's hormones have kicked in & that's not a pretty sight. His lino-munching baby sister refuses to walk or talk. His dad starts arresting farm animals & his mum suddenly won't stop crying. Right in the middle of this family shambles, an old flame comes scorching back into his life.

Lockie Leonard, Scumbuster. unabr. ed. Tim Winton. Read by Stig Weymess. 3 cass. (Running Time: 3 hrs.). (Lockie Leonard Ser.: Bk. 2). (YA). 1993. 28.00 (978-1-86442-367-9(6), 590374) Bolinda Pubng AUS.
Nothing's simple for Lockie. Dumped by his girlfriend he's back to being the loneliest kid in town until he makes friends with the wierdest human being he's ever met. As if that isn't enough, Lockie decides to save the planet, yes, he falls in love, he drops like a ton of bricks for a girl who's not even out of primary school yet & to make matters worse she surfs better than he ever will. Can a thirteen year old surfrat have a headbanger for a best friend, stay in love with an eleven year old frommet & still save his town from industrial pollution.

***Lockie Leonard, Scumbuster.** unabr. ed. Tim Winton. Read by Stig Wemyss. (Running Time: 3 hrs.). (YA). 2004. audio compact disk 54.95 (978-1-74093-398-8(2)) Pub: Bolinda Pubng AUS. Dist(s): Bolinda Pub Inc

Loco. unabr. ed. Lee Hoffman. Read by William Dufris. 4 cass. (Running Time: 5 hrs.). (Sagebrush Western Ser.). (J). 1999. 44.95 (978-1-57490-227-3(X)) Pub: ISIS Lrg Prnt GBR. Dist(s): Ulverscroft US

Loco for Latin: Alto Saxophone - Grade 3 - Book/CD Pack. Composed by James L. Hosay. 2003. pap. bk. 14.95 (978-90-431-1706-7(4), 9043117064) H Leonard.

Loco for Latin: Flute - Grade 3 - Book/CD Pack. Composed by James L. Hosay. 2003. pap. bk. 14.95 (978-90-431-1704-3(8), 9043117048) H Leonard.

Loco for Latin: Trombone - Grade 3 - Book/CD Pack. Composed by James L. Hosay. 2003. pap. bk. 14.95 (978-90-431-1708-1(0), 9043117080) H Leonard.

Loco for Latin: Trumpet - Grade 3 - Book/CD Pack. Composed by James L. Hosay. 2003. pap. bk. 14.95 (978-90-431-1707-4(2), 9043117072) H Leonard.

Locomotion. unabr. ed. Jacqueline Woodson. Read by J. D. Jackson. 1 cass. (Running Time: 1 hr. 30 mins.). (J). (gr. 4-6). 2003. 10.00 (978-1-4025-3949-7(5)) Recorded Bks.

Locust Songs see Poetry of Geoffrey

Lodger. Marie Belloc Lowndes & Lorna Raver. 6 cass. (Running Time: 8 hrs. 30 mins.). 2002. 44.95 (978-0-7861-2504-3(7), 3138) Blckstn Audio.

Lodger. Charles Nicholl. 2008. 61.95 (978-0-7531-3203-6(6)); audio compact disk 79.95 (978-0-7531-3204-3(4)) Pub: Isis Pubng Ltd GBR. Dist(s): Ulverscroft US

Lodger. unabr. ed. Marie Belloc Lowndes. Read by Lorna Raver. 7 CDs. (Running Time: 8 hrs. 30 mins.). 2000. audio compact disk 56.00 (978-0-7861-9026-3(4), 3138) Blckstn Audio.

Lodger: A Tale of the London Fog. unabr. ed. Marie Belloc Lowndes. Read by Lorna Raver. (Running Time: 8 hrs. 0 mins.). 2009. audio compact disk 19.95 (978-1-4332-7925-6(8)) Blckstn Audio.

Lodger: Story of Jack the Ripper. Perf. by Vincent Price & Cathy Lewis. (MM-5790) Natl Recrd Co.

Lodger Shakespeare: His Life on Silver Street. Charles Nicholl. Read by Simon Vance. (Playaway Adult Nonfiction Ser.). (ENG.). 2008. 64.99 (978-1-60514-851-9(2)) Find a World.

Lodger Shakespeare: His Life on Silver Street. unabr. ed. Charles Nicholl. Narrated by Simon Vance. (Running Time: 9 hrs. 0 mins. 0 sec.). (ENG.). 2008. audio compact disk 24.99 (978-1-4001-5628-3(9)); audio compact disk 69.99 (978-1-4001-3628-5(8)) Pub: Tantor Media. Dist(s): IngramPubServ

Lodger Shakespeare: His Life on Silver Street. unabr. ed. Charles Nicholl. Read by Simon Vance. (Running Time: 9 hrs. 0 mins. 0 sec.). (ENG.). 2008. audio compact disk 34.99 (978-1-4001-0628-8(1)) Pub: Tantor Media. Dist(s): IngramPubServ

Lodging for the Night see Bottle Imp & Other Stories

Log of a Cowboy: A Narrative of the Old Trail Days. abr. ed. Andy Adams. Read by Michael Martin Murphey. 2 cass. (Running Time: 3 hrs.). 1996. bk. 17.95 (978-1-57453-058-2(5)) Audio Lit.
Cowhand Adams tells of real cowboy life in the late 19th century: the dusty cattle drives, river crossings & meetings with Blackfoot, Oglala & Platte Indian tribes.

Logan's Choice, Level 2. Richard MacAndrew. Contrib. by Philip Prowse. (Running Time: 1 hr. 13 mins.). (Cambridge English Readers Ser.). (ENG.). 2001. 9.00 (978-0-521-79507-4(9)) Cambridge U Pr.

Logan's Fire. James R. Rada. 2 cass. 1996. 11.98 (978-1-55503-902-8(2), 07001290) Covenant Comms.
Three no-so-ordinary men on an extrordinary mission - to save a rebellious soul.

Logbook. 1 CD. Dramatization. (YA). 2004. audio compact disk 12.95 (978-0-9728150-2-4(3)) Ahquabi Hse.

Loggers. Rick Steber. Illus. by Don Gray. 1 cass. (Tales of the Wild West Ser.: Vol. 7). 1989. pap. bk. 9.95 (978-0-945134-57-2(6)) Bonanza Pub.

Logic & Mysticism. unabr. ed. Nathaniel Branden. 1 cass. (Running Time: 1 hr. 9 min.). (Basic Principles of Objectivism Ser.). 12.95 (563) J Norton Pubs.
Covers identity & causality; the validity of the senses; & reason vs. mysticism.

Logic & Theology: Paul's Use of Logic - Categorical Forms. John Robbins. 1 cass. (Introduction to Logic Ser.: No. 5). 5.00 Trinity Found.

Logic & Theology: Why Science Is Always False - Homework Review. John Robbins. 1 cass. (Introduction to Logic Ser.: No. 8). 5.00 Trinity Found.

Logic & Theology Pt. 1: The Westminster Confession - Informal Fallacies. John Robbins. 1 cass. (Introduction to Logic Ser.: No. 2). 5.00 Trinity Found.

Logic of International Diplomacy. unabr. ed. David Friedman. 1 cass. (Running Time: 40 min.). 12.95 (739) J Norton Pubs.

Logic of Life: The Rational Economics of an Irrational World. abr. ed. Tim Harford. Read by L. J. Ganser. (Running Time: 21600 sec.). (ENG.). 2008. audio compact disk 29.95 (978-0-7393-6556-4(8), Random AudioBks) Pub: Random Audio Pubg. Dist(s): Random

Logic of Pre-Electoral Coalition Formation. Sona Nadenichek Golder. (Parliaments & Legislatures Ser.). 2006. audio compact disk 9.95 (978-0-8142-9115-3(5)) Pub: Ohio St U Pr. Dist(s): Chicago Distribution Ctr

Logistics Pt. I: 1 Cor. 16:5-9. Ed Young. 1986. 4.95 (978-0-7417-1524-1(4), 524) Win Walk.

Logistics Pt. II: 1 Cor. 16:10-12. Ed Young. 1986. 4.95 (978-0-7417-1525-8(2), 525) Win Walk.

Logistics Products & Services in Hong Kong: A Strategic Reference 2007. Compiled by Icon Group International, Inc. Staff. 2007. ring bd. 195.00 (978-0-497-36000-9(4)) Icon Grp.

***Logos Latin 1 EFlashcards.** Julie Garfield. 2009. audio compact disk 19.00 (978-1-935000-20-4(9)) LogosPr.

***Logos Latin 2 EFlashcards.** Julie Garfield. Directed By Daniel Foucachon. 2010. audio compact disk 19.00 (978-1-935000-28-0(4)) LogosPr.

Logotherapy & Existentialism. unabr. ed. Viktor E. Frankl. 1 cass. (Running Time: 29 min.). 12.95 (29227) J Norton Pubs.
Examines logotherapy in relation to basic existential concepts, existential psychiatry in general & psycholanalysis.

Logra Vencer Tus Adicciones. Deepak Chopra. 1 cass. (Running Time: 1 hr. 30 mins.).Tr. of Succeed Against Drugs. (SPA.). 2001. Astran.

Logra Vencer Tus Adicciones. Deepak Chopra. 2 cass. (Running Time: 2 hrs.).Tr. of Succeed Against Drugs. (SPA.). 2002. (978-968-5163-12-5(X)) Taller del Exito.
Society has claimed its victims; dependency on food, drugs, caffeine, cigarettes, alcohol and sex has taken its toll on many. Explore the motivation behind these addictions and learn how to overcome them.

Loi du Desert, Pt. 1. Christian Jacq. Read by Pierre Forest. 4 cass. (Juge d'Egypte Ser.). (FRE.). 1996. 39.95 (1799-TH) Olivia & Hill.
In ancient Egypt, Juge Pazair pursues his investigation of the mysterious death of two guards of the Sphinx. The reader discovers the secrets of medicine, justice & life in that ancient civilization.

Loi du Desert, Pt. 2. Christian Jacq. Read by Pierre Forest. 4 cass. (Juge d'Egypte Ser.). (FRE.). 1996. 39.95 (1800-TH) Olivia & Hill.

Loi du Desert, Pts. 1 & 2. Christian Jacq. Read by Pierre Forest. 8 cass. (Juge d'Egypte Ser.: Vol. 2). (FRE.). 1996. 69.95 (1799/1800) Olivia & Hill.

Loint of Paw see Asimov's Mysteries

Lois Skiera-Zucek's Children's Songs about Saving Animals & the Rainforest with Help from a "Tree" Puppet & Members of Youth Audience; Fish Sampling & Native Rock Art. Hosted by Nancy Pearlman. 1 cass. (Running Time: 29 min.). 10.00 (1301) Educ Comm CA.

Loitering with Intent. unabr. ed. Muriel Spark. (Running Time: 18000 sec.). 2007. audio compact disk 19.95 (978-0-7861-6011-2(X)) Blckstn Audio.

Loitering with Intent. unabr. ed. Muriel Spark. Read by Nadia May. 4 CDs. (Running Time: 19800 sec.). 2007. audio compact disk 36.00 (978-0-7861-9432-2(4), 3002) Blckstn Audio.
"How wonderful to be an artist and a woman in the twentieth century," Fleur Talbot rejoices. Loitering about London, circa 1949, with intent to gather material for her writing, Fleur finds a job on the grubby edge of the literary world, as secretary to the odd Autobiographical Association. Are they mad egomaniacs, hilariously writing their memoirs in advance or poor fools ensnared by a blackmailer? Rich material, in any case. But when its pompous director, Sir Quentin, steals the manuscript of Fleur's new novel, fiction begins to appropriate life. The association's members begin to act out scenes exactly as Fleur herself had already written them in her missing manuscript. And as they meet darkly funny, pre-visioned fates, where does art start or reality end?.

Loitering with Intent. unabr. ed. Muriel Spark & Nadia May. 4 cass. (Running Time: 5 hrs. 30 mins.). 2002. 32.95 (978-0-7861-2316-2(8), 3002) Blckstn Audio.

Loitering with Intent. unabr. ed. Stuart Woods. Read by Tony Roberts. 6 CDs. (Running Time: 8 hrs.). (ENG.). (gr. 12 up). 2009. audio compact disk 29.95 (978-0-14-314451-9(0), PengAudBks) Penguin Grp USA.

Lola Haskins & Pattiann Rogers. unabr. ed. Read by Lola Hashkins & Pattiann Rogers. 1 cass. (Running Time: 29 min.). Incl. Castings; 1987. 10.00 New Letters.
Two poets read their from their works.

Lolita. abr. ed. Vladimir Nabokov. Perf. by James Mason. 1 cass. 1984. 12.95 (978-0-694-50951-5(5), SWC 1680) HarperCollins Pubs.

Lolita. abr. ed. Vladimir Nabokov. Perf. by James Mason. 1 cass. (Running Time: 1 hr. 01 min.). 1992. 12.00 (978-1-55994-634-6(2), DCN 1680, Harper Audio) HarperCollins Pubs.

Lolita. unabr. ed. Vladimir Nabokov. Read by Jeremy Irons. 8 cass. (Running Time: 12 hrs.). 2000. 39.95 (H860) Blckstn Audio.
Exhilarating, appallingly funny & hauntingly sad. For when the aging emigre Humbert Humbert falls in love with the precious nymphet Dolores Haze, all rules of desire, decency & literature are broken.

Lolita. unabr. ed. Vladimir Nabokov. Read by Jeremy Irons & Jeremy Irons. (Running Time: 12 hrs.). (ENG.). 2005. audio compact disk 30.00 (978-0-7393-2206-2(0), Random AudioBks) Pub: Random Audio Pubg. Dist(s): Random

Lolita. unabr. collector's ed. Vladimir Nabokov. Read by David Case. 10 cass. (Running Time: 15 hrs.). 1991. 80.00 (978-0-7366-1926-4(7), 2749) Books on Tape.
Lolita is the sensational best seller that blew away conventional restraints & took America by storm. Hubert Humbert is a middle age fantasist, still in love with Annabel, his first sweetheart. She was a beautiful & pure young woman who died years ago of typhus. Out of the blue Humbert finds a girl fatally reminiscent of Anabel. Her name is Dolores; he rechristens her Lolita. But instead of the innocence he expects, Lolita gives him steamy pubescence. She is greedily sensual, eager to earn her way into womanhood.

Lolita & Poems. unabr. ed. Vladimir Nabokov. Read by Vladimir Nabokov. 1 cass. (Running Time: 50 min.). 10.95 (978-0-8045-0902-2(6), SAC 43-1) Spoken Arts.

Lollipops & Spaghetti. Perf. by Jackie Silberg. 1 cass. (J). 1996. 10.95 (978-0-939514-13-7(3)) Miss Jackie.
Features fun-&-nonsense songs for children from 3 years old through primary grades.

***Lollipops Song.** Nita Buie. (ENG.). (J). 2010. audio compact disk 9.99 (978-1-61566-556-3(0)) Tate Pubng.

Lon Po Po. Ed Young. 1. 2006. 8.95 (978-0-439-87372-7(X)); audio compact disk 12.95 (978-0-439-87373-4(8)) Weston Woods.

Lon Po Po. unabr. ed. Ed Young. Narrated by B. D. Wong. 1 CD. (Running Time: 12 mins.). (J). (gr. k-4). 2006. pap. bk. 18.95 (978-0-439-87366-6(5), WPCD690) Weston Woods.

Lon Po Po. unabr. ed. Ed Young. Narrated by B. D. Wong. 1 CD. (Running Time: 12 mins.). (J). (gr. k-4). 2006. bk. 29.95 (978-0-439-87367-3(3),

WHCD690); pap. bk. 14.95 (978-0-439-87364-2(9), WPRA690); bk. 24.95 (978-0-439-87365-9(7), WHRA690) Weston Woods.
In this Chinese version of the classic fairy tale, a mother leaves her three children home alone while she goes to visit their grandmother. When the children are visited by a wolf, pretending to be their Po Po, or granny, they let him in the house, but ultimately are not fooled by his deep voice and hairy face. Combining ancient Chinese panel art techniques with a contemporary palette of watercolors and pastels, this powerful story brings lessons about strangers, trust and courage to a new generation.

Lon Po Po: A Red-Riding Hood Story from China. unabr. ed. Ed Young. Narrated by Christina Moore. 1 cass. (Running Time: 15 mins.). (gr. k up). 1989. 11.00 (978-0-7887-2496-1(7), 95571E7) Recorded Bks.
Three Chinese children outsmart a wolf who claims to be their grandmother. Valuable lessons about resourcefulness, teamwork & cultural differences.

Lon Po Po & Other Stories from the Asian Tradition: A Red-Riding Hood Story from China. Ed Young et al. Retold by Arlene Mosel. Narrated by B. D. Wong & Frances Kelley. (Playaway Children Ser.). (ENG.). (J). 2009. 44.99 (978-1-60812-564-7(5)) Find a World.

London, Pt. 1. unabr. collector's ed. Edward Rutherfurd. Read by David Case. 11 cass. (Running Time: 16 hrs. 30 min.). 1998. 88.00 (978-0-7366-4069-5(X), 4580-A) Books on Tape.
The historical epic follows the city's growth from Roman times throught the Victorian era.

London, Pt. 2. unabr. collector's ed. Edward Rutherfurd. Read by David Case. 11 cass. (Running Time: 16 hrs. 30 min.). 1998. 88.00 (978-0-7366-4070-1(3), 4580-B) Books on Tape.

London, Pt. 3. unabr. collector's ed. Edward Rutherfurd. Read by David Case. 10 cass. (Running Time: 15 hrs.). 1998. 80.00 (978-0-7366-4071-8(1), 4580-C) Books on Tape.

London: A History. unabr. ed. A. N. Wilson. Read by Christopher Kay. 4 cass. (Running Time: 6 hrs.). 2004. 49.75 (978-1-4193-0278-7(7)) Recorded Bks.

London: A Short History of the Greatest City in the Western World. Instructed by Robert Bucholz. 2009. 129.95 (978-1-59803-527-8(4)); audio compact disk 179.95 (978-1-59803-528-5(2)) Teaching Co.

London: The Inns & Outs of Court. unabr. ed. Gerald J. Morse. Read by Bernard Jacobson. 2 cass. (Running Time: 1 hr. 56 min.). (Talk-A-Walk Tours on Cassette Ser.). 1989. 17.50 (978-0-939969-05-0(X), LE9) Talk-a-Walk.
An historic walk through London's Inns of Court with commentary on the Lure of the Law. Detailed map included.

London: The Square Route - from Trafalgar Through Parliament to Queen Anne's Gate. Gerald J. Morse. Read by Bernard Jacobson. 1 cass. (Running Time: 1 hr. 25 min.). (Talk-A-Walk Tours on Cassette Ser.). 1989. 9.95 (978-0-939969-06-7(8), LE10) Talk-a-Walk.
A guided walk through London's core, its history, pageantry, architecture, & legend, reflecting the greatness of Britain. Detailed street map included.

London audio Guide. unabr. ed. Olivier Maisonneuve & Marlène Duroux. Read by Kate Gibbens & Ron Morris. (YA). 2007. 69.99 (978-2-35569-019-8(7)) Find a World.

London Bridge Is Falling Down! 2004. 8.95 (978-1-56008-958-2(X)); cass. & flmstrp 30.00 (978-1-56008-710-6(2)) Weston Woods.

London Bridges. unabr. ed. Read by Peter Jay Fernandez & Denis O'Hare. Adapted by James Patterson. 5 cass. (Running Time: 7 hrs. 30 min.). (Alex Cross Ser.: No. 10). 2004. 54.00 (978-1-4159-0491-6(X)) Books on Tape.

London Bridges. unabr. ed. James Patterson. Read by Peter Jay Fernandez & Denis O'Hare. 7 CDs. (Running Time: 7 hrs. 30 min.). (Alex Cross Ser.: No. 10). 2004. audio compact disk 72.00 (978-1-4159-0492-3(8)) Books on Tape.
From the author of Along Came a Spider and Kiss the Girls comes a new thriller featuring the detective Alex Cross. When terrorists seize London, Washington, DC, New York, and Frankfurt, threatening to destroy them unless their impossible demands are met,.

London Bridges. unabr. ed. James Patterson. Read by Peter Jay Fernandez & Denis O'Hare. (Alex Cross Ser.: No. 10). (ENG.). 2005. 14.98 (978-1-59483-137-9(8)) Pub: Hachet Audio. Dist(s): HachBkGrp

London Bridges. unabr. ed. James Patterson. Read by Peter Jay Fernandez & Denis O'Hare. (Running Time: 8 hrs.). (Alex Cross Ser.: No. 10). (ENG.). 2009. 59.98 (978-1-60024-896-2(9)) Pub: Hachet Audio. Dist(s): HachBkGrp

London Bridges. unabr. ed. Jane Stevenson. Narrated by Christopher Kay. 8 cass. (Running Time: 10 hrs. 45 mins.). 2000. 72.00 (978-1-84197-226-8(6), H1196L8, Clipper Audio) Recorded Bks.
When a young lawyer comes across a treasure lost in the Blitz, he becomes drawn into a series of crimes that have increasingly irreversible consequences. Eventually his crimes result in a murder. During these events, a contemporary assortment of characters seems to be assembling around him, leaving him in a state of confusion & bewilderment.

London Calling. unabr. ed. Edward Bloor. Read by Robertson Dean. 6 CDs. (Running Time: 7 hrs. 30 mins.). (YA). (gr. 6-9). 2006. audio compact disk 42.50 (978-0-7393-3788-2(2), Listening Lib) Pub: Random Audio Pubg. Dist(s): NetLibrary CO
Martin Conway comes from a family filled with heroes and disgraces. His grandfather was a statesman who worked at the US Embassy in London during WWII. His father is an alcoholic who left his family. His sister is an overachieving Ivy League graduate. And Martin? Martin is stuck in between - floundering. But during the summer after 7th grade, Martin meets a boy who will change his life forever. Jimmy Harker appears one night with a deceptively simple question: Will you help? Where did this boy come from, with his strange accent and urgent request? Is he a dream? It's the most vivid dream Martin's ever had. And he meets Jimmy again and again - but how can his dreams be set in London during the Blitz? How can he see his own grandfather, standing outside the Embassy? How can he wake up with a head full of people and facts and events that he certainly didn't know when he went to sleep - but which turn out to be verifiably real? The people and the scenes Martin witnesses have a profound effect on him. They become almost more real to him than his waking companions. And he begins to believe that maybe he can help Jimmy. Or maybe that he must help Jimmy, precisely because all logic and reason argue against it.

London Calling. unabr. ed. Edward Bloor. Read by Robertson Dean. (Running Time: 27000 sec.). (ENG.). (J). (gr. 5-7). 2006. audio compact disk 39.00 (978-0-7393-3666-3(5), Listening Lib) Pub: Random Audio Pubg. Dist(s): Random

London Child of The 1870s. Molly Hughes. Read by Celia Montague. 5 CDs. (Running Time: 5 hrs. 20 mins.). (Isis (CDs) Ser.). (J). 2004. audio compact disk 59.95 (978-0-7531-2273-0(1)) Pub: ISIS Lrg Prnt GBR. Dist(s): Ulverscroft US

London Child of the 1870s. unabr. ed. Molly Hughes. Read by Celia Montague. 5 cass. (Running Time: 7 hrs.). 2000. 49.95 (978-0-7531-0778-2(3), 000212) Pub: ISIS Audio GBR. Dist(s): Ulverscroft US
The author vividly evokes the small, everyday pleasures of a close family life in Victorian London: joyful Christmases, blissful holidays in Cornwall, escapades with her brothers, schooldays under the redoubtful Miss Buss.

London Eye Mystery. Siobhan Dowd. Read by Alex Kalajzic. (Playaway Children Ser.). (ENG.). (J). (gr. 3-7). 2008. 69.99 (978-1-60640-895-7(X)) Find a World.

London Eye Mystery. unabr. ed. Siobhan Dowd. Read by Alex Kalajzic. 1 MP3-CD. (Running Time: 6 hrs.). 2008. 39.25 (978-1-4233-7062-8(7), 9781423370628, Brlnc Audio MP3 Lib); 39.25 (978-1-4233-7064-2(3), 9781423370642, BADLE); 24.95 (978-1-4233-7061-1(9), 9781423370611, Brilliance MP3); 24.95 (978-1-4233-7063-5(5), 9781423370635, BAD); audio compact disk 74.25 (978-1-4233-7060-4(0), 9781423370604, BriAudCD Unabrid); audio compact disk 26.99 (978-1-4233-7059-8(7), 9781423370598, Bril Audio CD Unabri) Brilliance Audio.

London Girl of the 1870s. unabr. ed. Molly Hughes. Read by Celia Montague. 8 cass. (Running Time: 12 hrs.). 2001. 54.95 (000212) Pub: ISIS Audio GBR. Dist(s): Ulverscroft US

London Girl of The 1880s. Molly Hughes. Read by Celia Montague. 8 CDs. (Running Time: 8 hrs. 40 mins.). (Isis (CDs) Ser.). (J). 2004. audio compact disk 79.95 (978-0-7531-2323-2(1)) Pub: ISIS Lrg Prnt GBR. Dist(s): Ulverscroft US

London Girl of the 1880s. unabr. ed. Molly Hughes. Read by Celia Montague. 8 cass. (Running Time: 12 hrs.). 2000. 54.95 (978-0-7531-0871-0(2), 000613) Pub: ISIS Audio GBR. Dist(s): Ulverscroft US

London Home in the 1890s. Molly Hughes. Read by Celia Montague. 6 cass. (Running Time: 9 hrs.). 2001. 54.95 (000709) Pub: ISIS Audio GBR. Dist(s): Ulverscroft US

London Is the Best City in America. abr. ed. Laura Dave. Read by Renée Raudman. (Running Time: 4 hrs.). 2007. audio compact disk 14.99 (978-1-4233-2007-4(7), 9781423320074, BCD Value Price) Brilliance Audio.

London Is the Best City in America. unabr. ed. Laura Dave. Read by Renée Raudman. (Running Time: 7 hrs.). 2006. 39.25 (978-1-4233-2005-0(0), 9781423320050, BADLE); 24.95 (978-1-4233-2004-3(2), 9781423320043, BAD); 69.25 (978-1-4233-1999-3(0), 9781423319993, BrilAudUnabridg); audio compact disk 82.25 (978-1-4233-2001-2(8), 9781423320012, BriAudCD Unabrid); audio compact disk 39.25 (978-1-4233-2003-6(4), 9781423320036, Brlnc Audio MP3 Lib); audio compact disk 29.95 (978-1-4233-2000-5(X), 9781423320005); audio compact disk 24.95 (978-1-4233-2002-9(6), 9781423320029, Brilliance MP3) Brilliance Audio.
After making the difficult decision to call off her engagement, Emmy Everett left her life in New York City behind, and moved to a tiny fishing village in Rhode Island. She's been working on a documentary film, and generally avoiding the fact that she doesn't know what she wants to do with her life. But July 4th weekend has rolled around again, and Emmy is forced out of her self-imposed isolation - she has to return to her hometown (which is also the site of her failed romance with her ex-fiancé) for her brother Josh's wedding. Upon arrival, Emmy finds that Josh has a terrible case of cold feet. With less than twenty-four hours to go before the wedding, she takes him on an unforgettable road trip to help him figure out what he wants from life, and with whom he wants to spend it. Along the way Emmy learns some of her own lessons, and begins to realize that love, moving on, and happy endings that she thought were only found in movies, aren't a fantasy after all.

London Lass. Elizabeth Waite. Read by Annie Aldington. 12 cass. (Sound Ser.). (J). 2002. 94.95 (978-1-84283-224-0(7)) Pub: ISIS Lrg Prnt GBR. Dist(s): Ulverscroft US

London Lavender. unabr. ed. E. V. Lucas. Read by Peter Joyce. 5 cass. 1998. 49.95 (978-1-86015-451-5(4)) Pub: UlverLrgPrint GBR. Dist(s): Ulverscroft US
An entertaining portrait of life at the turn of the century. First published in 1912, the optimism of the new century is accurately depicted as it was before WWI.

London Life. unabr. ed. Henry James. Read by Flo Gibson. 3 cass. (Running Time: 4 hrs.). 1997. 16.95 (978-1-55685-438-5(2), 438-2) Audio Bk Con.
Contrasts in British & American manners & customs are cleverly drawn in this novella concerning an erupting marriage & an emerging love match & we are introduced to the marvelous Lady Davenant.

London Lodgings. unabr. ed. Claire Rayner. Read by Doreen Mantle. 12 cass. (Running Time: 13 hrs. 30 min.). (Quentin Quartet Ser.: Vol. 1). (J). 1996. 94.95 (978-1-85695-861-5(2), 9941106) Pub: ISIS Lrg Prnt GBR. Dist(s): Ulverscroft US

London Match, unabr. ed. Len Deighton. Read by Robert Whitfield. 9 cass. (Running Time: 13 hrs.). 1999. 62.95 (978-0-7861-1284-5(0), 2180) Blckstn Audio.
Here is the startling, conclusion in the game of defection begun in "Berlin Game" & intensified in "Mexico Set" with agent Bernard Samson enrolling his Soviet opposite number. The game reaches a new level of urgency when the treason epidemic in London Central comes to light.

London Match. unabr. ed. Len Deighton. Read by Paul Daneman. 10 cass. (Running Time: 15 hrs.). (Game, Set, & Match Ser.: Bk. 3). 2000. 69.95 (978-0-7451-4003-2(3), CAB 700) Pub: Chivers Audio Bks GBR. Dist(s): AudioGO
Bernard Samson hoped they'd put Elvira Miller behind bars, she was a KGB-trained agent whose carelessness had cost the agency a great deal of damage. But Mrs. Miller's confession was troubling: there were two code words where there should have only been one. Suspicions lead Samson back up to London where defector Erich Stinnes is locked up, refusing to speak. Samson had gotten him to London, now he had to get him to talk.

***London Match.** unabr. ed. Len Deighton. Read by Robert Whitfield. (Running Time: 12 hrs. 15 mins.). 2010. audio compact disk 29.95 (978-1-4417-0302-6(0)) Blckstn Audio.

London Match: Book 3 in the Samson Series. unabr. ed. Len Deighton. Read by Robert Whitfield. (Running Time: 12 hrs. 50 mins.). (ENG.). 2009. 29.95 (978-1-4417-0303-3(9)); audio compact disk 105.00 (978-1-4417-0300-2(4)) Blckstn Audio.

London Scene. (1787) Books on Tape.

London Tapes. Narrated by Juliet Stevenson. 2 cass. (Running Time: 2 hrs.). 1998. 16.95 incl. map. (978-1-900652-04-9(8)) Pub: Murchisons Pantheon GBR. Dist(s): Capital VA
Travel back in time to experience the sights, sounds & events of London's past at sixteen historic sites. In London, witness the execution of Charles I at the Banqueting House; join the crowds outside Buckingham Palace for a wedding tour; watch the Royal Barge bring Princess Elizabeth to the Tower; stand beside the river Thames & feel the terror of a Viking raid.

London to Ladysmith Via Pretoria. unabr. collector's ed. Winston L. S. Churchill. Read by David Case. 7 cass. (Running Time: 10 hrs. 30 min.). 1992. 56.00 (978-0-7366-2149-6(0), 2948) Books on Tape.
Churchill's experiences in the Boer War. True-life adventure.

London Town: A City Profile. Gerald J. Morse. 1 cass. (City Profiles Ser.). (J). 9.95 (978-0-939969-09-8(2), CP 1) Talk-a-Walk.
A general information reference especially for first time visitors to London.

Londonwalks. unabr. ed. Anton Powell. Read by Jean Marsh. Prod. by Carol Shapiro. 2 cass. (Running Time: 3 hrs.). 1997. 18.00 (978-1-890489-01-4(8)) Pub: Sound Trvl FRA. Dist(s): Penton Overseas
Listen to history, scandal and architectural curiosities while you stroll through one of the most magnificent cities of Europe. Maps included.

Lone Angler. abr. ed. Herb Curtis. Narrated by Richard Donat. 3 cass. (Running Time: 4 hrs.). (Between the Covers Collection). (ENG.). 2005. 19.95 (978-0-86492-242-7(6)) Pub: BTC Audiobks CAN. Dist(s): U Toronto Pr
In this entertaining comic novel rooted in New Brunswick's fabled Miramichi River region, two brothers set off to seek their fortunes in Texas and New York only to discover that they've taken the long route home. Stage and television actor Richard Donat has performed in more than fifty radio dramas.

Lone Calder Star. unabr. ed. Janet Dailey. Read by Anna Fields. 6 cass. (Running Time: 30000 sec.). (Calder Saga's Ser.). 2005. 54.95 (978-0-7927-3678-3(8), CSL 818); audio compact disk 74.95 (978-0-7927-3679-0(6), SLD 818) AudioGO.

Lone Cowboy: My Life Story. unabr. collector's ed. Will James. Read by Michael Prichard. 9 cass. (Running Time: 13 hrs. 30 mins.). 1985. 72.00 (978-0-7366-0800-8(1), 1750) Books on Tape.
James allows you to ride through the West with him while he experiences the sunshine, rains, blizzards & crosses of life on the range. He offers you a gentle horse to climb on & follow him.

Lone Eagle. Danielle Steel. 8 cass. (Running Time: 12 hrs.). 2001. 44.95 (978-0-7366-6740-1(7)) Books on Tape.

Lone Pine Canyon. Golana. (Running Time: 45 mins.). 2004. audio compact disk (978-1-891319-79-2(5)) Spring Hill CO.

Lone Ranger. 8 cass. (Running Time: 12 hrs.). 2003. 39.98 (978-1-57019-603-4(6), 4463) Radio Spirits.

Lone Ranger. Perf. by Brace Beemer & John Todd. 3 CDs. (Running Time: 3 hrs.). 2002. audio compact disk 19.98 (27602); 17.98 (27604) Radio Spirits.
The Lone Ranger thrilled radio listeners for more than 20 years as he and his faithful companion Tonto "led the fight for law and order." Return with us now to those thrilling days of yesteryear with the incredible collection of six never-before-release episodes from radio's longest-running Western series.

Lone Ranger. Old Radio Staff. 1995. audio compact disk 4.99 (978-0-88676-556-9(0)) Metacom Inc.

Lone Ranger. ltd. ed. 5 vols. (Running Time: 5 hrs.). (Limited Edition Chronical Ser.). 2003. bk. 39.95 (978-0-7413-0044-7(3), OTR49507) Pub: Great Am Audio. Dist(s): AudioGO

Lone Ranger. ltd. ed. 5 vols. (Running Time: 5 hrs.). (Limited Edition Chronical Ser.). 2002. bk. (978-0-7413-0042-3(7), OTR43507) Radio Spirits.
A fiery horse with the speed of light, a cloud of dust and a hearty Hi-Yo Silver! The Lone Ranger!" With his faithful Indian companion, the daring and resourceful masked rider of the plains led the fight for law and order in the early Western United States.

Lone Ranger. unabr. ed. 12 CDs. (Running Time: 12 hrs.). 2003. audio compact disk 39.98 (978-1-57019-604-1(4), 4464) Radio Spirits.

Lone Ranger, Vol. 1. collector's ed. Perf. by Brace Beemer. 6 cass. (Running Time: 9 hrs.). (J). 1998. bk. 34.98 (4046) Radio Spirits.
Return to those thrilling days of yesteryear with the masked man and Tonto in 18 great episodes of western adventure.

Lone Ranger, Vol. 2. collector's ed. Perf. by Brace Beemer. 6 cass. (Running Time: 9 hrs.). (J). 1998. bk. 34.98 (4016) Radio Spirits.
Who was that masked man? Find out with 18 exciting episodes.

Lone Ranger, Vol. 3. collector's ed. Perf. by Brace Beemer & John Todd. 6 cass. (Running Time: 9 hrs.). (J). 1998. bk. 34.98 (4002) Radio Spirits.
Return to those thrilling days of yesteryear with 18 fast-paced western adventures.

Lone Ranger, Vol. 4. collector's ed. Perf. by Earle Graser. 6 cass. (Running Time: 9 hrs.). (J). 1998. bk. 34.98 (4146) Radio Spirits.
18 exciting episodes from 1938.

Lone Ranger, Vol. 5. collector's ed. Fran Striker. Perf. by Brace Beemer & John Todd. Contrib. by George W. Trendle. 6 cass. (Running Time: 9 hrs.). (J). 1999. bk. 34.98 (4188) Radio Spirits.
18 episodes of this western adventure series.

Lone Ranger, Vol. 6. collector's ed. Perf. by Brace Beemer & John Todd. Narrated by Fred Foy. 6 cass. (Running Time: 9 hrs.). (J). 2000. bk. 34.98 (4429) Radio Spirits.
18 episodes of the classic western series.

Lone Ranger: An Alibi Cracked & Wagons Round the Mountain. Perf. by Brace Beemer & John Todd. 1 cass. (Running Time: 1 hr.). 2001. 6.98 (2482) Radio Spirits.

Lone Ranger: Bait for the Trap & The Train Robbery. Perf. by Brace Beemer & John Todd. 1 cass. (Running Time: 1 hr.). 2001. 6.98 (2522) Radio Spirits.

***Lone Ranger: Biography.** Perf. by Brace Beemer & John Todd. 2010. audio compact disk 31.95 (978-1-57019-923-3(X)) Radio Spirits.

Lone Ranger: Doc Robbins' Mosquitoes & Texas Justice. Perf. by Brace Beemer & John Todd. 1 cass. (Running Time: 1 hr.). 2001. 6.98 (2183) Radio Spirits.

Lone Ranger: For a Lost Cause & The Red Mark. Perf. by Brace Beemer & John Todd. 1 cass. (Running Time: 1 hr.). 2001. 6.98 (2557) Radio Spirits.

Lone Ranger: Guns Is Fer Fighting Men & In Its Place. Perf. by Brace Beemer & John Todd. 1 cas. (Running Time: 1 hr.). 2001. 6.98 (1768) Radio Spirits.

Lone Ranger: Holster Heritage & The Golden Link. Perf. by Brace Beemer & John Todd. 1 cass. (Running Time: 1 hr.). 2001. 6.98 (1769) Radio Spirits.

Lone Ranger: House & Home & Relief Train. Perf. by Brace Beemer & John Todd. 1 cass. (Running Time: 1 hr.). 2001. 6.98 (2541) Radio Spirits.

Lone Ranger: Landgrabber's Loss & Sixty Days for Life. Perf. by Brace Beemer & John Todd. 1 cass. (Running Time: 1 hr.). 2001. 6.98 (2346) Radio Spirits.

Lone Ranger: Last Laugh & Best Laid Plans. Perf. by Brace Beemer & John Todd. 1 cass. (Running Time: 1 hr.). 2001. 6.98 (2285) Radio Spirits.

Lone Ranger: Last of the Gang, Birthday for Billy & Gentle Tucson Thorpe. Perf. by Brace Beemer & John Todd. 1 cass. (Running Time: 1 hr.). 2001. 6.98 (1771) Radio Spirits.

Lone Ranger: Lawmen Pro Team & The Saddle. Perf. by Brace Beemer & John Todd. 1 cass. (Running Time: 1 hr.). 2001. 6.98 (1770) Radio Spirits.

Lone Ranger: Man Alive & Deadly Silver. Perf. by Brace Beemer & John Todd. 1 cass. (Running Time: 1 hr.). 2001. 6.98 (2162) Radio Spirits.

Lone Ranger: Murder Blooms at Night, Pt. 3 & Dan Goes to Jail, Pt. 4. Perf. by Brace Beemer & John Todd. 1 cass. (Running Time: 1 hr.). 2001. 6.98 (2442) Radio Spirits.

(978-1-60814-645-1(6)); audio compact disk 29.99 (978-1-59859-702-8(7)) Oasis Audio.

***Lonestar Sanctuary.** unabr. ed. Colleen Coble. Narrated by Aimee Lilly. (Running Time: 9 hrs. 0 mins. 0 sec.). (ENG.). 2011. audio compact disk 29.99 (978-1-59859-852-0(X)) Oasis Audio.

Lonestar Secrets. unabr. ed. Colleen Coble. Narrated by Aimee Lilly. (Running Time: 8 hrs. 30 mins. 35 sec.). (ENG.). 2009. 20.99 (978-1-60814-551-5(4)); audio compact disk 29.99 (978-1-59859-607-6(1)) Oasis Audio.

Long Acre. Claire Rayner. Read by Anne Cater. 9 cass. (Performers Ser.: Vol. 6). (J). 2005. 76.95 (978-1-84283-487-9(8)) Pub: ISIS Lrg Prnt GBR. Dist(s): Ulverscroft US

***Long after Midnight.** unabr. ed. Ray Bradbury. Narrated by Michael Prichard. (Running Time: 9 hrs. 0 mins.). 2010. 15.99 (978-1-4001-8820-8(2)); 24.99 (978-1-4001-6820-0(1)); audio compact disk 83.99 (978-1-4001-4820-2(0)); audio compact disk 34.99 (978-1-4001-1820-5(4)) Pub: Tantor Media. Dist(s): IngramPubServ

Long after Midnight & The Halloween Tree. unabr. collector's ed. Ray Bradbury. Read by Michael Prichard. 8 cass. (Running Time: 12 hrs.). 1990. 64.00 (978-0-7366-2201-1(2), 2996) Books on Tape.
Bradbury's imaginative field is boundless. In this collection of 32 stories he carries us from the cozy familiarity of small-town America to the frozen desert & double moon that has been part of our landscapes since The Martian Chronicles. Characters range from the "ordinary" - a rookie cop, an unhappy wife on vacation in Mexico, an old parish priest hearing confession - to the extraordinary: the parrot to whom Hemingway confided the plot of his last, greatest, never-put-down-on-paper novel & a woman who hangs out a sign in New York City reading "Melissa Toad, Witch".

Long Ago & Far Away. unabr. ed. David Ives. Perf. by Jane Brucker et al. 1 cass. (Running Time: 1 hr. 35 min.). 1995. 19.95 (978-1-58081-023-4(3)) L A Theatre.
A hard hat confesses his secret ties to the Russian Aristocracy on the 50th floor of a high rise construction project. These five short plays celebrate human foibles, romantic yearnings & most of all, the art of theatre.

Long Ago & Today/Moving from Place to Place. Steck-Vaughn Staff. 2002. (978-0-7398-5905-6(6)); (978-0-7398-5908-7(0)) SteckVau.

Long & Happy Life. Reynolds Price. Read by Reynolds Price. 1 cass. (Running Time: 1 hr. 20 min.). Incl. Names & Faces of Heroes. (2101); Permanent Errors. (2101); Source of Light. (2101); Surface of Earth. (2101); 13.95 (978-1-55644-051-9(0), 2101) Am Audio Prose.

Long-Arm Jurisdiction in Pennsylvania. Jeffrey M. Stopford. 1 cass. (Running Time: 1 hr.). 1984. 10.00 PA Bar Inst.

Long Arm of Love. Contrib. by Michael Olson. Prod. by Nate Sabin. 2005. audio compact disk 11.99 (978-5-559-07894-6(8)) Rocket.

Long as I Got King Jesus. Composed by James Cleveland. Contrib. by Lari Goss & Chris McDonald. 2007. audio compact disk 24.98 (978-5-557-49184-6(8), Word Music) Word Enter.

Long Ball. unabr. ed. Tom Adelman. 10 cass. (Running Time: 12 hrs. 30 mins.). 2003. 89.00 (978-1-4025-4209-1(7)) Recorded Bks.

Long Beach Lectures - 2 CD Set. rev. ed. Sydney Banks. 2003. audio compact disk (978-1-55105-420-9(5)) Lone Pine Publ CAN.

Long Before Forty. unabr. collector's ed. C. S. Forester. Read by Richard Green. 7 cass. (Running Time: 10 hrs. 30 mins.). 1981. 56.00 (978-0-7366-0360-7(3), 1346) Books on Tape.
This is the account of Forester's lonely struggle to learn to write. The concluding section is a memoir of his creation of Captain Hornblower.

***Long Bow Story.** Anonymous. 2009. (978-1-60136-583-5(7)) Audio Holding.

Long-Chain 3-Hydroxyacyl-Coenzyme A Dehydrogenase Deficiency - A Bibliography & Dictionary for Physicians, Patients, & Genome Researchers. Compiled by Icon Group International, Inc. Staff. 2007. ring bd. 28.95 (978-0-497-11375-9(9)) Icon Grp.

Long Cold Fall. unabr. ed. Sam Reaves. Read by Michael Hanson & Mary Dilts. 7 cass. (Running Time: 10 hrs. 13 mins.). (Cooper MacLeish Mystery Ser.: Vol. 1). 1994. 42.00 (978-0-9624010-7-7(2), 892560) Readers Chair.
Cooper tries to uncover the reason why an ex-girlfriend fell from her 23rd floor apartment. His investigation makes him the killer's next target & leads him to a teenager who might be his son.

Long Dark Tea-Time of the Soul. Douglas Adams. Read by Douglas Adams. 6 CDs. (Running Time: 6 hrs.). 2001. audio compact disk 39.95 (N Millennium Audio) New Millenn Enter.

Long Dark Tea-Time of the Soul. unabr. ed. Douglas Adams. Read by Douglas Adams. 6 CDs. (Running Time: 6 hrs.). 2004. audio compact disk 39.95 (978-1-59007-075-8(5)); 25.00 (978-1-59007-060-4(7)) Pub: New Millenn Enter. Dist(s): PerseuPGW
Kate Schechter would like to know why everyone she meets knows her name - & why Thor, the Norse god of thunder, keeps showing up on her doorstep. It takes the sardonic genius of Dirk Gently, detective & refrigerator wrestler, to get to the bottom of it all. Was the passenger check-in desk at Heathrow's blasting through the roof really an Act of God? What's going on at Woodshead Hospital? & why is a severed head spinning on a turntable, its body sitting amiably nearby? Only the sleuthing of Dirk Gently can uncover these mysteries.

***Long Day.** Anonymous. 2009. (978-1-60136-607-8(8)) Audio Holding.

Long Day in November see Bloodline

Long Day's Journey into War, Pt. 1. unabr. collector's ed. Stanley Weintraub. Read by Jonathan Reese. 10 cass. (Running Time: 15 hrs.). 1997. 80.00 (978-0-7366-3610-0(2), 4268-A) Books on Tape.
What was happening elsewhere when the Japanese bombed Pearl Harbor? Reconstructing world events on December 7th, 1941, Stanley Weintraub offers a bird's-eye view of the "day that will live in infamy".

Long Day's Journey into War, Pt. 2. collector's ed. Stanley Weintraub. Read by Jonathan Reese. 10 cass. (Running Time: 15 hrs.). 1997. 80.00 (978-0-7366-3611-7(0), 4268-B) Books on Tape.

Long Dimanche de Fiancailles see Very Long Engagement

***Long Distance Call.** (ENG.). 2010. audio compact disk (978-1-59171-255-8(6)) Falcon Picture.

Long Drift. abr. ed. Sam Brown. 1 cass. 1997. 17.00 (978-1-883268-45-9(1)) Spellbinders.

Long Exile see Great French & Russian Stories, Vol. 1, A Collection

Long Exile see Honest Thief & Other Stories

Long Fall. unabr. ed. Walter Mosley. Read by Mirron Willis. 7 CDs. (Running Time: 9 hrs.). No. 1. (ENG.). (gr. 12 up). 2009. audio compact disk 29.95 (978-0-14-314420-5(0), PengAudBks) Penguin Grp USA.

***Long Fall.** unabr. ed. Walter Mosley. Read by Mirron Willis. 7 CDs. (Running Time: 8 hrs. 45 mins.). (Leonid McGill Mystery Ser.). 2009. audio compact disk 100.00 (978-1-4159-6272-5(3), BksonTape) Pub: Random Audio Pubg. Dist(s): Random

Long Finish. Michael Dibdin. Read by Michael Kitchen. 8 vols. (Running Time: 12 hrs.). (Aurelio Zen Mystery Ser.). 2003. audio compact disk 79.95 (978-0-7540-5579-2(5)) Pub: Chivers Audio Bks GBR. Dist(s): AudioGO

Long Finish. unabr. ed. Michael Dibdin. Read by Michael Kitchen. 8 cass. (Aurelio Zen Mystery Ser.). 1999. 69.95 (978-0-7540-0362-5(0), CAB 1785) AudioGO.
Aurelio Zen finds himself back in Roome on a new assignment: to release the jailed scion of an important wine-growing family who is accused of brutal murder. Amid the quiet fields of Piedmont, Zen must penetrate a traditional culture in which family & soil are inextricably linked.

***Long for This World.** unabr. ed. Sonya Chung. (Running Time: 10 hrs. 0 mins. 0 sec.). (ENG.). 2010. audio compact disk 69.99 (978-1-4001-4643-7(7)) Pub: Tantor Media. Dist(s): IngramPubServ

***Long for This World.** unabr. ed. Jonathan Weiner. Read by Jim Meskimen. (ENG.). 2010. (978-0-06-201606-5(7), Harper Audio) HarperCollins Pubs.

***Long for This World: A Novel.** unabr. ed. Sonya Chung. (Running Time: 10 hrs. 0 mins.). 2010. 16.99 (978-1-4001-8643-3(9)); 24.99 (978-1-4001-6643-5(8)); audio compact disk 34.99 (978-1-4001-1643-0(0)) Pub: Tantor Media. Dist(s): IngramPubServ

***Long for This World: The Strange Science of Immortality.** unabr. ed. Jonathan Weiner. Read by Jim Meskimen. (ENG.). 2010. (978-0-06-201428-3(5), Harper Audio) HarperCollins Pubs.

***Long Fuse, Big Bang: Achieving Long-Term Success Through Daily Victories.** unabr. ed. Eric Haseltine. (Running Time: 9 hrs. 0 mins.). 2010. 15.99 (978-1-4001-8767-6(2)); 24.99 (978-1-4001-6767-8(1)); 34.99 (978-1-4001-9767-5(8)) Tantor Media.

***Long Fuse, Big Bang: Achieving Long-Term Success Through Daily Victories.** unabr. ed. Eric Haseltine. Narrated by Kirby Heyborne. (Running Time: 11 hrs. 30 mins. 0 sec.). (ENG.). 2010. audio compact disk 83.99 (978-1-4001-4767-0(0)); audio compact disk 34.99 (978-1-4001-1767-3(4)) Pub: Tantor Media. Dist(s): IngramPubServ

Long Goodbye. abr. ed. Raymond Chandler. Read by Elliott Gould. 2 cass. (Running Time: 3 hrs.). 2004. 18.00 (978-1-59007-095-6(X)); audio compact disk 21.95 (978-1-59007-096-3(8)) Pub: New Millenn Enter. Dist(s): PerseuPGW
Marlowe befriends a down on his luck war veteran with the scars to prove it. Then he finds out that Terry Lennox has a very wealthy nymphomaniac wife, who he's divorced and re-married and who ends up dead. and now Lennox is on the lam and the cops and a crazy gangster are after Marlowe.

Long Goodbye. unabr. ed. Patti Davis. Read by Staci Snell. 5 CDs. (Running Time: 6 hrs.). 2004. audio compact disk 63.00 (978-1-4159-0833-4(8)); 54.00 (978-1-4159-0538-8(X)) Books on Tape.
Patti Davis, the daughter of Ronald and Nancy Reagan, writes about losing her father to Alzheimer's disease and saying goodbye in stages, while watching the disease steal what is most precious-a person's memory. Past and present come together in this illuminating portrait of grief, of a man, a disease and a girl and her father.

Long Goodbye & The Little Sister. abr. ed. Raymond Chandler. 2 cass. (Running Time: 3 hrs.). 1999. 16.85 (978-0-563-55803-3(2)) BBC WrldWd GBR.
In "The Long Goodbye" Terry Lennox was a drunk with too much money, too much time & a wife who played the field in a big way. Trouble was, when she ended up dead, it wasn't money that took Lennox to Mexico. In "The Little Sister" the case of a missing brother from some two-bit Kansas town didn't look like Marlowe's best shot at the big time. This particular brother, though, tended to know guys who finished up on the wrong end of an ice pick.

Long Island's North Fork: From Riverhead to Orient Point Via Southold & Greenport. unabr. ed. Ed. by Bill McCoy. (Recorded Driving Tours Ser.). 2001. 19.95 (978-1-931739-05-4(6)) Travelog Corp.

Long John's One & Two. John Bird. 1 cass. 1998. 16.85 (978-1-897774-54-0(0)) Pub: LaughStockProd GBR. Dist(s): Random House

Long Journey Home. 1 cass., 1 CD. 9.58 Soundtrack. (RCA 68963); audio compact disk 14.38 (RCA 68963) NewSound.

Long Journey Home Audiotape. Richard Delaney. Narrated by David Rucker. (J). 1997. 10.95 (978-1-892194-99-2(6)) NW Media.

Long Knives Are Crying: Lakota Westerns. unabr. ed. Joseph M. Marshall III. Read by Joseph M. Marshall III. (Running Time: 19 hrs. 0 mins.). (ENG.). 2009. 44.95 (978-1-4332-2993-0(5)); 99.95 (978-1-4332-2989-3(7)); audio compact disk 120.00 (978-1-4332-2990-9(0)) Blckstn Audio.

Long Lavender Look. unabr. collector's ed. John D. MacDonald. Read by Michael Prichard. 6 cass. (Running Time: 9 hrs.). (Travis McGee Ser.: Vol. 12). 1984. 48.00 (978-0-7366-0705-6(6), 1668) Books on Tape.
While driving along a darkened stretch of Florida road, Travis McGee & friend encounter a young girl wearing little more than a frightened look as she leaps out from the shadows directly in line with their headlights. A skillful swerve saves the girl but finds McGee & friend upside down in 10 feet of swamp water. Not two minutes later they are dodging bullets from a speeding pickup. McGee reports these unusual events to the the local sheriff & finds himself arrested for murder!.

Long-Legged Fly see Dylan Thomas Reads the Poetry of W. B. Yeats & Others

Long-Legged Fly: A Lew Griffin Mystery. unabr. ed. James Sallis. (Running Time: 5 hrs. NaN mins.). 2008. 19.95 (978-1-4332-3001-1(1)); 34.95 (978-1-4332-2997-8(8)); audio compact disk 40.00 (978-1-4332-2998-5(6)) Blckstn Audio.

Long Life. collector's ed. Nigel Nicolson. Read by David Case. 9 cass. (Running Time: 13 hrs. 30 min.). 2000. 72.00 (978-0-7366-5437-1(2)) Books on Tape.
Nicolson has indeed led a long & eventful life. Here he shares with us his childhood in the heart of Bloomsbury as the son of Harold Nicolson & Vita Sackville-West.

***Long Live Walter Jameson.** (ENG.). 2010. audio compact disk (978-1-59171-261-9(0)) Falcon Picture.

***Long Lonesome.** H. A. DeRosso. 2009. (978-1-60136-447-0(4)) Audio Holding.

Long Lonesome. H. A. DeRosso. Read by Christopher Greybill. (Running Time: 1 hr. 30 mins.). 1999. 10.95 (978-1-60083-501-8(5)) Iofy Corp.

Long, Long Trail. unabr. collector's ed. Max Brand. Read by Jonathan Marosz. 7 cass. (Running Time: 7 hrs.). 1994. 42.00 (978-0-7366-2783-2(9), 3501) Books on Tape.
Eluding both the sheriff & bounty hunters, Jess Dreer follows a lone outlaw's trail after avenging his father's murder.

Long Lost. abr. ed. Harlan Coben. Read by Steven Weber. 4 CDs. (Running Time: 5 hrs.). (Myron Bolitar Ser.: No. 9). 2009. audio compact disk 24.99 (978-1-4233-2763-9(2), 9781423327639, BACD) Brilliance Audio.

Long Lost. abr. ed. Harlan Coben. Read by Steven Weber. (Running Time: 5 hrs.). (Myron Bolitar Ser.: No. 9). 2010. audio compact disk 14.99 (978-1-4233-2764-6(0), 9781423327646, BCD Value Price) Brilliance Audio.

Long Lost. abr. ed. David Morrell. Read by Neil Patrick Harris. (ENG.). 2005. 14.98 (978-1-59483-371-7(0)) Pub: Hachet Audio. Dist(s): HachBkGrp

Long Lost. unabr. ed. Harlan Coben. Read by Steven Weber. 1 MP3-CD. (Running Time: 9 hrs.). (Myron Bolitar Ser.: No. 9). 2009. 24.99 (978-1-4233-2759-2(4), 9781423327592, Brilliance MP3); 39.97 (978-1-4233-2762-2(4), 9781423327622, BADLE); 39.97 (978-1-4233-2760-8(8), 9781423327608, Brlnc Audio MP3 Lib); 24.99 (978-1-4233-2761-5(6), 9781423327615, BAD); audio compact disk 36.99 (978-1-4233-2757-8(8), 9781423327578, Bril Audio CD Unabri); audio compact disk 97.97 (978-1-4233-2758-5(6), 9781423327585, BriAudCD Unabrid) Brilliance Audio.

Long-Lost Map. unabr. ed. Pierdomenico Baccalario. Read by Michael Page. (Running Time: 18000 sec.). (Ulysses Moore Ser.: Bk. 2). (J). 2006. 62.25 (978-1-4233-1325-0(9), 9781423313250, BrilAudUnabridg); 24.95 (978-1-4233-1324-3(0), 9781423313243, BAU); audio compact disk 39.25 (978-1-4233-1329-8(1), 9781423313298, Brlnc Audio MP3 Lib); audio compact disk 24.95 (978-1-4233-1328-1(3), 9781423313281, Brilliance MP3); audio compact disk 24.95 (978-1-4233-1326-7(7), 9781423313267, Bril Audio CD Unabri) Brilliance Audio.
Please enter a Synopsis.

Long-Lost Map. unabr. ed. Pierdomenico Baccalario. Read by Michael Page. (Running Time: 5 hrs.). (Ulysses Moore Ser.: Bk. 2). 2006. 39.25 (978-1-4233-1331-1(3), 9781423313311, BADLE); 24.95 (978-1-4233-1330-4(5), 9781423313304, BAD); audio compact disk 69.25 (978-1-4233-1327-4(5), 9781423313274, BriAudCD Unabrid) Brilliance Audio.

Long March. unabr. collector's ed. William Styron. Read by Wolfram Kandinsky. 3 cass. (Running Time: 3 hrs.). 1984. 18.00 (978-0-7366-0930-2(X), 1874) Books on Tape.
Eight marines are killed almost casually by misfired mortar shells. Deciding that his platoon has been "doping off," Colonel Templeton calls for a 36-mile forced march to inculate discipline. "The Long March" is an account of this ordeal & of the two officers who resist.

Long March: How the Cultural Revolution of the 1960s Changed America. Roger Kimball. Read by Raymond Todd. (Running Time: 10 mins.). 2005. 59.95 (978-0-7861-3686-5(3)); audio compact disk 72.00 (978-0-7861-7647-2(4)) Blckstn Audio.

Long March: How the Cultural Revolution of the 1960s Changed America. unabr. ed. Roger Kimball. Read by Raymond Todd. (Running Time: 10 mins.). 2005. 29.95 (978-0-7861-7911-4(2)) Blckstn Audio.

Long March: The True History of Communist China's Founding Myth. Sun Shuyun. Read by Laural Merlington. (Playaway Adult Nonfiction Ser.). 2008. 64.99 (978-1-60514-999-8(3)) Find a World.

Long March: The True History of Communist China's Founding Myth. unabr. ed. Sun Shuyun. Read by Laural Merlington. (Running Time: 11 hrs. 0 mins. 0 sec.). (ENG.). 2007. audio compact disk 34.99 (978-1-4001-0452-9(1)); audio compact disk 69.99 (978-1-4001-3452-6(8)); audio compact disk 24.99 (978-1-4001-5452-4(9)) Pub: Tantor Media. Dist(s): IngramPubServ

Long March to Freedom. Thomas R. Hargrove. Narrated by Alan Sklar. (Running Time: 21 hrs.). 2005. 53.95 (978-1-59912-533-6(1)) Iofy Corp.

Long March to Freedom -Lib. Thomas R. Hargrove. Read by Alan Sklar. 15 cass. (Running Time: 22 hrs.). 2004. 95.95 (978-0-7861-2635-4(3), 3241); audio compact disk 136.00 (978-0-7861-8732-4(8), 3241) Blckstn Audio.

***Long Morrow.** 2010. audio compact disk (978-1-59171-197-1(5)) Falcon Picture.

Long Night of Winchell Dear. unabr. ed. Robert James Waller. Read by Richard McGonagle. 5 CDs. (Running Time: 6 hrs.). 2006. audio compact disk 38.25 (978-1-4159-3250-6(6)) Pub: Books on Tape. Dist(s): NetLibrary CO

Long Obedience in Same Direction: Discipleship in an Instant Society. unabr. ed. Eugene H. Peterson. 5 CDs. (Running Time: 5 hrs. 48 mins. 0 sec.). (ENG.). 2005. audio compact disk 23.98 (978-1-59644-121-7(6), Hovel Audio) christianaud.

***Long Obedience in the Same Direction: Discipleship in an Instant Society.** unabr. ed. Eugene H. Peterson. Narrated by Lloyd James. (ENG.). 2005. 14.98 (978-1-59644-119-4(4), Hovel Audio) christianaud.

Long Obedience in the Same Direction: Discipleship in an Instant Society. unabr. ed. Eugene H. Peterson. Narrated by Lloyd James. 1 MP3CD. (Running Time: 5 hrs. 48 mins. 0 sec.). (ENG.). 2005. lp 19.98 (978-1-59644-120-0(8), Hovel Audio) christianaud.
This world is no friend to grace. God has given us some resources, however. As we grow in character qualities like hope, patience, repentance and joy, we ill grow in our ability to persevere. The biblical passages in these studies offer encouragement to continue in the path Christ has set forth for us.

Long Pursuit. Jon Cleary. Read by Alan Dunbavan. 4 cass. (Running Time: 6 hrs.). 1999. 44.95 (60466) Pub: Soundings Ltd GBR. Dist(s): Ulverscroft US

Long Pursuit. unabr. ed. Jon Cleary. 4 cass. (Sound Ser.). 2004. 44.95 (978-1-85496-046-7(6)) Pub: UlverLrgPrint GBR. Dist(s): Ulverscroft US

Long Rain. unabr. ed. Peter Gadol. Narrated by Peter Francis James. 8 cass. (Running Time: 11 hrs. 30 mins.). 1997. 75.00 (978-0-7887-1314-9(0), 95172E7) Recorded Bks.
Atypical of the usual thriller, this book sneaks up on readers, lures them into beautiful California wine country, then surprises them with a terrible twist of fate & a hero who is forced to make an impossible choice.

Long Road Home. unabr. ed. Connie Monk. Read by Maggie Mash. 11 cass. (Running Time: 14 hrs. 35 mins.). (Story Sound Ser.). (J). 2006. 89.95 (978-1-85903-856-7(5)) Pub: Mgna Lrg Print GBR. Dist(s): Ulverscroft US

***Long Road Home.** unabr. ed. Mary Alice Monroe. Read by Sandra Burr. (Running Time: 13 hrs.). 2010. 24.99 (978-1-4418-9159-4(5), 9781441891594, BAD); 39.97 (978-1-4418-9160-0(9), 9781441891600, BADLE); 24.99 (978-1-4418-9157-0(9), 9781441891570, Brilliance MP3); 39.97 (978-1-4418-9158-7(7), 9781441891587, Brlnc Audio MP3 Lib); audio compact disk 29.99 (978-1-4418-9155-6(2), 9781441891556, Bril Audio CD Unabri); audio compact disk 79.97 (978-1-4418-9156-3(0), 9781441891563, BriAudCD Unabrid) Brilliance Audio.

Long Road Home. unabr. ed. Danielle Steel. 10 cass. (Running Time: 10 hrs.). 1998. 39.95 (Random AudioBks) Random Audio Pubg.

Long Road Home: A Story of War & Family. unabr. ed. Martha Raddatz. 8 CDs. (Running Time: 10 hrs. 0 mins. 0 sec.). (ENG.). 2007. audio compact disk 34.99 (978-1-4001-0446-8(7)) Pub: Tantor Media. Dist(s): IngramPubServ

Long Road Home: A Story of War & Family. unabr. ed. Martha Raddatz. Read by Joyce Bean. (Running Time: 10 hrs. 0 mins. 0 sec.). (ENG.). 2007. audio compact disk 24.99 (978-1-4001-5446-3(4)); audio compact disk 69.99 (978-1-4001-3446-5(3)) Pub: Tantor Media. Dist(s): IngramPubServ

Long Road to Freedom: Journey of the Hmong. (High Five Reading - Purple Ser.). (ENG.). (gr. 4-5). 2007. audio compact disk 5.95 (978-1-4296-1447-4(1)) CapstoneDig.

Long Road to Freedom: Journey of the Hmong. Linda Barr. (High Five Reading Ser.). (ENG.). (gr. 4 up). 2004. audio compact disk 5.95 (978-0-7368-3857-3(0)) CapstoneDig.

***Long Road to Gettysburg.** unabr. ed. Jim Murphy. Narrated by Ray Childs et al. 2 CDs. (Running Time: 2 hrs.). (YA). (gr. 5 up). 2010. audio compact disk 29.95 (978-1-935430-42-1(4)) Audio Bkshelf.

***Long Run: One Man's Attempt to Regain his Athletic Career-and His Life-by Running the New York City Marathon.** unabr. ed. Matthew Long & Charles Butler. Read by Matthew Del Negro. (ENG.). 2010. audio compact disk 35.00 (978-0-307-87748-2(5), Random AudioBks) Pub: Random Audio Pubg. Dist(s): Random

Long Sandy Hair of Neftoon Zamora. 2002. audio compact disk (978-1-56111-999-8(7)) Pac Arts Vid.

Long Secret. unabr. ed. Louise Fitzhugh. Read by Anne Bobby. 4 vols. (Running Time: 5 hrs. 56 mins.). (J). (gr. 3-7). 2004. pap. bk. 38.00 (978-0-8072-0666-9(0), LYA 303 SP, Listening Lib) Random Audio Pubg.
Harriet refuses to become ruffled when an unidentified person starts leaving disturbing notes, all over the quiet little beach town of Water Mill. Determined to discover the author of these notes, Harriet the Spy is on the case. But will she be ready to face the truth when she finds it.

Long Secret: Harriet the Spy Adventure. unabr. ed. Louise Fitzhugh. Read by Anne Bobby. 4 cass. (Running Time: 5 hrs. 56 mins.). (J). (gr. 3-7). 2004. 32.00 (978-0-8072-0498-6(6), Listening Lib) Random Audio Pubg.
Harriet the Spy refuses to become ruffled when an unidentified person starts leaving disturbing notes all over the quiet little beach town of Water Mill. She's determined to find the author of these notes & drags her best friend, mousy Beth Ellen, into all kinds of embarrassing situations trying to find the culprit. Harriet the Spy is on the case, but will she be ready to face the truth when she finds it?.

Long Shadow of the Ancient Greek World. Instructed by Ian Worthington. (ENG.). 2009. 249.95 (978-1-59803-541-4(X)); audio compact disk 359.95 (978-1-59803-542-1(8)) Teaching Co.

Long Shadows. Rowena Summers & Tanya Myers. 2009. 61.95 (978-1-84652-465-3(2)); audio compact disk 71.95 (978-1-84652-466-0(0)) Pub: Magna Story GBR. Dist(s): Ulverscroft US

Long Shot. Stephen Leather. (Isis (CDs) Ser.). 2007. audio compact disk 116.95 (978-0-7531-2622-6(2)) Pub: ISIS Lrg Prnt GBR. Dist(s): Ulverscroft US

Long Shot. Stephen Leather. Read by Martyn Read. 16 cass. (Running Time: 20 hrs. 40 mins.). (Isis Cassettes Ser.). 2007. 104.95 (978-0-7531-3590-7(6)) Pub: ISIS Lrg Prnt GBR. Dist(s): Ulverscroft US

***Long Shot.** unabr. ed. Mike Lupica. Contrib. by Keith Nobbs. (Running Time: 3 hrs.). (Comeback Kids Ser.). (J). 2010. audio compact disk 19.95 (978-0-14-314573-8(8), PengAudBks) Penguin Grp USA.

***Long Snapper.** unabr. ed. Jeffrey Marx. Read by Jeff Rechner. (ENG.). 2009. (978-0-06-190273-4(X), Harper Audio); (978-0-06-184552-9(3), Harper Audio) HarperCollins Pubs.

Long Spoon Lane. abr. ed. Anne Perry. Read by Michael Page. (Running Time: 21600 sec.). (Thomas Pitt Ser.). 2006. audio compact disk 16.99 (978-1-59737-340-1(0), 9781597373401, BCD Value Price) Brilliance Audio.
Anne Perry's bestselling Victorian novels offer readers an elixir as addictively rich as Devonshire cream and English ale - enticing millions into a literary world almost as real as the original. While flower sellers, costermongers, shopkeepers, and hansom drivers ply their trades, the London police watch over all. Or so people believe. . . . Early one morning, Thomas Pitt, dauntless mainstay of the Special Branch, is summoned to Long Spoon Lane, where anarchists are plotting an attack. Bombs explode, destroying the homes of many poor people. After a chase, two of the culprits are captured and the leader is shot . . . but by whom? As Pitt delves into the case, he finds that there is more to the terrorism than the destructive gestures of misguided idealists. The police are running a lucrative protection racket, and clues suggest that Inspector Wetron of Bow Street is the mastermind. As the shadowy leader of the Inner Circle, Wetron is using his influence with the press to whip up fears of more attacks - and to rush a bill through Parliament that would severely curtail civil liberties. This would make him the most powerful man in the country. To defeat Wetron, Pitt finds that he must run in harness with his old enemy, Sir Charles Voisey, and the unlikely allies are joined by Pitt's clever wife, Charlotte, and her great aunt, Lady Vespasia Cumming-Gould. Can they prevail? As they strive to prevent future destruction, nothing less than the fate of the British Empire hangs in precarious balance.

Long Spoon Lane. unabr. ed. Anne Perry. Read by Michael Page. (Running Time: 11 hrs.). (Thomas & Charlotte Pitt Ser.). 2005. 39.25 (978-1-59710-466-1(3), 9781597104661, BADLE); 24.95 (978-1-59710-467-8(1), 9781597104678, BAD); 39.25 (978-1-59335-980-5(2), 9781593359805, Brlnc Audio MP3 Lib); 24.95 (978-1-59335-979-9(9), 9781593359799, Brilliance MP3); 87.25 (978-1-59600-270-8(0), 9781596002708, BrilAudUnabridg); 34.95 (978-1-59600-269-2(7), 9781596002692, BAU); audio compact disk 102.25 (978-1-59600-272-2(7), 9781596002722, BriAudCD Unabrid); audio compact disk 36.95 (978-1-59600-271-5(9), 9781596002715, Bril Audio CD Unabri) Brilliance Audio.
Please enter a Synopsis.

Long Stay in a Distant Land. Chieh Chieng. Narrated by James Yaegashi. (Running Time: 6 hrs. 30 mins.). 2005. 25.95 (978-1-59912-394-3(0)) Iofy Corp.

Long Stay in a Distant Land: A Novel. unabr. ed. Chieh Chieng. 6 CDs. (Running Time: 023400 sec.). 2005. 44.95 (978-0-7861-2912-6(3)); reel tape 29.95 (978-0-7861-2911-9(5), E3388); audio compact disk 29.95 (978-0-7861-8237-4(7), ZE3388); audio compact disk 29.95 (978-0-7861-8312-8(8), ZM3388); audio compact disk 55.00 (978-0-7861-8236-7(9)) Blckstn Audio.

Long Stone's Throw. unabr. ed. Alphie McCourt. Read by Alphie McCourt. (Running Time: 11 hrs.). (ENG.). 2008. 24.98 (978-1-60024-503-9(X)); audio compact disk 29.98 (978-1-60024-502-2(1)) Pub: Hachet Audio. Dist(s): HachBkGrp

Long Surrender. unabr. ed. Burke Davis. Narrated by Ken Parker. 9 cass. (Running Time: 12 hrs. 30 mins.). 1993. 78.00 (978-1-55690-850-7(4), 93218E7) Recorded Bks.
The story of the last days of the Confederacy, focusing on its president, Jefferson Davis & its leading general, Robert E. Lee.

Long Surrender. unabr. collector's ed. Burke Davis. Read by Dick Estell. 8 cass. (Running Time: 12 hrs.). 1988. 64.00 (978-0-7366-1386-6(2), 2277) Books on Tape.
When Jefferson Davis & his cabinet fled Richmond during the closing days of the Confederacy, they sought to avoid capture & continue the war.

Long Tail: Why the Future of Business Is Selling Less of More. unabr. ed. Chris Anderson. Read by Christopher Nissley. 2006. 39.98 (978-1-4013-8504-0(4)); audio compact disk 39.98 (978-1-4013-8414-2(5), Hyperion Audio) Pub: Hyperion. Dist(s): HarperCollins Pubs

Long-Term Solutions to the Energy Crisis. unabr. ed. Milton Friedman et al. 1 cass. (Running Time: 1 hr. 55 min.). 12.95 (223) J Norton Pubs.
The authors discuss how government policy should be shaped to prevent any recurrence of the present energy crisis.

Long-term Solutions to the Energy Crisis (2-CD Set) Milton Friedman et al. (ENG.). 2007. audio compact disk 21.50 (978-1-57970-478-0(6), Audio-For) J Norton Pubs.

Long Time Ago Today. unabr. ed. 4 cass. (Running Time: 5 hrs. 15 min.). (J). 2003. 37.00 (978-1-4025-5736-1(1)) Recorded Bks.

Long Time Coming. unabr. ed. Sandra Brown. Read by Susan Denaker. 5 CDs. (Running Time: 21600 sec.). (ENG.). 2005. audio compact disk 29.95 (978-0-7393-2454-7(3), Random AudioBks) Pub: Random Audio Pubg. Dist(s): Random

Long Time Dead. abr. ed. Peter Chambers. Read by Garrick Hagan. 4 cass. (Running Time: 6 hrs.). (Sound Ser.). 2004. 44.95 (978-1-85496-351-2(1), 63511) Pub: UlverLrgPrint GBR. Dist(s): Ulverscroft US

***Long Time Gone.** abr. ed. J. A. Jance. Read by Harry Chase. (ENG.). 2005. (978-0-06-088465-9(7), Harper Audio) HarperCollins Pubs.

***Long Time Gone.** abr. ed. J. A. Jance. Read by Harry Chase. (ENG.). 2005. (978-0-06-079696-9(0), Harper Audio) HarperCollins Pubs.

Long Time Gone. abr. ed. J. A. Jance. Read by Harry Chase. (Running Time: 21600 sec.). (J. P. Beaumont Mystery Ser.). 2006. audio compact disk 14.95 (978-0-06-112656-7(X)) HarperCollins Pubs.

Long Time Gone. unabr. ed. Harry Chase. Read by Tim Jerome. (J. P. Beaumont Mystery Ser.). 2005. 29.95 (978-0-7927-3706-3(7), CMP 795); 69.95 (978-0-7927-3618-9(4), CSL 795); audio compact disk 89.95 (978-0-7927-3705-6(9), SLD 795) AudioGO.

Long Time Gone. unabr. ed. Harry Chase & J. A. Jance. Read by Tim Jerome. (J. P. Beaumont Mystery Ser.). 2005. audio compact disk 39.95 (978-0-06-079666-2(9)) HarperCollins Pubs.

***Long Time Gone.** unabr. ed. J. A. Jance. Read by Tim Jerome. (ENG.). 2005. (978-0-06-088467-3(3), Harper Audio); (978-0-06-088468-0(1), Harper Audio) HarperCollins Pubs.

Long Time Leaving. unabr. ed. Roy Blount, Jr.. Read by Roy Blount, Jr. (YA). 2007. 39.99 (978-1-60252-763-8(6)) Find a World.

Long Time Leaving: Dispatches from up South. unabr. abr. ed. Roy Blount, Jr.. Read by Roy Blount, Jr. 7 CDs. (Running Time: 8 hrs.). (ENG.). 2007. audio compact disk 32.95 (978-1-59887-095-4(5), 1598870955) Pub: HighBridge. Dist(s): Workman Pub

Long Time No See. Susan Isaacs. Narrated by Cristine McMurdo-Wallis. 10 cass. (Running Time: 14 hrs.). 2001. 88.00 (978-1-4025-0679-6(1), 96788) Recorded Bks.
If the truth be known, she still pines away for her former lover, Nelson Sharpe. When chaos strikes, her new focus leads her to danger. Offering her services in the murder investigation of the highly visible Courtney Logan, Judith finds herself in the midst of the world of mobsters.

Long Time No See. abr. ed. Susan Isaacs. Read by Susan Isaacs. 2004. audio compact disk 14.95 (978-0-06-074685-8(8)) HarperCollins Pubs.

***Long Time No See.** unabr. ed. Susan Isaacs. Read by Cristine Mcmurdo-wallis. (ENG.). 2005. (978-0-06-089331-6(1), Harper Audio); (978-0-06-089330-9(3), Harper Audio) HarperCollins Pubs.

Long Time No See. unabr. ed. Ed McBain, pseud. Read by Dan Lazar. 5 cass. (Running Time: 7 hrs. 30 min.). (87th Precinct Ser.: Bk. 32). 1986. 40.00 (978-0-7366-0823-7(0), 1773) Books on Tape.
Dectectives Carella & Meyer of the 87th Precinct examine the cold body of a murdered blind man, Jimmy Harris. Then they talk to his widow. She is blind too, but says she can identify the body anyway. She never does. The next day, her throat is cut.

***Long Time No See Low Price.** abr. ed. Susan Isaacs. Read by Susan Isaacs. (ENG.). 2005. (978-0-06-089332-3(X), Harper Audio); (978-0-06-089333-0(8), Harper Audio) HarperCollins Pubs.

Long Time to Freedom. Perf. by Ella Jenkins et al. 1 cass. (J). (gr. k up). 1992. (0-9307-45034-4-7) Smithsonian Folkways.
Adaptations of age-old African American traditions, songs sung on the long road toward freedom. For adults as well as children.

Long Trip. (Dovetales Ser.: Tape 4). pap. bk. 6.95 (978-0-944391-39-6(7)); 4.95 (978-0-944391-19-8(2)) DonWise Prodns.

Long Trousers see J. B. Priestley

Long Twilight, Lecture 4. Teaching Co.

Long Vacation: A Radio Play. Scripts. Garrett Vance & Birke Duncan. Based on a teleplay by Garrett Vance. Adapted by Birke Duncan. 1 CD. (Running Time: 46. mins.). Dramatization. 2005. audio compact disk (978-0-9710582-2-4(9)) NW Folklore.

Long Vowels. Steven Traugh & Susan Traugh. Ed. by Rozanne Lanczak Williams. Illus. by Diane Valko. (Fun Phonics Ser.: Vol. 8027). 1999. pap. bk. & tchr. ed. 13.99 (978-1-57471-641-2(7), 8027) Creat Teach Pr.

Long Vowels & Inflections Big Book: Level C, set. (Sing-along Songs Ser.). (ps-2). bk. 48.46 (978-0-7362-0421-7(0)) Hampton-Brown.

Long Vowels, R-Controlled Vowels, Inflections Big Book: Level E, set. (Sing-along Songs Ser.). (ps-2). bk. 48.46 (978-0-7362-0635-8(3)) Hampton-Brown.

***Long Walk.** unabr. ed. Stephen King. (Running Time: 9 hrs. 30 mins.). 2010. 29.95 (978-1-4417-3303-0(5)); 59.95 (978-1-4417-3299-6(3)); audio compact disk 50.00 (978-1-4417-3300-9(0)) Blckstn Audio.

Long Walk. unabr. ed. Stephen King. Read by Kirby Heyborne. 9 CDs. (Running Time: 11 hrs.). (ENG.). 2010. audio compact disk 39.95 (978-0-14-242783-5(7), PengAudBks) Penguin Grp USA.

Long Walk. unabr. ed. Slavomir Rawicz. Read by Bernard Mayes. 8 cass. (Running Time: 11 hrs. 30 mins.). 2003. 56.95 (978-0-7861-0197-9(0), 1173) Blckstn Audio.
In the spring of 1941, Slavomir Rawicz, a 26-year-old Polish lieutenant, escaped from a Soviet labor camp in Siberia with six fellow prisoners, including one American. They spent a year walking over 4,000 miles of the most forbidding terrain on Earth, to Freedom.

Long Walk: The True Story of a Trek to Freedom. unabr. ed. Slavomir Rawicz. Read by John Lee. (Running Time: 34200 sec.). 2006. 24.95 (978-0-7861-4685-7(0)); audio compact disk 24.95 (978-0-7861-6683-1(5)) Blckstn Audio.

Long Walk: The True Story of a Trek to Freedom. unabr. ed. Slavomir Rawicz. Read by John Lee. (Running Time: 34200 sec.). 2007. 59.95 (978-0-7861-0005-7(2)); audio compact disk 72.00 (978-0-7861-0038-5(9)) Blckstn Audio.

Long Walk: The True Story of Trek to Freedom. unabr. ed. Slavomir Rawicz. Read by John Lee. (Running Time: 34200 sec.). 2007. audio compact disk 29.95 (978-0-7861-7367-9(X)) Blckstn Audio.

Long Walk in Wintertime. unabr. ed. Libby Purves. Read by Lindsay Duncan. 8 cass. (Running Time: 8 hrs.). 1998. 69.95 (978-0-7540-0033-4(8), CAB1456) AudioGO.
At thirty-seven, Alice McDonald was content with her children & husband, Dan. But love is treacherous: Two months later, alone on a desperate quest through the bleak lanes of Norfolk, Alice cannot see how her life could ever be rebuilt. It takes a child, an old woman, & the glory of a Victorian fair to bring Alice & Daniel safely home from their long, cold, separate journeys.

Long Walk to Freedom: The Autobiography of Nelson Mandela. abr. ed. Nelson Mandela. Read by Danny Glover. 5 CDs. (Running Time: 6 hrs.). (ENG.). 2004. audio compact disk 31.98 (978-1-58621-688-7(0)) Pub: Hachet Audio. Dist(s): HachBkGrp

Long Walk to Freedom: The Autobiography of Nelson Mandela. abr. ed. Nelson Mandela. Read by Danny Glover. (ENG.). 2005. 14.98 (978-1-59483-318-2(4)) Pub: Hachet Audio. Dist(s): HachBkGrp

Long Walk to Freedom: The Autobiography of Nelson Mandela. abr. ed. Nelson Mandela. Read by Danny Glover. (Running Time: 6 hrs.). (ENG.). 2009. 49.98 (978-1-60024-922-8(1)) Pub: Hachet Audio. Dist(s): HachBkGrp

Long Walk to Freedom: The Autobiography of Nelson Mandela. unabr. ed. Nelson Mandela. Read by Morgan Duncan. 10 cass. (Running Time: 15 hrs.). 1996. 80.00 (4116-A); 72.00 (4116-B) Books on Tape.
To millions, Nelson Mandela personifies the ultimate triumph of those widely admired virtues in political activists: faith, hope & charity. But it wasn't always thus. In his youth, Mandela advocated active violence as a means to ending apartheid & for his pains spent 27 years in prison.

Long Walk to Freedom: The Autobiography of Nelson Mandela. unabr. ed. Nelson Mandela. Read by Duncan Morgan. 19 cass. (Running Time: 28 hrs. 30 min.). 1996. 152.00 (978-0-7366-3472-4(X), 4116A/B) Books on Tape.

Long Way: Exodus 13:14-18, A0110. Ed Young. (J). 1980. 4.95 (978-0-7417-1110-6(9)) Win Walk.

Long Way Down. unabr. ed. Collin Wilcox. Read by Larry McKeever. 8 cass. (Running Time: 8 hrs.). (Frank Hastings Ser.). 1996. 48.00 (978-0-7366-3474-8(6), 4117) Books on Tape.
Lt. Frank Hastings gets a case that has all the material to create a colorful tableau of a murder. Thomas King, a film maker, wealthy but profligate, ends up slashed & dead in the apartment of a girl who poses nude by day & sells sex by night. A trail of evidence leads to Arnold Clark. It figures: Clark has a rap sheet a mile long - & he's been keeping King's wife company.

Long Way from Chicago. Richard Peck. Read by Ron McLarty. 3 cass. (Running Time: 4 hrs. 30 mins.). (J). 2000. 24.00 (978-0-7366-5051-9(2)) Books on Tape.
When Joey & his sister, Mary Alice, travel from their home in Chicago to their grandmother's small town, they certainly don't expect the crazy adventures they encounter there. In the seven summers that they spend visiting her, the antics get even wackier & the children get an even bigger surprise than the year before.

Long Way from Chicago. unabr. ed. Richard Peck. 2 cass. (Running Time: 3 hrs.). (J). (gr. 1-8). 1999. 23.00 (LL 0153, Chivers Child Audio) AudioGO.

Long Way from Chicago. unabr. ed. Richard Peck. 2 cass. (Running Time: 3 hrs.). (YA). 1999. 16.98 (FS9-50966) Highsmith.

Long Way from Chicago. unabr. ed. Richard Peck. Read by Ron McLarty. 3 vols. (Running Time: 4 hrs. 17 mins.). (J). (gr. 5-9). 2004. pap. bk. 36.00 (978-0-8072-8126-0(3), Listening Lib); 30.00 (978-0-8072-8125-3(5), YA110CX, Listening Lib) Random Audio Pubg.
When Joey & his sister Mary Alice travel from their home in Chicago to their grandmother's small town, they certainly don't expect the crazy adventures they encounter there. In the seven summers that they visit her, the antics get more surprising than the year before.

Long Way from Chicago. unabr. ed. Richard Peck. Read by Ron McLarty. 4 CDs. (Running Time: 4 hrs. 17 mins.). (ENG.). (J). (gr. 3). 2005. audio compact disk 19.95 (978-0-307-24320-1(6), Listening Lib) Pub: Random Audio Pubg. Dist(s): Random

Long Way from Home. Connie Briscoe. Narrated by Peter Francis James. 10 cass. (Running Time: 14 hrs.). 1999. 93.00 (978-0-7887-4835-6(1), F0003E7) Recorded Bks.
A multigenerational story of slavery & freedom. It sings of the indestructible bonds of love & family witnessed through the lives of three unforgettable African-American women. Briscoe based one of the women on her great-great grandmother, who was a slave on Montpelier, President James Madison's Virginia plantation.

Long Way from Home. abr. ed. Connie Briscoe. Read by Audra McDonald. 2 cass. 1999. 18.00 (FS9-51004) Highsmith.

Long Way from Home: Growing up in the American Heartland. Tom Brokaw. Read by Dan Cashman. 2002. audio compact disk 72.00 (978-0-7366-8864-2(1)) Books on Tape.

Long Way from Home: Growing up in the American Heartland. abr. ed. Tom Brokaw. Read by Dan Cashman. 5 cass. (Running Time: 7 hrs. 30 mins.). 2002. 63.00 (978-0-7366-8863-5(3)) Books on Tape.
Brokaw writes a beautiful meditation on the enduring attraction of the American heartland for those who are forever influenced by its values.

Long Way Gone: Memoirs of a Boy Soldier. unabr. ed. Ishmael Beah. 7 CDs. (Running Time: 10 hrs. 30 mins.). 2007. audio compact disk 56.00 (978-1-4159-3803-4(2)) Books on Tape.

Long Way Gone: Memoirs of a Boy Soldier. unabr. ed. Ishmael Beah. Read by Ishmael Beah. 7 CDs. (Running Time: 8 hrs. 36 mins. 0 sec.). (ENG.). 2007. audio compact disk 34.95 (978-1-4272-0230-7(3)) Pub: Macmill Audio. Dist(s): Macmillan

Long Way Gone: Memoirs of a Boy Soldier. unabr. ed. Ishmael Beah. 7 CDs. (Running Time: 8 hrs. 36 mins. 0 sec.). (ENG.). 2008. audio compact disk 19.95 (978-1-4272-0646-6(5)) Pub: Macmill Audio. Dist(s): Macmillan

Long way Home. Janis Reams Hudson. Narrated by Ruth Ann Phimister. 8 cass. (Running Time: 10 hrs. 45 mins.). 72.00 (978-1-4025-2572-8(9)) Recorded Bks.

Long Way Home. Contrib. by Ginny Owens. Prod. by Will Hunt & Vincent. Contrib. by David Williams et al. 2005. audio compact disk 13.97 (978-5-558-78758-0(9)) Rocket.

Long Way Home. unabr. ed. Jessica Blair. Read by Marie McCarthy. 10 CDs. (Running Time: 12 hrs.). (Story Sound CD Ser.). (J). 2002. audio compact disk 89.95 (978-1-85903-588-7(4)) Pub: Mgna Lrg Print GBR. Dist(s): Ulverscroft US

Long Way Home. unabr. ed. Lydia Laube. Read by Deidre Rubenstein. 4 cass. (Running Time: 6 hrs.). 1998. (978-1-86340-659-8(X), 580131) Bolinda Pubng AUS.
In this sequel to "Behind the Veil" Lydia returns to Saudi Arabia, collects her pay, then decides to go home via Egypt, Sudan, Kenya & India. As eccentric & entertaining as ever, blithely she trots along, sunshade held aloft, while behind her ships sink, hotels explode, & wars erupt.

Long Way Home. unabr. ed. Michael Morpurgo. Read by Michael Maloney. 2 cass. (Running Time: 3 hrs.). (J). (gr. 1-8). 1999. 18.95 (CTC 794, Chivers Child Audio) AudioGO.

***Long Way Home.** unabr. ed. Michael Morpurgo. Read by Michael Moloney. 2 CDs. (Running Time: 2 hrs. 25 mins.). 2010. audio compact disk 21.95 (978-1-4056-5998-7(X)) AudioGO.

Long Way Home. unabr. ed. Robin Pilcher. (Running Time: 9 hrs. 0 mins. 0 sec.). (ENG.). 2010. audio compact disk 34.99 (978-1-4272-0963-4(4)) Pub: Macmill Audio. Dist(s): Macmillan

An Asterisk (*) at the beginning of an entry indicates that the title is appearing for the first time.

***Long Way Home: An American Journey from Ellis Island to the Great War.** unabr. ed. David Laskin. (Running Time: 14 hrs. 0 mins. 0 sec.). 2010. 29.99 (978-1-4001-6450-9(8)); 19.99 (978-1-4001-8450-7(9)); audio compact disk 39.99 (978-1-4001-1450-4(0)) Pub: Tantor Media. Dist(s): IngramPubServ

***Long Way Home: An American Journey from Ellis Island to the Great War.** unabr. ed. David Laskin. Narrated by Erik Synnestvedt. (Running Time: 14 hrs. 0 mins. 0 sec.). 2010. audio compact disk 79.99 (978-1-4001-4450-1(7)) Pub: Tantor Media. Dist(s): IngramPubServ

Long Way to a New Land. abr. ed. Joan Sandin. Illus. by Joan Sandin. 1 cass. (I Can Read Bks.). (J). (gr. k-3). 1991. cass. & cass. 8.99 (978-1-55994-494-6(3)) HarperCollins Pubs.

Long Ways to Travel: The Unreleased Folkways Masters, 1944-1949. Perf. by Woody Guthrie & Cisco Houston. Contrib. by Guy Logsdon et al. 1 cass. (0-9307-400460-9307-40046-2-3); audio compact disk (0-9307-40046-2-3) Smithsonian Folkways.
Includes "Harriet Tubman's Ballad," "Along in the Sun & the Rain" & "Talking Centralia".

Long Week-End Pt. 1: A Social History of Great Britain 1918-1939. collector's unabr. ed. Robert Graves. Read by Bill Kelsey. 7 cass. (Running Time: 10 hrs. 30 min.). 1988. 56.00 (978-0-7366-1454-2(0), 2336-A) Books on Tape.
A brilliant survey of the years between WW I & WW II in Great Britain. Explains why the democracies were asleep.

Long Week-End Pt. 2: A Social History of Great Britain, 1918-1939. unabr. collector's ed. Robert Graves. Read by Bill Kelsey. 6 cass. (Running Time: 9 hrs.). 1988. 48.00 (978-0-7366-1455-9(9), 2336-B) Books on Tape.
This survey of the interwar period in Great Britain includes surface aspects of the era, from current plays & novels being seen & read in London, to the latest dance fads & fashion imported from America in addition to the germinal & international influences at work in politics, business, science & the church.

Long Winter. unabr. ed. Laura Ingalls Wilder. Read by Cherry Jones. 6 CDs. (Running Time: 9 hrs.). (J). 2005. audio compact disk 25.95 (978-0-06-056502-2(0), HarperChildAud) HarperCollins Pubs.

Long 19th Century Vol. I-III: European History from 1789 To 1917. Instructed by Robert Weiner. 18 cass. (Running Time: 18 hrs.). bk. 79.95 (978-1-56585-993-7(6), 8190) Teaching Co.

Long 19th Century Vol. I-III: European History from 1789 To 1917. Instructed by Robert Weiner. 18 CDs. (Running Time: 18 hrs.). 2005. bk. 99.95 (978-1-56585-995-1(2), 8190) Teaching Co.

Longbows in the Far North: An Archer's Adventures in Alaska & Siberia. abr. ed. E. Donnall Thomas. Narrated by Michael Prichard. (Running Time: 16200 sec.). (Field & Stream Ser.). 2007. audio compact disk 28.00 (978-1-933309-24-8(5)) Pub: A Media Intl. Dist(s): Natl Bk Netwk

Longest Day: June 6, 1944. unabr. collector's ed. Cornelius Ryan. Read by Bill Kelsey. 6 cass. (Running Time: 9 hrs.). 1991. 48.00 (978-0-7366-1896-0(1), 2723) Books on Tape.
Through the hours before dawn on June 6, 1944, as paratroops fought in the hedgerows of Normandy, the greatest armada the world had ever known assembled off the beach - almost 5000 ships carrying more than 200,000 soldiers. In The Longest Day, Cornelius Ryan tells the story of the hours that preceded & followed H Hour of D-Day. It is not a military history but the story of people: the men of the Allied forces, the enemy & the civilians caught up in the confusion of battle. Besides researching published papers, Ryan tracked down 700 D-Day survivors. Their experiences are woven together into the breathtaking narrative of the Longest Day.

Longest Hair in the World. unabr. ed. Lois Duncan. Narrated by Christina Moore. 1 cass. (Running Time: 15 mins.). (J). (gr. 1 up). 1999. pap. bk. & stu. ed. 35.95 (978-0-7887-2661-3(7), 40821X4) Recorded Bks.
When Emily blows out the candles on her sixth birthday cake, she wishes for the longest hair in the world. Day by day, Emily's hair grows & grows. When will it Stop? Includes study guide.

Longest Hair in the World, Class Set. unabr. ed. Lois Duncan. Narrated by Christina Moore. 1 cass. (Running Time: 15 mins.). (gr. 1 up). 1999. 13.00 (978-0-7887-2632-3(3), 95636E7) Recorded Bks.

Longest Hair in the World, Class set. unabr. ed. Lois Duncan. Read by Christina Moore. 1 cass. (Running Time: 15 mins.). (J). (gr. 1 up). 1999. 180.80 (978-0-7887-3875-3(5), 47040) Recorded Bks.

Longest Journey. E. M. Forster. Narrated by Nadia May. (Running Time: 10 hrs.). 2000. 30.95 (978-1-59912-684-5(2)) Iofy Corp.

Longest Journey. unabr. ed. E. M. Forster. Read by Flo Gibson. 6 cass. (Running Time: 9 hrs.). 1997. 24.95 (978-1-55685-417-0(X), 417-X) Audio Bk Con.
The social & intellectual lives of Cambridge students are brilliantly pictured. Rickie's unfortunate marriage, his neglect of his old friends & his eventual willingness to cheat his half-brother are only redeemed when he loses his life saving Stephen Wondam's.

Longest Journey. unabr. ed. E. M. Forster. Read by Nadia May. 7 cass. (Running Time: 10 hrs.). 2001. 49.95 (978-0-7861-1993-6(4), 2763); audio compact disk 72.00 (978-0-7861-9732-3(3), 2763) Blckstn Audio.
A moving vision of a country split between pragmatism & imagination, sober conformity & redemptive eccentricity, upright Christianity & delirious paganism.

Longest Journey. unabr. collector's ed. E. M. Forster. Read by Jill Masters. 8 cass. (Running Time: 12 hrs.). 1993. 64.00 (978-0-7366-2589-0(5), 3334) Books on Tape.
Autobiographical novel centered on British public schools & universities from author of A Room with a View.

Longest Love see Monsarrat at Sea

Longest Night - A Personal History of Pan Am 103. Helen Engelhardt. Mem. of Helen Engelhardt. Directed By Jeffrey Hedquist. Engineer David Shinn. Prod. by Midsummer Sound Company Staff. 5 CDs. (Running Time: 6 hrs. 30 mins.). 2009. audio compact disk 34.95 (978-0-9802409-1-7(3)) Midsummer NY.

Longest Silence: A Life in Fishing. abr. ed. Thomas McGuane. Narrated by Grover Gardner. (Running Time: 16200 sec.). 2005. audio compact disk 28.00 (978-1-932378-74-0(X)) Pub: A Media Intl. Dist(s): Natl Bk Netwk

***Longest Trip Home.** unabr. ed. John Grogan. Read by John Grogan. (ENG.). 2008. (978-0-06-176943-6(6), Harper Audio) HarperCollins Pubs.

Longest Trip Home: A Memoir. unabr. ed. John Grogan. Narrated by John Grogan. (Running Time: 10 hrs. 45 mins.). (ENG.). 2008. (978-0-06-176944-3(4), Harper Audio) HarperCollins Pubs.

Longest Trip Home: A Memoir. unabr. ed. John Grogan. Read by John Grogan. 9 CDs. (Running Time: 11 hrs.). 2008. audio compact disk 34.95 (978-0-06-172629-3(X), Harper Audio) HarperCollins Pubs.

Longest Trip Home: A Memoir. unabr. ed. John Grogan. Read by John Grogan. 2009. audio compact disk 14.99 (978-0-06-190625-1(5), Harper Audio) HarperCollins Pubs.

Longest Trip Home: A Memoir. unabr. ed. John Grogan. Read by John Grogan. 9 CDs. (Running Time: 10 hrs. 45 mins.). 2007. audio compact disk 100.00 (978-1-4159-6230-5(8)) Random.

Longest Voyage see Award Winning Science Fiction

Longest Walk. unabr. ed. George Meegan. Narrated by Graeme Malcolm. 11 cass. (Running Time: 15 hrs. 15 mins.). 1990. 91.00 (978-1-55690-315-1(4), 90017E7) Recorded Bks.
The author's account of a 7 year, 19,000 mile trek from Tierra del Fuego to Alaska.

Longest Winter: The Battle of the Bulge & the Epic Story of World War II's Most Decorated Platoon. unabr. ed. Alex Kershaw & Grover Gardner. 7 cass. 2005. 59.95 (978-0-7927-3431-4(9), CSL 740); audio compact disk 89.95 (978-0-7927-3432-1(7), SLD 740) AudioGO.

Longfellow by Dancing Beetle. Perf. by Eugene Ely. 1 cass. (Running Time: 75 min.). (J). 1990. 10.00 Erthviibz.
Henry Wadsworth Longfellow, parody & nature sounds come together when Ms. Lemur & the spunky musical humans read & sing with Dancing Beetle.

Longing. 2 cass. 1999. 24.00 (978-1-887984-03-4(8)) The Gangaji Fnd.
A compilation of excerpts from public talks, exploring the core human desire of longing.

Longing. abr. ed. Beverly Lewis. Narrated by Aimee Lilly. (Running Time: 5 hrs. 49 mins. 0 sec.). (Courtship of Nellie Fisher Ser.: Bk. 3). (ENG.). 2008. 19.59 (978-1-60814-292-7(2)); audio compact disk 27.99 (978-1-59859-445-4(1)) Oasis Audio.

Longing for Death. Ed. by Alfred French. Intro. by Rene Wellek & Zdenek Pesat. 1 cass. (GER., (C). 1995. bk. 14.50 (978-0-930329-80-8(5)) Kabel Pubs.
The famous surgeon-musicologist's only available musical composition sung by a famous anonymous Alto Voice.

Longing for God: Seven Paths of Christian Devotion. abr. ed. Richard J. Foster & Gayle D. Beebe. (ENG.). 2009. audio compact disk 20.00 (978-0-8308-3526-3(1), IVP Bks) InterVarsity.

Longing for God: Seven Paths of Christian Devotion. unabr. ed. Richard J. Foster & Gayle D. Beebe. (Running Time: 12 hrs. 0 mins. 0 sec.). (ENG.). 2009. audio compact disk 28.98 (978-1-59644-627-4(7), Hovel Audio) christianaud.

***Longing for God: Seven Paths of Christian Devotion.** unabr. ed. Richard J. Foster & Gayle D. Beebe. Narrated by David Cochran Heath. (ENG.). 2009. 16.98 (978-1-59644-628-1(5), Hovel Audio) christianaud.

Longing for God: Seven Paths of Christian Devotion. unabr. ed. Richard J. Foster & Gayle D. Beebe. Narrated by David Cochran Heath. (Running Time: 12 hrs. 0 mins. 0 sec.). (ENG.). 2009. lp 19.98 (978-1-59644-626-7(9), Hovel Audio) christianaud.

Longing for His Appearing, Pt. 1. Derek Prince. 1 cass. (I-4133) Derek Prince.

Longing for His Appearing, Pt.1. Derek Prince. 1 cass. (Running Time: 60 min.). (I-132) Derek Prince.

Longing for His Appearing, Pt.2. Derek Prince. 1 cass. (Running Time: 60 min.). (I-133) Derek Prince.

Longing for Motherland-a Fraud see Classical Russian Poetry

Longing for the Divine. Swami Amar Jyoti. 1 cass. 1980. 9.95 (C-23) Truth Consciousness.
Finding our Center of Being. Truth, purity & longing for God are indispensable.

Longing, Lust, & Love: Black Lesbian Stories (Companion Piece) Poems. Prod. by Twinz DaWonda. Kiss Miss et al. 1 CD. (Running Time: 42 mins., 67 secs.). (ENG.). 2006. 14.95 (978-0-9785954-1-8(6), LLLAUDIO) Nghosi.

Longing to Go: Romans 15:22-23. Ed Young. 1984. 4.95 (978-0-7417-1405-3(1), 405) Win Walk.

Longinus: Book I of the Merlin Factor. (C). 2008. audio compact disk 19.95 (978-0-9773200-7-3(3)) Pub: Purple Haze Pr. Dist(s): AtlasBooks

Longitude. unabr. ed. Dava Sobel. Read by Kate Reading. 5 cass. (Running Time: 5 hrs.). 1996. 40.00 (978-0-7366-3420-5(7), 4066) Books on Tape.
Galileo & Sir Isaac Newton mapped the heavens for a celestial answer, but one man, John Harrison, figured out a mechanical one: a precise clock, known today as the chronometer. Full of heroism & chicanery, brilliance & the absurd, "Longitude" is also a fascinating brief history of astronomy & ocean navigation.

Longitudes & Attitudes: Exploring the World after September 11. abr. rev. ed. Thomas L. Friedman. Read by Thomas L. Friedman. (Running Time: 6 hrs. 0 mins. 0 sec.). (ENG.). 2006. audio compact disk 22.95 (978-1-4272-0138-6(2)) Pub: Macmill Audio. Dist(s): Macmillan

Longman Complete Course for the TOEFL Test: Preparation for the Computer & Paper Tests. Deborah Phillips. 5 cass. 2002. 49.95 (978-0-13-040898-3(0)); audio compact disk 49.95 (978-0-13-040897-6(2)) Longman.

Longman Introductory Course for the TOEFL Test, Set. Deborah Phillips. 2002. 50.15 (978-0-201-89853-8(5)) Longman.

Longman Preparation Series for the TOEIC Test. 3rd ed. Lin Lougheed. 2004. audio compact disk 29.27 (978-0-13-183884-0(9)) Longman.

Longshot. abr. ed. Dick Francis. Read by Kenneth Branagh. 2 cass. (Running Time: 3 hrs.). 2000. 7.95 (978-1-57815-047-2(7), 1019, Media Bks Audio) Media Bks NJ.

Longshot. unabr. ed. Dick Francis. Read by David Case. 7 cass. (Running Time: 10 hrs. 30 min.). 1994. 56.00 (978-0-7366-2739-9(1), 3465) Books on Tape.
John Kendall, a sometime-writer of survival guides for the hardiest of travelers, agrees to write the biography of Tremaine Vicers, a horse trainer. On the ride out, his Land Rover overturns in a ditch of freezing water, threatening the lives of the soaked party. Kendall uses his survival tactics to save everyone & soon after uses his skills of reason & survival on & off the race track when he finds himself involved with two murder investigations.

Longshot: A Novel. unabr. ed. Katie Kitamura. (Running Time: 7 hrs. 0 mins.). 2009. 29.95 (978-1-4417-1103-8(1)); 44.95 (978-1-4417-1099-4(X)); audio compact disk 69.00 (978-1-4417-1100-7(7)) Blckstn Audio.

Loo Sanction: A Novel. unabr. ed. Trevanian. Read by Joe Barrett. (Running Time: 10 hrs. 0 mins.). (ENG.). 2009. 29.95 (978-1-4332-5951-7(6)); 65.95 (978-1-4332-5947-0(8)); audio compact disk 100.00 (978-1-4332-5948-7(6)) Blckstn Audio.

Look Again. abr. ed. Lisa Scottoline. Read by Mary Stuart Masterson & Mary stuart Masterson. (Running Time: 6 hrs. 0 mins. 0 sec.). (ENG.). 2009. audio compact disk 29.95 (978-1-4272-0736-4(4)) Pub: Macmill Audio. Dist(s): Macmillan

Look Again. unabr. ed. Lisa Scottoline. Read by Mary Stuart Masterson. 9 CDs. (Running Time: 10 hrs. 0 mins. 0 sec.). (ENG.). 2009. audio compact disk 39.95 (978-1-4272-0658-9(9)) Pub: Macmill Audio. Dist(s): Macmillan

Look Again, for Hope. abr. ed. Eugene H. Peterson. Narrated by Kelly Ryan Dolan. (Running Time: 1 hr. 4 mins. 18 sec.). (ENG.). 2009. 9.99 (978-1-60814-547-8(6)); audio compact disk 9.99 (978-1-59859-603-8(9)) Oasis Audio.

Look Around Endangered Animals. unabr. ed. Ed Perez. 1 cass. (Running Time: 14 min.). (J). (gr. k-4). 1993. pap. bk. 13.45 (978-0-8045-6682-7(8), 6682) Spoken Arts.

Look At: "A Bright Future - Solar Box Cookers" & "Miracle of Guinope" in Hondorus. Hosted by Nancy Pearlman. 1 cass. (Running Time: 29 min.). 10.00 (908) Educ Comm CA.

Look At: "A River Cries" - Indians & Others Protest Cyanide Poisoning from Gold Mining on the Blackfoot River in Montana. Hosted by Nancy Pearlman. 1 cass. (Running Time: 29 min.). 10.00 (1314) Educ Comm CA.

Look At: "Abandoned" - Montana's Toxic Waste from Hard Rock Mining. Hosted by Nancy Pearlman. 1 cass. (Running Time: 28 min.). 10.00 (1418) Educ Comm CA.

Look At: "America's Wetlands - Resources at Risk," "Water Conservation in the City of Thousand Oaks" & "Population See-Saw" Hosted by Nancy Pearlman. 1 cass. (Running Time: 28 min.). 10.00 (1002) Educ Comm CA.

Look At: "Artic Refuge - Treasure of the North" Hosted by Nancy Pearlman. 1 cass. (Running Time: 29 min.). 10.00 (713) Educ Comm CA.

Look At: "Burros in the Desert" Hosted by Nancy Pearlman. 1 cass. (Running Time: 29 min.). 10.00 (209) Educ Comm CA.

Look At: "City of Thousand Oaks - Open Space Preservation;" "The Faceless Ones" Wildlife Tribute; The Penan's Forest Blockade in Borneo. Hosted by Nancy Pearlman. 1 cass. (Running Time: 28 min.). 10.00 (1003) Educ Comm CA.

Look At: "Dolphins of the Orange Coast" Hosted by Nancy Pearlman. 1 cass. (Running Time: 26 min.). 10.00 (410) Educ Comm CA.

Look At: "Garden of Eden" Hosted by Nancy Pearlman. 1 cass. (Running Time: 29 min.). 10.00 (109) Educ Comm CA.

Look At: "Kilowatts from Cowpies" Hosted by Nancy Pearlman. 1 cass. (Running Time: 28 min.). 10.00 (238) Educ Comm CA.

Look At: "Man of the Trees - Richard St. Barbe Baker" Hosted by Nancy Pearlman. 1 cass. (Running Time: 29 min.). 10.00 (905) Educ Comm CA.

Look At: "Mount Shasta - Cathedral of Wildness" Hosted by Nancy Pearlman. 1 cass. (Running Time: 28 min.). 10.00 (917) Educ Comm CA.

Look At: "Nimo's Garden" Hosted by Nancy Pearlman. 1 cass. (Running Time: 29 min.). 10.00 (307) Educ Comm CA.

Look At: "Nuclear Coverup: Chernousenko on Chernobyl" - A Nuclear Power Plant Accident in the Soviet Union. Hosted by Nancy Pearlman. 1 cass. (Running Time: 29 min.). 10.00 (1312) Educ Comm CA.

Look At: "Oasis in Time" - The Nature Conservancy's Coachella Valley Preserve. Hosted by Nancy Pearlman. 1 cass. (Running Time: 29 min.). 10.00 (417) Educ Comm CA.

Look At: "Planning the Global Family" Hosted by Nancy Pearlman. 1 cass. (Running Time: 28 min.). 10.00 (602) Educ Comm CA.

Look At: "Population Growth & the American Future" Hosted by Nancy Pearlman. 1 cass. (Running Time: 30 min.). 10.00 (329) Educ Comm CA.

Look At: Population Programs in Mexico & Iran. Hosted by Nancy Pearlman. 1 cass. (Running Time: 28 min.). 10.00 (328) Educ Comm CA.

Look At: "Rivers of the Deep South" Hosted by Nancy Pearlman. 1 cass. (Running Time: 29 min.). 10.00 (324) Educ Comm CA.

Look At: "Safe Water 2000" & Grasslands Resource Conservation District's Wetlands. Hosted by Nancy Pearlman. 1 cass. (Running Time: 29 min.). 10.00 (907) Educ Comm CA.

Look At: "Safeguarding the Future & the Urban Future" Hosted by Nancy Pearlman. 1 cass. (Running Time: 29 min.). 10.00 (604) Educ Comm CA.

Look At: "Sharing the Future" - The World Food Programme's Activities in India, Ethiopia & Peru. Hosted by Nancy Pearlman. 1 cass. (Running Time: 29 min.). 10.00 (1009) Educ Comm CA.

Look At: "So Large, So Small, Understanding Global Issues" Hosted by Nancy Pearlman. 1 cass. (Running Time: 27 min.). 10.00 (320) Educ Comm CA.

Look At: "Solar Promise" Hosted by Nancy Pearlman. 1 cass. (Running Time: 29 min.). 10.00 (231) Educ Comm CA.

Look At: "The Anchor-Outs of Richardson Bay" Hosted by Nancy Pearlman. 1 cass. (Running Time: 27 min.). 10.00 (715) Educ Comm CA.

Look At: "The Continental Ops" Hosted by Nancy Pearlman. 1 cass. (Running Time: 28 min.). 10.00 (310) Educ Comm CA.

Look At: "The Element of Doom" - Lead Mining in the Ozarks of Missouri. Hosted by Nancy Pearlman. 1 cass. (Running Time: 29 min.). 10.00 (1218) Educ Comm CA.

Look At: "The Future of Progress" - The Impact of Economic Development on Third-World Countries. Hosted by Nancy Pearlman. 1 cass. (Running Time: 29 min.). 10.00 (1025) Educ Comm CA.

Look At: "The Ninth Crusade - The Women Who Re-Won the West" Hosted by Nancy Pearlman. 1 cass. (Running Time: 28 min.). 10.00 (243) Educ Comm CA.

Look At: "The United Nations Population Fund Experience" Hosted by Nancy Pearlman. 1 cass. (Running Time: 28 min.). 10.00 (610) Educ Comm CA.

Look At: "Upper Newport Bay Ecological Reserve" Hosted by Nancy Pearlman. 1 cass. (Running Time: 29 min.). 10.00 (801) Educ Comm CA.

Look At: "What is the Limit?" Hosted by Nancy Pearlman. 1 cass. (Running Time: 29 min.). 10.00 (506) Educ Comm CA.

Look At: "Wind - Energy for the 90's & Beyond" Hosted by Nancy Pearlman. 1 cass. (Running Time: 28 min.). 10.00 (909) Educ Comm CA.

Look At: "Women for America, for the World" Hosted by Nancy Pearlman. 1 cass. (Running Time: 30 min.). 10.00 (510) Educ Comm CA.

Look At Pt. 1: "Earth First!, Radical Activism" Hosted by Nancy Pearlman. 1 cass. (Running Time: 30 min.). 10.00 (618) Educ Comm CA.

Look At Pt. 2: "Earth First!, Radical Activism" Hosted by Nancy Pearlman. 1 cass. (Running Time: 27 min.). 10.00 (619) Educ Comm CA.

Look At Pt. 2: "Our Finite World" Hosted by Nancy Pearlman. 1 cass. (Running Time: 30 min.). 10.00 (616); 10.00 (617) Educ Comm CA.

Look at an Historic Sierra Club Film: "The Grand Canyon" Depicting Rafting on the Colorado River Before the Dam. Hosted by Nancy Pearlman. 1 cass. (Running Time: 28 min.). 10.00 (1410) Educ Comm CA.

Look at Canada's Baby Harp Seals: Peace on Ice. Hosted by Nancy Pearlman. 1 cass. (Running Time: 28 min.). 10.00 (1115) Educ Comm CA.

Look at Day by Day Progressions. Edward Helin. 1 cass. 8.95 (150) Am Fed Astrologers.
Moving the moon for progressed year to time events and rectify.

Look at Ego States. Jeanne Avery. 8.95 (024) Am Fed Astrologers.
T. A. and aspects with group therapy demonstrations.

Look at "Family of the Great Mystery" - Navajo & Hopi Relocation on Big Mountain. Hosted by Nancy Pearlman. 1 cass. (Running Time: 29 min.). 10.00 (812) Educ Comm CA.

Look at Fighting Toxics in the Southwest: "No Time to Waste" Hosted by Nancy Pearlman. 1 cass. (Running Time: 28 min.). 10.00 (821) Educ Comm CA.

Look at Forest Regrowth after Fires: "Up from the Ashes" & Highway Deicing. Hosted by Nancy Pearlman. 1 cass. (Running Time: 29 min.). 10.00 (915) Educ Comm CA.

Look at Hazardous Waste Disposal from Massachusetts: "Inside Out's 'Waste Away'" Hosted by Nancy Pearlman. 1 cass. (Running Time: 29 min.). 10.00 (918) Educ Comm CA.

Look at India's Agricultural Changes: "Greening the Subcontinent" Hosted by Nancy Pearlman. 1 cass. (Running Time: 29 min.). 10.00 (1005) Educ Comm CA.

Look at Ladahk (Little Tibet) - Development in the Indian Himalayas. Hosted by Nancy Pearlman. 1 cass. (Running Time: 29 min.). 10.00 (1017) Educ Comm CA.

Look at Life from a Deer Stand: Hunting for the Meaning of Life. Steve Chapman. 1 cass. 1996. 11.98 (978-7-901442-59-7(X)) S&A Family.
Inspirational.

Look at Life from a Deer Stand: Hunting for the Meaning of Life. abr. ed. Steve Chapman. 2 cass. (Running Time: 3 hrs.). 2003. 16.99 (978-0-7369-1144-3(8)) Harvest Hse.

Look at Louisiana's Toxic Corridor: "For Our Children" Hosted by Nancy Pearlman. 1 cass. (Running Time: 28 min.). 10.00 (906) Educ Comm CA.

Look at Me. unabr. ed. Anita Brookner. Read by Judith Whale. 6 cass. (Running Time: 7 hrs. 15 min.). 2001. 54.95 (978-1-85695-455-6(2), 92084) Pub: ISIS Audio GBR. Dist(s): Ulverscroft US
During the course of her work in the reference library at a medical institute which specialized in the research of problems in human behavior, Frances Hinton is taken up by Nick & Alix, a dazzling & legendary couple. She abandoned most of her critical faculties, met new friends & discovered novel possibilities & impossibilities. Her sentimental education had begun.

Look at Mecklenburg County's "Planet Earth Save Me Now" Hosted by Nancy Pearlman. 1 cass. (Running Time: 28 min.). 10.00 (911) Educ Comm CA.

Look at New York's "The Altona Flat Rock" Hosted by Nancy Pearlman. 1 cass. (Running Time: 29 min.). 10.00 (811) Educ Comm CA.

Look at Non-Point Source Pollution along the Tualalin River: Oregon State University's "We All Live Downstream" Hosted by Nancy Pearlman. 1 cass. (Running Time: 29 min.). 10.00 (1509) Educ Comm CA.

Look at Plato. 10.00 Esstee Audios.
A view of the thinker as seen by Wilhelm Van Loon.

Look at Rainforests: "A Treasure in Jeopardy" Hosted by Nancy Pearlman. 1 cass. (Running Time: 28 min.). 10.00 (810) Educ Comm CA.

Look at SAS Files. Rick Aster. 2 cass. (Running Time: 95 min.). (Attitude Ser.: 1). 1994. pap. bk. 19.95 Set. (978-1-891957-00-0(7)) Brkfst Commn Corp.
Explains what is needed to use SAS software's special file types.

Look at Sweden's: "Acidification - The Invisible Enemy" Hosted by Nancy Pearlman. 1 cass. (Running Time: 29 min.). 10.00 (901) Educ Comm CA.

***Look at the Birdie.** unabr. ed. Kurt Vonnegut. Narrated by Barbara Rosenblat & Norman Dietz. 1 Playaway. (Running Time: 7 hrs. 15 mins.). 2009. 59.75 (978-1-4407-6231-4(7)); 67.75 (978-1-4407-6228-4(7)); audio compact disk 77.75 (978-1-4407-6229-1(5)) Recorded Bks.

***Look at the Birdie.** unabr. collector's ed. Kurt Vonnegut. Narrated by Barbara Rosenblat & Norman Dietz. 7 CDs. (Running Time: 7 hrs. 15 mins.). 2009. audio compact disk 44.95 (978-1-4407-6230-7(9)) Recorded Bks.

Look at the Book: Traveling the Original Route 66, Charles R. Swindoll. 7 cass. (Running Time: 13 hrs.). 1994. 34.95 (978-1-57972-032-2(3)) Insight Living.
Traveling through the Bible to gain an overall perspective of its message & purpose.

Look at the History of Wind Power: "Windsong" & Water Conservation in Phoenix, Arizona. Hosted by Nancy Pearlman. 1 cass. (Running Time: 29 min.). 10.00 (914) Educ Comm CA.

Look at the Masons. Stephen Mansfield. 1 cass. (Running Time: 90 mins.). (Studies in Church History Ser.: Vol. 4). 2000. 5.00 (SM02-004) Morning NC.
An in-depth look at different philosophies that have influenced church history, this series provides excellent keys for understanding how to effectively confront the important issues of our times.

Look at the Pacific Northwest Forests Through National Wildlife Federation's "In These Ancient Trees" Hosted by Nancy Pearlman. 1 cass. (Running Time: 30 min.). 10.00 (1001) Educ Comm CA.

Look at Toxic Discharges into the Mississippi River: "We All Live Downstream" Hosted by Nancy Pearlman. 1 cass. (Running Time: 29 min.). 10.00 (819) Educ Comm CA.

Look at UNDP's: "Borrowed from Our Future" & The 1990 International Whaling Commission Meeting. Hosted by Nancy Pearlman. 1 cass. (Running Time: 29 min.). 10.00 (820) Educ Comm CA.

Look Away. unabr. ed. Harold Coyle. Read by David Hilder. (Running Time: 13 hrs. 30 mins.). 2010. 29.95 (978-1-4417-2602-5(0)); audio compact disk 109.00 (978-1-4417-2599-8(7)) Blckstn Audio.

Look Away: A Novel. abr. ed. Harold Coyle. Read by Alex Chadwick. 4 cass. (Running Time: 5 hrs. 10 mins.). 1995. 19.95 (978-1-55935-168-3(3), 595948) Soundelux.
This first book in a major Civil War saga details the tension & agony of America's cruelest war.

Look Away: A Novel. abr. ed. Harold Coyle. 4 cass. (Running Time: 6 hrs.). 1995. 21.95 (978-1-55935-171-3(3)) Soundelux.

Look Away: A Novel. unabr. ed. Harold Coyle. Read by David Hilder. 13 cass. (Running Time: 19 hrs.). 1995. 85.95 (978-0-7861-0860-2(6), 1658) Blckstn Audio.
In this riveting Civil War adventure, Coyle's command of the battlefield brings home the grim reality of that wrenching conflict. At the heart of the story are two brothers, sons of a prosperous New Jersey businessman whose growing wealth & power are dependent on his ability to avoid choosing sides as the abolitionist movement takes hold. James & Kevin Bannon, who have always shielded each other from their father's tyrannical outbursts, see their fierce loyalty abruptly shattered by their rivalry over a woman...& her shocking, violent death. James is sent off to VMI to make something of himself, while Kevin attends college in the north. Soon they will find themselves on opposite sides in every great action of the war.

Look Back All the Green Valley: A Novel. unabr. ed. Fred Chappell. Narrated by Tom Stechschulte. 8 cass. (Running Time: 10 hrs. 15 mins.). 2000. 65.00 (978-0-7887-4863-9(7), 96083E7) Recorded Bks.
Jess Kirkman's mother is dying & he has come home to get family affairs in order. Now he faces the daunting task of sorting out the secret workshop his father left behind when he died 10 years ago. A journey through space & time & the story of a quest for perfect revenge, this reads like Mark Twain, Dante & Buck Rogers.

Look Better Naked Audio Book: Your Body's Owner's Manual. Speeches. Read by Norris Dendy. 1 CD. (Running Time: 75 min). 2003. audio compact disk 10.00 (978-0-9740292-1-4(1)) Real Firm.

Look Both Ways. Music by Frank Cappelli. (Running Time: 32 min.). (J). (ps-3). 1987. 8.98 (978-0-929304-00-7(4), CL1000) Peanut Heaven.
Features music designed to entertain & educate children.

Look Both Ways. Jacquelyn Mitchard. Read by Emily Durante. (Midnight Twins Ser.: No. 2). (J). 2009. 39.99 (978-1-60812-655-2(2)) Find a World.

Look Both Ways. unabr. ed. Jacquelyn Mitchard. Read by Emily Durante. 1 MP3-CD. (Running Time: 7 hrs.). (Midnight Twins Ser.: No. 2). 2009. 39.97 (978-1-4233-6501-3(1), 9781423365013, Brlnc Audio MP3 Lib); 24.99 (978-1-4233-6500-6(3), 9781423365006, Brilliance MP3); 39.97 (978-1-4233-6503-7(8), 9781423365037, BADLE); 24.99 (978-1-4233-6502-0(X), 9781423365020, BAD); audio compact disk 29.99 (978-1-4233-6498-6(8), 9781423364986, Bril Audio CD Unabri) Brilliance Audio.

Look Both Ways. unabr. ed. Jacquelyn Mitchard. Read by Emily Durante. 6 CDs. (Running Time: 7 hrs.). (Midnight Twins Ser.: No. 2). (YA). (gr. 6-9). 2009. audio compact disk 54.97 (978-1-4233-6499-3(6), 9781423364993, BriAudCD Unabrid) Brilliance Audio.

Look for the Silver Lining. June Francis. 2007. 84.95 (978-1-84652-109-6(2)) Pub: ISIS Audio GBR. Dist(s): Ulverscroft US

Look for the Silver Lining. June Francis. Read by Margaret Sircom. 11. (Running Time: 47700 sec.). 2007. audio compact disk 99.95 (978-1-84652-110-2(6)) Pub: ISIS Audio GBR. Dist(s): Ulverscroft US

Look Funebre, Homicide by night. Short Stories. Pierre Siniac. Read by J. Balutin. 1 cass. (FRE.). 1991. 21.95 (1123-VSL) Olivia & Hill.
Two short mystery stories.

Look Great, Feel Great: 12 Keys to Enjoying a Healthy Life Now. abr. unabr. ed. Joyce Meyer. Told to Rowan Jacobsen. (Running Time: 6 hrs.). (ENG.). 2006. 14.98 (978-1-59483-505-6(5)) Pub: Hachet Audio. Dist(s): HachBkGrp

Look Great, Feel Great: 12 Keys to Enjoying a Healthy Life Now. unabr. ed. Joyce Meyer. Read by Pat Lentz. Told to Rowan Jacobsen. (Running Time: 6 hrs.). (ENG.). 2009. 44.98 (978-1-60788-116-2(0)) Pub: Hachet Audio. Dist(s): HachBkGrp

Look Homeward, Angel, Pt. 1. unabr. collector's ed. Thomas Wolfe. Read by Jonathan Marosz. Intro. by Maxwell Perkins. 9 cass. (Running Time: 13 hrs. 30 min.). (J). 1996. 72.00 (978-0-7366-3223-2(9), 3885-A) Books on Tape.
Eugene Gant yearns to escape his tumultuous family & his small North Carolina town. Gant's experiences mirror Wolfe's.

Look Homeward, Angel, Pt. 2. unabr. collector's ed. Thomas Wolfe. Read by Jonathan Marosz. 9 cass. (Running Time: 13 hrs. 30 min.). (J). 1996. 72.00 (978-0-7366-3224-9(7), 3885-B) Books on Tape.
A young man escapes his tumultuous family & his claustrophobic town.

Look in Your Heart. Liz Von Seggen. 1 cass. (Running Time: 31 min.). Dramatization. 1996. 15.00 incl. script. (978-1-58302-043-2(8), STP-22) One Way St.
Includes song lyrics, production tips, & staging ideas for a puppet musical.

Look in Your Heart. Liz VonSeggen. Arranged by Mark Bradford. Contrib. by Todd Liebenow & Dave Privett. 2001. pap. bk. 15.00 (978-1-58302-189-7(2)) One Way St.

Look Inside. unabr. ed. Poems. Carolyn Ann O'Riley. 1 cass. (Running Time: 45 mins.). (J). 2000. 10.00 (978-1-891870-14-9(9)) Archangels Pen.
Archangel Michael divinely inspired lesson stories for children. Teaches about peace, self image, love, angels, The Creator & non-discrimination.

Look Me in the Eye: My Life with Asperger's. abr. ed. John Elder Robison. Read by John Elder Robison. Frwd. by Augusten Burroughs. 5 CDs. (Running Time: 21600 sec.). (ENG.). 2007. audio compact disk 29.95 (978-0-7393-5768-2(9), Random AudioBks) Pub: Random Audio Pubg. Dist(s): Random

Look Out, Doctor! unabr. ed. Robert Clifford. Read by Christopher Scott. 4 cass. (Running Time: 7 hrs. 30 min.). 2001. 49.95 (978-1-84283-002-4(3), 3-002-3) Pub: Soundings Ltd GBR. Dist(s): Ulverscroft US
Small though the town of Tadchester may be, nobody could accuse it of being sleepy. Not when the stream of patients flocking to the surgery include Mrs. Short with her secret addictions, Mick & Alice whose fifty years of successful marriage they put down to "a bloody good row" at least twice a week... not forgetting the entire rugby team from Drake's College who developed a mysterious & embarrassing ailment at a London night club after an away match.

Look Out, It's April Fools' Day. Frank Modell. (J). 1987. 40.88 (978-0-676-31441-0(4)) SRA McGraw.

Look Out, Secret Seven. unabr. ed. Enid Blyton. Read by Sarah Greene. 2 CDs. (Running Time: 3 hrs.). (J). 2002. audio compact disk 21.95 (978-0-7540-6536-4(7), CHCD 036, Chivers Child Audio) AudioGO.

Look to the Horizon. Scott Keyes. 1985. 10.00 (978-0-9633179-0-2(3)) D Scott Pubs.

Look to the Lady. unabr. ed. Margery Allingham. Read by Francis Matthews. 6 cass. (Running Time: 8 hrs. 57 min.). 1989. 54.95 (978-0-7451-5726-9(2), CAB 365) AudioGO.
When the security of a priceless artifact - -owned bu the Gyrth family for centuries - -is threatened by a greedy, ruthless ring of art collectors, Albert Campion springs to its defense. Enlisting the aid of young Valentine Gyrth and a few other associates, Campion embarks on an investigation that threatens to turn deadly.

Look to the Rainbow (from Finian's Rainbow) - ShowTrax. Arranged by Mark Brymer. 1 CD. 2000. audio compact disk 19.95 H Leonard.
Arrangement is designed with easily-learned parts & just a hint of the Celtic in the accompaniment.

Look to the Wolves. Alexander Fullerton. Read by Peter Wickham. 12 cass. (Running Time: 14 hrs.). (Sound Ser.). 2001. 94.95 (978-1-84283-082-6(1)) Pub: UlverLrgPrint GBR. Dist(s): Ulverscroft US

Look to the Wolves. unabr. ed. Alexander Fullerton. 12 CDs. (Soundings (CDs) Ser.). 2007. audio compact disk 99.95 (978-1-84559-535-7(1)) Pub: ISIS Lrg Prnt GBR. Dist(s): Ulverscroft US

Look to You. Contrib. by Hillsong United. 2005. audio compact disk 17.98 (978-5-559-07966-0(9)) Hillsong Pubng AUS.

Look up Sing Out ... by Faith: Volume 2. Prod. by Robert Swope & Michael Davis. Contrib. by Ken Pennell & Larry Blackwell. 2005. audio compact disk 12.98 (978-5-558-86596-7(2)) Pt of Grace Ent.

Look up Sing Out... Glory. 2006. 14.99 (978-5-558-40705-1(0)) Pt of Grace Ent.

Look What Happened While You Were Sleeping. A Friend of Medjugorje. 2008. audio compact disk 21.00 (978-1-878909-11-4(8)) St James Pub.

Look Younger - Better. Prod. by Betty L. Randolph. 1 cass. (Subliminal Plus Health Ser.). 12.98 (55) Randolph Tapes.
Tap the fountain of youth & de-age yourself.

Look Younger! Feel Younger! 1 cass. (Running Time: 45 min.). (Health Ser.). 9.98 (978-1-55909-062-9(6), 55); 15.98 90 min. extended length stereo music. (55X) Randolph Tapes.
Use your mind to tap the fountain of youth & "de-age" yourself. Subliminal messages are heard 3-5 minutes before becoming ocean sounds or music.

Lookin' Back Texas. unabr. ed. Leanna Ellis. Narrated by Pam Turlow. (Running Time: 10 hrs. 21 mins. 12 sec.). (ENG.). 2008. 19.59 (978-1-60814-293-4(0)); audio compact disk 27.99 (978-1-59859-423-2(0)) Oasis Audio.

Looking at Each Other see Poetry & Voice of Muriel Rukeyser

Looking at Fear, That Extraordinary Jewel. J. Krishnamurti. 1 cass. (Running Time: 75 min.). (Brockwood Park Talks - 1984 Ser.: No. 2). 8.50 (ABT842) Krishnamurti.
If all time is contained in the now, what is our relationship to each other & what is action? If there is no fear inwardly, would we have Gods?.

Looking at Government from the Inside. Read by Fred Schnaubelt & Dennis Brown. (Running Time: 60 min.). (Cal State Univ., Long Beach Ser.). 1981. 9.00 (F125) Freeland Pr.
Two elected officails discuss their efforts to work within the system to make those changes they think are necessary for our society. Panel discussion.

Looking at Love: With Guy de Maupassant. unabr. ed. Read by Adam Menken & Franette Liebow. 2 cass. (Running Time: 3 hrs.). 1996. 16.95 (978-1-882071-68-5(9)) B-B Audio.
Here is a delightful collection of tales by that superb master of the short story, Guy de Maupassant. In narratives that exhibit a brilliant simplicity and a gripping impact, de Maupassant evokes many moods and atmospheres and writes of a wide range of h.

Looking at Matter: Early Explorers Early Set B Audio CD. Mary Clare Goller. Adapted by Benchmark Education Staff. (J). 2007. audio compact disk 10.00 (978-1-4108-8222-6(5)) Benchmark Educ.

Looking at the Pieces Full Year & Music CD Pack. Zondervan Publishing Staff. (J). 2004. audio compact disk 909.99 (978-0-310-64417-0(8)) Zondervan.

Looking at the Pieces Music CD Pack Of 5. Willow Creek Association. (J). 2002. audio compact disk 64.95 (978-0-310-64382-1(1)) Zondervan.

Looking at the Sky Audio CD. Adapted by Benchmark Education Company Staff. Based on a work by Jeffrey B. Fuerst. (My First Reader's Theater Ser.). (J). (gr. k-1). 2008. audio compact disk 10.00 (978-1-60634-089-9(1)) Benchmark Educ.

Looking at the World Through Mundane Astrology. Zipporah P. Dobyns. 1 cass. 8.95 (089) Am Fed Astrologers.
An AFA Convention workshop tape.

Looking Back. Featuring Jack Benny. (J). 1950. audio compact disk 12.95 (978-1-57970-502-2(2), Audio-For) J Norton Pubs.

Looking Back. Belva Plain. Narrated by Kate Forbes. 10 CDs. (Running Time: 11 hrs. 30 mins.). audio compact disk 97.00 (978-1-4025-2068-6(9)) Recorded Bks.

Looking Back. unabr. ed. Perf. by Jack Benny. 1 cass. (Running Time: 38 min.). 12.95 (#490) J Norton Pubs.
Jack reminisces about his career. He reveals the origin of his celebrated feud with Fred Allen & comments on some of his best known gags.

Looking Back. unabr. ed. Belva Plain. Narrated by Kate Forbes. 8 cass. (Running Time: 11 hrs. 30 mins.). 2001. 76.00 (978-0-7887-8847-5(7)) Recorded Bks.
Cecile is a beautiful child of privilege; Amanda is ambitious but poor; Norma is the academic star, yet the least self-assured. They are inseparable at college. And when the three classmates graduate and move into careers and marriage, they remain close. But, secretly, one of them will begin a relationship that undermines their trust and alters the course of each life it touches.

Looking Back & Learning. George Eppley. 2005. audio compact disk 12.50 (978-0-9662805-2-4(0)) E & D Prodns.

Looking Back & Learning: From Three Score & Ten. 1996. 15.00 (978-0-9662805-0-0(4)) E & D Prodns.

Looking Back at Hiroshima. unabr. ed. Jacob Bester. 12.95 (19028) J Norton Pubs.
The man who dropped the first atomic bomb discusses the background, psychological implications & the ethical controversy of the explosion.

Looking Back with Captain Puget. Perf. by Captain Puget. 1 cass. (Don McCune Library). 1992. 8.95 Digitally Recorded. (A101) Don McCune Library.
Songs from the Captain Puget Show include: "Blow Ye Winds," "Santy Anno," "A-roving," "The Geoduck," "The Shark," "The Sea Squirt," "The Old Settler" ("Acres of Clams"), "The Whale," "Ode to Puget Sound," & "Looking Back".

Looking Backward. unabr. ed. Edward Bellamy. Read by Edward Lewis. 6 cass. (Running Time: 8 hrs. 30 mins.). Orig. Title: Looking Backward, 2000-1887. 2001. 44.95 (978-0-7861-2008-6(8), 2778); audio compact disk 56.00 (978-0-7861-9723-1(4), 2778) Blckstn Audio.
A blueprint of the "perfect society", in 1935 it was listed by several prominent thinkers as the most influential work written by an American in the preceding fifty years.

Looking Backward, 2000-1887 see Looking Backward

Looking Beyond the Mirror: 12 Steps to Overcoming Self Doubt. unabr. ed. Tricia Brennan. Read by Tricia Brennan. (Running Time: 32400 sec.). 2006. audio compact disk 87.95 (978-1-74093-701-6(5)) Pub: Bolinda Pubng AUS. Dist(s): Bolinda Pub Inc

Looking Deeply: Mindfulness & Meditation. Thich Nhat Hanh & Parallax Press Staff. 2 CDs. (Running Time: 2 hrs.). (ENG.). 2002. audio compact disk 19.00 (978-1-888375-26-8(4), 75264) Pub: Parallax Pr. Dist(s): PerseuPGW
Introducing a new Parallax CD Series: Classic Dharma Talks, Thich Nhat Hanh's seminal teachings on key topics, emphasizing on mindfulness and its importance to today's social and political issues. Being Peace is the original talk which inspired Thich Nha.

Looking Fabulous After 40: A woman's guide to fashin, makewup & Style. Speeches. Georgia Donovan. 3 CD's. (Running Time: 3 hours). 2007. audio compact disk 57.00 (978-0-9786891-3-1(5)) Austin Bay.

Looking for a Few Good Vars - Looking for a Few Good Vendors. 1 cass. 1990. 8.50 Recorded Res.

Looking for a Miracle: Weeping Icons, Relics, Stigmata, Visions & Healing Cures. Joe Nickell. Read by Joe Nickell. 2 pieces. (Running Time: 3 hrs.). (ENG.). 1996. 25.98 (978-1-57392-101-5(7)) Prometheus Bks.
Respected historical & paranormal investigator confronts such strange events, powers & objects such as the Shroud of Turin, bleeding statues, burning handprints, etc. & investigates the evidence relating to specific claims.

Looking for a Ship. John McPhee. Read by George Guidall. 4 Cass. (Running Time: 7.25 Hrs.). 19.95 (978-1-4025-2799-9(3)) Recorded Bks.

Looking for a Ship. unabr. ed. John McPhee. Read by Walter Zimmerman. 7 cass. (Running Time: 7 hrs.). 1990. 40.00 (978-0-7366-1862-5(7), 2693) Books on Tape.
The United States Merchant Marine, once a bold & thrusting institution, grows moribund. Reduced by international competition in ship building & a

scramble for cargos, the Merchant Marine has shrunk from more than 2000 ships to fewer than 400 in less than ten years.

Looking for a Ship. unabr. ed. John McPhee. Narrated by George Guidall. 5 cass. (Running Time: 7 hrs. 15 mins.). 1991. 44.00 (978-1-55690-316-8(2), 91128E7) Recorded Bks.
McPhee sails with first mate Andy Chase on an "exotic" run to South America aboard the "S.S. Stella Lykes." McPhee captures the excitement & the perilous dangers of the sea, of stowaways & cocaine heists, pirates & freak waves, apocryphal tales that could fill up several lifetimes, tinged with a barely-concealed regret for a way of life that is passing quickly away.

Looking for Alaska. John Green. Read by Jeff Woodman. (Playaway Young Adult Ser.). (J). 2008. 59.99 (978-1-60640-598-7(5)) Find a World.

Looking for Alaska. abr. ed. Short Stories. Peter Jenkins. Read by Peter Jenkins. Read by Rebekah Jenkins. 8 cass. (Running Time: 12 hrs. 33 min.). 2003. 39.95 (978-0-9725312-0-7(3)) Jenkins World Prod.
Best-selling author of "A Walk Across America", Peter Jenkins,spent 18 months in search of one of the most incredible places in the world, Alaska. Peter traveled over 20,000 miles in tiny bush planes, pulled by sled dogs, on snow machines and on snowshoes, in salmon fishing boats, on the Alaska Marine Highway and the Haul Road, searching for what defines Alaska. Hearing the stories of many real Alaskans, Peter gets to know this place in a way only he can. Also, he takes his family with him, renting a "home base" in Seward, Alaska, and coming and going from there. His family joins him at times on his unforgettable adventures, including Rebekah, his 20 year old daughter. She discovers her own wild Alaska, with and without her father, and writes a portion of this book. The resulting diary of discovery, a national best seller, is being called "one of the best books ever written about Alaska." Included are excerpts from interviews from the actual characters, along with nature sounds that Peter recorded throughout Alaska. Read by the authors.

Looking for Alaska. unabr. ed. John Green. Read by Jeff Woodman. (Running Time: 7 hrs.). 2006. 39.25 (978-1-4233-2449-2(8), 9781423324492, BADLE); 24.95 (978-1-4233-2448-5(X), 9781423324485, BAD); 39.25 (978-1-4233-2447-8(1), 9781423324478, Brlnc Audio MP3 Lib) Brilliance Audio.
Miles Halter is fascinated by famous last words - and tired of his safe life at home. He leaves for boarding school to seek what the dying poet Francois Rabelais called the "Great Perhaps." Much awaits Miles at Culver Creek, including Alaska Young. Clever, funny, screwed-up, and dead sexy, Alaska will pull Miles into her labyrinth and catapult him into the Great Perhaps. Looking for Alaska brilliantly chronicles the indelible impact one life can have on another. A stunning debut, it marks John Green's arrival as an important new voice in contemporary fiction.

Looking for Alaska. unabr. ed. John Green. Read by Jeff Woodman. 6 CDs. (Running Time: 25200 sec.). (YA). (gr. 8-12). 2006. audio compact disk 29.95 (978-1-4233-2444-7(7), 9781423324447, Bril Audio CD Unabri); audio compact disk 24.95 (978-1-4233-2446-1(3), 9781423324461, Brilliance MP3) Brilliance Audio.

Looking for Alaska. unabr. ed. John Green. Read by Jeff Woodman. 6 CDs. (Running Time: 7 hrs.). (YA). (gr. 9 up). 2006. audio compact disk 82.25 (978-1-4233-2445-4(5), 9781423324454, BriAudCD Unabrid) Brilliance Audio.

Looking for Alibrandi. Melina Marchetta. Read by Marcella Russo. (Running Time: 8 hrs.). (YA). 2009. 74.99 (978-1-74214-331-6(8), 9781742143316) Pub: Bolinda Pubng AUS. Dist(s): Bolinda Pub Inc

Looking for Alibrandi. unabr. ed. Melina Marchetta. Read by Marcella Russo. 6 cass. (Running Time: 9 hrs.). (YA). 1999. (978-1-86442-348-8(X), 581263) Bolinda Pubng AUS.

Looking for Alibrandi. unabr. ed. Melina Marchetta. Read by Marcella Russo. 7 CDs. (Running Time: 8 hrs.). (YA). 2001. audio compact disk 83.95 (978-1-74030-395-8(4)) Pub: Bolinda Pubng AUS. Dist(s): Bolinda Pub Inc

Looking for Alibrandi. unabr. ed. Melina Marchetta. Read by Marcella Russo. 6 cass. (Running Time: 8 hrs.). (YA). (gr. 7 up). 2004. 48.00 (978-1-74030-231-9(1)) Pub: Bolinda Pubng AUS. Dist(s): Bolinda Pub Inc

Looking for Alibrandi. unabr. ed. Melina Marchetta. Read by Marcella Russo. (Running Time: 27600 sec.). (J). 2007. audio compact disk 43.95 (978-1-921334-44-3(4), 9781921334443) Pub: Bolinda Pubng AUS. Dist(s): Bolinda Pub Inc

Looking for Chet Baker. Bill Moody. 6 cassettes. (Running Time: approx. 8 hours). 2003. 34.95 (978-0-9644138-2-5(5), Drk City Bks) OffByOne.

***Looking for Cover (Audio Cd)** Maria Fama. 2008. audio compact disk 6.00 (978-1-884419-96-6(8)) Pub: Bordighera. Dist(s): SPD-Small Pr Dist

Looking for Faith, Hope & Love. (Running Time: 48 mins.). audio compact disk (978-1-59076-202-8(9)) DscvrHlpPubng.

Looking for Gatsby: My Life. Faye Dunaway & Betsy Sharkey. 2 cass. 1996. 17.00 (978-1-56876-051-3(5)) Soundlines Ent.
The uncompromising & unaplogetic autobiography of one of Hollywood's most glamorous & enduring actress.

Looking for God: An Unexpected Journey Through Tattoos, Tofu, & Pronouns. unabr. ed. Nancy Ortberg. Narrated by Rebecca Gallagher. (ENG.). 2008. 13.99 (978-1-60814-294-1(9)) Oasis Audio.

Looking for God: An Unexpected Journey Through Tattoos, Tofu, & Pronouns. unabr. ed. Nancy Ortberg. Read by Nancy Ortberg. Narrated by Rebecca Gallagher. (ENG.). 2008. audio compact disk 19.99 (978-1-59859-380-8(3)) Oasis Audio.

Looking for Grandma's Teeth. Brenda Baker. (J). 1995. audio compact disk 12.95 (978-1-55050-092-9(9)) Pub: Coteau CAN. Dist(s): Fitzhenry W Ltd

Looking for Jamie Bridger, unabr. ed. Nancy Springer. Narrated by Alyssa Bresnahan. 4 cass. (Running Time: 5 hrs. 15 mins.). (gr. 8 up). 1997. 35.00 (978-0-7887-0749-0(3), 94926E7) Recorded Bks.
Fourteen-year-old Jamie has lived with her grandparents as long as she can remember. After her grandfather dies, leaving her alone & responsible for her now-childlike grandmother, Jamie starts looking for information about her mother & father.

Looking for JJ. Anne Cassidy. Read by Shirley Barthelmie. (Running Time: 6 hrs. 15 mins.). (YA). 2009. 69.99 (978-1-74214-307-1(5), 9781742143071) Pub: Bolinda Pubng AUS. Dist(s): Bolinda Pub Inc

Looking for JJ. unabr. ed. Anne Cassidy. Read by Shirley Barthelmie. 6 CDs. (Running Time: 22500 sec.). (J). (gr. 4-7). 2006. audio compact disk 77.95 (978-1-74093-729-0(5)) Pub: Bolinda Pubng AUS. Dist(s): Bolinda Pub Inc

Looking for Love: Building Right Relationships in a Not-So-Right World. Speeches. George G. Bloomer. 1 CD. (Running Time: 50 min). 2004. bk. 12.99 (978-0-88368-991-2(X), 77991X) Pub: Whitaker Hse. Dist(s): Anchor Distributors
Here's more insightful information on avoiding common relationship pitfalls in the words of Bishop Bloomer.

Looking for Love in All the Wrong Places: Genesis 24:1-67. Ed Young. 1994. 4.95 (978-0-7417-2039-9(6), 1039) Win Walk.

Looking for Mary: Or, the Blessed Mother & Me. Beverly Donofrio. Narrated by Christina Moore. 5 cass. (Running Time: 7 hrs. 15 mins.). 48.00 (978-1-4025-1772-3(6)) Recorded Bks.

Looking for Mary: Or, the Blessed Mother & Me. collector's ed. Beverly Donofrio. Narrated by Christina Moore. 5 cass. (Running Time: 7 hrs. 15 mins.). 2002. 32.95 (978-1-4025-1773-0(4), K1019) Recorded Bks.
Offers the universal story about a woman who - in a quest for the Blessed Mother - finds herself.

Looking for Mr. Goodbar. unabr. ed. Judith Rossner. Narrated by Susan Adams. 7 cass. (Running Time: 9 hrs. 30 mins.). 1980. 60.00 (978-1-55690-317-5(0), 80220E7) Recorded Bks.
Theresa Dunn teaches school by day & prowls the bars at night in search of sexual adventure.

Looking for Papito. Antonio Sacre. Perf. by Antonio Sacre. 1 cass. (Running Time: 1 hr.). (J). 1996. 10.00 (978-1-886283-09-1(5)) Woodside Ave Mus.
Cuban-American storyteller Antonio enthusiastically spins both traditional tales & stories from his own life & family. His stories are liberally sprinkled with music with a wide variety of whimsical self-produced sound effects. Be prepared to laugh at the repetition of his funniest words.

Looking for Peyton Place: A Novel. abr. ed. Barbara Delinsky. Read by Karen Ziemba. 2005. 15.95 (978-0-7435-5163-2(X)) Pub: S&S Audio. Dist(s): S and S Inc

Looking for Peyton Place: A Novel. unabr. ed. Barbara Delinsky. Read by Julia Gibson & Richard Ferrone. 11 cass. (Running Time: 15 hrs.). 2006. 109.75 (978-1-4193-6939-1(3), 98254) Recorded Bks.
Best-selling author Barbara Delinsky, best known for her steamy romance stories, expands her talent in this scintillating mystery set in the small New Hampshire town of Middle River. Residents are certain Grace Metalious' Peyton Place is based on their town - the two main characters are eerily similar to Annie Barnes' grandmother and mother - and they resent Metalious' sharing of their most scandalous secrets. But when her mother dies suddenly of mysterious causes and her sister Phoebe suffers from the same symptoms, Annie feels compelled to investigate.

Looking for Rachel Wallace. unabr. collector's ed. Robert B. Parker. Read by Michael Prichard. 6 cass. (Running Time: 6 hrs.). (Spenser Ser.). 1989. 48.00 (978-0-7366-1597-6(0), 2458) Books on Tape.
Rachel Wallace is a woman who writes & speaks her mind. She has made a lot of enemies - enemies who threaten her life. Spenser is the tough guy with a macho code of honor, hired to protect a woman who thinks that code is obsolete. Privately, they will never see eye to eye. That's why she fires him. But when Rachel vanishes Spenser rattles skeletons in blue-blooded family closets, tangles with the Klan & fights for her right to be exactly what she is. He is ready to lay his life on the line to find Rachel Wallace.

Looking for the Magic: How to Fall in Love, Lose Weight & Keep It Off Forever. Janet Greeson. 2 cass. (Magic of Recovery Ser.: Set, Vol. 1). 1994. 8.95 (978-0-9630955-1-0(X)) Greeson & Boyle.
Therapeutic mini workshops self help - how to lose weight.

Looking for the Muffin Man Audio CD. Adapted by Benchmark Education Company Staff. Based on a work by Francisco Blane. (Reader's Theater Nursery Rhymes & Songs Ser.). (J). (gr. k-1). 2008. audio compact disk 10.00 (978-1-60437-990-7(1)) Benchmark Educ.

Looking Glass. abr. ed. Richard Paul Evans. Read by Richard Thomas. 2 cass. 1999. 18.00 (FS9-51023) Highsmith.

Looking Glass. unabr. ed. Richard Paul Evans. Read by Barrett Whitener. 4 vols. (Running Time: 6 hrs.). 2001. bk. 39.95 (978-0-7927-2472-8(0), CSL 361, Chivers Sound Lib) AudioGO.
Hunter Bell is running from the bitter memories of his past, his ministry & ultimately, from his God. During a raging blizzard, Hunter finds a beautiful young woman in the snow, wounded by wolves & half dead with the cold. As Hunter nurses her back to health, he finds that his tender ministrations to Quaye have opened his heart to his greatest fear, that he might love again.

Looking Glass War. John le Carré & John le Carré. 2 cass. (Running Time: 3 hrs.). (George Smiley Ser.). 1999. (978-1-84032-108-1(3), HoddrStoughton) Hodder General GBR.
It has been too long since the department had mounted an operation. Soviet missiles were being put in place close to the German border.

***Looking Glass War.** unabr. ed. John le Carré. Narrated by Simon Russell Beale. 2 CDs. (Running Time: 2 hrs.). 2010. audio compact disk 29.95 (978-0-7927-6973-6(2), BBCD 313, Chivers Sound Lib) AudioGO.

Looking Glass War. unabr. ed. John le Carré & John le Carré. Read by Michael Jayston. 8 cass. (Running Time: 12 hrs.). (George Smiley Ser.: Bk. 4). 2000. 59.95 (978-0-7540-0105-8(9), CAB 1528) Pub: Chivers Audio Bks GBR. Dist(s): AudioGO
At one time, the Circus handled all political events while the Department dealt with military matters. But over the years the power had passed to the Circus. Suddenly the Department had a job on its hands: Soviet missiles on the German border, vital film is missing, and a courier is dead. Lacking active agents, the Department sends in Fred Leiser to the trouble brewing in the East.

Looking Glass War. unabr. ed. John le Carré & John le Carré. Narrated by Frank Muller. 6 cass. (Running Time: 7 hrs. 30 mins.). (George Smiley Novels Ser.). 1988. 51.00 (978-1-55690-318-2(9), 88250E7) Recorded Bks.
The director of an intelligence department attempts to restore its reputation.

Looking Glass War. unabr. collector's ed. John le Carré & John le Carré. Read by Wolfram Kandinsky. 8 cass. (Running Time: 8 hrs.). (George Smiley Novels Ser.). 1978. 48.00 (978-0-7366-0078-1(7), 1088) Books on Tape.
The story of a former military espionage department in London - a small, obsolete operation left over from World War II days, LeClerc, the department's obsessed director, struggles to keep his operation afloat. He sends a former agent, Polish defector Leiser, into East Germany to investigate a possible violation of the disarmament agreement.

Looking Glass War: A BBC Full-Cast Radio Drama. unabr. ed. John le Carré. Narrated by Simon Russell Beale & Full Cast Production Staff. 2 CDs. (Running Time: 2 hrs. 0 mins. 0 sec.). (ENG.). 2010. audio compact disk 19.95 (978-1-60283-859-8(3)) Pub: AudioGO. Dist(s): Perseus Dist

Looking Glass Wars. unabr. ed. Frank Beddor. Read by Gerard Doyle. (Looking Glass Wars Trilogy: Bk. 1). (J). 2007. 54.99 (978-1-60252-616-7(8)) Find a World.

Looking Glass Wars. unabr. ed. Frank Beddor. Read by Gerard Doyle. 7 CDs. (Running Time: 8 hrs. 41 mins.). (Looking Glass Wars Trilogy: Bk. 1). (YA). (gr. 7-12). 2006. 74.95 (978-0-439-89848-5(X)); audio compact disk 34.95 (978-0-439-89825-6(0), Scholastic) Scholastic Inc.

Looking into the Face of Death. Thomas Pinkson. 1 cass. 9.00 (A0270-84) Sound Photosyn.
A concentrated & personal ritual for healing.

Looking Inward: Examining Why You Do What You Do. Creflo A. Dollar. 2006. 8.00 (978-1-59944-054-5(7)); audio compact disk 11.00 (978-1-59944-055-2(5)) Creflo Dollar.

Looking Past the Fear. Sonya Shafer. (ENG.). 2009. 5.95 (978-1-61634-069-8(X)); audio compact disk 7.95 (978-1-61634-068-1(1)) Simply Char.

Looking Up. 1 CD. audio compact disk 15.98 (978-1-57908-279-6(3)); audio compact disk 15.98 (978-1-57908-278-9(5)) Platinm Enter.

Looking up from Upper Room: John 13:1-34. Ed Young. (J). 1982. 4.95 (978-0-7417-1221-9(0), 221) Win Walk.

Looking up Through the Darkness: Gen. 37:12-35. Ed Young. 1988. 4.95 (978-0-7417-1678-1(X), 678) Win Walk.

Looking with Jesus: The Practice of Forgiveness. Kenneth Wapnick. 3 CDs. 2005. audio compact disk 17.00 (978-1-59142-213-6(2), CD116) Foun Miracles.

***Looking with Jesus: The Practice of Forgiveness.** Kenneth Wapnick. 2009. 13.00 (978-1-59142-472-7(0)) Foun Miracles.

Looking Within: A Weekend Inquiry 7-CD Album. Exper. by Adyashanti. (ENG.). 2007. audio compact disk Rental 65.00 (978-1-933986-31-9(X)) Open Gate Pub.

Looks to Die For. unabr. ed. Janice Kaplan. Read by Renée Raudman. (Running Time: 9 hrs. 30 mins. 0 sec.). (ENG.). 2007. audio compact disk 34.99 (978-1-4001-0375-1(4)); audio compact disk 24.99 (978-1-4001-5375-6(1)); audio compact disk 69.99 (978-1-4001-3375-8(0)) Pub: Tantor Media. Dist(s): IngramPubServ

Looming Tower: Al Qaeda & the Road to 9/11. unabr. ed. Lawrence Wright. Read by Alan Sklar. (Running Time: 17 hrs. 30 mins. 0 sec.). (ENG.). 2006. audio compact disk 39.99 (978-1-4001-0305-8(3)) Pub: Tantor Media. Dist(s): IngramPubServ

Looming Tower: Al-Qaeda & the Road to 9/11. unabr. ed. Lawrence Wright. Narrated by Alan Sklar. (Running Time: 17 hrs. 30 mins. 0 sec.). (ENG.). 2006. audio compact disk 29.99 (978-1-4001-5305-3(0)); audio compact disk 79.99 (978-1-4001-3305-5(X)) Pub: Tantor Media. Dist(s): IngramPubServ

Looming Tower: Al-Qaeda & the Road To 9/11. unabr. ed. Lawrence Wright. Read by Alan Sklar. (YA). 2008. 64.99 (978-1-60514-594-5(7)) Find a World.

Loon & Raven Tales. unabr. ed. Read by Anne Cameron. (Running Time: 60 mins.). (ENG.). (J). 1996. 12.95 (978-1-55017-154-9(2)) Pub: Harbour Pub Co CAN. Dist(s): IngramPubServ

Loon at Northwood Lake. Elizabeth Ring. 1 cass. (Running Time: 35 min.). (J). (gr. k-4). 2001. 19.95 (SP 5013C) Kimbo Educ.
Watch loons nest & prepare to raise loonlings. Includes read along book.

Loon at Northwood Lake. Elizabeth Ring. Read by Alexi Komisar. Illus. by Taylor Oughton. 1 cass. (Running Time: 11 min.). (Smithsonian's Backyard Ser.). (J). (ps-2). 1997. 5.00 (978-1-56899-398-0(6), C5013) Soundprints.
Loon & his mate build a nest on a sheltered island & prepare for another summer of raising loonlings. One day, two fluffy chicks hatch & instantly become a handful.

Loon Family. Alice Damon. (YA). 1996. audio compact disk 10.00 (978-1-4276-1112-3(2)) AardGP.

Loon Magic. Tom Klein. Read by Denny Olson. 2 cass. (Running Time: 3 hrs.). 1994. 16.95 (978-0-939643-29-5(4), 0255, NrthWrd Bks) TandN Child.
History of the four species of North American loons. Transcends the scientific facts & figures to capture the incredible spirit of these remarkable birds. Interwoven with sounds from the northwoods.

Loon Talk. 1 cass. (Running Time: 60 min.). 1994. audio compact disk 15.95 CD. (0248, Creativ Pub) Quayside.
The loons' most haunting & beautiful calls.

Loon Talk. 1 cass. (Running Time: 60 min.). 1994. 9.95 (0244, NrthWrd Bks) TandN Child.

Looney Tunes: You Don't Know Doc! Acme Wise-Guy Edition. 1 cass. (Running Time: 1 hr. 30 mins.). (J). 2001. 5.98 (R4 79766); audio compact disk 9.98 (R2 79767) Rhino Enter.

Looney Tunes: You Don't Know Doc! Coast-to-Coast Edition. 1 cass. (Running Time: 1 hr. 30 mins.). (J). 2001. 5.98 (R4 79768); audio compact disk 9.98 (R2 79769) Rhino Enter.

Loon's Necklace. William Toye. Illus. by Elizabeth Cleaver. 2004. 8.95 (978-1-56008-959-9(8)); cass. & flmstrp 30.00 (978-1-56008-711-3(0)) Weston Woods.

Loons of Echo Pond. Bernie Krause. 1 cass. (Running Time: 60 min.). (Wild Sanctuary Ser.). 1994. audio compact disk 15.95 CD. (2340, Creativ Pub) Quayside.
A haunting harmony echoes across a pond in the rare wetland areas of the northeastern United States. The amazing loon & its incredible music.

Loons of Echo Pond. Bernie Krause. 1 cass. (Running Time: 60 min.). (Wild Sanctuary Ser.). 1994. 9.95 (2339, NrthWrd Bks) TandN Child.

Loop. unabr. ed. Joe Coomer. Read by Paul Michael Garcia. (Running Time: 6.5 hrs. NaN mins.). 2009. 29.95 (978-1-4332-6031-5(X)); audio compact disk 60.00 (978-1-4332-6028-5(X)); audio compact disk 44.95 (978-1-4332-6027-8(1)) Blckstn Audio.

Loop. unabr. ed. Nicholas Evans. Read by Michael Kramer. 10 cass. (Running Time: 15 hrs.). 1998. 80.00 (978-0-7366-4287-3(0), 4752) Books on Tape.
When a lone wolf kills a family dog, it marks the sudden & savage return of wolves to the Rocky Mountain ranching town of Hope, Montana.

Loop. unabr. ed. Nicholas Evans. Read by John Bedford Lloyd. 10 cass. 1999. 39.95 (FS9-43257) Highsmith.

Loop. unabr. ed. Nicholas Evans. Narrated by John B. Lloyd. 10 cass. (Running Time: 14 hrs. 30 mins.). 1998. 90.00 (978-0-7887-2281-3(6), 95532E7) Recorded Bks.
The author of "The Horse Whisperer" crafts another powerful story of healing and redemption set in magnificent Montana.

Loop. unabr. collector's ed. Nicholas Evans. Read by Michael Kramer. 12 CDs. (Running Time: 18 hrs.). 2001. audio compact disk 96.00 Books on Tape.
The return of wolves to the ranching town of Hope, Montana awakens ancient hatreds that threaten to tear a family and the town apart.

Loop Group. unabr. ed. Larry McMurtry. Read by C. J. Critt. 8. (Running Time: 7.5 hours). 2004. audio compact disk 34.99 (978-1-4193-1282-3(0)) Recorded Bks.

Loopholes of the Rich: How the Rich Legally Make More Money & Pay Less Tax. abr. ed. Diane Kennedy. Contrib. by Robert T. Kiyosaki. (Running Time: 3 hrs.). (ENG.). 2006. 14.98 (978-1-59483-858-3(5)) Pub: Hachet Audio. Dist(s): HachBkGrp

Loose Girl: A Memoir of Promiscuity. unabr. ed. Kerry Cohen. Narrated by Cynthia Holloway. (Running Time: 8 hrs. 30 mins. 0 sec.). (ENG.). 2008. audio compact disk 19.99 (978-1-4001-5670-2(X)) Pub: Tantor Media. Dist(s): IngramPubServ

Loose Girl: A Memoir of Promiscuity. unabr. ed. Kerry Cohen. Read by Cynthia Holloway. 7 CDs. (Running Time: 8 hrs. 30 mins. 0 sec.). (ENG.). 2008. audio compact disk 29.99 (978-1-4001-0670-7(2)) Pub: Tantor Media. Dist(s): IngramPubServ

Loose Girl: A Memoir of Promiscuity. unabr. ed. Kerry Cohen. Read by Cynthia Holloway. Narrated by Cynthia Holloway. (Running Time: 8 hrs. 30 mins. 0 sec.). (ENG.). 2008. audio compact disk 59.99 (978-1-4001-3670-4(9)) Pub: Tantor Media. Dist(s): IngramPubServ

Loose Him & Let Him Go. Kenneth E. Hagin. 1 cass. 4.95 (SH28) Faith Lib Pubns.

Loose Lips. unabr. ed. Claire Berlinski. Read by Cynthia Holloway. 5 cass. (Running Time: 7 hrs.). 2003. 27.95 (978-1-59086-804-1(8), 1590868048); 69.25 (978-1-59086-805-8(6), 1590868056) Brilliance Audio.
Loose Lips follows the story of Selena Keller who has just completed a doctorate in Oriental Studies. Living in Manhattan, unemployed, and dismayed by her dull job prospects, on a whim she sends her resume to the CIA. Within weeks she is contacted by a recruiter, who asks her how she would feel about convincing another human being to commit treason. Despite her checkered life history, she passes the background investigation, the polygraph, and a battery of bizarre CIA aptitude tests and begins duty as a Clandestine Service Trainee. Living undercover as a "government budget analyst", she is suddenly isolated from her family and her past. The loneliness and isolation of life undercover lead Selena into a romantic relationship with her classmate Stan, who cannot put a spy's habits aside, even in the bedroom. She learns that spies who fall in love with one another enter a wilderness of mirrors, where deception and betrayal are nothing less than professional obligations.

Loose Lips. unabr. ed. Claire Berlinski. Read by Cynthia Holloway. (Running Time: 7 hrs.). 2004. 39.25 (978-1-59335-383-4(9), 1593353839, Brlnc Audio MP3 Lib) Brilliance Audio.

Loose Lips. unabr. ed. Claire Berlinski. Read by Cynthia Holloway. (Running Time: 7 hrs.). 2004. 39.25 (978-1-59710-469-2(8), 1597104698, BADLE); 24.95 (978-1-59710-468-5(X), 159710468X, BAD) Brilliance Audio.

Loose Lips. unabr. ed. Claire Berlinski. Read by Cynthia Holloway. (Running Time: 7 hrs.). 2004. 24.95 (978-1-59335-103-8(8), 1593351038) Soulmate Audio Bks.

Loot, unabr. ed. Aaron Elkins. Narrated by Paul Hecht. 8 cass. (Running Time: 11 hrs. 15 mins.). 1999. 72.00 (978-0-7887-3472-4(5), 95688E7) Recorded Bks.
In 1945, while the Nazis are storing stolen art treasures in Austria, a truckload of the masterpieces is lost. Fifty years later in a seedy Boston pawn shop, art historian Ben Revere discovers a Velazquez from the missing truck. Hoping to find other works, he searches through Europe, only to confront lies, greed, and deadly violence.

Lopsided: How Having Breast Cancer Can Be Really Distracting. unabr. ed. Meredith Norton. Read by Carrington MacDuffie. (Running Time: 6 hrs. 0 mins.). 2008. 29.95 (978-1-4332-1485-1(7)); 24.95 (978-1-4332-1483-7(0)); 44.95 (978-1-4332-1481-3(4)); audio compact disk 50.00 (978-1-4332-1482-0(2)); audio compact disk & audio compact disk 24.95 (978-1-4332-1484-4(9)) Blckstn Audio.

Lord Arthur Savile's Crime & Other Stories. unabr. ed. Oscar Wilde. Read by Derek Jacobi. 6 cass. (Running Time: 9 hrs.). 2000. 49.95 (978-0-7540-0077-8(X), CAB 1500) Pub: Chivers Audio Bks GBR. Dist(s): AudioGO
Poison, explosive clocks and finally murder forerun married bliss.

Lord Arthur Savile's Crime, the Model Millionaire & the Ballad of Reading Gaol. unabr. ed. Oscar Wilde. Read by Flo Gibson. 2 cass. (Running Time: 2 hrs.). 1992. 14.95 (978-1-55685-257-2(6)) Audio Bk Con.
The twists & turns of a bizarre story of attempted murders, a charming tale of virtue rewarded, & a study of a man condemned to die are told with verve & compassion.

Lord Bacon's Interpretations of Classic Myths & Their Importance. Instructed by Manly P. Hall. 8.95 (978-0-89314-165-3(8), C771209) Philos Res.

Lord Break Me! unabr. ed. William MacDonald. Read by William MacDonald. 1 cass. (Running Time: 1 hr. 17 min.). (Upward Call Ser.: Vol. 6). 1995. 8.95 (978-0-9629152-9-1(7)) Lumen Prodns.
God won't use you until you are broken, yielded, & humble. This book-on-tape will help you to pray, "Lord, Break Me!".

Lord Buddha's Wisdom For Today. Swami Amar Jyoti. 1 cass. 1992. 9.95 (B-18) Truth Consciousness.
What is the answer to our present world situation? The higher vision of Lord Buddha. On desire, Dharma & evolution.

Lord, by Your Cross & Resurrection: The Chants of by Flowing Waters for Holy Week & Easter Sundays, Vol. 2. Paul F. Ford & Schola Cantorum of St. Peter the Apostle Staff. Directed By J. Michael Thompson. 1 CD. (Running Time: 1 hr. 30 mins.). 2005. audio compact disk 6.25 (978-0-8146-7951-7(X)) Liturgical Pr.

Lord Byron: Selected Poems. unabr. ed. Poems. Byron. Read by Frederick Davidson. 2 cass. (Running Time: 3 hrs.). 1992. 17.95 (978-0-7861-0341-6(8), 1298) Blckstn Audio.
This collection of 18 poems includes excerpts from English Bards & Scotch Reviewers, a satirical response to his critics, & from his epic "Don Juan." Also included is the ironic & colloquial "Beppo;" "The Vision of Judgement;" & "Epistle to Augusta," the half-sister whom Byron adored.

Lord Caitanya Appears as Lord Krsna. 1 cass. (Spiritual Stories Ser.). 5.00 Bhaktivedanta.

Lord Caitanya Cleanses Gundica Temple. 1 cass. (Spiritual Stories Ser.). 5.00 Bhaktivedanta.

Lord Caitanya Conquers the Kazi. 1 cass. (Spiritual Stories Ser.). 5.00 Bhaktivedanta.

Lord Caitanya Dances at Ratha-yatra. 1 cass. (Spiritual Stories Ser.). 5.00 Bhaktivedanta.

Lord Caitanya's Pastimes. 3 cass. vinyl bd. 15.00 Bhaktivedanta.
Portrays three of the most dramatic pastimes: His appearing as Lord Krsna (the Mahaprakasa or Grand Revelation pastime, derived from the Caitanya Bhagavata), conquering the Kazi (also from Caitanya Bhagavata), & dancing at Rathayatra (from Caitanya-caritamrta). By His example, Lord Caitanya inaugurated a revolution within the hearts of people towards a scientific understanding of their spiritual nature.

***Lord Edgware Dies.** Agatha Christie. Narrated by John Moffatt. 2 CDs. (Running Time: 2 hrs. 0 mins. 0 sec.). (ENG., 2010. audio compact disk 24.95 (978-0-563-51075-8(7)) Pub: AudioGO. Dist(s): Perseus Dist

Lord Edgware Dies. Agatha Christie. 1986. 90.00 (978-0-00-651411-4(1), 75608835) Pub: Brentwood Music. Dist(s): H Leonard

Lord Emsworth & Others. unabr. ed. P. G. Wodehouse. Read by Nigel Lambert. 8 CDs. (Running Time: 8 hrs.). 2000. audio compact disk 84.95 (978-0-7540-5375-0(X), CCD066) AudioGO.
Contained here are nine glorious episodes from the idyllic world of Wodehouse. There's a crime wave that was to rock Blandings Castle to its foundations; Ukridge appears on Corky's doorstep at three in the morning, wearing his yellow mackintosh & requesting a whiskey & soda; while the Oldest Member warns of the folly of driving into the father of the girl you love.

Lord Foulgrin's Letters: How to Strike Back at the Tyrant by Deceiving & Destroying His Human Vermin. Randy C. Alcorn. Read by Frank Muller. (Running Time: 24000 sec.). (ENG.). 2007. audio compact disk 26.99 (978-1-934384-02-2(X)) Pub: Treasure Pub. Dist(s): STL Dist NA

Lord GOD LORD God Revelation: Understanding the Mystery of the Godhead. Henry W. Wright. (ENG.). 2008. audio compact disk 17.95 (978-1-934680-45-2(1)) Be in Hlth.

Lord God Made Them All. unabr. ed. James Herriot. Read by Christopher Timothy. 8 cass. (Running Time: 12 hrs.). (Vet Ser.: Bk. 7). 2000. 59.95 (978-0-7451-6724-4(1), CAB 1340) Pub: Chivers Audio Bks GBR. Dist(s): AudioGO
The War is over, and the Royal Air Force uniform has been handed in and James Herriot goes back to work in the Yorkshire Dales. Plenty has changed in Darrowby, but the blunt-spoken local folk and their four-legged patients are still the same. So is their vet, who doesn't know that literary success is just around the corner.

Lord God Made Them All. unabr. ed. James Herriot. Narrated by Christopher Timothy. 9 CDs. (Running Time: 41220 sec.). (Vet Ser.). 2006. audio compact disk 89.95 (978-0-7927-4509-9(4), SLD1039) AudioGO.

Lord God Made Them All. unabr. ed. James Herriot & James Herriot. Read by Christopher Timothy. 9 CDs. (Running Time: 11 hrs. 30 mins. 0 sec.). (ENG.). 2005. audio compact disk 39.95 (978-1-59397-778-8(6)) Pub: Macmill Audio. Dist(s): Macmillan

Lord God Made Them All. unabr. rev. ed. James Herriot & James Herriot. Read by Christopher Timothy. 12 cass. (Running Time: 11 hrs. 30 mins. 0 sec.). Vol. 4. (ENG.). 1996. 49.95 (978-1-55927-402-9(6), 104430) Pub: Macmill Audio. Dist(s): Macmillan

Lord Hornblower. C. S. Forester. Read by Geoffrey Howard. 2001. audio compact disk 56.00 (978-0-7366-9117-8(0)) Books on Tape.

Lord Hornblower. unabr. collector's ed. C. S. Forester. Read by Richard Green. 8 cass. (Running Time: 8 hrs.). (Hornblower Ser.: No. 9). 1980. 48.00 (978-0-7366-0362-1(X), 1347-B) Books on Tape.
In "Lord Hornblower", Horatio concludes his private war with Napoleon. Never has the indomitable Sir Horatio put on a bolder front in a more ticklish situation; never had hindsight & seasickness caused him more inner qualms than in these adventures. This time mutiny is the problem, but not Hornblower's men, who remain devoted to him. Before the problem is solved the audacious Admiral has broadened the action & immeasureably aided by the faithful Captain Bush, secured a breach in Napoleon's defenses.

Lord Hornblower, Set. unabr. ed. C. S. Forester. Read by Christian Rodska. 8 cass. (Running Time: 8 hrs.). (Hornblower Ser.: No. 9). 1999. 69.95 (978-0-7540-0363-2(9), CAB1786) AudioGO.
The Admiral's face was grim as he gave Commodore Hornblower his orders. The situation was critical: mutiny was an infection that could spread through the fleet like the plague. Neither man dreamt on that day in 1813 that the mission would result in a death sentence for Horatio Hornblower.

Lord, I Believe CD. (CHI.). 2007. audio compact disk 15.00 (978-0-9721862-7-8(1)) Lamb Music & Min.

Lord I Believe in You. Contrib. by Lauren Talley. (Soundtraks Ser.). 2007. audio compact disk 8.99 (978-5-557-60859-6(1)) Christian Wrld.

Lord I Hurt. Charlotte Potter. Read by Charlotte Potter. 2 cass. (Running Time: 1 hr. 45 mins.). 2001. pap. bk. 9.95 (978-0-9716246-1-0(5)) Christian Min Inc.
Cassette and read along book.

Lord, I Would Follow Thee. Brent L. Top. 2 cass. 1998. 14.95 Set. (978-1-57008-542-0(0), Bkcraft Inc) Deseret Bk.

Lord Invader, Calypso in New York. Perf. by Lord Invader. 1 CD. (Running Time: 73 mins.). (YA). (gr. 9 up). 2000. audio compact disk 15.00 (40454) Smithsonian Folkways.

Lord Is Come. Bob Johnson. 1 cass. 1992. 8.00 (978-0-938612-25-4(5)) Destiny Image Pubs.

Lord Is Holy: Satb. Contrib. by Johnathan Crumpton & Marty Hamby. Prod. by Ed Kee. (ENG.). 2008. audio compact disk 24.99 (978-5-557-47019-3(0), Brentwood-Benson Music) Brentwood Music.

Lord Is My Shepherd. Dan Comer. 1 cass. 3.00 (104) Evang Outreach.

Lord Is My Shepherd. Read by Eknath Easwaran. 1 cass. (Running Time: 49 mins.). 1985. 7.95 (978-1-58638-562-0(3)) Nilgiri Pr.
Line-by-line commentary on the Twenty-third Psalm of David.

Lord Is My Shepherd American Psalmody, Vol. 3. audio compact disk 16.95 (978-1-55725-275-3(0), GDCD030) Paraclete MA.

Lord Is Risen. Composed by J. Paul Williams & Michael Barrett. (ENG.). 2009. audio compact disk 26.99 (978-1-4234-8730-2(3), 1423487303) Pub: Shawnee Pr. Dist(s): H Leonard

Lord Is There: Ezekiel 24:18. Ben Young. 2000. 4.95 (978-0-7417-6219-1(6), B0219) Win Walk.

Lord Jim see Heart of Darkness & Other Stories

Lord Jim. (Pacemaker Classics Ser.). (YA). (gr. 5-12). 2001. audio compact disk 18.95 (978-0-13-023743-9(4)) Globe Fearon.

Lord Jim. Joseph Conrad. Narrated by Flo Gibson. (ENG.). 2008. audio compact disk 36.95 (978-1-55685-978-6(3)) Audio Bk Con.

Lord Jim. Joseph Conrad. Read by Jim Killavey. 9 cass. (Running Time: 13 hrs.). 1989. 63.00 incl. album. (C-1) Jimcin Record.
One man's flight from his conscience.

Lord Jim. Alan Venable. Joseph Conrad. (Classic Adventures Ser.). 2001. audio compact disk 18.95 (978-1-4105-0175-2(2)) D Johnston Inc.

Lord Jim. unabr. ed. Joseph Conrad. Narrated by Flo Gibson. 9 cass. (Running Time: 12 hrs.). 2003. 28.95 (978-1-55685-709-6(8)) Audio Bk Con.
Haunted by an act of cowardice in the Merchant service, Jim finds himself at last by acts of courage and leadership in the Far East.

Lord Jim. unabr. ed. Joseph Conrad. Read by Frederick Davidson. 10 cass. (Running Time: 15 hrs.). (J). (gr. 9-12). 1993. 69.95 (978-0-7861-0404-8(X), 1356) Blckstn Audio.
This is a novel about a man's lifelong efforts to atone for an act of instinctive cowardice. The young Jim is the chief mate of the "Patna" who dreams of being a hero. When the "Patna" threatens to sink & the cowardly officers decide to save their own skins & escape in the few lifeboats, Jim despises them, but at the last moment, dazed by the horror & confusion of the moment, he joins them, deserting their passengers, eight hundred Muslim pilgrims, to apparently certain death.

Lord Jim. unabr. ed. Joseph Conrad. Read by Frederick Davidson. (Running Time: 50400 sec.). 2007. audio compact disk 19.95 (978-0-7861-5788-4(7)) Blckstn Audio.

Lord Jim. unabr. ed. Joseph Conrad. Read by Gene Engene. 12 cass. (Running Time: 13 hrs.). Incl. Lord Jim. Joseph Conrad. Read by Gene Engene. (160); Lord Jim. Joseph Conrad. Read by Gene Engene. (160); Lord Jim. Joseph Conrad. Read by Gene Engene. (160); 64.95 (978-1-55686-160-4(5), 112678) Books in Motion.
Young Jim, a member of the Merchant Marines, earns disgrace early in his career when he & his crew escape a sinking ship, leaving the passengers to die. Seeking to regain his self-respect, he redeems himself in a dangerous & exciting fashion.

Lord Jim. unabr. ed. Joseph Conrad. Read by Frederick Davidson. 10 cass. 1999. 69.95 (FS9-51106) Highsmith.

Lord Jim. unabr. ed. Joseph Conrad. Read by Nigel Graham. 10 cass. (Running Time: 14 hrs. 30 min.). 2001. 84.95 (978-1-85695-690-1(3), 93066) Pub: ISIS Audio GBR. Dist(s): Ulverscroft US
Lord Jim is the classic & tragic story of a young Englishman - "as unflinching as a hero in a book" - who disgraces himself by an act of cowardice, but who later compensates for his disgrace by becoming the effective & benevolent ruler of a Malay community.

Lord Jim, unabr. ed. Joseph Conrad. Narrated by Steven Crossley. 11 cass. (Running Time: 16 hrs.). 1997. 91.00 (978-0-7887-0922-7(4), 95062E7) Recorded Bks.
Focuses on a young seaman who travels to the tropics to lose himself, but comes to be worshipped as a god instead.

***Lord Jim.** unabr. ed. Joseph Conrad. Narrated by John Lee. (Running Time: 12 hrs. 30 mins. 0 sec.). (ENG.). 2010. 27.99 (978-1-4001-6585-8(7)); 18.99 (978-1-4001-8585-6(8)); audio compact disk 72.99 (978-1-4001-4585-0(6)); audio compact disk 35.99 (978-1-4001-1585-3(X)) Pub: Tantor Media. Dist(s): IngramPubServ

Lord Jim. unabr. collector's ed. Joseph Conrad. Read by Wolfram Kandinsky. 10 cass. (Running Time: 15 hrs.). 1979. 80.00 (978-0-7366-0254-9(2), 1249) Books on Tape.

Lord Jim, Vol. 9. Joseph Conrad. Ed. by Jerry Stemach et al. Retold by Alan Venable. Illus. by Jeff Ham & Susan Baptist. Narrated by Nick Sandys. Contrib. by Ted S. Hasselbring. (Start-to-Finish Books). 2001. 35.00 (978-1-58702-758-1(5)) D Johnston Inc.

Lord Jim, Vol. 9. Joseph Conrad. Ed. by Jerry Stemach et al. Retold by Alan Venable. Illus. by Jeff Ham & Susan Baptist. Narrated by Nick Sandys. Contrib. by Ted S. Hasselbring. (Start-to-Finish Books). 2002. 100.00 (978-1-58702-996-7(0)) D Johnston Inc.

Lord Jim, Vol. 9. abr. ed. Joseph Conrad. Ed. by Jerry Stemach et al. Retold by Alan Venable. Illus. by Jeff Ham & Susan Baptist. Narrated by Nick Sandys. Contrib. by Ted S. Hasselbring. 1 cass. (Running Time: 1 hr.). (Start-to-Finish Books). 2001. (978-1-58702-743-7(7)) D Johnston Inc.
Lord Jim is one of Joseph Conrad greatest novels. Set against a background of late 19th-century steamships, sailing ships, and Far Easter island civil wars, it tells the story of a young English sailor named Jim who at first could not imagine being anything less than always brave and heroic. But one impulsive, fearful act at sea leaves him stripped of his rank, reputation and self-respect. Guilty and ashamed that he had abandoned a leaking ship carrying hundreds of Moslem pilgrims.

Lord John & the Brotherhood of the Blade. Diana Gabaldon. Read by Jeff Woodman. 13. (Running Time: 15 hrs. 75 mins.). 2007. 113.75 (978-1-4281-5680-7(1)) Recorded Bks.

Lord John & the Brotherhood of the Blade. Diana Gabaldon. Narrated by Jeff Woodman. (Running Time: 56700 sec.). 2007. audio compact disk 39.99 (978-1-4281-5679-1(8)) Recorded Bks.

Lord John & the Brotherhood of the Blade. unabr. ed. Diana Gabaldon. Read by Jeff Woodman. 13 CDs. (Running Time: 15 hrs. 75 mins.). 2007. audio compact disk 123.75 (978-1-4281-5682-1(8)) Recorded Bks.

Lord John & the Hand of Devils. unabr. ed. Diana Gabaldon. Narrated by Jeff Woodman. 8 cass. (Running Time: 9 hrs. 45 mins.). 2007. 41.95 (978-1-4281-6625-7(4)); 67.75 (978-1-4281-6624-0(6)); audio compact disk 92.75 (978-1-4281-6626-4(2)) Recorded Bks.

Lord John & the Hand of Devils. unabr. ed. Diana Gabaldon. Read by Jeff Woodman. 9 CDs. (Running Time: 9 hrs.). 2007. audio compact disk 56.75 (978-1-4361-0249-0(9)) Recorded Bks.

Lord John & the Hand of Devils. unabr. ed. Diana Gabaldon. Narrated by Jeff Woodman. 8 CDs. (Running Time: 9 hrs. 45 mins.). (Recorded Books Unabridged Ser.). 2007. audio compact disk 34.99 (978-1-4281-6623-3(8)) Recorded Bks.

Lord John & the Private Matter. unabr. ed. Diana Gabaldon. Read by Jeff Woodman. 6 cass. (Running Time: 9 hrs. 45 mins.). 2004. 29.99 (978-1-4025-5811-5(2), 03304); audio compact disk 29.99 (978-1-4025-6884-8(3), 01292) Recorded Bks.
Although his cousin Olivia is engaged to marry the Honorable Joseph Trevelyan, Lord John has just observed something of a rather personal nature that, if confirmed, might put an end to any talk of marital bliss. Determined to investigate further, Lord John is distracted when the Crown calls for his services. A comrade in arms has been slain, and he may have been a traitor.

Lord Kapila Series. 16 cass. 44.00 Set, incl. 1 folder. Bhaktivedanta.
All the lectures on Lord Kapila's science of Sankhya yoga from Canto 3 of Srimad-Bhagavatam given in Bombay in 1974.

Lord Kirkle's Money. unabr. ed. Avi. Narrated by Simon Prebble. 9 pieces. (Running Time: 12 hrs. 45 mins.). (Beyond the Western Sea Ser.: Bk. 2). (gr. 6 up). 1997. 77.00 (978-0-7887-1160-2(1), 95120E7) Recorded Bks.
As 12-year-old Patrick O'Connell sails out of Liverpool on the "Robert Peel" with his older sister, he is in turmoil. His father is waiting in America, but his mother won't leave her homeland of Ireland. Even worse, if the captain discovers Patrick's young friend stowed away in the hold, they both will be arrested. The difficulties Irish immigrants faced in the mid 1800s vividly unfold.

Lord Looketh upon the Heart. Frost & Michael Anderson, Jr. 1 cass. 9.95 (978-1-57734-572-5(X), 06006132) Covenant Comms.
How Heavenly Father can help overcome eating disorders.

Lord Nelson: The Immortal Memory. unabr. ed. David Howarth & Stephen Howarth. Narrated by Ian Stuart. 12 cass. (Running Time: 16 hrs. 45 mins.). 1991. 97.00 (978-1-55690-319-9(7), 90099E7) Recorded Bks.
One of Britain's great sea heros profiled.

Lord of All Ages. Perf. by His Majesty's Musicians. 1 cass. (Running Time: 47 mins.). 1999. 9.95 (T8950); audio compact disk 14.95 (K6420) Liguori Pubns.
Songs include: "City of God," "You Are Mine," "Strength for the Journey" & more.

Lord of Chaos. Robert Jordan. Read by Kate Reading & Michael Kramer. (Wheel of Time Ser.: Bk. 6). 2004. 53.95 (978-1-59397-583-8(X)) Pub: Macmill Audio. Dist(s): Macmillan

Lord of Chaos. abr. ed. Scripts. Robert Jordan. Perf. by Mark Rolston. 2 cass. (Running Time: 3 hrs.). (Wheel of Time Ser.: Bk. 6). 2004. 16.95 (978-1-59007-332-2(0)); 20.95 (978-1-59007-333-9(9)) Pub: New Millenn Enter. Dist(s): PerseuPGW

Lord of Chaos. abr. ed. Robert Jordan. Read by Mark Rolston. 2 cass. (Running Time: 3 hrs.). (Wheel of Time Ser.: Bk. 6). 1994. 16.95 (978-1-879371-74-3(X)) Pub Mills.
As the Wheel turns, the winds of fate roll across the land, & Rand al'Thor sturggles to unite the nations for the Last Battle, when the Dark One will break free into the world, & to spring the snakes laid by the immortal Forsaken for unwary humankind.

Lord of Chaos. unabr. ed. Robert Jordan. Read by Kate Reading & Michael Kramer. 33 CDs. (Running Time: 43 hrs. 0 mins. 0 sec.). (Wheel of Time Ser.: Bk. 6). (ENG.). 2005. audio compact disk 89.95 (978-1-59397-683-5(6)) Pub: Macmill Audio. Dist(s): Macmillan

Lord of Chaos. unabr. ed. Scripts. Robert Jordan. Perf. by Michael Kramer & Kate Reading. 17 cass. (Running Time: 25 hrs.). (Wheel of Time Ser.: Bk. 6). 2004. 49.95 (978-1-59007-394-0(0)); audio compact disk 69.95 (978-1-59007-395-7(9)) Pub: New Millenn Enter. Dist(s): PerseuPGW

Lord of Chaos, Pt. 1. unabr. ed. Robert Jordan. Read by Kate Reading & Michael Kramer. 14 cass. (Running Time: 21 hrs.). (Wheel of Time Ser.: Bk. 6). 1998. 112.00 (978-0-7366-4171-5(8), 4672-A) Books on Tape.
Rand al'Thor & his comrades battle the forces of cosmic darkness.

Lord of Chaos, Pt. 2. unabr. ed. Robert Jordan. Read by Kate Reading & Michael Kramer. 15 cass. (Running Time: 22 hrs. 30 min.). (Wheel of Time Ser.: Bk. 6). 1998. 120.00 (978-0-7366-4172-2(6), 4672-B) Books on Tape.

Lord of Glory. Greg Skipper. 1993. 40.00 (978-0-7673-1836-5(6)) LifeWay Christian.

Lord of Glory. Greg Skipper. 1993. 8.00 (978-0-7673-1405-3(0)) LifeWay Christian.

Lord of Glory. Greg Skipper. (SPA.). 1995. 10.98 (978-0-7673-0686-7(4)) LifeWay Christian.

Lord of Glory. Greg Skipper & Gail Skipper. 1993. 11.98 (978-0-7673-1835-8(8)) LifeWay Christian.

Lord of Hawkfell Island. abr. ed. Catherine Coulter. Read by Shelley Hack. 2 cass. (Running Time: 3 hrs.). 1993. 16.95 (978-1-879371-76-7(6)) Pub Mills.

Lord of Hawkfell Island. abr. ed. Catherine Coulter. Read by Shelley Hack. 2 cass. (Running Time: 3 hrs.). 1994. 16.95 (978-1-879371-51-4(0), 40190) Pub Mills.
Mirana is kidnapped by Rorik, The Lord of Hawkfell Island, an island off the east coast of Britain. The moment Rorik brings Mirana to his Viking fortress, events are set in motion which leads to triumphs, tragedy & murder.

Lord of Misrule. unabr. ed. Rachel Caine. Narrated by Cynthia Holloway. (Running Time: 8 hrs. 0 mins. 0 sec.). (Morganville Vampires Ser.: Bk. 5). (ENG.). (YA). (gr. 9-13). 2009. audio compact disk 29.99 (978-1-4001-1194-7(3)); audio compact disk 19.99 (978-1-4001-6194-2(0)); audio compact disk 59.99 (978-1-4001-4194-4(X)) Pub: Tantor Media. Dist(s): IngramPubServ

Lord of My Life. Perf. by Lori Wilke. 1 cass. (Running Time: 6 min.). 1992. 9.98 Sound track. (978-1-891916-30-4(0)) Spirit To Spirit.

***Lord of the Changing Winds.** unabr. ed. Rachel Neumeier. Narrated by Emily Durante. (Running Time: 11 hrs. 0 mins. 0 sec.). (Griffin Mage Ser.). 2010. 24.99 (978-1-4001-6971-9(2)); 17.99 (978-1-4001-8971-7(3)); audio compact disk 34.99 (978-1-4001-1971-4(5)) Pub: Tantor Media. Dist(s): IngramPubServ

***Lord of the Changing Winds (Library Edition)** unabr. ed. Rachel Neumeier. Narrated by Emily Durante. (Running Time: 11 hrs. 0 mins.). (Griffin Mage Ser.). 2010. 34.99 (978-1-4001-9971-6(9)); audio compact disk 83.99 (978-1-4001-4971-1(1)) Pub: Tantor Media. Dist(s): IngramPubServ

Lord of the dead the secret history of Byron. Tom Holland. Read by Richard E. Grant. 2004. 10.95 (978-0-7435-4979-0(1)) Pub: S&S Audio. Dist(s): S and S Inc

Lord of the Deep. Graham Salisbury. Narrated by Robert Ramirez. 4 CDs. (Running Time: 4 hrs. 15 mins.). (gr. 5 up). audio compact disk 39.00 (978-1-4025-2316-8(5)) Recorded Bks.

Lord of the Deep. unabr. ed. Graham Salisbury. Narrated by Robert Ramirez. 3 pieces. (Running Time: 4 hrs. 15 mins.). (gr. 5 up). 2002. 28.00 (978-0-7887-9361-5(6)) Recorded Bks.
Vivid fishing adventure that takes place off of the great blue island of Hawaii.

***Lord of the Desert.** unabr. ed. Diana Palmer. (Running Time: 8 hrs.). 2011. audio compact disk 19.99 (978-1-4418-8316-2(9), 9781441883162, Bril Audio CD Unabri) Brilliance Audio.

Lord of the Fading Lands. C. Wilson. (Running Time: 17 mins.). (Tairen Soul Ser.). 2009. audio compact disk 39.95 (978-1-897304-59-4(5)) Dorch Pub Co.

***Lord of the Fading Lands.** C. L. Wilson. (Running Time: 17 mins.). (Tairen Soul Ser.). 2009. 19.95 (978-1-897331-12-5(6), AudioRealms) Dorch Pub Co.

Lord of the Flies. William Golding. Read by William Golding. 6 cass. (Running Time: 7 hrs.). (J). 2000. 56.00 (978-0-7366-9153-6(7)) Books on Tape.
About Lily.

Lord of the Flies. unabr. ed. William Golding. Read by William Golding. 6 cass. (Running Time: 9 hrs.). (J). (gr. 1-8). 1999. 40.00 (LL 0021, Chivers Child Audio) AudioGO.

Lord of the Flies. unabr. ed. William Golding. Read by William Golding. 6 cass. (Running Time: 5 hrs. 51 mins.). 44.95 (L142) Blckstn Audio.
Realistic account of a group of English schoolboys marooned on a tropical island & their struggle for survival.

Lord of the Flies. unabr. ed. William Golding. Read by William Golding. 6 cass. 44.95 (8013Q) Filmic Archives.
Hear this engaging reading by Golding himself, who is able to immerse us in his island world where young men have lost their moral compass, & where a primitive violence reigns. Use for reinforcement & review in the classroom, or for personal enjoyment & enhancement of this famous book.

Lord of the Flies. unabr. ed. William Golding. Read by William Golding. (J). 2006. 49.99 (978-0-7393-7509-9(1)) Find a World.

Lord of the Flies. unabr. ed. William Golding. Read by William Golding. 1 cass. (Running Time: 89 min.). (J). (gr. 7 up). 1988. 15.98 incl. bk. & guide. (978-0-8072-1818-1(9), JRH 109 SP, Listening Lib) Random Audio Pubg.

Lord of the Flies. unabr. ed. William Golding. Read by William Golding. 4 vols. (Running Time: 6 hrs. 51 mins.). (J). (gr. 7 up). 1977. pap. bk. 36.00 (978-0-8072-3176-0(2), CXL 503 SP, Listening Lib); 32.00 (978-0-8072-2914-9(8), CXL 503CX, Listening Lib) Random Audio Pubg.
Contains the complete novel as read by the author. This classic novel of primitive savagery & survival begins after a plane wreck deposits a group of boys, aged six to twelve, on an isolated tropical island. Their struggle to survive & impose order on their existence quickly evolves from a battle against nature into a batle against their own primitive instincts. A portrayal of the collapse of social order into chaos.

Lord of the Flies. unabr. ed. William Golding. Read by William Golding. 6 CDs. (Running Time: 6 hrs 51 mins.). (J). (gr. 7 up). 2004. audio compact disk 45.00 (978-0-8072-1617-0(8), S YA CXL 503 CD, Listening Lib) Random Audio Pubg.

Lord of the Flies. unabr. ed. William Golding. Read by William Golding. 6 CDs. (Running Time: 24720 sec.). (ENG.). (J). (gr. 7). 2005. audio compact disk 29.95 (978-0-307-28170-8(1), Listening Lib) Pub: Random Audio Pubg. Dist(s): Random

Lord of the Kongo. abr. ed. Peter Forbath. Read by Maxwell Caufield. 4 cass. (Running Time: 6 hrs.). 1996. 24.95 (978-1-57511-016-5(4)) Pub Mills.
An epic, historically accurate novel which follows the friendship between a Portuguese cabin boy & a Congo prince, & of the tragic events - the creation of a black Portuguese "kingdom", the fomenting of civil & religious wars, & the fatal introduction of the slave trade that dooms both young men. Based on real events & real people, this is a great, sweeping historical novel in the tradition of "Sho-Gun", about the collision of European culture with Africa.

Lord of the Nutcracker Men. unabr. ed. Iain Lawrence. Narrated by Steven Crossley. 6 CDs. (Running Time: 6 hrs. 30 mins.). (gr. 5 up). 2002. audio compact disk 58.00 (978-1-4025-2317-5(3)); 45.00 (978-0-7887-9788-0(3)) Recorded Bks.
Johnny's toymaker father has volunteered in the British Army during WWI. His spirits are hight as he completes basic training, but his tone becomes grim once he reaches the front. To ease his son's worries, Johnny's dad carves him little figurines that reflect his experiences in the war. Comprised of letters from his father, followed by Johnny's feelings.

Lord of the Rings: Complete Set. unabr. ed. J. R. R. Tolkien. 2002. (978-0-00-764816-0(2)) Zondervan.

Lord of the Rings: Radio Dramatization. unabr. ed. J. R. R. Tolkien. Perf. by Ian Holm et al. 11 CDs. (Running Time: 17 hrs. 30 mins.). (J). 2003. audio compact disk 99.95 (978-0-563-49614-4(2)) AudioGO.

Lord of the Rings: The Complete Trilogy. unabr. ed. J. R. R. Tolkien. Adapted by Brian Sibley & Michael Bakewell. 11 CDs. (Running Time: 13 hrs. 35 mins.). (ENG.). 2008. audio compact disk 49.95 (978-1-60283-492-7(X)) Pub: AudioGO. Dist(s): Perseus Dist

Lord of the Rings & the Hobbit Set. abr. ed. J. R. R. Tolkien. Contrib. by Ensemble Cast Staff. (ENG.). 2009. audio compact disk 59.95 (978-1-59887-892-9(1), 1598878921) Pub: HighBridge. Dist(s): Workman Pub

Lord of the Rings Box Set Cass. 2004. 49.99 (978-1-58926-327-7(8)) Domain Commns.

Lord of the Rings Box Set Cd. 2004. audio compact disk 59.99 (978-1-58926-328-4(6)) Domain Commns.

***Lord of the Silent.** abr. ed. Elizabeth Peters. Read by Barbara Rosenblat. (ENG.). 2005. (978-0-06-085321-1(2), Harper Audio); (978-0-06-085320-4(4), Harper Audio) HarperCollins Pubs.

Lord of the Silent. unabr. ed. Elizabeth Peters, pseud. Narrated by Barbara Rosenblat. 14 CDs. (Running Time: 16 hrs.). (Amelia Peabody Ser.: No. 13). 2001. audio compact disk 134.00 (978-1-4025-0477-8(2), C1533) Recorded Bks.
It is the autumn of 1916, and war has cast its long shadow across Egypt. Cairo is filled with soldiers, and the ancient tombs are filled with treasure hunters. Amidst this chaos, the Emersons have come for their yearly dig. When Amelia Peabody Emerson discovers a fresh corpse in an antique tomb, she knows this season will be a most intriguing one.

Lord of the Silent. unabr. ed. Elizabeth Peters, pseud. Narrated by Barbara Rosenblat. 11 cass. (Running Time: 16 hrs.). (Amelia Peabody Ser.: No. 13). 2001. 99.00 (978-0-7887-9359-2(4), 96726) Recorded Bks.

Lord of Thunder. unabr. ed. Andre Norton. Read by Richard J. Brewer. (Running Time: 6 hrs.). (Beast Master Chronicles Ser.). 2010. 24.99 (978-1-4233-9993-3(5), 9781423399933, Brilliance MP3); 24.99 (978-1-4233-9995-7(1), 9781423399957, BAD); 39.97 (978-1-4233-9994-0(3), 9781423399940, Brlnc Audio MP3 Lib); 39.97 (978-1-4233-9996-4(X), 9781423399964, BADLE); audio compact disk 24.99 (978-1-4233-9991-9(9), 9781423399919); audio compact disk 82.97 (978-1-4233-9992-6(7), 9781423399926, BriAudCD Unabrid) Brilliance Audio.

Lord Peter & l'Inconnu. 1 cass. (Running Time: 60 mins.). Dramatization. (Lord Peter Wimsey Mystery Ser.). (FRE.). 1996. 11.95 (1831-MA) Olivia & Hill.
Popular radio thriller, interpreted by France's best actors.

Lord Peter Views the Body. unabr. ed. Dorothy L. Sayers. Read by Ian Carmichael. 6 cass. (Running Time: 7 hrs. 9 mins.). (Lord Peter Wimsey Mystery Ser.). 2001. 29.95 (978-1-57270-218-9(4), N61218u) Pub: Audio Partners. Dist(s): PerseuPGW
Lord Peter views the body in 12 tantalizing and bizarre ways in this outstanding collection.

Lord Peter Views the Body. unabr. ed. Dorothy L. Sayers. Read by Ian Carmichael. 6 cass. (Running Time: 9 hrs.). (Lord Peter Wimsey Mystery Ser.). 2000. 49.95 (978-0-7451-6257-7(6), CAB 109) Pub: Chivers Audio Bks GBR. Dist(s): AudioGO
Aristocratic sleuth, Lord Peter Wimsey, rarely faces a seemingly unsoluble crime. Whether confronted with a severed head or a nasty case of blackmail, the upper-crust eccentric retains his sardonic sense of humor while unraveling the most bizarre cases.

Lord Randolph Churchill, Pt. 1. collector's ed. Winston S. Churchill. Read by David Case. 12 cass. (Running Time: 18 hrs.). 2000. 96.00 (978-0-7366-5619-1(7)) Books on Tape.
Randolph's involvement in the issues of his day & his accomplishments were legendary.

Lord Randolph Churchill, Pt. 2. collector's ed. Winston S. Churchill. Read by David Case. 9 cass. (Running Time: 13 hrs. 30 min.). 2000. 72.00 (978-0-7366-5663-4(4)) Books on Tape.

Lord Reigns. Created by Maranatha! Music. (Praise Ser.). 1999. audio compact disk 9.98 (978-7-01-610684-1(5)) Maranatha Music.

Lord Shiva the Great Transformer. Swami Amar Jyoti. 1 cass. 1995. 9.95 (K-145) Truth Consciousness.
Seeing the Terrible as a process of transformation. The perfection of God behind all appearances. Teaching the ego to bend.

Lord Shiva's Dance. Swami Amar Jyoti. 1 cass. 1982. 9.95 (O-19) Truth Consciousness.
That Great Being in Whom all particles dance in ecstatic love. Dancing with the Lord. Shanta Marga, the road of silence.

Lord, Stand by Me. Mark Chironna. 1 cass. 1992. 7.00 (978-1-56043-926-4(2)) Destiny Image Pubs.

Lord, Teach Me to Pray! Five Simple Secrets of Prevailing Prayer. Lynne Hammond. 5 Cds. (Running Time: 5 hrs). 2006. audio compact disk 25.00 (978-1-57399-303-6(4)) Mac Hammond.
If that's your heart's cry, this series will take you past the pat prescriptions and point you instead toward deeper levels of communion with God and release more prayer power than you've ever known.

Lord, Teach Me to Pray: Five Simple Secrets of Prevailing Prayer, 2 of Prayer Series. Lynne Hammond. 5 cass. (Running Time: 5 hrs.). 2005. 12.50 (978-1-57399-239-8(9)) Mac Hammond.

Lord Valentine's Castle. unabr. ed. Robert A. Silverberg. Read by Stefan Rudnicki. (Running Time: 19 hrs. 50 mins.). 2009. 44.95 (978-1-4332-5064-4(0)); 99.95 (978-1-4332-5061-3(6)); audio compact disk 123.00 (978-1-4332-5062-0(4)) Blckstn Audio.

Lord Vishnu's Love Handles. unabr. ed. Will Clarke. Read by William Dufris. (Running Time: 9 hrs. 0 mins. 0 sec.). (ENG.). 2005. audio compact disk 29.99 (978-1-4001-0175-7(1)) Pub: Tantor Media. Dist(s): IngramPubServ

Lord Vishnu's Love Handles: A Spy Novel (Sort Of) unabr. ed. Will Clarke. Read by William Dufris. (Running Time: 9 hrs. 0 mins. 0 sec.). (ENG.). 2005. audio compact disk 59.99 (978-1-4001-3175-4(8)); audio compact disk 19.99 (978-1-4001-5175-2(9)) Pub: Tantor Media. Dist(s): IngramPubServ

***Lord Your Healer.** abr. ed. Reinhard Bonnke. (ENG.). 2010. audio compact disk (978-1-936081-03-5(2)) Casscomm.

Lords & Ladies. Terry Pratchett. Read by Tony Robinson. 2 cass. (Running Time: 3 hrs.). (Discworld Ser.). 2000. 16.99 (978-0-552-14417-9(7), Corgi RHG) Pub: Transworld GBR. Dist(s): Trafalgar

Lords & Ladies. unabr. ed. Terry Pratchett. Read by Nigel Planer. 8 cass. (Running Time: 9 hr.). (Discworld Ser.). (J). 1996. 69.95 (978-0-7531-0018-9(5), 960703) Pub: ISIS Lrg Prnt GBR. Dist(s): Ulverscroft US
A Discwordl Novel. It's a hot Midsummer night. The crop circles are turning up everywhere-even on the mustard-&-cress of Pewseyy Ogg, aged four. And Magrat Garlick, witch, is going to be married in the morning... Everything ought to be going like a dream. But the Lancre All Comers Morris team have got drunk on a fairy mound & the elves have come back, bringing all those things traditionally associated with the magical, glittering realm of Faerie: cruelty, kidnapping, malice & evil, evil murder. Granny Weatherwas & her tiny argumentative coven have really got their work cut out this time... With full supporting cast of dwarfs, wizards, trolls, Morris Dancers & one orang-utan. And lots of hey-nonny-nonny & blood all over the place.

Lords & Ladies. unabr. ed. Terry Pratchett. Read by Nigel Planer. 8 CDs. (Running Time: 32400 sec.). (Discworld Ser.). 2007. audio compact disk 79.95 (978-0-7531-2316-4(9)) Ulverscroft US.

Lord's Day Seminar in Four Audio Cassettes: A Biblical Study of the Validity & Value of the Sabbath. unabr. ed. Samuele Bacchiocchi. Read by Samuele Bacchiocchi. 4 cass. (Running Time: 4 hrs.). (Biblical Perspectives Ser.: Vol. 1). 1995. 20.00 (978-1-930987-25-8(0), LDSA4) Biblical.

Lord's Invitation to Life. Andrew Cusack. 1 cass. (Running Time: 1 hr. 20 min.). 1996. 8.95 (TAH363) Alba Hse Comns.
Msgr. Cusack shows us how grace abounds when we allow the powerless to see the conviction that God is more in them than in ourselves. This precise formula for human wholeness allows us to bring God into the world through a thorough & effective witness.

Lords of Creation. unabr. collector's ed. Frederick L. Allen. Read by Walter Zimmerman. 12 cass. (Running Time: 18 hrs.). 1990. 96.00 (978-0-7366-1863-2(5), 2694) Books on Tape.
Our first golden age began about a century ago. Recovered from the Civil War, secure as a nation from coast to coast, fueled by millions of energetic immigrants (aka cheap labor), unrestrained by regulation, capital America gorged & fed. From 1890 to 1929 it could do no wrong. Those who controlled this growth, the Morgans, Rockefellers, Fords & Vanderbilts, lived far above the hoi polloi. They were the "lords of creation" about whom Frederick Lewis Allen has written.

***Lords of Discipline.** abr. ed. Pat Conroy. Read by Dan John Miller. (Running Time: 9 hrs.). 2010. audio compact disk 29.99 (978-1-4418-1505-7(8), 9781441815057, BACD) Brilliance Audio.

***Lords of Discipline.** abr. ed. Pat Conroy. Read by Dan John Miller. (Running Time: 9 hrs.). 2010. 9.99 (978-1-4418-9353-6(9), 9781441893536, BAD) Brilliance Audio.

***Lords of Discipline.** abr. ed. Pat Conroy. (Running Time: 6 hrs.). 2011. audio compact disk 14.99 (978-1-4418-1506-4(6), 9781441815064, BCD Value Price) Brilliance Audio.

Lords of Discipline. unabr. ed. Pat Conroy. Read by David Hilder. 13 cass. (Running Time: 19 hrs. 30 mins.). 1996. Rental 17.95 (1750) Blckstn Audio.
Here is Pat Conroy's powerful, captivating & highly acclaimed bestseller. He sweeps us into the turbulent world of four young men - friends, cadets & bloodbrothers - & their days of hazing, heartbreak, pride & betrayal. We go deeply into the heart of the novel's hero, Will McLean, a rebellious outsider with his own personal code of honor, who is battling into manhood the hard way. Immersed in a poignant love affair with a haunting beauty, Will must boldly confront the terrifying injustice of a corrupt institution as he struggles to expose a mysterious group known as "The Ten".

***Lords of Discipline.** unabr. ed. Pat Conroy. (Running Time: 22 hrs.). 2010. 29.99 (978-1-4418-1503-3(1), 9781441815033, BAD); 44.97 (978-1-4418-1504-0(X), 9781441815040, BADLE) Brilliance Audio.

***Lords of Discipline.** unabr. ed. Pat Conroy. Read by Dan John Miller. (Running Time: 21 hrs.). 2010. 29.99 (978-1-4418-1501-9(5), 9781441815019, Brilliance MP3); 44.97 (978-1-4418-1502-6(3), 9781441815026, Brlnc Audio MP3 Lib); audio compact disk 49.99 (978-1-4418-1499-9(X), 9781441814999, Bril Audio CD Unabri); audio compact disk 97.97 (978-1-4418-1500-2(7), 9781441815002, BriAudCD Unabrid) Brilliance Audio.

Lords of Discipline. unabr. ed. Pat Conroy. Read by David Hilder. 13 cass. 1999. 89.95 (FS9-51105) Highsmith.

Lords of Discipline. unabr. ed. Pat Conroy. Narrated by Tom Stechschulte. 15 cass. (Running Time: 22 hrs. 15 mins.). 1997. 120.00 (978-0-7887-0823-7(6), 94973E7) Recorded Bks.
A riveting portrait of life in a military school, follows one courageous cadet as he struggles to maintain a code of ethics in the face of time-honored rituals. The best-selling author, who graduated from the Citadel, based his novel on countless interviews of men in military schools across the country.

Lords of Discipline, Pt. A. unabr. ed. Pat Conroy. Read by Wolfram Kandinsky. 9 cass. (Running Time: 13 hrs. 30 mins.). 1989. 72.00 (978-0-7366-1666-9(7), 2515-A) Books on Tape.
Sweeps us into the world of a military school & four young men friends, cadets & blood brothers & their days of hazing, heartbreak, pride & betrayal. Conroy's hero, Will McLean, a rebellious outsider with his own personal code of honor, battles into manhood the hard way. Deeply in love with a beautiful, haunting young woman, Will boldly confronts the injustices of a corrupt institution. At the same time he takes on a shadow group known only as "The Ten".

Lords of Discipline, Pt. B. unabr. ed. Pat Conroy. Read by Wolfram Kandinsky. 9 cass. (Running Time: 13 hrs. 30 mins.). 1999. 72.00 (2515-B) Books on Tape.

Lords of Finance: The Bankers Who Broke the World. unabr. ed. Liaquat Ahamed. Narrated by Stephen Hoye. 2 MP3-CDs. (Running Time: 18 hrs. 30 mins. 0 sec.). (ENG.). 2009. audio compact disk 34.99 (978-1-4001-6179-9(7)) Pub: Tantor Media. Dist(s): IngramPubServ

Lords of Finance: The Bankers Who Broke the World. unabr. ed. Liaquat Ahamed. Read by Stephen Hoye. 15 CDs. (Running Time: 18 hrs. 30 mins. 0 sec.). (ENG.). 2009. audio compact disk 49.99 (978-1-4001-1179-4(X)); audio compact disk 99.99 (978-1-4001-4179-1(6)) Pub: Tantor Media. Dist(s): IngramPubServ

Lords of Kush. Stanley Burstein. Narrated by Larry A. McKeever. (Ancient Egyptian Mystery Ser.). (J). 2004. 10.95 (978-1-58659-123-6(1)); audio compact disk 14.95 (978-1-58659-357-5(9)) Artesian.

Lords of Light. abr. rev. ed. Deepak Chopra. Read by Michael Corbett. Created by Martin Greenberg. 2 cass. (Running Time: 3 hrs. 0 mins. 0 sec.). (ENG.). 1999. 17.95 (978-1-55927-546-0(4)) Pub: Macmill Audio. Dist(s): Macmillan

Lords of Misrule. unabr. ed. Nigel Tranter. Read by Joe Dunlop. 12 cass. (Running Time: 15 hr.). (House of Stewart Trilogy: Bk. 1). (J). 1998. 94.95

(978-0-7531-0223-7(4), 970809) Pub: ISIS Lrg Prnt GBR. Dist(s): Ulverscroft US
In turbulent 14th century Scotland, the ruling House of Stewart was a house divided, beset by hatred & jealousy. Descendants of the Bruce's daughter, they had only kept the throne by an astonishing genius for survival, or as many had said, the luck of the Devil. Their rivals were the Douglases & when the second Earl was slain in battle, the Stewarts were suspected of foul play. Young Jamie Douglas vowed to avenge his master.

Lords of Sipan, unabr. ed. Sidney D. Kirkpatrick. Narrated by John McDonough. 6 cass. (Running Time: 8 hrs. 30 mins.). 51.00 (978-0-7887-0492-5(3), 94684E7) Recorded Bks.
True story of grave robbers who discovered & plundered Sipan Temple & the archaeologist who attempts to excavate the remains while under siege by smugglers. Available to libraries only.

***Lords of Strategy: The Secret Intellectual History of the New Corporate World.** unabr. ed. Walter Kiechel, III. Read by Robertson Dean. (Running Time: 12 hrs.). 2010. 39.97 (978-1-4418-7239-5(6), 9781441872395, Brlnc Audio MP3 Lib); audio compact disk 29.99 (978-1-4418-7236-4(1), 9781441872364, Bril Audio CD Unabri) Brilliance Audio.

***Lords of Strategy: The Secret Intellectual History of the New Corporate World.** unabr. ed. Walter Kiechel, III. Walter Kiechel, III. (Running Time: 11 hrs.). 2010. 39.97 (978-1-4418-7241-8(8), 9781441872418, BADLE); 24.99 (978-1-4418-7240-1(X), 9781441872401, BAD) Brilliance Audio.

***Lords of Strategy: The Secret Intellectual History of the New Corporate World.** unabr. ed. Walter Kiechel, III. Read by Robertson Dean. (Running Time: 12 hrs.). 2010. 24.99 (978-1-4418-7238-8(8), 9781441872388, Brilliance MP3); audio compact disk 99.97 (978-1-4418-7237-1(X), 9781441872371, BriAudCD Unabrid) Brilliance Audio.

***Lords of the Earth.** unabr. ed. Don Richardson. Narrated by Raymond Todd. (ENG.). 2008. 16.98 (978-1-59644-560-4(2), Hovel Audio) christianaud.

Lords of the Earth. unabr. ed. Don Richardson. Read by Raymond Todd. (Running Time: 10 hrs. 30 mins. 0 sec.). (ENG.). 2008. audio compact disk 28.98 (978-1-59644-559-8(9)) christianaud.

Lords of the Golden Horn: From Suleiman the Magnificent to Kamal Ataturk. unabr. ed. Noel Barber. Narrated by Bill Mesnik. 6 cass. (Running Time: 9 hrs.). 1984. 51.00 (978-1-55690-323-6(5), 84010E7) Recorded Bks.
From the Golden Age of Suleiman the Magnificent to the "Sick Man Europe," it was an empire that refused to leave the state of European history. These are portraits of its rulers.

Lords of the North. abr. ed. Bernard Cornwell. Read by Jamie Glover. (Saxon Chronicles: No. 3). 2007. audio compact disk 29.95 (978-0-06-115578-9(0)) HarperCollins Pubs.

***Lords of the North.** abr. ed. Bernard Cornwell. Read by Jamie Glover. (ENG.). 2007. (978-0-06-125733-9(8), Harper Audio); (978-0-06-125732-2(X), Harper Audio) HarperCollins Pubs.

Lords of the North. unabr. ed. Bernard Cornwell. Read by Tom Sellwood. 11 CDs. (Running Time: 13 hrs. 8 mins.). (Saxon Chronicles: No. 3). 2007. audio compact disk 99.95 (978-0-7927-4729-1(1)) AudioGO.

***Lords of the North.** unabr. ed. Bernard Cornwell. Read by Tom Sellwood. (ENG.). 2007. (978-0-06-134912-6(7), Harper Audio); (978-0-06-137602-3(7), Harper Audio) HarperCollins Pubs.

Lords of the Rim. unabr. ed. Sterling Seagrave. Read by Geoffrey Howard. 8 cass. (Running Time: 12 hrs.). 1997. 64.00 (978-0-7366-3805-0(9), 4475) Books on Tape.
An examination of the complex web of Chinese operations that dominate the Far East's booming economics.

Lords of the Sea: The Epic Story of the Athenian Navy & the Birth of Democracy. unabr. ed. John R. Hale. Read by David Drummond. 11 CDs. (Running Time: 13 hrs. 0 mins. 0 sec.). (ENG.). 2009. audio compact disk 75.99 (978-1-4001-4188-3(5)) Pub: Tantor Media. Dist(s): IngramPubServ

Lords of the Sea: The Epic Story of the Athenian Navy & the Birth of Democracy. unabr. ed. John R. Hale. Read by David D. Drummond. 11 CDs. (Running Time: 13 hrs. 0 mins. 0 sec.). (ENG.). 2009. audio compact disk 37.99 (978-1-4001-1188-6(9)) Pub: Tantor Media. Dist(s): IngramPubServ

Lords of the Sea: The Epic Story of the Athenian Navy & the Birth of Democracy. unabr. ed. John R. Hale. Read by David Drummond. 2 MP3-CDs. (Running Time: 13 hrs. 0 mins. 0 sec.). (ENG.). 2009. audio compact disk 24.99 (978-1-4001-6188-1(6)) Pub: Tantor Media. Dist(s): IngramPubServ

Lords of the White Castle. unabr. ed. Elizabeth Chadwick. Read by Christopher Scott. 16 cass. (Running Time: 22 hrs. 30 min.). (Sound Ser.). (J). 2003. 104.95 (978-1-84283-388-9(X)) Pub: ISIS Lrg Prnt GBR. Dist(s): Ulverscroft US

Lord's Prayer. 1 cass. 1986. 7.95 (978-1-58638-563-7(1)) Nilgiri Pr.
Jesus' gift to spiritual aspirants.

Lord's Prayer. Eldon Taylor. 1 cass. (Running Time: 62 min.). (Inner Talk Ser.). 16.95 incl. script. (978-1-55978-159-6(9), 5385C) Progress Aware Res.
Soundtrack - Musical Themes with underlying subliminal affirmations.

Lord's Prayer. Warren W. Wiersbe. Read by Warren W. Wiersbe. 3 cass. (Running Time: 3 hrs. 45 min.). 1986. 14.95 (978-0-8474-2284-5(4)) Back to Bible.
Features twelve messages on the importance & the ingredients of prayer.

Lord's Prayer. unabr. ed. Jack Boland. Read by Jack Boland. 2 cass. (Running Time: 2 hrs.). 19.95 (978-0-88152-055-2(1), BA21) Master Mind.

Lord's Prayer: A Strategy for Living. Emmet Fox. 1 cass. (Running Time: 60 min.). (Sermon on the Mount Ser.). 9.95 HarperCollins Pubs.

Lord's Prayer: Accepting God's Will. Marianne Williamson. Read by Marianne Williamson. 1 cass. (Running Time: 90 mins.). (Lectures on a Course in Miracles). 1999. 10.00 (978-1-56170-242-8(0), M745) Hay House.

***Lord's Prayer: Insight & Inspiration to Draw You Closer to Him.** unabr. ed. R. T. Kendall. Narrated by R. T. Kendall. (Running Time: 6 hrs. 55 mins. 6 sec.). (ENG.). 2010. 16.09 (978-1-60814-675-8(8)); audio compact disk 22.99 (978-1-59859-724-0(8)) Oasis Audio.

Lord's Prayer: Integrating Eastern & Western Prayer. Louis Savary. Read by Louis Savary. 4 cass. (Running Time: 3 hrs. 20 min.). 32.95 incl. study guide in vinyl album. (AA0391); 7.95 music. Credence Commun.
Uses modern Scripture studies to anayze the seven petitions of the Our Father.

Lords Prayer: Millions Transformed by This Message. Larry Lea. 2 cass. 1991. 14.95 set. (978-1-879840-01-0(4)) Global AZ.
Practical guide to praying the Lords Prayer. A personal practical guide to assist the Christian in their prayer life. An audiotext with two audiocassettes.

Lord's Prayer: Ocean. Eldon Taylor. Read by Eldon Taylor. Ed. by Leslie Brice. 1 cass. (Running Time: 1 hr.). 1992. 16.95 (978-1-56705-354-8(8)) Gateways Inst.
Self improvement.

Lord's Prayer: Teachings on the Our Father in the Aramaic Language. Ron Roth. 3 cass. (Running Time: 3 hrs.). 1995. 24.95 (978-1-893869-02-8(4)) Celbrtng Life.
Brings the listener into a deeper knowledge of the sacred text.

Lord's Prayer Vol. 1: Christian Prayer. As told by Thomas Hopko. 4 CDs. 2004. audio compact disk 27.00 (978-0-88141-279-6(1)) St Vladimirs.
Volume One contains the topics of Christian prayer, Christ and prayer, The Lord's Prayer: Text and Context, and the opening phrase: Our Father Who Art in Heaven.

Lord's Prayer Vol. 2: The Kingdom Present. As told by Thomas Hopko. 4 CDs. 2004. audio compact disk 27.00 (978-0-88141-284-0(8)) St Vladimirs.
Volume Two looks at the phrases Hallowed Be Thy Name, Thy Kingdom Come, They Will Be Done on Earth as It is in Heaven, as well as a Q&A session.

Lord's Prayer Vol. 3: Provision & Purity. As told by Thomas Hopko. 4 CDs. 2004. audio compact disk 27.00 (978-0-88141-289-5(9)) St Vladimirs.
Volume Three: Provision and Purity explains the phrases Give Us This Day Our Daily Bread, Forgive Us Our Trespasses, Lead Us Not Into Temptation, as well as the second Q&A session.

Lord's Prayer - Complete Set. As told by Thomas Hopko. 12 CDs. 2004. audio compact disk 70.00 (978-0-88141-290-1(2)) St Vladimirs.
Fr Thomas Hopko deftly examines The Lord's Prayer given by Jesus to his disciples within the broader context of Christian prayer. The series offers hourse of sublime listening enjoyment from a renowned Orthodox theologian and lecturer.

Lord's Prayer & the Magnificat. Eugene LaVerdiere. 1 cass. (Running Time: 55 min.). 1999. 9.95 (TAH423) Alba Hse Comns.
Studied commentary of the most basic & universal of Christian prayers.

Lord's Prayer & the Magnificat. unabr. ed. Eugene LaVerdiere. 1 cass. (Running Time: 55 min.). 1999. 9.95 (TAH423) Alba Hse Comns.
Demonstrates finding parallels to the words of the Lord's Prayer in the words of the Magnificat.

Lord's Supper. John MacArthur, Jr. 4 cass. 15.95 (20154, HarperThor) HarpC GBR.

Lord's Supper. Ben Young. 2000. 4.95 (978-0-7417-6201-6(3), B0201) Win Walk.

Lore Segal. unabr. ed. Lore Segal. Read by Lore Segal. 1 cass. (Running Time: 29 min.). Incl. Her First American; 1987. 10.00 New Letters.
Austrian-born novelist reads from & talks about her work.

Loredo. unabr. ed. Hank Mitchum. Read by Charlie O'Dowd. 4 vols. No. 2. 2003. (978-1-58807-586-4(9)) Am Pubng Inc.

Lorenzo Thomas. unabr. ed. Read by Lorenzo Thomas. 1 cass. (Running Time: 29 min.). 1985. 10.00 New Letters.
Panama-born poet Lorenzo Thomas lives in Texas & is author of "Jambalaya" & "Chances Are Few".

***Loretta Lynn: Coal Miner's Daughter.** unabr. ed. George Vecsey & Loretta Lynn. Read by Sissy Spacek. (Running Time: 8 hrs.). (ENG.). 2010. audio compact disk 35.00 (978-0-307-91285-5(X), Random AudioBks) Pub: Random Audio Pubg. Dist(s): Random

Lorie Line Live! Perf. by Lorie Line & Pop Chamber Orchestra. 1 cass. or 1 CD. video.; 9.98; audio compact disk 15.98 Lifedance.
Live performance of original ("Threads of Love," "Heart & Soul") & traditional ("Amazing Grace," "Orange Blossom Special") pieces. Demo CD or cassette alive.

Lorinda Leigh. unabr. ed. Una Horne. Read by Margaret Sircom. 10 cass. (Running Time: 13 hrs. 15 min.). 1999. 98.95 (978-1-85903-282-4(6)) Pub: Magna Story GBR. Dist(s): Ulverscroft US

***Lorito Pelon.** Hilda Perera. Read by Gabriella Cavallero. Illus. by Rapi Diego & Martha Flores.Tr. of Featherless PArrot. (SPA.). (J). 2010. bk. 28.95 (978-0-9842981-8-1(5)) Lorito Bks.

Lorna Doone. R. D. Blackmore. Read by Anais 9000. 2008. 33.95 (978-1-60112-029-8(X)) Babblebooks.

Lorraine Hansberry: Raisin in the Sun, to Be Young, Gifted & Black & Lorraine Hansberry Speaks Out. abr. ed. Lorraine Hansberry. Read by Lorraine Hansberry. 5 CDs. (Running Time: 6 hrs.). 2009. audio compact disk 29.99 (978-0-06-176895-8(2), Caedmon) HarperCollins Pubs.

Lorraine Hansberry Speaks Out: Art & the Black Revolution. Read by Lorraine Hansberry. 1 cass. (Running Time: 60 mins.). 1999. 12.95 (CDSWC1352) African Am Imag.

Lorraine Hansberry Speaks Out: Art & the Black Revolution. unabr. ed. Lorraine Hansberry. Read by Lorraine Hansberry. Ed. by Robert Nemiroff. 1 cass. 1984. 12.95 (978-0-694-50224-0(3), SWC 1352) HarperCollins Pubs.

Lorre Wyatt: Roots & Branches. 1 cass. 9.98 (C-88) Folk-Legacy.
New songs & old from a highly talented performer.

Lorrie Goldensohn. unabr. ed. Read by Lorrie Goldensohn. 1 cass. (Running Time: 29 min.). 1985. 10.00 New Letters.
Lorrie Goldensohn reads from "Dreamwork" & "The Tether".

Lorrie Moore. unabr. ed. Ed. by Jim McKinley. Prod. by Rebekah Presson. 1 cass. (Running Time: 29 min.). (New Letters on the Air Ser.). 1994. 10.00 (011094) New Letters.
Moore is a young fiction writer whose work has been compared to Grace Paley's. Both writers have a sort of funny feminist sensibility, but Moore's heroines tend to be less wise & less political than Paley's. Here, young women see their options & recognize their consequences but still seem to make the "wrong" choices.

Los Alamos Contract. unabr. ed. Tom E. Neet. Read by Lynda Evans. 6 cass. (Running Time: 8 hrs. 24 min.). (Mel Tippet Mystery Ser.: Bk. 3). 1996. 39.95 (978-1-55686-648-7(8)) Books in Motion.
Mel is hired by Russia to secretly find the rogue Soviet agents who are attempting to sell Star Wars secrets, otherwise American loan guarantees could be lost.

Los Angeles Audio Tour by Scott's L. A. Perf. by Scott Carter. Narrated by Scott Carter. Des. by Paul Whitney. Music by Paul Whitney. (ENG.). 2009. audio compact disk 17.95 (978-0-9788500-2-9(5)) Scotts LA.

***Los Animales Y Las Estaciones Audio Cd.** Adapted by Benchmark Education Company, LLC. Based on a work by Margaret Mcnamara. (Content Connections Ser.). (SPA.). (J). 2009. audio compact disk 10.00 (978-1-935472-52-0(6)) Benchmark Educ.

***Los ayudantes de la comunidad Audio CD.** Cynthia Swain. Adapted by Benchmark Education Company, LLC. (My First Reader's Theater Ser.). (SPA.). (J). 2009. audio compact disk 10.00 (978-1-935470-81-6(7)) Benchmark Educ.

Los Bomberos: Spanish Learning CD for Children. Susy Dorn. 1 CD. (SPA.). (J). 2005. audio compact disk (978-0-9764010-3-2(7)) Susy Dorn Prodns.
Los Bomberos is a music CD with twenty short easy to learn songs in Spanish composed by Susy Dorn. This recording contains tracks that teach children various new Spanish vocabulary and give them an immersion opportunity as they hear fun songs about: Firefighters, Family, Opposites, Plants and Flowers, and songs that translate to familiar experiences like "Happy Birthday" and "Shoes." Many songs use rhyming, a proven effective way of learning. SONG TITLES AND DESCRIPTIONS: 1. Los Bomberos (The Firemen) 2. Rodeados de Color (Surrounded by Colors; A song rhyming objects with colors) 3. Cinco Monos (Five Monkeys; Rhyming and counting down monkeys doing things) 4. Quiero Cantar Rimas (I Want to Sing Rhymes; A fun rhyming song) 5. La Familia (The Family; Rhyming and singing about family) 6. Los Zapatos (The Shoes; Singing about shoes) 7. Cuantas cosas puedo hacer! (How Many Things I Can Do; eyes to see, ears to hear, etc...) 8. Barquito de Papel (Paper Boat) 9. Feliz Cumpleanos (Happy Birthday; A fun Birthday song for your child) 10. La Cara Rara (The Strange Face; Rhyming animals with facial features) 11. El Pirata (The Pirate; A fun song about a pirate and actions) 12. Pelos Diferentes (We All Have Different Hair) 13. El Castillo (The Castle) 14. El Baño (The Bathroom) 15. Mis Amigos Comilones 16. Los Opuestos (The Opposites) 17. El Campamento (Camping; A fun song about going camping) 18. Las Plantas y las Flores (The Plants and Flowers) 19. La Ronda (Making a Circle) 20. Un Canto por la Paz (A Song for Peace in the World) MORE ABOUT THE ARTIST: Besides a singer, author and song writer for children, Susy Dorn is a Spanish Immersion teacher in the Bay Area, CA. With a bachelor's degree in early childhood development, Susy has managed to develop very original and amazing Spanish Immersion materials that are fun and effective such as books, music CDs, and DVDs for her students to supplement the learning of Spanish in her program.

Los Bribones. (SPA.). (gr. k-1). 10.00 (978-0-7635-6266-3(1)) Rigby Educ.

***Los Cincos Idiomas del Amor: Como Expresar un Verdadero Compromiso a Tu Pareja.** abr. ed. Gary Chapman. Narrated by David Rojas. (SPA.). 2007. 12.59 (978-1-60814-660-4(X)) Oasis Audio.

los dos Anos: Audiocassette. (SPA.). (gr. k-1). 10.00 (978-0-7635-6260-1(2)) Rigby Educ.

Los Hermanos Karamazov. abr. ed. Fyodor Dostoyevsky. Read by Daniel Quintero. 3 CDs.Tr. of Brothers Karamazov. (SPA.). 2005. audio compact disk 17.00 (978-958-8218-52-6(7)) YoYoMusic.

Los Many Mundos of raulrsalinas: Un Poetic Jazz Viaje con Friends. Raul Salinas. Music by Mikey Figgins & Kevin Green. Text by Abel Salas. Illus. by Joyce DiBona. 2000. audio compact disk 15.00 (978-0-9660773-5-3(0)) Pub: Calaca Pr. Dist(s): SPD-Small Pr Dist

***Los Miserables.** abr. ed. Victor Hugo. Read by Fabio Camero. (SPA.). 2003. audio compact disk 17.00 (978-958-43-0199-4(3)) Pub: Yoyo Music COL. Dist(s): YoYoMusic

Los Negocios de Familia. unabr. ed. Basilio Balli et al.Tr. of Family Bussiness. (SPA.). audio compact disk 13.00 (978-958-43-0224-3(8)) YoYoMusic.

***Los niñOs Ayer Y Hoy Audio Cd.** Matthew Frank. Adapted by Benchmark Education Company, LLC. (Content Connections Ser.). (SPA.). (J). 2009. audio compact disk 10.00 (978-1-935472-56-8(9)) Benchmark Educ.

Los Novios. abr. ed. Alejandro Manzoni. Read by Laura Garcia. 3 CDs.Tr. of Betrothed. (SPA.). 2002. audio compact disk 17.00 (978-958-8161-29-7(0)) YoYoMusic.

***Los números hasta el 1,000 Audio CD.** April Barth. Adapted by Benchmark Education Co., LLC. (Content Connections Ser.). (SPA.). (J). 2010. audio compact disk 10.00 (978-1-61672-204-3(5)) Benchmark Educ.

Los Padres NF, CA Eastern 3-D. (California Historic & Recreation Ser.). audio compact disk 30.00 (978-0-7834-3090-4(6)) Map Link.

Los Principios del Exito. Jack L. Canfield. Narrated by Jose Duarte. (SPA.). 2009. 59.99 (978-1-61545-566-9(3)) Find a World.

Los Principios Que Gobierna el Reino de Dios. Daniel Peredo. 6 cass. (SPA.). 2003. 29.99 (978-0-89985-413-7(3)); audio compact disk 35.00 (978-0-89985-412-0(5)) Christ for the Nations.

Los Pueblos Indios de Mexico Hoy. Carlos Montemayor. Narrated by Alfredo Huereca. 3 cass. (Running Time: 5 hrs.). 28.00 (978-1-4025-1665-8(7)) Recorded Bks.

Los secretos de la buena Suerte. 3rd ed. Carlos Gonzalez. 1 CD. (Running Time: 32 mins).Tr. of Secrets for Good Luck. (SPA.). 2003. audio compact disk 15.00 (978-1-56491-099-8(7)) Imagine Pubs.

Los Secretos de la Buena Suerte. 6th ed. Carlos Gonzalez. 4 CDs. (Running Time: 2 hrs, 20 mins). (SPA.). 2004. audio compact disk 49.00 (978-1-56491-124-7(1)) Imagine Pubs.

Los Temporales de Aguililla Michoacan. Felipe Torres. 2008. audio compact disk 10.00 (978-1-4276-3146-6(8)) AardGP.

Los tres cerditos Audio CD. Benchmark Education Company. Based on a work by Brenda Parkes. (Shared Reading Classics Ser.). (J). (gr. k-2). 2009. audio compact disk 10.00 (978-1-60634-981-6(3)) Benchmark Educ.

Los tres chivos Gruñones Audio CD. Benchmark Education Company. Based on a work by Brenda Parkes. (Shared Reading Classics Ser.). (J). (gr. k-2). 2009. audio compact disk 10.00 (978-1-60634-977-9(5)) Benchmark Educ.

Los tres chivos Vivos. (SPA.). (gr. k-1). 10.00 (978-0-7635-6274-8(2)) Rigby Educ.

Los tres Cochinitos. (SPA.). (gr. k-1). 10.00 (978-0-7635-6275-5(0)) Rigby Educ.

Los Tres Deseos, EDL Level 20. (Fonolibros Ser.: Vol. 8). (SPA.). (J). 2003. 11.50 (978-0-7652-1029-6(0)) Modern Curr.

Los Tres Grandes Detectives. unabr. ed. Agatha Christie et al. Read by Fabio Camero & Hernando Ivan Cano. 3 CDs.Tr. of Three Great Detectives. (SPA.). 2003. audio compact disk 17.00 (978-958-8218-26-7(8)) YoYoMusic.

Los Tres Mosqueteros/Sandokan. Alejandro Dumas & Emilio Salgari. Read by Aron Rivera & Carlos Cvila. (SPA.). (YA). 2009. 64.99 (978-1-61545-959-9(6)) Find a World.

***Los Viajes de Gulliver.** abr. ed. Jonathan Swift. Read by Daniel Quintero. (SPA.). 2008. audio compact disk 17.00 (978-958-8318-29-5(7)) Pub: Yoyo Music COL. Dist(s): YoYoMusic

Los Zapaticos de Rosa. Jose Marti. Narrated by Jorge Pupo. (SPA.). (J). 2006. audio compact disk 9.99 (978-1-933032-12-2(X)) Lectorum Pubns.

Los 7 Habitos de la Gente Altamente Efectiva. abr. ed. Stephen R. Covey. Narrated by Alejo Felipe & Alberto Badillo. (SPA.). 2009. 59.99 (978-1-60847-837-8(8)) Find a World.

Los 7 Habitos para Gerentes. Stephen R. Covey. (Running Time: 7200 sec.). 2008. audio compact disk 24.95 (978-1-933499-70-3(2)) Fonolibro Inc.

Los 7 Pasos Para el Exito en el Amor. (Running Time: 4 hrs. 40 mins.). 2003. audio compact disk 16.95 (978-0-9721605-2-0(3)) Unicalibros.

Los 7 Pasos Para el Exito en la Vida. 4 CDs. 2003. audio compact disk 16.95 (978-0-9721605-5-1(8)) Unicalibros.

***Los 7 pasos para el éxito en la Vida.** Isabel Gomez-Bassols. Prod. by FonoLibro Inc.Tr. of 7 steps for the success in Life. (SPA.). 2009. audio compact disk 19.95 (978-1-933499-63-5(X)) Fonolibro Inc.

Los 7 Pasos para Ser Feliz: Como Liberarte del Estres, las Preocupaciones y las Angustias del Pasado. Isabel Gomez-Bassols. (SPA.). 2006. audio compact disk 22.95 (978-1-933499-21-5(4)) Fonolibro Inc.

Los 7 Pasos para Ser Mas Feliz. abr. ed. Isabel Gomez-Bassols. Read by Isabel Gomez-Bassols. (SPA.). 2009. 59.99 (978-1-60775-714-6(1)) Find a World.

Lose Fat, Stay Full Never Quit! Gary Coxe. 2 cass. (Running Time: 1 hrs. 30 min.). 1999. Set. (978-1-928926-00-9(2)) Coxes Ent.
Shows how to lose weight & at the same time, feel full. Answers questions most asked when a person begins a fitness program. Includes motivation & personal improvement & goal setting techniques.

Lose Ten Pounds in Ten Days. Stanley H. Title. Read by Stanley H. Title. Read by Marilyn Title. 1 cass. (Running Time: 1 hr.). (Self-Help Ser.). 1987. 9.95 (978-1-55569-194-3(3), SFH-6100) Great Am Audio.
Learn how to develop better eating habits, identify eating triggers & safely lose weight without fads or gimmicks. This is the proven method used on over 25,000 patients, successfully.

Lose Weight. 1 cass. (Running Time: 33 min.). 1985. L M Hersh.

Lose Weight. Lee Pulos. 2 cass. (Running Time: 60 min. per cass.). (Self Hypnosis & Subliminal Reinforcement Ser.). 14.95 (978-1-55569-225-4(7), SUB-8001) Great Am Audio.
Presents tools for positive self-change.

Lose Weight. Lee Pulos. Read by Lee Pulos. 1 cass. (Running Time: 60 min.). 9.95 (978-1-55569-421-0(7), 4010) Great Am Audio.
Subliminal self-help.

Lose Weight. Betty L. Randolph. Read by Betty L. Randolph. Read by Leonard Baron. Ed. by Success Education Institute International. 1 cass. (Running Time: 60 min.). (Health Ser.). 1989. bk. 9.98 90 min. extended length stereo music. (978-1-55909-001-8(4), 20X); 9.98 (978-1-55909-180-0(0), 20B) Randolph Tapes.
Designed to help you lose weight & maintain your ideal weight. Subliminal messages are heard 3-5 minutes before becoming ocean sounds or music.

Lose Weight. Shelley L. Stockwell. 1 cass. (Running Time: 60 min.). (Self Hypnosis Ser.). 1986. 10.00 (978-0-912559-02-5(0)) Creativity Unltd Pr.
Lose weight effortlessly, using the power of your mind.

Lose Weight. Dick Sutphen. 1 cass. (Running Time: 1 hr.). (Probe Seven Ser.). 14.98 (978-0-87554-370-3(7), P106) Valley Sun.
"You lose weight & take control of your life. Yes. You have self discipline...".

Lose Weight. unabr. ed. Dick Sutphen. Read by Dick Sutphen. 1 cass. (Running Time: 1 hr.). (Spirit Guide Meditations). 1999. 14.98 (978-0-87554-628-5(5), SG101) Valley Sun.
Your spirit guide assists you to eat less calories than you use. Maintain a dietary balance. Have the self-discipline to accomplish weight loss goals.

Lose Weight: Change Your Metabolism. 2 cass. (Running Time: 60 min. per cass.). (Self Hypnosis & Subliminal Reinforcement Ser.). 14.95 (978-1-55569-226-1(5), SUB-8002) Great Am Audio.
Presents tools for positive self-change.

Lose Weight: Subliminal. Lee Pulos. Read by Lee Pulos. 3 cass. (Running Time: 3 hrs.). 19.95 (978-1-55569-402-9(0), 7157) Great Am Audio.
Contains: Lose Weight - Change your Metabolism & Attain Your Goals.

Lose Weight - & Enjoy It! (audio CD) John Sears. (ENG.). 2007. audio compact disk 12.95 (978-1-57970-472-8(7), Audio-For) J Norton Pubs.

Lose Weight - Change Your Metabolism. Lee Pulos. Read by Lee Pulos. 1 cass. (Running Time: 60 min.). 9.95 (978-1-55569-422-7(5), 4011) Great Am Audio.
Subliminal self-help.

Lose Weight & Enjoy It! unabr. ed. John Sears. 1 cass. 12.95 (978-0-88432-230-6(0), AF0764) J Norton Pubs.
Demonstrates how to use proven psychological techniques that program your subconscious mind to replace an excessive craving for food with normal appetite.

Lose Weight & Keep It Off. Robert Speigel. (ENG.). 2003. 130.00 (978-0-937977-10-1(1)) Spiegel&Assoc.

Lose Weight & Perfect Your Body. 1 cass. 10.49 (978-0-87554-424-3(X), SS101) Valley Sun.
There is no easier, more convenient way to program your mind, any time, any place. No distracting ocean waves or music, Silent Subliminals contain just pure subliminals that bypass your conscious hearing to go directly to your brain.

Lose Weight Forever. Barry Tesar. 2 cass. 1998. 14.95 Set. (978-1-889800-12-7(0)) TNT Media Grp.

Lose Weight Hypnosis Program. Petrie Method Inc., Staff. 1 cass. 1990. bk. 49.95 (978-0-13-540360-0(X)) P-H.

***Lose Weight in Theta State: Guided Imagery for Weight Loss.** Kanta Bosniak. Narrated by Kanta Bosniak. Music by Joshua Bosniak. Carlos Gil. 2009. audio compact disk 16.99 (978-0-9843447-0-3(5)) K Bosniak.

Lose Weight Naturally. Michael P. Kelly. 1 cass. 1992. 14.95 (978-1-883700-01-0(9)) ThoughtForms.
Self help.

Lose Weight Now! Mel Gilley. Ed. by Steven C. Eggleston. 1 cass. (World of Hypnosis Ser.). 1987. 6.95 SCE Prod & List & Lrn.
Self-hypnosis for weight loss.

Lose Weight Now. Glenn Harrold. 1 cass. (Running Time: 1 hr. 30 mins.). 2002. 11.95 (978-1-901923-05-6(3)); audio compact disk 17.95 (978-1-901923-25-4(8)) Pub: Divinit Pubing GBR. Dist(s): Bookworld

Lose Weight Now with Self-Hypnosis: A New You in Thirty Days. unabr. ed. Clark Redwoods. Read by Diana Schneeman. Perf. by Amy J. Mews. 1 cass. (Running Time: 50 min.). 1994. 10.99 (978-1-892654-01-4(6), BET020) FutureLife.
Self-hypnosis techniques & exercises for weight control.

Lose Weight with Hypnosis. Christopher Crennen. Read by Christopher Crennen. 1 cass. (Running Time: 1 hr. 2 min.). 1991. 9.95 (978-0-9629733-0-7(0)) Rainbow Audio.
Side 1 is a discussion of hypnosis & dieting. Side 2 is three 10 minute hypnosis sessions, using imagery, affirmations & alternatives to overeating, to focus the listener's mind on the achievement of a weight-loss goal.

Lose Weight with Hypnosis: Nourishing Mind & Body for Healthy Weight. Scripts. Steven Gurgevich & Joy Kettler Gurgevich. Prod. by Steven Gurgevich & Joy Kettler Gurgevich. 6 CDs. (Running Time: 5 hrs). (ENG.). 2001. audio compact disk 79.95 (978-1-932170-02-3(2), HWH) Tranceformation.

***Lose Weight without Discipline or Willpower: Food Cravings Are the Reasons We Cheat on Our Diet.** unabr. ed. David J. Lieberman. Read by Sean Pratt. (Running Time: 40 mins.). (ENG.). 2010. 6.98 (978-1-59659-604-7(X), GildAudio) Pub: Gildan Media. Dist(s): HachBkGrp

Lose Your Accent in 28 Days. Scripts. Judy Ravin. 1 CD. (Running Time: 70 minutes). 2004. pap. bk. 49.95 (978-0-9725300-4-0(5)) Language Success Pr.

Loser. Ken McCoy. 2009. 69.95 (978-1-84652-505-6(5)); audio compact disk 84.95 (978-1-84652-506-3(3)) Pub: Magna Story GBR. Dist(s): Ulverscroft US

Loser. unabr. ed. Jerry Spinelli. Read by Steve Buscemi. (J). 2008. 54.99 (978-1-60514-735-2(4)) Find a World.

***Loser.** unabr. ed. Jerry Spinelli. Read by Steve Buscemi. (ENG.). 2008. (978-0-06-162872-6(7)); (978-0-06-162873-3(5)) HarperCollins Pubs.

***Losers Club: Lessons from the Least Likely Heroes of the Bible.** Zondervan. (Running Time: 4 hrs. 35 mins. 54 sec.). (ENG.). (YA). 2010. 14.99 (978-0-310-86989-4(7)) Zondervan.

Loser's Town. unabr. ed. Daniel Depp. Read by Don Leslie. 9 CDs. (Running Time: 7 hrs.). (ENG.). 2009. audio compact disk 29.95 (978-1-59887-871-4(9), 1598878719) Pub: HighBridge. Dist(s): Workman Pub

Losing Bin Laden: How Bill Clinton's Failures Unleashed Global Terror. Richard Miniter. Read by Alan Sklar. (Playaway Adult Nonfiction Ser.). (ENG.). 2009. 64.99 (978-1-60775-835-8(0)) Find a World.

Losing Bin Laden: How Bill Clinton's Failures Unleashed Global Terror. unabr. ed. Richard Miniter. Narrated by Alan Sklar. (Running Time: 10 hrs. 0 mins. 0 sec.). (ENG.). 2004. audio compact disk 69.99 (978-1-4001-3107-5(3)) Pub: Tantor Media. Dist(s): IngramPubServ

Losing Bin Laden: How Bill Clinton's Failures Unleashed Global Terror. unabr. ed. Richard F. Miniter. Narrated by Alan Sklar. 8 CDs. (Running Time: 10 hrs. 0 mins. 0 sec.). (ENG.). 2004. audio compact disk 34.99 (978-1-4001-0107-8(7)); audio compact disk 19.99 (978-1-4001-5107-3(4)) Pub: Tantor Media. Dist(s): IngramPubServ
Years before the public knew about bin Laden, Bill Clinton did. Bin Laden first attacked Americans during Clinton's presidential transition in December 1992. He struck again at the World Trade Center in February 1993. Over the next eight years the archterrorist's attacks would escalate killing hundreds and wounding thousands-while Clinton did his best to stymie the FBI and CIA and refused to wage a real war on terror. Why? The answer is here in investigative reporter Richard Miniter's stunning expose that includes exclusive interviews with both of Clinton's National Security Advisors, Clinton's counter-terrorism czar, his first CIA director, his Secretary of State, his Secretary of Defense, top CIA and FBI agents, lawmakers from both parties and foreign intelligence officials from France, Sudan, Egypt, and the United Arab Emirates, as well as on the-scene coverage from Sudan, Egypt, and elsewhere. Losing bin Laden is a dramatic, page-turning read, a riveting account of a terror war that bin Laden openly declared, but that Clinton left largely unfought. With a pounding narrative, up-close characters and detailed scenes, it takes you inside the Oval Office, the White House Situation Room and within some of the deadliest terrorist cells that America has ever faced. If Clinton had fought back, the attacks on September 11, 2001 might never have happened.

Losing Eddie. abr. ed. Deborah Joy Corey. Deborah Joy Corey. 2 CDs. (Running Time: 2 hrs.). (ENG.). 2004. audio compact disk 19.95 (978-0-86492-362-2(7)) Pub: BTC Audiobks CAN. Dist(s): U Toronto Pr

Losing Ground. Charles Murray. 1 cass. (Running Time: 60 min.). 1988. 9.95 (978-0-945999-08-9(9)) Independent Inst.
The Great Society's Social Welfare Programs Have Produced Disastrous Consequences for the Poor & Disadvantaged.

Losing Ground. unabr. ed. Charles Murray & Phillip J. Sawtelle. 7 cass. (Running Time: 10 hrs.). 1989. 49.95 (978-0-7861-0076-7(1), 1070) Blckstn Audio.
Using a remarkable array of research & analysis, Murray illustrates how the ambitious social programs of the Great Society to help the poor & disadvantaged have fallen far short of their intentions & in many cases, have actually made things worse.

Losing Isaiah. unabr. ed. Seth Margolis. Read by Sheila Hart. (Running Time: 12 hrs.). 2008. 39.25 (978-1-4233-5310-2(2), 9781423353102, BADLE); 24.95 (978-1-4233-5309-6(9), 9781423353096, BAD) Brilliance Audio.

Losing Isaiah. unabr. ed. Seth J. Margolis. Read by Sheila Hart. (Running Time: 13 hrs.). 2008. 24.95 (978-1-4233-5307-2(2), 9781423353072, Brilliance MP3); audio compact disk 39.25 (978-1-4233-5308-9(0), 9781423353089, Brinc Audio MP3 Lib) Brilliance Audio.

Losing It: And Gaining My Life Back One Pound at a Time. abr. ed. Valerie Bertinelli. Read by Valerie Bertinelli. (Running Time: 6 hrs. 0 mins. 0 sec.). (ENG.). 2009. audio compact disk 14.99 (978-0-7435-9879-8(2)) Pub: S&S Audio. Dist(s): S and S Inc

Losing It: And Gaining My Life Back One Pound at a Time. unabr. ed. Valerie Bertinelli. Read by Cassandra Campbell. (Running Time: 7.5 hrs. 0 mins.). 2008. 29.95 (978-1-4332-5081-1(0)); 54.95 (978-1-4332-5079-8(9)); audio compact disk 60.00 (978-1-4332-5080-4(2)) Blckstn Audio.

Losing Mum & Pup: A Memoir. unabr. ed. Christopher Buckley. Read by Christopher Buckley. (Running Time: 6 hrs. 30 mins.). (ENG.). 2009. 19.98 (978-1-60024-684-5(2)); audio compact disk 34.98 (978-1-60024-683-8(4)) Pub: Hachet Audio. Dist(s): HachBkGrp

Losing my Mind: An Intimate Look at Life with Alzheimer's. abr. ed. Thomas DeBaggio. 2004. 15.95 (978-0-7435-4980-6(5)) Pub: S&S Audio. Dist(s): S and S Inc

Losing Myth Consciousness: The Crisis of Post-Analytic Life. Read by Leland Roloff. 1 cass. (Running Time: 1 hr.). 1982. 9.95 (978-0-7822-0233-5(0), 098) C G Jung IL.

Losing Nelson. unabr. ed. Barry Unsworth. Narrated by Christopher Kay. 10 cass. (Running Time: 12 hrs. 45 mins.). 2000. 89.00 (978-1-84197-064-6(6), H1063E7) Recorded Bks.
Underway, in an old Victorian house, is the "best" biography of Nelson ever to be written. The author, Charles Cleasby, is Nelson's self-appointed "land shadow", a man who relives Nelson's life through its similarities to his own, who re-enacts each battle on the day it was fought & who is completely au fait with all aspects of his hero's life, except one. Helping him with his work is the opinionated Miss Lily, who can't see Nelson's heroism as he clearly deserves. Or is it clear? Charles, for all his vaunted knowledge, has great difficulty refuting his outspoken secretary's claims.

***Losing the Moon.** unabr. ed. Patti Callahan Henry. (Running Time: 11 hrs.). 2010. 24.99 (978-1-4418-6196-2(3), 9781441861962, BAD); 39.97 (978-1-4418-6197-9(1), 9781441861979, BADLE); 39.97 (978-1-4418-6195-5(5), 9781441861955, Brinc Audio MP3 Lib); 24.99 (978-1-4418-6194-8(7), 9781441861948, Brilliance MP3) Brilliance Audio.

***Losing the Moon.** unabr. ed. Patti Callahan Henry. Read by Janet Metzger. (Running Time: 11 hrs.). 2010. audio compact disk 29.99 (978-1-4418-6192-4(0), 9781441861924, Bril Audio CD Unabri); audio compact disk 79.97 (978-1-4418-6193-1(9), 9781441861931, BriAudCD Unabrid) Brilliance Audio.

Losing Weight Feeling Great: With Self Hypnosis & Meditation. Catherine Wiands. 2 cass. (Running Time: 2 hrs.). 2000. mass mkt. 20.00 (978-0-943262-26-0(7)) Chngng Attitudes.

Losing Weight Through Love. Edward Strachar. 1 cass. (Running Time: 55 mins.). 2002. 12.95 (978-0-9726941-2-4(9)); audio compact disk 14.95 (978-0-9726941-3-1(7)) InGenius Inc.

Losing Weight Using Hypnosis, Vol. 1. unabr. ed. Arlene V. Wayne. Read by Arlene V. Wayne. 4 cass. (Running Time: 2 hrs. 30 min.). 1998. 64.95 Set, incl. wkbk. (978-1-892789-00-6(0)) Positive Changes.

Losing You. abr. ed. Nicci French. Read by Anne Flosnik. (Running Time: 6 hrs.). 2009. audio compact disk 14.99 (978-1-4233-4367-7(0), 9781423343677, BCD Value Price) Brilliance Audio.

Losing You. unabr. ed. Nicci French. Read by Anne Flosnik. (Running Time: 9 hrs.). 2008. 24.95 (978-1-4233-4364-6(6), 9781423343646, BAD); 39.25 (978-1-4233-4365-3(4), 9781423343653, BADLE); audio compact disk 92.25 (978-1-4233-4361-5(1), 9781423343615, BriAudCD Unabrid); audio compact disk 39.25 (978-1-4233-4363-9(8), 9781423343639, Brinc Audio MP3 Lib); audio compact disk 34.95 (978-1-4233-4360-8(3), 9781423343608, Bril Audio CD Unabri); audio compact disk 24.95 (978-1-4233-4362-2(X), 9781423343622, Brilliance MP3) Brilliance Audio.

Losing Your Pounds of Pain. abr. ed. Doreen Virtue. 1 cass. (Running Time: 4 hrs.). 1999. 17.00 (55257) Courage-to-Change.
Often, overeating is the result of trying to relieve pain that is caused by abuse, stress, anxiety, or depression. Releasing the pain is the key to losing weight.

Loss & Grief, The Stressful Nature of..., Dealing with..., Implications of. John Thomas. 1986. 10.80 (0209A) Assn Prof Chaplains.

Loss for Words: The Story of Deafness in a Family. unabr. ed. Lou Ann Walker. Narrated by Barbara McCulloh. 5 cass. (Running Time: 6 hrs. 15 mins.). 1987. 44.00 (978-1-55690-324-3(3), 87440E7) Recorded Bks.
The author relates growing up as the hearing child of deaf parents. Her story brings new insight into a silent world.

Loss, Mourning & Creativity: Coming to Terms with the Past with the Help of Depth Psychology. Peter Homans. 1 cass. (Running Time: 40 min.). 1995. 8.95 (978-0-7822-0510-7(0), 584) C G Jung IL.
Mourning is one of the oldest & most widely known of all human experiences. This tape illustrates the resources of traditional cultures & then turns to contemporary society to examine experiences & representations of loss in literature, biography, & film. Throughout the lecture, he develops the view that the processes of loss, mourning, & individuation - drawn from depth psychology - provide a response to the contemporary problem of loss & offer the possibility of the creation of new meaning in one's life.

Loss of a Loved One. Barrie Konicov. 1 cass. 11.98 (978-0-87082-344-2(2), 081) Potentials.
Explains the meaning, the purpose & the mystery of the death of someone close to you & how to handle the pain, heal the hurt, put the pieces back together & heal the open wounds.

Loss of Innocence. unabr. ed. Rollo May & Sam Keen. 1 cass. (Running Time: 1 hr. 31 min.). 1974. 11.00 (04006) Big Sur Tapes.
Looks at myths of the West, focusing on death & tragedy as the elements that give a story the depth of mythology. Keen claims America has been trying to live without myth & without a past - in denial of death & the transcendent. The two esteemed teachers take this as a starting point to ask, "What does America need? What's the new myth".

Loss of Sammy Crockett see Martin Hewitt, Investigator

Loss of Sammy Crockett. unabr. ed. Arthur Morrison. Read by Walter Covell. 1 cass. (Running Time: 52 min.). Dramatization. 1981. 7.95 (S-12) Jimcin Record.
Matin Hewitt tracks down a missing athlete & solves the mystery of his disappearance.

Loss of the Sacred. abr. ed. Matthew O. Richardson. 1 CD. (Running Time: 2 Hours, 24 Mins.). 2003. audio compact disk 14.95 (978-1-59038-092-5(4)) Deseret Bk.

Lost. 1999. 15.95 (978-1-55927-173-8(6)) Pub: Macmill Audio. Dist(s): Macmillan

Lost. Michael Robotham. Narrated by Ray Lonnen. (Running Time: 45000 sec.). 2006. audio compact disk 34.99 (978-1-4193-7170-7(3)) Recorded Bks.

***Lost.** unabr. ed. Alice Lichtenstein & Alice Lichtenstein. (Running Time: 8 hrs. 30 mins.). 2010. 54.95 (978-1-4417-3718-2(9)); audio compact disk 76.00 (978-1-4417-3719-9(7)) Blckstn Audio.

Lost. unabr. ed. Jonathan Aycliffe. Narrated by Christopher Kay. 6 CDs. (Running Time: 6 hrs. 45 mins.). 2000. audio compact disk 62.00 (978-1-84197-135-3(9), C1205E7) Recorded Bks.
Although he comes from an aristocratic Romanian family, Michael Feraru knows nothing about his heritage. His paternal grandfather never spoke of the past & his father buried it when he married in Britain. Both are now dead, so when chance takes Michael to Romania, he means to satisfy his curiosity. As he uncovers old secrets, something long dormant is stirring, something his family emigrated to avoid.

Lost. unabr. ed. Jonathan Aycliffe. Narrated by Christopher Kay. 5 cass. (Running Time: 6 hrs. 45 mins.). 2000. 47.00 (978-1-84197-083-7(2), H1094E7) Recorded Bks.

***Lost.** unabr. ed. Alice Lichtenstein. (Running Time: 8 hrs. 30 mins.). 2010. 29.95 (978-1-4417-3722-9(7)); audio compact disk 29.95 (978-1-4417-3721-2(9)) Blckstn Audio.

Lost. unabr. ed. Gregory Maguire. Read by Jenny Sterlin. (Running Time: 41400 sec.). 2007. audio compact disk 39.95 (978-0-06-144027-4(2), Harper Audio) HarperCollins Pubs.

***Lost.** unabr. ed. Sarah Prineas. Narrated by Greg Steinbruner. 1 Playaway. (Running Time: 6 hrs. 30 mins.). (Magic Thief Ser.: Bk. 2). (YA). (gr. 5-8). 2009. 64.75 (978-1-4407-3132-7(2)); 51.75 (978-1-4407-3122-8(5)); audio compact disk 66.75 (978-1-4407-3126-6(8)) Recorded Bks.

Lost. unabr. ed. Michael Robotham. Read by Ray Lonnen. 11 CDs. (Running Time: 12 hrs.). 2006. audio compact disk 119.75 (978-1-4193-6897-4(4), C3516); 89.75 (978-1-4193-6895-0(8), 97949) Recorded Bks.
Michael Robotham's Suspect, hailed as "a lightning-paced debut" by Entertainment Weekly, was an international best-seller that raised the bar for thrillers. Now two characters from that acclaimed novel - Detective Vincent Ruiz and psychologist Joe O'Loughlin - return for the electrifying Lost. When Detective Ruiz is pulled from the Thames, he has a bullet in his leg, a photograph of a missing (and presumed dead) girl in his pocket, and absolutely no memory of what happened.

***Lost.** unabr. collector's ed. Sarah Prineas. Narrated by Greg Steinbruner. 6 CDs. (Running Time: 6 hrs. 30 mins.). (Magic Thief Ser.: Bk. 2). (YA). (gr. 5-8). 2009. audio compact disk 51.95 (978-1-4407-3130-3(6)) Recorded Bks.

***Lost: A Novel.** unabr. ed. Gregory Maguire. Read by Jenny Sterlin. (ENG.). 2007. (978-0-06-155603-6(3)); (978-0-06-155605-0(X)) HarperCollins Pubs.

Lost! Luke 15. Ed Young. 1992. 4.95 (978-0-7417-1932-4(0), 932) Win Walk.

Lost! On a Mountain in Maine. unabr. ed. Donn Fendler. Read by Amon Purinton. Music by Brent Thompson. Retold by Joseph B. Egan. 2 cass. (Running Time: 2 hrs.). (YA). 1993. reel tape 17.95 (978-1-883332-04-4(4), 390185) Audio Bkshelf.
The true account of a twelve-year-old's survival for nine days while lost on Mount Katahdin! Alone, starving & without shelter, yet determined to survive, Donn Fendler's story of his ordeal is a timeless adventure for listeners of all ages.

Lost @ Sea. 1 CD. 2000. audio compact disk 13.99 (978-1-58229-134-5(9), SO33210, Howard Bks) Pub: S and S. Dist(s): S and S Inc
Includes: "My Forever Smoochy Girl," "Unusual," "Coming Home," "Carry Me Through" & more.

***Lost & Forgotten Languages of Shanghai: A Novel.** unabr. ed. Ruiyan Xu. (Running Time: 9 hrs. 30 mins.). 2010. 16.99 (978-1-4001-8932-8(2)); 24.99 (978-1-4001-6932-0(1)) Pub: Tantor Media. Dist(s): IngramPubServ

***Lost & Forgotten Languages of Shanghai: A Novel.** unabr. ed. Ruiyan Xu. Narrated by Angela Dawe. (Running Time: 9 hrs. 30 mins. 0 sec.). 2010. audio compact disk 34.99 (978-1-4001-1932-5(4)) Pub: Tantor Media. Dist(s): IngramPubServ

***Lost & Forgotten Languages of Shanghai (Library Edition) A Novel.** unabr. ed. Ruiyan Xu. (Running Time: 9 hrs. 30 mins.). 2010. 34.99 (978-1-4001-9932-7(8)); audio compact disk 83.99 (978-1-4001-4932-2(0)) Pub: Tantor Media. Dist(s): IngramPubServ

Lost & Found. Andrew Clements. Read by Keith Nobbs. (Playaway Children Ser.). (ENG.). (J). 2009. 40.00 (978-1-60775-616-3(1)) Find a World.

Lost & Found. Perf. by Dietrick Haddon. 2002. audio compact disk Provident Mus Dist.

Lost & Found. Jayne Ann Krentz. 2009. audio compact disk 9.99 (978-1-4418-2652-7(1)) Brilliance Audio.

Lost & Found. Carolyn Parkhurst. Narrated by Anna Fields. 6 cass. (Running Time: 34560 sec.). (Sound Library). 2006. 54.95 (978-0-7927-4256-2(7), CSL 969); audio compact disk & audio compact disk 29.95 (978-0-7927-4257-9(5), CMP 969) AudioGO.

Lost & Found. Clair Poulson. 3 cass. 2004. 14.95 (978-1-59156-093-7(4)); audio compact disk 14.95 (978-1-59156-134-7(5)) Covenant Comms.

***Lost & Found.** Carl Sommer. (Quest for Success Ser.). (ENG.). (YA). 2009. bk. 19.95 (978-1-57537-330-0(0)); pap. bk. 11.95 (978-1-57537-379-9(3)) Advance Pub.

Lost & Found. abr. ed. AIO Team Staff. Contrib. by Paul Herlinger et al. (Running Time: 5 hrs.). (Adventures in Odyssey Ser.). (ENG.). (J). (gr. 8-12). 2006. audio compact disk 24.99 (978-1-58997-331-2(3)) Pub: Focus Family. Dist(s): Tyndale Hse

Lost & Found. abr. ed. Jayne Ann Krentz. Read by Sandra Burr. (Running Time: 6 hrs.). 2004. audio compact disk 16.99 (978-1-59355-695-2(0), 1593556950) Brilliance Audio.
Cady Briggs is very useful to Mack Easton - her expertise in art and antiques helps his shadowy, low-profile company, Lost and Found, find missing treasures for high-paying clients. But as Cady's beloved Aunt Vesta warns her, being useful to a client is one thing - being used is another. Still, Cady finds it hard to resist the magnetic pull Mack exerts, an attraction she felt from the first time she heard his voice on the phone. And as their work together puts them in an explosive situation, Cady wonders just how much she'd risk for the thrill of being with this man. When Aunt Vesta dies suddenly, and strange developments affect her family's prestigious gallery, Cady must turn to a man she isn't sure she can trust. And instead of tracking down missing masterpieces, they'll be hunting down a killer. .

Lost & Found. unabr. ed. Andrew Clements. Read by Keith Nobbs. (Running Time: 3 hrs. 0 mins. 0 sec.). (ENG.). (J). 2008. audio compact disk 19.95 (978-0-7435-7273-6(4)) Pub: S&S Audio. Dist(s): S and S Inc

Lost & Found. unabr. ed. Jayne Ann Krentz. Read by Sandra Burr. 7 cass. (Running Time: 10 hrs.). 2001. 78.25 (978-1-56740-940-6(7), 1567409407); 32.95 (978-1-56740-395-4(6), 1567403956, BAU) Brilliance Audio.

Lost & Found. unabr. ed. Jayne Ann Krentz. Read by Sandra Burr. (Running Time: 10 hrs.). 2005. 39.25 (978-1-59600-731-4(1), 9781596007314, BADLE); 24.95 (978-1-59600-730-7(3), 9781596007307, BAD); 39.25 (978-1-59600-729-1(X), 9781596007291, Brinc Audio MP3 Lib); 24.95 (978-1-59600-728-4(1), 9781596007284, Brilliance MP3) Brilliance Audio.

Lost & Found. unabr. ed. Jayne Ann Krentz. Read by Sandra Burr. (Running Time: 10 hrs.). 2007. audio compact disk 97.25 (978-1-4233-4094-2(9), 9781423340942, BriAudCD Unabrid) Brilliance Audio.

Lost & Found. unabr. ed. Jayne Ann Krentz. Read by Sandra Burr. (Running Time: 10 hrs.). 2010. audio compact disk 29.99 (978-1-4418-3582-6(2), 9781441835826, Bril Audio CD Unabri) Brilliance Audio.

Lost & Found. unabr. ed. Carolyn Parkhurst. Narrated by Anna Fields. 8 CDs. (Running Time: 34560 sec.). (Sound Library). 2006. audio compact disk 79.95 (978-0-7927-4062-9(9), SLD 969) AudioGO.

Lost & Found. unabr. ed. Carolyn Parkhurst. Read by Blair Brown. (Running Time: 10 hrs.). (ENG.). 2006. 14.98 (978-1-59483-523-0(3)) Pub: Hachet Audio. Dist(s): HachBkGrp

Lost & Found. unabr. ed. Carolyn Parkhurst. Read by Blair Brown. (Running Time: 10 hrs.). (ENG.). 2009. 59.98 (978-1-60788-158-2(6)) Pub: Hachet Audio. Dist(s): HachBkGrp

***Lost & Found.** unabr. ed. Jacqueline Sheehan. (Running Time: 8 hrs.). 2010. 24.99 (978-1-4418-6626-4(4), 9781441866264, Brilliance MP3); 24.99 (978-1-4418-6628-8(0), 9781441866288, BAD); 39.97 (978-1-4418-6627-1(2), 9781441866271, Brinc Audio MP3 Lib); 39.97 (978-1-4418-6629-5(9), 9781441866295, BADLE) Brilliance Audio.

***Lost & Found.** unabr. ed. Jacqueline Sheehan. Read by Sandra Burr. (Running Time: 9 hrs.). 2010. audio compact disk 29.99 (978-1-4418-6624-0(8), 9781441866240, Bril Audio CD Unabri); audio compact disk 79.97 (978-1-4418-6625-7(6), 9781441866257, BriAudCD Unabrid) Brilliance Audio.

***Lost & Found: The younger unchurched & the churches that reach Them.** unabr. ed. Ed Stetzer & Jason Hayes. Narrated by Marc Cashman. (ENG.). 2009. 14.98 (978-1-59644-794-3(X), Hovel Audio) christianaud.

Lost & Found: The younger unchurched & the churches that reach Them. unabr. ed. Ed Stetzer et al. (Running Time: 9 hrs. 36 mins. 0 sec.). (ENG.). 2009. audio compact disk 24.98 (978-1-59644-793-6(1), Hovel Audio) christianaud.

***Lost & Found: Unexpected Revelations about Food & Money.** Geneen Roth. (Running Time: 6 hrs.). (ENG.). 2011. audio compact disk 29.95 (978-0-14-242932-7(5), PengAudBks) Penguin Grp USA.

***Lost & Found / Perdida y Encontrada.** ed. Carl Sommer. (Quest for Success Bilingual Ser.). (ENG & SPA.). (YA). 2009. bk. 21.95 (978-1-57537-429-1(3)) Advance Pub.

Lost & Found in Alaska. Howard W. Gabriel, III. (J). (gr. k-12). 1987. 4.95 (978-0-936997-11-7(7), T87-09) M & H Enter.
Two Old Men Go Out to the Alaskan Seas in Very Different Boats, Both in Search of Something They May Have Missed in Their Lives. They Risk the Lives of Their Grandchildren.

Lost & Found Sound & Beyond: Stories from NPR's All Things Considered. unabr. ed. Kitchen Sisters Staff. Contrib. by Davia Nelson. (Running Time: 2 hrs. 30 mins.). (ENG.). 2004. audio compact disk 22.95 (978-1-56511-906-2(1), 1565119061) Pub: HighBridge. Dist(s): Workman Pub

Lost & Found/after Goldilocks. Created by Steck-Vaughn Staff. (Running Time: 327 sec.). (Primary Take-Me-Home Books Level A Ser.). 1998. 9.80 (978-0-8172-8660-6(8)) SteckVau.

Lost & Not Found. Teel McClanahan, 3rd. Narrated by Teel McClanahan, 3rd. 2009. audio compact disk 26.99 (978-1-934516-74-4(0)) Modern Evil.

Lost & Not Found. Teel McClanahan, III. Narrated by Teel McClanahan, III. 2009. 13.99 (978-1-934516-73-7(2)) Modern Evil.

Lost Angel. Mary Higgins Clark. 1 cass. 1998. 9.98 (978-0-671-58214-2(3), Audioworks) S&S Audio.
Psychological.

Lost Angel. abr. ed. Mary Higgins Clark. 2004. 7.95 (978-0-7435-4514-3(1)) Pub: S&S Audio. Dist(s): S and S Inc

Lost Angel. unabr. abr. ed. Cyrus Emerson. Read by Tom Weiner et al. (Running Time: 9000 sec.). 2007. 24.99 (978-1-4332-0385-5(5)); audio compact disk 27.00 (978-1-4332-0386-2(3)); audio compact disk 19.95 (978-1-4332-0387-9(1)) Blckstn Audio.

***Lost Ark of the Covenant.** unabr. ed. Tudor Parfitt. Read by Graeme Malcolm. (ENG.). 2008. (978-0-06-162960-0(X)); (978-0-06-162961-7(8)) HarperCollins Pubs.

Lost Ark of the Covenant: The Surprising Discovery of One of Civilization's Long-Vanished Treasures. unabr. ed. Tudor Parfitt. Read by Graeme Malcolm. (Running Time: 37800 sec.). 2008. audio compact disk 39.95 (978-0-06-146849-0(5), Harper Audio) HarperCollins Pubs.

***Lost Art of Gratitude.** unabr. ed. Ed. by Alexander McCall Smith. Narrated by Davina Porter. 1 Playaway. (Running Time: 8 hrs. 15 mins.). (Isabel Dalhousie Ser.: No. 6). 2009. 59.75 (978-1-4407-2814-3(3)); 67.75 (978-1-4407-2811-2(9)); audio compact disk 92.75 (978-1-4407-2812-9(7)); audio compact disk 34.99 (978-1-4407-4553-9(6)) Recorded Bks.

Lost Art of Intercession. abr. ed. Read by Jim W. Goll. 2 cass. (Running Time: 2 hrs.). 2001. 15.99 (978-0-7684-0202-5(6)); audio compact disk 19.99 (978-0-7684-0201-8(8)) Destiny Image Pubs.

Lost Art of War: The Recently Discovered Companion to the Bestselling "The Art of War" unabr. collector's ed. Sun-Tzu. Read by Bill Kelsey. 5 cass. (Running Time: 5 hrs.). 1996. 30.00 (978-0-7366-3396-3(0), 4044) Books on Tape.
In 1972, archaeologists made an exciting discovery in an ancient Chinese tomb: the first complete manuscript from Sun Tzu II, legendary military strategist & a direct descendant of Sun Tzu, author of "The Art of War".

Lost at Sea. Patrick Dillon. Read by Michael Kramer. 1999. audio compact disk 56.00 (978-0-7366-8046-2(2)) Books on Tape.

Lost at Sea. Prod. by Laraim Associates. (Barclay Family Adventure Ser.). (J). 2003. audio compact disk (978-1-56254-982-4(0)) Saddleback Edu.

Lost at Sea. unabr. collector's ed. Patrick Dillon. Read by Michael Kramer. 6 cass. (Running Time: 9 hrs.). 1999. 48.00 (978-0-7366-4670-3(1), 5052) Books on Tape.
Recounts the worst commercial fishing disaster in American history.

Lost Bird. unabr. ed. Margaret Coel. Read by Stephanie Brush. 8 cass. (Running Time: 8 hrs. 42 min). (Wind River Ser.). 2001. 49.95 (978-1-58116-003-1(8)); audio compact disk 52.00 (978-1-58116-179-3(4)) Books in Motion.
Hollywood star Sharon David travels to the Wind River Reservation with a feeling that somehow she was born in that area. During investigation, Arapahoe lawyer Vicki Holden finds clues that other babies might have been displaced.

***Lost Books of the Odyssey.** unabr. ed. Zachary Mason. Narrated by Simon Vance. 4 CDs. (Running Time: 4 hrs. 30 mins.). 2010. audio compact disk 64.95 (978-0-7927-7019-0(6)) AudioGO.

Lost Boy. unabr. ed. Robert Barnard. Read by Vincent Brimble. 1 cass. (Running Time: 1 hr.). (Isis Cassettes Ser.). (J). 1999. 14.00 (978-0-7531-0753-9(8), 991219) Pub: ISIS Lrg Prnt GBR. Dist(s): Ulverscroft US
As handsome Dick Randall buys his young son Malcolm an ice-cream, in a shopping precinct, he looks every inch the caring father. But Malcolm's mother is sitting by the phone at home waiting for frustratingly short calls from her missing son. Inspector Purley is following leads that take him zig-zagging across the country after the abducted boy & his criminal father, following trails of petty theft & brief telephone calls. Identities change, new lives begin & even happy reunions are not quite what they seem as this gifted crime writer questions our assumptions at every turn.

Lost Boy. unabr. ed. Robert Barnard. Read by Vincent Brimble. 1 CD. (Running Time: 1 hr. 30 mins.). (Isis (CDs) Ser.). (J). 2001. audio compact disk 17.95 (978-0-7531-0898-7(4), 108984) Pub: ISIS Lrg Prnt GBR. Dist(s): Ulverscroft US
As handsome Dick Randall buys his young son Malcolm an ice cream in a shopping precinct he looks every inch the caring father. But Malcolm's mother is sitting by the phone at home waiting for frustratingly short calls from her missing son. Inspector Purley is following leads that take him zig-zagging across the country after the abducted boy & his criminal father, following trails of petty thefts & brief telephone calls. Identities change, new lives begin & even happy reunions are not quite what they seem as this gifted crime writer questions our assumptions at every turn.

Lost Boy: A Foster Child's Search for the Love of a Family. Dave Pelzer. Narrated by Brian Keeler. 7 CDs. (Running Time: 7 hrs. 30 mins.). audio compact disk 69.00 (978-1-4025-1496-8(4)) Recorded Bks.

Lost Boy: A Foster Child's Search for the Love of a Family. Dave Pelzer. Narrated by Brian Keeler. 5 cass. (Running Time: 7 hrs. 30 mins.). 2000. 50.00 (978-1-4025-0677-2(5), 96920) Recorded Bks.
After surviving his abusive, alcoholic mother, Dave Pelzer lived in five different foster homes. A rebellious, defiant boy, Pelzer also spent time in juvenile detention before becoming a acclaimed motivational speaker he is today.

Lost Boy: A Foster Child's Search for the Love of a Family. Dave Pelzer. 4 cass. (Running Time: 7 hrs. 33 mins.). 2004. 19.99 (978-1-4025-0405-1(5), 00824) Recorded Bks.

***Lost Boy: The Next Chapter.** unabr. ed. Greg Laurie & Ellen Vaughn. Narrated by Greg Laurie. (Running Time: 1 hr. 11 mins. 11 sec.). 2010. 6.99 (978-1-60814-728-1(2)); audio compact disk 9.99 (978-1-59859-802-5(3)) Oasis Audio.

Lost Boy, Lost Girl. abr. ed. Peter Straub. Read by Ron McLarty. 2004. 15.95 (978-0-7435-4981-3(3)) Pub: S&S Audio. Dist(s): S and S Inc

Lost Boys. Orson Scott Card. Narrated by Stefan Rudnicki. (Running Time: 16 hrs.). (YA). 2004. 44.95 (978-1-59912-685-2(0)) Iofy Corp.

Lost Boys. unabr. ed. Orson Scott Card. 13 CDs. (Running Time: 16 hrs.). 2004. audio compact disk 104.00 (978-0-7861-8435-4(3), 3345) Blckstn Audio.

Lost Boys. unabr. ed. Orson Scott Card. Read by Stefan Rudnicki. 11 cass. (Running Time: 16 hrs.). 2004. 76.95 (978-0-7861-2854-9(2), 3345) Blckstn Audio.
Step Fletcher, his pregnant wife DeAnne, and their three children move to Steuben, North Carolina with high hopes. But Step?s new job with a software company turns out to be a snake pit, and eight-year-old Stevie?s school is worse. As Stevie retreats into himself, focusing more and more on a mysterious computer game and a growing troop of imaginary friends, the Fletchers? concern turns to terror. Young boys, whose names match a list of Stevie?s nonexistent friends, have mysteriously vanished from Steuben. And as evil strikes out from the most trusted corners, it?s suddenly clear that Stevie is next on the list.

Lost Boys: Why Our Sons Turn Violent & How We Can Save Them. James Garbarino. Read by Cotter Smith. 2004. 10.95 (978-0-7435-4982-0(1)) Pub: S&S Audio. Dist(s): S and S Inc

Lost Causes: Historical Consciousness in Victorian Literature. Jason B. Jones. (Victorian Critical Interventions Ser.). 2006. audio compact disk 9.95 (978-0-8142-9117-7(1)) Pub: Ohio St U Pr. Dist(s): Chicago Distribution Ctr

Lost Children. unabr. ed. Edith Pargeter. Read by Rosemary Davis. 10 cass. 1997. 84.95 Set. (961109) Eye Ear.
High on a rocky outcrop stands a Victorian gothic mansion, built by the ancient & aristocratic Rose family. In the lodge of the house lives the last of the fading line of the family. Rosalba Rose, at seventeen, has always been dutifully submissive to her ferocious eighty-year-old great-aunt Martine, but Rosalba's life contains little pleasure until she meets Eugene Seale, a young serviceman. Different as the two are, they fall in love, but is their passion, surrounded by upheaval, doomed.

Lost Children. unabr. ed. Edith Pargeter. Read by Rosemary Davis. 10 cass. (Running Time: 15 hrs.). 1997. 84.95 (978-0-7531-0105-6(X), 961109) Pub: ISIS Audio GBR. Dist(s): Ulverscroft US

Lost Choice. unabr. ed. Andy Andrews. Narrated by Andy Andrews. (ENG.). 2004. 16.09 (978-1-60814-296-5(5)) Oasis Audio.

Lost Choice: A Legend of Personal Discovery. Andy Andrews. Ed. by Andy Andrews. 5 cass. (Running Time: 6 hrs.). 2004. 40.00 (978-0-7861-8348-7(9), 3374) Blckstn Audio.

Lost Choice: A Legend of Personal Discovery. unabr. ed. Andy Andrews. 4 cass. (Running Time: 6 hrs.). 2004. 25.99 (978-1-58926-688-9(9), 6688) Oasis Audio.

Lost Choice: A Legend of Personal Discovery. unabr. ed. Andy Andrews. Narrated by Andy Andrews. 5 CDs. (Running Time: 6 hrs.). (ENG.). 2004. audio compact disk 22.99 (978-1-58926-689-6(7), 6689) Oasis Audio.

Lost Christianity. abr. ed. Jacob Needleman. Read by Jacob Needleman. 2 cass. (Running Time: 3 hrs.). 1997. 17.95 (978-1-57453-154-1(9)) Audio Lit.
An individual spiritual journey & a profound reexamination of the essence of Christianity & its power to transform the human heart & mind.

Lost City. abr. ed. Clive Cussler & Paul Kemprecos. 5 CDs. (Running Time: 6 hrs.). No. 5. (ENG.). (gr. k-8). 2005. audio compact disk 14.95 (978-0-14-305784-0(7), PengAudBks) Penguin Grp USA.

Lost City of Faar. D. J. MacHale. Read by William Dufris. (Pendragon Ser.: Bk. 2). (J). 2009. 59.99 (978-1-60775-675-0(7)) Find a World.

Lost City of Faar. unabr. ed. Read by William Dufris. (Running Time: 43200 sec.). (Pendragon Ser.: Bk. 2). (J). 2005. audio compact disk 39.25 (978-1-59737-248-0(X), 9781597372480, Brinc Audio MP3 Lib) Brilliance Audio.

Lost City of Faar. unabr. ed. D. J. MacHale. Read by William Dufris. (Running Time: 12 hrs.). (Pendragon Ser.: Bk. 2). 2005. 24.95 (978-1-59737-247-3(1), 9781597372473, Brilliance MP3); 39.25 (978-1-59737-250-3(1), 9781597372503, BADLE); 24.95 (978-1-59737-249-7(8), 9781597372497, BAD); 82.25 (978-1-59737-244-2(7), 9781597372442, BrilAudUnabridg); 29.95 (978-1-59737-243-5(9), 9781597372435, BAU) Brilliance Audio.
Fourteen-year-old Bobby Pendragon is not like other boys his age. His uncle Press is a Traveler, and, as Bobby has learned, that means Uncle Press is responsible, through his journeys, for solving interdimensional conflict wherever he encounters it. His mission is nothing less than to save the universe from ultimate evil. And he's taking Bobby along for the ride. Fresh from his first adventure on Denduron, Bobby finds himself in the territory of Cloral, a vast world that is entirely covered by water. Cloral is nearing a disaster of huge proportions. Reading the journals Bobby sends home, his friends learn that the desperate citizens of the endangered floating cities are on the brink of war. Can Bobby - suburban basketball star and all-around nice guy - help rid the area of marauders, and locate the legendary lost land of Faar, which may hold the key to Cloral's survival?.

Lost City of Faar. unabr. ed. D. J. MacHale. Read by William Dufris. (Running Time: 12 hrs.). (Pendragon Ser.: Bk. 2). 2009. audio compact disk 19.99 (978-1-4233-9897-4(1), 9781423398974); audio compact disk 49.97 (978-1-4233-9898-1(X), 9781423398981, BriAudCD Unabrid) Brilliance Audio.

Lost City of Z: A Tale of Deadly Obsession in the Amazon. unabr. ed. David Grann. Read by Mark Deakins. 8 CDs. (Running Time: 10 hrs.). 2009. audio compact disk 90.00 (978-1-4159-6024-0(0), BksonTape) Pub: Random Audio Pubg. Dist(s): Random

Lost City of Z: A Tale of Deadly Obsession in the Amazon. unabr. ed. David Grann. Illus. by David Grann. Read by Mark Deakins. (ENG.). 2009. audio compact disk 39.95 (978-0-7393-7698-0(5), Random AudioBks) Pub: Random Audio Pubg. Dist(s): Random

Lost City Search. Matt Oppenheimer. 1 cass. (Running Time: 1 hr.). (Wonder Tales Ser.). (J). (gr. k-5). 2000. 11.98 (978-1-930037-02-1(3), WT0003C) Inter Media Grp.
The listener discovers an ancient city.

Lost Civilizations: The Magnificent Maya. 1 cass. (Running Time: 1 hr. 30 min.). (J). 12.00 Hachet Audio.
Full-cast production based on the "Time Life Books" series.

Lost Civilizations: Egypt. abr. ed. Time-Life Books Editors. (Running Time: 35 mins.). (ENG.). 2006. 5.98 (978-1-59483-778-4(3)) Pub: Hachet Audio. Dist(s): HachBkGrp

Lost Civilizations: Greece: Temples, Tombs & Treasures. abr. ed. Time-Life Books Editors. (Running Time: 35 mins.). (ENG.). 2006. 5.98 (978-1-59483-779-1(1)) Pub: Hachet Audio. Dist(s): HachBkGrp

Lost Civilizations: Holy Land: The Landscape of the Testaments & the Koran. Read by Full Cast Production Staff. 1 cass. (Running Time: 90 min.). Dramatization. (Time Life Bks.). 12.00 Hachet Audio.

Lost Civilizations: Pompeii. abr. ed. Time-Life Books Editors. (ENG.). 2006. 5.98 (978-1-59483-782-1(1)) Pub: Hachet Audio. Dist(s): HachBkGrp

Lost Civilzations: The Magnificent Mayans Remnants of Glory & Genius. abr. ed. John Whitman. Read by Full Cast Production Staff. (ENG.). 2006. 5.98 (978-1-59483-846-0(1)) Pub: Hachet Audio. Dist(s): HachBkGrp

Lost Colony. Eoin Colfer. Read by Nathaniel Parker. 7. (Running Time: 8 hrs. 24 mins.). (Artemis Fowl Ser.: Bk. 5). 2006. audio compact disk 44.00 (978-0-7393-3773-8(4)) Books on Tape.

Lost Colony. Eoin Colfer. 5. (Running Time: 8 hrs. 24 mins.). (Artemis Fowl Ser.: Bk. 5). 2006. 32.00 (978-0-7393-3805-6(6), BksonTape) Pub: Random Audio Pubg. Dist(s): Random

Lost Colony. unabr. ed. Eoin Colfer. Read by Nathaniel Parker. (Running Time: 30240 sec.). (Artemis Fowl Ser.: Bk. 5). (J). (gr. 7-12). 2006. audio compact disk 37.00 (978-0-7393-3680-9(0), Listening Lib) Pub: Random Audio Pubg. Dist(s): Random

Lost Colony of Roanoke. unabr. ed. Brian Belval. Read by Jay Snyder. (Running Time: 1 hr.). (Primary Sources of the Thirteen Colonies Ser.). 2009. 14.99 (978-1-4233-9402-0(X), 9781423394020, Brilliance MP3); 39.97 (978-1-4233-9403-7(8), 9781423394037, Brinc Audio MP3 Lib); 39.97 (978-1-4233-9404-4(6), 9781423394044, BADLE); audio compact disk 14.99 (978-1-4233-9400-6(3), 9781423394006, Bril Audio CD Unabri);

audio compact disk 39.97 (978-1-4233-9401-3(1), 9781423394013, BriAudCD Unabrid) Brilliance Audio.

Lost Constitution. abr. ed. William Martin. Read by Phil Gigante. (Running Time: 6 hrs.). (Lost Constitution Ser.). 2008. audio compact disk 14.99 (978-1-4233-1278-9(3), 9781423312789, BCD Value Price) Brilliance Audio.

Lost Constitution. unabr. ed. William Martin. (Running Time: 19 hrs.). (Lost Constitution Ser.). 2007. 112.25 (978-1-4233-1270-3(8), 9781423312703, BrilAudUnabridg) Brilliance Audio.
Please enter a Synopsis.

Lost Constitution. unabr. ed. William Martin. Read by Phil Gigante. (Running Time: 19 hrs.). (Lost Constitution Ser.). 2007. 44.25 (978-1-4233-1276-5(7), 9781423312765, BADLE); 29.95 (978-1-4233-1275-8(9), 9781423312758, BAD); audio compact disk 44.25 (978-1-4233-1274-1(0), 9781423312741, Brlnc Audio MP3 Lib); audio compact disk 132.25 (978-1-4233-1272-7(4), 9781423312727, BriAudCD Unabrid); audio compact disk 29.95 (978-1-4233-1273-4(2), 9781423312734, Brilliance MP3); audio compact disk 38.95 (978-1-4233-1271-0(6), 9781423312710, Bril Audio CD Unabri) Brilliance Audio.

Lost Continent: Travels in Small-Town America. Bill Bryson. 2 cass. (Running Time: 90 min. per cass.). 1990. 15.95 (HarperChildAud) HarperCollins Pubs.

Lost Continent: Travels in Small-Town America. unabr. ed. Bill Bryson. Read by William Roberts. 8 cass. (Running Time: 12 hrs.). (Travels with Bill Bryson Ser.). 2000. 59.95 (978-0-7451-4121-3(8), CAB 804) Pub: Chivers Audio Bks GBR. Dist(s): AudioGO

Lost Continent: Travels in Small-Town America. unabr. ed. Bill Bryson. Read by William Roberts. 10 CDs. 2000. audio compact disk 94.95 (978-0-7540-5343-9(1), CCD 034) Pub: Chivers Audio Bks GBR. Dist(s): AudioGO
After ten years in England, Bill Bryson returns to America. He borrows his mother's old Chevrolet & travels through 38 states. He eats a lot of bad food, stays in cheap motels & visits Mark Twain's birthplace. This is a savagely funny portrait of contemporary America & a poignant memoir.

Lost Country Life. unabr. collector's ed. Dorothy Hartley. Read by Donada Peters. 8 cass. (Running Time: 12 hrs.). 1993. 64.00 (978-0-7366-2436-7(8), 3201) Books on Tape.
Heartfelt encyclopedia of rural life in the middle ages opens up a window on a vanished lifestyle.

Lost Days of Agatha Christie. unabr. ed. Carole Owens. Read by Nadia May. 3 cass. (Running Time: 4 hrs.). 1998. 23.95 (978-0-7861-1363-7(4), 2272) Blckstn Audio.
There was only one mystery she could not solve: her own disappearance in 1926. A practicing psychotherapist takes on Agatha Christie as a patient to diagnose her problem & at long last solve the mystery.

Lost Days of Agatha Christie. unabr. ed. Carole Owens. Read by Nadia May. 3 cass. (Running Time: 4 hrs. 30 min.). 1998. 19.95 (978-0-7861-1459-7(2)) Blckstn Audio.
The New York Times, seven decades after her disappearance, identified Agatha as "the town's (Harrogate's) most famous non-resident." It is an indication that the mystery of the lost days has never ceased to fascinate Christie fans. Time has not diminished their desire to find a solution.

Lost Decade see Great Gatsby & Other Stories

Lost Decade see Ten All Time Favorite Stories

Lost Decade see Fitzgerald Short Stories

Lost Destiny. abr. ed. Michael A. Stackpole. 2 cass. (Running Time: 3 hrs.). (Battletech: Vol. 3). 2003. 9.95 (978-1-931953-32-0(5)) Listen & Live.

Lost Dinosaurs of Egypt. unabr. ed. Josh Smith. 2002. 32.00 (978-0-8072-0732-1(2), Random AudioBks) Random Audio Pubg.

***Lost Dinosaurs of Egypt,Th(Dn)** abr. ed. Josh Smith. (Running Time: 5 hrs. 15 mins.). (ENG.). 2002. 14.95 (978-0-553-75548-0(X), Random AudioBks) Pub: Random Audio Pubg. Dist(s): Random

***Lost Dogs: Michael Vick's Dogs & Their Tale of Rescue & Redemption.** unabr. ed. Jim Gorant. Read by Paul Michael Garcia. (Running Time: 9.5 hrs. NaN mins.). (ENG.). 2010. 29.95 (978-1-4417-5833-0(X)); 59.95 (978-1-4417-5829-3(1)); audio compact disk 29.95 (978-1-4417-5832-3(1)); audio compact disk 90.00 (978-1-4417-5830-9(5)) Blckstn Audio.

Lost Dutchman O'Riley's Luck. Alan LeMay. (Running Time: 0 hr. 30 mins.). 1998. 10.95 (978-1-60083-449-3(3)) Iofy Corp.

***Lost Empire.** Clive Cussler & Grant Blackwood. (Running Time: 12 hrs.). (Fargo Adventure Ser.). (ENG.). 2010. audio compact disk 39.95 (978-0-14-242848-1(5), PengAudBks); audio compact disk 29.95 (978-0-14-242849-8(3), PengAudBks) Penguin Grp USA.

Lost Episodes. AIO Team Staff. Created by Focus on the Family. (Running Time: 5 hrs.). (Adventures in Odyssey Gold Ser.). (ENG.). (J). 2006. audio compact disk 24.99 (978-1-58997-363-3(1), Tyndale Ent) Tyndale Hse.

Lost Fleet, the: Dauntless: Dauntless. unabr. ed. Jack Campbell. Read by Christian Rummel. (Running Time: 10 hrs.). (Lost Fleet Ser.). 2009. 24.99 (978-1-4418-0646-8(6), 9781441806468, Brilliance MP3); 39.97 (978-1-4418-0647-5(4), 9781441806475, Brlnc Audio MP3 Lib); 39.97 (978-1-4418-0648-2(2), 9781441806482, BADLE); audio compact disk 97.97 (978-1-4418-0645-1(8), 9781441806451, BriAudCD Unabrid); audio compact disk 29.99 (978-1-4418-0644-4(X), 9781441806444, Bril Audio CD Unabri) Brilliance Audio.

Lost Fleet, the: Fearless: Fearless. unabr. ed. Jack Campbell. Read by Christian Rummel. (Running Time: 10 hrs.). (Lost Fleet Ser.). 2010. 24.99 (978-1-4418-0651-2(2), 9781441806512, Brilliance MP3); 39.97 (978-1-4418-0652-9(0), 9781441806529, Brlnc Audio MP3 Lib); 39.97 (978-1-4418-0653-6(9), 9781441806536, BADLE); audio compact disk 29.99 (978-1-4418-0649-9(0), 9781441806499, Bril Audio CD Unabri); audio compact disk 97.97 (978-1-4418-0650-5(4), 9781441806505, BriAudCD Unabrid) Brilliance Audio.

Lost Fleet, the: Relentless: Relentless. unabr. ed. Jack Campbell. Read by Christian Rummel. (Running Time: 10 hrs.). (Lost Fleet Ser.). 2009. 24.99 (978-1-4418-0641-3(5), 9781441806413, Brilliance MP3); 39.97 (978-1-4418-0642-0(3), 9781441806420, Brlnc Audio MP3 Lib); 39.97 (978-1-4418-0643-7(1), 9781441806437, BADLE); audio compact disk 97.97 (978-1-4418-0640-6(7), 9781441806406, BriAudCD Unabrid); audio compact disk 29.99 (978-1-4418-0639-0(3), 9781441806390, Bril Audio CD Unabri) Brilliance Audio.

Lost Fleet, the: Valiant: Valiant. unabr. ed. Jack Campbell. Read by Christian Rummel. (Running Time: 10 hrs.). (Lost Fleet Ser.). 2010. 39.97 (978-1-4418-0662-8(8), 9781441806628, Brlnc Audio MP3 Lib); 24.99 (978-1-4418-0661-1(X), 9781441806611, Brilliance MP3); audio compact disk 29.99 (978-1-4418-0659-8(8), 9781441806598, Bril Audio CD Unabri); audio compact disk 97.97 (978-1-4418-0660-4(1), 9781441806604, BriAudCD Unabrid) Brilliance Audio.

***Lost Fleet, the: Valiant: Valiant.** unabr. ed. Jack Campbell. Read by Christian Rummel. (Running Time: 10 hrs.). (Lost Fleet Ser.). 2010. 39.97 (978-1-4418-0663-5(6), 9781441806635, BADLE) Brilliance Audio.

Lost Gardens. unabr. ed. Anthony Eglin. Read by Gordon Griffin. 8 cass. (Soundings Ser.). (J). 2006. 69.95 (978-1-84559-324-7(3)) Pub: ISIS Lrg Prnt GBR. Dist(s): Ulverscroft US

***Lost Gate.** unabr. ed. Orson Scott Card. Read by Stefan Rudnicki & Emily Janice Card. (Running Time: 15 hrs.). (Mithermages Ser.). 2011. 29.95 (978-1-4417-7165-0(4)); 85.95 (978-1-4417-7162-9(X)); audio compact disk 29.95 (978-1-4417-7164-3(6)); audio compact disk 118.00 (978-1-4417-7163-6(8)) Blckstn Audio.

Lost Ghost see Wind in the Rose Bush & Other Stories of the Supernatural

Lost Girl. D. H. Lawrence. Narrated by Johanna Ward. (Running Time: 16 hrs. 30 mins.). 2002. 44.95 (978-1-59912-686-9(9)) Iofy Corp.

Lost Girl. unabr. ed. D. H. Lawrence. Read by Johanna Ward. 11 cass. (Running Time: 15 hrs. 30 min.). 2002. 76.95 (978-0-7861-2180-9(7)); audio compact disk 104.00 (978-0-7861-9541-1(X)) Blckstn Audio.
Charts the journey of a woman caught between two worlds and two lives - one mired in dreary, industrial England and a life of convention, the other set in the vibrant Italian landscape holding the promise of sensual liberation. Alvina Houghton is fading into spinsterhood when she meets Naples-born Cicio, a vaudeville dancer who draws her into a dance of seduction, reawakening her desire as she defies her stifling upper-class life.

Lost Gold of Red Canyon. William Russell. (ENG.). 2009. audio compact disk 24.95 (978-1-934965-23-8(5)) Dreamervision Pub.

Lost Gospel: The Quest for the Gospel of Judas Iscariot. unabr. ed. Herbert Krosney. Frwd. by Bart D. Ehrman. Narrated by Jason Culp. (Running Time: 36000 sec.). (ENG.). 2006. audio compact disk 44.95 (978-1-4262-0057-1(9), NatlGeo) Pub: Natl Geog. Dist(s): Random

Lost Gospel of Judas Iscariot: A New Look at Betrayer & Betrayed. unabr. ed. Bart D. Ehrman & Lew Grenville. Read by Dennis Boutsikaris. (YA). 2007. 44.99 (978-1-60252-764-5(4)) Find a World.

Lost Gospel Q: Original Sayings of Jesus. unabr. ed. Read by Jacob Needleman. Ed. by Marcus J. Borg. Afterword by Thomas Moore. 1 cass. (Running Time: 1 hr. 30 min.). 1997. 11.95 (978-1-57453-212-8(X)) Audio Lit.
Older than the four traditional Gospels, these are thought to be the original words of Jesus, preserved & written by his contemporaries.

Lost Heart of Asia. Colin Thubron. Read by Stuart Langton. 2001. 72.00 (978-0-7366-6097-6(6)) Books on Tape.

Lost Hearts. unabr. ed. M. R. James. Read by Walter Covell. 1 cass. (Running Time: 56 min.). Dramatization. 1981. 7.95 (S-19) Jimcin Record.
Strange rites seeking evil forces.

Lost Hearts & The Ash Tree. M. R. James. 1 cass. 1989. 7.95 (S-19) Jimcin Record.

***Lost Hero.** unabr. ed. Rick Riordan. (Running Time: 11 hrs.). (Heroes of Olympus Ser.: Bk. 1). (ENG.). (J). 2010. 22.00 (978-0-307-71178-6(1), Listening Lib) Pub: Random Audio Pubg. Dist(s): Random

***Lost Hero.** unabr. ed. Rick Riordan. Narrated by Joshua Swanson. 14 CDs. (Heroes of Olympus Ser.: Bk. 1). (J). (gr. 3-6). 2010. audio compact disk 50.00 (978-0-307-71179-3(X), Listening Lib) Pub: Random Audio Pubg. Dist(s): Random

***Lost Hero.** unabr. ed. Rick Riordan. Read by Joshua Swanson. (Running Time: 16 hrs. 36 mins.). (Heroes of Olympus Ser.: Bk. 1). (ENG.). (J). 2010. audio compact disk 50.00 (978-0-307-71177-9(3), Listening Lib) Pub: Random Audio Pubg. Dist(s): Random

Lost Highway. Richard Currey. Narrated by Ross Ballard. Music by Ross Ballard et al. 2005. audio compact disk 28.95 (978-0-9717801-5-6(3)) Mtn Whispers Pubng.

Lost History of Christianity: The Thousand-Year Golden Age of the Church in the Middle East, Africa, & Asia - And How It Died. unabr. ed. Philip Jenkins. Narrated by Dick Hill. (Running Time: 10 hrs. 30 mins. 0 sec.). (ENG.). 2008. audio compact disk 24.99 (978-1-4001-5971-0(7)); audio compact disk 69.99 (978-1-4001-3971-2(6)) Pub: Tantor Media. Dist(s): IngramPubServ

Lost History of Christianity: The Thousand-Year Golden Age of the Church in the Middle East, Africa, & Asia: And How It Died. unabr. ed. Philip Jenkins. Read by Dick Hill. (Running Time: 10 hrs. 30 mins. 0 sec.). (ENG.). 2008. audio compact disk 34.99 (978-1-4001-0971-5(X)) Pub: Tantor Media. Dist(s): IngramPubServ

***Lost Homestead.** Peter Dawson. 2009. (978-1-60136-400-5(8)) Audio Holding.

Lost Homestead. Peter Dawson. (Running Time: 2 hrs. 6 mins.). 2000. 10.95 (978-1-60083-546-9(5)) Iofy Corp.

Lost Honor: The Rest of the Story. collector's unabr. ed. John W. Dean. Read by Edward Holland. 10 cass. (Running Time: 15 hrs.). 2000. 80.00 (978-0-7366-5002-1(4)) Books on Tape.
Released from prison in January 1975, John Dean thought that the nightmare was over, that Watergate was behind him. He was wrong, because even as he tried to move away from the events of Watergate, he felt compelled to look deeper into the one remaining mystery of that era: the motives & identity of the man who had come to be known as Deep Throat.

Lost Horizon. James Hilton. 1 cass. (Running Time: 1 hr.). (Radiobook Ser.). 1987. 4.98 (978-0-929541-02-0(2)) Radiola Co.

Lost Horizon. James Hilton. Read by Christopher Kay. 5 cass. 1999. 49.95 (61195) Pub: Soundings Ltd GBR. Dist(s): ISIS Pub

Lost Horizon. unabr. ed. James Hilton. Read by Christopher Kay. 5 cass. (Running Time: 7 hrs. 30 mins.). (Sound Ser.). 2004. 49.95 (978-1-85496-119-8(5), 61195) Pub: UlverLrgPrint GBR. Dist(s): Ulverscroft US

Lost Horizon. unabr. collector's ed. James Hilton. Read by Richard Green. 7 cass. (Running Time: 7 hrs.). (J). 1978. 42.00 (978-0-7366-0144-3(9), 1146) Books on Tape.

Lost Hours. unabr. ed. Karen White. Read by Beth DeVries. 10 CDs. (Running Time: 13 hrs.). 2009. audio compact disk 29.95 (978-1-59316-170-5(0)) Listen & Live.

Lost in a Desert World: The Autobiography of Roland Johnson. As told by Karl Williams. 3 cass. (Running Time: 1 hrs. 30 mins.). (YA). (gr. 9 up). 2002. 18.00 (978-0-9672256-1-6(2)) Speaking Ourselves.
After spending half his childhood in Pennhurst State School and Hospital for the Mentally Retarded, Johnson emerged to become a captivating speaker and a respected leader of the self-advocacy movement. The book marks the first time that a person with developmental disabilities tells about his life in his own words.

Lost in a Good Book. abr. unabr. ed. Jasper Fforde. Read by Elizabeth Sastre. 10 CDs. (Running Time: 11 hrs. 30 mins.). (Thursday Next Ser.: No. 2). 2003. audio compact disk 36.95 (978-1-56511-757-0(3), 1565117573) Pub: HighBridge. Dist(s): Workman Pub

Lost in a Psychic Wonderland. Instructed by Manly P. Hall. 8.95 (978-0-89314-167-7(4), C820314) Philos Res.

Lost in Boggley Woods. Will Ryan. Ed. by Mary Becker. Illus. by David High et al. (J). (ps). 1986. bk. (978-0-318-60973-7(8)) Alchemy Comms.

Lost in Rooville. unabr. ed. Ray Blackston. Narrated by Andrew Petersen. (ENG.). 2005. 24.49 (978-1-60814-297-2(3)); audio compact disk 34.99 (978-1-59859-040-1(5)) Oasis Audio.

Lost in School. Lou Del Bianco. 1 cass. (Running Time: 1 hr.). (J). (gr. k-5). 2001. 10.00 (978-0-9642659-8-1(2)); audio compact disk 15.00 (978-0-9642659-7-4(4)) Story Maker.
Integrates 11 diverse musical moments with a storyline based on a true life experience.

Lost in Space. abr. ed. Joan D. Vinge. Read by Mimi Rogers. 2 cass. 1999. 18.00 (FS9-34624) Highsmith.

Lost in the Amazon: The True Story of Five Men & Their Desperate Battle for Survival. abr. ed. Stephen Kirkpatrick. Narrated by Kevin King. (ENG.). 2005. 15.39 (978-1-60814-298-9(1)) Oasis Audio.

Lost in the Barrens. unabr. ed. Farley Mowat. Read by Grover Gardner. 6 cass. (Running Time: 6 hrs.). 1994. 36.00 (978-0-7366-2850-1(9), 3558) Books on Tape.
Stranded in the wilderness, two boys face a challenge most men could not endure. With no food & little hope of rescue, they build a cabin, battle a grizzly, slaughter caribou for food & clothing. Two lost huskies offer companionship & maybe a way to get home.

Lost in the Blinded Blizzard. John R. Erickson. 2 cass. (Running Time: 2 hrs.). (Hank the Cowdog Ser.: No. 16). (J). (gr. 2-5). 1991. 16.95 Set. (978-0-87719-193-3(X), 9193) Lone Star Bks.

Lost in the Blinded Blizzard. unabr. ed. John R. Erickson. Read by John R. Erickson. 2 cass. (Running Time: 3 hrs.). (Hank the Cowdog Ser.: No. 16). (J). (gr. 2-5). 2001. 16.95 (978-0-7366-6905-4(1)) Books on Tape.
A raging blizzard shuts down the ranch. Someone must deliver medicine to Baby Molly & it's up to Hank to save the day.

Lost in the Blinded Blizzard. unabr. ed. John R. Erickson. Read by John R. Erickson. 2 cass. (Running Time: 3 hrs.). (Hank the Cowdog Ser.: No. 16). (J). 2002. 17.99 (978-1-59188-316-6(4)) Maverick Bks.
Hank and Drover listen to the wind howling outside and watch the snow piling up outside the window. Then the phone rings. It is High Loper telling Slim that baby Molly has a bad cough and needs some medicine. Can Hank go out into the blizzard and make it all the way to Headquarters with the cough medicine? Or will he be captured by Rip and Snort?.

Lost in the Blinded Blizzard. unabr. ed. John R. Erickson. Read by John R. Erickson. 3 CDs. (Running Time: Approx. 3 hours). (Hank the Cowdog Ser.: No. 16). (J). 2002. audio compact disk 19.99 (978-1-59188-616-7(3)) Maverick Bks.
As Head of Ranch Security, Hank the Cowdog has seen his share of though weather. So when a raging, swirling blizzard shuts down the ranch and Hank is stranded out at Slim?s cabin, he isn?t phased one bit. At least, not until a phone call from the ranch hose brings an emergency directive: someone?s got to deliver Slim?s cough medicine to Baby Molly. When Slim?s truck gets stuck in a snowdrift, it?s up to Hank to save the day. But a blinding blizzard is no place for a dog, even one as tough as Hank?Hear the coyote brothers sing ?We Don?t Give a Hoot? and Hank sing the touching ballad ?Oh Flee, My Love? in this hilarious adventure.

Lost in the Blinded Blizzard. unabr. ed. John R. Erickson. Read by John R. Erickson. 2 cass. (Hank the Cowdog Ser.: No. 16). (J). (gr. 2-5). 1998. 17.00 (21658) Recorded Bks.

Lost in the Blinded Blizzard. unabr. collector's ed. John R. Erickson. (Hank the Cowdog Ser.: Bk. 16). (J). 2001. audio compact disk 19.99 Books on Tape.
A raging blizzard shuts down the ranch. Someone must deliver medicine to Baby Molly and it's up to Hank to save the day.

Lost in the Blinded Blizzard. unabr. collector's ed. John R. Erickson. 2 cass. (Running Time: 3 hrs.). (Hank the Cowdog Ser.: No. 16). (J). 2001. 24.00 (978-0-7366-6149-2(2)); audio compact disk 28.00 (978-0-7366-7538-3(8)) Books on Tape.

Lost in the Cave - Book & Audio Cassette. 1 read-along cass. (J). (ps-3). 1986. bk. 9.98 (978-0-89544-157-7(8), NO. 157) Silbert Bress.
Tuffy learns that it is much wiser to do what he alone knows is right.

Lost in the Dark Unchanted Forest. John R. Erickson. Read by John R. Erickson. 2 cass. (Running Time: 2 hrs.). (Hank the Cowdog Ser.: No. 11). (J). (gr. 2-5). 1988. 15.95 (978-0-87719-127-8(1)) Lone Star Bks.

Lost in the Dark Unchanted Forest. unabr. ed. John R. Erickson. 2 cass. (Running Time: 3 hrs.). (Hank the Cowdog Ser.: No. 11). (J). (gr. 2-5). 2001. 24.00 (978-0-7366-6135-5(2)) Books on Tape.
Hank starts out to give Pete the Bamcat a little scare, but to his surprise, Pete turns out to be Sinister the Bobcat. Hank then finds himself on a mission in the Dark Unchanted Forest to save Little Alfred. Hank stumbles upon Madame Moonshine and gets trapped by Rip and Snort. Will Hank find a way out and will he rescue Little Alfred?.

Lost in the Dark Unchanted Forest. unabr. ed. John R. Erickson. Read by John R. Erickson. 2 cass. (Running Time: 3 hrs.). (Hank the Cowdog Ser.: No. 11). (J). (gr. 2-5). 2001. 16.95 (978-0-7366-6900-9(0)) Books on Tape.
Little Alfred runs away from home & Hank must save him from the monsters who lurk in the "dark unchanted forest".

Lost in the Dark Unchanted Forest. unabr. ed. John R. Erickson. Read by John R. Erickson. 2 cass. (Running Time: 3 hrs.). (Hank the Cowdog Ser.: No. 11). (J). 2002. 17.99 (978-1-59188-311-1(3)) Maverick Bks.
Hank starts out try to give Pete the Barncat a little scare, but to his surprise Pete turns out to be Sinister the Bobcat. Following that mishap, Hank finds himself on a mission in the Dark Unchanted Forest to save Little Alfred. Hank loses his way and stumbles upon Madame Moonshine and gets trapped by Rip and Snort.

Lost in the Dark Unchanted Forest. unabr. ed. John R. Erickson. Read by John R. Erickson. 3 CDs. (Running Time: Approx. 3 hours). (Hank the Cowdog Ser.: No. 11). (J). 2002. audio compact disk 19.99 (978-1-59188-611-2(2)) Maverick Bks.
When Little Alfred runs away from home and winds up in the Dark Unchanted Forest being trailed by a bobcat, Hank the Cowdog knows that it?s up to him to save his young master. So, mustering up all the courage that a Head of Ranch Security can come up with, he bravely makes his way into the forest. But before long, Hank is even more lost than Alfred. Can he find his master and get them both out of the woods? Or is he destined to pass the rest of his days going in circles?Hear the songs ?Disorientation,? ?I Love All Kinds of Stuff,? and ?The Storm? in this hilarious adventure for the whole family.

Lost in the Dark Unchanted Forest. unabr. ed. John R. Erickson. 2 cass. (Hank the Cowdog Ser.: No. 11). (J). (gr. 2-5). 1998. 17.00 (21653) Recorded Bks.

Lost in the Dark Unchanted Forest. unabr. collector's ed. John R. Erickson. 3 CDs. (Running Time: 4 hrs. 30 mins.). (Hank the Cowdog Ser.: No. 11). (J). (gr. 2-5). 2001. audio compact disk 28.00 Books on Tape.
Little Alfred runs away from home & Hank must save him from the monsters who lurk in the "dark unchanted forest".

Lost in the Dark Unchanted Forest & the Case of the Fiddle-Playing Fox. unabr. ed. John R. Erickson. Read by John R. Erickson. 4 cass,. (Running Time: 6 hrs.). (Hank the Cowdog Ser.: Nos. 11-12). (J). 2002. 26.99 (978-0-916941-66-6(3)); audio compact disk 31.99 (978-0-916941-86-4(8)) Maverick Bks.
When Little Alfred runs away from home and winds up in the Dark Unchanted Forest being trailed by a bobcat, Hank the Cowdog knows that it's up to him to save his young master. So, mustering up all the courage that a Head of Ranch Security can come up with, he bravely makes his way into the forest. But before long, Hank is even more lost than Alfred. Can he find his master and get them both out of the woods?.

Lost in the Fifties Tonight (Medley) - ShowTrax. Arranged by Ed Lojeski. 1 CD. (Running Time: 10 mins.). 2000. audio compact disk 45.00 (08201151) H Leonard.
Travel back in time to an age of young love, bobby socks & doo-wop! This charming medley, full of entertaining harmony & melody, will be a favorite. Includes: "Book of Love" (The Monotones, 1958); "Earth Angel" (The Crew-Cuts/The Penguins, 1955); "Graduation Day" (The Rover Boys/The Four Freshmen, 1956); "Lost in the Fifties Tonight" (In the Still of the Nite) (The Five Satins, 1956); & "Sh-Boom" (Life Could Be a Dream) (The Crew Cuts, 1954).

Lost in the Forest. unabr. ed. Sue Miller. Read by Blair Brown. (Running Time: 7 hrs. 30 mins.). (ENG.). 2005. audio compact disk 34.95 (978-0-7393-2023-5(8)) Pub: Random Audio Pubg. Dist(s): Random

Lost in the Middle: Audio Book. Paul Tripp. 2008. audio compact disk 35.00 (978-0-9815400-2-3(3)) Shepherd Pr PA.

Lost in the Solar System. Joanna Cole. Illus. by Bruce Degen. (Magic School Bus Ser.). (ENG.). (J). (gr. 2-5). 2010. 9.95 (978-0-545-22088-0(2)) Scholastic Inc.

Lost in the Woods: The Soundtrack & Read-along. Carl R. Sams, II. (J). (ps-3). 2006. audio compact disk 9.95 (978-0-9770108-2-0(1)) Carl R Sams.

Lost in Yonkers. Neil Simon. Perf. by Barbara Bain et al. 2 cass. (Running Time: 2 hrs.). Dramatization. 2001. 22.95; audio compact disk 24.95 L A Theatre.

Lost in Yonkers. Neil Simon. Contrib. by Barbara Bain et al. (Playaway Adult Fiction Ser.). (ENG.). 2009. 40.00 (978-1-60775-572-2(6)) Find a World.

Lost in Yonkers. unabr. ed. Neil Simon. Perf. by Barbara Bain et al. 2 CDs. (Running Time: 1 hr. 57 mins.). (L. A. Theatre Works). 2001. audio compact disk 25.95 (978-1-58081-226-9(0), CDTPT155) Pub: L A Theatre. Dist(s): NetLibrary CO
Set in Yonkers,New York in 1942, two boys, aged 13 and 16, must spend one year with their austere and demanding grandmother. While the war rages in Europe, jay and Arty learn the ropes from Uncle Louie and assorted relatives, all peculiar characters.

Lost in Yonkers. unabr. ed. Neil Simon. 2 cass. (Running Time: 2 hrs.). 2002. 22.95 (978-1-58081-212-2(0), TPT155) L A Theatre.
Set in Yonkers New York in 1942, two boys, aged 13 and 16, must spend one year with their austere and demanding grandmother. While the war rages in Europe, jay and Arty learn the ropes from Uncle Louie and assorted relatives, all peculiar characters.

Lost Island. unabr. ed. Phyllis A. Whitney. Read by Shelley Thompson. 8 cass. (Running Time: 12 hrs.). 2000. 69.95 (978-0-7540-0544-5(5), CAB 1967) Pub: Chivers Audio Bks GBR. Dist(s): AudioGO
They grew up together on a mist-shrouded island off the Georgia coast. Long ago & without Giles ever knowing it, Lacey gave birth to his son. But Elise, the beautiful, domineering one, got Giles. She got Lacey's child too, to bring up as her own. In ten years Lacey has not been able to forget, so she's going back. To see her son. To confront Elise. To exorcise the spell of the island & of Giles.

Lost King: Akhenaton. Kristi McCracken. Narrated by Larry A. McKeever. (Ancient Egyptian Mystery Ser.). (J). 2004. 10.95 (978-1-58659-121-2(5)); audio compact disk 14.95 (978-1-58659-355-1(2)) Artesian.

Lost Lake. abr. ed. Phillip Margolin. Read by Kristine Sutherland. 2005. audio compact disk 29.95 (978-0-06-075963-6(1)) HarperCollins Pubs.

***Lost Lake.** abr. ed. Phillip Margolin. Read by Sutherland Kristine. (ENG.). 2005. (978-0-06-083936-9(8), Harper Audio); (978-0-06-079675-4(8), Harper Audio) HarperCollins Pubs.

Lost Lake. unabr. ed. Phillip Margolin. Read by Deborah Hazlett. 2005. 29.95 (978-0-7927-3512-0(9), CMP 770); 49.95 (978-0-7927-3510-6(2), CSL 770); audio compact disk 64.95 (978-0-7927-3511-3(0), SLD 770) AudioGO.

Lost Lake. unabr. ed. Phillip Margolin. Read by Deborah Hazlett. 2005. audio compact disk & audio compact disk 39.95 (978-0-06-075962-9(3)) HarperCollins Pubs.

***Lost Lake.** unabr. ed. Phillip Margolin. Read by Deborah Hazlett. (ENG.). 2005. (978-0-06-083929-1(5), Harper Audio) HarperCollins Pubs.

***Lost Lake.** unabr. ed. Phillip Margolin. Read by Deborah Hazlett. (ENG.). 2005. (978-0-06-079674-7(X), Harper Audio) HarperCollins Pubs.

Lost Leader see Browning's Last Duchess

Lost Light. unabr. ed. Michael Connelly. Read by Len Cariou. 9 CDs. (Running Time: 10 hrs.). (Harry Bosch Ser.: No. 9). (ENG.). 2003. audio compact disk 46.98 (978-1-58621-489-0(6)) Pub: Hachet Audio. Dist(s): HachBkGrp

Lost Light. unabr. ed. Michael Connelly. Read by Len Cariou. (Harry Bosch Ser.: No. 9). (ENG.). 2005. 14.98 (978-1-59483-237-6(4)) Pub: Hachet Audio. Dist(s): HachBkGrp

Lost Light. unabr. ed. Michael Connelly. Read by Len Cariou. (Running Time: 10 hrs.). (Harry Bosch Ser.: No. 9). (ENG.). 2009. 70.98 (978-1-60024-961-7(2)) Pub: Hachet Audio. Dist(s): HachBkGrp

Lost Love Chronicles: Reunions & Memories of First Love. Nancy Kalish. (ENG.). 2008. (978-0-9787697-9-6(1)) N Kalish.

Lost Man's River. unabr. ed. Peter Mattiessen. Narrated by George Guidall. 19 cass. (Running Time: 27 hrs. 30 mins.). 1998. 154.00 (978-0-7887-1983-7(1), 95370E7) Recorded Bks.
Sequel to "Killing Mr. Watson," in which Lucius Watson is obsessed with learning the truth about his father, now that he's dead. Was he a man of progress & vision or an amoral opportunist?.

Lost Medal. Karen Jean Matsko Hood. (J). 2006. 29.95 (978-1-59434-758-0(1)) Whsprng Pine.

Lost Men: The Harrowing Saga of Shackleton's Ross Sea Party. abr. ed. Kelly Tyler-Lewis. Read by Graeme Malcolm. 2006. 17.95 (978-0-7435-5415-2(9), Audioworks) Pub: S&S Audio. Dist(s): S and S Inc

Lost Mode of Prayer. Gregg Braden. 2 CDs. 2004. audio compact disk 19.95 (978-1-59179-295-6(9), AW00408D) Sounds True.
Drawing on texts from the ancient Holy Land and other sources, Braden reveals an ancient prayer form for manifesting our highest visions in the outer world.

Lost Mother. unabr. ed. Mary McGarry Morris. Read by Judith Ivey. (YA). 2007. 49.99 (978-1-60252-648-8(6)) Find a World.

***Lost Music.** Illus. by Kathryn Meyrick. (Child's Play Library). (ENG.). (J). 2010. audio compact disk 21.98 (978-1-84643-402-0(5)) Childs Play GBR.

Lost Music: Gustav Mole's War on Noise. unabr. ed. Kathryn Meyrick. Illus. by Kathryn Meyrick. Read by Patrick Macnee. 1 cass. (Running Time: 040 min.). (Child's Play Library). (ENG.). (J). (ps-5). 1992. 6.99 (978-0-85953-378-2(6)) Childs Play GBR.
Feature Patrick Macnee once more as Gustav, & focuses on rare instruments introduced in the story.

Lost Ocean. Contrib. by Lost Ocean. Prod. by Nathan Dantzler. 2007. audio compact disk 13.99 (978-5-557-94920-0(8)) Sigma F RUS.

Lost! On a Mountain in Maine. Donn Fendler. Read by Amon Purinton. Retold by Joseph B. Egan. Music by Brent Thompson. 1 CD. (Running Time: 2 hrs.). (YA). (gr. 2 up). 1993. audio compact disk 24.95 (978-1-883332-65-5(6)) Audio Bkshelf.
The true account of a twelve-year-old's survival for nine days while lost on Mount Katahdin! Alone, starving & without shelter, yet determined to survive, Donn Fendler's story of his ordeal is a timeless adventure for listeners of all ages.

Lost! on a Mountain in Maine. Donn Fendler. Read by Amon Purinton. Told to Joseph B. Egan. (Playaway Children Ser.). (ENG.). (J). (gr. k). 2009. 39.99 (978-1-60812-572-2(6)) Find a World.

Lost on a Mountain in Maine. unabr. ed. 2 CDs. (Running Time: 2 hrs.). 2001. audio compact disk 24.95 Audio Bkshelf.

Lost on Dress Parade see Favorite Stories by O. Henry

Lost on Planet China: The Strange & True Story of One Man's Attempt to Understand the World's Most Mystifying Nation, or How He Became Comfortable Eating Live Squid. J. Maarten Troost. Read by Simon Vance. 2008. audio compact disk 19.95 (978-1-4332-4864-1(6)) Blckstn Audio.

Lost on Planet China: The Strange & True Story of One Man's Attempt to Understand the World's Most Mystifying Nation, or How He Became Comfortable Eating Live Squid. unabr. ed. J. Maarten Troost. Read by Simon Vance. (Running Time: 9 hrs. 0 mins.). 2008. 29.95 (978-1-4332-4865-8(4)); 59.95 (978-1-4332-4862-7(X)); audio compact disk 80.00 (978-1-4332-4863-4(8)) Blckstn Audio.

***Lost Peace: Leadership in a Time of Horror & Hope, 1945-1953.** unabr. ed. Robert Dallek. Read by Jonathan Davis. (ENG.). 2010. (978-0-06-200708-7(4), Harper Audio); (978-0-06-206237-6(9), Harper Audio) HarperCollins Pubs.

Lost Pirate: Early Explorers Early Set A Audio CD. Benchmark Education Staff. (J). 2006. audio compact disk 10.00 (978-1-4108-7620-1(9)) Benchmark Educ.

Lost Prince. Frances Hodgson Burnett. 9 Cds. (Running Time: 10 hours). (J). 2005. audio compact disk (978-0-9755663-4-3(2)) Alcazar AudioWorks.

Lost Prince. Frances Hodgson Burnett. Read by David Thorn. (Running Time: 39600 sec.). (J). (gr. 4-7). 2006. 65.95 (978-0-7861-4525-6(0)); audio compact disk 81.00 (978-0-7861-7179-8(0)) Blckstn Audio.

Lost Prince. unabr. ed. Frances Hodgson Burnett. Read by David Thorn. (Running Time: 39600 sec.). (J). (gr. 4-7). 2006. audio compact disk 29.95 (978-0-7861-7613-7(X)) Blckstn Audio.

***Lost Prosperity Secrets of Napoleon Hill: Newly Discovered Advice for Success in Tough Times from the Renowned Author of Think & Grow Rich.** unabr. ed. Napoleon Hill. Read by Erik Synnestvedt. (Running Time: 5 hrs. 30 mins.). (ENG.). 2011. 27.00 (978-1-59659-640-5(6), GildAudio); audio compact disk 29.98 (978-1-59659-625-2(2), GildAudio) Pub: Gildan Media. Dist(s): HachBkGrp

Lost Pueblo. unabr. collector's ed. Zane Grey. Read by Dan Lazar. 8 cass. (Running Time: 8 hrs.). 1998. 48.00 (978-0-7366-0326-3(3), 1312) Books on Tape.
An old-fashioned tale of romance in the Old West. The heroine is Jane Endicott, a rambunctious 20-year-old who travels to Arizona with her father for a wild west adventure. She becomes enthralled with the rough & rugged style of this new frontier, not to mention the eligible young cowboys vying for her attention.

Lost Race of Mars, Vol.1. unabr. ed. Michael D. Cooper. Read by Carol Eason. 2 cass. (Running Time: 3 hrs.). (Starman Ser.: No. 5). 2004. 18.00 (978-1-58807-478-2(1)) Am Pubng Inc.
The Starmen's search for the Benefactors leads them back to Mars. They must find the Benefactors before the vicious Xenobots destroy Earth in their search to destroy their 'ancient enemy'. But on Mars, people are strangely uncooperative, even though the same Starmen had been instrumental in saving Mars from Lurton Zimbardo's pirates. What the Starmen don't know is that the top organized crime boss on Mars has his own agenda, and he won't let the Starmen interfere with it.

Lost Race of Mars, Vol.2. unabr. ed. Michael D. Cooper. Read by Carol Eason. 2 cass. (Running Time: 3 hrs.). (Starman Ser.: No. 6). 2004. 18.00 (978-1-58807-479-9(X)) Am Pubng Inc.
While the Starmen are searching Mars for the lost race of Benefactors, an organized crime boss is getting the authorities to chase them down - by falsely accusing them of his own murder. He is also working for the Xenobots, who are searching for their 'ancient enemy' and who will stop at nothing until they find and destroy them. Zip, Mark, and Joe flee crooked cops, Xenobot robotic fighters, and Xenobots themselves in the Martian outback. Joe is captured by the mob boss, but Zip and Mark escape to hide in Martian caves. But they are trapped there. How can they escape to continue their search for the Benefactors, who hold the key to defeating the Xenobots and saving humanity?.

Lost Race of Mars, Vol.3. unabr. ed. Michael D. Cooper. Read by Carol Eason. 2 cass. (Running Time: 3 hrs.). (Starman Ser.: No. 7). 2004. 18.00 (978-1-58807-480-5(3)) Am Pubng Inc.
The Xenobots are searching for their 'ancient enemy' and will stop at nothing until they find and destroy them. Anyone who gets in their way, including the Starmen, will be destroyed as well. But the Starmen's search for the lost race of Benefactors has taken a strange turn. Zip and Mark now have help to rescue Joe, a prisoner of the Xenobots' human front man, and stop the mobster's illegal narcotics production. But Joe is locked in a cell deep underground with a nuclear time bomb. It's all a trap to destroy the Starmen and their leader, Richard Starlight. Can the Benefactors help?.

Lost Recipe for Happiness. unabr. ed. Barbara O'Neal. Read by Bernadette Dunne. 10 CDs. (Running Time: 12 hrs. 15 mins.). 2009. audio compact disk 110.00 (978-1-4159-5447-8(X), BksonTape) Pub: Random Audio Pubg. Dist(s): Random

***Lost Saint: A Dark Divine Novel.** unabr. ed. Bree Despain. (Running Time: 9 hrs.). (YA). 2010. audio compact disk 19.99 (978-1-61106-092-8(3), 9781611060928, Bril Audio CD Unabri) Brilliance Audio.

***Lost Saint, the: A Dark Divine Novel: A Dark Divine Novel.** unabr. ed. Bree Despain. (Running Time: 9 hrs.). (YA). 2010. 19.99 (978-1-61106-094-2(X), 9781611060942, Brilliance MP3); 39.97 (978-1-61106-096-6(6), 9781611060966, BADLE); 39.97 (978-1-61106-095-9(8), 9781611060959, Brlnc Audio MP3 Lib); audio compact disk 59.97 (978-1-61106-093-5(1), 9781611060935, BriAudCD Unabrid) Brilliance Audio.

Lost Scrolls, Vol. 6. Chris Heimerdinger. 4 cass. (Tennis Shoes Adventure Ser.). 2004. 19.95 (978-1-57734-419-3(7), 07001983) Covenant Comms.
Continuation of "Tennis Shoes & the Seven Churches.".

Lost Slipper. Tristan Davies & Nick Newman. Read by Peter Sallis & Gareth Armstrong. Characters created by Nick Park. (Running Time: 060 min.). (J). 2000. pap. bk. 10.95 (978-1-85998-903-6(9), HoddrStoughton) Pub: Hodder General GBR. Dist(s): Trafalgar
It's an ordinary day for Wallace, the fastidious inventor-handyman, and his dog-companion Gromit until Wallace discovers one of his slippers is missing. He crafts a Longlife Indoor Carpet Clog with Reinforced Everything as a replacement, but it's just not very comfortable. The only solution left is to aim the grandfather clock time machine back to where the missing slipper was last sighted. Wallace and Gromit believe they've set the coordinates for earlier that morning, 11:06 a.m. But alas, they zoom off to the year 1066 and land in the middle of the Battle of Hastings.

Lost Son see Twentieth-Century Poetry in English, No. 10, Recordings of Poets Reading Their Own Poetry

Lost Souls. abr. ed. Lisa Jackson. Read by Joyce Bean. (Running Time: 6 hrs.). (New Orleans Ser.: Bk. 5). 2009. audio compact disk 14.99 (978-1-4233-1532-2(4), 9781423315322, BCD Value Price) Brilliance Audio.

Lost Souls. unabr. ed. Lisa Jackson. Read by Joyce Bean. (Running Time: 15 hrs.). (New Orleans Ser.: Bk. 5). 2008. 39.25 (978-1-4233-1530-8(8), 9781423315308, BADLE); 24.95 (978-1-4233-1529-2(4), 9781423315292, BAD); 107.25 (978-1-4233-1524-7(3), 9781423315247, BrilAudUnabridg); audio compact disk 38.95 (978-1-4233-1525-4(1), 9781423315254, Bril Audio CD Unabri); audio compact disk 24.95 (978-1-4233-1527-8(8), 9781423315278, Brilliance MP3); audio compact disk 39.25 (978-1-4233-1528-5(6), 9781423315285, Brlnc Audio MP3 Lib); audio compact disk 112.25 (978-1-4233-1526-1(X), 9781423315261, BriAudCD Unabrid) Brilliance Audio.

***Lost Souls.** unabr. ed. Dean Koontz. Read by Christopher Lane. 1 Playaway. (Running Time: 9 hrs.). (Dean Koontz's Frankenstein Ser.: Bk. 4). 2010. 39.99 (978-1-4418-6896-1(8)) Brilliance Audio.

***Lost Souls.** unabr. ed. Dean Koontz. Read by Christopher Lane. (Running Time: 9 hrs.). 2010. 24.99 (978-1-4418-1833-1(2), 9781441818331, BAD) Brilliance Audio.

***Lost Souls.** unabr. ed. Dean Koontz. Read by Christopher Lane. 1 MP3-CD. (Running Time: 9 hrs.). (Dean Koontz's Frankenstein Ser.: Bk. 4). 2010. 39.97 (978-1-4418-1832-4(4), 9781441818324, Brlnc Audio MP3 Lib); 39.97 (978-1-4418-1834-8(0), 9781441818348, BADLE); 24.99 (978-1-4418-1831-7(6), 9781441818317, Brilliance MP3); audio compact disk 97.97 (978-1-4418-1830-0(8), 9781441818300, BriAudCD Unabrid); audio compact disk 34.99 (978-1-4418-1829-4(4), 9781441818294, Bril Audio CD Unabri) Brilliance Audio.

Lost Spy: An American in Stalin's Secret Service. unabr. ed. Andrew Meier. Narrated by David Chandler. (Running Time: 12 hrs.). 2008. 56.75 (978-1-4361-6511-2(3)) Recorded Bks.

Lost Spy: An American in Stalin's Secret Service. unabr. ed. Andrew Meier. Read by David Chandler. 10 cass. (Running Time: 12 hrs.). 2008. 82.75 (978-1-4361-0535-4(8)); audio compact disk 34.99 (978-1-4361-0534-7(X)); audio compact disk 123.75 (978-1-4361-0537-8(4)) Recorded Bks.

Lost Stage Valley. unabr. collector's ed. Frank Bonham. Read by Christopher Lane. 8 cass. (Running Time: 8 hrs.). 1995. 48.00 (978-0-7366-3065-8(1), 3747) Books on Tape.
Love of country drives Grif Holbrook into the most dangerous assignment of his career: save a stagecoach line from predatory bandits.

Lost Steps of Reiki: Transforming an Ancient Healing Art. Thomas A. Hensel & Kevin R. Emery. 2 cass. 1996. 19.95 (978-1-890405-01-4(9)) LightLines.
Channeled teachings based on the information of Wei Chi, designed to teach the Reiki practitioner how to make the system more holistic & cause-oriented.

Lost Stories of Louisa May Alcott. unabr. abr. ed. Short Stories. Louisa May Alcott. Ed. by Madeleine B. Stern et al. 2 cass. (Running Time: 3 hrs.). 1998. 16.95 (978-1-882071-53-1(0), 393003) B-B Audio.
The lost stories include many newly discovered tales. Written while she was completing LITTLE WOMEN, the thrillers that Alcott scribbled in her Boston attic were drawn from her experiences, from her reading, and even from her dreams. Her characters are.

Lost Stradivarius. John Meade Falkner. Read by Donna Barkman & Jim Killavey. 6 cass. (Running Time: 6 hrs.). 1989. 36.00 incl. album. (C-88) Jimcin Record.
A tale of the occult.

Lost Summer of Louisa May Alcott. unabr. ed. Kelly O'Connor McNees. Contrib. by Emily Janice Card. 7 CDs. (Running Time: 9 hrs.). (ENG.). 2010. audio compact disk 29.95 (978-0-14-242781-1(0), PengAudBks) Penguin Grp USA.

Lost Symbol. abr. ed. Dan Brown. Read by Paul Michael. (ENG.). 2009. audio compact disk 30.00 (978-0-7393-0956-8(0), Random AudioBks) Pub: Random Audio Pubg. Dist(s): Random

***Lost Symbol.** unabr. ed. Dan Brown. Read by Paul Michael. (Running Time: 17 hrs. 45 mins.). 2009. (978-0-307-70406-1(8), BksonTape); audio compact disk 100.00 (978-0-307-70405-4(X), BksonTape) Pub: Random Audio Pubg. Dist(s): Random

Lost Symbol. unabr. ed. Dan Brown. Read by Paul Michael. (ENG.). 2009. audio compact disk 50.00 (978-0-7393-1917-8(5), Random AudioBks) Pub: Random Audio Pubg. Dist(s): Random

Lost Tapes of Ian Mcharg: Collaboration with Nature, Ecological Planning Lecture. Ed. by Lynn Margulis et al. (Running Time: 1 hr. 14 mins.). (ENG.). 2006. audio compact disk 30.00 (978-1-933392-30-1(4)) Chelsea Green Pub.

Lost Teachings of Yoga. Georg Feuerstein. 2003. audio compact disk 69.95 (978-1-59179-009-9(3)) Sounds True.

Lost Testament. unabr. ed. Alan Gold. Read by James Condon. 14 cass. (Running Time: 21 hrs.). 2001. (978-1-86340-716-8(2), 570523) Bolinda Pubng AUS.
A cave deep in the Judean desert. A 2000 year old list. Tantalizing clues that Jesus Christ wrote a prophetic testament. The discovery galvanizes the world. Does the testament still exist? If so, what will be revealed if it is unearthed? Within hours, scholars, fortune tellers, religious groups & reporters are searching for the testament.

Lost, the Sick, the Sacred. Contrib. by Inhale Exhale. Prod. by Travis Wyrick. 2006. audio compact disk 16.99 (978-5-558-20692-0(6)) Solid State MO.

Lost Thing. unabr. ed. Shaun Tan. Read by Humphrey Bower. (Running Time: 900 sec.). (J). (ps-3). 2006. audio compact disk 39.95 (978-1-74093-705-4(8)) Pub: Bolinda Pubng AUS. Dist(s): Bolinda Pub Inc

Lost Throne. unabr. ed. Chris Kuzneski. Read by Dick Hill. (Running Time: 13 hrs.). (Payne & Jones Ser.: Bk. 4). 2009. 24.99 (978-1-4233-8958-3(1), 9781423389583, Brilliance MP3); 24.99 (978-1-4233-8960-6(3), 9781423389606, BAD); 39.97 (978-1-4233-8959-0(X), 9781423389590, Brlnc Audio MP3 Lib); 39.97 (978-1-4233-8961-3(1), 9781423389613, BADLE); audio compact disk 29.99 (978-1-4233-8956-9(5), 9781423389569, Bril Audio CD Unabri); audio compact disk 92.97

(978-1-4233-8957-6(3), 9781423389576, BriAudCD Unabrid) Brilliance Audio.

Lost Thyrsus see Widdershins: The First Book of Ghost Stories

Lost Tomb: This Is His Incredible Story of KV5 & Its Excavation. unabr. ed. Kent Weeks. Narrated by Richard M. Davidson. 8 cass. (Running Time: 11 hrs. 30 mins.). 1999. 72.00 (978-0-7887-2931-7(4), 95668E7) Recorded Bks.
When an American Egyptologist discovered the largest known tomb in the Valley of the Kings in 1995, the world was astonished. Dr. Weeks' chronicle of his risk-filled discovery reads like a thrilling adventure story.

Lost Tomorrow. Michael D. Cooper. Read by Carol Eason. 2 cass. (Running Time: 3 hrs.). (Starman Ser.: No. 8). 2004. 18.00 (978-1-58807-481-2(1)) Am Pubng Inc.

Lost Triumph: Lee's Real Plan at Gettysburg - and Why It Failed. unabr. ed. Tom Carhart. Narrated by Michael Prichard. (Running Time: 9 hrs. 30 mins. 0 sec.). (ENG.). 2005. audio compact disk 34.99 (978-1-4001-0157-3(3)); audio compact disk 19.99 (978-1-4001-5157-8(0)) Pub: Tantor Media. Dist(s): IngramPubServ

Lost Triumph: Lee's Real Plan at Gettysburg - and Why It Failed. unabr. ed. Tom Carhart. Read by Tom Carhart. Narrated by Michael Prichard. (Running Time: 9 hrs. 30 mins. 0 sec.). (ENG.). 2005. audio compact disk 69.99 (978-1-4001-3157-0(X)) Pub: Tantor Media. Dist(s): IngramPubServ

***Lost Truth.** unabr. ed. Dawn Cook. Read by Marguerite Gavin. (Running Time: 12 hrs.). (Truth Ser.). 2010. 29.95 (978-1-4417-5419-6(9)); 72.95 (978-1-4417-5415-8(6)); audio compact disk 29.95 (978-1-4417-5418-9(0)); audio compact disk 105.00 (978-1-4417-5416-5(4)) Blckstn Audio.

***Lost TV Episodes, 1964-1965, Vol. 1.** unabr. ed. Told to William Hartnell & Full Cast. (Running Time: 10 hrs. 45 mins. 0 sec.). (Doctor Who Ser.). (ENG.). 2010. audio compact disk 124.95 (978-1-4084-6751-0(8)) Pub: AudioGO. Dist(s): Perseus Dist

Lost Universe. 1 CD. (JPN.). 2003. audio compact disk 14.98 (978-1-57813-393-2(9), CLU/001) A D Vision.

Lost Victories: The Military Genius of Stonewall Jackson. unabr. ed. Bevin Alexander. Narrated by Nelson Runger. 9 CDs. (Running Time: 11 hrs.). 2000. audio compact disk 85.00 (978-0-7887-3395-6(8), C1001E7) Recorded Bks.
Challenges the sagacity attributed to one of the Civil War's most mythical heroes, General Robert E. Lee & presents evidence that it was actually the strategic vision of Stonewall Jackson that played the key role in the South's most dramatic battles.

Lost Victories: The Military Genius of Stonewall Jackson. unabr. ed. Bevin Alexander. Narrated by Nelson Runger. 8 cass. (Running Time: 11 hrs.). 1994. 70.00 (978-0-7887-0043-9(X), 94242E7) Recorded Bks.
The generalship of Stonewall Jackson is explored; with his death in battle early in the Civil War, the Southern cause lost perhaps its greatest leader.

Lost Wagon Train. unabr. ed. Zane Grey. Read by Brian O'Neill. 10 vols. (Running Time: 10 hrs.). 1999. bk. 84.95 (978-0-7927-2295-3(7), CSL 184, Chivers Sound Lib) AudioGO.
Civil War survivor Stephen Latch, a brigand with a ready gun, joins a raging Indian chief on a mission of terrifying revenge - to massacre a pioneer train of 160 wagons. But fate has a big surprise in store for big-hearted Latch.

Lost Weekend. Perf. by Ray Milland & Jane Wyman. (Running Time: 60 min.). 1946. 7.95 (DD-8430) Natl Recrd Co.
"The Lost Weekend" is a powerful radio presentation about a struggling writer who becomes an alcholic, but the love of a beautiful woman gives him hope. In "Sorry, Wrong Number" a bedridden, neurotic invalid, through a freak telephone connection, overhears two men plotting a murder...hers.

Lost Weekend. unabr. collector's ed. Charles Jackson. Read by Thomas H. Middleton. 6 cass. (Running Time: 9 hrs.). 1989. 48.00 (978-0-7366-1546-4(6), 2415) Books on Tape.
Don Dirnam is a sensitive, charming & well-read man. Yet when left alone for a few days by his brother, he struggles with his overwhelming desire for alcohol, succumbs to it & in the resulting prolonged agony goes over much of his life up to & including the lost weekend.

Lost Without You. Annette Lyon. 3 cass. 2004. 14.95 (978-1-59156-025-8(X)) Covenant Comms.

Lost Witness. unabr. ed. Robert Ellis. Read by Deanna Hurst. (Running Time: 14 hrs.). (Lena Gamble Ser.). 2009. 39.97 (978-1-4233-3701-0(8), 9781423337010, BADLE); 39.97 (978-1-4233-3699-0(2), 9781423336990, Brlnc Audio MP3 Lib); 24.99 (978-1-4233-3698-3(4), 9781423336983, Brilliance MP3); 24.99 (978-1-4233-3700-3(X), 9781423337003, BAD); audio compact disk 89.97 (978-1-4233-3697-6(6), 9781423336976, BriAudCD Unabrid); audio compact disk 38.99 (978-1-4233-3696-9(8), 9781423336969, Bril Audio CD Unabri) Brilliance Audio.

Lost Wolf. unabr. collector's ed. Max Brand. Read by Jonathan Marosz. 8 cass. (Running Time: 8 hrs.). 1995. 48.00 (978-0-7366-3067-2(8), 3749) Books on Tape.
The Cheyenne raised him, but Lost Wolf - born of white parents - can re-enter the white man's world if he wins a fight to the death.

***Lost Women of the Bible: Finding Strength & Significance through Their Stories.** Carolyn Custis James. (Running Time: 10 hrs. 24 mins. 0 sec.). (ENG.). 2008. 16.99 (978-0-310-30476-0(8)) Zondervan.

Lost Word: A Christmas Legend of Long Ago. Based on a story by Henry Van Dyke. (ENG.). 2007. 5.00 (978-1-60339-103-0(7)); audio compact disk 5.00 (978-1-60339-104-7(5)) Listenr Digest.

Lost World. unabr. ed. Michael Crichton. Read by Scott Brick. (Running Time: 55800 sec.). (ENG.). 2008. audio compact disk 34.95 (978-0-7393-5930-3(4), Random AudioBks) Pub: Random Audio Pubg. Dist(s): Random

Lost World. unabr. ed. Michael Crichton. Narrated by George Guidall. 9 cass. (Running Time: 13 hrs. 30 mins.). 1999. 80.00 (978-0-7887-3093-1(2), 95804E7) Recorded Bks.
Six years ago, in Central America, secret experiments at Jurassic Park went awry & the dinosaurs had to be destroyed. Now there are rumors that something survived.

Lost World. unabr. ed. Michael Crichton. Narrated by George Guidall. 12 CDs. (Running Time: 13 hrs. 30 mins.). 1999. audio compact disk 104.00 (978-0-7887-3725-1(2), C1082E7) Recorded Bks.

Lost World: Being an Account of the Recent Amazing Adventures of Professor George E. Challenger, Lord John Roxton, Professor Summerlee, & Mr E. D. Malone of the Daily Gazette. Arthur Conan Doyle. 2007. 16.95 (978-1-60112-018-2(4)) Babblebooks.

Lost World: Being an Account of the Recent Amazing Adventures of Professor George E. Challenger, Lord John Roxton, Professor Summerlee, & Mr E. D. Malone of the Daily Gazette. Arthur Conan Doyle. Read by Michael Prichard. (Running Time: 8 hrs. 15 mins.). 2003. 27.95 (978-1-60083-652-7(6), Audiofy Corp) Iofy Corp.

Lost World: Being an Account of the Recent Amazing Adventures of Professor George E. Challenger, Lord John Roxton, Professor Summerlee, & Mr E. D. Malone of the Daily Gazette. Arthur Conan Doyle. 2 cass. (Running Time: 2 hrs.). 2001. 17.95 (ALEN005); audio compact disk 19.95 (ALEN006) Lodestone Catalog.
Professor Challenger discovering a lost plateau in the Amazon, where ape-men have evolved beside dinosaurs & the fate of the human race hangs in the balance.

Lost World: Being an Account of the Recent Amazing Adventures of Professor George E. Challenger, Lord John Roxton, Professor Summerlee, & Mr E. D. Malone of the Daily Gazette. Arthur Conan Doyle. 2002. 12.95 (978-0-19-424361-2(3)) OUP.

Lost World: Being an Account of the Recent Amazing Adventures of Professor George E. Challenger, Lord John Roxton, Professor Summerlee, & Mr E. D. Malone of the Daily Gazette. Arthur Conan Doyle. Narrated by Michael Prichard. (ENG.). 2005. audio compact disk 78.00 (978-1-4001-3086-3(7)) Pub: Tantor Media. Dist(s): IngramPubServ

Lost World: Being an Account of the Recent Amazing Adventures of Professor George E. Challenger, Lord John Roxton, Professor Summerlee, & Mr E. D. Malone of the Daily Gazette. Arthur Conan Doyle. Adapted by Bob E. Flick. Engineer Bob E. Flick. Des. by Adam Mayefsky. 2 CDs. (Running Time: 2 hrs. 30 mins.). Dramatization. 1996. audio compact disk 19.00 (978-1-884214-15-8(0)) Ziggurat Prods.
Adapted from the original classic tale by Sir Arthur Conan Doyle! Travel with Professor Challenger to a secluded South American plateau, deep in the Amazon Jungle...where dinosaurs still roam! A stunningly powerful theatrical performance brought to new heights by a brilliant musical score. Enter a bold new world of sound that is rhythm-rich in dynamic melodies and compelling, progressivepercussion. The future of Audio Art has arrived!.

Lost World: Being an Account of the Recent Amazing Adventures of Professor George E. Challenger, Lord John Roxton, Professor Summerlee, & Mr E. D. Malone of the Daily Gazette. Arthur Conan Doyle. Perf. by Bob E. Flick & Perry Jacob. 2 cass. (Running Time: 2 hr. 30 min.). Dramatization. 1996. 18.00 (978-1-884214-02-8(9)) Ziggurat Prods.
An adventure to an isolated plateau where dinosaurs roam, with a full case, musical score & sound effects.

Lost World: Being an Account of the Recent Amazing Adventures of Professor George E. Challenger, Lord John Roxton, Professor Summerlee, & Mr E. D. Malone of the Daily Gazette. abr. ed. Arthur Conan Doyle. 1 cass. (Running Time: 55 min.). 10.95 (SAC 1097) Spoken Arts.

Lost World: Being an Account of the Recent Amazing Adventures of Professor George E. Challenger, Lord John Roxton, Professor Summerlee, & Mr E. D. Malone of the Daily Gazette. adpt. ed. Arthur Conan Doyle. 2 cass. (Running Time: 1 hr. 40 min.). 1998. 15.00 Set. (978-0-9661287-1-0(0)) Star Quest.
Explorers journey to a remote plateau where dinosaurs still roam.

Lost World: Being an Account of the Recent Amazing Adventures of Professor George E. Challenger, Lord John Roxton, Professor Summerlee, & Mr E. D. Malone of the Daily Gazette. unabr. ed. Arthur Conan Doyle. Read by Flo Gibson. 5 cass. (Running Time: 7 hrs.). 1998. 20.95 (978-1-55685-583-2(4)) Audio Bk Con.
Two eccentric professors, a plucky sportsman & an intrepid reporter explore the wilds of the Amazon valley in search of prehistoric animals. When their bridge to civilization collapses they are surrounded by vicious beasts, savage ape-men & dinosaurs.

Lost World: Being an Account of the Recent Amazing Adventures of Professor George E. Challenger, Lord John Roxton, Professor Summerlee, & Mr E. D. Malone of the Daily Gazette. unabr. ed. Arthur Conan Doyle. Read by Fred Williams. 6 cass. (Running Time: 9 hrs.). 1994. 44.95 (978-0-7861-0844-2(4), 1524) Blckstn Audio.
The account of a scientific expedition by four highspirited Englishmen deep into South America's Amazon jungle. In this region, which is cut off from the outside world by unscalable vertical cliffs & fetid swamps, they encounter a world where dinosaurs roam free & natives fight out a murderous war with the ape-men. Trapped with only hunting rifles as protection, they must use savvy & intellect to escape this primeval terror.

Lost World: Being an Account of the Recent Amazing Adventures of Professor George E. Challenger, Lord John Roxton, Professor Summerlee, & Mr E. D. Malone of the Daily Gazette. unabr. ed. Arthur Conan Doyle. Read by Jack Sondericker. 6 cass. (Running Time: 6 hrs. 30 min.). 1989. 39.95 (978-1-55686-294-6(6), 294) Books in Motion.
A small group of brave men venture into the heart of the South American forest in search of the plateau that the professor claims to exist - The Lost World.

Lost World: Being an Account of the Recent Amazing Adventures of Professor George E. Challenger, Lord John Roxton, Professor Summerlee, & Mr E. D. Malone of the Daily Gazette. unabr. ed. Arthur Conan Doyle. Read by Thomas Whitworth. 6 cass. (Running Time: 9 hrs.). 2001. 29.95 (978-0-7366-6803-3(9)) Books on Tape.
A South American scientific expedition encounters remnants of prehistory.

Lost World: Being an Account of the Recent Amazing Adventures of Professor George E. Challenger, Lord John Roxton, Professor Summerlee, & Mr E. D. Malone of the Daily Gazette. unabr. ed. Arthur Conan Doyle. Read by Michael Prichard. (YA). 2007. 64.99 (978-1-60252-566-5(8)) Find a World.

Lost World: Being an Account of the Recent Amazing Adventures of Professor George E. Challenger, Lord John Roxton, Professor Summerlee, & Mr E. D. Malone of the Daily Gazette. unabr. ed. Arthur Conan Doyle. Read by Glen McCready. 7 CDs. (Running Time: 8 hrs. 30 mins.). (Complete Classics Ser.). 2008. audio compact disk 34.98 (978-962-634-852-9(6), Naxos AudioBooks) Naxos.

Lost World: Being an Account of the Recent Amazing Adventures of Professor George E. Challenger, Lord John Roxton, Professor Summerlee, & Mr E. D. Malone of the Daily Gazette. unabr. ed. Arthur Conan Doyle. Narrated by Paul Hecht. 6 cass. (Running Time: 8 hrs.). 1999. 51.00 (978-0-7887-0474-1(5), 94667E7) Recorded Bks.
A scientific expedition sets out to explore an isolated South American plateau where it is rumored that dinosaurs are still alive.

Lost World: Being an Account of the Recent Amazing Adventures of Professor George E. Challenger, Lord John Roxton, Professor Summerlee, & Mr E. D. Malone of the Daily Gazette. unabr. ed. Arthur Conan Doyle. Narrated by Michael Prichard. 7 CDs. (Running Time: 8 hrs. 13 mins.). (ENG.). 2003. audio compact disk 39.00 (978-1-4001-0086-6(0)) Pub: Tantor Media. Dist(s): IngramPubServ
On a zoology expedition up the Amazon, Professor Challenger has made an inexplicable discovery. Back in London, his claims are ridiculed throughout the professional community. Reluctantly, he recounts to Journalist Edward Malone, "Curupuri is the spirit of the woods, something terrible, something malevolent, something to be avoided. None can describe its shape or nature, but it is a word of terror along the Amazon. Something terrible lay that way. It was my business to find out what it was."Professor Challenger vows to prove his tale at a Zoological meeting, and a party is formed to find the truth. Edward Malone joins adventurer Lord John Roxton, and staid professor Summerlee on the mission. They journey to the depths of the Amazon, well provisioned and armed to the teeth. But how little they are prepared for what they find there....Today, Arthur Conan Doyle is best known as the creator of Sherlock Holmes, but he was also the author of many other science fiction and mystery novels, and 'The Lost World' was one of his best. This original tale of the "living dinosaurs" was the inspiration for many of its kind, including Jurassic Park.

Lost World: Being an Account of the Recent Amazing Adventures of Professor George E. Challenger, Lord John Roxton, Professor Summerlee, & Mr E. D. Malone of the Daily Gazette. unabr. ed. Arthur Conan Doyle. Narrated by Michael Prichard. 1 MP3 CD. (Running Time: 8 hrs. 13 mins.). (ENG.). (YA). 2003. audio compact disk 20.00 (978-1-4001-5086-1(8)) Pub: Tantor Media. Dist(s): IngramPubServ

Lost World: Being an Account of the Recent Amazing Adventures of Professor George E. Challenger, Lord John Roxton, Professor Summerlee, & Mr E. D. Malone of the Daily Gazette. unabr. ed. Arthur Conan Doyle. Narrated by Michael Prichard. (Running Time: 8 hrs. 30 mins. 0 sec.). (ENG.). 2009. lab manual ed. 19.99 (978-1-4001-5926-0(1)); lab manual ed. 55.99 (978-1-4001-3926-2(0)); audio compact disk 27.99 (978-1-4001-0926-5(4)) Pub: Tantor Media. Dist(s): IngramPubServ

Lost World: Being an Account of the Recent Amazing Adventures of Professor George E. Challenger, Lord John Roxton, Professor Summerlee, & Mr E. D. Malone of the Daily Gazette. unabr. collector's ed. Arthur Conan Doyle. Read by Thomas Whitworth. 6 cass. (Running Time: 9 hrs.). (J). 1992. 48.00 (978-0-7366-2287-5(X), 3073) Books on Tape.
The account of a scientific expedition by four intrepid Englishmen into a remote plateau in the South American jungle. It is a region beyond time, cut off from the outside world by vertical cliffs & surrounded by swamps.

Lost World: Being an Account of the Recent Amazing Adventures of Professor George E. Challenger, Lord John Roxton, Professor Summerlee, & Mr E. D. Malone of the Daily Gazette, Stage 2. Arthur Conan Doyle & Susan Kingsley. (Dominoes Ser.). 2004. 14.25 (978-0-19-424428-2(8)) OUP.

Lost World: Na749312. Arthur Conan Doyle. Read by Glen McCready. 2008. audio compact disk 34.98 (978-962-634-493-4(8), Naxos AudioBooks) Naxos.

Lost World - the World that Perished in the Flood of Noah. 2005. 15.00 (978-1-933561-15-8(7)) BFM Books.

Lost World (A) abr. ed. Arthur Conan Doyle. (Running Time: 4 hrs.). 2009. audio compact disk 22.98 (978-962-634-941-0(7), Naxos AudioBooks) Naxos.

Lost World of the Kalahari. unabr. ed. Laurens Van der Post. Read by John Nettleton. 8 cass. (Running Time: 10 hrs. 40 min.). (Isis Ser.). 1995. 69.95 Set. (88041) Eye Ear.
Sir Laurens van der Post had always been fascinated by the Bushmen - the aboriginal inhabitants of Africa, who were rapidly becoming extinct. In 1957 he led an expedition over the Kalahari Desert in search of the remnants of this unique people. Natural obstacles, & certain human failings, nearly caused the expedition to come to grief. But, after arduous traveling & many setbacks, a community of Bushmen was discovered. Sir Laurens van der Post describes their circumstances, custom, lore & nature with affection, bringing home the remarkable qualities of these archaic, doomed, yet vividly alive survivors of an ancient world.

Lost World of the Kalahari. unabr. ed. Laurens Van der Post. Read by John Nettleton. 8 cass. (Running Time: 12 hrs.). 1995. 69.95 (978-1-85089-745-3(X), 88041) Pub: ISIS Audio GBR. Dist(s): Ulverscroft US

Lost Years. E. V. Thompson. 10 cass. (Sound Ser.). (J). 2003. 84.95 (978-1-84283-435-0(5)) Pub: ISIS Lrg Prnt GBR. Dist(s): Ulverscroft US

Lost Years. E. V Thompson. (Soundings (CDs) Ser.). (J). 2005. audio compact disk 89.95 (978-1-84559-016-1(3)) Pub: ISIS Lrg Prnt GBR. Dist(s): Ulverscroft US

Lost Years of Merlin. unabr. ed. T. A. Barron. Read by Michael Cumpsty. 6 cass. (Running Time: 9 hrs. 47 mins.). (Lost Years of Merlin Ser.: Bk. 1). (J). (gr. 5-9). 2004. 38.25 (978-0-8072-8765-1(2), YA261CX, Listening Lib); pap. bk. 46.00 (978-0-8072-8766-8(0), YA261SP, Listening Lib) Random Audio Pubg.
Spat out by the sea, the boy lay on the rocks, as still as death. Even if he survived the day, he had no home, no memory & no name. One day he will become the greatest wizard of all time, but he knows nothing of this now.

Lost Zoo. abr. ed. Countee Cullen. Perf. by Ruby Dee. 1 cass. (J). 1984. 9.95 (978-0-694-50816-7(0), CDL5 1539) HarperCollins Pubs.

Lost& Found Sound, Vol. 1. unabr. ed. Highbridge Audio Staff & Noah Adams. Contrib. by Davia Nelson. Prod. by Davia Nelson et al. 2 CDs. (Running Time: 2 hrs. 30 mins.). (ENG.). 2000. audio compact disk 24.95 (978-1-56511-402-9(7), 1565114027) Pub: HighBridge. Dist(s): Workman Pub

***Lostness of Man.** Featuring Ravi Zacharias. 1986. audio compact disk 9.00 (978-1-61256-025-0(3)) Ravi Zach.

Lost...The Devastating Word! Luke 15. Ed Young. (C). 1985. 4.95 (978-0-7417-1458-9(2), 458) Win Walk.

Lot No. 249 see Tales of the Supernatural

Lots & Lots of Trucks. Music by Jim Coffey. 1 cass. (Running Time: 35 min.). (J). (ps-6). 2001. 8.98 (978-1-58168-234-2(4)); audio compact disk 12.95 (978-1-58168-235-9(2)) Superior Home Vid.
Twelve sing-a-long songs about all kinds of trucks.

Lots of Laughs! unabr. ed. Neil Gaiman et al. (Selected Shorts Ser.: Vol. XVIII). (ENG.). 2005. audio compact disk 28.00 (978-0-9719218-2-5(2)) Pub: Symphony Space. Dist(s): IPG Chicago

Lots of Legs. (J). 2005. audio compact disk (978-1-933796-12-3(X)) PC Treasures.

Lotteries. 1 cass. (Running Time: 60 min.). 10.95 (L185) Psych Res Inst.
Pick winning numbers by mental powers.

Lottery & Seven Other Stories. unabr. ed. Shirley Jackson. Read by Carol Stewart. 2 cass. (Running Time: 3 hrs.). 2004. 17.95 (978-1-57270-051-2(3), M21051u) Pub: Audio Partners. Dist(s): PerseuPGW
Jackson reveals the hidden evils of the human mind & society in this compelling collection.

Lottery E.S.P. Prod. by Betty L. Randolph. 1 cass. (Subliminal Plus Success Ser.). 12.98 (111) Randolph Tapes.
This winner's tape helps you focus to win, using your mind-power to get what you want.

Lottery Rose. Irene Hunt. Narrated by George Guidall. 4 CDs. (Running Time: 4 hrs. 45 mins.). (gr. 6 up). audio compact disk 39.00 (978-1-4025-0467-9(5)) Recorded Bks.

Lottery Rose. unabr. ed. Irene Hunt. Narrated by George Guidall. 4 pieces. (Running Time: 4 hrs. 45 mins.). (gr. 6 up). 1997. 35.00 (978-0-7887-0679-0(9), 94851E7) Recorded Bks.
Georgie Burgess has known nothing but abuse & neglect all his life. When he is taken from his alcoholic mother & her brutal boyfriend & placed in a home for boys, he must learn to trust some people & forgive others. A moving story of a little boy's struggle to survive.

Lottery Ticket see Great French & Russian Stories, Vol. 1, A Collection

Lottery Ticket. 1981. (N-82) Jimcin Record.

Lottery Winner. Mary Higgins Clark. 2004. 13.95 (978-0-7435-4055-1(7)) Pub: S&S Audio. Dist(s): S and S Inc

Lottie Project. unabr. ed. Jacqueline Wilson. Read by Eve Karpf. 4 CDs. (Running Time: 17220 sec.). (J). 2002. audio compact disk 34.95 (978-0-7540-6530-2(8), CHCD 030, Chivers Child Audio) AudioGO.

Lottie Trago. E. V. Thompson. Read by Patricia Gallimore. 12 cass. (Running Time: 15 hrs.). (Sound Ser.). 2001. 94.95 (978-1-84283-031-4(7)) Pub: UlverLrgPrint GBR. Dist(s): Ulverscroft US
Cornwall 1864, Josh and Miriam Retallick return home from Africa. Josh soon becomes a new power in his native land, while Jane Trago, a sensual woman, but an unfeeling mother to Lottie, sweeps in like an ill-wind to take up her new trade in the local tavern. Against the fluctuating fortunes of the Sharptor mine, we follow Lottie Trago as she is drawn first to the dedicated trade unionist, Jethro Shovell, and then to the smooth talking aristocratic, Hawken Strike. Little knowing how heavily the sins of the mothers can fall - even on a daughter as wild as the moor.

Lottie Trago. unabr. ed. E. V. Thompson. Read by Patricia Gallimore. 12 CDs. (Running Time: 14 hrs.). (Sound Ser.). (J). 2003. audio compact disk 99.95 (978-1-84283-586-9(6)) Pub: ISIS Lrg Prnt GBR. Dist(s): Ulverscroft US
Cornwall 1864. Josh and Miriam Retallick return home from Africa. Josh soon becomes a new power in his native land, While Jane Trago, a sensual woman, but an unfeeling mother to Lottie, sweeps in like an ill-wind to take up her new trade in the local tavern. Against the fluctuating fortunes of the Sharptor mine, we follow Lottie Trago as she is drawn first to the dedicated trade unionist, Jethro Shovell, and then to the smooth talking aristocratic, Hawken Strike. Little knowing how heavily the sins of the mothers can fall - even on a daughter as wild as the moor.

Lotus & the Bottle see Great American Short Stories, Vol. II, A Collection

Lotus & the Bottle. O. Henry. 1983. (S-55) Jimcin Record.

Lotus & the Cross: Jesus Talks with Buddha. Ravi Zacharias. 2001. 9.99 (978-1-57673-855-9(8), Mltnmah) Doubday Relig.

Lotus & the Cross: Jesus Talks with Buddha. unabr. ed. Ravi Zacharias. Narrated by Simon Vance. 2 CDs. (Running Time: 2 hrs. 0 mins. 0 sec.). (ENG.). 2005. audio compact disk 15.98 (978-1-59644-240-5(9), Hovel Audio) christianaud.

***Lotus & the Cross: Jesus Talks with Buddha.** unabr. ed. Ravi Zacharias. Narrated by Simon Vance. (ENG.). 2005. 9.98 (978-1-59644-241-2(7), Hovel Audio) christianaud.

Lotus Eater. abr. ed. W. Somerset Maugham. Read by Alan Howard. 1 cass. 1984. 12.95 (978-0-694-50344-5(4), SWC 1663) HarperCollins Pubs.

Lotus Eaters see Treasury of Alfred Lord Tennyson

***Lotus Eaters.** unabr. ed. Tatjana Soli. (Running Time: 13 hrs. 0 mins.). 2010. 29.95 (978-1-4417-3714-4(6)); 79.95 (978-1-4417-3710-6(3)); audio compact disk 29.95 (978-1-4417-3713-7(8)); audio compact disk 109.00 (978-1-4417-3711-3(1)) Blckstn Audio.

***Lotus for You: Guided Meditations for Relaxation, Health, & Well-Being.** Carol J. Spears. Read by Carol J. Spears. (Playaway Adult Nonfiction Ser.). (ENG.). 2010. 39.99 (978-1-61587-633-4(2)) Find a World.

Lotus Seed Poems. Daniel Shanahan. 2003. audio compact disk 12.00 (978-0-9728423-0-3(6)) Lotus Seed.

Lotusland: A Story of Southern California. unabr. collector's ed. Ian Whitcomb. Read by Ian Whitcomb. 8 cass. (Running Time: 12 hrs.). 1984. 64.00 (978-0-7366-0508-3(8), 1482) Books on Tape.
A tour of the early dreams of Nirvana, beginning in the Venice of 1917. We see how Los Angeles has finally become the place where everything went.

Lou. Jane Coleman. (Running Time: 0 hr. 30 mins.). 1999. 10.95 (978-1-60083-503-2(1)) Iofy Corp.

***Lou.** Jane Candia Coleman. 2009. (978-1-60136-448-7(2)) Audio Holding.

Lou Adler's Basic One-Question Interview: The One-Question Performance-based Interview. Scripts. 1 CD. (Running Time: 59). 2005. audio compact disk 30.00 (978-1-59971-187-4(7)) AardGP.

Lou Brock: Base Stealing. Read by Lou Brock. 1 cass. 9.95 (7121) Lets Talk Assocs.
Lou Brock talks about the people & events which influenced his career, & his own approach to his speciality.

Lou Gehrig. unabr. ed. 4 cass. (Running Time: 6 hrs.). (Childhood of Famous Americans Ser.). (J). (gr. 1-3). 2001. 39.95 Blckstn Audio.
The inspiring story of one of the greatest professional baseball players who is remembered for playing 2,130 consecutive games in 14 seasons with the New York Yankees.

Lou Gehrig. unabr. ed. Guernsey Van Riper, Jr. Read by Lloyd James. 4 cass. (Running Time: 5 hrs. 30 mins.). 2006. 35.95 (978-0-7861-2062-8(2), K2823) Blckstn Audio.

Lou Gehrig: The Story of a Great Man. Short Stories. As told by Carol L. Birch. Created by Carol L. Birch. 1 cd. (Running Time: 58 mins,35 secs). 2002. audio compact disk 16.95 (978-0-9726932-0-2(3), sbp200) Silver Birch Prod.
Lou Gehrig's career is bigger than his stats. his spirit is more significant than the disease which destroyed him. His story is more than a baseball story, yet it brings to life an extraordinary time in baseball history.Gehrig's story is a study in contrasts. The son of impoverished immigrants, he went on to attend Columbia, an Ivy League university. One of the most powerful and distinguished baseball players of the Twentieth Century, he remained unassuming and modest throughout his career. Painfully shy and reticient, he avoided speaking publicly - yet in the end, he's remembered for a speech that reverberates in the American psyche to this day. In a world where winning is everything, Gehrig offered a more complex understanding of what it is to lose and what it is to win. His story - with humor and heart, grit and glory - resonates for diehard baseball fans and the uninitiated alike.Storyteller, Carol Birch may not have lived in Gehrig's era but like all compelling storytellers, she revitalizes Gehrig's world and life in the telling of his story. You'll want to join her for every step of this extra-ordinary journey.

Lou Stein Plays Sweet Georgia Brown. 1 cass. 1987. 12.95 (978-0-943748-20-7(8)) Ekay Music.

Lou Stratten: Shaggy Creature Productions Presents Lou Stratten. (YA). 2003. 18.42 (978-0-9747173-0-2(4)) L Stratten.

Lou the Prophet & Other Early Short Stories. unabr. ed. Willa Cather. Read by Marilyn Langbehn. 2 cass. (Running Time: 2 hrs. 30 min.). Dramatization. 1991. 16.95 (978-1-55686-374-5(8), 374) Books in Motion.
Included: Lou the Prophet, Nanette - An Aside, The Prodigies, The Resurrection, & The Conversion of Sung Loo.

Louanne Pig in Making the Team. Nancy Carlson. 1 read-along cass. (J). 1987. bk. 22.95; pap. bk. & instr.'s gde. ed. 31.95; 9.95 Live Oak Media.
Her tips to Arnie on how to improve his game & be selected for the football team are repaid by his constructive criticism of her cheerleading technique prior to tryouts. The result is that Louanne joins the school football team while Arnie finds himself leading the cheers from the sideline.

Louanne Pig in Making the Team. unabr. ed. Nancy Carlson. Illus. by Nancy Carlson. Read by Larry Robinson. 1 cass. (Running Time: 5 mins.). (J). (gr. k-3). 1987. bk. 24.95 (978-0-87499-040-9(8)); pap. bk. 15.95 (978-0-87499-038-6(6)); pap. bk. & tchr. ed. 31.95 Reading Chest. (978-0-87499-039-3(4)) Live Oak Media.
Louanne's tips to Arnie on how to improve his game & be selected for the football team are repaid by his constructive criticism of her cheerleading technique prior to tryouts. The result is that Louanne joins the school football team while Arnie finds himself leading the cheers from the sidelines.

Louanne Pig in the Mysterious Valentine. Nancy Carlson. 1 cass. (Running Time: 6 min.). (J). (ps-3). 1988. 9.95 Live Oak Media.
Though Louanne is unsuccessful in identifying the secret admirer who sent her the biggest, most beautiful valentine she's ever seen the observant reader will be quick to spot her father as the mysterious valentine.

Louanne Pig in the Mysterious Valentine. Nancy Carlson. Illus. by Nancy Carlson. Read by Peter Fernandez. 1 cass. (Running Time: 6 mins.). (J). 1988. bk. 24.95 (978-0-87499-087-4(4)) Live Oak Media.

Louanne Pig in the Mysterious Valentine. unabr. ed. Nancy Carlson. Illus. by Nancy Carlson. Read by Peter Fernandez. 1 cass. (Running Time: 6 mins.). (J). (gr. k-3). 1988. pap. bk. 15.95 (978-0-87499-086-7(6)); pap. bk. & tchr. ed. 31.95 Reading Chest. (978-0-87499-088-1(2)) Live Oak Media.

Louanne Pig in the Perfect Family. Nancy Carlson. Illus. by Nancy Carlson. Read by Larry Robinson. 14 vols. (Running Time: 8 mins.). (J). (gr. k-3). 1987. pap. bk. & tchr. ed. 31.95 Reading Chest. (978-0-87499-036-2(X)) Live Oak Media.
An only child, Louanne regrets not having brothers & sisters until she spends a hectic weekend with George & his five sisters & four brothers.

Louanne Pig in the Perfect Family. unabr. ed. Nancy Carlson. Illus. by Nancy Carlson. Read by Larry Robinson. 1 cass. (Running Time: 8 mins.). (J). (gr. k-3). 1987. bk. 24.95 (978-0-87499-037-9(8)); pap. bk. 15.95 (978-0-87499-035-5(1)) Live Oak Media.

Loud & Clear. unabr. ed. Anna Quindlen. Read by Kathe Mazur. 7 CDs. (Running Time: 10 hrs.). 2004. audio compact disk 76.50 (978-1-4159-9987-5(2)) Pub: Books on Tape. Dist(s): NetLibrary CO
Anna Quindlen, winner of the Pulitzer Prize for Commentary during her years as a columnist with the New York Times, takes a break from her stream of bestselling novels to present yet another volume of her collected columns. The readers of Newsweek got to see these ones first, but now the rest of us can enjoy her insightful, emotionally satisfying reflections on the impact public events have on ordinary lives. Quindlen is able to convey big ideas and trends in a way that makes them meaningful and relevant in human terms.

Louder! The Official James Scott Loud Reading Poetry. unabr. ed. James Scott. 1 cass. (Running Time: 47 min.). (J). (gr. 1-6). 1996. 9.95 (978-1-886080-01-0(1)) Loud Lit.
Hilarious reading by the Loud Poetry Guy of his equally-hilarious poetry book. Kids of all ages will laugh until their faces fall off!.

Louder: We Can't Hear You (Yet!) Marge Piercy. 1 CD. (Running Time: 90 min.). 2004. audio compact disk 15.95 (978-0-9728984-2-3(5)) Pub: Leapfrog Pr. Dist(s): Consort Bk Sales

Louder Than Thunder: A Contemporary Business Parable. Carol Dunitz. Read by Carol Dunitz. Illus. by Helen Gotlib. 2004. audio compact disk 15.00 (978-0-9748659-1-1(5)) Canterbury & Parks.

Louder Than Words: A Mother's Journey in Healing Autism. unabr. ed. Jenny McCarthy. Read by Tavia Gilbert. 4 CDs. 2007. audio compact disk 36.00 (978-1-4332-1175-1(0)) Blckstn Audio.
One morning, Jenny McCarthy sensed something was wrong and ran into her two-year-old son Evan's room to discover he was having a seizure. In that moment, Jenny was thrust into the midst of a medical odyssey. After numerous misdiagnoses and many harrowing, life-threatening episodes, Evan was finally diagnosed with autism. But Jenny didn't know what to do next and soon found herself alone, without any resources except for her determination to help her son. Realizing that she'd have to become a detective, Jenny spoke with many doctors, parents, governmental agencies, and private foundations and became an expert of Google research. At last, she discovered a combination of behavioral therapy, diet, and supplements that became the key to saving Evan from autism. Here, she shares her experiences and knowledge and offers a roadmap for other concerned parents.

Louder Than Words: A Mother's Journey in Healing Autism. unabr. ed. Jenny McCarthy. Read by Tavia Gilbert. (Running Time: 16200 sec.). 2007. 19.95 (978-1-4332-1176-8(9)); audio compact disk 19.95 (978-1-4332-1178-2(5)); audio compact disk 19.95 (978-1-4332-1177-5(7)) Blckstn Audio.

Loudest Noise in the World. 2004. 8.95 (978-1-56008-960-5(1)); cass. & flmstrp 30.00 (978-1-56008-712-0(9)) Weston Woods.

Loudest Noise in the World, the; Fish in the Air; Salt; Journey Cake, Ho! 2004. (978-0-89719-817-2(4)); cass. & flmstrp (978-0-89719-726-7(7)) Weston Woods.

Loudflower: Happy Now? 1997. 10.98 (978-0-7601-1031-7(X), C10004); audio compact disk 16.98 (978-0-7601-1032-4(8), CD10004) Pub: Brentwood Music. Dist(s): Provident Mus Dist
Combines elements of a stripped down punk pop trio of bass, drums & guitar with the sweet punch of a horn section. Packs satirical & challenging lyrics. Includes "Disaffected," "I Guess I Need You," Clouds," "Savior Business," & more.

Loudmouse see Roland the Minstrel Pig & Other Stories

Loudmouth George & the Fishing Trip. Nancy Carlson. Illus. by Nancy Carlson. Read by Linda Terheyden. 14 vols. (Running Time: 6 mins.). (J). (gr. k-3). 1986. pap. bk. & tchr. ed. 31.95 Reading chest. (978-0-87499-018-8(1)) Live Oak Media.

Loudmouth George & the Fishing Trip. unabr. ed. Nancy Carlson. Illus. by Nancy Carlson. Read by Linda Terheyden. 1 cass. (Running Time: 6 mins.). (J). (gr. k-3). 1986. bk. 24.95 (978-0-87499-019-5(X)); pap. bk. 15.95 (978-0-87499-017-1(3)) Live Oak Media.
George, the self-centered rabbit, suddenly loses his self-avowed prowess as a master angler when he actually hooks a fish.

Loudmouth George & the Fishing Trip. unabr. ed. Nancy Carlson. 1 cass. (Running Time: 6 min.). (J). (gr. k-3). 1986. pap. bk. 31.95 reading chest.; 9.95 Live Oak Media.

Loudmouth George & the Sixth Grade Bully. Nancy Carlson. Illus. by Nancy Carlson. Read by Linda Terheyden. 14 vols. (Running Time: 6 mins.). (J). (gr. k-3). 1986. pap. bk. & tchr. ed. 31.95 Reading Chest. (978-0-87499-015-7(7)) Live Oak Media.

Loudmouth George & the Sixth Grade Bully. unabr. ed. Nancy Carlson. Illus. by Nancy Carlson. Read by Linda Terheyden. 1 cass. (Running Time: 7 mins.). (J). (gr. k-3). 1986. bk. 24.95 (978-0-87499-016-4(5)); pap. bk. 15.95 (978-0-87499-014-0(9)) Live Oak Media.
A bully makes George give up his lunch everyday until his friend doctors his lunches with some unusual ingredients.

Loudmouth George & the Sixth Grade Bully. unabr. ed. Nancy Carlson. 1 cass. (Running Time: 7 min.). (J). (gr. k-3). 1986. pap. bk. 31.95 reading chest.; 9.95 Live Oak Media.

Loudmouth George Series. Nancy Carlson. Read by Linda Terheyden. 2 vols. (Running Time: 14 mins.). (J). (gr. k-3). 2000. pap. bk. 29.95 (978-0-87499-475-9(6)) Live Oak Media.
Includes: "Loudmouth George & the Fishing Trip" & "Loudmouth George & the Sixth Grade Bully.".

Louie: A Country Lady. unabr. ed. Doreen Louie West. Read by Tracey Lloyd. 6 cass. (Running Time: 8 hrs.). 1999. 54.95 (978-0-7531-0595-5(0), 990917) Pub: ISIS Audio GBR. Dist(s): Ulverscroft US
Set against the backcloth of two World Wars & farming life as it was in the rural Oxfordshire, this is the true story of Louie between 1910 & 1943, the wife of a prosperous Oxfordshire farmer & a country lady. Louie's amusing & tempestuous story is brought to life b her daughter Doreen, who vividly evokes a world of horse-drawn traps, milking by hand, clean-air, cottage hospitals & childhood innocence. She describes a rural community in which peopl's lives moved with the seasons, a hard life as farm help & midwife, but a life of fulfillment too.

***Louie the Layabout.** Nicholas M. Healy. Illus. by Sahin Erkocak. Contrib. by Arthor Noble. (Pfeffernut County Ser.). (ENG.). 2008. audio compact disk 11.93 (978-1-4048-5387-4(1)) CapstoneDig.

Louis & Allen Ginsberg. Read by Louis Ginsberg. Interview with Allen Ginsberg. 1 cass. (Running Time: 25 min.). 1970. 12.95 (L029) TFR.
Two poets, father & son talk about how the differences in the poetry reflect the gap in their generations. They read excerpts from their works.

Louis Armstrong: An Extravagant Life. unabr. ed. Laurence Bergreen. Read by Michael Kramer. 15 cass. (Running Time: 22 hrs. 30 min.). 1998. 120.00 (978-0-7366-4103-6(3), 4608) Books on Tape.
The first complete biography of a musical icon, one of the greatest figures in American social & cultural history.

Louis B. Jones: Ordinary Money. unabr. ed. Louis B. Jones. Read by Louis B. Jones. Read by Philip Hoosier. Interview with Rebekah Presson. 1 cass. 1991. 10.00 (031591) New Letters.
Jones' first novel, Ordinary Money, is the funny & touching story of a couple of blue collar friends who come onto $20 million in counterfeit money.

***Louis D. Brandeis: A Life.** unabr. ed. Melvin I. Urofsky. Read by Sean Pratt. (Running Time: 35 hrs.). (ENG.). 2010. 59.98 (978-1-59659-510-1(8), GildAudio) Pub: Gildan Media. Dist(s): HachBkGrp

Louis Edwards. unabr. ed. Louis Edwards. 1 cass. (Running Time: 29 min.). (New Letters on the Air Ser.). 1992. 10.00 (092091) New Letters.
Edwards talks about his impressive first novel, "Ten Seconds.".

Louis Farrakhan. Narrated by Louis Farrakhan. 1 cass. (Running Time: 1 hr.). 10.95 (K0180B090, HarperThor) HarpC GBR.

Louis L'Amour. Louis L'Amour. 2003. bk. 15.99 (978-1-57815-559-0(2), Media Bks Audio) Media Bks NJ.

Louis L'Amour: I Hate to Tell His Widow; Collect from a Corpse; Stay Out of My Nightmare; Street of Lost Corpses, abr. ed. Louis L'Amour. 4 cass. (Running Time: 4 hrs.). (Great Mysteries - Louis L'Amour Ser.). 2000. 12.99 (978-1-57815-152-3(X), 4401, Media Bks Audio) Media Bks NJ.

Louis L'Amour: McQueen of the Tumbling K; Law of the Desert. Louis L'Amour. 1 cass. 1993. 6.95 (978-1-877883-02-6(6)) Cimino Pub Grp.

Louis L'Amour Classic Westerns: His Brother's Debt; Trap of Gold; Lit a Shuck for Texas; Mistakes Can Kill You; Dutchman's Flat; Big Medicine. unabr. ed. Louis L'Amour. 4 cass. 1998. 19.95 incl. wooden gift box. (978-1-55935-150-8(0)) Soundelux.
Includes "Dutchman's Flat," "Big Medicine," "Four Card Draw," "Law of the Desert Born," "His Brother's Dept.," "Trap of Gold," "Lit a Shuck for Texas" & "Mistakes Can Kill You".

Louis L'Amour Collection. unabr. ed. Louis L'Amour. Read by Johnny Cash et al. (ENG.). 2007. audio compact disk 29.95 (978-1-59887-544-7(2), 1598875442) Pub: HighBridge. Dist(s): Workman Pub

Louis L'Amour Cowboy Stories. unabr. ed. Louis L'Amour. Read by Randy Travis. 2 cass. (Running Time: 3 hrs.). 1998. 17.95 Soundelux.
Includes: "Ride! You Tonto Raiders," "More Brains Than Bullets" & "The Lion Hunter & the Lady.".

Louis L'Amour Cowboy Stories. unabr. ed. Louis L'Amour. Read by Randy Travis. 2 cass. (Running Time: 3 hrs.). 1998. 17.95 (978-1-55935-294-9(9)) Soundelux.
Stories include: "Ride! You Tonto Raiders," "More Brains Than Bullets," "The Lion Hunter & the Lady".

Louis L'Amour Gift Set: A Man Called Trent & Riders of the Dawn. unabr. ed. 7 cass. (Running Time: 34200 sec.). 2006. 24.95 (978-0-7861-4549-2(8)) Blckstn Audio.

Louis L'Amour Trail Mix, Vol. 1. unabr. ed. Louis L'Amour. Read by Willie Nelson et al. (Running Time: 7200 sec.). (ENG.). 2002. audio compact disk 12.99 (978-1-56511-768-6(9), 1565117689) Pub: HighBridge. Dist(s): Workman Pub

Louis L'Amour Trail Mix, Vol. 2. unabr. ed. Louis L'Amour. Narrated by Willie Nelson. 2 CDs. (Running Time: 2 hrs.). Dramatization. (ENG.). 2002. audio compact disk 12.99 (978-1-56511-769-3(7), 1565117697) Pub: HighBridge. Dist(s): Workman Pub

Louis L'Amour's Desert Tales: Desert Death Song & Law of the Desert. unabr. ed. Stefan Rudnicki. (Running Time: 3600 sec.). 2007. audio compact disk 17.00 (978-1-4332-0507-1(6)) Blckstn Audio.

Louis L'Amour's Desert Tales: Desert Death Song & Law of the Desert. unabr. ed. Read by Stefan Rudnicki. (Running Time: 3600 sec.). 2007. 15.95 (978-1-4332-0506-4(8)); audio compact disk 19.95 (978-1-4332-0510-1(6)) Blckstn Audio.

Louis L'Amour's Desert Tales: Desert Death Song & Law of the Desert. unabr. ed. Read by Stefan Rudnicki. (Running Time: 3600 sec.). 2007. 9.95 (978-1-4332-0508-8(4)); audio compact disk 9.95 (978-1-4332-0509-5(2)) Blckstn Audio.

Louis L'Amour's Trio of Tales: McQueen of the Tumbling K; Big Medicine; Dutchman's Flat. unabr. ed. Louis L'Amour. (Running Time: 1.5 hr. NaN mins.). 2008. 19.95 (978-1-4332-1372-4(9)); cass. & audio compact disk 19.95 (978-1-4332-1373-1(7)) Blckstn Audio.

Louis L'Amour's Trio of Tales: McQueen of the Tumbling K; Big Medicine; Dutchman's Flat. unabr. ed. Louis L'Amour. Read by William Dufris. (Running Time: 7200 sec.). 2008. 22.95 (978-1-4332-1370-0(2)); audio compact disk 29.95 (978-1-4332-1374-8(5)); audio compact disk & audio compact disk 27.00 (978-1-4332-1371-7(0)) Blckstn Audio.

Louis L'Amour's Western Tales: Trap of Gold; Trail to Pie Town. unabr. ed. Read by William Dufris. (Running Time: 3600 sec.). 2008. 9.95

(978-1-4332-0903-1(9)); 15.95 (978-1-4332-0901-7(2)); audio compact disk & audio compact disk 19.95 (978-1-4332-0905-5(5)); audio compact disk & audio compact disk 17.95 (978-1-4332-0902-4(0)) Blckstn Audio.

Louis L'Amour's Western Tales: Trap of Gold; Trail to Pie Town. unabr. ed. Louis L'Amour. Read by William Dufris. (Running Time: 3600 sec.). 2008. audio compact disk 9.95 (978-1-4332-0904-8(7)) Blckstn Audio.

Louis Martin: Father of a Saint. Joyce R. Emert. 6 cass. 24.95 (317) Ignatius Pr.
Life of the saintly father of St. Therese of Lisieux.

Louis Pasteur. unabr. ed. Albert Keim & Louis Lumet. Read by David Mitchell. (YA). 2007. 34.99 (978-1-60252-846-8(2)) Find a World.

Louis Pasteur & Pasteurization. Jennifer Fandel et al. Illus. by Keith Wilson. (Inventions & Discovery Ser.). (ENG.). (gr. 3-4). 2007. audio compact disk 6.95 (978-1-4296-1117-6(0)) CapstoneDig.

Louis Pasteur & Pasteurization (INK Audiocassette) (Inventions & Discovery Ser.). (ENG.). 2007. audio compact disk 5.95 (978-0-7368-7988-0(9)) CapstoneDig.

Louis Simpson. unabr. ed. Read by Louis Simpson. 1 cass. (Running Time: 29 min.). 1985. 10.00 New Letters.
A reading by the Pulitzer Prize-winning poet.

Louis Wain: King of the Cat Artists, 1860-1939. Heather Latimer. Read by Heather Latimer. 3 cass. (Running Time: 4 hrs. 45 min.). 1990. 23.95 (978-0-943698-07-6(3)) Papyrus Letterbox.

Louisa see Great American Short Stories, Vol. III, A Collection

***Louisa May Alcott: A Personal Biography.** unabr. ed. Susan Cheever. (Running Time: 10 hrs. 0 mins. 0 sec.). 2010. 24.99 (978-1-4001-6790-6(6)); 16.99 (978-1-4001-8790-4(7)); 34.99 (978-1-4001-9790-3(2)); audio compact disk 83.99 (978-1-4001-4790-8(5)); audio compact disk 34.99 (978-1-4001-1790-1(9)) Pub: Tantor Media. Dist(s): IngramPubServ

Louisa May Alcott: The Woman Behind Little Women. unabr. ed. Harriet Reisen. Narrated by Harriet Reisen. 2 MP3-CDs. (Running Time: 13 hrs. 30 mins. 0 sec.). (ENG.). 2009. 24.99 (978-1-4001-6445-5(1)); audio compact disk 37.99 (978-1-4001-1445-0(4)); audio compact disk 75.99 (978-1-4001-4445-7(0)) Pub: Tantor Media. Dist(s): IngramPubServ

***Louisa May Alcott: The Woman Behind Little Women.** unabr. ed. Harriet Reisen. Narrated by Harriet Reisen. (Running Time: 13 hrs. 30 mins.). 2009. 18.99 (978-1-4001-8445-3(2)); 37.99 (978-1-4001-9445-2(8)) Tantor Media.

Louisa May Alcott Quartet: Little Women , Little Men , Eight Cousins & under the Lilacs. Louisa May Alcott. Narrated by Flo Gibson. (ENG.). 2008. 74.95 (978-1-60646-034-4(X)) Audio Bk Con.

Louisa May Alcott Unmasked: Collected Thrillers, unabr. ed. Louisa May Alcott. Ed. by Madeleine B. Stern. Intro. by Madeleine B. Stern. 2 cass. (Running Time: 3 hrs.). 1997. 16.95 (978-1-882071-63-0(8), 393916) B-B Audio.
Now one of Alcotts known thrillers is available. The tale called V.V. illuminates Alcotts versatility as a writer and her story telling talents. The sensational story, which features a succession of powerful and passionate heroines which also revea.

Louise Erdrich. Interview. Interview with Louise Erdrich & Kay Bonetti. 1 cass. 1986. 13.95 (978-1-55644-150-9(9), 6022) Am Audio Prose.
Erdrich, her husband & collaborator Michael Dorris, talk about how they work out of a unified vision based on their backgrounds as mixed-blood Native Americans.

Louise Erdrich. unabr. ed. Louise Erdrich. Read by Louise Erdrich. 1 cass. (Running Time: 29 min.). 1989. 10.00 (081189) New Letters.
The author of "Lore Medicine" & "The Beet Queen" reads from her acclaimed third novel, "Tracks".

Louise Erdrich Interview. 20.97 (978-0-13-090440-9(6)) P-H.

Louise L. Hay Gift Collection. Louise L. Hay. 4 cass. (Running Time: 4 hrs.). 1997. 25.00 (978-1-56170-465-1(2), 366) Hay House.
Includes Tape 1: "Meditations for Personal Healing"; Tape 2: "Morning & Evening Meditations"; Tape 3: "Self-Esteem Affirmations"; & Tape 4: "Receiving Prosperity".

***Louise, the Adventures of a Chicken.** Kate DiCamillo. Read by Barbara Rosenblat. 1 CD. (Running Time: 19 mins.). (J). (ps-2). 2009. bk. 28.95 (978-1-4301-0688-3(3)) Live Oak Media.

Louisiana! abr. ed. Dana Fuller Ross, pseud. Read by Lloyd James. Abr. by Mary Bevoni. 4 vols. (Wagons West Ser.: No. 16). 2003. 25.00 (978-1-58807-148-4(0)); (978-1-58807-617-5(2)) Am Pubng Inc.

Louisiana! abr. ed. Dana Fuller Ross, pseud. Read by Lloyd James. Abr. by Mary Bevoni. 5 vols. (Wagons West Ser.: No. 16). 2004. audio compact disk 30.00 (978-1-58807-383-9(1)); audio compact disk (978-1-58807-862-9(0)) Am Pubng Inc.

Louisiana: New Orleans - French Quarter. 2 cass. (Running Time: 90 min.). 1990. 21.95 (CC280) Comp Comms Inc.
Stroll at your own pace, listening to animated stories related by a native.

Louisiana Dawn: Poems of a Grafted Life (the amplified) Poems. Lisa Pertillar Brevard & Lisa Pertillar Brevard. Photos by Frank Lynn Brevard. 1 CD. (Running Time: 35 mins.). 2004. audio compact disk 15.95 (978-0-9749499-2-5(2)) Monarch Baby.
(The Amplified) Louisiana Dawn: Poems of a Grafted Life, by Lisa Pertillar Brevard explores natural themes...uniquely examining the miniscule in a city known the world over for its grandeur; honoring bits and pieces that flavor New Orleans; and recognizing jazz and blues themes found and expressed in the larger world of everyday life, love and loss. Includes selected poems from Brevard's softcover book, Louisiana Dawn: Poems of a Grafted Life, as well as original music, all written and performed by the author.

Louisiana Purchase. Kenneth Bruce. 1 cass. (Running Time: 68 min.). Dramatization. (Excursions in History Ser.). 12.50 Alpha Tape.

Louisiana Stories. Kate Chopin. Narrated by Jacqueline Kinlow. (Running Time: 12720 sec.). (Unabridged Classics in MP3 Ser.). (ENG.). 2008. audio compact disk 24.00 (978-1-58472-645-6(8), In Aud) Sound Room.

Loukoumi's Good Deeds. Nick Katsoris. Narrated by Jennifer Aniston & John Aniston. (J). (gr. 4-7). 2009. bk. 16.00 (978-0-9705100-9-9(8)) NK Pubns.

Lounge Freak. Perf. by John Janaq. 1997. 10.98 (978-0-7601-1564-0(8), C0300); audio compact disk 15.98 (978-0-7601-1199-4(5), CD0300) Brentwood Music.
Includes the biggest modern rock hits of the past year covered in an authentic lounge style.

Loup des Steppes. Hermann Hesse. Read by R. Bret. 6 cass. (FRE.). 1995. 46.95 (1747-LV) Olivia & Hill.
By constantly denying all that usually makes man happy, Harry Haller has become a "wolf of the steppes," a solitary fixture unable to relate to others. He contemplates suicide until he meets Hermine, his feminine counterpart.

Loup et la Chien see Fables de La Fontaine

Lousy Peter see Osbert Sitwell Reading His Poetry

Lovable Lulaby. Haynes. 1995. 6.98 (978-1-57042-328-4(8)) GrandCentral.

Lovable Lyle see Lyle, Lyle, Crocodile

Love see Great French & Russian Stories, Vol. 1, A Collection

Love see Charles Bell 1 & 2

Love. Leo F. Buscaglia. Read by Leo F. Buscaglia. 6 cass. 34.95 (131A) Nightingale-Conant.

Love. Linda Eyre & Richard Eyre. 2 cass. (Running Time: 3 hrs.). (Teaching Your Children Values Ser.). (J). (ps-7). 2000. bk. 16.95 (978-1-56015-786-1(0)) Penton Overseas.
Tape 1: a coaching, "how-to" program for parents; Tape 2: "Alexander's Amazing Adventures" program featuring stories, songs, sound effects & background music, that helps children ages 4-12 to develop social skills, communication skills & life skills. Includes activity cards.

Love. Francis Frangipane. 1 cass. (Running Time: 90 mins.). (Abide in Him Ser.: Vol. 4). 2000. 5.00 (FF08-004) Morning NC.
A subject Francis teaches on with great gifting, this series deals with the advantages of walking in the "abiding principle".

Love. Kenneth W. Hagin, Jr. 3 cass. (Faith's Firm Foundation Ser.). 12.00 (19J) Faith Lib Pubns.

Love. Osho Oshos. 1 cass. 9.00 (A0649-89) Sound Photosyn.

Love. unabr. ed. Toni Morrison. Read by Toni Morrison. 5 cass. (Running Time: 7 hrs. 30 min.). 2003. 43.20 (978-0-7366-9551-0(6)); audio compact disk 50.40 (978-0-7366-9620-3(2)) Books on Tape.
May, Christine, Heed, Junior, Vida, and L are women obsessed by Bill Cosey. More than the wealthy owner of the famous Cosey Hotel and Resort, he shapes their yearnings for father, husband, lover, guardian, and friend, yearnings that dominate these women's lives long after his death. Yet while he is both the void in, and the center of, their stories, he himself is driven by secret forces: a troubled past and a spellbinding woman named Celestial.

Love. unabr. ed. Toni Morrison. Read by Toni Morrison. (Running Time: 28800 sec.). (ENG.). 2007. audio compact disk 29.95 (978-0-7393-4228-2(2), Random AudioBks) Pub: Random Audio Pubg. Dist(s): Random

Love. unabr. ed. Elizabeth von Arnim. Narrated by Flo Gibson. 8 cass. (Running Time: 11 hrs.). 2002. 26.95 (978-1-55685-677-8(6),) Audio Bk Con.
A gentle romance that begins innocently enough in the stalls of a London theater where Catherine is enjoying her ninth & Christopher his thirty-sixth visit to the same play. There is an age difference & while Catherine is just a little bit older is flattered by the passionate attentions of youth.

Love. unabr. ed. Elizabeth von Arnim. Read by Eleanor Bron. 10 cass. (Running Time: 15 hrs.). 2001. 84.95 (978-0-7540-0584-1(4), CAB2007) AudioGO.

Love, Vol. 3. unabr. ed. Chris Yaw. Perf. by Scott Hiltzik. 1 cass. (Running Time: 1 hr.). (Living Words Ser.). 1998. 9.98 (978-1-893613-02-7(X)); audio compact disk 11.98 (978-1-893613-06-5(2)) Living Wds.

Love: God's Ability in You, Vol. 1. Speeches. Creflo A. Dollar. 4 cass. (Running Time: 5 hrs.). 2005. Rental 20.00 (978-1-59089-939-7(3)); audio compact disk 28.00 (978-1-59089-940-3(7)) Creflo Dollar.

Love: Guided Meditation for Well-Being. Catherine Sheen. 2 CDs. (Running Time: Depends on track). 2005. audio compact disk 22.95 (978-0-9773381-4-6(2)) Reach In.
Love Guided Meditation helps you feel the love you hold in your heart for your self and others. The more love you pour out, the more love you have. These meditations can help you release old pain and resentment and re-experience a natural feeling of love. There are 10, 15, 30 and 45 minute Love Guided Meditations on 2 CDs and the CDs include a Preparation for Meditation track.

Love: Songs for the Spirit. Compiled by Dean Diehl & Ed Kee. 1 CD. 2000. audio compact disk 9.99 (978-0-7601-3185-5(6), SO33210) Pub: Brentwood Music. Dist(s): Provident Mus Dist
Includes: "His Love Is Strong," "Give It Away," "One Love," "Mighty Love," "This Is Love" & more.

Love: The Foundation for the Annointing, Vol. 2. Speeches. Creflo A. Dollar. 6 cass. (Running Time: 5 hrs.). 2005. Rental 25.00 (978-1-59089-941-0(5)); audio compact disk 34.00 (978-1-59089-942-7(3)) Creflo Dollar.

Love: The Fruit of the Spirit - Loving One Another. Speeches. Creflo A. Dollar. 5 cass. (Running Time: 6 hrs.). 2003. Rental 25.00 (978-1-59089-770-6(6)); audio compact disk 34.00 (978-1-59089-771-3(4)) Creflo Dollar.

Love: The Fruit of the Spirit - Loving the Father. Speeches. Creflo A. Dollar. 5 cass. (Running Time: 6 hrs.). 2003. 25.00 (978-1-59089-768-3(4)); audio compact disk 34.00 (978-1-59089-769-0(2)) Creflo Dollar.

Love: The Fruit of the Spirit - Walking in Love. Speeches. Creflo A. Dollar. 5 cass. (Running Time: 6 hrs.). 2003. 25.00 (978-1-59089-772-0(2)); audio compact disk 34.00 (978-1-59089-773-7(0)) Creflo Dollar.

Love: The More Excellent Way Audio Book. Chuck Smith. Narrated by Peter Benson. (ENG.). 2008. audio compact disk 19.99 (978-1-59751-079-0(3)) Word For Today.

Love: The Way into Perfection. Kenneth Copeland. 4 cass. 1982. bk. 20.00 Set incl. study guide. (978-0-938458-30-2(2)) K Copeland Pubns.
How to live with God's love.

Love: The Way to Victory. Kenneth E. Hagin. 3 cass. 12.00 Set. (66H) Faith Lib Pubns.

Love-a-Byes. 1 cass. (Lullabies Ser.). (J). audio compact disk (978-0-7601-0077-6(2), CD-5081R, Brentwood Kids) Brentwood Music.
Combines soothing melodies with scriptural words that instill within your child the ultimate, eternal love of the Father. The instrumental side even allows you to sing these quiet, loving songs to your child.

Love, a Soul Force. Swami Amar Jyoti. 1 cass. 1976. 9.95 (K-5) Truth Consciousness.
The cosmic & intrinsic nature of the soul & its expression. Prophets are the inspirational examples of this true love.

Love Accepts. unabr. ed. Elisabeth Elliot. Read by Elisabeth Elliot. 1 cass. (Running Time: 1 hr.). 1990. 4.95 (978-0-8474-2173-2(2)) Back to Bible.
Elisabeth explains how to experience joy & harmony in the home through love & acceptance.

Love Addiction. Pia Mellody. Read by Pia Mellody. 1 cass. 10.00 (A9) Featuka Enter Inc.
How the addiction sets up uncomfortable relationships that you can't leave; valuable hints for recovery.

Love Affair with God: Ecc. 12:9-14. Ed Young. 1994. 4.95 (978-0-7417-2013-9(2), 1013) Win Walk.

Love Alters Not. Freda Lightfoot. Read by Trudy Harris. 7 cass. (Storysound Ser.). (J). 2000. 61.95 (978-1-85903-361-6(X)) Pub: Mgna Lrg Print GBR. Dist(s): Ulverscroft US

Love Alters Not. unabr. ed. Perf. by Eknath Easwaran. 1 cass. (Running Time: 1 hr.). 1985. 7.95 (978-1-58638-564-4(X)) Nilgiri Pr.

Love, Always. unabr. ed. Sally Brampton. Narrated by Diana Bishop. 8 cass. (Running Time: 10 hrs. 30 min.). 2000. 73.00 (H1090, Clipper Audio) Recorded Bks.
Life has always been difficult for Jane Rose. Moved from country to country as a child, she's still trying to find a place she can call home. England is latest of the friendless, lonely places in which she lives. All that changes when she meets the complex, fascinating Ben. Attraction is instant, but much too soon for insecure, youthful Jane. They slip through each other's fingers, only to meet again eight years later, when complications abound & the stakes are far greater than before.

Love among the Artists. unabr. ed. George Bernard Shaw. Read by Flo Gibson. 8 cass. (Running Time: 11 hrs. 30 min.). 1993. 26.95 (978-1-55685-291-6(6)) Audio Bk Con.
Musicians, composers, painters, actors & dilettantes comingle in London society frequently with passion & infrequently with love.

Love among the Chickens. P. G. Wodehouse. Read by Jonathan Cecil. 3 cass. 29.95 (978-0-7927-3820-6(9), CSL 876) AudioGO.

Love among the Chickens. P. G. Wodehouse. Read by Jonathan Cecil. 4 CDs. (Running Time: 18180 sec.). (Sound Library). 2006. audio compact disk 49.95 (978-0-7927-3821-3(7), SLD 876) AudioGO.

Love & Anger. John L. Bell & Graham Maule. 1 cass., 1 CD. 1998. 10.95 (CS-428); audio compact disk 15.95 (CD-428) GIA Pubns.

Love & Be Safe. unabr. ed. Carol Howe. 3 cass. (Running Time: 3 hrs. 15 min.). 1995. 21.95 (978-1-889642-11-6(8)) C Howe.
"Conventional wisdom" says this is impossible! However, if you are weary of living defensively & fearfully, you are urged to experience this process that leads you to safety & fulfillment as a daily, personal reality. This set explains: The process that guarantees safety in a world of fast-paced change. The beliefs we hold about danger, our attempts to protect ourselves, & why they fail. The experience of true power & security one gains through living defenselessly.

Love & Be Silent: King Lear, Defenselessness, & A Course in Miracles. Kenneth Wapnick. 4 CDs. 2005. audio compact disk 24.00 (978-1-59142-170-2(5), CD65) Foun Miracles.

Love & Compassion. Ganden Tripa-Rinpoche. 2 cass. 18.00 (OC48) Sound Horizons AV.

Love & Death. Carolyn G. Hart. 6 cass. (Running Time: 9 hrs.). 2000. 48.00 (978-0-7366-6042-6(9)) Books on Tape.
If you love a good mystery - or a mystery about lovers - you'll cherish this collection of fourteen seductively sinister tales. These original stories from today's finest crime & suspense writers prove that while love may be blind, it can still aim straight for the heart. Featuring fourteen tales from the most widely read, award-winning authors in the world of mystery, this is a special valentine. With authors such as Carolyn Hart, Nancy Pickard, Ed Gorman, Gar Anthony Haywood & ten others, these are tales of death and desire that any mystery fan will love.

Love & Death. Read by Kate Reading. Ed. by Carolyn G. Hart. 2001. audio compact disk 56.00 (978-0-7366-7138-5(2)) Books on Tape.

Love & Death: A Survivor's Journey into Healing Grief. Carla Czybora. 1 cass. 10.00 (978-1-877972-04-1(5)) New Bgnnngs.
Side 1: Original guided imagery & spoken word script. Side 2: Original subliminal messages.

Love & Desire: An Anthology of Love Poems. unabr. ed. Robert Burns. 2 cass. (Running Time: 3 hrs.). 2004. 18.00 (978-1-59007-126-7(3)) Pub: New Millenn Enter. Dist(s): PerseuPGW
Records the birth of a new science. This new science offers a way of seeing order and pattern where formerly only the random, the erratic, the unpredictable - in short, the chaotic - had been observed. Is a history of discovery. It chronicles, in the words of the scientists themselves, their conflicts and frustrations, their emotions and moments of revelation. After reading this, you will never look at the world in quite the same way again.

Love & Friendship: And Other Early Works. unabr. ed. Jane Austen. Read by Norma West. 4 cass. (Running Time: 4 hrs.). 1993. 44.95 (978-1-85089-687-6(9), 20292) Pub: ISIS Audio GBR. Dist(s): Ulverscroft US
This collection of Jane Austen's juvenilia includes "Love & Friendship," "The Three Sisters" & "Leslie Castle".

Love & Hope. unabr. ed. Thomas Merton. Read by Norman Merton. 2 cass. (Running Time: 1 hr. 23 min.). (Life & Prayer Ser.: No. 2). 1982. 19.95 Elec Paperback.
Discusses two topics of vital interest to today's men & women: human love as a reflection of God's love & the superiority of Christian hope to worldy optimism.

***Love & Infertility Survival Strategies for Balancing Infertility Marriage & Life Audio CD.** Kirsten A. Magnacca. 2010. audio compact disk (978-1-4507-1137-1(5)) Indep Pub IL.

Love & Inspiration: Songs of Romance to Open the Heart & Rekindle the Spirit. 1 CD. 1998. audio compact disk 11.98 (978-1-56826-953-5(6)) Rhino Enter.

Love & Inspiration: Songs of Romance to Open the Heart & Rekindle the Spirit. 1 cass. 1998. 7.98 (978-1-56826-952-8(8)) Rhino Enter.

Love & Intimacy. unabr. ed. Milton Diamond. 1 cass. (Running Time: 1 hr.). (Human Sexuality Ser.). 12.95 (34007) J Norton Pubs.

Love & Lies. unabr. ed. Kimberla Lawson Roby. Read by Tracey Leigh. 1 MP3-CD. (Running Time: 8 hrs. 5 mins.). (Reverend Curtis Black Ser.: Bk. 4). 2007. 44.95 (978-0-7927-4753-6(4)); audio compact disk 74.95 (978-0-7927-4520-4(5)); 59.95 (978-0-7927-4776-5(3)) AudioGO.
Best friends Charlotte and Janine have serious problems with their love lives. Charlotte's husband, the flashy preacher Curtis Black, may keep her living in luxury, but his book tours and evangelism mean he's never home. Charlotte's sure he's cheating and even hires a PI to follow him, but she's been known to have indiscretions herself. Her 12-year-old Matthew is another man's son and she suspects troubled 5-year-old Marissa, whom she swore was Curtis's child, might be the result of a tryst with a schizophrenic. Her friend Janine, a college professor, also is worried her boyfriend Antonio is cheating on her and getting heavily into drug dealing. She kicks him out but Antonio won't take no for an answer.

Love & Logic Magic for Early Childhood: Practical Parenting from Birth to Six Years. 2001. audio compact disk 24.95 (978-1-930429-16-1(9)) Love Logic.

Love & Logic Magic When Kids Drain Your Energy. 2004. audio compact disk 13.95 (978-1-930429-72-7(X)) Love Logic.

Love & Logic on the Bus. Bob Sornson. 2009. audio compact disk 13.95 (978-1-935326-03-8(1)) Love Logic.

Love & Marriage. Barry Tesar. 1 cass. (Running Time: 1 hr.). (Subliminal Inspiration Ser.). 1992. 9.98 (978-1-56470-020-9(8)) Success Cass.
Subliminal program.

Love & Philosophy: Aristotelian vs. Platonic. unabr. ed. Allan Gotthelf. 1 cass. (Running Time: 1 hrs. 40 min.). 1998. 13.95 (978-1-56114-524-9(6), CG51C) Second Renaissance.
Demonstrates how a person's view of love & his romantic choices are linked to his view of man & existence.

Love & Pleasure. J. Krishnamurti. 1 cass. (Running Time: 1 hr.). (Krishnamurti with Dr. Allan W. Anderson Ser.: No. 12). 8.50 (APA7412) Krishnamurti.
These 1974 dialogues cover the entire spectrum of Krishnamurti's teaching in a series highly regarded for its depth of inquiry into each particular subject.

Love, Groucho. Groucho Marx. Read by Miriam Marx Allen & Frank Ferrante. Ed. by Mariam Marx Allen. 1 cass. (Running Time: 90 min.). Dramatization. 1992. 10.95 (978-1-879371-38-5(3), 10020) Pub Mills.
Having saved virtually every letter her father wrote to her between the years 1938, when she was eleven, & 1967, Groucho's letters to his daughter Miriam show an extraordinary father-daughter relationship.

Love, Groucho: Letters from Groucho to His Daughter Miriam. abr. ed. Groucho Marx. Read by Frank Ferrante. Intro. by Dick Cavett. 2000. audio compact disk 16.98 (978-1-929243-22-8(7)) Uproar Ent.

Love Has a Face: Mascara, a Machete, & One Woman's Miraculous Journey with Jesus in Sudan. unabr. ed. Michele Perry. Narrated by Rebecca St. James. (Running Time: 5 hrs. 55 mins. 6 sec.). (ENG.). 2009. 16.09 (978-1-60814-570-6(0)); audio compact disk 22.99 (978-1-59859-617-5(9)) Oasis Audio.

***Love Has Always Been Our Song.** Composed by Joseph M. Martin. (Running Time: 3 mins.). (ENG.). 2010. audio compact disk 26.99 (978-1-4234-8603-9(X), 142348603X) H Leonard.

Love Hate Masquerade. Contrib. by Kids in the Way et al. Prod. by Kato Khandwala. 2007. audio compact disk 11.99 (978-5-557-60938-8(5)) Flicker.

Love Her Madly. unabr. ed. Mary-Ann Tirone Smith. Read by Susan Ericksen. 6 cass. (Running Time: 9 hrs.). 2002. 29.95 (978-1-58788-997-4(8), 1587889978, BAU); 69.25 (978-1-58788-998-1(6), 1587889986, Unabridge Lib Edns) Brilliance Audio.
Poppy Rice is home in her D.C. apartment with very little furniture and a stack of boxes she still hasn't unpacked after five years. It's three a.m. and she's suffering from her usual insomnia, so she watches a tape of the CBS Evening News. Dan Rather is interviewing convicted ax-murderer Rona Leigh Glueck who in ten days will be the first woman executed in Texas since the Civil War. Poppy pauses the tape on a close-up of Rona Leigh's delicate, child-like hands. So maybe it was a lightweight ax. Poppy digs out Rona Leigh's case file to find - along with the grisly crime-scene photos - a physician's testimony that glee, not muscle, gave her the strength to commit the crime. When her public defender asked the crime lab for help determining whether such a frail woman, only seventeen years old, could physically commit these murders, he was turned away for not filing the correct paperwork. With the reluctant support of her colleague and sometime lover, Joe Barnow, the impetuous and relentless Poppy reopens the investigation to find out if Rona Leigh deserves a certificate that will read: Death by Legal Homicide as Ordered by the State of Texas.

Love Her Madly. unabr. ed. Mary-Ann Tirone Smith. Read by Susan Ericksen. (Running Time: 9 hrs.). 2005. 39.25 (978-1-59600-735-2(4), 9781596007352, BADLE); 24.95 (978-1-59600-734-5(6), 9781596007345, BAD); 39.25 (978-1-59600-733-8(8), 9781596007338, Brinc Audio MP3 Lib); audio compact disk 24.95 (978-1-59600-732-1(X), 9781596007321, Brilliance MP3) Brilliance Audio.

Love Her to Death. Linda Palmer. Narrated by Celeste Lawson. (Running Time: 8 hrs.). 2005. 27.95 (978-1-59912-534-3(X)) Iofy Corp.

Love Her to Death. Linda Palmer. Read by Celeste Lawson. (Running Time: 8 hrs. 30 mins.). 2005. reel tape 54.95 (978-0-7861-3033-7(4)); audio compact disk 63.00 (978-0-7861-7838-4(8)) Blckstn Audio.

Love Her to Death. unabr. ed. Linda Palmer. Read by Celeste Lawson. 6 cass. (Running Time: 8 hrs. 30 mins.). 2005. 29.95 (978-0-7861-3049-8(0)) Blckstn Audio.

Love Her to Death. unabr. ed. Linda Palmer. Read by Celeste Lawson. 7 CDs. (Running Time: 28800 sec.). (Daytime Mysteries Ser.). 2005. audio compact disk 29.95 (978-0-7861-8026-4(9)); audio compact disk 29.95 (978-0-7861-8120-9(6)) Blckstn Audio.

Love Holds No Grievances (Selections) 3rd ed. Tara Singh. Read by Charles Johnson. 1 cass. (Running Time: 60 min.). (Books on Cassette Ser.). 1988. 9.95 Life Action Pr.
Deals with healing relationships by letting go of grievances.

***Love, Honor, & Betray.** unabr. ed. Kimberla Lawson Roby. Read by Paula Jai Parker-Martin. (Running Time: 8 hrs.). (ENG.). 2011. 24.98 (978-1-60788-680-8(4)) Pub: Hachet Audio. Dist(s): HachBkGrp

Love Hopes. (Paws & Tales Ser.: No. 37). 2002. 3.99 (978-1-57972-492-4(2)); audio compact disk 5.99 (978-1-57972-493-1(0)) Insight Living.

Love-Human & Divine Series. 3 cass. 23.00 (LS-14, ST52, 54, 55) Crystal Clarity.
Explains: The Meaning of Impersonal Love; The Importance of Human Relationships; How to Open Your Heart.

Love Hurts, Vol. 2. Cedering Fox. Read by Clarke Sarah. (WordTheatre Ser.). 2006. audio compact disk 9.95 (978-0-06-115424-9(5)) HarperCollins Pubs.

Love in a Dry Season. Shelby Foote. Narrated by Tom Parker. (Running Time: 8 hrs. 30 mins.). 2002. 27.95 (978-1-59912-535-0(8)) Iofy Corp.

Love in a Dry Season. unabr. ed. Shelby Foote. Read by Tom Parker. 6 cass. (Running Time: 8 hrs. 30 mins.). 2002. 44.95 (978-0-7861-2354-4(0), 3012); audio compact disk 56.00 (978-0-7861-9398-1(0), 3012) Blckstn Audio.
Describes an erotic and economic triangle, in which two wealthy and fantastically unhappy Mississippi families are joined by fortune hunter from the North.

Love in Action. unabr. ed. Eknath Easwaran. 1 cass. (Running Time: 64 min.). 1990. 7.95 (978-1-58638-566-8(6), LIA) Nilgiri Pr.
A general, introductory talk, with vivid stories & descriptions of many aspects of the spiritual life, including family relationships, detachment, faith, humility, & selflessness.

Love in Another Town. unabr. ed. Barbara Taylor Bradford. Read by Kate Reading. 5 cass. (Running Time: 5 hrs.). 1996. 40.00 (978-0-7366-3257-7(3), 3914) Books on Tape.
As he approaches his 29th birthday, Jake Cantrell believes his life has completely stalled. Saddened by the failure of his marriage to Amy, his childhood sweetheart, Jake moves to Kent, Connecticut to concentrate on his new business. Jake's a brilliant electrical engineer. He meets Maggie Sorrell, an interior designer, Maggie's renovating an old farmhouse for a client & she hires Jake as the electrical contractor. They fall in love & face obstacles: their age difference.

Love in Particular see Twentieth-Century Poetry in English, No. 4, Recordings of Poets Reading Their Own Poetry

***Love in the Afternoon.** abr. ed. Lisa Kleypas. Read by Rosalyn Landor. (Running Time: 5 hrs.). (Hathaways Ser.: No. 5). 2010. audio compact disk 14.99 (978-1-4418-4751-5(0), 9781441847515, BACD) Brilliance Audio.

***Love in the Afternoon.** unabr. ed. Lisa Kleypas. (Running Time: 10 hrs.). (Hathaways Ser.: No. 5). 2010. 39.97 (978-1-4418-4748-5(0), 9781441847485, Brinc Audio MP3 Lib); 24.99 (978-1-4418-4747-8(2), 9781441847478, Brilliance MP3); 39.97 (978-1-4418-4750-8(2), 9781441847508, BADLE); 24.99 (978-1-4418-4749-2(9), 9781441847492, BAD) Brilliance Audio.

***Love in the Afternoon.** unabr. ed. Lisa Kleypas. Read by Rosalyn Landor. (Running Time: 10 hrs.). (Hathaways Ser.: No. 5). 2010. audio compact disk 79.97 (978-1-4418-4746-1(4), 9781441847461, BriAudCD Unabrid); audio compact disk 29.99 (978-1-4418-4745-4(6), 9781441847454, Bril Audio CD Unabri) Brilliance Audio.

Love in the Air. Stella March. Read by Melissa Sinden. 4 cass. (Running Time: 6 hrs.). 1999. 44.95 (63937) Pub: Soundings Ltd GBR. Dist(s): Ulverscroft US

Love in the Asylum see Dylan Thomas Reading His Poetry

Love in the Driest Season: A Family Memoir. unabr. ed. Neely Tucker. 6 cass. (Running Time: 9 hrs.). 2004. 63.00 (978-0-7366-9861-0(2)) Books on Tape.

Love in the Ruins. unabr. ed. Walker Percy. Read by Tom Parker. 8 cass. (Running Time: 11 hrs. 30 mins.). 1994. 56.95 (978-0-7861-0481-9(3), 1433) Blckstn Audio.
The Auto Age is defunct. Buicks, Chryslers, & Pontiacs disfigure the landscape. Vines sprout in Manhattan. Wolves are seen in downtown Cleveland. And psychiatrist, mental hospital outpatient, & inventor Dr. Tom More has created a miraculous instrument - the Ontological Lapsometer, a kind of stethoscope of the human spirit. With it, he plans to cure mankind's spiritual flu. But first he must survive Moira, Lola, & Ellen - & discover why so many living people are actually dead.

***Love in the Time of Colic.** unabr. ed. Ian Kerner & Heidi Raykeil. Read by Ian Kerner & Heidi Raykeil. (ENG.). 2009. (978-0-06-171187-9(X)); (978-0-06-172977-5(9)) HarperCollins Pubs.

Love in the Western World. unabr. ed. Angeles Arrien & Robert Bly. 6 cass. (Running Time: 8 hrs. 13 min.). 1984. vinyl bd. 56.00 Big Sur Tapes.

Love in 90 Days: The Essential Guide to Finding Your Own True Love. unabr. ed. Diana Kirschner. Read by Diana Kirschner. (Running Time: 9 hrs.). (ENG.). 2009. 24.98 (978-1-59659-333-6(4), GildAudio) Pub: Gildan Media. Dist(s): HachBkGrp

Love in 90 Days: The Essential Guide to Finding Your Own True Love. unabr. ed. Diana Kirschner. Read by Diana Kirschner. (Running Time: 9 hrs.). (ENG.). 2010. audio compact disk 39.98 (978-1-59659-353-4(9), GildAudio) Pub: Gildan Media. Dist(s): HachBkGrp

Love Invents Us. unabr. collector's ed. Amy Bloom. Read by Tonya Jordan. 4 cass. (Running Time: 6 hrs.). 1998. 32.00 (978-0-7366-4161-6(0), 4664) Books on Tape.
Elizabeth Taube, shy & neglected, finds love & acceptance in mostly inappropriate places as she grows from girlhood to maturity.

Love Is a Circle. unabr. ed. Phyllis U. Hiller. Perf. by Emily Estes. 1 cass. (Running Time: 40 min.). (J). (gr. k-3). 1994. (978-1-884877-12-4(5)) Creat Mats Lib.
Eighteen songs about love, the earth, America, & being thankful.

Love Is a Fire & I Am Wood. 6 cass. (Running Time: 9 hrs.). 1999. 59.95 Set. (83-0056) Explorations.
Learn how Sufi prayer pulls you closer to God; what it means to drown in the ocean of divine love; how spiritual dreamwork guides you to the "heart of hearts," & other wisdom & teachings from the Sufi masters.

Love Is a Garden: Fulton J. Sheen. unabr. ed. Fulton J. Sheen. 3 cass. (Running Time: 30 min.). (Life Is Worth Living: 0008). 1986. 29.95 F Sheen Comm.
Inspirational talk from the late Bishop Fulton J. Sheen.

Love Is a Great Skill. Eknath Easwaran. 1 cass. (Running Time: 50 min.). 1989. 7.95 (978-1-58638-567-5(4), LGS) Nilgiri Pr.
The ideal of selfless love & how we can aspire to it. Includes inspiration from: The Buddha; Gandhi; Mother Teresa of Calcutta.

Love Is a Many Splendored Thing. Michael Ballam. 1 cass. 9.95 (119116); audio compact disk 14.95 (119122) Covenant Comms.
Ten of the world's great love songs.

Love Is a Many Splendored Thing: Fulton J. Sheen. unabr. ed. Fulton J. Sheen. 3 cass. (Running Time: 30 min.). (Life Is Worth Living: 0009). 1986. 29.95 F Sheen Comm.
Through poetry the late Bishop Sheen illustrates the splendor of love & the power it contains.

***Love Is a Many Trousered Thing.** unabr. ed. Louise Rennison. Narrated by Stina Nielsen. 1 Playaway. (Running Time: 5 hrs. 30 mins.). (Confessions of Georgia Nicolson Ser.: Bk. 8). (YA). (gr. 7 up). 2009. 54.75 (978-1-4407-6213-0(9)); 41.75 (978-1-4407-6204-8(X)); audio compact disk 51.75 (978-1-4407-6208-6(2)) Recorded Bks.

***Love Is a Many Trousered Thing.** unabr. collector's ed. Louise Rennison. Narrated by Stina Nielsen. 5 CDs. (Running Time: 5 hrs. 30 mins.). (Confessions of Georgia Nicolson Ser.: Bk. 8). (YA). (gr. 7 up). 2009. audio compact disk 39.95 (978-1-4407-6212-3(0)) Recorded Bks.

Love Is a Precious Skill. 1 cass. 7.00 Nilgiri Pr.
Based on St. Paul's Epistle to the Corinthians.

Love Is a Precious Skill. unabr. ed. Perf. by Eknath Easwaran. 1 cass. (Running Time: 1 hr.). 1979. 7.95 (978-1-58638-568-2(2)) Nilgiri Pr.

Love Is a Racket. John Ridley. Narrated by Peter Jay Fernandez. 10 CDs. (Running Time: 12 hrs. 15 mins.). 2001. audio compact disk 111.00 (978-1-4025-0517-1(5), C1573) Recorded Bks.
Jeffty Kittredge is a small-time Hollywood con in deep debt to a shark with a need to collect. If he can just come up with a plan - or maybe even only a partner - Jeffty is sure he'll be on his way to salvation. What he comes up with instead is Mona.

Love Is a Racket. unabr. ed. John Ridley. Narrated by Peter Jay Fernandez. 9 cass. (Running Time: 12 hrs. 15 mins.). 1998. 84.00 (978-0-7887-8835-2(3), F0047L8) Recorded Bks.

Love Is a Racket. unabr. ed. John Ridley. Narrated by Peter Jay Fernandez. 10 CDs. (Running Time: 12 hrs.). 2001. audio compact disk 111.00 Recorded Bks.

Love Is a Spanish Song. unabr. ed. Sara Blaine. Read by Margaret Holt. 3 cass. (Running Time: 4 hrs. 30 mins.). 2001. 34.95 (66839) Pub: Soundings Ltd GBR. Dist(s): Ulverscroft US

Love Is a Verb: Stories of What Happens When Love Comes Alive. unabr. ed. Gary Chapman. Narrated by Gary Chapman. (Running Time: 7 hrs. 15 mins. 0 sec.). (ENG.). 2009. audio compact disk 24.98 (978-1-59644-710-3(9), christianSeed) christianaud.

***Love Is a Verb: Stories of what happens when love comes Alive.** unabr. ed. Gary Chapman. Narrated by Grover Gardner. (ENG.). 2009. 14.98 (978-1-59644-711-0(7), christianSeed) christianaud.

Love Is All Around in Disguise: Meditations for Spiritual Seekers. Irene Dugan. Ed. by Avis Clendenen. Music by Jerri Greer. 2004. pap. bk. 19.95 (978-1-888602-29-6(5)) Pub: Chiron Pubns. Dist(s): SteinerBooks Inc

Love Is Anterior to Life see Poems & Letters of Emily Dickinson

Love Is Awake. Story Waters. Narrated by Story Waters. 1 CD. (Running Time: 54 mins). 2005. audio compact disk 15.95 (978-0-9765062-3-2(8)) Limitlessness.

Love Is Born: Favorite Christmas Carols from Around the World. Contrib. by Kurt Kaiser. 10.95 Pauline Bks.

Love Is Born: Favorite Christmas Carols from Around the World. Prod. by Kurt Kaiser. 1 cass. 1992. audio compact disk 14.95 (978-0-8198-4466-8(7), 332-165) Pauline Bks.
Includes: O Holy Night, Mary's Lullaby, What Child Is This?, Dindon, Dilin, Dindan, Pat-A-Pan, Some Children See Him, Gesu Bambino, Huron Carol, Come, Hear the Wonderful Tidings & Angelical Hymn (Medley), I Wonder As I Wander, Little Drummer Boy, Il Est Ne, le Divin Enfant, Will We Know Him?, Night of Silence, Silent Night, It Came upon the Midnight Clear, Sleep, O Holy Child, Mary's Boy Child, Kling, Glockchen, How Far Is It to Bethlehem?, Lo, How a Rose E'er Blooming.

Love Is Eternal: A Novel about Mary Todd & Abraham Lincoln, Pt. 1. unabr. ed. Irving Stone. Read by Flo Gibson. 10 cass. (Running Time: 15 hrs.). (Classic Books on Cassettes Collection). 1998. 80.00 Audio Bk Con.
Mary Todd was Lincoln's cross & foundation. An intimate portrait of a marriage.

Love Is Eternal: A Novel about Mary Todd & Abraham Lincoln, Pt. 1. unabr. ed. Irving Stone. Read by Flo Gibson. 8 cass. (Running Time: 12 hrs.). 1983. 64.00 (1634-A) Books on Tape.
This story of Mary Todd & Abraham Lincoln contrasts their occasional melancholia with their more frequent humor & love.

Love Is Eternal: A Novel about Mary Todd & Abraham Lincoln, Pt. 2. unabr. ed. Irving Stone. Read by Flo Gibson. 7 cass. (Running Time: 10 hrs. 30 min.). (Classic Books on Cassettes Collection). 1998. 56.00 Audio Bk Con.
Mary Tood was Lincoln's cross & foundation. An intimate portrait of a marriage.

Love Is Eternal: A Novel about Mary Todd & Abraham Lincoln, Pt. 2. unabr. ed. Irving Stone. Read by Flo Gibson. 7 cass. (Running Time: 10 hrs. 30 mins.). 1983. 56.00 (1634-B) Books on Tape.
This story of Mary Todd & Abraham Lincoln contrasts their occasional melancholia with their more frequent humor & love.

Love Is for the Rich. Contrib. by Surrogate. 2007. audio compact disk 17.99 (978-5-557-62807-5(X)) Tooth & Nail.

Love Is Here. Contrib. by Tenth Avenue North. (Mastertrax Ser.). 2008. audio compact disk 9.98 (978-5-557-39569-4(5)) Pt of Grace Ent.

Love Is His Word. Richard Proulx. 1 cass. 11.00 (978-1-58459-055-2(6)) Wrld Lib Pubns.

Love Is Letting Go of Fear. Gerald G. Jampolsky. Read by Gerald G. Jampolsky. 4 cass. 35.00 Set. (160A) Nightingale-Conant.

Love Is Murder. Linda Palmer. Read by Celeste Lawson. (Running Time: 7 hrs. 30 mins.). 2004. 27.95 (978-1-59912-536-7(6)) Iofy Corp.

Love Is Murder. unabr. ed. Linda Palmer. Read by Lorna Raver. (Running Time: 10 hrs.). 2004. audio compact disk 24.95 (978-0-7861-8502-3(3)) Blckstn Audio.

Love Is Murder. unabr. ed. Linda Palmer. Read by Lorna Raver. 6 cass. (Running Time: 8 hrs. 30 mins.). 2004. 44.95 (978-0-7861-2799-3(6), 3326); audio compact disk 46.00 (978-0-7861-8495-8(7), 3326) Blckstn Audio.

Love Is Murder. unabr. ed. Linda Palmer. Read by Celeste Lawson. 6 cass. (Running Time: 10 hrs.). 2005. 29.95 (978-0-7861-2736-8(8), E3305); audio compact disk 32.95 (978-0-7861-8478-1(7), ZE3305) Blckstn Audio.

Love Is Not All see Poetry of Edna St. Vincent Millay

Love Is Not Enough. Anne Herries. 2009. 61.95 (978-1-4079-0541-9(4)); audio compact disk 79.95 (978-1-4079-0542-6(2)) Pub: Soundings Ltd GBR. Dist(s): Ulverscroft US

Love Is the Answer Whatever the Question: Becoming Deep. Marianne Williamson. Read by Marianne Williamson. 1 cass. (Running Time: 90 mins.). (Lectures on a Course in Miracles). 1999. 10.00 (978-1-56170-244-2(7), M747) Hay House.

Love Is the Answer/Be Still & Know. Marianne Williamson. Read by Marianne Williamson. 1 cass. (Running Time: 90 mins.). (Lectures on a Course in Miracles). (ENG.). 1999. 10.00 (978-1-56170-704-1(X), M873) Hay House.

Love Is the Best Medicine: What Two Dogs Taught One Veterinarian about Hope, Humility, & Everyday Miracles. unabr. ed. Nick Trout. Read by Jonathan Cowley. (ENG.). 2010. audio compact disk 30.00 (978-0-307-70742-0(3), Random AudioBks) Pub: Random Audio Pubg. Dist(s): Random

Love Is the Heart of the Relationship. Lucile Johnson. 1 cass. 1996. 9.98 (978-1-57734-006-5(X), 06005349) Covenant Comms.
A truly inspiring message that is guaranteed to improve your relationship with your spouse.

Love Is the Key. Grace Goodwin. Read by Anne Cater. 4 cass. (Running Time: 6 hrs.). 1999. 44.95 (64100) Pub: Soundings Ltd GBR. Dist(s): Ulverscroft US

Love Is the Only Answer. Scripts. Created by Joan Marie Ambrose. Narrated by Joan Marie Ambrose. 1 CD. (Running Time: 68 mins). 2002. audio compact disk 15.95 (978-0-9718654-3-3(4)) Ser Hse.
Since the beginning of time, volumes and volumes of poems, reflections, stories and movies have been written about LOVE...the expression and feeling of love...yet, its true essence seems to elude most of us. Allow this CD to assist in uncovering the love that is within you. There is (8) minute grounding meditation;followed by a 60 minute teaching that will help you re-discover the love that you are.

Love Is the Target. Art Fettig. 1 cass. (Running Time: 44 min.). Dramatization. 1992. 9.95 (LTT) Growth Unltd.
Provides answers to help you lead a happier, healthier, more productive life.

Love Is the Victory! Gloria Copeland. Perf. by Kenneth Copeland. 1 cass. 1994. cass. & video 5.00 (978-0-88114-998-2(5)) K Copeland Pubns.
Biblical teaching on love.

Love Jones. Contrib. by Canton Jones et al. 2005. audio compact disk 11.98 (978-5-558-92012-3(2)) Pt of Grace Ent.

Love Joy & Pain. Mista & Taylor. (Running Time: 35 min.). 2004. audio compact disk 16.98 (978-5-559-50698-2(2)) Pub: Pt of Grace Ent. Dist(s): STL Dist NA

Love Knot. unabr. ed. Charlotte Bingham. Read by Judy Bennett. 12 cass. (Running Time: 18 hrs.). 2001. 96.95 (978-0-7540-0563-6(1), CAB1986) Pub: Chivers Audio Bks GBR. Dist(s): AudioGO
Three women decide to make their own way in the world, when to be independent was to risk social ostracism, or even tragedy. This is partly due to the influence each comes to have on the others' lives. The love knots that they face in their relationships finally unravel, but not before hearts have been broken & scandals risked.

Love Languages of God: How to Feel & Reflect Divine Love. Gary Chapman. (ENG.). 2003. 16.99 (978-1-881273-43-1(1)) Pub: Northfield Pub. Dist(s): Moody
Make the 'love connection' with Almighty GodThis is the book Gary Chapman was born to write...the one Chapman title EVERYONE should read, Christian and non-Christian alike. The best-selling author of The Five Love Languages books, Dr. Chapman says, 'The purpose of this book is to help people enjoy living, and have peace about dying. To love and be loved, what could be more important?'Once you discover your primary love language in human relationships, you can assume that will also be your primary love language in your relationship with God. Whether we are speaking to God or He is speaking to us - we are feeling God's love and presence strongest in one particular way! By teaching readers to tap into

divine love, Chapmen helps them relate to God in a way that will totally revolutionize their will to love one another.

Love Large. Joyce J. Rouse. 1 CD. (Running Time: 55 min.). (J). 1996. audio compact disk 14.95 (978-1-887712-02-6(X)) Rouse Hse Prodns.
Features global music for those who care about planet Earth & it's inhabitants.

Love Leadership: The New Way to Lead in a Fear-Based World. unabr. ed. John Hope Bryant. (Running Time: 5 hrs.). (ENG.). 2009. 24.98 (978-1-59659-472-2(1), GildAudio) Pub: Gildan Media. Dist(s): HachBkGrp

Love Letter. Contrib. by Brian Smith & Jazzy Jordan. 2007. audio compact disk 17.98 (978-5-557-63277-5(8), Verity) Brentwood Music.

Love Letter to Hans Christian Andersen see Carl Sandburg's Poems for Children

Love Letters from God. unabr. ed. Jim Cymbala. (Running Time: 6 hrs. 25 mins. 0 sec.). (ENG.). 2008. 18.99 (978-0-310-26508-5(8)) Zondervan.

Love Letters from Russia, No. 1. 2nd rev. ed. Weston Rodgers. Ed. by Pam Eversole. Photos by Curt Newbury. 1 CD. 1998. audio compact disk 29.00 (978-0-9668840-0-5(0)) Weston Prodn.
Romantic novel about an average American man's adventure to marry a Russian woman.

Love Letters of Great Men. unabr. ed. Ursula Doyle. Read by Anton Lesser. (Running Time: 3 hrs. 0 mins. 0 sec.). (ENG.). 2008. audio compact disk 14.95 (978-1-4272-0670-1(8)) Pub: Macmill Audio. Dist(s): Macmillan

Love Letters to the Bride of Christ. Read by Jean A. Flory. 2006. audio compact disk 15.00 (978-0-9792270-0-4(3)) Musicians Guild.

Love Lies Bleeding. Edmund Crispin. 2008. 54.95 (978-0-7531-3058-2(0)); audio compact disk 71.95 (978-0-7531-3059-9(9)) Pub: Isis Pubng Ltd GBR. Dist(s): Ulverscroft US

Love Life. Fred Andrie. (ENG.). 2008. pap. bk. 24.00 (978-1-880977-23-1(0)) Pub: XOXOX Pr. Dist(s): SPD-Small Pr Dist

Love Life. Jeremy Pearsons. (ENG.). (YA). 2006. audio compact disk 15.00 (978-1-57562-918-6(6)) K Copeland Pubns.

Love Life Pt. I: 1 Cor. 13:1-2. Ed Young. 1986. 4.95 (978-0-7417-1511-1(2), 511) Win Walk.

Love Life Pt. II: 1 Cor. 13:4-7. Ed Young. 1986. 4.95 (978-0-7417-1512-8(0), 512) Win Walk.

Love Life Pt. III: 1 Cor. 13:8-13. Ed Young. 1986. 4.95 (978-0-7417-1514-2(7), 514) Win Walk.

Love Lifted Me. 1 cass., 1 CD. 10.98 (978-1-57908-357-1(9), 5309); audio compact disk 15.98 (978-1-57908-356-4(0)) Platinm Enter.

Love, Light & Life. Eldon Taylor. Read by Eldon Taylor. Ed. by Leslie Brice. 1 cass. (Running Time: 1 hr.). 1992. 16.95 (978-1-56705-330-2(0)) Gateways Inst.
Self improvement.

Love, Light & Life. Eldon Taylor. 1 cass. (Running Time: 62 min.). (Inner Talk Ser.). 16.95 incl. script. (978-1-55978-014-8(2), 5414C) Progress Aware Res.
Soundtrack - Musical Themes with underlying subliminal affirmations.

Love, Light & Life: Babbling Brook. Eldon Taylor. 1 cass. 16.95 (978-1-55978-758-1(9), 5414F) Progress Aware Res.

Love Live. Scriptual Counsel Staff. 1 cass. 1979. 19.95 (978-0-00-497853-6(6)) Script Coun.

Love, Lost & Renewed. unabr. ed. Zev Wanderer. Read by Zev Wanderer. 1 cass. (Running Time: 1 hr. 2 min.). 12.95 J Norton Pubs.

***Love, Lust & Faking It: The Naked Truth about Sex, Lies, & True Romance.** unabr. ed. Jenny McCarthy. (ENG.). 2010. (978-0-06-204139-5(8), Harper Audio); (978-0-06-206468-4(1), Harper Audio) HarperCollins Pubs.

Love Lust & Lunacy. Henry Sosnowski. Voice by Henry Sosnowski. Ed. by Ivy Antonowitsch. Rev. by Ivy Antonowitsch. (ENG.). 2008. pap. bk. 15.00 (978-0-9815565-2-9(3)) Three Leg Dog.

Love, Magic, & Mudpies: Raising Your Kids to Feel Loved, Be Kind, & Make a Difference. rev. unabr. ed. Bernie S. Siegel. Read by Bernie S. Siegel. (Running Time: 5 hrs.). (ENG.). 2008. audio compact disk 29.98 (978-1-59659-133-2(1), GildAudio) Pub: Gildan Media. Dist(s): HachBkGrp

Love, Magic, & Mudpies: Raising Your Kids to Feel Loved, Be Kind, & Make a Difference. unabr. ed. Bernie S. Siegel. (Running Time: 5 hrs.). (ENG.). 2007. 29.98 (978-1-59659-116-5(1), GildAudio) Pub: Gildan Media. Dist(s): HachBkGrp

Love Magnetics. abr. ed. Roger W. Bretemitz. 1 cass. (Running Time: 45 min.). 1985. pap. bk. 9.95 (978-1-893417-13-7(1)) Vector Studios.
Side A gives facts about attraction & relationships, things to help a person become more attractive. Side B has relaxation script with suggestions to help a person's subliminal ability to attract opposite sex.

Love-Makers. abr. ed. Judith Gould. Read by Katey Segal. 3 vols. (YA). 2001. audio compact disk 11.99 (978-1-57815-521-7(5), Media Bks Audio) Media Bks NJ.

Love Makes the Astrological Wheel Go Around. Pauline Hassell. 1 cass. 8.95 (672) Am Fed Astrologers.
An AFA Convention workshop tape.

Love Makes the Difference: 1 Peter 4:8, 704. Ed Young. 1989. 4.95 (978-0-7417-1704-7(2), 704) Win Walk.

Love Mates Aquarius. Richard Hack. 1 cass. 1995. 5.99 (978-1-57375-028-8(X)) Audioscope.

Love Mates Libra. Richard Hack. 1 cass. 1995. 5.99 (978-1-57375-033-2(6)) Audioscope.

Love Me Enough to Set Some Limits: Building Your Child's Self-Esteem with Thoughtful Limit Setting. 1CD. (Running Time: 60 mins.). 2002. audio compact disk 13.95 (978-1-930429-26-0(6)) Pub: Love Logic. Dist(s): Penton Overseas

Love Me Enough to Set Some Limits: Building Your Child's Self-Esteem with Thoughtful Limit Setting. Jim Fay. Read by Jim Fay. Ed. by Bert Gurule Mizke. 1 cass. (Running Time: 1 hr.). 1996. 11.95 (978-0-944634-35-6(4)) Pub: Love Logic. Dist(s): Penton Overseas
Children-from babies to teenagers-need parents to set firm limits. Limits are the foundation for self-confidence & high self-esteem. Yet it seems many children have to pleas through their out of-control behavior. you'll hear practical examples that will help you practice setting your own limits.

Love Me Forever. abr. ed. Johanna Lindsey. Read by Michael Page. (Running Time: 3 hrs.). (Sherring Cross Ser.). 2008. audio compact disk 14.99 (978-1-4233-6592-1(5), 9781423365921, BCD Value Price) Brilliance Audio.

Love Me Forever. unabr. ed. Johanna Lindsey. Read by Frances Cassidy. 7 cass. (Running Time: 10 hrs. 30 mins.). 1996. 56.00 (978-0-7366-3308-6(1), 3962) Books on Tape.
Kimberly Richards, English heiress, needs a husband to escape the tyranny of her father, an earl. Unexpectedly, Lachlan, the laird of the impoverished Clan MacGregor, steals Kimberly's heart. But the two clash from the first. Their squabbling isn't the only strike against marriage: someone frames Lachlan for stealing & the couple must team up to clear his name. Will they catch the real culprit.

Love Me Forever. unabr. ed. Johanna Lindsey. Read by Michael Page. (Running Time: 9 hrs.). (Sherring Cross Ser.). 2008. 24.95 (978-1-4233-6590-7(9), 9781423365907, BAD); 24.95 (978-1-4233-6588-4(7), 9781423365884, Brilliance MP3); 39.25 (978-1-4233-6591-4(7), 9781423365914, BADLE); 39.25 (978-1-4233-6589-1(5), 9781423365891, Brlnc Audio MP3 Lib); audio compact disk 29.95 (978-1-4233-6586-0(0), 9781423365860, Bril Audio CD Unabri); audio compact disk 92.25 (978-1-4233-6587-7(9), 9781423365877, BriAudCD Unabrid) Brilliance Audio.

Love Me Forever, Say You Love Me. unabr. abr. ed. Johanna Lindsey. Read by Michael Page. (Running Time: 6 hrs.). 2010. audio compact disk 19.99 (978-1-4418-4984-7(X), 9781441849847, BACD) Brilliance Audio.

Love Me Good. Perf. by Michael W. Smith. 1 cass., 1 CD. 1998. 3.49 (978-0-7601-2318-8(7)); audio compact disk 3.49 CD. (978-0-7601-2319-5(5)) Provident Mus Dist.

***Love Me If You Dare.** unabr. ed. Carly Phillips. Read by Coleen Marlo. (Running Time: 8 hrs.). (Most Eligible Bachelor Ser.). 2010. 24.99 (978-1-4233-5226-6(2), 9781423352266, BAD); 24.99 (978-1-4233-5224-2(6), 9781423352242, Brilliance MP3); 39.97 (978-1-4233-5227-3(0), 9781423352273, BADLE); 39.97 (978-1-4233-5225-9(4), 9781423352259, Brlnc Audio MP3 Lib); audio compact disk 34.99 (978-1-4233-5222-8(X), 9781423352228, Bril Audio CD Unabri); audio compact disk 87.97 (978-1-4233-5223-5(8), 9781423352235, BriAudCD Unabrid) Brilliance Audio.

Love Me, Love My Broccoli. unabr. ed. Julie Anne Peters. Narrated by Julie Dretzin. 3 pieces. (Running Time: 3 hrs. 45 mins.). (gr. 5 up). 2001. 32.00 (978-0-7887-4558-4(1), 96244E7) Recorded Bks.
Chloe Mankewicz spends her free time working for animal rights. But everything changes after Brett, a charming football player, asks her out.

Love Me, Love My Broccoli. unabr. ed. Julie Anne Peters. Narrated by Julie Dretzin. 3 cass. (Running Time: 3 hrs. 45 mins.). (YA). 2001. pap. bk. & stu. ed. 45.24 Recorded Bks.

Love Me or Leave Me. unabr. ed. Josephine Cox. Read by Carole Boyd. 8 cass. (Running Time: 8 hrs.). 1999. 69.95 (978-0-7540-0237-6(3), CAB1660) AudioGO.
Eva & her mother support each other despite the abuse of her bitter, crippled father. But when a tragic accident robs Eva of both parents, she turns to her friend Patsy for support. Then tragedy strikes again.

Love Me Tender, Level 1. (Yamaha Clavinova Connection Ser.). 2004. disk 1.04 (978-0-634-09579-5(X)) H Leonard.

Love Me Tomorrow. unabr. ed. Patricia Robins. Read by Carolyn Oldershaw. 5 cass. (Running Time: 6 hr. 35 min.). 1998. 63.95 (978-1-85903-232-9(X)) Pub: Magna Story GBR. Dist(s): Ulverscroft US
Samantha finds she must decide who she really cares for, Andrew, her love from student days, or Ronnie, her husband.

Love Medicine. Louise Erdrich. Read by Louise Erdrich. 1 cass. (Running Time: 90 min.). (American Audio Prose Library: Series VI). 1986. 13.95 (978-1-55644-149-3(5), 6021) Am Audio Prose.
Erdrich reads selections from both novels.

***Love Mercy.** unabr. ed. Earlene Fowler. Narrated by Joanna Parker. 1 Playaway. (Running Time: 12 hrs.). 2009. 59.75 (978-1-4407-4938-4(8)); 61.75 (978-1-4281-9435-9(5)); audio compact disk 77.75 (978-1-4281-9437-3(1)) Recorded Bks.

***Love Mercy.** unabr. collector's ed. Earlene Fowler. Narrated by Joanna Parker. 10 CDs. (Running Time: 12 hrs.). 2009. audio compact disk 44.95 (978-1-4281-9438-0(X)) Recorded Bks.

***Love Mercy: A Mother & Daughter's Journey from the American Dream to the Kingdom of God.** Lisa Samson & Ty Samson. (Running Time: 5 hrs. 49 mins. 46 sec.). (ENG.). 2010. 15.99 (978-0-310-39577-5(1)) Zondervan.

Love Must Be Tough: New Hope for Families in Crisis. James C. Dobson. Narrated by Rick Rohan. 5 cass. (Running Time: 6 hrs. 45 mins.). 48.00 (978-0-7887-6087-7(4)) Recorded Bks.

Love Must Be Tough: New Hope for Families in Crisis. unabr. collector's ed. James C. Dobson. Read by Dick Estell. 8 cass. (Running Time: 8 hrs.). 1988. 48.00 (978-0-7366-1307-1(2), 2214) Books on Tape.
An examination of the causes of failed marriages, focusing on 'mutual disrespect' as the central problem. Offers advice on avoiding or settling marital conflicts.

Love Myself: Self-Esteem Programming. Dick Sutphen. 1 cass. (Running Time: 1 hr.). (RX17 Ser.). 1986. 14.98 (978-0-87554-313-0(8), RX122) Valley Sun.
You love & believe in yourself. You have high self-esteem. Your positive self-image generates success & happiness. Every day, you love yourself more. You are true to yourself. You are at peace with yourself, the world & everyone in it. You love yourself. You believe in yourself. You are proud of yourself. You do things that make you proud of yourself. "Self-love" are your key words for conditioned response.

Love Never Ends: Sacred Sounds. Elisabeth Von Trapp. (Running Time: 3600 sec.). 2005. audio compact disk 18.00 (978-0-89869-483-3(3)) Church Pub Inc.

Love No Conditions. 1 CD. (Running Time: 41 mins.). 2002. audio compact disk 6.99 (978-1-57583-531-0(2), 3002CD) Twin Sisters.
This is love: not that we loved God, but that he loved us and sent his Son as an atoning sacrifice for our sins. Amazing but true, there are no conditions with God's love! Kids will celebrate the deep love of Christ with these all-new, contemporary praise and worship songs.

Love Not the World. 4 cass. stu. ed. 15.95 (20129, HarperThor) HarpC GBR.

Love Not Your Life. Gloria Copeland. 1 cass. 1986. 5.00 (978-0-88114-724-7(9)) K Copeland Pubns.
Biblical teaching on Christian living.

Love Notes: 101 Lessons from the Heart. Jim Brickman & Cindy Pearlman. 1 CD. 2005. bk. 17.95 (978-1-4019-0608-5(7), 6087) Hay House.

Love of a Good Woman: Stories. Alice Munro. Read by Paula Parker. 10 CDs. 2004. audio compact disk 47.95 (978-0-7927-3247-1(2), SLD 205, Chivers Sound Lib) AudioGO.

Love of a Good Woman: Stories. unabr. ed. Short Stories. Alice Munro. Read by Paula Parker. 8 vols. (Running Time: 12 hr.). 1999. bk. 69.95 (978-0-7927-2316-5(3), CSL 205, Chivers Sound Lib) AudioGO.
In eight new stories, a master of the form extends & magnifies her great themes: the vagaries of love; the passion that leads down unexpected paths; the chaos hovering just under the surface of things; & the strange, often comical desires of the human heart.

Love of Christ Constrains Us. 1985. (0272) Evang Sisterhood Mary.

Love of Creator & Creation. unabr. ed. Swami Amar Jyoti. 1 cass. (Running Time: 1 hr. 30 min.). (Satsangs of Swami Amar Jyoti Ser.). 1998. 9.95 (978-0-933572-35-5(2), K163) Truth Consciousness.
The basis of all creation is pure Divine Love. Prophets & Realized Souls are it's embodiments. Coming home.

Love of Eternal Wisdom. Saint Louis Grignon de Montfort. 5 cass. 22.95 (924) Ignatius Pr.
A powerful guide to help in the spiritual life.

Love of Fat Men. Helen Dunmore. (Isis (CDs) Ser.). (J). 2005. audio compact disk 51.95 (978-0-7531-2404-8(1)) Pub: ISIS Lrg Prnt GBR. Dist(s): Ulverscroft US

Love of Fat Men. unabr. ed. Short Stories. Helen Dunmore. Read by Carole Boyd. 4 cass. (Running Time: 5 hr.). (Isis Ser.). (J). 1997. 44.95 (978-0-7531-0295-4(1), 971208) Pub: ISIS Lrg Prnt GBR. Dist(s): Ulverscroft US
Reveals a harsh, sensuous world of endless winters & midnight sun. Set as far apart as Finland, the Austrian Tyrol & upstate New York.

Love of God. Perf. by Campus Crusade Singers. Prod. by Randy Ray. 1 cass. 1992. 10.98 (978-1-57919-111-5(8)); audio compact disk 14.98 (978-1-57919-112-2(6)) Randolf Prod.

Love of God. Derek Prince. 3 cass. 17.85 Set. (103-104-105); 5.95 (4348) Derek Prince.
Love is the goal of all Christian instructions, the one sure evidence that we know God, but all too many Christians have never come to know the One who saved them.

Love of God: John 3:16; Eph. 3:14-19. Ed Young. 1990. 4.95 (978-0-7417-1826-6(X), 826) Win Walk.

Love of God: Logos October 5, 1997. Ben Young. 1997. 4.95 (978-0-7417-6050-0(9), B0050) Win Walk.

Love of God & Master. Swami Amar Jyoti. 1 cass. 1976. 9.95 (C-37) Truth Consciousness.
Love as the expression of creation. Total dependence upon God.

Love of God for You. Mac Hammond. 1 cass. (Running Time: 1 hr.). 2005. 5.00 (978-1-57399-212-1(7)); audio compact disk 5.00 (978-1-57399-261-9(5)) Mac Hammond.

Love of God in Christian Science Nursing. unabr. ed. Myrtle Smith. Prod. by David Keyston. 1 cass. (Running Time: 1 hrs. 31 min.). (Myrtle Smyth Audiotapes Ser.). 1998. , CD. (978-1-893107-14-4(0), M14, Cross & Crown) Healing Unltd.

Love of Life. unabr. ed. Jack London. Read by Walter Zimmerman & Jim Killavey. 1 cass. (Running Time: 82 min.). Dramatization. Incl. Law of Life. 1981. (N-64); Man with the Gash. 1981. (N-64); 1981. 8.95 (N-64) Jimcin Record.
Stories of the harsh life in the frozen North.

Love of My Own. unabr. ed. E. Lynn Harris. 7 cass. (Running Time: 10 hrs. 30 mins.). 2002. 56.00 (978-0-7366-8666-2(5)); audio compact disk 72.00 (978-0-7366-8667-9(3)) Books on Tape.
Takes on the universal issue of class and how changes in economic status among family and friends can often disrupt, confuse, and wound. But love, a signature Harris theme, abounds in this novel. As a band of close-knit characters (old and new) navigates life's challenges and tries to find their place in the world, each person goes on a journey of the heart in search of the one thing everyone wants: a love of their own.

Love of the God-Man. Read by Adi Da Samraj. 1 cass. 1986. 11.95 (978-0-918801-64-7(8)) Dawn Horse Pr.
In these three Talks, Sri Da Avabhasa Speaks ecstatically of the true secret of Spiritual life, the great love-relationship between the Enlightened God-Man & His devotee.

Love of the Prophets. unabr. ed. Swami Amar Jyoti. 1 cass. (Satsangs of Swami Amar Jyoti Ser.). (C). 1996. 9.95 (K-158) Truth Consciousness.
The tremendous, unconditional love & selfless being of the Prophets. In our drama, they suffer. Leaving false identification.

Love of Truth. Swami Amar Jyoti. 1 cass. 1976. 9.95 (K-75) Truth Consciousness.
There is no greater religion than Truth, it teaches us to love, it releases us. True service in relationships.

Love of Truth: A Dialogue on Reality, Reason, & Religion. Huston Smith & Jacob Needleman. 2 cass. 18.00 (A0472-89) Sound Photosyn.
A stimulating exchange between two of the most honored & respected thinkers of our time: Huston Smith, author of "The Religions of Man," each with long careers as professors of philosophy. They focus on examining the relationship between philosophy & religion & the spiritual search. Informative, inspiring, & well worth the listen.

Love on the Air - Gundell. A. J. Gundell. 1 cass. 1994. 17.95 (978-0-89524-807-7(7)) Cherry Lane.

Love on the Nile. abr. ed. Katrina Wright. Read by Margaret Holt. 2 cass. (Running Time: 3 hrs.). 1994. 24.95 (97[illegible]5496-211-9(6), 62116) Pub: Soundings Ltd GBR. Dist(s): Ulverscro[illegible]

Love One Another. Ed Pinegar. 1 cass. 9.[illegible] [illegible]78-1-57734-296-0(8), 06005829) Covenant Comms.
An entertaining & inspirational talk for youth.

Love One Another: A Talk on Living the Gospel. Speeches. Perf. by Catherine Doherty. 1 cass. (Running Time: 1 hr.). 2001. 9.95 (978-0-921440-70-3(7)) Madonna Hse CAN.
Catherine Doherty meditates on the Gospel message from St. John the Beloved-"Little children, love one another." She explains that love doesn't know the pronoun "I." Love understands, love forgives, love knows how to wait, love crosses all barriers. Love knows how to act and when. It has an intuition that comes directly from the Source-that source is God. This lecture introduces us to the love that casts out all fear, that urges us to live the gospel passionately.

***Love One Another: The Importance & Power of Christian Relationships.** Gordon Ferguson. 2009. 10.00 (978-0-9842006-5-8(7)) Illumination MA.

Love One Zero One: To Love Oneself is the Beginning of a Lifelong Romance. Peter McWilliams. 8 cass. (Running Time: 12 hrs.). 1995. 24.95 Mary Bks.

Love Only Once. abr. ed. Johanna Lindsey. Read by Alana Windsor. 1 cass. (Running Time: 90 min.). (Malory Ser.). 1994. 5.99 (978-1-57096-017-8(8), RAZ 918) Romance Alive Audio.
In 1817 London, Regina Ashton will never forget her handsome yet arrogant seducer, Nicholas Eden. She must unravel the dark secret of his past before they can enjoy their blazing destiny together.

Love Only Once. unabr. ed. Johanna Lindsey. Read by Laural Merlington. (Running Time: 8 hrs.). (Malory Ser.). 2008. 39.25 (978-1-4233-5092-7(8), 9781423350927, BADLE); 24.95 (978-1-4233-5091-0(X), 9781423350910, BAD); 82.25 (978-1-4233-5086-6(3), 9781423350866, BrilAudUnabridg); audio compact disk 87.25 (978-1-4233-5088-0(X), 9781423350880, BriAudCD Unabrid); audio compact disk 39.25 (978-1-4233-5090-3(1), 9781423350903, Brlnc Audio MP3 Lib); audio compact disk 29.95 (978-1-4233-5087-3(1), 9781423350873, Bril Audio CD Unabri); audio compact disk 24.95 (978-1-4233-5089-7(8), 9781423350897, Brilliance MP3) Brilliance Audio.

Love or Lust: What's the Difference (Panel Discussion) Judges 14:1-3. Ed Young. 1993. 4.95 (978-0-7417-1964-5(9), 964) Win Walk.

Love over Scotland. Alexander McCall Smith. (44 Scotland Street Ser.: Bk. 3). 2007. audio compact disk 34.99 (978-1-4281-5532-9(5)) Recorded Bks.

Love over Scotland. unabr. ed. Alexander McCall Smith. Read by Robert Ian MacKenzie. 12 cass. (Running Time: 14 hrs. 30 mins.). (44 Scotland Street Ser.: Bk. 3). 2007. 98.75 (978-1-4281-5533-6(3)) Recorded Bks.

***Love Overboard.** unabr. ed. Janet Evanovich. Read by C. J. Critt. Orig. Title: Ivan Takes a Wife. (ENG.). 2005. (978-0-06-083499-9(4), Harper Audio); (978-0-06-083500-2(1), Harper Audio) HarperCollins Pubs.

Love Overboard. unabr. ed. Janet Evanovich. Read by C. J. Critt. Orig. Title: Ivan Takes a Wife. 2005. 14.95 (978-0-06-079129-2(2)); audio compact disk 14.95 (978-0-06-073695-8(X)) HarperCollins Pubs.

Love Philtre of Iky Schoenstein see Favorite Stories by O. Henry

Love Poems. unabr. ed. Poems. Robert Bly. 2 cass. (Running Time: 2 hrs. 15 min.). 1986. 18.00 Set. (00311) Big Sur Tapes.

Love Poems. unabr. ed. Lawrence Durrell. Read by Lawrence Durrell. 10.95 (978-0-8045-0818-6(6), SAC 818) Spoken Arts.

LOVE Poems for the Romantic Heart Audio Cassette. D. N. Sutton. Read by D. N. Sutton. (ENG.). 2001. 6.00 (978-0-940361-30-0(2)) Sherwood-Spencer Pub.

LOVE Poems for the Romantic Heart CD. D. N. Sutton. Read by D. N. Sutton. (ENG.). 2001. audio compact disk 12.00 (978-0-940361-40-9(X)) Sherwood-Spencer Pub.

Love Poems for the Romantic Heart CD & Book. D. N. Sutton. Read by D. N. Sutton. (ENG.). 2001. per. 18.00 (978-0-940361-50-8(7)) Sherwood-Spencer Pub.

Love Poems of John Donne. abr. ed. John Donne. Read by Richard Burton. 1 cass. (Running Time: 37 min.). Incl. Anniversary. (CPN 1141); Apparition. (CPN 1141); Canonization. (CPN 1141); Curse. (CPN 1141); Elegy I: Jealosie. (CPN 1141); Elegy VII: Natures Lay Ideot. (CPN 1141); Elegy VIII: The Comparison. (CPN 1141); Extasie. (CPN 1141); Feaver. (CPN 1141); Flea. (CPN 1141); Funeral. (CPN 1141); Good-Morrow. (CPN 1141); Legacie. (CPN 1141); Nocturnal. (CPN 1141); Relique. (CPN 1141); Rising Sun. (CPN 1141); Song: Go & Catch a Falling Star. (CPN 1141); Song: Sweetest Love, I Do Not Go. (CPN 1141); Valediction: Forbidding Mourning. (CPN 1141); 1994. 12.00 (978-0-89845-248-8(1), CPN 1141) HarperCollins Pubs.

Love Poems World-Wide by Dancing Beetle. Perf. by Eugene Ely et al. 1 cass. (Running Time: 81 min.). (J). 1993. 10.00 Erthviibz.
Love poems world-wide & nature sounds come together when Ms. Ladybug & the spunky musical humans read & sing with Dancing Beetle.

Love Project. Interview with Arleen Lorrance & Diane K. Pike. 1 cass. (Running Time: 60 min.). 6.95 Teleos Inst.

Love Real. Marianne Williamson. Read by Marianne Williamson. 1 cass. (Running Time: 90 mins.). (Lectures on a Course in Miracles). (ENG.). 1998. 10.00 (978-1-56170-565-8(9), M854) Hay House.

Love Recognized see Robert Penn Warren Reads Selected Poems

Love Response. Eva Selhub. 2008. audio compact disk 19.98 (978-1-55961-979-0(1)) Pub: Relaxtn Co. Dist(s): S and S Inc

Love Response: Your Prescription to Transform Fear, Anger & Anxiety into Vibrant Health & Well-Being. unabr. ed. Divina Infusino & Eva Selhub. Read by Eva Selhub. (Running Time: 8 hrs.). 2009. 39.97 (978-1-4233-7789-4(3), 9781423377894, Brlnc Audio MP3 Lib); audio compact disk 87.97 (978-1-4233-7787-0(7), 9781423377870, BriAudCD Unabrid) Brilliance Audio.

Love Response: Your Prescription to Transform Fear, Anger & Anxiety into Vibrant Health & Well-Being. unabr. ed. Eva M. Selhub & Divina Infusino. Read by Eva M. Selhub. (Running Time: 8 hrs.). 2009. 24.99 (978-1-4233-7788-7(5), 9781423377887, Brilliance MP3); audio compact disk 29.99 (978-1-4233-7786-3(9), 9781423377863, Bril Audio CD Unabri) Brilliance Audio.

Love Response: Your Prescription to Turn off Fear, Anger, & Anxiety to Achieve Vibrant Health & Transform Your Life. unabr. ed. Eva M. Selhub. Read by Eva M. Selhub. (Running Time: 8 hrs.). 2009. 24.99 (978-1-4233-7790-0(7), 9781423377900, BAD) Brilliance Audio.

Love Response: Your Prescription to Turn off Fear, Anger, & Anxiety to Achieve Vibrant Health & Transform Your Life. unabr. ed. Eva M. Selhub & Divina Infusino. Read by Eva M. Selhub & Emily Durante. (Running Time: 8 hrs.). 2009. 39.97 (978-1-4233-7791-7(5), 9781423377917, BADLE) Brilliance Audio.

Love Revolution. unabr. ed. Joyce Meyer. Read by Sandra McCollom. (Running Time: 8 hrs.). (ENG.). 2009. 24.98 (978-1-60024-736-1(9)); audio compact disk 29.98 (978-1-60024-735-4(0)) Pub: Hachet Audio. Dist(s): HachBkGrp

Love, Ruby Lavender. Deborah Wiles. Read by Judith Ivey. 3 vols. (Running Time: 3 hrs. 58 mins.). (J). (gr. 3-7). 2004. pap. bk. 36.00 (978-0-8072-2096-2(5), Listening Lib); audio compact disk 35.00 (978-1-4000-8997-0(2), Listening Lib) Random Audio Pubg.

Love, Ruby Lavender. unabr. ed. Deborah Wiles. 3 cass. (Running Time: 3 hrs. 58 mins.). (J). (gr. 3-7). 2004. 30.00 (978-0-8072-0718-5(7), Listening Lib) Random Audio Pubg.

Love Scenes. Perf. by Diana Krall. 1 cass., 1 CD. 8.78 (IMP 233); audio compact disk 13.58 CD Jewel box. (IMP 233) NewSound.

Love Secret Spoken: An Exploration of Rumi's Poetry. unabr. ed. Gangaji Foundation Staff. Read by Christopher Mohr. Ed. by Christopher Mohr. 1 CD. (Running Time: 80 mins.). 2000. audio compact disk 15.00 (978-1-887984-06-5(2)) The Gangaji Fnd.
Presents American spiritual teacher, Gangaj: reading selected Rumi poetry, combined with spontaneous interview segments. It explores the sublime truth Rumi masterfully evokes, through poetry.

Love Secret Spoken: An Exploration of Rumi's Poetry. unabr. ed. Gangaji Foundation Staff. Read by Gangaji Foundation Staff. Read by Christopher Mohr. 1 cass. (Running Time: 80 mins.). 2000. 12.00 (978-1-887984-07-2(0)) The Gangaji Fnd.
Presents American spiritual teacher, Gangaji: reading from selected Rumi poetry, completed with spontaneous interview segments. It explores the sublime truth Rumi masterfully evokes.

Love Secrets. Brett Bravo. 1 cass. 1992. 8.95 (1011) Am Fed Astrologers.

***Love, Sex & Marriage.** Contrib. by Phillip D. Jensen. 2004. audio compact disk 13.99 (978-1-876326-81-4(6)) Matthias MediaAUS AUS.

Love, Sex & Marriage: Straight Talk to Generation X. abr. ed. Dennis Rainey. Ed. by Keith Lynch. 3 cass. (Running Time: 3 hrs.). 1996. 14.95 Set. (978-1-57229-033-4(1)) FamilyLife.

Love, Sex & Romance. unabr. ed. Leonard Peikoff. 1 cass. (Running Time: 1 hrs. 40 min.). 1998. 14.95 (978-1-56114-523-2(8), LP51C) Second Renaissance.
A wide-ranging discussion in a question & answer format.

Love, Sex, Romance in Your Chart. Mohan Koparkar. 1 cass. 8.95 (200) Am Fed Astrologers.
An AFA Convention workshop tape.

Love Smart: Find the One You Want - Fix the One You Got. abr. ed. Phil McGraw. Read by Phil McGraw. 2005. 15.95 (978-0-7435-5527-2(9)); audio compact disk 29.95 (978-0-7435-5189-2(3)) Pub: S&S Audio. Dist(s): S and S Inc

Love Somebody, Love Yourself. Poet's Workshop Staff. 1 cass. (Running Time: 20 min.). (YA). (gr. 10-12). 1991. 11.95 (37 SOR 700) Sell Out Recordings.
Poetry on loving & being kind to yourself.

Love Song. Nikki Gemmell. Read by Caroline Lee. (Running Time: 11 hrs.). 2009. 89.99 (978-1-74214-230-2(3), 9781742142302) Pub: Bolinda Pubng AUS. Dist(s): Bolinda Pub Inc

Love Song. unabr. ed. Charlotte Bingham. Read by Judy Bennett. 10 cass. 1999. 84.95 (978-0-7540-0305-2(1), CAB1728) AudioGO.

Love Song. unabr. ed. Nikki Gemmell. Read by Caroline Lee. 10 CDs. (Running Time: 39600 sec.). 2005. audio compact disk 98.95 (978-1-74093-577-7(2)) Pub: Bolinda Pubng AUS. Dist(s): Bolinda Pub Inc

Love Song. unabr. ed. Nikki Gemmell. Read by Caroline Lee. (Running Time: 11 hrs.). 2009. 43.95 (978-1-74214-128-2(5), 9781742141282) Pub: Bolinda Pubng AUS. Dist(s): Bolinda Pub Inc

Love Song: I & Thou see Twentieth-Century Poetry in English, No. 29, Recordings of Poets Reading Their Own Poetry

Love Song of J. Alfred Prufrock. 10.00 Esstee Audios.
A reading with analysis.

Love Song of J. Edgar Hoover. unabr. ed. Kinky Friedman. Read by Edward Lewis. 6 cass. (Running Time: 6 hrs.). 1998. 36.00 (978-0-7366-3661-2(7), 4335) Books on Tape.
For gumshoe Kinky Friedman, a simple missing person case turns into an FBI conspiracy to get him. Funny & irreverent.

Love Songs. Michael Taylor. Read by Julia Sands. 12 cass. (Running Time: 14 hrs.). (Storysound Ser.). (J). 2003. 94.95 (978-1-85903-599-3(X)) Pub: Mgna Lrg Print GBR. Dist(s): Ulverscroft US

Love Songs: Spread My Wings & Fly. Paul Sybert. 1 CD. (Running Time: 50 mins.). (ENG.). 2005. audio compact disk 15.00 (978-0-9767842-4-1(6)) Paul Syb.
1. What You?re Gonna? Do2. I?m Leaving the Neighborhood3. Call Me Anytime From Dixieland4. MoFo?s Guitar5. North Texas Day6. Parking Lot Picker7. I Want To Spread My Wings and Fly8. Love In Reverse9. Every Once In A While10. Hello Old Friend11. Your Roads Lead Back To Me12. Love Keeps Me Coming Back13. Every Time We Said Goodbye14. He Said I Love You2.3.4.5.6.7.8.9.10.11.12.13.14.

Love Songs: The Ultimate Collection. Contrib. by Steve Blair. 2006. audio compact disk 19.99 (978-5-558-54362-9(0)) Pt of Grace Ent.

Love Songs & Lullabyes for Daddy's Little Dreamer. J. Aaron Brown. Perf. by Tom Wurth. Illus. by Tina Blanck. 1 cass. (Running Time: 50 min.). (J). (gr. 3). 1995. bk. 15.95 (978-0-927945-14-1(2)) Someday Baby.
Collection of eight original lullabies with a full color lyric book.

Love Songs & Lullabyes for Daddy's Little Dreamer. J. Aaron Brown. Perf. by Tom Wurth. Illus. by Tina Blanck. 1 cass. (Running Time: 50 min.). (J). (ps). 1995. bk. 12.95 (978-0-927945-13-4(4)) Someday Baby.

Love Songs by Paul M Sutton CD: Romantic Songs by Paul M Sutton. Composed by Paul M. Sutton. Lyrics by Paul M. Sutton. Prod. by Marti Amado. Arranged by Marti Amado. Voice by Anthony Bollotta. (ENG.). 2009. audio compact disk 9.95 (978-0-940361-80-5(9)) Sherwood-Spencer Pub.

Love Songs for Solo Singers: 12 Contemporary Settings of Favorites from the Great American Songbook for Solo Voice & Piano (Medium High Voice) Composed by Jay Althouse. (For Solo Singers Ser.). (ENG.). 2008. audio compact disk 13.95 (978-0-7390-5342-3(6)) Alfred Pub.

Love Songs for Solo Singers: 12 Contemporary Settings of Favorites from the Great American Songbook for Solo Voice & Piano (Medium Low Voice) Composed by Jay Althouse. (For Solo Singers Ser.). (ENG.). 2008. audio compact disk 13.95 (978-0-7390-5345-4(0)) Alfred Pub.

Love Songs from Stage & Screen. Friedman-Fairfax and Sony Music Staff. 1 CD. (CD Ser.). 1994. pap. bk. 15.98 (978-1-56799-124-6(6), Friedman-Fairfax) M Friedman Pub Grp Inc.

Love Songs of Robert Burns. unabr. ed. Robert Burns. Perf. by Ann Moray. 10.95 (978-0-8045-0754-7(6), SAC 754) Spoken Arts.

Love, Stargirl. unabr. ed. Jerry Spinelli. Read by Mandy Siegfried & Mandy Siegfried. (Running Time: 22740 sec.). (ENG.). (J). (gr. 7-8). 2007. audio compact disk 28.00 (978-0-7393-5623-4(2), Listening Lib) Pub: Random Audio Pubg. Dist(s): Random

Love, Stargirl. unabr. ed. Jerry Spinelli. Read by Mandy Siegfried. 5 CDs. (Running Time: 6 hrs. 20 mins.). (YA). (gr. 6-10). 2007. audio compact disk 45.00 (978-0-7393-6103-0(1), Listening Lib) Pub: Random Audio Pubg. Dist(s): Random
Stargirl has moved and left everything behind: Arizona, Mica High, enchanted desert places - and Leo. He's all she can think about, and her life begins to feel like a parade of unhappy anniversaries. Then Stargirl meets her wonderfully bizarre new neighbors: Dootsie, the curly-headed five-year-old "human bean"; Betty Lou, who hasn't stepped outside her house for nine years; Charlie, who sits among the tombstones; hot-tempered Alvina with that one glittery nail; and Perry Delloplane, the blue-eyed thief who soon lays his own claim to Stargirl's heart. In letters to Leo over the course of a year, Stargirl comes to find hope in new places: mockingbirds, donut angels, moon flowers, and the Winter Solstice. But what's life without Leo? Will he - can he - answer that one crucial question she asks every morning to the rising sun?.

Love Stories. unabr. ed. Henry James et al. Read by Flo Gibson. 6 cass. (Running Time: 8 hrs.). 1998. 24.95 (978-1-55685-561-0(3)) Audio Bk Con.
Various works by well known authors, "A Day of Days", "The Parson's Daughter of Oxney Colne", "Right at Last", "The Captain's Love", "Her Last Appearance", "The Son's Veto", "Samson & Delilah", "The Nightingale & the Rose", "Trial of Love", "Dennis Haggerty's Wife", "The End of Her Journey", comprise a mixed bag of love, lust, laughter & tragedy.

Love Stories for Fathers & Sons. 2006. audio compact disk 26.50 (978-1-890246-55-6(7)) B Katie Int Inc.

Love Story see Robert Graves Reads from His Poetry & the White Goddess

Love Story Classics. unabr. ed. Short Stories. Kate Chopin et al. Read by J. P. Linton. Ed. by Love Story Classics Staff. 2 cass. (Running Time: 3 hrs.). (YA). (gr. 8 up). 1993. 16.95 (978-0-9637488-1-2(5)) Love Story Class.
The premiere volume of an anthology of short stories on the theme of love by famous authors.

Love Struck. unabr. ed. Melanie La'Brooy. Read by Louise Crawford. (Running Time: 10 hrs.). 2007. audio compact disk 93.95 (978-1-74093-922-5(0), 9781740939225) Pub: Bolinda Pubng AUS. Dist(s): Bolinda Pub Inc

Love Tactics: How to Win the One You Want. unabr. ed. Thomas W. McKnight & Robert H. Phillips. Read by Franette Liebow. 2 cass. (Running Time: 3 hrs.). 1999. 16.95 (978-1-882071-62-3(X)) B-B Audio.
Is there anything you can do to make that special someone want you as much as you want them? Absolutely! With Love Tactics, you will learn the most effective ways of developing meaningful relationships, intimacy, and ultimately - love. The authors eff.

Love Talk. abr. ed. Parrott Les, III & Leslie Parrott. (Running Time: 2 hrs. 41 mins. 0 sec.). (ENG.). 2005. 17.99 (978-0-310-26691-4(2)) Zondervan.

Love Talk & Lullabies. unabr. ed. 1 cass. (Running Time: 1 hr.). (J). 2002. 9.95 (978-0-9713895-0-2(0)); audio compact disk 14.95 Storytoons.

Love Talk Small Group Edition. unabr. ed. Les Parrott & Leslie Parrott. 2005. audio compact disk 8.99 (978-0-310-26469-9(3)) Zondervan.

Love Talker, unabr. ed. Elizabeth Peters, pseud. Read by Grace Conlin. 6 cass. (Running Time: 8 hrs. 30 mins.). 1995. 44.95 (978-0-7861-0709-4(X), 1586) Blckstn Audio.
There might be worse fates than spending a few months at Idlewood, Laurie thought as the Chicago winter howled around her. Certainly her Aunt Ida's invitation was well intentioned, & she couldn't really have meant what she said: "I have nothing of which to complain, considering my age. I only hope I will be taken before my mind fails. Fairies in the woods, indeed!" But when Laurie & her brother, Doug, arrive at the family home in the Maryland countryside, they discover that Aunt Ida may have reason to fear & that something is indeed in the woods.

Love Talker. unabr. ed. Elizabeth Peters, pseud. Read by Grace Conlin. (Running Time: 28800 sec.). 2007. audio compact disk 29.95 (978-0-7861-0337-9(X)) Blckstn Audio.

Love Tennis. abr. ed. Robert A. Monroe. Read by Robert A. Monroe. (Mine Food Ser.). 1980. 14.95 (978-1-56102-408-7(2)) Inter Indus.
Visualization exercises & training for a better tennis score.

Love That Cat. Ingrid Newkirk. 1. (Running Time: 80 mins.). (ENG.). 2002. audio compact disk (978-1-59056-042-6(6)) Lantern Books.

Love That Cat. Ingrid Newkirk. Read by Ingrid Newkirk. 1. (Running Time: 90 mins.). 2002. cass. & audio compact disk 5.00 (978-1-59056-041-9(8)) Pub: Lantern Books. Dist(s): SteinerBooks Inc

***Love That Dog.** abr. ed. Sharon Creech. Read by Scott Wolf. (ENG.). 2005. (978-0-06-084843-9(X)); (978-0-06-084844-6(8)) HarperCollins Pubs.

Love That Dog. unabr. ed. Sharon Creech. Read by Scott Wolf. (J). 2008. 34.99 (978-1-60514-654-6(4)) Find a World.

Love That Dog. unabr. ed. Sharon Creech. Read by Scott Wolf. (Running Time: 3600 sec.). (J). (gr. 4-7). 2006. audio compact disk 13.95 (978-0-06-085278-8(X), HarperChildAud) HarperCollins Pubs.

Love That Lasts: For Couples. Chuck Smith. Crystal Cooper. (ENG.). 2006. audio compact disk 2.99 (978-1-932941-90-6(8)) Word For Today.

Love That Will Not Let Go Part 1: Hos.11:1-12:15. Ed Young. 1988. 4.95 (978-0-7417-1661-3(5), 661) Win Walk.

Love That Will Not Let Go Pt. 11: Hos. 12:1-14. Ed Young. 1988. 4.05 (978-0-7417-1662-0(3), 662) Win Walk.

Love That Works: The Art & Science of Giving. Bruce Brander. Read by Tom Richards & Ruth Weisberg. 6 CDS. (Running Time: 20400 sec.). 2006. audio compact disk 19.95 (978-1-59947-092-4(6)) Pub: Templeton Pr. Dist(s): Chicago Distribution Ctr

Love, the Most Mysterious of Human Emotions. Instructed by Manly P. Hall. 8.95 (978-0-89314-173-8(9), C800141) Philos Res.

Love the One You're With. abr. ed. Emily Giffin. Read by Kathleen McInerney. 4 CDs. (Running Time: 5 hrs. 0 mins. 0 sec.). (ENG.). 2008. audio compact disk 24.95 (978-1-4272-0421-9(7)) Pub: Macmill Audio. Dist(s): Macmillan

Love the Wild Swan see Poetry of Robinson Jeffers

Love the Work, Hate the Job: Why America's Best Workers are Unhappier than Ever. unabr. ed. David Kusnet. (Running Time: 9 hrs. 0 mins.). 2008. 19.95 (978-1-4332-1559-9(4)); audio compact disk 19.95 (978-1-4332-1560-5(8)) Blckstn Audio.

Love the Work, Hate the Job: Why America's Best Workers Are Unhappier than Ever. unabr. ed. David Kusnet. Read by Tom Weiner. (Running Time: 8.5 hrs. 0 mins.). 2008. 54.95 (978-1-4332-1557-5(8)); audio compact disk 70.00 (978-1-4332-1558-2(6)) Blckstn Audio.

Love the Work, Hate the Job: Why America's Best Workers are Unhappier Than Ever. unabr. ed. David Kusnet. Read by Tom Weiner. (Running Time: 8.5 hrs. 0 mins.). 2008. 29.95 (978-1-4332-1561-2(6)) Blckstn Audio.

***Love This! Learning to Make It a Way of Life, Not Just a Word.** Zondervan. (Running Time: 3 hrs. 58 mins. 47 sec.). (ENG.). (YA). 2010. 14.99 (978-0-310-86993-1(5)) Zondervan.

Love Thy Neighbor: A Story of War. unabr. ed. Peter Maass. Narrated by George Guidall. 9 cass. (Running Time: 12 hrs. 30 mins.). 1996. 78.00 (978-0-7887-3536-3(5), 95923E7) Recorded Bks.
Peter Maass writes with passion & conviction about the nightmare in Bosnia.

Love to Last Forever. abr. ed. Tracie Peterson. Narrated by Aimee Lilly. (Running Time: 6 hrs. 40 mins. 54 sec.). (Brides of Gallatin County Ser.: No. 2). (ENG.). 2009. audio compact disk 27.99 (978-1-59859-527-7(X)) Oasis Audio.

Love to Last Forever. abr. ed. Tracie Peterson. Narrated by Aimee Lilly. (Running Time: 7 hrs. 15 mins. 0 sec.). (Brides of Gallatin County Ser.). (ENG.). 2009. 19.59 (978-1-60814-541-6(7)) Oasis Audio.

Love to Save the World. Created by Lillenas Publishing Company. 2007. audio compact disk 60.00 (978-5-557-69973-0(2)) Lillenas.

Love to Save the World: A Christmas Celebration of Invitation & Redemption. Contrib. by Cliff Duren. Created by Cliff Duren. 2007. audio compact disk 90.00 (978-5-557-69972-3(4)); audio compact disk 90.00 (978-5-557-69971-6(6)); audio compact disk 12.00 (978-5-557-69970-9(8)); audio compact disk 12.00 (978-5-557-69968-6(6)) Lillenas.

Love to the Highest Bidder. Rachel Ann Nunes. 2 cass. 12.95 (978-1-57734-279-3(8), 07001819) Covenant Comms.

Love Triangle - Love Class. Frank L. Natter. 1 cass. (Running Time: 90 min.). (Improving Your Personal Problem-Solving Ser.: Pt. II: Relati). 1989. 10.00 (978-1-878287-67-0(2), ATA-10) Type & Temperament.
Anyone in a relationship about which they care deeply (good-shape relationships/difficult relationships) learn of new insights & ways to appreciate & improve those relationships. Natter's comments on the work of Leo Buscaglia & others.

Love Under Pressure. Elbert Willis. 1 cass. (Patience & Long-Suffering Ser.). 4.00 Fill the Gap.

Love Unmasked. unabr. ed. Cherie Claire & Faith Garner. 1 cass. (Running Time: 90 min.). (Afterglow Romantic Walks Ser.). 1999. 10.99 (978-1-892026-04-0(X)) Afterglow.
Two brand-new, direct-to-audio romance stories with masquerade themes.

Love Walked In. Marisa de los Santos. 2007. audio compact disk 34.99 (978-1-4281-8966-9(1)) Recorded Bks.

Love Was the Reason. Stella March. Read by Anne Cater. 4 cass. 1999. 44.95 (63724) Pub: Soundings Ltd GBR. Dist(s): ISIS Pub

Love Wife. unabr. ed. Jen Gish. 13 cds. (Running Time: 15.75 hrs.). 2005. audio compact disk 119.75 (978-1-4193-1276-2(6)) Recorded Bks.

Love Wife. unabr. ed. Jen Gish. 12 cass. (Running Time: 15 hrs. 45 mins.). 2004. 109.75 (978-1-4193-1274-8(X), 97896MC) Recorded Bks.

Love Wife. unabr. ed. Jen Gish. 13 CDs. (Running Time: 15 hrs. 45 min.). 2004. audio compact disk 34.99 (978-1-4193-0481-1(X)) Recorded Bks.
Chinese-American Carnegie Wong and his WASPy wife Blondie have two adopted children of Asian descent, Lilly and Wendy. The girls are a handful, but they are nothing compared to Carnegie¿s mother. Mama Wong¿s dislike for Blondie is relentless¿so much so that she introduces a Chinese woman named Lan to the household. When Lilly and Wendy begin to favor Lan over their white mother, Blondie clings ever more tightly to her biological son, Bailey.

Love Without Conditions: Reflections of the Christ Mind. unabr. ed. Paul Ferrini. Read by Paul Ferrini. 2 cass. (Running Time: 3 hrs. 25 min.). 1997. 19.95 Set. (978-1-879159-24-2(4)) Heartways Pr.

Love You Forever. Robert Munsch. (J). (ps-3). 1992. 10.95 (978-0-920903-63-6(0), Gold Bks) RH Chldrns.

***Love You Hate You Miss You.** unabr. ed. Elizabeth Scott. Read by Tracy Pfau. (ENG.). 2009. (978-0-06-182555-2(7)); (978-0-06-190202-4(0)) HarperCollins Pubs.

Love You Madly. Linda Palmer. Read by Celeste Lawson. (Running Time: 32400 sec.). (Daytime Mysteries Ser.). 2006. 59.95 (978-0-7861-4558-4(7)); audio compact disk 72.00 (978-0-7861-7083-8(2)) Blckstn Audio.

Love You Madly. unabr. ed. Linda Palmer. Read by Celeste Lawson. (Running Time: 32400 sec.). (Daytime Mysteries Ser.). 2006. audio compact disk 29.95 (978-0-7861-7565-9(6)) Blckstn Audio.

***Love You More.** unabr. ed. Lisa Gardner. (ENG.). 2011. audio compact disk 40.00 (978-0-7393-6670-7(X), Random AudioBks) Pub: Random Audio Pubg. Dist(s): Random

Love Your Body Its Your Best Friend Learn to Relax, Scripts. 2 cass. (Running Time: 60 mins).Tr. of Quiera Su Cuerpo, Es Su Mejor Amigo Aprenda a Relajarse. (SPA.). 2003. 25.00 (978-0-9744786-5-4(2)) A Nogales.
Doctor Nogales is pleased to offer this important series of psychological self-help cassettes. Although they don't replace psychological therapy, they will give you the necessary information to find your own answers and possible solutions to common difficulties and life challenges. They also include practical exercises that can help to guide listeners to a healthier life. "Love Your Body?It?s Your Best Friend"?Learn to Relax?.

Love Your Enemy: The Gospel Call to Nonviolence. Richard Rohr. 1 cass. (Running Time: 1 hr.). 2001. 8.95 (A6661) St Anthony Mess Pr.
Jesus, unlike all other revolutionaries, does not justify the creation of victoms. He says, "Love your enemy." Examine three pivotal questions about violence and our response to them.

Love Your First Priority. Kenneth Copeland. 2 cass. 2006. (978-1-57562-842-4(2)); audio compact disk (978-1-57562-843-1(0)) K Copeland Pubns.

Love Your God with All Your Mind: The Role of Reason in the Life of the Soul. unabr. ed. Read by Grover Gardener. 6 CDs. (Running Time: 7 hrs. 30 mins. 0 sec.). (ENG.). 2005. audio compact disk 24.98 (978-1-59644-156-9(9), Hovel Audio) christianaud.
The mind plays an important role in Christianity. Unfortunately, many of us leave our minds behind when it comes to our faith. In Love Your God with All Your Mind, J.P. Moreland presents a logical case for the role of the mind in spiritual transformation. He challenges us to develop a Christian mind and to use our intellect to further God's kingdom through evangelism, apologetics, worship, and vocation.This is an invaluable book aiding the concerned Christian in the battle for the Christian intellect, Love Your God With All Your Mind offers a no-holds-barred approach to fixing what's gone wrong in the Church. The author brilliantly identifies the reasons for the loss of the Christian intellect and how the Christian mind has been lost to the ever-growing popularity of anti-intellectualism.

***Love Your God with All Your Mind: The Role of Reason in the Life of the Soul.** unabr. ed. J. P. Moreland. Narrated by Grover Gardner. (ENG.). 2005. 14.98 (978-1-59644-157-6(7), Hovel Audio) christianaud.

Love Your God with All Your Mind: The Role of Reason in the Life of the Soul. unabr. ed. J. P. Moreland. Narrated by Grover Gardner. 1 MP3 CD. (Running Time: 7 hrs. 30 mins. 0 sec.). (ENG.). 2005. lp 19.98 (978-1-59644-155-2(0), Hovel Audio) christianaud.

Love Your Life: Living Happy, Healthy, & Whole. unabr. ed. Victoria Osteen. Read by Victoria Osteen. (Running Time: 6 hrs. 30 mins. 0 sec.). (ENG.). 2010. audio compact disk 14.99 (978-1-4423-0095-8(7)) Pub: S&S Audio. Dist(s): S and S Inc

Love Your Life (the Ultimate Healer Subliminal Series, 1 Of 6) Be comfortable - & happy - with who you are & your place in the World. Kyrah Malan. 1. (Running Time: 27 mins). 2006. audio compact disk 39.95 (978-0-9787324-1-7(3), SPS1) K Malan.
The ultimate in subliminal affirmations. Music, messages and binaural beats are specifically designed to work together to assist you in becoming comfortable - and happy - with who you are and your place in the world.What you hear is beautiful music that has been proven in university studies or harmonize and organize your energy field, putting you in a calm, receptive state quickly and easily.What your subconscious hears are specially designed affirmations and suggestions, designed to rewrite subconscious beliefs and change behavior faster and more effectively than any subliminal program available today.The Foundation set is designed to be used in order, each CD building on the effects of the previous CDs, and includes Love Your Life, Release & Relax, Energy & Power, Manifest & Magnetize, Live Your Life, and Spirit & Soul. Can be used independently.Unlike typical subliminal programs which recommend you listen to them for at least 30 days, Ultimate healer CDs help create positive results in only 17 days; some people report results in as little as 2 or 3 days!You can play them during everyday activities, while driving, reading, or at work, or listen to them with headphones. You have freedom and flexibility with The Ultimate Healer Subliminal Series.

Love Your Way to Happiness. Created by Anne H. Spencer-Beacham. 1. 2003. audio compact disk (978-1-932163-50-6(6)) Infinity Inst.

Love Yourself Action Kit. unabr. ed. Judith L. Powell. Read by Judith L. Powell. 2 cass. (Running Time: 80 min.). 1997. pap. bk. 19.95 (978-0-914295-80-8(2)) Top Mtn Pub.
Step-by-step procedure to the secrets of overcoming shyness, developing personal power, a sense of humor & a winning personality. Also how to love yourself.

Love Yourself Thin Affirmations. 1. (Running Time: 29 mins). 2002. audio compact disk (978-0-9726482-0-2(8)) Energy Way.
Affirmations to help create an internal image of a healthy slim trim body.

Love Yourself to Prosperity & Financial Freedom: Affirmations. 1CD. (Running Time: 1hr.8min). 2003. audio compact disk (978-0-9726482-4-0(0)) Energy Way.
Motivational introduction with 50 minutes of affirmations to create the internal image to be one of Prosperity & Financial Freedom.

Love 101: Learning to Love More Meaningfully. Speeches. Laura M. Brotherson. 1 CD. (Running Time: 40 mins.). 2006. audio compact disk 12.95 (978-0-9785867-0-6(0)) Inspire Bk.

Love 101: To Love Oneself Is the Beginning of a Lifelong Romance. unabr. ed. Peter McWilliams. Read by Peter McWilliams. 8 cass. (Running Time: 12 hrs.). (Life 101 Ser.). 1995. 24.95 6 tapes. (978-0-931580-71-0(4)) Pub: Mary Bks. Dist(s): APG

Love 3:16. Walter Hallam. 4 cass. (Running Time: 4 hrs.). 2000. 20.00 (978-1-930663-09-1(9)) W Hallam Minist.
For God so LOVED...the world...that He GAVE...His only Son. In this series you will learn about God's love & how His love can be a foundation in your life.

Lovecraft Tapes. unabr. ed. Featuring Thomas E. Fuller & William Jackson. 1 cass. (Running Time: 90 min.). Dramatization. 2002. 12.95 (978-0-929483-05-4(7)) Centauri Express Co.

Loved by You. Contrib. by Jaci Velasquez. (Soundtraks Ser.). 2007. audio compact disk 8.99 (978-5-557-52866-5(0)) Christian Wrld.

Loved Dog: The Playful, Nonaggressive Way to Teach Your Dog Good Behavior. unabr. ed. Tamar Geller & Andrea Cagan. Read by Renée Raudman. (Running Time: 5 hrs. 30 mins. 0 sec.). (ENG.). 2007. audio compact disk 24.99 (978-1-4001-0439-0(4)); audio compact disk 19.99 (978-1-4001-5439-5(1)); audio compact disk 49.99 (978-1-4001-3439-7(0)) Pub: Tantor Media. Dist(s): IngramPubServ

Loved One. unabr. collector's ed. Evelyn Waugh. Read by David Case. 4 cass. (Running Time: 4 hrs.). 1992. 24.00 (978-0-7366-2108-3(3), 2912) Books on Tape.
What goes on at a mortuary for Hollywood's departed stars. Waugh's funniest & most broadly popular success.

Loveland: Music for Dreaming & Awakening. Jai Uttal & Ben Leinbach. 1 CD. (Running Time: 3600 sec.). 2006. audio compact disk 16.98 (978-1-59179-413-4(7), M997D) Sounds True.
Enter Loveland - a place where time dissolves, and the heart within your heart is awakened, where world music visionary Jai Uttal merges the pulsing beat of the universe with the flowing source of energy through sacred melodies to the Divine. Here, the Grammy(r) Award-nominated multi-instrumentalist and vocalist joins Ben Leinbach to create six extended tracks of evocative compositions that celebrate the breath of life, revel in the power of infinite love, and invite you to deeply experience the numinous. Also available by Jai Uttal: Yoga for Music and Other Joys and Kirtan! The Art and Practice of Ecstatic Chant.

Lovely Bones. Alice Sebold. 10 CDs. (Running Time: 11 hrs. 45 mins.). 2004. audio compact disk 29.99 (978-1-4025-3290-0(3), 00642) Recorded Bks.

Lovely Bones. unabr. ed. Alice Sebold. (Running Time: 10 hrs. 30 mins.). (ENG.). 2007. 19.98 (978-1-60024-069-0(0)) Pub: Hachet Audio. Dist(s): HachBkGrp

Lovely Bones. unabr. ed. Alice Sebold. Read by Alice Sebold. 9 CDs. (Running Time: 10 hrs. 30 mins.). (ENG.). 2009. audio compact disk 19.98 (978-1-60024-842-9(X)) Pub: Hachet Audio. Dist(s): HachBkGrp

Lovely Bones. unabr. ed. Alice Sebold. Read by Alice Sebold. (Running Time: 10 hrs. 30 mins.). 2009. audio compact disk 39.99 (978-1-60788-298-5(1)) Pub: Hachet Audio. Dist(s): HachBkGrp

Lovely Bones. unabr. ed. Alice Sebold. Narrated by Alyssa Bresnahan. 7 cass. (Running Time: 11 hrs. 45 mins.). 2002. 29.99 (978-1-4025-2115-7(4), 01414) Recorded Bks.
The Lovely Bones will take you on a journey you've never been on before. It will leave you transformed and filled with a deeper love of both life and family. When we first meet 14-year old Susie Salmon,she is already in heaven, she recounts her brutal rape and murder at the hands of a neighbor. Spanning nearly 20 years, Susie from heaven describes heaven for us as she watches her family struggle to come to grips with her death.

Lovely Bones. unabr. ed. Alice Sebold. Narrated by Alyssa Bresnahan. 9 cass. (Running Time: 11 hrs. 45 mins.). 2002. 77.00 (978-1-4025-2406-6(4)) Recorded Bks.
In the first chapter of this haunting novel, 14-year-old Susie Salmon looks down from heaven and describes the horrifying events of her murder. As time goes on, Susie continues her curious observations while her family struggles to cope with the pain of her death.

Lovely Illusion. unabr. ed. Tessa Barclay. Read by Judith Porter. 10 cass. (Running Time: 14 hrs.). 2001. 84.95 (978-1-84283-060-4(0)) Pub: Soundings Ltd GBR. Dist(s): Ulverscroft US

Lovely Me: The Life of Jacqueline Susann. unabr. collector's ed. Barbara Seaman. Read by Mary Woods. 10 cass. (Running Time: 15 hrs.). 1989. 80.00 (978-0-7366-1502-0(4), 2375) Books on Tape.
Jacqueline Susann's life was flamboyant, outrageous, a mile-a-minute trip through the gossip columns & casting couches of the entertainment world. At 50, she felt that she was failure. It was then that she wrote the novel that would become one of the all-time best sellers - Valley of the Dolls.

Lovemakers. abr. ed. Judith Gould. Read by Katey Sagal. 2 cass. (Running Time: 3 hrs.). 2000. 7.95 (978-1-57815-060-1(4), 1052, Media Bks Audio) Media Bks NJ.
About wealth, power & passion.

Lovemakers. abr. ed. Judith Gould. Read by Katey Sagal. 2 cass. (Running Time: 3 hrs.). 1991. 15.95 set. (978-1-879371-08-8(1), 40050) Pub Mills.
Elizabeth-Anne Hale, stunning & sensual, came out of Texas to found a hotel empire & to try to find happiness with a man she could not resist & children she could not control. She is the first of four generations of daring, desiring Hale women who fight with passion for what they want - love, sex, power, wealth - only to learn that trying to "have it all" carries a powerful price of its own. Based on The New York Times bestselling book!.

Lovemaking. Read by Mary Richards & Dennis MacMillan. 1 cass. (Running Time: 83 min.). (Series Two Thousand). 2007. audio compact disk 19.95 (978-1-56136-102-1(X)) Master Your Mind.

Lover. unabr. ed. Amanda Brookfield. Narrated by Briony Sykes. 7 cass. (Running Time: 9 hrs. 30 mins.). 2001. 63.00 (978-1-84197-175-9(8), H1159E7) Recorded Bks.
Numb with shock, Frances Copeland has to face the fact that her husband has died horrifyingly early. After being a wife & mother for over twenty years, she suddenly finds herself adrift & insecure. Life for her grown up children is not straightforward either. However, when Daniel Groves makes a somewhat untoward entry into their lives, things become at once easier & more complicated.

Lover: The Love Poetry of Carl Sandburg. Michael Hopp. 1 CD. (Running Time: 47 mins. 42 secs.). audio compact disk Spring Hill CO.

Lover Avenged. unabr. ed. J. R. Ward, pseud. (Running Time: 16 hrs.). (Black Dagger Brotherhood Ser.: Bk. 7). (ENG.). (gr. 12 up). 2009. audio compact disk 49.95 (978-0-14-314462-5(6), PengAudBks) Penguin Grp USA.

***Lover Avenged.** unabr. ed. J. R. Ward, pseud. Narrated by Jim Frangione. 1 Playaway. (Running Time: 23 hrs. 15 mins.). 2009. 69.75 (978-1-4407-5234-6(6)); 113.75 (978-1-4361-8053-5(8)) Recorded Bks.

***Lover Avenged.** unabr. ed. J. R. Ward, pseud. Narrated by Jim Frangione. 19 CDs. (Running Time: 23 hrs. 15 mins.). (Black Dagger Brotherhood Ser.: Bk. 7). 2009. audio compact disk 123.75 (978-1-4361-8054-2(6)) Recorded Bks.

***Lover Avenged.** unabr. collector's ed. J. R. Ward, pseud. Narrated by Jim Frangione. 19 CDs. (Running Time: 23 hrs. 15 mins.). 2009. audio compact disk 81.95 (978-1-4361-8055-9(4)) Recorded Bks.

Lover in the Rough. abr. ed. Elizabeth Lowell. Read by Laural Merlington. (Running Time: 10800 sec.). 2008. audio compact disk 14.99 (978-1-4233-2389-1(0), 9781423323891, BCD Value Price) Brilliance Audio.

Lover in the Rough. unabr. ed. Elizabeth Lowell. Read by Laural Merlington. (Running Time: 7 hrs.). 2007. 39.25 (978-1-4233-2385-3(8), 9781423323853, Brlnc Audio MP3 Lib); 24.95 (978-1-4233-2384-6(X), 9781423323846, Brilliance MP3); 39.25 (978-1-4233-2387-7(4), 9781423323877, BADLE); 24.95 (978-1-4233-2386-0(6), 9781423323860, BAD); 69.25 (978-1-4233-2381-5(5), 9781423323815, BrilAudUnabridg); audio compact disk 82.25 (978-1-4233-2383-9(1), 9781423323839, BriAudCD Unabrid); audio compact disk 29.95 (978-1-4233-2382-2(3), 9781423323822, Bril Audio CD Unabri) Brilliance Audio.

Lover Mine. unabr. ed. J. R. Ward, pseud. (Running Time: 23 hrs.). 2010. audio compact disk 49.95 (978-0-14-314578-3(9), PengAudBks) Penguin Grp USA.

Lover of the Grave. unabr. ed. Andrew Taylor. Read by Julia Franklin. 9 cass. (Running Time: 11 hrs.). (Sound Ser.). 2002. 76.95 (978-1-86042-590-5(9)) Pub: UlverLrgPrint GBR. Dist(s): Ulverscroft US
After the coldest night of the year, they find a man's body dangling from the Hanging Tree on the outskirts of a village near Lydmouth. Is it suicide, murder, or accidental death? Journalist Jill Francis and Detective Inspector Thornhill become involved in the case in separate ways. Meanwhile a Peeping Tom is preying upon Lydmouth; Jill has just moved into her own house and is afraid she is being watched. And there are more distractions, on a personal level, for both policeman and reporter.

Lover Within: A Study in Masculine Psychology. Read by Robert Moore. 8 cass. (Running Time: 7 hrs.). 1990. 48.95 (978-0-7822-0199-4(7), 403S) C G Jung IL.
The archetype of the Lover is the archetype men find most difficult to access without experiencing frightening emotional states. Without dis-identification from this archetype - & without a dynamic connection to it - a man may find himself alternately promiscuous & isolated, emotionally vulnerable & interpersonally exploitative, impulsive & addictive, yet afraid of his passion. Topics include the archetypal Lover in myth, folklore & religion; the Lover's role in masculine selfhood; psychopathology & the Boy Lover; & resources for healing the Lover.

Loverboy. Michele Jaffe. Read by Liz Sazzi. 11 vols. 2004. bk. 49.95 (978-0-7927-3243-3(X), SLD 664, Chivers Sound Lib) AudioGO.

Lovers. Heather Macauley. 1 cass. (Running Time: 78 min.). 1996. 9.99 (978-0-9648093-8-3(9)) HOME Pubng.
Relationships.

Lovers. abr. ed. John Connolly. Read by Jay O. Sanders. 6 CDs. (Running Time: 6 hrs. 0 mins. 0 sec.). (ENG.). 2009. audio compact disk 29.99 (978-0-7435-8210-0(1)) Pub: S&S Audio. Dist(s): S and S Inc

Lovers. unabr. ed. Judith Krantz. Read by Liza Ross. 14 cass. (Running Time: 17 hr. 45 min.). (Isis Ser.). (J). 2001. 99.95 (978-1-85695-924-7(4), 950304) Pub: ISIS Lrg Prnt GBR. Dist(s): Ulverscroft US

***Lovers.** unabr. ed. Vendela Vida. Read by Suzanne Toren. (ENG.). 2010. (978-0-06-201607-2(5), Harper Audio); (978-0-06-197866-1(3), Harper Audio) HarperCollins Pubs.

***Lovers: A Thriller.** abr. ed. John Connolly. Read by Jay O. Sanders. (Running Time: 6 hrs. 0 mins. 0 sec.). (ENG.). 2011. audio compact disk 14.99 (978-1-4423-3816-6(4)) Pub: S&S Audio. Dist(s): S and S Inc

Lovers & Liars. abr. ed. Sally Beauman. Read by Michael Page. 2 cass. (Running Time: 3 hrs.). 2000. 7.95 (978-1-57815-018-2(3), 1065, Media Bks Audio) Media Bks NJ.
A romantic, spellbinding suspenseful journey into the mysteries of the heart, where love can sustain the soul or twist it cruelly.

Lovers & Liars. unabr. ed. Josephine Cox. Read by Carole Boyd. 7 cass. 2005. 59.95 (978-0-7927-3463-5(7), CSL 754); audio compact disk 79.95 (978-0-7927-3464-2(5), SLD 754) AudioGO.

Lovers & Players. Jackie Collins. 2006. audio compact disk 29.95 (978-0-7927-3960-9(4), CMP 896) AudioGO.

Lovers & Players. Jackie Collins. Read by Isabel Keating. 10 CDs. (Running Time: 64500 sec.). (Sound Library). 2006. audio compact disk 94.95 (978-0-7927-3889-3(6), SLD 896) AudioGO.

Lovers & Players. abr. ed. Jackie Collins. 2006. 14.95 (978-1-59397-855-6(3)) Pub: Macmill Audio. Dist(s): Macmillan

Lovers & Players. abr. ed. Jackie Collins. Read by Jackie Collins. Read by Jack Scalia et al. 4 CDs. (Running Time: 5 hrs. 0 mins. 0 sec.). (ENG.). 2006. audio compact disk 24.95 (978-1-59397-854-9(5)) Pub: Macmill Audio. Dist(s): Macmillan

Lovers & Players. abr. ed. Jackie Collins. Read by Jackie Collins. Read by Sydney Tamila Poitier et al. 4 CDs. (Running Time: 5 hrs. 0 mins. 0 sec.). (ENG.). 2008. audio compact disk 14.95 (978-1-4272-0480-6(2)) Pub: Macmill Audio. Dist(s): Macmillan

***Lovers & Players.** abr. ed. Jackie Collins. Read by Sydney Tamiia Poitier et al. (Running Time: 5 hrs. 0 mins. 0 sec.). (ENG.). 2011. audio compact disk 14.99 (978-1-4272-1189-7(2)) Pub: Macmill Audio. Dist(s): Macmillan

Lovers & Players. unabr. ed. Jackie Collins. Read by Isabel Keating. 10 CDs. (Running Time: 18 hrs. 0 mins. 0 sec.). (ENG.). 2006. audio compact disk 49.95 (978-1-59397-874-7(X)) Pub: Macmill Audio. Dist(s): Macmillan

Lover's Complaint. (SWC 240) HarperCollins Pubs.

Lover's Gift: From Her to Him in Poetry, Prose & Music. Read by Laura Paton. 1 cass. (Running Time: 1 hr. 17 mins.). 2000. 9.98 (978-962-634-688-4(4), NA118814) Naxos.
A collection of poetry and music expressing the romantic feelings, from a women's perspective, of poets, writers and composers through the ages, including Elizabeth Barrett Browning, Katherine Mansfield, Shakespeare's Juliet and the music of Mendelssohn, Tchaikovsky, Puccini and Elgar.

Lover's Gift: From Her to Him in Poetry, Prose & Music. unabr. ed. Read by Laura Paton. 1 CD. (Running Time: 1 hr. 17 mins.). 2000. audio compact disk 11.98 (978-962-634-188-9(2), NA118812) Naxos.

Lover's Gift: From Him to Her in Poetry, Prose & Music. Read by Michael Sheen. 1 cass. (Running Time: 1 hr. 17 mins.). 2000. 9.98 (978-962-634-687-7(6), NA118714) Naxos.
A collection of poetry and music expressing the romantic feelings, from a man's perspective, of poets, writers and composers through the ages, including William Shakespeare, Robert Burns, Lord Byron, Puccini, Grieg, Faure and Elgar.

Lover's Gift: From Him to Her in Poetry, Prose & Music. unabr. ed. Read by Michael Sheen. 1 CD. (Running Time: 1 hr. 17 mins.). 2000. audio compact disk 11.98 (978-962-634-187-2(4), NA118712) Naxos.

Lover's Gift from Her to Him: Poetry, Prose & Music. abr. ed. Read by Laura Paton. (Running Time: 4667 sec.). 2006. audio compact disk 14.98 (978-962-634-388-3(5), Naxos AudioBooks) Naxos.

Lover's Gift from Him to Her: Poetry-Prose Music. Read by Michael Sheen. (Running Time: 4510 sec.). 2006. audio compact disk 14.98 (978-962-634-389-0(3), Naxos AudioBooks) Naxos.

Lover's Lane. unabr. ed. Jill Marie Landis. Read by Sandra Burr. (Running Time: 11 hrs.). 2004. 39.25 (978-1-59335-501-2(7), 1593355017, Brlnc Audio MP3 Lib) Brilliance Audio.
For six years Carly Nolan has built a life for herself and her son Christopher, never getting too close to anyone. Nobody in the sleepy little beach community suspects she is running - from the mistakes she made in her youth, the memory of her fiancé Rick and his unexpected death, and the rich, powerful people who want to take away her child. She has carefully concealed her troubled past from the folks in the isolated haven of Twilight Cove. Until now. Private investigator Jake Montgomery has been looking for elusive Caroline Graham since the day she disappeared with Rick's baby. All Jake wants is answers. He finally finds her living under an assumed name, no longer a wild teenager, but a beautiful, devoted single mother who captivates him like no one ever has before. As Carly cautiously allows Jake into her life, she begins to trust another person for the first time in a long while. She never imagines that Jake, caught between his mission and his growing passion, poses a threat to her protected world. For if her secrets are revealed, she might lose the child she holds so dear - and the man who possesses the key to her heart.

Lover's Lane. unabr. ed. Jill Marie Landis. Read by Sandra Burr. (Running Time: 11 hrs.). 2004. 39.25 (978-1-59710-470-8(1), 1597104701, BADLE); 24.95 (978-1-59710-471-5(X), 159710471X, BAD) Brilliance Audio.

Lover's Lane. unabr. ed. Jill Marie Landis. Read by Sandra Burr. (Running Time: 11 hrs.). 2004. 24.95 (978-1-59335-227-1(1), 1593352271) Soulmate Audio Bks.

Lovers' Room. Steven Carroll & Stan Pretty. 2009. 61.95 (978-1-84652-346-5(X)); audio compact disk 79.95 (978-1-84652-347-2(8)) Pub: Magna Story GBR. Dist(s): Ulverscroft US

Love's Awakening see Great French & Russian Stories, Vol. 1, A Collection

Love's Awakening see Favorite Stories by Guy de Maupassant

Love's Emerald Flame. unabr. ed. Willa Lambert. Read by Denise S. Utter. 8 cass. (Running Time: 9 hrs. 24 min.). 1994. 49.95 (978-1-55686-536-7(8)) Books in Motion.
All reporter Diana Green was required to do was go to some remote Incan ruins & snap a few pictures. But what was meant to be a simple job became a deadly jungle trek.

***Love's Encore.** abr. ed. Sandra Brown. Read by Natalie Ross. (Running Time: 3 hrs.). 2010. 14.99 (978-1-4418-8085-7(2), 9781441880857, BAD); audio compact disk 14.99 (978-1-4418-2691-6(2), 9781441826916, BACD) Brilliance Audio.

***Love's Encore.** unabr. ed. Sandra Brown. Read by Natalie Ross. (Running Time: 6 hrs.). 2010. audio compact disk 29.99 (978-1-4418-2685-5(8), 9781441826855, Bril Audio CD Unabri); audio compact disk 74.97 (978-1-4418-2686-2(6), 9781441826862, BriAudCD Unabrid) Brilliance Audio.

***Love's Encore.** unabr. ed. Sandra Brown. Read by Natalie Ross. (Running Time: 6 hrs.). 2010. 24.99 (978-1-4418-2687-9(4), 9781441826879, Brilliance MP3); 39.97 (978-1-4418-2688-6(2), 9781441826886, Brlnc Audio MP3 Lib); 39.97 (978-1-4418-2690-9(4), 9781441826909, BADLE); 24.99 (978-1-4418-2689-3(0), 9781441826893, BAD) Brilliance Audio.

Love's Humility. 8 cass. 24.95 (20128, HarperThor) HarpC GBR.

Love's Labors. 1 cass. (Running Time: 1 hr.). 1983. 7.95 (978-1-58638-569-9(0)) Nilgiri Pr.
The facts behind the poetry of love.

Love's Labor's Lost. unabr. ed. William Shakespeare. Narrated by Greg Wise et al. (Arkangel Shakespeare Ser.). (ENG.). 2005. audio compact disk 19.95 (978-1-932219-19-7(6)) Pub: AudioGO. Dist(s): Perseus Dist
Young King Ferdinand and his courtiers agree to dedicate three years to ascetic and celibate study. But when the fetching Princess of France and her ladies arrive on a diplomatic mission, the men's resolve is put to an arduous - and witty - test. The tension between their vow and their passion forms the subject of this charming, sparkling early comedy. Performed by Greg Wise, Samantha Bond, and the Arkangel cast.

Love's Labor's Lost. unabr. ed. William Shakespeare. Read by Audio Partners Staff. 2 cass. (Running Time: 2 hrs. 27 mins.). (Arkangel Shakespeare Ser.). 2004. 17.95 (978-1-932219-59-3(5), Atlntc Mnthly) Pub: Grove-Atltc. Dist(s): PerseuPGW

Love's Labor's Lost. unabr. ed. William Shakespeare. Perf. by Anna Massey et al. Music by Derek Oldfield. 3 cass. 19.95 (SCN 141) J Norton Pubs.
Lyrical play in which three young men take a vow of chastity to pursue academics but are soon overcome by the charms of three young women.

Love's Labour's Lost. William Shakespeare. Read by Lister Sinclair et al. 1 CD. (Running Time: 3600 sec.). Dramatization. 2006. audio compact disk 15.95 (978-0-660-19551-3(8), CBC Audio) Canadian Broadcasting CAN.

***Love's Labour's Lost.** abr. ed. William Shakespeare. Read by Ian Richardson & (null) Cast. (ENG.). 2005. (978-0-06-088641-7(2), Caedmon); (978-0-06-112607-9(1), Caedmon) HarperCollins Pubs.

Love's Labours Lost. unabr. ed. William Shakespeare. 2 cass. (Running Time: 3 hrs.). (Arkangel Complete Shakespeare Ser.). 2001. 17.95 (PengAudBks) Penguin Grp USA.

Love's Laws. (BI06) Master Mind.

Love's Light: The Human Aura. Stan Kendz. 1 cass. (Running Time: 090 min.). 1999. 17.95 (978-1-893527-48-5(4)) Namaste Pr NY.

Love's Long Journey. unabr. ed. Janette Oke. Narrated by Ruth Ann Phimister. 6 cass. (Running Time: 8 hrs. 15 mins.). (Love Comes Softly Ser.: Vol. 3). 1982. 59.75 (978-1-4193-0348-7(1), K1112MC) Recorded Bks.

Love's Melody. Perf. by Kim Waters. 1 cass., 1 CD. 7.98 (SH 5042); audio compact disk 12.78 (SH 5042) NewSound.

Loves Music, Loves to Dance. Mary Higgins Clark. Read by Kate Burton. 2004. 10.95 (978-0-7435-4515-0(X)) Pub: S&S Audio. Dist(s): S and S Inc

Loves Music, Loves to Dance. unabr. ed. Mary Higgins Clark. Read by Donada Peters. 8 cass. (Running Time: 8 hrs.). 1992. 48.00 (978-0-7366-2066-6(4), 2874) Books on Tape.
Erin Kelley & Darcy Scott, best friends since college, move to New York City for the glitz. Their timing is perfect, & life, wonderful. Then, on a lark, they help a friend prep a documentary on "boy wants girl" personal ads. It looks like fun.

Loves Music, Loves to Dance. unabr. ed. Mary Higgins Clark. Narrated by Christina Moore. 6 cass. (Running Time: 8 hrs. 30 mins.). 2005. 59.75 (978-1-4025-3531-4(7), 97234) Recorded Bks.
Number one New York Times best-selling author and Queen of Suspense, Mary Higgins Clark never falters to thrill her readers and keep them on the edge of their seats. The Washington Post calls her:a born storyteller." When they graduate from college, best friends Erin and Darcy move to New York to pursue their careers. But then Erin goes missing after placing a personal ad in a magazine. Now Darcy fears that she may be next.

Loves of Charles II. unabr. ed. Cornelia Otis Skinner. Read by Cornelia Otis Skinner. 1 cass. (Running Time: 50 min.). 10.95 (978-0-8045-0813-1(5), SAC 44-6) Spoken Arts.
Charles as reflected by six of the women who either loved him or worked at loving him for pay.

Love's Pure Light: A Celebration of Christmas. Perf. by His Majesty's Musicians. 1 cass. (Running Time: 50 mins.). 1999. 9.95 (T8958) Liguori Pubns.
In celebration of the light of God, talented artists sing of the birth of Jesus Christ. Breathes new life into some traditional carols.

Love's Several Faces. Gary F. Hutchison. 1 cass. (Running Time: 90 min.). 1994. 7.50 (978-1-885631-02-2(2)) G F Hutchison.
Discusses several types of love, how each operates, & what to expect (& not to) from each kind.

Love's Shadow. unabr. ed. Ada Leverson. Narrated by Flo Gibson. 4 cass. (Running Time: 6 hrs.). 2003. 19.95 (978-1-55685-728-7(4)) Audio Bk Con.
Bruce Ottley, a hypochondriac and crashing bore, and his delightful wife Edith introduce us to many characters in Edwardian London.

Love's Shadow. unabr. ed. Ada Leverson. Read by Shaela Connor. 6 cass. (Running Time: 6 hrs. 42 min.). Dramatization. 1992. 39.95 (978-1-55686-444-5(2), 444) Books in Motion.
To love, or not to love, that is the question, or at least that is the question posed by Hyacinth Verney, the charming, frivolous & somewhat confused heroine. Leverson turns her amused & penetrating eye to the foibles & follies of the British "leisured" class.

Love's Tangled Web. Joy St. Clair. Read by Angela Down. 4 cass. (Running Time: 6 hrs.). 1999. 44.95 (65611) Pub: Soundings Ltd GBR. Dist(s): Ulverscroft US

Love's Transforming Power. Gary V. Whetstone. 4 cass. (Running Time: 6 hrs.). (Freedom Ser.). 1994. pap. bk. 35.00 (978-1-58866-219-4(5), VROO7A) Gary Whet Pub.
God's love for us is awesome. This series will anchor you in the revelation of God's love that will transform you to become secure, moldable, & pliable in God's hands.

Lovesick: A Novel. abr. ed. Angeles Mastretta. Read by Liz Torres. 3 cass. (Running Time: 4 hrs. 30 min.). 1997. 21.95 (978-1-57453-178-7(6)) Audio Lit.
Story encompassing fifty years in the history of a nation, a family & a love affair.

Lovewords, Vol. 1. Millie Lee et al. Ed. by Chelley Kitzmiller & Steven Sanders. Intro. by Patricia Matthews. (Running Time: 1 hr. 24 min.). (Lovewords Romantic Audio Drama Ser.). 1987. 9.95 (978-0-929536-00-2(2)) Emb Cassettes.
Short, dramatized, romantic stories designed for an adult female audience.

Lovewords, Vol. 2. Patricia Matthews et al. Ed. by Steven Sanders. Intro. by Rita Rainville. 1 cass. (Running Time: 1 hr. 41 min.). (Lovewords Romantic Audio Drama Ser.). 9.95 (978-0-929536-01-9(0)) Emb Cassettes.
Features short, dramatized, romantic stories designed for an adult female audience.

Lovey Mary. Based on a book by Alice Caldwell Hegan Rice. (J). Audio Bk Con.

Love2U. Mark Victor Hansen. 4 cass. 60.00 (4) M V Hansen.
Enhance your own & everyone else's self-esteem.

Lovin' Life. Contrib. by Gaither Vocal Band & Bill Gaither. Prod. by Bill Gaither et al. 2008. audio compact disk 13.99 (978-5-557-44622-8(2)) Gaither Music Co.

Loving. Michael Ballam. 2 cass. (Running Time: 3 hrs.). 14.98 (978-1-55503-882-3(4), 1100750) Covenant Comms.
A sensitive look at the wondrous effects of loving.

Loving a Man, Loving a Woman. 4 CDs. 2005. audio compact disk 28.00 (978-1-933207-04-9(3)) Ransomed Heart.

Loving a Woman in Two Worlds. Robert Bly. Ed. by William Booth. 1 cass. (Running Time: 40 min.). 1986. 7.95 Ally Pr.
Bly reads poems from the book of the same title.

Loving a Woman in Two Worlds. Robert Bly. 1 cass. 9.00 (A0604-86) Sound Photosyn.
In this session he is evocative, patient & poetically articulate.

Loving & Healing Your Inner Adolescent. Martha B. Beveridge. 1 cass. (Running Time: 60 min.). 1994. 9.95 (978-1-889237-28-2(0)) Options Now.
Discover what the teenager in you has to teach you about yourself. Great for parents & teens.

Loving Chloe. unabr. ed. Jo-Ann Mapson. Read by Kate Forbes. 8 vols. (Running Time: 12 hrs.). 2000. bk. 69.95 (978-0-7927-2260-1(4), CSL 149, Chivers Sound Lib) AudioGO.
34-year-old Chloe Morgan appears on Hank Oliver's doorstep in Arizona pregnant with his child. Meanwhile, a local Navajo legend named Junior Whitebear returns home to collect his father's ashes and renew his spirit. Upon his arrival, he meets newcomer Chloe Morgan, and quickly begins to fall in love.

Loving Christ. Joseph M. Stowell. 2 cass. (Running Time: 2 hrs.). 2000. 16.99 Zondervan.

Loving Christ. unabr. ed. Joseph M. Stowell. 2000. 17.99 (978-0-310-22976-6(6)) Zondervan.

Loving Communication: Giving & Receiving Energy. unabr. ed. Galexis. 2 cass. (Running Time: 3 hrs.). 1997. 19.95 Set. (978-1-56089-050-8(9), G131) Visionary FL.
Practical living of spiritual principles through understanding & utilizing energies & frequencies in communication. Meditation included.

Loving Communications. Barry Tesar. 1 cass. (Running Time: 1 hr.). (Subliminal Inspiration Ser.). 1992. 9.98 (978-1-56470-012-4(7)) Success Cass.
Subliminal program.

Loving Daughters. unabr. l.t. ed. Olga Masters. Read by Beverly Dunn. 8 cass. (Running Time: 12 hrs.). 1998. pap. bk. (978-1-86340-591-1(7), 551004) Bolinda Pubng AUS.
Set in a tiny farming township south of Sydney after World War I, two lively young women, Una & Enid Herbert, keep house for their father & brothers. Family matters fill both their lives until the Reverend Colin Edwards moves into the district. Hungry for love, both women are drawn to him, & he to them, in a rapidly developing triangle of love & tension.

***Loving Dead.** unabr. ed. Amelia Beamer. (Running Time: 9 hrs.). 2010. 24.99 (978-1-4418-6837-4(2), 9781441868374, BAD); 39.97 (978-1-4418-6838-1(0), 9781441868381, BADLE) Brilliance Audio.

***Loving Dead.** unabr. ed. Amelia Beamer. Read by Emily Durante. (Running Time: 8 hrs.). 2010. 39.97 (978-1-4418-6836-7(4), 9781441868367, Brlnc Audio MP3 Lib); 24.99 (978-1-4418-6835-0(6), 9781441868350, Brilliance MP3); audio compact disk 29.99 (978-1-4418-6833-6(X), 9781441868336, Bril Audio CD Unabri); audio compact disk 79.97 (978-1-4418-6834-3(8), 9781441868343, BriAudCD Unabrid) Brilliance Audio.

Loving Each Other. Leo F. Buscaglia. Read by Leo F. Buscaglia. 4 cass. (Running Time: 90 min.). 44.95 (978-1-55525-219-9(2), 139A) Nightingale-Conant.
Analyzes the importance of such factors as the ability to communicate, the need for compassion, the healing power of forgiveness.

Loving Enemies. Jeannie Johnson. 2007. 84.95 (978-1-84559-792-4(3)) Pub: ISIS Audio GBR. Dist(s): Ulverscroft US

Loving Enemies. Jeannie Johnson. Read by Penelope Freeman. (Running Time: 46800 sec.). 2007. audio compact disk 99.95 (978-1-84559-793-1(1)) Pub: ISIS Audio GBR. Dist(s): Ulverscroft US

Loving Frank. Nancy Horan. Read by Joyce Bean. (Playaway Adult Fiction Ser.). 2008. 104.99 (978-1-60640-918-3(2)) Find a World.

Loving Frank. abr. ed. Nancy Horan. Read by Joyce Bean. (Running Time: 6 hrs.). 2008. audio compact disk 14.99 (978-1-4233-3293-0(8), 9781423332930, BCD Value Price) Brilliance Audio.

Loving Frank. unabr. ed. Nancy Horan. Read by Joyce Bean. (Running Time: 15 hrs.). 2007. 39.25 (978-1-4233-3291-6(1), 9781423332916, BADLE); 24.95 (978-1-4233-3290-9(3), 9781423332909, BAD); 97.25 (978-1-4233-3285-5(7), 9781423332855, BrilAudUnabridg); audio compact disk 38.95 (978-1-4233-3286-2(5), 9781423332862, Bril Audio CD Unabri); audio compact disk 24.95 (978-1-4233-3288-6(1), 9781423332886, Brilliance MP3); audio compact disk 39.25 (978-1-4233-3289-3(X), 9781423332893, Brlnc Audio MP3 Lib); audio compact disk 112.25 (978-1-4233-3287-9(3), 9781423332879, BriAudCD Unabrid) Brilliance Audio.

Loving God & Hating Evil Series. Jack Deere. 2 cass. (Running Time: 3 hrs.). 2000. 10.00 (JD05-000) Morning NC.
"Satan's Counterfeit Strategy" & "God's Army." The teaching contained in this miniseries can change your life & strengthen your relationship with God.

Loving Group Vol. 1: Breaking down Walls & Building up the Body. Perf. by Cecilia Yau. 1 cass. (Running Time: 90 mins.). (CHI.). (C). 2000. 5.00 (978-1-930490-01-7(1), 10B-201A) CCM Pubs.
Why are there walls among men? Is it possible to break them down? God's eternal plan is to unify all things in the universe thru Christ who first built the loving group on earth, namely: the church. The church building method is based on saving individual's souls & through these individuals to break down barriers of human relations for loving unity.

Loving Group Vol. 2: Centering in Christ. Perf. by Cecilia Yau. 1 cass. (Running Time: 90 mins.). (CHI.). (C). 2000. 5.00 (978-1-930490-02-4(X), 10B-201B) CCM Pubs.
How do we know a church's growth is based on God's blueprint? Chapter 3 of the Epistle to the Ephesians shows us the rules of church development: Christ as center, believer's mutual love as circumference with the great power of the Holy Spirit operating in their hearts, overcoming human weaknesses to accomplish God's plan.

Loving Group Vol. 3: Truth in Love. Perf. by Cecilia Yau. 1 cass. (Running Time: 90 mins.). (CHI.). (C). 2000. 5.00 (978-1-930490-03-1(8), 10B-201C) CCM Pubs.
Christians' self-centered nature & individual differences create tension in churches. Chapter 4 of Ephesians & Chapter 14 of Romans teach us to hold on to the unity of the basic doctrines, to accept differences in non-essential matters & to tell the truth in love.

Loving Group Vol. 4: Mutual Submission. Perf. by Cecilia Yau. 1 cass. (Running Time: 90 mins.). (CHI.). (C). 2000. 5.00 (978-1-930490-04-8(6), 10B-201D) CCM Pubs.
If Christians adopt the worldly system of hierarchy to handle human relations, it will create conflict & become difficult to serve one another genuinely. Chapter 5 of Ephesians points out the break-through path that one must have a heart of willingness to submit to others & reverence for Christ in order to serve one another successfully.

Loving Guidance: Setting Limits Without Guilt. 2. 2001. audio compact disk 15.00 (978-1-889609-20-1(X)) Loving Guidnce.

Loving Heart. Swami Amar Jyoti. 1 cass. 1981. 9.95 (K-47) Truth Consciousness.
Preparing the ground for love. Love is far beyond gratifications, philosophy & blueprints. Understanding born from a loving heart is infallible.

***Loving Jack.** unabr. ed. Nora Roberts. Read by Angela Dawe. (Running Time: 6 hrs.). 2010. 39.97 (978-1-4418-5428-5(2), 9781441854285, Brlnc Audio MP3 Lib); 24.99 (978-1-4418-5427-8(4), 9781441854278, Brilliance MP3); audio compact disk 79.97 (978-1-4418-5426-1(6), 9781441854261, BriAudCD Unabrid); audio compact disk 24.99 (978-1-4418-5425-4(8), 9781441854254, Bril Audio CD Unabri) Brilliance Audio.

***Loving Jack.** unabr. ed. Nora Roberts. Read by Angela Dawe. (Running Time: 7 hrs.). 2010. 39.97 (978-1-4418-5429-2(0), 9781441854292, BADLE) Brilliance Audio.

Loving Jesus. unabr. ed. Mother Teresa of Calcutta. Ed. by Jose Luis Gonzalez-Balado. Narrated by Ruth Ann Phimister. 3 cass. (Running Time: 3 hrs. 30 min.). 1991. 28.00 (K0086L8) Recorded Bks.
Truly a saint for the 20th century, Mother Teresa taught compassion not only for the sick & destitute, but also for the lonely, neglected & unappreciated, who surround us everyday.

Loving-Kindness Meditation. Sujatha Peradeniye. Prod. by Taldish Castle Films. Narrated by Kurt Piepenbrok. 1 CD. (Running Time: 50 mins.). 2006. audio compact disk 16.00 (978-0-9793525-0-8(9)) Taldish.

Loving Leadership: Rekindling the Human Spirit in Business, Relationships & Life. Christopher Loving. Read by Christopher Loving. 1 cass. (Running Time: 1 hr.). 1996. 12.95 (978-1-885408-14-3(5), LL007) Listen & Live.
Chris Loving shares a unique & thought-provoking perspective on leadership in business, relationships & life.

Loving Little Ones. Douglas Wilson. (ENG.). 2008. audio compact disk 16.00 (978-1-59128-394-2(9)) Canon Pr ID.

Loving Marriage. Rand H. Packer. 1 cass. 1998. 9.95 (978-1-57008-403-4(3), Bkcraft Inc) Deseret Bk.

Loving Matters. Bill Kerley. 6 cass. 2000. 59.95 (978-1-886298-06-4(8)) Bayou Pubng.
For people who want to ensure that love is exchanged & experienced in health & useful ways in the relationships they have.

Loving Memories from Dog to Dog Two Adventures with Shivers the Hamsters. Howard W. Gabriel, III. (J). (gr. k-8). 1987. 3.95 (978-0-936997-07-0(9), T85-07) M & H Enter.
In the First Story, a Man Dwells on All the Good Times Shared with His Old Dog. But Long after the Dog Dies, the Man's Daughter Struggles to Get Another Puppy. In the Second Story, a Wimpy Little Hamster Has to Learn to Try in Order to Save His Own Life & Rescue His Family. Later He Acquires a New Friend Through Misadventure.

***Loving Monday Audio Book: Succeeding in Business Without Selling Your Soul.** John D. Beckett. (ENG.). 2009. 16.00 (978-0-8308-5564-3(5), IVP Bks) InterVarsity.

Loving My Inner Child. 2007. audio compact disk 19.95 (978-1-56136-086-4(4)) Master Your Mind.

Loving Myself. Rick Brown. Read by Rick Brown. Ed. by John Quatro. 1 cass. (Running Time: 30 min.). (Subliminal - Soft Sounds Ser.). 1993. 10.95 (978-1-57100-073-6(9), S104); 10.95 (978-1-57100-097-2(6), W104); 10.95 (978-1-57100-121-4(2), H104) Sublime Sftware.
Builds self respect & self esteem.

Loving Myself, No. E104. Rick Brown. Read by Rick Brown. Ed. by John Quatro. 1 cass. (Running Time: 30 min.). (Subliminal - Easy Listening Ser.). 1993. 10.95 (978-1-57100-001-9(1)) Sublime Sftware.
"Loving Myself" builds self respect & self esteem.

Loving Myself, No. J104. Rick Brown. Read by Rick Brown. Ed. by John Quatro. 1 cass. (Running Time: 30 min.). (Subliminal - Easy Listening Ser.). 1993. 10.95 (978-1-57100-025-5(9)) Sublime Sftware.

Loving Myself, No. N104. Rick Brown. Read by Rick Brown. Ed. by John Quatro. 1 cass. (Running Time: 30 min.). (Subliminal - New Age Ser.). 1993. 10.95 (978-1-57100-049-1(6)) Sublime Sftware.

Loving Not Wisely but Too Well: Othello, Specialness, & a Course in Miracles. Kenneth Wapnick. 4 CDs. 2003. audio compact disk 26.00 (978-1-59142-116-0(0), CD90) Foun Miracles.
Shakespeare's "Othello," looked at through the lens of "A Course in Miracles," offers a penetrating if not painful insight into the nature of guilt; its origins in our special relationship with God, and its shadowy expression in our personal life of special relationships. Othello's choice to believe in Iago's lies-the ego's thought system-rather than Desdemona's innocence-the Atonement-is discussed from the perspective of our need to destroy love, and then experience the horrible consequences of the ensuing guilt. Othello's decision to trust his "friend" and murder his wife on the grounds of infidelity is irrevocable; not so, however, our decision for the ego, which can be undone in the instant we choose to trust our true friend and practice his lessons of forgiveness. Thus does Jesus add a "sixth act" to Shakespeare's five-act tragedy.

Loving Ourselves Free. Jane E. Latimer. Read by Jane E. Latimer. 4 cass. (Running Time: 73 min.). (Filling the Void Ser.). 1990. 9.95 (978-1-882109-02-9(3)) CoreWay Media.
Compulsive-addictive behavior is an attempt to love ourselves. The guided healing meditations include: "Meeting Your Non-Judgemental Observer," "Meeting Your Higher Power" & "An Experience in Self-Acceptance & Forgiveness".

Loving Personality. Rick Brown. Read by Rick Brown. Ed. by John Quatro. 1 cass. (Running Time: 30 min.). (Subliminal - New Age Ser.). 1993. 10.95 (978-1-57100-069-9(0), N149); 10.95 (978-1-57100-093-4(3), S149); 10.95 (978-1-57100-117-7(4), W149); 10.95 (978-1-57100-141-2(7), H149) Sublime Sftware.
Enhances natural warmth & love.

Loving Personality, No. E149. Rick Brown. Read by Rick Brown. Ed. by John Quatro. 1 cass. (Running Time: 30 min.). (Subliminal - Easy Listening Ser.). 1993. 10.95 (978-1-57100-021-7(6)) Sublime Sftware.
"Loving Personality" enhances natural warmth & love.

Loving Personality, No. J149. Rick Brown. Read by Rick Brown. Ed. by John Quatro. 1 cass. (Running Time: 30 min.). (Subliminal - Jazz Ser.). 1993. 10.95 (978-1-57100-045-3(3)) Sublime Sftware.

Loving Relationship. Read by Mary Richards. 12.95 (403) Master Your Mind.
Allows loving experiences to flow into the heart.

Loving Relationship-Subliminal. Read by Mary Richards. 1 cass. (Running Time: 60 min.). (Subliminal Impact Ser.). 2007. audio compact disk 19.95 (978-1-56136-049-9(X)) Master Your Mind.

Loving Relationships. Stuart Wilde. Read by Stuart Wilde. 1 cass. (Running Time: 1 hr.). 1996. 10.95 (978-1-56170-289-3(7), 299) Hay House.
Nurture the relationships that support you, & ditch the ones that don't!.

Loving Scoundrel. abr. ed. Johanna Lindsey. Read by Laural Merlington. 5. (Running Time: 21600 sec.). (Malory Ser.). 2007. audio compact disk 14.99 (978-1-4233-1954-2(0), 9781423319542, BCD Value Price) Brilliance Audio.

Loving Scoundrel. unabr. ed. Johanna Lindsey. 9 CDs. (Running Time: 10 hrs.). (Malory Ser.). 2004. audio compact disk 97.25 (978-1-59086-391-6(7), 1590863917, BriAudCD Unabrid) Brilliance Audio.

Loving Scoundrel. unabr. ed. Johanna Lindsey. Read by Laural Merlington. 7 cass. (Running Time: 10 hrs.). (Malory Ser.). 2004. 32.95 (978-1-59086-387-9(9), 1590863879, BAU); 82.25 (978-1-59086-388-6(7), 1590863887, BrilAudUnabridg); audio compact disk 36.95 (978-1-59086-390-9(9), 1590863909, Bril Audio CD Unabri) Brilliance Audio.
Enter the privileged world of English aristocrats and experience the passion, intrigue, and romantic pleasures of the incomparable Malorys - a family of dashing rogues, rakehell adventurers, and spirited ladies. Now Jeremy, the son of gentleman pirate James Malory, falls in love. . . . When Danny, a young woman who grew up on the streets of London with no memory of her real family, is banished from her gang because she helped handsome rakehell Jeremy Malory steal back the jewels his friend lost in a card game, Danny demands that Jeremy give her a job. She is determined to become respectable in order to fulfill her dream of marrying and starting a family. Intrigued by her beauty and spunk, Jeremy hires Danny as his upstairs maid, although he wants her as his mistress. Under the tutelage of Jeremy and his cousin Regina, Danny blossoms into a lady. Although she is drawn to Jeremy by passionate feelings she has never experienced before, she refuses to be anything more than a servant to him because she knows he is not the marrying kind. When Danny undergoes a Cinderella-like transformation and poses as Jeremy's new love in an attempt to help him avert a scandal, a few highly placed members of the ton remark on how familiar Danny looks. Now tongues are wagging, raising the question of her true identity, which threatens not only Danny's chances of capturing Jeremy's heart but her very life.

Loving Scoundrel. unabr. ed. Johanna Lindsey. Read by Laural Merlington. (Running Time: 10 hrs.). (Malory Ser.). 2004. 24.95 (978-1-59335-308-7(1), 1593353081, Brilliance MP3); 39.25 (978-1-59335-466-4(5), 1593354665, Brlnc Audio MP3 Lib) Brilliance Audio.

Loving Scoundrel. unabr. ed. Johanna Lindsey. Read by Laural Merlington. (Running Time: 10 hrs.). (Malory Ser.). 2004. 39.25 (978-1-59710-472-2(8), 1597104728, BADLE); 24.95 (978-1-59710-473-9(6), 1597104736, BAD) Brilliance Audio.

Loving the Body of Christ. Read by Wayne Monbleau. 2 cass. (Running Time: 2 hrs.). 1993. 10.00 (978-0-944648-24-7(X), LGT-1203) Loving Grace Pubns.
Religious.

Loving the Mentally Ill. (ENG.). 2006. audio compact disk 16.50 (978-1-890246-53-2(0)) B Katie Int Inc.

Loving Through Heartsongs. unabr. ed. Mattie J. T. Stepanek. Read by Mattie J. T. Stepanek. 1 cass. (Running Time: 1 hr.). 2003. 12.98 (978-1-4013-9694-7(1)) Pub: Hyperion. Dist(s): HarperCollins Pubs

Loving Time. Leslie Glass. Read by Jane E. Lawder. 4 cass. (Running Time: 360 min.). No. 3. 2000. 25.00 (978-1-58807-058-6(1)) Am Pubng Inc.

Loving Time. abr. ed. Leslie Glass. Read by M. J. Wilde. 4 vols. No. 3. 2003. (978-1-58807-733-2(0)) Am Pubng Inc.

Loving Will Shakespeare. unabr. ed. Carolyn Meyer. Read by Katherine Kellgren. 6 cass. (Running Time: 6 hrs. 50 mins.). (YA). (gr. 8 up). 2007. 51.75 (978-1-4281-4498-9(6)); audio compact disk 66.75 (978-1-4281-4503-0(6)) Recorded Bks.

Loving Your Child Is Not Enough: Positive Discipline That Works. abr. ed. Nancy Samalin & Martha Moraghan Jablow. Read by Nancy Samalin. (Running Time: 5400 sec.). (ENG.). 2006. audio compact disk 16.95 (978-1-59887-053-4(X), 159887053X) Pub: HighBridge. Dist(s): Workman Pub

Loving Your Long-Distance Relationship, Vol. 1. Stephen Blake. 2 cass. 1998. bk. 13.95 Set. (978-0-9680971-1-3(1)) Anton Publng CAN.

***Loving Your Mate Through the Seasons of Life (Part 1)** 2010. audio compact disk (978-0-9826360-8-4(3)) Mid A Bks & Tapes.

***Loving Your Mate Through the Seasons of Life (Part 2)** 2010. audio compact disk (978-0-9826360-9-1(1)) Mid A Bks & Tapes.

Loving Yourself & Others. Osho Oshos. Read by Osho Oshos. 1 cass. (Running Time: 90 min.). 10.95 (DCM-0003) Oshos.
Answers Questions such as "Can we love more than one person?" &"Why is love so painful"?.

Lovingkindness Meditation. Sharon Salzberg. 2 CDs. 2004. audio compact disk 24.95 (978-1-59179-268-0(1), AW00287D) Sounds True.
Salzberg teaches metta practice, the classic Buddhist meditation for using love to heal ourselves and the world.

Low Carb Yo-Yo: Why Low Carb Diets Dont' Work. unabr. ed. Barry Sears. Narrated by Barry Sears. (ENG.). 2004. 15.39 (978-1-60814-300-9(7)); audio compact disk 21.99 (978-1-58926-691-9(9), 6691) Oasis Audio.

Low Country. Anne Rivers Siddons. Read by Kate Reading. 1998. audio compact disk 80.00 (978-0-7366-5146-2(2)) Books on Tape.

Low Country. unabr. ed. Anne Rivers Siddons. Read by Kate Reading. 8 cass. (Running Time: 12 hrs.). 1998. 64.00 (978-0-7366-4236-1(6), 4733) Books on Tape.
Caroline Venable has everything her Southern heritage promised: money, prestige, a rich husband, a magnificent home & above all her island in the Low country that her beloved Granddaddy left her.

Low Country. unabr. ed. Anne Rivers Siddons. Read by Kate Reading. 10 CDs. (Running Time: 15 hrs.). 2001. audio compact disk 80.00 Books on Tape.

Low Country. unabr. ed. Anne Rivers Siddons. Narrated by Cristine McMurdo-Wallis. 10 CDs. (Running Time: 11 hrs. 45 mins.). 1999. audio compact disk 89.00 (978-0-7887-3444-1(X), C1050E7) Recorded Bks.
Whenever troubles overcome her, Caroline Venable flees to the South Carolina island her granddaddy left her. When those nearest her threaten the pristine hideaway, she is forced to make the toughest decision of her life.

Low Country. unabr. ed. Anne Rivers Siddons. Narrated by Cristine McMurdo-Wallis. 8 cass. (Running Time: 11 hrs. 45 mins.). 1998. 70.00 (978-0-7887-2163-2(1), 95459E7) Recorded Bks.

***Low Country Low Price.** abr. ed. Anne Rivers Siddons. Read by Debra Monk. (ENG.). 2005. (978-0-06-087903-7(3), Harper Audio); (978-0-06-087902-0(5), Harper Audio) HarperCollins Pubs.

Low down on the Low Back. Robert Lieberson. 1 cass. (Running Time: 30 min.). 1997. bk. 15.00 (978-1-58111-000-5(6)) Contemporary Medical.
Covers general anatomy of spine, causes of back & leg pain, various treatment & surgical interventions, preventative principles.

Low Immune. 1 cass. (Running Time: 1 hr.). 2001. 9.95 (CA610) Pub: VisnQst Vid Aud. Dist(s): TMW Media

Low Profile Selling. Tom Hopkins. 6 cass. (Running Time: 6 hrs.). 1995. 69.95 (12690A) Nightingale-Conant.

Low Profile Selling. Tom Hopkins. Read by Tom Hopkins. 6 cass. 1994. 79.95 (978-0-938636-30-4(8), 1465) T Hopkins Intl.
A low key approach to selling products & services.

Low Self Esteem: To Improve Self Image. rev. ed. Robert B. Speigel. 2 cass. (Audio-Suggestion Bedtime Story Tapes Ser.). (J). (gr. k-6). 1993. 19.95 set. (978-0-937977-03-3(9), 97703) Speigel&Assoc.
Therapeutic audio-cassette bedtime stories to treat low self esteem in children. Includes parent's information tape.

Lowboy. unabr. ed. John Wray. (Running Time: 8 hrs. 0 mins.). (ENG.). 2009. 29.95 (978-1-4332-8802-9(8)); 54.95 (978-1-4332-8798-5(6)); audio compact disk 70.00 (978-1-4332-8799-2(4)) Blckstn Audio.

***Lowcountry Summer.** unabr. ed. Dorothea Benton Frank. Read by Robin Miles. (ENG.). 2010. (978-0-06-201608-9(3), Harper Audio); audio compact disk 39.99 (978-0-06-200851-0(X), Harper Audio) HarperCollins Pubs.

***Lowcountry Summer: A Plantation Novel.** unabr. ed. Dorothea Benton Frank. Read by Robin Miles. (ENG.). 2010. (978-0-06-198877-6(4), Harper Audio) HarperCollins Pubs.

Lowell Ponte: Science & Socialism. (Running Time: 60 min.). (Long Beach City College). 1983. 9.00 (F157) Freeland Pr.
Giving historical examples, Ponte brings us through the evolution of Science vs. the State.

Lower Blood Pressure. 1 cass. (Running Time: 45 min.). (Health Ser.). 9.98 (978-1-55909-061-2(8), 54) Randolph Tapes.
Helps you to relax & make changes. Subliminal messages are heard 3-5 minutes before becoming ocean sounds or music.

Lower Blood Pressure. Barrie Konicov. 1 cass. 11.98 (978-0-87082-345-9(0), 082) Potentials.
Discusses how hypnosis can treat high blood pressure & how self-hypnosis can result in lowering blood pressure.

Lower Blood Pressure Drug Free: Guided Breathing for Low Blood Pressure. Concept by Andy Krals. Composed by Andy Krals. (ENG.). 2008. audio compact disk 29.95 (978-0-9821947-0-6(6)) Green Line Az.

Lower High Blood Pressure. Barrie Konicov. 1 CD. 2003. audio compact disk 16.98 (978-0-87082-975-8(0)) Potentials.
Many people who suffer from high blood pressure and other related serious illnesses don't realize that self-hypnosis is an effective treatment.You will find the self-hypnosis on track 1 and the subliminal on track 2. The easy-listening music of the subliminal, together with the self-hypnosis, is the original format which most people love and with which they are most familiar.

Lower Manhattan: From Customs House to South St. Seaport. unabr. ed. Gerald J. Morse. Read by Brooks Baldwin. 1 cass. (Running Time: 85 min.). (Talk-A-Walk Tours on Cassette Ser.). 1982. 9.95 (978-0-939969-01-2(7), LM3-4) Talk-a-Walk.
A guided tour through the historic areas of lower Manhattan, including the refurbished, cobblestoned South St. Seaport. Detailed street map included.

Lower Manhattan: From South Street Seaport to World Trade Center. unabr. ed. Gerald J. Morse. Read by Brooks Baldwin. 1 cass. (Running Time: 85 min.). (Talk-A-Walk Tours on Cassette Ser.). 1982. 9.95 (978-0-939969-02-9(5), LM5-6) Talk-a-Walk.
A guided walk through the historic area of lower Manhattan with emphasis on the wind, steam, electric power that made it great. Detailed street map included.

Lower Manhattan: From World Trade Center to Bowling Green. unabr. ed. Gerald J. Morse. Read by Brooks Baldwin. 1 cass. (Running Time: 85 min.). (Talk-A-Walk Tours on Cassette Ser.). 1982. 9.95 (978-0-939969-00-5(9), LM1-2) Talk-a-Walk.
A historical walk through lower Manhattan with emphasis on its food, commodities & financial markets. Detailed street map included.

Lower Tanana Athabaskan Listening & Writing Exercises. Isabel Charlie et al. 1 cass. (Running Time: 1 hr.). 1991. 4.00 (978-1-55500-040-0(1)) Alaska Native.

Lowered Blood Pressure. Eldon Taylor. 1 cass. (Running Time: 62 min.). (Inner Talk Ser.). 16.95 (978-1-55978-318-7(4), 5344A) Progress Aware Res.
Soundtrack - Tropical Lagoon with underlying subliminal affirmations.

Lowered Blood Pressure: Babbling Brook. Eldon Taylor. 1 cass. 16.95 (978-1-55978-478-8(4), 5344F) Progress Aware Res.

Lowered Blood Pressure: Classic. Eldon Taylor. Read by Eldon Taylor. Ed. by Leslie Brice. 1 cass. (Running Time: 1 hr.). 1992. 16.95 (978-1-56705-121-6(9)) Gateways Inst.
Self improvement.

Lowered Blood Pressure: Harmonies. Eldon Taylor. Read by Eldon Taylor. Ed. by Leslie Brice. 1 cass. (Running Time: 1 hr.). 1992. 16.95 (978-1-56705-122-3(7)) Gateways Inst.

Lowered Blood Pressure: Music Theme. Eldon Taylor. 1 cass. 16.95 (978-1-55978-078-0(9), 5344C) Progress Aware Res.

Lowered Blood Pressure: Ocean. Eldon Taylor. Read by Eldon Taylor. Ed. by Leslie Brice. 1 cass. (Running Time: 1 hr.). 1992. 16.95 (978-1-56705-123-0(5)) Gateways Inst.

Lowered Blood Pressure: Stream. Eldon Taylor. Read by Eldon Taylor. Ed. by Leslie Brice. 1 cass. (Running Time: 1 hr.). 1992. 16.95 (978-1-56705-124-7(3)) Gateways Inst.

Lowering Blood Pressure, Vol. 133. 2 cass. (Running Time: 2 hrs). 2001. 24.95 (978-1-58557-038-6(9)) Dynamic Growth.

Lowering Cholesterol. Barrie Konicov. Read by Barrie Konicov. 1 cass. 11.98 (978-0-87082-088-5(5), 158) Potentials.
You can lower your cholesterol in three easy steps. One, begin an exercise program. Two, change your diet. Three, relax. This tape is designed to promote changes in you that will make exercise, diet & relaxation an automatic part of your life.

Lowering Your Blood Pressure Naturally. Earl Mindell. Read by Earl Mindell. 1 cass. (Running Time: 1 hr.). (Stay Healthy Audio Ser.). 1991. 10.95 (978-1-56170-012-7(6), 241) Hay House.
Dr. Mindell discusses the causes of high blood pressure & its relationship to heart disease. He also gives you positive dietary solutions that can help lower your blood pressure the natural way.

Loyalist: Power of the Enneagram Individual Type Audio Recording. Scripts. Based on a work by Enneagram Institute Staff. 1 CD. (Running Time: 60 mins.). 2004. audio compact disk 10.00 (978-0-9755222-5-7(6)) Enneagr.
Type Six Individual Type Audio Recording (ITAR) in CD format from the audio tapeset The Power of the Enneagram. Includes a 25 minute introduction to the system as a whole, as well as a 35 minute exposition on Type Six. An excellent way for therapists or business consultants to introduce the Enneagram to clients, or to work with the Enneagram in ongoing situations.

Loyalties. unabr. ed. John Galsworthy. Read by Flo Gibson. 2 cass. (Running Time: 2 hrs. 30 min.). (gr. 9 up). 1998. 14.95 (978-1-55685-544-3(3)) Audio Bk Con.
A theft at a houseparty causes turmoil with an exposure of prejudices & straining of loyalties.

Loyalty & Dependability. Linda Eyre & Richard Eyre. 2 cass. (Running Time: 3 hrs.). (Teaching Your Children Values Ser.). (J). (ps-7). 2000. bk. 16.95 (978-1-56015-792-2(5)) Penton Overseas.
Tape 1: a coaching, "how-to" program for parents; Tape 2: "Alexander's Amazing Adventures" program featuring stories, songs, sound effects & background music, that helps children ages 4-12 to develop social skills, communication skills & life skills. Includes activity cards.

Loyalty, Betrayal & Other Contact Sports: Alpha. abr. ed. Brown Bear Staff. 1 cass. 1999. 20.00 (978-0-9673933-1-5(0)) Erzse.
Military aviation, aerial combat, space technology & international crime & terrorism.

Loyalty, Betrayal & Other Contact Sports: (Bravo) Brown Bear, pseud. 1 cass. 2000. (978-0-9673933-3-9(7)) Erzse.

Loyalty Defiled. unabr. ed. Alison Stuart. Read by Anne Dover. 10 cass. (Running Time: 13 hrs.). (Storysound Ser.). (J). 2002. 84.95 (978-1-85903-514-6(0)) Pub: Mgna Lrg Print GBR. Dist(s): Ulverscroft US

Loyalty Disloyalty. unabr. ed. Jeffrey Ashford. Read by Graham Padden. 5 cass. (Storysound Ser.). (J). 2000. 49.95 (978-1-85903-403-3(9)) Pub: Mgna Lrg Print GBR. Dist(s): Ulverscroft US

Loyalty in Death. abr. ed. J. D. Robb, pseud. Read by Susan Ericksen. 4 cass. (Running Time: 6 hrs.). (In Death Ser.:). 2003. 62.25 (978-1-58788-446-7(1), 1587884461) Brilliance Audio.
#9 in the Bestselling Series Eve Dallas Returns to Face Her Most Ingenious Foe - a "Secret Admirer" Who Taunts Her With Letters . . . And Kills Without Mercy An unknown bomber is stalking New York City. He is sending Eve Dallas taunting letters promising to wreak mass terror and destruction among the "corrupt masses." And when his cruel web of deceit and destruction threatens those she cares for most, Eve fights back. It's her city . . . it's her job . . . and it's hitting too close to home. Now, in a race against a ticking clock, Eve must make the pieces fit - before the city falls.

Loyalty in Death. abr. ed. J. D. Robb, pseud. Read by Susan Ericksen. (Running Time: 21600 sec.). (In Death Ser.). 2007. audio compact disk 14.99 (978-1-4233-1724-1(6), 9781423317241, BCD Value Price) Brilliance Audio.

Loyalty in Death. unabr. ed. J. D. Robb, pseud. Read by Susan Ericksen. (Running Time: 11 hrs.). (In Death Ser.). 2007. 39.25 (978-1-4233-0124-0(2), 9781423301240, BADLE); 24.95 (978-1-4233-0123-3(4), 9781423301233, BAD) Brilliance Audio.

Loyalty in Death. unabr. ed. J. D. Robb, pseud. Read by Susan Ericksen. (Running Time: 11 hrs.). (In Death Ser.). 2007. 39.25 (978-1-4233-0122-6(6), 9781423301226, Brlnc Audio MP3 Lib); 24.95 (978-1-4233-0121-9(8), 9781423301219, Brilliance MP3); 82.25 (978-1-4233-3722-5(0), 9781423337225, BrilAudUnabridg); audio compact disk 102.25 (978-1-4233-1722-7(X), 9781423317227, BriAudCD Unabrid); audio compact disk 36.95 (978-1-4233-1721-0(1), 9781423317210, Bril Audio CD Unabri) Brilliance Audio.

Lær at Tale Dansk see Learn to Speak Danish CDs, Text & Learner's Guide

LSD: My Problem Child. Albert Hoffman. 1 cass. 9.00 (A0043-83) Sound Photosyn.
The Swiss chemist discoverer of LSD in a rare public statement, at the Psychedelics Conference '83 in Santa Barbara.

LSD & the Nature of Reality. unabr. ed. Albert Hofmann. 1 cass. (Running Time: 1 hr. 10 min.). 1978. 11.00 (03501) Big Sur Tapes.
The chemist-scientist who discovered LSD-25 tells his story.

LSD Therapy. unabr. ed. Stanislav Grof. 1 cass. (Running Time: 54 min.). 1968. 11.00 (00808) Big Sur Tapes.
For many years Grof conducted numerous studies with LSD subjects in Czechoslovakia. His analysis of records from more than 2600 sessions with patients, scientists, philosophers & persons facing death, gives unique insights related to basic metaphysical questions.

LSU Dogfish Jones. 1 CD. audio compact disk 15.98 (978-1-57908-302-1(1), 1291) Platinm Enter.

LT's Theory of Pets. abr. ed. Stephen King. Read by Stephen King. 2006. 8.98 (978-0-7435-6336-9(0), Audioworks) Pub: S&S Audio. Dist(s): S and S Inc

LT's Theory of Pets. unabr. abr. ed. Stephen King. Read by Stephen King. 1 CD. (Running Time: 10 hrs. 0 mins. 0 sec.). (ENG.). 2001. audio compact disk 15.00 (978-0-7435-2005-8(X), Audioworks) Pub: S&S Audio. Dist(s): S and S Inc
A Rare Live Stephen King Recording! Stephen King delivers a haunting, heartfelt performance as he shares a story about the bonds between husbands, wives and pets. LT has a theory about pets, particularly his Siamese cat. It had been their cat not just his cat, but that was until he came home one day to a note on the fridge. His wife had left him. The cat stayed behind... Recorded live at London's Royal Festival Hall, LT's Theory of Pets demonstrates yet again that Stephen King is a master storyteller.

Luau Celebration Songs Music CD: A Song & Hula for Every Popular Occasion. Created by Vicki Corona. Lyrics by Vicki Corona. 1 CD. (Luau Celebration Ser.). 1988. 16.96 (978-1-58513-090-0(7)) Dance Fantasy.
A Hawaiian music CD containing songs and hulas for important luau events, i.e. birthdays, weddings, Father's Day, Mother's Day, anniversary, Christmas, and any congratulatory event. Written choreographies for each of the songs are sold separately.

Lucas: A Story of Love & Hate. unabr. ed. Kevin Brooks. Read by Stina Nielsen. 9 cass. (Running Time: 11hrs. 30 mins.). (YA). 2004. 71.75 (978-1-4025-9932-3(3)) Recorded Bks.
One summer, a boy named Lucas mysteriously appears on the small island where 15-year-old Caitlin lives. Lucas lives in the wild, and his freedom is just one thing Caitlin loves about him. They quickly become friends, but other islanders grow suspicious and even afraid of Lucas. When Lucas is falsely accused of a brutal knife attack, the manhunt is on and Caitlin is stuck in the middle.

Lucas on Life 2. Jeff Lucas. Read by Jeff Lucas. (ENG.). 2008. audio compact disk 20.99 (978-1-86024-563-3(3)) Pub: AuthenticMedia. Dist(s): STL Dist NA

Lucasfilm's the Alien Chronicles, Bk. 1. abr. ed. Deborah Chester. 2 cass. (Running Time: 2 hrs.). 1998. 16.95; audio compact disk 24.95 HarperCollins Pubs.

Luci Tapahonso. unabr. ed. Read by Luci Tapahanso & Rebekah Presson. Ed. by James McKinley. 1 cass. (Running Time: 29 min.). (New Letters on the Air Ser.). 1992. 10.00 (100292); 18.00 2-sided cass. New Letters.
Tapahanso is interviewed by Rebekah Presson & reads from Saanii Dahataal: The Women Are Singing.

Lucia: A Venetian Life in the Age of Napoleon. unabr. ed. Andrea Di Robilant. Read by Stephen Hoye. (Running Time: 12 hrs. 0 mins. 0 sec.). (ENG.). 2008. audio compact disk 34.99 (978-1-4001-0705-6(9)); audio compact disk 24.99 (978-1-4001-5705-1(6)); audio compact disk 69.99 (978-1-4001-3705-3(5)) Pub: Tantor Media. Dist(s): IngramPubServ

Lucia in London. unabr. ed. E. F. Benson. Read by Geraldine McEwan. 9 cass. (Running Time: 9 hrs. 20 min.). (Isis Ser.). (J). 1993. 76.95 (978-1-85089-532-9(5), 92033) Pub: ISIS Lrg Prnt GBR. Dist(s): Ulverscroft US

Lucia in London. unabr. ed. E. F. Benson. Read by Geraldine McEwan. 9 CDs. (Running Time: 9.5 hrs.). (Isis Ser.). (J). 2002. audio compact disk 84.95 (978-0-7531-1537-4(9)) Pub: ISIS Lrg Prnt GBR. Dist(s): Ulverscroft US
Pepino's Aunt dies, and all of Riseholme is curious as to what she has left her sole surviving relative. Lucia gradually lets slip that there is a house in Brompton Square, London, with a quantity of furniture, and an annual income of three thousand pounds. Her great rival Olga Braceley also reveals that she is taking a house in London for the summer. Lucia leaves for London, seen off only by Georgie. The papers are soon giving news of all her doings there, but Georgie still has no invitation to stay. Meanwhile Daisy has a great idea: to set up a Riseholme Museum with various Roman coins and bits of old brickwork; others in the village could also contribute items of interest. She immediately contacts Georgie who promptly agrees to help, a committee is assembled, and the exhibits considered. But Lucia has not been asked to take part, and her revenge on Georgie is sharp.

Lucia in Wartime. unabr. ed. Tom Holt. 5 cass. (Isis Ser.). (J). 2003. 49.95 (978-0-7531-1681-4(2)); audio compact disk 64.95 (978-0-7531-1707-1(X)) Pub: ISIS Lrg Prnt GBR. Dist(s): Ulverscroft US

Lucia Triumphant. unabr. ed. Tom Holt. Read by Norma West. 6 cass. (Running Time: 8 hrs. 37 min.). (Isis Ser.). (J). 2003. 54.95 (978-0-7531-1680-7(4)); audio compact disk 71.95 (978-0-7531-2203-7(0)) Pub: ISIS Lrg Prnt GBR. Dist(s): Ulverscroft US
Lucia, twice-elected Mayor of Tilling, with her dearest arch-enemy, Elizabeth Mapp-Flint, ousted from the Council, is strangely wearied of her mortal span. She feels she has accomplished everything - what else is there for her to do?But the times, and Elizabeth Mapp-Flint, have events of catastrophic proportion in store.

Luciano's Luck. unabr. ed. Jack Higgins. Read by Patrick Macnee. 6 cass. 1999. 29.95 (FS9-34530) Highsmith.

Luciano's Luck. unabr. ed. Jack Higgins. Perf. by Patrick Macnee. 6 cass. (Running Time: 3 hrs.). 2004. 34.95 (978-1-59007-197-7(2)) Pub: New Millenn Enter. Dist(s): PerseuPGW
From the bestselling author of The Eagle Has Landed comes a heart-stopping, gripping tale set in the dark, violent storm of World War II. In 1943, a British intelligence operative, two American Rangers, an extraordinary woman, and an American Mafia overlord parachute into Nazi-occupied Sicily to convince the Sicilian Mafian king to back invading American forces.

***Luciano's Luck.** unabr. ed. Jack Higgins. Read by Michael Page. (Running Time: 7 hrs.). 2011. audio compact disk 29.99 (978-1-4418-4475-0(9), 9781441844750, Bril Audio CD Unabri) Brilliance Audio.

Lucid Dreaming. Bruce Goldberg. (ENG.). 2005. audio compact disk 17.00 (978-1-57968-070-1(4)) Pub: B Goldberg. Dist(s): Baker Taylor

Lucid Dreaming. Scripts. Bruce Goldberg. Read by Bruce Goldberg. 1 cass. (Running Time: 25 mins.). (ENG.). 2007. 13.00 (978-1-885577-88-7(5)) B Goldberg.
Learn to be aware that you are dreaming, direct your dreams & explore other dimensions.

Lucid Dreaming. Stephen LaBerge. (Running Time: 1 hr. 15 mins.). 2006. bk. 19.95 (978-1-59179-150-8(2), K783D) Sounds True.

Lucid Dreaming. Eldon Taylor. 2 cass. (Running Time: 62 min. per cass.). (Omniphonics Ser.). 29.95 incl. script . (978-1-55978-804-5(6), 4005) Progress Aware Res.
3-D soundtrack with underlying subliminal affirmations, night & day versions.

Lucid Dreaming & Dream Programming see Futureshaping

Lucid Dreaming Series. unabr. ed. 4 cass. (Running Time: 6 hrs.). 1999. 44.85 (978-1-56102-938-9(6)) Inter Indus.
Helps teach someone how to program & consciously participate in their own personal dreamscape.

Lucid Eye in Silver Town see Assorted Prose

Lucid Intervals. unabr. ed. Stuart Woods. Read by Tony Roberts. 7 CDs. (Running Time: 8 hrs.). (Stone Barrington Ser.: No. 18). 2010. audio compact disk 29.95 (978-0-14-242772-9(1), PengAudBks) Penguin Grp USA.

Lucie Brock-Broido. unabr. ed. Lucie Brock-Broido. Read by Lucie Brock-Broido. 1 cass. (Running Time: 29 min.). 1987. 10.00 (18) New Letters.
The 1986 New Letters literary award winner reads & talks about her work & life.

Lucien Stryk. unabr. ed. Lucien Stryk. 1 cass. (Running Time: 29 min.). 1984. 10.00 (062284) New Letters.
Stryk is a poet who does not consider his work a part of any particular school of poetry & an oriental literature instructor. He has co-authored several translations of Zen poetry & thought from the Japanese. Taken from a Folkway recording.

Lucifer's Child. unabr. ed. William Luce. Read by Julie Harris. 2 cass. (Running Time: 2 hrs.). Dramatization. 2004. 16.95 (978-0-945353-80-5(4), D20380a) Pub: Audio Partners. Dist(s): PerseuPGW
Based on the life & writings of Isak Dinesen, author of Out of Africa.

Lucifer's Hammer, Pt. 1. collector's ed. Larry Niven & Jerry Pournelle. Read by Connor O'Brien. 8 cass. (Running Time: 12 hrs.). 1999. 64.00 (978-0-7366-4516-4(0), 4947-A) Books on Tape.
The newly discovered Hammer-Brown comet is on a collision course with the one major obstacle in its path: Earth.

Lucifer's Hammer, Pt. 2. unabr. collector's ed. Larry Niven & Jerry Pournelle. Read by Connor O'Brien. 8 cass. (Running Time: 12 hrs.). 1999. 64.00 (978-0-7366-4716-8(3), 4947-B) Books on Tape.
For millionaire Tim Hamner, the comet he helped discover is a ticket to immortality. For filmmaker Harvey Randall, it's a shot to redeem a flagging career. And for astronauts John Baker & Rick Delanty, it's a second chance for glory in outer space. But for a world gripped by comet fever, fascination quickly turns to fear. And only those who survive the impact will know the even greater terror, as the remnants of humanity grow savage to battle for what little remains.

Lucille: The Life of Lucille Ball. unabr. ed. Kathleen Brady. Read by C. M. Herbert. 9 cass. (Running Time: 13 hrs.). 1996. 62.95 (978-0-7861-1059-9(7), 1830) Blckstn Audio.
This definitive biography presents an extraordinary portrait of the Lucille that her fans have never known, based on recollections of fellow performers like Milton Berle, Ginger Rogers, Bob Hope & Katherine Hepburn; her closest friends & family; & Lucille herself.

Lucille Ball Set: My Favorite Husband, Perf. by Richard Denning. 6 cass. (Running Time: 1 hr. 30 mins. per cass.). 1999. 34.98 (Q109) Blckstn Audio.
This funny radio sitcom that aired from 1948-1951 is about "two people who live together & like it."

Lucille Clifton. unabr. ed. Lucille Clifton. Read by Lucille Clifton. 1 cass. (Running Time: 29 min.). 1989. 10.00 New Letters.
Clifton reads poetry from Good Women & is interviewed.

***Lucinda's Secret.** unabr. ed. Holly Black & Tony DiTerlizzi. Read by Mark Hamill. (Running Time: 1 hr. 7 mins.). (Spiderwick Chronicles: Bk. 3). (ENG.). (J). 2007. 7.50 (978-0-7393-6243-3(7), Listening Lib) Pub: Random Audio Pubg. Dist(s): Random

Lucinda's Secret & the Ironwood Tree. Tony DiTerlizzi & Holly Black. Read by Mark Hamill. 2 cass. (Running Time: 2 hrs.). (Spiderwick Chronicles: Bks. 3-4). (J). (gr. 1-5). 2004. 19.55 (978-0-8072-2311-6(5), Listening Lib) Pub: Random Audio Pubg. Dist(s): NetLibrary CO

***Lucinda's Secret & the Ironwood Tree.** unabr. ed. Holly Black & Tony DiTerlizzi. Read by Mark Hamill. (Running Time: 2 hrs.). (Spiderwick Chronicles: Bks. 3-4). (ENG.). (J). 2004. 8.95 (978-0-8072-2312-3(3), Listening Lib) Pub: Random Audio Pubg. Dist(s): Random

Luck: The Story of a Sandhill Crane. Jean Craighead George. Read by Wendell Minor. Illus. by Wendell Minor. 1 CD. (Running Time: 14 mins.). (J). (gr. k-4). 2008. bk. 28.95 (978-1-4301-0332-5(9)) Live Oak Media.

Luck: The Story of a Sandhill Crane. Jean Craighead George. Read by Wendell Minor. Illus. by Wendell Minor. 1 cass. (Running Time: 14 mins.). (J). (ps-3). 2007. bk. 25.95 (978-1-4301-0329-5(9)) Live Oak Media.

Luck Be a Lady. Anna King. 12 cass. (Soundings Ser.). 2007. 94.95 (978-1-84283-131-1(3)) Pub: ISIS Lrg Prnt GBR. Dist(s): Ulverscroft US

Luck Be a Lady. unabr. ed. Anna King. 11 CDs. (Soundings (CDs) Ser.). 2007. audio compact disk 99.95 (978-1-84559-532-6(7)) Pub: ISIS Lrg Prnt GBR. Dist(s): Ulverscroft US

Luck Factor: How to Take the Chance Out of Becoming a Success. Brian S. Tracy. 6 cass. (Running Time: 6 hrs.). 1997. (978-1-55525-071-3(8), 15360A); audio compact disk (978-1-55525-072-0(6), 15360cd) Nightingale-Conant.
Attract more luck in your life.

Luck Factor: How to Take the Chances Out of Becoming a Success. 1997. audio compact disk 69.95 (978-1-55525-104-8(8)) Nightingale-Conant.

Luck in the Shadows. Lynn Flewelling. Read by Raymond Todd. (Running Time: 18 hrs.). 2004. 48.95 (978-1-59912-537-4(4)) Iofy Corp.

Luck in the Shadows. unabr. ed. Lynn Flewelling. Read by Todd Raymond. 13 cass. (Running Time: 19 hrs.). 2004. 85.95 (978-0-7861-2719-1(8)); audio compact disk 120.00 (978-0-7861-8678-5(X)); audio compact disk 39.95 (978-0-7861-8569-6(4)) Blckstn Audio.

Luck of Roaring Camp. 1984. (SWC 1166) HarperCollins Pubs.

Luck of Roaring Camp. Bret Harte. 10.00 (LSS1108) Esstee Audios.

Luck of Roaring Camp. unabr. ed. Bret Harte. Read by Jack Benson. 1 cass. (Running Time: 52 min.). Dramatization. 1979. 7.95 (N-22) Jimcin Record.
Two famous "local color" stories of the wild west.

Luck of Roaring Camp, unabr. ed. Bret Harte. Narrated by Victor Raider-Wexler. 3 cass. (Running Time: 4 hrs. 15 mins.). 1989. 26.00 (978-1-55690-326-7(X), 89920E7) Recorded Bks.
Deaths were common in Roaring Camp, but a birth was something new. Stumpy, self-appointed godfather, decided on the name of Cherokee Sal's baby & took up a collection for the mite. A silver tobacco-box, a doubloon & a navy revolver were among the gifts laid at this young fellow's feet, but his greatest gift was surely in the name his well-wisher laid on him: Thomas Luck.

Luck of Roaring Camp & Other Stories. collector's ed. Bret Harte. Read by Jack Bensen. 6 cass. (Running Time: 6 hrs.). 1983. 36.00 (978-0-7366-3866-1(0), 9073) Books on Tape.
A prostitute dies, leaving a newborn son in the care of hardbitten miners. Named "Luck," the child unlocks emotions the miners never knew they had.

Luck of Roaring Camp & Other Stories. unabr. ed. Bret Harte. Read by Gene Engene. 3 cass. (Running Time: 3 hrs.). Dramatization. 1990. 21.95 (978-1-55686-099-7(4), 099) Books in Motion.
Three short stories; The Luck of Roaring Camp, The Outcasts of Poker Flat, Tennessee's Partner.

Luck of Roaring Camp & Other Stories. unabr. ed. Bret Harte. Read by Jack Benson et al. 4 cass. (Running Time: 6 hrs.). Dramatization. Incl. Brown of Calaveras. 1982. (C-73); Four Guardians of La Grange. 1982. (C-73); Ghost of the Sierras. 1982. (C-73); Idyll of Red Gulch. 1982. (C-73); Outcast of Poker Flat. 1982. (C-73); Passage in the Life of Mr. John Oakhurst. 1982. (C-73); Poet of Sierra Flat. 1982. (C-73); Right Eye of the Commander. 1982. (C-73); Salomy Jane's Kiss. 1982. (C-73); Tennessee's Partner. 1982. (C-73); 1982. 28.00 (C-73) Jimcin Record.
In "The Luck of Roaring Camp" a prostitute dies, leaving a new born son in the care of hardbitten miners. Named "Luck" the childs unlocks emotions the miners never knew they had.

***Luck of the Buttons.** unabr. ed. Anne Ylvisaker. (Running Time: 3 hrs.). 2011. 39.97 (978-1-61106-501-5(1), 9781611065015, Candlewick Bril); 19.99 (978-1-61106-497-1(X), 9781611064971, Candlewick Bril); 39.97 (978-1-61106-498-8(8), 9781611064988, Candlewick Bril); audio compact disk 44.97 (978-1-61106-496-4(1), 9781611064964, Candlewick Bril); audio compact disk 19.99 (978-1-61106-495-7(3), 9781611064957, Candlewick Bril) Brilliance Audio.

Luck...Good, Bad, or No Such Thing? Ecc.9:11-18. Ed Young. 1994. 4.95 (978-0-7417-2000-9(0), 1000) Win Walk.

Luckiest Girl in the World, unabr. ed. Steven Levenkron. Narrated by Barbara Caruso. 4 pieces. (Running Time: 5 hrs. 45 mins.). (gr. 8 up). 1997. 35.00 (978-0-7887-0894-7(5), 95032E7) Recorded Bks.
Fifteen-year old Katie Roskova's goal is to skate in the Olympics, but she can't seem to please both her coach & her mother. Soon she discovers a secret way to deal with her problems.

Luckiest Man: The Life & Death of Lou Gehrig. abr. ed. Jonathan Eig. Jonathan Eig. Read by Edward Herrmann. 2005. 15.95 (978-0-7435-5151-9(6)) Pub: S&S Audio. Dist(s): S and S Inc

Lucky. Jackie Collins. (Lucky Santangelo Ser.: Bk. 2). 2004. 10.95 (978-0-7435-4983-7(X)) Pub: S&S Audio. Dist(s): S and S Inc

***Lucky: How the Kingdom Comes to Unlikely People.** unabr. ed. Glenn Packiam. (Running Time: 5 hrs. 0 mins. 0 sec.). (ENG.). 2011. audio compact disk 19.99 (978-1-59859-853-7(8)) Oasis Audio.

***Lucky Baby: A Novel.** unabr. ed. Meredith Efken. Narrated by Cassandra Campbell. (Running Time: 11 hrs. 13 mins. 27 sec.). (ENG.). 2010. 24.49 (978-1-60814-670-3(7)); audio compact disk 34.99 (978-1-59859-719-6(1)) Oasis Audio.

Lucky Bastard. unabr. ed. Charles McCarry. Read by Tom Weiner. (Running Time: 52200 sec.). 2007. 89.95 (978-1-4332-1075-4(4)); audio compact disk 108.00 (978-1-4332-1076-1(2)) Blckstn Audio.

Lucky Bastard. unabr. ed. Charles McCarry & Tom Weiner. (Running Time: 52200 sec.). 2007. audio compact disk 44.95 (978-1-4332-1077-8(0)) Blckstn Audio.

Lucky Bastard: A Novel. unabr. ed. Charles McCarry. Read by Barrett Whitener. 12 cass. (Running Time: 18 hrs.). 1998. 96.00 (978-0-7366-4254-5(4), 4753) Books on Tape.
John Fitzgerald Adams, known by the voters as Jack, has good reason to believe he is the illegitimate son of JFK.

Lucky Break. unabr. ed. Carly Phillips. Read by Renée Raudman. (Running Time: 8 hrs.). (Lucky Ser.). 2009. 24.99 (978-1-4233-4745-3(5), 9781423347453, Brilliance MP3); 39.97 (978-1-4233-4746-0(3), 9781423347460, Brlnc Audio MP3 Lib); 24.99 (978-1-4233-4747-7(1), 9781423347477, BAD); 39.97 (978-1-4233-4748-4(X), 9781423347484, BADLE); audio compact disk 34.99 (978-1-4233-4743-9(9), 9781423347439, Bril Audio CD Unabri); audio compact disk 87.97 (978-1-4233-4744-6(7), 9781423347446, BriAudCD Unabrid) Brilliance Audio.

***Lucky Breaks.** unabr. ed. Susan Patron. Read by Cassandra Campbell. 4 CDs. (Running Time: 4 hrs. 35 mins.). (J). (gr. 4-6). 2009. audio compact disk 38.00 (978-0-7393-7954-7(2), Listening Lib) Pub: Random Audio Pubg. Dist(s): Random

Lucky Breaks. unabr. ed. Susan Patron. Read by Cassandra Campbell. (ENG.). (J). (gr. 3). 2009. audio compact disk 28.00 (978-0-7393-7952-3(6), Listening Lib) Pub: Random Audio Pubg. Dist(s): Random

Lucky Charm. unabr. ed. Carly Phillips. Read by Renée Raudman. (Running Time: 9 hrs.). 2008. 39.25 (978-1-4233-4730-9(7), 9781423347309, BADLE); 24.95 (978-1-4233-4729-3(3), 9781423347293, BAD); 39.25 (978-1-4233-4728-6(5), 9781423347286, Brinc Audio MP3 Lib); 24.95 (978-1-4233-4727-9(7), 9781423347279, Brilliance MP3); audio compact disk 87.25 (978-1-4233-4726-2(9), 9781423347262, BriAudCD Unabrid); audio compact disk 29.99 (978-1-4233-4725-5(0), 9781423347255, Bril Audio CD Unabri) Brilliance Audio.

Lucky Day. abr. ed. Mary Higgins Clark. Read by Greer Allison. 2004. 7.95 (978-0-7435-4516-7(8)) Pub: S&S Audio. Dist(s): S and S Inc

Lucky Dog. Max Brand. (Running Time: 1 hr. 36 mins.). 1999. 10.95 (978-1-60083-515-5(5)) Iofy Corp.

***Lucky Dog.** Max Brand. 2009. (978-1-60136-385-5(0)) Audio Holding.

Lucky Dog Days. unabr. ed. Judy Delton. Narrated by Christina Moore. 1 cass. (Running Time: 45 mins.). (Pee Wee Scouts Ser.: No. 3). (gr. 2-5). 1997. 10.00 (978-0-7887-0753-7(1), 94930E7) Recorded Bks.
August is Help-a-Pet month for Molly & the other Pee Wee Scouts. They're going on a trip to the animal shelter & hold a big rummage sale to earn money for homeless pets. But after the sale, a surprise is waiting for them - a small but lucky one.

Lucky Dog Days. unabr. ed. Judy Delton. Read by Christina Moore. 1 cass. (Running Time: 45 min.). (Pee Wee Scouts Ser.: No. 3). (J). (gr. 2-5). 1997. pap. bk. 22.24 (978-0-7887-1700-0(6), 40568); Rental 6.50 Recorded Bks.

Lucky Duck. Created by Kane Press. (Let's Read Together Ser.). 2005. audio compact disk 4.25 (978-1-57565-174-3(2)) Kane Pr.

*__Lucky for Good.__ unabr. ed. Susan Patron. (ENG.). (J). 2011. audio compact disk 28.00 (978-0-307-74589-7(9), Listening Lib) Pub: Random Audio Pubg. Dist(s): Random

Lucky Goes to the Hospital. Short Stories. Joy Frost. 1 CD. (Running Time: 20 Minutes). (J). 2004. audio compact disk 14.00 (978-0-9745977-8-2(3)) Joy Stories.
About the Story: Lucky, a newborn squirrel, falls from a tree before he is ready to survive on his own. He is rescued by Lauren, a nature loving eight year old, and is nurtured until he is well and capable of living on his own in his natural habitat. A child can relate to Lucky's dilemma,as he must endure shots and a hospital stay to restore good health. Lucky's example provides a model for a child to accept doctor's visits; hospital stays and the illness of loved ones. Suggested age 4-9 years old.Through ?Lucky Goes To The Hospital? a child learns: ?That having empathy for all creatures is important.?That hospital care and doctor visits are necessary for good health.?That providing care for a loved one is rewarding.?That good health can be restored with good care.?Factual information about squirrels and trees.

Lucky Goes to the Hosptial CD with Finger Puppet. Short Stories. Joy Frost. 1 CD. (Running Time: 20 Minutes). (J). 2005. audio compact disk 20.00 (978-0-9745977-9-9(1)) Joy Stories.

Lucky Jim. unabr. collector's ed. Kingsley Amis. Read by Richard Green. 6 cass. (Running Time: 9 hrs.). 1981. 48.00 (978-0-7366-0195-5(3), 1195) Books on Tape.
Describes, through one young adventurer in particular, the attempt of England's postwar generation to break from that country's traditional class structure.

Lucky Larribee. unabr. collector's ed. Max Brand. Read by Jonathan Marosz. 7 cass. (Running Time: 7 hrs.). 1996. 42.00 (978-0-7366-3497-7(5), 4137) Books on Tape.
Alfred Larribee likes drinking, not working. He likes gambling, too. Maybe that's what drives him to risk his easy-going life for Sky Blue, the horse of a lifetime.

Lucky Man: A Memoir. Michael J. Fox. 2002. 63.00 (978-0-7366-8654-9(1)) Books on Tape.

Lucky Man: A Memoir. abr. ed. Michael J. Fox. (Running Time: 5 hrs. 30 mins. 0 sec.). (ENG.). 2009. audio compact disk 14.99 (978-0-7435-7908-7(9)) Pub: S&S Audio. Dist(s): S and S Inc

Lucky Man: A Memoir. unabr. ed. Michael J. Fox. 2002. audio compact disk 81.00 (978-0-7366-8655-6(X)) Books on Tape.
Since being diagnosed with Parkinson's Disease some years ago, Michael J. Fox has held it at bay with passion, humor and energy.

Lucky One. abr. ed. Nicholas Sparks. Read by John Bedford Lloyd. (Running Time: 5 hrs.). (ENG.). 2008. 14.98 (978-1-60024-368-4(1)) Pub: Hachet Audio. Dist(s): HachBkGrp

Lucky One. abr. ed. Nicholas Sparks. Read by John Bedford Lloyd. 4 CDs. (Running Time: 5 hrs.). (ENG.). 2009. audio compact disk 14.98 (978-1-60024-613-5(3)) Pub: Hachet Audio. Dist(s): HachBkGrp

Lucky One. unabr. ed. Nicholas Sparks. Read by John Bedford Lloyd. (Running Time: 7 hrs. 30 mins.). (ENG.). 2008. 26.98 (978-1-60024-370-7(3)); audio compact disk 39.98 (978-1-60024-371-4(1)) Pub: Hachet Audio. Dist(s): HachBkGrp

Lucky One. unabr. ed. Nicholas Sparks. Read by John Bedford Lloyd. 9 CDs. (Running Time: 10 hrs. 30 mins.). 2008. audio compact disk 70.00 (978-1-4159-5966-4(8), BksonTape); 70.00 (978-1-4159-5968-8(4), BksonTape) Pub: Random Audio Pubg. Dist(s): Random
When U.S. Marine Logan Thibault finds a photograph of a smiling young woman half-buried in the dirt during his third tour of duty in Iraq, his first instinct is to toss it aside. Instead, he brings it back to the base for someone to claim, but when no one does, he finds himself always carrying the photo in his pocket. Soon Thibault experiences a sudden streak of luck, winning poker games and even surviving deadly combat that kills two of his closest buddies. Only his best friend, Victor, seems to have an explanation for his good fortune: the photograph - his lucky charm. Back home in Colorado, Thibault can't seem to get the photo - and the woman in it - out of his mind. Believing that she somehow holds the key to his destiny, he sets out on a journey across the country to find her, never expecting the strong but vulnerable woman he encounters in Hampton, North Carolina - - lizabeth - to be the girl he's been waiting his whole life to meet. Caught off guard by the attraction he feels, Thibault keeps the story of the photo, and his luck, a secret. As he and Elizabeth embark upon a passionate and all-consuming love affair, the secret he is keeping will soon threaten to tear them apart - destroying not only their love, but also their lives.

Lucky Ones. unabr. ed. Doris Mortman. Read by Kathleen O'Malley. 12 cass. (Running Time: 18 hrs.). 1997. 96.00 (978-0-7366-4051-0(7), 4550) Books on Tape.
Four women are bound by friendship, secrets & an invincible will to succeed. Zoe Vaughn, Georgie Hughes, Celia Porter & Kate Siegel are all big-league players in Washington politics & media. But with the approach of the Betway's biggest event, the Presidential election, their success won't protect them from their love affairs, double-deals & the demands of their careers. Pitted against each other in the high-stakes game of power & politics, only one woman can win. But what price will she pay for her triumph.

Lucky or Smart? Bo Peabody. Narrated by Bo Peabody. 2 CDs. (Running Time: 2 hrs. 30 mins.). 2005. audio compact disk 19.95 (978-1-59316-045-6(3)) Listen & Live.
Luck is a part of life, and everyone, at one point or another, gets lucky. But luck is a big part of business life and perhaps that biggest part of entrepreneurial life. At the very least, entrepreneurs must believe in luck. Ideally, they can recognize it when they see it. And over time, the best entrepreneurs can actually learn to create luck.As Bo Peabody, entrepreneur extraordinaire, explains: ?My formula for getting lucky in business is reasonably simple: Start a company that fundamentally innovative, morally compelling, and philosophically positive. Create and aura of authenticity around your start-up by carefully crafting your mission and communicating it with charisma and passion.?Our company will quickly attract smart, inspired people who will work very hard. Treat all these people fairly. Provide them with a clear action plan and give them the latitude to exercise their creativity. The result: serendipity, luck, success, and, ultimately, money. And the only smart thing about this formula is that I understand that on a day-to-day basis my brain has very little to do with any of it.?.

Lucky Spot. unabr. ed. Beth Henley. Perf. by Jack Black et al. 1 cass. (Running Time: 1 hr. 42 min.). 1997. 19.95 (978-1-58081-036-4(5), TPT53) L A Theatre.
It's Christmas Eve, 1938, & fifteen year old Cassidy Smith is very, very pregnant with the child of 40-ish Reed Hooker. Cassidy is desperate to marry Reed. Reed is desperate to open Louisiana's hottest new taxi-dancing emporium. Neither are prepared for the arrival of Reed's wife, Sue Jack Hooker, a dangerous beauty who has just been let out of the penitentiary.

Lucky Streak. unabr. ed. Carly Phillips. Read by Renée Raudman. (Running Time: 9 hrs.). 2009. 39.97 (978-1-4233-4737-8(4), 9781423347378, Brinc Audio MP3 Lib); 39.97 (978-1-4233-4739-2(0), 9781423347392, BADLE); 24.99 (978-1-4233-4738-5(2), 9781423347385, BAD); 24.99 (978-1-4233-4736-1(6), 9781423347361, Brilliance MP3); audio compact disk 29.99 (978-1-4233-4734-7(X), 9781423347347, Bril Audio CD Unabri); audio compact disk 87.97 (978-1-4233-4735-4(8), 9781423347354, BriAudCD Unabrid) Brilliance Audio.

Lucky You. abr. ed. Carl Hiaasen. Read by Edward Asner. (Running Time: 4 hrs.). (ENG.). 2008. 10.00 (978-0-7393-7639-3(X), Random AudioBks) Pub: Random Audio Pubg. Dist(s): Random

Lucky You. unabr. ed. Carl Hiaasen. Narrated by George Wilson. 13 CDs. (Running Time: 15 hrs.). 2001. audio compact disk 124.00 (978-0-7887-7177-4(9), C1427) Recorded Bks.
Quiet, reclusive JoLayne Lucks holds a winning ticket to the $28 million-dollar Florida state lottery. Unfortunately, the other winning ticket belongs to Bodean Gazzer & his buddy Chub Grungy, militant white supremacists. Now the chase for the tickets is on, & the path to the finish line is sure to be a twisted one. With liberal dashes of dark humor & vivid, loony characters, this is a best-selling author at his best.

Lucky You, unabr. ed. Carl Hiaasen. Narrated by George Wilson. 11 cass. (Running Time: 15 hrs.). 1998. 96.00 (978-0-7887-1869-4(X), 95291E7) Recorded Bks.
JoLayne Luck holds a winning lottery ticket for 28 million-dollars. Unfortunately, the other winning ticket belongs to two grungy, militant white supremacists. The chase is on.

Lucrezia Borgia: Life, Love, & Death in Renaissance Italy. unabr. ed. Sarah Bradford. Read by Lorna Raver. (Running Time: 15 hrs. 5 mins.). 2009. 29.95 (978-1-4332-2473-7(9)); audio compact disk 85.95 (978-1-4332-2469-0(0)); audio compact disk 110.00 (978-1-4332-2470-6(4)) Blckstn Audio.

Lucy Rose: Here's the Thing About Me. 2 CDs. (Running Time: 2:20 hrs.). 2004. audio compact disk 20.40 (978-1-4000-9503-2(4), Listening Lib) Pub: Random Audio Pubg. Dist(s): NetLibrary CO

Lucy Rose: Here's the Thing About Me. unabr. ed. 2 cass. (Running Time: 2:20 hrs.). 2004. 23.00 (978-1-4000-9151-5(9), Listening Lib) Random Audio Pubg.

Lucy Sullivan Is Getting Married. unabr. ed. Marian Keyes. Read by Julia Franklin. 17 CDs. (Running Time: 18 hrs.). (Isis Ser.). (J). 2002. audio compact disk 109.95 (978-0-7531-1577-0(8)) Pub: ISIS Lrg Prnt GBR. Dist(s): Ulverscroft US
Lucy doesn't even have a boyfriend (To be honest, she isn't that lucky in love). But Mrs Nolan has read her tarot cards and predicted that Lucy will walk up the aisle before the leaves have fallen again. Or, in layman's language, within the year. Lucy's flatmates Karen and Charlotte are appalled. If Lucy leaves it could interrupt them eating takeaways, drinking too much wine, bringing men home and never hoovering.

Lucy Sullivan Is Getting Married. unabr. ed. Marian Keyes. Read by Julia Franklin. 14 cass. (Running Time: 18 hrs.). (Isis Ser.). (J). 2002. 99.95 (978-0-7531-1223-6(X)) Pub: ISIS Lrg Prnt GBR. Dist(s): Ulverscroft US

Luddites & Friends. Paul Kennedy. 2005. audio compact disk 19.95 (978-0-660-19291-8(8)) Canadian Broadcasting CAN.

Ludwig Van Beethoven. Lene Mayer-Skumanz. Tr. by Alexis L. Spry from GER. Illus. by Winfried Opgenoorth. (Musical Picture Book Ser.). (ENG.). (J). (gr. 1-5). 2007. audio compact disk 20.00 (978-0-7358-2123-1(2)) Pub: North-South Bks NYC. Dist(s): IngramPubServ

Ludwig van Beethoven. Jeremy Siepmann. 4 CDs. (Running Time: 5 hrs.). 2002. pap. bk. 35.99 (978-1-930838-13-0(1), 8.558024-27) Naxos.
Narrated biography illustrated with extensive examples of musical works, companion booklet including word-for-word transcript of spoken text and detailed historical background, graded listening plan and more.

Ludwig Van Beethoven. Read by Jeremy Siepmann & Bob Peck. 4 CDs. (Running Time: 5 hrs.). (Life & Works Ser.). 2003. pap. bk. 35.99 (978-1-84379-091-4(2)) Naxos.

Ludwig von Mises. unabr. ed. Eamonn Butler. Read by Jeff Riggenbach. 7 cass. (Running Time: 10 hrs.). 1994. 49.95 (978-0-7861-0486-4(4), 1438) Blckstn Audio.
The Austrian economist is increasingly recognized as one of the most important originators of modern economic thought. This book studies his ideas in a clear & systematic way & pulls out from Mises's own writings the main themes of his work.

Ludwig von Mises: Fountainhead of the Modern Microeconomics Revolution. unabr. ed. Eamonn Butler. Read by Jeff Riggenbach. (Running Time: 10 hrs. 30 mins.). 2010. 29.95 (978-1-4417-1311-7(5)); audio compact disk 100.00 (978-1-4417-1308-7(5)) Blckstn Audio.

Luella Miller see Wind in the Rose Bush & Other Stories of the Supernatural

Lugarno. unabr. ed. Peter Corris. 4 cass. (Running Time: 5 hrs. 5 mins.). (Cliff Hardy Mystery: Ser.). 2002. 32.00 (978-1-74030-693-5(7)) Pub: Bolinda Pubng AUS. Dist(s): Bolinda Pub Inc

Lugarno. unabr. ed. Peter Corris. 5 CDs. (Running Time: 5 hrs. 5 mins.). (Cliff Hardy Mystery: Ser.). 2002. audio compact disk 63.95 (978-1-74030-855-7(7)) Pub: Bolinda Pubng AUS. Dist(s): Bolinda Pub Inc

Luigi Pirandello from Novelle Vol. 11: Multilingual Books Literature. Ed. by Maurizio Falyhera & Cristina Giocometti. 1 cass. (Audio Anthology of Italian Literature Ser.: 11). (ITA.). 1999. spiral bd. 19.95 (978-1-58214-120-6(7)) Language Assocs.

Luigo Pirardello from Novelle: Multilingual Books Literature. Excerpts. Luigo Pirardello. Ed. by Maurizio Falyhera & Cristina Giocometti. 1 CD. (Running Time: 90 mins.). (Audio Anthology of Italian Literature Ser.: 11). (ITA.). 1999. spiral bd. 29.95 (978-1-58214-121-3(5)) Language Assocs.

Luis Rodriguez. unabr. ed. Luis Rodriguez. 1 cass. (Running Time: 29 min.). (New Letters on the Air Ser.). 1992. 10.00 (012492) New Letters.
Rodriguez reads poems from "The Concrete River" & talks about trying to save his son from gang life.

Luis Valdez: The Making of a Mexican American Playwright. 1 cass. (Running Time: 30 min.). 9.95 (F0110B090, HarperThor) HarpC GBR.

Luisa Valenzuela. unabr. ed. Ed. by Jim McKinley. Prod. by Rebekah Presson. 1 cass. (Running Time: 29 min.). (New Letters on the Air Ser.). 1994. 10.00 (021293) New Letters.
The Argentinian novelist reads from her new book, "Black Novel with Argentines," a dark murder - love story set in the most sordid neighborhoods of New York. Valenzuela compares the dark elements of her book to its ultimate search for love & redemption, relating them to her own life.

Luisterband Vir HIGCSE Afrikaans Eerste Taal. University of Cambridge Local Examinations Syndication Staff. (Cambridge Open Learning Project in South Africa Ser.). (AFR.). 1999. 14.40 (978-0-521-65467-8(X)) Cambridge U Pr.

Luisterband Vir HIGCSE Afrikaans Tweede Taal. University of Cambridge Local Examinations Syndication Staff. (Cambridge Open Learning Project in South Africa Ser.). (AFR.). 2000. 14.40 (978-0-521-65466-1(1)) Cambridge U Pr.

*__Luka & the Fire of Life.__ Salman Rushdie. 2010. audio compact disk 29.99 (978-1-4498-4316-8(6)) Recorded Bks.

Luka Ke'elikolani. Ku'ulei Higashi. 1 cass. (HAW., (J). (gr. 2). 1999. pap. bk. 5.95 (978-1-58191-065-0(7)) Aha Punana Leo.

Luke I. (LifeLight Bible Studies: Course 22). 13.95 (20-2742) Concordia.

Luke II. (LifeLight Bible Studies: Course 23). 13.95 Set. (20-2747) Concordia.

Luke's Story. unabr. ed. Jerry B. Jenkins & Tim LaHaye. (Running Time: 13 hrs.). Bk. 3. (ENG.). (gr. 12 up). 2009. audio compact disk 34.95 (978-0-14-314414-4(6), PengAudBks) Penguin Grp USA.

Lukewarm No More. George Verwer. 2 cass. (Running Time: 3 hrs.). 2000. 12.99 (978-1-886463-79-0(4)) Oasis Audio.

Lukewarmness. Dan Corner. 1 cass. 3.00 (54) Evang Outreach.

LullaBible: A Musical Treasury for Mother & Baby. Stephen Elkins. 2 vols. (Running Time: 1 hr.). (J). 2004. bk. 21.99 (978-0-8054-2390-7(7)) BH Pubng Grp.

LullaBible: A Musical Treasury for Mother & Baby. Stephen Elkins. 2 CDs. (J). 2004. audio compact disk 12.99 (978-0-8054-2392-1(3)) BH Pubng Grp.

Lullabies. Perf. by Cedarmont Kids. 1 cass. 1999. 3.99 (978-0-00-546334-5(3)) Provident Music.

Lullabies. Perf. by Cedarmont Kids. 1 CD. (J). 1999. audio compact disk 5.99 (978-0-00-507230-1(1)) Provident Music.

Lullabies: A Songbook Companion. Richard Kapp. 1 cass., 1 CD. (J). 7.98 (ESSAY 1054); audio compact disk 12.98 CD. (ESSAY 1054) NewSound.
Thirty-five lullabies, some classic, some less than familiar, along with four pieces that are played & not sung, but which offer a kind of soothing beauty of their own. Songs represent a wide variety of musical styles & traditions, ranging from lullabies by famous composers & poets to simple, anonymous folk songs.

Lullabies & Bedtime Stories. Friedman-Fairfax and Sony Music Staff. 1 cass. (CD Ser.). (ps-3). 1994. pap. bk. 15.98 (978-1-56799-080-5(0), Friedman-Fairfax) M Friedman Pub Grp Inc.

Lullabies & Daydreams. 2nd ed. Suzanne Siegel Zenkel. Compiled by Lois L. Kaufman. Illus. by Amy Dietrich. (BookNotes Ser.). 1998. bk. 13.99 (978-0-88088-411-2(8)) Peter Pauper.

Lullabies & Love Songs. unabr. ed. Perf. by Tanja Solnik. 1 cass. (Running Time: 40 min.). 1996. 10.00 (978-0-9638749-1-7(8), DS102); audio compact disk 16.00 CD. (978-0-9638749-2-4(6)) DreamSong Recs.
Traditional folk songs, story songs & lullabies in Yiddish, Hebrew & Ladino. 1997 ALA Notable Children's Recording & NAPPA Honors Award Winner.

Lullabies & Lovesongs: For Children Around the World. unabr. ed. Mira J. Spektor. Perf. by Mira J. Spektor. 1 cass. (Running Time: 1 hr.). (J). 1996. 9.95 (978-1-885608-08-6(X)) Airplay.
Classic recording of songs sung to children throughout the world will be a joy for listeners of all ages, also well-loved & lesser known lullabies sung in ten languages.

Lullabies & Night Songs. unabr. ed. Perf. by Jan De Gaetani. Ed. by William Engvick. Contrib. by Alec Wilder & Maurice Sendak. 1 cass. (Running Time: 53 min.). (J). (ps-3). 1965. 9.95 (978-0-89845-897-8(8), HarperChildAud) HarperCollins Pubs.
With music newly composed or arranged for the piano, here are 48 nursery rhymes; poems by Blake, de la Mare, & others; & lullabies from different lands.

Lullabies & Night Songs. unabr. ed. Alex Wilder. 1 cass. (J). (gr. 2-4). 1985. 19.95 (978-0-89845-649-3(5), Z 1777) HarperCollins Pubs.
A selection of lullabies, nursery rhymes & poems set to music.

Lullabies Around the World. 1 cass. (Running Time: 1 hr.). (J). (ps-2). 2001. pap. bk. 14.95 (RT115C); pap. bk. 16.95 (RT 115CD) Kimbo Educ.
Traditional lullabies sung by native singers, with translated verses in English. Great activities representing each culture are included in the lyrics book. Flip side of cassette has music tracks for class performances.

Lullabies Around the World. Sara Jordan. Prod. by Sara Jordan. 1 CD. (Running Time: 30 min.). (Songs of Celebration Ser.). (UND.). (J). 1996. audio compact disk 13.95 (978-1-894262-27-9(1), JMP 115CD) Pub: S Jordan Publ. Dist(s): CrabtreePubCo

Lullabies for a Small World: Bedtime Songs from Around the World. Prod. by Ellipsis Arts Staff. 1 CD. (Running Time: 54 min.). (J). 2003. audio compact disk 15.98 (978-1-55961-715-4(2), Ellipsis Arts) Relaxtn Co.
Irresistibly sleepy collection of lullabies from around the worldMusicians from Italy, Mexico, Brazil, Russia, The United States, France, Denmark, Argentina, Cameroon, Ukraine, and Spain will ease your little ones to sleep with original and traditional lullabies sung in their native tongues.A musical welcome to a world of rich cultural diversity where the love for our children is universal.

Lullabies for Babies see Canciones para Bebe

Lullabies for Beautiful Dreamers. Prod. by Sara Jordan. Arranged by Sara Jordan. 1 CD. (Running Time: 30 min.). (Songs of Celebration Ser.). (J). 1996. audio compact disk (978-1-894262-26-2(3), JMP 110CD) S Jordan Publ.

Lullabies for Language & Learning. Perf. by Peter Wilder et al. Composed by Peter Wilder. Prod. by Linda Stoler. Lyrics by Linda Stoler. Composed by Meg Chambers & Tracy Tomasi. Prod. by Will Stoler. Des. by Gaelan Kelly. (J). 2008. audio compact disk (978-1-932354-21-8(2), Sign Two Me) Northlight Commns.

Lullabies for Little Dreamers. Rhino Records Staff. 1 cass. (J). (ps-3). 1998. 7.99 (978-1-56826-635-0(9)) Rhino Enter.

Lullabies for Little Dreamers. Kevin Roth. Perf. by Kevin Roth. 1 cass. (Running Time: 30 min.). (J). 1992. 8.98 (978-1-56406-557-5(X)); 8.98 Incl. sleeve pack. (978-1-56406-583-4(9)); audio compact disk 13.98 CD. (978-1-56406-570-4(7)) Sony Music Ent.

Lullabies for Little Dreamers. Perf. by James Taylor et al. 1 cass. (Running Time: 1 hr.). (J). 2002. 7.98 (978-1-56826-637-4(5), 72265); audio compact disk 11.98 (978-1-56826-636-7(7), 72265) Rhino Enter.
This compilation of quiet folk and soft pop tunes lets parents soothe the baby while enjoying performances by legendary artists.

Lullabies for Little Worshippers. Created by Maranatha! Music. Contrib. by Thomas Vegh. (ps). 2004. audio compact disk 5.99 (978-5-559-39285-1(5)) Maranatha Music.

Lullabies for Lovers: A Romantic Nightcap for Cuddlers. 1 cass., 1 CD. (Set Your Life to Music Ser.). 5.58 (PHI 462277); audio compact disk 10.38 CD Jewel box. (PHI 462277) NewSound.

Lullabies from Around the World. Contrib. by Beijing Angelic Choir. 1 CD. (Running Time: 52 mins.). (J). 1996. audio compact disk 16.95 (978-1-57606-065-0(9)) Pub: Wind Recs. Dist(s): Shens Bks

Lullabies from the Cozy Cottage. Read by Clair LeBear. Perf. by Clair LeBear. 1 CD. (Running Time: 1 hr.). (Clair's Cozy Cottage Music Ser.). 2000. audio compact disk 14.95 (978-0-9706321-4-2(2), CC002) Cozy Cottage.
A variety of lullabies for children.

Lullabies of Broadway. Read by Mimi Bessette. 1 cass. (J). (gr. 3 up). 1991. 9.98 (978-1-877737-80-0(1), MLP 244) MFLP CA.
Collection of soothing show tunes gathered from famous Broadway musicals & Hollywood films.

Lullabies of Latin America. Perf. by Maria Del Ray. 1 cass. (SPA & ENG.). (J). 1999. 9.98; 15.98 CD. MFLP CA.
Features bilingual collection of Latin lullabies & poems performed in Spanish & English. Listeners of all ages will appreciate the celebration of a rich culture, especially those of Latin American heritage, who will treasure this recording.

Lullabies of Love. Perf. by Shanda Lear. Prod. by Graziano Mandozzi & Gian Carlo Bertelli. 1 cass. (Running Time: 36 min.). (J). 1985. 10.00 (978-0-9648110-0-3(6)) Applause Intl.
Lullabies sung by Shanda Lear, for parent(s) & baby.

Lullaby see Twentieth-Century Poetry in English, No. 12, Recordings of Poets Reading Their Own Poetry

Lullaby see Twentieth-Century Poetry in English, No. 12, Recordings of Poets Reading Their Own Poetry

Lullaby. Ed McBain, pseud. Read by Jonathan Marosz. 6 cass. (Running Time: 9 hrs.). (87th Precinct Ser.: Bk. 41). 1989. 48.00 (5096) Books on Tape.
The savage of a baby & babysitter shocks even the veteran cops.

Lullaby. Ed McBain, pseud. Read by Jonathan Marosz. (87th Precinct Ser.: Bk. 41). 1999. 48.00 (978-0-7366-4872-1(0)) Books on Tape.

Lullaby. Chuck Palahniuk. Narrated by Richard Poe. 5 cass. (Running Time: 7 hrs. 30 mins.). 2004. 59.00 (978-1-4025-3038-8(2)) Recorded Bks.

Lullaby. Mike D. Zachary. 2004. audio compact disk 11.95 (978-1-60171-023-9(2), 831-010) Pub: N Valley Pubns. Dist(s): Bookworld

Lullaby. abr. ed. Ed McBain, pseud. Read by Len Cariou. 2 cass. (Running Time: 3 hrs.). (87th Precinct Ser.: Bk. 41). 2000. 7.95 (978-1-57815-050-2(7), 1014, Media Bks Audio) Media Bks NJ.
Detective mystery.

Lullaby. unabr. ed. Chuck Palahniuk. Narrated by Richard Poe. 5 cass. (Running Time: 7 hrs. 30 mins.). 2004. 24.99 (978-1-4025-2497-4(8), 01784) Recorded Bks.
Carl Streator, a 40-something widower and newspaper reporter, has lived a reclusive life since the death of his wife. His latest assignment is to write a series of articles on Sudden Infant Death Syndrome. In doing so, he discovers that there is an underlying commonality in the deaths. A children's book, Poems and Rhymes Around the World, containing an African Death chant, is found at the scene of the cases he investigates.

Lullaby, a Collection. 1 cass. (Running Time: 60 min.). (J). 1994. 9.98 (978-1-56628-053-2(2), MLP 2286B/WBMLP 2286/WB MLP D2286/WB 42565-2); 9.98 Norelco. (978-1-56628-052-5(4), MLP 2286/WB MLP D2286/WB 42565-2); audio compact disk 15.98 CD. (978-1-56628-054-9(0), MLP D2286/WB 42565-2) MFLP CA.
A compilation of lullabies from around the world.

Lullaby Album. Classics for Newborn Staff. 1 cass. (J). 1996. 10.98 Consort Bk Sales.

Lullaby & Goodnight. 4 cass. (Running Time: 4 hrs.). (Wood Cassette Toys Ser.). (J). 1991. 19.95 (978-1-55569-488-3(8), 8335) Great Am Audio.
Soothing lullabies for baby's sweet dreams, contains all the classic lullabies. Side 1 of each tape contains a vocal performance & musical background. Side 2 of each tape contains instrumental music only.

Lullaby & Goodnight. Great American Audio. 1 cass. (Running Time: 1 hr.). (Children's Audio Ser.). (J). 1990. 9.95 (978-1-55569-382-4(2), CSP-7092) Great Am Audio.
Listen to or sing-along with 14 classic lullabies. Complete lyric booklet included.

Lullaby & Goodnight. abr. ed. Nina Mattikow. Perf. by Purple Balloon Players. 3 cass. (Running Time: 3 hrs.). (Triple Packs Ser.). (J). 1992. 11.95 Set. (978-1-55569-535-4(3), 23001) Great Am Audio.
A precious collection of the most beloved lullabies of all time, guaranteed to make bedtime a warm & wonderful experience.

Lullaby & Goodnight Rocking Chair. 1 cass. 1995. 19.95 (978-1-55569-741-9(0)) Great Am Audio.

Lullaby Berceuse. Perf. by Connie Kaldor & Carmen Campagne. 1 cass. (Running Time: 30 min.). (ENG & FRE.). (J). (gr. 3 up). 1990. 9.98 (978-1-877737-65-7(8), MLP 2206) MFLP CA.
Collection of lullabies in English & French. Gentle harmonies with piano & guitar.

Lullaby Cradle. 1 cass. (Wood Toys Ser.). 1995. 19.95 (978-1-55569-639-9(2)) Great Am Audio.

Lullaby Cradle. Great American Audio. Read by Sherri Huffman et al. 4 cass. (Running Time: 4 hrs.). (Wood Cassette Toy Ser.). (J). (gr. k-8). 1989. 19.95 (978-1-55569-322-0(9), CWP-7065) Great Am Audio.
Four cassettes containing all the classic lullabies such as "Twinkle, Twinkle Little Star", "Rock-a-bye Baby", "Frere Jacques". Side one of each cassette contains a vocal performance with orchestrated background. Side Two of each cassette contains the orchestrated background music only so you can sing-along. Complete lyric booklet included. Packaged in a little wooden cradle.

Lullaby Cradle. abr. ed. Nina Mattikow. Perf. by Purple Balloon Players. 4 cass. (Running Time: 4 hrs.). (Wood Cassette Toys Ser.). (J). (gr. 4). 1992. 19.95 Set. (978-1-55569-566-8(3), 24004) Great Am Audio.
Make sleeptime a warm & wonderful experience! Our precious little cradle contains all the classic lullabies.

Lullaby Favorites. 1 cass.; 1 CD. 1998. 7.98 (978-1-56628-127-0(X), 72746); audio compact disk 11.98 CD. (978-1-56628-126-3(1), 72746D) MFLP CA.

Lullaby Favorites. abr. ed. Nina Mattikow. Perf. by Purple Balloon Players. 1 cass. (Running Time: 60 min.). (Cassettes for Kids Ser.). (J). 1992. 5.95 (978-1-55569-525-5(6), 20001) Great Am Audio.
Listen to or sing-along with 14 of your favorite lullabies.

Lullaby for Adults. 2004. audio compact disk 15.00 (978-0-9755843-5-4(9)) Dream Theater.

Lullaby Land. Linda Arnold. 1 cass. (Running Time: 48 min.). (J). 1994. 9.98 Incl. lyrics. (978-1-889212-05-0(9), CAAR5); audio compact disk 14.98 CD Incl. lyrics. (978-1-889212-06-7(7), CDAR5) Ariel Recs.
Traditional, Celtic & original lullabies performed by Linda Arnold with classical arrangements.

Lullaby Land. Perf. by Linda Arnold. 1 cass. (J). 10.98 (978-1-57471-435-7(X), YM125-CN); audio compact disk 13.98 (978-1-57471-438-8(4), YM125-CD) Youngheart Mus.
Songs include: "Lullaby Land"; "Starlight, Starbright"; "Teddy Bear King's Waltz"; "For Baby"; "All the Pretty Horses"; "Tender Shepherd"; "The Gartan Mother's Lullaby"; "Twinkle, Twinkle Little Star"; "Goodnight" & more.

Lullaby Magic. Read by Joanie Bartels. Prod. by David Wohlstadter et al. 1 cass. (Running Time: 50 min.). (Magic Ser.). (J). (ps). 1985. 9.95 (DM1) Discov Music.
Traditional & contemporary songs.

Lullaby Magic. Read by Joanie Bartels. 1 cass. (Running Time: 43 min.). (Magic Ser.). (J). 1985. pap. bk. 8.95 incl. lyric bk. (978-1-881225-01-0(1)) Discov Music.
New packaging includes full length audio cassette & complete full color lyric book with words to lullaby songs & photos of Joanie & kids.

Lullaby Magic 2. Read by Joanie Bartels. 1 cass. (Running Time: 46 min.). (Magic Ser.). (J). 1987. pap. bk. 8.95 incl. lyric bk. (978-1-881225-03-4(8)) Discov Music.

Lullaby Magic 2. Read by Joanie Bartels. 1 cass. (J). (ps). 1987. 9.95 Discov Music.

Lullaby Moon. 2003. audio compact disk 21.00 (978-0-89610-603-1(9)) Island Heritage.

Lullaby Music. 2001. audio compact disk 18.99 (978-0-89610-933-9(X)) Island Heritage.

Lullaby Songs. 1 cass. (My First Sing-Alongs Ser.). (J). bk. 7.99 (978-1-55723-604-3(6)) W Disney Records.

Lullaby Time for Little People. 1 cass. (Running Time: 1 hr.). (J). 2001. pap. bk. 10.95 incl. song sheet. (KIM 0850C); pap. bk. 11.95 (KIM 0850) Kimbo Educ.
These traditional lullabies have comforted & quieted children for generations. Brahm's Lullaby, Sweet & Low, Rock-a-Bye Baby & 17 more. Includes song sheet.

Lullaby Town. abr. ed. Robert Crais. Read by James Daniels. (Running Time: 6 hrs.). (Elvis Cole Ser.). 2001. 53.25 (978-1-58788-510-5(7), 1587885107, Lib Edit) Brilliance Audio.
Hollywood's newest wunderkind is Peter Alan Nelson, the brilliant, erratic director known as the King of Adventure. His films make billions, but his manners make enemies. What the boy king wants, he gets, and what Nelson wants is for Elvis to comb the country for the airhead wife and infant child the film-school flunkout dumped en route to becoming the third biggest filmmaker in America. It's the kind of case Cole can handle in his sleep - until it turns out to be a nightmare. For when Cole finds Nelson's wife in a small Conneticut town, she's nothing like what he expects. The lady has some unwanted - and very nasty - mob connections, which means Elvis could be opening the East Coast branch of his P.I. office . . . at the bottom of the Hudson River.

Lullaby Town. abr. ed. Robert Crais. Read by James Daniels. (Running Time: 6 hrs.). (Elvis Cole Ser.). 2006. 24.95 (978-1-4233-0127-1(7), 9781423301271, BAD) Brilliance Audio.

Lullaby Town. unabr. ed. Robert Crais. Read by Mel Foster. (Running Time: 9 hrs.). (Elvis Cole Ser.). 2008. 39.25 (978-1-4233-5644-8(6), 9781423356448, BADLE); 24.95 (978-1-4233-5643-1(8), 9781423356431, BAD); audio compact disk 39.25 (978-1-4233-5642-4(X), 9781423356424, Brlnc Audio MP3 Lib); audio compact disk 87.25 (978-1-4233-5640-0(3), 9781423356400, BriAudCD Unabrid); audio compact disk 34.95 (978-1-4233-5639-4(X), 9781423356394, Bril Audio CD Unabri); audio compact disk 24.95 (978-1-4233-5641-7(1), 9781423356417, Brilliance MP3) Brilliance Audio.

Lullaby Train Wood Toys. 1 cass. 1995. 19.95 (978-1-55569-598-9(1)) Great Am Audio.

Lulu & the Ant: A Message of Love. Louise L. Hay & Dan Olmos. Read by Louise L. Hay. Illus. by J. J. Smith-Moore. Music by Randall Leonard. 1 cass. (Running Time: 12 min.). (J). (ps-3). 1991. bk. 8.00 cass. & coloring bk. (978-1-56170-029-5(0), 256) Hay House.
Lulu meets a wise little ant who teaches her that everyone has the ability to do great things.

Lulu & the Dark: Conquering Fears. Louise L. Hay & Dan Olmos. Read by Louise L. Hay. Illus. by J. J. Smith-Moore. Music by Randall Leonard. 1 cass. (Running Time: 12 min.). (J). (ps-3). 1991. bk. 8.00 cass. & coloring bk. (978-1-56170-030-1(4), 257) Hay House.
Lulu visualizes a beautiful garden where a kindly owl teaches her a musical affirmation to feel safe in the dark.

Lulu & Willy the Duck: Learning Mirror Work. Louise L. Hay & Dan Olmos. Read by Louise L. Hay. Illus. by J. J. Smith-Moore. Music by Randall Leonard. 1 cass. (Running Time: 12 min.). (J). (ps-3). 1991. bk. 8.00 cass. & coloring bk. (978-1-56170-031-8(2), 258) Hay House.
Lulu shows Willy the Duck the power of loving yourself & teaches him that the best friend he has is within himself.

Lulu in Marrakech. abr. unabr. ed. Diane Johnson. Read by Justine Eyre. (ENG.). 2008. audio compact disk 39.95 (978-0-7393-0797-7(5), Random AudioBks) Pub: Random Audio Pubg. Dist(s): Random

Lulubelle & Her Bones. unabr. ed. Vashti Farrer. Read by Nicky Talacko. (Running Time: 4500 sec.). (J). (gr. 2-7). 2006. audio compact disk 39.95 (978-1-74093-731-3(7)) Pub: Bolinda Pubng AUS. Dist(s): Bolinda Pub Inc

Lum & Abner. Perf. by Chester Lauck & Norris Goff. 2 cass. (Running Time: 2 hrs.). 10.95 Set in vinyl album. (978-1-57816-062-4(6), LA2401) Audio File.
Includes: "November 11, 1948" Lum brags about his experience as a cowhand & winds up in a Rodeo bulldogging contest. "1948" Lum pretends he has a broken leg so he can avoid seeing the Widow Abernathy. "January 30, 1949" The boys start their own collection agency business. "1949" Lum tries to borrow some money so he can travel to his lodge convention in Leavenworth, Kansas.

Lum & Abner. Perf. by Chester Lauck & Norris Goff. (ENG.). 2009. audio compact disk 35.95 (978-1-57019-878-6(0)) Radio Spirits.

Lum & Abner, Vol. 1. 6 cass. 24.98 Set. Moonbeam Pubns.

Lum & Abner, Vol. 2. 6 cass. 24.98 Set. Moonbeam Pubns.

Lum & Abner, Vol. 3. 6 cass. 24.98 Set. Moonbeam Pubns.

Lum & Abner: Balancing the Books & Wanting to Buy a House. Perf. by Chester Lauck & Norris Goff. 1 cass. (Running Time: 1 hr.). 2001. 6.98 (2378) Radio Spirits.

Lum & Abner: Bulldogging Lum & Boat Launch Blues. Perf. by Chester Lauck & Norris Goff. 1 cass. (Running Time: 1 hr.). 2001. 6.98 (2558) Radio Spirits.

Lum & Abner: Income Taxes, Plus a Prize for Honesty. Perf. by Chester Lauck & Norris Goff. 1 cass. (Running Time: 1 hr.). 2001. 6.98 (1685) Radio Spirits.

Lum & Abner: Lum Abner & Smith Write Pamphlets. Perf. by Chester Lauck & Norris Goff. 1 cass. (Running Time: 1 hr.). 2001. 6.98 (1686) Radio Spirits.

Lum & Abner: Lum & Abner Open a Bakery. Perf. by Chester Lauck & Norris Goff. 1 cass. (Running Time: 1 hr.). 2001. 6.98 (1571) Radio Spirits.

Lum & Abner: Lum & Cedrick Force Smith to Confess to Counterfeiting. Perf. by Chester Lauck & Norris Goff. 1 cass. (Running Time: 1 hr.). 2001. 6.98 (1913) Radio Spirits.

Lum & Abner: Lum Catches Abner & Cedrick with Counterfeiting Machine. Perf. by Chester Lauck & Norris Goff. 1 cass. (Running Time: 1 hr.). 2001. 6.98 (1912) Radio Spirits.

Lum & Abner: Lum Is Appointed Circulation Manager. Perf. by Chester Lauck & Norris Goff. 1 cass. (Running Time: 1 hr.). 2001. 6.98 (1909) Radio Spirits.

Lum & Abner: Lum Is On Trial for Breaking into the Store. Perf. by Chester Lauck & Norris Goff. 1 cass. (Running Time: 1 hr.). 2001. 6.98 (1684) Radio Spirits.

Lum & Abner: Lum Is Out of a Job. Perf. by Chester Lauck & Norris Goff. 1 cass. (Running Time: 1 hr.). 2001. 6.98 (1574) Radio Spirits.

Lum & Abner: Lum the Mind Reader & Who Telephoned Lum? Perf. by Chester Lauck & Norris Goff. 1 cass. (Running Time: 1 hr.). 2001. 6.98 (1985) Radio Spirits.

Lum & Abner: Lum Wants to Be Mousey's Manager. Perf. by Chester Lauck & Norris Goff. 1 cass. (Running Time: 1 hr.). 2001. 6.98 (1573) Radio Spirits.

Lum & Abner: Lum Wants to Send a Valentine to His Girlfriend Rowena. (CC-8514) Natl Recrd Co.

Lum & Abner: Lum's Afraid Cedrick is Trying to Steal His Job. Perf. by Chester Lauck & Norris Goff. 1 cass. (Running Time: 1 hr.). 2001. 6.98 (1910) Radio Spirits.

Lum & Abner: Lum's Misadventures When Abner Won't Let Him in the Store. Perf. by Chester Lauck & Norris Goff. 1 cass. (Running Time: 1 hr.). 2001. 6.98 (1683) Radio Spirits.

Lum & Abner: Lum's Suspicious of the Money Cedrick Is Spending. Perf. by Chester Lauck & Norris Goff. 1 cass. (Running Time: 1 hr.). 2001. 6.98 (1911) Radio Spirits.

Lum & Abner: Snake Thinks Lum Wants to Marry His Sister. Perf. by Chester Lauck & Norris Goff. 1 cass. (Running Time: 1 hr.). 2001. 6.98 (1572) Radio Spirits.

Lum & Abner: The Hillbilly Talent & Abner Forgets Who Called Lum. Perf. by Chester Lauck & Norris Goff. 1 cass. (Running Time: 1 hr.). 2001. 6.98 (1682) Radio Spirits.

Lum & Abner: The Surprise Party & Moving the Store. Perf. by Chester Lauck & Norris Goff. 1 cass. (Running Time: 1 hr.). 2001. 6.98 (2376) Radio Spirits.

Lum & Abner: Traditional Christmas Show & Exchanging a Paperweight. Perf. by Chester Lauck & Norris Goff. 1 cass. (Running Time: 1 hr.). 2001. 6.98 (2377) Radio Spirits.

***Lum & Abner: Volume 2.** Perf. by Chester Lauck & Norris Goff. 2010. audio compact disk 35.95 (978-1-57019-913-4(2)) Radio Spirits.

Lum 'n' Abner, Vol. 1. collector's ed. Perf. by Chester Lauck & Norris Goff. 6 cass. (Running Time: 8 hrs.). 1999. bk. 34.98 (4001) Radio Spirits.
Lum Edwards and Abner Peabody, proprietors of "The Jot 'Em Down Store" located in Pine Ridge, Arkansas. Thirty-six consecutive episodes (#198 through #233) from the mid 1940s.

Lum 'n' Abner, Vol. 2. collector's ed. Perf. by Chester Lauck & Norris Goff. 6 cass. (Running Time: 8 hrs.). 1999. bk. 34.98 (4398) Radio Spirits.
Series set in the mythical Arkansas community of Pine Ridge located on the fringes of the Ouachita Mountain ranges. Thirty-six consecutive episodes from the mid 1940s.

Lumber Room see Saki: Strange Tales

Lumber Room, Vol. 6. unabr. ed. Saki. Read by Nelita B. Castillo. Narrated by Nelita B. Castillo. 1 cass. (Running Time: 35 min.). (Fantasies Ser.). (J). 1984. 17.95 Incl. holder, scripts, lesson plans, & tchr's. guide. (978-0-86617-047-5(2)) Multi Media TX.
Comprehensive lesson plans that use classic short stories to develop skills in listening, reading, vocabulary, following details, making inferences, visualization, drawing conclusions, critical appreciation & comparison. This module's objective is to identify the point of view represented.

Lumen de Lumine: Light of Light. Joseph Michael Levry. 1999. 19.00 (978-1-885562-16-6(0)) Root Light.

Lumen De Lumine: Light of Light. 3rd ed. Joseph Michael Levry. 1998. audio compact disk 19.00 Root Light.

Lumen Gentium: Vat. II's Constitution on the Church. James Kehoe. 7 cass. (Running Time: 60 min. per cass.). 28.00 Set. (96D) IRL Chicago.

Lumiere du Soir. l.t. ed. Brigitte LeTreut. (French Ser.). 1995. bk. 30.99 (978-2-84011-107-8(1)) Pub: UlverLrgPrint GBR. Dist(s): Ulverscroft US

Luminocity. Perf. by Scott Huckabay. 2007. audio compact disk 19.25 (978-0-923550-02-8(X)) Tetrahedron Pub.

Luminous Mind Workshop. Marianne Williamson. 4 cass. (Running Time: 5 hrs. 30 min.). 29.95 Set. (978-1-879323-47-6(8)) Sound Horizons AV.
The bestselling author takes us on an exploration of the mystery of human possibility with this workshop. In-depth exercises, meditations, prayers, & incredibly thought-provoking lectures are accompanied by beautifully produced therapeutic background music. The prayers & exercises were designed to have a profound effect on our day-to-day lives by helping us find & remain in our "Serene Center," with the courage & presence of mind to look at our lives in a new, "luminous" light.

Luminous Mysteries / Misterios Luminosos: The Holy Rosary Audio CD / el Santo Rosario Audio CD, Vol. 2. Kenneth L. Davison, Jr. & Shana Buck. Kenneth L. Davison, Jr. Prod. by Brian Shields. Music by William Straub. (ENG & SPA.). (J). 2008. audio compact disk 15.00 (978-0-9801121-1-5(7)) Holy Heroes.

***Lump of Coal.** unabr. ed. Lemony Snicket, pseud. Read by Neil Patrick Harris. Illus. by Brett Helquist. (ENG.). 2008. (978-0-06-166898-2(2)); (978-0-06-170740-7(6)) HarperCollins Pubs.

Lumpy Bumpy Pumpkin: A Halloween Tale. 1 cass. (Running Time: 32 min.). (See-More Ser.). (J). (ps-3). 1993. 5.50 (978-1-882601-20-2(3)) See-Mores Wrkshop.
Created for children based on Shadow Box Theatre's Production. Side 1 - word for word rendition of companion book with musical accompaniment. Side 2 - guided activity (movement, acting, singing) rendition of story with musical.

Lumpy Bumpy Pumpkin: A Halloween Tale. Sandra Robbins. Illus. by Richard Davis. (See-More's Stories Ser.). (J). (ps-4). 1993. pap. bk. 11.95 (978-1-882601-18-9(1)) See-Mores Wrkshop.

Lumpy Bumpy Pumpkin: Halloween. Sandra Robbins. Music by Jeff Olmsted. 1 CD. (Running Time: 32 mins). (See-More's Stories Ser.). (J). 1993. pap. bk. 16.95 (978-1-882601-41-7(6)) See-Mores Wrkshop.

Lumurian Echoes-Inner Peace Music. 2007. audio compact disk 16.95 (978-1-56136-411-4(8)) Master Your Mind.

Luna Adormecedora. Steck-Vaughn Staff. 1 cass. (Running Time: 1 hr. 30 min.). (SPA.). 1999. (978-0-7398-0747-7(1)) SteckVau.

Luna y Seis Peniques. abr. ed. Somerset Maugham. Read by Carlos Zambrano. 3 CDs.Tr. of Moon & Sixpence. (SPA.). 2002. audio compact disk 17.00 (978-958-8161-24-2(X)) YoYoMusic.

Lunar Nodes. Robert Donath. 1 cass. 8.95 (519) Am Fed Astrologers.
Use constructively in natal & comparison.

Lunar Nodes. Mohan Koparkar. 1 cass. (Running Time: 90 min.). 1994. 8.95 (1149) Am Fed Astrologers.

Lunar Nodes - Bridge Between Past & Future. Mohan Koparkar. 1 cass. 8.95 (201) Am Fed Astrologers.
An AFA Convention workshop tape.

Lunar Park. unabr. ed. Bret Easton Ellis. Read by James Van Der Beek. 8 cass. (Running Time: 12 hrs.). 2005. 72.00 (978-1-4159-2401-3(5)) Books on Tape.
Imagine becoming a bestselling novelist, and almost immediately famous and wealthy, while still in college, and before long seeing your insufferable father reduced to a bag of ashes in a safety-deposit box, while after American Psycho your celebrity drowns in a sea of vilification, booze, and drugs. Then imagine having a second chance ten years later, as the Bret Easton Ellis of this remarkable novel is given, with a wife, children, and suburban sobriety - only to watch this new life shatter beyond recognition in a matter of days. At a fateful Halloween party he glimpses a disturbing (fictional) character driving a car identical to his late father's, his stepdaughter's doll violently "malfunctions," and their house undergoes bizarre transformations both within and without. Connection these aberrations to graver events - a series of grotesque murders that no longer seem random and the epidemic disappearance of boys his son's age - Ellis struggles to defend his family against this escalating menace even as his wife, their therapists, and the police insist that his apprehensions are rooted instead in substance abuse and egomania.

Lunar Returns. Joan Titsworth. 1 cass. (Running Time: 90 min.). 1990. 8.95 (719) Am Fed Astrologers.

Lunatic. unabr. ed. Ted Dekker & Kaci Hill. Narrated by Tim Gregory. (Running Time: 7 hrs. 24 mins. 50 sec.). (Books of History Chronicles: Bk. 5). (ENG.). 2009. 16.09 (978-1-60814-566-9(2)); audio compact disk 22.99 (978-1-59859-530-7(X)) Oasis Audio.

Lunatic Café. abr. ed. Laurell K. Hamilton. Read by Kimberly Alexis. (Running Time: 7 hrs.). (Anita Blake, Vampire Hunter Ser.: No. 4). (ENG.). (gr. 12 up). 2009. audio compact disk 29.95 (978-0-14-314516-5(9), PengAudBks) Penguin Grp USA.

Lunatic Café. unabr. ed. Laurell K. Hamilton. Read by Kimberly Alexis. (Running Time: 12 hrs.). (Anita Blake, Vampire Hunter Ser.: No. 4). (ENG.). (gr. 12 up). 2009. audio compact disk 39.95 (978-0-14-314404-5(9), PengAudBks) Penguin Grp USA.

Lunatics. unabr. ed. Bradley Denton. Read by Michael Prichard. 8 cass. (Running Time: 12 hrs.). 1998. 64.00 (978-0-7366-4036-7(3), 4535) Books on Tape.
One man's moon-craziness is catching - his friends are getting loonier all the time.

Lunatics, Lovers & a Poet: A Collection of Poems & Sonnets. Thelma Homer. 2008. 29.95 (978-1-59434-268-4(7)); audio compact disk 24.95 (978-1-59434-263-9(6)) Whsprng Pine.

Lunatics, Lovers & a Poet - Book 2: A Collection of Poems. Thelma Holmer. 2006. 29.95 (978-1-59434-441-1(8)) Whsprng Pine.

Lunatics, Lovers & a Poet - Book 2: A Collection of Poems. Thelma Homer. 2006. audio compact disk 24.95 (978-1-59434-448-0(5)) Whsprng Pine.

Lunations & Weather. Alice Smith. 1 cass. (Running Time: 90 min.). 1984. 8.95 (317) Am Fed Astrologers.

Lunations in Geopolitical Astrology. Alice Smith. 1 cass. 8.95 (318) Am Fed Astrologers.
Role of lunations with examples.

Lunch Money. collector's unabr. ed. Andrew Clements. 4 cass. (Running Time: 6 hrs.). (YA). 2005. 30.00 (978-0-307-28297-2(X), Listening Lib); audio compact disk 32.30 (978-0-307-28298-9(8), Listening Lib) Pub: Random Audio Pubg. Dist(s): NetLibrary CO

Lunch Money. unabr. ed. Andrew Clements. Read by John H. Mayer. 5 CDs. (Running Time: 18120 sec.). (ENG.). (J). (gr. 5). 2005. audio compact disk 30.00 (978-0-307-28232-3(5), Listening Lib) Pub: Random Audio Pubg. Dist(s): Random

Lunch Time Specials. Brooks & Kleinsinger. 1 CD. (Running Time: 1 hr. 30 mins.). 2005. audio compact disk 12.95 (978-0-660-18831-7(7)) Pub: Canadian Broadcasting CAN. Dist(s): Georgetown Term

Lunch with Little Miss Muffet Audio CD. Adapted by Benchmark Education Company Staff. Based on a work by Jeffrey B. Fuerst. (Reader's Theater Nursery Rhymes & Songs Ser.). (J). (gr. k-1). 2008. audio compact disk 10.00 (978-1-60437-985-3(5)) Benchmark Educ.

***Luncheon.** Susan Dunlap. 2009. (978-1-60136-546-0(2)) Audio Holding.

Luncheon: Dr. Thomas P. Stanley. 1 cass. 1990. 8.50 Recorded Res.

Luncheon of the Boating Party. unabr. ed. Susan Vreeland. Read by Karen White. 14 CDs. (Running Time: 17 hrs.). 2007. audio compact disk 100.00 (978-1-4159-3973-4(X)) Books on Tape.

Luncheon Presentation: Tax Reform '86 - Plans, Prospects, & Potential Impacts. James J. Salmon. 1 cass. 9.00 (TAPE 4) Recorded Res.

Luncheon Presentation: The Malpractice Crisis - Current Status & Options for Reform. Orrin G. Hatch. 1 cass. 9.00 (TAPE 13) Recorded Res.

***Lunchmeat & Life Lessons.** Mary B. Lucas. 2010. 19.00 (978-0-9791234-2-9(9)) MBL Pr.

Lunchroom Rap Up. Mary Blakely. 1 cass. Azuray Learn.
Multi-sensory education, workbook incl.

Lunchroom Tales: A Natural History of the Cafetorium. unabr. ed. Read by Bill Harley. 1 cass. (Running Time: 50 min.). (J). (gr. 4-8). 1996. 9.95 (978-1-878126-19-1(9), RRR110); audio compact disk 15.00 CD. (978-1-878126-20-7(2), RRR110J) Round Riv Prodns.
When Bill returns to elementary school after 30 years, he finds that some things are the same & some are very different. A celebratory mixture of music & story sure to please kids & their grown-up companions. Intercom-Morning Announcements; Everyone's a Little Bit Different; Saturday; Mr. Anderson - Bus Driver; In the Back of the Bus; Happy Birthday, Mrs. Nottingham; Looking in the Mirror; I'm Gonna Do It Tomorrow; Kevin's Story; We've Been Friends; & Something Happened to Her.

Lungs: Repairs & Maintenance. abr. ed. Robert A. Monroe. Read by Robert A. Monroe. (Running Time: 30 min.). (Human Plus Ser.). 1989. 14.95 (978-1-56102-018-8(4)) Inter Indus.
Improve lung tissues & enhance oxygen exchange.

Lupus Disease & Women. 1 cass. (Running Time: 30 min.). 10.95 (I0370B090, HarperThor) HarpC GBR.

Lure of the Dim Trails. unabr. ed. B. M. Bower. Read by Jack Sondericker. 3 cass. (Running Time: 3 hrs.). 1987. 21.95 (978-1-55686-256-4(3), 256) Books in Motion.
Phil Thurston, writer, goes west to gather "Local Color" & a plot or two for a western novel. He is welcomed to the west at the point of a gun. Realizing his own shortcomings amid a land of rugged individualism, he seeks to learn the ways of the westerner. Phil takes a job at the Lazy Eight & his adventures begin.

Lure of the Labrador Wild. Dillon Wallace. Read by Jody Richardson. (Running Time: 32400 sec.). 2005. audio compact disk 29.95 (978-0-9734223-9-9(4)) Rattling Bks CAN.

Lush Life. unabr. ed. Richard Price. Read by Bobby Cannavale. 11 CDs. (Running Time: 13 hrs. 0 mins. 0 sec.). (ENG.). 2008. audio compact disk 44.95 (978-1-4272-0320-5(2)) Pub: Macmill Audio. Dist(s): Macmillan

Lusiades: The Lusiades (Excerpts) Luis Vaz de Camoes. 1 cass. (Running Time: 1 hrs.). (POR.). 1997. pap. bk. 19.50 (978-1-58085-675-1(6)) Interlingua VA.

Lust for Life: A Novel of Vincent Van Gogh. unabr. collector's ed. Irving Stone. Read by Michael Prichard. 12 cass. (Running Time: 18 hrs.). 1979. 96.00 (978-0-7366-0188-7(0), 1188) Books on Tape.
A fictionalized biography of the Dutch painter, Vincent Van Gogh, based primarily on his 3 volumes of letters to his brother Theo.

Lust Lizard of Melancholy Cove. unabr. ed. Christopher Moore. (Running Time: 11 hrs. 0 mins.). 2009. 29.95 (978-1-4332-9313-9(7)); 65.95 (978-1-4332-9309-2(9)); audio compact disk 100.00 (978-1-4332-9310-8(2)) Blckstn Audio.

Lust Lizard of Melancholy Cove. unabr. ed. Christopher Moore. Read by Oliver Wyman. 7 CDs. (Running Time: 8 hrs. 45 mins.). 2009. audio compact disk 24.99 (978-0-06-177051-7(5), Harper Audio) HarperCollins Pubs.

***Lust Lizard of Melancholy Cove.** unabr. ed. Christopher Moore. Read by Oliver Wyman. (ENG.). 2009. (978-0-06-190258-1(6), Harper Audio); (978-0-06-190260-4(8), Harper Audio) HarperCollins Pubs.

***Lust, Violence, Religion: Life in Historic Waco.** Compiled by Bradley Turner. Narrated by Mike Jones. (ENG.). 2010. audio compact disk 9.99 (978-1-934302-97-2(X)) TX State Tech.

Lustige Dialoge. Walbruck. 1 cass. (GER.). 2001. 15.00 (978-0-8442-2134-2(1)) Glencoe.
Beginning students will enjoy these brief, humorous dialogues. 30 dialogues with a vocabulary of high-frequency words.

Lustige Geschichten. 2 cass. (GER.). 2001. 25.00 (978-0-8442-2149-6(X)) Glencoe.
Designed to motivate advanced beginners & intermediate students through original & very funny stories. Questions follow each story.

Luther: Gospel, Law, & Reformation, I-II. Instructed by Phillip Cary. 12 cass. (Running Time: 12 hrs.). bk. 54.95 (978-1-56585-955-5(3), 6633) Teaching Co.

Luther: Gospel, Law, & Reformation, I-II. Instructed by Phillip Cary. 12 CDs. (Running Time: 12 hrs.). 2004. bk. 69.95 (978-1-56585-957-9(X), 6633) Teaching Co.

***Luther for Armchair Theologians.** unabr. ed. Steven Paulson. Narrated by Simon Vance. (ENG.). 2005. 12.98 (978-1-59644-201-6(8), Hovel Audio) christianaud.

Luther for Armchair Theologians. unabr. ed. Steven Paulson. Narrated by Simon Vance. 4 CDs. (Running Time: 5 hrs. 18 mins. 0 sec.). (ENG.). 2005. audio compact disk 21.98 (978-1-59644-200-9(X), Hovel Audio) christianaud.

Lutheran Visits Medjugorje. Interview with Mother Angelica & Wayne Weible. 1 cass. (Running Time: 60 min.). (Mother Angelica Live Ser.). 1987. 10.00 (978-1-55794-092-6(4), T43) Eternal Wrd TV.

***Luthien's Gamble.** unabr. ed. R. A. Salvatore. Narrated by David Drummond. (Running Time: 11 hrs. 0 mins.). (Crimson Shadow Ser.). 2010. 17.99 (978-1-4001-8356-2(1)) Tantor Media.

***Luthien's Gamble.** unabr. ed. R. A. Salvatore. Narrated by David Drummond. (Running Time: 11 hrs. 30 mins. 0 sec.). (Crimson Shadow Ser.). (ENG.). 2010. 24.99 (978-1-4001-6356-4(0)); audio compact disk 34.99 (978-1-4001-1356-9(3)); audio compact disk 69.99 (978-1-4001-4356-6(X)) Pub: Tantor Media. Dist(s): IngramPubServ

Lux Classics Presents Best of Lux Radio Theatre. Radio Spirits Publishing Staff. Read by Cary Grant. 2006. audio compact disk 39.98 (978-1-57019-819-9(5)) Radio Spirits.

Lux Radio, Vol. 1. 6 cass. 24.98 Set. Moonbeam Pubns.

Lux Radio, Vol. 2. 6 cass. 24.98 Set. Moonbeam Pubns.

***Lux Radio Theatre.** RadioArchives.com. (Running Time: 600). (ENG.). 2008. audio compact disk 29.98 (978-1-61081-076-0(7)) Radio Arch.

Lux Radio Theatre: After the Thin Man. Perf. by William Powell & Myrna Loy. 1 cass. (Running Time: 1 hr.). 2001. 6.98 (2123) Radio Spirits.

Lux Radio Theatre: Christmas in July with Dick Powell & Linda Darnell. Perf. by Dick Powell & Linda Darnell. 1 cass. (Running Time: 1 hr.). 2001. 6.98 (2560) Radio Spirits.

Lux Radio Theatre: Criminal Code with Edward G. Robinson & Beverly Roberts. Perf. by Edward G. Robinson & Beverly Roberts. 1 cass. (Running Time: 1 hr.). 2001. 6.98 (2401) Radio Spirits.

Lux Radio Theatre: Day the Earth Stood Still. Perf. by Michael Rennie et al. 1 cass. (Running Time: 60 min.). (Old Time Radio Classic Singles Ser.). 4.95 (978-1-57816-094-5(4), LR113) Audio File.
Includes: (1/4/54) Plus Exploring Tomorrow: "Martian Queen" complete short sci fi adventure.

Lux Radio Theatre: Flight Command. Perf. by Walter Pidgeon & Robert Taylor. 1 cass. (Running Time: 1 hr.). 2001. 6.98 (1514) Radio Spirits.

Lux Radio Theatre: If I Were King. Perf. by Douglas Fairbanks, Jr. & Cedric Hardwicke. 1 cass. (Running Time: 1 hr.). 2001. 6.98 (1773) Radio Spirits.

Lux Radio Theatre: It's a Wonderful Life. Perf. by Jimmy Stewart et al. 1 cass. (Running Time: 60 min.). (Old Time Radio Classic Singles Ser.). 4.95 (978-1-57816-111-9(8), WL114) Audio File.
Radio version of Frank Capra's classic film (1947).

Lux Radio Theatre: Jane Eyre with Ingrid Bergman & Robert Montgomery. Perf. by Ingrid Bergman & Robert Montgomery. 1 cass. (Running Time: 1 hr.). 2001. 6.98 (2201) Radio Spirits.

Lux Radio Theatre: Johnny Eager with Robert Taylor, Susan Peters & Van Heflin. Perf. by Robert Taylor et al. 1 cass. (Running Time: 1 hr.). 2001. 6.98 (2606) Radio Spirits.

Lux Radio Theatre: Little Woman. Perf. by June Allyson et al. 1 cass. (Running Time: 1 hr.). 2001. 6.98 (2103) Radio Spirits.

Lux Radio Theatre: Miracle on Thirty-Fourth Street. Perf. by Edmund Gwenn. 1 cass. (Running Time: 60 min.). (Old Time Radio Classic Singles Ser.). 4.95 (978-1-57816-115-7(0), LR115) Audio File.
(12/20/48).

Lux Radio Theatre: National Velvet. Perf. by Mickey Rooney et al. 1 cass. (Running Time: 1 hr.). 2001. 6.98 (2086) Radio Spirits.

Lux Radio Theatre: Now, Voyager. Perf. by Bette Davis et al. 1 cass. (Running Time: 1 hr.). 2001. 6.98 (2483) Radio Spirits.

Lux Radio Theatre: O.S.S. Perf. by Alan Ladd & Veronica Lake. 1 cass. (Running Time: 1 hr.). 2001. 6.98 (2583) Radio Spirits.

Lux Radio Theatre: Our Town. Perf. by Frank Craven et al. 1 cass. (Running Time: 1 hr.). 2001. 6.98 (2499) Radio Spirits.

Lux Radio Theatre: Pardon My Past. Perf. by Fred MacMurray et al. 1 cass. (Running Time: 1 hr.). 2001. 6.98 (1986) Radio Spirits.

Lux Radio Theatre: Pride of the Marines. Perf. by John Garfield et al. 1 cass. (Running Time: 1 hr.). 2001. 6.98 (2020) Radio Spirits.

Lux Radio Theatre: The Egg & I. Perf. by Claudette Colbert & Fred MacMurray. 1 cass. (Running Time: 1 hr.). 2001. 6.98 (2423) Radio Spirits.

Lux Radio Theatre: The Magnificent Dope. Perf. by Henry Fonda & Don Ameche. 1 cass. (Running Time: 1 hr.). 2001. 6.98 (2247) Radio Spirits.

Lux Radio Theatre: Treasure of Sierra Madre. Perf. by Humphrey Bogart et al. 1 cass. (Running Time: 60 min.). (Old Time Radio Classic Singles Ser.). 4.95 (978-1-57816-129-4(0), TS116) Audio File.
Radio version of the 1947 film (4/18/49).

Lux Radio Theatre: Undercurrent. Perf. by Katharine Hepburn & Robert Taylor. 1 cass. (Running Time: 1 hr.). 2001. 6.98 (2620) Radio Spirits.

Lux Radio Theatre: Wake Up & Live. Perf. by Frank Sinatra. 1 cass. (Running Time: 1 hr.). 2001. 6.98 (2184) Radio Spirits.

Lux Radio Theatre: Young Tom Edison. Perf. by Mickey Rooney & Beulah Bondi. 1 cass. (Running Time: 1 hr.). 2001. 6.98 (2559) Radio Spirits.

Lux Radio Theatre: 1930s. Perf. by Gary Cooper et al. 10 CDs. (Running Time: 10 hrs.). 2002. audio compact disk 39.98 (4486); 34.98 (4485) Radio Spirits.
AMC has carefully selected 10 of the all-time greatest performances from the Radio Spirits silver screen library for your listening enjoyment. Now you can hear a group of superstars in their famous movie roles. These 1930s radio adaptations, which were directed by Hollywood legend Cecil DeMille, used original scores and brilliant sound effects to reate an incredible audio version of film classics.

***Luxe.** unabr. ed. Anna Godbersen. Read by Nina Siemaszko. (ENG.). 2008. (978-0-06-169892-7(X)); (978-0-06-170609-7(4)) HarperCollins Pubs.

Luxuriate in the Life of Contemplation: A Conversation with the Incarnate Divine Person. Adi Da Samraj. 4 cass. 1997. 29.95 (978-1-57097-035-1(1)) Dawn Horse Pr.

Luxurious Hearses (A Story from Say You're One of Them) unabr. ed. Uwem Akpan. Read by Kevin Free. (Running Time: 4 hrs.). (ENG.). 2009. 7.98 (978-1-60788-494-1(1)) Pub: Hachet Audio. Dist(s): HachBkGrp

Luz: El es Grande. unabr. ed. José Medero. 1 cass. (Running Time: 30 min.). 2001. 4.99 (978-0-8297-3387-7(6)) Zondervan.

Luz de Vela en Quintero. David A. Petreman. (ENG.). 2007. 4.00 (978-1-933675-23-7(3)) Dos Madres Pr.

Luz en Mi Vida. Pablo Olivares. 2004. audio compact disk 16.99 (978-0-8297-4082-0(1)) Zondervan.

LUZ (Grupo Luz) 1. (YA). 1999. audio compact disk 5.00 (978-1-59305-045-0(3)) Good News Prod Intl.

***Luzhin Defense.** unabr. ed. Vladimir Nabokov. (Running Time: 8 hrs.). 2010. 24.99 (978-1-4418-7309-5(0), 9781441873095, BAD); 39.97 (978-1-4418-7296-8(5), 9781441872968, BADLE) Brilliance Audio.

***Luzhin Defense.** unabr. ed. Vladimir Nabokov. Read by Mel Foster. (Running Time: 8 hrs.). 2010. 24.99 (978-1-4418-7294-4(9), 9781441872944, Brilliance MP3); 39.97 (978-1-4418-7295-1(7), 9781441872951, Brlnc Audio MP3 Lib); audio compact disk 29.99 (978-1-4418-7292-0(2), 9781441872920, Bril Audio CD Unabri); audio compact disk 74.97 (978-1-4418-7293-7(0), 9781441872937, BriAudCD Unabrid) Brilliance Audio.

L.V.F., Set. Henri Amouroux. 2 cass. (Francais sous l'occupation Ser.). 1991. 26.95 (1231-RF) Olivia & Hill.
The first antisemitic measures.

LXXX Sermons see Cambridge Treasy Malory

Lycian Shore. unabr. collector's ed. Freya Stark. Read by Donada Peters. 7 cass. (Running Time: 7 hrs.). 1991. 42.00 (978-0-7366-1953-0(4), 2774) Books on Tape.
The Lycian Shore is an account of a single journey in a sailing yacht along the coast of Turkey in the earlier 1950s. The author & her companions followed the trail of Greek & Persian traders, the men who prepared the scene for Alexander the Great. Just as the ancient voyagers did, they landed as the tides & winds allowed. It was no ordinary journey & Freya Stark is no ordinary guide. The exciting, imaginative quality of her writing & her grasp of antiquity bring to life an ancient civilization with brilliance & intensity.

Lycidas see Treasury of John Milton

Lycidas see Hearing Great Poetry: From Chaucer to Milton

Lycidas see Poetry of John Milton

Lyddie. unabr. ed. Katherine Paterson. Narrated by Alyssa Bresnahan. 5 pieces. (Running Time: 6 hrs. 45 mins.). (gr. 7 up). 1993. 44.00 (978-1-55690-851-4(2), 93219E7) Recorded Bks.
Paints an authentic portrait of life in the mill towns of the Industrial Revolution. Lyddie Worthen is one of the girls who work in the mills of Lowell, Massachusetts. When the conditions at the mill begin to affect her friends' health, Lyddie risks her job to fight for better working conditions.

Lydia Cassatt Reading the Morning Paper. unabr. ed. Harriet Scott Chessman. Read by Harriet Scott Chessman. 3 cass. (Running Time: 3 hrs. 40 min.). 2002. 21.95 (978-1-57270-288-2(5)) Pub: Audio Partners. Dist(s): PerseuPGW
Lydia narrates as she poses for five of her sister's paintings. Ill with Bright's disease and conscious of impending death, Lydia contemplates her narrowing world.

Lydia Cassatt Reading the Morning Paper. unabr. ed. Harriet Scott Chessman. Read by Harriet Scott Chessman. 3 CDs. (Running Time: 3 hrs. 40 min.). 2002. audio compact disk 24.95 (978-1-57270-289-9(3)) Pub: Audio Partners. Dist(s): PerseuPGW
Lydia narrates as she poses for five of her sister's paintings. Ill with Bright's disease and conscious of impending death, Lydia contemplates her narrowing world.

Lydia Fielding. Susan Sallis. Read by Nicolette McKenzie. 10 cass. (Running Time: 11 hrs.). (Soundings Ser.). (J). 2005. 84.95 (978-1-84283-559-3(9)) Pub: ISIS Lrg Prnt GBR. Dist(s): Ulverscroft US

***Lydia's Charm: An Amish Widow Starts over in Charm, Ohio.** unabr. ed. Wanda Brunstetter. Narrated by Brooke Sanford. (Running Time: 9 hrs. 23 mins. 53 sec.). 2010. 24.49 (978-1-60814-727-4(4)) Oasis Audio.

***Lydia's Charm: An Amish Widow Starts over in Charm, Ohio.** unabr. ed. Wanda E. Brunstetter. Narrated by Brooke Sanford. (Running Time: 9 hrs. 23 mins. 53 sec.). 2010. audio compact disk 34.99 (978-1-59859-768-4(X)) Oasis Audio.

Lying. unabr. ed. Wendy Perriam. Narrated by Gerri Halligan. 9 cass. (Running Time: 12 hrs.). 2001. 82.00 (H1180E7, Clipper Audio) Recorded Bks.
An assistant & general dogsbody for a literary agency, Alison Ward has become used to lurching from one crisis to the next. One evening, in the crush of the crowded London tube, she arrives home with someone else's briefcase. Alison is soon swallowed up into a new world where faith & belief are tantamount to everything. However, she is soon to discover that beyond every facade, it's all too easy for everyone to be living a lie.

Lying Awake. Mark Salzman. 4 cass. (Running Time: 5 hrs. 30 mins.). 2004. 19.99 (978-1-4025-0174-6(9), 00604) Recorded Bks.

Lying Awake. unabr. ed. Mark Salzman. Narrated by Linda Stephens. 4 cass. (Running Time: 4 hrs. 30 mins.). 2001. 32.00 (978-0-7887-5321-3(5), 96568x7) Recorded Bks.
Sister John has devoted her life to serving God. She experiences religious visions of such intensity that she is revered by the other nuns. But these visions also bring on excruciating headaches. Offered a cure, she realizes

that it may also stop the visions & Sister John wonders how any change will affect her faith. Lying Awake is an eloquent examination of religious experience that transcends the boundaries of church & doctrine.

Lying Awake: A Novel see Twentieth-Century Poetry in English, No. 27, Recordings of Poets Reading Their Own Poetry

***Lying Carpet.** unabr. ed. David Lucas. Read by Nicholas Bell. (Running Time: 43 mins.). (J). 2010. audio compact disk 39.95 (978-1-74214-653-9(8), 9781742146539) Pub: Bolinda Pubng AUS. Dist(s): Bolinda Pub Inc

Lying in a Hammock see Poetry & Voice of James Wright

Lying in Wait. collector's ed. J. A. Jance. Read by Jonathan Marosz. 6 cass. (Running Time: 9 hrs.). (J. P. Beaumont Mystery Ser.). 2000. 48.00 (978-0-7366-5584-2(0)) Books on Tape.
Else Didriksen's husband was found mutilated on board the charred remains of their fishing boat. J. P. Beaumont dismisses no suspect as he tracks a killer whose vicious determination is fueled by a haunting, decades-old murder.

Lying in Wait. unabr. ed. J. A. Jance. Read by Gene Eugene. 8 cass. (Running Time: 11 hrs.). (J. P. Beaumont Mystery Ser.). 1994. 49.95 (978-1-55686-563-3(5), 102592) Books in Motion.

Lying Low. Diane Johnson. Read by Diane Johnson. 1 cass. (Running Time: 48 min.). 13.95 (978-1-55644-016-8(2), 1091) Am Audio Prose.
Contains closing sections of novel about Vietnam protest era fugitive & the lives she touches & is touched by.

lying Postman. unabr. ed. Darrel and Sally Odgers. Read by Alan King. (Running Time: 50 mins.). (Jack Russell: Dog Detective Ser.). (J). 2007. audio compact disk 39.95 (978-1-74093-915-7(8), 9781740939157) Pub: Bolinda Pubng AUS. Dist(s): Bolinda Pub Inc

lying postman / the awful Pawful. Darrel and Sally Odgers. Read by Alan King. (Running Time: 1 hr. 20 mins.). (Jack Russell: Dog Detective Ser.). (J). 2009. 39.99 (978-1-74214-418-4(7), 9781742144184) Pub: Bolinda Pubng AUS. Dist(s): Bolinda Pub Inc

Lying, Secrecy & Privacy. unabr. ed. Mary Mahowald. Read by Cliff Robertson. (Running Time: 10800 sec.). (Morality in Our Age Ser.). 2006. audio compact disk 25.95 (978-0-7861-6533-9(2)) Pub: Blckstn Audio. Dist(s): NetLibrary CO

Lying, Secrecy & Privacy. unabr. ed. Mary Mahowald. Read by Cliff Robertson. Ed. by John Lachs & Mike Hassell. 2 cass. (Running Time: 3 hrs.). Dramatization. (Morality in Our Age Ser.). 1995. 17.95 Set. (978-1-56823-025-2(7), 10504) Knowledge Prod.
Most people think it's wrong to lie, but sometimes telling the truth seems more hurtful than lying. Secrecy protects the truth & maintains our privacy, but it also can be a way of covering up lies. In an age of instant communication & information glut, what are the limits of privacy? Do public figures forfeit their privacy? Are some people - such as doctors, lawyers, & clergy - more obligated to keep secrets than others?.

Lying, the Nature of Satan & the Old Self. Dan Corner. 1 cass. 3.00 (56) Evang Outreach.

Lying Together: My Russian Affair. unabr. ed. Jennifer Beth Cohen. Read by Kimberly Breault. 7 CDs. (Running Time: 7 hrs. 30 mins.). 2005. audio compact disk 47.95 (978-1-59758-006-9(6)) Audis Libros Pub.

Lying with Strangers. unabr. ed. James Grippando. Read by Alyssa Bresnahan. (Running Time: 46800 sec.). 2007. audio compact disk 39.95 (978-0-06-125640-0(4), Harper Audio) HarperCollins Pubs.

***Lying with Strangers.** unabr. ed. James Grippando. Read by Alyssa Bresnahan. (ENG.). 2007. (978-0-06-145002-0(2), Harper Audio); (978-0-06-145003-7(0), Harper Audio) HarperCollins Pubs.

Lyle Alzado. 1 cass. (Reading With Winners: Ser. 1). 1984. 32.95 (978-0-89811-126-2(9), 8806C); Lets Talk Assocs.

Lyle Alzado: Defensive End. Read by Lyle Alzado. 1 cass. 9.95 (978-0-89811-108-8(0), 7159) Lets Talk Assocs.
Lyle Alzado talks about the people & events which influenced his career & his approach to his specialtiy.

Lyle & the Birthday Party see Lyle, Lyle, Crocodile

Lyle, Lyle, Crocodile. unabr. ed. Bernard Waber. Illus. by Bernard Waber. 1 cass. (Running Time: 15 min.). Dramatization. (Lyle the Crocodile Ser.). (ENG.). (J). (gr. k-3). 1993. pap. bk. 9.95 (978-0-395-66502-2(7), 497530, W Lorraine) HM Harcourt.

Lyle, Lyle, Crocodile. unabr. ed. Bernard Waber. Perf. by Gwen Verdon. 1 cass. (Running Time: 54 min.). Incl. House on East Eighty-Eighth Street. Bernard Weber. (Lyle the Crocodile Ser.). (J). (ps-3). 1989. (CPN 1350); Lovable Lyle. Based on a book by Bernard Waber. (Lyle the Crocodile Ser.). (J). (ps-3). 1989. (CPN 1350); Lyle & the Birthday Party. Based on a book by Bernard Waber. (Lyle the Crocodile Ser.). (J). (ps-3). 1989. (CPN 1350); (Lyle the Crocodile Ser.). (J). (gr. 3-5). 1989. 12.00 (978-0-89845-864-0(1), CPN 1350) HarperCollins Pubs.

Lyme Disease: Program from the Award Winning Public Radio Series. Interview. Hosted by Fred Goodwin. Comment by John Hockenberry. 1 CD. (Running Time: 1 hr). 2000. audio compact disk 21.95 (978-1-932479-62-1(7), LCM 110) Lichtenstein Creat.
Lyme disease is usually thought of as a relatively benign illness, causing a rash and flu-like symptoms. But when left untreated, this tick-borne illness can become serious, and can cause neurological and psychological symptoms, including facial paralysis, memory loss, and mood changes. We?ll talk to Dr. Patricia Coyle, professor of neurology at the School of Medicine at the State University of New York at Stony Brook, and Dr. Brian Fallon, the Director of the Lyme Disease Research program at the New York State Psychiatric Institute at Columbia Presbyterian Medical Center. Plus, a first person account of living with chronic Lyme Disease, an update on the West Nile Virus which sickened dozens of New Yorkers last year, some with deadly encephalitis, and commentary from John Hockenberry.

Lyn Lifshin. unabr. ed. Read by Lyn Lifshin. 1 cass. (Running Time: 29 min.). 1985. 10.00 New Letters.
A reading by a prolific poet from New York state, Lyn Lifshin.

Lynch Law in America. 1 cass. 10.00 (HV203) Esstee Audios.
How the idea of lynching began & what it has done to American justice.

Lynda Barry Experience. abr. ed. Narrated by Lynda Barry. 1 cass. (Running Time: 1 hr. 4 min.). 1999. 11.95 (978-1-57453-083-4(6)) Audio Lit.
Cartoonist, painter & writer Lynda Barry lets loose a fusillade of stories about her childhood. Some parts of these stories are made up, some parts are true.

Lynda Randle Christmas. Contrib. by Lynda Randle. Prod. by Michael Tait. 2005. audio compact disk 13.98 (978-5-558-77741-3(9)) Gaither Music Co.

Lyndon Johnson & the American Dream. unabr. ed. Doris Keams Goodwin. Read by Mary Woods. 12 cass. (Running Time: 17 hrs. 30 mins.). 1994. 83.95 (978-0-7861-0414-7(7), 1366) Blckstn Audio.
Lyndon Johnson - brilliant, formidable, troubled - is captured here in one of the most revealing portraits of an American President ever written. It is the story of Johnson's life from the farmhouse on the Pedernales where he was born, to the White House where he lived under siege during the last period of his term, terrified by dreams of paralysis, wandering at night through the mansion with a small flashlight. It is a brilliant analysis of the private man & his recurrent patterns of behavior, which allows us to understand some of the complexities of the public figure.

Lyon's Gate. abr. ed. Catherine Coulter. Read by Anne Flosnik. (Running Time: 21600 sec.). (Bride Ser.). 2006. audio compact disk 16.99 (978-1-59600-807-6(5), 9781596008076, BCD Value Price) Brilliance Audio.
Please enter a Synopsis.

***Lyon's Gate.** abr. ed. Catherine Coulter. 2010. audio compact disk 9.99 (978-1-4418-5636-4(6)) Brilliance Audio.

Lyon's Gate. abr. unabr. ed. Catherine Coulter. Read by Anne Flosnik. 5 CDs. (Running Time: 36000 sec.). (Bride Ser.). 2005. audio compact disk 97.25 (978-1-59086-911-6(7), 9781590869116, BACDLib Ed) Brilliance Audio.

Lyon's Gate. unabr. ed. Catherine Coulter. Read by Anne Flosnik. (Running Time: 10 hrs.). (Bride Ser.). 2005. 39.25 (978-1-59710-855-3(3), 9781597108553, BADLE); 24.95 (978-1-59710-854-6(5), 9781597108546, BAD); 82.25 (978-1-58788-906-6(4), 9781587889066, BrilAudUnabridg); 32.95 (978-1-58788-905-9(6), 9781587889059, BAU); audio compact disk 36.95 (978-1-59086-910-9(9), 9781590869109, BACD); audio compact disk 39.25 (978-1-59335-804-4(0), 9781593358044, Brlnc Audio MP3 Lib); audio compact disk 24.95 (978-1-59335-670-5(6), 9781593356705, Brilliance MP3) Brilliance Audio.

Lyon's Pride. abr. ed. Anne McCaffrey. Read by Jean Reed Bahle. 2 cass. (Running Time: 3 hrs.). 2000. 7.95 (978-1-57815-019-9(1), 1026, Media Bks Audio) Media Bks NJ.
Saga of the Rowan, Damia & their unforgettable families continues, as the powerful yet peaceful telepaths face an alien threat to their existence.

Lyon's Pride. unabr. ed. Anne McCaffrey. Read by Jean Reed Bahle. (Running Time: 11 hrs.). (Rowan/Damia Ser.). 2008. 39.97 (978-1-4233-8283-6(8), 9781423382836, BADLE); 39.97 (978-1-4233-8281-2(1), 9781423382812, Brlnc Audio MP3 Lib); 24.99 (978-1-4233-8282-9(X), 9781423382829, BAD); 24.99 (978-1-4233-8280-5(3), 9781423382805, Brilliance MP3); audio compact disk 84.97 (978-1-4233-8279-9(X), 9781423382799, BriAudCD Unabrid); audio compact disk 29.99 (978-1-4233-8278-2(1), 9781423382782, Bril Audio CD Unabri) Brilliance Audio.

Lyra's Oxford. Philip Pullman. (Running Time: 48 mins.). (His Dark Materials Ser.). (J). (gr. 7 up). 2004. audio compact disk 17.00 (978-0-8072-1997-3(5), Listening Lib) Pub: Random Audio Pubg. Dist(s): NetLibrary CO

Lyra's Oxford. Philip Pullman. Perf. by Philip Pullman. (Running Time: 48 mins.). (His Dark Materials Ser.). (J). (gr. 7 up). 2004. audio compact disk 18.00 (978-0-8072-8351-6(7), Listening Lib) Random Audio Pubg.

Lyra's Oxford. unabr. ed. Philip Pullman. Read by Philip Pullman. Read by Full Cast Production Staff. (Running Time: 48 mins.). (His Dark Materials Ser.). (ENG.). (J). 2003. audio compact disk 14.95 (978-0-8072-1996-6(7), Listening Lib) Pub: Random Audio Pubg. Dist(s): Random

Lyre of Orpheus. Robertson Davies. Read by Robertson Davies. (Running Time: 30 min.). 8.95 (AMF-203) Am Audio Prose.
Features talks on opera, academia and Rabelais.

Lyre of Orpheus. unabr. ed. Robertson Davies. Read by Frederick Davidson. 11 cass. (Running Time: 16 hrs.). (gr. 9-12). 1997. 76.95 (978-0-7861-1100-8(3), 1864) Blckstn Audio.
There is an important decision to be made. The Cornish Foundation, set up with money left by the late Francis Cornish, art expert, collector, connoisseur, & notable eccentric, must choose a worthy undertaking upon which to expend a portion of its considerable funds. And so it is decided: the Foundation will fund the doctoral work of one Hulda Schnakenburg, a grumpy, grimy, thoroughly difficult, & extraordinarily talented music student.

Lyre of Orpheus: The Cornish Trilogy, Book 3. unabr. ed. Robertson Davies. Read by Frederick Davidson. (Running Time: 15 hrs. 0 mins.). 2010. 29.95 (978-1-4417-0984-4(3)); audio compact disk 118.00 (978-1-4417-0981-3(9)) Blckstn Audio.

Lyrebirds see Gathering of Great Poetry for Children

Lyric Language: More Bilingual Live Action Video. unabr. ed. 1 cass. (Running Time: 35 min.). (J). cass. & video 19.95 ea. Penton Overseas.
Presents a fun-filled & easy way for kids of all ages to learn a new language. Inclues lyric book with "Family Circus" characters.

Lyric Language Italian: Interactive Music & Video Language Program. Penton. (Lyric Language Series 1). (ITA.). (J). 1996. audio compact disk 39.95 (978-1-56015-901-8(4)) Penton Overseas.

Lyrical Earth Science: Geology. Doug Elda & Dorry Elda. Illus. by Sally Raskauskas. Music by Bobby Harton. (YA). (gr. 5-10). 2003. pap. bk. 25.50 (978-0-9741635-2-9(X)) Lyrical Lrng.

Lyrical Earth Science: Geology. Doug Elda & Dory Elda. Illus. by Sally Raskauskas. Music by Bobby Harton. (YA). (gr. 5-10). 2003. pap. bk. 19.95 (978-0-9741635-7-4(0)) Lyrical Lrng.

Lyrical Earth Science: Geology. Doug Eldon. Perf. by Bobby Harton. Arranged by Bobby Harton. (YA). (gr. 5-10). 2003. audio compact disk 14.00 (978-0-9741635-0-5(3)) Lyrical Lrng.

Lyrical Earth Science: Geology. Doug Eldon & Dorry Eldon. Perf. by Bobby Harton. Illus. by Sally Raskavskas. Music by Bobby Harton. (YA). (gr. 5-10). 2003. pap. bk. 23.95 (978-0-9741635-8-1(9)) Lyrical Lrng.

Lyrical Life Science. Doug Eldon. Illus. by Eric Altenderf. Music by Bobby Harton. 2 cass. (Running Time: 3 hrs.). (YA). (gr. 5-10). 1995. pap. bk. 29.50 (978-0-9741635-4-3(6)) Lyrical Lrng.
"CD text workbook set biological information is set to old time camp, folk and patriotic tunes or CD text amplifies, explains and illustrates (with line drawings.) Workbook has essay questions and fill in-the-blank type questions based on the text and songs.".

Lyrical Life Science. Douglas C. Eldon. Perf. by Bobby Horton. Contrib. by Bobby Horton. 1 cass. (Running Time: 30 min.). (J). (gr. 3-10). 1995. 9.95 (978-0-9646367-1-2(9)) Lyrical Lrng.
Scientific information is set to traditional tunes & performed by acclaimed Civil War recording artist Bobby Horton. The 94p. accompanying text amplifies the songs. Also included are nearly 200 original illustrations & sheet music. A Parents' Choice 1995 Gold Award Winner. 1996 Notable Recording for Children (American Library Association, Association for Library Service to Children).

Lyrical Life Science. Douglas C. Eldon. Perf. by Bobby Horton. Contrib. by Bobby Horton. Illus. by Eric Altendorf. 1 cass. (Running Time: 30 min.). (J). (gr. 3-10). 1995. pap. bk. 19.95 (978-0-9646367-0-5(0)) Lyrical Lrng.

Lyrical Life Science: The Human Body, Vol. 3. Dorry Eldan. Illus. by Eric Altenderf & Sally Raskauskas. Music by Bobby Hartan. (YA). (gr. 5-10). 1998. pap. bk. 29.50 (978-0-9646367-6-7(X)) Lyrical Lrng.

Lyrical Life Science Vol. 2: Mammals, Ecology & Biomes. Dorry Eldon et al. Perf. by Bobby Horton. Contrib. by Bobby Horton. Illus. by Eric Altendorf. 1 cass. (Running Time: 44 min.). (J). (gr. 3-10). 1996. pap. bk. 19.95 (978-0-9646367-2-9(7)) Lyrical Lrng.
More scientific information set to old-time tunes to help students remember/learn vocabulary. 112p. text amplifies lyrics; includes zoo line drawings; also sheet music & guitar chords.

Lyrical Life Science Vol. 2: Mammals, Ecology & Biomes. Douglas C. Eldon et al. Perf. by Bobby Horton. Contrib. by Bobby Horton. 1 cass. (Running Time: 44 min.). (J). (gr. 3-10). 1996. pap. bk. 9.95 Incl. lyric sheet. (978-0-9646367-3-6(5)) Lyrical Lrng.

Lyrical Life Science Vol. 2: Mammals, Ecologyr Biomes. Doug Eldon & Dorry Eldon. Illus. by Eric Altendorf. Music by Bobby Harton. (YA). (gr. 5-10). 1996. bk. 29.50 (978-0-9741635-9-8(7)) Lyrical Lrng.

Lyrical Life Science Vol. 3: The Human Body. Dorry Eldon. Perf. by Bobby Horton. 1 cass. (Running Time: 33 min.). (J). (gr. 5-10). 1998. 9.95 cass. (978-0-9646367-5-0(1)) Lyrical Lrng.
Scientific information about eleven human body systems is set to old-time tunes.

Lyrical Life Science Vol. 3: The Human Body. Dorry Eldon. Perf. by Bobby Horton. Contrib. by Bobby Horton. Illus. by Eric Altendorf & Sally Raskauskas. 1 cass. (Running Time: 33 min.). (YA). (gr. 4-9). 1998. pap. bk. 19.95 (978-0-9646367-4-3(3)) Lyrical Lrng.

Lyrical Movements - Poetry CD. Composed by Lyrical Movements. (ENG.). 2009. audio compact disk (978-0-9823109-1-5(9)) Lyrical Move.

Lyrically Speaking, Vol. 1. 1 CD. 1998. audio compact disk (978-0-9673648-1-0(7)) Daniel Connell.

Lyricode 256. Perf. by Marc Lacy. Prod. by Canita Rogers. 2009. audio compact disk 14.00 (978-0-9749712-5-4(1)) AVO Pubng.

Lyrocal Earth Science: Geology. Doug Eldan. Perf. by Bobby Harton. Music by Bobby Harton. 1 cass. (Running Time: 1 hr.). (YA). (gr. 5-10). 2003. 10.00 (978-0-9741635-6-7(2)) Lyrical Lrng.
"Audiocassette only science songs, 18 geology songs of foundational information 2003 parents' choice silver award.".

Lysis see Phaedrus

M

M & M: Motivation & Marketing for Therapists. Bill Kerley. 2000. 14.95 (978-1-886298-01-9(7)) Bayou Pubng.

M. Balamurali Krishna: Vocal. 1 cass. (Maestro's Choice Series One). 1991. (C91015); audio compact disk (CD C91015) Multi-Cultural Bks.
Karnatic classical music.

M. Balamurali Krishna: Vocal. 1 cass. (Thyagaraja Masterpieces Ser.: Vol. 2). 1992. (C92045) Multi-Cultural Bks.

M Boogie Blue Cassette. Stephen Cosgrove. 2004. 5.00 (978-1-58804-425-9(4)) PCI Educ.

M. Butterfly. unabr. ed. David Henry Hwang. Perf. by David Dukes et al. 2 CDs. (Running Time: 1 hr. 54 mins.). (L. A. Theatre Works). 2000. audio compact disk 25.95 (978-1-58081-177-4(9), CDTPT73) Pub: L A Theatre. Dist(s): NetLibrary CO

M. Butterfly. unabr. ed. David Henry Hwang. Perf. by John Lithgow et al. 2 cass. (Running Time: 1 hr. 54 mins.). 2000. 23.95 (978-1-58081-006-7(3), TPT73) L A Theatre.
Inspired by an actual espionage scandal, a French diplomat discovers that his beautiful Chinese mistress of twenty years is actually a man & communist spy. In 1960's Beijing the married Rene Gallimard lusts for Song Liling, a seductive Chinese opera star.

M. C. Higgins, the Great. Virginia Hamilton. (J). 1985. 34.66 SRA McGraw.

M. C. Higgins, the Great. unabr. ed. Virginia Hamilton. Narrated by Roscoe Lee Browne. 6 pieces. (Running Time: 8 hrs. 30 mins.). (gr. 8 up). 1993. 51.00 (978-1-55690-647-3(1), 93134E7) Recorded Bks.
Growing up on an Appalachian mountain in country still beautiful yet ravaged by coal mining, M.C. Higgins struggles with growing up, his own perception that his family must get off the mountain & his father's desire to stay.

M. C. Higgins, the Great. unabr. ed. Virginia Hamilton. Narrated by Roscoe Lee Browne. 7 CDs. (Running Time: 8 hrs. 30 mins.). (gr. 8 up). 2000. audio compact disk 72.00 (978-0-7887-4215-6(9), C1154E7) Recorded Bks.
On an Appalachian mountain in a country still beautiful yet ravaged by coal mining, M.C. Higgins struggles with growing up, his own perception that his family must get off the mountain & his father's desire to stay.

M. Dupin au Secours de la Police. Edgar Allan Poe. 2 cass. (FRE.). 1992. 27.95 (1271-LV) Olivia & Hill.
A group of actors read two mysteries solved by Detective Dupin: "Le Double Assassinat Dans la Rue Morgue" & "La Lettre Volee.".

M. E. Beverly Hunter Great Masterpiece. 3rd ed. Marjorie E. Hunter. Illus. by Mark Williams. Intro. by H. Carson Hunter, Jr. 50.00 (978-0-685-35654-8(X)) MH & Pr.

M. E. Beverly Hunter Great Masterpiece: Beverly Entertaining & Interesting Thoughts & Beverly Entertaining Melody. Marjorie B. Hunter. Illus. by Marjorie B. Hunter. Illus. by Mark Williams. (J). (gr. 5 up). 1986. 10.00 (978-0-317-93274-4(8)) MH & Pr.

***M-factor: Why the Millennial Generation Is Rocking the Workplace & How You Can Turn Their Great Expectations into Even Greater Results.** unabr. ed. Lynne Lancaster & David Stillman. (Running Time: 10 hrs. 0 mins.). 2010. 16.99 (978-1-4001-8667-9(6)) Tantor Media.

***M-factor: Why the Millennial Generation Is Rocking the Workplace & How You Can Turn Their Great Expectations into Even Greater Results.** unabr. ed. Lynne Lancaster & David Stillman. Narrated by Susan Ericksen. (Running Time: 11 hrs. 30 mins. 0 sec.). (ENG.). 2010. 24.99 (978-1-4001-6667-1(5)); audio compact disk 34.99 (978-1-4001-1667-6(8)) Pub: Tantor Media. Dist(s): IngramPubServ

***M-Factor: Why the Millennial Generation Is Rocking the Workplace & How You Can Turn Their Great Expectations into Even Greater Results.** unabr. ed. Lynne Lancaster & David Stillman. (Running Time: 10 hrs. 0 mins.). 2010. 34.99 (978-1-4001-9667-8(1)) Tantor Media.

***M-Factor: Why the Millennial Generation Is Rocking the Workplace & How You Can Turn Their Great Expectations into Even Greater Results.** unabr. ed. Lynne Lancaster & David Stillman. Narrated by Susan Ericksen. (Running Time: 11 hrs. 30 mins. 0 sec.). (ENG.). 2010. audio compact disk 69.99 (978-1-4001-4667-3(4)) Pub: Tantor Media. Dist(s): IngramPubServ

M. I. T. Lectures. unabr. ed. Aldous Huxley. 5 cass. (Running Time: 7 hrs.). 1961. 46.00 Set. (01106) Big Sur Tapes.

M Is for Magic. unabr. ed. Neil Gaiman. Read by Neil Gaiman. (J). 2008. 54.99 (978-1-60514-527-3(0)) Find a World.

***M Is for Magic.** unabr. ed. Neil Gaiman. Read by Neil Gaiman. 2007. (978-0-06-147582-5(3)); (978-0-06-147581-8(5)) HarperCollins Pubs.

M Is for Magic. unabr. ed. Neil Gaiman. Read by Neil Gaiman. (Running Time: 18000 sec.). (J). (gr. 5-9). 2007. audio compact disk 25.95 (978-0-06-125459-8(2), HarperChildAud) HarperCollins Pubs.

M Is for Malice. abr. ed. Sue Grafton. Read by Judy Kaye. 4 CDs. (Running Time: 4 hrs.). (Kinsey Millhone Mystery Ser.). (ENG.). 2002. audio compact

disk 30.00 (978-0-553-71340-4(X)) Pub: Random Audio Pubg. Dist(s): Random
4 CDs 4 hours Read by Judy Kaye "There are few writers able to sustain the solid mixture of detection, narrative energy and cultural observations that one finds in Grafton." - Washington Post Book World "M" is for money. Lots of it. "M" is for Malek Construction, the $40 million company that grew out of modest soil to become one of the big three in California construction, one of the few still in family hands. "M" is for the Malek family: four sons now nearing middle age who stand to inherit a fortune - four men with very different outlooks, temperaments, and needs, linked only by blood and money. Eighteen years ago, one of them - angry, troubled, and in trouble - went missing. "M" is for Millhone, hired to trace that missing black sheep brother. "M" is for memories, none of them happy. The bitter memoirs of an embattled family. This prodigal son will find no welcome at his family's table. "M" is for malice. And in brutal consequence, "M" is for murder, the all-too-common outcome of familiar hatreds. "M" is for malice . . . and malice kills.

M Is for Malice. unabr. collector's ed. Sue Grafton. Read by Mary Peiffer. 7 cass. (Running Time: 10 hrs. 30 min.). (Kinsey Millhone Mystery Ser.). 1997. 56.00 (978-0-913369-70-8(5), 4322) Books on Tape.
"M" is for the Malik family: four sons now nearing middle age who stand to inherit a fortune. Eighteen years ago, one of them went missing. Kinsey Millhone is hired to trace the black sheep brother & finds malice & murder.

M. S. - Improving Mental & Physical Mobilities. Norman J. Caldwell. Read by Norman J. Caldwell. Ed. by Achieve Now Institute Staff. 1 cass. (Running Time: 20 min.). (Health-Imaging Ser.). 1988. 9.97 (978-1-56273-071-0(1)) My Mothers Pub.
Move ahead mentally & physically.

Ma Mere. Georges Bataille. Read by Pierre Arditi. 4 cass. (FRE.). 1992. 56.95 (1523-EF) Olivia & Hill.
This well-known contemporary writer describes the mother whom he adored. A violent & scandalously beautiful text.

Ma Perkins see Great Soap Operas: Selected Episodes

Ma Shakti, the Primal Energy. Swami Amar Jyoti. 1 dolby cass. 1986. 9.95 (K-86) Truth Consciousness.
The all pervading radiation of Reality, the source of all. Her pristine power & manifestation. Invoking help of Divine Mother.

Mac Hammond on Leadership: Keys to Becoming a Person of Influence. Mac Hammond. 8 CDs. (Running Time: 7 hours). 2002. audio compact disk 40.00 (978-1-57399-149-0(X)) Mac Hammond.
In this powerful teaching series, you'll discover the practical spiritual truths for advancing on th ejob, growing your business, managing people and increasing God's way.

Mac Hammond on Leadership: Keys to Becoming a Person of Influence. Mac Hammond. 8 cass. (Running Time: 8 hrs). 1999. (978-1-57399-085-1(X)) Mac Hammond.
Discover the practical spiritual truths for advancing on the job, growing your business & managing people.

Mac Hanan's Strategies for World-Class Sales Performance. Mack Hanan. 1 cass. (Running Time: 90 mins.). 1999. pap. bk. & wbk. ed. 30.00 (80241CHDG) AMACOM.

Macady. Jennie L. Hansen. 2 cass. 9.98 (978-1-55503-821-2(2), 07001193) Covenant Comms.
A contemporary romance about learning to trust again.

Macarena & the Train. 1 cass. (J). 2001. pap. bk. 5.95 (KIM 9145C); pap. bk. 7.95 (KIM 9145CD) Kimbo Educ.
The craze is here to stay! They're everyone's favorite dances! Simple, easy-to-follow instructions included. Let's dance! Ideal for all ages.

MacArthur: A Biography. unabr. ed. Richard B. Frank. Read by Tom Weiner. Frwd. by Wesley K. Clark. (Running Time: 25200 sec.). (Great Generals Ser.). 2007. 19.95 (978-1-4332-0047-2(3)); 44.95 (978-1-4332-0045-8(7)); audio compact disk 19.95 (978-1-4332-0048-9(1)); audio compact disk 29.95 (978-1-4332-0049-6(X)); audio compact disk 55.00 (978-1-4332-0046-5(5)) Blckstn Audio.

MacArthur's Farewell Address. Douglas MacArthur. Read by Douglas MacArthur. 1 cass. 1998. (978-0-912986-23-4(9)) Am Media.

MacArthur's Undercover War. unabr. ed. William B. Breuer. Read by Jonathan Marosz. 7 cass. (Running Time: 10 hrs. 30 mins.). 2001. 56.00 (978-0-7366-8376-0(3)) Books on Tape.
When General Douglas MacArthur made his escape from the Philippines, vowing "I shall return," it took a massive covert effort to make his return a reality. MacArthur established the super-secret Allied Intelligence Bureau (AIB), to gather intelligence and carry out undercover warfare against the Japanese on an enormous scale.

Macbeth see Shakespeare

Macbeth. Perf. by John Barrymore. Ed. by William Shakespeare. 1 cass. (Running Time: 60 min). 7.95 (DD-7080) Natl Recrd Co.
Includes scenes & dialogue selected by Barrymore from these two famous plays.

Macbeth. Perf. by Stephen Dillane & Fiona Shaw. Ed. by William Shakespeare. 3 cass. (Running Time: 2 hrs. 20 mins.). Dramatization. (Plays of William Shakespeare Ser.). 1998. 17.98 (978-962-634-662-4(0), NA316214, Naxos AudioBooks); audio compact disk 22.98 (978-962-634-162-9(9), NA316212, Naxos AudioBooks) Naxos.
The tragic story of the rise and fall of an ambitious prince. This version uses the text of The New Cambridge Shakespeare, used by The Royal Shakespeare Company and educational institutions across the world.

MacBeth. Read by Flo Gibson. Ed. by William Shakespeare. 2 cass. (Running Time: 2 hrs. 30 min.). 1995. 14.95 (978-1-55685-354-8(8)) Audio Bk Con.
In this great tragedy Macbeth's ambition to fullfill the witches' prophecy that he will be King of Scotland spurs him & his wife to murder King Duncan &, later, Banquo. Banquo's ghost, Lady Macbeth's conscience, & the march of Birnam Wood leads to their downfall.

Macbeth. Ed. by William Shakespeare et al. Illus. by Bob Stotts. Narrated by Nick Sandys. Contrib. by Ted S. Hasselbring. (Start-to-Finish Books). (J). (gr. 2-3). 2002. 100.00 (978-1-58702-966-0(9)) D Johnston Inc.

Macbeth. William Shakespeare. (Running Time: 2 hrs. 15 mins.). 2002. 23.95 (978-1-60083-835-4(9)) Iofy Corp.

Macbeth. Ed. by William Shakespeare & Jerry Stemach. Retold by Jerry Stemach. Illus. by Bob Stotts. Retold by Gail Portnuff Venable. 2000. audio compact disk 200.00 (978-1-58702-488-7(8)) D Johnston Inc.

Macbeth. Retold by Jerry Stemach. William Shakespeare. (Classic Literature Ser.). 2000. audio compact disk 18.95 (978-1-4105-0154-7(X)) D Johnston Inc.

Macbeth. Cedric Watts. Ed. by William Shakespeare. 2001. audio compact disk 21.45 (978-1-903342-15-2(5)) Wordsworth Educ GBR.

Macbeth. abr. ed. Perf. by Dublin Gate Theatre Staff. Ed. by William Shakespeare. 1 cass. (Running Time: 55 min.). Dramatization. 10.95 (978-0-8045-0782-0(1), SAC 782) Spoken Arts.

Macbeth. abr. ed. Ed. by William Shakespeare. 3 CDs. (Running Time: 1 hr.). 2005. audio compact disk 12.95 (978-0-660-18961-1(5)) Pub: Canadian Broadcasting CAN. Dist(s): Georgetown Term

Macbeth. abr. ed. Ed. by William Shakespeare et al. Illus. by Bob Stotts. Narrated by Nick Sandys. Contrib. by Ted S. Hasselbring. 1 cass. (Running Time: 1 hr.). (Start-to-Finish Books). (J). (gr. 2-3). 2000. (978-1-58702-324-8(5), F27K2) D Johnston Inc.
One stormy night in Scotland, General Macbeth a and his friend, General Banquo, meet three witches. The witches tell Macbeth that he will become the King of Scotland. They tell Banquo that he will be the father of kinds. This prophecy plants the seeds of tragedy in the life of Macbeth, who suddenly cannot stop envisioning himself as king. Spurred on by his greedy wife, Macbeth murders King Duncan and ascends the throne.

***Macbeth.** abr. ed. William Shakespeare. Read by Anthony Quayle & (null) Cast. (ENG.). 2003. (978-0-06-074326-0(3), Caedmon) HarperCollins Pubs.

***Macbeth.** abr. ed. William Shakespeare. Read by Anthony Quayle & (null) Cast. (ENG.). 2004. (978-0-06-081331-4(8), Caedmon) HarperCollins Pubs.

Macbeth. unabr. ed. Read by Audio Partners Staff. Ed. by William Shakespeare. 2 cass. (Running Time: 2 hrs. 19 mins.). (Arkangel Shakespeare Ser.). 2004. 17.95 (978-1-932219-60-9(9), Atlntc Mnthly) Pub: Grove-Atltic. Dist(s): PerseuPGW

Macbeth. unabr. ed. Read by Anthony Quale & Stanley Holloway. Ed. by William Shakespeare. 2 cass. (Running Time: 3 hrs.). Dramatization. 17.95 (H144) Blckstn Audio.
Three witches hail McBeth, a Scottish nobleman, as "one that shall be king hereafter," setting him off on a course of murder & ultimate self-destruction.

Macbeth. unabr. ed. Perf. by Anthony Quayle & Gwen Ffrangcon-Davies. Ed. by William Shakespeare. 2 cass. (Running Time: 2 hrs. 30 mins.). Dramatization. 2000. pap. bk. 37.20 (40743E5); 24.00 (21511E5) Recorded Bks.

Macbeth. unabr. ed. William Shakespeare. Narrated by Hugh Ross et al. (Arkangel Shakespeare Ser.). (ENG.). 2005. audio compact disk 19.95 (978-1-932219-20-3(X)) Pub: AudioGO. Dist(s): Perseus Dist

Macbeth. unabr. ed. Ed. by William Shakespeare. 2 CDs. (Running Time: 3 hrs.). 2001. audio compact disk 30.00 Books on Tape.
Seduced by ambition into a bloody cycle of fear, vengeance and murder, Macbeth unleashes a wave of bloody war that will destroy all he loves.

Macbeth. unabr. ed. William Shakespeare. Read by Full Ensemble Cast. (YA). 2006. 39.99 (978-1-59895-346-6(X)) Find a World.

Macbeth. unabr. ed. Ed. by William Shakespeare. 2 cass. 1999. 16.95 (FS9-51073) Highsmith.

Macbeth. unabr. abr. ed. William Shakespeare. Read by Anthony Quayle. Perf. by Stanley Holloway. 2 CDs. (Running Time: 2 hrs.). Dramatization. (Caedmon Shakespeare Ser.: Vol. 2). (gr. 9-12). 1995. 25.00 (978-0-694-51584-4(1), CD 231, Harper Audio) HarperCollins Pubs.

Macbeth, Set. unabr. ed. William Shakespeare & Naxos Audiobooks Staff. (Running Time: 2 hrs. 24 mins. 18 sec.). (New Cambridge Shakespeare Audio Ser.). (ENG.). 1998. audio compact disk 29.99 (978-0-521-62539-5(4)) Cambridge U Pr.

Macbeth, Vol. 3. Ed. by William Shakespeare et al. Illus. by Bob Stotts. Narrated by Nick Sandys. Contrib. by Ted S. Hasselbring. (Start-to-Finish Books). (J). (gr. 2-3). 2000. 35.00 (978-1-58702-489-4(6)) D Johnston Inc.

Macbeth: An A+ Audio Study Guide. unabr. ed. William Shakespeare. Read by Roger Rees. (Running Time: 1 hr. 25 mins.). (ENG.). 2006. 5.98 (978-1-59483-549-0(7)) Pub: Hachet Audio. Dist(s): HachBkGrp

Macbeth: An A+ Audio Study Guide. unabr. ed. William Shakespeare. Read by Roger Rees. (Running Time: 1 hr.). (ENG.). 2009. 14.98 (978-1-60788-265-7(5)) Pub: Hachet Audio. Dist(s): HachBkGrp

Macbeth & His Wife. unabr. ed. George B. Harrison. 1 cass. (Running Time: 50 min.). (Shakespeare's Critics Speak Ser.). 1965. 12.95 (23102) J Norton Pubs.
A demonstration lecture on the essential meaning of the tragedy of Macbeth as worked out in the relationship between Macbeth & his wife.

Macbeth, the Musical Comedy. Scripts. 1 cass. or 1 CD. (Running Time: 35 mins.). (YA). (gr. 6-9). 2000. pap. bk. & tchr. ed. 29.95 Bad Wolf Pr.
Our Macbeth, a tad confused, keeps spouting lines from "Hamlet," much to the annoyance of the other characters. Lady Macbeth is obsessed with dry-cleaning the castle drapes & King Duncan boasts that he invented plaid. Singing parts are equally distributed among a large cast. Sheet music available.

MacBride Discusses the Libertarian Party. unabr. ed. Roger Lea MacBride. 1 cass. (Running Time: 47 min.). 12.95 (446) J Norton Pubs.

MacBride Talks to Conservatives. unabr. ed. Roger Lea MacBride. 1 cass. (Running Time: 45 min.). 12.95 (447) J Norton Pubs.

MacDonald Murder Case. Elayne J. Manago. 1 cass. 8.95 (221) Am Fed Astrologers.
Potential for murder in natal chart.

Mach II Gift Set. Richard B. Brooke. Read by Richard B. Brooke. (ENG., 2008. lib. bdg. 29.95 (978-0-9700399-3-4(X)) High Perform.

MACH 1 Speed Reading Course. Robert Sandstrom. Read by Robert Sandstrom. Read by Jeff Steele. 2 cass. (Running Time: 3 hrs.). (YA). (gr. 7 up). 1991. 15.95 (978-0-9626918-8-1(7)) Stepping CA.
Shows reader how to increase their reading speed as much as 500% with better comprehension. Applies to any form of reading.

Machel Study 10-Year Strategic Review: Children & Conflict in a Changing World see Examen stratégique décennal de l'Etude Machel: Les enfants et les conflits dans un monde en Mutation

Machiavelli & the Mandrake (Then & Now) see Maquiavelo y la Mandragora

Machiavelli & the Mandrake (Then & Now) W. Somerset Maugham. Read by Santiago Munéra. (Running Time: 3 hrs.). 2002. 16.95 (978-1-60083-246-8(6), Audiofy Corp) Iofy Corp.

Machiavelli in Context. Instructed by William R. Cook. 12 cass. (Running Time: 12 hrs.). 2006. 129.95 (978-1-59803-168-3(6)); audio compact disk 69.95 (978-1-59803-170-6(8)) Teaching Co.

Machiavellians: Defenders of Freedom. unabr. ed. James Burnham. Read by Jeff Riggenbach. 7 cass. (Running Time: 10 hrs.). 1999. 49.95 (978-0-7861-1670-6(6), 2498) Blckstn Audio.
An account of the modern Machiavellians, a remarkable group who have been influential in Europe & practically unknown in the United States. A classic work of political theory & practice.

Machiavellians: Defenders of Freedom: A Defense of Political Truth Against Wishful Thinking. unabr. ed. James Burnham. Intro. by Sidney Hook. (Running Time: 32400 sec.). 2007. audio compact disk 72.00 (978-0-7861-0366-9(3)); audio compact disk 29.95 (978-0-7861-0369-0(8)) Blckstn Audio.

Machine Crusade. unabr. ed. Brian Herbert. Read by Kevin J. Anderson. 9 cass. (Running Time: 13 hrs. 30 mins.). 2001. 56.00 (978-0-7366-8432-3(8)) Books on Tape.
Emperor Shaddam Corrino, foolish and egoistic, seizes on a discovery that could grant him complete dominion over the galaxy. His advisor, Count Fenring, has stumbled on a Tleilaxu plan to manufacture synthetic spice, called amal, on the planet Ix. The real spice, melange, is used by interstellar navigators to ply their courses around the galaxy, and has hitherto only been found on the planet Dune. The Emperor hopes to make Dune irrelevant by making amal the sole narcotic of choice for interstellar transport. Meanwhile, Duke Leto Atreides is planning to attack Ix, to install his friend Rhombur Vernius as rule.

Machine Crusade. unabr. ed. Brian Herbert et al. Read by Michael Prichard. 9 cass. (Running Time: 13 hrs. 30 mins.). 2001. 72.00 (978-0-7366-8329-6(1)) Books on Tape.

Machine Crusade. unabr. rev. ed. Brian Herbert et al. Read by Scott Brick & Scott Sowers. 18 CDs. (Running Time: 28 hrs. 0 mins. 0 sec.). (Dune Ser.). (ENG., 2003. audio compact disk 59.95 (978-1-55927-945-1(1)) Pub: Macmill Audio. Dist(s): Macmillan

Machine Gun in the Clown's Hand. Jello Biafra. 1 CD. (Running Time: 1 hr. 30 min.). (ENG.). 2002. audio compact disk 19.98 (978-1-902593-66-1(9)) Pub: AK Pr GBR. Dist(s): Consort Bk Sales

Machine Gunners. Robert Westall. Read by James Bolam. 4 cass. (Running Time: 5 hrs. 10 min.). (J). (gr. 6 up). 35.00 (CC/034) C to C Cassettes.
Chas MacGill has the second-best collection of war souvenirs in Garmouth & he desperately wants it to be the best. His chance comes when he finds a crashed German Heinkel with a machine gun & all its ammunition intact. All he has to do is to remove it from the plane.

Machine Gunners. unabr. ed. Robert Westall. Read by James Bolam. 4 cass. (Running Time: 4 hrs.). (J). (gr. 1-8). 1999. 32.95 (CTC 034, Chivers Child Audio) AudioGO.
With Nazi planes raining bombs on England night after night, every boy in Garmouth has a collection of shrapnel & other war souvenirs. But nothing comes close to the working machine gun Chas McGill pulls out of a downed bomber. While the police search frantically for the missing gun, Chas & his friends build a secret fortress to fight the Germans themselves.

Machine Trans Spec. 2nd ed. Edith E. Ennis et al. (C). 1987. bk. 454.50 (978-0-15-551198-9(X)) Dryden Pr.

Machine Transcription. 2nd ed. Blanche Ettinger & Edda Perfetto. 1 cass. 1992. bk. 150.00 (978-1-56118-067-7(X), 25091) Paradigm MN.

Machinery & Mankind. unabr. ed. Frank Lloyd Wright. 1 cass. (Running Time: 30 min). 1951. 12.95 (11022) J Norton Pubs.
Wright feels that man's sense of moral obligation has not developed to keep pace with his technological might. Includes question & answer discussion.

***Machinery of the Mind.** L. Ron Hubbard. (RUS.). 2010. audio compact disk 15.00 (978-1-4031-7424-6(5)); audio compact disk 15.00 (978-1-4031-7415-4(6)); audio compact disk 15.00 (978-1-4031-7417-8(2)); audio compact disk 15.00 (978-1-4031-7413-0(X)); audio compact disk 15.00 (978-1-4031-7423-9(7)); audio compact disk 15.00 (978-1-4031-7414-7(8)); audio compact disk 15.00 (978-1-4031-7418-5(0)); audio compact disk 15.00 (978-1-4031-7425-3(3)); audio compact disk 15.00 (978-1-4031-7427-7(X)); audio compact disk 15.00 (978-1-4031-7421-5(0)); audio compact disk 15.00 (978-1-4031-7419-2(9)); audio compact disk 15.00 (978-1-4031-7426-0(1)); audio compact disk 15.00 (978-1-4031-7420-8(2)); audio compact disk 15.00 (978-1-4031-7428-4(8)); audio compact disk 15.00 (978-1-4031-7422-2(9)); audio compact disk 15.00 (978-1-4031-7416-1(4)) Bridge Pubns Inc.

***Machinery of the Mind.** L. Ron Hubbard. (ENG.). 2010. audio compact disk 15.00 (978-1-4031-0490-8(5)) Bridge Pubns Inc.

Machinery'S Handbook Guide, 27Th Edition - Ebook Activation Key. John M. Amiss et al. 2004. cd-rom 14.50 (978-0-8311-2788-6(0)) Indus Pr.

Macho! unabr. collector's ed. Victor Villaseñor. Read by Michael Prichard. 6 cass. (Running Time: 9 hrs.). 1996. 48.00 (978-0-7366-3352-9(9), 4003) Books on Tape.
For Roberto Garcia, age 17, crossing into California illegally is not just a dangerous trek to find work; it's also a journey into manhood. The back-breaking work in the vegetable fields shows him a reality he hadn't imagined. When Cesar Chavez campaigns to unionize the workers, Roberto must decide whether to support the common cause or to look out for his job & for himself.

Mach's Gut! Gwen Berwick & Sydney Thorne. 5 cass. (J). 1998. 300.00 Set. (978-0-7487-3571-6(2)) St Mut.

Macht oder Ohnmacht: Erziehung zum Missbrauch. Pierre F. Walter. (GER., 2010. 12.00 (978-0-9760433-3-1(5), IPUBLICA_ICK) Sirius C Media.

Macintosh Ilife 05: An Interactive Guide to iTunes, iPhoto, iMovie, iDVD, & GarageBand. Jim Heid. 1 CD-ROM. (ENG., 2005. audio compact disk 34.99 (978-0-321-33537-1(6)) Pub: Peachpit Pr. Dist(s): Pearson Educ

Mack Bolan 100: Devil's Bargain. Don Pendleton. (Mack Bolan Ser.: No. 100). 2006. audio compact disk 19.99 (978-1-59950-190-1(2)) GraphicAudio.

Mack Bolan 101: False Front. Don Pendleton. (Mack Bolan Ser.: No. 101). 2007. audio compact disk 19.99 (978-1-59950-198-7(8)) GraphicAudio.

Mack Bolan 101: False Front. Don Pendleton. (Mack Bolan Ser.: No. 101). 2007. audio compact disk 19.99 (978-1-59950-311-0(5)) GraphicAudio.

Mack Bolan 102: Lethal Tribute. Don Pendleton. Directed By Bob Supan. Contrib. by David Coyne et al. (Running Time: 25200 sec.). (Mack Bolan Ser.: No. 102). 2007. audio compact disk 19.99 (978-1-59950-196-3(1)) GraphicAudio.

Mack Bolan 102: Lethal Tribute. Don Pendleton. (Mack Bolan Ser.: No. 102). 2007. audio compact disk 19.99 (978-1-59950-320-2(4)) GraphicAudio.

Mack Bolan 103: Season of Slaughter. Don Pendleton. (Mack Bolan Ser.: No. 103). 2007. audio compact disk 19.99 (978-1-59950-337-0(9)) GraphicAudio.

Mack Bolan 104: Point of Betrayal. Don Pendleton. (Mack Bolan Ser.: No. 104). 2007. audio compact disk 19.99 (978-1-59950-355-4(7)) GraphicAudio.

Mack Bolan 105: Ballistic Force. Don Pendleton. (Mack Bolan Ser.: No. 105). 2007. audio compact disk 19.99 (978-1-59950-220-5(8)) GraphicAudio.

Mack Bolan 105: Ballistic Force. Based on a novel by Don Pendleton. (Mack Bolan Ser.: No. 105). 2007. audio compact disk 19.99 (978-1-59950-382-0(4)) GraphicAudio.

Mack Bolan 106: Renegade. Based on a novel by Don Pendleton. (Mack Bolan Ser.: No. 106). 2007. audio compact disk 19.99 (978-1-59950-221-2(6)) GraphicAudio.

Mack Bolan 106: Renegade. Based on a novel by Don Pendleton. (Mack Bolan Ser.: No. 106). 2008. audio compact disk 19.99 (978-1-59950-390-5(5)) GraphicAudio.

Mack Bolan 107: Survival Reflex. Based on a novel by Don Pendleton. (Mack Bolan Ser.: No. 107). 2008. audio compact disk 19.99 (978-1-59950-417-9(0)) GraphicAudio.

Mack Bolan 108: Path to War. Based on a novel by Don Pendleton. 2008. audio compact disk 19.99 (978-1-59950-460-5(X)) GraphicAudio.

Mack Bolan 80: A Dying Evil. Based on a novel by Don Pendleton. (Mack Bolan Ser.: No. 80). 2005. audio compact disk 19.99 (978-1-59950-017-1(5)) GraphicAudio.

Mack Bolan 80-89: MP3 CD Long Haul Boxset. Based on a book by Don Pendleton. (ENG.). 2007. 110.00 (978-1-59950-485-8(5)) GraphicAudio.

Mack Bolan 81: Deep Treachery. Based on a novel by Don Pendleton. (Mack Bolan Ser.: No. 81). 2006. audio compact disk 19.99 (978-1-59950-034-8(5)) GraphicAudio.

Mack Bolan 82: War Load. Based on a novel by Don Pendleton. (Mack Bolan Ser.: No. 82). 2005. audio compact disk 19.99 (978-1-59950-076-8(0)) GraphicAudio.

Mack Bolan 83: Sworn Enemies. Based on a novel by Don Pendleton. (Mack Bolan Ser.: No. 83). 2005. audio compact disk 19.99 (978-1-59950-077-5(9)) GraphicAudio.

Mack Bolan 84: Dark Truth. Don Pendleton. (Running Time: 25200 sec.). (Mack Bolan Ser.: No. 84). 2006. audio compact disk 19.99 (978-1-59950-078-2(7)) GraphicAudio.

Mack Bolan 85: Breakaway. Based on a novel by Don Pendleton. (Mack Bolan Ser.: No. 85). 2006. audio compact disk 19.99 (978-1-59950-092-8(2)) GraphicAudio.

Mack Bolan 87: Caged. Based on a novel by Don Pendleton. (Mack Bolan Ser.: No. 87). 2006. audio compact disk 19.99 (978-1-59950-113-0(9)) GraphicAudio.

Mack Bolan 88: Sleepers. Based on a novel by Don Pendleton. (Mack Bolan Ser.: No. 88). 2006. audio compact disk 19.99 (978-1-59950-114-7(7)) GraphicAudio.

Mack Bolan 90: Age of War. Based on a novel by Don Pendleton. (Mack Bolan Ser.: No. 90). 2006. audio compact disk 19.99 (978-1-59950-127-7(9)) GraphicAudio.

Mack Bolan 91: Line of Control. Don Pendleton. (Mack Bolan Ser.: No. 91). 2006. audio compact disk 19.99 (978-1-59950-134-5(1)) GraphicAudio.

Mack Bolan 92: Breached. Don Pendleton. (Mack Bolan Ser.: No. 92). 2006. audio compact disk 19.99 (978-1-59950-135-2(X)) GraphicAudio.

Mack Bolan 93: Retaliation. Based on a novel by Don Pendleton. (Mack Bolan Ser.: No. 93). 2006. audio compact disk 19.99 (978-1-59950-142-0(2)) GraphicAudio.

Mack Bolan 95: Silent Running. Don Pendleton. (Mack Bolan Ser.: No. 95). 2006. audio compact disk 19.99 (978-1-59950-167-3(8)) GraphicAudio.

Mack Bolan 97: Zero Option. Don Pendleton. (Mack Bolan Ser.: No. 98). 2006. audio compact disk 19.99 (978-1-59950-179-6(1)) GraphicAudio.

Mack Bolan 98: Predator Paradise. Don Pendleton. (Mack Bolan Ser.: No. 98). 2006. audio compact disk 19.99 (978-1-59950-180-2(5)) GraphicAudio.

Mack Bolan 99: Circle of Deception. Don Pendleton. (Mack Bolan Ser.: No. 99). 2006. audio compact disk 19.99 (978-1-59950-189-5(9)) GraphicAudio.

Mack Made Movies. Don Brown. Illus. by Don Brown. Narrated by George Guidall. 1 CD. (Running Time: 17 mins.). (J). (gr. 2-5). 2008. pap. bk. 39.95 (978-1-4301-0436-0(8)) Live Oak Media.

Mack Made Movies. Don Brown. Illus. by Don Brown. Read by George Guidall. (J). 2008. bk. 28.95 (978-1-4301-0435-3(X)); pap. bk. 18.95 (978-1-4301-0434-6(1)) Live Oak Media.

Mack Made Movies. Don Brown. Illus. by Don Brown. Read by George Guidall. 1 CD. (Running Time: 17 mins.). (J). (gr. 2-5). 2008. bk. 25.95 (978-1-4301-0432-2(5)); pap. bk. 16.95 (978-1-4301-0431-5(7)) Live Oak Media.

Mack Made Movies, Set. Don Brown. Illus. by Don Brown. Narrated by George Guidall. 1 cass. (Running Time: 17 mins.). (J). (gr. 2-5). 2008. pap. bk. 37.95 (978-1-4301-0433-9(3)) Live Oak Media.

MacKenna's Gold. unabr. collector's ed. Will Henry. Read by Christopher Lane. 6 cass. (Running Time: 9 hrs.). 1995. 48.00 (978-0-7366-3100-6(3), 3776) Books on Tape.
On his quest, Mackenna is followed by 10 deadly robbers, relentlessly pursued by the U.S. Cavalry, & trapped by a dangerous renegade. But Mackenna endures, ever mindful of a dazzling fortune waiting in the uncharted desert.

***Mackenzie's Mission.** unabr. ed. Linda Howard. Read by Dennis Boutsikaris. (Running Time: 6 hrs.). (Mackenzie's Legacy Ser.). 2010. 39.97 (978-1-4418-7101-5(2), 9781441871015, BADLE); 19.99 (978-1-4418-7099-5(7), 9781441870995, Brilliance MP3); 39.97 (978-1-4418-7100-8(4), 9781441871008, Brinc Audio MP3 Lib); audio compact disk 19.99 (978-1-4418-7097-1(0), 9781441870971, Bril Audio CD Unabri); audio compact disk 69.97 (978-1-4418-7098-8(9), 9781441870988, BriAudCD Unabrid) Brilliance Audio.

***Mackenzie's Mountain.** unabr. ed. Linda Howard. Read by Christina Traister. (Running Time: 8 hrs.). (Mackenzie's Legacy Ser.). 2010. 19.99 (978-1-4418-7094-0(6), 9781441870940, Brilliance MP3); 39.97 (978-1-4418-7096-4(2), 9781441870964, BADLE); 39.97 (978-1-4418-7095-7(4), 9781441870957, Brinc Audio MP3 Lib); audio compact disk 19.99 (978-1-4418-7092-6(X), 9781441870926, Bril Audio CD Unabri); audio compact disk 69.97 (978-1-4418-7093-3(8), 9781441870933, BriAudCD Unabrid) Brilliance Audio.

***Mackenzie's Pleasure.** unabr. ed. Linda Howard. Read by Dennis Boutsikaris. (Running Time: 7 hrs.). 2011. 39.97 (978-1-4418-7105-3(5), 9781441871053, Brinc Audio MP3 Lib); 39.97 (978-1-4418-7106-0(3), 9781441871060, BADLE); audio compact disk 69.97 (978-1-4418-7103-9(9), 9781441871039, BriAudCD Unabrid) Brilliance Audio.

***Mackenzie's Pleasure.** unabr. ed. Linda Howard & Linda Howard. Read by Dennis Boutsikaris. (Running Time: 7 hrs.). 2011. 19.99 (978-1-4418-7104-6(7), 9781441871046, Brilliance MP3); audio compact disk 19.99 (978-1-4418-7102-2(0), 9781441871022, Bril Audio CD Unabri) Brilliance Audio.

MacKinnon's Machine. unabr. ed. S. K. Wolf. Narrated by John Randolph Jones. 9 cass. (Running Time: 12 hrs. 30 mins.). 1992. 78.00 (978-1-55690-688-6(9), 92216E7) Recorded Bks.
A retired special forces trooper is hired to assemble an assassination team. The target: Moammar Qaddafy.

Macon County, North Carolina, Delayed Birth Records CD. Merrell J. Riddle. 2005. cd-rom & audio compact disk 20.00 (978-1-932671-16-2(1)) Riddle Gene Enter.

MacPherson's Lament. unabr. ed. Sharyn McCrumb. Narrated by Barbara Rosenblat. 5 cass. (Running Time: 6 hrs. 45 mins.). (Elizabeth MacPherson Ser.: No. 7). 2000. 46.00 (978-0-7887-3109-9(2), 95820E7) Recorded Bks.
When Elizabeth's brother Bill starts a law practice in Virginia, a simple case lands him with criminal charges. As she confronts her panicked sibling, Elizabeth wonders if even she can untangle this web of deceit.

Macrobiotics. Cecile T. Levin. 1 cass. 9.00 (A0293-90) Sound Photosyn.
A world-class expert speaks with Roy about the philosophies, recipes, & benefits of macrobiotics.

Macromedia Dreamweaver MX 2004: Design & Application; Instructor Resources; Instructor's Guide CD. John Marshall Baker. (Performance Ser.). 2005. audio compact disk 69.00 (978-0-7638-1989-7(1)) EMC-Paradigm.

Macromedia Flash MX: Design & Application; Instructor Resources; Instructor's Guide CD. Denise Seguin. (Performance Ser.). 2005. audio compact disk 69.00 (978-0-7638-1941-5(7)) EMC-Paradigm.

Macroshift: Navigating the Transformation to a Sustainable World. unabr. ed. Ervin Laszlo. 4 cass. (Running Time: 6 hrs.). 2001. 25.00 (978-1-57453-438-2(6)) Audio Lit.
We are in the midst of a macroshift - a transformation of practically all aspects of life, from individual lifestyles to the global economy. Macroshift describes the nature and dynamics of today's macroshift and points to the values that could bring it to a breakthrough, rather than allow it to drift to a breakdown.

***MacroWikinomics: Rebooting Business & the World.** unabr. ed. Don Tapscott & Anthony D. Williams. (Running Time: 20 hrs. 30 mins.). 2010. 23.99 (978-1-4001-8730-0(3)); 44.99 (978-1-4001-9730-9(9)) Tantor Media.

***MacroWikinomics: Rebooting Business & the World.** unabr. ed. Don Tapscott & Anthony D. Williams. Narrated by Alan Sklar. 2 MP3-CDs. (Running Time: 20 hrs. 30 mins. 0 sec.). 2010. 34.99 (978-1-4001-6730-2(2)); audio compact disk 44.99 (978-1-4001-1730-7(5)); audio compact disk 119.99 (978-1-4001-4730-4(1)) Pub: Tantor Media. Dist(s): IngramPubServ

Mad about the Boy? Dolores Gordon-Smith. 2009. 69.95 (978-1-4079-0690-4(9)) Pub: Soundings Ltd GBR. Dist(s): Ulverscroft US

Mad about the Boy? Dolores Gordon-Smith. 2009. audio compact disk 84.95 (978-1-4079-0691-1(7)) Pub: Soundings Ltd GBR. Dist(s): Ulverscroft US

***Mad about the Boy.** unabr. ed. Maggie Alderson. Read by Stephanie Daniel. (Running Time: 9 hrs. 50 mins.). 2004. audio compact disk 87.95 (978-1-74093-321-6(4)) Pub: Bolinda Pubng AUS. Dist(s): Bolinda Pub Inc

***Mad as Hell: How the Tea Party Movement Is Fundamentally Remaking Our Two-Party System.** unabr. ed. Scott Rasmussen. Read by Mike Chamberlain. (Running Time: 10 hrs. NaN mins.). (ENG.). 2010. 29.95 (978-1-4417-8424-7(1)); 59.95 (978-1-4417-8421-6(7)); audio compact disk 29.95 (978-1-4417-8423-0(3)); audio compact disk 90.00 (978-1-4417-8422-3(5)) Blckstn Audio.

Mad at the World: World History. 1 cass. 1999. 10.98 (KMGC8647); audio compact disk 16.98 (KMGD8647) Provident Mus Dist.

Mad Carew. unabr. ed. Ken McCoy. Read by Ken McCoy. 7 cass. (Running Time: 9 hrs. 15 mins.). (Story Sound Ser.). (J). 2005. 61.95 (978-1-85903-864-2(6)) Pub: Mgna Lrg Print GBR. Dist(s): Ulverscroft US

***Mad Church Disease: Overcoming the Burnout Epidemic.** Anne Jackson. (Running Time: 4 hrs. 42 mins. 0 sec.). (ENG.). 2009. 16.99 (978-0-310-32594-9(3)) Zondervan.

Mad Cows. unabr. ed. Kathy Lette. Read by Fiona Macleod. 6 cass. (Running Time: 9 hrs. 15 mins.). 2005. 48.00 (978-1-74093-556-2(X)); audio compact disk 87.95 (978-1-74093-572-2(1)) Pub: Bolinda Pubng AUS. Dist(s): Bolinda Pub Inc

Mad Dash. abr. ed. Patricia Gaffney. Read by Laural Merlington. (Running Time: 6 hrs.). 2008. audio compact disk 14.99 (978-1-4233-3012-7(9), 9781423330127, BCD Value Price) Brilliance Audio.

Mad Dash. unabr. ed. Patricia Gaffney. Read by Laural Merlington. (Running Time: 12 hrs.). 2007. 39.25 (978-1-4233-3010-3(2), 9781423330103, BADLE); 24.95 (978-1-4233-3009-7(9), 9781423330097, BAD); 87.25 (978-1-4233-3004-2(8), 9781423330042, BrilAudUnabridg); audio compact disk 24.95 (978-1-4233-3007-3(2), 9781423330073, Brilliance MP3); audio compact disk 36.95 (978-1-4233-3005-9(6), 9781423330059, Bril Audio CD Unabri); audio compact disk 107.25 (978-1-4233-3006-6(4), 9781423330066, BriAudCD Unabrid); audio compact disk 39.25 (978-1-4233-3008-0(0), 9781423330080, Brinc Audio MP3 Lib) Brilliance Audio.

Mad Desire to Dance. unabr. ed. Elie Wiesel. Read by Mark Bramhall & Kirsten Potter. Tr. by Catherine Temerson. 8 CDs. (Running Time: 10 hrs.). (ENG.). 2009. audio compact disk 34.95 (978-0-7393-8206-6(3), Random AudioBks) Pub: Random Audio Pubg. Dist(s): Random

Mad Dogs. unabr. ed. James Grady. Read by William Dufris. (YA). 2007. 64.99 (978-1-60252-915-1(9)) Find a World.

Mad Dogs. unabr. ed. James Grady. Read by William Dufris. (Running Time: 12 hrs. 30 mins. 0 sec.). (ENG.). 2006. audio compact disk 37.99 (978-1-4001-0318-8(5)); audio compact disk 75.99 (978-1-4001-3318-5(1)); audio compact disk 24.99 (978-1-4001-5318-3(2)) Pub: Tantor Media. Dist(s): IngramPubServ

Mad Girls in Love. Michael Lee West. 1 cass. 2005. 25.95 (978-0-694-52275-0(9)) HarperCollins Pubs.

***Mad Girls in Love.** abr. ed. Michael Lee West. Read by Michael Lee West. (ENG.). 2005. (978-0-06-085609-0(2), Harper Audio); (978-0-06-085610-6(6), Harper Audio) HarperCollins Pubs.

Mad Jack. abr. ed. Catherine Coulter. Read by Anne Flosnik. (Running Time: 21600 sec.). (Bride Ser.). 2007. audio compact disk 14.99 (978-1-59737-818-5(6), 9781597378185, BCD Value Price) Brilliance Audio.

Mad Jack. unabr. ed. Catherine Coulter. Read by Christopher Lane. 6 cass. (Running Time: 9 hrs.). 56.00 (978-0-7366-4583-6(7), 4962) Books on Tape.
Mad Jack arrives in London with the aunts, Mathilda & Maude, to beg the assistance of Lord Cliffe, Grayson St. Cyre. He welcomes the aunts, briefly spots the valet, Jack & proceeds very quickly after their arrival to fall down the rabbit hole. He catches the valet, Jack, stealing his horse, Durban, chases Jack down & then all sorts of interesting things happen. Amidst all the laughter, however, there lurks a deadly secret that's ready to leap out & crush both Jack & Gray.

Mad Jack. unabr. ed. Catherine Coulter. Read by Anne Flosnik. (Running Time: 10 hrs.). (Bride Ser.). 2006. 39.25 (978-1-59737-816-1(X), 9781597378161, BADLE); 24.95 (978-1-59737-815-4(1), 9781597378154, BAD); 82.25 (978-1-59737-810-9(0), 9781597378109, BrilAudUnabridg); audio compact disk 39.25 (978-1-59737-814-7(3), 9781597378147, Brinc Audio MP3 Lib); audio compact disk 97.25 (978-1-59737-812-3(7), 9781597378123, BriAudCD Unabrid); audio compact disk 24.95 (978-1-59737-813-0(5), 9781597378130, Brilliance MP3); audio compact disk 36.95 (978-1-59737-811-6(9), 9781597378116) Brilliance Audio.
Dear Reader: Mad Jack is lots of fun. You're going to meet two of the neatest people in 1811 London. In addition, you'll revisit the Sherbrookes - Douglas and Ryder, and see what's going on with them eight years after you first met them. As for Sinjun, she and Colin Kinross have been married for four years and Colin is in a real tizzy. Mad Jack is in reality Winifrede Levering Bascombe, who, happily, has her name changed very quickly in the story. She arrives in London with the aunts, Mathilda and Maude, to beg the assistance of Lord Cliffe, Grayson St. Cyre. He welcomes the aunts, briefly spots the valet, Jack, and proceeds very quickly after their arrival to fall down the rabbit hole. He catches the valet, Jack, stealing his horse, Durban, chases Jack down, and then all sorts of interesting things happen. Enter Sinjun with her frantic husband, Colin, on her trail. Amidst all the laughter, however, there lurks a deadly secret that's ready to leap out and crush both Jack and Gray. You'll hold your breath when a tough-brained Jack and a furious Gray get together and discover the truth of the accusation that could do them in before they can even get started with their lives. Do write to me at P.O. Box 17, Mill Valley, CA 94942, or email me at ReadMoi@aol.com, and tell me what you think of Mad Jack, a novel I very much enjoyed writing. Catherine Coulter.

Mad Lab. Perf. by Daniel Sjerven. Created by Daniel Sjerven. Prod. by Braun Media. (ENG.). 2008. (978-1-59987-669-6(8)) Braun Media.

Mad Melly Masters Her Moods. Pamela M. Goldberg. Illus. by Jimmy Boring. (J). 2008. pap. bk. (978-0-9778941-3-0(4)) Camp MakeBelieve.

Mad Ones: Crazy Joe Gallo & the Revolution at the Edge of the Underworld. unabr. ed. Tom Folsom. Read by Josh Clark. 5 CDs. (Running Time: 6 hrs.). 2009. audio compact disk 29.95 (978-1-61573-022-3(2), 1615730222) Pub: HighBridge. Dist(s): Workman Pub

Mad River Road. abr. ed. Joy Fielding. Read by Judith West. (Running Time: 21600 sec.). 2006. audio compact disk 16.99 (978-1-59737-654-9(X), 9781597376549, BCD Value Price) Brilliance Audio.
After spending a year in prison, Ralph Fisher has explicit plans for his first night of freedom: tonight, someone will be held accountable. He goes to murderous lengths to obtain the address of his former wife - the woman he blames for his fate and against whom he has sworn vengeance. Determined to bring her to his idea of justice, Ralph's next step is to travel from Florida's sandy beaches to Dayton, Ohio, where his ex-wife is struggling to make ends meet on Mad River Road. Also in Florida, Jamie Kellogg wakes from an agonizing nightmare of her mother's funeral, and assesses her life: a pretty but unaccomplished twenty-nine-year-old woman in a dead-end job, with an ex-husband in Atlanta, a married lover in the hospital, and a virtual stranger in her bed. But this stranger is everything the previous men in her life weren't: tender, attentive, and adventurous. After convincing Jamie to quit her miserable job and ditch her judgmental, perfectionist sister, he proposes a romantic getaway. While Jamie wonders if this thrilling man might finally be her Prince Charming, they plan a road trip to visit his son, who lives with his mother on a street called Mad River Road.

Mad River Road. unabr. ed. Joy Fielding. Read by Judith West. 8 cass. (Running Time: 39600 sec.). 2005. 34.95 (978-1-59737-645-7(0), 9781597376457) Brilliance Audio.

Mad River Road. unabr. ed. Joy Fielding. Read by Judith West. (Running Time: 11 hrs.). 2006. 39.25 (978-1-59737-652-5(3), 9781597376525, BADLE); 24.95 (978-1-59737-651-8(5), 9781597376518, BAD); 87.25 (978-1-59737-646-4(9), 9781597376464, BrilAudUnabridg); audio compact disk 36.95 (978-1-59737-647-1(7), 9781597376471, Bril Audio CD Unabri); audio compact disk 39.25 (978-1-59737-650-1(7), 9781597376501, Brinc Audio MP3 Lib); audio compact disk 97.25 (978-1-59737-648-8(5), 9781597376488, BriAudCD Unabrid); audio compact disk 24.95 (978-1-59737-649-5(3), 9781597376495, Brilliance MP3) Brilliance Audio.

Mad Scientists of Sound Gravikords, Whirlies & Pyrophones: Experimental Musical Instruments. Bart Hopkin. 1 CD. (Running Time: 1 hr.). 1996. pap. bk. 28.95 (978-1-55961-382-8(3), Ellipsis Arts) Relaxtn Co.

***Mad Ship.** unabr. ed. Robin Hobb. Narrated by Anne Flosnik. (Running Time: 33 hrs. 0 mins.). (Liveship Traders Ser.). 2010. 32.99 (978-1-4001-8438-5(X)); 44.99 (978-1-4001-6438-7(9)); 69.99 (978-1-4001-9438-4(5)); audio compact disk 139.99 (978-1-4001-4438-9(8)); audio compact disk 69.99 (978-1-4001-1438-2(1)) Pub: Tantor Media. Dist(s): IngramPubServ

Madam & the Census Man **see Poetry of Langston Hughes**

Madam & the Rent Man **see Poetry of Langston Hughes**

Madam President. Lane Smith. Narrated by Anna Chiodo. 1 CD. (Running Time: 9 mins.). (J). (gr. 1-4). 2008. bk. 29.95 (978-0-545-10688-7(5)); audio compact disk 12.95 (978-0-545-10684-9(2)) Weston Woods.

Madam Secretary: A Memoir. abr. rev. ed. Madeleine Albright. Read by Madeleine Albright. 6 CDs. (Running Time: 6 hrs. 30 mins.). 2003. audio compact disk 31.98 (978-1-4013-9745-6(X)) Pub: Hyperion. Dist(s): HarperCollins Pubs

Madam, Will You Talk? unabr. ed. Mary Stewart. Read by Nyree Dawn Porter. 6 cass. (Running Time: 9 hrs.). 2000. 49.95 (978-0-7451-6303-1(3), CAB 103) Pub: Chivers Audio Bks GBR. Dist(s): AudioGO
Charity Selborne and her friend Louise arrived at the enchanting city of Avignon, anticipating their summer vacation with pleasure. Not a cloud was in the sky as they made their way to the hotel. But how was Charity to know that a stranger in the crowded hotel was moving in the dark circle of his own personal hell, with murder on his mind.

Madama Butterfly. rev. ed. Composed by Giacomo Puccini. Comment by William Berger. Text by Daniel S. Brink. 2 vols. (ENG., 2005. audio compact disk 19.95 (978-1-57912-510-3(7), 1579125107) Pub: Blck Dog & Leventhal. Dist(s): Workman Pub

Madama Butterfly: An Introduction to Puccini's Opera. Thomson Smillie. Read by David Timson. 1 CD. (Running Time: 1 hr. 30 min.). (Opera Explained Ser.). 2003. audio compact disk 8.99 (978-1-84379-041-9(6)) NaxMulti GBR.

Madame Bovary **see Treasury of French Prose**

Madame Bovary. 10 CDs. (Running Time: 13 hours). Dramatization. 2005. audio compact disk (978-0-9755663-0-5(X)) Alcazar AudioWorks.
Emma Bovary lived in a world of romantic dreams. Her selfish and demanding ways led to a gradual corruption that showed her to be an utterly shallow and quite stupid woman, but her escapades and caprices draw us into her story until the tragic end.

Madame Bovary. Gustave Flaubert. Narrated by Walter Zimmerman. (Running Time: 12 hrs. 30 mins.). 1983. 20.95 (978-1-59912-836-8(5)) Iofy Corp.

Madame Bovary. Gustave Flaubert. Read by Carlos J. Vega. (Running Time: 3 hrs.). 2002. 16.95 (978-1-60083-194-2(X), Audiofy Corp) Iofy Corp.

Madame Bovary. Gustave Flaubert. Read by Imogen Stubbs. (Running Time: 4 hrs. 45 mins.). 2003. 28.95 (978-1-60083-836-1(7)) Iofy Corp.

Madame Bovary. Gustave Flaubert. Read by Walter Zimmerman. 9 cass. (Running Time: 12 hrs.). 1989. 59.00 incl. album. (C-129) Jimcin Record.
Masterpiece of French realism.

Madame Bovary. Gustave Flaubert. Read by Imogen Stubbs. 4 cass. (Running Time: 4 hrs. 45 mins.). (Classic Fiction Ser.). 1999. 22.98 (978-962-634-678-5(7), NA216814, Naxos AudioBooks); audio compact disk 28.98 (978-962-634-178-0(5), NA417814, Naxos AudioBooks) Naxos.
A woman, who having married a country doctor & found herself unhappy with a rural, genteel existence, longs for love & excitement. Her aspirations & desires lead her in a tragic downward spiral.

Madame Bovary. Gustave Flaubert. Read by G. Bejean et al. 8 cass. 1991. 59.95 (1645-46) Olivia & Hill.
A gem of French literature depicting the life of Emma Bovary brought up with dreams of romance & luxury & who ends up married to a loutish country doctor living in a small provincial town.

Madame Bovary. Gustave Flaubert. Read by Donada Peters. (Running Time: 41400 sec.). (Unabridged Classics in Audio Ser.). (ENG.). 2006. audio compact disk 24.99 (978-1-4001-5274-2(7)) Pub: Tantor Media. Dist(s): IngramPubServ

Madame Bovary. Gustave Flaubert. Read by Donada Peters. (Running Time: 41400 sec.). (Unabridged Classics in Audio Ser.). (ENG.). 2006. audio compact disk 69.99 (978-1-4001-3274-4(6)) Pub: Tantor Media. Dist(s): IngramPubServ

Madame Bovary. abr. ed. Gustave Flaubert. (Running Time: 7200 sec.). 2007. audio compact disk 16.95 (978-1-933499-18-5(4)) Fonolibro Inc.

Madame Bovary. abr. ed. Gustave Flaubert. Read by Emilia Fox. 2 cass. (Running Time: 3 hrs.). 2001. 13.95 (978-1-84032-496-9(1), HoddrStoughton) Pub: Hodder General GBR. Dist(s): Trafalgar

Madame Bovary. abr. ed. Gustave Flaubert. Perf. by Glenda Jackson. 4 cass. (Running Time: 6 hrs.). 2004. 25.00 (978-1-59007-128-1(X)) New Millenn Enter.

This exquisite novel tells the story of one of the most compelling heroines in modern literature-Emma Bovary. Unhappily married to a devoted, clumsy provincial doctor, Emma revolts against the ordinariness of her life by pursuing voluptuous dreams of ecstasy and love. But her sensuous and sentimental desires lead her only to suffering corruption and downfall. A brilliant psychological portrait, Madame Bovary searingly depicts the human mind in search of transcendence.

Madame Bovary. abr. ed. Gustave Flaubert. Read by Emilia Fox. 2 cass. (Running Time: 3 hrs.). (Hodder Headline Ser.). 2001. Trafalgar.

Madame Bovary. unabr. ed. Gustave Flaubert. Narrated by Flo Gibson. 8 cass. (Running Time: 12 hrs.). (Classic Books on Cassettes Ser.). 1988. 26.95 (978-1-55685-099-8(9)) Audio Bk Con.

Emma Bovary's quest for love & romance leads her into deeper & deeper financial & moral degradation.

Madame Bovary. unabr. ed. Gustave Flaubert. Read by Ronald Pickup. 10 cass. (Running Time: 15 hrs. 20 mins.). (gr. 9-12). 2004. 39.95 (978-1-57270-056-7(4), F91056u) Pub: Audio Partners. Dist(s): PerseuPGW

Painting a brilliant psychological portrait of a woman, this novel ushered in a new age of realism in literature. Emma, married to a clumsy country doctor, pursues her voluptuous dreams of ecstasy & love, leading to corruption & downfall.

Madame Bovary. unabr. ed. Gustave Flaubert. Narrated by Ronald Pickup. 12 CDs. (Running Time: 15 hrs. 21 mins.). 2008. audio compact disk 110.95 (978-0-7927-5260-8(0)) AudioGO.

Unhappily married to a devoted, clumsy provincial doctor, Emma revolts against the ordinariness of her life by pursuing dreams of ecstasy and love. But her sensuous and sentimental desires lead her only to suffering, corruption, and downfall. A brilliant psychological portrait, Madame Bovary searingly depicts the human mind in search of transcendence. Acclaimed as a masterpiece upon its publication in 1857, this classic is still revered today as one of the finest novels of English literature.

Madame Bovary. unabr. ed. Gustave Flaubert. Read by Anthony Heald. (Running Time: 12 hrs. 0 mins.). 2008. 29.95 (978-1-4332-5028-6(4)); audio compact disk 90.00 (978-1-4332-5027-9(6)) Blckstn Audio.

Madame Bovary. unabr. ed. Gustave Flaubert. Read by Simon Vance. Tr. by Margaret Mauldon. (Running Time: 12 hrs. 5 mins.). (Classic Collection Ser.). 2009. 29.95 (978-1-4332-5440-6(9)); audio compact disk 19.95 (978-1-4332-5521-2(9)) Blckstn Audio.

Madame Bovary. unabr. ed. Gustave Flaubert. Read by Donada Peters. (YA). 2008. 59.99 (978-1-60514-595-2(5)) Find a World.

Madame Bovary. unabr. ed. Gustave Flaubert. Narrated by Davina Porter. 9 cass. (Running Time: 13 hrs.). 1989. 78.00 (978-1-55690-328-1(6), 89393E7) Recorded Bks.

The bored wife of a French country physician seeks to invest her life with some excitement & brings down tragedy.

Madame Bovary. unabr. ed. Gustave Flaubert. Read by Donada Peters. (Running Time: 11 hrs. 30 mins. 0 sec.). (ENG.). 2009. 22.99 (978-1-4001-5904-8(0)) Pub: Tantor Media. Dist(s): IngramPubServ

Madame Bovary. unabr. abr. ed. Gustave Flaubert. Read by Carlos J. Vega. 3 CDs. (Running Time: 3 hrs.). (SPA.). 2002. audio compact disk 17.00 (978-958-9494-73-8(0)) YoYoMusic.

Flaubert logró en su retrato de Madame Bovary una de las mayores creaciones de toda la literatura, por que mostró un personaje universal, una mujer nunca satisfecha y cuyo errado ideal la lleva al adulterio y a su propia destrucción. A ella se la ha comparado con Don Quijote, a quien sus lecturas llevan a sueños que van más allá de la realidad de todos los días y que a la larga son víctimas de esos ideales inalcanzables. Pero precisamente por ser Emma Bovary una mujer corriente, el personaje se vuelve más universal, ya que con él es más fácil la identificación.

Madame Bovary. unabr. collector's ed. Gustave Flaubert. Read by Donada Peters. 8 cass. (Running Time: 12 hrs.). 1994. 64.00 (978-0-7366-2632-3(8), 3371) Books on Tape.

A good woman seeks adventure in romance but only finds tragedy.

Madame Bovary, Pts. 1 & 2. Gustave Flaubert. Read by G. Bejean et al. 8 cass. 34.95 Pt. 1. (1645-VSL); 34.95 Pt. 2. (1646-VSL) Olivia & Hill.

A gem of French literature depicting the life of Emma Bovary brought up with dreams of romance & luxury & who ends up married to a loutish country doctor living in a small provincial town.

Madame Bovary: Classic Collection. unabr. ed. Gustave Flaubert. Read by Simon Vance. (Running Time: 12 hrs. 5 mins.). 2009. audio compact disk 72.95 (978-1-4332-5438-3(7)); audio compact disk 90.00 (978-1-4332-5439-0(5)) Blckstn Audio.

Madame Bovary, with EBook. unabr. ed. Gustave Flaubert. Narrated by Donada Peters. (Running Time: 11 hrs. 30 mins. 0 sec.). (ENG.). 2009. audio compact disk 32.99 (978-1-4001-0904-3(3)) Pub: Tantor Media. Dist(s): IngramPubServ

Madame Bovary, with eBook. unabr. ed. Gustave Flaubert. Narrated by Donada Peters. (Running Time: 11 hrs. 30 mins. 0 sec.). (ENG.). 2009. audio compact disk 65.99 (978-1-4001-3904-0(X)) Pub: Tantor Media. Dist(s): IngramPubServ

Madame Cleo's Girls. unabr. ed. Lucianne Goldberg. Read by Roger Ellis. (Running Time: 16 hrs.). 2008. 39.25 (978-1-4233-5818-3(X), 9781423358183, BADLE); 39.25 (978-1-4233-5816-9(3), 9781423358169, Brinc Audio MP3 Lib); 24.95 (978-1-4233-5815-2(5), 9781423358152, Brilliance MP3); 24.95 (978-1-4233-5817-6(1), 9781423358176, BAD) Brilliance Audio.

Madame Crowl's Ghost & Ghost Stories of the Tiled House see Great Ghost Stories - Volume 1

Madame de Treymes. unabr. ed. Edith Wharton. Read by Anna Fields. 6 cass. 1999. 44.95 (FS9-43216) Highsmith.

Madame de Treymes & the Touchstone. unabr. ed. Edith Wharton. Narrated by Flo Gibson. 4 cass. (Running Time: 6 hrs.). 1984. 19.95 (978-1-55685-016-5(6)) Audio Bk Con.

A remarkable story depicting the differences between French and American traditions, values, and family relationships. In the second novella, a young man publishes, without identifying that he was the recipient, love letters written to him by a deceased and brilliant authoress and he becomes consumed with guilt.

Madame de Treymes & Two Novellas. unabr. ed. Edith Wharton. Read by Anna Fields. 6 cass. (Running Time: 8 hrs. 30 mins.). 1998. 44.95 (978-0-7861-1268-5(9), 2204) Blckstn Audio.

Follows the fortunes of two innocents abroad: Fanny Frisbee of New York, unhappily married to the Marquis de Malrive; & John Durham, her childhood friend, who arrives in Paris intent on persuading Fanny to divorce her husband & marry him instead. A scintillating picture of American & French culture at the turn of the century. Also contains "Sanctuary" (1903) & "Bunner Sisters" (1906).

Madame de Treymes & Two Novellas. unabr. ed. Edith Wharton. Read by Anna Fields. (Running Time: 28800 sec.). 2007. audio compact disk 29.95 (978-0-7861-5918-5(9)); audio compact disk 63.00 (978-0-7861-5917-8(0)) Blckstn Audio.

Madame Hillary: The Dark Road to the White House. R. Emmett Tyrrell, Jr. & Mark W. Davis. Narrated by Richard Rohan. 6 CDs. (Running Time: 6 hrs. 45 mins.). 2004. audio compact disk 29.99 (978-1-4025-8314-8(1), 02382) Recorded Bks.

Madame Hillary: The Dark Road to the White House. unabr. ed. R. Emmett Tyrrell & Mark W. Davis. 5 cass. (Running Time: 6 hrs. 45 min.). 2004. 69.75 (978-1-4025-8831-0(3)) Recorded Bks.

After the tremendous success of her book, Living History, Senator Clinton was sharply criticized by conservative personalities. But the objections to her and her book lacked cohesiveness. Now Tyrrell, Jr. delivers a persuasive argument that Senator Clinton is a power-hungry radical with a hidden agenda who seduces voters with her intelligence, charm, and carefully crafted public persona. Madame Hillary promises to open eyes and become one of the most hotly debated books in recent history.

Madame Imbert's Safe see Extraordinary Adventures of Arsene Lupin

Madame Mirabou's School of Love. unabr. ed. Barbara Samuel. 6 cass. (Running Time: 10 hrs.). 2006. 63.00 (978-1-4159-2628-4(X), BksonTape); audio compact disk 81.00 (978-1-4159-2629-1(8), BksonTape) Pub: Random Audio Pubg. Dist(s): Random

Madame Mouse Trots see Gathering of Great Poetry for Children

Madame Recamier: An Opera see Gertrude Stein Reads from Her Works

Madapple. unabr. ed. Christina Meldrum. Read by Kirsten Potter. 9 CDs. (Running Time: 11 hrs. 11 mins.). (YA). (gr. 9 up). 2008. audio compact disk 55.00 (978-0-7393-6731-5(5), Listening Lib) Pub: Random Audio Pubg. Dist(s): Random

THE SECRETS OF the past meet the shocks of the present.Aslaug is an unusual young woman. Her mother has brought her up in near isolation, teaching her about plants and nature and language - but not about life. Especially not how she came to have her own life, and who her father might be. When Aslaug's mother dies unexpectedly, everything changes. For Aslaug is a suspect in her mother's death. And the more her story unravels, the more questions unfold. About the nature of Aslaug's birth. About what she should do next. About whether divine miracles have truly happened. And whether, when all other explanations are impossible, they might still happen this very day.

Madapple. unabr. ed. Christina Meldrum. Read by Kirsten Potter. (ENG.). (J). (gr. 9). 2008. audio compact disk 55.00 (978-0-7393-6729-2(3), Listening Lib) Pub: Random Audio Pubg. Dist(s): Random

MADD Presents: Honor Them All. 1 cass., 1 CD. 8.78 (WH 11339); audio compact disk 13.58 (WH 11339) NewSound.

Conceived to increase awareness of the devastating problem of drunk driving, as well as to help support the foundation & to honor the victims & their families.

***Made by Hand: Searching for Meaning in a Throwaway World.** unabr. ed. Mark Frauenfelder. Narrated by Kirby Heyborne. (Running Time: 8 hrs. 0 mins.). 2010. 15.99 (978-1-4001-8781-2(8)); 19.99 (978-1-4001-6781-4(7)); audio compact disk 71.99 (978-1-4001-4781-6(6)); audio compact disk 29.99 (978-1-4001-1781-9(X)) Pub: Tantor Media. Dist(s): IngramPubServ

Made for His Pleasure. unabr. ed. Alistair Begg. 4 CDs. (Running Time: 4 hrs. 45 mins. 0 sec.). (ENG.). 2005. audio compact disk 21.98 (978-1-59644-324-2(3), Hovel Audio) christianaud.

Are You Living For God's Pleasure Or For Your Own?Pleasing God is not a matter of personal choice, but an imperative that must be taken seriously. In a world of self, we must give way to the priority of God if we want to experience His joy.In the popular book, Alistair identifies ten benchmarks from Scripture that will prove invaluable as you seek to live a life that is pleasing to God. His clear, personal message will challenge and revitalize your faith.

***Made for His Pleasure.** unabr. ed. Alistair Begg. Narrated by David Cochran Heath. (ENG.). 2005. 12.98 (978-1-59644-325-9(1), Hovel Audio) christianaud.

Made for Praise. 2003. audio compact disk 84.95 (978-0-633-09317-4(3)); audio compact disk 12.00 (978-0-633-09279-5(7)) LifeWay Christian.

Made for Praise. Barny Robertson. 2000. 79.95 (978-0-633-01234-2(3)) LifeWay Christian.

Made for Praise, Vol. 9. Genevox Music Staff. 2003. audio compact disk 16.98 (978-0-633-09274-0(6)) LifeWay Christian.

Made for Praise for Older Children Listening, Vol. 4. 1998. audio compact disk 16.98 (978-0-7673-3396-2(9)) LifeWay Christian.

Made for Praise for Younger Children. 1996. 40.00 (978-0-7673-0838-0(7)) LifeWay Christian.

Made for Praise for Younger Children. 1996. 40.00 (978-0-7673-0839-7(5)) LifeWay Christian.

Made for Praise Older Children. Barney Robertson. 2000. 11.98 (978-0-633-00895-6(8)) LifeWay Christian.

Made for Praise Older Children. Barny Robertson. 2000. audio compact disk 16.98 (978-0-633-00894-9(X)) LifeWay Christian.

Made for Praise Older Children, Vol. 3. 1997. 11.98 (978-0-7673-3580-5(5)) LifeWay Christian.

Made for Praise Older Children, Vol. 5. 1999. 11.98 (978-0-7673-9717-9(7)) LifeWay Christian.

Made for Praise Older Children, Vol. 7. Barny Robertson. 2001. 79.95 (978-0-633-01612-8(8)) LifeWay Christian.

Made for Praise Older Children Cassette Promo Pak, Vol. 5. 1999. 8.00 (978-0-7673-9649-3(9)) LifeWay Christian.

Made for Praise Older Children Listening, Vol. 3. 1997. audio compact disk 16.98 (978-0-7673-3582-9(1)) LifeWay Christian.

Made for Praise Older Children Listening, Vol. 4. 1998. 11.98 (978-0-7673-3395-5(0)) LifeWay Christian.

Made for Praise Older Children Listening, Vol. 5. 1999. audio compact disk 16.98 (978-0-7673-9708-7(8)) LifeWay Christian.

Made for Praise Older Children Promo Pak, Vol. 5. 1999. audio compact disk 12.00 (978-0-7673-9659-2(6)) LifeWay Christian.

Made for Praise Volume 7 Older Children. Barny Robertson. 2001. 11.98 (978-0-633-01610-4(1)); audio compact disk 16.98 (978-0-633-01611-1(X)) LifeWay Christian.

Made for Praise Volume 7 Younger Children Choral Cassette. Chris Marion. 2001. 11.98 (978-0-633-01618-0(7)) LifeWay Christian.

Made for Praise Volume 7 Younger Children Choral Cd. Chris Marion. 2001. audio compact disk 16.98 (978-0-633-01619-7(5)) LifeWay Christian.

Made for Praise V9 Cass. Genevox Music Staff. 2003. 11.98 (978-0-633-09275-7(4)) LifeWay Christian.

Made for Praise Younger Children. Chris Marion. 2000. 11.98 (978-0-633-00911-3(3)); audio compact disk 84.95 (978-0-633-00914-4(8)); audio compact disk 16.98 (978-0-633-00912-0(1)) LifeWay Christian.

Made for Praise Younger Children, Vol. 3. 1997. 11.98 (978-0-7673-3579-9(1)) LifeWay Christian.

Made for Praise Younger Children, Vol. 4. 1998. 11.98 (978-0-7673-3393-1(4)) LifeWay Christian.

Made for Praise Younger Children, Vol. 5. 1999. 11.98 (978-0-7673-9718-6(5)) LifeWay Christian.

Made for Praise Younger Children Cd Promo Pak, Vol. 5. 1999. audio compact disk 12.00 (978-0-7673-9661-5(8)) LifeWay Christian.

Made for Praise Younger Children Listening, Vol. 3. 1997. audio compact disk 16.98 (978-0-7673-3581-2(3)) LifeWay Christian.

Made for Praise Younger Children Listening, Vol. 4. 1998. audio compact disk 16.98 (978-0-7673-3394-8(2)) LifeWay Christian.

Made in America. Linda Cline Chandler. Prod. by Ko Hayashi. (ENG.). 2009. 150.00 (978-0-9639400-5-6(8)) Lrning Two-Thousand.

Made in America Pt. 1: Creating Success in Your Business & Personal Life in the 21st Century, 6 cass. (Leadership & Empowerment Ser.). 2001. 149.95 (978-1-58292-027-6(3)) Lrning Two-Thousand.

Made in Germany: What to Do & Not Do When Doing Business with Germany. Francis M. Brunetto. Read by Francis McGowan Brunetto. 1 cass. (Running Time: 60 min.). 1993. 19.95 Peregrine Media.

Made in Germany: What to Do & What Not to Do When Doing Business with Germany. Read by Francis M. Brunetto. 1 cass. (Running Time: 45 min.). 1992. 19.95 Peregrine Media.

An excellent briefing of vital facts..inside market advice..from major market players on today's reunified German business landscape. Ideal for both the first-time & seasoned business person.

Made in Japan: What to Do & Not Do When Doing Business with Japanese. Francis M. Brunetto. Read by Francis McGowan Brunetto. 1 cass. (Running Time: 60 min.). 1993. 19.95 Peregrine Media.

Made in Japan: What to Do & What Not to Do When Doing Business with Japanese. Read by Francis M. Brunetto. 1 cass. (Running Time: 1 hr.). 1993. 19.95 Peregrine Media.

An excellent panorama of today's Japanese business environment for the business traveller together with tips & insights from major market players.

Made in Mexico: What to Do & What Not to Do When Doing Business with Mexico. 1 cass. (Running Time: 1 hr.). 1994. 19.95 Peregrine Media.

A richly informative program that prepares the listener to understand & handle the often intricate Mexican business behaviors from crosstable negotiating tactics to proper protocol.

Made in the U. S. A. unabr. ed. Billie Letts. Read by Cassandra Morris. (Running Time: 9 hrs.). (ENG.). 2008. 14.98 (978-1-60024-208-3(1)) Pub: Hachet Audio. Dist(s): HachBkGrp

Made in the U. S. A. unabr. ed. Billie Letts. Read by Cassandra Morris. (Running Time: 9 hrs.). (ENG.). 2009. audio compact disk 14.98 (978-1-60024-584-8(6)) Pub: Hachet Audio. Dist(s): HachBkGrp

Made Praise Older Children Piano Accompaniment, Vol. 5. 1999. 19.95 (978-0-633-00290-9(9)) LifeWay Christian.

Made Praise Younger Children Printed Piano Accompaniment, Vol. 5. 1999. 19.95 (978-0-633-00291-6(7)) LifeWay Christian.

***Made to Crave: Satisfying Your Deepest Desire with God, Not Food.** Zondervan. (ENG.). 2010. 14.99 (978-0-310-41238-0(2)) Zondervan.

Made to Stick: Why Some Ideas Survive & Others Die. unabr. ed. Chip Heath & Dan Heath. Read by Charles Kahlenberg. (Running Time: 30600 sec.). (ENG.). 2007. audio compact disk 29.95 (978-0-7393-4134-6(0), Random AudioBks) Pub: Random Audio Pubg. Dist(s): Random

Made to Worship. Contrib. by Chris Tomlin. (Mastertrax Ser.). 2006. audio compact disk 9.98 (978-5-558-16012-3(8)) Pt of Grace Ent.

Made to Worship. Contrib. by Chris Tomlin. (Worship Tracks (Word Tracks) Ser.). 2007. audio compact disk 8.98 (978-5-558-10879-8(7), Word Records) Word Enter.

Made Whole Through Our Marriage to God. abr. ed. Helen M. Wright. Read by Alan Young & Michael Sutton. 7 cass. (Running Time: 8 hrs. 15 mins.). (Mary Baker Eddy - God's Great Scientist Ser.: Vol. 6). 1998. 22.95 (978-1-886505-13-1(6)) H M Wright.

The struggle for health, holiness & heaven is dissolved in the desire to know oneself as God does. Brings forth wonderful insights to Scripture.

Madeleine DeFrees. unabr. ed. Madeline DeFrees. Read by Madeline DeFrees. 1 cass. (Running Time: 29 min.). 1989. 10.00 New Letters.

DeFrees, a former Roman Catholic nun, reads her poetry & is interviewed.

Madeleine's Ghost: A Novel of New York, New Orleans & the Next World. unabr. ed. Robert Girardi. Narrated by [illegible] Magee. 10 cass. (Running Time: 14 hrs.). 1997. 85.00 (978-0-78[illegible]2-6(1), 95072E7) Recorded Bks.

Ned Conti, an unemployed historian, has a ghost in his New York apartment. He has also been hired by a local priest to research a long-dead sister who may qualify for sainthood.

Madeline. 1 cass. (Running Time: 35 min.). (SPA.). (J). 2001. 15.95 (VXS-32C) Kimbo Educ.

Madeline. Ludwig Bemelmans. Illus. by Ludwig Bemelmans. (Running Time: 8 mins.). (J). (ps-3). 1982. 9.95 (978-1-59112-086-5(1)); 12.95 (978-1-59112-804-5(8)) Live Oak Media.

Madeline & Other Bemelmans. abr. ed. Ludwig Bemelmans. Perf. by Carol Channing. 1 cass. Incl. Fifi. Ludwig Bemelmans. (J). (CPN 1113); Happy Place. (J). (CPN 1113); Madeline & the Bad Hat. Ludwig Bemelmans. (Madeline Ser.). (J). (ps-3). (CPN 1113); Madeline's Rescue. Ludwig Bemelmans. (Madeline Ser.). (J). (ps-3). (CPN 1113); (Madeline Ser.). (J). (ps-3). 1984. 9.95 (978-0-89845-820-6(X), CPN 1113) HarperCollins Pubs.

Madeline & the Bad Hat see Madeline & Other Bemelmans

Madeline & the Bad Hat. Ludwig Bemelmans. Illus. by Ludwig Bemelmans. 14 vols. (Running Time: 12 mins.). 1985. pap. bk. 39.95 (978-1-59112-815-1(3)) Live Oak Media.

Madeline & the Bad Hat. Ludwig Bemelmans. Illus. by Ludwig Bemelmans. (Running Time: 12 mins.). (J). (ps-3). 1985. 12.95 (978-1-59112-812-0(9)) Live Oak Media.

Madeline & the Bad Hat. Read by Linda Terheyden. 11 vols. (Running Time: 12 mins.). (J). 2004. pap. bk. 18.95 (978-1-59112-813-7(7)) Pub: Live Oak Media. Dist(s): AudioGO

Madeline & the Bad Hat. unabr. ed. Ludwig Bemelmans. Illus. by Ludwig Bemelmans. Read by Linda Terheyden. 11 vols. (Running Time: 12 mins.). (Madeline Ser.). (J). (ps-3). 1975. bk. 25.95 (978-0-670-44620-9(3)); pap. bk. 16.95 (978-0-670-44621-6(1)); pap. bk. & tchr. ed. 37.95 Reading Chest. (978-0-670-44616-2(5)) Live Oak Media.

Madeline & the Gypsies. Ludwig Bemelmans. Illus. by Ludwig Bemelmans. 11 vols. (Running Time: 15 mins.). 1982. bk. 28.95 (978-1-59112-822-9(6)); 9.95 (978-1-59112-088-9(8)); audio compact disk 12.95 (978-1-59112-820-5(X)) Live Oak Media.

Madeline & the Gypsies. unabr. ed. Ludwig Bemelmans. Illus. by Ludwig Bemelmans. Read by Jean Richards. 11 vols. (Running Time: 15 mins.). (Madeline Ser.). (J). (ps-3). 1982. bk. 25.95 (978-0-670-44689-6(0)); pap. bk. 16.95 (978-0-670-44688-9(2)); pap. bk. & tchr. ed. 37.95 Reading Chest. (978-0-670-44684-1(X)) Live Oak Media.
Madeline flourishes when she teams up with a Gypsy circus troup.

Madeline DeFrees. unabr. ed. Madeline DeFrees. Read by Madeline DeFrees. 1 cass. (Running Time: 29 min.). 1991. 8.00 (031789) New Letters.

Madeline in London. Ludwig Bemelmans. Illus. by Ludwig Bemelmans. 11 vols. (Running Time: 13 mins.). 1988. bk. 28.95 (978-1-59112-818-2(8)); pap. bk. 39.95 (978-1-59112-302-6(X)); 9.95 (978-1-59112-089-6(6)); audio compact disk 12.95 (978-1-59112-816-8(1)) Live Oak Media.

Madeline in London. unabr. ed. Ludwig Bemelmans. Illus. by Ludwig Bemelmans. Read by Jean Richards. 11 vols. (Running Time: 13 mins.). (Madeline Ser.). (J). (ps-3). 1978. bk. 25.95 (978-0-670-44651-3(3)); pap. bk. & tchr. ed. 37.95 Reading Chest. (978-0-670-44650-6(5)) Live Oak Media.
Madeline & Pepito, the Bad Hat, take a wild ride on horseback through London.

Madeline in London. unabr. ed. Ludwig Bemelmans. Illus. by Ludwig Bemelmans. Read by Jean Richards. 11 vols. (Running Time: 13 mins.). (Madeline Ser.). (J). (ps-3). 1995. pap. bk. 16.95 (978-0-670-44655-1(6)) Live Oak Media.

Madeline Series. Ludwig Bemelmans. Illus. by Ludwig Bemelmans. 55 vols. (Running Time: 57 mins.). 1985. pap. bk. 85.95 (978-1-59112-844-1(7)) Live Oak Media.

Madeline 72-Copy Mixed Floor Display. Ludwig Bemelmans. Illus. by Ludwig Bemelmans. (J). 9.95 (978-1-59112-286-9(4)) Live Oak Media.

Madeline 72-Copy Mixed Floor Display. Ludwig Bemelmans. Illus. by Ludwig Bemelmans. (Running Time: 8 mins.). 1997. 9.95 (978-1-59112-085-8(3)); audio compact disk 12.95 (978-1-59519-183-0(6)) Live Oak Media.

Madeline 72-Copy Mixed Floor Display. unabr. ed. Ludwig Bemelmans. 1 read-along cass. (Running Time: 8 min.). (Madeline Ser.). (J). (ps-3). 1975. 9.95 Live Oak Media.

Madeline's Rescue see Madeline & Other Bemelmans

Madeline's Rescue. 2004. bk. 24.95 (978-0-89719-890-5(5)); pap. bk. 32.75 (978-1-55592-260-3(0)); pap. bk. 32.75 (978-1-55592-261-0(9)); pap. bk. 14.95 (978-1-56008-063-3(9)); pap. bk. 14.95 (978-1-55592-662-5(2)); 8.95 (978-0-89719-928-5(6)); 8.95 (978-1-56008-147-0(3)) Weston Woods.

Madeline's Rescue. Ludwig Bemelmans. 1 read-along cass. (Running Time: 10 min.). (Madeline Ser.). (J). (ps-3). 1978. 9.95 Live Oak Media.
Madeline tumbles into the Seine & is rescued by a dog who comes back to school with Madeline & her little girl friends.

Madeline's Rescue. Ludwig Bemelmans. Illus. by Ludwig Bemelmans. Read by Jean Richards. 11 vols. (Running Time: 10 mins.). (Madeline Ser.). (J). (ps-3). 1978. bk. 25.95 (978-0-670-44719-0(6)) Live Oak Media.

Madeline's Rescue. Ludwig Bemelmans. Illus. by Ludwig Bemelmans. 14 vols. (Running Time: 10 mins.). 1985. pap. bk. 39.95 (978-1-59112-811-3(0)); audio compact disk 12.95 (978-1-59112-808-3(0)) Live Oak Media.

Madeline's Rescue. Ludwig Bemelmans. 1 cass. (Running Time: 7 min.). (Madeline Ser.). (J). (ps-3). bk. 24.95; pap. bk. 15.95 (PRA030); pap. bk. 32.75 Weston Woods.
One side with page turn signals, one side without.

Madeline's Rescue. Ludwig Bemelmans. Illus. by Ludwig Bemelmans. (Running Time: 10 mins.). (J). (ps-3). 1985. 9.95 (978-1-59112-090-2(X)) Live Oak Media.

Madeline's Rescue. Ludwig Bemelmans & Judi Barrett. Read by Jean Richards. 1 cass. (Running Time: 30 mins.). (Madeline Ser.). (J). (ps-3). 2000. pap. bk. 19.97 (978-0-7366-9205-2(3)) Books on Tape.
Madeline tumbles into the Seine & is rescued by a dog who comes back to school with Madeline & her little girl friends.

Madeline's Rescue. Read by Jean Richards. 11 vols. (Running Time: 10 mins.). (J). 2004. pap. bk. 18.95 (978-1-59112-809-0(9)) Pub: Live Oak Media. Dist(s): AudioGO

Madeline's Rescue. unabr. ed. Ludwig Bemelmans. Illus. by Ludwig Bemelmans. Read by Jean Richards. 11 vols. (Running Time: 10 mins.). (Madeline Ser.). (J). (ps-3). 1978. pap. bk. 16.95 (978-0-670-44723-7(4)); pap. bk. & tchr. ed. 37.95 Reading Chest. (978-0-670-44718-3(8)) Live Oak Media.

Mademoiselle Fifi et Autres Nouvelles, Guy de Maupassant. Read by G. Faraoun & C. Deis. 2 cass. (Running Time: 1 hr. 20 min.). (FRE.). 1991. 26.95 (1256-VSL) Olivia & Hill.
A collection of stories.

Mademoiselle, Voulez-vous Danser? Franco-American Music from the New England Borderlands. Ted Levin. Perf. by Maria Perrault et al. 1 CD. (Running Time: 57 min.). 1999. 14.00 Smithsonian Folkways.
Notes & photos included.

Madensky Square. unabr. ed. Eva Ibbotson. Narrated by Juanita McMahon. 8 cass. (Running Time: 11 hrs. 15 mins.). 2001. 72.00 (978-1-84197-188-9(X), H1172E7) Recorded Bks.
Susanna Weber is the best dressmaker in Imperial Vienna. Through skill & hard work, she now owns her own dress shop, looking out over the beautiful Madensky Square. To do so, she has left her past behind, if not without regret, at least resolutely. Looking around her, at her customers & friends, Susanna is aware that she has more than most - but a few small changes cause her to realize just how precarious her situation is.

Madhu Vidya Upasana. Swami Jyotirmayananda. Read by Swami Jyotirmayananda. 1 cass. (Running Time: 60 min.). 12.99 (716) Yoga Res Foun.

Madhu Vidya Upasana, No. 2. Swami Jyotirmayananda. 1 cass. (Running Time: 1 hr.). 1990. 12.99 Yoga Res Foun.

Madison the Manipulator Learns Fairness. Pamela M. Goldberg. Illus. by Jimmy Boring. (J). 2008. pap. bk. (978-0-9778941-2-3(6)) Camp MakeBelieve.

Madman's Manuscript see Complete Ghost Stories

Madness: A Bipolar Life. unabr. ed. Marya Hornbacher. (Running Time: 9 hrs. 0 mins.). 2008. audio compact disk 29.95 (978-1-4332-1237-6(4)) Blckstn Audio.

Madness: A Bipolar Life. unabr. ed. Marya Hornbacher. Read by Tavia Gilbert. (Running Time: 34200 sec.). 2008. 29.95 (978-1-4332-1236-9(6)); 65.95 (978-1-4332-1234-5(X)); audio compact disk 29.95 (978-1-4332-1238-3(2)); audio compact disk & audio compact disk 80.00 (978-1-4332-1235-2(8)) Blckstn Audio.

Madness for God. Swami Amar Jyoti. 1 cass. 1979. 9.95 (P-26) Truth Consciousness.
"Seek ye Divine first." Why did we will to enter this illusion? True seekers must assume responsibility for their blocks.

Madness for the Goal. Swami Amar Jyoti. 1 cass. 1976. 9.95 (C-5) Truth Consciousness.
The plunge that finishes karmas. That joy of madness leads to ecstasy. Being one pointed, time & energy only for That.

Madness in the Mountains. Kaye Umansky. Read by Nigel Lambert. 2 CDs. (Running Time: 3 hrs.). (J). 2003. audio compact disk 21.95 (978-0-7540-6585-2(5), CHCD 085) AudioGO.

Madness of George III: A BBC Radio Full-Cast Dramatization. Alan Bennett. (Running Time: 2 hrs. 0 mins. 0 sec.). (ENG.). 2009. audio compact disk 24.95 (978-1-60283-737-9(6)) Pub: AudioGO. Dist(s): Perseus Dist

Madness of Hamlet. (23285-A) J Norton Pubs.

Madness, Religious Experience, & the Wisdom to Know the Difference. Thomas P. Lavin. Read by Thomas P. Lavin. 6 cass. (Running Time: 6 hrs. 30 min.). 1993. 45.95 (978-0-7822-0439-1(2), 517) C G Jung IL.

Madness under the Royal Palms: Love & Death Behind the Gates of Palm Beach. unabr. ed. Laurence Leamer. Narrated by Todd McLaren. (Running Time: 11 hrs. 30 mins. 0 sec.). (ENG.). 2009. audio compact disk 34.99 (978-1-4001-1071-1(8)); audio compact disk 24.99 (978-1-4001-6071-6(5)); audio compact disk 69.99 (978-1-4001-4071-8(4)) Pub: Tantor Media. Dist(s): IngramPubServ

Madonna. abr. ed. Andrew Morton. Read by Ian Peakes. 4 CDs. (Running Time: 4 hrs.). 2001. audio compact disk 27.95 (978-1-58788-812-0(2), 1587888122, CD); audio compact disk 61.25 (978-1-58788-813-7(0), 1587888130, CD Lib Edt) Brilliance Audio.
At the age of forty-three, with a career that spans two decades and ranges from the scandalous to the transcendent, Madonna is a bigger phenomenon than ever. But who is the private woman behind the public image? Andrew Morton, whose #1 New York Times bestsellers about Princess Diana and Monica Lewinsky have proved his ability to gain access to insiders who won't talk to anyone else, answers that question in this decidedly unauthorized biography. Morton's extensive, in-depth interviews with members of Madonna's inner circle - lovers, friends (even as far back as school friends), and business connections, many of whom have never spoken before now - allow him to go behind the carefully constructed myths to unmask the real Madonna. Andrew Morton is able to make startling revelations, among them the real story of Madonna's family background; the events behind the violent attack that changed her views on sex and men; her relationships with Michael Jackson, Prince, John F. Kennedy Jr., Vanilla Ice, and other rock and Hollywood stars; the mystery man she wanted to marry; and the darkest days of her career when she threatened to quit show business. From motherless child to wife and mother, from "boy toy" to fiercely independent diva, Madonna is one of the most remarkable women of our time.

Madonna. unabr. ed. Andrew Morton. Read by Ian Peakes. 7 cass. Library ed. (Running Time: 10 hrs.). 2001. 78.25 (978-1-58788-809-0(2), 1587888092, Unabridge Lib Edns); 32.95 (978-1-58788-808-3(4), 1587888084, BAU) Brilliance Audio.

Madonna. unabr. ed. Andrew Morton. Read by Ian Peakes. (Running Time: 10 hrs.). 2004. 39.25 (978-1-59335-374-2(X), 159335374X, Brinc Audio MP3 Lib) Brilliance Audio.

Madonna. unabr. ed. Andrew Morton. Read by Ian Peakes. (Running Time: 10 hrs.). 2004. 39.25 (978-1-59710-475-3(2), 1597104752, BADLE); 24.95 (978-1-59710-474-6(4), 1597104744, BAD) Brilliance Audio.

Madonna. unabr. ed. Andrew Morton. Read by Ian Peakes. (Running Time: 10 hrs.). 2004. 24.95 (978-1-59335-111-3(9), 1593351119) Soulmate Audio Bks.

***Madonna of the Future.** Henry James. Narrated by William Coon. (Running Time: 102). (ENG.). 2009. 6.95 (978-0-9844138-3-6(9)) Pub: Eloq Voice. Dist(s): OverDrive Inc

Madonna 5 Bk. 5: Audio Books for Children. Madonna. (Running Time: 1 hr. 15 mins.). (ENG.). (J). (ps-6). 2005. audio compact disk 16.99 (978-0-670-06047-4(X)) Pub: Callaway Edns. Dist(s): Penguin Grp USA

Madre. abr. ed. Maximo Gorky. Read by Laura García. 3 CDs. (SPA.). 2002. audio compact disk 17.00 (978-958-8161-50-1(9)) YoYoMusic.

madre de Jesús. P. Juan Rivas. (SPA.). (YA). 2005. audio compact disk 18.95 (978-1-935405-87-0(X)) Hombre Nuevo.

Madre Monte. unabr. ed. Abuelo Historias Del. (SPA.). 2007. audio compact disk 13.00 (978-958-8318-04-2(1)) Pub: Yoyo Music COL. Dist(s): YoYoMusic

Madrigal for Charlie Muffin. Brian Freemantle. Read by Hayward Morse. 6 cass. (Sound Ser.). (J). 2003. 54.95 (978-1-84283-272-1(7)) Pub: ISIS Lrg Prnt GBR. Dist(s): Ulverscroft US

Mae Gen i Gan. Leah Owen et al. (Caneuon A Cherddoriaeth Song & Music Ser.). 2005. 5.25 (978-1-897664-70-4(2)) Cyhoeddiadau GBR.

Maelstrom. Taylor Anderson. Read by William Dufris. Narrated by William Dufris. (Running Time: 18 hrs. 0 mins. 0 sec.). (Destroyermen Ser.). (ENG.). 2009. lab manual ed. 79.99 (978-1-4001-4046-6(3)) Pub: Tantor Media. Dist(s): IngramPubServ

Maelstrom. unabr. ed. Taylor Anderson. Read by William Dufris. Narrated by William Dufris. (Running Time: 18 hrs. 0 mins. 0 sec.). (Destroyermen Ser.). (ENG.). 2009. audio compact disk 39.99 (978-1-4001-1046-9(7)); audio compact disk 29.99 (978-1-4001-6046-4(4)) Pub: Tantor Media. Dist(s): IngramPubServ

Maelstrom. unabr. ed. Keith Douglass. Read by David Hilder. 7 cass. (Running Time: 10 hrs.). (Carrier Ser.: No. 5). 2001. 29.95 (978-0-7366-6791-3(1)) Books on Tape.
When the Soviets crush Finland & eye all of Europe, Carrier Battle Group Fourteen heads them off. Can Tomstone Magruder keep pace?.

Maelstrom. unabr. ed. Sam Llewellyn. Read by Jonathon Oliver. 12 cass. (Running Time: 16 hrs.). (Isis Ser.). (J). 1997. 94.95 (978-1-85695-860-8(4), 940905) Pub: ISIS Lrg Prnt GBR. Dist(s): Ulverscroft US

Maelstrom. unabr. ed. Michael MacConnell. Read by Sean Mangan. (Running Time: 43200 sec.). (Sarah Reilly Ser.: Bk. 1). 2008. audio compact disk 103.95 (978-1-921334-76-4(2), 9781921334764, Bolinda AudioAUS) Pub: Bolinda Pubng AUS. Dist(s): Bolinda Pub Inc

***Maelstrom.** unabr. ed. Michael MacConnell. Read by Sean Mangan. (Running Time: 12 hrs.). 2010. 43.95 (978-1-74214-514-3(0), 9781742145143) Pub: Bolinda Pubng AUS. Dist(s): Bolinda Pub Inc

Maelstrom. unabr. ed. Anne McCaffrey & Elizabeth Ann Scarborough. Read by Robert Ramirez. 8 cass. (Running Time: 9 hrs.). (Twins of Petaybee Ser.: Bk. 2). 2007. 72.75 (978-1-4281-3242-9(2)) Recorded Bks.

Maelstrom. unabr. collector's ed. Keith Douglass. Read by David Hilder. 7 cass. (Running Time: 10 hrs. 30 mins.). (Carrier Ser.: No. 5). 1995. 56.00 (978-0-7366-3204-1(2), 3868) Books on Tape.
A Soviet invasion force obliterates Finland, occupies Norway, threatens Sweden & all of Europe. The U.S. president authorizes DEFCON 2. But short of nukes, can the outnumbered Carrier Battle Group Fourteen mount an effective response? It's up to Tombstone Magruder to keep pace. He & his team must fly wingtip to wingtip with the threat of a total war looming.

Maestosa & Magica Città see ARTineraries Tour Torino: Majestic & Magical City

Maestria del Amor: Una guia practica para el arte de las Relaciones. Don Miguel Ruiz. (SPA.). 2009. audio compact disk 18.95 (978-1-878424-66-2(1)) Pub: Amber-Allen Pub. Dist(s): Hay House

Maestro: A Surprising Story about Leading by Listening. unabr. ed. Roger Nierenberg. Contrib. by Oliver Wyman. (Running Time: 4 hrs.). (ENG.). (gr. 12 up). 2009. audio compact disk 25.95 (978-0-14-314525-7(8)) Penguin Grp USA.

Maestro: Greenspan's Fed & the American Boom. abr. ed. Bob Woodward. Epil. by Bob Woodward. Read by James Naughton. 2006. 18.95 (978-0-7435-6141-9(4)) Pub: S&S Audio. Dist(s): S and S Inc

Maestro's Choice: Series One. Music by Kishori Amonkar. 1 cass. 1991. (A91006); audio compact disk (CD A91006) Multi-Cultural Bks.

Maestro's Choice: Series One. Music by Bhimsen Joshi. 1 cass. 1991. (A91004); audio compact disk (CD A91004) Multi-Cultural Bks.

Maestro's Choice: Series One. Music by Amjad Ali Khan. 1 cass. 1991. (A91019); audio compact disk (CD A91019) Multi-Cultural Bks.

Maestro's Choice: Series One. Music by Asad Ali Khan. 1 cass. 1991. (A91012); audio compact disk (CD A91012) Multi-Cultural Bks.

Maestro's Choice: Series One. Music by Bismillah Khan. 1 cass. 1991. (A91001); audio compact disk (CD A91001) Multi-Cultural Bks.

Maestro's Choice: Series One. Music by Imrat Khan. 1 cass. 1991. (A91018); audio compact disk (CD A91018) Multi-Cultural Bks.

Maestro's Choice: Series One. Music by Mallikarjun Mansur. 1 cass. 1991. (A91002); audio compact disk (CD A91002) Multi-Cultural Bks.

Maestro's Choice: Series One. Music by Ram Narayan. 1 cass. 1991. (A91009); audio compact disk (CD A91009) Multi-Cultural Bks.

Maestro's Choice: Series One. Music by N. Rajam. 1 cass. 1991. (A91020); audio compact disk (CD A91020) Multi-Cultural Bks.

Maestro's Choice: Series One. Music by Alla Rakha & Zakir Hussain. 1 cass. 1991. (A91013); audio compact disk (CD A91013) Multi-Cultural Bks.

Maestro's Choice: Series One. Music by Ravi Shankar. 1 cass. 1991. (A91003); audio compact disk (CD A91003) Multi-Cultural Bks.

Maestro's Choice Series Two, Vol. 1. Music by Vilayat Khan. 1 cass. 1995. (A95001); audio compact disk (CD A95001) Multi-Cultural Bks.

Maestro's Choice Series Two, Vol. 2. Music by Bhimsen Joshi. 1 cass. 1995. (A95002); audio compact disk (CD A95002) Multi-Cultural Bks.

Maestro's Choice Series Two, Vol. 3. Music by Pandit Jasraj. 1 cass. 1995. (A95003); audio compact disk (CD A95003) Multi-Cultural Bks.

Maestro's Choice Series Two, Vol. 4. Music by Hari P. Chaurasia. 1 cass. 1995. (A95004); audio compact disk (CD A95004) Multi-Cultural Bks.

Maestro's Choice Series Two, Vol. 5. Music by Shiv K. Sharma. 1 cass. 1995. (A95005); audio compact disk (CD A95005) Multi-Cultural Bks.

Maestro's Choice Series Two, Vol. 6. Music by Zakir Hussain. 1 cass. 1995. (A95006); audio compact disk (CD A95006) Multi-Cultural Bks.

***Maeve Binchy: A Radio Collection: Four BBC Full-Cast Story Collections.** Maeve Binchy. Narrated by Full Cast. (Running Time: 6 hrs. 0 mins. 0 sec.). (ENG.). 2010. audio compact disk 74.95 (978-1-4084-6828-9(X)) Pub: AudioGO. Dist(s): Perseus Dist

***Mafia Principle of Global Hegemony: The Middle East, Empire, & Activism.** Noam Chomsky. (PM Audio Ser.). (ENG.). 2011. audio compact disk 14.95 (978-1-60486-304-8(8)) Pub: Pm Pre. Dist(s): IPG Chicago

Mafia Son: The Scarpa Mob Family, the FBI, & a Story of Betrayal. unabr. ed. Sandra Harmon. Read by Oliver Wyman. (Running Time: 10 hrs. 0 mins. 0 sec.). (ENG.). 2009. audio compact disk 39.95 (978-1-4272-0702-9(X)) Pub: Macmill Audio. Dist(s): Macmillan

Mafia to Mormon - in My Own Words. Mario Facione. 2005. audio compact disk 12.99 (978-1-55517-986-1(X), Cedar Fort) CFI Dist.

***Magazine Publishing Industry Report: Direct Mail & Email Marketing Trends, Statistics & Analysis.** North American Publishing Company. (ENG.). 2010. 197.00 (978-1-931068-40-6(2)) North Am Pub Co.

Magazine U. S. A. Edwin T. Cornelius et al. Illus. by John Odam. 1984. bk. 75.00 (978-0-89209-270-3(X)) Pace Grp Intl.

***Magdalen Martyrs.** Ken Bruen. 2010. 44.95 (978-1-4450-0160-9(8)); audio compact disk 59.95 (978-1-4450-0161-6(6)) Pub: Isis Pubng Ltd GBR. Dist(s): Ulverscroft US

Magdalene & the Other Mary: Songs of Holy Women. Lady Chapel Singers. 1. 2005. audio compact disk 18.00 (978-0-89869-491-8(4)) Church Pub Inc.

Magdallan - End of the Age. 1 CD. (Running Time: 60 mins.). 1999. audio compact disk Brentwood Music.
Songs include: "Caves of Hercules," "Soul Child," "Dome of the Rock," "Love to the Rescue," "Danger in Your Eyes" & more.

***Mage in Black.** unabr. ed. Jaye Wells. Narrated by Cynthia Holloway. (Running Time: 9 hrs. 30 mins.). (Sabina Kane Ser.). 2010. 16.99 (978-1-4001-8903-8(9)); 24.99 (978-1-4001-6903-0(8)); audio compact disk 34.99 (978-1-4001-1903-5(0)) Pub: Tantor Media. Dist(s): IngramPubServ

***Mage in Black (Library Edition)** unabr. ed. Jaye Wells. Narrated by Cynthia Holloway. (Running Time: 9 hrs. 30 mins.). (Sabina Kane Ser.). 2010. 34.99 (978-1-4001-9903-7(4)); audio compact disk 83.99 (978-1-4001-4903-2(7)) Pub: Tantor Media. Dist(s): IngramPubServ

Magestad de Hijo de Dios, DS. Charles R. Swindoll.Tr. of Majesty of God's Son. (SPA.). 2007. audio compact disk Rental 46.00 (978-1-57972-778-9(6)) Insight Living.

Magga Birds of Ranatan. unabr. ed. Herbert L. McClelland. Read by Herbert L. McClelland. Read by May Davenport. 1 cass. (Running Time: 40 min.). (J). (gr. 3-5). 1986. pap. bk. 6.95 (978-0-943864-51-8(8)) Davenport.
Kerri wanders the magic land of Ranatan where the Magga Birds shoot paralyzing rays. The only way to stop them is to destroy their birdbath, & bring joy to Ranatan. Learning tool for remedial readers & adults learning English as a second language.

Maggi Peirce-Live. Short Stories. Perf. by Maggi Peirce. 1 cass. (Running Time: 1 hr.). 1981. 9.95 (978-0-938756-07-1(9), 020) Yellow Moon.
Irish jokes, folktales & stories from the author's childhood in Belfast, Northern Ireland.

Maggie: A Girl of the Streets. Stephen Crane. Read by Jim Killavey. 3 cass. (Running Time: 3 hrs.). 1989. 24.00 incl. album. (C-140) Jimcin Record.
Realistic study of poverty.

Maggie: A Girl of the Streets. unabr. ed. Stephen Crane. Read by Jean DeBarbieris. 2 cass. (Running Time: 2 hrs. 30 min.). 16.95 (978-1-55686-136-9(2), 136) Books in Motion.
This story tries to show that environment is a tremendous thing in the world & frequently shapes people's lives, regardless of other influences. Set in the 1890's the story touches many lives but it is Maggie, the street girl, who endures the ultimate hardships.

Maggie: A Girl of the Streets. unabr. collector's ed. Stephen Crane. Read by Jim Killavey. 3 cass. (Running Time: 3 hrs.). 1985. 18.00 (978-0-7366-3907-1(1), 9140) Books on Tape.
Crane's first novel, "Maggie: A Girl of the Streets," is an unflinching picture of the New York slums & is a landmark of literary naturalism.

Maggie: A Girl of the Streets & Other New York Stories. unabr. ed. Stephen Crane. Read by Terry Bregy & Melissa Hughes. 2 cass. (Running Time: 3 hrs.). (Voices Ser.: Vol. 4). (J). 1997. 22.95 (978-1-883332-27-3(3)) Audio Bkshelf.
Includes "An Experiment in Misery," "A Desertion," & "The Reluctant Voyagers".

Maggie Set: A Girl of the Streets, Stephen Crane. Read by Flo Gibson. 3 cass. (Running Time: 4 hrs. 30 min.). 1996. 16.95 (978-1-55685-421-7(8)) Audio Bk Con.
Hailed as the first realistic American novel, this tragic tale & its companion piece are set in the slums of New York. The product of a brutal father, drunken mother, & faithless lover, we follow Maggie's degeneration.

Maggie & the Ferocious Beast: The Big Carrot. unabr. ed. Betty Paraskevas. Narrated by John McDonough. 1 cass. (Running Time: 15 mins.). (ps up). 2002. 10.00 (978-1-4025-1414-2(X)) Recorded Bks.
While bird-watching in Nowhere Land, Ferocious Beast, Maggie and Hamilton Hocks are stopped in their tracks. Before them, a most amazing sight - a rabbit struggling to dig up a carrot! 'Why is that so amazing?" you ask? Well, it's the carrot of all carrots - the most enormous carrot of all time! Nedley the rabbit refuses their offer of help, even as he grows grumpier with each shovelful of dirt. Soon realizing that there is no way he can accomplish such a humongous task on his own, he accepts help. Working as a team, they get the carrot out! But, there is one problem, a very big problem.

Maggie & the Ferocious Beast: The Big Scare. unabr. ed. Betty Paraskevas. Narrated by John McDonough. 1 cass. (Running Time: 15 mins.). (ps up). 2004. 10.00 (978-0-7887-6085-3(8)) Recorded Bks.
A terrible secret is making the Ferocious Beast sit next to the River of Dreams and cry. Maggie and Hamilton Hocks want to help. "Tell us your secret and then you¿ll feel better," they urge their sad friend. "Sometimes I get scared," the Ferocious Beast finally admits. But what could frighten a big, ferocious beast? Is it something worse than sea monsters, ghosts, and spaceships from another galaxy? These are the things that scare Maggie and Hamilton - even though they¿ve never seen them.

Maggie & the Pirate. 2004. bk. 24.95 (978-1-56008-008-4(6)); pap. bk. 14.95 (978-1-56008-064-0(7)); 8.95 (978-0-7882-0050-2(X)); cass. & flmstrp 30.00 (978-0-89719-606-2(6)) Weston Woods.

Maggie Jordan. unabr. ed. Emma Blair. Read by Eve Karpf. 12 cass. (Running Time: 16 hrs.). (Audio Ser.). 1991. 96.95 (978-0-7451-5793-1(9)) AudioGO.
When most of Maggie Jordan's family are killed in a freak flood in the small coastal village of Heymouth, she is forced to find work in one of Glasgow's carpet mills. She becomes engaged to Nevil Sanderson, an impetuous & highly political man, who suddenly decides to go to Spain & join the Republicans in their fight against Franco. Maggie resolutely struggles on without him, but when her own life is threatened, she realizes that her place is by his side. Stunned by the conditions in Spain, Maggie joins the Republican cause as well, but when Nevil is promoted to platoon commander he becomes distant & ruthless, & fiercely jealous of her friendship with an American journalist.

Maggie of Moss Street. unabr. ed. Pamela Evans. Read by Annie Aldington. 12 cass. (Running Time: 18 hrs.). 2001. 85.46 (978-1-86042-730-5(8), 27308) Pub: Soundings Ltd GBR. Dist(s): Ulverscroft US

Maggie Rowan. unabr. ed. Catherine Cookson. Read by Elizabeth Henry. 9 cass. (Running Time: 13 hrs. 30 min.). (Sound Ser.). 2004. 76.95 (978-1-85496-511-0(5), 23736) Pub: UlverLrgPrint GBR. Dist(s): Ulverscroft US
In the mining town of Fellburn in County Durham, the Rowans & the Taggarts are neighbors, fighting, laughing & enduring adversity together. All except Maggie Rowan, who is consumed with two ambitions - to become a mother, & to escape life in a miner's cottage.

Maggie's Door. Patricia Reilly Giff. Read by Fionnula Flanagan. 3 CDs. (Running Time: 3 hrs. 31 mins.). (J). (gr. 4-7). 2004. audio compact disk 30.00 (978-0-8072-2000-9(0), Listening Lib) Random Audio Pubg.
Story of the journey from Ireland to America told by both Nory and her neighbor and friend Sean Red Mallon, two different stories with the same destination the home of Nory?s sister Maggie, at 416 Smith Street, Brooklyn, America.

Maggie's Door. unabr. ed. Patricia Reilly Giff. Read by Fionnula Flanagan. 2 cass. (Running Time: 3 hrs. 31 mins.). (J). (gr. 4-7). 2004. 23.00 (978-0-8072-1798-6(0), Listening Lib) Random Audio Pubg.

Maggie's Market. unabr. ed. Dee Williams. Read by Roe Kendall. 7 cass. (Running Time: 10 hrs.). 1998. 49.95 (978-0-7861-1451-1(7), 2313) Blckstn Audio.
It's 1935 & Maggie Ross loves her life among the stallholders in Kelvin Market where husband Tony has a bric-a-brac stall & where she lives, with her young family, above Mr. Goldman's bespoke tailors. But one fine spring day her husband disappears into thin air & her world collapses, in this moving story full of intrigue & surprises.

Maggies Rainbows: Action Songs. Kingdom Karactors. Prod. by Palm Tree Productions. (ENG.). (J). 2007. audio compact disk (978-0-9795480-8-6(X)) Palm Tree.

Maggies Rainbows: Santa Songs. Maggie. (ENG.). (J). 2006. audio compact disk (978-0-9799879-4-6(6)) Palm Tree.

Maggie's Rainbows - Christmas Carols. Maggie. 1 CD. (J). 2006. audio compact disk (978-0-9787128-6-0(2)) Palm Tree.

Maggie's Way. Jessie Fallon. Perf. by High Sierra Players Staff. Narrated by Kerry Gies. Score by David Fabrizio. Directed By David Fabrizio. Illus. by Katrina Kirkpatrick. 2 CDs. (Running Time: 1 hr. 30 mins.). Dramatization. (ENG.). 2004. audio compact disk 16.95 (978-1-58124-018-4(X)) Pub: Fiction Works. Dist(s): Brodart

Magi Chronicles: Josh's Daring Summer Adventure. Loretto Livingston. (Running Time: 7320 sec.). (J). 2008. audio compact disk 17.99 (978-1-60604-366-0(8)) Tate Pubng.

Magic see Secret Garden: A Young Reader's Edition of the Classic Story

Magic. unabr. ed. Trenna Daniells. Read by Trenna Daniells. 4 cass. Dramatization. (One to Grow on Ser.). (J). (gr. k-6). 1982. 29.95 Trenna Prods.
Six stories & 2 subliminal programs promote human potential concepts in a manner that will stimulate your child's imagination & creativity.

Magic: White, Gray, & Black. Manly P. Hall. 8.95 (978-0-89314-174-5(7), C880710) Philos Res.
Beliefs of nature.

Magic & Miracles: Getting Your Needs Met. Marianne Williamson. Read by Marianne Williamson. 1 cass. (Running Time: 90 mins.). (Lectures on a Course in Miracles). 1999. 10.00 (978-1-56170-245-9(5), M748) Hay House.

Magic & Mystery of Angels. unabr. ed. Stephan Hoeller. 1 cass. (Running Time: 1 hr. 30 min.). 1991. 11.00 (40023) Big Sur Tapes.
Hoeller considers reacquainting ourselves with archetypes from our own culture, such as angel myths, a vitally important step in assimilating new experiences. As our culture becomes more complex & specialized, a "crisis of fragmentation of life in general" makes us increasingly susceptible to something ini the character of magic, & we should know how to respond.

Magic & Other Misdemeanors. unabr. ed. Michael Buckley. Narrated by L. J. Ganser. 6 CDs. (Running Time: 6 hrs. 30 mins.). (Sisters Grimm Ser.: Bk. 5). (J). (gr. 4-6). 2008. audio compact disk 66.75 (978-1-4281-8217-2(9)); 51.75 (978-1-4281-8212-7(8)) Recorded Bks.
New York Times best-selling author Michael Buckley has earned critical praise from publications like Kirkus Reviews and the Washington Post. His Sisters Grimm books are full of magical adventures and colorful fairy tale characters. In their fifth exploit, Sabrina and Daphne Grimm are on their own while investigating the theft of enchanted items from the Ever Afters. And if they don't solve the case, the villain behind the crimes will unleash chaos upon the residents of Ferryport Landing.

Magic & Power of Nature. Swami Amar Jyoti. 1 cass. 1989. 9.95 (K-118) Truth Consciousness.
The enticing spell of Maya, mystery of relativity, good & evil, man & woman, illusion & the way to freedom.

Magic & the Animal Powers. unabr. ed. Stephan Hoeller. 1 cass. (Running Time: 1 hr. 30 min.). 1988. 11.00 (40016) Big Sur Tapes.
"The overwhelming preoccupations of the Western mind bear the stamp of magic - to bring things out of the dark into the light, to bring the unconscious into consciousness." Joseph Campbell's work "The Way of the Animal Powers" provides Hoeller a starting point for this exploration of the role of magic in Western culture, & the importance of animals in mythology & in our psyches.

Magic Animal: Mankind Revisited. unabr. collector's ed. Philip Wylie. Read by Ron Shoop. 8 cass. (Running Time: 12 hrs.). 1983. 64.00 (978-0-7366-0548-9(7), 1522) Books on Tape.
Christianity, American materialism, behaviorist psychology, "Now" Generation...Wylie targets each of these & other conventions & prejudices that have dominated human conduct for more than 2000 years. He contends that man's growing depradation of his natural environment, his superstitions, his chosen ignorance of the basic laws of ecology & science have left him unfit to live in the 20th century.

Magic Apple Tree: A Country Year. unabr. ed. Susan Hill. Read by Delia Corrie. 6 cass. (Running Time: 9 hrs.). 1986. 54.95 (978-1-85496-117-4(9), 61179) Ulvrscrft Audio.

Magic Ark. Lao She. Adapted by Peggy Wang. 1 cass. (Running Time: 90 mins.). (CHI.). (YA). (gr. 10-12). 1986. pap. bk. 34.50 (978-0-614-01439-6(5), SCH210) J Norton Pubs.
Well-known story is retold in simple Chinese for students of advanced first-year or second-year Chinese. Text in Hanyu pinyin serves a a guide to pronunciation & an aid in using a pinyin Chinese-English dictionary.

Magic Ark. Peggy Wang. 1 cass. (Running Time: 60 min.). (J). 8.95 (978-0-88710-161-8(5)) Yale Far Eastern Pubns.
Charming children's story, 700 character level.

Magic Ark CDs & Book. Lao She. Adapted by Peggy Wang. (CHI.). 2006. audio compact disk 34.50 (978-1-57970-429-2(8), Audio-For) J Norton Pubs.

Magic Barrel. unabr. ed. Bernard Malamud & Isaac Bashevis Singer. Perf. by Shelly Berman. 1 cass. (Running Time: 55 min.). 1992. 19.95 (978-1-58081-074-6(8)) L A Theatre.
A story of a shy rabbinical student's struggle to find a wife through a matchmaker. In fate, a writer encounters a blustering, self-pitying matron at a party who spins a woeful tale about being abandoned by her family. Through the writer's sly reactions, the audience begins to suspect she is not telling the whole story.

Magic Bike. Green Chili Jam Band. 1 CD. (J). (ps-5). 1992. audio compact disk 14.98 (978-0-9638680-3-9(9)) Squeaky Wheel.

Magic Bike. Perf. by Green Chili Jam Band. 1 cass. (J). (ps-5). 1992. 9.98 (978-0-9638680-0-8(4), GC001) Squeaky Wheel.
Self esteem & imagination.

Magic Bites. unabr. ed. Ilona Andrews. Narrated by Renée Raudman. (Running Time: 9 hrs. 0 mins. 0 sec.). (Kate Daniels Ser.). (ENG.). 2009. lab manual ed. 69.99 (978-1-4001-4030-5(7)); audio compact disk 24.99 (978-1-4001-6030-3(8)); audio compact disk 34.99 (978-1-4001-1030-8(0)) Pub: Tantor Media. Dist(s): IngramPubServ

***Magic Bleeds.** unabr. ed. Ilona Andrews. Narrated by Renée Raudman. 2 MP3-CDs. (Running Time: 13 hrs. 30 mins. 0 sec.). (Kate Daniels Ser.). 2010. 24.99 (978-1-4001-6731-9(0)); 18.99 (978-1-4001-8731-7(1)); audio compact disk 37.99 (978-1-4001-1731-4(3)); audio compact disk 90.99 (978-1-4001-4731-1(X)) Pub: Tantor Media. Dist(s): IngramPubServ

Magic Burns. unabr. ed. Ilona Andrews. Narrated by Renée Raudman. (Running Time: 9 hrs. 30 mins. 0 sec.). (Kate Daniels Ser.). (ENG.). 2009. lab manual ed. 69.99 (978-1-4001-4031-2(5)); audio compact disk 34.99 (978-1-4001-1031-5(9)); audio compact disk 24.99 (978-1-4001-6031-0(6)) Pub: Tantor Media. Dist(s): IngramPubServ

Magic by the Book. unabr. ed. Nina Bernstein. Narrated by Katie Firth. 4 cass. (Running Time: 5 hrs. 30 mins.). (J). 2005. bk. 63.75 (978-1-4193-3607-2(X), 42048); 39.75 (978-1-4193-3605-8(3), 98019) Recorded Bks.
Staff reporter for The New York Times and National Book Award finalist, Nina Bernstein pens an engaging story about the magical adventures found inside books. Anne, Emily, and Will don't remember picking the book up at the library; but as soon as they start reading it, they come under its spell. Transported to Sherwood Forest with Robin Hood, then to an enchanted land of giant bugs, and later to a winter fest in Russia where they help save the world, the children discover a magic they've always dreamed of.

Magic Candle to Find Treasure see Graveyard of Ghost Tales

Magic Circle Pilates Matwork: Basic-Intermediate. Instructed by Aliesa George. (ENG.). 2009. 12.00 (978-0-9771576-6-2(0)) Ctr Pilates.

Magic City. unabr. ed. James W. Hall. Read by Richard Allen. (YA). 2007. 59.99 (978-1-60252-847-5(0)) Find a World.

Magic City. unabr. ed. James W. Hall. Read by Richard Allen. 9 CDs. (Running Time: 11 hrs. 30 mins. 0 sec.). (Thorn Ser.). (ENG.). 2007. audio compact disk 34.99 (978-1-4001-0406-2(8)); audio compact disk 24.99 (978-1-4001-5406-7(5)); audio compact disk 69.99 (978-1-4001-3406-9(4)) Pub: Tantor Media. Dist(s): IngramPubServ

Magic City. unabr. ed. E. Nesbit. Read by Flo Gibson. 4 cass. (Running Time: 5 hrs. 30 min.). (J). (gr. 1-3). 1998. 19.95 (978-1-55685-526-9(5)) Audio Bk Con.
Phillip & Lucy are suddenly transported into a magic city he built from toys. Winged horses, talking animals, magic islands & ancient buildings are threatened with disaster if the children cannot save them through valiant deeds, always contending with the evil Prentenderette.

Magic Cooking Pot: The Shoemaker & the Elves. Sue Arengo. (Classic Tales Ser.). 2001. 14.75 (978-0-19-422075-0(3)) OUP.

Magic Cottage. rev. ed. James Herbert. Read by Robert Powell. (Running Time: 3 hrs. 0 mins. 0 sec.). (ENG., 2007. audio compact disk 27.95 (978-0-230-52851-2(1)) Pub: Macmillan UK GBR. Dist(s): IPG Chicago

Magic Crossbow. unabr. ed. Alice Lucas. Read by Chung Hoang Chuong & Aurora Wetzel. 1 cass. (Running Time: 8 min.). (Voices of Liberty Ser.). (ENG & VIE.). (J). (gr. 5-8). 1990. 7.00 (978-0-936434-50-6(3)) SF Study Ctr.
Traditional Vietnamese folktale told in English & Vietnamese.

Magic Dulcimer. Lorraine Lee. Perf. by Lorraine Lee. 1 cass. (Running Time: 45 min.). (J). 1983. 9.95 (978-0-938756-08-8(7), 041) Yellow Moon.
A chance to hear Lorraine sing & play 17 of her favorites from the book of the same name. You can play along, learn the tunes by ear or listen to Lorraine's only solo release to date.

Magic Dulcimer. Lorraine Lee. Perf. by Lorraine Lee. 1 cass. (Running Time: 45 min.). (J). 1983. pap. bk. 20.95 (978-0-938756-10-1(9), 042) Yellow Moon.

Magic, Faith, Superstition & the Supernatural. Richard D. Dobbins. 3 cass. 14.95 (978-1-890329-58-7(4)) Totally Alive.
Dr. Dobbins exposing many of the lies & superstitions that have become mixed with the Christian faith. The series establishes a firm Scriptural foundation for the Christian believer.

Magic Finger see Roald Dahl

Magic Finger. Roald Dahl. (J). (gr. 4-6). 1988. (CPN 1633) HarperCollins Pubs.

Magic Fish. Freya Littledale. 1 cass. (Easy-to-Read Folktales Ser.). (J). (ps-2). 5.95 incl. bk. (978-0-590-63064-1(4)) Scholastic Inc.

Magic Fish: The Fisherman & His Wife. Jan Callner & Bill Wheeler. 1 cass. (Running Time: 49 min.). (J). (gr. k-4). 1999. 10.95 (978-1-928851-03-5(7), CK0002-4); audio compact disk 15.95 (978-1-928851-02-8(9), CK0002-2) Mike & Me.
A musical play for children based on Grimm's tale.

Magic Fish: Theater Package. unabr. ed. Jan Callner & Bill Wheeler. 1 CD. (Running Time: 45 mins.). (J). (ps-4). 2001. audio compact disk 19.95 (978-1-928851-07-3(X)) Mike & Me.
Musical play with dialogue & 7 songs, with 6 characters. Feature Broadway actors & recording artists. Tales are based on the Brothers Grimm stories. Includes puppet theatre and puppet.

Magic Fish: Theater Package. unabr. ed. Bill Wheeler. 1 cass. (Running Time: 45 mins.). Dramatization. (J). (ps-4). 2001. 14.95 (978-1-928851-09-7(6)) Mike & Me.

Magic Fishbone see Favorite Children's Stories: A Collection

Magic Fishbone. Charles Dickens. 1980. (N-41) Jimcin Record.

Magic Flute: An Alchemical Allegory. M. F. M van den Berk. 3 vols. 2004. bk. 322.00 (978-90-04-13099-9(3)) Pub: Brill Academic NLD. Dist(s): Brill Acad Pub

Magic Flute: An Introduction to Mozart's Opera. Thomson Smillie. Read by David Timson. 1 CD. (Running Time: 1 hr. 30 min.). (Opera Explained Ser.). 2003. audio compact disk 8.99 (978-1-84379-075-4(0)) NaxMulti GBR.

Magic Flute of Forgiveness. Kenneth Wapnick. 1 CD. (Running Time: 3 hrs. 56 mins. 41 secs.). 2006. 19.00 (978-1-59142-297-6(3), 3m135); audio compact disk 24.00 (978-1-59142-296-9(5), CD135) Foun Miracles.

Magic French for Kids. Beth Manners. 1 cass. (Running Time: 30 min.). (FRE.). (J). (ps-1). 2000. 9.98 (978-0-9662876-4-6(9)) Future Boomers.
A magical story with songs & games. Introduces French to 2-6 year olds from the producers of award winning tapes for French. French intructional, education, teaching or languag art.

Magic Hill see Prince Rabbit & Other Stories

Magic Hill, Peter Cottontail & Adventures of Buster Bear. unabr. ed. A. A. Milne. Narrated by Flo Gibson. 2 cass. (Running Time: 3 hrs.). (J). (gr. k-2). 2001. 14.95 (978-1-55685-648-8(2)) Audio Bk Con.
Princess Daffodil's gift of spreading flowers wherever she goes had its drawback until the king finds the magic hill. The adventure stories bring us into the war whimsical world of the Green Forest, the Smiling Pool & the Purple Mountains where the Merry Little Breezes, Reddy fox, Johnny Chuck, Buster Bear & Peter Cottontail among others romp & tease each other through many escapades.

Magic Hoofbeats. Ellen Verenieks & Josepha Sherman. (Running Time: 4 mins. 37 sec.). (ENG.). (J). 2006. audio compact disk 19.99 (978-1-84686-023-2(7)) BarefootBksMA.

Magic Hour. abr. ed. Kristin Hannah. Read by Suzanne Toren. 6. (Running Time: 25200 sec.). 2007. audio compact disk 14.99 (978-1-59600-851-9(2), 9781596008519, BCD Value Price) Brilliance Audio.
Please enter a Synopsis.

***Magic Hour.** abr. ed. Susan Isaacs. Read by Ken Howard. (ENG.). 2005. (978-0-06-089337-8(0), Harper Audio); (978-0-06-089336-1(2), Harper Audio) HarperCollins Pubs.

Magic Hour. unabr. ed. Kristin Hannah. Read by Suzanne Toren. (Running Time: 14 hrs.). 2006. 39.25 (978-1-59710-900-0(2), 9781597109000, BADLE); 24.95 (978-1-59710-901-7(0), 9781597109017, BAD); 34.95 (978-1-59355-510-8(5), 9781593555108, BAU); 87.25 (978-1-59355-511-5(3), 9781593555115, BrilAudUnabridg); audio compact disk 112.25 (978-1-59355-514-6(8), 9781593555146, BriAudCD Unabrid); audio compact disk 38.95 (978-1-59355-513-9(X), 9781593555139, Bril Audio CD Unabri); audio compact disk 39.25 (978-1-59335-863-1(6), 9781593358631, Brlnc Audio MP3 Lib); audio compact disk 24.95 (978-1-59335-729-0(X), 9781593357290, Brilliance MP3) Brilliance Audio.
Until recently, Dr. Julia Cates was one of the preeminent child psychiatrists in the country, but a scandal shattered her confidence, ruined her career, and made her a media target. When she gets a desperate call from her estranged sister, Ellie, a police chief in their small western Washington hometown, she jumps at the chance to escape. In Rain Valley, nothing much ever happens-until a girl emerges from the deep woods and walks into town. She is a victim unlike any Julia has ever seen: a child locked in a world of unimaginable fear and isolation. When word spreads of the "wild child" and the infamous doctor who is treating her, the media descend on Julia and once again her competence is challenged. State and federal authorities want to lock the girl away in an institution until an identification can be made. But to Julia, who has come to doubt her own ability, nothing is more important than saving the girl she now calls Alice. To heal this child, Julia will have to understand that she cannot work alone and must look to others-the people in the town she left long ago, the sister she barely knows, and Dr. Max Cerrasin, a handsome, private man with secrets of his own. Then a shocking revelation forces Julia to risk everything to discover the truth about

Alice. The ordeal that follows will test the limits of Julia's faith, forgiveness, and love, as she struggles to ascertain where Alice ultimately belongs.

Magic Hour. unabr. ed. Kristin Hannah. Read by Suzanne Toren. (YA). 2008. 99.99 (978-1-60514-817-5(2)) Find a World.

Magic in the Mountains. (J). 2003. audio compact disk (978-1-930429-46-8(0)) Love Logic.

Magic Island: Relaxation for Kids. Betty Mehling. Prod. by Betty Mehling. Perf. by Max Highstein. Composed by Max Highstein. Narrated by Radha Delamarter. (Running Time: 26 mins.). (J). (ps-8). 1990. 12.00 (978-0-917306-05-1(8)) Calif Pubns.

Magic Island: Relaxation for Kids. Betty Mehling. Prod. by Betty Mehling. Perf. by Max Highstein. Composed by Max Highstein. Narrated by Radha Delamarter. (Running Time: 52 mins.). (J). (ps-8). 2003. audio compact disk 16.95 (978-0-917306-06-8(6)) Calif Pubns.

Magic Island: Relaxation for Kids. Betty Mehling et al. 1 cass. (Running Time: 25 min.). (J). 1999. 12.00 (30374) Courage-to-Change.
A journey by hot air balloon to a magic island. Guided imagery helps to quiet the mind, soothe the emotions & expand the imagination.

Magic Johnson. 1 cass. (Running Time: 1 hr. 30 mins.). (SmartReader Ser.). (J). 1999. pap. bk. & tchr. ed. 19.95 (978-0-7887-0119-1(3), 79307T3) Recorded Bks.
He has shattered sports records, won awards & dominated professional basketball during his career. But Magic Johnson has also contributed priceless time & energy to promoting health education.

Magic Journey. John Nichols. Read by John Nichols. 1 cass. (Running Time: 1 hr.). 12.95 (978-1-55644-049-6(9), 2091) Am Audio Prose.
Nichols reads excerpts from his works "Magic Journey" & "Nirvana Blues".

***Magic Kettle.** Anonymous. 2009. (978-1-60136-579-8(9)) Audio Holding.

Magic Kingdom. unabr. ed. Stanley Elkin. Narrated by Graeme Malcolm. 8 cass. (Running Time: 11 hrs.). 1985. 72.00 (978-0-7887-3497-7(0), 95899E7) Recorded Bks.
When Eddy Bale loses his 12-year old son to a rare disease, he embarks on a campaign to take a group of terminally-ill children on a trip to Disney's Magic Kingdom.

Magic Kingdom for Sale - Sold! abr. ed. Terry Brooks. Read by Dick Hill. (Running Time: 6 hrs.). (Magic Kingdom of Landover Ser.: No. 1). 2006. 24.95 (978-1-4233-0131-8(5), 9781423301318, BAD) Brilliance Audio.

Magic Kingdom for Sale - Sold! abr. ed. Terry Brooks. Read by Dick Hill. (Running Time: 21600 sec.). (Magic Kingdom of Landover Ser.: No. 1). 2007. audio compact disk 14.99 (978-1-4233-5019-4(7), 9781423350194, BCD Value Price) Brilliance Audio.

Magic Kingdom for Sale - Sold! unabr. ed. Terry Brooks. (Running Time: 14 hrs.). (Magic Kingdom of Landover Ser.: No. 1). 2007. 39.25 (978-1-4233-5017-0(0), 9781423350170, BADLE); 24.95 (978-1-4233-5016-3(2), 9781423350163, BAD) Brilliance Audio.

Magic Kingdom for Sale - Sold! unabr. ed. Terry Brooks. Read by Dick Hill. (Running Time: 50400 sec.). (Magic Kingdom of Landover Ser.: No. 1). 2007. 107.25 (978-1-4233-5011-8(1), 9781423350118, BrilAudUnabridg); audio compact disk 39.25 (978-1-4233-5015-6(4), 9781423350156, Brinc Audio MP3 Lib); audio compact disk 112.25 (978-1-4233-5013-2(8), 9781423350132, BriAudCD Unabrid); audio compact disk 29.95 (978-1-4233-5012-5(X), 9781423350125, Bril Audio CD Unabri); audio compact disk 24.95 (978-1-4233-5014-9(6), 9781423350149, Brilliance MP3) Brilliance Audio.

***Magic Ladder to Success: The Wealth-Builder's Concise Guide to Winning!** unabr. ed. Napoleon Hill. Read by Sean Pratt. (Running Time: 5 hrs.). (ENG.). 2011. 27.00 (978-1-59659-639-9(2), GildAudio); audio compact disk 29.98 (978-1-59659-624-5(4), GildAudio) Pub: Gildan Media. Dist(s): HachBkGrp

Magic Looking Glass. unabr. ed. 36 cass. (Running Time: 7 hrs. 20 min.). Dramatization. (J). (gr. 2-6). 1989. 9.95 (978-0-7810-0013-0(0), NIM-CW-125-C) NIMCO.
A series made up of 6 units. Each unit is made up of 6 stories from another country. The stories are public-domain children's stories dramatized by various readers.

Magic Mandolin: 30 Folk Songs & Melodies from Around the World. Jozef Scales. 2002. bk. 17.95 (978-0-7866-5823-7(1), 98625BCD) Mel Bay.

Magic Michael. 2004. 8.95 (978-1-56008-961-2(X)); cass. & flmstrp 30.00 (978-1-56008-713-7(7)) Weston Woods.

Magic Mountain see Montaña Magica

Magic Mountain. Tomas Mann. Read by Daniel Quintero. (Running Time: 3 hrs.). 2003. 16.95 (978-1-60083-284-0(9), Audiofy Corp) Iofy Corp.

Magic Mushroom & Maria Sabina. unabr. ed. R. Gordon Wasson. 2 cass. (Running Time: 2 hrs. 38 min.). 1975. 18.00 (10801) Big Sur Tapes.
Wasson describes, in intimate detail, his journey to the village of Huautla de Jimenez & his work there with Curandera Maria Sabina.

Magic Music Man. Andy Drummond. 1990. 11.75 (978-0-19-458260-5(4)) OUP.

Magic of Believing. Claude M. Bristol. 2004. 7.95 (978-0-7435-1885-7(3)) Pub: S&S Audio. Dist(s): S and S Inc

Magic of Believing. abr. ed. Claude M. Bristol. Read by William Cane. (Running Time: 10 hrs. 0 mins. 0 sec.). (ENG.). 2005. audio compact disk 15.00 (978-0-7435-3948-7(6), Sound Ideas) Pub: S&S Audio. Dist(s): S and S Inc
*BELIEVE IN YOURSELF AND ALMOST ANYTHING CAN HAPPEN! Mystical, motivating and inspiring, The Magic of Believing is an extraordinary self-improvement program which draws on the philosophy that the energy of the subconscious mind can help individuals achieve any goal. With a step-by-step system for tapping and unleashing the powers of the mind, listeners will learn: * How to think more clearly and effectively to attain their highest goals * How to activate these goals and put them to work * The powers of self-suggestion and self-affirmation - keys to creating new ways of thinking and believing * How to combine mental pictures with the power of the subconscious so that any goal you imagine can be realized in the real world Written in 1948, The Magic of Believing has helped thousands attain both personal and professional goals and the appeal of its philosophy remains a powerful tool for change. Now you can turn your thoughts into real achievements too! WHY WAIT FOR BETTER TIMES WHEN YOU CAN MAKE THEM HAPPEN NOW? Leaders of government and industry...stars of stage and screen...giants of science and the business world agree...These clear, easy-to-follow principles changed their lives and they can change yours, too! Formulated by a successful businessman and world traveler, this method has been used by millions for over three decades. The Magic of Believing offers the key to a world of unlimited opportunity. Now you can discover: * How to become the person you believe yourself to be * How to use your imagination to set your goals * Three sure-fire steps to getting what you want * The power of suggestion: How to use your thoughts to make things happen * Mental picture: The art of turning thoughts into action, results and rewards * Why and how believing makes it so Make your job work for you. Start your own business. Increase your income. Lose weight. Add love to your life. Whatever your goal, you can make it happen through The Magic of Believing!.*

Magic of Color Dynamics Action Kit. unabr. ed. Judith L. Powell. Read by Judith L. Powell. 2 cass. (Running Time: 80 min.). (Powell Life Improvement Programs Ser.). 1987. pap. bk. 29.95 Incl. color cards & plastic album. (978-0-914295-81-5(0)) Top Mtn Pub.
Tape 1: Side A presents a step-by-step lecture to using color in everyday life; clothing, home, office. Also, how to "Color Breath" for better health, youthfulness & vitality. Side B presents a Mental Training Exercise designed to discover "subjective color" which can be used for obtaining high energy, protection & courage. Tape 2: Side A presents a Mental Training Exercise with a step-by-step mental process of "Color Healing." Side B presents Mental Training Exercise to use color visualization in the systematic "Color Balancing of the Chakras".

Magic of Color Energy. Judith L. Powell. 2 cass. 21.95 set. (978-1-56087-123-1(7)) Top Mtn Pub.
Enjoy the benefits of Dr. Judith Powell's famous "Color Dynamics Seminar" without leaving your home. This Action Kit contains a lecture & 3 beautifully guided visualization mental training exercises from this most popular, worldwide seminar.

Magic of Conflict Workshop: Your Personal Guidance System. Thomas F. Crum. 1989. 69.95 Aiki Works.
Includes: Conflict resolution: An Aiki approach beyond the gold Aiki energizer, the magic of conflict workbook & the magic of conflict.

Magic of Fairy Falls. Veronica Huston. Narrated by Veronica Huston. Prod. by Blue Kiss Audio. (ENG.). (J). 2008. (978-0-9725297-1-6(3)) Blue Kiss.

Magic of Forgiveness. unabr. ed. Jack Boland. Read by Jack Boland. 1 cass. (Running Time: 1 hr.). 9.95 (978-0-88152-062-0(4), BI16) Master Mind.

Magic of Getting What You Want. David J. Schwartz. Intro. by A. E. Whyte. 1 cass. (Running Time: 53 min.). (Listen & Learn USA! Ser.). 8.95 (978-0-88684-061-7(9)) Listen USA.
Shows how not to settle for less when you want more.

Magic of Giving. Marcus C. Cherry. Read by Marcus C. Cherry. 1 cass. (Running Time: 1 hr.). 1985. pap. bk. 21.99; 10.99 Ntl Underwriter.
The author discusses & gives answers to such questions as: What can be expected for the time & work involved & are there great amounts of money to be made in this area?; What is the underlying concept of the charitable giving market?; What has the life insurance industry done to promote charitable giving through life insurance?; Are some policies better for charitable giving market & if so, why?; What are some common problems to avoid & situations to look for?.

Magic of Happiness: Secrets to Living a Joyful Life. Barry Neil Kaufman. 6 cass. (Running Time: 6 hrs.). 1997. (978-1-55525-073-7(4), 17330A) Nightingale-Conant.
Choose happiness.

Magic of Living. Betty Neels. Read by Julia Sands. 4 cass. (Running Time: 6 hrs.). (978-1-84283-101-4(1)) Soundings Ltd GBR.
She stood no chance with Gideon Arabella Birch has a less than happy introduction to Holland when she becomes involved in a road accident. It seems providential that the first person on the scene should be Dr Gideon van der Vorst, who takes charge of the situation and Arabella! In a very masterful way. After that Arabella finds herself involved, in a professional way, with the imposing doctor, and begins to wonder if Providence had known what it was doing! For once her glamorous cousin Hilary caught sight of Gideon, it was no use Arabella falling in love with him.

Magic of Love. unabr. ed. Barbara Cartland. Read by Marie McCarthy. 4 cass. (Running Time: 5 hrs. 15 min.). 1999. 57.95 (978-1-85903-262-6(1)) Pub: Magna Story GBR. Dist(s): Ulverscroft US
Melita finds her happiness threatened by the jealousy of the cousin to the man she adores and the rituals of Voodoo which cast their dark shadow over slaves and plantation alike.

Magic of Love: How to Fall in Love, Lose Weight & Keep It off Forever. Janet Greeson. 4 cass. (Magic of Recovery Ser.: Vol. 2). 1994. 29.95 Set. (978-0-9630955-5-8(2)) Greeson & Boyle.
Therapeutic mini workshops. Self-help - how to lose weight.

***Magic of Metaphor Audiobook: Stories for Teachers, Trainers & Thinkers.** Short Stories. Nick Owen. Narrated by Nick Owen. 2 CDs. (Running Time: 2 hrs.). 2010. 34.95 (978-1-84590-405-0(2)) Crown Hse GBR.

Magic of Method Selling: Revolutionary New Sales Ideas Based on Old World Truth. James L. Rankin. Read by James L. Rankin. 1 cass. 1995. 6.95 (978-0-9641729-3-7(3)) eDream Pubng.
Based on the teachings of Stanislavski.

Magic of Real Moments: Living Your Life with Purpose & Passion. Barbara De Angelis. 6 cass. (Running Time: 6 hrs.). 1995. 59.95 incl. reminders. (13120AT) Nightingale-Conant.
A powerful invitation to transform your life, & a practical guide for nourishing your spirit. Also, it shows you how to tap into your own source of spiritual power & wisdom.

Magic of Recovery: How to Fall in Love, Lose Weight & Keep It off Forever. Janet Greeson. 14 cass. (Magic of Recovery Ser.: Vols. 1-4). 1994. 98.80 Set. (978-0-9630955-0-3(1)) Greeson & Boyle.
Therapeutic mini workshops. Self-help - how to lose weight.

Magic of Selling. Dan Hollis. 1. 2008. audio compact disk 12.95 (978-1-932226-66-9(4)) Wizard Acdmy.

Magic of the Heart: Weaving the Black Thread of African Shamanism in the New Age. Elie Hien. 1 cass. 7.00 (A0041-85) Sound Photosyn.
A masterful African shaman speaking & singing.

Magic of Thinking Big. abr. ed. David J. Schwartz. Read by David J. Schwartz. 4 CDs. (Running Time: 40 hrs. 0 mins. 0 sec.). (ENG., 2003. audio compact disk 30.00 (978-0-7435-2903-7(0), Sound Ideas) Pub: S&S Audio. Dist(s): S and S Inc

Magic of Thinking Big. unabr. ed. David J. Schwartz. Read by David J. Schwartz. 6 cass. (Running Time: 4 hrs. 30 min.). 1988. 59.95 Set. (978-0-671-64512-0(9)) S&S Audio.

Magic of Why. Read by Lynne Harden. 1999. audio compact disk 14.99 (978-0-9725506-2-8(3)) L Hardin.

Magic of Why, Musical Meditation. Lynne Harden. 1999. audio compact disk 12.99 (978-0-9725506-1-1(5)) L Hardin.

Magic of Willingness: Why Willingness Works Better Than Willpower. David Grudermeyer & Rebecca Grudermeyer. 2 cass. suppl. ed. 18.95 (T-07) Willingness Wrks.

Magic of You. Johanna Lindsey. Read by Laural Merlington. (Playaway Adult Fiction Ser.). (ENG.). 2009. 69.99 (978-1-60812-681-1(1)) Find a World.

Magic of You. abr. ed. Johanna Lindsey. Read by Sherilynn Cooke. 1 cass. (Running Time: 90 min.). (Malory Ser.). 1996. 6.99 (978-1-57096-036-9(4), RAZ 940) Romance Alive Audio.
Beautiful & headstrong Amy Malory is determined that wealthy American shipping magnate Warren Anderson will be hers. She pursues him shamelessly, but he resists his attraction to the tempestuous beauty, until Amy is taken hostage by Warren's bitter enemy & he must risk his life to recover her.

Magic of You. unabr. ed. Johanna Lindsey. (Running Time: 8 hrs.). (Malory Ser.). 2008. 39.25 (978-1-4233-5111-5(8), 9781423351115, Brinc Audio MP3 Lib) Brilliance Audio.

Magic of You. unabr. ed. Johanna Lindsey. Read by Laural Merlington. (Running Time: 8 hrs.). (Malory Ser.). 2008. 39.25 (978-1-4233-5113-9(4), 9781423351139, BADLE); 24.95 (978-1-4233-5112-2(6), 9781423351122, BAD); 24.95 (978-1-4233-5110-8(X), 9781423351108, Brilliance MP3); audio compact disk 97.25 (978-1-4233-5109-2(6), 9781423351092, BriAudCD Unabrid); audio compact disk 36.95 (978-1-4233-5108-5(8), 9781423351085, Bril Audio CD Unabri) Brilliance Audio.

Magic Orange Tree. Diane Wolkstein. Read by Diane Wolkstein. Perf. by Shirley Keller. 1 cass. (Running Time: 30 min.). 1991. Cloudstone NY.
8 stories freshly told from the book by its author. Sad, silly & touching Haitian songs weave between stories.

Magic Pasta Pot. 2004. 8.95 (978-0-7882-0300-8(2)) Weston Woods.

Magic Pill. Short Stories. G. Saul Snatsky. 1. (Running Time: 29 mins.). Dramatization. (ENG.). 2005. audio compact disk (978-0-9761674-3-3(3)) Sauls Audio.
A story of the diet craze taken to an interstellar extreme. Two worlds, Earth and Xyxgia, unaware of each other, have opposite, complementary problems, but with dramatic consequences for each. Sometimes you get what you wish for.

Magic Power Scouts Musical Adventures: Soundtrack from the Magic Power Scouts. Prod. by David Scott Harris. Based on a musical by David Scott Harris & Steven Durflinger. Score by Eric Monsanty. 1 CD. (Running Time: Approx. 35 Minutes). 2001. audio compact disk 8.95i (978-0-9715400-0-2(4)) Blue Giraffe Prod.

Magic Presence (Vol 2 Audio Cass. Tape Album), Vol. 2. unabr. ed. Godfre Ray King. Read by Gerald A. Craig. 12 cass. (Running Time: 10 hrs. 44 min.). (Saint Germain Ser.: Vol. 2). (ENG.). 1935. 55.00 (978-1-878891-10-5(3), St Germain Ser) St Germain.
Contains the second group of the author's experiences with the Ascended Master Saint Germain, & also includes instruction on the Great Laws of Life.

***Magic Presence (Vol 2-CD audio Book), Vol. 2.** Godfre Ray King. 2011. audio compact disk (978-1-878891-09-9(X), Law of Life) St Germain.

Magic Realism. unabr. ed. Ray Bradbury. 1 cass. (Running Time: 1 hr. 33 min.). 1967. 11.00 (11302) Big Sur Tapes.
Discusses his own development as a writer, his writing process, influences, & attitudes. He continually remarks on the emotional basis of the major decisions in his life.

Magic Ring. 1 cass. (Running Time: 53 mins.). 1999. Art of Hearing.
Charlie Crossioux is suddenly orphaned with his 8-year old twin brother & sister. Forced to provide for his siblings in the midst of the depression, he turns to boxing. A full cast of actors brings t his intense drama to life. You'll find yourself on the edge of your seat as this tale unfolds.

Magic Seed: Courage. Roxanne E. Daleo. 1 cass. (J). 1999. 12.95 Hlth Jmys.

Magic Seeds. unabr. ed. V. S. Naipaul. Narrated by Aasif Mandvi. 7 cass. (Running Time: 9 hrs. 30 mins.). 2004. 59.75 (978-1-4193-0729-4(0), 97865MC) Recorded Bks.

Magic Seeds. unabr. ed. V. S. Naipaul. Read by Aasif Mandvi. 8 CDs. (Running Time: 9.5). 2004. audio compact disk 29.99 (978-1-4193-0731-7(2)) Recorded Bks.

Magic Shop Book Series: Juliet Dove, Queen of Love; & the Monsters Ring. unabr. ed. Bruce Coville. Read by Full Cast Production Staff. (J). 2006. 44.99 (978-1-59895-507-1(1)) Find a World.

Magic Shop Series. unabr. ed. Bruce Coville. 7 cass. (Running Time: 10 hrs. 30 mins.). (J). 1999. 45.00 (5063) Books on Tape.
Young Thatcher, buys a mysterious, shining ball at a magic shop that turns out to be a dragon's egg. Jennifer buys a talking toad from the man at Elives Magic Shop. When Charlie Eggleston stumbles in Mr. Elives strange store & departs with the "skull of truth.".

Magic Signature Act - a spiritual journey in the magical worlds of name, lines & Shapes ! Anthony M. Benjamin, Sr. (ENG., 2008. audio compact disk 300.00 (978-0-9764590-6-4(X)) A M Benjamin.

Magic Skin. Honoré de Balzac. Read by John Bolen. (Running Time: 10 hrs.). 2001. 29.95 (978-1-60083-602-2(X), Audiofy Corp) Iofy Corp.

Magic Skin. Honoré de Balzac. Read by John Bolen. (ENG.). 2005. audio compact disk 90.00 (978-1-4001-3030-6(1)) Pub: Tantor Media. Dist(s): IngramPubServ

Magic Skin. unabr. ed. Honoré de Balzac. Narrated by John Bolen. 9 CDs. (Running Time: 10 hrs. 2 mins.). (ENG.). 2001. audio compact disk 45.00 (978-1-4001-0030-9(5)); audio compact disk 23.00 (978-1-4001-5030-4(2)) Pub: Tantor Media. Dist(s): IngramPubServ

Magic Skin. unabr. ed. Honoré de Balzac. Narrated by John Bolen. (Running Time: 10 hrs. 0 mins. 0 sec.). (ENG.). 2009. audio compact disk 65.99 (978-1-4001-4086-2(2)); audio compact disk 32.99 (978-1-4001-1086-5(6)) Pub: Tantor Media. Dist(s): IngramPubServ

Magic Skin. unabr. ed. Honoré de Balzac. Tr. by Honoré de Balzac. Narrated by John Bolen. (Running Time: 10 hrs. 0 mins. 0 sec.). (ENG.). 2009. audio compact disk 22.99 (978-1-4001-6086-0(3)) Pub: Tantor Media. Dist(s): IngramPubServ

Magic Sleeptime. Created by Wendy Leigh. 1 cass. (Running Time: 60 min.). (Smart Baby Ser.). 1997. 9.99 (978-1-890680-05-3(2)) Smart Baby.
Quality recordings of white noise to calm babies, featuring washer/dryer & hair dryer.

Magic Spring: My Year Learning to be English. Richard Lewis. Read by Michael Tudor Barnes. 8 cass. 2005. 69.95 (978-1-84559-171-7(2)) Pub: UlverLrgPrint GBR. Dist(s): Ulverscroft US

Magic Square. Jim Gross. 1 cass. 1992. 8.95 (1035) Am Fed Astrologers.

Magic Stone: And Other Stories. Michael Mish. 1 cass. (J). (gr. 2 up). 9.95 (978-0-9622465-6-2(5), MMM 2007) Mish Mash Music.
Compelling narratives reflecting on themes of self-esteem & the world of imagination; richly woven orchestrations make it a masterpiece. The educating that occurs is so subtle that children, generally, aren't even aware that they're learning...& that is mainly because the messages are so entertainingly presented.

Magic Story. unabr. ed. Frederic Van Rensselaer Day. (ENG.). 2005. 1.98 (978-1-59659-053-3(X), GildAudio) Pub: Gildan Media. Dist(s): HachBkGrp

Magic Street. Orson Scott Card. Read by Mirron Willis. (Running Time: 54000 sec.). 2005. 79.95 (978-0-7861-3525-7(5)) Blckstn Audio.

Magic Street. Orson Scott Card. Read by Mirron Willis. (Running Time: 48600 sec.). 2005. audio compact disk 99.00 (978-0-7861-7826-1(4)) Blckstn Audio.

Magic Street. unabr. ed. Orson Scott Card. Read by Mirron E. Willis. (Running Time: 13 hrs. 30 mins.). 2010. audio compact disk 29.95 (978-0-7861-8018-9(8)) Blckstn Audio.

***Magic Street.** unabr. ed. Orson Scott Card. Read by Mirron E. Willis. (Running Time: 13 hrs. 30 mins.). 2010. audio compact disk 29.95 (978-1-4417-4759-4(1)) Blckstn Audio.

Magic Strikes. unabr. ed. Ilona Andrews. Narrated by Renée Raudman. (Running Time: 11 hrs. 0 mins. 0 sec.). (Kate Daniels Ser.). (ENG.). 2009. 24.99 (978-1-4001-6289-5(0)); audio compact disk 34.99 (978-1-4001-1289-0(3)); audio compact disk 69.99 (978-1-4001-4289-7(X)) Pub: Tantor Media. Dist(s): IngramPubServ

Magic Swan see Favorite Children's Stories: A Collection

Magic Theater. Perf. by Shadowfax. 1 cass. (Running Time: 49 min.). 1994. 9.98 (978-1-56628-018-1(4), EB2199/WB42548-4) MFLP CA.
This imaginative collection of all new compositions comes on the heels of Shadowfax's 1992 Grammy-nominated Esperanto. Produced by Chuck Greenberg & Harry Andronis, the team responsible for the band's most successful projects, Magic Theater is vibrant with surprises yet faithful to the signature sound that has made Shadowfax an internationally acclaimed touring band.

***Magic Thief.** unabr. ed. Sarah Prineas. Read by Greg Steinbruner. Illus. by Antonio Javier Caparo. (ENG.). 2010. (978-0-06-200943-2(5)); (978-0-06-201609-6(1)) HarperCollins Pubs.

Magic Thief. unabr. ed. Sarah Prineas. Narrated by Greg Steinbruner. 7 cass. (Running Time: 7 hrs. 45 mins.). (Magic Thief Ser.: Bk. 1). (YA). (gr. 5-8). 2008. 61.75 (978-1-4361-3735-5(7)); audio compact disk 77.75 (978-1-4361-3740-9(3)) Recorded Bks.

***Magic Thief: Found.** unabr. ed. Sarah Prineas. Read by Greg Steinbruner. Illus. by Antonio Javier Caparo. (ENG.). 2010. (978-0-06-200945-6(1)); (978-0-06-201610-2(5)) HarperCollins Pubs.

***Magic Thief: Lost.** unabr. ed. Sarah Prineas. Read by Greg Steinbruner. Illus. by Antonio Javier Caparo. (ENG.). 2010. (978-0-06-200944-9(3)); (978-0-06-201611-9(3)) HarperCollins Pubs.

Magic Time. unabr. ed. Marc Scott Zicree. Read by Barbara Hambley. 11 cass. (Running Time: 16 hrs.). 2003. 76.95 (978-0-7861-2440-4(7), 3119) Blckstn Audio.
For young lawyer Cal Griffin, it's just another New York day, full of stress, screw-ups, deadlines, and anxiety. That is, until the city is rocked by a series of bizarre tremors and he is engulfed in the surreal chaos of a new world of nightmare and wonder.

Magic Time. unabr. ed. Marc Scott Zicree & Barbara Hambley. Read by Armin Shimmerman. 12 CDs. (Running Time: 16 hrs.). 2003. audio compact disk 96.00 (978-0-7861-9235-9(6), 3119); audio compact disk 24.95 (978-0-7861-8974-8(6), 3119) Blckstn Audio.

Magic Time. unabr. ed. Marc Scott Zicree & Barbara Hambly. Read by Armin Shimmerman. 11 pieces. 2004. reel tape 44.95 (978-0-7861-2470-1(9)); audio compact disk 49.95 (978-0-7861-9286-1(0)) Blckstn Audio.

Magic Time: Angel Fire. Marc Scott Zicree. Narrated by Mark Bramhall. (Running Time: 14 hrs.). 2004. 41.95 (978-1-59912-538-1(2)) Iofy Corp.

Magic Time: Angelfire -Lib. Maya Kaathryn Bonhoff. 12 CDs. (Running Time: 14 hrs. 30 mins.). 2004. audio compact disk 96.00 (978-0-7861-8379-1(9), 3337) Blckstn Audio.

Magic Time: Ghostlands. unabr. ed. Marc Scott Zicree & Robert C. Wilson. Read by Lloyd James. (Running Time: 15 mins. 30 sec.). (Magic Times Ser.). 2005. 29.95 (978-0-7861-7913-8(9)) Blckstn Audio.

Magic Time Library Edition: Angelfire. unabr. ed. Maya Kaathryn Bonhoff. 10 cass. (Running Time: 14 hrs. 30 mins.). 2004. 69.95 (978-0-7861-2807-5(0), 3337) Blckstn Audio.

Magic Time: Ghostlands: The Magic Times Series. Marc Scott Zicree & Robert C. Wilson. Read by Lloyd James. (Running Time: 15 mins. 30 sec.). 2005. 85.95 (978-0-7861-3688-9(X)); audio compact disk 108.00 (978-0-7861-7649-6(0)) Blckstn Audio.

Magic Time 1. Kathleen Kampa. 2008. audio compact disk 39.95 (978-0-19-436183-5(7)) OUP.

Magic Time 1. Kathleen Kampa & Charles Vilina. 2008. 39.95 (978-0-19-436182-8(9)) OUP.

Magic Time 2. Kathleen Kampa. 2008. 39.95 (978-0-19-436189-7(6)) OUP.

Magic Time 2. Kathleen Kampa. 2008. audio compact disk 39.95 (978-0-19-436190-3(X)) OUP.

Magic Toyshop. unabr. ed. Angela Carter. Read by Miriam Margolyes. 6 cass. (Running Time: 9 hrs.). 2000. 54.95 (978-0-7540-0448-6(1), CAB 1871) AudioGO.
One night, Melanie walks through the garden in her mother's wedding dress. The next morning the world is shattered & she's forced to leave her childhood home. She is sent to London to live with relatives she has never met. There, she meets Aunt Margaret, beautiful & speechless; brooding Uncle Philip, who loves only the life-sized wooden puppets he creates in his toyshop.

Magic Tree House. unabr. ed. Mary Pope Osborne. Read by Mary Pope Osborne. 5 CDs. (Running Time: 5 hrs. 30 mins.). (Magic Tree House Ser.: Nos. 9-16). (ENG.). (J). 2003. audio compact disk 30.00 (978-0-8072-1870-9(7), ImaginStudio) Pub: Random Audio Pubg. Dist(s): Random

Magic Tree House. unabr. ed. Mary Pope Osborne. Read by Mary Pope Osborne. 5 CDs. (Running Time: 5 hrs. 25 mins.). (Magic Tree House Ser.: Nos. 9-16). (J). (gr. 2-5). 2004. audio compact disk 38.25 (978-0-8072-1611-8(9), S YA 432 CD, Listening Lib) Pub: Random Audio Pubg. Dist(s): NetLibrary CO

***Magic Tree House, Bks. 40-41.** unabr. ed. Mary Pope Osborne. Read by Mary Pope Osborne. 2 CDs. (Running Time: 2 hrs. 35 mins.). (J). (gr. 1-3). 2009. audio compact disk 24.00 (978-0-7393-7409-2(5), Listening Lib) Pub: Random Audio Pubg. Dist(s): Random

Magic Tree House, Vol. 8. unabr. ed. Mary Pope Osborne. 3 CDs. (Running Time: 3:46 hrs.). (Magic Tree House Ser.: Nos. 30-32). 2004. audio compact disk 30.00 (978-1-4000-9481-3(X), Listening Lib) Random Audio Pubg.

Magic Tree House, Vol. 9. unabr. ed. Mary Pope Osborne. Illus. by Mary Pope Osborne. 3 CDs. (Running Time: 3 hrs. 48 mins.). (Magic Tree House Ser.: Nos. 33-35). (J). (ps-3). 2006. audio compact disk 30.00 (978-0-7393-3130-9(2), Listening Lib) Pub: Random Audio Pubg. Dist(s): Random

Magic Tree House: Carnival at Candlelight - Season of the Sandstorms - Night of the New Magicians - Blizzard of the Blue Moon. unabr. ed. Mary Pope Osborne. Read by Mary Pope Osborne. (Running Time: 18540 sec.). (Magic Tree House Ser.: Nos. 33-36). (ENG.). (J). (gr. 1). 2008. audio compact disk 28.00 (978-0-7393-6274-7(7), Listening Lib) Pub: Random Audio Pubg. Dist(s): Random

Magic Tree House Vol. 7: Stage Fright on a Summer Night; Good Morning, Gorillas; Thanksgiving on Thursday; High Tide in Hawaii. unabr. ed. Mary Pope Osborne. Read by Mary Pope Osborne. (Running Time: 9900 sec.). (Magic Tree House Ser.: Nos. 25-28). (ENG.). (J). (gr. 1-4). 2007. audio compact disk 25.00 (978-0-7393-3876-6(5), Listening Lib) Pub: Random Audio Pubg. Dist(s): Random

Magic Tree House Vol. 8, Bks. 29-32: Christmas in Camelot; Haunted Castle on Hallows Eve; Summer of the Sea Serpent; Winter of the Ice Wizard. unabr. ed. Mary Pope Osborne. Read by Mary Pope Osborne. (Running Time: 18480 sec.). (Magic Tree House Ser.: Nos. 29-32). (ENG.). (J). (gr. 1). 2007. audio compact disk 28.00 (978-0-7393-5622-7(4), Listening Lib) Pub: Random Audio Pubg. Dist(s): Random

Magic Tree House Collection. gif. unabr. ed. Mary Pope Osborne. Read by Mary Pope Osborne. 5 CDs. (Running Time: 5 hrs. 40 mins.). (Magic Tree House Ser.: Nos. 1-8). (ENG.). (gr. k-2). 2001. audio compact disk 30.00 (978-0-8072-0612-6(1), ImaginStudio) Pub: Random Audio Pubg. Dist(s): Random

Magic Tree House Collection. unabr. ed. Mary Pope Osborne. Read by Mary Pope Osborne. 5 CDs. (Running Time: 18240 sec.). (Magic Tree House Ser.: Nos. 17-24). (ENG.). (J). (gr. 1-3). 2005. audio compact disk 30.00 (978-0-307-24526-7(8), ImaginStudio) Pub: Random Audio Pubg. Dist(s): Random

Magic Tree House Collection, Set. unabr. gif. ed. Mary Pope Osborne. Read by Mary Pope Osborne. 5 CDs. (Running Time: 5 hrs. 40 mins.). (Magic Tree House Ser.: Nos. 1-8). (J). (gr. 2-5). 2004. 38.25 (978-0-8072-0613-3(X), S YA 330 CD, Listening Lib) Pub: Random Audio Pubg. Dist(s): NetLibrary CO
"These eight stories, currently available as two separate volumes on cassette with a combined price of $46.00, are being offered now along with the interview in a 5-CD set at a special price of $40.00 in library packaging. Don't miss this opportunity to own the special gift collection of these bestselling, well-loved stories.".

Magic Tree House Collection: Carnival at Candlelight; Season of the Sandstorms; Night of the New Magicians, Vol. 9. unabr. ed. Mary Pope Osborne. Read by Mary Pope Osborne. 3 cass. (Running Time: 3 hrs. 48 mins.). (Magic Tree House Ser.: Nos. 33-35). (J). (ps-3). 2006. 30.00 (978-0-7393-3131-6(0), Listening Lib) Pub: Random Audio Pubg. Dist(s): Random

Magic Tree House Collection: Civil War on Sunday; Revolutionary War on Wednesday; Twister on Tuesday; Earthquake in the Early Morning, Vol. 6. unabr. ed. Mary Pope Osborne. Read by Mary Pope Osborne. 2 cass. (Running Time: 2 hrs. 34 mins.). (Magic Tree House Ser.: Nos. 21-24). (J). (gr. 2-5). 2004. 23.00 (978-0-8072-0914-1(7), S YA 399 CX, Listening Lib) Random Audio Pubg.

Magic Tree House Collection: Dinosaurs Before Dark; The Knight at Dawn; Mummies in the Morning; Pirates Past Noon, Vol. 1. unabr. ed. Mary Pope Osborne. Read by Mary Pope Osborne. 3 CDs. (Running Time: 10140 sec.). (Magic Tree House Ser.: Nos. 1-4). (ENG.). (J). (gr. 1-3). 2006. audio compact disk 22.00 (978-0-307-28417-4(4), ImaginStudio) Pub: Random Audio Pubg. Dist(s): Random

Magic Tree House Collection: Dolphins at Daybreak; Ghost Town at Sundown; Lions at Lunchtime; Polar Bears Past Bedtime, Vol. 3. unabr. ed. Mary Pope Osborne. Read by Mary Pope Osborne. 2 cass. (Running Time: 2 hrs. 49 mins.). (Magic Tree House Ser.: Nos. 9-12). (J). (gr. 2-5). 2004. 23.00 (978-0-8072-0517-4(6), LL0216, Listening Lib) Random Audio Pubg.
Jack & Annie return for four more fun-filled adventures. Come along with Jack & Annie as they explore the ocean, visit a haunted town, wander the vast African plains & investigate the frozen arctic. Includes "Dolphins at Daybreak," "Ghost Town at Sundown," "Lions at Lunchtime" & "Polar Bears Past Bedtime".

Magic Tree House Collection: Night of the Ninjas; Afternoon on the Amazon; Sunset of the Sabertooth; Midnight on the Moon, Vol. 2. unabr. ed. Mary Pope Osborne. Read by Mary Pope Osborne. 2 cass. (Running Time: 2 hrs. 9 mins.). (Magic Tree House Ser.: Nos. 5-8). (J). (gr. 2-5). 2004. 23.00 (978-0-8072-8845-0(4), LL0215, Listening Lib) Random Audio Pubg.
Jack & Annie learn the secrets of the Ninjas, explore the rainforests of the Amazon, go back to the Ice Age, and travel forward in time to visit a moon base. Includes "Night of the Ninjas," "Afternoon on the Amazon," "Secret of the Sabertooth" & "Midnight on the Moon".

Magic Tree House Collection: Stage Fright on a Summer Night; Good Morning, Gorillas; Thanksgiving on Thursday; High Tide in Hawaii, Vol. 7. unabr. ed. Mary Pope Osborne. Read by Mary Pope Osborne. 2 cass. (Running Time: 1 hr. 30 mins.). (Magic Tree House Ser.: Nos. 25-28). (J). (gr. 2-5). 2004. 23.00 (978-0-8072-8734-7(2), LL0214, Listening Lib) Random Audio Pubg.
Popular time-travel beginning reader series includes: "Dinosaurs Before Dark," "The Knight at Dawn," "Mummies in the Morning," & "Pirates Past Noon".

Magic Tree House Collection: Vacation Under the Volcano; Day of the Dragon King; Viking Ships at Sunrise; Hour of the Olympics, Vol. 5. Mary Pope Osborne. Read by Mary Pope Osborne. 2 cass. (Running Time: 2 hrs. 49 mins.). (Magic Tree House Ser.: Nos. 17-20). (J). (gr. 2-5). 2004. 23.00 (978-0-8072-0805-2(1), Listening Lib) Random Audio Pubg.
Jack and Annie return with four more adventures: Tonight on the Titanic, Buffalo Before Breakfast, Tigers at Twilight, Dingoes at Dinnertime.

***Magic Tree House Collection: Books 41-44: #41 Moonlight on the Magic Flute; #42 A Good Night for Ghosts; #43 Leprechaun in Late Winter; #44 A Ghost Tale for Christmas Time.** unabr. ed. Mary Pope Osborne. Read by Mary Pope Osborne. (ENG.). (J). 2011. audio compact disk 30.00 (978-0-307-74668-9(2), Listening Lib) Pub: Random Audio Pubg. Dist(s): Random

Magic Tree House #35: Night of the New Magicians. unabr. ed. Mary Pope Osborne. Read by Mary Pope Osborne. (Running Time: 4620 sec.). (Magic Tree House Ser.: No. 35). (ENG.). (J). (gr. 1-7). 2006. audio compact disk 14.99 (978-0-307-28387-0(9), ImaginStudio) Pub: Random Audio Pubg. Dist(s): Random

Magic Tree House 40/7-CD Audio Collection Ppk. Mary Pope Osborne. (ENG.). 2009. audio compact disk, audio compact disk, audio compact disk 201.00 (978-0-7393-5260-1(1), ImaginStudio) Pub: Random Audio Pubg. Dist(s): Random

***Magic Tree House #44: A Ghost Tale for Christmas Time.** unabr. ed. Mary Pope Osborne. Read by Mary Pope Osborne. (ENG.). (J). 2010. audio compact disk 15.00 (978-0-7393-7298-2(X), Listening Lib) Pub: Random Audio Pubg. Dist(s): Random

***Magic Tree House #45: A Crazy Day with Cobras.** unabr. ed. Mary Pope Osborne. Read by Mary Pope Osborne. (ENG.). (J). 2011. audio compact disk 15.00 (978-0-307-74660-3(7), Listening Lib) Pub: Random Audio Pubg. Dist(s): Random

Magic Vessels. Vayu Naidu. 1 cass. (Running Time: 022 min.). (Under the Banyan Ser.). (YA). (gr. 2 up). 1998. bk. 11.99 (978-81-86838-29-7(5)) APG.
Fairy tales & folklore.

Magic Water. unabr. ed. Alison Uttley. 1 cass. (Running Time: 6 min.). (J). (gr. 2-5). 1987. bk. 16.95 (978-0-8045-6579-0(1), 6579) Spoken Arts.

Magic Within: How to Fall in Love, Lose Weight & Keep It off Forever. Janet Greeson. 4 cass. (Magic of Recovery Ser.: Vol. 3). 1994. 29.95 Set. (978-0-9630955-4-1(4)) Greeson & Boyle.
Therapeutic mini workshops. Self-help - how to lose weight.

Magic Word: Attitude. Earl Nightingale. 2 cass. 95.00 (584VX) Nightingale-Conant.
A powerful program by the Dean of Self-Development, Presenting a unique, memorable look at attitude, this program shows you the most crucial element of success. Go on location with some true masters of attitude implementation & see what winning really takes. Includes 43-minute VHS videocassette & two listener's guides.

Magic World. E. Nesbit. Read by Flo Gibson. 4 cass. (Running Time: 5 hrs. 30 min.). (J). (gr. 2-5). 1997. 19.95 (978-1-55685-471-2(4)) Audio Bk Con.
At her imaginative best we go through such tales as "The Cat-hood of Maurice," "The Mixed Mine," "Accidental Magic," "The Princess & the Hedge-pig," "The Related Muff," "Justnowland," "Kenneth & the Garp" & more.

Magic World. unabr. ed. Short Stories. E. Nesbit. Read by Johanna Ward. 5 cass. (Running Time: 7 hrs.). 1994. 39.95 (978-0-7861-0729-2(4), 1486) Blckstn Audio.
The magical stories in this book contain some of the best things ever written in the realm of fairy tales. A favorite is the tale of Princess Belinda, who was condemned to be ugly during the week & beautiful on Sunday.

Magical Blend Interview with Sound Photosynthesis. Faustin Bray & Brian Wallace. 1 cass. 9.00 (A0321-88) Sound Photosyn.
The tables are turned on Faustin & Brian. Richard Daab interviews.

Magical Child. Joseph C. Pearce. 2 cass. (Running Time: 2 hrs. 34 min.). 1975. 18.00 (09091) Big Sur Tapes.
The original nature of the child is very open to all kinds of possibilities, which become narrowed as acculturation occurs.

Magical Child Magical Adult. Joseph C. Pearce. 2 cass. 1995. 16.95 (978-1-879323-24-7(9)) Sound Horizons AV.
In this compelling program Joseph Chilton Pearce best-selling author of "The Magical Child" & "The Crack in the Cosmic Egg" speaks to the concerns of parents eager to give their offspring a good start in the world, explaining that the key to tapping the unlimited potential within each child is to develop the heart-brain connection.

Magical Chinese Characters. Wendy Da & Steven Da. (Eazychin Series for Learning Chinese Ser.). (CHI & ENG.). 2005. audio compact disk 19.95 (978-7-5619-1373-4(7), MACHCH1) Pub: Beijing Lang CHN. Dist(s): China Bks

Magical Chinese Characters, Vol. 2. Wendy Da & Steven Da. (Eazy Chinese Series for Learning Chinese Ser.). (CHI & ENG.). 2005. audio compact disk 19.95 (978-7-5619-1531-8(4), MACHCH2) Pub: Beijing Lang CHN. Dist(s): China Bks

Magical Classroom: Creating Effective, Brain-Friendly Environments for Learning. F. Noah Gordon. 2 cass. (Running Time: 60 min. per cass.). (YA). (gr. k-12). 1995. 12.00 Set, incl. manual. (1604-F3, ZephPr) Chicago Review.
Use imagery exercises to reaccess the intrinsic state of the brain that is receptive to learning.

Magical Concentration. Edward Strachar. 2000. (978-0-9717185-5-5(5)) InGenius Inc.

Magical Concentration. unabr. ed. Edward Strachar. 7 cass. (Running Time: 7 hrs.). 2000. 79.95 (978-1-55525-015-7(7), 21290A) Nightingale-Conant.
Magical Concentration will help you concentrate more effectively than you ever thought possible & it doesn't require you to do anything extra or put in a lot of effort. It's about accomplishing more & doing far less than you'd imagine.

Magical Earth. Sarah Pirtle. 1 cass. (Running Time: 50 min.). (J). (gr. 2-6). 1993. 9.95 (978-0-939065-54-7(1), GW1058) Gentle Wind.
Songs about children all over the world, & about nature.

Magical Earth. Sarah Pirtle. Perf. by Sarah Pirtle. 1 cass. (Running Time: 50 min.). (J). (gr. 2-6). 1993. audio compact disk 14.95 (978-0-939065-58-5(4)) Gentle Wind.

Magical Earth. Sarah Pirtle. 1 cass. (J). NewSound.
International rhythms, songs about best friends, pillow fights, the Rain Forest & more.

Magical Garden-Music. 2007. audio compact disk 16.95 (978-1-56136-415-2(0)) Master Your Mind.

Magical Illness & Its Treatment among Mestizo Ayahuasca Practitioners of the Peruvian Amazonas. Luis E. Luna. 1 cass. 9.00 (A0078-85) Sound Photosyn.
From ICSS '85.

Magical Journeys. unabr. ed. Michael Rosenbaum & Cindy Rosenbaum. Perf. by Jonathan Hatch & Kathy Flaherty. 1 cass. (Running Time: 38 min.). (J). (ps-2). 1990. 6.95 (978-1-881567-01-1(X)) Happy Kids Prods.
Five personalized, original songs that takes children on a series of different adventures. Songs include"Taking a Walk", "Farm Animal Blues", "Space Shuttle Boogie" & two others. Name sung over 40 times throughout the tape. Over 230 names available.

Magical Life. Thomas Moore. 2 cass. (Running Time: 2 hrs. 30 min.). 1996. 18.95 (978-1-879323-48-3(6)) Sound Horizons AV.
The modern tendency to consider life an exercise in problem solving & be ever vigilant about health & correctness stands in the way of enchantment. Thomas Moore restates the principals of magicians of the past, who advised tapping into the less obvious, less mechanical, less literal potencies of nature. In this magic, we bring the heart into play & regard the most ordinary aspects of daily life in their sacredness.

Magical Meditations. Alexandra Delis-Abrams. Read by Alexandra Delis-Abrams. Music by Jack Lee. 1 cass. (Running Time: 56 min.). 1993. 11.00 (978-1-879889-08-8(0)) Adage Pubns.
Four guided meditations for relaxation. Softly spoken with original music background. Will assist in reaching new levels of awareness & energization.

Magical Melodies. Pamala Ballingham & Timothy Ballingham. Perf. by Pamala Ballingham. 1 cass. (Running Time: 45 min.). (J). (ps up). 1991. 9.95 Norelco box. (978-0-922104-10-9(7), EMP 06B); 9.95 Bookpack pkg. (978-0-922104-11-6(5), EMP 06B6) Earth Mother Prodns.
A collection of songs from Broadway & motion pictures for children with musical themes which recognize some of the common concerns that all children share. Handled with understanding, tenderness & heart-warming inspiration, this recording supports the spirit of young, optimistic minds.

Magical Mind, Magical Body: Mastering the Mind/Body Connection for Perfect Health & Total Well-Being. Deepak Chopra. 1 CD. (Running Time: 1 hr.). 1990. stu. ed. 69.95 (978-1-55525-021-8(1), 879cd) Nightingale-Conant.

Magical Mind, Magical Body: Mastering the Mind/Body Connection for Perfect Health & Total Well-Being. unabr. ed. Deepak Chopra. Read by Deepak Chopra. 6 cass. (Running Time: 6 hrs.). 1990. stu. ed. 59.95 (978-1-55525-001-0(7), 879A) Nightingale-Conant.
Mastering the Mind/Body Connection for Perfect Health & Total Well-Being.

Magical Mind, Magical Body: Mastering the Mind/Body Connection for Perfect Health & Total Well-Being. unabr. ed. Deepak Chopra. Read by Deepak Chopra. 5 cass. (Running Time: 50 hrs. 0 mins. 0 sec.). (ENG.). 2003. audio compact disk 35.00 (978-0-7435-3013-2(6), Nightgale) Pub: S&S Audio. Dist(s): S and S Inc
Dr. Chopra helps listeners to uncover the healing power of the mind and utilize th epower of quantum healing to gain a perfect balance of mind, body and spirit.

Magical Mind/Magical Body see Mente-Cuerpo Magico

Magical Moments. unabr. ed. Contrib. by Susan Musleh. 1 cass. (Running Time: 3 min.). (Susan's Romantic Adventures - A Secret Admirer's Kit Ser.). (C). 1998. 24.95 (978-1-893494-01-5(2), MM-100) Susans Romantic Adv.
Kit that ladies use to invite the man of their dreams to a mysterious romantic rendezvous.

Magical Mouse see Gathering of Great Poetry for Children

Magical Music of Disney. Perf. by Erich Kunzel et al. 1 cass., 1 CD. (J). 7.98 (TA 30381); audio compact disk 12.78 (TA 80381); 7.98 (TA 30381); audio compact disk 12.78 (TA 80381) NewSound.
Featuring music from "The Lion King," "The Little Mermaid," "Alladin" & "Beauty & the Beast".

Magical Musical Spiraled Seashell & Friends. Dick Bozung. Illus. by Dick Bozung. (YA). 1989. (978-0-9622341-5-6(X)) Seven Arrows.

Magical, Mystical Money! Created by Louise LeBrun. (Women & Power Ser.: Vol. 2). 1999. 10.95 (978-0-9685566-1-0(2)) Par3tners Renewal CAN.

Magical Relationships: How to Get 'em - How to Have 'em - How to Keep 'em. Ariel Kane & Shya Kane. Contrib. by Helene DeLillo. 2 cass. (Running Time: 1 hrs. 51 min.). (Being in the Moment Ser.). 1995. (978-1-888043-06-8(7)) ASK Prodns.
Discusses the essence of creating magical relationships & teaches the listener vital keys for getting, having & keeping them.

Magical Science Adventure. 1 cass, 1 CD. (Twin Sisters Ser.). (J). 7.18 (TWIN 195); audio compact disk 10.38 (TWIN 196) NewSound.
Explore the world of outer space, learn how dolphins communicate, go on a dinosaur dig or learn about the weather.

Magical Thinking. unabr. ed. 6 cass. 54.95 (978-0-7927-3343-0(6)); audio compact disk 74.95 (978-0-7927-3344-7(4)) AudioGO.

Magical Thinking: True Stories. unabr. rev. ed. Augusten Burroughs. Read by Augusten Burroughs. Ed. by Jennifer Enderlin. 7 CDs. (Running Time: 9 hrs. 0 mins. 0 sec.). (ENG.). 2004. audio compact disk 29.95 (978-1-59397-421-3(3)) Pub: Macmill Audio. Dist(s): Macmillan

Magical Worlds of the Wizard of Ads on CD. Roy H. Williams, 3rd. Read by Roy H. Williams, 3rd. 7 CDs. (Running Time: 7hours 20minutes). 2001. audio compact disk 29.95 (978-0-9714769-3-6(4)) Wizard Academy.
Book three in the Wizard of Ads Trilogy on CD. Wizard of Ads books have become known for their unique blend of principle, practicality, and lore. Now here's the third book in the series, with yet more sage guidance and dozens of fascinating true stories. Drawing on the teachings of his renowned Academy, the Wizard shares his unique perspectives on the roles neuroscience, chaos theory, poetry, and art play in the field of human persuasion. His practical guidance will show you: How the right and left hemispheres of the brain process information differently and how to sneak past the rational left brain to deliver messages to the more open right brain; How to access long-term memory to powerfully brand your company, product, or service and avoid the one fatal error that can cost you mountains of advertising money; How to achieve quick sales miracles with advertising hype and why you should avoid doing so at all costs; How to create your own gravity well that gently draws customers in and gradually persuades them to commit. Includes: 7 Audio CDs. Total running time: 7hours 20minutes.

Magician. unabr. ed. Read by Frederick Davidson. Ed. by W. Somerset Maugham. 6 cass. (Running Time: 8 hrs. 30 mins.). 1999. 44.95 (978-0-7861-1654-6(4), 2482) Blckstn Audio.
Arthur Burdon & his beautiful fiancee disliked the enormously fat & eccentric Oliver Haddo, but they were fascinated by his stories of black magic, by his demonstrations of a power that seemed inhuman. Soon their dislike turned to loathing. A month later Margaret disappeared. She left a note saying she had married Oliver & was moving to London.

Magician. unabr. ed. Michael Scott. Read by Erik Singer. (Secrets of the Immortal Nicholas Flamel Ser.: Bk. 2). (ENG.). (J). (gr. 7). 2008. audio compact disk 44.00 (978-0-7393-6491-8(X), Listening Lib) Pub: Random Audio Pubg. Dist(s): Random

Magician. unabr. ed. Read by Erik Singer. Ed. by Michael Scott. 9 CDs. (Running Time: 10 hrs. 59 mins.). (Secrets of the Immortal Nicholas Flamel Ser.: Bk. 2). (YA). (gr. 6-9). 2008. audio compact disk 60.00 (978-0-7393-6493-2(6), Listening Lib) Pub: Random Audio Pubg. Dist(s): Random
After fleeing Ojai, Nicholas, Sophie, Josh, and Scatty emerge in Paris, the City of Lights. Home for Nicholas Flamel. Only this homecoming is anything but sweet. Perenell is still locked up back in Alcatraz and Paris is teeming with enemies. Nicollo Machiavelli, immortal author and celebrated art collector, is working for Dee. He's after them, and time is running out for Nicholas and Perenell. For every day spent without the Book of Abraham the Mage, they age one year - their magic becoming weaker and their bodies more frail. For Flamel, the Prophesy is becoming more and more clear. It's time for Sophie to learn the second elemental magic: Fire Magic. And there's only one man who can teach it to her: Flamel's old student, the Comte de Saint-Germain - alchemist, magician, and rock star. Josh and Sophie Newman are the world's only hope - if they don't turn on each other first.

Magician. unabr. ed. Sol Stein. Read by Grover Gardner. 6 CDs. (Running Time: 7 hrs.). 2003. audio compact disk 48.00 (978-0-7861-9348-6(4), 3038); 39.95 (978-0-7861-2330-8(3), 3038) Blckstn Audio.
This is a tale of two magicians, of high school extortion and violence, and of a criminal trial in which the guilty go free.

Magician of Lublin. Isaac Bashevis Singer. 2009. (978-1-60136-131-8(9)) Audio Holding.

Magician of Lublin. unabr. ed. Isaac Bashevis Singer. Read by Larry Keith. 6 cass. (Running Time: 9 hrs.). 2001. 39.95 (978-1-893079-07-6(4), JCCAUDIOBOOKS) Jewish Contempry Classics.
A brilliant magician, as successful with women as he is on stage, is caught between loves & cultures in the colorful world of 19th century Poland.

Magician of Samarkand. Alan Temperley. Read by Andrew Sachs. 3 CDs. (J). 2003. audio compact disk 24.95 (978-0-7540-6612-5(6), Chivers Child Audio) AudioGO.

Magician Within: A Study in Masculine Psychology. Read by Robert Moore. 4 cass. (Running Time: 6 hrs.). 1990. 34.95 (978-0-7822-0204-5(7), 406) C G Jung IL.
The archetype of the magician is the archetype of awareness, inner work, initiation, & healing. Without adequate access to this psychological resource a man will sleepwalk through his life, never asking the questions which can liberate him from his credulity & naivete.

Magicians. unabr. ed. Lev Grossman. Read by Mark Bramhall. 14 CDs. (Running Time: 17 hrs.). (gr. 12 up). 2009. audio compact disk 39.95 (978-0-14-314439-7(1), PengAudBks) Penguin Grp USA.

***Magicians.** unabr. ed. Lev Grossman. Read by Mark Bramhall. 14 CDs. (Running Time: 17 hrs. 30 mins.). 2009. audio compact disk 100.00 (978-1-4159-6245-9(6), BksonTape) Pub: Random Audio Pubg. Dist(s): Random

***Magician's Apprentice.** Illus. by Alison Edgson. (Flip-up Fairy Tales Ser.). (ENG.). (J). 2011. audio compact disk 7.99 (978-1-84643-409-9(2)) Childs Play GBR.

Magician's Apprentice. unabr. abr. ed. Trudi Canavan. Read by Rosamund Pike. (Running Time: 6 hrs.). (ENG.). 2009. 24.98 (978-1-60024-536-7(6)) Pub: Hachet Audio. Dist(s): HachBkGrp

Magician's Assistant. unabr. ed. Ann Patchett. Read by Karen Ziemba. 10 CDs. (Running Time: 12 hrs.). 2008. audio compact disk 39.95 (978-0-06-143833-2(2), Harper Audio) HarperCollins Pubs.

***Magician's Assistant.** unabr. ed. Ann Patchett. Read by Karen Ziemba. (ENG.). 2008. (978-0-06-163255-6(4)); (978-0-06-163256-3(2)) HarperCollins Pubs.

***Magician's Elephant.** unabr. ed. Kate DiCamillo. Read by Juliet Stevenson. (Running Time: 3 hrs.). 2010. 19.99 (978-1-4418-8908-9(6), 9781441889089, Candlewick Bril) Brilliance Audio.

***Magician's Elephant.** unabr. ed. Kate DiCamillo. Read by Juliet Stevenson. (Running Time: 3 hrs.). 2010. 39.97 (978-1-4418-8909-6(4), 9781441889096, Candlewick Bril); 39.97 (978-1-4418-8907-2(8), 9781441889072, Candlewick Bril); 19.99 (978-1-4418-8906-5(X), 9781441889065, Candlewick Bril); audio compact disk 49.97 (978-1-4418-8905-8(1), 9781441889058, Candlewick Bril); audio compact disk 24.99 (978-1-4418-4903-8(3), 9781441849038, Candlewick Bril) Brilliance Audio.

magicians' Guild. Trudi Canavan. Read by Richard Aspel. (Running Time: 15 hrs. 45 mins.). (Black Magician Trilogy). 2009. 114.99 (978-1-74214-197-8(8), 9781742141978) Pub: Bolinda Pubng AUS. Dist(s): Bolinda Pub Inc

Magicians' Guild. unabr. ed. Trudi Canavan. Read by Richard Aspel. (Running Time: 56700 sec.). (Black Magician Trilogy). 2007. audio compact disk 43.95 (978-1-921334-03-0(7), 9781921334030) Pub: Bolinda Pubng AUS. Dist(s): Bolinda Pub Inc

Magicians' Guild. unabr. ed. Trudi Canavan. Read by Richard Aspel. 10 cass. (Running Time: 15 hrs. 45 mins.). 2005. 80.00 (978-1-74093-555-5(1)) Pub: Bolinda Pubng AUS. Dist(s): Bolinda Pub Inc

Magician's Nephew see Complete Chronicles of Narnia

Magician's Nephew see Chronicles of Narnia Super-Soundbook

Magician's Nephew. C. S. Lewis. Read by Kenneth Branagh. 2 cass. (Running Time: 4 hrs.). (Chronicles of Narnia Ser.). (J). 2001. 24.00 (PH193) Blckstn Audio.
When Digory and Polly are tricked by Degory's peculiar Uncle Andrew into becoming part of an experiment, they set off on an adventure of a lifetime. At last, they find themselves in the magical land of Narnia, Narnia before the Talking Beasts, before the Dwarfs, before all but the great Lion, Aslan.

Magician's Nephew. C. S. Lewis. 2 cass. (Running Time: 2 hrs.). (Chronicles of Narnia Ser.). (J). (gr. 4-8). 2001. 18.00 (BMDD013) Lodestone Catalog.

Magician's Nephew. C. S. Lewis. 2 cass. (Chronicles of Narnia Ser.). (J). (gr. 4-8). 18.00 (BMDD013, Random AudioBks) Random Audio Pubg.

Magician's Nephew. unabr. ed. C. S. Lewis. Contrib. by Kenneth Branagh. (Running Time: 014400 sec.). (Chronicles of Narnia Ser.). 2005. audio compact disk 29.95 (978-0-06-079334-0(1)) HarperCollins Pubs.

Magician's Nephew. abr. ed. C. S. Lewis. 2 cass. (Running Time: 3 hrs.). (Chronicles of Narnia Ser.). (J). (gr. 4-8). 18.00 (D105) Blckstn Audio.
Young Digory embarks on Andre's experimental travels to unique & enchanted worlds.

Magician's Nephew. abr. ed. C. S. Lewis. Read by Claire Bloom. Illus. by Pauline Baynes. 1 cass. (Running Time: 1 hr. 04 min.). (Chronicles of Narnia Ser.). (J). (gr. 3 up). 1989. 12.00 (978-0-89845-877-0(3)) HarperCollins Pubs.

Magician's Nephew. adpt. ed. C. S. Lewis. (Running Time: 240 hrs. 0 mins.). (Chronicles of Narnia Ser.). (ENG.). (J). (gr. 3). 2007. audio compact disk 14.97 (978-1-58997-505-7(7), Tyndale Ent) Tyndale Hse.

Magician's Nephew. unabr. ed. C. S. Lewis. Read by Kenneth Branagh. 4 CDs. (Running Time: 4 hrs.). (Chronicles of Narnia Ser.). (J). (gr. 6-8). 2001. audio compact disk 27.50 (978-0-694-52620-8(7)) HarperCollins Pubs.

***Magician's Nephew.** unabr. ed. C. S. Lewis. Read by Kenneth Branagh. 2005. (978-0-06-085443-0(X)) HarperCollins Pubs.

Magician's Nephew. unabr. ed. C. S. Lewis. 4 cass. (Running Time: 6 hrs.). (Chronicles of Narnia Ser.). 2002. (978-0-00-712611-8(5)) Zondervan.
When Digory and Polly discover Uncle Andrew's secret workshop, they are tricked into touching the magic rings which transport them to the Other Place.

***Magician's Nephew.** unabr. ed. C. S. Lewis. Read by Kenneth Branagh. (ENG.). 2005. (978-0-06-085444-7(8)) HarperCollins Pubs.

Magician's Nephew. unabr. abr. ed. C. S. Lewis. Read by Kenneth Branagh. 3 cass. (Chronicles of Narnia Ser.). (J). (gr. 6-8). 2001. 24.00 (978-0-694-52619-2(3)) HarperCollins Pubs.

Magician's Wife. unabr. ed. Brian Moore. Narrated by Graeme Malcolm. 5 cass. (Running Time: 7 hrs. 30 mins.). 1997. 44.00 (978-0-7887-1980-6(7), 95367E7) Recorded Bks.
Emperor Napoleon III has sent a famous magician to Algeria to dazzle and deceive its Arab leaders. But as the magician's young wife discovers the layers of deception involved in the Emperor's plan, she sets out to change the results.

Magick of Israel Regardie. Christopher S. Hyatt. Ed. by Nick Tharcher. (ENG.). 2008. audio compact disk 31.00 (978-1-935150-00-8(6)) Orig Falcon.

MagicNet. John DeChancie. 3 cass. (Running Time: 3 hrs.). 2001. 21.95 (HHIR001) Lodestone Catalog.
The internet takes on a whole new demension as English professor "Skye" King finds reality crumbling around him & his dead friend Grant talking to him through a souped-up lap top.

Magna Carta of the Home: Deut. 6:4-9, 722. Ed Young. 1989. 4.95 (978-0-7417-1722-1(0), 722) Win Walk.

Magna Charta. James Daugherty. Narrated by Geoffrey Howard. (Running Time: 4 hrs.). 2002. 22.95 (978-1-59912-687-6(7)) Iofy Corp.

Magna Charta. unabr. ed. James Daugherty. Read by Geoffrey Howard. 3 cass. (Running Time: 4 hrs.). 2002. 23.95 (978-0-7861-2238-7(2), 2962); audio compact disk 24.00 (978-0-7861-9498-8(7), 2962) Blckstn Audio.
In the rich turbulence of English history, one day stands magnificently apart-June 15, 1215, the day of the signing of the Magna Charta. On this day, the first blow for English freedom was struck and forever affected the Western world. Here is the true story of three men, Stephen Langton, Williams Marshall, and Hubert de Burgh, whose heroic deeds opposed those of the ever deceitful and crafty King John.

Magnetic Fields of the Human Body & Their Functions. Manly P. Hall. 1 cass. 8.95 (978-0-89314-175-2(5), C890423) Philos Res.

Magnetic Mansion. Forrest Haskell, Jr. & Forrest Haskell. (Running Time: 28800 sec.). (Return to Eden Ser.). (ENG.). 2007. audio compact disk 29.95 (978-1-929976-43-0(7), TOP USA) Top Pubns.

***Magnetic Partners: How to Save Your Relationship by Discovering What Pulled You Together Is Now Pushing You Apart.** unabr. ed. Stephen Betchen. Narrated by Danny Campbell. (Running Time: 7 hrs. 0 mins.). 2010. 14.99 (978-1-4001-8665-5(X)); 19.99 (978-1-4001-6665-7(9)); audio compact disk 29.99 (978-1-4001-1665-2(1)); audio compact disk 59.99 (978-1-4001-4665-9(8)) Pub: Tantor Media. Dist(s): IngramPubServ

Magnetic Personality. Eldon Taylor. 1 cass. (Running Time: 62 min.). (Inner Talk Ser.). 16.95 incl. script. (978-1-55978-516-7(0), 53793F) Progress Aware Res.
Soundtrack - Brook with underlying subliminal affirmations.

Magnetic Personality: Music Theme. Eldon Taylor. 1 cass. 16.95 (978-0-940699-18-2(4), 53793C) Progress Aware Res.

Magnetic Resonance Imaging in a Flash! Judy Wells. 2008. audio compact disk 32.95 (978-0-7668-4339-4(4)) Pub: Delmar. Dist(s): CENGAGE Learn

Magnetic Sex Appeal. 1 cass. 10.00 (978-1-58506-025-2(9), 55) New Life Inst OR.
Learn to attract the opposite sex like a human magnet. For sale only to adults.

Magnetism & Personal Growth. 2 cass. (Running Time: 2 hrs.). (Personal Growth Ser.). 14.95 (ST-20) Crystal Clarity.
Includes: why magnetism begins in the heart; how discipline & focus increase magnetism; examples of magnetic attitudes; magnetism & inspiration.

Magnetizing Your Marriage. John Novak & Devi Novak. 1 cass. (Ananda Talks about Marriage Ser.). 9.95 (DM-4) Crystal Clarity.
Discusses: why couples need to have fun together; how to transform your marriage by serving your partner; strengthening the love bond through sexual transmutation.

Magnets/Imanes: Pulling Together, Pushing Apart/Atraen y Rechazan. abr. ed. Natalie M. Rosinsky. Tr. by Sol Robledo. Illus. by Sheree Boyd. (Running Time: 650 sec.). (Ciencia Asombrosa Ser.). (SPA.). (gr. k). 2008. audio compact disk 14.60 (978-1-4048-4474-2(0)) CapstoneDig.

Magnificence of St. Mark's Square: Venice, Italy. Scripts. Created by WhiteHot Productions. 3 CDs. (Running Time: 23520 sec.). (Great Discoveries Personal Audio Guides: Venice Ser.). 2006. audio compact disk 24.95 (978-1-59971-138-6(9)) AardGP.
Three hours and three minutes of playtime provide today's independent traveler with an unparalleled audio tour of this beautiful Byzantine-Gothic building that was the residence of the Venetian doges (rulers of the Venice) from 1340 up to the fall of the Republic in I797. The Doge Palace was also Venice's public palace, the seat of its government, its legislative body's and its courts. The palace remains the richest symbol of Venetian civilization, of its cultural, military, political, and economic history. Today, visitors view the Great Council Hall, the Chamber of the Council of Ten, the Chamber of the Senate, the torture chamber, prison cells, a remarkable armory, and other rooms. The famous Bridge of Sighs connects the Doge's Palace with the state prisons, which once confined the renowned 18th century Venetian adventurer, Casanova. If the Basilica of St. Mark's was the spiritual soul of Venice, then the Doge's Palace was its heart; pumping political, legal, financial, and military lifeblood to the body of the Republic. Earlier Venetian buildings were built on pilings, poles, supports and rafts. The final version of the Palace, that you see today, seems to mimic that construction. It is unlike a typical gothic building that featured a sturdy substructure supporting thinner, more graceful arches and spires. One could almost call this architecture reverse or inverted gothic, in that thicker arcade columns support thinner loggia columns, which in turn, support a massive upper structure. It is gravity defying and open to the world. All historic periods are visible in an extraordinary stratification of structural and decorative elements: from the antique foundations of the original Gothic complex, to the great halls dedicated to political life and decorated by the canvases of Veronese, Titian, Tintoretto and others. Even today, over two hundred years after the fall of the Republic and the last doge, the palace is still Venice's premier building and its address remains 1, San Marco. This 42 track audio tour is in standard CD format, on 3 CD's, ready for play on any CD player. Not for use on MP3 players.

Magnificent Ambersons. Booth Tarkington. 1 cass. (Running Time: 1 hr.). (Radiobook Ser.). 1987. 4.98 (978-0-929541-15-0(4)) Radiola Co.

Magnificent Ambersons. unabr. ed. Booth Tarkington. Read by Flo Gibson. 7 cass. (Running Time: 9 hrs. 46 mins.). 1993. 25.95 (978-1-55685-258-9(4)) Audio Bk Con.
A Pulitzer Prize-winner about greed, materialism & the changing fortunes of a mid-western family in the early 20th century, when horseless carriages were first appearing on the scene.

Magnificent Ambersons. unabr. ed. Booth Tarkington. Read by Geoffrey Blaisdell. (Running Time: 34200 sec.). 2007. 59.95 (978-1-4332-0266-7(2)); audio compact disk 29.95 (978-1-4332-0268-1(9)); audio compact disk 72.00 (978-1-4332-0267-4(0)) Blckstn Audio.

***Magnificent Ambersons.** unabr. ed. Booth Tarkington. Narrated by Peter Berkrot. (Running Time: 11 hrs. 30 mins. 0 sec.). 2010. 22.99 (978-1-4526-5023-4(3)); 17.99 (978-1-4526-7023-2(4)); audio compact disk 32.99 (978-1-4526-0023-9(6)); audio compact disk 78.99 (978-1-4526-3023-6(2)) Pub: Tantor Media. Dist(s): IngramPubServ

***Magnificent Ambersons (Library Edition)** unabr. ed. Booth Tarkington. Narrated by Peter Berkrot. (Running Time: 11 hrs. 30 mins.). 2010. 32.99 (978-1-4526-2023-7(7)) Tantor Media.

Magnificent Basilicas of Florence. Scripts. Created by WhiteHot Productions. 2 CDs. (Running Time: 27960 sec.). (Great Discoveries Personal Audio Guides: Florence Ser.). 2006. audio compact disk 21.95 (978-1-59971-116-4(8)) AardGP.
One hour and forty-three minutes of playtime provide today's independent traveler with an unparalleled audio tour of the Palazzo Vecchio, the centuries old home to Florence's many governments. Professional narrators delight, inform and amuse the listener as they explain the palaces great history and the wonderful works of art contained therein. This 29 track audio tour is in standard CD format, on 2 CD's, ready for play on any CD player. Not for use on MP3 players.

Magnificent Century. unabr. collector's ed. Thomas B. Costain. Read by David Case. 10 cass. (Running Time: 15 hrs.). (History of the Plantaganets Ser.). 1993. 80.00 (978-0-7366-2548-7(8), 3299) Books on Tape.
Second volume in A History of the Plantagenets covering the turbulent reign of England's Henry III, from 1216 to 1272.

Magnificent Desolation: The Long Journey Home from the Moon. unabr. ed. Buzz Aldrin, Jr. & Ken Abraham. Read by Patrick Egan. (ENG.). 2009. audio compact disk 35.00 (978-0-307-57746-7(5), Random AudioBks) Pub: Random Audio Pubg. Dist(s): Random

Magnificent Heritage: The Golden Age of Islamic Civilization; Decay or Rebirth? The Plight of Islamic Art Today. unabr. ed. Julian C. Hollick. 1 cass. (Running Time: 60 min.). (World of Islam Ser.). 1985. 15.00 (978-1-56709-055-0(9), 1029) Indep Broadcast.
Side A: This program explores the Golden Age of Islamic civilization, c. 800-1500, & the arts & sciences that it produced & developed. Side B: This program examines whether it is possible for the Muslim artist or scientist of today to work within his or her Islamic heritage or if markets & patronage dictate abandoning that heritage in favor of Western styles & tastes.

***Magnificent Mind at Any Age: Natural Ways to Unleash Your Brain's Maximum Potential.** unabr. ed. Daniel G. Amen. Read by Marc Cashman. 10 CDs. (Running Time: 12 hrs. 30 mins.). 2009. audio compact disk 100.00 (978-1-4159-6015-8(1), BksonTape) Pub: Random Audio Pubg. Dist(s): Random

Magnificent Mind at Any Age: Natural Ways to Unleash Your Brain's Maximum Potential. unabr. ed. Daniel G. Amen. 2008. audio compact disk 34.95 (978-0-7393-7721-5(3), Random AudioBks) Pub: Random Audio Pubg. Dist(s): Random

Magnificent Misfit: Vincent Van Gogh. unabr. ed. Louis Untermeyer. 1 cass. (Running Time: 23 min.). (Makers of the Modern World Ser.). 1968. 12.95 (11002) J Norton Pubs.
Traces the life of Van Gogh, an artist frenzied & tormented by a troubled humanity, whose creative madness added to the immortal gallery of art.

Magnificent Mummy Maker. 2005. 22.95 (978-0-7861-4444-0(0)); audio compact disk 27.00 (978-0-7861-7339-6(4)) Blckstn Audio.

Magnificent Mummy Maker. unabr. ed. Elvira Woodruff. Read by Lloyd James. 2005. 29.95 (978-0-7861-7720-2(9)) Blckstn Audio.

Magnificent Mummy Maker. unabr. ed. Elvira Woodruff. Read by Lloyd James. (J). 2007. 34.99 (978-1-59895-934-5(4)) Find a World.

Magnificent Obsession: Embracing the God-Filled Life. unabr. ed. Anne Graham Lotz. (Running Time: 9 hrs. 59 mins. 42 sec.). (ENG.). 2009. audio compact disk 24.99 (978-0-310-28903-6(3)) Zondervan.

***Magnificent Obsession: Embracing the God-Filled Life.** unabr. ed. Anne Graham Lotz. (Running Time: 8 hrs. 58 mins. 0 sec.). (ENG.). 2009. 19.99 (978-0-310-28904-3(1)) Zondervan.

Magnificent Recycling Machine Adventure: With Buffalo Biff & Farley's Raiders. unabr. ed. Joe Loesch. Ed. by Cheryl J. Hutchinson. Illus. by Ott Denney. 1 cass. (Running Time: 1 hr. 06 min.). (Backyard Adventure Ser.: Vol. 3). (J). (gr. 1-5). 1996. pap. bk. 14.95 (978-1-887729-04-8(6)); pap. bk. 16.95 (978-1-887729-05-5(4)) Toy Box Prods.
Their school needs to raise funds to plant trees in honor of "Earth Day." Biff, being the inventor he is & with the help of his magic buffalo horns, invents a recycling machine.

Magnificent Seven: SoundTrax. Mary Kay Beall & John Carter. (ENG.). 1995. audio compact disk 29.95 (978-0-7390-2133-0(8)) Alfred Pub.

Magnificient Obsession. Lloyd C. Douglas. Perf. by Irene Dunne & Willard Waterman. 1938. (DD-8120) Natl Recrd Co.

Magnify the Lord, Vols. 1 & 2. Compiled by Ken Bible. Contrib. by Tom Fettke. 1986. 19.99 (978-0-685-68425-2(3), TA-9077B) Lillenas.

Magnifying Your Spirituality. Richard G. Moore. 2006. audio compact disk 12.99 (978-1-55517-057-8(9)) CFI Dist.

Magnolia Grove. unabr. ed. Harvey Rosenfeld. Read by Patrick Cullen. 6 cass. (Running Time: 8 hrs. 30 mins.). 2001. 44.95 (978-0-7861-2001-7(0), 2771) Blckstn Audio.
When the Spanish American War was not going well for the U. S., Hobson survived a "suicide mission," sinking the "Merrimac" in an ironically failed attempt to block Santiago Harbor in Cuba & was instantly hailed as a hero. But unlike a stereotypical hero, he proved to be a complicated man with controversial political beliefs & he attracted as much criticism as praise.

***Magnolia Grove: The Story of Rear Admiral Richmond Pearson Hobson.** unabr. ed. Harvey Rosenfeld. Read by Patrick Cullen. (Running Time: 8.5 hrs. NaN mins.). (ENG.). 2011. 29.95 (978-1-4417-8474-2(8)); audio compact disk 76.00 (978-1-4417-8472-8(1)) Blckstn Audio.

Mago de Oz. 1 cass. (Running Time: 1 hr. 30 min.).Tr. of Wizard of Oz. (SPA.). (YA). (gr. 5-8). 2000. bk. 12.95 (978-84-207-6731-4(X)) Pub: Grupo Anaya ESP. Dist(s): Distribks Inc

Mago de Oz. abr. ed. L. Frank Baum. Read by Santiago Munevar. 3 CDs.Tr. of Wizard of Oz. (SPA.). 2002. audio compact disk 17.00 (978-958-8161-16-7(9)) YoYoMusic.

Magog Invasion. Chuck Missler. 2 CD's. (Running Time: 2 hrs.). (Briefing Packages by Chuck Missler). 2006. audio compact disk 19.95 (978-1-57821-351-1(7)) Koinonia Hse.
Ezekiel Chapters 38 and 39 describe the occasion in which God Himself intervenes to quell the ill-fated invasion of Israel by Magog and its allies (Persia, Cush, Phut, Libya, Gomer, Togarmah, Meshech, and Tubal). This passage also appears to anticipate the use of nuclear weapons.Why does the Bible use such strange names? It has to - we keep changing the names of things: Petrograd = St. Petersburg = Leningrad = St. Petersburg again. (My friends in Russia remind me that "in Russia, even the past is uncertain!") Byzantium = Constantinople = Istanbul. Cape Canaveral = Cape Kennedy, etc. But we don?t change the names of our ancestors!.

Magpies. Tom King. 1 CD. (Running Time: 1 hr. 30 mins.). 2005. audio compact disk 12.95 (978-0-660-18920-8(8)) Pub: Canadian Broadcasting CAN. Dist(s): Georgetown Term

Magwort & the Master. Read by Michael McCoy. 1 CD. (Running Time: 38 mins.). (J). 2003. audio compact disk 5.00 (978-0-9745431-2-3(8)) scholia.

Magyk. unabr. ed. Angie Sage. Read by Allan Corduner. (Septimus Heap Ser.: Bk. 1). (J). 2008. audio compact disk 14.95 (978-0-06-156306-5(4), HarperChildAud) HarperCollins Pubs.

Maha Mantra. unabr. ed. Yogi Hari. (Mantra Ser.). 2000. audio compact disk 14.95 (978-1-57777-031-2(5), 407-007) Pub: Nada Prodns. Dist(s): Bookworld

Mahalia Jackson: Gospel Singer & Civil Rights Champion. Montrew Dunham. Read by Pam Ward. (Running Time: 7200 sec.). (Young Patriots Ser.). (J). (gr. 3-7). 2007. 22.95 (978-1-4332-0155-4(0)); audio compact disk 24.00 (978-1-4332-0156-1(9)) Blckstn Audio.

Mahalia Jackson: Gospel Singer & Civil Rights Champion. unabr. ed. Montrew Dunham. Read by Pam Ward. (Young Patriots Ser.). (J). 2007. 34.99 (978-1-60252-666-2(4)) Find a World.

Mahamaya, Mother of the Buddha. Instructed by Manly P. Hall. 8.95 (978-0-89314-176-9(3), C840513) Philos Res.

Mahamudra Tantra: The Supreme Heart Jewel Nectar. Geshe Kelsang Gyatso. Read by Michael Sington. 4 CDs. (Running Time: 5 hrs. 0 mins. 0 sec.). (ENG., 2007. audio compact disk 24.95 (978-0-9548790-3-7(1)) Pub: Tharpa Pubns GBR. Dist(s): IPG Chicago

Mahamudra Teachings. Ole Nydahl. 2 cass. 18.00 Set. (A0409-89) Sound Photosyn.

Maharajapuram Santhanam: Vocal. 1 cass. (Maestro's Choice Series One). 1991. (C91016); audio compact disk (CD C91016) Multi-Cultural Bks.
Karnatic classical music.

Maharajapuram Santhanam: Vocal. 1 cass. (Thyagaraja Masterpieces Ser.: Vol. 3). 1992. (C92046) Multi-Cultural Bks.

Mahatma Gandhi: Fashion Designer. unabr. ed. Perf. by Eknath Easwaran. 1 cass. (Running Time: 1 hr.). 1983. 7.95 (978-1-58638-570-5(4)) Nilgiri Pr.

Mahatma Gandhi & His Apostles. unabr. ed. Ved Mehta. Read by Sheryl Dold. 8 cass. (Running Time: 12 hrs.). 1988. 64.00 (978-0-7366-1317-0(X), 2223) Books on Tape.
A biography of Gandhi compiled from interviews with his family & his followers.

Mahayana Buddhism. 4 cass. 45.00 set. (411) MEA A Watts Cass.

Mahogany Row. Scripts. Wayne J. Keeley. Perf. by Dave Hamilton. Score by David Fabrizio. Directed By David Fabrizio. Illus. by Rickey R. Mallory. 4 CDs. (Running Time: 4 hrs. 40 mins.). Dramatization. (ENG.). 2004. audio compact disk 24.95 (978-1-58124-680-3(3)) Pub: Fiction Works. Dist(s): Brodart

Mahuts & Annwm Aval: 2 Full-Length Video Theatre Plays. David Seals. Tr. by Arthwyr A. Meurig & Pierre Jakez-Helias from CHY. Intro. by Pierre Jakez-Helias. Photos by Alice Johnson. (7 Council Fires of Sweet Medicine Ser.: Acts 4 & 5). (C). 1996. 17.00 (978-1-887786-30-0(9)) Sky & Sage Bks.

Maia, Vol. 1. unabr. collector's ed. Richard Adams. Read by Bill Kelsey. 12 cass. (Running Time: 18 hrs.). 1987. 96.00 (978-0-7366-1165-7(7), 2090A) Books on Tape.
Maia, eldest daughter in a poor fisherman's family, grows up in a remote corner of the Belkan Empire. She leads a quiet, sheltered life until through an act of terrible deceit she finds herself en route to Belka, sold as a concubine.

Maia, Vol. 2. collector's ed. Richard Adams. Read by Bill Kelsey. 12 cass. (Running Time: 18 hrs.). 1987. 96.00 (978-0-7366-1166-4(5), 2090-B) Books on Tape.

Maia, Vol. 3. collector's ed. Richard Adams. Read by Bill Kelsey. 9 cass. (Running Time: 13 hrs. 30 min.). 1987. 72.00 (978-0-7366-1167-1(3), 2090-C) Books on Tape.

Maid in Waiting. unabr. ed. John Galsworthy. Read by David Case. (Running Time: 36000 sec.). (Forsyte Chronicles Ser.). 2007. 65.95 (978-1-4332-0215-5(8)); audio compact disk 29.95 (978-1-4332-0217-9(4)); audio compact disk 72.00 (978-1-4332-0216-2(6)) Blckstn Audio.

Maid in Waiting. unabr. collector's ed. John Galsworthy. Read by David Case. 7 cass. (Running Time: 10 hrs. 30 min.). (Forsyte Saga Ser.). 1999. 56.00 (978-0-7366-4382-5(6), 4848) Books on Tape.
Detailed picture of the British propertied class, from the wealth & security of the mid-Victorian era through Edwardian high-noon to a post-WW I world of change, strikes & social malaise. By showing the Forsytes in all their strengths & weaknesses against a detailed background of English life.

Maid of Buttermere. unabr. ed. Melvyn Bragg. Read by Joan Walker. 12 cass. (Running Time: 16 hrs. 19 min.). 2001. 94.95 (978-1-85695-565-2(6), 93014) Pub: ISIS Audio GBR. Dist(s): Ulverscroft US
"This is the story of an impostor & bigamist, a self-styled Colonel Hope, who travels to the North, where eventually he marries 'the Maid of Buttermere,' a young woman whose natural beauty inspired the dreams & confirmed the theories of various early nineteenth century writers...It is a fine story." - The Times.

Maiden: The Unauthorized Biography of Iron Maiden. Mark Crampton. (Maximum Ser.). (ENG.). 2001. audio compact disk 14.95 (978-1-84240-083-8(5)) Pub: Chrome Dreams GBR. Dist(s): IPG Chicago

Maiden Bride. Linda Needham. Narrated by Steven Crossley. 6 cass. (Running Time: 9 hrs.). 54.00 (978-0-7887-9550-3(3)); audio compact disk 78.00 (978-1-4025-2930-6(9)) Recorded Bks.

Maiden King: The Reunion of Masculine & Feminine. abr. ed. Robert Bly & Marion Woodman. Read by Robert Bly. 2 cass. (Running Time: 3 hrs.). 1998. 17.95 (978-1-55935-288-8(4)) Soundelux.

Maiden, Mother, Wise Woman: Reclaiming Our Sexuality. Savage. (ENG.). 2008. 20.00 (978-0-9753369-1-5(6)) Divine Fem Pubns.

Maiden Voyage. Alex Stuart. Read by Alexander Hall. 5 cass. 1999. 49.95 (63023) Pub: Soundings Ltd GBR. Dist(s): Ulverscroft US

Maiden's Grave. unabr. ed. Jeffery Deaver. Read by Connor O'Brien. 9 cass. (Running Time: 13 hrs. 30 min.). 1999. 72.00 (978-0-7366-4300-9(1), 4637) Books on Tape.
A school bus carrying eight deaf young girls & their teachers are taken hostage by three escaped killers. The FBI's senior hostage negotiator, Arthur Potter, attempts to secure their release, a situation made more difficult because the leader of the convicts, Lou Handy is as brilliant in his way as Potter is in his. With Handy threatening to kill one hostage an hour unless their demands are met, a terrifying game of cat & mouse begins.

***Maidhc Stiofainin Seoighe.** Tomas Ban. (ENG.). 1990. 11.95 (978-0-8023-7029-7(2)) Pub: Clo Iar-Chonnachta IRL. Dist(s): Dufour

Maigret a New York. Georges Simenon. Read by Marc Moro. 2 cass. (FRE.). 1996. 21.95 (1846-LQP) Olivia & Hill.
The pipe smoking detective solves another mystery.

Maigret à Vichy. Georges Simenon. Perf. by Jean Negroni & Francois Maistre. 3 cass. (FRE.). 1992. 32.95 (1672-RF) Olivia & Hill.
Maigret vacationing in Vichy with his wife solves a mystery in this well-known water town. A performance broadcast on French radio.

Maigret & the Bum. unabr. ed. Georges Simenon. Read by Michael Prichard. 4 cass. (Running Time: 6 hrs.). 2001. 17.95 (978-0-7366-5729-7(0)) Books on Tape.
When Maigret learns that a bum's death is really an assassination, he demands justice.

Maigret & the Bum. unabr. collector's ed. Georges Simenon. Read by Michael Prichard. 4 cass. (Running Time: 4 hrs.). 1984. 24.00 (978-0-7366-0540-3(1), 1514) Books on Tape.
When Maigret learns that a bum's murder is in reality an assassination, he becomes deeply involved.

Maigret & the Killer. Georges Simenon. Narrated by Full Cast Production Staff. (Running Time: 3 hrs.). 2006. 14.95 (978-1-60083-053-2(6)) Iofy Corp.

Maigret & the Killer. unabr. ed. Georges Simenon. Read by Andrew Sachs. 4 cass. (Running Time: 4 hrs.). (Inspector Maigret Mystery Ser.). 1993. 39.95 (978-0-7451-6284-3(3), CAB 600) AudioGO.

Maigret & the Killer. unabr. ed. Georges Simenon. Read by Andrew Sachs. 4 cass. (Running Time: 6 hrs.). (Inspector Maigret Mystery Ser.). 2000. 34.95 (CAB 600) Pub: Chivers Audio Bks GBR. Dist(s): AudioGO
Superintendent Maigret is called in when a man is found fatally wounded in the streets of Paris. This case intrigues the Press, for the victim is the son of a wealthy perfume manufacturer, a lonely student with a strange passion for collecting human voices. As Maigret tracks the killer with the aid of a tape recorder's testimony, he uncovers a link to a gang of art thieves and the bizarre motive for the killing.

Maigret & the Madwoman. unabr. ed. Georges Simenon. Read by Andrew Sachs. 3 cass. (Running Time: 4 hrs. 20 min.). 1999. 21.95 (978-1-57270-125-0(0), N31125u) Pub: Audio Partners. Dist(s): PerseuPGW
An elderly widow complains to the Parisian police that an intruder is following her & shifting things about in her tidy apartment. At first the police believe she's paranoid, but out of kindness, Chief Superintendent Jules Maigret agrees to follow up on her story. Before he can, however, the woman is murdered. Maigret sets out to find out why & by whom.

Maigret & the Minister. Georges Simenon. 2004. audio compact disk 39.95 (978-0-563-52404-5(9)) BBC Worldwide.

Maigret & the Pickpocket. unabr. ed. Georges Simenon. Read by Andrew Sachs. 4 cass. (Running Time: 6 hrs.). (Inspector Maigret Mystery Ser.). 2000. 34.95 (CAB 727) Pub: Chivers Audio Bks GBR. Dist(s): AudioGO
In a curious chain of events, a missing wallet and badge turn up when the thief contacts Maigret, which in turn results in the finding of the pickpocket's dead wife. Is the young robber, who works as a film director, a victim of circumstances or playing the role of his life?.

Maigret & the Reluctant Witness. Georges Simenon. Narrated by Full Cast Production Staff. (Running Time: 2 hrs. 30 mins.). 2006. 14.95 (978-1-60083-054-9(4)) Iofy Corp.

Maigret & the Toy Village. unabr. ed. Georges Simenon. Read by Andrew Sachs. 3 cass. (Running Time: 3 hrs. 45 mins.). 2001. 21.95 (978-1-57270-215-8(X), N31215u) Pub: Audio Partners. Dist(s): PerseuPGW
Peg Leg Lapie, a crusty old sailor, is found mysteriously murdered in a most incongruous setting: a picturesque cottage near Paris, where he lived attended only by his young housekeeper, Felicie. But Lapie was not alone, Maigret, chief inspector of the Paris police, is sure of it.

Maigret & the Wine Merchant. unabr. ed. Georges Simenon. Read by Michael Prichard. 4 cass. (Running Time: 5 hrs). 2001. 17.95 (978-0-7366-5731-0(2)) Books on Tape.
Why would anyone in Paris want to kill one of its finest wine merchants? Maigret asks the question... and finds the answer.

Maigret & the Wine Merchant. unabr. collector's ed. Georges Simenon. Read by Michael Prichard. 5 cass. (Running Time: 5 hrs.). 1984. 30.00 (978-0-7366-0544-1(4), 1518) Books on Tape.
While interrogating a penniless delinquent about a sordid crime, Maigret is called to the scene of an utterly different murder: one of the richest wine merchants in Paris is dead. Thus begins another Maigret probe into his chief preoccupation: the idea of guilt.

Maigret Bides His Time. unabr. ed. Georges Simenon. Read by Clifford Norgate. 3 cass. (Running Time: 4 hrs. 15 mins.). 2002. 19.95 (978-1-57270-241-7(9)) Pub: Audio Partners. Dist(s): PerseuPGW

Maigret Collection: Radio Dramatization. unabr. ed. Georges Simenon. 5 CDs. (Running Time: 7 hrs. 30 mins.). 2003. audio compact disk 59.95 (978-0-563-49598-7(X), BBCD 021) BBC Worldwide.

Maigret et le Clochard. Georges Simenon. Read by Mouloudji & Fabienne Nourbat. 2 cass. (FRE.). 1995. 28.95 (1625-LQP) Olivia & Hill.
Another mystery solved by Inspector Maigret.

Maigret Sets a Trap. unabr. ed. Georges Simenon. Read by Andrew Sachs. 3 cass. (Running Time: 4 hrs.). 2000. 21.95 (978-1-57270-152-6(8), N31152u) Pub: Audio Partners. Dist(s): PerseuPGW
Inspector Jules Maigret baits a cunning trap to lure the murderer of five women, each of whom has been brutally knifed in the streets of Montmartre.

Maigret Sets a Trap. unabr. ed. Georges Simenon. Read by Michael Prichard. 4 cass. (Running Time: 5 hrs.). 2001. 17.95 (978-0-7366-5726-6(6)) Books on Tape.
A human life is the bait as the famous Parisian police inspector, Jules Maigret, prepares to trap the murderer of five women. The homicidal pattern followed is identical: The victims all have been women of the same build; all were knifed at night in the streets of Montmartre; all had their clothes slashed.

Maigret Sets a Trap. unabr. collector's ed. Georges Simenon. Read by Michael Prichard. 5 cass. (Running Time: 5 hrs.). 1983. 30.00 (978-0-7366-0534-2(7), 1508) Books on Tape.

Maigret's Boyhood Friend. unabr. ed. Georges Simenon. Read by Michael Prichard. 4 cass. (Running Time: 6 hrs.). 2001. 17.95 (978-0-7366-5730-3(4)) Books on Tape.
Maigret receives a visit from a former schoolmate whose detailed account of a murder he has witnessed leaves Maigret curiously puzzled.

Maigret's Boyhood Friend. unabr. collector's ed. Georges Simenon. Read by Michael Prichard. 6 cass. (Running Time: 6 hrs.). 1984. 36.00 (978-0-7366-0543-4(6), 1517) Books on Tape.

Maigret's Christmas. unabr. collector's ed. Georges Simenon. Read by Grover Gardner. 10 cass. (Running Time: 15 hrs.). 1979. 80.00 (978-0-7366-0226-6(7), 1223) Books on Tape.
A collection of nine stories, Inspector Maigret appears in eight of them. Maigret, unlike any other stock detective, works by enveloping himself in the psychological atmosphere of the case in which he is engaged.

Mail. abr. ed. Mameve Medwed. 2006. 14.98 (978-1-59483-681-7(7)) Pub: Hachet Audio. Dist(s): HachBkGrp

Mail Comes to Main Street: Early Explorers Early Set A Audio CD. Benchmark Education Staff. (J). 2006. audio compact disk 10.00 (978-1-4108-7629-4(2)) Benchmark Educ.

Mail Myself to You. Perf. by John McCutcheon et al. 1 cass. (J). (ps-5). 9.98 (2137); audio compact disk 17.98 (D2137) MFLP CA.
Includes folk tunes by Woody Guthrie & Malvina Reynolds - rich hammered dulcimers, banjos, fiddles, & mandolins that we expect from folk music. It may not be traditional, but also includes hot saxophones, electric guitars joined by drums & even Caribbean rhythms.

Mail Myself to You. John McCutcheon. 1 cass. (Running Time: 40 min.). (J). 1988. 9.98 (978-1-886767-26-3(2), 8016); audio compact disk 14.98 (978-1-886767-27-0(0), 8016) Rounder Records.
The songs of John's second children's recording are for dancing & singing, for going to sleep & waking up, for remembering & imagining, for thinking about the future & the past. Songs include "New Car", "Barnyard Dance", "Teddy Bear", & "Kindergarten Wall". John brings you new version of childhood standards mixed with some exciting new songs.

Mailbox. unabr. ed. Audrey Shafer. Read by Nick Landrum. 5 cass. (Running Time: 5 hrs. 30 mins.). (J). (gr. 5-7). 2007. 41.75 (978-1-4281-4624-2(5)); audio compact disk 51.75 (978-1-4281-4629-7(6)) Recorded Bks.

Mailroom: Hollywood History from the Bottom Up. unabr. ed. David Rensin. Read by Dan Cashman. 12 cass. (Running Time: 12.00). 2004. 34.95 (978-1-59007-367-4(3)) Pub: New Millenn Enter. Dist(s): PerseuPGW

Maimonides. 10.00 Esstee Audios.
A Jewish renaissance man is looked at with respect to his impact on the world in which we live.

Maimonides: The Life & World of One of Civilization's Greatest Minds. unabr. ed. Joel L. Kraemer. Read by Sean Pratt. (Running Time: 20 hrs.). (ENG.). 2009. 49.98 (978-1-59659-363-3(6), GildAudio) Pub: Gildan Media. Dist(s): HachBkGrp

Maimonides & Medieval Jewish Philosophy. unabr. abr. ed. Read by Lynn Redgrave. (Running Time: 10800 sec.). (World of Philosophy Ser.). 2006. audio compact disk 25.95 (978-0-7861-6598-8(7)) Pub: Blckstn Audio. Dist(s): NetLibrary CO

Main Corpse. abr. ed. Diane Mott Davidson. Read by Mary Gross. 4 cass. (Goldy Schulz Culinary Mysteries Ser.: No. 6). 1996. 12.99 (978-1-57815-209-4(7), Media Bks Audio) Media Bks NJ.

Main Corpse. abr. ed. Diane Mott Davidson. Read by Mary Gross. 4 cass. (Running Time: 6 hrs.). (Goldy Schulz Culinary Mysteries Ser.: No. 6). 1996. 24.95 (978-1-57511-019-6(9), 694404) Pub Mills.

Main Corpse. unabr. ed. Diane Mott Davidson. Read by Mary Gross. 5 CDs. (Running Time: 6 hrs.). (Goldy Schulz Culinary Mysteries Ser.: No. 6). 2002. audio compact disk 14.99 (978-1-57815-547-7(9), 4423CD5, Media Bks Audio) Media Bks NJ.
Another irresistibel suspens and delectable humor.

Main Corpse. unabr. ed. Diane Mott Davidson. Perf. by Barbara Rosenblat. 7 cass. (Running Time: 9 hrs. 30 mins.). (Goldy Schulz Culinary Mysteries Ser.: No. 6). 2004. 32.95 (978-1-59007-349-0(5)) Pub: New Millenn Enter. Dist(s): PerseuPGW

Main Corpse. unabr. ed. Diane Mott Davidson. Read by Barbara Rosenblat. 9 CDs. (Running Time: 9 hrs. 30 min.). (Goldy Schulz Culinary Mysteries Ser.: No. 6). 2004. audio compact disk 55.00 (978-1-59007-441-1(6)) Pub: New Millenn Enter. Dist(s): PerseuPGW

Main Corpse. unabr. ed. Diane Mott Davidson. Narrated by Barbara Rosenblat. 7 cass. (Running Time: 9 hrs. 30 mins.). (Goldy Schulz Culinary Mysteries Ser.: No. 6). 1996. 60.00 (978-0-7887-0788-9(4), 94931E7) Recorded Bks.
Goldy is busy whipping up a sumptuous dinner for two wealthy clients when one of the men disappears, & her best friend is accused of murder.

Main Corpse. unabr. ed. Diane Mott Davidson. Read by Barbara Rosenblat. 7 cass. (Running Time: 9 hrs. 30 min.). (Goldy Schulz Culinary Mysteries Ser.: No. 6). 1996. Rental 16.50 (92931) Recorded Bks.

Main Street. unabr. ed. Sinclair Lewis. Read by Flo Gibson. 12 cass. (Running Time: 17 hrs.). 1995. 39.95 (978-1-55685-339-5(4)) Audio Bk Con.
In this once extraordinarily popular novel the provincialism & prejudice in the small town of Gopher Prairie are depicted as almost more than Carol Kennicot can bear. As the bored wife of the local doctor, her efforts to beautify the town & add cultural activities are met with ridicule & derision.

***Main Street.** unabr. ed. Sinclair Lewis. Narrated by Paul Garcia. (Running Time: 19 hrs. 0 mins.). 2010. 95.99 (978-1-4001-4982-7(7)); 39.99 (978-1-4001-1982-0(0)); 29.99 (978-1-4001-6982-5(8)) Tantor Media.

***Main Street.** unabr. ed. Sinclair Lewis. Narrated by Paul Michael Garcia. (Running Time: 19 hrs. 0 mins.). 2010. 22.99 (978-1-4001-8982-3(9)) Tantor Media.

Main Street: The Story of Carol Kennicott. Sinclair Lewis. Narrated by Brian Emerson. (Running Time: 18 hrs.). 2000. 48.95 (978-1-59912-539-8(0)) Iofy Corp.

Main Street: The Story of Carol Kennicott. unabr. ed. Sinclair Lewis. Read by Brian Emerson. 12 cass. (Running Time: 18 hrs.). 2001. 83.95 (978-0-7861-2002-4(9), 2772); audio compact disk 112.00 (978-0-7861-9727-9(7), z2772) Blckstn Audio.
The lonely predicament of Carol Kennicott, caught between her desires for social reform & individual happiness, reflects the position in which America's turn-of-the-century "emancipated woman" found herself.

Main Street: The Story of Carol Kennicott. unabr. ed. Sinclair Lewis. Narrated by Barbara Caruso. 13 cass. (Running Time: 18 hrs. 30 mins.). 1999. 104.00 (978-0-7887-0572-4(5), 94749E7) Recorded Bks.
Well-educated & sophisticated, Carol Kennicott is frustrated by life in her husband's small Midwestern town.

Main Street: The Story of Carol Kennicott, Pt. A. unabr. collector's ed. Sinclair Lewis. Read by Dick Estell. 6 cass. (Running Time: 9 hrs.). 1987. 48.00 (978-0-7366-1102-2(9), 2028-A) Books on Tape.
An allegory of exile & return, Main Street attacks those who resist change, who are under the illusion that they have chosen their tradition.

Main Street: The Story of Carol Kennicott, Pt. B. collector's ed. Sinclair Lewis. Read by Dick Estell. 7 cass. (Running Time: 10 hrs. 30 min.). 1987. 56.00 (978-0-7366-1103-9(7), 2028-B) Books on Tape.

***Main Street (Library Edition)** unabr. ed. Sinclair Lewis. Narrated by Paul Michael Garcia. (Running Time: 19 hrs. 0 mins.). 2010. 39.99 (978-1-4001-9982-2(4)) Tantor Media.

Main Tests of Life: What They Are & How You Can Pass Them. 6. (Running Time: 6 hrs.). (Passing the Test Ser.: 2). 2003. 30.00 (978-1-57399-150-6(3)) Mac Hammond.
Sadly, many of God's children are failing to pass the tests of life. In Volume II of his series on Passing the Test, you will learn what the main tests are, the answer key to each, and the difference between faith and trust. Get this series and start learning how to recognize and pass the main tests of life.

Main-Travelled Roads. Hamlin Garland. Read by Walter Zimmerman & D. White. 6 cass. (Running Time: 7 hrs. 30 min.). 1989. 36.00 incl. album. (C-100) Jimcin Record.
Stories of the Mississippi Valley.

***Maine.** unabr. ed. J. Courtney Sullivan. (ENG.). 2011. audio compact disk 40.00 (978-0-307-91729-4(0), Random AudioBks) Pub: Random Audio Pubg. Dist(s): Random

Maine Massacre. unabr. ed. Janwillem Van de Wetering. Narrated by George Guidall. 6 cass. (Running Time: 8 hrs. 45 mins.). (Grijpstra & DeGier Mystery Ser.). 1998. 51.00 (978-0-7887-2025-3(2), 95400E7) Recorded Bks.
When Grijpstra, the Commissaris of the Amsterdam police force gets a call from his newly-widowed sister, he flies to a snowy village in Maine to comfort her. When Sergeant De Gier joins him, De Gier quickly discovers that the man's death is one in a series of mysteriously fatal "accidents.".

Maine Mutiny. unabr. ed. Jessica Fletcher & Donald Bain. Read by Cynthia Darlow. 7 CDs. (Murder, She Wrote Ser.). 2005. audio compact disk 74.95 (978-0-7927-3527-4(7), SLD 777) AudioGO.

Maine Mutiny. unabr. ed. Jessica Fletcher et al. Read by Cynthia Darlow. 5 cass. (Running Time: 25680 sec.). (Murder, She Wrote Ser.). 2005. 49.95 (978-0-7927-3526-7(9), CSL 777) AudioGO.

Maine Pot-Hellion. Narrated by Alan Bemis et al. 1 cass. 8.95 (2) Bert and I Inc.
Comic tales from DownEast.

Maine Roustabout see Richard Eberhart Reading His Poetry

Mains Propres. 1 cass. (Running Time: 60 mins.). Dramatization. (Maitres du Mystere Ser.). (FRE.). 1996. 11.95 (1841-MA) Olivia & Hill.
Popular radio thriller, interpreted by France's best actors.

Maintain Weight Loss: Hypnotic & Subliminal Learning. David Illig. 1985. 14.99 (978-0-86580-043-4(X)) Success World.

Maintaining Balance During Loss & Beyond. Diane Y. Chapman. Read by Diane Y. Chapman. 1 cass. (Running Time: 58 min.). 1996. 12.95 (978-0-9653239-2-5(7)) Pub: Wrds to Yr Adv. Dist(s): Penton Overseas
Adult discussion about grief & loss - motivational, inspirational.

Maintaining Our Joy. unabr. ed. Myrtle Smith. Prod. by David Keyston. 1 cass. (Running Time: 1 hrs.). (Myrtle Smyth Audiotapes Ser.). 1998. , CD. (978-1-893107-06-9(X), M6, Cross & Crown) Healing Unltd.

Maintaining Professional Competence: Approaches to Career Enhancement, Vitality & Success Throughout a Work Life. Sherry L. Willis et al. (Higher & Adult Education Ser.). 1990. bk. 38.45 (978-1-55542-227-1(6), Jossey-Bass) Wiley US.

Maintaining Spiritual Health in Ministry: Over the Long Haul. 1 cass. (Care Cassettes Ser.: Vol. 20, No. 5). 1993. 10.80 Assn Prof Chaplains.

Maintaining Spirituality. 1 cass. 1987. 6.50 (978-0-933685-14-7(9), TP-34) A A Grapevine.
Articles selected from the AA Grapevine Magazine on how AA members practice the spiritual way of life.

Maintaining the Spirit of Faith. Gloria Copeland. Perf. by Gloria Copeland. 1 cass. (Ingredients for Success: Faith, Patience & Love Ser.: Tape 2). 1995. cass. & video 5.00 (978-1-57562-018-3(9)) K Copeland Pubns.
Biblical teaching on success.

***Maire Mhor.** Sean Choilin O. Conaire. (ENG.). 1987. 11.95 (978-0-8023-7004-4(7)) Pub: Clo Iar-Chonnachta IRL. Dist(s): Dufour

***Maire Rua - an Sean Agus an Nua.** Dara Ban Macdonnchadha. (ENG.). 1990. 11.95 (978-0-8023-7027-3(6)) Pub: Clo Iar-Chonnachta IRL. Dist(s): Dufour

Maisie Dobbs. unabr. ed. Jacqueline Winspear. Read by Rita Barrington. 6 cass. (Maisie Dobbs Mystery Ser.: Bk. 1). 2005. 54.95 (978-0-7927-3459-8(9), CSL 752); audio compact disk 79.95 (978-0-7927-3460-4(2), SLD 752) AudioGO.

Maison de Jade. Madeleine Chapsal. Read by Madeleine Chapsal. 1 cass. (FRE.). 1991. 24.95 (1030-EF) Olivia & Hill.
Popular novel about a woman who experiences passion & pain at the end of a relationship. Contemplating suicide, the desire to tell her story gives her a will to live.

Maison des Aravis. l.t. ed. Francoise Bourain. (French Ser.). 2001. bk. 30.99 (978-2-84011-410-9(0)) Pub: UlverLrgPrint GBR. Dist(s): Ulverscroft US

Maison Tellier. Guy de Maupassant. Read by Claude Beauclair. 1 cass. (FRE.). 1991. 13.95 (1257-OH) Olivia & Hill.
One day, when the men of a small Normandy village come for their evening at the "maison Tellier," they find the door closed & the house empty. Where have the Madame & her five girls gone?.

Maitraya - Christ: Alive & Living Well, in England. Benjamin Creme. 1 cass. (Roy Tuckman Interview Ser.). 9.00 (A0630-90) Sound Photosyn.
Tuckman interviewed Benjamin Creme live on KPFK. Benjamin has been talking about the Maitraya or Christ living in England as a Man getting ready to reveal Himself, & recent events including Gorbachev's & the Vatacan's private validation of His presence.

Majestic Palaces & Museums of Venice. Scripts. Created by WhiteHot Productions. 2 CDs. (Running Time: 37560 sec.). (Great Discoveries Personal Audio Guides: Venice Ser.). 2006. audio compact disk 21.95 (978-1-59971-139-3(7)) AardGP.
One hour and twenty-eight minutes of playtime provide today's independent traveler with an unparalleled audio tour of the church of Santa Maria della Salute, the most brilliant architectural jewel in the Venetian crown. La salute is a soaring baroque structure unlike any other. She lifts her gleaming drum of white istrian stone high above the city's tiled rooftops and her silhouette dominates the southern terminus of the Grand Canal. The church sits at the entrance to Venice Italy like some great lady, on the threshold of her salon. Her domes, scrolls, scalloped buttresses and statues form a pompous crown while her wide steps are placed on the ground like the train of a great robe. Throughout history, great plagues, wars, and disease have stimulated great art and architecture. La Salute is a case in point. In 1630, a plague had struck Venice taking some 45,000 people, over a quarter of its citizens, to early graves. In the midst of this horror, the Venetian Senate made a pact with God, "Stop the plague and we will build a church to honor the Virgin Mary." The pact worked, the plague came to a sudden end, most likely due to cooler weather, and the Senate set about honoring their promise to God by building the Basilica di Santa Maria della Salute or the Basilica of St. Mary of Good Health. Professional narrators delight, inform and amuse as they guide the listener through this magnificent cathedral, while discribing her remarkable history and magnificent art. La Salute contains masterpieces and great works aplenty including two of Titian's greatest paintings, "the Pentecost" and "St. Mark Enthroned with Other Saints." The large Sacristy contains an additional wealth of unforgettable Titian paintings as well as the work of other artists. Outstanding among these is one of Tintoretto's most famous paintings, the "Wedding at Cana." This 17 track audio tour is in standard CD format, on 2 CD's, ready for play on any CD player. Not for use on MP3 players.

Majestic Palaces & Piazzas of Florence. Scripts. Created by WhiteHot Productions. 4 CDs. (Running Time: 24720 sec.). (Great Discoveries Personal Audio Guides: Florence Ser.). 2006. audio compact disk 26.95 (978-1-59971-122-5(2)) AardGP.
Three hours and forty minutes of playtime provide today?s independent traveler with an unparalleled audio tour of Italy?s grandest Renaissance palace. Now one of the world?s great museums, the Pitti Palace was, from the 16th century on, home to the ruling families of Florence, Tuscany and Italy. The Medici?s, the Lorraine?s, the Bourbon's, the Bonaparte?s and the Savoy?s resided here. Professional narrators delight, inform and amuse as they present the palaces history, its great works of art, and the lives of the people, while guiding the listener through the Palatine Galleries and Royal Apartments. Its countless rambling rooms house several museums, the most important of which is the Palatine Gallery, whose beautiful salons are filled from floor to ceiling with paintings from the Medici private collection. It was in these rooms that the Medici accumulated the collections of great and not so great works of art that create the unique character of the Palatine Galleries. It is one of the largest and most important collections in the world containing works by Michelangelo, Raphael, Titian, Botticelli, Lippi, Tintoretto, Peter Paul Rubins, and others. This 42 track audio tour is in standard CD format, on 4 CD?s, ready for play on any CD player. Not for use on MP3 players.

***Majestie: The King Behind the King James Bible.** unabr. ed. David Teems. Narrated by Roger Mueller & Bob Souer. (Running Time: 7 hrs. 31 mins. 26 sec.). (ENG.). 2010. 19.59 (978-1-60814-778-6(9)); audio compact disk 27.99 (978-1-59859-806-3(6)) Oasis Audio.

Majesty: Piano & Flute. 1 cass. (Instrumental Praise Ser.). 1999. 7.99 (978-0-7601-2667-7(4), 83061-0501-483061-0501-2); audio compact disk 10.99 (978-0-7601-2668-4(2), 83061-0501-2) Provident Music.
Favorite praise choruses & cherished hymns performed by solo instruments & full orchestra. Includes: "All Hail the Power," "Be Exalted," "Be Thou My Vision," "Blessed Be the Lord God Almighty," "Great & Mighty," "How Great Thou Art," "How Majestic Is Your Name," "I Sing the Mighty Power of God," "Joyful, Joyful, We Adore Thee," "Lamb of God," "Majesty," "My Tribute," "Soon & Very Soon," "This is the Day," & "When I Survey the Wondrous Cross".

Majesty & the Glory: Psalm 8. Ed Young. 1989. 4.95 (978-0-7417-1759-7(X), 759) Win Walk.

Majesty of Calmness. unabr. ed. William George Jordan. (ENG.). 2005. 2.98 (978-1-59659-056-4(4), GildAudio) Pub: Gildan Media. Dist(s): HachBkGrp

Majesty of Calmness: Bonus the Sayings of Confucius. William George Jordan. Narrated by Ross M. Armetta. 1 CD. (Running Time: 70 Mins. Aprox.). 2005. audio compact disk 12.99 (978-1-59733-001-5(9), Trans Greats) InfoFount.
Life-transforming wisdom: INCREASE YOUR PRODUCTIVITY AND REDUCE YOUR STRESS.?Calmness is the rarest quality in human life. It is the poise of a great nature, in harmony with itself and its ideals. It is the moral atmosphere of a life self-centered, self-reliant, and self-controlled. Calmness is singleness of purpose, absolute confidence, and conscious power; ready to be focused in an instant to meet any crisis.??Hurry has ruined more Americans than has any other word in the vocabulary of life. It is the scourge of America; and is both a cause and a result of our high-pressure civilization. Hurry always pays the highest price for everything, and, usually the goods are not delivered. In the race for wealth we often sacrifice time, energy, health, home, happiness and honor, - everything that money cannot buy, the very things that money can never bring back. ? The Majesty of Calmness by William George Jordan has been recognized for almost 100 years as a truthful, practical book that helps focus an individual?s thoughts, energies, and attitudes to aid in self-transformation. It is written in an inspiring somewhat poetical and metaphorical style. The Majesty of Calmness describes how our lifestyle and character directly influence our total health (mind, body, spirit). The book also details how our lifestyle affects our outer health and success in life. It provides powerful suggestions on how a person may influence and better their life by controlling, their actions and circumstances with their attitude and lifestyle. Topics (partial) in the audiobook include; Hurry, the Scourge of America; The Power of Personal Influence; The Dignity of Self-Reliance; Failure as a Success; Doing Our Best at All Times and a Bonus: The Sayings of Confucius ? a biography of Confucius and highlights of his most famous sayings. Imagine, multiplying your productivity and effectiveness; finding greater depth and happiness in your relationships; greater respect, joy, and love for yourself and life; turning failure into success; and fulfillment in this hectic world. This audiobook can help you get there.?Self-confidence without self-reliance is as useless as a cooking recipe-without food. Self-confidence sees the possibilities of the individual; self-reliance realizes them. Self-confidence sees the angel in the unhewn block of marble; self-reliance carves it out for himself.??One who is self-reliant says ever: "No one can realize my possibilities for me, but me; no one can make me good or evil but myself." They work out their own salvation, financially, socially, mentally, physically, and morally. Life is an individual problem that must be solved by one self. Nature accepts no vicarious sacrifice, no vicarious service. Nature never recognizes a proxy vote. She has nothing to do with middle-men; she deals only with the individual. Nature is constantly seeking to show us that we are our own best friend, or our own worst enemy.?This audiobook is also available discounted as part of the ?7 Motivational Greats? audiobook combination pack. The pack includes this and 6 other audiobooks on CD for under $23.More information on the individual titles and complete Motivational and Transformational audiobook sets is available at www.InfoFount.com.

Majesty of God. 1 cass. (Music Machine Ser.). (J). 9.95 (AMOG) Brdgstn Multimed Grp.
In this special, Stevie & Nancy learn about the love of their Heavenly Father. Includes zippy tunes like "Here, There, Everywhere," & the beautiful "Some Invisible Things Are Real".

Majesty of God. Bridgestone Staff. 2004. audio compact disk 7.98 (978-1-56371-024-7(2)) Brdgstn Multimed Grp.

Majesty of God Cassette. Bridgestone Staff. 2004. 5.98 (978-1-56371-002-5(1)) Brdgstn Multimed Grp.

Majesty of God's Son see Magestad de Hijo de Dios, DS

Majesty of God's Son. 10 cass. 1999. 48.95 (978-1-57972-327-9(6)) Insight Living.

Majic Man. Max Allan Collins. Narrated by Jeff Woodman. 9 CDs. (Running Time: 10 hrs. 30 mins.). audio compact disk 89.00 (978-0-7887-4917-9(X)) Recorded Bks.

Majic Man. Max Allan Collins. Narrated by Jeff Woodman. 9 CDs. (Running Time: 10 hrs. 45 min.). 2000. audio compact disk 89.00 (C1298E7) Recorded Bks.
Detective Nathan Heller tackles one of postwar America's most controversial mysteries. When a case leads Heller to an alleged UFO crash site in Roswell, New Mexico, he finds himself on a twisted trail of conspiracy theories, top-secret agencies & an agenda of government disinformation.

Majic Man. unabr. ed. Max Allan Collins. Narrated by Jeff Woodman. 7 cass. (Running Time: 10 hrs. 30 mins.). 2000. 65.00 (978-0-7887-4417-4(8), 96109E7) Recorded Bks.

***Majipoor Chronicles.** unabr. ed. Robert Silverberg. Read by A. Full cast. (Running Time: 13 hrs. 30 mins.). 2011. 29.95 (978-1-4332-5076-7(4)); 79.95 (978-1-4332-5073-6(X)); audio compact disk 109.00 (978-1-4332-5074-3(8)) Blckstn Audio.

Major Alcoholic Beverages Wholesalers of the World. 6th rev. ed. BIA. (J). 2006. audio compact disk 289.00 (978-1-4187-5135-7(9)) Bus Info Agency.

Major Alcoholic Beverages Wholesalers of the World. 6th rev. ed. BIA. (J). 2006. audio compact disk 249.00 (978-1-4187-5134-0(0)) Bus Info Agency.

Major Amendment to the Divorce Code. John C. Howett. 1 cass. 1988. 20.00 PA Bar Inst.

Major Amendments to the Divorce Code. John C. Howett. 1 cass. (Running Time: 1 hr.). 1988. 20.00 PA Bar Inst.

Major & Minor Themes. 2 CDs. 2006. audio compact disk 17.00 (978-1-933207-12-4(4)) Ransomed Heart.

Major Andre. unabr. ed. Anthony Bailey. Narrated by Ron Keith. 5 cass. (Running Time: 6 hrs. 45 mins.). 44.00 (978-1-55690-329-8(4), 90097E7) Recorded Bks.
Recreates the time & manners of that crucial point of America's war of independence to recall to life America's most infamous traitor: General Benedict Arnold. Available to libraries only.

Major Automobile Dealers of the World. 6th rev. ed. BIA. (J). 2006. audio compact disk 289.00 (978-1-4187-5158-6(8)) Bus Info Agency.

Major Automobile Dealers of the World. 6th rev. ed. BIA. (J). 2006. audio compact disk 249.00 (978-1-4187-5157-9(X)) Bus Info Agency.

Major Bakery, Candy & Chocolate Manufacturers of the World. 6th rev. ed. BIA. (J). 2006. audio compact disk 289.00 (978-1-4187-5083-1(2)) Bus Info Agency.

Major Bakery, Candy & Chocolate Manufacturers of the World. 6th rev. ed. BIA. (J). 2006. audio compact disk 249.00 (978-1-4187-5082-4(4)) Bus Info Agency.

Major Banking, Financial, & Insurance Companies of Eastern Europe. 6th rev. ed. BIA. (J). 2006. audio compact disk 289.00 (978-1-4187-4601-8(0)) Bus Info Agency.

Major Banking, Financial, & Insurance Companies of Eastern Europe. 6th rev. ed. BIA. (J). 2006. audio compact disk 249.00 (978-1-4187-4600-1(2)) Bus Info Agency.

Major Barbara. George Bernard Shaw. Narrated by Flo Gibson. 3 CDs. (Running Time: 3 hrs. 35 mins.). Dramatization. 2006. audio compact disk Rental 19.95 (978-1-55685-878-9(7)) Audio Bk Con.

Major Barbara. unabr. ed. George Bernard Shaw. Read by Flo Gibson. 3 cass. (Running Time: 4 hrs.). 1993. 16.95 (978-1-55685-278-7(9)) Audio Bk Con.
Barbara, the granddaughter of an earl, is busy saving souls in the Salvation Army while her father, maintaining that poverty is the worst of crimes, runs a munitions factory.

Major Barbara. unabr. ed. George Bernard Shaw. Read by Kate Burton & Roger Rees. Adapted by Dakin Matthews. 2 CDs. (Running Time: 2 hrs.). 2008. audio compact disk 25.95 (978-1-58081-381-5(X)) L A Theatre.

Major Beverage Manufacturers of the World. 6th rev. ed. BIA. (J). 2006. audio compact disk 289.00 (978-1-4187-5081-7(6)) Bus Info Agency.

Major Beverage Manufacturers of the World. 6th rev. ed. BIA. (J). 2006. audio compact disk 249.00 (978-1-4187-5080-0(8)) Bus Info Agency.

Major Block to Realization. Swami Amar Jyoti. 1 cass. 1981. 9.95 (R-35) Truth Consciousness.
The "sleeping bag" of our personality. Giving it up to shoot like an arrow to the target, the solution for the New Age.

Major Building Materials Wholesalers of the World. 6th rev. ed. BIA. (J). 2006. audio compact disk 289.00 (978-1-4187-5160-9(X)) Bus Info Agency.

Major Building Materials Wholesalers of the World. 6th rev. ed. BIA. (J). 2006. audio compact disk 249.00 (978-1-4187-5159-3(6)) Bus Info Agency.

Major Candy & Chocolate Wholesalers of the World. 6th rev. ed. BIA. (J). 2006. audio compact disk 289.00 (978-1-4187-5137-1(5)) Bus Info Agency.

Major Candy & Chocolate Wholesalers of the World. 6th rev. ed. BIA. (J). 2006. audio compact disk 249.00 (978-1-4187-5136-4(7)) Bus Info Agency.

Major Chemical Manufacturers of the World. 6th rev. ed. BIA. (J). 2006. audio compact disk 289.00 (978-1-4187-5105-0(7)) Bus Info Agency.

Major Chemical Manufacturers of the World. 6th rev. ed. BIA. (J). 2006. audio compact disk 249.00 (978-1-4187-5104-3(9)) Bus Info Agency.

Major Chemical Wholesalers of the World. 6th rev. ed. BIA. (J). 2006. audio compact disk 289.00 (978-1-4187-5156-2(1)) Bus Info Agency.

Major Chemical Wholesalers of the World. 6th rev. ed. BIA. (J). 2006. audio compact disk 249.00 (978-1-4187-5155-5(3)) Bus Info Agency.

Major Communication Companies. 6th rev. ed. BIA. (J). 2006. audio compact disk 289.00 (978-1-4187-5127-2(8)) Bus Info Agency.

Major Communication Companies. 6th rev. ed. BIA. (J). 2006. audio compact disk 249.00 (978-1-4187-5126-5(X)) Bus Info Agency.

Major Companies of Argentina. 6th rev. ed. BIA. (J). 2006. audio compact disk 249.00 (978-1-4187-5164-7(2)) Bus Info Agency.

Major Companies of Argentina. 6th rev. ed. BIA. (J). 2006. audio compact disk 219.00 (978-1-4187-5163-0(4)) Bus Info Agency.

Major Companies of Asia. 6th rev. ed. BIA. (J). 2006. audio compact disk 289.00 (978-1-4187-4828-9(5)) Bus Info Agency.

Major Companies of Asia. 6th rev. ed. BIA. (J). 2006. audio compact disk 249.00 (978-1-4187-4827-2(7)) Bus Info Agency.

Major Companies of Austria. 6th rev. ed. BIA. (J). 2006. audio compact disk 289.00 (978-1-4187-4705-3(X)) Bus Info Agency.

Major Companies of Austria. 6th rev. ed. BIA. (J). 2006. audio compact disk 249.00 (978-1-4187-4704-6(1)) Bus Info Agency.

Major Companies of Belgium. 6th rev. ed. BIA. (J). 2006. audio compact disk 289.00 (978-1-4187-4719-0(X)) Bus Info Agency.

Major Companies of Belgium. 6th rev. ed. BIA. (J). 2006. audio compact disk 249.00 (978-1-4187-4718-3(1)) Bus Info Agency.

Major Companies of Brazil. 6th rev. ed. BIA. (J). 2006. audio compact disk 289.00 (978-1-4187-4603-2(7)) Bus Info Agency.

Major Companies of Brazil. 6th rev. ed. BIA. (J). 2006. audio compact disk 249.00 (978-1-4187-4602-5(9)) Bus Info Agency.

Major Companies of Bulgaria. 6th rev. ed. BIA. (J). 2006. audio compact disk 289.00 (978-1-4187-5272-9(X)) Bus Info Agency.

Major Companies of Bulgaria. 6th rev. ed. BIA. (J). 2006. audio compact disk 249.00 (978-1-4187-5271-2(1)) Bus Info Agency.

Major Companies of Canada. 6th rev. ed. BIA. (J). 2006. audio compact disk 289.00 (978-1-4187-5242-2(8)) Bus Info Agency.

Major Companies of Canada. 6th rev. ed. BIA. (J). 2006. audio compact disk 249.00 (978-1-4187-5241-5(X)) Bus Info Agency.

Major Companies of China. 6th rev. ed. BIA. (J). 2006. audio compact disk 289.00 (978-1-4187-4844-9(7)) Bus Info Agency.

Major Companies of China. 6th rev. ed. BIA. (J). 2006. audio compact disk 249.00 (978-1-4187-4843-2(9)) Bus Info Agency.

Major Companies of Croatia. 6th rev. ed. BIA. (J). 2006. audio compact disk 289.00 (978-1-4187-5270-5(3)) Bus Info Agency.

Major Companies of Croatia. 6th rev. ed. BIA. (J). 2006. audio compact disk 249.00 (978-1-4187-5269-9(X)) Bus Info Agency.

Major Companies of Denmark. 6th rev. ed. BIA. (J). 2006. audio compact disk 289.00 (978-1-4187-4733-6(5)) Bus Info Agency.

Major Companies of Denmark. 6th rev. ed. BIA. (J). 2006. audio compact disk 249.00 (978-1-4187-4732-9(7)) Bus Info Agency.

Major Companies of Estonia. 6th rev. ed. BIA. (J). 2006. audio compact disk 99.00 (978-1-4187-4614-8(2)) Bus Info Agency.

Major Companies of Estonia. 6th rev. ed. BIA. (J). 2006. audio compact disk 219.00 (978-1-4187-4613-1(4)) Bus Info Agency.

Major Companies of Finland. 6th rev. ed. BIA. (J). 2006. audio compact disk 259.00 (978-1-4187-5290-3(8)) Bus Info Agency.

Major Companies of Finland. 6th rev. ed. BIA. (J). 2006. audio compact disk 259.00 (978-1-4187-5289-7(4)) Bus Info Agency.

Major Companies of France. 6th rev. ed. BIA. (J). 2006. audio compact disk 289.00 (978-1-4187-4751-0(3)) Bus Info Agency.

Major Companies of France. 6th rev. ed. BIA. (J). 2006. audio compact disk 249.00 (978-1-4187-4750-3(5)) Bus Info Agency.

Major Companies of Germany. 6th rev. ed. BIA. (J). 2006. audio compact disk 289.00 (978-1-4187-4767-1(X)) Bus Info Agency.

Major Companies of Germany. 6th rev. ed. BIA. (J). 2006. audio compact disk 249.00 (978-1-4187-4766-4(1)) Bus Info Agency.

Major Companies of Greece. 6th rev. ed. BIA. (J). 2006. audio compact disk 289.00 (978-1-4187-4782-4(3)) Bus Info Agency.

Major Companies of Greece. 6th rev. ed. BIA. (J). 2006. audio compact disk 249.00 (978-1-4187-4781-7(5)) Bus Info Agency.

Major Companies of Hong Kong. 6th rev. ed. BIA. (J). 2006. audio compact disk 289.00 (978-1-4187-4850-0(1)) Bus Info Agency.

Major Companies of Hong Kong. 6th rev. ed. BIA. (J). 2006. audio compact disk 249.00 (978-1-4187-4849-4(8)) Bus Info Agency.

Major Companies of Hungary. 6th rev. ed. BIA. (J). 2006. audio compact disk 289.00 (978-1-4187-5274-3(6)) Bus Info Agency.

Major Companies of Hungary. 6th rev. ed. BIA. (J). 2006. audio compact disk 249.00 (978-1-4187-5273-6(8)) Bus Info Agency.

Major Companies of India. 6th rev. ed. BIA. (J). 2006. audio compact disk 289.00 (978-1-4187-4852-4(8)) Bus Info Agency.

Major Companies of India. 6th rev. ed. BIA. (J). 2006. audio compact disk 249.00 (978-1-4187-4851-7(X)) Bus Info Agency.

Major Companies of Ireland. 6th rev. ed. BIA. (J). 2006. audio compact disk 289.00 (978-1-4187-4785-5(8)) Bus Info Agency.

Major Companies of Ireland. 6th rev. ed. BIA. (J). 2006. audio compact disk 249.00 (978-1-4187-4784-8(X)) Bus Info Agency.

Major Companies of Israel. 6th rev. ed. BIA. (J). 2006. audio compact disk 289.00 (978-1-4187-4870-8(6)) Bus Info Agency.

Major Companies of Israel. 6th rev. ed. BIA. (J). 2006. audio compact disk 249.00 (978-1-4187-4869-2(2)) Bus Info Agency.

Major Companies of Italy. 6th rev. ed. BIA. (J). 2006. audio compact disk 289.00 (978-1-4187-4788-6(2)) Bus Info Agency.

Major Companies of Italy. 6th rev. ed. BIA. (J). 2006. audio compact disk 249.00 (978-1-4187-4787-9(4)) Bus Info Agency.

Major Companies of Japan. 6th rev. ed. BIA. (J). 2006. audio compact disk 289.00 (978-1-4187-4854-8(4)) Bus Info Agency.

Major Companies of Japan. 6th rev. ed. BIA. (J). 2006. audio compact disk 249.00 (978-1-4187-4853-1(6)) Bus Info Agency.

Major Companies of Latvia. 6th rev. ed. BIA. (J). 2006. audio compact disk 289.00 (978-1-4187-4624-7(X)) Bus Info Agency.

Major Companies of Latvia. 6th rev. ed. BIA. (J). 2006. audio compact disk 249.00 (978-1-4187-4623-0(1)) Bus Info Agency.

Major Companies of Liechtenstein. 6th rev. ed. BIA. (J). 2006. audio compact disk 249.00 (978-1-4187-5169-2(3)) Bus Info Agency.

Major Companies of Liechtenstein. 6th rev. ed. BIA. (J). 2006. audio compact disk 219.00 (978-1-4187-5168-5(5)) Bus Info Agency.

Major Companies of Lithuania. 6th rev. ed. BIA. (J). 2006. audio compact disk 249.00 (978-1-4187-4626-1(6)) Bus Info Agency.

Major Companies of Lithuania. 6th rev. ed. BIA. (J). 2006. audio compact disk 219.00 (978-1-4187-4625-4(8)) Bus Info Agency.

Major Companies of Luxembourg. 6th rev. ed. BIA. (J). 2006. audio compact disk 289.00 (978-1-4187-4806-7(4)) Bus Info Agency.

Major Companies of Luxembourg. 6th rev. ed. BIA. (J). 2006. audio compact disk 249.00 (978-1-4187-4805-0(6)) Bus Info Agency.

Major Companies of Mexico. 6th rev. ed. BIA. (J). 2006. audio compact disk 249.00 (978-1-4187-5171-5(5)) Bus Info Agency.

Major Companies of Mexico. 6th rev. ed. BIA. (J). 2006. audio compact disk 219.00 (978-1-4187-5170-8(7)) Bus Info Agency.

Major Companies of Moscow, Volume 1. 6th rev. ed. BIA. (J). 2006. audio compact disk 289.00 (978-1-4187-5184-5(7)) Bus Info Agency.

Major Companies of Moscow, Volume 1. 6th rev. ed. BIA. (J). 2006. audio compact disk 249.00 (978-1-4187-5183-8(9)) Bus Info Agency.

Major Companies of Moscow, Volume 2. 6th rev. ed. BIA. (J). 2006. audio compact disk 289.00 (978-1-4187-5189-0(8)) Bus Info Agency.

Major Companies of Moscow, Volume 2. 6th rev. ed. BIA. (J). 2006. audio compact disk 249.00 (978-1-4187-5188-3(X)) Bus Info Agency.

Major Companies of Norway. 6th rev. ed. BIA. (J). 2006. audio compact disk 289.00 (978-1-4187-5293-4(2)) Bus Info Agency.

Major Companies of Norway. 6th rev. ed. BIA. (J). 2006. audio compact disk 249.00 (978-1-4187-5292-7(4)) Bus Info Agency.

Major Companies of Poland. 6th rev. ed. BIA. (J). 2006. audio compact disk 289.00 (978-1-4187-5278-1(9)) Bus Info Agency.

Major Companies of Poland. 6th rev. ed. BIA. (J). 2006. audio compact disk 249.00 (978-1-4187-5277-4(0)) Bus Info Agency.

Major Companies of Portugal. 6th rev. ed. BIA. (J). 2006. audio compact disk 289.00 (978-1-4187-4944-6(3)) Bus Info Agency.

Major Companies of Portugal. 6th rev. ed. BIA. (J). 2006. audio compact disk 249.00 (978-1-4187-4943-9(5)) Bus Info Agency.

Major Companies of Romania. 6th rev. ed. BIA. (J). 2006. audio compact disk 249.00 (978-1-4187-4616-2(9)) Bus Info Agency.

Major Companies of Romania. 6th rev. ed. BIA. (J). 2006. audio compact disk 219.00 (978-1-4187-4615-5(0)) Bus Info Agency.

Major Companies of Serbia & Montenegro. 6th rev. ed. BIA. (J). 2006. audio compact disk 289.00 (978-1-4187-5280-4(0)) Bus Info Agency.

Major Companies of Serbia & Montenegro. 6th rev. ed. BIA. (J). 2006. audio compact disk 249.00 (978-1-4187-5279-8(7)) Bus Info Agency.

Major Companies of Singapore. 6th rev. ed. BIA. (J). 2006. audio compact disk 289.00 (978-1-4187-5276-7(2)) Bus Info Agency.

Major Companies of Singapore. 6th rev. ed. BIA. (J). 2006. audio compact disk 249.00 (978-1-4187-5275-0(4)) Bus Info Agency.

Major Companies of Slovakia. 6th rev. ed. BIA. (J). 2006. audio compact disk 289.00 (978-1-4187-5282-8(7)) Bus Info Agency.

Major Companies of Slovakia. 6th rev. ed. BIA. (J). 2006. audio compact disk 249.00 (978-1-4187-5281-1(9)) Bus Info Agency.

Major Companies of Slovenia. 6th rev. ed. BIA. (J). 2006. audio compact disk 289.00 (978-1-4187-5284-2(3)) Bus Info Agency.

Major Companies of Slovenia. 6th rev. ed. BIA. (J). 2006. audio compact disk 249.00 (978-1-4187-5283-5(5)) Bus Info Agency.

Major Companies of South America. 6th rev. ed. BIA. (J). 2006. audio compact disk 289.00 (978-1-4187-5288-0(6)) Bus Info Agency.

Major Companies of South America. 6th rev. ed. BIA. (J). 2006. audio compact disk 249.00 (978-1-4187-5287-3(8)) Bus Info Agency.

Major Companies of South Korea. 6th rev. ed. BIA. (J). 2006. audio compact disk 289.00 (978-1-4187-4858-6(7)) Bus Info Agency.

Major Companies of South Korea. 6th rev. ed. BIA. (J). 2006. audio compact disk 249.00 (978-1-4187-4857-9(9)) Bus Info Agency.

Major Companies of Spain. 6th rev. ed. BIA. (J). 2006. audio compact disk 289.00 (978-1-4187-4926-2(5)) Bus Info Agency.

Major Companies of Spain. 6th rev. ed. BIA. (J). 2006. audio compact disk 249.00 (978-1-4187-4925-5(7)) Bus Info Agency.

Major Companies of Sweden. 6th rev. ed. BIA. (J). 2006. audio compact disk 289.00 (978-1-4187-4915-6(X)) Bus Info Agency.

Major Companies of Sweden. 6th rev. ed. BIA. (J). 2006. audio compact disk 249.00 (978-1-4187-4914-9(1)) Bus Info Agency.

Major Companies of Switzerland. 6th rev. ed. BIA. (J). 2006. audio compact disk 289.00 (978-1-4187-4900-2(1)) Bus Info Agency.

Major Companies of Switzerland. 6th rev. ed. BIA. (J). 2006. audio compact disk 249.00 (978-1-4187-4899-9(4)) Bus Info Agency.

Major Companies of Thailand. 6th rev. ed. BIA. (J). 2006. audio compact disk 249.00 (978-1-4187-5173-9(1)) Bus Info Agency.

Major Companies of Thailand. 6th rev. ed. BIA. (J). 2006. audio compact disk 219.00 (978-1-4187-5172-2(3)) Bus Info Agency.

Major Companies of the Central Federal District of Russia. 6th rev. ed. BIA. (J). 2006. audio compact disk 289.00 (978-1-4187-4971-2(0)) Bus Info Agency.

Major Companies of the Central Federal District of Russia. 6th rev. ed. BIA. (J). 2006. audio compact disk 249.00 (978-1-4187-4970-5(2)) Bus Info Agency.

Major Companies of the Czech Republic. 6th rev. ed. BIA. (J). 2006. audio compact disk 289.00 (978-1-4187-4612-4(6)) Bus Info Agency.

Major Companies of the Czech Republic. 6th rev. ed. BIA. (J). 2006. audio compact disk 249.00 (978-1-4187-4611-7(8)) Bus Info Agency.

Major Companies of the Far Eastern Federal District of Russia. 6th rev. ed. BIA. (J). 2006. audio compact disk 289.00 (978-1-4187-4969-9(9)) Bus Info Agency.

Major Companies of the Far Eastern Federal District of Russia. 6th rev. ed. BIA. (J). 2006. audio compact disk 249.00 (978-1-4187-4968-2(0)) Bus Info Agency.

Major Companies of the Netherlands. 6th rev. ed. BIA. (J). 2006. audio compact disk 289.00 (978-1-4187-4810-4(2)) Bus Info Agency.

Major Companies of the Netherlands. 6th rev. ed. BIA. (J). 2006. audio compact disk 249.00 (978-1-4187-4809-8(9)) Bus Info Agency.

Major Companies of the Northwestern Federal District of Russia. 6th rev. ed. BIA. (J). 2006. audio compact disk 289.00 (978-1-4187-4973-6(7)) Bus Info Agency.

Major Companies of the Northwestern Federal District of Russia. 6th rev. ed. BIA. (J). 2006. audio compact disk 249.00 (978-1-4187-4972-9(9)) Bus Info Agency.

Major Companies of the Siberian Federal District of Russia. 6th rev. ed. BIA. (J). 2006. audio compact disk 289.00 (978-1-4187-4961-3(3)) Bus Info Agency.

Major Companies of the Siberian Federal District of Russia. 6th rev. ed. BIA. (J). 2006. audio compact disk 249.00 (978-1-4187-4960-6(5)) Bus Info Agency.

Major Companies of the Southern Federal District of Russia. 6th rev. ed. BIA. (J). 2006. audio compact disk 289.00 (978-1-4187-4963-7(X)) Bus Info Agency.

Major Companies of the Southern Federal District of Russia. 6th rev. ed. BIA. (J). 2006. audio compact disk 249.00 (978-1-4187-4962-0(1)) Bus Info Agency.

Major Companies of the United Kingdom. 6th rev. ed. BIA. (J). 2006. audio compact disk 289.00 (978-1-4187-4879-1(X)) Bus Info Agency.

Major Companies of the United Kingdom. 6th rev. ed. BIA. (J). 2006. audio compact disk 249.00 (978-1-4187-4878-4(1)) Bus Info Agency.

Major Companies of the Urals Federal District of Russia. 6th rev. ed. BIA. (J). 2006. audio compact disk 289.00 (978-1-4187-4965-1(6)) Bus Info Agency.

Major Companies of the Urals Federal District of Russia. 6th rev. ed. BIA. (J). 2006. audio compact disk 249.00 (978-1-4187-4964-4(8)) Bus Info Agency.

Major Companies of the USA. 6th rev. ed. BIA. (J). 2006. audio compact disk 289.00 (978-1-4187-5268-2(1)) Bus Info Agency.

Major Companies of the USA. 6th rev. ed. BIA. (J). 2006. audio compact disk 249.00 (978-1-4187-5267-5(3)) Bus Info Agency.

Major Companies of the Volga Federal District of Russia. 6th rev. ed. BIA. (J). 2006. audio compact disk 289.00 (978-1-4187-4967-5(2)) Bus Info Agency.

Major Companies of the Volga Federal District of Russia. 6th rev. ed. BIA. (J). 2006. audio compact disk 249.00 (978-1-4187-4966-8(4)) Bus Info Agency.

Major Companies of the World. 6th rev. ed. BIA. (J). 2006. audio compact disk 289.00 (978-1-4187-5073-2(5)) Bus Info Agency.

Major Companies of the World. 6th rev. ed. BIA. (J). 2006. audio compact disk 249.00 (978-1-4187-5072-5(7)) Bus Info Agency.

Major Companies of Turkey. 6th rev. ed. BIA. (J). 2006. audio compact disk 289.00 (978-1-4187-4866-1(8)) Bus Info Agency.

Major Companies of Turkey. 6th rev. ed. BIA. (J). 2006. audio compact disk 219.00 (978-1-4187-4865-4(X)) Bus Info Agency.

Major Companies of Venezuela. 6th rev. ed. BIA. (J). 2006. audio compact disk 249.00 (978-1-4187-5175-3(8)) Bus Info Agency.

Major Companies of Venezuela. 6th rev. ed. BIA. (J). 2006. audio compact disk 219.00 (978-1-4187-5174-6(X)) Bus Info Agency.

Major Companies of Western Europe. 6th rev. ed. BIA. (J). 2006. audio compact disk 289.00 (978-1-4187-4635-3(5)) Bus Info Agency.

Major Companies of Western Europe. 6th rev. ed. BIA. (J). 2006. audio compact disk 249.00 (978-1-4187-4634-6(7)) Bus Info Agency.

Major Concrete Manufacturers. 6th rev. ed. BIA. (J). 2006. audio compact disk 289.00 (978-1-4187-5111-1(1)) Bus Info Agency.

Major Concrete Manufacturers. 6th rev. ed. BIA. (J). 2006. audio compact disk 249.00 (978-1-4187-5110-4(3)) Bus Info Agency.

Major Construction Companies of Eastern Europe. 6th rev. ed. BIA. (J). 2006. audio compact disk 289.00 (978-1-4187-4594-3(4)) Bus Info Agency.

Major Construction Companies of Eastern Europe. 6th rev. ed. BIA. (J). 2006. audio compact disk 249.00 (978-1-4187-4593-6(6)) Bus Info Agency.

Major Construction Companies of France. 6th rev. ed. BIA. (J). 2006. audio compact disk 289.00 (978-1-4187-4757-2(2)) Bus Info Agency.

Major Construction Companies of France. 6th rev. ed. BIA. (J). 2006. audio compact disk 249.00 (978-1-4187-4756-5(4)) Bus Info Agency.

Major Construction Companies of Germany. 6th rev. ed. BIA. (J). 2006. audio compact disk 289.00 (978-1-4187-4773-2(4)) Bus Info Agency.

Major Construction Companies of Germany. 6th rev. ed. BIA. (J). 2006. audio compact disk 249.00 (978-1-4187-4772-5(6)) Bus Info Agency.

Major Cycle Charts. Theresa Gurlacz. 1 cass. 8.95 (744) Am Fed Astrologers.

Major Dairy Manufacturers of the World. 6th rev. ed. BIA. (J). 2006. audio compact disk 289.00 (978-1-4187-5079-4(4)) Bus Info Agency.

Major Dairy Manufacturers of the World. 6th rev. ed. BIA. (J). 2006. audio compact disk 249.00 (978-1-4187-5078-7(6)) Bus Info Agency.

Major Dairy Wholesalers of the World. 6th rev. ed. BIA. (J). 2006. audio compact disk 289.00 (978-1-4187-5133-3(2)) Bus Info Agency.

Major Dairy Wholesalers of the World. 6th rev. ed. BIA. (J). 2006. audio compact disk 249.00 (978-1-4187-5132-6(4)) Bus Info Agency.

Major Depression & Its Treatment. unabr. ed. Mercedes Leidlich. Read by Mercedes Leidlich. 1 cass. (Running Time: 1 hr.). 1992. 10.95 in Norelco box. (978-1-882174-03-4(8), MLL-004) UFD Pub.
Major depression is epidemic in North America. Many people suffer from this very treatable mood disorder without knowing what is wrong with them. This tape teaches the listener about the off-kilter brain neurotransmission present in depression, the treatments available, & a message of hope for recovery. Side B is a deep relaxation exercise set to soothing harp sound.

Major Dog & Pet Food Manufacturers of the World. 6th rev. ed. BIA. (J). 2006. audio compact disk 289.00 (978-1-4187-5087-9(5)) Bus Info Agency.

Major Dog & Pet Food Manufacturers of the World. 6th rev. ed. BIA. (J). 2006. audio compact disk 249.00 (978-1-4187-5086-2(7)) Bus Info Agency.

Major Drug & Medicine Wholesalers of the World. 6th rev. ed. BIA. (J). 2006. audio compact disk 289.00 (978-1-4187-5154-8(5)) Bus Info Agency.

Major Drug & Medicine Wholesalers of the World. 6th rev. ed. BIA. (J). 2006. audio compact disk 249.00 (978-1-4187-5153-1(7)) Bus Info Agency.

Major Electronic & Electrical Equipment Manufacturers of Asia. 6th rev. ed. BIA. (J). 2006. audio compact disk 289.00 (978-1-4187-4836-4(6)) Bus Info Agency.

Major Electronic & Electrical Equipment Manufacturers of Asia. 6th rev. ed. BIA. (J). 2006. audio compact disk 249.00 (978-1-4187-4835-7(8)) Bus Info Agency.

Major Electronic & Electrical Equipment Wholesalers of the World. 6th rev. ed. BIA. (J). 2006. audio compact disk 289.00 (978-1-4187-5162-3(6)) Bus Info Agency.

Major Electronic & Electrical Equipment Wholesalers of the World. 6th rev. ed. BIA. (J). 2006. audio compact disk 249.00 (978-1-4187-5161-6(8)) Bus Info Agency.

Major Electronic & Electrical Manufacturers of the World. 6th rev. ed. BIA. (J). 2006. audio compact disk 289.00 (978-1-4187-5119-7(7)) Bus Info Agency.

Major Electronic & Electrical Manufacturers of the World. 6th rev. ed. BIA. (J). 2006. audio compact disk 249.00 (978-1-4187-5118-0(9)) Bus Info Agency.

Major Fabricated Metal Companies of the World. 6th rev. ed. BIA. (J). 2006. audio compact disk 289.00 (978-1-4187-5115-9(4)) Bus Info Agency.

Major Fabricated Metal Companies of the World. 6th rev. ed. BIA. (J). 2006. audio compact disk 249.00 (978-1-4187-5114-2(6)) Bus Info Agency.

Major Farm Products Wholesalers of the World. 6th rev. ed. BIA. (J). 2006. audio compact disk 289.00 (978-1-4187-5152-4(9)) Bus Info Agency.

Major Farm Products Wholesalers of the World. 6th rev. ed. BIA. (J). 2006. audio compact disk 249.00 (978-1-4187-5151-7(0)) Bus Info Agency.

Major Farms of Eastern Europe. 6th rev. ed. BIA. (J). 2006. audio compact disk 289.00 (978-1-4187-4590-5(1)) Bus Info Agency.

Major Farms of Eastern Europe. 6th rev. ed. BIA. (J). 2006. audio compact disk 249.00 (978-1-4187-4589-9(8)) Bus Info Agency.

Major Fish & Seafood Manufacturers of the World. 6th rev. ed. BIA. (J). 2006. audio compact disk 289.00 (978-1-4187-5077-0(8)) Bus Info Agency.

Major Fish & Seafood Manufacturers of the World. 6th rev. ed. BIA. (J). 2006. audio compact disk 249.00 (978-1-4187-5076-3(X)) Bus Info Agency.

Major Fish & Seafood Wholesalers of the World. 6th rev. ed. BIA. (J). 2006. audio compact disk 289.00 (978-1-4187-5131-9(6)) Bus Info Agency.

Major Fish & Seafood Wholesalers of the World. 6th rev. ed. BIA. (J). 2006. audio compact disk 249.00 (978-1-4187-5130-2(8)) Bus Info Agency.

Major Footwear Wholesalers of the World. 6th rev. ed. BIA. (J). 2006. audio compact disk 289.00 (978-1-4187-5146-3(4)) Bus Info Agency.

Major Footwear Wholesalers of the World. 6th rev. ed. BIA. (J). 2006. audio compact disk 249.00 (978-1-4187-5145-6(6)) Bus Info Agency.

Major Fruit & Vegetable Product Manufacturers of the World. 6th rev. ed. BIA. (J). 2006. audio compact disk 289.00 (978-1-4187-5085-5(9)) Bus Info Agency.

Major Fruit & Vegetable Product Manufacturers of the World. 6th rev. ed. BIA. (J). 2006. audio compact disk 249.00 (978-1-4187-5084-8(0)) Bus Info Agency.

Major Fruits & Vegetables Wholesalers of the World. 6th rev. ed. BIA. (J). 2006. audio compact disk 289.00 (978-1-4187-5139-5(1)) Bus Info Agency.

Major Fruits & Vegetables Wholesalers of the World. 6th rev. ed. BIA. (J). 2006. audio compact disk 249.00 (978-1-4187-5138-8(3)) Bus Info Agency.

Major Furniture & Fixtures Manufacturers. 6th rev. ed. BIA. (J). 2006. audio compact disk 289.00 (978-1-4187-5099-2(9)) Bus Info Agency.

Major Furniture & Fixtures Manufacturers. 6th rev. ed. BIA. (J). 2006. audio compact disk 249.00 (978-1-4187-5098-5(0)) Bus Info Agency.

Major Furniture & Fixtures Wholesalers of the World. 6th rev. ed. BIA. (J). 2006. audio compact disk 289.00 (978-1-4187-5150-0(2)) Bus Info Agency.

Major Furniture & Fixtures Wholesalers of the World. 6th rev. ed. BIA. (J). 2006. audio compact disk 249.00 (978-1-4187-5149-4(9)) Bus Info Agency.

Major Health Care Offices & Clinics of Russia. 6th rev. ed. BIA. (J). 2006. audio compact disk 289.00 (978-1-4187-5179-1(0)) Bus Info Agency.

Major Health Care Offices & Clinics of Russia. 6th rev. ed. BIA. (J). 2006. audio compact disk 249.00 (978-1-4187-5178-4(2)) Bus Info Agency.

Major Industrial Machinery & Computer Manufacturers of the World. 6th rev. ed. BIA. (J). 2006. audio compact disk 289.00 (978-1-4187-5117-3(0)) Bus Info Agency.

Major Industrial Machinery & Computer Manufacturers of the World. 6th rev. ed. BIA. (J). 2006. audio compact disk 249.00 (978-1-4187-5116-6(2)) Bus Info Agency.

Major Leather Manufacturers of the World. 6th rev. ed. BIA. (J). 2006. audio compact disk 289.00 (978-1-4187-5109-8(X)) Bus Info Agency.

Major Leather Manufacturers of the World. 6th rev. ed. BIA. (J). 2006. audio compact disk 249.00 (978-1-4187-5108-1(1)) Bus Info Agency.

Major Lumber & Wood Manufacturers. 6th rev. ed. BIA. (J). 2006. audio compact disk 289.00 (978-1-4187-5097-8(2)) Bus Info Agency.

Major Lumber & Wood Manufacturers. 6th rev. ed. BIA. (J). 2006. audio compact disk 249.00 (978-1-4187-5096-1(4)) Bus Info Agency.

Major Lumber & Wood Wholesalers of the World. 6th rev. ed. BIA. (J). 2006. audio compact disk 289.00 (978-1-4187-5148-7(0)) Bus Info Agency.

Major Lumber & Wood Wholesalers of the World. 6th rev. ed. BIA. (J). 2006. audio compact disk 249.00 (978-1-4187-5147-0(2)) Bus Info Agency.

Major Manufacturers of Asia. 6th rev. ed. BIA. (J). 2006. audio compact disk 289.00 (978-1-4187-4830-2(7)) Bus Info Agency.

Major Manufacturers of Asia. 6th rev. ed. BIA. (J). 2006. audio compact disk 249.00 (978-1-4187-4829-6(3)) Bus Info Agency.

Major Manufacturers of Azerbaijan, Armenia, & Georgia. 6th rev. ed. BIA. (J). 2006. audio compact disk 249.00 (978-1-4187-4842-5(0)) Bus Info Agency.

Major Manufacturers of Azerbaijan, Armenia, & Georgia. 6th rev. ed. BIA. (J). 2006. audio compact disk 219.00 (978-1-4187-4841-8(2)) Bus Info Agency.

Major Manufacturers of Kazakhstan. 6th rev. ed. BIA. (J). 2006. audio compact disk 289.00 (978-1-4187-4856-2(0)) Bus Info Agency.

Major Manufacturers of Kazakhstan. 6th rev. ed. BIA. (J). 2006. audio compact disk 249.00 (978-1-4187-4855-5(2)) Bus Info Agency.

Major Manufacturers of Measuring, Analyzing, & Controlling Instrument of the World. 6th rev. ed. BIA. (J). 2006. audio compact disk 289.00 (978-1-4187-5123-4(5)) Bus Info Agency.

Major Manufacturers of Measuring, Analyzing, & Controlling Instrument of the World. 6th rev. ed. BIA. (J). 2006. audio compact disk 249.00 (978-1-4187-5122-7(7)) Bus Info Agency.

Major Meat Manufacturers of the World. 6th rev. ed. BIA. (J). 2006. audio compact disk 289.00 (978-1-4187-5075-6(1)) Bus Info Agency.

Major Meat Manufacturers of the World. 6th rev. ed. BIA. (J). 2006. audio compact disk 249.00 (978-1-4187-5074-9(3)) Bus Info Agency.

Major Meat Product Wholesalers of the World. 6th rev. ed. BIA. (J). 2006. audio compact disk 289.00 (978-1-4187-5129-6(4)) Bus Info Agency.

Major Meat Product Wholesalers of the World. 6th rev. ed. BIA. (J). 2006. audio compact disk 249.00 (978-1-4187-5128-9(6)) Bus Info Agency.

Major Men's & Boys' Clothing Manufacturers of the World. 6th rev. ed. BIA. (J). 2006. audio compact disk 289.00 (978-1-4187-5089-3(1)) Bus Info Agency.

Major Men's & Boys' Clothing Manufacturers of the World. 6th rev. ed. BIA. (J). 2006. audio compact disk 249.00 (978-1-4187-5088-6(3)) Bus Info Agency.

Major Men's & Boy's Clothing Wholesalers of the World. 6th rev. ed. BIA. (J). 2006. audio compact disk 289.00 (978-1-4187-5142-5(1)) Bus Info Agency.

Major Men's & Boy's Clothing Wholesalers of the World. 6th rev. ed. BIA. (J). 2006. audio compact disk 249.00 (978-1-4187-5141-8(3)) Bus Info Agency.

Major Men's & Women's Footwear Manufacturers of the World. 6th rev. ed. BIA. (J). 2006. audio compact disk 289.00 (978-1-4187-5093-0(X)) Bus Info Agency.

Major Men's & Women's Footwear Manufacturers of the World. 6th rev. ed. BIA. (J). 2006. audio compact disk 249.00 (978-1-4187-5092-3(1)) Bus Info Agency.

Major Metallurgical Companies of the World. 6th rev. ed. BIA. (J). 2006. audio compact disk 289.00 (978-1-4187-5113-5(8)) Bus Info Agency.

Major Metallurgical Companies of the World. 6th rev. ed. BIA. (J). 2006. audio compact disk 249.00 (978-1-4187-5112-8(X)) Bus Info Agency.

Major Mining Companies of Eastern Europe: Oil, Gas, Ores, & Coal. 6th rev. ed. BIA. (J). 2006. audio compact disk 289.00 (978-1-4187-4592-9(8)) Bus Info Agency.

Major Mining Companies of Eastern Europe: Oil, Gas, Ores, & Coal. 6th rev. ed. BIA. (J). 2006. audio compact disk 249.00 (978-1-4187-4591-2(X)) Bus Info Agency.

Major Mining Companies of the World. 6th rev. ed. BIA. (J). 2006. audio compact disk 289.00 (978-1-4187-5125-8(1)) Bus Info Agency.

Major Mining Companies of the World. 6th rev. ed. BIA. (J). 2006. audio compact disk 249.00 (978-1-4187-5124-1(3)) Bus Info Agency.

Major Paper Manufacturers of the World. 6th rev. ed. BIA. (J). 2006. audio compact disk 289.00 (978-1-4187-5101-2(4)) Bus Info Agency.

Major Paper Manufacturers of the World. 6th rev. ed. BIA. (J). 2006. audio compact disk 249.00 (978-1-4187-5100-5(6)) Bus Info Agency.

***Major Pettigrew's Last Stand.** unabr. ed. Helen Simonson. Read by Peter Altschuler. 11 CDs. 2010. audio compact disk 100.00 (978-0-307-71286-8(9), BksonTape) Pub: Random Audio Pubg. Dist(s): Random

Major Pettigrew's Last Stand. unabr. ed. Helen Simonson. Read by Peter Altschuler. (ENG.). 2010. audio compact disk 40.00 (978-0-307-71284-4(2), Random AudioBks) Pub: Random Audio Pubg. Dist(s): Random

Major Presidential Speeches 1933-1998. unabr. ed. Read by Original Recorded Speeches. (YA). 2006. 54.99 (978-1-59895-350-3(8)) Find a World.

Major Printing & Publishing Companies of the World. 6th rev. ed. BIA. (J). 2006. audio compact disk 289.00 (978-1-4187-5103-6(0)) Bus Info Agency.

Major Printing & Publishing Companies of the World. 6th rev. ed. BIA. (J). 2006. audio compact disk 249.00 (978-1-4187-5102-9(2)) Bus Info Agency.

Major Rubber & Plastic Manufacturers of the World. 6th rev. ed. BIA. (J). 2006. audio compact disk 289.00 (978-1-4187-5107-4(3)) Bus Info Agency.

Major Rubber & Plastic Manufacturers of the World. 6th rev. ed. BIA. (J). 2006. audio compact disk 249.00 (978-1-4187-5106-7(5)) Bus Info Agency.

Major Textile Manufacturers of the World. 6th rev. ed. BIA. (J). 2006. audio compact disk 289.00 (978-1-4187-5095-4(6)) Bus Info Agency.

Major Textile Manufacturers of the World. 6th rev. ed. BIA. (J). 2006. audio compact disk 249.00 (978-1-4187-5094-7(8)) Bus Info Agency.

Major Transportation Companies of Eastern Europe. 6th rev. ed. BIA. (J). 2006. audio compact disk 289.00 (978-1-4187-4596-7(0)) Bus Info Agency.

Major Transportation Companies of Eastern Europe. 6th rev. ed. BIA. (J). 2006. audio compact disk 249.00 (978-1-4187-4595-0(2)) Bus Info Agency.

Major Transportation Equipment Manufacturers of the World. 6th rev. ed. BIA. (J). 2006. audio compact disk 289.00 (978-1-4187-5121-0(9)) Bus Info Agency.

Major Transportation Equipment Manufacturers of the World. 6th rev. ed. BIA. (J). 2006. audio compact disk 249.00 (978-1-4187-5120-3(0)) Bus Info Agency.

Major Trends Today & How a Christian Should View Them. unabr. ed. R. J. Rushdoony. 1 cass. (Running Time: 1 hr. 21 min.). 12.95 (711) J Norton Pubs.

Major Wholesalers & Retailers in Asia. 6th rev. ed. BIA. (J). 2006. audio compact disk 289.00 (978-1-4187-4838-8(2)) Bus Info Agency.

Major Wholesalers & Retailers in Asia. 6th rev. ed. BIA. (J). 2006. audio compact disk 249.00 (978-1-4187-4837-1(4)) Bus Info Agency.

Major Wholesalers & Retailers in Austria. 6th rev. ed. BIA. (J). 2006. audio compact disk 289.00 (978-1-4187-4714-5(9)) Bus Info Agency.

Major Wholesalers & Retailers in Austria. 6th rev. ed. BIA. (J). 2006. audio compact disk 249.00 (978-1-4187-4713-8(0)) Bus Info Agency.

Major Wholesalers & Retailers in Belgium. 6th rev. ed. BIA. (J). 2006. audio compact disk 289.00 (978-1-4187-4728-2(9)) Bus Info Agency.

Major Wholesalers & Retailers in Belgium. 6th rev. ed. BIA. (J). 2006. audio compact disk 249.00 (978-1-4187-4727-5(0)) Bus Info Agency.

Major Wholesalers & Retailers in Denmark. 6th rev. ed. BIA. (J). 2006. audio compact disk 289.00 (978-1-4187-4744-2(0)) Bus Info Agency.

Major Wholesalers & Retailers in Denmark. 6th rev. ed. BIA. (J). 2006. audio compact disk 249.00 (978-1-4187-4743-5(2)) Bus Info Agency.

Major Wholesalers & Retailers in France. 6th rev. ed. BIA. (J). 2006. audio compact disk 289.00 (978-1-4187-4762-6(9)) Bus Info Agency.

Major Wholesalers & Retailers in France. 6th rev. ed. BIA. (J). 2006. audio compact disk 249.00 (978-1-4187-4761-9(0)) Bus Info Agency.

Major Wholesalers & Retailers in Germany. 6th rev. ed. BIA. (J). 2006. audio compact disk 289.00 (978-1-4187-4778-7(5)) Bus Info Agency.

Major Wholesalers & Retailers in Germany. 6th rev. ed. BIA. (J). 2006. audio compact disk 249.00 (978-1-4187-4777-0(7)) Bus Info Agency.

Major Wholesalers & Retailers in Israel. 6th rev. ed. BIA. (J). 2006. audio compact disk 289.00 (978-1-4187-4875-3(7)) Bus Info Agency.

Major Wholesalers & Retailers in Israel. 6th rev. ed. BIA. (J). 2006. audio compact disk 249.00 (978-1-4187-4874-6(9)) Bus Info Agency.

Major Wholesalers & Retailers in Italy. 6th rev. ed. BIA. (J). 2006. audio compact disk 289.00 (978-1-4187-4801-2(3)) Bus Info Agency.

Major Wholesalers & Retailers in Italy. 6th rev. ed. BIA. (J). 2006. audio compact disk 249.00 (978-1-4187-4800-5(5)) Bus Info Agency.

Major Wholesalers & Retailers in Portugal. 6th rev. ed. BIA. (J). 2006. audio compact disk 289.00 (978-1-4187-4955-2(9)) Bus Info Agency.

Major Wholesalers & Retailers in Portugal. 6th rev. ed. BIA. (J). 2006. audio compact disk 249.00 (978-1-4187-4954-5(0)) Bus Info Agency.

Major Wholesalers & Retailers in Sweden. 6th rev. ed. BIA. (J). 2006. audio compact disk 289.00 (978-1-4187-4922-4(2)) Bus Info Agency.

Major Wholesalers & Retailers in Sweden. 6th rev. ed. BIA. (J). 2006. audio compact disk 249.00 (978-1-4187-4921-7(4)) Bus Info Agency.

Major Wholesalers & Retailers in Switzerland. 6th rev. ed. BIA. (J). 2006. audio compact disk 289.00 (978-1-4187-4908-8(7)) Bus Info Agency.

Major Wholesalers & Retailers in Switzerland. 6th rev. ed. BIA. (J). 2006. audio compact disk 249.00 (978-1-4187-4907-1(9)) Bus Info Agency.

Major Wholesalers & Retailers of Eastern Europe. 6th rev. ed. BIA. (J). 2006. audio compact disk 289.00 (978-1-4187-4599-8(5)) Bus Info Agency.

Major Wholesalers & Retailers of Eastern Europe. 6th rev. ed. BIA. (J). 2006. audio compact disk 249.00 (978-1-4187-4598-1(7)) Bus Info Agency.

Major Wholesalers & Retailers of the Netherlands. 6th rev. ed. BIA. (J). 2006. audio compact disk 289.00 (978-1-4187-4822-7(6)) Bus Info Agency.

Major Wholesalers & Retailers of the Netherlands. 6th rev. ed. BIA. (J). 2006. audio compact disk 249.00 (978-1-4187-4821-0(8)) Bus Info Agency.

Major Wholesalers of China. 6th rev. ed. BIA. (J). 2006. audio compact disk 289.00 (978-1-4187-4848-7(X)) Bus Info Agency.

Major Wholesalers of China. 6th rev. ed. BIA. (J). 2006. audio compact disk 249.00 (978-1-4187-4847-0(1)) Bus Info Agency.

Major Wholesalers of Western Europe. 6th rev. ed. BIA. (J). 2006. audio compact disk 289.00 (978-1-4187-4698-8(3)) Bus Info Agency.

Major Wholesalers of Western Europe. 6th rev. ed. BIA. (J). 2006. audio compact disk 249.00 (978-1-4187-4697-1(5)) Bus Info Agency.

Major Women's & Children's Clothing Manufacturers of the World. 6th rev. ed. BIA. (J). 2006. audio compact disk 289.00 (978-1-4187-5091-6(3)) Bus Info Agency.

Major Women's & Children's Clothing Manufacturers of the World. 6th rev. ed. BIA. (J). 2006. audio compact disk 249.00 (978-1-4187-5090-9(5)) Bus Info Agency.

Major Women's, Children's, & Infants' Clothing Wholesalers of the World. 6th rev. ed. BIA. (J). 2006. audio compact disk 289.00 (978-1-4187-5144-9(8)) Bus Info Agency.

Major Women's, Children's, & Infants' Clothing Wholesalers of the World. 6th rev. ed. BIA. (J). 2006. audio compact disk 249.00 (978-1-4187-5143-2(X)) Bus Info Agency.

Major Wood & Lumber Manufacturers of Eastern Europe. 6th rev. ed. BIA. (J). 2006. audio compact disk 289.00 (978-1-4187-4543-1(X)) Bus Info Agency.

Major Wood & Lumber Manufacturers of Eastern Europe. 6th rev. ed. BIA. (J). 2006. audio compact disk 249.00 (978-1-4187-4542-4(1)) Bus Info Agency.

Majorie Daw see Great American Short Stories, Vol. II, A Collection

Majorie Daw. Thomas Bailey Aldrich. 1 cass. 1989. 7.95 (S-42) Jimcin Record.
Story of a manufactured mistress.

Majoring on Minors: Matthew 23:24. Ed Young. (J). 1979. 4.95 (978-0-7417-1070-3(6), A0070) Win Walk.

Majors. unabr. collector's ed. W. E. B. Griffin. Read by Michael Russotto. 10 cass. (Running Time: 15 hrs.). (Brotherhood of War Ser.: No. 3). 1995. 80.00 (978-0-7366-2981-2(5), 3672) Books on Tape.
Polished veterans of WWII & the Korean War face off against Ho Chi Minh's guerillas. The glory of battle still reigns in a secret war.

Majors: In Pursuit of Golf's Holy Grail. John Feinstein. Read by Michael Kramer. 1999. audio compact disk 120.00 (978-0-7366-7126-2(9)) Books on Tape.

Majors: In Pursuit of Golf's Holy Grail. unabr. ed. John Feinstein. Read by Michael Kramer. 12 cass. (Running Time: 18 hrs.). 1999. 96.00 (978-0-7366-4509-6(8), 4942) Books on Tape.
John Feinstein returns to his most popular subject, golf. He dispenses his usual complement of insights & observations, & displays a copius knowledge of golfing lore & legend.

Make a Decision to Win. Gail Kasper & Gail Kasper. 5 CDs. 2004. audio compact disk (978-0-9761061-0-4(8)) G Kasper.
4 audio CDs and 1 computer workbook CDDo you have goals that you want to attain? Do you believe you are capable of accomplishing more in your life? In Make a Decision to Win, Gail identifies what separates those who have success from those who don't and demonstrates how "extraordinary preparation" and "strategy" must become a way of life. She targets key areas that will lead to an increased level of personal confidence and peace of mind. Her formulas provide solutions to tackle the obstacles that interfere with our personal and professional success so that you consistently maintain a positive attitude, beat procrastination, manager your time more effectively, and make choices that result in success.

Make a Joyful Noise: A Worship Choir Collection. Contrib. by Lari Goss & Regi Stone. Created by Regi Stone. 2007. audio compact disk 16.98 (978-5-557-49725-1(0), Word Music); audio compact disk 10.00 (978-5-557-49690-2(4), Word Music) Word Enter.

Make a Joyful Noise! Music, Movement, & Creative Play to Teach Bible Stories. abr. ed. Contrib. by Heather Robbins & Hannah Robbins. (ENG.). 2007. 12.99 (978-0-9789056-9-9(5)) Pub: New Day NC. Dist(s): STL Dist NA

Make a Joyful Shout to Yahweh. 1 cass. (Running Time: 1 hr. 03 min.). 1990. 8.00 (978-1-890967-30-7(0)) Hse of Yahweh.
These Psalms inspire the listener to joyfully shout praise to Yahweh & proclaim His Name throughout all the earth that it will never be forgotten.

Make Your Miracle: Exceed Your Wildest Expections in 90 Days. Speeches. Joan Hangarter. 1 CD. (Running Time: 52 mins.). 2004. audio compact disk 15.99 (978-0-9745590-2-5(4), 33-202) Mir Makers Cl.
Dr Joan teaches you five steps to make your impossible dreams come true. Step One, commit to action and take your vibrational meter. Find your mission, and create the action plan and take the steps to the life of your dreams.

Make Your Own Family Tree (Astrologically) Theresa Gurlacz. 1 cass. 8.95 (136) Am Fed Astrologers.
Compile astrological genealogy with chart history.

Make Your Own Market: Seminar on Audio. Hosted by Tony DiCello. (ENG.). 2007. audio compact disk 50.00 (978-1-932649-07-9(7)) Relleck Pubng.

Make Your Own Market: Seminar on Audio. Hosted by Tony DiCello. (ENG.). 2007. 50.00 (978-1-932649-09-3(3)) Relleck Pubng.

Make Your Own Market Audio Scripts. Hosted by Tony DiCello. (ENG.). 2006. audio compact disk 50.00 (978-1-932649-05-5(0)) Relleck Pubng.

Make Yourself a Millionaire: How to Sleep Well & Stay Sane on the Road to Wealth. Charles C. Zhang. 3 CDs. (Running Time: 4 hrs. 30 min.). 2003. audio compact disk 28.00 (978-1-932378-13-9(8)); 24.00 (978-1-932378-12-2(X)) Pub: A Media Intl. Dist(s): Natl Bk Netwk
Easy to follow personal finance guidelines from American Express's #1 rated financial advisor.

Make Yourself Unforgettable: The Dale Carnegie Class-Act System. unabr. ed. Dale Carnegie and Associates Staff. (Running Time: 6 hrs. 0 mins. 0 sec.). (ENG.). 2006. audio compact disk 29.95 (978-0-7435-6390-1(5), Nightgale) Pub: S&S Audio. Dist(s): S and S Inc

Makeover. Kate Petty. 4 CDs. 2006. audio compact disk 34.95 (978-0-7540-6720-7(3), Chivers Child Audio) AudioGO.

Makeover Murders. unabr. ed. Jennifer Rowe. Read by Brenda Addie. 8 cass. (Running Time: 12 hrs.). 1998. (978-1-86340-569-0(0), 571230) Bolinda Pubng AUS.
At discreet Deepdene, the guests are ready to test for themselves the makeover mansion's claim that every woman can - with expensive encouragement -realize her full beauty. Soon it is clear to Verity Birdwood that all is not what it seems. But even she does not suspect that within the Deepdene's silk-lined walls is an enemy with murder in mind.

Maker of Gargoyles. Clark Ashton Smith. 2007. audio compact disk 27.95 (978-0-8095-7172-7(2)) Diamond Book Dists.

Maker of Heaven & Earth. Francis P. O'Brien. 2000. 10.95 (CS-492); audio compact disk 15.95 (CD-492) GIA Pubns.

***Makers: A Novel of the Whirlwind Changes to Come.** unabr. ed. Cory Doctorow. Read by Bernadette Dunne. 15 CDs. (Running Time: 18 hrs. 30 mins.). 2009. audio compact disk 100.00 (978-0-307-71453-4(5), BksonTape) Pub: Random Audio Pubg. Dist(s): Random

Makers & Takers: Why Conservatives Work Harder, Feel Happier, Have Closer Families, Take Fewer Drugs, Give More Generously, Value Honesty More, Are Less Materialistic & Envious, Whine Less... & Even Hug Their Children More Than Liberals. unabr. ed. Peter Schweizer. Read by Johnny Heller. (Running Time: 5 hrs. 30 mins. 0 sec.). (ENG.). 2008. audio compact disk 29.99 (978-1-4001-0748-3(2)) Pub: Tantor Media. Dist(s): IngramPubServ

Makers & Takers: Why Conservatives Work Harder, Feel Happier, Have Closer Families, Take Fewer Drugs, Give More Generously, Value Honesty More, Are Less Materialistic & Envious, Whine Less... & Even Hug Their Children More Than Liberals. unabr. ed. Peter Schweizer. Read by Johnny Heller. Narrated by Johnny Heller. (Running Time: 5 hrs. 30 mins. 0 sec.). (ENG.). 2008. audio compact disk 19.99 (978-1-4001-5748-8(X)); audio compact disk 59.99 (978-1-4001-3748-0(9)) Pub: Tantor Media. Dist(s): IngramPubServ

Maker's Diet. 2004. video & audio compact disk 29.95 (978-0-9759561-5-1(9)); audio compact disk 14.95 (978-0-9759561-7-5(5)) Garden of Life.

Maker's Diet DVD & CD Bundle. 2004. DVD & audio compact disk (978-0-9761382-1-1(2)) Garden of Life.

Maker's Diet Success Kit. 2004. mass mkt. 199.99 (978-0-9759561-9-9(1)) Garden of Life.

Makes Me Feel Like Singing. Darrell House. 2005. audio compact disk 16.95 (978-0-9663276-6-3(7)) Red Engine Pr.

Makin Music! Chris Patella & Eileen Oddo. Illus. by Kevin Schoonover. (J). (gr. k-2). 1989. cass. & lp (978-0-318-64483-7(5)) Musical Munchkins.

Makin' Music. Chris Patella & Eileen Oddo. Read by Chris Patella. Illus. by Kevin Schoonover. (Running Time: 45 min.). (Musical Munchkins Are...Ser.). (J). (gr. k-2). 1989. bk. & tchr. ed. 9.95 (978-0-944333-02-0(8)) Musical Munchkins.
Features songs, dramatic plays, games & activities designed for children.

Makin' Music. Chris Patella & Eileen Oddo. Read by Chris Patella. (Running Time: 45 min.). (J). (ps-3). 1989. pap. bk. 15.95 Musical Munchkins.

Makin' Whoopee. Perf. by Sam Pilafian & Frank Vignola. 1 cass., 1 CD. 7.98 (TA 33324); audio compact disk 12.78 NewSound.

Making. Creflo A. Dollar & Taffi L. Dollar. 25.00 (978-1-59089-032-5(9)) Pub: Creflo Dollar. Dist(s): STL Dist NA

Making a Call see Brian Patten Reading His Poetry

Making A Difference in the World -the Orange Collection: Developing A Child's Relationship with the World. Trenna Daniells. Narrated by Trenna Daniells. (ENG.). (J). 2009. audio compact disk (978-0-918519-66-5(7)) Trenna Prods.

Making a Friend of the Unknown. Speeches. Featuring David Whyte. one. 1997. audio compact disk 15.00 (978-1-932887-00-6(8)) Many Rivers Pr.
The people, places, communities and events in our lives can be gateways to the unknown, wherever we make our home in the world. On "Making a Friend of the Unknown", David Whyte looks at a long tradition that suggests that creation is breathlessly waiting for us to take our place in the conversation, whether on the grand stage of political events or in the humble kitchen garden of our own home.

Making a Good Brain Great: The Amen Clinic Program for Achieving & Sustaining Optimal Mental Performance. abr. ed. Daniel G. Amen. Read by Daniel G. Amen. (Running Time: 18000 sec.). (ENG.). 2005. audio compact disk 27.50 (978-0-7393-2229-1(X), Random AudioBks) Pub: Random Audio Pubg. Dist(s): Random

Making a Good Script Great. 1 cass. 19.95 (978-0-929536-19-4(3)) Emb Cassettes.

Making a Habit of Success. Samuel A. Cypert. 6 cass. (Running Time: 6 hrs.). 1995. 39.95 (12650AM) Nightingale-Conant.
Now you can unlock the secrets of greatness & achieve success by developing the positive everyday habits that produce significant results. Making a Habit of Success tells you how to get what you want from your career, your relationships - your life! Includes 4 free issues of Think & Grow Rich Newsletter.

Making a Life, Making a Living: Reclaiming Your Purpose & Passion in Business & in Life. Read by Mark Albion. 2000. (978-1-57042-983-5(9)) Hachet Audio.
Entrepreneur Albion robustly exhorts listeners to fulfill their own & society's interests so that life becomes more socially & financially satisfying.

Making a Life, Making a Living: Reclaiming Your Purpose & Passion in Business & in Life. abr. ed. Mark Albion. (ENG.). 2005. 14.98 (978-1-59483-479-0(2)) Pub: Hachet Audio. Dist(s): HachBkGrp

Making a Living by the Written Word. A. C. Greene. Read by A. C. Greene. 1 cass. (Running Time: 50 min.). (Texas Writers on Writing Ser.). 1989. 12.95 (978-1-880717-23-3(9),) Writers AudioShop.
Insight, advice & humor from the Dean of Texas letters.

Making a Man of God. unabr. ed. R. Edward Miller. Read by R. Edward Miller. 6 cass. (Running Time: 9 hrs.). 1997. 25.00 Set. (978-0-945818-12-0(2)) Peniel Pubns.
Ways & means God uses for the development of His ministers & servants.

Making a Managable Move, Vol. 4. unabr. ed. Juliette Becker. 1 cass. (Running Time: 25 min.). Dramatization. 1999. 19.95 incl. script. Postcards MindsEye.
Whether it's across the country or across the world, there is a way to move without stress.

Making a Second Marriage Succeed. A. Lynn Scoresby. 2 cass. 11.95 (978-1-57734-227-4(5), 07001681) Covenant Comms.
A unique seminar for those ready to try again.

Making All Things New. 9 cass. Incl. Making All Things New: A Capacity to Celebrate. Nancy B. Beck. 1983.; Making All Things New: Dreamworking: Creative Reconciliation Between Myth & Morning. Deborah Longmaid. 1983.; Making All Things New: Humour: A Tool for Friendly Renewal. Elizabeth House. 1983.; Making All Things New: Imagination Agitation. Mark W. Bailey. 1983.; Making All Things New: Love as the Kindling of Imagination. Peter Blood & Annie Patterson. 1983.; Making All Things New: Making Magic: A Mixed Media Meal. Andy Schloss. 1983.; Making All Things New: The Creative Word. Mary Morrison. 1983.; Making All Things New: The Irrepressible Yearning. Wallace Collett. 1983.; Making All Things New: The Urge to Create. James H. Ewing. 1983.; 1983. 28.00; 4.50 ea. Pendle Hill.

Making All Things New: A Capacity to Celebrate see Making All Things New

***Making All Things New: An Invitation to the Spiritual Life.** unabr. ed. Henri Nouwen. Narrated by Dan Cashman. (ENG.). 2007. 9.98 (978-1-59644-518-5(1), Hovel Audio) christianaud.

Making All Things New: An Invitation to the Spiritual Life. unabr. ed. Henri J. M. Nouwen. Read by Dan Cashman. (Running Time: 2 hrs. 30 mins. 0 sec.). (ENG.). 2007. audio compact disk 15.98 (978-1-59644-517-8(3), Hovel Audio) christianaud.

Making All Things New: Dreamworking: Creative Reconciliation Between Myth & Morning see Making All Things New

Making All Things New: Humour: A Tool for Friendly Renewal see Making All Things New

Making All Things New: Imagination Agitation see Making All Things New

Making All Things New: Love as the Kindling of Imagination see Making All Things New

Making All Things New: Making Magic: A Mixed Media Meal see Making All Things New

Making All Things New: The Creative Word see Making All Things New

Making All Things New: The Irrepressible Yearning see Making All Things New

Making All Things New: The Urge to Create see Making All Things New

Making an Executive Job Change in the 90's. Tom Mitchell. 5 cass. (Running Time: 3 hrs.). 1991. 59.95 Set. Audio Prof Grp.
Seminar presentation. Original production.

Making an Incredible Day. Shad Helmstetter. 1 cass. (Self-Talk Ser.). 10.95 (978-0-937065-64-8(1)) Grindle Pr.
Companion Self-Talk Cassettes as mentioned in the book, "What To Say When You Talk To Your Self".

Making Beautiful Music Together (Part 1) 1 Cor. 1:10. Ed Young. 1986. 4.95 (978-0-7417-1546-3(5), 546) Win Walk.

Making Beautiful Music Together (Part 11) 1 Cor. 13. Ed Young. 1986. 4.95 (978-0-7417-1547-0(3), 547) Win Walk.

Making Best Use of the Internet to Enhance Classroom Instruction. Phil Reinhardt. 6 cass. (Running Time: 4 hr. 21 min.). (J). (gr. 3-6). 1998. 75.00 Incl. handbk. (978-1-886397-17-0(1)) Bureau of Educ.

Making Career Advising Integral to Academic Advising: NACADA Webinar Series 15. Featuring Kenneth Hughey & Joanne Damminger. 2008. audio compact disk 140.00 (978-1-935140-57-3(4)) Nat Acad Adv.

***Making Change Work.** Created by CareerTrack. 2010. audio compact disk 199.95 (978-1-60959-017-8(1)) P Univ E Inc.

Making Changes. Betty L. Randolph. 1 stereo cass. (Running Time: 45 min.). (Self-Hypnosis Ser.). 9.98 (978-1-55909-155-8(X), 817) Randolph Tapes.
Teaches how to make decisions & changes in your personal life. Music background & spoken word.

Making Children Mind Without Losing Yours. unabr. ed. Kevin Leman. Narrated by Chris Fabry. (ENG.). 2009. 16.09 (978-1-60814-479-2(8)) Oasis Audio.

Making Children Mind Without Losing Yours. unabr. ed. Kevin Leman. Narrated by Chris Fabry. (Running Time: 7 hrs. 10 mins. 12 sec.). (ENG.). 2009. audio compact disk 22.99 (978-1-59859-561-1(X)) Oasis Audio.

Making Choices. 1 cass. (Running Time: 1 hr.). 1981. 7.95 (978-1-58638-572-9(0)) Nilgiri Pr.
Explains how to learn to see what will help most permanently.

Making Choices: True Healing. Michael P. Marshall. Read by Michael P. Marshall. Ed. by Jonathan C. Renaud. Music by Ted Crook. 1 cass. (Running Time: 52 min.). 1995. 9.00 (978-0-912403-19-9(5)) Prod Renaud.
True healing comes from within. Techniques & affirmations to heal body, soul, spirit & mind.

Making Connections: Companion Recording. Compiled by William M. Anderson & Marvelene C. Moore. 1 CD. (Running Time: 40 Min.). 1998. audio compact disk 15.00 (978-1-56545-107-0(4)) MENC.
Music for classroom listening for thirteen of the lessons are featured which includes African American children's game songs and gospel music, Balinese vocal gamelan music, Mexican American mariachi music and Native American music.

Making Connections: Enhance Your Listening Comprehension in Chinese. Madeline K. Spring. 1 CD. (Running Time: 1 hr. 30 mins.). 2002. audio compact disk (978-0-88727-367-4(X)) Cheng Tsui.

Making Contact with the Other Side. Sylvia Browne. 2 cass. (Running Time: 2 hrs.). 1998. 16.95 (978-1-56170-513-9(6), 379) Hay House.
How to get in touch with your spiritual self & reach those on the other side.

Making Conversation. 2001. (978-0-9704029-4-3(5)) NewsMax Media.

Making Decisions. Shad Helmstetter. 1 cass. (Self-Talk Ser.). 10.95 (978-0-937065-53-2(6)) Grindle Pr.
Companion Self-Talk Cassettes as mentioned in the book, "What To Say When You Talk To Your Self".

Making Do with Little. H. Douglas Miller. 1 cass. 8.95 (232) Am Fed Astrologers.
Good readings without birth time: Johndro locality & more.

Making Effective Choices in the Study Process. Edwin Locke. 1 cass. (Running Time: 1 hr. 30 min.). 1995. 12.95 (978-1-56114-435-8(5), IL09C) Second Renaissance.
Application of the theory of volition to the process of efficient studying.

Making Effective Presentations. Lidstone. 1985. 78.95 (978-0-566-02382-8(2)) Ashgate Pub Co.

Making Effective Use of the Internet to Enhance Your Classroom Instruction. Larry Lewin. 6 cass. (Running Time: 4 hr. 37 min.). 1998. 75.00 (978-1-886397-22-4(8)) Bureau of Educ.

Making Every Student a More Successful Reader Set: Practical Strategies for Improving Reading Skills, unabr. ed. Susan Finney. 6 cass. (J). (gr. 3-6). 1999. 75.00 (978-1-886397-24-8(4)) Bureau of Educ.

Making Everyday Extraordinary. Interview with Mother Angelica & Harold Cohen. 1 cass. (Running Time: 60 min.). 10.00 (978-1-55794-063-6(0), T14) Eternal Wrd TV.

Making Friends. Heinle.

Making Friends by Being Yourself: Matthew's New Jungle Friends. unabr. ed. Trenna Sutphen. 12 cass. (Running Time: 30 min.). (One to Grow On Ser.). (J). 1982. 9.95 (978-0-918519-05-4(5), 12004) Trenna Prods.
A great tool for parents to help their child to explore feelings in a very non-threatening way.

Making Friends by Being Yourself- Matthew's New Jungle Friends. Trenna Daniells. Narrated by Trenna Daniells. (ENG.). (J). 2009. (978-0-918519-31-3(4)) Trenna Prods.

Making Friends with All Your Feelings. Lois F. Timmins. 1 cass. (Running Time: 50 min.). (Feelings & How to Cope with Them Ser.: Vol. I). 1984. 12.95 (978-0-931814-03-7(0)) Comn Studies.
Emphasizes the universality of feelings & the importance of accepting all feelings, both comfortable & uncomfortable. It explains how feelings & actions are different, pointing up the significance of accepting feelings while controlling actions, & developing "the wisdom to know the difference.".

Making Friends with Your Shadow. Maureen Schuler. 1 cass. (Running Time: 44 min.). 1990. 7.95 (TAH231) Alba Hse Comns.
This tape shows how we make the greatest contribution to peace & justice by establishing peace within ourselves.

Making Fun! Patricia Shih. Perf. by Patricia Shih. 1 cass. (Running Time: 48 min.). (J). (ps-6). 1996. 9.00 (GR0030) Shih Ents.
Shows sparks of originality & humor while dealing with songs about self-esteem.

Making God Number One in Our Life. Swami Amar Jyoti. 2 cass. 1982. 12.95 (A-24) Truth Consciousness.
A searching appraisal - what is really number one for us, God or His creation? Building this world anew.

Making Great Decisions: For a Life Without Limits. abr. ed. T. D. Jakes. Read by T. D. Jakes. (Running Time: 6 hrs. 0 mins. 0 sec.). (ENG.). 2009. audio compact disk 14.99 (978-0-7435-9911-5(X)) Pub: S&S Audio. Dist(s): S and S Inc

Making Headway: Talking in Pairs Intermediate. Tania Bastow. 1999. 17.50 (978-0-19-435556-8(X)) OUP.

Making Headway: Talking in Pairs Pre-Intermediate. Tania Bastow & Ceri Jones. 1999. 17.50 (978-0-19-435549-0(7)) OUP.

Making History: How Great Historians Interpret the Past. Instructed by Allen C. Guelzo. 2008. 129.95 (978-1-59803-505-6(3)); audio compact disk 69.95 (978-1-59803-506-3(1)) Teaching Co.

***Making Ideas Happpen: Overcoming the Obstacles Between Vision & Reality.** unabr. ed. Scott Belsky. Read by Scott Peterson. (Running Time: 7 hrs.). (ENG.). 2010. 27.98 (978-1-59659-577-4(9), GildAudio) Pub: Gildan Media. Dist(s): HachBkGrp

Making Intimate Connections: 7 Guidelines for Better Couple Communication. abr. ed. Albert Ellis & Ted Crawford. Read by Stephen O'Hara. 2 cass. (Running Time: 3 hrs.). 2001. 18.00 (978-1-57453-398-9(3)) Audio Lit.
A highly influential psychotherapist, created two breakthrough cognitive therapies still widely used today. One of these, REBT, is the basis for "Making Intimate Connections" shows how REBT can improve intimacy where it exists or create intimacy where it is lacking.

Making It All Work: Winning at the Game of Work & the Business of Life. unabr. ed. David Allen. (Running Time: 9 hrs.). (ENG.). (gr. 12 up). 2009. audio compact disk 34.95 (978-0-14-314357-4(3), PengAudBks) Penguin Grp USA.

Making It Connect Full Year & Music CD Pack. Zondervan Publishing Staff. (J). 2004. audio compact disk 909.99 (978-0-310-64418-7(6)) Zondervan.

Making It Connect Music CD Pack Of 5. Willow Creek Association. (J). 2003. audio compact disk 64.95 (978-0-310-64383-8(X)) Zondervan.

Making It in America. unabr. collector's ed. Barry Minkow. Read by Ron Shoop. 5 cass. (Running Time: 5 hrs.). 1987. 30.00 (978-0-7366-1137-4(1), 2062) Books on Tape.
Barry Minkow & ZZZZ Best, now disgraced, were corporate darlings.

Making It in High Heels: Inspiring Stories by Women for Women of All Ages. unabr. ed. Kimberlee MacDonald. (Running Time: 4 hrs. 30 mins.). (ENG.). 2008. 19.98 (978-1-59659-318-3(0), GildAudio) Pub: Gildan Media. Dist(s): HachBkGrp

Making Jack Falcone: An Undercover FBI Agent Takes down a Mafia Family. unabr. ed. Joaquin Garcia. Read by Dick Hill. Told to Michael Levin. 8 CDs. (Running Time: 10 hrs. 0 mins. 0 sec.). (ENG.). 2008. audio compact disk 34.99 (978-1-4001-0872-5(1)) Pub: Tantor Media. Dist(s): IngramPubServ

Making Jack Falcone: An Undercover FBI Agent Takes down a Mafia Family. unabr. ed. Joaquin Garcia & Michael Levin. Narrated by Paul Boehmer & Dick Hill. (Running Time: 10 hrs. 0 mins. 0 sec.). (ENG.). 2008. audio compact disk 69.99 (978-1-4001-3872-2(8)) Pub: Tantor Media. Dist(s): IngramPubServ

Making Jack Falcone: An Undercover FBI Agent Takes down a Mafia Family. unabr. ed. Joaquin Garcia & Michael Levin. Narrated by Paul Boehmer. (Running Time: 10 hrs. 0 mins. 0 sec.). (ENG.). 2008. audio compact disk 24.99 (978-1-4001-5872-0(9)) Pub: Tantor Media. Dist(s): IngramPubServ

Making Jesus Your Jubilee. As told by Markus Bishop. 4 cass. (Running Time: 1 hr. 30 mins.). 2000. 20.00 (978-0-9628301-4-3(3)) M Bishop Minis.

Making Jubilee a Reality in Your Life. Creflo A. Dollar. 15.00 (978-1-59089-034-9(5)) Pub: Creflo Dollar. Dist(s): STL Dist NA

Making Life Work: Putting God's Wisdom into Action. abr. ed. Bill Hybels. 2 cass. (Running Time: 2 hrs. 60 mins.). (ENG.). 2005. 15.00 (978-0-8308-1790-0(5)) InterVarsity.

Making Lite of Myself. Contrib. by John Pinette. 2007. audio compact disk 16.98 (978-1-929243-76-1(6)) Uproar Ent.

***Making Love.** Barry Long. 2006. 24.95 (978-1-899324-23-1(2)) Pub: B Long Bks. Dist(s): AtlasBooks

Making Love: Sexual Love the Divine Way. rev. ed. Barry Long. 2 cass. (Running Time: 2 hrs. 28 mins.). (ENG.). 1996. audio compact disk 17.95 (978-1-899324-02-6(X)) Pub: B Long Bks. Dist(s): AtlasBooks

A life changing encounter with real love; a way to keep love constantly fresh & a love through honest, pure & conscious love making.

Making Love: The Chapman Guide to Making Sex an Act of Love. unabr. ed. Gary Chapman. Narrated by Maurice England. (Running Time: 9000 sec.). (Marriage Savers Ser.). (ENG.). 2008. audio compact disk 12.99 (978-1-59859-330-3(7)) Oasis Audio.

Making Love: The Chapman Guide to Making Sex an Act of Love (Marriage Saver) unabr. ed. Gary Chapman. Narrated by Maurice England. (Marriage Savers Ser.). (ENG.). 2008. 9.09 (978-1-60814-301-6(5)) Oasis Audio.

Making Love Last. Created by Barry Neil Kaufman. 1 CD. (Running Time: 60 min.). 2005. audio compact disk 17.50 (978-1-887254-16-8(1)) Epic Century.

Everyone is lovable. Everyone can give love. There are no exceptions to this possibility. One loving person, one truly loving person, changes the world. From this unflinchingly optimistic perspective, Barry Neil Kaufman presents an unusually refreshing and instructive guide which allows us to easily harness our natural abilities to generate love, to experience love, and to stay in love.

Making Love Last: Eight Crucial Factors for Staying Together. David Grudermeyer & Rebecca Grudermeyer. 2 cass. suppl. ed. 18.95 (T-47) Willingness Wrks.

Making Love Last: How to Sustain Intimacy & Nurture Genuine Connection. David Richo. (ENG.). 2008. audio compact disk 24.95 (978-1-59030-574-4(4)) Pub: Shambhala Pubns. Dist(s): Random

Making Love Work. Barbara De Angelis. 5 cass. pap. bk. 79.95 (12420PAM) Nightingale-Conant.

Dr. De Angelis has helped millions of people attract the right partner (& avoid the wrong one), rekindle & keep marital love & passion alive year after year, & create greater closeness between children & parents of all ages.

Making Magic in the World. Maya Angelou & Michael Toms. 1 cass. (Running Time: 1 hr.). 1998. 10.95 (978-1-56170-508-5(X), 376) Hay House.

Shares the memories of the mentors & teachers who profoundly influenced her life. Travel from the Deep South to the heart of Africa, & learn how you too can make magic in the world.

Making Managers into Leaders Learning System. Ed Oakley. Created by Enlightened Leadership Solutions. 2008. spiral bd. (978-0-9628255-1-4(4)) Enl Leadr Pub.

***Making Meaning Vocabulary Classroom Package for First Edition Users, Grade 2.** Developmental Studies Center Staff. 2009. pap. bk. & spiral bd. 245.00 (978-1-57621-666-8(7)) Develop Studie.

***Making Meaning Vocabulary Classroom Package for First Edition Users, Grade 3.** Developmental Studies Center Staff. 2009. pap. bk. & spiral bd. 250.00 (978-1-57621-662-0(4)) Develop Studie.

***Making Meaning Vocabulary Classroom Package for First Edition Users, Grade 4.** Developmental Studies Center Staff. 2005. pap. bk. & spiral bd. 310.00 (978-1-59892-001-7(4)) Develop Studie.

Making Millions in Direct Sales: The 8 Essential Activities Direct Sales Managers Must Do Every Day to Build a Successful Team & Earn More Money. abr. ed. Michael G. Malaghan. Read by Lloyd James. (Running Time: 16200 sec.). 2006. audio compact disk 28.00 (978-1-933309-08-8(3)) Pub: A Media Intl. Dist(s): Natl Bk Netwk

Making Models In 3D Studio R4: Interactive for Windows 3.1 & 95. AutoDesk Press Staff. (C). 1997. audio compact disk 63.95 (978-0-7668-0085-4(7)) Pub: Delmar. Dist(s): CENGAGE Learn

Making Money. unabr. ed. Terry Pratchett. Read by Stephen Briggs. (Running Time: 39600 sec.). (Discworld Ser.). 2007. audio compact disk 39.95 (978-0-06-136353-5(7), Harper Audio) HarperCollins Pubs.

***Making Money.** unabr. ed. Terry Pratchett. Read by Stephen Briggs. (ENG.). 2007. (978-0-06-155445-2(6), Harper Audio); (978-0-06-155444-5(8), Harper Audio) HarperCollins Pubs.

Making Money on the Web: How to Bootstrap Yourself to Online Profits. Seth Godin. 6 cass. (Running Time: 9 hrs.). 2000. wbk. ed. 69.95 (978-1-55525-022-5(X), 20850CD) Nightingale-Conant.

If you've got a company, an interest, or even just a hobby, you've got what it takes to start an easy, profitable online business.

Making Money on the Web: How to Bootstrap Yourself to Online Profits. unabr. ed. Seth Godin. 6 cass. (Running Time: 9 hrs.). 2000. wbk. ed. 59.95 (978-1-55525-005-8(X), 20850a) Nightingale-Conant.

Making Moosic. Perf. by Anna Moo. 1 cass. (Running Time: 34 min.). (J). 1993. 9.98 (978-1-877737-08-4(9), MLP227) MFLP CA.

Original songs by new children's artist, Anna Moo. Fun & funny mix of calypso, folk, reggae & more.

Making Movies, unabr. ed. Sidney Lumet. Narrated by Richard M. Davidson. 5 cass. (Running Time: 7 hrs. 15 mins.). 1999. 44.00 (978-0-7887-0452-9(4), 94643E7) Recorded Bks.

An honest & unflinching look at the business & craft of movie making. Lumet reveals the ingredients for the potion that brings movie magic to life & assures one thing: you will never look at movies the same way again.

Making Musical Kids: A Complete Music Program That Any Parent Can Teach. Dawn Hoebee. 2003. pap. bk. 24.99 (978-0-9732852-0-8(6)) Musical Kids Pr CAN.

Making Mystery Movies. unabr. ed. Alfred Hitchcock. 1 cass. (Running Time: 15 min.). 1964. 12.95 (11016) J Norton Pubs.

Hitchcock talks about the fact that solving a mystery is not the only element important in making of a suspense film.

Making New Discoveries. 1998. 16.95 (978-1-57972-279-1(2)) Insight Living.

Making Not Breaking: The First Year under Saddle. Cherry Hill. Prod. by Rick Lamb. 1 cass. (Running Time: 1 hr. 30 min.). 1998. 14.95 (978-0-9679487-1-3(1)) Horse Show.

Award-winning author Cherry Hill outlines a safe and effective training method for starting English and Western horses under saddle. Abridged from the best-selling book.

Making of a Blockbuster: How Wayne Huizenga Built a Sports & Entertainment Empire from Trash, Grit, & Videotape. abr. ed. Gail DeGeorge. Read by Joseph Campanella. 4 cass. (Running Time: 6 hrs.). 2004. 25.00 (978-1-59007-127-4(1)) Pub: New Millenn Enter. Dist(s): PerseuPGW

The inside story of the multimillionaire behind Blockbuster Video and the major player in the Viacom/Paramount/Blockbuster deal. Thirty-five years ago, Wayne Huizenga rose before the sun to run his garbage collection route. This audio chronicles the transformation of this ambitious entrepreneur into a corporate titan.

Making of a Chef: Mastering Heat at the Culinary Institute of America. unabr. ed. Michael Ruhlman. Read by Jeff Riggenbach. 11 CDs. (Running Time: 13 hrs.). 2001. audio compact disk 88.00 (978-0-7861-9712-5(9), 2290) Blckstn Audio.

Joins the students in Skills One at the Culinary Institute of America, the most influential cooking school in the country. Documents the training of America's chefs from the first classroom to the Culinary's final kitchen, the American Bounty Restaurant. Be propelled through a score of kitchens & classrooms, from Asian & American regional cuisines to lunch cookery & even table waiting, in search of the elusive, unnameable elements of great cooking.

Making of a Chef: Mastering Heat at the Culinary Institute of America. unabr. ed. Michael Ruhlman. Read by Jeff Riggenbach. 9 cass. (Running Time: 13 hrs.). 1998. 62.95 (978-0-7861-1414-6(2), 2290) Blckstn Audio.

Making of a Country Lawyer: An Autobiography. unabr. ed. Gerry Spence. Read by Jonathan Marosz. 14 cass. (Running Time: 21 hrs.). 1997. 89.50 (978-0-7366-3571-4(8), 4222) Books on Tape.

Gerry Spence grew up in Wyoming, where he memorized scripture, sold fresh bouquets door to door & herded sheep. And before he was 15, he had prowled the brothels of the Old West.

Making of a Giant Killer: Psalm 78. Ed Young. 1982. 4.95 (978-0-7417-1227-1(X), 227) Win Walk.

Making of a Man: Psalm 115:18. Ben Young. 2000. 4.95 (978-0-7417-6213-9(7), B0213) Win Walk.

Making of a Marchioness & the Methods of Lady Walderhurst. Frances Hodgson Burnett. 8 Cds. (Running Time: 8 hrs. 40 min.). Dramatization. 2003. audio compact disk (978-0-9746806-2-0(1)) Alcazar AudioWorks.

In early 1901, fifteen years after Little Lord Fauntleroy and ten years before the Secret Garden, Frances Hodgson Burnett wrote The Making of a Marchioness. She followed this short novel in the spring of the same year with the sequel, The Methods of Lady Walderhurst. The satisfying "Cinderella" quality of the first book which illustrates the harsh realism of Edwardian society, combines with the exciting melodramatic developments in the second book to create an intriguing story that continues to entertain us today.

Making of a Marchioness; The Methods of Lady Walderhurst. Frances Hodgson Burnett. Read by Susan McCarthy et al. (Running Time: 30600 sec.). (J). (gr. 4-7). 2006. 54.95 (978-0-7861-4524-9(2)); audio compact disk 63.00 (978-0-7861-7180-4(4)) Blckstn Audio.

Making of a Marchioness; The Methods of Lady Walderhurst. unabr. ed. Frances Hodgson Burnett. Read by Susan McCarthy et al. (Running Time: 30600 sec.). (J). (gr. 4-7). 2006. audio compact disk 29.95 (978-0-7861-7614-4(8)) Blckstn Audio.

Making of a Philosopher: My Journey Through Twentieth-Century Philosophy. Colin McGinn. Narrated by Colin McPhillamy. 5 cass. (Running Time: 6 hrs. 30 mins.). 2002. 48.00 (978-1-4025-0633-8(3)) Recorded Bks.

Making of a Saint. abr. ed. Michael Higgins. Prod. by Kevin Burns. 3. (Running Time: 10800 sec.). 2007. audio compact disk 34.95 (978-0-660-19679-4(4), CBC Audio) Pub: Canadian Broadcasting CAN. Dist(s): Georgetown Term

A saint is someone whom the church has formally acknowledged as a model of holiness and worthy of veneration. There are about six thousand officially recognized saints in the Roman Catholic Church. In this engaging three-part series by scholar and biographer, Michael Higgins, hear about the long and rigorous process of identifying who will be a saint and who will not. There is a lot at stake and the issues that revolve around saint making are often contentious.Michael Higgins? book, Stalking the Holy is published by House of Anansi Press, and is available in bookstores across North America.

Making of a Saint. unabr. collector's ed. W. Somerset Maugham. Read by Octavius Black. 6 cass. (Running Time: 9 hrs.). 1986. 48.00 (978-0-7366-1006-3(5), 1939) Books on Tape.

A story of 15th century Italy. Intrigue & assassination were standard & targets as likely to be clerical as courtly.

Making of a Surgeon, unabr. ed. William A. Nolen. Narrated by Richard Poe. 7 cass. (Running Time: 9 hrs. 30 mins.). 1992. 60.00 (978-1-55690-760-9(5), 92423E7) Recorded Bks.

William A. Nolen, M.D., reminisces on his five years as an intern at New York's Bellevue Hospital in the 1960s. A classic among medical memoirs.

Making of a Surgeon. unabr. collector's ed. William A. Nolen. Read by Bob Erickson. 8 cass. (Running Time: 8 hrs.). 1983. 48.00 (978-0-7366-0736-0(6), 1693) Books on Tape.

Dr. Nolen opens to us the process that trains & tests a doctor becoming a surgeon. The operation is a success, he removes the mystery found in similar accounts & shows the humanity & humor in the very real world where he was intern & chief resident for 5 years, Bellevue Hospital in New York City.

Making of Americans: Pts. I & II see Gertrude Stein Reads from Her Works

Making of Charles Dickens. unabr. collector's ed. Christopher Hibbert. Read by David Case. 7 cass. (Running Time: 10 hrs. 30 mins.). 2001. 56.00 (978-0-7366-6184-3(0)) Books on Tape.

In this extensive study of Dickens' childhood & youth, Hibbert sets down all that is known of those early years...over & above the blacking factory & the school we all know. In revealing how Dickens transferred the smallest fragments of his experience to his fiction, how he interpreted his youth to his readers & himself, & how those crucial years affected him as a writer and as a man, Hibbert throws a clear light on the creative process & the sources of literary imagination. His book illuminates a complex & baffling man without at any point suggesting that his writing & his actions explain his inner life entirely. Tracing Dickens through his thirty-third year, an epilogue completes the story of his life.

Making of Hayward Sanitarium. Prod. by Richard Fish. 1 cass. 5.95 (978-1-57677-082-5(6), LMPD301) Lodestone Catalog.

Making of June. unabr. ed. Annie Ward. Read by Aasne Vigesaa. 8 cass. (Running Time: 11 hrs.). 2002. 87.25 (978-1-59086-054-0(3), 1590860543, CD Unabrid Lib Ed); 34.95 (978-1-59086-053-3(5), 1590860535, BAU) Brilliance Audio.

At first, June appears to be the ideal California girl - blond hair, blue eyes, a production assistant at a film company, and married to a hot property about to get his doctorate - but she abandons her home and job to follow her husband to Bulgaria. Within a month of their arrival, June turns thirty and her husband leaves her for a young local girl. As difficult as it is for her to be without him and virtually friendless in a country on the verge of civil war, June doesn't run home. She drinks too much, falls into the arms of a Mafia kingpin, gets caught up in the revolution, and little by little revels in her new vision of the world outside the American periscope. She survives and learns that loss can be an opportunity and that loneliness gives a person time to change her life.

Making of June. unabr. ed. Annie Ward. Read by Aasne Vigesaa. (Running Time: 11 hrs.). 2004. 39.25 (978-1-59335-379-7(0), 1593353790, Brinc Audio MP3 Lib) Brilliance Audio.

Making of June. unabr. ed. Annie Ward. Read by Aasne Vigesaa. (Running Time: 11 hrs.). 2004. 39.25 (978-1-59710-477-7(9), 1597104779, BADLE); 24.95 (978-1-59710-476-0(0), 1597104760, BAD) Brilliance Audio.

Making of June. unabr. ed. Annie Ward. Read by Aasne Vigesaa. (Running Time: 11 hrs.). 2004. 24.95 (978-1-59335-115-1(1), 1593351151) Soulmate Audio Bks.

Making of May. unabr. ed. Gwyneth Rees. Read by Gillian Walton. 6 CDs. (Running Time: 22500 sec.). (J). (gr. 3-6). 2007. audio compact disk 59.95 (978-1-4056-5579-8(8), Chivers Child Audio) AudioGO.

Making of Mia. Ilana Fox. 2008. 69.95 (978-0-7531-3094-0(7)); audio compact disk 84.95 (978-0-7531-3095-7(5)) Pub: Isis Pubng Ltd GBR. Dist(s): Ulverscroft US

Making of Modern Britain: From Queen Victoria to V. E. Day. Andrew Marr. Read by Andrew Marr. (Running Time: 7 hrs.). (ENG.). 2009. audio compact disk 37.95 (978-0-230-71312-3(2), Macmillan) Pub: Pan Macmillan GBR. Dist(s): Trans-Atl Phila

Making of Modern Economics: The Lives & Ideas of the Great Thinkers. unabr. ed. Mark Skousen. Read by Patrick Cullen. 14 cass. (Running Time: 20 hrs. 30 mins.). 2002. 89.95 (978-0-7861-2295-0(1), 2984) Blckstn Audio.

The new history of economics - the story of how the great economic thinkers built a rigorous social science without peer.

Making of Modern Economics: Second Edition: The Lives & Ideas of the Great Thinkers. unabr. ed. Mark Skousen. (Running Time: 22 hrs.). (ENG.). 2009. 44.95 (978-1-4332-9400-6(1)); audio compact disk 32.95 (978-1-4332-9399-3(4)) Blckstn Audio.

Making of Modern Economics, Second Edition: The Lives & Ideas of the Great Thinkers. unabr. ed. Mark Skousen. (Running Time: 22 hrs. 0 mins.). (ENG.). 2009. 109.95 (978-1-4332-9396-2(X)); audio compact disk 123.00 (978-1-4332-9397-9(8)) Blckstn Audio.

Making of Modern Medicine: A BBC Radio Production. Read by Andrew Cunningham. (Running Time: 6 hrs. 0 mins. 0 sec.). (ENG.). 2009. audio compact disk 49.95 (978-1-60283-771-3(6)) Pub: AudioGO. Dist(s): Perseus Dist

***Making of Music, Vol. 1.** Read by James Naughtie. 6. (Running Time: 6 hrs. 0 mins. 0 sec.). (ENG., 2010. audio compact disk 49.95 (978-1-4056-7778-3(3)) Pub: AudioGO. Dist(s): Perseus Dist

***Making of Music, Vol. 2.** Read by James Naughtie. (Running Time: 6 hrs. 45 mins. 0 sec.). (ENG., 2010. audio compact disk 49.95 (978-1-4056-7779-0(1)) Pub: AudioGO. Dist(s): Perseus Dist

Making of Music: Volumes One & Two: A BBC Radio Production. Read by James Naughtie. (Running Time: 12 hrs. 0 mins. 0 sec.). (ENG.). 2009. audio compact disk 79.95 (978-1-60283-772-0(4)) Pub: AudioGO. Dist(s): Perseus Dist

Making of the Achiever. Allan Cox. 1 cass. 1987. 11.00 (978-0-89811-265-8(6), SP100070) Meyer Res Grp.

Learn the four winning qualities of successful executives: centered, courageous, judicious, & resourceful.

Making of the Achiever. Allan Cox. 1 cass. 10.00 (SP100070) SMI Intl.

If you want to advance in your current executive capacity, or if you are ambitious for an executive career, you will welcome the practical principles presented here. Four winning qualities of success executives are discussed - other-centered, courageous, judicious & resourceful. The successful executive is characterized by substance & performance.

Making of the Atomic Bomb see Richard Rhodes

Making of the Atomic Bomb. Richard Rhodes. Read by Grover Gardner. 1992. 96.00 (978-0-7366-2182-3(2)) Books on Tape.

Making of the Atomic Bomb, Pt. 1. unabr. ed. Richard Rhodes. Read by Grover Gardner. 12 cass. (Running Time: 18 hrs.). 1992. 96.00 (978-0-7366-2181-6(4), 2978-A) Books on Tape.

Here in rich detail, alive with human, political & scientific drama, is the complete story of how "the bomb" was developed. Pulitzer Prize winner.

Making of the Atomic Bomb, Pt. 2. unabr. ed. Richard Rhodes. Read by Grover Gardner. 12 cass. (Running Time: 18 hrs.). 1992. 96.00 (2978-B) Books on Tape.

Making of the Fittest: DNA & the Ultimate Forensic Record of Evolution. unabr. ed. Sean B. Carroll. Read by Patrick G. Lawlor. 10 CDs. (Running Time: 8 hrs. 0 mins. 0 sec.). (ENG.). 2007. audio compact disk 69.99 (978-1-4001-3315-4(7)); audio compact disk 24.99 (978-1-4001-5315-2(8)); audio compact disk 34.99 (978-1-4001-0315-7(0)) Pub: Tantor Media. Dist(s): IngramPubServ

Making of the President Pt. 1: 1960 (Kennedy vs. Nixon), unabr. collector's ed. Theodore H. White. Read by Grover Gardner. 7 cass. (Running Time: 10 hrs. 30 min.). 1987. 56.00 (978-0-7366-1191-6(6), 2110-A) Books on Tape.

Takes a look at the political campaign of Kennedy vs. Nixon.

Making of the President Pt. 2: 1960 (Kennedy vs. Nixon), collector's ed. Theodore H. White. Read by Grover Gardner. 6 cass. (Running Time: 9 hrs.). 1987. 48.00 (978-0-7366-1192-3(4), 2110-B) Books on Tape.

White, a journalist who makes contemporary history come alive, takes the cold ashes of political campaign & injects such a sense of immediacy that one feels again the tensions, uncertainties & emotional partisanship, a permanent contribution to the study of our democratic procedures.

Making of Toro. unabr. ed. Mark Sundeen. Read by Robertson Dean. 4 CDs. (Running Time: 5 hrs. 30 mins.). 2003. audio compact disk 32.00 (978-0-7861-9098-0(1), 3162); 32.95 (978-0-7861-2555-5(1), 3162) Blckstn Audio.

A brilliant and hilarious story of what happens when you try too hard to make life into high art.

Making Organizations Competitive: Enhancing Networks & Relationships Across Traditional Boundaries. Ralph H. Kilmann et al. (Management Ser.). 1990. bk. 43.95 (978-1-55542-285-1(3), Jossey-Bass) Wiley US.

Making Peace Heart Uprising. Laura Sim[illegible] Read by Laura Simms. Music by Steve Gorn et al. Prod. by Michael R. [illegible] 1 cass. (Running Time: 1 hr. 06 min.). (YA). (gr. 8 up). 1993. 10.00 (978-[illegible]6929-10-4(6), EW-C4925); audio compact disk 14.00 (978-1-886929-09-8(2), EW-CE4925) Earwig.

Some stories are ancient myths from Asia & Africa, others reveal the magic in every day moments in the turbulent urban environments. Many of the stories are accompanied by hypnotic music on an eclectic range of instruments.

Making Peace with Your Past. Martha B. Beveridge. 1 cass. (Running Time: 60 min.). 1994. 9.95 (978-1-889237-30-5(2)) Options Now.

A step-by-step process helps you discover the most interesting history lesson you can learn...the history of "you".

Making Progress in Meditation. unabr. ed. Perf. by Eknath Easwaran. 1 cass. (Running Time: 1 hr.). 1991. 7.95 (978-1-58638-573-6(9)) Nilgiri Pr.

Making Progress in Russian. Patricia Anne Davis & Donald V. Oprendek. (ENG.). (C). 1984. 226.95 (978-0-471-51793-1(3), JWiley) Wiley US.

Making Progress to First Certificate: A Pre-First Certificate Course, Set. Leo Jones. (Running Time: 2 hrs. 40 mins.). (ENG., 2005. audio compact disk 42.00 (978-0-521-53708-7(8)) Cambridge U Pr.

Making Quality a Way of Life. (Running Time: 48 mins.). audio compact disk (978-1-59076-204-2(5)) DscvrHlpPubng.

Making Relationships Work. Laurie Brady. 1 cass. 8.95 (033) Am Fed Astrologers.
Problems and solutions based on Venus aspects.

Making Relationships Work for You. Hal Stone & Sidra Stone. 2 cass. (Running Time: 2 hrs.). (Voice Dialogue Tapes Ser.). 1994. 16.95 (978-1-56557-022-1(7), T41) Delos Inc.
In these two tapes "Meeting Yourselves" & "The Dance of Selves in Relationships," Drs. Hal & Sidra Stone introduce you to the amazing family of selves that lives within you. In the first tape you will see how these selves developed & how they affect your life. In the second, you will see the impact they have on your relationships.

Making Room for Life: Trading Chaotic Lifestyles for Connected Relationships. unabr. ed. Randy Frazee. 1 cass. 2004. 24.99 (978-0-310-25685-4(2)) Zondervan.

Making Room for Life: Trading Chaotic Lifestyles for Connected Relationships. unabr. ed. Zondervan Publishing Staff & Randy Frazee. (Running Time: 4 hrs. 30 mins. 0 sec.). (ENG.). 2003. 14.99 (978-0-310-26162-9(7)) Zondervan.

Making Room for Yourself. unabr. ed. Keith A. Butler. 1 cass. (Running Time: 1 hr. 30 mins.). 2001. 5.00 (A107) Word Faith Pubng.

Making Room to Pray. unabr. ed. Terry Teykl. 1 cass. 1996. 5.00 (978-1-57892-036-5(1)) Prayer Pt Pr.
How to start a pray room in your church.

Making Rounds with Oscar: The Extraordinary Gift of an Ordinary Cat. unabr. ed. David Dosa. (Running Time: 8 hrs. 30 mins.). 2010. audio compact disk 34.95 (978-1-4417-2120-4(7)) Blckstn Audio.

Making Rounds with Oscar: The Extraordinary Gift of an Ordinary Cat. unabr. ed. David Dosa. Read by Ray Porter. (Running Time: 8 hrs. 30 mins.). 2010. 29.95 (978-1-4417-2121-1(5)); 54.95 (978-1-4417-2117-4(7)); audio compact disk 76.00 (978-1-4417-2118-1(5)) Blckstn Audio.

Making Rules Audio CD. Adapted by Benchmark Education Company Staff. Based on a work by Vickey Herold. (Early Explorers Set C Ser.). (J). (gr. 2). 2008. audio compact disk 10.00 (978-1-60437-548-0(5)) Benchmark Educ.

Making Schools Safe for Students: Creating a Proactive School Safety Plan. Peter D. Blauvelt. 2000. 59.95 (978-0-7619-7735-3(X)) Pub: Corwin Pr. Dist(s): SAGE

Making Sense of Gospel Symbols. Alonzo Gaskill. 2004. audio compact disk 11.95 (978-1-57734-888-7(5)) Covenant Comms.

Making Sense of Sensory Integration. Interview with Jane Koomar et al. 1 cass. (Running Time: 1 hr. 15 min.). (Belle Curve Information Ser.). 1998. (978-1-893601-26-0(9)) Sensory Res.
Informed conversation with recognized experts.

Making Sense of Suffering. Carole Riley. 2 cass. (Running Time: 2 hrs.). 2001. vinyl bd. 18.95 (A6350) St Anthony Mess Pr.
Speaks directly and sensitively about the mystery of human suffering; offers spiritual and psychological helps to spiritual growth for the one suffering and for the caregiver.

Making Sense of Wine. unabr. ed. Matt Kramer. Read by Frederick Davidson. 5 cass. (Running Time: 7 hrs.). 1994. 39.95 (978-0-7861-0776-6(6), 1504) Blckstn Audio.
Here you will find a sensibility about wine. Where others talk jargon about centrifuges, stainless steel tanks, & levels of acidity, author Matt Kramer talks about wine. A much-needed reminder that wine is an expression of the Earth, a revelation of site & grape to which we are witnesses & cultivators. You will discover a satisfaction that goes far beyond knowing how to read a label or impress a waiter.

Making Sense of Wine. unabr. ed. Matt Kramer. Read by Frederick Davidson. (Running Time: 23400 sec.). 2007. audio compact disk 55.00 (978-0-7861-6196-6(5)); audio compact disk 29.95 (978-0-7861-7274-0(6)) Blckstn Audio.

Making Small Groups Work. unabr. ed. Henry Cloud & John Townsend. 2003. 29.99 (978-0-310-25512-3(0)) Zondervan.

Making Small Groups Work: What Every Small Group Leader Needs to Know. unabr. ed. Henry Cloud & John Townsend. (Running Time: 7 hrs. 30 mins. 0 sec.). (ENG.). 2003. 20.99 (978-0-310-26163-6(5)) Zondervan.

Making Standards Work, 3rd Edition - 6 cd Set: How to Implement Standards-Based Assessments in the Classroom, School, & District. Douglas B. Reeves. 2005. audio compact disk 30.00 (978-0-9747343-4-7(9)) Pub: LeadplusLrn. Dist(s): Natl Bk Netwk

Making Technology Strategic. Contrib. by Gene Swearinger et al. (Transforming Local Government Ser.). Alliance Innov.

Making the Best Possible Use of Available Time. Instructed by Manly P. Hall. 8.95 (978-0-89314-177-6(1), C821212) Philos Res.

Making the Case for Yourself. unabr. ed. Susan Estrich. 4 cass. (Running Time: 6 hrs.). 1998. 24.95 (978-1-57511-038-7(5)) Pub Mills.
Well-known attorney, Estrich is a self-proclaimed "chronic diet failure" who finally succeeded at losing weight by applying her skills as a lawyer to dieting.

Making the Character Connection Vol. 1: Parenting to Cultivate Caring, Self Reliant, Productive Children, unabr. ed. Laurie Hacking & JoAnne Barge. 1 cass. (Running Time: 1 hr.). (YA). 2000. 14.95 (978-0-9700082-1-3(X)) Charac Conn.
Series of conversations in "radio play" format, with parents & a psychologist discussing parenting issues & character development.

Making the Character Connection Vol. 2: Parenting to Cultivate Caring, Self Reliant, Productive Children, unabr. ed. Laurie Hacking & JoAnne Barge. 1 cass. (Running Time: 1 hr.). (YA). (gr. 6-10). 2000. 14.95 (978-0-9700082-0-6(1)) Charac Conn.
A series of conversations in "radio play" format, with parents & a psychologist discussing parenting issues & character development. Covers infant & toddler years.

Making the Connection: Scaling Telecenters for Development. Barbara Fillip & Dennis R. Foote. 2007. per. (978-0-89492-020-2(0)) Acad Educ Dev.

Making the Grade: What Advisors & Administrators Need to Know to Better Assist Students with Disabilities. Featuring Marilyn Kaff. (ENG.). 2009. audio compact disk 140.00 (978-1-935140-66-5(3)) Nat Acad Adv.

Making the Heart Whole Again: Stories for a Wounded World. Perf. by Milbre Burch. As told by Milbre Burch. (ENG.). (J). 2007. audio compact disk 15.00 (978-0-9795271-8-0(X)) Kind Crone.

Making the Holy Spirit Special. Kenneth Wapnick. 2009. 48.00 (978-1-59142-350-8(3)) Foun Miracles.

Making the Holy Spirit Special: The Arrogance of the Ego. Kenneth Wapnick. 2008. audio compact disk 54.00 (978-1-59142-349-2(X)) Foun Miracles.

Making the List: A Cultural History of the American Bestseller 1900-1999. unabr. ed. Michael Korda. Narrated by Richard M. Davidson. 6 cass. (Running Time: 8 hrs.). 2002. 78.00 (978-1-4025-1872-0(2)) Recorded Bks.
The author is uniquely suited to produce a witty and informed look at publishing and American culture through a decade-by-decade study of the bestseller lists of the twentieth century. But his format creatures a peculiar problem for a narrator, as Korda's analyses are followed by the lists for each year in question. Ingeniously, Davidson handles these as if he were broadcasting a sporting event, with sometimes a hint of Howard Cosell or even of Walter Winchell in the delivery. Interesting book; very clever performance.

Making the Marathon Your Event. abr. ed. Richard Benyo. Read by Jason MacDonald. 2 cass. (Running Time: 3 hrs.). Dramatization. bk. 15.95 set. (978-1-56703-026-6(2)) High-Top Sports.

Making the Mind One-Pointed. Eknath Easwaran. 1 cass. (Running Time: 49 min.). 1991. 7.95 (978-1-58638-574-3(7), MMO) Nilgiri Pr.
From Chapter 6 of the Bhagavad Gita, inspirational & practical tips for mastering the mind.

Making the Most of a Site Visit with a Member of Congress (CD) Featuring Robert McLean. Prod. by TheCapitol.Net. 2006. 107.00 (978-1-58733-039-1(3)) TheCapitol.

***Making the Most of Crystal Reports.** PUEI. 2010. audio compact disk 199.00 (978-1-935041-94-8(0), CareerTrack) P Univ E Inc.

Making the Rough Places Plain: Living Larger Than Hardships & Creating the Future You Deserve. unabr. ed. Asha Tyson. 1 cass. (Running Time: 30 min.). (YA). 1998. 12.00 (978-0-9677420-0-7(5)) ATD Pub.
A 30 minute motivation speech about overcoming disappointments & regrets.

***Making the Shift: How to Live Your True Divine Purpose.** unabr. ed. Wayne W. Dyer. 2010. audio compact disk 45.00 (978-1-4019-2816-2(1)) Hay House.

Making the Transition. Read by Mary Richards. 1 cass. (Running Time: 60 min.). (Series Two Thousand). 2007. audio compact disk 19.95 (978-1-56136-107-6(0)) Master Your Mind.

Making the World We Want. Robert Thurman. 4 cass. (Running Time: 5 hrs.). 2001. 29.95 (AB00139, Audio Wisdom) ElectronicUniv.

Making Things Happen; Balance Your Life & Achieve Your Goals. Susan Pazak. 2 Cassettes. (Running Time: 50 minutes each). 2003. 24.95 (978-0-9749961-1-0(4)); audio compact disk 24.95 (978-0-9749961-0-3(6)) S Pazak.
The 2 CD and workbook series helps others to overcome barriers and attain success in any area of life. It is a mind, body and spiritual approach to attaining and maintaining all that one desires. The audio series and workbook gives a step-by-step outline to assist in making goals and dreams become reality!.

Making Time Work for You. Rebecca L. Morgan. Read by Rebecca L. Morgan. 1 cass. (Running Time: 37 min.). 1993. 12.95 incl. script. (978-0-9660740-5-5(X)) Morgan Seminar.
Essentials of time management offers entertaining insights into human nature.

Making Time Work for You. Harold L. Taylor. 1 cass. (Running Time: 50 min.). 11.00 (978-0-89811-207-8(9), 9449) Meyer Res Grp.
Discusses time management techniques in the field & the office for goal accomplishment.

Making Time Work for You. Harold L. Taylor. 1 cass. 10.00 (SP100064) SMI Intl.
Start managing your life - your time - right now. As a manager learn how to organize, delegate, & design your own systems. Practical suggestions for managing your activities, attitudes, productivity, & reducing frustration.

Making Toast: A Family Story. unabr. ed. Roger Rosenblatt. Read by Roger Rosenblatt. (Running Time: 6 hrs. 0 mins.). 2010. 29.95 (978-1-4417-2137-2(1)); 44.95 (978-1-4417-2133-4(9)); audio compact disk 29.95 (978-1-4417-2136-5(3)); audio compact disk 55.00 (978-1-4417-2134-1(7)) Blckstn Audio.

Making UNIX & Windows NT Talk: Object-Oriented Inter-Platform Communications. Mark Nadelson & Thomas Hagan. 1999. pap. bk. 44.95 (978-0-87930-584-0(3)) Sci Tech Bks.

***Making Vision Stick.** Zondervan. (Running Time: 1 hr. 6 mins. 32 sec.). (Leadership Library). (ENG.). 2010. 9.99 (978-0-310-86907-8(2)) Zondervan.

Making War to Keep Peace: Trials & Errors in American Foreign Policy from Kuwait to Baghdad. abr. ed. Jeane J. Kirkpatrick. 2007. audio compact disk 29.95 (978-0-06-123076-9(6)) HarperCollins Pubs.

Making Waves. Casandra King. Read by Colleen Delaney et al. (Running Time: 6 hrs.). 2006. 19.95 (978-1-59912-902-0(7)) Iofy Corp.

Making Waves. abr. ed. Cassandra King. 5 CDs. (Running Time: 6 hrs.). (What's New Ser.). 2004. audio compact disk 29.95 (978-1-59316-024-1(0), LL116) Listen & Live.
In a small Alabama town in Zion County, life is finally looking up for twenty-year-old Donnette Sullivan.Having just inherited her aunt's old house and beauty shop, she's taken over the business, and her husband Tim, recently crippled in an accident, is beginning to cope not just with his disabilities but also with the loss of his dreams. Once a promising artist who gave up art for sports, Tim paints a sign for Donnette's shop, Making Waves. The raising of the sign causes ripples through the town.In a sequence of events-sometimes funny, sometimes tragic-leading up to the surprise denouement, the lives of Donnette, Tim, and others in their small circle of family and friends are unavoidably affected.Making Waves is about love and friendship and betrayal, unfulfilled desires and heartbreaking losses. Once the waves of change surge through Zion County, the lives of its people are inextricably altered.

Making Waves: Young People at Their Best. unabr. ed. Christina Clement. Read by Thomas Amshay. 1 cass. (Running Time: 45 min.). (YA). (gr. 10-12). 1989. 9.00 (978-0-939401-02-4(9)) RFTS Prod.
Teaches the necessity of not doing things the way the majority of people do.

Making Wise Choices. Speeches. Joel Osteen. 10 audio cass. (J). 2002. 40.00 (978-1-931877-16-9(5), JAS013); audio compact disk 40.00 (978-1-931877-34-3(3), JCS013) J Osteen.

Making Wise Choices, Pt. 1. Short Stories. Told to Joel Osteen. 1 Cass. (Running Time: 30 Mins.). 2002. 6.00 (978-1-59349-128-4(X), JA0128) J Osteen.

Making Wise Choices: Having Godly Wisdom. Speeches. Joel Osteen. 1 Cass. (Running Time: 30 Mins.). 2002. 6.00 (978-1-59349-129-1(8), JA0129) J Osteen.

Making Wise Choices Pt. 3: Having the Right Priorities. Speeches. Joel Osteen. 1 Cass. (Running Time: 30 Mins.). 2002. Rental 6.00 (978-1-59349-130-7(1), JA0130) J Osteen.

Making Wise Choices Pt. 4: Living a Life of Integrity. Short Stories. Joel Osteen. 1 cass. (Running Time: 30 Mins.). 2002. Rental 6.00 (978-1-59349-131-4(X), JA0131) J Osteen.

Making Wise Choices Pt. 5: Staying in God's Timing. Speeches. Joel Osteen. 1 Cass. (Running Time: 30 Mins). 2002. 6.00 (978-1-59349-132-1(8), JA0132) J Osteen.

Making Wise Choices Pt. 6: Discipline & Self-Control. Speeches. Joel Osteen. 1 Cass. (Running Time: 30 Mins). 2002. 6.00 (978-1-59349-133-8(6), JA0133) J Osteen.

Making Wise Choices Pt. 7: Living a Life of Hope. Short Stories. Told to Joel Osteen. 1 Cass. (Running Time: 30 Mins.). 2002. 6.00 (978-1-59349-134-5(4), JA0134) J Osteen.

Making Wise Choices Pt. 8: The Dangers of Reasoning. Speeches. As told by Joel Osteen. 1 Cass. (Running Time: 30 Mins). 2002. 6.00 (978-1-59349-135-2(2), JA0135) J Osteen.

Making Wise Choices Pt. 9: Choosing Faith Instead of Fear. Speeches. Joel Osteen. 1 Cass. (Running Time: 30 Mins.). 2002. Rental 6.00 (978-1-59349-136-9(0), JA0136) J Osteen.

Making Wise Choices Pt. 10: Choosing the Right Thoughts. Speeches. Joel Osteen. 1 Cass. (Running Time: 30 Mins). 2002. 6.00 (978-1-59349-137-6(9), JA0137) J Osteen.

Making Wise Decisions about College: And Life after Home School. Douglas W. Phillips. 1 cass. (Running Time: 2 hrs.). 1999. 12.00 (978-0-9665233-1-7(8)) Pub: Vsn Forum. Dist(s): STL Dist NA

Making Wise Decisions about College: And Life after Home School. Douglas W. Phillips. 1 CD. (Running Time: 2 hrs.). 1999. audio compact disk 10.00 (978-1-929241-33-0(X)) Pub: Vsn Forum. Dist(s): STL Dist NA

***Making Work Work.** abr. ed. Julie Morgenstern. Read by Julie Morgenstern. (ENG.). 2005. (978-0-06-085614-4(9), Harper Audio); (978-0-06-085613-7(0), Harper Audio) HarperCollins Pubs.

Making Work Work: New Strategies for Surviving & Thriving at the Office. unabr. abr. ed. Julie Morgenstern. Read by Julie Morgenstern. 4 CDs. (Running Time: 6 hrs.). 2004. audio compact disk 22.00 (978-0-06-075178-4(9)) HarperCollins Pubs.

***Making Your Case: The Art of Persuading Judges an unabridged reading by the authors on audio CD.** 2009th rev. ed. Antonin Scalia & Bryan A. Garner. 2009. 44.00 (978-0-314-24216-7(3)) Pub: West Pub. Dist(s): West

***Making Your Children's Ministry the Best Hour of Every Kid's Week.** David Staal & Sue Miller. (Running Time: 4 hrs. 32 mins. 0 sec.). (ENG.). 2008. 14.99 (978-0-310-30478-4(4)) Zondervan.

Making Your Dreams Come True: A Plan for Easily Discovering & Achieving the Life You Want! unabr. ed. Marcia Wieder. Read by Marcia Wieder. (Running Time: 5 hrs.). (ENG.). 2009. 24.98 (978-1-59659-368-8(7), GildAudio) Pub: Gildan Media. Dist(s): HachBkGrp

Making Your Dreams Work for You. Hal Stone & Sidra Stone. 2 cass. (Running Time: 2 hrs.). 1997. 16.95 (978-1-56557-052-8(9), T43) Delos Inc.
Wouldn't it be wonderful to have a wise & objective friend, someone who could give you accurate, non-judgmental feedback & impartial guidance as you explored your many selves? Your unconscious is just that friend! It is an invaluable support; a treasure trove of information & wisdom. Its gifts are relayed to you nightly through your dreams. In "Decoding Your Dreams" & "Exploring the Dark Side of Dreams" Drs. Hal & Sidra Stone help you to understand the messages carried by your dreams. Hal's many years as a Jungian analyst give additional depth to the many years of dream work that are summarized.

Making Your Fourth Grade the Best It Can Be, Set. Rick Kilcup. 6 cass. (Running Time: 4 hr. 26 min.). (J). (gr. 4). 1998. 75.00 Incl. handbk. (978-1-886397-19-4(8)) Bureau of Educ.

Making Your House a Home. Mac Hammond. 1 cass. (Happily Ever after Ser.: Vol. 3). 1996. 18.00 (978-1-57399-029-5(9)) Mac Hammond.
Teaching on cultivating an atmosphere of God & love in the home.

Making Your House a Home: Building a Sanctuary of God's Comfort, Strength, & Joy. Mac Hammond & Lynne Hammond. 3 CDs. 2007. audio compact disk 15.00 (978-1-57399-326-5(3)) Mac Hammond.

Making Your Kindergarten the Best It Can Be. Valerie Welk. Read by Valerie Welk. 6 cass. (Running Time: 4 hr. 30 min.). 1996. 75.00 Incl. handbk. (978-1-886397-06-4(6)) Bureau of Educ.
Live audio seminar & a comprehensive resource handbook.

Making Your Marriage Work. unabr. ed. Elisabeth Elliot. Read by Elisabeth Elliot. 1 cass. (Running Time: 1 hr.). 1990. 4.95 (978-0-8474-2172-5(4)) Back to Bible.
Elisabeth talks about what it really takes to make a lasting marriage - through sacrifice.

Making Your Mind Up. Jill Mansell. (Isis (CDs) Ser.). 2006. audio compact disk 99.95 (978-0-7531-2559-5(5)) Pub: ISIS Lrg Prnt GBR. Dist(s): Ulverscroft US

Making Your Mind Up. unabr. ed. Jill Mansell. Read by Julia Franklin. 11 cass. (Running Time: 13 hrs. 50 mins.). (Isis Cassettes Ser.). 2006. 89.95 (978-0-7531-3542-6(6)) Pub: ISIS Lrg Prnt GBR. Dist(s): Ulverscroft US

Making Your Thoughts Work for You. abr. ed. Wayne W. Dyer & Byron Katie. 5 CDs. 2007. audio compact disk 23.95 (978-1-4019-1189-8(7)) Hay House.

Making Yourself Heard: A Guide to Assertiveness. unabr. ed. Robert E. Alberti. 3 cass. 39.50 (S1930) J Norton Pubs.
Discusses how to develop an assertive personality without becoming overbearing or aggressive.

Makings of a Philanthropic Fundraiser: The Instructive Example of Milton Murray. Ronald A. Knott. (Nonprofit Sector-Public Administration Ser.). 1992. bk. 40.50 (978-1-55542-424-4(4), Jossey-Bass) Wiley US.

Makso's Farm (book & Tape) Maude Heurtelou. (ENG.). (J). 2006. 19.00 (978-1-58432-306-8(X)) Educa Vision.

***Malacca Conspiracy.** Zondervan. (Running Time: 12 hrs. 36 mins. 14 sec.). (ENG.). 2010. 14.99 (978-0-310-41177-2(7)) Zondervan.

Malachi Martin: Gods Messenger. Brian Doran. 1 cass. (Running Time: 2 hrs. 30 mins.). 2000. 19.95 (978-0-9707796-0-1(7)) Mark IX.
Life & words of exorcist, Vatican diplomat & New York Times best-seller, Malachi Martin. Filled with many moments of Martin, himself, close friends & fellow priests, recalling his own words & predictions of what lies ahead in the new millennium.

Malachi Martin: God's Messenger. unabr. ed. Contrib. by Bernard Janzen et al. 3 cass. (Running Time: 2 hrs. 30 mins.). 2000. 24.95 (978-1-885692-08-5(0), 20230) Cath Treas.
Fascinating bio of priest, exorcist, author & one of America's top ten most popular talk radio guest.

Malade Imaginaire. 2 cass. (FRE.). 1991. 26.95 (1094-H) Olivia & Hill.
In this comedy, medicine & particularly those who purport to practice it, are the target of Moliere's ridicule. Argan, our hypochondriac, surrounds himself with two doctors, Purgon & Diafoirus, who manage to keep him believing that he is on the brink of death.

maladie cherche à me Guérir. unabr. ed. Philippe Dransart. Read by Philippe Dransart. Read by Thierry Aveline. (YA). 2007. 69.99 (978-2-35569-067-9(7)) Find a World.

Malagasy Newspaper Reader & Grammar, Set. Thomas P. Jedele & Lucien E. Randrianarivelo. 2 cass. (Running Time: 60 min. per cass.). (MLA.). 1998. 13.00 (3149) Dunwoody Pr.
Designed to take students with little or no knowledge to a moderately advanced level. Forty-four reading selections by three native speakers, are varied in form, context, & vocabulary & provide snapshots of the cultural life of the country.

Malakand Field Force. unabr. collector's ed. Winston L. S. Churchill. Read by David Case. 7 cass. (Running Time: 10 hrs. 30 min.). 1992. 56.00 (978-0-7366-2109-0(1), 2913) Books on Tape.
As a young officer, the author journeyed to India to subdue an insurrection. Churchill's first book.

Malaria Dreams. unabr. collector's ed. Stuart Stevens. Read by Bill Whitaker. 6 cass. (Running Time: 9 hrs.). 1990. 48.00 (978-0-7366-1828-1(7), 2664) Books on Tape.
It started off innocently. Stevens & his companion, a former fashion model, purchased an ancient Toyota & set out for Algiers via the Sahara. It took them three months. To get there, they battled killer ants in Cameroon, pacified revolutionary soldiers in the middle of Lake Chad & coaxed the always reluctant Toyota across the world's hottest desert. But they made it, battered & scathed, to the shores of the Mediterranean.

Malataverne. Bernard Clavel. 3 cass. (FRE.). 1991. 34.95 (1506-LV) Olivia & Hill.
In a small mountain village three adolescents involved in petty crimes decide to steal the savings of an old woman. The young men represent the social ladder of the village: Serge, the son of an affluent engineer, Christophe, the son of the village shopkeeper & Robert, the son of a laborer, who goes along halfheartedly.

Malay Survival. 3 cass. (Running Time: 2 hrs. 30 mins.). 1993. pap. bk. 55.00 (978-0-88432-617-5(9), AFMA20) J Norton Pubs.
Features basic vocabulary of topics: introductions, food & drink, accommodations, money, communications & transportation. Reference cards help reinforce newly acquired vocabulary & expressions.

Malay, Survival. unabr. ed. 3 cass. (Running Time: 2 hrs. 30 min.). (MAY.). (J). (gr. 10-12). pap. bk. 55.00 (978-0-88432-608-3(X), AFMA20) J Norton Pubs.
Basic vocabulary & pronunciation for travel & day-to-day living.

Malcolm Forsyth. Malcolm Forsyth. 2004. audio compact disk 15.95 (978-0-662-33317-3(9)) Pub: Canadian Broadcasting CAN. Dist(s): Georgetown Term

Malcolm Gladwell Box Set. unabr. ed. Malcolm Gladwell. Read by Malcolm Gladwell. (Running Time: 24 hrs. 30 mins.). (ENG.). 2010. 49.99 (978-1-60788-208-4(6)); audio compact disk 79.98 (978-1-60788-207-7(8)) Pub: Hachet Audio. Dist(s): HachBkGrp

Malcolm Glass: In the Shadow of the Gourd. unabr. ed. Malcolm Glass. Read by Malcolm Glass. Interview with Rebekah Presson. 1 cass. (Running Time: 29 min.). 1991. 10.00 (032991) New Letters.
Glass is the author of two books of poems & a text on writing poetry. Here, he reads from his most recent book, "In the Shadow of the Gourd". Glass directs the writing program at Austin Peay University in Tennessee.

Malcolm Muggeridge. unabr. ed. Malcolm Muggeridge. 1 cass. (Author Speaks Ser.). 1991. 14.95 J Norton Pubs.
Archival recordings of 20th-century authors.

Malcolm X. unabr. ed. 1 cass. (Running Time: 1 hr. 30 mins.). (J). 1999. pap. bk. & tchr. ed. 19.95 (978-0-7887-0121-4(5), 79309T3) Recorded Bks.
Malcolm X led the Nation of Islam during one of the most turbulent periods of recent American history. Follow this courageous man's life, from his early years in the Klan-ruled south to his last speech in Harlem.

Malcolm X. unabr. ed. Jack Rummel. Read by Steven A. Jones. 2 cass. (Running Time: 2 hrs.). (Black Americans of Achievement Ser.). 1993. 15.95 set. (978-1-879557-04-8(5)) Audio Scholar.
Biography of Malcolm X for all ages. From critically acclaimed book published by Chelsea House Publishers.

***Malcolm X: A Life of Reinvention.** Manning Marable. (Running Time: 13 hrs.). (ENG.). 2011. audio compact disk 39.95 (978-0-14-242844-3(2), PengAudBks) Penguin Grp USA.

***Malcolm X: A Life of Reinvention.** unabr. ed. Manning Marable. (Running Time: 21 hrs. NaN mins.). (ENG.). 2011. 44.95 (978-1-4417-6684-7(7)); 105.95 (978-1-4417-6681-6(2)); audio compact disk 123.00 (978-1-4417-6682-3(0)) Blckstn Audio.

Malcolm X: Portrait of the "Black Shining Prince" 1 cass. (Running Time: 30 min.). 9.95 (F0120B090, HarperThor) HarpC GBR.

Malcolm X: Words from the Frontlines. 1 cass. (Running Time: 72 min.). 1992. 9.98 RCA Recs Label.
This compilation of Malcolm X's speeches from the years 1963-1965, assembled with the assistance of his widow, Dr. Betty Shabazz, is full of powerful material. Those who have read the black leader's autobiography or seen Spike Lee's film account of his life may still be unprepared for the forceful immediacy of X's public speaking style.

Malcolm X in Dialogue. 1 cass. 10.00 (HB267) Esstee Audios.
In a vibrant & highly emotional dialogue with a Black moderate, Malcolm X gives his views of the Black-White relationship.

Malcolm X Speaks! 1 cass. 10.00 (HB267) Esstee Audios.
Malcolm X in dialogue on subjects of Black interest.

Male - Female Principles within the Self. unabr. ed. Robert A. Monroe. Read by Robert A. Monroe. (Running Time: 45 min.). (Explorer Ser.). 1983. 12.95 (978-1-56113-015-3(X), 16) Monroe Institute.
The effects of auditory signals on the brain.

Male & Female. Margaret Mead. 2 cass. (Running Time: 2 hrs. 30 min.). 1995. 17.95 (978-1-879557-27-7(4)) Audio Scholar.
Margaret Mead's landmark studies on the relations between the sexes fascinated readers & stirred lasting debate. In "Male & Female," she applies her findings to American society.

Male Brain: A Breakthrough Understanding of How Men & Boys Think. unabr. ed. Louann Brizendine. Read by Kimberly Farr. (ENG.). 2010. audio compact disk 30.00 (978-0-7393-8401-5(5), Random AudioBks) Pub: Random Audio Pubg. Dist(s): Random

Male Chauvinism! How it Works. unabr. collector's ed. Michael Korda. Read by Wanda McCaddon. 7 cass. (Running Time: 10 hrs. 30 min.). 1983. 56.00 (978-0-7366-0639-4(4), 1598) Books on Tape.
Michael Korda writes about what male chauvinism means, why men act the way they do toward women in business, marriage & sex & ways men are finally being asked to, forced to, abandon.

Male Choir of Clwyd. unabr. ed. 1 cass. 10.95 (C11053) J Norton Pubs.
Songs in Welsh & English.

Male Homemakers Handbook: Or Never Kiss a Kid Who's Just Eaten a Toad. Tom Pinnock. Read by Tom Pinnock. 2 cass. (Running Time: 3 hrs.). 1997. 12.95 (978-1-882467-19-8(1)) Wildstone Media.
Describes what it was like to abandon an exciting job as a reporter for the Orlando Sentinel to be a househusband.

Male Multiple Orgasm: Step-by-Step. Jack L. Johnston. 1 cass. (Running Time: 45 min.). bk. 14.95 (A5484) Lghtwrks Aud & Vid.
This breakthrough seminar teaches you how to separate orgasm from the physical limitations of ejaculation, without using "squeeze techniques" or other forms of holding back. Instead, you'll learn to bring on & express incredible orgasms as often as you want. This powerful information offers you a dramatic expansion of your erotic life!.

Male Multiple Orgasm: Step-by-Step. 4th ed. Jack L. Johnston. 1 CD. (Running Time: 1 hr. 10 min.). 2001. audio compact disk 19.95 (978-1-882899-06-7(7), MMO4-CD) J Johnston Seminars.
This breakthrough discovery, now in its globally popular Fourth Edition, offers step by step instruction teaching men how to experience multiple orgasms without using any artificial means such as squeeze techniques or other "hold-back" methods. Supported by extensive followup information and support on our website at www.malemultipleorgasm.com.

Male Sexual Dysfunction. Bruce Goldberg. (ENG.). 2005. audio compact disk 17.00 (978-1-57968-047-3(X)) Pub: B Goldberg. Dist(s): Baker Taylor

Male Sexual Dysfunction. Bruce Goldberg. Read by Bruce Goldberg. 1 cass. (Running Time: 25 min.). (ENG.). 2005. 13.00 (978-1-885577-36-8(2)) Pub: B Goldberg. Dist(s): Baker Taylor
Through self-hypnosis overcome premature ejaculation and/or impotency, and increase sexual desire and enjoyment.

Male Sexual Power. 1 cass. 10.00 (978-1-58506-022-1(4), 52) New Life Inst OR.
Sexual problems are a common concern for many people. These problems have been found to respond very well to subconscious suggestion. For sale only to adults.

Male Virility. Dick Sutphen. 1 cass. (Running Time: 1 hr.). (RX17 Ser.). 14.98 (978-0-87554-422-9(3), RX167) Valley Sun.

Malefactor. E. Phillips Oppenheim. Read by John Bolen. (ENG.). 2005. audio compact disk 78.00 (978-1-4001-3042-9(5)) Pub: Tantor Media. Dist(s): IngramPubServ

Malefactor. unabr. ed. E. Phillips Oppenheim. Narrated by John Bolen. 7 CDs. (Running Time: 7 hrs. 38 mins.). (ENG.). 2002. audio compact disk 39.00 (978-1-4001-0042-2(9)); audio compact disk 20.00 (978-1-4001-5042-7(6)) Pub: Tantor Media. Dist(s): IngramPubServ
Sir Wingrave Seton has been imprisoned for nine years rather than betraying a lady's honor. He seeks revenge by acquiring immense wealth for the sole purpose of destroying the lives of others. A lonely housewife, a young stockbroker and an orphaned daughter are on the brink of disaster when a mysterious benefactor saves them. He ultimately goes after the woman who conspired to betray him with her husband. Seton takes great pleasure in the pain that he inflicts on the couple until a new lover thaws the malefactor's icy heart.

Malefactor. unabr. ed. E. Phillips Oppenheim. Narrated by John Bolen. (Running Time: 7 hrs. 30 mins. 0 sec.). (ENG.). 2009. audio compact disk 19.99 (978-1-4001-6107-2(X)); audio compact disk 55.99 (978-1-4001-4107-4(9)); audio compact disk 27.99 (978-1-4001-1107-7(2)) Pub: Tantor Media. Dist(s): IngramPubServ

Malenkiy Geroy. Fyodor Dostoyevsky. 3 cass. (Running Time: 3 hrs.). (RUS.). 1996. 39.50 (978-1-58085-554-9(7)) Interlingua VA.
One of Dostoevsky's early short novels & few love stories.

M'Aleph V'ad Tav: Spirit Duplicating Reading Primer. Avivia Langsam. (HEB., 1997. tchr. ed. 18.00 (978-0-915152-02-5(9), A040) Pub: Langsam Publishing Co. Dist(s): Torah Umesorah

Malheurs de Sophie. Sophie Comtesse De Segur. Read by Christine Authier. 2 cass. (FRE.). 1991. bk. 35.95 (1GA059) Olivia & Hill.
The adventures of four-year-old Sophie have delighted generations since the 19th-century. Brought up in aristocratic surroundings, Sophie is a little devil who is constantly getting into mischief. Good fun for everybody.

Malheurs de Sophie. Adapted by Anne-Marie Deraspe. Illus. by Anne Cote. 1 CD . (Running Time: 1 hr. 30 mins.).Tr. of Sophie's Misfortune. (FRE.). (J). (gr. 1-7). 1998. 16.95 (978-2-921997-46-1(0)); cass. & audio compact disk 12.95 (978-2-921997-47-8(9)) Pub: Coffragants CAN. Dist(s): Penton Overseas
Features classic children's fables recorded completely in French by well-known artists.

Malice. Robert K. Tanenbaum. Read by Mel Foster. (Playaway Adult Fiction Ser.). (ENG.). 2009. 85.00 (978-1-60775-543-2(2)) Find a World.

Malice. abr. ed. Lisa Jackson. Read by Joyce Bean & Mel Foster. 5 CDs. (Running Time: 6 hrs.). (New Orleans Ser.: Bk. 6). 2009. audio compact disk 26.99 (978-1-4233-1541-4(3), 9781423315414, BACD) Brilliance Audio.

Malice. abr. ed. Lisa Jackson. Read by Joyce Bean & Mel Foster. (Running Time: 6 hrs.). (New Orleans Ser.: Bk. 6). 2010. audio compact disk 14.99 (978-1-4233-1542-1(1), 9781423315421, BCD Value Price) Brilliance Audio.

Malice. abr. ed. Robert K. Tanenbaum. Read by Mel Foster. (Running Time: 21600 sec.). (Butch Karp/Marlene Ciampi Ser.). 2008. audio compact disk 14.99 (978-1-4233-4102-4(3), 9781423341024, BCD Value Price) Brilliance Audio.

Malice. unabr. ed. Lisa Jackson. Read by Mel Foster & Joyce Bean. 1 MP3-CD. (Running Time: 15 hrs.). (New Orleans Ser.: Bk. 6). 2009. 24.99 (978-1-4233-1537-7(5), 9781423315377, Brilliance MP3) Brilliance Audio.

Malice. unabr. ed. Lisa Jackson. Read by Joyce Bean & Joyce Mel Foster. (Running Time: 15 hrs.). (New Orleans Ser.: Bk. 6). 2009. 39.97 (978-1-4233-1540-7(5), 9781423315407, BADLE) Brilliance Audio.

Malice. unabr. ed. Lisa Jackson. Read by Joyce Bean & Mel Foster. 1 MP3-CD. (Running Time: 15 hrs.). (New Orleans Ser.: Bk. 6). 2009. 39.97 (978-1-4233-1538-4(3), 9781423315384, Brlnc Audio MP3 Lib) Brilliance Audio.

Malice. unabr. ed. Lisa Jackson. Read by Joyce Bean & Joyce Mel Foster. (Running Time: 15 hrs.). (New Orleans Ser.: Bk. 6). 2009. 24.99 (978-1-4233-1539-1(1), 9781423315391, BAD) Brilliance Audio.

Malice. unabr. ed. Lisa Jackson. Read by Joyce Bean & Mel Foster. 13 CDs. (Running Time: 15 hrs.). (New Orleans Ser.: Bk. 6). 2009. audio compact disk 36.99 (978-1-4233-1535-3(9), 9781423315353, Bril Audio CD Unabri); audio compact disk 97.97 (978-1-4233-1536-0(7), 9781423315360, BriAudCD Unabrid) Brilliance Audio.

Malice. unabr. ed. Robert K. Tanenbaum. Read by Mel Foster. (Running Time: 17 hrs.). (Butch Karp/Marlene Ciampi Ser.). 2007. 24.95 (978-1-4233-4100-0(7), 9781423341000, BAD); 97.25 (978-1-4233-4095-9(7), 9781423340959, BrilAudUnabridg); audio compact disk 117.25 (978-1-4233-4097-3(3), 9781423340973, BriAudCD Unabrid); audio compact disk 39.25 (978-1-4233-4099-7(X), 9781423340997, Brlnc Audio MP3 Lib); audio compact disk 24.95 (978-1-4233-4098-0(1), 9781423340980, Brilliance MP3); audio compact disk 38.95 (978-1-4233-4096-6(5), 9781423340966, Bril Audio CD Unabri) Brilliance Audio.

Malice. unabr. ed. Robert K. Tanenbaum. Read by Mel Foster. (Running Time: 17 hrs.). (Butch Karp/Marlene Ciampi Ser.). 2009. 39.97 (978-1-4418-5033-1(3), 9781441850331, BADLE) Brilliance Audio.

Malice Domestic. unabr. ed. Elizabeth Peters, pseud. Read by Loretta Swit. 4 cass. (Running Time: 6 hrs.). 2001. 25.00 (978-1-59040-142-2(5), Phoenix Audio) Pub: Amer Intl Pub. Dist(s): PerseuPGW

Malice Domestic No. 4: An Anthology of Original Traditional Mystery Stories, No. 4. unabr. ed. Carolyn G. Hart. Read by Robert Forster. 4 cass. (Running Time: 6 hrs.). 2001. 25.00 (978-1-59040-144-6(1), Phoenix Audio) Pub: Amer Intl Pub. Dist(s): PerseuPGW

Malice Domestic No. 5: An Anthology of Original Traditional Mystery Stories. unabr. ed. Phyllis A. Whitney. Read by Roger Rees. 4 cass. (Running Time: 6 hrs.). 2001. 25.00 (978-1-59040-145-3(X), Phoenix Audio) Pub: Amer Intl Pub. Dist(s): PerseuPGW

Malice Domestic Vol. 3: An Anthology of Original Traditional Mystery Stories. unabr. ed. Nancy Pickard. Read by Linda Hamilton. 4 cass. (Running Time: 6 hrs.). 2001. 25.00 (978-1-59040-143-9(3), Phoenix Audio) Pub: Amer Intl Pub. Dist(s): PerseuPGW

Malice Domestic Vol. 6: An Anthology of Original Traditional Mystery Stories. unabr. ed. Anne Perry. Read by Patrick Macnee. 4 cass. (Running Time: 6 hrs.). 2001. 25.00 (978-1-59040-146-0(8), Phoenix Audio) Pub: Amer Intl Pub. Dist(s): PerseuPGW

Malice in Miniature, unabr. collector's ed. Jeanne M. Dams. Read by Kate Reading. 5 cass. (Running Time: 7 hrs. 30 min.). (Dorothy Martin Mystery Ser.: Bk. 4). 1999. 40.00 (978-0-7366-4506-5(3), 4919) Books on Tape.
Now married to her constable, Alan, Dorothy is settling in for a life of peace, quiet & domestic bliss. That last a month, until Ada Finch calls on them: Bob, Ada's gardener son with the wee problem with the bottle, is being accused of the attempted theft of a tea set from the toy museum at Brocklesby Hall & she doesn't know what to do. Of course, Dorothy agrees to help, even if her investigation takes her from a doll house to the doors of hte morgue to the big secrets hidden in the rooms filled with miniatures. After all, Alan didn't forbid her to look around, did he?.

Malice Poetic. unabr. ed. Betty Rowlands. 5 cass. 1998. 63.95 (978-1-85903-090-5(4)) Pub: Magna Story GBR. Dist(s): Ulverscroft US

Malice Prepense. unabr. ed. Kate Wilhelm. Read by Anna Fields. 13 CDs. (Running Time: 15 hrs. 30 mins.). 2000. audio compact disk 104.00 (978-0-7861-8632-7(1), 3290) Blckstn Audio.

Malice Prepense. unabr. ed. Kate Wilhelm. Read by Anna Fields. 11 cass. (Running Time: 15 hrs. 30 mins.). 2001. 76.95 (978-0-7861-2757-3(0), 3290) Blckstn Audio.

Malidittu la Lingua (Damned Language) Vincenzo Ancona. Tr. by Gaetano Cipolla. 1991. pap. bk. 16.00 (978-0-921252-14-6(5)) LEGAS CAN.

Malik & the Fairy Rasta. Jessica M. Alarcon. Perf. by Jessica M. Alarcon. (ENG., (J). 2009. pap. bk. 20.00 (978-0-9792197-3-3(6)) Torkwase.

Malinche. unabr. ed. Laura Esquivel. Read by Lucía Méndez. 5 CDs. (Running Time: 21600 sec.). (SPA.). 2006. audio compact disk 24.95 (978-1-933499-38-3(9)) Fonolibro Inc.

Malinche. unabr. ed. Laura Esquivel. Read by Maria Conchita Alonso. 2006. 17.95 (978-0-7435-6455-7(3), Audioworks) Pub: S&S Audio. Dist(s): S and S Inc

Malinche's Conquest. unabr. ed. Anna Lanyon. Narrated by Deidre Rubenstein. 4 cass. (Running Time: 6 hrs. 45 mins.). 2004. 32.00 (978-1-74030-566-2(3)) Pub: Bolinda Pubng AUS. Dist(s): Lndmrk Audiobks

Mallawindy. unabr. ed. Joy Dettman. Read by Deidre Rubenstein. (Running Time: 14 hrs.). 2009. audio compact disk 108.95 (978-1-921334-39-9(8), 9781921334399) Pub: Bolinda Pubng AUS. Dist(s): Bolinda Pub Inc

Mallen Girl. unabr. ed. Catherine Marchant, pseud. Read by Elizabeth Henry. 8 cass. (Running Time: 12 hrs.). 2001. 69.95 (978-1-85496-274-4(4), 62744) Pub: Soundings Ltd GBR. Dist(s): Ulverscroft US

Mallen Streak. unabr. ed. Catherine Marchant, pseud. Read by Elizabeth Henry. 8 cass. (Running Time: 12 hrs.). 1997. 79.95 (978-1-85496-267-6(1), 62671) Pub: Soundings Ltd GBR. Dist(s): Ulverscroft US
Thomas Mallen of High Banks had many sons, most of them illegitimate. But to all of them he passed on his mark; this was a distinctive flash of white hair running down to the left temple, & known as "the Mallen streak". It was said in the surrounding Northumberland countryside that those who bore the streak seldom reached old age or died in bed & that nothing good ever came of a Mallen.

Mallets Aforethought. Sarah Graves. Read by Lindsay Ellison. 7 vols. (Home Repair Is Homicide Mystery Ser.). 2004. 59.95 (978-0-7927-3194-8(8), CSL 646, Chivers Sound Lib); audio compact disk 89.95 (978-0-7927-3195-5(6), SLD 646, Chivers Sound Lib) AudioGO.

Mallikarjun Mansur (Vocal), Vol. 1. Music by Mallikarjun Mansur. 1 cass. (Music Today Presents Ser.). 1992. (A92020) Multi-Cultural Bks.

Mallikarjun Mansur (Vocal), Vol. 2. Music by Mallikarjun Mansur. 1 cass. (Music Today Presents Ser.). 1992. (A92021) Multi-Cultural Bks.

Mallorca Connection. Peter Kerr. Read by James Bryce. (Running Time: 34200 sec.). 2007. 61.95 (978-1-84559-655-2(2)); audio compact disk 79.95 (978-1-84559-697-2(8)) Pub: ISIS Audio GBR. Dist(s): Ulverscroft US

Mallory Keep. unabr. ed. Aileen Armitage. Read by Karen Cass. 8 cass. (Running Time: 10 hrs. 30 mins.). 2000. 69.95 (978-0-7531-0552-8(7), 990914) Pub: ISIS Audio GBR. Dist(s): Ulverscroft US
Amity Lucas hopes to escape a life of dreariness by accepting the post of companion to Regina Fairfax in the isolated manor of Mallory Keep. But on discovering that Mallory Keep is cursed, Amity is struck with fear at the prospect of living with these strange people. When she is forced to agree to a marriage to Regina's brother Damian against her wishes, she finds herself trapped in a maelstrom of unhappiness & longing.

Mallow Years. unabr. ed. Audrey Howard. Read by Carole Boyd. 16 cass. (Running Time: 16 hrs.). 1998. 124.95 (978-0-7540-0140-9(7), CAB1563) AudioGO.
Kit Chapman is the daughter of a ruthless mill owner. She will inherit the business, but only if she can prove herself worthy of it. Joss Greenwood is a weaver, driven into abject poverty by the new machinery. Now his life is a constant struggle with the factory owners. Kit & Joss meet by chance & it is the start of a friendship that turns into love during times of complete distress.

Malone Dies. Samuel Beckett. Read by Sean Barrett. (Running Time: 6 hrs.). 2006. 31.95 (978-1-60083-837-8(5)) Iofy Corp.

Malone Dies. Samuel Beckett. Read by Sean Barrett. 2004. pap. bk. 34.98 (978-962-634-319-7(2), Naxos AudioBooks) Naxos.

Malonyl-Coenzyme A Decarboxylase Deficiency - A Bibliography & Dictionary for Physicians, Patients, & Genome Researchers. Compiled by Icon Group International, Inc. Staff. 2007. ring bd. 28.95 (978-0-497-11252-3(3)) Icon Grp.

Malpractice & the Ethical Aspects of Estate Planning Practice. Read by Michael C. Ferguson. (Running Time: 3 hrs.). 1990. 65.00 Incl. Ethics: 2 hrs., & 146p. tape materials. (ES-53238) Cont Ed Bar-CA.
Covers problems & pitfalls, from conflicts of interest through referral fees, dealing with difficult clients, qualifying clients for public benefits, & choosing whether to avoid probate.

Malpractice Crisis of the 80's: Is No Fault the Solution? 2 cass. (General Sessions Ser.: C85-GS2). 15.00 (8537) Am Coll Surgeons.

Maltese Angel. unabr. ed. Catherine Cookson. Read by Elizabeth Henry. 12 cass. (Running Time: 18 hrs.). (Sound Ser.). 2004. 94.95 (978-1-85496-716-9(9), 67169) Pub: UlverLrgPrint GBR. Dist(s): Ulverscroft US

Maltese Falcon see Maltese Falcon

Maltese Falcon. Perf. by Humphrey Bogart et al. 1 cass. (Running Time: 60 min.). 1946. 7.95 (MM-5740) Natl Recrd Co.

Maltese Falcon. Dashiell Hammett. Contrib. by Tom Wilkinson et al. 2 CDs. (Running Time: 1 hr. 55 mins.).Tr. of Maltese Falcon. 2005. audio compact disk 29.95 (978-0-7927-3590-8(0), BBCD 104) AudioGO.

Maltese Falcon. Dashiell Hammett. Read by Michael Prichard.Tr. of Maltese Falcon. 1980. audio compact disk 48.00 (978-0-7366-6047-1(X)) Books on Tape.

Maltese Falcon. abr. ed. Dashiell Hammett. Narrated by Daniel Chodos. 2 cass. (Running Time: 2 hrs. 54 min.).Tr. of Maltese Falcon. 12.95 (978-0-89926-141-6(8), 829) Audio Bk.

Maltese Falcon. unabr. ed. Dashiell Hammett. Read by Daniel Chodos. 6 cass.Tr. of Maltese Falcon. 35.70 (B-131) Audio Bk.

Maltese Falcon. unabr. ed. Dashiell Hammett. Read by William Dufris. 5 cass. (Running Time: 6 hrs. 30 mins.).Tr. of Maltese Falcon. 2004. 27.95 (978-1-57270-363-6(6)) Pub: Audio Partners. Dist(s): PerseuPGW

Maltese Falcon. unabr. ed. Dashiell Hammett. Read by William Dufris. 6 CDs. (Running Time: 6 hrs. 30 mins.). (Mystery Masters Ser.).Tr. of Maltese Falcon. (ENG.). 2004. audio compact disk 29.95 (978-1-57270-364-3(4)) Pub: AudioGO. Dist(s): Perseus Dist

Story introduces detective Sam Spade, a man of few words who displays little emotion. Hired by a woman - Miss Wonderly - to locate her sister, Spade gives the assignment to his partner Miles Archer. Archer tails the missing sister's companion, and within a single evening both Archer and the man have been shot dead. As Spade pursues the mystery of his partner's death, he is drawn into a circle of colorful characters: Miss Wonderly, who lies prettily and pathologically about everything; a fat, well-dressed man named Gutman; a jumpy man named Cairo; and an extremely stupid, impulsive gunman.

Maltese Falcon. unabr. ed. Dashiell Hammett. Read by Michael Prichard. 7 cass. (Running Time: 7 hrs.).Tr. of Maltese Falcon. 1980. 56.00 (978-0-7366-0263-1(1), 1258) Books on Tape.

Sam Spade's partner is murdered while working on a case, & it is Spade's job to find the killer. In his search, Spade runs mortal risks as he comes closer to the answer.

Maltese Falcon. unabr. ed. Dashiell Hammett. Read by Michael Prichard. 7 cass. (Running Time: 10 hrs.).Tr. of Maltese Falcon. 2001. 29.95 (978-0-7366-6754-8(7)) Books on Tape.

A colorful cast of characters includes the antiheroic detective Sam Spade, a slightly shop-worn private eye with his own solitary code of ethics; Brigid O'Shaughnessy, a deceptive beauty whose loyalties shift at the drop of a dime; Joel Cairo, an effete Levantine whose gun gives him courage; the very fat & jovial but sinister Casper Gutman; & Gutman's "gunsel" Wilmer, eager to be feared. All of them are looking for the Maltese falcon, a fabulously valuable 16th-century artifact.

Maltese Falcon. unabr. ed. Dashiell Hammett. 6 cass. (Running Time: 6 hrs. 30 min.).Tr. of Maltese Falcon. 1997. 54.95 Eye Ear.

A Landmark in American crime fiction, the search for the coveted jewel-encrusted falcon.

Maltese Falcon. unabr. ed. Dashiell Hammett. Read by William Dufris. 6 cass. (Running Time: 6 hrs. 30 min.). (Isis Ser.).Tr. of Maltese Falcon. (J). 1997. 54.95 (978-1-85695-796-0(9), 940305) Pub: ISIS Lrg Prnt GBR. Dist(s): Ulverscroft US

Maltese Falcon. unabr. ed. Dashiell Hammett. Read by William Dufris. 6 CDs. (Running Time: 6 hrs. 30 min.). (Isis Ser.).Tr. of Maltese Falcon. (J). 2001. audio compact disk 64.95 (978-0-7531-0700-3(7), 107007) Pub: ISIS Lrg Prnt GBR. Dist(s): Ulverscroft US

Maltese Falcon. unabr. ed. Dashiell Hammett & A. Full Cast. (Running Time: 5 hrs. NaN mins.).Tr. of Maltese Falcon. 2008. 34.95 (978-1-4332-5247-1(3)); audio compact disk 40.00 (978-1-4332-5248-8(1)) Blckstn Audio.

Maltese Falcon. unabr. ed. Dashiell Hammett & Yuri Rasovsky. Read by Full Cast Production Staff. (Running Time: 5 hrs. NaN mins.).Tr. of Maltese Falcon. 2008. audio compact disk 19.95 (978-1-4332-5250-1(3)) Blckstn Audio.

Maltese Falcon. unabr. ed. Dashiell Hammett & Yuri Rasovsky. Read by Michael Madsen et al. 3 CDs. (Running Time: 3 hrs. 30 mins.).Tr. of Maltese Falcon. 2008. audio compact disk 19.95 (978-1-4332-5249-5(X)) Blckstn Audio.

Maltese Falcon. unabr. collector's ed. Dashiell Hammett. Read by Michael Prichard. 6 CDs. (Running Time: 9 hrs.).Tr. of Maltese Falcon. 2001. audio compact disk 48.00 Books on Tape.

Sam Spade's partner is murdered while working on a case, and it is Spade's responsibility to find the killer. In his search, Spade runs mortal risks as he comes closer to the answer.

Maltese Goddess. Thomas M. Lopez. 1 cass. (Running Time: 76 min.). 1996. 12.95 (978-1-57677-065-8(6)) Lodestone Catalog.

A tremendous tribute-&-spoof of film noir, telling a gripping mystery story with musical numbers in the great tradition of American musical theatre. This is a cosmic mystery story, set in the late 1930s. A detective dies, & his daughter picks up the pieces - including his last case: a search for mysterious 5000 year old stature, reputed to have mystical powers. The storyline encounters Eastern mysticism, voodoo, snake poison, & some truly unsavory mobsters.

Maltese Goddess. unabr. ed. Meatball Fulton. Read by Ida Faiella et al. 1 cass. (Running Time: 75 min.). Dramatization. 1994. 12.50 (978-1-881137-37-5(6)); audio compact disk 15.00 (978-1-881137-93-1(7)) ZBS Found.

A 3-D detective story, set in the late 1930's. Recorded in binaural sound. The daughter of a dead detective tries to solve his last case, The Maltese Goddess, a stolen statue originally from Malta.

***Mam Cheoil - from There to Here.** Mary O'Sullivan. (ENG.). 1992. 11.95 (978-0-8023-7076-1(4)) Pub: Clo Iar-Chonnachta IRL. Dist(s): Dufour

Mama see Momma

Mama & Daughter see Poetry & Reflections

Mama Day. unabr. ed. Gloria Naylor. Read by Multivoice Production Staff. (Running Time: 12 hrs.). 2008. 39.25 (978-1-4233-5914-2(3), 9781423359142, BADLE); 39.25 (978-1-4233-5912-8(7), 9781423359128, Brilnc Audio MP3 Lib); 24.95 (978-1-4233-5913-5(5), 9781423359135, BAD); 24.95 (978-1-4233-5911-1(9), 9781423359111, Brilliance MP3) Brilliance Audio.

Mama Don't Allow. Read by Tom Chapin. Perf. by Tom Chapin. 11 vols. (Running Time: 11 mins.). (Live Oak Readalong Ser.). (J). (ps-4). 2001. pap. bk. 16.95 (978-0-87499-743-9(7)) Pub: Live Oak Media. Dist(s): AudioGO

Picturebook based on a traditional songs, about misfit musicians who form the Swamp Band and whose music is soon in demand - from the sharp-toothed alligators.

Mama Don't Allow. Thacher Hurd. Illus. by Thacher Hurd. 14 vols. (Running Time: 11 mins.). 2001. pap. bk. 33.95 (978-0-87499-745-3(3)); 9.95 (978-0-87499-742-2(9)) Live Oak Media.

Mama Don't Allow. Thacher Hurd. Illus. by Thacher Hurd. 11 vols. (Running Time: 11 mins.). (Live Oak Readalong Ser.). (J). 2001. pap. bk. 18.95 (978-1-59112-135-0(3)) Pub: Live Oak Media. Dist(s): AudioGO

Mama Don't Allow. Thacher Hurd. Illus. by Thacher Hurd. (Running Time: 11 mins.). (J). (ps-3). 2001. 12.95 (978-1-59112-131-2(0)) Live Oak Media.

Mama Don't Allow. Photos by Thacher Hurd. (J). 1985. 18.66 (978-0-676-31471-7(6)) SRA McGraw.

Mama Flora's Family. Alex Haley & David Stevens. 2000. 15.99 (978-0-7435-0549-9(2), Audioworks) S&S Audio.

Mama flora's Family: A Novel. David Stevens & Alex Haley. 2004. 15.95 (978-0-7435-4987-5(2)) Pub: S&S Audio. Dist(s): S and S Inc

Mama Gone & Other Stories to Trouble Your Sleep. Perf. by Milbre Burch. Retold by Milbre Burch. Based on a story by Connie Regan-Blake et al. (ENG.). 2007. audio compact disk 15.00 (978-0-9795271-7-3(1)) Kind Crone.

Mama Learns to Drive. Read by Donald Davis. Created by Donald Davis. 1 CD. (Running Time: 54 mins.). 2002. audio compact disk 14.95 (978-0-87483-687-5(5)) Pub: August Hse. Dist(s): Natl Bk Netwk

Learning to drive has occasioned emotions ranging from reasonable caution to unbridled terror. Learning under the watchful eye of one's spouse is an added challenge. Undertaking the task with anxious children in the backseat can only heighten the sensory richness of the moment. Davis recalls his mother's driving lessons through the objective eye of a patient and restrained child, in contrast with his little brother, whose oft-shouted refrain. "You're going to kill us all" rings in memory.

Mama Learns to Drive. unabr. ed. Donald Davis. Read by Donald Davis. (J). 2007. 34.99 (978-1-59895-935-2(2)) Find a World.

Mama Maria's Dance & Pasta Party. Cimino. 1998. 5.95 (978-1-878427-63-2(6)); audio compact disk 9.95 (978-1-878427-62-5(8)) Cimino Pub Grp.

Mama One, Mama Two. unabr. ed. Patricia MacLachlan. Perf. by Glenn Close. 1 cass. (Running Time: 31 mins.). (J). 1987. 9.95 (978-0-89845-661-5(4), CPN 1803) HarperCollins Pubs.

Three stories by the 1986 Newbery Award winner include "Mama One, Mama Two," "The Sick Day" & "Through Grandpa's Eyes.".

***Mama Rides the Norther.** Lewis B. Patten. 2009. (978-1-60136-449-4(0)) Audio Holding.

Mama Rides the Norther. Lewis B. Patten. (Running Time: 0 hr. 30 mins.). 1998. 10.95 (978-1-60083-456-1(6)) Iofy Corp.

Mama Rock's Rules: Ten Lessons for Raising a Houseful of Successful Children. abr. unabr. ed. Rose Rock & Valerie Graham. Read by Rose Rock. Frwd. by Chris Rock. (Running Time: 21600 sec.). 2008. audio compact disk 29.95 (978-0-06-157115-2(6), Harper Audio) HarperCollins Pubs.

***Mama Rock's Rules: Ten Lessons for Raising Ten (or Less) Successful Children.** abr. ed. Rose Rock & Valerie Graham. Read by Rose Rock. (ENG.). 2008. (978-0-06-163254-9(6)) HarperCollins Pubs.

***Mama Rock's Rules: Ten Lessons for Raising Ten (Or Less) Successful Children.** abr. ed. Rose Rock & Valerie Graham. Read by Rose Rock. (ENG.). 2008. (978-0-06-163263-1(5)) HarperCollins Pubs.

Mamaji. unabr. ed. Ved Mehta. Read by David Case. 6 cass. (Running Time: 9 hrs.). 1989. 48.00 (978-0-7366-1598-3(9), 2459) Books on Tape.

Mamaji is the second installment in Ved Mehta's autobiographical series. It is the story of his mother, Shanti Devi Mehta & of her high-caste Hindu forebears. Even in India ambition has its rewards. Mamaji's grandfather started by hawking lengths of cheap cloth. Her father rose to be a lawyer in the Punjab High Court, a Senate Fellow of Punjab University & was honored by the British. Mamaji became the shy, orthodox wife of a British & American trained physician who held high posts under the raj. The book is a layering of the stories of all those whose lives touched Mamaji's - her parents & grandparents, her friends & neighbors - & so brings to life from another point of view India in the late 19th & early 20th centuries.

Mama's Coming Home. Andrea Steffens. 1 cass. 9.00 (A0137-84) Sound Photosyn.

Music-accompanied poetry.

Mama's Family: Ruth 4:13-15. Ed Young. 1991. 4.95 (978-0-7417-1855-6(3), 855) Win Walk.

Mama's Hand: Bluegrass & Mountain Songs about Mother. audio compact disk 17.98 Provident Mus Dist.

Mama's Torah (Audio) The Role of Women. Batya Ruth Wootten. Voice by Batya Ruth Wootten. (ENG.). 2009. cd-rom 1.95 (978-1-886987-31-9(9)) KeyofDavid.

Mambo Kings Play Songs of Love. Óscar Hijuelos. Read by Óscar Hijuelos. (Running Time: 30 min.). 8.95 (AMF-205) Am Audio Prose.

Talks about music, memory and Cuban-American culture.

Mambo Tonight! (Medley) - ShotTrax. Arranged by Paula Foley Tillen. 1 CD. (Running Time: 7 mins.). 2000. audio compact disk 35.00 (08201232) H Leonard.

Here's a fun medley just for girls! Super staging possibilities! Includes: "Papa Loves Mambo," "Cuban Pete" & "Mambo Italiano.".

Mamloshen. Perf. by Mandy Patinkin. 1 cass., 1 CD. 8.78 (NONE 79459); audio compact disk 13.58 (NONE 79459) NewSound.

A collection of songs from turn-of-the century Europe. Sung entirely in Yiddish.

Mammals. Bev Harvey. 1 cass. Dramatization. (J). pap. bk. 6.95 (978-0-86545-100-1(1)) Spizzirri.

Information about everything from The aardvark to the manatee.

Mammon & the Archer see Favorite Stories by O. Henry

Mammoth Cheese. unabr. ed. Sheri Holman. Read by Laural Merlington. (Running Time: 16 hrs.). 2003. 97.25 (978-1-59355-113-1(4), 1593551134, BrilAudUnabridg); 34.95 (978-1-59355-112-4(6), 1593551126, BAU); audio compact disk 112.25 (978-1-59355-115-5(0), 1593551150, BriAudCD Unabrid); audio compact disk 38.95 (978-1-59355-114-8(2), 1593551142, Bril Audio CD Unabri) Brilliance Audio.

Beautifully crafted and driven by warm, vibrant characters, The Mammoth Cheese follows the residents of rural Three Chimneys, Virginia, on their historic journey to re-create the making of the original Thomas Jefferson-era, 1,235-pound "Mammoth Cheese." As the book opens, the town is joyously celebrating the birth of the Frank Eleven (eleven babies simultaneously born to Manda and James Frank after fertility treatments) and enjoying the thrill of notoriety as reform-minded presidential hopeful Adams Brooke visits the newborns. But as autumn progresses and the babies start to die, the community seeks to redeem itself through the making and transporting of a symbolic Mammoth Cheese to Washington, as a gift for the newly elected President Brooke. The cheese is the brainchild of August Vaughn, a farmhand by day and a President Jefferson impersonator by night, and the creation of Margaret Prickett, a single mother and cheese maker trying to save her century-old family farm. As Margaret slips deeper into debt and desperation, her thirteen-year-old daughter, Polly, slides closer to an inappropriate relationship with her radical, attentive history teacher.

Mammoth Cheese. unabr. ed. Sheri Holman. Read by Laural Merlington. (Running Time: 16 hrs.). 2004. 39.25 (978-1-59335-610-1(2), 1593356102, Brlnc Audio MP3 Lib) Brilliance Audio.

Mammoth Cheese. unabr. ed. Sheri Holman. Read by Laural Merlington. (Running Time: 16 hrs.). 2004. 39.25 (978-1-59710-478-4(7), 1597104787, BADLE); 24.95 (978-1-59710-479-1(5), 1597104795, BAD) Brilliance Audio.

Mammoth Cheese. unabr. ed. Sheri Holman. Read by Laural Merlington. (Running Time: 16 hrs.). 2004. 24.95 (978-1-59335-220-2(4), 1593352204) Soulmate Audio Bks.

Mammoth Hunters. Jean M. Auel. Read by Sandra Burr. (Playaway Adult Fiction Ser.). 2008. 119.99 (978-1-60640-810-0(0)) Find a World.

Mammoth Hunters. collector's ed. Jean M. Auel. Read by Donada Peters. 10 cass. (Running Time: 15 hrs.). (Earth's Children Ser.: Vol. 3). 1986. 80.00 (978-0-7366-0815-2(X), 1764-B) Books on Tape.

Ayla sets out from the valley on Whinney, the horse she tamed, with Jondalar, the man she nursed back to health & came to love. Together they meet the Mamutoi - the Mammoth Hunters - among them is Ranec, an artistic, magnetic master carver of ivory. Ayla finds herself torn between Ranec & Jondalar, but it is not until the great mammoth hunt, when Ayla's life is threatened, that a fateful decision is made.

Mammoth Hunters. unabr. ed. Jean M. Auel. Read by Sandra Burr. 18 cass. (Running Time: 26 hrs.). (Earth's Children Ser.: Vol. 3). 1986. 162.55 (978-1-56100-023-4(X), 156100023X, Unabridge Lib Edns) Brilliance Audio.

An epic novel of love, knowledge, jealousy, and hard choices. Ayla, the independent heroine of the Earth's Children (TM) series, sets out from the valley on Whinney, the horse she tamed. With her is Jondalar, the tall handsome, yellow-haired man she nursed back to health and came to love. Together they meet Mamutoi - the Mammoth Hunters - people like Ayla. But to Ayla, who was raised by the Clan of the Cave Bear, they are the "Others." She approaches them with a mixture of fear and curiosity. It is the Mamutoi master carver of ivory - dark skinned Ranec, flirtatious, artistic, magnetic - who Ayla finds herself drawn to the most. Because of her uncanny control over animals, her healing skills, and the magic firestone she discovers, Ayla is adopted into the Mammoth Hearth by Mamut, the ancient shaman of the Great Earth Mother. Ayla finds herself torn between her strong feelings for Ranec and her powerful love for the wildly jealous and unsure Jondalar. It is not until after the great mammoth hunt, when Ayla's life is threatened, that a fateful decision is made.

Mammoth Hunters. unabr. ed. Jean M. Auel. Read by Sandra Burr. 17 cass. (Running Time: 26 hrs.). (Earth's Children Ser.: Vol. 3). 1999. 49.95 (978-1-56740-472-2(3), 1567404723, BAU) Brilliance Audio.

Mammoth Hunters. unabr. ed. Jean M. Auel. Read by Sandra Burr. 24 CDs. (Running Time: 26 hrs.). (Earth's Children Ser.: Vol. 3). 2002. audio compact disk 59.95 (978-1-59086-090-8(X), 159086090X, CD Unabridged); audio compact disk 165.25 (978-1-59086-091-5(8), 1590860918, CD Unabrid Lib Ed) Brilliance Audio.

Mammoth Hunters. unabr. ed. Jean M. Auel. Read by Sandra Burr. (Running Time: 26 hrs.). (Earth's Children Ser.). 2004. 29.95 (978-1-59335-318-6(9), 1593353189, Brilliance MP3) Brilliance Audio.

Mammoth Hunters. unabr. ed. Jean M. Auel. Read by Sandra Burr. (Running Time: 93600 sec.). (Earth's Children Ser.: Vol. 3). 2004. audio compact disk 44.25 (978-1-59335-476-3(2), 1593354762, Brlnc Audio MP3 Lib) Brilliance Audio.

Mammoth Hunters. unabr. ed. Jean M. Auel. Read by Sandra Burr. (Running Time: 26 hrs.). (Earth's Children Ser.). 2004. 44.25 (978-1-59710-481-4(7), 1597104817, BADLE); 24.99 (978-1-59710-480-7(9), 1597104809, BAD) Brilliance Audio.

***Mammoth Hunters.** unabr. ed. Jean M. Auel. Read by Sandra Burr. (Running Time: 26 hrs.). (Earth's Children Ser.). 2011. 19.99 (978-1-61106-455-1(4), 9781611064551, Brilliance MP3); audio compact disk 29.99 (978-1-61106-453-7(8), 9781611064537, Bril Audio CD Unabri); audio compact disk 99.97 (978-1-61106-454-4(6), 9781611064544, BriAudCD Unabrid) Brilliance Audio.

Mammoth Hunters. unabr. ed. Jean M. Auel. Read by Sandra Burr. 18 cass. (Earth's Children Ser.: Vol. 3). 1999. 162.55 (FS9-51033) Highsmith.

Mammoth Hunters, Pt. 1. unabr. collector's ed. Jean M. Auel. Read by Donada Peters. 11 cass. (Running Time: 16 hrs. 30 min.). (Earth's Children Ser.: Vol. 3). 1986. 88.00 (978-0-7366-0814-5(1), 1764A) Books on Tape.

Ayla sets out from the valley on Whinney, the horse she tamed, with Jondalar, the man she nursed back to health & came to love. Together they meet the Mamutoi - the Mammoth Hunters - among them is Ranec, an artistic, magnetic master carver of ivory. Ayla finds herself torn between Ranec & Jondalar, but it is not until the great mammoth hunt, when Ayla's life is threatened, that a fateful decision is made.

Mammy. Brendan O'Carroll. Read by Donada Peters. 1999. audio compact disk 40.00 (978-0-7366-5196-7(9)) Books on Tape.

Mammy. Brendan O'Carroll. Read by Donada Peters. 4 cass. (Running Time: 6 hrs.). 2000. 24.95 (978-0-7366-4691-8(4)) Books on Tape.

Brendan O'Carroll chronicles with raw humor & great affection the comic misadventures of a large North Dublin family in the 1960s.

Mammy. abr. ed. Brendan O'Carroll. Read by Donada Peters. 4 cass. (Running Time: 9 hrs.). 2000. 29.95 (978-0-7366-4696-3(5)) Books on Tape.

Agnes Browne, a widowed mother of seven in 1960s Dublin, runs a fruit & vegetable stall, so no one is starving in her family. Agnes's adventures include fending off the advances of a smitten French pizzeria owner, whacking a nun with a cucumber, & when three funerals accidentally overlap at the funeral parlor, vainly trying to figure out which coffin contains her late husband.

Mammy. collector's ed. Brendan O'Carroll. Read by Donada Peters. 4 cass. (Running Time: 6 hrs.). 1999. 32.00 (978-0-7366-4657-4(4), 5039) Books on Tape.

Agnes Browne, a widowed mother of seven in 1960's Dublin, runs a fruit & vegetable stall, so no one is starving in her family. Agnes's adventures include fending off the advances of a smitten French pizzeria owner, whacking a nun with a cucumber, & when three funerals accidentally overlap at the funeral parlor, vainly trying to figure out which coffin contains her late husband.

Mammy. unabr. collector's ed. Brendan O'Carroll. Read by Donada Peters. 5 CDs. (Running Time: 7 hrs. 30 mins.). 2001. audio compact disk 40.00 Books on Tape.

Seven kids. One dead husband called "Redser." And not a chance that she'll be defeated. Not by Sister Magdalene, her daughter's tyrannical teacher. Not by the amorous overtures of the French proprietor of the local pizza parlour. Not by the medical crisis that threatens her best pal, Marion. Every morning at five, Agnes Browne leaves her tenement flat and sets up her produce stall on Moore Street, in the teeming heart of the Jarro - home to Dublin's dealers, dockers, draymen, and those on the dole. But to the fatherless Browne brood, Agnes is more than a beloved mother and neighborhood character. She's just about everything there is.

Mamur Zapt & the Camel of Destruction. unabr. ed. Michael Pearce. Narrated by Simon Prebble. 5 cass. (Running Time: 6 hrs. 15 mins.). (Mamur Zapt Mystery Ser.: Vol. 7). 1996. 44.00 (978-0-7887-0508-3(3), 94701E7) Recorded Bks.
If Captain Gareth Owen, the head of the Cairo Secret Police, fails to uncover certain powerful people, corruption will surely trample the hapless city in its path.

Mamur Zapt & the Donkey-Vous. unabr. ed. Michael Pearce. Read by Stuart Langton. 5 cass. (Running Time: 7 hrs. 30 min.). 1998. 40.00 (978-0-7366-3830-2(X), 4546) Books on Tape.
It is 1908 in British-ruled Cairo, & a wealthy Frenchman has vanished from the terrace of Shepheard's Hotel.

Mamur Zapt & the Donkey-Vous. unabr. ed. Michael Pearce. Narrated by Simon Prebble. 6 cass. (Running Time: 8 hrs.). (Mamur Zapt Mystery Ser.: Vol. 3). 1994. 51.00 (978-0-7887-0044-6(8), 94243E7) Recorded Bks.
When a wealthy Frenchman vanishes from the terrace of Shepherd's Hotel, one of the busiest places in the city, the Mamur Zapt thinks it should be a routine case, but surprisingly, witnesses are conspicuously absent.

Mamur Zapt & the Girl in the Nile. unabr. ed. Michael Pearce. Read by Stuart Langton. 5 cass. (Running Time: 7 hrs.). 1998. 42.00 (978-0-7366-4028-2(2), 4527) Books on Tape.
Chief of Police Owen Cadwallader discovers that a young woman's murder leads to high places. Set in turn-of-the-century Cairo.

Mamur Zapt & the Girl in the Nile. unabr. ed. Michael Pearce. Narrated by Simon Prebble. 6 cass. (Running Time: 7 hrs. 45 mins.). (Mamur Zapt Mystery Ser.: Vol. 5). 2000. 51.00 (978-0-7887-0320-1(X), 94512E7) Recorded Bks.
When a mysterious young woman plummets off a royal boat & her drowned body disappears, Mamur Zapt must discover her identity.

Mamur Zapt & the Men Behind. unabr. ed. Michael Pearce. Read by Stuart Langton. 7 cass. (Running Time: 7 hrs.). 1997. 42.00 (978-0-7366-3572-1(6), 4223) Books on Tape.
The Mamur Zapt turns the tables on mysterious men who follow Cairo's civil servants.

Mamur Zapt & the Men Behind. unabr. ed. Michael Pearce. Narrated by Simon Prebble. 6 cass. (Running Time: 8 hrs.). (Mamur Zapt Mystery Ser.: Vol. 4). 1994. 51.00 (978-0-7887-0090-3(1), 94330E7) Recorded Bks.
In the Cairo of 1909, a seeming reign of terror against British & Egyptian civil servants has the Mamur Zapt struggling with what appears to be a political uprising.

Mamur Zapt & the Men Behind. unabr. ed. Michael Pearce. Read by Simon Prebble. 6 cass. (Running Time: 8 hrs.). 1994. Rental 13.50 Set. (94330) Recorded Bks.

Mamur Zapt & the Night of the Dog. Michael Pearce. Read by Stuart Langton. 7 cass. (Running Time: 7 hrs.). 1997. 42.00 (978-0-7366-3573-8(4), 4224) Books on Tape.
Odd crimes point to a pattern that the Mamur Zapt sees. Can he prevent a catastrophe?.

Mamur Zapt & the Night of the Dog. unabr. ed. Michael Pearce. Narrated by Simon Prebble. 5 cass. (Running Time: 6 hrs. 30 mins.). (Mamur Zapt Mystery Ser.: Vol. 2). 1993. 44.00 (978-1-55690-824-8(5), 93125E7) Recorded Bks.
Gareth Cadwallader Owen, head of the Cairo CID at the turn of the century, must cope with a potentially explosive situation when a Coptic grave is desecrated.

Mamur Zapt & the Return of the Carpet. Michael Pearce. Read by Stuart Langton. 8 cass. (Running Time: 12 hrs.). 1997. 48.00 (978-0-7366-3574-5(2), 4225) Books on Tape.
The Mamur Zapt looks for terrorists after someone tries to assassinate a politician. Can he avert a disaster before a big religious event.

Mamur Zapt & the Return of the Carpet. unabr. ed. Michael Pearce. Narrated by Simon Prebble. 5 cass. (Running Time: 7 hrs. 30 mins.). (Mamur Zapt Mystery Ser.: Vol. 1). 1992. 44.00 (978-1-55690-795-1(8), 92416E7) Recorded Bks.
The Mamur Zapt - the British Head of the Cairo CID - investigates a mystery within a growing Egyptian Nationalist movement in 1908.

Mamur Zapt & the Spoils of Egypt. unabr. ed. Michael Pearce. Narrated by Simon Prebble. 5 cass. (Running Time: 6 hrs. 15 mins.). (Mamur Zapt Mystery Ser.: Vol. 6). 2000. 44.00 (978-0-7887-0389-8(7), 94581E7) Recorded Bks.
After the niece of the future President of the U. S. inspects some mummified crocodiles, someone tries to kill her. As Owen investigates the attempt, he suspects the woman has deadly motives for visiting Cairo.

Man. unabr. ed. Alexander Pope. Read by Robert L. Halvorson. 2 cass. (Running Time: 180 min.). 14.95 (39) Halvorson Assocs.

Man: A Tri-Unity. Richard Hall. Read by Richard Hall. 1 cass. (Running Time: 1 hr.). 1993. 6.00 (978-1-57838-023-7(5)) CrossLife Express.
Biblical doctrine.

Man: God or Beast. unabr. ed. Rene Jules Dubos & Robert Claiborne. 1 cass. (Running Time: 56 min.). 12.95 (40094) J Norton Pubs.
A discussion on the evolution of human nature with the theme: what makes the human species better than the beast & less than a god?.

Man: God or Beast? CD. Interview. Rene Dubos. Interview with Heywood Hale Broun, Jr. 1 CD. (Running Time: 50 mins.). (Heywood Hale Broun Ser.). 2006. audio compact disk 12.95 (978-1-57970-412-4(3), C40094D, Audio-For) J Norton Pubs.

Man - The Moral Dimension: Moral Prejudice in Human Opinion & Judgment & Other Lectures. 1 cass. (Running Time: 37 min.). (Of Man; The Island & the Continent Ser.: Vol. 1). 1996. 9.00 (978-1-889954-57-8(8)) J Cassidy Prodns.
Opening lecture for Workshop in Ethics on Human Prejudice.

Man about Town see Favorite Stories by O. Henry

Man after God's Heart. abr. ed. Jim George. Read by Greg Wheatley. 2 cass. (Running Time: 3 hrs.). 2003. 17.99 (978-1-58926-157-0(7), H61L-0140) Oasis Audio.
Will help you realize the tremendous joy and confidence that come from pursuing God in every area of your life.

Man After God's Own Heart. abr. ed. Jim George & Elizabeth George. Read by Greg Wheatley. 2003. 29.99 (978-1-58926-304-8(9)) Oasis Audio.

Man after God's Own Heart: Devoting Your Life to What Really Matters. abr. ed. Jim George. Narrated by Greg Wheatley. 3 CDs. (Running Time: 3 hrs.). (ENG.). 2003. audio compact disk 14.99 (978-1-58926-158-7(5), H61L-014D) Oasis Audio.

Man after God's Own Heart: Devoting Your Life to What Really Matters. abr. ed. Jim George. Narrated by Greg Wheatley. (ENG.). 2003. 10.49 (978-1-60814-019-0(9)) Oasis Audio.

Man after God's Own Heart: The Life of David. Speeches. 4 CDS. (Running Time: 4 hours). 2005. audio compact disk 20.00 (978-0-9767583-2-7(6)) Illumination MA.

Man Alive: The CBC Winnipeg Comedy Festival. Prod. by Jason Andrich. Directed By Al Rae. 1 CD. (Running Time: 3600 sec.). 2006. audio compact disk 15.95 (978-0-660-19549-0(6), CBC Audio) Canadian Broadcasting CAN.

Man & Boy. Tony Parsons. Narrated by Gerard Doyle. 8 CDs. (Running Time: 9 hrs. 30 mins.). audio compact disk 78.00 (978-0-7887-9897-9(9)) Recorded Bks.

Man & Boy. unabr. ed. Tony Parsons. Narrated by Gerard Doyle. 7 cass. (Running Time: 9 hrs. 30 mins.). 2000. 63.00 (978-1-84197-146-9(4), H1140E7) Recorded Bks.
Harry Silver has everything that money can buy & everything it can't. Yet something is niggling Harry. He is about to turn 30 & the end of his youth seems to be looming. In defiance to all good sense, he splashes out on a expensive red sports car & finds himself yearning to turn back the clock.

Man & Boy. unabr. ed. Tony Parsons. Ed. by Gerard Doyle. 6 cass. (Running Time: 9 hrs. 30 mins.). 2004. 29.99 (978-0-7887-8949-6(X), 00334) Recorded Bks.

Man & Boy: A Novel. abr. ed. Tony Parsons. 2004. 10.95 (978-0-7435-4988-2(0)) Pub: S&S Audio. Dist(s): S and S Inc

Man & God. 10.00 (RJ122) Esstee Audios.

Man & His Planet. unabr. ed. Aldous Huxley. 1 cass. (Running Time: 1 hr.). (Human Situation Ser.). 1959. 11.00 (01107) Big Sur Tapes.

Man & His Symbols. C. G. Jung. 2 cass. (Running Time: 2 hrs. 30 min.). 1994. 17.95 (978-1-879557-17-8(7)) Audio Scholar.
This was the last work undertaken by Swiss psychologist Carl Jung. Its catalyst was a dream Jung had in which he recognized the need to explain his theories to the lay public. Jung was a prolific writer with a wide following.

Man & Miracles. Kenneth E. Hagin. 1 cass. 4.95 (SH14) Faith Lib Pubns.

Man & Religion. unabr. ed. Aldous Huxley. 1 cass. (Running Time: 1 hr.). (Human Situation Ser.). 1959. 11.00 (01119) Big Sur Tapes.
Illustrates what he calls the two main kinds of religion: religion of immediate experience or direct acquaintance with the divine, & religion of symbols or knowledge about the divine. He finds no conflict between the mystical approach to religion & the scientific approach.

Man & the Devil. unabr. ed. Gilbert Highet. Read by Gilbert Highet. 1 cass. (Running Time: 30 min.). 9.95 (23313-A) J Norton Pubs.

Man & the Donkey; The Host: Flows of Inspiration. Ann Ree Colton & Jonathan Murro. 1 cass. 7.95 A R Colton Fnd.

Man & the Fox. Idries Shah. Illus. by Sally Mallam. (J). (ps). 2006. pap. bk. 28.95 (978-1-933779-01-0(2), Hoopoe Books) ISHK.

Man & the Snake see Great American Short Stories

Man & the Snake see Horseman in the Sky

Man As An Evolving Universe; Jesus as World Power. Ann Ree Colton & Jonathan Murro. 1 cass. 7.95 A R Colton Fnd.

Man at the Window. Betty Rowlands. Read by Diana Bishop. 6 cass. (Running Time: 8 hrs.). (Sound Ser.). 2001. 54.95 (978-1-84283-012-3(0)) Pub: UlverLrgPrint GBR. Dist(s): Ulverscroft US
Graham Shipley has come to the Cotswolds to take up a new teaching appointment and to make a fresh start after the break-up of his marriage. He is made welcome by the Head of the school and by his new neighbor in Upper Benbury, crime writer Melissa Craig. But shortly after his arrival a young girl is found drowned. Foul play is suspected and when Graham's past threatens to catch up with him, he asks for Melissa's help.

Man Called Cash: The Life, Love, & Faith of an American Legend. Steve Turner. Read by Rex Linn. (Running Time: 10 mins.). 2005. 59.95 (978-0-7861-3671-1(5)) Blckstn Audio.

Man Called Cash: The Life, Love, & Faith of an American Legend. Steve Turner. Read by Rex Linn. Frwd. by Kris Kristofferson. (Running Time: 32400 sec.). 2005. DVD, audio compact disk, audio compact disk 72.00 (978-0-7861-7696-0(2)) Blckstn Audio.

***Man Called Cash: The Life, Love, & Faith of an American Legend.** Steve Turner. Read by Rex Linn. Frwd. by Kris Kristofferson. (Playaway Adult Fiction Ser.). (ENG.). 2010. 59.99 (978-1-4417-1813-6(3)) Find a World.

Man Called Cash: The Life, Love, & Faith of an American Legend. movie tie-in unabr. ed. Steve Turner. Read by Rex Linn. Frwd. by Kris Kristofferson. 7 cass. (Running Time: 32400 sec.). 2005. 29.95 (978-0-7861-3548-6(4), E3518); audio compact disk 29.95 (978-0-7861-7776-9(4), ZE3518); audio compact disk 29.95 (978-0-7861-7974-9(0), ZM3518) Blckstn Audio.

Man Called Peter. unabr. collector's ed. Catherine Marshall. Read by Alice Ian. 7 cass. (Running Time: 10 hrs. 30 mins.). 1986. 56.00 (978-0-7366-0561-8(4), 1533) Books on Tape.

***Man Called Peter: The Story of Peter Marshall.** unabr. ed. Catherine Marshall. Narrated by Renee Ertl. (Running Time: 10 hrs. 27 mins. 44 sec.). (ENG.). 2010. 24.49 (978-1-60814-712-0(6)); audio compact disk 34.99 (978-1-59859-757-8(4)) Oasis Audio.

Man Called Trent. abr. unabr. ed. Louis L'Amour. Read by Jim Gough. 4 cass. (Running Time: 18000 sec.). 2006. 19.95 (978-0-7861-4468-6(8)); audio compact disk 19.95 (978-0-7861-7284-9(3)) Blckstn Audio.

Man Called Trent. unabr. ed. (Running Time: 18000 sec.). 2006. audio compact disk 36.00 (978-0-7861-6595-7(2)) Blckstn Audio.

Man Called Trent. unabr. ed. Read by Jim Gough. (Running Time: 18000 sec.). 2006. 34.95 (978-0-7861-4699-4(0)); audio compact disk 29.95 (978-0-7861-7706-6(3)) Blckstn Audio.

Man Called Trent: And Riders of the Dawn. unabr. ed. (Running Time: 34200 sec.). 2006. audio compact disk 29.95 (978-0-7861-7569-7(9)) Blckstn Audio.

Man Called Trent: And Riders of the Dawn. unabr. ed. Read by Jim Gough. 8 CDs. (Running Time: 34200 sec.). 2006. audio compact disk 25.95 (978-0-7861-7129-3(4)) Blckstn Audio.

Man Called Trouble. unabr. ed. Jeffrey A. Poston. Read by Rusty Nelson. 6 cass. (Running Time: 6 hrs. 6 min.). 1999. 36.95 (978-1-55686-857-3(X)) Books in Motion.
Young Jason kills a man in self defense, & soon finds himself hunted by the friends of the dead man.

Man Called X. Herbert Marshall. 3 CDs. (Running Time: 3 cass.). 2002. audio compact disk 19.98 Radio Spirits.

Man Called X. Perf. by Herbert Marshall. 2 cass. (Running Time: 3 hrs.). 2002. 17.98 (27654) Radio Spirits.
Wherever there is mystery, intrigue, romance, ina all the strange and dangerous places of the world, there you will find The Man Called X. For eight years, listeners followed the adventures of agent Ken Thurston, jet-seeking man of mystery.

Man Called X. Contrib. by Herbert Marshall. (Running Time: 10800 sec.). 2004. 9.98 (978-1-57019-526-6(9)) Radio Spirits.

Man Called X, collector's ed. Perf. by Herbert Marshall. 6 cass. (Running Time: 9 hrs.). 1998. bk. 17.49 (4024) Radio Spirits.
Globetrotting secret agent Ken Thurston, along with his sidekick Pagan Zeldschmidt, solves mysteries for the U.S. government in 18 original episodes.

Man Called X: Blue Unicorn Inn & Indian Land Reclamation. Perf. by Herbert Marshall. 1 cass. (Running Time: 1 hr.). 2001. 6.98 (1776) Radio Spirits.

Man Called X: Chasing a Dead Agent & Assassination by Zombies. Perf. by Herbert Marshall. 1 cass. (Running Time: 1 hr.). 2001. 6.98 (1779) Radio Spirits.

Man Called X: Cholera Epidemic in Malaysia & Foot-in-Mouth Disease. Perf. by Herbert Marshall. 1 cass. (Running Time: 1 hr.). 2001. 6.98 (1785) Radio Spirits.

Man Called X: Cobalt Conspiracy in Tanganyika & Stolen Nerve Gas. Perf. by Herbert Marshall. 1 cass. (Running Time: 1 hr.). 2001. 6.98 (1783) Radio Spirits.

Man Called X: Japanese Weather Station & The Clicking Buddha. Perf. by Herbert Marshall. 1 cass. (Running Time: 1 hr.). 2001. 6.98 (1782) Radio Spirits.

Man Called X: Journey to Zenophon & Missing Scientists. Perf. by Herbert Marshall. 1 cass. (Running Time: 1 hr.). 2001. 6.98 (2041) Radio Spirits.

Man Called X: Medicine Smuggling in Red China & Spy in Bucharest. Perf. by Herbert Marshall. 1 cass. (Running Time: 1 hr.). 2001. 6.98 (1780) Radio Spirits.

Man Called X: Missing Deciphering Machine Plans & Stolen Cholera Virus. Perf. by Herbert Marshall. 1 cass. (Running Time: 1 hr.). 2001. 6.98 (1515) Radio Spirits.

Man Called X: Murder on the French Riviera & Gun Running in Syria. Perf. by Herbert Marshall. 1 cass. (Running Time: 1 hr.). 2001. 6.98 (1778) Radio Spirits.

Man Called X: Operation Fifty & Cargo Contraband. Perf. by Herbert Marshall. 1 cass. (Running Time: 1 hr.). 2001. 6.98 (1774) Radio Spirits.

Man Called X: Rubber Sabotage & Grain Black Market in India. Perf. by Herbert Marshall. 1 cass. (Running Time: 1 hr.). 2001. 6.98 (1781) Radio Spirits.

Man Called X: Sicilian Farmland & The Desert of Death. Perf. by Herbert Marshall. 1 cass. (Running Time: 1 hr.). 2001. 6.98 (1784) Radio Spirits.

Man Called X: Student Riots at Leiden & Missing Informer in Ecuador. Perf. by Herbert Marshall. 1 cass. (Running Time: 1 hr.). 2001. 6.98 (1775) Radio Spirits.

Man Called X: Thurston's Christmas Story & Belgian Congo Uranium Mine. Perf. by Herbert Marshall. 1 cass. (Running Time: 1 hr.). 2001. 6.98 (2226) Radio Spirits.

Man Called X: Treason at White Sands & Race Against Death. Perf. by Herbert Marshall. 1 cass. (Running Time: 1 hr.). 2001. 6.98 (1777) Radio Spirits.

Man Coming Toward You see Twentieth-Century Poetry in English, No. 26, Recordings of Poets Reading Their Own Poetry

Man Eater. unabr. ed. Ted Willis. 6 cass. 1998. 69.95 (978-1-872672-76-2(0)) Pub: Magna Story GBR. Dist(s): Ulverscroft US

Man for Others. unabr. ed. Patricia Treece. Read by Patricia Treece. Read by Al Covaia. 6 cass. 24.95 set. (765) Ignatius Pr.
A moving & intimate account of St. Maximilian Kolbe's life & death through letters & documents written by those who knew him best, his mother, Franciscan brothers & associates, & the survivors of Auschwitz whose lives he touched so deeply.

Man from Beijing. unabr. ed. Henning Mankell. Read by Rosalyn Landor. Tr. by Laurie Thompson.Tr. of Kinesen. (ENG.). 2010. audio compact disk 45.00 (978-0-307-71235-6(4), Random AudioBks) Pub: Random Audio Pubg. Dist(s): Random

Man from Iron Bark. 2004. 8.95 (978-1-56008-963-6(6)); cass. & flmstrp 30.00 (978-1-56008-715-1(3)) Weston Woods.

Man from Laramie. unabr. collector's ed. T. T. Flynn. Read by John MacDonald. 7 cass. (Running Time: 7 hrs.). 1996. 42.00 (978-0-7366-3258-4(1), 3915) Books on Tape.
Down from Wyoming comes a lone rider, cutting across the blizzard-swept rim of the Rockies, through the scorched wastes of the desert & finally into New Mexico Territory. His name is Lockhart & he carries with him a driving hate for a man he doesn't know a gun-runner who paid Apaches to kill Lockhart's brother. Now Lockhart vows to make the man pay again this time with his life. Will their first meeting be the last?.

***Man from Macedonia: My life of service, struggle, faith, & Hope.** Aaron Johnson. Mem. of Aaron Johnson. Read by Sherman Mason. Told to Deb Cleveland. Frwd. by Chuck Colson. Prod. by The Deborah. (ENG.). 2010. audio compact disk 26.95 (978-0-615-35086-8(0)) D n D Walsh.

Man from Nowhere, Level 2. Bernard Smith. Contrib. by Philip Prowse. (Running Time: 1 hr. 5 mins.). (Cambridge English Readers Ser.). (ENG.). 2000. 9.45 (978-0-521-78362-0(3)) Cambridge U Pr.

Man from Odessa. unabr. ed. Greville Wynne. Read by Joe Dunlop. 8 cass. (Running Time: 10 hrs. 45 min.). (Isis Ser.). (J). 1995. 69.95 (978-1-85089-612-8(7), 90121) Pub: ISIS Lrg Prnt GBR. Dist(s): Ulverscroft US

***Man from Saigon: A Novel.** unabr. ed. Marti Leimbach. Narrated by Susan Ericksen. (Running Time: 12 hrs. 0 mins.). 2010. 17.99 (978-1-4001-8633-4(1)); 34.99 (978-1-4001-9633-3(7)); 24.99 (978-1-4001-6633-6(0)); audio compact disk 69.99 (978-1-4001-4633-8(X)); audio compact disk 34.99 (978-1-4001-1633-1(3)) Pub: Tantor Media. Dist(s): IngramPubServ

Man from Snowy River. unabr. ed. Elyne Mitchell. Read by Richard Aspel. 4 cass. (Running Time: 5 hrs. 30 mins.). 2004. 32.00 (978-1-74030-086-5(6), 500114) Pub: Bolinda Pubng AUS. Dist(s): Lndmrk Audiobks
From Banjo Paterson's immortal ballad comes the stirring tale of the boy who became the man from Snowy River.

Man from St. Petersburg. Ken Follett. 2 cass. (Running Time: 3 hrs.). 2001. (978-0-333-73531-2(5)) Macmillan UK GBR.

Man from St. Petersburg. abr. ed. Ken Follett. 2 cass. 12.95 (978-0-89926-198-0(1), 868) Audio Bk.
Thriller about World War I intrigue.

Man from St. Petersburg. unabr. ed. Ken Follett. Read by Sean Morgan. 8 cass. (Running Time: 11 hrs. 30 mins.). 1985. 49.95 (978-1-55686-216-8(4), 102597) Books in Motion.
His name is Feliks & he came to London to commit a murder that would change history. He had many weapons at his command. The most dangerous were the love of a beautiful young woman longing for the end of innocence & the passion of a high-born lady demanding satisfaction at any price.

Man from St. Petersburg. unabr. ed. Ken Follett. Read by Richard Green. 8 cass. (Running Time: 12 hrs.). 64.00 (978-0-7366-0606-6(8), 1572) Books on Tape.
The year is 1914, the season summer & Europe is tottering toward the first World War. That encounter, taken so casually, will destroy the flower of English, French & German manhood, free Russia from Czars, but chain her ineluctably to a new tyranny, setting the stage for World War II.

Man from St. Petersburg. unabr. ed. Ken Follett. Narrated by Simon Prebble. 9 cass. (Running Time: 12 hrs. 30 mins.). 1992. 78.00 (978-1-55690-751-7(6), 92117E7) Recorded Bks.
One man can accomplish the impossible - persuade the Russians into the war on the side of the allies.

Man from Stone Creek. abr. ed. Linda Lael Miller. Read by Buck Schirner. (Running Time: 14400 sec.). (Stone Creek Ser.: Bk. 1). 2007. audio compact disk 14.99 (978-1-4233-2151-4(0), 9781423321514, BCD Value Price) Brilliance Audio.

Man from Stone Creek. unabr. ed. Linda Lael Miller. Read by Buck Schirner. (Running Time: 11 hrs.). (Stone Creek Ser.: Bk. 1). 2006. 39.25 (978-1-4233-2149-1(9), 9781423321491, BADLE); 24.95 (978-1-4233-2148-4(0), 9781423321484, BAD); 87.25 (978-1-4233-2143-9(X), 9781423321439, BrilAudUnabridg); audio compact disk 102.25 (978-1-4233-2145-3(6), 9781423321453, BriAudCD Unabrid); audio compact disk 39.25 (978-1-4233-2147-7(2), 9781423321477, Brlnc Audio MP3 Lib); audio compact disk 36.95 (978-1-4233-2144-6(8), 9781423321446, Bril Audio CD Unabri); audio compact disk 24.95 (978-1-4233-2146-0(4), 9781423321460, Brilliance MP3) Brilliance Audio.
Please enter a Synopsis.

Man from the Sky. unabr. ed. Avi. Narrated by George Guidall. 2 pieces. (Running Time: 1 hr. 45 mins.). (gr. 5 up). 1999. 19.00 (978-0-7887-2897-6(0), 95704E7) Recorded Bks.
While spending the summer with his grandparents, young Jamie sees a man parachute down through the Pennsylvania sky. The man is very real & very dangerous. How can he convince his grandparents that the man is not part of his imagination?.

Man Highly Esteemed by God. Dan Corner. 1 cass. 3.00 (10) Evang Outreach.

Man, I Need a Job! 2 cass. (Running Time: 3 hrs.). (Information Ser.). 1995. 17.95 set. (978-1-878436-16-0(3)) OPEN TX.
Designed specifically for people with a record! Not the advice you find in a traditional job search workbook. Helps offenders successfully disclose their criminal history & conquer fear of rejection. A strong motivational tool covering traditional job search procedures along with the coping skills needed to overcome stigma in the workplace.

Man in a Case see Chelovek v Futlyare

Man in Full Pt. 1: A Novel. abr. ed. Tom Wolfe. Read by David Ogden Stiers. 6 cass. (Running Time: 9 hrs.). 1999. 27.50 (FS9-43294) Highsmith.

Man in Full Pt. 1: A Novel. unabr. ed. Tom Wolfe. Read by Michael Prichard. 12 cass. (Running Time: 18 hrs.). 1999. 96.00 (978-0-7366-4374-0(5), 4814-B) Books on Tape.
Set in Atlanta, examines a racially mixed late-century boomtown full of fresh wealth, speculation and world-wise politicians.

Man in Full Pt. 1: A Novel. unabr. ed. Tom Wolfe. Read by Michael Prichard. 13cass. (Running Time: 19 hrs. 30 min.). 1999. 104.00 (978-0-7366-4373-3(7), 4814-A) Books on Tape.
Set in Atlanta, A Man in Full examines a racially mixed late-century boomtown full of fresh wealth, speculators & world-wise politicans.

Man in Lower Ten. Mary Roberts Rinehart. Read by Rebecca C. Burns. (Running Time: 7 hrs.). 2004. 27.95 (978-1-59912-688-3(5)) Iofy Corp.

Man in Lower Ten. Mary Roberts Rinehart. Read by Jim Killavey. 5 cass. (Running Time: 8 hrs.). 1989. 35.00 incl. album. (C-163) Jimcin Record.
Murder & love on a speeding train.

Man in Lower Ten. unabr. ed. Mary Roberts Rinehart. Read by Lynda Evans. 6 cass. (Running Time: 6 hrs. 48 min.). 2001. 39.95 (978-1-55686-943-3(6)) Books in Motion.
When a young lawyer decides to carry case-winning evidence by train from New York to Pittsburgh, death and a train wreck follow with the lawyer being charged for murder.

Man in Lower Ten. unabr. ed. Mary Roberts Rinehart. Narrated by Rebecca C. Burns. (Running Time: 6 hrs. 30 mins. 0 sec.). (ENG.). 2008. audio compact disk 27.99 (978-1-4001-0800-8(4)); audio compact disk 19.99 (978-1-4001-5800-3(1)); audio compact disk 55.99 (978-1-4001-3800-5(0)) Pub: Tantor Media. Dist(s): IngramPubServ

Man in Lower Ten. unabr. collector's ed. Mary Roberts Rinehart. Read by Rebecca C. Burns. 5 cass. (Running Time: 7 hrs. 30 min.). 1998. 40.00 (978-0-7366-4152-4(1), 4655) Books on Tape.
An attorney sets off to deliver documents by train, & along the way is implicated in a murder.

Man in Lower Ten, Set. unabr. ed. Mary Roberts Rinehart. Read by Grover Gardner. 4 cass. (Running Time: 6 hrs.). 1991. 19.95 (978-1-55685-205-3(3)) Audio Bk Con.
A young lawyer survives a ghastly train wreck only to be accused of murdering a man who accidentally fell asleep in the wrong berth. Another classic whodunit by the author of "The Circular Staircase".

Man in My Basement. unabr. ed. Walter Mosley. Read by Ernie Hudson. (ENG.). 2005. 14.98 (978-1-59483-172-0(6)) Pub: Hachet Audio. Dist(s): HachBkGrp

Man in My Basement. unabr. ed. Walter Mosley. Read by Ernie Hudson. (Running Time: 5 hrs.). (ENG.). 2009. 49.98 (978-1-60024-564-0(1)) Pub: Hachet Audio. Dist(s): HachBkGrp

Man in That Airplane see Twentieth-Century Poetry in English, No. 26, Recordings of Poets Reading Their Own Poetry

Man in the Black Suit: 4 Dark Tales. unabr. ed. Stephen King. Narrated by Becky Ann Baker et al. 4 CDs. (Running Time: 40 hrs. 0 mins. 0 sec.). (ENG.). 2002. audio compact disk 29.95 (978-0-7435-2585-5(X), Audioworks) Pub: S&S Audio. Dist(s): S and S Inc
THE MAN IN THE BLACK SUIT FOUR UNABRIDGED DARK TALES FROM STEPHEN KING The Man in the Black Suit Read by John Cullum "...the face of the man in the black suit grows ever clearer, ever closer, and I remember every word he said. I don't want to think of him, but I can't help it, and sometimes at night my old heart beats so hard and so fast I think it will tear itself right clear of my chest." A haunting recollection of a mysterious boyhood event, The Man in Black Suit read by John Cullum leads off this masterful collection from Stephen King. Other dark tales include: All That You Love Will Be Carried Away read by Peter Gerety, in which a man checks into a Lincoln, Nebraska Motel 6 to find the meaning in his life; That Feeling, You Can Only Say What It Is in French read by Becky Ann Baker presents the ultimate case of déejàa vu; and The Death of Jack Hamilton read by Arliss Howard - a blistering tale of Depression-era outlaws on the run. Whether writing about encounters with the dead, the near dead, or about the mundane dreads of life, Stephen King's The Man In The Black Suit: Four Dark Tales is intense, eerie and instantly compelling.

Man in the Black Suit: 4 Dark Tales. unabr. ed. Stephen King. Read by John Cullum et al. 2006. 17.95 (978-0-7435-6340-6(9), Audioworks) Pub: S&S Audio. Dist(s): S and S Inc

***Man in the Bottle.** 2010. audio compact disk (978-1-59171-153-7(3)) Falcon Picture.

Man in the Bottle. unabr. ed. Bill Knox. Read by James Bryce. 5 cass. (Running Time: 22200 sec.). (Isis Ser.). 2003. 49.95 (978-0-7531-1665-4(0)) Pub: ISIS Lrg Prnt GBR. Dist(s): Ulverscroft US
Chief Detective Inspector Colin Thane and his second-in-command D.I. Moss regarded it as little more than unpleasant routine when they were asked to identify the body of a salmon poacher. He had apparently blown himself up while illegally dynamiting a river pool. But two surprises await them: first, the dead man had a companion, now missing; second, the case has a connection with an assassination bid on a visiting politician from Moscow.

Man in the Brown Suit. unabr. ed. Agatha Christie. Read by Flo Gibson. 5 cass. (Running Time: 7 hrs.). 1999. 20.95 (978-1-55685-595-5(8)) Audio Bk Con.
Anne Beddingfeld, seeking adventure, becomes involved in a murder mystery & a case of missing diamonds. While in Africa her life is threatened, but she only can solve the case.

Man in the Brown Suit. unabr. ed. Agatha Christie. Read by Emilia Fox. (Running Time: 30360 sec.). 2005. 31.95 (978-1-57270-481-7(0)) Pub: Audio Partners. Dist(s): PerseuPGW

Man in the Brown Suit. unabr. ed. Agatha Christie. Narrated by Emilia Fox. (Running Time: 30360 sec.). (Mystery Masters Ser.). (ENG.). 2005. audio compact disk 31.95 (978-1-57270-482-4(9)) Pub: AudioGO. Dist(s): Perseus Dist
Yearning for a little adventure in life, Anne Beddingfeld gets far more than she bargained for: while at the tube station, she sees a man fall to the tracks and die. A man dressed in brown, claiming to be a doctor, pronounces him dead and hurries away, dropping a scrap of paper with the peculiar words "17-122 Kilmorden Castle." The police conclude the death was an accident, but Anne suspects otherwise. Lord Nasby, the press tycoon, agrees to hire her to investigate the matter. Armed with a small inheritance and the scrap of paper the mysterious man in the brown suit left behind, she sets off on her mission - a mission that takes her from England to South Africa, and that leads to the discovery of missing diamonds, another murder, and attempts on Anne's own life.

Man in the Ceiling. unabr. ed. Jules Feiffer. Narrated by Jules Feiffer. Narrated by L. J. Ganser. 3 pieces. (Running Time: 3 hrs. 30 mins.). (gr. 4 up). 1993. 45.00 (978-0-7887-5345-9(2), 96436) Recorded Bks.
Jimmy Jibbett feels almost worthless - a daydreamer in class, not especially talented on the ball field, and a big disappointment to his busy father. In this highly enjoyable story, Jimmy struggles to overcome his non-artistic father's notions of success and failure. Jimmy spends all of his time drawing and writing super-hero cartoons - and he's really good, too! There's just one thing Jimmy can't seem to draw: the human hand. Despite this, Jimmy is sure that one day he will be a great cartoonist - he's not sure, however, if his father will ever notice him. Before Jimmy can draw the perfect hand, he has to learn that success takes time and perseverance, and there is no such thing as absolute failure.

Man in the Dark. unabr. ed. Paul Auster. (Running Time: 4 hrs. 30 mins.). 2008. 29.95 (978-0-7927-5912-6(5), Chivers Sound Lib); audio compact disk 49.95 (978-0-7927-5642-2(8), Chivers Sound Lib) AudioGO.

Man in the Dark. unabr. ed. Paul Auster. Read by Paul Auster. 5 CDs. (Running Time: 4 hrs. 30 mins. 0 sec.). 2008. audio compact disk 24.95 (978-1-4272-0551-3(5)) Pub: Macmill Audio. Dist(s): Macmillan

***Man in the Gray Flannel Skirt.** abr. ed. Jon-Jon Goulian. (ENG.). 2011. audio compact disk 30.00 (978-0-307-87674-4(8), Random AudioBks) Pub: Random Audio Pubg. Dist(s): Random

***Man in the Gray Flannel Suit.** unabr. ed. Sloan Wilson. Narrated by Patrick Lawlor. (Running Time: 12 hrs. 0 mins. 0 sec.). (ENG.). 2010. 24.99 (978-1-4001-6872-9(4)); 18.99 (978-1-4001-8872-7(5)); 34.99 (978-1-4001-9872-6(0)); audio compact disk 34.99 (978-1-4001-1872-4(7)); audio compact disk 83.99 (978-1-4001-4872-1(3)) Pub: Tantor Media. Dist(s): IngramPubServ

Man in the Gray Flannel Suit. unabr. collector's ed. Sloan Wilson. Read by Dan Lazar. 10 cass. (Running Time: 10 hrs.). 1981. 60.00 (978-0-7366-0422-2(7), 1394) Books on Tape.
This speaks for a whole generation of Americans. They were the ones who suffered through the Depression, fought World War II & found themselves non-coms in America's corporate army. The strains of conformity, the straits of marriage, the stress of children & the striving for success are all recounted here.

Man in the Green Chevy. abr. ed. Susan Rogers Cooper. 1 cass. 1997. 17.00 (978-1-883268-46-6(X)) Spellbinders.

Man in the High Castle. unabr. ed. Philip K. Dick. Read by Tom Weiner. (Running Time: 30600 sec.). 2008. 24.95 (978-1-4332-1453-0(9)); audio compact disk 29.95 (978-1-4332-1455-4(5)); audio compact disk & audio compact disk 24.95 (978-1-4332-1454-7(7)) Blckstn Audio.

Man in the High Castle. unabr. ed. Philip K. Dick. Read by Tom Weiner. (Running Time: 8.5 hrs. 0 mins.). 2008. 54.95 (978-1-4332-1451-6(2)); audio compact disk 70.00 (978-1-4332-1452-3(0)) Blckstn Audio.

Man in the High Castle. unabr. ed. Philip K. Dick. Narrated by George Guidall. 7 cass. (Running Time: 9 hrs. 45 mins.). 1997. 60.00 (978-0-7887-1756-7(1), 95234E7) Recorded Bks.
In this Hugo Award-winning science fiction thriller, Dick rewrites history, creating a harrowing nightmare of the way things could have been. It is 1962. World War II victors Japan & Germany are occupying a sinister America.

Man in the Iron Mask. Alexandre Dumas. Read by Bill Homewood. (Running Time: 2 hrs. 30 mins.). 1999. 20.95 (978-1-60083-838-5(3)) Iofy Corp.

Man in the Iron Mask. Alexandre Dumas. Narrated by Walter Covell. (Running Time: 7 hrs.). 2006. 30.95 (978-1-59912-147-5(6)) Iofy Corp.

Man in the Iron Mask. Alexandre Dumas. Read by Bill Homewood. 2 cass. (Running Time: 2 hrs. 30 mins.). (Works of Alexandre Dumas). 1996. 13.98 (978-962-634-569-6(1), NA206914, Naxos AudioBooks) Naxos.
The continuation of adventures of the dauntless heroes of The Three Musketeers - Aramis, Athos, Porthos and d'Artagan. The veteran warriors find themselves at the center of a plot in which hearts and heads are broken.

Man in the Iron Mask. Alexandre Dumas. Read by Geoffrey Sherman. (Playaway Young Adult Ser.). (ENG.). (J). (gr. 6-12). 2008. 79.99 (978-1-60640-599-4(3)) Find a World.

Man in the Iron Mask. Alan Venable. Alexandre Dumas. (Classic Adventures Ser.). 2007. audio compact disk 18.95 (978-1-4105-0862-1(5)) D Johnston Inc.

Man in the Iron Mask. abr. ed. Alexandre Dumas. Read by Walter Covell. 6 cass. (Running Time: 8 hrs.). 1985. 42.00 (C-137) Jimcin Record.
Last adventure of The Three Musketeers.

Man in the Iron Mask. abr. ed. Alexandre Dumas. Read by Bill Homewood. 2 CDs. (Running Time: 2 hrs. 30 mins.). (Works of Alexandre Dumas). 1995. audio compact disk 17.98 (978-962-634-069-1(X), NA206912, Naxos AudioBooks) Naxos.
The continuation of adventures of the dauntless heroes of The Three Musketeers - Aramis, Athos, Porthos and d'Artagan. The veteran warriors find themselves at the center of a plot in which hearts and heads are broken.

Man in the Iron Mask. abr. ed. Alexandre Dumas. Perf. by Christopher Cazenove. 4 cass. (Running Time: 6 hrs.). 2004. 25.00 (978-1-59007-005-5(4)) Pub: New Millenn Enter. Dist(s): PerseuPGW
This novel is based on the historical legend of "Phillippe", a youthful prisoner who has languished in the dank, dismal depths of the Bastille for eight long years. Aramis, with characteristic derring-do, has bribed his way into Phillippe's cell to reveal a shocking secret unknown even to the boy himself - a closely guarded truth that could topple Louis XIV, King of France. As he swirls his way through a death-defying jailbreak, a brilliant masquerade and a terrifying fight for the throne, Aramis faces the most appalling threat of all: the possibility that he must break his sacred vow of "All for one, and one for all".

Man in the Iron Mask. abr. ed. Alexandre Dumas. Read by Reg Green. 2 cass. 1998. 17.95 Set. (978-1-55935-267-3(1)) Soundelux.
Final episode of Alexandre Dumas' swashbuckling classic.

Man in the Iron Mask. abr. adpt. ed. Alexandre Dumas. (Bring the Classics to Life: Level 3 Ser.). (ENG.). (gr. 6-12). 2008. audio compact disk 12.95 (978-1-55576-475-3(4)) EDCON Pubng.

Man in the Iron Mask. unabr. ed. Alexandre Dumas. Read by Geoffrey Sherman. (Running Time: 16 hrs.). 2006. 44.25 (978-1-4233-1087-7(X), 9781423310877, BADLE); audio compact disk 112.25 (978-1-4233-1083-9(7), 9781423310839, BriAudCD Unabrid); audio compact disk 44.25 (978-1-4233-1085-3(3), 9781423310853, Brlnc Audio MP3 Lib); audio compact disk 29.95 (978-1-4233-1084-6(5), 9781423310846, Brilliance MP3); audio compact disk 44.95 (978-1-4233-1082-2(9), 9781423310822, Bril Audio CD Unabri) Brilliance Audio.
Deep inside the dreaded Bastille, a twenty-three-year-old prisoner called merely "Philippe" has languished for eight long, dark years. He does not know his real name or what crime he is supposed to have committed. But Aramis, one of the original Three Musketeers, has bribed his way into the cell to reveal the shocking secret that has kept Philippe locked away from the world. That carefully concealed truth could topple Louis XIV, king of France, which is exactly what Aramis is plotting to do! A daring jailbreak, a brilliant masquerade, and a terrifying fight for the throne may make Aramis betray his sacred vow, "All for one, and one for all!" In this concluding episode of the Three Musketeers saga, the actions of Aramis and the other Musketeers - Athos, Porthos, and the most dashing of them all, D'Artagnan - bring either honor or disgrace...and a horrifying punishment for the final loser in the battle royal.

Man in the Iron Mask. unabr. ed. Alexandre Dumas. Perf. by Christopher Cazenove. 12 cass. (Running Time: 18 hrs.). 2004. 39.95 (978-1-59007-011-6(9)) Pub: New Millenn Enter. Dist(s): PerseuPGW
This novel is based on the historical legend of "Phillippe", a youthful prisoner who has languished in the dank, dismal depths of the Bastille for eight long years. Aramis, with characteristic derring-do, has bribed his way into Phillippe's cell to reveal a shocking secret unknown even to the boy himself - a closely guarded truth that could topple Louis XIV, King of France. As he swirls his way through a death-defying jailbreak, a brilliant masquerade and a terrifying fight for the throne, Aramis faces the most appalling threat of all: the possibility that he must break his sacred vow of "All for one, and one for all".

Man in the Iron Mask. unabr. ed. Alexandre Dumas. Read by Simon Vance. (Running Time: 28 hrs. 30 mins.). 2010. 44.95 (978-1-4417-2470-0(2)); 109.95 (978-1-4417-2465-6(6)); audio compact disk 123.00 (978-1-4417-2467-0(2)) Blckstn Audio.

Man in the Iron Mask. unabr. ed. Alexandre Dumas. Read by Geoffrey Sherman. (Running Time: 16 hrs.). 2006. 29.95 (978-1-4233-1086-0(1), 9781423310860, BAD) Brilliance Audio.

Man in the Iron Mask. unabr. collector's ed. Alexandre Dumas. Read by Walter Covell. 6 cass. (Running Time: 9 hrs.). (J). 1985. 48.00 (978-0-7366-3904-0(7), 895784) Books on Tape.
Louis XIII's queen produced twin male heirs - two sons of equal age with equal pretensions. Louis feared for France. One prince is peace & safety for the state, two are civil war & anarchy. One son had to go. Louis could not kill him, but he could hide him in an iron mask.

Man in the Iron Mask, Pt. 1. unabr. ed. Alexandre Dumas. Read by Frederick Davidson. 10 cass. (Running Time: 27 hrs. 30 mins.). 1994. 69.95 (978-0-7861-0487-1(2), 1439A,B) Blckstn Audio.
"Mystery! that was the charm. That speechless tongue, those prisoned features, that heart so freighted with unspoken troubles, & the breast so oppressed with its piteous secret had been there. These dank walls had known the man whose dolorous story is a sealed book forever! There was fascination in the spot." Thus Mark Twain described his enchantment with the historical legend of the man in the iron mask. Alexandre Dumas took a different tack. He chose to write a historical romance filled with "l'action et l'amour" & incorporating his epic characters whom he introduced in "The Three Musketeers": the romantic Athos; Aramis, the intellectual cynic; the strong & energetic Porthos; & their dashing leader, D'Artagnan. The suspense starts on the first page with the secret meeting between Aramis & Mme de Chevreuse, & thereafter the pace never slackens.

Man in the Iron Mask, Pt. 2. unabr. ed. Alexandre Dumas. Read by Frederick Davidson. 9 cass. (Running Time: 27 hrs. 30 mins.). 1994. 62.95 (978-0-7861-0641-7(7), 1439A,B) Blckstn Audio.
The suspense starts on the first page with the secret meeting between Aramis & Mme de Chevreuse & thereafter the pace never slackens.

***Man in the Iron Mask: Bring the Classics to Life.** adpt. ed. Alexandre Dumas. (Bring the Classics to Life Ser.). 2008. pap. bk. 21.95 (978-1-55576-505-7(X)) EDCON Pubng.

Man in the Iron Mask Read Along. Prod. by Saddleback Educational Publishing. (Saddleback's Illustrated Classics Ser.). (YA). 2006. 24.95 (978-1-56254-921-3(9)) Saddleback Edu.

Man in the Middle. Brian Haig. 2007. audio compact disk 39.99 (978-1-4193-7537-8(7)) Recorded Bks.

Man in the Mirror. abr. unabr. ed. Patrick Morley. 2001. 17.99 (978-0-310-24207-9(X)) Zondervan.

***Man in the Mirror: Solving the 24 Problems Men Face.** abr. ed. Patrick Morley. (Running Time: 2 hrs. 0 mins. 0 sec.). (ENG.). 2003. 10.99 (978-0-310-26077-6(9)) Zondervan.

Man in the Queue. unabr. ed. Josephine Tey. Read by Stephen Thorne. 6 cass. (Running Time: 7 hrs. 45 min..). 2000. 29.95 (978-1-57270-167-0(6), N61167u) Pub: Audio Partners. Dist(s): PerseuPGW
A smash hit musical comedy in London has drawn a standing-room-only crowd & a murderer. A man standing in the queue with a mass of other theatergoers is suddenly stabbed to death. It is baffling that he lacks all clues about his identity & no one comes forward to claim knowledge of him. Dapper detective Alan Grant skillfully probes the London theater community to learn the motives of both the victim & the murderer.

Man in the Saddle. unabr. collector's ed. Ernest Haycox. Read by Christopher Lane. 6 cass. (Running Time: 9 hrs.). 1995. 48.00 (978-0-7366-3024-5(4), 3707) Books on Tape.
One man wants another's spread on a lonely Western frontier far from the law. It's kill or be killed in a dramatic gunfight.

***Man in the Woods.** unabr. ed. Scott Spencer. Read by Christopher Burns. 2010. (978-0-06-204716-8(7), Harper Audio); (978-0-06-206233-8(6), Harper Audio) HarperCollins Pubs.

Man in the Yellow Raft. unabr. collector's ed. C. S. Forester. Read by Stuart Courtney. 6 cass. (Running Time: 6 hrs.). 1985. 36.00 (978-0-7366-0659-2(9), 1621) Books on Tape.
Collection of eight stories about the American destroyer Boon & the men who served on her during World War II. They remind us that courage & clear-thinking in the midst of great danger go hand in hand with & are the keys to survival. Not only is cowardice disgraceful, it is frequently lethal.

Man is That He Might Have Joy. Ed Pinegar. 1 cass. 5.98 (978-1-55503-192-3(7), 06003915) Covenant Comms.
Two talks about happiness, everday life & the gospel.

Man Is That He Might Have Joy. Ed Pinegar. 1 cass. 2004. 3.95 (978-1-57734-396-7(4), 34441379) Covenant Comms.

Man Lay Dead. unabr. ed. Ngaio Marsh. Read by James Saxon. 4 cass. (Running Time: 5 hrs. 30 mins). (Medical Intelligence Unit Ser.). 2000. 24.95 (978-1-57270-169-4(2), N41169u) Pub: Audio Partners. Dist(s): PerseuPGW
Guests gather at Sir Hubert Handesley's country house party for the uproarious parlor game of "Murder." But they aren't laughing when the lights come up on an actual corpse. Then Scotland Yard's Inspector Roderick Alleyn arrives & finds an intricate puzzle of betrayal. Thus begins a search for the key player in this deadly game.

Man Lay Dead. unabr. ed. Ngaio Marsh. Read by James Saxon. 6 cass. (Running Time: 9 hrs.). (Inspector Roderick Alleyn Mysteries Ser.). 2000. 49.95 (978-0-7451-4288-3(5), CAB 971) Pub: Chivers Audio Bks GBR. Dist(s): AudioGO
Sir Hubert was famous for his amusing house parties, always filled with games to entertain his guests. He devises a new form of the Murder Game, but when the lights go on, a real corpse with a real dagger in its back is found. And all seven suspects had ample time to concoct amusing alibis.

Man, Liberty & Government. unabr. ed. Robert LeFevre. 14 cass. (Running Time: 24 hrs.). 140.00 (1001-1014) J Norton Pubs.

Man Most Worthy. Narrated by Caroline Clay. 8 cass. (Running Time: 11 hrs. 15 mins.). 2003. 74.00 (978-1-4025-3800-1(6)) Recorded Bks.

Man Named Dave: A Story of Triumph & Forgiveness. Dave Pelzer. Narrated by Brian Keeler. 8 cass. (Running Time: 10 hrs. 45 mins.). 74.00 (978-0-7887-9562-6(7)); audio compact disk 97.00 (978-1-4025-3505-5(8)) Recorded Bks.

Man of Contradictions: A Life of A. L. Rowse. unabr. ed. Richard Ollard. Read by Geoffrey Howard. 9 cass. (Running Time: 13 hrs. 30 mins.). 2001. 72.00 (978-0-7366-8381-4(X)) Books on Tape.
The life of a fearless, obstreperous, admirable man of letters.

Man of Faith: The Spiritual Journey of George W. Bush. abr. ed. David Aikman. Read by David Aikman. 5 CDs. (Running Time: 5 hrs.). 2004. audio compact disk 27.99 (978-1-58926-621-6(8)); 24.99 (978-1-58926-619-3(6)) Oasis Audio.
More than any other world leader in recent times, George W. Bush is a man of faith...a conservative Christian who has brought the power of prayer and the search for God's will into the Oval Office. His faith has proven to be a bedrock of strength and resolve during two of the most tumultuous years in our nation's history.According to Newsweek magazine, "this presidency is the most resolutely faith based in modern times. An enterprise founded, supported and guided by trust in the temporal and spiritual power of God.

Man of Faith: The Spiritual Journey of George W. Bush. unabr. ed. David Aikman. Read by David Aikman. 6 cass. (Running Time: 8 hrs.). 2004. 29.99 (978-1-58926-623-0(4)); audio compact disk 34.99 (978-1-58926-650-6(1)) Oasis Audio.

Man of Faith: The Spiritual Journey of George W. Bush. unabr. ed. David Aikman. Narrated by David Aikman. (ENG.). 2004. 24.49 (978-1-60814-020-6(2)) Oasis Audio.

Man of Faith: The Spiritual Journey of George W. Bush. unabr. ed. David Aikman. Read by David Aikman. Prod. by Oasis Audio Staff. 8 CDs. (Running Time: 8 hrs. 30 mins.). 2006. audio compact disk 64.00 (978-0-7861-8635-8(6), 3287) Blckstn Audio.

Man of Faith: The Spiritual Journey of George W. Bush. unabr. ed. David Aikman. Read by David Aikman. Prod. by Oasis Audio Staff. 6 cass. (Running Time: 8 hrs. 30 mins.). 2006. 44.95 (978-0-7861-2754-2(6), 3287) Blckstn Audio.

Man of Her Dreams. unabr. ed. Tami Hoag. Narrated by Deanna Hurst. 5 CDs. (ENG.). 2008. audio compact disk 19.95 (978-1-60283-543-6(8)) Pub: AudioGO. Dist(s): Perseus Dist

Man of Mode: Epilogue see Poetry of John Dryden

Man of Property. unabr. ed. John Galsworthy. Read by David Case. (Running Time: 50400 sec.). 2006. 79.95 (978-0-7861-4576-8(5)); audio compact disk 99.00 (978-0-7861-7038-8(7)); audio compact disk 29.95 (978-0-7861-7552-9(4)) Blckstn Audio.

Man of Property, unabr. ed. John Galsworthy. Narrated by Neil Hunt. 10 cass. (Running Time: 15 hrs.). (Forsyte Saga Ser.: Vol. 1). 1988. 85.00 (978-1-55690-183-6(6), 88030E7) Recorded Bks.
The first of three novels charting the history of the Forsyte family in turn-of-the-century England. There are passion & lust in these pages, high art & low comedy & unthinking violence that ride alongside ever-correct manners.

Man of Property, Set. John Galsworthy. Narrated by Flo Gibson. 8 cass. (Running Time: 11 hrs. 30 min.). (Forsyte Saga Ser.: Bk. I). 1987. 26.95 (978-1-55685-092-9(1)) Audio Bk Con.
Galsworthy paints a vivid portrait of a wealthy & ambitious family in London at the turn of the century interwoven with the ill-starred romance of Irene & Bossiney.

Man of Property & Indian Summer of a Forsyte, unabr. collector's ed. John Galsworthy. Read by David Case. 10 cass. (Running Time: 15 hrs.). 1998. 80.00 (978-0-7366-4030-5(4), 4529) Books on Tape.
An upper-middle-class family resists change in turn-of-the-century England.

Man of the Crowd. unabr. ed. Edgar Allan Poe. Read by Ralph Cosham. 2 cass. (Running Time: 3 hrs.). 1994. lib. bdg. 18.95 Set. (978-1-883049-44-7(X)) Sound Room.
An unusual collection of Poe's best works spanning the range of his extraordinary talent - from the haunting poem, "Annabel Lee," to the dream-like love story, "Eleonora," to the whimsical "The Man That Was Used Up".

Man of the Crowd, Set. unabr. ed. Edgar Allan Poe. Read by Ralph Cosham. 2 cass. (Running Time: 3 hrs.). (Poe Ser.). 1994. bk. 16.95 (978-1-883049-38-6(5), 391134) Sound Room.

Man of the Family. unabr. ed. Ralph Moody. Read by Cameron Beierle. 8 CDs. (Running Time: 8 hrs. 48 min.). 2001. audio compact disk 52.00 (978-1-58116-185-4(9)) Books in Motion.
At age eleven, Ralph becomes man of the family and an entrepreneur. He continues his horse riding, cattle driving, and the Moody's start a cooking business.

Man of the Family. unabr. ed. Ralph Moody. Read by Cameron Beierle. 8 cass. (Running Time: 8 hrs. 48 min.). (Little Britches Ser.). 2001. 39.95 (978-1-58116-164-9(6)) Books in Motion.

Man of the Forest. Zane Grey. Read by John Bolen. (Playaway Adult Fiction Ser.). (ENG.). 2009. 89.99 (978-1-60775-793-1(1)) Find a World.

Man of the Forest. Zane Grey. Read by John Bolen. (Running Time: 12 hrs.). 2002. 29.95 (978-1-60083-610-7(0), Audiofy Corp) Iofy Corp.

Man of the Forest. Zane Grey. Read by John Bolen. (ENG.). 2005. audio compact disk 96.00 (978-1-4001-3039-9(5)) Pub: Tantor Media. Dist(s): IngramPubServ

Man of the Forest. unabr. ed. Zane Grey. Narrated by John Bolen. 1 CD (MP3). (ENG.). 2002. audio compact disk 23.00 (978-1-4001-5039-7(6)) Pub: Tantor Media. Dist(s): IngramPubServ

Man of the Forest. unabr. ed. Zane Grey. Narrated by John Bolen. 10 CDs. (Running Time: 12 hrs.). (ENG.). 2002. audio compact disk 48.00 (978-1-4001-0039-2(9), 110305) Pub: Tantor Media. Dist(s): IngramPubServ

Man of the Forest. unabr. ed. Zane Grey. Read by John Bolen. Narrated by John Bolen. (Running Time: 12 hrs. 0 mins. 0 sec.). (Tantor Unabridged Classics Ser.). (ENG.). 2009. audio compact disk 32.99 (978-1-4001-0942-5(6)); audio compact disk 65.99 (978-1-4001-3942-2(2)); audio compact disk 22.99 (978-1-4001-5942-0(3)) Pub: Tantor Media. Dist(s): IngramPubServ

Man of the Hour. abr. ed. Peter Blauner. 2000. (978-1-57042-878-4(6)) Hachet Audio.

Man of the Hour, unabr. ed. Peter Blauner. Read by Edward Lewis. 9 cass. (Running Time: 13 hrs. 30 mins.). 1999. 72.00 (978-0-7366-4450-1(4), 4895) Books on Tape.
When David Fitzgerald, a teacher in a Brooklyn high school, keeps his students from boarding a bus that turns out to have a bomb on it, he is hailed as a modern day hero. His fortunes change, however, when the police reveal that he is considered a suspect in the bombing & everything turns upside down. His media appearances are made to look sinister. His livelihood is taken away. Even his right to see his own son is threatened. Transformed from hero to pariah, finding the real bomber appears to be his only way out.

Man of the Hour. unabr. ed. Peter Blauner. 2000. (978-1-57042-879-1(4)) Hachet Audio.

Man of the House, Set. unabr. ed. Joan Jonker. 6 cass. 1998. 69.95 (978-1-85903-174-2(9)) Pub: Magna Story GBR. Dist(s): Ulverscroft US

Man of the Moment. unabr. ed. Alan Ayckbourn. Perf. by Rosalind Ayres et al. 1 cass. (Running Time: 1 hr. 57 min.). 1997. 22.95 (978-1-58081-096-8(9)) L A Theatre.
Jill, an ambitious TV reporter, reunites on the air two men who should be natural enemies. She hopes that fireworks will ensure when Douglas, a poor but hones man, arrives at the opulent villa of Vie, a bank robber he one foiled.

Man of the Thirties. unabr. ed. A. L. Rowse. Read by Bill Kelsey. 6 cass. (Running Time: 9 hrs.). 1992. 48.00 (978-0-7366-2288-2(8), 3074) Books on Tape.
The Gulf War rekindled our interest in the 1930s, that appalling decade of appeasement that led to WW II. A. L. Rowse observed it at the time in his diaries & journals, later calling on them for this portion of his autobiography.

Man on a Donkey, Pt. 1. unabr. collector's ed. Hilda Prescott. Read by Dan Lazar. 9 cass. (Running Time: 13 hrs. 30 min.). 1986. 72.00 (978-0-7366-0956-2(3), 1900-A) Books on Tape.
The Pilgrimage of Grace occurred in the midst of Reformation, a time of great torment & passion. The story is humanized, told through the experiences of characters who are historically accurate, made real to us by our identification with them.

Man on a Donkey, Pt. 2. collector's ed. Hilda Prescott. Read by Dan Lazar. 10 cass. (Running Time: 15 hrs.). 1986. 80.00 (978-0-7366-0957-9(1), 1900-B) Books on Tape.

Man on Mao's Right: From Harvard Yard to Tiananmen Square, My Life Inside China's Foreign Ministry. Ji Chaozhu. Read by Norman Dietz. (Playaway Adult Nonfiction Ser.). (ENG.). 2009. 69.99 (978-1-60812-553-1(X)) Find a World.

Man on Mao's Right: From Harvard Yard to Tiananmen Square, My Life Inside China's Foreign Ministry. unabr. ed. Ji Chaozhu. Narrated by Norman Dietz. (Running Time: 14 hrs. 0 mins. 0 sec.). (ENG.). 2008. audio compact disk 29.99 (978-1-4001-5823-2(0)); audio compact disk 39.99 (978-1-4001-0823-7(3)); audio compact disk 79.99 (978-1-4001-3823-4(X)) Pub: Tantor Media. Dist(s): IngramPubServ

Man on Platform Five. abr. ed. Robert Llewellyn. Read by Chris Barrie. 2 cass. (Running Time: 3 hrs.). 1999. (978-1-84032-148-7(2), HoddStoughton) Hodder General GBR.
From dud to dude in six weeks. Two sisters' battle over one man - a trainspotter called Ian.

Man on the Balcony. unabr. ed. Maj Sjöwall & Per Wahlöö. Read by Tom Weiner. (Running Time: 3 hrs. NaN mins.). 2009. audio compact disk 24.95 (978-1-4332-6051-3(4)); audio compact disk 33.00 (978-1-4332-6052-0(2)) Blckstn Audio.

Man on the Balcony. unabr. ed. Maj Sjöwall & Per Wahlöö. Read by Tom Weiner. (Running Time: 3 hrs. NaN mins.). (Martin Beck Police Mystery Ser.: No. 3). 2009. 19.95 (978-1-4332-6055-1(7)); audio compact disk 19.95 (978-1-4332-6054-4(9)) Blckstn Audio.

Man on the Moon. 1 cass. (Running Time: 30 min.). 14.95 (CBC644) MMI Corp.
Panel discussion on political, scientific & economic issues in manned space flight to the moon.

Man on the Moon Pt. 1: The Voyages of the Apollo Astronauts, collector's ed. Andrew Chaikin. Read by Michael Kramer. 9 cass. (Running Time: 13 hrs. 30 min.). 1999. 72.00 (978-0-7366-4586-7(1), 4979-A) Books on Tape.
On the night of July 20, 1969, two Americans, Neil Armstrong & Buzz Aldrin, walked on the moon. Now the greatest event of the twentieth century is retold through the eyes of people who were there.

Man on the Moon Pt. 2: The Voyages of the Apollo Astronauts, collector's ed. Andrew Chaikin. Read by Michael Kramer. 7 cass. (Running Time: 10 hrs. 30 min.). 1999. 56.00 (978-0-7366-4720-5(1), 4979-B) Books on Tape.
On the night of July 20, 1969, two Americans, Neil Armstrong & Buzz Aldrin, walked on the moon. Now the greatest event of the twentieth century is retold through the eyes of people who were there.

Man Out at First, unabr. ed. Matt Christopher. Narrated by Kerin McCue. 1 cass. (Running Time: 1 hr.). (Peach Street Mudders Ser.). (gr. 2 up). 10.00 (978-0-7887-0899-2(6), 95037E7) Recorded Bks.
Eight-year-old Turtleneck Jones handles first base for the Peach Street Mudders. But when he is accidentlly knocked out by a wild throw, he can't seem to catch the ball anymore. Available to libraries only.

Man Outside the Church: Luke 7:9. 1978. Rental 4.95 (978-0-7417-1015-4(3)) Win Walk.

Man Ray: American Artist. unabr. collector's ed. Neil Baldwin. Read by Michael Mitchell. 12 cass. (Running Time: 18 hrs.). 1996. 96.00 (978-0-7366-3520-2(3), 4157) Books on Tape.
The quintessential modernist figure - painter, sculptor & collagist; filmmaker & printmaker; poet, essayist & philosopher. He was also the most enigmatic of the Dada-Surrealists who transformed the Paris art world during the ferment of the 1920s & beyond.

***Man Riding West; Grub Line Rider; Down the Pogonip Trail.** unabr. ed. Louis L'Amour. 2010. 14.99 (978-0-307-74875-1(8), Random AudioBks) Pub: Random Audio Pubg. Dist(s): Random

Män Som Hatar Kvinnor see Girl with the Dragon Tattoo

Man That Corrupted Hadleyburg. Mark Twain. 10.00 (LSS1129) Esstee Audios.

Man That Corrupted Hadleyburg, unabr. ed. Short Stories. Mark Twain. Narrated by Norman Dietz. 3 cass. (Running Time: 4 hrs.). 1994. 26.00 (978-1-55690-988-7(8), 94127E7) Recorded Bks.
The title story of this collection of short stories features the tale of the "most honest & upright" town of Hadleyburg, whose residents boast of their unsmirched moral character. A stranger, offended by the pious reputation of the town, devises a plan to bring it's honored residents to shame. Is there even one righteous man in Hadleyburg? A biting satire filled with Twain's inimitable wit & penetrating insights into the follies of human nature. The third cassette features two other Twain favorites: "The Invalid's Story" & "The Stolen White Elephant".

Man That Corrupted Hadleyburg: And Other Stories. Mark Twain. Read by Full Cast Production Staff. (Running Time: 27000 sec.). 2006. 54.95 (978-0-7861-4533-1(1)); audio compact disk 63.00 (978-0-7861-7144-6(8)) Blckstn Audio.

Man That Corrupted Hadleyburg: And Other Stories. unabr. ed. Mark Twain. Read by Full Cast Production Staff. (Running Time: 27000 sec.). 2006. audio compact disk 29.95 (978-0-7861-7612-0(1)) Blckstn Audio.

Man That Corrupted Hadleyburg & Other Stories. unabr. ed. Mark Twain. Read by Cindy Hardin et al. 7 cass. (Running Time: 1 hr. per cass.). 24.00 Set. (9091) Books on Tape.
One of the demons Twain always set out to slay was the legend that the citizens of this republic are inherently more virtuous than others. By the invention of an elaborate hoax, a kind of giant practical joke, Twain has his hero turn Hadleyburg inside out & in the process teach the hypocrites who dwelt there a lesson in humility & moral realism. Also includes: "Baker's Bluejay Yarn," "The Story of the Bad Little Boy," "The Notorious Jumping Frog of Calaveras County," "Extracts from Adam's Diary," "Eve's Diary," "How I Edited An Agricultural Paper," "The Man Who Put up at Gadsby's," "Journalism in Tennessee," "The Joke That Made Ed's Fortune," "Edward Mills & George Benton: A Tale" & "Cannibalism in the Cars".

Man That Corrupted Hadleyburg & Other Stories. unabr. ed. Mark Twain. Read by Walter Zimmerman et al. 6 cass. (Running Time: 8 hrs. 30 min.). Incl. Baker's Bluejay Yarn. 1982. (C-91); Cannibalism in the Cars. 1982. (C-91); Edward Mills & George Benton: A Tale. 1982. (C-91); Extracts from Adam's Diary. 1982. (C-91); How I Edited an Agricultural Paper. 1982. (C-91); Joke That Made Ed's Fortune. 1982. (C-91); Journalism in Tennessee. 1982. (C-91); Man Who Put Up at Gadsby's. 1982. (C-91); Notorious Jumping Frog of Calaveras County. 1982. (C-91); Story of the Bad Little Boy. 1982. (C-91); 1982. 42.00 (C-91) Jimcin Record.
Mark Twain's satirical wit at its best.

Man that Put Up at Gadsby's see Favorite Stories by Mark Twain

Man: the Human Feelings Dimension: "Poetry, Music, & Freedom" & Other Lectures. 1 cass. (Running Time: 84 min.). (Of Man; the Island & the Continent Ser.: Vol. 2). 1996. 15.00 (978-1-889954-64-6(0)); 12.00 (978-1-889954-65-3(9)); 15.00 (978-1-889954-66-0(7)); 49.00 Set. (978-1-889954-67-7(5)) J Cassidy Prodns.
Introductory lecture on Man; on Religion & Humanism. Then three lectures in Aesthetics on Poetry & Music. Lecture One: Opening lecture in poetry & song, entitled, "Poetry, Music, & Freedom".

Man: The Moral & Human Feelings Dimension, Introductory Lecture: On Man; the Island, the Continent, & the Kingdom. 1 cass. (Running Time: 44 min.). (Of Man; The Island & the Continent Ser.: Vols. 1 & 2). 1996. 9.50 (978-1-889954-56-1(X)) J Cassidy Prodns.
Introductory lecture on Man; on Religion & Humanism.

Man: the Moral Dimension: "Moral Prejudice in Human Opinion & Judgment," & Other Lectures. 1 cass. (Running Time: 29 min.). (Of Man; the Island & the Continent Ser.: Vol. 1). 1996. 9.00 (978-1-889954-58-5(6)); 9.50 (978-1-889954-59-2(4)); 17.00 (978-1-889954-60-8(8)); 18.00 (978-1-889954-61-5(6)) J Cassidy Prodns.
Introductory lecture on Man; on Religion & Humanism. Then three lectures in Ethics-the first two on Human Prejudice, the final one on Our Humanity. Lecture Two: Follow-up lecture in ethics on human prejudice entitled "National Prejudice & Ethnic/Religious Persecution".

Man: The Moral Dimension: "Moral Prejudice in Human Opinion & Judgment" & Other Lectures. 2 cass. (Running Time: 2 hrs. 36 min.). (Of Man; The Island & the Continent Ser.: Vol. 1). 1996. 35.00 Set. (978-1-889954-62-2(4)); 38.00 Set. (978-1-889954-63-9(2)) J Cassidy Prodns.
Introductory lecture on Man; on Religion & Humanism. Then three lectures in Ethics - the first two on Human Prejudice, the final one on Our Humanity.

Man to Call My Own. Johanna Lindsey. Read by Laural Merlington. (Playaway Adult Fiction Ser.). (ENG.). 2009. 64.99 (978-1-60775-681-1(1)) Find a World.

Man to Call My Own. abr. ed. Johanna Lindsey. Read by Laural Merlington. (Running Time: 6 hrs.). 2007. audio compact disk 14.99 (978-1-4233-1953-5(2), 9781423319535, BCD Value Price) Brilliance Audio.

Man to Call My Own. unabr. ed. Johanna Lindsey. Read by Laural Merlington. 6 cass. (Running Time: 9 hrs.). 2003. 32.95 (978-1-59086-381-7(X), 159086381X, BAU); 74.25 (978-1-59086-382-4(8), 1590863828, Unabridge Lib Edns); audio compact disk 33.95 (978-1-59086-384-8(4), 1590863844);

audio compact disk 92.25 (978-1-59086-385-5(2), 1590863852, Unabridge Lib Edns) Brilliance Audio.

A Man to Call My Own introduces us to a charismatic pair of twins, Amanda and Marian Laton, who, after the sudden death of their father, are sent to live with their aunt on a sprawling Texas ranch. As the twin sisters - one of whom is nasty, the other nice - both find themselves pursuing Chad Kinkaid, the cowboy son of a neighboring ranching family, Lindsey skillfully charts the intoxicating course of first love - and all of love's attendant twists and turns - that ends in one of the Laton twins winning the heart of a man she can call her own.

Man to Call My Own. unabr. ed. Johanna Lindsey. Read by Laural Merlington. (Running Time: 9 hrs.). 2004. 39.25 (978-1-59335-638-5(2), 1593356382, Brinc Audio MP3 Lib) Brilliance Audio.

Man to Call My Own. unabr. ed. Johanna Lindsey. Read by Laural Merlington. (Running Time: 9 hrs.). 2004. 39.25 (978-1-59710-482-1(5), 1597104825, BADLE); 24.95 (978-1-59710-483-8(3), 1597104833, BAD) Brilliance Audio.

Man to Call My Own. unabr. ed. Johanna Lindsey. Read by Laural Merlington. (Running Time: 9 hrs.). 2004. 24.95 (978-1-59335-214-1(X), 159335214X) Soulmate Audio Bks.

Man to man: surviving prostate Cancer. Michael Korda. 2004. 10.95 (978-0-7435-4989-9(9)) Pub: S&S Audio. Dist(s): S and S Inc

Man Upstairs & Other Stories. unabr. ed. P. G. Wodehouse. Read by Frederick Davidson. 7 cass. (Running Time: 10 hrs.). 1997. 49.95 (978-0-7861-1225-8(5), 1968) Blckstn Audio.

A collection of stories written by Sir Wodehouse before the First World War. But such was Wodehouse's amiable genius that they have aged not a jot. Like ancient crusted port, they have matured with age, & perhaps only now can their timeless humor be savored with its full bouquet.

Man Upstairs & Other Stories. unabr. ed. P. G. Wodehouse. Read by Frederick Davidson. (Running Time: 10 hrs. 0 mins.). 2009. 29.95 (978-1-4417-0802-1(2)); audio compact disk 90.00 (978-1-4417-0799-4(9)) Blckstn Audio.

Man Upstairs & Other Stories, unabr. ed. Short Stories. P. G. Wodehouse. Read by Robin Browne. 8 cass. (Running Time: 11 hrs. 42 min.). (Isis Ser.). (J). 1995. 69.95 (978-1-85089-563-3(5), 92042) Pub: ISIS Lrg Prnt GBR. Dist(s): Ulverscroft US

Man Who Came Back see Isaac Bashevis Singer Reader

Man Who Came Back see Isaac Bashevis Singer

Man Who Came Early see Award Winning Science Fiction

Man Who Came to Dinner see Sound of Modern Drama: The Crucible

Man Who Came to Dinner. 1 cass. 10.95 (978-0-8045-0725-7(2), SAC 7146) Spoken Arts.

Man Who Cancelled Himself: A Stewart Hoag Mystery. unabr. ed. David Handler. Narrated by Tom Stechschulte. 10 cass. (Running Time: 14 hrs. 45 mins.). (Stewart Hoag Mystery Ser.: Vol. 6). 1999. 85.00 (978-0-7887-1992-9(0), 95379E7) Recorded Bks.

Hoagy's newest & richest client is in trouble. Uncle Chubby is a popular television celebrity, but his personal life is a mess. Now Uncle Chubby hopes Hoagy can write a glowing biography that will restore his tattered reputation.

Man Who Could Work Miracles see Tales of Space & Time

Man Who Could Work Miracles. unabr. ed. H. G. Wells. Read by Walter Zimmerman. 1 cass. (Running Time: 78 min.). Dramatization. 1977. 7.95 (N-9) Jimcin Record.

H. G. Wells is at his humorous best in this story of a man whose every wish is granted - & the incredible problems this causes for him.

Man Who Cried. unabr. ed. Catherine Cookson. Read by Gordon Griffin. 8 cass. (Running Time: 12 hrs.). 2001. 69.95 (978-1-85496-397-0(X), 6397X) Pub: Soundings Ltd GBR. Dist(s): Ulverscroft US

Abel's fate was interwoven with the conflicting lives of four women: his shrewish wife, his mistress, his unlawful wife with her warped view of love & her sister whom he loves most of all but cannot marry, even though she carries his child.

Man Who Didn't Wash His Dishes. 2004. 8.95 (978-1-56008-964-3(4)); cass. & flmstrp 30.00 (978-0-89719-537-9(X)) Weston Woods.

Man Who Didn't Wash His Dishes, the see Hombre Que No Lavabo Los Platos

Man Who Died. unabr. ed. D. h. Lawrence. Narrated by Flo Gibson. 2 cass. (Running Time: 2 hrs.). 2003. 14.95 (978-1-55685-701-0(2)) Audio Bk Con.

This erotic tale is about a man risen from death who has a love affair with a priestess.

Man Who Died on Friday. unabr. ed. Michael Underwood. Read by John Hendry. 6 cass. (Running Time: 9 hrs.). (Sound Ser.). 2004. 54.95 (978-1-85496-810-4(6), 68106) Pub: UlverLrgPrint GBR. Dist(s): Ulverscroft US

Man Who Fell in Love with a Chicken. David B. Axelrod. Ed. by Stanley H. Barkan. (Cross-Cultural Review Chapbook Ser.: No. 2). 1980. 10.00 (978-0-89304-826-6(7)) Cross-Cultrl NY.

Man Who Fell in Love with the Moon: A Novel. unabr. ed. Tom Spanbauer. Read by Kenneth Martines. 10 cass. (Running Time: 13 hrs. 30 min.). 1996. 59.95 Set. (978-1-888348-03-3(8), HCB203) Hall Closet.

An American epic of the Old West for our own times. Although laced with the ugliness & cruelty of the frontier West, the love & acceptance that tie this family together provide the true heart of this novel. A beautifully told, mythic tale that is as well a profound meditation on sexuality, race & man's relationship to himself & the natural world.

Man Who Fell to Earth. unabr. ed. Walter Tevis. Narrated by George Guidall. 5 cass. (Running Time: 6 hrs. 30 mins.). 1990. 44.00 (978-1-55690-330-4(8), 90062E7) Recorded Bks.

Thomas Newton "Falls to Earth" from his home planet of Anthea on a rescue mission.

Man Who Had All the Luck. Arthur Miller. Contrib. by Graham Hamilton. (Running Time: 7560 sec.). 2007. audio compact disk 25.95 (978-1-58081-372-3(0)) Pub: L A Theatre. Dist(s): NetLibrary CO

Man Who Had Everything Episode 1. unabr. ed. Simon R. Green. Narrated by Richard Rohan & Nanette Savard. 2 cass. (Running Time: 3 hrs.). (Deathstalker Ser.: Bk. 1). 2002. 9.95 (978-1-931953-18-4(X)) Listen & Live.

Outlawed by the ruthless Lionstone XIV, Owen Deathstalker is left with no allies, as even his oldest companions turn against him for the promise of fortune. Just as he is sure his life is coming to an imminent close, out of the sky falls Hazel d'Ark.

***Man Who Invented Florida.** unabr. ed. Randy Wayne White. Narrated by Dick Hill. (Running Time: 11 hrs. 30 mins.). (Doc Ford Ser.). 2010. 17.99 (978-1-4001-8670-9(6)); 24.99 (978-1-4001-6670-1(5)); audio compact disk 34.99 (978-1-4001-1670-6(8)); audio compact disk 69.99 (978-1-4001-4670-3(4)) Pub: Tantor Media. Dist(s): IngramPubServ

Man Who Killed the Deer. Frank Waters. Read by Frank Waters. 1 cass. (Running Time: 40 min.). 13.95 (978-1-55644-085-4(5), 3131) Am Audio Prose.

Reading of Pueblo Council meeting scene by vintage chronicler of the American West & Indian mysticism, author of "People of the Valley," "Book of the Hopi," & "Masked Gods".

Man Who Killed Too Soon. Michael Underwood. Read by Peter Barker. 5 cass. (Running Time: 7 hrs. 30 min.). 1999. 49.95 (67738) Pub: Soundings Ltd GBR. Dist(s): Ulverscroft US

Man Who Knew How. Perf. by Charles Laughton. 1 cass. (Running Time: 1 hr.). 7.95 (DD8865) Natl Recrd Co.

Man Who Knew Infinity: A Life of the Genius Ramanujan. unabr. ed. Robert Kanigal. Read by Humphrey Bower. (Running Time: 63000 sec.). 2007. audio compact disk 120.00 (978-1-4332-1034-1(7)); audio compact disk 44.95 (978-1-4332-1035-8(5)) Blckstn Audio.

Man Who Knew Infinity: A Life of the Genius Ramanujan. unabr. ed. Robert Kanigal & Humphrey Bower. (Running Time: 63000 sec.). 2007. 95.95 (978-1-4332-1033-4(9)) Blckstn Audio.

***Man Who Knew Too Much.** Gilbert Keith Chesterton. (ENG.). 2009. audio compact disk 18.95 (978-1-936231-09-6(3)) Cath Audio.

Man Who Laughs. Víctor Hugo. Read by Laura García. (Running Time: 3 hrs.). 2002. 16.95 (978-1-60083-252-9(0), Audiofy Corp) Iofy Corp.

***Man Who Lied to His Laptop: What Machines Teach Us about Human Relationships.** unabr. ed. Clifford Nass & Corina Yen. Read by Sean Pratt. (Running Time: 8 hrs.). (ENG.). 2010. 26.98 (978-1-59659-666-5(X), GildAudio) Pub: Gildan Media. Dist(s): HachBkGrp

Man Who Lied to His Laptop: What Machines Teach Us about Human Relationships. unabr. ed. Clifford Nass & Corina Yen. Read by Sean Pratt. (Running Time: 7 hrs. 30 mins.). (ENG.). 2010. audio compact disk 29.98 (978-1-59659-461-6(6), GildAudio) Pub: Gildan Media. Dist(s): HachBkGrp

Man Who Liked to Look at Himself & The Blank Page. unabr. ed. K. C. Constantine. Read by Lloyd James. 8 cass. (Running Time: 12 hrs.). (Mario Balzic Ser.: Vol. 2 & 3). 1997. 64.00 (978-0-7366-3612-4(9), 4271) Books on Tape.

Mario Balzic is hunting pheasants when he finds the remains of Frank Gallic, a butcher. Everyone suspects Gallic's business partner, who certainly had a wide choice of murder weapons.

Man Who Listens to Horses. unabr. ed. Monty Roberts. Read by Jonathan Marosz. 7 cass. (Running Time: 10 hrs. 30 min.). 1998. 56.00 (978-0-7366-4223-1(4), 4723) Books on Tape.

Man Who Listens to Horses, unabr. ed. Monty Roberts. Narrated by Ed Sala. 8 cass. (Running Time: 11 hrs. 15 mins.). 1998. 70.00 (978-0-7887-2210-3(7), 95509E7) Recorded Bks.

Life of Monty Roberts, who has traveled the world working with difficult horses. He has trained Queen Elizabeth's yearlings, jittery stallions on movie sets & million-dollar race horses.

Man Who Lived Alone. Donald Hall. 1986. 38.16 (978-0-676-31447-2(3)) SRA McGraw.

***Man Who Loved Books Too Much: The True Story of a Thief, a Detective, & a World of Literary Obsession.** unabr. ed. Allison Hoover Bartlett. Narrated by Judith Brackley. (Running Time: 6 hrs. 0 mins.). 2010. 29.99 (978-1-4001-9343-1(5)); 13.99 (978-1-4001-8343-2(X)) Tantor Media.

Man Who Loved Books Too Much: The True Story of a Thief, a Detective, & a World of Literary Obsession. unabr. ed. Allison Hoover Bartlett. Narrated by Judith Brackley. 1 MP3-CD. (Running Time: 6 hrs. 0 mins. 0 sec.). (ENG.). 2010. 19.99 (978-1-4001-6343-4(9)); audio compact disk 29.99 (978-1-4001-1343-9(1)); audio compact disk 59.99 (978-1-4001-4343-6(8)) Pub: Tantor Media. Dist(s): IngramPubServ

Man Who Loved Cat Dancing. unabr. collector's ed. Marilyn Durham. Read by Dan Lazar. 8 cass. (Running Time: 8 hrs.). 1977. 48.00 (978-0-7366-0008-8(6), 1018) Books on Tape.

This story blazes through Wyoming Territory in the 1880's. It plunges into the live of a fugitive U.S. Army Officer planning a desperate train robbery & his three accomplices.

Man Who Loved Children. unabr. ed. Christina Stead. Read by C. M. Herbert. 14 cass. (Running Time: 20 hrs. 30 mins.). 1997. 89.95 (978-0-7861-1073-5(2), 1843) Blckstn Audio.

Sam & Henny Pollit have too many children, too little money, & too much loathing for one another. As Sam uses the children's adoration to feed his own voracious ego, Henny watches in bleak despair, knowing the bitter reality that lies just below his mad visions. A chilling novel of family life, this work is acknowledged as a contemporary classic.

Man Who Loved Children. unabr. ed. Christina Stead. Read by C. M. Hebert. (Running Time: 70200 sec.). 2007. audio compact disk 120.00 (978-0-7861-5961-1(8)); audio compact disk 44.95 (978-0-7861-5962-8(6)) Blckstn Audio.

Man Who Loved Children. unabr. ed. Christina Stead. Read by Fiona Press. 17 cass. (Running Time: 19 hrs.). 2001. (978-1-74030-340-8(7)) Bolinda Pubng AUS.

Man Who Loved China: The Fantastic Story of the Eccentric Scientist Who Unlocked the Mysteries of the Middle Kingdom. unabr. ed. Simon Winchester. Read by Simon Winchester. 8 CDs. (Running Time: 9 hrs.). 2008. audio compact disk 39.95 (978-0-06-155627-2(0), Harper Audio) HarperCollins Pubs.

***Man Who Loved Extinct Mammals: A Selection from the John Updike Audio Collection.** unabr. ed. John Updike. Read by John Updike. (ENG.). 2009. (978-0-06-196247-9(3), Caedmon); (978-0-06-196248-6(1), Caedmon) HarperCollins Pubs.

Man Who Loved God. unabr. collector's ed. William X. Kienzle. Read by Edward Holland. 7 cass. (Running Time: 10 hrs. 30 min.). (Father Koesler Mystery Ser.: No. 19). 2000. 56.00 (978-0-7366-5927-7(7)) Books on Tape.

During Fr. Koesler's absence, Lt. Tully & his visiting half-brother, Fr. Tully, investigate the death of a bank manager.

Man Who Loved Women to Death. unabr. ed. David Handler. Narrated by Tom Stechschulte. 7 cass. (Running Time: 10 hrs.). (Stewart Hoag Ser.). 2001. 61.00 (978-0-7887-4877-6(7), 96453x7) Recorded Bks.

Hoagy has just received an unsolicited manuscript in the mail. The first chapter of an epistolary novel, it is a detailed account of a murder. Two days later, Hoagy is shocked & alarmed. To identify & stop the grisly writer, the ghost-writing sleuth will need lots of help from his perceptive canine companion, Lulu.

Man Who Made Lists: Love, Death, Madness, & the Creation of Roget's Thesaurus. unabr. ed. Joshua Kendall. (Running Time: 9 hrs. 0 mins. 0 sec.). (ENG.). 2008. audio compact disk 24.99 (978-1-4001-5653-5(X)) Pub: Tantor Media. Dist(s): IngramPubServ

Man Who Made Lists: Love, Death, Madness, & the Creation of Roget's Thesaurus. unabr. ed. Joshua Kendall. Read by Stephen Hoye. (Running Time: 9 hrs. 0 mins. 0 sec.). (ENG.). 2008. audio compact disk 34.99 (978-1-4001-0653-0(2)); audio compact disk 69.99 (978-1-4001-3653-7(9)) Pub: Tantor Media. Dist(s): IngramPubServ

Man Who Mistook His Wife for a Hat. abr. ed. Oliver Sacks. Read by Oliver Sacks. 1 cass. (Running Time: 1 hr. 23 min.). 1987. 11.95 (978-0-8045-1175-9(6), SAC 1175) Spoken Arts.

Selected chapters from Sacks' book telling cases of patients whose abnormalities from brain dysfunctions are remarkably integrated into their personalities.

Man Who Never Was. unabr. ed. Ewen Montagu. Read by Peter Joyce. 2 cass. 1997. 27.95 Set. T T Beeler.

True story of an Allied attempt to mislead the Germans during a 1943 invasion.

Man Who Owned Cars. Poems. Eliot Fried. Read by Eliot Fried. 1 cass. (Running Time: 40 min.). 1994. 8.95 (978-1-881903-07-9(9)) DW Artworks.

This collection features the poetry-as-humor, poetry-as-social commentary & poetry-as-reflection of this well-known West Coast poet & author. Twelve of the poems in this collection are also found in the author's "Marvel Mystery Oil".

Man Who Owns the News: Inside the Secret World of Rupert Murdoch. abr. ed. Michael Wolff. Read by Michael Wolff. (ENG.). 2008. audio compact disk 29.95 (978-0-7393-8184-7(9), Random AudioBks) Pub: Random Audio Pubg. Dist(s): Random

Man Who Owns the News: Inside the Secret World of Rupert Murdoch. unabr. ed. Michael Wolff. Read by Don Leslie. 13 CDs. (Running Time: 15 hrs. 45 mins.). 2009. audio compact disk 129.00 (978-1-4159-6030-1(5), BksonTape) Pub: Random Audio Pubg. Dist(s): Random

Man Who Planted Trees. Jean Giono. Read by Robert J. Lurtsema. Illus. by Michael McCurdy. Contrib. by Paul Winter. Music by Paul Winter Consort. 1 cass. (Running Time: 40 min.). (J). 1990. bk. 21.95 (978-0-930031-35-0(0)) Chelsea Green Pub.

This special recording beautifully captures the spirit of the story & reinforces its powerful message of hope.

Man Who Planted Trees. 20th anniv. ed. Jean Giono & Jean Giono. (Running Time: 1 hr.). (Helen & Scott Nearing Titles Ser.). (ENG., 1985. 16.00 (978-0-930031-76-3(8)) Chelsea Green Pub.

Man Who Played with Fire Readalong. Janet Lorimer. 1 cass. (Running Time: 1 hr.). (Ten-Minute Thrillers Ser.). (YA). (gr. 6-12). 1995. pap. bk. 12.95 (978-0-7854-1078-2(3), 40813) Am Guidance.

Man Who Presumed. unabr. ed. Byron Farwell. Read by Bill Kelsey. 10 cass. (Running Time: 15 hrs.). 80.00 (978-0-7366-2946-1(7), 3640) Books on Tape.

Stanley ("Dr. Livingston, I presume") roamed the globe for stories with a twist.

Man Who Put Up at Gadsby's see Man That Corrupted Hadleyburg & Other Stories

***Man Who Shot the Favourite.** Edgar Wallace. 2009. (978-1-60136-526-2(8)) Audio Holding.

Man Who Smiled. unabr. ed. Henning Mankell. Read by Dick Hill. (Running Time: 45000 sec.). (Kurt Wallander Ser.). 2006. 32.95 (978-0-7861-4730-4(X)); audio compact disk 34.95 (978-0-7861-6541-4(3)); audio compact disk 29.95 (978-0-7861-7311-2(4)) Blckstn Audio.

Man Who Smiled. unabr. ed. Henning Mankell. Read by Dick Hill. (Running Time: 34200 sec.). (Kurt Wallander Ser.). 2006. 72.95 (978-0-7861-4828-8(4)); audio compact disk 90.00 (978-0-7861-6141-6(8)) Blckstn Audio.

Man Who Walked Between the Towers. Mordicai Gerstein. Narrated by Mordicai Gerstein. (J). 2005. audio compact disk 12.95 (978-1-59519-423-7(1)) Live Oak Media.

Man Who Walked Between the Towers. Mordicai Gerstein. Read by Mordicai Gerstein. (Live Oak Readalong Ser.). (J). 2005. bk. 25.95 (978-1-59519-421-3(5)); bk. 28.95 (978-1-59519-425-1(8)) Pub: Live Oak Media. Dist(s): AudioGO

Man Who Walked Like a Bear. unabr. ed. Stuart M. Kaminsky. Narrated by Mark Hammer. 5 cass. (Running Time: 7 hrs. 30 mins.). (Inspector Porfiry Rostnikov Mystery Ser.: No. 7). 1994. 44.00 (978-0-7887-0049-1(9), 94248E7) Recorded Bks.

A giant of a man crashing dazed into a hospital room causes Inspector Rostnikov to begin an investigation that leads ultimately to the KGB itself.

Man Who Walked Through Time. unabr. collector's ed. Colin Fletcher. Read by Scott Forbes. 7 cass. (Running Time: 7 hrs.). 1976. 42.00 (978-0-7366-0041-5(8), 1052) Books on Tape.

Colin Fletcher, equipped with a backpack, purpose & stamina, takes on the Grand Canyon of Colorado & conquers it singlehandedly.

Man Who Wanted a Mark IX see Ship That Died of Shame

Man Who Was Nobody. Edgar Wallace. Read by Hernando Iván Cano. (Running Time: 3 hrs.). 2002. 16.95 (978-1-60083-255-0(5), Audiofy Corp) Iofy Corp.

Man Who Was Poe. Avi. Narrated by Case David. (ENG.). (YA). 2009. audio compact disk 44.95 (978-0-9814890-3-2(6)) Audio Bkshelf.

Man Who Was Poe. Avi. Narrated by George Guidall. 5 CDs. (Running Time: 5 hrs. 15 mins.). (gr. 6 up). audio compact disk 48.00 (978-1-4025-2318-2(1)) Recorded Bks.

Man Who Was Poe. unabr. ed. Avi. Read by David Case. 4 cass. (Running Time: 5 hrs. 30 min.). (YA). (gr. 5 up). 1995. 24.95 (978-1-883332-18-1(4), 592827) Audio Bkshelf.

The murky streets of Providence, Rhode Island in 1848 lend no hand to frantic young Edward as he searches for his missing mother, aunt & now his younger sister. Acclaimed author Avi spins a tale of dark intrigue. Is the mysterious stranger friend or foe? Help or hindrance? Things are never what they seem to be at first. Or are they?.

Man Who Was Poe. unabr. ed. Avi. Read by David Case. (J). 2008. 54.99 (978-1-60514-808-3(3)) Find a World.

Man Who Was Poe, unabr. ed. Avi. Narrated by George Guidall. 4 pieces. (Running Time: 5 hrs. 15 mins.). (gr. 6 up). 1997. 35.00 (978-0-7887-0202-0(5), 94427E7) Recorded Bks.

A tale of a young boy who asks Edgar Allan Poe to help him escape a plot of murder, calculation & deception.

Man Who Was Thursday. G. K. Chesterton. Read by Walter Covell. 5 cass. (Running Time: 7 hrs. 30 min.). 1989. 29.00 incl. album. (C-141) Jimcin Record.

Allegorical detective story.

Man Who Was Thursday. G. K. Chesterton. Narrated by Ron Keith. 5 cass. (Running Time: 7 hrs. 15 mins.). 46.00 (978-0-7887-3752-7(X)) Recorded Bks.

Man Who Was Thursday. unabr. ed. G. K. Chesterton. Read by Walter Covell. 5 cass. (Running Time: 7 hrs.). 1985. 39.95 (978-0-7861-0528-1(3), 2027) Blckstn Audio.

A poet named Gabriel Syme, hearing of a Council of Anarchists bent on the destruction of society, law, & religion, vows to fight this monstrous conspiracy. He joins a chapter of detectives whose sole purpose is to track down & destroy the anarchists. By accident, however, he is introduced into the Council of Seven Days, the very anarchist group he has been seeking.

When Syme boldly asks to be made a replacement for a recently deceased member, Thursday, he is welcomed into the group.

Man Who Was Thursday. unabr. ed. G k Chesterton. Narrated by Simon Vance. 1 MP3 CD. (Running Time: 5 hrs. 54 mins. 0 sec.). (ENG.). 2005. lp 19.98 (978-1-59644-084-5(8), Hovel Audio) christianaud.
This is quite possibly, Chesterton's most famous novel. All that G.K. Chesterton's critics labeled him- devotional, impious, confounding, intelligent, humorous, bombastic- he wove into The Man Who Was Thursday. This page-turner sends characters bobbing around a delightfully confusing plot of mythic proportions. The story begins when two poets meet. Gabriel Syme is a poet of law. Lucian Gregory is a poetic anarchist. As the poets protest their respective philosophies, they strike a challenge. In the ruckus that ensues, the Central European Council of Anarchists elects Syme to the post of Thursday, one of their seven chief council positions. Undercover. On the run, Syme meets with Sunday, the head of the council, a man so outrageously mysterious that his antics confound both the law-abiding and the anarchist. Who is lawful? Who is immoral? Such questions are strangely in the presence of Sunday. He is wholly other. He is above the timeless questions of humanity and also somehow behind them.

Man Who was Thursday. unabr. ed. G. K. Chesterton. Narrated by Simon Vance. 5 CDs. (Running Time: 5 hrs. 54 mins. 0 sec.). (ENG.). 2005. audio compact disk 23.98 (978-1-59644-085-2(6), Hovel Audio) christianaud.

***Man Who was Thursday.** unabr. ed. G k Chesterton. Narrated by Simon Vance. (ENG.). 2005. 14.98 (978-1-59644-083-8(X), Hovel Audio) christianaud.

Man Who Was Thursday, Set. unabr. ed. G. K. Chesterton. Read by Flo Gibson. 4 cass. (Running Time: 6 hrs.). 1992. 19.95 (978-1-55685-220-6(7)) Audio Bk Con.
Imaginative, philosophical, wild & hilarious describe this account of man's pursuit of the understanding of God & the nature of evil. Who are the anarchists & who are the law abiding citizens in the bizarre chase?.

Man Who was Thursday: A Nightmare. G. K. Chesterton. Prod. by Alcazar AudioWorks. Narrated by David Thorn. Engineer Scott Weiser. B. J. Bedford. Music by Hans Bisner. (ENG.). 2009. audio compact disk 27.95 (978-0-9821853-9-1(1)) Alcazar AudioWorks.

***Man Who Was Thursday: A Nightmare.** Gilbert Keith Chesterton. (ENG.). 2009. audio compact disk 18.95 (978-1-936231-10-2(7)) Cath Audio.

Man Who Went up in Smoke. Maj Sjöwall & Per Wahlöö. (Martin Beck Police Mystery Ser.: No. 2). 2008. audio compact disk 19.95 (978-1-4332-4900-6(6)) Blckstn Audio.

Man Who Went up in Smoke. unabr. ed. Maj Sjöwall & Per Wahlöö. Tr. by Lois Roth & Tom Weiner. (Running Time: 6 hrs. NaN mins.). (Martin Beck Police Mystery Ser.: No. 2). 2008. 29.95 (978-1-4332-4901-3(4)); 44.95 (978-1-4332-4898-6(0)); audio compact disk 50.00 (978-1-4332-4899-3(9)) Blckstn Audio.

Man Who Would Be F. Scott Fitzgerald. unabr. ed. David Handler. Narrated by Tom Stechschulte. 6 cass. (Running Time: 7 hrs. 45 mins.). (Stewart Hoag Mystery Ser.: Vol. 3). 1998. 51.00 (978-0-7887-0929-6(1), 95069E7) Recorded Bks.
Stewart 'Hoagy' Hoag, once the Golden Boy of the publishing world, is now resigned to ghost-writing for a young celebrity. He suddenly finds more danger than dialogue developing in his life.

Man Who Would Be King. Rudyard Kipling. Read by Richard Midgley. (Running Time: 1 hr.). 2005. 16.95 (978-1-59912-941-9(8)) Iofy Corp.

Man Who Would be King. Rudyard Kipling. Read by Rebecca C. Burns. (Running Time: 4 hrs. 30 mins.). 2005. 25.95 (978-1-60083-617-6(8), Audiofy Corp) Iofy Corp.

Man Who Would Be King: And Other Stories. unabr. ed. Rudyard Kipling. Read by Rebecca C. Burns. (Running Time: 14400 sec.). (Unabridged Classics in Audio Ser.). (ENG.). 1997. audio compact disk 24.99 (978-1-4001-0046-0(1)) Pub: Tantor Media. Dist(s): IngramPubServ

Man Who Would Be King: And Other Stories. unabr. ed. Rudyard Kipling. Read by Rebecca C. Burns. (Running Time: 14400 sec.). (Unabridged Classics in Audio Ser.). (ENG.). 2005. audio compact disk 19.99 (978-1-4001-5046-5(9)) Pub: Tantor Media. Dist(s): IngramPubServ

Man Who Would Be King & Other Stories. unabr. ed. Rudyard Kipling. Read by Fred Williams. 9 cass. (Running Time: 13 hrs. 30 min.). 1996. 62.95 (978-0-7861-0968-5(8), 1745) Blckstn Audio.
The story of two British vagabonds who set off to establish a small kingdom among primitive tribesmen in Afghanistan. Only one of the men returns, & his condition is so bad that the newspaperman-narrator barely recognizes him. This collection brings together seventeen of Kipling's early stories, written between 1885 & 1888, when Kipling was working as a journalist in India. The stories include: "The Phantom Rickshaw," "Baa Baa, Black Sheep," "At the Pit's Mouth," "A Wayside Comedy," "Gemini," "The Strange Ride of Morrowbie Jukes," "At Twenty-Two," & "With the Main Guard".

Man Who Would Be King & Other Stories. unabr. ed. Short Stories. Rudyard Kipling. Narrated by George Taylor. 3 cass. (Running Time: 3 hrs. 30 mins.). 1989. 26.00 (978-1-55690-331-1(6), 89890E7) Recorded Bks.
Two British soldiers set themselves up as rulers in the Indian highlands.

Man Who Would Be King & Other Stories. unabr. ed. Rudyard Kipling. Read by Rebecca C. Burns. (Running Time: 14400 sec.). (Unabridged Classics in Audio Ser.). (ENG.). 2005. audio compact disk 49.99 (978-1-4001-3046-7(8)) Pub: Tantor Media. Dist(s): IngramPubServ

Man Who Would Be King & Other Stories. unabr. collector's ed. Rudyard Kipling. Read by Rebecca C. Burns. 4 cass. (Running Time: 4 hrs.). (J). 1997. 24.00 (978-0-7366-3767-1(2), 4440) Books on Tape.
"The Man Who Would Be King" is the story of two British adventurers who set off to conquer a small kingdom in Afghanistan. Only one of the men returns. Also includes: "The Drums of the Fore & Aft," "Wee Willie Winkie," "Baa, Baa, Black Sheep," "Namgay Doola," "Moti Guj-Mutineer," "A Conference of the Powers" & "The Head of the District".

Man Who Would be King & Other Stories, with EBook. unabr. ed. Rudyard Kipling. Narrated by Rebecca Burns. (Running Time: 4 hrs. 30 mins. 0 sec.). (ENG.). 2009. audio compact disk 19.99 (978-1-4001-6110-2(X)); audio compact disk 19.99 (978-1-4001-1110-7(2)) Pub: Tantor Media. Dist(s): IngramPubServ

Man Who Would be King & Other Stories, with eBook. unabr. ed. Rudyard Kipling. Narrated by Rebecca Burns. (Running Time: 4 hrs. 30 mins. 0 sec.). (ENG.). 2009. audio compact disk 39.99 (978-1-4001-4110-4(9)) Pub: Tantor Media. Dist(s): IngramPubServ

Man with a Plan: Neh. 2:1-11. Ed Young. 1990. 4.95 (978-0-7417-1804-4(9), 804) Win Walk.

Man with a Squirrel. unabr. ed. Nicholas Kilmer. Read by Patrick Cullen. 6 cass. (Running Time: 8 hrs. 30 mins.). 1997. 44.95 (978-0-7861-1226-5(3), 1969) Blckstn Audio.
Oona, a Boston art shop proprietress, offers Fred a painting, the image of a common grey squirrel on a chain, which he discovers has been cut from a larger canvas. Believing it to be the work of an important eighteenth-century American master, he snaps up the fragment & then sets out to find the rest of the painting. Murder, mayhem, & other forms of vandalism soon join the violence already associated with the painting.

Man with Bad Manners. Idries Shah. Read by Michael Ashcraft. Illus. by Rose Mary Santiago. (Sounds of Afghanistan Ser.). (J). (ps-3). 2005. bk. 28.95 (978-1-883536-75-6(8), Hoopoe Books) ISHK.
This Afghani folktale has been recast in a modern Western setting, though Santiago's brilliantly hued, naive paintings give it a timeless quality. In a quaint village with well-cultivated gardens, everyone is courteous except for one man. He babbles "blah, blah, blah" in response to others' greetings, and in the night, bangs cans loudly. Everyone is happy when he leaves to visit friends in another village. A clever boy points out, though, that their problems aren't over yet, since the man will return. He has an idea that may make the rude fellow change his ways. This ingenious plan, carried out with the villagers' full cooperation, results in a happy ending for one and all. The tale's mild didacticism is leavened by Shah's gentle retelling and Santiago's artfully lighthearted illustrations.

Man with No Eyes & Other Stories. abr. ed. Fay Weldon. Read by Julie Christie. 2 cass. 1998. 16.85 Set. (978-1-901768-19-0(8)) Pub: CSA Telltapes GBR. Dist(s): Ulverscroft US

Man with No Name: Turn Lemons into Lemonade. Wally Amos. 2 cass. 1994. 16.95 set. (978-1-879323-37-7(0)) Sound Horizons AV.
The inspiring & wonderful voice of Wally Amos, whose name has become virtually synonymous with chocolate chip cookies, is featured in all its warmth & exuberance in this live reading of his best-seller "Man with No Name." Hear the amazing story of how Wally lost his business, his money, & even the use of his name - & how he turned it into the comeback story of the decade.

Man with the Bag (Ev'rybody's Waitin' for) - ShowTrax. Perf. by Kaye Starr. Arranged by Roger Emerson. 1 CD. (Running Time: 5 mins.). 2000. audio compact disk 19.95 (08742381) H Leonard.
"Yule be jammin'" with this fun song from the Big Band era!.

Man with the Gash see Love of Life

Man with the Gash see Call of the Wild & Other Stories

Man with the Getaway Face, unabr. collector's ed. Richard Stark, pseud. Read by Michael Kramer. 4 cass. (Running Time: 6 hrs.). 1999. 32.00 (978-0-7366-4410-5(5), 4871) Books on Tape.
Master thief Parker comes to a plastic surgeon in Nebraska with a face that the Outfit - the New York syndicate - wants to decorate with a bullet. But nothing can keep Parker away from his old life of crime - & the major heist of an armored car somewhere in New Jersey.

Man with the Golden Arm. collector's ed. Nelson Algren. Read by Barrett Whitener. 11 cass. (Running Time: 16 hrs. 30 min.). 2000. 88.00 (978-0-7366-5435-7(6)) Books on Tape.
Frankie Machine is a once-shrewd card sharp, now a junkie, whose "golden arm" shakes as he relies on morphine to overcome the pain of a war injury & to numb the guilt he feels for a drunken spree that put his wife, Sophie, in a wheelchair. Much of the psychological action centers on Sophie's attempts to manipulate Frankie. After Frankie kills his drug dealer & flees, he hangs himself in a seedy hotel.

Man with the Golden Arm. unabr. ed. Nelson Algren. (Running Time: 16 hrs. 0 mins.). 2009. 89.95 (978-1-4332-9676-5(4)); audio compact disk 118.00 (978-1-4332-9677-2(2)) Blckstn Audio.

Man with the Golden Arm. unabr. ed. Nelson Algren. Read by Malcolm Hillgartner. (Running Time: 14 hrs. 30 mins.). 2009. 29.95 (978-1-4332-9680-2(2)); audio compact disk 34.95 (978-1-4332-9679-6(9)) Blckstn Audio.

Man with the Golden Gun. unabr. ed. Ian Fleming. Read by David Rintoul. 4 cass. (Running Time: 4 hrs.). 1993. bk. 39.95 (978-0-7451-5933-1(8), CAB 266) AudioGO.

Man with the Golden Gun. unabr. ed. Ian Fleming. Narrated by Robert Whitfield. 4 cass. (Running Time: 5 hrs. 30 mins.). 2001. 32.95 (978-0-7861-2145-8(9), 2896); audio compact disk 32.00 (978-0-7861-9594-7(0), 2896) Blckstn Audio.
In a highly secret office somewhere in London, a murder is to be attempted. M is to be the victim... and the assassin is to be James Bond. Bond, believed dead for a year following the events of You Only Live Twice, returns to England. Brainwashed by the KGB, he believes his mission is to assassinate M. After his mind is "scrubbed," he is given a chance to redeem himself. The mission, to go to the Caribbean and track down Francisco Scaramanga, the one they call the "Man with the Golden Gun." He has built a deadly laser for the express purpose of killing. With his single-action, gold-plated Colt .45 and his deadeye accuracy, Scaramanga is deemed too deadly to live.

Man with the Golden Gun. unabr. ed. Ian Fleming. Read by Simon Vance. (Running Time: 4.5 hrs. 0 mins.). (James Bond Ser.: No. 13). 2009. audio compact disk 19.95 (978-1-4332-6136-7(7)) Blckstn Audio.

Man with the Golden Gun: James Bond Series #13. unabr. ed. Ian Fleming. Read by Simon Vance. (Running Time: 1 hr. 0 mins.). (ENG.). 2009. 19.95 (978-1-4332-9040-4(5)) Blckstn Audio.

Man with the Hoe see Classic American Poetry

Man with the Hoe see Favorite American Poems

Man with the Iron Heart. unabr. ed. Harry Turtledove. Narrated by William Dufris. (Running Time: 21 hrs. 0 mins. 0 sec.). (ENG.). 2008. audio compact disk 34.99 (978-1-4001-5804-1(4)); audio compact disk 99.99 (978-1-4001-3804-3(3)) Pub: Tantor Media. Dist(s): IngramPubServ

Man with the Iron Heart. unabr. ed. Harry Turtledove. Narrated by William Dufris. (Running Time: 21 hrs. 0 mins. 0 sec.). (ENG.). 2008. audio compact disk 49.99 (978-1-4001-0804-6(7)) Pub: Tantor Media. Dist(s): IngramPubServ

Man with the Red Tattoo. unabr. ed. Raymond Benson. Read by Robert Whitfield. 6 cass. (Running Time: 8 hrs. 30 mins.). 2002. 44.95 (978-0-7861-2325-4(7), 3032); audio compact disk 56.00 (978-0-7861-9380-6(8), 3032) Blckstn Audio.
When an important British businessman and his family are killed in Tokyo by a virulent form of West Nile disease, James Bond suspects a mass assassination. His mission to Japan reunites him with his old friend Tiger Tanaka. It's been years since they worked together, but the dangers they faced then are nothing compared with what awaits them today.

Man with the Twisted Lip see Adventures of Sherlock Holmes

Man with the Twisted Lip. unabr. ed. Arthur Conan Doyle. Read by Walter Covell. 1 cass. (Running Time: 50 min.). Dramatization. 1981. 7.95 (S-37) Jimcin Record.
A classic Sherlock Holmes adventure.

Man with Two Left Feet. P. G. Wodehouse. Read by Anais 9000. 2008. 27.95 (978-1-60112-196-7(2)) Babblebooks.

Man with Two Left Feet & Other Stories. unabr. ed. P. G. Wodehouse. Read by Frederick Davidson. 5 cass. (Running Time: 7 hrs.). 1997. 39.95 (978-0-7861-1117-6(8), 1885) Blckstn Audio.
It is here that Jeeves makes his first appearance. In the story "Extricating Young Gussie" we find Bertie Wooster's redoubtable Aunt Agatha, "who had an eye like a man-eating fish & had got a moral suasion down to a fine point." The other stories: the romance between a lovely girl & a would-be playwright, the rivalry between the ugly policeman & Alf the Romeo milkman, the plight of Henry in the title piece who fell in love with a dance hostess.

Man Within. Neville Goddard. 1 cass. (Running Time: 62 min.). 1968. 8.00 (5) J & L Pubns.
Neville taught Imagination Creates Reality. He was a powerfully influential teacher of God as Consciousness.

Man Without a Country. Edward E. Hale. Read by Jim Killavey. 3 cass. (Running Time: 3 hrs.). 1989. 21.00 incl. album. (C-37) Jimcin Record.
Also includes two short stories.

Man Without a Country. Edward E. Hale. 10.00 (LSS1113) Esstee Audios.

Man Without a Country. abr. ed. Kurt Vonnegut. Narrated by Norman Dietz. (Running Time: 9000 sec.). 2005. audio compact disk 14.99 (978-1-4193-6411-2(1)) Recorded Bks.

Man Without a Country. abr. adpt. ed. Edward Everett Hale. (Bring the Classics to Life: Level 2 Ser.). (ENG.). 2008. audio compact disk 12.95 (978-1-55576-461-6(4)) EDCON Pubng.

Man Without a Country. unabr. ed. Edward E. Hale. Read by Jim Killavey. 2 cass. (Running Time: 3 hrs.). Incl. Last Voyage of the "Resolute" 1989. (C-37); My Double & How He Undid Me. 1989. (C-37); 1989. 21.00 (C-37) Jimcin Record.
Famous story of a man's yearning for the country be once spurned.

Man Without a Country. unabr. ed. Kurt Vonnegut. 2 CDs. (Running Time: 2 hrs.). 2005. audio compact disk 29.75 (978-1-4193-6457-0(X), C3473) Recorded Bks.

Man Without a Country. unabr. ed. Kurt Vonnegut. Narrated by Norman Dietz. 2 cass. (Running Time: 2 hrs.). 2005. 19.75 (978-1-4193-6455-6(3), 98222) Recorded Bks.
One of the greatest minds in American writing, Kurt Vonnegut has left an indelible impression on literature with such inventive novels as Cat's Cradle, Slaughterhouse- Five and Breakfast of Champions. Now this iconic figure shares his often hilarious and always insightful reflections on America, art, politics and life in general. No matter the subject, Vonnegut will have you considering perspectives you may never have regarded. A Man without a Country showcases Vonnegut at his wittiest, most acerbic, and most concerned. Beyond the humor and biting satire is an appeal to all readers to give careful thought to the world around them and the people they share it with.

Man Without a Country: Abridged. (ENG.). 2007. (978-1-60339-001-9(4)); cd-rom & audio compact disk (978-1-60339-002-6(2)) Listenr Digest.

***Man without a Country: Bring the Classics to Life.** adpt. ed. Edward Everett Hale. (Bring the Classics to Life Ser.). 2008. pap. bk. 21.95 (978-1-55576-498-2(3)) EDCON Pubng.

Man Without Equal. Bill Bright. 1 cass. (Running Time: 081 min.). 1995. 4.99 (978-1-56399-017-5(2)) CampCrus.

Man-Woman Relationships, Set. Nathaniel Branden. 6 CDs. (Running Time: 4 hrs.). 2005. audio compact disk 50.00 (978-1-57970-253-3(8), AFNB04D, Audio-For) J Norton Pubs.
An interesting and informative collection with everything you always wanted to ask Nathaniel Branden about sex, man-woman relationships, marriage, and the various problems men and women encounter in the process of dealing with and relating to one another.

Man-Woman Relationships, Discussions Of. unabr. ed. Nathaniel Branden. 6 cass. (Running Time: 4 hrs.). 50.00 (534-39) J Norton Pubs.

Man You'll Marry. Debbie Macomber. 2009. audio compact disk 14.99 (978-1-4418-1639-9(9)) Brilliance Audio.

Man You'll Marry. unabr. ed. Debbie Macomber. Read by Kate Rudd. (Running Time: 7 hrs.). 2009. 24.99 (978-1-4418-1635-1(6), 9781441816351, Brilliance MP3); 14.99 (978-1-4418-4798-0(7), 9781441847980, Brilliance MP3); 14.99 (978-1-4418-4799-7(5), 9781441847997, BAD); 24.99 (978-1-4418-1637-5(2), 9781441816375, BAD); 39.97 (978-1-4418-1636-8(4), 9781441816368, Brinc Audio MP3 Lib); 39.97 (978-1-4418-1638-2(0), 9781441816382, BADLE); audio compact disk 29.99 (978-1-4418-1633-7(X), 9781441816337, Bril Audio CD Unabri); audio compact disk 14.99 (978-1-4418-4797-3(9), 9781441847973, Bril Audio CD Unabri); audio compact disk 97.97 (978-1-4418-1634-4(8), 9781441816344, BriAudCD Unabrid) Brilliance Audio.

Man Young & Old: First Love, Human Dignity, The Mermaid (poem) see Poetry of William Butler Yeats

Manage Your Anger. abr. ed. Gael Lindenfield. Read by Polly Adams. 1 cass. (Running Time: 090 min.). 1998. 9.95 (978-0-694-51910-1(3), CPN10135, Harper Audio) HarperCollins Pubs.

Manage your Dyslexia: Track 1 Powerful suggestions to boost confidence Track2 Listen, focus, organise thinking & Planning. Lynda Hudson. Eleanor May. (YA). 2007. audio compact disk 33.90 (978-1-905557-26-4(4)) First Way Forward GBR.

Manage Your Time to Reduce Your Stress: A Handbook for the Overworked, Overscheduled, & Overwhelmed. unabr. ed. Rita Emmett. Read by Rita Emmett. 4 CDs. (Running Time: 4 hrs. 30 mins. 0 sec.). (ENG.). 2008. audio compact disk 24.95 (978-1-4272-0648-0(1)) Pub: Macmill Audio. Dist(s): Macmillan

Management. abr. rev. ed. Peter F. Drucker. Read by Sam Tsoutsouvas. 2008. audio compact disk 59.95 (978-0-06-168768-6(5), Harper Audio) HarperCollins Pubs.

Management Advantage: Lessons from America's Top Business Schools, Set. 12 cass. 149.95 (859AX) Nightingale-Conant.
In this definitive management program, Tom Peters & Brian Tracy - along with 24 experts from America's leading business schools - share with you personal insights & ideas for business success. Learn to master the art of crisis management, use conflict as a positive force & manage your company for innovation. Discover nine ways to unlock office creativity, seven secrets for effective leadership & ten steps that can help you earn ten times your current salary! Includes 32-page booklet.

Management & Leadership Skills for Women. Susan Dellinger. 5 cass. 64.95 set. (V10117) CareerTrack Pubns.
This program deals with real problems that many women face as they move up the career ladder. Problems like dealing with people who resent your success ... don't like being told what to do by a woman ... or think women managers are pushovers.

Management & Supervisory Skills for Women, Set. abr. ed. Perf. by Lori Giovannoi. 6 cass. 1990. bk. 69.95 (978-1-929874-03-3(0)) SkillPath Pubns.

Management by Design: The Principles of Design for the New Enterprise. unabr. ed. D. W. Rasmus. (Running Time: 7 hrs.). 2008. 39.25 (978-1-4233-6039-1(7), 9781423360391, Brinc Audio MP3 Lib); 39.25 (978-1-4233-6041-4(9), 9781423360414, BADLE); 24.95 (978-1-4233-6040-7(0), 9781423360407, BAD); audio compact disk 82.25 (978-1-4233-6037-7(0), 9781423360377, BriAudCD Unabrid) Brilliance Audio.

Management by One Hundred Percent Responsibility. abr. ed. Linda L. McNeil. Read by Linda L. McNeil. 3 cass. (Running Time: 3 hrs.). 1991. pap. bk. 49.95 Set. (978-1-891446-03-0(7)) Open Mind.
Powerful presentation about attitudes in the workplace. Introduction to the roles & requirements of management with real world examples by someone who has been there, Linda McNeil. Demonstrates how different personalities communicate & tend to deal with stress & change.

Management by Responsibility. abr. ed. G. Michael Durst. Read by G. Michael Durst. 1 cass. (Running Time: 45 min.). 1987. 10.00 Train Sys.

Management by Responsibility. unabr. ed. G. Michael Durst. Read by G. Michael Durst. 6 cass. (Running Time: 4 hrs.). 1987. 80.00 Train Sys.

***Management Challenges for the 21St Century.** abr. ed. Peter F. Drucker. Read by Mark Blum. (ENG.). 2005. (978-0-06-088686-8(2), Harper Audio); (978-0-06-089414-6(8), Harper Audio) HarperCollins Pubs.

Management Challenges for the 21st Century. unabr. ed. Peter F. Drucker. Narrated by Mark Blum. 4 cass. (Running Time: 6 hrs. 15 mins.). 2000. 37.00 (978-0-7887-4951-3(X), 96466E7) Recorded Bks.
The evolving paradigms & management challenges businesses face as the new century begins. The author offers practical suggestions for improving productivity, handling the influx of information technology & leading in the modern workplace.

Management Excellence. Jack Kinder et al. Read by Jack Kinder et al. 6 cass. 59.95 Set. (525AD) Nightingale-Conant.
You'll discover the brass-tacks musts for transforming today's challenges into bottom-line results. You'll learn how to build on strength & "manage around" weakness & how to recognize & exploit the "teachable moment.".

Management for Intelligent People in A-E-P & Environmental Consulting Firms. 3 cass. 1998. 95.00 Set. (978-1-885002-47-1(5)) ZweigWhite.

Management Methods of Jesus: Ancient Wisdom for Modern Business. abr. ed. Bob Briner. 2 cass. (Running Time: 3 hrs.). 1998. bk. 15.99 (978-0-8054-1265-9(4)) BH Pubng Grp.
Provides today's managers with timeless wisdom from the life of Jesus.

Management Myth: Management Consulting Past, Present, & Largely Bogus. unabr. ed. Matthew Stewart. (Running Time: 10 hrs. 30 mins.). (ENG.). 2009. 29.95 (978-1-4332-9141-8(X)); 65.95 (978-1-4332-9137-1(1)); audio compact disk 29.95 (978-1-4332-9140-1(1)); audio compact disk 100.00 (978-1-4332-9138-8(X)) Blckstn Audio.

Management of Angina Pectoris. Read by Elliot Rapaport. 1 cass. (Running Time: 90 min.). 1985. 12.00 (C8542) Amer Coll Phys.

Management of Breast Cancer. Read by Philip S. Schein. 1 cass. (Running Time: 90 min.). 1985. 12.00 (C8536) Amer Coll Phys.

Management of Breast Cancer That May Not Behave Like Cancer. Moderated by Alfred S. Ketcham. 2 cass. (General Sessions Ser.: GS-1). 1986. 19.00 (8629) Am Coll Surgeons.

Management of Difficult Non-Malignant Esophageal Problems. 2 cass. (General Sessions Ser.: C84-GS5). 1984. 15.00 (8408) Am Coll Surgeons.

Management of Difficult Perineal Wounds after Treatment of Inflammatory Bowel Disease: Interdisciplinary Panel Discussion. Moderated by Luis O. Vasconez. 2 cass. (Plastic & Maxillofacial Surgery Ser.: PL-1). 1986. 19.00 (8660) Am Coll Surgeons.

Management of Equity Investments. Dimitris N. Chorafas. (ENG., 2005. 113.00 (978-0-7506-6456-1(8), Butter Sci Hein) Sci Tech Bks.

Management of Flexor Tendon Injuries of the Hand: Interdisciplinary Panel Discussion. Moderated by Elvin G. Zook. 2 cass. (Plastic & Maxillofacial Surgery Ser.: PL-5). 1986. 19.00 (8664) Am Coll Surgeons.

Management of Gastrointestinal Cancer. Read by Philip S. Schein. 1 cass. (Running Time: 90 min.). 1986. 12.00 (C8617) Amer Coll Phys.

Management of Infectious Disease Problems. Read by Robert C. Moellering, Jr. 1 cass. (Running Time: 90 min.). 1985. 12.00 (C8534) Amer Coll Phys.

Management of Intraabdominal Sepsis. 2 cass. (General Sessions Ser.: C85-GS4). 15.00 (8539) Am Coll Surgeons.

Management of Neurovascular Problems of the Upper Extremity. 2 cass. (Plastic & Maxillofacial Surgery Ser.: C85-PL5). 1985. 15.00 (8584) Am Coll Surgeons.

Management of Obstetrics & its Related Problem. Varma. 2004. cd-rom & audio compact disk 15.00 (978-81-8061-244-2(9)) Jaypee Brothers IND.

Management of Parotid Tumors Ser. Instructed by Nicholas J. Cassisi. 2 cass. (Otorhinolaryngology Ser.: OT-6). 1986. 19.00 (8658) Am Coll Surgeons.

Management of Patients with Secretory Pituitary Tumors. Read by Joseph B. Martin. 1 cass. (Running Time: 9 min.). 1985. 12.00 (C8545) Amer Coll Phys.

Management of Pediatric Surgical Emergencies. Moderated by Graham C. Fraser. 2 cass. (General Sessions Ser.: Spring 1986). 1986. 15.00 (8606) Am Coll Surgeons.
Discusses management of cardiothoracic emergencies, management of abdominal emergencies, management of airway emergencies.

Management of Periodontal Disease in the 90's. Planned Marketing Staff. 1 cass. 1994. 75.00 (978-1-882306-05-3(8)) Planned Mktg.
Training.

Management of Prostate Cancer. 2 cass. (Urologic Surgery Ser.: C85-UR1). 1985. 15.00 (8588) Am Coll Surgeons.

Management of Rectal Pain. Moderated by Ernestine Hambrick. 2 cass. (Colon & Rectal Surgery Ser.: CR-3). 1986. 19.00 (8638) Am Coll Surgeons.

Management of Severe & Refractory Hypertension. Read by John A. Oates. 1 cass. (Running Time: 90 min.). 1986. 12.00 (C8662) Amer Coll Phys.

Management of Sexually Transmitted Diseases. Read by Michael F. Rein. 1 cass. (Running Time: 90 min.). 1986. 12.00 (C8658) Amer Coll Phys.

Management of the absurd: paradoxes in leadership Cassette: Paradoxes in Leadership. Richard Farson. 2004. 10.95 (978-0-7435-4068-1(9)) Pub: S&S Audio. Dist(s): S and S Inc

Management of Venous Thromboembolism. Read by Kenneth M. Moser. 1 cass. (Running Time: 90 min.). 1986. 12.00 (C8663) Amer Coll Phys.

Management Practices in Canadian Forests - Perspectives of an American Journalist & an American Law Professor. Hosted by Nancy Pearlman. 1 cass. (Running Time: 29 min.). 10.00 (1505) Educ Comm CA.

Management Problems of the Technical Person in a Leadership Role. Fred Pryor. 6 cass. (Running Time: 6 hrs.). 1995. 59.95 Set. (12160A); 59.95 Set incl. wkbk. (12160AM) Nightingale-Conant.
Ideal for use as a training or reference tool.

***Management Rev Ed.** abr. ed. Peter F. Drucker. Read by Sam Tsoutsouvas. (ENG.). 2008. (978-0-06-176947-4(9), Harper Audio); (978-0-06-176945-0(2), Harper Audio) HarperCollins Pubs.

Management Series. Jerry Johnson & Glenn Swogger. Read by Jerry Johnson & Glenn Swogger. Ed. by Patricia Magerkurth. 2 cass. (Running Time: 1 hr. 04 min.). 1992. 20.00 set. (978-1-56948-011-3(7)) Menninger Clinic.

Management Skills for New Supervisors, Set. abr. ed. Jim Temme. Read by Jim Temme. 2 cass. (Running Time: 3 hrs.). 1996. bk. 21.95 (978-1-57294-073-4(5),) SkillPath Pubns.
Shows how an organization can benefit from acquiring or sharpening important management skills such as leading, motivating, coaching & guiding.

Management Skills for Secretaries, Administrative Assistants, & Support Staff: Even If Your Title Doesn't Say "Manager", You Can Still Harness the Power of Management Skills. 6 cass. 59.95 Set incl. wkbk. (12850AS) Pryor Resources.
This breakthrough seminar gives you high-impact approaches to gaining the confidence, power, & knowledge to handle whatever the workplace throws at you.

Management Support Plan: the next generation business Management see Het Management Support Plan: De volgende generatie Bedrijfsvoering

Managerial Data Processing. (13180) J Norton Pubs.

Managerial Skills for A Country in Conflict. Luis Tayron Lozada. Read by Luis Tayron Lozada Pedraza. (Running Time: 1 hr.). 2003. 14.95 (978-1-60083-305-2(5), Audiofy Corp) Iofy Corp.

Manager's Balancing Act: Paradoxical Management. Ben Bissell. 1 cass. (Running Time: 44 min.). 15.00 C Bissell.
Believing that managing paradoxes is the key for succeeding in the 90's, Dr. Bissell maps out ways to meet the challenges in the future.

Manager's Role As Coach. Bob Norton. 6 cass. 59.95 Set, incl. wkbk. (131-C47); 22.95 business user's manual, 200p. (456-C47) Natl Seminars.
Forget about being "the boss." Today's successful managers are - first & foremost - outstanding cheerleaders & coaches, people who can motivate teams to top performance, to winning! This program teaches you how to motivate teams, taught by the most inspiring business-world coaches of our day.

Managers' Roundtable. Contrib. by Jim Keene et al. 1 cass. Alliance Innov.

Managing. Harold Geneen. 1 cass. 8.95 Listen USA.
Covers what performance really means & managing for the best results.

Managing a Corporation's Law Department. 7 cass. (Running Time: 8 hrs. 30 min.). 1990. 175.00 Set. (T7-9312) PLI.

Managing a Local Area Network. Pinnacle Communications, Inc. Staff. Ed. by Jacqueline Jonas & Patricia A. Menges. 4 cass. (C). pap. bk. 245.00 set, incl. study guide. (978-0-917792-80-9(7), 152) OneOnOne Comp Trng.

Managing & Maintaining a Server Environment Classroom-to-Go: Windows Server 2003 Edition: Self-paced Instructional Training Course. abr. ed. William Stanek. Narrated by Ron Knowles. (Running Time: 1 hr. 56 mins.). 2006. audio compact disk 14.99 (978-1-57545-347-7(9), Classroom) Pub: Reagent Press. Dist(s): OverDrive Inc

Managing & Maintaining Network Resources Classroom-to-Go: Self-paced Instructional Training Course. abr. ed. William Stanek. Narrated by Ron Knowles. (Running Time: 1 hr. 12 mins.). (ENG.). 2006. 14.99 (978-1-57545-348-4(7), Classroom) Pub: Reagent Press. Dist(s): OverDrive Inc

Managing Brand You: 7 Steps to Creating Your Most Successful Self. unabr. ed. Jerry S. Wilson & Ira Blumenthal. Read by Jerry S. Wilson & Ira Blumenthal. (Running Time: 6 hrs. 5 mins.). (ENG.). 2008. 24.98 (978-1-59659-265-0(6), GildAudio) Pub: Gildan Media. Dist(s): HachBkGrp

Managing by Values: How to Put Your Values into Action for Extraordinary Results. unabr. ed. Ken Blanchard & Michael O'Connor. Read by Mitchell Ryan. 2 cass. (Running Time: 3 hrs.). (Right Livelihood Ser.). 1996. 17.95 (978-1-57453-146-6(8)) Audio Lit.
Today's business world is marked by increasing technological, social & economic change. Provides a practical & proven new solution for addressing these issues.

Managing Change & Transition. Ben Bissell. 1 cass. (Running Time: 44 min.). 15.00 C Bissell.
Each day changes take place in both our personal & professional lives. The successful manager must understand the 5 dynamic steps of change & how to guide his/her staff through them.

Managing Chronic Pain. 1 cass. (Care Cassettes Ser.: Vol. 15, No. 1). 1988. 10.80 Assn Prof Chaplains.

Managing Conflict. unabr. ed. Charlotte Eliopoulos. Read by Charlotte Eliopoulos. 1 cass. (Running Time: 20 min.). 1991. 15.00 (978-1-882515-11-0(0)) Hlth Educ Netwk.
Discusses sources of conflict in the health care facility & methods to manage conflict.

Managing Conflict, Set. 3 cass. pap. bk. & wbk. ed. 30.00 (978-0-7612-0813-6(5), 80187) AMACOM.
You'll learn how to: Zero in on the real causes of conflicts; Use leadership techniques that prevent power plays; Negotiate disagreements on a Win/Win basis; Employ the seven basic steps of rational problem solving in conflict resolution; Communicate in a way that encourages openness & cooperation; Deal effectively with the two different types of group conflicts; Put a stop to destructive, time-consuming game playing.

Managing Devices & Implementing Disaster Recovery Classroom-to-Go Windows Server 2003 Edition: Self-paced Instructional Training Course. abr. ed. William Stanek. Narrated by Ron Knowles. (Running Time: 1 hr. 41 mins.). (ENG.). 2006. 14.99 (978-1-57545-349-1(5), Classroom) Pub: Reagent Press. Dist(s): OverDrive Inc

Managing Economic Development: A Guide to State & Local Leadership Strategies. Jeffrey S. Luke et al. (Public Administration Ser.). 1988. bk. 47.00 (978-1-55542-092-5(3), Jossey-Bass) Wiley US.

Managing Ego Energy: The Transformation of Personal Meaning into Organizational Success. Ralph H. Kilmann & Ines Kilmann. (Management Ser.). 1994. bk. 39.95 (978-1-55542-618-7(2), Jossey-Bass) Wiley US.

Managing Elephants in Captivity & Protecting Them in the Wild. Hosted by Nancy Pearlman. 1 cass. (Running Time: 29 min.). 10.00 (1310) Educ Comm CA.

Managing for Increased Creativity. Featuring Charlie M. Leighton. 1995. audio compact disk 10.00 (978-1-880931-51-6(6)) KBA LLC.

Managing for the Future. unabr. ed. Peter F. Drucker. Read by Bill Weideman. (Running Time: 11 hrs.). 2010. 39.97 (978-1-4418-1866-9(9), 9781441818669, Brinc Audio MP3 Lib); 24.99 (978-1-4418-1865-2(0), 9781441818652, Brilliance MP3); 39.97 (978-1-4418-1868-3(5), 9781441818683, BADLE); 24.99 (978-1-4418-1867-6(7), 9781441818676, BAD) Brilliance Audio.

Managing for the Future. unabr. ed. Peter F. Drucker. Read by Joseph Campanella. 2 cass. (Running Time: 4 hrs.). 2004. 18.00 (978-1-59007-018-5(6)) Pub: New Millenn Enter. Dist(s): PerseuPGW
Offers clear-sighted analysis on a wide array of topics, including the end of the blue collar worker, the myths about the Japanese economic juggernaut, the formula for excellence in American exports and much more.

***Managing God's Money: A Biblical Guide.** unabr. ed. Randy Alcorn. (Running Time: 6 hrs. 0 mins. 0 sec.). (ENG.). 2011. audio compact disk 22.99 (978-1-59859-916-9(X)) Oasis Audio.

Managing Group Policy Classroom-to-Go: Self-paced Instructional Training Course. abr. ed. William Stanek. Narrated by Ron Knowles. (Running Time: 1 hr. 43 mins.). (ENG.). 2008. 14.99 (978-1-57545-350-7(9), Classroom) Pub: Reagent Press. Dist(s): OverDrive Inc

Managing Health Care Costs: The Continuing Challenge. 1 cass. (America's Supermarket Showcase '96 Ser.). 1996. 11.00 (NGA96-029) Sound Images.

Managing in a Time of Great Change. Peter F. Drucker. Narrated by Peter F. Drucker. 8 cass. (Running Time: 10 hrs. 30 mins.). 74.00 (978-1-4025-1576-7(6)) Recorded Bks.

Managing in a Time of Great Change. abr. ed. Peter F. Drucker. Read by Joseph Campanella. 4 cass. (Running Time: 6 hrs.). 2004. 25.00 (978-1-59007-019-2(4)) Pub: New Millenn Enter. Dist(s): PerseuPGW
Explores such topics as the new cost savings revolution in retailing, the urgent requirement for each company to have a "theory of the business" & the need for executives to seek new kinds of information through new technology. Other chapters examine the building rules for managing family-owned business, the 5 deadliest business sins, the rapid power shift of the U.S. economy & the opportunities & challenges of doing business with China & Japan.

Managing in the Face of Ever-Changing Requirements. Speeches. Kevin Aguanno. 1 CD. (Running Time: 72 mins). 2005. audio compact disk 14.87 (978-1-895186-32-1(3)) Multi-Media ON CAN.
1000% over budget. 2 years late. We've all heard about projects where the original budget and schedule were exceeded by orders of magnitude. How could this happen given competent project management? Whether in government or private industry, project managers face a huge challenge when confronted with continually-changing requirements. How can you plan when the WBS keeps changing? Traditional project management approaches suggest that we take a snapshot of the requirements as a baseline, and then use change control in an attempt to minimize the impact of any shifting requirements. Sometimes, however, these changes are a reality that the project sponsor has to accommodate. The new Agile Project Management methods help deal with these situations.Listeners of this session will learn the founding principles and techniques of Agile Project Management with examples from real-world projects that used these methods to control changing requirements.

Managing Infectious Waste. 1989. bk. 35.00 (AC-486) PA Bar Inst.

Managing Information Overload for Sales Professionals. Jeff Davidson. 2005. 13.95 (978-1-60729-225-8(4)) Breath Space Inst.

Managing Information Overload for Sales Professionals. Jeff Davidson. 2005. audio compact disk 14.95 (978-1-60729-117-6(7)) Breath Space Inst.

Managing Investment: 25 Keys to Profitable Capital Investment. unabr. ed. Robert Taggart. Read by Grover Gardner. 2 cass. (Running Time: 3 hrs.). (New York Times Pocket MBA Ser.). 2000. pap. bk. 27.95 Listen & Live.
Learn the 25 keys to finding, selecting, funding & managing outside investment & R&D internal investment for long-term success. Includes mergers & acquisitions.

Managing Investment: 25 Keys to Profitable Capital Investment. unabr. ed. Robert Taggart. Narrated by Grover Gardner. 2 cass. (Running Time: 2 hrs. 30 mins.). (New York Times Pocket MBA Ser.). 2000. 16.95 (978-1-885408-47-1(1), LL040) Listen & Live.

Managing iPhone Security Issues with Your Workforce ¿ What Companies Are Doing to Protect Themselves & Why They Are Establishing iPhone Policies. David Addis. 2009. 250.00 (978-1-59701-515-8(6)) ReedLogic.

Managing Knock Your Socks off Service. unabr. ed. Chip R. Bell et al. Read by Sean Pratt. (Running Time: 7 hrs. 30 mins.). (ENG.). 2008. 24.98 (978-1-59659-188-2(9), GildAudio) Pub: Gildan Media. Dist(s): HachBkGrp

Managing Law Firm Income. 1985. bk. 50.00; 35.00 PA Bar Inst.

Managing Madness: Program from the Award Winning Public Radio Series. Interview. Hosted by Fred Goodwin. Comment by John Hockenberry. 1 CD. (Running Time: 1hr). 1999. audio compact disk 21.95 (978-1-932479-63-8(5), LCM 85) Lichtenstein Creat.
In this hour, we look at how managed care is managing mental illness, with the suggestion that perhaps it isn't managing very well at all. We talk to doctors and therapists, and investigate managed care decision-making and its sometimes-fatal consequences. We also visit a unique health care program in Minnesota that bypasses insurance companies altogether. With commentary by John Hockenberry.

Managing Meetings That Get Results. Brian S. Tracy. Read by Brian S. Tracy. 2 cass. (Effective Manager Seminar Ser.: No. 8). 95.00 Set, incl. 1-hr. videotape & 2 wkbks., program notes & study guide. (750VD) Nightingale-Conant.
How to keep 'em short, to the point & productive.

Managing Messaging Security using Microsoft Exchange Server 2007 Training Course. 2008. 199.00 (978-1-60540-021-1(1)) K Alliance.

Managing Money. Shad Helmstetter. 1 cass. (Self-Talk Ser.). 10.95 (978-0-937065-51-8(X)) Grindle Pr.
Companion Self-Talk Cassettes as mentioned in the book, "What To Say When You Talk To Your Self".

Managing Multiple Projects, Priorities & Deadlines. Jim Temme. Read by Jim Temme. 6 cass. (Running Time: 5 hrs. 3 min.). 1990. 59.95 Set, incl. wkbk. (978-1-878542-17-5(6), 11-0606) SkillPath Pubns.
Action program that guides listener step-by-step through the process of tackling multiple projects, identifying & eliminating time-wasting activities, & effectively handling the pressures of juggling people, paper & priorities.

Managing Network Infrastructure Classroom-to-Go: Windows Server 2003 Edition: Self-paced Instructional Training Course. abr. ed. William Stanek. Narrated by Ron Knowles. (Running Time: 2 hrs. 33 mins.). 2007. audio compact disk 16.99 (978-1-57545-351-4(7), Classroom) Pub: Reagent Press. Dist(s): OverDrive Inc

Managing off-Site Employees. PUEI. 2007. audio compact disk 199.00 (978-1-934147-13-9(3), CareerTrack) P Univ E Inc.

Managing Older Employees. Gordon F. Shea. (Management Ser.). 1991. bk. 37.95 (978-1-55542-391-9(4), Jossey-Bass) Wiley US.

Managing Pain Before It Manages You. abr. ed. Margaret A. Caudill. Read by Margaret A. Caudill. 4 cass. (Running Time: 5 hrs.). 1996. 29.95 Set. (978-0-9652943-0-0(7)) M A Caudill.
Patient oriented workbook on audiotape which instructs individuals with chronic pain in pain management skills including relaxation techniques, exercise, nutrition, cognitive therapy, communication & problem-solving skills.

Managing People & Problems. Quentin De la Bedoyere. (Gower Audio Manual Ser.). 1989. 61.95 (978-0-566-02763-5(1), Gower Pubng) Pub: Ashgate Pub GBR. Dist(s): Ashgate Pub

Managing People Is Like Herding Cats: Warren Bennis on Leadership. Warren Bennis. Read by Warren Bennis. 2 cass. (Running Time: 2 hrs.). 1999. 14.95 (978-1-890009-10-6(5)) Exec Excell.

Managing Professionals in Research & Development. Donald B. Miller. (Management Ser.). 1986. bk. 47.95 (978-1-55542-000-0(1), Jossey-Bass) Wiley US.

Managing Projects as a Consultant: How to Quickly Succeed in an Unknown Environment. Speeches. Casey Worthington & Bruce Robertson. 1 CD. (Running Time: 44 mins). 2005. audio compact disk 14.87 (978-1-895186-51-2(X)) Multi-Media ON CAN.
This recording is designed for project managers who are interested in transitioning to the world of consultative project management. It includes - the differences between internal-, vendor-, and independent-based project management - the psychology of consulting as a project manager - how to adapt to customer environments - the politics and culture as a consultant - survival techniques (especially what not to do!) - plus, various tricks, tips and techniques to rapidly establish yourself in a new and unknown environment.

Managing Stress. American Institute for Preventive Medicine Staff. (For Your Information Ser.). 1993. 16.00 (978-1-56420-026-6(4)) New Readers.

Managing Stress. Ben Bissell. 1 cass. (Running Time: 1 hr. 36 min.). 15.00 C Bissell.
If you don't manage stress, your stress will manage you. Ben gives clear-cut directions & practical steps to reduce negative stress.

***Managing Stress.** Bob Griswold. Voice by Bob Griswold. (Running Time: 73). 2010. 15.98 (978-1-55848-159-6(1), Love Tapes) EffectiveMN.

Managing Stress. Read by Robert E. Griswold. 1 cass. 1992. 10.95 (978-1-55848-030-8(7)) EffectiveMN.
Relieving yourself from harmful stress may be one of the most important things you'll ever do for yourself & your family.

Managing Stress. Jennifer James. Read by Jennifer James. 1 cass. (Running Time: 58 min.). 1985. 9.95 (978-0-915423-13-2(8)) Jennifer J.
There is more to life than increasing its speed. Find out why you are not taking good care of yourself & learn how to change.

Managing Stress. Sanford G. Kulkin. 8 cass. (Running Time: 4 hrs.). 1992. bk. & ring bd. 295.00 Set. (978-1-58034-006-9(7)) IML Pubns.
Identifies sources of stress & shows how each of the four behavioral styles instinctively react to stress. Teaches how to administer a unique instrument that graphs stress levels in ten areas of one's life & develops a strategy to overcome stress.

Managing Stress. 2nd ed. Brian Luke Seaward. (C). 1998. audio compact disk 123.95 (978-0-7637-0751-4(1), 0751-1) Jones Bartlett.

Managing Stress. 3rd ed. Brian Luke Seaward. (C). 2001. tchr. ed. 124.95 (978-0-7637-1653-0(7), 1653-7); audio compact disk 12.95 (978-0-7637-1877-0(7), 1877-7) Jones Bartlett.

Managing Stress in Ministry. 1 cass. (Care Cassettes Ser.: Vol. 16, No. 1). 1989. 10.80 Assn Prof Chaplains.

Managing Stress on the Project Team. Speeches. Lou Russell. 1 CD. (Running Time: 70 mins). 2005. audio compact disk 14.87 (978-1-895186-41-3(2)) Multi-Media ON CAN.
According to recent research done by Cutter (12/2002), more than 60% of people claim that they are not only more burned out than they ever have been, but as soon as they are able, will do something about it. Employees under stress increase costs through ineffective work and health issues. Many companies are also concerned that as the economy improves, retention will suffer. The solution is complicated, since the very managers who must lead their staff through pressure, change and uncertainty are also struggling with the same issues. This recording is designed to help managers and staff change behaviors and leverage tools to help them be more flexible and resilient, reducing the business cost of stress. After listening to this recording, you will be able to:- Identify the origins of stress in your life. - Use your own personal vision and values as a means of managing stress. - Navigate change more effectively. - Prioritize activities integrating your work and personal priorities. - Set short and long term goals to improve personal productivity. - Learn to say ?No? to say ?Yes?.

Managing Stress Successfully. unabr. ed. James Richard. 1 cass. (Running Time: 50 min.). 1985. 9.95 Newtown Psychological Ctr.
Provides a lecture describing the nature of stress, stressor, & some strategies for dealing with stress. Side 2 is a guided relaxation exercise.

Managing Successful Software Development Projects. Speeches. John Rakos. 1 CD. (Running Time: 44 mins). 2005. audio compact disk 14.87 (978-1-895186-47-5(1)) Multi-Media ON CAN.
Managing the development of software projects presents several challenges. This presentation discusses the unique methodology required: approaching the development using specific phased activities and milestones. The project team has to be chosen and organized around technical skills as well as team communication. The project plan is unique because planning is a large part of the development. The greatest challenge is getting the correct requirements and keeping them current. Activities such as prototyping, iterative approaches, validation and client involvement are necessary. Risk management in software projects requires thoughtful approaches to a unique set of risks that historically have increased project cost and time by up to 50%. Most important, estimating a software development effort is difficult. Specific work breakdowns, formulas, templates, and historical data must be used. This presentation steers you through this maze of issues, giving specific, practical advice.

Managing Technological Innovation: Organizational Strategies for Implementing Advanced Manufacturing Technologies. Donald D. Davis et al. (Management Ser.). 1986. bk. 44.95 (978-1-55542-008-6(7), Jossey-Bass) Wiley US.

Managing the Networking Experience. Speeches. Michael J. Hughes. 1 CD. (Running Time: 32 mins). 2005. audio compact disk 18.47 (978-1-895186-34-5(X)) Multi-Media ON CAN.
In this second installment from the Four Cornerstones of Networking Success, author Michael J. Hughes, known as Canada?s Networking Guru, discusses the specifics of the networking experience. Specific topics include the business drivers behind the need to network, the realities of today?s networking environment, and how to network with others in this environment. This recording will uncover networking success secrets that will drive results and help you develop meaningful relationships. Guaranteed.

***Managing the Nonprofit Organization.** abr. ed. Peter F. Drucker. Read by Peter F. Drucker. (ENG.). 2005. (978-0-06-088690-5(0), Harper Audio); (978-0-06-089426-9(1), Harper Audio) HarperCollins Pubs.

Managing the Nonprofit Organization: Principles & Practices. abr. ed. Peter F. Drucker. Read by Peter F. Drucker. (Running Time: 10800 sec.). 2007. audio compact disk 14.95 (978-0-06-123207-7(6)) HarperCollins Pubs.

Managing the Pace with Grace. Jeff Davidson. 2008. audio compact disk 14.95 (978-1-60729-121-3(5)) Breath Space Inst.

Managing the Pace with Grace. Jeff Davidson. 1994. 17.95 (978-1-60729-343-9(9)) Breath Space Inst.

Managing the Private Law Library: Management Challenges, New Technology & Planning for the 1990's. 8 cass. (Running Time: 10 hrs. 30 min.). 125.00 (T7-9331) PLI.

Managing the Problem Employee: Turning Losers into Winners. Clay Sherman. Read by Clay Sherman. 6 cass. 69.95 Set incl. printed guide. (471AD) Nightingale-Conant.
How to cope with problem employees.

Managing the Quality Revolution. Philip B. Crosby. 4 cass. (Running Time: 4 hrs.). 1993. 49.95 set. (776A) Nightingale-Conant.

Managing the Stresses in Your Life. unabr. ed. Jack N. Singer. 1 cass. (Running Time: 1 hr.). (How to Change Your Life Ser.: Vol. 3). 1998. bk. 9.95 (978-0-9700694-2-9(1)) Psychologically Speak.
Listeners will learn the causes of their stress & how to prevent it. They will also learn a relaxation technique that will make a huge difference in their lives!.

Managing the Training Enterprise: High-Quality, Cost-Effective Employee Training in Organizations. Manuel London. (Management Ser.). 1989. bk. 38.95 (978-1-55542-183-0(0), Jossey-Bass) Wiley US.

Managing the Workforce of the 1990s. unabr. ed. Jennifer James. Read by Jennifer James. 2 cass. (Running Time: 2 hrs.). 14.95 set. Jennifer J.
In this tape, Jennifer outlines the elements that create a framework for management: perspective, energy & safety. Perspective is the ability to see what is happening. Increasing human energy is the cutting edge of productivity. Creating safety for yourself & colleagues is the essential base for perspective & energy.

Managing Thought. Mary Lore. 2008. audio compact disk 29.95 (978-1-933916-32-3(X)) Pub: Nelson Pubg MI. Dist(s): Partners Pubs Grp

Managing Time & Priorities, Set. abr. ed. Reich Gardner. Read by Reich Gardner. 2 cass. 1996. bk. 21.95 (978-1-57294-072-7(7),) SkillPath Pubns.
Learning together how to get more done faster & with better results than ever before.

Managing to Succeed: How Service Businesses Are Building Winning Teams, Vol. I. 2 cass. (Running Time: 29 min. per cass.). 1990. 27.95 Resource Direction.

Managing to Succeed: Success Stories from The Wall Street Journal. unabr. collector's ed. Read by Bob Erickson. Ed. by Lawrence A. Armour. 7 cass. (Running Time: 10 hrs. 30 min.). 1984. 56.00 (978-0-7366-0245-7(3), 1241) Books on Tape.
This is about executives who are making a success of running their businesses. Through these case studies Armour strips the terms "success" & "management of generalities" & presents them as concrete examples that help us see how one can truly manage to succeed.

Managing Today's Nonprofit Organization. Loren Ankarlo. 4 cass. 79.95 set. (C10123) CareerTrack Pubns.
This program gives you practical ways to: increase contributions in a declining market; maximize your board's contribution; meld the contributions of paid personnel & volunteers into a cohesive, effective staff & provide a predictable revenue stream to your organization.

Managing Transitions: Making the Most of Change. 2nd rev. unabr. ed. William Bridges. Read by Sean Pratt. (Running Time: 6 hrs.). (ENG.). 2007. audio compact disk 29.98 (978-1-59659-094-6(7), GildAudio) Pub: Gildan Media. Dist(s): HachBkGrp

Managing Users, Computers, & Groups Classroom-to-Go Windows Server 2003 Edition: Self-paced Instructional Training Course. abr. ed. William Stanek. Narrated by Ron Knowles. (Running Time: 1 hr. 53 mins.). (ENG.). 2006. 16.99 (978-1-57545-352-1(5), Classroom) Pub: Reagent Press. Dist(s): OverDrive Inc

Managing work in Life: A seven step plan to achieve your goals & master your new life business Plan. (ENG., 2008. audio compact disk 47.00 (978-1-933437-20-0(0)) Exe H & W Inc.

Managing Your Anger. Ben Bissell. 1 cass. (Running Time: 1 hr. 11 min.). 15.00 C Bissell.
This presentation introduces the cycles of anger & how to avoid the destructive ways anger affects one's life.

Managing Your Business: Milady's Guide to the Salon. Leslie Edgerton. 1 cass. (SalonOvations Ser.). 1995. 14.95 (978-1-56253-305-2(3), Milady) Pub: Delmar. Dist(s): CENGAGE Learn

Managing Your Client's Personal Injury Settlement: A Legal & Economic Analysis. (Running Time: 4 hrs.). 1999. bk. 99.00 (ACS-2226) PA Bar Inst.
After spending three years litigating a claim for a severely injured client, the insurance company has finally made a generous offer. Now what? Guide through the settlement process, explain guardianships & alternatives, discuss settlement options, including issues involved in choosing a form of settlement & identify estate planning techniques available to the client.

Managing Your Finances. Mark Crow. 5 cass. (Running Time: 5 hrs.). 2001. (978-1-931537-03-2(8)) Vision Comm Creat.

Managing Your Goals. Alec Mackenzie & Mel M. Brown. 6 cass. 59.95 Set incl. 40p. wkbk. (248AB) Nightingale-Conant.
With Managing Your Goals, you'll create your own destiny - as well as the route you'll take to get there. You'll learn the difference between just being busy & being truly effective. And you'll discover how to prioritize tasks & enhance your performance.

Managing Your Memory. Geraldine Markel. 2005. audio compact disk 12.95 (978-0-9791279-3-9(9)) Managing Mind.

Managing Your Money. abr. ed. Robert Heady. 2004. 25.99 (978-1-58926-822-7(9), 6822) Pub: Oasis Audio. Dist(s): TNT Media Grp

Managing Your Money. abr. ed. Robert Heady & Christy Heady. Narrated by Grover Gardner. (Complete Idiot's Guides). (ENG.). 2004. audio compact disk 27.99 (978-1-58926-823-4(7), 6823) Oasis Audio.

***Managing Your Money: CD add-on Set.** Perf. by Millmark Education Staff. (ConceptLinks Ser.). 2009. audio compact disk 50.00 (978-1-61618-359-2(4)) Millmark Educ.

***Managing Your Money Audio CD.** Perf. by Millmark Education Staff. (ConceptLinks Ser.). 2009. audio compact disk 28.00 (978-1-4334-0660-7(8)) Millmark Educ.

***Managing Your Money Audio CD: Be a Wise Consumer.** Perf. by Millmark Education Staff. (Content Literacy Libraries Ser.). 2009. audio compact disk (978-1-61618-144-4(3)) Millmark Educ.

***Managing Your Money Audio CD: Investing in Your Future.** Perf. by Millmark Education Staff. (Content Literacy Libraries Ser.). 2009. audio compact disk (978-1-61618-140-6(0)) Millmark Educ.

***Managing Your Money Audio CD: Planning Your Budget.** Perf. by Millmark Education Staff. (Content Literacy Libraries Ser.). 2009. audio compact disk (978-1-61618-136-9(2)) Millmark Educ.

***Managing Your Money Audio CD: Spend or Save?** Perf. by Millmark Education Staff. (Content Literacy Libraries Ser.). 2009. audio compact disk (978-1-61618-132-1(X)) Millmark Educ.

Managing Your Negative Emotions. Ginger Chalford. 4 cass. (Metaphysicsl-Psychological Ser.). 1986. bk. 34.95 (978-1-56089-015-7(0)) Visionary FL.
Explains how to identify, understand, express & release angers, fears, hurt & other difficult feelings.

Managing Your Point-of-Care Testing for Success. 3 cass. (Running Time: 75 min. per cass.). 90.00 (310118) Am Assn Clinical Chem.
The latest information on POCT management, instrument evalutions & inspections directly to you.

Managing Your Point-of-Care Testing, 1999. 3 cass. (Running Time: 90 min.). 1999. 95.00 Set, inclu. manual. (310013) Am Assn Clinical Chem.
Audioconferences that will provide you with solutions to all of your pressing POCT concerns.

Managing Your Self Esteem & Inner Power, Set. Carol Reynolds. Read by Carol Reynolds. 4 cass. (Running Time: 3 hrs. 47 min.). 1993. 34.95 set. (978-1-878542-47-2(8), 11-0401) SkillPath Pubns.
Learn secrets of developing high self-esteem & assertiveness training by using self renewal exercises & creative visualization.

Managing Your Stress. unabr. ed. Jerry V. Teplitz. Read by Jerry V. Teplitz. 6 cass. (Running Time: 6 hrs.). 1987. pap. bk. 70.00 (978-0-939372-00-3(2)); 60.00 (103) Happiness Unltd.
This album includes insomnia exercises, treatments for lower back pain, eyes, headaches, sinus colds, nutritional insights & Kinesiology.

Managing Your Time As a Director. Dora C. Fowler. 1 cass. (Running Time: 60 min.). 9.95 (978-1-57323-011-7(1)) Natl Inst Child Mgmt.

Managing Your Time to Achieve Your Goals, Set. 4 cass. pap. bk. & wbk. ed. 139.00 Incl. 2 multiple choice tests. (978-0-7612-0823-5(2), 80196); pap. bk. & wbk. ed. 30.00 (978-0-7612-0824-2(0), 80197) AMACOM.
You'll learn how to: Eliminate your personal time wasters; Minimize interruptions that occur during the day; Set long- & short-term goals & stick to them; Use planning & scheduling tools to accomplish your goal priorities; Reduce the time-consuming paperwork that confronts you every day; Delegate assignments as frequently as possible.

Managing Yourself, Relationships, & Situations. unabr. ed. Read by Dianne Webster. Ed. by Dennis E. Murphy. 4 cass. (Running Time: 4 hrs.). (Seminars on Tape Ser.). 1986. pap. bk. 49.95 Prof Train TX.
Discusses one's own work style, assesses the styles of others, enhancing one's manager's effectiveness & blending with organizination's "corporate culture".

***Manalive.** G k Chesterton. 2009. audio compact disk 34.95 (978-1-58617-421-7(5)) Pub: Ignatius Pr. Dist(s): Midpt Trade

Manana see Poesia y Drama de Garcia Lorca

Manana de Sol. Serafin Quinteros & Joaquin Quinteros. 1 cass. (Spanish Literature Ser.). (SPA.). 11.95 (978-0-8045-0851-3(8), SAC 851) Spoken Arts.
A One-act Spanish comedy in four scenes.

Manana de Sol. unabr. ed. Joaquin Alvarez Quinteros & Serafin Quinteros. 1 cass. (Running Time: 90 mins.). (SPA.). pap. bk. 16.95 (SSP375) J Norton Pubs.
Famous one-act comedy in four scenes.

***Manana, Iguana.** Ann Whitford Paul & Ethan Long. Narrated by Brian S. Amador & Rosi Amador. (ENG & SPA.). (J). (gr. k-3). 2009. bk. 28.95 (978-1-4301-0716-3(2)); pap. bk. 18.95 (978-1-4301-0715-6(4)) Live Oak Media.

Manana Para Los Ninos. Perf. by Batachanga Staff. 1 cass. 1989. 9.98 incl. Norelco pkg. (978-1-877737-37-4(2), EB 2557); audio compact disk 12.98 CD. (978-1-877737-52-7(6)) MFLP CA.
Afro-Caribbean culture & musical traditions.

Manassas. unabr. ed. James Reasoner. Read by Lloyd James. 8 CDs. (Running Time: 10 hrs.). (Civil War Battle Ser.: Bk. 1). 2003. audio compact disk 64.00 (978-0-7861-9178-9(3), 3099); 49.95 (978-0-7861-2464-0(4), 3099) Blckstn Audio.
Storm clouds are approaching Culpeper County, Virginia, in early January 1861. The troublesome Fogarty brothers have been raising havoc across the countryside, and when the local lawman, Will Brannon, returns from another futile attempt to track them down, he finds the townspeople abuzz. South Carolina has seceded from the Union, and rumor has it more states will follow, perhaps even Virginia. Will enlists, but so, too, do the Fogartys. All know that men die in battle and that these deaths are never investigated.

Manatee Winter. Kathleen Weidner Zoehfeld. (J). (ps-2). 2001. bk. 19.95 (SP 4003C) Kimbo Educ.
Mother & Little Calf head southward to a river along the Florida coast. Includes book.

Manatee Winter. unabr. ed. Kathleen Weidner Zoehfeld. Read by Peter Thomas. Illus. by Steven James Petruccio. Narrated by Peter Thomas. 1 cass. Dramatization. (Smithsonian Oceanic Collection). (J). (ps-2). 1994. 5.00 (978-1-56899-080-4(4), C4003) Soundprints.
Cassette is a dramatized readalong of the storybook, with authentic sound effects added. It consists of two sides - one with & one without page turning signals.

Mance Lipscomb/Texas Blues Guitar Solos. Transcribed by Dan Bowden. 1994. pap. bk. 25.95 (978-0-7866-1237-6(1), 95239CDP) Mel Bay.

Manchester Affair. unabr. ed. Elizabeth Elgin. Read by Shirley Dixon. 4 cass. (Running Time: 5 hr.). (Isis Ser.). (J). 1998. 44.95 (978-0-7531-0375-3(3), 980604) Pub: ISIS Lrg Prnt GBR. Dist(s): Ulverscroft US
When Anne Parker was convicted of shoplifting, Rachel, her adoptive mother knew she had no alternative but to make a promise that would change the whole course of her life. The distressing incident, said their doctor, had been a cry for help & had sprung from the need for Anne to meet her natural mother. When her wealthy, seemingly uncaring husband left for a business trip on the Continent, Rachel was determined, against his repeated warnings, to go ahead with the search. However, seeking a woman who does not want to be found is not easy at the best of times. How could she know that their lives, before it was all over, would become heartbreakingly entangled or that she would uncover a secret that had lain hidden for so long?.

Manchester Fourteen Miles. unabr. ed. Margaret Penn. Read by Elizabeth Proud. 8 cass. (Running Time: 8 hrs. 30 min.). 2001. 69.95 (978-1-85089-807-8(3), 21191) Pub: ISIS Audio GBR. Dist(s): Ulverscroft US
Margaret Penn was brought up in a village fourteen miles from Manchester at the end of the nineteenth century. This book describes her childhood & recreates a vivid sense of the frustrations as well as the warmth of a rural working class community. This is the first in a series of autobiographical novels.

Manchu Palaces. abr. ed. Jeanne Larsen. Read by Susan Clark. 3 cass. (Running Time: 4 hrs. 30 min.). 1997. 21.95 (978-1-57453-133-6(6)) Audio Lit.
It is the time of the Manchus. Lotus readies herself to secure a position in the imperial palaces of Beijing's Forbidden City. Told from a Buddhist perspective, this enchanting tale examines human loss & human folly.

Manchurian Candidate. Richard Condon. 2009. (978-1-60136-161-5(0)) Audio Holding.

Manchurian Candidate. unabr. ed. Richard Condon. Read by Christopher Hurt. 7 cass. (Running Time: 10 hrs.). 1995. 49.95 Set. (978-0-7861-0903-6(3), 1707) Blckstn Audio.
Buried deep within the consciousness of Sergeant Raymond Shaw is the mechanism of an assassin - a time bomb ticking toward explosion, controlled by the delicate skill of its Communist masters. Shaw returns from the Korean War to an idolizing & unsuspecting country. In a farcical, uproarious scene, he is greeted amid flashbulbs & frock coats by his power-hungry, domineering mother & her politician husband, who have decided to use Shaw's fame to further their own unscrupulous ambitions. What follows is a spy story, a love story, & a sobering, yet outrageously funny satire on demagoguery in American politics. Two tender love stories provide an undercurrent theme - the powers of light against the powers of dark.

Manchurian Candidate. unabr. ed. Richard Condon. Read by Christopher Hurt. 8 CDs. (Running Time: 10 hrs.). 2001. audio compact disk 64.00 (978-0-7861-8394-4(2), 1707) Blckstn Audio.

Manchurian Candidate. unabr. ed. Richard Condon. Read by Christopher Hurt. 8 CDs. (Running Time: 10 hrs.). 2004. audio compact disk 32.95 (978-0-7861-8525-2(2)) Blckstn Audio.

Manchurian Candidate. unabr. ed. Richard Condon. Read by Robert Vaughn. 2 cass. 34.95 Incl. transcript bk. & learner's guide. (S23910) J Norton Pubs.

Manchurian Candidate. unabr. collector's ed. Richard Condon. Read by Daniel Grace. 7 cass. (Running Time: 10 hrs. 30 min.). 1976. 56.00 (978-0-7366-0036-1(1), 1048) Books on Tape.
The fictional account of a far-from-ordinary G.I. who is brainwashed while held as a Korean P.O.W. He returns to the United States as a programmed, remote-controlled killer.

Manchurian Candidate. unabr. movie tie-in ed. Richard Condon. Read by Christopher Hurt. 7 cass. (Running Time: 10 hrs.). 2004. 29.95 (978-0-7861-2791-7(0)) Blckstn Audio.

***Manchurian President: Barack Obama's Ties to Communists, Socialists & Other Anti-American Extremists.** unabr. ed. Aaron Klein. Read by Sara Runnette. (Running Time: 10 hrs. 30 mins.). 2010. 29.95 (978-1-4417-6857-5(2)); 85.95 (978-1-4417-6854-4(8)); audio compact disk 32.95 (978-1-4417-6856-8(4)); audio compact disk 118.00 (978-1-4417-6855-1(6)) Blckstn Audio.

Mandala. Osel Tendzin. 4 cass. 1977. 45.00 Vajradhatu.
Includes: Nondual Confusion; Birth of the Samsaric Mandala; Using Samsara to Look at Itself; Dharmata.

Mandala. unabr. ed. Jose Arguelles & Miriam Arguelles. 1 cass. (Running Time: 1 hr. 30 min.). 1970. 11.00 (12901) Big Sur Tapes.

Mandala: Luminous Symbols for Healing. Judith Cornell. Read by Judith Cornell. 2 cass. (Running Time: 1 hr. 20 min.). 1994. 7.95 (978-0-8356-2101-4(4), 2101, Quest) Pub: Theos Pub Hse. Dist(s): Natl Bk Netwk

Mandala of the Enlightened Feminine: Awaken the Wisdom of the Five Dakinis. Tsultrim Allione. 2003. audio compact disk 59.95 (978-1-59179-062-4(X)) Sounds True.

Mandala of the Five Buddhas. Vajracarya. 6 cass. 1974. 56.50 (A020) Vajradhatu.
Six talks: 1)Nondualistic Ground from which Mandala Arises; 2) Birth of the Path; 3) Basic Intelligence; 4) Five Buddha Principles; 6) Awareness & Appreciation.

Mandala Principle. Read by Osel Tendzin. 4 cass. 1977. 45.00 (A064) Vajradhatu.
Four talks: 1) Nondual Confusion; 2) Birth of the Samsaric Mandala; 3) Using Samsara to Look at Itself; 4) Dharmata.

Mandala Principle & the Three Yanas. Vajracarya. Read by Chogyam Trungpa. 4 cass. 1976. 36.00 (A027) Vajradhatu.
Four talks: 1) The Charnel Ground; 2) Discrimination; 3) Working with Others; 4) The Vajra Castle.

Mandarin see Mandarin

Mandarin. Eca De Queiroz. Read by Carlos J. Vega. (Running Time: 3 hrs.). 2001. 16.95 (978-1-60083-175-1(3), Audiofy Corp) Iofy Corp.

Mandarin. Wei Jin et al. Contrib. by Rosi McNab. (Running Time: 3 hrs. 0 mins. 0 sec.). (Collins Easy Learning Audio Course Ser.). (ENG.). 2009. audio compact disk 13.95 (978-0-00-727176-4(X)) Pub: HarpC GBR. Dist(s): IPG Chicago

Mandarin. unabr. ed. Eça De Queiroz. Read by Carlos J. Vega. 3 CDs.Tr. of Mandarin. (SPA.). 2001. audio compact disk 17.00 (978-958-9494-36-3(6)) YoYoMusic.

Mandarin Chinese. Ed. by Berlitz Publishing Staff. (Berlitz iPhrase Ser.). (ENG.). 2008. audio compact disk 12.95 (978-981-268-489-9(1)) Pub: APA Pubns Serv SGP. Dist(s): IngramPubServ

Mandarin Chinese. Ed. by Berlitz Publishing Staff. 6 CDs. (Basic Ser.). (CHI & ENG., 2009. audio compact disk 29.95 (978-981-268-508-7(1)) Pub: Berlitz Pubng. Dist(s): Langenscheidt

Mandarin Chinese. unabr. ed. Ed. by Charles Berlitz. 2 cass. (Running Time: 1 hr. 30 mins.). (Language/30 Brief Course Ser.). pap. bk. 21.95 (AF1021) J Norton Pubs.
Quick, highly condensed introduction to the words & phrases you'll need to communicate effectively in the country you're visiting. Cassettes & phrase guide book are in a vinyl album.

Mandarin Chinese. unabr. ed. Oasis Audio Staff & Linguistics Staff. Narrated by Oasis Audio Staff & Linguistics Staff. (Running Time: 4 hrs. 15 mins. 30 sec.). (Complete Idiot's Guide Ser.). (ENG.). 2005. audio compact disk 19.99 (978-1-59859-059-3(6)) Oasis Audio.

Mandarin Chinese, Set, study guide. Paul Pimsleur. 6 cass. (Pimsleur Language Learning Ser.). 1991. 345.00 Set, incl. study guide. (0671-57911-8) SyberVision.

Mandarin Chinese: Learn to Speak & Understand Mandarin Chinese with Pimsleur Language Programs. 2nd unabr. ed. Pimsleur Staff. 5 CDs. (Running Time: 50 hrs. 0 mins. 0 sec.). (Basic Ser.). (CHI & ENG.). 2005. audio compact disk 24.95 (978-0-7435-5075-8(7), Pimsleur) Pub: S&S Audio. Dist(s): S and S Inc

Mandarin Chinese: The Simplest, Most Effective Language Course Ever Developed! Pimsleur Staff. 8 cass. (Running Time: 800 hrs. 0 mins. NaN sec.). (Instant Conversation Ser.). (ENG.). 2002. 49.95 (978-0-7435-2912-9(X), Pimsleur) Pub: S&S Audio. Dist(s): S and S Inc
Speak Chinese Mandarin Instantly! The Pimsleur® Method provides the most effective language - learning program ever developed. More than one million people every year use it to gain real conversational skills in new languages quickly and easily - without books, written exercises, or drills. Easy and Practical This package contains sixteen lessons that will get you started speaking today! Simply listen, follow the instructions, and then respond out loud, just as you would in an actual conversation. Complete one lesson each day, in consecutive order. When you've finished this program, you'll be thrilled to realize you can hold a real conversation in Chinese Mandarin! Go beyond the 8-lesson Quick & Simple - and double your language skills Simple, step-by-step instruction No classes to attend - learn at your own convenience and pace No books, written exercises, or memory drills Listen-and-respond method lets you self-test your mastery Increase Your Language Skills Learning a new language is a tremendously rewarding achievement. Once you see how much you've learned in these sixteen lessons, we think you'll want to continue with the complete 30-lesson Pimsleur® Program. To help you, we'll give you a rebate of $150.00 when you purchase the Level I Chinese Mandarin Comprehensive Program. Please see bottom of package for details.

Mandarin Chinese Guaranteed: The All-Audio Beginner's Course. Qiuxia Shao et al. (Berlitz Guaranteed Ser.). (CHI & ENG., 2007. audio compact disk 19.95 (978-981-268-184-3(1)) Pub: APA Pubns Serv SGP. Dist(s): IngramPubServ

Mandarin Chinese in 30 Days: Course Book. 2nd rev. abr. ed. De-An Wu Swihart. Created by Berlitz Guides. (Berlitz in 30 Days Ser.). (CHI & ENG., 2007. audio compact disk 21.95 (978-981-268-224-6(4)) Pub: APA Pubns Serv SGP. Dist(s): Langenscheidt

Mandarin Chinese in 60 Minutes. Created by Berlitz. (Berlitz in 60 Minutes Ser.). (CHI & ENG., 2007. audio compact disk 9.95 (978-981-268-205-5(8)) Pub: APA Pubns Serv SGP. Dist(s): Langenscheidt

Mandarin Chinese Travel Pack. Created by Berlitz Guides. (Berlitz Phrase Book & Dictionary Ser.). (CHI & ENG., 2007. audio compact disk 14.95 (978-981-268-208-6(2)) Pub: APA Pubns Serv SGP. Dist(s): Langenscheidt

Mandarin Cypher. unabr. collector's ed. Adam Hall. Read by Grover Gardner. 8 cass. (Running Time: 8 hrs.). (Quiller Ser.). 1987. 48.00 (978-0-7366-1164-0(9), 2089) Books on Tape.
Fast-moving thriller set in Hong Kong, featuring secret agent Quiller.

Mandarin Pearl. R. Austin Freeman. Perf. by Walter Covell. 1 cass. (Running Time: 82 min.). Dramatization. 1986. 7.95 (S-61) Jimcin Record.
A thief steals a pearl that has a curse on it.

Mandarin's Jade & Other Stories. abr. ed. Raymond Chandler. Perf. by Elliott Gould. 4 cass. (Running Time: 6 hrs.). 2004. 25.00 (978-1-59007-061-1(5)) Pub: New Millenn Enter. Dist(s): PerseuPGW
Raymond Chandler created the hard-boiled private eyes that rule American crime fiction, and this collection traces the genesis of Chandler's style in such stories as "Mandarin's Jade," "The Man Who Liked Dogs" and "Try the Girl".

Mandarin's Pearl see Classic Detective Stories, Vol. III, A Collection

Mandarin's Pearl. R. Austin Freeman. 1 cass. 1989. 8.95 (S-61) Jimcin Record.
Murder follow a cursed jewel.

***Mandate 1 & 2, the (2 CDs)** (ENG.). 2006. audio compact disk 17.99 (978-92-822-6082-1(8)) Pub: Kingsway Pubns GBR. Dist(s): STL Dist NA

Mandates of the Pastoral Ministry. Rick Joyner. 1 cass. (Running Time: 90 mins.). (Ministry of The Pastor Ser.: Vol. 1). 2000. 5.00 (RJ08-001) Morning NC.
"The Mandates of the Pastoral Ministry" & "The Shepherd's Heart." This brief series gives a revolutionary understanding of this most misunderstood ministry.

Mandatum Novum. (J). 1996. 39.95 (978-1-886412-12-5(X)) Preserv Press.

Mande Music: Traditional & Modern Music of the Maninka & Mandinka of Western Africa. Eric S. Charry. (Chicago Studies in Ethnomusicology). 2000. audio compact disk 19.00 (978-0-226-10163-7(0)) Pub: U Ch Pr. Dist(s): Chicago Distribution Ctr

Mandela's Way: Fifteen Lessons on Life, Love, & Courage. unabr. ed. Richard Stengel. Read by Richard Stengel. (ENG.). 2010. audio compact disk 27.00 (978-0-7393-8333-9(7), Random AudioBks) Pub: Random Audio Pubg. Dist(s): Random

Mandelbaum Gate. unabr. ed. Muriel Spark. Read by Frederick Davidson. 9 cass. (Running Time: 13 hrs.). 1994. 62.95 (978-0-7861-0649-3(2), 1462) Blckstn Audio.
When a young English woman, a half-Jewish Catholic convert, insists upon crossing over from Israel into Jordan, she sets off a series of bizarre situations. A British foreign service officer becomes so concerned for her safety amid the Arabs that he rescues her from a nunnery in the middle of the night, & a variety of characters are brought into surprising play, among them, a blue-eyed Arab girl, her father - an old-world patriarch - & an English spinster headmistress. Out of the complexities of this scene, on both sides of the Mandelbaum Gate, while the Eichmann trial is being conducted & the ancient sites & shrines of the Holy Land are visited, Mrs. Spark has created a many-faceted novel: a seriousness of purpose underlies the comic element & a wealth of information enriches a superb story.

Mandeville Talent. unabr. collector's ed. George V. Higgins. Read by John MacDonald. 7 cass. (Running Time: 10 hrs. 30 min.). 1992. 56.00 (978-0-7366-2228-8(4), 3018) Books on Tape.
Joe Corey gets drawn into the 23-year-old murder of his wife's grandfather. It's up to Corey to reheat cold leads, & when he does, things turn hotter than anyone ever expected.

Mandiani Drum & Dance: Aural Examples. Mark Sunkett. 1 cass., 1 CED. (Performance in World Music Ser.). 1995. 12.95 (978-0-941677-76-6(X)); audio compact disk 15.95 CD. (978-0-941677-82-0(6)) White Cliffs Media.

Mandibular Problems in Head & Neck Surgery: Interdisciplinary Panel Discussion. Moderated by William Lawson. 2 cass. (Otorhinolaryngology Ser.: OT-4). 1986. 19.00 (8656) Am Coll Surgeons.

Mandie & the Cherokee Legend. unabr. ed. Lois Gladys Leppard. Narrated by Kate Forbes. 3 pieces. (Running Time: 3 hrs. 30 mins.). (Mandie Bks.: No. 2). (gr. 3 up). 2001. 32.00 (978-0-7887-4559-1(X), 96005E7) Recorded Bks.
Mandie Shaw is nervous about her trip to visit her Cherokee relatives. The journey is full of danger & she wonders if her dead father's kinspeople will even like her once she arrives. The trip to the Indian reservation is only the beginning of Mandie's adventures.

Mandie & the Cherokee Legend. unabr. ed. Lois Gladys Leppard. Narrated by Kate Forbes. 3 cass. (Running Time: 3 hrs. 30 mins.). (Mandie Bks.: No. 2). (J). (gr. 4-7). 2001. pap. bk. & stu. ed. 46.24 Recorded Bks.

Mandie & the Secret Tunnel. unabr. ed. Lois Gladys Leppard. Narrated by Kate Forbes. 3 pieces. (Running Time: 3 hrs. 30 mins.). (Mandie Bks.: No. 1). (gr. 3 up). 2000. 29.00 (978-0-7887-4238-5(8), 96006E7) Recorded Bks.
When 11-year-old Mandie Shaw's father dies, her life reaches a low point. Longing for a home where she will be truly loved, Mandie seeks out an uncle she has never met. After a perilous journey, she finds herself in the middle of luxury she can scarcely believe & a mystery that will take all her brains & courage to solve.

M&M Conference. Featuring Bill Winston. 11 cass. 2005. 55.00 (978-1-59544-110-2(7)); audio compact disk 40.00 (978-1-59544-100-3(X)) Pub: B Winston Min. Dist(s): Anchor Distributors

M&M Conference 2005. Featuring Bill Winston. 5 cass. 2005. 25.00 (978-1-59544-099-0(2)) Pub: B Winston Min. Dist(s): Anchor Distributors

Mando. unabr. ed. Gary McCarthy. Read by Maynard Villers. 6 cass. (Running Time: 6 hrs. 42 min.). 1995. 39.95 (978-1-55686-577-0(5)) Books in Motion.
Mando Killion's world was shattered by Santa Anna's brutal invasion of Texas, his family killed, his sister taken hostage, & now he must summon the courage to wage a personal war to save his sister.

Mandolin Chords. Contrib. by Joe Carr. (Running Time: 30 mins.). 2005. 9.95 (978-5-558-08949-3(0)) Mel Bay.

Mandolin for Beginners. Morton Manus. (ENG.). 2001. audio compact disk 10.00 (978-0-7390-1099-0(9)) Alfred Pub.

***Mandolin for Seniors Book/CD Set.** Joe Carr. 2010. lib. bdg. 14.99 (978-0-7866-8161-7(6)) Mel Bay.

Mandolin Gospel Tunes. Joe Carr. 2008. pap. bk. 14.95 (978-0-7866-7047-5(9)) Mel Bay.

Mandolin Hymns. Butch Baldassari. 2008. pap. bk. 19.95 (978-1-59773-254-3(0), 1597732540) Pub: Homespun Video. Dist(s): H Leonard

***Mandolin Picker's Guide to Bluegrass Improvisation Book/CD Set.** Jasper Rubner-Peterson. 2010. lib. bdg. 24.99 (978-0-7866-8237-9(X)) Mel Bay.

Mandolin Player's Guide to Jamming. Carl Yaffey. (ENG., 2004. bk. 14.95 (978-0-7866-5736-0(7), 20818BCD) Mel Bay.

Mandolin Technique Studies, Volume 2. Matt Raum. 2008. spiral bd. 14.95 (978-0-7866-7353-7(2)) Mel Bay.

Mandy. abr. ed. Julie Andrews. Perf. by Julie Andrews. 2 cass. (Running Time: 2 hrs.). 2004. 18.00 (978-1-59007-020-8(8)) Pub: New Millenn Enter. Dist(s): PerseuPGW

Mandy & Pandy Visit China. Chris Lin. Read by Jiao Jing et al. Tr. by Shih-Wen Wu. Illus. by Ingrid Villalta. (Mandy & Pandy Ser.). (CHI & ENG.). (J). (ps-3). 2008. bds. 12.95 (978-0-9800156-2-1(6)) Pub: Mandy Pandy. Dist(s): China Bks

Maneater. abr. ed. Gigi Levangie Grazer. Read by Uma Thurman. 2006. 17.95 (978-0-7435-6221-8(6)) Pub: S&S Audio. Dist(s): S and S Inc

Manet: Music of His Time. Hugh Griffith. 1 CD. (Running Time: 1 hr. 30 min.). (Art & Music Ser.). 2003. audio compact disk (Naxos AudioBooks) Naxos.

Manga. abr. ed. James Patterson. Read by Evan Rachel Wood. (Maximum Ride Ser.: No. 1). (ENG.). (J). (gr. 5-17). 2005. 9.98 (978-1-59483-162-1(9)) Pub: Hachet Audio. Dist(s): HachBkGrp

Manga. abr. ed. James Patterson. Read by Evan Rachel Wood. (Running Time: 5 hrs.). (Maximum Ride Ser.: No. 1). (ENG.). 2009. 34.98 (978-1-60788-037-0(7)) Pub: Hachet Audio. Dist(s): HachBkGrp

Manga. abr. ed. James Patterson. Read by Evan Rachel Wood. (Running Time: 5 hrs.). No. 1. (ENG.). 2008. audio compact disk 9.98 (978-1-60024-226-7(X)) Pub: Little Brn Bks. Dist(s): HachBkGrp

Manga. unabr. ed. James Patterson. 8 CDs. (Running Time: 9 hrs. 45 mins.). (Maximum Ride Ser.: No. 1). 2005. audio compact disk 69.75 (978-1-4193-3844-1(7), C3276); 62.75 (978-1-4193-3629-4(0), 98023) Recorded Bks.
Number one New York Times best-selling suspense author James Patterson pens an amazing fantasy novel for young adults. Fourteen-year-old Max and her winged friends are the outcome of a strange experiment splicing human and bird DNA. Now one of their flock has been kidnapped by genetically engineered wolfmen. So the flying friends launch a rescue mission to save her that will lead them on an actionpacked journey across America.

Manga Design. Masanao Amano. (ENG, FRE, GER & MUL., 2004. 39.99 (978-3-8228-2591-4(3)) Pub: Taschen DEU. Dist(s): IngramPubServ

Mangala (Mars) Dulal C. Koley. 1 cass. 8.95 (432) Am Fed Astrologers.

Manger - Ne Pas Manger. unabr. ed. Robert A. Monroe. Read by Roland Simon. 1 cass. (Running Time: 30 min.). (Human Plus Ser.). (FRE.). 1993. 14.95 (978-1-56102-063-8(X)) Inter Indus.
Control your appetite.

Mango Plum's Earth Adventure. Compiled by Encyclopaedia Britannica, Inc. (gr. 5-10). 2008. audio compact disk 19.95 Ency Brit Inc.

Mango Plum's Space Adventure. Compiled by Encyclopaedia Britannica, Inc. (gr. 5-10). 2008. audio compact disk 19.95 Ency Brit Inc.

Mango Plum's Weather Adventure. Compiled by Encyclopaedia Britannica, Inc. (gr. 5-10). 2008. audio compact disk 19.95 Ency Brit Inc.

Mango-Shaped Space. unabr. ed. Wendy Mass. Read by Danielle Ferland. 6 cass. (Running Time: 7 hrs.). (YA). (gr. 5-8). 2007. 51.75 (978-1-4281-4923-6(6)); audio compact disk 66.75 (978-1-4281-4928-1(7)) Recorded Bks.

***Mango Tango.** Perf. by R. A. Zuckerman. Composed by R. A. Zuckerman. (ENG.). 2010. 12.95 (978-1-891083-19-8(8)) ConcertHall.

Mangrove Coast. Randy Wayne White. Narrated by Ron McLarty. 8 cass. (Running Time: 11 hrs. 15 mins.). (Doc Ford Ser.: No. 6). 1998. 77.00 (978-1-4025-2408-0(0)) Recorded Bks.

Mangrove Squeeze. unabr. ed. Laurence Shames. Narrated by Richard Ferrone. 7 cass. (Running Time: 10 hrs.). 1998. 60.00 (978-0-7887-2037-6(6), 95401E7) Recorded Bks.
When Suki Sperakis decides to write an expose on the Key West black market, she is strangled & left for dead. Her only chance at survival rests on the senile Sam Katz & ex-mobster Bert the Shirt, who must infiltrate the russian Mafia posing as a gay couple from New York.

Mangrove Squeeze. unabr. collector's ed. Laurence Shames. Read by Rob McQuay. 7 cass. (Running Time: 10 hrs. 30 min.). 1998. 56.00 (978-0-7366-4261-3(7), 4760) Books on Tape.
Suki Sperakis came to town with one thing in mind & ended up doing something completely different.

***Manhattan Beach Project: A Novel.** unabr. ed. Peter Lefcourt. Read by Tom Weiner. (Running Time: 10 hrs. 0 mins.). 2010. 29.95 (978-1-4417-2421-2(4)); 59.95 (978-1-4417-2417-5(6)); audio compact disk 90.00 (978-1-4417-2418-2(4)) Blckstn Audio.

Manhattan Hunt Club. unabr. ed. John Saul. Read by David Daoust. 10 CDs Library ed. (Running Time: 11 hrs.). 2001. audio compact disk 107.25 (978-1-58788-590-7(5), 1587885905, CD Unabrid Lib Ed); 32.95 (978-1-58788-571-6(9), 1587885719, BAU); 78.25 (978-1-58788-572-3(7), 1587885727, Unabridge Lib Edns); audio compact disk 39.95 (978-1-58788-589-1(1), 1587885891, CD Unabridged) Brilliance Audio.
John Saul is at his terrifying best as he takes readers into the vast, dark labyrinth of tunnels beneath Manhattan, home to a bizarre collection of outcasts, and introduces a secret society that uses (and stocks) this underworld as a private hunting ground, with its residents as their prey. When twenty-one year old NYU student Jeff Converse is convicted of a brutal rape and murder that he did not commit, his nightmare has just begun. Jeff is just the latest innocent man to be made a target of the society that controls that underground hell - the Manhattan Hunt Club. A prestigious club near Wall Street, its membership includes many of the city's political and financial elite. Bored with more conventional sport, some of the MHC members can't resist secretly indulging their desire to hunt the most dangerous game in the world - humans.

Manhattan Hunt Club. unabr. ed. John Saul. Read by David Daoust. (Running Time: 11 hrs.). 2005. 39.25 (978-1-59600-739-0(7), 9781596007390, BADLE); 24.95 (978-1-59600-738-3(9), 9781596007383, BAD); 39.25 (978-1-59600-737-6(0), 9781596007376, Brlnc Audio MP3 Lib); 24.95 (978-1-59600-736-9(2), 9781596007369, Brilliance MP3) Brilliance Audio.

Manhattan Magic. Jean Davidson. Read by Judith Porter. 4 cass. (Running Time: 6 hrs.). 1999. 44.95 (64925) Pub: Soundings Ltd GBR. Dist(s): Ulverscroft US

Manhattan Magic. Jean Davidson. 4 cass. (Sound Ser.). 2004. 44.95 (978-1-85496-492-2(5)) Pub: UlverLrgPrint GBR. Dist(s): Ulverscroft US

Manhattan Real Estate Leadership Seminar: Leading New York City Real Estate Advisors on Best Practices & Successful Client Relationships. Ed. by ReedLogic Staff. 2006. pap. bk. 249.95 (978-1-59701-082-5(0)) Aspatore Bks.

Manhattan Transfer. unabr. collector's ed. John Dos Passos. Read by Michael Prichard. 10 cass. (Running Time: 15 hrs.). 1983. 80.00 (978-0-7366-0354-6(9), 1340) Books on Tape.
A tapestry of many fragments of the New York scene. Characters appear & disappear, like threads in a design & like any respectable composition the whole is much more than the sum of its parts.

Manhattan Transfer Meets Tubby the Tuba. Paul Tripp et al. (J). 1994. pap. bk. (978-0-9642066-0-1(9)) MK Prods.

Manhattans & Murder. unabr. ed. Jessica Fletcher & Donald Bain. Read by Beth Porter. 6 cass. (Running Time: 7 hrs. 30 mins.). (Murder, She Wrote Ser.). 2000. 29.95 (978-1-57270-148-9(X), N61148u) Pub: Audio Partners. Dist(s): PerseuPGW
Jessica Fletcher, well-loved from the TV series starring Angela Lansbury, is in Manhattan to promote her new book. While there, a sidewalk Santa, who is actually a notorious drug smuggler & former citizen of Cabot Cove, recognizes her & asks her to meet with him the next day. When she does, she witnesses his murder in broad daylight. Who would want to kill Santa at Christmas time? Jessica Fletcher & her pals, Doc Hazelett & Sheriff Metzger, piece the puzzle together.

Manhattans & Murder. unabr. ed. Jessica Fletcher & Donald Bain. Read by Beth Porter. 6 vols. (Running Time: 9 hrs.). (Murder, She Wrote Ser.). 2000. bk. 54.95 (978-0-7927-2278-6(7), CSL 167, Chivers Sound Lib) AudioGO.
Promoting her latest book brings Jessica Fletcher to New York for Christmas. Her schedule includes book signings, Larry King Live, restaurants.. and murder? It all begins with a sidewalk Santa staring at Jessica with fear and recognition. Behind the beard is Waldo Morse, a former drug smuggler in Cabot Cove, Maine. Jessica agrees to meet with him the next day. But in no time at all Santa is dead, and Jessica is on the trail of a murderer.

Manheim Steamroller Meets the Mouse. Prod. by Walter Elias Disney. 1 cass. (J). (ps-3). 1998. 22.50 (978-0-7634-0509-0(4)) W Disney Records.

***Manhood for Amateurs.** unabr. ed. Michael Chabon. Read by Michael Chabon. (ENG.). 2009. (978-0-06-196654-5(1), Harper Audio); (978-0-06-196716-0(5), Harper Audio) HarperCollins Pubs.

Manhood for Amateurs: The Pleasures & Regrets of a Husband, Father, & Son. unabr. ed. Michael Chabon. Read by Michael Chabon. 7 CDs. (Running Time: 8 hrs.). 2009. audio compact disk 34.99 (978-0-06-184237-5(0), Harper Audio) HarperCollins Pubs.

***Manhunt.** unabr. ed. Janet Evanovich. Read by C. J. Critt. (ENG.). 2005. (978-0-06-112408-2(7), Harper Audio); (978-0-06-112409-9(5), Harper Audio) HarperCollins Pubs.

Manhunt. unabr. ed. Janet Evanovich. Read by C. J. Critt. (Running Time: 16200 sec.). 2005. 14.95 (978-0-06-087631-9(X)); audio compact disk 14.95 (978-0-06-073700-9(X)) HarperCollins Pubs.

Manhunt: The 12-Day Chase for Lincoln's Killer. James L. Swanson. 2006. cd-rom 39.99 (978-1-59895-488-3(1)) Find a World.

Manhunt: The 12-Day Chase for Lincoln's Killer. abr. ed. James L. Swanson. Read by Richard Thomas. 7 CDs. (Running Time: 32400 sec.). 2006. audio compact disk 34.95 (978-0-06-073835-8(9)) HarperCollins Pubs.

***Manhunt: The 12-Day Chase for Lincoln's Killer.** abr. ed. James L. Swanson. Read by Richard Thomas. 2006. (978-0-06-113468-5(6), Harper Audio); (978-0-06-113467-8(8), Harper Audio) HarperCollins Pubs.

Manhunter. unabr. ed. Matt Braun. Read by Gene Engene. 6 cass. (Running Time: 7 hrs. 36 min.). (Luke Starbuck Ser.: Bk. 3). 2001. 39.95 (978-1-58116-063-5(1)) Books in Motion.
Luke's paymasters want the bankrobbing habits of the James Gang to end. So Luke picks up the trail into Indian Territory, without knowing that there are others on the hunt for Frank and Jesse James.

Manhunting. unabr. ed. Jennifer Crusie, pseud. Read by Renée Raudman. (Running Time: 7 hrs.). 2007. 39.25 (978-1-4233-0502-6(7), 9781423305026, BADLE); 24.95 (978-1-4233-0501-9(9), 9781423305019, BAD); 69.25 (978-1-4233-0496-8(9), 9781423304968, BrilAudUnabridg); audio compact disk 82.25 (978-1-4233-0498-2(5), 9781423304982, BriAudCD Unabrid); audio compact disk 39.25 (978-1-4233-0500-2(0), 9781423305002, Brlnc Audio MP3 Lib); audio compact disk 29.95 (978-1-4233-0497-5(7), 9781423304975, Bril Audio CD Unabri); audio compact disk 24.95 (978-1-4233-0499-9(3), 9781423304999, Brilliance MP3) Brilliance Audio.

Maniac Commodity Trader's Guide to Making a Fortune: A Not-So Crazy Roadmap to Riches. rev. unabr. ed. Kevin Kerr. Read by Erik Synnestvedt. (Running Time: 7 hrs.). (ENG.). 2007. audio compact disk 29.98 (978-1-59659-129-5(3), GildAudio) Pub: Gildan Media. Dist(s): HachBkGrp

Maniac Magee. unabr. ed. Jerry Spinelli. Read by S. Epatha Merkerson. 3 vols. (Running Time: 3 hrs. 45 mins.). (J). (gr. 4-7). 2004. pap. bk. 36.00 (978-0-8072-0667-6(9), Listening Lib); audio compact disk 32.30 (978-0-8072-1166-3(4), S YA 331 CD, Listening Lib); 30.00 (978-0-8072-0596-9(6), Listening Lib) Random Audio Pubg.
He wasn't born with the name Maniac Magee. He came into this world named Jeffrey Lionel Magee, but when his parents died and his life changed, so did his name. And Maniac Magee became a legend. Even today kids talk about how fast he could run; about how he hit an inside-the-park "frog" homer; how no knot, no matter how snarled, would stay that way once he began to untie it. But the thing Maniac Magee is best known for is what he did for the kids from the East Side and those from the West Side.

Maniac Magee. unabr. ed. Jerry Spinelli. Read by S. Epatha Merkerson. 4 CDs. (Running Time: 4 hrs. 23 mins.). (ENG.). (J). (gr. 7). 2005. audio compact disk 19.95 (978-0-307-24318-8(4), Listening Lib) Pub: Random Audio Pubg. Dist(s): Random

Manic Depression. Prod. by Michelle Trudeau. 1 cass. (Running Time: 30 min.). 9.95 (I0290B090, HarperThor) HarpC GBR.

Manic Depression: Program from the Award Winning Public Radio Series. Hosted by Fred Goodwin. Comment by John Hockenberry. Contrib. by Jack Raglin et al. 1 cass. (Running Time: 1 hr.). (Infinite Mind Ser.). 1998. audio compact disk 21.95 (978-1-888064-30-8(7), LCM 32) Lichtenstein Creat.
With an untreated suicide rate of 20 to 25 percent, manic-depressive illness (also called bipolar disorder) ranks among the most fatal diseases in medicine.Why is it such a killer? For one thing, it's a long way down for a person falling from the HEIGHTs of mania to the depths of depression.We'll talk to top experts about this, and about new research that could narrow the gap between "average" and "optimal" treatments. Plus, a whole range of brand-new diagnoses that may leave you wondering whether everybody isn't a little bit bipolar.Host Dr. Fred Goodwin is joined by Donna, 26, who has been living with manic-depressive illness for 10 years; Dr. Joseph Hibbeln, a psychiatrist, lipid biologist and chief of the outpatient clinic at the National Institute on Alcohol and Alcohol Abuse, part of the National Institutes of Health, who studied epidemiological data about the rates of diseases and average diets in different parts of the world, and learned of an astonishing link between Omega 3 fatty acids in our diet, and mood disorders like manic depression and depression; Congresswoman Lynn Rivers, from Ann Arbor, who has represented Michigan's 13th District since 1994, and has grappled with bipolar disorder for more than 20 years; and Dr. J. Raymond DePaulo, professor of psychiatry and director of the affective disorders clinic at Johns Hopkins School of Medicine in Baltimore.

Manic Depression: Voices of an Illness. Lichtenstein Creative Media, Inc. Staff. Narrated by Patty Duke. 1 cass. (Running Time: 1 hr.). 1992. 29.00 incl. script Lib. & inst. Lichtenstein Creat.
The first major documentary to feature those with manic depressive illness telling their own stories - in their own words. It features nine people with the illness - including a fortune 500 executive, a nurse, a therapist & Patty Duke herself - describing their efforts to stabilize the disorder's effect on their lives. Also features leading mental health experts & advocates. Winner of eight broadcasting & mental health awards. Includes transcript & educational material written in conjunction with the National Institute of Mental Health.

Manic Depression: Voices of an Illness. P.e.r. 1942. 95.00 (978-0-8002-4384-5(6)) Taylor and Fran.

Manichini. Tiziana Merani. pap. bk. 21.95 (978-88-7754-813-9(4)) Pub: Cideb ITA. Dist(s): Distribks Inc

Manics X-Posed: An Interview with the Angriest Rock Group Around Today. Chrome Dreams. (ENG., 2002. audio compact disk 14.95 (978-1-84240-148-4(3)) Pub: Chrome Dreams GBR. Dist(s): IPG Chicago

***Manifest: A Meditation CD.** David Elliott. (ENG.). 2005. 15.00 (978-0-9753910-2-0(X)) Hawk Pr CA.

Manifest a Loving Relationship: Create & Establish a Loving Relationship in Your Life. Mark Bancroft. Read by Mark Bancroft. 1 CD, 1 bklet. (Running Time: 1 hr.). (Relationships/Family/Parenting Ser.). 2006. audio compact disk 20.00 (978-1-58522-049-6(3)) EnSpire Pr.
Two complete sessions plus printed instructionmanual/guidebook. With healing music soundtrack.

Manifest a Loving Relationship: Create & Experience a Loving Relationship in Your Life. Mark Bancroft. Read by Mark Bancroft. 1 cass., bklet. (Running Time: 1 hr.). (Relationships/Family/Parenting Ser.). 1999. 12.95 (978-1-58522-033-5(7), 602) EnSpire Pr.

Manifest a Miracle in Life. Dick Sutphen. 1 cass. (Running Time: 1 hr.). (RX17 Ser.). 14.98 (978-0-87554-397-0(9), RX161) Valley Sun.

Manifest & Magnetize (the Ultimate Healer Subliminal Series, 4 Of 6) Draw to yourself prosperity, health, love, & More. Kyrah Malan. 1 CD. (Running Time: 27 mins). 2006. audio compact disk 39.95 (978-0-9787324-4-8(8), SPS4) K Malan.
The ultimate in subliminal affirmations. Music, messages and binaural beats are specifically designed to work together to help you discover - and create - what you really want in life. Release unconscious limitations and allow yourself to have more.What you hear is beautiful music that has been proven in university studies or harmonize and organize your energy field, putting you in a calm, receptive state quickly and easily.What your subconscious hears are specially designed affirmations and suggestions, designed to rewrite subconscious beliefs and change behavior faster and more effectively than any subliminal program available today.The Foundation set is designed to be used in order, each CD building on the effects of the previous CDs, and includes Love Your Life, Release & Relax, Energy & Power, Manifest & Magnetize, Live Your Life, and Spirit & Soul. Can be used independently. Unlike typical subliminal programs which recommend you listen to them for at least 30 days, Ultimate healer CDs help create positive results in only 17 days; some people report results in as little as 2 or 3 days!You can play them during everyday activities, while driving, reading, or at work, or listen to them with headphones. You have freedom and flexibility with The Ultimate Healer Subliminal Series.

Manifest Destiny: The Oregon Trail. Kenneth Bruce. 1 cass. (Running Time: 56 min.). Dramatization. (Excursions in History Ser.). 12.50 Alpha Tape.

***Manifest Your Destiny.** abr. ed. Wayne W. Dyer. Read by Wayne W. Dyer. (ENG.). 2005. (978-0-06-084571-1(6), Harper Audio); (978-0-06-084570-4(8), Harper Audio) HarperCollins Pubs.

Manifest Your Destiny: The Nine Spiritual Principles for Getting Everything You Want. abr. ed. Wayne W. Dyer. Read by Wayne W. Dyer. 2 cass. (Running Time: 3 hrs.). 1997. 18.00 (978-0-694-51778-7(X), CPN 2620) HarperCollins Pubs.

Manifest Your Destiny: The Nine Spiritual Principles for Getting Everything You Want. abr. ed. Wayne W. Dyer. Read by Wayne W. Dyer. 2 CDs. (Running Time: 3 hrs.). 2001. 22.00 (978-0-694-52547-8(2)) HarperCollins Pubs.

Manifestatacion de los Hijos de Dios. Paty Camu. (SPA.). 2004. 25.00 (978-0-89985-430-4(3)) Christ for the Nations.

Manifestation Course: Advanced Techniques for Creating Abundance in Love & Money, Set. Gay Hendricks. Read by Gay Hendricks. 2 cass. (Running Time: 1 hr. 30 mins.). 1999. 16.95 (978-1-891323-02-7(4)) Hendricks Inst.
This rich program of clear explanations & experiential exercises, Hendricks reveals how we create our lives unconsciously - by default conditioning.

Manifestation of Love. Swami Amar Jyoti. 1 cass. 1987. 9.95 (K-93) Truth Consciousness.
The continuity of infinity & the multiplicity of forms. Forgetting that, we suffer. We are blocking our own way. The uniting of Kundalini with the Lord.

Manifestation of Love. Elbert Willis. 1 cass. (Faithfulness Through Love Ser.). 4.00 Fill the Gap.

Manifestation Process. unabr. ed. Stan Kendz. Read by Stan Kendz. 1 cass. (Running Time: 50 min.). 1994. 10.00 (978-1-57582-005-7(6)) HAPPE Progs.
Learn how to manifest your heart's desires.

Manifested Victory. Kenneth Copeland. Perf. by Kenneth Copeland. 1 cass. (Take Hold of Your Victory! Ser.: Tape 3). 1995. cass. & video 5.00 (978-1-57562-002-2(2)) K Copeland Pubns.
Biblical teaching on victory.

Manifesting. unabr. ed. Galexis. 2 cass. (Running Time: 3 hrs.). 1997. 19.95 Set. (978-1-56089-051-5(7), G132) Visionary FL.
Practical living of spiritual principles through releasing the victim/martyr self & dreaming up the new successful self. Meditation included.

Manifesting Abundance: Talks on Spirituality & Modern Life. Marianne Williamson. 4 CDs. 2004. audio compact disk 23.95 (978-1-4019-0395-4(9)) Hay House.

***Manifesting Change: It Couldn't Be Easier.** unabr. ed. Mike Dooley. Read by Mike Dooley. (Running Time: 6 hrs. 30 mins. 0 sec.). (ENG.). 2010. audio compact disk 29.99 (978-1-4423-3643-8(9)) Pub: S&S Audio. Dist(s): S and S Inc

Manifesting Enlightenment. Chogyam Trungpa. 1 cass. 1983. 10.00 Vajradhatu.
A workshop at the 1983 Conference on Christian & Buddhist Meditation.

Manifesting Miracles: Crucifixion & Resurrection. Marianne Williamson. Read by Marianne Williamson. 1 cass. (Running Time: 90 mins.). (Lectures on a Course in Miracles). 1999. 10.00 (978-1-56170-246-6(3), M749) Hay House.

Manifesting Money Abundance. Christopher Love. Read by Christopher Love. 1 cass. (Running Time: 30 min.). 1997. 10.95 (978-1-891820-10-6(9)) World Sangha Pubg.
Self-hypnosis meditation for healing, self-improvement & realizing our full & powerful potential as spiritual beings.

Manifesting the Life of Your Dreams. abr. ed. Robert A. Robinson. Read by Robert Anthony Robinson. Narrated by J. P. Daiu. 1 cass. (Running Time: 20 min.). (Magic Magnifying Mind Ser.). 1991. pap. bk. 8.95 (978-1-884780-02-8(4)) Phoenix Pubng.
Personal achievement, motivational & self help related sound recording.

Manifesting Victorious Dharma. Vajracarya. 2 cass. 1982. 22.50 Vajradhatu.
Topics include: The Conviction to Tame One's Mind; Dharma As Freedom from Neurosis; Meditation As Clarity; The Teacher.

Manifesting What You Want. Rhegina Sinozich. 2008. audio compact disk 14.95 (978-0-9706297-2-2(9)) Abrezia Pr.

Manifesting with the Angels: Allowing Heaven to Help You While You Fulfill Your Life's Purpose. Doreen Virtue. 1 cass. (Running Time: 1 hr.). 1999. 10.95 (978-1-56170-643-3(4), 484) Hay House.
A lecture invoking the angels to help with life.

Manifesting with the Angels: Allowing Heaven to Help You While You Fulfill Your Life's Purpose. Doreen Virtue. 1 CD. 2003. audio compact disk 10.95 (978-1-4019-0143-1(3), 1433) Hay House.

Manifesting Your Desires: Guided Excercises, Processes & Meditation. abr. ed. Victoria Loveland-Coen. Read by Victoria Loveland-Coen. Perf. by Joe Romano. 1 cass. (Running Time: 60 min.). 1997. 9.95 (978-0-9644765-1-6(7), 1002) Love Blessings.

Manifesting Your Inner Sanctuary with Archangel Raphael. Elisabeth Constantine. (Running Time: 53 mins.). (Light Meditations Series I Ser.). (ENG.). 2004. audio compact disk 17.99 (978-1-84409-039-6(6)) Pub: Findhorn Pr GBR. Dist(s): IPG Chicago

Manifesting Your Life Purpose. 1996. 12.50 (978-1-893027-27-5(9)) Path of Light.

Manifesting Your Vision. Eldon Taylor. 1 CD. (Running Time: 52 min.). (Whole Brain Innertalk Ser.). 1998. audio compact disk (978-1-55978-875-5(5)) Progress Aware Res.

Manifesto of Capitalism, 9th Edition: An Analysis & Summary of Adam Smith's the Wealth of Nations. 9th ed. Light Brigade Publishing House. (ENG.). 2008. pap. bk. 10.00 (978-0-9625163-6-8(8)) Light Brigade Pub Hse.

Manifesto of our King: The Sermon on the Mount. Chuck Missler. 2 CD's. (Running Time: 2 hrs.). (Briefing Packages by Chuck Missler). 2006. audio compact disk 19.95 (978-1-57821-342-9(8)) Koinonia Hse.
The Sermon on the Mount is the manifesto of our King and the platform of the Prince of Peace. And it's the Law! It goes vastly beyond the Law of Moses. It is the Ten Commandments amplified and expanded. It raises the law to the nth degree.As the Law of the Kingdom, it is the highest ethical teaching in the Bible. It will be the law of this world during the Millennium, and then it will find full fruition. Christ will reign on earth in person and will enforce every word of it. The Sermon on the Mount will finally prevail when He whose right it is to rule shall come.

Manipulateurs. Perf. by Isabelle Nazare-Aga. 2 CDs. (Running Time: 2 hrs. 30 mins.). 2003. audio compact disk 18.95 (978-2-89558-060-7(X)) Pub: Coffragants CAN. Dist(s): Penton Overseas

Manipulative Behavior Can Be OK. Arynne Simon. 1 cass. 1995. 14.95 (978-1-882389-15-5(8)) Wilarvi Communs.
An in-depth look at some specialized techniques of living life like a pro. Other topics: How to stay in control of your own life; Putting your feelings into perspective.

Manitou. Donald Clayton Porter. Read by Lloyd James. 4 vols. 2004. 25.00 (978-1-58807-232-0(0)) Am Pubng Inc.

Manitou. Donald Clayton Porter. Read by Lloyd James. 4 vols. No. 16. 2004. (978-1-58807-763-9(2)); audio compact disk 30.00 (978-1-58807-416-4(1)); audio compact disk (978-1-58807-880-3(9)) Am Pubng Inc.

Mankiewicz Brothers. unabr. ed. Read by Heywood Hale Broun et al. 1 cass. (Heywood Hale Broun Ser.). 12.95 (40352) J Norton Pubs.
Talks with Richard Merryman ("The Wit, World & Life of Herman Mankiewicz) & Kenneth R. Geist ("Pictures Will Talk: The Life & Films of Joseph L. Mankiewicz).

Mankiller. unabr. ed. Collin Wilcox. Read by Larry McKeever. 8 cass. (Running Time: 8 hrs.). (Frank Hastings Ser.). 1997. 48.00 (978-0-7366-3788-6(5), 4462) Books on Tape.
The night Rebecca Carlton was murdered,the world of rock'n'roll stood still. Lt. Frank Hastings has a job to do.

Mankiller: A Chief & Her People. abr. ed. Wilma P. Mankiller & Michael Wallis. Read by Joy Harjo. 2 cass. (Running Time: 3 hrs.). 1995. 16.95 (978-0-944993-89-7(3)) Audio Lit.
The principle chief of the Cherokee Nation tells the story of her life & the history of her people.

Manner of Death. Stephen White. Read by Michael Kramer. (Dr. Alan Gregory Ser.). 1999. audio compact disk 88.00 (978-0-7366-5158-5(6)) Books on Tape.

Manner of Death. unabr. ed. Stephen White. Read by Michael Kramer. 9 cass. (Running Time: 13 hrs. 30 min.). (Dr. Alan Gregory Ser.). 1999. 72.00 (978-0-7366-4403-7(2), 4864) Books on Tape.
Attending the funeral of a former colleague, psychologist Alan Gregory learns from two FBI agents that this is the latest in a string of clueless murders targeting the entire group of students, supervisors & staff who shared Alan's clinical psychology residency some years earlier. Only Alan & his former lover, Dr. Sawyer Sackett, now survive & they are undoubtedly next on the killer's hit list. Reuniting with Sawyer to investigate the string of murders, Alan finds not only his life, but his marriage endangered.

Manner of Death. unabr. collector's ed. Stephen White. Read by Michael Kramer. 11 CDs. (Running Time: 16 hrs. 30 mins.). (Dr. Alan Gregory Ser.). 2001. audio compact disk 88.00 Books on Tape.

Manners Can Be Fun. Perf. by Linda Sparks and The Oops Group Kids. (Oops Your Manners are Showing). (J). (gr. k-2). 4.95 (978-0-9660287-3-7(2)) Oops Grp.

Manners Minutes. 4 cass. 1999. 39.95 (978-0-9644556-4-1(1)) ETICON.

Mannings: Football's Famous Family. (High Five Reading - Blue Ser.). (ENG.). (gr. 1-2). 2007. audio compact disk 5.95 (978-1-4296-1410-8(2)) CapstoneDig.

Mannings: Football's Famous Family. Joe Worthington. (High Five Reading Ser.). (ENG., (gr. 4-5). 2005. audio compact disk 5.95 (978-0-7368-5751-2(6)) CapstoneDig.

Manny. unabr. ed. Holly Peterson. Read by Karen Ziemba. (Running Time: 41400 sec.). 2007. audio compact disk 39.95 (978-0-06-137612-2(4), Harper Audio) HarperCollins Pubs.

***Manny.** unabr. ed. Holly Peterson. Read by Karen Ziemba. (ENG.). 2007. (978-0-06-147337-1(5), Harper Audio); (978-0-06-147336-4(7), Harper Audio) HarperCollins Pubs.

Manny & the Holy Spirit. Randy Calhoun. Perf. by Jon Von Seggen. 1 cass. (Running Time: 28 min.). Dramatization. 1996. 15.00 incl. script. (978-1-58302-046-3(2), STP-19) One Way St.
Nine two to four minute puppet performance monologues featuring a young boy named Emmanuel.

Manny & the Holy Spirit. Randy Calhoun. Voice by Jon VonSeggen. Prod. by Dale Liz VonSeggen. 2001. audio compact disk 15.00 (978-1-58302-187-3(6)) One Way St.

Manny Files. unabr. ed. Christian Burch. Read by Daryl Anderson. 5 CDs. (Running Time: 6 hrs. 9 mins.). (J). 2006. audio compact disk 45.00 (978-0-7393-3623-6(1), Listening Lib); 35.00 (978-0-7393-3626-7(6), Listening Lib) Pub: Random Audio Pubg. Dist(s): Random
Manny: A male nanny or babysitter, known to be handsome, fabulous, and a lover of eighties music. "Be interesting." That's what the manny tells Keats Dalinger the first time he packs Keats' school lunch, but for Keats that's not always the easiest thing to do. Even though he's the only boy at home, it always feels like no one ever remembers him. His sisters are everywhere! Lulu is the smart one, India is the creative one, and Belly... well, Belly is the naked one. And the baby. School isn't much better. There, he's the shortest kid in the entire class. But now the manny is the Dalinger's new babysitter, and things are starting to look up. It seems as though the manny always knows the right thing to do. Not everyone likes the manny as much as Keats does, however. Lulu finds the manny embarrassing, and she's started to make a list of all the crazy things that he does, such as serenading the kids with "La Cucaracha" from the front yard or wearing underwear on his head or meeting the school bus with Belly, dressed as limo drivers. Keats is worried. What if Lulu's "Manny Files" makes his parents fire the manny? Who will teach him how to be interesting then?.

Manny y El Espiritu Santo. Randy Calhoun. Perf. by Todd Smith. Tr. by Veronica V. Smith. 1 cass. (Running Time: 33 min.). Dramatization. (SPA.). 1997. 15.00 incl. script. (978-1-58302-047-0(0), STP-19) One Way St.
Nine two to four minute puppet performance monologues featuring a young boy named Emmanuel.

Manny y el Espiritu Santo. Randy Calhoun. Tr. by Veronica Villafana Smith. Voice by Todd Smith. (SPA.). 2001. audio compact disk 15.00 (978-1-58302-186-6(8)) One Way St.

Mano a Mano. abr. ed. Matthew S. Hart. Read by Charlton Griffin. Abr. by Odin Westgaard. 2 vols. No. 5. 2003. 18.00 (978-1-58807-247-4(9)); (978-1-58807-742-4(X)) Am Pubng Inc.

Mano Grande. unabr. ed. Will McCann. Read by Rusty Nelson. 4 cass. (Running Time: 5 hrs. 24 min.). 2001. 26.95 (978-1-55686-757-6(3)) Books in Motion.
Tired of seeking revenge for his former partner's hand in placing him in prison for four years, circumstances bring Frank McGonagle back to Texas, and to old partner Diego Rivas.

***Manolo Franco: Aljibe.** Manolo Franco. Contrib. by Claude Worms. (Flamenco: Concierto Ser.). (ENG, FRE & SPA., 2009. audio compact disk 49.99 (978-84-936260-2-0(3)) AcordesCon ESP.

Manon. Prevost. Read by Santiago Munévar. (Running Time: 3 hrs.). 2002. 16.95 (978-1-60083-241-3(5), Audiofy Corp) Iofy Corp.

Manon. abr. ed. Prevost. 3 CDs. (SPA.). 2002. audio compact disk 17.00 (978-958-8161-32-7(0)) YoYoMusic.

Manon Lescaut. unabr. collector's ed. Abbe Prevost. Read by Walter Covell. 7 cass. (Running Time: 7 hrs.). 1983. 42.00 (978-0-7366-3971-2(3), 9516) Books on Tape.
The young Chevalier des Grieux, a student of philosophy at Amiens, meets Manon as she is entering a convent. He frees her & they flee to Paris where they live extravagantly, he as a card cheat, she as a mistress to an old & wealthy nobleman. They run away with the money & jewels, are apprehended by the police, imprisoned & exiled to the penal colony in Louisiana.

Manor. unabr. ed. Isaac Bashevis Singer. Read by Noah Waterman. 9 cass. (Running Time: 13 hrs.). 1995. 62.95 (978-0-7861-0704-9(9), 1581) Blckstn Audio.
Among those Poles who fought in the unsuccessful insurrection against Russia in 1863 was Count Wladislaw Jampolski. Because of his treason, he suffered imprisonment & confiscation of his lands. But Jampolski's disgrace turned out to be Calman Jacoby's good fortune. Calman, a pious Jew who made his living as a grain merchant, was given the opportunity to lease the manor lands of the Count.

Manor House. unabr. ed. Paige Rense. Read by Grace Conlin. 5 cass. (Running Time: 7 hrs.). 1997. 39.95 (978-0-7861-1155-8(0), 1925) Blckstn Audio.
This seemed like just another wild exaggeration from the myriad designers & decorators for whom the ultimate accolade is to be featured in the pages of the world's most exclusive, most sumptuous, most discriminating design magazine-until late one night in Hollywood when a dark figure put a bullet through the head of Beau Paxton, Manor House's flamboyant editor in chief.

Manpower, Pt. 1. 1 cass. 1997. 20.00 (978-1-57855-004-3(1)) T D Jakes.

Manpower, Pt. 2. 1 cass. 1997. 20.00 (978-1-57855-005-0(X)) T D Jakes.

Manpower, Pt. 3. 1 cass. 1997. 20.00 (978-1-57855-011-1(4)) T D Jakes.

Manpower: Challenge to the Man. Gary V. Whetstone. 6 cass. (Running Time: 9 hrs.). (Family & Relationships Ser.). 1995. bk. 50.00 (978-1-58866-229-3(2), VA002A) Gary Whet Pub.
This series will give you the wisdom to know what a man is to be in Christ. Find out how to overcome frustrations in finances, how to prevail in mental warfare.

Manpower Pt. 4: Reach behind Bar. Contrib. by T. D. Jakes Ministries Staff. 1 cass. 1997. 20.00 (978-1-57855-173-6(0)) T D Jakes.

Manpower Pt. 6, set: Armed & Dangerous. T. D. Jakes. 6 cass. 1999. 30.00 (978-1-57855-408-9(X)) T D Jakes.

Manpower 2000 Maximized Cass. 2004. 30.00 (978-1-57855-532-1(9)) T D Jakes.

Man's a Man: Bertolt Brecht. unabr. ed. New Repertory Theater Company. 10.95 (978-0-8045-0870-4(4), SAC 870) Spoken Arts.

Man's Approach to God: Four Talks on Male Spirituality. Richard Rohr. 4 cass. (Running Time: 6 hrs.). 2001. 29.95 (A2800) St Anthony Mess Pr.
Talks include: The Hero's Journey; Creators of Life; The Boy and the Old Man; The Grand Father.

Man's Field Guide to Dating. Robert A. Wray. 2 cass. (Running Time: 3 hrs.). 1999. bk. 17.95 Set. (978-0-9669723-1-3(7)) net Image.

Man's Greatest Problem: Logos May 17,1998. Ben Young. 1998. 4.95 (978-0-7417-6082-1(7), B0082) Win Walk.

Man's Head. unabr. ed. Georges Simenon. 3 vols. (Running Time: 3 hrs.). Dramatization. 2003. audio compact disk 39.95 (978-0-563-49664-9(9)) BBC Worldwide.
New adaptations of classic stories.

***Man's Heart.** Lori Copeland. (Running Time: 8 hrs. 7 mins. 13 sec.). (ENG.). 2010. 12.99 (978-0-310-77333-7(4)) Zondervan.

Man's Identity in a Mass Society. unabr. ed. Bruno Bettelheim. 1 cass. (Running Time: 48 min.). 12.95 (29124) J Norton Pubs.
Bettelheim responds to critics of our mass society who believe it is destroying man's dignity & individuality. He maintains the contrary is true & that our technology makes true self-realization & autonomy possible for the majority of the population for the first time in human history.

Man's Identity in a Mass Society CD. Bruno Bettelheim. 1 CD. (Running Time: 48 mins.). (Sound Seminars Ser.). 2006. audio compact disk 12.95 (978-1-57970-369-1(0), C29124D, Audio-For) J Norton Pubs.
Bettelheim responds to critics of our mass society who believe it is destroying our dignity and individuality. He maintains that the contrary is true, and that our new technology makes true human self-realization and autonomy for the majority of the population possible for the first time in human history.

Man's Journey to Simple Abundance. Sarah Ban Breathnach. Sarah Ban Breathnach. Read by Murphy Guyer. 2006. 17.95 (978-0-7435-6219-5(4)) Pub: S&S Audio. Dist(s): S and S Inc

Man's Mind. George King. 2006. audio compact disk (978-0-937249-34-5(3)) Aetherius Soc.

Man's Place. unabr. collector's ed. Annie Emaux. Read by Mary Peiffer. 6 cass. (Running Time: 6 hrs.). 1995. 36.00 (978-0-7366-3066-5(X)) Books on Tape.
Three semi-autobiographical works, tenderly dealing with tangled relationships.

Man's Prayer. Short Stories. Composed by Michael John Poirier. 1 cd. 1998. audio compact disk 17.00 (978-1-58459-192-4(7)) Wrld Lib Pubns.

***Man's Relentless Search.** L. Ron Hubbard. (ENG.). 2002. audio compact disk 15.00 (978-1-4031-1108-1(1)) Bridge Pubns Inc.

***Man's Relentless Search.** L. Ron Hubbard. (HEB.). 2010. audio compact disk 15.00 (978-1-4031-7617-2(5)); audio compact disk 15.00 (978-1-4031-7624-0(8)); audio compact disk 15.00 (978-1-4031-7613-4(2)); audio compact disk 15.00 (978-1-4031-7614-1(0)); audio compact disk 15.00 (978-1-4031-7623-3(X)); audio compact disk 15.00 (978-1-4031-7616-5(7)); audio compact disk 15.00 (978-1-4031-7622-6(1)); audio compact disk 15.00 (978-1-4031-7615-8(9)); audio compact disk 15.00 (978-1-4031-7612-7(4)); audio compact disk 15.00 (978-1-4031-7626-4(4)); audio compact disk 15.00 (978-1-4031-7619-6(1)); audio compact disk 15.00 (978-1-4031-7621-9(3)); audio compact disk 15.00 (978-1-4031-7627-1(2)); audio compact disk 15.00 (978-1-4031-7625-7(6)); audio compact disk 15.00 (978-1-4031-7618-9(3)); audio compact disk 15.00 (978-1-4031-7620-2(5)) Bridge Pubns Inc.

Man's Search for Meaning. unabr. ed. Viktor E. Frankl. Narrated by Simon Vance. 4 CDs. (Running Time: 6 hrs.). 2004. audio compact disk 25.95 (978-0-7861-9146-8(5), 750615) Blckstn Audio.

Man's Search for Meaning. unabr. ed. Viktor E. Frankl. Read by Simon Vance. 4 pieces. 2004. reel tape 25.95 (978-0-7861-2507-4(1)) Blckstn Audio.

Man's Search for Meaning: An Introduction to Logotherapy. unabr. ed. Viktor E. Frankl. Read by Simon Vance. 4 cass. (Running Time: 5 hrs. 30 mins.). 2003. 32.95 (978-0-7861-0867-1(3), 1665) Blckstn Audio.
The internationally renowned psychiatrist endured years of unspeakable horror in Nazi death camps. During & partly because of his suffering, Dr. Frankl developed a revolutionary approach to psychotherapy known as logotherapy. At the core of his theory is the belief that man's primary motivational force is his search for meaning.

Man's Search for Meaning: An Introduction to Logotherapy. unabr. ed. Viktor E. Frankl. Read by Simon Vance. 4 CDs. (Running Time: 5 hrs. 30 mins.). 2000. audio compact disk 32.00 (978-0-7861-9895-5(8), 1665) Blckstn Audio.

Man's Search for Meaning: An Introduction to Logotherapy. unabr. ed. Viktor E. Frankl. Read by Simon Vance. (Running Time: 18000 sec.). 2008. audio compact disk 17.95 (978-1-4332-1042-6(8)) Blckstn Audio.

Man's Search for Ultimate Meaning. rev. unabr. ed. Viktor E. Frankl & Viktor E. Frankl. Read by Grover Gardner. 6 CDs. (Running Time: 4 hrs. 30 mins.). (ENG.). 2008. audio compact disk 29.98 (978-1-59659-138-7(2)) Pub: Gildan Media. Dist(s): HachBkGrp

Man's Search for Ultimate Meaning. unabr. ed. Viktor E. Frankl. Read by Grover Gardner. (Running Time: 4 hrs. 30 mins.). (ENG.). 2008. 24.95 (978-1-59659-183-7(8), GildAudio) Pub: Gildan Media. Dist(s): HachBkGrp

Man's World, Woman's Place. unabr. collector's ed. Elizabeth Janeway. Read by Nancy Dannevik. 9 cass. (Running Time: 13 hrs. 30 min.). 1980. 72.00 (978-0-7366-0215-0(1), 1213) Books on Tape.
A study of the role of women in our modern society. She finds the isolation of women as household drudges barely three centuries old & confined largely to the middle class. She examines why society is so reluctant to abandon this notion & finds the answer lies in a number of well-established social & psychological patterns.

Mansfield Park. Jane Austen. 2007. audio compact disk 49.95 (978-1-57270-860-0(3)) Pub: AudioGO. Dist(s): Perseus Dist

Mansfield Park. Jane Austen. (Running Time: 15 hrs. 30 mins. 0 sec.). (Cover to Cover Ser.). (ENG.). 2010. audio compact disk 29.95 (978-1-60283-801-7(1)) Pub: AudioGO. Dist(s): Perseus Dist

Mansfield Park. Jane Austen. Read by Juliet Stevenson. (Running Time: 4 hrs.). 1999. 24.95 (978-1-60083-839-2(1)) Iofy Corp.

Mansfield Park. Jane Austen. Read by Juliet Stevenson. 3 CDs. (Running Time: 4 hrs.). (Works of Jane Austen). 1995. audio compact disk 22.98 (978-962-634-067-7(3), NA306712, Naxos AudioBooks) Naxos.
The story of two families living in rural prosperity at the beginning of the nineteenth century. Able to see beyond the selfishness and hypocrisy of both, Fanny embodies virtue and constancy in a world wracked by change and scandal.

Mansfield Park. Jane Austen. Read by Juliet Stevenson. 3 cass. (Running Time: 4 hrs.). (Works of Jane Austen). 2000. 17.98 (978-962-634-567-2(5), NA306714, Naxos AudioBooks) Naxos.

Mansfield Park. Jane Austen. Read by Juliet Stevenson. 14. (Running Time: 60625 sec.). (Complete Classics Ser.). 2007. audio compact disk 89.98 (978-962-634-467-5(9), Naxos AudioBooks) Naxos.

Mansfield Park. abr. ed. Jane Austen. Read by Anna Massey. Contrib. by Virginia Browne. 5 cass. 25.95 (SCN 076) J Norton Pubs.
The ordered calm of Mansfield Park is almost destroyed by the intrusion of the Crawfords, while the Bertroms find only misery in London. Fanny Price alone is clear-sighted enough to judge aright, proving herself to be the true heir of Mansfield Park.

Mansfield Park. unabr. ed. Jane Austen. Read by Maureen O'Brien. 12 cass. (Running Time: 16 hrs. 25 mins.). (gr. 9-12). 1999. 44.95 (978-1-57270-095-6(5), F91095u) Pub: Audio Partners. Dist(s): PerseuPGW

Mansfield Park. unabr. ed. Jane Austen. Read by Johanna Ward. 12 cass. (Running Time: 17 hrs. 30 mins.). 1994. 83.95 (978-0-7861-0675-2(1), 1463) Blckstn Audio.
The study of three families - the Bertrams, the Crawfords, & the Prices. The story's heroine, Fanny Price, is at its center. She is adopted into the family of her rich uncle Thomas Bertram, & is condescendingly treated as a poor relation by "Aunt Norris." Of her cousins, only Edmund, a young clergyman, appreciates her find qualities, & she falls in love with him. Unfortunately, however, he is drawn to the shallow & worldly Mary Crawford. Fanny's quiet passivity, steadfast loyalty, & natural goodness are matched against the wit & brilliance of her lovely rival. Jane Austen skillfully uses her characters' emotional relationships to explore the social & moral values by which they attempt or order their lives.

Mansfield Park. unabr. ed. Jane Austen. Read by Johanna Ward. (Running Time: 61200 sec.). 2008. audio compact disk & audio compact disk 49.95 (978-0-7861-6265-9(1)); audio compact disk & audio compact disk 120.00 (978-0-7861-6264-2(3)) Blckstn Audio.

Mansfield Park. unabr. ed. Jane Austen. Read by Juliet Stevenson. (YA). 2008. 109.99 (978-1-60514-900-4(4)) Find a World.

Mansfield Park, unabr. ed. Jane Austen. Narrated by Flo Gibson. 12 cass. (Running Time: 17 hrs.). 1984. 97.00 (978-1-55690-332-8(4), 84140E7) Recorded Bks.
Miss Fanny Price can offer little competition to the sparkling Mary Crawford in affairs of the heart. But true love must find a way.

Mansfield Park. unabr. ed. Jane Austen. Read by Wanda McCaddon. Narrated by Wanda McCaddon. (Running Time: 15 hrs. 0 mins. 0 sec.). (Tantor Unabridged Classics Ser.). (ENG.). 2008. audio compact disk 35.99 (978-1-4001-0691-2(5)); audio compact disk 27.99 (978-1-4001-5691-7(2)); audio compact disk 72.99 (978-1-4001-3691-9(1)) Pub: Tantor Media. Dist(s): IngramPubServ

Mansfield Park. unabr. collector's ed. Jane Austen. Read by Jill Masters. 9 cass. (Running Time: 13 hrs. 30 mins.). 1983. 72.00 (978-0-7366-3972-9(1), 9518) Books on Tape.
A comic epic, "Joseph Andrews" is a vivid picture of English life in the 18th century. Andrews is a footman to Lady Booby after Sir Thomas Booby's death. When Andrews rejects the widow Booby's advances, she discharges him. He sets out for London to see his sweetheart, Fanny. On the way he is robbed & beaten, but a charitable parson comes to his aid & travels with him. Their tribulations on the journey provide the theme of the story.

Mansfield Park. unabr. collector's ed. Jane Austen. Read by Jill Masters. 13 cass. (Running Time: 19 hrs. 30 mins.). 1983. 104.00 (978-0-7366-3983-5(7), 9530) Books on Tape.
During an era when upbringing was nearly everything, Fanny has the bad luck to be the poor relation in a wealthy family. Against a lovely & witty rival, she brings only natural goodness as a weapon in her battle for the man she loves.

Mansfield Park, Set. unabr. ed. Jane Austen. Read by Johanna Ward. 12 cass. 1999. bk. 83.95 (FS9-34249) Highsmith.

Mansfield Park, Vols. 1 & 2. Jane Austen. Read by Maureen O'Brien. Prod. by Helen Nicoll. 12 cass. (Running Time: 16 hrs. 25 min.). 69.95 C to C Cassettes.
It is a novel that harks back to a popular theme in 18th century literature - that of a central character whose place & role in society is neither defined nor assured.

Mansion in the Mist, unabr. ed. John Bellairs. Narrated by Betty Low. 4 pieces. (Running Time: 5 hrs. 15 mins.). (Anthony Monday Mystery Ser.: No. 4). (gr. 5 up). 1994. 35.00 (978-0-7887-0175-7(4), 94400E7) Recorded Bks.
Anthony Monday discovers an old wooden trunk that leads to another world. A world where evil powers are plotting to destroy the people of earth.

Mantalk Cass. 2004. 10.00 (978-1-57855-622-9(8)) T D Jakes.

Manticore. unabr. ed. Robertson Davies. Read by Dan Lazar. 6 cass. (Running Time: 9 hrs.). 48.00 (978-0-7366-0296-9(8), 1284) Books on Tape.
David Staunton, a Canadian, enters Jungian analysis in Switzerland to help him cope with his father's strange death. As the analysis proceeds, David learns surprising things not only about himself but also about his father, the schoolmaster Dustin Ramsay, the libidinous Liesl, & the warped & gifted Magnus Eisengrim.

Mantis & the Moon: A Story from Nelson Mandela's Favorite African Folktales. Read by Forest Whitaker. Compiled by Nelson Mandela. (Running Time: 8 mins.). (ENG.). 2009. 1.99 (978-1-60024-796-5(2)) Pub: Hachet Audio. Dist(s): HachBkGrp

Mantra. Kriyananda, pseud. 2001. audio compact disk 15.95 (978-1-56589-755-7(2)) Pub: Crystal Clarity. Dist(s): Natl Bk Netwk

Mantra: A Scientific Study. B. Purohit. Read by B. Purohit. 1 cass. (Running Time: 90 min.). 1994. 8.95 (1121) Am Fed Astrologers.

Mantra: Sacred Words of Power. Thomas Ashley-Farrand. 6 CDs. 2004. audio compact disk 69.95 (978-1-59179-147-8(2), AF00780D) Sounds True.
In 1978, Thomas Ashley-Farrand traveled to India for the first time, where he astonished the spiritual community there with his perfect command of mantra, the practice of using specific "sacred sound syllables" for spiritual and material transformation. Now, 20 years later, he shares for the first time his mastery of this ancient spiritual art on Mantra: Sacred Words of Power. Here is the first English language audio curriculum that teaches you how to use mantras to enhance the powers of your mind, influence the environment around you, and deepen your spiritual practice. According to the Vedic tradition of India, the universe was birthed from pure sound. This symphony of vibrational energy continues to unfold at this moment, creating everything that we hear, see, and touch. In 12 fascinating sessions, Thomas Ashley-Farrand teaches you a library of traditional mantras with relevance to every area of your life. From work and health, to love and enlightenment ? here are dozens of authentic chants that are used every day by millions of people to activate the energy of creation. "The power of mantras comes not from the meaning of the syllables," teaches Ashley-Farrand, "but from their direct vibrational effect on our body?s physiological and energetic systems." He also teaches, "Sanskrit is an energy-based language, and mantras are spiritual formulas for working with this energy. They are designed to eliminate obstacles as we progress spiritually, and to help us make energetic progress toward the good." With Mantra: Sacred Words of Power, you can begin practicing these powerful chants to heal and change your own life ? with the very first mantra that you chant. Includes a 36-page study guide.

Mantra, A Path to Spiritual & Material Attainment. Voice by Thomas Ashley-Farrand. Thomas Ashley-Farrand. Prod. by Saraswati Publications. (ENG.). 2007. audio compact disk 125.00 (978-0-9825238-6-5(6)) SaraswaPubns.

Mantra Healing Collection. Shri Anandi Ma. 3 CDs. 2004. audio compact disk 29.95 (978-1-59179-191-1(X), AW00845D) Sounds True.

Mantra Meditation for Attracting & Healing Relationships. Thomas Ashley-Farrand. 2003. audio compact disk 15.95 (978-1-59179-116-4(2)) Sounds True.

Mantra Meditation for Creating Abundance. Thomas Ashley-Farrand. 2003. audio compact disk 15.95 (978-1-59179-114-0(6)) Sounds True.

Mantra Meditation for Physical Health. Thomas Ashley-Farrand. 2003. audio compact disk 15.95 (978-1-59179-115-7(4)) Sounds True.

Mantra of Eternity: Aum. Kriyananda, pseud. 2003. audio compact disk 15.95 (978-1-56589-763-2(3)) Pub: Crystal Clarity. Dist(s): Natl Bk Netwk

Mantra Therapy for Prosperity: Healing Intensive 8. Thomas Ashley-Farrand. Voice by Thomas Ashley-Farrand. Saraswati Publications. (ENG.). (J). 2006. audio compact disk 18.00 (978-0-9825238-4-1(X)) SaraswaPubns.

Mantra Therapy for Restoration of Dharma & World Peace: Healing Intensive 7. Thomas Ashley-Farrand. Voice by Thomas Ashley-Farrand. Saraswati Publications. 2005. audio compact disk 18.00 (978-0-9825238-3-4(1)) SaraswaPubns.

Mantra Therapy, Healing Intensive 1, 2: Systemic Disorders, Mental-Emotional Difficulties. Thomas Ashley-Farrand. Voice by Thomas Ashley-Farrand. Saraswati Publications. (ENG.). 2001. audio compact disk 25.00 (978-0-9825238-2-7(3)) SaraswaPubns.

Mantramotion: The Next Step in Mind-Body Fitness. Hal F. Atkinson, III. 1 cass. (Running Time: 1 hrs.). 1997. pap. bk. 14.95 (978-0-9667003-0-5(9)) Mantramotion Inc.
Music to listen to while exercising. Booklet combines meditation & exercise simultaneously.

Mantrapped. Fay Weldon. Read by Fay Weldon. Read by Rula Lenska. 6 cass. 54.95 (978-0-7927-3802-2(0), CSL 867) AudioGO.

Mantrapped. Fay Weldon. Read by Fay Weldon. Read by Rula Lenska. 8 CDs. (Running Time: 33060 sec.). 2005. audio compact disk 79.95 (978-0-7927-3803-9(9), SLD 867) AudioGO.

Mantras. Steven Zdenek Eckels. 1 cass. (Running Time: 46 min.). 1996. 11.95 (978-1-57025-136-8(3)) Whole Person.
Escape to a journey that will bring relaxation, inner peace & rejuvenation. Resonate with the wisdom & "musical prayers of healing." Each side has 12 mantras separated by 45 seconds of seamless musical interlude.

Mantras: Songs of Yoga. Sivananda Radha. 1 cass. (Running Time: 60 min.). (ITA.). 1994. 9.95 (978-0-931454-33-2(6)) Timeless Bks.
Mantras are sacred sounds which lead you, through their repetition, to expanded awareness. They create harmony & purity at all levels of your being.

Mantras for Abundance. Shri Anandi Ma & Shri Dileepji Pathak. 1 CD. (Running Time: 1 hr. 25 mins.). 2002. audio compact disk 15.95 (978-1-59179-013-6(1), AW00648D) Sounds True.
For more than 5,000 years, the science of kundalini maha yoga has identified specific sound syllables for influencing the links between our internal and external conditions. In this tape the author chants specific mantras intended to help attract abundance in matters of personal relationship, material sustenance, creativity, and spiritual fulfillment. Simply listening to these chants is said to effect change by restoring the flow of prana (vital energy) between the body and its surrounding environment.

Mantras for Ascension. Tom Kenyon & Virginia Essene. Perf. by S. P. Madrigals. Prod. by Maureen J. St. Germain. 2 CDs. (Running Time: 3 hrs.). 2002. audio compact disk 15.95 (978-0-9721799-2-8(5)) M StGermain.
Contains two sung Mantras. First chant comes from the books titled The Hathor Material. it is a powerful chant to connect one to mother earth and the energies of earth, air, fire and water. The second (chant) or Mantra is a well known Hebrew chant sung to connect one directly to God, clearing all the mis-qualified energy between the individual and God.

Mantras for Releasing Fear. Shri Anandi Ma & Shri Dileepji Pathak. 1 CD. (Running Time: 1 hr. 25 mins.). 2002. audio compact disk 15.95 (978-1-59179-027-3(1), AW00566D) Sounds True.
What is fear? Kundalini maha yoga postulates that this emotion arises from a disturbance in the human energy field. These authors offer four authentic chants meant to dissipate fear and encourage a peaceful spiritual state. The sacred chants found here are said to work by subtly unblocking rigid thought patterns and redistributing prana among the body's chakra centers. According to the practice, allowing these sacred sounds to wash over the listener will help to release fear and calm the emotions.

Mantras of the Goddess: By Thomas Ashley-Farrand (Namadeva) Voice by Thomas Ashley-Farrand. Thomas Ashley-Farrand. Saraswati Publications. (ENG.). 2003. audio compact disk 18.00 (978-0-9825238-0-3(7)) SaraswaPubns.

Mantras Songs of Yoga: A Sampling of Traditional Mantras. Voice by Sivananda Radha. 1 CD. (Running Time: 61 mins.). 1997. audio compact disk 14.95 (978-0-931454-89-9(1)) Pub: Timeless Bks. Dist(s): Baker Taylor
Mantras are sacred sounds which lead you, through their repitition, to expanded awareness. They create harmony on all levels of your being. Swami Radha chants a variety of ancient mantras.

Manual & Freedom, Set. unabr. ed. Epictetus. Read by Robert L. Halvorson. 4 cass. (Running Time: 360 min.). 28.95 (2) Halvorson Assocs.

***Manual de Carreo para Nios: Cuentos para Fomentar los Buenos Habitos en Sus Hijos.** Gretel Garcia & Eduardo Torrijos. (SPA.). 2010. audio compact disk 15.99 (978-607-457-017-5(5)) Lectorum MEX.

Manual de lectura del medidor ElÉctrico. Virgil Johnson. Tr. by Leonel & Nancy Figueroa from ENG. (SPA.). 2005. audio compact disk 149.99 (978-0-9755301-4-6(3)) V Johnson Tech.

Manual del exito Familiar. Elizabeth Rodriguez. Narrated by Francisco Rivela. 4 cass. (Running Time: 5 hrs.). 38.00 (978-1-4025-1673-3(8)) Recorded Bks.

Manual Dexterity Exercises. 1 cass. (Running Time: 1 hr.). 2000. 15.95 Prof Pride.
Arrange cards according to complex directions. Taking directions. Fun games.

***Manual Flamenco para Cajon Flamenco Tools I: Alegrias y Seguiriyas.** Miguel Reyes Jimenez. (Flamenco: Didactica Ser.). (ENG & SPA., 2009. 49.99 (978-84-936260-4-4(X)) AcordesCon ESP.

Manual of Detection. unabr. ed. Jedediah Berry. Read by Pete Larkin. 8 CDs. (Running Time: 9 hrs. 15 mins.). 2009. audio compact disk 34.95 (978-1-59887-870-7(0), 1598878700) Pub: HighBridge. Dist(s): Workman Pub

Manuel d'Application de la Convention Relative aux Droits de L'Enfant: Edition Entièrement Révisée. United Nations Children's Fund. (FRE.). 2002. pap. bk. 50.00 (978-92-806-3785-4(1)) Pub: UNICEF. Dist(s): Untd Nat Pubns

Manuel Klausner: Keynote Speech. (Running Time: 60 min.). (Cal State Univ., Long Beach). 1984. 9.00 (F159) Freeland Pr.

Manufacturing & Automation Technology: Teaching Package. R. Thomas Wright. (gr. 9-12). tchr. ed. 36.00 (978-1-59070-214-7(X)) Goodheart.

Manufacturing Consent: The Art of Manipulating American Thought. Alexander Cockburn. Read by Alexander Cockburn. 1 cass. (Running Time: 1 hr.). 10.95 (L0020B090, HarperThor) HarpC GBR.

***Manufacturing Depression: The Secret History of an American Disease.** unabr. ed. Gary Greenberg. Narrated by Kirby Heyborne. (Running Time: 14 hrs. 30 mins. 0 sec.). (ENG.). 2010. 29.99 (978-1-4001-6544-5(X)); 19.99 (978-1-4001-8544-3(0)); audio compact disk 39.99 (978-1-4001-1544-0(2)); audio compact disk 79.99 (978-1-4001-4544-7(9)) Pub: Tantor Media. Dist(s): IngramPubServ

***Many Bloody Returns.** unabr. ed. Toni L. P. Kelner et al. Read by Teri Clark Linden. (Running Time: 13 hrs.). 2010. audio compact disk 79.97 (978-1-4418-6257-0(9), 9781441862570, BriAudCD Unabrid) Brilliance Audio.

***Many Bloody Returns: Tales of Birthdays with Bite.** unabr. ed. Read by Luke Daniels & Teri Clark Linden. Ed. by Charlaine Harris & Toni L. P. Kelner. (Running Time: 13 hrs.). 2010. audio compact disk 29.99 (978-1-4418-6256-3(0), 9781441862563, Bril Audio CD Unabri) Brilliance Audio.

***Many Bloody Returns: Tales of Birthdays with Bite.** unabr. ed. Ed. by Charlaine Harris & Toni L. P. Kelner. (Running Time: 12 hrs.). 2010. 24.99 (978-1-4418-6260-0(9), 9781441862600, BAD); 39.97 (978-1-4418-6261-7(7), 9781441862617, BADLE) Brilliance Audio.

***Many Bloody Returns: Tales of Birthdays with Bite.** unabr. ed. Read by Teri Clark Linden. Ed. by Charlaine Harris & Toni L. P. Kelner. (Running Time: 12 hrs.). 2010. 24.99 (978-1-4418-6258-7(7), 9781441862587, Brilliance MP3); 39.97 (978-1-4418-6259-4(5), 9781441862594, Brlnc Audio MP3 Lib) Brilliance Audio.

Many Called - Few Chosen: Matthew 22:11-14. Ed Young. (J). 1982. 4.95 (978-0-7417-1208-0(3), A0208) Win Walk.

***Many-Colored Land: Volume 1 of the Saga of Pliocene Exile.** unabr. ed. Julian May. (Running Time: 14 hrs. 30 mins.). (Saga of Pliocene Exile Ser.). 2010. 29.95 (978-1-4332-2409-6(7)); 85.95 (978-1-4332-2405-8(4)); audio compact disk 118.00 (978-1-4332-2406-5(2)) Blckstn Audio.

Many Deadly Returns. unabr. ed. Patricia Moyes. Read by Nadia May. 7 cass. (Running Time: 10 hrs.). (Henry Tibbett Mystery Ser.). 1994. 49.95 (978-0-7861-0433-8(3), 1385) Blckstn Audio.
The aged but indomitable Lady Crystal Balaclava, famous in her younger days for sybaritic socials, is celebrating a birthday at Foxes Trot, her country estate. Detective Inspector Henry Tibbett & his wife Emily are on hand because Lady Balaclava, for reasons known only to herself & the Ouija board she frequently consults, feels her life is in imminent danger. Henry watches her receive presents from her three daughters - a large cake specially baked in Switzerland, a case of French champagne, & a handsome bouquet of roses. Seconds later, before his amazed eyes, Lady Balaclava gasps, clutches her throat, & collapses - dead from an apparent heart attack. Here, with her usual deft touch, Patricia Moyes offers one of her best puzzles ever, an amazing & amusing intrigue that will surely captivate all Henry Tibbett fans.

***Many Deaths of the Firefly Brothers.** unabr. ed. Thomas Mullen. Narrated by William Dufris. (Running Time: 12 hrs. 0 mins.). 2010. 17.99 (978-1-4001-8559-7(9)) Tantor Media.

***Many Deaths of the Firefly Brothers.** unabr. ed. Thomas Mullen. Narrated by William Dufris. (Running Time: 16 hrs. 0 mins. 0 sec.). (ENG.). 2010. 24.99 (978-1-4001-6559-9(8)); audio compact disk 34.99 (978-1-4001-1559-4(0)); audio compact disk 69.99 (978-1-4001-4559-1(7)) Pub: Tantor Media. Dist(s): IngramPubServ

Many Faces of Islam. Nabeel Jabbour. 2004. audio compact disk 11.99 (978-1-58926-282-9(4), JA01-0200) Oasis Audio.

Many Faces of Islam. unabr. ed. Nabeel Jabbour. Read by Nabeel Jabbour. Prod. by Oasis Audio Staff. (Running Time: 1 hr.). 2000. 14.95 (978-0-7861-2644-6(2), 3250); audio compact disk 15.00 (978-0-7861-8731-7(X), 3250) Blckstn Audio.

Many Faces of Islam. unabr. ed. Nabeel T. Jabbour. 1 cass. (Running Time: 1 hr.). (Rapid Response Ser.). 2001. 8.99 (978-1-58926-058-0(9)) Oasis Audio.
Islam is the world's second largest religion and arguably it's least understood. With objectivity, the author outlines the tenets of Islam, addressing the issues of compassion and understanding between faiths.

Many Faces of John Donne. 1 cass. 10.00 Esstee Audios.

Many Faces of Mary, the Eternal One. Tricia McCannon. Read by Tricia McCannon. 1 cass. 1997. 20.00 (978-1-886932-07-4(7)) Hrzns Unltd.

Many Faces to Many Places. Judy Azar LeBlanc. Narrated by Dave Giorgio. 3 CDs. (Running Time: 3 hrs 12 mins). 2006. audio compact disk 17.95 (978-1-60031-001-0(X)) Spoken Books.
A spiritual allegory best described as a children's book for the grown up soul, this is a story full of beautifully descriptive moments that take the listener on a journey of spiritual awakening. The female protagonist, Many Faces, is guided by her Eyes Of Faith, as she communicates with nature and her surrounding elements in order to find truth, self awareness, and love. Lovingly narrated by Dave Giorgio.

Many Forms of God. Swami Amar Jyoti. 1 cass. 1975. 9.95 (R-73) Truth Consciousness.
Supreme Godhead & changing phenomena. Maya, the mother. Fear of Satan.

Many Furred Creature. unabr. ed. 1 cass. (Running Time: 20 min.). Dramatization. (Magic Looking Glass Ser.). (J). (gr. 2-6). 1989. 9.95 (978-0-7810-0027-7(0), NIM-CW-127-6-C) NIMCO.
A folk tale of German descent.

Many Griefs of Death. 1 cass. (Care Cassettes Ser.: Vol. 17, No. 1). 1990. 10.80 Assn Prof Chaplains.

Many Influences of T. S. Eliot: A Light & Enlightening Lecture, Featuring Elliot Engel. 2001. bk. 15.00 (978-1-890123-45-1(5)) Media Cnslts.

Many Kinds of Animals. Bobbie Kalman & Molly Aloian. (What Kind of Animal Is It? Ser.). (ENG.). (J). 2005. audio compact disk 10.00 (978-0-7787-7596-6(8)) CrabtreePubCo CAN.

Many Lives & Secret Sorrows of Josephine B. abr. ed. Sandra Gulland. Narrated by Louise Pitre. 3 CDs. (Running Time: 14400 sec.). (ENG.). 2007. audio compact disk 24.95 (978-0-86492-472-8(0)) Pub: Goose Ln Eds CAN. Dist(s): U Toronto Pr

Many Lives, Many Masters: The True Story of a Prominent Psychiatrist, His Young Patient, & the Past-Life Therapy That Changed Both Their Lives. Brian L. Weiss. 2004. 7.95 (978-0-7435-4069-8(7)) Pub: S&S Audio. Dist(s): S and S Inc

Many Lives, Many Masters: The True Story of a Prominent Psychiatrist, His Young Patient, & the Past-Life Therapy That Changed Both Their Lives. abr. ed. Brian L. Weiss. Read by Brian L. Weiss. 2 CDs. (Running Time: 13 hrs. 0 mins. 0 sec.). (ENG.). 2004. audio compact disk 19.95 (978-0-7435-3842-8(0), Sound Ideas) Pub: S&S Audio. Dist(s): S and S Inc

Many Lives of Ministry Wives. Sharon Hoffman. Ed. by Cindy G. Spear. 2 cass. 1997. bk. 19.95 Set, incl. printed intro. & outlines. (978-1-57052-086-0(0)) Chrch Grwth VA.
Addresses the joys, pains & challenges of being a minister's wife.

Many Luscious Lollipops. unabr. ed. Ruth Heller. 1 cass. (Running Time: 7 min.). (J). (gr. k-5). 1989. pap. bk. 17.95 (978-0-8045-6563-9(5), 6563) Spoken Arts.
Learning about adjectives can be fun! Reading Rainbow Review title. American Bookseller Pick of the Lists.

Many Mansions. Neville Goddard. 1 cass. (Running Time: 62 min.). 1969. 8.00 (60) J & L Pubns.
Neville taught Imagination Creates Reality. He was a powerfully influential teacher of God as Consciousness.

Many Miles: Mary Oliver Reads Mary Oliver. unabr. ed. Mary Oliver. (ENG.). 2010. audio compact disk (978-0-8070-6895-3(0)) Beacon Pr.

Many Moons. abr. ed. James Thurber. Read by Peter Ustinov. 1 cass. (J). 1984. 9.95 (978-0-694-50903-4(5), CDL5 1410) HarperCollins Pubs.

Many Others see J. B. Priestley

Many Stones. unabr. ed. Carolyn Coman. Read by Mandy Siegfried. 3 cass. (Running Time: 3 hrs. 40 mins.). (J). (gr. 7 up). 2004. 30.00 (978-0-8072-0518-1(4), Listening Lib) Random Audio Pubg.
Berry Morgan and her father set out on a two week trip to South Africa to attend her sister Laura's funeral. While coming to terms with their own grief they bear witness to a country's own search for truth and reconciliation.

Many Things Invisible. unabr. ed. Carrington MacDuffie. 1 CD. (Running Time: 1 hrs.). 2008. audio compact disk & audio compact disk 20.00 (978-1-4332-2686-1(3)) Blckstn Audio.

Many Troubles of Andy Russell. David A. Adler. Read by Oliver Wyman. Illus. by Will Hillenbrand. 2 CDs. (Running Time: 2 hrs. 28 mins.). (Andy Russell Ser.). (J). (gr. 2-5). 2008. pap. bk. 28.95 (978-1-4301-0480-3(5)) Live Oak Media.

Many Troubles of Andy Russell. David A. Adler. Narrated by Oliver Wyman. 2 cass. (Running Time: 2 hrs. 28 mins.). (J). (gr. 2-4). 2008. pap. bk. 24.95 (978-1-4301-0479-7(1)); 18.95 (978-1-4301-0477-3(5)) Live Oak Media.

Many Troubles of Andy Russell. David A. Adler. Read by Oliver Wyman. Illus. by Will Hillenbrand. 2 CDs. (Running Time: 2 hrs. 28 mins.). (Andy Russell Ser.). (J). (gr. 2-4). 2008. audio compact disk 22.95 (978-1-4301-0478-0(3)) Live Oak Media.

Many Voices. . . Wise Choices. Dave Privett. Prod. by Dale Liz VonSeggen. (YA). 1999. audio compact disk 15.00 (978-1-58302-194-1(9)) One Way St.

Many Voices... Wise Choices. Liz VonSeggen et al. 1 cass. (Running Time: 23 min.). 1999. 15.00 (978-1-58302-138-5(8), STP-27) One Way St.

Many Waters. Madeleine L'Engle. Read by Ann Marie Lee. (ENG.). (J). (gr. 5). 2008. audio compact disk 37.00 (978-0-7393-7197-8(5), Listening Lib) Pub: Random Audio Pubg. Dist(s): Random

Many Waters. unabr. ed. Madeleine L'Engle. Read by Ann Marie Lee. 7 CDs. (Running Time: 8 hrs. 55 mins.). (YA). (gr. 6 up). 2008. audio compact disk 55.00 (978-0-7393-7199-2(1), Listening Lib) Pub: Random Audio Pubg. Dist(s): Random

Many Waters, Set. Pamela Street. Read by Jane Jermyn. 4 cass. 1999. 44.95 (6187X) Pub: Soundings Ltd GBR. Dist(s): ISIS Pub

Many Ways to Learn: Young People's Guide to Learning Disabilities. Judith Stern & Uzi Ben-Ami. 1 cass. (Running Time: 1 hr. 30 min.). (J). (gr. 4-7). 1996. 14.95 (978-0-945354-75-8(4)) Am Psychol.
Suggestions for coping with learning disabilities, narrated by a boy with learning disabilities. Tells kids what to expect & strategies for school, homework, & social life.

Many Ways to Say I Love You: Wisdom for Parents & Children from Mister Rogers. unabr. abr. ed. Fred Rogers & Fred Rogers. Read by Jill Clayburgh et al. 1 CD. (Running Time: 4500 sec.). 2006. audio compact disk 16.98 (978-1-4013-8416-6(1), Hyperion Audio) Pub: Hyperion. Dist(s): HarperCollins Pubs

Mao: The Unknown Story. unabr. ed. Jung Chang & Jon Halliday. Read by Robertson Dean. 25 CDs. (Running Time: 30 hrs.). 2006. audio compact disk 149.00 (978-1-4159-3006-9(6)); 129.00 (978-1-4159-3005-2(8)) Books on Tape.
Based on a decade of research and on interviews with many of Mao's close circle in China who have never talked before - and with virtually everyone outside China who had significant dealings with him - this is the most authoritative life of Mao ever written. It is full of startling revelations, exploding the myth of the Long March, and showing a completely unknown Mao: he was not driven by idealism or ideology; his intimate and intricate relationship with Stalin went back to the 1920s, ultimately bringing him to power; he welcomed Japanese occupation of much of China; and he schemed, poisoned and blackmailed to get his way. After Mao conquered China in 1949, his secret goal was to dominate the world. In chasing this dream he caused the deaths of 38 million people in the greatest famine in history. In all, well over 70 million Chinese perished under Mao's rule - in peacetime.

Mao II. collector's ed. Don DeLillo. Read by Michael Prichard. 6 cass. (Running Time: 9 hrs.). 2000. 48.00 (978-0-7366-5087-8(3)) Books on Tape.
Bill Gray is a famous reclusive writer who escapes the failed novel he has been working on for many years & enters the world of political violence when he gets the chance to aid a hostage trapped in a basement in war-torn Beirut, a nightscape of Semtex explosives.

Mao Tse-Tung. unabr. ed. 1 cass. (Running Time: 1 hr. 5 min.). (History Maker Ser.). 12.95 (41030) J Norton Pubs.

Mao Zedong. Jonathan D. Spence. Read by Alexander Adams. 4 cass. (Running Time: 6 hrs.). 2000. 24.95 (978-0-7366-4943-8(3)) Books on Tape.

Mao Zedong. collector's ed. Jonathan D. Spence. Read by Alexander Adams. 4 cass. (Running Time: 6 hrs.). 2000. 32.00 (978-0-7366-4854-7(2)) Books on Tape.
Drawing from his expertise in Chinese politics & culture, the author penetrates Mao's rhetoric & infamous self-will to distill an intimate portrait of a man as withdrawn & mysterious as the emperors he disdained. The author superbly illuminates Mao, a leader who, at a watershed moment in history, turned the classic Chinese concept of reform through reversal into an endless adventure in upheaval.

Mao Zedong. collector's ed. Jonathan D. Spence. Read by Alexander Adams. 5 cass. (Running Time: 7 hrs. 30 min.). 2000. 40.00 (978-0-7366-5217-9(5)) Books on Tape.

Mao Zedong. unabr. ed. Delia Davin. Read by Michael Tudor Barnes. 2 cass. (Running Time: 2 hrs.). (Isis Ser.). (J). 1998. 24.95 (978-0-7531-0334-0(6), 980816) Pub: ISIS Lrg Prnt GBR. Dist(s): Ulverscroft US
Mao Zedong was active in Chinese politics for most of his 82 years & became one of the most important figures of the twentieth century. He was the first chairman of the People's Republic of China, one of the founders of the Chinese Communism Party & the architect of the Cultural Revolution, selling over 740 million copies of his Little Red Book. His struggle to build the Party & bring it to power, called the disastrous Great Leap Forward resulted in millions of deaths.

Mao Zedong. unabr. ed. Jonathan D. Spence. Read by Alexander Adams. 4 CDs. (Running Time: 4 hrs. 48 mins.). 2001. audio compact disk Books on Tape.
Drawing from his expertise in Chinese politics & culture, the author penetrates Mao's rhetoric & infamous self-will to distill an intimate portrait of a man as withdrawn & mysterious as the emperors he disdained. The author superbly illuminates Mao, a leader who, at a watershed moment in history, turned the classic Chinese concept of reform through reversal into an endless adventure in upheaval.

Mao's Last Dancer. Li Cunxin. Read by Paul English. (Running Time: 8 hrs. 55 mins.). 2009. 104.99 (978-1-74214-220-3(6), 9781742142203) Pub: Bolinda Pubng AUS. Dist(s): Bolinda Pub Inc

Mao's Last Dancer. unabr. ed. Li Cunxin. Read by Paul English. 12 CDs. (Running Time: 15 hrs. 30 mins.). 2004. audio compact disk 113.95 (978-1-74093-376-6(1)) Pub: Bolinda Pubng AUS. Dist(s): Bolinda Pub Inc

Mao's Last Dancer. unabr. ed. Li Cunxin. Read by Paul English. 13 cass. (Running Time: 15 hrs. 30 mins.). 2004. 96.00 (978-1-74093-294-3(3)) Pub: Bolinda Pubng AUS. Dist(s): Bolinda Pub Inc
The true story of a poor Chinese peasant boy who, plucked unsuspectingly at age 10 from millions of others across the land to be trained as a ballet dancer, turned the situation to his advantage to become one of the world's greatest ballet stars. Li tells his story with simplicity and charm, with humor and compassion, and at times with great drama. His childhood is drawn, despite the terrible hardships, with love and affection, as we share in the lives of Li and his large family.

Mao's Last Dancer. unabr. ed. Li Cunxin. Read by Paul English. (Running Time: 55800 sec.). 2005. audio compact disk 43.95 (978-1-74093-675-0(2)) Pub: Bolinda Pubng AUS. Dist(s): Bolinda Pub Inc

Mao's Last Dancer. unabr. ed. Li Cunxin. Read by Paul English. 8 CDs. (Running Time: 8 hrs. 55 mins.). (J). (gr. 4-7). 2006. audio compact disk 87.95 (978-1-74093-820-4(8)) Pub: Bolinda Pubng AUS. Dist(s): Bolinda Pub Inc

Mao's Last Dancer. unabr. ed. Li Cunxin. Read by Paul English. (Running Time: 8 hrs. 55 mins.). (YA). 2008. 43.95 (978-1-921415-89-0(4), 9781921415890) Pub: Bolinda Pubng AUS. Dist(s): Bolinda Pub Inc

Mao's Last Dancer. unabr. ed. Li Cunxin & Elyne Mitchell. Read by Paul English & Richard Aspel. (Running Time: 32100 sec.). (Classic Ser.). 2008. audio compact disk 63.95 (978-1-921415-90-6(8)) Pub: Bolinda Pubng AUS. Dist(s): Bolinda Pub Inc

Mao's Last Dancer. unabr. movie tie-in ed. Li Cunxin. Read by Paul English. (Running Time: 17 hrs. 7 mins.). 2009. audio compact disk 118.95 (978-1-74214-528-0(0), 9781742145280) Pub: Bolinda Pubng AUS. Dist(s): Bolinda Pub Inc

***Mao's Last Dancer.** unabr. movie tie-in ed. Li Cunxin. Read by Paul English. (Running Time: 17 hrs. 7 mins.). 2010. 43.95 (978-1-74214-750-5(X), 9781742147505) Pub: Bolinda Pubng AUS. Dist(s): Bolinda Pub Inc

Mao's Last Dancer: Young Readers Edition. Li Cunxin. Read by Paul English. (Running Time: 8 hrs. 55 mins.). (YA). 2009. 64.99 (978-1-74214-312-5(1), 9781742143125) Pub: Bolinda Pubng AUS. Dist(s): Bolinda Pub Inc

Map: The Way of All Great Men. unabr. ed. David Murrow. Narrated by Wayne Shepherd. (Running Time: 5 hrs. 49 mins. 37 sec.). (ENG.). 2010. 18.19 (978-1-60814-642-0(1)); audio compact disk 25.99 (978-1-59859-699-1(3)) Oasis Audio.

Map of All Things. unabr. ed. Kevin J. Anderson. Read by Scott Brick. (Running Time: 20 hrs.). (Terra Incognita Ser.). (ENG.). 2010. 29.98 (978-1-60788-236-7(1)) Pub: Hachet Audio. Dist(s): HachBkGrp

***Map of Bones.** unabr. ed. James Rollins. Read by John Meagher. (ENG.). 2009. (978-0-06-198542-3(2), Harper Audio); (978-0-06-197915-6(5), Harper Audio) HarperCollins Pubs.

Map of Glass. Jane Urquhart. Read by Hillary Huber. (Running Time: 41400 sec.). 2006. 79.95 (978-0-7861-4555-3(2)); audio compact disk 99.00 (978-0-7861-7086-9(7)) Blckstn Audio.

Map of Glass. unabr. ed. Jane Urquhart. Read by Hillary Huber. (Running Time: 41400 sec.). 2006. audio compact disk 29.95 (978-0-7861-7566-6(4)) Blckstn Audio.

Map of Life: A Simple Study of the Catholic Faith. Francis J. Sheed. 5 cass. 22.95 (901) Ignatius Pr.
Short statement of the Catholic faith.

Map of My House: Early Explorers Emergent Set B Audio CD. Katherine Scraper. Adapted by Benchmark Education Staff. (J). 2007. audio compact disk 10.00 (978-1-4108-8199-1(7)) Benchmark Educ.

Map of the Universe. Margaret Geller & John Huchra. Read by Margaret Geller & John Huchra. 1 cass. (Running Time: 30 min.). 1996. 10.95 (978-1-57511-011-0(3)) Pub Mills.
A radio documentary of the Smithsonian Institution & Soundprint. Using advanced instruments ranging from an array of mirror telescopes mounted in a rotating building high above the Arizona desert, to x-ray images from orbiting telescopes in space, the two are painstakingly pinpointing galaxies millions of light years across time & space from earth. In the process, Geller & Huchra have discovered a remarkable structure to the arrangement of galaxies: they are arranged as though on the surface of great "soap bubbles," separated by vast areas of other mysterious phenomena: dark matter. Their virtual adventure through space is as tantalizing as any on earth.

Map of the World. Jane Hamilton. Narrated by C. J. Critt & Frank Muller. 15 CDs. (Running Time: 17 hrs. 30 mins.). audio compact disk 142.00 (978-0-7887-4481-5(X)) Recorded Bks.

Map of the World. unabr. ed. Jane Hamilton. Narrated by C. J. Critt & Frank Muller. 12 cass. (Running Time: 17 hrs. 30 mins.). 1995. 97.00 (978-0-7887-0195-5(9), 94419K8) Recorded Bks.
Thirty-two-year-old Alice Goodwin begins the unremarkable June day much as every other on the small dairy farm. Suddenly, within the span of minutes, Alice's map of her world is forever altered when her neighbor's two-year-old, left with Alice for the morning, wanders away & drowns in the farm pond.

***Map of True Places.** unabr. ed. Brunonia Barry. Narrated by Alyssa Bresnahan. 1 Playaway. (Running Time: 12 hrs. 38 mins.). 2010. 110.95 (978-0-7927-7276-7(8)); 69.95 (978-0-7927-7204-0(0)); audio compact disk 110.95 (978-0-7927-7203-3(2)) AudioGO.

***Map of True Places.** unabr. ed. Brunonia Barry. Read by Alyssa Bresnahan. (ENG.). 2010. (978-0-06-199305-3(0), Harper Audio); (978-0-06-198870-7(7), Harper Audio) HarperCollins Pubs.

***MAP Plus Assessment Links: Individual CD.** Continental Press Staff. 2008. stu. ed. 49.95 (978-0-8454-5793-1(4)); stu. ed. 49.95 (978-0-8454-5788-7(8)); stu. ed. 49.95 (978-0-8454-5791-7(8)); stu. ed. 49.95 (978-0-8454-5790-0(X)); stu. ed. 49.95 (978-0-8454-5792-4(6)); stu. ed. 49.95 (978-0-8454-5789-4(6)) Continental Pr.

Map Search/Peanut Butter & Jelly. Steck-Vaughn Staff. (J). 2002. (978-0-7398-5989-6(7)) SteckVau.

Map Skills Audio CD. Adapted by Benchmark Education Company Staff. Based on a work by Margaret McNamara. (Content Connections Ser.). (J). (gr. k-2). 2008. audio compact disk 10.00 (978-1-60634-912-0(0)) Benchmark Educ.

***Map That Changed the World.** unabr. ed. Simon Winchester. Read by Simon Winchester. (ENG.). 2004. (978-0-06-079979-3(X), Harper Audio) HarperCollins Pubs.

***Map That Changed the World: William Smith & the Birth of Modern Geology.** unabr. ed. Simon Winchester. Read by Simon Winchester. (ENG.). 2004. (978-0-06-074607-0(6), Harper Audio) HarperCollins Pubs.

Map Tutor Cd-West Civil. 4th ed. (C). 2000. audio compact disk 21.95 (978-0-534-56860-3(2)) Pub: Wadsworth Pub. Dist(s): CENGAGE Learn

MAP Workshop. 3 cass. (Running Time: 4 hrs. 50 mins.). 2004. 19.95 (978-0-927978-17-0(2), WT-108) Perelandra Ltd.
Workshop includes lots of questions and answers about MAP, plus discussions on the Emergency MAP Process, using MAP with children and much more.

Mapa del Creador see Creator's Map

Mapaches y Mapachitos, EDL Level 14. (Fonolibros Ser.: Vol. 22). (SPA.). 2003. 11.50 (978-0-7652-1011-1(8)) Modern Curr.

***Mapas de Mi Escuela Audio Cd.** Matthew Frank. Adapted by Benchmark Education Company, LLC. (Content Connections Ser.). (SPA.). (J). 2009. audio compact disk 10.00 (978-1-935472-61-2(5)) Benchmark Educ.

Maple Syrup Urine Disease - A Bibliography & Dictionary for Physicians, Patients, & Genome Researchers. Compiled by Icon Group International, Inc. Staff. 2007. ring bd. 28.95 (978-0-497-11253-0(1)) Icon Grp.

Mapp & Lucia. unabr. ed. E. F. Benson. Read by Prunella Scales. 8 CDs. (Running Time: 11 hrs.). (Isis (CDs) Ser.). 2000. audio compact disk 79.95 (978-0-7531-0784-3(8)) Pub: ISIS Audio GBR. Dist(s): Ulverscroft US

Mapp & Lucia. unabr. ed. E. F. Benson. Read by Prunella Scales. 10 cass. (Running Time: 11 hrs. 15 min.). (Isis Ser.). (J). 1990. 84.95 (978-1-85089-748-4(4), 90084) Pub: ISIS Lrg Prnt GBR. Dist(s): Ulverscroft US

Mapping American History: Interactive Explorations. 2nd ed. Created by Prentice-Hall Staff. 2000. audio compact disk 24.20 (978-0-13-091368-5(5), P-H) Pearson Educ CAN CAN.

***Mapping of Love & Death.** unabr. ed. Jacqueline Winspear. Read by Orlagh Cassidy. 1 Playaway. (Running Time: 10 hrs.). 2010. 94.95 (978-0-7927-7122-7(2)); 59.95 (978-0-7927-7121-0(4)); audio compact disk 94.95 (978-0-7927-7120-3(6)) AudioGO.

***Mapping of Love & Death.** unabr. ed. Jacqueline Winspear. Read by Orlagh Cassidy. (ENG.). 2010. (978-0-06-197753-4(5), Harper Audio) HarperCollins Pubs.

***Mapping of Love & Death: A Maisie Dobbs Novel.** unabr. ed. Jacqueline Winspear. Read by Orlagh Cassidy. (ENG.). 2010. (978-0-06-197750-3(0), Harper Audio) HarperCollins Pubs.

Mapping the End of History. Terence McKenna. 5 cass. 1992. 45.00 set. (OC288-64) Sound Horizons AV.

Mapping the End of History. Terence McKenna. 4 cass. 1993. 36.00 set. (OC348-73) Sound Horizons AV.

Mapping the Spiritual Path. Frances Vaughan. 5 cass. 45.00 (OC81) Sound Horizons AV.

Mapping the Way: Early Explorers Early Set A Audio CD. Benchmark Education Staff. (J). 2006. audio compact disk 10.00 (978-1-4108-7617-1(9)) Benchmark Educ.

Mapping Tomorrow's Planet: Ecological Reverence in the Global Village. J. Edward Barrett. 1 cass. 1999. 14.00 (978-0-9660325-3-6(5)) Trillium Bks.

Mapping Your Road to Recovery. Pia Mellody. Read by Pia Mellody. 1 cass. 10.00 (A10) Featuka Enter Inc.
Covers the stages of recovery as well as recovery from the standpoint of five concurrent processes.

Maps of My School Audio CD. Adapted by Benchmark Education Company Staff. Based on a work by Margaret McNamara. (Content Connections Ser.). (J). (gr. k-2). 2008. audio compact disk 10.00 (978-1-60634-910-6(4)) Benchmark Educ.

Maps on File: 2006 Edition. (gr. 6-12). 2005. audio compact disk 199.95 (978-0-8160-6140-2(8)) Facts On File.

Maquiavelo y la Mandragora. abr. ed. Somerset Maugham. Read by Santiago Munevar. 3 CDs.Tr. of Machiavelli & the Mandrake (Then & Now). (SPA.). 2002. audio compact disk 17.00 (978-958-8161-28-0(2)) YoYoMusic.

Máquina Del Tiempo. abr. ed. H. G. Wells. 3 CDs. (SPA.). 2002. audio compact disk 17.00 (978-958-8161-06-8(1)) YoYoMusic.

Maranatha! Even So Come Quickly Lord Jesus, Prophecy Series. Chuck Smith et al. (ENG.). 2006. DVD 19.99 (978-1-932941-77-7(0)) Word For Today.

Marathon of Life. Emmett Smith. 1 cass. 9.95 (978-1-57734-270-0(4), 06005748) Covenant Comms.
Winning the race that matters most.

Marauder. unabr. ed. Cynthia Haseloff. Read by Sky Vogel. 6 vols. (Running Time: 9 hrs.). 2000. bk. 54.95 (978-0-7927-2248-9(5), CSL 137, Chivers Sound Lib) AudioGO.
During the bitter winter of 1862 the people of the Arkansas frontier were the victims of Confederate guerrillas and Yankee renegades. Most feared were the crazed raider Crysop, who stained the land with the blood-trails of his burning, thieving, murdering gang. Heroically, one lone woman thundered out of the war-scarred hills to defend her home and become the woman they called Marauder.

Maravilloso Es. unabr. ed. Jocelyn Arias. (SPA.). 2001. 9.99 (978-0-8297-3594-9(1)) Pub: Vida Pubs. Dist(s): Zondervan

Marble Faun. unabr. ed. Nathaniel Hawthorne. Read by Flo Gibson. 9 cass. (Running Time: 13 hrs. 30 min.). 1996. 28.95 (978-1-55685-411-8(0)) Audio Bk Con.
From Donatello (the faun) & Miriam's joyous romp in the Villa Borghese gardens to the gloom of the catacombs & from the glory of love to a ghastly murder, we run the gamut in this gripping tale. There are beautiful descriptions of Rome & the Italian countryside.

Marbleface. unabr. ed. Max Brand. (Running Time: 7 hrs.). 2007. 24.95 (978-1-4233-3497-2(3), 9781423334972, BAD) Brilliance Audio.

Marbleface. unabr. ed. Max Brand. Read by Multivoice Production Staff. (Running Time: 7 hrs.). 2007. 39.25 (978-1-4233-3498-9(1), 9781423334989, BADLE); audio compact disk 24.95 (978-1-4233-3495-8(7), 9781423334958, Brilliance MP3) Brilliance Audio.

Marbleface. unabr. ed. Max Brand. Read by Full Cast Production Staff. (Running Time: 25200 sec.). 2007. audio compact disk 39.25 (978-1-4233-3496-5(5), 9781423334965, Brinc Audio MP3 Lib) Brilliance Audio.

***Marbleface.** unabr. ed. Max Brand. Read by multivoice. (Running Time: 8 hrs.). 2009. audio compact disk 59.97 (978-1-4418-0484-6(6), 9781441804846, BriAudCD Unabrid) Brilliance Audio.

***Marbury Lens.** unabr. ed. Andrew Smith. Read by Mark Boyett. (Running Time: 11 hrs.). (YA). 2010. 24.99 (978-1-4418-8841-9(1), 9781441888419, Brilliance MP3); 39.97 (978-1-4418-8842-6(X), 9781441888426, Brinc Audio MP3 Lib); 39.97 (978-1-4418-8843-3(8), 9781441888433, BADLE); audio compact disk 29.99 (978-1-4418-8839-6(X), 9781441888396, Bril Audio CD Unabri); audio compact disk 74.97 (978-1-4418-8840-2(3), 9781441888402, BriAudCD Unabrid) Brilliance Audio.

Marc Brown Arthur: King Arthur; Francine, Believe it or Not; Arthur & the Cootie-Catcher;, Vol. 5. unabr. ed. Marc Brown. Read by Mark Linn-Baker. Text by Stephen Krensky. 1 cass. (Running Time: 38 mins.). (Arthur Chapter Bks.: No. 5). (J). (gr. 2-4). 1998. pap. bk. 17.00 (978-0-8072-0385-9(8), FTR191SP, Listening Lib) Random Audio Pubg.
Buster helps Arthur solve the mystery of the missing quarters.

Marc Brown Arthur Chapter Books. unabr. ed. Marc Brown. Read by Mark Linn-Baker. 2 cass. (Running Time: 1 hr. 46 mins.). (Arthur Chapter Bks.: No. 1). (J). (gr. 2-4). 1998. 23.00 (978-0-8072-8009-6(7), YA966CX, Listening Lib) Random Audio Pubg.
Adventures of Arthur the aardvark.

Marc Brown Arthur Chapter Books, Vol. 5. unabr. ed. Marc Brown. Read by Mark Linn-Baker. 2 cass. (Running Time: 1 hr. 59 mins.). (J). (gr. 2-4). 2004. 23.00 (978-0-8072-8881-8(0), Listening Lib) Random Audio Pubg.
In "King Arthur," Arthur and his third-grade classmates compete against Glenbrook Academy during the middle Ages Fair. Despite their attempts to win the pie-eating contest and other events, the gang is not having any success. In "Francine, Believe It or Not," after Francine's selfish play during a hockey game, Muffy bets her Princess Peach watch that Francine can't be nice for an entire week. In "Arthur and the Cootie Catcher," a series of correct predictions by Prunella's cootie catcher convinces the gang that it can foretell the future and place a curse on any nonbelievers.

Marc Brown's Arthur: Arthur & the Crunch Cereal Contest; Arthur Accused!; Locked in the Library. Marc Brown. Read by Mark Linn-Baker. 2 cass. (Running Time: 2 hrs.). (Arthur Chapter Bks.: No. 2). (J). (gr. 3-6). 2000. 18.00 (978-0-7366-9080-5(8)) Books on Tape.
This second collection includes "Arthur and the Crunch Cereal Contest," Arthur Accused!" & "Locked in the Library.".

Marc Brown's Arthur: Arthur & the Scare-Your-Pants-off Club; Arthur Makes the Team. Marc Brown. Read by Mark Linn-Baker. 2 cass. (Running Time: 2 hrs. 14 mins.). (Arthur Chapter Bks.: No. 1). (J). (gr. 3-6). 2000. 18.00 (978-0-7366-9079-9(4)) Books on Tape.
Adventures of an aardvark.

Marc Brown's Arthur: Arthur & the Scare-Your-Pants-off Club; Arthur Makes the Team. Marc Brown. Text by Stephen Krensky. 1 cass. (Arthur Chapter Bks.: No. 1). (J). (gr. 3-6). bk. 12.78 Blisterpack. (BFTR 187) NewSound.

Marc Brown's Arthur: Buster's Dino Dilemma; the Mystery of the Stolen Bike; Arthur & the Lost Diary. Marc Brown. Read by Mark Linn-Baker. 2 cass. (Running Time: 2 hrs.). (Arthur Chapter Bks.: No. 3). (J). (gr. 3-6). 2000. 18.00 (978-0-7366-9081-2(6)) Books on Tape.
Includes: "Buster's Dino Dilemma," "The Mystery of the Stolen Bike," & "Arthur and the Lost Diary.".

Marc Brown's Arthur: Buster's Dino Dilemma; the Mystery of the Stolen Bike; Arthur & the Lost Diary. Marc Brown. Text by Stephen Krensky. 1 cass. (Arthur Chapter Bks.: No. 3). (J). (gr. 3-6). 12.78 Blisterpack. (BFTR 189) NewSound.
It's baseball season, & Arthur & the gang all sign up to play. Coach Frensky's challenge is to work with a team where everyone wants to pitch - & no one knows the meaning of the word "teamwork".

Marc Brown's Arthur Anniversary Collection. unabr. ed. Marc Brown. Read by Mark Linn-Baker. 2 CDs. (Running Time: 2 hrs. 25 mins.). (Middle Grade Cassette Librariestm Ser.). (J). (gr. 2-4). 2004. audio compact disk 24.00 (978-0-8072-0527-3(3), S YA 291 CD, Listening Lib) Random Audio Pubg.

Marc Brown's Arthur Chapter Books: Arthur & the Crunch Cereal Contest; Arthur Accused!; Locked in the Library, Vol. 2. unabr. ed. Marc Brown. Read by Mark Linn-Baker. 2 cass. (Running Time: 1 hr. 58 mins.). (Arthur Chapter Bks.: No. 2). (J). (gr. 2-4). 1998. 23.00 (978-0-8072-8025-6(9), YA970CX, Listening Lib) Random Audio Pubg.
Three Arthur stories: "Arthur & the Crunch Cereal Contest," "Arthur Accused" & "Locked in the Library".

Marc Brown's Arthur Chapter Books: Buster's Dino Dilemma; the Mystery of the Stolen Bike; Arthur & the Lost Diary, Vol. 3. unabr. ed. Marc Brown. Read by Mark Linn-Baker. 2 cass. (Running Time: 1 hr. 54 mins.). (Arthur Chapter Bks.: No. 3). (J). (gr. 2-4). 1999. 23.00 (978-0-8072-8053-9(4), YA988CX, Listening Lib) Random Audio Pubg.
Arthur & his irrepressible frineds, Buster, Francine & Muffy once more embark on adventures & problem solving.

Marc Brown's Arthur Chapter Books: Who's in Love with Arthur?; Arthur Rocks with Binky; Arthur & the Popularity Test. collector's ed. Marc Brown. Read by Mark Linn-Baker. 2 cass. (Running Time: 2 hrs.). (Arthur Chapter Bks.: No. 4). (J). (gr. 3-6). 1999. 18.00 (978-0-7366-9008-9(5)) Books on Tape.
Includes: "Who's in Love with Arthur," "Arthur Rocks with Binky," & " Arthur and the Popularity Test.".

Marc Brown's Arthur Chapter Books: Who's in Love with Arthur?; Arthur Rocks with Binky; Arthur & the Popularity Test, Vol. 4. unabr. ed. Marc Brown. Read by Mark Linn-Baker. 2 cass. (Running Time: 2 hrs. 1 min.). (Arthur Chapter Bks.: No. 4). (J). (gr. 2-4). 2004. 23.00 (978-0-8072-8115-4(8), YA107CX, Listening Lib) Random Audio Pubg.
Arthur & the gang are back again in a brand new collection of their irrepressible adventures. Includes "Who's in Love with Arthur," "Arthur Rocks with BINKY" & "Arthur & the Popularity Contest".

Marca Terror. Doctor Who. 2 CDs. (Running Time: 1 hr. 35 mins.). 2001. audio compact disk 15.99 (978-0-563-47756-3(3)) London Brdge.

Marcel Dadi & Jean-Felix LaLanne Concert Solo. Marcel Dadi. Ed. by Jean-Felix Lalanne. Compiled by Jean-Felix Lalanne. 2001. bk. 22.95 (978-0-7866-4790-3(6)) Mel Bay.

Marcel Dadi/Fingerpicking Guitar Legend, Vol. 1. Marcel Dadi. 1997. spiral bd. 22.95 (978-0-7866-3142-1(2), 94851BCD) Mel Bay.

Marcel Dadi/Fingerpicking Guitar Legend, Vol. 2. Marcel Dadi. 1997. spiral bd. 22.95 (978-0-7866-3143-8(0), 95115BCD) Mel Bay.

Marcel Marceau Speaks in English. unabr. ed. Marcel Marceau. Perf. by Marcel Marceau. Perf. by William Fifield. 1 cass. 1984. 12.95 (978-0-694-50181-6(6), SWC 1255) HarperCollins Pubs.

Marcel Proust. Edmund White. Read by David Case. 1999. audio compact disk 32.00 (978-0-7366-5191-2(8)) Books on Tape.

Marcel Proust. unabr. ed. Edmund White. Read by David Case. 3 cass. (Running Time: 4 hrs.). 2000. 17.95 (978-0-7366-4692-5(2)) Books on Tape.
A clear & thorough history of Proust's life & then connects it to his writings. He fashions a monument of Proust the human being & helps us to much better understand his books.

Marcel Proust. unabr. ed. Edmund White. Read by David Case. 2001. audio compact disk Books on Tape.

Marcel Proust. unabr. collector's ed. Edmund White. Read by David Case. 3 cass. (Running Time: 4 hrs. 30 mins.). 1999. 28.00 (978-0-7366-4608-6(6), 4994) Books on Tape.

Marcel Proust a Paris, Set. Marcel Proust. Contrib. by Roland Barthes & Jean Montalbetti. 3 cass. (FRE.). 1991. 32.95 (1390-RF) Olivia & Hill.
Roland Barthes & Jean Montalbetti take us on three tours with Marcel Proust.

***Marcello: Sonata for Flute & Basso Continuo Op. 2 No. 7 in B-flat Major.** Composed by Benedetto Marcello. (ENG.). 2008. pap. bk. 19.95 (978-1-4234-5864-7(8), 1423458648) Pub: Dowani Intl LIE. Dist(s): H Leonard

***Marcelo in the Real World.** unabr. ed. Francisco X. Stork. Read by Lincoln Hoppe. 8 CDs. (Running Time: 10 hrs.). (YA). (gr. 8 up). 2009. audio compact disk 60.00 (978-0-7393-7991-2(7), Listening Lib) Pub: Random Audio Pubg. Dist(s): Random

Marcelo in the Real World. unabr. ed. Francisco X. Stork. Read by Lincoln Hoppe. (J). (gr. 9). 2009. audio compact disk 40.00 (978-0-7393-7989-9(5), Listening Lib) Pub: Random Audio Pubg. Dist(s): Random

March. E. L. Doctorow. 6 cds. 2005. audio compact disk 45.90 (978-1-4159-2420-4(1)) Pub: Books on Tape. Dist(s): NetLibrary CO

March. unabr. ed. E. L. Doctorow. 4 cass. 2005. 36.00 (978-1-4159-2419-8(8)) Books on Tape.

March. unabr. ed. E. L. Doctorow. Read by Joe Morton. 10 CDs. (Running Time: 40200 sec.). (ENG.). 2005. audio compact disk 39.95 (978-0-7393-2135-5(8)) Pub: Random Audio Pubg. Dist(s): Random

March: A Novel. unabr. ed. Geraldine Brooks. Read by Richard Easton. 2005. 29.95 (978-0-7927-3489-5(0), CMP 760); 29.95 (978-0-7927-3506-9(4), CMP 755); 54.95 (978-0-7927-3487-1(4), CSL 760); 59.95 (978-0-7927-3472-7(6), CSL 755); audio compact disk 89.95 (978-0-7927-3473-4(4), SLD 755) AudioGO.

March: A Novel. unabr. ed. Geraldine Brooks. (Running Time: 7 hrs.). (ENG.). (gr. 12 up). 2005. audio compact disk 39.95 (978-0-14-280092-8(9), PengAudBks) Penguin Grp USA.

***March in Country.** unabr. ed. E. E. Knight. Read by Christian Rummel. (Running Time: 11 hrs.). (Vampire Earth Ser.). 2010. 24.99 (978-1-4418-6810-7(0), 9781441868107, Brilliance MP3); 39.97 (978-1-4418-6811-4(9), 9781441868114, Brlnc Audio MP3 Lib); 39.97 (978-1-4418-6812-1(7), 9781441868121, BADLE) Brilliance Audio.

***March in Country.** unabr. ed. E. E. Knight. Read by Christian Rummel. (Running Time: 11 hrs.). (Vampire Earth Ser.). 2010. audio compact disk 92.97 (978-1-4418-6809-1(7), 9781441868091, BriAudCD Unabrid) Brilliance Audio.

***March in Country.** unabr. ed. E. E. Knight. Read by Christian Rummel. (Running Time: 11 hrs.). (Vampire Earth Ser.). 2010. audio compact disk 29.99 (978-1-4418-6808-4(9), 9781441868084, Bril Audio CD Unabri) Brilliance Audio.

March Melodies: Alto Saxophone. Arranged by Clark. (Playing with the Band Ser.). 2004. audio compact disk 12.95 (978-0-8258-5322-7(2)) Fischer Inc NY.

March Melodies: Clarinet. Arranged by Clark. (Playing with the Band Ser.). 2004. audio compact disk 12.95 (978-0-8258-5321-0(4)) Fischer Inc NY.

March Melodies: Trombone. Arranged by Clark. (Playing with the Band Ser.). 2004. audio compact disk 12.95 (978-0-8258-5324-1(9)) Fischer Inc NY.

March Melodies: Trumpet. Arranged by Clark. (Playing with the Band Ser.). 2004. audio compact disk 12.95 (978-0-8258-5323-4(0)) Fischer Inc NY.

March of Dimes Show. Perf. by Jack Benny et al. Hosted by Eddie Cantor. 1 cass. (Running Time: 1 hr.). 2001. 6.98 (2062) Radio Spirits.

March of Foll: From Troy to Vietnam. unabr. ed. Barbara W. Tuchman. Read by Grover Gardner. 12 cass. (Running Time: 18 hrs.). 1990. 96.00 (978-0-7366-1771-0(X), 2610) Books on Tape.
The folly of the title is a staple in human affairs. It would be of less concern were it restricted to mongoloids & geriatrics. But alas, it flourishes everywhere, not least in the halls of government. It is institutionalized folly against which the author inveighs. She quotes enough examples throughout history to make us uncomfortable in our own time, quickly running out, & very pessimistic about our children's. To make her case, Tuchman analyses the Trojan War, the splintering of Christendom, King George's misrule of his colonies in the 1770s, plus our own desperately inept Vietnamese War. What emerges is a chronicle of self-hypnosis, cynicism & concern about the competence of government, no matter whose & no matter where.

March of Folly: From Troy to Vietnam. unabr. ed. Barbara W. Tuchman. Read by Nadia May. (Running Time: 16 hrs. 50 mins.). (ENG.). 2009. 44.95 (978-1-4332-9510-2(5)); 89.95 (978-1-4332-9506-5(7)); audio compact disk 118.00 (978-1-4332-9507-2(5)) Blckstn Audio.

March of the Movies. 10.00 (MC1000) Esstee Audios.

March On! The Day My Brother Martin Changed the World. Christine King Farris. Narrated by Lynn Whitfield. Illus. by London Ladd. 1 CD. (Running Time: 18 mins.). (J). (gr. 2-7). 2008. bk. 29.95 (978-0-545-10689-4(3)); audio compact disk 12.95 (978-0-545-10685-6(0)) Weston Woods.

... March! the American Civil War: The 25 Unknown Battles. Short Stories. Gary C. Martin. Narrated by Luke Behan. 2 CDs. (Running Time: 2 hrs., 40 mins.). Dramatization. 2002. audio compact disk 9.95 (978-0-9721444-4-5(7)) Audio History.
From March 1 to March 15, 1862 the Blue & Gray engaged in 25, mostly unknown, battles in every theatre of the American Civil War. From the shores of Florida, Georgia & the Carolinas to the pine forests of Virginia all the way to Arkansas, the sounds of attack & defense shook the hopelessly divided population. ...march! tells the stories of these conflicts in the words of the participants themselves with sound effect & music background.

March to Glory. unabr. ed. Robert Leckie. Narrated by Tom West. 4 cass. (Running Time: 5 hrs. 30 mins.). 1981. 35.00 (978-1-55690-333-5(2), 81090E7) Recorded Bks.
In 1950 North Korea at the Chosin Reservoir were the date & site of one of the U. S. Marine's history's darkest chapters.

March to Glory. unabr. ed. Robert Leckie. Narrated by Tom West. 4 cass. (Running Time: 5 hrs. 30 mins.). 2002. 29.95 (978-0-7887-6448-6(9), RC997) Recorded Bks.
In November of 1950, the First Marine Division was trapped along a 75-mile corridor leading to Korea's Chosin Reservoir and had to fight its way out in one of the bloodiest and most miserable campaigns in American military history. This is their story.

March to the Sea. unabr. ed. David Weber & John Ringo. Read by Stefan Rudnicki. (Running Time: 68400 sec.). (March Upcountry Ser.). 2006. 85.95 (978-0-7861-4751-9(2)); audio compact disk 108.00 (978-0-7861-6335-9(6)); audio compact disk 29.95 (978-0-7861-7254-2(1)) Blckstn Audio.

March to the Stars. unabr. ed. David Weber & John Ringo. Read by Stefan Rudnicki. (Running Time: 17 mins. 30 sec.). (J). 2006. 89.95 (978-0-7861-4757-1(1)); audio compact disk 120.00 (978-0-7861-6341-0(0)) Blckstn Audio.

March to the Stars. unabr. ed. David Weber & John Ringo. Read by Stefan Rudnicki. (Running Time: 63000 sec.). (March Upcountry Ser.). 2006. audio compact disk 44.95 (978-0-7861-7260-3(6)) Blckstn Audio.

March to Tunis, Pt. I. unabr. ed. Alan Moorehead. Read by Ian Whitcomb. 10 cass. (Running Time: 10 hrs.). 1976. 60.00 (978-0-7366-0018-7(3), 1029) Books on Tape.
Brilliant, contempory history of WWII & the greatest tank battles of all time, in the North African desert.

March to Tunis, Pt. II. unabr. ed. Alan Moorehead. Read by Ian Whitcomb. 8 cass. (Running Time: 12 hrs.). 1976. 64.00 (978-0-7366-0023-1(X), 1034) Books on Tape.

March to Tunis, Pt. III. unabr. ed. Alan Moorehead. Read by Ian Whitcomb. 6 cass. (Running Time: 9 hrs.). 1976. 48.00 (978-0-7366-0025-5(6), 1037) Books on Tape.

March Upcountry. 2005. audio compact disk 120.00 (978-0-7861-7577-2(X)) Blckstn Audio.

March Upcountry. David Weber & John Ringo. Read by Stefan Rudnicki. (Running Time: 63000 sec.). (March Upcountry Ser.). 2005. 89.95 (978-0-7861-3793-0(2)) Blckstn Audio.

March Upcountry. unabr. ed. David Weber & John Ringo. Read by Stefan Rudnicki. (Running Time: 63000 sec.). (March Upcountry Ser.). 2005. audio compact disk 44.95 (978-0-7861-7852-0(3)) Blckstn Audio.

Marchen see Fairy Tale

***Marching for Freedom: Walk Together Children & Don't You Grow Weary: Walk Together Children & Don't You Grow Weary.** unabr. ed. Elizabeth Partridge. (Running Time: 2 hrs.). (YA). 2010. 24.99 (978-1-4418-6881-7(X), 9781441868817, BAD) Brilliance Audio.

***Marching for Freedom: Walk Together Children & Don't You Grow Weary: Walk Together Children & Don't You Grow Weary.** unabr. ed. Elizabeth Partridge. (Running Time: 2 hrs.). (YA). 2011. audio compact disk 49.97 (978-1-4418-6878-7(X), 9781441868787, BriAudCD Unabrid) Brilliance Audio.

***Marching for Freedom: Walk Together Children & Don't You Grow Weary: Walk Together Children & Don't You Grow Weary.** unabr. ed. Elizabeth Partridge. Read by Alan Bomar Jones. (Running Time: 2 hrs.). (YA). 2011. 24.99 (978-1-4418-6879-4(8), 9781441868794, Brilliance MP3); 39.97 (978-1-4418-6880-0(1), 9781441868800, Brlnc Audio MP3 Lib) Brilliance Audio.

***Marching for Freedom: Walk Together Children & Don't You Grow Weary: Walk Together Children & Don't You Grow Weary.** unabr. ed. Elizabeth Partridge. Read by Alan Bomar Jones. (Running Time: 2 hrs.). (YA). 2011. 39.97 (978-1-4418-6882-4(8), 9781441868824, BADLE) Brilliance Audio.

***Marching for Freedom: Walk Together Children & Don't You Grow Weary: Walk Together Children & Don't You Grow Weary.** unabr. ed. Elizabeth Patridge & Elizabeth Partridge. Read by Alan Bomar Jones. (Running Time: 2 hrs.). (YA). 2011. audio compact disk 24.99 (978-1-4418-6877-0(1), 9781441868770, Bril Audio CD Unabri) Brilliance Audio.

Marching On: Acts 13:16-52. Ed Young. 1998. 4.95 (978-0-7417-2180-8(5), A1180) Win Walk.

Marching Out of Time: The Fifes & Drums of Colonial Williamsburg. 1 CD. 2004. audio compact disk (978-1-931592-04-8(7)) Colonial Williamsburg.
The Fifes and Drums of Colonial Williamsburg are easily recognizable as the embodiment of Colonial Williamsburg's living history programs. The ensemble of Fifers and Drummers was raised in 1958 to support the military programs presented in the historic area. The young members usually spend nine years learning their art, both formally and phonetically, and graduate from the senior group when they graduate from high school. The music on this recording has been documented and researched as authentic to the colonial period, and has been arranged by staff members and members of the Fifes and Drums of Colonial Williamsburg.

***Marching Powder.** unabr. ed. Rusty Young. Read by Adrian Mulraney. (Running Time: 14 hrs. 1 min.). 2010. audio compact disk 103.95 (978-1-74214-743-7(7), 9781742147437) Pub: Bolinda Pubng AUS. Dist(s): Bolinda Pub Inc

Marching Season, unabr. ed. Daniel Silva. Narrated by Frank Muller. 8 cass. (Running Time: 11 hrs. 15 mins.). 1999. 75.00 (978-0-7887-3097-9(5), 95808E7) Recorded Bks.
Terrorists are moving to shatter the fragile Good Friday peace accord through a series of brutal assassinations. CIA officer Michael Osbourne's job is to stop their deadliest hit man.

Marching Season. unabr. ed. Daniel Silva. Narrated by Frank Muller. 10 CDs. (Running Time: 11 hrs. 15 mins.). 2000. audio compact disk 90.00 (978-0-7887-3972-9(7), C1009E7) Recorded Bks.

Marching Through Georgia: My Walk with Sherman. abr. ed. Jerry Ellis. Read by Jerry Ellis. (Running Time: 3 hrs.). 2008. 24.95 (978-1-4233-5941-8(0), 9781423359418, BAD); 24.95 (978-1-4233-5939-5(5), 9781423359395, Brilliance MP3); 39.25 (978-1-4233-5942-5(9), 9781423359425, BADLE); 39.25 (978-1-4233-5940-1(2), 9781423359401, Brlnc Audio MP3 Lib) Brilliance Audio.

***Marching to a Different Drummer.** Featuring Ravi Zacharias. 1996. audio compact disk 9.00 (978-1-61256-054-0(7)) Ravi Zach.

Marcia Southwick. unabr. ed. Read by Marcia Southwick. 1 cass. (Running Time: 29 min.). 1985. 10.00 New Letters.
One of a weekly half-hour radio program with authors talking & presenting their own works. Marcia Southwick reads from "What the Trees Go Into".

Marco Polo: From Venice to Xanadu. abr. ed. Laurence Bergreen. Read by Paul Boehmer. (Running Time: 36000 sec.). (ENG.). 2007. audio compact disk 34.95 (978-0-7393-5741-5(7), Random AudioBks) Pub: Random Audio Pubg. Dist(s): Random

Marco Polo, If You Can. unabr. collector's ed. William F. Buckley, Jr. Read by Michael Prichard. 8 cass. (Running Time: 8 hrs.). (Blackford Oakes Mystery Ser.). 1982. 48.00 (978-0-7366-0683-7(1), 1643) Books on Tape.
Oakes has just been cashiered from the Agency, when his boss decides he is the only man for an exceptionally dirty piece of work. Oakes agrees to return, but in short order finds himself standing before a secret soviet military tribunal which has as its subject his execution for spying.

Marco Polo, If You Can: A Blackford Oakes Mystery. unabr. ed. William F. Buckley Jr. Read by Geoffrey Blaisdell. (Running Time: 8 hrs. 0 mins.). 2009. 29.95 (978-1-4332-1617-6(5)); 54.95 (978-1-4332-1613-8(2)); audio compact disk 76.00 (978-1-4332-1614-5(0)) Blckstn Audio.

Marcos Dynasty. unabr. ed. Sterling Seagrave. Read by Geoffrey Howard. 13 cass. (Running Time: 19 hrs. 30 min.). 1997. 104.00 (978-0-7366-4055-8(X), 4566) Books on Tape.
This meticulously documented study reveals the criminality of the ex-dictator of the Phillippines & his wife.

Marcus Garvey. 1 cass. 10.00 (HB258) Esstee Audios.
The back to Africa movement.

mare au Diable. unabr. ed. George Sand. Read by Béatrice Pasquier. 2007. 69.99 (978-2-35569-027-3(8)) Find a World.

Mare au Diable, Set. George Sand. Read by Isabelle Bucaile. 2 cass. (FRE.). 1991. 26.95 (1287-H) Olivia & Hill.
This work published in 1846 represents George Sand's desire to bring the rural world into that of literature.

Mare au Diable: Level 1. George Sand. (FRE.). bk. 14.95 (978-2-09-032979-7(3), CL9793E) Pub: Cle Intl FRA. Dist(s): Continental Bk

Mare on the Hill. Thomas Locker. (J). 1987. bk. 42.60 (978-0-676-31615-5(8)) SRA McGraw.

Maressa & Merlone: A Musical Fairy Tale. unabr. ed. 2 cass. (Running Time: 1 hr. 45 mins.). (J). (gr. 1 up). 2001. 16.95 (978-0-9711377-0-7(6)) Heartfull Prod.
Princess Maressa is called on adventure to find a magical healing flower. Along the way she meets Merlone. Together they learn the magic of following your heart.

Marfan Syndrome - A Bibliography & Dictionary for Physicians, Patients, & Genome Researchers. Compiled by Icon Group International, Inc. Staff. 2007. ring bd. 28.95 (978-0-497-11254-7(X)) Icon Grp.

Marga, Comtesse de Palmyre. l.t. ed. Marie-Cecile De Tailac. (French Ser.). 2000. bk. 30.99 (978-2-84011-362-1(7)) Pub: UlverLrgPrint GBR. Dist(s): Ulverscroft US

Margaret Atwood. Interview with Margaret Atwood & Jan Castro. 1 cass. (Running Time: 55 min.). 1983. 13.95 (978-1-55644-063-2(4), 3012) Am Audio Prose.
Castro, editor of "River Styx", conducted this interview which covers a variety of issues pertinent to Atwood's Canadian Nationalism, feminism, themes & craft of individual novels & short stories.

Margaret Atwood Interview. 20.97 (978-0-13-090499-7(6)) P-H.

Margaret Atwood Presents: Stories by Canada's Best New Women Writers. unabr. ed. Ed. by Margaret Atwood. Contrib. by Canada's Best New Women Writers. 2 CDs. (Running Time: 2 hrs.). (ENG.). 2004. audio compact disk 19.95 (978-0-86492-388-2(0)) Pub: BTC Audiobks CAN. Dist(s): U Toronto Pr
Seven stories by seven up-and-coming Canadian women writers, handpicked by Canada's leading lady of fiction and read by noted women actors - this is the idea behind a compelling audio compilation of the best new short fiction. Margaret Atwood Presents features stories by Annabel Lyon, Caroline Adderson, Nancy Lee, Elise Levine, Lisa Moore, Kristi-Ly Green, and Sheila Heti. Brilliant, daring, funny, and frequently, these writers pull no punches when it comes to depicting society as they see it. In "Sally, In Parts," Nancy Lee from Vancouver explores a young woman's unusual relationship with her body. In "Cancer," Toronto writer Kristi-Ly Green describes a primary-school class's ambivalent responses towards a poor little rich girl. Lisa Moore of St. John's, Newfoundland, brings a haunting, sensuous intensity to a tale of love in "Haloes," while Toronto's Sheila Heti upends traditional forms in the sharp urban parable "The Princess and the Plumber." Vividly brought to life through the voices of Liisa Repo-Martell, Meg Ruffman, Chapelle Jaffe, Genevieve Steele, Sandra Oh, Juno Mills-Cockell, and Mary Lewis, these stories herald an exciting new generation of Canadian women writers.

Margaret Atwood's Textual Assassinations: Recent Poetry & Fiction. Ed. by Sharon Rose Wilson. 2003. audio compact disk 9.95 (978-0-8142-9012-5(4)) Pub: Ohio St U Pr. Dist(s): Chicago Distribution Ctr

Margaret Mead. Interview with Margaret Mead. 1 cass. (Running Time: 25 min.). 1969. 10.95 (L048) TFR.
The late anthropologist & social thinker talks about alternatives to war & states her view that there would be no truces if women were running them.

Margaret Mead. unabr. ed. Margaret Mead. 1 cass. (Author Speaks Ser.). 1991. 14.95 J Norton Pubs.
Archival recordings of 20th-century authors.

Margaret Mitchell's Atlanta: An Audio Driving Tour. Marianne L. Gardner. 1 cass. (Running Time: 90 mins.). 1999. 12.95 (978-0-9676290-0-1(4)) Ghost Tours.
Includes a map packaged like an audiobook. Describes places that Margaret Mitchell knew & the legendar Atlanta that she helped create.

Margaret O'Brien & Thomas Mitchell: The Angel with the Cold Nose & The Miracle at Christmas. unabr. ed. 1 cass. (Running Time: 60 min.). Dramatization. 7.95 Norelco box. (DD-8110) Natl Recrd Co.
The Angel with the Cold Nose: This is a Christmas story of a little girl who believes that angels don't have just wings...sometimes they have a cold nose. Add a lot of faith, mix with a good Christmas story & a miracle is certain to appear. The Miracle of Christmas: An auto accident leaves a wealthy man a cripple. George, his friend & neighbor has a little girl that is also a cripple. The two become very good friends & because of this close friendship, a miracle happens. A very happy ending to an emotional Christmas story.

Margaret Thatcher Pt. 1&2: The Downing Street Years 1979-1990. unabr. ed. Margaret Thatcher. Read by Donada Peters. 27 cass. (Running Time: 40 hrs. 30 mins.). 216.00 (978-0-7366-3303-1(0)) Books on Tape.
This gutsy memoir reveals the author's thoroughness, tenacity & passion for change.

Margaret Thatcher Pt. 2: The Downing Street Years. unabr. ed. Margaret Thatcher. Read by Donada Peters. 14 cass. (Running Time: 21 hrs.). 1996. 112.00 (3958-A); 104.00 (3958-B) Books on Tape.
Not since Winston Churchill has a British head of state had as influential a role in U.S. politics & world events as Margaret Thatcher. This gutsy memoir reveals her thoroughness, her tenacity & her passion for change. It reads like a thriller.

Margarita, Esta Linda la Mar. unabr. ed. Sergio Ramirez. Narrated by Francisco Rivela. 8 cass. (Running Time: 10 hrs. 30 mins.).Tr. of Margarita, How Beautiful the Sea. (ENG & SPA.). 1998. 79.75 (978-1-4025-7632-4(3), E1054MC, Griot Aud) Recorded Bks.

Margarita, How Beautiful the Sea see Margarita, Esta Linda la Mar

Margaritas & Murder. unabr. ed. Jessica Fletcher & Donald Bain. 5 cass. (Murder, She Wrote Ser.). 2005. 49.95 (978-0-7927-3544-1(7), Chivers Sound Lib) AudioGO.

Margaritas & Murder. unabr. ed. Jessica Fletcher et al. Read by Cynthia Darlow. 7 CDs. (Running Time: 24180 sec.). (Murder, She Wrote Ser.). 2005. audio compact disk 74.95 (978-0-7927-3828-2(4), Chivers Sound Lib) AudioGO.

Marge Piercy. Interview. Interview with Marge Piercy & Kay Bonetti. 1 cass. 1986. 13.95 (978-1-55644-168-4(1), 6112) Am Audio Prose.
Piercy talks about the structure of her novels, her soon-to-be-published holocaust novel & how plot develops for her out of her characters.

Marge Piercy. unabr. ed. Marge Piercy. Read by Marge Piercy. Interview with Robert Stewart. Prod. by Rebekah Presson. 1 cass. (Running Time: 29 min.). 1989. 10.00 (102789) New Letters.
Piercy is probably best-known as a fiction writer with such titles as" Woman on the Edge of Time" & "Gone to Soldiers". However, Piercy is also the author of 11 books of poetry. Here, she reads poems & talks about her dedication to social justice.

Margin of Error. abr. ed. Edna Buchanan. Read by Sandra Burr. 2 cass. (Running Time: 3 hrs.). (Britt Montero Mystery Ser.). 2000. 7.95 (978-1-57815-174-5(0), 1117, Media Bks Audio) Media Bks NJ.
A film crew is shooting on location, but more than one real killer is on the loose & stalking the films star, through the streets of Los Angeles.

Margin of Error. abr. ed. Edna Buchanan. Read by Sandra Burr. 3 CDs. (Running Time: 3 hrs.). (Britt Montero Mystery Ser.). (YA). 2000. audio compact disk 11.99 (978-1-57815-508-8(8), 1117 CD3, Media Bks Audio) Media Bks NJ.
A film crew is shooting on location but more than one real killer is on the loose & stalking the films star through the streets of Los Angeles.

Margin of Error. unabr. ed. Edna Buchanan. Narrated by Barbara Caruso. 9 CDs. (Running Time: 10 hrs. 45 mins.). (Britt Montero Mystery Ser.). 1999. audio compact disk 79.00 (978-0-7887-3424-3(5), C1030E7) Recorded Bks.
A staged explosion on a movie set misfires, sending Britt & the handsome leading man on a perilous search for the culprit.

Margin of Error. unabr. ed. Edna Buchanan. Narrated by Barbara Caruso. 8 cass. (Running Time: 10 hrs. 45 mins.). (Britt Montero Mystery Ser.). 1997. 75.00 (978-0-7887-1777-2(4), 95251E7) Recorded Bks.

Margin of Error. unabr. collector's ed. Edna Buchanan. Read by Anna Fields. 7 cass. (Running Time: 10 hrs. 30 min.). (Britt Montero Mystery Ser.). 1997. 56.00 (978-0-7366-3832-6(6), 4552) Books on Tape.
Brit Montero is a Miami reporter who suffers the effects of post-traumatic stress syndrome, reliving the moment she was forced to kill a man.

Marginal People. Michael A. Smith. Read by Andrew Nance. 7 cass. (Running Time: 9 hrs.). 2002. audio compact disk 34.95 (978-0-9724564-1-8(4)) First Coast Prod.
By circumstances of birth and choice, some people are on the outside, with their noses pressed against the glass of life. Richey Stanton is an aspiring actor who never made it beyond regional theater. His artist girlfriend, Carmen Salazar, bears the childhood scars inflicted by an alcoholic father. Marshon Johnson has overcome poverty and racism to become a criminal kingpin of the poverty-stricken East Side. He plans to liquidate his business and begin life anew in the Caribbean along with his girlfriend, Gail Thomas. Kandie Givens is a single mother of three recently transplanted to the city, where she ekes out a living as a waitress, and waits for her "prince on a white horse." She mistakenly thinks that a new arrival in town, Ace Semanski, will love and care for her and her children. Semanski, an ex-con and racist, is the catalyst who uses guile, blackmail, and murder to force the others to participate in a kidnapping/ransom plot. The efforts of these marginalized people to extricate themselves from this maelstrom makes some of them stronger, and cost others their lives.Marginal People is a psychological thriller and an examination of our society's values, and their impact on individual lives.

Marginal People. unabr. ed. Michael A. Smith. Read by Andrew Nance. 7 cass. (Running Time: 9 hrs.). 2002. 39.95 (978-0-9724564-0-1(6)) First Coast Prod.

Marginal Utility. John Robbins. 1 cass. (Introduction to Economics Ser.: No. 6). 5.00 Trinity Found.

Marguerite: Message of Merciful Love to Little Souls. 10 cass. 39.95 (914) Ignatius Pr.
Messages of Our Lord to a Belgian woman.

Marguerite Young. Interview. Interview with Marguerite Young & Kay Bonetti. 1 cass. (Running Time: 1 hr. 21 min.). 13.95 (978-1-55644-090-8(1), 3152) Am Audio Prose.
Young is completing a 2-volume biography of Eugene Debs. Interview includes discussion of Debs' biography; history & method of composition of "Miss MacIntosh" & Young's debt to the psychology & philosophy of William James.

Mari. unabr. ed. Jane Valentine Barker. Read by Juanita Parker. 6 cass. (Running Time: 7 hrs. 36 min.). 2001. 39.95 (978-1-55686-900-6(2)) Books in Motion.
Mari is a Nebraska Sandhills farm girl who seeks to carve a place for herself in a world ruled by the iron hand of her pioneer rancher-father.

Mari, Set. unabr. ed. Jane Valentine Barker. Read by Juanita Parker. 6 cass. 1999. 36.96 Books in Motion.
The true story of the turbulent relationship between famed Western author Mari Sandoz & her pioneering father, Jules Sandoz. Set in the Sandhills of northwest Nebraska in the early 1900's, the story brings to life the struggles between free-spirited Mari & her violent father as Mari seeks to carve a place for herself in a man's world.

Mari Gayatri - Meditation Towards Wholeness. Mari Gayatri. 1 cass. (Running Time: 1 hr.). 1987. 12.00 Gypsy Dog.
Guided meditation, breathing exercises, positive imagery, relaxation techniques, with uplifting music.

Maria. Jorge Isaacs. Read by Fabio Camero. (Running Time: 3 hrs.). 2001. 16.95 (978-1-60083-150-8(8), Audiofy Corp) Iofy Corp.

Maria. abr. ed. Scripts. Jorge Isaac. Read by Mayra Alejandra & Miguel De Leon. 2 CDs. (Running Time: 7200 sec.). Dramatization. (SPA.). 2006. audio compact disk 16.95 (978-1-933499-23-9(0)) Fonolibro Inc.
FonoLibro se enorgullece al presentar Maria, la obra cumbre de la novela romantica latinoamericana del prestigioso escritor colombiano Jorge Isaac.Maria fue publicada originalmente en 1867 y se convirtio en una de las novelas mas vendidas para su epoca. Hoy es una de las joyas de la literatura en espa?ol y latinoamericana que nadie debe dejar de conocer.

Maria. abr. ed. Jorge Isaacs. Read by Fabio Camero. 3 CDs.Tr. of Maria. (SPA.). 2001. audio compact disk 17.00 (978-958-9494-17-2(X)) YoYoMusic.

Maria Callas: The Scala Years. Vittoria Crespi Morbio. Told to Georges Pretre. 2008. bk. 70.00 (978-88-422-1560-8(0)) Pub: U Allemandi GBR. Dist(s): Natl Bk Netwk

Maria Callas - The 1958 Los Angeles Concert. Perf. by Maria Callas. Conducted by Nicola Rescigno. 1 cass. 16.99 (VAIA 1182) VAI Audio.

Maria Oliveira's Conversational Portuguese. Maria L. Oliveira. Read by Maria Oliveira & Keith Hezmahalch. 2 cass. (Running Time: 2 hrs.). (Series 2). (POR & ENG.). 1996. 19.95 Set. (978-1-888165-23-4(5)); 19.95 Set. (978-1-888165-25-8(1)) M Oliveira.
Covers greeting & farewell expressions, names of kitchen utensils, rooms of the house, women's & men's clothing as well as ar, er, & ir verb conjugations in the present of the indicative, direct object & complete sentences.

Maria Oliveira's Conversational Spanish, Series 1. unabr. ed. Maria L. Oliveira. Read by Maria Oliveira & Keith Hezmahaleh. 4 cass. (Running Time: 5 hrs.). 1994. 49.95 Set. (978-1-888165-00-5(6)) M Oliveira.
This bilingual album consists of five hours of basic Spanish vocabulary & grammar as well as basic greeting & farewell expressions, phrases & sentences.

Maria Oliveira's Conversational Spanish, Series 2. unabr. ed. Maria L. Oliveira. Read by Maria Oliveira & Keith Hezmahaleh. 4 cass. (Running Time: 4 hrs.). 1995. 39.95 Set. (978-1-888165-10-4(3)) M Oliveira.
This bilingual album consists of four hours of intermediate Spanish vocabulary & grammar. It covers verb conjugations in the present & preterit, positive & negative statements, idiomatic expressions & many irregular verbs.

Maria Oliveira's Ingles Basico. Maria L. Oliveira. Read by Maria L. Oliveira. Read by Norm Gonsalves. 2 cass. (Running Time: 2 hrs.). (Series 1). (POR & ENG.). 1997. 19.95 Set. (978-1-888165-33-3(2)) M Oliveira.
This bilingual album teaches basic English vocabulary to Portuguese speakers. Its content consists of numbers 1-1000, the names of the days, months & seasons, how to tell time & time expressions.

Maria Oliveira's Ingles Basico. Maria L. Oliveira. Read by Maria L. Oliveira. Read by Glen Cordon. 2 cass. (Running Time: 2 hrs.). (Series 2). (POR & ENG.). 1997. 19.95 Set. (978-1-888165-34-0(0)) M Oliveira.
Teaches basic English vocabulary & grammar to Portuguese speakers. Its content consists of the name of basic colors, family relationships, foods & beverages. The grammar consists of adjectives, nouns, articles, subject pronouns & verbs - to be & to have conjugated in the present. Sentence formation & a quiz are part of the oral practice exercises.

Maria Oliveira's Portuguese Vocabulary. Maria L. Oliveira. Read by Maria L. Oliveira. Read by Keith Hezmahalch. 2 cass. (Running Time: 2 hrs.). (Series 1). (POR & ENG.). 1996. 19.95 Set. (978-1-888165-20-3(0)) M Oliveira.
The oral lessons & exercises cover the letters of the alphabet, numbers 1-1000, the names of the days, months & seasons as well as how to tell time in Portuguese.

Mariachi Philharmonic (Mariachi in the Traditional String Orchestra) John Nieto & Bob Phillips. (ENG.). 2005. audio compact disk 10.95 (978-0-7390-3784-3(6)) Alfred Pub.

Mariachi... y Mas. Lonnie Dai Zovi. 1994. pap. bk. 31.50 (978-0-935301-77-9(1)) Vibrante Pr.

Mariachis! An Introduction to Mexican Mariachi Music. Patricia Harpole. Narrated by Patricia Harpole. Perf. by Mark Fogelquist. Contrib. by Mark Fogelquist. 1991. pap. bk. 16.95 (978-0-937203-79-8(3)) World Music Pr.

Mariachis! An Introduction to Mexican Mariachi Music. Patricia Harpole & Mark Fogelquist. Read by Patricia Harpole & Mark Fogelquist. Read by Mariachi Uclatan. 1 cass. (Running Time: 55 min.). (J). (gr. 4 up). 1989. 7.95 (978-0-937203-29-3(7)) World Music Pr.
Features narrative & performance by El Mariachi Uclatan of a wide variety of styles illustrating the range of music the typical mariachi plays & commenting on the instrumentation & history of the tradition. Must be purchased as set.

Mariachis! An Introduction to Mexican Mariachi Music. Patricia Harpole & Mark Fogelquist. Read by Patricia Harpole & Mark Fogelquist. Read by Mariachi Uclatan. 1 cass. (Running Time: 55 min.). (J). (gr. 4 up). 1989. pap. bk. 12.95 (978-0-937203-31-6(9)) World Music Pr.

Mariage. Diane Johnson. Narrated by Suzanne Toren. 10 CDs. (Running Time: 12 hrs.). 2001. audio compact disk 97.00 (978-0-7887-5167-7(0), C1329E7) Recorded Bks.
Struggling American writer Tim Nolinger pursues his journalism career in Paris while Frenchwoman Anne-Marie plans their wedding. Tim covers the theft of a valuable manuscript, which leads the couple to the local home of a reclusive American film director & his actress wife. Once there, Tim & Anne-Marie find themselves in the midst of a murder investigation, a French-American feud & a reckless love affair that threatens to destroy their marriage before it even begins.

Mariage. unabr. ed. Diane Johnson. Narrated by Suzanne Toren. 9 cass. (Running Time: 12 hrs.). 2000. 81.00 (978-0-7887-4365-8(1), 96343E7) Recorded Bks.
Comedy of Americans abroad & Parisians at home. When American journalist Tim Nolinger follows up a stolen manuscript, the story leads him & his French fiancee to the home of a film director. Suddenly they are plunged into a murder investigation & a reckless love affair that threaten to destroy their marriage before it begins.

Marian Devotion in the Catechism. Frederick Jelly. 1 cass. (Inspiring Presentations from the National Rosary Congress Ser.). 2.50 (978-1-56036-092-6(5)) AMI Pr.

Marian Doctrine in the Catechism. James McCurry. 1 cass. (Inspiring Presentations from the National Rosary Congress Ser.). 2.50 (978-1-56036-091-9(7)) AMI Pr.

Marian Mcpartland's Jazz World: All in Good Time. Marian McPartland. Read by Marian McPartland. (Running Time: 28800 sec.). 2006. 54.95 (978-0-7861-4554-6(4)); audio compact disk 55.00 (978-0-7861-7087-6(5)) Blckstn Audio.

Marian Mcpartland's Jazz World: All in Good Time. unabr. ed. Marian McPartland. Read by Marian McPartland. 6 cass. (Running Time: 28800 sec.). 2006. 29.95 (978-0-7861-4397-9(5)); audio compact disk 29.95 (978-0-7861-7441-6(2)); audio compact disk 29.95 (978-0-7861-7772-1(1)) Blckstn Audio.

Marian McPartland's Piano Jazz. Marian McPartland. 25 cass. (Running Time: 60 min. per cass.). 348.00 set. (HarperThor); 13.95 ea. (HarperThor) HarpC GBR.

Mariana. unabr. ed. Monica Dickens. Read by Jane Asher. 10 cass. (Running Time: 12 hrs. 45 min.). 1994. 84.95 (978-1-85089-497-1(3), 92023) Pub: ISIS Audio GBR. Dist(s): Ulverscroft US
It is feared that three of the seven officers, & twenty of the crew on the British destroyer Phantom have lost their lives. For a woman, waiting is the hardest part of war...As Mary waits to hear if her husband is alive, she remembers the startling joy of meeting Sam & the years that have led up to this evening - the crisis of her life.

Mariane Rust. unabr. ed. Mariane Rust. Ed. by James McKinley. Prod. by Rebeah Presson. 1 cass. (Running Time: 29 min.). (On the Air Ser.). 1993. 10.00 New Letters.
Interview, reads from Gatherings, novel based on Marshall Fields Family by granddaughter of Fields.

Marianela. Galdos. audio compact disk 12.95 (978-0-8219-3822-5(3)) EMC-Paradigm.

Marianela. Galdos Perez. (SPA.). pap. bk. 20.75 (978-88-7754-809-2(6)) Pub: Cideb ITA. Dist(s): Distribks Inc

Marianela. Benito Pérez Galdós. Read by Laura García. (Running Time: 3 hrs.). 2002. 16.95 (978-1-60083-247-5(4), Audiofy Corp) Iofy Corp.

Marianela. unabr. abr. ed. Benito Pérez Galdós. Read by Laura García. 3 CDs. (Running Time: 3 hrs.). (SPA.). 2002. audio compact disk 17.00 (978-958-8161-37-2(1)) YoYoMusic.
Uno de los más grandes escritores españoles del siglo XIX, Pérez Galdós creó en "Marianela" la triste historia de una muchacha campesina, lazarillo de un joven ciego, que cree que ella reúne todas las bondades y la belleza, cuando lo cierto es que Marianela es bastante fea. En una intervención quirúrgica el muchacho logra recobrar la vista y eso hace que el mundo de la joven caiga en ruin.

Marianne, Level 3. (Yamaha Clavinova Connection Ser.). 2004. disk 0.82 (978-0-634-09599-3(4)) H Leonard.

Marianne Moore. Contrib. by Unapix Inner Dimension Staff. 1 cass. 1997. 10.95 (978-1-57523-166-2(2)) Unapix Enter.

Marianne Moore. unabr. ed. Marianne Moore. 1 cass. (Author Speaks Ser.). 1991. 14.95 J Norton Pubs.
Archival recordings of 20th-century authors.

Marianne Moore Reading Her Poems & Fables from La Fontaine. abr. ed. Marianne Moore. 1 cass. 1984. 12.95 (978-0-694-50021-5(6), SWC 1025) HarperCollins Pubs.

Marianne Moore Reads Her Poetry. unabr. ed. Marianne Moore. Read by Marianne Moore. 1 cass. (Running Time: 22 min.). 1965. 12.95 (23044) J Norton Pubs.

Marianne Williamson Collection, Set. unabr. ed. Marianne Williamson. Read by Marianne Williamson. 4 cass. (Running Time: 6 hrs.). 1993. 39.00 (978-1-55994-974-3(0), BGS 002, Harper Audio) HarperCollins Pubs.

Marianne Williamson Live! Marianne Williamson. 6 cass. (Running Time: 6 hrs.). 1995. 59.95 (978-1-55525-055-3(6), 10690A) Nightingale-Conant.
This series captures Williamson at her best - in front of a live audience - offering her uplifting interpretation of A Course in Miracles. This program teaches a shift in thinking which leads to radical inner transformation. Discover how to take responsibility for your own emotional support. Build self-esteem. Maintain a sense of connectedness. And improve interpersonal communications.

Marianne Williamson on Meditation & Prayer. unabr. ed. 1 cass. (Running Time: 80 min.). 1996. 12.00 (978-0-694-51635-3(X), DCN 10050) HarperCollins Pubs.

Marianne Williamson on Transforming Your Life. unabr. abr. ed. Marianne Williamson. Read by Marianne Williamson. 1 cass. (Running Time: 90 min.). 1996. 12.00 (978-0-694-51625-4(2), CPN 10074, Harper Audio) HarperCollins Pubs.

Marianne Williamson Relationships Workshop, Set. Marianne Williamson. 2 cass. (Running Time: 2 hrs.). 1994. 19.95 (978-1-879323-14-8(1)) Sound Horizons AV.
Meditations, exercises & Marianne lecturing at her best.

Marie. H. Rider Haggard. Read by Shelly Frasier. (Running Time: 10 hrs.). 2001. 29.95 (978-1-60083-595-7(3), Audiofy Corp) Iofy Corp.

Marie. H. Rider Haggard. Read by Shelly Frasier. (Zulu (Tantor) Ser.). (ENG.). 2005. audio compact disk 90.00 (978-1-4001-3023-8(9)) Pub: Tantor Media. Dist(s): IngramPubServ

Marie. unabr. ed. H. Rider Haggard. Read by Shelly Frasier. 9 CDs. (Running Time: 10 hrs. 7 mins). (Zulu (Tantor) Ser.). (ENG.). 2001. audio compact disk 45.00 (978-1-4001-0023-1(2)); audio compact disk 23.00 (978-1-4001-5023-6(X)) Pub: Tantor Media. Dist(s): IngramPubServ

Marie. unabr. ed. H. Rider Haggard. Narrated by Shelly Frasier. (Running Time: 10 hrs. 0 mins. 0 sec.). (Zulu Ser.). (ENG.). 2009. audio compact disk 32.99 (978-1-4001-1098-8(X)); audio compact disk 65.99 (978-1-4001-4098-5(6)); audio compact disk 22.99 (978-1-4001-6098-3(7)) Pub: Tantor Media. Dist(s): IngramPubServ

Marie & Pierre Curie: A Concise Biography. unabr. ed. John E. Senior. Read by Anita Wright. 2 cass. (Running Time: 2 hrs. 20 min.). 1999. 24.95 (978-0-7531-0572-6(1), 990216) Pub: ISIS Audio GBR. Dist(s): Ulverscroft US
Marie & Pierre Curie were pioneers in the study of radioactivity, achieving world renown for their Nobel Prize-winning discovery of radium & polonium. After Pierre's death, Marie succeeded him in the chair of physics at the Sorbonne & was awarded a second Nobel Prize.

Marie Antoinette. unabr. ed. Antonia Fraser. Read by Donada Peters. 15 cass. (Running Time: 22 hrs. 30 mins.). 2001. 120.00 (978-0-7366-8308-1(9)) Books on Tape.
The Marie Antoinette of "Let them eat cake!" is no more. Then again, like much of what is common knowledge about her, that persona was the work of scandal-mongering pamphleteers who mocked and magnified the French queen's youth, her sexual liabilities, and her innocence. Antonia Fraser delivers a much more nuanced portrait of Marie Antoinette, which avoids turning her either into a romantic ingenue or into a misogynist's lurid fantasy.

Marie Antoinette: The Journey. unabr. ed. Antonia Fraser. Read by Donada Peters. (YA). 2006. 59.99 (978-0-7393-7511-2(3)) Find a World.

Marie Antoinette: The Journey. unabr. ed. Antonia Fraser. Read by Donada Peters. (Running Time: 73800 sec.). (ENG.). 2006. audio compact disk 39.95 (978-0-7393-4006-6(9), Random AudioBks) Pub: Random Audio Pubg. Dist(s): Random

Marie Antoinette: The Last Queen of France. abr. movie tie-in unabr. ed. Evelyne Lever. Read by Lorna Raver. 12 CDs. (Running Time: 52200 sec.). 2006. audio compact disk 24.95 (978-0-7861-7237-5(1)) Blckstn Audio.

Marie-Antoinette: The Last Queen of France. abr. movie tie-in unabr. ed. Evelyne Lever. Read by Lorna Raver. 9 cass. (Running Time: 52200 sec.). 2006. 24.95 (978-0-7861-4491-4(2)) Blckstn Audio.

Marie Antoinette: The Last Queen of France. unabr. ed. Evelyne Lever. Read by Lorna Raver. (Running Time: 52200 sec.). 2006. 72.95 (978-0-7861-4709-0(1)); audio compact disk 99.00 (978-0-7861-6584-1(7)) Blckstn Audio.

Marie Antoinette: The Last Queen of France. unabr. movie tie-in ed. Evelyne Lever. Read by Lorna Raver. (Running Time: 52200 sec.). 2006. audio compact disk 29.95 (978-0-7861-7665-6(2)) Blckstn Audio.

Marie Curie & Radioactivity. Connie Colwell Miller. Illus. by Scott Larson & Mark Heike. (Inventions & Discovery Ser.). (ENG.). (gr. 3-4). 2007. audio compact disk 6.95 (978-1-4296-1118-3(9)) CapstoneDig.

Marie Curie & Radioactivity (INK Audiocassette) (Inventions & Discovery Ser.). (ENG.). 2007. audio compact disk 5.95 (978-0-7368-7992-7(7)) CapstoneDig.

Marie, Dancing. Carolyn Meyer. Read by Carine Montbertrand. 6. (Running Time: 7 hrs. 25 mins.). 2007. 61.75 (978-1-4281-3507-9(3)); audio compact disk 87.75 (978-1-4281-3512-3(X)) Recorded Bks.

Marie Hare of Strathadam, NB, Canada. 1 cass. 9.98 (C-9) Folk-Legacy.
The broadside ballad tradition of the Maritimes.

***Mariel Hemingway's Healthy Living from the Inside Out.** abr. ed. Mariel Hemingway. Read by Mariel Hemingway. (ENG.). 2006. (978-0-06-134429-9(X), Harper Audio); (978-0-06-134430-5(3), Harper Audio) HarperCollins Pubs.

***Mariel Hemingway's Healthy Living from the Inside Out.** unabr. ed. Mariel Hemingway. Read by Mariel Hemingway. (ENG.). 2007. (978-0-06-137388-6(5), Harper Audio) HarperCollins Pubs.

Mariel Hemingway's Healthy Living from the Inside Out: Every Woman's Guide to Real Beauty, Renewed Energy, & a Radiant Life. abr. ed. Mariel Hemingway. Read by Mariel Hemingway. (Running Time: 21600 sec.). 2007. audio compact disk 29.95 (978-0-06-122727-1(7)) HarperCollins Pubs.

Mariel of Redwall. unabr. ed. Brian Jacques. 9 cass. (Running Time: 11 hrs. 45 mins.). (Redwall Ser.). (YA). 2004. 79.75 (978-1-4025-1793-8(9)) Recorded Bks.
In Mariel of Redwall, he tells the tale of two mice, Joseph the Bellmaker and his daughter who are separated when the rat pirate king, Gabool the Wild, raids their ship. Mariel vows to find her father and recover the prized bell Gabool stole from their treasure.

Mariel of Redwall. unabr. ed. Brian Jacques. Narrated by Brian Jacques. 10 CDs. (Running Time: 11 hrs. 30 mins.). (Redwall Ser.). 2004. audio compact disk 29.99 (978-1-4025-8738-2(4), 02482) Recorded Bks.
The tale of two mice, Joseph the Bellmaker and his daughter Mariel, who are separated when the rat pirate king, Gabool the Wild, raids their ship. Mariel vows to find her father and recover the prized bell Gabool stole from their treasure.

Marienleben see Poetry of Rainer Maria Rilke

Marietta Becker: Blinde Eifersucht. unabr. ed. 3 cass. (Running Time: 3 hrs.). (GER.). 34.95 (SGE325) J Norton Pubs.
A young woman who cares for a rich old woman meets two men who pursue her in an atmosphere of live, lies & intrigue.

Mariette in Ecstasy: A Novel. unabr. ed. Ron Hansen. Narrated by Barbara Caruso. 5 cass. (Running Time: 6 hrs. 30 mins.). 1998. 44.00 (978-0-7887-1881-6(9), 95303E7) Recorded Bks.
Set in upstate New York at the turn of the century, this young woman's journey of faith will inspire listeners to examine their beliefs.

Marigold & Grandma on the Town. unabr. ed. Stephanie Calmenson. Narrated by Barbara Caruso. 1 cass. (Running Time: 15 mins.). (I Can Read Bks.). (gr. k up). 1999. 10.00 (978-0-7887-3204-1(8), 95654E7) Recorded Bks.
In spite of Marigold's best efforts to please her grandmother during their special day together in town, the young bunny keeps running into trouble. Will Grandma still think she is wonderful when the day is through?.

Marigold & Grandma on the Town. unabr. ed. Stephanie Calmenson. Narrated by Barbara Caruso. 1 cass. (Running Time: 15 mins.). (I Can Read Bks.). (J). (gr. 1-3). 1999. pap. bk. & stu. ed. 22.00 (978-0-7887-3172-3(6), 40907X4) Recorded Bks.

Marigold & Grandma on the Town, Class set. unabr. ed. Stephanie Calmenson. Read by Barbara Caruso. 1 cass. (Running Time: 15 mins.). (J). (gr. k up). 1999. 68.30 (978-0-7887-3218-8(8), 46874) Recorded Bks.

Marigold & the Dark. Annie O'Dowd. Read by Annie O'Dowd. (Running Time: 1 hr. 20 mins.). (seadog Adventure 2: Ser.). (J). 2009. 34.99 (978-1-74214-168-8(4), 9781742141688) Pub: Bolinda Pubng AUS. Dist(s): Bolinda Pub Inc

Marigold & the Dark. unabr. ed. Annie O'Dowd. Read by Annie O'Dowd. (Running Time: 1 hr. 20 mins.). (seadog Adventure 2: Ser.). (J). 2008. audio compact disk 39.95 (978-1-74214-038-4(6), 9781742140384) Pub: Bolinda Pubng AUS. Dist(s): Bolinda Pub Inc

Marigold Field. unabr. ed. Diane Pearson. Read by Patricia Gallimore. 10 cass. (Running Time: 11 hrs. 30 mins.). (Soundings Ser.). (J). 2006. 84.95 (978-1-84559-244-8(1)) Pub: ISIS Lrg Prnt GBR. Dist(s): Ulverscroft US

Marijuana. David L. Ohlms. Read by David L. Ohlms. Ed. by JoAnn Moore. 1 cass. (Running Time: 1 hr.). 1994. 10.95 (978-1-56168-002-3(8), A9403) GWC Inc.
Marijuana use is beginning to show an intractable stability in the 1990s. Some experts believe the drug has achieved a level of acceptability on a par with alcohol. Still the dangers of the drug remain, particularly to those with abuse & addiction problems. In this update, Dr. Ohlms explains the hazards of marijuana use with eye-opening references to potential physical & mental damage.

Marijuana: Pro & Con. unabr. ed. Alan N. Schoonmaker. 1 cass. (Running Time: 24 min.). 12.95 (35005) J Norton Pubs.
An analysis of the scientific evidence on the effects of marijuana & consequences of its legalization or prohibition.

Marijuana & the Goddess. unabr. ed. Stephen Post. 1 cass. 1987. 9.00 (978-1-56964-164-4(1), A0103-86) Sound Photosyn.
A scholarly tribute from a geomancer.

Marilyn Hacker. Read by Marilyn Hacker. (Running Time: 29 min.). 1985. 10.00 New Letters.
The author reads from "Presentation Pieces" & "Separations".

Marilyn Monroe. collector's ed. Barbara Leaming. Read by Julia Delfino. 12 cass. (Running Time: 18 hrs.). 1999. 96.00 (978-0-7366-4730-4(9), 5068) Books on Tape.
A sympathetic portrait that will totally change the view & the most enduring icon of American sexuality & the complexities in Marilyn's life.

Marilyn Monroe: A Concise Biography. unabr. ed. Sheridan Morley & Ruth Leon. Read by Sheridan Morley. 2 cass. (Running Time: 2 hrs. 15 mins.). (Pocket Biography Ser.). (J). 2001. 24.95 (978-0-7531-0333-3(8), 980516) Pub: ISIS Lrg Prnt GBR. Dist(s): Ulverscroft US
Marilyn Monroe was born Norma Jean Baker in Los Angeles in 1926, the illegitimate child of a salesman; when she died aged 36, from a drug overdose, she was perhaps the greatest star in the history of motion pictures. After an unhappy childhood, Marilyn became a photographer's model & spotted by Howard Hughes, was signed up by Twentieth Century Fox. In the 1950's she played in a series of highly successful comedies, but exploited as a sex symbol, her personal life deteriorated. Her marriage to baseball player Joe DiMaggio quickly collapsed & her relationship with playwright Arthur Miller (who wrote "The Misfits" for her) came under severe strain as her bent for self-destruction, which would end with her death, began to overwhelm both.

Marilyn Monroe: The Biography. unabr. ed. Donald Spoto. Read by Anna Fields. 16 cass. (Running Time: 23 hrs. 30 mins.). 1996. 99.95 (978-0-7861-0984-5(X), 1761) Blckstn Audio.
More than thirty years after her death, Marilyn Monroe still beguiles the world & her image enthralls millions. Many books have attempted to explain her allure & tell her story, but none has succeeded...until this.

Marilyn Monroe: The Biography. unabr. ed. Donald Spoto. Read by Anna Fields. 16 cass. (Running Time: 24 hrs.). 1996. 99.95 (1761) Blckstn Audio.
Exhaustive research uncovers a conspiracy of silence, which allows the facts to be presented free from often-repeated myths & speculation. The truth emerges & provides a moving, often shocking picture of the real Monroe - including the horrifying, bizarre truth about how she really died.

Marilynne Robinson. unabr. ed. Marilynne Robinson. Read by Marilynne Robinson. 1 cass. (Running Time: 29 min.). 1989. 10.00 New Letters.
Robinson reads from the novel Housekeeping & is interviewed.

Marilynne Robinson: Interview with Marilynne Robinson & Kay Bonetti. unabr. ed. Marilynne Robinson. 1 cass. 1989. 13.95 (978-1-55644-329-9(3), 9032) Am Audio Prose.

Marina Rust. unabr. ed. Ed. by Jim McKinley. Prod. by Rebekah Presson. 1 cass. (Running Time: 29 min.). (New Letters on the Air Ser.). 1994. 10.00 (043093) New Letters.
Rust's first novel, "Gatherings," has the world of high society in a flutter. Based loosely on her own life as heiress to the Marshall Fields family fortune, Rust's novel has been critically acclaimed as "an elegant, perfectly controlled novel," & the story has caught the attention of "Vanity Fair" & other magazines.

Marine! The Life of Lt. General Lewis B. "Chesty" Puller. unabr. collector's ed. Burke Davis. Read by Dick Estell. 10 cass. (Running Time: 15 hrs.). 1990. 80.00 (978-0-7366-1691-1(8), 2538) Books on Tape.
General Puller's story is one of the great narratives of our military history as well as one of the most instructive. No modern American general has been so candid in his criticism of our military posture, policy, aims & equipment. Thus this book is as much memoir as biography, based largely on a series of interviews with the general.

Marine Biologist. 1 cass. (Science Ser.). (J). bk. Incl. 24p. bk. (TWIN 423) NewSound.
Learn about whales, dolphins, sea turtles, manatees & other animals that live in the ocean.

Marine Corps Way: Using Maneuver Warfare to Lead a Winning Organization. Eric K. Clemons. 4 CDs. 2004. audio compact disk 28.00 (978-1-932378-59-7(6)) Pub: A Media Intl. Dist(s): Natl Bk Netwk

Marine Mammals & Bighorn Sheep. Hosted by Nancy Pearlman. 1 cass. (Running Time: 29 min.). 10.00 (407) Educ Comm CA.

Marine One. unabr. ed. James W. Huston. (Running Time: 10 hrs. 0 mins.). 2009. 29.95 (978-1-4332-2745-5(2)); audio compact disk 24.95 (978-1-4332-2744-8(4)) Blckstn Audio.

Marine One. unabr. ed. W. James Huston. (Running Time: 10 hrs. 0 mins.). (ENG.). 2009. 59.95 (978-1-4332-2741-7(X)); audio compact disk 80.00 (978-1-4332-2742-4(8)) Blckstn Audio.

Marine Planarians of the World. R. Sluys. 1996. audio compact disk 137.00 (978-3-540-14192-1(8)) Spri.

Marine Sniper. unabr. ed. Charles Henderson. Read by Kevin Foley. 8 cass. (Running Time: 10 hrs. 30 min.). 2001. 49.95 (978-1-55686-887-0(1)) Books in Motion.
As an expert marksman, Marine Gunnery Sergeant Carlos Hathcock is assigned to disrupt the Viet Cong behind enemy lines.

Marines Don't Hold Their Horses. unabr. collector's ed. Ian Skidmore. Read by Bill Kelsey. 5 cass. (Running Time: 5 hrs.). 1987. 30.00 (978-0-7366-1185-5(1), 2105) Books on Tape.
World War II produced many heroes whose exploits were little known to the public. One of these was Alan Warren, a Colonel of British marines. He took the war behind enemy lines & when captured, was a thorn in the flesh of his Japanese guards.

Mario & the Magician see Mario y el Mago

Mario & the Magician. Thomas Mann. Read by Laura García. (Running Time: 3 hrs.). 2002. 16.95 (978-1-60083-242-0(3), Audiofy Corp) Iofy Corp.

***Mario Escudero - the Glory of Flamenco Guitar: Mario Escudero Gloria de la Guitarra Flamenca.** Mario Escudero. (ENG., 2009. pap. bk. 49.99 (978-84-934729-9-3(9)) AcordesCon ESP.

Mario y el Mago. abr. ed. Thomas Mann. Read by Laura García. 3 CDs.Tr. of Mario & the Magician. (SPA.). 2002. audio compact disk 17.00 (978-958-8161-27-3(4)) YoYoMusic.

Marion Fay. Anthony Trollope. Narrated by Flo Gibson. 2007. 42.95 (978-1-55685-889-5(2)) Audio Bk Con.

Marion Weinstein Stand-up Witch: Live at the Village Gate! unabr. ed. Marion Weinstein. Read by Marion Weinstein. 1 cass. (Running Time: 51 min.). 1989. 9.95 (978-0-9604128-8-4(3)) Earth Magic.
Live performance of Marion Weinstein's unique comedy act. Includes stories about being a witch in the public eye for over 25 years.

Marion Winik Live: Advice & Inspiration for Personal Essayists. Marion Winik. Read by Marion Winik. 3 CDs. (Running Time: 3 hrs.). 2001. audio compact disk 21.95 Penton Overseas.

Marion Winik Live: Advice & Inspiration for Personal Essayists. Marion Winik. 3 CDs. (Running Time: 3 hrs.). 2001. audio compact disk 21.95 (978-1-880717-46-2(8), 829-040) Writers AudioShop.
Teaches you to transform your (possibly) self-indulgent, boring collection of words into literature that achieves universality.

Marion Winik Live: Advice & Inspiration for Personal Essayists. Marion Winik. Read by Marion Winik. 2 cass. (Running Time: 3 hrs.). (ENG.). 2001. 18.95 (978-1-880717-44-8(1)) Writers AudioShop.

Marion Zimmer Bradley's Sword of Avalon. unabr. ed. Diana L. Paxson. Narrated by Lorna Raver. 2 MP3-CDs. (Running Time: 17 hrs. 0 mins. 0 sec.). (Avalon Ser.). (ENG.). 2009. 29.99 (978-1-4001-6187-4(8)); audio compact disk 79.99 (978-1-4001-4187-6(7)); audio compact disk 39.99 (978-1-4001-1187-9(0)) Pub: Tantor Media. Dist(s): IngramPubServ

***Marion Zimmer Bradley's Sword of Avalon.** unabr. ed. Diana L. Paxson. Narrated by Lorna Raver. (Running Time: 17 hrs. 0 mins.). 2009. 39.99 (978-1-4001-9187-1(4)); 21.99 (978-1-4001-8187-2(9)) Tantor Media.

Marionettes, Inc. see Fantastic Tales of Ray Bradbury

Mariposa. Perf. by Juanita Newland Ulloa. 1 CD. (Running Time: 90 mins.). (SPA & ENG.). 2000. audio compact disk 17.00 Ulloa Prods.
Bilingual collection of original songs & traditional lullabies from various Latin American cultures.

***Mariposa: A Quantico Novel.** unabr. ed. Greg Bear. Narrated by Charles Leggett. 1 Playaway. (Running Time: 11 hrs. 27 mins.). 2009. 94.95 (978-0-7927-6816-6(7)); 59.95 (978-0-7927-6815-9(9)); audio compact disk 94.95 (978-0-7927-6814-2(0)) AudioGO.

Marital Check-up. Steven G. Pittman. 1 cass. (Running Time: 20 min.). 1994. bk. & wbk. ed. 149.95 (978-0-9670678-0-3(4)) S G Pittman.
Used by couples to enhance their relationship & improve communication.

Marital Deduction Trusts. 1 cass. (Running Time: 50 min.). 1993. 95.00 Incl. study guide. (Y506) Am Law Inst.
Examines the types, structure, & drafting plus related complex tax issues.

Marital Privileges: 1 Cor. 7:1-7. Ed Young. 1986. 4.95 (978-0-7417-1495-4(7), 495) Win Walk.

Marital Relationships Seminar. Douglas A. Brinley. 4 cass. 16.98 incl. 24-page booklet. (978-1-55503-532-7(9), 090050) Covenant Comms.
Best help available for couples.

Marital Relationships Seminar. Douglas E. Brinley. 4 cass. 2004. 19.95 (978-1-57734-779-8(X)); audio compact disk 24.95 (978-1-57734-780-4(3)) Covenant Comms.

Marital Relationships Seminar, Set. Douglas A. Brinley. 4 cass. 19.95 (978-1-57734-150-5(3), 0900133) Covenant Comms.
Updated release for this popular marriage enrichment seminar.

Marjorie Daw. unabr. ed. Thomas Bailey Aldrich. Read by Walter Zimmerman & Jim Killavey. 1 cass. (Running Time: 47 min.). Dramatization. 1983. 7.95 (S-42) Jimcin Record.
Humorous story of a manufactured mistress.

Marjorie Kinnan Rawlings Short Stories. unabr. ed. Short Stories. Marjorie Kinnan Rawlings. Read by Melissa Hughes. 4 cass. (Running Time: 4 hrs.). (Voices Ser.: Bk. 3). 1995. 26.95 (978-1-883332-16-7(8), 492854) Audio Bkshelf.
Here is the only collection of Rawlings' short stories in audio format. In these eight stories, Rawlings paints a precise portrait of Florida in the 30's & 40's - a portrait brushed with humor, dignity & uncanny insightfulness.

Marjorie Morningstar, Pt. 1. unabr. ed. Herman Wouk. Read by Michael Prichard. 8 cass. (Running Time: 12 hrs.). Incl. Pt. 2. Marjorie Morningstar. 10 cass. (Running Time: 15 cass.). Herman Wouk. Read by Michael Prichard. 80.00 (1321-B); 1983. 64.00 (978-0-7366-0334-8(4), 1321-A) Books on Tape.
A boy & girl, both raised in Jewish families proud of their ancestry & culture, deny as young adults their background, symbolized by changing their names. Marjorie Morningstar falls in love with Noel Airman & struggles to become an actress: interwoven is her struggle against her environment, typical of adolescents everywhere.

Mark see Twentieth-Century Poetry in English, No. 2, Recordings of Poets Reading Their Own Poetry

Mark. Michael Pearl. 1 cd. (Running Time: 17 hrs). 2006. (978-1-892112-90-3(6)) No Greater Joy.

Mark: An Experience in Sound & Drama. unabr. adpt. ed. Tim LaHaye & Jerry B. Jenkins. 4 CDs. (Running Time: 4 hrs. 30 min.). (Left Behind Ser.: No. 8). (ENG., 2002. audio compact disk 19.99 (978-0-8423-4342-8(3)) Tyndale Hse.

Mark: The Beast Rules the World. Tim LaHaye & Jerry B. Jenkins. Narrated by Frank Muller. 7 CDs. (Running Time: 8 hrs. 45 mins.). (Left Behind Ser.: Bk. 8). 2001. audio compact disk 69.00 (978-0-7887-4969-8(2), C1314E7) Recorded Bks.
Now that the beast rules the world, everyone must decide whether to receive the mark of the beast, or die.

Mark: The Beast Rules the World. Tim LaHaye & Jerry B. Jenkins. Read by Frank Muller. 7 CDs. (Running Time: 8 hrs. 45 mins.). (Left Behind Ser.: Bk. 8). 2004. audio compact disk 39.95 (978-0-7887-4971-1(4), 00012) Recorded Bks.

Mark: The Beast Rules the World. unabr. ed. Tim LaHaye & Jerry B. Jenkins. Read by Jack Sondericker. 8 cass. (Running Time: 10 hrs.). (Left Behind Ser.: Bk. 8). 2001. 49.95 (978-1-58116-103-8(4)); audio compact disk 58.50 (978-1-58116-132-8(8)) Books in Motion.
Nicolae Carpathia returns to power. With the technological means of domination at his disposal, Carpathia has instituted a mandate that all subjects receive the mark to be able to buy, sell or trade in the new global economy. The Tribulation Force must race against the clock to outwit Carpathia's plan.

Mark: The Beast Rules the World. unabr. ed. Tim LaHaye & Jerry B. Jenkins. Read by Frank Muller. 1 cass. (Running Time: 1 hr. 30 mins.). (Left Behind Ser.: Bk. 8). 2001.; audio compact disk Books on Tape.

Mark: The Beast Rules the World. unabr. ed. Tim LaHaye & Jerry B. Jenkins. Narrated by Frank Muller. 6 cass. (Running Time: 8 hrs. 45 mins.). (Left Behind Ser.: Bk. 8). 2000. 59.00 (978-0-7887-4846-2(7), 96448E7) Recorded Bks.
The latest & greatest in the biggest selling inspirational series of all time. Now that the beast rules the world, everyone must decide whether to receive the mark of the beast or die. The Tribulation Force is pursued on every side as they fight for the faithful.

Mark: The Beast Rules the World. unabr. ed. Tim LaHaye & Jerry B. Jenkins. Read by Frank Muller. 5 cass. (Running Time: 8 hrs. 45 mins.). (Left Behind Ser.: Bk. 8). 2004. 29.95 (978-0-7887-4970-4(6), 00014) Recorded Bks.
Those who were left behind after the Rapture must now make a crucial decision. Each person must choose whether to receive the mark of the beast, or die.

Mark Amerika. unabr. ed. Ed. by Jim McKinley. Prod. by Rebeka Presson. 1 cass. (Running Time: 29 min.). (New Letters on the Air Ser.). 1994. 10.00 (050294) New Letters.
Amerika publishes a series of "experimental" novels under the "Black Ice" imprint. The Colorado author's own "ribald, caustic, controversial & inspirational" book, "The Kafka Chronicles" is part of the series. Amerika talks about it & his connections to "Generation X" writing.

Mark Commentary. Chuck Missler. 1 MP3 CD-ROM. (Running Time: 16 hours). (Chuck Missler Commentaries). 2001. cd-rom 39.95 (978-1-57821-164-7(6)) Koinonia Hse.
*And forthwith, when they were come out of the synagogue, they entered into the house of Simon and Andrew, with James and John. But Simon's wife's mother lay sick of a fever, and anon they tell him of her. And he came and took her by the hand, and lifted her up; and immediately the fever left her, and she ministered unto them.- Mark 1:29-31"Quiet on the set and...Action!" The Gospel of Mark reads like a shooting script, taking us from one encounter to another. It is commonly thought that Mark is writing this gospel for Peter and that Mark's house was the location for the first church. This rich gospel gives us a perspective unique from the others and seems to fit with Peter's action-oriented personality.This MP3 CD-ROM is self-contained and includes: * Over 20 hours of Verse-by-Verse audio teaching through the Gospel of Mark as MP3 files. * Extensive searchable study notes as PDF files. * A special message from Chuck Missler. * Listings of other MP3 resources. * Real? Player and Real? Juke Box. This program will play MP3 audio files. * Adobe Acrobat? Reader.This program will read the PDF notes.This CD-ROM contains the following audio files: * Mark Chapter 1 - Introduction. The meaning of Baptism. Jesus heals a leper. * Mark Chapter 2 - Raising the roof. Healing. Fasting. Jesus is Lord of the Sabbath. * Mark Chapter 3 - Jesus chooses the Twelve. Beelzebub. * Mark Chapter 4 - Why parables? Jesus calms the storm. * Mark Chapter 5 - The case of the deviled ham. Raising Jairus' daughter. Woman with issue of blood. * Mark Chapter 6 - The mission of the Twelve. Feeding the five thousand. * Mark Chapter 7 - God's command or man's tradition? Evil comes from the heart. * Mark Chapter 8 - Peter's declaration. Jesus predicts his death and resurrection. * Mark Chapter 9 - The transfiguration. The greatness of humility. Entrapments. * Mark Chapter 10 - Divorce. The first shall be last. The poor become rich. * Mark Chapter 11 - The triumphal entry. Cursed fig tree. A lesson on prayer. * Mark Chapter 12 - Money talks. Priorities. Money reveals. A question of authority. * Mark Chapter 13 - Jesus' confidential briefing. The last days. The second coming. * Mark Chapter 14 - In Bethany. The Upper Room. The Garden. The Palace. * Mark Chapter 15 - The trials. Jesus is crucified. The Garden Tomb.* Mark Chapter 16 - Jesus is risen. Jesus appears to Mary. The last 12 verses of Mark.*

Mark Costello. Interview with Mark Costello. 1 cass. (Running Time: 51 min.). 13.95 (978-1-55644-041-0(3), 2042) Am Audio Prose.
Discusses autobiographical aspects of his work & related matters.

Mark Dalton: Highway Robbery & Other Tales of the Open Road. Edo Van Belkom. (ENG.). 2007. audio compact disk 19.99 (978-1-59950-424-7(3)) GraphicAudio.

Mark Dalton No. 2: Reefer Madness & Other Stories. Edo Van Belkom. 2008. audio compact disk 19.99 (978-1-59950-539-8(8)) GraphicAudio.

Mark Eric Ely-Chatlain: The Free Territory of Chatlain. (Running Time: 60 min.). (Freeland III Ser.). 1985. 9.00 (FL14) Freeland Pr.
The nature of governments is examined as a preface to the main theme.

Mark Gungor Worship You. Composed by Mark Gungor. 2005. audio compact disk 15.99 (978-1-935519-07-2(7)) Laugh Your Way.

Mark Harris. Interview with Mark Harris. 1 cass. (Running Time: 35 min.). 1981. 12.95 (L033) TFR.
Harris talks on "Bang the Drum Slowly" & his other works.

Mark Hayes: Christmas, Med-Hi. Mark Hayes. (Mark Hayes Vocal Solo Collection). (ENG.). 1999. audio compact disk 11.95 (978-0-7390-1555-1(9), 18917) Alfred Pub.

Mark Hayes: Spirit. Mark Hayes. 1 CD. (Running Time: 1 hr. 30 mins.). (Mark Hayes Vocal Solo Collection). (ENG.). 1998. audio compact disk 16.95 (978-0-7390-1307-6(6), 18022) Alfred Pub.

Mark Hayes: Spirit, Med-Hi. Mark Hayes. 1 CD. (Running Time: 1 hr. 30 mins.). (Mark Hayes Vocal Solo Collection). (ENG.). 1998. audio compact disk 11.95 (978-0-7390-1308-3(4), 17956) Alfred Pub.

Mark Hayes: Spirit, Med-Lo. Mark Hayes. (Mark Hayes Vocal Solo Collection). (ENG.). 1998. audio compact disk 11.95 (978-0-7390-1615-2(6), 17961) Alfred Pub.

Mark Hayes' Sing Praise Project: An Anthology of His Most Popular Anthems for SATB (Choir Kit), CD Pack. Composed by Mark Hayes. (ENG.). 2009. audio compact disk 60.00 (978-0-7390-6412-2(6)) Alfred Pub.

Mark Hayes' Sing Praise Project: An Anthology of His Most Popular Anthems for SATB (InstruTrax Accompaniment/Performance) Composed by Mark Hayes. (ENG.). 2009. audio compact disk 69.95 (978-0-7390-6410-8(X)) Alfred Pub.

Mark Hayes' Sing Praise Project: An Anthology of His Most Popular Anthems for SATB (Listening) Composed by Mark Hayes. (ENG.). 2009. audio compact disk 15.95 (978-0-7390-6411-5(8)) Alfred Pub.

Mark Hayes Vocal Solo Collection - 10 Christmas Songs for Solo Voice: Medium Low Voice. Composed by Mark Hayes. (Mark Hayes Vocal Solo Collection). (ENG.). 1999. audio compact disk 11.95 (978-0-7390-2246-7(6)) Alfred Pub.

Mark Hayes Vocal Solo Collection - 10 Folk Songs for Solo Voice: Medium High Voice. Composed by Mark Hayes. (Mark Hayes Vocal Solo Collection). (ENG.). 2002. audio compact disk 11.95 (978-0-7390-2391-4(8)) Alfred Pub.

Mark Hayes Vocal Solo Collection - 10 Folk Songs for Solo Voice: Medium Low Voice. Composed by Mark Hayes. (Mark Hayes Vocal Solo Collection). (ENG.). 2002. audio compact disk 10.95 (978-0-7390-2394-5(2)) Alfred Pub.

Mark Hayes Vocal Solo Collection - 10 Folk Songs for Solo Voice: Mixed Voicings. Composed by Mark Hayes. (Mark Hayes Vocal Solo Collection). (ENG.). 2002. audio compact disk 16.95 (978-0-7390-2395-2(0)) Alfred Pub.

Mark Hayes Vocal Solo Collection - 7 Praise & Worship Songs for Solo Voice: Medium High Voice. Composed by Mark Hayes. (Mark Hayes Vocal Solo Collection). (ENG.). 2005. audio compact disk 15.95 (978-0-7390-3723-2(4)) Alfred Pub.

Mark Hayes Vocal Solo Collection - 7 Praise & Worship Songs for Solo Voice: Medium Low Voice. Composed by Mark Hayes. (Mark Hayes Vocal Solo Collection). (ENG.). 2005. audio compact disk 15.95 (978-0-7390-3726-3(9)) Alfred Pub.

Mark Hayes Vocal Solo Collection - 7 Praise & Worship Songs for Solo Voice: Mixed Voicings. Composed by Mark Hayes. (Mark Hayes Vocal Solo Collection). (ENG.). 2005. audio compact disk 19.95 (978-0-7390-3727-0(7)) Alfred Pub.

Mark Hayes Vocal Solo Collection - 7 Psalms & Spiritual Songs for Solo Voice: Medium High Voice. Composed by Mark Hayes. (Mark Hayes Vocal Solo Collection). (ENG.). 2004. audio compact disk 11.95 (978-0-7390-3494-1(4)) Alfred Pub.

Mark Hayes Vocal Solo Collection - 7 Psalms & Spiritual Songs for Solo Voice: Medium Low Voice. Composed by Mark Hayes. (Mark Hayes Vocal Solo Collection). (ENG.). 2004. audio compact disk 11.95 (978-0-7390-3497-2(9)) Alfred Pub.

Mark Hayes Vocal Solo Collection - 7 Psalms & Spiritual Songs for Solo Voice: Mixed Voicings. Composed by Mark Hayes. (Mark Hayes Vocal Solo Collection). (ENG.). 2004. audio compact disk 16.95 (978-0-7390-3498-9(7)) Alfred Pub.

Mark Hubbard & the United Voices for Christ. Mark Hubbard & United Voices for Christ staff. 1 cass.; 1 CD. 9.98 (978-1-57908-361-8(7), 1430); audio compact disk 15.98 CD. (978-1-57908-360-1(9)) Platinm Enter.

Mark Lane: Warren Commission Report see Buckley's Firing Line

Mark of a Killer. unabr. ed. A. L. McWilliams. Read by Maynard Villers. 6 cass. (Running Time: 7 hrs. 6 min.). 1996. 39.95 (978-1-55686-709-5(3)) Books in Motion.
Catlin Myers returns home to Fort Griffin after a lengthy absence as a secret, hired gun & finds the town sinking deeper & deeper into a murky pool of deceit, politics & murder.

Mark of a Man. unabr. ed. Elisabeth Elliot. Read by Elisabeth Elliot. 6 cass. (Running Time: 5 hrs. 25 min.). 1989. 25.95 (978-0-8474-2013-1(2)) Back to Bible.
This series examines the many characteristics of manhood exemplified in the life of Christ.

Mark of the Angel. unabr. ed. Nancy Huston. Read by Richard Aspel. 6 CDs. (Running Time: 7 hrs. 30 mins.).Tr. of Empreinte de L'Ange. 2004. audio compact disk 77.95 (978-1-74093-439-8(3)) Pub: Bolinda Pubng AUS. Dist(s): Bolinda Pub Inc

Mark of the Angel. unabr. ed. Nancy Huston. 5 cass. (Running Time: 7 hrs. 30 mins.).Tr. of Empreinte de l'Ange. 2004. 40.00 (978-1-74030-740-6(2)) Pub: Bolinda Pubng AUS. Dist(s): Bolinda Pub Inc

Mark of the Assassin. abr. ed. Daniel Silva. Read by Christopher Lane & Phil Gigante. (Running Time: 5 hrs.). 2009. audio compact disk 26.99 (978-1-4233-6828-1(2), 9781423368281, BACD) Brilliance Audio.

Mark of the Assassin. abr. ed. Daniel Silva. Read by Christopher Lane. (Running Time: 6 hrs.). 2010. audio compact disk 14.99 (978-1-4233-6829-8(0), 9781423368298, BCD Value Price) Brilliance Audio.

Mark of the Assassin. unabr. ed. Daniel Silva. Read by Christopher Lane. (Running Time: 11 hrs.). 2009. 24.99 (978-1-4233-6826-7(6), 9781423368267, Brilliance MP3); 24.99 (978-1-4233-6857-1(6), 9781423368571, BAD); 39.97 (978-1-4233-6827-4(4), 9781423368274, Brlnc Audio MP3 Lib); 39.97 (978-1-4233-6858-8(4), 9781423368588, BADLE); audio compact disk 38.99 (978-1-4233-6824-3(X), 9781423368243, Bril Audio CD Unabri); audio compact disk 99.97 (978-1-4233-6825-0(8), 9781423368250, BriAudCD Unabrid) Brilliance Audio.

Mark of the Assassin, Set. abr. ed. Daniel Silva. Read by Frank Runyeon. 4 cass. (Running Time: 6 hrs.). 1999. 25.00 (FS9-36019) Highsmith.

Mark of the Beast see Tales of Adventure & Suspense

Mark of the Beast. Rick Joyner. 1 cass. (Running Time: 90 mins.). (Foundation Ser.: Vol. 10). 2000. 5.00 (RJ04-010) Morning NC.
Firmly establishing basic Christian principles, these messages also illuminate some of the primary enemies of truth, such as legalism & the control spirit.

***Mark of the Christian.** unabr. ed. Francis A. Schaeffer. Narrated by Robertson Dean. (ENG.). 2007. 8.98 (978-1-59644-478-2(9), Hovel Audio) christianaud.

Mark of the Christian. unabr. ed. Francis A. Schaeffer. Narrated by Robertson Dean. 1 CD. (Running Time: 1 hr. 0 mins. 0 sec.). (ENG.). 2007. audio compact disk 12.98 (978-1-59644-477-5(0), Hovel Audio) christianaud.

Mark of the Dragon: Ruin Mist Chronicles, Book 4. unabr. ed. Robert Stanek, pseud. Narrated by Karl Fehr. (Running Time: 11 hrs. 47 mins.). (Ruin Mist Chronicles Ser.). 2008. audio compact disk 59.95 (978-1-57545-353-8(3), RP Audio Pubng) Reagent Press.

Mark of the Lion Trilogy, Set. abr. ed. Francine Rivers. Read by Wayne Shepherd. 2 cass. (Running Time: 3 hrs.). (Mark of the Lion Ser.: Vols. 1-3). 1999. 15.99 (978-1-886463-51-6(4)) Oasis Audio.

Mark of Zorro. Johnston McCulley. Read by Anais 9000. 2008. 27.95 (978-1-60112-013-7(3)) Babblebooks.

***Mark of Zorro.** Johnston McCulley. Read by Val Kilmer. (Running Time: 3 hrs. NaN mins.). (ENG.). 2011. 19.95 (978-1-4417-2890-6(2)); 34.95 (978-1-4417-2886-9(4)); audio compact disk 19.95 (978-1-4417-2889-0(9)); audio compact disk 40.00 (978-1-4417-2887-6(2)) Blckstn Audio.

Mark the Wind's Power. unabr. ed. George R. Cerveny. Read by Gene Engene. 8 cass. (Running Time: 10 hrs.). 49.95 (978-1-55686-173-4(7), 173) Books in Motion.
Set in northern Idaho in the Bitterroot mountains during the early workers' Union era. There are six principal characters in this true-to-life novel. The main force in their lives is their need to come to terms with the agonizingly beautiful & yet terrifying Idaho mountain & lake country.

Mark Twain. abr. ed. Mark Twain. Read by Ed Begley. 6 CDs. (Running Time: 6 hrs.). (ps-4). 2001. audio compact disk 29.95 (978-0-06-000271-8(9)) HarperCollins Pubs.

Mark Twain. unabr. ed. Mark Twain. 4 cass. (Running Time: 6 hrs.). Dramatization. (Classic Author Ser.). 1995. 16.95 Set. (978-1-55935-170-6(5)) Soundelux.
Includes "The Adventures of Huckleberry Finn" & "The Celebrated Frog of Calaveras County".

Mark Twain. unabr. ed. Geoffrey C. Ward et al. Read by Bill Meisle. 5 CDs. (Running Time: 8 hrs.). (ENG.). 2001. audio compact disk 35.00 (978-0-375-42048-1(7)) Pub: Random Audio Pubg. Dist(s): Random

Mark Twain: A Life. abr. ed. Ron Powers. Read by Ron Powers. 2005. 21.95 (978-0-7435-5218-9(0)) Pub: S&S Audio. Dist(s): S and S Inc

Mark Twain: Letters from the Earth. abr. ed. McAvoy Layne. Read by McAvoy Layne. 1 cass. (Running Time: 1 hr.). 2004. 12.95 (978-1-57270-023-9(8), D11023a) Pub: Audio Partners. Dist(s): PerseuPGW
The most controversial of Twain's works, not published until 1962 when it was a NYT bestseller, as interpreted by the man who has portrayed Twain in more than 1000 performances internationally.

Mark Twain: The Eternal Boy. unabr. ed. Louis Untermeyer. 1 cass. (Running Time: 27 min). (Makers of the Modern World Ser.). 1968. 12.95 (23038) J Norton Pubs.
Analyzes of the views of Mark Twain on society.

Mark Twain: Wild Humorist of the West. Mark Twain. Read by McAvoy Layne. 2 cass. (Running Time: 2 hrs. 25 min.). Dramatization. 2004. 16.95 (978-1-57270-009-3(2), D20009a) Pub: Audio Partners. Dist(s): PerseuPGW
A one-man performance that highlights Twain's humor, wisdom, & perpetual struggle between boyhood & social order. Based on the writings of Mark Twain, this emphasizes the great author's Western years.

Mark Twain Set: Short Stories. abr. ed. Short Stories. Mark Twain. Perf. by David Wayne. 3 cass. (Running Time: 4 hrs. 30 min.). 1984. 27.95 (978-0-694-50447-3(5), SWC 3007) HarperCollins Pubs.

Mark Twain Set: The Humor of Mark Twain. unabr. ed. Mark Twain. Read by Thomas Becker. 6 cass. (Running Time: 7 hrs.). (Great Authors Ser.). 1997. 34.95 Set, incl. literary notes, author's picture, author's biography & collector's box. (978-1-883049-72-0(5), Commuters Library) Sound Room.
Twenty-two of Twain's best tall tales, stories & essays.

Mark Twain & the Laughing River. (Running Time: 34 min.). 10.00; audio compact disk 15.00 CD. Woodside Ave Mus.
The music evokes a period in our history when steamboat traveled the Mississippi.

Mark Twain Collection. Mark Twain. Ed. by Jerry Stemach et al. Retold by Alan Venable. Illus. by Jack Nichols. Contrib. by Ed Smaron & Ted S. Hasselbring. 1 cass. (Running Time: 1 hr.). (Start-to-Finish Books: Vol. 1). (J). (gr. 2-3). 1999. (978-1-893376-48-9(6), F09K2) D Johnston Inc.
In this classic Gold Rush tall tale, '49er Jim will bet on anything that moves. After swindling his fellows with other wild gambles, Jim trains a frog as a champion jumper. But the last laugh is on Jim. And to this day, Calaveras County still holds an annual frog-jumping contest.

Mark Twain Collection. Mark Twain. Ed. by Jerry Stemach et al. Retold by Alan Venable. Illus. by Jack Nichols. Contrib. by Ed Smaron & Ted S. Hasselbring. (Start-to-Finish Books: Vol. 1). 2000. 35.00 (978-1-58702-444-3(6)) D Johnston Inc.

Mark Twain Collection. Mark Twain. Ed. by Jerry Stemach et al. Retold by Alan Venable. Illus. by Jack Nichols. Contrib. by Ed Smaron & Ted S. Hasselbring. (Start-to-Finish Books: Vol. 1). 2002. 100.00 (978-1-58702-963-9(4)) D Johnston Inc.

Mark Twain Collection. Mark Twain. Read by Garrick Hagon. (Running Time: 10 hrs.). 2002. 61.95 (978-1-60083-840-8(5)) Iofy Corp.

Mark Twain Collection. Retold by Alan Venable. Mark Twain. (Famous Short Stories Ser.). 1999. audio compact disk 18.95 (978-1-4105-0136-3(1)) D Johnston Inc.

Mark Twain Collection. unabr. ed. Mark Twain. Read by Garrick Hagon & Kenneth Jay. 8 cass. (Running Time: 10 hrs.). 2002. 49.98 (978-1-930838-21-5(2), NA802114, Naxos AudioBooks) Naxos.
Mark Twain's delightful adventures on the Mississippi River and magical journeys set in old England are especially popular among younger listeners and continue to fascinate and entertain the young and young at heart over 100 years after originally published in book form. In this exceptional collection you'll join Tom Sawyer, Huck Finn, Hank Morgan, Tom Canty and so many others on exciting trips that you will never tire of.

Mark Twain Collection. unabr. ed. Mark Twain. Read by Garrick Hagon & Kenneth Jay. 8 CDs. (Running Time: 10 hrs.). 2002. audio compact disk 55.98 (978-1-930838-22-2(0), NA802212, Naxos AudioBooks) Naxos.

Mark Twain Sampler. unabr. ed. Short Stories. Mark Twain. Read by Blair Einstein. 2 CDs. (Running Time: 3 hrs.). 1994. audio compact disk 29.95 (978-1-883332-51-8(6)) Audio Bkshelf.
Collection includes stories, memoirs, letter & speeches from Mark Twain, one of the best-loved American writers of the 19th century.

Mark Twain Sampler. unabr. ed. Short Stories. Mark Twain. Read by Blair Einstein. 2 cass. (Running Time: 3 hrs.). 1994. 19.95 (978-1-883332-07-5(9), 391142) Audio Bkshelf.

Mark Twain Short Stories. Mark Twain. Read by Jack Whitaker. 2 cass. (Running Time: 2 hrs.). 19.95 set. (8017Q) Filmic Archives.
Eleven entertaining stories from one of America's most popular authors. Your students will enjoy these yarns, including "The Celebrated Jumping Frog of Calaveras County", which first brought Twain to the attention of Eastern readers.

Mark Twain Short Stories. unabr. ed. Mark Twain. Read by Jack Sondericker. 4 cass. (Running Time: 3 hrs. 30 min.). 1988. 26.95 (978-1-55686-249-6(0), 249) Books in Motion.
Features 4 short stories by Mark Twain: Nos. 1 & 2 Extract from Captain Stormfield's Visit to Heaven & Nos. 3 & 4 Extracts from Adam & Eve's Diary.

Mark Twain Short Stories, Set. unabr. ed. Mark Twain. Read by Jack Whitaker. 2 cass. (Running Time: 1 hr. 52 min.). (Cassette Bookshelf Ser.). 1984. 15.98 (978-0-8072-3406-8(0), CB 102CX, Listening Lib) Random Audio Pubg.

Mark Twain Short Stories, Set. unabr. ed. Mark Twain. Read by Jack Whitaker. 2 cass. (Running Time: 1 hr. 52 min.). (Cassette Bookshelf Ser.). 1999. 15.95 trade pkg. (978-0-8072-3491-4(5), CB102CXR, Listening Lib) Random Audio Pubg.

Mark Twain Stories. unabr. ed. Mark Twain. Read by Jack Sondericker. 2 cass. (Running Time: 2 hrs.). Dramatization. 1990. 16.95 (978-1-55686-093-5(5), 093) Books in Motion.
Two Mark Twain stories; The Private History of a Campaign That Failed & The One Million Pound Banknote.

Mark Twain Tonight. Mark Twain & Hal Holbrook. 2 cass. (Running Time: 1 hr. 40 min.). 19.95 set. (8011Q) Filmic Archives.
We hear the American spirit in Holbrook's performance of excerpts from one of America's most popular authors.

Mark Twain Tonight! abr. ed. Hal Holbrook. Perf. by Hal Holbrook. 2 cass. (Running Time: 1 hr. 40 mins.). 2004. 16.95 (978-0-88690-272-8(X), D20162a) Pub: Audio Partners. Dist(s): PerseuPGW
The great American humorist is brought to life in this one-man show.

Mark Twain Tonight! unabr. ed. Mark Twain & Hal Holbrook. (Running Time: 6000 sec.). (Audio Editions Ser.). (ENG.). 2006. audio compact disk 24.95 (978-1-57270-562-3(0)) Pub: AudioGO. Dist(s): Perseus Dist

Mark Twain's America, Set. abr. ed. Mark Twain. Perf. by Will Geer. 2 cass. 1984. 19.95 (978-0-694-50419-0(X), SWC 2064) HarperCollins Pubs.

***Mark Twain's Book for Bad Boys & Girls.** Ed. by R. Kent Rasmussen. Narrated by Richard Henzel. (ENG.). 2010. audio compact disk 29.99 (978-0-9826688-4-9(8)) R Henzel.

Mark Twain's Letters from Hawaii. unabr. abr. ed. Mark Twain. Read by McAvoy Layne. 3 CDs. (Running Time: 3 hrs. 45 mins.). (ENG.). 2004. audio compact disk 24.95 (978-1-57270-428-2(4)) Pub: AudioGO. Dist(s): Perseus Dist
Mark Twain arrived in Honolulu on Sunday, March 18, 1866, to write a series of travel letters to be published in the Sacramento Union. His letters about "the loveliest fleet of islands that lies anchored in any ocean" show Twain's keen ability to detail and portray what life was really like in Hawaii in the nineteenth century. McAvoy Layne's dramatic reading beautifully conveys the strength and spirit of both Twain and early Hawaii, an unspoiled paradise to which Twain always longed to return.

Mark Twain's Library of Humor. unabr. ed. Mark Twain. Ed. by Mark Twain et al. Read by Marsh McCandless et al. 4 cass. (Running Time: 6 hrs.). 2004. 21.95 (978-1-57270-027-7(0), F41027u) Pub: Audio Partners. Dist(s): PerseuPGW
Tall tales, regional dialects, puns & witty ripostes fill this generous sampling of humor. Stories selected by Twain himself, by such authors as Frederick W. Cozzens; Oliver Wendell Holmes; Harriet Beecher Stowe; Joel Chandler Ward; Katherine Kent Walker; Artemus Ward & others.

Mark Twain's Own Autobiography. unabr. collector's ed. Michael Kiskis. Read by Wolfram Kandinsky. 10 cass. (Running Time: 15 hrs.). 1992. 80.00 (978-0-7366-2289-9(6), 3075) Books on Tape.
When Mark Twain died in 1910, he left behind half a million words of autobiographical writing. The question of how to organize this wealth of material continues to bedevil editors. But there is one text, published under Twain's supervision, that can be considered authentic.

Mark Twain's World. unabr. ed. Mark Twain. Read by Hiram Sherman. 6 cass. (Running Time: 4 hrs.). 1987. 55.00 (978-0-8045-0018-0(5), PCC 18) Spoken Arts.

Mark Vinz. Read by Mark Vinz. 1 cass. (Running Time: 29 min.). 1985. 10.00 New Letters.
North Dakota's Mark Vinz is author of Letters to The Poetry Editor & Red River Blues.

Marked. P. C. Cast & Kristin Cast. Read by Edwina Wren. (Running Time: 9 hrs. 30 mins.). (House of Night Ser.). (YA). 2009. 79.99 (978-1-74214-186-2(2), 9781742141862) Pub: Bolinda Pubng AUS. Dist(s): Bolinda Pub Inc

Marked. unabr. ed. P. C. Cast & Kristin Cast. Read by Edwina Wren. (Running Time: 9 hrs. 30 mins.). (House of Night Ser.: No. 1). (YA). 2008. audio compact disk 87.95 (978-1-74214-061-2(0), 9781742140612) Pub: Bolinda Pubng AUS. Dist(s): Bolinda Pub Inc

***Marked.** unabr. ed. P. C. Cast & Kristin Cast. Read by Edwina Wren. (Running Time: 9 hrs. 30 mins.). (House of Night Ser.). (YA). 2010. 43.95 (978-1-74214-652-2(X), 9781742146522) Pub: Bolinda Pubng AUS. Dist(s): Bolinda Pub Inc

Marked for Murder. William X. Kienzle. 7 cass. (Running Time: 10.5 hrs.). (Father Koesler Mystery Ser.: No. 10). 2001. 56.00 (978-0-7366-6357-1(6)) Books on Tape.

***Marked Man.** unabr. ed. William Lashner. Read by Richard Rohan. (ENG.). 2006. (978-0-06-113524-8(0), Harper Audio); (978-0-06-113525-5(9), Harper Audio) HarperCollins Pubs.

Marked Man. unabr. ed. William Lashner. Read by Richard Rohan. 12 CDs. (Running Time: 50400 sec.). 2006. audio compact disk 44.95 (978-0-06-112630-7(6), Harper Audio) HarperCollins Pubs.

Marker. unabr. ed. Robin Cook. Read by George Guidall. Contrib. by George Guidall. (Running Time: 057600 sec.). No. 5. (ENG.). (gr. k-8). 2005. audio compact disk 39.95 (978-0-14-305773-4(1), PengAudBks) Penguin Grp USA.

Market & Prospect for Real Estate Like Crazy! Bernice L. Ross. 10 CDs. (Running Time: 10 hrs). 2003. spiral bd. 299.00 (978-0-9725081-0-0(4)) RossdalePress.

Market & Prospect for Real Estate Like Crazy Audio Scripts. Bernice Ross. 2006. audio compact disk 149.00 (978-0-9725081-3-1(9)) RossdalePress.

Market Cycles, How to Profit From. unabr. ed. Donald J. Hoppe. 1 cass. (Running Time: 36 min.). 12.95 (1115) J Norton Pubs.
Cycle analyses are explored, covering many commodities, & basic types of cycles, such as Kitchin & Business. Examines how cycles reflect historical events, & difference between trends & cycles.

Market Forces. unabr. ed. Richard K. Morgan. Read by Simon Vance. 12 CDs. (Running Time: 16 hrs. 0 mins. 0 sec.). (ENG.). 2005. audio compact disk 79.99 (978-1-4001-3139-6(1)) Pub: Tantor Media. Dist(s): IngramPubServ

Market Forces. unabr. ed. Richard K. Morgan. Read by Todd McLaren. Narrated by Simon Vance. (Running Time: 16 hrs. 0 mins. 0 sec.). (ENG.). 2005. audio compact disk 25.99 (978-1-4001-5139-4(2)); audio compact disk 39.99 (978-1-4001-0139-9(5)) Pub: Tantor Media. Dist(s): IngramPubServ

Market Forecasts for Russia. 6th rev. ed. BIA. (J). 2006. audio compact disk 359.00 (978-1-4187-5367-2(X)) Bus Info Agency.

Market Forecasts for the Central Federal District of Russia. 6th rev. ed. BIA. (J). 2006. audio compact disk 359.00 (978-1-4187-5372-6(6)) Bus Info Agency.

Market Forecasts for the Far Eastern Federal District of Russia. 6th rev. ed. BIA. (J). 2006. audio compact disk 359.00 (978-1-4187-5366-5(1)) Bus Info Agency.

Market Forecasts for the Northwestern Federal District of Russia. 6th rev. ed. BIA. (J). 2006. audio compact disk 359.00 (978-1-4187-5373-3(4)) Bus Info Agency.

Market Forecasts for the Siberian Federal District of Russia. 6th rev. ed. BIA. (J). 2006. audio compact disk 359.00 (978-1-4187-5368-9(8)) Bus Info Agency.

Market Forecasts for the Southern Federal District of Russia. 6th rev. ed. BIA. (J). 2006. audio compact disk 359.00 (978-1-4187-5371-9(8)) Bus Info Agency.

Market Forecasts for the Urals Federal District of Russia. 6th rev. ed. BIA. (J). 2006. audio compact disk 359.00 (978-1-4187-5369-6(6)) Bus Info Agency.

Market Forecasts for the Volga Federal District of Russia. 6th rev. ed. BIA. (J). 2006. audio compact disk 359.00 (978-1-4187-5370-2(X)) Bus Info Agency.

Market Research see Investigacion de Mercados

Market Research. Flavio Vera. Read by Flavio Vera Lizarazo. (Running Time: 1 hr.). 2003. 14.95 (978-1-60083-303-8(9), Audiofy Corp) Iofy Corp.

Market Square. Miss Read Staff. Narrated by June Barrie. 4 cass. (Running Time: 22800 sec.). (Sound Library). 2006. 39.95 (978-0-7927-4248-7(6), CSL 983) AudioGO.

Market Square. Miss Read. Narrated by June Barrie. 5 CDs. 2006. audio compact disk 59.95 (978-0-7927-4076-6(9), SLD 983) AudioGO.

Market with Articles. Interview. Christopher Knight et al. 1 CD. (Running Time: 1 hour). 2005. audio compact disk 39.00 (978-1-888983-16-6(7)) Spec Intrsts Pub.
Publishing articles online is easy, it?s free . . . and it is one of the most effective ways to market. Even if you believe you can?t write, you can create short articles (250 - 1000 words) that can bring you better results than many ad campaigns costing thousands of dollars.As the author of online articles, you get:Exposure. Your article may be viewed by thousands of potential customers. Credibility. Being published makes you the expert. Web Site Traffic. Live links in your articles bring customers to your Web site. Higher Search Engine Positioning. "Link popularity" is one of the things the search engines consider when ranking Web pages. Your online articles give you quality links and enhance your standing in the search engines. More Sales! Customers know and trust you before they get to your Web site. More credibility and trust, plus more Web site traffic, add up to more customers, more sales and greater profit for you. Listen to Christopher Knight and Cathy Stucker tell how you can use free online articles as an important part of your marketing strategy. You will learn:Why you should market with articles; How to choose great topics for your articles; What makes a powerful article title; What word length is best; How to write a resource box (author bio) that maximizes your results; How to use articles to improve your search engine position; The secret to make your links more effective; What you should NOT do in your articles; How to promote yourself as an expert on multiple topics; and How to develop and implement your strategy to market with articles NOW!.

Market Wizards: Interview with Bruce Kovner, Vol. 2. Bruce Kovner & Jack Schwager. (ENG.). 2006. audio compact disk 12.95 (978-1-59280-284-5(2)) Marketplace Bks.

Market Wizards: Interview with Dr. Van K. Tharp, Vol. 12. Van K. Tharp & Jack Schwager. (ENG.). 2006. audio compact disk 12.95 (978-1-59280-250-0(8)) Marketplace Bks.

Market Wizards: Interview with Marty Schwartz, Vol. 8. Marty Schwartz & Jack Schwager. (ENG.). 2006. audio compact disk 12.95 (978-1-59280-278-4(8)) Marketplace Bks.

Market Wizards: Interview with Michael Marcus, Vol. 1. Michael Marcus & Jack Schwager. (ENG.). 2006. audio compact disk 12.95 (978-1-59280-285-2(0)) Marketplace Bks.

Market Wizards: Interview with Michael Steinhardt, Vol. 6. Michael Steinhardt & Jack Schwager. (ENG.). 2006. audio compact disk 12.95 (978-1-59280-280-7(X)) Marketplace Bks.

Market Wizards: Interview with Richard Dennis, Vol. 3. Richard Dennis & Jack Schwager. (ENG.). 2006. audio compact disk 12.95 (978-1-59280-283-8(4)) Marketplace Bks.

Market Wizards: Interviews with Ed Seykota & Larry Hite, Vol. 5. Ed Seykota et al. (ENG.). 2006. audio compact disk 12.95 (978-1-59280-281-4(8)) Marketplace Bks.

Market Wizards: Interviews with Mark Weinstein & Brian Gelber, Vol. 10. Mark Weinstein et al. 2006. audio compact disk 12.95 (978-1-59280-276-0(1)) Marketplace Bks.

Market Wizards: Interviews with Paul Tudor Jones & Gary Bielfeldt, Vol. 4. Paul Tudor Jones et al. (ENG.). 2006. audio compact disk 12.95 (978-1-59280-282-1(6)) Marketplace Bks.

Market Wizards: Interviews with Tom Baldwin & Tony Saliba, Vol. 11. Tom Baldwin et al. 2006. audio compact disk 12.95 (978-1-59280-275-3(3)) Marketplace Bks.

Market Wizards: James B. Rogers, Jr: Buying Value & Selling Hysteria, Vol. 9. abr. ed. Jack Schwager. Contrib. by James B. Rogers, Jr. (Running Time: 3858 sec.). (ENG.). 2006. audio compact disk 12.95 (978-1-59280-277-7(X)) Marketplace Bks.

Market Wizards: William O'Neil, David Ryan: The Art of Stock Selection/Stock Investment as a Treasure Hunt, Vol. 7. abr. ed. Jack Schwager. Contrib. by William J. O'Neil & David Ryan. (Running Time: 4091 sec.). (ENG.). 2006. audio compact disk 12.95 (978-1-59280-279-1(6)) Marketplace Bks.

Market Yourself for Success. Cynthia L. Schoeppel. 1 cass. 1995. 9.95 (978-1-887608-02-2(8)) HRC Pub.

Marketing. 2nd abr. ed. Alexander Hiam. Read by Brett Barry. (Running Time: 12600 sec.). 2007. audio compact disk 14.95 (978-0-06-137432-6(6), Harper Audio) HarperCollins Pubs.

Marketing Blunders of the Century, Five Greatest. unabr. ed. Center for Entrepreneurial Management Staff. 1 cass. (Running Time: 1 hr. 24 min.). 12.95 (1360) J Norton Pubs.
Talks about the problems encountered by five large companies that faced either dissolution or abandonment of a product into which a lot of market research, promotional effort & money had been invested.

Marketing Chaplaincy. 1 cass. (Care Cassettes Ser.: Vol. 13, No. 9). 1986. 10.80 Assn Prof Chaplains.

Marketing Edge: Six Pros Tell You How to Get It. George Lazarus. 6 cass. (Running Time: 4 hrs. 30 min.). (Success Clinic Ser.). 1987. 49.95 incl. Listener's Guide. (2006) Dartnell Corp.
Six marketing greats share with marketing expert/columnist George Lazarus & the listener the marketing strategies that lead to their success.

Marketing Financial Services to Seniors CD Superpack: A Program for Tapping the Most Affluent Market in America Today. 6 CDs. 2004. audio compact disk 24.95 (978-0-9662062-6-5(6)) NF Comns.

***Marketing for Dummies 2nd Ed.** 2nd abr. ed. Alexander Hiam. Read by Brett Barry. (ENG.). 2007. (978-0-06-155597-8(5)); (978-0-06-155598-5(3)) HarperCollins Pubs.

Marketing for Law Firms. Moderated by Edward J. Burke & Susan Raridon. (Running Time: 24 hrs.). 1992. 295.00 NY Law Pub.
Designed to help law firms take the steps to succeed in marketing to expand their businesses. Includes planning; case studies; working with the press; building the marketing infrastructure; putting the marketing plan into action; & establishing & building relationships with corporate legal departments.

Marketing for Next Level Ministry CD. Gary Hawkins, Sr. 2005. audio compact disk 15.95 (978-0-9774291-6-5(4)) Mall Pub Co.

Marketing for People Who Hate to Sell! Andrew Wood. 1 CD, 1 Cass. 2000. 79.95 Personal Quest.
Program designed to make business come to you! Covers all major marketing methods, including publicity, networking, referrals, customer service, speaking, newsletters, sales letters, brochures, the telephone & fax, the Internet, advertising & sales.

Marketing for Speakers & Seminar Promoters. Randy Gage et al. 1 cass. (Running Time: 90 mins.). 1994. 149.00 (978-1-884667-06-0(6)) Prime Concepts Grp.
Business training.

Marketing Fundamentals. Somers H. White. 4 cass. (Running Time: 4 hrs.). 100.00 set. S White.

Marketing Imagination. Ted Levitt. Intro. by A. E. Whyte. 1 cass. (Listen & Learn U. S. A.! Ser.). 8.95 (978-0-88684-027-3(9)) Listen USA.

***Marketing in the Moment: The Practical Guide to Using Web 3. 0 Marketing to Reach Your Customers First.** unabr. ed. Michael Tasner. Read by Don Hagen. (Running Time: 6 hrs.). (ENG.). 2010. 24.98 (978-1-59659-606-1(6), GildAudio) Pub: Gildan Media. Dist(s): HachBkGrp

Marketing Internacional - Creatividad E Innovacion. unabr. ed. Basilio Balli Morales.Tr. of International Marketing - Creativity & Innovation. (SPA.). audio compact disk 13.00 (978-958-43-0228-1(0)) YoYoMusic.

***Marketing Lessons from the Grateful Dead: What Every Business Can Learn from the Most Iconic Band in History.** unabr. ed. David Meerman Scott et al. (Running Time: 3 hrs.). (ENG.). 2010. 24.98 (978-1-59659-655-9(4), GildAudio) Pub: Gildan Media. Dist(s): HachBkGrp

Marketing Made Easy. 2004. audio compact disk (978-1-932163-57-5(3)) Infinity Inst.

***Marketing of Evil: How Radicals, Elitists, & Pseudo-Experts Sell Us Corruption Disguised as Freedom.** David Kupelian. 2009. audio compact disk 24.99 (978-1-935071-25-9(4), WND Bks) Pub: Cumberland Hse. Dist(s): Midpt Trade

Marketing of Managed Accounts Series. Incl. Marketing of Managed Accounts Series: Building Your "PR" - Your Public Reputation. L. Rose.; Marketing of Managed Accounts Series: Changing Nature of Managed Money Marketing. G. Booth.; Marketing of Managed Accounts Series: Marketing Commodity Money Management. R. Walsh & R. Filler.; Marketing of Managed Accounts Series: Marketing Money Management in 1985: Panel Discussion. 2 cass. 25.00; Marketing of Managed Accounts Series: Marketing the CTA. P. Verrill & S. Gregory.; Marketing of Managed Accounts Series: Marketing the Limited Partnership; Training & Motivating AE's. D. Kelly & L. Murphy.; Marketing of Managed Accounts Series: Merger, Sale or Acquisition of a CTA. M. Mitchell & R. Cornew.; Marketing of Managed Accounts Series: The Marketing of Managed Accounts. J. Krass.; Marketing of Managed Accounts Series: Using the CME-Simex Link-up. J. Wederits.; 100.00 Set. (Mngd Acct Reprts); 15.00 ea. Futures Pub.

Marketing of Managed Accounts Series: Building Your "PR" - Your Public Reputation see Marketing of Managed Accounts Series

Marketing of Managed Accounts Series: Changing Nature of Managed Money Marketing see Marketing of Managed Accounts Series

Marketing of Managed Accounts Series: Marketing Commodity Money Management see Marketing of Managed Accounts Series

Marketing of Managed Accounts Series: Marketing Money Management in 1985: Panel Discussion see Marketing of Managed Accounts Series

Marketing of Managed Accounts Series: Marketing the CTA see Marketing of Managed Accounts Series

Marketing of Managed Accounts Series: Marketing the Limited Partnership; Training & Motivating AE's see Marketing of Managed Accounts Series

Marketing of Managed Accounts Series: Merger, Sale or Acquisition of a CTA see Marketing of Managed Accounts Series

Marketing of Managed Accounts Series: The Marketing of Managed Accounts see Marketing of Managed Accounts Series

Marketing of Managed Accounts Series: Using the CME-Simex Link-up see Marketing of Managed Accounts Series

Marketing Strategy for Fast Growth. Brian S. Tracy. Read by Brian S. Tracy. 2 cass. (Effective Manager Seminar Ser.: No. 13). 95.00 Set, incl. 1-hr. videotape & 2 wkbks., program notes & study guide. (753VD) Nightingale-Conant.
Defining where you are, where you want to go, & how to get there.

Marketing the Church: National Association of Evangelicals, 47th Annual Convention, Columbus, Ohio, March 7-9, 1989. Norman Wilson. 1 cass. (Workshops Ser.: No. 19-Wednesd). 1989. 4.25 ea. 1-8 tapes.; 4.00 ea. 9 tapes or more. Nat Assn Evan.

Marketing to Multicultural Customers. 1 cass. (America's Supermarket Showcase '96 Ser.). 1996. 11.00 (NGA96-046) Sound Images.

Marketing up in a down Economy: Best Practices for Marketing Executives. Steve Cone. 2009. 250.00 (978-1-59701-464-9(8)) ReedLogic.

Marketing Warfare. Al Trout & Jack Ries. 1 cass. (Running Time: 50 min.). 8.95 (978-0-88684-082-2(1)) Listen USA.
Elements of war may be applied to successful marketing techniques.

Marketing Without Money for Small Businesses! Excerpts. Based on a book by Nicholas E. Bade. 1 cassette. (Running Time: 48 mins.). 2003. 14.95 (978-1-882923-14-4(6)) Halle Hse Pub.
Marketing Without Money! is for anyone trying to build a small business on a small budget. It's packed with practical, proven ways to increase sales fast - at low or NO cost. It's ideal for businesses of all kinds and sizes. Best of all, you don't need any marketing experience.

Marketing Your Forensic Practice. unabr. ed. Dan Poynter. Read by Dan Poynter. 1 cass. (Running Time: 1 hr.). 1993. 9.95 (978-0-915516-78-0(0), E-102) Para Pub.
You will learn how to select a field of practice, define your geographical area, assemble your promotion package & build a professional image. Poynter will share the ten ways to let lawyers know you are available to assist them. Includes resources.

Marketing Your Law Firm's Services. 1987. bk. 35.00; 25.00 PA Bar Inst.

Marketing Your MLM Business: A One-Day Marketing Bootcamp. Randy Gage. 1 cass. 1994. 99.00 (978-1-884667-03-9(1)) Prime Concepts Grp.
Business training.

Marketing Your Sewing Business. Barbara Wright Sykes. 1 CD. 2004. audio compact disk 16.95 (978-0-9632857-4-4(2)) Pub: Collins Pubns. Dist(s): Baker Taylor

Marketing Your Small Business. Ed. by Socrates Media Editors. 2005. audio compact disk 29.95 (978-1-59546-099-8(3)) Pub: Socrates Med LLC. Dist(s): Midpt Trade

Marketing Yourself for Success: The Product Is You. unabr. ed. Ronald Goldstein & Allegra Kessler. 1 cass. (Running Time: 50 min.). 1984. 9.95 Newtown Psychological Ctr.
An instructional presentation dealing with the skills & techniques necessary to present oneself to the fullest advantage in both the interview situation & the workplace itself.

Marketing Yourself in a Competitive World. Patricia Smith-Pierce. 2 cass. (Running Time: 2 hrs. 30 min.). 25.00 Set. (5008) Natl Inst Child Mgmt.
Successful child care directors will effectively position themselves with a strong positive approach as they communicate with others. This includes Marketing daily on a variety of fronts: with parents, other executives, staff & the public. A strong, confident voice is coercive power, a fundamental base of personal power to be used in assuring the success of this marketing. Provides the tools to successfully market yourself.

Marketmaker. unabr. ed. Michael Ridpath. Read by Neil Conrich. 10 cass. (Running Time: 12 hrs.). (Isis Ser.). (J). 1999. 84.95 (978-0-7531-0464-4(4), 981004) Pub: ISIS Lrg Prnt GBR. Dist(s): Ulverscroft US
Disgruntled academic Nick Eliot is the greenest trader on the stand at a tough firm of brokers in the city. Dekker Ward created, & now dominates, the turbulent market in Latin American bonds. But can they stay on top & still play by the rules? Dekker's South American business is run by Ricardo Ross - the most successful trader the region has ever seen. He is the Marketmaker. At first the new boy is content to ride his luck until strange things start happening to Dekker employees.

***Marketplace of Ideas: Reform & Reaction in the American University.** unabr. ed. Louis Menand. Narrated by Michael Prichard. (Running Time: 4 hrs. 0 mins.). 2010. 12.99 (978-1-4001-8419-4(3)); 24.99 (978-1-4001-9419-3(9)) Tantor Media.

Marketplace of Ideas: Reform & Reaction in the American University. unabr. ed. Louis Menand. Narrated by Michael Prichard. (Running Time: 4 hrs. 0 mins. 0 sec.). (ENG.). 2010. 19.99 (978-1-4001-6419-6(2)); audio compact disk 49.99 (978-1-4001-4419-8(1)); audio compact disk 24.99 (978-1-4001-1419-1(5)) Pub: Tantor Media. Dist(s): IngramPubServ

Markheim see Great Ghost Stories - Volume 1

Markheim see Suicide Club & Other Stories

Markheim. 1977. (D-8) Jimcin Record.

Markheim. Robert Louis Stevenson. Ed. by Raymond Harris. Illus. by Robert J. Pailthorpe. (Classics Ser.). (YA). (gr. 6-12). 1982. pap. bk. 13.00 (978-0-89061-252-1(8), 456) Jamestown.

Marking & Tracing Lives Within the Christ; Sensitivity Development. Ann Ree Colton & Jonathan Murro. 1 cass. 7.95 A R Colton Fnd.

Marking & Tracing Reincarnation; Vows & Visualizations. Ann Ree Colton & Jonathan Murro. 1 cass. 7.95 A R Colton Fnd.

Marking Time. Elizabeth Jane Howard. 4 cass. (Running Time: 6 hrs.). (ENG., 2001. (978-0-333-67559-5(2)) Macmillan UK GBR.

Marking Time. unabr. ed. Elizabeth Jane Howard. Read by Jill Balcon. 16 CDs. (Running Time: 24 hrs.). 2002. audio compact disk 119.95 (978-0-7540-5521-1(3), CCD 212) Pub: Chivers Pr GBR. Dist(s): AudioGO

Marking Time. unabr. collector's ed. Elizabeth Jane Howard. Read by Donada Peters. 12 cass. (Running Time: 18 hrs.). (Cazalet Chronicles: Vol. 2). 1997. 96.00 (978-0-7366-4021-3(5), 4519) Books on Tape.
Sixteen year old Louise, Edward & Villy's daughter, moves out into the world, discovering at drama school a casualness towards language & sex that would shock her parents, as much as their secret lives would shock her & Polly, now fourteen, finds that war cannot forestall the pangs of adolescence, while another fourteen year old, Clary, is the one hit hardest by the war, her father, Rupert, has been reported missing after Dunkirk. While the rest of the family gradually accepts that he must be dead, Clary clings to the belief that he is alive.

Markiss, King of the Liars see Best of Mark Twain

Markmanship: Babbling Brook. Eldon Taylor. 1 cass. 16.95 (978-1-55978-534-1(9), 53893F) Progress Aware Res.

Markology. Mark O'Connor. Tr. by John Carlini. 1997. spiral bd. 31.95 (978-0-7866-1656-5(3), 95695CDP) Mel Bay.

Marks of a Christian. Kenneth W. Hagin, Jr. 16.00 (C8126) Faith Lib Pubns.
Believers should be imitators of Christ.

Marks of a True Believer. 6 cass. 19.95 (20145, HarperThor) HarpC GBR.

Marks of Discipleship Thematic. 1998. pap. bk. 35.00 (978-0-933173-82-8(2)) Chging Church Forum.

Marks of Jesus. Neville Goddard. 1 cass. (Running Time: 62 min.). 1965. 8.00 (90) J & L Pubns.
Neville taught Imagination Creates Reality. He was a powerfully influential teacher of God as Consciousness.

Marks of the Master. 1978. 4.95 (978-0-7417-1005-5(6)) Win Walk.

Mark's Story: The Gospel According to Peter. unabr. ed. Tim LaHaye & Jerry B. Jenkins. Read by Robertson Dean. (Running Time: 10 hrs.). No. 2. (ENG.). (gr. 8). 2007. audio compact disk 34.95 (978-0-14-314247-8(X), PengAudBks) Penguin Grp USA.

Marksmanship: Soundtrack: Synthesized Moments. Eldon Taylor. 1 cass. (Running Time: 62 min.). 16.95 incl. script. (978-0-940699-23-6(0), 53893D) Progress Aware Res.
Musical soundtrack with underlying subliminal affirmations.

Marktchance Wirtschaftsdeutsch Level 2: Lehrbuch. Juergen Bolten. (GER.). (C). 1993. 29.75 (978-3-12-675141-4(5)) Pub: Klett Ernst Verlag DEU. Dist(s): Intl Bk Import

Marky & the Cat: Story Book. Deanna Luke. Adapted by East Wind Productions Staff. (Marky Ser.: Vol. 2). (J). 2001. 4.95 (978-1-928777-18-2(X), BOW Bks) Blessing Our Wrld.

Marky & the Fish: Story Book. Deanna Luke. Adapted by East Wind Productions Staff. (Marky Ser.: Vol. 4). (J). 2001. 4.95 (978-1-928777-28-1(7), BOW Bks) Blessing Our Wrld.

Marky & the Mouse Vol. 1: Story Book. Deanna Luke. Adapted by East Wind Productions Staff. (Marky Ser.: Vol. 1). (J). 2001. 4.95 (978-1-928777-17-5(1), BOW Bks) Blessing Our Wrld.

Marky & the Rat. Deanna Luke. Adapted by East Wind Productions Staff. (Marky Ser.: Vol. 3). (J). 2001. audio compact disk 5.95 (978-1-928777-22-9(8), BOW Bks) Blessing Our Wrld.

Marky & the Rat: Story Book. Deanna Luke. Adapted by East Wind Productions Staff. (Marky Ser.: Vol. 3). (J). 2001. 4.95 (978-1-928777-19-9(8), BOW Bks) Blessing Our Wrld.

Marky & the Rooster: Story Book. Deanna Luke. Adapted by East Wind Productions Staff. (Marky Ser.: Vol. 5). (J). 2001. 4.95 (978-1-928777-29-8(5), BOW Bks) Blessing Our Wrld.

Marky & the Seagull: Story Book. Deanna Luke. Adapted by East Wind Productions Staff. (Marky Ser.: Vol. 6). (J). 2001. 4.95 (978-1-928777-30-4(9), BOW Bks) Blessing Our Wrld.

Marlborough Bk. 1: His Life & Times. unabr. collector's ed. Winston L. S. Churchill. Read by David Case. 9 cass. (Running Time: 13 hrs. 30 min.). 1989. 72.00 (978-0-7366-1641-6(1), 2496-A) Books on Tape.
Winston Churchill's biography of his ancestor, John Churchill, Duke of Marlborough, provides a unique picture of author & subject. Both men, the 18th century military commander & the 20th century prime minister were gruff & outspoken, fine soldiers & easy aristocrats. Both were devoted servants of England. Marlborough, like Churchill, led victorious Allied forces against the threat of tyranny in Europe. Marlborough's great program was to counter Louis XIV's bid for hegemony. The Duke's military successes were unmatched even by Napoleon. Churchill's original Marlborough, in six volumes, was published in the 1930s. This revised account, edited by Henry Steele Commanger, preserved the sweep & magnificence of the original, including Churchill's grand prose where, in a reviewer's words, "...great figures strut & march; you can hear the horses galloping & bugles blowing".

Marlborough Bk. 2: His Life & Times. collector's ed. Winston L. S. Churchill. Read by David Case. 9 cass. (Running Time: 13 hrs. 30 min.). 1989. 72.00 (978-0-7366-1642-3(X), 2496-B) Books on Tape.

Marlborough Bk. 3: His Life & Times. collector's ed. Winston L. S. Churchill & David Case. 7 cass. (Running Time: 10 hrs. 30 min.). 1989. 56.00 (978-0-7366-1643-0(8), 2496-C) Books on Tape.

Marlene Springer. unabr. ed. Read by Marlene Springer. 1 cass. (Running Time: 29 min.). 1985. 10.00 New Letters.
Springer talks about a book she edited, "What Manner of Woman: Essays on English & American Life & Literature".

***Marley.** unabr. ed. John Grogan. Read by Neil Patrick Harris. (ENG.). 2007. (978-0-06-145071-6(5), Harper Audio); (978-0-06-145070-9(7), Harper Audio) HarperCollins Pubs.

Marley: A Dog Like No Other. John Grogan. Contrib. by Neil Patrick Harris. (Playaway Children Ser.). (J). 2008. 59.99 (978-1-60640-617-5(5)) Find a World.

Marley: A Dog Like No Other. unabr. ed. John Grogan. Read by Neil Patrick Harris. (J). 2008. audio compact disk 21.95 (978-0-06-175576-7(1), Harper Audio) HarperCollins Pubs.

***Marley & Me.** abr. ed. John Grogan. Read by John Grogan. (ENG.). 2005. (978-0-06-089756-7(2), Harper Audio); (978-0-06-089755-0(4), Harper Audio) HarperCollins Pubs.

Marley & Me: Life & Love with the World's Worst Dog. John Grogan. 2006. cd-rom 34.99 (978-1-59895-490-6(3)) Find a World.

Marley & Me: Life & Love with the World's Worst Dog. abr. ed. John Grogan. Read by John Grogan. 5 CDs. (Running Time: 6 hrs.). 2008. audio compact disk 14.95 (978-0-06-167132-6(0), Harper Audio) HarperCollins Pubs.

Marley & Me: Life & Love with the World's Worst Dog. unabr. ed. John Grogan. Read by Johnny Heller. 7 cass. (Running Time: 9 hrs. 75 mins.). 2006. 72.75 (978-1-4193-9628-1(5)); audio compact disk 102.75 (978-1-4193-9630-4(7)) Recorded Bks.

Marley & Me: The World's Worst Dog Will Bring Out the Best in Their Family. movie tie-in abr. ed. John Grogan. Read by John Grogan. 5 CDs. (Running Time: 6 hrs.). 2008. audio compact disk 14.95 (978-0-06-175486-9(2), Harper Audio) HarperCollins Pubs.

***Marley Goes to School.** unabr. ed. John Grogan. Read by Fred Berman. (ENG.). 2009. (978-0-06-177613-7(0)); (978-0-06-190233-8(0)) HarperCollins Pubs.

Marley Magic: Celebrating the Natural Mystic. Perf. by Ziggy Marley et al. 2 cass. 1997. 15.98 Set. (978-1-56896-169-9(3), 54186-4); cass. & video 19.98 (978-1-56896-171-2(5), 54078-3); audio compact disk 24.98 Double CD. (978-1-56896-170-5(7), 54186-2) Lightyear Entrtnmnt.
Recorded & filmed live in Central Park at Summerstage.

Marlon Brando. Patricia Bosworth. Read by Edward Holland. 2001. audio compact disk 48.00 (978-0-7366-8530-6(8)) Books on Tape.

Marlon Brando. unabr. ed. Patricia Bosworth. 1 cass. (Running Time: 1 hr. 30 mins.). 2001. 40.00 (978-0-7366-7623-6(6)) Books on Tape.

Marlon Brando. unabr. ed. Patricia Bosworth. 4 cass. (Running Time: 6 hrs.). 2001. 24.95 (978-0-7366-6813-2(6)) Books on Tape.
From rebellious unknown to reluctant idol to falling star, acclaimed biographer Patricia Bosworth reveals the complex, charismatic genius who changed the face of acting.

Marmara Contract. unabr. ed. Alan Gold. Narrated by Sean Mangan. 13 cass. (Running Time: 19 hrs.). 2001. (978-1-74030-338-5(5)) Bolinda Pubng AUS.

Marni Speaks, Marni Seeks Truth. Poems. 1. (Running Time: 31 mins, 1 sec.). 2003. audio compact disk 14.00 (978-0-9727687-2-6(6), 003) Williams Enterprise.
This long-awaited CD consists of poems from the book, "My Little Book of Poetry: Marni Speaks, Marni Seeks Truth" with and exquisite accompaniment of jazz, blues and hip-hop.

Marooned off Vesta see Asimov's Mysteries

Marooned off Vesta see Best of Isaac Asimov

Marooned on Tim's Island. Tim Cain. 1 cass. (J). (ps-3). 1996. 9.95 (978-1-884115-05-9(5)); audio compact disk 14.95 CD. Tims Tunes.

Marpa: The Fruition of Mahamudra in Everyday Life. Osel Tendzin. Read by Osel Tendzin. 5 cass. 1977. 45.00 Vajradhatu.
"Situation as teacher is not thinking that a thunderstorm is a message from Thor. Situation as teacher means every situation in your life brings you back to discipline, basic teaching, to what is going on".

Marpa I. Vajracarya. 4 cass. 1973. 38.50 Vajradhatu.
Explores: The Style of Kagyu Lineage; Marpa's Approach; Mahamudra Awareness Through Intellect; Mahamudra As Ground Tantra.

Marpa II. Vajracarya. 3 cass. 1975. 27.00 Vajradhatu.
Discusses: Marpa's Style & Beginning Practitoners; Marpa & his Students; Becoming a Member of the Lineage.

Marque & Reprisal. Based on a novel by Elizabeth Moon. 2010. audio compact disk 19.99 (978-1-59950-647-0(5)) GraphicAudio.

***Marque & Reprisal.** Elizabeth Moon. 2010. audio compact disk 19.99 (978-1-59950-656-2(4)) GraphicAudio.

Marque & Reprisal. unabr. ed. Elizabeth Moon. Narrated by Cynthia Holloway. (Running Time: 14 hrs. 30 mins. 0 sec.). (Vatta's War Ser.). (ENG.). 2008. audio compact disk 75.99 (978-1-4001-3828-9(0)); audio compact disk 24.99 (978-1-4001-5828-7(1)); audio compact disk 37.99 (978-1-4001-0828-2(4)) Pub: Tantor Media. Dist(s): IngramPubServ

Marquesa 2: Heroines of the Golden West. Stephen Bly. Narrated by Linda Stephens. 6 cass. (Running Time: 8 hrs. 15 mins.). 59.00 (978-1-4025-0253-8(2)) Recorded Bks.

Marquise see Women in Literature, the Short Story: A Collection

Marquise. unabr. ed. George Sand. Read by Walter Zimmerman. 1 cass. Dramatization. 1982. 7.95 (S-21) Jimcin Record.
An old world intrigue in this classic of French Literature.

Marrakech see Richard Eberhart Reading His Poetry

Marrakesh One-Two. unabr. ed. Richard Grenier. Read by Michael Prichard. 8 cass. (Running Time: 12 hrs.). 1986. 64.00 (978-0-7366-1002-5(2), 1935) Books on Tape.
It all begins as Burt Nelson, struggling with the mysteries of the Arab mind, tries to complete a film version of the life of Mohammed. But things keep getting in the way - a bloody but failed coup in Morocco, a confrontation with Colonel Kaddafi & a hijacking. The novel refracts Arab character & customs both sinister & hilarious.

Marriage see Robert Lowell: A Reading

Marriage. 3 CDs. 2005. audio compact disk (978-0-9767967-8-7(3)) Family Discipleship.

Marriage. unabr. ed. Oasis Audio. Read by Kelly Ryan Dolan. Narrated by Jill Shellabarger. (Running Time: 1 hr. 16 mins. 30 sec.). (What the Bible Says Ser.). (ENG.). 2008. audio compact disk 9.99 (978-1-59859-407-2(9)) Oasis Audio.

Marriage. unabr. ed. H. G. Wells. Narrated by Flo Gibson. (Running Time: 16 hrs.). 2001. 34.95 (978-1-55685-778-2(0)) Audio Bk Con.

Marriage, Set. unabr. ed. Susan Ferrier. Read by Flo Gibson. 10 cass. (Running Time: 15 hrs.). 1994. 44.95 (978-1-55685-322-7(X)) Audio Bk Con.
In this hilarious social satire the authoress, happily influenced by Jane Austen, contrasts the joys of happy marriage with the evils that arise from an imprudent match. The varied, complex & comic characters play out their lives in the Scottish Highlands & the environs of London.

Marriage: Bonding or Binding. 1 cass. 1997. 20.00 (978-1-57855-006-7(8)) T D Jakes.

Marriage: Covenant or Contract. Creflo A. Dollar. (ENG.). 2006. 15.00 (978-1-59944-133-7(0)); audio compact disk 21.00 (978-1-59944-134-4(9)) Creflo Dollar.

Marriage: From Surviving to Thriving. 2006. 34.00 (978-1-57972-716-1(6)); audio compact disk 34.00 (978-1-57972-715-4(8)) Insight Living.

Marriage: Hit or Myth? Lynn Scoresby. 1 cass. 6.98 (978-1-55503-312-5(1), 061939) Covenant Comms.
See through myths, grapple with reality, make marriage better!.

Marriage: How to Make it Work. Voddie Baucham, Jr. (YA). 2002. audio compact disk 20.00 (978-0-633-09031-9(X)) LifeWay Christian.

Marriage: Now & Forever. A. Lynn Scoresby. 1 cass. 9.95 (978-1-57734-229-8(1), 06005764) Covenant Comms.
True foundations of a happy marriage.

Marriage: Program from the Award Winning Public Radio Series. Hosted by Fred Goodwin. Comment by John Hockenberry. 1 CD. (Running Time: 1 hr). (Infinite Mind Ser.). 2002. audio compact disk 21.95 (978-1-932479-12-6(0), LCM 245) Lichtenstein Creat.
In this hour, we explore Marriage. Guests include Dr. Howard Markman, a professor of psychology at the University of Denver, whose books include the bestseller Fighting for Your Marriage; psychologist Dr. Shirley Glass, a marital and family therapist and a leading expert on infidelity; Dr. James Coyne, a professor of psychology at the University of Pennsylvania, who researches the differing effects of good and bad marriages on health and mental health; historian Dr. Nancy Cott of Harvard University who is the author of Public Vows: A History of Marriage and the Nation; Pamela Holm, author of The Toaster Broke, So We're Getting Married; and novelist Anne Bernays and her husband of forty-eight years, Pulitzer-Prize winning biographer Justin Kaplan. Commentary by John Hockenberry.

Marriage: The Ultimate Fix? Ed Young. 1994. 4.95 (978-0-7417-2014-6(0), 1014) Win Walk.

Marriage - Learning to Love Yourself. Kenneth W. Hagin, Jr. 1 cass. 4.95 (3J06) Faith Lib Pubns.

Marriage: a Curse or Blessing: Judges 14:1-20. Ed Young. 1998. 4.95 (978-0-7417-2172-3(4), A1172) Win Walk.

Marriage: A Private Castle: 1 Cor. 11:13. Ed Young. 1991. 4.95 (978-0-7417-1836-5(7), 836) Win Walk.

Marriage & Divorce: Exposing the Lies Myths, & Misconceptions, Vol. 1. Mac Hammond & Lynne Hammond. (ENG.). 2007. audio compact disk 10.00 (978-1-57399-334-0(4)) Mac Hammond.

Marriage & Divorce: New Beginnings & Healing for the Brokenhearted. 2007. audio compact disk 17.99 (978-1-934570-04-3(4)) Lanphier Pr.

Marriage & Divorce: 1 Cor. 7:8-16. Ed Young. 1986. 4.95 (978-0-7417-1496-1(5), 496) Win Walk.

Marriage & Divorce, Vol 1 of the Happily Ever after Series: Exposing the Lies, Myths & Misconceptions. Mac Hammond & Lynne Hammond. 2 cass. 1992. 10.00 (978-1-57399-142-1(2)) Mac Hammond.
Is a Christian bound to stay in an abusive relationship? Does a divorce disqualify a person for ministry? What are the right and wrong reasons for marrying? Let this practical series turn your confusion into confidence.

Marriage & Family. 2004. audio compact disk (978-1-931713-95-5(2)) Word For Today.

Marriage & Family, Volume 1 2004. audio compact disk (978-1-931713-93-1(6)) Word For Today.

Marriage & Family, Volume 1 2003. (978-1-931713-68-9(5)) Word For Today.

Marriage & Family, Volume 2. 2004. audio compact disk (978-1-931713-94-8(4)) Word For Today.

Marriage & Family, Volume 2. 2003. (978-1-931713-69-6(3)) Word For Today.

Marriage & Family: Gospel Insights. Covey & Madsen. 4 cass. 1984. 19.95 Set. (978-1-57008-045-6(3), Bkcraft Inc) Deseret Bk.

Marriage & Mary Ann. unabr. ed. Catherine Marchant, pseud. Read by Susan Jameson. 4 cass. (Running Time: 4 hrs.). 1993. bk. 39.95 (978-0-7451-5853-2(6), CAB 026) AudioGO.

Marriage & Other Acts of Charity: A Memoir. unabr. ed. Kate Braestrup. Read by Kate Braestrup. (Running Time: 6 hrs.). (ENG.). 2010. 24.98 (978-1-60024-780-4(6)); audio compact disk 29.98 (978-1-60024-778-1(4)) Pub: Hachet Audio. Dist(s): HachBkGrp

Marriage & Relationships. David T. Demola. 12 cass. 48.00 (S-1054) Faith Fellow Min.

Marriage & the Blended Family: Re-Establishing the Family Unit God's Way. Alfred D. Harvey, Jr. 10 cass in album. (Running Time: 9 hrs. 10 mins.). 2003. 50.00 (978-1-932508-22-2(8)) Doers Pub.
Understanding the dynamics involved in properly preparing for a successful blended union of families with children, or improving the one you're already in.

Marriage & the Seventh House. Pat Strickland. 1 cass. 8.95 (464) Am Fed Astrologers.
Determine relationship potential.

Marriage & the Tree of Life: God's Plan for Prosperity, Dominion & Blessing. Mac Hammond. 1 cass. (LAWS That Govern Prosperity Ser.: Vol. 1). 1996. 30.00 (978-1-57399-019-6(1)) Mac Hammond.
Teaching on marriage union.

Marriage as Manifest Glory: Vol. 1. Read by Douglas Wilson. 8. 2004. 22.00 (978-1-59128-416-1(3)); 28.00 (978-1-59128-418-5(X)) Canon Pr ID.

Marriage as Manifest Glory: Vol. 3. Read by Douglas Wilson. 6 cass. 2005. 20.00 (978-1-59128-424-6(4)) Canon Pr ID.

Marriage as Manifest Glory-CD-Vol. 4: Vol. 4. Read by Douglas Wilson. 8 cass. 2005. (978-1-59128-427-7(9)) Canon Pr ID.

Marriage as Manifest Glory-CD-Vol. 5: Vol. 5. Read by Douglas Wilson. 5. 2005. 23.00 (978-1-59128-431-4(7)) Canon Pr ID.

Marriage as Manifest Glory-mp3-Vol. 1: Vol. 1. Read by Douglas Wilson. 6 cass. 2004. 22.00 (978-1-59128-223-5(3)) Canon Pr ID.

Marriage as Manifest Glory-mp3-Vol. 2: Vol. 2. Read by Douglas Wilson. 5. 2005. 14.00 (978-1-59128-419-2(8)) Canon Pr ID.

Marriage as Manifest Glory-mp3-Vol. 3: Vol. 3. Read by Douglas Wilson. 6. 2005. 16.00 (978-1-59128-422-2(8)) Canon Pr ID.

Marriage as Manifest Glory-tape-Vol. 1: Vol. 1. Read by Douglas Wilson. 5 cass. 2004. 28.00 (978-1-59128-421-5(X)) Canon Pr ID.

Marriage as Manifest Glory-tape-Vol. 3: Vol. 3. Read by Douglas Wilson. 8. 2005. 20.00 (978-1-59128-425-3(2)) Canon Pr ID.

Marriage as Manifest Glory-tape-Vol. 4: Vol. 4. Read by Douglas Wilson. 7. 2005. (978-1-59128-428-4(7)) Canon Pr ID.

Marriage as Manifest Glory-tape-Vol. 5: Vol. 5. Read by Douglas Wilson. 7 cass. 2005. 23.00 (978-1-59128-430-7(9)) Canon Pr ID.

Marriage as Manifest Glory-tape-Vol. 6: Vol. 6. Read by Douglas Wilson. 5 cass. 2005. 18.00 (978-1-59128-433-8(3)) Canon Pr ID.

Marriage Charts. Emylu Hughes. 1 cass. 8.95 (537) Am Fed Astrologers.
New look at relationships - case studies.

Marriage Charts. Mary L. Lewis. 1 cass. 8.95 (212) Am Fed Astrologers.
How timing influences the future of the marriage.

Marriage Code: Discovering Your Own Secret Language of Love. unabr. ed. Bill Farrel & Pam Farrel. Narrated by Bill Farrel & Pam Farrel. (Running Time: 6 hrs. 35 mins. 55 sec.). (ENG.). 2009. 18.19 (978-1-60814-539-3(5)); audio compact disk 25.99 (978-1-59859-599-4(7)) Oasis Audio.

Marriage Contract. Cathy Maxwell. Narrated by Virginia Leishman. 6 cass. (Running Time: 9 hrs.). 56.00 (978-0-7887-5978-9(7)); audio compact disk 78.00 (978-1-4025-3482-9(5)) Recorded Bks.

Marriage Contract. unabr. ed. Cathy Maxwell. 2001. 54.00 (L1003L8) Recorded Bks.
In this Regency-set historical romance, a pretty but penniless debutante is forced into marriage with a man she's never met.

Marriage Covenant. Derek Prince. 1 cass. (B-4182) Derek Prince.

Marriage, Divorce, Remarriage or Celibacy. Derek Prince. 5 cass. (Running Time: 60 min.). 24.95 Album. (B-MD1) Derek Prince.

Marriage Enrichment Conference. Featuring Bill Winston. 4 cass. (Running Time: 4 hrs.). 2001. 20.00 (978-1-59544-071-6(2)) Pub: B Winston Min. Dist(s): Anchor Distributors
As God's covenant partners, discover how you and your spouse can enjoy days of heaven on the earth in every area of life.

Marriage: from Surviving to Thriving see Matrimonio: De Sobrevivir a Prosperar

Marriage Game. Fern Michaels. Read by Laural Merlington. (Playaway Adult Fiction Ser.). 2008. 84.99 (978-1-60640-791-2(0)) Find a World.

Marriage Game. abr. ed. Fern Michaels. Read by Laural Merlington. (Running Time: 21600 sec.). 2007. audio compact disk 14.99 (978-1-59737-481-1(4), 9781597374811, BCD Value Price) Brilliance Audio.
Please enter a Synopsis.

Marriage Game. unabr. ed. Fern Michaels. (Running Time: 10 hrs.). 2007. 39.25 (978-1-59737-477-4(6), 9781597374774, Brlnc Audio MP3 Lib); 24.95 (978-1-59737-476-7(8), 9781597374767, Brilliance MP3); 82.25 (978-1-59737-473-6(3), 9781597374736, BrilAudUnabridg) Brilliance Audio.

Marriage Game. unabr. ed. Fern Michaels. Read by Laural Merlington. (Running Time: 10 hrs.). 2007. 39.25 (978-1-59737-479-8(2), 9781597374798, BADLE); 24.95 (978-1-59737-478-1(4), 9781597374781, BAD); audio compact disk 92.25 (978-1-59737-475-0(X), 9781597374750, BriAudCD Unabrid); audio compact disk 34.95 (978-1-59737-474-3(1), 9781597374743, Bril Audio CD Unabri) Brilliance Audio.

Marriage in the Lord, Marriage in America. Featuring Deacon James Keating. Interview with Kris McGregor. Prod. by Kvss. 2008. audio compact disk 25.00 (978-0-9800455-4-3(1)) IPF Publns.

Marriage in the Self-Genesis Age; The Dharma. Jonathan Murro & Ann Ree Colton. Read by Jonathan Murro. 1 cass. 7.95 A R Colton Fnd.
Discusses the goal of God-Realization.

Marriage Is a Contract/NSM. George Bloomer. 2004. audio compact disk 14.99 (978-0-88368-450-4(0)) Whitaker Hse.

Marriage Is Murder. unabr. ed. Nancy Pickard. Read by Norah Bernard. 6 vols. (Running Time: 9 hrs.). (Jenny Cain Mystery Ser.). 2000. bk. 54.95 (978-0-7927-2202-1(7), CSL 091, Chivers Sound Lib) AudioGO.
Jenny Cain and police detective Geof Bushfield already have pre-nuptial jitters. Then a sudden wave of domestic violence rocks placid Port Frederick: in just two weeks, the husbands of three battered wives are shot dead. None of the wives confess, and none of the guns are found. As Geof searches for clues, Jenny uncovers a dangerous secret that threatens to tear Port Frederick apart!.

Marriage Is Murder. unabr. ed. Nancy Pickard. Read by Norah Bernard. 6 CDs. (Running Time: 9 hrs.). (Jenny Cain Mystery Ser.). 2000. audio compact disk 64.95 (978-0-7927-9969-6(0), SLD 020, Chivers Sound Lib) AudioGO.
Jenny Cain & police detective Geof Bushfield already had nuptial jitters. Then in just two weeks, the husbands of three battered wives were shot dead. None of the wives confessed & none of the guns can be found.

Marriage Made in Heaven. Bill Winston. 6 cass. (C). 1994. 25.00 (978-1-931289-49-8(2)) Pub: B Winston Min. Dist(s): Anchor Distributors

Marriage Made in Heaven: Or Too Tired for an Affair. unabr. ed. Erma Bombeck. Read by C. M. Herbert. 4 cass. (Running Time: 5 hrs. 30 mins.). 2003. 32.95 (978-0-7861-0663-9(8), 1566) Blckstn Audio.
Since the sunny day in 1949 when Erma & Bill Bombeck first plighted their troth, their marriage has weathered the advent of televised football & the dark side of Donna Reed. They've grappled with teenagers & technology, the women's movement & the sexual revolution & have patented their own course in Creative Arguing.

Marriage Made in Heaven: Or Too Tired for an Affair. unabr. ed. Erma Bombeck. Read by C. M. Herbert. 5 CDs. (Running Time: 5 hrs. 30 mins.). 2000. audio compact disk 40.00 (978-0-7861-9922-8(9), 1566) Blckstn Audio.

Marriage Made in Heaven: Or Too Tired for an Affair. unabr. ed. Erma Bombeck. Read by Kate Reading. 6 cass. (Running Time: 9 hrs.). 1996. 48.00 (978-0-7366-3326-0(X), 3978) Books on Tape.
These two titles offer an intimate look at Ms. Bombeck's enduring marriage & inspiration from children with cancer. Poignant & witty.

Marriage Made in Heaven: Or Too Tired for an Affair. unabr. ed. Erma Bombeck. Read by Celeste Lawson. 4 cass. (Running Time: 6 hrs.). 2001. 24.95 Penton Overseas.

Marriage Made in Heaven: Or Too Tired for an Affair. unabr. ed. Erma Bombeck. Narrated by Barbara Rosenblat. 4 cass. (Running Time: 5 hrs. 15 mins.). 1996. 35.00 (978-0-7887-0619-6(5), 94790E7) Recorded Bks.
The witty columnist turns her keen eye on what it takes to have a happy marriage.

Marriage Made in Heaven: Or Too Tired for an Affair. unabr. ed. Erma Bombeck. Narrated by Barbara Rosenblat. 5 CDs. (Running Time: 5 hrs. 30 min.). 2000. audio compact disk 48.00 (C1167E7) Recorded Bks.

Marriage Maps from the Scriptures. Charles Beckert. 1 cass. 2004. 3.95 (978-1-57734-372-1(7), 34441107) Covenant Comms.

Marriage Maps from the Scriptures. Charles B. Beckert. 1 cass. 6.98 (978-1-55503-368-2(7), 069104) Covenant Comms.
New ways to apply scriptures to marriage!.

Marriage Matters: A Seminar Providing a Practical & Spiritual Guide for Marriage, 13 CD Set. 13. (Running Time: 13 hours). 2005. audio compact disk 69.95 (978-0-9769068-2-7(1)) Mid A Bks & Tapes.

Marriage Matters: A Seminar Providing a Practical & Spiritual Guide for Marriage, 16 cassette Tapes. 16 cass. (Running Time: 16 hours). 2005. 59.95 (978-0-9769068-4-1(8)) Mid A Bks & Tapes.

Marriage Most Scandalous. abr. unabr. ed. Johanna Lindsey. Read by Anne Flosnik. (Running Time: 32400 sec.). 2005. DVD, audio compact disk, audio compact disk 97.25 (978-1-59600-229-6(8), 9781596002296, BACDLib Ed) Brilliance Audio.
For Sebastian Townshend, son of the eighth Earl of Edgewood, England is a distant and bitter memory. After unintentionally killing his best friend in a duel and being disowned by his family, Sebastian left, vowing never to return, and forged a reputation for himself on the continent as a mercenary - the deadly soldier of fortune known as the Raven. Now, eleven years later, Lady Margaret Landor pays a visit to his ruined castle in the north of France, intent on hiring the Raven to investigate suspicious occurrences back in England. But she can barely conceal her shock upon meeting the handsome killer face to face - for the Raven is none other than her former neighbor, Sebastian Townshend. The mission for which she intends to hire him involves investigating death threats against his estranged father. Though unmoved, Sebastian agrees to accompany Margaret back to England posing as her husband, which will facilitate his reentry to society - but only if she pays him an exorbitant fee - a fee that, once he learns of the lady's inability to pay, is eventually changed to a sexual trade. As the unlikely "newlyweds" uncover the intrigue at Edgewood, a love begins to blossom that neither Sebastian nor Margaret anticipated - and that neither of them can resist.

Marriage Most Scandalous. unabr. ed. Johanna Lindsey. Read by Anne Flosnik. (Running Time: 9 hrs.). 2005. 39.25 (978-1-59710-907-9(X), 9781597109079, BADLE); 24.95 (978-1-59710-906-2(1), 9781597109062, BAD); 39.25 (978-1-59335-963-8(2), 9781593359638, Brlnc Audio MP3 Lib); 24.95 (978-1-59335-962-1(4), 9781593359621, Brilliance MP3); 32.95 (978-1-59600-225-8(5), 9781596002258, BAU); 82.25 (978-1-59600-226-5(3), 9781596002265, BrilAudUnabridg); audio compact disk 36.95 (978-1-59600-839-7(3), 9781596008397, Bril Audio CD Unabri) Brilliance Audio.
Lady Margaret Landor first met Sebastian Townshend as a child, when he caught her peeking into her older sister's engagement ball. Tall, dashing, and charming, Sebastian was one of the most sought-after bachelors in Kent and cut a romantic figure she would not soon forget. Never did she dream that one day she would be living at his family's magnificent estate with Sebastian's father, the eighth Earl of Edgewood, as her guardian and Sebastian banished from his family due to the tragic results of a duel. When life at Edgewood takes a sinister turn with the earl suffering a suspicious number of life-threatening accidents, Margaret wonders if Sebastian's younger brother and his wife have grown impatient to inherit the earldom. Setting out to find the one man she believes can set the situation to rights, she discovers that Sebastian Townshend has forged a new identity for himself on the continent. Now known as The Raven, a deadly mercenary, notorious for accomplishing any mission no matter how seemingly impossible, he has vowed never to return to England. Not until Margaret meets his outrageous monetary demands does Sebastian agree to return home, reluctantly posing as her husband in order to facilitate his return to society. When he learns she cannot afford to pay his fee, he suggests a scandalous trade. As Margaret and Sebastian work to uncover the intrigue at his father's estate, a fierce passion blooms that neither of them anticipated and neither can resist. But can Margaret persuade Sebastian to abandon the dark path he believes is his fate and claim the life - and love - he deserves? Breathtaking in scope and wondrously passionate, Marriage Most Scandalous is Johanna Lindsey at her finest.

Marriage Most Scandalous-Abr. Johanna Lindsey & Romance Historical. 2010. audio compact disk 9.99 (978-1-4418-4190-2(3)) Brilliance Audio.

Marriage Myths: 11 Samuel 24:12-19. Ed Young. 1986. 4.95 (978-0-7417-1536-4(8), 536) Win Walk.

Marriage of Figaro. rev. ed. Composed by Wolfgang Amadeus Mozart. Comment by William Berger. Text by Robert Levine. 2 vols.Tr. of Nozze Di Figaro. (ENG., 2005. audio compact disk 19.95 (978-1-57912-512-7(3), 1579125123) Pub: Blck Dog & Leventhal. Dist(s): Workman Pub

Marriage of Figaro: An Introduction to Mozart's Opera. Thomson Smillie. Read by David Timson. (Opera Explained Ser.). 2003. audio compact disk 8.99 (978-1-84379-083-9(1)) NaxMulti GBR.

Marriage of Phaedra see Troll Garden

Marriage of the Personality & the Soul, Set. unabr. ed. Jacquelyn Small. 2 cass. 16.00 (978-0-939344-11-6(4)) Eupsychian.
Tells the myth of Psyche & Eros, our highest love affair, the union of spirit & matter. With music & imagery, the author takes on a journey into the collective unconscious, psyche's archetypal realm.

Marriage on the Rock, Set. Jimmy Evans. 12 cass. 1996. 60.00 (978-0-00-519041-8(X)) Majestic Mda.

Marriage on the Rock Curriculum Kit: God's Design for Your Dream Marriage. Jimmy Evans. (Marriage on the Rock Ser.). 2009. 169.95 (978-1-931585-10-1(5)) Majestic Mda.

Marriage on the Rocks & Home Away from Home. unabr. collector's ed. Janet Geringer Woititz. Read by Ruth Stokesberry. 7 cass. (Running Time: 10 hrs. 30 min.). 1988. 56.00 (978-0-7366-1425-2(7), 2311) Books on Tape.
How families of alcoholics can help themselves.

Marriage Records of Cherokee County Texas 1905-1931. Ed. by Gordon Bennett. Compiled by Sylvia Booth Acker et al. 2001. audio compact disk 15.00 (978-1-931167-16-1(8)) Cherok Cty Genealog.

Marriage Relationship. Mary L. Lewis. 1 cass. 8.95 (773) Am Fed Astrologers.

Marriage Repertoire Assumption of the Blessed Virgin Mary Catholic Church Middlebury, Vermont: 1845-1930. 2004. audio compact disk 45.00 (978-0-9761263-1-7(1)) Vermont French.

***Marriage Risk.** unabr. ed. Debbie Macomber. Read by Dan John Miller. (Running Time: 5 hrs.). (Midnight Sons Ser.: Bk. 2). 2010. 14.99 (978-1-4418-5299-1(9), 9781441852991, Brilliance MP3); 14.99 (978-1-4418-5301-1(4), 9781441853011, BAD) Brilliance Audio.

***Marriage Risk, Vol. 1.** unabr. ed. Debbie Macomber. Read by Dan John Miller. (Running Time: 5 hrs.). (Midnight Sons Ser.: Bk. 2). 2010. audio compact disk 14.99 (978-1-4418-5298-4(0), 9781441852984, Bril Audio CD Unabri) Brilliance Audio.

Marriage Seminar: How to Walk by the Spirit in Your Marriage. Paul D. Norcross. 6 cassettes. (Running Time: 9.5 hrs). 2000. 50.00 (978-0-9671353-2-8(X), ST09) Kingdom Presence.
This is a power-packedteaching series with instruction manual on how to have a dynamic marriage as God intended by the power of the Holy Spirit.

MARRIAGE SPIRIT FINDING PASSION JOY of SOUL CE: Finding the Passion & Joy of Soul-Centered Love. Evelyn Moschetta & Paul Moschetta. 2004. 10.95 (978-0-7435-4070-4(0)) Pub: S&S Audio. Dist(s): S and S Inc

Marriage You've Always Wanted. Gary Chapman. 2005. 19.99 (978-1-59859-009-8(X)) Oasis Audio.

Marriage You've Always Wanted. unabr. ed. Gary Chapman. Narrated by Gary Chapman. (ENG.). 2005. 18.19 (978-1-60814-302-3(3)); audio compact disk 25.99 (978-1-59859-008-1(1)) Oasis Audio.

Marriages Made in Heaven; Is God Permissive? Jonathan Murro. 1 cass. 7.95 A R Colton Fnd.

***Married by Morning.** abr. ed. Lisa Kleypas. Read by Rosalyn Landor. (Running Time: 5 hrs.). (Hathaways Ser.: No. 4). 2010. audio compact disk 14.99 (978-1-4418-4744-7(8), 9781441847447, BACD) Brilliance Audio.

***Married by Morning.** unabr. ed. Lisa Kleypas. Read by Rosalyn Landor. (Running Time: 10 hrs.). (Hathaways Ser.). 2010. 39.97 (978-1-4418-4741-6(3), 9781441847416, Brlnc Audio MP3 Lib); audio compact disk 29.99 (978-1-4418-4738-6(3), 9781441847386, Bril Audio CD Unabri) Brilliance Audio.

***Married by Morning.** unabr. ed. Lisa Kleypas. Read by Rosalyn Landor. (Running Time: 10 hrs.). (Hathaways Ser.: No. 4). 2010. 24.99 (978-1-4418-4740-9(5), 9781441847409, Brilliance MP3); 24.99 (978-1-4418-4742-3(1), 9781441847423, BAD); 39.97 (978-1-4418-4743-0(X), 9781441847430, BADLE) Brilliance Audio.

***Married by Morning.** unabr. ed. Lisa Kleypas. Read by Rosalyn Landor. (Running Time: 10 hrs.). (Hathaways Ser.: No. 5). 2010. audio compact disk 79.97 (978-1-4418-4739-3(1), 9781441847393, BriAudCD Unabrid) Brilliance Audio.

Married Couple Group Therapy. unabr. ed. Martin G. Blinder & Martin Kirschenbaum. 1 cass. (Running Time: 40 min.). 12.95 (29102) J Norton Pubs.
Explores the causes of marital conflict & demonstrates techniques suitable for work with couples or groups of couples by which such conflict may be resolved.

Married in Haste. Cathy Maxwell. Narrated by Virginia Leishman. 7 cass. (Running Time: 9 hrs. 45 mins.). 64.00 (978-0-7887-9502-2(3)) Recorded Bks.

Married in Seattle: First Comes Marriage; Wanted: Perfect Partner. unabr. ed. Debbie Macomber. Read by Angela Dawe. (Running Time: 9 hrs.). 2010. audio compact disk 29.99 (978-1-4418-1950-5(9), 9781441819505, Bril Audio CD Unabri) Brilliance Audio.

***Married in Seattle: First Comes Marriage; Wanted: Perfect Partner.** unabr. ed. Debbie Macomber. Read by Angela Dawe. (Running Time: 9 hrs.). 2010. 24.99 (978-1-4418-1952-9(5), 9781441819529, Brilliance MP3); 39.97 (978-1-4418-1953-6(3), 9781441819536, Brlnc Audio MP3 Lib); 24.99 (978-1-4418-1954-3(1), 9781441819543, BAD); 39.97 (978-1-4418-1955-0(X), 9781441819550, BADLE); audio compact disk 87.97 (978-1-4418-1951-2(7), 9781441819512, BriAudCD Unabrid) Brilliance Audio.

Married Lovers. abr. ed. Jackie Collins. Read by Jackie Collins. Read by Ilyana Kadushin et al. 6 CDs. (Running Time: 7 hrs. 0 mins. 0 sec.). (ENG.). 2008. audio compact disk 29.95 (978-1-4272-0406-6(3)) Pub: Macmill Audio. Dist(s): Macmillan

Married Lovers. unabr. ed. Jackie Collins. Read by John Bedford Lloyd. 14 CDs. (Running Time: 12 hrs. 0 mins. 0 sec.). (ENG.). 2008. audio compact disk 39.95 (978-1-4272-0405-9(5)) Pub: Macmill Audio. Dist(s): Macmillan

Married Man. Piers Paul Read. Read by Piers Paul Read. 1 cass. (Running Time: 30 min.). 8.95 (AMF-10) Am Audio Prose.
Read discusses moral fiction & reads from "A Married Man".

Married Men. Carl Weber. 10 cass. (Running Time: 15 hrs.). 88.00 (978-1-4025-0605-5(8)) Recorded Bks.

Married to Distraction: Restoring Intimacy & Strengthening Your Marriage in an Age of Interruption. abr. ed. Edward Hallowell. (ENG.). 2010. audio compact disk 30.00 (978-0-307-71299-8(0), Random AudioBks) Pub: Random Audio Pubg. Dist(s): Random

***Married with Zombies.** Jesse Petersen. Read by Cassandra Campbell. 2010. audio compact disk 34.99 (978-1-61120-003-4(2)) Dreamscap OH.

Married Without Baggage: How to Activate Lasting Passionate Love by Unpacking Your Emotional Baggage. abr. ed. Charles Rivers. (ENG.). 2009. audio compact disk 17.95 (978-0-9758984-5-1(0)) Falling Love.

Marrieds. unabr. ed. Milton Diamond. 1 cass. (Running Time: 1 hr.). (Human Sexuality Ser.). 12.95 (34024) J Norton Pubs.
Ramifications of four marriage styles explored: interdependent; dominant & submissive; mutually aggressive; independent or open.

Marrow of Flame: Poems of the Spiritual Journey. Dorothy Walters. Read by Andrew Harvey. 2001. cass. & audio compact disk 12.00 (978-1-890772-13-0(5)) Hohm Pr.

Marrow of Tradition. abr. ed. Charles Waddell Chesnutt. 3 cass. (Running Time: 3 hrs. 30 mins.). 2002. 24.95 (978-0-9645593-0-1(7)) MasterBuy Audio Bks.
Based upon the Wilmington, NC, race riot of 12898 and written in 1901, this historical novel makes a plea for racial justice. A group of powerful white men continue to run the fictional town of Wellington and their households as though the Civil War had never occurred. Complicated matters even further, Olivia Carteret, wife of the white newspaper editor, discovers she and Janet Miller, wife of the town's black doctor, have the same father. As the town's residents battle their way through the social and racial issues resulting from the war, Olivia and Janet work their way through racial, social and family issues.

Marrow of Tradition. abr. ed. Charles Waddell Chesnutt. Read by Michael Collins. 2 cass. (Running Time: 3 hrs.). 2000. 16.95 MasterBuy Audio Bks.

***Marry Him.** unabr. ed. Lori Gottlieb. Read by Mia Barron. (ENG.). 2010. (978-0-06-200577-9(4), Harper Audio) HarperCollins Pubs.

***Marry Him: The Case for Settling for Mr. Good Enough.** unabr. ed. Lori Gottlieb. Read by Mia Barron. (ENG.). 2010. (978-0-06-199894-2(X), Harper Audio) HarperCollins Pubs.

Marry Me. unabr. collector's ed. John Updike. Read by Wolfram Kandinsky. 7 cass. (Running Time: 10 hrs. 30 min.). 1978. 56.00 (978-0-7366-0127-6(9), 1133) Books on Tape.
The theme is the cliche of adultery in the suburbs. Jerry Conant & Sally Mathias are the couple. Inevitably their affair has repercussions on themselves, their spouses & their children.

Marry YourSelf First Audio Edition. (ENG.). 2009. 49.97 (978-0-9771756-4-2(2)) Kenilee Ink.

***Marrying Daisy Bellamy.** abr. ed. Susan Wiggs. (Running Time: 6 hrs.). (Lakeshore Chronicles Ser.). 2011. 9.99 (978-1-4418-9407-6(1), 9781441894076, BAD) Brilliance Audio.

***Marrying Daisy Bellamy.** abr. ed. Susan Wiggs. Read by Joyce Bean. (Running Time: 6 hrs.). (Lakeshore Chronicles Ser.). 2011. audio compact disk 14.99 (978-1-4418-5989-1(6), 9781441859891, BACD) Brilliance Audio.

***Marrying Daisy Bellamy.** unabr. ed. Susan Wiggs. (Running Time: 12 hrs.). (Lakeshore Chronicles Ser.). 2011. 24.99 (978-1-4418-5987-7(X), 9781441859877, BAD); 39.97 (978-1-4418-5988-4(8), 9781441859884, BADLE) Brilliance Audio.

***Marrying Daisy Bellamy.** unabr. ed. Susan Wiggs. Read by Joyce Bean. (Running Time: 12 hrs.). (Lakeshore Chronicles Ser.). 2011. 39.97 (978-1-4418-5986-0(1), 9781441859860, Brlnc Audio MP3 Lib); 24.99 (978-1-4418-5985-3(3), 9781441859853, Brilliance MP3); audio compact disk 79.97 (978-1-4418-5984-6(5), 9781441859846, BriAudCD Unabrid); audio compact disk 29.99 (978-1-4418-5983-9(7), 9781441859839, Bril Audio CD Unabri) Brilliance Audio.

Marrying Kind. Debbie Macomber. Read by Sandra Burr. (Playaway Adult Fiction Ser.). (ENG.). 2009. 49.99 (978-1-4418-0280-4(0)) Find a World.

Marrying Kind. abr. ed. Debbie Macomber. Read by Serena Daniels. 1 cass. (Running Time: 90 min.). 1996. 6.99 (978-1-57096-044-4(5), RAZ 945) Romance Alive Audio.
Jason Ingram finds himself face to face with his high school sweetheart Katie on the eve of his wedding to another woman. Brutally separated as teen newlyweds, both harbor lingering resentment, but in one night of passion their lives are changed forever & Jason must make the most difficult decision of his life.

Marrying Kind. unabr. ed. Debbie Macomber. Read by Sandra Burr. (Running Time: 2 hrs.). 2009. 24.99 (978-1-4418-0079-4(4), 9781441800794, BAD); 39.97 (978-1-4418-0080-0(8), 9781441800800, BADLE); audio compact disk 14.99 (978-1-4418-0077-0(8), 9781441800770, Bril Audio CD Unabri); audio compact disk 69.97 (978-1-4418-0078-7(6), 9781441800787, BriAudCD Unabrid) Brilliance Audio.

Marrying Malcolm Murgatroyd, unabr. ed. Mame Farrell. Narrated by Alyssa Bresnahan. 3 pieces. (Running Time: 4 hrs.). (gr. 5 up). 1997. 27.00 (978-0-7887-0705-6(1), 94879E7) Recorded Bks.
Ever since she can remember, Hannah Billings has been sticking up for Malcolm Murgatroyd. Not only are they growing up together, but they will probably grow old together as well. A story of family, friendship & coming of age.

Marrying Miss Martha. Anna Jacobs. (Soundings (CDs) Ser.). 2007. audio compact disk 84.95 (978-1-84559-589-0(0)) Pub: ISIS Lrg Prnt GBR. Dist(s): Ulverscroft US

Marrying Miss Martha. Anna Jacobs. Read by Nicolette McKenzie. 8 cass. (Soundings Ser.). 2007. 69.95 (978-1-84559-339-1(1)) Pub: ISIS Lrg Prnt GBR. Dist(s): Ulverscroft US

Marrying off Mother & Other Stories. unabr. ed. Gerald Durrell. Read by Nigel Davenport. 6 cass. (Running Time: 9 hrs.). 2000. 49.95 (978-0-7451-4123-7(4), CAB 806) Pub: Chivers Audio Bks GBR. Dist(s): AudioGO
When mother shows an interest in passion flowers, the children decide it's time she get married again. The candidates on the island of Corfu are the 18-year-old who runs the fish market, Professor Euripides Androtheomatacottopolous, and the dashing actor, Antoine de Vere. Meanwhile young Gerald is more concerned about the marital affairs of his toads than those of his mother!.

Marrying the Mistress. unabr. ed. Joanna Trollope. Read by Lindsay Duncan. 8 cass. (Running Time: 12 hrs.). 2000. 69.95 (978-0-7540-0543-8(7), CAB 1966) Pub: Chivers Audio Bks GBR. Dist(s): AudioGO

Marrying the Mistress. unabr. ed. Joanna Trollope. Read by Lindsay Duncan. 8 CDs. (Running Time: 12 hrs.). 2000. audio compact disk 79.95 (978-0-7540-5394-1(6), CCD 085) Pub: Chivers Audio Bks GBR. Dist(s): AudioGO
Simon Stockdale spells it out for his son Jack: "Your grandfather is proposing to leave your grandmother to whom he has been married for forty years & marry a woman with whom has been having an affair for seven years." What can this mean to Jack in the throes of his first love affair?.

Mars. unabr. ed. Ben Bova. Read by Stefan Rudnicki. (Running Time: 19 hrs. 0 mins.). 2009. 44.95 (978-1-4332-6373-6(4)); audio compact disk 99.95 (978-1-4332-6369-9(6)); audio compact disk 120.00 (978-1-4332-6370-5(X)) Blckstn Audio.

Mars - Jupiter: Guided Visualizations. Luisa De La Lama. Narrated by Leila Gomez Bear & Jaques Bourquin. Music by Summa. 1 cass. (Running Time: 30 min.). (Power Planets Inner Journeys Ser.). 1994. 11.95 set. (978-1-883381-02-8(9)) White Dragon.
Guided visualizations to contact the archetypal powers of Mars & Jupiter using Greek mythological figures. Theme narrated from the book "Power Planets".

Mars & Pluto. Gwen Steifbold. 1 cass. (Running Time: 90 min.). 8.95 (732) Am Fed Astrologers.

An Asterisk (*) at the beginning of an entry indicates that the title is appearing for the first time.

Mars & the Mind of Man. Read by Ray Bradbury et al. 1 cass. (Running Time: 57 min.). 14.95 (35897) MMI Corp.
A tribute to the first popularizer of Mars, Edgar Rice Burroughs & a discussion of the relationship between science & science fiction.

Mars & Venus. Compiled by Benchmark Education Staff. 2006. audio compact disk 10.00 (978-1-4108-6696-7(3)) Benchmark Educ.

Mars & Venus - Connecting with Your Soul Mate: Find True & Lasting Love - John Gray's Live Seminar. abr. ed. John Gray. 2 cass. (Running Time: 3 hrs.). 1999. 17.95 Set. (978-1-55935-316-8(3)) Soundelux.
Learn how past relationships affect your future. What is necessary for making your soul mate connection.

Mars & Venus Diet & Exercise Solution: Create the Brain Chemistry of Health, Happiness, & Lasting Romance. abr. rev. ed. John Gray & John Gray. Frwd. by Daniel G. Amen. 3 CDs. (Running Time: 10 hrs. 0 mins. 0 sec.). (ENG.). 2003. audio compact disk 22.00 (978-1-55927-920-8(6)) Pub: Macmill Audio. Dist(s): Macmillan

Mars & Venus Diet & Exercise Solution: Create the Brain Chemistry of Health, Happiness, & Lasting Romance, Set. abr. ed. John Gray. Read by John Gray. 3 cass. (Running Time: 6 hrs.). 1995. 39.00 (978-0-694-51589-9(2), BGS 007, Harper Audio) HarperCollins Pubs.

*__Mars & Venus in Love.__ abr. ed. John Gray. Read by John Gray. (ENG.). 2005. (978-0-06-085653-3(X), Harper Audio); (978-0-06-085652-6(1), Harper Audio) HarperCollins Pubs.

Mars & Venus in Love: Inspiring & Heartfelt Stories of Relationships That Work. abr. ed. John Gray. Read by John Gray. 2 cass. (Running Time: 3 hrs.). 1996. 18.00 (978-0-694-51713-8(5), CPN 2579) HarperCollins Pubs.

Mars & Venus in Love: Inspiring & Heartfelt Stories of Relationships That Work. abr. ed. John Gray. Read by John Gray. 5 cass. (Running Time: 7 hrs. 30 min.). 2000. 39.95 (978-0-694-52298-9(8)) HarperCollins Pubs.

Mars & Venus in Love: Inspiring & Heartfelt Stories of Relationships That Work. unabr. ed. John Gray. Read by Connor O'Brien. 6 cass. (Running Time: 6 hrs.). 1996. 36.00 (978-0-7366-3475-5(4), 4118) Books on Tape.

Mars & Venus in the Bedroom see Marte y Venus en el Dormitorio: Una Guia para Hacer Durar el Romance y la Pasion

*__Mars & Venus in the Bedroom.__ abr. ed. John Gray. Read by John Gray. (ENG.). 2005. (978-0-06-085659-5(9), Harper Audio); (978-0-06-085658-8(0), Harper Audio) HarperCollins Pubs.

Mars & Venus in the Bedroom: A Guide to Lasting Romance & Passion. unabr. ed. John Gray. Read by Alexander Adams. 5 cass. (Running Time: 5 hrs.). 1995. 30.00 (978-0-7366-3135-8(6), 3810) Books on Tape.
Sex in a long-term relationship can get stale & routine. How do we keep it fresh?

Mars & Venus in the Bedroom: A Guide to Lasting Romance & Passion, unabr. ed. John Gray. Narrated by George Guidall. 4 cass. (Running Time: 5 hrs. 45 mins.). 1995. 35.00 (978-0-7887-0341-6(2), 94533E7) Recorded Bks.
Offers straightforward, reassuring advice for couples on how to keep the fires of passion burning & achieve greater intimacy in their relationships.

*__Mars & Venus in the Workplace.__ abr. ed. John Gray. Read by John Gray. (ENG.). 2005. (978-0-06-085630-4(0), Harper Audio); (978-0-06-085631-1(9), Harper Audio) HarperCollins Pubs.

*__Mars & Venus in the Workplace.__ unabr. ed. John Gray. Read by John Gray. (ENG.). 2005. (978-0-06-085628-1(9), Harper Audio); (978-0-06-085629-8(7), Harper Audio) HarperCollins Pubs.

Mars & Venus in the Workplace: A Practical Guide for Improving Communication & Getting Results at Work. unabr. ed. John Gray. Narrated by George Guidall. 6 cass. (Running Time: 9 hrs.). 2004. 59.00 (978-1-4025-1608-5(8)) Recorded Bks.

*__Mars & Venus on a Date.__ abr. ed. John Gray. Read by John Gray. (ENG.). 2005. (978-0-06-085655-7(6), Harper Audio); (978-0-06-085654-0(8), Harper Audio) HarperCollins Pubs.

Mars & Venus on a Date: A Guide for Navigating the 5 Stages of Dating to Create a Loving & Lasting Relationship. abr. ed. John Gray. Read by John Gray. 2 cass. (Running Time: 3 hrs.). 1997. 18.00 (978-0-694-51845-6(X), CPN 2658) HarperCollins Pubs.

Mars & Venus on a Date: A Guide for Navigating the 5 Stages of Dating to Create a Loving & Lasting Relationship. unabr. ed. John Gray. Read by Alexander Adams. 7 cass. (Running Time: 10 hrs. 30 min.). 1998. 56.00 (978-0-7366-4096-1(7), 4601) Books on Tape.
Bestselling psychologist turns to the special difficulties of single life, including finding & sustaining a fulfilling relationship.

*__Mars & Venus Starting Over.__ abr. ed. John Gray. Read by John Gray. (ENG.). 2005. (978-0-06-085636-6(X), Harper Audio); (978-0-06-085637-3(8), Harper Audio) HarperCollins Pubs.

Mars & Venus Starting Over: A Practical Guide for Finding Love Again after a Painful Breakup, Divorce, or the Loss of a Loved One. abr. ed. John Gray. Read by John Gray. 2 cass. (Running Time: 3 hrs.). 1998. 18.00 (978-0-694-51976-7(6), JG19R) HarperCollins Pubs.

Mars & Venus Starting Over: A Practical Guide for Finding Love Again after a Painful Breakup, Divorce, or the Loss of a Loved One. unabr. ed. John Gray. Read by Connor O'Brien. 8 cass. (Running Time: 12 hrs.). 1999. 64.00 (978-0-7366-4306-1(0), 4797) Books on Tape.
Offers insights carefully selected from his years of experience for those of us who are starting over. Whether newly single after a death, a divorce, or other serious break-up. The author makes it clear that, although the pain of loss is an inevitable part of life, suffering is not. And while the healing process is fundamentally the same, starting over on Venus is light years away from starting over on Mars. Venus explores the common challenges women face, the pressures of dating, glorifying the past, fear of intimacy & putting children first. Mars deals with sex on the rebound, work, money, impatience, & other self-defeating tendencies. Based on three decades of counseling.

Mars & Venus Starting Over: A Practical Guide for Finding Love Again after a Painful Breakup, Divorce, or the Loss of a Loved One. unabr. ed. John Gray. Narrated by Simon Prebble. 6 cass. (Running Time: 8 hrs. 45 mins.). 1998. 51.00 (978-0-7887-2165-6(8), 95461E7) Recorded Bks.
With his step-by-step process, Dr. Gray shows how those hurting can work through pain and anger to heal themselves & move on to new love with confidence.

Mars & Venus Starting Over: A Practical Guide for Finding Love Again after a Painful Breakup, Divorce, or the Loss of a Loved One, Set. abr. ed. John Gray. Read by John Gray. 2 cass. 1999. 18.00 (FS9-43205) Highsmith.

Mars Daybreak Soundtrack #1. (YA). 2006. 14.98 (978-1-59409-610-5(4)) Bandai Ent.

Mars Daybreak Soundtrack #2. (YA). 2005. 14.98 (978-1-59409-611-2(2)) Bandai Ent.

Mars et Venus sur l'Oreiller. Audio. 1 cass., bklet. (Running Time: 90 mins.). (FRE., cass. & audio compact disk 14.95 (978-2-89517-023-5(1)) Pub: Coffragants CAN. Dist(s): Penton Overseas
Recorded completely in international French language by well-known actors or speakers.

Mars Is Heaven & The Crowd. Ray Bradbury. 1 cass. (Running Time: 1 hr.). (Radiobook Ser.). 1987. 4.98 (978-0-929541-46-4(4)) Radiola Co.
Two complete stories.

Mars Is Heaven; And the Moon Be Still As Bright. Ray Bradbury. 1 cass. (Running Time: 60 min.). Dramatization. (X Minus One Ser.). 1955. 6.00 Once Upon Rad.
Radio broadcasts - fantasy & science fiction.

Mars-Jupiter Aspects in Writer's Charts. Lawrence A. Williams. 1 cass. (Running Time: 90 min.). 1984. 8.95 (367) Am Fed Astrologers.

Mars Life: Third in the Mars Series. unabr. ed. Ben Bova. Read by Stefan Rudnicki. (Running Time: 12 hrs. 0 mins.). (ENG.). 2009. 29.95 (978-1-4332-3129-2(8)); 72.95 (978-1-4332-3125-4(5)); audio compact disk 90.00 (978-1-4332-3126-1(3)) Blckstn Audio.

Mars Observer Hijacking. Interview with Richard C. Hoagland. Hosted by Bruce Stephen Holmes. 1 cass. (Running Time: 50 min.). 9.95 (AT5482) Lghtwrks Aud & Vid.
Richard Hoagland is interviewed about the disappearance of the Mars Observer probe on August 21, 1993. Hoagland reports whistle-blowers inside NASA have told him that a small rogue group within the space agency deliberately "pulled the plug" in order to avoid re-photographing the Pyramids & Face on Mars, as part of a decades-old plan to keep the existence of extraterrestrials secret.

Mars Tapes. unabr. ed. Roger Zelaney et al. Read by Amy Bruce. Ed. by Allan Kaster. 4 cass. (Running Time: 6 hrs.). 1999. 25.99 (978-1-884612-30-5(X)) AudioText.
Collection of Mars stories, including: "A Rose for Ecclesiastes," "The Man Who Lost the Sea," "A Martian Ricorso," "In the Hall of the Martian Kings" & "Live from the Mars Hotel".

Mars, Venus & Pro Wrestling's Wacky World, Pt. I. Roger Mock. Read by Roger Mock. 1 cass. (Running Time: 90 min.). 1994. 8.95 (1164) Am Fed Astrologers.

Mars, Venus & Pro Wrestling's Wacky World, Pt. II. Roger Mock. Read by Roger Mock. 1 cass. (Running Time: 90 min.). 1994. 8.95 (1165) Am Fed Astrologers.

Marsh Island, Set. Sarah Orne Jewett. Read by Flo Gibson. 4 cass. (Running Time: 5 hrs. 30 min.). 1996. 19.95 (978-1-55685-415-6(3)) Audio Bk Con.
The author's gift of giving local color to these scenes on the coast of Maine gives a charming backdrop to a tender romance.

Marsh King's Daughter. Elizabeth Chadwick. Narrated by Gerri Halligan. 11 cass. (Running Time: 15 hrs.). 98.00 (978-1-84197-331-9(9)); audio compact disk 124.00 (978-1-4025-2084-6(0)) Recorded Bks.

Marsha Martinez Meets the Stars. Jenny Oldfield. Read by India Fisher. (Running Time: 11280 sec.). (J). 2001. audio compact disk 29.95 (978-0-7540-6766-5(1)) AudioGo GBR.

Marshal from Deadwood. unabr. ed. Todhunter Ballard. Read by William Dufris. 6 cass. (Running Time: 9 hrs.). (Sagebrush Western Ser.). (J). 2005. 44.95 (978-1-57490-317-1(9)) Pub: ISIS Lrg Prnt GBR. Dist(s): Ulverscroft US

Marshmallows & Wieners. unabr. ed. Chief Little Summer. Contrib. by Warm Night Rain. 1 CD. (Marshmallows & Wieners). (J). (gr. k-6). 1999. audio compact disk 11.95 CD. (978-1-880440-22-3(9)) Piqua Pr.
Grandfather & grandmother relate Indian stories.

*__Marte Y Venus en el Dormitorio.__ abr. ed. John Gray. Read by Francisco Rivela. (ENG.). 2006. (978-0-06-128748-0(2), Harper Audio); (978-0-06-128747-3(4), Harper Audio) HarperCollins Pubs.

Marte y Venus en el Dormitorio: Una Guia para Hacer Durar el Romance y la Pasion. unabr. ed. John Gray. Narrated by Francisco Rivela. 4 cass. (Running Time: 5 hrs. 45 mins.).Tr. of Mars & Venus in the Bedroom. 2003. 38.00 (978-1-4025-1260-5(0)) Recorded Bks.
Gives frank and explicit advice on how to satisfy your partner in the bedroom.

Martha see Secret Garden: A Young Reader's Edition of the Classic Story

Martha Jane & Me: A Girlhood in Wales. Read by Diana Bishop. Perf. by Mavis Nicholson. 6 cass. (Running Time: 9 hrs.). 2001. 54.95 (000414) Pub: ISIS Audio GBR. Dist(s): Ulverscroft US

Martha McFerren. unabr. ed. Ed. by Jim McKinley. Prod. by Rebekah Presson. 1 cass. (Running Time: 29 min.). (New Letters on the Air Ser.). 1994. 10.00 (022693) New Letters.
McFerren won last year's Marianne Moore poetry prize & reads from her award-winning collection, "Women in Cars." McFerren's work is hilarious & biting as it chronicles the lives of southern women who drive around naked out of boredom & men who form clubs in order to fight each other.

Martha Peake: A Novel of the American Revolution. unabr. ed. Patrick McGrath. Read by Tom Sellwood. 8 cass. (Running Time: 45600 sec.). 2005. 69.95 (978-0-7927-3699-8(0), CSL 826); audio compact disk 84.95 (978-0-7927-3700-1(8), SLD 826) AudioGO.

Martha Rules: 10 Essentials for Achieving Success As You Start, Build, or Manage a Business. unabr. ed. Martha Stewart. Read by Martha Stewart. 4 cass. (Running Time: 5 hrs. 30 mins.). 2005. 54.00 (978-1-4159-2810-3(X)); audio compact disk 61.20 (978-1-4159-2811-0(8)) Pub: Books on Tape. Dist(s): NetLibrary CO
Now, for the first time, Martha Stewart shares her business knowledge and advice in this handbook for success. Tapping into her years of experience in building a thriving business, Martha will help listeners identify their own entrepreneurial voice and channel their skills and passions into a successful business venture. Her advice and insight is applicable to anyone who is about to start or expand a venture of any size, whether it is a business or philanthropic endeavor, but also to individuals who want to apply the entrepreneurial spirit to a job or corporation to increase innovation and maintain a competitive edge. Featuring Martha's top principles for success, as well as stories and anecdotes from her own experiences, MARTHA'S RULES is sure to appeal to business readers, fans, and anyone who admires her for her style, taste, and great advice - and who have great business ideas of their own!.

Martha Stewart Baby: Sleepytime. Perf. by Linda Ronstadt et al. (J). 2002. 7.98 (978-0-7379-0183-2(7), 76777) Rhino Enter.
Martha Stewart Baby has created a unique treasury of songs for parents and children to share. Featuring a diverse assortment of contemporary artists. Sleepytime provides music to soothe and music to sing. Together with the editors of MS Baby, Martha has overseen this comprehensive collection, providing parents with music they can enjoy over and over again. Packaging also includes Martha's signature "how to" advice and project ideas on preparing baby's room, creating keepsake memories, milk/formula options and quiet time suggestions.

Martha Stewart Baby: Sleepytime. Perf. by Linda Ronstadt et al. Contrib. by Martha Stewart. (J). 2002. audio compact disk 11.98 (978-0-7379-0184-9(5), 76778) Rhino Enter.

Martha Stewart Living: Spooky Scary Sounds for Halloween. Martha Stewart. 1 cass. (Running Time: 1 hr. 30 mins.). 2001. 5.99 (R4 79975); audio compact disk 9.98 (R2 79975) Rhino Enter.

Martha Stewart Living: Spooky Scary Sounds for Halloween. Perf. by Martha Stewart. 1 cass. (Running Time: 1 hr.). 2002. 5.99 (978-0-7379-0159-7(4), 79975); audio compact disk 9.98 (978-0-7379-0218-1(3), 79975); audio compact disk 9.98 (79975) Rhino Enter.
Created and overseen by Martha directly, this special collection contains the actual eerie sound effects she uses at Halloween in her own home. In addition to the movie-quality spooky sounds, the package contains three of her "how-to" projects for Halloween fun.

Martial Arts. Eldon Taylor. 1 cass. (Running Time: 62 min.). (Inner Talk Ser.). 16.95 incl. script. (978-1-55978-524-2(1), 53809F) Progress Aware Res.
Soundtrack - Brook with underlying subliminal affirmations.

Martial Arts: Contemporary Moment. Eldon Taylor. 1 cass. 16.95 (978-1-55978-608-9(6), 53809N) Progress Aware Res.

Martial Arts: Rhythm. Eldon Taylor. Read by Eldon Taylor. Ed. by Leslie Brice. 1 cass. (Running Time: 1 hr.). 1992. 16.95 (978-1-56705-248-0(7)) Gateways Inst.
Self improvement.

Martial Arts: Stream. Eldon Taylor. Read by Eldon Taylor. Ed. by Leslie Brice. 1 cass. (Running Time: 1 hr.). 1992. 16.95 (978-1-56705-249-7(5)) Gateways Inst.

Martial Arts History. James S. Benko. 1986. 12.95 (TC-4) ITA Inst.
An overview of the major martial arts system of martial arts practiced throughout the world. Some countries featured are: China, Okinawa, Japan & Korea.

Martial Arts Philosophy Made Easy. Sid Campbell. (Running Time: 4 hrs. 30 min.). 29.95 (978-0-682-87108-2(7)) Gong Prods.

Martial Strategist's Master Strategy Pack Samurai , Art of War , Book of Five Rings , Zen Mind Control & More. SunZi et al. Tr. by Urara Tsukamoto. Narrated by Ross M. Armetta. 10 CDs. (Running Time: 11 hours approx.). 2005. audio compact disk 44.99 (978-1-59733-206-4(2), Martial Strat) InfoFount.
Learn the strategy and discipline of martial arts ? KNOW HOW TO WIN ! The "Strategy Master Pack" (10CD) set consists of popular Strategy and related titles in a discounted package. These strategy titles provide crucial knowledge that is useful for business, sports, and virtually any competitive situation.The Art of War Deluxe (3CD) provides strategies, and tactics for conventional war / competition. Learn what not to do and how to avoid traps by the competition / enemy and develop external and internal psychology and strategy. Bonus The Sayings of Confucius.Bushido ?The Soul of Japan (3CD) outlines the fundamentals of Oriental marital training, virtue, and philosophy. This audiobook explains the discipline, physical, and moral training of the Japanese warrior and its integration into Japanese culture. It can help you create successful, honorable, and respectable, actions and campaigns.Starting at 13 years old, Musashi Miyamoto fought over 60 life and death battles - never losing! Gorin No Sho - The Book of 5 Rings (1CD) describes the fundamentals of Kendo and marital training as proven successful in actual combat by Japan's Greatest Samurai - Musashi Miyamoto. Learn about black spots, rhythms, positioning, psyching your opponent out and much more - you?ll know winning strategies.Zen Mind Control (1CD) is chapter 8 (Zen Mind Training) from Zen, The Religion of the Samurai. It is a straightforward, non dogmatic and practical study of Zen Buddhism that is accessible and USEFUL. This audiobook can change your life. The Art of War Applied (1CD) is the story of George Washington and how the principles of the Art of War were used to beat the vastly superior British Army. Military Giants of the Early Republic (1CD) includes John Paul Jones, Robert E. Lee, Stonewall Jackson, George G. Meade, David Farragut, and Oliver Perry. It tells of their exploits and the qualities that made them renowned.Martial Strategists are strategy specialists. They obtain, translate, and make the most useful military and strategy editions - unequaled for practical application, and value.More information on the individual titles and complete audiobook sets is available at www.InfoFount.com.

Martial's Epigrams: A Selection. unabr. ed. Read by Garry Wills. (Running Time: 5 hrs.). 2008. audio compact disk 25.95 (978-0-14-314355-0(7), PengAudBks) Penguin Grp USA.

Martian Child: A Novel about a Single Father Adopting a Son. David Gerrold. Read by Scott Brick. (Running Time: 18000 sec.). 2006. 34.95 (978-0-7861-4570-6(6)); audio compact disk 36.00 (978-0-7861-7044-9(1)) Blckstn Audio.

Martian Child: A Novel about a Single Father Adopting a Son. Short Stories. David Gerrold. Read by David Gerrold. Prod. by Jeremy Bloom. 1 CD. (Running Time: 70 mins). 2002. audio compact disk 9.95 (978-0-9707056-9-3(7), 61-1) Frquency Pubng.
Haven't we all felt, at times when we just don't seem to fit into the normal world, that we must be from another planet? David Gerrold's autobiographical tale takes us on a journey of discovery as a single gay man adopts a misfit child who says he's from Mars. Winner of both the Nebula and Hugo Awards.

Martian Child: A Novel about a Single Father Adopting a Son. unabr. movie tie-in ed. David Gerrold. Read by Scott Brick. (Running Time: 18000 sec.). 2006. audio compact disk 29.95 (978-0-7861-7764-6(0)) Blckstn Audio.

Martian Child: A Novel about a Single Father Adopting a Son. unabr. movie tie-in ed. David Gerrold. Read by Scott Brick. 8 cass. (Running Time: 18000 sec.). 2006. 24.95 (978-0-7861-4409-9(2)); audio compact disk 25.95 (978-0-7861-7427-0(7)) Blckstn Audio.

Martian Chronicles see SF Soundbook

Martian Chronicles. unabr. ed. Ray Bradbury. (Running Time: 5.5 hrs. 0 mins.). (ENG.). 2009. 34.95 (978-1-4332-9348-1(X)); audio compact disk 55.00 (978-1-4332-9349-8(8)) Blckstn Audio.

*__Martian Chronicles.__ unabr. ed. Ray Bradbury. Narrated by Scott Brick. 1 MP3-CD. (Running Time: 9 hrs. 30 mins. 0 sec.). 2010. 19.99 (978-1-4001-6824-8(4)); 15.99 (978-1-4001-8824-6(5)); audio compact disk 71.99 (978-1-4001-4824-0(3)); audio compact disk 29.99 (978-1-4001-1824-3(7)) Pub: Tantor Media. Dist(s): IngramPubServ

Martian Chronicles. unabr. collector's ed. Ray Bradbury. Read by Michael Prichard. 8 cass. (Running Time: 8 hrs.). 1987. 48.00 (978-0-7366-1209-8(2), 2127) Books on Tape.
Classic science-fiction stories of man's colonization of Mars.

Martian Chronicles, Set. unabr. ed. Ray Bradbury. Read by Ray Bradbury. 6 cass. (Running Time: 7 hrs. 14 min.). 1991. 44.98 (978-0-8072-2907-1(5), CSL 501 CX, Listening Lib) Random Audio Pubg.

Martian Chronicles: Modern Classic Collection. unabr. ed. Ray Bradbury. (Running Time: 5 hrs. 30 mins.). (ENG.). 2009. 29.95 (978-1-4332-9352-8(8)); audio compact disk 19.95 (978-1-4332-9351-1(X)) Blckstn Audio.

Martian Odyssey. Stanley G. Weinbaum. 1 cass. (Running Time: 1 hr.). 2001. 12.95 (STAR001) Lodestone Catalog.
On the first manned Mars missions, a scout ship crashes into a vast meteor crater. Jarvis' perilous journey back to the others & meet his new-found Martian companion.

Martian Odyssey. unabr. ed. Stanley G. Weinbaum. 1 cass. (Running Time: 45 min.). Dramatization. 1997. 15.00 (978-0-9661287-0-3(2)) Star Quest.
About the first men to land on Mars. Science-Fiction of the year award.

Martian Successor Nadesico: Prince of Darkness. 1 CD. (JPN.). 2003. audio compact disk 14.98 (978-1-57813-399-4(8), CND/001) A D Vision.

Martian Time-Slip. unabr. ed. Philip K. Dick. Read by Tom Parker. 6 cass. (Running Time: 9 hrs.). 2003. 44.95 (978-0-7861-1352-1(9), 2255) Blckstn Audio.

Martian Time-Slip & the Golden Man. Philip K. Dick. Read by Grover Gardner. (Running Time: 34200 sec.). 2007. audio compact disk 24.95 (978-1-4332-0068-7(6)) Blckstn Audio.

Martian Time-Slip & the Golden Man. unabr. ed. Philip K. Dick. Read by Grover Gardner. (Running Time: 34200 sec.). 2007. audio compact disk 29.95 (978-1-4332-0069-4(4)) Blckstn Audio.

Martian Time-Slip & the Golden Man. unabr. ed. Philip K. Dick. Read by Grover Gardner. (Running Time: 34200 sec.). 2007. 59.95 (978-1-4332-0065-6(1)) Blckstn Audio.

Martian Time-Slip & the Golden Man: Philip K. Dick Boxed Set. Philip K. Dick. Read by Grover Gardner. 7. (Running Time: 34200 sec.). 2007. 24.95 (978-1-4332-0067-0(8)) Blckstn Audio.

Martian Time-Slip/the Golden Man. unabr. ed. Philip K. Dick. Read by Grover Gardner. (Running Time: 34200 sec.). 2007. audio compact disk 72.00 (978-1-4332-0066-3(X)) Blckstn Audio.

Martian Way see Best of Isaac Asimov

Martin & Lewis Show. 18 episodes on 6 ca. (Running Time: 9 hrs.). 1998. 26.98 Boxed set. (4109); audio compact disk 32.98 CD Boxed set. (4110) Radio Spirits.
Never-before-released programs that illustrate the vocal talent of Dean Martin & the comedic genius of Jerry Lewis.

Martin & Lewis Show. Perf. by Dean Martin & Jerry Lewis. 2 cass. (Running Time: 3 hrs.). 2002. 17.98 (27614) Radio Spirits.
Dean Martin and Jerry Lewis were drawing rave reviews for their hilarious stage show when they were lured to NBC Radio in 1949. For three seasons the show featured the vocal stylings of Dean sprinkled liberally with the screwball antics of his screeching sidekick. Relive the fun with six great episodes including shows that are being released for the first time ever.

Martin & Lewis Show, Set. Perf. by Lucille Ball et al. 6 cass. (Running Time: 1 hr. 30 mins. per cass.). 34.98 Set. Blckstn Audio.
Eighteen never-before-released programs from the collection of Jerry Lewis. Illustrates the vocal talent of Dean & the comedic genius of Jerry.

Martin Chuzzlewit. Charles Dickens. Narrated by David Case. (Running Time: 3 hrs.). 2006. 14.95 (978-1-59912-993-8(0)) Iofy Corp.

Martin Chuzzlewit. abr. ed. Charles Dickens. 6 cass. (Running Time: 9 hrs.). 1999. 31.80 Set. (978-0-563-39321-4(1)) BBC WrldWd GBR.
Martin is the grandson of the wealthy Martin Chuzzlewit & is in love with his grandfather's adopted daughter, Mary Graham. His Grandfather, however, has been made cynical by the greed of the family & distrusts Martin. So Martin decides to go & make his fortune in America.

Martin Chuzzlewit. abr. ed. Charles Dickens. Perf. by Paul Scofield. 4 cass. (Running Time: 6 hrs.). (Ultimate Classics Ser.). 2004. 25.00 (978-1-931056-66-3(8), N Millennium Audio) New Millenn Enter.
In the squalor of a textile town, successful businessman & arch-pragmatist Thomas Gradshed, proclaiming that he is a self-made man, teaches his children to suppress their imagination & embrace hard facts.

Martin Chuzzlewit. abr. ed. Charles Dickens. Read by Paul Scofield. 5 CDs. (Running Time: 6 hrs.). 2004. audio compact disk 34.95 (978-1-59007-575-3(7)) Pub: New Millenn Enter. Dist(s): PerseuPGW

Martin Chuzzlewit. unabr. ed. Charles Dickens & Frederick Davidson. (Running Time: 19 hrs. 5 mins.). 2008. 59.95 (978-1-4332-5402-4(6)); audio compact disk 120.00 (978-1-4332-5403-1(4)); audio compact disk 110.00 (978-1-4332-5401-7(8)) Blckstn Audio.

Martin Chuzzlewit, Pt. 1. unabr. ed. Charles Dickens. Read by Frederick Davidson. 13 cass. (Running Time: 36 hrs. 30 mins.). 1995. 85.95 (978-0-7861-0754-4(5), 1605A,B) Blckstn Audio.
Wealthy & old, Martin Chuzzlewit, Sr. is surrounded by greedy relatives hoping to obtain a portion of his estate upon his death. The story relates the contrasting destinies of two descendants of the brothers Chuzzlewit. Although both are born & bred selfish, one, Martin Jr., has the good fortune to transform, while the other, Jonas, does not & receives a fatal penalty. With such notable characters as Seth Pecksniff, Mrs. Gamp, Montague Tiggs, Chevy Slyme, & Poll Sweedlepipe, "Martin Chuzzlewit" is one of Charles Dickens' great comic masterpieces.

Martin Chuzzlewit, Pt. 2. unabr. ed. Charles Dickens. 11 cass. (Running Time: 15 hrs. 30 min.). 1992. 71.95 Set. Audio Bk Con.

Martin Chuzzlewit, Pt. 2. unabr. ed. Charles Dickens. 11 cass. (Running Time: 15 hrs. 30 min.). 2000. 71.95 Audio Bk Con.
The vast cast of diverse characters includes, among many others, the hypocrite Mr. Pecksniff, the undertaker Mr. Mould, the jolly Mark Tapley, the gentle Tom Pinch, the nurse who enjoys her bottled comforts, Mrs. Gamp, & the lovely Mary Graham, over whom the disagreements of the young & old Martin Chuzzlewits cause the younger to go to America to seek his fortune. Dickens' depictions of the United States are amusing & scathing, to say the least!.

Martin Chuzzlewit, Pt. 2. unabr. ed. Charles Dickens. Read by Frederick Davidson. 2 cass. (Running Time: 36 hrs. 30 mins.). 1995. 83.95 (978-0-7861-0755-1(3), 1605A,B) Blckstn Audio.
Wealthy & old, Martin Chuzzlewit, Sr., is surrounded by greedy relatives hoping to obtain a portion of his estate upon his death. The story relates the contrasting destinies of two descendants of the brothers Chuzzlewit. Both are born & bred in the same heritage of selfishness; one has the good fortune to transform while the other does not & receives a fatal penalty.

Martin Chuzzlewit: Radio Dramatization. unabr. ed. Charles Dickens. 7 CDs. (Running Time: 10 hrs. 30 mins.). 2003. audio compact disk 74.95 (978-0-563-49612-0(6), BBCD 014) BBC Worldwide.

Martin Chuzzlewit (Part 1), Vol. 1. unabr. ed. Charles Dickens. Read by Flo Gibson. 12 cass. (Running Time: 18 hrs.). 1992. 39.95 (978-1-55685-250-3(9)) Audio Bk Con.
Among the vast cast of divergent characters are Mr. Pecksniff, the hypocrite, the undertaker Mr. Mould, the jolly Mark Tapley, gentle Tom Pinch, the nurse Mrs. Gamp, who enjoys her bottled comforts, the lovely Mary Graham, over whom the young Martin Chuzzlewits' disagreements cause the younger to go to America to seek his fortune. Dickens' depictions of the United States are amusing & scathing to say the least!.

Martin Chuzzlewit (Part 2), Vol. 2. unabr. ed. Charles Dickens. Narrated by Flo Gibson. (Running Time: 14 hrs. 52 mins.). 1991. 34.95 (978-1-55685-818-5(3)) Audio Bk Con.

Martin Chuzzlewit (Parts 1 And 2) unabr. ed. Charles Dickens. Narrated by Flo Gibson. (Running Time: 34 hrs. 15 mins.). 1991. 63.95 (978-1-55685-819-2(1)) Audio Bk Con.

Martin Dressler: The Tale of an American Dreamer. unabr. ed. Steven Millhauser. Narrated by George Guidall. 6 cass. (Running Time: 9 hrs.). 1997. 56.00 (978-0-7887-1757-4(X), 95235E7) Recorded Bks.
At the turn of the century, young Martin rises from the shadows of his father's cigar shop in New York City to become a powerful entrepreneur & builder of hotels.

Martin Eden. Jack London. Narrated by Jim Killavey. (Running Time: 14 hrs.). 1986. 37.95 (978-1-59912-861-0(6)) Iofy Corp.

Martin Eden. Jack London. Read by Carlos Zambrano. (Running Time: 3 hrs.). 2002. 16.95 (978-1-60083-249-9(0), Audiofy Corp) Iofy Corp.

Martin Eden. Jack London. Read by Jim Killavey. 10 cass. (Running Time: 15 hrs.). 1989. 49.00 incl. album. (C-151) Jimcin Record.
Semi-autobiographical novel.

Martín Edén. abr. ed. Jack London. Read by Carlos Zambrano. 3 CDs. (SPA.). 2002. audio compact disk 17.00 (978-958-8161-40-2(1)) YoYoMusic.

Martin Eden. unabr. collector's ed. Jack London. Read by Jim Killavey. 10 cass. (Running Time: 15 hrs.). (Jimcin Recording Ser.). 1986. 80.00 (978-0-7366-3913-2(6), 9151) Books on Tape.
Eden grows up poor in San Francisco, takes to the sea, struggles for an education & literary fame.

Martin Hewitt, Investigator. unabr. ed. Arthur Morrison. Read by Walter Covell. 4 cass. (Running Time: 6 hrs.). Incl. Case of the Dixon Torpedo. 1989. (C-50); Case of the Missing Hand. 1989. (C-50); Holford Will Case. 1989. (C-50); Lenton Croft Robberies. 1989. (C-50); Loss of Sammy Crockett. 1989. (C-50); Stanway Cameo Mystery. 1989. (C-50); 1989. 21.00 (C-50) Jimcin Record.
Six adventures of Sherlock Holmes' closest rival.

Martin L. King on Leadership. Donald T. Phillips. 2002. (978-1-57042-962-0(6)) Hachet Audio.

Martin Luther. unabr. ed. 1 cass. (Running Time: 1 hr. 2 min.). (History Maker Ser.). 12.95 (41008) J Norton Pubs.
Traces the effect upon subsequent centuries of this humble, rebellious monk who changed the religious thinking of Europe.

Martin Luther. unabr. ed. Martin E. Marty. Read by Paul Michael. 4 cassettes. (Running Time: 6 hrs). 2005. 36.00 (978-1-4159-0137-3(6)) Books on Tape.

Martin Luther. unabr. ed. J. A. Morrison. Narrated by Edward Lewis. 2 cass. (Running Time: 2 hrs. 30 mins.). 2002. 17.95 (978-0-7861-2158-8(0), 2908) Blckstn Audio.
When a boy who has poverty for his companion is inclined to find fault with the company that he is forced to keep, he should comfort himself by reading about the boyhood days of Martin Luther.

Martin Luther: A Faithful Servant of God. Mandy Frantti. Read by Carl Kangas. Ed. by Paul Waaraniemi. Illus. by Liisa Koski. Des. by Ruth Roiko. Ruth Roiko. (J). 2008. pap. bk. 16.00 (978-1-887034-05-0(6)) Laestadian Lutheran.

Martin Luther: In His Own Words. unabr. ed. Martin Luther. 2 CDs. (Running Time: 2 hrs. 15 mins. 0 sec.). (ENG.). 2006. audio compact disk 15.98 (978-1-59644-405-8(3), Hovel Audio) christianaud.
Most all Christians know the name Martin Luther. Less familiar, however, are his words. This compilation of many of Luther's most important writings serves as an excellent introduction to those new to Luther. It also provides a fresh medium for people familiar with his writing.

***Martin Luther: in His Own Words.** unabr. ed. Martin Luther. Narrated by David Cochran Heath. (ENG.). 2006. 9.98 (978-1-59644-406-5(1), Hovel Audio) christianaud.

Martin Luther King. Harry Harmer. Read by Garrick Hogan. 2 cass. (Running Time: 3 hrs.). 2001. 24.95 (990817) Pub: ISIS Audio GBR. Dist(s): Ulverscroft US

Martin Luther King Set: A Concise Biography. unabr. ed. Harry Harmer. Read by Garrick Hogan. 2 cass. (Running Time: 2 hrs. 20 mins.). (Isis Ser.). (J). 2001. 24.95 (978-0-7531-0643-3(4), 990817) Pub: ISIS Lrg Prnt GBR. Dist(s): Ulverscroft US
In 1963, Martin Luther King led 250,000 followers to the Lincoln Memorial in Washington & began to tell the assembled mass of all races & creeds of his vision of the future, "I have a dream..." The following year the Civil Rights Act became law & then the Voting Rights Act, but as effectiveness of peaceful demonstration was called into question by activists demanding more militant action, he turned to a wider front, attacking the Vietnam war & the conditions of the poor generally. Increasingly controversial & criticized by some for his milder tactics, in April 1968 he was assassinated by James Earl Ray.

Martin Luther King Set: The Landmark Speeches & Sermons of Martin Luther King, Jr. unabr. ed. Clayborne Carson et al. Read by Keith David et al. (Running Time: 16 hrs.). (ENG.). 2009. 32.98 (978-1-60024-891-7(8)) Pub: Hachet Audio. Dist(s): HachBkGrp

Martin Luther King Day. Linda Lowery. Illus. by Hetty Mitchell. 1 cass. (Running Time: 17 min.). (J). (ps-4). 1987. 9.95 Live Oak Media.
Presents an introduction to the life & times of Dr. King & an appreciation of the works & goals of the man.

Martin Luther King Day. Linda Lowery. Read by Peter Fernandez. Illus. by Hetty Mitchell. 11 vols. (Running Time: 18 mins.). (J). (gr. 1-6). 1987. pap. bk. 16.95 (978-0-87499-070-6(X)) Pub: Live Oak Media. Dist(s): AudioGO

Martin Luther King Day. unabr. ed. Linda Lowery. Read by Peter Fernandez. Illus. by Hetty Mitchell. 1 cass. (Running Time: 17 mins.). (J). (gr. 1-6). 1987. bk. 24.95 (978-0-87499-071-3(8)) Live Oak Media.

Martin Luther King Day, Grades 1-6. unabr. ed. Linda Lowery. Read by Peter Fernandez. Illus. by Hetty Mitchell. 14 vols. (Running Time: 18 mins.). (J). 1987. pap. bk. & tchr. ed. 37.95 Reading Chest. (978-0-87499-072-0(6)) Live Oak Media.

Martin Luther King, Jr. 2 cass. (Running Time: 3 hrs.). (Black Americans of Achievement Ser.). 1993. 15.95 set. (978-1-879557-06-2(1)) Audio Scholar.

Martin Luther King, Jr. 4 cass. (Running Time: 6 hrs.). (Childhood of Famous Americans Ser.). (J). (gr. 1-3). 2001. pap. bk. 39.95 Blckstn Audio.

Martin Luther King, Jr. 10.00 Esstee Audios.

Martin Luther King, Jr. unabr. ed. Marshall Frady. Read by Marshall Frady. 5 cass. (Running Time: 7 hrs. 30 mins.). 2001. 40.00 (978-0-7366-8491-0(3)) Books on Tape.
An analytical, sometimes revisionist, succinct biography of Dr. Martin Luther King, Jr.

Martin Luther King, Jr. unabr. ed. Dharathula H. Millender. Read by Lloyd James. 4 cass. (Running Time: 5 hrs. 30 mins.). 2004. 35.95 (978-0-7861-2058-1(4), K2819) Blckstn Audio.

Martin Luther King, Jr. Facing the Challenge of a New Age. 1 cass. (Running Time: 60 mins.). 1999. 12.95 (SPA-1201) African Am Imag.

Martin Luther King, Jr. I Have a Dream. Ed. by Pent. 1 cass. (Running Time: 61 min.). 1994. cass. & audio compact disk 10.98 (978-1-885959-05-8(2), JRCS 7021) Jerden Recs.
Excerpted highlights of the major speeches given by the Rev. Martin Luther King, Jr., from 1963 to 1968.

***Martin Luther King, Jr. The Essential Box Set: The Landmark Speeches & Sermons of Martin Luther King, Jr.** unabr. ed. Martin Luther King, Jr. 2 MP3-CDs. (Running Time: 16 hrs.). 2010. 69.99 (978-1-60788-342-5(2)); audio compact disk 117.99 (978-1-60788-338-8(4)) Pub: Hachet Audio. Dist(s): HachBkGrp

Martin Luther King, Jr. The Prolonged Dream. 1 cass. (Running Time: 30 min.). 9.95 (F0140B090, HarperThor) HarpC GBR.

Martin Luther King, Jr. The Prolonged Dream. unabr. ed. Interview with Coretta Scott King. 1 cass. (Running Time: 45 min.). 1989. 10.95 (978-0-8045-1181-0(0), SAC 1181) Spoken Arts.

Martin Luther King Jr. , on Leadership: Inspiration & Wisdom for Challenging Times. abr. ed. Donald T. Phillips. (Running Time: 3 hrs.). (ENG.). 2006. 14.98 (978-1-59483-739-5(2)) Pub: Hachet Audio. Dist(s): HachBkGrp

Martin Luther King Jr. , on Leadership: Inspiration & Wisdom for Challenging Times. abr. ed. Donald T. Phillips. Read by Donald T. Phillips. 3 CDs. (Running Time: 3 hrs.). (ENG.). 2009. audio compact disk 17.98 (978-1-60024-801-6(2)) Pub: Hachet Audio. Dist(s): HachBkGrp

Martin Luther King Jr Day. Linda Lowery. Illus. by Hetty Mitchell. (Running Time: 18 mins.). 1987. 9.95 (978-1-59112-130-5(2)) Live Oak Media.

Martin Luther King Jr. Day. Linda Lowery. Illus. by Hetty Mitchell. Narrated by Peter Fernandez. (J). (gr. k-3). 1987. 12.95 (978-1-59519-327-8(8)) Live Oak Media.

Martin Luther King Jr. Day. Linda Lowery. Read by Peter Fernandez. Illus. by Hetty Mitchell. (On My Own Holidays (Live Oak Media) Ser.). (J). (ps-3). 2006. pap. bk. 39.95 (978-1-59519-329-2(4)) Live Oak Media.

Martin Luther King, Jr. on Leadership: Inspiration & Wisdom for Challenging Times. Donald T. Phillips. 2002. 17.98 (978-1-58621-011-3(4)) Hachet Audio.

Martin Luther King, Jr. on Leadership: Inspiration & Wisdom for Challenging Times. Donald T. Phillips. Narrated by Nelson Runger. 12 CDs. (Running Time: 14 hrs.). 2000. audio compact disk 116.00 (978-0-7887-4918-6(8), C1299E7) Recorded Bks.
Uses lessons culled from Dr. King's written words & speeches to provide practical advice for leading in the home, the community & the office.

Martin Luther King, Jr. on Leadership: Inspiration & Wisdom for Challenging Times. unabr. ed. Donald T. Phillips. Narrated by Nelson Runger. 10 cass. (Running Time: 14 hrs.). 2000. 91.00 (978-0-7887-4418-1(6), 96101E7) Recorded Bks.

Martin Luther King Jr./Sports Around the World. Steck-Vaughn Staff. 2002. 9.00 (978-0-7398-5991-9(9)) SteckVau.

***Martin Luther, the Lion-Hearted Reformer.** unabr. ed. J. A. Morrison. Read by Edward Lewis. (Running Time: 2.5 hrs. NaN mins.). (ENG.). 2011. 19.95 (978-1-4417-8371-4(7)); audio compact disk 28.00 (978-1-4417-8369-1(5)) Blckstn Audio.

Martin Luther's Here I Stand: The Speech That Launched the Protestant Reformation. Narrated by Max McLean. 1 CD. 2006. audio compact disk 10.95 (978-1-931047-55-5(3)) Fellow Perform Arts.

Martin Memorial Lecture. 1 cass. (Named Lectures: C85-NL5). 1985. 7.50 (8535) Am Coll Surgeons.

Martin Misunderstood. unabr. ed. Karin Slaughter. Narrated by Wayne Knight. (Running Time: 2 hrs. 30 mins.). 2008. 19.95 (978-0-7927-5575-3(8)); audio compact disk 29.95 (978-0-7927-5485-5(9)) AudioGO.
Martin Reed is thoroughly average in every way. So how has he wound up with such a pathetic existence? Martin has no friends, no lovers, and no respect. Working as a senior accountant at Southern Toilet Supply and still living with his nagging mother, his sole source of excitement is the crime novels he cherishes. So immersed is Martin in these escapes that he fails to notice the crimes going on all around him. When first one, then another, of his co-workers is brutally murdered, Martin is shocked to become the fetching female investigator's prime suspect. Center stage at last, Martin basks not in the glow of the spotlight, but in the harsh glare of interrogation.

Martin Misunderstood. unabr. ed. Karin Slaughter. Narrated by Wayne Knight. (ENG.). 2008. audio compact disk 19.95 (978-1-60283-434-7(2)) Pub: AudioGO. Dist(s): Perseus Dist

Martin Misunderstood. unabr. ed. Karin Slaughter. Read by Wayne Knight. 2 CDs. (Running Time: 2 hrs.). 2008. audio compact disk 19.95 (978-1-60283-411-8(3)) AudioGO.

Martin Simpson-Smoked Mirrors. Martin Simpson. 1997. pap. bk. 24.95 (978-0-7866-3094-3(9), 95717CDP) Mel Bay.

Martin the Warrior. Brian Jacques. Read by Brian Jacques. 2 cass. (Running Time: 3 hrs.). Dramatization. (Redwall Ser.: Bk. 2). (J). (gr. 4-8). 1998. 17.95 (L193) Blckstn Audio.
In this final installment of the great mouse epic, the good-hearted defenders of Redwall Abbey have stood against the wrath of Cluny the Scourge & his horde of rats. But now his minions are digging a tunnel under the thick walls of the Abbey. One mouse remains missing - the stalwart Matthias. Following his own destiny, as he seeks the sword of Martin the Warrior, a quest that will lead him into the lair of the great adder Asmodeus, & a horrifying confrontation with hypnotic evil. Will Redwall stand? Will Mathias return? And as the final battle rages, who will live, & who will die. Read by a full cast.

Martin the Warrior. Brian Jacques. 8 cass. (Running Time: 90 mins. per cass.). (Redwall Ser.). (J). (gr. 4-8). 2000. 50.00 (5162) Books on Tape.
This prequel gives the details of the early life of Redwall's founder & most glorious hero.

Martin the Warrior. collector's ed. Brian Jacques. Read by Brian Jacques. 8 cass. (Running Time: 12 hrs.). (Redwall Ser.). (J). (gr. 4-8). 1999. 50.00 (978-0-7366-9002-7(6)) Books on Tape.
Tale of how the mouse warrior of Redwall gained his title & his fame.

Martin the Warrior. unabr. ed. Brian Jacques. Read by Full Cast Production Staff. 8 cass. (Running Time: 12 hrs.). (Redwall Ser.). (J). (gr. 4-8). 1999. 52.00 (LL 0148, Chivers Child Audio) AudioGO.

Martin the Warrior. unabr. ed. Brian Jacques. Read by Brian Jacques. Read by Full Cast Production Staff. (Running Time: 36420 sec.). (Redwall Ser.). (ENG.). (J). (gr. 3-7). 2007. audio compact disk 40.00 (978-0-7393-5614-2(3), Listening Lib) Pub: Random Audio Pubg. Dist(s): Random

Martin the Warrior Bk. 1: The Prisoner & the Tyrant. unabr. ed. Brian Jacques. Read by Brian Jacques. 3 cass. (Redwall Ser.). (J). (gr. 4-8). 1999. 19.95 Set; trade pkg. (978-0-8072-8150-5(6), BWYA111CXR, Listening Lib); 23.98 Set; library album pkg. (978-0-8072-8128-4(X), BWYA111CX, Listening Lib) Random Audio Pubg.

Martin the Warrior Bk. 2: Actors & Searchers. unabr. ed. Brian Jacques. Read by Brian Jacques. 3 cass. (Redwall Ser.). (J). (gr. 4-8). 1999. 23.98 Library album pkg. (BWYA119CX, Listening Lib) Random Audio Pubg.

Martin the Warrior Bk. 3: The Battle of Marshank. unabr. ed. Brian Jacques. Read by Brian Jacques. 3 cass. (Redwall Ser.). (J). (gr. 4-8). 1999. 23.98 Set; library album pkg. (978-0-8072-8159-8(X), BWYA122CX, Listening Lib) Random Audio Pubg.

Martin the Warrior Bks. 1-3: The Prisoner & the Tyrant; Actors & Searchers; The Battle of Marshank. unabr. ed. Brian Jacques. 3 cass. (Redwall Ser.). (J). (gr. 4-8). 1999. 59.98 (FS9-50961) Highsmith.

Martin the Warrior Bks. 1-3: The Prisoner & the Tyrant; Actors & Searchers; The Battle of Marshank. unabr. ed. Brian Jacques. Read by Brian Jacques. 8 vols. (Running Time: 10 hrs. 10 mins.). Dramatization. (Redwall Ser.). (J). (gr. 4-7). 2004. pap. bk. 50.00 (978-0-8072-8177-2(8), YA124CX, Listening Lib); pap. bk. 58.00 (978-0-8072-8178-9(6), YA124SP, Listening Lib) Random Audio Pubg.

Jacques & a full cast relate the long awaited tale of how the mouse warrior of Redwall gained his title & his fame.

Martin Van Buren. rev. unabr. ed. Edward L. Widmer & Ted Widmer. (ENG.). 2003. audio compact disk 29.95 (978-1-55927-880-5(3)) Pub: Macmill Audio. Dist(s): Macmillan

Martina the Beautiful Cockroach: A Cuban Folktale. unabr. ed. Carmen Agra Deedy. Perf. by Carmen Agra Deedy. Illus. by Michael Austin. 1 CD. (Running Time: 37 mins.). (ENG & SPA.). (J). (gr. k-3). 2008. audio compact disk 6.95 (978-1-56145-467-9(2)) Peachtree Pubs.

Martina the Beautiful Cockroach: A Cuban Folktale. unabr. ed. Carmen Agra Deedy. Illus. by Michael Austin. 1 CD. (Running Time: 10 mins.). (ENG & SPA.). (J). (gr. k-3). 2008. bk. 19.95 (978-1-56145-468-6(0)) Peachtree Pubs.

Martine a l'Ecole. 1 cass. (FRE.). (J). (gr. 3 up). bk. 13.95 (1CA048) Olivia & Hill.

Martine goes to school.

Martine au Zoo. 1 cass. (FRE.). (J). (gr. 3 up). 1991. bk. 13.95 (1CA051) Olivia & Hill.

Martine dans la Foret. 1 cass.Tr. of Martine in the Forest. (FRE.). (J). (gr. 3 up). bk. 13.95 (1CA050) Olivia & Hill.

Martine decouvre la Musique. 1 cass. (FRE.). (J). (gr. 3 up). 1991. bk. 13.95 (1CA049) Olivia & Hill.

Martine discovers music.

Martine est Malade. 1 cass. (FRE.). (J). (gr. 3 up). bk. 13.95 (1CA047) Olivia & Hill.

Martine is sick & has to stay in bed.

Martine et le Cadeau d'Anniversaire. 1 cass. (FRE.). (J). (gr. 3 up). 1991. bk. 13.95 (1CA052) Olivia & Hill.

Martine's birthday party.

Martine Fait de la Bicyclette. 1 cass. (My Friend, Martine Ser.). (FRE.). (J). 1995. bk. 13.95 (1CA056) Olivia & Hill.

The adventures of 8-year-old Martine.

Martine Fait du Camping. 1 cass. (FRE.). (J). (gr. 3 up). 1991. bk. 13.95 (1CA053) Olivia & Hill.

Martine on a camping trip.

Martine Fait Du Cheval. 1 cass. (My Friend, Martine Ser.). (FRE.). (J). 1995. bk. 13.95 (1CA055) Olivia & Hill.

The adventures of 8-year-old Martine.

Martine in the Forest see Martine dans la Foret

Martine Petit Rat de l'Opera. 1 cass. (FRE.). (J). (gr. 3 up). 1991. bk. 13.95 (1CA054) Olivia & Hill.

Martine takes ballet lessons.

Martine, Petite Maman. 1 cass. (FRE.). (J). (gr. 3 up). 1991. bk. 13.95 (1CA045) Olivia & Hill.

Martine takes care of her baby brother.

Martin's Big Words. 2004. pap. bk. 38.75 (978-1-55592-637-3(1)); pap. bk. 32.75 (978-1-55592-367-9(4)); pap. bk. 14.95 (978-1-55592-169-9(8)) Weston Woods.

Martin's Big Words. 1 cass. (Running Time: 10 mins.). (J). (gr. k-6). 2004. bk. 24.95 (978-1-55592-092-0(6)); 8.95 (978-1-55592-960-2(5)); audio compact disk 12.95 (978-1-55592-934-3(6)) Weston Woods.

Dr. Martin Luther King, Jr. comes to life in this biography about beliefs and dreams and following one's heart.

Marty Aardvark. Created by Kane Press. (Let's Read Together Ser.). 2005. audio compact disk 4.25 (978-1-57565-180-4(7)) Kane Pr.

Marty Brennaman: Voice of the Reds. Janell Hughes. (ENG.). 2006. audio compact disk 16.00 (978-0-9818365-2-2(6)) Baseball Voice.

***Marty Mcguire - Audio.** Kate Messner. (ENG.). 2011. audio compact disk 19.99 (978-0-545-32144-0(1)) Scholastic Inc.

***Marty Mcguire - Audio Library Edition.** Kate Messner. (ENG.). 2011. audio compact disk 29.99 (978-0-545-32146-4(8)) Scholastic Inc.

Martyr. unabr. ed. Rory Clements. Narrated by Todd McLaren & Simon Vance. 10 CDs. (Running Time: 12 hrs. 30 mins. 0 sec.). (ENG.). 2009. audio compact disk 75.99 (978-1-4001-4066-4(8)); audio compact disk 37.99 (978-1-4001-1066-7(1)) Pub: Tantor Media. Dist(s): IngramPubServ

Martyr. unabr. ed. Rory Clements. Read by Simon Vance. Narrated by Todd McLaren. (Running Time: 12 hrs. 30 mins. 0 sec.). (ENG.). 2009. audio compact disk 24.99 (978-1-4001-6066-2(9)) Pub: Tantor Media. Dist(s): IngramPubServ

Martyr (James) Acts 12:1-2. Ed Young. 1985. 4.95 (978-0-7417-1467-1(1), 467) Win Walk.

Martyr of the Catacombs. unabr. ed. Read by Frederick Davidson. 3 cass. (Running Time: 4 hrs.). 2000. 23.95 (978-0-7861-2432-9(6), 3111) Blckstn Audio.

Martyr of the Catacombs. unabr. ed. Read by Frederick Davidson. 3 CDs. (Running Time: 4 hrs.). 2001. audio compact disk 24.00 (978-0-7861-8830-7(8), 3111) Blckstn Audio.

Martyrs' Day: Chronicle of a Small War. unabr. collector's ed. Michael Kelly. Read by Jonathan Reese. 10 cass. (Running Time: 15 hrs.). 1995. 80.00 (978-0-7366-3101-3(1), 3777) Books on Tape.

As bombs fell on Baghdad & the Gulf War erupted, journalist Thomas Kelly was there. Cruising in a 4X4, he witnessed it all: the ground war in Saudi Arabia, the missile attacks in Israel, shadows of torture & rape in Kuwait, & highways strewn with twisted torsos - grisly remnants of the Iraqi retreat.

Martyr's Dying Words to You: Focus: Logos December 12, 1999. Ben Young. 1999. 4.95 (978-0-7417-6161-3(0), B0161) Win Walk.

Martyr's Dying Words to You: Power: Logos December 12, 1999. Ben Young. 1999. 4.95 (978-0-7417-6160-6(2), B0161) Win Walk.

Martyrs to Madness. abr. ed. Vonnie Lindsell. Read by Lew Nelson et al. 1 cass. 1996. 26.95 (978-0-9651882-4-1(8)) Ace Enter.

Story about a serial killer who terrorizes citizens of a small town when their power is cut off by a slide during an earthquake.

Maruzen International Organic Modeling Kit #1013. audio compact disk (978-0-8400-5325-1(8)) Pearson Higher.

Marva Collins Interview. 1 cass. (Leonard Peikoff Show Ser.). 1996. 12.95 (LPXXC11) Second Renaissance.

Marvel. Perf. by Lads. 2002. audio compact disk 17.98 Provident Music.

Marvel of the Real, Program 11. Read by Alejo Carpentier. (F007FB090) Natl Public Radio.

Marvellous Land of Oz. abr. ed. L. Frank Baum. (Running Time: 2 hrs. 30 mins.). 2009. audio compact disk 17.98 (978-962-634-950-2(6), Naxos AudioBooks) Naxos.

Marvelous Effect. unabr. ed. Troy Cle. Read by Malcolm-Jamal Warner. 7 CDs. (Running Time: 8 hrs. 9 mins.). (J). (gr. 4-7). 2007. audio compact disk 50.00 (978-0-7393-5100-0(1), Random Hse Audible) Pub: Random Audio Pubg. Dist(s): Random

Marvelous Effect. unabr. ed. Troy Cle. Read by Malcolm-Jamal Warner. (Running Time: 29340 sec.). (Marvelous World Ser.). (ENG.). (J). (gr. 5-12). 2007. audio compact disk 37.00 (978-0-7393-5047-8(1), Listening Lib) Pub: Random Audio Pubg. Dist(s): Random

Marvelous Inventions of Alvin Fernald. unabr. ed. Clifford B. Hicks. Narrated by Johnny Heller. 2 cass. (Running Time: 2 hrs. 30 mins.). (YA). 1999. pap. bk. & stu. ed. 32.24 (978-0-7887-3648-3(5), 41014X4) Recorded Bks.

Marvelous Inventions of Alvin Fernald. unabr. ed. Clifford B. Hicks. Narrated by Johnny Heller. 2 cass. (Running Time: 2 hrs. 30 mins.). (gr. 7 up). 1999. 19.00 (978-0-7887-3517-2(9), 95909E7) Recorded Bks.

If you'd like to own an automatic bed maker or a foolproof burglar alarm, Alvin is the man for you. His 12-year-old brain is constantly inventing contraptions to make life easier. When old Mrs. Huntley disappears, Alvin investigates.

Marvelous Inventions of Alvin Fernald, Class set. Clifford B. Hicks. Read by Johnny Heller. 2 cass. (Running Time: 2 hrs. 30 mins.). (YA). 1999. stu. ed. 89.70 (978-0-7887-3678-0(7), 46981) Recorded Bks.

Marvelous Journey Home. John M. Simmons. Read by Alan Peterson. 1 cass, 10 CDs. (Running Time: 39600 sec.). Dramatization. (ENG.). 2008. audio compact disk 29.95 (978-0-9725916-4-5(8)) WhiteKnight.

Marvelous Land of Oz, Set. unabr. ed. L. Frank Baum. Read by Flo Gibson. 3 cass. (Running Time: 4 hrs. 30 min.). (Oz Ser.). (YA). (gr. 5-8). 1993. 16.95 (978-1-55685-290-9(8)) Audio Bk Con.

Tip escapes from the wicked witch Mombi with the companions he created, Jack Pumpkinhead & the Saw-Horse. They join forces with the Scarecrow, the Tin Woodman & Glinda the Good to recapture the Emerald City from General Ginjur.

Marvelous Mentors. Dave Johnson. (Dave Johnson Educational Library). D Johnson.

An Anthology of first person stories that are designed for inspiration.

***Marvelous Motion CD.** Nadia Higgins. Illus. by Andres Martinez Ricci. (Science Rocks! Set 2 CD Ser.). 2010. cd-rom 27.07 (978-1-60270-965-2(3)) ABDO Pub Co.

***Marvelous Motion Site CD.** Nadia Higgins. Illus. by Andres Martinez Ricci. (Science Rocks! Set 2 Site CD Ser.). 2010. cd-rom 57.07 (978-1-60270-979-9(3)) ABDO Pub Co.

***Marvelous Mouth Music: Songames for Speech Development.** Suzanne Evans Morris et al. (ENG.). 2010. audio compact disk 21.95 (978-1-935567-09-7(8)) Pub: Sensory Res. Dist(s): IngramPubServ

Marvelous Mouth Music: Songames for Speech Therapy & Beyond. Aubrey Londe et al. 1 cass., 1 CD. (Running Time: 1 hr. 15 min.). (Belle Curve Clinical Ser.). (J). (ps-3). 1998. bk. 20.00 (978-1-893601-05-5(6), BCRI-6B); 22.00 bklet. (978-1-893601-04-8(8), BCRI-6A) Sensory Res.

Twenty-one activity-based song games enhance speech development & language acquisition.

Marvelous Musical Adventures. 1 cass. (J). (ps-2). 1987. bk. 7.95; bk. 15.95; 9.95 Musical Munchkins.

Marvelous Musical Adventures for Developing Early Musicianship. Chris Patella & Eileen Oddo. Illus. by Karen Hanley. (Musical Munchkins Presents Ser.). 1987. cass. & lp 9.95 (978-0-685-19315-0(2)) Musical Munchkins.

Marvelous Toy. Tom Paxton. (Metro Reading Ser.). (J). (gr. k). 2000. 8.46 (978-1-58120-993-8(2)) Metro Teaching.

Marvelous Work & a Wonder, Set. LeGrand Richards. Narrated by Rex Campbell. 10 cass. 20.97 (978-1-55503-575-4(2), 03997) Covenant Comms.

Marvin Bell, Set, Pts. 1 & 11. unabr. ed. Read by Marvin Bell. 2 cass. (Running Time: 29 min.). 1985. 10.00 ea. One-sided cass.; 18.00 Two-sided cass. New Letters.

Marvin Bell of the Iowa Writers Workshop reads from several of his poetry books.

Marvin One Too Many. Katherine Paterson. Illus. by Jane Clark Brown. 11 vols. (Running Time: 13 mins.). 2003. bk. 25.95 (978-1-59112-254-8(6)); bk. 28.95 (978-1-59112-635-5(5)); pap. bk. 31.95 (978-1-59112-636-2(3)); 9.95 (978-1-59112-252-4(X)); audio compact disk 12.95 (978-1-59112-633-1(9)) Live Oak Media.

Marvin One Too Many. Katherine Paterson. Illus. by Jane Clark Brown. 14 vols. (Running Time: 13 mins.). (Readalongs for Beginning Readers Ser.). (J). 2003. pap. bk. 29.95 (978-1-59112-255-5(4)) Live Oak Media.

Marwan: The Autobiography of a 9/11 Terrorist. Aram Schefrin. (Running Time: 16 hrs). 2005. audio compact disk 0.00 (978-1-4276-0039-4(2)) AardGP.

How did an Egyptian city planner, a Yemeni religious fanatic, a boy from the United Arab Emirates who worshipped sex, not Allah, and a young student of aircraft design who went to a Christian school in Lebanon- four very different men with very different ideas- get involved in flying the 9/11 planes? How did the plot develop, and who developed it? "Marwan," a podcast novel by Aram Schefrin, puts the reported facts together and fills in the details - from the group's first coming together in Hamburg, Germany, to the moments before the jets they were to hijack took off. You'll come to know the participants, and how they were motivated, what their personal lives were like and the roles they played in the plan. You will learn to know them as people- not simply as "terrorists"- because, as the author sees it, you have to understand your enemies if you want to defend yourself. The novel can be subscribed to or downloaded chapter by chapter at iTunes and most other podcatchers, or directly at libsyn.com or podiobooks.com.

Marx in Soho: A Play on History. Howard Zinn. Brian Jones. (ENG.). 2009. audio compact disk 16.00 (978-1-931859-80-6(9)) Pub: Haymarket Bks. Dist(s): Consort Bk Sales

Marx in 90 Minutes. unabr. ed. Paul Strathern. Read by Robert Whitfield. (Running Time: 5400 sec.). (Philosophers in 90 Minutes Ser.). 2006. 14.95 (978-0-7861-3684-1(7)); audio compact disk 16.00 (978-0-7861-5944-4(8)) Blckstn Audio.

Marxism: Philosophy & Economics. unabr. ed. Thomas Sowell. Read by Louis Lotorto. 6 cass. (Running Time: 8 hrs. 30 mins.). 1988. 44.95 (978-0-7861-0007-1(9), 1006) Blckstn Audio.

Shatters some existing interpretations of Marx - interpretations that have become standard through repetition, rather than scholarship. Topics include: Marx's concept of capitalist "exploitation," Marxian morality, Marx's business cycle theory, Communism in Marx & in the Soviet Union & Marx the man.

Marx's das Kapital: A Biography. unabr. ed. Francis Wheen. Narrated by Simon Vance. (Running Time: 3 hrs. 30 mins. 0 sec.). (Books That Changed the World Ser.). (ENG.). 2007. audio compact disk 24.99 (978-1-4001-0392-8(4)); audio compact disk 19.99 (978-1-4001-5392-3(1)) Pub: Tantor Media. Dist(s): IngramPubServ

Marx's das Kapital: A Biography. unabr. ed. Francis Wheen. Read by Simon Vance. (Running Time: 3 hrs. 30 mins. 0 sec.). (Books That Changed the World Ser.). (ENG.). 2007. audio compact disk 49.99 (978-1-4001-3392-5(0)) Pub: Tantor Media. Dist(s): IngramPubServ

Marx's General: The Revolutionary Life of Friedrich Engels. unabr. ed. Tristram Hunt. Narrated by Norman Dietz. 2 MP3-CDs. (Running Time: 17 hrs. 0 mins. 0 sec.). 2010. 29.99 (978-1-4001-6372-4(2)); audio compact disk 79.99 (978-1-4001-4372-6(1)); audio compact disk 39.99 (978-1-4001-1372-9(5)) Pub: Tantor Media. Dist(s): IngramPubServ

***Marx's General: The Revolutionary Life of Friedrich Engels.** unabr. ed. Tristram Hunt. Narrated by Norman Dietz. (Running Time: 17 hrs. 0 mins.). 2010. 21.99 (978-1-4001-8372-2(3)); 39.99 (978-1-4001-9372-1(9)) Tantor Media.

Mary. Mary Wollstonecraft. Read by Anais 9000. 2008. 27.95 (978-1-60112-186-8(5)) Babblebooks.

***Mary.** unabr. ed. Vladimir Nabokov. (Running Time: 4 hrs.). 2010. 39.97 (978-1-4418-7253-1(1), 9781441872531, BADLE); 19.99 (978-1-4418-7252-4(3), 9781441872524, BAD); audio compact disk 59.97 (978-1-4418-7249-4(3), 9781441872494, BriAudCD Unabrid) Brilliance Audio.

***Mary.** unabr. ed. Vladimir Nabokov. Read by Christopher Lane. (Running Time: 4 hrs.). 2010. 19.99 (978-1-4418-7250-0(7), 9781441872500, Brilliance MP3); 39.97 (978-1-4418-7251-7(5), 9781441872517, Brinc Audio MP3 Lib); audio compact disk 19.99 (978-1-4418-7248-7(5), 9781441872487, Bril Audio CD Unabri) Brilliance Audio.

Mary: A Gospel Portrait. Francis J. Moloney. 3 cass. 24.95 incl. shelf-case. (TAH100) Alba Hse Comns.

Reflections upon the gospel materials about Mary.

Mary: Full of Grace. Megan McKenna. 3 cass. (Running Time: 3 hrs.). 2001. 26.95 (A6460) St Anthony Mess Pr.

Discusses the different images of Jesus' mother found in the Gospels, tells of Mary's focus on loving others and suggests Mary is the mother of all who are outcasts.

Mary: Gifted by the Spirit. Carole Riley. 2 cass. (Running Time: 2 hrs. 39 min.). 1997. 18.95 Set. (TAH384) St Pauls Alba.

The insights derived from this superb program can be applied across the spectrum of contemporary life to help develop an integration which celebrates the gifts of the Holy Spirit.

Mary: Her Life, Her Story, Her Destiny. Terri Copeland Pearsons. (ENG.). 2006. audio compact disk 5.00 (978-1-57562-928-5(3)) K Copeland Pubns.

Mary: Light & Temple. Thomas Merton. 1 cass. 8.95 (AA2367) Credence Commun.

Mary: Our Mother & Advocate. Jeff Cavins. 2006. audio compact disk 9.95 (978-1-934567-03-6(5)) Excorde Inc.

Mary - Her Honor & Her Dignity. 1 cass. (Running Time: 60 min.). (Mother Angelica Live Ser.). 10.00 (978-1-55794-082-7(7), T33) Eternal Wrd TV.

Mary & Elisabeth: Noble Daughters of God. Kent Brown. 2 cass. 2004. 14.95 (978-1-59156-101-9(9)) Covenant Comms.

Mary & the Holy Spirit. Fred Jelly. 2 cass. (Running Time: 2 hrs.). 1992. 15.95 set. (TAH267) Alba Hse Comns.

Perfect for meditation, preparation for Pentecost, monthly recollection, prayer groups, discussion groups.

Mary & the Holy Spirit in St. John of the Cross. Emmanuel Sullivan. 1 cass. (Running Time: 56 min.). 8.95 I C S Pubns.

Fr. Emmanuel Sullivan, O.C.D. gives a timely reflection on Mary as exemplar of one moved in all things by the Spirit of God.

Mary & the New Millennium. abr. ed. Fred Jelly. 1 cass. (Running Time: 1 hrs. 26 min.). 1998. 9.95 (TAH401) Alba Hse Comns.

Fr. Jelly explores Mary's special role in preparing for the coming of the third millennium.

Mary & the Spiritual Life. Frederick L. Miller. Read by Frederick L. Miller. 5 cass. (Running Time: 5 hrs.). 1991. 19.95 (978-1-56036-024-7(0), 362502) AMI Pr.

Tapes include: The Spiritual Motherhood of Mary (Parts 1 & 2); Mary, Model & Mother of Faith; Mary's Journey of Faith; the Meaning of Consecration to Mary. Recorded at Fatima, Portugal.

Mary Ann & Bill. unabr. ed. Catherine Cookson. Read by Susan Jameson. 4 cass. (Running Time: 4 hrs.). 1993. 39.95 (978-0-7451-5854-9(4), CAB 030) AudioGO.

***Mary Ann in Autumn.** unabr. ed. Armistead Maupin. 2010. audio compact disk 34.99 (978-0-06-200849-7(8), Harper Audio) HarperCollins Pubs.

***Mary Ann in Autumn: A Tales of the City Novel.** unabr. ed. Armistead Maupin. Read by Armistead Maupin. 2010. (978-0-06-200713-1(0), Harper Audio); (978-0-06-206190-4(9), Harper Audio) HarperCollins Pubs.

Mary-Anne see Osbert Sitwell Reading His Poetry

Mary Anne. unabr. ed. Daphne Du Maurier. Read by Carole Boyd. 10 cass. (Running Time: 15 hrs.). 2003. 84.95 (978-0-7540-0923-8(8), CAB 2345) AudioGO.

Mary Ann's Angels. unabr. ed. Catherine Cookson. Read by Susan Jameson. 4 cass. (Running Time: 4 hrs.). 1993. 39.95 (978-0-7451-5855-6(2), CAB 029) AudioGO.

Mary As Catechist at Fatima. Frederick L. Miller. 1 cass. 1989. 2.50 (978-1-56036-069-8(0)) AMI Pr.

Mary at Fatima, Image & Model of the Church. Frederick L. Miller. 1 cass. 1992. 2.50 (978-1-56036-044-5(5)) AMI Pr.

Mary Baker Eddy. Helen M. Wright. Read by Alan Young & Michael Sutton. 4 cass. (Running Time: 4 hrs. 30 mins.). (God's Great Scientist Ser.: Vol. 2). 1999. 14.95 (978-1-886505-17-9(9)) H M Wright.

Addresses the chapter "Imposition & Demonstration" in Eddy's first edition of Science & Health.

Mary Baker Eddy. collector's ed. Gillian Gill. Read by Donada Peters. 11 cass. (Running Time: 16 hrs. 30 min.). 2000. 88.00 (978-0-7366-5506-4(9)); 80.00 (978-0-7366-5553-8(0)) Books on Tape.

Mary Baker Eddy (1821-1910) rose, in mid-life, from poverty, illness & obscurity to found the Christian Science Church, a national newspaper & to become one of the most influential women in America.

Mary Baker Eddy. unabr. ed. 1 cass. (Running Time: 54 min.). (History Maker Ser.). 12.95 (41023) J Norton Pubs.

Describes the upheaval created by her new religion & the criticism & challenges that arose as its influence spread through the world.

Mary Baker Eddy Vol. 1: Leader Forever. abr. ed. Helen M. Wright. Read by Alan Young. 4 cass. (Running Time: 2 hrs. 45 min.). 1997. pap. bk. 12.95 Set. (978-1-886505-07-0(1)) H M Wright.

Dynamite information that has been hidden from Christian Scientists concerning the history of Eddy's church.

Mary Baker Eddy Vol. 3: God's Great Scientist. Helen M. Wright. Read by Alan Young. 4 cass. (Running Time: 4 hrs. 30 mins.). 1999. 15.50 (978-1-886505-26-1(8)) H M Wright.

Focuses on Chapter III, "Spirit & Matter," which proclaims Spirit is All; matter is illusion. This core teaching leads us out of materiality, translating human

consciousness from matter beliefs back into Spirit, our true & right God-being & identity.

Mary Baker Eddy Vol. 3: God's Great Scientist. abr. ed. Helen M. Wright. Read by Alan Young & Michael Sutton. 4 cass. (Running Time: 4 hrs. 30 mins.). 1998. 15.50 (978-1-886505-15-5(2)) H M Wright.
Explores Mrs. Eddy's vital early teaching, before Science & Health was written, which enabled her students to go forth & heal every manner of disease & discord, then delves into Chapter 1 of the first edition of Science & Health to reveal the all-power of Mind, the true & real Mind of the reader.

Mary Baker Eddy Reveals Your Divinity. abr. ed. Helen M. Wright. Read by Alan Young. 6 cass. (Running Time: 8 hrs.). (Mary Baker Eddy - God's Great Scientist Ser.: Vol. 4). 1998. pap. bk. 19.95 (978-1-886505-10-0(1)) H M Wright.
Explores Chapter IV to reveal how Mary Baker Eddy, God's divinely prophesied messenger to this age, lifts the veil, the hypnotism of the five physical senses that hides your divinity. "The kingdom of God is within you," needing only spiritual education to set you free to enjoy your infinite harmonious Christ-expressing selfhood.

Mary Barton: A Tale of Manchester Life. unabr. ed. Elizabeth Gaskell. Read by Flo Gibson. 10 cass. (Running Time: 14 hrs. 30 min.). 1996. 44.95 (978-1-55685-402-6(1)) Audio Bk Con.
A social history of the appalling results of the "hungry" 1840's in Manchester, a love story & a murder, involving Mary, her father & Jem Wilson, are vividly told as we witness individual responses to poverty & injustice.

Mary, Behold Thy Son, Set. Roxcy Jeppson. 2 cass. 11.95 (978-1-57734-231-1(3), 07001711) Covenant Comms.

Mary Called Magdalene: A Novel. unabr. ed. Margaret George. Read by Melissa Hughes. 3 CDs. (Running Time: 30 hrs,). 2002. audio compact disk 69.95 (978-0-7927-2660-9(X), CMP 456, Chivers Sound Lib) AudioGO.
Brilliantly grounded in both biblical and secular historical research, it depicts Mary of Magdala in the first hundred years of the first millennium, even as it peels away layers of legend. Testaments, letters, and narrative convincingly capture Mary's immediate and moving voice as she becomes part of the circle of disciples and comes to grips with the divine.

Mary, Did You Know? Satb. Contrib. by Bruce Greer. Created by Bruce Greer. Created by David Guthrie. 1998. audio compact disk 16.98 (978-7-01-985759-7(0), Word Music) Word Enter.

***Mary Ellen Edmunds Collection, Cd Set.** Mary Ellen Edmunds. 2010. audio compact disk 39.99 (978-1-60641-263-3(9)) Deseret Bk.

Mary Engelbreit's Mother Goose. unabr. ed. Mary Engelbreit. Read by Lynn Redgrave & Leonard S. Marcus. 1 cd. (Running Time: 30 mins). (J). 2005. 13.95 (978-0-06-082399-3(2), HarperChildAud) HarperCollins Pubs.

***Mary Engelbreit's Mother Goose: One-Hundred Best Loved Verses.** unabr. ed. Mary Engelbreit. Read by Lynn Redgrave. (ENG.). 2005. (978-0-06-088975-3(6)); (978-0-06-088976-0(4)) HarperCollins Pubs.

Mary for Today. Hans Urs Von Balthasar. Read by Andrea Pruseau. 2 cass. 1988. pap. bk. 7.95 (978-0-89870-190-6(2), 120) Ignatius Pr.
A rich harvest of scripture and tradition about the Mother of God.

Mary Gordon. unabr. ed. Mary Gordon. 1 cass. (Running Time: 29 min.). 1991. 10.00 (010590) New Letters.
The Other Side.

Mary Gordon: The Second Coming. unabr. ed. Mary Gordon. Read by Mary Gordon. 1 cass. (Running Time: 30 min.). 1990. 10.00 (NL 40) New Letters.
The writer reads from her highly acclaimed fourth novel, "The Second Coming," & talks about the effect Catholicism has had on her work & ideas.

Mary Had a Little Lamb. (YA). 2003. audio compact disk 60.00 (978-1-58302-240-5(6)) One Way St.
This 30-minute musical tells the Christmas story from the viewpoint of the stable animals. God's plan of replacing the sacrifice of an unblemished lamb with the Messiah, who would eventually die for man's sin, is presented so beautifully that children and adults can each understand at their own level. There are twelve speaking parts: ten animals, a male and female narrator.Written by Dan Barker.

Mary Had a Little Lamb. 2004. bk. 24.95 (978-0-7882-0582-8(X)); pap. bk. 14.95 (978-0-7882-0650-4(8)); 8.95 (978-0-89719-952-0(9)); cass. & flmstrp 30.00 (978-0-89719-564-5(7)) Weston Woods.

Mary Had a Little Lamb. Dan Barker. (YA). 2003. audio compact disk 15.00 (978-1-58302-238-2(4)) One Way St.

Mary Had a Little Lamb. unabr. ed. Sarah Josephbuell Hale. Illus. by Tomie dePaola. 1 cass. (Running Time: 6 mins.). (J). (ps-2). 1989. bk. 22.95 Incl. cloth bk. (978-0-87499-125-3(0)); pap. bk. 15.95 (978-0-87499-124-6(2)) Live Oak Media.
The original nursery rhyme of 1830 in its entirety.

Mary Had a Little Lamb, unabr. ed. Sarah Josephbuell Hale. Illus. by Tomie dePaola. 14 vols. (Running Time: 6 mins.). (J). (ps-2). 1989. pap. bk. 33.95 4 bks. & guide. (978-0-87499-126-0(9)) Live Oak Media.

Mary Had a Little Lamb: Instrumental Only. (YA). 2003. audio compact disk 60.00 (978-1-58302-241-2(4)) One Way St.
This 30-minute musical tells the Christmas story from the viewpoint of the stable animals. God's plan of replacing the sacrifice of an unblemished lamb with the Messiah, who would eventually die for man's sin, is presented so beautifully that children and adults can each understand at their own level. There are twelve speaking parts: ten animals, a male and female narrator. Written by Dan Barker.

Mary Has a Little Lamb Audio CD. Adapted by Benchmark Education Company Staff. Based on a work by Carrie Smith. (Reader's Theater Nursery Rhymes & Songs Ser.). (J). (gr. k-1). 2008. audio compact disk 10.00 (978-1-60634-002-8(6)) Benchmark Educ.

Mary Higgins Clark Double Feature. abr. ed. Mary Higgins Clark. Read by Jessica Walter & Elizabeth Ashley. 4 cass. (Running Time: 4 hrs.). 25.00 Set. S&S Audio.

Mary Higgins Clark Presents Malice Domestic II: An Anthology of Original Mystery Stories. unabr. ed. Read by Mason Adams et al. 4 cass. (Running Time: 6 hrs.). 2001. 25.00 (978-1-59040-010-4(0), Phoenix Audio) Pub: Amer Intl Pub. Dist(s): PerseuPGW
A delightfully chilling collection of original mystery stories showcases a houseful of top contemporary writers at their very best.

Mary in Our Spiritual Life Today. Fred Jelly. 2 cass. (Running Time: 2 hrs.). 1992. 16.95 set. (TAH259) Alba Hse Comns.
These tapes should be very useful to everyone & to all groups who wish to come closer & closer to Christ through Mary.

Mary in the Catechism of the Catholic Church. Fred Jelly. 1 cass. (Running Time: 1 hr. 45 min.). 1995. 8.95 (TAH356) Alba Hse Comns.
Fr. Jelly has developed this program on the theology of Mary based on the new catechism of the Catholic church. This enlightening mini-course is a valuable tool for the study of the theology of Mary, & a great companion to the new catechism.

Mary in the Scripture & in the Teaching of the Church. Frederick L. Miller. Read by Frederick L. Miller. 5 cass. (Running Time: 5 hrs.). 16.95 (978-1-56036-008-7(9), 361574) AMI Pr.
This series includes presentations on the mystery of Mary & the Immaculate Conception, her Perpetual Virginity, Divine Maternity & her role as Model of the Church.

Mary in the Scriptures & Devotion to Mary: An Avenue to God. James C. Turro. Read by James C. Turro. 1 cass. (Running Time: 1 hr.). 2.50 (978-0-911988-87-1(4), 361564) AMI Pr.
A spiritual insight into the love & devotion of Our Lady.

Mary Joan Coleman. unabr. ed. Read by Mary J. Coleman. 1 cass. (Running Time: 29 min.). 1986. 10.00 New Letters.
The author read from her book "Take One Blood Red Rose", about the Appalachia region. Music is performed by Brian Lloyd.

Mary-Kate & Ashley's Greatest Hits. Perf. by Mary-Kate Olsen & Ashley Olsen. 1 CD. (Running Time: 1 hr.). (J). 2002. audio compact disk 15.98 (978-1-56896-425-6(0), 54363-2) Lightyear Entrtnmnt.
America has watched the Olsen twins grow up from their TV series "Full House" to their current series "So Little Time". The whole family can enjoy this series titles. Featuring Fashion Jr. High, We're Gonna Start Somethin' New, It's Not Me, it's You.

Mary-Kate & Ashley's Greatest Hits, Vol. I. 1 cass. (Running Time: 1 hr.). (J). 2002. 8.98 (978-1-56896-426-3(9), 54363-4) Lightyear Entrtnmnt.

Mary-Kate & Ashley's Greatest Hits, Vol. II. Perf. by Mary-Kate Olsen & Ashley Olsen. 1 cass. (Running Time: 1 hr.). (J). 2002. 8.98 (978-1-56896-562-8(1), 54441-4); audio compact disk 15.98 (978-1-56896-561-1(3), 54441-2) Lightyear Entrtnmnt.

Mary Kay: On People Management, unabr. ed. Mary Kay Ash. Narrated by Rita Knox. 4 cass. (Running Time: 5 hrs. 30 mins.). 1985. 35.00 (978-1-55690-334-2(0), 85120E7) Recorded Bks.
She built a multimillion dollar cosmetics business from a 500 square-foot Dallas storefront. Anyone in a leadership position would do well to listen to her story.

Mary Kay on People Management. unabr. ed. Mary Kay Ash. Read by Roses Prichard. 8 cass. (Running Time: 8 hrs.). 1985. 48.00 (978-0-7366-1019-3(7), 1950) Books on Tape.
Designed to encourage managers to treat staff, customers, suppliers & everyone with the same care, consideration & concern they would like to receive themselves.

Mary MacKillop Unveiled. unabr. ed. Lesley O'Brien. Read by Jenny Seedsman. 6 cass. (Running Time: 9 hrs.). 1998. (978-1-86340-609-3(3), 550702) Bolinda Pubng AUS.
A moving account of the life & times of Australia's first official saint, who let nothing stand in the way of her care for the underprivileged. Her determination brought her into conflict with the leading churchmen of the day.

***Mary MacKillop Unveiled.** unabr. ed. Lesley O'Brien. Read by Jenny Seedsman. (Running Time: 8 hrs. 25 mins.). 2010. audio compact disk 83.95 (978-1-74214-842-7(5), 9781742148427) Pub: Bolinda Pubng AUS. Dist(s): Bolinda Pub Inc

Mary Magdalene. 2 cass. (Running Time: 2 hrs.). 1997. 12.99 HARK Ent.

Mary Magdelene. Contrib. by Bible Games Company Staff. 1 cass. 1997. 14.99 (978-7-901288-77-5(9)) Bible Games Co.
Bible stories from the New Testament.

Mary, Mary. unabr. ed. Ed McBain, pseud. Read by Paul Shay. 9 cass. (Running Time: 13 hrs. 30 min.). (Matthew Hope Mystery Ser.: No. 10). 1993. 72.00 (978-0-7366-2480-0(5), 3242) Books on Tape.
Matthew Hope defends a former teacher charged with the murder of three young girls found buried in her garden.

Mary, Mary. unabr. ed. James Patterson. 7 CDs. (Running Time: 7 hrs. 30 mins.). (Alex Cross Ser.: No. 11). 2005. audio compact disk 63.00 (978-1-4159-2580-5(1)); 45.00 (978-1-4159-2579-9(8)) Books on Tape.
Several high-profile murders in LA have the whole district panicking. All the victims are perfect visions of motherhood, and when detailed, first-person accounts of the killings arrive at the LA Times, FBI agent Alex Cross is called in to investigate.

Mary, Mary. unabr. ed. James Patterson. Read by Peter Jay Fernandez et al. (Alex Cross Ser.: No. 11). (ENG.). 2005. 14.98 (978-1-59483-266-6(8)) Pub: Hachet Audio. Dist(s): HachBkGrp

Mary, Mary. unabr. ed. James Patterson. Read by Peter Jay Fernandez et al. (Running Time: 8 hrs.). (Alex Cross Ser.: No. 11). (ENG.). 2009. 59.98 (978-1-60788-105-6(5)) Pub: Hachet Audio. Dist(s): HachBkGrp

Mary McAnally. unabr. ed. Read by Mary McAnally. 1 cass. (Running Time: 29 min.). 1985. 10.00 New Letters.
A reading by the author of "We Will Make A River" & "Absence of The Father".

Mary McCarthy. Interview with Mary McCarthy. 1 cass. (Running Time: 25 min.). 1973. 11.95 (L046) TFR.
McCarthy talks about Watergate as a novel as this interview was conducted during the 1973 Ervin Committee hearings she was covering as a reporter. She says only Tolstoy or Dostoyevsky could have coped with the material & she ventures some guesses as to how they would have done it.

Mary Modern. unabr. ed. Camille DeAngelis. Read by Jenna Lamia et al. (YA). 2007. 44.99 (978-1-60252-765-2(2)) Find a World.

Mary Moon Is Missing. Patricia Reilly Giff. Illus. by Lynne Avril Cravath. 2000. 9.95 (978-0-87499-633-3(3)); 9.95 (978-0-87499-634-0(1)) Live Oak Media.

Mary Moon Is Missing. Patricia Reilly Giff. Read by Dana Lubotsky. Illus. by Lynne W. Cravath. 21 vols. (Running Time: 1 hr. 32 mins.). (Adventures of Minnie & Max Ser.). (J). (gr. 4). 2000. pap. bk. 23.95 (978-0-87499-636-4(8)) Live Oak Media.
Minnie isn't crazy about pigeons, but she likes to investigate mysteries with her best friend, Cash & her rather unusual cat, Max. So when a prize racing pigeon, Mary Moon, disappears, Minnie & her friends are on the case.

Mary Moon Is Missing. Patricia Reilly Giff. Read by Dana Lubotsky. Illus. by Lynne W. Cravath. 2 vols. (Running Time: 1 hr. 32 mins.). (Adventures of Minnie & Max Ser.). (J). (gr. 4-6). 2000. bk. 30.95 (978-0-87499-637-1(6)) Live Oak Media.

Mary Moon Is Missing. Patricia Reilly Giff. Read by Dana Lubotsky. Illus. by Lynne Avril Cravath. (Running Time: 5520 sec.). (Adventures of Minnie & Max Ser.). (J). 2006. audio compact disk 22.95 (978-1-59519-846-4(6)) Live Oak Media.

Mary Moon Is Missing. Patricia Reilly Giff. Read by Dana Lubotsky. Illus. by Lynne Avril Cravath. (Live Oak Mysteries Ser.). (J). 2006. pap. bk. 27.95 (978-1-59519-847-1(4)) Live Oak Media.

Mary Moon Is Missing. unabr. ed. Patricia Reilly Giff. Read by Dana Lubotsky. Illus. by Lynne W. Cravath. 24 vols. (Running Time: 1 hr. 32 mins.). (Adventures of Minnie & Max Ser.). (J). 2000. pap. bk. & tchr. ed. 32.95 Reading Chest. (978-0-87499-638-8(4)); 16.95 (978-0-87499-635-7(X), OAK004) Pub: Live Oak Media. Dist(s): AudioGO

Mary Morison see Poetry of Robert Burns & Border Ballads

Mary Morris. unabr. ed. Mary McGarry Morris. Read by Mary McGarry Morris. 1 cass. (Running Time: 29 min.). 1988. 10.00 New Letters.
Morris reads from her travel memoir Nothing to Declare & is interviewed.

Mary, Mother of Evangelization. John A. Hardon. 1 cass. (National Meeting of the Institute, 1992 Ser.). 4.00 (92N8) IRL Chicago.

Mary Mother of God. Edd Anthony. Read by Edd Anthony. 1 cass. (Running Time: 30 min.). 1989. 6.95 (978-1-881586-03-6(0)) Canticle Cass.
Meditation & music (spoken word meditation).

Mary Mother of God. Edd Anthony. Read by Edd Anthony. 2007. audio compact disk 16.95 (978-1-881586-19-7(7)) Canticle Cass.

Mary of Mile 18. 2004. 8.95 (978-1-56008-965-0(2)); cass. & flmstrp 30.00 (978-1-56008-716-8(1)) Weston Woods.

Mary Our Hope. John J. Wright. Read by Maureen O'Leary. 9 cass. 1988. 36.95 (937) Ignatius Pr.
Posthumous collection of sermons and writings by Cardinal John J. Wright on Our Lady.

Mary Poppins. (Classic Soundtrack Ser.). (J). (gr. k up). 1997. 11.99 (978-0-7634-0295-2(8)); 11.99 Norelco. (978-0-7634-0294-5(X)); audio compact disk 19.99 CD. (978-0-7634-0296-9(6)); audio compact disk 19.99 (978-0-7634-0297-6(4)) W Disney Records.

Mary Poppins. Pamela L. Travers. Read by Sophie Thompson. 3 cass. (Running Time: 4 hrs. 30 mins.). (J). 2000. 24.00 (978-0-7366-9108-6(1)) Books on Tape.
A blast of wind, a house-rattling bang & the beloved magical nanny, Mary Poppins, arrives in the Banks home. Quicker than she can close her umbrella, she takes charge of the Banks children Jane, Michael & twins John & Barbara & changes their lives forever.

Mary Poppins. Pamela L. Travers. Read by Maggie Smith. 1 cass. (Running Time: 90 min.). (J). (ps-3). 1992. 11.00 (978-1-55994-657-5(1), HarperChildAud) HarperCollins Pubs.
Chronicles the magical adventures of the unusual governess whose remarkable powers transform the lives of the Banks family. Also included is an interview with the author of this cherished tale.

Mary Poppins. unabr. ed. Pamela L. Travers. Read by Sophie Thompson. 3 cass. (Running Time: 4 hrs., 30 min.). (J). (gr. 1-8). 1999. 30.00 (LL 0136, Chivers Child Audio) AudioGO.

Mary Poppins. unabr. ed. Pamela L. Travers. Read by Sophie Thompson. 3 vols. (Running Time: 3 hrs. 49 mins.). (J). (gr. 4-7). 1999. pap. bk. 36.00 (978-0-8072-8082-9(8), YA997SP, Listening Lib); 30.00 (978-0-8072-8081-2(X), YA997CX, Listening Lib) Random Audio Pubg.
Beloved magical nanny arrives in the Banks home & takes charge of the children.

Mary Poppins. unabr. ed. Pamela L. Travers. Read by Sophie Thompson. (Running Time: 13620 sec.). (ENG.). (J). (gr. 5). 2008. audio compact disk 19.99 (978-0-7393-6679-0(3), Listening Lib) Pub: Random Audio Pubg. Dist(s): Random

Mary Poppins Read-Along. Read by Karen Dotrice. (Classic Soundtrack Ser.). (J). (gr. 3 up). 1997. bk. 7.99 (978-0-7634-0300-3(8)) W Disney Records.

Mary Queen of Scotland & the Isles. collector's unabr. ed. Margaret George. Read by Donada Peters. 15 cass. (Running Time: 22 hrs. 30 min.). 1998. 120.00 (978-0-7366-4232-3(3), 4738-A) Books on Tape.
An exhaustively researched novel weaves both historical fact & plausible fiction in bringing the story of Mary Queen of Scot to life.

Mary Queen of Scotland & the Isles. unabr. collector's ed. Margaret George. Read by Donada Peters. 15 cass. (Running Time: 22 hrs. 30 min.). 1998. 120.00 (978-0-7366-4231-6(5), 4738-B) Books on Tape.

Mary Queen of Scotland & the Isles: Abridged. (ENG.). 2007. (978-1-60339-013-2(8)); cd-rom & audio compact disk (978-1-60339-014-9(6)) Listenr Digest.

Mary, Queen of Scots, Pt. 1. unabr. ed. Antonia Fraser. Read by Flo Gibson. 11 cass. (Running Time: 16 hrs. 30 min.). (Classic Books on Cassettes Collection). 1998. 88.00 Audio Bk Con.
Mary Stuart is one of history's enigmas. She inspired devotion in her followers, but hatred in Elizabeth's court. She is revealed here as an intensely feminine, regal, yet tragic figure - a woman more moved about on history's stage than responsible for her own actions.

Mary, Queen of Scots, Pt. 1. unabr. collector's ed. Antonia Fraser. Read by Flo Gibson. 11 cass. (Running Time: 16 hrs. 30 min.). 1984. 88.00 (978-0-7366-0879-4(6), 1826-A) Books on Tape.
An intensely feminine, regal, yet tragic figure - a woman is revealed to the listener by the author.

Mary, Queen of Scots, Pt. 2. collector's ed. Antonia Fraser. Read by Flo Gibson. 10 cass. (Running Time: 15 hrs.). 1984. 80.00 (978-0-7366-0880-0(X), 1826-B) Books on Tape.

Mary, Queen of Scots, Pt. 2, set. unabr. ed. Antonia Fraser. Read by Flo Gibson. 10 cass. (Running Time: 15 hrs.). (Classic Books on Cassettes Collection). 1998. 80.00 Audio Bk Con.
Mary Stuart is one of history's enigmas. She inspired devotion in her followers, but hatred in Elizabeth's court. She is revealed here as an intensely feminine, regal, yet tragic figure - a woman more moved about on history's stage than responsible for her own actions.

Mary Robison: Seizing Control. unabr. ed. Mary Robison. Read by Mary Robison. Interview with Robert Stewart. 1 cass. (Running Time: 29 min.). 1991. 10.00 (051388) New Letters.

Mary Rose. J. M. Barrie. Read by Flo Gibson. 2 cass. (Running Time: 2 hrs. 30 min.). 1996. 14.95 (978-1-55685-416-3(1)) Audio Bk Con.
The mystery of Mary Rose's two disappearances on a little island in the Hebrides is a gripping part of this strange & mystical play.

Mary Shelley - in Her Own Words. Mara Purl & Sydney Swire. Perf. by Mara Purl. 1 CD. (Running Time: 45 minutes). Dramatization. 2003. audio compact disk 14.95 (978-1-58436-621-8(4)) Haven Bks CA.
Mary Shelley, a widow, looks back at the happy days during which she wrote her novel "Frankenstein." These are the private revelations from the author of the classic tale of horror. From the private letters, personal poetry, and public preface to her tale, Mary Shelley's own words describe her chastened ambition, her crippling loss, and the genesis of the tale that haunted even its author. Two modern women writers, fascinated by a woman writer from the past, honor the nineteenth-century author by presenting her thoughts in her own words.

Mary Shelley's Frankenstein. unabr. ed. Mary Wollstonecraft Shelley. 6 cass. (Running Time: 8 hrs.). (Horror Library). 1997. pap. bk. 26.95 (978-1-55656-255-6(1)) Pub: Dercum Audio. Dist(s): APG
Drama about a being who is judged as a monster because of his appearance, & who then spurns the society - & the maker - that rejects him.

Mary Stories. Milbre Burch. Perf. by Milbre Burch. (ENG.). 2005. audio compact disk 15.00 (978-0-9795271-1-1(2)) Kind Crone.

Mary Stuart. unabr. ed. 2 CDs. (Running Time: 7200 sec.). 2007. audio compact disk 25.95 (978-1-58081-375-4(5)) L A Theatre.

Mary Stuart, Queen of Scots. abr. ed. Alexandre Dumas. Read by Julie Christie. 4 cass. (Running Time: 6 hrs.). 2004. 25.00 (978-1-59007-021-5(6)) Pub: New Millenn Enter. Dist(s): PerseuPGW
Regal and dazzlingly beautiful, Mary was often misunderstood yet revered for the mystery of her life. Succumbing to the irresistible impulses of passion, she gambled away her throne for love. Unbelievable acts of abduction, rape & even murder were performed at her behest; she stopped at nothing. Ultimately, the deadly game of power she played and lost against her envious cousin, Elizabeth I, cost her not only her kingdom, but also her life. Betrayed by those she trusted most, pampered and adored even as she was led to her own beheading, she remained an enigma.

Mary System: Children & Marriages (Side 1); Jesus & Mary (Side 2) Jonathan Murro. 1 cass. 1990. 7.95 A R Colton Fnd.
Lectures by Jonathan Murro on the subject of spiritual childrearing.

Mary vs. Martha: Balancing the Demands of Loving People & Running a Household. Sono Harris. 2 cass. 1997. 13.95 Set. (978-1-56857-078-5(3), 1788) Noble Pub Assocs.
How to balance all the demands through a biblical approach.

Mary Wore Her Red Dress & Henry Wore His Green Sneakers. Merle Peek. (J). (gr. k-ps). 2005. audio compact disk 6.00 (978-0-618-70910-6(X), Clarion Bks) HM Harcourt.

Marya: A Life. Joyce Carol Oates. Read by Joyce Carol Oates. Prod. by Moveable Feast Staff. 1 cass. (Running Time: 30 min.). 8.95 (AMF-26) Am Audio Prose.
Oates talks about the unchanging author's voice & the autobiographical impulse in her own work.

Marya Mannes. Interview. Interview with Marya Mannes. 1980. (L043) TFR.

Maryknoll Golden Book: An Anthology of Mission Literature. Ed. by Albert Nevins. (J). 24.95 Part I, 6 cass. (513); 22.95 Part II, 5 cass. (514) Ignatius Pr.
Over 100 selections tell heroic stories of sanctity in mission lands.

Marys in the New Testament. Raymond E. Brown. 2004. 20.00 (978-1-904756-05-7(0)) STL Dist NA.

Mary's Lullaby. Wanda West Palmer. 1 cass. 9.95 (10001069); audio compact disk 14.95 (2800691) Covenant Comms.
Recorded with the London Philharmonic Symphony.

Mary's Lullaby & Other Favorites. Wanda West Palmer. 1 cass. 9.95 (119124) Covenant Comms.
10 original songs w/orchestra, solos & chorus.

Mary's Message of Hope. abr. ed. Annie Kirkwood. Read by Salome Jens. 2 cass. (Running Time: 2 hrs. 15 min.). 1998. 17.95 (978-1-57453-107-7(7)) Audio Lit.

Mary's Message to the World. abr. ed. Annie Kirkwood. Read by Salome Jens. 2 cass. (Running Time: 3 hrs.). 1997. bk. 17.95 (978-1-57453-106-0(9)) Audio Lit.
From 1987 to 1992, Annie Kirkwood received in the form of "interior locutions" a series of talks from Mary, the Mother of Jesus. Mary explains how to be more fully conscious of our presence & purpose here on Earth.

Mary's Message to the World. unabr. ed. Annie K. Wood. Read by Claire Applegate & Matthew Carlton. 5 cass. (Running Time: 7 hrs. 30 min.). 1993. 49.95 (978-0-931892-57-8(0)) B Dolphin Pub.
A series of "talks" as given by Mary, Mother of Jesus, to a woman in Texas from 1987 to 1991.

Mary's Prayer. unabr. ed. Martyn Waites. Read by Martyn Waites. 5 cass. (Running Time: 6 hrs. 35 mins.). (Story Sound Ser.). (J). 2004. 49.95 (978-1-85903-714-0(3)) Pub: Mgna Lrg Print GBR. Dist(s): Ulverscroft US

Mary's Story of Christmas. Don J. Black. 1 cass. 4.98 (978-1-55503-893-9(X), 06005179) Covenant Comms.
A new perspective of the greatest story ever told.

Mary's Vineyard: Prayers, Meditations, Inspirations for Bringing Mary into Your Life. Andrew Harvey. 2 cass. 1997. 5.95 (978-0-8356-2009-3(3), Quest) Pub: Theos Pub Hse. Dist(s): Natl Bk Netwk

Mary's World: Love, War, & Family Ties in Nineteenth-Century Charleston. Richard N. Cote. Narrated by Walter Edgar & Anita Rosenberg. Music by Kathleen Wilson. 8 CDs. (Running Time: 10 hrs. 30 mins.). 2003. audio compact disk 39.95 (978-1-929175-38-3(8), Corinthian Bks) Pub: Cote Lit Grp. Dist(s): Follett Librar
Born to affluence and opportunity in the South's Golden Age, Mary Motte Alston Pringle (1803-1884) represented the epitome of Southern white womanhood. Her husband was a wealthy rice planter who owned four plantations and 337 slaves. Her thirteen children included two Harvard scholars, seven world travelers, three socialite daughters, six Confederate soldiers, one possible Union collaborator, a Confederate firebrand trapped in the North, an expatriate bon vivant in France, and two California pioneers. How Mary, William, their children, and slaves lived before the Civil War, clung desperately to life in the eye of the maelstrom, and coped or failed to cope with its bewildering aftermath is the story of this book.

Mas Alla Complete, Bk. 3. Olga Gallego & Concepción B. Godev. (ENG.). (C). 2004. audio compact disk 68.95 (978-0-471-66999-9(7)) Wiley US.

Mas Alla de Las Palabras. 2nd ed. Olga Gallego & Concepción B. Godev. (ENG.). (C). 2009. audio compact disk 25.95 (978-0-470-50205-1(3), JWiley) Wiley US.

Más Allá de Las Palabras. 2nd ed. Olga Gallego et al. (SPA.). (C). 2009. cass. & cd-rom 38.95 (978-0-470-52380-3(8), JWiley) Wiley US.

Más Allá de las Palabras, Bk. 2. Olga Gallego & Concepción B. Godev. (ENG.). (C). 2004. audio compact disk 47.95 (978-0-471-67000-1(6)) Wiley US.

Más Allá de Las Palabras: A Complete Intermediate Spanish Program. Olga Gallego & Concepción B. Godev. (ENG.). (C). 2004. lab manual ed. 26.95 (978-0-471-48578-0(0)) Wiley US.

Más Allá de las Palabras: Intermediate Spanish. Olga Gallego & Concepción B. Godev. (ENG.). (C). 2004. 38.95 (978-0-471-48561-2(6)) Wiley US.

***Mas alla de tu Vida: Creado para hacer una Diferencia.** unabr. ed. Max Lucado. Narrated by David Rojas. (Running Time: 3 hrs. 57 mins. 51 sec.). (SPA.). 2010. 12.59 (978-1-60814-757-1(6)) Oasis Audio.

***Mas Alla de Tu Vida: Creado para Hacer una Diferencia.** unabr. ed. Max Lucado. Narrated by David Rojas. (Running Time: 3 hrs. 57 mins. 51 sec.). (SPA.). 2010. audio compact disk 17.99 (978-1-59859-836-0(8)) Oasis Audio.

Mas Alla Del Horizonte: Visiones del Nuevo Milenio. abr. ed. Walter Mercado.Tr. of Behind the Horizon. (ENG.). 2006. 9.99 (978-1-59483-683-1(3)) Pub: Hachet Audio. Dist(s): HachBkGrp

Mas Aventuras de Sherlock Holmes. unabr. ed. Arthur Conan Doyle. Read by Carlos Zambrano. 3 CDs.Tr. of More Adventures of Sherlock Holmes. (SPA.). 2002. audio compact disk 17.00 (978-958-9494-89-9(7)) YoYoMusic.

Mas Concentracion. Carlos González. Read by Carlos González. Ed. by Dina Gonzalez. 1 cass. (Running Time: 32 min.).Tr. of More Concentration. (SPA.). 1990. 10.00 (978-1-56491-019-6(9)) Imagine Pubs.
In Spanish. Mental drills to master concentration, to work & study better.

***¿Más corto o más largo? Audio CD.** April Barth. Adapted by Benchmark Education Co., LLC. (Content Connections Ser.). (SPA.). (J). 2010. audio compact disk 10.00 (978-1-61672-201-2(0)) Benchmark Educ.

Mas Cuentos de las 1001 Noches. unabr. ed. Read by Laura García. 3 CDs.Tr. of More Arabian Tales. (SPA.). 2001. audio compact disk 17.00 (978-958-9494-47-9(1)) YoYoMusic.

MÁS ESPAÑOL LIBRO 1 Audio CD (L1-8) Spanish language Teaching. 2006. audio compact disk (978-0-7428-1778-4(4)) CCLS Pubg Hse.

MÁS ESPAÑOL LIBRO 1 Audio CD (L9-15) Spanish language Teaching. (SPA.). 2006. audio compact disk (978-0-7428-1779-1(2)) CCLS Pubg Hse.

MÁS ESPAÑOL LIBRO 2 Audio CD (L1-8) Spanish language Teaching. (SPA.). 2006. audio compact disk (978-0-7428-1780-7(6)) CCLS Pubg Hse.

MÁS ESPAÑOL LIBRO 2 Audio CD (L9-15) Spanish language Teaching. (SPA.). 2006. audio compact disk (978-0-7428-1781-4(4)) CCLS Pubg Hse.

***¿Mas, menos, o lo mismo? Audio CD.** April Barth. Adapted by Benchmark Education Co., LLC. (Content Connections Ser.). (SPA.). (J). 2010. audio compact disk 10.00 (978-1-61672-202-9(9)) Benchmark Educ.

Mas Personal. Bani Munoz. 2008. audio compact disk 14.99 (978-0-8297-5480-3(6)) Pub: Vida Pubs. Dist(s): Zondervan

Mas Que Palabras. Todd Liebenow et al. Tr. by Veronica Smith. (SPA.). 2001. pap. bk. 15.00 (978-1-58302-197-2(3)) One Way St.

***más, uno menos Audio CD.** April Barth. Adapted by Benchmark Education Co., LLC. (Content Connections Ser.). (SPA.). (J). 2010. audio compact disk 10.00 (978-1-61672-196-1(0)) Benchmark Educ.

Masada. 1 cass. (Running Time: 43 min. per cass.). 1987. 10.00 (RME107) Esstee Audios.
The revolt of the Zealots & their eventual destruction during the Roman seige of the mountaintop fortress of Masada in A.D. 73.

Masculine Journey. 2 CDs. 2006. audio compact disk 17.00 (978-1-933207-13-1(2)) Ransomed Heart.

Masculine Power: Archetypal Potential & Planetary Challenge. Read by Robert Moore. 1 cass. (Running Time: 90 min.). 1988. 10.95 (978-0-7822-0181-9(4), 357) C G Jung IL.
Though it is not uncommon for masculine power to be equated with the culture of patriarchy, Dr. Moore shows how patriarchy itself - along with sexual violence, torture, & political oppression - is actually an expression of puer psychology & the acting out of the immature, fragmenting masculine.

Masculine Psychology. Read by Donald Sandner. 2 cass. (Running Time: 4 hrs.). 1987. 21.95 (978-0-7822-0243-4(8), 259) C G Jung IL.

Masculine Rage: Does Kali Stand Behind the Phenomenon? Read by Eugene Monick. 1 cass. (Running Time: 1 hr.). 1980. 9.95 (978-0-7822-0169-7(5), ND8006) C G Jung IL.

Masculine Spirituality. Martin W. Pable. 3 cass. (Running Time: 3 hrs. 23 min.). 1994. 26.95 (TAH312) Alba Hse Comns.
Excellent for any man searching for a genuine spirituality that works & not some sweet emotional unmasculine approach to God. Answers those questions that you so want answered. Especially good for the layman - but certainly of value for priests & brothers.

Masculinity: Masculine Spirituality. Stuart Wilde. 1 cass. (Subliminal Tape Ser.). 1992. 11.95 (978-0-930603-52-6(4)) White Dove NM.
The spiritual male is confident of his sexuality & sensitive to the needs of others. He knows that his ability to be magnanimous is the touchstone of his spiritual growth. He aligns with his power & pulls to himself what he needs to meet his obligations as the "out-going" creator of the earth plane.

Masculinity & Femininity, The Meaning Of. unabr. ed. Nathaniel Branden. 1 cass. (Running Time: 1 hr. 2 min.). 12.95 (606) J Norton Pubs.
Covers the psychological consequences & expression of man's & woman's biological differences & the criteria of authentic masculinity & Femininity.

Mask. unabr. ed. Dean Koontz. Read by Natalie Ross. (Running Time: 8 hrs.). 2010. audio compact disk 38.99 (978-1-4418-1722-8(0), 9781441817228, Bril Audio CD Unabri) Brilliance Audio.

***Mask.** unabr. ed. Dean Koontz. Read by Natalie Ross. (Running Time: 8 hrs.). 2010. 24.99 (978-1-4418-1724-2(7), 9781441817242, Brilliance MP3); 39.97 (978-1-4418-1725-9(5), 9781441817259, Brlnc Audio MP3 Lib); audio compact disk 97.97 (978-1-4418-1723-5(9), 9781441817235, BriAudCD Unabrid) Brilliance Audio.

Mask Making. Suki Rappaport. 1 cass. 9.00 (A0219-87) Sound Photosyn.
ICSS '87 with Lewis.

Mask Market. abr. ed. Andrew Vachss. Read by David Joe Wirth. (Running Time: 14400 sec.). (Burke Ser.: Bk. 16). 2007. audio compact disk 14.99 (978-1-4233-1708-1(4), 9781423317081, BCD Value Price) Brilliance Audio.

Mask Market. unabr. ed. Andrew Vachss. Read by David Joe Wirth. (Running Time: 8 hrs.). (Burke Ser.). 2006. 24.95 (978-1-4233-1705-0(X), 9781423317050, BAD) Brilliance Audio.

Mask Market. unabr. ed. Andrew Vachss. Read by David Joe Wirth. (Running Time: 8 hrs.). (Burke Ser.: Bk. 16). 2006. 39.25 (978-1-4233-1706-7(8), 9781423317067, BADLE) Brilliance Audio.

Mask Market. unabr. ed. Andrew Vachss. Read by David Wirth. (Running Time: 28800 sec.). (Burke Ser.: Bk. 16). 2006. 74.25 (978-1-4233-1700-5(9), 9781423317005, BrilAudUnabridg) Brilliance Audio.
In the latest Burke thriller, Burke is witness to a professional hit that sends him on a hunt to find a girl he had rescued years before, and leads him down some of the darkest warrens of his past. A must for fans of this popular series. Widespread acclaim for the Burke series: "The Burke books make the noir-film genre look practically pastel... The plot-driven stories churn with energy and a memorable gallery of the walking wounded." - The Philadelphia Inquirer "[Vachss] writes a hypnotically violent prose made up of equal parts broken concrete block and razor wire." - Chicago Sun Times.

Mask Market. unabr. ed. Andrew Vachss. Read by David Joe Wirth. 7 CDs. (Running Time: 28800 sec.). (Burke Ser.: Bk. 16). 2006. audio compact disk 34.95 (978-1-4233-1701-2(7), 9781423317012, Bril Audio CD Unabri) Brilliance Audio.

Mask Market. unabr. ed. Andrew Vachss. Read by David Wirth. (Running Time: 28800 sec.). (Burke Ser.: Bk. 16). 2006. audio compact disk 24.95 (978-1-4233-1703-6(3), 9781423317036, Brilliance MP3) Brilliance Audio.

Mask Market. unabr. ed. Andrew Vachss. Read by David Joe Wirth. (Running Time: 28800 sec.). (Burke Ser.: Bk. 16). 2006. audio compact disk 87.25 (978-1-4233-1702-9(5), 9781423317029, BriAudCD Unabrid) Brilliance Audio.

Mask Market. unabr. ed. Andrew Vachss. Read by David Wirth. (Running Time: 28800 sec.). (Burke Ser.: Bk. 16). 2006. audio compact disk 39.25 (978-1-4233-1704-3(1), 9781423317043, Brlnc Audio MP3 Lib) Brilliance Audio.

Mask of Apollo. unabr. ed. Mary Renault. Read by Peter McDonald. 10 cass. (Running Time: 15 hrs.). 1982. 80.00 (978-0-7366-0520-5(7), 1494) Books on Tape.
A gifted actor, Nikeratos, takes us through ancient Greece in which he supposedly lived. With him, we meet the leading playwrights & politicians. Ultimately we become involved with a larger story, that of Dion, a man of noble birth, a friend of Plato & one who for a time gives promise of becoming a philosopher king.

Mask of Command. unabr. collector's ed. John Keegan. Read by Bill Kelsey. 11 cass. (Running Time: 16 hrs. 30 min.). 1991. 88.00 (978-0-7366-2014-7(1), 2830) Books on Tape.
Dozens of names come to mind...Napoleon, Lee, Charlemagne, Hannibal, Castro, Hussein. From a wide array, Keegan chooses four commanders who profoundly influenced the course of history: Alexander, Wellington, Grant & Hitler. All powerful leaders, each cast in a different mold, each with diverse results.

Mask of the Andes, Jon Cleary. Read by Christopher Kay. 6 cass. (Running Time: 6 hrs.). 1999. 54.95 (60474) Pub: Soundings Ltd GBR. Dist(s): Ulverscroft US

Mask of the Andes. unabr. ed. Jon Cleary. 6 cass. (Sound Ser.). 2004. 54.95 (978-1-85496-047-4(4)) Pub: UlverLrgPrint GBR. Dist(s): Ulverscroft US

Mask of the Enchantress. unabr. ed. Victoria Holt. Read by Eva Haddon. 10 cass. (Running Time: 10 hrs.). 1997. 84.95 (978-0-7451-6623-0(7), CAB 1239) AudioGO.
From the moment Suewellyn saw the Mateland castle, she knew she wanted it. But how could an illegitimate child ever aspire to such a dream? The answer lay in a perilous deception that succeeded too well. Suewellyn now had to make a desperate choice: risk losing the man she loved, or face the terrifying chance that she would be trapped forever by the tragedy that haunted every Mateland bride.

Mask of the Enchantress. unabr. collector's ed. Victoria Holt. Read by Donada Peters. 8 cass. (Running Time: 12 hrs.). 1993. 64.00 (978-0-7366-2531-9(3), 3283) Books on Tape.
Masquerade forces a woman to choose between leaving the man she loves or accepting him with his tragic legacy.

Mask of the Medusa. Perf. by Peter Lorre. 1 cass. (Running Time: 60 min.). 1947. 7.95 (MM-8875) Natl Recrd Co.
In a museum are 46 fiendish & sadistic murderers. Their death & final resting place were due to their looking upon the Mask of the Medusa. The owner of the museum is fascinated by murderers & in the Goddess of Greek mythology...the evil Medusa. In "Beyond Good & Evil," an escaped prisoner takes the life of a minister & assumes his identity. Changes take place when the fake reverend becomes involved in pastoral work...a twist ending.

Mask of Zorro. abr. ed. Jim Lucino. Read by Catherine Zeta-Jones. 2 cass. 1998. 16.85 (978-1-85998-884-8(9)) Ulvrscrft Audio.
Swashbuckling adventure, romance, good triumphing over evil, all set in a turbulent revolutionary Mexico.

Masked Love, Katrina Wright. Read by Delia Corrie. 2 cass. (Running Time: 3 hrs.). 1999. 24.95 (62124) Pub: Soundings Ltd GBR. Dist(s): Ulverscroft US

Maskerade. Terry Pratchett. Read by Tony Robinson. 2 cass. (Running Time: 3 hrs. 0 mins. 0 sec.). (Discworld Ser.). (ENG.). 1996. 16.99 (978-0-552-14426-1(6), Corgi RHG) Pub: Transworld GBR. Dist(s): IPG Chicago

Maskerade. unabr. ed. Terry Pratchett. Read by Nigel Planer. 8 cass. (Running Time: 10 hrs.). (Discworld Ser.). 1999. 69.95 (978-0-7531-0518-4(7), 990504) Pub: ISIS Audio GBR. Dist(s): Ulverscroft US
The show must go on, as murder, music & mayhem run riot in the night. The Opera House, Ankh-Morpork a huge, rambling building where innocent young sopranos are lured to their destiny by a strangely familiar evil mastermind in a hideously deformed evening dress. At least, he hopes so, but Granny Weatherwax, Diseworld's most famous witch, is in the audience & she doesn't hold with that sort of thing.

Maskerade. unabr. ed. Terry Pratchett. Read by Nigel Planer. 10 CDs. (Running Time: 8 hrs. 49 min.). (Discworld Ser.). (J). 2001. audio compact disk 89.95 (978-0-7531-0743-0(0)) Pub: ISIS Lrg Prnt GBR. Dist(s): Ulverscroft US
The Opera House, Ankh-Morpork... a huge, rambling building, where innocent young sopranos are lured to their destiny by a strangely familiar evil mastermind in a hideously-deformed evening dress... At least, he hopes so. But Granny Weatherwax, Discworld's most famous witch, is in the audience and she doesn't hold with that sort of thing. So there's going to be trouble.

***Masks.** 2010. audio compact disk (978-1-59171-215-2(7)) Falcon Picture.

Mason & Dixon, Pt. 1. unabr. collector's ed. Thomas Pynchon. Read by Jonathan Reese. 10 cass. (Running Time: 15 hrs.). 1997. 80.00 (978-0-7366-3781-7(8), 4454-A) Books on Tape.
This comic novel follows the zany exploits of the eighteenth-century surveyors for whom the Mason-Dixon Line is named.

Mason & Dixon, Pt. 2. unabr. collector's ed. Thomas Pynchon. Read by Jonathan Reese. 10 cass. (Running Time: 15 hrs.). 1997. 80.00 (978-0-7366-3782-4(6), 4454-B) Books on Tape.
Follows Charles Mason & Jeremiah Dixon through a series of exploits that involves Native Americans, ripped bodices, naval warfare, political conspiracies, & major caffeine abuse.

Mason-Dixon Knitting Outside the Lines & Stories from the Nation?s Leading Bi-regional Knitting Blog. Kaye Gardiner & Ann Shayne. Narrated by Kaye Gardiner & Ann Shayne. (ENG.). 2009. audio compact disk 19.95 (978-0-9796073-8-7(8)) Pub: Knitting Out. Dist(s): Interweave

Masonic Movement & the Fatima Message. Robert I. Bradley. Read by Robert I. Bradley. 1 cass. (Running Time: 1 hr.). (Fatima Today! Ser.). 1990. 2.50 (978-1-56036-027-8(5), 361917) AMI Pr.
An explanation of the Masonic Movement & the Fatima message.

Masonic Mysteries. Perf. by John Thaw. 2 cass.: Set. (Running Time: 1 hr. 50 min.). (Inspector Morse Mystery Ser.). 1998. 14.95 (978-1-56938-259-2(X), AMP-8259) Acorn Inc.
Inspector Morse tops the list of suspects when his lady friend is found dead. Even his loyal sergeant sees all clues pointing to Morse.

Masque. F. Paul Wilson. Read by Michael Prichard. 2000. 72.00 (978-0-7366-5598-9(0)) Books on Tape.

Masque Making. Suki Rappaport. 1 cass. 9.00 (A0681-89) Sound Photosyn.
ICSS '89.

Masque of Reason see Robert Frost in Recital

Masque of the Red Death see Raven & Other Works

Masque of the Red Death see Best of Edgar Allan Poe

Masque of the Red Death see Edgar Allan Poe, Set, Short Stories and Poems

Masque of the Red Death see Mind of Poe

Masque of the Red Death. Edgar Allan Poe. Ed. by Raymond Harris. Illus. by Robert J. Pailthorpe. (Classics Ser.). (YA). (gr. 6-12). 1982. pap. bk. 17.96 (978-0-89061-273-6(0), 476) Jamestown.

Masque of the Red Death. unabr. ed. Edgar Allan Poe. Read by Walter Zimmerman & John Chatty. 1 cass. (Running Time: 58 min.). Dramatization. Incl. Black Cat. 1977. (N-3); Tell-Tale Heart. 1977. (N-3); 1977. 8.95 (N-3) Jimcin Record.
Poe's eerie genius at its best.

Masque of the Red Death. unabr. ed. Edgar Allan Poe. Read by Hurd Hatfield. 1 cass. 10.95 (992) Spoken Arts.

Masquerade. William X. Kienzle. Read by Edward Holland. (Father Koesler Mystery Ser.: No. 12). 2001. 64.00 (978-0-7366-7173-6(0)) Books on Tape.

Masquerade. Walter Satterthwait. Narrated by Jeff Woodman. 8 cass. (Running Time: 11 hrs. 30 mins.). 1998. 74.00 (978-0-7887-5452-4(1)) Recorded Bks.

Masquerade. unabr. ed. Janet Dailey. Read by Kate Harper. 8 cass. (Running Time: 12 hrs.). 2000. 59.95 (978-0-7451-6821-0(3), CAB 552) Pub: Chivers Audio Bks GBR. Dist(s): AudioGO
She knows she is beautiful, she can see it beneath the bruises that mar her face, and she knows she is wealthy by her expensive clothes and jewelry. But she doesn't know anything else. She is Remy Jardin, determined and intelligent; inexplicitly attacked and suffering from amnesia. When Cole Buchanan collects her from the hospital, he is furious with her, but she cannot think why. Remy embarks on a search for the truth, and discovers some startling and unpleasant things.

Masquerade. unabr. collector's ed. William X. Kienzle. Read by Edward Holland. 8 cass. (Running Time: 12 hrs.). (Father Koesler Mystery Ser.: No. 12). 2001. 64.00 Books on Tape.

***Masquerade Dance Suite.** Perf. by R. A. Zuckerman. Composed by R. A. Zuckerman. (ENG.). 2010. 12.95 (978-1-891083-16-7(3)) ConcertHall.

Masqueraders. unabr. ed. Georgette Heyer. Read by Rosemary Leach. 8 cass. (Running Time: 8 hrs.). 1993. 69.95 (978-0-7451-6013-9(1), CAB 410) AudioGO.

***Masques.** unabr. ed. Patricia Briggs. Read by Katherine Kellgren. (Running Time: 11 hrs.). 2010. 39.97 (978-1-4418-9228-7(1), 9781441892287, Brlnc Audio MP3 Lib) Brilliance Audio.

***Masques.** unabr. ed. Patricia Briggs. Read by Katherine Kellgren. (Running Time: 11 hrs.). 2010. 24.99 (978-1-4418-9227-0(3), 9781441892270, Brilliance MP3); 39.97 (978-1-4418-9229-4(X), 9781441892294, BADLE); audio compact disk 29.99 (978-1-4418-9225-6(7), 9781441892256, Bril Audio CD Unabri); audio compact disk 79.97 (978-1-4418-9226-3(5), 9781441892263, BriAudCD Unabrid) Brilliance Audio.

Mass: The Center of Our Faith. Jeff Cavins. (ENG.). 2006. audio compact disk 9.95 (978-1-934567-01-2(9)) Excorde Inc.

Mass & Charge Transport in Inorganic Materials III. Ed. by P. Vincenzini & V. Buscaglia. audio compact disk 113.00 (978-3-908158-02-8(8)) Trans T Pub CHE.

Mass Choir Gospel. abr. ed. 1 cass., 1 CD. 4.98 (978-1-57908-464-6(8), 5340); audio compact disk 5.98 (978-1-57908-463-9(X), 5340) Platinm Enter.

Mass Effect: Ascension. unabr. ed. Drew Karpyshyn. (Running Time: 9 hrs. 30 mins. 0 sec.). (Mass Effect Ser.). (ENG.). 2008. audio compact disk 34.99 (978-1-4001-1004-9(1)); audio compact disk 69.99 (978-1-4001-4004-6(8)); audio compact disk 24.99 (978-1-4001-6004-4(9)) Pub: Tantor Media. Dist(s): IngramPubServ

***Mass Effect: Retribution.** unabr. ed. Drew Karpyshyn. Narrated by David Colacci. (Running Time: 9 hrs. 30 mins.). (Mass Effect Ser.). 2010. 34.99 (978-1-4001-9680-7(9)); 16.99 (978-1-4001-8680-8(3)) Tantor Media.

***Mass Effect: Retribution.** unabr. ed. Drew Karpyshyn. Narrated by Stephen Hoye & David Colacci. (Running Time: 9 hrs. 30 mins. 0 sec.). (Mass Effect Ser.). (ENG.). 2010. 24.99 (978-1-4001-6680-0(2)); audio compact disk 83.99 (978-1-4001-4680-2(1)); audio compact disk 34.99 (978-1-4001-1680-5(5)) Pub: Tantor Media. Dist(s): IngramPubServ

Mass, Energy & Light. Swami Amar Jyoti. 2 cass. 1980. 12.95 (O-18) Truth Consciousness.
Beyond conceptions & perceptions to the answers about space, time, speed & the whole cosmic creation. Getting to Reality, the totality of Truth.

Mass of Creation. Marty Haugen. 1996. 10.95 (168); audio compact disk 15.95 (168) GIA Pubns.

Mass of St. Cyprian: A Live Recording. Kenneth W. Louis. 1 cass. 1999. 10.95 (CS-462); 10.95 (CS-462); audio compact disk 15.95 (CD-462) GIA Pubns.

Mass of the Nations. Donna Pena. 1 cass. (Running Time: 1 hr.). 1998. 10.95 (CS-423); audio compact disk 15.95 (CD-423) GIA Pubns.

Mass Transportation Security Equipment & Services in Japan: A Strategic Reference 2007. Compiled by Icon Group International, Inc. Staff. 2007. ring bd. 195.00 (978-0-497-82329-0(2)) Icon Grp.

Massachusetts: Boston Freedom Trail (Walking Tour) 1 cass. (Running Time: 60 min.). 12.95 (CC203) Comp Comms Inc.
Walk through some of America's oldest streets & historic places: The Park Street Church, King's Chapel, Old Corner Book Store, Old South Meeting House, Boston Tea Party, Faneuil Hall, Paul Revere's House & Old North Church.

Massacre. Read by William Hartnell. (J). 2001. audio compact disk 9.99 (978-0-563-55256-7(5)) London Brdge.

Massacre. Read by William Hartnell. 2 CDs. 2001. cd-rom 13.99 (978-0-563-55261-1(1)) London Brdge.

Massacre at Fall Creek. unabr. ed. Jessamyn West. Read by Roses Prichard. 9 cass. (Running Time: 13 hrs. 30 min.). 1980. 72.00 (978-0-7366-0255-6(0), 1250) Books on Tape.
This story concerns an America coming to terms with itself, specifically the conflict between whites & Indians in the wooded hills of the midwest.

Massacre at Malmedy. unabr. collector's ed. Charles Whiting. Read by Grover Gardner. 8 cass. (Running Time: 8 hrs.). 1984. 48.00 (978-0-7366-0694-3(7), 1657) Books on Tape.
At Malmedy the Germans extended battlefield victory to murdering their American prisoners.

Massage. Read by Nancy L. Tubesing & Donald Tubesing. Music by Steven Zdenek Eckels. 1 cass. (Running Time: 45 min.). 1995. 11.95 (978-1-57025-095-8(2)) Whole Person.
Reduce stress & enjoy the healing benefits of soothing touch as you're guided through revitalizing acupressure & shiatsu massage routines. Gently relieve tension from head to toe in a full-body sequence, or target typical tension-collecting spots.

Massey Lectures: the Ethical Imagination. Speeches. Margaret Somerville. 5 CDs. (Running Time: 18000 sec.). (Massey Lecture Ser.). 2006. audio compact disk 39.95 (978-0-660-19614-5(X), CBC Audio) Canadian Broadcasting CAN.

Massie. unabr. ed. Read by Cassandra Morris. Created by Lisi Harrison. (Running Time: 3 hrs. 30 mins.). (Clique Summer Collection: No. 1). (ENG.). 2009. 9.98 (978-1-60024-696-8(6)) Pub: Hachet Audio. Dist(s): HachBkGrp

Master. Colm Tóibín. Narrated by Geoffrey Howard. (Running Time: 13 hrs.). 2004. 41.95 (978-1-59912-689-0(3)) Iofy Corp.

Master. unabr. ed. Colm Tóibín. Read by Geoffrey Howard. 9 cass. (Running Time: 12 hrs. 30 mins.). 2004. 62.95 (978-0-7861-2797-9(X), 3324); audio compact disk 80.00 (978-0-7861-8498-9(1), 3324) Blckstn Audio.
In stunningly resonant prose, Tóibín captures the loneliness and longing, the hope and despair of a man who never married, never resolved his sexual identity, and whose forays into intimacy inevitably failed him and those he tried to love. The emotional intensity of Tóibin¿s portrait of James is riveting. Time and again, James, a master of psychological subtlety in his fiction, proves blind to his own heart.

Master. unabr. ed. Colm Tóibín. Read by Geoffrey Howard. 20 cass. (Running Time: 12 hrs. 30 mins.). 2004. reel tape 29.95 (978-0-7861-2920-1(4), E3324); audio compact disk 24.95 (978-0-7861-8505-4(8), 3324); audio compact disk 32.95 (978-0-7861-8275-6(X), ZE3324) Blckstn Audio.

Master: A Life of Jesus, unabr. ed. John Pollock. Read by Frederick Davidson. 5 cass. (Running Time: 7 hrs.). 1996. 39.95 (978-0-7861-1067-4(8), 1838) Blckstn Audio.
This absorbing narrative brings the New Testament story freshly alive. Seen as through the eyes of the disciple John, the life & work of Jesus are brought into clear & compelling focus: the interested bystander will be caught up in excitement & the Christian who is already familiar with the Bible will marvel anew at the miracle of the Incarnation.

Master Advan. French. E. J. Neather. 2 Cass. (Mastering Languages Ser.). (ENG.). 1995. 12.95 (978-0-7818-0313-7(6)) Hippocrene Bks.

Master & Bos'n Song see Dylan Thomas Reading

Master & Bos'n Song see Evening with Dylan Thomas

Master & Commander. Patrick O'Brian. Narrated by Simon Vance. (Running Time: 13 hrs. 30 mins.). (Aubrey-Maturin Ser.). (C). 2005. 41.95 (978-1-59912-540-4(4)) Iofy Corp.

Master & Commander. unabr. ed. Patrick O'Brian. Read by Simon Vance. 10 cass. (Running Time: 13 hrs. 30 mins.). (Aubrey-Maturin Ser.). 2004. 69.95 (978-0-7861-2669-9(8), 3227); audio compact disk 88.00 (978-0-7861-8837-6(5), 3227) Blckstn Audio.

Master & Commander. unabr. ed. Patrick O'Brian. Read by Simon Vance. 10 pieces. (Running Time: 14 hrs. 30 mins.). (Aubrey-Maturin Ser.). 2004. reel tape 44.95 (978-0-7861-2763-4(5)); audio compact disk 24.95 (978-0-7861-8713-3(1), 3227); audio compact disk 49.95 (978-0-7861-8629-7(1)) Blckstn Audio.

Master & Commander. unabr. ed. Patrick O'Brian. Read by Richard Brown. 11 cass. (Running Time: 16 hrs. 30 mins.). (Aubrey-Maturin Ser.). 1992. 88.00 (978-0-7366-2183-0(0), 2979) Books on Tape.
First in the splendid series of Jack Aubrey novels set against the backdrop of the Napoleonic wars. "The best historical novels ever written." (The New York Times).

Master & Commander. unabr. ed. Patrick O'Brian. Read by Richard Brown. 11 cass. (Running Time: 16 hrs.). (Aubrey-Maturin Ser.). 2001. 34.95 (978-0-7366-5713-6(4)) Books on Tape.
This, the first in the splendid series of Jack Aubrey novels, establishes the friendship between Captain Aubrey, R. N., & Stephen Maturin, ship's surgeon & intelligence agent, against the thrilling backdrop of the Napoleonic wars. Every ship action, every battle & landing, is based on careful research of Admiralty records.

Master & Commander. unabr. ed. Patrick O'Brian. Read by Richard Brown. 13 CDs. (Running Time: 19 hrs. 30 mins.). (Aubrey-Maturin Ser.: No. 1). 2001. audio compact disk 104.00 Books on Tape.
The friendship between Captain Aubrey, R.N., and Stephen Maturin, ship's surgeon and intelligence agent, against the thrilling backdrop of the Napoleonic wars. Every ship action, every battle and landing, is based on careful research of Admiralty records.

Master & Commander. unabr. ed. Patrick O'Brian. Narrated by Patrick Tull. 10 cassettes. (Running Time: 17 hrs.). (Aubrey-Maturin Ser.). 39.95 (978-1-4025-0220-0(6)) Recorded Bks.

Master & Commander. unabr. ed. Patrick O'Brian. Read by Patrick Tull. 15 Cds. (Running Time: 17 Hrs). (Aubrey-Maturin Ser.). audio compact disk 49.95 (978-1-4025-2608-4(3)) Recorded Bks.

Master & Commander. unabr. ed. Patrick O'Brian. Narrated by Patrick Tull. 15 CDs. (Running Time: 16 hrs. 45 mins.). (Aubrey-Maturin Ser.). 2001. audio compact disk 129.00 (978-0-7887-7201-6(5), C1442) Recorded Bks.
This first in the series introduces us to its two main characters: the ambitious & libidinous Jack Aubrey, anxious to have his own ship & make his fortune; & Stephen Maturin, an eccentric surgeon straight from the pages of Dickens.

Master & Commander. unabr. ed. Patrick O'Brian. Narrated by Patrick Tull. 12 cass. (Running Time: 16 hrs. 45 mins.). (Aubrey-Maturin Ser.: No. 1). 1991. 97.00 (978-1-55690-629-9(3), 91414E7) Recorded Bks.
Royal Navy Lieutenant Jack Aubrey & shipboard surgeon, Stephen Maturin sail out in the Sophie against Napoleon's fleet.

Master & Commander: Book. unabr. ed. Patrick O'Brian. Read by Simon Vance. (YA). 2007. 74.99 (978-1-59895-862-1(3)) Find a World.

Master & Man. (9059) Books on Tape.

Master & Man. 1981. (C-59) Jimcin Record.

Master & Margarita. abr. ed. Mikhail Afanasevich Bulgakov. Read by Julian Rhind-Tutt. 7 CDs. (Running Time: 8 hrs.). 2009. audio compact disk 34.98 (978-962-634-936-6(0), Naxos AudioBooks) Naxos.

Master Anthology of Fingerstyle Guitar Solos, Vol. 1. Mel Bay Staff. 2000. per. 39.95 (978-0-7866-5290-7(X), 98370BCD) Mel Bay.

Master Anthology of Jazz Guitar Solos, Vol. 2. 2001. per. 19.95 (978-0-7866-6071-1(6)) Mel Bay.

Master Anthology of Jazz Guitar Solos, Volume One. Mel Bay Publications. (ENG.). 2000. per. 39.95 (978-0-7866-5291-4(8), 98371BCD) Mel Bay.

Master Builder. unabr. ed. Henrik Ibsen. Narrated by Flo Gibson. (Running Time: 2 hrs. 59 mins.). 2001. 14.95 (978-1-55685-735-5(7)) Audio Bk Con.

Master Builder. unabr. ed. Henrik Ibsen. 2 cass. (Running Time: 3 hrs.). 2003. 20.95 Audio Bk Con.
Urged on by the lovely Hilda, Solness, a successful builder, goes a step too far.

Master Builder, unabr. ed. Henrik Ibsen. Perf. by Michael Redgrave & Maggie Smith. Ed. by Emlyn Williams. 2 cass. Dramatization. 1984. 19.95 (978-0-694-50772-6(5), SWC 307) HarperCollins Pubs.
Cast includes: Celia Johnson, Max Adrian, Derek Jacobi, Jeanne Hepple, Martin Boddey, & Rob Inglis.

Master Butcher's Singing Club. Louise Erdrich. Read by Louise Erdrich. 1975. 14.95 (978-0-06-074337-6(9)) HarperCollins Pubs.

***Master Butchers Singing Club.** unabr. ed. Louise Erdrich. Read by Louise Erdrich. (ENG.). 2004. (978-0-06-079795-9(9), Harper Audio); (978-0-06-082445-7(X), Harper Audio) HarperCollins Pubs.

Master Detectives. unabr. ed. Perf. by Gerald Mohr et al. 10 vols. (Running Time: 10 hrs.). (10-Hour Collections). 2001. bk. 39.98 (978-1-57019-364-4(9), OTR4467) Pub: Radio Spirits. Dist(s): AudioGO
Guess whodunit along with radio's greatest sleuths, including Gerald Mohr as Philip Marlowe, Howard Duff as Sam Spade, Chester Morris in Boston Blackie and Orson Welles as Sherlock Holmes.

Master Detectives. unabr. ed. Perf. by Gerald Mohr et al. 10 vols. (Running Time: 10 hrs.). (Old-Time Radio Blockbusters Ser.). 2002. bk. 34.98 (978-1-57019-363-7(0), OTR4466) Pub: Radio Spirits. Dist(s): AudioGO

Master Georgie. Beryl Bainbridge. Read by Paul McGann. (Running Time: 16320 sec.). 2003. audio compact disk 49.95 (978-0-7540-5578-5(7)) Pub: Chivers Audio Bks GBR. Dist(s): AudioGO

Master Georgie. unabr. ed. Beryl Bainbridge. Read by Paul McGann. 4 cass. (Running Time: 4 hrs.). 1998. 39.95 (978-0-7540-0224-6(1), CAB 1647) AudioGO.
Set during the Crimean War, four people lives are linked by incident to the past.

Master Georgie. unabr. ed. Beryl Bainbridge. Read by Paul McGann. 4 cass. (Running Time: 6 hrs.). 2001. 34.95 (CAB 1647) Pub: Chivers Audio Bks GBR. Dist(s): AudioGO
Master Georgie is the centerpiece of this novel set during the Crimean War. It unfolds through the narratives of three protagonists: the geologist Doctor Potter; Pompey Jones, the photographer's assistant; and Myrtle, a girl believed to be Georgie's sister. All four characters are linked by incident to the past which changed their lives forever.

Master Harold ... & the Boys. Athol Fugard. Contrib. by Leon Addison Brown et al. 2 CDs. (Running Time: 1 hr. 32 mins.). audio compact disk 25.95 (978-1-58081-289-4(9), CDTPT210) L A Theatre.

Master i Margarita. Mikhail Afanasevich Bulgakov. 2 cass. (Running Time: 2 hrs.). (RUS.). 1997. pap. bk. 29.50 (978-1-58085-584-6(9)) Interlingua VA.

Master Immersed in Meditation Must Not Be Unable to Endure Contact with Course Human Nature: Volume 19, Vol. 19. Speeches. As told by Bhagat Singh Thind. (Running Time: 60 mins.). (ENG., 2003. 6.50 (978-1-932630-43-5(0)) Pub: Dr Bhagat Sin. Dist(s): Baker Taylor

Master Immersed in Meditation Must Not Be Unable to Endure Contact with Course Human Nature: Volume 19, Vol. 19. Speeches. Singh Bhagat Thind. (Running Time: 60 mins.). (ENG., 2003. audio compact disk 12.00 (978-1-932630-20-6(1)) Pub: Dr Bhagat Sin. Dist(s): Baker Taylor

Master Key System. unabr. ed. Charles F. Haanel. Read by James Boles. Ed. by Ruth L. Miller. (Running Time: 7 hrs. 0 mins. 0 sec.). (ENG.). 2008. audio compact disk 29.95 (978-0-7435-7197-5(5)) Pub: S&S Audio. Dist(s): S and S Inc

Master Key System Audiobook: 28 Parts - Questions & Answers. Charles F. Haanel. Narrated by Philip Ives. (ENG.). 2006. 19.95 (978-0-9840646-1-8(3)) Thinking Stuff.

Master Key System Audiobook: 28 Parts - Questions & Answers. unabr. ed. Charles F. Haanel. Narrated by Philip Ives. (ENG.). 2006. audio compact disk 49.95 (978-0-9840646-0-1(5)) Thinking Stuff.

Master Key to Riches. Napoleon Hill. (Running Time: 4 hrs.). (ENG.). (gr. 12 up). 2009. audio compact disk 25.95 (978-0-14-314461-8(8), PengAudBks) Penguin Grp USA.

Master Leaders. unabr. ed. George Barna & Bill Dallas. (Running Time: 7 hrs. 15 mins. 0 sec.). (ENG.). 2009. audio compact disk 24.98 (978-1-59644-799-8(0), christianSeed) christianaud.

***Master Leaders: Revealing Conversations with 30 Leadership Greats.** unabr. ed. George Barna & Bill Dallas. (ENG.). 2009. 14.98 (978-1-59644-800-1(8), christianSeed) christianaud.

Master Mind Principle. Jack Boland. 3 cass. 1977. 27.95 (978-0-88152-000-2(4)) Master Mind.
Transcend human limitations. This system will transform you into a master problem solver by increasing your power & wisdom.

Master Minding...the Way to Success & Happiness. Jack Boland. 4 cass. 1982. 34.95 (978-0-88152-001-9(2)) Master Mind.
Learn more about the ancient concept of master minding.

***Master of All Masters.** Anonymous. 2009. (978-1-60136-594-1(2)) Audio Holding.

Master of Ashwood, Emma Stirling. Read by Elizabeth Henry. 4 cass. 1999. 44.95 (21342) Pub: Soundings Ltd GBR. Dist(s): ISIS Pub

Master of Ballantrae. unabr. ed. Robert Louis Stevenson. Read by Jack Sondericker. 8 cass. (Running Time: 9 hrs.). 1988. 49.95 (978-1-55686-253-3(9), 253) Books in Motion.
Tells of a life-long feud between Master Ballantrae & his younger brother, Henry. Thwarted at every turn & persecuted by his brother, Henry becomes obsessed with the desire for retribution.

Master of Ballantrae. unabr. collector's ed. Robert Louis Stevenson. Read by John Chatty. 6 cass. (Running Time: 9 hrs.). 1983. 48.00 (978-0-7366-3968-2(3), 9512) Books on Tape.

Master of Craft. unabr. ed. W. W. Jacobs. Read by Peter Joyce. 5 cass. (Running Time: 7 hrs. 40 min.). 1998. 49.95 (978-1-86015-456-0(5)) Pub: UlverLrgPrint GBR. Dist(s): Ulverscroft US
Written in 1900, this tale tells of the marital mishaps & misadventures among the mariners of London's East End.

Master of Dragons. Margaret Weis. Read by Suzanne Toren. (Dragonvarld Trilogy: Bk. 3). 2005. 23.95 (978-1-59397-809-9(X)) Pub: Macmill Audio. Dist(s): Macmillan

Master of Dragons. unabr. ed. Margaret Weis & Margaret Weis. Read by Suzanne Toren. 12 CDs. (Running Time: 15 hrs. 0 mins. 0 sec.). Bk. 3. (ENG.). 2005. audio compact disk 49.95 (978-1-59397-357-5(8)) Pub: Macmill Audio. Dist(s): Macmillan

Master of Harp. Rene Giessen. 2005. pap. bk. 24.95 (978-3-89922-005-6(6)) AMA Verlag DEU.

Master of Marshlands. l.t. ed. Miriam MacGregor. 1991. 18.95 (978-0-263-12718-8(4), Macmillan Ref) Gale.

Master of Morholm. unabr. ed. T. R. Wilson. 10 cass. (Running Time: 14 hrs.). (Soundings Ser.). (J). 2006. 84.95 (978-1-84283-880-8(6)) Pub: ISIS Lrg Prnt GBR. Dist(s): Ulverscroft US

Master of Petersburg. unabr. ed. J. M. Coetzee. Read by David Case. 6 cass. (Running Time: 9 hrs.). 1995. 48.00 (978-0-7366-3178-5(X), 3847); Rental 9.95 (3847) Books on Tape.
Coetzee's Dostoevsky leaves his self-imposed exile in Germany, seeking answers in St. Petersburg to the mystery of his beloved stepson's death. It's a torturous search for Dostoevsky, who faces his own battles: epileptic seizures, consuming guilt & an erotic, edgy obsession with his stepson's landlady. Coetzee's intense writing does justice to this troubled genius & the age in which he lived.

Master of Rain. unabr. ed. Tom Bradby. Read by Steven Pacey. 12 cass. (Running Time: 18 hrs.). 2002. 96.95 (978-0-7540-0895-8(9), CAB 2317) Pub: Chivers Audio Bks GBR. Dist(s): AudioGO

Master of Space & Time. unabr. ed. Rudy V. B. Rucker. (Running Time: 21600 sec.). 2007. 44.95 (978-1-4332-0769-3(9)); audio compact disk 29.95 (978-1-4332-0771-6(0)); audio compact disk 45.00 (978-1-4332-0770-9(2)) Blckstn Audio.

Master of the Ballantrae. Perf. by Orson Welles & Agnes Moorehead. 1 cass. 10.00 (MC1022) Esstee Audios.
Radio drama.

Master of the Game: Tales from a Republican Revolutionary. unabr. ed. Trent Lott. 6 cass. (Running Time: 9 hrs.). 2004. audio compact disk 25.95 (978-0-06-073869-3(3)) HarperCollins Pubs.

Master of the Game: Tales from a Republican Revolutionary. unabr. ed. Trent Lott. 6 CDs. (Running Time: 9 hrs.). 2005. audio compact disk 29.95 (978-0-06-073870-9(7)) HarperCollins Pubs.

Master of the Moor. unabr. ed. Ruth Rendell. Read by Michael Bryant. 6 cass. (Running Time: 6 hrs.). 1996. 54.95 (978-0-7451-6235-5(5), CAB061) AudioGO.

Master of the Senate Pt. 2: The Years of Lyndon Johnson. unabr. ed. Robert A. Caro. Read by Grover Gardner. 11 cass. (Running Time: 16 hrs. 30 min.). 2002. 104.00 (978-0-7366-8454-5(9)) Books on Tape.
Lyndon Johnson uses his finely honed political acumen to dominate the U.S. Senate.

Master of the Senate Pt. 3: The Years of Lyndon Johnson. Robert A. Caro. Read by Grover Gardner. 2002. 112.00 (978-0-7366-8696-9(7)) Books on Tape.

Master of the Senate Pt. I: The Years of Lyndon Johnson. Robert A. Caro. Read by Grover Gardner. 11 cass. (Running Time: 16 hrs. 30 min.). 2002. 88.00 (978-0-7366-8444-6(1)) Books on Tape.
Caro's third volume in his series on the life of Lyndon Johnson is as riveting as its predecessors; the series comprises the most admired and compelling political biography of our era. At the heart of the book is its unprecedented revelation of how legislative power works, how the U.S. Senate works, how Lyndon Johnson on his way to the presidency mastered both, and how he used his power to break Southern control of Capitol Hill and to pass the first civil rights legislation since Reconstruction.

Master of the World. Jules Verne. Read by Jim Killavey. 4 cass. (Running Time: 5 hrs.). 1989. 28.00 incl. album. (C-2) Jimcin Record.
A mad inventor & his terrifying machine!.

Master of This Vessel. unabr. ed. Gwyn Griffin. Read by Wolfram Kandinsky. 12 cass. (Running Time: 18 hrs.). 1982. 96.00 (978-0-7366-0242-6(9), 1238) Books on Tape.
This is a tale of conflict & adventure at sea. Seratino Ciccolanti, a 26-year old professional sailor who accepts a temporary post as chief officer on a small ship bound for Australia. When the Captain dies en route, Ciccolanti reluctantly takes command. A simmering brew of personal rivalries robs Ciccolanti of his effectiveness & when the ship is beset by storm, the crew mutinies.

Master of War: The Life of General George H. Thomas. unabr. ed. Benson Bobrick. Narrated by Norman Dietz. (Running Time: 14 hrs. 0 mins.). 2009. 8.91 (978-1-4001-8158-2(5)); audio compact disk 79.99 (978-1-4001-4158-6(3)) Pub: Tantor Media. Dist(s): IngramPubServ

Master of War: The Life of General George H. Thomas. unabr. ed. Benson Bobrick. Read by Norman Dietz. (Running Time: 14 hrs. 0 mins. 0 sec.). (ENG.). 2009. 29.99 (978-1-4001-6158-4(4)); audio compact disk 39.99 (978-1-4001-1158-9(7)) Pub: Tantor Media. Dist(s): IngramPubServ

Master Plan. Contrib. by James P. Connolly. Prod. by Steve North & Barb North. 2006. audio compact disk 16.98 (978-1-929243-74-7(X)) Uproar Ent.

***Master Plan of Evangelism.** unabr. ed. Robert Coleman. Narrated by Scott Grunden. (ENG.). 2008. 12.98 (978-1-59644-566-6(1), christianSeed) christianaud.

Master Plan of Evangelism. unabr. ed. Robert E. Coleman. Read by Scott Grunden. (Running Time: 2 hrs. 48 mins. 0 sec.). (ENG.). 2008. audio compact disk 21.98 (978-1-59644-565-9(3)) christianaud.

Master Quilter. Narrated by Jennifer Chiaverini. 6 cass. (Running Time: 10 hrs. 45 mins.). (Elm Creek Quilts Ser.: No. 6). 2004. 29.99 (978-1-4025-6957-9(2), 03834) Recorded Bks.

Master Reader. Edward Fritsch & Nate Rosenblatt. Read by Nate Rosenblatt & Edward Fritsch. (Running Time: 3 hrs.). (C). 2005. 35.95 (978-1-59912-165-9(4)) Iofy Corp.

Master Secret. Eldon Taylor. 16 cass. 239.95 (978-1-55978-392-7(3), A101) Progress Aware Res.

Master Self-Hypnosis. 2 cass. (Running Time: 60 min. per cass.). (Self Hypnosis & Subliminal Reinforcement Ser.). 14.95 (978-1-55569-232-2(X), SUB-8008) Great Am Audio.
Presents tools for positive self-change.

Master Skylark. unabr. ed. John Bennett. Read by Flo Gibson. 5 cass. (Running Time: 7 hrs. 30 min.). (J). 1995. 20.95 (978-1-55685-401-9(3)) Audio Bk Con.
A young lad, with the voice of a skylark, is spirited away from Stratford-on-Avon by a theatrical troup. After many adventures, both frightening & triumphant, including a performance at the palace for Queen Bess, he is rescued by William Shakespeare.

***Master Sniper.** abr. ed. Stephen Hunter. Read by Christopher Lane. (Running Time: 6 hrs.). 2010. audio compact disk 14.99 (978-1-4418-6148-1(3), 9781441861481, BACD) Brilliance Audio.

***Master Sniper.** unabr. ed. Stephen Hunter. Read by Christopher Lane. (Running Time: 11 hrs.). 2010. 39.97 (978-1-4418-6147-4(5), 9781441861474, BADLE); 24.99 (978-1-4418-6144-3(0), 9781441861443, Brilliance MP3); 39.97 (978-1-4418-6145-0(9), 9781441861450, Brinc Audio MP3 Lib); 24.99 (978-1-4418-6146-7(7), 9781441861467, BAD); audio compact disk 92.97 (978-1-4418-6143-6(2), 9781441861436, BriAudCD Unabrid) Brilliance Audio.

***Master Sniper.** unabr. ed. Stephen Hunter. Read by Christopher Lane. (Running Time: 11 hrs.). 2010. audio compact disk 29.99 (978-1-4418-6142-9(4), 9781441861429, Bril Audio CD Unabri) Brilliance Audio.

Master Strategies for Higher Achievement: Set Your Goals & Reach Them - Fast! Brian S. Tracy. Read by Brian S. Tracy. (Running Time: 6 hrs.). (C). 2005. 36.95 (978-1-59912-150-5(6)) Iofy Corp.

Master Strategies for Higher Achievement: Set Your Goals & Reach Them - Fast! Brian S. Tracy. 6 cass. (Running Time: 6 hrs.). 1995. 59.95 (12170A) Nightingale-Conant.

Master Strategies for Higher Achievement: Set Your Goals & Reach Them - Fast! unabr. ed. Brian S. Tracy. Read by Brian S. Tracy. 6 CDs. (Running Time: 6 hrs.). (ENG.). 2005. audio compact disk 19.98 (978-1-59659-001-4(7), GildAudio) Pub: Gildan Media. Dist(s): HachBkGrp

Master Swing Trader: Tools & Techniques to Profit from Outstanding Short-Term Trading Opportunities. Alan S. Farley. 4 cass. (Running Time: 6 hrs.). 2004. 24.00 (978-1-932378-34-4(0)); audio compact disk 28.00 (978-1-932378-35-1(9)) Pub: A Media Intl. Dist(s): Natl Bk Netwk
Contains a proven course for short-term traders that will help improve bottom lines, lessen risks - and increase confidence in building solid profits in todays volatile market.

Master T. T. Liang's T'ai Chi Music: 150-Posture Yang Style Long Form. Prod. by Valley Spirit Arts. (ENG.). 2006. audio compact disk 19.95 (978-1-889633-23-7(2)) Valley SpiritA.

Master Teachers: Perennial Wisdom for the 21st Century. Michael Toms. 6 cass. (Running Time: 5 hrs.). (New Dimensions Ser.). (ENG.). 2000. 59.95 (978-1-56170-733-1(3), 4035) Hay House.
Michael Toms has dialogues with a number of distinguished philosophers, metaphysicians and spititual leaders.

Master the American Accent. Judy Ravin et al. (ENG.). 2009. pap. bk. 79.95 (978-0-9817754-2-5(X)) Pub: Language Success Pr. Dist(s): Baker Taylor

***Master Your Debt: Slash Your Monthly Payments & Become Debt Free.** unabr. ed. Jordan E. Goodman. (Running Time: 7 hrs.). (ENG.). 2010. 27.98 (978-1-59659-513-2(2), GildAudio) Pub: Gildan Media. Dist(s): HachBkGrp

***Master Your Debt: Slash Your Monthly Payments & Become Debt Free.** unabr. ed. Jordan E. Goodman. (Running Time: 7 hrs.). (ENG.). 2010. audio compact disk 29.98 (978-1-59659-542-2(6), GildAudio) Pub: Gildan Media. Dist(s): HachBkGrp

Master Your Keyboard. unabr. rev. ed. 3 cass. (Running Time: 4 hrs.). 1994. pap. bk. 34.50 (978-0-88432-750-9(7), S17080) J Norton Pubs.

Master Your Metabolism: The 3 Diet Secrets to Naturally Balancing Your Hormones for a Hot & Healthy Body! abr. ed. Jillian Michaels & Mariska van Aalst. (ENG.). 2010. audio compact disk 20.00 (978-0-307-73727-4(6), Random AudioBks) Pub: Random Audio Pubg. Dist(s): Random

Master Your Mind, Children's Album # 1 No. 1: I Am a Happy Child; I Am a Healthy Child; I Am a Creative Child; I Am a Sleepy Child. Read by Mary Richards. 4 cass. (J). 2007. audio compact disk 59.85 (978-1-56136-166-3(6)) Master Your Mind.

Master Your Mind, Children's Album # 2 No. 2: I Am Smart; I Am a Friendly Child; I Am Whatever I Want to Be; I Am Thankful. Read by Mary Richards. 4 cass. (J). 2007. audio compact disk 59.85 (978-1-56136-167-0(4)) Master Your Mind.

Master Your Mind, Guided Relaxation: Autogenic Relaxation. Read by Mary Richards. 1 cass. (Running Time: 1 hr.). 2007. audio compact disk 19.95 (978-1-56136-024-6(4)) Master Your Mind.

Master Your Mind, Guided Relaxation: Be All That You Are. Read by Mary Richards. 1 cass. (Running Time: 1 hr. 3 min.). 2007. audio compact disk 19.95 (978-1-56136-007-9(4)) Master Your Mind.

Master Your Mind, Guided Relaxation: Be Slim... Think Slim. Read by Mary Richards. 1 cass. (Running Time: 1 hr. 23 min.). 2007. audio compact disk 19.95 (978-1-56136-004-8(X)) Master Your Mind.

Master Your Mind, Guided Relaxation: Beauty Rest - Sleep Tape. Read by Mary Richards. 1 cass. (Running Time: 1 hr. 44 min.). 2007. audio compact disk 19.95 (978-1-56136-034-5(1)) Master Your Mind.

Master Your Mind, Guided Relaxation: Change Eating Habits. Read by Mary Richards. 1 cass. (Running Time: 1 hr. 12 min.). 2007. audio compact disk 19.95 (978-1-56136-005-5(8)) Master Your Mind.

Master Your Mind, Guided Relaxation: Energy Chakra Meditation. Read by Mary Richards. 1 cass. (Running Time: 48 min.). 2007. audio compact disk 19.95 (978-1-56136-009-3(0)) Master Your Mind.

Master Your Mind, Guided Relaxation: Fighting the Cancer. Read by Mary Richards. 1 cass. (Running Time: 1 hr.). 2007. audio compact disk 19.95 (978-1-56136-023-9(6)) Master Your Mind.

Master Your Mind, Guided Relaxation: Financial Success - Sleep Tape. Read by Mary Richards. 1 cass. (Running Time: 1 hr. 10 min.). 2007. audio compact disk 19.95 (978-1-56136-032-1(5)) Master Your Mind.

Master Your Mind, Guided Relaxation: Find the Joy Within. Read by Mary Richards. 1 cass. (Running Time: 48 min.). 2007. audio compact disk 19.95 (978-1-56136-008-6(2)) Master Your Mind.

Master Your Mind, Guided Relaxation: Forgiveness Process. Read by Mary Richards. 1 cass. (Running Time: 1 hr.). 2007. audio compact disk 19.95 (978-1-56136-010-9(4)) Master Your Mind.

Master Your Mind, Guided Relaxation: Goal Achievement. Read by Mary Richards. 1 cass. (Running Time: 45 min.). 2007. audio compact disk 19.95 (978-1-56136-001-7(5)) Master Your Mind.

Master Your Mind, Guided Relaxation: Goal Achievement - Sleep Tape. Read by Mary Richards. 1 cass. (Running Time: 1 hr. 17 min.). 2007. audio compact disk 19.95 (978-1-56136-038-3(4)) Master Your Mind.

Master Your Mind, Guided Relaxation: Healing Energy - Sleep Tape. Read by Mary Richards. 1 cass. (Running Time: 1 hr. 12 min.). 2007. audio compact disk 19.95 (978-1-56136-036-9(8)) Master Your Mind.

Master Your Mind, Guided Relaxation: Healing the Child Within. Read by Mary Richards. 1 cass. (Running Time: 55 min.). 2007. audio compact disk 19.95 (978-1-56136-018-5(X)) Master Your Mind.

Master Your Mind, Guided Relaxation: High Mountain Meditation. Read by Mary Richards. 1 cass. (Running Time: 1 hr. 23 min.). 2007. audio compact disk 19.95 (978-1-56136-021-5(X)) Master Your Mind.

Master Your Mind, Guided Relaxation: High Performance. Read by Mary Richards. 1 cass. (Running Time: 1 hr.). 2007. audio compact disk 19.95 (978-1-56136-013-0(9)) Master Your Mind.

Master Your Mind, Guided Relaxation: Inner Peace Autogenic. Read by Mary Richards. 1 cass. (Running Time: 1 hr.). 2007. audio compact disk 19.95 (978-1-56136-027-7(9)) Master Your Mind.

Master Your Mind, Guided Relaxation: Inner Sanctuary. Read by Mary Richards. 1 cass. (Running Time: 1 hr. 5 min.). 2007. audio compact disk 19.95 (978-1-56136-025-3(2)) Master Your Mind.

Master Your Mind, Guided Relaxation: Inner Wisdom. Read by Mary Richards. 1 cass. (Running Time: 1 hr.). 2007. audio compact disk 19.95 (978-1-56136-002-4(3)) Master Your Mind.

Master Your Mind, Guided Relaxation: Inner Wisdom - Sleep Tape. Read by Mary Richards. 1 cass. (Running Time: 1 hr. 16 min.). 2007. audio compact disk 19.95 (978-1-56136-037-6(6)) Master Your Mind.

Master Your Mind, Guided Relaxation: Loving Relationship. Read by Mary Richards. 1 cass. (Running Time: 1 hr. 5 min.). 2007. audio compact disk 19.95 (978-1-56136-015-4(5)) Master Your Mind.

Master Your Mind, Guided Relaxation: Normal Blood Pressure. Read by Mary Richards. 1 cass. (Running Time: 1 hr.). 2007. audio compact disk 19.95 (978-1-56136-028-4(7)) Master Your Mind.

Master Your Mind, Guided Relaxation: Optimal Performance Autogenic. Read by Mary Richards. 1 cass. (Running Time: 1 hr.). 2007. audio compact disk 19.95 (978-1-56136-029-1(5)) Master Your Mind.

Master Your Mind, Guided Relaxation: Pre Surgery - Sleep Tape. Read by Mary Richards. 1 cass. (Running Time: 1 hr. 12 min.). 2007. audio compact disk 19.95 (978-1-56136-035-2(X)) Master Your Mind.

Master Your Mind, Guided Relaxation: Re Write Your Script. Read by Mary Richards. 1 cass. (Running Time: 1 hr. 5 min.). 2007. audio compact disk 19.95 (978-1-56136-012-3(0)) Master Your Mind.

Master Your Mind, Guided Relaxation: Relaxing into Sleep - Sleep Tape. Read by Mary Richards. 1 cass. (Running Time: 1 hr. 23 min.). 2007. audio compact disk 19.95 (978-1-56136-033-8(3)) Master Your Mind.

Master Your Mind, Guided Relaxation: Release Discomfort. Read by Mary Richards. 1 cass. (Running Time: 83 min.). 2007. audio compact disk 19.95 (978-1-56136-019-2(8)) Master Your Mind.

Master Your Mind, Guided Relaxation: Self Confident Self Assured - Sleep Tape. Read by Mary Richards. 1 cass. (Running Time: 1 hr.). 2007. audio compact disk 19.95 (978-1-56136-039-0(2)) Master Your Mind.

Master Your Mind, Guided Relaxation: Self Hypnosis. Read by Mary Richards. 1 cass. (Running Time: 48 min.). 2007. audio compact disk 19.95 (978-1-56136-011-6(2)) Master Your Mind.

Master Your Mind, Guided Relaxation: Spiritual Cleansing. Read by Mary Richards. 1 cass. (Running Time: 45 min.). 2007. audio compact disk 19.95 (978-1-56136-022-2(8)) Master Your Mind.

Master Your Mind, Guided Relaxation: Stop Smoking. Read by Mary Richards. 1 cass. (Running Time: 72 min.). 2007. audio compact disk 19.95 (978-1-56136-006-2(6)) Master Your Mind.

Master Your Mind, Guided Relaxation: Stop Smoking - Sleep Tape. Read by Mary Richards. 1 cass. (Running Time: 1 hr. 5 min.). 2007. audio compact disk 19.95 (978-1-56136-031-4(7)) Master Your Mind.

Master Your Mind, Guided Relaxation: Successful Surgery. Read by Mary Richards. 1 cass. (Running Time: 1 hr. 12 min.). 2007. audio compact disk 19.95 (978-1-56136-014-7(7)) Master Your Mind.

Master Your Mind, Guided Relaxation: Supporting Your Recovery. Read by Mary Richards. 1 cass. (Running Time: 1 hr. 8 min.). 2007. audio compact disk 19.95 (978-1-56136-016-1(3)) Master Your Mind.

Master Your Mind, Guided Relaxation: Tap Positive Energy. Read by Mary Richards. 1 cass. (Running Time: 1 hr. 5 min.). 2007. audio compact disk 19.95 (978-1-56136-026-0(0)) Master Your Mind.

Master Your Mind, Guided Relaxation: Weight Loss - Sleep Tape. Read by Mary Richards. 1 cass. (Running Time: 1 hr. 3 min.). 2007. audio compact disk 19.95 (978-1-56136-030-7(9)) Master Your Mind.

Master Your Mind, Guided Relaxation: Your Inner Healer. Read by Mary Richards. 1 cass. (Running Time: 1 hr. 12 min.). 2007. audio compact disk 19.95 (978-1-56136-020-8(1)) Master Your Mind.

Master Your Mind, Guided Relaxation -0000: Body Awareness. Read by Mary Richards. 1 cass. (Running Time: 1 hr.). 2007. audio compact disk 19.95 (978-1-56136-017-8(1)) Master Your Mind.

Master Your Mind, Inner Quest Album. 4 cass. 2007. audio compact disk 59.85 (978-1-56136-187-8(9)) Master Your Mind.

Master Your Mind, Realtor's Power Plus Pack: Successful Realtor; Stop Procrastinating; Financial Success; Self Esteem. 4 cass. 2007. audio compact disk 59.85 (978-1-56136-188-5(7)) Master Your Mind.

Master Your Mind, Relax & Live Longer Album: Rapid Stress Reduction; Relax & Let Go; Higher Self Meditation; Breathing Colors. Read by Mary Richards. 4 cass. 2007. audio compact disk 59.85 (978-1-56136-190-8(9)) Master Your Mind.

Master Your Mind, Short Strengthening Exercise: Build Your Energy Field. Read by Mary Richards. 1 cass. (Running Time: 12 min.). 2007. audio compact disk 19.95 (978-1-56136-164-9(X)) Master Your Mind.

Master Your Mind, Short Strengthening Exercise: Healing Your Inner Child. Read by Mary Richards. 1 cass. (Running Time: 20 min.). 2007. audio compact disk 19.95 (978-1-56136-165-6(8)) Master Your Mind.

Master Your Mind, the Course in Miracles: Forgiveness Sets Me Free. Read by Mary Richards. 1 cass. (Running Time: 60 min.). 2007. audio compact disk 19.95 (978-1-56136-088-8(0)) Master Your Mind.

Master Your Mind, the Course in Miracles: Song Remembered. Read by Mary Richards. 1 cass. (Running Time: 60 min.). 2007. audio compact disk 19.95 (978-1-56136-090-1(2)) Master Your Mind.

Master Your Mind, the Course in Miracles: Teach Only Love. Read by Mary Richards. 1 cass. (Running Time: 83 min.). 2007. audio compact disk 19.95 (978-1-56136-089-5(9)) Master Your Mind.

Master Your Money Audio Album. Instructed by Ron Blue. 2000. 29.95 (978-1-885447-58-6(2)) Walk Thru the Bible.
With the dynamic Bible-based teaching of financial consultant Ron Blue, the award-winning Master Your Money series teaches viewers to control their finances with clear-cut Biblical principles.

Master Your Money Type: Using Your Financial Personality to Create a Life of Wealth & Freedom. abr. ed. Jordan E. Goodman. Read by Geoffrey Wade. (Running Time: 7 hrs.). (ENG.). 2006. audio compact disk 29.95 (978-1-59887-012-1(2), 1598870122) Pub: Penguin-HghBrdg. Dist(s): Penguin Grp USA

Masterful Coach Vol. 1: Permission to Be. Leza Danly. (Running Time: 1 hr.). 1999. (978-0-9675727-0-3(3)) L Danly.
Self-help for professional coaches.

Masterful Content: How to Create Engaging & Transformational Content for Your Group Coaching Program. Wendy Y. Bailey. 1. (Running Time: 60 mins.). (ENG.). 2010. audio compact disk 197.00 (978-0-9749914-1-2(4), 0-9749914-1-4) Brilliance In Action.
Building a successful business involves making choices and decisions that move you forward and allow you to grow and develop. It's important to know you're on track about your choices as you consider all of the available opportunities. Order this one-hour audio CD so you can discover the Seven Steps of Choice. You'll learn to use these steps to create a Personal Model For Choice that will propel your business forward while you enjoy personal freedom. This TeleClass recording is ideal for women in business who want to gain a sense of clarity about choices and decisions. Includes Detailed TeleClass notes with challenge assignments.

Masterful Leadership: Leading Like Jesus. unabr. ed. Ken Blanchard. 2005. 29.99 (978-1-58926-844-9(X), 6844) Pub: Oasis Audio. Dist(s): TNT Media Grp

Masterful Leadership: Leading Like Jesus. unabr. ed. Ken Blanchard & John Ortberg. (ENG.). 2005. audio compact disk 19.99 (978-1-58926-845-6(8), 6845) Oasis Audio.

Masterful Leadership: Leading Like Jesus. unabr. ed. Ken Blanchard & John Ortberg. (ENG.). 2005. 13.99 (978-1-60814-303-0(1)) Oasis Audio.

***Mastergate.** unabr. ed. Larry Gelbart. Perf. by Walter Matthau & Edward Asner. 2 CDs. (Running Time: 2 hrs.). 2009. audio compact disk 25.95 (978-1-58081-646-5(0)) L A Theatre.

Mastergate. unabr. ed. Larry Gelbart. Perf. by Edward Asner et al. 1 cass. (Running Time: 1 hr. 35 mins.). 1992. 19.95 (978-1-58081-007-4(1), TPT55) L A Theatre.
Satire about the Iran-Contra Senate hearings & their participants.

Masterharper of Pern. unabr. ed. Anne McCaffrey. Read by Dick Hill. 10 cass. (Running Time: 13 hrs.). (Dragonriders of Pern Ser.). 1998. 89.25 (978-1-56740-566-8(5), 1567405665, Unabridge Lib Edns) Brilliance Audio.

Masterharper of Pern. unabr. ed. Anne McCaffrey. Read by Dick Hill. (Running Time: 13 hrs.). (Dragonriders of Pern Ser.). 2005. 39.25 (978-1-59737-020-2(7), 9781597370202, BADLE); 24.95 (978-1-59737-019-6(3), 9781597370196, BAD); audio compact disk 39.25 (978-1-59737-018-9(5), 9781597370189, Brinc Audio MP3 Lib); audio compact disk 24.95 (978-1-59737-017-2(7), 9781597370172, Brilliance MP3); audio compact disk 112.25 (978-1-59737-016-5(9), 9781597370165, BriAudCD Unabrid); audio compact disk 37.95 (978-1-59737-015-8(0), 9781597370158, Bril Audio CD Unabri) Brilliance Audio.
In a time when no Thread has fallen for centuries - when, indeed, many are beginning to dare to hope that Thread will never fall again - a boy is born to Harper Hall. His name is Robinton, and he is destined to be one of the most famous and beloved leaders Pern has ever known. It is a perilous time for harpers. They sing of Thread, yet more and more people are beginning to doubt the return of that deadly scourge. They teach reading, writing, history, but Fax - who hates the harpers in general - is determined to keep his

growing area of influence free of the learning that might sow unrest. And they extol the dragonriders, whom many view increasingly as a drain on the resources of the Holds. Now harpers are being turned away from the holds; and, worse yet, they are being derided, attacked, even beaten. It is the climate of unrest that Robinton will come into his own. For despite the tragedies that beset his own life, he continues to believe in music and in the dragons, and is determined to save his beloved Pern from itself . . .so that the dragonriders can be ready to fly against the dreaded Thread when it at last returns!.

Masterharper of Pern, unabr. ed. Anne McCaffrey. Read by Dick Hill. 10 cass. (Pern Ser.). 1999. 89.25 (FS9-34440) Highsmith.

Masteriing Effective English Communication Cassette Series see Mastering Effective English Communication (MEEC) CD Series

Mastering Acoustic Guitar. Greg Horne. 1 CD. (Running Time: 1 hr. 30 mins.). (ENG.). 2000. audio compact disk 11.00 (978-0-7390-0431-9(X), 19342) Alfred Pub.

Mastering Advanced Italian. N. Messora. 1 cass. (Running Time: 1 hr. 30 mins.). (ENG.). suppl. ed. 12.95 (978-0-7818-0334-2(9)) Hippocrene Bks.

Mastering Bluegrass Guitar: For the Intermediate & Advanced Player. Composed by Russ Barenberg. 2001. audio compact disk 59.95 (978-0-634-04097-9(9), 0634040979) Pub: Homespun Video. Dist(s): H Leonard

Mastering Blues Guitar. Wayne Riker. Ed. by Workshop Arts Staff. (ENG.). 1994. audio compact disk 10.95 (978-0-7390-0409-8(3), 11280) Alfred Pub.

Mastering Contemporary Rock. Chris Amelar. (ENG.). 1993. 8.95 (978-0-7390-1823-1(X)) Alfred Pub.

Mastering Effective English Communication (MEEC) CD Series. 4th ed. 13 CDs. (Running Time: 14 hrs 19 mins.). (Mastering Effective English Communication Ser.). Orig. Title: Masteriing Effective English Communication Cassette Series. 2004. spiral bd. 250.00 (978-1-883574-10-9(2), 1070) LDS & Asocs.
3 spiral bound workbooks and 13cds in a small CD album. Nothing speeds your speech goals like frequent oral practice - and no other fills your absence between sessions as well as our audio programs. Male/female speakers - You need both for the best role models. Lecture information is recorded, not just exercises Reinforces your key points Saves valuable contact time by allowing clients to preview new topics with solid information Lets you repeat as often as needed until it "sinks" in! CD markers and CD directories are graphically noted in workbooks Wastes little time in making appropriate home assignments via easy to use directories and indices Format suits the learning needs of adult, getting them up and running faster! PLUS: Volume Indexes. Clients now have one more aid to find the exact material they need. Instructors can quickly pinpoint exercises by length, sound combinations or key words, and more! Checkpoints! Beep tones on the CDs signal special messages: keeps listeners alert to the goals, provides usage hints, or suggests more challenging exercises. SMART CD use!! Many CD programs aren?t really functional for the immediate feedback loop you want to have for practicing oral skills: there are few (more often no -) tracks that you can skip to ? and they never tell you that! You have to listen to 30-35 minutes of continuous copy! We made liberal use of tracks on every CD: on average, you?re listening for only 3-5 minutes before you can replay the copy you really want. Feedback is far more immediate. Most exercises also have their own track!.

Mastering Electric Bass. David Overthrow. 1 CD. (ENG.). 2000. audio compact disk 10.00 (978-0-7390-0684-9(3), 19357) Alfred Pub.

Mastering Emotions. Barry Tesar. 1 cass. (Running Time: 1 hr.). (Subliminal Inspiration Ser.). 1992. 9.98 (978-1-56470-024-7(0)) Success Cass.
Subliminal program.

Mastering English Book 1 Listening Comprehension Test CD-A: Elt. 2003. audio compact disk (978-0-7428-0936-9(6)) CCLS Pubg Hse.

Mastering English Book 2 Listening Comprehension Test CD-A: Elt. 2003. audio compact disk (978-0-7428-0937-6(4)) CCLS Pubg Hse.

Mastering English Book 3 Listening Comprehension Test CD-A: Elt. 2002. audio compact disk (978-0-7428-0938-3(2)) CCLS Pubg Hse.

Mastering English Book 4 Listening Comprehension Test CD-A: Elt. 2003. audio compact disk (978-0-7428-0939-0(0)) CCLS Pubg Hse.

Mastering Essential Math Skills, Book One: Grades 4 And 5: 20 Minutes a Day to Success. Richard W. Fisher. (Mastering Essential Math Skills Ser.). (J). (gr. 6-13). 2007. pap. bk. 19.95 (978-0-9821901-0-4(7)) Math Essentials.

Mastering Essential Math Skills Book Two: Middle Grades/High School: 20 Minutes a Day to Success. America's Math Teacher. (Mastering Essential Math Skills Ser.). (J). (gr. 6-13). 2007. pap. bk. 39.95 (978-0-9821901-1-1(5)) Math Essentials.

Mastering Evidence: Using the Rules That Shape the Case. James McElhaney. 3 cass. (Running Time: 4 hrs.). (McElhaney's Master Advocate Ser.). 1988. 85.00 PEG MN.

Mastering Finnish. Aspasia Books & Borje Vahamaki. (ENG.). 1999. 16.00 (978-0-9685881-1-6(5)) Pub: Aspasia Bks CAN. Dist(s): U Toronto Pr

Mastering Finnish CDs: Set of 2 CDs. Aspasia Books & Borje Vahamaki. (ENG.). 2003. audio compact disk 18.00 (978-0-9689054-9-4(8)) Pub: Aspasia Bks CAN. Dist(s): U Toronto Pr

Mastering French. E. J. Neather. (Mastering Languages Ser.). (ENG., 1991. 12.95 (978-0-87052-060-0(1)) Hippocrene Bks.

Mastering High Probability Chart Reading Methods with John Murphy. Speeches. John A. Murphy. (Running Time: 82 Mins.). 2003. 19.95 (978-1-59280-101-5(3), Marketplc Aud) Marketplace Bks.
*Post big gains - even if the market is locked in a downward spiral - by following the powerful sector trading strategies of renowned technical analyst John Murphy. The Traders Hall of Fame honoree shows you step-by-step how to pinpoint the right sectors to play at the right time - and how to shift seamlessly from one to the other - with profits in tow. Citing key relationships among markets - from stocks to commodities, bonds to currencies - Murphy's methods help you determine when to move from one to the other so you're poised to capture the most lucrative opportunities available in any market climate. With a full online support manual available at www.traderslibrary.com/tradesecrets ttp://www.traderslibrary.com/tradesecrets, Murphy's on-target cues for rotating among sectors will keep you in the "hot" winning ones, at the best points in the business cycle - time after time. *Formally titled: "Simple Sector Trading Strategies: Profit by being in the right markets - at the right time".*

Mastering Italian. Noemi Messora. (Mastering Languages Ser.). (ENG., 1991. 12.95 (978-0-87052-066-2(0)) Hippocrene Bks.

Mastering Jazz Guitar - Chord/Melody. Jody Fischer. 1 CD. (FRE.). Date not set. pap. bk. (978-0-7390-0829-4(3), 19377) Alfred Pub.

Mastering Jazz Guitar Improv. Jody Fischer. 1 CD. (FRE.). Date not set. pap. bk. (978-0-7390-0828-7(5), 19376) Alfred Pub.

Mastering Korean. Park. 12 cass. (Running Time: 18 hrs.). (Foreign Service Institute Language Ser.). (KOR & ENG.). 1988. pap. bk. 79.95 (978-0-8120-7480-2(7)) Barron.

Mastering Leadership. Steve Sullivan. 1998. 11.95 (978-1-890522-06-3(6)) Pub: Motivat Resources. Dist(s): HRD Press

Mastering Life's Challenges: Introducing the Option Process(r) & the Option Institute. Barry Neil Kaufman. (ENG.). 2006. audio compact disk 4.00 (978-0-9798105-0-3(7)) Option Inst.

Mastering Memory in the Workshop of Life. Richard D. Dobbins. 3 cass. 14.95 (978-1-890329-60-0(6)) Totally Alive.
Learn how to retrain your memories so they give you the courage to face today & tomorrow secure in God's loving presence.

Mastering Modes for Guitar. Ed Lozano & Joe Dineen. 2004. audio compact disk 17.95 (978-0-8256-1903-8(3)) Pub: Music Sales. Dist(s): H Leonard

Mastering Monday: A Guide to Integrating Faith & Work. John D. Beckett. (Running Time: 18000 sec.). (ENG.). 2006. audio compact disk 25.00 (978-0-8308-3386-3(2)) InterVarsity.

Mastering Music. Ed. by Alfred Publishing. (ENG.). 2007. audio compact disk 199.00 (978-0-7390-5003-3(6)) Alfred Pub.

Mastering Our Difficulties: Zech. 4:7. Ed Young. (J). 1981. 4.95 (978-0-7417-1167-0(2), A0167) Win Walk.

Mastering Pain: Control Pain Without Medication. 2000. (978-1-893238-00-8(8)) Doc Borrie.

Mastering Personal Relationships. Pat Carroll. Read by Pat Carroll. Ed. by Tony Carroll. 1 cass. (Running Time: 30 min.). 10.00 Inner-Mind Concepts.
Teaches how to overcome the human fear of rejection through communication.

Mastering Reading & Language Skills with the Newspaper - The International Herald Tribune. Maxine Chernoff & Ethel Tiersky. 3 cass. (Running Time: 3 hrs.). 1993. 39.95 (Passport Bks) McGraw-Hill Trade.

Mastering Relaxation Series. Roderick Borrie. Music by Hugh Fraser. 1993. (978-1-893238-16-9(4)) Doc Borrie.

Mastering Russian. Erika Haber. (Mastering Languages Ser.). (ENG.). 1994. 12.95 (978-0-7818-0271-0(7)) Hippocrene Bks.

Mastering Safety Communication: Communication Skills for a Safe, Productive & Profitable Workplace. unabr. ed. John W. Drebinger, Jr. Read by Karen P. Drebinger. 4 cass. 1997. 47.77 Set. (978-1-890296-01-8(5)) Wulamoc Pub.
Communication skills for safety professionals.

Mastering Spanish. Robert Clarke. (Mastering Languages Ser.). (ENG.). 1991. 12.95 (978-0-87052-067-9(9)) Hippocrene Bks.

Mastering Stress Management. Speeches. Edward Strachar. 1 cass. (Running Time: 50 mins.). 2002. 14.95 (978-0-9719358-4-6(X)) InGenius Inc.

Mastering Stress Management. Speeches. Edward Strachar. 1 CD. (Running Time: 60 mins.). 2002. audio compact disk 14.95 (978-0-9726941-0-0(2)) InGenius Inc.

Mastering Stress Overnight. Instructed by Jane Ann Covington. 1 cass. (Running Time: 70 mins.). 2002. audio compact disk 23.95 (978-0-9726080-0-8(1)) CDM Prodns.

Mastering Telephone Skills for Sales Professionals. Dennis R. Kyle. Created by Dennis R. Kyle. Ed. by Marcella McMahon. 1998. 199.00i (978-0-9701329-0-1(5)) Kyle Pubng.

Mastering the Art of Cold Calling. Ron La Vine. 2 CD's. (Running Time: approximately 100 minutes). 2005. audio compact disk 195.00 (978-1-59971-016-7(1)) AardGP.
Complete Set of Two Audio CDs which cover all the materials in the 17 sections of the Workbook (they are about 45 minutes each) presented by Ron La Vine.

Mastering the Art of Cross Examination. 11 cass. (Running Time: 8 hrs. 28 min.). (Complete Audiotape Ser.). 195.00 (FAMAC0S); 20.00 ea. Natl Inst Trial Ad.

Mastering the Art of Cross Examination. Irving Younger. 11 cass. 1987. 210.00 (AUDMACOS) NITA.
Covers the cross examination of a variety of witnesses including: the well-prepared witness, eyewitness, child witness, expert witness, & more. Also available on videotape.

Mastering the Art of Neural Enhancement. Gary Coxe. 4 cass. (Running Time: 2 hrs.). 1992. 39.00 (978-1-928926-01-6(0)) Coxes Ent.
Make people remember who you are without even realizing it. Especially beneficial for sales representatives & entrepreneurs.

Mastering the Art of Voiceovers Audio CD's: Or What the Guys Who Make All That Money Won't Tell You. 4 CDs. (Running Time: 4 hrs). 2003. audio compact disk 189.00 (978-0-9766122-0-9(8)) D Balestrero.

Mastering the Attitude of Achievement. Lou Tice. Read by Lou Tice. 6 cass. 1991. 59.95 (791A) Nightingale-Conant.
Lou Tice teaches that beliefs & thoughts affect a person's quality & quantity of life & attitude affects your level of achievement. Learn to alter your attitude towards success & achievement.

Mastering the Cisco CCNA Audiobook. Awdeeo. Narrated by Awdeeo. 2008. 39.99 (978-0-9818187-1-9(4)) PrepLogic.

Mastering the CompTIA A+ Audiobook. Awdeeo. Narrated by Awdeeo. (ENG.). 2008. 39.99 (978-0-9818187-0-2(6)) PrepLogic.

Mastering the Craft of Modern Trial Advocacy. Michael E. Tigar. 6 cass. (Running Time: 6 hrs.). 1998. pap. bk. 185.00 (978-0-943380-57-5(X)) PEG MN.

Mastering the Fire Service Assessment Center. Anthony Kastros. Narrated by Keith Boscher. Frwd. by Alan V. Brunacini. 2008. audio compact disk 49.00 (978-1-59370-163-5(2), Fire Eng Bks & Vid) PennWell Corp.

Mastering the French Subjunctive: A Conversational Method. Scripts. Faye Halpern et al. 1 Cassette. (Running Time: 20 mins). Dramatization.Tr. of Subjonctif Par la Conversation. (FRE & ENG.). 2002. (978-0-9717944-1-2(3)) F Halpern Co.

Mastering the Gentle Art of Verbal Self-Defense. Suzette Haden Elgin. Read by Suzette Haden Elgin. 6 cass. (Running Time: 6 hrs.). 1988. pap. bk. 69.95 (978-0-13-559908-2(3)) P-H.
Techniques on how to defend yourself diplomatically in delicate family situations & in the hard-nosed business world.

Mastering the Gentle Art of Verbal Self Defense. Suzette Haden Elgin. Read by Suzette Haden Elgin. 1 cass. (Running Time: 90 min.). 9.95 S&S Audio.

Mastering the Gentle Art of Verbal Self Defense. unabr. ed. Suzette Haden Elgin. Read by Suzette Haden Elgin. 4 cass. (Running Time: 6 hrs.). 2001. 25.00 (978-1-59040-099-9(2), Phoenix Audio) Pub: Amer Intl Pub. Dist(s): PerseuPGW

Mastering the Guitar, Bk. 2A. William Bay & Mike Christiansen. 1998. pap. bk. 31.95 (978-0-7866-3651-8(3), 97195CDP) Mel Bay.

Mastering the Guitar, Bk. 2B. William Bay & Mike Christiansen. 1999. pap. bk. 29.95 (978-0-7866-3813-0(3), 97196CDP) Mel Bay.

Mastering the Guitar, Bk. 2C. William Bay & Mike Christiansen. 1999. pap. bk. 33.95 (978-0-7866-3815-4(X), 97197CDP) Mel Bay.

Mastering the Guitar: Class Method Level 1/Beginning 9th Grade & Higher Education. 2001. audio compact disk 19.95 (978-0-7866-5940-1(8)) Mel Bay.

Mastering the Guitar: Class Method Short Term Course. William Bay & Mike Christiansen. 2003. audio compact disk 9.98 (978-0-7866-7056-7(8)) Mel Bay.

Mastering the Guitar, Book 1a. William Bay & Mike Christiansen. 2008. pap. bk. 22.95 (978-0-7866-7921-8(2)) Mel Bay.

Mastering the Guitar: Book 1A: A Comprehensive Method for Today's Guitarist! 1997. audio compact disk 19.95 (978-0-7866-2805-6(7)) Mel Bay.

Mastering the Guitar Book 1A - Spiral Version: A Comprehensive Method for Today's Guitarist! William Bay & Mike Christiansen. 2008. spiral bd. 29.95 (978-0-7866-7839-6(9)) Mel Bay.

Mastering the Guitar Book: 1b: A Comprehensinve Method for Today's Guitarist! 1997. audio compact disk 19.95 (978-0-7866-2802-5(2)) Mel Bay.

Mastering the Guitar Book 1B Bk. 1B: Beginning-Intermediate Level. William Bay & Mike Christiansen. (ENG.). 1997. pap. bk. 24.95 (978-0-7866-2928-2(2), 96621BCD) Mel Bay.

Mastering the Guitar: Class Method: Class Method Level 1/Beginning Elementary Through 8th Grade. 2001. audio compact disk 19.95 (978-0-7866-5830-5(4)) Mel Bay.

Mastering the Information Age. Michael McCarthy. 6 cass. 1992. 59.95 (2661AX) Nightingale-Conant.
Now you can use your mind's unlimited capabilities for growth, expansion & increased levels of concentration to gather, access & process more of the information you're exposed to every day. Gain the thinking techniques that will empower your mind's true potential & take advantage of the amazing opportunities offered by today's information explosion - with Thinking Skills for the 21st Century! Includes workbook.

Mastering the Mental Game of Archery. Troy Bassham. Based on a work by Lanny Bassham. 6 CDs. (Running Time: 5 hrs). 2007. 150.00 (978-1-934324-04-2(3)) Mental Mgmnt.

Mastering the One Minute Relationship. Jonathan Robinson. Read by Jonathan Robinson. 1 cass. (Running Time: 1 hr. 30 min.). 1995. 9.95 (978-1-57328-798-2(9)) Focal Pt Calif.
Learn the 9 keys to meeting people & immediately "hit it off" with them. Get people to like & trust you, starting with the very first minute. Whether you're looking for a friend, lover, or a big sell, these techniques will tell you how to establish immediate rapport with people.

Mastering the Secrets of Permission to Succeed. unabr. ed. Noah St. John. (Running Time: 1 hr. 30 mins.). (ENG.). 2007. 14.98 (978-1-59659-143-1(9), GildAudio) Pub: Gildan Media. Dist(s): HachBkGrp

Mastering the Seven Decisions: That Determine Personal Success. unabr. ed. Andy Andrews. Narrated by Andy Andrews. (ENG.). 2008. 16.09 (978-1-60814-304-7(X)); audio compact disk 22.99 (978-1-59859-378-5(1)) Oasis Audio.

Mastering the Seven Decisions LIVE. (ENG.). 2008. audio compact disk 24.99 (978-0-9629620-2-8(3)) Lightning Crown Pub.

Mastering the Trade: Proven Techniques for Profiting from Intraday & Swing Trading Setups. John F. Carter. 2007. audio compact disk 28.00 (978-1-933309-62-0(8)) Pub: A Media Intl. Dist(s): Natl Bk Netwk

Mastering the Zone. abr. ed. Barry Sears. Read by Barry Sears. 2 cass. (Running Time: 3 hrs.). 1997. 18.00 (978-0-694-51777-0(1), CPN 10103, HarperFestival) HarperCollins Pubs.

***Mastering the Zone.** abr. ed. Barry Sears. Read by Barry Sears. (ENG.). 2005. (978-0-06-085672-4(6), Harper Audio); (978-0-06-085673-1(4), Harper Audio) HarperCollins Pubs.

Mastering Wealth. Liah Kraft-Kristaine. Read by Liah Kraft-Kristaine. 6 cass. (Running Time: 4 hrs. 35 min.). 1991. 39.95 (978-1-878095-18-3(8)) LMI Prodns.
Learn to uncover barriers holding you back from the wealth you desire, to clear away negative ideas about the nature of prosperity & to take positive action.

Mastering Wealth, Tape C. Liah Kraft-Kristaine. Read by Liah Kraft-Kristaine. 1 cass. (Running Time: 46 min.). 1991. 9.95 (978-1-878095-14-5(5)) LMI Prodns.
Defining your short & your long-term prosperity goals.

Mastering Wealth, Tape D. Liah Kraft-Kristaine. Read by Liah Kraft-Kristaine. 1 cass. (Running Time: 46 min.). 1991. 9.95 (978-1-878095-15-2(3)) LMI Prodns.
Developing skills to create increased willpower, concentration, & mental purpose.

Mastering Wealth, Tape A. Liah Kraft-Kristaine. Read by Liah Kraft-Kristaine. 1 cass. (Running Time: 45 min.). 1991. 9.95 (978-1-878095-12-1(9)) LMI Prodns.
Foundation for understanding the real nature of prosperity.

Mastering Wealth, Tape B. Liah Kraft-Kristaine. Read by Liah Kraft-Kristaine. 1 cass. (Running Time: 45 min.). 1991. 9.95 (978-1-878095-13-8(7)) LMI Prodns.
Creating a self-image as a wealth-deserving person.

Mastering Wealth, Tape E. Liah Kraft-Kristaine. Read by Liah Kraft-Kristaine. 1 cass. (Running Time: 46 min.). 1991. 9.95 (978-1-878095-16-9(1)) LMI Prodns.
Transforming desire into expectations.

Mastering Wealth, Tape F. Liah Kraft-Kristaine. Read by Liah Kraft-Kristaine. 1 cass. (Running Time: 46 min.). 1991. 9.95 (978-1-878095-17-6(X)) LMI Prodns.
Manifestation techniques.

Mastering What You Learn Easier, Faster... Smarter! Created by McGraw-Hill Staff. 2007. audio compact disk 17.75 (978-0-07-291689-8(3)) McGraw.

Mastering Women's Ministry: The Handbook for Organizing & Administering an Effective Ministry. Kathy Slamp. 2 cass. (Running Time: 3 hrs. 30 min.). 39.95 (354) Chrch Grwth VA.
Hands-on, practical guide for Women's Ministry in the local church.

Mastering Woodworking Machines. Mark Duginske. (Fine Woodworking Ser.). (ENG.). 2006. audio compact disk 19.95 (978-1-56158-703-2(6), Taunt) Pub: Taunton. Dist(s): IngramPubServ

Mastering Your Message. Tony Alessandra. Read by Tony Alessandra. 6 cass. (Running Time: 5 hrs.). 1997. 59.95 (978-1-57294-079-6(4), 11-0615) SkillPath Pubns.
Combination of real-life examples & practical instructions to help become a better listener, interpret body language, develop interpersonal skills, resolve conflicts, & make better presentations.

Mastering Your Way to the Top: Secrets for Success from the World's Greatest Salesman & America's Leading Businesspeople. abr. ed. Joe Girard & Robert Casemore. (ENG.). 2006. 5.98 (978-1-59483-781-4(3)) Pub: Hachet Audio. Dist(s): HachBkGrp

Masterjazz: John McNeil's Learn to Play Jazz. 2004. video & audio compact disk 29.95 (978-0-9714962-4-8(2), MJ10002); audio compact disk 19.95 (978-0-9714962-1-7(8), MJ10002) Pub: Inter Prod Grp. Dist(s): Music Sales

***Mastermind: Inside the Secret World of Khalid Shaikh Mohammed.** unabr. ed. Richard Miniter. (Running Time: 8 hrs. 0 mins.). 2011. 71.99

(978-1-4526-3055-7(0)); 29.99 (978-1-4526-0055-0(4)); 19.99 (978-1-4526-5055-5(1)); 15.99 (978-1-4526-7055-3(2)) Tantor Media.

***Mastermind (Library Edition) Inside the Secret World of Khalid Shaikh Mohammed.** unabr. ed. Richard Miniter. (Running Time: 8 hrs. 0 mins.). 2011. 29.99 (978-1-4526-2055-8(5)) Tantor Media.

***Masterpiece.** unabr. ed. Elise Broach. Read by Jeremy Davidson. (Running Time: 5 hrs. 30 mins. 0 sec.). (ENG.). (J). 2010. audio compact disk 14.99 (978-1-4272-1115-6(9)) Pub: Macmill Audio. Dist(s): Macmillan

Masterpiece & More. Contrib. by Anthony Burger & Luann Burger. Prod. by Lari Goss. (Gaither Gospel (Video) Ser.). 2008. 19.99 (978-5-557-42324-3(9)) Sprg Hill Music Group.

Masterpieces for the Koto. unabr. ed. 1 cass. 12.95 (7219) J Norton Pubs.

Masterpieces of Ancient Greek Literature. Instructed by David J. Schenker. 18 cass. (Running Time: 18 hrs.). 2007. 199.95 (978-1-59803-276-5(3)); audio compact disk 99.95 (978-1-59803-277-2(1)) Teaching Co.

Masterpieces of Short Fiction. Instructed by Michael Krasny. 2008. 129.95 (978-1-59803-438-7(3)); audio compact disk 69.95 (978-1-59803-439-4(1)) Teaching Co.

Masterpieces of the Imaginative Mind: Literature¿s Most Fantastic Works. Instructed by Eric S. Rabkin. 12 cass. (Running Time: 12 hrs.). 2007. 129.95 (978-1-59803-288-8(7)); audio compact disk 69.95 (978-1-59803-289-5(5)) Teaching Co.

Masterpieces Take Time. Elbert Willis. 1 cass. (Patience & Long-Suffering Ser.). 4.00 Fill the Gap.

Masters. Curt Sampson. Read by Barrett Whitener. (Running Time: 10 hrs.). 2002. 34.95 (978-1-59912-690-6(7)) Iofy Corp.

Masters. unabr. ed. Curt Sampson. Read by Barrett Whitener. 9 CDs. (Running Time: 11 hrs. 30 mins.). 2003. audio compact disk 72.00 (978-0-7861-9247-2(X), 3089); 56.95 (978-0-7861-2417-6(2), 3089) Blckstn Audio.
An amazing slice of history, a look at how the new South coexists with the old South: the relationships between blacks and whites, between Southerners and Northerners, between rich and poor.

Masters. unabr. ed. C. P. Snow. Read by David Case. 8 cass. (Running Time: 12 hrs.). (Strangers & Brothers Ser.: Vol. 5). 1994. 64.00 (978-0-7366-2633-0(6), 3372) Books on Tape.

Masters Audio Collection: The Ultimate Guide for Creating Success & True Happiness in Your Life. Jack L. Canfield et al. 2000. bk. 34.95 (978-0-9703652-0-0(9)) Daily Plnt.

Masters Audio Collection: The Ultimate Guide for Creating Success & True Happiness in Your Life. unabr. ed. 3 cass. (Running Time: 3 hrs. 30 min.). 2000. 29.95 (978-0-9703652-1-7(7)) Daily Plnt.
Audio compilation featuring the western worlds most successful spiritual authors each discuss their belief, philosophies & understanding of how the universe works. Includes Jack Canfield, Deepak Chopra MD, John Gray PhD, Marianne Williamson, Dan Millman & Neale Donald Walsch.

Master's Healing Temple I: A Guided Meditation Journey. Composed by Yana L. Freeman. 1 CD. (Running Time: 33mins., 00 sec). (ENG.). 2006. audio compact disk 15.00 (978-0-9768728-3-2(8), 72832) Sacred Path.
The Temple of The Master's is a Guided Imagery CD that was a gift for humanity to aid in healing of body, mind and spirit. It helps anyone to achieve inner peace and enables the listener to receive healing on many levels as they work with Spirit Healers, Angels, Masters, The Ancient Ones, Guides and Loved Ones who have crossed over. The meditation journey enables the listener to heal unresolved issues, past and present life issues, the inner child and much more. It is a wonderful relaxing meditation journey that thousands have taken over the past ten plus years with Hypnotherpist Yana Freeman as their guide.It is a 'must buy" for anyone who sells guided imagery, new age, metaphysical, sel-help, spirituality and related topics.

Master's Healing Touch. 2001. (978-1-59024-005-2(7)); (978-1-59024-008-3(1)); (978-1-59024-018-2(9)); audio compact disk (978-1-59024-017-5(0)) B Hinn Min.

Master's Healing Touch, Vol. 1. (SPA.). 2001. (978-1-59024-010-6(3)); (978-1-59024-013-7(8)); audio compact disk (978-0-9708141-9-7(4)) B Hinn Min.

Master's Healing Touch, Vol. 2. (SPA.). 2001. (978-1-59024-011-3(1)); (978-1-59024-014-4(6)) B Hinn Min.

Master's Healing Touch, Vol. II. 2001. (978-1-59024-006-9(5)); audio compact disk (978-1-59024-000-7(6)) B Hinn Min.

Master's Healing Touch, Vol. 3. (SPA.). 2001. (978-1-59024-012-0(X)); (978-1-59024-015-1(4)) B Hinn Min.

Master's Healing Touch, Vol. III. 2001. (978-1-59024-007-6(3)); audio compact disk (978-1-59024-001-4(4)) B Hinn Min.

Master's Healing Touch, Vols.1-3. 2001. audio compact disk (978-1-59024-002-1(2)) B Hinn Min.

Master's Men. 7 cass. 21.95 (2079, HarperThor) HarpC GBR.

Master's Message of Life Eternal - Hearing Jesus & the Apostles Present the Gospel. 2005. 15.00 (978-1-933561-16-5(5)) BFM Books.

Masters of Atlantis. Charles Portis. Narrated by Brian Emerson. (Running Time: 10 hrs.). (C). 2002. 30.95 (978-1-59912-541-1(2)) Iofy Corp.

Masters of Atlantis. unabr. ed. Charles Portis. Narrated by Brian Emerson. 8 CDs. (Running Time: 10 hrs.). 2002. audio compact disk 64.00 (978-0-7861-9576-3(2), 2892) Blckstn Audio.
This comic masterpiece centers on Lamar Jimmerson, the leader of the Gnomon Society, the international fraternal order dedicated to preserving the arcane wisdom of the lost city of Atlantis. Stationed in France in 1917, Jimmerson comes across a little book crammed with Atlantean puzzles, Egyptian riddles, and extended alchemical metaphors. It's the Codex Pappus-the sacred Gnomon text. Soon he is basking in the lore of lost Atlantis, convinced that his mission on earth is to administer to and extend the ranks of this noble brotherhood.

Masters of Atlantis. unabr. ed. Charles Portis. Narrated by Brian Emerson. 7 cass. (Running Time: 10 hrs.). 2002. 49.95 (978-0-7861-2141-0(6), 2892) Blckstn Audio.

Masters of Deception: The Gang That Ruled Cyberspace. unabr. ed. Michelle Slatalla & Joshua Quittner. Narrated by Richard Poe. 6 cass. (Running Time: 9 hrs.). 51.00 (978-0-7887-0584-7(9), 94762E7) Recorded Bks.
When isolated teenagers suddenly join together to form a high-tech computer-hacking gang, even AT&T's most heavily guarded records are no longer secure. Offers an unparalled look into the ongoing guerilla warfare between computer hackers & information super powers. Available to libraries only.

***Masters of Disaster.** unabr. ed. Gary Paulsen. (Running Time: 3 hrs.). (YA). 2011. 14.99 (978-1-4558-0142-8(9), 9781455801428, BAD); 39.97 (978-1-4558-0143-5(7), 9781455801435, BADLE); 14.99 (978-1-4558-0140-4(2), 9781455801404, Brilliance MP3); 39.97 (978-1-4558-0141-1(0), 9781455801411, Brlnc Audio MP3 Lib); audio compact disk 14.99 (978-1-4558-0138-1(0), 9781455801381, Bril Audio CD Unabri); audio compact disk 39.97 (978-1-4558-0139-8(9), 9781455801398, BriAudCD Unabrid) Brilliance Audio.

Masters of Greek Thought: Plato, Socrates, & Aristotle. Instructed by Robert C. Bartlett. 2008. 199.95 (978-1-59803-442-4(1)); audio compact disk 99.95 (978-1-59803-443-1(X)) Teaching Co.

Masters of Music. 1994. 17.00 (978-0-7692-5725-9(9), Warner Bro) Alfred Pub.

Masters of the Mountain Dulcimer. Prod. by Susan Trump. 1 cass. (Running Time: 1 hr. 30 min.). 9.98 (C-605); audio compact disk 14.98 CD. (CD-605) Folk-Legacy.

Masters of the Renaissance. Perf. by Gloriae Dei Cantores. 1 CD. 2006. audio compact disk 16.95 (978-1-55725-497-9(4)) Paraclete MA.
This release from Glori? Dei Cantores features sacred music from one of the most inspired periods in the arts ? the Renaissance. Each of the European schools of composition - Italian, Flemish, German, Spanish, and English - are represented by a total of 20 composers, offering a fascinating cross-section of styles and influences. Great masters such as Lassus, Byrd and Victoria are featured, as well as lesser-known composers such as Hassler, de Wert, and Nanino. The central work of this recording is the Missa super bell? amfitrit' altera? by Lassus, generally considered one of his finest works. Other selections include Anerio?s tender and stirring Requiem aeternum and William Byrd?s Terra tremuit, which has been described as ?one of the most dramatic texts in the whole of music.?.

Masters of the Renaissance: Michelangelo, Leonardo da Vinci... And More. unabr. ed. Narrated by Jim Weiss. 1 CD. (Running Time: 1 hr. 18 mins.). (YA). (gr. 5 up). 2006. audio compact disk 13.95 (978-1-882513-88-6(6)) Greathall Prods.
In true stories as vivid as the colors in which they painted, Jim Weiss brings to life the astounding Leonardo da Vinci; the volcanic genius Michelangelo; Brunelleschi, who changed the way we see the world; the lighthearted sculptor, Donatello; and other captivating characters. You will watch fierce Pope Julius II drive out invaders while supervising the painting of the Sistine Chapel, and dine in the palace of Lorenzo de Medici, swordsman, statesman and patron of the arts, as he faces treachery and turns war to peace. This recording will inspire a lifelong fascination with the arts - and with the riches and high aspirations of the Renaissance.

Master's Plan for the Church. 8 vols. 2000. 39.95 (978-1-57972-350-7(0)) Insight Living.

Master's Working. Swami Amar Jyoti. 2 cass. 1980. 12.95 (E-18) Truth Consciousness.
Swamiji frankly exposes aspects of His working that we do not see or understand. The classical ways of the Masters. The Guru-disciple relationship.

Masterthinker. Edward De Bono. 2004. 7.95 (978-0-7435-4071-1(9)) Pub: S&S Audio. Dist(s): S and S Inc

Masterworks of Early 20th-Century Literature. Instructed by David Thorburn. 109.95 (978-1-59803-318-2(2)) Teaching Co.

Masterworks of Early 20th-Century Literature. Instructed by David Thorburn. 2007. audio compact disk 69.95 (978-1-59803-319-9(0)) Teaching Co.

Masterworks of Japanese Painting: The Etsuko & Joe Price Collection. Robb Lazarus et al. 1994. audio compact disk 79.95 (978-1-886664-06-7(4)); audio compact disk 79.95 (978-1-886664-07-4(2)) Digital Collect.

Masterworks of Japanese Painting: The Etsuko & Joe Price Collection: Jewel Case. Robb Lazarus et al. 1994. audio compact disk 49.95 (978-1-886664-37-1(4)); audio compact disk 49.95 (978-1-886664-38-8(2)) Digital Collect.

Masterworks of Orson Wells. abr. ed. Rudyard Kipling et al. Perf. by Orson Welles et al. 4 cass. (Running Time: 6 hrs.). (Ultimate Classics Ser.). 2004. 25.00 (978-1-931056-51-9(X), N Millennium Audio) New Millenn Enter.
A legend of the American entertainment industry. Here is an historic recording of Welles' interpretations of excerpts from classic literature.

Mastery see Richard Eberhart Reading His Poetry

Mastery of Life Audio Course: A Step-by-Step Process for Having Life Work. Bill Ferguson. 8 CDs. 2004. audio compact disk 95.00 (978-1-878410-34-4(2)) Return Heart.

Mastery of Love: A Practical Guide to the Art of Relationship. abr. ed. Don Miguel Ruiz. Read by Jill Eikenberry & Michael Tucker. 2 cass. (Running Time: 2 hrs. 33 mins.). (Toltec Wisdom Ser.). (ENG.). 2003. 17.95 (978-1-878424-47-1(5)) Amber-Allen Pub.

Mastery of Love: A Practical Guide to the Art of Relationship. abr. ed. Don Miguel Ruiz. Read by Jill Eikenberry & Michael Tucker. 2 CDs. (Running Time: 2 hrs. 33 mins.). (ENG.). 2005. audio compact disk 18.95 (978-1-878424-57-0(2)) Amber-Allen Pub.

Mastery of Money. Stuart Wilde. 4 cass. 29.95 (978-0-930603-14-4(1)) White Dove NM.
This series looks at practical & esoteric techniques for consciousness alignment that allow you to step effortlessly into abundance.

Mastery of the Flamenco Guitar Series: Toques Libres: Volume 3: the Non-Rhythmic Flamenco Tradition. Ed. by Mario Congreve. Contrib. by Guillermo Rios. Prod. by Rose M. Samp. (Running Time: 1 hr. 25 mins.). (Mastery of the Flamenco Guitar Ser.). 2005. 39.95 (978-5-558-11114-9(3)) Mel Bay.

Mastery of the Flamenco Guitar Series, Volume 1: Mastery of Technique. Contrib. by Guillermo Rios. (Running Time: 1 hr. 35 mins.). (Mastery of the Flamenco Guitar Ser.). 2005. 39.95 (978-5-558-11116-3(X)) Mel Bay.

Mastery of the Flamenco Guitar Series, Volume 2: Soleares & Alegrias. Guillermo Rios. (Running Time: 1 hr. 16 mins.). 2005. 39.95 (978-5-558-11115-6(1)) Pub: Sigma F RUS. Dist(s): Destiny Image Pubs

Mastery Through Accomplishment: The Audio-Book. abr. ed. Khan Inayat. Read by Jay Sheridan & Jan Sheridan. 2 cass. (Running Time: 3 hrs. 10 min.). Dramatization. 1993. 24.95 (978-1-883388-00-3(7)) Add Venture.
A selection of readings to enhance listening. Brief musical interludes have been interspersed with the readings.

***Mastin de los Baskerville.** abr. ed. Arthur Conan Doyle. Read by Daniel Quintero. (SPA.). 2009. audio compact disk 17.00 (978-958-8318-95-0(5)) Pub: Yoyo Music COL. Dist(s): YoYoMusic

Mata Atlantica: A Rare Brazilian Rain Forest. Bernie Krause. 1 CD. (Running Time: 1 hr.). (Wild Sanctuary Ser.). 1994. audio compact disk 15.95 (2366, Creativ Pub) Quayside.
Dry rain forests in southeastern Brazil. Parakeets & parrots, spider monkeys & frogs, hummingbirds & cicadas. Beautifully unique sounds.

Mata Atlantica: A Rare Brazilian Rain Forest. Bernie Krause. 1 cass. (Running Time: 1 hr.). (Wild Sanctuary Ser.). 1994. 9.95 (2365, NrthWrd Bks) TandN Child.

Matador. unabr. ed. Barnaby Conrad. 5 CDs. (Running Time: 5 hrs. 30 mins.). 2003. audio compact disk 40.00 (978-0-7861-9244-1(5), 3086); 32.95 (978-0-7861-2420-6(2), 3086) Blckstn Audio.
It is the morning of Pacote's last fight, the finale of a great career. The city of Sevilla waits, heavy with anticipation. But Pacote finds he is afraid & fears disgrace in the ring. Time, once his friend, now presses him on to the moment when the gate opens & the first bull enters the ring. You are there in the stands with the screaming crowd & in the lonely emptiness at the center of the arena with only a red cape & a slender sword.

Matador. unabr. collector's ed. Barnaby Conrad. Read by Wolfram Kandinsky. 6 cass. (Running Time: 9 hrs.). 1989. 48.00 (978-0-7366-1644-7(6), 2497) Books on Tape.

Matanzas, Set. unabr. ed. Clint Custer. Read by John Keyworth. 3 cass. (Running Time: 75 min. per cass.). (Sound Ser.). 1988. 34.95 (978-1-85496-070-2(9), US0133) Pub: UlverLrgPrint GBR. Dist(s): Ulverscroft US
Cab Dunaway rode south from Ratan into a part of New Mexico from the moment three Mexican cowboys pointed a gun at this head, until he sat beneath the trees with a beautiful woman a month later, he lived through a great ordeals.

Matarese Circle. Robert Ludlum. Read by Martin Balsam. 2 cass. (Running Time: 3 hrs.). 1999. (391151, Random AudioBks) Random Audio Pubg.
Two men, who are sworn mortal enemies from opposite sides of the Iron Curtain, must cooperate to foil a plan to topple the world's government. The men must fight the Matarese Circle, a group of the world's most ruthless terrorists.

Matarese Circle. unabr. collector's ed. Robert Ludlum. Read by Michael Prichard. 14 cass. (Running Time: 21 hrs.). 1983. 112.00 (978-0-7366-2659-0(X), 3396) Books on Tape.
Russian & American secret agents have sworn to kill each other but they must become allies in order to destroy the Matarese, an international circle of killers.

Matarese Circle, Pt. 1. unabr. ed. Robert Ludlum. Read by Michael Prichard. 7 cass. (Running Time: 10 hrs. 30 min.). 1983. 56.00 (1759-A) Books on Tape.

Matarese Circle, Pt. 2. Robert Ludlum. Read by Michael Prichard. 7 cass. (Running Time: 10 hrs. 30 min.). 1983. 56.00 (1759-B) Books on Tape.

Matarese Countdown. unabr. ed. Robert Ludlum. Read by Michael Prichard. 14 cass. (Running Time: 21 hrs.). 1997. 112.00 (978-0-7366-3786-2(9), 4458) Books on Tape.
The Matarese dynasty is back in all its glory & evil, & there's only one man with enough knowledge to stop it: CIA case officer Cameron Pryce.

Match Made in Heaven. unabr. ed. Bob Mitchell. Read by Mel Foster. (Running Time: 25200 sec.). 2006. audio compact disk 82.25 (978-1-4233-1167-6(1), 9781423311676, BriAudCD Unabrid); audio compact disk 24.95 (978-1-4233-1168-3(X), 9781423311683, Brilliance MP3) Brilliance Audio.
Fifty-year-old Harvard literature professor Elliott Goodman, stricken by a heart attack, is rushed to the nearest emergency room and prepped for bypass surgery. Frightened and in pain, he cries out to God for help. Much to his surprise, God appears, suspended from the ceiling of the OR. He asks Elliott why his life deserves to be saved, and Elliott has no brilliant answer to offer. God, in his infinite wisdom and mercy, gives him a chance at salvation. He challenges Elliott to an eighteen-hole golf match. If Elliott wins, he will be saved; if he loses, he won't make it through the surgery. Much to his surprise, Elliott finds himself at his favorite golf course, Inwood Country Club on Long Island. At the first tee, an old, white-bearded man taking practice swings turns around to face Elliott. It is not God, as he'd expected, but Leonardo Da Vinci! The Renaissance Man explains that to be fair, God has sent down eighteen "substitutes" from heaven, one per hole, to play against Elliott. With his life hanging in the balance, Elliott proceeds to play against an unforgettable procession of substitutes, including Moses, John Lennon, Freud, Socrates, Joan of Arc, Marilyn Monroe, Picasso, Beethoven, Shakespeare, and Gandhi. As Elliott competes against this colorful cast of characters (each of whom comes to life with distinctive greatness), this witty, profound, suspenseful, funny, and wonderfully entertaining tale of golf is all about the life lessons he learns - from his amazing opponents and from the game of golf - and how he comes to an understanding of why, after all, his life deserves to be saved.

Match Made in Heaven. unabr. ed. Bob Mitchell. Read by Mel Foster. (Running Time: 7 hrs.). 2006. 39.25 (978-1-4233-1171-3(X), 9781423311713, BADLE); 24.95 (978-1-4233-1170-6(1), 9781423311706, BAD); audio compact disk 39.25 (978-1-4233-1169-0(8), 9781423311690, Brlnc Audio MP3 Lib) Brilliance Audio.

Match Made in Heaven. unabr. ed. Bob Mitchell. Read by Mel Foster. (Running Time: 7 hrs.). 2007. audio compact disk 14.99 (978-1-4233-3350-0(0), 9781423333500, BCD Value Price) Brilliance Audio.

Match Me If You Can. Susan Elizabeth Phillips. (Chicago Stars Bks.: No. 6). 2005. audio compact disk 24.95 (978-0-06-079414-9(3)) HarperCollins Pubs.

Match Me If You Can. unabr. ed. Susan Elizabeth Phillips. Read by Anna Fields. (Chicago Stars Bks.: No. 6). 2005. 29.95 (978-0-7927-3704-9(0), CMP 793); 59.95 (978-0-7927-3617-2(6), CSL 793); audio compact disk 89.95 (978-0-7927-3703-2(2), SLD 793) AudioGO.

***Match Me If You Can.** unabr. ed. Susan Elizabeth Phillips. Read by Anna Fields. (ENG.). 2005. (978-0-06-087918-1(1), Harper Audio); (978-0-06-087919-8(X), Harper Audio) HarperCollins Pubs.

Match Me If You Can. unabr. ed. Susan Elizabeth Phillips. Read by Anna Fields. (Chicago Stars Bks.: No. 6). 2005. audio compact disk 39.95 (978-0-06-082825-7(0)) HarperCollins Pubs.

Match Point. Robin Cruise. Narrated by Larry A. McKeever. (Sport Ser.). (J). 2000. audio compact disk 14.95 (978-1-58659-294-3(7)) Artesian.

Match Point. unabr. ed. Robin Cruise. Narrated by Larry A. McKeever. 1 cass. (Running Time: 40 min.). (Sport Ser.). (J). 2000. 10.95 (978-1-58659-040-6(5), 54120) Artesian.

Matchbreaker. Chris Manby. 2008. audio compact disk 79.95 (978-0-7531-3252-4(4)) Pub: ISIS Audio GBR. Dist(s): Ulverscroft US

Matchbreaker. unabr. ed. Chris Manby. Read by Julia Franklin. 7 cass. (Running Time: 9 hrs. 10 mins.). 2008. 61.95 (978-0-7531-3524-2(8)) Pub: ISIS Audio GBR. Dist(s): Ulverscroft US

***Matched.** Ally Condie. (Running Time: 10 hrs.). (ENG.). 2010. audio compact disk 29.95 (978-0-14-242863-4(9), PengAudBks) Penguin Grp USA.

Matchmaker. Lynne Haggerman. Orig. Title: Seven Hundred Fifty Plus Sure Fire Interview Questions. 1993. audio compact disk 139.00 (978-0-9727471-0-3(9)) Haggerman Assocs.

Matchmakers. unabr. ed. Debbie Macomber. Read by Tanya Eby. (Running Time: 5 hrs.). 2010. audio compact disk 14.99 (978-1-4418-1962-8(2), 9781441819628, Bril Audio CD Unabri) Brilliance Audio.

***Matchmakers.** unabr. ed. Debbie Macomber. Read by Tanya Eby. (Running Time: 5 hrs.). 2010. 24.99 (978-1-4418-1964-2(9), 9781441819642, Brilliance MP3); 39.97 (978-1-4418-1965-9(7), 9781441819659, Brlnc Audio MP3 Lib); 24.99 (978-1-4418-1966-6(5), 9781441819666, BAD); 39.97 (978-1-4418-1967-3(3), 9781441819673, BADLE); audio compact disk 87.97 (978-1-4418-1963-5(0), 9781441819635, BriAudCD Unabrid) Brilliance Audio.

Matchstick Men. unabr. abr. ed. Eric Garcia. Read by Stanley Tucci. 4 cass. (Running Time: 6 hrs.). 2003. 19.95 (978-0-06-056743-9(0)) HarperCollins Pubs.

Materia del Deseo. Edmundo Paz Soldan. 6 cass. (Running Time: 8 hrs.). (SPA.). 59.75 (978-1-4025-7665-2(X)) Recorded Bks.

Material del Instructor del Seminario de Auto-Estima. Scripts. Lilburn S. Barksdale. Tr. by George Teague from ENG. 5. (SPA.). 1994. pap. bk. & tchr. ed. 105.00 (978-0-918588-45-6(6), 201S) NCADD.
Information and affirmations for building self-esteem. This is a kit for an instructor to use in presenting the Barksdale Self-Esteem Workshop in Spanish. It includes 5 audio tapes, a script for the presenter, a Human Behavior Diagram, schedules, and a training packet for presenters.

Material del Participante del Seminario de Auto-Estima. Lilburn S. Barksdale. Tr. by George Teague from ENG. 3 cass. (SPA.). 1994. 39.95 (978-0-918588-47-0(2), 203S) NCADD.
Cassettes provide information and affirmations for building sound self-esteem.

Material Dreams: Southern California Through the 1920's, Pt. 1. collector's ed. Kevin Starr. Read by Lloyd James. 8 cass. (Running Time: 12 hrs.). 2000. 64.00 (978-0-7366-5648-1(0)) Books on Tape.
Reveals how Los Angeles arose almost defiantly on a site lacking many of the advantages normally required for urban development.

Material Dreams Pt. 2: Southern California Through the 1920's. collector's ed. Kevin Starr. Read by Lloyd James. 10 cass. (Running Time: 15 hrs.). 2000. 80.00 (978-0-7366-5664-1(2)) Books on Tape.
Reveals how Los Angeles arose almost defiantly on a site lacking many of the advantages normally required for urban development.

Material Witness. unabr. ed. Robert K. Tanenbaum. Read by Connor O'Brien. 8 cass. (Running Time: 12 hrs.). (Butch Karp Mystery Ser.). 1997. 64.00 (978-0-7366-3687-2(0), 4366) Books on Tape.
New York's top celebrity athlete is blown away in his white Caddie, with a huge stash of cocaine on hand. His good name vanishes in a hail of bullets. That's when A.D.A. Butch Karp grabs control of the case. On his side is his wife & partner, Marlene Ciampi & a burnt-out cop whose seen better days. Against him are mobsters, hitmen, city politics & an assortment of big shots, all working together as an enterprising terror team. When Karp & Ciampi get close to the truth behind the athlete's murder, they find that the movers & shakers in New York law enforcement don't like their work. And blowing the whistle might mean curtains for Butch & Marlene.

Materialism & Spirituality. Swami Amar Jyoti. 1 cass. 1991. 9.95 (K-128) Truth Consciousness.
What is materialism, what is spiritual? The role of Dharma in harmonizing the two.

Materiality Is the Glamorizing of Beauty. Manly P. Hall. 1 cass. 8.95 (978-0-89314-178-3(X), C891119) Philos Res.

Materials Degradation: Innovation, Inspection, Control & Rehabilitation. Ed. by G. P. Gu et al. 2005. bk. (978-1-894475-57-0(7)) CIM CAN.

Materials in Clinical Applications VII. Ed. by P. Vincenzini & R. Giardino. (Advances in Science & Technology Ser.: Vol. 49). audio compact disk 193.00 (978-3-908158-05-9(2)) Trans T Pub CHE.

Materials of the House. Rick Joyner. 1 cass. (Running Time: 90 mins.). (Foundation Ser.: Vol. 6). 2000. 5.00 (RJ05-006) Morning NC.
As an overview of God's plan for His church, this series contains essential truths for everyone who wants to see the church become all that she is called to be.

Materials Read-Aloud Audio Book. 2009. audio compact disk 5.95 (978-1-4329-3268-8(3), Acorn Read) Heinemann Rai.

Materials Rock-Audio Book. (Materials Ser.). (ENG.). 2009. audio compact disk 5.95 (978-1-4329-3252-7(7), AcornHR) Heinemann Rai.

Materials Rubber-Audio Book. (Materials Ser.). 2009. audio compact disk 5.95 (978-1-4329-3253-4(5), AcornHR) Heinemann Rai.

Materials Soil-Audio Book. (Materials Ser.). 2009. audio compact disk 5.95 (978-1-4329-3254-1(3), AcornHR) Heinemann Rai.

Materials Water-Audio Book. (Materials Ser.). 2009. audio compact disk 5.95 (978-1-4329-3255-8(1), AcornHR) Heinemann Rai.

Materials Wood-Audio Book. (Materials Ser.). 2009. audio compact disk 5.95 (978-1-4329-3256-5(X), AcornHR) Heinemann Rai.

Maternal Child, Pt. 1. Patricia Hoefler. (Complete Q & A Ser.). 2002. (978-1-56533-129-7(X)) MEDS Pubng.

Maternal Child, Pt. 2. Patricia Hoefler. (Complete Q & A Ser.). 2002. (978-1-56533-130-3(3)) MEDS Pubng.

Maternal Face of God. Richard Rohr. 1 cass. (Running Time: 1 hr.). 2001. 8.95 (A7071) St Anthony Mess Pr.
Brings us to recognize a tender compassionate God, the God who is beyond gender, yet gives the maternal love we hunger for.

Maternity Meditations Relaxation Exercises for Successful Breastfeeding & Breast Pumping. Crystina Hale. 2006. audio compact disk 12.00 (978-1-4276-0250-3(6)) AardGP.

***Mates, Dates & Chocolate Cheats.** Cathy Hopkins. Read by Nicky Talacko. (Running Time: 4 hrs. 9 mins.). (YA). 2010. 59.99 (978-1-74214-622-5(8), 9781742146225) Pub: Bolinda Pubng AUS. Dist(s): Bolinda Pub Inc

Mates, dates & chocolate Cheats. unabr. ed. Cathy Hopkins. Read by Nicky Talacko. (Running Time: 4 hrs. 9 mins.). (YA). 2009. audio compact disk 57.95 (978-1-74214-533-4(7), 9781742145334) Pub: Bolinda Pubng AUS. Dist(s): Bolinda Pub Inc

Mates, dates & cosmic Kisses. Cathy Hopkins. Read by Amanda Hulme. (Running Time: 3 hrs. 20 mins.). (Mates, Dates Ser.). (YA). 2009. 54.99 (978-1-74214-320-0(2), 9781742143200) Pub: Bolinda Pubng AUS. Dist(s): Bolinda Pub Inc

Mates, Dates, & Cosmic Kisses. unabr. ed. Cathy Hopkins. Read by Amanda Hulme. 3 CDs. (Running Time: 3 hrs. 20 mins.). (Mates, Dates Ser.). (YA). (gr. 7 up). 2005. audio compact disk 54.95 (978-1-74093-248-6(X)) Pub: Bolinda Pubng AUS. Dist(s): Bolinda Pub Inc

***Mates, dates & diamond Destiny.** Cathy Hopkins. Read by Nicky Talacko. (Running Time: 5 hrs.). (YA). 2010. 59.99 (978-1-74214-630-0(9), 9781742146300) Pub: Bolinda Pubng AUS. Dist(s): Bolinda Pub Inc

Mates, Dates & Diamond Destiny. unabr. ed. Cathy Hopkins. Read by Nicky Talacko. (Running Time: 5 hrs.). (YA). 2009. audio compact disk 57.95 (978-1-74214-535-8(3), 9781742145358) Pub: Bolinda Pubng AUS. Dist(s): Bolinda Pub Inc

***Mates, dates & great Escapes.** Cathy Hopkins. Read by Nicky Talacko. (Running Time: 4 hrs. 5 mins.). (YA). 2010. 59.99 (978-1-74214-621-8(X), 9781742146218) Pub: Bolinda Pubng AUS. Dist(s): Bolinda Pub Inc

Mates, dates & great Escapes. unabr. ed. Cathy Hopkins. Read by Nicky Talacko. (Running Time: 4 hrs. 5 mins.). (YA). 2009. audio compact disk 57.95 (978-1-74214-530-3(2), 9781742145303) Pub: Bolinda Pubng AUS. Dist(s): Bolinda Pub Inc

Mates, Dates, & Inflatable Bras. unabr. ed. Cathy Hopkins. Read by Amanda Hulme. 3 CDs. (Running Time: 3 hrs. 5 mins.). (Mates, Dates Ser.). 2005. audio compact disk 54.95 (978-1-74093-135-9(1)) Pub: Bolinda Pubng AUS. Dist(s): Bolinda Pub Inc

Mates, dates & mad Mistakes. Cathy Hopkins. Read by Shirley Barthelmie. (Running Time: 3 hrs. 15 mins.). (YA). 2009. 54.99 (978-1-74214-318-7(0), 9781742143187) Pub: Bolinda Pubng AUS. Dist(s): Bolinda Pub Inc

Mates, Dates & Mad Mistakes. unabr. ed. Cathy Hopkins & Cathy Hopkins. Read by Shirley Barthelmie. 3 CDs. (Running Time: 11700 sec.). (Mates, Dates Ser.). (YA). (gr. 7-12). 2006. audio compact disk 54.95 (978-1-74093-703-0(1)) Pub: Bolinda Pubng AUS. Dist(s): Bolinda Pub Inc

Mates, dates & Portobello Princesses. Cathy Hopkins. Read by Melissa Eccleston. (Running Time: 3 hrs. 40 mins.). (YA). 2009. 54.99 (978-1-74214-322-4(9), 9781742143224) Pub: Bolinda Pubng AUS. Dist(s): Bolinda Pub Inc

Mates, Dates & Portobello Princesses. unabr. ed. Cathy Hopkins & Cathy Hopkins. Read by Melissa Eccleston. 3 CDs. (Running Time: 13200 sec.). (Mates, Dates Ser.). (YA). (gr. 7-13). 2005. audio compact disk 54.95 (978-1-74093-562-3(4)) Pub: Bolinda Pubng AUS. Dist(s): Bolinda Pub Inc

Mates, dates & pulling Power. Cathy Hopkins. Read by Nicky Talacko. (Running Time: 4 hrs. 30 mins.). (YA). 2009. 59.99 (978-1-74214-319-4(9), 9781742143194) Pub: Bolinda Pubng AUS. Dist(s): Bolinda Pub Inc

Mates, Dates & Pulling Power. unabr. ed. Cathy Hopkins. Read by Nicky Talacko. (Running Time: 4 hrs. 30 mins.). (YA). 2007. audio compact disk 57.95 (978-1-74093-962-1(X), 9781740939621) Pub: Bolinda Pubng AUS. Dist(s): Bolinda Pub Inc

***Mates, dates & sizzling Summers.** Cathy Hopkins. Read by Nicky Talacko. (Running Time: 4 hrs. 50 mins.). (YA). 2010. 59.99 (978-1-74214-631-7(7), 9781742146317) Pub: Bolinda Pubng AUS. Dist(s): Bolinda Pub Inc

Mates, Dates & Sizzling Summers. unabr. ed. Cathy Hopkins. Read by Nicky Talacko. (Running Time: 4 hrs. 50 mins.). (YA). 2009. audio compact disk 57.95 (978-1-74214-541-9(8), 9781742145419) Pub: Bolinda Pubng AUS. Dist(s): Bolinda Pub Inc

***Mates, dates & sleepover Secrets.** Cathy Hopkins. Read by Shirley Barthelmie. (Running Time: 3 hrs. 10 mins.). (YA). 2009. 39.99 (978-1-74214-323-1(7), 9781742143231) Pub: Bolinda Pubng AUS. Dist(s): Bolinda Pub Inc

Mates, Dates & Sleepover Secrets. unabr. ed. Cathy Hopkins & Cathy Hopkins. Read by Shirley Barthelmie. 3 CDs. (Running Time: 11400 sec.). (Mates, Dates Ser.). (YA). (gr. 7-13). 2002. audio compact disk 54.95 (978-1-74093-626-2(4)) Pub: Bolinda Pubng AUS. Dist(s): Bolinda Pub Inc

***Mates, dates & sole Survivors.** Cathy Hopkins. Read by Shirley Barthelmie. (Running Time: 3 hrs. 25 mins.). (Mates, Dates Ser.). (YA). 2009. 39.99 (978-1-74214-324-8(5), 9781742143248) Pub: Bolinda Pubng AUS. Dist(s): Bolinda Pub Inc

Mates, Dates & Sole Survivors. unabr. ed. Cathy Hopkins & Cathy Hopkins. Read by Shirley Barthelmie. 3 CDs. (Running Time: 12300 sec.). (Mates, Dates Ser.). (YA). (gr. 7-12). 2006. audio compact disk 54.95 (978-1-74093-814-3(3)) Pub: Bolinda Pubng AUS. Dist(s): Bolinda Pub Inc

***Mates, dates & tempting Trouble.** Cathy Hopkins. Read by Nicky Talacko. (Running Time: 5 hrs. 40 mins.). (YA). 2009. 44.99 (978-1-74214-325-5(3), 9781742143255) Pub: Bolinda Pubng AUS. Dist(s): Bolinda Pub Inc

Mates, Dates & Tempting Trouble. unabr. ed. Cathy Hopkins & Cathy Hopkins. Read by Nicky Talacko. (Running Time: 20400 sec.). (YA). (gr. 7-12). 2008. audio compact disk 63.95 (978-1-74093-988-1(3), 9781740939881) Pub: Bolinda Pubng AUS. Dist(s): Bolinda Pub Inc

Mates-Jack & Charmian London. Willard Manus. 1 cass. (Running Time: 1 hr. 30 min.). 2001. W Manus.
The life of the great American writer, Jack London - and his wife Charmian.

Math: Count to Fractions, Vol. 1. l.t. ed. Scripts. Thomas B. Albright. Music by Robert E. Albright. 4 cass. (Running Time: 4 hrs. 24 min.). Dramatization. (Non-Specialty Lifetime Math Ser.: 1 of 4). 1993. 6.00 (978-1-888264-06-7(3)) Twty-Frst Ctry.
Included are: counting, math steps, fractions, square root, personal math, percentages, quadratics, algebra, shapes, & math look ahead.

Math: Decimals, Multiply, Divide, Square Root, Vol. 2. Scripts. Thomas B. Albright. Read by Thomas B. Albright. Music by Robert E. Albright. 4 cassettes. (Running Time: 4.31 hrs.). (Non-Specialty Lifetime Math Ser.: 2 of 4). 1993. (978-1-888264-07-4(1)) Twty-Frst Ctry.
Describes Math Signs (+, -, x, ./.) to include decimals and square root.

Math: Rules, Math-World, Things, Person, Algebra, Vol. 3. Scripts. Thomas B. Albright. Narrated by Thomas B. Albright. Music by Robert E. Albright. 4 cass. (Running Time: 4.31 hrs.). (Non-Specialty Lifetime Math Ser.: 3 of 4). 1993. (978-1-888264-08-1(X)) Twty-Frst Ctry.
Includes Rules, Math - World, Things, Person, Algebra.

Math Vol. 4: Algebra, Percentages, Math Ahead. Scripts. Thomas B. Albright. Narrated by Thomas B. Albright. Music by Robert E. Albright. 4 cass. (Running Time: 4.31 hrs.). (Non-Specialty Lifetime Math Ser.). 1993. 6.00 (978-1-888264-09-8(8)) Twty-Frst Ctry.
Includes Algebra, Percentages, Quadratics, Math Shapes, Math Ahead.

Math Activity Program: Standards-based, printable templates for hands-on money & number Exercises. 2004. spiral bd. 49.00 (978-1-57861-524-7(0), IEP Res) Attainment.

Math Book & Tapes: Live Book. 2nd unabr. l.t. ed. Scripts. Thomas B. Albright. Reviewed by Thomas B. Albright. 4 cass.; $7ea; $25 f. (Running Time: 4 hrs. 32 min.). Dramatization. 1998. pap. bk. 8.00 Set. (978-1-888264-03-6(9)) Twty-Frst Ctry.
Included are: counting, math steps, fractions, square root, personal math, percentages, quadratics, algebra, shapes, & math look ahead.

Math Connects, Grade 4, Math Songs CD. Macmillan/McGraw-Hill. (ENG.). 2007. audio compact disk 66.64 (978-0-02-106417-5(2), 0021064172) Pub: Macmillan McGraw-Hill Schl Div. Dist(s): McGraw

Math Connects, Grade 4, Spanish Math Songs CD. Macmillan/McGraw-Hill. (SPA.). 2008. audio compact disk 66.64 (978-0-02-107443-3(7), 9780021074433) Pub: Macmillan McGraw-Hill Schl Div. Dist(s): McGraw

Math Connects, Grades K-1, Math Songs CD. MacMillan/McGraw-Hill Staff. (ENG.). 2007. audio compact disk 66.64 (978-0-02-106404-5(0), 0021064040) Pub: Macmillan McGraw-Hill Schl Div. Dist(s): McGraw

Math Connects, Grades K-1, Spanish Math Songs CD. Macmillan/McGraw-Hill. (SPA.). 2008. audio compact disk 66.64 (978-0-02-107441-9(0), 9780021074419) Pub: Macmillan McGraw-Hill Schl Div. Dist(s): McGraw

Math Connects, Grades 2-3, Math Songs CD. MacMillan/McGraw-Hill Staff. (ENG.). 2007. audio compact disk 66.64 (978-0-02-106411-3(3), 0021064113) Pub: Macmillan McGraw-Hill Schl Div. Dist(s): McGraw

Math Connects, Grades 2-3, Spanish Math Songs CD. Macmillan/McGraw-Hill. (SPA.). 2008. audio compact disk 66.64 (978-0-02-107442-6(9), 9780021074426) Pub: Macmillan McGraw-Hill Schl Div. Dist(s): McGraw

Math Curse. Jon Scieszka. Illus. by Lane Smith. Narrated by Nancy Wu. Music by Scotty Huff & Robert Reynolds. Animated by Daniel Ivanick. 1 CD. (Running Time: 13 mins.). (J). (gr. 1-4). 2009. bk. 29.95 (978-0-545-13458-3(7)); pap. bk. 18.95 (978-0-545-13459-0(5)); audio compact disk 12.95 (978-0-545-15722-3(6)) Weston Woods.

Math Curse, Set. Jon Scieszka. Illus. by Lane Smith. Narrated by Nancy Wu. Music by Scotty Huff & Robert Reynolds. Animated by Daniel Ivanick. 1 CD. (Running Time: 13 mins.). (J). (gr. 1-4). 2009. pap. bk. 38.75 (978-0-545-13460-6(9)) Weston Woods.

Math Early Explorers Take Home Book: CD Rom. Compiled by Benchmark Education Staff. (J). 2007. audio compact disk 10.00 (978-1-4108-9487-8(8)) Benchmark Educ.

Math Explorers Set A Audio CD Set. Compiled by Benchmark Education Company Staff. (Math Explorers Ser.). (J). (gr. 3-8). 2008. audio compact disk 235.00 (978-1-60634-593-1(1)) Benchmark Educ.

Math for Everyday Living. Allan A. Schwartz & Ann Edson. 5 cass. (J). (gr. 4-6). 89.00 (978-0-89525-170-1(1), AKC 158) Ed Activities.
Teaches & develops the necessary basic math skills involved in real-life activities, such as shopping, traveling, banking, getting the best paying job, paying bills, using credit, etc. Includes 8 activity books.

***Math Games Galore: Fractions & Decimals, Gr. 3 Ebook: 10 Matching Games That Reinforce Basic Math Skills.** Stephen Davis. (J). 2009. 12.99 (978-1-60689-959-5(7)) Creat Teach Pr.

***Math Games Galore: Number Sense & Place Value, Gr. 3 Ebook: 10 Matching Games That Reinforce Basic Math Skills.** Stephen Davis. (J). 2009. 12.99 (978-1-60689-958-8(9)) Creat Teach Pr.

***Math Games Galore: Time & Money, Gr. 3 Ebook: 10 Matching Games That Reinforce Basic Math Skills.** Stephen Davis. (J). 2009. 12.99 (978-1-60689-960-1(0)) Creat Teach Pr.

Math Generator 3. (Timesaving Software Tools for Teachers Ser.). 2004. audio compact disk 19.99 (978-1-57690-704-7(X)) Tchr Create Ma.

Math Music: Sing Lowe - Score High. Amy Lowe. Perf. by Fifth Grade Students. 1 cass. (Running Time: 15 min.). (J). 1998. 9.98 (978-0-9660947-7-0(8), EKCT5004) Emphasis Ent.
Eight engaging songs that teach children basic rules for measuring length, capacity, temperature, perimeter, area, time, & the Metric System.

Math Music Vol. 1: Understanding Math Through Music. Amy Lowe. 1 CD. (Running Time: 17 mins.). (J). 2005. audio compact disk 18.98 (978-1-893967-25-0(5)) Emphasis Ent.
Includes: Lesson Plans; Printable Lyrics; Printable Classroom; posters; Amy Lowe Biography and Workshop Information; Additional Product and order information.

Math of Marriage: Gen. 1:27-2:25, 720. Ed Young. 1989. 4.95 (978-0-7417-1720-7(4), 720) Win Walk.

Math on File: Algebra. James Alexander. (gr. 9). 2004. audio compact disk 149.95 (978-0-8160-5002-4(3)) Facts On File.

Math on File: Calculus. James C. Alexander. (gr. 9). 2004. audio compact disk 149.95 (978-0-8160-5003-1(1)) Facts On File.

Math on File: Geometry. James C. Alexander. (gr. 9). 2004. audio compact disk 149.95 (978-0-8160-5004-8(X)) Facts On File.

Math Readiness: Addition & Subtraction. Hap Palmer. (J). 1972. 11.95 Ed Activities.

Math Readiness: Vocabulary & Concepts. Hap Palmer. (J). 1973. 11.95 Ed Activities.

Math Readiness Vocabulary & Concepts. Perf. by Hap Palmer. 1 cass. (Running Time: 35 min.). (J). 11.95 (EA 540C); lp 11.95 (EA 540) Kimbo Educ.
Count-up, Countdown - Movin' by Numerals - Make a Set - How Many Ways & more.

Math Stories. Sundance/Newbridge, LLC Staff. (Early Math Ser.). (gr. k-1). 2000. 12.00 (978-1-58273-994-6(3)) Sund Newbrdge.

***Math Strands Assessment Links: Individual CD Level C.** Continental Press Staff. 2008. stu. ed. 49.95 (978-0-8454-5794-8(2)) Continental Pr.

***Math Strands Assessment Links: Individual CD Level D.** Continental Press Staff. 2008. stu. ed. 49.95 (978-0-8454-5795-5(0)) Continental Pr.

***Math Strands Assessment Links: Individual CD Level E.** Continental Press Staff. 2008. stu. ed. 49.95 (978-0-8454-5796-2(9)) Continental Pr.

***Math Strands Assessment Links: Individual CD Level F.** Continental Press Staff. 2008. stu. ed. 49.95 (978-0-8454-5797-9(7)) Continental Pr.

***Math Strands Assessment Links: Individual CD Level G.** Continental Press Staff. 2008. stu. ed. 49.95 (978-0-8454-5798-6(5)) Continental Pr.

***Math Strands Assessment Links: Individual CD Level H.** Continental Press Staff. 2008. stu. ed. 49.95 (978-0-8454-5799-3(3)) Continental Pr.

Math Take Home Book CD-ROM: Early. Benchmark Education Staff. (J). 2006. audio compact disk 10.00 (978-1-4108-7387-3(0)) Benchmark Educ.

Math Take Home Book CD-ROM: Emergent. Benchmark Education Staff. (J). 2006. audio compact disk 10.00 (978-1-4108-7384-2(6)) Benchmark Educ.

Math Take Home Book CD-ROM: Fluent. Benchmark Education Staff. (J). 2006. audio compact disk 10.00 (978-1-4108-7390-3(0)) Benchmark Educ.

Mathamusic One. Barbara Kronau-Sorensen. Ed. by Paul Sorensen. 1 cass. (J). (ps-12). 1994. 10.00 (978-1-892185-02-0(4)) FantabulPub.
Side A: The Substitution Principle (country/blues), Coordinate Geometry (rap), Naming Numbers with Operators (rock). Side B: Instrumental versions of all 3 songs for easy sing-along karaoke or playing along on instruments. Includes song & activity book.

Mathcue. 3rd ed. (C). 2005. audio compact disk 44.95 (978-0-324-32059-6(0)) Pub: South-West. Dist(s): CENGAGE Learn

Mathematics for the Managerial, Life, & Social Sciences. 6th ed. (C). 2005. audio compact disk 16.95 (978-0-495-01535-2(0)) Pub: Brooks-Cole. Dist(s): CENGAGE Learn

Mathematics Is Easy. Eldon Taylor. Read by Eldon Taylor. Ed. by Leslie Brice. 1 cass. (Running Time: 1 hr.). 1992. 16.95 (978-1-56705-152-0(9)) Gateways Inst.
Self improvement.

Mathematics Is Easy. Eldon Taylor. 1 cass. (Running Time: 1 hr. 2 min.). (Inner Talk Ser.). 16.95 (978-1-55978-130-5(0), 5372C) Progress Aware Res.
Soundtrack - Musical Themes with underlying subliminal affirmations. Includes script.

Mathematics is Easy: Babbling Brook. Eldon Taylor. 1 cass. 16.95 (978-1-55978-493-1(8), 5372F) Progress Aware Res.

Mathematics Is Easy: Ocean. Eldon Taylor. Read by Eldon Taylor. Ed. by Leslie Brice. 1 cass. (Running Time: 1 hr.). 1992. 16.95 (978-1-56705-153-7(7)) Gateways Inst.
Self improvement.

Mathematics Is Easy: Stream. Eldon Taylor. Read by Eldon Taylor. Ed. by Leslie Brice. 1 cass. (Running Time: 1 hr.). 1992. 16.95 (978-1-56705-154-4(5)) Gateways Inst.

Mathematics, Music, & Mysticism. Ralph H. Abraham. 1 cass. 9.00 (A0001-86) Sound Photosyn.
Ralph is a professor of mathematics at UC Santa Cruz & plays with visual music instruments & chaos.

Mathematics of Morality. Ed. by Marco A. V. Bitetto. 1 cass. 2000. (978-1-58578-338-0(2)) Inst of Cybernetics.

Mathematics Reprints. Ed. by Marco A. V. Bitetto. 1 cass. 2000. (978-1-58578-050-1(2)) Inst of Cybernetics.

Mathilda. Mary Wollstonecraft Shelley. Read by Anais 9000. 2009. 27.95 (978-1-60112-226-1(8)) Babblebooks.

Mathilda Savitch: A Novel. unabr. ed. Victor Lodato. Narrated by Cassandra Campbell. 1 MP3-CD. (Running Time: 8 hrs. 30 mins. 0 sec.). (ENG.). 2009. 19.99 (978-1-4001-6330-4(7)); audio compact disk 59.99 (978-1-4001-4330-6(6)); audio compact disk 29.99 (978-1-4001-1330-9(X)) Pub: Tantor Media. Dist(s): IngramPubServ

Matilda. Roald Dahl. Narrated by Sarah Greene. 3 cass. (Running Time: 1 hr. 40 mins.). (J). pap. bk. 29.95 (978-0-7540-6216-5(3)) AudioGO.
Poor, misunderstood Matilda fights back against an unappreciative world through a hidden talent: Matilda is the world's greatest practical joker! Little effort is needed to put one over on her obnoxious parents, but can shy little Matilda handle the formidable headmistress, Miss Trunchbull, and win the respect of every kid in school? Yes!.

Matilda. abr. ed. Roald Dahl. Illus. by Jean Marsh. 1 cass. (Running Time: 1 hr. 30 min.). (Stand Alone Ser.). (J). (gr. 4-6). 1993. 12.00 (978-1-55994-792-3(6), HarperChildAud) HarperCollins Pubs.

***Matilda.** unabr. ed. Roald Dahl. Read by Joely Richardson. (ENG.). 2004. (978-0-06-079980-9(3)); (978-0-06-074604-9(1)) HarperCollins Pubs.

Matilda, unabr. ed. Roald Dahl. Narrated by Ron Keith. 4 pieces. (Running Time: 5 hrs. 15 mins.). (gr. 6 up). 1994. 35.00 (978-0-7887-0139-9(8), 94364E7) Recorded Bks.
Meet Matilda, book lover & child genius. When she decides to match wits with school head-mistress Miss Trunchbull (200 pounds of mean, kid-hating bully), get ready for lots of laughs.

Matilda. unabr. ed. Roald Dahl. Narrated by Ron Keith. 5 CDs. (Running Time: 5 hrs. 15 mins.). (gr. 6 up). 2000. audio compact disk 39.00 (978-0-7887-3450-2(4), C1056E7) Recorded Bks.

Matilda. unabr. abr. ed. Roald Dahl. Read by Joely Richardson. 4 CDs. (Running Time: 6 hrs.). (J). 2004. audio compact disk 27.50 (978-0-06-058254-8(5)) HarperCollins Pubs.

Matilda Bone. unabr. ed. Karen Cushman. Read by Janet McTeer. 3 vols. (Running Time: 4 hrs. 1 min.). (Middle Grade Cassette Librariestm Ser.). (J). (gr. 5-9). 2004. pap. bk. 36.00 (978-0-8072-1725-2(5), S YA 252 SP, Listening Lib); 30.00 (978-0-8072-8737-8(7), YA252CX, Listening Lib) Random Audio Pubg.
To Blood & Bone Alley, home of leech, barber-surgeon & apothecary, comes Matilda, raised by a priest to be pious & learned & now destined to dismay, her work will not involve Latin or writing, but lighting the fire, going to market, mixing plasters & poultices & helping Peg treat patients.

Matin Latin 1. Featuring Karen L. Craig. (Mars Hill Textbook Ser.). (YA). 2000. 10.00 (978-1-885767-81-3(1)) Canon Pr ID.

Matin Latin 1: Pronunciation Aid. Read by J. T. Grauke. (ENG & LAT.). (YA). 2008. audio compact disk 10.00 (978-1-59128-021-7(4)) Canon Pr ID.

Matin Latin 2. Featuring Karen L. Craig. (YA). 2000. 10.00 (978-1-885767-82-0(X)) Canon Pr ID.

Matin Latin 2: Pronunciation Aid. Read by J. T. Grauke. (ENG & LAT.). (YA). 2008. audio compact disk 10.00 (978-1-59128-022-4(2)) Canon Pr ID.

***Matinee with Bob & Ray, Volume 1.** RadioArchives.com. (ENG.). 2006. audio compact disk 29.98 (978-1-61081-045-6(7)) Radio Arch.

***Mating in Captivity: In Search of Erotic Intelligence.** unabr. ed. Esther Perel. Read by Esther Perel. (ENG.). 2006. (978-0-06-124359-2(0), Harper Audio); (978-0-06-124360-8(4), Harper Audio) HarperCollins Pubs.

Mating in Captivity: Reconciling the Erotic & the Domestic. unabr. ed. Esther Perel. Read by Esther Perel. (Running Time: 28800 sec.). 2006. audio compact disk 34.95 (978-0-06-114235-2(2)) HarperCollins Pubs.

***Mating in Captivity: Introduction.** abr. ed. Esther Perel. Read by Esther Perel. (ENG.). 2006. (978-0-06-134112-0(6), Harper Audio) HarperCollins Pubs.

Mating Season. P. G. Wodehouse. Narrated by Frederick Davidson. (Running Time: 8 hrs. 30 mins.). 1995. 27.95 (978-1-59912-691-3(5)) Iofy Corp.

Mating Season. unabr. ed. P. G. Wodehouse. Read by Frederick Davidson. 6 cass. (Running Time: 8 hrs. 30 mins.). 1995. 44.95 (978-0-7861-0761-2(8), 1610) Blckstn Audio.
When Gussie Fink-Nottle, after a convivial evening with "Catsmeat" Pinbright, was sentenced to 14 days without the option for wading in the fountain at Trafalgar Square, Bertie Wooster saw the red light. For Gussie was an expected guest at Deverill Hall and clearly his enforced absence would give rise to immediate inquiries. From this point it would be but a short step to a complete revelation of the scandalous details of his escapade and Bertram well knew what would be the effect of this intelligence on Gussie's fiance, Madeline. As always when a rift appeared in her love affairs, Madeline would transfer her simpering affection to Bertram.

Mating Season. unabr. ed. P. G. Wodehouse. Read by Jonathan Cecil. 8 cass. (Running Time: 12 hrs.). (Jeeves & Wooster Ser.). 2000. 59.95 (978-0-7451-6374-1(2), CAB 667) Pub: Chivers Audio Bks GBR. Dist(s): AudioGO
With a visit to Deverill Hall, the home of Esmond Haddock's Headache Hokies and his five aunts, Bertie is drafted for the village concert! But thanks to Jeeves, the balance sheet of sundered hearts and reunited hearts is even at the end of his visit!.

***Mating Season.** unabr. ed. P. g. Wodehouse. Read by Frederick Davidson. (Running Time: 8 hrs. 30 mins.). 2010. 29.95 (978-1-4417-4505-7(X)); audio compact disk 76.00 (978-1-4417-4502-6(5)) Blckstn Audio.

Matisse see Gertrude Stein Reads from Her Works

Matisse Stories. unabr. ed. A. S. Byatt. Read by Nadia May. 2 cass. (Running Time: 2 hrs. 30 mins.). 1995. 17.95 (978-0-7861-0805-3(1), 1628) Blckstn Audio.
This elegant collection contains three stories, each touched in a different way by the paintings of Henri Matisse. Their subjects' lives unravel from simple beginnings - a trip to the hair-dresser, a cleaning woman's passion for knitting, lunch in a Chinese restaurant - but gradually the veneer of ordinariness is peeled back to expose pain, reveal desire, or express the intensity of joy in color & creation.

Matisse Stories, unabr. ed. A. S. Byatt. Read by Nadia May. 2 cass. 1999. 17.95 (FS9-51102) Highsmith.

Matisse Stories. unabr. ed. A. S. Byatt. Read by Virginia Leishman. 3 cass. (Running Time: 3 hrs.). 1997. 26.00 (95117) Recorded Bks.
Three elegant stories that catch the subtle interplays between mind & eye.

Matisse Stories. unabr. ed. Short Stories. A. S. Byatt. Narrated by Virginia Leishman. 3 cass. (Running Time: 3 hrs.). 1999. 26.00 (978-0-7887-1149-7(0), 95117E7) Recorded Bks.
Three elegant stories that catch the subtle interplays between mind & eye. In the first story, a fashionable woman watches her life change in the mirror of a beauty salon. In another, an eccentric housekeeper cultivates a disturbing eye for color.

Matisse Stories. unabr. ed. A. S. Byatt. Read by Nadia May. (Running Time: 9000 sec.). 2007. audio compact disk 27.00 (978-0-7861-5827-0(1)); audio compact disk 19.95 (978-0-7861-6968-9(0)) Blckstn Audio.

Matlock Bath see Sir John Betjeman Reading His Poetry

Matlock Paper. unabr. collector's ed. Robert Ludlum. Read by Michael Prichard. 7 cass. (Running Time: 10 hrs. 30 mins.). 1984. 56.00 (978-0-7366-0803-9(6), 1753) Books on Tape.
This assignment was to cause Matlock & his loved ones pain. But the soundless machines & the faceless men who monitored them didn't care as long as a conspiracy called Nimrod was destroyed, even if he should be destroyed with it.

Matou, Yves Beauchemin. Read by Albert Millaire. 4 cass. (FRE.). 1996. 36.95 (1811-LV) Olivia & Hill.
More than a million copies have been sold of this popular Quebecois novel full of touching characters: Florent, a young man who lives in Montreal & dreams of owning a restaurant, his wife who dreams of having a child & of M. Emile, a strange 6-year-old boy who dreams of being adopted, with his cat Dejeuner, etc.

Matri, Letters from the Mother. Read by Zoe Ann Nicholson. 1 CD. (Running Time: 58 mins). 2005. audio compact disk 19.95 (978-0-9723928-8-4(2)) Lune Soleil.

Matricide at St. Martha's. unabr. ed. Ruth Dudley Edwards. Read by Bill Wallis. 6 cass. (Running Time: 9 hrs.). (Robert Amiss Mystery Ser.). 2000. 54.95 (978-0-7540-0435-6(X), CAB 1858); audio compact disk 64.95 (978-0-7540-5329-3(6), CCD 020) Pub: Chivers Audio Bks GBR. Dist(s): AudioGO
When an enormous bequest is left to St. Martha's College, the dons split into three factions: the Virgins, the Dykes & the Old Women. As the factions fight over how to spend the money, one of the Virgins is found dead. Once again, Robert Amiss finds himself with a murder investigation.

Matrimonial Appellate Practice. 1997. bk. 99.00 (ACS-1264) PA Bar Inst.
You may have tried dozens of family law cases & feel comfortable with all aspects of local procedure & developing case law. But if you can't handle an appeal, you may disappoint your formerly happy client. Even if you choose not to appeal, the other side may do so. You must be prepared to navigate the treacherous waters of appeallate procedure at a moment's notice. This prepares you to handle any aspect of an appeal of a family law case.

Matrimonial Litigation Across State Lines. 1986. 25.00; 25.00; bk. 50.00 PA Bar Inst.
Includes book.

Matrimonio: De Sobrevivir a Prosperar. Charles R. Swindoll.Tr. of Marriage: from Surviving to Thriving. 2009. audio compact disk 31.00 (978-1-57972-828-1(6)) Insight Living.

Matrimonio Niños Resolver. Ronald Hubbard. 2007. audio compact disk 17.00 (978-958-8218-99-1(3)) Centro de Literatura COL.

Matrimonio y Vida. P. Juan Rivas. (SPA.). (YA). 2007. audio compact disk 18.95 (978-1-935405-98-6(5)) Hombre Nuevo.

Matrimonios Felices: Para mantener el amor Encendido. Mariano de Blas.Tr. of Happily Married. (SPA.). 2009. audio compact disk 25.00 (978-1-935405-18-4(7)) Hombre Nuevo.

Matrix Energetics Experience. Richard Bartlett. 2009. audio compact disk 99.95 (978-1-59179-677-0(6)) Sounds True.

***Matt Jensen: Deadly Trail: the Last Mountain Man 2.** William W. Johnstone. 2010. audio compact disk 19.99 (978-1-59950-699-9(8)) GraphicAudio.

***Matt Jensen 1: The Last Mountain Man.** William W. Johnstone & J. A. Johnstone. (Matt Jensen: No. 1). 2010. audio compact disk 19.99 (978-1-59950-674-6(2)) GraphicAudio.

Matt Talbot & His Times. Mary Purcell. 6 cass. 24.95 (306) Ignatius Pr.
Story of the converted Irish alcoholic who became very saintly.

Mattawa Song Cycle: Music by Carolyn Brown Senier. Composed by Carolyn Brown Senier. (ENG.). 2004. 10.95 (978-1-884540-74-5(0)) Haleys.

Matter. unabr. abr. ed. Iain M. Banks. Read by Toby Longworth. (Running Time: 6 hrs.). (ENG.). 2009. 24.98 (978-1-60024-504-6(8)) Pub: Hachet Audio. Dist(s): HachBkGrp

Matter Audio CD Theme Set: Set of 6 Set A. Adapted by Benchmark Education Staff. (English Explorers Ser.). (J). (gr. 3-6). 2007. audio compact disk 60.00 (978-1-4108-9831-9(8)) Benchmark Educ.

Matter, Energy & the Black Hole. John Lilly. 1 cass. 10.00 (A0072-78) Sound Photosyn.
From Dr. Lilly's personal collection.

Matter Is Everywhere: Solids, Liquids, & Gases. Compiled by Benchmark Education Staff. 2005. audio compact disk 10.00 (978-1-4108-5487-2(6)) Benchmark Educ.

Matter of Chance, Set, Level 4. David A. Hill. Contrib. by Philip Prowse. (Running Time: 2 hrs. 12 mins.). (Cambridge English Readers Ser.). (ENG.). 2000. 15.75 (978-0-521-77546-5(9)) Cambridge U Pr.

***Matter of Character.** Robin Lee Hatcher. (Running Time: 7 hrs. 42 mins. 28 sec.). (Sisters of Bethlehem Springs Ser.). (ENG.). 2010. 14.99 (978-0-310-77280-4(X)) Zondervan.

***Matter of Class.** Mary Balogh. Contrib. by Anne Flosnik. (Playaway Adult Fiction Ser.). (ENG.). 2009. 49.99 (978-1-4418-3332-7(3)) Find a World.

Matter of Class. unabr. ed. Mary Balogh. Read by Rosalyn Landor & Anne Flosnik. (Running Time: 4 hrs.). 2009. 19.99 (978-1-4418-2639-8(4), 9781441826398, Brilliance MP3); 19.99 (978-1-4418-2641-1(6), 9781441826411, BAD); 39.97 (978-1-4418-2640-4(8), 9781441826404, Brlnc Audio MP3 Lib); 39.97 (978-1-4418-2642-8(4), 9781441826428, BADLE) Brilliance Audio.

Matter of Class. unabr. ed. Mary Balogh. Read by Anne Flosnik. (Running Time: 4 hrs.). 2009. audio compact disk 19.99 (978-1-4418-2637-4(8), 9781441826374, Bril Audio CD Unabri) Brilliance Audio.

Matter of Class. unabr. ed. Mary Balogh. Read by Anne Flosnik. (Running Time: 4 hrs.). 2009. audio compact disk 69.97 (978-1-4418-2638-1(6), 9781441826381, BriAudCD Unabrid) Brilliance Audio.

Matter of Destiny: How to Find & Marry Your Soulmate: A Beginner's Spiritual Guide. Joanne Parrotta. Narrated by Maria d'Alleva. (ENG.). 2008. audio compact disk 19.99 (978-1-60031-026-3(5)) Spoken Books.

Matter of Fat. unabr. ed. Sherry Ashworth. Read by Paddy Glynn. 6 cass. (Running Time: 9 hrs.). 2001. 54.95 (978-0-7531-1043-0(1)) Pub: ISIS Audio GBR. Dist(s): Ulverscroft US

Matter of Honor. 10.00 Esstee Audios.
A dramatization of the events leading up to the Hamilton-Burr duel & the final days of Hamilton.

Matter of Honor. Jeffrey Archer. 2 cass. (Running Time: 3 hrs.). 2001. 16.99 (978-0-00-104766-2(3)) Pub: HarpC GBR. Dist(s): Trafalgar
In 1966, Adam Scott, an unemployed British ex-army officer with an uncertain future, attends the reading of his disgraced father's will. Part of his inheritance is a letter detailing the events of Hermann Goering's suicide and two unopened letters from the Nazi general giving him access to a Swiss bank vault and the valuable Russian icon it contains. However, a veritable state secret is concealed in the painting and the KGB and the CIA both want it before the expiry of a crucial deadline. Scott's perilous journey across Europe to the questionable safety of England is by plane, car, foot, bus, ambulance, van, and ferry as he stays one step ahead of death with the assistance of farmers, salesmen, racing cyclists, hoodlums, and an entire orchestra.

Matter of Honor. abr. rev. ed. Jeffrey Archer. Read by Martin Jarvis. 3 CDs. (Running Time: 3 hrs. 0 mins. 0 sec.). 2004. audio compact disk 14.95 (978-1-59397-515-9(5)) Pub: Macmill Audio. Dist(s): Macmillan

Matter of Honor. unabr. ed. Jeffrey Archer. Read by David Rintoul. 8 cass. (Running Time: 8 hrs). 1993. 69.95 (978-0-7451-5751-1(3), CAB 450) AudioGO.

Matter of Honor. unabr. ed. Jeffrey Archer. Read by David Rintoul. 8 cass. (Running Time: 12 hrs.). 2001. 59.95 (CAB 450) Pub: Chivers Audio Bks GBR. Dist(s): AudioGO
When Adam Scott opens the letter from his father's will, he realizes life can never be the same again. The letter had brought dishonor to the family and forced his father out of the regiment in disgrace. Now it leads Adam to a priceless Russian icon left hidden in a Swiss bank vault since World War II, and to an explosive revelation that could change the balance of power between Russia and the U.S.

Matter of Honor. unabr. collector's ed. Jeffrey Archer. Read by Dick Estell. 8 cass. (Running Time: 12 hrs.). 1987. 64.00 (978-0-7366-1093-3(6), 2017) Books on Tape.
When Colonel Scott dies, his will points the way to clearing the unspoken secret that shadowed his retirement & turned him from a WW II hero into a disgraced & broken man. It is up to Adam to follow. As he works to clear his father's name, he stumbles across a revelation so explosive, so charged, so unexpected that it could change the balance of power between America & the Soviet Union.

Matter of Justice. unabr. ed. Charles Todd. Narrated by Simon Prebble. 9 CDs. (Running Time: 11 hrs. 30 mins.). (Inspector Ian Rutledge Mystery Ser.: Bk. 11). 2009. audio compact disk 89.95 (978-0-7927-5954-6(0), Chivers Sound Lib) AudioGO.

Matter of Justice: Claiming the Treasure in the Field. Megan McKenna. 4 cass. (Running Time: 4 hrs.). 2001. vinyl bd. 33.95 (A6360) St Anthony Mess Pr.
Challenges us through parables and Scripture to taste God's justice and commit our lives to community.

Matter of Life & Death: Relationship & Self-Preservation. Read by Peter Mudd. 1 cass. (Running Time: 1 hr. 30 min.). 1988. 10.95 (978-0-7822-0212-0(8), 349) C G Jung IL.

Matter of Loyalty. Sandra Howard. 2009. 84.95 (978-0-7531-4301-8(1)); audio compact disk 99.95 (978-0-7531-4302-5(X)) Pub: Isis Pubng Ltd GBR. Dist(s): Ulverscroft US

***Matter of Matter.** L. Ron Hubbard. Read by Michael Yurchak et al. Narrated by R. F. Daley. (YA). 2010. audio compact disk 9.95 (978-1-59212-239-4(6)) Gala Pr LLC.

***Matter of Trust.** unabr. ed. Sydney Bauer. Read by Bill Ten Eyck. (Running Time: 16 hrs. 58 mins.). 2010. audio compact disk 118.95 (978-1-74214-742-0(9), 9781742147420) Pub: Bolinda Pubng AUS. Dist(s): Bolinda Pub Inc

***Matterhorn: A Novel of the Vietnam War.** unabr. ed. Karl Marlantes. (Running Time: 20 hrs. 0 mins.). 2010. 44.95 (978-1-4417-4231-5(X)); 105.95 (978-1-4417-4227-8(1)) Blckstn Audio.

***Matterhorn: A Novel of the Vietnam War.** unabr. ed. Karl Marlantes. Read by Bronson Pinchot. 16 CDs. (Running Time: 20 hrs.). 2010. audio compact disk 39.95 (978-1-4417-4230-8(1)); audio compact disk 123.00 (978-1-4417-4228-5(X)) Blckstn Audio.

Matter/la Materia: See It, Touch It, Taste It, Smell It/Mirca, Toca, Prueba, Huele. abr. ed. Darlene Stille. Tr. by Sol Robledo. Illus. by Sheree Boyd. (Amazing Science Ser.). (SPA.). (gr. k). 2008. audio compact disk 14.60 (978-1-4048-4477-3(5)) CapstoneDig.

***Matters Arising.** Sarah Harrison. 2010. 54.95 (978-1-4450-0051-0(2)); audio compact disk 71.95 (978-1-4450-0052-7(0)) Pub: Isis Pubng Ltd GBR. Dist(s): Ulverscroft US

Matters of Life & Death: Risks vs. Benefits of Medical Care. unabr. collector's ed. Eugene D. Robin. Read by Michael Prichard. 6 cass. (Running Time: 9 hrs.). 1985. 48.00 (978-0-7366-1061-2(8), 1988) Books on Tape.
This is a thoughtful, well-reasoned explanation of the practice of medicine & it will help you make sensible decisions about medicine & medical care.

Matters of the Blood. Maria Lima. 2007. audio compact disk 45.95 (978-0-8095-7218-2(4)) Diamond Book Dists.

Matters of the Heart. abr. ed. Danielle Steel. Read by Mel Foster. (Running Time: 5 hrs.). 2010. audio compact disk 14.99 (978-1-4233-2067-8(0), 9781423320678, BCD Value Price) Brilliance Audio.

Matters of the Heart. unabr. ed. Danielle Steel. Read by Mel Foster. 1 MP3-CD. (Running Time: 10 hrs.). 2009. 24.99 (978-1-4233-2062-3(X), 9781423320623, Brilliance MP3); 39.97 (978-1-4233-2063-0(8), 9781423320630, Brlnc Audio MP3 Lib); 39.97 (978-1-4233-2065-4(4), 9781423320654, BADLE); 24.99 (978-1-4233-2064-7(6), 9781423320647, BAD); audio compact disk 38.99 (978-1-4233-2060-9(3), 9781423320609, Bril Audio CD Unabri); audio compact disk 99.97 (978-1-4233-2061-6(1), 9781423320616, BriAudCD Unabrid) Brilliance Audio.

Matters of the Heart: How to Experience Lasting & Positive Change. Mac Hammond. 3 CDs. 2004. audio compact disk 15.00 (978-1-57399-125-4(2)) Mac Hammond.
If you have constant problems in your life or lingering contrary circumstances which need to change, get this series by Mac Hammond and learn how to initiate and experience lasting and positive change.

Matters of the Heart: Stop Trying to Fix the Old - Let God Give You Something New. abr. ed. Juanita Bynum. Read by Sandra Burr. (Running Time: 10800 sec.). 2002. audio compact disk 24.95 (978-1-4233-0361-9(X), 9781423303619, Brilliance MP3) Brilliance Audio.
God began to deal with me...As the tears rolled down my face, God said, You are thinking like a man. You are always concerned about the outward appearance...but what is the condition of your heart toward Me and toward My people? I sat there confused and said to the Lord, 'MY HEART?'... This groundbreaking message will open your eyes to the truth about your own heart. Whether you are new to the faith or have been doing great things for God's kingdom for years, you still need a new heart. This Word from the Lord has changed Juanita Bynum's life, and it will change yours as well! Find out how you can be doing good works for God and not even know Him as you should. Uncover areas where your old heart deceived you, and learn why it can't be fixed. Explore the heart/mind connection and see why this key to intimacy with God is so vital to a healthy, satisfying and effective life. God wants to do some major heart surgery and give you a permanent and improved life. Are you ready to receive?.

Matters of the Heart: Stop Trying to Fix the Old - Let God Give You Something New. unabr. ed. Juanita Bynum. Read by Sandra Burr. 3 CDs. (Running Time: 3 hrs.). 2003. audio compact disk 19.95 (978-1-59355-271-8(8), 1593552718); 17.95 (978-1-59355-269-5(6), 1593552696); 44.25 (978-1-59355-270-1(X), 159355270X); audio compact disk 62.25 (978-1-59355-272-5(6), 1593552726) Brilliance Audio.

Matters of the Heart: Stop Trying to Fix the Old - Let God Give You Something New. abr. ed. Juanita Bynum. Read by Sandra Burr. (Running Time: 3 hrs.). 2006. 39.25 (978-1-4233-0364-0(4), 9781423303640, BADLE); 24.95 (978-1-4233-0363-3(6), 9781423303633, BAD); audio compact disk 39.25 (978-1-4233-0362-6(8), 9781423303626, Brlnc Audio MP3 Lib) Brilliance Audio.

Matters of the Heart Vol. 1. Told to Mac Hammond. 3 cass. 2003. 15.00 (978-1-57399-174-2(0)) Mac Hammond.

Matthew. Michael Pearl. (ENG.). 2008. (978-1-934794-25-8(2)) No Greater Joy.

Matthew. Perf. by Visual Entertainment Staff. Prod. by Charles K. Robertson. 4 cass. (Running Time: 240 min.). 1998. 24.95 (978-1-889710-12-9(1)) Visual Entnmnt.

Matthew: A Gospel for the Church. Donald Senior. 4 cass. (Running Time: 4 hrs.). 2001. vinyl bd. 31.95 (A6550) St Anthony Mess Pr.
In our own time of transition Matthew's message of change and continuity is one we need to hear.

Matthew Pt. 1: Audio Dramatization Based Word for Word on the Visual Bible's Epic Motion Picture. (LifeLight Ser.). audio compact disk 15.00 (978-0-570-07817-3(2), 20-3302) Concordia.

Matthew Pt. 2: Audio Dramatization Based Word for Word on the Visual Bible's Epic Motion Picture. audio compact disk 15.00 (978-0-570-07849-4(0), 20-3312) Concordia.

Matthew Commentary. Chuck Missler. 24 audio CDs. (Running Time: 24 hours aprox). 2006. audio compact disk 89.95 (978-1-57821-332-0(0)) Koinonia Hse.

Matthew Commentary: Verse-by-Verse with Chuck Missler. Chuck Missler. 1 CD-ROM. (Running Time: 30 hrs.). 2000. cd-rom 44.95 (978-1-57821-111-1(5)) Koinonia Hse.
Matthew presents Jesus Christ as the Messiah of Israel, the Lion of the tribe of Judah. It was written by a Jew, to Jews, about a Jew. This book of the Bible uses more Old Testament quotes than any other. The Gospel of Matthew emphasizes the sayings of Jesus, including ten parables not found in any other Gospel.

***Matthew Flinders' Cat.** Bryce Courtenay. Read by Humphrey Bower. (Running Time: 17 hrs. 33 mins.). 2009. 114.99 (978-1-74214-205-0(2), 9781742142050) Pub: Bolinda Pubng AUS. Dist(s): Bolinda Pub Inc

Matthew Flinders' Cat. unabr. ed. Bryce Courtenay. Read by Humphrey Bower. 12 cass. (Running Time: 17 hrs. 33 mins.). 2003. 96.00 (978-1-74030-984-4(7)) Pub: Bolinda Pubng AUS. Dist(s): Bolinda Pub Inc

Matthew Flinders' Cat. unabr. ed. Bryce Courtenay. Read by Humphrey Bower. (Running Time: 17 hrs. 33 mins.). 2004. audio compact disk 113.95 (978-1-74093-512-8(8)) Pub: Bolinda Pubng AUS. Dist(s): Bolinda Pub Inc

***Matthew Flinders' Cat.** unabr. ed. Bryce Courtenay. Read by Humphrey Bower. (Running Time: 17 hrs. 33 mins.). 2010. 43.95 (978-1-921415-18-0(5), 9781921415180) Pub: Bolinda Pubng AUS. Dist(s): Bolinda Pub Inc

Matthew I. (LifeLight Bible Studies: Course I). 13.95 (20-2237) Concordia.

Matthew II. (LifeLight Bible Studies: Course 2). 13.95 (20-2247) Concordia.

Matthew Kelly. . . Live. Speeches. M. J. Kelly. 2 cass. (Running Time: 2hrs. 30mins.). 2000. 15.00 (978-1-929266-03-6(0)) Beacon OH.
Two and one half - hours of Matthew Kelly's most notable talks captured on audio tape. With his keen sense of humor and heart - warming charm, he elevates and energizes his audience to pursue the highest values of the human spirit.

Matthew, The Apostle. Dan Corner. 1 cass. 3.00 (105) Evang Outreach.

Matthew Traveled Around the World. Connie K. McHugh. 1 cass. (Running Time: 50 mins.). (J). (ps-4). 1997. pap. bk. 12.95 (978-0-9657351-3-1(3)) Pub: Music Fantasy. Dist(s): Penton Overseas
Introduces very young children to different cultures of people & places around the world. It includes art work done in bright markers showing a touch of traditional costumes, flash cards for learning to count in the languages, listening tape set for general information about several countries, continents & states.

Matthew's Gospel: Embracing Our Jewish Roots. Carolyn Osiek. 2 cass. (Running Time: 2 hrs.). 2001. 24.95 (A7060) St Anthony Mess Pr.
Emphasizes the challenge and insight offered for preachers, teachers, catechists and liturgists.

Matthew's Story. unabr. ed. Tim LaHaye & Jerry B. Jenkins. Contrib. by Robertson Dean. (Running Time: 10 hrs.). Bk. 4. (ENG.). (gr. 12 up). 2010. audio compact disk 39.95 (978-0-14-314543-1(6), PengAudBks) Penguin Grp USA.

Mattie. unabr. ed. Judy Alter. Narrated by Pam Hyatt. 8 cass. (Running Time: 10 hrs. 45 mins.). 1992. 70.00 (978-1-55690-681-7(1), 92333E7) Recorded Bks.
The daughter of a fallen woman, Mattie Armstrong's life should have ended in poverty & failure. But at 17, Mattie escaped her gossiping neighbors & her loneliness & went to work for Dr. Dinsmore. There, she began to nurture a dream that would take her to the Nebraska prairies as the state's first woman doctor.

Mattimeo. unabr. ed. Brian Jacques. 10 cass. (Running Time: 13 hrs. 30 min.). (Redwall Ser.). 2003. 85.00 (978-1-4025-6513-7(5)) Recorded Bks.

Mattimeo. unabr. ed. Brian Jacques. 8 cass. (Running Time: 13 hrs. 30 mins.). (Redwall Ser.). 2004. 29.99 (978-1-4025-0522-5(1), 00864) Recorded Bks.

Mature Church. Kelley Varner. 1 cass. 25.00 Destiny Image Pubs.

Mature, Glorious Church. Kelley Varner. 4 cass. 1992. 25.00 (978-0-938612-83-4(2)) Destiny Image Pubs.

Mature Relationship: Knowing Who We Are & Who We Aren't. Leland Roloff. Read by Leland Roloff. 3 cass. (Running Time: 4 hrs.). 1992. 24.95 (978-0-7822-0404-9(X), 495) C G Jung IL.
Part of the set The Questions & Meanings of Intimate Relationship (catalog No. INTIMATE).

Maturing of a Secret: Ideas on How to Turn the Shame & Secrecy of Sexual Abuse into a Successful Process for Coping With Daily Life. Dennis E. Williams & Norma R. Atwood. 2002. audio compact disk 29.95 (978-0-9722905-0-0(8)) Atwill Pubns.
Self-help workbook format with poetry and reflective scenic photography to help elicit feelings. Can be printed to use the journal lines that are supplied on each page. Has 25 relevant questions that will help incest survivors process their life event.

Maturity & Twenty-Four Hours. 1 cass. (Recovery Is Forever Ser.). 1981. 8.95 (1533G) Hazelden.

Maturity is the Grand Illusion. Instructed by Manly P. Hall. 8.95 (978-0-89314-179-0(8), C851124) Philos Res.

Maud see Brian Patten Reading His Poetry

Maui Beaches. Kirsten Whatley. 2004. audio compact disk 4.95 (978-1-57306-174-2(3)) Bess Pr.

Maui Millionaires: Discover the Secrets Behind the World's Most Exclusive Wealth Retreat & Become Financially Free. unabr. ed. Diane Kennedy & David Finkel. Read by Ellen Archer. (Running Time: 7 hrs. 0 mins. 0 sec.). (ENG.). 2001. audio compact disk 59.99 (978-1-4001-3341-3(6)) Pub: Tantor Media. Dist(s): IngramPubServ

Maui Millionaires: Discover the Secrets Behind the World's Most Exclusive Wealth Retreat & Become Financially Free. unabr. ed. Diane Kennedy & David Finkel. Read by Alan Sklar. (Running Time: 7 hrs. 0 mins. 0 sec.). (ENG.). 2001. audio compact disk 19.99 (978-1-4001-5341-1(7)) Pub: Tantor Media. Dist(s): IngramPubServ

Maui Millionaires: Discover the Secrets Behind the World's Most Exclusive Wealth Retreat & Become Financially Free. unabr. ed. Diane Kennedy & David Finkel. Read by Ellen Archer. (Running Time: 7 hrs. 0 mins. 0 sec.). (ENG.). 2007. audio compact disk 29.99 (978-1-4001-0341-6(X)) Pub: Tantor Media. Dist(s): IngramPubServ

Maum Chrish' Chaa'stun, a Gullah Story. Virginia Mixson Geraty. 1 cass. (Running Time: 30 min.). (978-0-9652170-0-2(0)) Cabb Row Co.

Maundy Thursday. Monks of Solesmes Staff. 1 CD. (Running Time: 1 hr. 30 min.). 1990. audio compact disk 16.95 (978-1-55725-120-6(7), 930-072) Paraclete MA.

Maupassant's Best Known Stories. abr. ed. Guy de Maupassant. Narrated by Charlotte Harrison & Mary McDonald-Lewis. 2 cass. (Running Time: 1 hr. 38 min.). Incl. Babette. (860); In the Moonlight. (860); Necklace. (860); Passion. (860); Piece of String. (860); Wedding Night. (860); 12.95 (978-0-89926-165-2(5), 860) Audio Bk.

Maureen Freely. unabr. ed. Read by Maureen Freely. 1 cass. (Running Time: 29 min.). 1985. 10.00 New Letters.
Readings from the first chapter of Maureen Freely's novel, "The Life of The Party", about a group of expatriots in Turkey.

Maurer Power: Discover the Secret to Get Lean, Strong & Energized, George P. Maurer. Perf. by Martah Rebecca. 4 CD. (Running Time: 3 hr. 0 min.). 1998. audio compact disk 59.95 (978-1-891542-00-8(1)) Maurer Power.

Maurice. unabr. collector's ed. E. M. Forster. Read by David Case. 8 cass. (Running Time: 8 hrs.). 1995. 48.00 (978-0-7366-2992-8(0), 3681) Books on Tape.
A conventional young English businessman comes to grips with his sexuality. Revealing & intelligent.

Maurice Sendak. Interview with Maurice Sendak. 1 cass. (Running Time: 45 min.). 13.95 (L067) TFR.
The artist-writer of many prize-winning children's books talks about his works, particularly "In the Night Kitchen".

Maurice Sendak. abr. ed. Maurice Sendak. 4 cass. Incl. Higglety Pigglety Pop! Or There Must Be More to Life. (J). (SBC 124); Kenny's Window. (J). (SBC 124); Really Rosie. (J). (SBC 124); Where the Wild Things Are & Other Stories. Maurice Sendak. (J). (SBC 124); (J). 1985. 29.95 incl. program bklet. (978-0-89845-029-3(2), SBC 124) HarperCollins Pubs.

Maurice Sendak Audio Collection. abr. ed. Maurice Sendak. Illus. by Tammy Grimes. Music by Carole King. 4 cass. (Running Time: 3 hrs.). (Stand Alone Ser.). (J). (ps-1). 1992. 29.95 (978-1-55994-674-2(1), 393506) HarperCollins Pubs.

Mauritius Command. Patrick O'Brian. Narrated by Simon Vance. (Running Time: 10 hrs. 30 mins.). (Aubrey-Maturin Ser.). 2004. 30.95 (978-1-59912-692-0(3)) Iofy Corp.

Mauritius Command. Patrick O'Brian. Narrated by Patrick Tull. 12 CDs. (Running Time: 13.75 hrs.). (Aubrey-Maturin Ser.). audio compact disk 44.95 (978-1-4025-2833-0(7)) Recorded Bks.

Mauritius Command. Patrick O'Brian. Narrated by Patrick Tull. 12 CDs. (Running Time: 13 hrs. 45 mins.). (Aubrey-Maturin Ser.: Vol. 4). audio compact disk 116.00 (978-0-7887-9876-4(6)) Recorded Bks.

Mauritius Command. Patrick O'Brian. Read by Patrick Tull. 8 Cass. (Running Time: 13.75 Hrs.). (Aubrey-Maturin Ser.). 34.95 (978-1-4025-3709-7(3)) Recorded Bks.

Mauritius Command. Patrick O'Brian & Simon Vance. 9 CDs. (Running Time: 10 hrs. 30 mins.). (Aubrey-Maturin Ser.). 2002. audio compact disk 72.00 (978-0-7861-8385-2(3), 3340) Blckstn Audio.

Mauritius Command. unabr. ed. Patrick O'Brian. Read by Simon Vance. 8 cass. (Running Time: 10 hrs. 30 mins.). (Aubrey-Maturin Ser.). 2000. 56.95 (978-0-7861-2828-0(3), 3340) Blckstn Audio.

Mauritius Command. unabr. ed. Patrick O'Brian. Read by Simon Vance. 9 pieces. (Running Time: 13 hrs.). (Aubrey-Maturin Ser.). 2004. reel tape 39.95 (978-0-7861-2816-7(X)); audio compact disk 49.95 (978-0-7861-8449-1(3)) Blckstn Audio.
Captain Jack Aubrey is ashore on half pay without a command, until Stephen Maturin arrives with secret orders for Aubrey to take a frigate to the Cape of Good Hope under a commodore's pennant, there to mount an expedition against the French-held islands of Mauritius and La Reunion. But the difficulties of carrying out his orders are compounded by two of his own captains-Lord Clonfert, a pleasure-seeking dilettante, and Captain Corbett, whose severity pushes his crew to the verge of mutiny.

Mauritius Command. unabr. ed. Patrick O'Brian. Read by Simon Vance. (Running Time: 10 hrs. 30 mins.). (Aubrey-Maturin Ser.). 2004. audio compact disk 24.95 (978-0-7861-8459-0(0), 3340) Blckstn Audio.

Mauritius Command. unabr. ed. Patrick O'Brian. Read by Richard Brown. 9 cass. (Running Time: 13 hrs. 30 min.). (Aubrey-Maturin Ser.). 1992. 72.00 (978-0-7366-2248-6(9), 3037) Books on Tape.
Maturin brings secret orders for Aubrey to sail to the Cape of Good Hope to mount an expedition against French-held islands.

Mauritius Command. unabr. ed. Patrick O'Brian. Narrated by Patrick Tull. 10 cass. (Running Time: 13 hrs. 45 mins.). (Aubrey-Maturin Ser.: No. 4). 1993. 85.00 (978-1-55690-804-0(0), 93113E7) Recorded Bks.
Aubrey escapes the burdens of domesticity when he is appointed to the post of Admiral for an expedition to the coast of Madagascar where French frigates are threatening one of England's valued trade routes.

Mauritius Command, Vol. 3. unabr. ed. Patrick O'Brian. Read by Simon Vance. (Running Time: 13 hrs.). (Aubrey-Maturin Ser.). 2004. audio compact disk 24.95 (978-0-7861-8562-7(7), 3289) Blckstn Audio.

Mauritius Command: Book. unabr. ed. Patrick O'Brian. Read by Simon Vance. (YA). 2007. 64.99 (978-1-59895-863-8(1)) Find a World.

Maury Wills: Base Running. Read by Maury Wills. 1 cass. 9.95 (978-0-89811-067-8(X), 7118) Lets Talk Assocs.
Maury Wills talks about the people & events which influenced his career & his own approach to his speciality.

Maury Wills: Base Stealing. Read by Maury Wills. 1 cass. 9.95 (978-0-89811-089-0(0), 7140) Lets Talk Assocs.

Maushop Tales. Medicine Story. 1 cass. (Running Time: 1 hr.). 6.00 Story Stone.
More Wampanoag creation tales of Maushop.

Mausoleum: A Ben Abbott Mystery. unabr. ed. Justin Scott. Read by Joe Barrett. (Running Time: 28800 sec.). 2008. 54.95 (978-1-4332-1309-0(5)); audio compact disk & audio compact disk 29.95 (978-1-4332-1311-3(7)); audio compact disk & audio compact disk 60.00 (978-1-4332-1310-6(9)) Blckstn Audio.

Mauve Gloves & Madmen, Clutter & Vine. unabr. collector's ed. Tom Wolfe. Read by Michael Prichard. 5 cass. (Running Time: 7 hrs. 30 min.). 1991. 40.00 (978-0-7366-2067-3(2), 2875) Books on Tape.
If generals prepare for the last war, then politicians run on yesterday's issues. Never was this truer than in the 1970s. Our elected elite couldn't get a handle on the times. But Tom Wolfe could. In fact he gave the era its name - "The Me Decade." And like an artist briskly painting the passing scene, he captured it in stories & essays. This collection includes the best - "Pornoviolence," "Funky Chic," "The Man Who Always Peaked Too Soon," plus the story for which this collection is named.

Maverick Selling Method. Brian Burns. 2009. audio compact disk 18.95 (978-1-60031-068-3(0)) Infinity PubPA.

***Mavericks at Work.** abr. ed. William C. Taylor. Read by Barrett Whitener. (ENG.). 2006. (978-0-06-122999-2(7), Harper Audio); (978-0-06-123000-4(6), Harper Audio) HarperCollins Pubs.

Mavericks at Work. abr. ed. William C. Taylor. Read by Barrett Whitener. (Running Time: 21600 sec.). 2007. audio compact disk 14.95 (978-0-06-137417-3(2), Harper Audio) HarperCollins Pubs.

Mavreen Part 3: Harvest Moon. unabr. ed. Claire Lorrimer. Read by Patricia Gallimore. 6 cass. 1998. 69.95 (978-1-85903-072-1(6)) Pub: Magna Story GBR. Dist(s): Ulverscroft US

Max & Maddy & the Chocolate Money Mystery. unabr. ed. Alexander McCall Smith. 1 cass. (Running Time: 1 hr.). (J). 2007. 15.95 (978-1-4281-8153-3(9)); 15.75 (978-1-4281-8152-6(0)); audio compact disk 15.75 (978-1-4281-8157-1(1)) Recorded Bks.

Max Brand's Best Western Stories. unabr. ed. Short Stories. Max Brand. Read by Jack Clancy. Ed. by William F. Nolan. 6 cass. (Running Time: 6 hrs.). 1995. 54.95 (CAB 254) AudioGO.
Chosen by leading Western authority, William F. Nolan, these six stories are true classics of the American West. The collection includes: "Wine on the Desert," "MacDonald's Dream," "Dust Across the Range," "Virginia Creeper," "Partners" & "The Bells of San Carlos.".

Max Brod Discusses Franz Kafka. unabr. ed. 1 cass. (Running Time: 55 mins.). (GER.). 14.95 (C23142) J Norton Pubs.

Max Ferguson: Fifty Years & a Day. 1 CD. (Running Time: 1 hr.). 2005. audio compact disk 15.95 (978-0-660-18901-7(1)) Canadian Broadcasting CAN.

Max Goes to School. Adria F. Klein. Illus. by Mernie Gallagher-Cole. (Read-It! Readers: Purple Level Ser.). (ENG & SPA.). (J). (ps-4). 2007. audio compact disk 30.65 (978-1-4048-5353-9(7)) CapstoneDig.

Max Goes to School/Max Va a la Escuela. abr. ed. Adria F. Klein. Illus. by Mernie Gallagher-Cole. (Read-It! Readers: the Life of Max Purple Level Ser.). (J). (gr. k). 2008. audio compact disk 9.27 (978-1-4048-4457-5(0)) CapstoneDig.

Max Goes to the Barber. Adria F. Klein. Illus. by Mernie Gallagher-Cole. (Read-It! Readers: Purple Level Ser.). (ENG & SPA.). (J). (ps-4). 2007. audio compact disk 30.65 (978-1-4048-5354-6(5)) CapstoneDig.

Max Goes to the Barber/Max Va a la Peluqueria. abr. ed. Adria F. Klein. Illus. by Mernie Gallagher-Cole. (Read-It! Readers: the Life of Max Audio Ser.). (J). (gr. k). 2008. audio compact disk 9.27 (978-1-4048-4461-2(9)) CapstoneDig.

Max Goes to the Dentist. Adria F. Klein. Illus. by Mernie Gallagher-Cole. (Read-It! Readers: Purple Level Ser.). (ENG & SPA.). (J). (ps-4). 2007. audio compact disk 30.65 (978-1-4048-5355-3(3)) CapstoneDig.

Max Goes to the Dentist/Max Va Al Dentista. abr. ed. Adria F. Klein. Illus. by Mernie Gallagher-Cole. (Read-It! Readers: the Life of Max Audio Ser.). (J). (gr. k). 2008. audio compact disk 9.27 (978-1-4048-4463-6(5)) CapstoneDig.

Max Goes to the Doctor. Adria F. Klein. Illus. by Mernie Gallagher-Cole. (Read-It! Readers: Purple Level Ser.). (ENG & SPA.). (J). (ps-3). 2007. audio compact disk 30.65 (978-1-4048-5356-0(1)) CapstoneDig.

Max Goes to the Doctor/Max Va Al Doctor. abr. ed. Adria F. Klein. Illus. by Mernie Gallagher-Cole. (Read-It! Readers: the Life of Max Audio Ser.). (J). (gr. k). 2008. audio compact disk 9.27 (978-1-4048-4492-6(9)) CapstoneDig.

Max Goes to the Library. Adria F. Klein. Illus. by Mernie Gallagher-Cole. (Read-It! Readers: Purple Level Ser.). (ENG.). (J). (ps-4). 2007. audio compact disk 30.65 (978-1-4048-5352-2(9)) CapstoneDig.

Max Goes to the Library/Max Va a la Biblioteca. Adria F. Klein. Illus. by Mernie Gallagher-Cole. (Picture Window Books Interactive Ser.). (ENG & SPA.). (J). 2007. audio compact disk 30.65 (978-1-4048-5370-6(7)) CapstoneDig.

Max Goes to the Zoo. Adria F. Klein. Illus. by Mernie Gallagher-Cole. (Read-It! Readers: Purple Level Ser.). (ENG & SPA.). (J). (ps-3). 2007. audio compact disk 30.65 (978-1-4048-5357-7(X)) CapstoneDig.

Max Goes to the Zoo/Max Va Al Zoologico. Adria F. Klein. Illus. by Mernie Gallagher-Cole. (Read-It! Readers: Purple Level Ser.). (J). (gr. k). 2008. audio compact disk 9.27 (978-1-4048-4493-3(7)) CapstoneDig.

Max Hunter: Ozark Songs & Ballads. 1 cass. 9.98 (C-11) Folk-Legacy.
Ballads & songs from an Ozark singer & collector.

Max Perkins: Editor of Genius. unabr. ed. A. Scott Berg. Read by Walter Zimmerman. 14 cass. (Running Time: 21 hrs.). 112.00 (978-0-7366-1897-7(X), 2724) Books on Tape.
F. Scott Fitzgerald, Ernest Hemingway, Thomas Wolfe, Ring Lardner, Erskine Caldwell. They all knew Max Perkins. They worked with him, fought with him, challenged him, worshipped him. He was their editor & he helped make them great.

Max Trescott's G1000 Glass Cockpit Handbook. Max Trescott, 8th. (YA). 2006. per. 34.95 (978-0-9777030-0-5(2)) Glass Cockpit.

Max und Mortiz: A Boys Story. Created by Wilhelm Busch. 2007. 25.00 (978-0-9602456-5-9(0)) Colman Pubs.

Maximes. Francois de La Rochefoucauld. Read by M. Petit. 1 cass. (FRE.). 1991. 21.95 (1416-VSL) Olivia & Hill.
The maxims of this 17th-century moralist are known for their merciless analysis of human conduct & for their clear & elegant style.

Maximilian Affair in Mexico. Kenneth Bruce. 1 cass. (Running Time: 1 hr.). Dramatization. (Excursions in History Ser.). 12.50 Alpha Tape.

Maximize the Moment! How to Have More Fun & Happiness in Life. Ray DiGiuseppe. 1 cass. (Running Time: 59 min.). 9.95 (C041) A Ellis Institute.
"Grab the goodies & damn the consequences" is not the REBT approach to life. Learn how to be a responsible hedonist, using today's actions, thoughts & feelings to make tomorrow's pleasures long-lasting & satisfying.

Maximize the Moment! How to Have More Fun & Happiness in Life. Ray DiGiuseppe. 1 cass. (Running Time: 59 min.). 9.95 (C041) Inst Rational-Emotive.
Learn how to be a responsible hedonist, using today's actions, thoughts & feelings to make tomorrow's pleasures long-lasting & satisfying.

Maximize the Moment V1 Audio S. T. D. Jakes. 2004. 19.99 (978-1-57855-562-8(0)) T D Jakes.

Maximize the Moment V2 Audio S. T. D. Jakes. 2004. 19.99 (978-1-57855-555-0(8)) T D Jakes.

Maximize Your Potential. 8 cass. (Running Time: 8 hrs.). 69.95 (MP-1) Psych Res Inst.
This success set builds upon individual effectiveness, enthusiasm & direction toward leadership abilities. Winners imagine what they wish to become & transform it into fact.

Maximized Sex. Ed Young. 1994. 4.95 (978-0-7417-2010-8(8), 1010) Win Walk.

Maximizing Customer Satisfaction. Read by Arlene Farber Sirkin. Ed. by Carl Birkmeyer. 1 cass. (Running Time: 45 min.). 1994. 12.00 (978-1-56641-015-1(0), 10150M) Library Video.
Prominent lecturer & consultant, Arlene Farber Sirkin, gives concrete examples of how to better serve customers. Her topics include the benefits of having satisfied customers, how to keep the customers happy when you don't have what they want & knowing what quality service really means. If you already have a customer base, she reveals the essentials of keeping them.

Maximizing Networking Relationships. Speeches. Michael J. Hughes. 1 CD. (Running Time: 26 mins). 2005. audio compact disk 18.47 (978-1-895186-36-9(6)) Multi-Media ON CAN.
In the last installment from the Four Cornerstones of Networking Success, author Michael J. Hughes, known as Canada?s Networking Guru, looks at how to make the most out of your existing networking relationships to find work, to locate the best resources for your team, or to contact the right subject matter experts to help solve a problem. If you are involved in sales, or are a project management consultant, you will also find tremendous value in this recording, as the author shares with you his secrets on how to use networking to double repeat and referral business. This recording will present you with a proven strategy to develop and leverage centers of influence to create advocates and on-going referral sources. Guaranteed.

Maximizing the Arthritis Cure. Jason Theodosakis. Read by Brenda D. Adderly. 2 cass. (Running Time: 4 hrs.). 1999. 18.00 (978-0-694-51954-5(5), CPN2754, Harper Audio) HarperCollins Pubs.

Maximizing the Learning of Your Third Graders, unabr. ed. Pamela Haack. Read by Pamela Haack. 6 cass. (Running Time: 4 hr. 13 min.). 1998. 75.00 (978-1-886397-15-6(5)) Bureau of Educ.

Maximizing Your Leadership Potential. Frank Damazio. 8 cass. (Running Time: 12 hrs.). 2000. (978-1-886849-41-9(2)) CityChristian.

Maximizing Your Money Freeway Guide. Peter Bielagus. Contrib. by Peter Bielagus. (Freeway Guides: Practical Audio for People on the Go Ser.). (ENG.). 2009. 34.99 (978-1-60812-506-7(8)) Find a World.

Maximizing Your Potential. Myles Munroe. 12 cass. 1992. 58.00 (978-1-56043-907-3(6)) Destiny Image Pubs.

Maximizing Your Potential: How to Boost Your IQ - How to Stop Worrying & Start Living. unabr. ed. Shmuel Irons. Read by Shmuel Irons. 2 cass. (Running Time: 3 hrs.). 19.95 (978-1-889648-13-2(2)) Jwish Her Fdtn.
Applies the timeless truths found in the Bible & Talmud to gain knowledge, peace of mind & the practical tools to live a happier life.

Maximizing Your Vision Potential. Frank Damazio. 8 cass. (Running Time: 12 hrs.). 2000. (978-1-886849-44-0(7)) CityChristian.

Maximizing Your Warfare Potential. Frank Damazio. 8 cass. (Running Time: 12 hrs.). 2000. (978-1-886849-46-4(3)) CityChristian.

Maxims, Morals, & Metaphors: A Primer on Venture Capital. Scott Chou. Read by David Brower. 2008. audio compact disk 19.95 (978-1-4276-3385-9(1)) AardGP.

Maxims of Life & Business: With Selected Prayers. John Wanamaker. Read by Charlie Tremendous Jones. (Life-Changing Classics Ser.). (ENG.). 2007. audio compact disk 19.95 (978-1-933715-34-6(0)) Executive Bks.

Maximum Achievement. Brian Tracy. 2004. 11.95 (978-0-7435-4104-6(9)) Pub: S&S Audio. Dist(s): S and S Inc

Maximum Alanis Morissette: The Unauthorised Biography of Alanis Morissette. Ben Graham. (Maximum Ser.). (ENG., 2003. audio compact disk 14.95 (978-1-84240-187-3(4)) Pub: Chrome Dreams GBR. Dist(s): IPG Chicago

Maximum Bob. unabr. ed. Elmore Leonard. Read by Alexander Adams. 8 cass. (Running Time: 8 hrs.). 1992. 64.00 (978-0-7366-2256-1(X), 3045) Books on Tape.
Someone puts a ten-foot alligator in the backyard of Bob Gibbs, the redneck judge known as "Maximum Bob." Someone shoots into the judge's house. It figures that someone's out to get Maximum Bob. Kathy Baker, a nifty young probation officer, gets herself in the middle.

Maximum Coldplay: The Unauthorised Biography of Coldplay. Michael Sumsion. (Maximum Ser.). (ENG., 2003. audio compact disk 14.95 (978-1-84240-204-7(8)) Pub: Chrome Dreams GBR. Dist(s): IPG Chicago

Maximum Confidence: Ten Secrets of Extreme Self-Esteem. unabr. ed. Jack L. Canfield. Read by Jack L. Canfield. 5 CDs. (Running Time: 5 hrs. 0 mins. 0 sec.). (ENG.). 2007. audio compact disk 29.95 (978-0-7435-7001-5(4), Nightgale) Pub: S&S Audio. Dist(s): S and S Inc

Maximum Doors: The Unauthorized Biography of the Doors. Alan Clayson. (Maximum Ser.). (ENG.). 2002. audio compact disk 14.95 (978-1-84240-185-9(8)) Pub: Chrome Dreams GBR. Dist(s): IPG Chicago

Maximum Freddie Mercury. Ben Graham. As told by Nancy McClean. 1 CD. (Running Time: 60 mins). (Maximum Ser.). 2005. audio compact disk (978-1-84240-323-5(0)) Chrome Dreams GBR.
More than 15 years since his untimely death, Freddie Mercury remains amongstthe best-loved performer of the rock era. Lead singer and driving forcebehind Queen's musical and visual style, Freddie is sadly missed but notforgotten. Gifted with one of most distinctive voices ever, he is also agreat inspiration and influence to many current bands.'Maximum Freddie Mercury' is the complete and unauthorised biography of thistruly legendary, flamboyant and charismatic front man who captured thehearts of millions and retains a fanatical following to this day. This CD isan absolute must for all Freddie fans everywhere.

Maximum Goo Goo Dolls: The Unauthorized Biography of the Goo Goo Dolls. Andrea Thorn. (Maximum Ser.). (ENG.). 2001. audio compact disk 14.95 (978-1-84240-045-6(2)) Pub: Chrome Dreams GBR. Dist(s): IPG Chicago

Maximum Gwen Stefani. Michael Sumsion. 1 CD. (Maximum Ser.). 2005. audio compact disk (978-1-84240-316-7(8)) Chrome Dreams GBR.
One of contemporary pop's most dynamic forces, Gwen Stefani is a genuinemaverick talent responsible for producing some of the finest work of themodern era. She is a living and breathing testament to perseverance,enthusiasm and swaggering style and a natural high-octane bundle of energy.Her recent solo outing has now eclipsed the recognition she received as amember of 90's Pop / Ska outfit No Doubt, and a long career in the spotlightnow seems a certainty.Maximum Gwen Stefani charts the rise and rise of Gwen. It tells the storyfrom her unusual childhood to fronting the record breaking No Doubt and onto her going successfully solo on her own merit. With a huge worldwide fanbase growing bigger daily, this unique title is sure to be a big hit amongstthe dedicated many.

Maximum Impact Strategies for Life Fitness. Frederick Elias. 2005. audio compact disk 39.95 (978-1-881241-02-7(5)) ODC Pub.

Maximum Janet Jackson: The Unauthorised Biography of Janet Jackson. Sally Wilford. (Maximum Ser.). (ENG.). 2001. audio compact disk 14.95 (978-1-84240-109-5(2)) Pub: Chrome Dreams GBR. Dist(s): IPG Chicago

Maximum Jennifer Lopez: The Unauthorized Biography of Jennifer Lopez. William Drysdale-Wood. 1 CD. (Running Time: 1 hr.). (Maximum Ser.). (ENG.). 2001. audio compact disk 14.95 (978-1-84240-032-6(0)) Pub: Chrome Dreams GBR. Dist(s): IPG Chicago
Jennifer Lopez has risen from the backstreets of the Bronx to the golden hills of Hollywood. Thoughout her career she has combined beauty and talent to become the highest-paid Latino actress of all time and a million-dollar pop performer.This audio-biog includes exclusive interview clips and comments from Jennifer plus a free poster.

Maximum Kurt Cobain: The Unauthorised Biography of Kurt Cobain. Ben Graham. (Maximum Ser.). (ENG., 2003. audio compact disk 14.95 (978-1-84240-216-0(1)) Pub: Chrome Dreams GBR. Dist(s): IPG Chicago

Maximum leadership the world's leading ceos share their five strategies for Succ: The World's Leading CEOs Share Their Five Strategies for Success. Charles M. Farkas. 2004. 10.95 (978-0-7435-4103-9(0)) Pub: S&S Audio. Dist(s): S and S Inc

Maximum Lennon: The Unauthorised Biography of John Lennon. abr. ed. Sally Wilford & Alan Clayson. (Maximum Ser.). (ENG.). 2001. audio compact disk 14.95 (978-1-84240-108-8(4)) Pub: Chrome Dreams GBR. Dist(s): IPG Chicago

Maximum Linkin Park: The Unauthorized Biography of Linkin Park. Ben Graham. (Maximum Ser.). (ENG., 2001. audio compact disk 14.95 (978-1-84240-151-4(3)) Pub: Chrome Dreams GBR. Dist(s): IPG Chicago

Maximum Matchbox 20: The Unauthorised Biography of Matchbox 20. Tim Sayer & Kath Sayer. (Maximum Ser.). (ENG.). 2001. audio compact disk 14.95 (978-1-84240-100-2(9)) Pub: Chrome Dreams GBR. Dist(s): IPG Chicago

Maximum Mcfly. Micheal Sumsion. As told by Sian Jones. 1 CD. (Running Time: 60 Minutes). (Maximum Ser.). 2005. audio compact disk (978-1-84240-321-1(4)) Chrome Dreams GBR.
With the recent news that Busted are all but finished, the doors are wide open for their natural successors. McFly, please take a bow! Having stormed the UK charts over the past 12 months with 3 no.1 singles - including the current hit All About You / You've Got A Friend that kept even Elvis off the top spot - and their debut album Room On The Third Floor entering the album chart at the top, the future looks increasingly bright for these cheeky young chappies, already poised top take the mantle of the country's foremost pop act.Now, for the first time, 'Maximum McFly' tells the complete and unauthorised story of how these showbiz giants became so successful in the fickle world of Pop. An absolute must for every crazed fan.

Maximum Monster Magnet: The Unauthorised Biography of Monster Magnet. Michael Sumsion. (Maximum Ser.). (ENG.). 2001. audio compact disk 14.95 (978-1-84240-121-7(1)) Pub: Chrome Dreams GBR. Dist(s): IPG Chicago

Maximum Motivation. Eldon Taylor. Read by Eldon Taylor. Ed. by Leslie Brice. 1 cass. (Running Time: 1 hr.). 1992. 19.95 (978-1-56705-013-4(1)) Gateways Inst.
Self improvement.

Maximum Nelly: The Unauthorised Biography of Nelly. Andy Brewer. (Maximum Ser.). (ENG., 2003. audio compact disk 14.95 (978-1-84240-215-3(3)) Pub: Chrome Dreams GBR. Dist(s): IPG Chicago

Maximum New Order. Ben Graham. As told by Nancy McClean. 1 CD. (Maximum Ser.). 2005. audio compact disk (978-1-84240-320-4(6)) Chrome Dreams GBR.
The 1980 suicide of Ian Curtis and the subsequent demise of Joy Division wasat the time rightfully seen as a tragedy,. But as one of the most importantgroups of the era split another emerged and tragedy led to triumph as thethree remaining members formed New Order and became one of the mostinfluential and acclaimed bands of the 1980's. As the pioneers of BritishElectronic music, mixing dance and rock with disco beats, their sound andstyle is so unique that they remain at the top of their game four decadesinto their career. Now with the release of their eighth album Waiting ForThe Siren's To Call, they continue to stimulate fans everywhere and are aninspiration to many of today's most promising new artists.'Maximum New Order' charts the success of their outstanding career spanningfour decades, from the bedsits of Manchester to stadiums worldwide; fromtragedy to triumph this CD reveals all. An essential purchase for all NewOrder fans old and new!.

Maximum Nightwish. Micheal Sumsion. As told by Sian Jones. 1 CD. (Running Time: 60 min). (Maximum Ser.). 2005. audio compact disk (978-1-84240-326-6(5)) Chrome Dreams GBR.
Having achieved enormous success in their native Finland over the past 8years, Nightwish are now virtually household names right across Europe aswell. And with a massive fan base already established and new converts beingadded daily, the Goth / Metal crossover sounds they create look sure to beone of 2005s most interesting and popular genres, ensuring further successacross the world. Hot on the heels of contemporaries such as Evanescence andH.I.M., global domination beckons for this strange but exciting collective.Maximum Nightwish is the complete and unauthorised biography, charting thephenomenal success of this extraordinary band. This CD is essentiallistening for all Nightwish fans everywhere!.

Maximum Nirvana: The Unauthorised Biography of Nirvana. Ben Graham. (Maximum Ser.). (ENG., 2003. audio compact disk 14.95 (978-1-84240-176-7(9)) Pub: Chrome Dreams GBR. Dist(s): IPG Chicago

Maximum Pantera: The Unauthorized Biography of Pantera. Scott Gigney. (Maximum Ser.). (ENG.). 2001. audio compact disk 14.95 (978-1-84240-081-4(9)) Pub: Chrome Dreams GBR. Dist(s): IPG Chicago

Maximum Phish: The Unauthorised Biography of Phish. Martin Harper. (Maximum Ser.). (ENG.). 2001. audio compact disk 14.95 (978-1-84240-099-9(1)) Pub: Chrome Dreams GBR. Dist(s): IPG Chicago

Maximum Pink: The Unauthorised Biography of Pink. Ben Graham. (Maximum Ser.). (ENG., 2003. audio compact disk 14.95 (978-1-84240-212-2(9)) Pub: Chrome Dreams GBR. Dist(s): IPG Chicago

Maximum Pixies. Tim Footman. As told by Sian Jones. 1. (Running Time: 60 mins). (Maximum Ser.). 2005. audio compact disk (978-1-84240-312-9(5)) Chrome Dreams GBR.
The Pixies were pretty unlikely rockers; misfits in more ways than many,they provided a deliriously off-kilter perspective to the music scene in thelate 1980s and early 1990s. Arguably the most influential band of theirgeneration; they have become an inspiration to many since. Having split in1992, everybody thought that that was the end. But last year, after a breakof over ten years they came back to rave reviews and more fans than ever!'Maximum Pixies' tells the complete and unauthorised story of thisphenomenal group. Revealing where it all began, their journey to the top,break-up, successful solo careers, reunification and then their return tothe top once again. Telling the story of how it really happened, this is anessential CD for any Pixies fan.

Maximum Puff Daddy: The Unauthorised Biography of Puff Daddy. Andy Brewer. (Maximum Ser.). (ENG., 2003. audio compact disk 14.95 (978-1-84240-211-5(0)) Pub: Chrome Dreams GBR. Dist(s): IPG Chicago

Maximum Queen: The Unauthorised Biography of Queen. Keith Rodway. (Maximum Ser.). (ENG., 2003. audio compact disk 14.95 (978-1-84240-213-9(7)) Pub: Chrome Dreams GBR. Dist(s): IPG Chicago

Maximum Radiohead: The Unauthorised Biography of Radiohead. Harry Drysdale-Wood. (Maximum Ser.). (ENG.). 2001. audio compact disk 14.95 (978-1-84240-093-7(2)) Pub: Chrome Dreams GBR. Dist(s): IPG Chicago

Maximum Ride. abr. ed. James Patterson. Read by Valentina de Angelis. (Running Time: 5 hrs.). (Maximum Ride Ser.: No. 3). (J). (gr. 5-17). 2007. 9.98 (978-1-59483-909-2(3)) Pub: Hachet Audio. Dist(s): HachBkGrp

Maximum Santana: The Unauthorised Biography of Santana. Michael Sumsion. (Maximum Ser.). (ENG.). 2001. audio compact disk 14.95 (978-1-84240-107-1(6)) Pub: Chrome Dreams GBR. Dist(s): IPG Chicago

Maximum Security. unabr. ed. Rose Connors. 5 cass. (Running Time: 6 hrs. 30 mins.). 2004. 44.95 (978-0-7861-2746-7(5), 3293); audio compact disk 56.00 (978-0-7861-8536-8(8), 3293) Blckstn Audio.

Maximum Security. unabr. ed. Rose Connors. Read by Bernadette Dunne. 5 cass. (Running Time: 8 hrs. 30 mins.). 2005. reel tape 29.95 (978-0-7861-2774-0(0), E3293); audio compact disk 24.95 (978-0-7861-8552-8(X), 3293); audio compact disk 32.95 (978-0-7861-8591-7(0), ZE3293) Blckstn Audio.

Maximum Snoop Dogg. Michael Sumsion. As told by Nancy McClean. 1. (Running Time: 60 mins). (Maximum Ser.). 2005. audio compact disk (978-1-84240-306-8(0)) Chrome Dreams GBR.
Snoop Dogg, notorious for creating G-Funk and putting the West Coast firmlyon the map, adding an izzle to everything, and not just being gansta butalso breaking through as an actor in mainstream films. Introduced to themasses by Dr Dre, Snoop came into his own with the release of hissensational debut album Doggystyle and has had many successful hitsworldwide since then. More than ten years later, he continues to win overnew fans with every release and is truly one of the most significant Rapartists of our time.'Maximum Snoop Dogg' tells the complete and unauthorised story of thisphenomenal talent. Revealing where it all began, his journey to the top anddetails what was behind his inspiration to become one of the mostinfluential and successful Hip-Hop artists of our time. An essential CD forany Snoop Dogg fan.

Maximum Stone Age: The Unauthorised Biography of Queens of the Stone Age. Michael Sumsion. (Maximum Ser.). (ENG., 2001. audio compact disk 14.95 (978-1-84240-129-3(7)) Pub: Chrome Dreams GBR. Dist(s): IPG Chicago

Maximum White Stripes: The Unauthorised Biography of the White Stripes. Ben Graham. (Maximum Ser.). (ENG., 2003. audio compact disk 14.95 (978-1-84240-209-2(9)) Pub: Chrome Dreams GBR. Dist(s): IPG Chicago

Maximum Who: The Unauthorised Biography of the Who. Keith Rodway. (Maximum Ser.). (ENG., 2003. audio compact disk 14.95 (978-1-84240-202-3(1)) Pub: Chrome Dreams GBR. Dist(s): IPG Chicago

Maxine Hong Kingston. Interview. Interview with Maxine Hong Kingston. 1 cass. 1986. 13.95 (978-1-55644-162-2(2), 6082) Am Audio Prose.

Maxine Hong Kingston Interview. 20.97 (978-0-13-090309-9(4)) P-H.

Maxine Kumin, No. 11. unabr. ed. Maxine Kumin. Read by Maxine Kimin. 1 cass. (Running Time: 29 min.). 1987. 10.00 (122587) New Letters.
Pulitzer Prize-winning poet reads & talks about how tough it was to be a woman writer in the '50's & how her sex has developed into an asset in the literary world.

Max's Chocolate Chicken. 2004. bk. 24.95 (978-0-89719-893-6(X)); pap. bk. 18.95 (978-1-55592-439-3(5)); pap. bk. 18.95 (978-1-55592-442-3(5)); pap. bk. 38.75 (978-1-55592-441-6(7)); pap. bk. 38.75 (978-1-55592-443-0(3)); pap. bk. 32.75 (978-1-55592-264-1(3)); pap. bk. 32.75 (978-1-55592-265-8(1)); pap. bk. 14.95 (978-0-7882-0586-6(2)); pap. bk. 14.95 (978-1-55592-087-6(X)); 8.95 (978-1-56008-966-7(0)); 8.95 (978-1-56008-149-4(X)); cass. & flmstrp 30.00 (978-0-89719-629-1(5)); audio compact disk 12.95 (978-1-55592-916-9(8)) Weston Woods.

Max's Chocolate Chicken. Rosemary Wells. 1 cass. (Max & Ruby Ser.). (J). (gr. k-2). bk. 24.95 (HRA344); pap. bk. 32.75; 8.95 (RAC344) Weston Woods.

Max's Chocolate Chicken. Rosemary Wells. 1 cass. (Running Time: 15 min.). (Max & Ruby Ser.). (J). (gr. k-2). 2000. pap. bk. 12.95 Weston Woods.
Will Max or will Ruby find the most Easter eggs to win the chocolate chicken? Only the Easter Bunny knows for sure.

Max's Christmas. 2004. bk. 24.95 (978-0-89719-781-6(X)); pap. bk. 14.95 (978-0-7882-0661-0(3)); 8.95 (978-1-56008-395-5(6)); cass. & flmstrp 30.00 (978-0-89719-580-5(9)); audio compact disk 12.95 (978-1-55592-876-6(5)) Weston Woods.

Max's Christmas. Rosemary Wells. 1 cass. (Max & Ruby Ser.). (J). (gr. k-2). 12.95 (PRA322) Weston Woods.
Ruby can't get her little brother Max to go to sleep on Christmas Eve. He wants to see Santa & doesn't understand why he can't stay up.

Max's Christmas. Rosemary Wells. 1 cass. (Running Time: 15 min.). (Max & Ruby Ser.). (J). (gr. k-2). 2000. bk. 24.95 Weston Woods.

Max's Christmas. Rosemary Wells. 1 cass. (Max & Ruby Ser.). (J). (gr. k-2). 2004. pap. bk. 8.95 (978-0-89719-968-1(5), RAC322) Weston Woods.

Max's Job: Early Explorers Emergent Set A Audio CD. Benchmark Education Staff. (J). 2006. audio compact disk 10.00 (978-1-4108-7600-3(4)) Benchmark Educ.

Max's Words. Kate Banks. 1 cass. (Running Time: 10 mins.). (J). (gr. k-2). 2007. bk. 24.95 (978-0-545-04374-8(3)) Weston Woods.

Max's Words. Kate Banks. 1 CD. (Running Time: 10 mins.). (J). (gr. k-2). 2008. bk. 29.95 (978-0-545-04373-1(5)) Weston Woods.

Maxwell Perkins: Editor of Genius. unabr. ed. Comment by A. Scott Berg. 1 cass. 12.95 (ECN 183) J Norton Pubs.
Berg talks about Perkin's work which seems to encompass most of the history of 20th century American literature.

Maxwell's Chain. M. J. Trow. 2009. 69.95 (978-1-4079-0060-5(9)); audio compact disk 84.95 (978-1-4079-0061-2(7)) Pub: Soundings Ltd GBR. Dist(s): Ulverscroft US

Maxwell's Curse. unabr. ed. M. J. Trow. Read by Peter Wickham. 8 cass. (Running Time: 9 hrs.). (Peter Maxwell Mystery Ser.: No. 5). 2001. (978-1-84283-107-6(0)) ISIS Audio GBR.
Peter Maxwell is about to celebrate the millennium mathematically and historically correct version, December 2000. But when the doorbell rings, it's no new year reveller; it's the body of an old woman, who of unseasonal mildness, has been frozen to death.

Maxwell's Flame. M. J. Trow. Read by Peter Wickham. 7 cass. (Peter Maxwell Mystery Ser.: No. 2). (J). 2006. 61.95 (978-1-84559-185-4(2)) Pub: ISIS Lrg Prnt GBR. Dist(s): Ulverscroft US

Maxwell's Grave. unabr. ed. M. J. Trow. 10 cass. (Running Time: 11 hrs.). (Peter Maxwell Mystery Ser.: No. 10). (J). 2005. 84.95 (978-1-84559-102-1(X)) Pub: ISIS Lrg Prnt GBR. Dist(s): Ulverscroft US

Maxwell's House. unabr. ed. M. J. Trow. Read by Peter Wickham. 7 cass. (Running Time: 9 hrs.). (Peter Maxwell Mystery Ser.: No. 1). (J). 2006. 61.95 (978-1-84559-183-0(6)) Pub: ISIS Lrg Prnt GBR. Dist(s): Ulverscroft US

Maxwell's Inspection. M. J. Trow. 8 cass. (Running Time: 10 hrs. 30 mins.). (Peter Maxwell Mystery Ser.: No. 9). (J). 2005. 69.95 (978-1-84559-065-9(1)) Pub: ISIS Lrg Prnt GBR. Dist(s): Ulverscroft US

Maxwell's Match. M. J. Trow. Read by Peter Wickham. 9 cass. (Running Time: 11 hrs. 30 mins.). (Peter Maxwell Mystery Ser.: No. 8). (J). 2004. 76.95 (978-1-84283-605-7(6)) Pub: ISIS Lrg Prnt GBR. Dist(s): Ulverscroft US

Maxwell's Movie. M. J. Trow & M. J. Trow. (Peter Maxwell Mystery Ser.: No. 3). (J). 2007. 61.95 (978-1-84559-184-7(4)) Pub: ISIS Lrg Prnt GBR. Dist(s): Ulverscroft US

Maxwell's Reunion. M. J. Trow. Read by Peter Wickham. 7 cass. (Peter Maxwell Mystery Ser.: No. 7). (J). 2002. 61.95 (978-1-84283-208-0(5)) Pub: ISIS Lrg Prnt GBR. Dist(s): Ulverscroft US

May Bell's Daughter / the Story of Esther. Featuring Eva Whittington Self. 2006. audio compact disk 15.00 (978-0-9767407-3-5(7)) Serv Heart Pub.

May Bird & the Ever After. unabr. ed. Jodi Lynn Anderson. Read by Bernadette Dunne. 6 cass. (Running Time: 8 hrs. 52 mins.). (J). (gr. 4-7). 2005. 45.00 (978-0-307-28344-3(5), BksonTape); audio compact disk 55.00 (978-0-307-28345-0(3), BksonTape) Random Audio Pubg.

May I Bring a Friend? 2004. bk. 24.95 (978-1-56008-150-0(3)); pap. bk. 32.75 (978-1-55592-266-5(X)); pap. bk. 32.75 (978-1-55592-267-2(8)); 8.95 (978-1-56008-967-4(9)) Weston Woods.

May I Bring a Friend. 2004. cass. & flmstrp 30.00 (978-0-89719-538-6(8)) Weston Woods.

May I Bring A Friend? Beatrice Schenk De Regniers. Illus. by Beni Montresor. 1 cass., 5 bks. (Running Time: 7 min.). (J). pap. bk. 32.75 Weston Woods.
An imaginative boy graciously accepts invitations from the King & Queen.

May I Bring A Friend? Beatrice Schenk De Regniers. Illus. by Beni Montresor. 1 cass. (Running Time: 7 min.). (J). (ps-3). bk. 24.95 Weston Woods.

May I Bring a Friend? Beatrice Schenk de Rogniers. 1 cass. (Running Time: 7 min.). (J). (ps-3). 1993. 8.95 (978-1-56008-119-7(8), RAC164) Weston Woods.
From the book by Beatrice Schenk de Rogniers. An imaginative boy graciously accepts invitations from the King & Queen.

May I Bring a Friend? Beatrice Schenk De Regniers. Illus. by Beni Montresor. 1 cass. (Running Time: 7 min.). (J). (ps-3). 1993. pap. bk. 14.95 (978-1-56008-151-7(1), PRA164) Weston Woods.

May I Have This Dance? Guided Meditations. Joyce Rupp. (Running Time: 8220 sec.). 2007. audio compact disk 24.95 (978-1-59471-167-1(4)) Ave Maria Pr.

May Queen. unabr. ed. Alison Uttley. 1 cass. (Running Time: 6 min.). (J). (gr. 2-5). 1987. bk. 16.95 (978-0-8045-6578-3(3), 6578) Spoken Arts.

May Sarton. Interview. Interview with May Sarton & Kay Bonetti. 1 cass. (Running Time: 58 min.). 1982. 13.95 (978-1-55644-056-4(1), 2122) Am Audio Prose.
Sarton gives a fascinating review of her life & work & reveals great wisdom in talking about her own perfect blending of life & art.

May Sarton: Excerpts from a Life - Journals & Memoirs. abr. ed. Read by Andrea Itkin. Ed. by H. Frederick. Intro. by May Sarton. 4 cass. (Running Time: 4 hrs.). 1994. 29.95 (978-1-883332-09-9(5)) Audio Bkshelf.
This award-winning overview of May Sarton's life is introduced by the author herself. Picked as the best biographical audio production by PW, & winner of the Earphones Award by Audiofile.

May Swenson. abr. ed. Poems. May Swenson. 1 cass. Incl. Bison Crossing Near Mt. Rushmore. (SWC 1500); Bleeding. (SWC 1500); Blue Bottle. (SWC 1500); Cause & Effect. (SWC 1500); DNA Molecule. (SWC 1500); Fountains of Aix. (SWC 1500); How Everything Happens (Based on a Study of the Wave) (SWC 1500); In Navajoland. (SWC 1500); Key to Everything. (SWC 1500); Lightning. (SWC 1500); Naked in Borneo. (SWC 1500); Orbiter 5 Shows How Earth Looks from the Moon. (SWC 1500); Out of the Sea, Early. (SWC 1500); Overboard. (SWC 1500); Pure Suit of Happiness. (SWC 1500); Speed. (SWC 1500); Stone Gullets. (SWC 1500); Survey of the Whole. (SWC 1500); Trance. (SWC 1500); Unconscious Came a Beauty. (SWC 1500); Watch. (SWC 1500); While Sitting in the Tuileries & Facing the Slanting Sun. (SWC 1500); 1976. 14.00 (978-0-694-50278-3(2), SWC 1500) HarperCollins Pubs.

***May the Force Go Through You.** Created by Uncommon Sensing LLC. (ENG.). 2008. audio compact disk 60.00 (978-0-9826724-8-8(9)) Uncommon Sens.

May We Never Forget. Contrib. by Martins. (Studio Tracks Plus Ser.). 2005. audio compact disk 9.98 (978-5-558-71558-3(8)) Sprg Hill Music Group.

May Your Kingdom Come CD. (CHI.). 2003. audio compact disk 15.00 (978-0-9721862-6-1(3)) Lamb Music & Min.

Maya & Freedom - Teacher of Spirituality. unabr. ed. Vivekananda. Read by Robert Adjemian & John Batiste. 1 cass. (Running Time: 45 min.). 1990. 7.95 (978-1-882915-11-8(9)) Vedanta Ctr Atlanta.
Maya (illusion) & how it affects our lives; Qualifications for a true teacher of spirituality.

Maya Angelou. Maya Angelou. 2 cass. (Running Time: 2 hrs. 15 min.). 1993. 15.95 set. (8276Q) Filmic Archives.
Civil Rights activist, writer & poet, Maya Angelou has inspired the hearts & minds of a generation with her honesty & eloquence. Her voice speaks to the challenges of personal growth & social progress.

Maya Angelou. Interview with Maya Angelou. 1 cass. (Running Time: 30 min.). 1979. 13.95 (L004) TFR.
Angelou reads her poetry, talks about her memoir, "I Know Why the Caged Bird Sings," & discusses a three year period in her childhood during which she refused to speak.

Maya Angelou. unabr. ed. Miles Shapiro. Read by Joyce Diamond. 2 cass. (Running Time: 2 hrs. 30 min.). (Black Americans of Achievement Ser.). 1993. 15.95 (978-1-879557-08-6(8)) Audio Scholar.
Biography - for all ages - from critically acclaimed series Black Americans of Achievement Series by Chelsea House Publishers.

Maya Angelou: A Glorious Celebration. Marcia Ann Gillespie et al. Read by Dion Graham. Frwd. by Oprah Winfrey. (Playaway Adult Nonfiction Ser.). (ENG.). 2009. 74.99 (978-1-60812-653-8(6)) Find a World.

Maya Angelou: A Glorious Celebration. unabr. ed. Marcia Ann Gillespie et al. Read by Dion Graham. (Running Time: 3 hrs.). 2008. 39.25 (978-1-4233-6489-4(9), 9781423364894, BADLE); 24.95 (978-1-4233-6488-7(0), 9781423364887, BAD) Brilliance Audio.

Maya Angelou: A Glorious Celebration. unabr. ed. Marcia Ann Gillespie et al. Read by Dion Graham. Frwd. by Oprah Winfrey. 1 MP3-CD. (Running Time: 10800 sec.). 2008. audio compact disk 24.95 (978-1-4233-6486-3(4), 9781423364863, Brilliance MP3); audio compact disk 26.95 (978-1-4233-6484-9(8), 9781423364849, Bril Audio CD Unabri); audio compact disk 74.25 (978-1-4233-6485-6(6), 9781423364856, BriAudCD Unabrid); audio compact disk 39.25 (978-1-4233-6487-0(2), 9781423364870, Brlnc Audio MP3 Lib) Brilliance Audio.

Maya Angelou: Survival of the African-American Artist. Rex A. Barnett. (Running Time: 58 min.). (YA). 1990. 9.99 (978-0-924198-16-8(8)) Hist Video.
Talks about contribution of black writers & their relevance.

Maya Moon. Retold by Marianne Mitchell. (SPA.). 2001. (978-1-56801-796-9(0)) Sund Newbrdge.

Maya World. Compiled by Benchmark Education Staff. 2005. audio compact disk 10.00 (978-1-4108-5509-1(0)) Benchmark Educ.

Mayan. John Whitman. (Lost Civilizations Ser.). 1999. (978-1-57042-727-5(5)) Hachet Audio.

Mayan Factor. Jose Arguelles. 5 cass. 45.00 (OC67) Sound Horizons AV.

Mayan Landing 2012 CD. Music by ThunderBeat ThunderVision Records. 2008. (978-0-9814651-5-9(3), ThundrBeat) ThunderVision.

Mayan Mysteries. Sam Keen. 2 cass. 18.00 (OC38) Sound Horizons AV.

Maybe see Carl Sandburg's Poems for Children

Maybe I'll Pitch Forever. unabr. ed. LeRoy Paige & David Lipman. Read by Edward Lewis. Frwd. by John B. Holway. 5 cass. (Running Time: 7 hrs.). 1999. 39.95 (978-0-7861-1527-3(0), 2377) Blckstn Audio.
For twenty-two years, beginning in 1926, Satchel Paige dazzled throngs with his performance in the Negro Baseball Leagues. He was forty-two years old in 1948 when he became the first black pitcher in the American League & outlasted everyone by playing professional baseball, in & out of the majors, until 1965. The struggle, fast living & a humorous point of view were part of his story.

***Maybe I'll Pitch Forever: A Great Baseball Player Tells the Hilarious Story behind the Legend.** unabr. ed. LeRoy (Satchel) Paige. Read by Edward Lewis. (Running Time: 7 hrs.). 2010. 29.95 (978-1-4417-6704-2(5)); audio compact disk 69.00 (978-1-4417-6702-8(9)) Blckstn Audio.

***Maybe the Moon.** abr. ed. Armistead Maupin. Read by Armistead Maupin. (ENG.). 2007. (978-0-06-123763-8(9), Harper Audio); (978-0-06-123764-5(7), Harper Audio) HarperCollins Pubs.

Maybe This Time. abr. ed. Jennifer Crusie, pseud. (Running Time: 6 hrs.). 2009. audio compact disk 14.99 (978-1-4233-0661-0(9), 9781423306610, BCD Value Price) Brilliance Audio.

Maybe This Time. unabr. ed. Jennifer Crusie, pseud. Read by Angela Dawe. (Running Time: 11 hrs.). 2010. 39.97 (978-1-59710-860-7(X), 9781597108607, BADLE); 24.99 (978-1-59710-861-4(8), 9781597108614, BAD); 39.97 (978-1-59335-853-2(9), 9781593358532, Brlnc Audio MP3 Lib); 24.99 (978-1-59335-719-1(2), 9781593357191, Brilliance MP3); audio compact disk 36.99 (978-1-59355-379-1(X), 9781593553791, Bril Audio CD Unabri); audio compact disk 97.97 (978-1-59355-380-7(3), 9781593553807, BriAudCD Unabrid) Brilliance Audio.
Please enter a Synopsis.

***Maybe You Never Cry Again.** abr. ed. Bernie Mac. Read by Bernie Mac. (ENG.). 2006. (978-0-06-078270-2(6), Harper Audio); (978-0-06-122927-5(X), Harper Audio) HarperCollins Pubs.

Maybe You Never Cry Again. abr. ed. Bernie Mac. Read by Bernie Mac. 2008. audio compact disk 14.95 (978-0-06-177242-9(9), Harper Audio) HarperCollins Pubs.

Maybe You Never Cry Again: A True Story. Bernie Mac. 2003. audio compact disk 89.82 (978-0-06-053464-6(8)) HarperCollins Pubs.

Mayday! 1 cass. 1984. 9.95 incl. script. (978-0-9670805-0-5(9)) PDQ Prods.
Actual aircraft distress calls; aviations; flight instruction.

Mayday. Nelson DeMille & Thomas Block. Read by Michael Prichard. 1997. audio compact disk 96.00 (978-0-7366-6060-0(7)) Books on Tape.

Mayday. abr. ed. Nelson DeMille & Thomas Block. 2002. (978-1-58621-009-0(2)) Hachet Audio.

Mayday. abr. ed. Nelson DeMille & Thomas Block. (ENG.). 2006. 14.98 (978-1-59483-684-8(1)) Pub: Hachet Audio. Dist(s): HachBkGrp

Mayday. unabr. ed. Nelson DeMille. Read by Michael Prichard. 1 CD. (Running Time: 1 hr. 30 mins.). 2001. audio compact disk Books on Tape.
Begins twelve miles above the Pacific Ocean, where a jumbo jet is about to meet disaster.

Mayday. unabr. ed. Nelson DeMille & Thomas Block. Read by Michael Prichard. 10 cass. (Running Time: 15 hrs.). 1997. 80.00 (978-0-7366-3835-7(0), 4555) Books on Tape.

Mayday. unabr. ed. Nelson DeMille & Thomas Block. 2002. 44.98 (978-1-58621-010-6(6)) Hachet Audio.

Mayday. unabr. ed. Nelson DeMille & Thomas Block. (ENG.). 2005. 26.98 (978-1-59483-673-2(6)) Pub: Hachet Audio. Dist(s): HachBkGrp

Mayday on Holderness see Poetry & Voice of Ted Hughes

Mayflower. Nathaniel Philbrick. 2006. cd-rom 49.99 (978-1-59895-487-6(3)) Find a World.

Mayflower: A Story of Courage, Community, & War. unabr. ed. Nathaniel Philbrick. Read by George Guidall. 11 CDs. (Running Time: 13 hrs.). (ENG.). (gr. 12 up). 2006. audio compact disk 44.95 (978-0-14-305875-5(4), PengAudBks) Penguin Grp USA.

Mayhem: The Invasion. unabr. ed. Tim Robbins. Perf. by Tim Robbins. Perf. by Starr Andreeff et al. 1 cass. (Running Time: 1 hr. 21 min.). 1992. 19.95 (978-1-58081-067-8(5)) L A Theatre.
A biting political satire which challenges the myth of Columbus as heroic explorer. Tim Robbins plays an expert debating this issue within the inane context of the television talk show, "Conflagration." A strange hybrid of Crossfire & Wheel of Fortune, "Conflagration" is constantly being interrupted by late-breaking news on the impending Gulf War.

Mayhem Dressed Like an Eight Point Buck. Bil Lepp. 2003. 9.95 (978-1-891852-31-2(0)); audio compact disk 12.95 (978-1-891852-30-5(2)) Pub: Quarrier Pr. Dist(s): WV Book Co

Maylene & the Sons of Disaster. Contrib. by Maylene & the Sons of Disaster. Prod. by Jason Elgin. 2005. audio compact disk 13.98 (978-5-558-77733-8(8)) Mono Vs Ster.

Maynard Moose: Sleeping Beastly. Willy Claflin. (Running Time: 41 mins.). 1992. audio compact disk 14.95 (978-0-87483-703-2(0)) Pub: August Hse. Dist(s): Natl Bk Netwk

Maynard Moose Tales. Perf. by Willy Claflin. Created by Willy Claflin. 1 CD. (Running Time: 41 mins.). 2002. audio compact disk 14.95 (978-0-87483-699-8(9)) Pub: August Hse. Dist(s): Natl Bk Netwk
Mother Moose Tales?, The creation myth of Mother Moose?, The Big Bad Pig?, Rumbleshirtskin?, Handsome and Gristle? All of those and more are served up here in the voice of Maynard Moose, the alter-ego of storyteller Willy Claflin. Willy launches first into a cautionary tale, Maynard's not-so-traditional retelling of Big Bad Pig, in which the innocent little wolves set out to seek their fortune only to be attacked by, you guessed it, Big Bad Pig.

Mayo Clinic: Heart Book. Bernard J. Gersh. Narrated by L. J. Ganser. 10 cass. (Running Time: 13 hrs. 30 mins.). 99.00 (978-1-4025-2883-5(3)) Recorded Bks.

Mayo Clinic on Alzheimer's. unabr. ed. Ronald C. Peterson. Narrated by Nelson Runger. 5 cass. (Running Time: 7 hrs. 30 min.). 2003. 32.95 (978-1-4025-4685-3(8)) Recorded Bks.
Mayo Clinic presents a concise, easy-to-understand book on the critical subject of Alzheimer's Disease. This resource thoroughly covers the possible causes and available treatments of the disease.

Mayo Clinic on Arthritis. Gene G. Hunder. Narrated by Robert O'Keefe. 5 cass. (Running Time: 7 hrs.). 1999. 48.00 (978-0-7887-8855-0(8), 96748) Recorded Bks.
Focuses on arthritis, one of the most common medical problems in the world today. The causes of osteoarthritis and rheumatoid arthritis are thoroughly examined and helpful situations based on the proven practices of Mayo Clinic doctors are offered. You will learn how to better manage your condition today or prepare for tomorrow with the invaluable resource.

Mayo Clinic on Digestive Health. John E. King. Narrated by Rick Rohan. 4 cass. (Running Time: 6 hrs.). 52.00 (978-1-4025-3354-9(3)) Recorded Bks.

Mayo Clinic on Healthy Aging. Edward T. Creagan. Narrated by John McDonough. 7 cass. (Running Time: 10 hrs.). 2001. 69.00 (978-1-4025-3887-2(1)) Recorded Bks.

Mayo Clinic on Healthy Weight. unabr. ed. Donald D. Hensrud. Ed. by Donald D. Hensrud. Narrated by Barbara Caruso. 5 cass. (Running Time: 6 hrs.). 2001. 48.00 (978-0-7887-5471-5(8), 96606x7) Recorded Bks.
Weight is an issue of health as well as appearance. Following the tips in this book will help you achieve & maintain the weight that's healthiest for you & reduce your risk of weight-related diseases. Dr. Hensrud is an assistant professor of preventative medicine & nutrition at the Mayo Clinic.

Mayo Clinic on High Blood Pressure. Sheldon G. Sheps. Narrated by Nelson Runger. 5 cass. (Running Time: 7 hrs. 15 mins.). 48.00 (978-1-4025-1874-4(9)) Recorded Bks.

Mayo Clinic on Prostate Health. unabr. ed. David M. Barrett. Ed. by David M. Barrett. Narrated by Simon Prebble. 4 cass. (Running Time: 5 hrs.). 2001. 38.00 (978-0-7887-9572-5(4)) Recorded Bks.
Helps identify and understand prostate problems, and make well-informed decisions on how to treat them.

Mayor for a Day. Short Stories. Carl Sommer. Narrated by Carl Sommer. 1 cass. Dramatization. (Another Sommer-Time Story Ser.). (J). (gr. 1-4). 2003. bk. 16.95 (978-1-57537-562-5(1)) Advance Pub.

Mayor for A Day Read-along. Carl Sommer. Narrated by Carl Sommer. 1 cass. Dramatization. (Another Sommer-Time Story Ser.). (J). 2003. lib. bdg. 23.95 (978-1-57537-763-6(2)) Advance Pub.
Character Education story with character song by Karacter Kidz.

***Mayor for the Day / Alcalde Por un Dia.** ed. Carl Sommer. Illus. by Dick Westbrook. (Another Sommer-Time Story Bilingual Ser.). (ENG & SPA.). (J). 2009. bk. 26.95 (978-1-57537-184-9(7)) Advance Pub.

Mayor of Casterbridge. Thomas Hardy. Contrib. by John Nettles et al. 3 CDs. (Running Time: 3 hrs. 30 mins.). 2006. audio compact disk 39.95 (978-0-7927-4331-6(8), BBCD 158) AudioGO.

Mayor of Casterbridge. Thomas Hardy. Read by John Rowe. 9 cass. (Running Time: 12 hrs. 30 min.). 59.95 (CC/028) C to C Cassettes.
Micheal Henchard has through abstinence & application striven to become a respected & successful corn merchant. For years a secret horror on his early life was suppressed but when his secret becomes known his energies fail & he is ruined by drink & despair.

Mayor of Casterbridge. Thomas Hardy. Narrated by Jenny Sterlin. 10 cass. (Running Time: 14 hrs.). 1886. 91.00 (978-1-4025-4022-6(1)) Recorded Bks.

Mayor of Casterbridge. unabr. ed. Thomas Hardy. Read by Flo Gibson. 8 cass. (Running Time: 11 hr.). 1995. 26.95 (978-1-55685-315-9(7)) Audio Bk Con.
After auctioning off his wife & daughter during a drinking bout, Henchard suffers pangs of deep remorse. When they reappear eighteen years later, he tries to make amends only to learn that the young girl is not his. This is followed by a number of surprising & embittering experiences.

Mayor of Casterbridge. unabr. ed. Thomas Hardy. Read by John Rowe. 8 cass. (Running Time: 12 hrs. 30 mins.). 2004. 34.95 (978-1-57270-072-7(6), F81072u) Pub: Audio Partners. Dist(s): PerseuPGW

Mayor of Casterbridge. unabr. ed. Thomas Hardy. 10 cass. (Running Time: 14 hrs. 30 mins.). 2001. 69.95 (978-0-7861-2100-7(9), 2862) Blckstn Audio.
Rooted in an actual case of wife-selling in early nineteenth-century England, the story builds into an awesome Sophoclean drama of guilt and revenge, in which the strong, willful Henchard rises to a position of wealth and power, only to achieve a most bitter downfall. Proud, obsessed, ultimately committed to his own destruction, Henchard is, as Albert Guerard has said, "Hardy's Lord Jim...his only tragic hero and one of the greatest tragic heroes in all fiction".

Mayor of Casterbridge. unabr. ed. Thomas Hardy. Read by Pamela Garelick. 12 CDs. (Running Time: 14 hrs. 30 mins.). 2001. audio compact disk 96.00 (978-0-7861-9649-4(1), 2862) Blckstn Audio.

Mayor of Casterbridge. unabr. ed. Thomas Hardy. Read by Tony Britton. 10 cass. (Running Time: 15 hrs.). 2000. 69.95 (SAB 152) Pub: Chivers Audio Bks GBR. Dist(s): AudioGO
Michael Henchard, successful corn-merchant and Mayor of Casterbridge, has striven to shake off his tainted past. But years of industry, abstinence and application cannot save him from his own history. The flaws that mar his great spirit serve only to drag him back into the mire of drink and despair.

***Mayor of Casterbridge.** unabr. ed. Thomas Hardy. Narrated by Simon Vance. (Running Time: 13 hrs. 0 mins.). 2010. 18.99 (978-1-4001-8613-6(7)); 24.99 (978-1-4001-6613-8(6)); audio compact disk 69.99 (978-1-4001-4613-0(5)); audio compact disk 34.99 (978-1-4001-1613-3(9)) Pub: Tantor Media. Dist(s): IngramPubServ

Mayor of Casterbridge. unabr. collector's ed. Thomas Hardy. Read by Jill Masters. 9 cass. (Running Time: 13 hrs. 30 mins.). 1983. 72.00 (978-0-7366-3975-0(6), 9521) Books on Tape.
A young farm laborer, dead drunk, sells his wife & child to another man for five pounds. Simultaneously freed of any restraints & goaded by a hidden guilt, he goes on to become a fabulously rich grain merchant & Mayor of Casterbridge in the bargain. At this point his wife & child reappear & his life, which he thought so secure, begins to unravel.

Mayor of Lexington Avenue. unabr. ed. James Sheehan. Narrated by Dick Hill. 11 CDs. (Running Time: 14 hrs. 0 mins. 0 sec.). (ENG.). 2008. audio compact disk 39.99 (978-1-4001-0663-9(X)); audio compact disk 29.99 (978-1-4001-5663-4(7)); audio compact disk 79.99 (978-1-4001-3663-6(6)) Pub: Tantor Media. Dist(s): IngramPubServ

Mayor Signo de Vida: Una Nueva Filosofia. Created by Martinez Roca. (Running Time: 4440 sec.). (Jorge Lis Coaching Ser.). 2005. audio compact disk 20.95 (978-84-609-6906-8(1)) EdicMart ESP.

Mayors. abr. ed. Isaac Asimov. 1 cass. 1984. 12.95 (978-0-694-50288-2(X), SWC 1527) HarperCollins Pubs.
The story of the first of the great mayors - Salvor Hardin & his adventures with the planet Anacreon.

Mayor's Wife: Genesis 19:26. Ed Young. 1982. 4.95 (978-0-7417-1245-5(8), 245) Win Walk.

Maytime. unabr. ed. Perf. by Jeanette MacDonald & Nelson Eddy. Hosted by Cecil B. DeMille. 1 cass. (Running Time: 1 hr.). Dramatization. 1950. 7.95 Norelco box. (DD-8786) Natl Recrd Co.
Lux Radio Theatre presents Sigmund Romberg's beautiful music performed by two of the finest singers of their time, or of anytime. Jeanette MacDonald was a great opera star when she first meets Nelson Eddy in Paris...a lazy young man with a very fine but "untrained" voice. It isn't too long before they are singing duets from opera, to "Sweetheart," to dialog, to "Sweetheart" once more. As they say, "it is some kind of singing." A love story, but also beautiful music that can be heard over-&-over again.

Maytrees. unabr. ed. Annie Dillard. Read by David Rasche. 5 CDs. (Running Time: 19800 sec.). 2007. audio compact disk 29.95 (978-0-06-128546-2(3), Harper Audio) HarperCollins Pubs.

***Maytrees.** unabr. ed. Annie Dillard. Read by David Rasche. (ENG.). 2007. (978-0-06-147289-3(1), Harper Audio); (978-0-06-147288-6(3), Harper Audio) HarperCollins Pubs.

Maze. Catherine Coulter. Read by Susan Ericksen. (FBI Thriller Ser.: No. 2). 2009. 69.99 (978-1-60775-685-9(4)) Find a World.

Maze. Will Hobbs. Narrated by Ed Sala. 5 CDs. (Running Time: 5 hrs. 30 mins.). (gr. 5 up). audio compact disk 48.00 (978-1-4025-2319-9(X)) Recorded Bks.

Maze, William Hobbs. Read by Ed Sala. 4 cass. (Running Time: 5 hrs. 30 mins.). (YA). 1999. stu. ed. 195.30 (978-0-7887-3991-0(3), 47057) Recorded Bks.
At 14, Rick Walker's life seems like a maze full of dead ends. But when he runs away, he enters a real maze - the enormous rocky expanse of Canyonlands National Park in Utah. Filled with riveting adventure in an unforgettable wilderness setting, this traces the young man's growing confidence.

Maze. abr. ed. Catherine Coulter. Read by Susan Ericksen. (Running Time: 21600 sec.). (FBI Thriller Ser.: No. 2). 2008. audio compact disk 14.99 (978-1-4233-6225-8(X), 9781423362258, BCD Value Price) Brilliance Audio.

Maze. unabr. ed. Larry Collins. Read by Brian Emerson. 11 cass. (Running Time: 16 hrs.). 1994. 76.95 (978-0-7861-0828-2(2), 1525) Blckstn Audio.
Working with KGB defectors, former top officials of the CIA, & scientists at the forefront of a revolution in brain research, Larry Collins has constructed a diabolically clever conspiracy. At its center are a beautiful Soviet scientist who has discovered the key to manipulating human emotions by remote means & the newly appointed head of the KGB. A ruthless man, he is determined to do anything to reverse his country's declining fortunes, to halt the onrush of Perestroika & check the tide of Islamic fundamentalism that threatens to split up the Soviet Empire in places like Azerbaijan. His target: the mind of the President of the United States.

Maze. unabr. ed. Catherine Coulter. Read by Susan Ericksen. 8 cass. (Running Time: 12 hrs.). (FBI Thriller Ser.: No. 2). 1997. 73.25 (978-1-56100-826-1(5), 1561008265, Unabridge Lib Edns) Brilliance Audio.

Maze. unabr. ed. Catherine Coulter. Read by Susan Ericksen. (Running Time: 12 hrs.). (FBI Thriller Ser.: No. 2). 2005. 39.25 (978-1-59335-929-4(2), 9781593359294, Brlnc Audio MP3 Lib); 39.25 (978-1-59710-484-5(1), 9781597104845, BADLE); 24.95 (978-1-59710-485-2(X), 9781597104852, BAD) Brilliance Audio.

Maze. unabr. ed. Catherine Coulter. Read by Susan Eriksen. (Running Time: 12 hrs.). (FBI Thriller Ser.: No. 2). 2005. 29.95 (978-1-59600-095-7(3), 9781596000957, BAU) Brilliance Audio.

Maze. unabr. ed. Catherine Coulter. Read by Susan Ericksen. (Running Time: 12 hrs.). (FBI Thriller Ser.: No. 2). 2005. 24.95 (978-1-59335-795-5(8), 9781593357955, Brilliance MP3) Brilliance Audio.
Lacey Sherlock's life is forever changed when her older sister's body is discovered in an abandoned warehouse. She is the fourth victim of the String Killer, the name given by the media to a murderer who leads his victims into a maze with a ball of twine. Seven years after Belinda's death, Lacey, now an FBI agent, is paired up with computer whiz Dillon Savitch, who has developed a predictive program to aid in the apprehension of serial killers. When the String Killer strikes again, Lacey spots his handiwork, resulting in his capture. The suspect confesses, but maintains that he did not kill Belinda. No sooner does Lacey confirm his innocence of that crime, than an attempt is made on her life. Suspecting her attacker is the same person who murdered her sister, Lacey and Dillon know they must solve the mystery - before they become the killer's next victims.

Maze. unabr. ed. Catherine Coulter. Read by Susan Ericksen. (Running Time: 39600 sec.). (FBI Thriller Ser.: No. 2). 2008. audio compact disk 29.95 (978-1-4233-6583-9(6), 9781423365839, Bril Audio CD Unabri); audio compact disk 97.25 (978-1-4233-6584-6(4), 9781423365846, BriAudCD Unabrid) Brilliance Audio.

Maze. unabr. ed. William Hobbs. Narrated by Ed Sala. 4 cass. (Running Time: 5 hrs. 30 mins.). (YA). 1999. pap. bk. & stu. ed. 59.00 (978-0-7887-3990-3(5), 41062X4) Recorded Bks.
At 14, Rick Walker's life seems like a maze full of dead ends. But when he runs away, he enters a real maze - the enormous rocky expanse of Canyonlands National Park in Utah. Filled with riveting adventure in an unforgettable wilderness setting, this traces the young man's growing confidence.

Maze, unabr. ed. William Hobbs. Narrated by Ed Sala. 4 pieces. (Running Time: 5 hrs. 30 mins.). (gr. 5 up). 1999. 37.00 (978-0-7887-3892-0(5), 95933E7) Recorded Bks.

Maze of Bones. Rick Riordan. Read by David Pittu. (39 Clues Ser.: Bk. 1). (J). 2008. 44.99 (978-1-60640-545-1(4)) Find a World.

Maze of Bones. unabr. ed. Rick Riordan. Read by David Pittu. 4 CDs. (Running Time: 5 hrs. 11 mins.). (39 Clues Ser.: Bk. 1). (J). (gr. 4-6). 2008. audio compact disk 49.95 (978-0-545-14290-8(3)) Scholastic Inc.

Maze of Bones. unabr. ed. Rick Riordan. Narrated by David Pittu. 4 CDs. (Running Time: 5 hrs. 11 mins.). (ENG.). (J). (gr. 4-7). 2008. audio compact disk 19.95 (978-0-545-09104-6(7)) Scholastic Inc.

Maze of Bones. unabr. ed. Rick Riordan. Read by David Pittu. 4 CDs. (39 Clues Ser.: No. 1). (ENG.). (J). (gr. 4-7). 2008. audio compact disk 49.95 (978-0-545-09108-4(X)) Scholastic Inc.

Maze of Mormonism. Walter Ralston Martin. 1 cass. 1997. 6.99 (978-7-5116-0033-2(6)) Gospel Lght.
Evangelism.

Maze of Mysteries. Prod. by Focus on the Family Staff. 6 cass. (Running Time: 6 hrs.). (Adventures in Odyssey Classics Ser.: Vol. 2). 1999. 24.99 (978-1-56179-685-4(9)) Pub: Focus Family. Dist(s): Nelson

Maze of Mysteries travel visor Pack. AIO Team Staff. Created by Focus on the Family Staff. (Running Time: 15 hrs.). (Adventures in Odyssey Ser.). (ENG.). (J). 2007. audio compact disk 19.97 (978-1-58997-425-8(5), Tyndale Ent) Tyndale Hse.

***Maze Runner.** unabr. ed. James Dashner. Read by Mark Deakins. 9 CDs. (Running Time: 10 hrs. 30 mins.). (Maze Runner Ser.: Bk. 1). (YA). (gr. 7 up). 2009. audio compact disk 65.00 (978-0-307-58290-4(6), BksonTape) Pub: Random Audio Pubg. Dist(s): Random

Maze Runner. unabr. ed. James Dashner. Read by Mark Deakins. (Maze Runner Ser.: Bk. 1). (ENG.). (J). (gr. 7). 2009. audio compact disk 44.00 (978-0-307-58288-1(4), Listening Lib) Pub: Random Audio Pubg. Dist(s): Random

Mazel & Shlimazel: Or the Milk of a Lioness. unabr. ed. Isaac Bashevis Singer. Narrated by George Guidall. 1 cass. (Running Time: 45 mins.). (gr. 1 up). 1997. 10.00 (978-0-7887-0698-1(5), 94872E7) Recorded Bks.
When Mazel, the spirit of good luck, meets Shlimazel, the spirit of bad luck, the fate of a peasant lad hangs in the balance.

MBA V. Alan Weiss. Perf. by Alan Weiss. 2008. bk. 295.00 (978-1-928611-14-1(1)) Summit Cons Grp.

Mbembe. unabr. ed. Read by Mbembe. 1 cass. (Running Time: 29 min.). 1985. 10.00 New Letters.
Young black poet from Kansas City reads his poems & others from an anthology "Four Black Poets".

Mbembe Memorial. unabr. ed. Mbembe. 1 cass. (Running Time: 29 min.). 1985. 10.00 New Letters.
A tribute to black poet Mbembe Milton Smith including readings by Walter & David Smith & jazz poems performed by Lloyd Daniel & Bill Russell.

MBGU: Jazz Moveable Shapes: Concepts for Reharmonizing II-V-I's. Sheryl Bailey. (ENG.). 2009. pap. bk. 9.95 (978-0-7866-7936-2(0)) Mel Bay.

MBGU Rock Curriculum: Chord-Lead Soloing for Guitar. Tim Quinn. (ENG.). 2009. pap. bk. 17.99 (978-0-7866-7281-3(1)) Mel Bay.

MBGU Rock Curriculum: Fluid Pentatonics, Book 2 84 Melodic Studies for Guitar. Quinn Tim. (ENG.). 2009. pap. bk. 19.99 (978-0-7866-7282-0(X)) Mel Bay.

MBGU Rock Curriculum: String Skipping & Wide Interval Soloing for Guitar: Fluid Soloing, Book 4. Tim Quinn. (ENG.). 2009. lib. bdg. 19.99 (978-0-7866-7296-7(X)) Mel Bay.

***MBGU Rock Guitar Curriculum: 60 Sweep Picking Licks for Contemporary Electric Guitar.** Ioannis Anastassakis. 2010. spiral bd. 24.99 (978-0-7866-7495-4(4)) Mel Bay.

Mbira: Healing Music of Zimbabwe. Erica Kundidzora Azim. 1 CD. (Running Time: 1:00:00). 2000. audio compact disk 15.95 (978-1-55961-612-6(1)) Sounds True.

Mbuti Pygmies of the Ituri Rainforest. Ed. by Michelle Kisliuk. Contrib. by Colin Turnbull & Francis S. Chapman. 1 cass. 1992. (0-9307-404010-9307-40401-2-6); audio compact disk (0-9307-40401-2-6) Smithsonian Folkways.
Captures the extraordinary variety & tonal quality of the solo & choral traditions of the Mbuti. Songs are primarily about the Mbuti's nomadic life & the forest.

MC - Our Path to Fulfillment. Annie Hershey. 1 cass. 8.95 (155) Am Fed Astrologers.
MC/IC axis with examples for each sign.

MCAT: The Best Test Preparation for the Medical College Admission Test with REA's TESTware. Joseph A. Alvarez. (Test Prep Ser.). 2002. bk. 52.95 (978-0-87891-350-3(5)) Res Educ.

MCAT Audiolearn: Medical College Admission Test Audiolearn. 3rd ed. Scripts. Shahrad Yazdani. 6 CDs & a CD-Rom. (Running Time: Over 4 Hours). (C). 2003. audio compact disk 124.00 (978-0-9704199-8-9(8)) AudioLearn.
Listen to a comprehensive, structured and well-organized review of the complete syllabus for the Medical College Admission Test (MCAT). We?ve made sure that MCAT AudioLearn is packed with every theory, formula and equation ? all the facts ? to ensure your complete success with a high-scoring result. Discover for yourself what a powerful method audiolearning can be for memorizing the massive amounts of information you?ll need. Dip into the revision notes from the comfort of home or while on the move. Improve your exam performance through the proven techniques of audio-learning.

McCain's Promise: Aboard the Straight Talk Express with John Mccain & a Whole Bunch of Actual Reporters, Thinking about Hope. unabr. ed. David Foster Wallace. Read by Henry Leyva. Frwd. by Jacob Weisberg. (Running Time: 3 hrs.). (ENG.). 2008. 12.98 (978-1-60024-533-6(1)) Pub: Hachet Audio. Dist(s): HachBkGrp

McCarthy & McCarthyism. Ernest Yaniger. Read by Tim O'Connor. 1 cass. (Running Time: 54 min.). 1982. 10.00 (HT345) Esstee Audios.
McCarthy desired personal success & recognition, no matter what the cost. This ambition ruled his every move, from young manhood to his position as senator, when he decided on a Communist witchhunt as a lightning-rod issue.

McCarthy the Poet. unabr. ed. Eugene McCarthy. Read by Eugene McCarthy. 1 cass. (Running Time: 1 hr.). 1970. 12.95 (23046) J Norton Pubs.
U. S. Senator reads his poetry.

McClairen's Isle: The Passionate One. collector's ed. Connie Brockway. Read by Donada Peters. 7 cass. (Running Time: 10 hrs. 30 min.). 1999. 56.00 (978-0-7366-4734-2(1), 5072) Books on Tape.
We are introduced to the Merrick family, two brothers & a sister, who are bound together by an evil father. Ashton, the eldest was a notorious rogue with a reputation for hell-raising & heartbreaking but family secrets forced him to do his ruthless father's bidding & escort Rhiannon Russell back to McClairen's Isle. Ashton suspected that his father intended to make the innocent beauty his fourth wife. But he didn't expect the passions she would ignite in his own wary heart.

McClairen's Isle: The Ravishing One. unabr. ed. Connie Brockway. Read by Donada Peters. 7 cass. (Running Time: 10 hrs. 30 mins.). 2001. 56.00 (978-0-7366-6191-1(3)) Books on Tape.
Fia Merrick gives her heart to no one, for love is a weakness she cannot afford. Once she would have given her soul to Thomas McClairen, until he shattered her innocent dreams. Now he is back, a convict returned to England in disguise to abduct Fia to Scotland, to McClairen's Isle. There, a passion is ignited that defies the past & cannot be denied.

McClairen's Isle: The Reckless One. collector's ed. Connie Brockway. Read by Donada Peters. 7 cass. (Running Time: 10 hrs. 30 min.). 2000. 56.00 (978-0-7366-5627-6(8)) Books on Tape.

McDougal Littell Algebra 1: Chapter Audio Summaries. (SPA.). (gr. 6-12). 2004. audio compact disk (978-0-618-35331-6(3), 2-91222); audio compact disk (978-0-618-39633-7(0), 2-05625) Holt McDoug.

McDougal Littell Algebra 1: Chapter Summaries. (gr. 6-12). 2004. audio compact disk (978-0-618-35329-3(1), 2-91220) Holt McDoug.

McDougal Littell Algebra 2: Chapter Audio Summaries. (gr. 6-12). 2004. audio compact disk (978-0-618-35335-4(6), 2-91226); audio compact disk (978-0-618-35337-8(2), 2-91228); audio compact disk (978-0-618-39641-2(1), 2-05628) Holt McDoug.

McDougal Littell Geometry: Chapter Audio Summaries. (ENG & SPA.). (gr. 6-12). 2004. audio compact disk (978-0-618-39642-9(X), 2-05629) Holt McDoug.

McDougal Littell Geometry: Chapter Summaries. (gr. 6-12). 2004. audio compact disk (978-0-618-35342-2(9), 2-91233); audio compact disk (978-0-618-35344-6(5), 2-91235) Holt McDoug.

McGraw-Hill Spanish Audio Program for Medical Terminology. McGraw-Hill Staff. (ENG.). (C). 2005. audio compact disk 29.33 (978-0-07-313405-5(8), 0073134058, Career Educ) Pub: McGrw-H Hghr Educ. Dist(s): McGraw

McIlhenny's Gold: How a Louisiana Family Built the Tabasco Empire. unabr. ed. Jeffrey Rothfeder. Read by Norman Dietz. (Running Time: 10 hrs. 0 mins. 0 sec.). (ENG.). 2007. audio compact disk 29.99 (978-1-4001-0569-4(2)); audio compact disk 19.99 (978-1-4001-5569-9(X)); audio compact disk 59.99 (978-1-4001-3569-1(9)) Pub: Tantor Media. Dist(s): IngramPubServ

***Mckettrick Legend: Sierra's Homecoming, the Mckettrick Way.** unabr. ed. Nora Roberts & Linda Lael Miller. (Running Time: 14 hrs.). 2010. 19.99 (978-1-61106-127-7(X), 9781611061277, Brilliance MP3) Brilliance Audio.

***McKettrick Way: A Selection from the McKettrick Legend.** unabr. ed. Linda Lael Miller. (Running Time: 7 hrs.). (McKettrick Ser.). 2010. 39.97 (978-1-4418-7116-9(0), 9781441871169, BADLE); audio compact disk 19.99 (978-1-4418-7112-1(8), 9781441871121, Bril Audio CD Unabri) Brilliance Audio.

***McKettrick Way: A Selection from the McKettrick Legend.** unabr. ed. Linda Lael Miller. Read by Natalie Ross. (Running Time: 7 hrs.). (McKettrick Ser.). 2010. 19.99 (978-1-4418-7114-5(4), 9781441871145, Brilliance MP3); 39.97 (978-1-4418-7115-2(2), 9781441871152, Brlnc Audio MP3 Lib); audio compact disk 69.97 (978-1-4418-7113-8(6), 9781441871138, BriAudCD Unabrid) Brilliance Audio.

McKinley Assassination. Narrated by Doug Tillett. 1 cass. (Running Time: 15 min.). 1981. 6.50 Esstee Audios.
Outlines the interplay between the opposing political forces in the U.S. at the beginning of the century. An eyewitness description of the assassination of President McKinley is included.

McKinley Years. (Presidency Ser.). 10.00 Esstee Audios.
A President running the nation during prosperity with a look at the nature of the times - including the war.

McL, No. 2. 1999. audio compact disk 4.50 (978-0-8297-2496-7(6)) Pub: Vida Pubs. Dist(s): Zondervan

McL, No. 4. 2000. audio compact disk 3.99 (978-0-8297-2551-3(2)) Vida Pubs.

McL, No. 5. 2001. audio compact disk 3.99 (978-0-8297-2554-4(7)) Pub: Vida Pubs. Dist(s): Zondervan

McMafia: A Journey Through the Global Criminal Underworld. abr. ed. Misha Glenny. Read by John Lee. (Running Time: 36000 sec.). (ENG.). 2008. audio compact disk 34.95 (978-0-7393-5926-6(6), Random AudioBks) Pub: Random Audio Pubg. Dist(s): Random

McMeen Acoustic Guitar Treasures. El McMeen. 1999. pap. bk. 26.95 (978-0-7866-4354-7(4), 97883CDP) Mel Bay.

McMummy, unabr. ed. Betsy Byars. Narrated by George Guidall. 2 pieces. (Running Time: 3 hrs.). (gr. 1 up). 1995. 19.00 (978-0-7887-0368-3(4), 94560E7) Recorded Bks.
Mozie has been looking after an eccentric scientist's greenhouse & discovers a large mummy-shaped pod on one of the plants. Christening the pod McMummy, Mozie involves his friend, Batty Batson & a beauty pageant hopeful named Valvoline, as he endeavors to assess & meet the needs of a humming, human-sized bean. Is Mozie's life turning into a bad horror movie? Or is he in real danger?.

McNally's Alibi. Vincent Lardo & Lawrence Sanders. Read by Boyd Gaines. (Archy McNally Mystery Ser.). 2004. 15.95 (978-0-7435-4084-1(0)) Pub: S&S Audio. Dist(s): S and S Inc

McNally's Bluff. abr. ed. Vincent Lardo & Lawrence Sanders. Read by Boyd Gaines. (Archy McNally Mystery Ser.). 2004. 15.95 (978-0-7435-5012-3(9)) Pub: S&S Audio. Dist(s): S and S Inc

McNally's Caper. Lawrence Sanders. (Archy McNally Mystery Ser.). 2004. 10.95 (978-0-7435-4072-8(7)) Pub: S&S Audio. Dist(s): S and S Inc

McNally's Chance. Vincent Lardo & Lawrence Sanders. Read by Adam Henderson. 6 vols. (Archy McNally Mystery Ser.). 2004. 54.95 (978-0-7927-3130-6(1), CSL 628, Chivers Sound Lib); audio compact disk 74.95 (978-0-7927-3131-3(X), SLD 628, Chivers Sound Lib); audio compact disk 29.95 (978-0-7927-3132-0(8), CMP 628, Chivers Sound Lib) AudioGO.

McNally's Chance. Vincent Lardo & Lawrence Sanders. Read by Boyd Gaines. (Archy McNally Mystery Ser.). 2004. 10.95 (978-0-7435-4105-3(7)) Pub: S&S Audio. Dist(s): S and S Inc

McNally's Dare. Vincent Lardo & Lawrence Sanders. Read by Boyd Gaines. (Archy McNally Mystery Ser.). 2004. 15.95 (978-0-7435-4106-0(5)) Pub: S&S Audio. Dist(s): S and S Inc

McNally's Dare. unabr. ed. Vincent Lardo & Lawrence Sanders. 6 cass. (Running Time: 9 hrs.). (Archy McNally Mystery Ser.). 2003. 78.00 (978-1-4025-5926-6(7)) Recorded Bks.

McNally's Dilemma. Lawrence Sanders & Vincent Lardo. Read by Boyd Gaines. (Archy McNally Mystery Ser.). 2004. 10.95 (978-0-7435-4073-5(5)) Pub: S&S Audio. Dist(s): S and S Inc

McNally's Dilemma. unabr. ed. Lawrence Sanders & Vincent Lardo. 12 CDs. (Running Time: 18 hrs.). (Archy McNally Mystery Ser.). 2001. audio compact disk 110.95 (978-0-7927-9904-7(6), SLD 055, Chivers Sound Lib) AudioGO.
After finding her second husband in a precarious position with an attractive young lady, Melva Williams pulls the trigger & admits to the crime passionately. To shield her daughter from the press, she turns to her friend Archy McNally. But the holes in the stories of both mother & daughter are too big to control.

McNally's Dilemma. unabr. ed. Lawrence Sanders & Vincent Lardo. Read by Adam Henderson. 8 vols. (Running Time: 12 hrs.). (Archy McNally Mystery Ser.). 2001. bk. 69.95 (978-0-7927-2436-0(4), CSL 325, Chivers Sound Lib) AudioGO.

McNally's Folly. unabr. ed. Vincent Lardo & Lawrence Sanders. Read by Adam Henderson. 8 vols. (Running Time: 12 hrs.). (Archy McNally Mystery Ser.). 2000. bk. 69.95 (978-0-7927-2392-9(9), CSL 281, Chivers Sound Lib) AudioGO.
When the Palm Beach Community Theater needs a director for its production of Arsenic & Old Lace, Archy tosses his megaphone into the ring. Desdemona Darling will lend her considerable talents to the show, while Lady Horowitz wants a little of the spotlight to fall on her latest love, Buzz Carr. For Archy, there's more drama backstage than on-stage, especially when an actor sips some prop wine & drops dead.

McNally's Folly. unabr. ed. Vincent Lardo & Lawrence Sanders. Read by Adam Henderson. 8 CDs. (Running Time: 12 hrs.). (Archy McNally Mystery Ser.). 2001. audio compact disk 79.95 (978-0-7927-9924-5(0), SLD 075, Chivers Sound Lib) AudioGO.
When the Palm Beach Community Theater needs a director for its production of Arsenic and Old Lace, Archy throws his megaphone into the ring. After all, Hollywood legend Desdemona Darling will lend her considerable talents to the show. But for Archy, there's more drama backstage than onstage - especially when an actor sips some prop wine and promptly drops dead.

McNally's Gamble. Lawrence Sanders. 1 cass. (Archy McNally Mystery Ser.). 1998. 9.98 (978-0-671-58153-4(8), Audioworks) S&S Audio.
Hardboiled mystery & detective.

McNally's Gamble. Lawrence Sanders. (Archy McNally Mystery Ser.). 2004. 10.95 (978-0-7435-4079-7(4)) Pub: S&S Audio. Dist(s): S and S Inc

McNally's Gamble. unabr. ed. Lawrence Sanders. Read by Adam Henderson. 6 vols. (Running Time: 12 hrs.). (Archy McNally Mystery Ser.). 2000. bk. 54.95 (978-0-7927-2373-8(2), CSL 262, Chivers Sound Lib) AudioGO.
Sun & sin in Palm Beach where the rich count their schemes before they're hatched. Well-to-do widow Edythe Westmore has announced her intent to invest a large part of her fortune in a Faberge Imperial egg. Horrified, her children argue about the financial risk & enlist Archy's services to put the kibosh on the deal. But when the sleuth sticks his nose in the widow's business, the whole case begins to smell like a rotten egg, but much harder to crack.

McNally's Gamble. unabr. ed. Lawrence Sanders. Read by Adam Henderson. 8 CDs. (Running Time: 12 hrs.). (Archy McNally Mystery Ser.). 2001. audio compact disk 79.95 (978-0-7927-9910-8(0), SLD 061, Chivers Sound Lib) AudioGO.

McNally's Luck. Lawrence Sanders. (Archy McNally Mystery Ser.). 2004. 10.95 (978-0-7435-4121-3(9)) Pub: S&S Audio. Dist(s): S and S Inc

McNally's Luck. unabr. ed. Lawrence Sanders. Read by Adam Henderson. 6 vols. (Running Time: 9 hrs.). (Archy McNally Mystery Ser.). 2001. bk. 54.95 (978-0-7927-2505-3(0), CSL 394, Chivers Sound Lib) Pub: AudioGO. Dist(s): AudioGO
Playboy/lover/sleuth Archy McNally is back - and the secrets of the filthy rich have never been filthier. What begins with a kidnapped cat leads to ransom and homicide. And if a sensuous psychic makes a believer out of McNally, he will learn that humans don't have nine lives, but scandals do.

McNally's Luck. unabr. ed. Lawrence Sanders. Read by Adam Henderson. 6 cass. (Running Time: 9 hrs.). (Archy McNally Mystery Ser.). 2002. 49.95 (CSL 394) AudioGO.
The irresistible Archy McNally returns in a masterful new thriller. The Palm Beach playboy/sleuth has taken on some odd jobs in his day, but nothing compares to his latest: catnapping. What starts as a simple investigation quickly opens a Pandora's box of lust, greed, and murder.

McNally's Puzzle. Lawrence Sanders. (Archy McNally Mystery Ser.). 2004. 10.95 (978-0-7435-4081-0(6)) Pub: S&S Audio. Dist(s): S and S Inc

McNally's Puzzle. unabr. ed. Lawrence Sanders. Read by Adam Henderson. 6 vols. (Running Time: 9 hrs.). (Archy McNally Mystery Ser.). 2001. bk. 54.95 (978-0-7927-2437-7(2), CSL 326, Chivers Sound Lib) AudioGO.
Hiram Gottschalk is a wealthy, elderly widower living in Palm Beach & the owner of Parrots Unlimited & he is convinced his life is in danger. After all, a photo of Hiram with his deceased wife has been slashed, a mass card is found taped inside his closet door & his pet mynah is discovered strangled. Hiram turns to McNally & son for answers. With his sidekick, Binky Watrous, in place posing as a salesman & cage cleaner in the bird store, Archy feels that his client's life will soon return to order. But Hiram Gottschalk is murdered in his sleep & McNally will use every ounce of his skill to put together the pieces of the puzzle & stay alive in the process.

McNally's Risk. Lawrence Sanders. Read by Adam Henderson. 6 cass. (Archy McNally Mystery Ser.). 2004. 54.95 (978-0-7927-3172-6(7), CSL 637, Chivers Sound Lib); audio compact disk 74.95 (978-0-7927-3173-3(5), SLD 637, Chivers Sound Lib) AudioGO.

McNally's Risk. Lawrence Sanders. (Archy McNally Mystery Ser.). 2004. 10.95 (978-0-7435-4082-7(4)) Pub: S&S Audio. Dist(s): S and S Inc

McNally's Secret. Lawrence Sanders. (Archy McNally Mystery Ser.). 2004. 10.95 (978-0-7435-4122-0(7)) Pub: S&S Audio. Dist(s): S and S Inc

McNally's Secret. abr. ed. Lawrence Sanders & Lawrence Sanders. Read by Nathan Lane. (Running Time: 3 hrs. 0 mins. 0 sec.). (ENG.). 2006. audio compact disk 9.95 (978-0-7435-6532-5(0), S&S Encore) Pub: S&S Audio. Dist(s): S and S Inc

McNally's Secret. unabr. ed. Lawrence Sanders. Read by Adam Henderson. 6 vols. (Running Time: 9 hrs.). (Archy McNally Mystery Ser.). 2002. bk. 54.95 (978-0-7927-2524-4(7), CSL 413, Chivers Sound Lib) AudioGO.
Archy McNally, freewheeling playboy who specializes in "Discreet Inquires" for the rich and not-so-discreet, has another mystery to solve. Beneath the glaring sun of Palm Beach and behind the lowest crimes of high society, McNally is paid to keep family skeletons in the closet. But when it comes to sex and scandal, McNally has a few secrets of his own.

McNally's Trial. Lawrence Sanders. (Archy McNally Mystery Ser.). 2004. 10.95 (978-0-7435-4083-4(2)) Pub: S&S Audio. Dist(s): S and S Inc

McNally's Trial. abr. ed. Lawrence Sanders & Lawrence Sanders. Read by Boyd Gaines. (Running Time: 30 hrs. 0 mins. 0 sec.). (ENG.). 2003. audio compact disk 9.95 (978-0-7435-3263-1(5), S&S Encore) Pub: S&S Audio. Dist(s): S and S Inc
As an investigator for his father's Palm Beach law firm, Archy McNally has discreetly handled scores of unusual cases for the firm's upscale clientele. But when Sunny Fogarty, the attractive comptroller for Whitcomb Funeral Homes, approaches McNally & Son to investigate an unexplained rise in her company's fortunes, Archy soon finds himself conducting a most peculiar investigation.

McNally's Trial. unabr. ed. Lawrence Sanders. Read by Edward Lewis. 8 cass. (Running Time: 8 hrs.). (Archy McNally Mystery Ser.). 1996. 48.00 (978-0-7366-3260-7(3), 3917) Books on Tape.
Ignorance isn't really bliss; still, it's better if one doesn't know too much. But when you're Archy McNally, Chief of Discreet Inquiries at a prestigious Palm Beach law firm, it's your job to know. The irrepressible private eye sets out to discover why there's a suspicious rise in business at the Whitcomb Funeral Home. McNally's faithful sidekick Binky Watrous helps him untangle a double-dealing, murderous criminal network that has infested the wealthy family. So far, this is his most enticing case - sinister, sexy, & scandalous - & he hopes to stay a Whitcomb vendor, not a client.

McNally's Trial, unabr. ed. Lawrence Sanders. Narrated by Richard M. Davidson. 6 cass. (Running Time: 9 hrs.). (Archy McNally Mystery Ser.). 51.00 (978-0-7887-0487-1(7), 94680E7) Recorded Bks.
The treasurer at a local funeral home reports suspicious funds, plunging P.I. Archy McNally into a case involving the nefarious criminal underworld. Available to libraries only.

***McNelly Knows a Ranger; A Job for a Ranger; Desert Death Song.** unabr. ed. Louis L'Amour. (ENG.). 2010. audio compact disk 14.99 (978-0-307-74874-4(X), Random AudioBks) Pub: Random Audio Pubg. Dist(s): Random

McQueen of the Tumbling K. unabr. ed. Louis L'Amour. Read by Dramatization Staff. (Running Time: 10800 sec.). (ENG.). 2008. audio compact disk 14.99 (978-0-7393-5886-3(3), Random AudioBks) Pub: Random Audio Pubg. Dist(s): Random

McReele. Stephen Belber. Directed By Jenny Sullivan. Contrib. by Eric Stoltz et al. (Running Time: 6360 sec.). 2006. audio compact disk 25.95 (978-1-58081-349-5(6)) L A Theatre.

MCSE CBT for Windows 2000 Directory Services Design. Course Technology Staff. 2001. audio compact disk 53.95 (978-0-619-06290-3(8)) Pub: Course Tech. Dist(s): CENGAGE Learn

MCSE TBT for Microsoft Windows 2000 Active Directory. Course Technology Staff. 2001. audio compact disk 53.95 (978-0-619-06291-0(6)) Pub: Course Tech. Dist(s): CENGAGE Learn

MCSE TBT for Microsoft Windows 2000 Networking. Course Technology Staff. 2001. audio compact disk 53.95 (978-0-619-06288-0(6)) Pub: Course Tech. Dist(s): CENGAGE Learn

***McTeague.** Frank Norris. Read by Alfred von Lecteur. 2010. 27.95 (978-1-60112-959-8(9)) Babblebooks.

McTeague. unabr. ed. Frank Norris. Read by Wolfram Kandinsky. (Running Time: 14 hrs. 0 mins.). 2008. 29.95 (978-1-4332-5000-2(4)); audio compact disk 110.00 (978-1-4332-4999-0(5)) Blckstn Audio.

McTeague: A Story of San Francisco. Frank Norris. Contrib. by Stacy Keach et al. 12 CDs. (Running Time: 12 hrs.). 2007. audio compact disk 25.95 (978-1-58081-323-5(2)) Pub: L A Theatre. Dist(s): NetLibrary CO

McTeague: A Story of San Francisco. collector's ed. Frank Norris. Read by Jonathan Reese. 8 cass. (Running Time: 12 hrs.). 2000. 64.00 (978-0-7366-5911-6(0)) Books on Tape.
Murder & mayhem move side by side with tender love & flashes of irresistible humor as we follow a dentist's gradual & harrowing decline.

McTeague: A Story of San Francisco. unabr. ed. Frank Norris. Read by Flo Gibson. 8 cass. (Running Time: 12 hrs.). (Classic Books on Cassettes Collection). 1998. 26.95 (978-1-55685-273-2(8)) Audio Bk Con.

McTeague: A Story of San Francisco. unabr. ed. Frank Norris. Read by Wolfram Kandinsky. 10 cass. (Running Time: 14 hrs. 30 mins.). 1993. 69.95 (978-0-7861-0462-8(7), 1414) Blckstn Audio.
When first published in 1899, "McTeague" shocked the reading public. It graphically revealed the seamy side of American urban life, specifically the human degradation in the turn-of-the-century San Francisco. Forbidden to practice dentistry when Marcus Schouler informs the authorities that he lacks both license & diploma, McTeague grows brutish & surly, while his wife, Trina, who had won 5,000 dollars in a lottery, becomes a miser & they sink into poverty. McTeague then deserts, commits a heinous crime & meets an inevitable end in the scorching heat of California's Death Valley.

McTeague: A Story of San Francisco. unabr. ed. Frank Norris. Perf. by Edward Asner et al. 12 cass. (Running Time: 12 hrs.). 1990. 80.95 (978-1-58081-104-0(3), RDP9) L A Theatre.
Frank Norris' seminal novel about the destructive effects of greed.

McVeigh Verdict. Leonard Peikoff. 1 cass. (Philosophy: Who Needs It? Ser.). 1997. 12.95 (LPXXC28) Second Renaissance.

McWilliams & the Burglar Alarm see Great American Short Stories, Vol. II, A Collection

McWilliams & the Burglar Alarm see Californian's Tale

Me. abr. ed. Katharine Hepburn. Read by Katharine Hepburn. (Running Time: 3 hrs.). (ENG.). 2003. audio compact disk 19.95 (978-0-7393-1076-2(3)) Pub: Random Audio Pubg. Dist(s): Random

Me & a Guy Named Elvis. unabr. ed. Jerry Schilling. Read by William Dufris. (Running Time: 14 hrs. 30 mins. 0 sec.). (ENG.). 2006. audio compact disk 39.99 (978-1-4001-0297-6(9)) Pub: Tantor Media. Dist(s): IngramPubServ

Me & a Guy Named Elvis: My Lifelong Friendship with Elvis Presley. unabr. ed. Jerry Schilling. Read by William Dufris. Told to Chuck Crisafulli. (Running Time: 14 hrs. 30 mins. 0 sec.). (ENG.). 2006. audio compact disk 29.99 (978-1-4001-5297-1(6)) Pub: Tantor Media. Dist(s): IngramPubServ

Me & a Guy Named Elvis: My Lifelong Friendship with Elvis Presley. unabr. ed. Jerry Schilling & Chuck Crisafulli. Read by William Dufris. (Running Time: 14 hrs. 30 mins. 0 sec.). (ENG.). 2006. audio compact disk 79.99 (978-1-4001-3297-3(5)) Pub: Tantor Media. Dist(s): IngramPubServ

Me & Belinda Gillis. S. A. Blackman. 1 cass. (J). (gr. 5-9). 2003. bk. 12.95 (978-1-929409-04-4(4)) Blade Pubg.
Educational program about 2 preteens battling obesity & clamoring for acceptance from family, friends, teacher & peers.

Me & Belinda Gillis. unabr. ed. S. A. Blackman. 1 cass. (Running Time: 90 min.). 2003. 13.95 (978-1-929409-05-1(2)) Blade Pubg.

Me & My Baby View the Eclipse. unabr. ed. Short Stories. Lee Smith. Narrated by Linda Stephens & Tom Stechschulte. 6 cass. (Running Time: 7 hrs. 30 mins.). 1998. 51.00 (978-0-7887-0841-1(4), 94987E7) Recorded Bks.
In each of nine powerful stories, ordinary people from the small-town South find inner strength as life's turbulent storms toss them about.

Me & My Bean Bag. 1 cass. (Running Time: 40 min.). (J). 2001. bk. 10.95 (978-0-937124-21-5(4), KIM 9111C); pap. bk. 14.95 (KIM 9111CD) Kimbo Educ.
Don't just pass that bean bag - balance it, juggle it, toss it, dance with it! Team up with The Learning Station & do "The Bean Bag Dance," "the Mexican Bean Bag Hop," "The Bean Bag Pretend," "The Bean Bag Boogie" & more. (Manipulatives - Bean Bags). Includes guide & bean bag.

Me & My Harmonica. 1 cass. 12.95 Musical I Pr.

Me & the Mule see Poetry of Langston Hughes

Me & the Orgone. unabr. ed. Orson Bean. 2 cass. (Running Time: 3 hrs.). 2002. 17.95 (978-0-7861-2187-8(4), 2946); audio compact disk 27.00 (978-0-7861-9582-4(7), 2946) Blckstn Audio.
After spending ten years and thousands of dollars for psychoanalysis, actor Orson Bean was divorced, depressed, and dissatisfied with life. Then he discovered medical orgone therapy. Wilhelm Reich, M.D., developed this unique method of treatment, which centers on the concept that sensual, sexual feelings must be integrated with tender feelings of love for an individual to achieve complete sexual satisfaction. One must be free of emotional and physical blocks to experience such feelings. Here is the candid, deeply personal story of Bean's experience with medical orgone therapy and how it triggered his own sexual revolution and well being.

Me Book: Activities for MeLand 2 (CD) Eva Thayer. 2000. bk. 10.95 (978-1-931228-00-8(0)) Tes Pub.

***Me gusta en mi ciudad Audio CD.** Francisco Blane. Adapted by Benchmark Education Company, LLC. (My First Reader's Theater Ser.). (SPA.). (J). 2009. audio compact disk 10.00 (978-1-935470-66-3(3)) Benchmark Educ.

***Me gusta jugar Audio CD.** Jeffrey B. Fuerst. Adapted by Benchmark Education Company, LLC. (My First Reader's Theater Ser.). (SPA.). (J). 2009. audio compact disk 10.00 (978-1-935470-82-3(5)) Benchmark Educ.

***Me gusta mi hogar Audio CD.** Jeffrey B. Fuerst. Adapted by Benchmark Education Company, LLC. (My First Reader's Theater Ser.). (SPA.). (J). 2009. audio compact disk 10.00 (978-1-935470-64-9(7)) Benchmark Educ.

Me Gustaria Tener. Alma Flor Ada. Illus. by Vivi Escrivá. (Libros Para Contar Ser.). (SPA.). (J). (gr. k-3). 4.95 (978-1-58105-255-8(3)) Santillana.

***Me I Want to Be.** unabr. ed. Thomas C. Oden. (Running Time: 6 hrs. 44 mins. 0 sec.). (ENG.). 2009. 19.99 (978-0-310-57246-6(0)) Zondervan.

Me I Want to Be: Redeeming My Time. unabr. ed. John Ortberg. (Running Time: 6 hrs. 44 mins. 0 sec.). (ENG.). 2009. audio compact disk 32.99 (978-0-310-32696-0(6)) Zondervan.

Me, Inc: How to Master the Business of Being You: A Personalized Program for Exceptional Living. rev. unabr. ed. Scott W. Ventrella. Read by Jonathan Marosz. (Running Time: 5 hrs.). (ENG.). 2007. audio compact disk 19.98 (978-1-59659-130-1(7), GildAudio) Pub: Gildan Media. Dist(s): HachBkGrp

Me, My Family & Friends. 1 CD. (Running Time: 27 min.). (J). 2005. audio compact disk 14.95 (978-0-9765887-3-3(0)) S Edu Res LLC.

***Me, Myself & Why?** unabr. ed. MaryJanice Davidson. Read by Renée Raudman. (Running Time: 12 hrs. 30 mins.). 2010. 29.95 (978-1-4417-5939-9(5)); 44.95 (978-1-4417-5935-1(2)); audio compact disk 69.00 (978-1-4417-5936-8(0)) Blckstn Audio.

***Me, Myself, & Why.** unabr. ed. MaryJanice Davidson. Read by Renée Raudman. (Running Time: 12 hrs. 30 mins.). 2010. audio compact disk 29.95 (978-1-4417-5938-2(7)) Blckstn Audio.

Me, Myself & You. 1986. (1539) Hazelden.

***Me of Little Faith.** Lewis Black. (Running Time: 6 hrs.). (ENG.). 2010. audio compact disk 14.95 (978-0-14-242867-2(1), PengAudBks) Penguin Grp USA.

Me Talk Pretty One Day. David Sedaris. 2001. 24.98 (978-1-58621-132-5(3)) Hachet Audio.

Me Talk Pretty One Day. abr. ed. David Sedaris. Read by David Sedaris. 5 CDs. (Running Time: 5 hrs.). (ENG.). 2001. audio compact disk 29.98 (978-1-58621-066-3(1)) Pub: Hachet Audio. Dist(s): HachBkGrp

Me Talk Pretty One Day. abr. unabr. ed. David Sedaris. (ENG.). 2006. 16.98 (978-1-59483-685-5(X)) Pub: Hachet Audio. Dist(s): HachBkGrp

Me Talk Pretty One Day. unabr. ed. David Sedaris. (Running Time: 5 hrs.). (ENG.). 2009. 44.98 (978-1-60024-947-1(7)) Pub: Hachet Audio. Dist(s): HachBkGrp

***Me, the Missing, & the Dead.** unabr. ed. Jenny Valentine. Narrated by John Keating. 4 CDs. (Running Time: 4 hrs.). (YA). (gr. 8 up). 2009. 33.75 (978-1-4361-6263-0(7)); audio compact disk 46.75 (978-1-4361-6268-5(8)) Recorded Bks.

***Me, the Mob, & the Music: One Helluva Ride with Tommy James & the Shondells.** unabr. ed. Tommy James & Martin Fitzpatrick. Narrated by David Colacci. (Running Time: 8 hrs. 0 mins. 0 sec.). (ENG.). 2010. 19.99 (978-1-4001-6632-9(2)); 14.99 (978-1-4001-8632-7(3)); audio compact disk 59.99 (978-1-4001-4632-1(1)); audio compact disk 29.99 (978-1-4001-1632-4(5)) Pub: Tantor Media. Dist(s): IngramPubServ

Me Times Three. Alex Witchel. Narrated by Alyssa Bresnahan. 10 CDs. (Running Time: 11 hrs. 30 mins.). audio compact disk 99.00 (978-1-4025-2907-8(4)) Recorded Bks.

Me Times Three. unabr. ed. Alex Witchel. Narrated by Alyssa Bresnahan. 8 cass. (Running Time: 11 hrs. 30 mins.). 2002. 78.00 (978-1-4025-0234-7(6), 96873) Recorded Bks.
During the 1980s, a disenchanted assistant editor at a women's magazine is devoted to her fiance, a Wall street moneyman who personifies all her yuppie lifestyle fantasies. However, her bubble bursts when she discovers he's secretly engaged to two other women. Crestfallen, the woman who hates her magazine job, becomes devoted to it.

***Me Unabridged CDs.** Ricky Martin. (Running Time: 8 hrs.). (ENG.). 2010. audio compact disk 29.95 (978-0-14-242930-3(9), PengAudBks) Penguin Grp USA.

Me vs. Myself. Prod. by Fourth Man Records Staff. 1 CD. (Running Time: 30 min.). 2004. audio compact disk 16.98 (978-5-559-59227-5(7)) Pub: Pt of Grace Ent. Dist(s): STL Dist NA

Meadow. Alison Cameron. Read by Alison Cameron. 1 cass. (Running Time: 20 min.). (J). (gr. 4). 1995. 6.95 (978-1-881903-09-3(5)) DW Artworks.
A sleep-time audio in the truest sense: it encourages visualization & relaxation of preschool & kindergarten aged children. The quiet music which accompanies the narration is played in full on side two.

Meadow. James Galvin. Narrated by Patrick G. Lawlor. (Running Time: 7 hrs. 30 mins.). 2003. 27.95 (978-1-59912-693-7(1)) Iofy Corp.

Meadow. unabr. ed. James Galvin. Read by Patrick G. Lawlor. 5 cass. (Running Time: 7 hrs.). 2000. 39.95 (978-0-7861-2593-7(4), 3194) Blckstn Audio.

Meadow. unabr. ed. James Galvin. Read by Patrick G. Lawlor. 6 CDs. (Running Time: 7 hrs.). 2001. audio compact disk 48.00 (978-0-7861-8946-5(0), 3194) Blckstn Audio.

Meadow in Summer see Carl Sandburg's Poems for Children

Mealey International Asbestos Conference Audiotape. Compiled by LexisNexis Staff. 2003. 399.00 (978-1-59579-358-4(5)) Pub: LexisNexis Mealey. Dist(s): LEXIS Pub

Mealey's Additional Insurance Conference (May 12-13) Audiotape. Compiled by LexisNexis Staff. 2005. reel tape 399.00 (978-1-59579-363-8(1)) Pub: LexisNexis Mealey. Dist(s): LEXIS Pub

Mealey's Additional Insurance Conference (May 16-17) Audiotape. Compiled by LexisNexis Staff. 2005. reel tape 399.00 (978-1-59579-366-9(6)) Pub: LexisNexis Mealey. Dist(s): LEXIS Pub

Mealey's Additional Insured Conference Audio CD (April 2007) 2007. 499.00 (978-1-59579-689-9(4)) Pub: LexisNexis Mealey. Dist(s): LEXIS Pub

Mealey's Additional Insured Conference Audio CD (June 2006) 2006. audio compact disk 399.00 (978-1-59579-545-8(6)) Pub: LexisNexis Mealey. Dist(s): LEXIS Pub

Mealey's Additional Insured Conference Audiotape. Compiled by LexisNexis Staff. 2004. reel tape 399.00 (978-1-59579-462-8(X)) Pub: LexisNexis Mealey. Dist(s): LEXIS Pub

Mealey's Additional Insured Conference Audiotape (December 2004) 2004. reel tape 399.00 (978-1-59579-521-2(9)) Pub: LexisNexis Mealey. Dist(s): LEXIS Pub

Mealey's Advanced Insurance Coverage Conference: Top 10 Issues Audiotape. Compiled by LexisNexis Staff. 2004. reel tape 399.00 (978-1-59579-438-3(7)) Pub: LexisNexis Mealey. Dist(s): LEXIS Pub

Mealey's Advanced Insurance Coverage Conference: Top 10 Issues for Practioners Audiotape. 3rd rev. ed. Compiled by LexisNexis Staff. 2003. reel tape 399.00 (978-1-59579-124-5(8)) Pub: LexisNexis Mealey. Dist(s): LEXIS Pub

Mealey's Advanced Insurance Coverage Conference Audiotape. Compiled by LexisNexis Staff. 2005. reel tape 399.00 (978-1-59579-332-4(1)) Pub: LexisNexis Mealey. Dist(s): LEXIS Pub

Mealey's Advanced Skills for Litigation Paralegals Conference Audiotape. Compiled by LexisNexis Staff. 2004. reel tape 225.00 (978-1-59579-485-7(9)) Pub: LexisNexis Mealey. Dist(s): LEXIS Pub

Mealey's Advanced Skills for Mass Tort Paralegals Conference Audiotape. Compiled by LexisNexis Staff. 2004. reel tape 225.00 (978-1-59579-475-8(1)) Pub: LexisNexis Mealey. Dist(s): LEXIS Pub

Mealey's All Sums: Reallocation & Settlement Credits Conference Audiotape. Compiled by LexisNexis Staff. 2004. reel tape 225.00 (978-1-59579-489-5(1)) Pub: LexisNexis Mealey. Dist(s): LEXIS Pub

Mealey's All Sums Conference Audiotape (November 2005) 2005. reel tape 225.00 (978-1-59579-665-3(7)) Pub: LexisNexis Mealey. Dist(s): LEXIS Pub

Mealey's Asbestos Bankruptcy Conference. 3rd rev. ed. Speeches. 2002. reel tape 299.00 (978-1-930146-80-8(9)) Pub: LexisNexis Mealey. Dist(s): LEXIS Pub
A compilation of select speaker presentations from Mealey's Asbestos Bankruptcy Conference, June 2002.

Mealey's Asbestos Bankruptcy Conference Audio CD (December 2007) 2007. 325.00 (978-1-59579-775-9(0)) Pub: LexisNexis Mealey. Dist(s): LEXIS Pub

Mealey's Asbestos Bankruptcy Conference Audio CD (June 2006) 2006. audio compact disk 399.00 (978-1-59579-548-9(0)) Pub: LexisNexis Mealey. Dist(s): LEXIS Pub

Mealey's Asbestos Bankruptcy Conference Audio CD (June 2007) 2007. 499.00 (978-1-59579-709-4(2)) Pub: LexisNexis Mealey. Dist(s): LEXIS Pub

Mealey's Asbestos Bankruptcy Conference Audiotape (December 2004) 2004. reel tape 399.00 (978-1-59579-493-2(X)) Pub: LexisNexis Mealey. Dist(s): LEXIS Pub

Mealey's Asbestos Bankruptcy Conference Audiotape (December 2005) 2005. reel tape 399.00 (978-1-59579-669-1(X)) Pub: LexisNexis Mealey. Dist(s): LEXIS Pub

Mealey's Asbestos Bankruptcy Litigation Conference. Compiled by LexisNexis Staff. 2003. 399.00 (978-1-59579-055-2(1)) LexisNexis Mealey.

Mealey's Asbestos Bankruptcy Litigation Conference Audiotape. Compiled by LexisNexis Staff. 2005. reel tape 399.00 (978-1-59579-370-6(4)) Pub: LexisNexis Mealey. Dist(s): LEXIS Pub

Mealey's Asbestos Conference: The New Face of Asbestos Litigation Audio CD (February 2007) 2007. 399.00 (978-1-59579-620-2(7)) Pub: LexisNexis Mealey. Dist(s): LEXIS Pub

Mealey's Asbestos Gaskets Teleconference: Exposure & State of the Art Audio CD (November 2007) 2007. 149.00 (978-1-59579-785-8(8)) Pub: LexisNexis Mealey. Dist(s): LEXIS Pub

Mealey's Asbestos Insurance Conference Audiotape (December 2005) 2005. reel tape 225.00 (978-1-59579-672-1(X)) Pub: LexisNexis Mealey. Dist(s): LEXIS Pub

Mealey's Asbestos Insurance Teleconference: Where We Stand in Light of Keasbey Audio CD (August 2007) 2007. audio compact disk 149.00 (978-1-59579-719-3(X)) Pub: LexisNexis Mealey. Dist(s): LEXIS Pub

Mealey's Asbestos Insurance Teleconference Audiotape (October 2005) 2005. reel tape 249.00 (978-1-59579-650-9(9)) Pub: LexisNexis Mealey. Dist(s): LEXIS Pub

Mealey's Asbestos Legislation Teleconference. Compiled by LexisNexis Staff. 2006. audio compact disk 225.00 (978-1-59579-060-6(8)) Pub: LexisNexis Mealey. Dist(s): LEXIS Pub

Mealey's Asbestos Liability Forum Audiotape (November 2005) 2005. reel tape 399.00 (978-1-59579-658-5(4)) Pub: LexisNexis Mealey. Dist(s): LEXIS Pub

Mealey's Asbestos Litigation 101 Conference. Compiled by LexisNexis Staff. 2003. 399.00 (978-1-59579-054-5(3)) LexisNexis Mealey.

Mealey's Asbestos Litigation 101 Conference Audiotape. Compiled by LexisNexis Staff. 2004. reel tape 399.00 (978-1-59579-470-3(0)) Pub: LexisNexis Mealey. Dist(s): LEXIS Pub

Mealey's Asbestos Litigation 101 Conference Audiotape. Compiled by LexisNexis Staff. 2005. reel tape 399.00 (978-1-59579-334-8(8)) Pub: LexisNexis Mealey. Dist(s): LEXIS Pub

Mealey's Asbestos Litigation 101 Conference Audiotape. Compiled by LexisNexis Staff. 2005. 399.00 (978-1-59579-381-2(X)) Pub: LexisNexis Mealey. Dist(s): LEXIS Pub

Mealey's Asbestos Medicine Conference. Compiled by LexisNexis Staff. 2006. audio compact disk 175.00 (978-1-59579-318-8(6)) Pub: LexisNexis Mealey. Dist(s): LEXIS Pub

Mealey's Asbestos Medicine Conference Audio CD (April 2007) 2007. 349.00 (978-1-59579-691-2(6)) Pub: LexisNexis Mealey. Dist(s): LEXIS Pub

Mealey's Asbestos Medicine Teleconference Audiotape (October 2005) 2005. reel tape 249.00 (978-1-59579-652-3(5)) Pub: LexisNexis Mealey. Dist(s): LEXIS Pub

Mealey's Asbestos Premises Liability Conference Audiotape. 3rd rev. ed. Compiled by LexisNexis Staff. 2003. reel tape 225.00 (978-1-59579-122-1(1)) Pub: LexisNexis Mealey. Dist(s): LEXIS Pub

Mealey's Asbestos Premises Liability Conference Audiotape (December 2004) 2004. reel tape 399.00 (978-1-59579-497-0(2)) Pub: LexisNexis Mealey. Dist(s): LEXIS Pub

Mealey's Asbestos Teleconference: Data Analysis, Fraudulent Filings Update, & Recovery Trends Audio CD (November 2007) 2007. 149.00 (978-1-59579-742-1(4)) Pub: LexisNexis Mealey. Dist(s): LEXIS Pub

Mealey's Asbestos 101 Conference Audiotape. Compiled by LexisNexis Staff. 2003. 399.00 (978-1-59579-355-3(0)) Pub: LexisNexis Mealey. Dist(s): LEXIS Pub

Mealey's Asbestos 101 Litigation Conference Audiotape. Compiled by LexisNexis Staff. 2004. reel tape 399.00 (978-1-59579-443-7(3)) Pub: LexisNexis Mealey. Dist(s): LEXIS Pub

Mealey's Avandia Litigation Conference Audio CD (July 2007) 2007. audio compact disk 325.00 (978-1-59579-716-2(5)) Pub: LexisNexis Mealey. Dist(s): LEXIS Pub

Mealey's Bad Faith Conference Audiotape. Compiled by LexisNexis Staff. 2004. reel tape 399.00 (978-1-59579-478-9(6)) Pub: LexisNexis Mealey. Dist(s): LEXIS Pub

Mealey's Bad Faith Conference Audiotape. 3rd rev. ed. Compiled by LexisNexis Staff. 2003. reel tape 399.00 (978-1-59579-143-6(4)) Pub: LexisNexis Mealey. Dist(s): LEXIS Pub

Mealey's Bad Faith Litigation Conference Audio CD (September 2007) 2007. 499.00 (978-1-59579-734-6(3)) Pub: LexisNexis Mealey. Dist(s): LEXIS Pub

Mealey's Bad Faith Litigation Conference Audiotape. Compiled by LexisNexis Staff. 2005. reel tape 399.00 (978-1-59579-385-0(2)) Pub: LexisNexis Mealey. Dist(s): LEXIS Pub

Mealey's Bad Faith Teleconference Series: Innovative & Emerging Theories, with a Duty to Defend Update Audio CD (October 2007) 2007. 149.00 (978-1-59579-753-7(X)) Pub: LexisNexis Mealey. Dist(s): LEXIS Pub

Mealey's Baycol Litigation Conference Audiotape. 3rd rev. ed. Compiled by LexisNexis Staff. 2003. reel tape 399.00 (978-1-59579-154-2(X)) Pub: LexisNexis Mealey. Dist(s): LEXIS Pub

Mealey's Baycol Litigation Conference Audiotape. 3rd rev. ed. Compiled by LexisNexis Staff. 2004. reel tape 225.00 (978-1-59579-127-6(2)) Pub: LexisNexis Mealey. Dist(s): LEXIS Pub

Mealey's Benzene Litigation Conference Audio CD (June 2006) 2006. audio compact disk 399.00 (978-1-59579-550-2(2)) Pub: LexisNexis Mealey. Dist(s): LEXIS Pub

Mealey's Benzene Litigation Conference Audiotape (October 2005) 2005. reel tape 399.00 (978-1-59579-625-7(8)) Pub: LexisNexis Mealey. Dist(s): LEXIS Pub

Mealey's Bextra & Celebrex Conference Audiotape. Compiled by LexisNexis Staff. 2005. reel tape 225.00 (978-1-59579-368-3(2)) Pub: LexisNexis Mealey. Dist(s): LEXIS Pub

Mealey's Bextra & Celebrex Teleconference. Compiled by LexisNexis Staff. 2006. audio compact disk 249.00 (978-1-59579-310-2(0)) Pub: LexisNexis Mealey. Dist(s): LEXIS Pub

Mealey's Birth Control Patch Litigation Teleconference. Compiled by LexisNexis Staff. 2006. 249.00 (978-1-59579-308-9(9)) LexisNexis Mealey.

Mealey's Business Interruption Insurance Conference Audiotape. Compiled by LexisNexis Staff. 2004. reel tape 225.00 (978-1-59579-464-2(6)) Pub: LexisNexis Mealey. Dist(s): LEXIS Pub

Mealey's C-8/PFOA Science, Risk & Litigation Conference Audiotape (October 2005) 2005. reel tape 399.00 (978-1-59579-647-9(9)) Pub: LexisNexis Mealey. Dist(s): LEXIS Pub

Mealey's California Bad Faith Conference Audio CD (March 2007) 2007. 499.00 (978-1-59579-628-8(2)) Pub: LexisNexis Mealey. Dist(s): LEXIS Pub

Mealey's California Section 17200 Conference Audiotape. Compiled by LexisNexis Staff. 2004. reel tape 399.00 (978-1-59579-491-8(3)) Pub: LexisNexis Mealey. Dist(s): LEXIS Pub

Mealey's Catastrophic Loss: Hurricane Katrina Teleconference Audiotape (October 2005) 2005. reel tape 249.00 (978-1-59579-649-3(5)) Pub: LexisNexis Mealey. Dist(s): LEXIS Pub

Mealey's Catastrophic Loss Conference. Compiled by LexisNexis Staff. 2006. audio compact disk 399.00 (978-1-59579-328-7(3)) Pub: LexisNexis Mealey. Dist(s): LEXIS Pub

Mealey's Catastrophic Loss Conference Audiotape (October 2005) 2005. reel tape 399.00 (978-1-59579-623-3(1)) Pub: LexisNexis Mealey. Dist(s): LEXIS Pub

Mealey's Catastrophic Loss Teleconference: Business Interruption Claims Analysis Audio CD (June 2007) 2007. 149.00 (978-1-59579-710-0(6)) Pub: LexisNexis Mealey. Dist(s): LEXIS Pub

Mealey's Class Certification Teleconference Audiotape (December 2005) 2005. reel tape 249.00 (978-1-59579-675-2(4)) Pub: LexisNexis Mealey. Dist(s): LEXIS Pub

Mealey's Concrete Litigation Conference. Compiled by LexisNexis Staff. 2006. audio compact disk 175.00 (978-1-59579-058-3(6)) Pub: LexisNexis Mealey. Dist(s): LEXIS Pub

Mealey's Conference: Food & Product Recall Business Strategies Audio CD (April 2008) 2008. 499.00 (978-1-59579-852-7(8)) Pub: LexisNexis Mealey. Dist(s): LEXIS Pub

Mealey's Construction Defect & Mold Litigation Conference Audiotape (December 2004) reel tape 399.00 (978-1-59579-495-6(6)) Pub: LexisNexis Mealey. Dist(s): LEXIS Pub

Mealey's Construction Defect & Mold Litigation Conference Audiotape (November 2005) 2005. reel tape 399.00 (978-1-59579-660-8(6)) Pub: LexisNexis Mealey. Dist(s): LEXIS Pub

Mealey's Construction Defect Teleconference: Building a Better WRAP Program Audio CD (December 2007) 2007. 149.00 (978-1-59579-791-9(2)) Pub: LexisNexis Mealey. Dist(s): LEXIS Pub

Mealey's Construction Litigation Conference Audio CD (May 2008) 2008. 499.00 (978-1-59579-866-4(8)) Pub: LexisNexis Mealey. Dist(s): LEXIS Pub

Mealey's Corporate E-Discovery Conference Audio CD (April 2007) 2007. 325.00 (978-1-59579-687-5(8)) Pub: LexisNexis Mealey. Dist(s): LEXIS Pub

Mealey's Courtroom Practices Teleconference Series: Best Practices for Surviving an Expert Admissibility Challenge Audio CD (February 2007) 2007. 249.00 (978-1-59579-621-9(5)) Pub: LexisNexis Mealey. Dist(s): LEXIS Pub

Mealey's D & O Litigation Teleconference Update: Global Warming Stock Options Backdating, Sub-Prime Lending Audio CD (August 2007) 2007. 149.00 (978-1-59579-727-8(0)) Pub: LexisNexis Mealey. Dist(s): LEXIS Pub

Mealey's Defense Strategies for Pharmaceutical & Medical Device Litigation Conference Audiotape (February 2003) reel tape 399.00 (978-1-59579-522-9(7)) Pub: LexisNexis Mealey. Dist(s): LEXIS Pub

Mealey's Drug & Medical Device Litigation Conference Audio CD (May 2007) 2007. 499.00 (978-1-59579-697-4(5)) Pub: LexisNexis Mealey. Dist(s): LEXIS Pub

Mealey's Drug & Medical Device Teleconference Series: HRT Update in light of Arlene Rowatt, et al. V. Wyeth Audio CD (January 2008) 2008. 149.00 (978-1-59579-796-4(3)) Pub: LexisNexis Mealey. Dist(s): LEXIS Pub

Mealey's Drug & Medical Device Teleconference Series: Trasylol (Aprotinin) Litigation Audio CD (December 2007) 2007. 149.00 (978-1-59579-780-3(7)) Pub: LexisNexis Mealey. Dist(s): LEXIS Pub

Mealey's Drug & Medical Device Teleconference Series: Trasylol (Aprotinin) Litigation Audio CD (February 2007) 2007. 249.00 (978-1-59579-622-6(3)) Pub: LexisNexis Mealey. Dist(s): LEXIS Pub

Mealey's Drug & Medical Device Teleconference Series: Zelnorm Audio CD (May 2007) 2007. 249.00 (978-1-59579-701-8(7)) Pub: LexisNexis Mealey. Dist(s): LEXIS Pub

Mealey's Email Discovery & Rentention Policies Conference Audio CD. Compiled by LexisNexis Staff. 2006. audio compact disk 225.00 (978-1-59579-361-4(5)) Pub: LexisNexis Mealey. Dist(s): LEXIS Pub

Mealey's Email Discovery & Retention Policies Conference. Compiled by LexisNexis Staff. 2006. audio compact disk 175.00 (978-1-59579-316-4(X)) Pub: LexisNexis Mealey. Dist(s): LEXIS Pub

Mealey's Email Discovery & Retention Policies for Corporate Counsel Teleconference Audiotape (October 2005) 2005. reel tape 249.00 (978-1-59579-655-4(X)) Pub: LexisNexis Mealey. Dist(s): LEXIS Pub

Mealey's Emerging Trends in Asbestos Litigation Conference Audio CD (March 2008) 2008. 499.00 (978-1-59579-843-5(9)) Pub: LexisNexis Mealey. Dist(s): LEXIS Pub

Mealey's Environmental Litigation Conference Audiotape. Compiled by LexisNexis Staff. 2005. reel tape 399.00 (978-1-59579-354-6(2)) Pub: LexisNexis Mealey. Dist(s): LEXIS Pub

Mealey's Ephedra & PPA Litigation Conference Audiotape. Compiled by LexisNexis Staff. 2005. reel tape 399.00 (978-1-59579-378-2(X)) Pub: LexisNexis Mealey. Dist(s): LEXIS Pub

Mealey's Ephedra Litigation Conference Audiotape. Compiled by LexisNexis Staff. 2004. reel tape 225.00 (978-1-59579-460-4(3)) Pub: LexisNexis Mealey. Dist(s): LEXIS Pub

Mealey's Ephreda Litigation Conference Audiotape. 3rd rev. ed. Compiled by LexisNexis Staff. 2003. reel tape 399.00 (978-1-59579-146-7(9)) Pub: LexisNexis Mealey. Dist(s): LEXIS Pub

Mealey's ERISA Litigation Conference Audiotape. 3rd rev. ed. Compiled by LexisNexis Staff. 2003. reel tape 399.00 (978-1-59579-133-7(7)) Pub: LexisNexis Mealey. Dist(s): LEXIS Pub

Mealey's Ethics Teleconference Series: Attorney Client Privilege in Mass Torts & Class Actions Audio CD (March 2007) 2007. 249.00 (978-1-59579-629-5(0)) Pub: LexisNexis Mealey. Dist(s): LEXIS Pub

Mealey's Finite Risk Reinsurance Teleconference Audiotape (December 2005) 2005. reel tape 249.00 (978-1-59579-681-3(9)) Pub: LexisNexis Mealey. Dist(s): LEXIS Pub

Mealey's Foodborne Illness Liability Teleconference Audiotape (November 2005) 2005. reel tape 249.00 (978-1-59579-661-5(4)) Pub: LexisNexis Mealey. Dist(s): LEXIS Pub

Mealey's Fundamental of Asbestos Conference. Compiled by LexisNexis Staff. 2006. audio compact disk 399.00 (978-1-59579-306-5(2)) Pub: LexisNexis Mealey. Dist(s): LEXIS Pub

Mealey's Fundamentals of Insurance Conference. Compiled by LexisNexis Staff. 2006. audio compact disk 399.00 (978-1-59579-063-7(2)) Pub: LexisNexis Mealey. Dist(s): LEXIS Pub

Mealey's Fundamentals of Insurance Conference Audio CD (February 2007) 2007. 399.00 (978-1-59579-617-2(7)) Pub: LexisNexis Mealey. Dist(s): LEXIS Pub

Mealey's Fundamentals of Insurance Coverage Law Conf Audiotape. 3rd rev. ed. Compiled by LexisNexis Staff. 2003. reel tape 399.00 (978-1-59579-167-2(1)) Pub: LexisNexis Mealey. Dist(s): LEXIS Pub

Mealey's Fundamentals of Insurance Coverage Law Conference Audiotape. 3rd rev. ed. Compiled by LexisNexis Staff. 2003. reel tape 225.00 (978-1-59579-165-8(5)) Pub: LexisNexis Mealey. Dist(s): LEXIS Pub

Mealey's Fundamentals of Reinsurance & Insolvency Conference Audiotape. 3rd rev. ed. Compiled by LexisNexis Staff. 2003. reel tape 349.00 (978-1-59579-166-5(3)) Pub: LexisNexis Mealey. Dist(s): LEXIS Pub

Mealey's Fundamentals of Reinsurance Conference Audio CD (March 2007) 2007. 499.00 (978-1-59579-631-8(2)) Pub: LexisNexis Mealey. Dist(s): LEXIS Pub

Mealey's Fundamentals of Reinsurance Litigation & Arbitration Conference. Compiled by LexisNexis Staff. 2006. 399.00 (978-1-59579-313-3(5)) LexisNexis Mealey.

Mealey's Gadolinium Litigation Teleconference Audio CD (August 2007) 2007. 149.00 (978-1-59579-728-5(9)) Pub: LexisNexis Mealey. Dist(s): LEXIS Pub

Mealey's Global Warming Insurance Litigation Conference Audio CD (June 2007) 2007. 325.00 (978-1-59579-707-0(6)) Pub: LexisNexis Mealey. Dist(s): LEXIS Pub

Mealey's Heart Device Litigation Teleconference Audio CD. Compiled by LexisNexis Staff. 2005. reel tape 249.00 (978-1-59579-379-9(8)) Pub: LexisNexis Mealey. Dist(s): LEXIS Pub

Mealey's High-Rise Condo Construction Defect Litigation Teleconference. Compiled by LexisNexis Staff. 2006. audio compact disk 249.00 (978-1-59579-323-2(2)) Pub: LexisNexis Mealey. Dist(s): LEXIS Pub

Mealey's Hurrican & Natural Disaster Conference Series - Affect on the INS & REI Industries Teleconference. Compiled by LexisNexis Staff. 2006. audio compact disk 249.00 (978-1-59579-309-6(7)) Pub: LexisNexis Mealey. Dist(s): LEXIS Pub

Mealey's Hurricane & Natural Disaster Conference Series - Business Interruption Claims Analysis Teleconference. Compiled by LexisNexis Staff. 2006. audio compact disk 249.00 (978-1-59579-320-1(8)) Pub: LexisNexis Mealey. Dist(s): LEXIS Pub

Mealey's Hurricane & Natural Disaster Conference Series - Claims Impact Teleconference. Compiled by LexisNexis Staff. 2006. audio compact disk 249.00 (978-1-59579-312-6(7)) Pub: LexisNexis Mealey. Dist(s): LEXIS Pub

Mealey's Insurance & Reinsurance Corporate Counsel's Conference Audiotape (December 2005) 2005. reel tape 399.00 (978-1-59579-663-9(0)) Pub: LexisNexis Mealey. Dist(s): LEXIS Pub

Mealey's Insurance Coverage Disputes Concerning Construction Defects Audiotape. Compiled by LexisNexis Staff. 2004. reel tape 399.00 (978-1-59579-481-9(6)) Pub: LexisNexis Mealey. Dist(s): LEXIS Pub

Mealey's Insurance Coverage Disputes Concerning Construction Defects Audiotape (October 2005) 2005. reel tape 399.00 (978-1-59579-641-7(X)) Pub: LexisNexis Mealey. Dist(s): LEXIS Pub

Mealey's Insurance Coverage Disputes Concerning Construction Defects Conference. Compiled by LexisNexis Staff. 2006. audio compact disk 399.00 (978-1-59579-322-5(4)) Pub: LexisNexis Mealey. Dist(s): LEXIS Pub

Mealey's Insurance Coverage Disputes Concerning Constructions Defects Conference Audiotape. 3rd rev. ed. Compiled by LexisNexis Staff. 2003. reel tape 399.00 (978-1-59579-117-7(5)) Pub: LexisNexis Mealey. Dist(s): LEXIS Pub

Mealey's Insurance Coverage for Financial Institution Exposures Conference Audiotape. Compiled by LexisNexis Staff. 2005. reel tape 225.00 (978-1-59579-348-5(8)) Pub: LexisNexis Mealey. Dist(s): LEXIS Pub

Mealey's Insurance Insolvency & Reinsurance Roundtable Audiotape. 3rd rev. ed. Compiled by LexisNexis Staff. 2003. reel tape 399.00 (978-1-59579-135-1(3)) Pub: LexisNexis Mealey. Dist(s): LEXIS Pub

Mealey's Insurance Insolvency & Reinsurance Roundtable Conference. Compiled by LexisNexis Staff. 2006. audio compact disk 175.00 (978-1-59579-317-1(8)) Pub: LexisNexis Mealey. Dist(s): LEXIS Pub

Mealey's Insurance Summit Audio CD (May 2008) 2008. 499.00 (978-1-59579-864-0(1)) Pub: LexisNexis Mealey. Dist(s): LEXIS Pub

Mealey's Insurance Teleconference Series: Global Warming & What Companies Need to Know to Avoid Liability Audio CD (September 2007) 2007. 149.00 (978-1-59579-730-8(0)) Pub: LexisNexis Mealey. Dist(s): LEXIS Pub

Mealey's Insurance 101 Conference Audiotape. Compiled by LexisNexis Staff. 2004. reel tape 399.00 (978-1-59579-450-5(6)) Pub: LexisNexis Mealey. Dist(s): LEXIS Pub

Mealey's Insurance 101 Conference Audiotape. Compiled by LexisNexis Staff. 2005. reel tape 399.00 (978-1-59579-337-9(2)) Pub: LexisNexis Mealey. Dist(s): LEXIS Pub

Mealey's Insurance/Reinsurance Company Run-off Conference. Compiled by LexisNexis Staff. 2006. audio compact disk 399.00 (978-1-59579-325-6(9)) Pub: LexisNexis Mealey. Dist(s): LEXIS Pub

Mealey's Lead Litigation: The Impact of the Rhode Island Decision. Compiled by LexisNexis Staff. 2006. audio compact disk 249.00 (978-1-59579-315-7(1)) Pub: LexisNexis Mealey. Dist(s): LEXIS Pub

Mealey's Lead Litigation Conference Audio CD (April 2007) 2007. 499.00 (978-1-59579-694-3(0)) Pub: LexisNexis Mealey. Dist(s): LEXIS Pub

Mealey's Lead Litigation Conference Audio CD (April 2008) 2008. 499.00 (978-1-59579-849-7(8)) Pub: LexisNexis Mealey. Dist(s): LEXIS Pub

Mealey's Lead Litigation Conference Audio CD (June 2006) 2006. audio compact disk 399.00 (978-1-59579-543-4(X)) Pub: LexisNexis Mealey. Dist(s): LEXIS Pub

Mealey's Lead Litigation Conference Audiotape. 3rd rev. ed. Compiled by LexisNexis Staff. 2003. reel tape 399.00 (978-1-59579-144-3(2)) Pub: LexisNexis Mealey. Dist(s): LEXIS Pub

Mealey's Lead Litigation Conference Audiotape (December 2005) 2005. reel tape 399.00 (978-1-59579-679-0(7)) Pub: LexisNexis Mealey. Dist(s): LEXIS Pub

Mealey's Life of a Reinsurance Claim Teleconference Audiotape (October 2005) 2005. reel tape 249.00 (978-1-59579-645-5(2)) Pub: LexisNexis Mealey. Dist(s): LEXIS Pub

Mealey's Litigation Management Guidelines Conference Audio CD (May 2007) 2007. 499.00 (978-1-59579-699-8(1)) Pub: LexisNexis Mealey. Dist(s): LEXIS Pub

Mealey's Mass Tort Insurance Coverage Conference Audio CD (March 2007) 2007. 499.00 (978-1-59579-633-2(9)) Pub: LexisNexis Mealey. Dist(s): LEXIS Pub

Mealey's Medicine for Lawyers Teleconference Series: Pulmonology Audio CD (January 2007) 2007. 249.00 (978-1-59579-614-1(2)) Pub: LexisNexis Mealey. Dist(s): LEXIS Pub

Mealey's Mold Litigation Conference Audiotape. Compiled by LexisNexis Staff. 2005. reel tape 399.00 (978-1-59579-376-8(3)) Pub: LexisNexis Mealey. Dist(s): LEXIS Pub

Mealey's Mold Litigation Conference Audiotape. 3rd rev. ed. Compiled by LexisNexis Staff. 2003. reel tape 399.00 (978-1-59579-168-9(X)) Pub: LexisNexis Mealey. Dist(s): LEXIS Pub

Mealey's Mold Litigation Teleconference Audiotape (December 2005) 2005. reel tape 249.00 (978-1-59579-680-6(0)) Pub: LexisNexis Mealey. Dist(s): LEXIS Pub

Mealey's Mold 101 Conference Audiotape. Compiled by LexisNexis Staff. 2004. reel tape 399.00 (978-1-59579-456-7(5)) Pub: LexisNexis Mealey. Dist(s): LEXIS Pub

Mealey's Motor Vehicle Liability Conference Audiotape. Compiled by LexisNexis Staff. 2005. reel tape 225.00 (978-1-59579-346-1(1)) Pub: LexisNexis Mealey. Dist(s): LEXIS Pub

Mealey's MTBE: New Groundbreaking Rulings in the Federal MDL Teleconference Audiotape (October 2005) 2005. reel tape 249.00 (978-1-59579-651-6(7)) Pub: LexisNexis Mealey. Dist(s): LEXIS Pub

Mealey's National Asbestos Conference Audiotape. Compiled by LexisNexis Staff. 2003. 399.00 (978-1-59579-357-7(7)) Pub: LexisNexis Mealey. Dist(s): LEXIS Pub

Mealey's National Asbestos Litigation Conference. Compiled by LexisNexis Staff. 2005. reel tape 399.00 (978-1-59579-382-9(8)) Pub: LexisNexis Mealey. Dist(s): LEXIS Pub

Mealey's National Asbestos Litigation Conference Audiotape. Compiled by LexisNexis Staff. 2004. reel tape 399.00 (978-1-59579-472-7(7)) Pub: LexisNexis Mealey. Dist(s): LEXIS Pub

Mealey's National Asbestos Litigation Conference Audiotape. Compiled by LexisNexis Staff. 2005. reel tape 399.00 (978-1-59579-383-6(6)) Pub: LexisNexis Mealey. Dist(s): LEXIS Pub

Mealey's National Asbestos SuperConference Audio CD (September 2007) 2007. 525.00 (978-1-59579-739-1(4)) Pub: LexisNexis Mealey. Dist(s): LEXIS Pub

Mealey's National Mold Litigation Conference Audiotape. Compiled by LexisNexis Staff. 2004. reel tape 399.00 (978-1-59579-468-0(9)) Pub: LexisNexis Mealey. Dist(s): LEXIS Pub

Mealey's Natural Resource Damages Conference Audio CD (March 2008) 2008. 325.00 (978-1-59579-847-3(1)) Pub: LexisNexis Mealey. Dist(s): LEXIS Pub

Mealey's Pacific Northwest Construction Defect Conference Audio CD (June 2006) 2006. audio compact disk 399.00 (978-1-59579-555-7(3)) Pub: LexisNexis Mealey. Dist(s): LEXIS Pub

Mealey's Perchlorate Teleconference: The Debate over a National Standard Audiotape (December 2005) 2005. reel tape 249.00 (978-1-59579-677-6(0)) Pub: LexisNexis Mealey. Dist(s): LEXIS Pub

Mealey's Pesticide Litigation Teleconference Audiotape (November 2005) 2005. reel tape 249.00 (978-1-59579-667-7(3)) Pub: LexisNexis Mealey. Dist(s): LEXIS Pub

Mealey's Pharmaceutical Litigation 101 Conference Audiotape. Compiled by LexisNexis Staff. 2005. reel tape 399.00 (978-1-59579-374-4(7)) Pub: LexisNexis Mealey. Dist(s): LEXIS Pub

Mealey's PPA Litigation Conference Audiotape. Compiled by LexisNexis Staff. 2004. reel tape 225.00 (978-1-59579-436-9(0)) Pub: LexisNexis Mealey. Dist(s): LEXIS Pub

Mealey's Practical Skills Series: Toxic Tort Litigation Conference Audiotape. 3rd rev. ed. Compiled by LexisNexis Staff. 2003. reel tape 399.00 (978-1-59579-142-9(6)) Pub: LexisNexis Mealey. Dist(s): LEXIS Pub

Mealey's Practical Training for the Claims Professional Conference Audiotape. Compiled by LexisNexis Staff. 2004. reel tape 225.00 (978-1-59579-445-1(X)) Pub: LexisNexis Mealey. Dist(s): LEXIS Pub

Mealey's Product Liability Teleconference: Lead Paint Toy Recalls Audio CD (November 2007) 2007. 149.00 (978-1-59579-779-7(3)) Pub: LexisNexis Mealey. Dist(s): LEXIS Pub

Mealey's Professional Teleconference: Understanding How a Multidistrict Litigation Works Audio CD (July 2006) 2006. audio compact disk 249.00 (978-1-59579-560-1(X)) Pub: LexisNexis Mealey. Dist(s): LEXIS Pub

Mealey's Public Nuisance Teleconference: An Evolving Theory of Tort Recovery & Its Implications for Insurance Audio CD (October 2007) 2007. 149.00 (978-1-59579-743-8(2)) Pub: LexisNexis Mealey. Dist(s): LEXIS Pub

Mealey's P2P Networks & Liability Teleconference: Protection of Digital Materials. Compiled by LexisNexis Staff. 2006. audio compact disk 249.00 (978-1-59579-324-9(0)) Pub: LexisNexis Mealey. Dist(s): LEXIS Pub

Mealey's Real World Application of Additional Insured Claims Teleconference Audiotape (November 2005) 2005. reel tape 249.00 (978-1-59579-656-1(8)) Pub: LexisNexis Mealey. Dist(s): LEXIS Pub

Mealey's Reinsurance Arbitration Teleconference: Comparison of US & UK Processes Audio CD (July 2007) 2007. 149.00 (978-1-59579-721-6(1)) Pub: LexisNexis Mealey. Dist(s): LEXIS Pub

Mealey's Reinsurance Litigation & Arbitration Conference Audio CD (February 2008) 2008. 499.00 (978-1-59579-837-4(4)) Pub: LexisNexis Mealey. Dist(s): LEXIS Pub

Mealey's Reinsurance 101 Conference Audiotape. Compiled by LexisNexis Staff. 2004. reel tape 399.00 (978-1-59579-441-3(7)) Pub: LexisNexis Mealey. Dist(s): LEXIS Pub

Mealey's Reinsurance 101 Conference Audiotape. Compiled by LexisNexis Staff. 2005. reel tape 399.00 (978-1-59579-340-9(2)) Pub: LexisNexis Mealey. Dist(s): LEXIS Pub

Mealey's Retail & Hospitality Liability Conference Audiotape (October 2005) 2005. reel tape 399.00 (978-1-59579-644-8(4)) Pub: LexisNexis Mealey. Dist(s): LEXIS Pub

Mealey's Retail Liability Conference Audiotape (December 2004) 2004. reel tape 399.00 (978-1-59579-499-4(9)) Pub: LexisNexis Mealey. Dist(s): LEXIS Pub

Mealey's Role of Paralegals in Mass Tort Litigation Conference Audiotape. Compiled by LexisNexis Staff. 2004. reel tape 225.00 (978-1-59579-466-6(2)) Pub: LexisNexis Mealey. Dist(s): LEXIS Pub

Mealey's Scope of Coverage Conference Audio CD (October 2007) 2007. 325.00 (978-1-59579-747-6(5)) Pub: LexisNexis Mealey. Dist(s): LEXIS Pub

Mealey's Silica Litigation Conference Audiotape. Compiled by LexisNexis Staff. 2004. reel tape 399.00 (978-1-59579-487-1(5)) Pub: LexisNexis Mealey. Dist(s): LEXIS Pub

Mealey's Silica Litigation conference Audiotape. 3rd rev. ed. Compiled by LexisNexis Staff. 2003. reel tape 399.00 (978-1-59579-147-4(7)) Pub: LexisNexis Mealey. Dist(s): LEXIS Pub

Mealey's Silica Medicine Conference Audiotape. Compiled by LexisNexis Staff. 2004. reel tape 399.00 (978-1-59579-452-9(2)) Pub: LexisNexis Mealey. Dist(s): LEXIS Pub

Mealey's Solvent Schemes & Part VII Transfers Conference Audio CD (January 2008) 2008. 499.00 (978-1-59579-767-4(X)) Pub: LexisNexis Mealey. Dist(s): LEXIS Pub

Mealey's Solvent Schemes of Arrangement Conference. Compiled by LexisNexis Staff. 2006. audio compact disk 399.00 (978-1-59579-059-0(4)) Pub: LexisNexis Mealey. Dist(s): LEXIS Pub

Mealey's SSRI's Teleconference Audiotape (December 2005) 2005. reel tape 249.00 (978-1-59579-670-7(3)) Pub: LexisNexis Mealey. Dist(s): LEXIS Pub

Mealey's Subprime Mortgage Litigation Conference Audio CD (October 2007) 2007. 499.00 (978-1-59579-755-1(6)) Pub: LexisNexis Mealey. Dist(s): LEXIS Pub

Mealey's Subprime Mortgage Teleconference: Coverage Issues Arising from Subprime Lending Audio CD (March 2008) 2008. 149.00 (978-1-59579-857-2(9)) Pub: LexisNexis Mealey. Dist(s): LEXIS Pub

Mealey's Teleconference: Are you Covered? Protecting Business from the Most Common Liabilities Audio CD (June 2006) 2006. audio compact disk 249.00 (978-1-59579-557-1(X)) Pub: LexisNexis Mealey. Dist(s): LEXIS Pub

Mealey's Teleconference: Asbestos Legislation - Is A Solution to the Crisis Around the Corner? Audio CD (July 2006) 2006. audio compact disk 249.00 (978-1-59579-559-5(6)) Pub: LexisNexis Mealey. Dist(s): LEXIS Pub

Mealey's Teleconference: Asbestos Litigation Update - Life after the FAIR Act Audio CD (June 2007) 2007. 149.00 (978-1-59579-713-1(0)) Pub: LexisNexis Mealey. Dist(s): LEXIS Pub

Mealey's Teleconference: Avandia Litigation Update Audio CD (October 2007) 2007. 149.00 (978-1-59579-750-6(5)) Pub: LexisNexis Mealey. Dist(s): LEXIS Pub

Mealey's Teleconference: Challenges of the Managing General Agents Model Audio CD (March 2008) 2008. 149.00 (978-1-59579-855-8(2)) Pub: LexisNexis Mealey. Dist(s): LEXIS Pub

Mealey's Teleconference: Climate Change & Insurance Exposures Audio CD (February 2008) 2008. 149.00 (978-1-59579-841-1(2)) Pub: LexisNexis Mealey. Dist(s): LEXIS Pub

Mealey's Teleconference: Contact Lens Solution Audio CD (June 2006) 2006. audio compact disk 249.00 (978-1-59579-556-4(1)) Pub: LexisNexis Mealey. Dist(s): LEXIS Pub

Mealey's Teleconference: Contact Lens Solution Litigation Audio CD (July 2007) 2007. 149.00 (978-1-59579-722-3(X)) Pub: LexisNexis Mealey. Dist(s): LEXIS Pub

Mealey's Teleconference: Discrimination Suits Facing the Retail Industry Audio CD (July 2006) 2006. audio compact disk 249.00 (978-1-59579-561-8(8)) Pub: LexisNexis Mealey. Dist(s): LEXIS Pub

Mealey's Teleconference: Emerging Issues in Reinsurance Arbitration Audio CD (June 2007) 2007. 149.00 (978-1-59579-714-8(9)) Pub: LexisNexis Mealey. Dist(s): LEXIS Pub

Mealey's Teleconference: Ethical Issues Arising in Class Actions Audio CD (September 2006) 2006. audio compact disk 175.00 (978-1-59579-579-3(0)) Pub: LexisNexis Mealey. Dist(s): LEXIS Pub

Mealey's Teleconference: Ethics in Class Actions Audio CD (June 2006) 2006. audio compact disk 249.00 (978-1-59579-551-9(0)) Pub: LexisNexis Mealey. Dist(s): LEXIS Pub

Mealey's Teleconference: Finite Reinsurance Update Audio CD (June 2006) 2006. audio compact disk 249.00 (978-1-59579-552-6(9)) Pub: LexisNexis Mealey. Dist(s): LEXIS Pub

Mealey's Teleconference: Fosamax Audio CD (June 2006) 2006. audio compact disk 249.00 (978-1-59579-553-3(7)) Pub: LexisNexis Mealey. Dist(s): LEXIS Pub

Mealey's Teleconference: Going for the Golden Ring - Tactics & Techniques for Moving Toward Partnership Audio CD (November 2007) 2007. 149.00 (978-1-59579-783-4(1)) Pub: LexisNexis Mealey. Dist(s): LEXIS Pub

Mealey's Teleconference: Insurance Coverage for Product Recalls Audio CD (February 2008) 2008. 149.00 (978-1-59579-771-1(8)) Pub: LexisNexis Mealey. Dist(s): LEXIS Pub

Mealey's Teleconference: Lead Litigation Update Audio CD (December 2007) 2007. 149.00 (978-1-59579-784-1(X)) Pub: LexisNexis Mealey. Dist(s): LEXIS Pub

Mealey's Teleconference: Litigation Management Guidelines I: Introduction Audio CD (October 2007) 2007. 149.00 (978-1-59579-725-4(4)) Pub: LexisNexis Mealey. Dist(s): LEXIS Pub

Mealey's Teleconference: Mold & Construction Defect Litigation in Public Buildings. Compiled by LexisNexis Staff. 2006. audio compact disk 249.00 (978-1-59579-307-2(0)) Pub: LexisNexis Mealey. Dist(s): LEXIS Pub

Mealey's Teleconference: Nanotechnology Audio CD (January 2007) 2007. 249.00 (978-1-59579-607-3(X)) Pub: LexisNexis Mealey. Dist(s): LEXIS Pub

Mealey's Teleconference: Overview of Managing General Agents & Program Writing Business Audio CD (December 2007) 2007. 149.00 (978-1-59579-777-3(7)) Pub: LexisNexis Mealey. Dist(s): LEXIS Pub

Mealey's Teleconference: PPA & Ephedra Audio CD (July 2006) 2006. audio compact disk 249.00 (978-1-59579-558-8(8)) Pub: LexisNexis Mealey. Dist(s): LEXIS Pub

Mealey's Teleconference: Preemption the FDA & Pharmaceutical Drug Litigation Audio CD (June 2006) 2006. audio compact disk 249.00 (978-1-59579-546-5(4)) Pub: LexisNexis Mealey. Dist(s): LEXIS Pub

Mealey's Teleconference: Procedural Issues in Reinsurance Disputes Audio CD (August 2007) 2007. audio compact disk 149.00 (978-1-59579-717-9(3)) Pub: LexisNexis Mealey. Dist(s): LEXIS Pub

Mealey's Teleconference: Update on Solvent Schemes & WFUM Audio CD (November 2007) 2007. 149.00 (978-1-59579-787-2(4)) Pub: LexisNexis Mealey. Dist(s): LEXIS Pub

Mealey's Teleconference: Wrap-up Insurance - Controlling Costs & Limiting Liability Audio CD (August 2007) 2007. 149.00 (978-1-59579-723-0(8)) Pub: LexisNexis Mealey. Dist(s): LEXIS Pub

Mealey's Teleconference - Tough Cases in Tough Places - Defensive Strategies in Plaintiff Friendly Jurisdictions. Compiled by LexisNexis Staff. 2006. audio compact disk 249.00 (978-1-59579-326-3(7)) Pub: LexisNexis Mealey. Dist(s): LEXIS Pub

Mealey's Teleconference on D & O Litigation Audiotape (December 2005) 2005. reel tape 249.00 (978-1-59579-676-9(2)) Pub: LexisNexis Mealey. Dist(s): LEXIS Pub

Mealey's Teleconference on Ethics: Attorney Advertising. Compiled by LexisNexis Staff. 2006. 249.00 (978-1-59579-061-3(6)) LexisNexis Mealey.

Mealey's Teleconference on Jurisdictional Issues: Fradulent Joinder. Compiled by LexisNexis Staff. 2006. audio compact disk 249.00 (978-1-59579-321-8(6)) Pub: LexisNexis Mealey. Dist(s): LEXIS Pub

Mealey's Toxic Tort Teleconference Series: Vapor Intrusion ... the Contamination Slipping Through the Cracks Audio CD (August 2007) 2007. 149.00 (978-1-59579-724-7(6)) Pub: LexisNexis Mealey. Dist(s): LEXIS Pub

Mealey's Toxic Tort Update: Texas. Compiled by LexisNexis Staff. 2006. audio compact disk 399.00 (978-1-59579-311-9(9)) Pub: LexisNexis Mealey. Dist(s): LEXIS Pub

Mealey's Toxic Torts Teleconference Series: Natural Resource Damages Audio CD (August 2007) 2007. audio compact disk 149.00 (978-1-59579-715-5(7)) Pub: LexisNexis Mealey. Dist(s): LEXIS Pub

Mealey's Trial Preparation Skills for Paralegals Conference Audiotape. 3rd rev. ed. Compiled by LexisNexis Staff. 2007. reel tape 399.00 (978-1-59579-155-9(8)) Pub: LexisNexis Mealey. Dist(s): LEXIS Pub

Mealey's VIOXX Litigation Conference. Compiled by LexisNexis Staff. 2006. audio compact disk 399.00 (978-1-59579-327-0(5)) Pub: LexisNexis Mealey. Dist(s): LEXIS Pub

Mealey's VIOXX Litigation Conference Audiotape. Compiled by LexisNexis Staff. 2005. reel tape 399.00 (978-1-59579-329-4(1)) Pub: LexisNexis Mealey. Dist(s): LEXIS Pub

Mealey's VIOXX Litigation Conference Audiotape. Compiled by LexisNexis Staff. 2005. reel tape 399.00 (978-1-59579-372-0(0)) Pub: LexisNexis Mealey. Dist(s): LEXIS Pub

Mealey's VIOXX Litigation Conference Audiotape (December 2005) 2005. reel tape 399.00 (978-1-59579-674-5(6)) Pub: LexisNexis Mealey. Dist(s): LEXIS Pub

Mealey's Water Contamination Conference Audiotape. Compiled by LexisNexis Staff. 2004. reel tape 399.00 (978-1-59579-437-6(9)) Pub: LexisNexis Mealey. Dist(s): LEXIS Pub

Mealey's Water Contamination Conference Audiotape. Compiled by LexisNexis Staff. 2005. reel tape 399.00 (978-1-59579-387-4(9)) Pub: LexisNexis Mealey. Dist(s): LEXIS Pub

Mealey's Webinar: Pooled Special Needs Trust Audio CD (November 2007) 2007. 149.00 (978-1-59579-781-0(5)) Pub: LexisNexis Mealey. Dist(s): LEXIS Pub

Mealey's Welding Rod Litigation Conference. Compiled by LexisNexis Staff. 2006. audio compact disk 225.00 (978-1-59579-319-5(4)) Pub: LexisNexis Mealey. Dist(s): LEXIS Pub

Mealey's Welding Rod Litigation Conference Audiotape. Compiled by LexisNexis Staff. 2004. reel tape 399.00 (978-1-59579-447-5(6)) Pub: LexisNexis Mealey. Dist(s): LEXIS Pub

Mealey's Welding Rod Litigation Conference Audiotape. Compiled by LexisNexis Staff. 2004. reel tape 399.00 (978-1-59579-483-3(2)) Pub: LexisNexis Mealey. Dist(s): LEXIS Pub

Mealey's Welding Rod Litigation Conference Audiotape. Compiled by LexisNexis Staff. 2005. reel tape 399.00 (978-1-59579-350-8(X)) Pub: LexisNexis Mealey. Dist(s): LEXIS Pub

Mealey's Welding Rod Litigation Teleconference Audiotape (December 2005) 2005. reel tape 249.00 (978-1-59579-682-0(7)) Pub: LexisNexis Mealey. Dist(s): LEXIS Pub

Mealey's Women in the Law Teleconference Series: The Keys to Successful Rainmaking Audio CD (April 2007) 2007. 249.00 (978-1-59579-637-0(1)) Pub: LexisNexis Mealey. Dist(s): LEXIS Pub

Mealey's Women in the Law Webinar: The Keys to Successful Rainmaking Audio CD (February 2008) 2008. 149.00 (978-1-59579-769-8(6)) Pub: LexisNexis Mealey. Dist(s): LEXIS Pub

Mealey's Working with Experts in Pharmaceutical Cases Teleconference. Compiled by LexisNexis Staff. 2006. audio compact disk 249.00 (978-1-59579-314-0(3)) Pub: LexisNexis Mealey. Dist(s): LEXIS Pub

Mealey's 12th Annual Insurance Insolvency & Reinsurance Roundtable Conference Audiotape. Compiled by LexisNexis Staff. 2005. reel tape 399.00 (978-1-59579-352-2(6)) Pub: LexisNexis Mealey. Dist(s): LEXIS Pub

Mealey's 14th Annual Insurance Insolvency & Reinsurance Roundtable Handbook on CD (April 2007) 2007. pap. bk. 275.00 (978-1-59579-696-7(7)) Pub: LexisNexis Mealey. Dist(s): LEXIS Pub

Mealey's 2nd Annual Solvent Schemes of Arrangement Conference Audio CD (March 2007) 2007. 499.00 (978-1-59579-626-4(6)) Pub: LexisNexis Mealey. Dist(s): LEXIS Pub

Mealey's 4th Annual Advanced Insurance Coverage Conference: Top 10 Issues. Compiled by LexisNexis Staff. 2006. audio compact disk 399.00 (978-1-59579-057-6(8)) Pub: LexisNexis Mealey. Dist(s): LEXIS Pub

Mealey's 5th Annual Advanced Insurance Coverage Conference: Top 10 Issues Audio CD (January 2007) 2007. 499.00 (978-1-59579-604-2(5)) Pub: LexisNexis Mealey. Dist(s): LEXIS Pub

***Meall Mor.** Dara Ban Macdonnchadha. (ENG.). 1987. 11.95 (978-0-8023-7005-1(5)) Pub: Clo Iar-Chonnachta IRL. Dist(s): Dufour

Mean Business: How I Save Bad Companies & Make Good Companies Great, unabr. ed. Albert J. Dunlap & Bob Andelman. Narrated by Richard M. Davidson. 8 cass. (Running Time: 11 hrs. 15 mins.). 2000. 70.00 (978-0-7887-1287-6(X), 95133K8) Recorded Bks.

When Al Dunlap became CEO of Scott Paper in 1994, the company had suffered a $277 million loss the previous year. After 19 months with "Chainsaw Al" at its helm, Scott was once again a world class competitor. Listeners involved in any aspect of the business world will profit from learning & using his "Four Simple Rules" for effective management & leadership.

Mean High Tide, unabr. ed. James W. Hall. Narrated by Frank Muller. 9 cass. (Running Time: 12 hrs. 30 mins.). (Thorn Ser.). 1994. 78.00 (978-0-7887-0026-2(X), 94225E7) Recorded Bks.

Having spent the better part of his life in Key Largo, Thorn knew all to well the perils of the coral reef & the seedy criminals on shore that fed on weekend tourists & so did Darcy. But neither one of them is prepared for Sylvie, homely, needy & sensual - a sexual piranha hidden in a waifish shell; a daddy's girl bent on childish revenge; a mysterious keeper of secrets.

Mean Margaret. Tor Seidler. Read by Jeff Woodman. 3 cass. (Running Time: 3 hrs. 45 mins.). (J). (gr. 2 up). 2000. stu. ed. 50.95 (978-0-7887-3649-0(3), 41015) Recorded Bks.

Woodchucks Fred & Phoebe are newlyweds just settling into their cozy burrow. But one morning, a rude, noisy problem shows up on their doorstep.

Mean Margaret, Tor Seidler. Read by Jeff Woodman. Illus. by Jon Agee. 3 cass. (Running Time: 3 hrs. 45 mins.). (YA). (gr. 2 up). 2000. stu. ed. 186.80 (978-0-7887-3650-6(7), 46982) Recorded Bks.

Mean Margaret. unabr. ed. Tor Seidler. Narrated by Jeff Woodman. 3 pieces. (Running Time: 3 hrs. 45 mins.). (gr. 2 up). 2000. 29.00 (978-0-7887-3523-3(3), 95863E7) Recorded Bks.

Mean Margaret. unabr. ed. Tor Seidler. Narrated by Jeff Woodman. 4 CDs. (Running Time: 3 hrs. 45 mins.). (gr. 2 up). 2001. audio compact disk 29.00 (978-0-7887-5224-7(3), C1372E7) Recorded Bks.
Woodchucks Fred & Phoebe are newlyweds just settling into their cozy burrow. But one morning a rude, noisy problem shows up on their doorstep.

Mean Streets. unabr. ed. Ron Ellis. Contrib. by Dave John. 7 cass. (Story Sound Ser.). (J). 2006. 61.95 (978-1-85903-872-7(7)) Pub: Mgna Lrg Print GBR. Dist(s): Ulverscroft US

Mean Streets. unabr. ed. Ron Ellis & Dave John. Contrib. by Dave John. 8 vols. (Story Sound CD Ser.). (J). 2006. audio compact disk 79.95 (978-1-85903-987-8(1)) Pub: Mgna Lrg Print GBR. Dist(s): Ulverscroft US

Mean Waters. Frank Woodson. Narrated by Larry A. McKeever. (Adventure Ser.). (J). 2000. audio compact disk 14.95 (978-1-58659-284-4(X)) Artesian.

Mean Waters. unabr. ed. Frank Woodson. Narrated by Larry A. McKeever. 1 cass. (Running Time: 40 min.). (Adventure Ser.). (J). (gr. 3-12). 2000. 10.95 (978-1-58659-020-8(0), 54110) Artesian.

Meanest Doll in the World. Ann M. Martin & Laura Godwin. Illus. by Brian Selznick. 4 CDs. (Running Time: 3 hrs. 55 mins.). (J). (gr. 3-7). 2004. audio compact disk 35.00 (978-0-8072-2005-4(1), Listening Lib) Pub: Random Audio Pubg. Dist(s): Random
The dolls take a trip outside the house in Kate's backpack by mistake. Unfortunately, there is a mix-up at school and the dolls wind up in the home of classmate BJ. Here they meet the evil Mimi, a doll who is convinced she shall be queen of all the dolls and has the demanding attitude to prove it. Annabelle and Tiffany, along with an assortment of other dolls, fend off Mimi and her wicked army before returning to their own home.

Meanest Doll in the World. unabr. ed. Ann M. Martin & Laura Godwin. Illus. by Brian Selznick. 3 cass. (Running Time: 3 hrs. 55 mins.). (J). (gr. 3-7). 2004. 30.00 (978-0-8072-1789-4(1), Listening Lib) Pub: Random Audio Pubg. Dist(s): Random

Meanest Doll in the World. unabr. ed. Ann M. Martin & Laura Godwin. Read by Lynn Redgrave. 3 cass. (Running Time: 3 hrs. 50 mins.). (Middle Grade Cassette Librariestm Ser.). (J). (gr. 3-7). 2004. 30.00 (978-0-8072-0512-9(5), S YA 309 CX, Listening Lib) Random Audio Pubg.
"The 100-year-old Doll family-beautifully crafted china dolls passed down through four generations of girls in one American family-meet their new neighbors, the Funcrafts, a doll family made completely of plastic and delivered straight from the factory shelves.".

Meanest Word: Proverbs 16:28. Ed Young. (J). 1980. 4.95 (978-0-7417-1117-5(6), A0117) Win Walk.

Meaning? What Is Meant By. unabr. ed. Viktor E. Frankl. 1 cass. (Running Time: 33 min.). 12.95 (25005) J Norton Pubs.
Clarifies the way in which meanings & values are relative & subjective, reaffirming the self-transcendent quality of human existence in the face of reductionism.

Meaning & Origins of Christian Devotion, Benedict J. Groeschel. 2 cass. (Running Time: 3 hrs. 33 min.). 1999. 19.95 (TAH419) Alba Hse Comns.
Surveys the historical significance, the Biblical foundations & the divine sources of our treasured but all-too-often dismissed devotions.

Meaning & Recognition of the Dark Night Experience. Constance FitzGerald. 4 cass. (Running Time: 4 hrs. 10 min.). 1991. 33.95 (TAH250) Alba Hse Comns.
This workshop endeavors to interpret the Dark Night experience with particular, though not exclusive emphasis on Books I & II of the Dark Night. In this way prayer-life development are understood better & light is thrown on contemporary experiences of darkness, personal & societal. This workshop shows how human desire - that great motivating power within the human heart - is purified & transformed in its movement through life toward God.

Meaning of Africa see Poems from Black Africa

Meaning of Christmas: Luke 2:1-16. Ed Young. 1997. 4.95 (978-0-7417-2164-8(3), A1164) Win Walk.

Meaning of Death. Vajracarya. 2 cass. 1973. 25.00 Vajradhatu.
This four talk seminar examines our relationships with the impermanence of both life & death.

Meaning of Dreams. Robert Stone. 1 cass. 1983. 10.00 (978-0-938137-07-8(7)) Listen & Learn.
Includes: Research on Dream Deprivation; Freud: the Dreamwork Process; The Meaning of Dreams; Dream Interpretation; Jung: the Function & Purpose of Dreams; Fritz Perls: A Gestalt Therapy Approach to Dream Interpretation & Integration.

***Meaning of Everything.** unabr. ed. Simon Winchester. Read by Simon Winchester. (ENG.). 2004. (978-0-06-079968-7(4), Harper Audio); (978-0-06-074403-8(0), Harper Audio) HarperCollins Pubs.

Meaning of Faith. Elbert Willis. 1 cass. (Faith School Ser.: Vol. 1). 4.00 Fill the Gap.

Meaning of Forgiveness. Kenneth Wapnick. 2 CDs. 2003. audio compact disk 15.00 (978-1-59142-106-1(3), CD53) Foun Miracles.
Forgiveness, the central teaching of "A Course in Miracles," has almost universally been misunderstood. In this workshop, its true meaning is explained in contrast to the distortions coming from the world's version, which has made forgiveness into a scourge rather than the path home to God. Through readings and examples, all forms of victimization are shown to be rooted in the projections of responsibility for our belief that we are separate from God's Love. Forgiveness begins with looking at our experiences of victimization with Jesus, who helps us see their cause and healing. These lie only in our mind's decision, either to be joined with his love or to remain separate from it.

Meaning of Forgiveness. Kenneth Wapnick. 2008. 12.00 (978-1-59142-363-8(5)) Foun Miracles.

***Meaning of Freedom.** Angela Davis. (PM Audio Ser.). (ENG.). 2011. audio compact disk 14.95 (978-1-60486-102-0(9)) Pub: Pm Pre. Dist(s): IPG Chicago

Meaning of Good Parent Relations. Dora C. Fowler. 1 cass. (Running Time: 1 hr.). 1990. 9.95 (978-1-57323-028-5(6)) Natl Inst Child Mgmt.
Staff training material for child care.

Meaning of Great Lent in the Modern World. Contrib. by Kallistos T. Ware. 1 cass. (Running Time: 0.30). 5.95 (978-1-891295-05-8(5), OakPubns) St Vladimirs.

Meaning of Hope to Severely Disabled Young People. Nina Donnelly. 1986. 10.80 (0812) Assn Prof Chaplains.

Meaning of Illness. John Sanford. 1 cass. (Running Time: 50 min.). 1993. 8.95 Credence Commun.
Some illnesses lead us to faith, others to compassion or contrition. The New Testament is rich & nuanced in its understanding of the role of sickness in our lives.

Meaning of Impersonal Love. 1 cass. (Love-Human & Divine Ser.). 9.95 (ST-53) Crystal Clarity.
Includes: The limitations of personal love; why impersonal love is more loving & selfless than personal love; increasing your awareness by offering the ego to God; giving loved ones the freedom to make mistakes.

Meaning of Inner Communion. 1 cass. (Yoga & Christianity Ser.). 9.95 (ST-48) Crystal Clarity.
Discusses Yogananda's teachings as a new expression of "original Christianity"; the need for inner communion in Christian churches; meditation as a doorway to inner silence; recent Holy Mother visions & her message of inner communion; the importance of turning each day (& each breath) into a new beginning.

Meaning of It All: Thoughts of a Citizen-Scientist. unabr. ed. Richard Phillips Feynman. (Running Time: 10800 sec.). 2007. 22.95 (978-1-4332-0284-1(0)); audio compact disk 27.00 (978-1-4332-0285-8(9)) Blckstn Audio.

Meaning of It All: Thoughts of a Citizen-Scientist. unabr. ed. Richard Phillips Feynman. Read by Raymond Todd. (Running Time: 10800 sec.). 2007. 19.95 (978-1-4332-0171-4(2)); audio compact disk 19.95 (978-1-4332-0172-1(0)); audio compact disk 19.95 (978-1-4332-0173-8(9)) Blckstn Audio.

Meaning of Judgment. Kenneth Wapnick. 2 CDs. 2006. audio compact disk 12.00 (978-1-59142-271-6(X), CD37) Foun Miracles.

Meaning of Judgment. Kenneth Wapnick. 1 CD. (Running Time: 1 hr. 59 mins. 44 secs.). 2006. 10.00 (978-1-59142-272-3(8), 3m37) Foun Miracles.

Meaning of Life. Read by Chogyam Trungpa. 1 cass. 1972. 12.50 (A200) Vajradhatu.

Meaning of Life: Buddhist Perspectives on Cause & Effect. abr. unabr. ed. Dalai Lama XIV. Read by Ken McLeod. Ed. by Jeffrey Hopkins. Tr. by Jeffrey Hopkins. 3 CDs. (Running Time: 3 hrs. 0 mins. 0 sec.). (ENG.). 2008. audio compact disk 19.95 (978-1-4272-0564-3(7)) Pub: Macmill Audio. Dist(s): Macmillan

Meaning of Monastic Spirituality. Thomas Merton. 1 cass. (Running Time: 1 hr.). (Monastic Spirituality Ser.). 8.95 (AA2085) Credence Commun.
Commentary on monastic spirituality being at the heart of the church & any spirituality.

Meaning of Morale. W. Walter Menninger. Read by W. Walter Menninger. 1 cass. (Running Time: 44 min.). (Executive Seminar Ser.). 1987. 10.00 (978-1-56948-008-3(7)) Menninger Clinic.
Dr. W. Walter Menninger discusses the impact new experiences have on morale. He suggests that a clear understanding of the predictable shifts in morale provides a useful framework for the successful management of organizational growth & change.

Meaning of Night: A Confession. Michael Cox. Narrated by David Timson. (Running Time: 81000 sec.). 2006. audio compact disk 49.99 (978-1-4281-2488-2(8)) Recorded Bks.

Meaning of Pastoral Intimacy. Myron Madden & Wilbur Schwartz. 1986. 10.80 (0210A) Assn Prof Chaplains.

Meaning of Tantra. unabr. ed. Ajit Mookerjee. 2 cass. (Running Time: 2 hrs. 42 min.). 1978. 18.00 (13101) Big Sur Tapes.
This in-depth exposition of tantra provides an excellent introduction to a subject so often misunderstood in the West.

Meaning of the Fourth of July for the Negro: Frederick Douglass's Fifth of July Speech. abr. ed. Frederick Douglass. Perf. by Fred Morsell. 1 cass. (Running Time: 47 min.). (Frederick Douglass's Greatest Speeches). (C). 1993. 11.99 (978-1-883210-00-7(3),); audio compact disk 13.99 (978-1-883210-01-4(1)) TBM Records.
The Rochester (New York) Ladies Anti-Slavery Society invited Frederick Douglass to give a 4th of July oration commemorating the United States' 76th birthday. "The Meaning of the Fourth of July for the Negro" is also known as "Frederick Douglass's Fifth of July Speech," & is considered the greatest anti-slavery speech leading to the Civil War.

Meaning of the Holy Instant. Kenneth Wapnick. 2 CDs. 2006. audio compact disk 13.00 (978-1-59142-286-0(8), CD62) Foun Miracles.

Meaning of the Holy Instant. Kenneth Wapnick. 1 CD. (Running Time: 2 hrs. 5 mins. 28 secs.). 2006. 10.00 (978-1-59142-287-7(6), 3m62) Foun Miracles.

Meaning of the Inner Voice Experience. Myrtle Heery. 1 cass. 9.00 (A0371-88) Sound Photosyn.

Meaning of Tradition in Science. Read by Werner Heisenberg. 1 cass. (Running Time: 56 min.). 14.95 (CBC998) MMI Corp.

Meaning of Truth. unabr. ed. William James. (Great Books in Philosophy). (ENG.). 1997. 15.98 (978-1-57392-138-1(6)) Prometheus Bks.

Meaning of Yoga. unabr. ed. Frederic Spiegelberg. 3 cass. (Running Time: 3 hrs. 58 min.). 1980. 26.00 (08803) Big Sur Tapes.
An attempt to straighten out the many misconceptions about what yoga is.

Meaning Versus Usage: Dilemma of the Dictionary. Instructed by Manly P. Hall. 8.95 (978-0-89314-180-6(1), C800139) Philos Res.

Meaning Well, Doing Well: Developing Intentional Effectiveness, David Grudermeyer & Rebecca Grudermeyer. 2 cass. 18.95 INCL. HANDOUTS. (T-64) Willingness Wrks.

Meanings into Words Upper-Intermediate (Drills) An Integrated Course for Students of English. Adrian Doff et al. (Running Time: 1 hr. 29 mins.). (Meanings into Words Ser.). (ENG.). 1984. 23.00 (978-0-521-24465-7(X)) Cambridge U Pr.

Means at Large: Cookin' Around. Anna Means. 1 CD. (Running Time: 52 mins.). 2002. audio compact disk 8.00 (978-0-9718320-0-8(5)) Deck Slug.
Stories of traveling in France with an adult friend and two teenagers.

Means at Large: French Files. unabr. ed. Anna Means. 1 CD. (Running Time: 52 mins.). 2002. audio compact disk 8.00 (978-0-9718320-1-5(3)) Deck Slug.
Stories of traveling in rance with an adult friend and two teenagers.

Means of Evil & Other Stories. unabr. ed. Short Stories. Ruth Rendell. Read by Nigel Anthony. 4 cass. (Running Time: 4 hrs.). (Inspector Wexford Mystery Short Story Collection). 1996. 39.95 (978-0-7451-6635-3(0), CAB 1251) AudioGO.
Here are five classic Inspector Wexford cases that display his remarkable ingenuity. Ranging from every day crimes of passion & violence in quite Kingsmarkham, to a bizarre murder in Yugoslavia.

Means of Evil & Other Stories. unabr. ed. Ruth Rendell. Read by Nigel Anthony. 4 cass. (Running Time: 6 hrs.). (Inspector Wexford Mystery Short Story Collection). 2000. 34.95 (CAB 1251) Pub: Chivers Audio Bks GBR. Dist(s): AudioGO
Ranging from everyday crimes of passion and violence in quiet Kingsmarkham, to a bizarre murder in Yugoslavia, each case challenges Detective Chief Inspector Wexford's imagination and resourcefulness, and the patient reasoning of Inspector Burden.

Means of Evil & Other Stories. unabr. collector's ed. Ruth Rendell. Read by Donada Peters. 6 cass. (Running Time: 6 hrs.). (Inspector Wexford Mystery Short Story Collection). 1990. 36.00 (978-0-7366-1740-6(X), 2580) Books on Tape.
According to the London Sunday Express, Ruth Rendell is "one of the best crime novelists writing today." For readers new to her work, this collection of five mysteries, all cases for Detective Chief Inspector Wexford, is a perfect introduction. In Wexford, Rendell has created a first-rate & endearing character. Like all memorable & remarkable individuals, Wexford is a man of great intuitive power. His best performances are flashes of insight, solutions that seem inspired more by instinct than intellect.

Means of Grace. unabr. ed. Edith Pargeter. Read by Marie McCarthy. 12 cass. (Running Time: 13 hrs. 30 min.). (Isis Ser.). (J). 1997. 94.95 (978-0-7531-0104-9(1), 970210) Pub: ISIS Lrg Prnt GBR. Dist(s): Ulverscroft US
Emmy's friends think she's crazy to go back, crazy to expect to find the same country, the same city, the same people. The country is divided by the Communism that has taken over after the ravages of a world war. But she does return. Emmy & the Ivanescue family will not allow politics to intervene in their friendship.

Means of Grace: August 2, 1998. Ben Young. 1998. 4.95 (978-0-7417-6091-3(6), B0091) Win Walk.

Means of Grace: Logos August 2, 1998. Ben Young. 1998. 4.95 (978-0-7417-6092-0(4), B0092) Win Walk.

Meant to Be. unabr. ed. Walter Anderson. Read by George Guidall. 5 cass. (Running Time: 7 hrs.). 2005. 49.75 (978-1-4193-1686-9(9)) Recorded Bks.
Anderson, longtime editor of "Parade," the Sunday newspaper magazine, had a wrong-side-of-the-tracks childhood and a loving mother who tried to protect him from a drunken, bullying father. He escaped his father's abuse through a stint in the Marines and volunteering for Vietnam, where his newspaper piece about the war initiated a writing career. After his father's funeral, Anderson confronted his mother about his paternity, and she confirmed his suspicions that the man who raised him was not his blood father. Left stateside while her husband served in World War II, the author's mother had had an affair with a Russian-Jewish man. Anderson, later a husband and father himself, eventually began to explore his Jewish d tracked down a half-brother, his only surviving sibling. The highlights of Anderson's life show him to be an ethical, strong-willed survivor capable of growing through adversity.

Meanwhile, in Another Part of Town. AIO Team Staff. Read by Hal Smith et al. (Running Time: 5 hrs.). (Adventures in Odyssey Gold Ser.). (ENG.). (J). (gr. 1-7). 2006. audio compact disk 24.99 (978-1-58997-290-2(2), Tyndale Ent) Tyndale Hse.

Measle & the Wrathmonk. unabr. ed. Ian Ogilvy. Read by Nickolas Grace. 3 cass. (Running Time: 4 hrs. 15 mins.). (J). (gr. 4-7). 2005. 30.00 (978-1-4000-9894-1(7), Listening Lib); audio compact disk 38.00 (978-0-307-24609-7(4), Listening Lib) Pub: Random Audio Pubg. Dist(s): Random

Measure & Compare: Early Explorers Fluent Set B Audio CD. Clare O'Brien. Adapted by Benchmark Education Staff. (J). 2007. audio compact disk 10.00 (978-1-4108-8253-0(5)) Benchmark Educ.

Measure & Cook/My Photo Journal. Steck-Vaughn Staff. 2002. (978-0-7398-5997-1(8)) SteckVau.

***Measure for Measure.** abr. ed. William Shakespeare. (ENG.). 2003. (978-0-06-079955-7(2), Caedmon); (978-0-06-074315-4(8), Caedmon) HarperCollins Pubs.

Measure for Measure. unabr. ed. William Shakespeare. Read by Arkangel Cast Staff. (Arkangel Shakespeare Ser.). (ENG.). 2006. audio compact disk 19.95 (978-1-932219-21-0(8)) Pub: AudioGO. Dist(s): Perseus Dist

Measure for Measure, unabr. ed. William Shakespeare. Read by John Gielgud et al. 2 cass. (Running Time: 3 hrs.). Dramatization. 17.95 (H172) Blckstn Audio.
A young woman is offered the choice of saving a man's life at the price of her chastity. What should she do?.

Measure for Measure. unabr. ed. William Shakespeare. Read by Audio Partners Staff. 2 cass. (Running Time: 2 hrs. 29 mins.). (Arkangel Shakespeare Ser.). 2004. 17.95 (978-1-932219-61-6(7), Atlntc Mnthly) Pub: Grove-Atltc. Dist(s): PerseuPGW

Measure for Measure, unabr. ed. William Shakespeare. Perf. by John Gielgud et al. 3 cass. Dramatization. 1984. pap. bk. 18.00 (978-0-694-50652-1(4), SWC 204) HarperCollins Pubs.
Cast includes: Ralph Richardson, Mark Dignam, Tony White, Alec McCowen, William Marlowe, Alexis Kanner, Christopher Burgess, Brian Murray, Paul Vieya, Ronald Barker, Lee Montague, Elric Hooper, Renee Asherson, Miranda Connell, & Hazel Hughes. Includes text.

Measure for Measure. unabr. ed. William Shakespeare. Narrated by Flo Gibson. (Running Time: 2 hrs. 50 mins.). 2004. 14.95 (978-1-55685-760-7(8)) Audio Bk Con.

Measure for Measure. unabr. abr. ed. William Shakespeare. Perf. by John Gielgud & Margaret Leighton. 2 cass. (Running Time: 3 hrs.). (gr. 9-12). 1995. 18.00 (978-1-55994-816-6(7), CPN 204, Harper Audio) HarperCollins Pubs.

Measure of a Leader. Aubrey Daniels. 2008. audio compact disk 28.00 (978-1-933309-58-3(X)) Pub: A Media Intl. Dist(s): Natl Bk Netwk

Measure of a Man. unabr. ed. Gene Getz. Read by Lloyd James. (Running Time: 4 hrs. 53 mins. 0 sec.). (ENG.). 2008. audio compact disk 26.98 (978-1-59644-557-4(2)) christianaud.

***Measure of a Man.** unabr. ed. Sidney Poitier. Read by Sidney Poitier. (ENG.). 2007. (978-0-06-137450-0(4), Harper Audio); (978-0-06-137449-4(0), Harper Audio) HarperCollins Pubs.

Measure of a Man: A Spiritual Autobiography. unabr. ed. Sidney Poitier. Read by Sidney Poitier. 7 CDs. (Running Time: 28800 sec.). (Oprah's Book Club Ser.). 2007. audio compact disk 24.95 (978-0-06-135543-1(7), Harper Audio) HarperCollins Pubs.

***Measure of a Man: Twenty Attributes of a Godly Man.** unabr. ed. Gene Getz. Narrated by James Lloyd. (ENG.). 2008. 16.98 (978-1-59644-558-1(0), christianSeed) christianaud.

Measure of All Things: The Seven-Year Odyssey & Hidden Error That Transformed the World. abr. ed. Ken Alder. Read by Brian Jennings. 2006. 17.95 (978-0-7435-6214-0(3)) Pub: S&S Audio. Dist(s): S and S Inc

Measure of Mercy. abr. ed. Lauraine Snelling. Narrated by Renee Ertl. (Running Time: 8 hrs. 1 mins. 4 sec.). (Home to Blessing Ser.: No. 1). (ENG.). 2009. 19.59 (978-1-60814-575-1(1)); audio compact disk 27.99 (978-1-59859-622-9(5)) Oasis Audio.

Measurement, Instrumentation & Sensors Handbook: CRCnetBASE 1999. John G. Webster. 1999. audio compact disk 199.95 (978-0-8493-2145-0(X), 2145) Pub: CRC Pr. Dist(s): Taylor and Fran

Measuring America. Andro Linklater. Read by Alan Sklar. (Running Time: 11 hrs. 30 mins.). (C). 2003. 29.95 (978-1-60083-656-5(9), Audiofy Corp) Iofy Corp.

Measuring America. unabr. ed. Andro Linklater. Narrated by Alan Sklar. 9 CDs. (Running Time: 11 hrs. 33 mins. 0 sec.). (ENG.). 2003. audio compact disk 39.99 (978-1-4001-0090-3(9)) Pub: Tantor Media. Dist(s): IngramPubServ

Measuring America: How an Untamed Wilderness Shaped the United States & Fulfilled the Promise of Democracy. Andro Linklater. Read by Alan Sklar. (ENG.). 2009. 69.99 (978-1-60775-788-7(5)) Find a World.

Measuring America: How an Untamed Wilderness Shaped the United States & Fulfilled the Promise of Democracy. unabr. ed. Andro Linklater. Narrated by Alan Sklar. (Running Time: 11 hrs. 33 mins. 0 sec.). (ENG.). 2003. audio compact disk 22.99 (978-1-4001-5090-8(6)) Pub: Tantor Media. Dist(s): IngramPubServ

Measuring America: How an Untamed Wilderness Shaped Then Hiunited States & Fulfilled the Promise of Democracy. unabr. ed. Andro Linklater. Narrated by Alan Sklar. (Running Time: 11 hrs. 33 mins. 0 sec.). (ENG.). 2003. audio compact disk 79.99 (978-1-4001-3090-0(5)) Pub: Tantor Media. Dist(s): IngramPubServ

***Measuring Angles.** Fred Johnston. (ENG.). 1992. 11.95 (978-0-8023-0015-7(4)) Pub: Clo Iar-Chonnachta IRL. Dist(s): Dufour

Measuring Matter: Solids, Liquids, & Gases. Compiled by Benchmark Education Staff. 2005. audio compact disk 10.00 (978-1-4108-5480-3(9)) Benchmark Educ.

Measuring the Universe. 1 cass. (Running Time: 30 min.). 14.95 (23350) MMI Corp.
Noted astronomers discuss celestial mechanics, "solar parallax," observing the sun, recent advances in astrophysics.

Measuring Theme Audio CD. ed. (J). 2004. audio compact disk (978-1-4108-1832-4(2)) Benchmark Educ.

Measuring Up. Sundance/Newbridge, LLC Staff. (Early Math Ser.). (gr. k-1). 2000. 12.00 (978-1-58273-317-3(1)) Sund Newbrdge.

Meat-Eating Plants & Other Extreme Plant Life. June Preszler. Contrib. by Patrick Olson & Charity Jones. (Extreme Life Ser.). (ENG.). (gr. 3-4). 2008. audio compact disk 12.99 (978-1-4296-3208-9(9)) CapstoneDig.

Mechanical & Electrical Systems CD-ROM. 2003. audio compact disk 45.00 (978-0-7931-8645-7(5)) Kaplan Pubng.

Mechanics' Liens. 1991. 45.00 (AC-602) PA Bar Inst.

Mechanics of a New Party. unabr. ed. Stephen Maltese et al. 1 cass. (Running Time: 1 hr. 24 min.). 12.95 (333) J Norton Pubs.

Mechanische Musikinstrumente, Volume 7: Joseph Haydn Samtliche Flotenuhren. Ed. by Helmut Kowar. (Tondokumente aus dem Phonogrammarchiv Mechanische Musikinstrumente Ser.). (GER.). (C). 2009. audio compact disk 23.00 (978-3-7001-6681-8(8)) Pub: Verlag Osterreich AUT. Dist(s): David Brown

Mechanisms & Management of Nephrotic Syndrome. Read by Richard J. Glassock. 1 cass. (Running Time: 9 min.). 1986. 12.00 (C8606) Amer Coll Phys.

***Med FAQs- Child: Interview with Dr. James Lee.** David Russ & Christopher T. McCarthy. Created by Informed Therapy Resources (ITR). Featuring James Lee. (ENG.). 2009. audio compact disk 15.95 (978-0-9822380-2-8(9)) Informed Ther Res.

Medea. Perf. by Judith Anderson. 1 cass. 10.00 (MC1019) Esstee Audios.
Radio drama.

Medea. Euripides. 2 CDs. (Running Time: 3 hrs.). 2005. audio compact disk 15.95 (978-0-660-18537-8(7)) Pub: Canadian Broadcasting CAN. Dist(s): Georgetown Term

Medea s Daughters: Forming & performing the woman who Kil. Jennifer Jones. 2003. audio compact disk 9.95 (978-0-8142-9020-0(5)) Pub: Ohio St U Pr. Dist(s): Chicago Distribution Ctr

Media. Standard Publishing Staff. 2006. cd-rom 24.99 (978-0-7847-1888-9(1)) Standard Pub.

Media: Influence & Education. Contrib. by Marjorie Hogan et al. 1 cass. (American Academy of Pediatrics UPDATE: Vol. 19, No. 1). 1998. 20.00 Am Acad Pediat.

***Media: Journalism in Crisis.** unabr. ed. Neal Cortell. Read by Morton Dean. (Running Time: 5 hrs.). 2010. 14.99 (978-1-4418-6600-4(0), 9781441866004, Brilliance MP3); 39.97 (978-1-4418-6601-1(9), 9781441866011, Brlnc Audio MP3 Lib); 39.97 (978-1-4418-6603-5(5), 9781441866035, BADLE); 14.99 (978-1-4418-6602-8(7), 9781441866028, BAD); audio compact disk 24.99 (978-1-4418-6598-4(5), 9781441865984, Bril Audio CD Unabri); audio compact disk 69.97 (978-1-4418-6599-1(3), 9781441865991, BriAudCD Unabrid) Brilliance Audio.

Media & the Mind. David Walsh. 2 cass. 17.90 (978-1-890423-02-5(5)) Natl Inst Media.
How electronic media influences the cognitive & emotional development of children.

Media Bias. unabr. ed. David Susskind. 1 cass. (Running Time: 1 hr.). 1967. 12.95 (32007) J Norton Pubs.
From William Buckley's "Firing Line" program, this is a debate with David Susskind on bias in the media.

Media Control: The Spectacular Achievements of Propaganda. Noam Chomsky. (Running Time: 45 mins.). (Open Media Ser.). (ENG., 2004. audio compact disk 14.95 (978-1-58322-664-3(8)) Pub: Seven Stories. Dist(s): Consort Bk Sales

Media Element Cd-Corp Fin Acct. 21st ed. Charles Warren. (C). 2005. audio compact disk 14.95 (978-0-324-30532-6(X)) Pub: South-West. Dist(s): CENGAGE Learn

Media Element Cd-Fin Acct. 21st ed. Charles Warren. (C). 2004. audio compact disk 14.95 (978-0-324-30528-9(1)) Pub: South-West. Dist(s): CENGAGE Learn

Media Element Cd-Mgrl Acct. 21st ed. Charles Warren. (C). 2004. audio compact disk 14.95 (978-0-324-30529-6(X)) Pub: South-West. Dist(s): CENGAGE Learn

Media Relations: Capitol Learning Audio Course. Bob McLean. Prod. by TheCapitol.Net. (ENG.). 2007. 47.00 (978-1-58733-067-4(9)) TheCapitol.

Media Relations: Capitol Learning Audio Course. Ed. by TheCapitol.Net. (ENG.). 2005. audio compact disk 47.00 (978-1-58733-022-3(9)) TheCapitol.

Media Relations: Secrets to Changing Nattering Nabobs of Negativism into Perky Purveyors of Positivism (CD) Featuring Brad Fitch. Prod. by TheCapitol.Net. 2006. 107.00 (978-1-58733-046-9(6)) TheCapitol.

Media Relations for the Newbie. 1 CD. (Running Time: 70 mins). 2005. audio compact disk 139.00 (978-1-58733-017-9(2)) TheCapitol.
This program will assist the new public or government affairs professional in learning how local, state and national media work and how to work the media. Topics to be covered include:- Tips for dealing with reporters- What the media can do for you- Getting the media interested in your organization- Deadlines and lead time- Different approaches to pitching to television, print, and radio reporters.

Media Services in Mexico: A Strategic Reference 2007. Compiled by Icon Group International, Inc. Staff. 2007. ring bd. 195.00 (978-0-497-82355-9(1)) Icon Grp.

Mediate on a Beautiful Scene of Nature. (135) Yoga Res Foun.

Mediation: Simulation of a Construction Dispute. Panel of Arbitrators. 2 cass. (Running Time: 1 hr. 30 min.). 1988. 250.00 (978-1-55917-454-1(4), 8214) Natl Prac Inst.
See how veteran attorneys & former governor settle a construction dispute involving hundreds of thousands of dollars & multitude of other pressing considerations.

Mediation: Simulation of a Personal Injury Case. Panel of Arbitrators. 2 cass. (Running Time: 1 hr. 30 min.). 1988. 195.00 (978-1-55917-451-0(X), 8212) Natl Prac Inst.
Learn the ins & outs of the hottest legal alternative to complex & costly litigation.

Mediation Advocacy. Contrib. by John W. Cooley. 6 cass. 1997. 73.95 (978-1-55681-543-0(3)) NITA.
Provides concrete guidance on how to achieve the best results for clients in mediation.

Mediation in Public Utility Commission Practice. 1997. bk. 99.00 (ACS-1350) PA Bar Inst.
PUC practice is changing with the rapidly-expanding use of alternative dispute resolution techniques, particularly mediation. Mandated under the Telecommunications Act & increasingly favored by the Commission to resolve disputes, utility practitioners must be prepared to mediate many of their cases.

Mediation in the Millennium. 1998. bk. 99.00 (ACS-2112) PA Bar Inst.
Mediation, among all of the alternatives to litigation, is emerging as the cornerstone of dispute resolution for the 21st century. Whether mandated by statute or court rule, demanded by economics or by sophisticated clients, or by increasing counsel recognizing its advantages, you will be handling cases in mediation.

Medical Astrology. Harish T. Dhutia. Read by Harish T. Dhutia. 1 cass. (Running Time: 90 min.). 1994. 8.95 (1128) Am Fed Astrologers.

Medical Astrology. Annie Hershey. 1 cass. (Running Time: 1 hr. 30 min.). 7.95 (156) Am Fed Astrologers.
Use astrological factors to promote good health.

Medical Astrology - Electional Charts - Surgery. John H. Goode. 1 cass. 8.95 (133) Am Fed Astrologers.
An AFA Convention workshop tape.

Medical Chemistry. Compiled by Benchmark Education Staff. 2006. audio compact disk 10.00 (978-1-4108-6691-2(2)) Benchmark Educ.

Medical-Dental Terminology: Syllabus. 2nd ed. LeGrand H. Woolley. (J). 1974. 179.15 (978-0-89420-162-2(X), 196700) Natl Book.

Medical Detectives, Vol. I. unabr. collector's ed. Berton Roueche. Read by Paul Shay. 10 cass. (Running Time: 15 hrs.). 1986. 80.00 (978-0-7366-0581-6(9), 1551) Books on Tape.
These research scientists, laboring alone or in teams, sift through the data supplied doctors from the front lines of disease. Their solutions are often intuitive & they rely as much on judgement as on what the test tubes show.

Medical Detectives, Vol. II. unabr. collector's ed. Berton Roueche. Read by Paul Shay. 11 cass. (Running Time: 16 hrs. 30 min.). 1986. 88.00 (978-0-7366-0592-2(4), 1559) Books on Tape.
All across America strange illnesses, rare diseases & the threat of contagion suddenly surface to bedevil an individual, a family or a seemingly unrelated group of people. The local health authorities can discover nothing to define the counteract the threat & the race is on. They are searching for the clue that leds to the source of infection & its destruction - before the victim worsens or the unknown & possibly fatal disease threatens to spread.

Medical Devices: Gadgets for the 1980s. 2 cass. (General Sessions Ser.: C84-SP4). 1984. 15.00 (8419) Am Coll Surgeons.

Medical Devices in Austria: A Strategic Reference 2007. Compiled by Icon Group International, Inc. Staff. 2007. ring bd. 195.00 (978-0-497-35817-4(4)) Icon Grp.

Medical Devices in France: A Strategic Reference 2006. Compiled by Icon Group International, Inc. Staff. 2007. ring bd. 195.00 (978-0-497-35953-9(7)) Icon Grp.

Medical Devices Panel Discussion: Devices, Dollars & Dictums. 2 cass. (General Sessions Ser.: C85-SP3). 15.00 (8545) Am Coll Surgeons.

Medical Diagnostics Laboratories in India: A Strategic Reference 2007. Compiled by Icon Group International, Inc. Staff. 2007. ring bd. 195.00 (978-0-497-36016-0(0)) Icon Grp.

Medical Dictation at Sixty - One Hundred Twenty WPM. unabr. ed. Conversa-Phone Institute Staff. 1 cass. (Running Time: 55 min.). (Secretarial Courses SEr.). 1992. 9.95 (978-1-56752-105-4(3)) Conversa-phone.
Dictation of letters given at different speeds. Manual for correcting work. These letters are medically oriented.

Medical Electional Charts, Geo & Helio. John H. Goode. 1 cass. 8.95 (408) Am Fed Astrologers.
Chart as a tool to determine best surgery time.

Medical Equipment & Products for the Aged & the Disabled in China: A Strategic Reference 2006. Compiled by Icon Group International, Inc. Staff. 2007. ring bd. 195.00 (978-0-497-35885-3(9)) Icon Grp.

Medical Equipment & Products in Vietnam: A Strategic Reference 2007. Compiled by Icon Group International, Inc. Staff. 2007. ring bd. 195.00 (978-0-497-82475-4(2)) Icon Grp.

Medical Equipment & Supplies for Cardiac Surgery in India: A Strategic Reference 2007. Compiled by Icon Group International, Inc. Staff. 2007. ring bd. 195.00 (978-0-497-36017-7(9)) Icon Grp.

Medical Equipment & Supplies for Infant Care in Ecuador: A Strategic Reference 2007. Compiled by Icon Group International, Inc. Staff. 2007. ring bd. 195.00 (978-0-497-35925-6(1)) Icon Grp.

Medical Equipment & Supplies in Egypt: A Strategic Reference 2007. Compiled by Icon Group International, Inc. Staff. 2007. ring bd. 195.00 (978-0-497-35931-7(6)) Icon Grp.

Medical Equipment & Supplies in Finland: A Strategic Reference 2006. Compiled by Icon Group International, Inc. Staff. 2007. ring bd. 195.00 (978-0-497-35938-6(3)) Icon Grp.

Medical Equipment & Supplies in Sweden: A Strategic Reference 2006. Compiled by Icon Group International, Inc. Staff. 2007. ring bd. 195.00 (978-0-497-82422-8(1)) Icon Grp.

Medical Equipment & Supplies in Thailand: A Strategic Reference 2006. Compiled by Icon Group International, Inc. Staff. 2007. ring bd. 195.00 (978-0-497-82442-6(6)) Icon Grp.

Medical Issues - Legal & Risk Management - Seizures. Steven Selbst & Gary Strange. (Pediatric Emergencies: The National Conference for Practioners Ser.). 1986. 9.00 (978-0-932491-75-6(8)) Res Appl Inc.

Medical Language. Layman. 1994. 107.25 (978-0-8273-6923-8(9)) Delmar.

Medical-Legal Laetrile Panel. unabr. ed. James Privitero. 1 cass. (Running Time: 1 hr. 5 min.). 12.95 (935) J Norton Pubs.

Medical Library Association Consumer Health Reference Service Handbook. Donald A. Barclay & Deborah D. Halsted. 2001. audio compact disk 75.00 (978-1-55570-418-6(2)) Neal-Schuman.

Medical Malpractice. Robert S. Sigman. Read by Robert S. Sigman. 1 cass. (Running Time: 1 hr.). (Law for the Layman Ser.). 1990. 16.95 (978-1-878135-01-8(5)) Legovac.
What you need to know before you see a lawyer!.

Medical Malpractice Crisis. 1 cass. (Care Cassettes Ser.: Vol. 14, No. 2). 1987. 10.80 Assn Prof Chaplains.

Medical Malpractice Litigation. (Running Time: 5 hrs.). 1994. 92.00 (20331) NYS Bar.
Addresses many aspects of medical malpractice litigation including the plaintiff's pre-suit activities & pleadings & discovery from both the plaintiff's & defendant's perspectives. The program also includes consideration of the judge's perspective & 187 page course book.

Medical Malpractice Litigation. 1988. bk. 110.00; 60.00 PA Bar Inst.

Medical Malpractice Litigation: A New Era. 1997. bk. 58.00 (ACS-1247) PA Bar Inst.
In November of 1996, the state legislature amended the Health Care Malpractice Act of 1975 to provide a stable funding source for the Medical Professional Liability Catastrophe Loss Fund. The amendments also redefine & extend informed consent, place caps on punitive damages, attempt to streamline the legal process relating to medical negligence & permit the periodic payment of future damages in certain circumstances.

Medical Microbiology AudioLearn. 2 CDs. (C). 2003. audio compact disk 34.99 (978-0-9704199-4-1(5)) AudioLearn.

Medical Myths That Can Kill You: And the 101 Truths That Will Save, Extend, & Improve Your Life. abr. ed. Nancy L. Snyderman. Read by Nancy L. Snyderman. (ENG.). 2009. audio compact disk 19.95 (978-0-7393-8432-9(5), Random AudioBks) Pub: Random Audio Pubg. Dist(s): Random

***Medical OSHA Compliance 2009.** PUEI. 2009. audio compact disk 199.00 (978-1-935041-61-0(4), CareerTrack) P Univ E Inc.

Medical Perspectives on the Value of Human Life. unabr. ed. Michael E. DeBakey. 1 cass. (Running Time: 18 min.). 12.95 (33013) J Norton Pubs.
A discussion of a physician's duty to relieve suffering & prolong life. The controversy over the right of the individual & of society, whose guidelines should govern today's physician - those of medicine, law, theology, philosophy.

Medical Procedure Relaxation for Adults: Guided Imagery for Well-Being. Catherine Sheen. 1 CD. (Running Time: 27 minutes). 2006. audio compact disk 14.95 (978-0-9773381-8-4(5)) Reach In.
Medical Procedure Relaxation for Adults CD is a Guided Imagery that helps slow your breathing and calm and relax your body to reduce fear and anxiety. You can gain confidence in your body?s ability to benefit from the medical procedure or surgery and have the best possible outcome. The CD includes Information for Family, Care Givers and Patients and Preparation for Guided Imagery tracks.

Medical Procedure Relaxation for Children: Guided Imagery for Well-Being. Catherine Sheen. 1 CD. (Running Time: 27 minutes). 2006. audio compact disk 14.95 (978-0-9773381-9-1(3)) Reach In.
Medical Procedure Relaxation for Children CD is a Guided Imagery that guides the child or adolescent to slow their breathing, calm and relax the body, express their fears and reduce anxiety. They can gain confidence in their body?s ability to benefit from the medical procedure or surgery and have the best possible outcome. The CD includes Information for Family and Care Givers and Preparation for Guided Imagery tracks.

Medical Reports. Research Panel Staff. 1 cass. 8.95 (791) Am Fed Astrologers.

Medical Review Criteria for Managing Care. 4th ed. Margaret Bischel. 2005. ring bd. 675.00 (978-1-893826-67-0(8), 1) Apollo Managed.

Medical Risks of Vitamin E "Therapy" H. J. Roberts. 2 cass. (Running Time: 3 hrs.). 1994. 19.95 (978-0-9633260-9-6(0)) Sunshine Sentinel.
An important "rest of the story" expose about the ignored, overlooked or suppressed potential hazards of excessive vitamin E - at a time when its consumption is escalating without restraint. They include hypertension thrombophlebitis breast tumors.

Medical School Libraries & Hospital Libraries Sections - Living on the Edge of Tension: The Library's Position in the Managed Care Environment. 2 cass. (Medical Library Association 1998 Annual Meeting & Exhibit Ser.). 1998. 12.00 (08) Med Lib Assn.

Medical School Libraries & Medical Informatics Sections - Evidence-based Medicine: The Library's Role in Twenty-first Century Medicine. 1 cass. (Medical Library Association 1998 Annual Meeting & Exhibit Ser.). 1998. 12.00 (16) Med Lib Assn.

Medical Science. unabr. ed. Roger White. Read by Edwin Newman. (Running Time: 10800 sec.). (Audio Classics: Science & Discovery Ser.). 2006. audio compact disk 25.95 (978-0-7861-6434-9(4)) Pub: Blckstn Audio. Dist(s): NetLibrary CO

Medical Spanish: A Conversational Approach. Maria A. Di Lorenzo-Kearon. 12 cass. (Running Time: 11 hrs. 30 mins.). (SPA.). 1982. pap. bk. 225.00 Incl. 29p. listener guide. (978-0-88432-079-1(0), AFMS20) J Norton Pubs.
Beginning course for doctors, nurses & medical & nursing students. Practice dialogs, mini-conversations & other activities help you develop conversational skills. Medical/technical vocabulary is always presented in context. Text includes reading comprehension & written exercises, medical questionnaires & anatomical diagrams in both Spanish & English. Assumes no previous knowledge of Spanish. Includes listener's guide.

Medical Spanish: Conversational Approach. 2nd ed. Kearon. bk. 80.95 (978-0-8384-7494-5(2)) Heinle.

Medical Spanish: Conversational Approach. 2nd ed. Kearon. (C). bk. 80.95 (978-0-8384-7161-6(7)); bk. 120.95 (978-0-8384-7877-6(8)); bk. 88.95 (978-0-8384-7879-0(4)) Heinle.

Medical Spanish CDs, text & listener's Guide. Maria DiLorenzo-Kearon & Thomas Kearon. 12 CDs. (Running Time: 11 hrs. 30 mins.). (SPA.). 2005. audio compact disk 225.00 (978-1-57970-244-1(9), AFMS20D, Audio-For) J Norton Pubs.

Medical Spanish, Disc I. 2003. ring bd. (978-0-9744783-1-9(8)) Spanish Acad Cu Inst.

Medical Spanish, Disc 2. 2004. audio compact disk (978-0-9747887-9-1(1)) Spanish Acad Cu Inst.

Medical Spanish, Disc 3. 2004. audio compact disk (978-0-9753143-0-2(0)) Spanish Acad Cu Inst.

Medical Staff Issues & Litigation: An Rx for the 1990s. 1990. 140.00 (AC-570) PA Bar Inst.

Medical Surgical, Pt. 1. Patricia Hoefler. (Complete Q & A Ser.). 2002. (978-1-56533-123-5(0)) MEDS Pubng.

Medical Surgical, Pt. 2. Patricia Hoefler. (Complete Q & A Ser.). 2002. (978-1-56533-124-2(9)) MEDS Pubng.

Medical Surgical, Pt. 3. Patricia Hoefler. (Complete Q & A Ser.). 2002. (978-1-56533-125-9(7)) MEDS Pubng.

Medical Surgical, Pt. 4. Patricia Hoefler. (Complete Q & A Ser.). 2002. (978-1-56533-126-6(5)) MEDS Pubng.

Medical-Surgical Emergencies I. unabr. ed. Instructed by JoAnn C. Tess-Pibum. 4 cass. (Running Time: 7 hrs.). 1990. pap. bk. 79.00 (HT29) Ctr Hlth Educ.
Be prepared to meet your next medical emergency with this power packed course. It has four audio tapes & a softbound text that gives you the latest facts on prevention, treatment & nursing care that can be used daily. This course helps you master the art of assessment & treatment for patients with: GI & esophageal bleeding; allergic reactions; pulmonary emboli; acute respiratory failure; hemorrhagic shock; bowel obstruction vs. an ileus. Includes soft bound book.

Medical-Surgical Emergencies II. unabr. ed. Instructed by JoAnn C. Tess-Pibum. 4 cass. (Running Time: 7 hrs.). 1990. 79.00 (HT6A) Ctr Hlth Educ.
This seminar is filled with hot tips. It will assist you in detecting early signs & symptoms of life threatening complications that you deal with frequently. Get advanced knowledge & down-to-earth solutions you can use daily. You will learn: how to identify patients in early state septic shock & prevention of further complications; how to treat accute MIs, CHF, & renal failure; what to look for in a rare crisis of thyroid storm; how to assist in medical procedures during emergency situations such as seizures, cardiac arrhythmias, & acute diabetic reactions. Includes soft-bound book.

Medical Terminology. 1994. 104.95 (978-0-8273-6920-7(4)) Delmar.

Medical Terminology: A Systems Approach. 4th rev. ed. Barbara A. Gylys & Mary E. Wedding. 2 vols. 2004. bk. 36.95 (978-0-8036-0396-7(7)) Davis Co.

Medical Terminology AudioLearn. Speeches. Created by Barbara Williams. 2 CDs. (C). 2003. audio compact disk 29.99 (978-0-9704199-6-5(1)) AudioLearn.

Medical Terminology Essentials: Student Courseware. Alice G. Ettinger & Pamala F. Burch. bk. 58.95 (978-0-7638-0308-7(1)); 48.95 (978-0-7638-0307-0(3)) EMC-Paradigm.

Medical Terminology for Health Careers. Alice G. Ettinger & Pamala F. Burch. bk. 79.95 (978-0-7638-0301-8(4)) EMC-Paradigm.

Medical Terminology for Health Careers. 2nd ed. Alice G. Ettinger & Pamala F. Burch. 2007. audio compact disk 56.95 (978-0-7638-2270-5(1)) EMC-Paradigm.

Medical Terminology for Health Professions. Ann Ehrlich & Carol L. Schroeder. 2 cass. (Running Time: 3 hrs.). 2001. 108.95 Includes duplication rights. (978-0-7668-1299-4(5)) Delmar.

Medical Terminology for Health Professions. 3rd ed. Ann Ehrlich. 1 cass. (Medical Terminology Ser.). 1997. bk. 99.95 (978-0-8273-7840-7(8)) Delmar.

Medical Terminology for Health Professions. 6th ed. Ann Ehrlich & Carol L. Schroeder. (Studyware Ser.). (ENG.). 2009. pap. bk. & spiral bd. 186.95 (978-1-4354-4307-5(1)) Delmar.

Medical Terminology Made Easy. 2nd ed. Jean T. Dennerll. 2 cass. 1997. 39.95 (978-0-8273-8138-4(7)) Delmar.

Medical Terminology Online to Accompany Exploring Medical Language: User Guide & Access Code. 6th ed. Myrna LaFleur Brooks & Mosby Staff. 2005. bk. 105.00 (978-0-323-03381-7(4), MosElsHlth) Elsevier HthSci.

Medical Terms Made Easy. Jean T. Dennerll. 1 cass. 1993. bk. 25.95 (978-0-8273-5907-9(1)); bk. 36.95 (978-0-8273-5918-5(7)) Delmar.

Medical Tourism in Philippines: A Strategic Reference 2007. Compiled by Icon Group International, Inc. Staff. 2007. ring bd. 195.00 (978-0-497-82389-4(6)) Icon Grp.

Medical Transcription. 2nd rev. ed. Blanche Ettinger & Alice G. Ettinger. 7 cass. 2005. 225.00 (978-0-7638-1411-3(3)); audio compact disk 225.00 (978-0-7638-1892-0(5)) EMC-Paradigm.

Medical Transcription: Instructor Resources; Instructor's Guide on CD. 2nd rev. ed. Blanche Ettinger & Alice G. Ettinger. 2005. audio compact disk 17.95 (978-0-7638-2007-7(5)) EMC-Paradigm.

Medical Transcription & Terminology: An Integrated Approach. Florence C. Maloney & Lois M. Burns. 6 cass. (Running Time: 9 hrs.). 1997. 217.95 Includes duplication rights. (978-0-7668-0323-7(6)) Delmar.

Medical Transcription Power Building: Student Key & Guide. Bruce Tennant. 1983. pap. bk. 111.95 (978-0-89420-224-7(3), 470000) Natl Book.

Medical Transcription Self-Assessment, No. 1. 1 cass. 1995. bk. & stu. ed. 35.00 (978-0-935229-28-0(0)) Am Assoc Med.
15 minutes of physician dictation & accompanying booklet of instructions, transcripts; a tool to help MTs evaluate their skills.

Medical Transcription Self-Assessment, No. 2. 1 cass. 1996. bk. & stu. ed. 35.00 (978-0-935229-30-1(2), MTSA-2) Am Assoc Med.
Tools to help MTs evaluate their skills. Derived from previously used core certification practical exam material, intended to simulate the exam process. CMTs may earn 3 CECs (1 medical, 2 nonmedical) for completion of assessment.

Medical Works, abr. ed. Hippocrates. Read by Robert L. Halvorson. 6 cass. (Running Time: 9 hrs.). 42.95 (57) Halvorson Assocs.

Medically Speaking RULES with Audio: Rules for Using Linguistic Elements of Speech-Teacher's Edition. Lynda Katz Wilner & Marjorie Feinstein-Whittaker. 2007. spiral bd. 90.00 (978-0-9717038-8-9(4)) Seccess Speaking.

Medication Safety for Nursing. Prod. by Lippincott Williams and Wilkins Staff. (ENG.). 2007. 20.00 (978-0-7817-9413-8(7)) Lppncott W W.

Medicinal & Pharmaceutical Products in Austria: A Strategic Reference 2007. Compiled by Icon Group International, Inc. Staff. 2007. ring bd. 195.00 (978-0-497-35818-1(2)) Icon Grp.

Medicine: Christian Identity & Community. 1 cass. (Care Cassettes Ser.: Vol. 15, No. 7). 1988. 10.80 Assn Prof Chaplains.

Medicine: Cure or Control. unabr. ed. Thomas Szasa. 1 cass. (Running Time: 1 hr. 30 min.). 1973. 11.00 (10701) Big Sur Tapes.
Sees the function of some psychiatrists as social control, determining who is "sick" & who is "normal" with no objective standards of mental health or illness. He explores psychiatric techniques defined as "treatment" as disguised forms of extra-legal punishment & confinement for those of whom society disapproves.

Medicine: The Death of a Profession. Leonard Peikoff. Read by Leonard Peikoff. 1 cass. (Running Time: 1 hr. 30 min.). 1985. 12.95 (978-1-56114-061-9(9), LP08C) Second Renaissance.
How government controls are destroying the ability & the desire of competent doctors to practice medicine.

Medicine: The Sick Man in a Mixed Economy (Panel Discussion) Tonkin et al. 1 cass. (Running Time: 1 hr. 30 min.). 1989. 12.95 (978-1-56114-136-4(4), HD01C) Second Renaissance.

Medicine Bow, Lauran Paine. Read by Tom Hunsinger. 3 cass. (Running Time: 4 hrs. 30 min.). 1999. 34.95 (62477) Pub: Soundings Ltd GBR. Dist(s): Ulverscroft US

Medicine Buddha Mandala & Revelation. Yeshi Donden. 4 cass. 18.00 (OC11L) Sound Horizons AV.

Medicine Garden. David Freudberg. Perf. by Andrew Weil et al. 2 cass. (Running Time: 2 hrs.). 1996. 15.95 (978-1-886373-06-8(X)) Human Media.
An introduction to natural herbal remedies - clearly explained by doctors & other health experts.

Medicine Garden, Pt. 1. unabr. ed. Interview with David Freudberg & Andrew Weil. 1 cass. (Running Time: 1 hr.). 1996. 10.95 (978-1-886373-07-5(8)) Human Media.
Introduction to natural herbal remedies - clearly explained by doctors & other health experts.

Medicine Heart. Black Bear. 1 cass. (Running Time: 1 hr. 45 mins.). 1998. 15.00 (978-0-9700042-1-5(4), DI006) Divine Ideas.
Sacred teaching from Black Bear's lineage, passed down to him from his teacher, Mountain Bear.

Medicine Heart Songs. Perf. by Thomas Pinkson. 1 cass. 9.00 (A0345-88) Sound Photosyn.
A psychologist singing & drumming pieces from the American Indian tradition.

Medicine Horn. unabr. ed. Jory Sherman. Read by Maynard Villers. 8 cass. (Running Time: 9 hrs. 30 min.). (Buckskinners Ser.: Bk. 1). 1996. 49.95 (978-1-55686-662-3(3)) Books in Motion.
Lemuel Hawke, a poor dirt farmer, follows a fierce craving for the freedom & opportunity found in the mountains beyond the boundaries of civilization.

***Medicine Man of Business: Unblocking the Profit Pathways.** unabr. ed. Terry Patryluk. (Running Time: 3 hrs. 30 mins.). (ENG.). 2010. 24.98 (978-1-59659-514-9(0), GildAudio) Pub: Gildan Media. Dist(s): HachBkGrp

Medicine, Meaning & Prayer. Interview with Larry Dossey & Michael Toms. 2 cass. (Running Time: 1 hr. 30 min.). 1997. 15.95 (978-1-56170-419-4(9), 338) Hay House.
Presents & evaluates the evidence that prayer plays a role in physical health & explores its implications for both medical practice & individual healing.

Medicine Path: Healing Songs & Stories of the Northwest Native Americans. unabr. ed. Read by Johnny Moses. 1 cass. (Running Time: 1 hr.). (Native American Storytime Ser.). 2001. 11.95 Parabola Bks.
Storyteller, healer and respected spiritual leader Johnny Moses shares the spiritual practices that cured his illness and sustain his people to this day. Full of chants and lore from the Northwest tribes, shows how stories and everyday acts can serve as the most powerful medicine of all. Includes the Indian Shaker song for soul loss, Healing of the Heart Song and more.

Medicine Woman. Lynn V. Andrews. Read by Lynn V. Andrews. 2 cass. (Running Time: 2 hrs.). 14.95 HarperCollins Pubs.

Medicus: A Novel of the Roman Empire. Ruth Downie. Read by Simon Vance. (Playaway Adult Fiction Ser.). 2008. 69.99 (978-1-60640-709-7(0)) Find a World.

Medicus: A Novel of the Roman Empire. unabr. ed. Ruth Downie. (Running Time: 12 hrs. 30 mins. 0 sec.). (Roman Empire Ser.). (ENG.). 2007. audio compact disk 29.99 (978-1-4001-5363-3(8)) Pub: Tantor Media. Dist(s): IngramPubServ

Medicus: A Novel of the Roman Empire. unabr. ed. Ruth Downie. Narrated by Simon Vance. (Running Time: 12 hrs. 30 mins. 0 sec.). (Roman Empire Ser.). (ENG.). 2007. audio compact disk 39.99 (978-1-4001-0363-8(0)) Pub: Tantor Media. Dist(s): IngramPubServ

Medicus: A Novel of the Roman Empire. unabr. ed. Ruth Downie. Narrated by Simon Vance. (Running Time: 12 hrs. 30 mins. 0 sec.). (Roman Empire Ser.). (ENG.). 2007. audio compact disk 79.99 (978-1-4001-3363-5(7)) Pub: Tantor Media. Dist(s): IngramPubServ

Medidas. 1 cass. (Primeros Pasos en Ciencia Ser.). (SPA.). (J). 12.00 (7454-0, Natl Textbk Co) M-H Contemporary.
Helps children in grades 1-4 discover the process of scientific investigation. Part of the First Steps in Science Program.

Medieval & Renaissance Dance Music for Acoustic Guitar. Jamey Bellizzi. 1998. pap. bk. 19.95 (978-0-7866-4036-2(7), 94847BCD) Mel Bay.

Medieval Bedazzle. Tecoa T. Washington. (Running Time: 31380 sec.). 2008. audio compact disk 37.99 (978-1-60604-499-5(0)) Tate Pubng.

Medieval Europe, Pts. I-II. Instructed by Teofilo Ruiz. 8 cass. (Running Time: 12 hrs.). 54.95 (978-1-56585-258-7(3)) Teaching Co.

Medieval Europe: Crisis & Renewal. Instructed by Teofilo F. Ruiz. 16 CDs. (Running Time: 12 hrs.). audio compact disk 69.95 (978-1-59803-193-5(7)) Teaching Co.

Medieval Europe Vol. 2: Crisis & Renewal. Instructed by Teofilo Ruiz. 4 cass. (Running Time: 6 hrs.). 1996. 129.95 (978-1-56585-259-4(1)) Teaching Co.

Medieval Heroines in History & Legend, Pt. I-II. Instructed by Bonnie Wheeler. 12 CDs. (Running Time: 12 hrs.). bk. 69.95 (978-1-56585-524-3(8)) Teaching Co.

Medieval Heroines in History & Legend, Pts. I-II. Instructed by Bonnie Wheeler. 12 cass. (Running Time: 12 hrs.). 2002. bk. 54.95 (978-1-56585-523-6(X)) Teaching Co.

Medieval People. unabr. ed. Eileen Power. Read by Roe Kendall. 5 cass. (Running Time: 7 hrs.). 2000. 39.95 (978-0-7861-1994-3(2), 2764) Blckstn Audio.
There are full-length portraits of Bodo, a Frankish peasant in the time of Charlemagne (ninth century); Marco Polo, the Venetian traveler, Madame Eglentyne, the Prioress of Chaucer's Canterbury Tales, the young (fifteen-year-old) wife of a fourteenth-century Parisian bourgeois, and two English merchants of the fifteenth century, Thomas Betson of the wool trade and Thomas Paycocke of Coggeshall, an Essex clothier.

Medieval People. unabr. ed. Eileen Power. Read by Roe Kendall. 6 CDs. (Running Time: 7 hrs.). 2003. audio compact disk 55.00 (978-0-7861-8128-5(1), 2764) Blckstn Audio.

Medieval Science. unabr. ed. John T. Sanders. Read by Edwin Newman. Ed. by Jack Sommer & Mike Hassell. 2 cass. (Running Time: 2 hrs. 45 min.). Dramatization. (Science & Discovery Ser.). (YA). (gr. 11 up). 1992. 17.95 (978-0-938935-67-4(4), 10402) Knowledge Prod.
Many believe the "Middle Ages" lacked progress, yet during this time algebra was developed, & Islamic scholars preserved & extended Greek thought (which otherwise was lost). Metallurgy (& its speculative counterpart, alchemy) led to a deeper understanding of materials. These advances set the stage for the Renaissance - & a scientific revolution.

***Medieval World.** Instructed by Dorsey Armstrong. 2009. 199.95 (978-1-59803-601-5(7)); audio compact disk 269.95 (978-1-59803-602-2(5)) Teaching Co.

Medigate: Dr. Strecker & the Rife Microscope. Robert Strecker. 2 cass. (Roy Tuckman Interview Ser.). 2001. 18.00 (A0187-87) Sound Photosyn.

Meditacion para lograr una mente clara: una fuente diferente de Felicidad: Meditaciones sencillas de la tradicion budista para la vida Diaria. Vive la Meditacion Staff & Tharpa Publications Staff. (Running Time: 0 hr. 30 mins. 0 sec.). (Meditations for Daily Life Ser.). (SPA.). 2010. audio compact disk 12.95 (978-84-936169-9-1(0)) Pub: Tharpa Pubns GBR. Dist(s): IPG Chicago

Meditaciones para el Alma. Deepak Chopra. 2006. bk. 34.99 (978-84-414-1702-1(4)) Edaf Edit ESP.

Meditaciones para la Relajacion: Tres meditaciones guiadas para relajar el cuerpo y la Mente. Living Meditation & Tharpa Publications Staff. (Running Time: 0 hr. 45 mins. 0 sec.). (Meditations for Daily Life Ser.). (SPA.). 2009. audio compact disk 12.95 (978-84-936169-8-4(2)) Pub: Tharpa Pubns GBR. Dist(s): IPG Chicago

Meditapes Eight: Your Healing Journey for Cancer. Stephanie Carter & JoAnn Lederman. 6 cass. (Running Time: 2 hrs. 45 min.). (YA). (gr. 7 up). 1998. 49.95 Set, incl. guidebk. (978-1-893868-07-6(9)) Meditapes.
Will comfort & guide through all phases of treatment.

Meditapes Five - Relax Pak. Stephanie Carter & JoAnn Lederman. 2 cass. (Running Time: 1 hr.). (YA). (gr. 7 up). 1995. 24.95 (978-1-893868-04-5(4)) Meditapes.
Helps to let go & unwind, using a tapestry of guided imagery & soothing music. Includes guidebook.

Meditapes Four - Getting a Good Night's Sleep. Stephanie Carter & JoAnn Lederman. 2 cass. (Running Time: 45 min.). (YA). (gr. 7 up). 1998. pap. bk. 24.95 (978-1-893868-03-8(6)) Meditapes.
Tape 1 - quickstart program. Tape 2 - relaxation program. Includes guidebook.

Meditapes One - For Your Surgery. Stephanie Carter & JoAnn Lederman. 2 cass. (Running Time: 45 min.). (J). 1998. pap. bk. 24.95 (978-1-893868-00-7(1)) Meditapes.
Reduce fear, diminish pain & promote healing before, during & after surgery. Tape 1 - quick start program. Tape 2 - relaxation program. lincl. guidebk.

Meditapes Seven - Chemotherapy Comfort. Stephanie Carter & JoAnn Lederman. 2 cass. (Running Time: 45 min.). (YA). (gr. 7 up). 1998. pap. bk. 24.95 (978-1-893868-06-9(0)) Meditapes.
Relax & enhance the beneficial effects of your treatment Tape 1 - quickstart program. Tape 2 - relaxation program. Incl. guidebk.

Meditapes Six - Fighting Cancer. Stephanie Carter & JoAnn Lederman. 2 cass. (Running Time: 45 min.). (YA). (gr. 7 up). 1998. pap. bk. 24.95 (978-1-893868-05-2(2)) Meditapes.
Learn to reduce anxiety, boost the immune system & triumph over cancer. Tape 1 - quickstart program. Tape 2 - relaxation program. Includes guidebook.

Meditapes Three - Thinking Thin & Healthy. Stephanie Carter & JoAnn Lederman. 2 cass. (Running Time: 45 min.). (YA). (gr. 7 up). 1998. pap. bk. 24.95 (978-1-893868-02-1(8)) Meditapes.
Tape 1 - quickstart program. Tape 2 - relaxation program. Includes guidebook.

Meditapes Two - Calming Your Child Night & Day. Stephanie Carter & JoAnn Lederman. 2 cass. (Running Time: 45 min.). 1998. pap. bk. 24.95 (978-1-893868-01-4(X)) Meditapes.
Contains a magical journey to help a child create inner tranquility. Tape 1 - quickstart program. Tape 2 - relaxation program. Includes guidebook.

Meditate on a Beautiful Scene of Nature. Swami Jyotirmayananda. 1 cass. (Running Time: 1 hr.). 1990. 12.99 Yoga Res Foun.

Meditate Through Menopause. unabr. ed. Mercedes Leidlich. Read by Mercedes Leidlich. 1 cass. (Running Time: 1 hr.). 1992. 10.95 (978-1-882174-13-3(5), MLL-014) UFD Pub.
This tape is geared toward the Baby Boomers who are now approaching middle age. Against a soothing background of harp & ocean wave, the listener is guided through gentle meditations to enhance self-esteem, accept what cannot be changed & to ease the transition into mid-life & beyond.

Meditate with Dr. Gayle Kimball. Gayle Kimball. 1 CD. (Running Time: 50 mins.). 2001. audio compact disk 12.00 (978-0-938795-95-7(3)) Equality Pr.
Includes: meditation, goal setting and gaining information from one's higher self.

Meditating Mind: Making Meditation a Part of Your Life. Thomas M. Sterner. Read by Thomas M. Sterner. Lin McDowell. 2006. audio compact disk 18.95 (978-0-9776572-2-3(1)) Mountain Sage.

Meditating with Children. Carlin Diamond. 1 cass. (Running Time: 1 hr.). 1986. 10.00 CPR San Rafael.
Stimulates the wonderful imagination of children. Rekindles their natural ability to meditate that they lose by modeling after us. With the use of a few images used by the author while meditating with children at home & in the classroom.

Meditating with Mary on the Seven Last Words. Fred Jelly. 1 cass. (Running Time: 1 hr. 30 min.). 1996. 9.95 (TAH373) St Pauls Alba.
Renew within yourself the promise of victory Christ has won for us as you stand, with Mary, on Calvary & discover anew his seven last words from the cross.

Meditating with the Body: Six Tibetan Buddhist Meditations for Touching Enlightenment with the Body. Interview. Reginald A. Ray. 4 CDs. (Running Time: 5 hours). 2003. audio compact disk 34.95 (978-1-59179-038-9(7)) Sounds True.
On "Meditating with the Body," listeners will learn to master a series of six Tibetan-based meditations to settle and calm the mind, channel vitalizing energy throughout the body, connect with the living, healing quality of the earth, and uncover the body's untapped powers of perception, intuition, and wisdom.

Meditation see Richard Eberhart Reading His Poetry

Meditation see Twentieth-Century Poetry in English, No. 25, Recordings of Poets Reading Their Own Poetry

Meditation. (714) Yoga Res Foun.

Meditation. James S. Benko. Read by James S. Benko. 1986. 12.95 (TC-9); 28.00 (TCR-1) ITA Inst.
Presentation which takes you into the world of the mind. How, why & where to meditate are discussed by Master Benko. Exercises are given to highten your awareness & ability to reach goals both in & out of the training hall.

Meditation. Swami Jyotirmayananda. 1 cass. (Running Time: 1 hr.). 1990. 12.99 Yoga Res Foun.

Meditation. Joyce Levine. Read by Joyce Levine. 1 cass. (Running Time: 50 min.). 1994. 11.95 (978-1-885856-00-5(8)) Vizualizations.
Side 1 - How meditation works; Side 2 - meditation.

Meditation. Read by Linda Ruth. Contrib. by Paul Brunton. 1 cass. (Running Time: 1 hr.). 9.95 Larson Pubns.
Excellent for learning about meditation & for meditative listening.

Meditation. Read by Chogyam Trungpa. 1 cass. 1986. 10.00 (A093) Vajradhatu.

Meditation. abr. rev. unabr. ed. Mark Thurston & Edgar Cayce. Read by Stanley Ralph Ross. 1 CD. (Running Time: 1 hr. 0 mins. 0 sec.). (ENG.). 2001. audio compact disk 14.95 (978-1-55927-664-1(9)) Pub: Macmill Audio. Dist(s): Macmillan

Meditation. rev. ed. Mary Ellen Flora. 2000. reel tape 10.00 (978-1-886983-12-0(7)) CDM Pubns.

Meditation, No. 1. J. Krishnamurti. 1 cass. (Running Time: 1 hr.). (Krishnamurti with Dr. Allan W. Anderson Ser.: No. 17). 8.50 (APA7417) Krishnamurti.
These 1974 dialogues cover the entire spectrum of Krishnamurti's teaching in a series highly regarded for its depth of inquiry into each particular subject.

Meditation, No. 2. J. Krishnamurti. 1 cass. (Running Time: 1 hr.). (Krishnamurti with Dr. Allan W. Anderson Ser.: No. 18). 8.50 (APA7418) Krishnamurti.

Meditation: A Complete Audio Guide to a Practical Eight Point Program. unabr. ed. Eknath Easwaran. Read by Eknath Easwaran. 2 vols. (Running Time: 3 hrs.). 1995. 16.95 (978-0-915132-81-2(8)) Nilgiri Pr.
Listen as Easwaran gives complete instructions in his Eight Point Program of meditation and supporting practices. Anyone can use this method to learn to meditate without dogma - within any religious tradition or outside them all.

Meditation: A Foundation for Living a Fearless Life. unabr. ed. Andrew Cohen. 2 CDs. (Running Time: 2 hrs.). 2006. audio compact disk 19.95 (978-1-883929-46-6(6)) Moksha Pr.

Meditation: A Guided Practice for Everyday. Featuring Swami Chetanananda. 2 CDs. (Running Time: 1 hr. 31 mins.). 2006. audio compact disk 20.00 (978-0-915801-24-4(8)) Rudra Pr.

Meditation: A Practical Survival for the 90's. Allen Holmquist. 1 cass. 1993. 6.99 CMH Records.

Meditation: A Practical Survival Kit for the Nineties. Allen Holmquist. 1 cass. 1993. 9.98 (978-5-555-77158-2(4)) CMH Records.

Meditation: A Simple Eight Point Program for Translating Spiritual Ideals into Daily Life. Eknath Easwaran. 2 CDs. (Running Time: 2 hrs. 40 mins. 0 sec.). Orig. Title: Meditation: Commonsense Directions for an Uncommon Life. (ENG.). 2004. audio compact disk 18.95 (978-1-58638-636-8(0)) Pub: Nilgiri Pr. Dist(s): PerseuPGW

Meditation: Key to Spiritual Awakening. Mary Ellen Flora. 1 cass. (Running Time: 1 hr. 8 min.). 1992. 9.95 (978-0-9631993-1-7(5)) CDM Pubns.
Learn 5 spiritual techniques followed by a guided meditation. Meditation is the process through which we can heal ourselves and our world. It is the path back to our spiritual awareness and our open relationship with all things.

Meditation: Maintaining Contact with Deep Psyche. Kenneth James. Read by Kenneth James. 4 cass. (Running Time: 4 hrs. 40 min.). 1997. 28.95 (978-0-7822-0530-5(5), 596) C G Jung IL.
Introduces the listener to various traditions of meditation to establish & maintain contact with deep layers of psychic material.

Meditation: On the Edge. Instructed by Stuart Wilde. 2 cass. (Self-Help Tape Ser.). 2001. 19.95 (978-0-930603-26-7(5)) White Dove NM.
Side one of this two-tape series discusses how to get real value from your meditations & gives you techniques for expanding contact with the inner worlds & your Higher Self. Sides two, three & four are unusual guided meditations centering on Pulling Instant Power, Spiritual Healing, & Contacting the Reservoirs of Talent Deep Within.

Meditation: Pandora's Box or Christ Treasures; The Joy of Mary Magdalene. Jonathan Murro. 1 cass. 7.95 A R Colton Fnd.
Discusses the goal of God-Realization.

Meditation: The Basics. Patricia J. Crane. Read by Patricia J. Crane. 1 cass. (Running Time: 54 min.). 1986. 10.00 (978-1-893705-02-9(1)) Hlth Horiz.
Discussion of basic meditation techniques. Instruction in four different techniques.

Meditation: The Music of Silence. Osho Oshos. Read by Osho Oshos. 1 cass. (Running Time: 1 hr. 30 min.). 2001. 10.95 (DCM-0011) Oshos.
Answers "Questions such as How to have technique to prepare meditation & Is it really possible to grow & flower in the harsh environment of the West".

Meditation: Week of June 22, 1998. Perf. by Philip Glass. Hosted by Fred Goodwin. Comment by John Hockenberry. Contrib. by Dalai Lama XIV et al. 1 cass. (Running Time: 1 hr.). (Infinite Mind Ser.). 1998. audio compact disk 15.00 (978-1-888064-39-1(0)) Lichtenstein Creat.
Why are many turning to the ancient practice of meditation & how does it affect the brain? Discussions with brain scientists & the latest news from "Psychology Today" magazine.

Meditation: Your First Steps. unabr. ed. Barbara J. Faison. 2004. audio compact disk 16.95 (978-0-9672081-1-4(4)) In Search Pubns.
"If you have ever thought about meditation. Meditation: Your First Steps by Barbara J. Faison is the CD for you. In this hectic hurried world Barbara's soothing voice guides listeners through four 10-minute meditations to help you relax your body, release your worries and recharge your spirit. Try the bonus track, Be Relaxed, to unwind at the end of the day. Choose one meditation a week to stress less and live more.".

Meditation - Quieting the Busy Mind. Michael Chojnacki. (ENG.). 2008. audio compact disk (978-0-9786006-2-4(2)) Infinite Wisdm.

Meditation & Contemplation. Gary Arnold. (ENG.). 2007. audio compact disk 24.95 (978-1-57867-055-0(1)) Pub: Windhorse Corp. Dist(s): New Leaf Dist

Meditation & Devotion. unabr. ed. Twin Sisters Productions. Read by Twin Sisters. (YA). 2007. 44.99 (978-1-60252-849-9(7)) Find a World.

Meditation & Discipline. unabr. ed. Osho Oshos. Read by Osho Oshos. 1 cass. (Running Time: 1 hr. 30 min.). 1987. 10.95 (CTI-083187B) Oshos.
An in-depth look at the most important contribution of the East to the world: Meditation.

Meditation & Guru's Grace. Swami Amar Jyoti. 1 cass. (Satsangs of Swami Amar Jyoti Ser.). 9.95 (I-19) Truth Consciousness.

Meditation & Hypnosis. 1 CD. (Running Time: 70 minutes). 2000. 14.95 (978-0-9779472-2-5(X)) Health Wealth Inc.
This program was created to easily, and effectively make the benefits of meditation available to everyone. Most people never relax enough mentally, or take long periods of effort to enter meditation. These recordings will help you to use the principles of hypnosis to aid in preparing you to meditate. Find out how easy meditation can be!.

Meditation & Motivation. Steven M. Kohn. 1 CD. 1999. audio compact disk Hlth Jrnys.

Meditation & Needs. Jackie Woods. 1 cass. (Running Time: 33 min.). 1999. 15.00 (978-0-9659665-1-1(8)) Adawehi Pr.

Meditation & Peace: The Goal of Inner Peace. Marianne Williamson. Read by Marianne Williamson. 1 cass. (Running Time: 1 hr. 30 min.). (Lectures on a Course in Miracles). 1999. 10.00 (978-1-56170-247-3(1), M750) Hay House.

Meditation & Prayer in The Buddhadharma. Vajracarya. Read by Chogyam Trungpa. 4 cass. 1976. 36.00 Vajradhatu.
Topics include: Theistic & Nontheistic Traditions, Empty Heart, Lineage & Heritage, The Basis of Trust, Practice & Workability.

***Meditation & Psychotherapy.** Tara Brach. (Running Time: 10:00:00). 2011. audio compact disk 79.95 (978-1-59179-970-2(8)) Sounds True.

Meditation & Reveries. Read by Jack Schwarz. 1 cass. 10.00 (#101) Aletheia Psycho.
A step-by-step meditation & two reveries.

Meditation & Selfless Service. Eknath Easwaran. 1 cass. (Running Time: 56 mins.). 1989. 7.95 (978-1-58638-575-0(5), MSS) Nilgiri Pr.
"The dynamic relationship between our inward life and outward work; here is inspiration from: Angelus Silesius, Eckhart, Ansari of Herat, Brother Lawrence, Mechthild of Magdeburg.".

Meditation & the Simple Life. Swami Amar Jyoti. 1 cass. 1982. 9.95 (I-15) Truth Consciousness.
Meditating on the Imperishable; prerequisite is simplifying life, mind & heart. Cause of our social ills.

Meditation & The Spiritual Life. Dalai Lama XIV. 1 cass. 1981. 10.00 Vajradhatu.
A talk by the fourteenth Dalai Lama.

Meditation as Medicine: Activate the Power of Your Natural Healing Force. Dharma Singh Khalsa & Cameron Stauth. 2004. 15.95 (978-0-7435-4124-4(3)) Pub: S&S Audio. Dist(s): S and S Inc

Meditation Bringing the Mind Home. Sogyal Rinpoche. 1 cass. 1996. 10.99 (978-0-9624884-5-0(3)) Rigpa Pubns.

Meditation: Commonsense Directions for an Uncommon Life see Meditation: A Simple Eight Point Program for Translating Spiritual Ideals into Daily Life

Meditation Crossroads; Three Kinds of Pain. Jonathan Murro & Ann Ree Colton. 1 cass. 7.95 A R Colton Fnd.
Discusses the goal of God-Realization.

Meditation Deck & Disc. Compass Labs Staff. 2002. pap. bk. 14.95 (978-1-931918-05-3(8)) Compass Labs.

Meditation Diciplines Can Cause Trouble. Instructed by Manly P. Hall. 8.95 (978-0-89314-181-3(X), C830731) Philos Res.

Meditation, Emotion & Healing: Connecting with the Source of Well Being Within You. William G. DeFoore. (ENG.). 2007. audio compact disk 29.99 (978-0-9814740-4-5(7)) Halcyon Life.

Meditation Experience, Vol. 1. Music by Gina Balducci. Judith A. Pennington. 2007. audio compact disk 16.00 (978-0-9799617-0-0(X)) Heart N.

Meditation Experience, Vol. 2. Judith A. Pennington. 2008. audio compact disk 16.00 (978-0-9799617-1-7(8)) Heart N.

Meditation for a Good Night's Sleep. Perf. by John Daniels. 1 cass. (Running Time: 1 hr. 30 min.). 7.98 (CMH 2014) NewSound.
Filled with calming thoughts & suggestions meant to ease any fears about reaching slumber.

Meditation for a Good Night's Sleep. Perf. by John Daniels. 1 CD. (Running Time: 1 hr. 30 min.). 2001. audio compact disk 9.58 (CMH 2014) NewSound.

Meditation for Beginners. unabr. ed. Jack Kornfield. 2 CDs. (Running Time: 2 hrs. 30 mins.). 2000. audio compact disk 24.95 (978-1-56455-867-1(3), W523D) Sounds True.
Kornfield teaches this ancient practice in its purest form, making meditation easy to understand and practice for even those with no previous experience or spiritual context. Clearly articulated and skillfully presented, Meditation for Beginners is designed to bring the peace and power of mindfulness into listener everyday lives. It is the definitive resource for anyone who ever thought about learning to meditate, but lacked the information they needed to start.

***Meditation for Beginners: 10th-Anniversary Edition.** anniv. ed. Jack Kornfield. (Running Time: 2:00:00). 2010. audio compact disk 19.95 (978-1-59179-784-5(5)) Sounds True.

Meditation for Christians. James Finley. 2003. audio compact disk 24.95 (978-1-59179-121-8(9)) Sounds True.

Meditation for Extremely Busy People, Vol. 1. Mike George. Illus. by George Edwards. Intro. by Chris Drake. 3 cass. 1997. bk. & wbk. ed. (978-1-886872-11-0(2)) Brahma Kumaris.

Meditation for Initiates. unabr. ed. Rama. Read by Rama. 1 cass. (Running Time: 27 mins.). 1990. 7.95 (978-0-89389-165-7(7), CS211MO) Himalayan Inst.
A practical guide for using mantra to lead us to the peaceful center of our being.

Meditation for Mastering Menopause. Belleruth Naparstek. Perf. by Belleruth Naparstek. Music by Steven Mark Kohn. 1 CD. (Running Time: 50 minutes). (Health Journeys Ser.: No. 2128). 2002. audio compact disk 17.98 (978-1-881405-55-9(9)) Hlth Jrnys.
Designed by Psychotherapist Belleruth Naparstek to help balance mood; harness energy, creativity and power; reinforce self-esteem and confidence; reduce anxiety and discomfort; redefine notions of beauty and aging; encourage restful sleep; reduce intensity and frequency of hot flashes; and foster love and gratitude for the body. With affirmations.

Meditation for Optimum Health: How to Use Mindfulness & Breathing to Heal. abr. ed. Andrew Weil & Jon Kabat-Zinn. Read by Andrew Weil. 2 CDs. (Running Time: 2 hrs. 30 mins.). 2001. audio compact disk 24.95 (978-1-56455-882-4(7), W531D) Sounds True.
The practice of meditation & its relevance in modern-day life & health.

Meditation for Peace & Happiness. Rajinder Singh. 1 cass. 1993. bk. 15.00 (978-0-918224-35-4(7)) S K Pubns.
Meditation, mysticism, philosophy, self-help, new age, spirituality, Yoga, near-death experiences.

Meditation for Peaceful Dying for End-of-Life Patients, Their Family & Friends. Belleruth Naparstek. Perf. by Belleruth Naparstek. Music by Steven Mark Kohn. 1 CD. (Running Time: 60 minutes). (Health Journeys Ser.). (ENG.). 2001. audio compact disk 16.98 (978-1-881405-41-2(9)) Hlth Jrnys.
Designed by Psychotherapist Belleruth Naparstek to help end-of-life patients find peace and acceptance; prepare for the journey; reduce pain; forgive self and others; bring closure to unresolved issues; say goodbye to loved ones. Made to help family and friends as well. Scored to exquisite, original music, composed and performed by Steven Mark Kohn. With affirmations.

Meditation for Peaceful Dying for End-of-Life Patients, Their Family & Friends. Belleruth Naparstek. Composed by Steven Mark Kohn. 1 cass. (Running Time: 1 hr.). (Health Journeys Ser.). 2001. 12.98 (978-1-881405-37-5(0)) Hlth Jrnys.
Designed to create relaxed feelings of safety, calm & reasurance; clear the mind & help prepare the spirit for the journey that is dying.

Meditation for Personal Growth. Steven Halpern & John Bradshaw. Read by Steven Halpern & John Bradshaw. 1 cass. (Running Time: 42 min.). (Soundwave 2000 AudioActive Subliminal Ser.). 1990. 9.98 (978-1-878625-14-4(4), SRXB 1211) Inner Peace Mus.
Relaxing, beautiful music with guided meditations to support individuals in recovery.

Meditation for Prosperity: I Give Myself Permission to Prosper! (ENG., 2009. audio compact disk 19.95 (978-0-9766735-7-6(6)) R Seals.

Meditation for Recovery from Alcohol & Other Drugs. Belleruth Naparstek. 1 cass. (Running Time: 1 hr. 1 min.). 1999. 12.00 (10249) Courage-to-Change.
Designed to reduce addictive craving, soften the discomfort of withdrawal, teach potent new relaxation skills, help reverse organ damage, restore vitality, increase self-esteem & reinforce 12-step programs.

Meditation for Relaxation: Guided Mediations from the Buddhist Tradition. Geshe Kelsang Gyatso et al. (Running Time: 0 hr. 70 mins. 0 sec.). (Meditations for Daily Life Ser.). (ENG.). 2010. audio compact disk 12.95 (978-0-9789067-9-5(9)) Pub: Tharpa Pubns GBR. Dist(s): IPG Chicago

Meditation for Relaxation: Simple meditations for everyday life derived from the Buddhist Tradition. Scripts. Geshe Kelsang Gyatso. Read by Kelsang Naljor. 1 CD. (Running Time: 30 mins). (ENG., 2008. audio compact disk 14.95 (978-0-9548790-5-1(8)) Pub: Tharpa Pubns GBR. Dist(s): Tharpa NY

Meditation for Relaxation & Wellness. Belleruth Naparstek. Perf. by Belleruth Naparstek. Music by Steven Mark Kohn. 1 CD. (Running Time: 38 minutes). (Health Journeys Ser.: No. 2135). 2001. audio compact disk 17.98 (978-1-881405-56-6(7)) Hlth Jrnys.
Designed by Psychotherapist Belleruth Naparstek to promote feelings of peace, calm, safety and support; reduce anxiety and stress; encourage hope, confidence, balance and optimism. To help face any stressful situation, or for general anxiety. With affirmations.

Meditation for Starters. (Running Time: 1 hr.). 2005. 15.95 (978-1-56589-759-5(5)) Pub: Crystal Clarity. Dist(s): Natl Bk Netwk

Meditation for Starters. unabr. ed. J. Donald Walters. 1996. audio compact disk 15.95 (978-1-56589-077-0(9)) Pub: Crystal Clarity. Dist(s): Natl Bk Netwk

***Meditation for Stress Release DVD.** Maoshing Ni. 2007. audio compact disk 10.95 (978-1-887575-15-7(4)) Pub: SevenStar Comm. Dist(s): AtlasBooks

Meditation for Success: Where Dreams Become Reality! (ENG., 2009. audio compact disk 19.95 (978-0-9766735-4-5(1)) R Seals.

Meditation in a New York Minute: Super Calm for the Super Busy. Mark Thornton. 2 CDs. (Running Time: 9000 sec.). 2006. audio compact disk 19.95 (978-1-59179-428-8(5), W1012D) Sounds True.

Meditation in Action. Daniel Goleman & Tata Bennett-Goleman. 4 cass. 18.00 (OC149) Sound Horizons AV.

Meditation in the Three Yanas. Read by Chogyam Trungpa & Osel Tendzin. 9 cass. 1979. 90.00 (A108) Vajradhatu.
Nine talks. The practice of meditation in the hinayana, mahayana & vajrayana.

Meditation Instruction: The Art & Practice. Isabella Alexandria Morgan. (YA). 2007. audio compact disk 19.95 (978-0-9792759-0-6(3)) Infinite Utp.

Meditation Is a Metaphor for Liberation. unabr. ed. Andrew Cohen. 1 cass. (Running Time: 1 hr. 6 min.). 10.95 (978-1-883929-18-3(0)) Moksha Pr.
Through inspired talks & guided meditations, you are taken beyond a fundamental sense of struggle with life to experience a deeper possiblity - what it could mean to live life truly at peace.

***Meditation Made Easy.** abr. ed. Lorin Roche. Read by Lorin Roche. (ENG.). 2004. (978-0-06-078329-7(X), Harper Audio) HarperCollins Pubs.

***Meditation Made Easy.** abr. ed. Lorin Roche. Read by Lorin Roche. (ENG.). 2004. (978-0-06-081413-7(6), Harper Audio) HarperCollins Pubs.

Meditation Magic: A Course in Freedom & Dreaming. Anami. Read by Anami. Illus. by Janine Johnston & Gayle Maddocks. 6 cass. (Running Time: 7 hrs.). 1996. pap. bk. 15.00 (978-0-9635756-0-9(0)) Beyond Bks.
Contains 3 hours of highlights from the book & over 5 hours of guided meditations & instruction.

Meditation Magic: A Course in Freedom & Dreaming. Anami. Read by Anami. 6 cass. (Running Time: 7 hrs.). 2001. 50.00 (978-0-9635756-1-6(9)) Beyond Bks.
Contains 3 hours of highlights from the book & over 5 hours of guided meditations & instruction. Includes case.

Meditation Manuscripts/the Subconscious Mind: Volume 23, Vol. 23. Speeches. As told by Bhagat Singh Thind. (Running Time: 60 mins.). (ENG., 2003. 6.50 (978-1-932630-47-3(3)) Pub: Dr Bhagat Sin. Dist(s): Baker Taylor

Meditation Music. Composed by Steven Mark Kohn. 1 cass. (Running Time: 54 mins.). (Health Journeys Ser.). 1995. 12.98 (978-1-881405-18-4(4)) Hlth Jrnys.
The soundtrack of the calming background music featured on our general wellness & stress tapes.

Meditation Music. Perf. by Steven Mark Kohn. 1 cass. (Running Time: 60 min.). (Health Journeys Ser.). 1995. 12.98 (978-1-881405-20-7(6), 23) Hlth Jrnys.
Second stand alone music tape is for inspiration & motivation. This is the more powerful & complex music that accompanies our health journeys tapes for weight loss, alcohol & drug recovery. Side B is the mellow music from the affirmations side of these tapes.

Meditation Music: Tamboura. unabr. ed. Rama Berch. 1 cass. (Running Time: 50 min.). (Relaxations Ser.: Vol. 3). 1992. (978-1-930559-04-2(6)); audio compact disk (978-1-930559-05-9(4)) STC Inc.
Tamboura music to set a deeply peaceful mood during meditation.

Meditation, Mysticism, Imagination. abr. ed. Leo J. Fishbeck. Read by Leo J. Fishbeck. 3 cass. (Running Time: 3 hrs. 36 min.). 1993. 30.00 R S Outreach.
Blends meditation techniques & explores the impact of the mystical experience on creativity.

Meditation of Transformation. unabr. ed. Carolyn Ann O'Riley. 1 cass. (Running Time: 30 mins.). 2000. audio compact disk 12.50 (978-1-891870-12-5(2)) Archangels Pen.
Two meditations inspired by Archangel Michael. Side A: "Meditation of Transformation"; Side B: "A Dance of Oneness" & "The Gift of the Solar Heart.".

Meditation on Healing the Inner Child, Vol. 1. abr. ed. Angela P. Trafford. 1 cass. (Running Time: 25 mins.). 2000. 10.00 (978-0-9677696-0-8(4)) APT-Self Heal.
Spiritual healing & self improvement.

Meditation on Loving the Self, Vol. 1. abr. ed. Angela P. Trafford. 1 cass. (Running Time: 24 mins.). 2000. (978-0-9677696-1-5(2)) APT-Self Heal.

Meditation on the A-Thirty see Sir John Betjeman Reading His Poetry

Meditation on the Compost Heap. Vilma Seelaus. 1 cass. 1988. 7.95 (TAH205) Alba Hse Comns.
Using the image of the compost heap, Sister Vilma opens with clarity, persuasiveness & depth the reality of God at work in human-life crisis. Dark times conditions us for God & elicit a deeper faith, hope & love.

Meditation on the Goddess Within: Meditation on the Chakras: The Rainbow. Featuring Diane Stein. 1988. 9.95 (978-1-59157-023-3(9)) Assn for Cons.

Meditation on the Perfect You. Chris Prentiss. 2008. audio compact disk 9.95 (978-0-943015-59-0(6)) Pub: Power Press. Dist(s): SCB Distributors

Meditation Retreat Weekend. Joseph Goldstein. 5 cass. 1992. 45.00 (OC283-63) Sound Horizons AV.

Meditation Smarts by Dancing Beetle. Perf. by Eugene Ely. 1 cass. (Running Time: 1 hr. 16 min.). (J). 1993. 10.00 Erthviibz.
Tone chants join animal voices & nature sounds to create these meditations with Ms. Grasshopper & the spunky musical humans & Dancing Beetle.

Meditation Techniques - Meditation for Healing. Voice by Marti Angel. 2006. 16.99 (978-0-9797102-0-9(0)) Angel Health.

Meditation That Transforms the Mind: Madras, India December 15, 1974. J. Krishnamurti. 1 cass. (Public Talk Ser.: No. 4). 8.50 (AMT744) Krishnamurti.

***Meditation to Connect with Archangel Gabriel.** Diana Cooper. Andrew Brel. (Running Time: 0 hr. 49 mins. 30 sec.). (Angel & Archangel Meditations Ser.). (ENG.). 2010. audio compact disk 14.95 (978-1-84409-513-1(4)) Pub: Findhorn Pr GBR. Dist(s): IPG Chicago

***Meditation to Connect with Archangel Michael.** Diana Cooper. Andrew Brel. (Running Time: 0 hr. 43 mins. 48 sec.). (Angel & Archangel Meditations Ser.). (ENG.). 2010. audio compact disk 14.95 (978-1-84409-514-8(2)) Pub: Findhorn Pr GBR. Dist(s): IPG Chicago

***Meditation to Connect with Archangel Raphael.** Diana Cooper. Andrew Brel. (Running Time: 0 hr. 44 mins. 30 sec.). (Angel & Archangel Meditations Ser.). (ENG.). 2010. audio compact disk 14.95 (978-1-84409-516-2(9)) Pub: Findhorn Pr GBR. Dist(s): IPG Chicago

***Meditation to Connect with Archangel Uriel.** Diana Cooper. Andrew Brel. (Running Time: 0 hr. 51 mins. 54 sec.). (Angel & Archangel Meditations Ser.). (ENG.). 2010. audio compact disk 14.95 (978-1-84409-515-5(0)) Pub: Findhorn Pr GBR. Dist(s): IPG Chicago

***Meditation to Connect with Your Guardian Angel.** Diana Cooper. Andrew Brel. (Running Time: 0 hr. 49 mins. 54 sec.). (Angel & Archangel Meditations Ser.). (ENG.). 2010. audio compact disk 14.95 (978-1-84409-517-9(7)) Pub: Findhorn Pr GBR. Dist(s): IPG Chicago

Meditation to Ease Grief. Belleruth Naparstek. Composed by Steven Mark Kohn. 1 cass. (Running Time: 50 mins.). 1992. 12.98 (978-1-881405-09-2(5)) Hlth Jrnys.
Designed to help listeners release grief, find peace & feel less isolated; accept feelings; regain energy & focus; encourage hope & inspiration for the future.

Meditation to Ease Grief. Belleruth Naparstek. Perf. by Belleruth Naparstek. Music by Steven Mark Kohn. 1 CD. (Running Time: 50 mins.). (Health Journeys Ser.). 1992. audio compact disk 16.98 (978-1-881405-43-6(5)) Hlth Jrnys.
Designed by Psychotherapist Belleruth Naparstek to help listeners release grief, find peace & feel less isolated; accept feelings; regain energy & focus; encourage hope & inspiration for the future. With Affirmations.

Meditation to Ease Pain. Belleruth Naparstek. Composed by Steven Mark Kohn. 1 cass. (Running Time: 45 mins.). (Health Journeys Ser.). 1995. 12.98 (978-1-881405-16-0(8)) Hlth Jrnys.
Designed to reduce pain by elevating seratonin levels, teaching relaxation skills, refocusing the mind, encouraging feelings of love, gratitude, safety & peace, marshaling courage, self-esteem & patience.

***Meditation to Help Ease Pain.** Belleruth Naparstek. Read by Belleruth Naparstek. (Playaway Adult Nonfiction Ser.). (ENG.). 2010. 39.99 (978-1-61587-381-4(3)) Find a World.

Meditation to Help Ease Pain. Belleruth Naparstek. Perf. by Belleruth Naparstek. Music by Steven Mark Kohn. 1 CD. (Running Time: 44 mins.). (Health Journeys Ser.: 2132). 1995. audio compact disk 16.98 (978-1-881405-36-8(2)) Hlth Jrnys.
Designed by Psychotherapist Belleruth Naparstek to reduce pain by elevating serotonin levels; teaching relaxation skils; refocusing the mind; encouraging feelings of love, gratitude, safety and peace; and marshalling courage and patience. With affirmations.

Meditation to Help Relieve Asthma. Belleruth Naparstek. Read by Belleruth Naparstek. Composed by Steven Mark Kohn. 1 cass. (Running Time: 1 hr. 30 mins.). (Health Journeys Ser.). 1992. 12.98 (978-1-881405-05-4(2)) Hlth Jrnys.
Designed to help reduce swollen linings in the lungs, dissolve mucous & loosen tightened muscle banks around airways; reduce anxiety; help neutralize a histamine response in mast cells.

Meditation to Help Relieve Asthma. Belleruth Naparstek. Read by Belleruth Naparstek. Music by Steven Mark Kohn. 1 CD. (Running Time: 45 minutes). 1992. audio compact disk 17.98 (978-1-881405-77-1(X)) Hlth Jrnys.
Designed by Psychologist Belleruth Naparstek to help reduce swollen lings in the lungs, dissolve mucous, and loosen tightened muscle bands around airways; help neutralize a histamine response in mast cells; reduce anxiety; and help the listener feel more protected from the environment. With affirmations.

Meditation to Help Relieve Headaches. Belleruth Naparstek. Composed by Steven Mark Kohn. 2 cass. (Running Time: 1 hr. 45 mins.). (Health Journeys Ser.). 1995. 17.98 (978-1-881405-10-8(9)) Hlth Jrnys.
Designed to help relax tense muscles in the head & neck; open & even out blood vessel caliber. Part 1 is to help relieve headaches & Part 2 is to help prevent them.

Meditation to Help Relieve Headaches. Belleruth Naparstek. Perf. by Belleruth Naparstek. Music by Steven Mark Kohn. 1 CD. (Running Time: 74 minutes). (Health Journeys Ser.). 1995. audio compact disk 17.98 (978-1-881405-70-2(2)) Hlth Jrnys.
An audio designed by Psychotherapist Belleruth Naparstek to help relax tense muscles in the head and neck; open and even out blood vessel caliber; elevate serotonin levels; reduce pain; clear out toxins; promote emotional balance. Part One is to help relieve headaches and Part Two is to help prevent them. With affirmations.

Meditation to Help with Anger & Forgiveness. 1 CD. (Running Time: 43 min.). 2001. audio compact disk 17.98 (978-1-881405-58-0(3)) Hlth Jrnys.
Designed by Psychotherapist Belleruth Naparstek to promote feelings of acceptance and forgiveness of self and others; motivate and heal; reduce anger and blame; evoke compassion and empathy; encourage feelings of safety and support; offer a preview of the emotionial liberation that comes with forgiveness. With affirmations.

Meditation to Help with Dialysis: For Listening Before, During & after Treatment. Belleruth Naparstek. Composed by Steven Mark Kohn. 1 cass. (Running Time: 58 mins.). (Health Journeys Ser.). 2001. 12.98 (978-1-881405-38-2(9)) Hlth Jrnys.
Designed to promote relaxation & peaceful perspective; ease discomfort; reduce fear of needles; reinforce optimism & motivation; help stabilize blood pressure; increase energy; counter depression & support a positive outlook.

Meditation to Help with Fibromyalgia & Chronic Fatigue. Belleruth Naparstek. Perf. by Belleruth Naparstek. Music by Steven Mark Kohn. 1 CD. (Running Time: 47 min.). (Health Journeys Ser.). 2001. audio compact disk 17.98 (978-1-881405-57-3(5)) Hlth Jrnys.
Designed by Psychotherapist Belleruth Naparstek to help with physical and emotional fatigue; help reduce depression; alleviate aches and pains; promote relaxation and the ability to sleep soundly; encourage deep, full breathing; increase circulation; support balanced functioning of the immune system; release toxicity; return muscle fibers to healthy resilience; help regulate digestive discomfort; heighten motivation and engender faith in the future. With affirmations.

Meditation to Help with Irritable Bowel Syndrome & Inflammatory Bowel Disease. Belleruth Naparstek. Perf. by Belleruth Naparstek. Music by Steven Mark Kohn. 1 CD. (Running Time: 39 minutes). (Health Journeys Ser.: No. 2126). 2001. audio compact disk 17.98 (978-1-881405-60-3(5)) Hlth Jrnys.
Designed by Psychotherapist Belleruth Naparstek to promote relaxation and calm; increase energy and stamina; encourage balanced, steady functioning of the digestive system; help the body return inflamed, irritated tissue to normal; reduce bloating and swelling; release toxins; alleviate pain and discomfort; assist with sleep; support a sense of saftey, hope strength and balance. With affirmations.

Meditation to Help You Be Relaxed & Awake During Medical Procedures. Belleruth Naparstek. Perf. by Belleruth Naparstek. Music by Steven Mark Kohn. 1 CD. (Running Time: 41 minutes). (Health Journeys Ser.: 2136). 2001. audio compact disk 17.98 (978-1-881405-72-6(9)) Hlth Jrnys.
Designed by Psychotherapist Belleruth Naparstek to promote relaxation and calm; release muscle tension; reduce discomfort; relieve fear; support a sense of mastery and control. For use before and during uncomfortable medical procedures. Followed by continuous music.

Meditation to Help You Combat Depression. Belleruth Naparstek. Perf. by Belleruth Naparstek. Music by Steven Mark Kohn. 1 CD. (Running Time: 44 min.). (Health Journeys Ser.). 1993. audio compact disk 17.98 (978-1-881405-61-0(3)) Hlth Jrnys.
The Health Journeys series audio programs are highly acclaimed, research-proven, physician-endorsed guided meditation combines healing imagery, powerful music and the most current understanding of the mind-body connection to help you counter the effects of depression. Belleruth Naparstek's imagery is designed to reduce despair and self-hatred; mobilize energy; reduce fatigue; elicit memories that inspire feelings of love, hope and gratitude; help the listener reconnect with inner strength; reduce anxiety and marshal spiritual support. With affirmations.

Meditation to Help You Control Diabetes. Belleruth Naparstek. Composed by Steven Mark Kohn. 1 cass. (Running Time: 50 mins.). (Health Journeys Ser.). 1991. 12.98 (978-1-881405-08-5(7)) Hlth Jrnys.
Designed to encourage insulin sensitivity at the cellular level; help the body metabolise food in a steady balanced way; help repair damage to organs & tissue; increase patience, self esteem & relaxation.

Meditation to Help You Control Diabetes. Belleruth Naparstek. Perf. by Belleruth Naparstek. Music by Steven Mark Kohn. 1 CD. (Running Time: 48 min.). (Health Journeys Ser.). 1991. audio compact disk 17.98 (978-1-881405-63-4(X)) Hlth Jrnys.
Designed by Psychotherapist Belleruth Naparstek to balance mood; relax the body; motivate and encourage adherence; support insulin sensitivity (either to the body's insulin or to medication) at the cellular level; help the body metabolize food in a steady, balanced way; help the body repair damage to organs and tissue; increase patience, self-esteem and confidence. With affirmations.

Meditation to Help You Fight Cancer. Belleruth Naparstek. Composed by Steven Mark Kohn. 1 cass. (Running Time: 45 mins.). (Health Journeys Ser.). 1991. 12.98 (978-1-881405-06-1(0)) Hlth Jrnys.
Designed to help mobilize a fighting response from immune cells, imagine tumors shrinking, engender a sense of support, safety & hope; reduce fear & encourage feelings of love, safety & support.

Meditation to Help You Fight Cancer. Belleruth Naparstek. Perf. by Belleruth Naparstek. Music by Steven Mark Kohn. 1 CD. (Running Time: 41 mins.). (Health Journeys Ser.). 1991. audio compact disk 16.98 (978-1-881405-35-1(4)) Hlth Jrnys.
Designed by Psychotherapist Belleruth Naparstek to help mobilize a fighting response from immune cells; imagine tumors shrinking, engender a sense of support, safety & hope; reduce fear & encourage feelings of love, safety & support. With affirmations.

Meditation to Help You Improve Self-Confidence & Reach Peak Performance. Belleruth Naparstek. Perf. by Belleruth Naparstek. Music by Steven Mark Kohn. 1 CD. (Running Time: 43 minutes). (Health Journeys Ser.: 2138). 2001. audio compact disk 16.98 (978-1-881405-33-7(8)) Hlth Jrnys.
Designed by Psychotherapist Belleruth Naparstek to increase feelings of self-esteem and confidence; improve mastery and performance; reduce anxiety and fear of failure; promote calm under pressure; heighten creativity, endurance and ability to focus within. With affirmations.

Meditation to Help You Stop Smoking. Belleruth Naparstek. Composed by Steven Mark Kohn. 1 cass. (Running Time: 1 hr.). (Health Journeys Ser.). 1997. 12.98 (978-1-881405-27-6(3)) Hlth Jrnys.
Designed to reduce craving for nicotine, increase self-esteem & confidence, help repair damaged lung tissue, help lungs clear away toxins, reduce withdrawal discomfort, teach relaxation skills.

Meditation to Help You Stop Smoking. Belleruth Naparstek. Perf. by Belleruth Naparstek. Music by Steven Mark Kohn. 1 CD. (Running Time: 60 minutes). (Health Journeys Ser.: 2139). 1997. audio compact disk 17.98 (978-1-881405-68-9(0)) Hlth Jrnys.
Designed by Psychotherapist Belleruth Naparstek to reduce the craving for nicotine, increase self-esteem and confidence; help repair damaged lung tissue; help the lungs clear away toxins; reduce the discomfort of nicotine withdrawal; teach potent relaxation skills. With affirmations.

***Meditation to Help You with Chemotherapy.** Belleruth Naparstek. Read by Belleruth Naparstek. (Playaway Adult Nonfiction Ser.). (ENG.). 2010. 39.99 (978-1-61587-380-7(5)) Find a World.

Meditation to Help You with Chemotherapy. Belleruth Naparstek. Composed by Steven Mark Kohn. 1 cass. (Running Time: 40 mins.). (Health Journeys Ser.). 1991. 12.98 (978-1-881405-07-8(9)) Hlth Jrnys.
Designed to show chemotherapy in a positive light; reduce aversive side effects; help the body's immune cells fight cancer; encourage hope, safety, support & peace.

Meditation to Help You with Chemotherapy. Belleruth Naparstek. Perf. by Belleruth Naparstek. Music by Steven Mark Kohn. 1 CD. (Running Time: 41 min.). (Health Journeys Ser.). 1991. audio compact disk 17.98 (978-1-881405-59-7(1)) Hlth Jrnys.
Designed by Psychotherapist Belleruth Naparstek to show chemotherapy in a positive light; reduce aversive side effects, such as fatigue and nausea; help the body's immune cells fight cancer; encourage hope, safety and calm. With affirmations.

Meditation to Help You with Fatigue. Belleruth Naparstek. Composed by Steven Mark Kohn. 1 cass. (Running Time: 40 mins.). (Health Journeys Ser.). 1998. 12.98 (978-1-881405-31-3(1)) Hlth Jrnys.
Guided imagery to help relieve tiredness from chemotherapy or radiation therapy; made to help combat symptoms created by the major cancer fighting treatment.

***Meditation to Help You with Healthful Sleep.** Belleruth Naparstek. Read by Belleruth Naparstek. (Playaway Adult Nonfiction Ser.). (ENG.). 2010. 39.99 (978-1-61587-383-8(X)) Find a World.

Meditation to Help You with Healthful Sleep. Belleruth Naparstek. Perf. by Belleruth Naparstek. Music by Steven Mark Kohn. 1 CD. (Running Time: 1 hr.). (Health Journeys Ser.). 2000. audio compact disk 16.98 (978-1-881405-32-0(X)) Hlth Jrnys.
Designed by Psychotherapist Belleruth Naparstek to promote peaceful sleep; create relaxed feelings of safety & calm; release muscular tension in the body; clear the mind of worry & obsessive thinking and heighten a sense of protection and support. With Music only on second track.

Meditation to Help You with HIV. Belleruth Naparstek. Composed by Steven Mark Kohn. 1 cass. (Running Time: 50 mins.). (Health Journeys Ser.). 1991. 12.98 (978-1-881405-14-6(1)) Hlth Jrnys.
Designed to alleviate depression & fatigue; help immune cells fight disease; generate energy & appetite; promote hope, love, gratitude & peace.

Meditation to Help You with Multiple Sclerosis. Belleruth Naparstek. Composed by Steven Mark Kohn. 1 cass. (Running Time: 45 mins.). (Health Journeys Ser.). 1991. 12.98 (978-1-881405-15-3(X)) Hlth Jrnys.
Designed to combat fatigue & depression; help the body reduce swelling & scarring along the myelin sheath; improve movement & balance; calm overactive misdirected immune cells.

Meditation to Help You with Multiple Sclerosis. Belleruth Naparstek. Perf. by Belleruth Naparstek. Music by Steven Mark Kohn. 1 CD. (Running Time: 38 min.). (Health Journeys Ser.: 2130). 1991. audio compact disk 17.98 (978-1-881405-76-4(1)) Hlth Jrnys.
Designed by Psychotherapist Belleruth Naparstek to combat fatigue and depression; help the body reduce swelling and scarring along the myelin sheath; improve movement and balance; reduce cramping and pain; promote comfort, hope and energy; and calm overactive, misdirected immune cells. With affirmations.

Meditation to Help You with Radiation Therapy. Belleruth Naparstek. Perf. by Belleruth Naparstek. Music by Steven Mark Kohn. 1 CD. (Running Time: 32 minutes). (Health Journeys Ser.: 2133). 1999. audio compact disk 17.98 (978-1-881405-71-9(0)) Hlth Jrnys.
Designed by Psychotherapist Belleruth Naparstek to help listeners see radiation treatment in a positive light; reduce adverse side effects, such as fatigue and nausea; help immune cells combat trouble spots; reduce anxiety; encourage feelings of hope, resiliency, safety and support. Followed by continuous music.

Meditation to Help You with Weight Loss. Belleruth Naparstek. Composed by Steven Mark Kohn. 1 cass. (Running Time: 1 hr.). (Health Journeys Ser.). 1997. 12.98 (978-1-881405-02-3(8), 37) Hlth Jrnys.
Designed to reduce the craving for food, increase confidence & self-esteem; encourage acceptance of the body; safely speed up the body's metabolism; help the body convert fat into energy; reinforce positive behavior change.

Meditation to Help You with Weight Loss. Belleruth Naparstek. Perf. by Belleruth Naparstek. Composed by Steven Mark Kohn. 1 CD. (Running Time: 60 minutes). (Health Journeys Ser.: 2143). 1997. audio compact disk 16.98 (978-1-881405-30-6(3)) Hlth Jrnys.
Designed by Psychotherapist Belleruth Naparstek to reduce the craving for food, increase confidence & self-esteem; encourage acceptance of the body; safely speed up the body's metabolism; help the body convert fat into energy; reinforce positive behavior change. With Affirmations.

Meditation to Promote a Healthy Heart. Belleruth Naparstek. Composed by Steven Mark Kohn. 1 cass. (Running Time: 50 mins.). (Health Journeys Ser.). 1999. 12.98 (978-1-881405-12-2(5)) Hlth Jrnys.
Designed to help the body restore wear on heart tissue; improve cholesterol & blood pressure, dissolve arterial plaque; reduce stress.

Meditation to Promote a Healthy Heart: Guided Imagery for Healthy Cholesterol, Open Arteries & a Strong Heart. Belleruth Naparstek. Perf. by Belleruth Naparstek. Music by Steven Mark Kohn. 1 CD. (Running Time: 50 minutes). (Health Journeys Ser.). 1999. audio compact disk 16.98 (978-1-881405-44-3(3)) Hlth Jrnys.
Designed by Psychotherapist Belleruth Naparstek to help the body relax and heal; improve cholesterol levels and blood pressure; maintain healthy arteries; reduce stress; and evoke feelings of love, gratitude, safety and connection. With affirmations.

Meditation to Promote General Wellness. Belleruth Naparstek. Perf. by Belleruth Naparstek. Music by Steven Mark Kohn. 1 CD. (Running Time: 42 min.). (Health Journeys Ser.). 1993. audio compact disk 16.98 (978-1-881405-64-1(8)) Hlth Jrnys.
Health Journeys series of audio programs are highly acclaimed, research-proven, physician-endorsed guided meditation that combines healing imagery, powerful music and the most current understanding of the mind-body connection to help you promote and maintain your good health. Belleruth Naparstek's imagery is designed to uplift and relax; help the body eliminate unhealthy cells and tissue, and replace them with strong, new growth; encourage psychological healing and growth; invoke a sense of connection with the universe to strengthen mind, body and spirit. With affirmations.

Meditation to Promote Successful Surgery. Belleruth Naparstek. Composed by Steven Mark Kohn. 2 cass. (Running Time: 1 hr. 30 mins.). (Health Journeys Ser.). 1992. 17.98 (978-1-881405-29-0(X)) Hlth Jrnys.
Tape one is designed to help imagine a successful surgery experience, surrounded by protection the body slowing down blood flow & speeding up its mending capacity. Tape 2 has continuous music to be taken into the operating room.

Meditation to Promote Successful Surgery. Belleruth Naparstek. Perf. by Belleruth Naparstek. Music by Steven Mark Kohn. 2 CDs. (Running Time: 93 minutes). (Health Journeys Ser.: 2142). 1992. audio compact disk 19.98 (978-1-881405-34-4(6)) Hlth Jrnys.
Designed by Psychotherapist Belleruth Naparstek to help mind and body anticipate a successful surgery experience, surrounded by protection and support, the body slowing down blood flow and speeding up its mending capacity. Affirmations are geared for post surgical recovery, and the continuous music that scored the imagery is for use in the operating room.

Meditation to Release & Let Go: Release All Cares & Worries While Letting Go of the Need to Keep Them! (ENG., 2009. audio compact disk 19.95 (978-0-9766735-2-1(5)) R Seals.

Meditation to Self Healing. Created by Anne H. Spencer-Beacham. 1. 2003. audio compact disk (978-1-932163-52-0(2)) Infinity Inst.

Meditation to Support Your Recovery from Alcohol & Other Drugs. Belleruth Naparstek. Composed by Steven Mark Kohn. 1 CD. (Running Time: 61 minutes). (Health Journeys Ser.). 1997. audio compact disk 17.98 (978-1-881405-73-3(7)) Hlth Jrnys.
Designed by Psychotherapist Belleruth Naparstek to reduce addictive craving, ease withdrawal, teach potent new relaxation skills, help the body reverse organ damage, restore vitality, increase self-esteem, and reinforce a 12-step program.

Meditation to Support Your Recovery from Alcohol & Other Drugs. Belleruth Naparstek. Read by Belleruth Naparstek. Composed by Steven Mark Kohn. 1 cass. (Running Time: 1 hr.). (Health Journeys Ser.). 1997. 12.98 (978-1-881405-04-7(4)) Hlth Jrnys.
Designed to reduce addictive craving, ease withdrawal, teach potent new relaxation skills, help the body reverse organ damage, restore vitality, increase self-esteem & reinforce a 12-step program.

Meditation to Support Your Recovery from Stroke. Belleruth Naparstek. Read by Belleruth Naparstek. Composed by Steven Mark Kohn. 1 cass. (Running Time: 50 mins.). (Health Journeys Ser.). 1991. 12.98 (978-1-881405-28-3(1)) Hlth Jrnys.
Designed to help the body repair arteries & reduce plaque; restore the body's optimal functioning; replace information routes from the brain.

Meditation to the Archangels: Rainbow Angel Meditation. Maureen J. St. Germain. Ed. by Maureen J. St. Germain. 2 CDs. (Running Time: 3 hrs.). 2001. audio compact disk 15.95 (978-0-9721799-1-1(7)) M StGermain.
Spoken meditation with background music. Features the seven archangels, (Michael, etc.), Their qualities, how to access them. Angels Featured: Michael, Uriel, Chamuel, Jodhiel, Gabriel, Raphael and Fadkeil.

Meditation Tool Kit. Steven Sadleir. 7. (Running Time: 5 hours). 2005. 20.00 (978-1-883544-09-6(2)) Self Awareness.
This CD set makes it easy for anyone to meditate. It includes (1) An overview of meditation, (2) a Quick Stress Releaf Meditation, (3) A 30 minute Guided Meditation, (4) A Deep Relaxation and Healing Meditation, (5) An Emotional Cleansing Breath Meditation, (6) An Introspection Meditation, and (7) an Shaktipat Energy Transmission.

Meditation 1 And 2: Volume 7, Vol. 7. Speeches. As told by Bhagat Singh Thind. Clark Walker. (Running Time: 60 mins.). 2003. audio compact disk 12.00 (978-1-932630-08-4(2)) Pub: Dr Bhagat Sin. Dist(s): New Leaf Dist

Meditation 101. Steven S. Sadleir. 6. (Running Time: 6 hours). 2005. 20.00 (978-1-883544-10-2(6)) Self Awareness.
This CD Course on meditation provides for talks providing a broad overview of the principal paths to enlightenment and includes four guided meditations including: (1) Kundalini Meditation, (2) Shaktipat Meditation, (3) Heart Meditation, and (4) Non-Duality/Jhana Meditation.

Meditations. Poems. Alphonse De Lamartine. Read by C. Deis & A. Deviegue. 1 cass. (FRE.). 1991. 22.95 (1415-VSL) Olivia & Hill.
This collection contains some of Lamartine's most famous poems, including "Isolement".

***Meditations.** abr. ed. Thomas Moore. Read by Thomas Moore. (ENG.). 2005. (978-0-06-089389-7(3), Harper Audio); (978-0-06-089390-3(7), Harper Audio) HarperCollins Pubs.

***Meditations.** unabr. ed. Marcus Aurelius. Narrated by Wanda McCaddon. (Running Time: 4 hrs. 30 mins.). 2009. 12.99 (978-1-4001-8549-8(1)) Tantor Media.

Meditations, unabr. ed. Marcus Aurelius. Read by Walter Covell. 6 cass. (Running Time: 8 hrs. 30 mins.). 1987. 44.95 (978-0-7861-0536-6(4), 2032) Blckstn Audio.
Marcus Aurelius was a contemplative & good man whose sense of duty & honor set an example for the ages that have followed. His Meditations reveal a mind possessing great stature & natural humility & many valuable lessons can be learned from his good writing.

***Meditations.** unabr. ed. Marcus Aurelius. Narrated by Wanda McCaddon. (Running Time: 4 hrs. 30 mins. 0 sec.). (ENG.). 2010. audio compact disk 55.99 (978-1-4001-4549-2(X)) Pub: Tantor Media. Dist(s): IngramPubServ

***Meditations.** unabr. ed. Marcus Aurelius. Narrated by Marcus Aurelius. Narrated by Wanda McCaddon. (Running Time: 4 hrs. 30 mins. 0 sec.). (ENG.). 2010. 19.99 (978-1-4001-6549-0(0)); audio compact disk 27.99 (978-1-4001-1549-5(3)) Pub: Tantor Media. Dist(s): IngramPubServ

Meditations. unabr. ed. Sylvia Browne. Music by Gary Raffanelli. 2 vols. 2002. audio compact disk 16.95 (978-1-4019-0108-0(5)) Hay House.

Meditations. unabr. ed. Shakti Gawain. Read by Shakti Gawain. 3 cass. (Running Time: 3 hrs. 0 mins. 0 sec.). (Gawain, Shakti Ser.). (ENG.). 2004. audio compact disk 21.95 (978-1-57731-477-6(8)) Pub: New Wrld Lib. Dist(s): PerseuPGW

Meditations. unabr. collector's ed. Marcus Aurelius. Read by Walter Covell. 6 cass. (Running Time: 6 hrs.). 1988. 36.00 (978-0-7366-3939-2(X), 9183) Books on Tape.
Marcus Aurelius was born to a good family, one related by blood & marriage to rulers & bankers. From birth he was destined to lead. Romans of that era had come through the debauchery of an earlier epoch & were usually a sober & respectable group. Those who inherited power & vast fortunes were expected to set an example. Marcus Aurelius did just that. He shouldered his responsibilities with a clear sense of honor. He was the first ombudsman in history & if his role as a legislator or conquerer was not great, he did set high standards for emulation.

Meditations, Bks. I-XIII unabr. ed. Marcus Aurelius. Read by Robert L. Halvorson. 4 cass. (Running Time: 6 hrs.). 28.95 (3) Halvorson Assocs.

Meditations: Angels Guide Audio with Music. Belinda Womack. 1 cass. 1998. 9.99 (978-0-9659850-8-6(3)) Pubng Joy.

Meditations: Angels Guide Audio with Music. Belinda Womack. 1 cass. 1999. 15.99 (978-0-9659850-6-2(7)) Pubng Joy.

Meditations: The Audio Collection I. Created by Patricia J. Crane. 3 CDs. 2004. audio compact disk 29.95 (978-1-893705-13-5(7), Cranes Nest) Hlth Horiz.
Meditations on CD.

Meditations: The Best of Flora Slosson Wuellner. Voice by Edwin D. Wilder. Based on a work by Flora Slosson Wuellner. Prod. by Prayerways. 1 CD. (Running Time: 52 mins.). 2003. audio compact disk 15.00 (978-0-9743728-0-8(3)) Prayerways.
Wuellner carefully selected these 9 Christian guided meditations from her many books, as being the most representative of her work in inner healing. This CD includes meditations for inner healing, healing of relationships, and healing for the community. Wilder has given them sensitive and heartfelt voice.

Meditations: Walk in the Mountains a Quiet Place. Jeanette Keil & Neva Duyndam. Read by Neva Duyndam. 1 cass. 1989. 9.95 (978-1-878159-04-5(6)) Duvall Media.
Beautifully & simply written, these meditations focus on the peace that can be found in nature.

Meditations Adapted from Ask Your Angels: Ground, Release, Relax. Alma Daniel. 2 cass. 1995. 16.95 (978-1-879323-36-0(2)) Sound Horizons AV.
Co-author of the best-selling & internationally-translated "Ask Your Angels," Alma Daniel guides the listener through peaceful meditations designed to bring forth deep clarity, well-being & inner balance. A wonderful gift, these tapes can also help you enlist the aid of your own guardian angels.

Meditations & Celebrations. John Bradshaw. (Running Time: 7200 sec.). 2008. audio compact disk 70.00 (978-1-57388-252-1(6)) J B Media.

Meditations & Music for Sound Healing: A Leading Oncologist Explores the Healing Power of Sound. unabr. ed. Mitchell L. Gaynor. (Running Time: 2:00:00). 2006. audio compact disk 19.98 (978-1-55961-728-4(4)) Sounds True.

Meditations & Stories: A Spiritual Resource. John E. Bradshaw. (Running Time: 14400 sec.). 2008. audio compact disk 100.00 (978-1-57388-270-5(4)) J B Media.

***Meditations for a Clear Mind: Finding Happiness from a Different Source.** Living Meditation Staff & Tharpa Publications Staff. (Meditations for Daily Life Ser.). (ENG.). 2010. audio compact disk 12.95 (978-0-9817277-3-8(5)) Pub: Tharpa Pubns GBR. Dist(s): IPG Chicago

***Meditations for a Kind Heart: The Healing Power of Cherishing Others.** Tharpa Publications. (Running Time: 0 hr. 35 mins. 0 sec.). (Meditations for Daily Life Ser.). (ENG.). 2011. audio compact disk 12.95 (978-1-61606-003-9(4)) Pub: Tharpa Pubns GBR. Dist(s): IPG Chicago

Meditations for a Miraculous Life. Marianne Williamson. 2 CDs. 2007. audio compact disk 16.95 (978-1-4019-1732-6(1)) Hay House.

Meditations for a New Earth. unabr. ed. Kim Eng. Intro. by Eckhart Tolle. 2008. audio compact disk 19.95 (978-1-59179-690-9(3)) Sounds True.

Meditations for a Peaceful Heart. Susie Levan. Read by Susie Levan. Perf. by Steven Halpern. 1 cass. (Running Time: 1 hr.). 1998. 12.00 (978-0-9668816-0-8(5)) Sanctuary Heal.
A channeled meditation tape unlike other journeys with an obvious beginning, middle & end. The words spring from the void.

Meditations for Children. Elizabeth Beyer. (Running Time: 2940 sec.). 2005. spiral bd. 15.95 (978-0-9757683-3-4(6), 425-015) Pub: Blue Angel AUS. Dist(s): Bookworld

Meditations for Courage & Compassion: Developing Resilience in Turbulent Times. Joan Borysenko. (ENG.). 2010. audio compact disk 15.00 (978-1-4019-2757-8(2)) Hay House.

Meditations for Creating True Prosperity. abr. ed. Shakti Gawain. Read by Shakti Gawain. 1 cass. (Running Time: 1 hr.). 1998. 11.95 (978-1-57731-033-4(0)) Pub: New Wrld Lib. Dist(s): PerseuPGW
Explains concepts from book & guides readers through a series of meditations.

Meditations for Daily Practice. Sai Maa Lakshmi Devi. 2004. audio compact disk 16.00 (978-0-9766664-5-5(6)) HIU Pr.

Meditations for Daily Practice, Vol. 2 Sai Maa Lakshmi Devi. 2005. audio compact disk 16.00 (978-0-9766664-6-2(4)) HIU Pr.

Meditations for Difficult Times: How to Survive & Thrive. Bernie S. Siegel. 1 cass. (Running Time: 1 hr.). 1999. 10.95 (978-1-56170-648-8(5), 481) Hay House.
A lecture on how to survive the tough times.

Meditations for Difficult Times: How to Survive & Thrive. Bernie S. Siegel. 1 CD. 2004. audio compact disk 10.95 (978-1-4019-0406-7(8)) Hay House.

Meditations for Emotional Healing: Finding Freedom in the Face of Difficulty. Tara Brach. (Running Time: 2:00:00). 2009. audio compact disk 19.95 (978-1-59179-741-8(1)) Sounds True.

Meditations for Enhancing Your Immune System: Strengthen Your Body's Ability to Heal. Bernie S. Siegel. Music by Robert Gass. 1 CD. (Running Time: 47 min.). (Prescriptions for Living Ser.). (ENG.). 1992. audio compact disk 10.95 (978-1-56170-534-4(9), 442) Hay House.

Meditations for Entering the Temples on the Other Side. Sylvia Browne. 4 CDs. 2008. audio compact disk 19.95 (978-1-4019-1749-4(6)) Hay House.

Meditations for Finding the Key to Good Health. unabr. abr. ed. Bernie S. Siegel. 1 CD. (Running Time: 90 min.). 2006. audio compact disk 10.95 (978-1-4019-0670-2(2)) Hay House.

Meditations for Finding the Key to Good Health: Open the Door to a Healthier You. Bernie S. Siegel. Read by Bernie S. Siegel. Music by Robert Gass. 1 cass. (Running Time: 48 min.). (Prescriptions for Living Ser.). 1992. 10.00 (978-1-56170-043-1(6), 262) Hay House.
These meditations will help you utilize your mind & empower you to create good health while motivating you to take control of your life.

Meditations for Forgiveness. Joan Borysenko. 1 cass. (Running Time: 1 hr.). 1999. 10.95 Courage-to-Change.
Will help to forgive yourself & others & help to find a new sense of acceptance & well-being.

Meditations for Healing & Spiritual Transformation with Elizabeth Foley. Created by Elizabeth J. Foley. (ENG.). 2008. audio compact disk 14.95 (978-0-9800806-1-2(4)) Angel Street.

Meditations for Healing Stress. Susie Levan. Read by Susie Levan. Perf. by Steven Halpern. 1 cass. (Running Time: 1 hr.). 1998. (978-0-9668816-1-5(3)) Sanctuary Heal.
Meditation for awareness, building your sense of control & mastery over stress.

Meditations for Healing Your Inner Child: Become Friends with the Creative, Playful Aspect of Your Self. Bernie S. Siegel. Read by Bernie S. Siegel. Music by Jerry Florence. 1 cass. (Running Time: 1 hr.). (Prescriptions for Living Ser.). 1990. 10.00 (978-0-937611-81-4(6), 224) Hay House.
Dr. Siegel provides us with an opportunity to recreate our experiences & to heal past hurts as well as taking us through the various stages of our life - past, present & future.

Meditations for Inner Peace. Toni Carmine Salerno. (Running Time: 4440 sec.). 2005. spiral bd. 15.95 (978-0-9752166-6-8(X), 425-016) Pub: Blue Angel AUS. Dist(s): Bookworld

Meditations for Manifesting: Morning & Evening Meditations to Literally Create Your Heart's Desire. Wayne W. Dyer. Read by Wayne W. Dyer. 1 cass. (Running Time: 1 hr.). 1995. 10.95 (978-1-56170-313-5(3), 690) Hay House.
Dr. Dyer brings you amazing effective techniques for creating what you want in life through manifestation meditations that really work!.

Meditations for Manifesting: Morning & Evening Meditations to Literally Create Your Heart's Desire. unabr. ed. Wayne W. Dyer. Read by Wayne W. Dyer. 1 CD. (Running Time: 1 hr.). 1995. audio compact disk 15.00 (978-1-56170-315-9(X), 890) Hay House.

Meditations for Morning & Evening: Start & End Your Day with Confidence & Ease. Bernie S. Siegel. 1 CD. 2005. audio compact disk 10.95 (978-1-4019-0415-9(7)) Hay House.

Meditations for Overcoming Depression. Joan Borysenko. 1 cass. (Running Time: 1 hr.). 1999. 10.95 (61223) Courage-to-Change.
Guided meditations that help you reduce anxiety & alleviate the symptoms of depression.

Meditations for Overcoming Life's Stresses & Strains: Meditations for Morning & Evening. Bernie S. Siegel. 1 cass. (Running Time: 1 hr.). 1994. audio compact disk 18.00 (978-1-56170-083-7(5), 821) Hay House.

Meditations for Overcoming Life's Stresses & Strains: Open Your Heart & Let Your Bloodstream Flow Freely. Bernie S. Siegel. 1 CD. 2004. audio compact disk 10.95 (978-1-4019-0410-4(6), 4106) Hay House.

Meditations for Overcoming Life's Stresses & Strains: Open Your Heart & Reduce Your Blood Pressure. Bernie S. Siegel. Read by Bernie S. Siegel. Music by Robert Gass. 1 cass. (Running Time: 53 min.). (Prescriptions for Living Ser.). 1992. reel tape 10.95 (978-1-56170-042-4(8), 261) Hay House.
Dr. Siegel takes listeners through a peaceful, relaxing journey that allows you to release stress & concentrate on your heart & blood pressure & how you can regulate them.

Meditations for Peace of Mind: Relax & Appreciate Your Uniqueness. Bernie S. Siegel. Read by Bernie S. Siegel. Music by Jerry Florence. 1 cass. (Running Time: 1 hr.). (Prescriptions for Living Ser.). 1990. 10.95 (978-0-937611-82-1(4), 225) Hay House.
Dr. Siegel helps us to recognize the qualities that make us unique, special & worthwhile while showing us that we can rejoice in ourselves despite whatever may be happening in our lives.

Meditations for Peace of Mind: Relax & Appreciate Your Uniqueness. Bernie S. Siegel. 1 CD. 2004. audio compact disk 10.95 (978-1-4019-0397-8(5)) Hay House.

Meditations for Personal Healing. abr. ed. Louise L. Hay. 1 CD. 2005. audio compact disk 10.95 (978-1-4019-0653-5(2)) Hay House.

Meditations for Personal Healing. unabr. ed. Louise L. Hay. Read by Louise L. Hay. 1 cass. (Running Time: 60 min.). 1993. 10.95 (978-1-56170-062-2(2), 273) Hay House.

Meditations for Personal Healing: Overcoming Fears. Louise L. Hay. 1 cass. 1994. 18.00 (978-1-56170-080-6(0)) Hay House.

Meditations for Receiving Divine Guidance, Support, & Healing, Set. Sonia Choquette. 2 CDs. 2007. audio compact disk 18.95 (978-1-4019-1751-7(8)) Hay House.

Meditations for Relaxation & Stress Reduction. Joan Borysenko. Read by Joan Borysenko. 1 cass. (Running Time: 1 hr. 11 min.). (Love Is the Lesson Tape Ser.). 1992. 10.95 (978-1-56170-052-3(5), 267) Hay House.
In these meditations, Joan guides you into balancing each part of your body as well as simple meditative stretches to restore body, mind & spirit.

Meditations for Relaxation & Stress Reduction. abr. ed. Joan Z. Borysenko. 1 x CD. 2005. audio compact disk 10.95 (978-1-4019-0446-3(7)) Hay House.

Meditations for Resting in God: From a Course in Miracles. Robert Perry. 2005. audio compact disk 12.95 (978-1-886602-31-1(X)) Pub: CirPubng. Dist(s): Midpt Trade

Meditations for Self-Healing & Inner Power. Joan Borysenko. Read by Joan Borysenko. 1 cass. (Running Time: 1 hr. 1 min.). (Love Is the Lesson Tape Ser.). 1992. 10.95 (978-1-56170-053-0(3), 268) Hay House.
These meditations help you acknowledge & express gratitude to your body. They also focus on the powers behind meditation, concentration & awareness.

Meditations for Self-Healing & Inner Power. abr. ed. Joan Z. Borysenko. 1 CD. (Running Time: 90 min.). 2005. audio compact disk 10.95 (978-1-4019-0449-4(1)) Hay House.

Meditations from a Hospital Bed. Bob Trotter & Martha Trotter. 1986. 10.80 (090) Assn Prof Chaplains.

Meditations from Remembering the Language of God: Divine Love & Healing Meditation. abr. ed. Angela P. Trafford. 1 cass. (Running Time: 25 min.). 1994. pap. bk. 12.00 (978-0-9674748-8-5(4)) APT-Self Heal.
Recommended for anyone interested in spiritual healing & self-improvement. Includes script.

Meditations from Remembering the Language of God: Forgiveness & Release of Anger. abr. ed. Angela P. Trafford. 1 cass. (Running Time: 25 min.). 1998. pap. bk. 12.00 (978-0-9674748-7-8(6)) APT-Self Heal.

Meditations from the Heroic Path: Butterfly Meditation - Transformation & Free Fall. abr. ed. Angela P. Trafford. 1 cass. (Running Time: 25 min.). 1993. pap. bk. 12.00 (978-0-9674748-3-0(3)) APT-Self Heal.

Meditations from the Heroic Path: Fountain of Healing Waters. abr. ed. Angela P. Trafford. 1 cass. (Running Time: 25 min.). 1993. 12.00 (978-0-9674748-5-4(X)) APT-Self Heal.
Recommended for anyone interested in spiritual healing. Includes script.

Meditations from the Heroic Path: Hammock of Light & Healing Addiction. abr. ed. Angela P. Trafford. 1 cass. (Running Time: 25 min.). 1993. pap. bk. 12.00 (978-0-9674748-4-7(1)) APT-Self Heal.
Recommended for anyone interested in spiritual & self-healing. Includes script.

Meditations from the Heroic Path: Healing Energy: Taking Back Your Power & Affirmations for Health. abr. ed. Angela P. Trafford. 1 cass. (Running Time: 25 min.). 1994. pap. bk. 12.00 (978-0-9674748-6-1(8)) APT-Self Heal.
Recommended for anyone interested in spiritual healing & self-improvement. Includes script.

Meditations from the Heroic Path: Recovering Creative Power & Morning Prayer. abr. ed. Angela P. Trafford. 1 cass. (Running Time: 25 min.). 1993. pap. bk. 12.00 (978-0-9674748-2-3(5)) APT-Self Heal.

Meditations from the Temple Within. Denise Iwaniw. 2002. per. 24.95 (978-0-9722002-0-2(7)) Temple With.

Meditations of Marcus Aurelius. Read by Walter Covell. 6 cass. (Running Time: 6 hrs.). 1989. pap. bk. 32.00 (C-183) Jimcin Record.
Ancient wisdom for today. Includes album.

Meditations on Energy & Power & Success: A Quest Audio. unabr. ed. Hari Nam Singh Khalsa. Read by Hari Nam Singh Khalsa. (Running Time: 2 hrs.). (Quest Ser.). 2009. 39.97 (978-1-4233-8018-4(5), 9781423380184, Brinc Audio MP3 Lib); 19.99 (978-1-4233-8017-7(7), 9781423380177, Brilliance MP3); audio compact disk 55.97 (978-1-4233-8016-0(9), 9781423380160, BriAudCD Unabrid) Brilliance Audio.

Meditations on Finding the Love You Want & Your Soulmate. unabr. ed. Hari Nam Singh Khalsa. Read by Hari Nam Singh Khalsa. (Running Time: 2 hrs.). (Quest Ser.). 2009. 39.97 (978-1-4233-8030-6(4), 9781423380306, Brinc Audio MP3 Lib); 19.99 (978-1-4233-8029-0(0), 9781423380290, Brilliance MP3); audio compact disk 55.97 (978-1-4233-8028-3(2), 9781423380283, BriAudCD Unabrid) Brilliance Audio.

Meditations on Hunting. unabr. collector's ed. José Ortega y Gasset. Read by Victor Rumbellow. 4 cass. (Running Time: 4 hrs.). 1982. 24.00 (978-0-7366-0305-8(0), 1293) Books on Tape.
Discusses the evolution of hunting & carefully examines its implications to the hunter...its total absorption of mind & body, its atavistic reverberations, its animalistic fulfillments & its tonic immersion in nature.

Meditations on Life~Death. 2001. bk. 25.00 (978-0-9713902-0-1(7)) Voces Novae.

Meditations on Living, Dying & Loss: The Essential Tibetan Book of the Dead. unabr. ed. Graham Coleman. Narrated by Stephen Hoye. (Running Time: 3 hrs. 30 mins. 0 sec.). (ENG.). 2009. 19.99 (978-1-4001-6297-0(1)); audio compact disk 49.99 (978-1-4001-4297-2(0)); audio compact disk 24.99 (978-1-4001-1297-5(4)) Pub: Tantor Media. Dist(s): IngramPubServ

***Meditations on Living, Dying & Loss: The Essential Tibetan Book of the Dead.** unabr. ed. Graham Coleman. Narrated by Stephen Hoye. (Running Time: 3 hrs. 30 mins.). 2009. 11.99 (978-1-4001-8297-8(2)) Tantor Media.

Meditations on the New Catechism, Pillars 1 & 2. Fr. Malcolm. 12 cass. (Running Time: 12 hrs.). 2001. 60.00 (94D) IRL Chicago.

Meditations on Zen by Osho. abr. rev. unabr. ed. Osho. Read by Osho. 2 cass. (Running Time: 3 hrs. 0 mins. 0 sec.). (ENG.). 1997. 17.95 (978-1-55927-428-9(X)) Pub: Macmill Audio. Dist(s): Macmillan

Meditations on Zodiac Signs. Louise Huber. 1 cass. 8.95 (167) Am Fed Astrologers.
Transformation of consciousness from exoteric to esoteric rulers.

Meditations to Awaken Superconsciousness. unabr. ed. J. Donald Walters. 1 cass. (Running Time: 40 min.). 2004. 10.95 (978-1-56589-139-5(2)) Pub: Crystal Clarity. Dist(s): Natl Bk Netwk

Meditations to Change Your Brain. unabr. ed. Rick Hanson & Richard Mendius. (Running Time: 3:43:31). 2009. audio compact disk 24.95 (978-1-59179-711-1(X)) Sounds True.

Meditations to Heal Your Life. unabr. ed. Louise L. Hay. Read by Louise L. Hay. Ed. by Jill Kramer. 2 cass. (Running Time: 3 hrs.). 1994. 17.00 (978-1-56170-111-7(4), 363) Hay House.
Louise presents treatments & meditations that explain her philosophy on life.

Meditations to Live to Be 100: Traditional Chinese Practices for Health, Vitality & Longevity. Maoshing Ni. (Running Time: 7200 sec.). 2008. audio compact disk 19.95 (978-1-59179-956-6(2)) Sounds True.

***Meditations to Promote Successful Surgery.** Belleruth Naparstek. Read by Belleruth Naparstek. (Playaway Adult Nonfiction Ser.). (ENG.). 2010. 39.99 (978-1-61587-386-9(4)) Find a World.

***Meditations to Relieve Stress.** Belleruth Naparstek. Read by Belleruth Naparstek. (Playaway Adult Nonfiction Ser.). (ENG.). 2010. 39.99 (978-1-61587-384-5(8)) Find a World.

Meditations to Relieve Stress. Belleruth Naparstek. Perf. by Belleruth Naparstek. 2 CD. (Running Time: 72 minutes). (Health Journeys Ser.: No. 2140). 1995. audio compact disk 19.98 (978-1-881405-62-7(1)) Hlth Jrnys.
Four section program designed by Psychotherapist Belleruth Naparstek. The first exercise alleviates anxiety; the second promotes a powerful sense of peace, love and protection; the third guides a soothing, walking meditaionl the fourth is positive affirmations.

Meditations to Support a Healthy Pregnancy & Successful Childbirth. Belleruth Naparstek. Composed by Steven Mark Kohn. 2 cass. (Running Time: 2 hrs.). (Health Journeys Ser.). 2000. 17.98 (978-1-881405-13-9(3)) Hlth Jrnys.
The pregnancy imagery inspires confidence & gratitude for the body; feelings of safety, relaxation, protection & support; sets the stage for labor; connection with the baby & the chain of life. The childbirth imagery eases discomfort, focuses breathing & promotes relaxation; increases feelings of confidence, safety & support; trust in the body & the birth process & connection to protective spiritual forces.

Meditations to Support a Healthy Pregnancy & Successful Childbirth. Belleruth Naparstek. Perf. by Belleruth Naparstek. Music by Steven Mark Kohn. 2 CDs. (Running Time: 2 hrs.). (Health Journeys Ser.). 2000. audio compact disk 19.98 (978-1-881405-45-0(1)) Hlth Jrnys.

Meditations to Support Successful Relationships. Belleruth Naparstek. Composed by Steven Mark Kohn. 2 cass. (Running Time: 1 hr. 10 mins.). (Health Journeys Ser.). 1992. 17.98 (978-1-881405-17-7(6)) Hlth Jrnys.
The first 2 exercises explore inner difficulty non-judgmentally while promoting empathy. The third exercise helps release grief. The 4th is designed to open the heart & promote feelings of unconditional love.

Meditations to Support Successful Relationships. Belleruth Naparstek. Perf. by Belleruth Naparstek. Music by Steven Mark Kohn. 2 CD. (Running Time: 68 minutes). (Health Journeys Ser.: No. 2134). 1992. audio compact disk 19.98 (978-1-881405-66-5(4)) Hlth Jrnys.
Four different imagery exercises designed by Psychotherapist Belleruth Naparstek to help explore inner difficulties non-judgmentally, promote empathy, release grief, and open the heart.

Meditations with a Difference. John Bradshaw. 2008. audio compact disk 85.00 (978-1-57388-148-7(1)) J B Media.

Meditations with Angels. Martine Salerno. 2005. spiral bd. 15.95 (978-81-610-0072-5(7), 425-019) Pub: Blue Angel AUS. Dist(s): Bookworld

Meditations with Music. Music by Sheldon Cohen. 1 cass. (Running Time: 30 min.). (Devotional Tape Ser.). 1997. 8.95 (978-0-914070-43-6(6), 307) ACTA Pubns.
Original 2-3 minute meditations for individual & small group prayer, sick & homebound, bible study groups, etc.

Meditations 1 And 2: Volume 7, Vol. 7. As told by Bhagat Singh Thind. (Running Time: 60). (ENG., 2003. 6.50 (978-1-932630-31-2(7)) Pub: Dr Bhagat Sin. Dist(s): Baker Taylor

Meditative Exercises. John Lilly. 1 cass. 10.00 (A0071-83) Sound Photosyn.
From Dr. Lilly's personal collection.

Meditative Life. Guy Finley. (ENG.). 2005. 19.95 (978-1-929320-46-2(9)); 19.95 (978-1-929320-23-3(X)); audio compact disk 24.95 (978-1-929320-24-0(8)) Life of Learn.
This extraordinary audio album, recorded live by best-selling self-realization author Guy Finley, is packed with perception-altering principles and gentle practices to help us realize the beauty and power of a meditative life. Includes 11 insight-filled talks, such as "Learn the First Step to True Inner Stillness" and "Find the Feeling of 'Now' - Anytime, Anywhere You Are.".

Meditative Mind: The Varieties of Meditative Experience. Daniel Goleman. 1 cass. 9.00 (OC148) Sound Horizons AV.

Meditative Ocean & Rainforest. abr. ed. Jeffrey Thompson. (Running Time: 2:00:00). 2008. audio compact disk 19.98 (978-1-55961-976-9(7)) Sounds True.

Meditative Prayer in Pastoral Care. 1 cass. (Care Cassettes Ser.: Vol. 18, No. 8). 1991. 10.80 Assn Prof Chaplains.

Meditative Relaxation: Find Inner Fulfillment & Strength. Lloyd Glauberman. 2000. 12.00 (978-1-929043-00-2(7)) Psycho-tech.

Mediterannean Lullaby. 1 CD. (Running Time: 1 hr.). 2001. audio compact disk 16.00 (93-0188) Relaxtn Co.
Soothe children to sleep with the heartfelt sound. Gathered from the shores of the Mediterranean Sea, gentle lullabies sung in sweet voices are accompanied by local instruments of the region.

Mediterranean, Pt. 2. collector's ed. Ernle Bradford. Read by Walter Zimmerman. 8 cass. (Running Time: 12 hrs.). 1985. 64.00 (978-0-7366-0774-2(9), 1728-B) Books on Tape.
Bradford cruised the Mediterranean for many years. For he believes that to understand its history one must first understand its geography & he sees the interplay between east & west across the Mediterranean as the yeast of our culture.

Mediterranean Basin. unabr. ed. Ralph Raico. Read by Richard C. Hottlet. Ed. by Wendy McElroy. 2 cass. (Running Time: 2 hrs. 50 min.). Dramatization. (World's Political Hot Spots Ser.). (YA). (gr. 11 up). 1992. 17.95 Set. (978-0-938935-47-6(X), 10365) Knowledge Prod.
History of the lands surrounding the Mediterranean Sea.

Mediterranean Basin. unabr. ed. Ralph Raico. Read by Richard C. Hottelet. Ed. by Wendy McElroy. Prod. by Pat Childs. (Running Time: 10800 sec.). (World's Political Hot Spots Ser.). 2006. audio compact disk 25.95 (978-0-7861-6445-5(X)) Pub: Blckstn Audio. Dist(s): NetLibrary CO

Mediterranean Beach see Robert Penn Warren Reads Selected Poems

Mediterranean Caper. unabr. ed. Clive Cussler. Read by Michael Prichard. 8 cass. (Running Time: 8 hrs.). (Dirk Pitt Ser.). 1992. 64.00 (978-0-7366-2257-8(8), 3046) Books on Tape.
On an isolated Greek Island, a WW I fighter plane attacks a modern U.S. Air Force base, a mysterious saboteur preys on an American scientific expedition & Dirk Pitt plays a deadly game of hunter & hunted with the elusive head of an international smuggling ring. Pitt is hot on the trail of a mammoth drug conspiracy controlled by a missing nazi war criminal. It's his most daring, desperate adventure yet.

Mediterranean Lullaby. 1 cass. (Running Time: 1 hr.). 9.95 (978-1-55961-626-3(1)) Relaxtn Co.

Mediterrannea. Savina Yannatou. 1 CD. (Running Time: 1 hr.). 2000. audio compact disk 16.98 (978-1-56455-722-3(7), MM00118D) Sounds True.
From the fertile landscape of the Mediterranean rim comes this shimmering mosaic of voice & rhythm from the ancient song traditions of Greece, Tunisia, Sicily, Corsica, Albania, the Holy Land & more.

Medium, Perf. by Marie Powers et al. Contrib. by Thomas Schippers. 2 CDs. 1998. audio compact disk 16.99 (VAIA1162-2) VAI Audio.
"The Medium (Menotti)" complete soundtract of the acclaimed 1950 film.

Medium-Chain Acyl-Coenzyme A Dehydrogenase Deficiency - A Bibliography & Dictionary for Physicians, Patients, & Genome Researchers. Compiled by Icon Group International, Inc. Staff. 2007. ring bd. 28.95 (978-0-497-11255-4(8)) Icon Grp.

Medium is the Marriage. unabr. ed. Murray Stein. 1 cass. (Running Time: 1 hr. 23 min.). 1983. 11.00 (11901) Big Sur Tapes.
Describes the typical "pristine" images of marriage, which are fantasies of what marriage will be like before actually experienced. He distinguishes differences between two types of marriages: those that are looked to as a place of well being, comfort & safety; & those that lead to a path of healing, a pilgrimage to individuation & meaning through struggle & conflict.

***Medium Raw: A Bloody Valentine to the World of Food & the People Who Cook.** unabr. ed. Anthony Bourdain. Read by Anthony Bourdain. (ENG.). 2010. (978-0-06-198876-9(6), Harper Audio); (978-0-06-201612-6(1), Harper Audio) HarperCollins Pubs.

Medium Term Assessment Resource CD-ROM Version - Year 9. Brian Seager & Mark Patmore. (Running Time: 4 hrs.). (J). 2004. audio compact disk 229.50 (978-0-340-85662-8(9), HodderMurray) Pub: Hodder Edu GBR. Dist(s): Trans-Atl Phila

Medjugorje. Interview with Mother Angelica et al. 1 cass. (Running Time: 1 hr.). (Mother Angelica Live Ser.). 10.00 (978-1-55794-081-0(9), T32) Eternal Wrd TV.

Medjugorje: The Message. abr. ed. Wayne Weible. Read by Wayne Weible. 1 cass. (Running Time: 6 hrs.). 1996. cass. & video 29.95 (978-1-55725-176-3(2)) Paraclete MA.
Wayne Weible's best seller recounts how he found peace & love in the tiny village of Medjugorje through God's message to seven young people.

Medley of Murder. unabr. ed. Dorothy R. Kliewer. Read by Denise S. Utter. 6 cass. (Running Time: 6 hrs.). 1996. 39.95 (978-1-55686-726-2(3)) Books in Motion.
Misty Hathaway, ward of Jacob Reynolds, finds herself embroiled in secrets & intrigue during a family will summons. Patriarch Jacob is re-making his will & it leads to murder.

Medley of Murders, Edgar Allan Poe et al. Narrated by Richard Brown et al. 3 cass. (Running Time: 4 hrs. 30 min.). 1987. 16.95 (978-1-55685-093-6(X)) Audio Bk Con.
These eerie tales include Poe's "Murders in the Rue Morgue", Boyle's "The Adventure of Silver Blaze", Riddell's "The Old House in Vauxhall Walk", Braddon's "Leyinson's Victim" & "The Woman with Yellow Hair".

Medley of New Insights. Nona G. Press. 1 cass. (Running Time: 1 hr. 30 min.). 1994. 8.95 (1114) Am Fed Astrologers.
New insights into astrology on various topics.

Medley of Tellers & Tales. Short Stories. Jackson Gilman & Laura Pershin. Perf. by Doug Lipman et al. 1 cass. (Running Time: 1 hr.). 1982. 9.95 (978-0-938756-06-4(0), 002) Yellow Moon.
A collection of 7 stories selected from the 1981 Fall series of "Storytellers in Concert." The stories range from an original story by Jay O'Callahan to a Jack tale from Appalachia to Irish folktales.

MedStudy Pediatrics Board-Style Questions & Answers CD-ROM, Volume 2, 2. MedStudy & J. Thomas Cross, Jr. (ENG.). 2006. audio compact disk (978-1-932703-11-5(X)) MedStudy.

Medusa. Clive Cussler & Paul Kemprecos. (Running Time: 6 hrs.). No. 8. (ENG.). (gr. 12 up). 2009. audio compact disk 29.95 (978-0-14-314455-7(3), PengAudBks) Penguin Grp USA.

Medusa. unabr. ed. Clive Cussler & Paul Kemprecos. Read by Scott Brick. 11 CDs. (Running Time: 14 hrs.). No. 8. (ENG.). (gr. 12 up). 2009. audio compact disk 39.95 (978-0-14-314454-0(5), PengAudBks) Penguin Grp USA.

***Medusa.** unabr. ed. Clive Cussler & Paul Kemprecos. Read by Scott Brick. 11 CDs. (Running Time: 13 hrs. 30 mins.). 2009. audio compact disk 100.00 (978-1-4159-6628-0(1), BksonTape) Pub: Random Audio Pubg. Dist(s): Random

Medusa. unabr. ed. Michael Dibdin. Read by Michael Tudor Barnes. 7 cass. (Running Time: 30600 sec.). (Isis Ser.). 2003. 61.95 (978-0-7531-1800-9(9)) Pub: ISIS Lrg Prnt GBR. Dist(s): Ulverscroft US
When a group of Austrian cavers, exploring a network of military tunnels in the Italian Alps, come across human remains at the bottom of a deep shaft, everyone assumes the death was accidental. But then the still unidentified body is stolen from the morgue and the Defence Ministry puts a news blackout on the case. The search for the answers leads Zen to Italy to uncover a crime that everyone thought was as dead and buried as the victim.

Medusa. unabr. ed. Michael Dibdin. Read by Michael Tudor Barnes. 8 CDs. (Running Time: 9 hrs. 30 min.). (Isis Ser.). (J). 2003. audio compact disk 79.95 (978-0-7531-2246-4(4)) Pub: ISIS Lrg Prnt GBR. Dist(s): Ulverscroft US

Medusa & the Snail. unabr. ed. Lewis Thomas. 3 cass. (Running Time: 4 hrs. 30 mins.). 2001. 28.00 (978-0-7366-8264-0(3)) Books on Tape.
Varying in length and topic, these essays address death, cloning, symbiotic relationships in nature, as well as a wide range of other subjects. There is an excellent essay on the failure of modem medical education, with Thomas's prescription to fix it.

Medusa & the Snail: More Notes of a Biology Watcher. unabr. ed. Lewis Thomas. Read by Jonathan Tindle. 3 cass. (Running Time: 4 hrs.). 2000. 23.95 (978-0-7861-1857-1(1), 2656); audio compact disk 32.00 (978-0-7861-9824-5(9), 2656) Blckstn Audio.
With the medusa as a metaphor for life, the author continues the exploration of the world. Among his offerings are essays on the genius of human error, cloning, disease & natural death & an an assessment of contemporary health care.

Medusa Stone. unabr. ed. Jack Du Brul. Read by J. Charles. (Running Time: 14 hrs.). 2008. 39.25 (978-1-4233-4006-5(X), 9781423340065, Brinc Audio MP3 Lib); 39.25 (978-1-4233-4008-9(6), 9781423340089, BADLE); 24.95 (978-1-4233-4005-8(1), 9781423340058, Brilliance MP3); 24.95 (978-1-4233-4007-2(8), 9781423340072, BAD) Brilliance Audio.

Medusa's Child. abr. ed. John J. Nance. Read by John J. Nance. 4 cass. Library ed. (Running Time: 6 hrs.). 2003. 62.25 (978-1-59086-668-9(1), 1590866681, CD Lib Edit); audio compact disk 74.25 (978-1-59086-830-0(7), 1590868307, BACDLib Ed) Brilliance Audio.
For thirty-year-old captain Scott McKay, the transport run from Miami to Denver will give him the money he desperately needs to keep his fledgling air cargo company flying. When a mysterious crate is discovered on his plane, however, McKay is ordered to abandon his present course and fly the crate and its owner, Vivian Henry, to Washington, D.C., before going to Denver. McKay takes the forced detour in stride - until a strange noise comes from deep inside the crate. It is the voice of Vivian's husband, Dr. Rogers Henry, warning that the shipment they are carrying is actually a fully armed Medusa device, a thermonuclear bomb that can destroy every computer chip over an entire continent, and blast the Silicon Age back to the Stone Age. And it is set to go off within hours. As panic spreads from the small community of nuclear scientists who used to work for Dr. Rogers Henry to the White House and eventually to the general public, a group of rogue military officers conspires to disobey the President's orders and secure the technology of the Medusa device, whatever the cost. Will Captain McKay and his crew trust their own instincts to dispose of the bomb, or will they let a misguided government dictate their actions?.

Medusa's Child. abr. ed. John J. Nance. Read by John J. Nance. (Running Time: 6 hrs.). 2006. 39.25 (978-1-4233-0136-3(6), 9781423301363, BADLE); audio compact disk 39.25 (978-1-4233-0134-9(X), 9781423301349, Brinc Audio MP3 Lib); audio compact disk 24.95 (978-1-4233-0133-2(1), 9781423301332, Brilliance MP3) Brilliance Audio.

Medusa's Child. abr. ed. John J. Nance. Read by John J. Nance. (Running Time: 6 hrs.). 2006. 24.95 (978-1-4233-0135-6(8), 9781423301356, BAD) Brilliance Audio.

Meeka & Her Cool Cousins. Perf. by Meeka. Contrib. by Art Halperin. 1 cass. (J). 1997. 10.98 (978-1-57471-441-8(4), YM111-CN); audio compact disk 13.98 (978-1-57471-444-9(9), YM111-CD) Youngheart Mus.
Songs include: "Un-Oh"; "Ice Cream Truck"; "Dove"; "Duet"; "Telephone"; "You Say Whatever I Say"; "ABC Family"; "Tickle Time"; "Take the 'A Side' Train, 'B Side' Arrival"; "Sun Shines for All"; "Peter Peter"; "P.I.G." & more.

Meerkats. Jody Sullivan Rake. Contrib. by Colleen Buckman. (African Animals Ser.). (ENG.). (gr. k-1). 2008. audio compact disk 14.65 (978-1-4296-3194-5(5)) CapstoneDig.

Meet a Time Traveler. Bruce Goldberg. (ENG.). 2005. audio compact disk 17.00 (978-1-57968-067-1(4)) Pub: B Goldberg. Dist(s): Baker Taylor

Meet a Time Traveler. Bruce Goldberg. Read by Bruce Goldberg. 1 cass. (Running Time: 25 min.). (ENG.). 2007. 13.00 (978-1-57968-001-5(1)) Pub: B Goldberg. Dist(s): Baker Taylor
Travel through the fifth dimension & communicate with a time traveler from our future. Includes script.

***Meet Abraham Lincoln: Inspirational Stories.** unabr. ed. Charles Margerison. Read by Markus Hayes. (Running Time: 8 mins.). (ENG.). 2010. 1.99 (978-1-921629-82-2(7)) Pub: CJMPub AUS. Dist(s): HachBkGrp

***Meet Albert Einstein: Inspirational Stories.** unabr. ed. Charles Margerison. Read by Charles Margerison. (Running Time: 25 mins.). (ENG.). 2010. 1.99 (978-1-921629-88-4(6)) Pub: CJMPub AUS. Dist(s): HachBkGrp

***Meet Amelia Earhart: Inspirational Stories.** unabr. ed. Charles Margerison. Read by Sarah Wintermeyer. (Running Time: 10 mins.). (ENG.). 2010. 1.99 (978-1-921629-79-2(7)) Pub: CJMPub AUS. Dist(s): HachBkGrp

***Meet Benjamin Franklin: Inspirational Stories.** unabr. ed. Charles Margerison. Read by Josh Bergman. (Running Time: 15 mins.). (ENG.). 2010. 1.99 (978-1-921629-84-6(3)) Pub: CJMPub AUS. Dist(s): HachBkGrp

***Meet Charles Darwin: Inspirational Stories.** unabr. ed. Charles Margerison. Read by Mark Smith. (Running Time: 14 mins.). (ENG.). 2010. 1.99 (978-1-921629-85-3(1)) Pub: CJMPub AUS. Dist(s): HachBkGrp

***Meet Christopher Columbus: Inspirational Stories.** unabr. ed. Charles Margerison. Read by Markus Hayes. (Running Time: 17 mins.). (ENG.). 2010. 1.99 (978-1-921629-87-7(8)) Pub: CJMPub AUS. Dist(s): HachBkGrp

***Meet Coco Chanel: Inspirational Stories.** unabr. ed. Charles Margerison. Read by Michelle Plum. (Running Time: 10 mins.). (ENG.). 2010. 1.99 (978-1-921629-71-6(1)) Pub: CJMPub AUS. Dist(s): HachBkGrp

***Meet Edith Piaf: Inspirational Stories.** unabr. ed. Charles Margerison. Read by Michelle Plum. (Running Time: 25 mins.). (ENG.). 2010. 1.99 (978-1-921629-77-8(0)) Pub: CJMPub AUS. Dist(s): HachBkGrp

***Meet Elvis Presley: Inspirational Stories.** unabr. ed. Charles Margerison. Read by Andrew Chaiken. (Running Time: 24 mins.). (ENG.). 2010. 1.99 (978-1-921629-91-4(6)) Pub: CJMPub AUS. Dist(s): HachBkGrp

***Meet Florence Nightingale: Inspirational Stories.** unabr. ed. Charles Margerison. Read by Hannah Davis. (Running Time: 7 mins.). (ENG.). 2010. 1.99 (978-1-921629-76-1(2)) Pub: CJMPub AUS. Dist(s): HachBkGrp

***Meet George Washington: Inspirational Stories.** unabr. ed. Charles Margerison. Read by Josh Bergman. (Running Time: 8 mins.). (ENG.). 2010. 1.99 (978-1-921629-83-9(5)) Pub: CJMPub AUS. Dist(s): HachBkGrp

***Meet Golda Meir: Inspirational Stories.** unabr. ed. Charles Margerison. Read by Hannah Davis. (Running Time: 9 mins.). (ENG.). 2010. 1.99 (978-1-921629-74-7(6)) Pub: CJMPub AUS. Dist(s): HachBkGrp

***Meet Issac Newton: Inspirational Stories.** unabr. ed. Charles Margerison. Read by Mark Smith. (Running Time: 7 mins.). (ENG.). 2010. 1.99 (978-1-921629-86-0(X)) Pub: CJMPub AUS. Dist(s): HachBkGrp

***Meet Ludvig Van Beethoven: Inspirational Stories.** unabr. ed. Charles Margerison. Read by James Rix. (Running Time: 13 mins.). (ENG.). 2010. 1.99 (978-1-921629-73-0(8)) Pub: CJMPub AUS. Dist(s): HachBkGrp

Meet M & M, Pat Ross. Read by C. J. Critt. 1 cass. (Running Time: 15 mins.). (J). (gr. 2 up). 1999. stu. ed. 70.70 (978-0-7887-3224-9(2), 46880) Recorded Bks.
Mandy & Mindy live in the same apartment building & even look alike. They always play together after school. But one day things begin to go wrong. Mandy & Mindy argue about what game to play & soon they aren't speaking to each other at all. What will it take to get the friends together again?.

Meet M & M. unabr. ed. Pat Ross. Narrated by C. J. Critt. 1 cass. (Running Time: 15 mins.). (gr. 2 up). 1999. 10.00 (978-0-7887-3159-4(9), 95832E7) Recorded Bks.

Meet M & M. unabr. ed. Pat Ross. Read by C. J. Critt. 1 cass. (Running Time: 15 mins.). (J). (gr. 2 up). 1999. pap. bk. & stu. ed. 22.24 (978-0-7887-3178-5(5), 40913X4) Recorded Bks.

***Meet Maria Montessori: Inspirational Stories.** unabr. ed. Charles Margerison. Read by Hannah Davis. (Running Time: 11 mins.). (ENG.). 2010. 1.99 (978-1-921629-75-4(4)) Pub: CJMPub AUS. Dist(s): HachBkGrp

***Meet Marie Curie: Inspirational Stories.** unabr. ed. Charles Margerison. Read by Hannah Davis. (Running Time: 8 mins.). (ENG.). 2010. 1.99 (978-1-921629-72-3(X)) Pub: CJMPub AUS. Dist(s): HachBkGrp

Meet Me at the Morgue. Ross MacDonald, pseud & Grover Gardner. 4 cass. (Running Time: 6 hrs.). 2002. 32.95 (978-0-7861-2693-4(0), 3268) Blckstn Audio.

Meet Me at the Morgue. unabr. ed. Ross MacDonald, pseud. Read by Grover Gardner. 5 CDs. (Running Time: 6 hrs.). 2003. audio compact disk 40.00 (978-0-7861-8683-9(6), 3268) Blckstn Audio.

Meet Me at the Savoy, Jean Nicol. Read by Jane Ballard. 4 cass. (Running Time: 6 hrs.). 1999. 44.95 (61705) Pub: Soundings Ltd GBR. Dist(s): ISIS Pub

Meet Me in St. Louis. Perf. by Judy Garland et al. 1 cass. (Running Time: 1 hr.). 1946. 7.95 (DD-5080) Natl Recrd Co.
A charming & sentimental tale about a family in St. Louis at the turn of the century. It takes place about the time of the 1904 St. Louis World's Fair & involves the romances, heartaches, laughs & problems of a family of three girls, a boy, a grandfather & of course a mother & a stern father. The father gets a promotion, but must move to New York City & that does cause quite an emotional situation. Cast also includes Gale Gordon.

Meet Me in St. Louis. Featuring Judy Garland. 2008. audio compact disk 12.95 (978-1-57970-510-7(3), Audio-For) J Norton Pubs.

Meet Me in St. Louis. Perf. by Judy Garland & Margaret O'Brien. 1 cass. (Running Time: 1 hr.). Dramatization. (Lux Radio Theater Ser.). 1946. 6.00 Once Upon Rad.
Radio broadcasts - drama.

Meet Me in St. Louis. unabr. ed. Perf. by Lux Theatre Cast et al. 1 cass. (Running Time: 55 min.). 12.95 (492) J Norton Pubs.
A radio adaptation of Meet Me in St. Louis. It includes the title number "The Trolley Song" & others. Cast also includes Tom Drake.

Meet Me Where I Am. Contrib. by Noelle Garcia. Prod. by Kevin Page. 2007. audio compact disk 17.00 (978-1-58459-340-9(7)) Wrld Lib Pubns.

***Meet Mother Teresa: Inspirational Stories.** unabr. ed. Charles Margerison. Read by Hannah Davis. (Running Time: 6 mins.). (ENG.). 2010. 1.99 (978-1-921629-78-5(9)) Pub: CJMPub AUS. Dist(s): HachBkGrp

***Meet Nancy Astor: Inspirational Stories.** unabr. ed. Charles Margerison. Read by Hannah Davis. (Running Time: 6 mins.). (ENG.). 2010. 1.99 (978-1-921629-70-9(3)) Pub: CJMPub AUS. Dist(s): HachBkGrp

Meet the Barkers: Morgan & Moffat Go to School. Tomie dePaola. 1 CD. (Running Time: 13 mins.). (J). (gr. k-3). 2005. pap. bk. 19.95 (978-0-8045-4129-9(9), SACD4129); pap. bk. 17.95 (978-0-8045-6934-7(7), SAC6934) Spoken Arts.
The Barker twins are about to go to school for the first time. Morgie and Moffie can¿t wait. First, it¿s off to buy backpacks and pencil boxes, and then it¿s off to school! As the week goes on, Moffie, who always has to be first, wins gold stars. Morgie, who loves everybody, makes friends. But by the end of the week each has helped the other understand how to make new friends and earn gold stars, and the Barker twins both LOVE school!.

Meet the Composer, No. 1. Maurice Hinson et al. (Learning Link Ser.). (ENG.). 1995. audio compact disk 10.95 (978-0-7390-1691-6(1), 11758) Alfred Pub.

Meet the Composer, No. 2. Harry Fox Agency Staff et al. (Learning Link Ser.). (ENG.). 1997. audio compact disk 10.95 (978-0-7390-1692-3(X), 16889) Alfred Pub.

Meet the Emmanuels. Contrib. by Emmanuels. Prod. by David Gough. (Running Time: 1 hr.). 2003. audio compact disk 16.98 (978-5-552-41381-2(4)) Pub: Pt of Grace Ent. Dist(s): STL Dist NA

Meet the Emmanuels. Emmanuels, The. (Running Time: 30 min.). 2003. 11.98 (978-5-552-41378-2(4)) Pub: Pt of Grace Ent. Dist(s): STL Dist NA

Meet the Gecko. Wendelin Van Draanen. Read by Daniel Young. (Shredderman Ser.: Bk. 3). (J). 2008. 34.99 (978-1-60640-650-2(7)) Find a World.

Meet the Gecko. unabr. ed. Wendelin Van Draanen. Read by Daniel Young. 2 CDs. (Running Time: 2 hrs. 2 mins.). (Shredderman Ser.). (J). (gr. 3-6). 2007. pap. bk. 28.95 (978-1-4301-0107-9(5)) Live Oak Media.

Meet the Gecko. unabr. ed. Wendelin Van Draanen. Read by Daniel Young. Illus. by Brian Biggs. 2 cass. (Running Time: 2 hrs. 2 mins.). (Shredderman Ser.). (J). (gr. 2-5). 2007. 18.95 (978-1-4301-0104-8(0)); 24.95 (978-1-4301-0105-5(9)) Live Oak Media.

Meet the Gecko. unabr. ed. Wendelin Van Draanen. Read by Daniel Young. Illus. by Brian Biggs. 2 CDs. (Running Time: 2 hrs. 2 mins.). (Shredderman Ser.). (J). (gr. 3-6). 2007. 22.95 (978-1-4301-0106-2(7)) Live Oak Media.

***Meet the Great Jazz Legends: Short Sessions on the Lives, Times & Music of the Great Jazz Legends.** Composed by Ronald C. McCurdy. (ENG.). 2009. audio compact disk 14.95 (978-0-7390-4436-0(2)) Alfred Pub.

Meet the Great Masters! Bb Clarinet - Grade 1-2. James Curnow. 2000. pap. bk. 12.95 (978-90-431-1020-4(5), 9043110205) H Leonard.

Meet the Great Masters! Eb Alto Saxophone - Grade 1-2. James Curnow. 2000. pap. bk. 12.95 (978-90-431-1021-1(3), 9043110213) H Leonard.

Meet the Great Masters! F/Eb Horn - Grade 1-2. James Curnow. 2000. pap. bk. 12.95 (978-90-431-1025-9(6), 9043110256) H Leonard.

Meet the Great Masters! Flute/Oboe - Grade 1-2. James Curnow. 2000. pap. bk. 12.95 (978-90-431-1019-8(1), 9043110191) H Leonard.

Meet the Great Masters! Trombone - Grade 1-2. James Curnow. 2000. pap. bk. 12.95 (978-90-431-1023-5(X), 904311023X) H Leonard.

Meet the Pusher. Hal Stone & Sidra Stone. 1 cass. (Mendocino Ser.). 1990. 10.95 (978-1-56557-004-7(9), T06) Delos Inc.
The Inner Pusher is a driving force in our lives. This is the self which creates your agenda, tells you what you should do, accomplish, finish, read, write, create, etc...It can accomplish much, but it can also keep you in a constant state of dissatisfaction & can even erode your health.

Meet the Superkids, No. 1. (J). 2005. audio compact disk (978-1-59833-950-5(8)) Rowland Reading.

Meet the Superkids, No. 2. (J). 2005. audio compact disk (978-1-59833-951-2(6)) Rowland Reading.

Meet the Superkids, No. 3. (J). 2005. audio compact disk (978-1-59833-952-9(4)) Rowland Reading.

Meet the Superkids, No. 4. (J). 2005. audio compact disk (978-1-59833-953-6(2)) Rowland Reading.

Meet the Superkids, No. 5. (J). 2005. audio compact disk (978-1-59833-954-3(0)) Rowland Reading.

Meet the Superkids, No. 6. (J). 2005. audio compact disk (978-1-59833-955-0(9)) Rowland Reading.

***Meet Thomas Edison: Inspirational Stories.** unabr. ed. Charles Margerison. Read by Markus Hayes. (Running Time: 9 mins.). (ENG.). 2010. 1.99 (978-1-921629-80-8(0)) Pub: CJMPub AUS. Dist(s): HachBkGrp

***Meet Thomas Jefferson: Inspirational Stories.** unabr. ed. Charles Margerison. Read by J. S. Gilbert. (Running Time: 13 mins.). (ENG.). 2010. 1.99 (978-1-921629-89-1(4)) Pub: CJMPub AUS. Dist(s): HachBkGrp

***Meet Wolfgang Mozart: Inspirational Stories.** unabr. ed. Charles Margerison. Read by Charles Margerison. (Running Time: 22 mins.). (ENG.). 2010. 1.99 (978-1-921629-90-7(8)) Pub: CJMPub AUS. Dist(s): HachBkGrp

Meet Your Angel. Created by Sunny Dawn Johnston. Music by Don Wehbey. (ENG.). 2007. audio compact disk 16.00 (978-0-9798119-0-6(2)) Sunlight.

Meet Your Inner Critic. Hal Stone & Sidra Stone. 1 cass. (Running Time: 1 hr.). (Mendocino Ser.). 1992. 10.95 (978-1-56557-002-3(2), T07) Delos Inc.
Everybody has an Inner Critic who is an authority on everything. It is the part of us that always has something critical to say. It is brilliant & accurate & when it whispers in our ears, it usually sounds absolutely accurate in its uncharitable view of us. Learn how to separate from yours.

Meet Your Inner Critic Two. Hal Stone & Sidra Stone. 1 cass. (Running Time: 1 hr. 30 mins.). (Mendocino Ser.). 1990. 10.95 (978-1-56557-003-0(0), T08) Delos Inc.
Further adventures with the Inner Critic! Hear it speak & gain greater understanding of its power in your life. Even if you know about your Inner Critic already, we suggest that you listen to "Meet Your Inner Critic" first.

Meet Your Spirit Guides: The Amethyst Mirror. unabr. ed. Kim Falcone & Steven Falcone. Read by Steven Falcone. 1 cass. (Running Time: 1 hr.). 1994. 10.95 (978-1-887799-02-7(8), 1-843-276) Creat Aware.
This program reflects on the subject of Angels & Spirit Guides.

Meeting Across the River: Stories Inspired by the Haunting Bruce Springsteen Song. Ed. by Jessica Kaye & Richard Brewer. (Running Time: 32400 sec.). 2005. 59.95 (978-0-7861-3760-2(6)); audio compact disk 72.00 (978-0-7861-7631-1(8)) Blckstn Audio.

Meeting Across the River: Stories Inspired by the Haunting Bruce Springsteen Song. unabr. ed. Ed. by Jessica Kaye & Richard Brewer. 8 CDs. (Running Time: 32400 sec.). 2005. audio compact disk 29.95 (978-0-7861-7632-8(6), ZE3554) Blckstn Audio.
"Meeting Across the River," from Bruce Springsteen's"Born to Run" album, is a song with an evocative melody and lyrics that unfold like a noir fable: a man down on his luck but desperate to make things right with his girl tells his buddy, Eddie, that they have to get across the river for a last-chance meeting with someone, all in the hopes of a big score: two grand. With that money, our hero can win back his girl and all will be right with the world. But if he and Eddie screw up, the consequences will be grave.

Meeting Across the River: Stories Inspired by the Haunting Bruce Springsteen Song. unabr. ed. Ed. by Jessica Kaye & Richard J. Brewer. 1 MP3. (Running Time: 8 hrs. 30 mins.). 2005. 29.95 (978-0-7861-7874-2(4), ZM3554) Blckstn Audio.

Meeting an Inner Advisor: A Step-by-Step Program for Learning to Relax Instantly. Created by David Bresler. (ENG.). 2007. audio compact disk 19.95 (978-1-887211-04-8(7), Imag Res) AlphaBks CA.

Meeting & Acquiring Women: The Average Man's Guide to Defensive Womanizing. unabr. ed. Will I. Boner. Read by Will I. Boner. 2 cass. (Running Time: 2 hrs. 30 mins.). 2000. 19.95 (978-0-9678847-1-4(3), Politically Incorrect) SafeHome.
"How-to" guide that uses scientific, systematic & results-oriented principles & techniques to help men of all ages find the right woman fast.

Meeting & Mastering Your Internal Saboteur. Martha B. Beveridge. 1 cass. (Running Time: 1 hr. 30 mins.). 1989. 9.95 (978-1-889237-25-1(6)) Options Now.
Stop pulling the plug on pleasure, intimacy & success. Get to the root of your self-sabotage patterns.

Meeting at Corvalis. S. M. Stirling. Read by Todd McLaren. (Playaway Adult Fiction Ser.). (ENG.). 2009. 89.99 (978-1-60775-794-8(X)) Find a World.

Meeting at Corvallis. unabr. ed. S. M. Stirling. Read by Todd McLaren. Narrated by Todd McLaren. (Running Time: 23 hrs. 30 mins. 0 sec.). (Emberverse Ser.). (ENG.). 2008. audio compact disk 49.99 (978-1-4001-0678-3(8)); audio compact disk 34.99 (978-1-4001-5678-8(5)); audio compact disk 99.99 (978-1-4001-3678-0(4)) Pub: Tantor Media. Dist(s): IngramPubServ

Meeting at Potsdam: The Origin of Our Present World Troubles? unabr. ed. Charles L. Mee & Drew Middleton. 1 cass. (Running Time: 56 min.). 12.95 (40099) J Norton Pubs.
Mee, author of "Meeting at Potsdam," & Middleton, of the New York Times, explore with Heywood Hale Broun the background & questionable results of the historic carving game at Potsdam, in 1945, where Truman, Stalin, & Churchill decided the political fate of the world.

Meeting Christ & His Friends in the Church. Rembert G. Weakland. 1 cass. (Running Time: 1 hr.). 2001. 7.95 (A6961) St Anthony Mess Pr.
We need to respect the peoples of various cultures that make up the Church, to be instruments of grace and to risk belief in the Church breaking all barriers.

Meeting Evil. unabr. collector's ed. Thomas Berger. Read by Michael Russotto. 8 cass. (Running Time: 8 hrs.). 1994. 48.00 (978-0-7366-2634-7(4), 3373) Books on Tape.
When John Felton meets Richie, there's no sense of alarm. But not for long because Richie, a cheerful psychopath, takes John with him in an expanding web of crime. With his flair for perfect detail, Thomas Berger constructs an ironic, modern drama exposing the banality of evil & the precariousness of reality, identity & truth.

Meeting God in Familiar Places see Encontrando a Dios en Lugares Conocidos

Meeting God in Familiar Places. Charles R. Swindoll. 2008. audio compact disk (978-1-57972-836-6(7)) Insight Living.

Meeting Half Way, Level 1. 2 cass. (Running Time: 1 hr. 30 mins.). (SmartReader Ser.). (J). 1999. pap. bk. & tchr. ed. 19.95 (978-0-7887-1157-2(1), 79418T3) Recorded Bks.
Fifteen-year-old Patty & her family moved from China to America just three months ago. Her mother works hard & relies on Patty to watch her baby brother at night. But already, Patty wants the same freedom her classmates enjoy.

Meeting Half Way, Level 2. 2 cass. (Running Time: 1 hr. 30 mins.). (SmartReader Ser.). (J). 1999. pap. bk. & tchr. ed. 19.95 (978-0-7887-0123-8(1), 79311T3) Recorded Bks.

Meeting of the Minds: Otto Kernberg, David Burns, Albert Ellis & Ethel Person. 10 cass. 89.95 (PC26-31) Inst Rational-Emotive.
Experience the excitement & controversy of this historic conference today!.

Meeting of the Minds: Otto Kernberg, David Burns, Albert Ellis & Ethel Person, Unit 1: Overview. 1 cass. (Running Time: 1 hr. 30 min.). 11.95 (PC26) Inst Rational-Emotive.

Meeting of the Minds: Otto Kernberg, David Burns, Albert Ellis & Ethel Person, Unit 2: Analysis vs. CBT - Differences. 2 cass. (Running Time: 3 hrs.). 17.95 (PC27) Inst Rational-Emotive.

Meeting of the Minds: Otto Kernberg, David Burns, Albert Ellis & Ethel Person, Unit 4: Responses of Panel to Videotaped Vignettes. 2 cass. (Running Time: 3 hrs.). 17.95 (PC29) Inst Rational-Emotive.

Meeting of the Minds: Otto Kernberg, David Burns, Albert Ellis & Ethel Person, Unit 5: Integrating Psychoanalysis & CBT. 2 cass. (Running Time: 3 hrs.). 17.95 (PC30) Inst Rational-Emotive.

Meeting of the Minds: Otto Kernberg, David Burns, Albert Ellis & Ethel Person, Unit 6: Summary by John Norcross. 1 cass. (Running Time: 1 hr. 30 min.). 11.95 (PC31) Inst Rational-Emotive.

Meeting of the Minds: Otto Kernberg, David Burns, Albert Ellis& Ethel Person, Unit 3: Analysis vs. CBT - Similarities. 2 cass. (Running Time: 3 hrs.). 17.95 (PC28) Inst Rational-Emotive.

***Meeting of the Waters: 7 Global Currents That Will Propel the Future Church.** unabr. ed. Fritz Kling. Narrated by Danny Campbell. (ENG.). 2010. 12.98 (978-1-59644-062-3(7)) christianaud.

Meeting Place. Janette Oke & T. Davis Bunn. Narrated by Suzanne Toren. 6 cass. (Running Time: 9 hrs.). (Song of Acadia Ser.: Vol. 1). 54.00 (978-0-7887-5112-7(3)) Recorded Bks.

Meeting the Challenge of Living in the World Series. 4 cass. (Running Time: 6 hrs.). 32.00 Crystal Clarity.
Topics includes: Generating a Positive Environment; How to Develop Your Inner Magenetism; How to Spiritualize Your Daily Life; How to Benefit From Changes in Your Life. Includes vinyl storage album.

Meeting the Mad Woman. Linda Leonard. 1 cass. 1993. 9.00 (OC327-70) Sound Horizons AV.

Meeting the President. unabr. ed. Gail Taylor. Read by Gail Taylor. Ed. by James B. Kirgan. 1 cass. (Running Time: 1 hr. 30 min.). (Essence of Nature Ser.: Vol. 9). (J). 1989. 12.99 stereo. (978-1-878362-09-4(7)) Emerald Ent.
On this tape Thumper, the adventure dog, explores Kennebunkport, Maine in search of the President. This tape includes the actual sounds one hears in this small New England town but, does not contain a real recording of President Bush.

Meeting the World - Seeing the World (Extraverts - Introverts, Sensing - Intuitives) Frank L. Natter. 1 cass. (Running Time: 1 hr. 30 mins.). (Improving Your Personal Problem-Solving Ser.: Pt. I). 1989. 10.00 (978-1-878287-62-5(1), ATA-6) Type & Temperament.
Basics of psychological Type related to problem-solving.

Meeting with Father Time. unabr. ed. Robert A. Monroe. Read by Robert A. Monroe. (Running Time: 45 min.). (Explorer Ser.). 1983. 12.95 (978-1-56113-020-7(6), 21) Monroe Institute.
Encounters with other forms of existence.

Meeting with Robert Anton Wilson. Featuring Robert Anton Wilson. 1986. 9.95 (978-1-59157-011-0(5)) Assn for Cons.

Meeting with Success: How to Make Every Meeting Count, Jim Cathcart. 4 cass. 49.95 (527AX) Nightingale-Conant.
Discover how to use each minute of every meeting to optimize the best interests of yourself & your company. In this series, you'll listen as renowned business expert Jim Cathcart teaches you how to master ways to elicit true cooperation among staff & co-workers.

Meeting Your Match: The Seven Keys for Finding Your Perfect Mate. abr. ed. Karen A. Bowen. Read by Karen A. Bowen. 1 cass. (Running Time: 1 hr. 30 min.). 1995. 9.95 (978-0-9649343-2-0(9)) Ariadne Pubs.
Seven keys for finding your perfect mate. Selections based on the book "Meeting Your Match, a Practical Guide for Finding Your Perfect Mate".

Meeting Your Needs for Faith & Worth. 1 cass. 1986. 10.00 Berringer Pub.
Explains how faith is a belief in oneself to achieve what one wants and also a belief in something greater than oneself.

Meeting Your Needs for Freedom & Belonging. 1 cass. 10.00 Berringer Pub.
Explains how to start to immediately reduce relationship and freedom conflicts.

Meeting Your Needs for Knowledge & Health. 1 cass. 1986. 10.00 Berringer Pub.
Explains how to not only talk or dream about a healthy body, but really have one forever.

Meeting Your Needs for Security & Fun. 1 cass. 1986. 10.00 Berringer Pub.
Discusses the most frequent misconceptions about security and asks what one needs to do to be totally secure in all situations.

Meeting Your Selves: An Introduction to the Psychology of Selves. Hal Stone & Sidra Stone. 1 cass. (Mendocino Ser.). 1990. 10.95 (978-1-56557-000-9(6), T01) Delos Inc.
Teaches how to recognize & understand the amazing family of selves that lives within each of us. It explores how they develop & how they influence our lives. A wonderful beginning to the study of "The Psychology of Selves".

Meetings: A Gower Audio Manual. Greville Janner. 1988. audio compact disk 49.95 (978-0-566-02720-8(8), Gower Pubng) Pub: Ashgate Pub GBR. Dist(s): Ashgate Pub

Meetings with a Remarkable Man: Personal Tales of Milton H. Erickson. Short Stories. Bill O'Hanlon. As told by Bill O'Hanlon. 1 cass. (Running Time: 50). 2009. audio compact disk 16.95 (978-0-9823573-0-9(3), 7309) Crown Hse GBR.

Meets the Hooded Fang. Mordecai Richler. 1 CD. (Running Time: 1 hr. 30 mins.). 2005. audio compact disk 12.95 (978-0-660-18925-3(9)) Pub: Canadian Broadcasting CAN. Dist(s): Georgetown Term

Meg & Mog. unabr. ed. Helen Nicoll & Jan Pienkowski. Read by Maureen Lipman. 1 cass. (Running Time: 35 mins.). (J). 1995. 9.95 (978-1-85549-210-3(5), CTC 086, Chivers Child Audio) AudioGO.

Meg & Mog & Meg's Eggs. Helen Nicoll & Jan Pienkowski. Read by Maureen Lipman. 1 cass. (J). (ps-1). 6.95 (CC/025) C to C Cassettes.

Meg at Sea & Meg on the Moon. Helen Nicoll & Jan Pienkowski. Read by Maureen Lipman. 1 cass. (J). (ps-1). 6.95 (CC/026) C to C Cassettes.

Mega Brain Zones. Perf. by Michael Hutchinson. 6 cass. (Running Time: 6 hrs.). 1999. pap. bk. 74.95 (83-0058) Explorations.
Awaken the mind's hidden reserves, stimulate higher order brain states & achieve peak performance. This course is designed to produce the complex patterns of brainwave activity associated with heightened states of consciousness, from profound serenity to transcendent release. Includes booklet with 37 pages.

Mega Learning. Betty L. Randolph. Read by Betty L. Randolph. Read by Leonard Baron. Ed. by Success Education Institute International Staff. 1 cass. (Educational Ser.). 1989. bk. 14.98 Ocean Format. (978-1-55909-242-5(4), 310P); bk. Music Format. (310PM) Randolph Tapes.
Features 60,000 messages with the left-right brain.

Mega Memory. 8 cass. 59.95 Set. (273-C47) Natl Seminars.
Designed to expand & stimulate your brain's natural memory functions. This approach to memory improvement will enable you to learn faster & retain information for a longer period of time.

Mega Memory. Kevin Trudeau. 8 cass. 2001. pap. bk. & wbk. ed. 69.95 (1060AS) Pryor Resources.
Imagine what you could accomplish if you had a perfect memory, if all the information you needed was always at your mental fingertips, if your brain was like a computer data base! You'll discover how easy it is to have total recall once you learn how to access your permanent memory bank. Includes workbook and pocket guide.

Mega Memory. Kevin Trudeau. Read by Kevin Trudeau. 2 cass. (Running Time: 2 hrs.). 1999. 16.85 (978-0-671-01112-3(X)) S and S Inc.
Teaches how to remember any number.

Mega Memory. Kevin Trudeau & Jeanne Jones. Read by Kevin Trudeau. 8 cass. (Running Time: 8 hrs.). 1991. wbk. ed. 69.95 (978-1-55525-056-0(4), 1060A) Nightingale-Conant.
Imagine meeting 50 people & remembering all of their names. Or giving a presentation & having facts, figures, & prices instantly at your mental fingertips. Imagine having an infallible, photgraphic memory. Kevin Trudeau will show you how to release your own perfect, "instant recall" memory to remember the things you read, hear, & think about...& give you the advantage in both your personal & professional life.

Mega Memory. abr. ed. Roger W. Breternitz. 1 cass. (Running Time: 45 min.). 1985. pap. bk. 9.95 (978-1-893417-22-9(0)) Vector Studios.
Hypnosis: Implants suggestions on memory retention, long & short term memory. Removes blocks, has suggestions & "tricks" to improve general memory.

Mega Memory. abr. ed. Kevin Trudeau. 2 CDs. (Running Time: 20 hrs. 0 mins. 0 sec.). (ENG., 2001. audio compact disk 20.00 (978-0-7435-0919-0(6), Nightgale) Pub: S&S Audio. Dist(s): S and S Inc

Mega Memory. unabr. ed. Kevin Trudeau. Read by Kevin Trudeau. (Running Time: 60 hrs. 0 mins. 0 sec.). (ENG.). 2003. audio compact disk 35.00 (978-0-7435-3028-6(4), Nightgale) Pub: S&S Audio. Dist(s): S and S Inc

Mega Power Learning Action Kit. unabr. ed. Tag Powell. Read by Tag Powell. 2 cass. (Running Time: 1 hr. 20 min.). (Powell Life Improvement Programs Ser.). 1997. pap. bk. 19.95 Set. (978-1-56087-044-9(3)) Top Mtn Pub.
Tape 1: Side A presents step-by-step procedure to learn math, data, languages, lessons, facts, formulas, etc. Side B presents Mental Training Exercise designed to open the speed learning level of mind. Tape 2: Side A presents Power Learning Music with musical subliminals to help with the mind-body relaxation effect. Side B presents Power Learning Pacer - metronome sound, set at one beat every four seconds, to be used as a background sound while studying or learning.

Mega Speed Reading. Kevin Trudeau & Howard Stephen Berg. 6 cass. (Running Time: 6 hrs.). 1996. wbk. ed. (978-1-55525-057-7(2), 13980AV) Nightingale-Conant.
Read at record speed.

MegaBrain Neurotek Talk. Michael Hutchison. 1 cass. 9.00 (A0044-87) Sound Photosyn.
Speaking of brain machines, isolation tanks, etc., Brian records Faustin interviewing the author of "MegaBrain".

Megaliths, Stars & Goddesses. Mimi Lobell. 1 cass. 9.00 (OC152) Sound Horizons AV.

MegaMath: The Human Calculator. Scott Flansburg & Kevin Trudeau. 4 cass. (Running Time: 4 hrs.). 1997. wbk. ed. (978-1-55525-058-4(0), 13990av) Nightingale-Conant.
Become a human calculator.

Megamunch: And Other Singable Songs. Brenda Baker. (J). 2005. audio compact disk 12.95 (978-1-55050-222-0(0)) Pub: Coteau CAN. Dist(s): Fitzhenry W Ltd

Megan Terry: "Couplings & Groupings" unabr. ed. Megan Terry. Interview with Megan Terry. 1 cass. (Running Time: 29 min.). 1985. 10.00 New Letters.
Megan Terry & actors read her chronicle of America's sexual revolution. The Obie-winning playwright also discusses her life in theater.

Megatrends: Job 1. Ed Young. 1983. 4.95 (978-0-7417-1314-8(4), 314) Win Walk.

Megatrends asia eight asian megatrends that are reshaping our World. John Naisbitt. 2004. 10.95 (978-0-7435-4130-5(8)) Pub: S&S Audio. Dist(s): S and S Inc

Megatrends 2010: The Rise of Conscious Capitalism: Seven New Trends That Will Transform How You Work, Live, & Invest. Patricia Aburdene. Read by Patricia Aburdene. 2 CDs. (Running Time: 8100 sec.). 2007. audio compact disk 19.95 (978-1-59179-587-2(7), AW01156D) Sounds True.
A change in business is coming-one that is far more important than advances in information technology or a shift in the economy. In Megatrends 2010, best-selling author and legendary social forecaster Patricia Aburdene charts the forces that will shape the way business is conducted in the next ten years. These trends will give rise to an economy driven by social responsibility, spirituality, and consciousness. Using the same proven methods of prediction used in her previous Megatrends books, Aburdene presents compelling evidence for a revolutionary shift towards enlightened business in the next decade-and shows why success for any business will hinge on merging capitalism and consciousness.

Megh Malhar, Vol. 3. Music by Hariprasad Chaurasia & Bhimsen Joshi. 1 cass. (Music of the Seasons Ser.). 1991. (A91027); audio compact disk (CD A91027) Multi-Cultural Bks.

Megh Malhar, Vol. 4. Music by Kishori Amonkar & Bismillah Khan. 1 cass. (Music of the Seasons Ser.). 1991. (A91028); audio compact disk (CD A91028) Multi-Cultural Bks.

Meghdutam, Vol. 1. Composed by Vishwa M. Bhatt. 1 cass. 1996. (M96009); audio compact disk (CD M96009) Multi-Cultural Bks.
The Forlorn Yaksha, Invocation to the Cloud, The Way of the Cloud, On Amrakuta Peak, Ripening Earth, Detour to Ujjain, The River Nirvindhya, The Mansions of Ujjain, The Majesty of Kailash, The Beautiful Yakshi, Farewell to the Cloud.

Meghlamotir Deshe. Nazrul Islam. Voice by Sheema Mohit. 1 cd. 1999. audio compact disk 10.00 (978-0-9647672-8-7(7)) Beacon Hse IN.

Mei-Lai-Gong. unabr. ed. James C. Glass. Read by Maynard Villers. 8 cass. (Running Time: 11 hrs. 36 min.). 2001. 49.95 (978-1-55686-792-7(1)) Books in Motion.
The Empress of Light and her brother Mengjai possess the power to move mass. Working to save a dying planet, the sister and brother duo are threatened by those more powerful.

Meilleures Chansons Pour Enfants. Kidzup Productions Staff. (French Ser.). (J). 2003. audio compact disk 17.99 (978-1-894677-45-5(5)) Pub: Kidzup Prodns. Dist(s): Penton Overseas

Meister Eckhart & Shankara Acharya. unabr. ed. Perf. by Eknath Easwaran. 1 cass. (Running Time: 1 hr.). 1974. 7.95 (978-1-58638-576-7(3)) Nilgiri Pr.

Mekong Dong Song Nghen Mach: Cau Chuyen Cua Dong Song. The Vinh Ngo. Narrated by Anh Nguyet Trinh. Music by Tuan Thao Nguyen. Doan Van Nghe Dan Toc Lac Hong. (VIE.). 2007. audio compact disk 16.00 (978-0-9793097-1-7(9)) Van Nghe Moi.

Mel Bay Presents English Carols for Piano Solo. 1995. audio compact disk 15.98 (978-0-7866-0393-0(3), 95040CD) Mel Bay.

Mel Bay presents Essential Jazz Lines in the Style of John Coltrane, Violin Edition. Corey Christiansen & Kim Bock. 2008. pap. bk. 19.95 (978-0-7866-7930-0(1)) Mel Bay.

Mel Bay's Complete Bluegrass Banjo Method. 1995. audio compact disk 15.98 (978-0-7866-1619-0(9), 93345CD) Mel Bay.

Mel Bay's Complete Modern Drum Set. Frank Briggs. 1995. audio compact disk 15.98 (978-0-7866-0261-2(9)) Mel Bay.

Mel Bay's Master Anthology of Blues Guitar Solos, Vol. 1. Compiled by Mel Bay Staff. 1 CD. (Running Time: 90 mins.). 2000. per. 29.95 (978-0-7866-4724-8(8), 98424BCD) Mel Bay.

Mel Bay's Modern Guitar Method: Grade 1. Narrated by Matthew Bay. Contrib. by William Bay. Prod. by William Bay. 1993. audio compact disk 10.95 (978-0-7866-0450-0(6), 93200CD) Mel Bay.

Mel Bay's Modern Guitar Method: Grade 1 Pop Version. Contrib. by William Bay. Prod. by Nori Kelley. 1995. audio compact disk 10.95 (978-0-7866-0433-3(6)) Mel Bay.

Mel Bay's Modern Guitar Method: Grade 2. Created by Mel Bay Publications Inc. 1995. audio compact disk 14.95 (978-0-7866-0424-1(7)) Mel Bay.

Mel Bay's Super Country/Flatpicking Guitar Techniques. Contrib. by Joe Carr. (Running Time: 30 mins.). 2006. 14.95 (978-5-558-08954-7(7)) Mel Bay.

Mel Blanc Fix-It Shop: Mr. Colby to Accept Mel & Engagement Mix-Up. Perf. by Mel Blanc. 1 cass. (Running Time: 1 hr.). 2001. 6.98 (1874) Radio Spirits.

Mel Blanc Show. collector's ed. Perf. by Mary Jane Croft et al. 6 cass. (Running Time: 9 hrs.). 1998. bk. 17.49 (4148) Radio Spirits.
The comedic genius that was also the voice of so many cartoon characters plays two characters: an addled young man who runs a fix-it shop & Zookie, Mel's helper in the shop. 18 episodes.

Mel Brooks & Carl Reiner: The Two Thousand Year Old Man in the Year Two Thousand. Mel Brooks & Carl Reiner. 1 cass. (Running Time: 1 hr. 30 min.). 1961. 10.98 (978-1-56826-855-2(6)); 16.98 (978-1-56826-856-9(4)) Rhino Enter.

Melancholy Astronomer. (23314-A) J Norton Pubs.

Meland: "It's a Joy to Be Me" Contrib. by Eva Thayer. 1 cass. (Running Time: 50 min.). (YA). (gr. k-9). 1998. 9.95 (978-0-9616432-5-6(0)) Tes Pub.

MeLand 2: Songs & Raps for Youth, Teens, Adults. Eva Thayer. 2000. bk. 12.95 (978-1-931228-01-5(9)) Tes Pub.

MeLand 3: Songs & Raps for 3-4-5 Year Olds. Eva Thayer. (J). 2001. bk. 12.95 (978-1-931228-02-2(7)) Tes Pub.

Melange: Short Stories by American, British & European Writers. Ed. by Gary Gabriel. 6 cass. (Running Time: 6 hrs.). (Audio-Drama 101 Ser.: Vol. 3). 1998. 14.95 (978-1-892077-02-8(7)) Lend-A-Hand Soc.

MELATONIN MIRACLE the NATURE's SEX-ENHANCING DISEASE-FIGHTING AGE-REVERSING HORM: Nature's Disease-Fighting, Sex-Enhancing, Age-Reversing Hormone. Walter Pierpaoli. 2004. 7.95 (978-0-7435-4131-2(6)) Pub: S&S Audio. Dist(s): S and S Inc

Melayu Music of Sumatra & the Riau Islands: Zapin, Mak Yong, Ronggeng. Anno. by Philip Yampolsky. 1 CD. (Running Time: 1 hr. 13 min.). (Music of Indonesia Ser.: Vol. 11). 1996. audio compact disk (0-9307-40427-2-4) Smithsonian Folkways.
Presents two widespread Melayu entertainment genres plus songs & instrumental music from two forms of Melayu theater. Among the instruments heard are gambus (a lute believed to have originated in Arabia), violin, several kinds of drums & accordion.

Melchizedek: Hebrews 7:1-10. Ed Young. 1992. 4.95 (978-0-7417-1898-3(7), 898) Win Walk.

Melchizedek: Satellites in Time; The Astonishing Doctrine of Jesus. Jonathan Murro & Ann Ree Colton. 1 cass. 7.95 A R Colton Fnd.

Mele Kalikimaka: Songs & Dances for Christmas Luaus. Perf. by Sybil Ku'uipo Pruett & Brandon Kane. Prod. by Vicki Corona. Music by Vicki Corona. 1 CD. (Celebrate the Cultures Ser.: 2Music). 2000. 16.95 (978-1-58513-197-6(0)) Dance Fantasy.
Songs and dances for career Hawaiian Luau Dancers. Includes Hawaiian Snowman, Polynesian Jingle Bells, Believe in Me, Silent Night, Here Comes Santa, Candy Cane Hula, Mele Kalikimaka, and Christmas in Tahiti. Songs and Instrumentals by Vikilani, the Rhythms of Polynesia Band, and guest artists, Brandoin Kane and Kumu Hula Sybil Ku'uipo Pruett. Individual written choreographies are sold separately for $6 each.

Mele Kalikimaka Choreography: Songs & Hulas for Christmas Luaus. Prod. by Vicki Corona. Choreography by Vicki Corona. 1 CD. (Running Time: 25 mins). (Luau Celebration Ser.: 2). 2005. pap. bk. 6.00 (978-1-58513-196-9(2)) Dance Fantasy.
A music CD for career Polynesian dancers. Perfect for Christmas Luaus. Contains the songs Hawaiian Snowman, Silent Night, Christmas in Tahiti, Here Comes Santa, Believe in Me, Polynesian Jingle Bells, Candy Cane Hula, and Mele Kalikimaka. The written choreographies for each hula are sold separately.

Mele Oli: Chants from Ancient Hawaii. Perf. by Kanilau Brothers. 1 cass. (Running Time: 1 hr. 30 min.). 7.98 (STA 7); audio compact disk 12.78 CD Jewel box. (STA 7) NewSound.

Mele the Crab Finds the Way Out. Gail Omoto & Jan and July Dill. Illus. by Garrett Omoto. Voice by Nina Keali'iwahamana. (ENG.). (J). 2007. audio compact disk (978-1-933835-10-5(9)) Part Dev.

Melelana. 1999. audio compact disk 18.99 (978-0-89610-949-0(6)) Island Heritage.

Melelana. 2000. audio compact disk (978-0-89610-948-3(8)) Island Heritage.

Melika & the Magic Leaf. unabr. ed. Pere Butter. Read by Kiwi Butter. 1 CD. (Running Time: 16 mins.). (Pseudonymous Ser.: Vol. P-1). (J). (gr. k-5). 2002. audio compact disk 6.00 (978-0-915090-91-4(0)) Firefall.
The restaurant game, played with leaves for props, leads young Melika to an artful mission. Protecting the forest against a false spring.

Melindres de Belisa. unabr. ed. Lope de Vega. Perf. by Radio Nacional de Espana Staff & Nela Conjiu. 1 cass. (Running Time: 90 mins.). (SPA.). pap. bk. 16.95 (SSP385) J Norton Pubs.
One of the greatest classical plays by Spain's foremost dramatic author.

Melindres de Belisa. unabr. ed. Lope de Vega. Perf. by Theatrical Company of Radio Nacional de Espana Staff. (Spanish Literature Ser.). (SPA.). 11.95 (978-0-8045-0843-8(7), SAC 843) Spoken Arts.
One of the classical plays of Spain by one of their foremost dramatic author.

Melisande, Goops & How to Be Them & Prince Prijio, unabr. ed. E. Nesbit et al. Read by Flo Gibson. 2 cass. (Running Time: 2 hrs. 30 min.). (J). (gr. 1-3). 1991. 14.95 (978-1-55685-207-7(X)) Audio Bk Con.
Magical, funny, & fanciful describes this treasure trove in prose & verse.

Mellon: An American Life. abr. ed. David Cannadine. Read by John H. Mayer & John H. Mayer. (Running Time: 37800 sec.). (ENG.). 2006. audio compact disk 39.95 (978-0-7393-4023-3(9), Random AudioBks) Pub: Random Audio Pubg. Dist(s): Random

Mellow Muscles. Read by Paul Fair. 1 cass. (Running Time: 45 min.). (Relaxation Ser.). 1996. 12.95 (978-1-889896-02-1(0), S4041) Strs Les Inc.
Stress reduction.

Mellow Out Baby. Perf. by Sherry Goffin Kondor. 1 cass. (Running Time: 40 min.). (J). (ps-2). 2001. 10.00 (978-1-888795-19-6(0)); audio compact disk 13.00 (978-1-888795-18-9(2)) Sugar Beats.
Traditional and contemporary classics like "Never Never Land" from Peter Pan, "The Inch Worm" from Hans Christian Anderson, "All Through the Night" and "Brahms Lullabye".

Melodic Arpeggios for Lead Guitar. Mark Galbo. 2004. pap. bk. 24.95 (978-0-8256-1951-9(3), Schirmer Trade Bks) Pub: Music Sales. Dist(s): H Leonard

Melodious Masterpieces. Ed. by Jane Magrath. Contrib. by Scott Price. (ENG.). 2001. audio compact disk 10.95 (978-0-7390-2226-9(1)); audio compact disk 10.95 (978-0-7390-2227-6(X)); audio compact disk 10.95 (978-0-7390-2225-2(3)) Alfred Pub.

Melody. unabr. ed. V. C. Andrews. Read by Laurel Lefkow. 10 CDs. (Running Time: 38700 sec.). (Isis (CDs) Ser.). 2005. audio compact disk 89.95 (978-0-7531-1038-6(5)) Pub: ISIS Lrg Prnt GBR. Dist(s): Ulverscroft US

Melody in Poetry, Pt. B. (23320) J Norton Pubs.

Melody Moth Cassette. Stephen Cosgrove. 2004. 5.00 (978-1-58804-363-4(0)) PCI Educ.

Melt Away: Sugar Series. 2006. audio compact disk 15.95 (978-0-9759671-3-3(4)) Sounds Pubng Inc.

Melt Stress: Relaxation & Peace of Mind, Vol. 17. Jonathan Parker. 2 cass. (Running Time: 1 hr. 45 min.). 1992. 17.00 (978-1-58400-016-7(3)) QuantumQuests Intl.

***Meltdown.** Ben Elton. 2010. 76.95 (978-1-4450-0307-8(4)); audio compact disk 99.95 (978-1-4450-0308-5(2)) Pub: Isis Pubng Ltd GBR. Dist(s): Ulverscroft US

Meltdown. abr. ed. James Powlik. 2 cass. (Running Time: 3 hrs.). 2000. 18.00 (978-1-55935-348-9(1)) Soundelux.
A new biological thriller from the author of "Sea Change." The Inuit of the Arctic Circle are dying, as industry reaps the natural resources around them.

Meltdown: A Free-Market Look at Why the Stock Market Collapsed, the Economy Tanked, & Government Bailouts Will Make Things Worse. unabr. ed. Thomas E. Woods, Jr. Narrated by Alan Sklar. 5 CDs. (Running Time: 6 hrs. 30 mins. 0 sec.). (ENG.). 2009. audio compact disk 49.99 (978-1-4001-4209-5(1)) Pub: Tantor Media. Dist(s): IngramPubServ

Meltdown: A Free-Market Look at Why the Stock Market Collapsed, the Economy Tanked, & Government Bailouts Will Make Things Worse. unabr. ed. Thomas E. Woods, Jr. Narrated by Alan Sklar. Frwd. by Ron Paul. 1 MP3-CD. (Running Time: 6 hrs. 30 mins. 0 sec.). (ENG.). 2009. audio compact disk 19.99 (978-1-4001-6209-3(2)) Pub: Tantor Media. Dist(s): IngramPubServ

Meltdown: A Free-Market Look at Why the Stock Market Collapsed, the Economy Tanked, & Government Bailouts Will Make Things Worse. unabr. ed. Thomas E. Woods, Jr. Read by Alan Sklar. Narrated by Alan Sklar. Frwd. by Ron Paul. 5 CDs. (Running Time: 6 hrs. 30 mins. 0 sec.). (ENG.). 2009. audio compact disk 24.99 (978-1-4001-1209-8(5)) Pub: Tantor Media. Dist(s): IngramPubServ

Melted into Air: A Comedy of Errors in the Umbrian Hills. Sandi Toksvig. Read by Sandi Toksvig. (Running Time: 3 hrs. 0 mins. 0 sec.). (ENG., 2006. audio compact disk 24.95 (978-1-4055-0086-9(7)) Pub: Little BrownUK GBR. Dist(s): IPG Chicago

Melting. unabr. ed. Anna Davis. Read by Annie Aldington. 8 cass. (Running Time: 10 hrs. 12 mins.). (Isis Ser.). (J). 2002. 69.95 (978-0-7531-1364-6(3)) Pub: ISIS Lrg Prnt GBR. Dist(s): Ulverscroft US
Jason, Fran and Eileen move listlessly from city to city, conning everyone they meet. For years they've been small-time. Now they're ready to take on something bigger. A chance meeting gives Jason the idea for a grand scam in Cardiff's Tiger Bay, centering on a restaurant called The Melt. The scammers have only each other to hold on to in their self-created world where nothing is solid and real. But these consummate actors are beginning to confuse fact and fiction. Can they really trust each other.

Melting Snow - Thirsty Flowers. Randall Leonard. 1 cass. (Running Time: 45 min.). 1994. 10.95 (610); audio compact disk 15.00 (616) Hay House.
Original piano solos that evoke the joy & wonder of nature.

Melting Stones. unabr. ed. Tamora Pierce. Read by Full Cast Production Staff. (Circle Reforged Ser.: Bk. 2). (J). 2007. 44.99 (978-1-60252-766-9(0)) Find a World.

Melting Stones. unabr. ed. Tamora Pierce. Read by Grace Kelly. 8 CDs. (Running Time: 30600 sec.). (Circle Reforged Ser.: Bk. 2). (J). (gr. 5-9). 2007. audio compact disk 55.00 (978-1-934180-12-9(2)) Full Cast Audio.

Melting the Ego. Swami Amar Jyoti. 1 cass. 1982. 9.95 (C-35) Truth Consciousness.
Willingly allowing the Sculptor to mold us to Divinity. Opening to higher evolution. True channels of the Lord.

Melville: Six Short Novels. unabr. collector's ed. Herman Melville. Read by Dan Lazar. 8 cass. (Running Time: 8 hrs.). Incl. Apple-Tree Table & Other Sketches. Herman Melville. 1984. (1008); Bartleby, the Scrivener. Herman Melville. 1984. (1008); Billy Budd, Sailor. Herman Melville. 1984. (1008); Happy Failure. 1984. (1008); I & My Chimney. 1984. (1008); Piazza. 1984. (1008); 1975. 48.00 (978-0-913369-98-2(5), 1008) Books on Tape.
Included in this selection are "Billy Budd," Bartleby the Scrivener," "The Apple Tree Table," "The Piazza," "I & My Chimney" & "The Happy Failure.".

Melvin B. Tolson Memorial: Gallery of Harlem Portraits. unabr. ed. Melvin B. Tolson. 1 cass. (Running Time: 29 min.). 1980. 10.00 (020480) New Letters.
The late Melvin B. Tolson was a writer & educator with roots in the Harlem Renaissance. This program of readings was presented to celebrate the posthumous publication of his "Gallery of Harlem Portraits".

Mem Fox Reads. 1 cass. (Running Time: 30 mins.). (J). 1999. 9.98 (T 4593 CX, Listening Lib) Random Audio Pubg.

Mem Fox Reads. Read by Mem Fox. 1 cass. (Running Time: 32 min.). (J). (ps-3). 1992. 10.00 (978-0-15-253173-7(4)) Harcourt CAN CAN.
On this unusual tape, odd sound effects & ethereal New Age music lend an air of other worldliness to six stories read by the Australian author. On Koala Lou, for example, the bear makes weird squeaky, scratchy, snuffly noises that are nonetheless endearing. Fox's mellifluous, expressive voice has a calming quality. Tough Boris is one of two offerings here (the other is Feathers & Fools). It is a simple tale of a pirate that revolves around the repetition of a short phrase structure - "He was scruffy. All pirates are scruffy." After replacing "scruffy" with other adjectives (e.g., "greedy" & "scary") the author concludes, "But when his parrot died, he cried & cried. All pirates cry. And so do I".

Member of the Family: Cesar Millan's Guide to a Lifetime of Fulfillment with Your Dog. abr. ed. Cesar Millan & Melissa Jo Peltier. (ENG.). 2008. audio compact disk 29.95 (978-0-7393-6958-6(X), Random AudioBks) Pub: Random Audio Pubg. Dist(s): Random

Member of the Family: Cesar Millan's Guide to a Lifetime of Fulfillment with Your Dog. unabr. ed. Cesar Millan & Melissa Jo Peltier. Read by John H. Mayer. 6 cass. 2008. 100.00 (978-1-4159-6092-9(5), BksonTape); audio compact disk 100.00 (978-1-4159-5767-7(3), BksonTape) Pub: Random Audio Pubg. Dist(s): Random

Member of the Wedding. unabr. ed. Carson McCullers. Perf. by Ruby Dee et al. 2 cass. (Running Time: 1 hr. 45 mins.). Dramatization. 2001. 23.95 (978-1-58081-206-1(6), TPT151) L A Theatre.
Twelve-year-old Frankie Adams, longing at once for escape & belonging, takes her role as "member of the wedding" to mean that when her older brother marries she will join the happy couple in their new life together. But Frankie is unlucky in love; her mother is dead & Frankie narrowly escapes being raped by a drunken soldier during a farewell tour of the town. Worst of all, "member of the wedding" doesn't mean what she thinks.

Members Only. unabr. ed. Craig Fraley. Read by Maynard Villers. 6 cass. (Running Time: 7 hrs. 24 min.). (Kiahawk Ser.). 1996. 39.95 (978-1-55686-666-1(6)) Books in Motion.
New York's Little Italy, circa 1953. Michael Savini is lured into the false glamor of organized crime. He decides on an explosive confrontation when his name is placed on a hit list.

Membership Has Its Privileges: Logos March 22, 1998. Ben Young. 1998. 4.95 (978-0-7417-6077-7(0), B0077) Win Walk.

***Membership Matters: Insights from Effective Churches on New Member Classes & Assimilation.** Chuck Lawless. (Running Time: 3 hrs. 46 mins. 0 sec.). (ENG.). 2009. 18.99 (978-0-310-30479-1(2)) Zondervan.

Membership to Ministry to Maturity. Dave Early & Steve Benninger. 4 cass. bk. 99.95 (455) Chrch Grwth VA.
A program proven to carry people from seeker to baptized believer to ministering member to maturing Christian.

Memento Mori. Muriel Spark. Read by Nadia May. (Running Time: 6 hrs. 30 mins.). 2003. 27.95 (978-1-59912-542-8(0)) Iofy Corp.

Memento Mori. unabr. ed. Muriel Spark. Read by Nadia May. 6 CDs. (Running Time: 9 hrs.). 2003. audio compact disk 48.00 (978-0-7861-9249-6(6)) Blckstn Audio.

Memento Mori. unabr. ed. Muriel Spark. Read by Nadia May. 6 CDs. (Running Time: 7 hrs.). 2003. audio compact disk 48.00 (978-0-7861-9127-7(9), 3072); 39.95 (978-0-7861-2395-7(8), 3072) Blckstn Audio.
A blackly comic masterwork that begins with a voice on the telephone warning, "Remember, you must die." The recipient of the grim message is elderly Dame Lettie Colston, but soon ten of Lettie's oldest friends also become targets of Death's anonymous herald. A bizarre investigation lays bare an intricate network of deception and disloyalty that binds together the vulnerable group of aging eccentrics.

Memento Mori. unabr. ed. Muriel Spark. Read by Edward Petherbridge. 6 cass. (Running Time: 9 hrs.). 2000. 49.95 (SAB 065) Pub: Chivers Audio Bks GBR. Dist(s): AudioGO
Letti Colston has much in common with the elderly residents of Maud Long Medical Center. All are united by resentment, boredom, and the maudlin humor that masks the awareness of death. Then the phone calls begin: "Remember, you must die!" echoes the anonymous voice. Their lives intertwine as they try to catch the mysterious caller.

Memo. Martin H. Muller et al. (Running Time: 1 hr. 40 mins.). (GER.). 1995. 24.95 (978-3-468-49792-6(X)) Langenscheidt.

***Memo to the President Elect.** unabr. ed. Madeleine Albright. Read by Madeleine Albright. (ENG.). 2008. (978-0-06-157965-3(3)); (978-0-06-162874-0(3)) HarperCollins Pubs.

Memo to the President Elect: How We Can Restore America's Reputation & Leadership. unabr. ed. Madeleine Albright. Read by Madeleine Albright. 8 CDs. (Running Time: 8 hrs. 30 mins.). 2008. audio compact disk 39.95 (978-0-06-145271-0(8), Harper Audio) HarperCollins Pubs.

Memoir Cuando Era Puertorriquena. unabr. ed. Esmeralda Santiago. Read by Esmeralda Santiago. 10 cass. (Running Time: 13 hrs. 30 mins.). 2005. 94.75 (978-1-4193-4337-7(8)) Recorded Bks.
From a three-room apartment in Brooklyn occupied by ten family members, Esmeralda Santiago begins a journey that is both a triumphant struggle for identity and independence, and a mother's worst nightmare. Challenged by language barriers, cultural stereotypes, and the fiercely protective Mami, Santiago continues the rollicking ascent she began in When I Was Puerto Rican. By day she perfects the role of Cleopatra at Performing Arts High School and interprets for the family at city welfare offices. At night she accompanies her mother and sisters to Latin dance halls, but on such a strict leash that she has her first date at the age of twenty. Undaunted, she makes up for lost time in a romantic apprenticeship at once hilarious and heartbreaking.

Memoir of Jane Austen. unabr. ed. James E. Austen-Leigh. Narrated by Flo Gibson. 4 cass. (Running Time: 6 hrs.). 1984. 19.95 (978-1-55685-017-2(4)) Audio Bk Con.
A picture of Jane Austen, her life & times, written by her adoring nephew. It includes some letters, verse & the alternate chapter of "Persuasion.".

Memoires, Pts. 1-2 Saint-Simon. Read by Philippe Millat-Carus. 4 cass. (FRE.). 1995. 47.95 (1675/76-VSL) Olivia & Hill.
A detailed look at late 17th-century life, not only events but other interesting incidents of high society.

Memoires Pt. 1: Le Roi et les Siens, Saint-Simon. Read by Philippe Millat-Carus. 2 cass. (FRE.). 1995. 26.95 (1675-VSL) Olivia & Hill.

Memoires Pt. 2: La Fin d'un Regne, Saint-Simon. Read by Philippe Millat-Carus. 2 cass. (FRE.). 1995. 26.95 (1676-VSL) Olivia & Hill.

Mémoires de la Mer. unabr. ed. Collectif. Read by Sonia Johnson et al. 2007. 69.99 (978-2-35569-063-1(4)) Find a World.

Memoires de Sherlock Holmes, Vol. 1 Arthur Conan Doyle. 2 cass.Tr. of Memoirs of Sherlock Holmes. (FRE.). 1995. 26.95 (1656-LV) Olivia & Hill.
"Flamme d'argent," "La Figure jaune" & "L'Employe de l'agent de change." Read by a cast of actors.

Memoires de Sherlock Holmes, Vol. 2 Arthur Conan Doyle. 2 cass.Tr. of Memoirs of Sherlock Holmes. (FRE.). 1995. 26.95 (1699-LV) Olivia & Hill.
"Le Gloria-Scott," "Le Rituel des Musgraves" & "Les Proprietairse de Reigate." Read by a cast of actors.

Memoires d'Hadrien, Vol. 2 Marguerite Yourcenar. Read by Jean-Claude Rey & Jean-Marie Fonbonne. 3 cass. (FRE.). 1995. 34.95 (1638-LV) Olivia & Hill.
Hadrian, the Roman Emperor (117-38 A.D.), ill & about to die, writes a letter to his 17-year-old successor, Marcus Aurelius, recounting the various experiences of his personal & public life.

Memoires d'Hadrien, Vols. 1 & 2. Marguerite Yourcenar. Read by Jean-Claude Rey & Jean-Marie Fonbonne. 7 cass. (FRE.). 38.95 Vol. 1: 4 cass. (1637-LV) Olivia & Hill.

Memoires d'Hadrien, Vols. 1 & 2 Marguerite Yourcenar. Read by Jean-Claude Rey & Jean-Marie Fonbonne. 7 cass. (FRE.). 1992. 64.95 (1627-38) Olivia & Hill.

Memoires D'un Tricheur, Sacha Guitry. Read by Henri Virlogeux. 2 cass. (FRE.). 1995. 26.95 (1671-RF) Olivia & Hill.
A young man, who has been taken in by a cousin only interested in his inheritance, tries to escape his fate by answering want ads. He becomes a groom, a croupier, a swindler & finally an honest player.

Memoirs see Treasury of French Prose

Memoirs of A Coxcomb. John Cleland. Read by Anais 9000. 2008. 27.95 (978-1-60112-171-4(7)) Babblebooks.

Memoirs of a Dangerous Alien. unabr. ed. Maggie Prince. Read by Dermot Crowley. 4 cass. (Running Time: 4 hrs.). (J). (gr. 1-8). 1997. 32.95 (CCA 3378, Chivers Child Audio) AudioGO.

Memoirs of a Fellwanderer. unabr. ed. A. Wainwright. Read by Timothy West. 3 cass. (Running Time: 3 hrs.). 1997. 31.95 (978-0-7451-4332-3(6), CAB 1015) AudioGO.
A. Wainwright was the author of over 50 guidebooks, with his most famous being the legendary "Pictorial Guides to the Lakeland Fells." In his delightful memoir, Wainwright tells of his childhood, his rise from a lowly office boy to Treasurer, his marriage & the foundation of his animal charity. His memoir also describes the secrets held by the mountains & valleys of beautiful Lakeland.

Memoirs of a Geisha. Arthur Golden. Read by Bernadette Dunne. 11 cass. (Running Time: 16 hrs. 30 min.). 2000. 49.95 (H372) Blckstn Audio.
Captures the geisha experience in the art of fiction.

Memoirs of a Geisha. Arthur Golden. Read by Bernadette Dunne. 1998. audio compact disk 120.00 (978-0-7366-6061-7(5)) Books on Tape.

Memoirs of a Geisha. abr. movie tie-in ed. Arthur Golden. Read by Elaina Erika Davis. (Running Time: 10800 sec.). (ENG.). 2005. audio compact disk 24.95 (978-0-7393-2421-9(7), Random AudioBks) Pub: Random Audio Pubg. Dist(s): Random

Memoirs of a Geisha. unabr. ed. Arthur Golden. Read by Bernadette Dunne. 1 CD. (Running Time: 1 hr. 30 mins.). 2001. audio compact disk Books on Tape.
The geisha world is brought alive through the life of one woman who serves as a window to a little known world of incredible beauty.

Memoirs of a Geisha, unabr. ed. Arthur Golden. Read by Bernadette Dunne. 13 cass. (Running Time: 19 hrs. 30 min.). 1998. 104.00 (978-0-7366-4186-9(6), 4684) Books on Tape.

Memoirs of a Geisha. unabr. ed. Arthur Golden. Read by Carole Boyd. 14 cass. (Running Time: 14 hrs.). 1999. 89.95 (978-0-7540-0365-6(5), CAB1788) Pub: Chivers Audio Bks GBR. Dist(s): AudioGO
Spanning a quarter century, from 1929 to the post-war years of Japan's dramatic history, it opens a window onto a half-hidden world of eroticism, enchantment & degradation. Sayuri tells her story, from her humble beginnings in a fishing port to her busy life as one of Gion's eight hundred Geisha.

Memoirs of a Geisha. unabr. movie tie-in ed. Arthur Golden. Read by Bernadette Dunne. 15 CDs. (Running Time: 64800 sec.). (ENG.). 2005. audio compact disk 45.00 (978-0-7393-2167-6(6), Random AudioBks) Pub: Random Audio Pubg. Dist(s): Random

Memoirs of a Teenage Amnesiac. unabr. ed. Gabrielle Zevin. Read by Caitlin Greer. 6 CDs. (Running Time: 6 hrs. 70 mins.). (YA). (gr. 9 up). 2007. audio compact disk 50.00 (978-0-7393-6130-6(9), Random AudioBks) Pub: Random Audio Pubg. Dist(s): Random

Memoirs of an American Citizen. Robert Herrick. Read by Anais 9000. 1 CD. (Running Time: 7.9 hours). 2006. 16.95 (978-1-60112-004-5(4)) Babblebooks.

Memoirs of an Orphan Boy. unabr. ed. Hugo Bergstrom. Read by Michael Tudor Barnes. 5 cass. (Running Time: 7 hrs.). (Sound Ser.). (J). 2003. 49.95 (978-1-84283-384-1(7)) Pub: ISIS Lrg Prnt GBR. Dist(s): Ulverscroft US

Memoirs of Barry Lyndon see Memorias de Barry Lindon

Memoirs of Barry Lyndon. William Makepeace Thackeray. Read by Pedro Montoya. (Running Time: 3 hrs.). 2002. 16.95 (978-1-60083-237-6(7), Audiofy Corp) Iofy Corp.

Memoirs of Cleopatra, Pt. 1. unabr. collector's ed. Margaret George. Read by Donada Peters. 13 cass. (Running Time: 19 hrs. 30 mins.). 1998. 104.00 (978-0-7366-4093-0(2), 4600-A) Books on Tape.
This novel allows the unscrupulous & proud Queen of the Nile to recount her own tale.

Memoirs of Cleopatra, Pt. 2. unabr. collector's ed. Margaret George. Read by Donada Peters. 11 cass. (Running Time: 16 hrs. 30 mins.). 1998. 88.00 (978-0-7366-4094-7(0), 4600-B) Books on Tape.

Memoirs of Cleopatra, Pt. 3. unabr. collector's ed. Margaret George. Read by Donada Peters. 11 cass. (Running Time: 16 hrs. 30 min.). 1998. 88.00 (978-0-7366-4095-4(9), 4600-C) Books on Tape.

Memoirs of General William T. Sherman, Pt. 1. collector's ed. William Tecumseh Sherman. Read by Jonathan Reese. 12 cass. (Running Time: 18 hrs.). 1992. 96.00 (978-0-7366-2290-5(X), 3076-A) Books on Tape.
Memoirs of the Union general who marched from Atlanta to the sea & gave us the concept of "total war".

Memoirs of General William T. Sherman, Pt. 2. unabr. collector's ed. William Tecumseh Sherman. Read by Jonathan Reese. 12 cass. (Running Time: 18 hrs.). 1992. 96.00 (978-0-7366-2291-2(8), 3076-B) Books on Tape.

Memoirs of Hecate County. unabr. ed. Edmund Wilson. Read by Wolfram Kandinsky. 10 cass. (Running Time: 15 hrs.). 1986. 80.00 (978-0-7366-0545-8(2), 1519) Books on Tape.
Defines the American experience during the 30's. "What it means to be at home in America" was one of the literary objective of the thirties.

***Memoirs of My Life as a russian Secret Agent: The true story of how an artist was burned alive & went on to create a life she never dreamed Possible.** Allison Massari. 2010. audio compact disk (978-1-61623-820-9(8)) Indep Pub IL.

Memoirs of Sherlock Holmes see Memoires de Sherlock Holmes

Memoirs of Sherlock Holmes, unabr. ed. Arthur Conan Doyle. Read by Walter Covell. 7 cass. (Running Time: 10 hrs.). 1981. 49.95 (978-0-7861-0604-2(2), 2094) Blckstn Audio.
Among the short stories included in this collection is "The Gloria Scott," an account of Holmes's very first case. These delightful stories of the famous hawk-eyed detective are told by his friend & foil, Dr. Watson.

***Memoirs of Sherlock Holmes.** unabr. ed. Arthur Conan Doyle. Read by Ralph Cosham. (Running Time: 7 hrs. 30 mins.). 2010. 29.95 (978-1-4417-2018-4(9)); 54.95 (978-1-4417-2014-6(6)); audio compact disk 69.00 (978-1-4417-2015-3(4)) Blckstn Audio.

Memoirs of Sherlock Holmes. unabr. ed. Arthur Conan Doyle. Read by Walter Covell. 7 cass. (Running Time: 10 hr.). Incl. Adventure of the Crooked Man. (C-40); Adventure of the Gloria Scott. (C-40); Adventure of the Greek Interpreter. (C-40); Adventure of the Musgrave Ritual. (C-40); Adventure of the Naval Treaty. Arthur Conan Doyle. (C-40); Adventure of the Reigate Squire. (C-40); Adventure of the Resident Patient. (C-40); Adventure of the Stockbroker's Clerk. (C-40); Adventure of the Yellow Face. (C-40); Adventures of Silver Blaze. (C-40); 49.00 (C-40) Jimcin Record.

Memoirs of Sherlock Holmes. unabr. ed. Arthur Conan Doyle. Narrated by Alexander Spencer. 7 cass. (Running Time: 10 hrs. 30 mins.). (Sherlock Holmes Mystery Ser.). (gr. 10 up). 1986. 60.00 (978-1-55690-335-9(9), 86960E7) Recorded Bks.
Sherlock Holmes & his assistant, Dr. Watson, are posed eleven mysteries to solve. Includes: "The Final Problem".

***Memoirs of Sherlock Holmes.** unabr. ed. Arthur Conan Doyle. Narrated by Simon Prebble. (Running Time: 9 hrs. 30 mins.). 2010. 16.99 (978-1-4001-8518-4(1)) Tantor Media.

***Memoirs of Sherlock Holmes.** unabr. e[illegible]ur Conan Doyle. Narrated by Simon Prebble. (Running Time: 8 hrs. [illegible]s. 0 sec.). (ENG.). 2010. 22.99 (978-1-4001-6518-6(0)); audio compact disk 65.99 (978-1-4001-4518-8(X)); audio compact disk 32.99 (978-1-4001-1518-1(3)) Pub: Tantor Media. Dist(s): IngramPubServ

Memoirs of Sherlock Holmes. unabr. collector's ed. Arthur Conan Doyle. Read by Richard Lancelyn Green. 8 cass. (Running Time: 8 hrs.). Incl. Adventures of Silver Blaze. 1984. (1308); Crooked Man. 1984. (1308); Final Problem. 1984. (1308); Gloria Scott. Arthur Conan Doyle. 1984. (1308); Greek Interpreter. 1984. (1308); Musgrave Ritual. 1984. (1308); Naval Treaty. 1984. (1308); Reigate Squires. 1984. (1308); Resident Patient. Arthur Conan Doyle. 1984. (1308); Stockbroker's Clerk. 1984. (1308); Yellow Face. 1984. (1308); (Sherlock Holmes Ser.). (J). 1980. 48.00 (978-0-7366-0320-1(4), 1308) Books on Tape.

Memoirs of the Forties. unabr. collector's ed. Julian Maclaren-Ross. Read by Ian Whitcomb. 9 cass. (Running Time: 13 hrs. 30 min.). 1992. 72.00 (978-0-7366-2292-9(6), 3077) Books on Tape.
Evoking a demolished era of incendiary bombs & rationing, Maclaren-Ross misses none of it & introduces us to the budding luminaries of the age, among them Dylan Thomas & Graham Greene.

Memoirs of William T. Sherman - Excerpts: Atlanta & the March to the Sea. unabr. ed. William Tecumseh Sherman. Narrated by Nelson Runger. 3 cass. (Running Time: 4 hrs. 30 mins.). 1989. 26.00 (978-1-55690-336-6(7), 89540E7) Recorded Bks.
He reveals his strategic planning for battles such as Bull Run, Shiloh, and Vicksburg and delivers classic lessons - and milatary philosophies - about the Civil War.

Memorabilia see Browning's Last Duchess

Memorable Scenes from Old Testament Homes. 2001. 20.95 (978-1-57972-364-4(0)) Insight Living.

Memoranda During the War: From Specimen Days. unabr. ed. Walt Whitman. Narrated by Robert Gorman. 3 cass. (Running Time: 4 hrs.). 1988. 26.00 (978-1-55690-337-3(5), 88740E7) Recorded Bks.
He spent time during the Civil War as a medical attendant. This is his memoir.

Memorial Day. abr. ed. Vince Flynn. Read by Armand Schultz. (Mitch Rapp Ser.: No. 5). 2004. 15.95 (978-0-7435-3940-1(0)) Pub: S&S Audio. Dist(s): S and S Inc

Memorial Day. abr. ed. Vince Flynn. Read by Armand Schultz. (Running Time: 5 hrs. 0 mins. 0 sec.). No. 5. (ENG.). 2007. audio compact disk 14.99 (978-0-7435-6655-1(6)) Pub: S&S Audio. Dist(s): S and S Inc

Memorial Day. unabr. ed. Vince Flynn. Read by George Guidall. 10 cass. (Running Time: 13 hrs.). (Mitch Rapp Ser.: No. 5). 2005. 94.75 (978-1-4193-0923-6(4), 97889) Recorded Bks.
Fearless counterterrorism operative Mitch Rapp is called upon to fight against the world's most deadly terrorists in this harrowing political thriller by New York Times best-selling author Vince Flynn. Memorial Day is packed with the heartstopping action and political intrigue that Vince Flynn's fans love.

Memorial for Joseph Campbell, & a Preview of "Goddess" Charles Muses. 1 cass. 9.00 (A0272-88) Sound Photosyn.

Memorial Hall Murder. unabr. ed. Jane Langton. Read by Michael Prichard. 8 cass. (Running Time: 8 hrs.). 1982. 48.00 (978-0-7366-0631-8(9), 1592) Books on Tape.
This story takes place during rehearsals for a Christmas performance of Handel's Messiah, & each chapter is introduced by a selection from his masterpiece. When someone bombs Memorial Hall, Hamilton Down, the corpulent & beloved choir master, disappears in the rubble. Fortunately on hand to help the local police set to work is Jane Langston's famous sleuth, Homer Kelly.

Memorial of the Convoy of Women Sent to Auschwitz on 24 January 1943, Excerpts. 2 cass. (FRE.). 1996. 26.95 (1810-RF) Olivia & Hill.
Charlotte Delbo was one of the few survivors of the convoy of 229 women deported to Auschwitz on 24 January 1943. Excerpts from Delbo's memoirs "Auschwitz & Apres".

Memorial to S. Hasegawa. 1 cass. (Running Time: 30 min.). 12.00 (L420) MEA A Watts Cass.

Memorias de Barry Lindon. abr. ed. William Makepeace Thackeray. Read by Pedro Montoya. 3 CDs.Tr. of Memoirs of Barry Lyndon. (SPA.). 2002. audio compact disk 17.00 (978-958-8161-19-8(3)) YoYoMusic.

Memorie. Lorenzo Da Ponte. Read by Elsa Proverbio. 2 cass. (Running Time: 2 hrs.). (Letterati, Memorialisti E Viaggiatori Del 700 Ser.). (ITA.). 1996. pap. bk. 29.50 (978-1-58085-461-0(3)) Interlingua VA.

Memorie Inutili. Carlo Gozzi. Read by Elsa Proverbio. 6 cass. (Running Time: 6 hrs.). (Letterati, Memorialisti E Viaggiatori Del 700 Ser.). (ITA.). 1996. pap. bk. 69.50 (978-1-58085-458-0(3)) Interlingua VA.

Memories. Frank Minirth & Paul Meier. Read by Frank Minirth & Paul Meier. 1 cass. (Running Time: 1 hr.). (Minirth & Meier Home Counseling Audio Library). 1994. 9.95 (978-1-56707-039-2(6)) Dallas Christ Recs.
Understanding & overcoming a painful past.

Memories: The Autobiography of Ralph Emery. abr. ed. Ralph Emery & Tom Carter. Read by Ralph Emery. 2 cass. (Running Time: 3 hrs.). 15.95 (978-1-881109-02-0(X)) Soundbks.

Memories & Adventures. unabr. ed. Arthur Conan Doyle. Read by Robert Whitfield. 10 cass. (Running Time: 14 hrs. 30 mins.). 1999. 69.95 (978-0-7861-1655-3(2), 2483) Blckstn Audio.
"I have been constrained to devote my latter years to telling the world the final result of thirty-six years' study of the occult...Such is the life which I have told in some detail." In his preface to this autobiography, Sir Arthur Conan Doyle makes bold claims for his life. His life, & his description of it, in no way fail to live up to those claims.

***Memories & Adventures.** unabr. ed. Arthur Conan Doyle. Read by Robert Whitfield. (Running Time: 14 hrs.). 2010. 29.95 (978-1-4417-1929-4(6)); audio compact disk 118.00 (978-1-4417-1926-3(1)) Blckstn Audio.

Memories Can Be Murder. unabr. ed. Connie Shelton. Read by Lynda Evans. 6 cass. (Running Time: 7 hrs. 2 min.). (Charlie Parker Mystery Ser.: No. 5). 2001. 39.95 (978-1-58116-100-7(X)) Books in Motion.
Upon returning home after visiting her fiancee in Hawaii, Charlie learns that her mother and father have been killed in a suspicious small plane crash.

Memories from the Wild. Barbara O'Donnell. 2001. audio compact disk 15.00 (978-0-89914-500-6(0)) Third Party Pub.

Memories Last... A Time to Grieve Catholic Edition. Karen Jean Matsko Hood. 2010. audio compact disk 24.95 (978-1-59210-998-2(5)) Whsprng Pine.

Memories Last... A Time to Grieve Christian Edition. Karen Jean Matsko Hood. 2010. audio compact disk 24.95 (978-1-59210-991-3(8)) Whsprng Pine.

Memories Last... A Time to Heal Catholic Edition. Karen Jean Matsko Hood. 2010. audio compact disk 24.95 (978-1-59210-957-9(8)) Whsprng Pine.

Memories Last... A Time to Heal Christian Edition. Karen Jean Matsko Hood. 2010. audio compact disk 24.95 (978-1-59210-950-0(0)) Whsprng Pine.

Memories of a Yellow Dog see Favorite Stories by O. Henry

Memories of an Invented City, Program 4. Read by Guillermo C. Infante. (F007BB090) Natl Public Radio.

Memories of Carl Gustav Jung, Corona W. Anderson. Read by Flo Gibson. 2 cass. (Running Time: 2 hrs. 30 min.). 1996. 14.95 (978-1-55685-432-3(3)) Audio Bk Con.
These intimate glimpses of Jung by the narrator's mother capture his humor, wisdom & deep kindness.

Memories of D. H. Lawrence. Aldous Huxley & Freda Lawrence. 1 cass. 1999. 11.00 (01130) Big Sur Tapes.

Memories of Heaven. unabr. ed. Gilbert Highet. Read by Gilbert Highet. 1 cass. (Running Time: 30 min.). 9.95 (23293-A) J Norton Pubs.

Memories of Maryhill. Roderick Wilkinson. Read by James Bryce. 4 cass. (Running Time: 6 hrs.). 2001. 44.95 (001012) Pub: ISIS Audio GBR. Dist(s): Ulverscroft US

Memories of Men & Women. unabr. ed. A. L. Rowse. Read by Bill Kelsey. 7 cass. (Running Time: 10 hrs. 30 mins.). 1988. 56.00 (978-0-7366-1402-3(8), 2291) Books on Tape.
Features a collection of the author's personal recollections of Sir Winston Churchill, Lady Astor, Admiral Nimitz, Agatha Christie, G. M. Trevelyan, Samuel Eliot Morison, Andre Maurois, Edmond Wilson, T. S. Eliot, W. H. Auden & Willa Cather.

Memories of Midnight. Sidney Sheldon. Contrib. by Steven Pacey. (Playaway Adult Fiction Ser.). 2008. 64.99 (978-1-60640-669-4(8)) Find a World.

Memories of Midnight. unabr. ed. Scripts. Sidney Sheldon. Read by Steven Pacey. 8 cass. (Running Time: 12 hrs.). 2004. 34.95 (978-1-59007-382-7(7)) Pub: New Millenn Enter. Dist(s): PerseuPGW

Memories of President Lincoln see Twentieth-Century Poetry in English, No. 16, Walt Whitman Speaks for Himself

Memories of Summer. Ruth White. Narrated by Kate Forbes. 3 CDs. (Running Time: 3 hrs. 30 mins.). (gr. 7 up). audio compact disk 29.00 (978-0-7887-6154-6(4)) Recorded Bks.

Memories of Summer. unabr. ed. Ruth White. Narrated by Kate Forbes. 3 CDs. (Running Time: 3 hrs. 30 min.). (YA). (gr. 5-8). 2001. audio compact disk 29.00 (C1378) Recorded Bks.
In 1955, thirteen-year-old Lyric, her older sister Summer & their widowed father pack the car. Poor yet hopeful, they move from the hills of Virginia to Flint, Michigan, where "Poppy" plans to find factory work. Once they are in Michigan, Lyric & Summer love the excitement of the city. Lyric makes friends at her new school, but Summer feels like an outcast. Soon, the close bond between the two sisters begins to dissolve. Lyric always knew that Summer was a bit odd, but now Summer withdraws more & more into a fantasy world. Filled with love & pain, Memories of Summer is Lyric's story of her sister's descent into mental illness.

Memories of Summer. unabr. ed. Ruth White. Narrated by Kate Forbes. 3 pieces. (Running Time: 3 hrs. 30 mins.). (gr. 7 up). 2001. 28.00 (978-0-7887-5030-4(5), 96528E7) Recorded Bks.

Memories of the Ford Administration. unabr. collector's ed. John Updike. Read by Michael Prichard. 10 cass. (Running Time: 15 hrs.). 1993. 80.00 (978-0-7366-2481-7(3), 3243) Books on Tape.
College instructor writes about his life during Gerald Ford's presidency, as well as about President James Buchanan.

Memories of West Street & Lepke see Robert Lowell: A Reading

Memories Past Ruling Today. Bonnie Smith. 1 cass. 8.95 (319) Am Fed Astrologers.
Work with the moon for a better life.

Memoriser, Se Rappeler, Se Liberer. unabr. ed. Robert A. Monroe. Read by Roland Simon. 1 cass. (Running Time: 30 min.). (Mind Food Ser.). 1992. 14.95 (978-1-56102-428-5(7)) Inter Indus.
Incorporates encoding cues to assist in memory process.

Memorist. unabr. ed. M. J. Rose. Read by Phil Gigante. (Running Time: 11 hrs.). (Reincarnationist Ser.). 2010. 24.99 (978-1-4233-9018-3(0), 9781423390183, Brilliance MP3); 24.99 (978-1-4233-9020-6(2), 9781423390206, BAD); 39.97 (978-1-4233-9019-0(9), 9781423390190, Brlnc Audio MP3 Lib); 39.97 (978-1-4233-9021-3(0), 9781423390213, BADLE) Brilliance Audio.

Memorist. unabr. ed. M. J. Rose. Read by Phil Gigante. (Running Time: 11 hrs.). (Reincarnationist Ser.). 2010. audio compact disk 29.99 (978-1-4233-9016-9(4), 9781423390169, Bril Audio CD Unabri); audio compact disk 92.97 (978-1-4233-9017-6(2), 9781423390176, BriAudCD Unabrid) Brilliance Audio.

Memory see Eudora Welty Reading from Her Works

Memory. Lois McMaster Bujold. Read by Grover Gardner. (Running Time: 52200 sec.). (Vorkosigan Ser.). 2007. 85.95 (978-1-4332-0113-4(5)); audio compact disk 99.00 (978-1-4332-0114-1(3)); audio compact disk 29.95 (978-1-4332-0115-8(1)) Blckstn Audio.

Memory, Level 1. (Yamaha Clavinova Connection Ser.). 2004. disk 1.04 (978-0-634-09584-9(6)) H Leonard.

Memory: Program from the Award Winning Public Radio Series. Interview. Hosted by Fred Goodwin. Comment by John Hockenberry. 1 CD. (Running Time: 1 hr). (Infinite Mind Ser.). 1999. audio compact disk 21.95 (978-1-932479-17-1(1), LCM 84) Lichtenstein Creat.
New memory research is teaching scientists how the brain remembers, why it forgets, and, potentially, how to improve memory. In this hour, we talk about the new research. We also dispel some common memory myths, talk to kids about memory, and visit a memory enhancement class. Plus, singer/songwriter Dar Williams remembers her childhood in song, and commentary from John Hockenberry.

Memory Advantage. unabr. ed. 2 cass. (Running Time: 2 hrs.). 2000. (978-1-931187-19-0(3), MAD); audio compact disk (978-1-931187-04-6(5), CDMAD) Word Success.

Memory & Dream. unabr. ed. Kate Reading. (Running Time: 73800 sec.). 2007. 95.95 (978-1-4332-1069-3(X)); audio compact disk 120.00 (978-1-4332-1070-9(3)) Blckstn Audio.

Memory & Dream. unabr. ed. Read by Kate Reading. (Running Time: 72000 sec.). 2007. audio compact disk 44.95 (978-1-4332-1071-6(1)) Blckstn Audio.

Memory & Recall. Rick Brown. Read by Rick Brown. Ed. by John Quatro. 1 cass. (Running Time: 30 min.). (Subliminal - Easy Listening Ser.). 1993. 10.95 (978-1-57100-008-8(9), E120); 10.95 (978-1-57100-032-3(1), J120); 10.95 (978-1-57100-056-9(9), N120); 10.95 (978-1-57100-080-4(1), S120); 10.95 (978-1-57100-104-7(2), W120); 10.95 (978-1-57100-128-3(X), H120) Sublime Sftware.
Enhances memory & improves recall.

Memory & Recall Made Fun (CD) Eric Jensen. 2002. 64.95 (978-1-890460-17-4(6)) Pub: Corwin Pr. Dist(s): SAGE

***Memory Bible: An Innovative Strategy for Keeping Your Brain Young.** unabr. ed. Gary Small. (Running Time: 6 hrs. 0 mins. 0 sec.). (ENG.). 2011. audio compact disk 16.99 (978-1-59859-915-2(1)) Oasis Audio.

Memory Book: A Benny Cooperman Mystery. abr. ed. Howard Engel. 3 CDs. (Running Time: 3 hrs. 30 mins.). (ENG.). 2006. audio compact disk 24.95 (978-0-86492-470-4(4)) Pub: BTC Audiobks CAN. Dist(s): U Toronto Pr

Memory Box. unabr. ed. Margaret Forster. Read by Clare Higgins. 8 cass. (Running Time: 33900 sec.). (Horatio Hornblower Adventures Ser.). 2000. 69.95 (978-0-7540-0436-3(8), CAB 1859) AudioGO.
Catherine's mother died when she was a child. Her father quickly remarried & Catherine attached herself to her stepmother, banishing her birth mother Susannah to a distant memory. Susannah, however, refused to be forgotten & has left a box of memories. Reluctantly, Catherine confronts the box & discovers Susannah was not the person everyone remembers.

Memory Church, unabr. ed. Tim Sebastian. Narrated by Simon Prebble. 6 cass. (Running Time: 7 hrs. 45 mins.). 1994. 51.00 (978-1-55690-984-9(5), 94123E7) Recorded Bks.
A startlingly realistic insider's look under the rocks of the crumbling Berlin Wall. Caught in the midst of the chaos is James Martin, British by birth, now living in East Berlin & considered a traitor even by his own mother. He knows he must flee, but to whom should he turn... the KGB, his employer for the past few years - his old friends in British Intelligence, or the woman whose touch he could still remember even after long years apart, the woman who may have betrayed him.

Memory Collector. unabr. ed. Meg Gardiner. Read by Susan Ericksen. 1 MP3-CD. (Running Time: 13 hrs.). (Jo Beckett Ser.). 2009. 39.97 (978-1-4233-6164-0(4), 9781423361640, Brlnc Audio MP3 Lib); 39.97 (978-1-4233-6166-4(0), 9781423361664, BADLE); 24.99 (978-1-4233-6163-3(6), 9781423361633, Brilliance MP3); 24.99 (978-1-4233-6165-7(2), 9781423361657, BAD); audio compact disk 97.97 (978-1-4233-6162-6(8), 9781423361626, BriAudCD Unabrid); audio compact disk 36.99 (978-1-4233-6161-9(X), 9781423361619, Bril Audio CD Unabri) Brilliance Audio.

Memory Cure: New Discoveries on How to Protect Your Brain Against Memory Loss & Alzheimer's Disease. Majid Fotuhi. 3 cass. (Running Time: 4 hrs. 30 min.). 2003. audio compact disk 28.00 (978-1-932378-02-3(2)); 24.00 (978-0-9724889-6-9(0)) Pub: A Media Intl. Dist(s): Natl Bk Netwk
In this book Dr Fotuhi outlines an exciting and highly effective plan that targets the 13 factors contributing to the development of memory loss.

Memory Doctor: Fun, Simple Techniques to Improve Memory & Boost Your Brain Power. abr. unabr. ed. Douglas J. Mason & Spencer Xavier Smith. Read by Erik Singer. (Running Time: 10800 sec.). 2008. audio compact disk 14.95 (978-0-06-155838-2(9), Harper Audio) HarperCollins Pubs.

Memory Game. unabr. ed. Nicci French. Read by Harriet Walter. 10 cass. (Running Time: 10 hrs.). 1997. 84.95 (978-0-7540-0005-1(2), CAB 1428) AudioGO.
On an autumn morning, the body of 16-year old Natalie Martello is found buried in a country house garden in Shropshire. She has been missing for 25 years. For her family, she represents lost hopes & a terrible crime long concealed. Who would kill an innocent teenage girl? Natalie's friend Jane investigates & uncovers a dark family secret which exceeds her most terrible fears.

Memory Game. unabr. ed. Nicci French. Read by Harriet Walter. 10 cass. (Running Time: 15 hrs.). 2000. 69.95 (CAB 1428) Pub: Chivers Audio Bks GBR. Dist(s): AudioGO
On an Autumn morning, the body of 16-year-old Natalie Martello is found buried in a country house garden in Shropshire. She has been missing for 25 years. For her family, she represents lost hopes & a terrible crime long concealed. Who would kill an innocent teenage girl? Natalie's friend Jane investigates and uncovers a dark family secret which exceeds her most terrible fears.

Memory I see George Seferis

Memory Improvement. Read by Robert E. Griswold. 1 cass. (Running Time: 1 hr.). 1988. 10.95 (978-1-55848-031-5(5)) EffectiveMN.
If you think you have a poor memory, this tape will provide you with techniques & positive programming to help you use your memory more effectively.

Memory Improvement. Barrie Konicov. 1 cass. (Video-Audio System Ser.). (YA). cass. & video 24.98 (978-0-87082-447-0(3), SYS 083) Potentials.

Memory Improvement, Barrie Konicov. 2 cass. (YA). 16.98 (978-1-56001-299-3(4), SCII 083) Potentials.
Rid yourself of both negative thoughts & the "I can't remember" syndrome & remember everything you have ever heard or learned. Enjoy full use of your facilities of memory, recall & retention - now.

Memory Improvement. Barrie Konicov. 1 CD. 2003. audio compact disk 16.98 (978-0-87082-958-1(0)) Potentials.
Your subconscious remembers everything you have ever heard. Play this program;enjoy full use of your faculties of memory, recall, and retention.You will find the self-hypnosis on track 1 and the subliminal on track 2. The easy-listening music of the subliminal, together with the self-hypnosis, is the original format which most people love and with which they are most familiar.

Memory Improvement. Barrie Konicov. 2 CDs. 2003. audio compact disk 27.98 (978-1-56001-981-7(6)) Potentials.
Your subconscious remembers everything you have ever heard. Play this program; enjoy full use of your faculties of memory, recall, and retention.This 2-CD program from our Super Consciousness series is our newest, most powerful format. On the self-hypnosis CD, SC programs have the Subliminal Persuasion soundtrack added under Barrie?s voice. And the 17th Century Baroque music on the Subliminal CD has the same beat as your body's natural rhythm, thereby allowing the suggestions to enter deeply and effortlessly.

Memory Improvement. Created by Anne H. Spencer-Beacham. 1. 2003. audio compact disk (978-1-932163-54-4(9)) Infinity Inst.

Memory Improvement: Mejore Su Memoria. Barrie Konicov. 1 cass. (Running Time: 1 hr. 30 min.). (Spanish-Language Audios Ser.). (SPA.). (YA). 1995. 11.98 (978-0-87082-806-5(1), 083) Potentials.
It is the nature of your subconscious mind to remember everything you have ever heard or learned; yet too often, by repeated unconscious negative self-suggestion, you can cripple your memory faculties. Rid yourself of both negative thoughts & the "I can't remember" syndrome.

Memory Improvement (Total Recall Improve Test Scores) Norman J. Caldwell. Read by Norman J. Caldwell. Ed. by Achieve Now Institute Staff. 1 cass. (Running Time: 20 min.). (Academic Achievement Ser.). 1988. 9.97 (978-1-56273-082-6(7)) My Mothers Pub.
Your mind stores everything, learn how to bring it out.

Memory in a Month. 2004. audio compact disk (978-0-9747212-1-7(2)) R White Train.

Memory in Death. abr. ed. J. D. Robb, pseud. Read by Susan Ericksen. (Running Time: 21600 sec.). (In Death Ser.). 2006. audio compact disk 16.99 (978-1-4233-0474-6(8), 9781423304746, BCD Value Price) Brilliance Audio.
Eve Dallas is one tough cop. She's got no problem dealing with a holiday reveler in a red suit who plunges thirty-seven stories and gives new meaning to the term "sidewalk Santa." But when she gets back to the station and Trudy Lombard shows up, it's all Eve can do to hold it together. Instantly, she's plunged back into the past, to the days when she was a vulnerable, traumatized girl - trapped in foster care with the twisted woman who now sits in front of her, smiling. Trudy claims she just wanted to see how Eve was doing. But Eve's husband, Roarke, suspects otherwise - and his suspicions prove correct when Trudy arrives at his office demanding money in exchange for keeping the ugly details of his wife's childhood a secret. Barely restraining himself, Roarke shows her the door - and makes it clear that she'd be wise to get out of New York and never bother him or his wife again. But just a few days later, Trudy's found on the floor of her hotel room, a mess of bruises and blood. A cop to the core, Eve is determined to solve the case, if only for the sake of Trudy's bereaved son. Unfortunately, Eve is not the only one to have suffered at this woman's hands, and she and Roarke will follow a circuitous, dangerous path to find out who turned this victimizer into a victim.

Memory in Death. unabr. ed. J. D. Robb, pseud. Read by Susan Ericksen. (Running Time: 11 hrs.). (In Death Ser.). 2006. 39.25 (978-1-4233-0470-8(5), 9781423304708, BADLE); 24.95 (978-1-4233-0469-2(1), 9781423304692, BAD); 87.25 (978-1-4233-0464-7(0), 9781423304647, BrilAudUnabridg); audio compact disk 36.95 (978-1-4233-0465-4(9), 9781423304654); audio compact disk 39.25 (978-1-4233-0468-5(3), 9781423304685, Brlnc Audio MP3 Lib); audio compact disk 97.25 (978-1-4233-0466-1(7), 9781423304661, BriAudCD Unabrid); audio compact disk 24.95 (978-1-4233-0467-8(5), 9781423304678, Brilliance MP3) Brilliance Audio.

Memory Jogger E-Book 1999 Series. Created by GOAL/QPC. (Memory Jogger Ser.). (ENG.). 1999. audio compact disk 37.25 (978-0-01-328701-8(X)) GOAL-QPC.

***Memory Keeper's Daughter.** Kim Edwards. Read by Ilyana Kadushin. (ENG.). 2006. (978-0-06-128478-6(5), Harper Audio) HarperCollins Pubs.

Memory Keeper's Daughter. abr. ed. Kim Edwards. Read by Martha Plimpton. 9 CDs. (Running Time: 11 hrs.). 2005. audio compact disk 19.95 (978-0-06-082580-5(4), Harper Audio) HarperCollins Pubs.

***Memory Keeper's Daughter.** abr. ed. Kim Edwards. Read by Martha Plimpton. (ENG.). 2006. (978-0-06-115796-7(1), Harper Audio); (978-0-06-115795-0(3), Harper Audio) HarperCollins Pubs.

***Memory Keeper's Daughter.** unabr. ed. Kim Edwards. Read by Ilyana Kadushin. (ENG.). 2006. (978-0-06-128479-3(3), Harper Audio) HarperCollins Pubs.

Memory Lane. unabr. ed. 1 cass. cass. & video 71.95 (86701) Books on Tape.
The fun & easy system for writing about your life, & producing a professional-looking book. Includes writing guides & book material (Memory Joggers guide, Writer's Companion, Topic Organizer, & book production pages).

Memory Lane: Share Your Thoughts & Memories with Those You Love. Lifescapes Staff. 1 cass. (Running Time: 1 hr.). 1995. cass. & video 79.95 (12320AVS) Nightingale-Conant.
A fun & easy system for writing about your life. You can honor your parents & grandparents by preserving priceless family memories & creating a family treasure that will last forever. Includes workbook.

Memory Made Easy. unabr. ed. Robert L. Montgomery. 3 cass. (Running Time: 3 hrs.). 1987. pap. bk. 39.95 (SO1805) J Norton Pubs.
Designed to dramatically increase your ability to remember. Topics include: three basic principles of memory & how to master them, the alphabet system for recalling numbers & how to improve your speechmaking & joke-telling.

Memory Made Easy: Remember Every Fact, figure & Detail. unabr. ed. 6 cass. (Running Time: 9 hrs.). 2001. pap. bk. & pupil's gde. ed. 59.95 (3183) Oasis Audio.
Imagine being to remember every name in a room full of people, recall phone numbers, dates & statistics with pinpoint accuracy. Discover the secrets that momory experts use to train their minds for instant recall.

Memory Magic, Hypnosis for Memory. Wendi Friesen. 4 CDs. 2002. audio compact disk 99.00 (978-1-929058-14-3(4)) Wendicom.
Six Hypnosis Sessions on CDs that will make your mind a more interesting place. I love this program, especially the mind machines. How much do I LOVE this new memory program? A LOT! Please order it and find out how cool it is to have a better memory and be able to focus and retain what you learn!.

Memory Maker. unabr. ed. JoAnne Lower. Read by JoAnne Lower. 1 cass. (Running Time: 1 hr.). 1994. (978-1-888940-00-8(X)) J Lower Ent.
Personal stories of a young girl growing up on an Iowa farm.

Memory of All That. unabr. ed. Bryan Forbes. Read by Vincent Marzello. 12 cass. (Running Time: 57600 sec.). 2004. 96.95 (978-0-7540-0409-7(0), CAB 1832) Pub: Chivers Audio Bks GBR. Dist(s): AudioGO
In the Hollywood of the 1950's, the major studios were very much in control & the price of success could be high. Robert Peterson, encouraged by the success of one novel, is a Hollywood innocent. But when a British producer introduces him to the enigmatic Amanda, Robert allows himself to be seduced along the first stages of corruption.

Memory of Earth. unabr. ed. Orson Scott Card. Read by Stefan Rudnicki. (Running Time: 10 hrs. 50 mins.). 2008. 29.95 (978-1-4332-1873-6(9)); 65.95 (978-1-4332-1869-9(0)); audio compact disk & audio compact disk 90.00 (978-1-4332-1870-5(4)) Blckstn Audio.

Memory of Old Jack. unabr. ed. Wendell Berry. 6 CDs. (Running Time: 7 hrs. 42 mins. 0 sec.). (ENG.). 2007. audio compact disk 23.98 (978-1-59644-446-1(0), christaudio) christianaud.

***Memory of Old Jack.** unabr. ed. Wendell Berry. Narrated by Paul Michael. (Yasmin Peace Ser.). (ENG.). 2007. 14.98 (978-1-59644-447-8(9), christaudio) christianaud.

Memory of Running: A Novel. Ron McLarty. Narrated by Ron McLarty. 12 CDs. (Running Time: 12 hrs. 30 mins.). 2001. audio compact disk 111.00 (978-0-7887-5194-3(8), C1351E7) Recorded Bks.
Forty-three years old & 279 pounds when his parents die in a accident, Smithson uncovers his old Raleigh bicycle in the garage & begins a cross country journey to find his sister - the beautiful but tragically psychotic Bethany.

Memory of Running: A Novel. unabr. ed. Ron McLarty. Narrated by Ron McLarty. 10 cass. (Running Time: 12 hrs. 30 mins.). 2000. 81.00 (978-0-7887-4391-7(0), 96322E7) Recorded Bks.
Journey on a quest to find hope & redemption with unlikely hero Smithson Ide. Forty-three years old & 279 pounds when his parents are in an accident, Smithson uncovers his old Raleigh bicycle in the garage & begins a cross-country journey to find his sister, the beautiful but tragically psychotic Bethany.

Memory of Running: A Novel. unabr. ed. Ron McLarty. 9 CDs. (Running Time: 11 hrs.). 2004. audio compact disk 34.99 (978-1-4025-9429-8(1), 01802) Recorded Bks.

Memory of Running: A Novel. unabr. collector's ed. Ron McLarty. Narrated by Ron McLarty. 10 cass. (Running Time: 12 hrs. 30 min.). 2003. 33.71 (978-0-7887-6904-7(9)) Recorded Bks.
Smithson Ide is 43 years old and weighs 279 pounds when his parents die in an accident. Lost in memories of childhood, Smithson uncovers his old Raleigh bicycle in the garage and begins a cross-country journey to find his beautiful, but tragically psychotic sister. Keenly aware of how ridiculous he must appear, Smithson nonetheless perseveres through a journey that is hilarious and horrifying. It is a trip, he soon realizes, that might provide his last chance to become the person he has always wanted to be.

Memory of Water. Karen White. Read by Susanna Burney. 2009. audio compact disk 29.95 (978-1-59316-469-0(6)) Listen & Live.

***Memory Palace: A Memoir.** unabr. ed. Mira Bartok. (Running Time: 9 hrs. 0 mins.). 2011. 24.99 (978-1-4526-5025-8(X)); 34.99 (978-1-4526-0025-3(2)); 83.99 (978-1-4526-3025-0(9)); 15.99 (978-1-4526-7025-6(0)) Tantor Media.

***Memory Palace (Library Edition) A Memoir.** unabr. ed. Mira Bartok. (Running Time: 9 hrs. 0 mins.). 2011. 34.99 (978-1-4526-2025-1(3)) Tantor Media.

Memory Power. 1 cass. 10.00 (978-1-58506-001-6(1), 02) New Life Inst OR.
Release your own perfect memory now - instantly & without effort.

Memory Power. 1 cass. (Running Time: 1 hr.). 10.95 (003) Psych Res Inst.
Learn faster & remember more by controlling the assimilation of facts & information.

Memory Power. Richard Jafolla & Mary-Alice Jafolla. Read by Richard Jafolla & Mary-Alice Jafolla. (Self-Improvement Ser.). 1986. 12.95 (250) Stppng Stones.
Motivational tapes that work on the subconscious mind (subliminal) & conscious mind to bring about self-improvement.

Memory Power. Steve Moidel. 6 cass. (Running Time: 5 hrs. 38 min.). 59.95 Set. (Q10121) CareerTrack Pubns.
Steve Moidel has spent years studying how the mind works. His proven methods can help you remember anything, without cumbersome mental tricks. You'll be more confident meeting people. You'll lose things less. You'll be more effective in your job.

Memory Power. Steve Moidel. 2 cass. (Running Time: 3 hrs.). 1995. 15.95 (978-1-55977-032-3(5)) CareerTrack Pubns.

Memory Quilt: A Christmas Story for Our Times. unabr. ed. T. D. Jakes. Read by T. D. Jakes. Read by C. C. H. Pounder. (Running Time: 4 hrs. 0 mins. 0 sec.). (ENG.). 2009. audio compact disk 29.99 (978-0-7435-9980-1(2)) Pub: S&S Audio. Dist(s): S and S Inc

Memory Stones. Kate O'Riordan. Read by Maureen O'Brien. 2003. 84.95 (978-0-7540-8418-1(3)) Pub: Chivers Audio Bks GBR. Dist(s): AudioGO

Memory Stretch for Adults, Vol. 2. 2001. 59.75i (978-1-883315-37-5(9)) Imaginart Intl.

Memory Stretch for Children. rev. ed. 2001. 52.75i (978-1-883315-36-8(0)) Imaginart Intl.

Memory Supercharger. Paul R. Scheele. 1 cass. (Running Time: 16 min.). (Paraliminal Tapes Ser.). 1989. 14.95 (978-0-925480-06-4(1)) Learn Strategies.
Designed to increase ones ability to remember facts principles, details and theories.

Memory Workshop; Memory Techniques That Will Help You Teach & Help Students to Learn. Robby Berman. 1 cass. (Running Time: 1 hr. 30 min.). 1999. 6.00 (W60SA) Torah Umesorah.

Memphis Ribs. abr. ed. Gerald Duff. 2 cass. (Running Time: 3 hrs.). 2004. 18.00 (978-1-58807-339-6(4)) Am Pubng Inc.
Memphis Ribs is a hard-boiled mystery about J.W. Ragsdale, Memphis Homicide Detective, who seeks the murderer of a tourist and a local society giant during the May International Barbecue Contest and the Cotton Carnival, two events spanning Memphis society and culture. Duff combines humor with what the Atlantic Monthly called a "grotesquely amusing and bloody version of the southern Gothic genre." Memphis Ribs pits the greed and arrogance of old money against the easy money of narcotics, masterfully capturing the intersection and dialect of both worlds.

Men, No. 1. 4 cass. (Running Time: 4 hrs.). 40.00 (978-1-893165-51-9(5)) Rational Isl.
Shared experiences of men, on being men & about using re-evaluation counseling.

Men, No. 2. 4 cass. (Running Time: 4 hrs.). 40.00 (978-1-893165-52-6(3)) Rational Isl.
Shared experiences of men, on being men & about men using re-evaluation counseling.

Men Against the Sea & Pitcairn's Island. unabr. ed. Charles Nordhoff & James Norman Hall. Read by Jonathan Reese. 11 cass. (Running Time: 16 hrs. 30 mins.). (Bounty Ser.: Pts. 2 & 3). 1978. 88.00 (1149-B) Books on Tape.
Set adrift, Captain Bligh sailed 3,600 miles. The mutineers remained aboard the "Bounty" & cast about for security. There was little respite for the crew.

Men & Cartoons. unabr. ed. Jonathan Lethem. 3 cass. (Running Time: 4 hrs. 30 min.). 2004. 36.00 (978-1-4159-0361-2(1)); audio compact disk 45.00 (978-1-4159-0782-5(X)) Books on Tape.
From Jonathan Lethem, author of the "New York Times" bestseller THE FORTRESS OF SOLITUDE, comes a new collection of stories that will be a feast for his fans and the perfect introduction for new listeners-a smorgasbord of fantastic, amusing, poignant tales written in a dizzying variety of styles. Lethem is a trailblazer of a new kind of literary fiction, sampling high and low culture to create fictional worlds that are utterly original.

Men & Depression (Suicide) Program from the Award Winning Public Radio Series. Hosted by Fred Goodwin. Comment by John Hockenberry. Contrib. by Gary Brooks et al. 1 cass. (Running Time: 1 hr.). (Infinite Mind Ser.). 1998. audio compact disk 21.95 (978-1-888064-33-9(1), LCM 29) Lichtenstein Creat.
Is our nation?s health care system able to help people suffering from depression? Tim Hogan, a Massachusetts newspaper publisher, repeatedly sought help but found none, and committed suicide. In an exclusive interview, his family speaks publicly for the first time. Experts and advocates say Hogan?s experience is common - and unacceptable.

Men & Dogs. unabr. ed. Katie Crouch. Read by Gabra Zackman. (Running Time: 9 hrs.). (ENG.). 2010. 24.98 (978-1-60788-184-1(5)); audio compact disk 29.98 (978-1-60788-183-4(7)) Pub: Hachet Audio. Dist(s): HachBkGrp

Men & Marriage, unabr. ed. George Gilder. Read by Michael Pocaro. 6 cass. (Running Time: 8 hrs. 30 mins.). 1988. 44.95 (978-0-7861-0006-4(0), 1005) Blckstn Audio.
Argues that "sexual liberation" leads inevitably to "social suicide" by desecrating the traditional family & fostering an onset of numerous pathologies including homosexuality, pornography, sexual license & violence.

Men & Songs. Perf. by James Taylor et al. 1 CD. Lifedance.

Men & the Girls. unabr. ed. Joanna Trollope. Read by Eleanor Bron. 8 cass. (Running Time: 12 hrs.). 2000. 59.95 (SAB 041) Pub: Chivers Audio Bks GBR. Dist(s): AudioGO
Lifelong friends now in their sixties, James and Hugh both live with women 25-years their junior! But the age gap is an inevitable complication, as Kate yearns for a life more suitable to her own age, while Julia's career blossoms. Both events threaten their relationships with James and Hugh, and the arrival of Beatrice Bachelor just fuels the fire.

Men & the Life of Desire. Robert Bly et al. Read by Robert Bly et al. 4 cass. (Running Time: 4 hrs.). 1991. 29.95 (978-1-880155-00-4(1), 796) Oral Trad Arch.
Digital/stereo live presentation addressing men's issues such as Initiation, The Hunger for the Father, Importance of Passion & Purpose. Includes story, poetry with sitar & tabla accompaniment & lively discussion.

Men & the Wound Pts. 1 & 2: The Iron John Story. Robert Bly. 1 cass. (Running Time: 1 hr. 30 min.). 1989. 10.00 (978-0-915408-39-9(2)) Ally Pr.
Discusses the subjects of male growth & healing ones own wounds in connection with the fairy tale "Iron John".

Men, & Their Fathers. Samuel Osherson. 3 cass. 27.00 (OC142) Sound Horizons AV.

Men & Their Feelings. Earnie Larsen. 1 cass. (Running Time: 1 hr.). 1989. 10.95 (978-1-56047-015-1(1), A119) E Larsen Enterprises.
Discusses what is the problem with men & their feelings.

***Men & Women: Enjoying the Difference.** abr. ed. Larry Crabb. (Running Time: 2 hrs. 0 mins. 0 sec.). (ENG.). 2003. 10.99 (978-0-310-26078-3(7)) Zondervan.

Men & Women: Talking Together. Deborah Tannen & Robert Bly. Read by Deborah Tannen. 2 cass. (Running Time: 2 hrs.). (Sound Horizons Presents Ser.). 1995. pap. bk. 16.95 (978-1-879323-09-4(5), SH10) Sound Horizons AV.
This live recording is based on an evening sponsored by the New York Open Center. The event paired Tannen & Bly, both best-selling authors whose recent books have examined gender-specific ideas about language & culture.

Men & Women: The Journey of Spiritual Transformation. Richard Rohr. 2 cass. (Running Time: 2 hrs. 43 mins.). 2001. 17.95 St Anthony Mess Pr.
Great spirituality shows us how to transform our pain and not inflict it on another. These talks explore how men and women approach that spiritualitydifferently in midlife.

Men & Women Are from Earth after All. John Bradshaw. 2 cass. (Running Time: 3 hrs.). 1999. 18.00 (70192) Courage-to-Change.
Clinical studies that offer extensive research on what factors constitute well-functioning relationships.

Men & Women Are from Earth after All: Effective Ways to Deal with Ten Problems Inherent in All Relationships. John Bradshaw. (Running Time: 10800 sec.). 2008. audio compact disk 100.00 (978-1-57388-070-1(1)) J B Media.

Men & Women Are from Earth, Afterall: Effective Ways to Deal with Ten Problems Inherent in All Relationships. John Bradshaw. Read by John Bradshaw. 2 cass. (Running Time: 3 hrs.). 1999. 18.00 (978-1-57388-069-5(8)) J B Media.
Identifies 10 reasons that destroy relationships, such as high expectations, inefficient communications, family rules, familiarity & need for parental-type of partner.

Men & Women Now. unabr. ed. Robert Bly. 5 cass. (Running Time: 1 hr. 22 min.). 1984. 46.00 (02804) Big Sur Tapes.
With music, myths, fairy stories & his great wit & humor, Bly explores the masculine & feminine archetype of men & women.

Men Are from GM, Women Are from Ford: Calls about Couples & Cars. abr. unabr. ed. Tom Magliozzi & Ray Magliozzi. 1 CD. (Running Time: 1 hr.). (ENG.). 2001. audio compact disk 13.95 (978-1-56511-562-0(7), 1565115627) Pub: HighBridge. Dist(s): Workman Pub

Men Are from GM...Women Are from Ford: Car Talk's Calls about Couples & Their Cars. Tom Magliozzi & Ray Magliozzi. 1 cass. 1998. 11.95 (978-1-55935-264-2(7)); audio compact disk 14.95 (978-1-55935-279-6(5)) Soundelux.
Probes the depths of our most intimate relationships under the guise of a weekly automotive repair call-in show.

***Men Are from Mars.** abr. ed. John Gray. Read by John Gray. (ENG.). 2005. (978-0-06-085648-9(3), Harper Audio); (978-0-06-085646-5(7), Harper Audio) HarperCollins Pubs.

Men Are from Mars, Women Are from Venus see Hombres Son de Marte, las Mujeres Son de Venus

Men Are from Mars, Women are from Venus see Hommes Viennent de Mars, les Femmes Viennent de Venus

Men Are from Mars, Women Are from Venus. abr. ed. John Gray & John Gray. Read by John Gray. (Running Time: 5400 sec.). 2007. audio compact disk 14.95 (978-0-06-123205-3(X)) HarperCollins Pubs.

***Men are from Mars, Women are from Venus.** unabr. ed. John Gray. Read by John Gray. (ENG.). 2005. (978-0-06-085644-1(0), Harper Audio); (978-0-06-085645-8(9), Harper Audio) HarperCollins Pubs.

Men Are from Mars, Women Are from Venus: A Practical Guide for Improving Communication & Getting What You Want in Your Relationships. John Gray. 12 cass. (Running Time: 12 hrs.). 99.98 set. (HA-2206) Gaiam Intl.

Men Are from Mars, Women Are from Venus: A Practical Guide for Improving Communication & Getting What You Want in Your Relationships. John Gray. 1 cass. (Running Time: 12 hrs.). 99.95 (A5490) Lghtwrks Aud & Vid.
John Gray's highly acclaimed, challenging, informative & uplifting seminar which illuminates such topics as: The Secrets of Passion; Understanding Martian & Venusian; Giving & Receiving Love; Lasting Intimacy & Fulfillment; Improving Communication; The Secrets of Great Sex.

Men Are from Mars, Women Are from Venus: A Practical Guide for Improving Communication & Getting What You Want in Your Relationships. John Gray. 12 cass. 99.95 Set. (11282PAM) Nightingale-Conant.
Uncover the seven secrets of creating & sustaining passionate relationships. Discover how to understand men's & women's intimacy cycles...communicate better in stressful times...& develop a balanced approach to loving based on respect & compassion. Men & women enter relationships looking to fill unique needs - needs you'll understand & appreciate with John Gray's revealing insights.

Men Are from Mars, Women Are from Venus: A Practical Guide for Improving Communication & Getting What You Want in Your Relationships. unabr. ed. John Gray. Read by Alexander Adams. 6 cass. (Running Time: 9 hrs.). 1995. 48.00 (978-0-7366-2917-1(3), 3614) Books on Tape.
Once upon a time Martians & venusians met, fell in love & were happy because they respected & accepted their differences. Then they came to Earth & amnesia set in: they forgot they were from different planets. Using this metaphor to illustrate common conflicts between men & women, Dr. John Gray shows how these differences can come between the sexes & strain loving relationships. His advice tells us how to counteract differences in communication styles, emotional needs & modes of behavior to promote a greater understanding between individual partners.

Men Are from Mars, Women Are from Venus: A Practical Guide for Improving Communication & Getting What You Want in Your Relationships, unabr. ed. John Gray. Narrated by George Guidall. 6 cass. (Running Time: 9 hrs. 15 mins.). 1994. 51.00 (978-0-7887-0084-2(7), 94324E7) Recorded Bks.
Based on over 20 years of successful counseling, Gray's proven, practical advice on understanding the different needs & communication styles of men & women is a step-by-step manual for creating deeper, more satisfying relationships.

Men Are from Mars, Women Are from Venus: A Practical Guide for Improving Communication & Getting What You Want in Your Relationships. unabr. ed. John Gray. Narrated by George Guidall. 8 CDs. (Running Time: 9 hrs. 15 mins.). 2000. audio compact disk 69.00 (978-0-7887-3400-7(8), C1006E7) Recorded Bks.

Men Are from Mars, Women Are from Venus: Secrets of Great Sex, Improving Communication, Lasting Intimacy & Fulfillment, Giving & Receiving Love. John Gray. 12 cass. (Running Time: 10 hrs.). (Secrets of Successful Relationships Ser.). 1995. 79.95 (978-1-886095-10-6(8)) Genesis Media Grp.
Interpersonal relations.

Men Are from Mars, Women Are from Venus; Children Are from Heaven, abr. ed. John Gray. Read by John Gray. 6 cass. 1999. 34.95 (FS9-51081) Highsmith.

Men Are from Mars, Women Are from Venus Reflections: Inspirations to Enrich Your Relationships, abr. ed. John Gray. Read by John Gray. 2 cass. 1999. 18.00 (FS9-43293) Highsmith.

Men Are Like Waffles Women Are Like Spaghetti: Understanding & Delighting in Your Differences. unabr. ed. Bill Farrel & Pam Farrel. (Running Time: 5 hrs. 43 mins. 37 sec.). (ENG.). 2008. 16.09 (978-1-60814-305-4(8)) Oasis Audio.

Men Are Like Waffles Women Are Like Spaghetti: Understanding & Delighting in Your Differences. unabr. ed. Bill Farrel & Pam Farrel. Read by Bill Farrel & Pam Farrel. (Running Time: 5 hrs. 43 mins. 37 sec.). (ENG.). 2008. audio compact disk 22.99 (978-1-59859-308-2(0)) Oasis Audio.

Men at Arms. unabr. ed. Terry Pratchett. Read by Nigel Planer. 9 CDs. (Running Time: 35100 sec.). (Discworld Ser.). 2007. audio compact disk 84.95 (978-0-7531-2256-3(1)) Pub: ISIS Audio GBR. Dist(s): Ulverscroft US

Men at Arms. unabr. ed. Terry Pratchett. Read by Nigel Planer. 8 cass. (Running Time: 10 hrs. 30 min.). (Discworld Ser.). (J). 1996. 69.95 (978-0-7531-0017-2(7), 960403) Pub: ISIS Lrg Prnt GBR. Dist(s): Ulverscroft US
Includes Corporal Carrot (technically a dwarf), Lance-constable Cuddy (really a dwarf), Lance-constable Detritus (a troll), Lance-constable Angua (a woman...most of the time) & Corporal Nobbs (disqualified from the human race for shoving). They need all the help they can get, because they've only got twenty-four hours to clean up the town & this is Ankh-Morpork we're talking about.

Men at Arms. unabr. collector's ed. Evelyn Waugh. Read by David Case. 6 cass. (Running Time: 9 hrs.). (World War II Trilogy). 1992. 48.00 (978-0-7366-2184-7(9), 2980) Books on Tape.
First volume in Waugh's masterful WW II trilogy about war, religion & politics. Meet Guy Crouchback, a 35-year-old, divorced Catholic, who joins the Royal Corps of Halberdiers.

Men at Work: The Craft of Baseball. unabr. collector's ed. George F. Will. Read by John MacDonald. 10 cass. (Running Time: 15 hrs.). 1990. 80.00 (978-0-7366-1798-7(1), 2635) Books on Tape.
Being an informed, observant baseball fan is a form of participation in that complex, subtle ritual. "Baseball," writes George F. Will, "is indeed a game, but one at which men work with admirable seriousness." It is best appreciated by those fans who understand the discipline & attention to detail practiced by players & managers. Based on his own extensive contacts with participants in this sport, Will treats the elements of the game by examining four men who are exemplars of its various crafts. The manager is Tony La Russa of the Oakland Athletics; the pitcher, Dodger Orel Hershiser, Tony Gwynn of the San Diego Padres represents batters, while Baltimore Orioles shortstop Cal Ripken exemplifies defense.

Men for All Seasons. Dick Rice. 6 cass. (Running Time: 6 hrs.). 1994. 44.95 (AA2610) Credence Commun.
Rice is conversant with the current men's issues (in the land of Robert Bly) & mixes them uncommonly well with sophisticated contemporary theology.

Men Healing Shame see Breaking the Shackles: Bringing Joy Into Our Lives

Men in Balance: The Mid-Life Make & the Healthy Psyche. John Lee. 2 cass. (Running Time: 2 hrs.). 1993. 16.95 Sound Horizons AV.

Men in Balance: The Mid-Life Male & the Healthy Psyche. John Lee. 2 cass. (Running Time: 2 hrs.). 1995. 16.95 (978-1-879323-13-1(3)) Sound Horizons AV.
The author of The Flying Boy & At My Father's Wedding posits the theory that the male psyche must be balanced between the masculine & feminine. It is the connection with both parts of himself that results in growth, change & healing.

Men in Black, unabr. ed. Spencer Scott. Narrated by Ron McLarty. 8 cass. (Running Time: 11 hrs.). 1999. 70.00 (978-0-7887-2936-2(5), 95677E7) Recorded Bks.
Is it possible to tell the truth in a culture of profitable lies? Such deeply serious themes are woven into this engaging story of a writer who becomes famous for all the wrong reasons. With his family in crisis due to his indiscretions, Sam Holland never dreams that his largely made-up primer on UFO's will become a best-seller.

Men in Black: How the Supreme Court Is Destroying America. Mark R. Levin. Intro. by Rush Limbaugh. (Running Time: 8 hrs. 0 mins.). 2005. audio compact disk 72.00 (978-0-7861-7898-8(1)) Blckstn Audio.

Men in Black: How the Supreme Court Is Destroying America. Mark R. Levin. Narrated by Jeff Riggenbach. (Running Time: 9 hrs.). 2005. 30.95 (978-1-59912-543-5(9)) Iofy Corp.

Men in Black: How the Supreme Court Is Destroying America. abr. ed. Mark R. Levin. Intro. by Rush Limbaugh. (Running Time: 8 hrs. 0 mins.). 2005. 59.95 (978-0-7861-3480-9(1)) Blckstn Audio.

Men in Black: How the Supreme Court Is Destroying America. unabr. ed. Mark R. Levin. Read by Jeff Riggenbach. Intro. by Rush Limbaugh. 8 CDs. (Running Time: 9 hrs.). 2005. audio compact disk 29.95 (978-0-7861-7925-1(2), ZE3461); 29.95 (978-0-7861-3482-3(8), E3461) Blckstn Audio.
These days the Constitution is no restraint on our out-of-control Supreme Court. The Court imperiously strikes down laws and imposes new ones purely on its own arbitrary whims. Even though liberals like John Kerry are repeatedly defeated at the polls, the majority on the allegedly "conservative" Supreme court reflects their views and wields absolute power. There's a word for this: tyranny. In Men in Black, radio talk show host and legal scholar Mark R. Levin dissects the judicial tyranny that is robbing us of our freedoms and stuffing the ballot box in favor of liberal policies. If you've ever wondered why no matter who holds political power American society always seems to drift to the left, Mark Levin has the answer: the black-robed justices of the Supreme Court, subverting democracy in favor of their own liberal agenda.

Men in Black: How the Supreme Court Is Destroying America. unabr. ed. Mark R. Levin. Read by Jeff Riggenbach. Intro. by Rush Limbaugh. 1 MP3. (Running Time: 9 hrs.). 2005. audio compact disk 29.95 (978-0-7861-8104-9(4), ZM3461) Blckstn Audio.

Men in Blue. unabr. collector's ed. W. E. B. Griffin. Read by Michael Prichard. 8 cass. (Running Time: 12 hrs.). (Badge of Honor Ser.: Vol. 1). 1993. 64.00 (978-0-7366-2482-4(1), 3244) Books on Tape.
City police force reels at the killing of a cop in the line of duty.

Men in Mid-Life Crisis. James C. Dobson. 1 cass. 1990. 10.99 (978-2-01-013973-4(9)) Nelson.
Discusses the book by Jim Conway entitled, "Men in Mid-life Crisis." Talks about the effect of mid-life crisis on a man's physical energy, job, wife, children & religious faith. Offers ten practical ideas that can help turn the crisis into opportunity for personal & spiritual growth.

Men in White Apparel: Revelations about Death & the Life after Death. Ann Ree Colton. 1 cass. (Running Time: 90 mins.). 2000. 18.95 (978-0-917189-28-9(0)) A R Colton Fnd.
Prepares individuals for the death experience & explains how they may sensitively minister to the dying, the dead & the bereaved. Also writes of the men in white apparel & other spiritual beings who watch over, instruct & shepherd the dead.

Men, Love & Sex: The Complete Users Guide for Women. unabr. ed. David Zinczenko. Read by Stephen Hoye. 5 CDs. (Running Time: 5 hrs. 0 mins. 0 sec.). (ENG.). 2006. audio compact disk 24.99 (978-1-4001-0317-1(7)) Pub: Tantor Media. Dist(s): IngramPubServ

Men, Love & Sex: The Complete Users Guide for Women. unabr. ed. David Zinczenko. Read by Stephen Hoye. Told to Ted Spiker. (Running Time: 5 hrs. 0 mins. 0 sec.). (ENG.). 2006. audio compact disk 49.99 (978-1-4001-3317-8(3)) Pub: Tantor Media. Dist(s): IngramPubServ

Men, Love & Sex: The Complete User's Guide for Women: Thousands of Men Confess Their Well-Guarded Secrets about How They Think, Feel, & Behave! unabr. ed. David Zinczenko. Read by Stephen Hoye. Told to Ted Spiker. (Running Time: 5 hrs. 0 mins. 0 sec.). (ENG.). 2006. audio compact disk 19.99 (978-1-4001-5317-6(4)) Pub: Tantor Media. Dist(s): IngramPubServ

Men of Brewster Place. unabr. ed. Gloria Naylor. Read by Richard Allen. 4 vols. (Running Time: 6 Hrs.). 2000. bk. 39.95 (978-0-7927-2415-5(1), CSL 304, Chivers Sound Lib) AudioGO.
Gloria Naylor brings alive the voices of the men of Brewster Place with her characteristic grace, humor & compassion.

Men of Brewster Place. unabr. ed. Gloria Naylor. 2004. 15.95 (978-0-7435-4132-9(4)) Pub: S&S Audio. Dist(s): S and S Inc

Men of Fire: Grant, Forrest, & the Campaign That Decided the Civil War. unabr. ed. Jack Hurst. Read by Tom Weiner. (Running Time: 48600 sec.). 2007. 79.95 (978-0-7861-6811-8(0)); audio compact disk 99.00 (978-0-7861-6810-1(2)) Blckstn Audio.

Men of Fire: Grant, Forrest & the Campaign That Decided the Civil War. unabr. ed. Jack Hurst. Read by Tom Weiner. (Running Time: 48600 sec.). (ENG.). 2007. audio compact disk 29.95 (978-0-7861-6960-3(5)) Blckstn Audio.

Men of Fire: Grant, Forrest & the Campaign That Decided the Civil War. unabr. ed. Jack Hurst. Read by Tom Weiner. (Running Time: 48600 sec.). (ENG.). 2007. 32.95 (978-0-7861-4977-3(9)); audio compact disk 32.95 (978-0-7861-5787-7(9)) Blckstn Audio.

Men of Forty Mile see Son of the Wolf

Men of God. (Dovetales Ser.: Tape 7). pap. bk. 6.95 (978-0-944391-42-6(7)); 4.95 (978-0-944391-22-8(2)) DonWise Prodns.

***Men of God.** 2010. audio compact disk (978-0-9769068-8-9(0)) Mid A Bks & Tapes.

Men of Gospo: Volume 1. Contrib. by Vicki Mack Lataillade & Claude Lataillade. 2005. audio compact disk 13.99 (978-5-558-69494-9(7)) Pt of Grace Ent.

Men of Gospo, Vol. 2. Contrib. by Vicki Mack Lataillade & Claude Lataillade. 2006. audio compact disk 13.99 (978-5-558-26034-2(3)) GospoCen.

Men of Iron. Howard Pyle. Read by Robert Whitfield. (Running Time: 7 hrs.). 2003. 27.95 (978-1-59912-544-2(7)) Iofy Corp.

Men of Iron. unabr. ed. Howard Pyle. Read by Robert Whitfield. 5 cass. (Running Time: 7 hrs.). 2003. 39.95 (978-0-7861-2421-3(0), 3087); audio compact disk 40.00 (978-0-7861-9241-0(0), 3087) Blckstn Audio.

Men of Iron. unabr. ed. Howard Pyle. Read by Ian Richardson. 1 cass. 1984. 12.95 (978-0-694-50359-9(2), SWC 1704) HarperCollins Pubs.
men.

Men of Men. Wilbur Smith. 2 cass. (Running Time: 3 hrs.). (ENG., 2001. (978-0-333-78239-2(9)) Macmillan UK GBR.

Men of Men. unabr. ed. Wilbur Smith. Read by Stephen Thorne. 16 cass. (Running Time: 24 hrs.). (Ballantyne Novel Ser.). 2000. 99.95 (978-0-7540-0316-8(7), CAB 1739) Pub: Chivers Audio Bks GBR. Dist(s): AudioGO
After the prospectors and hunters had opened the way to the African interior, the miners and adventurers followed. Watch the strange genius of Cecil Rhodes forging an empire based on diamonds and land, and the tragedy of a tribe dispossessed by greed and ambition.

Men of Men, Pt. 1. unabr. collector's ed. Wilbur Smith. Read by Richard Brown. 9 cass. (Running Time: 13 hrs. 30 min.). (Ballantyne Novels Ser.). 1989. 72.00 (978-0-7366-1645-4(4), 2498-A) Books on Tape.
During the reign of Queen Victoria, Englishmen answering the call of Empire voyaged out to take possession of half their known world. In Africa some pioneers headed north from the Cape in search of gold & loot or cattle & land. Others went for glory & the pursuit of a dream. For Zouga Ballantyne the dream of the north began in the danger & drudgery of the diamond pits of Kimberly & ended on the rich grasslands of Matabeleland below the Zambezi River - but not before a king had died & a nation of proud warriors had been shattered.

Men of Men, Pt. 2. collector's unabr. ed. Wilbur Smith. Read by Richard Brown. 9 cass. (Running Time: 13 hrs. 30 min.). (Ballantyne Novels Ser.). 1989. 72.00 (978-0-7366-1646-1(2), 2498-B) Books on Tape.

Men of the Open Range. Mike Logan. 9.95 (978-1-56044-343-8(X), Fal) Globe Pequot.

***Men of the Otherworld.** Kelley Armstrong. Narrated by Charles Leggett. (Running Time: 11 hrs. 5 mins. 0 sec.). (ENG.). 2011. audio compact disk 29.95 (978-1-60998-195-2(2)) Pub: AudioGO. Dist(s): Perseus Dist

Men of the Otherworld. unabr. ed. Kelley Armstrong. Narrated by Charles Leggett. 9 CDs. (Running Time: 11 hrs.). 2009. audio compact disk 89.95 (978-0-7927-6046-7(8)) AudioGO.

Men of Valor: The Powerful Impact of a Righteous Man. Robert Millet. 2008. audio compact disk 19.95 (978-1-59038-934-8(4)) Deseret Bk.

Men Talking about Women: Conversations & Teaching on Beauty & Sexuality. Featuring John Eldredge et al. 2007. audio compact disk 36.00 (978-1-933207-23-0(X)) Ransomed Heart.

Men That Don't Fit In see Poetry of Robert W. Service

Men to Match My Mountains: The Opening of the West 1840-1900. unabr. ed. Irving Stone. Read by John MacDonald. 14 cass. (Running Time: 21 hrs.). 1983. 112.00 (978-0-7366-0669-1(6), 1631) Books on Tape.

Men Who Hate Women & the Women Who Love Them. Susan Forward. 1 cass. 1987. 7.95 (978-0-553-45080-4(8), Random AudioBks) Random Audio Pubg.

***men who stare at Goats.** Jon Ronson. Read by Sean Mangan. (Running Time: 7 hrs. 20 mins.). 2010. 79.99 (978-1-74214-806-9(9), 9781742148069) Pub: Bolinda Pubng AUS. Dist(s): Bolinda Pub Inc

Men Who Stare at Goats. unabr. ed. Jon Ronson. Read by Sean Mangan. (Running Time: 26400 sec.). 2006. audio compact disk 83.95 (978-1-74093-728-3(7)) Pub: Bolinda Pubng AUS. Dist(s): Bolinda Pub Inc

***Men Who Stare at Goats.** unabr. movie tie-in ed. Jon Ronson. Read by Sean Mangan. 2009. audio compact disk 83.95 (978-1-74214-572-3(8), 9781742145723) Pub: Bolinda Pubng AUS. Dist(s): Bolinda Pub Inc

***Men Who Stare at Goats.** unabr. movie tie-in ed. Jon Ronson. Read by Sean Mangan. 2010. 43.95 (978-1-74214-590-7(6), 9781742145907) Pub: Bolinda Pubng AUS. Dist(s): Bolinda Pub Inc

***Men Who Would Be King: An Almost Epic Tale of Moguls, Movies, & a Company Called DreamWorks.** unabr. ed. Nicole LaPorte. (Running Time: 18 hrs. 30 mins.). 2010. 22.99 (978-1-4001-8647-1(1)) Tantor Media.

***Men Who Would Be King: An Almost Epic Tale of Moguls, Movies, & a Company Called DreamWorks.** unabr. ed. Nicole LaPorte. Narrated by Stephen Hoye. (Running Time: 18 hrs. 0 mins. 0 sec.). 2010. 34.99 (978-1-4001-6647-3(0)); audio compact disk 49.99 (978-1-4001-1647-8(3)); audio compact disk 99.99 (978-1-4001-4647-5(X)) Pub: Tantor Media. Dist(s): IngramPubServ

***Men, Women & Relationships.** abr. ed. John Gray. Read by John Gray. (ENG.). 2005. (978-0-06-085632-8(7), Harper Audio); (978-0-06-085633-5(5), Harper Audio) HarperCollins Pubs.

Men, Women & Relationships: Making Peace with the Opposite Sex. abr. ed. John Gray. Read by John Gray. 1 cass. (Running Time: 1 hr. 30 min.). 1995. 12.00 (978-0-694-51534-9(5), CPN 10052) HarperCollins Pubs.

Men, Women, Marriage & Sex. Asha Praver. 1 cass. (Running Time: 1 hr. 30 min.). (Relationship Ser.). 9.95 (AT-51) Crystal Clarity.
Includes: Why marriages fail; do we neccessarily marry our "soul-mates"?; the spiritual purposes of marriage; ways of measuring the success of marriage; harmonizing the magnetism between husband & wife.

Menace from Earth. unabr. ed. Robert A. Heinlein. Read by Rob McQuay. 5 cass. (Running Time: 7 hrs. 30 min.). 1997. 39.95 (978-0-7861-1158-9(5), 1928) Blckstn Audio.
Startling stories of time & space from a master of science fiction.

Menace from Earth & Other Stories. unabr. ed. Robert A. Heinlein. Read by Rob McQuay. (Running Time: 7 hrs.). 1998. 24.95 (978-0-7861-9320-2(4)) Blckstn Audio.

Menace in Europe: Why the Continent's Crisis Is America's, Too. unabr. ed. Claire Berlinski. Read by Nadia May. (Running Time: 34200 sec.). 2006. audio compact disk 81.00 (978-0-7861-6788-3(2)); audio compact disk 29.95 (978-0-7861-7420-1(X)) Blckstn Audio.

Menace in Europe: Why the Continent's Crisis Is America's Too. unabr. ed. Claire Berlinski. Read by Nadia May. (Running Time: 34200 sec.). 2006. 65.95 (978-0-7861-4648-2(6)) Blckstn Audio.

Menage Outre: The Jarabon. Lee Killough. 1 cass. (Running Time: 1 hr.). Dramatization. 1985. 7.95 (AS001) Audio Saga.
This cassette features two science fiction stories. "Menage Outre", takes place in Aventina, haven for the rich & famous; "The Jarabon," concerns a beautiful professional thief & her mission to secure a rare carved jewel, the Jarabon.

Menagerie. unabr. ed. Catherine Cookson. Read by Susan Jameson. 6 cass. (Running Time: 6 hrs.). 1993. bk. 54.95 (978-0-7451-5865-5(X), CAB 172) AudioGO.

Mencken: A Life. unabr. ed. Fred Hobson. Read by Alexander Adams. 15 cass. (Running Time: 22 hrs. 30 mins.). 1995. 120.00 (978-0-7366-2947-8(5), 3641) Books on Tape.
This landmark biography gives intimate details about H.L. Mencken's complex life. It wasn't all beer & skittles.

Mencken: the American Iconoclast: The Life & Times of the Bad Boy of Baltimore. unabr. ed. Marion Elizabeth Rodgers. Read by Anthony Heald. (Running Time: 2 hrs. 0 mins.). (ENG.). 2009. 44.95 (978-1-4332-2281-8(7)); audio compact disk 140.00 (978-1-4332-2278-8(7)) Blckstn Audio.

Mencken: the American Iconoclast Part A: The Life & Times of the Bad Boy of Baltimore. unabr. ed. Marion Elizabeth Rodgers. Read by Anthony Heald. 9 cass. (Running Time: 11 hrs. 30 mins.). 2009. 69.95 (978-1-4332-2277-1(9)) Blckstn Audio.

Mencken: the American Iconoclast Part B: The Life & Times of the Bad Boy of Baltimore. unabr. ed. Marion Elizabeth Rodgers. 8 cass. (Running Time: 12 hrs, 30 mins.). 2009. 45.00 (978-1-4332-8918-7(0)) Blckstn Audio.

***Mendacity of Hope: Barack Obama & the Betrayal of American Liberalism.** unabr. ed. Roger D. Hodge. 2010. (978-0-06-204713-7(2), Harper Audio) HarperCollins Pubs.

Mendeleyev & the Periodic Table. unabr. ed. Katherine White. Read by Jay A. Snyder. 1 MP3-CD. (Running Time: 1 hr.). (Primary Sources of Revolutionary Scientific Discoveries & Theories Ser.). 2009. 39.97 (978-1-4233-8216-4(1), 9781423382164, Brinc Audio MP3 Lib); 19.99 (978-1-4233-8215-7(3), 9781423382157, Brilliance MP3); 39.97 (978-1-4233-8217-1(X), 9781423382171, BADLE) Brilliance Audio.

Mendeleyev & the Periodic Table. unabr. ed. Katherine White. Read by Jay A. Snyder & Jay Snyder. 2 CDs. (Running Time: 1 hr.). (Primary Sources of Revolutionary Scientific Discoveries & Theories Ser.). 2009. audio compact disk 19.99 (978-1-4233-8213-3(7), 9781423382133, Bril Audio CD Unabri) Brilliance Audio.

Mendeleyev & the Periodic Table. unabr. ed. Katherine White. Read by Jay A. Snyder. 2 CDs. (Running Time: 1 hr.). (Primary Sources of Revolutionary Scientific Discoveries & Theories Ser.). 2009. audio compact disk 39.97 (978-1-4233-8214-0(5), 9781423382140, BriAudCD Unabrid) Brilliance Audio.

Mendelssohn - Violin Concerto in E Minor, Op. 64: 2-CD Set. Composed by Felix Mendelssohn. 2006. pap. bk. 34.98 (978-1-59615-098-0(X), 159615098X) Pub: Music Minus. Dist(s): H Leonard

Mendelssohn & Brahms: Sacred Motets. Gloriae Dei Cantores. 1 CD. 2000. audio compact disk 16.95 (978-1-55725-243-2(2), GDCD107) Paraclete MA.

Mending a Relationship. Richard Jafolla & Mary-Alice Jafolla. Read by Richard Jafolla & Mary-Alice Jafolla. (Relationships Ser.). 1986. 12.95 (340) Stppng Stones.
Motivational tapes that work on the subconscious mind (subliminal) & conscious mind to bring about self-improvement.

Mending at the Edge. unabr. ed. Jane Kirkpatrick. Read by Kirsten Potter. (Running Time: 13 hrs. 18 mins. 0 sec.). (ENG.). 2008. audio compact disk 28.98 (978-1-59644-571-0(8)) christianaud.

***Mending at the Edge: A Novel.** unabr. ed. Jane Kirkpatrick. Narrated by Potter Kirsten. (Yasmin Peace Ser.). (ENG.). 2008. 16.98 (978-1-59644-572-7(6), christaudio) christianaud.

***Mending Hearts & Minds: A Steo-by-Step Program that will Help you Guide your Children in Healing the Heartbreak of Divorce.** Jim Fogarty Ed.D. Ed. by Melissa Reinke. Prod. by Cross Country Publishing. Des. by Caryn Baker. (ENG.). 2010. pap. bk. 279.00 (978-0-615-41240-5(8)) CrossCountry.

***Mending the Broken Heart: After Your Child Dies.** (ENG.). 2008. audio compact disk 15.00 (978-0-9822444-0-1(1)) BKaminsky.

***Mending the Soul: Understanding & Healing Abuse.** Zondervan. (Running Time: 9 hrs. 53 mins. 40 sec.). (ENG.). 2010. 9.99 (978-0-310-86905-4(6)) Zondervan.

Mending Wall see Robert Frost Reads

Mending Your Heart in a Broken World. abr. ed. Patsy Clairmont. (ENG.). 2005. 14.98 (978-1-59483-397-7(4)) Pub: Hachet Audio. Dist(s): HachBkGrp

Menendez Murders. A. C. Torkle. Read by A. C. Torkle. 1 cass. (Running Time: 1 hr. 30 min.). 1994. 8.95 (1101) Am Fed Astrologers.
Examination of the Menendez murders.

Menkes Syndrome - A Bibliography & Dictionary for Physicians, Patients, & Genome Researchers. Compiled by Icon Group International, Inc. Staff. 2007. ring bd. 28.95 (978-0-497-11256-1(6)) Icon Grp.

Menninger Talks. Ram Dass. 3 cass. (Running Time: 4 hrs. 30 min.). 1970. 26.00 Big Sur Tapes.
In the Spring of 1970, the Menninger Foundation in Kansas, hosted an afternoon of conversations with Baba Ram Dass. The recordings will be of special interest to the intellectual community particularly because of provocative questions asked by Menninger staff members.

***Mennonite in a Little Black Dress: A Memoir of Going Home.** Rhoda Janzen. Read by Hillary Huber. (ENG.). 2009. 44.99 (978-1-61587-608-2(1)) Find a World.

Mennonite in a Little Black Dress: A Memoir of Going Home. unabr. ed. Rhoda Janzen. Read by Hillary Huber. (ENG.). 2009. audio compact disk 29.95 (978-1-59887-907-0(3), 1598879073) Pub: HighBridge. Dist(s): Workman Pub

Meno. (70) Halvorson Assocs.

Menopausal Lust: Poems by Sue Silvermarie. unabr. ed. Sue Silvermarie. Read by Sue Silvermarie. Ed. by Deby DeWeese. 1 cass. (Running Time: 59 min.). 1994. 10.00 (978-1-881926-03-0(6)) Lavender Tapes.
Erotic poetry by Milwaukee poet Sue Silvermarie.

Menopause. Read by David D. Federman. 1 cass. (Running Time: 1 hr. 30 min.). 1986. 12.00 (C8610) Amer Coll Phys.

Menopause. unabr. ed. Mercedes Leidlich. Read by Mercedes Leidlich. 1 cass. (Running Time: 1 hr.). 1992. 10.95 (978-1-882174-09-6(7), MLL-010) UFD Pub.
This tape explains the physiology of menopause, symptoms, & various available treatments.

Menopause: A Wholistic Approach. Perf. by Mariposa Bernstien. 1 cass. (Way of Life Lecture Ser.: Vol. 2). 6.95 (978-0-9657944-2-8(3)) Guinea Pig.
Live lecture covering all aspects from a health & wellness pespective.

Menopause: Initiation into Power. Joan Borysenko. 4 CDs. 2004. audio compact disk 29.95 (978-1-59179-187-4(1), AW00822D) Sounds True.
Perhaps there is no more significant time in a woman?s life than when she experiences menopause. Joan Borysenko, Ph.D. ? author of the classic New York Times Bestseller Minding the Body, Mending the Mind ? refers to this compelling time in the feminine life cycle as ?The Guardian? stage, when women become passionate protectors of their highest values. What are the essential steps we need to take at this crucial point in our lives?On Menopause: Initiation into Power, Joan Borysenko brings together her unique training as a medical scientist, clinical psychologist, and teacher at Harvard Medical School to examine the ?mid-life metamorphosis? from our 40s to our 60s. It is at this stage when a woman?s focus extends beyond family and friends into an expansive view of her place in the whole of life. It is a time when her authentic self boldly emerges.

Menopause - Emerging Issues. Contrib. by William C. Andrews et al. 1 cass. (American College of Obstetrics & Gynecologists UPDATE: Vol. 21, No. 3). 1998. 20.00 Am Coll Obstetric.

Menopause & Beyond: New Wisdom for Women. Christiane Northrup. 2 CDs. (ENG.). 2011. audio compact disk 18.95 (978-1-4019-1842-2(5)) Hay House.

Menopause & the Mind: Program from the Award Winning Public Radio Series. Interview. Hosted by Fred Goodwin. Comment by John Hockenberry. 1 CD. (Running Time: 1 hr). (Infinite Mind Ser.). 1999. audio compact disk 21.95 (978-1-932479-14-0(7), LCM 82) Lichtenstein Creat.
As thousands of boomers approach 50, we explore what happens to a woman's mind during menopause. Mood swings and memory loss are common complaints. With the latest science, menopause poetry and commentary by John Hockenberry.

Menopause Is No Longer a Mystery: How the Change Can Bring You Joy, Love & Laughter. Illus. by Angela Brown. Voice by Terri Malucci. Prod. by Les Lingle. 1 cass. (Running Time: 30 mins.). (Words of Wellness - Your Show for Simple Solutions Ser.: Vol. 327). 2000. 12.95 (978-1-930995-20-8(2)) Life Long Pubg.
Feeling bloated, sweaty & irritable doesn't have to wreck your day. Realize you are not going through "The Change" alone & learn what other women are doing to make the most of things.

Menorah Men. unabr. collector's ed. Lionel Davidson. Read by Rupert Keenlyside. 6 cass. (Running Time: 9 hrs.). 1982. 48.00 (978-0-7366-0342-3(5), 1328) Books on Tape.
Caspar Laing, a young British archeologist, is persuaded to travel to Israel to decipher a recently discovered scroll. Its contents set him hot on the trail of the long-lost Menorah. Accompanied by Shoshana, a dusky Yemenite soldier who is his chaffeuse, Laing scours the Holy Land in a dangerous search for a priceless buried treasure.

Men's Casual Fashion in Japan: A Strategic Reference 2003. Compiled by Icon Group International, Inc. Staff. 2007. ring bd. 195.00 (978-0-497-82330-6(6)) Icon Grp.

Men's Cosmetics & Toiletries in Taiwan: A Strategic Reference 2006. Compiled by Icon Group International, Inc. Staff. 2007. ring bd. 195.00 (978-0-497-82432-7(9)) Icon Grp.

Men's Dreams, Men's Healing. Robert H. Hopcke. Read by Tony Kahn. 2 cass. (Running Time: 2 hrs.). 2001. 16.95 (AZ00011, Shmbhala Lion) Pub: Shambhala Pubns. Dist(s): Sounds True

Men's Health in Action: Master Your Health for Personal & Business Success, Vol. 1. Gary S. Ross. Interview with Kathleen S. Ross. 2 cass. 1998. 24.00 (978-1-891875-07-6(8), NTS010) Creat Hlth Wrks.
Tells how to take action on: male menopause, prostate enlargement, low hormones, aches & pains, sexual function, brain function, atherscIerosis & more. Includes script & boxed set includes booklet.

Men's Private Parts. James H. Gilbaugh, Jr. Read by Robert Whitfield. (Running Time: 3 hrs. 30 mins.). 2004. 22.95 (978-1-59912-545-9(5)) Iofy Corp.

Men's Private Parts. unabr. ed. James H. Gilbaugh, Jr. Read by Jeff Riggenbach. 3 cass. (Running Time: 4 hrs.). 2004. 32.95 (978-0-7861-2795-5(3), 3322); audio compact disk 32.00 (978-0-7861-8481-1(7), 3322) Blckstn Audio.
Dr. James H. Gilbaugh, Jr., a board-certified urologist and fellow of the American College of Surgeons with twenty-five years of clinical practice, presents the latest medical information for men in a straightforward, friendly, and accessible style. In addition to putting locker-room misconceptions to rest he offers plain explanations of the workings of the unique male system and the best, most up-to-date medical advice.

Men's Work: How to Stop the Violence That Tears Our Lives Apart. Paul Kivel. 1 cass. (Running Time: 1 hr.). bk. 11.00 (978-0-89486-827-6(6), 5658) Hazelden.
Hear echoes of the past as a father chastises a son. Reassess relationships as a young man pushes a date for "more". Paul Kivel paints a vivid picture of the effects of violence in men's lives in this audio adaptation. You'll hear Kivel's new approach for changing abusive control to loving power.

Mensaje de Garcia. abr. ed. Charles Patrick Garcia. Narrated by Jose Duarte & Luis Perez Pons. (SPA.). 2009. 59.99 (978-1-61545-570-6(1)) Find a World.

Mensaje de Garcia. abr. ed. Charles Patrick Garcia. 4 CDs. (Running Time: 3.5 Hrs). (SPA.). 2005. audio compact disk 29.95 (978-0-9728598-7-5(X)) Fonolibro Inc.
Un verdadero triunfador en el mundo norteamericano de los negocios pone al alcance de todos, las ideas mas novedosas-aterrizadas en pasos concretos- para alcanzar el exito empresarial, la satisfaccion en la vida y la realizacion de los sue?os personales.?Que es lo mas importante para alcanzar el exito? El autor responde: ?Saber que es, donde se encuentra y como obtenerlo;? asi, nos explica que todas estas respuestas se encuentran dentro de nosotros mismos. El exito no es una oportunidad fortuita ni un acto del destino, ni un cumulo de sacrificios que producen ganancias materiales, como tampoco se trata de un titulo de reconocimiento publico. Todo lo anterior son productos colaterales inherentes al exito real y perdurable: lograr nuestros sue?os.

Mensaje de los Sabios. Camilo Cruz. 2 cass. (Running Time: 2 hrs.).Tr. of Unleashing the Power of the Subconscious Mind. (SPA.). 2002. (978-1-931059-29-9(2)) Taller del Exito.
Provides strategies for tapping into the limitless power of the subconscious mind. Discover how your internal dialog and your beliefs can program your mind for success or failure.

Mensaje De los Sabios: Descubra El Poder Ilimitado De la Mente Subconsciente. Camilo Cruz. 2003. (978-1-931059-35-0(7)) Taller del Exito.

***Mensajes de Navidad y Año Nuevo.** Charles R. Swindoll.Tr. of Christmas & New Year Messages. 2009. audio compact disk 15.00 (978-1-57972-870-0(7)) Insight Living.

Mensajes 1. Neus Sans & Lourdes Miguel. (SPA.). 2001. 10.00 (978-84-8323-240-8(5)) Cambridge U Pr.

Mensajes 1. Neus Sans & Lourdes Miguel. (Running Time: 24 mins.). (SPA.). 2001. audio compact disk 10.00 (978-84-8323-234-7(0)) Cambridge U Pr.

Mensajes 2. Neus Sans & Lourdes Miguel. 2 cass. (SPA.). 2001. 10.00 (978-84-8323-242-2(1)); audio compact disk 10.00 (978-84-8323-235-4(9)) Cambridge U Pr.

Mensajes 3. Neus Sans & Lourdes Miguel. 3 cass. (SPA.). 2002. 10.00 (978-84-8323-243-9(X)); audio compact disk 10.00 (978-84-8323-237-8(5)) Cambridge U Pr.

Mensajes 4. Neus Sans & Lourdes Miguel. (SPA.). 2002. (978-84-8323-245-3(6)); audio compact disk 14.00 (978-84-8323-239-2(1)) Cambridge U Pr.

Menschen um Mueller: Textbuch. E. Mueller. (GER., (C). 1978. 33.25 (978-3-12-558570-6(8)) Pub: Klett Ernst Verlag DEU. Dist(s): Intl Bk Import

Mental Alchemy - How to Handle Discordant Aspects. Joan Titsworth. 1 cass. 8.95 (468) Am Fed Astrologers.

Mental & Physical Purity. Swami Jyotirmayananda. 1 cass. (Running Time: 1 hr.). 1990. 12.99 Yoga Res Foun.

Mental Attitudes Affect Physical Health. Instructed by Manly P. Hall. 8.95 (978-0-89314-182-0(8), C861019) Philos Res.

Mental Balance. Carlos Gonzalez. 1 CD. (Running Time: 40 mins). 2003. audio compact disk 15.00 (978-1-56491-117-9(9)) Imagine Pubs.

Mental Bank Review. John G. Kappas. 1 cass. (Running Time: 2 hrs.). 1986. 49.95 (978-0-937671-66-5(5), 66-5) Panorama Van Nuys.
Success motivation concept based on reprogramming subconscious life scripting. Details a step-by-step process to help the user to achieve individual goals of success, happiness & prosperity.

Mental Cleanse Summer 2004. 2004. audio compact disk 40.00 (978-1-890246-89-1(1)) B Katie Int Inc.

Mental Codes 2-CD Set: Secret Powers of the Mind CD. Michael J. Duckett & Leslie P. Duckett. (ENG.). 2007. audio compact disk 19.95 (978-0-9800797-1-5(3)) Hyper Pub.

Mental Diseases. Swami Jyotirmayananda. 1 cass. (Running Time: 45 min.). 1990. 10.00 Yoga Res Foun.

Mental Disorders in Primary Care. Jeanne Miranda. (Health Ser.). 1994. bk. 62.50 (978-1-55542-660-6(3), Jossey-Bass) Wiley US.

Mental Edge MLM: How to Master Your Mind & Emotions & Influence the Actions of Your Prospects. Randy Gage & Peter Pearson. 6 CDs. 2004. audio compact disk 147.00 (978-0-9744363-2-6(1)) Prime Concepts Grp.

***Mental Floss: Cocktail Party Cheat Sheets.** abr. ed. Mental Floss Editors. (ENG.). 2006. (978-0-06-135556-1(9), Harper Audio) HarperCollins Pubs.

Mental Floss History of the World: An Irreverent Romp Through Civilization's Best Bits. unabr. ed. Steve Wiegand & Erik Sass. Narrated by Johnny Heller. (Running Time: 15 hrs. 0 mins. 0 sec.). (ENG.). 2008. audio compact disk 79.99 (978-1-4001-3970-5(8)) Pub: Tantor Media. Dist(s): IngramPubServ

Mental Floss History of the World: An Irreverent Romp Through Civilization's Best Bits. unabr. ed. Steve Wiegand & Erik Sass. Read by Johnny Heller. 12 CDs. (Running Time: 15 hrs. 0 mins. 0 sec.). (ENG.). 2008. audio compact disk 39.99 (978-1-4001-0970-8(1)); audio compact disk 29.99 (978-1-4001-5970-3(9)) Pub: Tantor Media. Dist(s): IngramPubServ

Mental Health & Primary Care: Program from the Award Winning Public Radio Series. Interview. Hosted by Fred Goodwin. 1 CD. (Running Time: 1 hr). 2003. audio compact disk 21.95 (978-1-932479-64-5(3), LCM 292) Lichtenstein Creat.
In this hour, we explore the connections and misconnections between Mental Health and Primary Care. Guests include Dr. Harold Pincus, executive vice chairman of the department of psychiatry at the University of Pittsburgh School of Medicine and national director of the Robert Wood Johnson Depression in Primary Care program; Dr. Allen Dietrich, a family physician and professor in the department of community and family medicine at Dartmouth College and co-chair of the MacArthur Initiative on Depression and Primary Care; Dr. Barbara Yawn, director of research at the Olmsted Medical Center, a multi-specialty medical clinic in Rochester, Minnesota; and Dr. Michael Jellinek, professor of psychiatry and pediatrics at Harvard Medical school, chief of the child psychiatry service at Massachusetts General Hospital and president of Newton Wellesley Hospital.

Mental Health Care for Latinos: Program from the Award Winning Public Radio Series. Hosted by Fred Goodwin. 1 CD. (Running Time: 1hr). 2003. audio compact disk 21.95 (978-1-932479-65-2(1), LCM 299) Lichtenstein Creat.
More than one in eight people in the United States are of Hispanic origin. The majority of children born in California are Latino. And yet, Latinos are falling through the cracks of the mental health system. As a caller on the program comments, "In my culture, in Mexico, going to a psychologist means I'm crazy, I'm loco." On this The Infinite Mind program, we go Between Two Worlds, to investigate Mental Health Care for Latinos. Language is often a barrier. Dr. Roberto Lewis-Fernandez, a psychiatrist at Columbia University says, "If someone thinks they're being attacked spiritually, you have to begin with an understanding of that language." Almost a third of all Latinos lack health insurance. As Alba Cuevas, who suffers from depression, puts it, "All they can do is stay at home and hope they'll get better by themselves." What needs to change? We'll visit a program in Dallas that works - patients never miss their appointments. Plus, we'll talk to Elena Avila, a curandera, or traditional folk healer, who tackles depression with rituals: "I finish with the rosemary that I pass all over the body, and the last thing I do is I pass the eagle feather or the condor feather." And writer Judith Ortiz Cofer discusses her new novel, a coming-of-age tale set in her native Puerto Rico, and describes how her own family dealt with her father's depression. (60 minutes).

Mental Health in Troubled Times: Program from the Award Winning Public Radio Series. Interview. Hosted by Fred Goodwin. 1 CD. (Running Time: 1 hr). 2001. audio compact disk 21.95 (978-1-932479-66-9(X), LCM 185) Lichtenstein Creat.
We explore Mental Health in Troubled Times with a compilation of common sense, science and psychology on topics such as courage, altruism, trauma, grieving, group psychology, and anxiety from some of our best programs.According to a recent study by the Pew Research Center, 7 out of 10 Americans feel depressed, nearly half have had trouble concentrating, and nearly one-third report having trouble sleeping at night. We offer insight into these reactions and perspective on a range of psychological issues now affecting all of our lives.Guests include members of Rescue Company One, the New York City Fire Department?s oldest rescue team; noted anxiety researcher Dr. Michael Davis of Emory University; Dr. Matthew Friedman, director of the National Center for Post Traumatic Stress Disorder; Dr. Daniel Goldhagen, author of Hitler's Willing Executioners; and a discussion about altruism with a Buddhist lama, an Episcopal priest, a Muslim imam and a Jewish rabbi.

Mental Illness - How to Get Rid of Evil Spirits & Restore Your Self to Sanity. Mary M. Harris. 2 cass. (Running Time: 2 hrs. 55 min.). (Heal Your Self Ser.). 1997. 10.00 BBCSPub.
For use by patients & counseling professionals to teach & guide in the causes of mental illness & how to overcome it & restore one's mental health. Includes workbook.

Mental Illness in the Family: Program from the Award Winning Public Radio Series. Hosted by Fred Goodwin. Comment by John Hockenberry. 1 CD. (Running Time: 1hr.). (Infinite Mind Ser.). 2002. audio compact disk 21.95 (978-1-888064-74-2(9), LCM 224) Lichtenstein Creat.
In this hour, we explore Mental Illness in the Family. Anger. Frustration. Resentment. Helplessness. If someone in your family has mental illness, may be feeling all of these things. What can you do to help yourself, and by doing so your loved one as well? Guests include: Dr. David Miklowitz, a professor of psychology at The University of Colorado-Boulder and author of The Bipolar Disorder Survival Guide: What You and Your Family Need to Know; Dr. Lisa Dixon, an associate professor of medicine and psychiatry at The University of Maryland, where her research focuses on schizophrenia and family treatment; Dr. William Beardslee, a professor of child psychiatry at Harvard Medical school, Psychiatrist-in-Chief at Boston's Children's Hospital, and author of Out of the Darkened Room: When a Parent is Depressed: Protecting the Children and Strengthening the Family. Julie Totten, founder of Families for Depression Awareness; and Rose Styron, wife of writer William Styron, who suffers from major depression. Sharon Lerner with a special report on parents that have had to give up custody of their ill children to foster care when their mental health insurance runs out. And commentary by John Hockenberry.

Mental Machine. Electrifying MoJo. 1 cass. (Running Time: 1 hr. 30 min.). (978-0-9639811-0-3(2)) C Johnson.
A spell binding, action packed, riveting, poetic tale of love & hate, peace & war, life & death, adversity & respect, in America's big cities. "The Mental Machine" is a collage of hundreds of graphic sound effects, ranging from uzi's to songbirds, from galloping horses to a spring rain, from the landing & departure of a spaceship to seagulls chasing a boat! A digital stroll through your mind. A fascinating, 21st century mental motion picture.

Mental Management for Shooting Sports. Lanny Bassham. 6 CDs. (Running Time: 7 hrs). 2003. 135.00 (978-1-934324-02-8(7)) Mental Mgmnt.

Mental Massage: Relaxing into a Perfect Body. Juliann Donnelly. Illus. by Lisa Infantino Nasuti. Music by David Snider. 1 cass. 1997. 9.95 (978-1-929632-02-2(9)) Julstro Pubns.

Mental, Physical & Spiritual Health. Gurdip Hari. (978-0-9766186-3-8(X)) Jasmin Publg.

Mental Power. unabr. ed. Judith L. Powell. Read by Judith L. Powell. 1 cass. (Running Time: 40 min.). (Successful Living Ser.). 1987. pap. bk. 12.95 (978-0-914295-24-2(1)) Top Mtn Pub.
Side A presents exercises designed to boost mental powers by tapping into inner thoughts, ideas, & experiences, & build these areas into a dynamic force. Side B presents subliminal mind-expanding suggestions hidden in New Age Music.

Mental Rehearsal. 2002. audio compact disk 14.95 (978-0-9728185-3-7(7)) InGenius Inc.

Mental Rehearsal. Edward Strachar. 2000. (978-0-9717185-6-2(3)) InGenius Inc.

Mental Self-Defense. James S. Benko. Read by James S. Benko. 1986. 12.95 (TC-13) ITA Inst.
You may "think" you can defend yourself in a self-defense situation, but are you mentally prepared? Master Benko takes you into the "real" world & dispells many of the myths about so-called practical defense techniques. Be ready, mentally.

Mental Serenity. (701) Yoga Res Foun.

Mental Shielding. Richard Driscoll. 1 cass. 1999. bk. 16.00 (20481) Courage-to-Change.
Learn how to protect yourself from irritable co-workers, an angry boss, an upset mate, or critical parents.

Mental Shielding to Brush off Hostility. 2nd unabr. ed. Richard Driscoll. Read by Richard Driscoll. 1 cass. (Running Time: 32 min.). 1994. pap. bk. 18.00 (978-0-9634126-1-4(2)) Westside Pubng.
Stress reduction training for hostile situations.

Mental Stress. Manly P. Hall. 1 cass. 8.95 (978-0-89314-183-7(6), C900819) Philos Res.

Mental Stress & Physical Illness. unabr. ed. Kenneth R. Pelletier. 1 cass. 12.95 (29287) J Norton Pubs.
Pelletier teaches listeners how to recognize illness-provoking stress reactions & suggests preventive & treatment methods for stress-induced illnesses.

Mental Toughness Training. James E. Loehr & Peter McLaughlin. Read by James E. Loehr & Peter McLaughlin. 6 cass. (Running Time: 9 hrs.). pap. bk. 59.95 (891AD) Nightingale-Conant.
Now you can undertake a total mind/body training program that teaches you how to alter your own brain & body chemistry so that you can move from low energy, anxiety & negative emotions to an "Ideal Performance State" in a matter of minutes. A revolutionary program utilizing recent discoveries in the sciences of biochemistry, brain physiology, psychology & medicine. Includes training log.

Mental Tranquility. 1 cass. (Running Time: 1 hr.). 12.99 (703) Yoga Res Foun.

Mente-Cuerpo Magico. Deepak Chopra. 1 cass. (Running Time: 1 hr. 30 mins.).Tr. of Magical Mind/Magical Body. (SPA.). 2001. Astran.

Mente Sin Tiempo/Cuerpo Sin Edad. Deepak Chopra. 1 cass. (Running Time: 1 hr. 30 mins.).Tr. of Ageless Body, Timeless Mind. (SPA.). 2001. Astran.

***Mentor Leader: Secrets to Building People & Teams That Win Consistently.** unabr. ed. Tony Dungy. (ENG.). 2010. audio compact disk 34.99 (978-1-4143-3805-7(8)) Tyndale Hse.

***Mentored by the King: Arnold Palmer's Success Lessons for Golf, Business, & Life.** Brad Brewer. (ENG.). 2011. 16.99 (978-0-310-58591-6(0)) Zondervan.

***Mentored by the King: Arnold Palmer's Success Lessons for Golf, Business, & Life.** unabr. ed. Brad Brewer. (ENG.). 2011. audio compact disk 21.99 (978-0-310-32666-3(4)) Zondervan.

Mentoring. Susan Fowler-Woodring. 2 cass. (Running Time: 3 hr.). 1995. 15.95 (978-1-55977-160-3(7)) CareerTrack Pubns.

Mentoring that Makes a Difference: What It Is & How You Can Do It. Featuring Linda Phillips-Jones. 2000. 20.00 (978-1-890608-06-4(8)) Coalition Cnsling.

Mephisto Club. abr. ed. Tess Gerritsen. Read by Carolyn McCormick. (Running Time: 18000 sec.). (Jane Rizzoli & Maura Isles Ser.: Bk. 6). (ENG.). 2007. audio compact disk 14.99 (978-0-7393-5397-4(7), Random AudioBks) Pub: Random Audio Pubg. Dist(s): Random

Mercedes Coffin. unabr. ed. Faye Kellerman. Read by George Guidall. (Running Time: 11 hrs.). (ENG.). 2008. (978-0-06-170246-4(3), Harper Audio); audio compact disk 39.95 (978-0-06-155586-2(X), Harper Audio) HarperCollins Pubs.

***Mercedes Coffin.** unabr. ed. Faye Kellerman. Read by George Guidall. (ENG.). 2008. (978-0-06-170245-7(5)) HarperCollins Pubs.

Mercenary. Cynthia Ozick. Read by Cynthia Ozick. 1 cass. 1986. 13.95 (978-1-55644-163-9(0), 6091) Am Audio Prose.
This blackly humorous story, read by the author herself centers of the enigma of Lushinski, a Polish holocaust survivor who has denied his Jewishness to the outrageous extent of becoming an African.

***Mercenary Cold Calling Tactics for the Sales Jungle-Situational Selling Tactics.** Joe Cole. 2010. 297.00 (978-1-4507-0070-2(5)) Indep Pub IL.

Mercenary Collector's. abr. ed. Axel Kilgore. Read by Carol Eason. 6 cass. (Running Time: 9 hrs.). 2004. 35.00 (978-1-58807-434-8(X)) Am Pubng Inc.
This special Collector's Edition includes the first three novels in Axel Kilgore's Mercenary series, covering the exploits of Hank Frost, the wise-craking, one-eyed, mercenary captain. In The Killer Genesis, Frost goes on a vicious blood-hunt into the jungles of war-torn Central Africa, carrying his vendetta against the kill-crazy rogue commander who massacred Frost's outfit down to the very last man. The trail leads him into a three-sided ground war between Communist terrorist butchers, a bloody-handed puppet dictator, and the CIA's own revolutionary army. Through an endless web of torture slayings, a bank heist commando raid, and deception, Frost never takes his remaining eye off his ultimate goal: Killing the man who killed his troops. In The Slaughter Run, there's assassination in the Swiss Alps, terrorism in the Central American jungle, treachery in Washington ... and Hank Frost is right in the middle. The wise-cracking mercenary captain is up to his eyepatch in brutal violence, torture, and betrayal. There's the presidential bodyguard force he'd be a fool to trust, the fighting right-wing general whose republic is aflame with revolt, the general's seductive wife who'll have Frost as her lover - or have Frost dead, and the Communist Terrorist Army that's out for a final bloodbath. In Fourth Reich Death Squad, a frightening ransom message and and a bloody finger are all Hank Frost finds after he loses his prize charge to terrorist kidnappers. And to get Professor Balsam back, the fast-talking, fast-shooting, one-eyed mercenary captain has to gut his way through a sadistic torture team, neo-Nazi gunmen, and a vastly powerful Fourth Reich conspiracy. To add to the already harrowing situation, the French police, Israeli Intelligence, and Marita, a beautiful Mossad agent claiming to be

Balsam's daughter, are all after him for one reason or another. From Chicago to Paris to the Bavarian Alps, from terrorist assaults to torture sessions, Hank Frost is in trouble - up to his eye patch.

Merchant of Death. D. J. MacHale. Read by William Dufris. (Pendragon Ser.: Bk. 1). (J). 2009. 60.00 (978-1-60775-515-9(7)) Find a World.

Merchant of Death. unabr. ed. D. J. MacHale. Read by William Dufris. (Running Time: 12 hrs.). (Pendragon Ser.: Bk. 1). 2005. 39.25 (978-1-59737-242-8(0), 9781597372428, BADLE); 24.95 (978-1-59737-241-1(2), 9781597372411, BAD); 29.95 (978-1-59737-235-0(8), 9781597372350, BAU); 39.25 (978-1-59737-240-4(4), 9781597372404, Brlnc Audio MP3 Lib); 24.95 (978-1-59737-239-8(0), 9781597372398, Brilliance MP3); 82.25 (978-1-59737-236-7(6), 9781597372367, BriAudUnabridg) Brilliance Audio.
Bobby Pendragon is a seemingly normal fourteen-year-old boy. He has a family, a home, and even Marley, his beloved dog. But there is something very special about Bobby. He is going to save the world. And not just Earth as we know it. Bobby is slowly starting to realize that life in the cosmos isn't quite what he thought it was. And before he can object, he is swept off to an alternate dimension known as Denduron, a territory inhabited by strange beings, ruled by a magical tyrant, and plagued by dangerous revolution. If Bobby wants to see his family again, he's going to have to accept his role as savior, and accept it wholeheartedly. Because, as he is about to discover, Denduron is only the beginning.

Merchant of Death. unabr. ed. D. J. MacHale. Read by William Dufris. (Running Time: 12 hrs.). (Pendragon Ser.: Bk. 1). 2009. audio compact disk 19.99 (978-1-4233-9895-0(5), 9781423398950); audio compact disk 49.97 (978-1-4233-9896-7(3), 9781423398967, BriAudCD Unabrid) Brilliance Audio.

Merchant of Illusion: James Rouse, American Salesman of the Businessman's Utopia. Nicholas Dagen Bloom. 2004. audio compact disk 9.95 (978-0-8142-9026-2(4)) Ohio St U Pr.

Merchant of Prato. unabr. collector's ed. Iris Origo. Read by Donada Peters. 10 cass. (Running Time: 15 hrs.). 1988. 80.00 (978-0-7366-1293-7(9), 2201) Books on Tape.
Historical interpretation of the life of Francesco di Marco Datini, a powerful & successful banker & trader in 14th Century Florence.

Merchant of Venice. William Shakespeare. Ed. by Cedric Watts. 2001. audio compact disk 21.45 (978-1-903342-17-6(1)) Wordsworth Educ GBR.

Merchant of Venice. William Shakespeare. Contrib. by Antony Sher et al. (Playaway Young Adult Ser.). (ENG.). 2009. 40.00 (978-1-60775-585-2(8)) Find a World.

Merchant of Venice. abr. ed. William Shakespeare. 3 CDs. (Running Time: 3 hrs.). 2005. audio compact disk 19.95 (978-0-660-18673-3(X)) Pub: Canadian Broadcasting CAN. Dist(s): Georgetown Term

Merchant of Venice. abr. ed. William Shakespeare. Perf. by Michael Redgrave & Peter Neil. 2 cass. Dramatization. 1984. 19.95 (978-0-694-50375-9(4), SWC 2013) HarperCollins Pubs.
Cast includes: Alan McNaughton, Ian Lubbock, John Westbrook, Paul Daneman, Geoffrey Wincott, Nicolette Bernard, Betty Linton, Errol John, Timothy Bateson, Wyndham Mulligan, Diana Olsson, Malcolm Hayes, David Price & Diana Poulton.

***Merchant of Venice.** abr. ed. William Shakespeare. Read by Hugh Griffith. (ENG.). 2003. (978-0-06-079959-5(5), Caedmon); (978-0-06-074319-2(0), Caedmon) HarperCollins Pubs.

Merchant of Venice. unabr. ed. William Shakespeare. Read by Hugh Griffith & Dorothy Tutin. 2 cass. (Running Time: 2 hrs. 20 mins.). Dramatization. 17.95 (H146) Blckstn Audio.
The Jewish moneylender Shylock demands - & gets - justice in this play about laws & lawyers that also focuses on the "quality of mercy.".

Merchant of Venice. unabr. ed. William Shakespeare. Read by Audio Partners Staff. 2 cass. (Running Time: 2 hrs. 17 mins.). (Arkangel Shakespeare Ser.). 2004. 17.95 (978-1-932219-62-3(5), Atlntc Mnthly) Pub: Grove-Atltic. Dist(s): PerseuPGW
Shylock the moneylender is determined to exact his pound of flesh when Antonio defaults on a loan. The persecuted Shylock, one of Shakespeare's most complex characters, dominates this dark comedy, which features a memorable courtroom climax. Performed by Hadyn Gwynne, Bill Nighy, and the Arkangel cast.

Merchant of Venice, unabr. ed. William Shakespeare. Perf. by Hugh Griffith & Dorothy Tutin. 3 cass. Dramatization. 1984. 26.94 (CDL5 209) HarperCollins Pubs.
Cast includes: Harry Andrews, Laurence Hardy, Mark Dignam, Basil Moskins, Jeremy Brett, Stephen Moore, Robin Philips, Derek Godfrey, Ian Holm, Ken Wynne, Ronnie Barker, Roy Dotrice, Frank Wood, Roy Marsden, Judith Stott, & Zena Walker. Includes text.

Merchant of Venice. unabr. ed. William Shakespeare. Perf. by Haydn Gwynne et al. 2 cass. (Running Time: 3 hrs.). 16.95 (879893, PengAudBks) Penguin Grp USA.
A pound of flesh is a lot for an unpaid loan - even a substantial one. But that is Shylock's price. Antonio, the merchant of Venice, fully expects to repay the debt incurred for his friend Bassanio. But when he can't, it is Bassanio's beloved Portia who saves the day in this romantic but often disturbing comedy.

Merchant of Venice. unabr. ed. William Shakespeare. 2 cass. (Running Time: 2 hrs. 30 mins.). Dramatization. 2000. pap. bk. 34.20 (40749E5); 22.00 (21517E5) Recorded Bks.
The earliest of Shakespeare's comedies, this play sets a generous Portia in sharp contrast to a memorable Shylock.

Merchant of Venice. unabr. ed. William Shakespeare. Perf. by Dublin Gate Theatre Staff. 1 cass. Dramatization. 10.95 (978-0-8045-0810-0(0), SAC 7009) Spoken Arts.

Merchant of Venice. unabr. ed. William Shakespeare. Narrated by Hadyn Gwynne et al. (Arkangel Shakespeare Ser.). 2005. audio compact disk 19.95 (978-1-932219-22-7(6)) Pub: AudioGO. Dist(s): Perseus Dist

Merchant of Venice. unabr. ed. William Shakespeare. Narrated by Flo Gibson. 2 cass. (Running Time: 3 hrs.). 2003. 14.95 (978-1-55685-715-7(2)) Audio Bk Con.

Merchant of Venice, Set. unabr. ed. William Shakespeare. 2 cass. 1999. 15.95 (FS9-51067) Highsmith.

Merchant's Prologue & Tale: From the Canterbury Tales by Geoffrey Chaucer. Geoffrey Chaucer. Ed. by A. C. Spearing. Contrib. by A. C. Spearing et al. (Running Time: 1 hr. 5 mins.). (Selected Tales from Chaucer Ser.). (ENG.). 1999. audio compact disk 28.25 (978-0-521-63528-8(4)) Cambridge U Pr.

Mercia Hymns see Poetry of Geoffrey

Mercies Anew. Created by Allegis Publications. 2007. audio compact disk 24.99 (978-5-557-63281-2(6)) Allegis.

Merciful God of Prophecy: His Loving Plan for You in the End Times. abr. ed. Tim LaHaye. Read by Richard Davidson. (ENG.). 2005. 14.98 (978-1-59483-358-8(3)) Pub: Hachet Audio. Dist(s): HachBkGrp

Merciful Mother. Perf. by Still Waters. 1 cass. (Running Time: 44 min.). 1995. 12.00 (978-1-884479-03-8(0)) Spirit Song.
Catholic hymns to Mary, sung by Still Waters family music ministry.

Mercury. 1 cass. (Running Time: 25 min.). 14.95 (23321) MMI Corp.
Mercury's year, how Mercury is photographed, temperature, other fascinating facts are discussed.

Mercury No. 4: Planet Novel. unabr. ed. Ben Bova & Ben Bova. Read by Arte Johnson et al. 10 CDs. (Running Time: 11 hrs. 0 mins. 0 sec.). (Grand Tour Ser.). (ENG.). 2005. audio compact disk 39.95 (978-1-59397-501-2(5)) Pub: Macmill Audio. Dist(s): Macmillan

Mercury - Venus: Guided Visualizations. Luisa De La Lama. Narrated by Leila Gomez Bear & Jaques Bourquin. Music by Summa. 6 cass. (Running Time: 9 hrs.). (Power Planets Inner Journeys Ser.). 1994. 11.95 White Dragon.
Guided visualizations to contact the archetypal powers of Mercury & Venus using Greek mythological figures. These narrated from the book "Power Planets".

Mercury in Retrograde. unabr. ed. Paula Froelich. Narrated by Marguerite Gavin. (Running Time: 7 hrs. 30 mins. 0 sec.). (ENG.). 2009. 19.99 (978-1-4001-6380-9(3)); audio compact disk 59.99 (978-1-4001-4380-1(2)); audio compact disk 29.99 (978-1-4001-1380-4(6)) Pub: Tantor Media. Dist(s): IngramPubServ

Mercury Rising. Ryne Douglas Pearson. Read by Joe Morton. 2004. 10.95 (978-0-7435-4133-6(2)) Pub: S&S Audio. Dist(s): S and S Inc

***Mercury Theatre on the Air.** RadioArchives.com. (Running Time: 600). (ENG.). 2008. audio compact disk 29.98 (978-1-61081-080-7(5)) Radio Arch.

Mercury Theatre on the Air. Perf. by Orson Welles et al. 2 cass. (Running Time: 2 hrs.). 10.95 (978-1-57816-068-6(5), MT2201) Audio File.
Includes: "The War of the Worlds" (10-30-38) The most famous radio broadcast of all time. Orson Welles' production of the H. G. Wells story of a Martian invasion, treated by the Mercury Players as a dramatization of unfolding news events. The program caused widespread panic throughout the United States. "Dracula" (7-11-38) A classic radio version of the vampire story by Bram Stoker. Orson Welles produced, directed & hosts the program & plays two roles: Dr. Steward & Count Dracula. Set in vinyl album.

Mercury Theatre on the Air. unabr. ed. Perf. by Orson Welles. 2 CDs. (Running Time: 2 Hrs.). bk. 15.95 (978-1-57816-160-7(6), DMT907) Audio File.
Orson Welles and his Mercury Players in two classic hour-long dramas exactly as broadcast on C.B.S.

Mercury Theatre on the Air: Adventures of Sherlock Holmes - Strange Case of Professor Moriarty. Perf. by Orson Welles. 1 cass. (Running Time: 1 hr.). 2001. 6.98 (2164) Radio Spirits.

Mercury Theatre on the Air: Around the World in Eighty Days. Perf. by Orson Welles. 1 cass. (Running Time: 1 hr.). 2001. 6.98 (2501) Radio Spirits.

Mercury Theatre on the Air: Hell on Ice. Perf. by Orson Welles. 1 cass. (Running Time: 1 hr.). 2001. 6.98 (1914) Radio Spirits.

Mercury Theatre on the Air: I'm a Fool, The Open Window & My Little Boy. Perf. by Orson Welles. 1 cass. (Running Time: 1 hr.). 2001. 6.98 (1516) Radio Spirits.

Mercury Theatre on the Air: The Affairs of Anatole. Perf. by Orson Welles. 1 cass. (Running Time: 1 hr.). 2001. 6.98 (2185) Radio Spirits.

Mercury Theatre on the Air: The Count of Monte Cristo. Perf. by Orson Welles. 1 cass. (Running Time: 1 hr.). 2001. 6.98 (1855) Radio Spirits.

Mercury Theatre on the Air: The Hitchhiker & The Search for Henri Lefevre. Perf. by Orson Welles. 1 cass. (Running Time: 1 hr.). 2001. 6.98 (2021) Radio Spirits.

Mercury Theatre on the Air: The War of the Worlds. Perf. by Orson Welles. 1 CD. (Running Time: 1 hr.). (Old-Time Radio Blockbusters Ser.). 2001. audio compact disk 4.98 (7709) Radio Spirits.

Mercury Theatre on the Air: The 39 Steps. Perf. by Orson Welles. 1 cass. (Running Time: 1 hr.). 2001. 6.98 (2584) Radio Spirits.

Mercury Theatre on the Air: Treasure Island. Perf. by Orson Welles. 1 cass. (Running Time: 1 hr.). 2001. 6.98 (1786) Radio Spirits.

Mercury Visions of Louis Daguerre. Dominic Smith. Read by Stephen Hoye. (Running Time: 37800 sec.). 2006. 72.95 (978-0-7861-4447-1(5)); audio compact disk 99.00 (978-0-7861-7336-5(X)) Blckstn Audio.

Mercury Visions of Louis Daguerre. unabr. ed. Dominic Smith. Read by Stephen Hoye. 11 CDs. (Running Time: 37800 sec.). 2006. audio compact disk 32.95 (978-0-7861-7449-2(8)) Blckstn Audio.

Mercury Visions of Louis Daguerre: A Novel. unabr. ed. Dominic Smith. 9 cass. (Running Time: 13 hrs.). (YA). 2006. 29.95 (978-0-7861-4385-6(1)) Blckstn Audio.

Mercy see James Dickey Reads His Poetry & Prose

Mercy. Julie Garwood. 2004. 15.95 (978-0-7435-4134-3(0)) Pub: S&S Audio. Dist(s): S and S Inc

Mercy. unabr. ed. Julie Garwood. Read by Johanna Rodriguez. 10 vols. (Running Time: 15 hrs.). 2002. bk. 84.95 (978-0-7927-2525-1(5), CSL 414, Chivers Sound Lib); audio compact disk 110.95 (978-0-7927-9948-1(8), SLD 099, Chivers Sound Lib) AudioGO.
Like his FBI-agent brother Nick, Theo Buchanan is devoted to his crime-fighting career. Only Theo works the other side of the desk as an esteemed Justice Department attorney. At a gala ceremony in New Orleans, he is suddenly struck ill and is rushed to a hospital where a brilliant and beautiful surgeon, Dr. Michelle Renard, saves his life. It is not the only life-and-death crisis that will ensnare Theo, for he is about to uncover a ring of criminals bent on preserving their secrecy at any cost.

Mercy. unabr. ed. Toni Morrison. Read by Toni Morrison. 4 cass. 2008. 40.00 (978-1-4159-6102-5(6), BksonTape) Pub: Random Audio Pubg. Dist(s): Random
A powerful tragedy distilled into a jewel of a masterpiece by the Nobel Prize-winning author of Beloved and, almost like a prelude to that story, set two centuries earlier. In the 1680s the slave trade was still in its infancy. In the Americas, virulent religious and class divisions, prejudice and oppression were rife, providing the fertile soil in which slavery and race hatred were planted and took root. Jacob is an Anglo-Dutch trader and adventurer, with a small holding in the harsh north. Despite his distaste for dealing in "flesh," he takes a small slave girl in part payment for a bad debt from a plantation owner in Catholic Maryland. This is Florens, "with the hands of a slave and the feet of a Portuguese lady." Florens looks for love, first from Lina, an older servant woman at her new master's house, but later from a handsome blacksmith, an African, never enslaved. There are other voices: Lina, whose tribe was decimated by smallpox; their mistress, Rebekka, herself a victim of religious intolerance back in England; Sorrow, a strange girl who's spent her early years at sea; and finally the devastating voice of Florens' mother. These are all men and women inventing themselves in the wilderness. A Mercy reveals what lies beneath the surface of slavery. But at its heart it is the ambivalent, disturbing story of a mother who casts off her daughter in order to save her, and of a daughter who may never exorcise that abandonment. Acts of mercy may have unforeseen consequences.

Mercy. unabr. ed. Toni Morrison. Read by Toni Morrison. 5 CDs. (Running Time: 6 hrs. 30 mins.). 2008. audio compact disk 29.95 (978-0-7393-3254-2(6), Random AudioBks); audio compact disk 40.00 (978-1-4159-5681-6(2), BksonTape) Pub: Random Audio Pubg. Dist(s): Random

Mercy. unabr. ed. Jodi Picoult. Narrated by Alyssa Bresnahan. (Running Time: 17 hrs.). 2009. 61.75 (978-1-4361-5729-2(3)); 113.75 (978-1-4193-8280-2(2)); audio compact disk 123.75 (978-1-4193-8282-6(9)) Recorded Bks.

Mercy. unabr. ed. Myrtle Smith. Prod. by David Keyston. 1 CD. (Running Time: 1 hrs. 6 min.). (Myrtle Smyth Audiotapes Ser.). 1998. audio compact disk (978-1-893107-07-6(8), M7, Cross & Crown) Healing Unltd.

Mercy. unabr. collector's ed. Jodi Picoult. Narrated by Alyssa Bresnahan. 15 CDs. (Running Time: 17 hrs.). 2009. audio compact disk 72.95 (978-1-4193-8283-3(7)) Recorded Bks.

Mercy: Based on the Chaplet of the Divine Mercy. Eugene Koshenina. Narrated by Robert DeGrandis. Music by Cecilia Kittley. Prod. by Eugene Chu Koshenina. 1. (Running Time: 60 mins.). 2002. audio compact disk Rental 14.95 (978-0-9722438-4-1(4)) Eugene Chu.
Stories, Songs, & Prayers featuring "The Chaplet of the Divine Mercy"More Music with Ave Maria.

MERCY - Based on the Chaplet of the Divine Mercy. Scripts. Eugene Peter Koshenina. Narrated by Robert DeGrandis. Music by Cecilia Kittley. 1. (Running Time: 60 mins). 2002. Rental 9.95 (978-0-9722438-5-8(2)) Eugene Chu.

***Mercy Clifton: Pilgrim Girl.** unabr. ed. Peter Marshall et al. Narrated by Aimee Lilly. (Running Time: 6 hrs. 41 mins. 45 sec.). (Crimson Cross Ser.). (ENG.). 2010. 18.19 (978-1-60814-762-5(2)); audio compact disk 25.99 (978-1-59859-780-6(9)) Oasis Audio.

Mercy in Action: Goodness. Elbert Willis. 1 cass. (Gentleness & Goodness Ser.). 4.00 Fill the Gap.

Mercy Kill. unabr. ed. Lori Armstrong. (Running Time: 11 hrs.). (Mercy Gunderson Ser.). 2011. audio compact disk 29.99 (978-1-4233-7756-6(7), 9781423377566, Bril Audio CD Unabri) Brilliance Audio.

***Mercy Kill.** unabr. ed. Lori Armstrong. (Running Time: 11 hrs.). (Mercy Gunderson Ser.). 2011. 24.99 (978-1-4233-7760-3(5), 9781423377603, BAD); 39.97 (978-1-4233-7761-0(3), 9781423377610, BADLE); 24.99 (978-1-4233-7758-0(3), 9781423377580, Brilliance MP3); 39.97 (978-1-4233-7759-7(1), 9781423377597, Brlnc Audio MP3 Lib); audio compact disk 79.97 (978-1-4233-7757-3(5), 9781423377573, BriAudCD Unabrid) Brilliance Audio.

Mercy of God. Kenneth Copeland. 4 cass. (Running Time: 6 hrs.). 1984. 20.00 (978-0-88114-692-9(7)) K Copeland Pubns.
Biblical teaching on God's mercy. Includes study guide.

Mercy of Thin Air. abr. ed. Ronlyn Domingue. Read by Rebecca Gayheart. 2005. 15.95 (978-0-7435-5241-7(5)) Pub: S&S Audio. Dist(s): S and S Inc

Mercy Papers: A Memoir of Three Weeks. unabr. ed. Robin Romm. Narrated by Ann Marie Lee. 5 CDs. 2009. audio compact disk 70.00 (978-1-4159-6257-2(X), BksonTape) Pub: Random Audio Pubg. Dist(s): Random

Mercy Rule. abr. ed. John Lescroart. Read by David Colacci. (Running Time: 6 hrs.). (Dismas Hardy Ser.: No. 5). 2010. audio compact disk 14.99 (978-1-4418-2539-1(8), 9781441825391, BCD Value Price) Brilliance Audio.

Mercy Rule. unabr. ed. John Lescroart. Read by David Colacci. (Running Time: 17 hrs.). (Dismas Hardy Ser.: No. 5). 2009. 44.97 (978-1-4233-8696-4(5), 9781423386964, Brlnc Audio MP3 Lib); 29.99 (978-1-4233-8695-7(7), 9781423386957, Brilliance MP3); 44.97 (978-1-4233-8698-8(1), 9781423386988, BADLE); 29.99 (978-1-4233-8697-1(3), 9781423386971, BAD); audio compact disk 97.97 (978-1-4233-8694-0(9), 9781423386940, BriAudCD Unabrid); audio compact disk 38.99 (978-1-4233-8693-3(0), 9781423386933, Bril Audio CD Unabri) Brilliance Audio.

Mercy Seat. Martyn Waites. (Story Sound Ser.). 2007. 76.95 (978-1-84652-083-9(5)); audio compact disk 99.95 (978-1-84652-084-6(3)) Pub: Mgna Lrg Print GBR. Dist(s): Ulverscroft US

Mercy Street. abr. ed. Mariah Stewart. Read by Joyce Bean. (Running Time: 6 hrs.). (Mercy Street Ser.: No. 1). 2009. audio compact disk 14.99 (978-1-4233-1928-3(1), 9781423319283, BCD Value Price) Brilliance Audio.

Mercy Street. unabr. ed. Mariah Stewart. Read by Joyce Bean. (Running Time: 10 hrs.). (Mercy Street Ser.: No. 1). 2008. 39.25 (978-1-4233-1926-9(5), 9781423319269, BADLE); 24.95 (978-1-4233-1925-2(7), 9781423319252, BAD); audio compact disk 24.95 (978-1-4233-1923-8(0), 9781423319238, Brilliance MP3); audio compact disk 34.95 (978-1-4233-1921-4(4), 9781423319214, Bril Audio CD Unabri); audio compact disk 92.25 (978-1-4233-1922-1(2), 9781423319221, BriAudCD Unabrid); audio compact disk 39.25 (978-1-4233-1924-5(9), 9781423319245, Brlnc Audio MP3 Lib) Brilliance Audio.

Mercy Watson Collection Vol. 1: Mercy Watson to the Rescue; Mercy Watson Goes For a Ride. unabr. ed. Kate DiCamillo. Read by Ron McLarty. 1 CD. (Running Time: 42 mins.). (Mercy Watson Ser.: Bks. 1-2). (J). (ps-3). 2006. audio compact disk 17.00 (978-0-7393-3557-4(X), Listening Lib) Pub: Random Audio Pubg. Dist(s): NetLibrary CO
Mercy Watson to the Rescue: To Mr. & Mrs. Watson, Mercy is not just a pig - she's a porcine wonder. And to the portly and good-natured Mercy, the Watson's are an excellent source of buttered toast, no to mention that buttery-toast feeling she gets when she snuggles in to bed with them. This is not, however so good for the Watsons' bed. BOOM! CRACK! Welcome to the wry and endearing world of Mercy Watson. [18:50 minutes]. Mercy Watson Goes for a Ride: Mr. and Mrs. Watson's porcine wonder, Mercy, loves nothing more than a ride in the car. It takes a fair amount of nudging and bribing and a "You are such a good sport, darling" to get the portly pig out of the driver's seat, but once the convertible is on the road, Mercy loves the feel of the wind tickling her ears and the sun on her snout. [22:58 minutes].

Mercy Watson Collection Vol. 2: Mercy Watson Fights Crime; Princess in Disguise. unabr. ed. Kate DiCamillo. Read by Ron McLarty. 1 CD. (Running Time: 43 mins.). (Mercy Watson Ser.: Bks. 3-4). (J). (gr. k-2). 2007. audio compact disk 24.00 (978-0-7393-5124-6(9), Listening Lib) Pub: Random Audio Pubg. Dist(s): Random

Mercy Watson Collection Vol. 2: Mercy Watson Fights Crime; Princess in Disguise. unabr. ed. Kate DiCamillo. Read by Ron McLarty. (Running Time: 2580 sec.). (Mercy Watson Ser.: Bks. 3-4). (J). (gr. 1-4). 2007. audio compact disk 14.95 (978-0-7393-3630-4(4), Listening Lib) Pub: Random Audio Pubg. Dist(s): Random

***Mercy Watson Collection Vol. 3: Mercy Watson Thinks Like a Pig; Something Wonky This Way Comes.** unabr. ed. Kate DiCamillo. Read by Ron McLarty. 1 CD. (Running Time: 49 mins.). (Mercy Watson Ser.: Bks. 5-6). (J). (gr. 1-3). 2009. audio compact disk 24.00 (978-0-7393-6266-2(6), Listening Lib) Pub: Random Audio Pubg. Dist(s): Random

Mercy Watson Collection Vol. 3: Mercy Watson Thinks Like a Pig; Something Wonky This Way Comes. unabr. ed. Kate DiCamillo. Read by Ron McLarty. (Mercy Watson Ser.: Bks. 5-6). (J). (gr. 1). 2009. audio compact disk 14.95 (978-0-7393-6050-7(7), Listening Lib) Pub: Random Audio Pubg. Dist(s): Random

Mercy Watson to the Rescue; Mercy Watson Goes for a Ride. unabr. ed. Kate DiCamillo. Read by Ron McLarty. 1 cd. (Running Time: 2520 sec.). (Mercy Watson Ser.: Bks. 1-2). (ENG.). (J). (gr. 1). 2006. audio compact disk 15.00 (978-0-307-28425-9(5), Listening Lib) Pub: Random Audio Pubg. Dist(s): Random

Mercy's Voice. Contrib. by Rose Leibundguth. 1998. 15.00 (978-1-931262-00-2(4)) Rose Leibund.

Mere Christianity. C. S. Lewis. Narrated by Geoffrey Howard. (Running Time: 7 hrs.). (C). 2000. 27.95 (978-1-59912-546-6(3)) Iofy Corp.

Mere Christianity. unabr. ed. Read by Geoffrey Howard. Ed. by C. S. Lewis. Compiled by C. S. Lewis. 5 cass. (Running Time: 7 hrs.). 2000. 39.95 (978-0-7861-1781-9(8), 2580); audio compact disk 40.00 (978-0-7861-9876-4(1), 2580) Blckstn Audio.
Forceful & accessible doctrine of Christian belief. First heard as informal radio broadcasts & brings together what Lewis sees as the fundamental truths of the religion & finds a common ground on which all those who have Christian faith can stand together.

Mere Christianity. unabr. ed. C. S. Lewis. Read by Geoffrey Howard. 5 CDs. (Running Time: 6 hrs.). 2003. audio compact disk 29.95 (978-0-06-057263-1(9)) HarperCollins Pubs.

Mere Christianity. unabr. ed. Read by Michael York. Ed. by C. S. Lewis. Compiled by C. S. Lewis. 8 cass. (Running Time: 8 hrs.). 1987. 48.00 (978-0-7366-1155-8(X), 2080) Books on Tape.
Incorporates the author's thoughts about the Christian faith. A strong current of warmth & affection run through it.

Mere Christianity: Abolition of Man (Bonus Feature) unabr. ed. Read by Robert Whitfield. 5 cass. (Running Time: 27000 sec.). 2006. 25.95 (978-0-7861-4402-0(5)); audio compact disk 25.95 (978-0-7861-7436-2(6)); audio compact disk 29.95 (978-0-7861-7767-7(5)) Blckstn Audio.

Mere Sauvage - Le Petit Soldat. Guy de Maupassant. Read by Georges Riquier. 1 cass. (FRE.). 1991. bk. 16.95 (1258-SA) Olivia & Hill.
Two tales set in the context of the Franco-Prussian war.

Mere Sauvage - Le Petit Soldat. unabr. ed. Guy de Maupassant. 1 cass. (Guy de Maupassant Ser.: Vol. IV). (FRE.). bk. 16.95 (SFR454) J Norton Pubs.

Meredith Gentry: A Stroke of Midnight, Mistral's Kiss, Lick of Frost. abr. ed. Laurell K. Hamilton. Read by Laural Merlington. (Running Time: 15 hrs.). 2009. audio compact disk 34.99 (978-1-4233-9728-1(2), 9781423397281) Brilliance Audio.

Meredith Gentry CD Collection: A Kiss of Shadows; A Caress of Twilight; Seduced by Moonlight. abr. ed. Laurell K. Hamilton. Read by Laural Merlington. (Running Time: 18 hrs.). (Meredith Gentry Ser.). 2008. audio compact disk 34.99 (978-1-4233-6214-2(4), 9781423362142, BACD) Brilliance Audio.

Mergers, Acquisitions & Affiliations of Health Care Institutions. 1988. 65.00 (AC-456) PA Bar Inst.

Mergers, Acquisitions & Buyouts October 1999: A Transactional Analysis of the Governing Tax, Legal & Accounting Considerations. Jack S. Levin & Martin D. Ginsburg. 2000. audio compact disk 350.00 (978-0-7355-1111-8(X), 1111X, Aspen) WoltersKlu.

Mergers Acquisitions Buying & Selling a Business. Somers H. White. 4 cass. (Running Time: 4 hrs.). 100.00 S White.

Mergers & Acquisitions. unabr. ed. Ronald G. Quintero, Jr. 6 cass. (Running Time: 8 hrs.). 1995. bk. 119.00 (752454EZ) Am Inst CPA.
Mergers & acquisitions continue to play a vital role in business strategy. Accounting professionals are indispensable participants in various stages of a process that annually results in the transfer of billions of dollars. This tape reveals the nuts & bolts of mergers & acquisitions, including sales & divestitures, pricing & structuring the transaction, accounting & tax considerations, financing the purchase & closing the transaction. Examples, analyses & checklists drawn from actual transactions give you fascinating insights into the entire process.

Mergers & Acquisitions 1989: Techniques & Strategies. unabr. ed. Contrib. by Melvin Katz & Ronald M. Loeb. 4 cass. (Running Time: 5 hrs. 30 min.). 1989. pap. bk. 95.00 (T6-9100) PLI.
Designed for corporate in-house counsel & other attorneys who advise corporations on business & financing strategy, this recording of PLI's February 1989 satellite program analyzes the practical & technical problems of structuring mergers & acquisitions. Topics include: friendly & unfriendly take-overs, leveraged buyouts & other asset-deployment transactions, business considerations affecting acquisitions & mergers, tax & accounting aspects of acquisitions & mergers, current regulatory environment, including federal & state securities regulations & ethical questions.

Merging Back into Oneness. Swami Amar Jyoti. 1 cass. 1980. 9.95 (R-31) Truth Consciousness.
What will solve our weeping & miseries? Why intellectual answers do not satisfy. Going back to the point where it all started.

Merging into Light. Swami Amar Jyoti. 1 cass. 1995. 9.95 (M-97) Truth Consciousness.
Invincible Light is within us, covered by illusion. When the floodgates of Light open, all darkness vanishes instantly.

Merging Psychiatry & Endocrinology: Screening & Managing Severely Mentally Ill Patients for Metabolic Disorders. Featuring Ramachandiran Cooppan & Stephen Stahl. 2005. audio compact disk (978-1-4225-0016-3(0)) NEI Pr.

Merging with Solar Light Vol. 1: Transforming Your Mind. 1992. 49.95 (978-1-893027-23-7(6)) Path of Light.

Merging with Solar Light Vol. 2: Transforming Your Emotions. 1992. 49.95 (978-1-893027-24-4(4)) Path of Light.

Merging with Solar Light Vol. 3: Transforming Your Body. 1994. 49.95 (978-1-893027-25-1(2)) Path of Light.

Merian C. Cooper's King Kong. Brad Strickland. Read by David Baker. (Running Time: 6 hrs. 30 mins.). 2005. 32.95 (978-1-60083-552-0(X)) Iofy Corp.

Merian C. Cooper's King Kong. unabr. ed. Brad Strickland. Read by Full Cast Production Staff. (YA). 2007. 44.99 (978-1-60252-567-2(6)) Find a World.

Meridel LeSueur. unabr. ed. Read by Meridel LeSueur. 1 cass. (Running Time: 29 min.). 1985. 10.00 New Letters.
The author of stories of the 30's Depression here reads poems from "The Rites of Ancient Ripening".

Meridians. Short Stories. (3081) Am Audio Prose.

Merinda & the Magic Mirror: A Program for Inner-Child Recovery. Scripts. Marjorie Baker Price. Narrated by Marjorie Baker Price. Illus. by Beth Price & David Price. 1. (Running Time: 30 minutes). 1995. spiral bd. 12.95 (978-0-9713013-1-3(X)) Centering Pubns.

Merkabah of Love. Created by Amazonah Elam. Lyrics by Amazonah Elam. Executive Producer MabyMuzik. 2007. 10.00 (978-0-9796605-7-3(2)) Bonzai Arts.

Merle Bleu. l.t. ed. Michele Gazier. (French Ser.). (FRE., 2000. bk. 30.99 (978-2-84011-356-0(2)) Pub: UlverLrgPrint GBR. Dist(s): Ulverscroft US

Merle Miller. Interview with Merle Miller. 1 cass. (Running Time: 15 min.). 1972. 9.95 (L052) TFR.
Miller speaks on his memoirs, "What Happened," the story of his awakening to his homosexuality & the resistance he found in society & himself.

Merle's Door: Lessons from a Freethinking Dog. unabr. ed. Ted Kerasote. 1 MP3-CD. (Running Time: 13 hrs. 0 mins. 0 sec.). (ENG.). 2007. audio compact disk 24.99 (978-1-4001-5357-2(3)); audio compact disk 69.99 (978-1-4001-3357-4(2)) Pub: Tantor Media. Dist(s): IngramPubServ

Merle's Door: Lessons from a Freethinking Dog. unabr. ed. Ted Kerasote. Read by Patrick G. Lawlor. 11 CDs. (Running Time: 13 hrs. 0 mins. 0 sec.). (ENG.). 2007. audio compact disk 34.99 (978-1-4001-0357-6(X)) Pub: Tantor Media. Dist(s): IngramPubServ

Merlin see Poetry of Geoffrey

Merlin, unabr. ed. Stephen R. Lawhead. Read by Frederick Davidson. 13 cass. (Running Time: 19 hrs. 30 min.). 1995. 85.95 (978-0-7861-0708-7(1), 1585) Blckstn Audio.
He was born to greatness, the son of a druid bard & a princess of lost Atlantis. A trained warrior, blessed with the gifts of prophecy & song, he grew to manhood in a Britain abandoned by its Roman conquerors - a land ravaged by the brutal greed of petty chieftains & barbarian invaders. Respected, feared & hated by many, he was to have a higher destiny: to prepare the way for the momentous event that would unite the Island of the Mighty - the coming of Arthur Pendragon, Lord of the Kingdom of Summer.

Merlin. unabr. ed. Stephen R. Lawhead. Read by Frederick Davidson. (Running Time: 19 hrs.). 1998. 39.95 (978-0-7861-9318-9(2)) Blckstn Audio.

Merlin & the Dragons. (What's a Good Story? Ser.). (YA). 1991. pap. bk. & stu. ed. 99.00 (60796) Phoenix Films.
Provides detailed information on both literature & the writing process.

Merlin & the Dragons. unabr. ed. Jane Yolen. Narrated by Kevin Kline. 1 cass. (Running Time: 37 min.). (Stories to Remember Ser.). (J). (gr. 1-5). 1991. 8.98 (978-1-879496-21-7(6)) Lightyear Entrtnmnt.
Kevin Kline is Merlin, reassuring young King Arthur about the true value of dreams in this story based on medieval Arthurian literature.

Merlin & the Dragons. unabr. ed. Jane Yolen. Narrated by Kevin Kline. 1 CD. (Running Time: 37 min.). (Stories to Remember Ser.). (J). (gr. 1-5). 1993. pap. bk. 13.98 (978-1-56896-035-7(2)) Lightyear Entrtnmnt.

Merlin I & II see Poetry of Ralph Waldo Emerson

Merlot Murders. unabr. ed. Ellen Crosby. 8 CDs. (Running Time: 32700 sec.). (Wine Country Mysteries Ser.). 2006. audio compact disk 79.95 (978-0-7927-4525-9(6), SLD 1055) AudioGO.

Mermaid: Fifth Section see Robert Lowell: A Reading

Mermaid Chair. Sue Monk Kidd. Read by Eliza Foss. 2005. audio compact disk 90.00 (978-1-4159-1625-4(X)) Books on Tape.

Mermaid Chair. unabr. ed. Sue Monk Kidd. Read by Eliza Foss. 9 CDs. (Running Time: 10 hrs.). (ENG.). (gr. 12 up). 2005. audio compact disk 39.95 (978-0-14-305742-0(1), PengAudBks) Penguin Grp USA.

Mermaid Magic. Gwyneth Rees. Read by Syan Blake. (Running Time: 9600 sec.). (J). 2001. audio compact disk 29.95 (978-0-7540-6754-2(8)) AudioGo GBR.

Mermaid of Edam. unabr. ed. 1 cass. (Running Time: 20 min.). Dramatization. (Magic Looking Glass Ser.). (J). (gr. 2-6). 1989. 9.95 (978-0-7810-0038-3(6), NIM-CW-129-3-C) NIMCO.
A Dutch folk tale.

Mermaids & Fairy Dust: Magical Meditations for Girls of All Ages. Christiane Kerr. (Calm for Kids Ser.). (ps-16). 2005. audio compact disk 17.95 (978-1-901923-91-9(6)) Divinit Pubing GBR.

***Mermaid's Mirror.** unabr. ed. L. K. Madigan. Read by Katie Schorr. 1 MP3-CD. (Running Time: 7 hrs.). (YA). 2010. 24.99 (978-1-4418-8251-6(0), 9781441882516, Brilliance MP3); 39.97 (978-1-4418-8252-3(9), 9781441882523, Brinc Audio MP3 Lib); 39.97 (978-1-4418-8253-0(7), 9781441882530, BADLE); audio compact disk 24.99 (978-1-4418-8249-3(9), 9781441882493, Bril Audio CD Unabri); audio compact disk 59.97 (978-1-4418-8250-9(2), 9781441882509, BriAudCD Unabrid) Brilliance Audio.

Mermaids Singing. Lisa Carey. 2004. 10.95 (978-0-7435-4135-0(9)) Pub: S&S Audio. Dist(s): S and S Inc

Mermaids Singing, unabr. ed. Val McDermid. Read by Graham Roberts. 14 CDs. (Running Time: 14 hrs. 15 min.). (Isis Ser.). (J). 2000. audio compact disk 104.95 (978-0-7531-0710-2(4), 107104) Pub: ISIS Lrg Prnt GBR. Dist(s): Ulverscroft US

Mermaids Singing. unabr. ed. Val McDermid. Read by Graham Roberts. 10 cass. (Running Time: 15 hrs.). (Isis Ser.). (J). 2004. 84.95 (978-0-7531-0075-2(4), 960808) Pub: ISIS Lrg Prnt GBR. Dist(s): Ulverscroft US
A serial killer is on the loose & four men have been brutally killed by savage knife wounds. In each case the men have been mutilated & tortured, though the mutilation are not identical & nothing obvious appears to connect the victims. Fear grips the city; no man feels safe. Clinical psychologist Tony Hill is brought in to profile the killer, to work alongside Detective Inspector Carol Jordan. Tony himself becomes embroiled in a battle of wits & wills where he has to use every ounce of his professional skill & personal nerve to survive.

Mermaid's Tale Plus Five More. unabr. ed. Read by Rebecca Macauley. (Running Time: 1 hr. 35 mins.). (Aussie Nibbles: Ser.). (J). 2001. 18.00 (978-1-74030-529-7(9)) Pub: Bolinda Pubng AUS. Dist(s): Bolinda Pub Inc

Mermaid's Tale Plus Five More. unabr. ed. Read by Rebecca Macauley. 1 cass. (Running Time: 1 hr. 35 mins.). (Aussie Nibbles: Ser.). (J). 2002. 18.00 (978-1-74030-731-4(3)) Pub: Bolinda Pubng AUS. Dist(s): Bolinda Pub Inc

Merman. unabr. ed. Dick King-Smith. Read by June Whitfield. 2 cass. (Running Time: 3 hrs.). (J). (gr. 1-8). 1999. 23.00 (LL 0158, Chivers Child Audio) AudioGO.

Merman, unabr. ed. Dick King-Smith. Read by June Whitfield. 2 cass. (YA). 1999. 16.98 (FS9-50962) Highsmith.

Merman. unabr. ed. Dick King-Smith. Read by June Whitfield. 2 vols. (Running Time: 1 hr. 32 mins.). (J). (gr. 3-7). 2004. pap. bk. 29.00 (978-0-8072-8132-1(8), Listening Lib); 23.00 (978-0-8072-8131-4(X), YA112CX, Listening Lib) Random Audio Pubg.
On her tenth birthday Zeta finds something that changes her life forever - a merman. The two become great friends & Zeta is left with two very special gifts.

Merriam-Webster's Collegiate Dictionary & Thesaurus. 11th rev. ed. Merriam-Webster, Inc. Staff. (gr. 7). 2003. audio compact disk 14.95 (978-0-87779-471-4(5), MER-471) Merriam-Webs.

Merriam-Webster's Collegiate Dictionary & Thesaurus, Deluxe Audio Edition. 11th deluxe rev. ed. Merriam-Webster, Inc. Staff. (gr. 7). 2003. audio compact disk 24.95 (978-0-87779-470-7(7), MER-470) Merriam-Webs.

Merriam-Webster's Spanish-English Dictionary. Ed. by Merriam-Webster, Inc. Staff. (SPA & ENG.). (gr. 7). 2003. audio compact disk 24.95 (978-0-87779-472-1(3), MER-472) Merriam-Webs.

Merrick. Anne Rice. Read by Graeme Malcolm. (Vampire Chronicles: Bk. 7). 2000. 56.00 (978-0-7366-5987-1(0)) Books on Tape.

Merrick. unabr. ed. Anne Rice. Read by Graeme Malcolm. 8 cass. (Running Time: 12 hrs.). (Vampire Chronicles: Bk. 7). 2000. 39.95 (H234) Blckstn Audio.
At the center is the beautiful, unconquerable witch Merrick. She is a descendant of the gens de couleur libres, a society of New Orleans octoroons & quadroons steeped in the lore & ceremony of voodoo, who reign in the shadowy world where African & French - the dark & the white - intermingle. Her ancestors are the great Mayfair witches, of whom she knows nothing & from whom she inherits the power & the magical knowledge of a Circe.

Merrick. unabr. ed. Anne Rice. Read by Graeme Malcolm. 7 cass. (Running Time: 10 hrs.30 min.). (Vampire Chronicles: Bk. 7). 2000. 35.95 Books on Tape.
At the center is Merrick, a beautiful unconquerable witch, raised with the lore & ceremony of voodoo. Her ancestors were the great Mayfair Witches from whom she has inherited certain powers & magical knowledge. Into this realm comes David Talbot, an almost mortal vampire. It is he who recounts Merrick's haunting tale, which takes us from present day New Orleans to Maya ruins of a century ago & to ancient civilization not yet explored. Here is an irresistible story of two worlds where magical powers & other worldly fascination are locked together in a dance of deduction, death & rebirth.

Merrily, Merrily, Greet the Morn! Ladybug Magazine Editors. 1 cass. (J). (ps-1). 1998. 10.95 (978-0-8126-0252-4(8)) Open Ct Pub.

Merrittorious Action. Arthur Pfister. Arthur Pfister. (ENG.). 2009. audio compact disk 19.95 (978-0-9824551-0-4(0)) Pub: Margaret Media. Dist(s): Forest Sales & Dist

Merry Adventures of Robin Hood see Childhood Legends

Merry Adventures of Robin Hood. Howard Pyle. Read by David Case. (Playaway Children Ser.). (ENG.). (J). 2009. 69.99 (978-1-60812-810-5(5)) Find a World.

Merry Adventures of Robin Hood. Howard Pyle. Narrated by John Chatty. (Running Time: 8 hrs. 30 mins.). 1982. 21.95 (978-1-59912-824-5(1)) Iofy Corp.

Merry Adventures of Robin Hood. Howard Pyle. Read by David Thorn. Engineer Bobbie Frohman. 10 cds. (Running Time: 11 hrs. 20 mins). (YA). 2006. audio compact disk (978-0-9755663-7-4(7)) Alcazar AudioWorks.
The traditional and exciting stories of Robin Hood and his merry band of outlaws in Sherwood Forest. Tales of adventure, skullduggery, archery matches, helping of the poor and downtrodden...all are part of the action packed life of Robin Hood. The merry minstrels sing and entertain.

Merry Adventures of Robin Hood. abr. ed. Howard Pyle. Narrated by Michael Rye. 2 cass. (Running Time: 2 hrs. 24 min.). (J). 12.95 (978-0-89926-127-0(2), 815) Audio Bk.

Merry Adventures of Robin Hood. abr. ed. Howard Pyle. Perf. by St. Charles Players. 1 cass. (Running Time: 1 hr. 30 min.). (Audio Theatre Ser.). (YA). (gr. 5 up). 2001. 16.95 (978-1-56994-534-6(9)) Monterey Media Inc.
A band of outlaws ride boldly against the Sheriff of Nottingham's men. They seek to overturn injustice - to rob from the rich and give to the poor.

Merry Adventures of Robin Hood. adpt. ed. Howard Pyle. (Bring the Classics to Life: Level 2 Ser.). (ENG.). 2008. audio compact disk 12.95 (978-1-55576-459-3(2)) EDCON Pubng.

Merry Adventures of Robin Hood, unabr. ed. Howard Pyle. Read by John Chatty. 8 cass. (Running Time: 11 hrs. 30 mins.). (gr. 6-8). 1980. 56.95 (978-0-7861-0580-9(1), 2069) Blckstn Audio.
Robin Hood brings the brave, good-humored outlaw & his cohorts to life as they romp about deep in the Sherwood Forest just for the fun of it. Here are all the exciting tales, including Robin Hood's breathtaking escapes from his arch enemy, the Sheriff of Nottingham, a villain who sees Robin Hood as competition.

Merry Adventures of Robin Hood. unabr. ed. Howard Pyle. Read by Christopher Cazenove. (Running Time: 12 hrs. 50 mins.). (ENG.). 2009. 72.95 (978-1-4332-7787-0(5)); audio compact disk 90.00 (978-1-4332-7788-7(3)) Blckstn Audio.

Merry Adventures of Robin Hood. unabr. ed. Howard Pyle. Read by John Chatty. 8 cass. (Running Time: 12 hrs.). 1980. 56.00 (C-44) Jimcin Record.
The adventures of Robin, Friar Tuck, Little John & the rest of the merry men in Sherwood Forest.

Merry Adventures of Robin Hood. unabr. ed. Howard Pyle. Read by David Case. (Running Time: 12 hrs. 0 mins. 0 sec.). (ENG.). 2008. 22.99 (978-1-4001-5915-4(6)); audio compact disk 32.99 (978-1-4001-0915-9(9)); audio compact disk 65.99 (978-1-4001-3915-6(5)) Pub: Tantor Media. Dist(s): IngramPubServ

Merry Adventures of Robin Hood. unabr. collector's ed. Howard Pyle. Read by David Case. 8 cass. (Running Time: 12 hrs.). (J). (gr. 4-7). 1993. 64.00 (978-0-7366-2341-4(8), 3120) Books on Tape.
Relive the adventures of Robin Hood & his cohorts - Friar Tuck, Little John, Will Scarlet - in Sherwood Forest.

***Merry Adventures of Robin Hood: Bring the Classics to Life.** adpt. ed. Howard Pyle. (Bring the Classics to Life Ser.). 2008. pap. bk. 21.95 (978-1-55576-496-8(7)) EDCON Pubng.

Merry Adventures of Robin Hood of Great Renown, in Nottinghamshire: Classic Collection. unabr. ed. Howard Pyle. Read by Christopher Cazenove. (Running Time: 12 hrs. 50 mins.). (ENG.). 2009. 29.95 (978-1-4332-7791-7(3)) Blckstn Audio.

Merry Adventures of Robin Hood of Great Renown, in Nottinghamshire: Classic Collection. unabr. ed. Howard Pyle. Read by Christopher Cazenove. (Running Time: 12 hrs. 50 mins.). 2009. audio compact disk 19.95 (978-1-4332-7790-0(5)) Blckstn Audio.

Merry Band of Murderers: An Original Mystery Anthology of Songs & Stories. Read by Tom Weiner et al. Ed. by Claudia Bishop & Don Bruns. (Running Time: 34200 sec.). 2007. 65.95 (978-1-4332-0076-2(7)); audio compact disk 81.00 (978-1-4332-0077-9(5)); audio compact disk 29.95 (978-1-4332-0078-6(3)) Blckstn Audio.

Merry Blackeyed Snowman. Silvia Silk. 1986. (978-0-938861-07-2(7)) Jasmine Texts.

Merry Christmas see Little Women: With Good Wives

Merry Christmas. Heinle.

Merry Christmas: Parang Style. 1 cass. (Running Time: 30 min.). 8.00 (C0590B090, HarperThor) HarpC GBR.

Merry Christmas - Joe Scruggs. Perf. by Joe Scruggs. 1 cass. (Running Time: 32 min.). (J). (ps-4). 1989. 9.95 (978-0-916123-10-9(3), SPR 150, Shadow Play Recs & Video) Ed Graphics Pr.
Contains nine all-time Christmas favorites as well as four Joe Scruggs originals. Fully orchestrated with no synthesized sounds.

Merry Christmas, Amelia Bedelia. unabr. ed. Peggy Parish. Read by Sally Darling. 1 cass. (Running Time: 36 mins.). (Amelia Bedelia Ser.). (J). (gr. k-3). 1988. pap. bk. 17.00 (978-0-8072-0154-1(5), FTR130SP, Listening Lib) Random Audio Pubg.
Join in on the fun as everyone's favorite maid celebrates Christmas in her own inimitable, literal-minded fashion.

Merry Christmas, Gus!/Feliz Navidad, Gus! Jacklyn Williams. Illus. by Doug Cushman. (Running Time: 1001 sec.). (Read-It! Readers: Gus the Hedgehog Orange Level Ser.). (J). (gr. k-4). 2008. audio compact disk 9.27 (978-1-4048-4459-9(7)) CapstoneDig.

Merry Christmas Happy Hanukkah: A Multilingual Songbook & CD. Elizabeth C. Axford. Compiled by Elizabeth C. Axford. (ENG, HEB, SPA, GER & FRE.). 1999. pap. bk. 24.95 (978-0-9673325-0-5(8), PP1001) Pub: Piano Pr. Dist(s): BkWhole

Merry Christmas Sled. Read by Charles Dickens & E. T. A. Hoffmann. 4 cass. (Running Time: 4 hrs.). (Wood Cassette Toys Ser.). (J). 1991. 19.95 (978-1-55569-484-5(5), 8320) Great Am Audio.
Tape-1, christmas carols, Tape-2, The Nutcracker, Tapes 3&4, filled with sing-a-longs & popular christmas songs.

Merry Christmas Songs. 2004. bk. 7.95 (978-0-7119-9570-3(2)) Music Sales.

Merry Christmas Space Case. 2004. pap. bk. 38.75 (978-1-55592-638-0(X)); pap. bk. 32.75 (978-1-55592-626-7(6)); pap. bk. 14.95 (978-1-55592-149-1(3)) Weston Woods.

Merry Christmas, Space Case. James Marshall. 1 cass. (Running Time: 13 mins.). (J). 2004. pap. bk. 14.95 (978-1-55592-156-9(6)); pap. bk. 14.95 (978-1-55592-093-7(4)); pap. bk. 18.95 (978-1-55592-150-7(7)) Weston Woods.
Buddy McGee eagerly awaits a promised Christmas visit from his friend, the thing from outer space.

Merry Christmas, Space Case. James Marshall. 1 CD. (Running Time: 13 mins.). (J). (ps-3). 2004. pap. bk. 32.75 (978-1-55592-157-6(4)); 8.95 (978-1-55592-961-9(3)); audio compact disk 12.95 (978-1-55592-892-6(7)) Weston Woods.

Merry Christmas, Space Case. unabr. ed. Edward Marshall. 1 cass. (Running Time: 7 min.). (J). (gr. k-4). 1992. pap. bk. 15.90 (978-0-8045-6598-1(8), 6598) Spoken Arts.

Merry Christmas, Strega Nona. unabr. ed. Tomie dePaola. Illus. by Tomie dePaola. Read by Celeste Holm. Illus. by Tom Glazer. 1 cass. (Running Time: 31 mins.). (Love to Listen Ser.). (J). 1987. 11.00 incl. six Christmas carols. (978-0-8072-0138-1(3), FTR125CX, Listening Lib) Random Audio Pubg.
The witch in the 1976 Caldecott Honor Book, Strega Nona, is back & cooking! But will her Christmas feast be ready in time? There is little hope, until Big Anthony calls upon the magic of love.

Merry Go-Round see Poetry & Reflections

Merry-Go-Round. Wendy Ann Kesselman. Perf. by Wendy Ann Kesselman. Perf. by Steven Weber & Mary Stuart Masterson. 1 cass. (Running Time: 53 mins.). 1997. 19.95 (978-1-58081-153-8(1), RDP29) L A Theatre.

Merry-Go-Round. collector's ed. W. Somerset Maugham. Read by Penelope Dellaporta. 10 cass. (Running Time: 15 hrs.). 1987. 80.00 (978-0-7366-2501-2(1), 3259) Books on Tape.
A story of London at the turn of the century.

Merry-Go-Round. unabr. ed. Ruth Heller. 1 cass. (Running Time: 16 min.). (J). (gr. k-5). 1989. pap. bk. 17.95 (978-0-8045-6582-0(1), 6582) Spoken Arts.
Concrete & abstract nouns, possessives, plurals & more are accompanied by stunning, realistic pictures of all sorts of people, places & things. Reading Rainbow Review title. American Bookseller Pick of the Lists.

Merry Heart Doeth Good, Vol. 1. 2004. audio compact disk 9.99 (978-5-550-02186-6(2)) Nairi ARM.

Merry Heart Doeth Good, Vol. 3. 2004. audio compact disk 9.99 (978-5-550-02174-3(9)) Nairi ARM.

Merry Little Christmas, 2 cass. 2.37 (978-1-57734-028-7(0), 07001444) Covenant Comms.

***Merry Love to Play.** Gerry Harrington. Peter Horan. (ENG.). 2008. audio compact disk 28.95 (978-0-8023-8167-5(7)) Pub: Clo Iar-Chonnachta IRL. Dist(s): Dufour

Merry Mistress. Judith Saxton. Read by Annie Aldington. 4 cass. (Soundings Ser.). (J). 2005. 44.95 (978-1-84283-472-5(X)) Pub: ISIS Lrg Prnt GBR. Dist(s): Ulverscroft US

Merry Month of May see Prisoner

Merry Night of Halloween see Spirits & Spooks for Halloween

***Merry Wives of Maggody.** Joan Hess. Narrated by C. J. Critt. (Running Time: 12 hrs. 7 mins. 0 sec.). (Arly Hanks Mystery Ser.). (ENG.). 2010. audio compact disk 29.95 (978-1-60283-907-6(7)) Pub: AudioGO. Dist(s): Perseus Dist

***Merry Wives of Windsor.** abr. ed. William Shakespeare. (ENG.). 2003. (978-0-06-079954-0(4), Caedmon); (978-0-06-074314-7(X), Caedmon) HarperCollins Pubs.

Merry Wives of Windsor. unabr. ed. William Shakespeare. Narrated by Dinsdale Landen et al. (Arkangel Shakespeare Ser.). (ENG.). 2005. audio compact disk 19.95 (978-1-932219-23-4(4)) Pub: AudioGO. Dist(s): Perseus Dist
The dissolute Sir John Falstaff plans to seduce Mistress Ford and Mistress Page, two "Merry Wives of Windsor," thereby gaining access to their husbands' wealth. The two women have the old rogue's measure, however, and Falstaff's plots lead only to his humiliation. But the Merry Wives themselves fall victim to plotting as their plans to prevent Mistress Page's daughter Anne from marrying the young man she loves are frustrated in their turn. This play is performed by Dinsdale Landen, Penny Downie, and the Arkangel Cast.

Merry Wives of Windsor. unabr. ed. William Shakespeare. Read by Anthony Quayle et al. 2 cass. (Running Time: 2 hrs. 30 mins.). Dramatization. 17.95 (H170) Blckstn Audio.
Falstaff, the stumbling, drunken scoundrel finds himself in need of funds & sets his sights on Mistress Ford & Mistress Page. His act of writing identical love letters to the two ladies - who are close friends - sets this farce in motion. It is as the "perennial bachelor" that he meets his fall.

Merry Wives of Windsor. unabr. ed. William Shakespeare. Read by Audio Partners Staff. 2 cass. (Running Time: 2 hrs. 15 mins.). (Arkangel Shakespeare Ser.). 2004. 17.95 (978-1-932219-63-0(3), Atlntc Mnthly) Pub: Grove-Atltic. Dist(s): PerseuPGW

Merry Wives of Windsor, unabr. ed. William Shakespeare. Perf. by Anthony Quayle & Michael MacLiammoir. 3 cass. Dramatization. 1984. HarperCollins Pubs.
Cast includes: Joyce Redman, Murray Melvin, Alec McCowen, John Laurie, Ernest Milton, Ronnie Stevens, Michael Hordern, Anthony Nicholls, Michael Howe, Aubrey Richards, Trevor Martin, Peter Bayliss, Gerald Rowlands, Eric Jones, June Jago, Judith Stott, & Hazel Hughes.

Merry Wives of Windsor. unabr. ed. William Shakespeare. Perf. by Anthony Quayle & Michael MacLiammoir. 3 cass. (Running Time: 4 hrs.). Dramatization. (J). (ps-3). 1988. 30.00 (978-0-694-50651-4(6), SWC 203) HarperCollins Pubs.

Merry Wives of Windsor. unabr. ed. William Shakespeare. 2 cass. (Running Time: 3 hrs.). (Arkangel Complete Shakespeare Ser.). 2001. 17.95 (PengAudBks) Penguin Grp USA.

Merry Wives of Windsor. unabr. ed. William Shakespeare. Narrated by Flo Gibson. (Running Time: 1 hr. 45 mins.). 2005. 14.95 (978-1-55685-757-7(8)) Audio Bk Con.

Mes Chansons Preferees. Kidzup Productions Staff. (French Ser.). (FRE.). (J). 2003. audio compact disk 17.99 (978-1-894677-42-4(0)) Pub: Kidzup Prodns. Dist(s): Penton Overseas

Mes Pensees et Celles des Autres. Sacha Guitry. 1 cass. (FRE.). 1995. 21.95 (1722-LQP) Olivia & Hill.
A long monologue filled with witticisms by Sacha Guitry. As with all of Guitry's recordings, it is a perfect example of the French language well spoken.

Mes Yeux de l'Interieur (Mes Yeux D'Enfant) see Miguel

Mesa Verde. Scripts. Hank Mitchum. 5 CDs. (Running Time: 6 hrs.). (Stagecoach Ser.: No. 24). 2005. 14.99 (978-1-58807-868-1(X)) Am Pubng Inc.
Laurel Fox, half Ute and half white, left her tribal homeland and, against all odds, became a physician. A desperate showdown looms at Mesa Verde, home to the troubled spirits of an ancient people and Laurel's grandfather, a revered medicine man with powers greater than the white man has ever known.

Mesa Verde. unabr. ed. Gary McCarthy. Narrated by Gene Engene. 12 cass. (Running Time: 14 hrs.). 1997. 64.95 (978-1-55686-777-4(8)) Books in Motion.
Historical fiction on the remains of the civilization & artifacts of the Anasazi tribe.

Mesa Verde Communities. Compiled by Benchmark Education Staff. 2005. audio compact disk 10.00 (978-1-4108-5508-4(2)) Benchmark Educ.

Mesh: A Journey Through Discrete Geometry. Beau Janzen & Konrad Polthier. (Running Time: 2340 sec.). (Springer VideoMATH Ser.). 2007. 29.95 (978-3-540-28484-0(2), 3540284842) Spri.

***Mesh: How Selling Less & Sharing More Is Redefining Business.** unabr. ed. Lisa Gansky. (Running Time: 4 hrs. 30 mins.). (ENG.). 2010. audio compact disk 29.98 (978-1-59659-532-3(9), GildAudio) Pub: Gildan Media. Dist(s): HachBkGrp

Mesivtos - A Fresh Perspective. Dovid Harris. 1 cass. (Running Time: 1 hr. 30 min.). 1999. 6.00 (P60F3) Torah Umesorah.

Message. Contrib. by Dennis Allen. 1997. 11.98 (978-0-00-513768-0(3), 75608662) Pub: Brentwood Music. Dist(s): H Leonard

Message. unabr. ed. Eugene H. Peterson. Read by Eugene H. Peterson. Narrated by Kelly Ryan Dolan. 14 cass. (Running Time: 20 hrs.). (Proven Wisdom Ser.). (ENG.). 2003. 39.99 (978-1-58926-087-0(2)) Oasis Audio.

Message. unabr. ed. Eugene H. Peterson. 4 cass. (Running Time: 8 hrs.). 2003. 24.99 (978-1-58926-278-2(6), N58L-0120, Oasis Kids) Oasis Audio.

Message. unabr. ed. Eugene H. Peterson. Narrated by Kelly Ryan Dolan. 45 cass. (Running Time: 75 hrs.). (Proven Wisdom Ser.). (ENG.). 2004. 79.99 (978-1-58926-696-4(X), 6696) Oasis Audio.

Message. unabr. ed. Eugene H. Peterson. Narrated by Kelly Ryan Dolan. (Running Time: 77 hrs. 51 mins. 48 sec.). (ENG.). 2008. audio compact disk 79.99 (978-1-59859-451-5(6)); audio compact disk 39.99 (978-1-59859-458-4(3)) Oasis Audio.

Message: A Story from Nelson Mandela's Favorite African Folktales. Read by Charlize Theron. Compiled by Nelson Mandela. (Running Time: 7 mins.). (ENG.). 2009. 1.99 (978-1-60024-805-4(5)) Pub: Hachet Audio. Dist(s): HachBkGrp

MESSAGE: Dear Slave , Be FREE. Featuring A. Lane. Prod. by JumpOff TVsm Staff. Directed By A. Fitzgerald. 2003. 12.00 (978-0-9745010-1-7(8)) AHHA Ent.
"FREE Slaves" , Captain Morgan , real "Caribbean Pirates" , "African - American" politicians of the 1800's , and much more packed in to this exciting little known TRUE story.

Message Bible. unabr. ed. Eugene H. Peterson. Narrated by Kelly Ryan Dolan. (Running Time: 77 hrs. 52 mins. 13 sec.). (ENG.). 2008. audio compact disk 79.99 (978-1-59859-454-6(0)); audio compact disk 79.99 (978-1-59859-453-9(2)) Oasis Audio.

Message Bible. unabr. ed. Eugene H. Peterson. Narrated by Kelly Ryan Dolan. (Running Time: 24 hrs. 0 mins. 0 sec.). (ENG.). 2008. audio compact disk 39.99 (978-1-59859-460-7(5)) Oasis Audio.

Message Bible: Complete Bible. unabr. ed. Eugene H. Peterson. Narrated by Kelly Ryan Dolan. (Running Time: 80 hrs. 0 mins. 0 sec.). (ENG.). 2004. 29.99 (978-1-60814-307-8(4)) Oasis Audio.

Message Bible: New Testament. unabr. ed. Eugene H. Peterson. Narrated by Kelly Ryan Dolan. (Running Time: 24 hrs. 0 mins. 0 sec.). (ENG.). 2003. 19.99 (978-1-60814-306-1(6)) Oasis Audio.

Message Bible Remix Psalms & Proverbs. unabr. ed. Eugene H. Peterson. Narrated by Kelly Ryan Dolan. (Running Time: 6 hrs. 0 mins. 0 sec.). (ENG.). 2007. 6.99 (978-1-60814-359-7(7)) Oasis Audio.

Message Bible Remix Psalms & Proverbs. unabr. ed. Eugene H. Peterson. Narrated by Kelly Ryan Dolan. (Running Time: 6 hrs. 0 mins. 0 sec.). (ENG.). 2008. audio compact disk 19.99 (978-1-59859-462-1(1)) Oasis Audio.

Message for Dads. Jeff Cavins. 2004. audio compact disk 7.95 (978-1-932927-43-6(3)) Ascensn Pr.

Message for Quick Verse. Findex Com Staff. 2004. audio compact disk 19.95 (978-1-930594-84-5(4)) Findex.

Message for the New Age. George King. 2009. audio compact disk (978-0-937249-54-3(8)) Aetherius Soc.

Message from Absalom. unabr. ed. Anne A. Thompson. Read by Nancy Dannevik. 7 cass. (Running Time: 7 hrs.). 42.00 (978-0-7366-0230-3(5), 1226) Books on Tape.
The heroine is an ex-CIA agent. The action begins when a CIA operative smuggles her a code message with instructions that she must take it to the President of the United States & trust no one else. This she does but not without horrifying obstacles - from near rape & torture in Communist Bulgaria, to being held hostage on a plane hijacked to the desert by Palestinian guerillas.

Message from Archbishop Desmond Tutu: An Excerpt from Nelson Mandela's Favorite African Folktales. Read by Desmond Tutu. Compiled by Nelson Mandela. Composed by Johnny Clegg. (Running Time: 3 mins.). (ENG.). 2009. 1.99 (978-1-60024-658-6(3)) Pub: Hachet Audio. Dist(s): HachBkGrp

Message from Hell: Luke 16:19-31. Ed Young. (J). 1982. 4.95 (978-0-7417-1219-6(9), A0219) Win Walk.

Message from Malaga. unabr. collector's ed. Helen MacInnes. Read by Wanda McCaddon. 11 cass. (Running Time: 16 hrs. 30 min.). 1982. 88.00 (978-0-7366-0395-9(6), 1372) Books on Tape.
To a background of clacking heels & hands, whirling skirts & the haunting cadences of flamenco guitars a drama of espionage begins to unfold in a cafe courtyard in Malaga. For Ian Ferrier, on a vacation visit to his old friend Jeff Reid, it means the startling discovery that Reid is more than just a wine exporter. He is in fact a CIA agent involved in smuggling Cuban refugees into Spain.

Message from the Masters. Brian L. Weiss. 2001. (978-1-58621-018-2(1)) Hachet Audio.

Message in a Bottle. Nicholas Sparks. Read by Kimberly Schraf. 1998. audio compact disk 72.00 (978-0-7366-5137-0(3)) Books on Tape.

Message in a Bottle. abr. ed. Nicholas Sparks. (ENG.). 2006. 14.98 (978-1-59483-687-9(6)) Pub: Hachet Audio. Dist(s): HachBkGrp

Message in a Bottle. unabr. ed. Nicholas Sparks. Read by Kimberly Schraf. 7 CDs. (Running Time: 8 hrs. 12 mins.). 2001. audio compact disk Books on Tape.
A single mother finds a message in a bottle that changes her entire life.

Message in a Bottle. unabr. ed. Nicholas Sparks. Read by Kimberly Schraf. 7 cass. (Running Time: 10 hrs. 30 min.). 1998. 56.00 (978-0-7366-4104-3(1), 4609) Books on Tape.
A thirty-six-year-old single mother is recovering from a failed marriage. As she jogs along the shores of Cape Cod, she comes upon a half-buried bottle containing a love letter. Heartfelt words from a man to his "darling Catherine" were written only three weeks earlier. After reading the note, she takes a daring leap into the unknown, changing her life forever. Boarding a plane, she faces an uncertain future. Yet it brims with the promise of wisdom gained through introspection & the possibility of finding a deep & long-lasting love.

Message in a Bottle. unabr. ed. Nicholas Sparks. Read by Kimberly Schraf. (Running Time: 7 hrs. 30 mins.). (ENG.). 2009. 44.98 (978-1-60788-151-3(9)) Pub: Hachet Audio. Dist(s): HachBkGrp

Message in a Bottle, unabr. ed. Nicholas Sparks. Read by Kimberly Schraf. 6 cass. (Running Time: 9 hrs.). 1999. 29.98 (FS9-43189) Highsmith.

Message Is: Pray, Love & Serve CD. Interview. Mother Teresa of Calcutta. 1 CD. (Running Time: 28 mins.). 2006. audio compact disk 12.95 (978-1-57970-420-9(4), ECN199D, Audio-For) J Norton Pubs.
Mother Teresa was born in Skopje, Yugoslavia of Albanian parents, and was educated in Ireland. Since becoming a nun in 1950, her work in Calcutta with the destitute and dying made her honored throughout the world. In 1979 she was awarded the Nobel Peace Prize. She says that without love there can be no peace, and without God there can be no love. Human dignity and happiness will depend, as it always has, on our recognition of our vocation to be holy. Her simple, unforgettable message is: pray, love, serve.

Message of Divali. Swami Jyotirmayananda. 1 cass. (Running Time: 45 min.). 1990. 10.00 Yoga Res Foun.

Message of Redemption & Revival in the Book of Ruth. Nancy Leigh DeMoss. 3 cass. 2003. (978-0-940110-50-2(4)) Life Action Publishing.

Message of Religion. Swami Amar Jyoti. 1 cass. 1989. 9.95 (Q-22) Truth Consciousness.
Fundamentals of religion. Cultures differ, but not true religion. Religion as a way of life.

***Message of Resurrection: Christ Is Risen!** abr. ed. Eugene H. Petersen. Narrated by Mark Lowry. (ENG.). 2008. 10.49 (978-1-60814-741-0(X)) Oasis Audio.

Message of Resurrection: Christ Is Risen! abr. ed. Eugene H. Peterson. Narrated by Mark Lowry. (Running Time: 1 hr. 15 mins. 44 sec.). (ENG.). 2008. audio compact disk 14.99 (978-1-59859-210-8(6)) Oasis Audio.

Message of the Anointed's Anointing. Kenneth Copeland. Perf. by Kenneth Copeland. 1 cass. (Anointed & His Anointing Ser.: Tape 4). 1995. cass. & video 5.00 (978-1-57562-031-2(6)) K Copeland Pubns.

Message of the Gita. 1 cass. Incl. Message of the Gita: How to Elevate the Mind. (153); 12.99 (153) Yoga Res Foun.

Message of the Gita: How to Elevate the Mind see Message of the Gita

Message of the Gita to Sri Aurobindo. Karan Singh. 1 cass. 9.00 (A0475-89) Sound Photosyn.
The former Indian Ambassador to the U.S. in a tight, evocative & poetic speech.

Message of the Sphinx: A Quest for the Hidden Legacy of Mankind. abr. ed. Graham Hancock & Robert Bauval. Read by Nick Ullett. 2 cass. (Running Time: 3 hrs.). (Alternative History Ser.). 1998. 17.95 (978-1-57453-256-2(1)) Audio Lit.
Clues to the ancient riddles posed by Egypt's great monuments of stone.

Message Psalms & Proverbs. unabr. ed. Eugene H. Peterson. Read by Kelly Ryan Dolan & Carol Nixon. 4 cass. (Running Time: 6 hrs.). 2003. 24.99; audio compact disk 26.99 Oasis Audio.

Message Remix Bible: Complete Bible. unabr. ed. Eugene H. Peterson. Narrated by Kelly Ryan Dolan. (Running Time: 77 hrs. 51 mins. 48 sec.). (ENG.). 2006. 29.99 (978-1-60814-308-5(2)) Oasis Audio.

Message Remix Bible: New Testament. unabr. ed. Eugene H. Peterson. Narrated by Kelly Ryan Dolan. (Running Time: 24 hrs. 0 mins. 0 sec.). (ENG.). 2003. 19.99 (978-1-60814-309-2(0)) Oasis Audio.

Message Sent: Meditations for Retrieving the Gift of Love. Narrated by Terri Amos. Music by Rashid Lanie. 1 cass. (Running Time: 1.10). 2003. audio compact disk 16.95 Pub: WorldofLite Pubng. Dist(s): DeVorss

Message to Garcia. Elbert Hubbard. 10.00 (LSS1123) Esstee Audios.

Message to Garcia. Elbert Hubbard. Read by Charlie Tremendous Jones. (Life-Changing Classics Ser.). (ENG.). 2007. audio compact disk 19.95 (978-1-933715-32-2(4)) Executive Bks.

Message to Garcia. unabr. ed. Elbert Hubbard. (ENG.). 2005. 0.98 (978-1-59659-055-7(6), GildAudio) Pub: Gildan Media. Dist(s): HachBkGrp

Message to Garcia: Being a Preachment by Fra Elbert Hubbard. unabr. ed. Elbert Hubbard. 1 cass. (Running Time: 15 mins.). 2000. 7.00 (978-0-7661-0838-7(4)) Kessinger Pub.
A marvelous story about a man who "went it alone & got it done." Translated into all languages, this story has become a model for success.

Message to the Planet. unabr. ed. Iris Murdoch. Perf. by Juliet Mills. 4 cass. (Running Time: 6 hrs.). 2003. 58.95 (978-1-931056-92-2(7), N Millennium Audio) Pub: New Millenn Enter. Dist(s): PerseuPGW
Explores the meaning of life in a story of love & betrayal, faith & doubt.

Message to the Seven Churches: A Biblical Interpretation. Concept by Ermance Rejebian. (ENG.). 2007. 5.99 (978-1-60339-147-4(9)); audio compact disk 5.99 (978-1-60339-148-1(7)) Listenr Digest.

Message to the World: An Audio Journey into the First World Conference of Indigenous Peoples. 2 cass. (Running Time: 2 hrs.). 1993. 19.95 (978-1-879323-18-6(4)) Sound Horizons AV.
One week before The Earth Summit in Rio, 1992 a groundbreaking conference of over 700 indigenous people from six different continents made history. The conference took place in Kari-Oka, a village consecrated & built for this event. You will hear inspiring music as well as learn about the plight of indigenous people around the globe. A significant portion of the sales of "Message to the World" will be donated to help the cause of indigenous people around the world.

Message/REMIX New Testament. unabr. ed. 20 CDs. (Running Time: 20 hrs.). 2003. audio compact disk 49.99 Oasis Audio.

***Message//REMIX Solo: An Uncommon Devotional.** unabr. ed. Eugene H. Peterson. Narrated by Kelly Ryan Dolan. (Running Time: 13 hrs. 0 mins. 0 sec.). (ENG.). 2010. 17.99 (978-1-60814-760-1(6)) Oasis Audio.

Messages see James Dickey Reads His Poetry & Prose

Messages: Angels Guide Audio with Music. Belinda Womack. 2 cass. 1999. 22.00 (978-0-9659850-3-1(2)) Pubng Joy.

Messages: Class 4. Diana Goodey et al. (Running Time: 3 hrs. 1 min.). (ENG., 2006. audio compact disk 40.00 (978-0-521-61444-3(9)) Cambridge U Pr.

Messages from Space. Read by James Pickering. (Running Time: 35 min.). 14.95 (13615) MMI Corp.
Discusses sounds from Jupiter, spectrum, messages from deep space, extraterrestrail life & more.

Messages from Spirit Set: Exploring Your Connection to Divine Guidance. Colette Baron-Reid. 4 CDs. 2008. audio compact disk 23.95 (978-1-4019-2281-8(3)) Hay House.

Messages from Your Angels. Doreen Virtue. 2 CDs. 2004. audio compact disk 18.95 (978-1-4019-0444-9(0)) Hay House.

Messages from Your Animal Spirit Guide: A Meditation Journey. Steven D. Farmer. 1 CD. 2007. audio compact disk 10.95 (978-1-4019-1768-5(2)) Hay House.

Messages of Rediscovering the Kingdom Vol 1. Myles Munroe. (Running Time: 4 hrs. 19 mins.). 2007. 24.99 (978-1-4245-0693-4(X)) Tre Med Inc.

Messages of Rediscovering the Kingdom Vol 2. Myles Munroe. (Running Time: 4 hrs. 18 mins.). 2007. 24.99 (978-1-4245-0694-1(8)) Tre Med Inc.

Messages of Rediscovering the Kingdom Vol 3. Myles Munroe. (Running Time: 3 hrs. 39 mins.). 2007. 24.99 (978-1-4245-0695-8(6)) Tre Med Inc.

Messages of Rediscovering the Kingdom Vol 4. Myles Munroe. (Running Time: 4 hrs. 37 mins.). 2007. 24.99 (978-1-4245-0696-5(4)) Tre Med Inc.

Messages of Rediscovering the Kingdom Vol 5. Myles Munroe. (Running Time: 5 hours, 38 minutes). 2007. 24.99 (978-1-4245-0697-2(2)) Tre Med Inc.

Messages of Rediscovering the Kingdom, Volume 2. Myles Munroe. (Running Time: 15480 sec.). 2006. audio compact disk 24.99 (978-0-7684-0252-0(2)) Destiny Image Pubs.

Messages 1. Diana Goodey & Noel Goodey. (Running Time: 2 hrs. 39 mins.). (ENG.). 2005. audio compact disk 42.00 (978-0-521-61428-3(7)) Cambridge U Pr.

Messages 1. Diana Goodey & Noel Goodey. Contrib. by James Dingle. (Running Time: 2 hrs. 39 mins.). (ENG.). 2005. 41.00 (978-0-521-61427-6(9)) Cambridge U Pr.

Messages 1 Class CDs Italian Version. Diana Goodey & Noel Goodey. (Running Time: 2 hrs. 39 mins.). 2006. audio compact disk 41.00 (978-0-521-61460-3(0)) Cambridge U Pr.

Messages 2. Diana Goodey & Noel Goodey. (ENG.). 2005. audio compact disk 41.00 (978-0-521-61432-0(5)) Cambridge U Pr.

Messages 2. Diana Goodey & Noel Goodey. Contrib. by James Dingle. 2 cass. (ENG.). 2005. 41.00 (978-0-521-61431-3(7)) Cambridge U Pr.

Messages 3. Diana Goodey et al. Contrib. by James Dingle. (Running Time: 2 hrs. 39 mins.). (ENG., 2006. 43.05 (978-0-521-61437-5(6)) Cambridge U Pr.

Messages 3: Class Audio CDs. Diana Goodey et al. (Running Time: 2 hrs. 39 mins.). (ENG., 2005. audio compact disk 43.05 (978-0-521-61438-2(4)) Cambridge U Pr.

Messages 3 Class CDs Italian Version. Diana Goodey et al. (Running Time: 2 hrs. 39 mins.). 2006. audio compact disk 41.00 (978-0-521-61462-7(7)) Cambridge U Pr.

Messages 4 Class Audio Cassettes. Diana Goodey & Noel Goodey. Contrib. by James Dingle. (Running Time: 2 hrs. 55 mins.). 2006. 41.00 (978-0-521-61443-6(0)) Cambridge U Pr.

Messe de l'Athee. Honoré de Balzac. 1 cass. (Running Time: 1 hr.). (FRE.). 1996. pap. bk. 19.50 (978-1-58085-363-7(3)) Interlingua VA.
Includes dual French-English transcription. The combination of written text & clarity & pace of diction will open the door for intermediate & advanced students to genuine comprehension & the use of literary texts for advancement in rapid understanding of written & oral language materials. The audio text plus written text concept makes foreign languages accessible to a much wider range of students than books alone.

Messenger. Lois Lowry. 3 CDs. (Running Time: 3 hrs.). (J). (gr. 5 up). 2004. audio compact disk 25.50 (978-1-4000-8620-7(5), Listening Lib) Pub: Random Audio Pubg. Dist(s): NetLibrary CO

Messenger. Daniel Silva. Read by Christopher Lane. (Gabriel Allon Ser.: No. 6). 2009. 70.00 (978-1-60775-544-9(0)) Find a World.

Messenger. abr. ed. Daniel Silva. Read by Christopher Lane. (Running Time: 21600 sec.). (Gabriel Allon Ser.: No. 6). 2007. audio compact disk 14.99 (978-1-59600-887-8(3), 9781596008878, BCD Value Price) Brilliance Audio.
Please enter a Synopsis.

Messenger. unabr. ed. J. R. Chabot. Read by Maynard Villers. 8 cass. (Running Time: 8 hrs. 42 min.). 2001. 49.95 (978-1-55686-827-6(8)) Books in Motion.
When aliens visit the earth, the visitors bring news of their planet's effect on the earth's evolution. 13 world citizens are chosen to receive this data, but the aliens have an ulterior motive for making this move.

Messenger. unabr. ed. Lois Lowry. 2 cass. (Running Time: 3 hrs.). (YA). (gr. 5 up). 2004. 30.00 (978-0-8072-2373-4(5), Listening Lib) Random Audio Pubg.

Messenger. unabr. ed. Lois Lowry. Read by David Morse. 4 CDs. (Running Time: 14640 sec.). (ENG.). (J). (gr. 7-12). 2006. audio compact disk 28.00 (978-0-307-28421-1(2), Listening Lib) Pub: Random Audio Pubg. Dist(s): Random

Messenger. unabr. ed. Daniel Silva. Read by Christopher Lane. (Running Time: 11 hrs.). (Gabriel Allon Ser.: No. 6). 2006. 39.25 (978-1-59710-935-2(5), 9781597109352, BADLE); 24.95 (978-1-59710-934-5(7), 9781597109345, BAD); 82.25 (978-1-59600-027-8(9), 9781596000278, BrilAudUnabridg); 32.95 (978-1-59600-026-1(0), 9781596000261, BAU); audio compact disk 36.95 (978-1-59600-029-2(5), 9781596000292, Bril Audio CD Unabri); audio compact disk 24.95 (978-1-59335-785-6(0), 9781593357856, Brilliance MP3); audio compact disk 39.25 (978-1-59335-919-5(5), 9781593359195, Brinc Audio MP3 Lib) Brilliance Audio.
Please enter a Synopsis.

Messenger. unabr. ed. Daniel Silva. Read by Christopher Lane. 9 CDs. (Running Time: 39600 sec.). (Gabriel Allon Ser.: No. 6). 2006. audio compact disk 97.25 (978-1-59600-030-8(9), 9781596000308, BriAudCD Unabrid) Brilliance Audio.

Messenger: The Legacy of Mattie J. T. Stepanek & Heartsongs. unabr. ed. Jeni Stepanek & Larry Lindner. Narrated by Jeni Stepanek. (Running Time: 11 hrs. 48 mins. 40 sec.). (ENG.). 2009. 25.89 (978-1-60814-606-2(5), SpringWater); audio compact disk 36.99 (978-1-59859-658-8(6), SpringWater) Oasis Audio.

Messenger of Truth. unabr. ed. Jacqueline Winspear. Narrated by Orlagh Cassidy. 6 cass. (Maisie Dobbs Mystery Ser.: Bk. 4). 2006. 59.95 (978-0-7927-4533-4(7), CSL 991); audio compact disk 89.95 (978-0-7927-4367-5(9), SLD 991) AudioGO.

Messenger of Truth. unabr. ed. Jacqueline Winspear. Read by Orlagh Cassidy. 9 CDs. (Running Time: 11 hrs. 0 mins. 0 sec.). (Maisie Dobbs Mystery Ser.: Bk. 4). (ENG.). 2006. audio compact disk 39.95 (978-1-59397-971-3(1)) Pub: Macmill Audio. Dist(s): Macmillan

Messengers from Mind at Large. Michael Grosso. 1 cass. (AA & A Symposium Ser.). 9.00 (A0251-87) Sound Photosyn.

Messer Marco Polo. unabr. ed. Donn Byrne. Read by Efrem Zimbalist & Efrem Zimbalist, Jr. (Running Time: 7200 sec.). (J). 2006. 22.95 (978-0-7861-4669-7(9)); audio compact disk 24.00 (978-0-7861-6738-8(6)); audio compact disk 19.95 (978-0-7861-7402-7(1)) Blckstn Audio.

Messerschmitts over Sicily. unabr. ed. Johannes Steinhoff. Narrated by George Guidall. 7 cass. (Running Time: 9 hrs. 30 mins.). 1992. 60.00 (978-1-55690-694-7(3), 92228E7) Recorded Bks.
A German fighter pilot recounts his part in the defense of Sicily, June 1943. His first-person account gets you inside a Messerschmitt 109 as it maneuvers through the air & offers a perspective on the political maneuvers taking place on the ground below.

***Messiah.** Compiled by Barbour Publishing, Inc. (ENG.). 2010. audio compact disk 9.99 (978-1-61626-059-0(9), Barbour Bks) Barbour Pub.

Messiah, Mormon Tabernacle Choir. 2 cass. 18.95 (1500139) Covenant Comms.

Messiah. Paul T. Smith. 8 cass. (New Testament Study Ser.). 19.98 (978-1-55503-764-2(X), 0900117) Covenant Comms.
Role & mission of Savior.

Messiah. Paul Thomas Smith. 6 cass. (New Testament Study Ser.). 2004. 21.95 (978-1-59156-149-1(3)); audio compact disk 21.95 (978-1-59156-150-7(7)) Covenant Comms.

Messiah. unabr. ed. Boris Starling. Read by Joe Dunlop. 13 CDs. (Running Time: 15 hrs. 15 mins.). (Isis (CDs) Ser.). (J). 2005. audio compact disk 99.95 (978-0-7531-2466-6(1)); 94.95 (978-0-7531-1214-4(0)) Pub: ISIS Lrg Prnt GBR. Dist(s): Ulverscroft US
London is in the grip of a heatwave: airless days, steamy nights and a killer stalking the streets. Women are being murdered to some mysterious pattern, clues left behind, only corpses with silver spoons their tongues.

Messiah, Set. Mormon Tabernacle Choir. 2 CDs. audio compact disk 37.95 (2800160) Covenant Comms.

Messiah: A New Testament, Paul Thomas Smith. 8 cass. 29.95 (978-1-57734-417-9(0), 0900176) Covenant Comms.
Improve your understanding of the Savior.

Messiah at Christmas: Bb Clarinet. Composed by George Frideric Handel. James Curnow. 2007. pap. bk. 12.95 (978-90-431-2592-5(X), 904312592X) H Leonard.

Messiah at Christmas: Bb Trumpet. Composed by George Frideric Handel. James Curnow. 2007. pap. bk. 12.95 (978-90-431-2594-9(6), 9043125946) H Leonard.

Messiah at Christmas: Eb Alto Saxophone. Composed by George Frideric Handel. James Curnow. 2007. pap. bk. 12.95 (978-90-431-2593-2(8), 9043125938) H Leonard.

Messiah at Christmas: F/Eb Horn. Composed by George Frideric Handel. James Curnow. 2007. pap. bk. 12.95 (978-90-431-2595-6(4), 9043125954) H Leonard.

Messiah at Christmas: Flute/Oboe/Mallet Percussion. Composed by George Frideric Handel. James Curnow. 2007. pap. bk. 12.95 (978-90-431-2591-8(1), 9043125911) H Leonard.

Messiah at Christmas: Trombone/Euphonium BC/TC/Bassoon. Composed by George Frideric Handel. James Curnow. 2007. pap. bk. 12.95 (978-90-431-2596-3(2), 9043125962) H Leonard.

Messiah at Easter: Flute/Oboe/Mallet Percussion. Composed by George Frideric Handel. James Curnow. 2007. pap. bk. 12.95 (978-90-431-2654-0(3), 9043126543) H Leonard.

Messiah Comes: Fourth Sunday of Advent. Carroll Stuhlmueller. Read by Carroll Stuhlmueller. 1 cass. (Running Time: 1 hr.). 7.95 (TAH221) Alba Hse Comns.

Messiah Comes: The Immaculate Conception. Carroll Stuhlmueller. Read by Carroll Stuhlmueller. 1 cass. (Running Time: 1 hr.). 7.95 (TAH219) Alba Hse Comns.

Messiah Comes: Third Sunday of Advent. Carroll Stuhlmueller. Read by Carroll Stuhlmueller. 1 cass. (Running Time: 45 min.). 7.95 (TAH220) Alba Hse Comns.

Messiah, History, & the Tribulation Period: 2005 Prophecy Conference (on CD) Speeches. Tim Cohen. Featuring Tim Cohen. 12 CDs. (Running Time: 12 hrs. 27 mins.). 2005. audio compact disk 144.95 (978-1-933689-20-3(X), CDPack01) Prophecy Hse.
In July, 2005, Tim introduced his forthcoming MESSIAH, HISTORY, AND THE TRIBULATION PERIOD multi-volume series - in seven prophecy conference sessions held over three days in Odessa, Texas. The following sessions are available on either eight DVDs (DVDPack01) or twelve CDs (CDPack01): Some Highlights (on "Messiah, History, and the Tribulation Period") • Some Hermeneutics (Biblical Interpretation) • The Real Rapture • "The AntiChrist and a Cup of Tea" (An Overview and An Update) • On Feasts and Prophecy • Question and Answer Session • The Passover: Israel Conformed to Yeshua's Crucifixion, Death, Burial, and Resurrection. The DVD set also includes a full-length live interview with God's Learning Channel on a ninth disc. Even the most seasoned bible and prophecy "veterans" will find that there is much to learn from Tim. Prophecy House is convinced that you will find Tim's prophetic teachings at this "Messiah, History, and the Tribulation Period" conference to be the most instructive, the most informative, and the most powerful relating to prophecy and the Person and work of Yeshua (Jesus) that you have ever heard. In fact, there has likely never before been a prophecy conference offering this much biblical understanding and knowledge. This is the one which you, as well as all the Church of God in Christ, truly cannot afford to miss!.

Messiah, History, & the Tribulation Period: 2005 Prophecy Conference: on Feasts & Prophecy (on CD) Speeches. Tim Cohen. Featuring Tim Cohen. 3 CDs. (Running Time: 3 hrs.). 2005. audio compact disk 44.95 (978-1-933689-27-2(7), CDPack06) Prophecy Hse.
In these two DVDs (DVDPack06) or three CDs (CDPack06), which are from Tim's 2005 "Messiah, History, and the Tribulation Period Prophecy" Conference, Tim demonstrates that all the biblical feasts are fulfilled in each of the major biblical weeks (i.e., the Crucifixion Week, the Week of History, and the coming Tribulation Week). This understanding will greatly impact your prophetic discernment, as well as that of the entire Church in days to come, related to God's Holy Days. For example, as Tim demonstrates, it is untrue that the relative timing of the coming rapture can be determined on the basis of the prophetic fulfillment of the feasts. Like Tim's "The Real Rapture," this too is revolutionary, and once again, Tim surprises and astonishes with the depth of the biblical knowledge and understanding he has received from God. What Tim offers here will further challenge and change the views of many who have been led astray by the common prophetic half-truths of our time. Catch this - you'll be glad you did!.

Messiah, History, & the Tribulation Period: 2005 Prophecy Conference: the Passover, Israel Conformed to Yeshua's Crucifixion, Death, Burial, & Resurrection. Speeches. Tim Cohen. Featuring Tim Cohen. 3 CDs. (Running Time: 3 hrs. 18 mins.). 2005. audio compact disk 44.95 (978-1-933689-28-9(5), CDPack07) Prophecy Hse.
Taken from Tim's 2005 "Messiah, History, and the Tribulation Period" Prophecy Conference, "The Passover: Israel Conformed to Yeshua's Crucifixion, Death, Burial, and Resurrection" is available on two DVDs (DVDPack07) or three CDs (CDPack07). What Tim shares herein will vastly enhance your understanding of Yeshua's (Jesus') crucifixion, death, burial, and resurrection; these central events to the Christian faith are more central to the work of God in all spheres than the saints yet know. Listen as Tim begins to unfold this great, transforming mystery for the Church. Not only will your understanding of the work of Christ be expanded and taken to new depths, but your apprehension of God's calling upon Israel as a nation and a people will begin to be just as transformed. This presentation is based upon the fourth day in Tim's "Messiah, History, and the Tribulation Period" volume entitled, "The Harmony of Weeks: God's Inspired 'Grand Unified Theology' Unveiled." This is the heart of all of Tim's work for Christ and the greatest example of what God has called him to accomplish for the saints and the Church; it is the "creme de la creme." Herein, Tim demonstrates that Israel as a nation suffers the typological equivalent of a national crucifixion, death, and burial at the midpoints of the Week of History (past) and the Tribulation Week (yet future); like Christ, Israel is biblically called God's "firstborn son." This has huge theological implications, and explains much about God's dealings with His chosen people throughout history. We are confident that this material will radically enhance your understanding of Christ, Israel, and God's dealings with both; it quite literally represents a quantum leap in biblical understanding and theology.

Messiah, History, & the Tribulation Period: 2005 Prophecy Conference: the Real Rapture (on CD) Speeches. Tim Cohen. Featuring Tim Cohen. 3 CDs. (Running Time: 3 hrs. 27 mins.). 2005. audio compact disk 44.95 (978-1-933689-26-5(9), CDPack05) Prophecy Hse.
Taken from Tim's 2005 "Messiah, History, and the Tribulation Period" Prophecy Conference, these two presentations on two DVDs (DVDPack05) or three CDs (CDPack05) will have you glued to the edge of your seat from start to finish. This material, which is derived from the corresponding volume in Tim's upcoming "Messiah, History, and the Tribulation Period" series of books, has changed the views of entire churches on the Tribulation Period and the timing of the coming rapture! It is revolutionary, and will leave you wondering how so many in the Church could have been so misled for so long by so-called "prophecy experts," "scholars," and "teachers!" Tim makes some startling and astonishing revelations; these presentations - the most powerful ever given to the Church on the rapture - will significantly affect your views on the subject of Jesus' return and its timing for the saints. Yes, Tim also covers all the "rapture bases," to include the pretribulational, midtribulational, pre-wrath, and posttribulational views, before offering the true biblical view and timings. This is the meat of The Word, and you will come away equipped to carefully test everything you've heard from scripture. (You may find yourself watching these two presentations several times over!) False "Christian" teachers and "Christian" prophets everywhere take heed: Tim is gunning for your lies, and his aim is lethal! Those who hear Tim will no longer have an excuse to walk in a dark haze of prophetic deception. This is a powerful call to repentance for the entire Church.

Messiah in a Manger - Donkeys. 1 cass. (J). 1995. 5.99 (978-1-886858-01-5(2)) Shepherds Tales.

Messiah Interviews. Narrated by John Herring. (ENG.). 2009. audio compact disk 31.99 (978-1-934814-07-9(5)) Red Planet Au.

Messiah of Morris Avenue. Tony Hendra. Narrated by John Bedford Lloyd. 6 CDs. (Running Time: 27060 sec.). (Sound Library). 2006. audio compact disk 64.95 (978-0-7927-4019-3(X), SLD 938) AudioGO.

Messiah of Morris Avenue: A Novel. Tony Hendra. 2006. 17.95 (978-1-59397-919-5(3)) Pub: Macmill Audio. Dist(s): Macmillan

Messiah Seed, Vol. I. Story Waters. 4 CDs. 2005. audio compact disk 29.95 (978-0-9765062-1-8(1)) Limitlessness.

Messiah True & Faithful. Beverly Darnall. 1994. 75.00 (978-0-7673-0692-8(9)); 11.98 (978-0-7673-0657-7(0)) LifeWay Christian.

Messiah True & Faithful. Beverly Darnall. 1994. audio compact disk 85.00 (978-0-7673-0720-8(8)) LifeWay Christian.

Messiah True & Faithful (Sterep Acc Cassette0. Beverly Darnall. 1994. 75.00 (978-0-7673-0696-6(1)) LifeWay Christian.

Messiah's Song of Love Vol. 1: The Psalms. Read by Joanne Sweetman. 1 CD. (Running Time: 1 hr. 14 min.). (Best of Ser.). 1998. audio compact disk 12.95 (978-0-9663621-1-4(X)) Sweetnote Rec.
Translation, with music accompaniment.

Messiah's Song of Love Vol. 1: The Psalms. Read by Joanne Sweetman. 5 CDs. (Running Time: 6 hrs. 15 min.). 1998. audio compact disk 49.95 (978-0-9663621-7-6(9)) Sweetnote Rec.
Reading of translation of the psalms, with musical accompaniment.

Messiah's Song of Love Vol. 1: The Psalms, Set. Scripts. Read by Joanne Sweetman. 1 cass. (Running Time: 1 hr. 14 min.). (Best of Ser.). 1998. 10.95 (978-0-9663621-0-7(1)) Sweetnote Rec.
Translation, with music accompaniment.

Messiah's Song of Love Vol. 1: The Psalms, Set. Scripts. Read by Joanne Sweetman. 5 cass. (Running Time: 6 hrs. 15 min.). 1998. 44.95 (978-0-9663621-2-1(8)) Sweetnote Rec.
Reading of translation of the psalms, with musical accompaniment.

Messiah's Song of Love Vol. 2: The Proverbs, Ecclesiastes & Song of Solomon, Scripts. Read by Joanne Sweetman. 3 cass. (Running Time: 3 hrs. 20 min.). 1998. 27.95 (978-0-9663621-5-2(2)); audio compact disk 24.95 (978-0-9663621-6-9(0)) Sweetnote Rec.
Reading of translation of the Proverbs, Ecclesiastes & Song of solomon, with an original music sound track.

Messiah's Song of Love Vol. 2: The Proverbs, Ecclesiastes & Song of Solomon. Scripts. Read by Joanne Sweetman. 1 cass. (Running Time: 55 min.). (Best of Ser.). 1998. 10.95 (978-0-9663621-3-8(6)); audio compact disk 12.95 (978-0-9663621-4-5(4)) Sweetnote Rec.

Messian. Read by James Hall. 1 cass . (Running Time: 1 hr.). 10.98 (978-1-57908-411-0(7), 1408); audio compact disk 15.98 CD. (978-1-57908-410-3(9), 1408) Platinm Enter.

***Messy Spirituality: God's Annoying Love for Imperfect People.** Mike Yaconelli. (Running Time: 4 hrs. 5 mins. 0 sec.). (ENG.). 2008. 14.99 (978-0-310-30480-7(6)) Zondervan.

Meta Music Artist Sampler. Eric Heberling et al. 1 cass. (Meta Music Ser.). 6.95 (978-1-56102-239-7(X)) Inter Indus.
The tape has excerpts from seven different tapes.

Metabolic Acidosis in the ICU. Read by Arnold Aberman. 1 cass. (Running Time: 1 hr. 30 min.). 1985. 12.00 (C8537) Amer Coll Phys.

Metafisica al Alcance de Todos. abr. ed. Conny Mendez. Read by Isabel Varas. (Running Time: 4200 sec.). 2006. audio compact disk 12.95 (978-1-933499-29-1(X)) Fonolibro Inc.

Metafisica 4 En 1. abr. ed. Scripts. Conny Mendez. 5 CDs. (Running Time: 21600 sec.). (SPA.). 2006. audio compact disk 24.95 (978-1-933499-01-7(X)) Fonolibro Inc.
FonoLibro se enorgullece en presentar el audiolibro en espanol del bestseller Metafisica 4 en 1 de la afamada Conny Mendez; titulo que ha atrapado los corazones y almas de millones de lectores de metafisica en Latinoamerica, Espana y la poblacion hispana en Estados Unidos, los cuales han comprobado que La Fe Mueve Montanas. Aunque muchos titulos han sido escritos basados en las Leyes del Pensamiento, muy pocos son los que combinan estas leyes con la Verdad Espiritual.Es precisamente la combinacion de libros que compone este titulo (Metafisica al Alcance de Todos, Te regalo lo que se te antoje, El maravilloso numero 7 y Quien es y quien fue el Conde de Saint Germain) lo que constituye una renovacion para la persona no especializada en el tema. El audiolibro Metafisica 4 en 1 lo ayudara a tomar el control de su vida al manejar asi mismo el poder interior dirigiendolo a traves de canales constructivos mientras la salud incrementa visiblemente. Conny Mendez siempre creyo que las verdades espirituales, filosoficas y metafisicas debian ser expuestas con las palabras mas claras y sencillas de manera que cualquier nino inteligente pudiera captarlas. FonoLibro les trae de una forma amena el audiolibro de su coleccion mas famosa en una magnifica produccion la cual puedes escuchar en todo momento y en cada capitulo encontrar una solucion a cualquier problema que estes pasando.

Metafisica 4 En 1: Volume II, Vol. 2. unabr. abr. ed. Conny Mendez. (Running Time: 18000 sec.). 2007. audio compact disk 24.95 (978-1-933499-46-8(X)) Fonolibro Inc.

***Metafisica 4 En 1 (Vol 3), vol. 3.** abr. ed. Conny Mendez. Prod. by FonoLibro Inc.Tr. of Metaphysics 4 In 1 (Vol 3). (SPA.). 2010. audio compact disk 24.95 (978-1-933499-98-7(2)) Fonolibro Inc.

Metal. (Materials Ser.). (ENG.). 2009. audio compact disk 5.95 (978-1-4329-3250-3(0), AcornHR) Heinemann Rai.

Metal: The Autumn Season. Ann Bailey. Read by Ann Bailey. Read by Jon Bailey. 1 cass. (Running Time: 50 min.). (Wellness Through the Seasons Ser.). 1994. 12.00 (978-1-889643-06-9(8)) SourcePoint.
Music, sounds & spoken word illustrate the connection between the autumn season & health within the body, mind & spirit. Includes script.

Metal Guitar, Vol. 2. Jason Beveridge. (Progressive Ser.). 2004. pap. bk. 24.95 (978-1-86469-180-1(8), 256-124) Kolala Music SGP.

Metal Swarm. Kevin J. Anderson, Jr. Read by David Colacci. (Playaway Adult Fiction Ser.). 2008. 94.99 (978-1-60640-808-7(9)) Find a World.

Metal Swarm. unabr. ed. Kevin J. Anderson. (Running Time: 19 hrs.). (Saga of Seven Suns Ser.: Bk. 6). 2007. 44.25 (978-1-59737-234-3(X), 9781597372343, BADLE); 29.95 (978-1-59737-233-6(1), 9781597372336, BAD) Brilliance Audio.

Metal Swarm. unabr. ed. Kevin J. Anderson. Read by David Colacci. (Running Time: 68400 sec.). (Saga of Seven Suns Ser.: Bk. 6). 2007. audio compact disk 42.95 (978-1-59737-227-5(7), 9781597372275, Bril Audio CD Unabri); 127.25 (978-1-59737-226-8(9), 9781597372268, BrilAudUnabridg); audio compact disk 132.25 (978-1-59737-228-2(5), 9781597372282, BriAudCD Unabrid); audio compact disk 44.25 (978-1-59737-232-9(3), 9781597372329, Brlnc Audio MP3 Lib) Brilliance Audio.
Please enter a Synopsis.

Metal Swarm, No. 2. unabr. ed. Kevin J. Anderson. Read by David Colacci. (Running Time: 68400 sec.). (Saga of Seven Suns Ser.: Bk. 6). 2007. audio compact disk 29.95 (978-1-59737-231-2(5), 9781597372312, Brilliance MP3) Brilliance Audio.

Metallica Collector's Box. Micheal Sumsion & Essi Berelian. As told by Weekley Louise & Sian Jones. 3 CDs. 2005. audio compact disk (978-1-84240-324-2(9)) Chrome Dreams GBR.
Now well into their third decade, Metallica are without doubt the biggestRock band on the planet. But despite tragedy, controversy and the normalstrains of Rock N' Roll excess mixed with gruelling touring schedules, thisextraordinary group battle on year after year always delighting theirdevoted millions.With new material rumoured to appear later in the year and some tracksalready available via the official website and getting rave reviews to boot,the signs are good for a full scale return to form over the coming monthsMetallica Collector's Box is the perfect opportunity for all fan's to getthe low down on this phenomenal band, the highs and the lows. This setcontains 3CDs of interviews and audio-biographies, posters, booklets,postcards and more.

Metallurgical Chemistry. unabr. ed. Read by Fathi Habashi. 5 cass. (Running Time: 5 hrs.). pap. bk. 430.00 (92) Am Chemical.

Metalworking Technology & Deterioration of Jin Bronzes from the Tianma-Qucun Site, Shanxi, China. Quanyu Wang. (BAR International Ser.: Vol. 1023). 2002. audio compact disk 112.50 (978-1-84171-404-2(6)) Pub: British Arch Reports GBR. Dist(s): David Brown

Metamorfosis: El Impulso Hacia El Cambio. Franco Soldi. 2003. (978-1-931059-14-5(4)) Taller del Exito.

Metamorfosis: Un Artista del Ayuno - Informe a una Academia. abr. ed. Franz Kafka. Read by Pedro Montoya. 3 CDs.Tr. of Metamorphosis - A Fasting Artist - A Report to an Academy. (SPA.). 2002. audio compact disk 17.00 (978-958-9494-68-4(4)) YoYoMusic.

Metamorphose, La Colonie Penitentiaire, Franz Kafka. Read by Daniel Mesguich. 3 CDs. (Running Time: 4 hrs. 30 min.). 1991. audio compact disk 29.95 (1063-AV) Olivia & Hill.

Metamorphoses. Ovid. Read by Barry Kraft. 2008. audio compact disk 19.95 (978-1-4332-4963-1(4)) Blckstn Audio.

Metamorphoses. unabr. ed. Ovid. Read by Barry Kraft. (Running Time: 55800 sec.). 2008. 85.95 (978-1-4332-1322-9(2)) Blckstn Audio.

Metamorphoses. unabr. ed. Ovid. Read by Barry Kraft. Tr. by Frank Justus Miller. (Running Time: 55800 sec.). 2008. audio compact disk & audio compact disk 99.00 (978-1-4332-1323-6(0)) Blckstn Audio.

Metamorphoses. unabr. ed. Ovid. Tr. by Frank Justus Miller. (Running Time: 55800 sec.). 2008. audio compact disk 29.95 (978-1-4332-1324-3(9)) Blckstn Audio.

Metamorphosis. Contrib. by J R et al. 2005. audio compact disk 17.98 (978-5-558-78755-9(4)) C Mason Res.

Metamorphosis. Franz Kafka. Read by Tom Whitworth. (Running Time: 5 hrs.). 2005. 25.95 (978-1-60083-616-9(X), Audiofy Corp) Iofy Corp.

Metamorphosis. Franz Kafka. Read by Martin Javis. (Running Time: 1 hr. 15 mins.).Tr. of Wervandlung. 2003. 20.95 (978-1-60083-841-5(3)) Iofy Corp.

Metamorphosis. Franz Kafka. Read by Martin Jarvis. Tr. by Richard Stokes. 2 CDs. (Running Time: 1 hr. 12 min.).Tr. of Wervandlung. (C). 2003. audio compact disk 17.98 (978-962-634-286-2(2), Naxos AudioBooks) Naxos.

Metamorphosis. abr. ed. Franz Kafka. Perf. by James Mason. 1 cass. 1984. 12.95 (SWC 1594) HarperCollins Pubs.

Metamorphosis. unabr. ed. Franz Kafka. Read by Martin Jarvis.Tr. of Wervandlung. (YA). 2008. 34.99 (978-1-60514-901-1(2)) Find a World.

Metamorphosis: And Other Stories. Franz Kafka & Guy de Maupassant. Read by Tom Whitworth. (Running Time: 16200 sec.). (Unabridged Classics in Audio Ser.). (ENG.). 2005. audio compact disk 49.99 (978-1-4001-3045-0(X)) Pub: Tantor Media. Dist(s): IngramPubServ

Metamorphosis - A Fasting Artist - A Report to an Academy see Metamorfosis: Un Artista del Ayuno - Informe a una Academia

Metamorphosis - A Fasting Artist - A Report to an Academy. Franz Kafka. Read by Pedro Montoya. (Running Time: 3 hrs.). 2002. 16.95 (978-1-60083-188-1(5), Audiofy Corp) Iofy Corp.

Metamorphosis Activity Fun Pack. Sally A. Bonkrude. Ed. by Karla Lange & Steve Bonkrude. Illus. by Terri Bahn. 1 cass. (J). (ps-2). 1988. bk. 12.95 (978-0-924829-00-0(1)); 5.95 (978-0-924829-08-6(7)) Musical Imag.
Metamorphosis of a tadpole & caterpillar.

Metamorphosis & Dragonfield. Milbre Burch. Perf. by Milbre Burch. Based on a story by Jane Yolen. (ENG.). 2007. audio compact disk 15.00 (978-0-9795271-4-2(7)) Kind Crone.

Metamorphosis & Other Stories. Franz Kafka. Read by George Guidall. 5 Cassettes. (Running Time: 8.75 Hours). 19.95 (978-1-4025-2791-3(8)) Recorded Bks.

Metamorphosis & Other Stories. Franz Kafka & Guy de Maupassant. Read by Tom Whitworth. (Playaway Young Adult Ser.). (ENG.). 2009. 50.00 (978-1-60775-630-9(7)) Find a World.

Metamorphosis & Other Stories, unabr. ed. Short Stories. Franz Kafka. Tr. by Joachim Neugroschel. Narrated by George Guidall. 6 cass. (Running Time: 8 hrs. 45 mins.). 1999. 51.00 (978-0-7887-0218-1(1), 94443E7) Recorded Bks.
Reveals the author's extraordinary talents in a variety of forms: prose poems, allegories & novelettes. Showcases the straight-faced humor, startling psychological insights & haunting imagination for which he is revered as a modern master.

Metamorphosis & Other Stories, with EBook. unabr. ed. Franz Kafka & Guy de Maupassant. Narrated by Tom Whitworth. (Running Time: 5 hrs. 0 mins. 0 sec.). (ENG.). 2009. audio compact disk 19.99 (978-1-4001-6109-6(6)); audio compact disk 19.99 (978-1-4001-1109-1(9)) Pub: Tantor Media. Dist(s): IngramPubServ

Metamorphosis & Other Stories, with eBook. unabr. ed. Franz Kafka & Guy de Maupassant. Narrated by Tom Whitworth. (Running Time: 5 hrs. 0 mins. 0 sec.). (ENG.). 2009. audio compact disk 39.99 (978-1-4001-4109-8(5)) Pub: Tantor Media. Dist(s): IngramPubServ

Metamorphosis & Short Stories. unabr. collector's ed. Franz Kafka & Guy de Maupassant. Read by Thomas Whitworth. 5 cass. (Running Time: 5 hrs.).Tr. of Wervandlung. 1992. 30.00 (978-0-7366-2229-5(2), 3019) Books on Tape.
Also included are stories by Guy de Maupassant: "The Englishman," "The Piece of String," "The Necklace," "A Crisis," "The Will," "Love," "The Inn" & "Was It a Dream".

Metamorphosis CD: Changing Bodies. Bobbie Kalman. (ENG.). (J). 2008. audio compact disk 10.00 (978-0-7787-7712-0(X)) CrabtreePubCo CAN.

***Metamorphosis: Junior Year: Junior Year.** unabr. ed. Betsy Franco. (Running Time: 2 hrs.). 2010. 39.97 (978-1-4418-9023-8(8), 9781441890238, Candlewick Bril); 19.99 (978-1-4418-9022-1(X), 9781441890221, Candlewick Bril) Brilliance Audio.

***Metamorphosis: Junior Year: Junior Year.** unabr. ed. Betsy Franco. Read by James Franco & David Franco. (Running Time: 2 hrs.). 2010. audio compact disk 19.99 (978-1-4418-9018-4(1), 9781441890184, Candlewick Bril) Brilliance Audio.

***Metamorphosis: Junior Year: Junior Year.** unabr. ed. Betsy Franco et al. (Running Time: 1 hr.). 2010. audio compact disk 19.99 (978-1-4418-9020-7(3), 9781441890207, Candlewick Bril); audio compact disk 39.97 (978-1-4418-9019-1(X), 9781441890191, Candlewick Bril); audio compact disk 39.97 (978-1-4418-9021-4(1), 9781441890214, Candlewick Bril) Brilliance Audio.

Metamorphosite. unabr. ed. Robert A. Monroe. Read by Robert A. Monroe. (Running Time: 45 min.). (Gateway Experience - Prospecting Ser.). 1984. 14.95 (978-1-56113-286-7(1)) Monroe Institute.
Hunter your gems of change.

Metaphor & the Short Story. unabr. ed. Walter Havighurst. 1 cass. (Running Time: 23 min.). 1953. 12.95 (23007) J Norton Pubs.
A short story which is approached as a technique for conveying a general truth through the presentation of specific instance in an entertaining way.

Metaphors & Butterflies. unabr. ed. Gregory Bateson. 1 cass. (Running Time: 1 hr. 30 min.). 1975. 11.00 Big Sur Tapes.
This is the first tape of the 12-tape archive or library edition of "The Informal Esalen Lectures, 1975-1980" recorded during the last five years of Gregory Bateson's life.

Metaphors & Symbols of Transformation. unabr. ed. Ralph Metzner. 1 cass. (Running Time: 1 hr. 30 min.). 1980. 11.00 (01601) Big Sur Tapes.
One needs to find words for one's experiences in order to bring them from the inner world through to the outer world. Metzner describes ten classic metaphors for transformation & evolution to other dimensions of being.

Metaphors of Identity: Operating Metaphors & Iconic Change. Charles Faulkner. 3 cass. 1991. pap. bk. (978-1-884605-02-4(8)) Genesis II.
Personal & professional development. Includes booklet.

Metaphors of Identity: Operating Metaphors¿& Iconic Change. Charles Faulkner. 4 CDs. 2005. audio compact disk 39.95 (978-1-884605-15-4(X)) Genesis II.
How do we know what to want? Our desires, deepest longings, even our hidden fears, are shaped (and revealed) by unconscious metaphors in our everyday language. Life is a Game. Life is a Problem. Life is an Uphill Struggle. Life is an Adventure. These Operating Metaphors? reveal what the world means to us. They determine our beliefs, values, actions, lifestyles, even our identities.Edited from a live seminar, this audio seminar presents a complete day of training and transformational experiences of this new metaphoric approach to awareness, change, and personal and professional development. Also included are follow-up interviews with two participants whose lives changed dramatically as a result.CD 1: Metaphors and the Mind How unconscious metaphors determine our desires, values, beliefs and identities.CD 2: Discovering Operating Metaphors? Part 1How to recognize an individual or company?s Operating Metaphors? from ordinary language.CD 3: Discovering Operating Metaphors? Part 2How to recognize an individual or company?s Operating Metaphors? from personal possessions, actions or lifestyles, and appreciate its importance.CD 4: Iconic ChangeProcesses to clarify, enrich, or totally transform your Operating Metaphors? for fuller and more satisfying experiences in your relationships, work and life.

Metaphors of Transformation. Ralph Metzner. 2 cass. (Running Time: 1 hr. 28 min.). 1982. 18.00 (01601) Big Sur Tapes.

Metaphysical Affirmations. 1 cass. (Running Time: 1 hr. 30 min.). 12.98 (978-0-87554-512-7(2), 1110) Valley Sun.
Universal laws & important metaphysical concepts as suggestions: You know that where your attention goes your energy flows & that you attract what you are & what you concentrate upon. So you focus your attention upon positive, loving things. All answers can be found in your higher mind. You attract what you feel worthy of receiving. You deserve the best life has to offer. Much more.

Metaphysical Club: A Story of Ideas in America. abr. ed. Louis Menand. Read by Henry Leyva. 6 CDs. (Running Time: 7 hrs.). (ENG.). 2001. audio compact disk 34.95 (978-1-56511-542-2(2), 1565115422) Pub: HighBridge. Dist(s): Workman Pub

Metaphysical Love Stories. Dick Sutphen. 2 cass. (Running Time: 3 hrs.). (C). 1992. 14.95 (978-0-87554-525-7(4)) Valley Sun.

Metaphysical Meditations. J. Donald Walters & Swami Kriyananda. 2003. audio compact disk 10.95 (978-1-56589-152-4(X)) Pub: Crystal Clarity. Dist(s): Natl Bk Netwk

Metaphysical Oneness. Eldon Taylor. Read by Eldon Taylor. Ed. by Leslie Brice. 1 cass. (Running Time: 1 hr.). 1992. 16.95 (978-1-56705-333-3(5)) Gateways Inst.
Self improvement.

Metaphysical Poetry. unabr. ed. Poems. Perf. by Cedric Hardwicke & Robert Newton. 1 cass. Incl. Metaphysical Poetry: Beauty. Abraham Cowley. (SWC 1049); Metaphysical Poetry: For Her Gait If She Be Walking. William Browne. (SWC 1049); Metaphysical Poetry: For Hope. Richard Crashaw. (SWC 1049); Metaphysical Poetry: Hope. George Herbert. (SWC 1049); Metaphysical Poetry: Jordan. George Herbert. (SWC 1049); Metaphysical Poetry: Love. George Herbert. (SWC 1049); Metaphysical Poetry: Man. George Herbert. (SWC 1049); Metaphysical Poetry: Man. Henry Vaughan. (SWC 1049); Metaphysical Poetry: Miserie. George Herbert. (SWC 1049); Metaphysical Poetry: No Platonique Love. William Cartwright. (SWC 1049); Metaphysical Poetry: Ode upon Doctor Harvey. Abraham Cowley. (SWC 1049); Metaphysical Poetry: On the Countess Dowager of Pembroke. William Browne. (SWC 1049); Metaphysical Poetry: Prayer. George Herbert. (SWC 1049); Metaphysical Poetry: Shadows in the Water. Thomas Traherne. (SWC 1049); Metaphysical Poetry: Signs & Grones. George Herbert. (SWC 1049); Metaphysical Poetry: The Flaming Heart. Richard Crashaw. (SWC 1049); Metaphysical Poetry: The Pulley. George Herbert. (SWC 1049); Metaphysical Poetry: The Retreate. Henry Vaughan. (SWC 1049); Metaphysical Poetry: The World. Henry Vaughan. (SWC 1049); Metaphysical Poetry: To Althea from Prison. Richard Lovelace. (SWC 1049); Metaphysical Poetry: To His Coy Mistress: The Garden. Andrew Marvell. (SWC 1049); Metaphysical Poetry: When Westwall Downes. Ralph Strode. (SWC 1049); Metaphysical Poetry: Why So Pale & Wan, Fond Lover. John Suckling. (SWC 1049); 1984. 12.95 (978-0-694-50038-3(0), SWC 1049) HarperCollins Pubs.

Metaphysical Poetry: Beauty see Metaphysical Poetry

Metaphysical Poetry: For Her Gait If She Be Walking see Metaphysical Poetry

Metaphysical Poetry: For Hope see Metaphysical Poetry

Metaphysical Poetry: Hope see Metaphysical Poetry

Metaphysical Poetry: Jordan see Metaphysical Poetry

Metaphysical Poetry: Love see Metaphysical Poetry

Metaphysical Poetry: Man see Metaphysical Poetry

Metaphysical Poetry: Miserie see Metaphysical Poetry

Metaphysical Poetry: No Platonique Love see Metaphysical Poetry

Metaphysical Poetry: Ode upon Doctor Harvey see Metaphysical Poetry

Metaphysical Poetry: On the Countess Dowager of Pembroke see Metaphysical Poetry

Metaphysical Poetry: Prayer see Metaphysical Poetry

Metaphysical Poetry: Shadows in the Water see Metaphysical Poetry

Metaphysical Poetry: Signs & Grones see Metaphysical Poetry

Metaphysical Poetry: The Flaming Heart see Metaphysical Poetry

Metaphysical Poetry: The Pulley see Metaphysical Poetry

Metaphysical Poetry: The Retreate see Metaphysical Poetry

Metaphysical Poetry: The World see Metaphysical Poetry

Metaphysical Poetry: To Althea from Prison see Metaphysical Poetry

Metaphysical Poetry: To His Coy Mistress: The Garden see Metaphysical Poetry

Metaphysical Poetry: When Westwall Downes see Metaphysical Poetry

Metaphysical Poetry: Why So Pale & Wan, Fond Lover see Metaphysical Poetry

Metaphysical Self-Sufficiency: Finding Your Own Answers. unabr. ed. Galexis. 2 cass. (Running Time: 3 hrs.). 1997. 19.95 (978-1-56089-053-9(3), G134) Visionary FL.
Practical living of spiritual principles workshop. How to self test yourself kinesiologically, read "omens" & "messages," trust your intuition. Meditation included.

Metaphysical Straight Talk: How to Avoid "Quacks" & Make Metaphysics Work for You. Ginger Chalford. 2 cass. (Metaphysical-Spiritual Ser.). 1988. bk. 17.95 (978-1-56089-017-1(7)) Visionary FL.
Features an explanation of the principles of metaphysics, what questions to ask astrologers, readers & healers etc. to receive benefit & avoid "Being taken".

Metaphysical Value-Judgments. unabr. ed. Gary Hull. 1 cass. (Running Time: 1 hrs. 40 min.). 1997. 12.95 (978-1-56114-406-8(1), CH46C) Second Renaissance.
The crucial role that metaphysical value-judgments play in all areas of life.

Metaphysics of Separation & Forgiveness see Metaphysik der Trennung und Vergebung

Metaphysics of Separation & Forgiveness. Kenneth Wapnick. 2 CDs. 2006. audio compact disk 12.00 (978-1-59142-269-3(8), CD34) Foun Miracles.

Metaphysics of Separation & Forgiveness. Kenneth Wapnick. 1 CD. (Running Time: 2 hrs. 2 mins. 53 secs.). 2006. 10.00 (978-1-59142-270-9(1), 3m34) Foun Miracles.

Metaphysics of Time. Kenneth Wapnick. 4 CDs. 2002. audio compact disk 24.00 (978-1-59142-306-5(6), CD139) Foun Miracles.

Metaphysics of Time. Kenneth Wapnick. 1 CD. (Running Time: 3 hrs. 57 mins. 4 secs.). 2007. 19.00 (978-1-59142-307-2(4), 3m139) Foun Miracles.

Metaphysics 4 In 1 (Vol 3) see Metafisica 4 En 1 (Vol 3)

Metaphysik der Trennung und Vergebung. 1 cass. (Running Time: 1 hr.).Tr. of Metaphysics of Separation & Forgiveness. 2001. (978-3-923662-53-1(X)) Foun Miracles.

Metas: Como Alcanzar Nuestros Objetivos Con Exito. Zig Ziglar. 2003. (978-1-931059-37-4(3)) Taller del Exito.

METAtropolis. unabr. ed. Jay Lake, Tobias Buckell, Elizabeth Bear, John Scalzi, Karl Schroeder. Read by Michael Hogan, Scott Brick, Kandyse McClure, Alessandro Juliani, Stefan Rudnicki, John Scalzi. (Running Time: 9 hrs.). 2009. 24.99 (978-1-4233-9495-2(X), 9781423394952, Brilliance MP3); 39.97 (978-1-4233-9496-9(8), 9781423394969, Brlnc Audio MP3 Lib); 39.97 (978-1-4233-9497-6(6), 9781423394976, BADLE); audio compact disk 29.99 (978-1-4233-9493-8(3), 9781423394938, Bril Audio CD Unabri); audio compact disk 92.97 (978-1-4233-9494-5(1), 9781423394945, BriAudCD Unabrid) Brilliance Audio.

Metcalf Testimony Series. unabr. ed. Earle Metcalf & Earle Metcalf. 2007. (978-1-60246-006-5(X)) Tucson Taber.

Meteor! Patricia Polacco. Narrated by Patricia Polacco. 1 cass. (Running Time: 15 min.). (J). (gr. k-4). 2001. pap. bk. 17.95 (978-0-8045-6857-9(X), 6857) Spoken Arts.
When a meteor crashes into their Michigan farmyard one summer, Grandma and Grandpa Gaw find their lives dramatically changed.

Meteor Man. 1943. (MM-7040) Natl Recrd Co.

Meteorologist: Science Series. 1 cass. (Science Ser.). (J). bk. (TWIN 426) NewSound.
Includes book.

Meteors. 1 cass. (Running Time: 26 min.). 14.95 (23335) MMI Corp.
Tells the story of "falling stars," Meteor showers, characteristics, historical meteors & more.

Method & Definitions; The Axiom of Scripture. John Robbins. 1 cass. (Introduction to Economics Ser.: No. 3). 5.00 Trinity Found.

Method of Grace. 1 CD. 2007. audio compact disk 10.95 (978-1-931047-57-9(X)) Fellow Perform Arts.

Methode de Guitare Jazz. Jean Bonal. Ed. by Michael Lefferts. (FRE.). (C). 1997. bk. 28.95 (978-0-7692-1321-7(9), 01010314, Warner Bro) Alfred Pub.

Methode de Synchronisation Hemispherique. unabr. ed. Robert A. Monroe. Read by Roland Simon. 1 cass. (Running Time: 30 min.). (Mind Food Ser.). 1992. 14.95 (978-1-56102-429-2(5)) Inter Indus.
An introduction & demonstration of benefits of Hemi-Sync.

Methode Orange. Reboullet et al. (Methode Orange Ser.). (FRE., (J). (gr. 7-12). 1979. wbk. ed. 85.00 (978-0-686-60844-8(5)) Prentice ESL.

Methods of Execution. unabr. ed. Frederick D. Huebner. Read by John MacDonald. 7 cass. (Running Time: 10 hrs. 30 min.). 1994. 56.00 (978-0-7366-2882-2(7), 3584) Books on Tape.
Attorney Matthew Riordan finds himself appealing the death sentence of a convicted serial killer he detests. How did this happen?.

Methylmalonic Acidemia - A Bibliography & Dictionary for Physicians, Patients, & Genome Researchers. Compiled by Icon Group International, Inc. Staff. 2007. ring bd. 28.95 (978-0-497-11258-5(2)) Icon Grp.

Metric System: Syllabus. Don H. Parker et al. (J). 1974. 18.15 (978-0-89420-163-9(8), 280000) Natl Book.

Metrics Are Coming! Janeen Brady. 1 cass. (J). (ps-4). 1980. 9.95 (978-0-944803-14-1(8)) Brite Music.

***Metro Girl.** abr. ed. Janet Evanovich. Read by C. J. Critt. (ENG.). 2004. (978-0-06-081801-2(8), Harper Audio); (978-0-06-081803-6(4), Harper Audio) HarperCollins Pubs.

Metro Girl. abr. ed. Janet Evanovich. Read by C. J. Critt. (Running Time: 21600 sec.). (Alex Barnaby Ser.: No. 1). 2006. audio compact disk 14.95 (978-0-06-112652-9(7)) HarperCollins Pubs.

***Metro Girl.** unabr. ed. Janet Evanovich. Read by C. J. Critt. (ENG.). 2004. (978-0-06-081814-2(X), Harper Audio); (978-0-06-081813-5(1), Harper Audio) HarperCollins Pubs.

Metro Girl. unabr. ed. Janet Evanovich. Read by C. J. Critt. (Alex Barnaby Ser.: No. 1). 2004. 29.95 (978-0-06-073839-6(1)) HarperCollins Pubs.

Metro Girl. unabr. ed. Janet Evanovich. Narrated by C. J. Critt. 6 cass. (Running Time: 9 hrs.). (Alex Barnaby Ser.: No. 1). 2004. 69.75 (978-1-4193-0733-1(9), 97866MC) Recorded Bks.

Metroland. unabr. ed. Julian Barnes. Read by Greg Wise. 6 cass. 1999. 54.95 (978-0-7540-0376-2(0), CAB 1799) AudioGO.
As adolescents, Christopher & Toni sneered at the stifling ennui of Metroland, their patch of suburbia on the Metropolitan Line. They longed for life to begin with sex & freedom & the ability to make their own decisions. Now thirty, Chris starts to settle comfortably into bourgeois contentment himself. Luckily, Toni is still around to challenge such backsliding.

Metronome Beats. Bruce Goldberg. (ENG.). 2005. 13.00 (978-1-57968-114-2(X)); audio compact disk 17.00 (978-1-57968-105-0(0)) Pub: B Goldberg. Dist(s): Baker Taylor

Metropolis. Based on a book by Thea Von Harbou. 2 cass. (Running Time: 2 hrs.). 2001. 19.95 (ZIGG001) Lodestone Catalog.

Metropolis. Thea Von Harbou. Adapted by Bob E. Flick. Engineer Bob E. Flick. Des. by Adam Mayefsky. 2 CDs. (Running Time: 2 hrs. 30 mins.). Dramatization. 1995. audio compact disk 19.00 (978-1-884214-17-2(7)) Ziggurat Prods.
A science-fiction classic! Journey to the eerie future of machine-dominated 2027, and witness first-hand as the evil Master of Metropolis feeds his machines...with human beings!.

Metropolis, abr. ed. Thea Von Harbou. Prod. by Bob E. Flick. Engineer Bob E. Flick. Prod. by Perry Jacob. 2 cass. (Running Time: 2 hr. 30 min.). Dramatization. 1995. 18.00 (978-1-884214-01-1(0), 1-884214-01-0) Ziggurat Prods.
Adaptation of the novel "Metropolis" to audio, with full cast, musical score & sound effects.

***Metropolis.** adpt. ed. Thea Von Harbou. (Bring the Classics to Life Ser.). (ENG.). 2008. audio compact disk 12.95 (978-1-55576-578-1(5)) EDCON Pubng.

Metropolis, unabr. ed. Upton Sinclair. Read by Flo Gibson. 6 cass. (Running Time: 9 hrs.). 1995. 24.95 (978-1-55685-384-5(X)) Audio Bk Con.
Montague, a young lawyer from Mississippi, is introduced to New York City in the early 1990's by his younger brother who has been accepted by "High Society." Glimpses of Wall Street, the Tenderloin, tenement districts, opulent entertainment & the lives of the very, very wealthy are described with bitterness & price tags that are meant to shock.

***Metropolis: Bring the Classics to Life.** adpt. ed. Thea Von Harbou. (Bring the Classics to Life Ser.). 2008. pap. bk. 21.95 (978-1-55576-622-1(6)) EDCON Pubng.

Metropolitan Life. Fran Lebowitz. Read by Fran Lebowitz. 1 cass. (Running Time: 30 min.). 8.95 (AMF-22) Am Audio Prose.
Lebowitz talks about wit & style in the 1980's as compared to the era of the Algonquin Round Table.

Metropolitan Murder. unabr. ed. Lee M. Jackson. Narrated by Joe Dunlop. 8 cass. (Running Time: 8 hrs. 45 mins.). 2004. 79.75 (978-1-84505-219-5(6), H1756MC, Clipper Audio) Recorded Bks.

Metropolitan Nightmare see Poetry of Benet

Metzger's Dog. unabr. ed. Thomas Perry. Narrated by Michael Kramer. (Running Time: 8 hrs. 0 mins. 0 sec.). (ENG.). 2009. audio compact disk 24.99 (978-1-4001-6023-5(5)) Pub: Tantor Media. Dist(s): IngramPubServ

Metzger's Dog. unabr. ed. Thomas Perry. Narrated by Michael Kramer. Intro. by Carl Hiaasen. (Running Time: 8 hrs. 0 mins. 0 sec.). (ENG.). 2009. audio compact disk 34.99 (978-1-4001-1023-0(8)) Pub: Tantor Media. Dist(s): IngramPubServ

Metzger's Dog. unabr. ed. Thomas Perry. Read by Michael Kramer. Intro. by Carl Hiaasen. (Running Time: 8 hrs. 0 mins. 0 sec.). (ENG.). 2009. audio compact disk 69.99 (978-1-4001-4023-7(4)) Pub: Tantor Media. Dist(s): IngramPubServ

Meurtre Chez Tante Leonie. l.t. ed. Estelle Monbrun. (French Ser.). 1995. bk. 30.99 (978-2-84011-105-4(5)) Pub: UlverLrgPrint GBR. Dist(s): Ulverscroft US

Meutre de R. Ackroyd. 1 cass. (Running Time: 1 hr.). Dramatization. (Maitres du Mystere Ser.). (FRE.). 1996. 11.95 (1825-MA) Olivia & Hill.
Popular radio thriller, interpreted by France's best actors.

Mexican-American War. unabr. ed. Jeffrey Rogers Hummel. Read by George C. Scott. (Running Time: 9000 sec.). (United States at War Ser.). 2006. audio compact disk 25.95 (978-0-7861-6381-6(X)) Pub: Blckstn Audio. Dist(s): NetLibrary CO

Mexican-American War, unabr. ed. Jeffrey Rogers Hummel. Ed. by Wendy McElroy. Narrated by George C. Scott. 2 cass. (Running Time: 2 hrs. 30 min.). Dramatization. (United States at War Ser.). (YA). (gr. 9 up). 1989. 17.95 (978-0-938935-54-4(2), 390279) Knowledge Prod.
Mexico lost one million square miles to a victorious United States in the Mexican-American War (1846-1847). America's borders expanded to the Rio Grande, to the Pacific & to the 49th parallel. But within this move toward empire would come the seeds of America's Civil War.

Mexican Folk Dance Booklet w/Music CD. Vicki Corona. (Celebrate the Cultures Ser.: 3-11A). 2004. pap. bk. 24.95 (978-1-58513-114-3(8)) Dance Fantasy.

Mexican Hat. unabr. ed. Michael McGarrity. Narrated by George Guidall. 6 cass. (Running Time: 8 hrs. 30 mins.). (Kevin Kerney Ser.: Bk. 2). 1998. 51.00 (978-0-7887-1892-2(4), 95314E7) Recorded Bks.
When retired Santa Fe detective Kerney discovers a mysterious body, his quiet summer in the Gila Wilderness is interrupted.

Mexican Literature since the 1960s. 1 cass. (Running Time: 30 min.). (SPA.). 9.95 (SA-82-04-21, HarperThor) HarpC GBR.

Mexican Spanish Phrase Book & Cd. (PHRASE BOOK & CD Ser.). (SPA & ENG., 2009. audio compact disk 12.95 (978-981-268-607-7(X)) Pub: Berlitz Pubng. Dist(s): Langenscheidt

Mexican Tree Duck. unabr. ed. James Crumley. Read by Rob McQuay. 6 cass. (Running Time: 9 hrs.). 1997. 48.00 (978-0-7366-3820-3(2), 4488) Books on Tape.
C.W. Sughrue is looking for Sarita Cisneros Pines because no one can find her which leads him to the Mexican border.

Mexican War: A Compact History 1846-1848. unabr. ed. Charles L. Dufour. Narrated by Tom West. 8 cass. (Running Time: 11 hrs.). 1981. 70.00 (978-1-55690-338-0(3), 81200E7) Recorded Bks.
This 1846 War added a roster of famous names to the country's roll of military heros: Lee, Grant, Beauregard, Jackson.

***Mexicano y Otros Cuentos.** abr. ed. Jack London. Read by Santiago Munevar. (SPA.). 2008. audio compact disk 17.00 (978-958-8318-46-2(7)) Pub: Yoyo Music COL. Dist(s): YoYoMusic

Mexico. Compiled by Benchmark Education Staff. 2006. audio compact disk 10.00 (978-1-4108-6648-6(3)) Benchmark Educ.

Mexico. James A. Michener. Read by Alexander Adams. 1993. 72.00 (978-0-7366-2395-7(7)); 64.00 (978-0-7366-2394-0(9), 3164-A/B) Books on Tape.
American journalist discovers Mexico's history while researching his family's past.

Mexico. unabr. ed. Joseph Stromberg. Read by Peter Hackes. Ed. by Wendy McElroy. Prod. by Pat Childs. (Running Time: 10800 sec.). (World's Political Hot Spots Ser.). 2006. audio compact disk 25.95 (978-0-7861-6476-9(X)) Pub: Blckstn Audio. Dist(s): NetLibrary CO

Mexico. unabr. ed. Joseph Stromberg. Read by Peter Hackes. Ed. by Wendy McElroy. 2 cass. (Running Time: 3 hrs.). Dramatization. (World's Political Hot Spots). (YA). (gr. 11 up). 1991. 17.95 (978-0-938935-94-0(1), 10359) Knowledge Prod.
In 1540, Mexico was declared to be New Spain. With a diverse culture & great natural resources, it should have prospered like its Northern neighbor. But Mexico's history includes political corruption, war, revolution & grinding poverty.

Mexico, Pt. 1. unabr. ed. James A. Michener. Read by Alexander Adams. 8 cass. (Running Time: 12 hrs.). 1993. 64.00 (3164A) Books on Tape.
American journalist discovers Mexico's history while researching his family's past.

Mexico, Pt. 2. unabr. ed. James A. Michener. Read by Alexander Adams. 8 cass. (Running Time: 12 hrs.). 1993. 72.00 set. (3164B) Books on Tape.

Mexico: The Land of Opportunity. Thomas M. Magee. 6 cass. (Running Time: 6 hrs.). 1993. 110.00 (978-1-56559-021-2(X)) Ret Knowledge.

Mexico City, Mexico. Compiled by Benchmark Education Staff. 2006. audio compact disk 10.00 (978-1-4108-6612-7(2)) Benchmark Educ.

Mexico Set. Len Deighton. Read by Robert Whitfield. 9 CDs. (Running Time: 11 hrs. 30 mins.). 2004. audio compact disk 81.00 (978-0-7861-8143-8(5), 2171) Blckstn Audio.

Mexico Set, unabr. ed. Len Deighton. Read by Robert Whitfield. 8 cass. (Running Time: 12 hrs.). 1998. 56.95 (2171) Blckstn Audio.
On the shadowy East-West battlefield of Mexico City, British intelligence agent Bernard Samson must entice his opposite number, a disaffected KGB major, to take the final, dramatic step - & defect. But the price of one Russian's freedom must be paid in blood - blood that Samson unexpectedly & incriminatingly finds on his own hands. On every side, he becomes dangerously enmeshed in an intricate web of suspicion & hatred. Yet how can he fight when he doesn't know where to find his most determined enemies - or even who they are.

Mexico Set. unabr. ed. Len Deighton. Read by Robert Whitfield. 8 cass. (Running Time: 11 hrs. 30 mins.). (Samson Ser.: Vol. 2). 2003. 56.95 (978-0-7861-1256-2(5), 2171) Blckstn Audio.

***Mexico Set.** unabr. ed. Len Deighton. Read by Robert Whitfield. (Running Time: 11 hrs.). 2010. audio compact disk 29.95 (978-1-4417-3572-0(0)) Blckstn Audio.

Mexico Smarts by Dancing Beetle. Perf. by Eugene Ely. 1 cass. (Running Time: 1 hr. 28 min.). (J). 1995. 10.00 Erthviibz.
Mexican science, myth, ecology & nature sounds come together when Ms. Tarantula & the spunky musical humans read & sing with Dancing Beetle.

Mexifornia. unabr. ed. Victor Davis Hanson. Read by Lloyd James. (Running Time: 7 hrs.). 2000. audio compact disk 24.95 (978-0-7861-8821-5(9), 3176) Blckstn Audio.

Mexifornia. unabr. ed. Victor Davis Hanson. Read by Lloyd James. 5 pieces. (Running Time: 7 hrs.). 2004. reel tape 29.95 (978-0-7861-2612-5(4)); audio compact disk 29.95 (978-0-7861-8927-4(4)) Blckstn Audio.

Mexifornia: A State of Becoming. unabr. ed. Victor Davis Hanson. 5 cass. (Running Time: 7 hrs.). 2004. 39.95 (978-0-7861-2544-9(6), 3176) Blckstn Audio.
While Mexifornia is a look at the ambition and vigor of people who have made California strong, it is also an indictment of the policies that got California into its present mess and that could also affect Americans who inhabit ¿Mexizona,¿ ¿Mexichusetts¿ and other states of becoming.

Mexifornia: A State of Becoming. unabr. ed. Victor Davis Hanson. Read by Lloyd James. 5 CDs. (Running Time: 7 hrs.). 2004. audio compact disk 40.00 (978-0-7861-9034-8(5), 3176) Blckstn Audio.

Mezzo Cammin see Best Loved Poems of Longfellow

Mezzo-Soprano Bk. 2: Alto Solos. Ed. by Joan Frey Boytim. Created by Hal Leonard Corporation Staff. (ENG.). 1997. audio compact disk 18.99 (978-0-7935-8648-6(8), 0793586488, G Schirmer) H Leonard.

Mezzotint. 1981. (S-18) Jimcin Record.

***MGM Theatre of the Air.** RadioArchives.com. (Running Time: 600). (ENG.). 2009. audio compact disk 29.98 (978-1-61081-083-8(X)) Radio Arch.

Mhurs. Composed by Jonathan Brian Maguire. 2008. audio compact disk 5.00 (978-1-4276-3220-3(0)) AardGP.

***Mi Alma Tiene Sed.** Composed by Pedro Rubalcava. (SPA.). 1995. audio compact disk (978-1-58459-250-1(8)) Wrld Lib Pubns.

Mi Casa es Su Casa: My House Is Your House. Perf. by Michele Valeri. 1 cass. (J). (ps-7). 9.98 (273) MFLP CA.
Take an energetic musical journey south of the border. This zesty collection of children's songs is a fun way to learn the music & customs of Latin America while picking up familiar Spanish phrases.

***Mi confianza esta en Ti.** (SPA.). 2009. audio compact disk 14.99 (978-0-8297-6147-4(0)) Pub: CanZion. Dist(s): Zondervan

Mi Corazon Te Espera: Interpretaciones de los Cantos Cosmicos de Paramahansa Yogananda. Composed by Paramhansa Yogananda. 2005. audio compact disk 19.50 (978-0-87612-508-3(9)) Self Realization.

Mi Deleite. Michael Rodriguez. 2008. audio compact disk 15.99 (978-0-8297-5426-1(1)) Pub: Vida Pubs. Dist(s): Zondervan

Mi Fortaleza. unabr. ed. Torre Fuerte & Heriberto Hermosillo. (SPA.). 1998. 7.99 (978-0-8297-2701-2(9)) Pub: Vida Pubs. Dist(s): Zondervan

Mi Fortaleza. unabr. ed. Heriberto Hermosillo. 1998. audio compact disk 11.99 (978-0-8297-2702-9(7)) Zondervan.

***Mi mundo necesita de Ti.** (SPA.). 2009. audio compact disk 14.99 (978-0-8297-6159-7(4)) Pub: CanZion. Dist(s): Zondervan

Mi Pais Inventado: Un Paseo Nostalgico por Chile see My Invented Country: A Nostalgic Journey Through Chile

Mi Paraguas Rojo. Tr. of My Red Umbrella. (SPA.). 2004. 8.95 (978-0-7882-0287-2(1)) Weston Woods.

Mi Proposito. Contrib. by Dario Navac. Directed By Dario Navac et al. 2005. audio compact disk 14.98 (978-5-559-01289-6(0)) Integrity Music.

Mi Regalo. unabr. ed. Marcos Vidal. 1998. audio compact disk 14.99 (978-0-8297-2638-1(1)) Zondervan.

Mi Vida Saxual. Paquito D'Rivera. Read by Paquito D'Rivera. 9 cass. (Running Time: 11 hrs. 75 mins.). (SPA.). 2004. 42.95 (978-1-4025-6679-0(4)) Recorded Bks.
In this book, Paquito counts on nostalgia, tenderness and humor. Considered by experts to be one of the best jazz instrumentalists in the world, his groups have included the Paquito D'Rivera Big Bar Quinteto Paquito D'Rivers and the Assembly Triangle.

MI 5: British Security Service. unabr. collector's ed. Nigel West. Read by Rupert Keenlyside. 10 cass. (Running Time: 15 hrs.). 1986. 80.00 (978-0-7366-0841-1(9), 1792) Books on Tape.
The enigmatic title, MI 5, stands in the public mind for the dark world of counter-intelligence. Its object is to combat espionage, sabotage & subversion directed against the United Kingdom. This traces the history of MI 5 & focuses on its role in W.W. II. Laced with true anecodotes, this book is based on interviews of Nazi & Soviet agents, counter-intelligence officers, case officers & more than a dozen of the double agents.

Miami. abr. ed. Pat Booth. Read by Morgan Fairchild. 2 cass. (Running Time: 3 hrs.). 2000. 7.95 (978-1-57815-058-8(2), 1042, Media Bks Audio) Media Bks NJ.
Mary's wrath consumes her & endangers the others as she vows that if she can't have Rob, no one will.

Miami. abr. ed. Pat Booth. Read by Morgan Fairchild. 2 cass. (Running Time: 3 hrs.). 1992. 15.95 (978-1-879371-21-7(9)) Pub Mills.
Christina Kenwood, a world famous ex-model, decides to open her own modeling agency in the sizzling heat of American's newest mecca, Miami. Soon her fast growing empire is threatened by the jealousy & tainted affairs of her stable of beautiful young models.

Miami Babylon: Crime, Wealth, & Power - -A Dispatch from the Beach. unabr. ed. Gerald Posner. Narrated by Alan Sklar. (Running Time: 18 hrs. 30 mins. 0 sec.). (ENG.). 2009. 29.99 (978-1-4001-6441-7(9)); audio compact disk 39.99 (978-1-4001-1441-2(1)); audio compact disk 79.99 (978-1-4001-4441-9(8)) Pub: Tantor Media. Dist(s): IngramPubServ

***Miami Babylon: Crime, Wealth, & Power - -A Dispatch from the Beach.** unabr. ed. Gerald Posner. Narrated by Alan Sklar. (Running Time: 18 hrs. 30 mins.). 2009. 22.99 (978-1-4001-8441-5(X)) Tantor Media.

Miami, It's Murder. unabr. collector's ed. Edna Buchanan. Read by Frances Cassidy. 6 cass. (Running Time: 9 hrs.). (Britt Montero Mystery Ser.). 1994. 48.00 (978-0-7366-2740-5(5), 3466) Books on Tape.
Crime journalist Britt Montero has a double dose of dirty work on her hands as she tracks a serial rapist while probing a string of murders. According to her mentor, a powerful politician got away with one of these murders.

Micah. unabr. ed. Laurell K. Hamilton. Read by Rey Colette. (Running Time: 4 hrs.). (Anita Blake, Vampire Hunter Ser.: No. 13). 2006. 39.25 (978-1-4233-1690-9(8), 9781423316909, BADLE); 24.95 (978-1-4233-1689-3(4), 9781423316893, BAD); audio compact disk 39.25 (978-1-4233-1688-6(6), 9781423316886, Brlnc Audio MP3 Lib); audio compact disk 69.25 (978-1-4233-1686-2(X), 9781423316862, BriAudCD Unabrid); audio compact disk 24.95 (978-1-4233-1687-9(8), 9781423316879, Brilliance MP3) Brilliance Audio.
A novella featuring Micah, the wereleopard from the Anita Blake series.

Micah. unabr. ed. Laurell K. Hamilton. Read by Rey Colette. (Running Time: 14400 sec.). (Anita Blake, Vampire Hunter Ser.: No. 13). 2007. audio compact disk 14.99 (978-1-4233-3366-1(7), 9781423333661, BCD Value Price) Brilliance Audio.

Micah Commentary. Chuck Missler. 1 MP3 CD-ROM. (Running Time: 8 hrs.). (Chuck Missler Commentaries). 2001. audio compact disk 29.95 (978-1-57821-171-5(9)) Koinonia Hse.
If you study Hosea, Joel, Amos, and Obadiah, you discover that their messages went unheeded. Their warnings were rejected; judgment came. In Micah's case, the message was heeded, repentance followed, and disaster was postponed for a century. Here was a prophet (like Jonah) who changed history! One man can make a difference.

Mice of the Herring Bone. abr. ed. Tim Davis. Perf. by Lonnie Polson. (Running Time: 057 min.). (J). (ps-5). 2000. 9.95 (978-0-89084-906-4(4), 092635) BJUPr.

Mice of the Herring Bone, Set. Tim Davis. (J). (ps-5). 2000. pap. bk. 14.98 (978-0-89084-907-1(2), 100263) BJUPr.

Mice of the Nine Lives. Tim Davis. 1 cass. (Running Time: 1 hr.). (J). (ps-5). 2000. 9.95 (978-1-57924-058-5(5), 092643) BJUPr.

Mice of the Nine Lives, Set. Tim Davis. (J). (ps-5). 2000. pap. bk. 14.98 (978-1-57924-089-9(5), 115048) BJUPr.

Michael. (41) Halvorson Assocs.

Michael & Natasha. unabr. ed. Rosemary Crawford & Donald Crawford. Read by Nadia May. 13 cass. (Running Time: 19 hrs.). 1999. 85.95 (978-0-7861-1625-6(0), 2453) Blckstn Audio.
Based on hundreds of letters which have long been hidden in the Russian state archive in Moscow & St. Petersburg, as well as on Michael's private diaries held by the Forbes Collection in New York, this is the story of one of the greatest & most dramatic love stories of this century, & sheds significant new light on the downfall of the Romanov dynasty.

Michael & Natasha: The Life & Love of Michael II, the Last of the Romanov Tsars. unabr. ed. Rosemary Crawford. (Running Time: 64800 sec.). 2007. audio compact disk 120.00 (978-0-7861-6009-9(8)); audio compact disk 44.95 (978-0-7861-6010-5(1)) Blckstn Audio.

Michael Anderson's Little Black Book of Songwriting: Audio Version. Michael Anderson. 2 CDs. (Running Time: 2 hrs. 30 mins.). 2007. audio compact disk 12.95 (978-0-9786025-2-9(8)) Cadillac Pink.

Michael Ballam Christmas. Michael Ballam. 1 cass. 9.95 (119117) Covenant Comms.
Music cassette-favorite holiday songs.

Michael Ballam Sings Religious Favorites. Michael Ballam. 1 cass. 9.95 (1000942); audio compact disk 14.95 (109110) Covenant Comms.

Michael Brooks & the Royal Priesthood. Michael Brooks and the Royal Priesthood Staff. 2005. audio compact disk 16.98 (978-5-558-95179-0(6)) Pub: Pt of Grace Ent. Dist(s): STL Dist NA

Michael Connelly: The Concrete Blonde, the Last Coyote, Trunk Music. abr. ed. Michael Connelly. Read by Dick Hill. (Running Time: 9 hrs.). (Harry Bosch Ser.: Nos. 3-5). 2006. audio compact disk 29.95 (978-1-59737-720-1(1), 9781597377201) Brilliance Audio.
The Concrete Blonde: This high-voltage thriller opens with Homicide Detective Bosch battling charges as the chief defendant in a civil suit against the LAPD. The family of a notorious serial killer whom Bosch shot during an arrest four years ago has accused Bosch of killing the wrong man. This allegation becomes horrifyingly plausible when a new murder occurs with all the hallmarks of the dead slayer's style. The Last Coyote: Harry attacked his commanding officer and is suspended indefinitely, pending a psychiatric evaluation. At first he resists the LAPD shrink, but finally recognizes that something is troubling him and has for a long time. In 1961, when Harry was twelve, his mother, a prostitute, was brutally murdered with no one ever accused of the crime. Trunk Music: Back on the job after an involuntary leave of absence, LAPD homicide detective Harry Bosch is ready for a challenge. But his first case is a little more than he bargained for. It starts with the body of a Hollywood producer in the trunk of a Rolls-Royce, shot twice in the head at close range - what looks like "trunk music", a Mafia hit.

Michael Connelly CD Collection: The Black Echo; The Black Ice. abr. ed. Michael Connelly. Read by Dick Hill. (Running Time: 43200 sec.). (Harry Bosch Ser.: Nos. 1-2). 2005. audio compact disk 29.95 (978-1-59737-701-0(5), 9781597377010) Brilliance Audio.
The Black Echo: For LAPD homicide cop Harry Bosch - hero, maverick, nighthawk - the body in the drainpipe at Mulholland Dam is more than another anonymous statistic. This one is personal. The dead man, Billy Meadows, was a fellow Vietnam "tunnel rat" who fought side by side with him in a nightmare underground war that brought them to the depths of hell. Now, Bosch is about to relive the horror of Nam. From a dangerous maze of blind alleys to a daring criminal heist beneath the city to the torturous link that must be uncovered, his survival instincts will once again be tested to their limit. The Black Ice: Narcotics officer Cal Moore's orders were to look into the city's latest drug killing. Instead, he ends up in a motel room with his head in several pieces and a suicide note stuffed in his back pocket. Years ago, Harry Bosch learned the first rule of the good cop: don't look for the facts, but the glue that holds them together. Now, Harry's making some very dangerous connections, starting with one dead cop and leading to a bloody string of murders that winds from Hollywood Boulevard's drug bazaar to the dusty back alleys south of the border and into the center of a complex and lethal game - one in which Harry is the next and likeliest victim.

Michael Connelly Collection: The Black Echo; The Poet. abr. ed. Michael Connelly. Narrated by Dick Hill & Buck Schirner. 6 cass. (Running Time: 9 hrs.). 2002. 19.95 (978-1-58788-755-0(X), 158788755X, Nova Audio Bks) Brilliance Audio.
The Black Echo (read by Dick Hill) For LAPD homicide cop Harry Bosch - hero, maverick, nighthawk - the body in the drainpipe at Mulholland Dam is more than another anonymous statistic. This one is personal. The dead man, Billy Meadows, was a fellow Vietnam "tunnel rat" who fought side by side with him in a nightmare underground war that brought them to the depths of hell. Now, Bosch is about to relive the horror of Nam. From a dangerous maze of blind alleys to a daring criminal heist beneath the city to the tortuous link that must be uncovered, his survival instincts will once again be tested to their limit. Joining with an enigmatic and seductive female FBI agent, pitted against enemies inside his own department, Bosch must make the agonizing choice between justice and vengeance, as he tracks down a killer whose true face will shock him. The Poet (read by Buck Schirner) Our hero is Jack McEvoy, a Rocky Mountain News crime-beat reporter. As the novel opens, Jack's twin brother, a Denver homicide detective, has just killed himself. Or so it seems. But when Jack begins to investigate the phenomenon of police suicides, a disturbing pattern emerges, and soon suspects that a serial murderer is at work - a devious cop killer who's left a coast-to-coast trail of "suicide notes" drawn from the poems of Edgar Allan Poe. It's the story of a lifetime - except that "the Poet" already seems to know that Jack is trailing him. .

Michael Connelly Collection: The Concrete Blonde; The Last Coyote; Trunk Music. abr. ed. Michael Connelly. Read by Dick Hill. 6 cass. (Running Time: 9 hrs.). (Harry Bosch Ser.: Nos. 3-5). 2001. 19.95 (978-1-58788-748-2(7), 1587887487, Nova Audio Bks) Brilliance Audio.
The Concrete Blonde This high-voltage thriller opens with Homicide Detective Bosch battling charges as the chief defendant in a civil suit against the LAPD. The family of a notorious serial killer whom Bosch shot during an arrest four years ago has accused Bosch of killing the wrong man. This allegation becomes horrifyingly plausible when a new murder occurs with all the hallmarks of the dead slayer's style. The Last Coyote Harry attacked his commanding officer and is suspended indefinitely, pending a psychiatric evaluation. At first he resists the LAPD shrink, but finally recognizes that something is troubling him and has for a long time. In 1961, when Harry was twelve, his mother, a prostitute, was brutally murdered with no one ever accused of the crime. Trunk Music Back on the job after an involuntary leave of absence, LAPD homicide detective Harry Bosch is ready for a challenge. But his first case is a little more than he bargained for. It starts with the body of a Hollywood producer in the trunk of a Rolls-Royce, shot twice in the head at close range - what looks like "trunk music", a Mafia hit.

Michael Cooney: The Cheese Stands Alone. 1 cass. 9.98 (C-35) Folk-Legacy.
Michael's first recording & a good one.

Michael Crichton Collection: Airframe - The Lost World - Timeline. abr. ed. Michael Crichton. Read by Blair Brown et al. (Running Time: 50400 sec.). (ENG.). 2006. audio compact disk 29.95 (978-0-7393-4033-2(6), Random AudioBks) Pub: Random Audio Pubg. Dist(s): Random

Michael Dorris, Vol. II. unabr. ed. Ed. by Jim McKinley. Prod. by Rebekah Presson. 1 cass. (Running Time: 29 min.). (New Letters on the Air Ser.). 1994. 10.00 (053094) New Letters.
Dorris is the founder of the Native American studies program at Dartmouth College & the author of many books of fiction & non-fiction, including the acclaimed look at Fetal Alcohol Syndrome, "The Broken Cord." Dorris also collaborates with his novelist-wife Louise Erdrich. Here, he reads from & talks about a new book of essays, "Paper Trail".

Michael Foot: Socialism see Buckley's Firing Line

Michael Gerber Masterclass. Michael Gerber. 2006. audio compact disk 225.00 (978-0-273-70994-7(1), FT Pren) Pearson EducLt GBR.

Michael Grossberg: Which Way for the Space Movement? (Running Time: 1 hr.). (Freeland Ser.). 1985. 9.00 (FL17) Freeland Pr.
Free enterprise is threatened by society's unwillingness to look to the private sector regarding space & its potential. According to the author, America's space program is still tied to the political structure.

Michael Harper. unabr. ed. Read by Michael Harper. 1 cass. (Running Time: 29 min.). 1985. 10.00 New Letters.
A reading from "Images of Kin, New & Selected Poems" which concerns jazz musicians & the Black American experience.

Michael Heffernan. Read by Michael Heffernan. 1 cass. (Running Time: 29 min.). 1985. 10.00 New Letters.
Kansas poet Michael Heffernan reads from The Cry of Oliver Hardy.

Michael Horovitz. unabr. ed. Read by Michael Horovitz. 1 cass. (Running Time: 29 min.). 1985. 10.00 New Letters.
English "experimental" poet reads & plays the kazoo.

***Michael Jackson: King of Pop 1958 - 2009.** unabr. ed. Emily Herbert. Read by Andre Blake & Colin Moody. 6 CDs. (Running Time: 6 hrs. 44 mins.). 2010. audio compact disk 77.95 (978-1-74214-584-6(1), 9781742145846) Pub: Bolinda Pubng AUS. Dist(s): Bolinda Pub Inc

Michael Jackson: the Final Years: An Excerpt from Michael Jackson: the Magic, the Madness, the Whole Story, 1958-2009. J. Randy Taraborrelli. Read by Robert Petkoff. (Running Time: 2 hrs.). (ENG.). 2009. 8.98 (978-1-60788-256-5(6)) Pub: Hachet Audio. Dist(s): HachBkGrp

Michael Jeneid Shares His Poems & Paintings of Birds from Walt Whitman. Hosted by Nancy Pearlman. 1 cass. (Running Time: 29 min.). 10.00 (1302) Educ Comm CA.

Michael Jordan: In His Own Words. abr. unabr. ed. Geoffrey Giuliano. 1 cass. (Running Time: 1 hr.). 1990. 12.95 (978-0-929071-62-6(X)); audio compact disk 14.95 (978-0-929071-63-3(8)) B-B Audio.
Michael Jordan is not only the greatest basketball player of all time, but also an international figure and genuine role model. Jordans inspirational story is one of intense personal struggle and unequaled success not only on the hardwood but also as a r.

Michael Jordan: Out of Thin Air, Level 1. 2 cass. (Running Time: 1 hr. 30 mins.). (SmartReader Ser.). (J). 1999. tchr. ed. 19.95 (978-0-7887-0780-3(9), 79342T3) Recorded Bks.
Sometimes, becoming a basketball star requires endless determination. During his career, Michael Jordan has worked hard to earn his success - with spectacular results.

Michael Jordan: Out of Thin Air, Level 2. 2 cass. (Running Time: 1 hr. 30 mins.). (SmartReader Ser.). (J). 1999. tchr. ed. 19.95 (978-0-7887-0782-7(5), 79343T3) Recorded Bks.

Michael Jordan: The Best Ever. Sarah Houghton. (High Five Reading - Purple Ser.). (ENG.). (gr. 4 up). 2001. audio compact disk 5.95 (978-0-7368-9507-1(8)) CapstoneDig.

Michael Jordan: The Best Ever. Sarah Houghton. (High Five Reading - Purple Ser.). (ENG.). (gr. 4-5). 2007. audio compact disk 5.95 (978-1-4296-1427-6(7)) CapstoneDig.

Michael Jordan: an Audio Tribute. Contrib. by Michael Jordan. (ENG.). 1999. audio compact disk 15.98 (978-5-559-38445-0(3), Speechworks) Jerden Recs.

Michael Jordan Look-Alike: Acts. 18:18-28. Ed Young. 2000. 4.95 (978-0-7417-2242-3(9), 1242) Win Walk.

Michael Jordan Speaks: Lessons from the World's Greatest Champion. abr. ed. Janet C. Lowe. 2 cass. (Running Time: 3 hrs.). 1999. 17.95 (978-1-55935-308-3(2)) Soundelux.
Sheds light on the incredible success of "His Royal Airness," by drawing on his own words culled from articles, newscasts & interviews. Free of self-editing & censorship, this offers a unique view of the American legend.

Michael Kincaid the Strangeseeker Complete Collection Volume One. Jim French. (ENG.). 2008. audio compact disk 34.95 (978-1-60245-089-9(7)) GDL Multimedia.

Michael Kincaid the Strangeseeker Volume 1. Short Stories. 2 CDs. (Running Time: 2 hrs.). Dramatization. 2006. audio compact disk 9.95 (978-1-60245-003-5(X)) GDL Multimedia.

Michael Kincaid the Strangeseeker Volume 2. Short Stories. 2 CDs. (Running Time: 2 hrs.). Dramatization. 2006. audio compact disk 9.95 (978-1-60245-004-2(8)) GDL Multimedia.

Michael Knott: Michael & LSU Definitive Collection. Perf. by Michael Knott. 1 CD. 1999. audio compact disk 16.98 (KMGD8695) Provident Mus Dist.

Michael Mish Presents a Kid's Eye View of the Environment. Michael Mish. Read by Michael Mish. (Running Time: 40 min.). (J). (ps-7). 1989. 9.95 (978-0-9622465-1-7(4)); audio compact disk 5.95 coloring bk. Mish Mash Music.
Features candid interviews with children about the environment with pop songs sung by children with Michael Mish. Includes coloring book.

Michael Mish Presents I'm Blue. Michael Mish. (Running Time: 40 min.). (J). (ps-8). 1991. 9.95 (978-0-9622465-5-5(7)) Mish Mash Music.
Quickly edited children's comments on the planet earth as it relates to the Solar System & galaxy. With songs about stars; gravity; planets etc.

Michael Mish Presents Sleepy Train. Michael Mish. Read by Michael Mish. 1 cass. (Running Time: 40 min.). (J). (gr. k up). 1989. 9.95 (978-0-9622465-2-4(2)) Mish Mash Music.
One narrated story & several songs designed for the parent at a child's bedtime. Winner Parent's Choice Award.

Michael Mish Presents We Love the Animals. Michael Mish. 1 cass. (Running Time: 40 min.). (J). (ps-7). 1990. 9.95 (978-0-9622465-4-8(9)) Mish Mash Music.
Whimsical & catchy songs about different animals & endangered species. Up-beat & poignant.

Michael O'Brien & Sharon Olds. unabr. ed. Read by Michael O'Brien & Sharon Olds. 1 cass. (Running Time: 29 min.). 1986. 10.00 New Letters.
Two New York poets presents a reading.

Michael O'Dorn in Concert. Contrib. by Michael O'Dorn. (Running Time: 47 mins.). 2006. 24.95 (978-5-558-09165-6(7)) Mel Bay.

Michael Palmer: The Fifth Vial, the First Patient, the Second Opinion. abr. ed. Michael Palmer. (Running Time: 18 hrs.). 2010. audio compact disk 29.99 (978-1-4418-4986-1(6), 9781441849861, BACD) Brilliance Audio.

Michael Palmer: The Sisterhood - Side Effects - The Society. abr. ed. Michael Palmer. (Running Time: 18 hrs.). 2006. audio compact disk 34.95 (978-1-59737-715-7(5), 9781597377157) Brilliance Audio.
The Sisterhood: Inside Boston Doctors Hospital, patients are dying. In the glare of the operating room, they survive the surgeon's knife. But in the dark, hollow silence of the night, they die. Suddenly, inexplicably, horribly. A tough, bright doctor will risk his very life for a dedicated young nurse who unknowingly holds the answers. Side Effects: Kate Bennett. A bright hospital pathologist with a loving husband and a solid future. Until one day her world turns dark. A strange, puzzling illness has killed two women. Now it endangers Kate's closest friend. Soon it will threaten Kate's marriage. Her sanity. Her life. Kate has uncovered a horrifying secret. Important people will stop at nothing to protect it. It is a terrifying medical discovery. And its roots lie in one of the greatest evils in the history of humankind. The Society: At the headquarters of Boston's Eastern Quality Health, the wealthy and powerful CEO is brutally murdered. A vicious serial killer is on the loose and the victims have one thing in common: they are all high-profile executives in the managed care industry. As a member of the Hippocrates Society, Dr. Will Grant seeks to reclaim the profession of medicine from the hundreds of companies profiting wildly by controlling the decisions that affect the delivery of care. But the doctor's determination has attracted a dangerous zealot who will stop at nothing to make Will his ally.

Michael Pettit: Cardinal Points. Michael Pettit. Read by Michael Pettit. Interview with Rebekah Presson. 1 cass. (Running Time: 29 min.). 1991. 10.00 (111888) New Letters.

Michael S. Harper. unabr. ed. Ed. by Jim McKinley. Prod. by Rebekah Presson. 1 cass. (Running Time: 29 min.). (New Letters on the Air Ser.). 1994. 10.00 (021494) New Letters.
Harper's poetry has long struggled with the questions posed by W.E.B. DuBois about the dualities of citizenship of African Americans. Harper, a professor at Brown University, writes about jazz, history, politics & family, among other subjects. Here, he reads "Advice to Bill Clinton" & talks about the difficulty of his role as a creative, educated, black American man.

Michael Shayne: Deadly Dough & Popular Corpse. Read by Jeff Chandler. 1 cass. (Running Time: 1 hr.). 2001. 6.98 (1881) Radio Spirits.

Michael Shayne: Return to Huxley & the Party. Read by Jeff Chandler. 1 cass. (Running Time: 1 hr.). 2001. 6.98 (2186) Radio Spirits.

***Michael Shepherd - Back to the Book, Vol. 3.** Arranged by Polishing the Pulpit. 2010. audio compact disk 25.00 (978-1-60644-121-3(3)) Heart Heart.

***Michael Shepherd - Back to the Book, Vol. 4.** Arranged by Polishing the Pulpit. 2010. audio compact disk 25.00 (978-1-60644-122-0(1)) Heart Heart.

Michael Straight. Interview with Michael Straight. 1 cass. (Running Time: 1 hr.). 1983. 13.95 (L072) TFR.
The author of "After Long Silence" describes his communist days at Cambridge, his contacts with Soviet spies in the U. S. & how he finally told all.

Michael Strogoff. Jules Verne. Read by John Bolen. (Running Time: 9 hrs. 45 mins.). 2002. 27.95 (978-1-60083-599-5(6), Audiofy Corp) Iofy Corp.

Michael Strogoff. Jules Verne. Read by John Bolen. (ENG.). 2005. audio compact disk 90.00 (978-1-4001-3027-6(1)) Pub: Tantor Media. Dist(s): IngramPubServ

Michael Strogoff. unabr. ed. Jules Verne. Narrated by John Bolen. 9 CDs. (Running Time: 9 hrs. 44 mins.). (ENG.). 2002. audio compact disk 45.00 (978-1-4001-0027-9(5)) Pub: Tantor Media. Dist(s): IngramPubServ

Michael Strogoff. unabr. ed. Jules Verne. Narrated by John Bolen. 1 CD (MP3). (Running Time: 9 hrs. 44 mins.). (ENG.). 2002. audio compact disk 20.00 (978-1-4001-5027-4(2)) Pub: Tantor Media. Dist(s): IngramPubServ

Michael Strogoff. unabr. ed. Jules Verne & Jules Verne. Narrated by John Bolen. (Running Time: 9 hrs. 30 mins. 0 sec.). (ENG.). 2009. lab manual ed. 65.99 (978-1-4001-4101-2(X)); audio compact disk 32.99 (978-1-4001-1101-5(3)); audio compact disk 22.99 (978-1-4001-6101-0(0)) Pub: Tantor Media. Dist(s): IngramPubServ

Michael Thelwell. Interview. Interview with Michael Thelwell & Kay Bonetti. 1 cass. (Running Time: 1 hr. 21 min.). 1981. 13.95 (978-1-55644-026-7(X), 1142) Am Audio Prose.
Discussion of Rastafarianism, the genesis of "The Harder They Come," its relation to the movie & place of Third World literature in the larger tradition.

Michael Tolliver Lives. unabr. ed. Armistead Maupin. Read by Armistead Maupin. 6 CDs. (Running Time: 25200 sec.). 2007. audio compact disk 34.95 (978-0-06-125641-7(2), Harper Audio) HarperCollins Pubs.

***Michael Tolliver Lives.** unabr. ed. Armistead Maupin. Read by Armistead Maupin. (ENG.). 2007. (978-0-06-147294-7(8), Harper Audio); (978-0-06-147293-0(X), Harper Audio) HarperCollins Pubs.

Michael W. Smith: Christmastime. Perf. by Michael W. Smith. 1 cass. 1999. (978-0-7601-2449-9(3)); audio compact disk (978-0-7601-2450-5(7)) Brentwood Music.

Michael W. Smith: Christmastime. Perf. by Michael W. Smith. 1 cass., 1 CD. 1998. 10.98 Provident Mus Dist.

Michael W. Smith 2. Perf. by Michael W. Smith & Amy Grant. 1 CD. 1984. audio compact disk Brentwood Music.
Features:" I am Sure," " Hosanna" & "Restless Heart," co-written with Amy Grant.

***Michaelmas Tribute.** Cora Harrison. 2010. 69.95 (978-1-4079-0787-1(5)); audio compact disk 84.95 (978-1-4079-0788-8(3)) Pub: Soundings Ltd GBR. Dist(s): Ulverscroft US

Micheif Maker/Nick the Knife. Featuring Ellery Queen. 1950. audio compact disk 12.95 (978-1-57970-505-3(7), Audio-For) J Norton Pubs.

Michel Bouquet dit Victor Hugo, Poems. Perf. by Michel Bouquet. 2 cass. (FRE.). 1991. 27.95 (1362-DI) Olivia & Hill.
The noted French actor, a teacher at the Conservatoire, interprets some of Victor Hugo's most famous poems.

Michel Strogoff: Level 1. Jules Verne. 1 cass. (Running Time: 1 hr. 30 min.). (FRE.). 2001. 9.95 (978-2-09-032921-6(1)) Pub: Cle Intl FRA. Dist(s): Continental Bk
Aids aural comprehension and includes music.

Michel Thomas Speak German for Beginners. Michel Thomas. 10 cds. (Michel Thomas Ser.). 2006. 79.95 (978-0-07-147985-1(6), 9780071479851) McGraw.

Michel Thomas Speak Italian for Beginners. Michel Thomas. 10 cds. (Michel Thomas Ser.). 2006. 79.95 (978-0-07-148007-9(2), 9780071480079) McGraw.

Michelangelo: A Biography, unabr. ed. George Bull. Read by Nadia May. 14 cass. (Running Time: 20 hrs. 30 mins.). 1998. 89.95 (978-0-7861-1367-5(7), 2275) Blckstn Audio.
Bull brings before the listener a towering genius whose versatility & originality are being rediscovered, not least through the revealing cleaning of the frescoes in the Sistine Chapel. Traces the life & spiritual quest of the man & artist & brings to the narrative an exceptional feel for the Italian Renaissance.

Michelangelo & the Pope's Ceiling. abr. ed. Ross King. Read by Alan Sklar. 6 CDs. (Running Time: 9 hrs.). 2003. audio compact disk 29.95 (978-1-57270-306-3(7)) Pub: Audio Partners. Dist(s): PerseuPGW

Michelangelo & the Pope's Ceiling. unabr. ed. Ross King. Read by Alan Sklar. 4 cass. (Running Time: 6 hrs.). 2003. 29.95 (978-1-57270-305-6(9)) Pub: Audio Partners. Dist(s): PerseuPGW

Michele Success: The Positive Pop. Perf. by Michele Blood. 1 cass. 1993. 10.95 (978-1-890679-23-1(2)) Micheles.
Michele?s hit album!.

Michele's Goal Setting Program: Find Out What You Want & How to Attract It. 4th rev. ed. Michele Blood. Ed. by Michele Blood. Illus. by Musivation International Staff. 1 cass. (Running Time: 1 hr.). 1993. 12.95 (978-1-890679-22-4(4)) Micheles.

Michele's Magnetic Creative Visualization Program: Accelerate Your Money Magnetism. Michele Blood. Ed. by Michele Blood. 2 cass. (Running Time: 2 hrs.). 2000. 19.95 (978-1-890679-19-4(4)) Micheles.

Michelle Wie: She's Got the Power. (High Five Reading - Blue Ser.). (ENG.). (gr. 1-2). 2007. audio compact disk 5.95 (978-1-4296-1411-5(0)) CapstoneDig.

Michelle Wie: She's Got the Power! Cynthia A. Dean. (High Five Reading Ser.). (ENG., (gr. 4-5). 2005. audio compact disk 5.95 (978-0-7368-5756-7(7)) CapstoneDig.

Michie's Historical Libraries, 1995 Edition. 2nd rev. ed. 1995. audio compact disk 595.00 (978-0-327-13284-4(1)) LEXIS Pub.

Michie's Tennessee Forms. 2nd rev. ed. 1994. audio compact disk 351.00 (978-0-327-10258-8(6), MICHIE) LEXIS Pub.

Michie's#8482; Jury Instructions#8482; on CD-ROM. 2nd rev. ed. audio compact disk 649.00 (978-0-327-10246-5(2)) LEXIS Pub.

Mick & Megan Visit London. N. J. Ross. 1 cass. (Running Time: 90 mins.). (J). 2000. bk. (978-1-930303-09-6(2)); bk. (978-1-930303-10-2(6)); (978-1-930303-04-1(1)); audio compact disk (978-1-930303-06-5(8)) Angelic Enter.
The story of how an ordinary Oklahoma puppy ends up in a London hotel room.

Mick & Megan Visit the French Riviera. N. J. Ross. 1 CD. (Running Time: 60 mins.). (J). 2000. bk. (978-1-930303-08-9(4)); (978-1-930303-03-4(3)); audio compact disk (978-1-930303-05-8(X)) Angelic Enter.
The story of how Mick's favorite red car is left behind on the airplane & how Mick & Megan find it again.

Mick & Megan Visit the French Riviera. N. J. Ross. Read by N. J. Ross. (J). (gr. k-4). 2000. bk. (978-1-930303-07-2(6)) Angelic Enter.

Mick Harte Was Here. Barbara Park. 2 cass. (J). 13.58 (BYA 922) NewSound.
Mick is a kid who would still be alive - if only he had worn his bicycle helmet. Phoebe's poignant story about her beloved brother, & how she struggles to deal with her grief.

Mick Harte Was Here. unabr. ed. Read by Dana Lubotsky. Ed. by Barbara Park. 2 vols. (Running Time: 1 hr. 42 mins.). (Middle Grade Cassette Librariestm Ser.). (J). (gr. 3-7). 2004. pap. bk. 29.00 (978-0-8072-7797-3(5), S YA 922 SP, Listening Lib) Random Audio Pubg.
"Mick Harte was one of the neatest kids you'd ever want to meet. Mick is also the kid who would still be alive-if only he had worn his bicycle helmet. Laughter will mingle with tears as listeners hear thirteen-year-old Phoebe's poignant story about her beloved brother and how she struggles to deal with her grief in this witty, touching narrative that will long be remembered.".

Mick Harte Was Here. unabr. ed. Barbara Park. Read by Dana Lubotsky. 2 cass. (YA). 1999. 16.98 (FS9-31553) Highsmith.

Mick Harte Was Here. unabr. ed. Barbara Park. Read by Dana Lubotsky. 2 cass. (Running Time: 1 hr. 42 mins.). (J). (gr. 3-7). 1997. 23.00 (978-0-8072-7796-6(7), YA922CX, Listening Lib) Random Audio Pubg.
Thirteen-year-old Phoebe endures the wrenching shock of her brother's death due to a bike accident & then must cope with the slow, painful process of dealing with her grief & that of her parents.

Mick Harte Was Here, unabr. ed. Barbara Park. Narrated by Christina Moore. 2 pieces. (Running Time: 1 hr. 45 mins.). (gr. 7 up). 1998. 19.00 (978-0-7887-1918-9(1), 95339E7) Recorded Bks.
Deals with the sometime fatal consequences when bicyclists fail to wear helmets. For 12 years, Phoebe & her younger brother Mick have been partners in everything, when they aren't fighting. Everything changes the day she refuses to ride his bike home for him after school.

Mick Harte Was Here, unabr. ed. Barbara Park. Read by Christina Moore. 2 cass. (Running Time: 1 hr. 45 min.). (J). (gr. 4-6). 1998. 31.75 Homework set. (978-0-7887-1946-2(7), 40653); 84.80 (978-0-7887-3603-2(5), 46340) Recorded Bks.
Phoebe & her younger brother Mick have been partners in everything when they aren't fighting. Everything changes the day she refuses to ride his bike home for him after school.

Mick Jagger Syndrome: Ecc. 6:1-12. Ed Young. 1993. 4.95 (978-0-7417-1987-4(8), 987) Win Walk.

Mickelsson's Ghosts. unabr. ed. John Gardner. Read by Jack Hrkach. 21 cass. (Running Time: 31 hrs. 30 mins.). Incl. Pt. 1. Mickelsson's Ghosts. 11 cass. (Running Time: 16 hrs. 30 mins.). John Gardner. Read by Jack Hrkach. 88.00 (1748-A); Pt. 2. Mickelsson's Ghosts. 10 cass. (Running Time: 15 hrs.). John Gardner. Read by Jack Hrkach. 80.00 (1748-B); 168.00 (978-0-7366-0797-1(8), 1748A/B) Books on Tape.
Once considered a brilliant philosopher in his own right, he has now slipped into debt & an alcohol-ridden state in which he is haunted by ghosts. In a desperate effort to escape the mounting chaos he buys a ramshackle farmhouse in the mountains. His own ghosts follow him & are soon joined by the real ghosts who inhabit the lonely farmhouse. Confronted with the ghosts of his past & the real ghosts of his newly aquired farmhouse, Mickelesson faces the ultimate test of his courage.

Mickey Mouse Disco. Walt Disney Productions Staff. 1 cass. (Retro Mickey Ser.). (J). 7.99 Norelco. (978-1-55723-943-3(6)) W Disney Records.

Mickey Mouse Disco. Walt Disney Productions Staff. 1 CD. (Retro Micky Ser.). (J). (ps-3). 1996. audio compact disk 13.99 (978-1-55723-944-0(4)) W Disney Records.

Mickey Sport Songs. 1 cass. (Classic Collections). (J). 10.99 (978-0-7634-0061-3(0)); 10.99 (978-0-7634-0060-6(2)); audio compact disk 16.99 (978-0-7634-0062-0(9)); audio compact disk 16.99 (978-0-7634-0063-7(7)) W Disney Records.

Mickey Unrapped. 1 cass. (Classic Collections). (J). 10.99 Norelco.; audio compact disk 16.99 (978-1-55723-698-2(4)) W Disney Records.

Mickey Unrapped. 1 cass. (Classic Collections). (J). (ps-3). 1994. 10.99 (978-1-55723-695-1(X)); audio compact disk 16.99 (978-1-55723-697-5(6)) W Disney Records.

Mickey's Christmas Around the World Pop-Up. 1 cass. (Running Time: 30 min.). (J). bk. 14.98 Disney Prod.

Mickey's Christmas Carol Read-Along. 1 cass. (Running Time: 15 min.). (J). bk. 5.98 Disney Prod.
The Charles Dickens story retold with Disney cartoon characters.

Mickey's Christmas Carol Read-Along. 1 cass. (J). (ps-3). 1991. bk. 6.98 (978-1-55723-250-2(4)) W Disney Records.

Mickey's Comedy for Kids. Prod. by Walter Elias Disney. 1 cass. (J). 1999. 3.89 (978-0-7634-0558-8(2)) W Disney Records.

Mickey's Favorites. 1 cass. (Sing-Along Ser.). (J). bk. 11.99 (978-1-55723-962-4(2)) W Disney Records.

Micro-Trading Tactics with Oliver Velez. Instructed by Oliver Velez. 1 cass. (Running Time: 90 mins). (Trade Secrets Audio Ser.). 2002. 19.95 (978-1-931611-72-5(6)) Marketplace Bks.
Unlike Swing Traders, who often hold positions for 2-5 days, astute Micro Traders jump on breakouts - and breakdowns - moving in and out of positions quickly each market day. They find opportunity in 5 or 15-minute charts, taking frequent, bite-sized profits out of the market. This technique can be immensely rewarding - but takes skill and training to survive such rapid-fire moves. Now, this groundbreaking new course presents powerful methods for mastering the art of Micro Trading with maximum precision. Find a complete listing of what you'll learn under the 'Jacket Description' section.

Microbe Hunters. unabr. ed. Paul De Kruif. Read by Andrew P. Cross. 8 cass. (Running Time: 12 hrs.). 1992. 39.00 (978-1-879884-01-4(1)) Sound Writs.
Dramatized history of development of microbiology & mankind's efforts against infectious disease - among the most widely read science books of all time.

Microbiology an Introduction: Computerized Test Bank. 8th rev. ed. Gerard J. Tortora et al. audio compact disk 49.97 (978-0-8053-7617-3(8)) Addson-Wesley Educ.

Microbiology an Introduction: Instructor's Resource CD. 8th rev. ed. Gerard J. Tortora et al. audio compact disk 14.97 (978-0-8053-7621-0(6)) Addson-Wesley Educ.

Microbiology with Diseases by Taxonomy: Computerized Test Bank. 2nd rev. ed. Zymunt Bauman. audio compact disk 49.97 (978-0-8053-7791-0(3)) Addson-Wesley Educ.

Microbiology with Diseases by Taxonomy: Media Manager. 2nd rev. ed. Zymunt Bauman. audio compact disk 18.97 (978-0-8053-7785-9(9)) Addson-Wesley Educ.

Microcomputer Hardware: Understanding & Expanding on the Basics. 2 cass. (Running Time: 3 hrs.). 1990. 16.00 Recorded Res.

Microcosm, unabr. ed. George Gilder. Read by John MacDonald. 10 cass. (Running Time: 14 hrs. 30 mins.). 1989. 69.95 (978-0-7861-0092-7(3), 1085) Blckstn Audio.
A visionary look into the future world that is being shaped by today's technological revolutions.

Microlatin: 20 Pieces Based on Latin Rhythms for the Beginner Pianist. Composed by Christopher Norton. 2008. pap. bk. 22.95 (978-0-85162-560-7(6), 0851625606) H Leonard.

Micromegas. Francois Voltaire, pseud. 1 cass. (Running Time: 1 hr.). (FRE.). 1996. pap. bk. 19.50 (978-1-58085-367-5(6)) Interlingua VA.
Includes dual French-English transcription. The combination of written text & clarity & pace of diction will open the door for intermediate & advanced students to genuine comprehension & the use of literary texts for advancement in rapid understanding of written & oral language materials. The audio text plus written text concept makes foreign languages accessible to a much wider range of students than books alone.

Micromegas. Francois Voltaire, pseud. Read by Claude Beauclair. 1 cass. (FRE.). 1991. 13.95 (1303-OH) Olivia & Hill.
Micromegas, 120,000 feet tall, an inhabitant of Saturn, visits the earth where he is surprised to find a group of philosophers able to measure the distance to the stars, but unable to define terms as simple as "soul" & "spirit.".

Microserfs, Douglas Coupland. Read by Matthew Perry. 2 cass. (Running Time: 1 hr. 80 min.). 1995. 17.00 (978-0-694-51560-8(4)) HarperCollins Pubs.

***Microsoft Access Database Security.** Created by Fred Pryor Seminars/CareerTrack. 2010. 199.95 (978-1-60959-006-2(6)) P Univ E Inc.

***Microsoft Access Forms & Reporting Made Easy.** PUEI. 2009. audio compact disk 199.00 (978-1-935041-71-9(1), CareerTrack) P Univ E Inc.

***Microsoft Access Queries Made Easy.** PUEI. 2009. audio compact disk 199.00 (978-1-935041-57-3(6), CareerTrack) P Univ E Inc.

Microsoft Access 2000 Core & Expert Certification: Microsoft Office Specialist Certification; Text with Microsoft Office Specialist Ready! CD. Meredith Flynn & Nita Rutkosky. (Benchmark Ser.). audio compact disk 58.95 (978-0-7638-0373-5(1)) EMC-Paradigm.

Microsoft Access 2002: Web Courses-Full Content Instruction; Core Text with iExperience Access 2002 CD Course. Nita Rutkosky & Denise Seguin. (Marquee Ser.). audio compact disk 44.00 (978-0-7638-1758-9(9)) EMC-Paradigm.

Microsoft Access 2002 Core & Expert Certification: Instructor Resources; Test Generator CD. Nita Rutkosky & Meredith Flynn. (Benchmark Ser.). audio compact disk 129.95 (978-0-7638-1914-9(X)) EMC-Paradigm.

Microsoft Access 2002 Core & Expert Certification: Web Courses-Full Content Instruction; Text with iExperience Access 2002 CD Course. Nita Rutkosky & Meredith Flynn. (Benchmark Ser.). audio compact disk 75.95 (978-0-7638-1745-9(7)) EMC-Paradigm.

Microsoft Access 2002 Core Certification: Student Courseware; Core Text with CD. Nita Rutkosky. (Benchmark Ser.). audio compact disk 21.95 (978-0-7638-1437-3(7)) EMC-Paradigm.

Microsoft Edge. Julie Bick & Susan O'Malley. 4 cass. (Running Time: 5 hrs. 30 mins.). 2002. 32.95 (978-0-7861-1904-2(7), 2697) Blckstn Audio.

***Microsoft Edge: Insider Strategies for Building Success.** unabr. ed. Julie Bick. Read by Susan O'Malley. (Running Time: 5.5 hrs. NaN mins.). (ENG.). 2011. 29.95 (978-1-4417-8456-8(X)); audio compact disk 55.00 (978-1-4417-8454-4(3)) Blckstn Audio.

Microsoft Edge: Insider Strategies for Building Success. unabr. ed. Julie Bick. Read by Susan O'Malley. 4 cass. (Running Time: 6 hrs.). 2001. 32.95 (2697) Blckstn Audio.
Behind the scenes at Microsoft, some of the nation's most savvy & successful managers are at work every day. How can their innovative perspectives & daily practices help guide your own journey on the road to success? Microsoft veteran Julie Bick reveals these insider strategies in this book.

***Microsoft Excel Charts & Graphs Made Easy.** PUEI. 2007. audio compact disk 199.00 (978-1-935041-90-0(8), CareerTrack) P Univ E Inc.

***Microsoft Excel Forms.** Created by Fred Pryor Seminars/CareerTrack. 2010. 199.95 (978-1-60959-005-5(8)) P Univ E Inc.

***Microsoft Excel PivotTables Made Easy.** PUEI. 2008. audio compact disk 199.00 (978-1-935041-00-9(2), CareerTrack) P Univ E Inc.

Microsoft Excel 2000 Core Certification: Instructor Resources; Instructor's Guide with CD. Nita Rutkosky. (Benchmark Ser.). audio compact disk 69.00 (978-0-7638-0237-0(9)) EMC-Paradigm.

Microsoft Excel 2000 Core Certification: Instructor Resources; Test Generator CD. Nita Rutkosky. (Benchmark Ser.). audio compact disk 78.95 (978-0-7638-0238-7(7)) EMC-Paradigm.

Microsoft Excel 2002: Web Courses-Full Content Instruction; Core Text with iExperience Excel 2002 CD Course. Nita Rutkosky & Denise Seguin. (Marquee Ser.). audio compact disk 43.50 (978-0-7638-1757-2(0)) EMC-Paradigm.

Microsoft Excel 2002 Core & Expert Certification: Web Courses-Full Content Instruction; Text with iExperience Excel 2002 CD Course. Nita Rutkosky & Meredith Flynn. (Benchmark Ser.). audio compact disk 77.95 (978-0-7638-1743-5(0)) EMC-Paradigm.

***Microsoft Excel 2007 Made Easy.** PUEI. 2009. audio compact disk 199.00 (978-1-935041-51-1(7), CareerTrack) P Univ E Inc.

Microsoft First Generation: The Success Secrets of the Visionaries Who Launched a Technology Empire. unabr. ed. Cheryl D. Tsang. Read by Mary Woods. 5 cass. (Running Time: 7 hrs.). 2000. 39.95 (978-0-7861-1801-4(6), 2600); audio compact disk 48.00 (978-0-7861-9870-2(2), 2600) Blckstn Audio.
What began as a modest start-up partnership only twenty-five years ago has already surpassed all the giants of contemporary capitalism, including General Electric & IBM & has achieved a market value estimated at nearly $500 billion. How did Microsoft achieve all of this in so short a time? What was the true nature of the Microsoft environment in the beginning & what are the secrets behind its triumph?.

Microsoft First Generation: The Success Secrets of the Visionaries Who Launched a Technology Empire. unabr. ed. Cheryl D. Tsang. Read by Mary Woods. 1 CD. (Running Time: 7 hrs. 30 mins.). 2001. audio compact disk 19.95 (2600) Blckstn Audio.

Microsoft Office Professional for Windows 95 Essentials: Virtual Tutor (Integration Exercises) Suzanne Weixel. 1996. suppl. ed. 29.33 (978-1-57576-108-4(4), Prentice Hall) P-H.

Microsoft Office Specialist Certification: Expert Text with Microsoft Office Specialist Ready! audio compact disk 46.95 (978-0-7638-1514-1(4)) Paradigm MN.

Microsoft Office XP: Instructor Resources; Test Generator CD. Nita Rutkosky & Denise Seguin. (Marquee Ser.). audio compact disk 129.95 (978-0-7638-1927-9(1)) EMC-Paradigm.

Microsoft Office XP: Microsoft Office Specialist Certification; Marquee Microsoft Office Specialist Ready! CD. Nita Rutkosky & Denise Seguin. (Marquee Ser.). audio compact disk 17.95 (978-0-7638-1692-6(2)) EMC-Paradigm.

Microsoft Office XP: Web Courses-Full Content Instruction; Brief Text with iExperience Office XP CD Course. Nita Rutkosky & Denise Seguin. (Marquee Ser.). audio compact disk 73.95 (978-0-7638-1755-8(4)) EMC-Paradigm.

Microsoft Office XP: Web Courses-Full Content Instruction; Core Text with iExperience Office XP CD Course. Nita Rutkosky & Denise Seguin. (Marquee Ser.). audio compact disk 88.00 (978-0-7638-1754-1(6)) EMC-Paradigm.

Microsoft Office XP Core Certification: Microsoft Office Specialist Certification; Benchmark Microsoft Office Specialist Ready! CD. Nita Rutkosky. (Benchmark Ser.). audio compact disk 20.95 (978-0-7638-1691-9(4)) EMC-Paradigm.

Microsoft Office XP Core Certification: Web Courses-Full Content Instruction; Core Text with iExperience Office XP CD Course. Nita Rutkosky. (Benchmark Ser.). audio compact disk 90.95 (978-0-7638-1740-4(6)) EMC-Paradigm.

Microsoft Office 2000: CD Courses-Full Content Instruction; Core Text with Core CD Course. Nita Rutkosky et al. (Marquee Ser.). audio compact disk 71.95 (978-0-7638-0360-5(X)) EMC-Paradigm.

Microsoft Office 2000: Instructor Resources; Instructor's CD. Nita Rutkosky et al. (Marquee Ser.). audio compact disk 69.00 (978-0-7638-0361-2(8)) EMC-Paradigm.

Microsoft Office 2000: Instructor Resources; Test Generator CD. Nita Rutkosky et al. (Marquee Ser.). audio compact disk 129.00 (978-0-7638-0526-5(2)) EMC-Paradigm.

Microsoft Office 2000 Core Certification: CD Courses-Full Content Instruction; Core Text & Core CD Course. Nita Rutkosky. (Benchmark Ser.). audio compact disk 68.95 (978-0-7638-0542-5(4)) EMC-Paradigm.

Microsoft Office 2000 Core Certification: Instructor Resources; Test Generator CD. Nita Rutkosky. (Benchmark Ser.). audio compact disk 129.00 (978-0-7638-0525-8(4)) EMC-Paradigm.

Microsoft Office 2003: Instructor Resources; Instructor's Guide CD. Nita Rutkosky & Denise Seguin. (Marquee Ser.). 2005. audio compact disk 69.00 (978-0-7638-2075-6(X)) EMC-Paradigm.

Microsoft Office 2003: Instructor Resources; Test Generator CD. Nita Rutkosky & Denise Seguin. (Marquee Ser.). 2005. audio compact disk 129.00 (978-0-7638-2076-3(8)) EMC-Paradigm.

Microsoft Office 2003 Specialist: Instructor Resources; Instructor's Guide CD. Nita Rutkosky. (Benchmark Ser.). 2005. audio compact disk 69.00 (978-0-7638-2054-1(7)) EMC-Paradigm.

Microsoft Office 2003 Specialist: Instructor Resources; Test Generator CD. Nita Rutkosky. (Benchmark Ser.). 2005. audio compact disk 129.00 (978-0-7638-2055-8(5)) EMC-Paradigm.

Microsoft Office 2007 Fundamentals Projects Binder, Pack. Laura Story & Dawna Walls. (C). 2010. audio compact disk 8.95 (978-0-538-45205-2(6)) Pub: Course Tech. Dist(s): CENGAGE Learn

Microsoft Outlook 2002: Microsoft Office Specialist Certification; Text with Microsoft Office Specialist Ready! Denise Seguin. (Benchmark Ser.). audio compact disk 49.95 (978-0-7638-1783-1(X)) EMC-Paradigm.

Microsoft PowerPoint 2002: Web Courses-Full Content Instruction; Text with iExperience PowerPoint CD Course. Nita Rutkosky & Denise Seguin. (Marquee Ser.). audio compact disk 43.50 (978-0-7638-1759-6(7)) EMC-Paradigm.

Microsoft PowerPoint 2002 Comprehensive Certification: Web Courses-Full Content Instruction; Text with iExperience PowerPoint CD Course. Nita Rutkosky. (Benchmark Ser.). audio compact disk 64.95 (978-0-7638-1744-2(9)) EMC-Paradigm.

***Microsoft Project Tips & Tricks.** Puei. 2010. (978-1-60959-001-7(5)) P Univ E Inc.

***Microsoft SharePoint Tips & Tricks.** PUEI. 2010. audio compact disk 199.00 (978-1-935041-92-4(4), CareerTrack) P Univ E Inc.

Microsoft Vision 2002. 2nd ed. 2001. audio compact disk 85.25 (978-0-619-06341-2(6)) Course Tech.

Microsoft Visual C++ 6.0 Compiler: Introductory Edition. Microsoft Official Academic Course Staff. (C). 2000. audio compact disk 13.95 (978-0-7637-1514-4(X), 076371514X) Jones Bartlett.

Microsoft Windows NT 4.0 Review. Steven Tate. 3 cass. (Running Time: 2 hrs. 30 min.). (C). 1998. pap. bk. 89.95 (978-1-892646-00-2(5), 1009801) Tate Cnsltng.
Provides a fast-paced review of key facts & concepts of Windows NT. Covers the objectives of Microsoft's NT workstation & NT server exams. Includes study guide.

***Microsoft Windows Server 2008: Enterprise Administration.** Richard Robb. (ENG.). 2010. 75.25 (978-1-4239-0288-1(2)) Pub: Course Tech. Dist(s): CENGAGE Learn

Microsoft Windows Vista Business Complete Training Course. Created by K-Alliance Staff. 2007. 129.00 (978-1-60540-006-8(8)) K Alliance.

Microsoft Windows XP Professional: Instructor Resources; Instructor's Guide CD Package. Michael D. Stewart. (Netability Ser.). 2005. audio compact disk 69.95 (978-0-7638-1963-7(8)) EMC-Paradigm.

Microsoft Windows 2000 Professional: Instructor Resources; Instructor's Guide CD Package. Michael D. Stewart. (Netability Ser.). 2005. audio compact disk 69.95 (978-0-7638-1962-0(X)) EMC-Paradigm.

Microsoft Windows 2000 Server: Instructor Resources; Instructor's Guide CD. Nancy Woolridge & Dale Craig. (Netability Ser.). audio compact disk 29.00 (978-0-7638-1332-1(X)) EMC-Paradigm.

Microsoft Windows 7 - Illustrated Essentials, Pack. 2010. audio compact disk 8.95 (978-0-538-75079-0(0)) Pub: Course Tech. Dist(s): CENGAGE Learn

MicroSoft with Macroeconomics Users Manual. Dornbusch. 1 CD. (Running Time: 90 min.). 2001. audio compact disk 21.00 (978-0-07-248000-9(9), Irwn McGrw-H) McGrw-H Hghr Educ.

Microsoft Word 2000 Core & Expert Certification: Instructor Resources; Test Generator CD. Nita Rutkosky. (Signature Ser.). audio compact disk 78.95 (978-0-7638-0253-0(0)) EMC-Paradigm.

Microsoft Word 2000 Core Certification: Instructor Resources; Test Generator CD. Nita Rutkosky. (Benchmark Ser.). audio compact disk 78.95 (978-0-7638-0346-9(4)) EMC-Paradigm.

Microsoft Word 2002: Web Courses-Full Content Instruction; Core Text with iExperience Word 2002 CD Course. Nita Rutkosky & Denise Seguin. (Marquee Ser.). audio compact disk 43.50 (978-0-7638-1756-5(2)) EMC-Paradigm.

Microsoft Word 2002 Core & Expert Certification: Instructor Resources; Test Generator CD. Nita Rutkosky. (Signature Ser.). audio compact disk 129.95 (978-0-7638-1930-9(1)) EMC-Paradigm.

Microsoft Word 2002 Core & Expert Certification: Microsoft Office Specialist Certification; Signature Microsoft Office Specialist Ready! CD. Nita Rutkosky. (Signature Ser.). audio compact disk 15.95 (978-0-7638-1690-2(6)) EMC-Paradigm.

Microsoft Word 2002 Core & Expert Certification: Web Courses-Full Content Instruction; Text with iExperience Word 2002 CD Course. Nita Rutkosky. (Benchmark Ser.). audio compact disk 78.95 (978-0-7638-1742-8(2)) EMC-Paradigm.

Microsoft Word 2002 Core & Expert Certification: Web Courses-Full Content Instruction; Text with iExperience Word 2002 Complete CD Course. Nita Rutkosky. (Signature Ser.). audio compact disk 88.95 (978-0-7638-1747-3(3)) EMC-Paradigm.

Microsoft Word 2003: Instructor Resources; Instructor's Guide CD. Nita Rutkosky. (Signature Ser.). 2005. audio compact disk 69.00 (978-0-7638-2085-5(7)) EMC-Paradigm.

Microsoft Word 2003: Instructor Resources; Test Generator CD. Nita Rutkosky. (Signature Ser.). 2005. audio compact disk 129.95 (978-0-7638-2086-2(5)) EMC-Paradigm.

Microsoft Word 97 Core Certification: Instructor Resources; Instructor's Software Package, CD. Nita Rutkosky. (Signature Ser.). audio compact disk 69.00 (978-0-7638-0148-9(8)) EMC-Paradigm.

Microsoft Word 97 Core Certification: Microsoft Office Specialist Certification; Microsoft Office Specialist Ready! CD. Nita Rutkosky. (Signature Ser.). audio compact disk 10.00 (978-0-7638-0309-4(X)) EMC-Paradigm.

Microsoft Works 4. D. Steer. 1997. audio compact disk 57.95 (978-1-889347-29-5(9)) Delmar.

Microtectonics. C. W. Passchier et al. 2000. audio compact disk 125.00 (978-3-540-14679-7(2)) Spri.

Microtrends: The Small Forces Behind Tomorrow's Big Changes. unabr. ed. Mark J. Penn & E. Kinney Zalesne. Read by Brett Barry. 10 CD. (Running Time: 12 hrs.). (ENG.). 2007. 26.98 (978-1-60024-024-9(0), Twelve) Pub: GrandCentral. Dist(s): HachBkGrp

Microtrends: The Small Forces Behind Tomorrow's Big Changes. unabr. ed. E. Kinney Zalesne & Mark J. Penn. Read by Brett Barry. 10 CD. (Running Time: 12 hrs.). (ENG.). 2007. audio compact disk 39.98 (978-1-60024-023-2(2), Twelve) Pub: GrandCentral. Dist(s): HachBkGrp

Mid-Country Blow see Gathering of Great Poetry for Children

Mid-Hudson Valley: Rhinebeck & the Mansions - From Beacon to Hudson. Bill McCoy. (Travelog Recorded Driving Tour Ser.). 2001. audio compact disk 19.95 (978-1-931739-02-3(1)) Travelog Corp.

Mid Letters Heaped upon the Floor see Classical Russian Poetry

Mid Life Allure - Feel as Great as You Look: Age Gracefully with Style. Illus. by Angela Brown. Voice by Jo Peddicord. Prod. by Les Lingle. 1 cass. (Running Time: 30 mins.). (Words of Wellness - Your Show for Simple Solutions Ser.: Vol. 371). 2001. 12.95 (978-1-930995-65-9(2), LLP371) Life Long Pubg.
Zip through Mid Life with zeal & zest with allure & style while feeling your best. Say goodbye to old age, you don't have to be an old foogie.

Mid Life Crazies. Maureen Schuler. 3 cass. (Running Time: 2 hrs. 52 min.). 1994. 26.95 (TAH311) Alba Hse Comns.
An excellent program for those who are confused by their own experience of the mid-life crazies, as well as those who have to cope with such a person. Good for those interested in personal development & emotional & spiritual growth.

Mid Life Make Over: Physical Wellness & Irresistible Tips. abr. ed. Featuring Bob Powers. Interview with Angela Brown. Prod. by Les Lingle. 1 cass. (Running Time: 30 mins.). (Words of Wellness Ser.). 2000. 12.95 (978-1-930995-00-0(8), LLP307) Life Long Pubg.
Why exercise is important in mid-life. Easy steps to take that can ensure youth, longevity & lasting health. How to look better, feel better & improve clarity of thinking.

Mid-Life Tragedy: Adultery: 11 Samuel 11. Ed Young. 1982. 4.95 (978-0-7417-1238-7(5), 238) Win Walk.

Midair. Frank Conroy. Read by Frank Conroy. 1 cass. (Running Time: 30 min.). 8.95 (AMF-19) Am Audio Prose.
Reads from his collection of stories "Midair" & talks about surrealism & the short story.

Midas. abr. ed. Russell Andrews. Read by Patrick G. Lawlor. (Running Time: 6 hrs.). 2005. audio compact disk 82.25 (978-1-59600-254-8(9), 9781596002548, BACDLib Ed) Brilliance Audio.
New York's Hamptons are the summer playground for Wall Street big shots, Hollywood starlets, and all species of glitterati in between. But when a Middle Eastern man rigged with explosives walks into a chic restaurant and blows himself up, all that glamour is shattered. And so is the security and safety of the entire United States. Drawn into this case is Justin Westwood, a local East End Harbor cop who is still haunted by the violent deaths of his wife and daughter years before. After meeting a beautiful woman whose hunger for human contact and comfort matches his own, he believes he is finally winning the battle with his old ghosts. Yet just as he is beginning to grasp hold of the new life he's been craving, he is saddled with this new murder investigation - one far more dangerous than any he's ever tackled. Soon after the restaurant explosion - the first suicide bombing ever to hit U.S. shores - a small plane crashes in the middle of East End Harbor. It is initially deemed an accident but after the pilot's body disappears, as do all traces of his identification, Justin realizes he's dealing with sabotage. When more terrorist strikes occur, each more devastating than the last, Justin also begins to understand that they all share an elusive, undeniable link - one that will plunge him into a terrifying journey leading to some of the country's most powerful figures and their darkest, most closely held secrets. If he is to survive, Justin must wend his way through a complicated maze of corruption and confront startling truths about big business and politics and, most of all, about himself. For a long time, Justin Westwood has wondered if he could ever truly be frightened again, or if anything could reclaim his soul. Some part of him hoped it was possible. He is about to get his wish.

Midas. unabr. ed. Russell Andrews. Read by Patrick G. Lawlor. (Running Time: 12 hrs.). 2005. 39.25 (978-1-59710-486-9(8), 9781597104869, BADLE); 24.95 (978-1-59710-487-6(6), 9781597104876, BAD); 39.25 (978-1-59335-974-4(8), 9781593359744, Brinc Audio MP3 Lib); 24.95 (978-1-59335-973-7(X), 9781593359737, Brilliance MP3); 87.25 (978-1-59600-252-4(2), 9781596002524, BrilAudUnabridg) Brilliance Audio.

Midas Mentality: Expecting & Accepting Your Abundance. Randy Gage. 2002. audio compact disk 477.00 (978-0-9744363-0-2(5)) Prime Concepts Grp.

Midas Touch: Boundless Good Luck, Vol. 13. Jonathan Parker. 2 cass. (Running Time: 1 hr. 45 min.). 1992. 17.00 (978-1-58400-012-9(0)) QuantumQuests Intl.

Midas Touch: The Strategies That Have Made Warren Buffet America's Pre-Eminent Investor. unabr. ed. John Train. Narrated by George Wilson. 4 cass. (Running Time: 5 hrs. 30 mins.). 1990. 35.00 (978-1-55690-339-7(1), 90018K8) Recorded Bks.
Train takes us close up, splicing financial analysis with straight scoop on Warren Buffett, "a cheerful vulture" who loves junk food & "winning the game".

Middle Age: A Romance. unabr. ed. Joyce Carol Oates. 8 cass. (Running Time: 12 hrs.). 2001. 64.00 (978-0-7366-7630-4(9)); 64.00 (978-0-7366-8008-0(X)) Books on Tape.
Death has curious side effects. For some people it is an impetus that awakens one's zest for living; for others it forces open doors to the past; for still others, death is a reminder of one's own mortality, the grief and anger giving way to fear and then eventual renewal. When Adam Berendt dies performing a selfless act, the community of Salt Hill is stunned. Adam was loved by women and respected by men, and his death has a profound impact on those left behind.

Middle Age: A Romance. unabr. ed. Joyce Carol Oates. 9 CDs. (Running Time: 12 hrs.l). 2001. audio compact disk 152.00 (978-0-7366-8009-7(8)) Books on Tape.
The unexpected death of a charismatic and mysterious sculptor has an unanticipated effect upon his friends.

Middle Age Crazies. John E. Bradshaw. (Running Time: 27000 sec.). 2008. audio compact disk 199.00 (978-1-57388-291-0(7)) J B Media.

Middle-Aged Man on the Flying Trapeze see Thurber Carnival

Middle-Aged Man on the Flying Trapeze. unabr. ed. James Thurber. Read by Wolfram Kandinsky. 6 cass. (Running Time: 9 hrs.). 2001. 29.95 (978-0-7366-6778-4(4)) Books on Tape.
Thirty-six stories including "Hell Only Breaks Loose Once" & "If Grant Had Been Drinking At Appomattox".

Middle-Aged Man on the Flying Trapeze. unabr. collector's ed. James Thurber. Read by Wolfram Kandinsky. 6 cass. (Running Time: 6 hrs.). Incl. Everything Is Wild. (1155); Gentleman Is Cold. (1155); Hell Only Breaks Loose Once. (1155); How to See a Bad Play. (1155); If Grant Had Been Drinking at Appomattox. (1155); Mr. Preble Gets Rid of His Wife. (1155); 1979. 36.00 (978-0-7366-0155-9(4), 1155) Books on Tape.

Middle Ages, Renaissance, & Reformation History. Marlin Detweiler & Laurie Detweiler. Perf. by Meshell Watt. 1998. 6.95 (978-1-930710-07-8(0)) Veritas Pr PA.

Middle Class Millionaire: The Rise of the New Rich & How They Are Changing America. Lewis Prince Schiff. Read by Lloyd James. (Playaway Adult Nonfiction Ser.). 2008. 59.99 (978-1-60640-860-5(7)) Find a World.

Middle-Class Millionaire: The Rise of the New Rich & How They Are Changing America. unabr. ed. Russ Alan Prince & Lewis Schiff. Narrated by Lloyd James. (Running Time: 8 hrs. 0 mins. 0 sec.). (ENG.). 2008. audio compact disk 29.99 (978-1-4001-0700-1(8)); audio compact disk 19.99 (978-1-4001-5700-6(5)) Pub: Tantor Media. Dist(s): IngramPubServ

Middle-Class Millionaire: The Rise of the New Rich & How They Are Changing America. 3rd unabr. ed. Russ Alan Prince & Lewis Schiff. Narrated by Lloyd James. (Running Time: 8 hrs. 0 mins. 0 sec.). (ENG.). 2008. audio compact disk 59.99 (978-1-4001-3700-8(4)) Pub: Tantor Media. Dist(s): IngramPubServ

Middle East. unabr. ed. Steve Halbrook et al. 1 cass. (Running Time: 1 hr. 11 min.). 12.95 (740) J Norton Pubs.

Middle East, unabr. ed. Wendy McElroy. Read by Harry Reasoner. 2 cass. (Running Time: 3 hrs.). (World's Political Hot Spots Ser.). 1991. 17.95 (978-0-938935-86-5(0), 390280) Knowledge Prod.
By the end of World War II, Britain had promised control of this area to no less than three groups: two of them were Arabs & Jews. Both of these people claimed a longstanding right to the same piece of land & violence was inevitable.

Middle East: A Brief History of the Last 2,000 Years. unabr. ed. Bernard Lewis. Narrated by Richard M. Davidson. 17 CDs. (Running Time: 19 hrs. 15 mins.). 2001. audio compact disk 160.00 (978-1-4025-0508-9(6), C1564) Recorded Bks.
Elegantly written and accessible, this comprehensive volume paints a varied and intriguing portrait of a region steeped in traditionalism even while geography and politics force change upon it. With wit and gravity, sympathy and objectivity, the author explores the cultural currents that for 2,000 years have flowed across the broad territory spanning Morocco to the Central Asian steppes. He covers fascinating details like transformations in clothing to earth-shaking events like the Mongol conquest. And he considers the future of the region where ancient patterns and conflicts seem destined to repeat themselves.

Middle East: A Brief History of the Last 2,000 Years. unabr. ed. Bernard Lewis. Narrated by Richard M. Davidson. 14 cass. (Running Time: 19 hrs. 15 mins.). 2001. 117.00 (978-0-7887-4997-1(8), 96413) Recorded Bks.
From the birth of Christianity to the modern era, renowned historian Bernard Lewis charts the fascinating history of the Middle East. Elegantly written & accessible, this comprehensive volume paints a varied & intriguing portrait of a region steeped in traditionalism, even while geography & politics force change upon it.

Middle East: Knowledge Products. unabr. ed. McElroy Wendy & Richman Sheldon. Read by Reasoner Harry. 2006. audio compact disk 25.95 (978-0-7861-6698-5(3)) Pub: Blckstn Audio. Dist(s): NetLibrary CO

Middle East & Gold. unabr. ed. Timothy S. Green. 1 cass. (Running Time: 40 min.). 12.95 (1102) J Norton Pubs.
Green points out that the Middle East, including Turkey, is now absorbing one third of all the new gold coming on the market, excluding speculative buying; that the sheer volume in jewelry investment there is much greater than the U.S. or Europe & that the people there will continue to buy in ever increasing number.

Middle East Conflict Roundtable discussion on CD: An LDS Perspective on the History of Hatred. Moderated by Richard Neitzel Holzapfel. 2007. audio compact disk 15.95 (978-1-59038-819-8(4)) Deseret Bk.

Middle East Perspective. unabr. ed. J. William Fulbright et al. 1 cass. (Running Time: 40 min.). 12.95 (451) J Norton Pubs.

Middle Eastern Candle Dancing w/Music CD. Vicki Corona. Prod. by Vicki Corona. (Celebrate the Cultures Ser.: 1-22A). 1980. 24.95 (978-1-58513-151-8(2)) Dance Fantasy.

Middle English Medical Texts. Irma Taavitsainen et al. Ed. by Irma Taavitsainen et al. 2005. cd-rom & audio compact disk 72.00 (978-90-272-3230-4(X)) Pub: J Benjamins Pubng NLD. Dist(s): J Benjamins Pubng Co

Middle Heart. collector's ed. Bette Bao Lord. Read by Penelope Dellaporta. 13 cass. (Running Time: 19 hrs. 30 mins.). 1997. 104.00 (978-0-7366-3644-5(7), 4306) Books on Tape.
In turbulent WWII China, three young people discover the perils of loyalty to ideals, country, family & self.

Middle of My Tether: Familiar Essays. unabr. ed. Joseph Epstein. Read by Michael Russotto. 6 cass. (Running Time: 9 hrs.). 1989. 48.00 (978-0-7366-1718-5(3), 2559) Books on Tape.
The trick, the charm, the magic of the familiar essay is to show what is uncommon about common things, & to make life itself seem more interesting. Epstein's point of view is humorous, skeptical, erudite. He calls into consultation the great writers of times past & present. His perspective changes your own.

Middle of Nowhere. unabr. ed. Ridley Pearson. Read by Ridley Pearson. 7 cass. (Running Time: 10 hrs.). (Lou Boldt/Daphne Matthews Ser.). 2000. 73.25 (978-1-56740-716-7(1), 1567407161, Unabridge Lib Edns); 32.95 (978-1-56740-498-2(7), 1567404987, BAU) Brilliance Audio.
The "blue flu" has struck the Seattle Police Force and the majority of officers are on an unofficial strike. Overworked and understaffed, detective Lou Boldt is committed to remaining on the job no matter what. But when a string of robberies and the brutal near-murder of a female cop descend on the city, the pressure of being a nearly one-man operation threatens Bodt's psyche and his marriage. With the help of Daphne Matthews and Sergeant John LaMoia, Boldt is able to make slow progress cracking the case and their work leads them to a Denver convict and his brother, a hardened criminal. Boldt and Daphne come to realize that the robberies, assaults, and strike are somehow connected - and that his life is now in very real danger. Filled with the fast-paced, spiraling action that has made his previous novels "irresistible" (The Los Angeles Times Book Review) works of suspense that "grip the imagination" (People), this latest offering from "the best thriller writer alive" (Booklist) is certain to win Ridley Pearson an even more enthusiastic audience.

Middle of Nowhere. unabr. ed. Ridley Pearson. Read by Ridley Pearson. (Running Time: 10 hrs.). (Lou Boldt/Daphne Matthews Ser.). 2005. 39.25 (978-1-59600-654-6(4), 9781596006546, BADLE); 24.95 (978-1-59600-653-9(6), 9781596006539, BAD); 39.25 (978-1-59600-652-2(8), 9781596006522, Brinc Audio MP3 Lib); audio compact disk 24.95 (978-1-59600-651-5(X), 9781596006515, Brilliance MP3) Brilliance Audio.

Middle of Nowhere. unabr. ed. Ridley Pearson. Read by Ridley Pearson. (Running Time: 12 hrs.). (Lou Boldt/Daphne Matthews Ser.). 2008. audio compact disk 97.25 (978-1-4233-3666-2(6), 9781423336662, BriAudCD Unabrid); audio compact disk 36.95 (978-1-4233-3665-5(8), 9781423336655, Bril Audio CD Unabri) Brilliance Audio.

Middle of Nowhere Readalong. Janet Lorimer. 1 cass. (Running Time: 1 hr.). (Ten-Minute Thrillers Ser.). (YA). (gr. 6-12). 1995. pap. bk. 12.95 (978-0-7854-1079-9(1), 40816) Am Guidance.

Middle of the Night. Paddy Chayefsky. Contrib. by Elliott Gould et al. (Running Time: 5580 sec.). 2007. audio compact disk 25.95 (978-1-58081-253-5(8)) L A Theatre.

Middle of the Night. Bob Hartman & Michael McGuire. 1 cass. (J). (ps-3). 1994. bk. 11.99 (3-1214) David C Cook.
Children's Bible story.

***middle parts of Fortune.** Frederic Manning. Read by Stanley McGeagh. (Running Time: 10 hrs. 15 mins.). 2010. 89.99 (978-1-74214-635-5(X), 9781742146355) Pub: Bolinda Pubng AUS. Dist(s): Bolinda Pub Inc

Middle Parts of Fortune. unabr. ed. Frederic Manning. Narrated by Stanley McGeagh. 8 cass. (Running Time: 10 hrs. 30 mins.). 2001. 64.00 (978-1-74030-352-1(0)) Pub: Bolinda Pubng AUS. Dist(s): Bolinda Pub Inc

***Middle Parts of Fortune.** unabr. ed. Frederic Manning. Read by Stanley McGeagh. 8 CDs. (Running Time: 10 hrs. 15 mins.). 2010. audio compact disk 87.95 (978-1-74214-571-6(X), 9781742145716) Pub: Bolinda Pubng AUS. Dist(s): Bolinda Pub Inc

Middle Passage. Charles Johnson. Narrated by Dion Graham. 6 CDs. (Running Time: 7 hrs. 15 mins.). 2002. audio compact disk 58.00 (978-1-4025-3826-1(X)) Recorded Bks.

Middle Passage. Charles R. Johnson. Narrated by Dion Graham. 5 cass. (Running Time: 7 hrs. 15 mins.). 45.00 (978-1-4025-2038-9(7)) Recorded Bks.

Middle Passage: From Misery to Meaning in Midlife. James Hollis. 4 CDs. (Running Time: 4 hours 45 minutes). 2004. audio compact disk 24.50 (978-0-9663401-4-3(0)) BMA Studios.
The Middle Passage is read by the author, noted Jungian analyst, Dr. James Hollis. It is an accessible and profound understanding of the midlife crisis.

Middle Passages & the Healing Place of History: Migration & Identity in Black Women's Literature. Elizabeth Brown-Guillory. 2006. audio compact disk 9.95 (978-0-8142-9116-0(3)) Pub: Ohio St U Pr. Dist(s): Chicago Distribution Ctr

Middle Place. unabr. ed. Kelly Corrigan. Read by Tavia Gilbert. 7 CDs. (Running Time: 8 hrs.). 2009. audio compact disk 29.95 (978-1-4332-1274-1(9)) Blckstn Audio.

Middle Place. unabr. ed. Kelly Corrigan. Read by Tavia Gilbert. 1 MP3-CD. (Running Time: 7 hrs. 30 mins.). 2008. 29.95 (978-1-4332-1275-8(7)); 29.95 (978-1-4332-1273-4(0)); 54.95 (978-1-4332-1271-0(4)); audio compact disk & audio compact disk 63.00 (978-1-4332-1272-7(2)) Blckstn Audio.

Middle School Math: Chapter Audio Summaries, Course 1. (gr. 6-9). 2004. audio compact disk (978-0-618-36390-2(4), 2-06514) Holt McDoug.

Middle School Math: Chapter Audio Summaries, Course 2. (gr. 6-12). 2004. audio compact disk (978-0-618-36379-7(3), 2-06503) Holt McDoug.

Middle School Math: Chapter Audio Summaries, Course 3. (gr. 6-12). 2004. audio compact disk (978-0-618-36385-8(8), 2-06509) Holt McDoug.

Middle School Math, Course 1: Chapter Audio Summaries. (SPA.). (gr. 6-9). 2004. audio compact disk (978-0-618-36399-5(8), 2-06523); audio compact disk (978-0-618-36376-6(9), 2-06500) Holt McDoug.

Middle School Math, Course 2: Chapter Audio Summaries. (SPA.). (gr. 6-12). 2004. audio compact disk (978-0-618-36380-3(7), 2-06504); audio compact disk (978-0-618-36378-0(5), 2-06502) Holt McDoug.

Middle School Math, Course 3: Chapter Audio Summaries. (SPA.). (gr. 6-12). 2004. audio compact disk (978-0-618-36386-5(6), 2-06510); audio compact disk (978-0-618-36384-1(X), 2-06508) Holt McDoug.

Middle Temple Murder. unabr. ed. Joseph Fletcher. Read by Flo Gibson. 5 cass. (Running Time: 7 hrs.). 1996. 20.95 (978-1-55685-449-1(8)) Audio Bk Con.
Frank Spargo, a young reporter, follows a chain of clues to a murder that has baffled the London police. This is considered to be one of the Edwardian era's greatest mysteries.

Middle Toe of the Right Foot see Classic Ghost Stories, Vol. 1, A Collection

Middle Toe of the Right Foot. unabr. ed. Ambrose Bierce. Read by Ivor Hugh & Jack Benson. 1 cass. (Running Time: 57 min.). 1977. 7.95 (N-13) Jimcin Record.
An extraordinary ghost story & a story of a man's last thoughts before his hanging.

Middle Way: The Story of Buddhism. Jinananda. Read by David Timson et al. 3 cass. (Running Time: 3 hrs. 30 mins.). 1997. 17.98 (978-962-634-646-4(9), NA314614, Naxos AudioBooks) Naxos.
Learn the Three Jewels of Buddhism - Buddha, a life of the historical figure; The Dharma, an account of the fundamental teachings and the Sangha, the disciplines, both lay and monastic throughout the world. Written for Naxos AudioBooks.

Middle Way: The Story of Buddhism. unabr. ed. Jinananda. Read by David Timson et al. 3 CDs. (Running Time: 3 hrs. 30 mins.). 1997. audio compact disk 22.98 (978-962-634-146-9(7), NA314612, Naxos AudioBooks) Naxos.
Learn the Three Jewels ofBbuddhism - The Buddha, a life of the historical figure; The Dharma, an account of the fundamental teachings; and The Sangha, the disciplines, both lay and monastic throughout the world. Written for Naxos AudioBooks.

Middle Way (the Story of Buddhism) Jinananda. Read by David Timson & Auston Lesser. (Running Time: 3 hrs. 30 mins.). (C). 2001. 24.95 (978-1-60083-842-2(1)) Iofy Corp.

Middle Window. unabr. collector's ed. Elizabeth Goudge. Read by Donada Peters. 7 cass. (Running Time: 10 hrs. 30 mins.). 1989. 56.00 (978-0-7366-1574-7(1), 2441) Books on Tape.
Judy Cameron is ever so bored with London & her glamorous, perfect life. Stifled, her imagination seizes on a picture she sees in a shop window, a picture of the Scottish wilds. It inspires her. Strong-willed, she prevails on her parents & fiance to change their summer plans & head for cold, damp Scotland sure that there she will find the freedom she craves.

Middlemarch. unabr. ed. George Eliot. Read by Nadia May. (Running Time: 113400 sec.). 2007. audio compact disk 44.95 (978-0-7861-6206-2(6)); audio compact disk & audio compact disk 160.00 (978-0-7861-6205-5(8)) Blckstn Audio.

Middlemarch. unabr. ed. George Eliot. Read by Kate Reading. (YA). 2008. 124.99 (978-1-60514-672-0(2)) Find a World.

Middlemarch. unabr. ed. George Eliot. Narrated by Kate Reading. (Running Time: 32 hrs. 0 mins. 0 sec.). (ENG.). 2008. 39.99 (978-1-4001-5863-8(X)); audio compact disk 54.99 (978-1-4001-0863-3(2)); audio compact disk 109.99 (978-1-4001-3863-0(9)) Pub: Tantor Media. Dist(s): IngramPubServ

Middlemarch: A Study of Provincial Life. George Eliot. Read by Carole Boyd. (Running Time: 7 hrs. 30 mins.). 2004. 38.95 (978-1-60083-843-9(X)) Iofy Corp.

Middlemarch: A Study of Provincial Life. George Eliot. Read by Carole Boyd. 6 cass. (Running Time: 7 hrs. 30 mins.). (Classic Literature with Classical Music Ser.). 2000. 32.98 (978-962-634-696-9(5), NA419614); audio compact disk 41.98 (978-962-634-196-4(3), NA619612) Naxos.
Story of the blighted marriage of Dorothea, a young idealistic woman, & Lyd Gate, who is betrayed by his wife's egoism.

Middlemarch: A Study of Provincial Life. unabr. ed. George Eliot. 4 cass. 29.95 (47342) Books on Tape.
The BBC's television production of "Middlemarch" mesmerized millions & elevated George Eliot to bestseller lists for the first time in over a century. Now, lovers of Eliot's classic text can rediscover all the excitement of the novel that inspired the sensational PBS series.

Middlemarch: A Study of Provincial Life, Pt. 1. unabr. ed. George Eliot. Read by Nadia May. 12 cass. (Running Time: 33 hrs. 30 mins.). 1994. 83.95 (978-0-7861-0725-4(1), 1489A,B) Blckstn Audio.
A brilliant portrait of 19th-century English provincial life, "Middlemarch" is a multilayered work centering around two expertly constructed characters: Dorothea Brooke, an ardent, intelligent, idealistic young woman who traps herself into a loveless marriage; & Tertius Lydgate, a well-connected & ambitious young doctor who comes to Middlemarch fired with the desire to spread the new science of medicine. Epic in scope of vision & unsurpassed in its depiction of human nature, "Middlemarch" is one of the greatest works in all of world literature.

Middlemarch: A Study of Provincial Life, Pt. 1. unabr. collector's ed. George Eliot. Read by Kate Reading. 12 cass. (Running Time: 18 hrs.). 2001. 96.00 (978-0-7366-6100-3(X)) Books on Tape.
Centered around the beautiful, spirited Dorothea Brooks, who marries an elderly cleric in the belief that by doing so she has devoted her life to a great cause. Instead, to her dismay, she finds herself committed to a petty, vindictive man and inept scholar - and dangerously drawn to Will Ladislaw, her husband's handsome young cousin.

Middlemarch: A Study of Provincial Life, Pt. 2. George Eliot. 12 cass. (Running Time: 16 hrs.). 2000. 77.95 Audio Bk Con.
This multi-layered novel concerns complex social relationships in a provincial Victorian neighborhood & the struggle to hold fast to personal integrity in a materialistic enviomment.

Middlemarch: A Study of Provincial Life, Pt. 2. collector's unabr. ed. George Eliot. Read by Kate Reading. 11 cass. (Running Time: 16 hrs. 30 mins.). 2001. 88.00 (978-0-7366-6101-0(8)) Books on Tape.
Centered around the beautiful, spirited Dorothea Brooks, who marries an elderly cleric in the belief that by doing so she has devoted her life to a great cause. Instead, to her dismay, she finds herself committed to a petty, vindictive man and inept scholar - and dangerously drawn to Will Ladislaw, her husband's handsome young cousin.

Middlemarch: A Study of Provincial Life, Pt. 2. unabr. ed. George Eliot. Read by Nadia May. 11 cass. (Running Time: 33 hrs. 30 mins.). 1994. 76.95 (978-0-7861-0726-1(X), 1489A,B) Blckstn Audio.
A brilliant portrait of 19th-century English provincial life, "Middlemarch" is a multilayered work centering around two expertly constructed characters: Dorothea Brooke, an ardent, intelligent, idealistic young woman who traps herself into a loveless marriage; & Tertius Lydgate, a well-connected & ambitious young doctor who comes to Middlemarch fired with the desire to spread the new science of medicine. Epic in scope of vision & unsurpassed in its depiction of human nature, "Middlemarch" is one of the greatest works in all of world literature.

Middlemarch: Classic Collection. unabr. ed. George Eliot. Read by Nadia May. (Running Time: 31 hrs. 50 mins.). 2008. audio compact disk 44.95 (978-1-4332-1497-4(0)) Blckstn Audio.

Middlemarch: Part 1 & Part 2. unabr. ed. George Eliot. Narrated by Kate Reading. (ENG.). 2006. audio compact disk 139.99 (978-1-4001-3216-4(9)); audio compact disk 44.99 (978-1-4001-5216-2(X)) Pub: Tantor Media. Dist(s): IngramPubServ

Middlemarch (Part 1) unabr. ed. George Eliot. Narrated by Flo Gibson. (Running Time: 15 hrs. 42 mins.). 2004. audio compact disk 44.95 (978-1-55685-771-3(3)) Audio Bk Con.

Middlemarch (Part 1), Vol. 1. unabr. ed. George Eliot. Read by Flo Gibson. 12 cass. (Running Time: 16 hrs. 30 min.). 1986. 39.95 (978-1-55685-018-9(2)) Audio Bk Con.
This novel explores the whole of provincial Victorian society & the struggle to hold fast to personal integrity in a materialistic & mean spirited age. The idealistic Dorothea, who is trapped in a loveless marriage & Lydgate, who is betrayed by his wife's egoism, are the main characters in this work concerning complex social interrelationship.

Middlemarch (Part 2), Vol. 2. unabr. ed. George Eliot. Narrated by Flo Gibson. (Running Time: 15 hrs. 11 mins.). 1986. 39.95 (978-1-55685-019-6(0)) Audio Bk Con.

Middlemarch (Part 2), Vol. 2. unabr. ed. George Eliot. Narrated by Flo Gibson. (Running Time: 15 hrs. 11 mins.). 2004. audio compact disk 44.95 (978-1-55685-772-0(1)) Audio Bk Con.

Middlemarch (Parts 1 And 2) unabr. ed. George Eliot. Narrated by Flo Gibson. (Running Time: 30 hrs. 53 mins.). 1986. 64.95 (978-1-55685-781-2(0)) Audio Bk Con.

Middlemarch, Parts 1 And 2. unabr. ed. George Eliot. Narrated by Flo Gibson. (Running Time: 30 hrs. 53 mins.). 2005. audio compact disk 68.95 (978-1-55685-780-5(2)) Audio Bk Con.

Middler Resources: Spring 1999. 1 cass. (J). (gr. 3-4). 1999. 10.99 Incl. tchr's. visuals. (978-1-57405-493-4(7)) CharismaLife Pub.

Middler Resources: Summer 99. 1 cass. (J). (gr. 3-4). 1999. 10.99 (978-1-57405-545-0(3)) CharismaLife Pub.
Includes teachers visuals.

Middler Resources: Winter 99-2000. 1 cass. (J). (gr. 3-4). 1999. pap. bk. 10.99 (978-1-57405-624-2(7)) CharismaLife Pub.

Middlesex. abr. ed. Jeffrey Eugenides. 2002. audio compact disk 30.00 (978-1-55927-781-5(5)) Pub: Macmill Audio. Dist(s): Macmillan

Middlesex. unabr. rev. ed. Jeffrey Eugenides. Read by Kristoffer Tabori. 17 CDs. (Running Time: 21 hrs. 0 mins. 0 sec.). (ENG.). 2004. audio compact disk 49.95 (978-1-59397-734-4(4)) Pub: Macmill Audio. Dist(s): Macmillan

Middlessence. Myron Madden & Mary B. Madden. 1986. 10.80 (0403) Assn Prof Chaplains.

Middletown, America: One Town's Passage from Grief to Recovery. abr. ed. Gail Sheehy. Read by Gail Sheehy. (Running Time: 6 hrs.). 2003. audio compact disk 26.95 (978-1-59355-226-8(2), 1593552262, BACD); audio compact disk 74.25 (978-1-59355-227-5(0), 1593552270, BACDLib Ed) Brilliance Audio.
Fifty people never came home to Middletown, New Jersey after September 11th. Wall Street fathers, young Port Authority police, single working moms, the beloved coach of the championship girls traveling basketball team. Three toddlers in one church pre-school lost their daddies. Dozens of widows, young and beautiful girls in their 20s and 30s, some still nursing newborns, watched their dreams literally go up in smoke in that amphitheater of death across the river. Gail Sheehy traveled to Middletown shortly after the disaster and began in-depth interviews with many of the bereaved. Middletown, America was written as the year progressed, following parallel and intertwining stories of selected individuals and their families. A mother who was doubly bereft when she lost her only son as he tried to fill the shoes of her absentee husband; the sole survivor in an office of 67 people who escaped the 88th floor of Tower 2 seconds before the floor was decimated. Here are the fire-fighters, rescue workers and front-line public health volunteers, now training to be soldiers in this new war. Of equal importance, however, is the way these very real individuals dealt with this disaster and the trauma that followed. Middletown, America is also a story of recovery and of the ways people finally learn to deal with seemingly insurmountable grief and an incomprehensible physical and financial disaster.

Middletown, America: One Town's Passage from Grief to Recovery. unabr. ed. Gail Sheehy. Read by Sandra Burr. 11 cass. (Running Time: 16 hrs.). 2003. 34.95 (978-1-59355-224-4(6), 1593552246, BAU); 97.25 (978-1-59355-225-1(4), 1593552254, BrilAudUnabridg) Brilliance Audio.

Middletown, America: One Town's Passage from Trauma to Hope. unabr. ed. Gail Sheehy. Read by Sandra Burr. (Running Time: 16 hrs.). 2004. 44.25 (978-1-59335-500-5(9), 1593355009, Brinc Audio MP3 Lib) Brilliance Audio.

Middletown, America: One Town's Passage from Trauma to Hope. unabr. ed. Gail Sheehy. Read by Sandra Burr. (Running Time: 16 hrs.). 2004. 39.25 (978-1-59710-489-0(2), 1597104892, BADLE); 24.95 (978-1-59710-488-3(4), 1597104884, BAD) Brilliance Audio.

Middletown, America: One Town's Passage from Trauma to Hope. unabr. ed. Gail Sheehy. Read by Sandra Burr. (Running Time: 16 hrs.). 2004. 29.95 (978-1-59335-226-4(3), 1593352263) Soulmate Audio Bks.

***Middleworld.** unabr. ed. Jon Voelkel & Pamela Voelkel. Narrated by Scott Brick. 9 CDs. (Jaguar Stones Trilogy: Bk. 1). (J). (gr. 3-6). 2010. audio compact disk 44.00 (978-0-307-71199-1(4), Listening Lib) Pub: Random Audio Pubg. Dist(s): Random

Middleworld. unabr. ed. Jon Voelkel & Pamela Voelkel. Read by Scott Brick. (Jaguar Stones Trilogy: Bk. 1). (ENG.). (J). 2010. audio compact disk 44.00 (978-0-307-71197-7(8), Listening Lib) Pub: Random Audio Pubg. Dist(s): Random

***Mide 'Wiwin or Grand Medicine Society of the Ojibway.** l.t. ed. W. J. Hoffman. (ENG., 2008. pap. bk. 23.95 (978-1-61033-188-3(5), TGSPubng) T G S.

Midi-Bacharach & David. 1998. 13.95 (978-1-85909-430-3(9), Warner Bro) Alfred Pub.

Midi-Michael George. 1998. 13.95 (978-1-85909-444-0(9), Warner Bro) Alfred Pub.

Midi-Pop Hits of The 90s. 1998. 13.95 (978-1-85909-058-9(3), Warner Bro) Alfred Pub.

Midi-Showtunes. 1998. 13.95 (978-1-85909-220-0(9), Warner Bro) Alfred Pub.

Midi-Sinatra & Nat King Cole. 1998. 13.95 (978-1-85909-057-2(5), Warner Bro) Alfred Pub.

Midlife: Program from the Award Winning Public Radio Series the Infinite Mind. Interview. Hosted by Petter Kramer & Peter Kramer. 1 CD. (Running Time: 1 hr.). (Infinite Mind Ser.: 382). 2005. 21.95 (978-1-933644-16-5(8), LCM 382) Lichtenstein Creat.
This week on The Infinite Mind: What do we mean when we talk about "midlife"? It depends on who you ask. Short of being that span of time between adolescence and old age, "midlife" can be the years of greatest contentment - then again, they may be times of unrelenting stress and discomfort. From songwriters to sociologists, poets to psychologists and even to comics, midlife offers an unusually vast panorama by which to witness and explore the human experience as we begin, in singer/songwriter Loudon Wainwright III's happy phrase, "to crunch the numbers."Joining Dr. Peter Kramer this week are members of the Mid-Life Crisis Comedy tour. Dr. Ronald Kessler from the MacArthur Foundation Midlife Network tells us that midlife can be the best of times and the worst of times - it just depends on the gender, the class, and the age of the person you're talking with. Dr. Margie Lachman, a psychologist at the Lifespan Lab at Brandeis University explains that even as mid-lifers start to experience some loss in "the mechanisms of cognition," years of knowledge make them invaluable additions to the workplace. Singer/songwriter Loudon Wainwright III offers a brand-new song touching on the "ancients" at your high school reunion. The Infinite Mind's Jackson Braider tells anxious midlifers that it's okay to worry - the world of work is indeed fraught with change, with very little benefit to the midlife employee. Finally, centenarian and former Poet Laureate Stanley Kunitz offers a vision of midlife from the vantage point of a lifetime of experience. Midlife - CD382-CD$18.00, 4/$54.00 Midlife - MP3 Audio File (Instant Download)382-MP3Price: $10.00Special price: $8.00, 4/$24.00 Midlife - Transcript (Instant Download)382-TrlDPrice: $10.00Special price: $8.00, 4/$24.00 This week on The Infinite Mind: What do we mean when we talk about "midlife"? It depends on who you ask. Short of being that span of time between adolescence and old age, "midlife" can be the years of greatest contentment - then again, they may be times of unrelenting stress and discomfort. From songwriters to sociologists, poets to psychologists and even to comics, midlife offers an unusually vast panorama by which to witness and explore the human experience as we begin, in singer/songwriter Loudon Wainwright III's happy phrase, "to crunch the numbers."Joining Dr. Peter Kramer this week are members of the Mid-Life Crisis Comedy tour. Dr. Ronald Kessler from the MacArthur Foundation Midlife Network tells us that midlife can be the best of times and the worst of times - it just depends on the gender, the class, and the age of the person you're talking with. Dr. Margie Lachman, a psychologist at the Lifespan Lab at Brandeis University explains that even as mid-lifers start to experience some loss in "the mechanisms of cognition," years of knowledge make them invaluable additions to the workplace. Singer/songwriter Loudon Wainwright III offers a brand-new song touching on the "ancients" at your high school reunion. The Infinite Mind's Jackson Braider tells anxious midlifers that it's okay to worry - the world of work is indeed fraught with change, with very little benefit to the midlife employee. Finally, centenarian and former Poet Laureate Stanley Kunitz offers a vision of midlife from the vantage point of a lifetime of experience.

Midlife & the Great Unknown. David Whyte. 2003. audio compact disk 24.95 (978-1-59179-069-3(7)) Sounds True.

Midlife Crisis. Heather Lawn. 1 cass. 8.95 (209) Am Fed Astrologers.
Change your life with major transits.

Midnight. Dean Koontz. Read by J. Charles. (Playaway Adult Fiction Ser.). 2008. 79.99 (978-1-60640-600-7(0)) Find a World.

Midnight. unabr. ed. Dean Koontz. Read by J. Charles. (Running Time: 15 hrs.). 2004. 29.95 (978-1-59355-324-1(2), 1593553242, BAU); 97.25 (978-1-59355-325-8(0), 1593553250, BrilAudUnabridg); audio compact disk 42.95 (978-1-59355-326-5(9), 1593553269, Bril Audio CD Unabri); audio compact disk 112.25 (978-1-59355-327-2(7), 1593553277, BriAudCD Unabrid) Brilliance Audio.

Midnight. unabr. ed. Dean Koontz. Read by J. Charles. (Running Time: 15 hrs.). 2004. 39.25 (978-1-59335-644-6(7), 1593356447, Brinc Audio MP3 Lib); 24.95 (978-1-59335-272-1(7), 1593352727, Brilliance MP3) Brilliance Audio.

Midnight. unabr. ed. Dean Koontz. Read by J. Charles. (Running Time: 15 hrs.). 2004. 49.97 (978-1-59710-490-6(6), 1597104906, BADLE); 24.95 (978-1-59710-491-3(4), 1597104914, BAD) Brilliance Audio.

Midnight Alley. unabr. ed. Rachel Caine. Narrated by Cynthia Holloway. (Running Time: 9 hrs. 0 mins. 0 sec.). (Morganville Vampires Ser.: Bk. 3). (ENG.). (YA). (gr. 7-12). 2009. audio compact disk 19.99 (978-1-4001-6192-8(4)); audio compact disk 29.99 (978-1-4001-1192-3(7)) Pub: Tantor Media. Dist(s): IngramPubServ

Midnight Alley. unabr. ed. Rachel Caine. Narrated by Cynthia Holloway. (Running Time: 9 hrs. 0 mins. 0 sec.). (Morganville Vampires Ser.: Bk. 3). (ENG.). (YA). (gr. 8-12). 2009. audio compact disk 59.99 (978-1-4001-4192-0(3)) Pub: Tantor Media. Dist(s): IngramPubServ

Midnight at the Casa Luna, Vol. 1. Thomas M. Lopez. 1 CD. (Running Time: 1 hr. 5 min.). (C). 1998. audio compact disk 15.95 (978-1-881137-58-0(9)) ZBS Found.
Hero Jack Flanders enters a transcendental coffee shop & is transported to another realm.

***Midnight Awakening.** unabr. ed. Lara Adrian. Narrated by Hillary Huber. (Running Time: 10 hrs. 0 mins. 0 sec.). (Midnight Breed Ser.). (ENG.). 2010. 24.99 (978-1-4001-6459-2(1)); 16.99 (978-1-4001-8459-0(2)); audio compact disk 69.99 (978-1-4001-4459-4(0)); audio compact disk 34.99 (978-1-4001-1459-7(4)) Pub: Tantor Media. Dist(s): IngramPubServ

Midnight Bayou. abr. ed. Nora Roberts. Read by James Daniels & Sandra Burr. (Running Time: 6 hrs.). 2004. audio compact disk 16.99 (978-1-59355-689-1(6), 1593556896, BCD Value Price) Brilliance Audio.
Declan Fitzgerald had always been the family maverick, but even he couldn't understand his impulse to buy a dilapidated mansion on the outskirts of New Orleans. All he knew was that ever since he saw Manet Hall, he'd been enchanted - and obsessed - with it. So when the opportunity to buy the house comes up Declan jumps at the chance to live out a dream. Determined to restore Manet Hall to its former splendor, Declan begins the daunting renovation room by room, relying on his own labor and skills. But the days spent in total isolation in the empty house take a toll. He is seeing visions of days from a century past, and experiencing sensations of terror and nearly unbearable grief - sensations not his own, but those of a stranger. Local legend has it that the house is haunted, and with every passing day Declan's belief in the ghostly presence grows. Only the companionship of the alluring Angelina Simone can distract him from the mysterious happenings in the house, but Angelina too has her own surprising connection to Manet Hall - a connection that will help Declan uncover a secret that's been buried for a hundred years.

***Midnight Bayou.** abr. ed. Nora Roberts. 2010. audio compact disk 9.99 (978-1-4418-5637-1(4)) Brilliance Audio.

Midnight Bayou. unabr. ed. Nora Roberts. Narrated by James Daniels. 7 cass. (Running Time: 9 hrs.). 2001. 32.95 (978-1-58788-778-9(9), 1587887789, BAU) Brilliance Audio.

Midnight Bayou. unabr. ed. Nora Roberts. Read by Sandra Burr. Narrated by James Daniels. 7 cass. Library ed. (Running Time: 9 hrs.). 2001. 78.25 (978-1-58788-779-6(7), 1587887797, Unabridge Lib Edns) Brilliance Audio.

Midnight Bayou. unabr. ed. Nora Roberts. Read by James Daniels. (Running Time: 9 hrs.). 2004. 39.25 (978-1-59335-411-4(8), 1593354118, Brlnc Audio MP3 Lib) Brilliance Audio.

Midnight Bayou. unabr. ed. Nora Roberts. Read by James Daniels & Sandra Burr. (Running Time: 9 hrs.). 2004. 39.25 (978-1-59710-493-7(0), 1597104930, BADLE); 24.95 (978-1-59710-492-0(2), 1597104922, BAD) Brilliance Audio.

Midnight Bayou. unabr. ed. Nora Roberts. Read by James Daniels & Sandra Burr. (Running Time: 9 hrs.). 2007. audio compact disk 97.25 (978-1-4233-3390-6(X), 9781423333906, BriAudCD Unabrid); audio compact disk 36.95 (978-1-4233-3389-0(6), 9781423333890, Bril Audio CD Unabri) Brilliance Audio.

Midnight Bayou. unabr. ed. Nora Roberts. Read by James Daniels & Sandra Burr. (Running Time: 9 hrs.). 2004. 24.95 (978-1-59335-113-7(5), 1593351135) Soulmate Audio Bks.

Midnight Before Christmas. William Bernhardt. Read by Jonathan Marosz. 3 cass. (Running Time: 4 hrs. 30 min.). 1999. 24.95 (5059); 28.00 (978-0-7366-4677-2(9)) Books on Tape.

Midnight Cab. James W. Nichol. Narrated by Scott Brick. (Running Time: 12 hrs.). 2005. 34.95 (978-1-59912-547-3(1)) Iofy Corp.

Midnight Cab. James W. Nichol. Read by Scott Brick. 9 cass. (Running Time: 43200 sec.). 2002. cass., cass., DVD 72.95 (978-0-7861-3012-2(1), 3421) Blckstn Audio.

Midnight Cab. James Nickoll. 3 CDs. (Running Time: 4 hrs. 30 mins.). 2005. audio compact disk 19.95 (978-0-660-18959-8(3)) Pub: Canadian Broadcasting CAN. Dist(s): Georgetown Term

Midnight Cab. unabr. ed. James W. Nichol. Read by Scott Brick. 8 cass. (Running Time: 43200 sec.). 2005. 29.95 (978-0-7861-3442-7(9)); audio compact disk 29.95 (978-0-7861-7992-3(9)) Blckstn Audio.

Midnight Cab. unabr. ed. James W. Nichol. Read by Scott Brick. 13 vols. (Running Time: 13 hrs.). 2005. audio compact disk 29.95 (978-0-7861-8201-5(6), 3421) Blckstn Audio.

Midnight Cab: Mystery of the Great Man. James W. Nichol. 2009. (978-1-60136-179-0(3)) Audio Holding.

Midnight Cab: Mystery of the Locked Room. James W. Nichol. 2009. (978-1-60136-181-3(5)) Audio Holding.

Midnight Cab: Mystery of the Screaming Woman. James W. Nichol. 2009. (978-1-60136-188-2(2)) Audio Holding.

Midnight Cab: Mystery of the Secret Letters. James W. Nichol. 2009. (978-1-60136-189-9(0)) Audio Holding.

Midnight Cab: Mystery of the White-Eyed Cat. James W. Nichol. 2009. (978-1-60136-193-6(9)) Audio Holding.

Midnight Cab -Lib. unabr. ed. James W. Nichol. Read by Scott Brick. 10 CDs. (Running Time: 12 hrs.). 2005. audio compact disk 90.00 (978-0-7861-8079-0(X), 3421) Blckstn Audio.

***Midnight Charter.** unabr. ed. David Whitley. Narrated by Simon Vance. 8 CDs. (Running Time: 10 hrs.). (YA). (gr. 6-9). 2009. audio compact disk 79.95 (978-0-7927-6457-1(9), Chivers Child Audio) AudioGO.

Midnight Clear. abr. ed. Dallas Jenkins. Narrated by Loren Lester. (ENG.). 2007. 13.99 (978-1-60814-310-8(4)) Oasis Audio.

Midnight Clear. abr. ed. Dallas Jenkins & Jerry B. Jenkins. Narrated by Loren Lester. (Running Time: 3 hrs. 11 mins. 14 sec.). (ENG.). 2007. audio compact disk 19.99 (978-1-59859-289-4(0)) Oasis Audio.

Midnight Club. James Patterson. Read by Michael Kramer. 1999. audio compact disk 64.00 (978-0-7366-7497-3(7)); 48.00 (978-0-7366-4547-8(0), 4954) Books on Tape.
Charming, urbane, but megalomaniacal Alexander St. Germain wanted nothing less than control of international organized crime. A sadistic psychotic as well, he shot & crippled a New York policeman & his wife. A few years later, during a purge of other New York crime lords, St. Germain is brutally murdered, or is he.

Midnight Club. abr. ed. James Patterson. (ENG.). 2006. 14.98 (978-1-59483-688-6(4)) Pub: Hachet Audio. Dist(s): HachBkGrp

Midnight Club. abr. ed. James Patterson. Read by Robert Forster. 4 cass. 1999. 24.00 (FS9-50898) Highsmith.

Midnight Club. unabr. ed. James Patterson. Read by Michael Kramer. 7 cass. (Running Time: 9 hrs.). 2000. 32.00 (978-1-57042-634-6(1)) Hachet Audio.

Midnight Club. unabr. ed. James Patterson. Read by Michael Kramer. 7 cass. 1999. 32.00 (FS9-43905) Highsmith.

Midnight Come Again. Dana Stabenow. Read by Marguerite Gavin. (Kate Shugak Ser.). 2000. audio compact disk 64.00 (978-0-7366-6298-7(7)) Books on Tape.

Midnight Come Again. collector's ed. Dana Stabenow. Read by Marguerite Gavin. 7 cass. (Running Time: 10 hrs. 30 min.). (Kate Shugak Ser.). 2000. 56.00 (978-0-7366-5085-4(7), 5299) Books on Tape.
She is spending the winter working under an assumed name in an effort to get over a grief she can't discuss. Her best friend, State Trooper Jim Chopin, needing her to help him work a new case, discovers her hiding out in Bering, a small fishing village on Alaska's western coast. Before they can even discuss Kate's last several months, or what Jim is doing looking for her in Bering, they are up to their eyebrows in Jim's case, which is suddenly more complicated & more dangerous than they suspected.

Midnight Come Again. unabr. ed. Dana Stabenow. Read by Marguerite Gavin. 7 CDs. (Running Time: 8 hrs. 12 mins). (Kate Shugak Ser.). 2001. audio compact disk Books on Tape.
While deck-handing on a fishing boat, Kate Shugak hauls in the dead body of the most disliked fisherman around. Kate's search for the killer isn't making her too popular in town - especially since he's being hailed as the catch of the day.

Midnight Come Again. unabr. ed. Dana Stabenow. Read by Marguerite Gavin. 7 cass. (Running Time: 10 hrs. 30 mins.). (Kate Shugak Ser.). 2000. 29.95 (978-0-7366-4934-6(4)) Books on Tape.
Kate Shugak and State Trooper Jim Chopin solve another murder in the Alaskan wilderness.

Midnight Comes at Noon. unabr. ed. Daniel Easterman. Read by Garrick Hagon. 12 cass. (Running Time: 16 hrs. 19 mins.). (Isis Cassettes Ser.). (J). 2004. 94.95 (978-0-7531-1907-5(2)); audio compact disk 104.95 (978-0-7531-2260-0(X)) Pub: ISIS Lrg Prnt GBR. Dist(s): Ulverscroft US

***Midnight Crystal.** abr. ed. Jayne Castle, pseud. Read by Tanya Eby. (Running Time: 5 hrs.). (Dreamlight Trilogy). 2010. 9.99 (978-1-4418-9387-1(3), 9781441893871, BAD) Brilliance Audio.

***Midnight Crystal.** abr. ed. Jayne Castle, pseud. Read by Joyce Bean & Tanya Eby. (Running Time: 4 hrs.). (Dreamlight Ser.). 2010. audio compact disk 14.99 (978-1-4418-1354-1(3), 9781441813541, BACD) Brilliance Audio.

***Midnight Crystal.** unabr. ed. Jayne Castle, pseud. Read by Joyce Bean & Tanya Eby. (Running Time: 9 hrs.). (Dreamlight Ser.). 2010. 39.97 (978-1-4418-1339-8(X), 9781441813398, Brlnc Audio MP3 Lib); 24.99 (978-1-4418-1338-1(1), 9781441813381, Brilliance MP3); 39.97 (978-1-4418-1341-1(1), 9781441813411, BADLE); 24.99 (978-1-4418-1340-4(3), 9781441813404, BAD); audio compact disk 92.97 (978-1-4418-1337-4(3), 9781441813374, BriAudCD Unabrid); audio compact disk 34.99 (978-1-4418-1336-7(5), 9781441813367, Bril Audio CD Unabri) Brilliance Audio.

Midnight Farm. 2004. pap. bk. 14.95 (978-0-7882-0687-0(7)) Weston Woods.

Midnight Farm. 2004. bk. 24.95 (978-1-56008-011-4(6)); 8.95 (978-0-7882-0059-5(3)); cass. & flmstrp 30.00 (978-0-89719-597-3(3)) Weston Woods.

Midnight Farm. Reeve Lindbergh. Illus. by Susan Jeffers. 1 cass., 5 bks. (Running Time: 5 min.). (J). pap. bk. 32.75 Weston Woods.
A mother & her child take a reassuring tour of their farm at night.

Midnight Farm. Reeve Lindbergh. Illus. by Susan Jeffers. 1 cass. (Running Time: 5 min.). (J). bk. 24.95 Weston Woods.

Midnight Farm. Reeve Lindbergh. Read by Lindsay Crouse. 1 cass. (Running Time: 5 min.). (J). (ps-4). 1989. pap. bk. 8.95 (978-0-89719-993-3(6), 337); pap. bk. 12.95 (PRA337) Weston Woods.

Midnight for Charlie Bone. Jenny Nimmo. Read by Simon Russell Beale. 7 CDs. (Running Time: 7 hrs. 9 mins.). (Children of the Red King Ser.: Bk. 1). (J). (gr. 3 up). 2004. audio compact disk 50.00 (978-1-4000-8614-6(0), Listening Lib) Random Audio Pubg.

Midnight for Charlie Bone. unabr. ed. Jenny Nimmo. Read by Simon Russell Beale. (Running Time: 25800 sec.). (Children of the Red King Ser.: Bk. 1). (ENG.). (J). (gr. 3). 2007. audio compact disk 28.00 (978-0-7393-3900-8(1), Listening Lib) Pub: Random Audio Pubg. Dist(s): Random

Midnight Fox. abr. ed. Betsy Byars. 1 cass. (Running Time: 55 mins.). Dramatization. (J). (gr. 4-7). 1973. 9.95 (978-0-670-47476-9(2)) Live Oak Media.
The study of a boy who, through concern over a fox, overcomes a sense of abandonment at being forced to spend a summer on his uncle's farm.

Midnight Fox. abr. ed. Betsy Byars. Illus. by Ann Grifalconi. 12 vols. (Running Time: 55 mins.). Dramatization. (J). (gr. 4-7). 1973. pap. bk. 15.95 (978-0-670-47478-3(9)) Live Oak Media.

Midnight Game. abr. ed. Engle & Barnes. (Running Time: 2 hrs.). (Strange Matter Ser.). 2006. 9.95 (978-1-4233-0860-7(3), 9781423308607, BAD) Brilliance Audio.

Midnight Game. abr. ed. Engle & Julian Barnes. Read by Multivoice Production Staff. (Running Time: 2 hrs.). (Strange Matter Ser.). 2006. 25.25 (978-1-4233-0861-4(1), 9781423308614, BADLE) Brilliance Audio.

Midnight Game. abr. ed. Engle & Engle. (Running Time: 7200 sec.). (Strange Matter Ser.). (J). (gr. 4-7). 2006. audio compact disk 25.25 (978-1-4233-0859-1(X), 9781423308591, BACDLib Ed); audio compact disk 9.95 (978-1-4233-0858-4(1), 9781423308584, BACD) Brilliance Audio.
Tyler Webb has been invited to attend a very special game. Someone has left him a ticket for a final showdown between two old football teams from Fairfield's past. The only problem is, the game is scheduled for midnight, and there's no way Tyler's parents will let him go. Curiosity gets the best of him, and Tyler sneaks out to see the game. Now he's sitting in the bleachers under the moonlight, waiting for the arrival of both sides. But the players are not running onto the field. They're crawling. Straight up from the ground. And they know they're being watched.

Midnight Hour. unabr. ed. Karen Robards. Narrated by Barbara Rosenblat. 9 cass. (Running Time: 12 hrs. 15 mins.). 1999. 83.00 (978-0-7887-3101-3(7), 95812E7) Recorded Bks.
A blend of suspense & smoldering romance, a nightmarish suburban crime story unfolds, with a vivid portrayal of the attraction of opposites.

Midnight House. unabr. ed. Alex Berenson. Contrib. by George Guidall. 9 CDs. (Running Time: 11 hrs.). (ENG.). (gr. 12 up). 2010. audio compact disk 39.95 (978-0-14-314539-4(8), PengAudBks) Penguin Grp USA.

Midnight Hunt see Childe Rowland & Other British Fairy Tales

Midnight in Death. unabr. ed. J. D. Robb, pseud. Read by Susan Ericksen. (Running Time: 3 hrs.). (In Death Ser.). 2005. 39.25 (978-1-4233-0996-3(0), 9781423309963, BADLE); 24.95 (978-1-4233-0995-6(2), 9781423309956, BAD); audio compact disk 19.95 (978-1-4233-0990-1(1), 9781423309901); audio compact disk 62.25 (978-1-4233-0991-8(X), 9781423309918); audio compact disk 39.25 (978-1-4233-1173-7(6), 9781423311737, Brlnc Audio MP3 Lib); audio compact disk 24.95 (978-1-4233-1172-0(8), 9781423311720, Brilliance MP3) Brilliance Audio.
The number-one New York Times bestselling In Death series explodes with intrigue, passion, and suspense. Now, Nora Roberts, writing as J. D. Robb, propels you into the darkest night of Lieutenant Eve Dallas's life - when a killer comes to call... Eve's name has made a Christmas list, but it's not for being naughty or nice. It's for putting a serial killer behind bars. Now the escaped madman has her in his sights. With her husband, Roarke, at her side, Eve must stop the man from exacting his bloody vengeance - or die trying... "Gritty and steamy." - Booklist "Very suspenseful." - The Literary Times.

Midnight in Death. unabr. ed. J. D. Robb, pseud. Read by Susan Ericksen. (Running Time: 10800 sec.). (In Death Ser.). 2007. 44.25 (978-1-4233-3723-2(9), 9781423337232, BrilAudUnabridg) Brilliance Audio.

Midnight in Death. unabr. ed. J. D. Robb, pseud. Read by Susan Ericksen. (In Death Ser.). (YA). 2008. 54.99 (978-1-60514-818-2(0)) Find a World.

Midnight in Death; Interlude in Death. unabr. ed. J. D. Robb, pseud. Read by Susan Ericksen. (Running Time: 6 hrs.). (In Death Ser.). 2007. audio compact disk 29.95 (978-1-4233-0994-9(4), 9781423309949, Bril Audio CD Unabri) Brilliance Audio.

***Midnight in Madrid.** Noel Hynd. (Running Time: 13 hrs. 42 mins. 0 sec.). (Russian Ser.). (ENG.). 2009. 14.99 (978-0-310-30258-2(7)) Zondervan.

***Midnight in Ruby Bayou.** unabr. ed. Elizabeth Lowell. Read by Robin Rowan. (ENG.). 2009. (978-0-06-196717-7(3), Harper Audio); (978-0-06-182979-6(X), Harper Audio) HarperCollins Pubs.

Midnight in the Garden of Good & Evil. abr. ed. John Berendt. Read by Anthony Heald. 3 CDs. (Running Time: 11400 sec.). (ENG.). 2005. audio compact disk 14.99 (978-0-7393-2150-8(1), RH Aud Price) Pub: Random Audio Pubg. Dist(s): Random

Midnight in the Garden of Good & Evil: A Savannah Story. John Berendt. 1 cass., 1 CD. 8.78 (WB 46829); audio compact disk 14.38 (WB 46829) NewSound.

Midnight in the Garden of Good & Evil: A Savannah Story. John Berendt. Narrated by Jeff Woodman. 13 CDs. (Running Time: 15 hrs. 15 mins.). 2001. audio compact disk 124.00 (978-0-7887-5303-9(7), C1344E7) Recorded Bks.
Shots rang out in Savannah's grandest mansion in the misty, early morning hours of May 2, 1981. Was it murder or self defense? The question captivated the city's society, high & low, for over a decade.

Midnight in the Garden of Good & Evil: A Savannah Story. abr. ed. John Berendt. 2 cass. (Running Time: 3 hrs.). 14.95 (43802) Books on Tape.
Meet some of the real residents of Savannah, Georgia who are religiously eccentric & who happily display each other's dirty laundry.

Midnight in the Garden of Good & Evil: A Savannah Story. unabr. ed. John Berendt. Read by Jeff Woodman. 10 cass. (Running Time: 15 hrs.). 2000. 39.95 (H802) Blckstn Audio.
An account of life in Savannah, interwoven with the unpredictable twists & turns of a landmark murder case & by a gallery of remarkable characters, from Southern belles to drag queens to voodoo priestess.

Midnight in the Garden of Good & Evil: A Savannah Story. unabr. ed. John Berendt. Narrated by Jeff Woodman. 13 CDs. (Running Time: 15 hrs.). 1997. audio compact disk 124.00 (978-0-7887-5187-5(5)) Recorded Bks.
Shots rang out in Savannah's grandest mansion in the misty, early morning hours of May 2, 1981. Was it murder or self defense? The question captivated the city's society, high & low, for over a decade.

Midnight in the Garden of Good & Evil: A Savannah Story, unabr. ed. John Berendt. Narrated by Jeff Woodman. 11 cass. (Running Time: 15 hrs.). 1996. 91.00 (978-0-7887-0439-0(7), 94631E7) Recorded Bks.

Midnight in the Sunken Cathedral. unabr. ed. Short Stories. Harlan Ellison. Read by Harlan Ellison. 4 cass. (Running Time: 5 hrs.). 2001. reel tape 25.00 (978-1-57453-412-2(2)) Audio Lit.
Includes: "Jeffrey Is Five," "Prince Myshkin." "Hold the Relish," "The End of the Time of Leinard," "Anywhere but Here" & more.

Midnight in the Sunken Cathedral. unabr. ed. Short Stories. Harlan Ellison. 5 CDs. (Running Time: 5 hrs.). 2001. audio compact disk 29.95 (978-1-57453-415-3(7)) Audio Lit.
This new collection of stories by award-winning author Harlan Ellison includes "Midnight in the Sunken Cathedral," "Jeffrey is Five," "Prince Myshkin," & "Hold the Relish." This is the first audio collection of one of the great American short story writers.

Midnight Is a Lonely Place. unabr. ed. Barbara Erskine. Read by Rula Lenska. 12 cass. (Running Time: 18 hrs.). 2000. 79.95 (978-0-7451-6535-6(4), CAB 1151) Pub: Chivers Audio Bks GBR. Dist(s): AudioGO
After a broken love affair, Kate Kennedy retires to a remote cottage to work on her new book. But when Alison, the daughter of the cottage's owner, uncovers an ancient Roman site nearby, long-buried passions are unleashed! Kate, Alison and her brother Greg find their lives overturned as a disturbing episode in East Angelia's violent past thrusts its way into present day reality.

***Midnight Magic.** Avi. (ENG.). 2010. audio compact disk 49.99 (978-0-545-03324-4(1)) Scholastic Inc.

***Midnight Magic.** Avi. Illus. by Jeff Woodman. (Running Time: 5 hrs.). (ENG.). 2010. audio compact disk 25.99 (978-0-545-15169-6(4)) Scholastic Inc.

Midnight Man. Loren D. Estleman. Read by Alan Zimmerman. 4 cass. (Running Time: 360 min.). (Amos Walker Ser.). 2000. 25.00 (978-1-58807-046-3(8)) Am Pubng Inc.

Midnight Mass & Other Great Vampire Stories. unabr. ed. Read by Susan Anspach et al. Ed. by Martin Greenberg. 4 cass. (Running Time: 6 hrs.). 2002. 25.00 (978-1-59040-245-0(6), Phoenix Audio) Pub: Amer Intl Pub. Dist(s): PerseuPGW
From the horrifying to the humorous, shared stories about one of mankind's oldest imagined evils, the vampire. The contents include "Bite Me Not, or Fleur de Fur" by Tanith Lee, "Food Chain" by Nina Kiriki Hoffman, "Moonlight in Vermont" by Esther Freisner, "Madeleine" by Barbara Hambly, "Victims" by Kristine Kathryn Rusch, "Seat Partner" by Chelsea Quinn Yarbro, and "Midnight Mass" by F. Paul Wilson.

Midnight Miracle: A Musical Christmas Story. Gene Grier & Lowell Everson. 3 cass. (Running Time: 4 hrs. 30 mins.). (gr. 2-6). 2004. bk. 12.00 (978-0-687-01525-2(1)) Abingdon.
Musical for 2-6 graders. Includes parts for 5-8, plus options for up to 26. Runs 30 minutes with 7 songs. Tells the story of Christmas through the eyes of the shepherds and animals.

Midnight Miracle: Accompanist Edition, Singer's Edition. unabr. ed. Gene Grier & Lowell Everson. 10 CDs. (Running Time: 6 hrs. 40 mins.). (gr. 2-6). 2004. bk. 40.00 (978-0-687-01535-1(9)) Abingdon.

Midnight Miracle: Singer's Edition. Gene Grier & Lowell Everson. 1 cass. (Running Time: 1 hr. 30 mins.). (gr. 2-6). 2004. bk. 10.00 (978-0-687-01565-8(0)) Abingdon.

***Midnight Never Comes.** unabr. ed. Jack Higgins. Read by Michael Page. (Running Time: 5 hrs.). 2011. 24.99 (978-1-4418-4532-0(1), 9781441845320, Brilliance MP3); 39.97 (978-1-4418-4533-7(X), 9781441845337, Brlnc Audio MP3 Lib); audio compact disk 29.99 (978-1-4418-4530-6(5), 9781441845306, Bril Audio CD Unabri); audio compact disk 87.97 (978-1-4418-4531-3(3), 9781441845313, BriAudCD Unabrid) Brilliance Audio.

Midnight Nineteen Eighty-Nine. Pauline Hassell. 1 cass. 8.95 (673) Am Fed Astrologers.
An AFA Convention workshop tape.

Midnight Noel. Mark Hayes. (Mark Hayes Vocal Solo Collection). (ENG.). 1999. audio compact disk 17.95 (978-0-7390-0817-1(X), 18922) Alfred Pub.

Midnight on the Moon. unabr. ed. Mary Pope Osborne. 1 cass. (Running Time: 48 mins.). (Magic Tree House Ser.: No. 8). (J). (gr. k-3). 2004. pap. bk. 17.00 (978-0-8072-0341-5(6), Listening Lib) Random Audio Pubg.

Midnight Outcry see Robert Penn Warren Reads Selected Poems

Midnight over Sanctaphrax. unabr. ed. Paul Stewart & Chris Riddell. Read by John Lee. 7 CDs. (Running Time: 8 hrs. 10 mins.). (Edge Chronicles Ser.: Bk. 3). (J). (gr. 4-7). 2006. audio compact disk 55.00 (978-0-307-28589-8(8), Listening Lib); 40.00 (978-0-307-28588-1(X), Listening Lib) Pub: Random Audio Pubg. Dist(s): Random
Far over the Edge, the Mother Storm is brewing - a storm more terrifying than any seen in the lifetime of any Edgelander. Sweeping in from the open sky, it must strike the source of the Edgewater River to bring new energy to the land. But in its way is Sanctaphrax, a magnificent city built on a floating rock and tethered to the land by a massive chain. Only one person can save the Edgelands from certain disaster: Twig, the young sky pirate captain who dared to sail over the Edge - and returned with his memory shattered and his crew flung far and wide. But to recover his memory and take action, Twig must first find his lost crew. And this means a journey back into the Deepwoods, and beyond.

***Midnight Palace.** unabr. ed. Carlos Ruiz Zafon. (Running Time: 8 hrs.). (ENG.). (YA). 2011. 19.98 (978-1-60941-098-8(X)); audio compact disk & audio compact disk 24.98 (978-1-60941-095-7(5)) Pub: Hachet Audio. Dist(s): HachBkGrp

Midnight Partner. abr. ed. Bart Davis. Read by Wally Fields & Jennifer Durand. 4 cass. 24.00 (978-1-886392-08-3(0), Parrot Bks) Walberg Pubng.

Midnight Pass. unabr. ed. Stuart M. Kaminsky. 5 cass. (Running Time: 7 hrs. 30 min.). (Lew Fonesca Mystery Ser.: Vol. 3). 2003. 45.00 (978-0-7366-9612-8(1)) Books on Tape.

Midnight Rambler. unabr. ed. James Swain. Read by Peter Jay Fernandez. (YA). 2008. 64.99 (978-1-60252-982-3(5)) Find a World.

***Midnight Rambler: Unabridged Value-Priced Edition.** James Swain. Narrated by Peter Jay Fernandez. (Running Time: 9 hrs. 45 mins. 0 sec.). (ENG.). 2010. audio compact disk 14.95 (978-1-60283-996-0(4)) Pub: AudioGO. Dist(s): Perseus Dist

***Midnight Rescue.** unabr. ed. Catherine Marshall. Adapted by C. Archer. Narrated by Jaimee Draper. (Catherine Marshall's Christy Ser.). (ENG.). 2010. 7.00 (978-1-60814-703-8(7), SpringWater) Oasis Audio.

***Midnight Ride of Blackwell Station.** Mary Peace Finley. (J). 2010. audio compact disk 10.95 (978-0-86541-111-1(5)) Filter.

***Midnight Rising.** unabr. ed. Lara Adrian. Narrated by Hillary Huber. (Running Time: 10 hrs. 0 mins.). (Midnight Breed Ser.). 2010. 16.99 (978-1-4001-8460-6(6)); 24.99 (978-1-4001-6460-8(5)); audio compact disk 34.99 (978-1-4001-1460-3(8)) Pub: Tantor Media. Dist(s): IngramPubServ

***Midnight Rising (Library Edition)** unabr. ed. Lara Adrian. Narrated by Hillary Huber. (Running Time: 10 hrs. 0 mins.). (Midnight Breed Ser.). 2010. 34.99 (978-1-4001-9460-5(1)); audio compact disk 83.99 (978-1-4001-4460-0(4)) Pub: Tantor Media. Dist(s): IngramPubServ

***Midnight Road.** unabr. ed. Tom Piccirilli. (Running Time: 12 hrs.). 2010. 29.95 (978-1-4417-6691-5(X)); 72.95 (978-1-4417-6688-5(X)); audio compact disk 105.00 (978-1-4417-6689-2(8)) Blckstn Audio.

Midnight Runner. Jack Higgins. Narrated by Patrick MacNee. 6 cass. (Running Time: 8 hrs. 30 mins.). (Sean Dillon Ser.). 2002. 54.00 (978-1-4025-1699-3(1), 96999) Recorded Bks.
British agent Sean Dillon returns in a sequel. Introducing the intriguing and powerful Arab/English Rashid family. Kate, the only Rashid left after an assassination attempt on the American president foiled by Dillon, has sworn to avenge her family and will do anything to humiliate the United States, including sabotage her own oil fields to cripple America's, and the world's, oil supplies.

Midnight Runner. Jack Higgins. Narrated by Patrick McNee. 7 CDs. (Running Time: 8 hrs. 30 mins.). (Sean Dillon Ser.). 2002. audio compact disk 69.00 (978-1-4025-2071-6(9), RF846) Recorded Bks.

Midnight Smile. unabr. ed. Aileen Armitage. Read by Diana Bishop. 8 cass. (Running Time: 10 hrs. 52 mins.). (Isis Ser.). (J). 2002. 69.95 (978-0-7531-0553-5(5)) Pub: ISIS Lrg Prnt GBR. Dist(s): Ulverscroft US
Suddenly left alone in the world, Joanna Forrest and her younger sister, are slowly coming to terms with their new life. But their routine is shattered one day, by the arrival of a charming yet totally unpredictable poet. As the girls become increasingly obsessed by him, he starts to take over their lives. Then violence and tragedy reach out, and the dream is shattered.

***Midnight Sons & Daughters.** Debbie Macomber. 2011. audio compact disk 9.99 (978-1-4418-5348-6(0)) Brilliance Audio.

***Midnight Sons & Daughters.** unabr. ed. Debbie Macomber. Read by Dan John Miller. (Running Time: 2 hrs.). 2010. 14.99 (978-1-4418-5346-2(4), 9781441853462, Brilliance MP3); 14.99 (978-1-4418-5347-9(2), 9781441853479, BAD); audio compact disk 14.99 (978-1-4418-5345-5(6), 9781441853455, Bril Audio CD Unabri) Brilliance Audio.

***Midnight Sun.** 2010. audio compact disk (978-1-59171-174-2(6)) Falcon Picture.

Midnight Twins. unabr. ed. Jacquelyn Mitchard. Read by Emily Durante. 1 MP3-CD. (Running Time: 6 hrs.). (Midnight Twins Ser.: No. 1). 2008. 24.95 (978-1-4233-6493-1(7), 9781423364931, Brilliance MP3); 39.25 (978-1-4233-6494-8(5), 9781423364948, Brlnc Audio MP3 Lib); 39.25 (978-1-4233-6496-2(1), 9781423364962, BADLE); 24.95 (978-1-4233-6495-5(3), 9781423364955, BAD); audio compact disk 26.95 (978-1-4233-6491-7(0), 9781423364917, Bril Audio CD Unabri) Brilliance Audio.

Midnight Twins. unabr. ed. Jacquelyn Mitchard. Read by Emily Durante. 5 CDs. (Running Time: 6 hrs.). (Midnight Twins Ser.: No. 1). (YA). (gr. 6-9). 2008. audio compact disk 54.97 (978-1-4233-6492-4(9), 9781423364924, BriAudCD Unabrid) Brilliance Audio.

Midnight Voices. unabr. ed. John Saul. Read by Aasne Vigesaa. 7 cass. (Running Time: 11 hrs.). 2002. 32.95 (978-1-59086-217-9(1), 1590862171, BAU); 82.25 (978-1-59086-218-6(X), 159086218X, Unabridge Lib Edns); audio compact disk 36.95 (978-1-59086-219-3(8), 1590862198, CD Unabridged); audio compact disk 92.25 (978-1-59086-220-9(1), 1590862201, CD Unabrid Lib Ed) Brilliance Audio.
Caroline Evans, a recently widowed mother of two, thinks things have finally fallen into place when she meets the charismatic Anthony Fleming. They are quickly married and she and her two children move into his luxury apartment in the legendary Rockwell on Central Park West. Despite her son's misgivings about the building and the people who dwell there, Caroline dismisses the oddities of their new neighbors as pleasant eccentricities. Until things begin to change. And behind the luxury and beauty of The Rockwell lurks a secret that Caroline can't possibly imagine.

Midnight Voices. unabr. ed. John Saul. Read by Aasne Vigesaa. (Running Time: 11 hrs.). 2004. 39.25 (978-1-59335-421-3(5), 1593354215, Brlnc Audio MP3 Lib) Brilliance Audio.

Midnight Voices. unabr. ed. John Saul. Read by Aasne Vigesaa. (Running Time: 11 hrs.). 2004. 39.25 (978-1-59710-494-4(9), 1597104949, BADLE); 24.95 (978-1-59710-495-1(7), 1597104957, BAD) Brilliance Audio.

Midnight Voices. unabr. ed. John Saul. Read by Aasne Vigesaa. (Running Time: 11 hrs.). 2004. 24.95 (978-1-59335-189-2(5), 1593351895) Soulmate Audio Bks.

Midnight Whispers, unabr. ed. V. C. Andrews. Read by Donada Peters. 9 cass. (Running Time: 13 hrs. 30 min.). 1993. 72.00 (978-0-7366-2532-6(1), 3284) Books on Tape.
Dawn's daughter, Christie, struggles to break the cruel bonds of the past that continue to haunt her family.

Midnight Whispers. unabr. ed. V. C. Andrews. Read by Laurel Lefkow. 10 cass. (Running Time: 12 hrs. 46 mins.). (Isis Cassettes Ser.). (J). 2004. 84.95 (978-0-7531-1775-0(4)) Pub: ISIS Lrg Prnt GBR. Dist(s): Ulverscroft US

***midnight Zoo.** unabr. ed. Sonya Hartnett. Read by Richard Aspel. (Running Time: 4 hrs. 33 mins.). (J). 2010. audio compact disk 57.95 (978-1-74214-824-3(7), 9781742148243) Pub: Bolinda Pubng AUS. Dist(s): Bolinda Pub Inc

Midnight's Choice. unabr. ed. Kate Thompson. 4 cass. (Running Time: 5 hrs. 1 min.). (J). 2000. 25.00 (Random AudioBks) Random Audio Pubg.
Since Tess's friend Kevin left the human world to become a phoenix, Tess has felt increasingly lonely & isolated. Soon it will be Tess's fifteenth birthday, the age at which she must finally decide what form she will take for the rest of her life. If she chooses, she too, can become a phoenix & join Kevin in his seemingly perfect existence but everything changes when Kevin is captured by a local zoo. Tess is introduced to a world unknown to her before, a world ruled by vampires, darkness & menacing forces that threaten to change her own life forever.

Midnight's Choice. unabr. ed. Kate Thompson. Read by Niamh Cusack. 4 vols. (Running Time: 4 hrs. 28 mins.). (Switchers Ser.: Vol. 2). (J). (gr. 5-9). 2004. pap. bk. 38.00 (978-0-8072-8769-9(5), Listening Lib); 32.00 (978-0-8072-8768-2(7), YA262CX, Listening Lib) Random Audio Pubg.

***Midnight's Daughter.** unabr. ed. Karen Chance. Narrated by Joyce Bean. (Running Time: 12 hrs. 0 mins.). (Dorina Basarab Ser.). 2010. 17.99 (978-1-4001-8738-6(9)) Tantor Media.

***Midnight's Daughter.** unabr. ed. Karen Chance. Narrated by Joyce Bean. (Running Time: 12 hrs. 0 mins. 0 sec.). (Dorina Basarab Ser.). (ENG.). 2010. 24.99 (978-1-4001-6738-8(8)); audio compact disk 34.99 (978-1-4001-1738-3(0)); audio compact disk 83.99 (978-1-4001-4738-0(7)) Pub: Tantor Media. Dist(s): IngramPubServ

Midnight's Smiling. unabr. ed. Alexandra Connor. Read by Gareth Armstrong. 8 cass. (Running Time: 12 hrs.). 1999. 69.95 (978-0-7531-0517-7(9), 990309) Pub: ISIS Audio GBR. Dist(s): Ulverscroft US
Dr. George Cochrane led a comfortable life with his wife & shy son, Michael, in their gracious old house on the outskirts of Pendleton. By day, he was Dr. to the worst streets of the nearby city. Then his wife died. Somehow, Michael could never make up for the loss. Although he followed in his father's footsteps, his brilliant friend Harry outshone him. One young rival was watching, biding her time, acknowledging his ambition & ability as her own. Michael's daughter, Mel.

***Midnights with the Mystic: A Little Guide to Freedom & Bliss.** unabr. ed. Cheryl Simone & Sadhguru Jaggi Vasudev. (Running Time: 7 hrs.). (ENG.). 2010. 27.98 (978-1-59659-673-3(2), GildAudio) Pub: Gildan Media. Dist(s): HachBkGrp

Midpoint Planet Dynamics in Relationships. Steve Pincus. 1 cass. 8.95 (280) Am Fed Astrologers.
Points of harmony & stress are revealed. Triggers shown.

Midpoints & Murder. Harry Darling. 1 cass. 8.95 (609) Am Fed Astrologers.
An AFA Convention workshop tape.

Midrashim. David Curzon. (Review Jewish Writers Chapbook Ser.: No. 5). 1991. 10.00 (978-0-685-49056-3(4)) Cross-Cultrl NY.

Midshipman Bolitho, unabr. ed. Alexander Kent, pseud. Read by Michael Jayston. 6 cass. (Running Time: 6 hrs.). (Richard Bolitho Ser.: Bk. 1). 1993. 54.95 (978-0-7451-4006-3(8), CAB 703) AudioGO.

Midsummer Meeting. Elvi Rhodes. 10 cass. (Running Time: 15 hrs.). 2001. 84.95 (978-1-86042-686-5(7)) Pub: Soundings Ltd GBR. Dist(s): Ulverscroft US

Midsummer Night. Ed. by Robert A. Monroe. 1 cass. (Running Time: 30 min.). (Meta Music Ser.). 1986. 12.95 (978-1-56102-215-1(2)) Inter Indus.
Crickets & a gentle thunderstorm begin this soft & restful meditative piece with music that serves to slow excess mental activity & take you to that calm, deep, & beautiful center inside you.

Midsummer Nights. Bernie Krause. 1 cass. (Running Time: 1 hr.). (Wild Sanctuary Ser.). 1994. audio compact disk 15.95 (2368, Creativ Pub) Quayside.
Cicadas & small insects in the eastern Adirondack Mountains. Cascade Mountains of northern California - bull frogs & great horned owls join the insect chorus.

Midsummer Nights. Bernie Krause. 1 cass. (Running Time: 1 hr.). (Wild Sanctuary Ser.). 1994. 9.95 (2367, NrthWrd Bks) TandN Child.

Midsummer Night's Dream see Gathering of Great Poetry for Children

Midsummer Night's Dream. William Shakespeare. (Running Time: 2 hrs. 30 mins.). 2001. 23.95 (978-1-60083-844-6(8)) Iofy Corp.

Midsummer Night's Dream. William Shakespeare. Perf. by Warren Mitchell et al. 3 cass. (Running Time: 2 hrs. 30 mins.). Dramatization. (Plays of William Shakespeare Ser.). (YA). 1997. 17.98 (978-962-634-650-1(7), NA315014, Naxos AudioBooks) Naxos.
A blend of comedy, magic, mystery and a satisfying set of contrasts make this one of shakespeare's most popular plays. Uses the text of the New Cambridge Shakespeare, used by the royal Shakespeare company and educational institutions worldwide.

Midsummer Night's Dream. William Shakespeare. Perf. by Warren Mitchell et al. 3 CDs. (Running Time: 2 hrs. 30 mins.). Dramatization. (Plays of William Shakespeare Ser.). (J). (gr. 9-12). 1997. audio compact disk 22.98 (978-962-634-150-6(5), NA315012) Naxos.

Midsummer Night's Dream. William Shakespeare. Read by Kimberly Schraf. 2 cass. (Running Time: 2 hrs. 30 mins.). 1995. 14.95 (978-1-55685-391-3(2)) Audio Bk Con.
In this, Shakespeare's most fantastical comedy, the fairy world wreaks havoc with the foolish mortal one & a lover's nightmare melts into an innocent dream. Under the canopy of a moonlit forest, four sets of lovers & five delightfully inept "mechanicals" weave a magic web.

Midsummer Night's Dream. Retold by Noe Venable. William Shakespeare. (Classic Literature Ser.). 2003. audio compact disk 18.95 (978-1-4105-0194-3(9)) D Johnston Inc.

Midsummer Night's Dream. abr. ed. William Shakespeare. 2 CDs. (Running Time: 2 hrs.). 2005. audio compact disk 12.95 (978-0-660-18968-0(2)) Pub: Canadian Broadcasting CAN. Dist(s): Georgetown Term

Midsummer Night's Dream. abr. ed. William Shakespeare. Read by Paul Scofield. Perf. by Joy Parker. 2 cass. (Running Time: 3 hrs.). Dramatization. (gr. 9-12). 1991. 18.00 (978-1-55994-086-3(7), CPN 208) HarperCollins Pubs.

***Midsummer Night's Dream.** abr. ed. William Shakespeare. Read by (null) Cast. (ENG.). 2003. (978-0-06-074318-5(2), Caedmon) HarperCollins Pubs.

***Midsummer Night's Dream.** abr. ed. William Shakespeare. Read by (null) Cast. (ENG.). 2004. (978-0-06-081330-7(X), Caedmon) HarperCollins Pubs.

Midsummer Night's Dream. unabr. ed. Ernest Schanzer. 1 cass. (Running Time: 19 min.). (Shakespeare's Critics Speak Ser.). 1965. 12.95 (23097) J Norton Pubs.
A discussion of the various aspects of "A Midsummer Night's Dream" emphasizing its central theme, but also including Shakespeare's treatment of the fairies, the play's unity of atmosphere & the artistry of its opening lines.

Midsummer Night's Dream. unabr. ed. William Shakespeare. Read by Paul Scofield & Joy Parker. 2 cass. (Running Time: 2 hrs. 20 mins.). Dramatization. 17.95 (H148) Blckstn Audio.
Shakespeare's most enchanting comedy features lovers chasing each other through a moonlit forest already teeming with rustics rehearsing a play - & regal fairies nursing a quarrel.

Midsummer Night's Dream. unabr. ed. William Shakespeare. 1 cass. (Running Time: 1 hr. 30 mins.). 2001.; audio compact disk Books on Tape.

Midsummer Night's Dream. unabr. ed. William Shakespeare. 2 cass. 1999. 18.00 (FS9-51069) Highsmith.

Midsummer Night's Dream. unabr. ed. William Shakespeare. 2 cass. (Running Time: 2 hrs.). Dramatization. 2000. pap. bk. 34.20 (40750E5); 22.00 (21518E5) Recorded Bks.

Midsummer Night's Dream. unabr. ed. William Shakespeare. Perf. by Folio Theatre Players. 1 cass. Dramatization. 10.95 (978-0-8045-0882-7(8), SAC 8013) Spoken Arts.

Midsummer Night's Dream. unabr. ed. William Shakespeare. Narrated by Roy Hudd et al. (Arkangel Shakespeare Ser.). (ENG.). 2005. audio compact disk 19.95 (978-1-932219-24-1(2)) Pub: AudioGO. Dist(s): Perseus Dist
Lysander loves Hermia, but Hermia is to be married to Demetrius, who is still the apple of Helena's eye. Hermia and Lysander plan to elope so they tell Helena, who warns Demetrius. Demetrius follows Hermia into the woods, then Helena follows Demetrius. When Oberon, king of the fairies, uses his magic to cast a spell on the four runaway lovers in a midsummer wood outside Athens, chaos ensues. This wonderful production is performed by Roy Hudd, Amanda Root, and the Arkangel cast.

Midsummer Night's Dream. unabr. ed. William Shakespeare. Read by Full Ensemble Cast. (YA). 2006. 34.99 (978-1-59895-619-1(1)) Find a World.

Midsummer Night's Dream, Set. William Shakespeare. Contrib. by Naxos Audiobooks Staff. Told to Warren Mitchell. As told by Michael Maloney & Sarah Woodward. 3 cass. or 3 CDs. (Running Time: 2 hrs. 19 mins. 12 sec.). (New Cambridge Shakespeare & Naxos AudioBooks Ser.). (ENG.). 1998. audio compact disk 29.99 (978-0-521-62487-9(8)) Cambridge U Pr.

Midsummer Night's Dream: Act III, Scene 1 see Hearing Great Poetry: From Chaucer to Milton

Midsummer Night's Dream: An A+ Study Guide. unabr. ed. Helen Mirren. (Running Time: 1 hr.). (ENG.). 2006. 5.98 (978-1-59483-705-0(8)) Pub: Hachet Audio. Dist(s): HachBkGrp

Midsummer Nights Dream Cd Audio. abr. ed. William Shakespeare. Read by Cast Staff. 2 cass. (Running Time: 3 hrs.). 1995. audio compact disk 25.00 (978-0-694-51585-1(X), Harper Audio) HarperCollins Pubs.

Midsummer Night's Dream Read Along. Prod. by Saddleback Educational Publishing. (Saddleback's Illustrated Classics Ser.). (YA). 2006. audio compact disk 24.95 (978-1-56254-923-7(5)) Saddleback Edu.

Midsummer Night's Scream. Jill Churchill. Read by Susan Ericksen. 4 cass. (Jane Jeffry Mystery Ser.). 39.95 (978-0-7927-3368-3(1), CSL 713); audio compact disk 59.95 (978-0-7927-3369-0(X), SLD 713) AudioGO.

Midsummer's Eve. unabr. ed. Philippa Carr. Read by Erica Grant. 14 cass. (Running Time: 15 hrs. 45 min.). 2001. 99.95 (978-1-85695-821-9(3), 940708) Pub: ISIS Audio GBR. Dist(s): Ulverscroft US
Annora Cadorson had lived a quiet & sheltered existence at the family home in Cador in Cornwall, until one fateful Midsummer's Eve when she witnessed a horrifying incident.

Midway: The Battle That Doomed Japan, the Japanese Navy's Story. unabr. ed. Mitsuo Fuchida & Masatake Okumiya. Ed. by Clarke H. Kawakami & Roger Pineau. 6 vols. (Running Time: 1 hr. 20 mins.). (Now Hear This Audiobooks Ser.). 2004. 29.95 (978-1-59114-293-5(8)) Naval Inst Pr.

Midwest Ramblin' The Goose Island Ramblers. Goose Island Ramblers. 2004. audio compact disk 16.00 (978-0-924119-20-0(9)) Pub: Max Kade. Dist(s): Chicago Distribution Ctr

Midwest Region. Compiled by Benchmark Education Staff. 2005. audio compact disk 10.00 (978-1-4108-5482-7(5)) Benchmark Educ.

Midwich Cuckoos. unabr. ed. John Wyndham. Narrated by Full Cast. (Running Time: 2 hrs. 0 mins. 0 sec.). (ENG.). 2010. audio compact disk 24.95 (978-1-60283-817-8(8)) Pub: AudioGO. Dist(s): Perseus Dist

Midwich Cuckoos: (Village of the Damned) John Wyndham. Read by Jeremy Clyde. 2002. pap. bk. (978-1-901768-48-0(1)) CSA Telltapes GBR.
Why did so many women in Midwich village give birth at the same time to identical children with strange telepathic powers and anti-social tendencies? An alien invasion of catastrophic proportions is imagined in this disturbing novel which has become a classic of literary science fiction.

Midwifery & Herbs. Willa Shaffer. (Woodland Health Ser.). 1987. 4.95 (978-0-913923-19-1(2)) Pub: Woodland UT. Dist(s): Midpt Trade

Midwife's Apprentice. Karen Cushman. Read by Charlotte Coleman. 2 cass. (Running Time: 2 hrs. 50 mins.). (J). 2000. 18.00 (978-0-7366-9030-0(1)) Books on Tape.
A sharp-tongued midwife makes the homeless orphan girl, known only as Brat, her apprentice. As the girl learns her craft, she develops her own identity & finds her place in the world.

Midwife's Apprentice. Karen Cushman. Narrated by Jenny Sterlin. 3 CDs. (Running Time: 2 hrs. 45 mins.). (gr. 6 up). audio compact disk 29.00 (978-1-4025-2320-5(3)) Recorded Bks.

Midwife's Apprentice, unabr. ed. Karen Cushman. Narrated by Jenny Sterlin. 2 pieces. (Running Time: 2 hrs. 45 mins.). (gr. 6 up). 1997. 19.00 (978-0-7887-0577-9(6), 94778E7) Recorded Bks.
Jane the Midwife finds a half-starved girl hiding in a dung heap. When she takes the girl home to her cottage, a unique relationship begins. Paints an unforgettable picture of village life in the Middle Ages & the midwife's craft.

Midwillow Martyrs. Janet Mary Tomson. Read by Anne Cater. 7 cass. (Soundings Ser.). (J). 2006. 61.95 (978-1-84559-261-5(1)) Pub: ISIS Lrg Prnt GBR. Dist(s): Ulverscroft US

Midwinter Blues see Poetry of Langston Hughes

Midwinter of the Spirit. Phil Rickman. (Merrily Watkins Ser.). 2008. 94.95 (978-0-7531-3824-3(7)); audio compact disk 104.95 (978-0-7531-2806-0(3)) Pub: ISIS Audio GBR. Dist(s): Ulverscroft US

Midwinter, Presolstice see Poetry & Voice of Margaret Atwood

Midwinter Turns to Spring - the Music CD. Prod. by Zendrik N/A. Arranged by Zendrik N/A. Lyrics by Maria Veloso. Based on a book by Maria Veloso. (ENG.). 2006. audio compact disk 12.99 (978-0-9770751-1-9(7)) Think Outside.

Midwinter's Tale. Andrew M. Greeley. Read by Jonathan Marosz. 9 cass. (Running Time: 13 hrs. 30 min.). (O'Malley Family Saga). 1999. 34.95 (978-0-7366-4596-6(9)) Books on Tape.
Saga of the O'Malley family of Chicago. It begins with the story of Charles Cronin O'Malley's coming of age, graduation from high school in 1946 & service with the Army in a still much traumatized Germany. He finds hunger everywhere, the black market booming, government agents hunting down refugees for the ruthless Russians, & streets filled with human suffering. All that O'Malley wants is to go to Notre Dame, become an accountant, & have a nice, orderly life... but the Deity seems to have other plans for him.

Midwinter's Tale. collector's ed. Andrew M. Greeley. Read by Jonathan Marosz. 9 cass. (Running Time: 13 hrs. 30 min.). (O'Malley Family Saga). 1999. 72.00 (978-0-7366-4930-8(1), 4893) Books on Tape.

Midwinter's Tale. collector's ed. Andrew M. Greeley. Read by Jonathan Marosz. 10 cass. (Running Time: 10 hrs.). (O'Malley Family Saga). 2000. 80.00 (978-0-7366-5163-9(2)) Books on Tape.

Midwinter's Tale, unabr. ed. Andrew M. Greeley. Read by Jonathan Marosz. 9 cass. (Running Time: 13 hrs. 30 mins.). (O'Malley Family Saga). 1999. 72.00 (978-0-7366-4448-8(2), 4893) Books on Tape.
Saga of the O'Malley family of Chicago. Beginnning with the story of Charles Cronin O'Mallye's, graduation from high school in 1946 & service with the Army in a still much traumatized Germany, finding hunger everywhere, the black market booming, government agents hunting down refugees for the ruthless Russians & streets filled with human suffering.

Midwinter's Tale. unabr. ed. Andrew M. Greeley. Read by Jonathan Marosz. 1 CD. (Running Time: 1 hr. 30 mins.). (O'Malley Family Saga). 2001. audio compact disk Books on Tape.
Saga of the O'Malley family of Chicago. It begins with the story of Charles Cronin O'Malley's coming of age, graduation from high school in 1946 & service with the Army in a still much traumatized Germany. He finds hunger everywhere, the black market booming, government agents hunting down refugees for the ruthless Russians, & streets filled with human suffering. All that O'Malley wants is to go to Notre Dame, become an accountant, & have a nice, orderly life... but the Deity seems to have other plans for him.

Midwives, unabr. ed. Chris Bohjalian. Read by Valerie Leonard. 8 vols. (Running Time: 11 hr.). 2000. bk. 69.95 (978-0-7927-2340-0(6), CSL 229, Chivers Sound Lib) AudioGO.
In an isolated house in rural Vermont, a midwife named Sibyl Danforth takes desperate measures to save a baby's life. She performs an emergency cesarean section on a mother she believes has died of a stroke. But what is Sibyl's patient wasn't dead & she inadvertently killed her? Sibyl faces the antagonism of the law, the hostility of traditional doctors & the accusations of her own conscience.

Midwives. unabr. ed. Chris Bohjalian. Read by Valerie Leonard. 12 CDs. (Running Time: 18 hrs.). 2001. audio compact disk 110.95 (978-0-7927-9965-8(8), SLD 016, Chivers Sound Lib) AudioGO.
On an icy winter night in Vermont, a seasoned midwife performs an emergency cesarean section to save a baby's life on a woman she believes has died of a stroke.

Mie Prigioni. Silvio Pellico. Read by Elsa Proverbio. 9 cass. (Running Time: 9 hrs.). (ITA.). 1996. bk. 99.50 (978-1-58085-454-2(0)) Interlingua VA.
Includes Italian transcription with notes in Italian. The combination of written text & clarity & pace of diction will open the door for intermediate & advanced students to genuine comprehension & the use of literary texts for advancement in rapid understanding of written & oral language materials. The audio text plus written text concept makes foreign languages accessible to a much wider range of students than books alone.

Miedo. abr. ed. L. Ron Hubbard. 3 CDs. (SPA.). 2003. audio compact disk 17.00 (978-958-43-0173-4(X)) YoYoMusic.

Miedo a Los Animales. Enrique Serna. Narrated by Francisco Rivela. 6 cass. (Running Time: 8 hrs. 45 mins.). 58.00 (978-1-4025-1264-3(3)) Recorded Bks.

Mientras tenga Vida. Read by Luis Campos. 2007. audio compact disk 14.99 (978-0-8297-5499-5(7)) Pub: Vida Pubs. Dist(s): Zondervan

Miernik Dossier. Charles McCarry. (Running Time: 34200 sec.). 2005. 59.95 (978-0-7861-3774-9(6)); audio compact disk 72.00 (978-0-7861-7592-5(3)) Blckstn Audio.

Miernik Dossier. unabr. ed. Charles McCarry. (Running Time: 34200 sec.). 2006. audio compact disk 29.95 (978-0-7861-7867-4(1)) Blckstn Audio.

Miernik Dossier. unabr. ed. Charles McCarry. Read by Stefan Rudnicki et al. 7 cass. (Running Time: 34200 sec.). 2006. 29.95 (978-0-7861-4413-6(0)); audio compact disk 32.95 (978-0-7861-7398-3(X)) Blckstn Audio.

Might As Well Be Dead. unabr. ed. Rex Stout. Read by Michael Prichard. 5 cass. (Running Time: 7 hrs.). (Nero Wolfe Ser.). 2004. 27.95 (978-1-57270-413-8(6)) Pub: Audio Partners. Dist(s): PerseuPGW
Eleven years ago, wealthy Nebraska businessman James Herrold unjustly threw his only son, Paul, out of the family business. Now he wants Nero Wolfe to find Paul so he can make amends. But what if the young man doesn't want to be found? And what if he's the same Paul Herrold on trial for murder? This case draws the great detective and his devoted sidekick into a web of deceit, one that even the master sleuth may regret taking on.

Might As Well Be Dead. unabr. ed. Rex Stout. Narrated by Michael Prichard. 6 CDs. (Nero Wolfe Ser.). (ENG.). 2004. audio compact disk 29.95 (978-1-57270-414-5(4)) Pub: AudioGO. Dist(s): Perseus Dist

Might As Well Be Dead. unabr. collector's ed. Rex Stout. Read by Michael Prichard. 7 cass. (Running Time: 7 hrs.). (Nero Wolfe Ser.). 1996. 56.00 (978-0-7366-3225-6(5), 3886) Books on Tape.
It's a noble idea: James Herold, a wealthy businessman, gave his son a very raw deal 11 years ago. Now he wants to make amends. But the son is long-gone & he wants to stay that way. Herold hires Nero Wolfe to track him down. It turns out the son is bad company, on trial for a cold-blooded murder. Wolfe gets caught in a web of lies & it will cost him dearly.

Might of Meekness Series, Elbert Willis. 4 cass. 13.00 Fill the Gap.

Mighty. Rodman Philbrick. Read by Elden Henson. 2 cass. (Running Time: 3 hrs. 15 mins.). (J). 2000. 18.00 (978-0-7366-9101-7(4)) Books on Tape.
Max Kane is a gentle soul who has been taunted all his life as stupid, dumb & slow. Struggling with loneliness & a dark secret, he hides from the world. Then he meets Kevin, a tiny Einstein in leg braces with more smarts & savvy than any other kid in town & together they become "Freak the Mighty." They defend the weak, right every wrong & finally solve the mystery of Max's past.

Mighty: (Based on Freak the Mighty) Rodman Philbrick. 2 cass. (J). 12.78 (BYA 959) NewSound.
About friendship, being different, & not feeling alone anymore.

Mighty Accordion: The Complete Guide to Mastering Left Hand Bass/Chord Patterns. David DiGiuseppe. (ENG.). 2009. lib. bdg. 29.99 (978-0-7866-6057-5(0)) Mel Bay.

Mighty Acts of God: A Family Bible Story Book. unabr. ed. Starr Meade. Narrated by Deborah Stromberg. (Running Time: 8 hrs. 48 mins. 18 sec.). (ENG.). 2010. 18.19 (978-1-60814-631-4(6)); audio compact disk 27.99 (978-1-59859-688-5(8)) Oasis Audio.

***Mighty & the Almighty.** unabr. ed. Madeleine Albright. Read by Madeleine Albright. (ENG.). 2006. (978-0-06-117239-7(1), Harper Audio); (978-0-06-117240-3(5), Harper Audio) HarperCollins Pubs.

Mighty & the Almighty: Reflections on America, God, & World Affairs. unabr. ed. Madeleine Albright. Read by Madeleine Albright. (Running Time: 36000 sec.). 2006. audio compact disk 39.95 (978-0-06-089789-5(9)) HarperCollins Pubs.

Mighty Boosh. unabr. ed. Read by Julian Barratt et al. (Running Time: 3 hrs. 0 mins. 0 sec.). (ENG.). 2009. audio compact disk 19.95 (978-1-60283-687-7(6)) Pub: AudioGO. Dist(s): Perseus Dist

***Mighty Casey.** 2010. audio compact disk (978-1-59171-242-8(4)) Falcon Picture.

Mighty Clouds of Joy: The Definitive Gospel Collection. Contrib. by Mighty Clouds of Joy. (Definitive Gospel Collection). 2008. audio compact disk 7.99 (978-5-557-49737-4(4), Word Records) Word Enter.

Mighty Fortress. unabr. ed. David Weber. Read by Oliver Wyman. (Running Time: 35 hrs. 0 mins. 0 sec.). (ENG.). 2010. audio compact disk 69.99 (978-1-4272-0900-9(6)) Pub: Macmill Audio. Dist(s): Macmillan

Mighty Fortress Is Our God: The Story of Martin Luther. J. Cromarty. 5 cass. (Running Time: 6 hrs. 37 mins.). (Champions of the Faith Ser.). 2004. 24.99 (978-0-85234-496-5(1)) Evangelical Pr GBR.

Mighty Hood. unabr. collector's ed. Ernle Bradford. Read by Walter Zimmerman. 6 cass. (Running Time: 9 hrs.). 1989. 48.00 (978-0-7366-1547-1(4), 2416) Books on Tape.
HMS Hood was the largest & fastest warship in the world. She represented British naval power & was the symbol of Britain's status as a world power. And yet, the Hood had a fatal flaw - deck armor had been sacrificed for speed. In her first & only major engagement she was sunk by a salvo from the Bismarck. She left only three survivors.

Mighty Joe Walker Soldier, Sheriff & Mountain Man, abr. ed. 3 cass. (Running Time: 4 hrs. 21 min.). (History As It Happens Ser.: Vol. 1). 2001. 19.95 (978-1-889252-07-0(7)) Photosensitive.

Mighty Johns & Other Stories. unabr. ed. David Baldacci et al. Read by Scott Brick & Martin Jarvis. Ed. by Otto Penzler. 5 cass. (Running Time: 7 hrs. 30 mins.). 2002. 29.95 (978-1-59007-231-8(6), N Millennium Audio) Pub: New Millenn Enter. Dist(s): PerseuPGW

Mighty Lord & His Coming; Ressurection Grace. Ann Ree Colton & Jonathan Murro. 1 cass. 7.95 A R Colton Fnd.

***Mighty Magnets CD.** Nadia Higgins. Illus. by Andres Martinez Ricci. (Science Rocks! Set 2 CD Ser.). 2010. cd-rom 27.07 (978-1-60270-966-9(1)) ABDO Pub Co.

***Mighty Magnets Site CD.** Nadia Higgins. Illus. by Andres Martinez Ricci. (Science Rocks! Set 2 Site CD Ser.). 2010. cd-rom 57.07 (978-1-60270-980-5(7)) ABDO Pub Co.

Mighty Men. (Dovetales Ser.: Tape 5). pap. bk. 6.95 (978-0-944391-40-2(0)); 4.95 (978-0-944391-20-4(6)) DonWise Prodns.

Mighty Men. unabr. ed. Terry Teykl. 6 cass. 1996. 25.00 (978-1-57892-033-4(7)) Prayer Pt Pr.
Sermon/teaching on mighty men.

Mighty Messengers Big Adventure: For Kids, for Christmas. 1 cass. (Running Time: 1 hr.). (J). (MU9302C) Lillenas.

Mighty Messengers Big Adventure: For Kids, for Christmas. 1 CD. (Running Time: 1 hr.). (J). 2001. audio compact disk (MU-9203T) Lillenas.

Mighty Messengers Big Adventure: For Kids, for Christmas. 1 cass. (Running Time: 1 hr.). (YA). 2001. 12.99 (TA-9302C); 54.99 (TA-9302PK) Lillenas.

***Mighty Queens of Freeville: A Mother, a Daughter, & the People Who Raised Them.** Amy Dickinson. (ENG.). 2009. 14.99 (978-1-4013-9250-5(4)); 14.99 (978-1-4013-9251-2(2)) Pub: Hyperion. Dist(s): HarperCollins Pubs

***Mighty Queens of Freeville: A Story of Surprising Second Chances.** unabr. ed. Amy Dickinson. Read by Amy Dickinson. 2010. audio compact disk 14.99 (978-1-4013-9514-8(7), Hyperion Audio) Pub: Hyperion. Dist(s): HarperCollins Pubs

Mighty to Save. Contrib. by Hillsong. 2006. audio compact disk 19.98 (978-5-558-20302-8(1)) Hillsong Pubng AUS.

Mighty to Save. Contrib. by Don Moen. Created by Integrity Music. (Iworship Ser.). 2008. 14.98 (978-5-557-51576-4(3)) Integrity Music.

Mighty to Save: Powerful Songs Transforming Worship. Contrib. by Don Moen. 2007. audio compact disk 13.99 (978-5-557-57588-1(X)) Integrity Music.

Migraine: Program from the Award Winning Public Radio Series. Interview. Hosted by Fred Goodwin. 1CD. (Running Time: 1 hr). (Infinite Mind Ser.). 2001. audio compact disk 21.95 (978-1-888064-97-1(8), LCM 154) Lichtenstein Creat.
When most of us get a headache, we take aspirin and wait for it to go away. But for the 30 million Americans who suffer from migraine headaches, the ?two aspirins and call me in the morning? approach isn?t a valid option. As recent studies have shown, migraine is a neurological condition, and too often it is debilitating. This show brings together scientists and ?migraineurs? to share the latest research on migraine and talk over what?s going on in the brains and lives of people with migraine.Guests include neurologist Dr. Stuart Tepper, the director at the New England Center for Headache in Stamford; Michael John Coleman, Executive Director and founder of MAGNUM, The National Migraine Association; Dr. Stephen J. Peroutka, a geneticist who has succeeded in pinpointing several of the genes associated with migraine; and Dr. Oliver Sacks, renowned as a neurologist and author, but perhaps less well-known as a migraine sufferer.

Migraine & Other Headaches. abr. ed. Stephen D. Silberstein & William B. Young. 2006. audio compact disk 22.95 (978-1-933310-11-4(1)) STI Certified.

Migraine Headaches. Bruce Goldberg. 1 cass. (Running Time: 20 min.). (ENG.). 2006. 13.00 (978-1-885577-11-5(7)) Pub: B Goldberg. Dist(s): Baker Taylor
This self hypnosis program trains the listener to overcome and prevent headaches.

Migraine Headaches & the Foods You Eat: 200 Recipes for Relief. Agnes P. Hartnell & G. Scott Tyler. 1997. pap. bk. 12.95 (978-1-56561-121-4(7)) Wiley US.

Migraine Relief. Barrie Konicov. 1 cass. 11.98 (978-0-87082-346-6(9), 084) Potentials.
The author tells how self-hypnosis can relieve the agony of headache pain.

Migrant see Poetry & Reflections

Migrant. unabr. ed. Nickolas Sheridan Stanton. Read by Paul Michael Garcia. (Running Time: 18800 sec.). 2007. audio compact disk 108.00 (978-0-7861-5836-2(0)); audio compact disk 44.95 (978-0-7861-6973-3(7)) Blckstn Audio.

Migrant Part I. unabr. ed. Nickolas Sheridan Stanton. Read by Paul Michael Garcia. (Running Time: 54000 sec.). 2007. 85.95 (978-0-7861-4957-5(4)) Blckstn Audio.

Migrant Part II. unabr. ed. Nickolas Sheridan Stanton. Read by Paul Michael Garcia. (Running Time: 48600 sec.). 2007. 79.95 (978-0-7861-4969-8(8)) Blckstn Audio.

Migration of Managerial Innovation: Diagnosis-Related Groups & Health Care Administration in Western Europe. John R. Kimberly & Gerard De Pouvourville. (Health Management Ser.). 1993. bk. 61.50 (978-1-55542-520-3(8), Jossey-Bass) Wiley US.

Migration Talk. 1 cass. (Running Time: 1 hr.). 1994. audio compact disk 15.95 CD. (2534, Creativ Pub) Quayside.
Sounds of tundra swans & sandhill cranes. Great blue heron's courtship calls & flock of over 300 Canada geese.

Migration Talk. 1 cass. (Running Time: 1 hr.). 1994. 9.95 (0253, NrthWrd Bks) TandN Child.

Migrations & Cultures: A World View. unabr. ed. Thomas Sowell. Read by Barrett Whitener. 13 cass. (Running Time: 19 hrs. 30 min.). 1997. 104.00 (978-0-7366-4465-5(2), 4915) Books on Tape.
To future generations, the late twentieth century may come to be known as the time of the DPs: Displaced Persons. Migration & relocation are raising inflammatory issues from Germany to the Tex-Mex border. Into this whirlpool of half-truths, sermons, prejudices & fears dives Hoover Institution economist & syndicated columnist, the author. It is not necessary to agree with all of the authors views to admire his imposing attempt to arrive at a theory of migration & culture. Or to succumb to his fascinating tales of how immigrants from Germany, Japan, China & other countries have coped - & excelled - on strange new shores.

Migrations of the Human Spirit. Manly P. Hall. 1 cass. 8.95 (978-0-89314-184-4(4), C890618) Philos Res.

Miguel. Francois Doucet. 1 cass. (Coffragants Ser.). Orig. Title: Mes Yeux de l'Interieur (Mes Yeux D'Enfant). (FRE.). 1998. cass. & audio compact disk 12.95 (978-2-921997-66-9(5)) Penton Overseas.

Miguel Mulligan Y Su Plal de Vapor. Tr. of Mike Mulligan & His Steam Shovel. (SPA.). 2004. 8.95 (978-0-7882-0253-7(7)) Weston Woods.

Miguel Robles: So Far. (SWC 1431) HarperCollins Pubs.

Miguel Strogoff. Jules Verne. Read by Carlos J. Vega. (Running Time: 3 hrs.). 2001. 16.95 (978-1-60083-174-4(5), Audiofy Corp) Iofy Corp.

Miguel Strogoff. abr. ed. Jules Verne. Read by Carlos J. Vega. 3 CDs. (SPA.). 2001. audio compact disk 17.00 (978-958-9494-50-9(1)) YoYoMusic.

Mikado see Gilbert & Sullivan: The D'Oyly Carte Opera Company

Mike & Mike's Rules for Sports & Life. unabr. ed. Mike Greenberg & Mike Golic. Narrated by Mike Greenberg & Mike Golic. (Running Time: 4 hrs. 25 mins. 7 sec.). (ENG.). 2010. 18.19 (978-1-60814-655-0(3), SpringWater); audio compact disk 25.99 (978-1-59859-712-7(4), SpringWater) Oasis Audio.

Mike Fink see American Tall Tales

Mike Fink & Stormalong, Vol. 3. unabr. ed. Adrien Stoutenburg. Read by Ed Begley. 1 cass. (J). 1984. 9.95 (978-0-89845-523-6(5), CDL5 1320) HarperCollins Pubs.
Mike Fink was acknowledged as the roughest, toughest & most reckless of all the fierce, feared rivermen. He became a legendary symbol of his breed, the "last of the boatmen". Also described on this recording is Stormalong, the hero of the deepwater men, in the days of the sailing ships.

Mike Mentzer's High Intensity Training Program: Secrets to Building Muscles in Minutes. Mike Mentzer. 4 cass. (Running Time: 3 hrs. 20 min.). 1997. bk. 39.95 (978-1-889462-02-8(0)) Advanced Research Pr.

Mike Mulligan & His Steam Shovel see Miguel Mulligan Y Su Plal de Vapor

Mike Mulligan & His Steam Shovel. 2004. bk. 24.95 (978-0-89719-895-0(6)); pap. bk. 32.75 (978-1-55592-268-9(6)); pap. bk. 14.95 (978-1-56008-208-8(9)); 8.95 (978-1-56008-968-1(7)); 8.95 (978-1-56008-416-7(2)); cass. & flmstrp 30.00 (978-0-89719-539-3(6)) Weston Woods.

Mike Mulligan & His Steam Shovel. Virginia Lee Burton. Read by Yadu. Composed by Stephen Simon. Conducted by Stephen Simon. (Stories in Music Ser.). (ENG.). (J). (ps-3). 2004. audio compact disk 19.99 (978-1-932684-08-7(5)) Simon Simon.

Mike Mulligan & His Steam Shovel. Virginia Lee Burton. Illus. by Virginia Lee Burton. Conducted by Stephen Simon. 1 CD. (Running Time: 3074 sec.). (Stories in Music Ser.). (J). (gr. k-5). 2008. audio compact disk 16.98 (978-1-932684-00-1(X)) Simon Simon.
In the tradition of Peter and the Wolf, Magic Maestro Music presents Virginia Lee Burton's beloved children's story, Mike Mulligan and his Steam Shovel with original music composed and conducted by Stephen Simon. Premiered on the Stories in Music children's series at the Kennedy Center in Washington, DC, this classic story is brought to life in a fresh, wondrous way.

Mike Mulligan & His Steam Shovel. Virginia Lee Burton. 1 read-along cass. (Running Time: 14 min.). (J). pap. bk. 12.95 (PRA004); 8.95 (RAC004); bk. 24.95; pap. bk. 12.95; pap. bk. 32.75 Weston Woods.
Big diesel machines threaten Mike Mulligan & his old steam shovel, Mary Anne. Determined to compete, they succeed in digging the cellar for the new Town Hall in just one day. But in so doing, they dig themselves into another dilemma which is resolved happily by a little boy.

Mike Mulligan & His Steam Shovel. Narrated by Yadu. Conducted by Stephen Simon. (Running Time: 51 mins.). (J). (ps-3). 2004. audio compact disk 16.98 (978-1-932684-02-5(6)) Simon Simon.

Mike Strickland Collection. 1 cass. (Running Time: 1 hr.). 7.98 (RVR 982); audio compact disk 12.78 (RVR 982) NewSound.

Mike's Election Guide. unabr. ed. Michael Moore. Read by Michael Moore. (Running Time: 3 hrs.). (ENG.). 2008. 14.98 (978-1-60024-527-5(7)) Pub: Hachet Audio. Dist(s): HachBkGrp

Mike's Mystery. Gertrude Chandler Warner. Read by Phyllis Newman. 2 cass. (Running Time: 2 hrs.). (Boxcar Children Ser.: No. 5). (J). (gr. 2-5). 2000. 18.00 (978-0-7366-9176-5(6)) Books on Tape.

Mike's Mystery. unabr. ed. Gertrude Chandler Warner. Read by Phyllis Newman. 2 vols. (Running Time: 1 hr. 47 mins.). (Boxcar Children Ser.: No. 5). (J). (gr. 3-7). 1994. pap. bk. 29.00 (978-0-8072-7438-5(0), YA859SP,

Listening Lib); 23.00 (978-0-8072-7437-8(2), YA859CX, Listening Lib) Random Audio Pubg.
The fifth book of the Boxcar Children Series, the Alden children return to Mystery Ranch where they encounter an extraordinary disaster & find themselves hot on the trail of a new mystery.

Mikhail Gorbachev. unabr. ed. (Biography Ser.). (J). (ps). 1988. bk. 27.90 (978-0-8045-6544-8(9), SAC 6544) Spoken Arts.

Mikuru Asahina Character CD. Perf. by Yuko Goto. (YA). 2007. 9.98 (978-1-59409-844-4(1)) Bandai Ent.

Milady's Salon Receptionist's Handbook. Judy Ventura. 1 cass. (SalonOvations Ser.). 1995. 14.95 (978-1-56253-307-6(X), Milady) Pub: Delmar. Dist(s): CENGAGE Learn

Milady's Standard: Nail Technology. 2nd ed. Milady. (C). 2006. audio compact disk 99.95 (978-1-4180-1627-2(6), Milady) Pub: Delmar. Dist(s): CENGAGE Learn

Milagro Beanfield War: A Novel, abr. ed. John Nichols. Perf. by Cheech Marin. 2 cass. (Running Time: 2 hrs. 30 min.). (J). 1986. 15.95 (978-0-88690-126-4(X), M20023) Audio Partners.
In a land where irrigation rights & grazing permits are serious social & political issues, a simple act like watering a beanfield can have dramatic repercussions.

Milarepa, Pt. 1. Read by Chogyam Trungpa. 7 cass. (Running Time: 10 hrs. 30 min.). 1973. 65.50 (A039) Vajradhatu.
Seven talks: 1) Surrender & Devotion; 2) One Upmanship; 3) Renunciation; 4) Search; 5) Letting Go of Ego; 6) Mahamudra & Poetry; 7) Mahamudra & Milarepa's Songs.

Milarepa, Pt. 2. Read by Chogyam Trungpa. 12 cass. 1970. 124.00 (A040) Vajradhatu.
Twelve talks: 1) Relationship to the Guru; 2) Challenge from a Wise Demoness; 3) Song of Realization; 4) Women in the Dharma; 5) Challenge from the Logicians; 6) Realization of Megom Repa; 7) Sahle Aui; 8) Story of the Yak Horn; 9) Rechungpa's Repentance; 10) Conversaion with the Scholar Lodun; 11) Beer Drinking son; 12) Farewell to Gampopa.

Milarepa: The Yogic Songs. Read by Chogyam Trungpa. 9 cass. (Running Time: 13 hrs. 30 min.). 1976. 85.50 (A041) Vajradhatu.
Ten talks: 1) Milarepa & Marpa; 2) Attitude toward Spirituality; 3) Discovery of the Guru; 4) Dealing with Samsara; 5) Ego & Its Renunciation; 6) Discipline & Aloneness; 7) Breakthrough; 8) Mahamudra; 9) Mahamudra II; 10) Buddha Activity.

Milarepa, His Life & Example. Read by Chogyam Trungpa. 4 cass. 1976. 36.00 (A104) Vajradhatu.
Four talks. Milarepa's example of extraordinary exertion & devotion proclaims the workability of our lives.

Milarepa I. Vajracarya. 7 cass. 1973. 65.50 Vajradhatu.
Deals with: Surrender & Devotion; One Upmanship; Renunciation; Letting Go of Ego; Mahamudra & Poetry; Mahamudra's & Milarepa's Songs.

Milarepa II. Vajracarya. 12 cass. 1970. 108.00 Vajradhatu.
Topics Include: Relationship to the Guru; Challenge from a Wise Demoness; Women in the Dharma; Challenge from the Logicians; Realization of Megom Repa; Sahle Aui, Story of the Yak Horn; Rechungpa's Repentance.

Milbre Burch: Touch Magicpass It on- Jane Yolen Stories-the Ballad of the Mage's Birth; the Cat Bride; Sans Soleil; Sleeping Ugly; Princess Heart O'stone; the King's Dragon; the Lady & the Merman; L'Envoi. 2004. 8.95 (978-0-89719-948-3(0)) Weston Woods.

***Mildred & Sam.** unabr. ed. Sharleen Collicott. (ENG.). 2008. (978-0-06-169476-9(2)); (978-0-06-171323-1(6)) HarperCollins Pubs.

Mildred Pierce. James M. Cain. Read by Christine Williams. (Running Time: 36000 sec.). 2007. 59.95 (978-0-7861-4898-9(4)); audio compact disk 72.00 (978-0-7861-5775-4(5)) Blckstn Audio.

Mildred Pierce. unabr. ed. James M. Cain. Read by Christine Williams. (Running Time: 36000 sec.). 2007. 24.95 (978-0-7861-4861-5(6)); audio compact disk 24.95 (978-0-7861-6047-1(0)); audio compact disk 29.95 (978-0-7861-7153-8(7)) Blckstn Audio.

Mile Dath - A Cloak of Many Colours. Contrib. by Eilin Ni Bheaglaoich. (ENG.). 1992. 12.95 (978-0-8023-7079-2(9)); audio compact disk 21.95 (978-0-8023-8079-1(4)) Pub: Clo Iar-Chonnachta IRL. Dist(s): Dufour

Mile End Girl. unabr. ed. Elizabeth Lord. Read by Patricia Gallimore. 10 cass. (Running Time: 13 hrs. 56 mins.). (Isis Ser.). (J). 2003. 84.95 (978-0-7531-1291-5(4)) Pub: ISIS Lrg Prnt GBR. Dist(s): Ulverscroft US
When Jenny Pullan discovers her great grandmother Jessie's diary in the loft, she is enthralled by it. Jessie had dreams of better life and being bright at school is her salvation. It enables her to get a job at the Telephone Exchange. Joining the choir at the People Palace, she attracts the attention of James Medway. But married life isn't a bed of roses. With only her diary to confide in, can Jessie weather the storm and make a good life for herself and her baby?.

Mile of River. Judith Allnatt. 2008. 61.95 (978-0-7531-3207-4(9)); audio compact disk 84.95 (978-0-7531-3208-1(7)) Pub: Isis Pubng Ltd GBR. Dist(s): Ulverscroft US

Mile Zero. Thomas Sanchez. Read by Thomas Sanchez. 13.95 (978-1-55644-354-1(4), 10031) Am Audio Prose.
The author reads from his novel "Mile Zero" which focuses on St. Cloud, a burned out, alcoholic anti-war activist, who has gradually lost the wife of his youth & finds himself falling in love with a much younger woman.

Mileoidean Scaoilte. Contrib. by Johnny Connolly. (ENG.). 2004. audio compact disk 23.95 (978-0-8023-8157-6(X)) Pub: Clo Iar-Chonnachta IRL. Dist(s): Dufour

Miles: The Autobiography. unabr. ed. Miles Davis & Quincy Troupe. Read by LeVar Burton. 2 cass. (Running Time: 3 hrs.). 1995. bk. 16.95 (978-0-944993-62-0(1)) Audio Lit.
The life story of master jazz artist Miles Davis in his own words & with no punches pulled.

Miles Between. unabr. ed. Mary E. Pearson. Read by Jeannie Stith. (Running Time: 6 hrs.). 2009. 24.99 (978-1-4233-9939-1(0), 9781423399391, Brilliance MP3); 39.97 (978-1-4233-9940-7(4), 9781423399407, Brinc Audio MP3 Lib); 24.99 (978-1-4233-9941-4(2), 9781423399414, BAD); 39.97 (978-1-4233-9942-1(0), 9781423399421, BADLE); audio compact disk 24.99 (978-1-4233-9937-7(4), 9781423399377) Brilliance Audio.

Miles Between. unabr. ed. Mary E. Pearson. Read by Jeannie Stith. 5 CDs. (Running Time: 6 hrs.). (YA). (gr. 7-10). 2009. audio compact disk 54.97 (978-1-4233-9938-4(2), 9781423399384, BriAudCD Unabrid) Brilliance Audio.

Miles Davis: The Man with the Horn. Prod. by Ross Porter. Hosted by Ross Porter. 5 CDs. (Running Time: 5 hrs.). 2005. audio compact disk 39.95 (978-0-660-19224-6(1)) Pub: Canadian Broadcasting CAN. Dist(s): Georgetown Term

Miles from Nowhere. unabr. collector's ed. Barbara Savage. Read by Dick Estell. 11 cass. (Running Time: 16 hrs. 30 mins.). 1987. 88.00 (978-0-7366-1089-6(8), 2013) Books on Tape.
An around-the-world bicycle trip taken by two young people, Barbara & Larry Savage, started as a sort of joke-a fantasy-to relieve the tedium of the daily routine & of careers that had hit plateaus. It took them two years & 25 countries.

Miles from Nowhere: A Round-the-World Bicycle Adventure, unabr. ed. Barbara Savage. Narrated by Alexandra O'Karma. 10 cass. (Running Time: 14 hrs.). 1988. 85.00 (978-1-55690-340-3(5), 88260E7) Recorded Bks.
Join the husband & wife cycling team on a zainy, courageous, good-humored odyssey around the world.

Miles Gone By: A Literary Autobiography. William F. Buckley, Jr.. Read by William F. Buckley, Jr. (Running Time: 18 mins. 30 sec.). 2005. 95.95 (978-0-7861-3038-2(5)); audio compact disk 120.00 (978-0-7861-7942-8(2)) Blckstn Audio.

Miles Gone By: A Literary Autobiography. unabr. ed. William F. Buckley, Jr.. Read by William F. Buckley, Jr. 11 cass. (Running Time: 16 hrs.). 2005. 32.95 (978-0-7861-3434-2(8)) Blckstn Audio.

Miles Gone By: A Literary Autobiography. unabr. ed. William F. Buckley, Jr. 13 vols. (Running Time: 66600 sec.). 2005. audio compact disk 29.95 (978-0-7861-8118-6(4)) Blckstn Audio.

Miles Gone By: A Literary Autobiography. unabr. ed. William F. Buckley, Jr.. Read by William F. Buckley, Jr. 12 CDs. (Running Time: 66600 sec.). 2005. audio compact disk 34.95 (978-0-7861-7984-8(8)) Blckstn Audio.

Miles of Smiles. Scooter & Jim Kimball. (J). 1992. 11.98 (978-1-881214-02-1(8)) J Jangle Ent.

Miles to Go. Chris Murphy. Read by Patrick G. Lawlor. (Running Time: 28800 sec.). 2006. audio compact disk 63.00 (978-0-7861-7088-3(3)) Blckstn Audio.

***Miles to Go.** unabr. ed. Richard Paul Evans. (Running Time: 5 hrs. 0 mins. 0 sec.). (ENG.). 2011. audio compact disk 29.99 (978-1-4423-3759-6(1)) Pub: S&S Audio. Dist(s): S and S Inc

Miles to Go: The Lost Years: an Intimate Memoir of Life on the Road with Miles Davis 1973-1983. Chris Murphy. Read by Patrick G. Lawlor. (Running Time: 28800 sec.). 2006. 59.95 (978-0-7861-4553-9(6)) Blckstn Audio.

Miles to Go: The Lost Years: an Intimate Memoir of Life on the Road with Miles Davis 1973-1983. unabr. ed. Chris Murphy. Read by Patrick G. Lawlor. 7 cass. (Running Time: 28800 sec.). 2006. 29.95 (978-0-7861-4391-7(6)); audio compact disk 29.95 (978-0-7861-7447-8(1)); audio compact disk 29.95 (978-0-7861-7803-2(5)) Blckstn Audio.

Milestones: Normal Speech & Language Development Across the Lifespan. John W. Oller et al. Orig. Title: Introducing Normal Speech & Language Development: Milestones Across the Lifespan. (C). 2006. pap. bk. 79.95 (978-1-59756-036-8(7)) Plural Pub Inc.

***Miley Cyrus CD.** Sarah Tieck. (Big Buddy Biographies CD Ser.). 2010. cd-rom 27.07 (978-1-61613-070-1(9)) ABDO Pub Co.

***Miley Cyrus Site CD.** Sarah Tieck. (Big Buddy Biographies Site CD Ser.). 2010. cd-rom 57.07 (978-1-61613-250-7(7)) ABDO Pub Co.

Military Defense Without a State. unabr. ed. Jarret B. Wollstein. 1 cass. (Running Time: 45 min.). 12.95 (986) J Norton Pubs.

Military Parks: Chickamauga (GA) 1 cass. (Running Time: 1 hr.). 11.95 (CENP307) Comp Comms Inc.
One of the bloodiest battles of the war was fought along the banks of Chickamauga Creek on September 19-20, 1863. Prepared in cooperation with the National Park Service to help you more fully understand the tactics & strategies used by each General during the battles. Comes with its own map.

Military Parks: Fredericksburg, Wilderness, Spotslyvania (VA), May 5-21, 1864. 1 cass. (Running Time: 1 hr.). 11.95 (CENP308) Comp Comms Inc.
The first battles that led to final Union victory in Virginia & the end of the Civil War. The tour transports visitors to scenes of battle, from the burning woods of the Wilderness Area to the blood-soaked trenches at Spotsylvania, the highlights of the two battlefields are interpreted.

Military Parks: Gettysburg National Military Park (PA) 1 cass. (Running Time: 1 hr. 30 min.). 11.95 (CC1-306) Comp Comms Inc.
At Gettysburg was fought one of the most violent & controversial battles of the Civil War on July 1, 2 & 3, 1863. This tour gives you a complete picture of what happened, where it happened & why.

Military Parks: Valley Forge. 1 cass. (Running Time: 45 min.). 11.95 (CC309) Comp Comms Inc.
Valley Forge (Dec. 19, 1777-June 19, 1778). This tour route takes you past extensive remains & reconstructions of major forts & lines of earthworks, the Artillery Park, Washington's Headquarters & the Grand Parade where General von Steuben rebuilt the army & where the French alliance was announced on May 6, 1778.

Milk - the Deadly Poison. abr. ed. Robert Cohen. 2 cass. (Running Time: 1 hr. 30 min.). 1998. 16.95 Set. (978-0-9659196-7-8(6)) Argus Pub.

Milk & Honey. unabr. ed. Faye Kellerman. Read by Mitchell Greenberg. 6 CDs. (Running Time: 7 hrs.). 2009. audio compact disk 19.99 (978-0-06-144178-3(3), Harper Audio) HarperCollins Pubs.

***Milk & Honey.** unabr. ed. Faye Kellerman. Read by Mitchell Greenberg. (ENG.). 2009. (978-0-06-172484-8(X)); (978-0-06-172487-9(4)) HarperCollins Pubs.

Milk from the Bull's Horn: Tales of Nurturing Men. Short Stories. Perf. by Doug Lipman. 1 cass. (Running Time: 1 hr). (J). (gr. 4 up). 1986. 9.95 (978-0-938756-14-9(1), 011) Yellow Moon.
A collection of folktales from various cultures that provide images of nurturing men. This much needed collection fills a gap in the world of images for men today. Images other than that of Prince Charming or the competitive & often violent man. The stories come from Ireland, Israel, Japan & the Appalachian Mountains.

Milk in My Coffee. Eric Jerome Dickey. Narrated by Ezra Knight & Robin Miles. 9 cass. (Running Time: 13 hrs. 30 mins.). 1998. 84.00 (978-0-7887-5333-6(9)) Recorded Bks.

Milk My Ewes & Weep. unabr. ed. Joyce Fussey & Anita Wright. 4 cass. (Isis Audio Reminiscence Ser.). (J). 2003. 44.95 (978-0-7531-1179-6(9)) Pub: ISIS Lrg Prnt GBR. Dist(s): Ulverscroft US

Milk of Human Kindness. unabr. ed. E. X. Ferrars. Read by Eva Haddon. 6 cass. (Running Time: 6 hrs.). 1996. 54.95 (978-0-7451-6653-7(9), CAB 1269) AudioGO.
Marabelle had no idea of the chain of events that would follow from a visit by her self-centered sister, Susan. She has come to ask Marabelle a favor. Marabelle reluctantly agrees & she is thrust into a maelstrom of tangled relationships & strange coincidences. Her feelings of repressed jealousy soon reach a pitch that can only lead to one grizzly conclusion: Murder!.

Milk-White Moon see Gathering of Great Poetry for Children

Milk White Moon, Put the Cows to Sleep see Carl Sandburg's Poems for Children

Milking Jug. George Wallace. Ed. by Stanley H. Barkan. Illus. by Peggy Wallace. (Review Long Island Writers Chapbook Ser.: No. 1). 1989. 10.00 (978-0-89304-254-7(4)) Cross-Cultrl NY.

Milkmaid & Her Pail. Carol Barnett. 1 cass. (Bilingual Fables). (J). 59.95 (978-0-8442-7582-6(4), Natl Textbk Co) M-H Contemporary.
Presents a story in Spanish & English.

Milkweed see Poetry & Voice of James Wright

Milkweed. Jerry Spinelli. Read by Ron Rifkin. 3 cass. (Running Time: 5 hrs. 16 mins.). (J). (gr. 4-7). 2004. 30.00 (978-0-8072-1859-4(6), Listening Lib); audio compact disk 40.00 (978-0-8072-2001-6(9), Listening Lib) Random Audio Pubg.

Milky Floor. Sheila E. Murphy & John M. Bennett. Read by Sheila E. Murphy & John M. Bennett. 1 cass. (Running Time: 1 hr. 30 min.). 1996. 7.00 (978-0-935350-62-3(4)) Luna Bisonte.

***Mill House.** Paul McCusker. (Running Time: 12 hrs. 9 mins. 0 sec.). (ENG.). 2009. 14.99 (978-0-310-30481-4(4)) Zondervan.

Mill on the Floss see Cambridge Treasury of English Prose: Dickens to Butler

Mill on the Floss. George Eliot. Read by Eileen Atkins. 14 cass. (Running Time: 19 hrs. 20 min.). 83.95 (CC/009) C to C Cassettes.
Miller Tulliver's vendetta with Lawyer Wakeham is disasterous for him & his family. Only at the end are children Maggie & Tom reconciled.

Mill on the Floss. George Eliot. Read by Emily Watson. (Running Time: 3 hrs. 0 mins. 0 sec.). (ENG., 2003. 14.99 (978-1-84032-777-9(4), HoddrStoughton) Pub: Hodder General GBR. Dist(s): IPG Chicago

Mill on the Floss. George Eliot. Read by Sara Kestelman. (Running Time: 5 hrs.). 2002. 28.95 (978-1-60083-845-3(6)) Iofy Corp.

Mill on the Floss. abr. ed. George Eliot. 3 CDs. (Running Time: 4 Hrs. 30 Mins.). 2004. audio compact disk 9.99 (978-1-57050-042-8(8)) Multilingua.

Mill on the Floss. abr. ed. George Eliot. Read by Sara Kestelman. 4 CDs. (Running Time: 18180 sec.). 2006. audio compact disk 28.98 (978-962-634-371-5(0), NA437112) Naxos.

Mill on the Floss. unabr. ed. George Eliot. Read by Nadia May. 14 cass. (Running Time: 20 hrs. 30 mins.). (gr. 9-12). 2003. 89.95 (978-0-7861-0441-3(4), 1393) Blckstn Audio.
Set in nineteenth century England, the charm of this great novel of domestic realism lies chiefly in the magic by which the commonplace lives of the principal characters are transformed into lively pictures full of vital appeal. Maggie Tulliver, whose father owns a mill perched on the banks of the River Floss, is intelligent & richly imaginative beyond the understanding of her relatives & in particular of her brother Tom, a boy of limited intelligence. Despite their opposite temperaments, Maggie & Tom are united by a strong bond. When Maggie is pursued by Philip Wakem, the deformed son of the lawyer responsible for the ruin of her father, Tom forbids Maggie's friendship with Philip to which Maggie reluctantly complies. Later, she falls in love with Stephen Guest, the handsome & passionate fiance of her cousin Lucy Deane. They go off together on impulse, & although Maggie repents before it is too late, her return is misconstrued & her life is made desperately unhappy.

Mill on the Floss. unabr. ed. George Eliot. Read by Nadia May. (Running Time: 19 hrs. 50 mins.). 2008. 44.95 (978-1-4332-4996-9(0)); audio compact disk 120.00 (978-1-4332-4995-2(2)) Blckstn Audio.

Mill on the Floss. unabr. ed. George Eliot. Read by Alec McCowen. Contrib. by Gabriel Woolf. 5 cass. 25.95 (SCN 008) J Norton Pubs.
Eliot depicted the character of Stephen Guest, which some male commentators found difficult to accept. Rebuttal of such expressed fundamental belief in the novelist's duty to present characters in a truthful manner.

Mill on the Floss, Pt. 2. George Eliot. 6 cass. (Running Time: 8 hrs. 30 min.). 2000. 41.95 Audio Bk Con.
The childhood of Maggie & her brother, Tom & their conflicts & growth in a narrow, tradition-bound society lead to tragedy.

Mill on the Floss, Pt. 2. unabr. ed. George Eliot. 6 cass. (Running Time: 8 hrs. 30 min.). 1988. 41.95 Audio Bk Con.

Mill on the Floss, Set. abr. ed. George Eliot. Read by Sara Kestelman. 4 cass. (Running Time: 5 hr. 3 min.). 1998. 22.98 (415414, Naxos AudioBooks) Naxos.
Maggie has two lovers - Philip, son of her father's enemy, Stephan, already promised to her cousin. But the love she wants most is that of her brother, Tom. Her struggle against passionate & sensual nature leads her to a deeper understanding & to eventual tragedy.

Mill on the Floss (Part 1), Vol. 1. unabr. ed. George Eliot. Read by Flo Gibson. 8 cass. (Running Time: 11 hrs. 30 min.). (gr. 8 up). 1988. 26.95 (978-1-55685-128-5(6)) Audio Bk Con.
Depicts the childhood of Maggie Tulliver & her brother, Tom. Their conflicts & growth in a narrow tradition bound society lead to scandal & tragedy.

Mill on the Floss (Part 2), Vol. 2. unabr. ed. George Eliot. Narrated by Flo Gibson. (Running Time: 8 hrs. 22 mins.). 1988. 24.95 (978-1-55685-782-9(9)) Audio Bk Con.

Mill on the Floss (Parts 1 And 2) unabr. ed. George Eliot. Narrated by Flo Gibson. (Running Time: 19 hrs. 11 mins.). 1988. 42.95 (978-1-55685-783-6(7)) Audio Bk Con.

Mill Race, Pamela Street. Read by Jane Jermyn. 4 cass. 1999. 44.95 (61888) Pub: Soundings Ltd GBR. Dist(s): ISIS Pub

Mille et un Poemes. Poems. Text by Andre Breton et al. 1 CD. (FRE.). 1991. bk. 32.95 (1387-RF) Olivia & Hill.
A collection of French poems of the 20th century broadcast on France-Culture.

Mille et un Poemes, Vol. 2. Poems. 1 CD, text. (FRE.). 1995. audio compact disk 29.95 (1479-RF) Olivia & Hill.
More French poetry of the 20th century broadcast on France-Culture: Cesaire, Queneau, Supervielle, Saint-John Perse, Michaud & others.

Millennium. FSP Choir Staff. 1996. audio compact disk 14.95 (978-0-8198-4787-4(9), 332-202) Pauline Bks.

Millennium: Eternal Societies on Earth. Finis J. Dake, Sr. (J). (gr. k up). 5.95 (978-1-55829-038-9(9)) Dake Publishing.
Bible study.

Millennium: Gehenna. 2nd abr. ed. Lewis Gannett. Narrated by Bill Smitrovich. Created by Chris Carter. 2 cass. (Running Time: 3 hrs.). 1997. 18.00 (978-0-694-51872-2(7), CPN 2697, Harper Audio) HarperCollins Pubs.

Millennium: The Greater Works. unabr. ed. Myrtle Smyth. 1 cass. (Running Time: 1 hrs. 1 min.). (Myrtle Smyth Audiotapes Ser.: Vol. 25). 1999. 8.95 (978-1-893107-27-4(2), M25) Healing Unltd.
Lecture on the "Greater Works" that we are all capable of & should be doing.

Millennium: Tribal Wisdom & the Modern World. unabr. ed. David Maybury-Lewis. Read by Hans Zimmer. 1 cass. (Running Time: 54 min.). 1992. pap. bk. 9.98 (978-0-934245-21-0(5)); audio compact disk 10.98 (978-0-934245-20-3(7)) Narada Prodns.
The book reflects the essence of the acclaimed 10-part television series of the same name. It looks at the people of tribal, "indigenous" societies - the

Aborigines of Australia; the Dogon & Gabra of Africa; the Navajo of the United States, among others - & asks: Who is more comfortable? We in "modem societies, with computers, health care, air transportation, mechanised food production; or those in less anxious, less lonesome, more tradition-bound tribal societies? The series initiates a mutually beneficial exchange of outlooks. The recording's booklet includes striking photography, plus tribal perspectives on issues such as personal identity, love & sex, art, death, & the natural world.

Millennium Atlas - Book Only: Petroleum Geology of the Central & Northern North Sea. Ed. by D. Evans et al. 2003. bk. 435.00 (978-1-86239-119-2(X)) Pub: Geol Soc Pub Hse GBR. Dist(s): AAPG

Millennium Celebration. (J). (ps-3). 1999. 12.98 (978-0-7634-0636-3(8)); audio compact disk 22.46 (978-0-7634-0638-7(4)) W Disney Records.

Millennium Chorus. 1 cass. 2000. (978-0-9678004-1-7(2)); audio compact disk (978-0-9678004-0-0(4)) Ascentmusic.

Millennium Falcon. unabr. ed. James Luceno. Read by Marc Thompson. (Star Wars Ser.). (ENG.). 2008. audio compact disk 39.95 (978-0-7393-7713-0(2), Random AudioBks) Pub: Random Audio Pubg. Dist(s): Random

Millennium Meltdown. Grant R. Jeffrey. 1 cass. 1999. 15.99 (978-0-921714-35-4(1)) Spring Arbor Dist.

Millennium Rising. unabr. ed. Jane Jensen. Read by Dick Hill. (Running Time: 18 hrs.). 2009. 44.97 (978-1-4233-9079-4(2), 9781423390794, Brlnc Audio MP3 Lib); 29.99 (978-1-4233-9078-7(4), 9781423390787, Brilliance MP3); 29.99 (978-1-4233-9080-0(6), 9781423390800, BAD); 44.97 (978-1-4233-9081-7(4), 9781423390817, BADLE) Brilliance Audio.

Miller, His Son & Their Donkey. Aesop. 2004. 8.95 (978-1-56008-969-8(5)); cass. & flmstrp 30.00 (978-1-56008-717-5(X)) Weston Woods.

Miller Williams. unabr. ed. Read by Miller Williams. 1 cass. (Running Time: 29 min.). 1985. 10.00 New Letters.

Arkansas poet Miller Williams was recorded at a public reading.

Miller's Court: An Original Radio Drama. (ENG.). 2005. audio compact disk 12.99 (978-0-9817573-3-9(2)) Scene Unseen.

Miller's Daughter see Three by Zola

Miller's Daughter. unabr. ed. Emile Zola. Read by Walter Covell. (Running Time: 48 min.). 1981. 7.95 (N-84) Jimcin Record.

Also known as "An Attack on the Mill," this is a classic French short story.

Miller's Prologue & Tale: From the Canterbury Tales by Geoffrey Chaucer. Geoffrey Chaucer. Ed. by James Winney & James Winny. Contrib. by M. Hussey et al. (Running Time: 40 mins.). (Selected Tales from Chaucer Ser.). (ENG.). 1999. audio compact disk 28.25 (978-0-521-63529-5(2)) Cambridge U Pr.

Millicent Min, Girl Genius. unabr. ed. Lisa Yee. Read by Keiko Agena. Prod. by Listening Library Staff. 4 cass. (Running Time: 5 hrs. 27 min.). (J). (gr. 4-7). 2004. 32.00 (978-0-8072-1931-7(2), Listening Lib) Random Audio Pubg.

Million - Dollar Wound. Max Allan Collins. Read by Yuri Rasovsky. (Running Time: 12 mins.). 2005. 65.95 (978-0-7861-3696-4(0)) Blckstn Audio.

Million - Dollar Wound. Max Allan Collins. Read by Yuri Rasovsky. (Running Time: 41400 sec.). (Nathan Heller Ser.). 2005. DVD, audio compact disk, audio compact disk 90.00 (978-0-7861-7683-0(0)) Blckstn Audio.

Million - Dollar Wound. unabr. ed. Max Allan Collins. Read by Yuri Rasovsky. (Running Time: 12 mins.). 2005. 29.95 (978-0-7861-7921-3(X)) Blckstn Audio.

Million a Minute. unabr. ed. Hillary Davis. Read by Nadia May. 7 cass. (Running Time: 10 hrs.). 1999. 49.95 (978-0-7861-1555-6(6), 2385) Blckstn Audio.

The inside story of the mysterious & wildly influential world of trading.

Million a Minute. unabr. ed. Hillary Davis. Read by Nadia May. 6 CDs. (Running Time: 8 hrs. 30 mins.). 1999. audio compact disk 29.95 (978-0-7861-1699-7(4)) Pub: Blckstn Audio. Dist(s): Penton Overseas

The former portfolio manager shows us who & what front-line free-market warriors are, what motivates them & how they came to be so powerful.

Million Dollar: Effective Sales Procedure. Dave Johnson. (Dave Johnson Educational Library). 65.00 D Johnson.

Includes steps to build rapport & a friend & immediately double & triple product sales.

Million Dollar Habits: Proven Power Practices to Double & Triple Your Income. unabr. abr. ed. Brian Tracy. 2 CDs. (Running Time: 23 hrs. 0 mins. 0 sec.). (ENG.). 2001. audio compact disk 20.00 (978-0-7435-0934-3(X), Nightgale) Pub: S&S Audio. Dist(s): S and S Inc

Million Dollar Kick. unabr. ed. Dan Gutman. Narrated by Christina Moore. 3 pieces. (Running Time: 3 hrs. 30 mins.). (gr. 3 up). 2002. 28.00 (978-0-7887-5509-5(9)) Recorded Bks.

The great news: The prize is $1 million! With it, 13-year-old Whisper Nelson could buy jewelry, clothes, and pay for college. She could even send her sister to college! To win, she must kick a goal past a professional soccer player. The bad news: She hates sports - all sports - with a passion! After her infamous soccer goal four years ago, to the other team's advantage, Whisper vowed to never play sports again. Afraid of, yet again, looking like a total failure in front of a crowd of people, Whisper has a tough choice to make. Will she try the kick?.

Million Dollar Media Rep: How to Become a Television & Radio Superstar. Michael Guld. 2008. audio compact disk 45.00 (978-0-9766470-1-0(X)) Guld Resource.

Million-Dollar Mortgage Radio. Blaine Parker. Read by Blaine Parker. 2 CDs. (Running Time: 2hours 17min). 2004. audio compact disk 12.95 (978-1-932226-31-7(1)) Pub: Wizard Acdmy. Dist(s): Baker Taylor

You?re a mortgage broker. You want to make more deals. What if you had access to a marketing consultant who?s helped your competitors sell millions of dollars worth of residential mortgages? How much would you pay for that information? Hundreds? Thousands? How about the cover price of this book? For the first time, a successful Los Angeles radio creative director shares trade secrets with you?applying an irreverent sense of humor, a pithy, take-no-prisoners prose, and notions that will frustrate both your competitors and the big advertising agencies. Bottom line: if you know just what to say and just how to say it, radio advertising can dramatically increase your business. You too can do Million-Dollar Mortgage Radio.?Name a big ad agency, I?ve probably worked for them. And this is absolutely not how I was taught to do advertising. So why am I quoting this book to my clients??- Helene CohnFreelance Copywriter and former V.P. Creative, Grey AdvertisingBlaine Parker is an award-winning creative director for radio advertising. However, despite the trophies and occasional cash prizes, he maintains that no advertising award equals the thrill of an ecstatic client. When not busy working to make his clients rich, he can be found at his home in the super-heated Los Angeles real estate market, where he?s perpetually considering new and interesting ways to refinance.

Million Dollar Personal Success Plan. Paul J. Meyer. 1 cass. (Running Time: 31 min.). 11.00 (978-0-89811-030-2(0), 5173) Meyer Res Grp.

Accept personal responsibility for your motivation & you can overcome obstacles & achieve your personal & professional goals. Also available in Spanish.

Million Dollar Personal Success Plan: Who Motivates the Motivator? Paul J. Meyer. 1 cass. 10.00 (SP100015) SMI Intl.

Five single concepts - applied consistently - brought Paul J. Meyer outstanding success. They will work for you, too. Accept personal responsibility for your own motivation & you can overcome obstacles & achieve your personal & professional goals.

Million Dollar Personal Success Plan/Who Motivates the Motivator? 1965. audio compact disk (978-0-89811-285-6(0)) Meyer Res Grp.

Million Dollar Shot. unabr. ed. Dan Gutman. Narrated by Johnny Heller. 2 pieces. (Running Time: 2 hrs.). (gr. 4 up). 2001. 19.00 (978-0-7887-8840-6(X)) Recorded Bks.

Million-Dollar Tattoo. unabr. ed. Earl Emerson. Narrated by Richard Poe. 6 cass. (Running Time: 8 hrs. 15 mins.). (Thomas Black Mystery Ser.: Vol. 9). 1997. 51.00 (978-0-7887-0813-8(9), 94963E7) Recorded Bks.

An early call from a panicked detective buddy plunges Thomas Black into an out-of-this-world case.

Million Dollar Vocabulary Personal Learning Course: Sharpen Your Verbal Edge for Success, J. Michael Bennett & Paul R. Scheele. Read by J. Michael Bennett & Paul R. Scheele. 6 cass. (Running Time: 6 hrs.). 1999. pap. bk. 129.95 (978-0-925480-64-4(9), 9VLC) Learn Strategies.

Million Little Pieces. abr. ed. James Frey. Read by Oliver Wyman. 8 CDs. (Running Time: 10 hrs.). (ENG.). 2003. audio compact disk 34.95 (978-1-56511-778-5(6), 1565117786) Pub: HighBridge. Dist(s): Workman Pub

Million Shades of Gray. unabr. ed. Cynthia Kadohata. Read by Keith Nobbs. (Running Time: 4 hrs. 30 mins. 0 sec.). (ENG.). (J). 2010. audio compact disk 29.99 (978-0-7435-8196-7(2)) Pub: S&S Audio. Dist(s): S and S Inc

Millionaire by Thirty: The Quickest Path to Early Financial Independence. unabr. ed. Douglas R. Andrew et al. Read by Douglas R. Andrew et al. (Running Time: 7 hrs.). (ENG.). 2008. 24.98 (978-1-60024-150-5(6)); audio compact disk 29.98 (978-1-60024-149-9(2)) Pub: Hachet Audio. Dist(s): HachBkGrp

Millionaire Course Seminar: A Visionary Plan for Creating the Life of Your Dreams. unabr. ed. Marc Allen. 3 cass. (Running Time: 3 hrs. 0 mins. 0 sec.). (ENG.). 2004. audio compact disk 21.95 (978-1-57731-465-3(4)) Pub: New Wrld Lib. Dist(s): PerseuPGW

An easy in-depth guide to accomplishing one's dreams in life. Structured in results-minded lessons and interwoven with keys that offer sudden moments of understanding, the book helps the reader grasp new ways of thinking of, and attaining, wealth and fulfillment by doing what we love and adhering to compassionate values.

Millionaire Maker: Act, Think, & Make Money the Way the Wealthy Do. abr. ed. Loral Langemeier. Read by Bernadette Dunne. (Running Time: 16200 sec.). 2007. audio compact disk 28.00 (978-1-933309-29-3(6)) Pub: A Media Intl. Dist(s): Natl Bk Netwk

Millionaire Mentality: As a Man Thinks, So Is He. Gary V. Whetstone. 4 cass. (Running Time: 6 hrs.). (Finance Ser.). 1995. 35.00 (978-1-58866-238-5(1), V1004A) Gary Whet Pub.

Discover the key to generating millions of dollars for the Kingdom of God! Learn how to create a cash pump of perpetual wealth & spark creative ideas for business.

Millionaire Mind. abr. ed. Thomas J. Stanley. Read by Cotter Smith. 2 CDs. (Running Time: 20 hrs. 0 mins. 0 sec.). (ENG.). 2000. audio compact disk 18.00 (978-0-7435-1786-7(5), Sound Ideas) Pub: S&S Audio. Dist(s): S and S Inc

Millionaire Mind. abr. ed. Thomas J. Stanley. Read by Cotter Smith. 2006. 10.95 (978-0-7435-6115-0(5)) Pub: S&S Audio. Dist(s): S and S Inc

Millionaire Mind. unabr. ed. Thomas J. Stanley. Narrated by Cotter Smith. 9 cass. (Running Time: 12 hrs.). 2000. 78.00 (978-0-7887-5463-0(7), T1006L8) Recorded Bks.

Shows you where to find America's wealthy. Takes you inside their minds to explore the unique ideas & approaches to life that make them so amazingly prosperous.

Millionaire Mind. unabr. ed. Thomas J. Stanley. Narrated by Cotter Smith. 10 CDs. (Running Time: 12 hrs.). 2001. audio compact disk 111.00 (978-1-4025-1051-9(9), C1597) Recorded Bks.

Author, lecturer, and researcher Thomas J. Stanley has studied the wealthy since 1973. His unexpected findings show many of America's financial elite got that way in only one generation - sometimes astonishing the teachers who years ago had predicted mediocre futures for them. So what sets millionaires apart from everyone else? Is it the schools they attend, their choices of vocation, or the way they run their households? Or is it just plain luck?.

Millionaire Mind. unabr. ed. Thomas J. Stanley. Read by Cotter Smith. 12 CDs. (Running Time: 123 hrs. 0 mins. 0 sec.). (ENG.). 2000. audio compact disk 49.95 (978-0-7435-1788-1(1), Sound Ideas) Pub: S&S Audio. Dist(s): S and S Inc

Do you have the millionaire mind? The runaway bestseller The Millionaire Next Door told us who America's wealthy really are. The Millionaire Mind tells how they got there, and how to become one of them. Inside, you'll discover the surprising answers to questions such as... What success factors made them wealthy in one generation? What part did luck and school play? How did they find the courage to take financial risks? How did they find their ideal vocations? What are they spouses like and how did they choose them? How do they run their households? How do they buy and sell their homes? What are their favorite leisure activities? To become a millionaire, you have to think like one. The Millionaire Mind tells you how.

Millionaire Mind. unabr. ed. Thomas J. Stanley. Read by Cotter Smith. 2006. 29.95 (978-0-7435-6128-0(7)) Pub: S&S Audio. Dist(s): S and S Inc

Millionaire Mondays: Season 1. Prod. by Millionaire Systems. 2005. audio compact disk 39.00 (978-1-932649-01-7(8)) Relleck Pubng.

Millionaire Mondays: Season 2. Created by Millionaire Systems. (ENG.). 2005. audio compact disk 39.00 (978-1-932649-03-1(4)) Relleck Pubng.

Millionaire Mondays: The 3Ls. Prod. by Millionaire Systems. (ENG.). 2005. audio compact disk 19.00 (978-1-932649-02-4(6)) Relleck Pubng.

Millionaire Next Door. Thomas J. Stanley. 2002. audio compact disk 18.00 (978-0-7435-2766-8(6), Sound Ideas) S&S Audio.

Millionaire Next Door: The Surprising Secrets of America's Wealthy. Thomas J. Stanley & William D. Danko. Narrated by Cotter Smith. 7 CDs. (Running Time: 8 hrs. 15 mins.). audio compact disk 71.00 (978-0-7887-9855-9(3)) Recorded Bks.

Millionaire Next Door: The Surprising Secrets of America's Wealthy. abr. ed. Thomas J. Stanley & William D. Danko. Read by Cotter Smith. 2 CDs. (Running Time: 20 hrs. 0 mins. 0 sec.). (ENG.). 2000. audio compact disk 19.95 (978-0-7435-1782-9(2), Sound Ideas) Pub: S&S Audio. Dist(s): S and S Inc

Millionaire Next Door: The Surprising Secrets of Americas Wealthy. abr. ed. Thomas J. Stanley & William D. Danko. Read by Cotter Smith. 2006. 10.95 (978-0-7435-6114-3(7)) Pub: S&S Audio. Dist(s): S and S Inc

Millionaire Next Door: The Surprising Secrets of America's Wealthy. unabr. ed. Thomas J. Stanley & William D. Danko. Narrated by Cotter Smith. 6 cass. (Running Time: 8 hrs. 15 mins.). 2001. 58.00 (978-0-7887-5008-3(9), 96513L8) Recorded Bks.

Change your life & join the ranks of how to think & handle your money like a millionaire.

Millionaire Next Door: The Surprising Secrets of America's Wealthy. unabr. ed. Thomas J. Stanley & William D. Danko. Read by Cotter Smith. 8 CDs. (Running Time: 80 hrs. 0 mins. 0 sec.). (ENG.). 2000. audio compact disk 39.95 (978-0-7435-1784-3(9), Sound Ideas) Pub: S&S Audio. Dist(s): S and S Inc

Millionaire Next Door: The Surprising Secrets of Americas Wealthy. unabr. ed. Thomas J. Stanley & William D. Danko. Read by Cotter Smith. 2006. 23.95 (978-0-7435-6127-3(9)) Pub: S&S Audio. Dist(s): S and S Inc

Millionaire Orbit. Eldon Taylor. 1 cass. (Running Time: 1 hr. 2 min.). (Inner Talk Ser.). 16.95 incl. script. (978-1-55978-510-5(1), 5399F) Progress Aware Res.

Soundtrack - Brook with underlying subliminal affirmations.

Millionaire Orbit: Contemporary Moments. Eldon Taylor. 1 cass. 16.95 (978-1-55978-606-5(X), 5399N) Progress Aware Res.

Millionaire Real Estate Agent Digital Audio. Gary Keller. Narrated by Kyle Hebert. 2007. 59.00 (978-1-932649-11-6(5)) Relleck Pubng.

Millionaire Real Estate Investor Audio Book. Gary Keller. Narrated by Cliff Haby. (ENG.). 2005. audio compact disk 59.00 (978-1-932649-04-8(2)) Relleck Pubng.

Millionaire Real Estate Investor Digital Audio Product. Gary Keller. Narrated by Cliff Haby. 2007. 59.00 (978-1-932649-12-3(3)) Relleck Pubng.

Millionaire Zone: Seven Winning Steps to a Seven-Figure Fortune. unabr. ed. Jennifer Openshaw. Read by Marguerite Gavin. (Running Time: 7 hrs. 0 mins. 0 sec.). (ENG.). 2007. audio compact disk 34.99 (978-1-4001-0414-7(9)); audio compact disk 24.99 (978-1-4001-5414-2(6)) Pub: Tantor Media. Dist(s): IngramPubServ

Millionaire Zone: 7 Winning Steps to a Seven-Figure Fortune. unabr. ed. Jennifer Openshaw. (Running Time: 7 hrs. 0 mins. 0 sec.). (ENG.). 2007. audio compact disk 69.99 (978-1-4001-3414-4(5)) Pub: Tantor Media. Dist(s): IngramPubServ

Millionaires. abr. ed. Brad Meltzer. Read by Tony Goldwyn. (ENG.). 2005. 14.98 (978-1-59483-377-9(X)) Pub: Hachet Audio. Dist(s): HachBkGrp

Millionaires. unabr. ed. Brad Meltzer. Read by Scott Brick. 10 cass. (Running Time: 15 hrs.). 2001. 44.98 (978-0-7366-8495-8(6)) Books on Tape.

When Charlie and Oliver Caruso take three million dollars from an abandoned account at their bank, they're in a lot of trouble.

Millionaires. unabr. ed. Brad Meltzer. Read by Scott Brick. (YA). 2007. 49.99 (978-1-60252-768-3(7)) Find a World.

Millionaires. unabr. ed. Brad Meltzer. Read by Scott Brick. (ENG.). 2005. 16.98 (978-1-59483-378-6(8)) Pub: Hachet Audio. Dist(s): HachBkGrp

Millionaires. unabr. ed. Brad Meltzer. Read by Scott Brick. (Running Time: 15 hrs.). (ENG.). 2009. 59.98 (978-1-60788-101-8(2)) Pub: Hachet Audio. Dist(s): HachBkGrp

Millionaires, Mansions, & Motor Yachts: An Era of Opulence. unabr. ed. Ross MacTaggart. Read by Ross MacTaggart. 9 cass. (Running Time: 13 hrs.). 2004. 36.95 (978-1-59007-459-6(9), 110353); audio compact disk 65.00 (978-1-59007-460-2(2), 130360) Pub: New Millenn Enter. Dist(s): PerseuPGW

Millionaires' Unit: The Aristocratic Flyboys Who Fought the Great War & Invented American Air Power. unabr. ed. Marc Wortman. Read by Patrick G. Lawlor. 12 CDs. (Running Time: 13 hrs. 30 mins. 0 sec.). (ENG.). 2006. audio compact disk 39.99 (978-1-4001-0250-1(2)); audio compact disk 79.99 (978-1-4001-3250-8(9)); audio compact disk 29.99 (978-1-4001-5250-6(X)) Pub: Tantor Media. Dist(s): IngramPubServ

***Millions.** unabr. ed. Frank Cottrell Boyce. Read by Simon Jones. (ENG.). 2008. (978-0-06-085889-6(3), Harper Audio); (978-0-06-085890-2(7), Harper Audio) HarperCollins Pubs.

Millions: How Would You Spend a Million in Cash? unabr. ed. Frank Cottrell Boyce. Read by Simon Jones. (Running Time: 16200 sec.). (J). 2008. audio compact disk 14.95 (978-0-06-145126-3(6), HarperChildAud) HarperCollins Pubs.

Millions of Cats see Millones de Gatoe

Millions of Cats. 2004. bk. 24.95 (978-1-56008-227-9(5)); pap. bk. 14.95 (978-0-7882-0594-1(3)); pap. bk. 14.95 (978-1-55592-663-2(0)); 8.95 (978-1-56008-970-4(9)); cass. & flmstrp 30.00 (978-0-89719-540-9(X)) Weston Woods.

Millions of Cats. Wanda Gag. 1 cass. (Running Time: 10 min.). (J). 2000. pap. bk. 12.95 Weston Woods.

This is the classic story about the gentle old man, who looks for one car for his lonely wife & returns wife "millions & billions & trillions of cats.

Millones de Gatoe. Tr. of Millions of Cats. (SPA.). 2004. 8.95 (978-0-7882-0254-4(5)) Weston Woods.

Millroy the Magician, unabr. ed. Paul Theroux. Read by Christopher Hurt. 12 cass. (Running Time: 18 hrs.). 1999. 83.95 (1522) Blckstn Audio.

Jilly Farina is fourteen. Her father is drunk on the day of the Barnstable County Fair, so she goes by herself & by that night her life has been transformed. When she walks into a tent to see Millroy the Magician, his eyes lighten from brown to green & fasten upon her. He performs miracles in front of Jilly's spellbound eyes & tells her he wants to eat her. He tells her that he will train her to be his assistant. But Millroy is a healer, too, a vegetarian & health fanatic with a mission to change the eating habits of the Untied States.

Millroy the Magician. unabr. ed. Paul Theroux. Read by Christopher Hurt. 12 cass. (Running Time: 17 hrs. 30 mins.). 1994. 83.95 Set. (978-0-7861-0792-6(8), 1522) Blckstn Audio.

Jilly Farina is fourteen. Her father is drunk on the day of the Barnstable County Fair, so she goes by herself, & by that night her life has been transformed. When she walks into a tent to see Milroy the Magician, his eyes lighten from brown to green & fasten upon her. He performs miracles in front of Jilly's spellbound eyes & tells her he wants to eat her. He tells her that he will train her to be his assistant, & that he will give her a sequined costume.

Mills of God Grind Slowly. Instructed by Manly P. Hall. 8.95 (978-0-89314-185-1(2), C800148) Philos Res.

Mill's on Liberty. Scripts. Read by Albert A. Anderson. Ed. by Albert A. Anderson. Lieselotte Anderson. 5 Cds. (Running Time: 6 hours). 2003. audio compact disk 30.00 (978-1-887250-32-0(8)) Agora Pubns.

***Milo Hamilton, A Call for the Ages.** 2009. audio compact disk 16.00 (978-0-9818365-6-0(9)) Baseball Voice.

Milo's Great Invention/Inventors. Steck-Vaughn Staff. 1997. (978-0-8172-7384-2(0)) SteckVau.

Milo's Hat Trick. Jon Agee. 1 cass. (Running Time: 10 mins.). (J). (gr. k-3). 2002. 26.90 (978-0-8045-6889-0(8)) Spoken Arts.

Milo the Magician has a bear in his hat. All Milo has to do is whistle and the bear will jump out, astonishing the crown at the Rialto Theatre.

Milton see Poetry of William Blake

***Milton Berle Show.** RadioArchives.com. (Running Time: 600). (ENG.). 2004. audio compact disk 29.98 (978-1-61081-017-3(1)) Radio Arch.

Milton Berle Show: A Salute to Automobiles & A Salute to Brooklyn. Hosted by Milton Berle. 1 cass. (Running Time: 1 hr.). 2001. 6.98 (2402) Radio Spirits.

Milton Berle Show: Salute to Railroads & Salute to South America. Hosted by Milton Berle. 1 cass. (Running Time: 1 hr.). 2001. 6.98 (2042) Radio Spirits.

Milton Berle Show: Saluting Farmers & Saluting Radio. Hosted by Milton Berle. 1 cass. (Running Time: 1 hr.). 2001. 6.98 (2145) Radio Spirits.

Milton Berle Show: The Night Before Christmas & Highlights of 1947 Season. Hosted by Milton Berle. 1 cass. (Running Time: 1 hr.). 2001. 6.98 (2228) Radio Spirits.

Milton by Dancing Beetle. Eugene Ely. 1 cass. (Running Time: 1 hr. 25 min.). (J). 1990. 10.00 Erthviibz.
John Milton, parody & nature sounds come together when Ms. Earwig & the spunky musical humans read & sing with Dancing Beetle.

Milton Friedman: A Guide to His Economic Thought, unabr. ed. Eamonn Butler. Read by Jeff Riggenbach. 6 cass. (Running Time: 8 hrs. 30 mins.). 1993. 44.95 (978-0-7861-0456-7(2), 1408) Blckstn Audio.
Butler's clear, systematic, perceptive study is the first book that describes Friedman's ideas & explains their significance. Starting with a short survey of Friedman's career, Dr. Butler goes on to analyze the main elements in this thought: the quantity theory of money; the supply of money; the factors that influence demand; the practical & theoretical problems of using monetary policy; Friedman's contribution to market economic thought; & methodological questions that arise from Friedman's approach.

Milton Friedman: The Economic Crisis see Buckley's Firing Line

Milton in America. unabr. collector's ed. Peter Ackroyd. Read by David Case. 6 cass. (Running Time: 9 hrs.). 1999. 48.00 (978-0-7366-4390-0(7), 4853) Books on Tape.
What if the poet John Milton had come to Puritan America in 1660? Fleeing the restoration of the hated monarchy in England, the aging, blind Milton crosses the ocean & soon becomes the leader of a community of Puritan settlers in New England. Insisting on strict & merciless application of Puritan justice, he becomes as much a tyrant as the despots from whom he has sought refuge.

Milton the Puritan: Portrait of a Mind. unabr. ed. A. L. Rowse. Read by Stuart Courtney. 10 cass. (Running Time: 15 hrs.). 1986. 80.00 (978-0-7366-0980-7(6), 1921) Books on Tape.
Study of John Milton - his intellectual outfit - the line he took about the issues that led to the English Civil War & its consequences.

Milton's Vision of Paradise Lost & Regained. Manly P. Hall. 1 cass. 8.95 (978-0-89314-186-8(0), C830313) Philos Res.

Milwaukee. unabr. ed. Bernice Rubens. Read by Judith Porter. 6 cass. (Running Time: 6 hrs. 34 min.). (Isis Ser.). (J). 2001. 54.95 (978-0-7531-1238-0(8)) Pub: ISIS Lrg Prnt GBR. Dist(s): Ulverscroft US
Milwaukee - Is it a place? A person? Or the painful memory of a night to forget? It could be any of them. For Mary, it is the name of her father. For Annie, her mother, it is an anonymous American GI. For her grandmother, it is a place in Wisconsin and an opportunity for revenge. Each clings to her illusions, and the result is an explosion of lies that fragments and destroys a family.

Milwaukee. unabr. ed. Bernice Rubens. Read by Judith Porter. 6 CDs. (Running Time: 6 hrs. 34 mins.). (Isis Ser.). (J). 2002. audio compact disk 64.95 (978-0-7531-1393-6(7)) Pub: ISIS Lrg Prnt GBR. Dist(s): Ulverscroft US

Mimic: 1 Cor. 4:6-21. Ed Young. 1985. Rental 4.95 (978-0-7417-1490-9(6), 490) Win Walk.

Mimi's Guide. unabr. ed. Doris Baizley. Perf. by Powers Boothe et al. 1 cass. (Running Time: 1 hr. 31 min.). 1996. 19.95 (978-1-58081-037-1(3)) L A Theatre.
The sensuality of Louisiana's humid, jasmine-scented air permeates this love triangle about three people who are haunted by memories of war. Encountering each other at a university in the deep South, they find their old demons are awakened by the lush climate & each other.

Mimosoideae of SE Asia: Macintosh/Windows Version. Ed. by J. W. A. Ridder-Numan & I. De Kort. 2000. audio compact disk 71.95 (978-3-540-14705-3(5)) Spri.

Mimsy Were the Borogoves see SF Soundbook

Mimus. unabr. ed. Lilli Thal. Read by Maxwell Caulfield. Tr. by John Brownjohn. 10 CDs. (Running Time: 10 hrs. 28 mins.). (YA). (gr. 7 up). 2007. audio compact disk 70.00 (978-0-7393-4865-9(5)) Pub: Random Audio Pubg. Dist(s): Random

Mina und Otto: Lehrerhandbuch. J. Douvitsas-Gamst & S. Xanthos-Kretzschmer. (GER.). (J). 1989. 22.50 (978-3-12-675034-9(6)) Pub: Klett Ernst Verlag DEU. Dist(s): Intl Bk Import

Minarat of DJAM & Perseus in the Wind. unabr. ed. Freya Stark. Read by Donada Peters. 8 cass. (Running Time: 8 hrs.). 1991. 48.00 (2876) Books on Tape.
An excursion through Afghanistan reported by this century's finest traveler-historian.

Minaret of Djam & Perseus in the Wind. collector's ed. Freya Stark. Read by Donada Peters. 8 cass. (Running Time: 8 hrs.). 1991. 48.00 (978-0-7366-2068-0(0)) Books on Tape.

Minas Del Rey Salomón. abr. ed. H. Rider Haggard. 3 CDs.Tr. of Mines of King Salomon. (SPA.). 2002. audio compact disk 17.00 (978-958-9494-98-1(6)) YoYoMusic.

Mind. Osho Oshos. 1 cass. 9.00 (A0653-89) Sound Photosyn.

Mind, Pt. 1. Ben Young. 1997. 4.95 (978-0-7417-6041-8(X)) Win Walk.

Mind: The Power of the Subconscious Mind. Instructed by Stuart Wilde. 1 cass. (Self-Help Tape Ser.). 9.95 (978-0-930603-44-1(3)) White Dove NM.
So much of your personal power lies dormant in the inner mind waiting for you to reclaim it. Listen to author Stuart Wilde talk to you about unleashing the awesome power of the shamanistic mind. Use the practical techniques he offers to whip-saw life into giving you what you want.

Mind Pt. 2: 07/1997. Ben Young. 1997. 4.95 (978-0-7417-6042-5(8)) Win Walk.

Mind - Body Communication. Robert Stone. Read by Robert Stone. 6 cass. (Running Time: 6 hrs.). 1993. 59.95 (607AB) Nightingale-Conant.
Right now you possess the power & resources to maintain your good health & prevent any future sickness. Bob Stone explores your innate ability to affect your body's healing processes through cyberphysiology - the science of self-regulation. Learn to activate your mental imaging powers, communicate with cells in your body to promote healing, boost your immune system, "see" your body as a unified whole, access higher mental abilities & much more. Includes wellness guide.

Mind - Body Connection; Death & Afterlife; Psychics & Prophets, Vol. 1. abr. ed. Neale Donald Walsch. Read by Neale Donald Walsch. Read by Edward Asner & Ellen Burstyn. 2 cass. (Running Time: 3 hrs.). 1999. 17.95 Audio Lit.
The relationship between body, mind & soul, the nature of psychic power & the truth of falsehood of prophecies of doom.

Mind Aesthetics I. Julian Cauceglia. 1 CD. (Running Time: 1 hr). 2002. audio compact disk 29.95 (978-0-9717407-0-9(4)) J Cauceglia.
A unique utilization of Hypnotic and NLP techniques that will bring the listener to the deepest level of relaxation, fill them with the overwhelming abundance of positive energy and instill the feeling of being ?beautiful inside?. Dr. Julian Cauceglia who has degrees in Clinical Hypnotherapy and Psychology, has developed Mind Aesthetics for use in the Salon and Spa industry during the application of services such as facials, massages and wraps, etc, as well as by individuals at home who desire to reach new levels of relaxation and emerge feeling positive, new and beautiful.

Mind & Body Tune Up. 1 cass. (Running Time: 1 hr.). 10.95 (022) Psych Res Inst.
A totally positive approach where health is a glowing vitality with feelings of continuous physical & mental growth.

Mind & Cancer. unabr. ed. Carl Simonton. 1 cass. (Running Time: 1 hr. 30 min.). 1979. 11.00 (08001) Big Sur Tapes.
Speaks on the interrelatedness of mind & body in health & illness.

Mind & Meditation. Osel Tendzin. 5 cass. 1978. 47.50 Vajradhatu.
Discussion on: Examining the Karmic Chain; Dispelling Ignorance; Intelligence without Identity; Developing Kindness.

Mind & Reality. Daniel Clement Dennett et al. 2 cass. (Running Time: 2 hrs. 30 mins.). 1996. 17.95 (978-1-879557-42-0(8)) Pub: Audio Scholar. Dist(s): Penton Overseas
Selections from the MIT Press. Authors present mind-stretching speculations on the nature of human intelligence. Subjects discussed in this anthology include: consciousness & its place in nature, the emergence of language & reflection, the meaning of mental representations & in a coda exploding with possibilities, the expansion of consciousness by theoretical revelation.

Mind & the Book: Planned Reading Can Enrich Your Life. Instructed by Manly P. Hall. 8.95 (978-0-89314-187-5(9), C800119) Philos Res.

***Mind & the Matter.** 2010. audio compact disk (978-1-59171-224-4(6)) Falcon Picture.

Mind & the True Self. Swami Amar Jyoti. 1 cass. 1991. 9.95 (J-56) Truth Consciousness.
Sharanagati: by quieting the mind, the Self, Infinite Being, is seen.

Mind & Time, Spirit & Matter: Santa Fe Lecture & Workshop. Terence McKenna. 8 cass. 80.00 (A0444-90) Sound Photosyn.
Packaged in a padded album, the edited eight-tape audio set includes the Friday evening introductory lecture, as well as the weekend workshop.

Mind & Time, Spirit & Matter: Santa Fe Lecture Only. Terence McKenna. 2 cass. (Running Time: 3 hrs.). 18.00 set. (A0608-90); 35.00 (V0206-90) Sound Photosyn.
In Santa Fe, an inspired lecture before the latest & greatest workshop.

Mind & Time, Spirit & Matter: Santa Fe Workshop. Terence McKenna. 7 cass. 63.00 (A0609-90) Sound Photosyn.
Author & explorer, shamanologist & philosopher, Terence McKenna brings a unique perspective to the idea of a spiritual path for each of us & an impending total transformation of the human world. We will examine human attitudes toward the other, discuss time & its mysteries, the nature of language, & the techniques of ecstasy that have developed in non-Western societies to navigate to & from invisible worlds. The role of hallucinogenic plants will be discussed in depth.

Mind As Hero in "Atlas Shrugged" Andrew Bernstein. 2 cass. (Running Time: 2 hrs.). 1994. 19.95 (978-1-56114-285-9(9), MB03D) Second Renaissance.
Lecture on the theme of "Atlas Shrugged.".

Mind at A Time. Mel Levine. 2004. 15.95 (978-0-7435-4136-7(7)) Pub: S&S Audio. Dist(s): S and S Inc

Mind Attuned to God. Marianne Williamson. (ENG.). 2000. 10.00 (978-1-56170-755-3(4)) Hay House.

Mind-Beauty Connection: 9 Days to Reverse Stress Aging & Reveal More Youthful, Beautiful Skin. unabr. ed. Amy Wechsler. Narrated by Renée Raudman. (Running Time: 9 hrs. 30 mins. 0 sec.). 2008. audio compact disk 29.99 (978-1-4001-0880-0(2)) Pub: Tantor Media. Dist(s): IngramPubServ

Mind-Beauty Connection: 9 Days to Reverse Stress Aging & Reveal More Youthful, Beautiful Skin. unabr. ed. Amy Wechsler. Narrated by Paul Boehmer & Renée Raudman. 8 CDs. (Running Time: 9 hrs. 30 mins. 0 sec.). 2008. audio compact disk 59.99 (978-1-4001-3880-7(9)) Pub: Tantor Media. Dist(s): IngramPubServ

Mind-Beauty Connection: 9 Days to Reverse Stress Aging & Reveal More Youthful, Beautiful Skin. unabr. ed. Amy Wechsler. Read by Renée Raudman. Narrated by Paul Boehmer. (Running Time: 9 hrs. 30 mins. 0 sec.). (ENG.). 2008. audio compact disk 19.99 (978-1-4001-5880-5(X)) Pub: Tantor Media. Dist(s): IngramPubServ

Mind-Body Code: How the Mind Wounds & Heals the Body. unabr. ed. Mario Martinez. 6 CDs. (Running Time: 6 mins). 2009. audio compact disk 69.95 (978-1-59179-710-4(1)) Sounds True.

Mind-Body Communication in Hypnosis. Milton H. Erickson. Ed. by Ernest L. Rossi & Margaret O. Ryan. (Seminars, Workshops & Lectures of Milton H. Erickson Ser.: Vol. 3). 1986. 20.00 (978-0-8290-3161-4(8)) Irvington.

Mind-Body Dance. abr. ed. Tammie Fowles. Read by Tammie Fowles. Read by Kevin Fowles. 4 cass. (Running Time: 6 hrs.). 1998. 22.95 SagePlace.
Explores the unity of our physical, emotional & spiritual selves, offering valuable insights & tools for creating life styles that foster health & well-being.

***Mind-Body Exercises for Stress Hardiness Optimization.** Belleruth Naparstek. Read by Belleruth Naparstek. (Playaway Adult Nonfiction Ser.). (ENG.). 2010. 39.99 (978-1-61587-385-2(6)) Find a World.

***Mind Body Healing.** unabr. ed. Kelly Howell. Read by Kelly Howell. 2 CDs. (Running Time: 2 hrs.). 2008. audio compact disk 24.00 (978-1-4159-5576-5(X), BksonTape) Pub: Random Audio Pubg. Dist(s): Random

Mind-Body Healing: Facilitate & Enhance Physical Healing. Mark Bancroft. Read by Mark Bancroft. 1 cass., bklet. (Running Time: 1 hr.). (Alternative Health & Healing Ser.). 1999. 12.95 (978-1-58522-014-4(0), 201, EnSpire Aud) EnSpire Pr.
Two complete sessions plus printed instruction manual/guidebook. With healing music soundtrack.

Mind-Body Healing: Facilitate & Enhance Physical Healing. Mark Bancroft. Read by Mark Bancroft. 1 CD, bklet. (Running Time: 1 hr.). (Alternative Health & Healing Ser.). 2006. audio compact disk 20.00 (978-1-58522-046-5(9)) EnSpire Pr.
Two complete sessions plus printed instructionmanual-guidebook. With healing music soundtrack.

Mind Body Healing: Meditations to Focus the Mind & Heal the Body: Healing Meditation & Sound Healing. Kelly Howell. 2 CDs. (Running Time: 7200 sec.). 2006. audio compact disk 24.95 (978-1-881451-52-5(6)) Brain Sync.
If you are preparing for surgery or if you need to heal on any level, Mind Body Healing will help. Delta waves are woven into soothing music to induce deeply restorative states ideal for healing. These are blissful states of reverie that are proven to enhance immune function, reduce pain and activate the body's natural healing abilities. In this quantum state of renewal, recovery is often swifter: blood loss is reduced, less pain is perceived, and fewer analgesics are needed. Moreover, the immune system seems to respond better, and hospital stays can be shortened.

Mind, Body, Miracles! Patricia J. Crane. Read by Patricia J. Crane. 1 cass. (Running Time: 1 hr. 2 min.). 1996. 11.95 (978-1-893705-06-7(4)) Hlth Horiz.
Overview of the mind-body connection & two guided meditations.

Mind Catcher. unabr. ed. John Darnton. Read by Dick Hill. 9 cass. Library ed. (Running Time: 13 hrs.). 2002. 92.25 (978-1-59086-222-3(8), 1590862228, Unabridge Lib Edns); audio compact disk 42.95 (978-1-59086-268-1(6), 1590862686, CD Unabridged); audio compact disk 107.25 (978-1-59086-270-4(8), 1590862708, CD Unabrid Lib Ed) Brilliance Audio.
New York City: A thirteen-year-old boy named Tyler lies in a hospital, his brain damaged in a tragic accident. By his bedside, his father stands helplessly, as two very different scientists take charge of the boy's fate. One is a neurosurgeon, whose unorthodox experiments use computers to control a patient's physical responses during surgery. The other is a researcher with experiments of his own, ones so secret he can reveal them to no one: his attempts to find the spark of human consciousness...and capture it forever. Together, they will produce a result beyond anything they could have conceived, sending Tyler far beyond the frontiers of medical science into an astonishing netherworld of man and machine - a place no living person has gone before and from which one desperate person will try to bring him back.

Mind Catcher. unabr. ed. John Darnton. Read by John Darnton. Read by Dick Hill. 9 cass. (Running Time: 13 hrs.). 2002. 34.95 (978-1-59086-221-6(X), 159086221X, BAU) Brilliance Audio.

Mind Catcher. unabr. ed. John Darnton. Read by Dick Hill. (Running Time: 13 hrs.). 2004. 39.25 (978-1-59335-422-0(3), 1593354223, Brlnc Audio MP3 Lib) Brilliance Audio.

Mind Catcher. unabr. ed. John Darnton. Read by Dick Hill. (Running Time: 13 hrs.). 2004. 39.25 (978-1-59710-497-5(3), 1597104973, BADLE); 24.95 (978-1-59710-496-8(5), 1597104965, BAD) Brilliance Audio.

Mind Catcher. unabr. ed. John Darnton. Read by Dick Hill. (Running Time: 13 hrs.). 2004. 24.95 (978-1-59335-190-8(9), 1593351909) Soulmate Audio Bks.

Mind Change: A Biblical Path to Overcoming Life's Challenges. Thomas A. Jones. Read by Thomas A. Jones. 2008. audio compact disk 16.00 (978-1-57782-227-1(7)) Discipleshp.

Mind Coach Series Part 1: The Story of Jaren: Keeper of the Clean Heart Grid. Short Stories. Marilyne Woodsmall, 8th. 3 CDs. (Running Time: 2 hrs.30 min). Dramatization. 2004. audio compact disk 66.33 (978-1-892876-09-6(4)) Next Step Pr.
Join the Mind Coach as she gives instruction to an aspiring athlete on how to prepare his mind, body, soul and spirit to participate in the "great games." This is both educational and inspirational.

Mind Control: The Ultimate Weapon. William E. Mayer. Read by William E. Mayer. 1 cass. 1999. (978-0-912986-34-0(4)) Am Media.

Mind Control in America. Steven Jacobson. 1 cass. (Running Time: 1 hr.). 11.95 (A5498) Lghtwrks Aud & Vid.
Psychological warfare is being waged against an unsuspecting public through the control of mass media & the altering of public education. You will learn about brainwashing techniques employed like "backward masking". More importantly, you will gain a greater understanding of who is behind these manipulative efforts & what you can do to become aware of how they are influencing our society.

Mind Control Relaxation. unabr. ed. Ed Foreman. 2 cass. (Running Time: 1 hr. 10 min.). 1989. 29.95 (978-1-893603-06-6(7)) Exec Dev Syst.
Helps you let go of stress, anxiety & frustration & enjoy peaceful rejuvenation of your mind & body. Instructs & leads you into a restful alpha level to lower your blood pressure, decrease your heart rate, relieve tension & replenish you with energy & vitality. Also included is "Positive Self-Talk," for daily follow-through conversations with yourself.

Mind Controlled Analgesia: A Step-by-Step Program for Learning to Relax Instantly. Created by David Bresler. (ENG.). 2007. audio compact disk 19.95 (978-1-887211-01-7(2), Imag Res) AlphaBks CA.

Mind Detox. Deborah Marshall Warren. 1 cass. (Running Time: 1 hr.). 2001. (978-0-7225-9922-8(6), HarperThor) HarpC GBR.

Mind Electronics: Beta-to-Theta - Hypnagogic. 1 cass. 14.98 (978-0-87554-284-3(0), NX501) Valley Sun.

***Mind Expanding Flesh Machines: Konan the Cosmic Rhythm Master.** Prod. by Ziggurat Productions. Arranged by Ziggurat Productions. (Running Time: 52). (YA). 2010. audio compact disk 15.00 (978-1-884214-62-2(2)) Ziggurat Prods.

Mind Fields. unabr. ed. W. Bartow Wright. Read by Rusty Nelson. 6 cass. (Running Time: 7 hrs. 56 min.). (Bucky Dolan Ser.: Bk. 3). 2001. 39.95 (978-1-55686-966-2(5)) Books in Motion.
Bucky is asked to investigate the mysterious deaths of government officials at a meeting arranged through a think-tank, which also houses a parapsychology lab.

Mind Game. unabr. ed. Hector MacDonald. 6 cass. (Running Time: 9 hrs.). 2001. 29.95 (978-1-57511-087-5(3)) Pub Mills.
Ben Ashurst is a student at Oxford. He leads a fairly placid life, befriending shy girls, playing "keep up with the Joneses" with his crowd of wealthy (and nasty) friends and trying to impress his tutor, the brilliant and controversial behavioral scientist James Fieldhead. A single day, however, is enough to turn his calm existence upside down. When he meets the beautiful and enigmatic Cara and when Fieldhead requests Ben's participation in a ground-breaking research experiment, Ben will find himself thrust into a life where every measure of normality is rent asunder.

Mind Game of Chess, Vol. 42. 1 cass. (Running Time: 56 min.). 1998. 15.00 (978-1-891826-41-2(7)) Introspect.
Teaches how to use the mind to its fullest. Be aware of all that goes on within the game & beyond. Helps to prepare & recall the positive moves.

Mind Games. Prod. by Jeanna Gabellini & MasterPeace Coaching and Training. Susan Johnson. (ENG.). 2008. audio compact disk 19.99 (978-0-9710787-4-1(2)) Mstr Pce Coach Train.

Mind Games. Chuck Webb. 1 CD. (Running Time: 30 mins). 2002. audio compact disk 14.98 (978-1-893967-17-5(4)) Emphasis Ent.

Mind Games. unabr. ed. Hilary Norman. Read by Hilary Norman. 10 cass. (Running Time: 13 hrs. 15 mins.). (Storysound Ser.). (J). 2002. 84.95 (978-1-85903-507-8(8)) Pub: Mgna Lrg Print GBR. Dist(s): Ulverscroft US

***Mind Games in a World of Images.** Featuring Ravi Zacharias. 1993. audio compact disk 9.00 (978-1-61256-057-1(1)) Ravi Zach.

An Asterisk (*) at the beginning of an entry indicates that the title is appearing for the first time.

Mind in Meditation, 1971. J. Krishnamurti. Read by J. Krishnamurti. 1 cass. (Running Time: 1 hr.). 8.50 (AMM71) Krishnamurti.

Mind in Yoga Philosophy. 1 cass. (Running Time: 1 hr.). 12.99 (610) Yoga Res Foun.

Mind Is a Child. 2006. audio compact disk 15.00 (978-1-890246-35-8(2)) B Katie Int Inc.

Mind Juice. Jimmy Robinson. (ENG.). 2008. audio compact disk 14.97 (978-0-9792672-9-1(3)) Jimmyland.

Mind Magic. Donna Seebo. Read by Donna Seebo. 2 cass. bk. 20.00 (978-1-883164-00-3(1)) Delphi Intl.
A personal story of how to develop intuitive talents.

Mind, Mantra & Unity. Swami Amar Jyoti. 1 cass. 1991. 9.95 (J-57) Truth Consciousness.
As the flame & its glow, mind is never seperate from the Totality. Nature & God are One.

Mind Mapping: How to Liberate Your Natural Genius. Michael J. Gelb. Read by Michael J. Gelb. 4 cass. (Running Time: 4 hrs.). 1993. 49.95 (10400A) Nightingale-Conant.

Mind Mapping: How to Liberate Your Natural Genius. unabr. abr. ed. Michael J. Gelb. Read by Michael J. Gelb. 2 CDs. (Running Time: 20 hrs. 0 mins. 0 sec.). 2003. audio compact disk 19.95 (978-0-7435-2907-5(3), Nightgale) Pub: S&S Audio. Dist(s): S and S Inc
THE BREAKTHROUGH AUDIOBOOK BY THE AUTHOR OF HOW TO THINK LIKE LEONARDO DA VINCI TAP INTO THE GENIUS WITHIN Your thinking process is free-flowing and highly individualized, so you need a method of organizing your thoughts that is uniquely your own. It's time you discovered Mind Mapping, a marriage of logic and imagination that allows you to balance the formation and organization of ideas while encouraging a full range of mental expression. A Mind Map® begins with a symbol or picture representing your topic and serving as the home base for creative associations. Completed, a Mind Map is colorful, imaginative and expressive of what is distinctively you. Use the breakthrough tool of Mind Mapping to: Think faster and more creatively Get more work done in far less time Develop an "I Can" attitude Awaken your power to learn Identify talents you never knew you had.

Mind Mapping Made Easy! Speeches. 1 CD. (Running Time: 55 mins.). 2002. audio compact disk 14.95 (978-0-9726941-9-3(6)) InGenius Inc.

Mind Mapping Made Easy! Edward Strachar. 2002. (978-0-9717185-9-3(8)) InGenius Inc.

Mind Matters in Selling. unabr. ed. Jeffrey Offenburger & Nancy Constant. 6 cass. pap. bk. 69.50 (978-0-88432-175-0(4), S29600) J Norton Pubs.
Helps you unlock your own creativity, enthusiasm & motivation. This program is based on self-hypnosis & has been used as a training program by many corporations. Includes booklet and album.

Mind Mint. 2004. audio compact disk (978-0-9755937-7-6(3)) TheraScapes.

Mind of Plato, unabr. ed. A. E. Taylor. Read by Frederick Davidson. 3 cass. (Running Time: 4 hrs.). 1993. 23.95 (978-0-7861-0458-1(9), 1410) Blckstn Audio.
Examines the philosopher's theory of knowledge & doctrine of ideas; the ideal of the philosopher-king; social system advocated in Republic; judgments on democracy; & belief in the immortality of the soul. Also considered: Plato's relationship with his master, Socrates; contribution to the idea of university education; attack on art; abstention from public life.

Mind of Poe. unabr. ed. Edgar Allan Poe. Read by Hurd Hatfield et al. 6 cass. (Running Time: 4 hrs. 19 min.). Incl. Black Cat. 1987. (PCC 51); Cask of Amontillado. 1987. (PCC 51); Descent into the Maelstrom. 1987. (PCC 51); Fall of the House of Usher. 1987. (PCC 51); Masque of the Red Death. 1987. (PCC 51); Pit & the Pendulum. Edgar Allan Poe. 1987. (PCC 51); Tell-Tale Heart. 1987. (PCC 51); 1987. 55.00 (978-0-8045-0051-7(7), PCC 51) Spoken Arts.
Poe's short stories & poems.

Mind of the Maker, unabr. ed. Dorothy L. Sayers. Read by Nadia May. 5 cass. (Running Time: 7 hrs.). 1991. 39.95 (978-0-7861-0219-8(5), 1193) Blckstn Audio.
This classic is by turns an entrancing meditation on language; a piercing commentary on the nature of art & why so much of what we read, hear & see falls short; and a brilliant examination of the fundamental tenets of Christianity.

Mind of the Soul: Responsible Choice. abr. unabr. ed. Gary Zukav & Linda Francis. Read by Gary Zukav & Linda Francis. 5 CDs. (Running Time: 60 hrs. 0 mins. 0 sec.). (ENG.). 2003. audio compact disk 30.00 (978-0-7435-3326-3(7), Sound Ideas) Pub: S&S Audio. Dist(s): S and S Inc

Mind over Illness. Norman Cousins. Read by Norman Cousins. 6 cass. 45.00 (510A) Nightingale-Conant.

Mind over Matter. unabr. ed. Steven Rose et al. 2 cass. (Running Time: 2 hrs. 30 min.). 19.95 (29368-29369) J Norton Pubs.
Researching into psychosomatic illness, especially via feedback & drugs has altered the orthodox Western medical model of the mind-body relation. It challenges the reductionist approach & our views of parapsychological phenomena.

Mind over Matter: The Epic Crossing of the Antarctic Continent. unabr. ed. Ranulph Fiennes. Read by Ranulph Fiennes. 6 cass. (Running Time: 9 hrs.). 2000. 49.95 (978-0-7451-4360-6(1), CAB 1043) Pub: Chivers Audio Bks GBR. Dist(s): AudioGO
In 1992, Ranulph Fiennes and Dr. Michael Stroud set out from the Filchner Ice Shelf to attempt the first unassisted crossing of the Antarctic Continent. For 97 days they encountered starvation, equipment failure, and hypothermia while dragging their 500 pound sleds towards the South Pole.

Mind over Money. unabr. ed. Mark E. Matson & Donn Burrows. 4 cass. (Running Time: 3 hrs. 30 min.). 1998. 39.95 (978-0-9650376-8-6(1)) McGriff Pubng.

Mind over Money, Vol. 1. Dennis B. Stevenson. Ed. by Kevin Frazier. 8 cass. 1997. bk. 175.00 (978-1-892479-01-3(X)) Focus Educ.

Mind over Money: Overcoming the Money Disorders that Threaten our Financial Health. abr. ed. Brad Klontz & Ted Klontz. Read by Brad Klontz. (ENG.). 2009. audio compact disk 18.00 (978-0-307-71291-2(5), Random AudioBks) Pub: Random Audio Pubg. Dist(s): Random

Mind over Murder. unabr. collector's ed. William X. Kienzle. Read by Edward Holland. 8 cass. (Running Time: 12 hrs.). (Father Koesler Mystery Ser.: No. 3). 1997. 64.00 (978-0-7366-4064-0(9), 4575) Books on Tape.
A Monsignor vanishes from his car, & Father Koesler finds a trail of the cleric's enemies. the scene of the disappearances the local Catholic school's parking lot, where the police find the ambitious clergyman's Cadillac. Inside the car are traces of blood & a shell from a .32 automatic. The Monsignor is nowhere to be found, but he has left some interesting details behind.

Mind over Myths: Managing Difficult Situations in the Workplace. 6 cass. wbk. ed. 89.95 (C016) Inst Rational-Emotive.
Includes: Introduction to Self-Management; Pinpointing Self-Defeating Behaviors; Overcoming Procrastination; Getting along with Colleagues & Supervisors; & Handling Performance Reviews. Includes workbook.

Mind over Myths: Managing Difficult Workplace Situations, 6 cass. (Running Time: 30 min. per cass.). bk. & wbk. ed. 44.99 (C016) A Ellis Institute.
Includes "Introduction to Self-Management"; "Pinpointing Self-Defeating Behaviors"; "Overcoming Procrastination"; "Getting Along with Colleagues & Supervisors"; & "Handling Performance Reviews." Includes workbook & book.

Mind over Pain. 1 cass. (Running Time: 1 hr.). 10.95 (021) Psych Res Inst.
A drug-free approach to minor pain relief through natural healing & relaxation techniques.

Mind Power: Visualizing Your Success in Business. Gini G. Scott. 4 cass. 1989. 59.95 (978-0-13-583550-0(X)) P-H.
Directed to business managers, executives and any self-improvement buyer who wants to develop their mental imaging skills (positive visualization) to achieve personal and professional success.

Mind Power for Memory & Study. Pat Carroll. Read by Pat Carroll. Ed. by Tony Carroll. 1 cass. (Running Time: 30 min.). 10.00 Inner-Mind Concepts.
Instructs how to train the mind to learn faster & remember more.

Mind Power for Weight Loss, Vol. 25. Jonathan Parker. 2 cass. (Running Time: 1 hr. 45 min.). 1992. 17.00 (978-1-58400-024-2(4)) QuantumQuests Intl.

Mind Power Is Energy. 2004. audio compact disk (978-1-932163-63-6(8)) Infinity Inst.

Mind Power to Better Golf. unabr. ed. Robert J. Rotella & Coop. 3 cass. pap. bk. 34.50 (978-0-88432-187-3(8), S01820) J Norton Pubs.
Helps you perfect your mental control of your game.

Mind Power to Better Golf. unabr. ed. Robert J. Rotella et al. 3 cass. 39.95 (S1820) J Norton Pubs.
Discusses & explains how golfers can compete better & win more by following certain strategies to mental readiness.

Mind Power to Reach Your Goals & Dreams, Vol. 16. Jonathan Parker. 2 cass. (Running Time: 1 hr. 45 min.). 1992. 17.00 (978-1-58400-015-0(5)) QuantumQuests Intl.

Mind, Prana & Mother Shakti. Swami Amar Jyoti. 1 cass. 1990. 9.95 (K-121) Truth Consciousness.
Greatness & benevolence of Divine Mother: "See if you can find Her, touch Her; She will be always present".

Mind Prey. John Sandford, pseud. Read by John Shea. (Prey Ser.). 2004. 10.95 (978-0-7435-4137-4(5)) Pub: S&S Audio. Dist(s): S and S Inc

Mind Prey. John Sandford, pseud. Read by John Shea. (Running Time: 30 hrs. 0 mins. 0 sec.). (ENG.). 2003. audio compact disk 9.95 (978-0-7435-3276-1(7), S&S Encore) Pub: S&S Audio. Dist(s): S and S Inc
John Sandford's acclaimed Prey novels featuring the brilliant Lucas Davenport have plunged millions of readers into the darkest recesses of the criminal mind. Now Lucas has met his match. His newest nemesis is more intelligent, more deadly, than any he has tracked before: a kidnapper, a violator, and a cruel, wanton killer who knows more about mind games than Lucas himself.

Mind Prey, unabr. ed. Ed. by John Sandford, pseud. Narrated by Richard Ferrone. 9 cass. (Running Time: 12 hrs. 30 mins.). (Prey Ser.). 1995. 78.00 (978-0-7887-0387-4(0), 94578K8) Recorded Bks.
When a brutal kidnapper nabs a therapist & her two young daughters, Deputy Chief Davenport begins to feel like a character in one of his computer games. He must figure out clues to the kidnapper's identity before he can find where he is holding his prey.

Mind Prey. unabr. ed. Ed. by John Sandford, pseud. Narrated by Richard Ferrone. 11 CDs. (Running Time: 12 hrs. 30 mins.). (Prey Ser.). 2000. audio compact disk 96.00 (978-0-7887-3403-8(2), C1009E7) Recorded Bks.

Mind Reading: An Interactive Guide to Emotions. Cd Rom. (YA). 2004. audio compact disk 129.95 (978-1-932565-14-0(0)) Fut Horizons.

Mind Robber. unabr. ed. Peter Ling. Narrated by Derek Jacobi. (Running Time: 6 hrs. 0 mins. 0 sec.). (ENG.). 2010. audio compact disk 39.95 (978-1-60283-825-3(9)) Pub: AudioGO. Dist(s): Perseus Dist

***Mind Set!** abr. ed. John Naisbitt. Read by Eric Conger. (ENG.). 2006. (978-0-06-123035-6(9), Harper Audio); (978-0-06-123036-3(7), Harper Audio) HarperCollins Pubs.

Mind Set! Reset Your Thinking & See the Future. abr. ed. John Naisbitt. Read by Eric Conger. (Running Time: 12600 sec.). 2006. audio compact disk 22.95 (978-0-06-114262-8(X)) HarperCollins Pubs.

***Mind the Gap.** Featuring Ravi Zacharias. 2005. audio compact disk 9.00 (978-1-61256-061-8(X)) Ravi Zach.

Mind to Murder. unabr. ed. P. D. James. Read by Penelope Dellaporta. 7 cass. (Running Time: 10 hrs. 30 min.). (Adam Dalgliesh Mystery Ser.). 1993. 56.00 (978-0-7366-2396-4(5), 3165) Books on Tape.
Psychiatric clinic's head dies with a chisel driven through her heart. Superintendent Adam Dalgliesh gets the call.

Mind to Murder. unabr. ed. P. D. James. Read by Roy Marsden. 6 cass. (Running Time: 9 hrs.). (Adam Dalgliesh Mystery Ser.). 2000. 49.95 (978-0-7451-6062-7(X), CAB 131) Pub: Chivers Audio Bks GBR. Dist(s): AudioGO
A call from Scotland Yard to investigate a brutal murder interrupts Superintendent Adam Dalgliesh from his publishers' annual sherry party. In the elegant Steen Psychiatric Clinic, which caters to the upper-class, sprawled the body of Enid Bolam - a chisel through her heart. It was a vicious, calculated thrust, suggesting that the killer had confident knowledge of anatomy and unusual strength. It's now up to Dalgliesh to find the killer.

Mind Travel: Radical Ways to Use Your Mind for Healing, Improving Relationships & Inner Calm. unabr. ed. Dick Sutphen. 6 cass. (Running Time: 9 hrs.). 2000. pap. bk. & suppl. ed. 59.95 (978-1-55525-012-6(2), 19610a) Nightingale-Conant.
Takes you on an amazing journey into the unexplored realms of perception that exist all around you.

Mind Tripping: How to Use Your Head to Reduce Your Body. Frances M. Stern. Read by Frances Meritt Stern. 1 cass. (Running Time: 58 min.). 1975. 12.95 (978-1-884435-07-2(6)) Inst Behavior.
Techniques for weight reduction.

Mind Wide Open: Your Brain & the Neuroscience of Everyday Life. unabr. ed. Steven Johnson. Narrated by Alan Sklar. (Running Time: 8 hrs. 9 mins. 0 sec.). (ENG.). 2004. audio compact disk 59.99 (978-1-4001-3116-7(2)); audio compact disk 19.99 (978-1-4001-5116-5(3)); audio compact disk 29.99 (978-1-4001-0116-0(6)) Pub: Tantor Media. Dist(s): IngramPubServ

Mind Your Health. Betty L. Randolph. Read by Betty L. Randolph. Read by Leonard Baron. Ed. by Success Education Institute International Staff. 1 cass. (Health Ser.). 1989. bk. 14.98 Ocean Format. (978-1-55909-250-0(5), 380P); bk. Music Format. (380PM) Randolph Tapes.
Features 60,000 messages with the left-right brain.

Mind Your Own Business. Murray Raphel. 4 cass. 39.95 (01-03MRM) Nat Grocers Assn.
Includes: I'm Gonna Sit Right down & Write Myself a Letter; Quest to Be Best; The Headline Book; & Five Ways Advertising Works.

Mind Your Weight. Ormond McGill. 1 cass. 2000. (978-1-933332-06-2(9)) Hypnotherapy Train.

Mindbend. unabr. ed. Robin Cook. Read by Donada Peters. 6 cass. (Running Time: 9 hrs.). 1993. 48.00 (978-0-7366-2397-1(3), 3166) Books on Tape.
Man questions his drug firm employer & their clinic when his wife's pregnancy goes wrong.

Mindful Brain. Daniel J. Siegel. 2008. audio compact disk 29.95 (978-1-59179-952-8(X)) Sounds True.

***Mindful Eating: How to Change the Habits That Sabotage Your Health.** Mary Ann Wallace. (ENG.). 2009. pap. bk. 19.95 (978-1-59299-445-8(8)) Inkwater.

Mindful Leader: Ten Principles for Bringing Out the Best in Ourselves & Others. abr. ed. Michael Carroll. Read by Michael Carroll. 2007. 39.99 (978-1-60252-809-3(8)) Find a World.

Mindful Living. Thich Nhat Hanh. 5 cass. (Running Time: 7 hrs.). 2003. 40.00 (56263) Parallax Pr.

Mindful Living. unabr. ed. Gary Arnold. 1 cass. (Running Time: 1 hr.). 1997. pap. bk. 12.95 (978-1-57867-096-3(9)) Windhorse Corp.
Experience quantum transformation beyond traditional ideas of achievement & success.

Mindful Meditation: Cultivating the Wisdom of Your Body & Mind. Jon Kabat-Zinn. 6 cass. (Running Time: 6 hrs.). 1995. 59.95 incls. pamphlet & bonus cass. (978-1-55525-059-1(9), 12330A) Nightingale-Conant.
This insightful program offers a unique, exhilarating & powerful approach that can add new levels of depth, meaning & color to your life. Cultivating mindfulness can help you access deep states of inner calmness & stillness...while turning life's trials into a source of inner strength, wisdom, kindness & self-acceptance.

Mindful of You the Sodden Earth in Spring see Poetry of Edna St. Vincent Millay

Mindful Way Through Depression: Freeing Yourself from Chronic Unhappiness. abr. ed. Jon Kabat-Zinn et al. 4 CDs. (Running Time: 5 hrs.). 2008. audio compact disk 29.95 (978-1-59179-665-7(2)) Sounds True.

Mindfulness. rev. unabr. ed. Ellen J. Langer. Read by Bernadette Dunne. 5 CDs. (Running Time: 6 hrs.). (ENG.). 2008. audio compact disk 29.98 (978-1-59659-136-3(6)) Pub: Gildan Media. Dist(s): HachBkGrp

Mindfulness @ Work: A Leading with Emotional Intelligence Conversation with Jon Kabat-Zinn. unabr. ed. Daniel Goleman & Jon Kabat-Zinn. (Running Time: 1 hr. 0 mins. 0 sec.). (ENG.). 2007. audio compact disk 14.95 (978-1-4272-0067-9(X)) Pub: Macmill Audio. Dist(s): Macmillan

Mindfulness & Awareness. Read by Chogyam Trungpa. 3 cass. 1974. 29.50 (A006) Vajradhatu.
Three talks. This seminar lays the ground for an understanding of the Buddhist practice of meditation & the attitude towards enlightenment.

Mindfulness & Awareness, NYC. Vajracarya. 3 cass. 1974. 27.00 Vajradhatu.
A three talk seminar that lays the ground work for a fundamental understanding of the Buddhist practice of meditation & the attitude towards enlightenment.

Mindfulness & Psychotherapy. Thich Nhat Hanh. 2 cass. (Running Time: 180 min.). 2003. 19.00 (56328) Parallax Pr.
This breakthrough workshop, designed especially for psychotherapists, teaches how to find and nourish an inner peacefulness and maintain it throughout the day - no matter what your caseload is.

Mindfulness & Psychotherapy. unabr. ed. Thich Nhat Hanh. 3 CDs. (Running Time: 9900 sec.). 2006. audio compact disk 24.95 (978-1-59179-436-3(6), AW00103D) Sounds True.

***Mindfulness & the Brain: A Professional Training in the Science & Practice of Meditative Awareness.** Jack Kornfield & Daniel J. Siegel. (Running Time: 6:00:00). 2010. audio compact disk 69.95 (978-1-59179-774-6(8)) Sounds True.

Mindfulness for Beginners. Jon Kabat-Zinn. Read by Jon Kabat-Zinn. (Playaway Adult Nonfiction Ser.). (ENG.). 2009. 39.99 (978-1-60812-775-7(3)) Find a World.

Mindfulness for Beginners. Jon Kabat-Zinn. (Running Time: 8100 sec.). 2006. audio compact disk 19.95 (978-1-59179-464-6(1)) Sounds True.

Mindfulness Meditation: Cultivating the Wisdom of Your Body & Mind. abr. ed. Jon Kabat-Zinn. 2 CDs. (Running Time: 20 hrs. 0 mins. 0 sec.). (ENG.). 2002. audio compact disk 20.00 (978-0-7435-2068-3(8), Nightgale) Pub: S&S Audio. Dist(s): S and S Inc
Offers an inside look at how you can raise your awareness level for maximum personal and professional achievement.

Mindfulness Meditation for Pain Relief: Guided Practices for Reclaiming Your Body & Your Life. Jon Kabat-Zinn. (Running Time: 1:55:49). 2009. audio compact disk 19.95 (978-1-59179-740-1(3)) Sounds True.

Mindfulness Meditation in Everyday Life. Jon Kabat-Zinn. 2 cass. (Running Time: 1 hr. 30 min.). 1994. 16.95 (978-1-879323-33-9(8)) Sound Horizons AV.

Mindfulness Meditation Workshop: Exercises & Meditations. Jon Kabat-Zinn. 4 cass. 1995. 24.95 (978-1-879323-34-6(6)) Sound Horizons AV.
Listeners are guided by the best-selling author of "Wherever You Go, There You Are" through gentle meditation techniques & stimulating exercises designed to create spiritual attunement & mindful behavior.

Mindfulness Practice with Marsha Linehan Vol. 1: From Suffering to Freedom Through Acceptance. Featuring Marsha M. Linehan. 2 CDs. 2002. audio compact disk 15.95 (978-0-9710837-1-4(1)) Behavioral Tech.
Marsha guides listeners through 10 mindfulness practices, including: Awareness Will Set You Free, Just This Breath, and Watching Your Mind. Each track includes a Description of the exercise followed by 5 minutes of silent practice time. Marsha rings a bell three times when you're to start each practice, and once again to conclude. This is a 2-CD volume.

Mindfulness Practice with Marsha Linehan, Vol. 2 **see Walking Like Buffalo: Reflections on Mindfulness & DBT**

Mindhunter: Inside the FBI's Elite Serial Crime Unit. John E. Douglas. 2004. 10.95 (978-0-7435-4138-1(3)) Pub: S&S Audio. Dist(s): S and S Inc

Mindhunter: Inside the FBI's Elite Serial Crime Unit. abr. ed. John Douglas & Mark Olshaker. 2 cass. 14.95 Set. (53604) Books on Tape.
Here's a behind-the-scenes look at the most famous murder cases in history. You'll learn what makes a serial killer tick.

Mindhunter: Inside the FBI's Elite Serial Crime Unit. unabr. ed. John Douglas. Narrated by Richard M. Davidson. 11 cass. (Running Time: 15 hrs. 15 mins.). 1996. 91.00 (978-0-7887-0626-4(8), 94800E7) Recorded Bks.
For 25 years, John Douglas & his FBI colleagues pursued notorious & sadistic serial killers. Douglas creates surprisingly accurate profiles by examining each crime scene & portraying both the killer's & the victim's actions in his mind. Chilling, at times grisly, but always insightful & inspired, this recounts Douglas' legendary career.

***Minding Frankie.** abr. ed. Maeve Binchy. (ENG.). 2011. audio compact disk 30.00 (978-0-307-71360-5(1), Random AudioBks) Pub: Random Audio Pubg. Dist(s): Random

Minding the Body, Mending the Mind. Joan Z. Borysenko. 5 CDs. 2005. audio compact disk 23.95 (978-1-4019-0440-1(8)) Hay House.

Minding the Body, Mending the Mind. unabr. rev. ed. Joan Borysenko. Read by Joan Borysenko. 5 CDs. (Running Time: 8 hrs. 30 mins.). (ENG.). 2009. audio compact disk 29.98 (978-1-59659-217-9(6)) Pub: Gildan Media. Dist(s): HachBkGrp

Minding the Body, Mending the Mind, Set. unabr. ed. Joan Borysenko. Read by Joan Borysenko. 5 cass. (Running Time: 7 hrs.). 1995. 25.00 (978-1-56170-107-0(6), 313) Hay House.
Dr. Borysenko shows how you can take an active role in healing yourself.

Minding the Soul. 1 cass. (Care Cassettes Ser.: Vol. 20, No. 5). 1993. 10.80 Assn Prof Chaplains.

Mindless. unabr. ed. Joe Bright. Read by Ron Varela. 12 cass. (Running Time: 12 hrs. 18 min.). 2001. 64.95 (978-1-55686-927-3(4)) Books in Motion.
Dave Tschanz, an average 29 year-old working man, unknowingly becomes a subject in a breakthrough experiment when an elderly scientist successfully changes his mentality and talents to an intellectual.

Mindless Eating: Why We Eat More Than We Think. abr. ed. Brian Wansink. Read by Brian Wansink. (Running Time: 19800 sec.). (ENG.). 2006. audio compact disk 29.95 (978-0-7393-4037-0(9), Random AudioBks) Pub: Random Audio Pubg. Dist(s): Random

Mindlessness & Mindfulness. unabr. ed. Charles Tart. 1 cass. (Running Time: 1 hr. 29 min.). 1988. 11.00 (05204) Big Sur Tapes.
Discusses antidotes to mindlessness & the "consensus trance" of ordinary consciousness, drawing from Gurdjieff's Self-Remembering practice & Buddhist methods of developing concentration & insight.

Mindlessness, Mindfulness, Meditation & the Psychopathology of Everyday Life. unabr. ed. Charles Tart. 2 cass. 1988. 18.00 (978-1-56964-803-2(4), A0275-88) Sound Photosyn.
A fascinating look at possibilities of release from cultural hypnotism.

Mind's Eye. Perf. by James Reynolds. 1 cass. 9.98 (MPC2901); audio compact disk 14.98 Miramar Images.
Progressive & driving at times, soft & melodic during others. This music was inspired by the computer animated video album of the same name.

***Mind's Eye.** unabr. ed. Oliver Sacks. Read by Oliver Sacks. Read by Richard Davidson. (Running Time: 8 hrs. 30 mins.). 2010. audio compact disk 35.00 (978-0-7393-8391-9(4), Random AudioBks) Pub: Random Audio Pubg. Dist(s): Random

Mind's Sky: Human Intelligence in a Cosmic Context. abr. unabr. ed. Timothy Ferris. Read by Timothy Ferris. 4 cass. (Running Time: 6 hrs.). 2004. 25.00 (978-1-931056-21-2(8), N Millennium Audio) New Millenn Enter.
Timothy Ferris explores inner as well as outer space in these essays on the human mind, the search for extraterrestrial intelligence & their intersection. Other chapters look at near-death experience; apocalyptic prophecies.

Mind's Window. 1 cass. (Running Time: 1 hr.). 10.95 (OP-76-10-08, HarperThor) HarpC GBR.

Mindset: The New Psychology of Success. unabr. ed. Carol Dweck. Read by Marguerite Gavin. (Running Time: 8 hrs. 30 mins.). (ENG.). 2009. 24.98 (978-1-59659-371-8(7), GildAudio) Pub: Gildan Media. Dist(s): HachBkGrp

Mindset of a Champion. David L. Cook. (ENG.). 2004. audio compact disk 34.95 (978-0-9742650-2-5(0)) Sacred Story.

MindShift: The Steve Chandler Success Course. Steve Chandler. Read by Steve Chandler. (ENG.). 2008. audio compact disk 249.00 (978-1-60025-086-6(0)) M Bassett.

Mindsight: The New Science of Personal Transformation. unabr. ed. Daniel J. Siegel. Read by Daniel J. Siegel. (Running Time: 11 hrs.). 2010. 24.99 (978-1-4418-0783-0(7), 9781441807830, BAD); 24.99 (978-1-4418-0781-6(0), 9781441807816, Brilliance MP3); 39.97 (978-1-4418-0782-3(9), 9781441807823, Brlnc Audio MP3 Lib); 39.97 (978-1-4418-0784-7(5), 9781441807847, BADLE); audio compact disk 29.99 (978-1-4418-0779-3(9), 9781441807793, Bril Audio CD Unabri); audio compact disk 92.97 (978-1-4418-0780-9(2), 9781441807809, BriAudCD Unabrid) Brilliance Audio.

Mindsurfing Basics: The Cool New Way to Higher Awareness. unabr. ed. Johnny Rockit et al. Read by Johnny Rockit et al. 1 cass. (Running Time: 1 hr.). (Mindsurfing Ser.). 1998. 14.99 (978-1-892654-15-1(6)) FutureLife.
Explains techniques for increasing a person's mental clarity & acuity.

***Mindswap.** unabr. ed. Robert Sheckley. Read by Tom Weiner. (Running Time: 7 hrs. 30 mins.). 2010. 29.95 (978-1-4417-3650-5(6)); 54.95 (978-1-4417-3646-8(8)); audio compact disk 69.00 (978-1-4417-3647-5(6)) Blckstn Audio.

MindWalks with Music: Audio Walks to Relieve Stress, Stay Motivated & Nourish Your Soul. Mary H. Frakes. 1 cass. (Running Time: 1 hr.). (MindPaths Ser.). 1999. 9.95 (978-0-9667879-3-1(5)) Life Lessons.
Four narrated segments with musical interludes let users tailor a walk to fit their mood & use it to motivate, relax or energize themselves.

MindWorks for Children: Guided Imagery & Relaxation Journeys. unabr. ed. Roxanne E. Daleo. Read by Roxanne E. Daleo. 4 cass. (Running Time: 2 hrs. 4 min.). (MindWorks for Children Ser.). (J). (ps-6). 1988. 44.95 (978-1-889447-10-0(2)) Mindwrks Chldrn.
Designed to give children skills they need to relax body & mind, develop self-confidence & a healthy mental attitude, improve concentration & problem solving abilities & stimulate creativity.

Mine Be a Cot Beside the Hill see Palgrave's Golden Treasury of English Poetry

***Mine Is the Night: A Novel.** unabr. ed. Liz Curtis Higgs. Read by Liz Curtis Higgs. (ENG.). 2011. audio compact disk 35.00 (978-0-307-74740-2(9), Random AudioBks) Pub: Random Audio Pubg. Dist(s): Random

Mine till Midnight. abr. ed. Lisa Kleypas. Read by Rosalyn Landor. (Running Time: 5 hrs.). (Hathaways Ser.: No. 1). 2009. audio compact disk 24.99 (978-1-4418-0719-9(5), 9781441807199, BACD) Brilliance Audio.

Mine till Midnight. unabr. ed. Lisa Kleypas. Read by Rosalyn Landor. (Running Time: 10 hrs.). (Hathaways Ser.: No. 1). 2009. 24.99 (978-1-4233-8988-0(3), 9781423389880, Brilliance MP3); 24.99 (978-1-4233-8990-3(5), 9781423389903, BAD); 39.97 (978-1-4233-8989-7(1), 9781423389897, Brlnc Audio MP3 Lib); 39.97 (978-1-4233-8991-0(3), 9781423389910, BADLE); audio compact disk 29.99 (978-1-4233-8986-6(7), 9781423389866, Bril Audio CD Unabri); audio compact disk 92.97 (978-1-4233-8987-3(5), 9781423389873, BriAudCD Unabrid) Brilliance Audio.

Mineral Palace. unabr. ed. Heidi Julavits. Read by Susan Ericksen. 7 cass. (Running Time: 10 hrs.). 2000. 32.95 (978-1-56740-389-3(1), 1567403891, BAU); 73.25 (978-1-56740-991-8(1), 1567409911, Unabridge Lib Edns) Brilliance Audio.
In a bold debut novel of the Great Depression, a young doctor's wife uncovers the sordid secrets of a withering Colorado mining town, even as she struggles with the ravaging truths about her marriage and her child. In the drought-ridden spring of 1934, Bena Jonnsen, her husband Ted, and their newborn baby relocate from their home in Minnesota to Pueblo, a Western plains town plagued by suffocating dust storms and equally suffocating social structures. Little can thrive in this bleak environment, neither Bena and Ted's marriage nor the baby, whom Bena believes - despite her husband's constant assurances - is slipping away from her. To distract herself from worrying, Bena accepts a part-time position at Pueblo's daily newspaper, The Chieftain, reporting on the "good works" of the town's elite Ladies' Club leaders, women such as Reimer Lee Jackson and her plans to restore the town's crumbling monument tot he mining industry - the Mineral Palace - to its turn-of-the-century grandeur. Bena is drawn to the Mineral Palace and to the lurid hallways of Pueblo's brothel, befriending a prostitute, Maude, and Red, a reticent cowpoke. Through these new emotional entanglements, Bena slowly exposes not only the sexual corruption on which the entire town is founded, but also the lies enclosing her own marriage and the sanctity of motherhood. She returns again and again to the decaying architecture of the Mineral Palace; within its eroding walls she is forced to confront her most terrifying secret, which becomes her only means for salvation. With her gritty and magical prose, Heidi Julavits elegantly examines the darker side of paternity and maternity, as well as the intersection of parental love and merciful destruction. The Mineral Palace is a startling and authentic story of survival in a world of decadence and depravity.

Mineral Palace. unabr. ed. Heidi Julavits. Read by Susan Ericksen. (Running Time: 10 hrs.). 2005. 39.25 (978-1-59600-658-4(7), 9781596006584, BADLE); 24.95 (978-1-59600-657-7(9), 9781596006577, BAD); audio compact disk 39.25 (978-1-59600-656-0(0), 9781596006560, Brlnc Audio MP3 Lib); audio compact disk 24.95 (978-1-59600-655-3(2), 9781596006553, Brilliance MP3) Brilliance Audio.

Mineral Water in Bedrooms of Foreign Hotels see J. B. Priestley

Minerals. Compiled by Benchmark Education Staff. 2006. audio compact disk 10.00 (978-1-4108-6684-4(X)) Benchmark Educ.

Minerat of Djam & Perseus in the Wind. unabr. ed. Freya Stark. Read by Donada Peters. 8 cass. (Running Time: 8 hrs.). 1970. 48.00 (2876); Rental 9.95 (2876) Books on Tape.
An excursion through Afghanistan by this century's finest traveler-historian.

Miners. Rick Steber. Illus. by Don Gray. 1 cass. (Tales of the Wild West Ser.: Vol. 9). 1990. pap. bk. 9.95 (978-0-945134-59-6(2)) Bonanza Pub.

Minerva Holmes in the Case of the Golden Key. unabr. ed. Ian McTavish. Ed. by Kenneth Thomas. 1 cass. (Running Time: 1 hr. 30 min.). Dramatization. (Adventures of Sherlock Holmes' Daughter Ser.). (YA). (gr. 7 up). 1994. 11.00 (978-1-884262-00-5(7), IGA53219) IDA Games.
17 episodes of Minerva Holmes, Sherlock Holmes daughter.

Minerva Lane. unabr. ed. Judith Glover. Read by Margaret Sircom. 7 cass. (Running Time: 9 hrs. 15 mins.). 1999. 76.95 (978-1-85903-265-7(6)) Pub: Magna Story GBR. Dist(s): Ulverscroft US
Wolverhampton, 1885. After Lizzie Gallimore marries handsome Jack McShane, her young daughter Ruby is drawn to the experienced older man. A traumatic event reveals Jack in his true colours & Ruby realizes that he has been playing with both her own & her mother's happiness. Seeking independence, she finds different & dubious means of earning money to support her epileptic younger brother. When Lizzie dies, the truth emerges. Ruby must fight to save her brother from Jack's clutches & to win back the one man who ever truly loved her.

Minerva's Dream/Gail Devers. Steck-Vaughn Staff. 1997. (978-0-8172-7381-1(6)) SteckVau.

Mines of King Salomon see Minas Del Rey Salomón

Mines of King Salomon. H. Rider Haggard. Read by Carlos J. Vega. (Running Time: 3 hrs.). 2002. 16.95 (978-1-60083-207-9(5), Audiofy Corp) Iofy Corp.

***Mine's the Best.** unabr. ed. Crosby Bonsall. (ENG.). 2008. (978-0-06-169478-3(9)); (978-0-06-171006-3(7)) HarperCollins Pubs.

Ming Lo Moves the Mountain. Arnold Lobel. Read by Lionel Wilson & Jean Richards. 1 cass. (J). 1986. 5.95 Scholastic Inc.
Includes book.

Ming Lo Moves the Mountain. Arnold Lobel. 1 cass. (Running Time: 15 min.). (J). (gr. k-3). 2001. pap. bk. 16.90 (978-0-8045-6846-3(4), 6846) Spoken Arts.
When Ming Lo's wife insists that he move the mountain that is damaging their house, he seeks the advice of the village wise man.

Mini-Masterpieces of Science Fiction. Stephen Baxter et al. Ed. by Allan Kaster. Narrated by Vanessa Hart & Tom Dheere. (ENG.). 2008. audio compact disk 23.99 (978-1-884612-79-4(2)) AudioText.

Mini-Module, No. MS1: Skillbuilding in Medicine-Surgery. Ed. by American Association for Medical Transcription Staff. 1 cass. (Running Time: 30 min.). (Exploring Transcription Practices Ser.). (C). 1993. bk. & stu. ed. 30.00 (978-0-935229-18-9(3)) Am Assoc Med.
For skillbuilding or classroom. Includes transcripts.

Mini-Module, No. MS3: Skillbuilding in Medicine-Surgery. Ed. by American Association for Medical Transcription Staff. 1 cass. (Running Time: 30 min.). (Exploring Transcription Practices Ser.). (C). 1995. bk. & stu. ed. 30.00 (978-0-935229-26-4(4)) Am Assoc Med.
Physician dictation with transcripts; for skillbuilding/classroom use.

Mini-Module, No. R1: Skillbuilding in Radiology. Ed. by American Association for Medical Transcription Staff. 1 cass. (Running Time: 30 min.). (Exploring Transcription Practices Ser.). (C). 1993. bk. & stu. ed. 30.00 (978-0-935229-19-6(1)) Am Assoc Med.

Mini-Module, No. R2: Skillbuilding in Radiology. Ed. by American Association for Medical Transcription Staff. 1 cass. (Running Time: 30 min.). (Exploring Transcription Practices Ser.). (C). 1994. bk. & stu. ed. 30.00 (978-0-935229-24-0(8)) Am Assoc Med.

***Mini Shopaholic.** abr. ed. Sophie Kinsella, pseud. Read by Rosalyn Landor. 2010. audio compact disk 30.00 (978-0-7393-8326-1(4), Random AudioBks) Pub: Random Audio Pubg. Dist(s): Random

***Miniature.** 2010. audio compact disk (978-1-59171-240-4(8)) Falcon Picture.

Miniature Murder Mystery. unabr. ed. Peter Chambers. Read by John Keyworth. 3 cass. (Running Time: 4 hrs. 30 min.). (Sound Ser.). 1993. 34.95 (978-1-85496-038-2(5), 60385) Pub: UlverLrgPrint GBR. Dist(s): Ulverscroft US
Honoria Lockhart's death was termed "accidental", & besides there was no reason why anyone should want to murder her. Her younger husband had nothing to gain, & the only other relative was an older sister. But the next death was murder, & the wrong people would suffer unless Mark Preston solved the puzzle.

MiniBike Mystery. unabr. ed. Gutman & Steve Johnson. 1 cass. (Running Time: 20 min.). (Adventure Abounds Ser.). (J). (gr. 3-6). 1984. bk. 16.99 (978-0-934898-67-6(7)); pap. bk. 9.95 (978-0-934898-76-8(6)) Jan Prods.
Their excitement & anticipation of the upcoming bike race are brought to a sharp halt when two young entrants find that their bike is missing.

Minimally Invasive Surgery. Contrib. by Keith Georgeson et al. 1 cass. (American Academy of Pediatrics UPDATE: Vol. 16, No. 4). 1998. 20.00 Am Acad Pediat.

Minimum Design Loads for Buildings & Other Structures: SEI/ASCE 7-02. (SEI/ASCE Standard Ser.: No. 7-02). 2003. audio compact disk 108.00 (978-0-7844-0667-0(7), 40667) Am Soc Civil Eng.

Minimum of Two. unabr. ed. Tim Winton. Read by Stig Wemyss. 4 cass. (Running Time: 3 hrs. 45 mins.). 2001. 32.00 (978-1-74030-351-4(2)) Pub: Bolinda Pubng AUS. Dist(s): Bolinda Pub Inc

Minimum of Two. unabr. ed. Tim Winton. Read by Stig Wemyss. 4 CDs. (Running Time: 3 hrs. 45 mins.). 2002. audio compact disk 57.95 (978-1-74030-896-0(4)) Pub: Bolinda Pubng AUS. Dist(s): Bolinda Pub Inc

Minimum Wages & Poverty: An Evaluation of Policy Alternatives. Ed. by J. P. Formby et al. 2005. 128.95 (978-0-444-52029-6(5)) Pub: E G Pubng GBR. Dist(s): TurpinDistUSA

Minimus: Starting Out in Latin. Barbara Bell. 1 cass. (Running Time: 90 mins.). (Minimus Ser.). (LAT & ENG.). 2002. 23.00 (978-0-521-00511-1(6)) Cambridge U Pr.

Minimus: Starting Out in Latin. abr. ed. Barbara Bell. (Minimus Ser.). (ENG.). 2006. audio compact disk 23.00 (978-0-521-68146-9(4)) Cambridge U Pr.

Minimus Secundus: Moving on in Latin. Barbara Bell. (Minimus Ser.). (ENG.). 2004. 23.00 (978-0-521-75547-4(6)) Cambridge U Pr.

Minimus Secundus: Moving on in Latin. abr. ed. Barbara Bell. (Minimus Ser.). (ENG.). 2006. audio compact disk 23.00 (978-0-521-68147-6(2)) Cambridge U Pr.

Minister & His Family (2001) 12 cass. 2001. 40.00 (978-1-59128-370-6(1)) Canon Pr ID.

Minister & Mission Conference. Featuring Bill Winston. 5. 2004. 25.00 (978-1-59544-011-2(9)); 60.00 (978-1-59544-012-9(7)) Pub: B Winston Min. Dist(s): Anchor Distributors

Minister As Negotiator. Wesley Monfalcone. 1986. 10.80 (0201B) Assn Prof Chaplains.

Minister Everyone Would Respect: A Study of 2 Corinthians 8-13. 2001. 34.95 (978-1-57972-374-3(8)) Insight Living.

Minister of Others Affairs. Jay O'Callahan. Perf. by Jay O'Callahan. 1 cass. (Running Time: 53 min.). (J). (gr. 2 up). 1984. bk. 10.00 (978-1-877954-03-0(9)) Artana Prodns.
Politics in the magical land of Artana. Wildly funny for kids and adults.

Ministering Angel. unabr. ed. Anthea Cohen. Read by Julia Sands. 5 cass. (Storysound Ser.). (J). 2001. 49.95 (978-1-85903-421-7(7)) Pub: Mgna Lrg Print GBR. Dist(s): Ulverscroft US

Ministering Angels. Kenneth Copeland. 1 cass. 1986. 5.00 (978-0-88114-755-1(9)) K Copeland Pubns.
Biblical teaching on ministering angels.

Ministering Healing. Tim N. Enloe. 2006. audio compact disk 17.99 (978-0-9749739-9-9(8)) E M Pubns.

Ministering in the Marketplace. 1 cass. (Care Cassettes Ser.: Vol. 10, No. 7). 1983. 10.80 Assn Prof Chaplains.

Ministering (Side 1); Dharmic Principles & the Messiah (Side 2) Jonathan Murro. 1 cass. 1990. 7.95 A R Colton Fnd.
Lectures by Jonathan Murro, a teacher of the Higher Life for nearly 40 years.

Ministering to Abortion's Aftermath. unabr. ed. William D. Banks. Read by William D. Banks. 3 cass. (Running Time: 3 hrs. 30 min.). 1990. 19.95 (978-0-89228-107-7(3)) Impact Christian.
Contains a message that UPI says should be in every home to give hope to those who had abortions.

Ministering to Minority Groups. 1 cass. (Care Cassettes Ser.: Vol. 10, No. 1). 1983. 10.80 Assn Prof Chaplains.

Ministering to the Brokenhearted. Kenneth W. Hagin, Jr. 3 cass.Tr. of Ministrando los Quebrantados De Corazon. 1995. 12.00 (32J) Faith Lib Pubns.

Ministering to the Lord. Kenneth E. Hagin. 4 cass. 16.00 (33H) Faith Lib Pubns.

Ministering to the Sexual Concerns of the Ostomy Patient. Kenneth Reed et al. 1986. 10.80 (0402) Assn Prof Chaplains.

Ministerio, Dinero, y Trabajo... Que Dice Dios? Palemon Camu. 6 cass. (SPA.). 2003. 29.99 (978-0-89985-407-6(9)); audio compact disk 35.00 (978-0-89985-406-9(0)) Christ for the Nations.

Ministers & Missions. Featuring Bill Winston. 7 cass. 2006. 25.00 (978-1-59544-124-9(7)); audio compact disk 40.00 (978-1-59544-125-6(5)) Pub: B Winston Min. Dist(s): Anchor Distributors

Ministers & Missions Conference: Workshop. Featuring Bill Winston. 9 cass. 2006. 45.00 (978-1-59544-178-2(6)) Pub: B Winston Min. Dist(s): Anchor Distributors

Ministers & Missions Conference 2003. Hosted by Bill Winston. 13 cass. (Running Time: 17hr.57min.). (C). 2003. 45.00 (978-1-931289-30-6(1)) Pub: B Winston Min. Dist(s): Anchor Distributors

Minister's Black Veil see Great American Short Stories

Minister's Black Veil. Nathaniel Hawthorne. 10.00 (LSS1104) Esstee Audios.

Minister's Black Veil. unabr. ed. Nathaniel Hawthorne. Read by Walter Zimmerman & John Chatty. 1 cass. (Running Time: 1 hr. 22 min.). Dramatization. 1980. 7.95 (N-34) Jimcin Record.
Famous stories of hidden evil.

Minister's Black Veil. unabr. ed. Nathaniel Hawthorne. 10.95 (7029) Spoken Arts.

Ministers Compensation Pkg Aud. B. J. Worth. (Running Time: 1 hr.). 2004. reel tape 10.99 (978-1-928915-41-6(8)) Evangel Pub Hse.

Minister's Daughter. unabr. ed. Julie Hearn. Read by Heather O'Neill. 5 cass. (Running Time: 7 hrs.). (YA). 2005. 40.00 (978-0-307-24599-1(3), Listening Lib); audio compact disk 55.00 (978-0-307-24625-7(6), Listening Lib) Pub: Random Audio Pubg. Dist(s): Random

Minister's Mental Health. Joe Abbott. 1986. 10.80 (0305A) Assn Prof Chaplains.

Ministrando los Quebrantados De Corazon see Ministering to the Brokenhearted

***Ministries of Mercy: The Call of the Jericho Road.** unabr. ed. Tim Keller. Narrated by Sean Runnette. (ENG.). 2010. 14.98 (978-1-59644-382-2(0), Hovel Audio) christianaud.

***Ministries of Mercy: The Call of the Jericho Road.** unabr. ed. Timothy J. Keller & Tim Keller. Narrated by Sean Runnette. (Running Time: 9 hrs. 30 mins. 0 sec.). (ENG.). 2010. audio compact disk 24.98 (978-1-59644-381-5(2), Hovel Audio) christianaud.

Ministries of the Holy Spirit. Derek Prince. 1 cass. (Running Time: 1 hr.). 1991. 5.95 (I-4329) Derek Prince.
The Holy Spirit, as Christ's personal representative, wishes to give believers supernatural gifts. What must you do to prepare to receive these gifts?.

Ministries of the Holy Spirit. Lester Sumrall. 16 cass. (Running Time: 24 hrs.). 1999. 64.00 (978-1-58568-050-4(8)) Sumrall Pubng.

Ministro al que Cualquiera puede Respetar. 2004. audio compact disk 42.00 (978-1-57972-615-7(1)) Insight Living.

Ministry & Human Sexuality. 1 cass. (Running Time: 1 hr. 30 min.). (Care Cassettes Ser.: Vol. 11, No. 6). 1984. 10.80 Assn Prof Chaplains.

Ministry Anyone Could Trust. 1998. 39.95 (978-1-57972-265-4(2)) Insight Living.

Ministry Anyone Could Trust: A Study of 2 Corinthians 1-7. 2001. 39.95 (978-1-57972-372-9(1)) Insight Living.

Ministry Essentials see Elementos Esencales del Ministerio

Ministry Essentials. Charles R. Swindoll. 1 cass. 1998. 20.95 (978-1-57972-239-5(3)) Insight Living.

Ministry Explosion: Putting the Layman to Work: National Association of Evangelicals, 47th Annual Convention, Columbus, Ohio, March 7-9,1989. L. Lynn Hood. 1 cass. (Running Time: 1 hr. 30 min.). (Workshops Ser.: No. 26-Thursda). 1989. 4.25; 36.00 Nat Assn Evan.

Ministry Gifts. Kenneth E. Hagin. 8 cass. 32.00 (14H) Faith Lib Pubns.

Ministry Gifts & His Church. Gary V. Whetstone. (New Testament Ser.). 1996. 80.00 (978-1-928774-93-8(8), NT203) Gary Whet Pub.

Ministry in the Emergency Room. Donald Thomas & Mary Bennett. 1986. 10.80 (0706) Assn Prof Chaplains.

Ministry Is a Many Peopled Thing: Church Growth Strategy That Works: Proceedings of the 45th Annual Convention National Association of Evangelicals Buffalo, New York. Read by James L. Nicodem. 1 cass. (Running Time: 1 hr.). 1987. 4.00 (323) Nat Assn Evan.

Ministry Kids on Drugs: When Love Isn't Enough, Set. John Vawter et al. 6 cass. 1999. vinyl bd. 39.95 (978-1-57052-155-3(7)) Chrch Grwth VA.
Conference for parents who are in Christian Ministry & whose child/children have substance abuse problems.

Ministry of Angels. Nathaniel Holcomb. 9 cass. (Running Time: 13 hrs. 30 mins.). 1988. (978-1-930918-20-7(8)) Its All About Him.

Ministry of Angels - Harvesting Generation. Bill Winston. 4 cass. (Running Time: 3hr.06min.). (C). 1999. 20.00 (978-1-931289-45-0(X)) Pub: B Winston Min. Dist(s): Anchor Distributors

Ministry of Archers. Contrib. by Joy Electric. 2005. audio compact disk 13.98 (978-5-558-87067-1(2)) Tooth & Nail.

Ministry of Healing. Ellen G. White. Narrated by Eric Martin. 13 CDs. 2004. audio compact disk 39.95 (978-1-883012-21-2(X)) Remnant Pubns.

Ministry of Intercession. Derek Prince. 1 cass. 5.95 (021) Derek Prince.
No higher or more powerful ministry is open to man, raising us to the realm of divine possibilities.

Ministry of Prayer: The Key to Building the Local Church. Mac Hammond. 1 cass. (Running Time: 1 hr). 2005. 5.00 (978-1-57399-207-7(0)) Mac Hammond.

Ministry of Serving. Gary V. Whetstone. Instructed by Gif Wilson. 4 cass. (Running Time: 6 hrs.). (Practics Ser.: PR103). 1996. pap. bk. 80.00 (978-1-58866-059-6(1), BR103 A00) Gary Whet Pub.
This course is designed to show the establishment of the Ministry of Helps through its application to situations.

Ministry of Special Cases. unabr. ed. Nathan Englander. Read by Arthur Morey. 12 CDs. (Running Time: 15 hrs.). 2007. audio compact disk 120.00 (978-1-4159-3642-9(0)); 100.00 (978-1-4159-3980-2(2)) Books on Tape.
From its unforgettable opening scene in the darkness of a forgotten cemetery in Buenos Aires, THE MINISTRY OF SPECIAL CASES casts a powerful spell. In the heart of Argentina's Dirty War, Kaddish Poznan struggles with a son who won't accept him; strives for a wife who forever saves him; and spends his nights protecting the good name of a community that denies his existence - and denies a checkered history that only Kaddish holds dear.

Ministry of the Holy Spirit. Taffi L. Dollar. 10.00 (978-1-59089-079-0(5)) Pub: Creflo Dollar. Dist(s): STL Dist NA

Ministry of the Holy Spirit, Vol. 2. Creflo A. Dollar. 25.00 (978-1-59089-081-3(7)) Pub: Creflo Dollar. Dist(s): STL Dist NA

Ministry of the Pastor Series. Rick Joyner. 2 cass. (Running Time: 3 hrs.). 2000. 10.00 (RJ08-000) Morning NC.
"The Mandates of the Pastoral Ministry" & "the Shepherd's Heart." This brief series gives a revolutionary understanding of this most misunderstood ministry.

Ministry of the Spirit in Acts, Chapters 1-9. Jack Deere. 1 cass. (Running Time: 1 hr. 30 min.). 2000. 5.00 (JD10-001) Morning NC.
An insightful study on the development of the early church & her dependence on the Holy Spirit, this series offers timely applications for our day.

Ministry of the Spirit in Acts, Chapters 10-19. Jack Deere. 1 cass. (Running Time: 1 hr. 30 min.). 2000. 5.00 (JD10-002) Morning NC.

Ministry of the Spirit in Acts, Chapters 20-23. Jack Deere. 1 cass. (Running Time: 1 hr. 30 min.). 2000. 5.00 (JD10-003) Morning NC.

Ministry of the Spirit in Acts, Chapters 24-28. Jack Deere. 1 cass. (Running Time: 1 hr. 30 min.). 2000. 5.00 (JD10-004) Morning NC.

Ministry of the Spirit in Acts Series. Jack Deere. 4 cass. (Running Time: 6 hrs.). 2000. 20.00 (JD10-000) Morning NC.

Ministry Potential Discerner Program: Fr. Lauerman & Panel Discussion. 1 cass. (National Meeting of the Institute, 1992 Ser.). 4.00 (92N4) IRL Chicago.

Ministry Staff Member: A Contemporary, Practical Handbook to Equip, Encourage, & Empower. unabr. ed. Douglas L. Fagerstrom. (Running Time: 11 hrs. 34 mins. 0 sec.). (ENG.). 2009. 19.99 (978-0-310-77163-0(3)) Zondervan.

Ministry to Clergy & Their Families. G. Lloyd Rediger. 1986. 10.80 (0806) Assn Prof Chaplains.

Ministry to Gays & Gays in Ministry. 1 cass. (Care Cassettes Ser.: Vol. 11, No. 9). 1984. 10.80 Assn Prof Chaplains.

Ministry to Parents of Chronically Ill Children. 1 cass. (Care Cassettes Ser.: Vol. 16, No. 3). 1989. 10.80 Assn Prof Chaplains.

Ministry to Patients with Personality Disorders. 1 cass. (Care Cassettes Ser.: Vol. 14, No. 1). 1987. 10.80 Assn Prof Chaplains.

Ministry to Survivors of Suicide. 1 cass. (Care Cassettes Ser.: Vol. 9, No. 9). 1982. 10.80 Assn Prof Chaplains.

Ministry to the Alcoholic. John McCann. 1986. 10.80 (0309) Assn Prof Chaplains.

Ministry to the Cancer Patient. Edward Mahnke et al. 1986. 10.80 (0502B) Assn Prof Chaplains.

Ministry to the Dying Patient. Leroy Joesten. 1986. 10.80 (0606) Assn Prof Chaplains.

Ministry to the Young Alcoholic. R. Patterson et al. 1986. 10.80 (0701) Assn Prof Chaplains.

Ministry to Unconscious Patients. A. L. Toews. 1986. 10.80 (0106A) Assn Prof Chaplains.

Ministry to Victims of Violent Crime & Trauma. 1 cass. (Care Cassettes Ser.: Vol. 14, No. 9). 1987. 10.80 Assn Prof Chaplains.

Mink & Red Herring: The Wayward Pressman's Casebook. unabr. ed. A. J. Liebling. Read by Wolfram Kandinsky. 9 cass. (Running Time: 9 hrs.). 1987. 54.00 (978-0-7366-1076-6(6), 2003) Books on Tape.
Discusses the inadequacies of the American press, especially during the late 1940's.

Minneapolis Poem see Poetry & Voice of James Wright

Minnesota Polka: Dance Music from Four Traditions. James P. Leary. 1 cass. (Running Time: 42 min.). (Minnesota Musical Traditions Ser.). 1990. pap. bk. 9.95 (C-004) Minn Hist.
Sampler of obereks, laendlers, waltzes, & polkas performed by German, Polish, Bohemian & Slovenian bands - four of Minnesota's polka-loving ethnic groups. Includes booklet.

Minnie & Moo: Minnie & Moo & the Musk of Zorro. Denys Cazet. Illus. by Denys Cazet. Read by Barbara Caruso. 11 vols. (Running Time: 20 mins.). (Live Oak Readalong Ser.). (J). 2002. pap. bk. 18.95 (978-1-59112-388-0(7)) Pub: Live Oak Media. Dist(s): AudioGO

Minnie & Moo: Minnie & Moo & the Thanksgiving Tree. Denys Cazet. Illus. by Denys Cazet. Read by Barbara Caruso. 11 vols. (Running Time: 18 mins.). (Live Oak Readalong Ser.). (J). 2002. pap. bk. 18.95 (978-1-59112-386-6(0)) Pub: Live Oak Media. Dist(s): AudioGO

Minnie & Moo: Minnie & Moo Go Dancing. Denys Cazet. Illus. by Denys Cazet. Read by Barbara Caruso. 11 vols. (Running Time: 16 mins.). (Live Oak Readalong Ser.). (J). 2001. pap. bk. 18.95 (978-1-59112-390-3(9)) Pub: Live Oak Media. Dist(s): AudioGO

Minnie & Moo: Minnie & Moo Go to Paris. Denys Cazet. Illus. by Denys Cazet. Read by Barbara Caruso. 11 vols. (Running Time: 17 mins.). (Live Oak Readalong Ser.). (J). 2001. pap. bk. 18.95 (978-1-59112-394-1(1)) Pub: Live Oak Media. Dist(s): AudioGO

Minnie & Moo: Minnie & Moo Go to the Moon. Denys Cazet. Illus. by Denys Cazet. Read by Barbara Caruso. (Live Oak Readalong Ser.). (J). bk. 18.95 (978-1-59112-392-7(5)) Pub: Live Oak Media. Dist(s): AudioGO

Minnie & Moo: Minnie & Moo Save the Earth. Denys Cazet. Illus. by Denys Cazet. Read by Barbara Caruso. 11 vols. (Running Time: 17 mins.). (Live Oak Readalong Ser.). (J). 2001. pap. bk. 18.95 (978-1-59112-396-5(8)) Pub: Live Oak Media. Dist(s): AudioGO

Minnie & Moo: The Case of the Missing Jelly Donut. Denys Cazet. Illus. by Denys Cazet. Read by Barbara Caruso. 1 cass. (Running Time: 16 mins.). (Minnie & Moo Ser.). (J). (ps-3). 2007. 25.95 (978-1-4301-0087-4(7)) Live Oak Media.

Minnie & Moo: The Case of the Missing Jelly Donut. Denys Cazet. Read by Denys Cazet. Read by Barbara Caruso. 1 CD. (Running Time: 16 mins.). (Minnie & Moo Ser.). (J). (ps-3). 2007. bk. 28.95 (978-1-4301-0090-4(7)); audio compact disk 18.95 (978-1-4301-0089-8(3)) Live Oak Media.

Minnie & Moo: The Case of the Missing Jelly Donut. Denys Cazet. Illus. by Denys Cazet. Read by Barbara Caruso. 1 cass. (Running Time: 16 mins.). (Minnie & Moo Ser.). (J). (ps-3). 2007. pap. bk. 16.95 (978-1-4301-0086-7(9)); pap. bk. 29.95 (978-1-4301-0088-1(5)) Live Oak Media.

Minnie & Moo: The Case of the Missing Jelly Donut, Set. Denys Cazet. 1 CD. (Running Time: 16 mins.). (J). (gr. k-2). 2007. pap. bk. 31.95 (978-1-4301-0091-1(5)) Live Oak Media.

Minnie & Moo: The Night Before Christmas. Denys Cazet. Illus. by Denys Cazet. 11 vols. (Running Time: 16 mins.). (Readalongs for Beginning Readers Ser.). 2004. bk. 25.95 (978-1-59112-884-7(6)) Live Oak Media.

Minnie & Moo: The Night Before Christmas. Denys Cazet. Illus. by Denys Cazet. 14 vols. (Running Time: 16 mins.). (Readalongs for Beginning Readers Ser.). (J). 2004. pap. bk. 31.95 (978-1-59112-889-2(7)); pap. bk. 29.95 (978-1-59112-885-4(4)) Live Oak Media.

Minnie & Moo: Will You Be My Valentine? Read by Denys Cazet. 11 vols. (Running Time: 18 mins.). (Read-Alongs for Beginning Readers Ser.). (J). (ps-3). 2004. bk. 25.95 (978-1-59112-892-2(7)); pap. bk. 31.95 (978-1-59112-897-7(8)); pap. bk. 29.95 (978-1-59112-893-9(5)) Live Oak Media.

Minnie & Moo Adventure Series. Denys Cazet. Illus. by Denys Cazet. 33 vols. (Running Time: 54 mins.). 2004. pap. bk. 45.95 (978-1-59112-849-6(8)); pap. bk. 51.95 (978-1-59112-850-2(1)) Live Oak Media.

Minnie & Moo & the Musk of Zorro. Denys Cazet. 9.95 (978-1-59112-295-1(3)) Live Oak Media.

Minnie & Moo & the Musk of Zorro. Denys Cazet. Illus. by Denys Cazet. 11 vols. (Running Time: 20 mins.). 2002. bk. 28.95 (978-1-59112-589-1(8)); pap. bk. 31.95 (978-1-59112-588-4(X)) Live Oak Media.

Minnie & Moo & the Musk of Zorro. Denys Cazet. Illus. by Denys Cazet. (Running Time: 20 mins.). (J). (gr. k-4). 2002. 12.95 (978-1-59112-387-3(9)) Live Oak Media.

Minnie & Moo & the Musk of Zorro. Denys Cazet. Illus. by Denys Cazet. 14 vols. (Running Time: 20 mins.). (J). (ps-3). 2002. pap. bk. & tchr.'s planning gde. ed. 29.95 (978-0-87499-920-4(0)) Live Oak Media.
It's Zorro del Moo and her sidekick Dolores del Zorro del Minnie to the rescue when the bovine buddies masquerade to set things right on the farm.

Minnie & Moo & the Musk of Zorro. Denys Cazet. Illus. by Denys Cazet. 11 vols. (Running Time: 20 mins.). (J). (ps-4). 2002. bk. 25.95 (978-0-87499-919-8(7)) Live Oak Media.

Minnie & Moo & the Musk of Zorro. Denys Cazet. Illus. by Denys Cazet. Read by Barbara Caruso. 11 vols. (Running Time: 20 mins.). (Live Oak Readalong Ser.). (J). (ps-3). 2002. pap. bk. 16.95 (978-0-87499-918-1(9)) Pub: Live Oak Media. Dist(s): AudioGO

Minnie & Moo & the Night Before Christmas. Denys Cazet. Illus. by Denys Cazet. (Running Time: 16 mins.). (J). 2004. 9.95 (978-1-59112-882-3(X)); audio compact disk 12.95 (978-1-59112-886-1(2)) Live Oak Media.

Minnie & Moo & the Potato from Planet X. Denys Cazet. Illus. by Denys Cazet. (Running Time: 17 mins.). 2004. 9.95 (978-1-59112-256-2(2)) Live Oak Media.

Minnie & Moo & the Potato from Planet X. Denys Cazet. Illus. by Denys Cazet. (Running Time: 17 mins.). (J). 2004. audio compact disk 12.95 (978-1-59112-878-6(1)) Live Oak Media.

Minnie & Moo & the Potato from Planet X. Read by Denys Cazet. 11 vols. (Running Time: 17 mins.). (Readalongs for Beginning Readers Ser.). (J). (ps-3). 2004. bk. 25.95 (978-1-59112-258-6(9)); bk. 28.95 (978-1-59112-880-9(3)); pap. bk. 29.95 (978-1-59112-259-3(7)) Live Oak Media.

Minnie & Moo & the Potato from Planet X. Denys Cazet. Illus. by Denys Cazet. Read by Barbara Caruso. 11 vols. (Running Time: 17 mins.). (Readalongs for Beginning Readers Ser.). (J). 2005. pap. bk. 16.95 (978-1-59112-257-9(0)) Pub: Live Oak Media. Dist(s): AudioGO

Minnie & Moo & the Potato from Planet X. Read by Denys Cazet. 11 vols. (Running Time: 17 mins.). (Readalongs for Beginning Readers Ser.). (J). (ps-3). 2005. pap. bk. 18.95 (978-1-59112-879-3(X)) Pub: Live Oak Media. Dist(s): AudioGO

Minnie & Moo & the Thanksgiving Tree. Denys Cazet. Illus. by Denys Cazet. 11 vols. (Running Time: 18 mins.). 2002. bk. 28.95 (978-1-59112-587-7(1)) Live Oak Media.

Minnie & Moo & the Thanksgiving Tree. Denys Cazet. Illus. by Denys Cazet. (Running Time: 18 mins.). 2002. 9.95 (978-0-87499-913-6(8)) Live Oak Media.

Minnie & Moo & the Thanksgiving Tree. Denys Cazet. Illus. by Denys Cazet. (Running Time: 18 mins.). (J). 2002. audio compact disk 12.95 (978-1-59112-385-9(2)); pap. bk. & tchr.'s planning gde. ed. 29.95 (978-0-87499-916-7(2)) Live Oak Media.
The intrepid cows Minnie and Moo attempt to hide the turkeys, and other farm animals on the food chain, from the farmer since it's Thanksgiving.

Minnie & Moo & the Thanksgiving Tree. Denys Cazet. Illus. by Denys Cazet. 11 vols. (Running Time: 18 mins.). (J). (ps-4). 2002. bk. 25.95 (978-0-87499-915-0(4)) Live Oak Media.

Minnie & Moo & the Thanksgiving Tree. Denys Cazet. Illus. by Denys Cazet. Read by Barbara Caruso. 11 vols. (Running Time: 18 mins.). (Live Oak Readalong Ser.). (J). 2002. pap. bk. 16.95 (978-0-87499-914-3(6)) Pub: Live Oak Media. Dist(s): AudioGO

Minnie & Moo Go Dancing. Denys Cazet. 11 vols. (Running Time: 16 mins.). (Live Oak Readalong Ser.). (J). (ps-4). 2001. pap. bk. 16.95 (978-0-87499-721-7(6)) Pub: Live Oak Media. Dist(s): AudioGO
The bovine friends attend a dance at the farmer's home, where they are mistaken for his twin sisters and introduced to a couple of country boys.

Minnie & Moo Go Dancing. Denys Cazet. Illus. by Denys Cazet. 11 vols. (Running Time: 16 mins.). 2001. bk. 25.95 (978-0-87499-722-4(4)); bk. 28.95 (978-1-59112-591-4(X)); pap. bk. 29.95 (978-0-87499-723-1(2)); pap. bk. 31.95 (978-1-59112-590-7(1)) Live Oak Media.

Minnie & Moo Go Dancing. Denys Cazet. Illus. by Denys Cazet. (Running Time: 16 mins.). (J). 2001. audio compact disk 12.95 (978-1-59112-389-7(5)) Live Oak Media.

Minnie & Moo Go to Paris. Denys Cazet. 9.95 (978-1-59112-431-3(X)) Live Oak Media.

Minnie & Moo Go to Paris. Denys Cazet. 11 vols. (Running Time: 17 mins.). (J). (gr. 1-3). 2001. bk. 25.95 (978-0-87499-767-5(4)); pap. bk. 16.95 (978-0-87499-766-8(6)) Pub: Live Oak Media. Dist(s): AudioGO
The bovine buddies travel past a crane they think is the Eiffel Tower, picking up a busload of animal friends from Africa World, careening through a car wash that resembles China, and trading stories under a night sky in what they hope is America.

Minnie & Moo Go to Paris. Denys Cazet. Illus. by Denys Cazet. 11 vols. (Running Time: 17 mins.). 2001. bk. 28.95 (978-1-59112-595-2(2)); pap. bk. 29.95 (978-0-87499-768-2(2)); pap. bk. 31.95 (978-1-59112-594-5(4)); audio compact disk 12.95 (978-1-59112-393-4(3)) Live Oak Media.

Minnie & Moo Go to Paris. Denys Cazet. Illus. by Denys Cazet. (Running Time: 17 mins.). (J). (gr. k-4). 2001. 9.95 (978-0-87499-765-1(8)) Live Oak Media.

Minnie & Moo Go to the Moon. Denys Cazet. 9.95 (978-1-59112-167-1(1)) Live Oak Media.

Minnie & Moo Go to the Moon. Denys Cazet. 11 vols. (Running Time: 15 mins.). (Live Oak Readalong Ser.). (J). (ps-4). 2001. pap. bk. 16.95 (978-0-87499-717-0(8)) Pub: Live Oak Media. Dist(s): AudioGO
The bovine "Thelma and Louise" take the farmer's tractor for a joyride and believe they land on the moon.

Minnie & Moo Go to the Moon. Denys Cazet. Illus. by Denys Cazet. 11 vols. (Running Time: 15 mins.). 2001. bk. 25.95 (978-0-87499-718-7(6)); pap. bk. 29.95 (978-0-87499-719-4(4)); pap. bk. 31.95 (978-1-59112-592-1(8)); pap. bk. 18.95 (978-1-59112-593-8(6)); 9.95 (978-0-87499-716-3(X)) Live Oak Media.

Minnie & Moo Go to the Moon. Denys Cazet. Illus. by Denys Cazet. (Running Time: 15 mins.). (J). 2001. audio compact disk 12.95 (978-1-59112-391-0(7)) Live Oak Media.

Minnie & Moo Holiday Series. Denys Cazet. Illus. by Denys Cazet. 33 vols. (Running Time: 52 mins.). 2004. pap. bk. 45.95 (978-1-59112-851-9(X)); pap. bk. 51.95 (978-1-59112-852-6(8)) Live Oak Media.

Minnie & Moo Meet Frankenswine. Denys Cazet. Illus. by Denys Cazet. 11 vols. (Running Time: 18 mins.). (Readalongs for Beginning Readers Ser.). 2004. bk. 28.95 (978-1-59112-876-2(5)); audio compact disk 12.95 (978-1-59112-874-8(9)) Live Oak Media.

Minnie & Moo Meet Frankenswine. Denys Cazet. Illus. by Denys Cazet. 11 vols. (Running Time: 18 mins.). (Readalongs for Beginning Readers Ser.). (J). 2004. bk. 25.95 (978-1-59112-262-3(7)); pap. bk. 29.95 (978-1-59112-263-0(5)); 9.95 (978-1-59112-260-9(0)) Live Oak Media.

Minnie & Moo Meet Frankenswine. Denys Cazet. Illus. by Denys Cazet. 11 vols. (Running Time: 18 mins.). (Readalongs for Beginning Readers Ser.). (J). 2005. pap. bk. 18.95 (978-1-59112-875-5(7)) Pub: Live Oak Media. Dist(s): AudioGO

Minnie & Moo Meet Frankenswine. Denys Cazet. Illus. by Denys Cazet. Read by Barbara Caruso. 11 vols. (Running Time: 18 mins.). (Readalongs for Beginning Readers Ser.). (J). 2005. pap. bk. 16.95 (978-1-59112-261-6(9)) Pub: Live Oak Media. Dist(s): AudioGO

Minnie & Moo on the Go Series. Denys Cazet. Illus. by Denys Cazet. 44 vols. (Running Time: 65 mins.). 2001. pap. bk. 61.95 (978-0-87499-996-9(0)); pap. bk. 68.95 (978-1-59112-848-9(X)) Live Oak Media.

Minnie & Moo Save the Earth. Denys Cazet. 11 vols. (Running Time: 17 mins.). (Live Oak Readalong Ser.). (J). (ps-4). 2001. pap. bk. 16.95 (978-0-87499-770-5(4)) Pub: Live Oak Media. Dist(s): AudioGO
Space invaders - in the form of large "bugs" - attack the farm and it's up to Minnie and Moo to fight back.

Minnie & Moo Save the Earth. Denys Cazet. Illus. by Denys Cazet. 11 vols. (Running Time: 17 mins.). 2001. bk. 25.95 (978-0-87499-771-2(2)); bk. 28.95 (978-1-59112-597-6(9)); pap. bk. 29.95 (978-0-87499-772-9(0)); pap. bk. 31.95 (978-1-59112-596-9(0)); 9.95 (978-0-87499-769-9(0)) Live Oak Media.

Minnie & Moo Save the Earth. Denys Cazet. Illus. by Denys Cazet. (Running Time: 17 mins.). (J). (gr. k-4). 2001. 12.95 (978-1-59112-395-8(X)) Live Oak Media.

Minnie & Moo the Case of the Missing Jelly Donut. Denys Cazet. Narrated by Barbara Caruso. (J). (gr. k-4). 2007. 12.95 (978-1-4301-0085-0(0)) Live Oak Media.

Minnie & Moo Would You Be My Valentine? Denys Cazet. Illus. by Denys Cazet. (Running Time: 18 mins.). 2004. audio compact disk 12.95 (978-1-59112-894-6(3)) Live Oak Media.

Minnie & Moo Would You Be My Valentine? Denys Cazet. Illus. by Denys Cazet. (Running Time: 18 mins.). (J). 2004. 9.95 (978-1-59112-890-8(0)) Live Oak Media.

Minor Aspects. Emma B. Donath. 1 cass. (Running Time: 1 hr. 30 min.). 1988. 8.95 (653) Am Fed Astrologers.

Minor Aspects - Natal. Emma B. Donath. 1 cass. 8.95 (095) Am Fed Astrologers.
An AFA Convention workshop tape.

Minor in Possession. unabr. ed. J. A. Jance. Read by Gene Engene. 8 cass. (Running Time: 9 hrs. 12 mins.). Dramatization. (J. P. Beaumont Mystery Ser.). 1993. 49.95 (978-1-55686-475-9(2), 892536) Books in Motion.
Beaumont's trip to an Arizona alchohol rehab ranch turns into a nightmare when he is framed for the murder of a sleazy teen-age drug dealer.

Minor in Possession. unabr. collector's ed. J. A. Jance. Read by Connor O'Brien. 7 cass. (Running Time: 10 hrs. 30 min.). (J. P. Beaumont Mystery Ser.). 1997. 56.00 (978-0-7366-3824-1(5), 4492) Books on Tape.
The Arizona alcohol rehab ranch is no picnic for J.P. Beaumont, but the weather's fine.

Minor Litany see Poetry of Benet

Minor Prophets. (LifeLight Bible Studies: Course 19). 13.95 (20-2547) Concordia.

Minorities in America Series: World Events over Time Collection. Eugene Lieber. (ENG.). 2006. audio compact disk 160.00 (978-1-935069-14-0(4)) IAB Inc.

Minority Funding Workshop 2012: How to Prepare & Present AI Funding Request! Mervin L. Evans. 6 Audio CD. (Running Time: 410 Minutes). 2010. spiral bd. & wbk. ed. 69.99 (978-0-914391-21-0(6)) Comm People Pr.

***Minority Report.** unabr. ed. Philip K. Dick. Read by Keir Dullea. (ENG.). 2003. (978-0-06-079947-2(1), Harper Audio) HarperCollins Pubs.

***Minority Report & Other Stories.** unabr. ed. Philip K. Dick. Read by Keir Dullea. (ENG.). 2003. (978-0-06-074246-1(1), Harper Audio) HarperCollins Pubs.

Minority Shareholders: Rights & Remedies. 1 cass. (Running Time: 1 hr. 30 min.). 1985. 30.00; bk. 65.00 PA Bar Inst.
Includes book.

Minority Shareholders: Rights & Remedies. 1989. 50.00 (AC-500) PA Bar Inst.

Minority Western. (ENG.). (YA). 2010. DVD 14.95 (978-0-9841748-8-1(5), Fad Prod) Vizzie CA.

Minotaur see Tanglewood Tales

Minotaur. unabr. ed. Stephen Coonts. Read by Michael Prichard. 11 cass. (Running Time: 16 hrs. 30 min.). (Jake Grafton Novel Ser.: Vol. 3). 1990. 88.00 (978-0-7366-1830-4(9), 2666) Books on Tape.
After flying A-6 Intruders in Vietnam & commanding an air wing in the Mediterranean, Jake Grafton is grounded. He draws assignment to the Pentagon where he takes on development of the Navy's new top-secret stealth attack plane - the A-12. At every turn, Jake encounters political & technical problems. Before long he learns of Minotaur, a mole hidden in the Pentagon, who is funneling American defense secrets to the Russians. Who can he be? Jake sets out to find him.

Minotaur. unabr. ed. Nathaniel Hawthorne. Read by Walter Zimmerman. (Running Time: 82 min.). Dramatization. 1981. 7.95 (N-67) Jimcin Record.
Theseus battles a terrible monster in this adaptation of a Greek myth.

Minotaur & the Golden Fleece. unabr. ed. Nathaniel Hawthorne. Read by Mary Starkey. 2 cass. (Running Time: 2 hrs. 30 min.). 16.95 (978-1-55686-147-5(8), 147) Books in Motion.
Two stories from Hawthorne's Tanglewood Tales; both are taken from Greek fairy tales and rewritten.

Minstrel. Perf. by Ben Tankard. 1 cass. 1999. 10.98 (978-0-7601-2944-9(4)); audio compact disk 16.98 (978-0-7601-2943-2(6)) Provident Music.

Minstrels of Bremen. Narrated by Ed Begley Jr. (Running Time: 1 hr.). 2006. 14.95 (978-1-60083-007-5(2)) Iofy Corp.

***Minstrels of Brementown.** Anonymous. 2009. (978-1-60136-587-3(X)) Audio Holding.

Mint Julep Murder. unabr. ed. Carolyn G. Hart. Read by Kate Reading. 6 cass. (Running Time: 9 hrs.). (Death on Demand Mystery Ser.: No. 9). 1996. 48.00 (978-0-7366-3498-4(3), 4138) Books on Tape.
When more than 70 Southern authors gather at the Dixie Book Festival to compete for the coveted Medallion awards, you would expect wounded egos, but not the murder of a publisher.

Minus Stress. George E. Soroka. 1 cass. (Running Time: 1 hr. 30 min.). 1997. 15.00 (978-1-889122-51-9(3)) Ariel Starr.
Self-help tape on how to rid yourself of stress.

Minute Manna. Denny Brownlee et al. 2000. pap. bk. 15.00 (978-1-58302-161-3(2)) One Way St.

Minute Manna for the Holidays. Denny Brownlee & Sandy Brownlee. 2002. pap. bk. 20.00 (978-1-58302-209-2(0)) One Way St.

Minute Meditations: Guided Imagery Meditations to Relieve Stress & Enhance Wellness. abr. ed. Jane Pernotto Ehrman. Read by Jane Pernotto Ehrman. (Playaway Adult Nonfiction Ser.). (ENG.). 2009. 39.99 (978-1-60812-741-2(9)) Find a World.

Minute Motivational Messages: To Help You Have a Great Day. Bernard H. Petrina. Read by Bernard Hugh Petrina. 6 progs. on 3 cass. (Running Time: 1 hr. 30 min.). 1995. 19.95 Set. (978-0-940799-05-9(7)) Exec Mgmt Renew Prog.
The only way to have more good days than bad days is to take personal control of your life with a positive attitude & a full appreciation of your talents & abilities. These messages will help you: Deal with changes you face; Maintain a positive attitude in times of adversity; Implement techniques to overcome anger; Understand simple principles for making better decisions; Pull out of depression & discouragement; Find the keys for taking charge of your own life; & see the blessings in disguise we miss everyday.

Minutos de Sabiduria (Minutes of Wisdom), Vol. 1. Carlos Torres Pastorino. 1 cass. (Running Time: 1 hrs. 30 mins.). (SPA.). 8.95 Pub: Sociedad de San Pablo COL. Dist(s): St Pauls Alba

Minutos de Sabiduria (Minutes of Wisdom), Vol. 2. Carlos Torres Pastorino. 1 cass. (Running Time: 1 hr. 30 mins.). (SPA.). 8.95 Pub: Sociedad de San Pablo COL. Dist(s): St Pauls Alba

Minutos de Sabiduria (Minutes of Wisdom), Vol. 3. Carlos Torres Pastorino. 1 cass. (Running Time: 1 hr. 30 mins.). (SPA.). 8.95 Pub: Sociedad de San Pablo COL. Dist(s): St Pauls Alba

Minutos de Sabiduria (Minutes of Wisdom), Vol. 4. Carlos Torres Pastorino. 1 cass. (Running Time: 1 hr. 30 mins.). (SPA.). 8.95 Pub: Sociedad de San Pablo COL. Dist(s): St Pauls Alba

Minutos de Sabiduria (Minutes of Wisdom), Vol. 5. Carlos Torres Pastorino. 1 cass. (Running Time: 1 hr. 30 mins.). (SPA.). 8.95 Pub: Sociedad de San Pablo COL. Dist(s): St Pauls Alba

Minyan. unabr. ed. Alan Gold. 7 cass. (Running Time: 9 hrs. 30 mins.). 2004. 56.00 (978-1-74030-582-2(5)) Pub: Bolinda Pubng AUS. Dist(s): Lndmrk Audiobks

Mira Y Habla. Tr. of See & Say. (SPA.). 2004. 8.95 (978-0-7882-0270-4(7)) Weston Woods.

Miracle. Neville Goddard. 1 cass. (Running Time: 1 hr. 2 min.). 8.00 (53) J & L Pubns.
Neville taught Imagination Creates Reality. He was a powerfully influential teacher of God as Consciousness.

***Miracle.** Gilbert Morris. (Running Time: 9 hrs. 7 mins. 0 sec.). (Singing River Ser.). (ENG.). 2009. 14.99 (978-0-310-30526-2(8)) Zondervan.

Miracle. unabr. ed. Danielle Steel. 4 cass. (Running Time: 6 hrs.). 2005. 36.00 (978-1-4159-2013-8(3)); audio compact disk 45.00 (978-1-4159-2128-9(8)) Books on Tape.

Miracle. unabr. ed. Danielle Steel. Read by Glenn Fitzgerald. (Running Time: 18000 sec.). (Danielle Steel Ser.). (ENG.). 2005. audio compact disk 27.50 (978-0-553-75721-7(0)) Pub: Random Audio Pubg. Dist(s): Random

Miracle. unabr. ed. Irving Wallace. Read by Multivoice Production Staff & Luke Daniels. (Running Time: 16 hrs.). 2009. 39.97 (978-1-4233-8575-2(6), 9781423385752, Brlnc Audio MP3 Lib); 39.97 (978-1-4233-8577-6(2), 9781423385776, BADLE); 24.99 (978-1-4233-8574-5(8), 9781423385745, Brilliance MP3); 24.99 (978-1-4233-8576-9(4), 9781423385769, BAD); audio compact disk 87.97 (978-1-4418-0161-6(8), 9781441801616, BriAudCD Unabrid) Brilliance Audio.

Miracle. unabr. ed. Irving Wallace. Read by Luke Daniels. (Running Time: 17 hrs.). 2009. audio compact disk 29.99 (978-1-4418-0160-9(X), 9781441801609, Bril Audio CD Unabri) Brilliance Audio.

Miracle. unabr. collector's ed. Katherine Sutcliffe. Read by Kate Reading. 9 cass. (Running Time: 13 hrs. 30 min.). 1996. 72.00 (978-0-7366-3521-9(1), 4158) Books on Tape.
Imagine how much more you could accomplish if you could duplicate yourself. Trey Hawthorne, a busy duke, has this happy advantage in his twin brother, Clayton. To handle the time-consuming business of courting a wife, Trey sends Clayton to the island home of the beautiful Miracle Cavendish. Trey figures that once Miracle's enticed, she'll fall into his arms none the wiser.

Miracle Activation Meditation Music. Composed by Gail Muldrow. 1 CD. (Running Time: 34 mins.). 2005. audio compact disk 19.99 (978-0-9745590-4-9(0), 33-204) Mir Makers Cl.
Tune into the energy of your own personal frequency and inner being with this CD of soothing music for quiet reflection.

Miracle at Midway. unabr. collector's ed. Gordon W. Prange. Read by Grover Gardner. 11 cass. (Running Time: 16 hrs. 30 min.). 1987. 88.00 (978-0-7366-1146-6(0), 2070) Books on Tape.
The Battle of Midway put our Navy back into the war in the Pacific. Seven months after savaging our ships at Pearl Harbor the Japanese commander, Admiral Yamamoto, prepared to finish his work. He targeted a smaller U.S. force. Given the superiority of the Japanese fleet, there was no reason to believe the outcome would be different.

Miracle at Philadelphia. Catherine Drinker Bowen. Narrated by Tom Teti. 12 cass. (Running Time: 10 hrs.). 2002. 50.00 (978-0-7567-5567-6(0)) DIANE Pub.

Miracle at Philadelphia, unabr. ed. Catherine Drinker Bowen. Read by Kristen Underwood. 9 cass. (Running Time: 13 hrs.). 1995. 62.95 (978-0-7861-0710-0(3), 1587) Blckstn Audio.
The story of the stormy, brilliant session of 1787 in Philadelphia which saw the birth of the Constitution of the United States. Here is the fascinating record of the months of debate & decision when ideas clashed & tempers flared.

Miracle at Philadelphia. unabr. ed. Catherine Drinker Bowen. 12 pieces. (Running Time: 10 hrs.). (Classic Literature Ser.). 1997. 49.95 (978-1-55656-265-5(9)) Pub: Dercum Audio. Dist(s): APG
In the summer of 1787, 55 men from differing backgrounds & beliefs came together in Philadelphia to draft our Constitution. James Madison, their secretary, describes in detail the conflict & contributions of Patrick Henry, Benjamin Franklin, Alexander Hamilton & George Washington, to name a few of these men of different upbringing & philosophies.

Miracle at Philadelphia: The Story of the Constitutional Convention May to September 1787. unabr. ed. Catherine Drinker Bowen & Kristen Underwood. (Running Time: 13 hrs. 5 mins.). 2008. audio compact disk 99.00 (978-1-4332-5417-8(4)) Blckstn Audio.

Miracle at Philadelphia: The Story of the Constitutional Convention May to September 1787. unabr. ed. Catherine Bowen & Kristen Underwood. (Running Time: 13 hrs. 5 mins.). 2008. 29.95 (978-1-4332-5418-5(2)) Blckstn Audio.

Miracle at Speedy Motors. unabr. ed. Alexander McCall Smith. Narrated by Lisette Lecat. 8 cass. (Running Time: 8 hrs. 30 mins.). (No. 1 Ladies' Detective Agency Ser.: No. 9). 2008. 41.95 (978-1-4281-8541-8(0)); 67.75 (978-1-4281-0414-3(3)); audio compact disk 29.99 (978-1-4281-8540-1(2)); audio compact disk 92.75 (978-1-4281-0415-0(1)) Recorded Bks.

Miracle at St. Anna. unabr. ed. James McBride. Read by Ted Daniel. 6 cass. (Running Time: 9 hrs.). 2001. 48.00 (978-0-7366-8499-6(9)); audio compact disk 56.00 (978-0-7366-8515-3(4)) Books on Tape.
Four African-American soldiers in Italy during WW II come to the site of a massacre but find a miracle.

Miracle at St. Bruno's. unabr. ed. Philippa Carr. Read by Anne White. 14 CDs. (Running Time: 21 hrs.). 2001. audio compact disk 89.96 (978-0-7531-1051-5(2), 110512) Pub: ISIS Audio GBR. Dist(s): Ulverscroft US

Miracle at St. Bruno's. unabr. ed. Philippa Carr. Read by Anne White. 12 cass. (Running Time: 18 hrs.). (Isis Ser.). (J). 2001. 94.95 (978-1-85695-268-2(1), 951011) Pub: ISIS Lrg Prnt GBR. Dist(s): Ulverscroft US

Miracle Course: A Way of Life. unabr. ed. Carol Howe. 3 cass. (Running Time: 4 hrs. 30 min.). 1992. 23.95 (978-1-889642-13-0(4)) C Howe.
The message becomes simple & attainable as its principles of love & forgiveness are clarified. Proven very helpful for both beginners & experienced students of spirituality, this set provides: Specific application of the "Course's" wisdom & teachings to relationship issues, as well as to health & wellness, & those many problems which seem to be beyond control. The understanding of how changing your mind guarantees a new & happier way of life.

Miracle Cure. abr. ed. Michael Palmer. Read by Scott Bryce. 4 cass. (Running Time: 6 hrs.). 1998. 23.95 (978-0-553-47816-7(8), Random AudioBks) Random Audio Pubg.
Gripping medical suspense thriller, featuring a doctor whose promising new job in a state-of-the art cardiology center turns into a diabolical trap.

Miracle Cure. unabr. ed. Michael Palmer. Read by Michael Kramer. 8 cass. (Running Time: 12 hrs.). 1998. 64.00 (978-0-7366-4158-6(0), 4661) Books on Tape.
The prestigious Boston Heart Institute has offered cardiologist Brian Holbrook the chance to participate in trials of a dazzling new drug that could revolutionize medicine. As the study progresses, Brian begins to question his superior's motives & suspects that knowing too much may be the quickest way to the morgue.

Miracle Cure. unabr. ed. Michael Palmer. Narrated by Ron McLarty. 9 cass. (Running Time: 12 hrs. 30 mins.). 1998. 78.00 (978-0-7887-1897-7(5), 95319E7) Recorded Bks.
When patients testing an experimental heart drug start dying unexpectedly, it's up to Dr. Holbrook to uncover the truth before his father becomes the next victim.

Miracle Eyesight Method. Meir Schneider. 3 CDs. (Running Time: 2 hrs 45 mins). 2005. audio compact disk 24.95 (978-1-59179-390-8(4), AW00312D) Sounds True.
Meir Schneider can see - and that's a miracle. Born without sight, he refused to give into his blindness and instead began an intensive exploration of sight and self-healing systems. Miracle Eyesight Method is Meir Schneider's original bestselling audio program for better eye health. Covers the full theoretical foundations of natural eyesight improvement plus Schneider's complete set of techniques for exercising your eyes back to health.

Miracle in the Andes: 72 Days on the Mountain & My Long Trek Home. abr. ed. Nando Parrado. Read by Josh Davis. 5 CDs. (Running Time: 21600 sec.). (ENG.). 2006. audio compact disk 29.95 (978-0-7393-3258-0(9), Random AudioBks) Pub: Random Audio Pubg. Dist(s): Random

Miracle in the Making. (BI09A) Master Mind.

Miracle in the Middle East. 2003. 30.00 (978-0-9742635-8-8(3)) TSEA.

Miracle Is You. Short Stories. Created by Debbie Milam. As told by Jan Sheer. Based on a story by Shellie Berkelhammer. 1 CD. (Running Time: 78 mins.). Dramatization. 2002. audio compact disk 18.00 (978-0-9723082-0-5(2)) Unlimited Inspir.
The Miracle is You CD is a magical combination of story, song, and meditation to help your children discover the extraordinary possibilities that are within them. In this imaginative adventure your children will learn how to let go of fear and anger, overcome obstacles and sadness and embrace the miracles within them to create a more peaceful, loving world. This CD will inspire your children to soar to their greatest potential. A portion of the proceeds will be donated to Camp Fiesta, Children?s Cancer Caring Camps.

Miracle Land Series, Elbert Willis. 4 cass. 13.00 Fill the Gap.

Miracle Life of Edgar Mint: A Novel. Brady Udall. Narrated by Scott Shina. 12 cass. (Running Time: 16 hrs.). 99.00 (978-1-4025-1625-2(8)) Recorded Bks.

Miracle-Making Decisions. Elbert Willis. 1 cass. (Miracle Mentality Ser.). 4.00 Fill the Gap.

Miracle Mentality. Elbert Willis. 1 cass. 4.00 Fill the Gap.

Miracle Mentality Exhortation. Elbert Willis. 1 cass. (Miracle Mentality Ser.). 4.00 Fill the Gap.

Miracle Mentality Series, Elbert Willis. 4 [illegible] 13.00 Fill the Gap.

Miracle Mindedness. Eldon Taylor. 1 cas[illegible]nning Time: 1 hr. 2 min.). (Inner Talk Ser.). 16.95 (978-1-55978-770-3(8), [illegible]876F); 29.95 (978-1-55978-801-4(1), 4002) Progress Aware Res.
3-D soundtrack with underlying subliminal affirmations, night & day versions. Includes script.

Miracle Mindedness. Eldon Taylor. 1 CD. (Running Time: 52 min.). (Whole Brain Innertalk Ser.). 1998. audio compact disk (978-1-55978-777-2(5)) Progress Aware Res.

Miracle Mindedness. Eldon Taylor. 1 CD. (Running Time: 52 min.). (Whole Brain Innertalk Ser.). 1999. audio compact disk (978-1-55978-924-0(7)) Progress Aware Res.

Miracle Mindedness (Building A Foundation Of) The Fundamentals of A Course in Miracles. Brian Sheen. 2004. audio compact disk 99.00 (978-1-928787-08-2(8)) Quan Pubg.

Miracle Next Door. Malka Adler & Yona T. Yacobowicz. 2004. bk. 26.99 (978-1-56871-328-1(2)) Pub: Targum Pr. Dist(s): Feldheim

Miracle of a Changed Heart. JoAnn Hibbert Hamilton. 2004. 9.95 (978-1-59156-224-5(4)); audio compact disk 11.95 (978-1-59156-225-2(2)) Covenant Comms.

Miracle of Believing. Mary M. Slappey. Read by Mary M. Slappey. 1 cass. (Running Time: 1 hr.). 9.95 bk. Interspace Bks.
Relating principles of art & science to success in life & work.

Miracle of Debt Release. Creflo A. Dollar. 20.00 (978-1-59089-095-0(7)) Pub: Creflo Dollar. Dist(s): STL Dist NA

Miracle of Dunkirk. unabr. ed. Walter Lord. Read by John MacDonald. 7 cass. (Running Time: 10 hrs. 30 min.). 1986. 56.00 (978-0-7366-1020-9(0), 1951) Books on Tape.
Tells of the greatest rescue of all time. On May 24, 1940, some 400,000 Allied troups lay pinned against the coast of Flanders near the French port of Dunkirk. Hitler's advancing tanks were only ten miles away. By June 4 more than 338,000 of these men had been evacuated safely to England. Contains fresh information from the British archives, new material uncovered in France & Germany & above all, the reports of some 500 participants.

Miracle of Dunkirk. unabr. ed. Walter Lord. Read by Jeff Cummings. (Running Time: 10 hrs. 0 mins.). (ENG.). 2009. 29.95 (978-1-4332-2377-8(5)); 65.95 (978-1-4332-2373-0(2)); audio compact disk 90.00 (978-1-4332-2374-7(0)) Blckstn Audio.

Miracle of Forgiveness, Spencer W. Kimball. Narrated by Rex Campbell. 9 cass. (Running Time: 13 hrs. 30 min.). 2004. 29.95 (978-1-55503-920-2(0), 030058) Covenant Comms.

Miracle of Forgiveness. Spencer W. Kimball. Narrated by Rex Campbell. 9 cass. (Running Time: 13 hrs. 30 min.). 49.95 (978-1-55503-209-8(5), 030058) Covenant Comms.
Includes plastic tote.

Miracle of Forgiveness, Spencer W. Kimball. Narrated by Rex Campbell. 11 CDs. (Running Time: 16 hrs. 30 min.). audio compact disk 39.95 (978-1-57734-293-9(3), 0300152) Covenant Comms.

Miracle of Forgiveness. Spencer W. Kimball. Narrated by Rex Cambell. 11 CDs. 2004. audio compact disk 29.95 (978-1-59156-021-0(7)) Covenant Comms.

Miracle of Hope. Contrib. by Brooklyn Tabernacle Choir. 2008. 14.98 (978-5-557-46117-7(5)) Integrity Music.

Miracle of Life. Eldon Taylor. Read by Eldon Taylor. Interview with XProgress Aware Staff. 1 cass. (Running Time: 1 hr. 2 min.). (Child Guidance Ser.). 16.95 (978-1-55978-668-3(X), 3003) Progress Aware Res.
Story & soundtrack with underlying subliminal affirmations. Includes script.

Miracle of Life Change CD Series. 2005. audio compact disk 32.00 (978-1-59834-008-2(5)) Walk Thru the Bible.

Miracle of Love. Matthew Manning. 1 cass. 11.95 (MM-106) White Dove NM.
Forgiveness is a powerful message for allowing love to flow more freely in our lives. When you begin to forgive & release all hurts & resentments, be prepared for miracles to happen. Try it! Let love heal your life & peace of mind prevails.

Miracle of Mindfulness: A Manual on Meditation. abr. ed. Thich Nhat Hanh. Read by Peter Thomas. 2 cass. (Running Time: 150 min.). 2003. 18.00 (14624) Parallax Pr.
A classic introductory manual on meditation, concentration, and relaxation.

Miracle of Miracles: John 1:1-14. Ed Young. 1999. 4.95 (978-0-7417-2240-9(2), 1240) Win Walk.

Miracle of Purun Bhagat. Rudyard Kipling. (J). 1983. (S-43) Jimcin Record.

Miracle of Starvation Flat. Giff Cheshire. (Running Time: 1 hr.). 2000. 10.95 (978-1-60083-537-7(6)) Iofy Corp.

***Miracle of Starvation Flat.** Gifford Cheshire. 2009. (978-1-60136-450-0(4)) Audio Holding.

Miracle of the Maccabees: The Story of Chanukah. Prod. by Jewish Educational Media. 1 cass. (Running Time: 30 mins.). 2004. 9.00 (978-0-8266-9999-2(5)) Kehot Pubn Soc.
"This action-filled and well-researched dramatization portrays the miracle of Chanukah as a victory of Jewish spirit over the forces of assimilation and

spiritual annihilation, as well as over the armies of Antiochus. The drama and exciting narration make this a thrilling audiocassette from Jewish Educational Media.".

Miracle of Trust: Overcoming the One Obstacle to Love's Infinite Presence. Nouk Sanchez & Tomas Vieira. 2009. audio compact disk 69.95 (978-1-59179-735-7(7)) Sounds True.

Miracle on the 17th Green. unabr. ed. James Patterson & Peter de Jonge. Read by Hal Linden. (Running Time: 3 hrs.). (ENG.). 2010. 16.98 (978-1-60788-203-9(5)); audio compact disk 24.98 (978-1-60788-202-2(7)) Pub: Hachet Audio. Dist(s): HachBkGrp

Miracle on Thirty Fourth Street. Perf. by Edmund Gwenn. 1 cass. (Running Time: 1 hr.). (J). 7.95 (LS-7789) Natl Recrd Co.

This is the radio adaption of the 1947 film about the Macy's Department Store Santa Claus who goes on trial to prove that he is indeed the real Santa. The radio version closely follows the story as presented on the screen. This is a classical story that will be enjoyed every year at Christmas time.

Miracle on 34th Street. adpt. collector's ed. Perf. by Edmund Gwenn & Maureen O'Hara. Based on a movie by George Seaton. 1 CD. (Running Time: 1 hr.). (Adventures in Old-Time Radio Ser.). 1999. audio compact disk 4.98 (978-1-57019-342-2(8), OTR7011) Pub: Radio Spirits. Dist(s): AudioGO

Miracle on 34th Street. adpt. collector's ed. Perf. by Edmund Gwenn & Maureen O'Hara. Based on a movie by George Seaton. 1 cass. (Running Time: 1 hr.). (Adventures in Old-Time Radio Ser.). 2002. 4.98 (978-1-57019-173-2(5), OTR4158) Pub: Radio Spirits. Dist(s): AudioGO

Miracle on 49th Street. unabr. ed. Mike Lupica. Read by Michele Santopietro. (Running Time: 21840 sec.). (ENG.). (J). (gr. 9-9). 2006. audio compact disk 30.00 (978-0-7393-3861-2(7), Listening Lib) Pub: Random Audio Pubg. Dist(s): Random

Miracle Power of the Word. David T. Demola. 1 cass. 4.00 (2-138) Faith Fellow Min.

Miracle Worker. Perf. by Voices of Binghampton. 1 cass. 1997. audio compact disk 15.99 (D2036) Diamante Music Grp.

This is the Voices of Binghampton's second album on New Haven, & their finest to date, displaying energetic vocal performances & dynamic songs filled with spirit. Kevin Davidson, the choir's director, has been with the group since 1989, & has written all of the songs on this latest project. If you want high-energy gospel music, this is the album for you.

Miracle Worker: Abridged. (ENG.). 2007. (978-1-60339-025-5(1)); cd-rom & audio compact disk (978-1-60339-026-2(X)) Listenr Digest.

Miracle Worker Soundtrack-on Cd. Prod. by Myattic Studio. (YA). 2000. audio compact disk 89.95 (978-0-7365-3272-3(2)) Films Media Grp.

Miracles see Gathering of Great Poetry for Children

Miracles. (Dovetales Ser.: Tape 12). pap. bk. 6.95 (978-0-944391-47-1(8)); 4.95 (978-0-944391-27-3(3)) DonWise Prodns.

Miracles. C. S. Lewis. Read by Robert Whitfield. 5 cass. (Running Time: 7 hrs.). 2000. 39.95 (978-0-7861-1813-7(X), 2612) Blckstn Audio.

The central miracle asserted by Christians is the Incarnation. They say that God became Man. Every other miracle prepares the way for this or results from this. The author shows that a Christian must not only accept but rejoice in miracles as a testimony of the unique personal involvement of God in his creation. Using his characteristic lucidity & wit to develop his argument, he challenges the rationalists, agnostics & deists on their own grounds.

Miracles. Eldon Taylor. Read by Eldon Taylor. Ed. by Leslie Brice. 1 cass. (Running Time: 1 hr.). 1992. 16.95 (978-1-56705-334-0(3)) Gateways Inst.

Self improvement.

Miracles. Stuart Wilde. Read by Stuart Wilde. 2 CDs. 2006. audio compact disk 18.95 (978-1-4019-0667-2(2)) Hay House.

Miracles. unabr. ed. C. S. Lewis. Read by Robert Whitfield. 6 CDs. (Running Time: 7 hrs.). 2000. audio compact disk 48.00 (978-0-7861-9818-4(4), 2612) Blckstn Audio.

The central miracle asserted by Christians is the Incarnation. They say that God became Man. Every other miracle prepares the way for this, or results from this. This is the key statement of Miracles in which the author shows that a Christian must not only accept but rejoice in miracles as a testimony of the unique personal involvement of God in his creation. Using his characteristic lucidity & wit to develop his argument, he challenges the rationalists, agnostics & deists on their own grounds.

Miracles: An Introduction to Using "The Course". Diane B. Gusic. 2 cass. 1994. 16.95 (978-1-879323-29-2(X)) Sound Horizons AV.

A riveting introduction to newcomers as well as long time students of A.C.I.M. Diane Brook Gusic, MA presents A Course in Miracles workshops across the country. She has been an astrologer, numerologist, spirtual psychotherapist & lecturer for over two decades.

Miracles: Babbling Brook. Eldon Taylor. 1 cass. 16.95 (978-1-55978-539-6(X), 5419F) Progress Aware Res.

Miracles! Vol. 3: How to Flow in the Wonder-Working Power of the Anointing. Mac Hammond. 7 cass. (Running Time: 1 hr.). (Annointing Ser.: Vol. 3). 1998. 42.00 (978-1-57399-067-7(1)) Mac Hammond.

Miracles & Earning the Right to Brag: Collector's Edition. Matthew Cowley. 1 cass. 9.95 (978-1-55503-066-7(1), 0600408); audio compact disk 10.98 (978-1-57734-114-7(7), 2500809) Covenant Comms.

Miracles & Wonders: Musicals for Chanukah & Purim. Debbie Friedman. Frwd. by Randee Friedman. 1992. 6.95 (978-1-890161-15-6(2)) Sounds Write.

Miracles & Wonders: Musicals for Chanukah & Purim. Debbie Friedman. Frwd. by Randee Friedman. Illus. by Andy Friedman. 1 cass. (Running Time: 40 min.). 1992. 9.95 (978-1-890161-14-9(4)) Sounds Write.

Debbie's well-loved original Purim & Chanukah musicals for children of all ages.

Miracles & Wonders: Musicals for Chanukah & Purim. Debbie Friedman. Frwd. by Randee Friedman. Illus. by Andy Friedman. 1 CD. (Running Time: 40 min.). 1995. audio compact disk 15.95 (978-1-890161-16-3(0)) Sounds Write.

Miracles Are Guaranteed: A Handbook for Living. abr. ed. Bill Ferguson. Read by Bill Ferguson. (Running Time: 8040 sec.). 2006. audio compact disk 21.95 (978-1-878410-39-9(3)) Return Heart.

Miracle's Boys. unabr. ed. Jacqueline Woodson. Read by Dule Hill. 2 vols. (Running Time: 2 hrs. 27 mins.). (J). (gr. 7 up). 2004. pap. bk. 29.00 (978-0-8072-0789-5(6), LYA 322 SP, Listening Lib); 23.00 (978-0-8072-0525-9(7), Listening Lib) Random Audio Pubg.

A moving tale of one family's struggle to make a better life for themselves despite overwhelming odds and terrible tragedy.

Miracles Can Happen to You: Power of Visual Imagery. Lew Miller. 1 cass. (Running Time: 1 hr.). 1989. 12.00 (978-0-9615752-1-2(2)) Milbeck Pr.

Your own private instruction cassette on the development of vivid imagination. A disciplined conditioning program emphasizing the listener's active participation, the quickest & most successful method to engage & train the mind. Includes practical exercises, meditative practices & techniques designed to help you build "creative muscles".

Miracles for the Earth. Sandra Ingerman. 2 CDs. 2004. audio compact disk 19.95 (978-1-59179-201-7(0), AW00851D) Sounds True.

Combining Shamanic principles for merging with your pure essence with the measuring tools of modern science, this internationally respected shaman demonstrates how to harness your spiritual power to generate changes in your own health, in your relationships, and in the natural surroundings where you live. This program includes many guided visualizations, rituals, and chants.

Miracles in Maggody. Joan Hess & Mary Lechter. 5 cass. (Running Time: 7 hrs.). (Arly Hanks Mystery Ser.). 2002. 39.95 (978-0-7861-1034-6(1), 1809) Blckstn Audio.

Miracles in Maggody, unabr. ed. Joan Hess. Read by Mary Lechter. 5 cass. (Running Time: 7 hr. 30 mins.). (Arly Hanks Mystery Ser.). 1999. 39.95 (1809) Blckstn Audio.

Chief of Police Arly Hanks handles all the crime that comes her way in Maggody, Arkansas, inlcuding a motorcade of televangelists & faith healer Malachi Hope who come rolling into town. This results in greed growing in the hearts of the town's citizens. But what not even the chief knows yet is that this is a prelude to a double murder.

Miracles of God Experienced Today. Read by Basilea Schlink. 1 cass. (Running Time: 30 min.). 1985. (0207) Evang Sisterhood Mary.

Includes God's Intervention in the Darkest Hours; Learning True Dependence on the Father; Through Suffering to Heavenly Joy.

Miracles of Healing, Vol. 1. Kenneth E. Hagin. 1 cass. 1997. 24.00 (C716) Faith Lib Pubns.

Examines God's willingness to heal everyone who comes to Him in faith! Both volumes explore in detail specific healings recorded under Jesus' earthly ministry.

Miracles of Healing, Vol. 2. Kenneth E. Hagin. 1 cass. 1997. 24.00 (C717) Faith Lib Pubns.

Miracles of Healing Series. Kenneth E. Hagin. 24.00 (C8127) Faith Lib Pubns.

Believers can mix their faith with the power of God to receive their healing.

Miracles of Jesus. Lester Sumrall. 7 cass. (Running Time: 10 hrs. 30 mins.). 1999. 28.00 (978-1-58568-089-4(3)) Sumrall Pubng.

Miracles of Santo Fico. D. L. Smith. Read by William Hope. 10 vols. 2004. 84.95 (978-0-7927-3123-8(9), CSL 625, Chivers Sound Lib); audio compact disk 94.95 (978-0-7927-3124-5(7), SLD 625, Chivers Sound Lib) AudioGO.

Miracles of St. Pio of Pietrelcina. C. Bernard Ruffin. Read by Johnnette Benkovic. 2 cass. (Running Time: 180 mins.). 2002. 14.95 (978-1-931709-61-3(0)) Our Sunday Visitor.

St Pio was the greatest miracle worker of the modern age. Even before he was canonized, two popes called him a saint. Now stories of his miracles come to life in the voice of Johnnette Benkovic, host of EWTN's hit series, Living His Life Abundantly.

Miracles of the Master: An in-Depth Look at the Healing Ministry of Jesus. Lynne Hammond. 2008. audio compact disk 30.00 (978-1-57399-404-0(9)) Mac Hammond.

Miracles on Maple Hill. Joan W. Blos. (J). 1988. 20.00 (978-0-394-77062-8(5)) SRA McGraw.

Miracles on Maple Hill. Virginia Sorenson. 3 cass. (Running Time: 4 hrs 40 min). (J). 2004. audio compact disk Rental 24.00 (978-1-932076-67-7(0)) Full Cast Audio.

Miracles on Maple Hill. unabr. ed. Virginia Sorensen. Read by Full Cast Production Staff. (J). 2007. 39.99 (978-1-59895-936-9(0)) Find a World.

Miracles, Relationships & the Course. Diane B. Gusic. 2 cass. 1995. 16.95 (978-1-879323-44-5(3)) Sound Horizons AV.

This audio program deals with relationship...physiologically, metaphysically & practically. This album explores the many insanities, & misperceptions that we cherish in the name of love, & helps us to move from a sense of fear & scarcity to more peaceful & holy relationships.

Miracles versus Magic. Kenneth Wapnick. 1 CD. (Running Time: 2 hrs. 36 mins. 14 secs.). 2006. 12.00 (978-1-59142-265-5(5), 3m128); audio compact disk 16.00 (978-1-59142-264-8(7), CD128) Foun Miracles.

Miraculous Count-Down see Christmas with Ogden Nash

Miraculous Jackass. unabr. ed. Gilbert Highet. Read by Gilbert Highet. 1 cass. (Running Time: 30 min.). 9.95 (23309-A,B) J Norton Pubs.

Concerns a discussion of the "Golden Ass" by Apuleius. Has it any meaning, or is it only a cheap thriller.

Miraculous Journey of Edward Tulane. unabr. ed. Kate DiCamillo. Read by Judith Ivey. 2 CDs. (Running Time: 1 hr. 56 mins.). (J). (gr. 4-7). 2006. audio compact disk 20.40 (978-0-307-24595-3(0), Listening Lib); 23.00 (978-0-307-24594-6(2), Listening Lib) Pub: Random Audio Pubg. Dist(s): Random

Once, in a house on Egypt Street, there lived a china rabbit named Edward Tulane. The rabbit was very pleased with himself, and for good reason: he was owned by a girl named Abilene, who treated him with the utmost care and adored him completely. And then, one day, he was lost. Kate DiCamillo takes us on an extraordinary journey, from the depths of the ocean to the net of a fisherman, from the top of a garbage heap to the fireside of a hoboes' camp, from the bedside of an ailing child to the bustling streets of Memphis. And along the way, we are shown a true miracle - that even a heart of the most breakable kind can learn to love, to lose, and to love again.

Miraculous Journey of Edward Tulane. unabr. ed. Kate DiCamillo. Read by Judith Ivey. 3 CDs. (Running Time: 1 hr. 56 mins.). (J). (gr. 3). 2006. audio compact disk 19.95 (978-0-307-24593-9(4), Listening Lib) Pub: Random Audio Pubg. Dist(s): Random

Miraculous Revolt of the Maccabees: First & Second Book of Maccabees. 2 CDs. 2006. audio compact disk 14.95 (978-0-9774914-3-8(9)) Archangel Audio.

Follow Mattathias Maccabee and his five sons as they seek to overthrow the mad King Antiochus Epiphanies. Against all odds the Maccabees remain faithful to the Jewish laws and with God's help gain victory over pagan armies. Miraculously, the Maccabees are able to seize control of the Temple, purify it and rededicate it in a celebration that is still remembered today. (Hanukkah) Circa 260 B.C. to 60 B.C.Complete text of the First and Second Book of Maccabees from the Revised Standard Version of the Bible read by Richard L. Gaskell.

Mirage see Twentieth-Century Poetry in English, No. 26, Recordings of Poets Reading Their Own Poetry

Mirage: Napoleon's Scientists & the Unveiling of Egypt. unabr. ed. Nina Burleigh. Read by Cassandra Campbell. 9 CDs. (Running Time: 10 hrs.). 2007. audio compact disk 90.00 (978-1-4159-4514-8(4)) Random.

Mirage of Peace. unabr. ed. David Aikman. (Running Time: 10 hrs. 0 mins. 0 sec.). (ENG.). 2009. audio compact disk 24.98 (978-1-59644-819-3(9), Hovel Audio) christianaud.

***Mirage of Peace: Why the Conflict in the Middle East Never Ends.** unabr. ed. David Aikman. (ENG.). 2009. 14.98 (978-1-59644-820-9(2), Hovel Audio) christianaud.

Mirame, Puedo Cantar! Look I Can Sing, Vol. 6. unabr. ed. Gale Mackey. 1 cass. (Running Time: 35 min.). (Look, I Can Talk! Ser.). (J). (gr. 7-12). 1998. 11.95 INCLD. LYRICS. (978-0-929724-40-9(2)) Command Performance.

Songs for first-year Spanish students based on stories in the TPR Storytelling book "Mirame, puedo hablar!".

Mirame, Puedo Cantar Mas!, Vol. 2. Gale Mackey. 1 cass. (SPA.). (YA). (gr. 7-12). 1997. 12.95 (978-0-929724-29-4(1)) Command Performance.

Songs for second-year Spanish students, based on the TPR storytelling book Mirame, puedo hablar mas!.

Mirame, Puedo Cantar Mas! Vol. 5: Look, I Can Sing More! Gale Mackey & Contee Seely. Perf. by Pete Butler & Safi Madain. 1 cass. (Look, I Can Talk! Ser.: Vol. 5). (SPA.). (gr. 4-12). 1997. pap. bk. 19.95 (978-0-929724-31-7(3), 31-3) Command Performance.

Intended for learning Spanish but entertaining to anyone who understands Spanish.

Miranda Rites: My Life as the Mysterious Hollywood Sweet Talker. Miranda. 4 cass. (Running Time: 6 hrs.). 2001. 25.25 (978-0-694-52538-6(3), Harper Audio) HarperCollins Pubs.

Miranda the Great. Eleanor Estes. Read by Lyssa Browne. (Running Time: 10800 sec.). (J). (ps-7). 2005. audio compact disk 19.95 (978-1-59316-066-1(6)) Listen & Live.

Miranda the Great & the Curious Adventures of Jimmy Mcgee. unabr. ed. Eleanor Estes. Read by Lyssa Browne & Jane Jacobs. (J). 2006. 44.99 (978-1-59895-200-1(5)) Find a World.

Miranda's Magic Garden. Linda Atnip. 1 cass. 2004. 9.98 (978-1-885394-24-8(1)) Amber Lotus.

Miranda's Magic Garden. Linda Atnip. 1 cass. (Running Time: 1 hr. 30 min.). (J). 7.98 (ORE 25); audio compact disk 12.78 CD Jewel box. (ORE 25) NewSound.

A little girl lives in a big city with no prospects for friends except the plants in her garden. Guided by her dreams & imagination, Miranda embarks on a courageous journey of self-discovery to face her deepest fears.

***Mirando el cielo Audio CD.** Jeffrey B. Fuerst. Adapted by Benchmark Education Company. (My First Reader's Theater Ser.). (SPA.). (J). 2009. audio compact disk 10.00 (978-1-935470-74-8(4)) Benchmark Educ.

Miranon: Human Existence. unabr. ed. Robert A. Monroe. Read by Robert A. Monroe. (Running Time: 45 min.). (Explorer Ser.). 1983. 12.95 (978-1-56113-012-2(5), 13) Monroe Institute.

Miranon discusses health & energy.

Miranon: Levels & Planes of Existence. unabr. ed. Robert A. Monroe. Read by Robert A. Monroe. (Running Time: 45 min.). (Explorer Ser.). 1983. 12.95 (978-1-56113-005-4(2), 6) Monroe Institute.

Miranon explains the "Cosmology of Seven".

Miranon: The Brain & Higher Consciousness. unabr. ed. Robert A. Monroe. Read by Robert A. Monroe. (Running Time: 45 min.). (Explorer Ser.). 1983. 12.95 (978-1-56113-013-9(3), 14) Monroe Institute.

Left & Right hemispheres of the brain.

***Miri, Who Charms.** Joanne Greenberg. Narrated by Diana Andrade. Engineer Derek Whitacre. Prod. by Brook Forest Voices LLC. (Running Time: 620). (ENG.). 2010. 12.99 (978-0-9830872-0-5(2)) BrookFor Voic.

***Miri, Who Charms.** Joanne Greenberg. Read by Diana Andrade. Engineer Brook Forest Voices LLC Staff. (Running Time: 705). 2010. 14.99 (978-0-9830872-1-2(0)) BrookFor Voic.

Miriam Halliday. Read by Miriam Halliday. 1 cass. (Running Time: 29 min.). 1985. 10.00 New Letters.

Halliday reads intense litanies & talks about her work & her world.

Miriam's Healing. unabr. ed. Cynthia Davis. Read by M. J. Wilde. 4 cass. (Running Time: 6 hrs.). (Footprints from the Bible Ser.: No. 3). 2004. 27.00 (978-1-58807-036-4(0), 691168) Am Pubng Inc.

Mirror see Isaac Bashevis Singer Reader

***Mirror.** 2010. audio compact disk (978-1-59171-289-3(0)) Falcon Picture.

Mirror. unabr. ed. Marlys Millhiser. Read by Lynda Evans. 12 cass. (Running Time: 13 hrs. 12 min.). 1999. 64.95 (978-1-55686-892-4(8)) Books in Motion.

On the eve of her wedding, Shay Garrett stands before the antique mirror in her family's home, the famed Victorian Gingerbread House in Boulder & suddenly falls unconscious. She wakes in the body of her own grandmother Brandy on the eve of her wedding in 1900, while Brandy awakes in Shay's body in the present.

***Mirror Crack'D from Side to Side.** Agatha Christie. Narrated by June Whitfield & Full Cast Production Staff. 2 CDs. (Running Time: 1 hr. 30 mins. 0 sec.). (ENG., 2010. audio compact disk 24.95 (978-0-563-51085-7(4)) Pub: AudioGO. Dist(s): Perseus Dist

Mirror Crack'D from Side to Side. unabr. ed. Agatha Christie. Read by Rosemary Leach. 6 cass. (Running Time: 8 hrs. 40 min.). (Miss Marple Ser.: No. 11). 2002. 29.95 (978-1-57270-277-6(X)) Pub: Audio Partners. Dist(s): PerseuPGW

This whodunit of movies, mayhem, and murder features fading film actress Marina Gregg. When Gregg hosts a charity event in her new home, high spirits take a tumble when one of the guests is poisoned.

Mirror Dance. unabr. ed. Lois McMaster Bujold. Read by Grover Gardner. (Running Time: 64800 sec.). (Vorkosigan Ser.). 2007. 99.95 (978-1-4332-0568-2(8)); audio compact disk 44.95 (978-1-4332-0570-5(X)); audio compact disk 120.00 (978-1-4332-0569-9(6)) Blckstn Audio.

Mirror Dance. unabr. ed. Lois McMaster Bujold. Read by Michael Hanson & Carol Cowan. 1 cass. (Running Time: 1 hr.). (Vorkosigan Ser.). 2001. (978-1-885585-08-0(X)); audio compact disk (978-1-885585-11-0(X)) Readers Chair.

Mark Vorkosigan (Mile's clone) impersonates Admiral Naismith & tries to rescue the clones on Jackson's Whole.

***Mirror Effect.** unabr. ed. Drew Pinsky & S. Mark Young. Read by Drew Pinsky. (ENG.). 2009. (978-0-06-170742-1(2)); (978-0-06-170754-4(6)) HarperCollins Pubs.

***Mirror Image.** 2010. audio compact disk (978-1-59171-195-7(9)) Falcon Picture.

Mirror Image. abr. ed. Sandra Brown. Read by Dick Hill. (Running Time: 6 hrs.). 2008. audio compact disk 14.99 (978-1-4233-2499-7(4), 9781423324997, BCD Value Price) Brilliance Audio.

Mirror Image. unabr. ed. Sandra Brown. Read by Dick Hill. (Running Time: 15 hrs.). 2007. 39.25 (978-1-4233-2497-3(8), 9781423324973, BADLE); 24.95 (978-1-4233-2496-6(X), 9781423324966, BAD); 97.25 (978-1-4233-2491-1(9), 9781423324911, BrilAudUnabridg); audio compact disk 39.95 (978-1-4233-2492-8(7), 9781423324928, Bril Audio CD Unabri); audio compact disk 24.95 (978-1-4233-2494-2(3), 9781423324942, Brilliance MP3); audio compact disk 117.25 (978-1-4233-2493-5(5), 9781423324935, BriAudCD Unabrid); audio compact disk 39.25

(978-1-4233-2495-9(1), 9781423324959, Brlnc Audio MP3 Lib) Brilliance Audio.

***Mirror Image.** unabr. ed. Dennis Palumbo. (Running Time: 8 hrs. 30 mins.). 2010. 29.95 (978-1-4417-5435-6(0)); 54.95 (978-1-4417-5431-8(8)); audio compact disk 76.00 (978-1-4417-5432-5(6)) Blckstn Audio.

Mirror Image. unabr. ed. Danielle Steel. Read by John Fleming. 12 cass. (Running Time: 12 hrs.). 1999. 39.95 (FS9-43282) Highsmith.

Mirror Image/How Many Pennies? Steck-Vaughn Staff. 2002. 9.00 (978-0-7398-5995-7(1)) SteckVau.

Mirror Images see Best of Isaac Asimov

Mirror Lake. Golana. 2007. audio compact disk (978-1-891319-82-2(5)) Spring Hill CO.

Mirror Lake. unabr. ed. Thomas Christopher Greene. Read by Christopher Burns. (YA). 2007. 39.99 (978-1-59895-937-6(9)) Find a World.

Mirror Mirror. unabr. ed. Gregory Maguire. Read by John McDonough. 9 cass. (Running Time: 12 hrs.). 2003. 34.95 (978-0-06-056767-5(8), ReganBooks) HarperCollins Pubs.

Mirror Mirror. unabr. ed. Gregory Maguire. Read by John Mcdonough. 2008. audio compact disk 34.95 (978-0-06-176183-6(4), Harper Audio) HarperCollins Pubs.

***Mirror Mirror.** unabr. ed. Gregory Maguire. Read by John Mcdonough. (ENG.). 2008. (978-0-06-176284-0(9), Harper Audio); (978-0-06-176283-3(0), Harper Audio) HarperCollins Pubs.

Mirror, Mirror. unabr. ed. Patricia Scanlan. Read by Marie McCarthy. 12 cass. (Running Time: 18 hrs.). (Isis Ser.). (J). 2000. 94.95 (978-0-7531-0584-9(5), 990603) Pub: ISIS Lrg Prnt GBR. Dist(s): Ulverscroft US

Mirror Mirror on the Wall. Maritha Pottenger. 1 cass. 8.95 (285) Am Fed Astrologers.
What chart reveals about challenges, learning in relationships.

Mirror of Fire & Dreaming. unabr. ed. Chitra Banerjee Divakaruni. Read by James Langton. 5 cass. (Running Time: 8 hrs. 9 mins.). (Brotherhood of the Conch Ser.). (J). (gr. 4-7). 2005. 40.00 (978-0-307-28336-8(4), Listening Lib) Pub: Random Audio Pubg. Dist(s): Random

Mirror of Merlin. unabr. ed. T. A. Barron. Read by Kevin Isola. 6 CDs. (Running Time: 7 hrs. 41 mins.). (Lost Years of Merlin Ser.: Bk. 4). (YA). (gr. 6-9). 2006. audio compact disk 50.00 (978-0-7393-3579-6(0), Listening Lib); 40.00 (978-0-7393-3578-9(2), Listening Lib) Pub: Random Audio Pubg. Dist(s): Random
Strange wickedness is rising from a remote swamp on the magical isle of Fincayra. To save his homeland, as well as his own destiny, young Merlin must voyage to frightening places - both on the land and in himself. Joined by Hallia, the deer-woman he has grown to love, and by his own mischievous shadow, Merlin discovers a magical mirror that can alter anyone's fate. But when he looks into it, the person he sees is the person he least expects to find.

Mirror of the Sea. unabr. collector's ed. Joseph Conrad. Read by Wolfram Kandinsky. 5 cass. (Running Time: 7 hrs. 30 mins.). 1984. 40.00 (978-0-7366-1021-6(9), 1952) Books on Tape.
In 1878, Joseph Conrad took berth on a British freighter & began a 17 year odyssey. Conrad's story reflects the sea's force & grandeur. He describes the ocean's moods, her anger & charm & how men deal with her.

Mirror of the Sky: Songs of the Bauls of Bengal. Compiled by Deben Bdattacharya. 1999. audio compact disk 14.95 (978-0-934252-98-0(X)) Hohm Pr.

***Mirror Test: Is Your Business Really Breathing?** unabr. ed. Jeffrey W. Hayzlett. Read by Jeffrey W. Hayzlett. Told to Jim Eber. (Running Time: 6 hrs.). (ENG.). 2010. 27.98 (978-1-59659-584-2(1), GildAudio) Pub: Gildan Media. Dist(s): HachBkGrp

Mirror to America: The Autobiography of John Hope Franklin. abr. ed. John Hope Franklin. 2005. 17.95 (978-1-59397-820-4(0)) Pub: Macmill Audio. Dist(s): Macmillan

***Mirror to the Church: Resurrecting Faith after Genocide in Rwanda.** Emmanuel M. Katongole & Jonathan Wilson-Hartgrove. (Running Time: 4 hrs. 3 mins. 0 sec.). (ENG.). 2009. 15.99 (978-0-310-77312-2(1)) Zondervan.

Mirrormask. unabr. ed. Neil Gaiman. Read by Stephanie Leonidas. 1 CD. (Running Time: 1 hr. 30 mins.). (YA). (gr. 6-9). 2006. audio compact disk 12.75 (978-1-4281-1093-9(3)); 12.75 (978-1-4281-1088-5(7)) Recorded Bks.
This is the tale of Helena, a young girl growing up in the circus who longs to know what "normal" life is like. After she sees a girl who looks remarkably like her in a mirror, she is transported to a mystical land where very little makes sense. There, she befriends the mischievous Valentine, and together they attempt to get her home.

***MirrorMask.** unabr. ed. Neil Gaiman. Read by Stephanie Leonidas. (ENG.). 2006. (978-0-06-113059-5(1), Harper Audio); (978-0-06-113060-1(5), Harper Audio) HarperCollins Pubs.

MirrorMask: The Illustrated Film Script of the Motion Picture from the Jim Henson Company. unabr. ed. Neil Gaiman. Read by Stephanie Leonidas. 2006. audio compact disk 13.95 (978-0-06-089932-5(8)) HarperCollins Pubs.

Mirrors Inside You. Lois F. Timmins. 1 cass. (Running Time: 55 min.). (Feelings & How to Cope with Them Ser.: Vol. II). 1984. 12.95 (978-0-931814-04-4(9)) Comn Studies.
Deals with what self-awareness consists of, how it is achieved, what is lost by not striving for it & what is gained by doing so.

Mirrorscape. unabr. ed. Mike Wilks. Read by Paul English. (Running Time: 10 hrs.). 2009. 24.99 (978-1-4233-8464-9(4), 9781423384649, Brilliance MP3); 24.99 (978-1-4233-8466-3(0), 9781423384663, BAD); 39.97 (978-1-4233-8465-6(2), 9781423384656, Brlnc Audio MP3 Lib); 39.97 (978-1-4233-8467-0(9), 9781423384670, BADLE); audio compact disk 29.99 (978-1-4233-8462-5(8), 9781423384625, Bril Audio CD Unabri); audio compact disk 79.97 (978-1-4233-8463-2(6), 9781423384632, BriAudCD Unabrid) Brilliance Audio.

Mirrorshade. unabr. ed. Mike Wilks. 2011. (978-1-4233-8477-9(6), 9781423384779, Brlnc Audio MP3 Lib); (978-1-4233-8479-3(2), 9781423384793, BADLE); (978-1-4233-8476-2(8), 9781423384762, Brilliance MP3); (978-1-4233-8478-6(4), 9781423384786, BAD); audio compact disk (978-1-4233-8475-5(X), 9781423384755, BriAudCD Unabrid); audio compact disk (978-1-4233-8474-8(1), 9781423384748, Bril Audio CD Unabri) Brilliance Audio.

Mirrorstorm. unabr. ed. Mike Wilks. 2010. (978-1-4233-8470-0(9), 9781423384700, Brilliance MP3); (978-1-4233-8472-4(5), 9781423384724, BAD); (978-1-4233-8471-7(7), 9781423384717, Brlnc Audio MP3 Lib); (978-1-4233-8473-1(3), 9781423384731, BADLE); audio compact disk (978-1-4233-8469-4(5), 9781423384694, BriAudCD Unabrid) Brilliance Audio.

Mirrorstorm. unabr. ed. Mike Wilks. Read by Paul English. (Running Time: 12 hrs.). 2010. audio compact disk 29.99 (978-1-4233-8468-7(7), 9781423384687, Bril Audio CD Unabri) Brilliance Audio.

***Mirth of a Nation.** unabr. ed. Michael J. Rosen. Read by Tony Roberts. (ENG.). 2006. (978-0-06-115371-6(0), Harper Audio); (978-0-06-115368-6(0), Harper Audio) HarperCollins Pubs.

Mirth of a Nation: Laff Tracks from America's Most Trusted Humor Anthology. unabr. ed. Michael J. Rosen. Read by Tony Roberts & Susie Essman. 6 CDs. (Running Time: 6 hrs.). 2002. audio compact disk 29.95 (978-0-06-051319-1(5)) HarperCollins Pubs.

Mirthmaking: The Value of Humor. unabr. ed. 1 cass. (Running Time: 1 hr. 10 mins.). 1998. (978-0-9700349-3-9(8)) Mayfield Present.

Mis Canciones Favoritas. Michael Rodriguez. 2002. audio compact disk 14.99 (978-0-8297-3732-5(4)) Pub: Vida Pubs. Dist(s): Zondervan

Mis Canciones Favoritas. Michael Rodriguez. 2002. 2.00 (978-0-8297-3735-6(9)); audio compact disk 3.60 (978-0-8297-3733-2(2)) Zondervan.

Mis Canciones Favoritas. unabr. ed. Michael Rodriguez. (SPA.). 2002. 9.99 (978-0-8297-3734-9(0)) Pub: Vida Pubs. Dist(s): Zondervan

Mis-Education of the Negro. Rodney Wayne Davis. 5 cd. (Running Time: 5 hrs). 2005. audio compact disk Rental 30.00 (978-0-9759849-0-1(X)) Heru Inc.

Mis-Education of the Negro Audiobook. Carter/Goodwin Woodson. Read by Anthony Stewart. (ENG.). 2007. audio compact disk 29.95 (978-0-615-22043-7(6)) A Stewart.

***Mis-Education of the Negro-Audiobook Edition.** unabr. ed. Carter G. Woodson. Narrated by Roderick Prior. (ENG.). 2010. audio compact disk 24.95 (978-0-9845406-1-7(X)) AMENTAM.

Mis Primeras Canciones en Ingles. Tr. of My First Songs in English. (SPA.). 2001. (978-84-305-8656-1(3)) Astran.

Misadventures in the (213). abr. ed. Dennis Hensley. Read by Dennis Hensley. Perf. by Kathy Griffin et al. 2 cass. (Running Time: 3 hrs.). Dramatization. 1999. 18.00 (978-1-57511-063-9(6)) Pub Mills.
In Los Angeles, this tale follows a struggling screenwriter & his circle of celebrity-seeking friends as they attempt to make it in "the biz.".

Misadventures of Benjamin Bartholomew Piff. unabr. ed. Jason Lethcoe. Read by Roy Dotrice. 4 CDs. (Running Time: 4 hrs. 2 mins.). (J). (gr. 4-6). 2007. audio compact disk 30.00 (978-0-7393-5151-2(6), Random AudioBks) Pub: Random Audio Pubg. Dist(s): Random

Misadventures of Benjamin Bartholomew Piff. unabr. ed. Jason Lethcoe. Read by Roy Dotrice. (ENG.). (J). (gr. 5). 2007. audio compact disk 28.00 (978-0-7393-5109-3(5), Listening Lib) Pub: Random Audio Pubg. Dist(s): Random

Misadventures of Maude March. unabr. ed. Audrey Couloumbis. Read by Lee Adams. 7 CDs. (Running Time: 8 hrs. 12 mins.). (J). (gr. 4-7). 2006. audio compact disk 55.00 (978-0-7393-3610-6(X), Listening Lib); 40.00 (978-0-7393-3609-0(6), Listening Lib) Pub: Random Audio Pubg. Dist(s): Random
Eleven-year-old Sallie March is a whip-smart tomboy and voracious reader of Western adventure novels. When she and her ladylike older sister Maude are orphaned for the second time, they decide to take matters into their own hands and escape their self-serving guardians for the wilds of the frontier and an adventure the likes of which Sallie has only read about. This time however, the wanted woman isn't a villain out of a dime novel - it's Sallie's very own sister! Narrated by the irrepressible Sallie, what follows is the rollicking, edge-of-your-seat story of what really happened out there on the range. Not the lies the papers printed, but the honest-to-goodness truth of how things went from bad to worse and how two very different sisters went from being orphans to being outlaws and lived to tell the tale!.

Misadventures of Maude March. unabr. ed. Audrey Couloumbis. Read by Lee Adams. (Running Time: 29520 sec.). (J). (gr. 5-9). 2006. audio compact disk 45.00 (978-0-7393-3545-1(6), Listening Lib) Pub: Random Audio Pubg. Dist(s): Random

Misadventures of Silk & Shakespeare. unabr. ed. Winfred Blevins. Narrated by John Randolph Jones. 5 cass. (Running Time: 6 hrs. 15 mins.). 1992. 44.00 (978-1-55690-696-1(X), 92113E7) Recorded Bks.
Tal Jones & Mountain Man, Shakespeare, form an unlikely partnership in America's frontier. Tal Jones first spotted Shakespeare stalking a grizzly bear. In dirtiness & ugliness, man & bear were about equal, so it wasn't always clear to Tal who actually had the upper hand. But by day's end, Tal was wearing the bear's head as a trophy, Shakespeare had a nasty hole in the side of his head & the two of them were howling at each other's jokes as if they'd known each other for years.

Misalliance. unabr. ed. Anita Brookner. Narrated by Margaret Hilton. 6 cass. (Running Time: 7 hrs. 30 mins.). 1988. 51.00 (978-1-55690-341-0(3), 88510E7) Recorded Bks.
A woman starts life anew after a divorce.

Misalliance. unabr. ed. George Bernard Shaw. Read by Flo Gibson. 3 cass. (Running Time: 4 hrs.). 1993. 16.95 (978-1-55685-279-4(7)) Audio Bk Con.
Witty, wacky & wonderful are the characters in this debate in one sitting. The Tarleton conservatory is the scene of many a Shavian skirmish: parents versus children, sibling rivalry & the battle of the sexes. An airplane crashes into their greenhouse & a gunner & Polish daredevil complicate affairs further.

Misalliance. unabr. ed. George Bernard Shaw. Contrib. by Roger Rees et al. 2 CDs. (Running Time: 6540 sec.). 2005. audio compact disk 25.95 (978-1-58081-275-7(9), CDTPT186) Pub: L A Theatre. Dist(s): NetLibrary CO
Taking place on a single day in May 1909, a self-made millionaire and his family invite their future nobleman in-law for a visit to their estate in Surrey, England. In this delightfully clever play, issues of gender, class, politics, and family are all targets for Shaw's keen wit.

Misanthrope. unabr. ed. Molière. Perf. by Kevin Gudahl et al. 1 cass. (Running Time: 1 hr. 44 min.). 1990. 22.95 (978-1-58081-053-1(5), CTA48) L A Theatre.
Neil Barlett's version of the play is both extremely faithful to the original & very contemporary.

Misanthrope, Set. Molière. Read by Michel Duchaussoy. 2 cass. (FRE.). 1991. 26.95 (1096-RF) Olivia & Hill.
In this play Moliere portrays Alceste as intolerant of society, its rules & conventions. Comedy is inevitable when Alceste falls in love with Celimene, who is the personification of all that he loathes in society.

Miscarriage: The After Effects. Barrie Konicov. 1 cass. 11.98 (978-0-87082-347-3(7), 085) Potentials.
The author says the miscarriage you experienced needs to be addressed physically, mentally & emotionally. Failure to do so may put future pregnancies in jeopardy. This program creates an atmosphere for healing & guides you to the cause of your miscarriage which may be found in your family tree.

Miscarriage - A Neglected Area for Ministry. Frank Moyer & Debbie Saban. 1986. 10.80 (0706) Assn Prof Chaplains.

Miscellaneous Lectures. Gordon Clark. 5 cass. 25.00 Set. Trinity Found.

Mischa elman favorite encores (2 CD Set) Daniela Stereva. 2 vols. 1999. pap. bk. 34.98 (978-1-59615-191-8(9), 586-066) Pub: Music Minus. Dist(s): Bookworld

Mischa Kuball. Ed. by Ulrich Krempel. (ENG & GER., pap. bk. (978-3-89322-255-1(3)) Edition Cantz DEU.

Mischief. Amanda Quick, pseud. Read by Mary Peiffer. 8 cass. (Running Time: 12 hrs.). 1996. 64.00 (978-0-7366-3540-0(8), 4187) Books on Tape.
In Regency England, a wealthy woman falls for a man she hires to dupe an enemy.

Mischief. abr. ed. Ed McBain, pseud. Read by Len Cariou. 2 cass. (Running Time: 3 hrs.). (87th Precinct Ser.: Bk. 45). 2000. 7.95 (978-1-57815-051-9(5), 1043, Media Bks Audio) Media Bks NJ.
A detective finds himself racing against time in a game of wits & an onslaught of dirty tricks by one of the masters of underworld mischief.

Mischief. unabr. ed. Ed McBain, pseud. Read by Paul Shay. 8 cass. (Running Time: 12 hrs.). (87th Precinct Ser.: Bk. 45). 1993. 64.00 (978-0-7366-2591-3(7), 3336) Books on Tape.
The Deaf Man is back. He taunts Steve Carella with advance notice of his crimes.

Mischief. unabr. ed. Amanda Quick, pseud. Narrated by Barbara Rosenblat. 9 cass. (Running Time: 12 hrs.). Rental 17.50 (94806) Recorded Bks.

Mischief. unabr. ed. Amanda Quick, pseud. Narrated by Barbara Rosenblat. 9 cass. (Running Time: 12 hrs.). 78.00 (978-0-7887-0631-8(4), 94806E7) Recorded Bks.
Beautiful, headstrong Imogen Waterstone has recruited the darkly infamous Earl of Colchester to help her seek revenge for the murder of her best friend. As they set a perilous trap for the villain, they are unprepared for the dizzying passion sparked by their partnership. Available to libraries only.

Mischief. unabr. ed. Ben Travers. Read by Flo Gibson. 6 cass. (Running Time: 9 hrs.). (Classic Books on Cassettes Coll.). 1998. 48.00 Audio Bk Con.
When a middle-aged man marries a younger woman, the results are calamitous & funny.

Mischief. unabr. collector's ed. Ben Travers. Read by Flo Gibson. 6 cass. (Running Time: 9 hrs.). 1984. 48.00 (978-0-7366-0822-0(2), 1771) Books on Tape.
Farcical story of the calamitous marriage between Reggy, the middle-aged protective husband & his impulsive young wife.

***Mischief Low Priced: Low Price.** abr. ed. Ed Mcbain. Read by Len Cariou. (ENG.). 2006. (978-0-06-114065-5(1), Harper Audio); (978-0-06-114064-8(3), Harper Audio) HarperCollins Pubs.

Mischief Maker see Ellery Queen

Mischievous Bugs. 1 CD. (Running Time: 40:54 min.). (J). 2003. audio compact disk 14.95 (978-0-9722673-3-5(6)) Audrey Prods.

***Mischievous Bugs.** Audrey Smith. (ENG., (J). 2005. pap. bk. 12.68 (978-0-9722673-5-9(2)) Audrey Prods.

***Misconception: One Couple's Journey from Embryo to Mix-up to Miracle Baby.** unabr. ed. Shannon Morell & Angela Hunt. Narrated by Tavia Gilbert. (ENG.). 2010. 12.98 (978-1-59644-937-4(3)); audio compact disk 21.98 (978-1-59644-936-7(5)) christianaud.

Misconceptions about Masculinity & Femininity. unabr. ed. Nathaniel Branden. 1 cass. (Running Time: 1 hr. 12 min.). 12.95 (605) J Norton Pubs.
Covers: common fallacies about the nature of man & woman; the Freudian view; the conspiracy against woman.

Miserable Mill. unabr. ed. Lemony Snicket, pseud. 3 pieces. (Running Time: 3 hrs.). (Series of Unfortunate Events Ser.: Bk. 4). (gr. 5 up). 2000. 30.00 (978-1-4025-3729-5(8)) Recorded Bks.

Miserable Mill. unabr. abr. ed. Lemony Snicket, pseud. Read by Lemony Snicket, pseud. 3 cass. (Running Time: 180 min.). (Series of Unfortunate Events Ser.: Bk. 4). (J). (gr. 3-8). 2001. 20.00 (978-0-694-52543-0(X)) HarperCollins Pubs.

Miserable Mill. unabr. abr. ed. Lemony Snicket, pseud. Read by Lemony Snicket, pseud. 3 CDs. (Running Time: 3 hrs.). (Series of Unfortunate Events Ser.: Bk. 4). (J). (gr. 3-8). 2003. audio compact disk 25.99 (978-0-06-056618-0(3)) HarperCollins Pubs.

***Miserable Millie.** Carl Sommer. Illus. by Enrique Vignolo. (Another Sommer-Time Story Ser.). (ENG.). (J). 2007. bk. 23.95 (978-1-57537-721-6(7)) Advance Pub.

***Miserable Millie / la Pobrecita Mili.** ed. Carl Sommer. Illus. by Enrique Vignolo. (Another Sommer-Time Story Bilingual Ser.). (ENG & SPA.). (J). 2009. bk. 26.95 (978-1-57537-185-6(5)) Advance Pub.

Misérables see Treasury of French Prose

Miserables. Hugo. audio compact disk 12.95 (978-0-8219-3775-4(8)) EMC-Paradigm.

Miserables. Scripts. Based on a novel by Victor Hugo. Adapted by FonoLibro Inc. 4 CDs. (Running Time: 4 Hrs). Dramatization. (SPA.). 2009. audio compact disk 21.95 (978-0-9728598-4-4(5)) Pub: Fonolibro Inc. Dist(s): Lectorum Pubns
Audiobook dramatized in Spanish based on the original story of Victor Hugo. Cataloged as the first social literary work of its time, Les Miserables is one of the most famous novels of all times. It is the story of Jean Valjean, a convict that was unjustly imprisoned for 19 years for stealing a loaf of bread. After being released, Valjean tries to escape from his past full of depravation and badness to live a normal and honest life. However, his past returns when inspector Javert recognizes him, and begins obsessively to pursue Valjean to put him back in prison. This pursuit consumes the life of both men, and concludes in an unexpected end. FonoLibro brings you this excellent dramatization of Victor Hugo's masterpiece, with a full cast, original music, and sound effects that will shake you and reach your heart.

Misérables. Victor Hugo. pap. bk. 21.95 (978-88-7754-700-2(6)) Pub: Cideb ITA. Dist(s): Distribks Inc

Misérables. Victor Hugo. Narrated by Charles E. Wilbur. (Running Time: 33 hrs. 30 mins.). 1989. 51.95 (978-1-59912-860-3(8)) Iofy Corp.

Misérables. Victor Hugo. Read by Homewood, Bill Homewood. (Running Time: 5 hrs.). 2000. 28.95 (978-1-60083-808-8(1)) Iofy Corp.

Misérables. Victor Hugo. Read by Fabio Camero. (Running Time: 3 hrs.). 2003. 16.95 (978-1-60083-282-6(2), Audiofy Corp) Iofy Corp.

Misérables. Victor Hugo. Perf. by Orson Welles. 3 cass. (Running Time: 1 hr. ea.). Dramatization. 23.85 Set. (DD8460) Natl Recrd Co.
Jean Valjean is a convict imprisoned for 5 years for stealing a loaf of bread & another 14 years for attempting to escape. After being released he steals the cherished silver plates of a gracious Bishop. He repents & is transformed into a man of honesty & honor. He adopts a 7-year-old abused orphan, Cosette, & gives her a place in the sunshine.

Misérables. Victor Hugo. Read by Bill Homewood. 4 cass. (Running Time: 5 hrs.). 1996. 22.98 (978-962-634-605-1(1), NA410514, Naxos AudioBooks) Naxos.

Misérables. Victor Hugo. 3 cass. (Running Time: 3 hrs. 30 min.). (Radiola 3-CMR 5). 1987. 16.95 set. (978-0-929541-48-8(0)); 4.98 (978-0-929541-22-8(7)) Radiola Co.

Misérables. abr. ed. Victor Hugo. Read by Frederick Davidson. 9 cass. (Running Time: 13 hrs. 30 min.). 62.95 (1900) Blckstn Audio.

Misérables. abr. ed. Victor Hugo. Read by Christopher Cazenove. (Running Time: 10800 sec.). 2007. audio compact disk 19.95 (978-1-4332-0698-6(6)); audio compact disk & audio compact disk 27.00 (978-1-4332-1346-5(X)) Blckstn Audio.

Misérables. abr. ed. Victor Hugo. Read by David Case. (YA). 2006. 59.99 (978-1-59895-684-9(1)) Find a World.

Misérables. abr. ed. Victor Hugo. Read by Ben Cross. 2 cass. (Running Time: 3 hrs.). 2000. 7.95 (978-1-57815-117-2(1), 1079, Media Bks Audio) Media Bks NJ.
An ex-convict is on the run during the battle of Waterloo & the July Revolution in 19th century France.

Misérables. abr. ed. Victor Hugo. Read by Bill Homewood. 4 CDs. (Running Time: 5 hrs.). 1996. audio compact disk 28.98 (978-962-634-105-6(X), NA410512, Naxos AudioBooks) Naxos.
After 19 years of unjust imprisonment, Jean Valjean changes his name & sets out to restart his life & become a respected member of society. Unfortunately, his struggle to shake off his criminal reputation threatens every opportunity for happiness.

Misérables. abr. ed. Victor Hugo. Perf. by Christopher Cazenove. 2 cass. (Running Time: 3 hrs.). 2004. 18.00 (978-1-59007-123-6(9)); audio compact disk 25.00 (978-1-59007-124-3(7)) Pub: New Millenn Enter. Dist(s): PerseuPGW
Trying to forget his past and live an honest life, escaped convict Jean Valjean risks his freedom to take care of a motherless young girl during a period of political unrest in Paris.

Misérables. abr. ed. Victor Hugo. Read by Mark McKerracher. Tr. by Lee Fahnestock & Norman MacAfee. 5 CDs. (Running Time: 6 hrs.). (ENG.). 1998. audio compact disk 34.95 (978-0-453-00966-9(2), 0453009662) Pub: Penguin-HghBrdg. Dist(s): Workman Pub

Misérables. abr. ed. Victor Hugo. Narrated by Michael York. 4 cass. (Running Time: 6 hrs.). 1998. 22.95 (978-1-55935-273-4(6)) Soundelux.
Classical tale on the political upheaval in 19th-century France.

Misérables. abr. ed. Victor Hugo. Read by David Case. (Running Time: 45000 sec.). (Abridged Classics in Audio Ser.). (ENG.). 2006. audio compact disk 24.99 (978-1-4001-5275-9(5)); audio compact disk 69.99 (978-1-4001-3275-1(4)) Pub: Tantor Media. Dist(s): IngramPubServ

Misérables. adpt. ed. Victor Hugo. Contrib. by Full Cast Production Staff. Adapted by Philip Glassborow. Prod. by Focus on the Family Staff. (Running Time: 2 hrs. 49 mins.). (Radio Theatre Ser.). (ENG.). 2007. audio compact disk 14.97 (978-1-58997-394-7(1), Tyndale Ent) Tyndale Hse.

Misérables. adpt. collector's ed. Victor Hugo & Michael Dawson. Perf. by Orson Welles et al. Contrib. by Smithsonian Institution Staff. 3 CDs. (Running Time: 5 hrs.). Dramatization. (Smithsonian Historical Performances Ser.). 1998. bk. & pap. bk. 24.98 (978-1-57019-066-7(6), 4035) Radio Spirits.
Booklet details the production of the broadcasts and the cast of each of the 7 episodes. Digitally restored and remastered.

Misérables. adpt. unabr. collector's ed. Victor Hugo & Michael Dawson. Perf. by Orson Welles et al. Contrib. by Smithsonian Institution Staff. 3 cass. (Running Time: 3 hrs. 30 mins.). Dramatization. (Smithsonian Historical Performances Ser.). 1998. bk. & pap. bk. 9.99 (978-1-57019-065-0(8), 4034) Radio Spirits.

Misérables. unabr. ed. Victor Hugo. Read by David Case. 1993. 72.00 (3118) Books on Tape.
The story of Jean-Valjean, a convict struggling against his past.

Misérables. unabr. ed. Victor Hugo & Frederick Davidson. Tr. by Charles E. Wilbour. (Running Time: 58 hrs. NaN mins.). 2008. 69.95 (978-0-7861-8854-3(5)); audio compact disk 160.00 (978-1-4332-5460-4(3)); audio compact disk 160.00 (978-1-4332-5459-8(X)) Blckstn Audio.

Misérables. unabr. ed. Victor Hugo & Frederick Davidson. Tr. by Charles E. Wilbour. (Running Time: 12 hrs. NaN mins.). 2008. 29.95 (978-1-4332-5392-8(5)); audio compact disk 99.00 (978-1-4332-5391-1(7)) Blckstn Audio.

Misérables. unabr. collector's ed. Victor Hugo. Read by David Case. 9 cass. (Running Time: 13 hrs. 30 mins.). (J). 1993. 72.00 (978-0-7366-2339-1(6), 116013) Books on Tape.
The story of Jean-Valjean, a convict struggling to escape his past, became a gospel of the poor & oppressed.

Misérables, Pt. 3. unabr. ed. Victor Hugo. Read by Frederick Davidson. 12 cass. (Running Time: 18 hrs.). 83.95 (1810-C) Blckstn Audio.

Miserables: Parts I & II. abr. ed. Victor Hugo. Read by Walter Covell. 24 cass. (Running Time: 36 hrs.). 1989. 120.00 (C202A, C202B) Jimcin Record.
The Story of the convict Jean Valjean's struggle to escape his past & reaffirm his humanity. Superb adventure & powerful social document.

Miserables: Radio Dramatization. unabr. ed. Victor Hugo. 5 CDs. (Running Time: 7 hrs. 30 mins.). 2003. audio compact disk 59.95 (978-0-563-49602-1(9), BBCD 019) BBC Worldwide.

Misérables (abridged) abr. ed. Victor Hugo. Read by Frederick Davidson. (Running Time: 12 hrs.). 1998. 62.95 (978-0-7861-1038-4(4)) Blckstn Audio.

Miserables (Choral Selections) - ShowTrax. Arranged by Roger Emerson. 1 CD. (Running Time: 7 mins.). 2000. audio compact disk 45.00 (08551441) H Leonard.
For the first time young choirs can perform this music in this moving & dramatic medley.

Misérables Part 1. unabr. ed. Victor Hugo. Read by Frederick Davidson. (Running Time: 17 hrs.). 1998. 99.95 (978-0-7861-1035-3(X)) Blckstn Audio.

Misérables Part 2. unabr. ed. Victor Hugo. Read by Frederick Davidson. (Running Time: 14 hrs.). 1998. 85.95 (978-0-7861-1036-0(8)) Blckstn Audio.

Misérables Part 3. unabr. ed. Victor Hugo. Read by Frederick Davidson. (Running Time: 13 hrs.). 1998. 83.95 (978-0-7861-1037-7(6)) Blckstn Audio.

Misery. unabr. ed. Stephen King. Read by Lindsay Crouse. (ENG.). 2009. audio compact disk 36.95 (978-1-59887-874-5(3), 1598878743) Pub: Penguin-HghBrdg. Dist(s): Workman Pub

Misery: Folktales Retold by George Pilling. unabr. ed. Perf. by George Pilling. 1 cass. (Running Time: 36 min.). (J). (gr. 3-12). 1998. 11.95 (978-0-9665930-1-3(4), 13919CS); audio compact disk 14.95 (978-0-9665930-0-6(6), 13919CD) Sound Stories.
Folktales of many cultures told by a master storyteller. Includes: "The Monkey Who Wanted Misery" (Haiti), "The Caged Bird" (Sufi), "The Wise Old Woman" (Japan), "The Three Suitors" (Somalia), "The Four Grains of Rice" (China), & "The Princess with Horns" (Italy).

Misery & Pity/ Hope. C. J. Henderson. 1 CD. (Running Time: 51 min.). 2003. audio compact disk (978-0-9731596-3-9(4)) AudioRealms CN CAN.

Misery Guts. unabr. ed. Morris Gleitzman. Read by Morris Gleitzman. 2 cass. (Running Time: 2 hrs. 10 mins.). (J). 2003. 24.00 (978-1-74030-976-9(6)) Pub: Bolinda Pubng AUS. Dist(s): Bolinda Pub Inc

Misery Guts. unabr. ed. Morris Gleitzman. Read by Morris Gleitzman. 2 CDs. (Running Time: 2 hrs. 10 mins.). (J). 2003. audio compact disk 43.95 (978-1-74093-123-6(8)) Pub: Bolinda Pubng AUS. Dist(s): Bolinda Pub Inc

Misery Loves Maggody. Joan Hess. Narrated by C. J. Critt. 9 CDs. (Running Time: 10 hrs.). (Arly Hanks Mystery Ser.). audio compact disk 89.00 (978-1-4025-2933-7(3)) Recorded Bks.

Misery Loves Maggody. Joan Hess. Narrated by C. J. Critt. 7 cass. (Running Time: 10 hrs.). (Arly Hanks Mystery Ser.). 1998. 65.00 (978-0-7887-9495-7(7), 96798) Recorded Bks.
Maggody Police Chief Arly Hanks is all shook up when she hears that her mother collapsed during a pilgrimage to Graceland and is in a Memphis hospital. Arly's suspicious mind tells her to snap into action, it's now or never.

Misfit Returns, Vol. 1. unabr. ed. Chief Little Summer. Interview with Warm Night Rain. 2 CDs. (J). (gr. 6-12). 1999. audio compact disk 14.95 CD Set. (978-1-880440-12-4(1)) Piqua Pr.
Indian philosophy, historical education/teaching with humor.

Misfits. James Howe. 3 cassettes. 2002. lib. bdg. 24.00 (978-1-932076-12-7(3), 02010A) Full Cast Audio.

Misfits. unabr. ed. James Howe. Read by Full Cast Production Staff. (J). 2007. 39.99 (978-1-60252-534-4(X)) Find a World.

Misfortune's Daughters. Joan Collins & Joan Collins. 9 cass. (Running Time: 12 hrs. 5 mins.). (Isis Cassettes Ser.). (J). 2005. 76.95 (978-0-7531-2199-3(9)) Pub: ISIS Lrg Prnt GBR. Dist(s): Ulverscroft US

Misfortune's Daughters. unabr. ed. Joan Collins & Joan Collins. Read by Lorelei King. 10 CDs. (Running Time: 12 hrs. 4 mins.). (Isis (CDs) Ser.). (J). 2005. audio compact disk 89.95 (978-0-7531-2451-2(3)) Pub: ISIS Lrg Prnt GBR. Dist(s): Ulverscroft US

***Misguided Angel.** Melissa De la Cruz. Narrated by Christina Moore. 6 CDs. (Running Time: 7 hrs.). (Blue Bloods Ser.: Bk. 5). (YA). (gr. 9 up). 2009. audio compact disk 77.75 (978-1-4407-2221-9(8)) Recorded Bks.

***Misguided Angel.** unabr. ed. Melissa De La Cruz. Narrated by Christina Moore. 1 Playaway. (Running Time: 7 hrs.). (Blue Bloods Ser.: Bk. 5). (YA). (gr. 9 up). 2009. 59.75 (978-1-4407-2226-4(9)); 56.75 (978-1-4407-2217-2(X)) Recorded Bks.

***Misguided Angel.** unabr. collector's ed. Melissa De la Cruz. Narrated by Christina Moore. 6 CDs. (Running Time: 7 hrs.). (Blue Blood Ser.: Bk. 5). (YA). (gr. 9 up). 2009. audio compact disk 44.95 (978-1-4407-2566-1(7)) Recorded Bks.

Misguided Mercy: Euthanasia & Physician Assisted Suicide. Catholic Ministry of Health Care Professionals Staff. 2 cass. (Running Time: 2 hrs. 27 min.). 1997. 18.95 (TAH386) St Pauls Alba.
Presents a colloquium of professionals from four disciplines who explore a number of pressing issues that together fuel the current debate which rages within the heart of our cultural identity. Covers many controversies surrounding euthanasia & assisted suicide in our nation.

Mision: Exito! Og Mandino. 1 cass. (Running Time: 1 hr.).Tr. of Mission: Success. (SPA.). 2003. 17.98 (978-1-931059-07-7(1)) Taller del Exito.
The gripping story of a World War II bombardier who is granted a very special gift - the gift of success - which he now shares with us all.

Misión Posible. unabr. ed. Ronny Huffman. 2003. 9.99 (978-0-8297-3174-3(1)) Pub: Vida Pubs. Dist(s): Zondervan

Mismatch. unabr. ed. Tami Hoag. Narrated by Jen Taylor. 5 CDs. (Running Time: 5 hrs. 37 mins.). (Loveswept Romance Ser.). (ENG.). 2008. audio compact disk 19.95 (978-1-60283-420-0(2)) Pub: AudioGO. Dist(s): Perseus Dist

Mismatch: Luke 11:21-23, 636. Ed Young. 1987. 4.95 (978-0-7417-1636-1(4), 636) Win Walk.

Mismatch: 1 Samuel 17. Ed Young. 1982. 4.95 (978-0-7417-1230-1(X), 230) Win Walk.

Mismeasure of Man. unabr. collector's ed. Stephen Jay Gould. Read by Larry McKeever. 10 cass. (Running Time: 15 hrs.). 1995. 80.00 (978-0-7366-2918-8(1), 3615) Books on Tape.
National Book Critics' Circle Award winner dissects scientific racism & IQ theories.

Misplaced Spy Audiobook. unabr. ed. Elizabeth Altham. Read by Colleen Hammond. Voice by Colleen Hammond. B. J. Nartker. Des. by Sebrina Higdon. (ENG.). (YA). 2010. audio compact disk 24.95 (978-0-9824787-3-8(9)) Blue n Gold IL.

Misrables, with EBook. abr. unabr. ed. Victor Hugo. Narrated by David Case. (Running Time: 12 hrs. 30 mins. 0 sec.). (ENG.). 2008. audio compact disk 32.99 (978-1-4001-0900-5(0)) Pub: Tantor Media. Dist(s): IngramPubServ

Misrables, with EBook. unabr. ed. Victor Hugo. Narrated by David Case. (Running Time: 12 hrs. 30 mins. 0 sec.). (ENG.). 2008. audio compact disk 22.99 (978-1-4001-5900-0(8)) Pub: Tantor Media. Dist(s): IngramPubServ

Misrables, with eBook. unabr. ed. Victor Hugo. Narrated by David Case. (Running Time: 12 hrs. 30 mins. 0 sec.). (ENG.). 2008. audio compact disk 65.99 (978-1-4001-3900-2(7)) Pub: Tantor Media. Dist(s): IngramPubServ

Miss. unabr. ed. L. E. Usher. 5 cass. (Running Time: 6 hrs.). 2004. 40.00 (978-1-74030-534-1(5)) Pub: Bolinda Pubng AUS. Dist(s): Lndmrk Audiobks

Miss Ambar Regrets. unabr. ed. Jon Cleary. Read by Brian Hewlett. 7 cass. (Story Sound Ser.). (J). 2006. 61.95 (978-1-85903-875-8(1)) Pub: Mgna Lrg Print GBR. Dist(s): Ulverscroft US

Miss Ambar Regrets. unabr. ed. Jon Cleary & Jon Cleary. 8 CDs. (Running Time: 33300 sec.). (Story Sound CD Ser.). 2006. audio compact disk 79.95 (978-1-85903-937-3(5)) Pub: Mgna Lrg Print GBR. Dist(s): Ulverscroft US

Miss America 1945: Bess Myerson & the Year That Changed Our Lives. abr. ed. Susan Dworkin. Read by Bess Myerson & Adam Grupper. Intro. by Hal Linden. 4 cass. (Running Time: 5 hrs. 10 min.). 1998. bk. 19.95 (978-1-893079-00-7(7), JCCAUDIOBOOKS) Jewish Contempry Classics.
Bess Myerson & Adam Grupper read altemately her memoirs & the political & social history of her time, as a young girl & as Miss America 1945.

Miss Bridie Chose a Shovel. Leslie Connor. Narrated by Katherine Kellgren. (Running Time: 15 mins.). (J). 2004. 10.75 (978-1-4193-2029-3(7)) Recorded Bks.

Miss Bridie Chose a Shovel. unabr. ed. Leslie Connor. Illus. by Mary Azarian. 1 CD. (Running Time: 8 mins.). (J). (gr. k-3). 2005. bk. 29.95 (978-0-8045-4135-0(3), SACD4135); bk. 27.95 (978-0-8045-6936-1(3), SAC6936) Spoken Arts.
Here is a lyrical tribute to the millions of immigrants who left their homes to begin anew in America, and an enchanting look at how one woman carves out a life with the help of a common shovel.

Miss Bun, the Baker's Daughter. unabr. ed. D. E. Stevenson. Read by Hilary Neville. 7 cass. 2007. 61.95 (978-1-84559-416-9(9)) Pub: ISIS Audio GBR. Dist(s): Ulverscroft US

Miss Clare Remembers. unabr. ed. Miss Read. Read by Gwen Watford. 6 cass. (Running Time: 6 hrs.). (Fairacre Chronicles). 1994. 54.95 (978-0-7451-4234-0(6), CAB 917) AudioGO.
Born into a home where food & clothing were well-earned, Miss Dolly Clare, a retired schoolmistress, looks back on a rich & rewarding life. From vivid details of her childhood, life in the classroom & the sadness of the war years, Miss Clare remembers with amusement, clarity & affection.

Miss Daisy. Donald Davis. 1 cass. (Running Time: 58 mins.). (American Storytelling Ser.). (J). (gr. 3 up). 1993. 12.00 audiobk. pkg. (978-0-87483-320-1(5)) August Hse.
Miss Daisy, an elementary school teacher, didn't use established methods or materials: piles of textbooks lined her closets - their brown paper wrappers never removed. What Miss Daisy did employ was the imagination of her fourth-graders as she lead them on a year-long world tour. Includes Miss Annie.

Miss Daisy. Donald Davis. (Running Time: 58 mins.). 1993. audio compact disk 16.95 (978-0-87483-717-9(0)) Pub: August Hse. Dist(s): Natl Bk Netwk

Miss Daisy. unabr. ed. Donald Davis. Read by Donald Davis. (J). 2007. 34.99 (978-1-59895-879-9(8)) Find a World.

Miss Dulane & My Lord see Classic Ghost Stories, Vol. 3, A Collection

Miss Fannie's Hat. Jan Karon. Read by Jan Koran. Interview with Toni Goffe. 1 cass. (J). 1999. pap. bk. 17.00 Augsburg Fortress.
Miss Fannie donates one of her most dazzling hats to the church.

Miss Fannie's Hat. Jan Karon. Illus. by Toni Goffe. (ps-2). 2003. cd-rom 17.99 (978-0-8066-4585-8(7), Augsburg Bks) Augsburg Fortress.

Miss Fontenot 3: Heroines of the Golden West. Stephen Bly. Narrated by Linda Stephens. 6 cass. (Running Time: 8 hrs. 45 mins.). 54.00 (978-0-7887-7223-8(6)) Recorded Bks.

Miss Harper Can Do It. unabr. ed. Jane Berentson. Read by Jeannie Stith. 1 MP3-CD. (Running Time: 11 hrs.). 2009. 39.97 (978-1-4233-8923-1(9), 9781423389231, Brinc Audio MP3 Lib); 39.97 (978-1-4233-8925-5(5), 9781423389255, BADLE); 24.99 (978-1-4233-8922-4(0), 9781423389224, Brilliance MP3); 24.99 (978-1-4233-8924-8(7), 9781423389248, BAD); audio compact disk 97.97 (978-1-4233-8921-7(2), 9781423389217, BriAudCD Unabrid); audio compact disk 28.99 (978-1-4233-8920-0(4), 9781423389200) Brilliance Audio.

Miss Helga Grissel. (Paws & Tales Ser.: No. 39). 2002. 3.99 (978-1-57972-496-2(5)); audio compact disk 5.99 (978-1-57972-497-9(3)) Insight Living.

Miss Hickory. abr. ed. Carolyn Sherwin Bailey. 1 cass. (Running Time: 49 min.). Dramatization. (J). 1972. pap. bk. 15.95 Live Oak Media.
The tale of the simple doll who, with help from her animal friends, lives through a harsh New Hampshire winter.

Miss Hickory. abr. ed. Carolyn Sherwin Bailey. 1 cass. (Running Time: 49 mins.). Dramatization. (J). (gr. 4-7). 1972. 9.95 (978-0-670-47943-6(8)) Live Oak Media.

Miss Hickory, abr. ed. Carolyn Sherwin Bailey. Illus. by Ruth Gannett. 1 cass. (Running Time: 49 mins.). Dramatization. (J). (gr. 4-7). 1972. bk. 24.95 (978-0-670-47944-3(6)) Live Oak Media.

Miss Hickory, Set. abr. ed. Carolyn Sherwin Bailey. Illus. by Ruth Gannett. 11 vols. (Running Time: 49 mins.). Dramatization. (J). (gr. 4-7). 1972. pap. bk. 15.95 Incl. paper bk. in bag. (978-0-670-47945-0(4)) Live Oak Media.
The adventures of a doll made from an apple branch with a hickory nut head. Newbery Award winner, 1947.

Miss Honoraria West. unabr. ed. Ruth Hamilton. Read by Marlene Sidaway. 10 cass. (Running Time: 15 hrs.). 2001. 84.95 (000505) Pub: ISIS Audio GBR. Dist(s): Ulverscroft US

Miss Honoria West. Ruth Hamilton. (Isis (CDs) Ser.). 2007. audio compact disk 99.95 (978-0-7531-2686-8(9)) Pub: ISIS Lrg Prnt GBR. Dist(s): Ulverscroft US

Miss Honoria West. unabr. ed. E. F. Benson. Read by Prunella Scales. 8 cass. (Running Time: 12 hrs.). (Isis Ser.). (J). 1992. 69.95 (978-1-85089-537-4(6), 92072) Pub: ISIS Lrg Prnt GBR. Dist(s): Ulverscroft US

Miss Honoria West. unabr. ed. E. F. Benson. Read by Prunella Scales. 8 CDs. (Isis (CDs) Ser.). 2001. audio compact disk 79.95 (978-0-7531-1050-8(4)) Pub: ISIS Lrg Prnt GBR. Dist(s): Ulverscroft US

Miss Honoria West. unabr. ed. E. F. Benson & Ruth Hamilton. Read by Prunella Scales. 10 cass. (Running Time: 12 hrs.). (Isis Ser.). (J). 2000. 84.95 (978-0-7531-0869-7(0), 108690) Pub: ISIS Lrg Prnt GBR. Dist(s): Ulverscroft US
Early twentieth-century England, its mores & class struggles, both social & personal, are all vividly brought to life. Scales portrays both men & women with equal grace. The main characters are instantly recognizable as they exchange slights, slurs & maudlin compliments. The content & delivery are laugh-out-loud funny.

Miss Is Good As a Mile: Mark 12:28-34. Ed Young. (J). 1983. 4.95 (978-0-7417-1296-7(2), 296) Win Walk.

Miss Julia Delivers the Goods. Ann B. Ross. 2009. audio compact disk 34.99 (978-1-4407-1161-9(5)) Recorded Bks.

Miss Julia Hits the Road. unabr. ed. Ann B. Ross. Read by Claudia Hughes. 6 cass. (Running Time: 9 hrs.). 2003. 34.95 (978-0-06-053225-3(4)) HarperCollins Pubs.

Miss Julia Meets Her Match. Ann B. Ross. Read by Claudia Hughes. 9 CDs. 2004. audio compact disk 44.95 (978-0-7927-3233-4(2), SLD 660, Chivers Sound Lib) AudioGO.

Miss Julia Paints the Town. unabr. ed. Ann B. Ross. Narrated by Cynthia Darlow. 8 CDs. (Running Time: 9 hrs. 45 mins.). 2008. audio compact disk 34.99 (978-1-4281-9818-0(0)) Recorded Bks.

Miss Julia Speaks Her Mind. unabr. ed. Ann B. Ross. Read by Karen White. 7 cass. (Running Time: 10 hrs. 30 mins.). 2001. 42.00 Books on Tape.
When a proper Southern widow must look after her dead husband's bastard, she becomes enraged and decides to tell it like it is.

Miss Julia Speaks Her Mind. unabr. ed. Ann B. Ross. Read by Karen White. 7 cass. (Running Time: 10 hrs. 30 mins.). 2001. 56.00 (978-0-7366-8082-0(9)) Books on Tape.
Miss Julia Springer, a proper Southern woman, is the principal figure of this Southern comic novel. Recently widowed by the death of her husband, the late Wesley Springer, she is busy with the distribution of his estate when she is visited by Wesley's hitherto unknown mistress and a young boy, Wesley's hitherto unknown bastard. Disappointed in the results of the will, the mistress leaves the boy with Julia, forcing Julia to exercise "good Christian charity." Julia is incensed at these events and at the scandal that follows, and she rips into everyone and everything in her way with true "Steel Magnolias" poise. She speaks her mind about all the unsavory activities her husband left behind, and about much more.

Miss Julia Stands Her Ground. Ann B. Ross. Read by Cynthia Darlow. (Running Time: 33300 sec.). 2006. audio compact disk 34.99 (978-1-4193-9403-4(7)) Recorded Bks.

Miss Julia Strikes Back. Ann B. Ross. Narrated by Cynthia Darlow. (Running Time: 34200 sec.). 2007. audio compact disk 34.99 (978-1-4281-4779-9(9)) Recorded Bks.

Miss Julia Takes Over. Ann B. Ross. Read by Karen White. 2002. 64.00 (978-0-7366-8569-6(3)) Books on Tape.

Miss Julia Throws a Wedding. Ann B. Ross. 2002. 64.00 (978-0-7366-8627-3(4)) Books on Tape.

Miss Julia Throws a Wedding. unabr. ed. Ann B. Ross. 10 CDs. (Running Time: 12 hrs.). 2002. audio compact disk 80.00 (978-0-7366-8692-1(4)) Books on Tape.
Miss Julia Springer, who combines Southern grace, the dignity of a woman "of a certain age," an encyclopedic knowledge of etiquette, and a bitingly sharp tongue, is at a loss. Her late husband's former illicit squeeze, who is now her best friend, is going to live in sin with her friend Mr. Pickens instead of with her. Fortunately, a wedding is on the horizon. The happy couple was planning to have a perfunctory courthouse wedding, but Miss Julia has plans of her own for a real honest-to-goodness ceremony, albeit with some shortcuts on the etiquette side. Miss Julia's caustic wit and unstoppable drive mean that the couple is going to get married the right way.

Miss Julia's School of Beauty. Ann B. Ross. 2005. 29.99 (978-1-4193-2673-8(2)) Recorded Bks.

Miss Julia's School of Beauty. unabr. ed. Ann B. Ross. 2005. audio compact disk 34.99 (978-1-4193-2906-7(5)) Recorded Bks.

Miss Keen Needs Help: Early Explorers Early Set A Audio CD. Benchmark Education Staff. (J). 2006. audio compact disk 10.00 (978-1-4108-7624-9(1)) Benchmark Educ.

Miss Lily's Fabulous Pink Feather Boa. unabr. ed. Margaret Wild. Read by Rebecca Macauley. (Running Time: 10 mins.). (J). 2005. audio compact disk 39.95 (978-1-74093-604-0(3)) Pub: Bolinda Pubng AUS. Dist(s): Bolinda Pub Inc

Miss Lizzie. Walter Satterthwait. Narrated by Christina Moore. 8 CDs. (Running Time: 10 hrs.). 2000. audio compact disk 78.00 (C1258E7) Recorded Bks.
While spending the summer of 1921 on the Massachusetts shore with her parents, Amanda Burton befriends her elderly neighbor. She is none other than the infamous Lizzie Borden, who was tried & acquitted of the brutal ax-murders of her parents 30 years before. When Amanda's stepmother is found murdered in a similar fashion, the police are sure they know whom to blame. Together, Amanda & Lizzie set out to find the truth & clear her name once & for all.

Miss Lizzie. unabr. ed. Walter Satterthwait. Narrated by Christina Moore. 7 cass. (Running Time: 9 hrs. 30 mins.). 2000. 62.00 (978-0-7887-4068-8(7), 96032E7) Recorded Bks.

Miss Lonelyhearts. Nathanael West. 2005. pap. bk. 24.95 (978-1-86015-478-2(6)) Ulverscroft US.

***Miss Lonelyhearts.** unabr. ed. Nathanael West. Read by L. J. Ganser and Kevin Pariseau. (Running Time: 3 hrs.). 2010. 19.99 (978-1-4418-8583-8(8), 9781441885838, Brilliance MP3); 39.97 (978-1-4418-8584-5(6), 9781441885845, Brlnc Audio MP3 Lib); 39.97 (978-1-4418-8585-2(4), 9781441885852, BADLE); audio compact disk 19.99 (978-1-4418-8581-4(1), 9781441885814, Bril Audio CD Unabri); audio compact disk 49.97 (978-1-4418-8582-1(X), 9781441885821, BriAudCD Unabrid) Brilliance Audio.

Miss Lopez see Osbert Sitwell Reading His Poetry

Miss Macintosh, My Darling. Marguerite Young. Read by Marguerite Young. Prod. by AAPL Staff. 2 cass. (Running Time: 2 hrs. 33 min.). 13.95 (978-1-55644-089-2(8), 3151) Am Audio Prose.
Skillful & dramatic reading by one of America's most legendary & learned writers.

Miss Mackenzie. unabr. ed. Anthony Trollope. Read by Flo Gibson. 8 cass. (Running Time: 12 hrs.). 1997. 26.95 (978-1-55685-482-8(X), 482-X) Audio Bk Con.
A middle-aged spinster, temporarily heiress to a small fortune, is wooed by three suitors. Who will she wed? A satirical portrait of evangelical Little Bath & a frantic bazaar are part of the comedy.

Miss Mackenzie. unabr. collector's ed. Anthony Trollope. Read by Donada Peters. 9 cass. (Running Time: 13 hrs. 30 min.). 1995. 72.00 (978-0-7366-2994-2(7), 3683) Books on Tape.
When an ordinary woman inherits a fortune, she's importuned by distant family, willing suitors & swindlers. Biting portrait of Victorian culture.

Miss Mapp. E. F. Benson. Narrated by Nadia May. (Running Time: 10 hrs. 30 mins.). 2001. 30.95 (978-1-59912-548-0(X)) Iofy Corp.

Miss Mapp. unabr. ed. E. F. Benson. Read by Flo Gibson. 6 cass. (Running Time: 9 hrs.). 1999. 24.95 (978-1-55685-587-0(7)) Audio Bk Con.
In the delightful town of Tilling the nosy Miss Mapp & her fellow busybodies deal deftly in one-upmanship.

Miss Mapp. unabr. ed. E. F. Benson. Read by Nadia May. 7 cass. (Running Time: 8 hrs. 30 mins.). (Make Way for Lucia: Vol. 3). 2001. 49.95 (978-0-7861-2054-3(1), 2814); audio compact disk 64.00 (978-0-7861-9699-9(8), 2814) Blckstn Audio.
Miss Elizabeth Mapp, magnificent grande dame and heiress, is always on the lookout lest her neighbors fall outside the bounds of perfect, exemplary manners. But her tightly controlled world is soon beset on all sides by interlopers, first in the disturbingly masculine form of two very different retired army officers, both of whom are anything but retiring in their conflicting aims upon her heart. Second, there appears the elegant, insidiously evil Contessa possessed of dazzling charm and diabolical designs.

Miss Mapp. unabr. ed. E. F. Benson. Read by Prunella Scales. 8 cass. (Running Time: 9 hrs. 5 min.). (J). 2001. 69.95 (978-1-85089-769-9(7), 90113) Pub: ISIS Audio GBR. Dist(s): Ulverscroft US
Miss Mapp is an arch schemer, a woman of fine habits who spends her days in the bow windows of her home noting the affairs of her neighbors with the aid of her light opera-glasses.

Miss Marjoribanks. unabr. ed. Margaret Oliphant. Narrated by Flo Gibson. 14 cass. (Running Time: 20 hrs. 30 mins.). 2003. 42.95 (978-1-55685-748-5(9)) Audio Bk Con.
When her mother dies, and after a broad education on the Continent, Lucilla returns to Carlingford to "be a comfort to dear Papa" and to become a leader in the community. She takes hold of these challenges with admirable zest determined to solve such mysteries as the Archdeacon's past.

Miss McKenzie Had a Farm/Farm Life. Steck-Vaughn Staff. (J). 1997. (978-0-8172-7365-1(4)) SteckVau.

Miss Misery: A Novel. Andy Greenwald. 2005. audio compact disk 39.99 (978-1-4193-6547-8(9)) Recorded Bks.

Miss Mole. unabr. ed. E. H. Young. Narrated by Flo Gibson. 7 cass. (Running Time: 11 hrs. 30 mins.). 2003. 25.95 (978-1-55685-718-8(7)) Audio Bk Con.
Hannah Mole, a delightful housekeeper and governess, copes with adversity and a dysfunctional clergyman's family with compassion, kindness and sometimes biting wit. A charming book full of humor.

Miss Nelson Has a Field Day. 2004. bk. 24.95 (978-1-56008-646-8(7)); pap. bk. 18.95 (978-1-55592-747-9(5)); pap. bk. 18.95 (978-1-55592-748-6(3)); pap. bk. 38.75 (978-1-55592-754-7(8)); pap. bk. 38.75 (978-1-55592-755-4(6)); pap. bk. 32.75 (978-1-55592-269-6(4)); pap. bk. 32.75 (978-1-55592-270-2(8)); pap. bk. 14.95 (978-1-56008-647-5(5)); pap. bk. 14.95 (978-1-55592-664-9(9)); 8.95 (978-0-7882-0097-7(6)); audio compact disk 12.95 (978-1-55592-734-9(3)) Weston Woods.

Miss Nelson Has a Field Day. Harry Allard. Illus. by James Marshall. Narrated by Diana Canova. Music by Robert Reynolds et al. 1 cass., 5 bks. (Running Time: 13 min.). (Miss Nelson Ser.). (J). (ps-3). pap. bk. 32.75 Weston Woods.
Nothing seems to help the hapless football team at the Horace B. Smedley School. Not the depressed Mr. Blandsworth or the ineffective Coach Armstrong. Everyone is down in the dumps until the arrival of the notorious Viola Swamp who takes it upon herself to ship the team into shape for the big Thanksgiving Day game. Do the Smedley Tornadoes dare lose again?.

Miss Nelson Has a Field Day. Harry Allard. Illus. by James Marshall. Narrated by Diana Canova. Music by Robert Reynolds et al. 1 cass. (Running Time: 13 min.). (J). bk. 24.95 Weston Woods.

Miss Nelson Has a Field Day. Harry Allard. Music by Robert Reynolds et al. Narrated by Diana Canova. 1 cass. (Running Time: 13 min.). (J). (gr. 1-5). 2000. pap. bk. 12.95 (QPRA384) Weston Woods.

Miss Nelson Has a Field Day & Other Back-to-School Stories. Created by Playaway. (Playaway Children Ser.). (ENG.). (J). 2009. 44.99 (978-1-60812-598-2(X)) Find a World.

Miss Nelson Is Back. 2004. bk. 24.95 (978-1-56008-643-7(2)); pap. bk. 18.95 (978-1-55592-808-7(0)); pap. bk. 18.95 (978-1-55592-775-2(0)); pap. bk. 38.75 (978-1-55592-758-5(0)); pap. bk. 38.75 (978-1-55592-722-6(X)); pap. bk. 32.75 (978-1-55592-271-9(6)); pap. bk. 32.75 (978-1-55592-272-6(4)); pap. bk. 14.95 (978-1-56008-644-4(0)); pap. bk. 14.95 (978-1-55592-665-6(7)); 8.95 (978-0-7882-0095-3(X)); audio compact disk 12.95 (978-1-55592-877-3(3)) Weston Woods.

Miss Nelson Is Back. Ed. by Harry Allard. Illus. by James Marshall. Narrated by Diana Canova. 1 cass. (Running Time: 13 min.). (J). bk. 24.95 Weston Woods.
When the kids in Room 207 find out that their teacher, Miss Nelson, will be away for a few days, they prepare to act up, despite the likely appearance of Miss Viola Swamp, the meanest substitute in the whole world. Luckily, the unexciting Mr. Blandsworth, their principal, takes over instead. Soon the bored-to-tears kids send up a Miss Nelson look-alike to relieve him of his duties. Then it's fun & games until the real Viola Swamp shows up. What would Miss Nelson say if she knew?.

Miss Nelson Is Back. Ed. by Harry Allard. Illus. by James Marshall. Music by Diana Canova & Ernest V. Troost. 1 cass. (Running Time: 13 min.). (J). (ps-4). 2000. pap. bk. 12.95 (QPRA383) Weston Woods.

Miss Nelson Is Back. Ed. by Harry Allard. Illus. by James Marshall. Narrated by Diana Canova. 1 cass., 5 bks. (Running Time: 13 min.). (Miss Nelson Ser.). (J). (ps-3). 2000. pap. bk. 32.75 Weston Woods.

Miss Nelson Is Missing! 2004. bk. 24.95 (978-0-89719-896-7(4)); pap. bk. 32.75 (978-1-55592-273-3(2)); pap. bk. 32.75 (978-1-55592-274-0(0)); pap. bk. 14.95 (978-1-56008-066-4(3)); 8.95 (978-1-56008-971-1(7)); 8.95 (978-1-56008-417-4(0)) Weston Woods.

Miss Nelson Is Missing. 2004. cass. & flmstrp 30.00 (978-0-89719-616-1(3)) Weston Woods.

Miss Nelson Is Missing! Harry Allard. 1 cass., 5 bks. (Running Time: 7 min.). (Miss Nelson Ser.). (J). (ps-3). pap. bk. 32.75; 8.95 (RAC290) Weston Woods.
One side with page turn signals, one side without.

Miss Nelson Is Missing! Harry Allard. 1 cass. (Running Time: 7 min.). (Miss Nelson Ser.). (J). (ps-3). bk. 24.95 Weston Woods.

Miss Nelson Is Missing! Harry Allard. Illus. by James Marshall. 1 read-along cass. (Running Time: 7 min.). (Miss Nelson Ser.). (J). (ps-3). 2000. pap. bk. 12.95 (PRA290) Weston Woods.

Miss Nelson Is Missing & Other Storybook Classics: No Roses for Harry; Miss Nelson Is Missing; the Story about Ping; the Little House; Mike Mulligan & His Steam Shovel. unabr. ed. Gene Zion et al. Read by Bruce Johnson et al. (J). 2007. 44.99 (978-1-60252-630-3(3)) Find a World.

Miss O'Dell: My Hard Days & Long Nights with the Beatles, the Stones, Bob Dylan, Eric Clapton, & the Women They Loved. unabr. ed. Chris O'Dell & Katherine Ketcham. Narrated by Renée Raudman. 2 MP3-CDs. (Running Time: 14 hrs. 0 mins. 0 sec.). 2009. 29.99 (978-1-4001-6491-2(5)); audio compact disk 79.99 (978-1-4001-4491-4(4)); audio compact disk 39.99 (978-1-4001-1491-7(8)) Pub: Tantor Media. Dist(s): IngramPubServ

***Miss O'Dell: My Hard Days & Long Nights with the Beatles,the Stones, Bob Dylan, Eric Clapton, & the Women They Loved.** unabr. ed. Chris O'Dell & Katherine Ketcham. Narrated by Renée Raudman. (Running Time: 14 hrs. 0 mins.). 2009. 19.99 (978-1-4001-8491-0(6)) Tantor Media.

Miss or Mrs. ? unabr. ed. Wilkie Collins. Read by Flo Gibson. 2 cass. (Running Time: 2 hrs. 59 mins.). 2003. 14.95 (978-1-55685-658-7(X)) Audio Bk Con.
Fast-paced novella about attempted murder, clandestine marriage & fraud.

Miss Pettigrew Lives for a Day. Winifred Watson. Read by Frances McDormand. (Running Time: 22080 sec.). (ENG.). 2008. audio compact disk 30.00 (978-1-906462-06-2(2)) Pub: Persephone Bks Ltd GBR. Dist(s): Consort Bk Sales

Miss Route 66. Michael Lund. 2004. audio compact disk 24.95 (978-1-888725-12-4(5), BeachHouse Bks) Sci & Human Pr.

Miss Rumphius see Senorita Runfio

Miss Rumphius. 2004. audio compact disk 12.95 (978-1-55592-948-0(6)) Weston Woods.

Miss Rumphius. 2004. bk. 24.95 (978-1-55592-061-6(6)); bk. 24.95 (978-1-55592-163-7(9)); pap. bk. 18.95 (978-1-55592-110-1(8)); pap. bk. 18.95 (978-0-7882-0328-2(2)); pap. bk. 38.75 (978-1-55592-639-7(8)); pap. bk. 32.75 (978-1-55592-275-7(9)); pap. bk. 38.75 (978-0-7882-0330-5(4)); pap. bk. 32.75 (978-0-7882-0329-9(0)); pap. bk. 14.95 (978-1-55592-062-3(4)); pap. bk. 14.95 (978-1-55592-086-9(1)); pap. bk. 14.95 (978-0-7882-0327-5(4)) Weston Woods.

Miss Rumphius. unabr. ed. Barbara Cooney. Narrated by Christina Moore. 1 cass. (Running Time: 15 mins.). (gr. k up). 1998. 10.00 (978-0-7887-1901-1(7), 95322 E7) Recorded Bks.
Follows an intrepid librarian from childhood to old age. When she is a little girl, Miss Rumphius promises her grandfather that she will do something to make the world more beautiful. Conveys all the glowing curiosity & wonder that fill Miss Rumphius' colorful life as she searches for a way to keep her promise.

Miss Rumphius. unabr. ed. Barbara Cooney. Read by Christina Moore. 1 cass. (Running Time: 15 min.). (J). (gr. 2). 1998. 24.24 (978-0-7887-1929-5(7), 40636) Recorded Bks.
This tale follows an intrepid librarian from childhood to old age.Includes homework set.

Miss Silver Intervenes. Patricia Wentworth. Read by Diana Bishop. (Running Time: 26700 sec.). (Isis Cassettes Ser.). 2007. 61.95 (978-0-7531-3724-6(0)); audio compact disk 79.95 (978-0-7531-2691-2(5)) Pub: ISIS Lrg Prnt GBR. Dist(s): Ulverscroft US

Miss Smith's Incredible Storybook. Michael Garland. 2007. bk. 27.95 (978-0-8045-6945-3(2)); bk. 29.95 (978-0-8045-4159-6(0)) Spoken Arts.

Miss Spider's Tea Party. unabr. ed. David Kirk. (Scholastic Bookshelf Ser.). (J). (ps-3). 2008. pap. bk. 18.95 (978-0-545-02979-7(1)) Scholastic Inc.
All Miss Spider wants is to invite some friends to tea, but the other bugs are afraid of her!.

Miss Spitfire: Reaching Helen Keller. unabr. ed. Sarah Miller. Narrated by Terry Donnelly. 6 CDs. (Running Time: 6 hrs. 45 mins.). (YA). (gr. 5-9). 2008. audio compact disk 66.75 (978-1-4361-1320-5(2)); 51.75 (978-1-4361-1318-2(0)) Recorded Bks.
Sarah Miller's accomplished debut presents a fictionalized account of Anne Sullivan's life and her time as Helen Keller's teacher. Arriving at Ivy Green in 1887, Anne was a partially blind orphan who had been tasked with teaching the difficult blind, deaf, and mute girl to communicate. Anne quickly learned, along with Helen, that words are a miracle.

Miss Switch Online. unabr. ed. Barbara Brooks Wallace. Narrated by Jeff Woodman. 3 pieces. (Running Time: 3 hrs. 45 mins.). (gr. 4 up). 2002. 28.00 (978-1-4025-2278-9(9)) Recorded Bks.
Rupert P. Brown's biggest worry about sixth grade is it might be well, a little bit dull. After all, how can a fellow be expected to top a fifth-grade year in which his best friend was kidnapped and he found out his best teacher ever was a real, honest-to-goodness witch? But when Rupert types the word "computowitch" in an e-mail message, his screen goes all green, and then his parakeet starts giving him math lessons. He knows it can only mean one thing: Miss Switch is back!.

Miss Switch to the Rescue. Barbara Brooks Wallace. Narrated by Jeff Woodman. 3 cass. (Running Time: 3 hrs. 15 mins.). (gr. 5 up). 28.00 (978-0-7887-9528-2(7)) Recorded Bks.

Miss Tempe's Watchers. Kate Chopin. Sound Room.

Miss Tempy's Watchers. unabr. ed. Sarah Orne Jewett. Read by Tana Hicken. 2 cass. (Running Time: 2 hrs. 30 mins.). 1994. lib. bdg. 18.95 (978-1-883049-48-5(2)) Sound Room.
The stories: "Miss Tempy's Watchers," "Miss Esther's Guest," "Going to Shrewsbury," "The Flight of Betsey Lane" (the favorite story of Willa Cather). This collection of stories deals with the tribulations & reminiscences of elderly women & is a delight.

Miss Tempy's Watchers, unabr. ed. Short Stories. Sarah Orne Jewett. Read by Tana Hicken. 2 cass. (Running Time: 2 hrs. 30 mins.). (Jewett Ser.). 1994. bk. 16.95 (978-1-883049-42-3(3), 390232, Commuters Library) Sound Room.
This delightful collection of short stories includes: "Miss Tempy's Watchers," "Miss Esther's Guest," "Going to Shrewsbury," "The Flight of Betsey Lane" (the favorite story of Willa Cather). Stories that deal with the tribulations & reminiscences of elderly women.

Miss Wyoming. unabr. ed. Douglas Coupland. Read by Sharon Williams & Aaron Fryc. 6 cass. (Running Time: 8 hrs.). 2000. 29.95 (978-1-56740-350-3(6), 1567403506, BAU) Brilliance Audio.
She is a former child beauty pageant contender. He is a hard-living movie producer. She walks away from a plane crash without so much as a scratch. He comes away from a near-death experience with a unique, vivid plan. She, refusing to spend one more day peddling herself for cheesy TV sitcom parts, disappears. He turns his back on a hedonistic life making blockbuster action flicks with names like Mega Force. Shedding their self-made identities, each sets out on an uncharted course across the Gap-clogged, strip-mall landscape of Los Angeles, searching for the one thing, love, that neither has ever really known, but that they now think they just might, actually, desperately want. How could they not find each other?.

Miss Wyoming. unabr. ed. Douglas Coupland. Read by Sharon Williams and Aaron Fryc. (Running Time: 9 hrs.). 2008. 24.95 (978-1-4233-5971-5(2), 9781423359715, Brilliance MP3); 24.95 (978-1-4233-5973-9(9), 9781423359739, BAD); 39.25 (978-1-4233-5972-2(0), 9781423359722, Brlnc Audio MP3 Lib); 39.25 (978-1-4233-5974-6(7), 9781423359746, BADLE) Brilliance Audio.

Miss You Forever. Josephine Cox. Narrated by Carole Boyd. (ENG., 1997. 16.99 (978-1-85998-878-7(4)) Pub: Headline Bk Pub GBR. Dist(s): IPG Chicago

Miss You Forever. unabr. ed. Josephine Cox. Read by Carole Boyd. 8 cass. (Running Time: 8 hrs.). 1998. 69.95 (978-0-7540-0168-3(7), CAB 1591) AudioGO.
One winter's night Rosie finds a severely beaten woman in her yard. At a glance, Kathleen looks like a vagabond; the sum of her life is in the diaries she so jealously guards. In the hospital & fighting for her life, Kathleen entrusts the precious diaries to Rosie. They reveal a tale of undying love & loss. But will this be the end for Kathleen?.

Missa cum Jubilo: From The Abbey of St. Michael's Gregorian Chant. 1 cass. (Running Time: 50 mins.). 1999. 9.95 (T8990); audio compact disk 15.95 (K6520) Liguori Pubns.
Includes: "Dominus Dixit," "Kyrie," "Gloria," "Alleluia" & more.

Missa Luba & Kenyan Folk Melodies. Perf. by Muungano National Choir of Kenya. 1 cass. (J). (gr. 2 up). 9.98 (2139); audio compact disk 15.98 (D2139) MFLP CA.
The first strains of this captivating African mass transport you to the plains & jungles of a world mingling ancient tribal traditions with Western culture. Includes secular songs handed down from generation to generation & haunting Kenyan folk tunes.

Missed Fortune 101: A Starter Kit to Becoming a Millionaire. abr. ed. Douglas R. Andrew. (Running Time: 3 hrs.). (ENG.). 2006. 14.98 (978-1-59483-871-2(2)) Pub: Hachet Audio. Dist(s): HachBkGrp

Missed Fortune 101: A Starter Kit to Becoming a Millionaire. abr. ed. Douglas R. Andrew. (Running Time: 3 hrs.). (ENG.). 2009. 39.98 (978-1-60788-289-3(2)) Pub: Hachet Audio. Dist(s): HachBkGrp

Misserables. abr. ed. Victor Hugo & Ben Cross. 2 CDs. (Running Time: 3 Hours). 2004. audio compact disk 11.99 (978-1-57050-031-2(2)) Multilingua.

Missing. Cath Staincliffe. 2008. 54.95 (978-1-84559-716-0(8)); audio compact disk 64.95 (978-1-84559-717-7(6)) Pub: Soundings Ltd GBR. Dist(s): Ulverscroft US

Missing. abr. ed. Beverly Lewis. Narrated by Aimee Lilly. (Running Time: 5 hrs. 34 mins. 8 sec.). (Seasons of Grace Ser.). (ENG.). 2009. 18.19 (978-1-60814-577-5(8)); audio compact disk 25.99 (978-1-59859-624-3(1)) Oasis Audio.

Missing Cat. Created by Berlitz Publishing. 1. (Running Time: 1 hr.). (Berlitz Adventures with Nicholas Ser.). (ENG & ITA., (gr. 4-7). 2006. audio compact disk 9.95 (978-981-246-822-2(6)) Pub: Berlitz Pubng. Dist(s): Langenscheidt

Missing Cat: French. Created by Berlitz Publishing. 1. (Running Time: 1 hr.). (Berlitz Adventures with Nicholas Ser.). (ENG & FRE., (ps-3). 2006. audio compact disk 9.95 (978-981-246-820-8(X)) Pub: Berlitz Pubng. Dist(s): Langenscheidt

Missing Cat: Spanish. Illus. by Chris L. Demarest. Created by Berlitz Publishing. (Running Time: 1 hr.). (Berlitz Adventures with Nicholas Ser.). (ENG & SPA.). (ps-3). 2006. audio compact disk 9.95 (978-981-246-823-9(4)) Pub: Berlitz Pubng. Dist(s): Langenscheidt

Missing Cat/la Gata Perdida. Chris L. Demarest. Illus. by Chris L. Demarest. 1. (Running Time: 1 hr.). (Berlitz Adventures with Nicholas Ser.). (ENG & SPA.). (ps). 2006. audio compact disk 9.95 (978-981-246-821-5(8)) Pub: Berlitz Pubng. Dist(s): Langenscheidt

Missing Chums, unabr. ed. Franklin W. Dixon. Read by Bill Irwin. 2 cass. (Running Time: 3 hrs. 25 mins.). (Hardy Boys Ser.: No. 4). (J). (gr. 4-7).

2004. 23.00 (978-0-8072-0776-5(4), S YA 409 CX, Listening Lib) Random Audio Pubg.
"When the Hardy Boys set out to solve the mystery of their missing chums, they discover a gang hide-out on an island along the way.".

Missing Dates see Caedmon Treasury of Modern Poets Reading Their Own Poetry

Missing Dates see Twentieth-Century Poetry in English: Recordings of Poets Reading Their Own Poetry

Missing from the Record, unabr. ed. Clive Egleton. Narrated by Simon Prebble. 6 cass. (Running Time: 9 hrs.). 1994. 51.00 (978-1-55690-995-5(0), 94134E7) Recorded Bks.
Sarah Cartwright, wife & mother of two & former employee of the Foreign Service, has disappeared, leaving behind only a series of conflicting messages. Her husband, Tom, a staff officer in the British Army, begins a methodical international search for his missing wife. Unaware that her most important message has not reached her husband, Sarah leads him on a chase from Europe to the Far East.

Missing in Death. abr. unabr. ed. J. D. Robb, pseud. (Running Time: 3 hrs.). (In Death Ser.). 2010. audio compact disk 9.99 (978-1-4233-8367-3(2), 9781423383673, BCD Value Price) Brilliance Audio.

Missing in Death. unabr. ed. J. D. Robb, pseud. Read by Susan Ericksen. (Running Time: 3 hrs.). (In Death Ser.). 2009. 19.99 (978-1-4233-8363-5(X), 9781423383635, Brilliance MP3); 39.97 (978-1-4233-8364-2(8), 9781423383642, Brlnc Audio MP3 Lib); 19.99 (978-1-4233-8365-9(6), 9781423383659, BAD); 39.97 (978-1-4233-8366-6(4), 9781423383666, BADLE); audio compact disk 19.99 (978-1-4233-8361-1(3), 9781423383611, Bril Audio CD Unabri); audio compact disk 62.97 (978-1-4233-8362-8(1), 9781423383628, BriAudCD Unabrid) Brilliance Audio.

Missing Ingredient. Elbert Willis. 1 cass. (Joy & Peace Ser.). 4.00 Fill the Gap.

Missing Ingredient in Marriage: 1 Cor. 13:3-7. Ed Young. (J). 1981. 4.95 (978-0-7417-1162-5(1), A0162) Win Walk.

Missing Jew: New & Selected Poems. rev. ed. Rodger Kamenetz. 1992. 12.95 (978-1-877770-59-3(0)) Time Being Bks.

Missing Joseph. unabr. ed. Elizabeth George. Read by Donada Peters. 13 cass. (Running Time: 19 hrs. 30 min.). (Inspector Lynley Ser.). 1993. 104.00 (978-0-7366-2533-3(X), 3285) Books on Tape.
Deborah St. James & her husband Simon take a holiday in Lancashire to see the vicar of Winslough, a close friend. But the vicar dies before they arrive. Simon suspects murder. With Detective Inspector Thomas Lynley's assistance, he means to find out why no charges were brought against the sensual herbalist who fed the vicar a dinner laced with death.

Missing Justice. Alafair Burke. Read by Betty Bobbitt. (Running Time: 11 hrs.). 2009. 84.99 (978-1-74214-196-1(X), 9781742141961) Pub: Bolinda Pubng AUS. Dist(s): Bolinda Pub Inc

Missing Justice. unabr. ed. Alafair Burke. Read by Betty Bobbitt. 11 CDs. (Running Time: 39600 sec.). (Samantha Kincaid Mysteries). 2005. audio compact disk 103.95 (978-1-74093-714-6(7)) Pub: Bolinda Pubng AUS. Dist(s): Bolinda Pub Inc

Missing Link. Joyce Holms. 2007. 69.95 (978-1-84559-639-2(0)) Pub: Soundings Ltd GBR. Dist(s): Ulverscroft US

***Missing Links.** unabr. ed. Rick Reilly. Read by Bronson Pinchot. (Running Time: 8 hrs. 30 mins.). 2010. 29.95 (978-1-4417-4017-5(1)); 54.95 (978-1-4417-4013-7(9)); audio compact disk 19.95 (978-1-4417-4016-8(3)); audio compact disk 76.00 (978-1-4417-4014-4(7)) Blckstn Audio.

Missing Marlene. abr. ed. Evan Marshall. Read by M. J. Wilde. 6 vols. 2003. 25.00 (978-1-58807-433-1(1)) Am Pubng Inc.

***Missing Max.** unabr. ed. Karen Young. Narrated by Laural Merlington. (Running Time: 9 hrs. 23 mins. 10 sec.). (ENG.). 2010. 20.99 (978-1-60814-677-2(4)); audio compact disk 29.99 (978-1-59859-726-4(4)) Oasis Audio.

Missing May. Cynthia Rylant. Read by Frances McDormand. 2 cass. (Running Time: 2 hrs. 24 mins.). (J). 2000. 18.00 (978-0-7366-9061-4(1)) Books on Tape.
About twelve year old heroine named Summer.

Missing May, abr. ed. Cynthia Rylant. Read by Frances McDormand. 2 cass. (Running Time: 3 hrs.). (J). (978-0-553-47682-8(3), 394036, Random AudioBks) Random Audio Pubg.
May was always " a big barrel of nothing but love." May had been Summer's mother for the last six happy years. May was dead. But only Ob, her sorrowing husband, sensed her visitation when she stopped by the trailer. Newbery Award Winner.

Missing May. unabr. ed. Cynthia Rylant. Read by Frances McDormand. 2 vols. (Running Time: 1 hr. 58 mins.). (J). (gr. 5-9). 2004. pap. bk. 29.00 (978-0-8072-8701-9(6), YA240SP, Listening Lib); 23.00 (978-0-8072-8700-2(8), YA240CX, Listening Lib) Random Audio Pubg.
After being passed among relatives, Summer joins her aunt & uncle & marvels at the couple's deep love for one another. But after Aunt May dies, Summer & Uncle Ob are brought together in their struggles to come to terms with her death.

Missing May, unabr. ed. Cynthia Rylant. Narrated by Angela Jayne Rogers. 2 pieces. (Running Time: 2 hrs.). (gr. 5 up). 1997. 19.00 (978-0-7887-0377-5(3), 94568E7) Recorded Bks.
As twelve-year-old Summer tries to understand her loneliness after a beloved aunt dies, she searches for some sign that the old woman is still watching over her. A gentle tale of grief & friendship.

Missing Mom. unabr. ed. Joyce Carol Oates. 1 CD. 2005. 29.95 (978-0-7927-3838-1(1), Chivers Sound Lib) AudioGO.

Missing Mom. unabr. ed. Joyce Carol Oates. Read by Anna Fields. 8 cass. (Running Time: 52140 sec.). 2005. 69.95 (978-0-7927-3766-7(0), Chivers Sound Lib); audio compact disk 89.95 (978-0-7927-3767-4(9), Chivers Sound Lib) AudioGO.

Missing Mom. unabr. ed. Joyce Carol Oates. Read by Anna Fields. (YA). 2007. 79.99 (978-1-60252-850-5(0)) Find a World.

Missing Person see Chamber Music

Missing Person Mystery. Julianna Anastasiadis. 1 cass. 8.95 (605) Am Fed Astrologers.
An AFA Convention workshop tape.

Missing Persons. abr. ed. Stephen White. Read by Dick Hill. (Running Time: 6 hrs.). (Dr. Alan Gregory Ser.). 2005. audio compact disk 74.25 (978-1-59355-565-8(2), 9781593555658, BACDLib Ed) Brilliance Audio.
Please enter a Synopsis.

Missing Persons. abr. ed. Stephen White. Read by Dick Hill. (Running Time: 6 hrs.). (Dr. Alan Gregory Ser.). 2010. audio compact disk 9.99 (978-1-4418-4184-1(9), 9781441841841) Brilliance Audio.

Missing Persons. unabr. ed. Stephen White. Read by Dick Hill. (Running Time: 12 hrs.). (Dr. Alan Gregory Ser.). 2005. 49.97 (978-1-59710-498-2(1), 9781597104982, BADLE); 24.95 (978-1-59710-499-9(X), 9781597104999, BAD); 24.95 (978-1-59335-739-9(7), 9781593357399); 39.25 (978-1-59335-873-0(3), 9781593358730, Brlnc Audio MP3 Lib) Brilliance Audio.

***Missing Persons.** unabr. ed. Stephen White. Read by Dick Hill. (Running Time: 13 hrs.). (Dr. Alan Gregory Ser.). 2010. audio compact disk 29.99 (978-1-4418-4051-6(6), 9781441840516, Bril Audio CD Unabri); audio compact disk 89.97 (978-1-4418-4052-3(4), 9781441840523, BriAudCD Unabrid) Brilliance Audio.

Missing Pet/A Pet for You. Steck-Vaughn Staff. 1997. (978-0-8172-7366-8(2)) SteckVau.

Missing Pieces, Level 1. (J). 2002. audio compact disk (978-0-7398-5318-4(X)) SteckVau.

Missing Pieces Level 1. (J). 2002. (978-0-7398-5087-9(3)) SteckVau.

Missing, Presumed Dead. unabr. ed. J. M. Gregson. Read by Robbie MacNab. 5 cass. (Running Time: 6 hrs. 35 min.). 1998. 63.95 (978-1-85903-187-2(0)) Pub: Magna Story GBR. Dist(s): Ulverscroft US
Detective Inspector Percy Peach, bouncy & aggressive, is unimpressed to find his new detective sergeant is to be a woman, especially when the capable & resourceful Lucy Blake proves to be more than a match for her formidable boss. Two years after a nineteen-year-old girl disappeared from her home, her body is found at the bottom of a deep pond on the North Lancashire golf course. Peach & Blake, while investigating the circumstances of those who were close to the girl, find the truth behind the mystery is as unexpected as it is chilling.

Missing Racehorse & Reuben Calloway. Perf. by Jack Webb. 1 cass. (Running Time: 1 hr.). Dramatization. (Pat Novak for Hire Ser.). 1949. 6.00 Once Upon Rad.
Mystery & suspense radio broadcasts.

Missing Secret: How to Use the Law of Attraction to Easily Attract What You Want... Every Time. abr. ed. Joe Vitale, Jr.. Read by Joe Vitale, Jr. 2 CDs. (Running Time: 2 hrs. 0 mins. 0 sec.). (ENG.). 2008. audio compact disk 19.99 (978-0-7435-7617-8(9), Nightgale) Pub: S&S Audio. Dist(s): S and S Inc

***Missing Sisters.** unabr. ed. Gregory Maguire. Read by Angela Goethals. (ENG.). 2009. (978-0-06-190236-9(5)); (978-0-06-176105-8(2)) HarperCollins Pubs.

Missing Susan. unabr. ed. Sharyn McCrumb. Narrated by Barbara Rosenblat. 6 cass. (Running Time: 8 hrs. 45 mins.). (Elizabeth MacPherson Ser.: No. 6). 1998. 51.00 (978-0-7887-1993-6(9), 95380E7) Recorded Bks.
When a British tour director is offered $50,000 to murder a particularly obnoxious client, he surprises himself by accepting the offer. But one of the other tourists is super sleuth Elizabeth MacPherson. Will she spoil the plot or unwittingly help it along.

Missing Three-Quarter see Return of Sherlock Holmes

Missing Three-Quarter. Arthur Conan Doyle. 1 cass. 1989. 7.95 (S-36) Jimcin Record.

Missing Virtue - Integrity: Dan. 6:1-13. Ed Young. (J). 1982. 4.95 (978-0-7417-1216-5(4), A0216) Win Walk.

Missing You. Meg Cabot. Read by Johanna Parker. 5. (Running Time: 6 hrs.). (1-800-Where-R-You Ser.: No. 5). 2007. 49.75 (978-1-4281-3437-9(9)); audio compact disk 77.75 (978-1-4281-3442-3(5)) Recorded Bks.

Mission: Black List No. 1 - The Inside Story of the Search for Saddam Hussein - As Told by the Soldier Who Masterminded His Capture. unabr. ed. Eric Maddox & Davin Seay. Read by Bernie Mcinerney. 6 CDs. (Running Time: 7 hrs. 30 mins.). 2008. audio compact disk 34.95 (978-0-06-171907-3(2), Harper Audio) HarperCollins Pubs.

Mission: Possible. Mark Bradford. 1 CD. (Running Time: 1 hr.). Dramatization. (Target Trax Ser.). 1997. pap. bk. 15.00 (978-1-58302-131-6(0), DTT-06) One Way St.
Collection of religious musical puppetry performance pieces. Six segments included with script.

Mission: Success! The Anthology of Achievement. Og Mandino. Read by Og Mandino. 6 cass. Dramatization. 59.95 (788AD) Nightingale-Conant.
Each story is a full-cast production with musical score, bringing you inspiring principles of success & achievement along with a thoroughly entertaining story. You'll be provided with principles, techniques, & good habits that will virtually "guarantee" your success & help you profit many times over.

Mission Accomplished: Neh. 6:15-19. Ed Young. 1990. 4.95 (978-0-7417-1813-6(8), 813) Win Walk.

Mission: Accomplished: Terrific Tales, Mysterious Missions. Marshal Younger. Created by Focus on the Family Staff. 6 cass. (Adventures in Odyssey Gold Ser.). (ENG.). (J). 2005. audio compact disk 24.99 (978-1-58997-232-2(5)) Pub: Focus Family. Dist(s): Tyndale Hse

***Mission: Black List #1.** unabr. ed. Eric Maddox & Davin Seay. Read by Bernie Mcinerney. (ENG.). 2008. (978-0-06-172674-3(5)); (978-0-06-172675-0(3)) HarperCollins Pubs.

Mission: Black List #1: The Inside Story of the Search for Saddam Hussein - As Told by the Soldier Who Masterminded His Capture. Eric Maddox. Read by Bernie McInerney. Told to Davin Seay. (ENG.). 2009. 59.99 (978-1-60812-711-5(7)) Find a World.

Mission Canyon. unabr. ed. Meg Gardiner. Read by Tanya Eby Sirois. 1 MP3-CD. (Running Time: 10 hrs.). (Evan Delaney Ser.). 2008. 39.25 (978-1-4233-6127-5(X), 9781423361275, Brlnc Audio MP3 Lib) Brilliance Audio.

Mission Canyon. unabr. ed. Meg Gardiner. Read by Tanya Eby Sirois. (Running Time: 10 hrs.). (Evan Delaney Ser.). 2008. 24.95 (978-1-4233-6128-2(8), 9781423361282, BAD) Brilliance Audio.

Mission Canyon. unabr. ed. Meg Gardiner. Read by Tanya Eby Sirois. 1 MP3-CD. (Running Time: 10 hrs.). (Evan Delaney Ser.). 2008. 24.95 (978-1-4233-6126-8(1), 9781423361268, Brilliance MP3) Brilliance Audio.

Mission Canyon. unabr. ed. Meg Gardiner. Read by Tanya Eby Sirois. (Running Time: 10 hrs.). (Evan Delaney Ser.). 2008. 39.25 (978-1-4233-6129-9(6), 9781423361299, BADLE) Brilliance Audio.

Mission Canyon. unabr. ed. Meg Gardiner. Read by Tanya Eby Sirois. 8 CDs. (Running Time: 10 hrs.). (Evan Delaney Ser.). 2008. audio compact disk 97.25 (978-1-4233-6125-1(3), 9781423361251, BriAudCD Unabrid); audio compact disk 36.95 (978-1-4233-6124-4(5), 9781423361244, Bril Audio CD Unabri) Brilliance Audio.

Mission Compromised: A Novel. abr. ed. Oliver North & Joe Musser. 6 cass. 2002. 24.99 (978-0-8054-2636-6(1)) BH Pubng Grp.

Mission Day. unabr. ed. Robert A. Monroe. Read by Robert A. Monroe. (Running Time: 45 min.). (Gateway Experience - Exploring Ser.). 1984. 14.95 (978-1-56113-276-8(4)) Monroe Institute.

Mission Earth 1: The Invaders Plan. 3 CDs. audio compact disk 25.00 (978-1-59212-192-2(6)) Gala Pr LLC.

Mission Earth 2: Black Genesis. 3 CDs. audio compact disk 25.00 (978-1-59212-193-9(4)) Gala Pr LLC.

Mission Earth 3: The Enemy Within. 3 CDs. audio compact disk 25.00 (978-1-59212-194-6(2)) Gala Pr LLC.

Mission Earth 4: An Alien Affair. 3 CDs. audio compact disk 25.00 (978-1-59212-195-3(0)) Gala Pr LLC.

Mission Earth 5: Fortune of Fear. 3 CDs. audio compact disk 25.00 (978-1-59212-196-0(9)) Gala Pr LLC.

Mission Earth 6: Death Quest. 3 CDs. audio compact disk 25.00 (978-1-59212-197-7(7)) Gala Pr LLC.

Mission Earth 7: Voyage of Vengeance. 3 CDs. audio compact disk 25.00 (978-1-59212-198-4(5)) Gala Pr LLC.

Mission Earth 8: Disaster. 3 CDs. audio compact disk 25.00 (978-1-59212-199-1(3)) Gala Pr LLC.

Mission Earth 9: Villainy Victorious. 3 CDs. audio compact disk 25.00 (978-1-59212-200-4(0)) Gala Pr LLC.

Mission Earth 10: The Doomed Planet. 3 CDs. audio compact disk 25.00 (978-1-59212-201-1(9)) Gala Pr LLC.

Mission Field Tours for Key Leaders & Supporters: National Association of Evangelicals, 47th Annual Association, Columbus, Ohio, March 7-9, 1989. Kermit Yoder. 1 cass. (Workshops Ser.: No. 9-Wednesda). 1989. 4.25 ea. 1-8 tapes.; 4.00 ea. 9 tapes or more. Nat Assn Evan.

Mission I Missed. Troy Dunn. 1 cass. 2004. 9.95 (978-1-55503-732-1(1), 069401) Covenant Comms.
Encourages youth to get their priorities straight.

Mission Night. unabr. ed. Robert A. Monroe. Read by Robert A. Monroe. (Running Time: 45 min.). (Gateway Experience - Exploring Ser.). 1984. 14.95 (978-1-56113-277-5(2)) Monroe Institute.
Make the most of your sleeping hours.

***Mission of God's People: A Biblical Theology of the Church's Mission.** unabr. ed. Christopher J. H. Wright. (Running Time: 14 hrs. 18 mins. 28 sec.). (Biblical Theology for Life Ser.). (ENG.). 2010. 24.99 (978-0-310-78244-5(9)) Zondervan.

***Mission of Honor.** unabr. ed. David Weber. Read by Allyson Johnson. (Running Time: 24 hrs.). (Honor Harrington Ser.). 2010. 44.97 (978-1-4418-6726-1(0), 9781441867261, Brlnc Audio MP3 Lib); 29.99 (978-1-4418-6725-4(2), 9781441867254, Brilliance MP3); 44.97 (978-1-4418-6727-8(9), 9781441867278, BADLE); audio compact disk 99.97 (978-1-4418-6724-7(4), 9781441867247, BriAudCD Unabrid) Brilliance Audio.

***Mission of Honor.** unabr. ed. David Weber. Read by Allyson Johnson. (Running Time: 24 hrs.). (Honor Harrington Ser.: Bk. 12). 2010. audio compact disk 39.99 (978-1-4418-6723-0(6), 9781441867230, Bril Audio CD Unabri) Brilliance Audio.

Mission of Jane see Women in Literature, the Short Story: A Collection

Mission of Jane see Selected American Short Stories

Mission of Jane. unabr. ed. Edith Wharton. Read by Walter Zimmerman. 1 cass. (Running Time: 1 hr.). Dramatization. 1982. 7.95 (S-23) Jimcin Record.
Life in high society.

Mission of Jane, unabr. ed. Edith Wharton. 2 cass. (Running Time: 2 hrs. 30 mins.). (Edith Wharton Ser.). 1994. bk. 16.95 (978-1-883049-15-7(6), 390233) Sound Room.
In "The Mission of Jane" an awkward couple adopt & raise a daughter & gain something unexpected when she marries. An inherent pitfall of an open marriage comes to light in "The Reckoning" & in "Les Metteurs en Scene" a young couple learn the cruelty of irony.

Mission of Jane. unabr. ed. Edith Wharton. Read by Susan McInerney. 2 cass. Library ed. (Running Time: 2 hrs. 25 min.). 1994. lib. bdg. 18.95 (978-1-883049-36-2(9)) Sound Room.
A collection of three stories: "The Mission of Jane", "Les Metteurs en Scene", & "The Reckoning".

Mission of Lord Buddha. Swami Amar Jyoti. 1 cass. 1991. 9.95 (K-130) Truth Consciousness.
Many glowing episodes from the life of Lord Buddha. Embodiment of perfect Peace, Kindness & Compassion, He changed the lives of millions.

Mission of the Messiah. Timothy Gray. 6 cass. (Running Time: 6 hrs.). 1998. 22.95 (978-0-9663223-2-3(0)) Emmaus Rd Pubng.
Catholic Bible study on the Gospel of Luke.

Mission of Women. Alice Von Hildebrand. 1 cass. 1992. 2.50 (978-1-56036-046-9(1)) AMI Pr.

Mission Possible. Contrib. by Don Marsh & Lorie Marsh. 1997. 11.98 (978-0-7601-1520-6(6), 75602086) Pub: Brentwood Music. Dist(s): H Leonard

Mission Possible. Contrib. by Don Marsh & Lorie Marsh. 1997. audio compact disk 85.00 (978-0-7601-1525-1(7), 75606311) Pub: Brentwood Music. Dist(s): H Leonard

Mission Possible. Contrib. by Don Marsh & Lorie Marsh. 1997. 85.00 (978-0-7601-1524-4(9), 75606310) Pub: Brentwood Music. Dist(s): H Leonard

Mission Possible: Adventures in Faith Teaching Unit. Liz VonSeggen et al. Ed. by Liz VonSeggen. Prod. by One Way Street. Orig. Title: Mission Possible: Adventures in Faith. (J). 2002. audio compact disk 40.00 (978-1-58302-221-4(X)) One Way St.
This ten-week unit will thrill your children as they become F.B.I. cadets (Faith Building Interns). Sacred Agent Man introduces them to bible and modern day heros and then issues fith challenges to each cadet. All takes place in the Hall of Faith with puppets, drama, music, Bible memory, and fun detective work! This NEW CD includes special music for this unit.

Mission Possible: Becoming a World Class Organization While There's Still Time, abr. ed. Ken Blanchard & Terry Waghorn. Read by Richard Beebe. 2 cass. (Running Time: 3 hrs.). 1999. 16.95 (978-1-55935-242-0(6), 394632) Soundelux.
How a manager can concentrate on improving the existing organization, while at the same time keeping focused & creating an all important future plan. It covers quality, benchmarking, strategic planning, empowerment, core competencies & more.

Mission Possible: Spiritual Covering. Deborah McCarragher. (ENG.). 2009. audio compact disk 9.95 (978-0-615-28584-9(8)) Ala Box Pub.

Mission Possible: Adventures in Faith see Mission Possible: Adventures in Faith Teaching Unit

Mission Primer: Four Steps to an Effective Mission Statement. Richard D. O'Hallaron & David R. O'Hallaron. Voice by Richard D. O'Hallaron. (ENG.). 2008. 19.00 (978-0-9676635-1-7(2)) Mission Inc.

Mission Song. abr. ed. John le Carré. Read by David Oyelowo. (Running Time: 6 hrs. 30 mins.). (ENG.). 2006. 14.98 (978-1-59483-565-0(9)) Pub: Hachet Audio. Dist(s): HachBkGrp

Mission Song. abr. ed. John le Carré. Read by David Oyelowo. (Running Time: 6 hrs. 30 mins.). (ENG.). 2008. audio compact disk 14.98 (978-1-60024-276-2(6)) Pub: Hachet Audio. Dist(s): HachBkGrp

Mission Song. unabr. ed. John le Carré. John le Carré. 12 cass. (Running Time: 18 hrs.). 2006. 96.00 (978-1-4159-3464-7(9)); audio compact disk 120.00 (978-1-4159-3465-4(7)) Books on Tape.

Mission Song. unabr. ed. John le Carré. Read by David Oyelowo. (Running Time: 11 hrs. 30 mins.). (ENG.). 2006. 16.98 (978-1-59483-567-4(5)) Pub: Hachet Audio. Dist(s): HachBkGrp

Mission Song: A Novel. unabr. ed. John le Carré. Read by David Oyelowo. (Running Time: 11 hrs. 30 mins.). (ENG.). 2009. 59.98 (978-1-60788-148-3(9)) Pub: Hachet Audio. Dist(s): HachBkGrp

Mission: Success see Mision: Exito!

Mission 10. unabr. ed. Robert A. Monroe. Read by Robert A. Monroe. (Running Time: 45 min.). (Gateway Experience - Exploring Ser.). 1984. 14.95 (978-1-56113-274-4(8)) Monroe Institute.
Discover more powerful & effective focus 10.

Mission 12. unabr. ed. Robert A. Monroe. Read by Robert A. Monroe. (Running Time: 45 min.). (Gateway Experience - Exploring Ser.). 1984. 14.95 (978-1-56113-275-1(6)) Monroe Institute.
Expand your possibilities with Free Flow 12.

Missionaries Need to Know God. Grant Von Harrison. Read by Ted Gibbons. 1 cass. (Missionary Success Ser.). 6.95 (978-0-929985-37-4(0)) Jackman Pubng.
Knowing God through true obedience & spiritual success.

Missionary & Temple Work for the Dead. unabr. ed. Duane S. Crowther. Read by Duane S. Crowther. 1 cass. (Running Time: 1 hr. 30 min.). 1989. 13.98 (978-0-88290-356-9(X), 1828) Horizon Utah.
This tape focuses on the great missionary work going on beyond the veil. Vivid descriptions of after-death missionary work are explained, & an excellent explanation is given of the meanings & purposes of vicarious temple work for the dead who accept the missionary message.

Missionary Stew, unabr. ed. Ross Thomas. Narrated by Frank Muller. 6 cass. (Running Time: 7 hrs. 45 mins.). 1986. 51.00 (978-1-55690-342-7(1), 86470E7) Recorded Bks.
The gold links in the band of Morgan Citron's Rolex had enabled him to survive the prison of the Emperor-President. After that, he wanted nothing more than a desert island to spend his life on. So how did he become involved in shady presidential politics, a cocaine war & the overthrow of a South American dictatorship.

Missionary's Little Book of Answers. Gilbert Scharffs. 3 cass. 2004. 14.95 (978-1-59156-039-5(X)); audio compact disk 14.95 (978-1-59156-040-1(3)) Covenant Comms.

Missions Chairman's Training Institute. unabr. ed. Tom Telford. 3 cass. (Running Time: 50 mins. ea. cass.). 2000. 17.98 (ACMC) Caleb Res.
Seminar given at an ACMC National Conference.

Mississippi! abr. ed. Dana Fuller Ross, pseud. Read by Lloyd James. Abr. by Mary Bevoni. 4 vols. (Wagons West Ser.: No. 15). 2003. 25.00 (978-1-58807-147-7(2)); (978-1-58807-616-8(4)) Am Pubng Inc.

Mississippi! abr. ed. Dana Fuller Ross, pseud. Read by Lloyd James. Abr. by Mary Bevoni. 5 vols. (Wagons West Ser.: No. 15). 2004. audio compact disk 30.00 (978-1-58807-382-3(3)); audio compact disk (978-1-58807-861-2(2)) Am Pubng Inc.

Mississippi: River of Song. annot. ed. Perf. by Soul Asylum et al. Anno. by Elijah Wald. Compiled by Elijah Wald. 2 CDs. (Running Time: 2 hrs. 11 min.). 1998. audio compact disk 24.95 Smithsonian Folkways.
Artists featured in a 4 part TV series that aired on PBS.

Mississippi Jack: Being an Account of the Further Waterborne Adventures of Jacky Faber, Midshipman, Fine Lady, & Lily of the West. unabr. ed. Steve Jenkins. Read by Katherine Kellgren. (YA). 2009. audio compact disk 29.95 (978-1-59316-445-4(9)) Listen & Live.

***Mississippi Memories Lead to New Beginnings: An Nccu Arts & Humanities Documentary Dvd.** rev. ed. North Carolina Central University, Museum of Art Staff. 2010. audio compact disk 98.38 (978-0-7575-2697-8(7)) Kendall-Hunt.

Mississippi Morning. 1 cass. (Running Time: 12 mins.). (J). (gr. 3-5). 2008. 27.95 (978-0-8045-6963-7(0)); audio compact disk 29.95 (978-0-8045-4186-2(8)) Spoken Arts.

Mississippi Pirates. unabr. ed. Douglas Hirt. Read by Rusty Nelson. 8 cass. (Running Time: 10 hrs. 12 min.). (Riverboat Ser.: Bk. 2). 2001. 49.95 (978-1-55686-893-1(6)) Books in Motion.
Captain Hamilton's Tempest Queen steams the Mississippi facing danger from river pirate Deke Saunders, as the ambitions and stories of the passengers unfold.

Mississippi Vistas: Volume One of A Mississippi Trilogy. Louis Daniel Brodsky. (Mississippi Trilogy). 1990. pap. bk. 19.95 (978-1-877770-15-9(9)); 12.95 (978-1-877770-14-2(0)) Time Being Bks.

Missouri! abr. ed. Dana Fuller Ross, pseud. Read by Lloyd James. 4 vols. (Wagons West Ser.: No. 14). 2003. (978-1-58807-615-1(6)) Am Pubng Inc.

Missouri! abr. ed. Dana Fuller Ross, pseud. Read by Lloyd James. 4 cass. (Running Time: 360 mins.). (Wagon West Ser.: No. 14). 2003. 25.00 (978-1-58807-002-9(6)) Am Pubng Inc.

Missouri! abr. ed. Dana Fuller Ross, pseud. Read by Lloyd James. 5 vols. (Wagons West Ser.: No. 14). 2004. audio compact disk 30.00 (978-1-58807-381-5(5)); audio compact disk (978-1-58807-860-5(4)) Am Pubng Inc.

Missouri Guns. unabr. ed. Larry D. Names. Read by Maynard Villers. 8 cass. (Running Time: 9 hrs. 36 min.). (Creed Ser.: Bk. 6). 2001. 49.95 (978-1-55686-809-2(X)) Books in Motion.
Seeking to find those who framed him as an outlaw, Slate Creed find himself in Missouri, where he's heading straight into a deadly snare plotted by none other than outlaw Cole Younger.

Missouri Mule (Thomas) John 20:24-28. Ed Young. 1985. 4.95 (978-0-7417-1471-8(X), 471) Win Walk.

Mist. 1 CD. audio compact disk 15.95 (MIST002) S & S.

Mist. 1 cass. 12.95 (MIST001) S&S Audio.

Mist: In 3-D Sound. Stephen King. 1 cass. (Running Time: 1 hr.). 2001. 12.95 (MIST001); audio compact disk 15.95 (MIST002) Lodestone Catalog.

Mist: In 3-D Sound. Stephen King. 1 cass. (Running Time: 1 hr. 30 min.). 12.50 (TM) ZBS Ind.
Includes:The Making of the Mist, 15-minute documentary about the special sound effects.

Mist: In 3-D Sound. abr. ed. Stephen King. Read by Stephen King. Read by Full Cast Production Staff. 1 cass. (Running Time: 20 hrs. 0 mins. 0 sec.). (ENG.). 1986. 12.00 (978-0-671-62138-4(6), Audioworks) Pub: S&S Audio. Dist(s): S and S Inc

Mist: In 3-D Sound. abr. movie tie-in ed. Stephen King. Contrib. by Full Cast Production Staff. (Running Time: 13 hrs. 0 mins. 0 sec.). (ENG.). 2007. audio compact disk 15.00 (978-0-7435-7128-9(2)) Pub: S&S Audio. Dist(s): S and S Inc

Mist & Stone. Maggie Sansone. 1993. pap. bk. 19.95 (978-0-7866-1181-2(2), 95025P); pap. bk. 24.95 (978-0-7866-1180-5(4), 95025CDP) Mel Bay.

Mist-ery. unabr. ed. Liese C. Reich. Read by Liese C. Reich. Perf. by Cynthia Stacey. 1 cass. (Running Time: 1 hr. 10 min.). 1996. 9.95 (978-0-9654137-0-1(5), MW1207) Mystic Wave.
Stories/myths (fiction) with themes of nature, spirit, journey, desire, mystery & grace.

Mistake Free Grammar & Proofreading. PUEI. 2005. audio compact disk 89.95 (978-1-933328-25-6(8), CareerTrack) P Univ E Inc.

Mistake of Mind over Matter: Embodied Spirituality. Read by Julia Jewett. 1 cass. (Running Time: 1 hr. 30 min.). 1987. 10.95 (978-0-7822-0101-7(6), 273) C G Jung IL.

Mistaken Identity. Lisa Scottoline. Read by Kate Harper. 12 CDs. 2004. audio compact disk 110.95 (978-0-7927-3205-1(7), SLD 243, Chivers Sound Lib) AudioGO.

Mistaken Identity, abr. ed. Lisa Scottoline. Read by Kate Burton. 2 cass. 1999. 18.00 (FS9-43405) Highsmith.

Mistaken Identity. unabr. ed. Lisa Scottoline. Read by Kate Harper. 14 vols. (Running Time: 21 hrs.). 2000. bk. 110.95 (978-0-7927-2354-7(6), CSL 243, Chivers Sound Lib) AudioGO.
Bennie Rosato, head of her own Philadelphia law firm, specializes in police misconduct cases. Her new client, Alice Connolly, is accused of murdering her lover, a highly decorated police officer. What shocks Bennie is that Connolly looks just like her. "Pleased to meet you. I'm your twin. Your identical twin," Connolly tells Bennie, who grew up an only child, or so she thought. Bennie plunges into the mystery of the murder & her family's dark secrets.

Mistaken Identity. unabr. ed. Lisa Scottoline. Read by Kate Harper. 2 CDs. (Running Time: 6 hrs.). 2002. audio compact disk 49.95 (978-0-7927-2766-8(5), CMP 243, Chivers Sound Lib) AudioGO.

***Mistaken Identity Low Price.** abr. ed. Lisa Scottoline. Read by Kate Burton. (ENG.). 2005. (978-0-06-088655-4(2), Harper Audio); (978-0-06-088656-1(0), Harper Audio) HarperCollins Pubs.

Mistakenly in Mallorca. unabr. ed. Roderic Jeffries. Narrated by Patrick Tull. 6 cass. (Running Time: 7 hrs. 45 mins.). 2000. 56.00 (978-0-7887-4933-9(1), H1105E7) Recorded Bks.
John Tatham, devastated by the loss of his wife, escapes his sorrow by visiting his Aunt Alvina in Mallorca, where she is considered the most eccentric of the Englishwomen on the island. However, when Alvina dies, Tatham finds himself deep in an elaborate coverup.

***Mistakes Are Normal Audio CD.** Susan Diane Matz. (ENG.). 2010. 15.95 (978-0-9841054-9-6(2)) Abriev Ent.

Mistakes I Made My First Five Years in Business. Elizabeth K. Fischer. 2002. (978-0-9721255-3-6(1)) Monarch Tree.

Mistakes Were Made CD. Bill Harley. 2003. audio compact disk 15.00 (978-1-878126-45-0(8)) Round Riv Prodns.
A collection of stories and songs about the trials and tribulations of being an adult from Bill Harley.

Mister & Me. Kimberly Willis Holt. Read by Andrea Johnson. 2 cass. (Running Time: 1 hr. 30 mins.). (J). (gr. 2 up). 2000. pap. bk. & stu. ed. 39.99 (978-0-7887-4341-2(4), 41135) Recorded Bks.
Jolene's daddy died when she was a baby, but Momma & Grandpa are all the family she needs. Now Momma's talking about marrying again & Jolene is worried & scared. Does this mean she could lose Momma, too?.

Mister & Me, Kimberly Willis Holt. Read by Andrea Johnson. 2 cass. (Running Time: 1 hr. 30 mins.). (J). (gr. 2 up). 2000. stu. ed. 167.20 (978-0-7887-4441-9(0), 47132) Recorded Bks.

Mister & Me. unabr. ed. Kimberly Willis Holt. Narrated by Andrea Johnson. 2 pieces. (Running Time: 1 hr. 30 mins.). (gr. 2 up). 2000. 19.00 (978-0-7887-4225-5(6), 96203E7) Recorded Bks.

***Mister B. Gone.** unabr. ed. Clive Barker. Read by Doug Bradley. (ENG.). 2007. (978-0-06-155574-9(6)); (978-0-06-155575-6(4)) HarperCollins Pubs.

Mister B. Gone. unabr. ed. Clive Barker. Read by Doug Bradley. 2008. audio compact disk 14.95 (978-0-06-167290-3(4), Harper Audio) HarperCollins Pubs.

Mister Candid. Jules Hardy. 10 CDs. (Running Time: 12 hrs. 33 mins.). (Isis (CDs) Ser.). (J). 2004. audio compact disk 89.95 (978-0-7531-2349-2(5)) Pub: ISIS Lrg Prnt GBR. Dist(s): Ulverscroft US

Mister Candid. unabr. ed. Jules Hardy. Read by William Dufris. 9 cass. (Running Time: 12 hrs. 33 mins.). (Isis Cassettes Ser.). (J). 2004. 76.95 (978-0-7531-1950-1(1)) Pub: ISIS Lrg Prnt GBR. Dist(s): Ulverscroft US

Mister God, this Is Anna. Read by Colin Moody. (Running Time: 6 hrs.). (YA). 2009. 64.99 (978-1-74214-315-6(6), 9781742143156) Pub: Bolinda Pubng AUS. Dist(s): Bolinda Pub Inc

Mister God, This Is Anna. unabr. ed. Fynn. Read by Colin Moody. 6 CDs. (Running Time: 21600 sec.). 2005. audio compact disk 63.95 (978-1-74093-690-3(6)) Pub: Bolinda Pubng AUS. Dist(s): Bolinda Pub Inc

Mister Monday. Garth Nix. 5 cass. (Running Time: 8 hrs. 4 mins.). (Keys to the Kingdom Ser.: No. 1). (J). (gr. 4-7). 2004. 40.00 (978-0-8072-1657-6(7), Listening Lib) Random Audio Pubg.

Mister Rogers' Neighborhood: 1 Sam. 1:21-28. Ed Young. 1991. 4.95 (978-0-7417-1858-7(8), 858) Win Walk.

Mister Rogers Won't You Be My Neighbor? Mister Rogers. 1 cass. (MusicTivity Ser.). (J). 1994. pap. bk. 9.95 (978-0-7935-2927-8(1), 00815023) H Leonard.
Performing Arts - Music.

Mister Rural Dean. unabr. ed. Fred Secombe. Read by Fred Secombe. 7 cass. (Running Time: 9 hrs. 30 mins.). 1999. 61.95 (978-1-86042-471-7(6), 24716) Pub: Soundings Ltd GBR. Dist(s): Ulverscroft US
Begins with an amateur performance of the "Pirates of Penzance" by the newly created Church Gilbert & Sullivan Society & ends with a highly professional midnight matinee featuring the Vicar's brother. In between these two events life is hectic for the incumbent of Abergelly. He has to cope with the elopement of the Church Warden of St. David's with an eighteen-years-old schoolgirl, an unexpected visit to the Parish of the Earl of Duffryn & the sudden death of the organist at St. Mary's. Then there is a gypsy wedding where the only participation of the congregation in the service is the recitation of the Lord's Prayer. At another wedding the local bookmaker is married to a young bride whose day is spoilt by the desecration of the wedding cake by children while the couple are in church.

Mister St. John. unabr. ed. Loren D. Estleman. Narrated by Richard Ferrone. 6 cass. (Running Time: 8 hrs. 45 mins.). 1992. 51.00 (978-1-55690-674-9(9), 92328E7) Recorded Bks.
St. John is called out of retirement to stop the Bruichner Gang's most daring bank heist yet. The renewed lawman & his posse ride to a showdown in Wyoming's famed Hole in the Wall.

Mister Wolf & Little Red Riding Hood Bk/Cass. Dulcie Colby & John Harrison. (Canada Is... Music Ser.). (ENG.). 2000. audio compact disk 139.95 (978-0-7119-7517-0(5)) Alfred Pub.

Misterio en Tuluca. M. J. Oliver. (C). bk. & stu. ed. 152.95 (978-0-8384-8247-6(3)) Heinle.

Misterios Gozosos see Joyful Mysteries / Misterios Gozosos: The Holy Rosary Audio CD / el Santo Rosario Audio CD

Mistery of God's Will: Knowing God's Will Series, Sept. Ben Young. 2000. 4.95 (978-0-7417-6196-5(3), B0196) Win Walk.

Mistik Lake. unabr. ed. Martha Brooks. Read by Katie MacNichol. 4 CDs. (Running Time: 4 hrs. 52 mins.). (YA). (gr. 8 up). 2008. audio compact disk 38.00 (978-0-7393-6472-7(3), Listening Lib) Pub: Random Audio Pubg. Dist(s): Random

Mistler's Exit. unabr. ed. Louis Begley. Narrated by Paul Hecht. 5 cass. (Running Time: 6 hrs. 45 mins.). 1999. 44.00 (978-0-7887-2497-8(5), 95572E7) Recorded Bks.
Diagnosed with terminal cancer, Thomas Mistler feels a sense of liberation. Now the hard-driving Madison Avenue mogul has an excuse to live for the moment. As growing evidence of his physical decline intrudes, he boldly plans his exit on his own terms.

Mistral's Kiss. abr. ed. Laurell K. Hamilton. Read by Laural Merlington. (Running Time: 10800 sec.). (Meredith Gentry Ser.: No. 5). 2007. audio compact disk 14.99 (978-1-4233-2236-8(3), 9781423322368, BCD Value Price) Brilliance Audio.

Mistral's Kiss. unabr. ed. Laurell K. Hamilton. Read by Laural Merlington. (Running Time: 7 hrs.). (Meredith Gentry Ser.: No. 5). 2006. 39.25 (978-1-4233-2234-4(7), 9781423322344, BADLE); 24.95 (978-1-4233-2233-7(9), 9781423322337, BAD); 69.25 (978-1-4233-2228-3(2), 9781423322283, BrilAudUnabridg); audio compact disk 82.25 (978-1-4233-2230-6(4), 9781423322306, BriAudCD Unabrid); audio compact disk 39.25 (978-1-4233-2232-0(0), 9781423322320, Brinc Audio MP3 Lib); audio compact disk 24.95 (978-1-4233-2231-3(2), 9781423322313, Brilliance MP3); audio compact disk 29.95 (978-1-4233-2229-0(0), 9781423322290, Bril Audio CD Unabri) Brilliance Audio.

Mistress. Philippe Tapon. Read by Roe Kendall. 5 cass. (Running Time: 7 hrs. 30 mins.). 2000. 27.95 (978-0-7861-1778-9(8)) Blckstn Audio.

Mistress. unabr. ed. Amanda Quick, pseud. Narrated by Barbara Rosenblat. 9 cass. (Running Time: 12 hrs. 30 mins.). 1994. 78.00 (978-0-7887-0158-0(4), 94380E7) Recorded Bks.
A woman pursuing a blackmailer by pretending to be the mistress of a handsome, wealthy English Lord is caught in her charade.

Mistress. unabr. ed. Philippe Tapon. Read by Roe Kendall. 5 cass. (Running Time: 7 hrs.). 2003. 39.95 (978-0-7861-1730-7(3), 2535) Blckstn Audio.
She is called Simone, the illicit lover of Dr. Emile Bastien who practices medicine on the rue de Maubeuge, treating Parisians & Germans alike. But Simone is more than his mistress; she is the guardian of all of his most dangerous secrets.

Mistress. unabr. ed. Philippe Tapon. Read by Roe Kendall. 6 CDs. (Running Time: 7 hrs.). 2000. audio compact disk 48.00 (978-0-7861-9907-5(5), 2535) Blckstn Audio.

Mistress. unabr. ed. Philippe Tapon. Read by Roe Kendall. 1 CD. (Running Time: 6 hrs. 30 mins.). 2001. audio compact disk 19.95 (zm2535) Blckstn Audio.

Mistress. unabr. ed. Philippe Tapon. Read by Roe Kendall. 5 cass. (Running Time: 7 hrs.). 2000. 27.95 Penton Overseas.

Mistress Anne: The Exceptional Life of Anne Boleyn. Carolly Erickson. Narrated by Simon Prebble. 7 cass. (Running Time: 9 hrs. 15 mins.). 2000. 61.00 (978-0-7887-2519-7(X), 95592E7) Recorded Bks.
A powerful ruler, an attractive young woman, a scandal that would rock the nation. This is the full fascinating story of the enigmatic Anne Boleyn, a powerful ruler.

Mistress Mary Quite Contrary see Secret Garden: A Young Reader's Edition of the Classic Story

Mistress of Blackstone Castle. unabr. ed. Patricia Werner. Narrated by Nadia May. 6 cass. (Running Time: 8 hrs. 30 mins.). 2001. 44.95 (978-0-7861-2146-5(7), 2897) Blckstn Audio.
Taught the art of lace-making during her orphanage childhood, Heather Blackstone manages to earn her living in a Nottingham factory, but the legend of her ancestry haunts her dreams. When a gypsy fortune teller predicts a journey to Northumberland, Heather knows that her destiny is clear: she must find a way to reclaim the castle that bears her family name and the fortune that is rightfully hers. But when she approaches the castle, her determination falters. Sir Byron Worthington only laughs when she tells him her name, but behind his cold gray eyes she senses her. Braving his strange household, vowing to find the lost document that will prove her claim, Heather accepts Sir Byron's offer of a job as secretary, only to learn that she is being watched, followed & stalked. And as the danger escalates, Heather knows that she must make a heartbreaking decision: give up her search or risk her life to become Mistress of Blackstone.

***Mistress of Blackstone Castle.** unabr. ed. Patricia Werner. Read by Nadia May. (Running Time: 8.5 hrs. NaN mins.). (ENG.). 2011. 29.95 (978-1-4417-8376-9(8)); audio compact disk 76.00 (978-1-4417-8374-5(1)) Blckstn Audio.

Mistress of Dragons. unabr. rev. ed. Margaret Weis & Margaret Weis. Read by Gigi Marceau-Clark. 9 CDs. (Running Time: 11 hrs. 0 mins. 0 sec.). Bk. 1. (ENG., 2003. audio compact disk 44.95 (978-1-55927-894-2(3)) Pub: Macmill Audio. Dist(s): Macmillan

Mistress of Lamberly Grange, Stella March. Read by Anne Cater. 4 cass. (Running Time: 6 hrs.). 1999. 44.95 (64828) Pub: Soundings Ltd GBR. Dist(s): Ulverscroft US

Mistress of Manningtor. Connie Monk. Read by Marie McCarthy. 9 cass. (Running Time: 12 hrs.). (Story Sound Ser.). (J). 2004. 76.95 (978-1-85903-709-6(7)) Pub: Mgna Lrg Print GBR. Dist(s): Ulverscroft US

Mistress of Marymoor. Anna Jacobs. (Story Sound Ser.). (J). 2005. 61.95 (978-1-85903-727-0(5)) Pub: Mgna Lrg Print GBR. Dist(s): Ulverscroft US

Mistress of Mellyn, unabr. ed. Victoria Holt. Read by Felicity Kendal. 6 cass. 1999. 54.95 (CAB 082) AudioGO.

Mistress of Mellyn. unabr. ed. Victoria Holt. Read by Felicity Kendal. 6 cass. (Running Time: 9 hrs.). 2000. 49.95 (978-0-7451-6028-3(X), CAB 082) Pub: Chivers Audio Bks GBR. Dist(s): AudioGO
Martha hated the very idea of becoming a governess at Mount Mellyn. And upon her arrival, her anxiety grows when she learns that three governess' had already left the eerie mansion due to strange accidents, infidelity and death. It was not long before Martha's own life was in danger.

***Mistress of Nothing: A Novel.** unabr. ed. Kate Pullinger. (Running Time: 8 hrs. 30 mins.). 2011. 29.95 (978-1-4417-7158-2(1)); 54.95 (978-1-4417-7155-1(7)); audio compact disk 29.95 (978-1-4417-7157-5(3)); audio compact disk 76.00 (978-1-4417-7156-8(5)) Blckstn Audio.

Mistress of the Art of Death. Ariana Franklin, pseud. Read by Rosalyn Landor. (ENG.). (gr. 8). 2008. audio compact disk 19.95 (978-0-14-314343-7(3), PengAudBks) Penguin Grp USA.

Mistress Shakespeare. unabr. ed. Karen Harper. Read by Anne Flosnik. 1 MP3-CD. (Running Time: 12 hrs.). 2009. 39.97 (978-1-4233-8159-4(9), 9781423381594, Brinc Audio MP3 Lib); 39.97 (978-1-4233-8161-7(0), 9781423381617, BADLE); 24.99 (978-1-4233-8158-7(0), 9781423381587, Brilliance MP3); 24.99 (978-1-4233-8160-0(2), 9781423381600, BAD); audio compact disk 89.97 (978-1-4233-8157-0(2), 9781423381570, BriAudCD Unabrid); audio compact disk 29.99 (978-1-4233-8156-3(4), 9781423381563, Bril Audio CD Unabri) Brilliance Audio.

Mists of Avalon. abr. ed. Marion Zimmer Bradley. (ENG.). 2006. 14.98 (978-1-59483-759-3(7)) Pub: Hachet Audio. Dist(s): HachBkGrp

Mists of Avalon. unabr. ed. Marion Zimmer Bradley. Narrated by Davina Porter. 10 cass. (Running Time: 13 hrs. 45 mins.). 1993. 85.00 (978-1-55690-868-2(7), 93310E7) Recorded Bks.
A retelling of the Arthurian legend, focusing on the women behind the throne; Book One begins with the high priestess Viviane arranging the match between Igraine & Uther Pendragon, & ends just after the coronation of Arthur as King.

Mists of Avalon. unabr. ed. Marion Zimmer Bradley. Narrated by Davina Porter. 9 cass. (Running Time: 12 hrs. 30 mins.). 1993. 78.00 (978-1-55690-903-0(9), 93345E7) Recorded Bks.
In Book Two of The Mists of Avalon, King Arthur marries Gwenhwyfar & the new queen struggles with her growing attraction to her husband's knight, Lancelot.

Mists of Avalon. unabr. ed. Marion Zimmer Bradley. Narrated by Davina Porter. 8 cass. (Running Time: 11 hrs. 30 mins.). 1993. 70.00 (978-1-55690-917-7(9), 93413E7); 78.00 (978-1-55690-938-2(1), 93434E7) Recorded Bks.
In Book 4, King Arthur's illegitimate son challenges him for the throne of England.

Misty of Chincoteague. Marguerite Henry. Read by Edward Herrmann. (Playaway Children Ser.). (ENG.). (J). (gr. 4-7). 2009. 40.00 (978-1-60775-617-0(X)) Find a World.

Misty of Chincoteague. unabr. ed. Marguerite Henry. 1 cass. (Running Time: 1 hr. 30 mins.). 2003. 7.99 (978-0-06-058442-9(4)) HarperCollins Pubs.

Misty of Chincoteague. unabr. ed. Marguerite Henry. Narrated by John McDonough. 3 pieces. (Running Time: 3 hrs. 15 mins.). (gr. 2 up). 1997. 27.00 (978-0-7887-0793-3(0), 94943E7z) Recorded Bks.
Each year, some of the wild ponies of Assateague Island are rounded up & coaxed across a narrow strip of ocean to Chincoteague Island to be sold at auction. The Phantom is the wildest pony on Assateague Island, but Paul & Maureen have their hearts set on buying & training her.

Misty of Chincoteague. unabr. ed. Marguerite Henry. Narrated by John McDonough. 3 CDs. (Running Time: 3 hrs. 15 mins.). (gr. 2 up). 2000. audio compact disk 29.00 (978-0-7887-3733-6(3), C1104E7) Recorded Bks.

Misty of Chincoteague. unabr. ed. Marguerite Henry. Read by Edward Herrmann. (Running Time: 2 hrs. 30 mins. 0 sec.). (ENG.). (J). 2008. audio compact disk 14.99 (978-0-7435-7250-7(5)) Pub: S&S Audio. Dist(s): S and S Inc

Misty's Twilight. unabr. ed. Marguerite Henry. Narrated by Barbara Caruso. 2 pieces. (Running Time: 2 hrs. 45 mins.). (gr. 5 up). 1994. 19.00 (978-0-7887-0080-4(4), 94313E7) Recorded Bks.
A young doctor from Florida & her two children go to Chincoteague, Virginia, for Pony Penning Day & adopt "Twilight," one of the descendants of the famous "Misty".

Misunderstood Characteristics. Elbert Willis. 1 cass. (Might of Meekness Ser.). 4.00 Fill the Gap.

Mit Erfolg zum Zertifikat: Testheft. Hubert L. Eichheim & G. Storch. (GER.). (C). 1992. 29.00 (978-3-12-675368-5(X)) Pub: Klett Ernst Verlag DEU. Dist(s): Intl Bk Import

Mit Erfolg zum Zertifikat Deutsch als Fremdsprache: Uebungsbuch. Hubert L. Eichheim & G. Storch. (GER.). (C). 1992. 32.00 (978-3-12-675366-1(3)) Pub: Klett Ernst Verlag DEU. Dist(s): Intl Bk Import

***Mitch & Amy.** unabr. ed. Beverly Cleary. Read by Kathleen Mcinerney. (ENG.). 2009. (978-0-06-180565-3(3)); (978-0-06-174468-6(9)) HarperCollins Pubs.

Mitchell Goodman. unabr. ed. Mitchell Goodman. Read by Mitchell Goodman. 1 cass. (Running Time: 29 min.). 1986. 10.00 New Letters.
Also known as a political activist & novelist, Mitchell Goodman reads poetry from "A Life in Common".

Mitchell Is Moving. 1 cass. (Running Time: 35 min.). (J). (ps-3). 2001. pap. bk. 15.95 (VX-425C) Kimbo Educ.
Mitchell, the Dinosaur, thinks that 60 years in one place is long enough. He decides to move & his neighbor threatens to stop him. Includes read along book.

Mitchell Is Moving. 9.95 (978-1-59112-168-8(X)) Live Oak Media.

Mitchell Is Moving. Marjorie Weinman Sharmat. Read by Robert Sevra. Illus. by Jose Aruego & Ariane Dewey. 1 cass. (Running Time: 30 mins.). (J). 2000. pap. bk. 19.97 (978-0-7366-9209-0(6)) Books on Tape.
Margo, a spotted orange dinosaur & her next door neighbor, Mitchell, a spotted aqua dinosaur who has decided to move two weeks away.

Mitchell Is Moving. Marjorie Weinman Sharmat. Illus. by Jose Aruego & Ariane Dewey. 14 vols. (Running Time: 17 mins.). 1998. pap. bk. 31.95 (978-1-59112-658-4(4)); 9.95 (978-0-87499-424-7(1)); audio compact disk 12.95 (978-1-59112-656-0(8)) Live Oak Media.

Mitchell Is Moving. Marjorie Weinman Sharmat. Read by Bob Sevra. Illus. by Jose Aruego & Ariane Dewey. 14 vols. (Running Time: 17 mins.). 1998. pap. bk. & tchr. ed. 29.95 (978-0-87499-427-8(6)) Live Oak Media.
Mitchell the dinosaur thinks that sixty years in one place is long enough, but when he decides to move, his neighbor, Margo, threatens drastic measures to stop him. Two weeks later, Mitchell is satisfied with his move but misses his best friend until she makes a move to join him.

Mitchell Is Moving. unabr. ed. Marjorie Weinman Sharmat. Read by Bob Sevra. Illus. by Jose Aruego & Ariane Dewey. 11 vols. (Running Time: 17 mins.). (J). (gr. k-3). 1998. pap. bk. 16.95 (978-0-87499-425-4(X)) Live Oak Media.

Mitigar el Estres. Betty L. Randolph. 1 cass. (Health Ser.). 1989. bk. 12.98 (978-1-55909-185-5(1), 25E) Randolph Tapes.
Presents a program in Spanish. Features male-female voice tracks with the right-left brain.

Mitigating Circumstances. unabr. ed. Nancy Taylor Rosenberg. Read by Frances Cassidy. 9 cass. (Running Time: 13 hrs. 30 min.). 1996. 72.00 (978-0-7366-3476-2(2), 4119) Books on Tape.
Put yourself in this picture: you're at home with your teenage daughter when suddenly an intruder appears, attacks you both & escapes after doing real damage. The authorities are no help, but you learn how you might find the intruder. Would you revenge the assault yourself, risking your career, your marriage - maybe even your life.

Mitigating Circumstances. unabr. ed. Nancy Taylor Rosenberg. Narrated by Barbara Rosenblat. 9 cass. (Running Time: 12 hrs. 30 mins.). 1997. 78.00 (978-0-7887-0822-0(8), 94972E7) Recorded Bks.
When her failing marriage evolves into a fiery office romance, Assistant D. A. Lily Forester moves into her own home for a fresh start. But her life takes an unexpected direction when she & her daughter endure a savage attack & Lily takes up vengeance.

***Mitlesen Mitt.** 3rd ed. Rosmarie T. Morewedge. (ENG.). (C). 2003. 22.95 (978-1-4130-0166-2(1)) Pub: Heinle. Dist(s): CENGAGE Learn

Mitochondrial Trifunctional Protein Deficiency - A Bibliography & Dictionary for Physicians, Patients, & Genome Researchers. Compiled by Icon Group International, Inc. Staff. 2007. ring bd. 28.95 (978-0-497-11376-6(7)) Icon Grp.

Mitsie the Meekest Mouse. Irene Sheehan. Illus. by Irene Sheehan. (J). 2001. audio compact disk 4.50 (978-0-9711768-7-4(6), 28282) Red Reef Pubng.

Mitten. 1 cass. (Blue-Ribbon Listen-and-Read Ser.). (J). (ps-2). pap. bk. 5.95 (978-0-590-63092-4(X)) Scholastic Inc.
Read along book included.

Mitten. Jan Brett. Narrated by Frances Sternhagen. 1 cass. (Running Time: 15 min.). (J). (gr. k-3). 2001. bk. 27.95 (978-0-8045-6862-3(6), 6862) Spoken Arts.
Nicki, a little boy, drops his mitten in the snow and magically the wild animals crowd into it for shelter.

Mitten. Alvin R. Tresselt. Illus. by Frances Sternhagen. 1 cass. (Running Time: 15 min.). (J). (gr. k-3). 2001. pap. bk. 16.90 (6689) Spoken Arts.
A Ukrainian folktale in which a little boy loses his mitten and magically the wild animals crowd into it for shelter.

Mitten Strings for God: Reflections for Mothers in a Hurry. abr. ed. Katrina Kenison. (ENG.). 2005. 14.98 (978-1-59483-469-1(5)) Pub: Hachet Audio. Dist(s): HachBkGrp

Mitz: The Marmoset of Bloomsbury. unabr. ed. Sigrid Nunez. Read by Nadia May. 3 cass. (Running Time: 4 hrs.). 1998. 23.95 (978-0-7861-1436-8(3), 2322) Blckstn Audio.
Provides a glimpse of what Virginia Woolf once described as "the private side of life - the play side," which she believed one's pets represented. Through skillful storytelling, an intimate portrait of a most uncommon household emerges.

Mitzi & the Muscletones. M M T, Inc. International Staff. 1 CD. (Running Time: 27 min.). (J). (gr. 1-6). 2000. audio compact disk 19.99 (978-0-9705024-0-7(0)) M M T Inc.
Nine song soundtrack combined with audio instruction gives children a explanation of each exercise and how to follow along while listening to the music.

Mixed Blessings. Elvi Rhodes. 12 cass. 2005. 94.95 (978-1-84559-260-8(3)); audio compact disk 99.95 (978-1-84559-265-3(4)) Pub: UlverLrgPrint GBR. Dist(s): Ulverscroft US

Mixed-up Mask Mystery. unabr. ed. Elizabeth Levy. Read by William Dufris & Christine Marshall. Illus. by Mordicai Gerstein. 1 CD. (Running Time: 3600 sec.). (First Chapter Bks.). (YA). (gr. 7-11). 2006. audio compact disk 15.95 (978-1-59519-709-2(5)); 12.95 (978-1-59519-708-5(7)) Live Oak Media.
Fletcher is upset when someone tries to ruin the masked ball celebrating the opening of a new park. Everything seems to point to the young park ranger who's always getting mysterious calls on her cell phone, but Fletcher is sure she's innocent. Can Fletcher's trusty nose sniff out the real culprit?.

Mixed-Up Mask Mystery: A Fletcher Mystery. unabr. ed. Elizabeth Levy. Read by William Dufris. Illus. by Mordicai Gorstein. 1 CD. (Running Time: 1 hr.). (First Chapter Bks.). (J). (gr. 2-4). 2006. pap. bk. 20.95 (978-1-59519-711-5(7)) Live Oak Media.

Mixed-Up Mask Mystery: A Fletcher Mystery. unabr. ed. Elizabeth Levy. Read by William Dufris. Illus. by Mordicai Gorstein. 1 cass. (Running Time: 1 hr.). (First Chapter Bks.). (J). (gr. 2-4). 2006. pap. bk. 17.95 (978-1-59519-710-8(9)) Live Oak Media.

***Mixed-up Morning Blues.** Mark Ross. Illus. by Nathan Mellott. (ENG.). (J). 2010. bk. 17.99 (978-1-936172-13-9(5)) Eifrig Pubg.

Mixing with Murder: A Fran Varady Crime Novel. unabr. ed. Ann Granger. Narrated by Kim Hicks. 6 cass. (Running Time: 31680 sec.). (Poldark Ser.). 2006. 59.95 (978-0-7927-4543-3(4), CSL 1057); audio compact disk 79.95 (978-0-7927-4527-3(2), SLD 1057) AudioGO.

Mixture of Frailties. unabr. ed. Robertson Davies. Read by Frederick Davidson. 9 cass. (Running Time: 13 hrs.). 1997. 62.95 (978-0-7861-1171-8(2), 1958) Blckstn Audio.
"It's a muddle," thought Monica. "A muddle & I can't get it straight. I wish I knew what I should do. I wish I even knew what I want to do...I want to go on in the life that has somehow or other found me & claimed me. And I want so terribly to be happy. Oh god, don't let me slip under the surface of all the heavy-hearted dullness that seems to claim so many people...".

Mixture of Frailties: The Salterton Trilogy, Book 3. unabr. ed. Robertson Davies. Read by Frederick Davidson. (Running Time: 13 hrs. 0 mins.). 2010. 29.95 (978-1-4417-0967-7(3)); audio compact disk 109.00 (978-1-4417-0964-6(9)) Blckstn Audio.

Mizlansky - Zilinsky. unabr. ed. Jon Robin Baitz. Perf. by Nathan Lane et al. 2 CDs. (Running Time: 1 hr. 46 mins.). 2000. audio compact disk 25.95 (978-1-58081-189-7(2), CDTPT105) Pub: L A Theatre. Dist(s): NetLibrary CO

Mizlansky-Zilinsky. unabr. ed. Jon Robin Baitz. Perf. by Samantha Bennett et al. 2 cass. (Running Time: 1 hr. 46 mins.). 2000. 25.95 (978-1-58081-108-8(6), TPT105) Pub: L A Theatre. Dist(s): NetLibrary CO
Larry has it all: a house in the Hollywood Hills, a sprinkler system that transforms his dry canyon into a lush oasis & a personal assistant who removes the scallions from his Szechwan noodles. So why does everything keep going so terribly wrong.

Mizz Buggly Cassette. Stephen Cosgrove. 2004. 5.00 (978-1-58804-394-8(0)) PCI Educ.

Mkt Scales Hndbk Comp Multi-It, Vol. 4. Nick Jones et al. 2006. bk. 189.95 (978-0-324-30083-3(2)) Pub: South-West. Dist(s): CENGAGE Learn

M'Liss see Great American Short Stories, Vol. III, A Collection

M'Liss. Bret Harte. Read by Donna Barkman. 1 cass. (Running Time: 1 hr. 20 min.). Dramatization. 1985. 7.95 (S-67) Jimcin Record.

MLM Marketing War College. Randy Gage. 8. 2001. 147.00 (978-0-9673164-7-5(2)) Prime Concepts Grp.

Mmadipetsane: A Story from Nelson Mandela's Favorite African Folktales. Read by Alfre Woodard. Compiled by Nelson Mandela. (Running Time: 10 mins.). (ENG.). 2009. 1.99 (978-1-60788-011-0(3)) Pub: Hachet Audio. Dist(s): HachBkGrp

Mo Chuid den TSaol. Contrib. by Peadar O. Ceannabhain. (ENG.). 1997. 13.95 (978-0-8023-7131-7(0)); audio compact disk 21.95 (978-0-8023-8131-6(6)) Pub: Clo Iar-Chonnachta IRL. Dist(s): Dufour

Mo Ghrasa Thall na Deise. Contrib. by Ann Mulqueen. (ENG.). 1992. audio compact disk 21.95 (978-0-8023-8080-7(8)) Pub: Clo Iar-Chonnachta IRL. Dist(s): Dufour

Mo Ghrasa Thall Na Deise. Contrib. by Ann Mulqueen. (ENG.). 1992. 13.95 (978-0-8023-7080-8(2)) Pub: Clo Iar-Chonnachta IRL. Dist(s): Dufour

Mob: Stories of Death & Betrayal from Organized Crime. unabr. ed. Read by Terence Aselford et al. Ed. by Clint Willis. 4 cass. (Running Time: 6 hrs.). (Adrenaline Ser.). 2002. 24.95 (978-1-885408-66-2(8), LL058) Listen & Live.
The Mafia. La Cosa Nostra. The underground, & often not-so-underground, organization & syndicate of criminal activity that has been part of American history for the past century. Hear the true stories of the inner workings of this chaotic, violent, & suprisingly human world, a world of respect, tradition, & honor.

***Mob & Me: Wiseguys & the Witness Protection Program.** unabr. ed. John Partington & Arlene Violet. (Running Time: 9 hrs. 30 mins.). 2010. 34.99 (978-1-4001-9892-4(5)); 24.99 (978-1-4001-6892-7(9)); 16.99 (978-1-4001-8892-5(X)); audio compact disk 83.99 (978-1-4001-4892-9(8)); audio compact disk 34.99 (978-1-4001-1892-2(1)) Pub: Tantor Media. Dist(s): IngramPubServ

Mobilizing Believers. Gary V. Whetstone. 7 cass. (Running Time: 10 hrs. 30 mins.). (Empowerment Ser.). 1994. pap. bk. 50.00 (978-1-58866-192-0(X), VEO14A) Gary Whet Pub.
This series will empower you to effectively touch others through ministering salvation, baptism of the Holy Spirit, leading people in forgiveness & reconciliation, healing.

Mobilizing Laity for Home Missions: National Association of Evangelicals, 47th Annual Convention, Columbus, Ohio, March 7-9, 1989. Lamar Headley. 1 cass. (Workshops Ser.: No. 10-Wednesd). 1989. 4.25 ea. 1-8 tapes.; 4.00 ea. 9 tapes or more. Nat Assn Evan.

Mobius West. abr. ed. Robert A. Monroe. Read by Robert A. Monroe. (Running Time: 30 min.). (Human Plus Ser.). 1989. 14.95 (978-1-56102-020-1(6)) Inter Indus.
Plan or change your personal reality.

Mobs, Messiahs, & Markets: Surviving the Public Spectacle in Finance & Politics. William Bonner & Lila Rajiva. Read by Erik Synnestvedt. (Playaway Adult Nonfiction Ser.). 2008. 59.99 (978-1-60640-504-8(7)) Find a World.

Mobs, Messiahs, & Markets: Surviving the Public Spectacle in Finance & Politics. unabr. ed. William Bonner & Lila Rajiva. Read by Erik Synnestvedt. (Running Time: 13 hrs. 30 mins.). (ENG.). 2007. 29.98 (978-1-59659-176-9(5), GildAudio) Pub: Gildan Media. Dist(s): HachBkGrp

Moby-Dick. Herman Melville. Contrib. by F.Murray Abraham. 3 CDs. (Running Time: 3 hrs.). 2006. audio compact disk 39.95 (978-0-7927-3981-4(7), BBCD 132) AudioGO.

Moby-Dick. Herman Melville. Read by Paul Boehmer. 2002. audio compact disk 160.00 (978-0-7366-8792-8(0)) Books on Tape.

Moby-Dick. Herman Melville. Read by Pedro Montoya. (Running Time: 3 hrs.). 2001. 16.95 (978-1-60083-161-4(3), Audiofy Corp) Iofy Corp.

Moby-Dick. Herman Melville. Read by Bill Bailey. 4 cass. (Running Time: 4 hrs. 45 mins.). (Classic Literature with Classical Music Ser.). 1995. 22.98 (978-962-634-526-9(8), NA402614, Naxos AudioBooks) Naxos.
The Nantucket whaling ship, the Pequod, spirals the globe in search of Moby Dick, the mythical white whale of the southern oceans. Join Ishmael & the crew as they deal with the obsessive revenge of Captain Ahab.

Moby-Dick. Herman Melville. 1 cass. (Running Time: 1 hr.). (Radiobook Ser.). 1987. 4.98 (978-0-929541-38-9(3)) Radiola Co.

Moby-Dick. Herman Melville. Read by Frank Muller. 12 Cass. (Running Time: 21 Hrs.). 34.95 (978-1-4025-3693-9(3)) Recorded Bks.

Moby-Dick. Herman Melville. 2004. pap. bk. 44.95 (978-1-4025-9422-9(4)) Recorded Bks.

Moby Dick. Herman Melville. Read by Brian Keeler. 15 cass. 2005. 29.95 (978-1-56585-989-0(8)); audio compact disk 44.95 (978-1-59803-005-1(1)) Teaching Co.

Moby Dick. abr. ed. Bob Harvey. 2. (Running Time: 7200 sec.). 2007. audio compact disk 16.95 (978-1-933499-14-7(1)) Fonolibro Inc.

Moby-Dick. abr. ed. Herman Melville. Read by Charlton Heston et al. 2 cass. (Running Time: 93 min.). (J). 1991. 17.00 Set. (978-1-55994-394-9(7), DCN 2077) HarperCollins Pubs.
This recording, dating from 1975, comes from Caedmon's rich trove of vintage literary readings. The excerpts are carefully chosen, suggesting the breadth of Melville's archetypal American novel.

Moby-Dick. abr. ed. Herman Melville. Perf. by St. Charles Players. 2 cass. (Running Time: 2 hrs.). Dramatization. (Adventure Theatre Ser.). 1999. 16.95 (978-1-56994-505-6(5), 331514, Monterey SoundWorks) Monterey Media Inc.
The challenge of a man against the wonders of nature's ocean, of man against a demon, or perhaps his God, as he searches for his nemisis, the great white whale.

Moby-Dick. abr. ed. Herman Melville. Read by Bill Bailey. 4 CDs. (Running Time: 4 hrs. 45 mins.). (Classic Fiction Ser.). (J). (gr. 9-12). 1995. audio compact disk 28.98 (978-962-634-026-4(6), NA402612) Naxos.
The Nantucket whaling ship, the Pequod, spirals the globe in search of Moby Dick, the mythical white whale of the southern oceans. Join Ishmael & the crew as they deal with the obsessive revenge of Captain Ahab.

Moby-Dick. abr. ed. Herman Melville. Read by Burt Reynolds. 4 cass. (Running Time: 6 hrs.). 2004. 25.00 (978-1-59007-022-2(4)) Pub: New Millenn Enter. Dist(s): PerseuPGW
The epic story of Captain Ahab's incredible quest for the elusive great whale.

Moby-Dick. abr. ed. Herman Melville. 1 cass. (Monarch Notes Ser.). 1984. 7.95 (978-0-671-54405-8(5)) S&S Audio.
Intended as a supplement to classroom study, offering plot summary, interpretive themes, information on literary theme & style. The flashcards outline the author's life.

Moby-Dick. abr. ed. Herman Melville. (Classic Stage Ser.). 2005. audio compact disk 14.99 (978-1-894003-32-2(2)) Pub: Scenario Prods CAN. Dist(s): Baker Taylor

Moby-Dick. abr. ed. Herman Melville. Read by Pedro Montoya. 3 CDs. (SPA.). 2001. audio compact disk 17.00 (978-958-9494-41-7(2)) YoYoMusic.

Moby-Dick. abr. ed. Herman Melville & William Hootkins. (Running Time: 6 hrs.). (ENG.). (gr. 12 up). 2005. audio compact disk 16.95 (978-0-14-305809-0(6), PengAudBks) Penguin Grp USA.

Moby-Dick. rev. ed. Herman Melville. Ed. by Robert James Dixson. (American Classics: Bk. 2). (J). (gr. 9 up). 1987. 65.00 (978-0-13-024662-2(X), 58219) Prentice ESL.

Moby-Dick. unabr. ed. Herman Melville. Read by Anthony Heald. (Running Time: 24 hrs. 0 mins.). 2009. 44.95 (978-1-4332-5745-2(9)); audio compact disk 29.95 (978-1-4332-5744-5(0)); audio compact disk 130.00 (978-1-4332-5742-1(4)) Blckstn Audio.

Moby-Dick. unabr. ed. Herman Melville. 17 cass. (Running Time: 25 hrs. 30 mins.). 2002. 136.00 (978-0-7366-8891-8(9)) Books on Tape.

Moby-Dick. unabr. ed. Herman Melville. Read by William Hootkins. (YA). 2006. 99.99 (978-1-59895-630-6(2)) Find a World.

Moby-Dick. unabr. ed. Herman Melville. Read by Robert L. Halvorson. 17 cass. (Running Time: 25 hrs.). 119.95 (77) Halvorson Assocs.

Moby-Dick. unabr. ed. Herman Melville. 2 cass. (Read-along Ser.). bk. 34.95 Set, incl. learner's guide & exercises. (S23908) J Norton Pubs.

Moby-Dick. unabr. ed. Herman Melville. Narrated by Frank Muller. 15 cass. (Running Time: 21 hrs.). 1987. 120.00 (978-1-55690-343-4(X), 87370E7) Recorded Bks.
A young man joins Captain Ahab's quest for the white whale.

Moby-Dick. unabr. ed. Herman Melville. Read by Frank Muller. 18 CDs. (Running Time: 21 Hrs). 2005. audio compact disk 44.95 (978-1-4193-2393-5(8)) Recorded Bks.

Moby-Dick. unabr. ed. Herman Melville. Read by Robert H. Chapman. 10.95 (978-0-8045-0850-6(X), SAC 850) Spoken Arts.

***Moby-Dick.** unabr. ed. Herman Melville. Narrated by Norman Dietz. (Running Time: 25 hrs. 0 mins. 0 sec.). (ENG.). 2010. 34.99 (978-1-4001-6601-5(2)); 26.99 (978-1-4001-8601-3(3)); audio compact disk 45.99 (978-1-4001-1601-0(5)); audio compact disk 91.99 (978-1-4001-4601-7(1)) Pub: Tantor Media. Dist(s): IngramPubServ

Moby Dick. unabr. abr. ed. Bob Harvey. Read by Burt Reynolds. (Running Time: 25200 sec.). 2007. audio compact disk 36.00 (978-1-4332-0549-1(1)) Blckstn Audio.

Moby Dick. unabr. abr. ed. Bob Harvey. Read by Burt Reynolds. (Running Time: 25200 sec.). 2007. audio compact disk 19.95 (978-1-4332-0550-7(5)) Blckstn Audio.

Moby-Dick, Part A. unabr. ed. Herman Melville. Read by Anthony Heald. (Running Time: 13 hrs. 0 mins.). (Classic Collection Ser.). 2009. audio compact disk 72.95 (978-1-4332-5741-4(6)) Blckstn Audio.

Moby-Dick, Part B. unabr. ed. Herman Melville. Read by Anthony Heald. (Running Time: 11 hrs. 0 mins.). 2009. audio compact disk 65.95 (978-1-4332-6156-5(1)) Blckstn Audio.

Moby-Dick, Pt. 2. collector's ed. Herman Melville. Read by Walter Zimmerman. 9 cass. (Running Time: 13 hrs. 30 min.). (J). 1984. 72.00 (978-0-7366-1001-8(4), 1934-B) Books on Tape.
Captain Ahab, driven by rage & revenge, pursues the great white whale & only Ishmael remains to tell the tale.

Moby-Dick, Pt. A. collector's ed. Herman Melville. Read by Walter Zimmerman. 9 cass. (Running Time: 13 hrs. 30 mins.). (J). 1984. 72.00 (978-0-7366-1000-1(6), 1934-A) Books on Tape.

Moby-Dick, Set. abr. ed. Herman Melville. Perf. by St. Charles Players. 13 cass. Dramatization. 1999. 85.95 (FS9-34217) Highsmith.

***Moby Dick: Bring the Classics to Life.** adpt. ed. Herman Melville. (Bring the Classics to Life Ser.). 2008. pap. bk. 21.95 (978-1-55576-655-9(2)) EDCON Pubng.

Moby Dick: The Audio BookNotes Guide. (Audio BookNotes Guide). (C). 2002. audio compact disk 9.95 (978-1-929011-05-6(9)) Scholarly Audio.

Moby Dick & Rime of the Ancient Mariner. abr. ed. Herman Melville & Samuel Taylor Coleridge. 2 cass. (Running Time: 120 min.). 2001. (978-1-894003-22-3(5)) Scenario Prods CAN.

Moby Dick Audio CD: Bring the Classics to Life-Level 5. adpt. ed. Herman Melville. (Bring the Classics to Life Ser.). (ENG.). 2008. audio compact disk 12.95 (978-1-55576-585-9(8)) EDCON Pubng.

Mockingbird. Contrib. by Derek Webb. Prod. by Cason Cooley. 2005. audio compact disk 13.97 (978-5-558-63166-1(X)) INO Rec.

***Mockingjay.** Suzanne Collins. (ENG.). 2010. audio compact disk 84.99 (978-0-545-10144-8(1)) Scholastic Inc.

***Mockingjay.** unabr. ed. Suzanne Collins. Narrated by Carolyn McCormick. (Hunger Games Ser.: Bk. 3). (YA). 2010. audio compact disk 39.99 (978-0-545-10142-4(5)) Scholastic Inc.

Mod Marches. Hap Palmer. 1 cass. (J). 11.95 (EA527C) Kimbo Educ.
Includes It's a Small World, Yellow Submarine, Penny Lane, Love Is Blue & more.

Modal Method Play along Tape. Chris Theriault. Ed. by Byron Duckwall. 1 cass. (Running Time: 30 min.). (Getting into the Guitar Ser.). 1992. 8.00 (978-1-883617-03-5(0)) Evergreen Music.
Twenty-five chord progressions from the "Popular Chord Progressions" section in the back of the Modal Method Music Book. It is designed for the reader to play along.

Modal Music Composition. Stephen M. Cormier. Composed by Stephen M. Cormier. 1 CD. (Running Time: 55 mins). 2004. pap. bk. 25.00 (978-0-9754318-0-1(3)) Inman Artz.
Audio CD contains sound recordings of 50 music examples and 3 study compositions.

Mode of Intergration in Sabian Astrology. Dick Degeiso. 1 cass. 8.95 (081) Am Fed Astrologers.

Model. abr. ed. Michael Gross. Read by Sheila Hart. 2 cass. (Running Time: 3 hrs.). 2000. 7.95 (978-1-57815-002-1(7), 1061, Media Bks Audio) Media Bks NJ.
The ugly business of beautiful women.

Model for Murder. Jack Bates. Read by Erik Parker. (ENG.). 2009. audio compact disk 5.49 (978-0-9821192-9-7(1)) Mind Wings Aud.

Model for Murder. unabr. ed. Alan Geoffrey Yates & Carter Brown. Read by Sean Mangan. 4 cass. (Running Time: 3 hrs. 15 mins.). 2004. 32.00 (978-1-876584-30-6(0), 590790) Pub: Bolinda Pubng AUS. Dist(s): Lndmrk Audiobks
When Nigel Barrett, a strikingly handsome male model, was found stabbed to death in his elegant apartment, the case landed on Al Wheeler's desk. Al soon discovered that Nigel was the object of passion & jealousy from many quarters. There was Madeline, who had discovered the body & claimed to be Nigel's "friend" but she was heavily involved with Pete, a macho type with a shady past. Then there was Lou, spoiled, beauty & wealthy, who had posed for certain pictures with Nigel, pictures that could be very damaging if they fell into the wrong hands. Al knew the murderer wouldn't hesitate to kill again to prevent discovery & Al Wheeler was Target #1.

***Model for Murder: A Harry Landers Episode.** Jack Bates. Read by Erik Parker. (Running Time: 55). (ENG.). 2009. 2.99 (978-1-61114-010-1(2)) Mind Wings Aud.

***Model Home.** unabr. ed. Eric Puchner. Narrated by David Colacci. (Running Time: 15 hrs. 30 mins. 0 sec.). (ENG.). 2010. audio compact disk 79.99 (978-1-4001-4652-9(6)) Pub: Tantor Media. Dist(s): IngramPubServ

***Model Home: A Novel.** unabr. ed. Eric Puchner. Narrated by David Colacci. (Running Time: 14 hrs. 0 mins.). 2010. 39.99 (978-1-4001-9652-4(3)); 29.99 (978-1-4001-6652-7(7)); 19.99 (978-1-4001-8652-5(8)); audio compact disk 39.99 (978-1-4001-1652-2(X)) Pub: Tantor Media. Dist(s): IngramPubServ

Modeling the Healing Process. John Grinder. Read by John Grinder. Read by Finbar Nolan. 7 cass. (Running Time: 10 hrs. 30 min.). 1988. 120.00 Metamorphous Pr.
This series features John Grinder leading participants through the latest exercises in NLP modeling technology. Methods of creating optimal states for responding to healing interventions are also demonstrated. Finbar Nolan, internationally respected touch healer, Stephanie Alt, & Herbert Lustig each discuss the development & practice of their healing work. Written descriptions of preparatory exercises are included.

Modelling & Detailing German Armour. Graham Dunbar-Brown. 2007. 24.95 (978-1-905573-98-1(7)) Pub: Compendium GBR. Dist(s): Casemate Pubs

Modelos y Recurso Para la Unidad: Proceedings of the 45th Annual Convention National Association of Evangelicals Buffalo, New York. Read by Luciano Padilla. 1 cass. (Running Time: 1 hr.). (SPA.). 1987. 4.00 (336) Nat Assn Evan.

Models & Beliefs. John Lilly. 1 cass. 10.00 (A0070-79) Sound Photosyn.
From Dr. Lilly's personal collection.

Models of Manifestation. Rick Jarow. 3 cass. 1993. 27.00 (OC333-71) Sound Horizons AV.

Modem. Ed. by Robert A. Monroe. 1 cass. (Running Time: 30 min.). (Meta Music Ser.). 1985. 12.95 (978-1-56102-216-8(0)) Inter Indus.
Take advantage of the communication aspects of your consciousness. Lie back, relax & allow Modem to assist you in establishing rapport with your inner self & possibly with other reality systems.

Moderation see Custom

Modern African Literature: Its Challenge & Changing Direction. unabr. ed. Claude Wauthier. 1 cass. (Running Time: 22 min.). 1968. 12.95 (23145) J Norton Pubs.
Mr. Wauthier analyzes the contribution of native South African writers to the gradual evolution of the African continent. Beginning with the period directly after World War II, he depicts, through the voices of African writers, the rise of the anti-colonial movement.

Modern American English. Robert James Dixson. (YA). (gr. 7-12). 1987. 100.00 (978-0-13-543190-0(5)) Prentice ESL.

Modern American English, Level 2. 4th ed. Steven J. Molinsky et al. 2002. 177.80 (978-0-13-593989-5(5)) Longman.

Modern American English, Level 3. 4th ed. Robert James Dixson. 2002. 177.80 (978-0-13-594052-5(4)) Longman.

Modern American English, Level 4. 4th ed. Robert James Dixson. 2002. 177.80 (978-0-13-594094-5(X)) Longman.

Modern American Life. 1 cass. (Urban Problems Ser.). 10.00 (UP707) Esstee Audios.
How rising expectations have changed American thinking.

Modern American Square Dance Series. Narrated by Dick Leger. 2 CDs. (Running Time: 1 hr.). (J). 2001. pap. bk. 24.95 (KIM 4060CD) Kimbo Educ.
Based on a graded progression of skills & combined with qualities of traditional style. Includes Dos a Dos, Promenade, Circle, Fwd & Back, Allemande L, Star & more. Includes dance manual.

Modern American Square Dance Series, Vol. 1. 2 cass. (J). 2001. 18.95 (KIM 4060C) Kimbo Educ.
American square dancing is combined with qualities of the traditional style. Albums are based on a graded progression of skills (with & without calls). Formation: Circle/square. Musical Field: Tijuana Brass. Includes manual.

Modern American Square Dance Series, Vol. 2. 2 cass. 2001. pap. bk. 18.95 (KIM 5080C) Kimbo Educ.

Modern American Square Dance Series, Vol. 3. 2 cass. 2001. pap. bk. 18.95 (KIM 8070C) Kimbo Educ.

Modern Approach to Classical Guitar Repertoire - Part 1. Charles Duncan. (ENG.). 1985. pap. bk. 14.99 (978-1-4234-7456-2(2), 1423474562) H Leonard.

Modern Arabic Complete. rev. ed. Ernest T. Abdel-Massih. 7 cass. 1982. 60.26 U MI Lang Res.

Modern Arabic 2. Samar Attar. 17 cass. (Running Time: 1530 min.). (ARA.). 180.00 (978-0-86685-822-9(9)) Intl Bk Ctr.

Modern Art: Is Meaning Necessary? unabr. ed. Sylvia Angus. 1 cass. (Running Time: 21 min.). 1968. 12.95 (11003) J Norton Pubs.
The current emphasis of the arts on technique & sense perception rather than on content is examined & related to the social dislocations of our time.

Modern Automotive Technology: Teaching Package Instructor's Resource CD. James E. Duffy. (gr. 9-13). tchr. ed. 220.00 (978-1-59070-192-8(5)) Goodheart.

Modern Automotive Technology: Teaching Package Powerpoint Presentations Individual License. James E. Duffy. 2 CDs. (gr. 9-13). audio compact disk 240.00 (978-1-59070-193-5(3)) Goodheart.

Modern Biology, Set. 2nd ed. Towle. 2004. audio compact disk 598.33 (978-0-03-038064-8(2)) Holt McDoug.

Modern Biology: Guided Reading Program. 2nd ed. Holt, Rinehart and Winston Staff. 2001. audio compact disk 247.13 (978-0-03-064271-5(X)) Holt McDoug.

Modern British Drama. 4 cass. (Running Time: 6 hrs.). 1994. 39.95 (978-1-56585-060-6(2)) Teaching Co.

Modern Carpentry: Teaching Package Exam View(r) Test Generator Software Windows. Willis H. Wagner & Howard Bud Smith. (gr. 9-13). audio compact disk 140.00 (978-1-59070-206-2(9)) Goodheart.

Modern Chemistry, Set. 2nd ed. Wayne R. Davis. 2004. audio compact disk 598.33 (978-0-03-038077-8(4)) Holt McDoug.

Modern Chinese: A Basic Course. Peking University staff. 3 cass. (Running Time: 1 hr. 30 min.). Dover.
Self-study course in modern Mandarin, Pin yin transcription used with conversion table for Yale & Wade systems.

Modern Cinderella & A Matter-of-Fact Fairy Tale. (J). 2005. audio compact disk (978-1-933796-45-1(6)) PC Treasures.

Modern Consciousness Research: Applications for Psychiatry & Psychology. Read by Stanislav Grof. 2 cass. (Running Time: 2 hrs.). 1982. 16.95 (978-0-7822-0082-9(6), 099) C G Jung IL.

Modern Cult of Efficiency. Thomas Merton. 1 cass. (Running Time: 1 hr.). (Poverty Ser.). 4.50 (AA2101) Credence Commun.
Discusses sins against poverty in our society & the demands of poverty in the monastery.

Modern Day Heroes for Youth & Our Spiritual Needs. Randall Bird. 1 cass. 1996. 2.97 (978-1-57734-082-9(5), 06005454) Covenant Comms.
Stories of the true heroes among us.

Modern-Day Martyr. Mother Angelica & Father Michael. 1 cass. (Running Time: 1 hr.). (Mother Angelica Live Ser.). 1989. 10.00 (978-1-55794-114-5(9), T65) Eternal Wrd TV.
Anti-Abortion Activist describes the prison experiences she suffered for taking a stand against abortion.

***Modern Drum Method Grade 2.** Steve Fidyk. 2010. pap. bk. 14.99 (978-0-7866-8257-7(4)) Mel Bay.

Modern Economic Issues. unabr. ed. Instructed by Robert Whaples. 18 cass. (Running Time: 18 hrs.). 2008. 199.95 (978-1-59803-378-6(6)); audio compact disk 99.95 (978-1-59803-379-3(4)) Teaching Co.

Modern Electric Bass. rev. ed. Jaco Pastorius. (SPA & ITA.). audio compact disk 24.95 (978-88-7207-553-1(X), ML1445) Nuova Carisch ITA.

Modern Era. Abr. by iSummaries Staff. 2007. audio compact disk 79.95 (978-1-934488-29-4(1)) L England.

Modern European History Series: World Events over Time Collection. Eugene Lieber. (ENG.). 2006. audio compact disk 140.00 (978-1-935069-22-5(5)) IAB Inc.

Modern Fiddling Method Grade 1. Mary Ann Willis. 2008. spiral bd. 14.95 (978-0-7866-7824-2(0)) Mel Bay.

Modern Flight History. unabr. ed. John Stollery. 1 cass. 1990. 12.95 (ECN066) J Norton Pubs.

Modern Garde Manger: A Global Perspective-Cd Rom. (C). 2006. audio compact disk 14.95 (978-1-4018-5011-1(1)) Pub: Delmar. Dist(s): CENGAGE Learn

Modern Gladiator. Hyrum W. Smith. Read by Hyrum W. Smith. 2 cass. (Running Time: 3 hrs.). 2001. 12.95; audio compact disk 12.95 Franklin Covey.
Many years of training and experience are the equivalent of the ancient gladiator's shield, and the tools of personal productivity are the short sword which led to the rising of the Roman Empire. The Modern Gladiator will not only help you deflect the onslaught of today's life-overload but will also take you to a higher level of inner peace and increased personal productivity.

Modern Greek, Set. 1963rd ed. Paul Pimsleur. 10 cass. (Pimsleur Language Learning Ser.). 1963. pap. bk. & stu. ed. 345.00 (0671-57928-2) SyberVision.

Modern Greek: Learn to Speak & Understand Greek with Pimsleur Language Programs. 2nd unabr. ed. Pimsleur. Created by Pimsleur. 5 CDs. (Running Time: 50 hrs. 0 mins. 0 sec.). (Basic Ser.). (GRE & ENG.). 2005. audio compact disk 24.95 (978-0-7435-5077-2(3), Pimsleur); audio compact disk 49.95 (978-0-7435-5051-2(X), Pimsleur) Pub: S&S Audio. Dist(s): S and S Inc

Modern Greek: Learn to Speak & Understand Modern Greek. 2nd ed. Pimsleur Staff. 4 cds. (Running Time: 400 hrs. 0 mins. NaN sec.). (Pimsleur Language Program Ser.). (ENG.). 2001. audio compact disk 19.95 (978-0-684-87428-9(8), Pimsleur) Pub: S&S Audio. Dist(s): S and S Inc
You're not just learning "phrases" with The Pimsleur® Method, you're acquiring essential, conversational Modern Greek! You'll be thrilled to discover you can hold a real conversation in Modern Greek when you have finished these eight, 30-minute lessons! Dr. Paul Pimsleur's original and unique method enables you to acquire Modern Greek as effortlessly as children absorb their native language. You will succeed because the Pimsleur program makes sure that you learn vocabulary and grammar correctly and easily in conversational settings without mindless repetition. Pimsleur is the only language program that includes exclusive, copyrighted memory training that ensures you always will remember what you have learned. When you finish these lessons you'll be so delighted with your fast-growing spoken language skills, you'll want to continue with the full 30-lesson Pimsleur® Program. And to make it easier, we've included in this package a trade-up coupon that gives you a $50.00 savings when you purchase the Level I Modern Greek Comprehensive Program. Learn at your own pace, comfortably and conveniently.

Modern Greek Poetry, Reader 1. unabr. ed. 1 cass. (Running Time: 52 mins.). 1994. pap. bk. 34.95 (978-0-88432-525-3(3), SGR175) J Norton Pubs.

Modern Guitar Method: Grade 1. Bay, Mel, Publications, Inc. Staff. 1980. 9.98 (978-0-87166-355-9(4), 93200C) Mel Bay.

Modern Guitar Method: Grade 1. Mel Bay Staff. 1993. bk. 14.95 (978-0-87166-356-6(2), 93200P) Mel Bay.

Modern Guitar Method: Grade 1. Mel Bay Staff & William Bay. 1948. pap. bk. 19.95 (978-0-7866-0906-2(0), 93200CDP) Mel Bay.

Modern Guitar Method: Grade 2. Mel Bay Staff. 1993. bk. 22.95 (978-0-87166-359-7(7), 93201P) Mel Bay.

Modern Guitar Method: Grade 2. Mel Bay Staff & William Bay. 1 CD. (Running Time: 90 mins.). (J). (gr. 2). 1949. pap. bk. 29.95 (978-0-7866-1385-4(8), 93201CDP) Mel Bay.

Modern Guitar Method: Grade 3. Bay, Mel, Publications, Inc. Staff. 1992. 9.98 (978-0-87166-361-0(9), 93202C) Mel Bay.

Modern Guitar Method: Grade 3. Mel Bay Staff. 1993. bk. 14.95 (978-0-87166-362-7(7), 93202P) Mel Bay.

Modern Guitar Method Grade 1 - Rock Studies. Stuart Bull. 2008. pap. bk. 12.95 (978-0-7866-7591-3(8)) Mel Bay.

Modern Guitar Method Grade 1, Play All-Time Favorite Hits by Ear. Collin Bay. 2008. pap. bk. 14.95 (978-0-7866-7590-6(X)) Mel Bay.

***Modern Guitar Method Grade 1, Playing Chords Book/CD Set.** William Bay. 2010. pap. bk. 14.95 (978-0-7866-7876-1(3)) Mel Bay.

Modern Guitar Method Grade 3. Bay, Mel, Publications, Inc. Staff. 2003. pap. bk. 14.95 (978-0-7866-9679-6(6), 93202BCD) Mel Bay.

Modern Guitar Method Grade 4, Rock Studies. Compiled by Mel Bay Publications. 2008. pap. bk. 19.95 (978-0-7866-7874-7(7)) Mel Bay.

***Modern Guitar Method Grade 7, Expanded Edition Book/2-CD Set.** William Bay & Mel Bay. (ENG.). 2010. spiral bd. 19.95 (978-0-7866-7643-9(4)) Mel Bay.

Modern Guitar Method Jammin' the Blues, #1. Frank Vignola. (ENG.). 2008. pap. bk. 14.95 (978-0-7866-7969-0(7)) Mel Bay.

Modern Guitar Method Jammin' the Blues, #3. Frank Vignola. (ENG.). 2008. pap. bk. Rental 14.95 (978-0-7866-7972-0(7)) Mel Bay.

Modern Guitar Method Rhythm Changes, #3. Frank Vignola. (ENG.). 2008. pap. bk. 14.95 (978-0-7866-3706-5(4)) Mel Bay.

Modern Hebrew II: Learn to Speak & Understand Hebrew with Pimsleur Language Programs. unabr. ed. Pimsleur Staff. (Running Time: 16 hrs. 0 mins. 0 sec.). (Comprehensive Ser.). (HEB & ENG.). 2007. audio compact disk 345.00 (978-0-7435-5254-7(7), Pimsleur) Pub: S&S Audio. Dist(s): S and S Inc

Modern Idea of Man. unabr. ed. Joseph Wood Krutch. 1 cass. (Running Time: 23 min.). 12.95 (25012) J Norton Pubs.
Discusses the paradox of what man is & what he ought to be that enables both democracy & totalitarianism to develop.

Modern Indian Spirituality. Ramchandra Gandhi. 14 cass. (Running Time: 14 hrs.). 120.00 (A0312-88) Sound Photosyn.
The entire lecture series: Ramu is a witty & profound thinker & dramatic orator replete with reverberations from his grandfather, Mahatma Gandhi. He is, by personal or deeply intuitive contact, familiar with these great modern teachers & generously introduces us.

Modern Indian Spirituality Vol. 1: Sri Ramakrishna, Sri Sarada Devi, Swami Vivekananda, Sri Ramana Maharshi, & Alagamma. Ramchandra Gandhi. 5 cass. (Running Time: 7 hrs. 30 min.). 45.00 (A0322-88) Sound Photosyn.

Modern Indian Spirituality Vol. 2: Sri Aurobindo & the Mother, Mira, & Sri J. Krishnamurti. Ramchandra Gandhi. 5 cass. (Running Time: 7 hrs. 30 min.). 45.00 (A0313-88) Sound Photosyn.

Modern Indian Spirituality Vol. 4: In the West Today. Ramchandra Gandhi. 2 cass. (Running Time: 3 hrs. 30 min.). 18.00 (A0314-88) Sound Photosyn.

Modern Indian Spirituality, Vol. 3: On Mahatma Gandhi. Ramchandra Gandhi. 2 cass. (Running Time: 3 hrs.). 18.00 (A0314-88) Sound Photosyn.
Ramchandra shares an intimate & personal reminiscence of his grandfather.

Modern Instance, unabr. ed. William Dean Howells. Read by Flo Gibson. 10 cass. (Running Time: 14 hrs.). (J). (gr. 10 up). 1997. 44.95 (978-1-55685-461-3(7), 461-7) Audio Bk Con.
The turbulent marriage of Bartley Hubbard, a philanderer, opportunist & dishonest journalist, & naive, possessive Mary Gaylord ends in divorce. At the time of its publication this socially realistic novel was considered daring for its handling of the divorce question.

***Modern Intellectual Tradition: From Descartes to Derrida.** Instructed by Lawrence Cahoone. 2010. audio compact disk 269.95 (978-1-59803-664-0(5)) Teaching Co.

Modern Irish Literature. unabr. ed. Maurice Harmon. 1 cass. (Running Time: 25 min.). 1968. 12.95 (23086) J Norton Pubs.
Covers the growth of Irish writing from 1800 to the present. Discusses & illustrates the main periods & the principal writers, including the leading figures of the Irish Literary Revival.

Modern Italian, Pt. A. 185.00 (1972, Lm Inc) Oasis Audio.
Features methods in learning a second language.

Modern Italian, Pt. B. 185.00 (1973, Lm Inc) Oasis Audio.
Presents methods in learning a second language.

Modern Jazz Voicings: Arranging for Small & Medium Ensembles. Ted Pease & Ken Pullig. (Music Reference Ser.). (ENG., 2001. 24.95 (978-0-634-01443-7(9), 0634014439) H Leonard.

Modern Left-Handed Rock Guitar Method Grade 1. William Bay. 2008. pap. bk. 14.95 (978-0-7866-7782-5(1)) Mel Bay.

Modern Liquid Chromatography: A Practical Course in MLC Theory, Methods & Interpretation. 2nd ed. Instructed by Lloyd R. Snyder & J. J. Kirkland. 12 cass. (Running Time: 8 hrs. 6 min.). pap. bk. 305.00 (62) Am Chemical.
This course provides an approach to modern liquid chromatography. Includes manual.

Modern Liquid Chromatography - Special Topics. Instructed by Lloyd R. Snyder & J. J. Kirkland. 7 cass. (Running Time: 6 hrs. 42 min.). pap. bk. 275.00 (68) Am Chemical.
This Special Topics course supplements "Modern Liquid Chromatography, 2nd Ed.". Includes manual.

Modern Logistics Products & Services in China: A Strategic Reference 2006. Compiled by Icon Group International, Inc. Staff. 2007. ring bd. 195.00 (978-0-497-35886-0(7)) Icon Grp.

Modern Management of Ectopic Pregnancy. Moderated by A. Brian Little. 2 cass. (Gynecology & Obstetrics Ser.: GO-4). 1986. 19.00 (8643) Am Coll Surgeons.

Modern Mephistopheles. unabr. ed. Louisa May Alcott. Read by C. M. Herbert. 4 cass. (Running Time: 5 hrs. 30 mins.). 1996. 32.95 (978-0-7861-1041-4(4), 1813) Blckstn Audio.
This chilling tale of greed, lust & deception opens on a midwinter night when Felix Canaris, a despairing writer about to take his own life, is saved by a knock at the door. The mysterious visitor, a Jasper Helwyze, promises Felix fame & fortune in return for his complete devotion. Helwyze then plots to corrupt the overly ambitious Felix by cleverly manipulating the beautiful & innocent Gladys. And when Helwyze decides that he wants Gladys for himself, Felix must defend the adoring young woman from the destructive influence of his diabolical patron.

Modern Mephistopheles. unabr. ed. Louisa May Alcott. Read by C. M. Hebert. (Running Time: 6 hrs. 0 mins.). 2010. 29.95 (978-1-4417-0597-6(X)); audio compact disk 55.00 (978-1-4417-0594-5(5)) Blckstn Audio.

Modern Method Advanced Spanish. unabr. ed. Conversa-Phone Institute Staff. 3 cass. (Running Time: 3 hrs. 5 min.). (Modern Method Language Sets Ser.). 1991. 21.95 (978-1-56752-082-8(0)) Conversa-phone.
This program provides a full study of advanced Spanish. Longer sentences, phrases, conversation & a special section on grammar. These programs are for the serious student or persons wanting a more indepth study of the language.

Modern Method for Guitar, Vol. 1. Composed by William Leavitt. 1995. pap. bk. 22.95 (978-0-7935-4511-7(0), 50449404, Berklee Pr) H Leonard.

Modern Method for Guitar: Beginner. William G. Leavitt. 1995. audio compact disk 22.95 (978-0-87639-014-6(9)) Berklee Pr Pubns.

Modern Method French. unabr. ed. Conversa-Phone Institute Staff. 3 cass. (Running Time: 3 hrs. 5 min.). (Modern Method Language Sets Ser.). 1991. 21.95 (978-1-56752-042-2(1)) Conversa-phone.
This program provides a full study of French alphabet thru sentences, phrases, conversation & a special section on grammar. These programs are for the serious student or persons wanting a more indepth study of the language.

Modern Method German. unabr. ed. Conversa-Phone Institute Staff. 3 cass. (Running Time: 3 hrs. 5 min.). (Modern Method Language Sets Ser.). 1991. 21.95 (978-1-56752-043-9(X)) Conversa-phone.
This program provides a full study of German alphabet thru sentences, phrases, conversation & a special section on grammar. These programs are for the serious student or persons wanting a more indepth study of the language.

Modern Method Greek. unabr. ed. Conversa-Phone Institute Staff. 2 cass. (Running Time: 2 hrs. 5 min.). (Modern Method Language Sets Ser.). 1991. 21.95 (978-1-56752-048-4(0), COC-3025) Conversa-phone.
This program provides a full study of Modern Greek. Alphabet thru sentences phrases, conversation & a special section on grammar. These programs are for the serious student or persons wanting a more in depth study of the language.

Modern Method Italian. unabr. ed. Conversa-Phone Institute Staff. 3 cass. (Running Time: 3 hrs. 5 min.). (Modern Method Language Sets Ser.). 1991. 21.95 (978-1-56752-044-6(8)) Conversa-phone.
This program provides a full study of Italian alphabet thru sentences, phrases, conversation & a special section on grammar. These programs are for the serious student or persons wanting a more indepth study of the language.

Modern Method Mandarin Chinese. unabr. ed. Conversa-Phone Institute Staff. 3 cass. (Running Time: 3 hrs. 5 min.). (Modern Method Language Sets Ser.). 1991. 21.95 (978-1-56752-081-1(2)) Conversa-phone.
This program provides a full study of Chinese alphabet thru sentences, phrases, conversation & a special section on grammar. These programs are for the serious student or persons wanting a more indepth study of the language.

Modern Method Russian. unabr. ed. 2 cass. (Running Time: 2 hrs. 5 min.). (Modern Method Language Sets Ser.). 1991. 21.95 (978-1-56752-045-3(6), COC-3013) Conversa-phone.
This program provides a full study of Russian. Alphabet thru sentences phrases, conversation & a special section on grammar. These programs are for the serious student or persons wanting a more in depth study of the language.

Modern Method Spanish. unabr. ed. Conversa-Phone Institute Staff. 3 cass. (Running Time: 3 hrs. 5 min.). (Modern Method Language Sets Ser.). 1991. 21.95 (978-1-56752-041-5(3)) Conversa-phone.
This program provides a full study of Spanish alphabet thru sentences, phrases, conversation & a special section on grammar. These programs are for the serious student or persons wanting a more indepth study of the language.

Modern Method Swedish. unabr. ed. Conversa-Phone Institute Staff. 2 cass. (Running Time: 2 hrs. 5 min.). (Modern Method Language Sets Ser.). 1991. 21.95 (978-1-56752-046-0(4), COC-3016) Conversa-phone.
This program provides a full study of Swedish. Alphabet thru sentences phrases, conversation & a special section on grammar. These programs are for the serious student or persons wanting a more in depth study of the language.

Modern Mongolian: Cassette. Gaunt. 2004. bk. 56.95 (978-0-415-31512-8(3)) Pub: Routledge. Dist(s): Taylor and Fran

Modern Oral Amdo Tibetan: A Language Primer. Kalsang Norbu et al. (Studies in Linguistics & Semiotics: Vol. 5). 2000. audio compact disk 119.95 (978-0-7734-7895-4(7)) E Mellen.

Modern Painters see Cambridge Treasury of English Prose: Dickens to Butler

Modern Parables, Volume 1: Living in the Kingdom of God. Thomas Purifoy & Jonathan Rogers. 2007. DVD & audio compact disk 129.00 (978-0-9798524-0-4(4)) Comp Cin.

Modern Persian: Elementary. Gernot L. Windfuhr & Hassan Teranisa. 8 cass. (Running Time: 12 hrs.). 1979. 68.88 U MI Lang Res.

Modern Persian: Intermediate Level I. Gernot L. Windfuhr & Shapur Bostanbakhsh. 3 cass. (Running Time: 4 hrs. 30 min.). 1980. 40.99 U MI Lang Res.

Modern Persian: Intermediate Level II. Gernot L. Windfuhr. 7 cass. (Running Time: 10 hrs. 30 min.). 1982. 63.58 U MI Lang Res.

Modern Persian Complete. Gernot L. Windfuhr et al. 18 cass. 121.39 U MI Lang Res.

Modern Persian Course Book Cass. Abrahams. 2007. audio compact disk 49.95 (978-0-415-33446-4(2)) Pub: Routledge. Dist(s): Taylor and Fran

Modern Philosophy Vol. 2: Kant to the Present. Leonard Peikoff. 24 cass. (Running Time: 33 hrs.). (History of Philosophy Ser.). 1994. 295.00 (978-1-56114-341-2(3), LP38D) Second Renaissance.
Presents the ideas that shaped Western Philosophy.

Modern Political Philosophy: The Ideas of Hobbes, Locke & Rousseau. Darryl Wright. 6 cass. (Running Time: 7 hrs.). 59.95 Second Renaissance.
This course contrasts Hobbes' & Rouseau's respective forms of political absolutism with Locke's intransigent defense of individual rights.

Modern Real Estate Practice in New York: Keypoint Review. 1 cass. 1995. 27.00 (978-0-7931-1497-9(7)) Kaplan Pubng.

Modern Real Estate Practice in Texas, Keypoint Review Audio Tapes. C. Nance. 1995. 27.00 (978-0-7931-1496-2(9), 1518-0901, Dearbm Real Est Ed) Kaplan Pubng.

Modern Real Estate Transactions. 15 cass. (Running Time: 22 hrs. 50 min.). 1997. 395.00 (MC11) Am Law Inst.
Discusses & analyzes the techniques & substantive law of modern commercial real estate practice. Designed for lawyers representing developers, construction & term lenders, investors, ground lessors & lessees & space tenants. Includes 1996 resource materials & 1977 supplemental course materials.

Modern Real Estate Transactions. 1 cass. (Running Time: 23 hrs.). 1999. 595.00 (AE15) Am Law Inst.
Includes resource marts.

Modern Rock Sessions for Guitar. Ed. by Ed Lazano. Contrib. by Randy Young & Peter Marunzak. 1 CD. (Running Time: 1 hr.). 1998. pap. bk. 12.95 (978-0-8256-1626-6(3), AM945164) Music Sales.

Modern Russian One. Clayton Dawson et al. 24 cass. (Multilingual Books Intensive Language Courses). (RUS.). (C). 2004. per. 225.00 (978-1-58214-362-0(5)) Language Assocs.

Modern Russian One. Clayton Dawson et al. 31 CD's. (RUS.). 2004. per. 269.00 (978-1-58214-361-3(7)) Language Assocs.

***Modern Russian Vol 2 Cds & Book.** Clayton L. Dawson & Assya Humesky. (ENG & RUS.). 2005. pap. bk. 295.00 (978-1-57970-204-5(X), Audio-For) J Norton Pubs.

Modern Science of Thief-Taking. unabr. ed. Charles Dickens. Read by Tom Teti. 2 cass. (Running Time: 3 hrs. 10 min.). 16.95 (978-1-55656-015-6(X)) Dercum Audio.
Dickens is one of the pioneers of detective fiction. His many revolutionary concepts include the first use of the plain clothes detective. Included here are: Dr. Manette's Manuscript; Hunted Down; & Household Words - Three Detective Anecdotes. Includes library case.

Modern Short Stories in English, Set. Lolita Dixson. (C). 1987. 105.00 (978-0-13-597659-3(6)) Longman.

Modern Spoken Italian Part B CDs & Text. Elaine Vertucci Baran. 8 CDs. (Running Time: 8 hrs. 30 mins.). (ITA.). 2005. audio compact disk 225.00 (978-1-57970-260-1(0), AFZ551D, Audio-For) J Norton Pubs.
The second part of a two-volume course designed specifically for the beginner, focusing on practical, easy-to-use, everyday conversational Italian. Part B extends the scope of the course through additional vocabulary, the use of the past tense, and more comprehensive drill and exercise materials.

Modern Tap Dancing. 2 LPs. (Running Time: 3 hrs.). stu. ed. 27.00 (KIM 4070); 27.00 (KIM 4070C); audio compact disk 31.00 CD. (KIM 4070CD) Kimbo Educ.
Short piano & orchestrated selections for teaching tap technique.

Modern Tibetan Language, Vol. 1. Lobsang Thonden. 4 cass. 2000. pap. bk. 60.00 (978-81-85102-28-3(7)) Laurier Bks CAN.

Modern Tibetan Language, Vol. II. Lobsang Thonden. 3 cass. 1998. pap. bk. 58.00 (978-81-85102-49-8(X)) Laurier Bks CAN.

Modern Times. unabr. ed. Paul Johnson. Read by Nadia May. 3 pieces. (Running Time: 154800 sec.). 2007. audio compact disk 54.95 (978-0-7861-8963-2(0), 1004A,B) Blckstn Audio.

Modern Times, Pt. 1. unabr. ed. Paul Johnson. Read by Nadia May. 14 cass. (Running Time: 42 hrs. 30 mins.). 1991. 89.95 (978-0-7861-0003-3(6), 1004A,B) Blckstn Audio.
Paul Johnson has written an historical account of the past 7 decades (commencing with WWI) that not only reports the events & supporting facts, but also analyzes how & why much of this history came to be.

Modern Times, Pt. 2. unabr. ed. Paul Johnson. Read by Nadia May. 15 cass. (Running Time: 42 hrs. 30 mins.). 1991. 95.95 (978-0-7861-0004-0(4), 1004A,B) Blckstn Audio.

Modern Times: Part II: the World from the Twenties to the Eighties. unabr. ed. Paul Johnson. Read by Nadia May. (Running Time: 59400 sec.). 2007. audio compact disk 120.00 (978-0-7861-0108-5(3)) Blckstn Audio.

Modern Times: The World Form the Twenties to the Nineties, Part 1. unabr. ed. Paul Johnson. Read by Nadia May. (Running Time: 59400 sec.). 2007. audio compact disk 130.00 (978-0-7861-4996-4(5)) Blckstn Audio.

Modern Times: The World from the Twenties to the Eighties. Paul Johnson. Read by Larry McKeever. 29 cass. (Running Time: 43 hrs. 30 mins.). 1989. 232.00 (978-0-7366-1503-7(2)) Books on Tape.
A comprehensive narrative history of the world in the six decades since the end of WW I.

Modern Times Pt. 2: The World from the Twenties to the Eighties. unabr. ed. Paul Johnson. Read by Larry McKeever. 10 cass. (Running Time: 15 hrs.). 1989. 80.00 (2377-B) Books on Tape.
This comprehensive narrative history of the modern world covers all the great events, ideas & personalities of the six decades since the end of WWI.

Modern Trial Advocacy. Steven Lubet. 10 cass. (Running Time: 15 hrs.). 1995. 139.95 (AUDZ250S) NITA.
A thorough discussion of trial law, tactics & strategies as they apply to all phases of presenting the case. Includes case analysis, persuasion, direct examination, cross examination, impeachment, expert testimony, objections, foundations & exhibits, final arguments & jury selection.

Modern Trial Advocacy. Steven Lubet. 11 cass. (Running Time: 10 hrs.). 1995. 99.95 (FAZ250S) Natl Inst Trial Ad.
Case analysis, persuasion, direct examination, cross examination, impeachment, expert testimony, objections, foundations & exhibits, final arguments, & jury selection.

Modern Ukrainian. Assya Humesky. 12 cass. (Running Time: 18 hrs.). 93.18 Set. U MI Lang Res.

Modern Utopia. H. G. Wells. Read by Anais 9000. 2008. 27.95 (978-1-60112-165-3(2)) Babblebooks.

Modern World History: Patterns of Interaction: Chapter Summaries. (ENG & SPA.). (gr. 6-12). 2003. audio compact disk (978-0-618-18466-8(X), 2-10105) Holt McDoug.

Modern World History: Patterns of Interaction: Chapter Summary. (ENG & SPA.). (gr. 6-12). 2001. (978-0-395-93904-8(6), 2-81065) Holt McDoug.

Modern World History: Patterns of Interaction: Reading Study Guide. (gr. 6-12). 2005. audio compact disk (978-0-618-42720-8(1), 2-00705); audio compact disk (978-0-618-42721-5(X), 2-00706) Holt McDoug.

Modern World History: Patterns of Interaction: Voices from the Past. (gr. 6-12). 2005. audio compact disk (978-0-618-43165-6(9), 2-00800) Holt McDoug.

Modern Written Arabic FSI CDs & Text, Vol. 1. 19 CDs. (Running Time: 30 hrs.). (Foreign Service Institute Basic Course Ser.). (ARA.). 2005. audio compact disk 325.00 (978-1-57970-274-8(0), AFA269D, Audio-For) J Norton Pubs.

Modern Written Arabic FSI CDs & Text, Vol. 2. 8 CDs. (Running Time: 8 hrs.). (Foreign Service Institute Basic Course Ser.). (ARA.). 2005. audio compact disk 225.00 (978-1-57970-275-5(9), AFA320D, Audio-For) J Norton Pubs.

Modernism & Madness. Leonard Peikoff. 1 cass. (Running Time: 1 hr. 30 min.). 1994. 14.95 (978-1-56114-371-9(5), LP28C) Second Renaissance.
Connecting modern culture with schizophrenia.

Modesty: Does God Really Care What I Wear. Nancy Leigh DeMoss. (ENG.). 2003. audio compact disk 16.00 (978-0-940110-72-4(5)) Life Action Publishing.

***Modified Rapture: Comedy in W. S. Gilbert's Savoy Operas.** Alan Fischler. (Victorian Literature & Culture Ser.). (ENG.). 27.50 (978-0-8139-2933-0(4)) U Pr of Va.

Modigliani Scandal. abr. ed. Ken Follett. Perf. by Michael York. 2 cass. (Running Time: 3 hrs.). 2004. 18.00 (978-1-59007-183-0(2)) Pub: New Millenn Enter. Dist(s): PerseuPGW

Modigliani Scandal. unabr. ed. Read by Ken Follett & David Case. 8 cass. (Running Time: 8 hrs.). 1988. 42.00 (978-0-7366-1426-9(5), 2312) Books on Tape.
It was a hoax from which the art world might never recover. It started with a rumor that set dealers & art historians at each other's throats: the only surviving canvas from a great 20th century painter's brief experiment with drugs was hidden away in a remote corner of Europe.

Modules: Physical Science; Earth Science. (McDougal Littell Science Ser.). (gr. 6-12). 2005. audio compact disk (978-0-618-43176-2(4), 2-01192); audio compact disk (978-0-618-43173-1(X), 2-01189) Holt McDoug.

Modules: Physical Science; Life Science. (gr. 6-12). 2005. audio compact disk (978-0-618-43177-9(2), 2-01193); audio compact disk (978-0-618-43174-8(8), 2-01190) Holt McDoug.

Modules: Physical Science; Physical Science. (gr. 6-12). 2005. audio compact disk (978-0-618-43178-6(0), 2-01194); audio compact disk (978-0-618-43175-5(6), 2-01191) Holt McDoug.

Moe Levine: The Historic Recordings. Moe Levine. (ENG.). 2009. audio compact disk 95.00 (978-1-934833-10-0(X)) Trial Guides.

Moeurs Contemporaines see Caedmon Treasury of Modern Poets Reading Their Own Poetry

Moffats. unabr. ed. Eleanor Estes. Read by Full Cast Production Staff. (J). 2007. 39.99 (978-1-59895-880-5(1)) Find a World.

Moffats. unabr. ed. Eleanor Estes. Read by Cynthia Bishop. 3 cass. (Running Time: 4 hrs. 30 mins.). 2002. lib. bdg. 24.00 (978-1-932076-01-1(8)) Full Cast Audio.

Mohawk Baronet. unabr. collector's ed. James Thomas Flexner. Read by Jonathan Reese. 10 cass. (Running Time: 15 hrs.). 1995. 80.00 (978-0-7366-2948-5(3), 3642) Books on Tape.
In this sweeping biography, Sir William Johnson, a powerful, romantic figure who was both a British Baronet & a savvy Mohawk leader, comes into his own. Stranger than fiction.

Moises: El hombre que libero a su pueblo: Serie Heroes de la fe. 2000. (978-1-57697-839-9(7)) Untd Bible Amrcas Svce.

Moisés, el hombre que liberó a su Pueblo. (SPA.). (J). 2004. audio compact disk (978-1-933218-02-1(9)) Untd Bible Amrcas Svce.

Moises: Padre de una nacion: Serie Heroes de la fe. 2000. (978-1-57697-840-5(0)) Untd Bible Amrcas Svce.

Mojave. Hank Mitchum. Read by Charlie O'Dowd. 4 vols. 2004. 25.00 (978-1-58807-199-6(5)) Am Pubng Inc.

Mojave. Hank Mitchum. Read by Charlie O'Dowd. 4 vols. No. 16. 2004. (978-1-58807-959-6(7)) Am Pubng Inc.

Mojave. unabr. ed. Scripts. Hank Mitchum. 5 CDs. (Running Time: 6 hrs.). (Stagecoach Ser.: No. 16). 2005. audio compact disk 14.99 (978-1-58807-301-3(7)) Am Pubng Inc.

Mojave Crossing. unabr. ed. Read by Louis L'Amour & David Strathairn. (Running Time: 14400 sec.). (Louis L'Amour Ser.). (ENG.). 2006. audio compact disk 25.95 (978-0-7393-2115-7(3), Random AudioBks) Pub: Random Audio Pubg. Dist(s): Random

Mojave Showdown. Larry J. Martin. 1 cass. 1994. (978-1-885339-01-0(1)) Wolfpack Pub.
Western fiction.

Mojo: How to Get It, How to Keep It, & How to Get It Back If You Lose It. abr. unabr. ed. Marshall Goldsmith & Mark Reiter. Read by Marshall Goldsmith. 2010. audio compact disk 29.99 (978-1-4013-9260-4(1), Harper Audio) Pub: Hyperion. Dist(s): HarperCollins Pubs

Mojo Plays Morocco. unabr. ed. Read by George Schultz. 1 cass. (Running Time: 1 hr.). 1977. 9.00 (978-1-881137-22-1(8)) ZBS Found.
The haunting piano music from "Moon over Morocco." Blended with authentic Moroccan sound effects.

Molders of Twentieth Century Religious Thought. Linwood Urban. 10 cass. (Running Time: 10 hrs.). Incl. Molders of Twentieth Century Religious Thought: Martin Buber: Judaism & the Covenant. 1981.; Molders of Twentieth Century Religious Thought: Martin Buber: The Eclipse of God. 1981.; Molders of Twentieth Century Religious Thought: Paul Tillich: Faith in

Moment Mal!, Vol. 1.3, Level I. unabr. ed. Martin Müller et al. 1 CD. (Running Time: 1 hr. 30 min.). (Moment Mal Ser.). (GER.). 1998. audio compact disk 24.00 (978-3-468-47809-3(7)) Langenscheidt.

Moment Mal!, Vol. 1.3, Level I. unabr. ed. Martin Müller et al. 1 cass. (Running Time: 1 hr. 30 min.). (Moment Mal Ser.). (GER.). 2005. 16.50 (978-3-468-47758-4(9)) Langenscheidt.

Moment Mal!, Vol. 1.4, Level I. unabr. ed. Martin Müller et al. 1 cass. (Moment Mal Ser.). (GER.). 2005. 23.95 (978-3-468-47759-1(7)) Langenscheidt.

Moment Mal!, Vol. 2.1. unabr. ed. Martin Müller et al. 2 cass. (Running Time: 1 hr. 30 min.). (Moment Mal Ser.). (GER.). 2005. 39.50 (978-3-468-47776-8(7)) Langenscheidt.

Moment Mal!, Vol. 2.2, Level II. unabr. ed. Martin Müller et al. 1 cass. (Running Time: 1 hr. 30 min.). (Moment Mal Ser.). (GER.). 2005. 17.50 (978-3-468-47777-5(5)) Langenscheidt.

Moment Mal!, Vol. 2.3, Level II. unabr. ed. Martin Müller et al. 1 CD. (Running Time: 1 hr. 30 min.). (Moment Mal Ser.). (GER.). 1998. audio compact disk 24.00 (978-3-468-47810-9(0)) Langenscheidt.

Moment Mal!, Vol. 2.3, Level II. unabr. ed. Martin Müller et al. 1 cass. (Running Time: 1 hr. 30 min.). (Moment Mal Ser.). (GER.). 2005. 23.95 (978-3-468-47779-9(1)) Langenscheidt.

Moment Mal!, Vol. 3.1, Level III. unabr. ed. Martin Müller et al. 2 CDs. (Running Time: 1 hr. 30 min.). (Moment Mal Ser.). (GER.). 2005. audio compact disk 36.50 (978-3-468-47807-9(0)) Langenscheidt.

Moment Mal!, Vol. 3.2, Level III. unabr. ed. Martin Müller et al. 1 CD. (Running Time: 1 hr. 30 min.). (Moment Mal Ser.). (GER.). 2005. 17.50 (978-3-468-47797-3(X)) Langenscheidt.

Moment Mal!, Vol. 3.3, Level III. unabr. ed. Martin Müller et al. 1 CD. (Running Time: 1 hr. 30 min.). (Moment Mal Ser.). (GER.). 1998. audio compact disk 24.00 (978-3-468-47811-6(9)) Langenscheidt.

Moment Mal!, Vol. 3.3, Level III. unabr. ed. Martin Müller et al. 1 cass. (Running Time: 1 hr. 30 min.). (Moment Mal Ser.). (GER.). 2005. 23.95 (978-3-468-47798-0(8)) Langenscheidt.

Moment Mal! Level III, Vol. 3.1. unabr. ed. Martin Müller et al. 2 cass. (Running Time: 1 hr.). (Moment Mal Ser.). (GER.). 2005. 39.50 (978-3-468-47796-6(1)) Langenscheidt.

Moment Mal! Level III, Vol. 3.2. unabr. ed. 1 cass., 1 CD. (GER.). audio compact disk 18.95 CD. Langenscheidt.

Moment of Discovery. abr. ed. Told to Steven Harrison. 4 cass. (Running Time: 6 hrs.). 2002. 24.95 (978-1-59181-004-9(3)) Pub: Sentient Pubns. Dist(s): Natl Bk Netwk

Moment of Glory: The Year Underdogs Ruled Golf. unabr. ed. John Feinstein. Read by L. J. Ganser. (Running Time: 12 hrs.). (ENG.). 2010. 24.98 (978-1-60788-201-5(9)); audio compact disk 34.98 (978-1-60788-200-8(0)) Pub: Hachet Audio. Dist(s): HachBkGrp

Moment of Madness. unabr. ed. Una-Mary Parker. Read by Liz Holliss. 12 cass. (Running Time: 14 hrs. 45 mins.). (Isis Ser.). (J). 2002. 94.95 (978-0-7531-1352-3(X)) Pub: ISIS Lrg Prnt GBR. Dist(s): Ulverscroft US
When Lucinda Farrell's father, Miles Scott-Forbes, suddenly dies at the age of 77, there is a natural sense of grief; but it is touched with a hint of relief on the part of Lucinda and her brothers. Miles was an eccentric, brilliant mathematician who hovered on the brink of madness, driving his family, sometimes cruelly, to distraction. But it seems, although he is now dead, that Lucinda is not going to escape his Machiavellian nature. He has left Lucinda a sealed box along with instructions to open it alone. Her brothers are in a fever of curiosity, tinged with jealousy. But for Lucinda, the opening of the box will have shocking consequences.

Moment of Revelation. abr. ed. Robert A. Monroe. Read by Robert A. Monroe. (Mind Food Ser.). 1983. 14.95 (978-1-56102-409-4(0)) Inter Indus.
Help to achieve a peak experience.

Moment of Silence. Anna Dean. 2009. 54.95 (978-1-4079-0700-0(X)); audio compact disk 71.95 (978-1-4079-0701-7(8)) Pub: Soundings Ltd GBR. Dist(s): Ulverscroft US

Moment of Truth. Lisa Scottoline. Narrated by Barbara Rosenblat. 10 CDs. (Running Time: 11 hrs. 30 mins.). 2000. audio compact disk 97.00 (978-0-7887-4741-0(X), C1228E7) Recorded Bks.
Mary DiNunzio is a lawyer with an unusual problem. Her new client, Jack Newlin, is an innocent man claiming to be guilty. Now she finds herself risking her own life to discover why a man would frame himself for his wife's murder.

***Moment of Truth.** unabr. ed. Lisa Scottoline. Read by Barbara Rosenblat. (ENG.). 2006. (978-0-06-088851-0(2), Harper Audio); (978-0-06-088852-7(0), Harper Audio) HarperCollins Pubs.

Moment of Truth. unabr. ed. Lisa Scottoline. Narrated by Barbara Rosenblat. 8 cass. (Running Time: 11 hrs. 30 mins.). 1999. 75.00 (978-0-7887-4152-4(7), 96182E7) Recorded Bks.

Moment of Truth: 12 Stories On - Grace, Acting on Faith & More! AIO Team Staff. Created by Focus on the Family Staff. (Running Time: 4 hrs.). (Adventures in Odyssey Ser.). (ENG.). (J). (gr. 1-7). 2007. audio compact disk 24.99 (978-1-58997-447-0(6), Tyndale Ent) Tyndale Hse.

***Moment of Truth Low Price.** abr. ed. Lisa Scottoline. Read by Kate Burton. (ENG.). 2005. (978-0-06-088657-8(9), Harper Audio); (978-0-06-088659-2(5), Harper Audio) HarperCollins Pubs.

Moment of War. unabr. ed. Laurie Lee. Read by Stephen Thorne. 4 cass. (Running Time: 4 hrs. 35 min.). 2001. 44.95 (978-1-85089-873-3(1), 92051) Pub: ISIS Audio GBR. Dist(s): Ulverscroft US
In December 1937, a naive & romantic young man walked over the Pyrenees into Spain to join the International Brigade. In this new volume of his autobiographical trilogy Laurie Lee describes the bitter winter leading to the Republican army's defeat.

Moment She Was Gone. unabr. ed. Evan Hunter. Read by Michael Rafkin. 4 vols. (Running Time: 6 hrs.). 2002. bk. 39.95 (978-0-7927-2723-1(1), CSL 509, Chivers Sound Lib); audio compact disk 64.95 (978-0-7927-2754-5(1), SLD 509, Chivers Sound Lib) AudioGO.
Twenty-four hours is all Evan Hunter's disaffected urban hero has to find the woman who is closer to his heart than anyone - his schizophrenic twin. His quest takes him into the history of their entwined past as he comes to terms with his sister's illness and his own tenuous sense of identity.

Moment Towards the End of the Play. unabr. ed. Timothy West. 10 cass. (Running Time: 15 hrs.). 2002. 84.95 (978-0-7540-0847-7(9), CAB 2269) Pub: Chivers Pr GBR. Dist(s): AudioGO

***Moment Where We Begin... An Exploration Between Intention & Action.** Created by Uncommon Sensing LLC. (ENG.). 2000. audio compact disk 60.00 (978-0-9826724-2-6(X)) Uncommon Sens.

Moments in Our Lives: A Woman's Eye View. 2005. audio compact disk 12.95 (978-0-9771894-4-1(9)) Town & Country Repro.

Moments of Being: Unpublished Autobiographical Writings. Virginia Woolf. Read by Peggy Ashcroft. Adapted by Michael Voysey. 3 cass. 19.95 (SCN 135) J Norton Pubs.
As well as her diaries & collected letters, there are a number of more formal autobiographical essays, published. This selection of memories ranges from her childhood at St. Ives, Cornwall, to her first ventures into 'society'.

Moments of Being: Unpublished Autobiographical Writings. unabr. collector's ed. Virginia Woolf. Read by Penelope Dellaporta. 8 cass. (Running Time: 12 hrs.). 1989. 64.00 (978-0-7366-1668-3(3), 2516) Books on Tape.
The author was well born & in "Reminiscenses," the first of five pieces, she focuses on the death of her mother, "the greatest disaster that could happen" & "A Sketch of the Past" is the most significant of the pieces. It gives an account of Woolf's early years & illuminates her relationship with her father, who played such a vital role in her development as a writer.

Moments Out of Time: Childhood As Memory & Archetype. Daniel Lindley. 1 cass. (Running Time: 58 min.). 1995. 9.95 (978-0-7822-0485-8(6), 561) C G Jung IL.
This lecture is an exploration of the connections between real childhood - imaged in memory & photographs - & archetypal childhood seen in images from poetry, art, & dream.

Moment's Peace: Reducing Stress & Creating Balance through Guided Visualization. 1 CD. (Running Time: 1 hr). 2004. audio compact disk 15.95 (978-0-9753279-0-6(9)) InVision.
Included are the essentials for creating a personal stress reduction practice, including 3 powerful visualizations, an introduction to stress reduction and guidelines for an effective visualization practice.

Moments Together for Couples. unabr. ed. Dennis Rainey & Barbara Rainey. (Running Time: 14 hrs. 0 mins. 0 sec.). (ENG.). 2009. audio compact disk 28.98 (978-1-59644-801-8(6), christianSeed) christianaud.

***Moments Together for Couples: Devotions for Drawing near to God & One Another.** unabr. ed. Barbara Rainey. Narrated by Adam Verner. (ENG.). 2009. 18.98 (978-1-59644-802-5(4), christianSeed) christianaud.

Momentum. Contrib. by Tobymac. 2002. 9.99 (978-5-552-52772-4(0)) FF Rcds.

Momma. unabr. ed. Terry McMillan. Read by Marjorie Johnson. 8 vols. (Running Time: 12 hrs.).Tr. of Mama. 2000. bk. 69.95 (978-0-7927-2239-7(6), CSL 128, Chivers Sound Lib) AudioGO.
"It ain't that I don't believe in God. I just don't trust his judgement." Mildred Peacock is the rough feisty heroine, a survivor who will do anything to keep her family together. In Mildred's life, men disappear as quickly as paychecks.

Momma. unabr. ed. Terry McMillan. Read by Jennifer Wydra. 8 CDs. (Running Time: 12 Hrs.).Tr. of Mama. 2000. audio compact disk 79.95 (978-0-7927-9977-1(1), SLD 028, Chivers Sound Lib) AudioGO.
"It ain't that I don't believe in God. I just don't trust his judgment." Mildred Peacock is a survivor who will do anything to keep her family together.

Mommies Who Drink: Sex, Drugs, & Other Distant Memories of an Ordinary Mom. unabr. ed. Brett Paesel. Read by Brett Paesel. (YA). 2007. 39.99 (978-1-60252-769-0(5)) Find a World.

Mommy. Max Allan Collins. Read by Patty McCormack. 2 cass. (Running Time: 3 hrs.). 1996. bk. 16.95 Set. (978-1-882071-87-6(5)) B-B Audio.
The ultimate protective mother, who will go to any lengths necessary to keep her daughter at the top of her class, resorts to murder. Young Jessica Ann comes to the conclusion that her loving "mommy" may, in fact, be a deranged killer.

Mommy Bunny's Going to Work. Shelley L. Stockwell. 1 cass. (Running Time: 25 min.). (Self-Hynosis Ser.). (J). (gr. 4). 1986. 10.00 (978-0-912559-06-3(3)) Creativity Unltd Pr.
Story tape for children of working mothers. Two versions-one for general population, one for flight attendants.

Mommy, Buy Me a China Doll. 2004. 8.95 (978-1-56008-972-8(5)); cass. & flmstrp 30.00 (978-1-56008-718-2(8)) Weston Woods.

Mommy, Daddy, Where Do Babies Come From? unabr. ed. Grace Ayad & Richard Panzer. Perf. by Christine Libon et al. 1 cass. (Running Time: 8 min.). (Wonderful World of True Love Ser.). (J). 1997. pap. bk. 18.90 (978-1-888933-10-9(0)); 5.95 (978-1-888933-09-3(7)) Ctr Educ Media.
Discussions about love, weddings, marriage, pregnancy & dangers involved in the misuse of love when Jenny asks her parents where babies come from.

Mommy Dressing: A Love Story, After a Fashion. collector's ed. Lois Gould. Read by Mary Peiffer. 4 cass. (Running Time: 6 hrs.). 1999. 32.00 (978-0-7366-4747-2(3), 5085) Books on Tape.
The story of Jo Copeland, fashion designer to the stars & the daughter who struggled to please her. From the viewpoint of an isolated girl acutely conscious that she would never enter her mother's glittering domain, Lois Gould paints a mesmerizing picture of the kingdom of movie stars, fashion show & steamer trunks that her mother ruled. Not only a personal history of her family, it is also a fascinating portrayal of New York's emergence as the world's fashion & glamour capital.

Mommy, Gimme a Drinka Water! Perf. by Didi Conn. 1 cass. (Running Time: 1 hr. 30 min.). (J). 1995. 9.95 (1903-4); audio compact disk 12.95 (1903-2) Kultur NJ.
Sung from the viewpoint of children in different situations. Kids of all ages will love the way the words mirror the way a young child sees the world.

Mommy, Is God a Super Hero? Beverly Lozier Jackson. (J). 2007. audio compact disk 9.99 (978-1-60247-051-4(0)) Tate Pubng.

Mommy Tracked. unabr. ed. Whitney Gaskell. (Running Time: 43200 sec.). 2007. 59.95 (978-1-4332-0775-4(3)); audio compact disk 72.00 (978-1-4332-0776-1(1)); audio compact disk 29.95 (978-1-4332-0777-8(X)) Blckstn Audio.

Mommy You've Always Wanted. Vivian King. Music by Jim Oliver. 1 cass. (Running Time: 1 hr.). 1995. (978-0-9641043-1-0(8)) Spirit Mtn.
In your Inner Theatre - the theatre of your mind - there is a cast of characters as rich & varied as actors on a Broadway Stage. One of these actors is the Mommy you've always wanted.

Mommy...I'm a Big Girl Now! Lewis Carroll, pseud. 2005. audio compact disk 9.99 (978-0-9763798-0-5(5)) Lions Crest Pr.

Mommy's Lullabies. Twin Sisters Productions Staff. 1 CD. (Running Time: 59 mins). (Growing Minds with Music Ser.). (J). 2004. audio compact disk 12.99 (978-1-57583-719-2(6)) Twin Sisters.
Twelve traditional and original lullabies for Mommy to sing to her little one. Tracks 1-12 feature soothing vocals to help her learn the lullabies; tracks 13-24 are instrumental so baby will hear only Mommy's voice!.

Mommy's Office. unabr. ed. Barbara Shook Hazen. 1 cass. (Running Time: 6 min.). (J). (gr. k-2). 1994. bk. 24.90 (978-0-8045-6824-1(3), 6824) Spoken Arts.

Mommywood. unabr. ed. Tori Spelling. Read by Tori Spelling. 6 CDs. (Running Time: 6 hrs. 30 mins. 0 sec.). (ENG.). 2009. audio compact disk 29.99 (978-0-7435-8237-7(3)) Pub: S&S Audio. Dist(s): S and S Inc

Mom's Life. unabr. ed. Kathryn Grody. Read by Kathryn Grody. 2 CDs. (Running Time: 2 hrs.). 2000. audio compact disk 15.00 (978-1-885608-43-7(8)) Airplay.
A recounting of just how it was being a first time mom, along with her husband & first time dad.

Mom's Life. unabr. ed. Kathryn Grody. Read by Kathryn Grody. 2 cass. (Running Time: 2 hrs. 20 min.). Dramatization. 1995. 14.95 (978-1-885608-03-1(9)) Airplay.
The actress/author reads her book based on how it is being a first time mom.

Moms Like Us Too, Volume 1. Compiled by Jonathan Dunn. 2008. 9.99 (978-5-557-50317-4(X)) Tooth & Nail.

Mom's Rules: What Mom Really Taught Us. Short Stories. As told by Mark Mayfield. 4 Cassettes. (Running Time: 5 hours). 2000. 25.00 (978-0-9700349-1-5(1)) Mayfield Present.
Compilation of 40 phrases that all moms say....and what they REALLY mean as read by the author.

Moms That Cook. 1 cass. (Running Time: 48 mins.). (J). 2000. 10.98 (978-0-9647786-3-4(7)); audio compact disk 15.98 (978-0-9647786-2-7(9)) Baby Music.
Twelve popular performers, who also happen to be moms, serve up a recipe for listening fun. Mix of mostly original tunes (with two traditional lullabies stirred in) ranges in style from blues to bluegrass.

Mom's the Word: A Journey in Meter & Centimeters. Milbre Burch. Perf. by Milbre Burch. (ENG.). 2009. audio compact disk 20.00 (978-0-9795271-9-7(8)) Kind Crone.

***Moms' Ultimate Guide to the Tween Girl World.** Zondervan. (Running Time: 7 hrs. 35 mins. 55 sec.). (ENG.). 2010. 16.99 (978-0-310-41287-8(0)) Zondervan.

Momzillas. abr. ed. Jill Kargman. Read by Renée Raudman. (Running Time: 10800 sec.). 2008. audio compact disk 14.99 (978-1-4233-2746-2(2), 9781423327462, BCD Value Price) Brilliance Audio.

Momzillas. unabr. ed. Jill Kargman. Read by Renée Raudman. (Running Time: 8 hrs.). 2007. 39.25 (978-1-4233-2742-4(X), 9781423327424, Brinc Audio MP3 Lib); 24.95 (978-1-4233-2741-7(1), 9781423327417, Brilliance MP3); 39.25 (978-1-4233-2744-8(6), 9781423327448, BADLE); 24.95 (978-1-4233-2743-1(8), 9781423327431, BAD); 69.25 (978-1-4233-2738-7(1), 9781423327387, BrilAudUnabridg); audio compact disk 87.25 (978-1-4233-2740-0(3), 9781423327400, BriAudCD Unabrid); audio compact disk 29.95 (978-1-4233-2739-4(X), 9781423327394, Bril Audio CD Unabri) Brilliance Audio.

Mon Ami Godefroy (My Friend Godefroy) Helene Vachon. 1 cass. (Running Time: 50 mins.). (Best-Sellers Ser.). (FRE.). (J). (ps-2). 2000. cass. & audio compact disk 9.95 (978-2-921997-37-9(1)) Pub: Coffragants CAN. Dist(s): Penton Overseas

Mon Ami Maigret, Georges Simenon. Read by Marc Moro. 2 cass. (FRE.). 1996. 28.95 (1847-LQP) Olivia & Hill.
The pipe smoking detective solves yet another mystery.

Mon imagier des Amuset. pap. bk. 34.95 (978-2-07-054653-4(5)) Pub: Gallimard Edns FRA. Dist(s): Distribks Inc

Mon imagier Sonore. pap. bk. 34.95 (978-2-07-054393-9(5)) Pub: Gallimard Edns FRA. Dist(s): Distribks Inc

Mon Moulin, Lettres De. unabr. ed. 2 cass. (Running Time: 3 hrs.). 1992. bk. 19.95 (978-0-88432-480-5(X), SFR130) J Norton Pubs.
Foreign Language Instruction. Three stories from Daudet's classic.

Mon Oncle Jules see Contes de Maupassant

Mon Oncle Jules et Le Parapluie. Short Stories. Guy de Maupassant. Read by Georges Riquier. 1 cass. (FRE.). 1991. bk. 16.95 (1082-SA) Olivia & Hill.
Two short stories.

Mon Oncle Jules et Le Parapluie. unabr. ed. Guy de Maupassant. 1 cass. (Guy de Maupassant Ser.: Vol. 2). (FRE.). bk. 16.95 (SFR452) J Norton Pubs.

Mon Pere Avant Raison, Sacha Guitry. Perf. by Michel Etchevery & Catherine Samie. 2 cass. Dramatization. (FRE.). 1996. 26.95 (1819-RF) Olivia & Hill.
The Comedie Francaise performance of a typical, fast-moving play by one of France's most popular playwrights who, once again, deals with the theme of adultery & deceit.

Mona Lisa Stratagem: The Art of Women, Age, & Power. abr. ed. Harriet Rubin. (Running Time: 5 hrs.). (ENG.). 2007. 14.98 (978-1-59483-907-8(7)) Pub: Hachet Audio. Dist(s): HachBkGrp

Mona Mousa Code Set, Bks. 15&16: A Cheese-Colored Camper. Illus. by Geronimo Stilton. Narrated by Bill Lobley. (Running Time: 9780 sec.). (Geronimo Stilton Ser.). (J). (gr. 2-5). 2008. audio compact disk 19.95 (978-0-545-02881-3(7)) Scholastic Inc.

Mona Mousa Code, A Cheese-Colored Camper. unabr. ed. Geronimo Stilton. Read by Bill Lobley. (Geronimo Stilton Ser.). (J). 2008. 34.99 (978-1-60514-638-6(2)) Find a World.

Mona Simpson. unabr. ed. Mona Simpson. Read by Mona Simpson. 1 cass. (Running Time: 29 min.). 1988. 10.00 (011588) New Letters.
Author of "Anywhere But Here" reads from her novel & talks about the current literary brat pack.

Mona Van Duyn. unabr. ed. Read by Mona Van Duyn. 1 cass. (Running Time: 29 min.). 1985. 10.00 New Letters.
National Book Award winning poet Mona Van Duyn was recorded at a public reading.

Mona Van Duyn II. Mona Van Duyn. 1 cass. (Running Time: 29 min.). (New Letters on the Air Ser.). 1992. 10.00 (100491) New Letters.
Van Duyn reads from "Near Changes" & comments on the state of poetry & her general sense of optimism.

Monarch Butterfly of Aster Way. 1 cass. (Running Time: 35 min.). (J). (ps-2). 2001. bk. 19.95 (SP 5017C) Kimbo Educ.
Journey with this butterfly across the U. S. & down into Mexico to spend the winter. Includes book.

Monarch of Deadman Bay: The Life & Death of a Kodiak Bear. unabr. ed. Roger A. Caras. Narrated by Norman Dietz. 4 cass. (Running Time: 6 hrs.). 35.00 (978-1-55690-947-4(0), 93437E7) Recorded Bks.
With a naturalist's careful eye, Caras vividly captures the spirit of the last symbol of the shrinking American wilderness, the Kodiak bear, giving the listener new insight into his savage & tragic encounters with sportsmen & scientists, alike. Available to libraries only.

Monarch of the Glen. unabr. ed. Compton Mackenzie. Read by David Rintoul. 8 cass. (Running Time: 8 hrs.). 2001. 69.95 (978-0-7540-0627-5(1)) Pub: Chivers Audio Bks GBR. Dist(s): AudioGO
It was perhaps inevitable that the Monarch of Glen would not put up with any interference with the life of his Castle & the Drumcockie Grouse Moor. So on the sacred 12th, when interference arrives in the form of the National Union of Hikers, a bitter feud culminates in a pitched battle. Taking part are Ben Nevis's two daughters who are hefty young women standing no nonsense; Kilwhillie, a neighborly lesser laird who is doleful but very effective; & Chester Royde who shows that the spirit of Wall Street is not dead.

Monarch of the Glen, unabr. ed. Compton Mackenzie. Read by Gabriel Woolf. 8 cass. (Running Time: 10 hrs. 45 min.). 1995. 69.95 (978-1-85089-452-0(3), 20492) Pub: ISIS Audio GBR. Dist(s): Ulverscroft US

Monarch of the Glen. unabr. ed. Read by David Rintoul. 8 CDs. (Running Time: 36960 sec.). (Alo Nudger Mysteries Ser.). 2001. audio compact disk 79.95 (978-0-7540-5419-1(5), CCD 110) Pub: Chivers Audio Bks GBR. Dist(s): AudioGO

Monarchs on Audio. Alison Deming. (ENG.). 2009. audio compact disk 18.00 (978-1-888553-14-7(6)) Pub: Kore Pr. Dist(s): Chicago Distribution Ctr

Monastic Spirituality, Pt. II. Thomas Merton. 1 cass. (Running Time: 60 min.). 8.95 (AA2084) Credence Commun.
Commentary on monastic spirituality being at the heart of the church & any spirituality.

Monastic Spirituality - Citeaux. Thomas Merton. 1 cass. (Running Time: 60 min.). 8.95 (AA2083) Credence Commun.

Monday Girl. Doris Davidson. 2009. 84.95 (978-1-4079-0737-6(9)); audio compact disk 99.95 (978-1-4079-0738-3(7)) Pub: Soundings Ltd GBR. Dist(s): Ulverscroft US

Monday Morning Faith. unabr. ed. Lori Copeland. (Running Time: 9 hrs. 0 mins. 0 sec.). (ENG.). 2008. 13.99 (978-0-310-27820-7(1)) Zondervan.

Monday Morning Leadership. 2 cass. (Running Time: 3 hrs.). 2003. audio compact disk 19.95 (978-0-9719424-6-2(3)) CornerStone Leader.

Monday Morning Leadership for Women. 2003. audio compact disk 19.95 (978-0-9746403-1-0(X)) CornerStone Leader.

Monday Mourning. abr. ed. Kathy Reichs. Read by Michele Pawk. (Temperance Brennan Ser.: No. 7). 2004. 18.95 (978-0-7435-3999-9(0)); audio compact disk 30.00 (978-0-7435-3642-4(8), Audioworks) Pub: S&S Audio. Dist(s): S and S Inc
Temperance Brennan, forensic anthropologist for both North Carolina and Quebec, has come from Charlotte to Montreal during the bleak days of December to testify as an expert witness at a murder trial. She should be going over her notes, but instead she's digging in the basement of a pizza parlor. Not fun. Freezing cold. Crawling rats. And now, the skeletonized remains of three young women. How did they get there? When did they die?.

Monday Mourning. unabr. ed. Kathy Reichs. Read by Michele Pawk. (Temperance Brennan Ser.: No. 7). 2004. 23.95 (978-0-7435-3998-2(2)) Pub: S&S Audio. Dist(s): S and S Inc

Monday or Tuesday, Kew Gardens & More, unabr. ed. Virginia Woolf. Read by Flo Gibson. 2 cass. (Running Time: 2 hrs. 30 min.). 1996. 14.95 (978-1-55685-414-9(5)) Audio Bk Con.
Herein we find the wonders of great writing. In addition to the title stories, the author's remarkable talents are displayed in "The Mark on the Wall," "A Haunted House," "The Mysterious Case of Miss V.," "The Journal of Mistress Joan Martyn" & "Memoirs of a Novelist".

Monday the Rabbi Took Off. unabr. ed. Harry Kemelman. Narrated by George Guidall. 6 cass. (Running Time: 9 hrs.). (Rabbi Small Mystery Ser.). 1998. 51.00 (978-0-7887-1926-4(2), 95347E7) Recorded Bks.
While on vacation in Jerusalem, Rabbi Small faces off with the formidable Israeli intelligence & anonymous Arab terrorists intent on murder.

Monday with a Mad Genius. unabr. ed. Mary Pope Osborne. Read by Mary Pope Osborne. (Running Time: 4680 sec.). (Magic Tree House Ser.: No. 38). (ENG.). (J). (gr. 1-7). 2007. audio compact disk 14.95 (978-0-7393-5646-3(1), Listening Lib) Pub: Random Audio Pubg. Dist(s): Random

Monday with a Mad Genius; Dark Day in the Deep Sea. unabr. ed. Mary Pope Osborne. Read by Mary Pope Osborne. 2 CDs. (Running Time: 2 hrs. 35 mins.). (Magic Tree House Ser.: Nos. 38-39). (J). (gr. 3-5). 2008. audio compact disk 24.00 (978-0-7393-6394-2(8), Listening Lib) Pub: Random Audio Pubg. Dist(s): Random
Monday with a Mad Genius: Jack and Annie know they have to search for one of the four secrets of happiness to help Merlin the magician find joy in his life again. And so they head off in the magic tree house for Florence, Italy, in the early 1500s to spend the day with one of the greatest artists and inventors of all time - Leonardo da Vinci! Dark Day in the Deep Sea: Jack and Annie know they have to find one of the four secrets of happiness to help save Merlin. But when the magic tree house whisks them off to a misty island in the middle of nowhere, they wonder how they will find anything. As the fog lifts, they see a huge ship that turns out to be the world's first floating science laboratory. The ship's crew is searching for undiscovered sea creatures - and for the giant sea monster that seems to be following them!.

Monday's Child. Rowena Summers. Read by Trudy Harris. 9. 2007. audio compact disk 84.95 (978-1-84652-142-3(4)) Pub: ISIS Audio GBR. Dist(s): Ulverscroft US

Monday's Child. Rowena Summers. Read by Trudy Harris. 7. 2007. 61.95 (978-1-84652-141-6(6)) Pub: Magna Story GBR. Dist(s): Ulverscroft US

Monday's Troll. unabr. ed. Jack Prelutsky. Read by Jack Prelutsky. 1 cass. (Running Time: 40 min.). (J). (gr. 4-7). 1996. 9.95 (978-0-8072-0240-1(1), FTR175CXR, Listening Lib) Random Audio Pubg.
Jack Prelutsky has done it again with this latest collection of poems & music to enthrall young listeners. Includes "If I Were Not a Wizard," "We're Seven Grubby Goblins," & "Ogrebrag".

Monday's Troll. unabr. ed. Jack Prelutsky. Read by Jack Prelutsky. 1 cass. (Running Time: 51 mins.). (J). (ps-3). 1996. 11.00 (978-0-8072-0234-0(7), FTR175CX, Listening Lib) Random Audio Pubg.

Mondsteinmaerchen. Roland Kuebler. Read by Otto Mellies. 1 CD. (Running Time: 60 min.). (GER.). 2000. audio compact disk (978-3-15-120014-7(1)) P Reclam DEU.

***Moner Manush by Sunil Gangopadhyay - Audiobook.** Prod. by Bangla Beyond Borders. (BEN.). 2010. audio compact disk 29.99 (978-0-9829884-0-4(0)) Bangla Beyon.

Monet: Music of His Time. Hugh Griffith. 1 CD. (Running Time: 1 hr. 30 min.). (Art & Music Ser.). 2003. audio compact disk (Naxos AudioBooks) Naxos.

Monetarism & Supply Side Economics. abr. ed. Arjo Klamer. Ed. by Israel M. Kirzner & Mike Hassell. Narrated by Louis Rukeyser. 2 cass. (Running Time: 2 hrs. 40 min.). Dramatization. (Great Economic Thinkers Ser.). (YA). (gr. 10 up). 1988. 17.95 (978-0-938935-43-8(7), 10213) Knowledge Prod.
Countering the prevailing Keynesian view of economics in the 20th century are monetarists, who believe markets are efficient if government does not exercise discretionary power over the nation's money supply. Supply siders emphasize incentives for individual workers & investors & they advocate lower rates to improve economic performance.

Monetarism & Supply Side Economics: Free Market Thought in the Late 20th Century. Arlo Klamer & Alan Reynolds. Read by Louis Rukeyser. (Running Time: 10800 sec.). (Great Economic Thinkers Ser.). 2006. audio compact disk 25.95 (978-0-7861-6945-0(1)) Pub: Blckstn Audio. Dist(s): NetLibrary CO

Monetary Manipulation: Its Structural Effects. unabr. ed. Walter E. Grinder. 1 cass. (Running Time: 25 min.). (Symposium on the Geographical Aspects of Inflation Ser.: Tape 5 of 5). 12.95 (465) J Norton Pubs.

Monetary Reform & the Fight Against Inflation. unabr. ed. Henry Hazlitt. 1 cass. (Running Time: 1 hr. 12 min.). 12.95 (284) J Norton Pubs.

Monetary Value in Particular Value in General. unabr. ed. John Hospers. 1 cass. (Running Time: 1 hr.). 12.95 (251) J Norton Pubs.
Hospers provides an analysis of the concept of value & discusses the value destruction fostered by collectivism & paternalism through slave labor, inflation, confiscatory taxation & prohibition of gold ownership.

***Money.** Ernest Haycox. 2009. (978-1-60136-451-7(2)) Audio Holding.

Money. Ernest Haycox. (Running Time: 1 hr. 18 mins.). 1999. 10.95 (978-1-60083-513-1(9)) Iofy Corp.

***Money.** L. Ron Hubbard. (FRE.). 2010. audio compact disk 15.00 (978-1-4031-7630-1(2)); audio compact disk 15.00 (978-1-4031-7629-5(9)); audio compact disk 15.00 (978-1-4031-7632-5(9)); audio compact disk 15.00 (978-1-4031-7643-1(4)); audio compact disk 15.00 (978-1-4031-7637-0(X)); audio compact disk 15.00 (978-1-4031-7642-4(6)); audio compact disk 15.00 (978-1-4031-7628-8(0)); audio compact disk 15.00 (978-1-4031-7640-0(X)); audio compact disk 15.00 (978-1-4031-7633-2(7)); audio compact disk 15.00 (978-1-4031-7639-4(6)); audio compact disk 15.00 (978-1-4031-7641-7(8)); audio compact disk 15.00 (978-1-4031-7634-9(5)); audio compact disk 15.00 (978-1-4031-7638-7(8)); audio compact disk 15.00 (978-1-4031-7635-6(3)); audio compact disk 15.00 (978-1-4031-0506-6(5)); audio compact disk 15.00 (978-1-4031-7636-3(1)); audio compact disk 15.00 (978-1-4031-7631-8(0)) Bridge Pubns Inc.

Money. Vajracarya. Read by Chogyam Trungpa. 1 cass. 1970. 12.50 (A078) Vajradhatu.
A seminar by the scholar & meditation master trained in the philosophical & meditative traditions of Buddhism in Tibet.

Money. rev. ed. Sandra Block et al. (ENG.). 2009. audio compact disk 19.99 (978-1-4133-0958-4(5)) Nolo.

Money. unabr. ed. Martin Amis. Read by Richard Green. 12 cass. (Running Time: 18 hrs.). 1998. 96.00 (978-0-7366-4048-0(7), 4547) Books on Tape.
Sex, drugs & fast-cash distract a British film-maker in this send-up of Reagan's America & Thatcher's England.

Money. unabr. ed. Oasis Audio. Read by Kelly Ryan Dolan. Narrated by Jill Shellabarger. (Running Time: 1 hr. 9 mins. 49 sec.). (What the Bible Says Ser.). (ENG.). 2008. audio compact disk 9.99 (978-1-59859-408-9(7)) Oasis Audio.

Money: An Owner's Manual. Perf. by Dennis Deaton. 4 CDs. (Running Time: 3 hrs. 55 min.). 2005. audio compact disk 59.95 (978-1-881840-20-6(4)) Quma Learning.

Money: The Great Mirror of Consciousness. John-Roger & John Morton. 4 cass. (Running Time: 2 hrs.). 1997. 30.00 (978-0-914829-46-1(7)) Mandeville LA.
Explains how to shift your attitude and awareness to attract more money, use it as a tool for greater upliftment, and create greater balance, happiness, and well-being.

Money - Prosperity. Betty L. Randolph. 1 cass. (Running Time: 45 min.). (Success Ser.). 1989. bk. 9.98 90 mins. extended length stereo music. (978-1-55909-018-6(9), 29X); 9.98 (978-1-55909-253-1(X), 29S) Randolph Tapes.
Learn to use your total mind power to attract riches! Subliminal messages are heard for 3-5 minutes before becoming ocean sounds or music.

Money, A Memoir: Women, Emotions, & Cash. abr. ed. Liz Perle. 2006. 14.95 (978-1-59397-888-4(X)) Pub: Macmill Audio. Dist(s): Macmillan

Money & Financial Freedom. Shad Helmstetter. 1 cass. (Self-Talk Cassettes Ser.). 10.95 (978-0-937065-00-6(5)) Grindle Pr.

Money & Marriage God's Way. unabr. ed. Howard Dayton. Narrated by Howard Dayton. (Running Time: 3 hrs. 27 mins. 56 sec.). (ENG.). 2009. audio compact disk 19.99 (978-1-59859-556-7(3)) Oasis Audio.

Money & Marriage God's Way. unabr. ed. Howard Dayton. Narrated by Howard Dayton. (Running Time: 3 hrs. 27 mins. 56 sec.). (ENG.). 2009. 13.99 (978-1-60814-474-7(7)) Oasis Audio.

Money & Prices. unabr. ed. Murray Newton Rothbard. 1 cass. (Running Time: 1 hr. 21 min.). (Introduction to Free Market Economics Ser.). 12.95 (314) J Norton Pubs.
Topics include: the evolution of money; gold & silver; depreciation of the currency; prices & price levels.

Money & Prosperity Are Yours. Created by Anne H. Spencer-Beacham. 1. 2003. audio compact disk (978-1-932163-56-8(5)) Infinity Inst.

***Money & Spirit Workshop.** Brent Kessel CFP & Spencer Sherman CFP, MBA. (Running Time: 8:00:00). 2011. pap. bk. 99.95 (978-1-60407-089-7(7)) Sounds True.

Money & Success. Barry Tesar. 1 cass. (Running Time: 1 hr.). (Subliminal Inspiration Ser.). 1992. 9.98 (978-1-56470-006-3(2)) Success Cass.
Subliminal program.

Money & the Balance of Payments. unabr. ed. Murray Newton Rothbard. 1 cass. (Running Time: 1 hr. 30 min.). (Introduction to Free Market Economics Ser.). 12.95 (315) J Norton Pubs.
Analyzes the foreign exchange market & the balance of payments.

Money & the Balance of Payments: CD Set. ed. Murray N. Rothbard. 2 CDs. (Running Time: 88 mins.). (Introduction to Free Market Economics Ser.). 2006. audio compact disk 14.95 (978-1-57970-397-4(6), AF0315D, Audio-For) J Norton Pubs.
Dr. Rothbard lectures on the foreign exchange market and the balance of payments. (from Dr. Rothbard's series, "Introduction to Free-Market Economics").

Money & the Christian Seminar. Caleb McAfee. 16 cass. (Running Time: 16 hrs.). 69.95 (978-0-9656010-2-3(1)) Dimensn Four.

Money, & the Law of Attraction: Learning to Attract Wealth, Health, & Happiness. unabr. ed. Esther Hicks & Jerry Hicks. Read by Esther Hicks & Jerry Hicks. 8 CDs. (Running Time: 10 hrs.). 2008. audio compact disk 39.95 (978-1-4019-1877-4(8)) Hay House.

Money & the Meaning of Life. abr. ed. Jacob Needleman. Read by Jacob Needleman. 2 cass. (Running Time: 3 hrs.). 1997. bk. 17.95 (978-1-57453-213-5(8)) Audio Lit.
Introduces the radical idea that money is a means toward self-knowledge. Drawing on sages & scholars from across the ages, Needleman weaves a tapestry of tales & ideas that gives the listener a new way of looking not only at money but at the very nature of human life itself.

Money & the Mind: Program from the Award Winning Public Radio Series. Interview. Hosted by Fred Goodwin. 1 CD. (Running Time: 1hr.). (Infinite Mind Ser.). 2002. audio compact disk 21.95 (978-1-888064-76-6(5), LCM 222) Lichtenstein Creat.
Guests include: behavioral economists Dr. Eldar Shafir, Professor of Psychology and Public Affairs at Princeton University, Dr. Robert Frank, Professor of Economics, Ethics and Public Policy at Cornell University, and Dr. Andrew Oswald, Professor of Economics at the University of Warwick in England; James Cramer, co-founder of TheStreet.com and SmartMoney magazine; and writer Sandra Cisneros.

Money & the People You Love. Bruce Helmer. (ENG.). 2009. audio compact disk 12.95 (978-0-9817491-7-4(8)) Holton Hse.

Money & the Related. Dan Comer. 1 cass. 3.00 (58) Evang Outreach.

Money Attraction. 1 cass. (Running Time: 1 hr.). 10.95 (016) Psych Res Inst.
Use natural intuitive powers to be aware of opportunites & develop confidence to take advantage of opportunities.

Money Book. Sundance/Newbridge, LLC Staff. (Early Math Ser.). (gr. k-1). 2000. 12.00 (978-1-58273-875-8(0)) Sund Newbrdge.

Money Book for the Young, Fabulous & Broke. abr. ed. Suze Orman. 5 CDs. (Running Time: 6 hours). (ENG.). (gr. 8). 2005. audio compact disk 29.95 (978-0-14-305736-9(7), PengAudBks) Penguin Grp USA.

Money Book for the Young, Fabulous & Broke 1 Audio CDfor QVC/PBS. Suze Orman. 2005. audio compact disk 14.95 (978-1-59448-916-7(5), RivhdHC) Penguin Grp USA.

Money Book of Dreams. William Eaton. 1 cass. (Running Time: 30 min). 2003. 6.95 (978-0-9713693-4-4(8)); audio compact disk 9.95 (978-0-9713693-5-1(6)) W Eaton.

***Money Class.** abr. ed. Suze Orman. (Running Time: 6 hrs.). (ENG.). 2011. audio compact disk 30.00 (978-0-307-91317-3(1), Random AudioBks) Pub: Random Audio Pubg. Dist(s): Random

***Money Class 12-copy CD Pre-Pack.** Suze Orman. (ENG.). 2011. audio compact disk 360.00 (978-0-7393-5282-3(2), Random AudioBks) Pub: Random Audio Pubg. Dist(s): Random

Money Cometh! Leroy Tompson, Sr. 2002. 55.00 (978-1-931804-00-4(1)) Ever Increase Wd Min.

Money Culture. unabr. collector's ed. Michael Lewis. Read by Jonathan Reese. 6 cass. (Running Time: 9 hrs.). 1992. 48.00 (978-0-7366-2230-1(6), 3020) Books on Tape.
Michael Lewis instructs us in the moral codes of Donald Trump, Leona Helmsley, Ivan Boesky, & sundry other luminaries in this tour of the 1980's world of high finance.

Money, Food & Sex. Adi Da Avatar. 1 cass. (Method of the Siddhas Ser.). 11.95 (978-0-918801-61-6(3)) Dawn Horse Pr.
Da Avabhasa explains that money, food & sex represent the basic life-functions that must be understood & transcended by anyone who is serious about Spiritual life.

***Money for Nothing: How the Failure of Corporate Boards Is Ruining American Business & Costing Us Trillions.** unabr. ed. John Gillespie & David Zweig. Narrated by Mel Foster. (Running Time: 10 hrs. 0 mins.). 2010. 16.99 (978-1-4001-8553-5(X)) Tantor Media.

***Money for Nothing: How the Failure of Corporate Boards Is Ruining American Business & Costing Us Trillions.** unabr. ed. Gillespie, John & David Zweig. Narrated by Mel Foster. (Running Time: 10 hrs. 0 mins. 0 sec.). (ENG.). 2010. 24.99 (978-1-400[illegible]-7(9)); audio compact disk 69.99 (978-1-4001-4553-9(8)); audio compact disk 34.99 (978-1-4001-1553-2(1)) Pub: Tantor Media. Dist(s): IngramPubServ

Money for Nothing: One Man's Journey Through the Dark Side of Lottery Millions. unabr. ed. Edward Ugel. Read by Arthur Morey. (Running Time: 9 hrs. NaN mins.). 2009. 29.95 (978-1-4332-5630-1(4)); audio compact disk 59.95 (978-1-4332-5626-4(6)); audio compact disk 80.00 (978-1-4332-5627-1(4)) Blckstn Audio.

Money, Freedom, & the Bible. John Robbins. 1 cass. (Christianity & Economics Ser.: Pt. 1). 5.00 Trinity Found.

Money Hunt Guide to Growing Your Own Business. unabr. ed. Clifford R. Ennico. 5 cass. (Running Time: 5 hrs.). 1998. 29.95 (978-0-9632835-7-3(X)) Pub: Biennix. Dist(s): Penton Overseas
Starting & managing a successful small business, real world advice from the PBS television series "Money Hunt." Ennico challenges the conventional wisdom about entrepreneurship & talks with brutal honesty about what makes the difference between success & failure.

Money, Inflation & the Business Cycle. unabr. ed. Walter Block. 1 cass. (Running Time: 40 min.). 12.95 (430) J Norton Pubs.
Block discusses the significance of money, its advantages over barter & the necessary qualities of a monetary medium. He discusses cause & consequences of inflation & answers arguments against the gold standard. Finally, he talks about the business cycle, contrasting the Keynesian "fine-tuning" approach with the Austrian School's theory of time preference.

Money Is God in Action. Terry Cole-Whittaker. Read by Terry Cole-Whittaker. 1 cass. (Running Time: 1 hr.). 1991. 10.95 (978-1-56170-036-3(3), 260) Hay House.
Terry explains the true meaning of money & how to fully appreciate it's worth & usefulness in our lives. She ends with two powerful meditations.

Money Issues & Self-Esteem. Earnie Larsen. Read by Earnie Larsen. 1 cass. (Running Time: 1 hr.). 1993. 10.95 (978-1-56047-057-1(7), A123) E Larsen Enterprises.
Discusses what is at the core of money issues with concrete steps for healing.

Money Laundering & Forfeiture. Moderated by Charles Carberry & Gary P. Naftalis. (Running Time: 11 hrs.). 1992. pap. bk. 295.00 NY Law Pub.
A practical look at the "RICO of the '90's" through an analysis of current law enforcement initiatives; regulations affecting financial institutions; sentencing guidelines; defending against sting operations; litigation techniques; civil & criminal forfeiture & freeze orders; corporate compliance programs; & increased prosecutions for failure to file IRS Form 8300. Includes course book.

Money Lessons for a Lifetime: Stories, Observations & Tips on Living a Prosperous Life. abr. ed. Jim Jorgensen. 2 cass. (Running Time: 117 min.). 1998. 15.95 (978-1-55977-879-4(2)) CareerTrack Pubns.

Money Magnetics. Carol Rios. 2007. audio compact disk 18.95 (978-1-4276-2339-3(2)) AardGP.

Money Magnetics. abr. ed. Roger W. Bretemitz. 1 cass. (Running Time: 45 min.). 1985. pap. bk. 9.95 (978-1-893417-15-1(8)) Vector Studios.
Hypnosis: Side A talks about money making techniques & what it takes. Side B hypnosis implants the desires & drive to carry out goal attaining duties to draw money to a person.

Money Magnetism. 1 cass. 10.00 (978-1-58506-032-0(1), 64) New Life Inst OR.
Tune your inner mind to financial success & watch it attract money like a magnet.

Money Making Trends. Grace K. Morris. 1 cass. 1992. 8.95 (1070) Am Fed Astrologers.

Money Management. Mac Hammond. 4 cass. (Running Time: 4 hrs.). (Simplify Your Life Ser.: Vol. 3). 1997. 24.00 (978-1-57399-060-8(4)) Mac Hammond.

Money Manager. Eldon Taylor. 2 cass. (Running Time: 1 hr. 2 min.). (Inner Talk Ser.). 16.95 (978-0-940699-89-2(3), 5306A) Progress Aware Res.
Soundtrack - Tropical Lagoon with underlying subliminal affirmations.

Money Manager: Soundtrack: Leisure Listening. Eldon Taylor. 1 cass. (Running Time: 1 hr. 2 min.). 16.95 (978-0-940699-12-0(5), 5306B) Progress Aware Res.
Musical soundtrack with underlying subliminal affirmations.

Money Manager: Soundtrack: Musical Themes. Eldon Taylor. 1 cass. (Running Time: 1 hr. 2 min.). 16.95 (978-0-940699-13-7(3), 5306C) Progress Aware Res.
Musical soundtrack with underlying subliminal affirmations. Includes script.

Money Managers & Deal Makers. Narrated by Louis Rukeyser. 2 cass. (Running Time: 2 hrs. 30 mins.). (Secrets of the Great Investors Ser.: Vol. 11). 2003. 17.95 (978-1-56823-063-4(X)) Pub: Knowledge Prod. Dist(s): APG
Learn about the timeless strategies, tactics, judgments & principles that have produced great wealth. Hear history's great figures & personalities - in their own words - describe their techniques & achievements in finance & investing. Now you can listen to these great lessons while commuting, traveling, walking...anytime your hands are busy, but your mind is not.

Money Managers & Mutual Funds. unabr. ed. Donald J. Christensen. Read by Louis Rukeyser. (Running Time: 10800 sec.). (Secrets of the Great Investors Ser.). 2006. audio compact disk 25.95 (978-0-7861-6525-4(1)) Pub: Blckstn Audio. Dist(s): NetLibrary CO

Money Masters: Investment Wizards. unabr. ed. John Train. Narrated by Adrian Cronauer. 6 cass. (Running Time: 8 hrs.). 1985. 51.00 (978-1-55690-345-8(6), 85170E7) Recorded Bks.
Profiles of investment pros Warren Buffet, Paul Cabot, Ken Graham, Larry Tisch & five other leaders of the pack.

Money Mastery: Principle-Based Money Management. Peter Jeppson & Alan Williams. 1 cass. 99.00 (145-C47) Natl Seminars.
You probably have more money than you realize. Surprised? You just need the knowledge, tools, & skills that this program provide to find it! This system explains the 10 fundamental principles you need to understand how to become empowered by the money you're already earning. Follow Jeppson's & Williams' plan & you'll increase your reserves by at least half a million dollars by the time you retire.

Money Men: Capitalism, Democracy, & the Hundred Years' War over the American Dollar. unabr. ed. H. W. Brands. Read by Lloyd James. (YA). 2007. 44.99 (978-1-60252-916-8(7)) Find a World.

Money Men: Capitalism, Democracy, & the Hundred Years' War over the American Dollar. unabr. ed. H. W. Brands. Read by Lloyd James. (Running Time: 5 hrs. 30 mins. 0 sec.). (ENG.). 2006. audio compact disk 24.99 (978-1-4001-0293-8(6)); audio compact disk 49.99 (978-1-4001-3293-5(2)); audio compact disk 19.99 (978-1-4001-5293-3(3)) Pub: Tantor Media. Dist(s): IngramPubServ

Money Mischief: Episodes in Monetary History. unabr. ed. Milton Friedman. Read by Nadia May. 5 cass. (Running Time: 7 hrs.). 1992. 39.95 (978-0-7861-0339-3(6), 1296) Blckstn Audio.
Dr. Friedman discusses the creation of value: from stones to feathers to gold. He explains what the present monetary system in the United States - a system without historical precedent - means for your paycheck & savings book as well as for the global economy.

Money, Money, Money. Ed McBain, pseud. (87th Precinct Ser.: Bk. 51). 2004. 15.95 (978-0-7435-4141-1(3)) Pub: S&S Audio. Dist(s): S and S Inc

Money, Money, Money. unabr. ed. Ed McBain, pseud. Read by Garrick Hagon. 8 vols. (Running Time: 12 hrs.). (87th Precinct Ser.: Bk. 51). 2002. bk. 69.95 (978-0-7927-2533-6(6), CSL 422, Chivers Sound Lib); audio compact disk 94.95 (978-0-7927-9858-3(9), SLD 109, Chivers Sound Lib) AudioGO.
It is Christmas in the city. A retired Gulf War pilot, a careless second-story man, a pair of angry Mexicans, and an equally shady pair of Secret Service agents are in town after a large stash of money. Steve Carella and Fat Ollie Weeks catch the squeal when the lions in the city zoo get an unauthorized feeding of a young woman's body. And then there's a trash can stuffed with a book salesman carrying a P-38 Walther and a wad of big bills.

Money, Possessions & Eternity. abr. ed. Randy C. Alcorn. Narrated by Randy C. Alcorn. (Running Time: 9 hrs. 46 mins. 54 sec.). (ENG.). 2009. 20.99 (978-1-60814-554-6(9)); audio compact disk 29.99 (978-1-59859-472-0(9)) Oasis Audio.

Money-Prosperity. Barrie Konicov. 1 cass. (Video-Audio System Ser.). cass. & video 24.98 (978-0-87082-448-7(1), SYS 086); 11.98 (978-0-87082-436-4(8), 086) Potentials.
Prosperity is 98 percent mental preparation & 2 percent outer action. Begin preparing your consciousness to attract the riches you deserve today.

Money-Prosperity. Barrie Konicov. 1 CD. 2003. audio compact disk 16.98 (978-0-87082-956-7(4)) Potentials.
Awaken the financial genius within you now! Develop a prosperity consciousness to attract the riches you deserve. After all, prosperity is 98% mental preparation and 2% outer action.You will find the self-hypnosis on track 1 and the subliminal on track 2. The easy-listening music of the subliminal, together with the self-hypnosis, is the original format which most people love and with which they are most familiar.

Money Prosperity. Barrie Konicov. 1 cass. 2000. 16.98 (978-1-56001-306-8(0)) Potentials.

Money-Prosperity. Betty L. Randolph. 1 stereo cass. (Running Time: 45 min.). (Self-Hypnosis Ser.). 9.98 (978-1-55909-157-2(6), 903) Randolph Tapes.
Discusses how to find the financial genius within the subconscious. Music background & spoken word.

Money Prosperity: Dinero-Prosperidad. Barrie Konicov. 1 cass. (Running Time: 1 hr. 30 min.). (Spanish-Language Audios Ser.). (SPA.). 1995. 11.98 (978-0-87082-805-8(3), 086) Potentials.
Learn to become rich in your mind, the prerequisite to the riches. Learn the "consciousness of prosperity" to attract the riches you deserve; awaken the financial genius in you today.

Money: Relax & Retire! Financing the Best Years of Your Life. abr. ed. Money Magazine. (ENG.). 2006. 9.99 (978-1-59483-689-3(2)) Pub: Hachet Audio. Dist(s): HachBkGrp

Money Remittance Services in Philippines: A Strategic Reference 2007. Compiled by Icon Group International, Inc. Staff. 2007. ring bd. 195.00 (978-0-497-82390-0(X)) Icon Grp.

Money Revival. 2009. audio compact disk 10.00 (978-0-9819971-2-4(0)) TSEA.

Money Sense. 2001. 26.95 (978-1-888992-25-0(5)) Catholic Answers.

Money, Sex & Power. Richard Foster. 1 cass. (Running Time: 1 hr.). 1988. bk. 8.95 (978-0-06-062838-3(3)) HarperCollins Pubs.
Explores the three great ethical themes crucial to business, marriage, & government. Using practical examples, guides us in day-to-day ethical decision making & helps us determine the proper place in Christian life of money, sex & power.

Money Smarts: 15 Laws of Managing Money & Creating Wealth. unabr. ed. Larry Koenig. Narrated by Jon Gauger. (Running Time: 2 hrs. 58 mins. 4 sec.). (Crash Course Ser.). (ENG.). 2007. audio compact disk 12.99 (978-1-59859-254-2(8)) Oasis Audio.

Money Smarts: 15 Laws of Managing Money & Creating Wealth. unabr. ed. Larry J. Koenig. Narrated by Jon Gauger. (Crash Course Ser.). (ENG.). 2007. 9.09 (978-1-60814-162-3(4)) Oasis Audio.

Money Smarts by Dancing Beetle. Eugene Ely et al. 1 cass. (Running Time: 1 hr. 18 min.). (J). 1993. 10.00 Erthviibz.
Our society's excessive career & monetary expectations can be controlled. Create your own expectations & reward systems for freedom, balance, love & fulfillment. Infotainment by Ms. Mantaray & Dancing Beetle.

Money Station: Standards-based Instruction. 2002. spiral bd. 79.00 (978-1-57861-156-0(3), IEP Res) Attainment.

Money Supply Causes of Price Inflation. unabr. ed. Norman Bailey et al. 1 cass. (Running Time: 1 hr. 43 min.). 12.95 (282) J Norton Pubs.

Money Supply Explained: We Are the Krill. Nicholas B. Jaszewski. Voice by Nicholas Jaszewski & Ephraim McCormick. (ENG.). (YA). 2009. audio compact disk 15.00 (978-0-9818619-5-1(4)) TBT Pub.

Money: Take Charge of Your Life: Making More of Your Money & Your Life. abr. ed. Money Magazine. (ENG.). 2006. 9.99 (978-1-59483-690-9(6)) Pub: Hachet Audio. Dist(s): HachBkGrp

Money Tape: The Way to Abundance. Shelley L. Stockwell & Joan Lessin. Music by Ed Seykota. 1 cass. (Running Time: 1 hr.). 1990. pap. bk. 10.00 (978-0-945596-01-1(4)) Creativity Unltd Pr.
Create & realize money goals. Uses self-hypnosis, subliminal suggestion, music & fun!.

***Money to Burn.** unabr. ed. James Grippando. Narrated by Jonathan Davis. 1 Playaway. 2010. 94.95 (978-0-7927-7029-9(3)); audio compact disk 94.95 (978-0-7927-7027-5(7)) AudioGO.

***Money to Burn.** unabr. ed. James Grippando. Narrated by Jonathan Davis. 1 MP3-CD. 2010. 59.95 (978-0-7927-7028-2(5)) AudioGO.

***Money to Burn.** unabr. ed. James Grippando. Read by Jonathan Davis. (ENG.). 2010. (978-0-06-198543-0(0), Harper Audio) HarperCollins Pubs.

Money to Burn. unabr. ed. Gloria White. (Running Time: 30600 sec.). (Ronnie Ventana Mystery Ser.). 2007. 54.95 (978-1-4332-0733-4(8)); audio compact disk 63.00 (978-1-4332-0734-1(6)); audio compact disk 29.95 (978-1-4332-0735-8(4)) Blckstn Audio.

Money to Burn. unabr. ed. Gloria White. Read by Carol Cowan. 6 cass. (Running Time: 8 hrs. 12 mins.). (Ronnie Ventana Mystery Ser.). 1993. 36.00 (978-0-9624010-6-0(4), 752466) Readers Chair.
This is the second Ronnie Ventana mystery. Ronnie searches for a woman whose lovers have all come into sudden riches & sudden death. Ronnie races to catch the killer, before the killer catches her.

***Money to Burn: A Novel of Suspense.** unabr. ed. James Grippando. Read by Jonathan Davis. (ENG.). 2010. (978-0-06-195358-3(X), Harper Audio) HarperCollins Pubs.

Money Tree. Sarah Stewart. Read by Randye Kaye. 1 CD. (Running Time: 10 mins.). (J). (ps-2). 2007. bk. 28.95 (978-1-4301-0046-1(X)); bk. 25.95 (978-1-4301-0043-0(5)); pap. bk. 18.95 (978-1-4301-0045-4(1)); pap. bk. 16.95 (978-1-4301-0042-3(7)) Live Oak Media.

Money Tree. Sarah Stewart. Read by Randye Kaye. Illus. by David Small. 1 CD. (Running Time: 10 mins.). (J). (ps-2). 2007. pap. bk. 37.95 (978-1-4301-0047-8(8)) Live Oak Media.

Money Tree, Set. Sarah Stewart. Read by Randye Kaye. 1 cass. (Running Time: 10 mins.). (J). (ps-2). 2007. pap. bk. 34.15 (978-1-4301-0044-7(3)) Live Oak Media.

Money Wagon Info Business: Seminar. Francis Whalen. 2004. (978-1-932551-31-0(X)) High King Pub.
SEMINAR FORMAT.

Money: who has how much & why Cassette: Who Has How Much & Why. Andrew Hacker. 2004. 10.95 (978-0-7435-4140-4(5)) Pub: S&S Audio. Dist(s): S and S Inc

Money Wisdom. Suze Orman. Interview with Suze Orman. Interview with Michael Toms. 1 cass. (Running Time: 1 hr.). (New Dimensions Ser.). 1999. 10.95 (978-1-56170-700-3(7), 4025) Hay House.
Discusses how to be wise with money.

Money Wise & Spiritually Rich. Dennis R. Deaton. 2 cass. (Running Time: 2 hrs.). 1998. 14.95 Set. (978-1-57008-541-3(2), Bkcraft Inc) Deseret Bk.

Money with a Mission. Creflo A. Dollar. cass. & video 25.00 (978-1-59089-126-1(0)) Pub: Creflo Dollar. Dist(s): STL Dist NA

***Money 911.** unabr. ed. Jean Chatzky. Read by Jean Chatzky. (ENG.). 2009. (978-0-06-196760-3(2), Harper Audio) HarperCollins Pubs.

***Money 911: Your Most Pressing Money Questions Answered, Your Money Emergencies Solved.** unabr. ed. Jean Chatzky. Read by Jean Chatzky. (ENG.). 2009. (978-0-06-195375-0(X), Harper Audio) HarperCollins Pubs.

***Money 911: Budgeting & Cutting Spending.** unabr. ed. Jean Chatzky. Read by Jean Chatzky. (ENG.). 2009. (978-0-06-200046-0(2), Harper Audio); (978-0-06-200339-3(9), Harper Audio) HarperCollins Pubs.

***Money 911: Careers/Work.** unabr. ed. Jean Chatzky. Read by Jean Chatzky. (ENG.). 2009. (978-0-06-200047-7(0), Harper Audio); (978-0-06-200340-9(2), Harper Audio) HarperCollins Pubs.

***Money 911: Credit.** unabr. ed. Jean Chatzky. Read by Jean Chatzky. (ENG.). 2009. (978-0-06-200048-4(9), Harper Audio); (978-0-06-200341-6(0), Harper Audio) HarperCollins Pubs.

***Money 911: Debt.** unabr. ed. Jean Chatzky. Read by Jean Chatzky. (ENG.). 2009. (978-0-06-200049-1(7), Harper Audio); (978-0-06-200342-3(9), Harper Audio) HarperCollins Pubs.

***Money 911: Identity Theft & Scams.** unabr. ed. Jean Chatzky. Read by Jean Chatzky. (ENG.). 2009. (978-0-06-200050-7(0), Harper Audio); (978-0-06-200343-0(7), Harper Audio) HarperCollins Pubs.

***Money 911: Insurance.** unabr. ed. Jean Chatzky. Read by Jean Chatzky. (ENG.). 2009. (978-0-06-200344-7(5), Harper Audio); (978-0-06-200051-4(9), Harper Audio) HarperCollins Pubs.

***Money 911: Marriage.** unabr. ed. Jean Chatzky. Read by Jean Chatzky. (ENG.). 2009. (978-0-06-200345-4(3), Harper Audio); (978-0-06-200052-1(7), Harper Audio) HarperCollins Pubs.

***Money 911: Milestones.** unabr. ed. Jean Chatzky. Read by Jean Chatzky. (ENG.). 2009. (978-0-06-200346-1(1), Harper Audio); (978-0-06-200053-8(5), Harper Audio) HarperCollins Pubs.

***Money 911: Money & Life.** unabr. ed. Jean Chatzky. Read by Jean Chatzky. (ENG.). 2009. (978-0-06-200347-8(X), Harper Audio); (978-0-06-200054-5(3), Harper Audio) HarperCollins Pubs.

***Money 911: Paying for College.** unabr. ed. Jean Chatzky. Read by Jean Chatzky. (ENG.). 2009. (978-0-06-200348-5(8), Harper Audio); (978-0-06-200055-2(1), Harper Audio) HarperCollins Pubs.

***Money 911: Protecting Your Family.** unabr. ed. Jean Chatzky. Read by Jean Chatzky. (ENG.). 2009. (978-0-06-200056-9(X), Harper Audio); (978-0-06-200349-2(6), Harper Audio) HarperCollins Pubs.

***Money 911: Real Estate/Mortgages.** unabr. ed. Jean Chatzky. Read by Jean Chatzky. (ENG.). 2009. (978-0-06-200057-6(8), Harper Audio); (978-0-06-200350-8(X), Harper Audio) HarperCollins Pubs.

***Money 911: Retirement.** unabr. ed. Jean Chatzky. Read by Jean Chatzky. (ENG.). 2009. (978-0-06-200351-5(8), Harper Audio); (978-0-06-200058-3(6), Harper Audio) HarperCollins Pubs.

***Money 911: Saving & Investing.** unabr. ed. Jean Chatzky. Read by Jean Chatzky. (ENG.). 2009. (978-0-06-200352-2(6), Harper Audio); (978-0-06-200059-0(4), Harper Audio) HarperCollins Pubs.

***Money 911: Taxes.** unabr. ed. Jean Chatzky. Read by Jean Chatzky. (ENG.). 2009. (978-0-06-200353-9(4), Harper Audio); (978-0-06-200060-6(8), Harper Audio) HarperCollins Pubs.

Moneyball: The Art of Winning an Unfair Game. abr. ed. Michael Lewis. Read by Michael Lewis. 3 CDs. (Running Time: 6 hrs.). (ENG.). 2004. audio compact disk 14.99 (978-0-7393-1774-7(1), Random AudioBks) Pub: Random Audio Pubg. Dist(s): Random

Moneyball: The Art of Winning an Unfair Game. unabr. ed. Michael Lewis. 7 cass. (Running Time: 10 hrs. 30 min.). 2003. 72.00 (978-0-7366-9533-6(8)) Books on Tape.

Money/Prosperity. Barrie Konicov. 2 CDs. 2003. audio compact disk 27.98 (978-1-56001-982-4(4)) Potentials.
Awaken the financial genius within you now! Develop a prosperity consciousness to attract the riches you deserve. After all, prosperity is 98% mental preparation and 2% outer action.This 2-CD program from our Super Consciousness series is our newest, most powerful format. On the self-hypnosis CD, SC programs have the Subliminal Persuasion soundtrack added under Barrie?s voice. And the 17th Century Baroque music on the Subliminal CD has the same beat as your body's natural rhythm, thereby allowing the suggestions to enter deeply and effortlessly.

Mongane Wally-Serote. Read by Mongane Wally-Serote. 1 cass. (Running Time: 29 min.). 1985. 10.00 New Letters.
South African poet, who has suffered under Apartheid, reads & discusses his work with Jan Munro.

Mongol. Barry Sadler. Read by Charlton Griffin. 2 vols. (Casca Ser.: No. 22). 2004. 18.00 (978-1-58807-122-4(7)); (978-1-58807-562-8(1)) Am Pubng Inc.

Mongolian. 9 cass. (Running Time: 6 hrs.). pap. bk. 225.00 (AFMN10) J Norton Pubs.
Introductory course in the Khalka dialect, spoken in the Mongolian People's Republic (traditionally known as Outer Mongolia). the course which uses the Cyrillic alphabet consists of 24 units containing basic sentences, notes on pronunciation or grammar, drills & exercises.

Mongolian CDs & Text. 7 CDs. (Running Time: 7 hrs.). (MON.). 2005. audio compact disk 275.00 (978-1-57970-196-3(5), AFMN10D) J Norton Pubs.

Mongolian Parallel Text, William Rozycki. 2 cass. (Running Time: 3 hrs.). (MON.). 1994. 19.00 (3119) Dunwoody Pr.
Intended for the advanced beginner & intermediate student. Includes thirty-five selections from 1992 Mongolian newspapers & English translations.

Mongoose R. I. P. collector's ed. William F. Buckley, Jr. Read by Michael Prichard. 8 cass. (Running Time: 12 hrs.). (Blackford Oakes Mystery Ser.). 1988. 64.00 (978-0-7366-1377-4(3), 2271) Books on Tape.
Blackford Oakes plays pointman in President Kennedy's strike to eliminate Fidel Castro.

Mongoose R. I. P., unabr. ed. William F. Buckley, Jr. Read by John MacDonald. 8 cass. (Running Time: 11 hrs. 30 mins.). (Blackford Oakes Mystery Ser.). 1992. 56.95 (978-0-7861-0097-2(4), 1090) Blckstn Audio.
The year is 1963. Fidel Castro is seeking revenge for his humiliation during the missile crisis. President Kennedy & his brother Robert have their own plan for ending the menace of the Caribbean dictator. In the documents, it's called Operation Mongoose. Blackford Oakes, the CIA's urbane, handsome ace agent, becomes point man in the secret maneuverings. Again he works with the wise, enigmatic spymaster Rufus, & with his resourceful, rowdy, & loyal classmate, Anthony Trust. Headquarters: Miami, seething with anti-Castro intrigues & counterintelligence agents from Cuba. Oakes is, as he is meant to be, a pawn, the agent of a purpose designed by the highest officials. Then he learns that there is a counterplan, one that only incidentally calls for the death of Oakes himself.

Monitoring Serum Levels of Drugs: Pitfalls & Problems. Read by David J. Greenblatt. 1 cass. (Running Time: 1 hr. 30 min.). 1986. 12.00 (C8614) Amer Coll Phys.

Monk. Matthew G. Lewis. Read by Anais 9000. 2008. 27.95 (978-1-60112-020-5(6)) Babblebooks.

Monk Rock. Contrib. by John Michael Talbot. 2005. audio compact disk 16.98 (978-5-558-92013-0(0)) TroubadorPub GBR.

Monk Swimming. Malachy McCourt. Read by David Case. 6 cass. (Running Time: 9 hrs.). 1999. 29.95 (978-0-7366-4427-3(X)) Books on Tape.
What a monk brought with him & what he left behind. He left a childhood of poverty in Limerick, Ireland & headed for the promises of America.

Monk Swimming. collector's ed. Malachy McCourt. Read by David Case. 7 cass. (Running Time: 10 hrs. 30 min.). 2000. 56.00 (978-0-7366-5144-8(6)) Books on Tape.
What a monk brought with him & what he left behind. He left a childhood of poverty in Limerick, Ireland & headed for the promises of America.

Monk Swimming. unabr. ed. Malachy McCourt. Read by David Case. 6 CDs. (Running Time: 7 hrs. 12 mins.). 2001. audio compact disk Books on Tape.

Monk Swimming. unabr. collector's ed. Malachy McCourt. Read by David Case. 6 cass. (Running Time: 9 hrs.). 1998. 48.00 (978-0-7366-4523-2(3), 4724) Books on Tape.

Monkeewrench. unabr. ed. P. J. Tracy. Read by Buck Schirner. 7 cass. (Running Time: 10 hrs.). (Monkeewrench Ser.). 2003. 32.95 (978-1-59086-626-9(6), 1590866266, BAU); 82.25 (978-1-59086-627-6(4), 1590866274, CD Unabrid Lib Ed) Brilliance Audio.
Haunted by a series of horrifying and violent episodes in their past, Grace McBride and the oddball crew of her software company, Monkeewrench, create a computer game where the killer is always caught, where the good guys always win. But their game becomes a nightmare when someone starts duplicating the fictional murders in real life, down to the last detail. By the time the police realize what's happening, three people are dead, and with seventeen more murder scenarios available online, there are seventeen more potential victims. While the authorities scramble to find the killer in a city paralyzed by fear, the Monkeewrench staff are playing their own game, analyzing victim profiles in a frantic attempt to discover the murderer's next target. In a thriller populated by characters both hilarious and heartbreaking, a rural Wisconsin sheriff, two Minneapolis police detectives, and Grace's gang are caught in a web of decades-old secrets that could get them all killed.

Monkeewrench. unabr. ed. P. J. Tracy. Read by Buck Schirner. (Running Time: 10 hrs.). (Monkeewrench Ser.). 2004. 39.25 (978-1-59335-597-5(1), 1593355971, Brinc Audio MP3 Lib) Brilliance Audio.

Monkeewrench. unabr. ed. P. J. Tracy. Read by Buck Schirner. (Running Time: 10 hrs.). (Monkeewrench Ser.). 2004. 39.25 (978-1-59710-500-2(7), 1597105007, BADLE); 24.95 (978-1-59710-501-9(5), 1597105015, BAD) Brilliance Audio.

Monkeewrench. unabr. ed. P. J. Tracy. Read by Buck Schirner. (Running Time: 10 hrs.). (Monkeewrench Ser.). 2004. 24.95 (978-1-59335-138-0(0), 1593351380) Soulmate Audio Bks.

Monkey. unabr. ed. Jeff Stone. Read by Kiki Barrera. 3 cass. (Running Time: 4 hrs. 15 mins.). (Five Ancestors Ser.: Bk. 2). (J). 2005. 30.00 (978-0-307-28334-4(8), BksonTape); audio compact disk 32.30 (978-0-307-28335-1(6), BksonTape) Pub: Random Audio Pubg. Dist(s): NetLibrary CO

Monkey & the Crocodile. Naseeruddin Shah. 1 cass. (Running Time: 22 min.). (Karadi Tales Ser.). (YA). (gr. 1 up). 1998. bk. 9.99 (978-81-86838-35-8(X)) APG.
Fairy tales & folklore.

Monkey & the Crocodile CD: Scripts for Young Readers. Read by Patrick Feehan. Retold by Heather McDonald. (J). 2009. 9.95 (978-1-60184-165-0(5)) Primry Concpts.

***Monkey & the Fish: Liquid Leadership for a Third-Culture Church.** Zondervan. (Running Time: 5 hrs. 28 mins. 40 sec.). (Leadership Network Innovation Ser.). (ENG.). 2010. 9.99 (978-0-310-86910-8(2)) Zondervan.

Monkey Business. unabr. ed. David Attenborough. 1 cass. (Running Time: 54 min.). (Animal Language Ser.). 12.95 J Norton Pubs.

Monkey House. unabr. ed. John Fullerton. Read by J. Charles. (Running Time: 9 hrs.). 2008. 39.25 (978-1-4233-5350-8(1), 9781423353508, BADLE); 24.95 (978-1-4233-5349-2(8), 9781423353492, BAD); audio compact disk 39.25 (978-1-4233-5348-5(X), 9781423353485, Brlnc Audio MP3 Lib); audio compact disk 24.95 (978-1-4233-5347-8(1), 9781423353478, Brilliance MP3) Brilliance Audio.

Monkey Island. unabr. ed. Paula Fox. Narrated by George Guidall. 3 pieces. (Running Time: 3 hrs. 45 mins.). (gr. 5 up). 1994. 27.00 (978-0-7887-0019-4(7), 94218E7) Recorded Bks.
When 11-year-old Clay's father loses his job & walks out on Clay & his mother, mother & son take refuge in a welfare hotel. Then Clay's mother disappears & Clay takes to the streets where he is befriended by two homeless men.

Monkey King. Saeed Jaffrey. 1 cass. (Running Time: 22 min.). (Karadi Tales Ser.). (YA). (gr. 1 up). 1998. bk. 9.99 (978-81-86838-12-9(0)) APG.
Asian fairy tales & folklore.

Monkey Moves. unabr. ed. Stephen Rosenholtz. Read by Stephen Rosenholtz. 1 cass. (Running Time: 22 min.). (J). (ps-3). 1993. pap. bk. 14.95 (978-0-9630979-2-7(X)) Rosewd Pubns.
A developmental movement awareness program for children. The songs, read-along stories, whimsical Japanese brush drawings & movements in the packages encourage children in important motor-development skills including balance, coordination & sequencing.

Monkey People. Read by Raul Julia. Music by Lee Ritenour. 1 cass. (Running Time: 25 min.). (J). 1995. 19.95 (SSChildren) SandS Childrens.
The story tells of a lazy society that uses monkeys - cut from leaves & miraculously brought to life - to do whatever is distasteful; eventually the animals end up performing all of the tasks. Side B contains the score without narration.

Monkey Town: The Summer of the Scopes Trial. unabr. ed. Ronald Kidd. Read by Ashley Albert. 5 CDs. (Running Time: 5 hrs. 58 mins.). (YA). (gr. 6 up). 2006. audio compact disk 38.25 (978-0-7393-3795-0(5)) Pub: Books on Tape. Dist(s): NetLibrary CO

Monkey Trix. unabr. ed. Raewyn Caisley. (Aussie Bites Ser.). (YA). 2003. audio compact disk 39.95 (978-1-74030-961-5(8)) Pub: Bolinda Pubng AUS. Dist(s): Bolinda Pub Inc

Monkey Wars. unabr. collector's ed. Deborah Blum. Read by Mary Peiffer. 9 cass. (Running Time: 13 hrs. 30 min.). 1995. 72.00 (978-0-7366-3102-0(X), 3778) Books on Tape.
Human life vs. animal life. Extremists on both sides would have us believe that's the bottom-line tradeoff for medical progress. But in "The Monkey Wars," Deborah Blum, winner of the Pulitzer prize for a series of articles that inspired her book, explores a complex middle ground in which a respectful, open dialogue replaces bombast. She suggests radically different ways to conduct science, to serve life.

Monkey Wrench Gang. unabr. collector's ed. Edward Abbey. Read by Paul Shay. 11 cass. (Running Time: 16 hrs. 30 mins.). 1988. 88.00 (978-0-7366-1329-3(3), 2233) Books on Tape.
The bridge is decked with bunting & Day-Glo, ready for christening. Suddenly its center rises & splits along a jagged line. A sheet of red flames streaks skyward. The Monkey Wrench Gang Strikes again!.

Monkey's Paw see Tales of Terror

Monkey's Paw. 10.00 Esstee Audios.
The W. W. Jacobs classic.

Monkey's Paw. (ENG.). 2007. (978-1-60339-055-2(3)); cd-rom & audio compact disk (978-1-60339-056-9(1)) Listenr Digest.

Monkey's Paw. 1 cass. (Running Time: 1 hr. 30 mins.). (SmartReader Ser.). (J). 1999. pap. bk. & tchr. ed. 19.95 (978-0-7887-2850-1(4), 79667T3) Recorded Bks.
An adaptation from the original text by W.W. Jacobs. The Whites have a magical monkey's paw that makes wishes come true. But when Mister White makes a wish, the result is horrible. Travel to England of long ago & discover the frightening power of the monkey's paw.

Monkey's Paw. Jacobs. (J). 1984. Multi Media TX.

Monkey's Paw. W. W. Jacobs. 10.95 (SAC 1090) Spoken Arts.

Monkey's Paw. unabr. ed. Jacobs. 1 cass. (Running Time: 32 min.). (Creative Short Story Audio Library Ser.). (YA). (gr. 7-12). 1995. 11.00 (978-0-8072-6100-2(9), CS900CX, Listening Lib) Random Audio Pubg.
Presents the impact of man's greedy desire for riches.

Monkey's Paw. unabr. ed. W. W. Jacobs. (Running Time: 45 min.). Dramatization. 1977. 7.95 (D-7) Jimcin Record.
A horror story about the three wishes.

Monkey's Paw: A Collection of Short Stories. unabr. ed. Short Stories. W. W. Jacobs. Read by Peter Joyce. 4 cass. (Running Time: 6 hrs.). 1996. 44.95 (978-1-86015-427-0(1)) Pub: UlverLrgPrint GBR. Dist(s): Ulverscroft US
Ten entertaining yarns set in 19th century England.

***Monkey's Paw: A Tale of Terror.** W. W. Jacobs. 2009. (978-1-60136-517-0(9)) Audio Holding.

Monkey's Paw: And Other Classic Tales of Terror. unabr. ed. 2 cass. (Running Time: 2 hrs. 20 min.). (YA). (gr. 7-12). 1995. 15.95 (978-0-8072-3545-4(8), CB135CXR, Listening Lib) Random Audio Pubg.
Includes: Monkey's Paw by W. W. Jacobs; A Watcher by the Dead by Ambrose Bierce; The Damned Thing by Ambrose Bierce; The Pit & the Pendulum by Edgar Allan Poe; Was It a Dream? by Guy de Maupassant.

Monkey's Paw - The Three Sisters. W. W. Jacobs. Read by John Jascoll. 1999. 10.00 (978-0-9643012-9-0(6)) Hazelwood Pr.

Monkey's Paw & Other Stories. Victor Garber. Narrated by Walter Covell. (Running Time: 3 hrs. 30 mins.). 1978. 21.95 (978-1-59912-870-2(5)) Iofy Corp.

Monkey's Paw & Other Tales of Terror see Pata del Mono y Otros Grandes Cuentos de Terror

Monkey's Paw & other Tales of Terror. Narrated by Victor Garber. (Running Time: 1 hr. 30 mins.). 2006. 14.95 (978-1-60083-027-3(7)) Iofy Corp.

Monkey's Paw & Other Tales of Terror. W. W. Jacobs. Read by Fabio Camero. (Running Time: 3 hrs.). 2003. 16.95 (978-1-60083-291-8(1), Audiofy Corp) Iofy Corp.

Monkey's Raincoat. abr. ed. Robert Crais. Read by David Stuart. (Running Time: 6 hrs.). (Elvis Cole Ser.). 2006. 24.95 (978-1-4233-0139-4(0), 9781423301394, BAD) Brilliance Audio.

Monkey's Raincoat. abr. ed. Robert Crais. Read by David Stuart. (Running Time: 21600 sec.). (Elvis Cole Ser.). 2006. audio compact disk 16.99 (978-1-4233-1821-7(8), 9781423318217) Brilliance Audio.
When Ellen Lang's husband disappears with their son, she hires Elvis Cole to track him down. A quiet and seemingly submissive wife, Ellen can't even write a check without him. All she wants is to get him and her son back - no questions asked. The search for Ellen's errant husband leads Elvis into the seamier side of Hollywood. He soon learns that Mort Lang is a down-on-his-luck talent agent who associates with a schlocky movie producer, and the last place he was spotted was at a party thrown by a famous and very well-connected ex-Matador. But no one has seen him since - including his B-movie girlfriend. At the same time the police find Mort in his parked car with four gunshots in his chest - and no kid in sight - Ellen disappears. Now nothing is what it seems, and the heat is on. It's up to Elvis Cole and his partner Joe Pike to find the connection between sleazy Hollywood players and an ex-Matador. "Far and away the most satisfying private eye novel in years. Grab this one - it's a winner!" - Lawrence Block "Is Bob Crais good? Put it this way: if they're taking you out to put you against the firing squad wall, and you want to enjoy your last moments on earth, pass on the last cigarette and ask for an Elvis Cole novel." - Harlan Ellison "Robert B. Parker has some competition on his hands....Elvis Cole is an appealing character and Crais' style is fresh and funny." - Sue Grafton.

Monkey's Raincoat. unabr. ed. Robert Crais. Read by Patrick G. Lawlor. (Running Time: 8 hrs.). (Elvis Cole Ser.). 2008. 39.25 (978-1-4233-5612-7(8), 9781423356127, BADLE); 24.95 (978-1-4233-5611-0(X), 9781423356110, BAD); 82.25 (978-1-4233-5757-5(4), 9781423357575, BriAudUnabridg); audio compact disk 87.25 (978-1-4233-5608-0(X), 9781423356080, BriAudCD Unabrid); audio compact disk 39.25 (978-1-4233-5610-3(1), 9781423356103, Brlnc Audio MP3 Lib); audio compact disk 24.95 (978-1-4233-5609-7(8), 9781423356097, Brilliance MP3); audio compact disk 34.95 (978-1-4233-5607-3(1), 9781423356073, Bril Audio CD Unabri) Brilliance Audio.

Monkey's Shoes: Audiocassette. (Sails Literacy Ser.). (gr. k up). 10.00 (978-0-7578-2653-5(9)) Rigby Educ.

Monkeyshines On: How Are Things with You? 1 cass. (J). 1999. 16.95; audio compact disk 16.95 Allosaurus Pubs.
Includes original songs on feelings, respect, self-esteem, responsibility & much more. Also includes 16 read along poems about current & pressing issues affecting young people.

Monkeyshines on How Are Things with You. Phyllis B. Goldman. Illus. by John Grigni. (J). 1995. audio compact disk 12.95 (978-0-9620900-8-0(5)) Allosaurus Pubs.

Monkeywrenching the New World Order: Global Capitalism & Its Discontents. Noam Chomsky. Contrib. by Howard Zinn et al. 1 CD. (Running Time: 1 hr. 30 min.). (ENG.). 2001. audio compact disk 20.00 (978-1-902593-35-7(9)) Pub: AK Pr GBR. Dist(s): Consort Bk Sales

Monk's Hood. Ellis Peters, pseud. Perf. by Derek Jacobi & Sean Pertwee. 1 cass. (Running Time: 1 hr. 20 min.). Dramatization. (Chronicles of Brother Cadfael Ser.: Vol. 3). 1999. 9.95 (978-1-56938-266-0(2), AMP-2662) Acorn Inc.
A wealthy landowner is poisoned while at the abbey, just before leaving his inheritance to the church. Cadfael is shocked to learn that the landowner's wife is his childhood sweetheart.

Monk's Hood. unabr. ed. Ellis Peters. Read by Johanna Ward. 6 cass. (Running Time: 8 hrs. 30 mins.). 2006. 44.95 (978-0-7861-1029-2(5), 1804) Blckstn Audio.

Monk's Hood. unabr. ed. Ellis Peters, pseud. Read by Johanna Ward. 6 cass. (Running Time: 9 hrs.). (Chronicles of Brother Cadfael Ser.: Vol. 3). 1999. 44.95 (1804) Blckstn Audio.
When Gervase Bonel, a guest at Shrewsbury Abbey of St. Peter & St. Paul is suddenly taken ill, Brother Cadfael, a skilled herbalist is called to his bedside. He discovers that Master Bonel's wife is Richildis, whom he loved many years ago before he took his Benedictine vows & that Bonel has been fatally poisoned. The Sheriff is convinced that the murderer is Richildis' son, Edwin. Relying upon his knowledge of both herbal medicines & the human heart, Cadfael deciphers this deadly recipe for murder.

Monk's Hood. unabr. ed. Ellis Peters, pseud. Read by Stephen Thorne. 6 cass. (Running Time: 9 hrs.). (Chronicles of Brother Cadfael Ser.: Vol. 3). 2000. 49.95 (CAB 524) Pub: Chivers Audio Bks GBR. Dist(s): AudioGO
At the Benedictine monastery in Shrewsbury in 1138, the gardens are flourishing under the expert tending of Brother Cadfael. His shelves boast all sorts of medication for every kind of ailment. But then a local landowner is poisoned with Cadfael's own concoction intended for aching joints. As the monk investigates, he finds a web of family intrigue, where suspicion has fallen on someone he is certain is innocent.

Monk's Hood. unabr. ed. Ellis Peters, pseud. Narrated by Patrick Tull. 7 cass. (Running Time: 9 hrs. 30 mins.). (Chronicles of Brother Cadfael Ser.: Vol. 3). 1991. 60.00 (978-1-55690-630-5(7), 91409E7) Recorded Bks.
When a fatal draught of Monk's Hood turns up in the dinner plate of a guest at the Shrewsbury abbey, fingers point at half a dozen likely suspects, including an abashed and bewildered Cadfael.

***Monk's Hood: The Third Chronicle of Brother Cadfael.** unabr. ed. Ellis Peters. Read by Johanna Ward. (Running Time: 7 hrs. 30 mins.). 2010. 29.95 (978-1-4332-5818-3(8)); audio compact disk 76.00 (978-1-4332-5815-2(3)) Blckstn Audio.

Mono Lake - Fight for Survival. Hosted by Nancy Pearlman. 1 cass. (Running Time: 29 min.). 10.00 (304) Educ Comm CA.

Monocled Mutineer. unabr. ed. William Thomas Allison & John Fairley. Read by Raymond Sawyer. 6 cass. (Running Time: 8 hrs.). (Isis Ser.). (J). 1991. 54.95 (978-1-85089-640-1(2), 91012) Pub: ISIS Lrg Prnt GBR. Dist(s): Ulverscroft US

Monogamist. unabr. ed. Thomas Gallagher. Read by John MacDonald. 6 cass. (Running Time: 6 hrs.). 36.00 (978-0-7366-0280-8(1), 1270) Books on Tape.
John Wisher is a man who can not bring himself to live a double life he has to be one man, the same at home or abroad, or he is nothing. He has been married for 25 years, his family is grown & his business has prospered. Then he meets a young woman & realizes he has oversimplified his life. He falls in love, yet he still loves his wife.

Monologos de Dante Gebel: Relatos de la Vida Cotidiana. unabr. ed. Dante Gebel. (SPA & ENG.). 2009. audio compact disk 14.99 (978-0-8297-5731-6(7)) Pub: Vida Pubs. Dist(s): Zondervan

Monopolize Your Marketplace: Separate Your Business From the Competition. Then Eliminate Them. abr. ed. Richard C. Harshaw & Edward A. Earle. 2 CDs. (Running Time: 2 hrs.). 2000. audio compact disk 24.95 (978-0-9666505-3-2(0)) MSI Mktg.
The authoritative, hands-on, real-life, 'here's-how-you-do-it,'make more money right now. Guide to success in marketing, advertising & business.

Monopoly & Competition. unabr. ed. Murray Newton Rothbard. 1 cass. (Running Time: 1 hr. 25 min.). (Introduction to Free Market Economics Ser.). 12.95 (313) J Norton Pubs.
Topics explored include: cartels; the airlines; fair trade laws; antitrust.

Monotonia Chronicles: Step into a Magical Kingdom, Where Brave Princesses Face Wicked Wizards & Royal Traitors. As told by Cynthia Marcucci. (Running Time: 4380 sec.). (J). (gr. k-6). 2006. audio compact disk 12.95 (978-1-933781-04-4(1)) TallTales Aud.

Monsarrat at Sea. unabr. ed. Nicholas Monsarrat. Read by Richard Green. 10 cass. (Running Time: 15 hrs.). Incl. HMS Marlborough Will Enter Harbour. 1984. (1127); I Was There. 1984. (1127); It Was Cruel. 1984. (1127); Longest Love. 1984. (1127); Ship That Died of Shame. 1984. (1127); Ship to Remember. 1984. (1127); Three Corvettes: H.M. Corvette, East Coast Corvette, Corvette Command. 1984. (1127); 1978. 80.00 (978-0-7366-0120-7(1), 1127) Books on Tape.
An anthology that brings together all the author's short stories of the sea.

Monsieur Beaucaire. unabr. ed. Booth Tarkington. Read by Flo Gibson. 2 cass. (Running Time: 2 hrs.). (gr. 6 up). 1989. 14.95 (978-1-55685-157-5(X)) Audio Bk Con.
The cousin of Louis XV arrives disguised as a barber; he forces his rival for the lovely Mary Carlisle to introduce him as the Duc de Chateamrien, but the evil Winterset soon announces his trade. When his true identity is revealed, it is too late for those who have scorned him.

Monsieur Beaucaire & Other Stories. unabr. ed. Booth Tarkington. Read by Jim Killavey. 3 cass. (Running Time: 4 hrs. 30 min.). Dramatization. Incl. Beautiful Lady. 1982. (C-66); Mrs. Protheroe. 1982. (C-66); 1982. 21.00 (C-66) Jimcin Record.
Early swashbuckling novel.

Monsieur Maurice & The Phantom Lover. Amelia B. Edwards & Vernon Lee. Read by Cindy Hardin & Walter Covell. 4 cass. (Running Time: 5 hrs. 30 min.). 1989. 28.00 (C-93); 33.00 incl. album. Jimcin Record.
Two supernatural thrillers.

Monsieur Pamplemousse. unabr. ed. Michael Bond. Narrated by George Guidall. 4 cass. (Running Time: 5 hrs. 45 mins.). (Monsieur Pamplemousse Mystery Ser.: Vol. 1). (gr. 10 up). 1991. 35.00 (978-1-55690-346-5(4), 91225E7) Recorded Bks.
Gourmet sleuth, Monsieur Pamplemousse & his canine sidekick, Pommes Frites, solve a menu of mysteries.

Monsieur Pamplemousse & the Secret Mission. unabr. ed. Michael Bond. Narrated by George Guidall. 4 cass. (Running Time: 6 hrs.). (Monsieur Pamplemousse Mystery Ser.: Vol. 3). 1991. 35.00 (978-1-55690-327-4(8), 91311E7) Recorded Bks.
Monsieur Pamplemousse, food critic for Le Guide, uncovers some unsavory business in the Loire.

Monsieur Pamplemousse Investigates. unabr. ed. Michael Bond. Narrated by George Guidall. 5 cass. (Running Time: 6 hrs. 30 mins.). (Monsieur Pamplemousse Mystery Ser.: Vol. 7). 1991. 44.00 (978-1-55690-698-5(6), 91408E7) Recorded Bks.
The guide's director is dead. Only Pamplemousse can uncover the mystery.

Monsieur Pamplemousse Rests His Case. unabr. ed. Michael Bond. Narrated by George Guidall. 4 cass. (Running Time: 6 hrs.). (Monsieur Pamplemousse Mystery Ser.: Vol. 8). 1992. 35.00 (978-1-55690-759-3(1), 92415E7) Recorded Bks.
Six of the most famous mystery writers in America are set to meet in Vichy to reenact a famous meal from the days of Dumas. But Monsieur Pamplemousse & his canine collaborator, Pommes Frites, have a new mystery on their hands when the sumptious banquet becomes an invitation to death.

Monsieur Rene. unabr. ed. Peter Ustinov. Read by Peter Ustinov. 10 cass. (Running Time: 15 hrs.). 2000. 84.95 (978-0-7540-0559-9(3), CAB 1982) Pub: Chivers Audio Bks GBR. Dist(s): AudioGO
As a retired, widowed & meticulously organized Monsieur Rene's life seems entirely in order. But, despite a sharp & active mind, he is suffering from late life depression & finally decides that he must find a new diversion.

Monsieur Rene. unabr. ed. Peter Ustinov. Read by Peter Ustinov. 10 CDs. (Running Time: 15 hrs.). 2001. audio compact disk 94.95 (978-0-7540-5398-9(9), CCD089) Pub: Chivers Audio Bks GBR. Dist(s): AudioGO
As a retired, widowed & meticulously organized hotelier Monsieur Rene's life seems entirely in order. Despite a sharp & active mind, he is suffering from late life depression & finally decides that he must find a new diversion. This a wonderfully engaging novel about a sharp-witted man discovering a new lease on life in his twilight years.

Monsignor Quixote. unabr. ed. Graham Greene. Read by Daniel Grace. 8 cass. (Running Time: 8 hrs.). 1988. 48.00 (978-0-7366-1273-9(4), 2182) Books on Tape.
A late novel by Greene, based on Cervantes' Don Quixote, in which a descendant of the comic hero sets out on a pilgrimage across modern-day Spain.

Monsignor Quixote. unabr. ed. Graham Greene. Read by Cyril Cusack. 6 cass. (Running Time: 9 hrs.). 2000. 49.95 (CSL 027) Pub: Chivers Audio Bks GBR. Dist(s): AudioGO
The locals had doubts that Father Quixote was a descendant of the fictional character. But it seemed that he was, and he was promoted to the rank of Monsignor. So Quixote and his friend Sancho, the ex-mayor of El Toboso, set off on their travels in the rusty old car they call Rocinante. And where Don Quixote wore his sword, helmut and spurs, Sancho insisted that his descendant rig himself out in the socks and bib that befitted his new rank.

Monsignor Ronald Knox. Evelyn Waugh. 9 cass. 22.95 (308) Ignatius Pr.
Life of one of England's greatest Catholic preachers & writers.

Monsoon. Di Morrissey. Read by Kate Hood. (Running Time: 13 hrs. 30 mins.). 2009. 94.99 (978-1-74214-181-7(1), 9781742141817) Pub: Bolinda Pubng AUS. Dist(s): Bolinda Pub Inc

Monsoon. abr. ed. Wilbur Smith. Perf. by Christopher Cazenove. 4 cass. (Running Time: 6 hrs.). 2001. 25.00 (978-1-59040-055-5(0), Phoenix Audio) Pub: Amer Intl Pub. Dist(s): PerseuPGW
A tremendous epic of adventure, mystery and intrigue set in 18th-century Africa.

Monsoon. unabr. ed. Di Morrissey. Read by Kate Hood. (Running Time: 13 hrs. 30 mins.). 2008. audio compact disk 103.95 (978-1-921334-89-3(3), 9781921334849) Pub: Bolinda Pubng AUS. Dist(s): Bolinda Pub Inc

Monsoon. unabr. ed. Di Morrissey. Read by Kate Hood. (Running Time: 13 hrs. 30 mins.). 2009. 43.95 (978-1-74214-138-1(2), 9781742141381) Pub: Bolinda Pubng AUS. Dist(s): Bolinda Pub Inc

Monsoon. 3rd abr. ed. Wilbur Smith. Read by Tim Piggott-Smith. 4 CDs. (Running Time: 4 hrs.). (ENG.). 1985. audio compact disk 6.50 (978-0-333-90354-4(4)) Asia Bk Corp.

Monsoon, Pt. 1. unabr. collector's ed. Wilbur Smith. Read by David Case. 11 cass. (Running Time: 16 hrs. 30 min.). (Courtney Novels). 1999. 88.00 (978-0-7366-4566-9(7), 4973-A) Books on Tape.
Continues the story begun in "Birds of Prey." Set in the dawn of the eighteenth century in England, East Africa & Arabia, it relates the lives & loves of the three sons of Hal Courteney.

Monsoon, Pt. 2. collector's ed. Wilbur Smith. Read by David Case. 10 cass. (Running Time: 15 hrs.). (Courtney Novels). 1999. 80.00 (978-0-7366-4718-2(X), 4973-B) Books on Tape.

Monster. Jonathan Kellerman. Read by Alexander Adams. (Alex Delaware Ser.: No. 13). 1999. audio compact disk 88.00 (978-0-7366-5206-3(X)) Books on Tape.

Monster. Walter Dean Myers. Narrated by Peter Francis James. 4 CDs. (Running Time: 4 hrs.). (gr. 10 up). 2001. audio compact disk 39.00 (978-0-7887-5219-3(7), C1367E7) Recorded Bks.
Steve Harmon is 16 years old. He's a good student with a stable & loving family. In an attempt to cope with the brutality & degradation of jail & the helplessness he feels at trial, Steve writes down his experiences & feelings as though it were a script for a movie.

Monster, abr. ed. Jonathan Kellerman. 3 cass. (Running Time: 5 hrs.). (Alex Delaware Ser.: No. 13). 1999. 29.95 (Random AudioBks) Random Audio Pubg.
How can a nonfunctional psychotic locked up in a supposedly secure institution for homicidal madmen predict brutal murders in the outside world? This is the enigma that Dr. Alex Delaware & Detective Milo Sturgis must penetrate in order to stop these horrific killings. First, a marginal actor is found dead in a car trunk, sawn in half. Months later, a psychologist at Starkweather Hospital for the Criminally Insane is discovered murdered & mutilated in a tantalizingly similar way.

Monster. abr. ed. Frank E. Peretti. (Running Time: 4 hrs. 30 mins.). 2005. audio compact disk 26.99 (978-1-59554-020-1(2)) Nelson.
Miles away from the hectic city, Reed and Rebecca hike into the beautiful Northwestern woods. They're surrounded by gorgeous mountains, waterfalls, and hundreds of acres of unspoiled wilderness. But something-or someone-begins closing in on them. Something no human has ever seen. And it's killing everyone in its path without remorse. Best-selling author Frank Peretti has sold more than 12 million novels about angels, demons, and dragons. That was just the warm-up. From the master of suspense and supernatural thrillers comes the season's hottest page-turner. Be warned: this monster's got teeth.

Monster. unabr. ed. Jonathan Kellerman. Read by Alexander Adams. 9 cass. (Running Time: 13 hrs. 30 min.). (Alex Delaware Ser.: No. 13). 1999. 72.00 (978-0-7366-4793-9(7), 5141); audio compact disk 88.00 Books on Tape.
Alex Delaware must discover how an institutionalized madman can predict brutal murders in the outside world. The climactic discovery Delaware & Sturgis make as they race to prevent more killings gives fresh & terrifying meaning to the concept of monstrosity.

***Monster.** unabr. ed. Walter Dean Myers. 2 CDs. (YA). (gr. 7-12). 2010. audio compact disk 24.00 (978-0-7393-3592-5(8), Listening Lib) Pub: Random Audio Pubg. Dist(s): Random

Monster. unabr. ed. Walter Dean Myers. 2 vols. (Running Time: 3 hrs. 34 mins.). (J). (gr. 7 up). 2004. pap. bk. 29.00 (978-0-8072-8363-9(0), YA188CX, Listening Lib); 23.00 (978-0-8072-8362-2(2), LL0194, Listening Lib) Random Audio Pubg.
A Harlem drugstore owner was shot & killed in his store & the word is out that 16-year-old Steve Harmon served as the lookout. Was he involved or was he simply in the wrong place at the wrong time? Steve transcribes his trial into a movie script, showing how his life was turned around in an instant.

Monster. unabr. ed. Walter Dean Myers. Narrated by Peter Francis James. 3 pieces. (Running Time: 4 hrs.). (gr. 10 up). 2001. 32.00 (978-0-7887-4564-5(6), 96335B7) Recorded Bks.
Steve Harmon is sixteen years old, a good student with a stable & loving family. And he's on trial for murder. Steve is writing down his experiences & feelings.

Monster. unabr. ed. Walter Dean Myers. Narrated by Peter Francis James. 3 cass. (Running Time: 4 hrs.). (YA). 2001. pap. bk. & stu. ed. 54.95 Recorded Bks.

Monster. unabr. ed. Walter Dean Myers & Full Cast Production Staff. (Running Time: 9240 sec.). (ENG.). (J). (gr. 7). 2007. audio compact disk 19.95 (978-0-7393-5556-5(2), Listening Lib) Pub: Random Audio Pubg. Dist(s): Random

***Monster.** unabr. ed. Frank Peretti. Narrated by Frank Peretti. (ENG.). 2005. 24.49 (978-1-60814-658-1(8)) Oasis Audio.

Monster. unabr. ed. Frank E. Peretti. Read by Frank E. Peretti. (Running Time: 41400 sec.). 2006. audio compact disk 99.00 (978-0-7861-6776-0(9)) Blckstn Audio.

Monster. unabr. ed. Frank E. Peretti. Read by Frank E. Peretti. 8 pieces. 29.99 (978-1-58926-895-1(4)) Oasis Audio.

Monster. unabr. ed. Frank E. Peretti. Narrated by Frank E. Peretti. 12 CDs. (Running Time: 11 hrs. 19 mins. 45 sec.). (ENG.). 2005. audio compact disk 34.99 (978-1-58926-896-8(2)) Oasis Audio.

Monster All-Stars. Lavaille Lavette. Narrated by Brent Barry. 1 cass. (Running Time: 840 sec.). (Adventures of Roopster Roux Ser.). (ENG.). (J). (ps-3). 1998. 5.95 (978-1-56554-403-1(X)) Pelican.
Roopster's team, the Vikings, plays Tegore's Monster All-Stars in a high-stakes Halloween basketball game.

Monster & the Tailor. unabr. ed. Paul Galdone. 1 cass. (Running Time: 9 min.). (J). (gr. k-4). 1987. pap. bk. 15.90 (978-0-8045-6555-4(4), 6555) Spoken Arts.
A poor tailor is ordered by the Grand Duke to make a pair of trousers, but he has to make them in a graveyard where a spooky monster lives.

Monster at Moonridge & The Shooting of Carl Neilson. Perf. by John Dehner. 1 cass. (Running Time: 1 hr.). Dramatization. (Have Gun, Will Travel Ser.). 6.00 Once Upon Rad.
Radio broadcasts - westerns.

Monster Blood for Breakfast! R. L. Stine. Read by Charlie McWade. (Goosebumps HorrorLand Ser.: No. 3). (J). 2008. 34.99 (978-1-60640-844-5(5)) Find a World.

Monster Blood for Breakfast! R. L. Stine. (Goosebumps HorrorLand Ser.: No. 3). (ENG.). (J). (gr. 4-7). 2008. audio compact disk 29.95 (978-0-545-11327-4(X)) Scholastic Inc.

Monster Blood for Breakfast! R. L. Stine. Narrated by Charlie McWade. (Goosebumps HorrorLand Ser.: No. 3). (J). (gr. 4-7). 2008. audio compact disk 9.95 (978-0-545-11152-2(8)) Scholastic Inc.

***Monster High.** unabr. ed. Lisi Harrison. Read by Rebecca Soler. (Running Time: 6 hrs.). (ENG.). (YA). 2010. 16.98 (978-1-60788-636-5(7)); audio compact disk 24.98 (978-1-60788-635-8(9)) Pub: Hachet Audio. Dist(s): HachBkGrp

Monster in a Box. abr. ed. Spalding Gray. Read by Spalding Gray. 2 cass. (Running Time: 1 hr. 41 min.). 1996. 17.95 (978-1-57453-082-7(8)) Audio Lit.

***Monster in the Box.** Ruth Rendell. Read by Nicolas Coster. (Playaway Adult Fiction Ser.). (ENG.). 2010. 59.99 (978-1-61637-709-0(7)) Find a World.

Monster in the Third Dresser Drawer, Janice Lee Smith. Read by Johnny Heller. 1 cass. (Running Time: 1 hr.). (Adam Joshua Capers Ser.). (J). (gr. 2 up). 1999. stu. ed. 73.30 (978-0-7887-3876-0(3), 47041) Recorded Bks.
Adam Joshua is moving. And a strange house is only one of his problems. Soon he must deal with a baby sister, Great-aunt Emily & even a monster.

Monster in the Third Dresser Drawer. unabr. ed. Janice Lee Smith. Narrated by Johnny Heller. 1 cass. (Running Time: 1 hr.). (Adam Joshua Capers Ser.). (J). (gr. 2 up). 1999. pap. bk. & stu. ed. 22.50 (978-0-7887-3850-0(X), 41048X4) Recorded Bks.

Monster in the Third Dresser Drawer. unabr. ed. Janice Lee Smith. Narrated by Johnny Heller. 1 cass. (Running Time: 1 hr.). (Adam Joshua Capers Ser.). (J). (gr. 2 up). 1999. 10.00 (978-0-7887-3813-5(5), 96058E7) Recorded Bks.

Monster in the Woods: A Musical Adventure in Learning & Fun. unabr. ed. James Comey. Contrib. by Larry McKenna & Christopher McGovern. 1 cass. (Running Time: 1 hr. 7 min.). (Stages Audio Bks.: Vol. 1). (J). (ps-5). 1996. 7.99 (978-0-9652093-0-4(X)) Stages Imag.
Story with music about seeing past superficial differences, courage & the power of love.

Monster Madness. 1 CD. (Running Time: 30 min.). (Halloween Party Ser.). (J). (gr. k-5). 2001. pap. bk. 5.98 (9687-2) Peter Pan.
Spooky songs, sounds and stories with holiday spirit. Includes Halloween Party Tip Guide.

Monster Mansion. Perf. by Daniel Sjerven. Created by Daniel Sjerven. Prod. by Braun Media. (ENG.). 2008. (978-1-59987-670-2(1)) Braun Media.

Monster Mix: Non-Stop Halloween Horror. (J). 1997. 10.00 (978-1-57375-547-4(8)) Audioscope.

Monster Mother. Deanna R. LuBin. Tr. by Tom Fosten. (J). (ps-9). 1991. pap. bk. (978-0-318-67147-5(6)) Lubin Pr.

Monster of Florence. unabr. ed. Douglas Preston. Read by Dennis Boutsikaris. Told to Mario Spezi. (Running Time: 9 hrs. 30 mins.). (ENG.). 2008. 19.98 (978-1-60024-210-6(3)) Pub: Hachet Audio. Dist(s): HachBkGrp

Monster of Florence. unabr. ed. Douglas Preston. Read by Dennis Boutsikaris. Told to Mario Spezi. (Running Time: 9 hrs. 30 mins.). (ENG.). 2009. audio compact disk 19.98 (978-1-60024-664-7(8)) Pub: Hachet Audio. Dist(s): HachBkGrp

Monster of the Maze. Jeffrey Lord. Read by Lloyd James. Abr. by Odin Westgaard. 2 vols. 2004. 18.00 (978-1-58807-361-7(0)) Am Pubng Inc.

Monster of the Maze. abr. ed. Jeffrey Lord. Read by Lloyd James. Abr. by Odin Westgaard. 2 vols. No. 6. 2004. (978-1-58807-779-0(9)) Am Pubng Inc.

Monster of the Maze. abr. ed. Jeffrey Lord. Read by Carol Eason. Abr. by Odin Westgaard. 3 CDs. (Running Time: 3 hrs.). (Richard Blade Adventure Ser.: No. 6). 2004. audio compact disk 25.00 (978-1-58807-497-3(8)) Am Pubng Inc.
British secret agent Blade once again ventures into a parallel dimension seeking knowledge and resources. This time he arrives only to find himself trapped in a baby's body, helpless. Will he be rescued, or will this visit to Dimension X be his last?.

Monster of the Month Club, unabr. ed. Dian Curtis Regan. Narrated by Christina Moore. 3 pieces. (Running Time: 3 hrs. 15 min.). (gr. 3 up). 1998. 29.00 (978-0-7887-2222-6(0), 95521E7) Recorded Bks.
How do you stop monsters from arriving in the mail? Rilla has already gotten a seven-eyed monster in the mail & someone has signed her up to receive a new one every month.

Monster of the Month Club, unabr. ed. Dian Curtis Regan. Read by Christina Moore. 3 cass. (Running Time: 3 hrs. 15 min.). (J). 1998. bk. 38.24 (978-0-7887-2239-4(5), 40723) Recorded Bks.
Rilla has received a seven-eyed monster in the mail & someone has signed her up to receive a new monster on the first of each month!.

Monster of the Month Club, unabr. ed. Dian Curtis Regan. Read by Christina Moore. 3 cass. (Running Time: 3 hrs. 15 min.). (J). (gr. 4). 1998. bk. 89.70 (978-0-7887-2544-9(0), 46714) Recorded Bks.

Monster Stickers. (Art Rom Create Your Own... Ser.). (J). 2004. pap. bk. 9.99 (978-1-84229-734-6(1)) Top That GBR.

Monster Truck Racing. Leeanne Trimble Spalding. (Rourke Discovery Library (CD-ROM) Ser.). (J). 2008. audio compact disk 24.95 (978-1-60472-772-2(1)) Rourke FL.

Monsters & Monstrous Things! 1 cass. (Running Time: 1 hr.). (J). 2001. pap. bk. 10.95 (KUB 0003C); pap. bk. & pupil's gde. ed. 11.95 (KUB 0003) Kimbo Educ.
Friendly "monsters" teach children important basic skills in an imaginative way. Kids will think these irresistable monsters are "cool" & you'll be pleased how quickly they will learn concepts such as shapes, manners, colors, counting, following direction & more. Includes Dragon Achoo, Monster Mash, Monster Color Game, Boogie Man Boogie, Dinosaurs, Monstery ABC's & more. Includes guide.

***Monsters are Due on Maple St.** 2010. audio compact disk (978-1-59171-165-0(7)) Falcon Picture.

Monsters in the Bathroom. Bill Harley. (Running Time: 42 mins.). (J). 2000. audio compact disk 15.00 (978-1-878126-35-1(0)) Round Riv Prodns.
Bill's first recording: songs & stories recorded live at an elementary school & in the studio. Black Socks; What's the Matter With You; Monsters in the Bathroom; When I Grow Up; That's What Friends Are For; Freddy the Fly-Eating Frog; The Billboard Song; The Freedom Bird; Abiyoyo; I'm Not Small.

Monsters in the Bathroom. unabr. ed. Bill Harley. Read by Bill Harley. 1 cass. (Running Time: 39 min.). (J). (gr. k-6). 1984. 10.00 (978-1-878126-00-9(8), RRR101) Round Riv Prodns.

Monsters Inc. Read Along. 1 CD. (Running Time: 1 hr. 30 mins.). (J). 2001. pap. bk. 9.98 (978-0-7634-1828-1(5)) W Disney Records.

***Monsters of Men.** unabr. ed. Patrick Ness. (Running Time: 14 hrs.). (Chaos Walking Ser.). 2010. 39.97 (978-1-4418-8957-7(4), 9781441889577, Candlewick Bril); 19.99 (978-1-4418-8956-0(6), 9781441889560, Candlewick Bril) Brilliance Audio.

***Monsters of Men.** unabr. ed. Patrick Ness. Read by Nick Andrews. 1 MP3-CD. (Running Time: 14 hrs.). (Chaos Walking Ser.). 2010. audio compact disk 39.97 (978-1-4418-8955-3(8), 9781441889553, Candlewick Bril) Brilliance Audio.

***Monsters of Men.** unabr. ed. Patrick Ness. Read by MacLeod Andrews et al. 12 CDs. (Running Time: 15 hrs.). (Chaos Walking Ser.). 2010. audio compact disk 24.99 (978-1-4418-8952-2(3), 9781441889522, Candlewick Bril); audio compact disk 19.99 (978-1-4418-8954-6(X), 9781441889546, Candlewick Bril) Brilliance Audio.

***Monsters of Men.** unabr. ed. Patrick Ness. Read by Nick Podehl et al. 12 CDs. (Running Time: 15 hrs.). (Chaos Walking Ser.). 2010. audio compact disk 74.97 (978-1-4418-8953-9(1), 9781441889539, Candlewick Bril) Brilliance Audio.

Monsters of Morley Manor. unabr. ed. Bruce Coville. Read by Full Cast Production Staff. (J). 2007. 39.99 (978-1-60252-568-9(4)) Find a World.

Monsters of Otherness. unabr. ed. Kaza Kingsley. Read by Simon Jones. (Running Time: 10 hrs. 0 mins. 0 sec.). (Erec Rex Ser.). (ENG.). (J). 2009. audio compact disk 39.99 (978-0-7435-8141-7(5)) Pub: S&S Audio. Dist(s): S and S Inc

Monsters of Templeton. unabr. ed. Lauren Groff. Read by Nicole Roberts. (Running Time: 46800 sec.). 2008. audio compact disk 39.95 (978-1-4013-8892-8(2)) Pub: Hyperion. Dist(s): HarperCollins Pubs

Monsters of the Deep: Deep Sea Adaptation. Kelly Regan Barnhill. Contrib. by Patrick Olson & Charity Jones. (Extreme Life Ser.). (ENG.). (gr. 3-4). 2008. audio compact disk 12.99 (978-1-4296-3210-2(0)) CapstoneDig.

Monster's Ring. Bruce Coville. Read by Bruce Coville. 2 cassettes. (Magic Shop Bks.). 2002. lib. bdg. (978-1-932076-10-3(7), 02009) Full Cast Audio.

Monster's Ring, unabr. ed. Bruce Coville. Narrated by Mark Hammer. 2 pieces. (Running Time: 2 hrs. 15 mins.). (Magic Shop Bks.). (gr. 4 up). 1992. 19.00 (978-1-55690-640-4(4), 92324E7) Recorded Bks.
Russell buys a "Monster's Ring" in a mysterious magic shop, only to discover it actually can turn him into a real monster.

Monstre sur le seuil. H. P. Lovecraft. Read by Jacques Dufilho. 1 cass. (FRE.). 1991. 21.95 (1075-VSL) Olivia & Hill.
A horror story by a modern Edgar Allan Poe.

Monstrous Memoirs of a Mighty McFearless. unabr. ed. Ahmet Zappa. Read by Katherine Kellgren. 4 CDs. (Running Time: 5 hrs. 6 mins.). (J). (gr. 4-6). 2007. audio compact disk 38.00 (978-0-7393-4820-8(5), Listening Lib) Pub: Random Audio Pubg. Dist(s): Random

Monstrous Regiment. Terry Pratchett. Read by Stephen Briggs. (Discworld Ser.). 1975. 14.95 (978-0-06-074373-4(5)) HarperCollins Pubs.

Monstrous Regiment. abr. unabr. ed. Terry Pratchett. Read by Stephen Briggs. (Discworld Ser.). 2003. 39.95 (978-0-06-056996-9(4)) HarperCollins Pubs.

***Monstrous Regiment.** unabr. ed. Terry Pratchett. Read by Stephen Briggs. (ENG.). 2004. (978-0-06-082456-3(5), Harper Audio); (978-0-06-079882-6(3), Harper Audio); (978-0-06-082457-0(3), Harper Audio) HarperCollins Pubs.

Monstrous Regiment of Women. unabr. ed. Laurie R. King. Narrated by Jenny Sterlin. 9 cass. (Running Time: 12 hrs.). (Mary Russell Mystery Ser.: Vol. 2). 1996. 78.00 (978-0-7887-0493-2(1), 94685E7) Recorded Bks.
Followers of the New Temple of God - all well-bred, well-heeled young women - are becoming targets for murder. Mary & Holmes plunge headlong into a dangerous investigation.

***Monstrumologist.** unabr. ed. Rick Yancey. Narrated by Steven Boyer. 1 Playaway. (Running Time: 11 hrs. 45 mins.). (YA). (gr. 9 up). 2009. 59.75 (978-1-4407-3570-7(0)); 78.75 (978-1-4407-3560-8(3)); audio compact disk 108.75 (978-1-4407-3564-6(6)) Recorded Bks.

***Monstrumologist.** unabr. collector's ed. Rick Yancey. Narrated by Steven Boyer. 10 CDs. (Running Time: 11 hrs. 45 mins.). (YA). (gr. 9 up). 2009. audio compact disk 51.95 (978-1-4407-3568-4(9)) Recorded Bks.

Monstruo Debajo de la Cama, EDL Level 28. (Fonolibros Ser.: Vol. 9). (SPA.). (J). 2003. 11.50 (978-0-7652-1030-2(4)) Modern Curr.

Montage: Deuxième Niveau. 3rd ed. Lucia F. Baker. 1 cass. (Running Time: 90 min.). (C). 1996. stu. ed. 52.50 (978-0-07-913240-6(5), 9780079132406, Mc-H Human Soc) Pub: McGrw-H Hghr Educ. Dist(s): McGraw

Montana! abr. ed. Dana Fuller Ross, pseud. Read by Bruce Watson. 4 vols. (Wagons West Ser.: No. 10). 2003. (978-1-58807-536-9(2)) Am Pubng Inc.

Montana! abr. ed. Dana Fuller Ross, pseud. Read by Bruce Watson. 4 vols. (Running Time: 6 hrs.). (Wagon West Ser.: No. 10). 2003. 25.00 (978-1-58807-015-9(8)) Am Pubng Inc.
MONTANA! With the deep wounds of the Civil War freshly healed, America's bravest ride westward to unite the continent into one great nation. Toby Holt, son of the legendary wagonmaster Whip Holt, courageously accepts a presidential mandate to take the Northwest Railroad into hazardous Montana Territory. But, Sioux war drums beat a dire warning to stay out of this Indian land. Under Montana's azure skies, daring men and women steel themselves with new valor to fight for America's richest lands!.

Montana! abr. ed. Dana Fuller Ross, pseud. Read by Bruce Watson. 5 vols. (Running Time: 6 hrs.). (Wagons West Ser.: No. 10). 2004. audio compact disk 30.00 (978-1-58807-377-8(7)); audio compact disk (978-1-58807-856-8(6)) Am Pubng Inc.

Montaña Magica. abr. ed. Tomas Mann. 3 CDs.Tr. of Magic Mountain. (SPA.). 2003. audio compact disk 17.00 (978-958-8218-21-2(7)) YoYoMusic.

Montana Moon Lady. rev. ed. Gina Beth Clark. 1 cass. (Running Time: 1 hr. 30 min.). 2001. (978-0-9712681-3-5(4)) G B C Audio Bk.

Montana Moon Lady. rev. ed. Gina Beth Clark. 1 CD. (Running Time: 1 hr. 30 mins.). 2002. audio compact disk (978-0-9712681-7-3(7), 043-015) G B C Audio Bk.

montana que Llora. (Saludos Ser.: Vol. 1). (SPA.). (gr. 3-5). 10.00 (978-0-7635-1849-3(2)) Rigby Educ.

Montana Rides. unabr. collector's ed. Max Brand. Read by Wolfram Kandinsky. 7 cass. (Running Time: 10 hrs. 30 mins.). 1991. 56.00 (978-0-7366-2015-4(X), 2831) Books on Tape.
He didn't even have a name. They called him "Kid," "Montana," "Mexico" or "Punch." But manacled in the sheriff's office, he chose Montana. It looked to be the farthest away. The one thing Montana did have was a reputation. He said he was only crooked with crooks. The sheriff thinks different, but can't prove it. He lets him go. Then a cattle baron's long-lost son shows up to claim his inheritance - he looks amazingly like Montana.

Montana Rides Again. unabr. collector's ed. Max Brand. Read by Wolfram Kandinsky. 6 cass. (Running Time: 9 hrs.). 1992. 48.00 (978-0-7366-2293-6(4), 3078) Books on Tape.
The Montana Kid, "El Keed" south of the border, slips a marriage noose to join Mateo Rubriz, prince of Mexican outlaws, in a wild cross-border raid. The target: a gold & emerald crown stolen by the governor of Duraya from the church under his protection.

Montana Showdown, Level 1. 2 cass. (Running Time: 1 hr. 30 mins.). (SmartReader Ser.). (J). 1999. pap. bk. & tchr. ed. 19.95 (978-0-7887-0768-1(X), 79349T3) Recorded Bks.
With the help of a legendary character, one lonesome stranger learns to stand up to racism in the old West.

Montana Showdown, Level 2. 2 cass. (Running Time: 1 hr. 30 mins.). (SmartReader Ser.). (J). 1999. pap. bk. & tchr. ed. 19.95 (978-0-7887-0543-4(1), 79330T3) Recorded Bks.

Montana Sky. abr. ed. Nora Roberts. Read by Erika Leigh. (Running Time: 10800 sec.). 2007. audio compact disk 14.99 (978-1-4233-2463-8(3), 9781423324638, BCD Value Price) Brilliance Audio.

Montana Sky. unabr. ed. Nora Roberts. Read by Anna Fields. 11 cass. (Running Time: 16 hrs. 30 min.). 1997. 88.00 (978-0-913369-43-2(8), 4226) Books on Tape.

When Jack Mercy dies, his three daughters - unknown to each other & each conceived through different mothers - gather at his Montana ranch to hear the reading of his will. They're shocked to learn that they must live together on the ranch for one year before they can inherit their shares. Sisters yet strangers, they'll have to shelve their bitterness & unite like a family. If they don't, a sily enemy could destroy them & drain their newly found wealth.

Montana Sky. unabr. ed. Nora Roberts. Read by Erika Leigh. (Running Time: 15 hrs.). 2006. 39.25 (978-1-4233-2461-4(7), 9781423324614, BADLE); 24.95 (978-1-4233-2460-7(9), 9781423324607, BAD); audio compact disk 38.95 (978-1-4233-2456-0(0), 9781423324560); audio compact disk 117.25 (978-1-4233-2457-7(9), 9781423324577, BriAudCD Unabrid); audio compact disk 39.25 (978-1-4233-2459-1(5), 9781423324591, Brinc Audio MP3 Lib); audio compact disk 24.95 (978-1-4233-2458-4(7), 9781423324584, Brilliance MP3) Brilliance Audio.

When Jack Mercy died, he left behind a lot of enemies . . .and a ranch worth nearly twenty million dollars. Now his three daughters - each born of a different marriage, and each unknown to the others - are gathered to hear the reading of the will. Willa, the only one who knew her father, boldly expects that everything will be hers. Tess, who has reluctantly flown in from Hollywood, just hopes to fly back with as much cash as possible - as soon as possible. And Lily Mercy would be grateful for anything; she has learned to expect disappointment, even cruelty, from men. But the women are shocked to learn that before any of them can inherit, they must live together on the ranch for one year. They are sisters . . .and strangers. Now they face a challenge: to put their bitterness aside and live like family. To protect each other from danger - and unite against an enemy who threatens to destroy all. And finally, to weave together three very different worlds in this beautiful and isolated place called Montana . .

Montana 1948. unabr. ed. Larry Watson. Narrated by Beau Bridges. 4 CDs. (Running Time: 4 hrs.). 1999. audio compact disk 36.00 (C1023) Recorded Bks.

Montana 1948. unabr. ed. Larry Watson. Narrated by Beau Bridges. 4 CDs. (Running Time: 4 hrs.). 2000. audio compact disk 36.00 (978-0-7887-3417-5(2), C1023E7) Recorded Bks.

Set in an archetypal western town, this remarkable coming-of-age story also contains the elements of a gripping mystery. As a 12-year-old boy watches his father, the town sheriff, investigate a series of old crimes, he learns much about his family by what is left unsaid.

Montana 1948. unabr. ed. Larry Watson. Narrated by Beau Bridges. 3 cass. (Running Time: 4 hrs.). 1997. 26.00 (978-0-7887-0816-9(3), 94966E7) Recorded Bks.

As a twelve year-old boy watches his father, the town sheriff, investigate a series of old crimes, he learns much about this family by what is left unsaid.

Montana 1948. unabr. ed. Larry Watson. 2004. 12.95 (978-0-7435-4142-8(1)) Pub: S&S Audio. Dist(s): S and S Inc

Montclair Unity Church Meditation. unabr. ed. Phyllis Crichlow. Read by Phyllis Crichlow. 1 cass. (Running Time: 30 mins.). (Metamusic Meditation Ser.). 2001. 6.39 (978-1-56102-903-7(3)) Inter Indus.

A verbally guided meditation.

Monte Walsh, Pt. 1 unabr. collector's ed. Jack Schaefer. Read by Walter Zimmerman. 7 cass. (Running Time: 10 hrs. 30 min.). 1988. 56.00 (978-0-7366-1330-9(7), 2234-A) Books on Tape.

Monte Walsh was the kind of man who preferred coffee to whiskey & horseback to an easy chair. Living in a routine where every day would seem alike if the weather weren't so cantankerous, Monte & his friends at the Slash Y Ranch typify what was strongest, most honest & most admirable about the cowboys at the turn of the century.

Monte Walsh, Pt. 2. collector's ed. Jack Schaefer. Read by Walter Zimmerman. 8 cass. (Running Time: 12 hrs.). 1988. 64.00 (978-0-7366-1331-6(5), 2234-B) Books on Tape.

Monterant Affair. Richard Grayson. Read by Gordon Griffin. 5 cass. (Running Time: 7 hrs. 30 mins.). (Sound Ser.). 2004. 49.95 (978-1-85496-777-0(0), 64615) Pub: UlverLrgPrint GBR. Dist(s): Ulverscroft US

Monterey Deathsong. unabr. ed. Steve Hailes. Read by Maynard Villers. 4 cass. (Running Time: 5 hrs. 36 min.). 1996. 26.95 (978-1-55686-729-3(8)) Books in Motion.

Ex-Texas Ranger Matt Janzene is persuaded to lend his fists & his colts in support of California's first constitutional convention which is being threatened by subversive elements.

Monterey Shorts/Book. Short Stories. Byron Merritt, Sr. 5 CDs. (Running Time: 4 hrs. 45 mins). Dramatization. 2004. audio compact disk 21.95 (978-0-9760096-8-9(4)) Pub: FWOMP Pubng. Dist(s): Sunbelt Pubns

Montezuma Castle National Monument: Walkabout Audio Tours. Patrick T. Houlihan & Betsy Houlihan. 1 cass. (Running Time: 1 hr). 2000. 9.00 (978-1-931544-01-6(8)); audio compact disk 16.00 (978-1-931544-00-9(X)) Walkabout Audio.

An historical description of cultural geological, archaeological floral & fauna facts of Montezuma Castle National Monument. Also an explanation of prehistoric Native American occupation.

Montezuma Well National Monument: Walkabout Audio Tours. Patrick T. Houlihan & Betsy Houlihan. 1 cass. (Running Time: 1 hr). 2000. 9.00 (978-1-931544-03-0(4)); audio compact disk 16.00 (978-1-931544-02-3(6)) Walkabout Audio.

An historical description of cultural geological, archaeological floral & fauna facts of Montezuma Castle Well National Monument. Also an explanation of prehistoric Native American occupation.

Montgomery. unabr. collector's ed. Alan Moorehead. Read by Bill Kelsey. 7 cass. (Running Time: 10 hrs. 30 mins.). 1988. 56.00 (978-0-7366-1450-4(8), 2332) Books on Tape.

Examines the early life & career of this English Officer from the battlefields ow W W II.

Montgomery/Howard Cos, MD Atlas. (Maryland Cities & Counties Ser.). audio compact disk 15.95 (978-0-528-99702-0(5)) Pub: Rand McNally. Dist(s): Map Link

Month in the Country. unabr. ed. J. L. Carr. Read by Nick Rawlinson. 4 CDs. (Running Time: 3 hrs. 46 min.). (Isis Ser.). (J). 2003. audio compact disk 51.95 (978-0-7531-2222-8(7)); 34.95 (978-0-7531-1684-5(7)) Pub: ISIS Lrg Prnt GBR. Dist(s): Ulverscroft US

A haunting story of two war veterans, who meet in the quiet English countryside of the north, in 1920.Living inside the church, one, the narrator, is uncovering and restoring an historic wall painting; the other, Moon, is in search of a lost grave in the field next door.

Month of Miracles. Charlene Bunas. Ed. by Rennie Mau. 1989. pap. bk. (978-0-318-66307-4(4)) Media Bridge.

***Month of Summer.** unabr. ed. Lisa Wingate. Read by Johanna Parker. 12 CDs. (Running Time: 13:50). 2008. audio compact disk 49.95 (978-1-4361-5531-1(2)) Recorded Bks.

Month of Sundays. unabr. collector's ed. John Updike. Read by Wolfram Kandinsky. 5 cass. (Running Time: 7 hrs. 30 min.). 1981. 40.00 (978-0-7366-0291-4(7), 1279) Books on Tape.

After years of dutifully ministering to his flock, the Reverand Thomas Marshfield, 41, begins fleecing the ewes. When his fervid trysts are exposed, the errant preacher is shipped off for a month's retreat at a desert spa for troubled clergyman. The rules of this "enforced" rest demand that afternoons be spent alone at an obligatory typewriter, where he confesses orgies of oriental voluptuousness.

Month of Sundays: Thanksgiving & Praise. Contrib. by Jan Sanborn. (Sacred Performer Collections Ser.). (ENG.). 2003. audio compact disk 9.95 (978-0-7390-2876-6(6)) Alfred Pub.

Monthly Forecast: Lunar Returns, New Moons. Joan Titsworth. 1 cass. (Running Time: 1 hr. 30 min.). 8.95 (346) Am Fed Astrologers.

Monticello. Leroy Aarons. Perf. by Shana Blake Hill & Christopher Schuman. Music by Glenn Paxton. 2 CDs. (Running Time: 1 hr. 35 mins.). 2000. audio compact disk 25.95 (978-1-58081-168-2(X), TPT144) Pub: L A Theatre. Dist(s): NetLibrary CO

Montmartre Murders. Richard Grayson. Read by Gordon Griffin. 5 cass. (Running Time: 7 hrs. 30 mins.). (Sound Ser.). 1991. 49.95 (978-1-85496-461-8(5), 64615) Pub: UlverLrgPrint GBR. Dist(s): Ulverscroft US

Montreal Stories. Mavis Gallant. Read by Margot Dionne. (Running Time: 39600 sec.). 2006. audio compact disk 29.95 (978-0-9737586-4-1(3)) Rattling Bks CAN.

Monty Moudlyn: Founder of the Hug Brigade. Birke R. Duncan. Based on a book by Birke R. Duncan. Hosted by Bob McAllister. Directed By Kevin Veatch. Narrated by Michael J. Leonard. Photos by Garrett W. Vance. 2009. audio compact disk 11.50 (978-0-9710582-5-5(3)) NW Folklore.

Monty Python's Flying Circus. Interview with Monty Python. 1 cass. (Running Time: 1 hr.). 1998. 11.25 (978-0-563-55815-6(6)) BBC WrldWd GBR.

Its sketches, songs & catchphrases are legendary: the dead parrot, the Ministry of Silly Walks, The Lumberjack Song & Now for Something Completely Different & many more.

Monty Python's Flying Circus Greatest Skits. abr. ed. Monty Python. Contrib. by Graham Chapman et al. (Running Time: 3300 sec.). (ENG.). 2007. audio compact disk 14.95 (978-1-60283-056-1(8)) Pub: AudioGO. Dist(s): Perseus Dist

Monty Python's Tunisian Holiday: My Life with Brian. unabr. ed. Kim Howard Johnson. Narrated by Johnny Heller & Simon Vance. (Running Time: 6 hrs. 30 mins. 0 sec.). (ENG.). 2008. audio compact disk 69.99 (978-1-4001-4043-5(9)); audio compact disk 24.99 (978-1-4001-6043-3(X)); audio compact disk 34.99 (978-1-4001-1043-8(2)) Pub: Tantor Media. Dist(s): IngramPubServ

Monument Rock. Louis L'Amour. 1 cass. (Running Time: 1 hr.). 2001. 10.95 (BMDD003) Lodestone Catalog.

Monuments: Sacred or Profane? Chuck Missler. 2 cass. (Running Time: 3 hrs.). (Briefing Packages by Chuck Missler). 1991. vinyl bd. 14.95 (978-1-880532-77-5(8)) Koinonia Hse.

 # Are the recent discoveries on the Planet Mars really monuments built by some other culture?# Is the mile-wide "Face" a carefully crafted monument, or simply a natural aberration?# Is there a link between the "pyramids" on Mars, and the Great Pyramid of Egypt?# Has all this been described in the Bible?

Monuments - Sacred or Profane? Chuck Missler. 2 CD's. (Running Time: 120 mins.). (Briefing Packages by Chuck Missler). 1991. audio compact disk 19.95 (978-1-57821-307-8(X)) Koinonia Hse.

Are the recent discoveries on the Planet Mars really monuments built by some other culture?Is the mile-wide "Face" a carefully crafted monument, or simply a natural aberration?Is there a link between the "pyramids" on Mars, and the Great Pyramid of Egypt?Has all this been described in the Bible?Chuck Missler is an internationaly recognized authority, and was a consultant on several CBS prime-time television specials.

Monuments Men: Allied Heroes, Nazi Thieves, & the Greatest Treasure Hunt in History. abr. ed. Robert M. Edsel. Read by Jeremy Davidson. Told to Bret Witter. 6 CDs. (Running Time: 7 hrs. 30 mins. 0 sec.). (ENG.). 2009. audio compact disk 29.99 (978-1-4272-0691-6(0)) Pub: Macmill Audio. Dist(s): Macmillan

Monuments of Mars - A Mythic Link? Richard C. Hoagland. 1 cass. (AA & A Symposium Ser.). 9.00 (A0258-87) Sound Photosyn.

Moo. unabr. ed. Jane Smiley. Narrated by Suzanne Toren. 10 cas. (Running Time: 16.25 hrs.). 39.95 (978-1-4025-3935-0(5)); audio compact disk 49.95 (978-1-4025-3936-7(3)) Recorded Bks.

Moo. unabr. ed. Jane Smiley. Narrated by Suzanne Toren. 12 cass. (Running Time: 16 hrs. 15 mins.). 2000. 99.00 (978-0-7887-2933-1(0), 95536E7) Recorded Bks.

A hilarious tour through the inner sanctums of a Midwestern university. Although the story focuses a sharp eye on academia, its satire is tempered by loveable characters who ring absolutely true.

Moobli. unabr. ed. Mike Tomkies. Read by Joe Dunlop. 8 cass. (Running Time: 11 hrs.). (Isis Ser.). (J). 1991. 69.95 (978-1-85089-617-3(8), 91022) Pub: ISIS Lrg Prnt GBR. Dist(s): Ulverscroft US

***Mooched.** unabr. ed. Carol Higgins Clark. (Running Time: 6 hrs. 0 mins. 0 sec.). (ENG.). 2011. audio compact disk 29.99 (978-1-4423-3757-2(5)) Pub: S&S Audio. Dist(s): S and S Inc

Mood Control. unabr. collector's ed. Gene Bylinsky. Read by Michael Prichard. 8 cass. (Running Time: 8 hrs.). 1980. 48.00 (978-0-7366-0265-5(8), 1260) Books on Tape.

Traveling through this book the reader encounters aphrodisiacs, psychopharmocology, memory aids & drugs for controlling aggresion & rage. While their proposed use is beguiling, & may even bring about the end of madness, our concern is the harmful use to which such potent drugs can be put.

Mood Management. abr. ed. 2 CDs. (Running Time: 3600 sec.). (Medical Information Ser.). 2007. audio compact disk 15.95 (978-0-660-19676-3(X), CBC Audio) Pub: Canadian Broadcasting CAN. Dist(s): Georgetown Term

Mood is an integral part of our lives. Mood extremes can lead to psychosis, hallucinations and delusional thinking. For the past 30 years, we?ve assumed that medications can fix mood disorders. Scholar and broadcaster Monique Dull takes us on a fascinating journey and shows us that taking the right medications brings things totally back to normal for only about 1 in 4 patients with manic-depressive illness. Mood hygiene captures the new tension in clinical thinking. The new theory for controlling mood is based on the idea of controlling behaviour to keep the illness at bay.

Mood Stabilizers & Atypical Antipsychotics. Interview. Interview with Stephen M. Stahl. Featuring Ronnie Swift. 1. 2005. audio compact disk (978-1-4225-0038-5(1)) NEI Pr.

Moods & Modes: Recorder Music for Beginning Ensembles. Robert a. Amchin. Ed. by Brent M. Holl. Brent M. Holl. Karen Holl. Michael R. Nichols. Traci Batchelor. (ENG., (J). 2010. pap. bk. 19.95 (978-0-9797522-8-5(0)) Pub: Beatin Path. Dist(s): West Music

Moody Broadcasting, 'Open Line' Christian Rock. Read by David Benoit & Glen Kaiser. (Running Time: 1 hr.). 1988. 6.00 (978-0-923105-09-9(3)) Glory Ministries.

Glen Kaiser of the heavy metal Christian group "Rez Band" and David Benoit confront the major issues surrounding the contemporary "Christian" music debate, in particular heavy metal "Christian" music.

Moon. Compiled by Benchmark Education Staff. 2006. audio compact disk 10.00 (978-1-4108-6667-7(X)) Benchmark Educ.

Moon. James Herbert. Read by James Frain. 3 CDs. (Running Time: 3 hrs. 0 mins. 0 sec.). (ENG.). 2008. audio compact disk 24.95 (978-0-230-70434-3(4)) Pub: Macmillan UK GBR. Dist(s): IPG Chicago

Moon & Beyond. 2002. (978-0-7398-5193-7(4)) SteckVau.

Moon & Beyond. Steck-Vaughn Staff. 2002. pap. bk. 41.60 (978-0-7398-6978-9(7)) SteckVau.

Moon & Beyond Level 4. (J). 2002. audio compact disk (978-0-7398-5349-8(X)) SteckVau.

Moon & Saturn. Buz Myers. 1 cass. 8.95 (567) Am Fed Astrologers.

An AFA Convention workshop tape.

Moon & Sixpence see Luna y Seis Peniques

Moon & Sixpence. (ENG.). 2007. (978-1-60339-081-1(2)); cd-rom & audio compact disk (978-1-60339-082-8(0)) Listenr Digest.

Moon & Sixpence. W. Somerset Maugham. Read by Anais 9000. 2008. 27.95 (978-1-60112-180-6(6)) Babblebooks.

Moon & Sixpence. W. Somerset Maugham. Read by Frederick Davidson. 1995. 27.95 (978-1-59912-694-4(X)) Iofy Corp.

Moon & Sixpence. W. Somerset Maugham. Read by Carlos Zambrano. (Running Time: 3 hrs.). 2002. 16.95 (978-1-60083-245-1(8), Audiofy Corp) Iofy Corp.

Moon & Sixpence, unabr. ed. W. Somerset Maugham. Read by Michael Russotto. 6 cass. (Running Time: 7 hrs. 55 mins.). 1996. 24.95 (978-1-55685-407-1(2)) Audio Bk Con.

An enigmatic, but brilliant Englishman, Charles Strickland, gives up his successful, bourgeois existence at age forty to become an artist. As a painter, his selfish, soul-searching efforts to express himself on canvas lead to tragedy in his travels from London to Paris & ultimately, to the South Seas. This novel is closely based on the life of Paul Gauguin.

Moon & Sixpence. unabr. ed. W. Somerset Maugham. Read by Frederick Davidson. 6 cass. (Running Time: 8 hrs. 30 mins.). 1994. 44.95 (978-0-7861-0797-1(9), 1526) Blckstn Audio.

This is the story of an artist who was willing to sacrifice everything for the sake of art. In much of its general outline, this famous novel follows the life of Paul Gauguin, famous French post-impressionist painter, but it is not a novelized biography of Gauguin. Rather it is a sharply delineated, carefully wrought "private life", written by one of the most vivid & penetrating contemporary literary masters.

Moon & Sixpence. unabr. ed. W. Somerset Maugham. Read by Frederick Davidson. 7 CDs. (Running Time: 8 hrs. 30 mins.). 2000. audio compact disk 56.00 (978-0-7861-9888-7(5), 1526) Blckstn Audio.

Moon & Sixpence. unabr. ed. W. Somerset Maugham. Read by Frederick Davidson. (Running Time: 8 hrs. 30 mins.). 2001. audio compact disk 24.95 (978-0-7861-9268-7(2), 1526) Blckstn Audio.

Moon & Sixpence. unabr. ed. W. Somerset Maugham. Read by Michael Page. (Running Time: 7 hrs.). 2007. 39.25 (978-1-4233-3674-7(7), 9781423336747, Brinc Audio MP3 Lib); 39.25 (978-1-4233-3676-1(3), 9781423336761, BADLE); 24.95 (978-1-4233-3675-4(5), 9781423336754, BAD); audio compact disk 82.25 (978-1-4233-3672-3(0), 9781423336723, BriAudCD Unabrid); audio compact disk 29.95 (978-1-4233-3671-6(2), 9781423336716, Bril Audio CD Unabri); audio compact disk 24.95 (978-1-4233-3673-0(9), 9781423336730, Brilliance MP3) Brilliance Audio.

Moon & Sixpence, unabr. ed. W. Somerset Maugham. Narrated by Neil Hunt. 6 cass. (Running Time: 8 hrs.). 1999. 51.00 (978-0-7887-1288-3(8), 95139E7) Recorded Bks.

Thinly-disguised account of the passionate career of Paul Gauguin, creating a powerful image of primitive life that captured a generation.

***Moon & Sixpence.** unabr. ed. W. Somerset Maugham. Narrated by Steven Crossley. (Running Time: 8 hrs. 30 mins. 0 sec.). (ENG.). 2010. 19.99 (978-1-4001-6758-6(2)); 15.99 (978-1-4001-8758-4(3)); audio compact disk 27.99 (978-1-4001-1758-1(5)); audio compact disk 66.99 (978-1-4001-4758-8(1)) Pub: Tantor Media. Dist(s): IngramPubServ

Moon & Sixpence. unabr. collector's ed. W. Somerset Maugham. Read by Richard Green. 8 cass. (Running Time: 8 hrs.). 1977. 48.00 (978-0-7366-0068-2(X), 1079) Books on Tape.

Maugham portrays a 19th century gentleman who abandons his lucrative profession & family to pursue a bohemian existence in Paris.

Moon & the Mistypips. 1 cass. (Running Time: 25 min.). (Hopewell Stories Ser.). (J). (ps-4). 1992. 8.95 (978-0-9631215-3-0(7)) Hopewell Stories.

Hopewell Stories are enchanting musical tales. Children learn about character values like responsibility, loyalty, respect & caring, through examples set by warm heroic characters who, by the way, kids love...& what better place to start.

Moon & the Sun, unabr. ed. Vonda N. McIntyre. Read by Anna Fields. 11 cass. (Running Time: 16 hrs. 30 min.). 1999. 76.95 (978-0-7861-1637-9(4), 2465) Blckstn Audio.

In seventeenth-century France, Louis XIV rules with flamboyant ambition. In his domain, wealth & beauty take all; frivolity begets cruelty; science & alchemy collide. A tale of alternate history.

Moon & the Sun. unabr. ed. Vonda N. McIntyre & Anna Fields. (Running Time: 15 hrs. NaN mins.). 2008. 29.95 (978-1-4332-5492-5(1)); audio compact disk 110.00 (978-1-4332-5491-8(3)) Blckstn Audio.

Moon Blood. unabr. ed. Alastair MacNeill. Read by Simon J. Williamson. 8 cass. (Running Time: 10 hrs. 35 min.). 1999. 83.95 (978-1-85903-267-1(2)) Pub: Magna Story GBR. Dist(s): Ulverscroft US

Donald Brennan has stumbled on a terrible secret in the deepest Amazon jungle. If his pursuers catch up with him his death is a certainty.

Moon for the Misbegotten, unabr. ed. Eugene O'Neill. Perf. by Salome Jens & Michael Ryan. 3 cass. Dramatization. 1984. 27.95 (978-0-694-50877-8(2), SWC 333) HarperCollins Pubs.

Cast includes: W. B. Brydon, Jack Kehoe, Garry Mitchell.

Moon in Relationships. Ingrid Naiman. 2 cass. (Running Time: 2 hrs. 15 min.). 20.00 (978-1-882834-92-1(5)) Seventh Ray.

How the unconscious affects basic assumptions & contentment in relationships - what we seek from others.

Moon Is a Harsh Mistress. Robert A. Heinlein. Read by Lloyd James. 12 CDs. (Running Time: 14 hrs. 45 mins.). 2000. audio compact disk 96.00 (978-0-7861-9885-6(0), z2566) Blckstn Audio.
The master of modern Sci-Fi tells the strange story of an even stranger world, Twenty-first century Luna, a harsh penal colony where a revolt is plotted between a bashful computer & a ragtag collection of maverick humans. A revolt that goes beautifully until the inevitable happens. Heinlein draws many historical parallels with the War of Independence & clearly shows his own libertarian political views.

Moon Is a Harsh Mistress. unabr. ed. Robert A. Heinlein. Read by Lloyd James. 8 cass. (Running Time: 11 hrs. 30 mins.). 2000. 56.95 (978-0-7861-1764-2(8), 2567) Blckstn Audio.

Moon Is a Harsh Mistress. unabr. ed. Robert A. Heinlein. Narrated by George Wilson. 11 cass. (Running Time: 15 hrs. 30 mins.). 1998. 93.00 (978-0-7887-1987-5(4), 95374 E7) Recorded Bks.
On the moon in 2075, residents live like sharecroppers, kept prisoners of the mother planet. But a small group of dissidents are planning a revolution that will change this relationship.

Moon Is a Harsh Mistress. unabr. ed. Robert A. Heinlein. Read by Lloyd James. (Running Time: 14 hrs. 30 mins.). 2000. 24.95 (978-0-7861-9221-2(6)) Blckstn Audio.

***Moon Is a Harsh Mistress.** unabr. ed. Robert A. Heinlein. Read by Lloyd James. (Running Time: 14 hrs. 15 mins.). 2010. audio compact disk 29.95 (978-1-4417-4005-2(8)) Blckstn Audio.

Moon Is Down. unabr. ed. John Steinbeck. Narrated by George Guidall. 3 cass. (Running Time: 4 hrs. 30 mins.). 1999. 26.00 (978-0-7887-3479-3(2), 95792E7) Recorded Bks.
When invaders take over a peaceful European village, it seems like an easy victory. As the days & weeks wear on, however, the occupying force wonders who really controls the village.

Moon Is My Witness. Alexandra Connor. (Isis (CDs) Ser.). 2006. audio compact disk 84.95 (978-0-7531-2567-0(6)) Pub: ISIS Lrg Prnt GBR. Dist(s): Ulverscroft US

Moon Is My Witness. unabr. ed. Alexandra Connor. Read by Gordon Griffin. 8 cass. (Running Time: 12 hrs.). 2000. 69.95 (978-0-7531-0772-0(4), 000108) Pub: ISIS Audio GBR. Dist(s): ISIS Pub
Expanding his empire, John Crossworth turns from coal to cotton, founding a business dynasty which dominates the Lancashire town. But as time passes the co-inheritors of the fortune, the Crossworth twins, become enemies & the dream that their father made reality is threatened by greed, envy & revenge.

Moon Is Our Witness. unabr. ed. Alexandra Connor. Read by Gordon Griffin. 8 cass. (Running Time: 12 hrs.). 2001. 69.95 (000108) Pub: ISIS Audio GBR. Dist(s): Ulverscroft US

Moon Is the Muse: La Lune e' la Musa. (ITA.). 2007. audio compact disk 14.95 (978-0-9785535-2-4(7)) C Di Sanzo.

Moon Island. Rosie Thomas. Read by Bonnie Hurren. (Chivers Audio Bks.). 2003. audio compact disk 110.95 (978-0-7540-8784-7(0)) Pub: Chivers Audio Bks GBR. Dist(s): AudioGO

Moon Island. unabr. ed. Rosie Thomas. Read by Bonnie Hurren. 10 cass. (Running Time: 15 hrs.). 1999. 84.95 (978-0-7540-0291-8(8), CAB 1714) AudioGO.

Moon Lady. unabr. ed. Amy Tan. 1 CD. (Running Time: 1.5 hrs.). 2004. audio compact disk 15.00 (978-1-931056-94-6(3), N Millennium Audio) New Millenn Enter.
Relates what happened when Ying Ying was seven & celebrated the Moon Festival in China.

Moon Lady. unabr. abr. ed. Amy Tan. Read by Amy Tan. 1 cass. (Running Time: 1.5 hrs.). 2004. 15.00 (978-1-931056-39-7(0), N Millennium Audio) New Millenn Enter.
A haunting tale, about three sisters that listen to their grandmother recount a mesmerizing childhood memory on a rainy afternoon. The long, complex story, filled with danger and excitement, relates what happened when Ying-ying was seven and celebrating the Moon Festival in China. On that long-ago night of the Moon Festival, she encountered the Moon Lady, who grants the secret wishes of those who ask.

Moon Man. 2004. bk. 24.95 (978-0-7882-0576-7(5)); 8.95 (978-1-56008-973-5(3)); cass. & flmstrp 30.00 (978-1-56008-719-9(6)) Weston Woods.

Moon Man; Crictor; Two of Them, the; Three Little Pigs. 2004. (978-0-89719-849-3(2)); cass. & flmstrp (978-0-89719-705-2(4)) Weston Woods.

Moon Medicine. Mike Blakely. Narrated by Joel Leffert. 10 cass. (Running Time: 14 hrs.). 2002. 92.00 (978-1-4025-1603-0(7)) Recorded Bks.

Moon Mouse. Ed. by Adelaide Hull. Illus. by Adelaide Hull. (J). 1989. 14.96 (978-0-394-03887-2(8)) McGraw.

Moon Music. Faye Kellerman. Read by Bernadette Dunne. 1999. audio compact disk 104.00 (978-0-7366-8012-7(8)); 88.00 (978-0-7366-4408-2(3), 4869) Books on Tape.
While investigating the mutilation murder of a young girl, Detective Romulus Poe is struck by its similarities to another case.

Moon Music. Faye Kellerman. 2004. 15.95 (978-0-7435-4143-5(X)) Pub: S&S Audio. Dist(s): S and S Inc

Moon Music, abr. ed. Faye Kellerman. Read by Keith Szarabajka. 4 cass. (Running Time: 6 hrs.). 1999. 25.00 (FS9-43228) Highsmith.

Moon of First Snow. Golana. 1 CD. (Running Time: 54 mins.). 2002. audio compact disk (978-1-891319-71-6(X)) Spring Hill CO.

Moon of Gomrath. Alan Garner. Read by Philip Madoc. (Running Time: 16297 sec.). (Classic Literature with Classical Music Ser.). 2007. audio compact disk 28.98 (978-962-634-470-5(9), Naxos AudioBooks) Naxos.

Moon of Gomrath. unabr. ed. Alan Garner. Read by Philip Madoc. (J). 2007. 39.99 (978-1-60252-770-6(9)) Find a World.

Moon of the Alligators. unabr. ed. Jean Craighead George. Narrated by Barbara Caruso. 1 cass. (Running Time: 30 mins.). (Thirteen Moons Ser.). (gr. 3 up). 1997. 10.00 (978-0-7887-1231-9(4), 95155E7) Recorded Bks.
Captures the animals in their natural environments & chronicles their fight for survival. Explores the intricate relationships among animals, plants & the ever-changing environment in which we live.

Moon of the Bears. unabr. ed. Jean Craighead George. Narrated by Barbara Caruso. 1 cass. (Running Time: 30 mins.). (Thirteen Moons Ser.). (gr. 3 up). 1997. 10.00 (978-0-7887-1232-6(2), 95156E7) Recorded Bks.

Moon of the Chickarees. unabr. ed. Jean Craighead George. Narrated by Barbara Caruso. 1 cass,. (Running Time: 30 mins.). (Thirteen Moons Ser.). (gr. 3 up). 1997. 10.00 (978-0-7887-1233-3(0), 95157E7) Recorded Bks.

Moon of the Deer. unabr. ed. Jean Craighead George. Narrated by Barbara Caruso. 1 cass. (Running Time: 30 mins.). (Thirteen Moons Ser.). (gr. 3 up). 1997. 10.00 (978-0-7887-1234-0(9), 95158E7) Recorded Bks.

Moon of the Fox Pups. unabr. ed. Jean Craighead George. Narrated by Barbara Caruso. 1 cass. (Running Time: 30 mins.). (Thirteen Moons Ser.). (gr. 3 up). 1997. 10.00 (978-0-7887-1235-7(7), 95159E7) Recorded Bks.

Moon of the Gray Wolves. unabr. ed. Jean Craighead George. Narrated by Barbara Caruso. 1 cass. (Running Time: 30 mins.). (Thirteen Moons Ser.). (gr. 3 up). 1997. 10.00 (978-0-7887-1236-4(5), 95160E7) Recorded Bks.

Moon of the Moles. unabr. ed. Jean Craighead George. Narrated by Barbara Caruso. 1 cass. (Running Time: 30 mins.). (Thirteen Moons Ser.). (gr. 3 up). 1997. 10.00 (978-0-7887-1237-1(3), 95161E7) Recorded Bks.

Moon of the Monarch Butterflies. unabr. ed. Jean Craighead George. Narrated by Barbara Caruso. 1 cass. (Running Time: 30 mins.). (Thirteen Moons Ser.). (gr. 3 up). 1997. 10.00 (978-0-7887-1238-8(1), 95162E7) Recorded Bks.

Moon of the Mountain Lions. unabr. ed. Jean Craighead George. Narrated by Barbara Caruso. 1 cass. (Running Time: 30 mins.). (Thirteen Moons Ser.). (gr. 3 up). 1997. 10.00 (978-0-7887-1239-5(X), 95163E7) Recorded Bks.

Moon of the Owls. unabr. ed. Jean Craighead George. Narrated by Barbara Caruso. 1 cass. (Running Time: 30 mins.). (Thirteen Moons Ser.). (gr. 3 up). 1997. 10.00 (978-0-7887-1240-1(3), 95164E7) Recorded Bks.

Moon of the Salamanders. unabr. ed. Jean Craighead George. Narrated by Barbara Caruso. 1 cass. (Running Time: 30 mins.). (Thirteen Moons Ser.). (gr. 3 up). 1997. 10.00 (978-0-7887-1241-8(1), 95165E7) Recorded Bks.

Moon of the Wild Pigs. unabr. ed. Jean Craighead George. Narrated by Barbara Caruso. 1 cass. (Running Time: 30 mins.). (Thirteen Moons Ser.). (gr. 3 up). 1997. 10.00 (978-0-7887-1242-5(X), 95166E7) Recorded Bks.

Moon of the Winter Bird. unabr. ed. Jean Craighead George. Narrated by Barbara Caruso. 1 cass. (Running Time: 30 mins.). (Thirteen Moons Ser.). (gr. 3 up). 1997. 10.00 (978-0-7887-1243-2(8), 95167E7) Recorded Bks.

Moon on Fire. Read by Laura Simms. 1 cass. (Running Time: 1 hr). (J). 1987. 9.95 (978-0-938756-15-6(X), 030) Yellow Moon.
A collection of folktales from around the world that focuses on the ideas of spirit & transformation. Laura's stories express aspects of the awakening of the feminine in men & women, as well as ways in which the Feminine Principle awakens us in the world.

Moon on the Water. Stan Richardson. 2 CDs. (Running Time: 7020 sec.). 2005. audio compact disk 18.98 (978-1-59179-280-2(0), M927D) Sounds True.
What is the sound of the moon on the water? It is the music of utter stillness and complete spaciousness-the perfect reflection of self within the universe, and the universe within the self. There is no finer instrument for capturing this music of Zen than the shakuhachi bamboo flute, the instrument which Stan Richardson has dedicated his life to master. With Moon on the Water, Richardson offers two musical experiences. On the first CD, listeners enjoy the pure tones of the solo shakuhachi, as it has been played for centuries. For the second CD, Stan Richardson combines natural sounds recorded during his travels across the Japanese countryside-the rushing of water, the wind over waves, the singing of cranes-with the beauty of the bamboo flute. Pure and elegant, intricate and subtle-Moon on the Water invokes the Zen mind, and makes for the perfect musical complement to massage and bodywork, yoga, and any moment of peaceful contemplation.

Moon over Manhattan: A Novel of Mystery & Mayhem. unabr. ed. Larry King. Read by Larry King. Read by Thomas H. Cook. 5 CDs. (Running Time: 6 hrs.). 2004. audio compact disk 34.95 (978-1-59007-077-2(1)) Pub: New Millenn Enter. Dist(s): PerseuPGW

Moon over Manhattan: A Novel of Mystery & Mayhem. unabr. ed. Scripts. Larry King & Thomas H. Cook. 4 cass. (Running Time: 6 hrs.). 2004. 24.95 (978-1-59007-235-6(9)) Pub: New Millenn Enter. Dist(s): PerseuPGW

Moon over Morocco. Meatball Fulton. Read by Robert Lesser et al. 7 cass. (Running Time: 10 hrs.). (Jack Flanders Ser.). 40.00 (ZBSF011) ZBS Ind.

Moon over Morocco. Thomas M. Lopez. 7 cass. (Running Time: 10 hrs.). 2001. 40.00 (ZBSF011); audio compact disk 45.00 (ZBSF012) Lodestone Catalog.
Once in a far away land there existed a knowledge of natural magic that has been lost to modern man. Jack Flanders travels to Morocco, where magic remains an integral part of daily life & then discovers far more than he expected.

Moon over Morocco. unabr. ed. Meatball Fulton. Read by Robert Lorick et al. 7 cass. (Running Time: 10 hrs.). Dramatization. 1974. 40.00 (978-1-881137-10-8(4)) ZBS Found.
Moon over Morocco finds Jack on a quest for the natural magic that has been lost to modern man. Our hero seeks the knowledge of that magic in modern Morocco.

Moon over Morocco, unabr. ed. Meatball Fulton. Read by Robert Lorick et al. 8 CDs. (Running Time: 10 hrs.). Dramatization. 1974. audio compact disk 45.00 (978-1-881137-86-3(4), ZBSF012) ZBS Found.

Moon Phase & Its Significance, Pt. I. Marilyn Busteed. 1 cass. (Running Time: 1 hr. 30 min.). 8.95 (496) Am Fed Astrologers.
Easy to figure & interpret.

Moon Phase & Its Significance, Pt. II. Marilyn Busteed. 1 cass. (Running Time: 1 hr.). 8.95 (496A) Am Fed Astrologers.
An AFA Convention workshop tape.

Moon Pool. Abraham Merritt. Read by Anais 9000. 2008. 27.95 (978-1-60112-178-3(4)) Babblebooks.

Moon Racists. Mark Paul Sebar. Voice by Mark Paul Sebar. Voice by Arlene Francis et al. 2 CD. (Running Time: 120 mins.). 2001. audio compact disk 9.99 (978-1-930246-07-2(2), 1930246072) Sebar Pubng.
College students lock a bunch of racists up in a room together on the dark side of the moon. Will they learn to survive together.

Moon Racists MP3. Mark Paul Sebar. 2001. audio compact disk 9.99 (978-1-930246-26-3(9), 1930246269) Sebar Pubng.

Moon River, Level 1. (Yamaha Clavinova Connection Ser.). 2004. disk 1.04 (978-0-634-09583-2(8)) H Leonard.

Moon River & Me: A Memoir. unabr. ed. Andy Williams. Read by Andy Williams. 5 CDs. (Running Time: 5 hrs.). (ENG.). (gr. 12 up). 2009. audio compact disk 34.95 (978-0-14-314500-4(2), PengAudBks) Penguin Grp USA.

Moon Shell Beach. unabr. ed. Nancy Thayer. Narrated by Renée Raudman. (Running Time: 9 hrs. 30 mins. 0 sec.). (ENG.). 2008. audio compact disk 34.99 (978-1-4001-0775-9(X)); audio compact disk 24.99 (978-1-4001-5775-4(7)) Pub: Tantor Media. Dist(s): IngramPubServ

Moon Song. unabr. ed. Byrd Baylor. Read by Byrd Baylor. 1 cass. (Running Time: 4 min.). (Byrd Baylor: Storyteller Ser.). (J). (gr. k-6). 1990. 5.95 (978-0-929937-21-2(X)) SW Series.
Pima Indian legend on the creation of the coyote.

Moon Tiger. unabr. ed. Penelope Lively. Read by Sheila Mitchell. 6 cass. (Running Time: 7 hr. 30 min.). (Isis Ser.). (J). 1997. 54.95 (978-1-85089-663-0(1), 88011) Pub: ISIS Lrg Prnt GBR. Dist(s): Ulverscroft US

Moon Tiger, unabr. ed. Penelope Lively. Read by Sheila Mitchell. 6 cass. (Running Time: 7 hrs. 30 min.). 1988. 49.00 (978-1-55690-347-2(2), 88560) Recorded Bks.
A woman lies dying in hospital, remembering her life.

Moonbeam Stream: The Legend of Annie Oakleaf & Buble O'Bill. unabr. ed. J. D. Isaacs. Read by J. D. Isaacs. 1 cass. (Running Time: 50 min.). Dramatization. (J). (gr. 1-6). 1995. 10.00 (978-0-9647834-0-9(1), NWA9501T); audio compact disk 15.00 CD. (978-0-9647834-1-6(X), NWA9501C) New Water Audio.
Storytelling with original music of a fictional tale woven around the very real problem of toxic waste flowing into our natural waterways.

Moonbeams & Gentle Dreams: Favorite Lullabies for Children. 1 cass. (J). (ps). 1988. 6.98 Norelco. (978-1-877737-13-8(5), MLP 261) MFLP CA.
Musical lullabies for children. "Sampler.".

Moondreamer. Priscilla Herdman. 1 cass. (Running Time: 1 hr. 30 min.). (J). 1998. 9.98; audio compact disk 15.98 Rounder Kids Mus Dist.
These songs are good lullabies for little ones, & soothing listening experience for adults.

Moondreamer, No. 3. Priscilla Herdman. 1 cass. (Running Time: 1 hr. 30 min.). (J). 7.98 (RWM 5401); audio compact disk 12.78 (RWM 5401) NewSound.
A collection of lullabies which includes: "Howl at the Moon," "A Velveteen Love Song," "One Thousand Pairs of Pajamas" & more.

Moonfleet. John Meade Falkner. 1999. pap. bk. 79.95 (978-1-86015-004-3(7)) Ulverscroft US.

Moonfleet. unabr. ed. J. Meade Falkner. Narrated by Full Cast. (Running Time: 2 hrs. 0 mins. 0 sec.). (ENG.). 2010. audio compact disk 24.95 (978-1-60283-847-5(X)) Pub: AudioGO. Dist(s): Perseus Dist

Moonfleet. unabr. ed. John Meade Falkner. Read by Peter Joyce. 6 cass. 1999. 49.95 (978-1-86015-460-7(3)) Ulverscroft US.

Moongobble & Me Series. unabr. ed. Bruce Coville. Read by Bruce Coville. Read by Full Cast Production Staff. (J). 2006. 44.99 (978-1-59895-620-7(5)) Find a World.

Moonheart. unabr. ed. Charles de Lint & Paul Michael Garcia. (Running Time: 20 hrs. NaN mins.). 2008. 44.95 (978-1-4332-3073-8(9)); 105.95 (978-1-4332-3069-1(0)); audio compact disk 120.00 (978-1-4332-3070-7(4)) Blckstn Audio.

Moonless Night. B. A. James. Read by Terry Wale. 6 cass. (Running Time: 8 hrs.). (Soundings Ser.). (J). 2004. 54.95 (978-1-84283-227-1(1)) Pub: ISIS Lrg Prnt GBR. Dist(s): Ulverscroft US

Moonlight. abr. ed. Suzanne Forster. Perf. by Kim Zimmer & Robert Newman. 2 cass. (Running Time: 3 hrs.). (My Romance Ser.: 3). 1999. 14.95 (978-0-9661644-2-8(3)) Renaiss Prodns.
Romance performed by daytime television stars of "Guiding Light.".

***Moonlight.** unabr. ed. Cynthia Rylant. Read by Suzanne Toren. (ENG.). 2009. (978-0-06-178456-9(7)); (978-0-06-190264-2(0)) HarperCollins Pubs.

Moonlight becomes Her. Meagan McKinney. Narrated by Richard Ferrone. 9 cass. (Running Time: 13 hrs. 15 mins.). 82.00 (978-1-4025-3445-4(0)) Recorded Bks.

Moonlight Becomes You. abr. ed. Mary Higgins Clark. Read by Megan Gallagher. (Running Time: 30 hrs. 0 mins. 0 sec.). (ENG.). 2009. audio compact disk 9.99 (978-0-7435-8352-7(3)) Pub: S&S Audio. Dist(s): S and S Inc

Moonlight Becomes You. unabr. ed. Mary Higgins Clark. Read by Mary Peiffer. 7 cass. (Running Time: 10 hrs. 30 min.). 1996. 56.00 (978-0-7366-3522-6(X), 4159) Books on Tape.
It's a pleasant surprise for Maggie Holloway, a photographer, when she's re-united with her former stepmother, Nuala Moore, at a Manhattan party. But happiness turns to tragedy when Maggie finds Nuala dead in her Newport, Rhode Island house.

Moonlight Express. Perf. by Fred Penner. 1 cass. (Running Time: 1 hr. 30 min.). (J). (ps-5). 1998. 10.98 (978-0-945267-52-2(5), YM084-CN); audio compact disk 13.98 (978-0-945267-53-9(3), YM084-CD) Youngheart Mus.
Songs include:"A Wish to Grow on"; "Moonlight Express"; "Stories Live"; "Music Is Everywhere"; "Don't Be Afraid"; "Family of Man"; "From the Heart"; "Growing"; "Build a Fort"; "It's No Secret"; "Tears"; "I'm Going to Go Back There Someday"; "Stardust" & "Simply Because of You.".

Moonlight Madness. John R. Erickson. Illus. by Gerald L. Holmes. 2 cass. (Running Time: 3 hrs.). (Hank the Cowdog Ser.: No. 23). (J). (gr. 2-5). 1994. 16.95 (978-0-87719-253-4(7), 9253) Lone Star Bks.

Moonlight Madness. unabr. ed. John R. Erickson. 1 cass. (Running Time: 1 hr. 30 mins.). (Hank the Cowdog Ser.: No. 23). (J). 2001. 24.00 (978-0-7366-6156-0(5)) Books on Tape.
Hank's efforts to keep Eddy, the orphaned raccoon, out of trouble causes him to land in hot water.

Moonlight Madness. unabr. ed. John R. Erickson. Read by John R. Erickson. 2 cass. (Running Time: 3 hrs.). (Hank the Cowdog Ser.: No. 23). (J). (gr. 2-5). 2001. 16.95 (978-0-7366-6912-2(4)) Books on Tape.

Moonlight Madness. unabr. ed. John R. Erickson. 2 CDs. (Running Time: 2 hrs.). (Hank the Cowdog Ser.: No. 23). 2001. audio compact disk 28.00 (978-0-7366-7545-1(0)) Books on Tape.
Hank's efforts to keep Eddy, the orphaned raccoon, out of trouble causes him to land in hot water.

Moonlight Madness. unabr. ed. John R. Erickson. Read by John R. Erickson. 2 cass. (Running Time: 3 hrs.). (Hank the Cowdog Ser.: No. 23). (J). 2002. 17.99 (978-1-59188-323-4(7)) Maverick Bks.
Slim rescues an orphan raccoon, and much to Hank's dismay, everyone on the ranch is enchanted with the "cute" baby coon with the beady little eyes and amazing little hands. Yet, little do they know that every midnight rolls around, Eddy the Rac is seized with uncontrollable fits and it's Hank's responsibility to guard the crafty masked bandit every moment!.

Moonlight Madness. unabr. ed. John R. Erickson. Read by John R. Erickson. 3 CDs. (Running Time: Approx. 3 hours). (Hank the Cowdog Ser.: No. 23). (J). 2002. audio compact disk 19.99 (978-1-59188-623-5(6)) Maverick Bks.
Hank the Cowdog could have told Slim that bringing an orphaned raccoon back to the ranch was not the best idea. But since Slim never pays any attention to Hank, Loper and Sally May soon find themselves housing an adolescent coon with a mischievous streak a mile wide. As the Head of Ranch Security, Hank?s got to keep an eye on Eddy the Rac. So when Eddy starts claiming ?Moonlight Madness??a crazed restlessness brought on by the light of the moon?it?s up to Hank to find a way to keep him from getting into trouble. The only problem is, whenever Hank tries to stop Eddy, he?s the one who ends up in hot water!New songs in this hilarious adventure for the whole family include ?Cowboy Transfusion? and ?Free the Cookies.?.

Moonlight Madness. unabr. ed. John R. Erickson. Read by John R. Erickson. 2 cass. (Hank the Cowdog Ser.: No. 23). (J). (gr. 2-5). 1998. 17.00 (21662) Recorded Bks.

***Moonlight Mile.** unabr. ed. Dennis Lehane. 2010. (978-0-06-206418-9(5), Harper Audio); (978-0-06-202362-9(4), Harper Audio); audio compact disk 34.99 (978-0-06-201086-5(7), Harper Audio) HarperCollins Pubs.

Moonlight on the Magic Flute. unabr. ed. Mary Pope Osborne. Read by Mary Pope Osborne. (Magic Tree House Ser.: No. 41). (J). (gr. 1). 2009. audio compact disk 14.95 (978-0-7393-7292-0(0), Listening Lib) Pub: Random Audio Pubg. Dist(s): Random

Moonlight on the Millpond. Lori Wick. Read by Barbara Rosenblat. (Running Time: 8 hrs.). (Tucker Mills Trilogy). 2005. audio compact disk 63.00 (978-0-7861-7834-6(5)) Blckstn Audio.

Moonlight on the Millpond. unabr. ed. Lori Wick. Narrated by Barbara Rosenblat. (Tucker Mills Trilogy). (ENG.). (YA). 2005. 24.49 (978-1-60814-311-5(2)); audio compact disk 25.99 (978-1-58926-894-4(6)) Oasis Audio.

Moonlighters. unabr. ed. Ray Hogan. Read by William Dufris. 4 cass. (Running Time: 4 hrs.). (Sagebrush Western Ser.). (J). 1998. 44.95 (978-1-57490-222-8(9)) Pub: ISIS Lrg Prnt GBR. Dist(s): Ulverscroft US

***Moonlit Earth.** unabr. ed. Christopher Rice. (Running Time: 12 hrs. 0 mins.). 2010. 29.95 (978-1-4417-4276-6(X)); 72.95 (978-1-4417-4272-8(7)); audio compact disk 29.95 (978-1-4417-4275-9(1)); audio compact disk 105.00 (978-1-4417-4273-5(5)) Blckstn Audio.

Moonlit Eyes. unabr. ed. Emma Blair. Read by Rowena Cooper. 10 cass. (Running Time: 15 hrs.). 2003. 84.95 (978-0-7540-0879-8(7)) AudioGO.

Moonlit Road see Classic Ghost Stories, Vol. 1, A Collection

Moonlit Road see Horseman in the Sky

Moonlit Road: And Other Stories. abr. ed. Ambrose Bierce et al. Read by Clare Anderson. 2. (Running Time: 8782 sec.). (Classic Fiction Ser.). 2007. audio compact disk 17.98 (978-962-634-494-1(6), Naxos AudioBooks) Naxos.

Moonpool. unabr. ed. P. T. Deutermann. Read by Mel Foster. (Running Time: 12 hrs.). 2008. 39.25 (978-1-4233-3621-1(6), 9781423336211, BADLE); 24.95 (978-1-4233-3620-4(8), 9781423336204, BAD) Brilliance Audio.

Moonpool. unabr. ed. Peter T. Deutermann. Read by Mel Foster. 12 CDs. (Running Time: 43200 sec.). 2008. audio compact disk 36.95 (978-1-4233-3616-7(X), 9781423336167, Bril Audio CD Unabri); audio compact disk 24.95 (978-1-4233-3618-1(6), 9781423336181, Brilliance MP3); audio compact disk 39.25 (978-1-4233-3619-8(4), 9781423336198, Brinc Audio MP3 Lib); audio compact disk 112.25 (978-1-4233-3617-4(8), 9781423336174, BriAudCD Unabrid) Brilliance Audio.

Moonraker. unabr. ed. Ian Fleming. Read by Robert Whitfield. 5 cass. (Running Time: 7 hrs.). (James Bond Ser.). 2000. 39.95 (978-0-7861-1898-4(9), 2691); audio compact disk 48.00 (978-0-7861-9796-5(X), 2691) Blckstn Audio.
Bond is back...facing a deadly countdown in this fast-paced thriller about a sadistic genius, a beautiful lady spy & a super rocket that can blow the world sky high.

Moonraker. unabr. ed. Ian Fleming. Read by Simon Vance. 6 CDs. (Running Time: 7 hrs.). 2009. audio compact disk 19.95 (978-1-4332-5854-1(4)) Blckstn Audio.

Moonraker. unabr. ed. Ian Fleming. Read by David Rintoul. 6 cass. (Running Time: 9 hrs.). (James Bond Ser.: Bk. 3). 1998. 49.95 (978-0-7451-5931-7(1), CAB 147) Pub: Chivers Audio Bks GBR. Dist(s): AudioGO
James Bond is asked to settle an ungentlemanly dispute. The accused is Sir Hugo Drax, business tycoon and head of the million dollar Moonraker missile program. Soon, however, the dispute takes on serious implications, and Bond finds out the bizarre truth about Drax and Moonraker. Truth that could prove fatal for 007 and millions of people.

Moonraker Mutiny. Antony Trew. 2007. 69.95 (978-1-84559-668-2(4)) Pub: Soundings Ltd GBR. Dist(s): Ulverscroft US

Moonrise to Mourning: Memoir. Short Stories. (3071) Am Audio Prose.

Moon's Nodes. Karl A. Jensen. 1 cass. (Running Time: 1 hr. 30 min.). 1992. 8.95 (1049) Am Fed Astrologers.

Moon's the North Wind's Cooky see Poetry of Vachel Lindsay

Moonshine: A Life in Pursuit of White Liquor. unabr. collector's ed. Alec Wilkinson. Read by Grover Gardner. 4 cass. (Running Time: 4 hrs.). 1987. 24.00 (978-0-7366-1193-0(2), 2111) Books on Tape.
Features a portrait of an American original - a modern day "revenuer," Garland Bunting.

***Moonshine War.** unabr. ed. Elmore Leonard. Read by Mark Hammer. (ENG.). 2010. (978-0-06-199758-7(7), Harper Audio); (978-0-06-199366-4(2), Harper Audio) HarperCollins Pubs.

Moonshine War. unabr. ed. Elmore Leonard. Narrated by Mark Hammer. 5 cass. (Running Time: 7 hrs. 30 mins.). 1996. 44.00 (978-0-7887-0504-5(0), 94696E7) Recorded Bks.
Leonard, master of the gangster thriller, takes the listener out of the city & into the heart of the Kentucky moonshine country. When a resourceful bootlegger tries to outwit a determined federal marshal during Prohibition, the result is a potent, 100-proof adventure.

Moonshine War. unabr. collector's ed. Elmore Leonard. Read by Alexander Adams. 6 cass. (Running Time: 6 hrs.). 1995. 36.00 (978-0-7366-3068-9(6), 3750) Books on Tape.
In prohibition, Son Martin will shoot, scratch, claw, kick & connive to keep a huge stash of Kentucky whiskey. Who'll take him on.

Moonshiner's Gold. unabr. ed. John R. Erickson. Read by Rooster Morris. 4 cass. (Running Time: 6 hrs.). (Tales of Wolves Ser.: Vol. #2). (J). 2001. 32.00 (978-0-7366-8096-7(9)) Books on Tape.
Riley McDaniels lives with his mother and brother in the panhandle of Texas during the time of Prohibition. One day, he discovers that moonshiners have built a still in a lonely canyon on his family's land, and are making whiskey. When he tries to report this to the law, he finds that no one will help him. Then he receives an eviction notice from his Aunt Mattie, who rents the family its house and land. Riley and his entire family must go to the corrupt boomtown of Sparrow. They discover that Aunt Mattie is being poisoned and manipulated, but this is just the first thread in a web of crime that they must try to tear down.

***Moonshot: The Flight of Apollo 11.** Brian Floca. Illus. by Brian Floca. Narrated by Asa Dorfman. 1 CD. (Running Time: 14 mins.). (J). (gr. 2-5). 2009. audio compact disk 29.95 (978-0-8045-4206-7(6)) Spoken Arts.

***Moonshot: The Flight of Apollo 11.** Brian Floca. Illus. by Brian Floca. Narrated by Asa Dorfman. 1 cass. (Running Time: 14 mins.). (J). (gr. 2-7). 2009. 27.95 (978-0-8045-6981-1(9)) Spoken Arts.

Moonstick: The Seasons of the Sioux. unabr. ed. Eve Bunting. Narrated by Peter Frances James. 1 cass. (Running Time: 15 mins.). (gr. k up). 1998. 10.00 (978-0-7887-1791-8(X), 95263E7) Recorded Bks.
A young Native-American boy discovers the marvelous changes in the world around him, as his father explains each of the 13 moons in the Sioux calendar.

Moonstick: The Seasons of the Sioux. unabr. ed. Eve Bunting. Read by Peter Francis James. 1 cass. (Running Time: 15 min.). (J). 1997. bk. 31.70 (978-0-7887-1832-8(0), 40612); bk. 167.80 (978-0-7887-3927-9(1), 46348) Recorded Bks.

Moonstone. Wilkie Collins. Read by Ian Holm. 14 cass. (Running Time: 20 hrs.). 1988. 87.95 C to C Cassettes.

Moonstone. Wilkie Collins. (Running Time: 4 hrs.). 1999. 24.95 (978-1-60083-850-7(2)) Iofy Corp.

Moonstone. Wilkie Collins. Adapted by Brian Gear. 6 cass. 29.95 (SCN 140) J Norton Pubs.
THe publication of this book in 1868 established Collins as the father of English fiction. Sergeant Cuff sets out to find the missing Moonstone.

Moonstone. Wilkie Collins. 15 cass. (Running Time: 25 hrs.). 1989. 89.00 (C-127) Jimcin Record.
Great detective story. Includes album.

Moonstone. Wilkie Collins. Read by Clive Swift et al. 3 cass. (Running Time: 4 hrs.). 1995. 17.98 (978-962-634-527-6(6), NA302714, Naxos AudioBooks) Naxos.
When Rachel Verinder inherits the moonstone, a huge & priceless diamond, her delight turns to dismay when the gem disappears mysteriously. Drama & suspense fill this first & magnificent English detective novel.

Moonstone. Narrated by David Thom. Prod. by Alcazar AudioWorks. Engineer Scott Weiser. Wilkie Collins. B. J. Bedford. (ENG.). 2009. audio compact disk 49.95 (978-0-9821853-5-3(9)) Alcazar AudioWorks.

Moonstone. abr. ed. Wilkie Collins. Read by Clive Swift et al. 3 CDs. (Running Time: 4 hrs.). 1995. audio compact disk 22.98 (978-962-634-027-1(4), NA302712, Naxos AudioBooks) Naxos.
When Rachel Verinder inherits the moonstone, a huge & priceless diamond, her delight turns to dimay when the gem disappears mysteriously. Drama & suspense fill this first & magnificent English detective novel.

Moonstone. unabr. ed. Wilkie Collins. Read by Flo Gibson. 12 cass. (Running Time: 17 hrs. 30 min.). 1998. 39.95 (978-1-55685-553-5(2)) Audio Bk Con.
This detective story, traces an enormous Indian diamond through theft, murder & baffling situations which are narrated by various fascinating characters.

Moonstone. unabr. ed. Wilkie Collins. Narrated by Wilkie Collins. 14 cass. (Running Time: 21 hrs.). 1989. 112.00 (978-1-55690-348-9(0), 89300E7) Recorded Bks.
A priceless, yellow diamond is missing. Police Sgt. Cuff must recover it & catch the thief.

***Moonstone.** unabr. ed. Wilkie Collins. Narrated by James Langton. (Running Time: 21 hrs. 30 mins.). 2010. 24.99 (978-1-4001-8944-1(6)); 29.99 (978-1-4001-6944-3(5)); 39.99 (978-1-4001-9944-0(1)); audio compact disk 95.99 (978-1-4001-4944-5(4)); audio compact disk 39.99 (978-1-4001-1944-8(8)) Pub: Tantor Media. Dist(s): IngramPubServ

Moonstone, Pt. 1. unabr. ed. Wilkie Collins. Read by Walter Zimmerman et al. 8 cass. (Running Time: 12 hrs.). 1986. 56.95 (978-0-7861-0553-3(4), 2047-A) Blckstn Audio.
The moonstone - originally stolen from an Indian shrine - is given to an English girl on her eighteenth birthday but disappears that same night. What follows is a spellbinding mystery full of danger & suspense.

Moonstone, Pt. 1. unabr. collector's ed. Wilkie Collins. Read by Walter Covell & Jill Masters. 8 cass. (Running Time: 12 hrs.). 1984. 64.00 (978-0-7366-3896-8(2), 9127-A) Books on Tape.
Classic early mystery novel, published in 1868, concerning the disappearance of a large diamond.

Moonstone, Pt. 2. collector's ed. Wilkie Collins. Read by Walter Zimmerman. 7 cass. (Running Time: 10 hrs. 30 min.). (J). 1984. 56.00 (978-0-7366-3897-5(0), 9127-B) Books on Tape.

Moonstone, Pt. 2. unabr. ed. Wilkie Collins. Read by Walter Zimmerman et al. 7 cass. (Running Time: 10 hrs. 30 mins.). 1986. 49.95 (978-0-7861-0554-0(2), 2047-B) Blckstn Audio.
The moonstone - originally stolen from an Indian shrine - is given to an English girl on her eighteenth birthday but disappears that same night. What follows is a spellbinding mystery full of danger & suspense.

***Moopy the Underground Monster.** Cari Meister. Illus. by Dennis Messner. (Monster Friends Ser.). (ENG.). 2010. audio compact disk 14.60 (978-1-4342-2590-0(9)) CapstoneDig.

Moor. Laurie R. King. Narrated by Jenny Sterlin. 9 CDs. (Running Time: 10 hrs. 45 mins.). (Mary Russell Mystery Ser.: Vol. 4). audio compact disk 89.00 (978-0-7887-4477-8(1)) Recorded Bks.

Moor. unabr. ed. Laurie R. King. Narrated by Jenny Sterlin. 8 cass. (Running Time: 10 hrs. 45 mins.). (Mary Russell Mystery Ser.: Vol. 4). 1998. 75.00 (978-0-7887-1979-0(3), 95366E7) Recorded Bks.
Mary Russel-Sherlock Holmes adventure in which a ghostly coach & giant dog have been spotted on Dartmoor - the chilling landscape of the "Hound of the Baskervilles".

Moor. unabr. ed. Laurie R. King & Walter Satterthwait. Narrated by Jenny Sterlin & Christian Moore. 8 CDs. (Running Time: 9 hrs. 30 mins.). (Mary Russell Mystery Ser.: Vol. 4). 2000. audio compact disk 78.00 (978-0-7887-4765-6(7), C1174E7) Recorded Bks.
A ghostly coach & a giant dog have been spotted on Dartmoor - the chilling landscape of the Hound of the Baskervilles.

Moorchild. unabr. ed. Eloise Jarvis McGraw. Narrated by Virginia Leishman. 5 pieces. (Running Time: 6 hrs.). (gr. 6 up). 1998. 44.00 (978-0-7887-1920-2(3), 95341E7) Recorded Bks.
Newberry's Medal Winning story of Saaski, a changeling, half human, half fairy, who manages in her own way to come to terms with both of the worlds which reject her & to make her own place in the human world.

Moorchild. unabr. ed. Eloise Jarvis McGraw. Read by Virginia Leishman. 5 cass. (Running Time: 6 hrs.). (YA). (gr. 5). 1998. 67.00 (978-0-7887-1948-6(3), 40655) Recorded Bks.
Mogl's mother is one of the Folk, one of those tiny faires who live hidden from mere mortals, but her father is human.

Moore's Rules of Federal Practice Teleconference: Recent Developments in Class Actions & the Impact of the Class Action Fairness Act Audio CD (November 2007) 2007. 149.00 (978-1-59579-778-0(5)) Pub: LexisNexis Mealey. Dist(s): LEXIS Pub

Moore's Rules of Federal Practice Teleconference: Tutorial of Procedural Federal Practice in Light of the Recent Rules Changes Audio CD (January 2008) 2008. 149.00 (978-1-59579-757-5(2)) Pub: LexisNexis Mealey. Dist(s): LEXIS Pub

Moose Tracks. Mary Casanova. Narrated by Johnny Heller. 2 CDs. (Running Time: 2 hrs. 15 mins.). (gr. 4 up). audio compact disk 22.00 (978-1-4025-0466-2(7)) Recorded Bks.

Moose Tracks. Mary Casanova. Narrated by Johnny Heller. 2 pieces. (Running Time: 2 hrs. 15 mins.). (gr. 4 up). 2001. 19.00 (978-0-7887-5365-7(7)) Recorded Bks.
While following animal tracks into the woods. Seth discovers a moose and her calf. Gunshots ring out. The calf is wounded and its mother killed. Seth has found the poachers his father warned him about. But the poachers have found him, too.

Moose Who Wanted to Be a Dragon; Luke & the Christmas Reindeer. unabr. ed. Ned Ackerman. Read by Leitha Christie. 1 cass. (Running Time: 58 min.). (J). (ps-4). 1994. 9.95 (978-1-889112-00-8(3)) Earbks.
Two Christmas stories set in Maine.

Moot Court Success. 2nd unabr. rev. ed. Matthew Moffett. 3 cass. (Running Time: 3 hrs. 30 mins.). (Outstanding Professors Ser.). 1996. 55.00 (978-1-57793-026-6(6), 28420, West Lglwrks) West.
Lecture on moot court techniques given by an outstanding American law school professor.

Mop Top. Don Freeman. Illus. by Don Freeman. (Running Time: 14 mins.). 1982. audio compact disk 12.95 (978-1-59519-058-1(9)) Live Oak Media.

Mop Top. Don Freeman. Illus. by Don Freeman. (Running Time: 14 mins.). (J). (ps-2). 1982. 9.95 (978-1-59112-093-3(4)) Live Oak Media.

Mop Top. unabr. ed. Don Freeman. 1 read along cass. (Running Time: 14 min.). (J). 1982. 9.95 Live Oak Media.
Moppy's disregard for his personal appearance, epitomized by his shaggy, unkempt hair, vanishes when he finally sees himself as others see him.

Mop Top. unabr. ed. Don Freeman. Read by Jerry Terheyden. 1 read along cass. (Running Time: 14 mins.). (J). (gr. k-3). 1982. pap. bk. 16.95 (978-0-941078-12-2(4)); pap. bk. & tchr. ed. 33.95 (978-0-941078-13-9(2)) Live Oak Media.

Mopwater Files. unabr. ed. John R. Erickson. 1 cass. (Running Time: 1 hr. 30 mins.). (Hank the Cowdog Ser.: No. 28). (J). 2001. 24.00 (978-0-7366-6161-4(1)) Books on Tape.
Despite drinking a bucket full of mop water, Hank still has the strength to take on a Dobert Pinscher who is after Beulah.

Mopwater Files. unabr. ed. John R. Erickson. Read by John R. Erickson. 2 cass. (Running Time: 3 hrs.). (Hank the Cowdog Ser.: No. 28). (J). (gr. 2-5). 2001. 16.95 (978-0-7366-6917-7(5)) Books on Tape.
Despite drinking a bucket full of mop water, Hank still has the strength to take on a Doberman Pinscher who is after Beulah.

Mopwater Files. unabr. ed. John R. Erickson. 2 CDs. (Running Time: 2 hrs.). (Hank the Cowdog Ser.: No. 28). (J). 2001. audio compact disk 28.00 (978-0-7366-7550-5(7)) Books on Tape.
Despite drinking a bucket full of mop water, Hank still has the strength to take on a Dobert Pinscher who is after Beulah.

Mopwater Files. unabr. ed. John R. Erickson. Read by John R. Erickson. 2 cass. (Running Time: 3 hrs.). (Hank the Cowdog Ser.: No. 28). (J). 2002. 17.99 (978-1-59188-328-9(8)) Maverick Bks.
Hank discovers an elixir that gives him a huge burst of energy-Sally May's bucket of root stimulator. It gives him such a kick, he challenges Rufus, the Doberman Pincher to a fight, only to discover that Sally May has filled the bucket with mopwater. Big trouble for the Head of Ranch Security.

Mopwater Files. unabr. ed. John R. Erickson. Read by John R. Erickson. 3 CDs. (Running Time: Approx. 3 hours). (Hank the Cowdog Ser.: No. 28). (J). 2002. audio compact disk 19.99 (978-1-59188-628-0(7)) Maverick Bks.
Rufus the Doberman Pinscher has come to the ranch, and he?s harassing the girl of Hank?s dreams?the beautiful Miss Beulah the Collie. Meanwhile, Hank is suffering a serious case of mopwater poisoning. In his weakened condition, he enlists the help of that crafty little owl, Madame Moonshine. But before he knows it, Madame Moonshine is trapped in Rufus? clutches. Can Hank find a way to overcome the deadly poison and save the day?Hank sings ?The Mopwater Song? and Rip and Snort sing ?We?re Proud to be Ignoramuses? in this hilarious adventure for the whole family.

Mopwater Files. unabr. ed. John R. Erickson. Read by John R. Erickson. 2 cass. (Running Time: 3 hrs.). (Hank the Cowdog Ser.: No. 28). (J). (gr. 2-5). 1998. 17.00 (21667) Recorded Bks.

Moral & Religious Ideas CD: Davies Memorial Address. Speeches. Adlai E. Steven, Jr. 1 CD. (Running Time: 55 mins.). 2006. audio compact disk 12.95 (978-1-57970-407-0(7), C27006D, Audio-For) J Norton Pubs.
First memorial service for Rev. A. Powell Davies, in which Stevenson talks on the interrelations of moral and religious ideas with the realm of politics. Rev. Davies was a noted Unitarian minister who was a staunch advocate of free speech and the right to dissent.

Moral Aspects of Foreign Policy. unabr. ed. Eugene McCarthy. 1 cass. (Running Time: 43 min.). 12.95 (27012) J Norton Pubs.

Moral Compass: Stories for a Life's Journey, Vol. 1. William J. Bennett. 2004. 15.95 (978-0-7435-4144-2(8)) Pub: S&S Audio. Dist(s): S and S Inc

Moral Courage: Effecting Positive Change Through Our Moral & Spiritual Choices. Daya Mata. 1 cass. (Running Time: 1 hr. 30 min.). 1991. 6.50 (2128) Self Realization.
In this talk, Daya Mata speaks with candor & deep compassion about our need to understand & live in harmony with the eternal principles of happiness. Topics include: The causes of today's moral crisis; repercussions of the "sexual revolution"; the power of a positive example - in the home, school & community; the most effective way to help people; learning to trust in God's unconditional forgiveness.

Moral Courage: How Do We Obtain It? unabr. ed. Myrtle Smith. Prod. by David Keyston. 1 CD. (Running Time: 1 hrs. 20 min.). (Myrtle Smyth Audiotapes Ser.). 1998. audio compact disk (978-1-893107-02-1(7), M2, Cross & Crown) Healing Unltd.

Moral Dilemmas in the Professions. 3 cass. Incl. Moral Dilemmas in the Professions: Moral Dilemmas in Business. Oliver E. Rodgers. 1978.; Moral Dilemmas in the Professions: Moral Dilemmas in Education. Dulany Seaver. 1978.; Moral Dilemmas in the Professions: Moral Dilemmas in the Medical Field. William P. Camp. 1978.; 1978. 12.00; 4.50 ea. Pendle Hill.

Moral Dilemmas in the Professions: Moral Dilemmas in Business see Moral Dilemmas in the Professions

Moral Dilemmas in the Professions: Moral Dilemmas in Education see Moral Dilemmas in the Professions

Moral Dilemmas in the Professions: Moral Dilemmas in the Medical Field see Moral Dilemmas in the Professions

Moral Disorder. unabr. ed. Margaret Atwood. 5 cass. (Running Time: 7 hrs.). 2006. 45.00 (978-1-4159-3344-2(8)) Books on Tape.

Moral Disorder: And Other Stories. unabr. ed. Margaret Atwood. Read by Susan Denaker. 7 CDs. (Running Time: 7 hrs.). 2006. audio compact disk 68.85 (978-1-4159-3345-9(6)) Pub: Books on Tape. Dist(s): NetLibrary CO

Moral Disorder: And Other Stories. unabr. ed. Margaret Atwood. Read by Susan Denaker. (Running Time: 27000 sec.). (ENG.). 2006. audio compact disk 34.95 (978-0-7393-4051-6(4), Random AudioBks) Pub: Random Audio Pubg. Dist(s): Random

Moral Economics: Classical Political Economy & Cultural Authority in Nineteenth-Century England. Claudia C. Klaver. 2003. audio compact disk 9.95 (978-0-8142-9021-7(3)) Pub: Ohio St U Pr. Dist(s): Chicago Distribution Ctr

Moral Essays. abr. ed. Seneca. Read by Robert L. Halvorson. 4 cass. (Running Time: 3 hrs.). 28.95 (18) Halvorson Assocs.

Moral Factor. Ayn Rand. Read by Ayn Rand. 1 cass. (Running Time: 1 hr. 30 min.). 12.95 (978-1-56114-009-1(0), AR22C) Second Renaissance.
Ayn Rand depicts the people's desperate quest for genuine moral guidance - & the intellectuals' refusal to provide anything other than mildewed "public-interest" bromides. The highlight of this lecture is a penetrating portrait of the psychology of the welfare state. She describes how Sweden, the model of allegedly benign collectivism, is driven, by envy, to inculcate

"the spirit of serfdom & of chronic guilt," as it seeks to prevent any individual from rising above mass mediocrity.

Moral Intelligence of Children: How to Raise a Moral Child. unabr. ed. Robert Coles. Read by Arthur Addison. 8 cass. (Running Time: 8 hrs.). 1997. 48.00 (978-0-913369-85-2(3), 4381) Books on Tape.

***Moral Landscape: How Science Can Determine Human Values.** unabr. ed. Sam Harris. Read by Sam Harris. (Running Time: 7 hrs. 0 mins. 0 sec.). (ENG.). 2010. audio compact disk 29.99 (978-1-4423-0014-9(0)) Pub: S&S Audio. Dist(s): S and S Inc

Moral Meaning of the Bible: The What, How, & Why of Biblical Ethics, Vol. II. Reuven Kimelman. Ed. by Sergiu Simmel. Des. by Joanne Tarlin Franklin. Engineer David Sparr. 2007. per. 120.00 (978-0-9769330-3-8(9)) O Learn Co.

Moral Meaning of the Bible: The What, How, & Why of Biblical Ethics, Vol.I. Reuven Kimelman. Ed. by Sergiu Simmel. Des. by Joanne Tarlin Franklin. Engineer David Sparr. (ENG., 2006. per. 120.00 (978-0-9769330-2-1(0)) O Learn Co.

Moral of the Story: Folktales for Character Development. Bobby Norfolk & Sherry Norfolk. 1 CD. (Running Time: 58 mins.). 2000. audio compact disk 16.95 (978-0-87483-597-7(6)) Pub: August Hse. Dist(s): Natl Bk Netwk
Award-winning storytellers tell tales they use in character education programs in classrooms and with other groups.

Moral of the Story: Folktales for Character Development. Bobby Norfolk & Sherry Norfolk. 1 cass. (Running Time: 58 mins.). (World Storytelling from August House Ser.). (gr. 3-7). 2000. 12.00 (978-0-87483-595-3(X)) Pub: August Hse. Dist(s): Natl Bk Netwk

Moral or Less: An Adventure in Addition & Subtraction. Maxine Nodel. Illus. by Norman Nodel. (Arithmetic Math Ser.). (J). (ps-3). 1990. 9.00 (978-0-922613-28-1(1)) Hachai Pubng.

Moral Sense. James Q. Wilson. Read by Nadia May. 2000. audio compact disk 19.95 (2757) Blckstn Audio.
Wilson admits in the preface of his book that "virtue has acquired a bad name." However, people make some kind of reference to morality whenever they discuss whether or not someone is kind, dependable, or decent; whether they have a good character; and the aspects of friendship, loyalty, and moderation that are all informed by morality. Although we may disguise this language of morality as a language of personality, it is, in Wilson's words, "the language of virtue and vice," which he uncovers in his book. He goes on to say, "This book is an effort to clarify what ordinary people mean when they speak of their moral feelings and to explain, insofar as one can, the origins of those feelings.

Moral Sense. James Q. Wilson. Narrated by Nadia May. (Running Time: 12 hrs.). 2000. 34.95 (978-1-59912-695-1(8)) Iofy Corp.

Moral Sense. unabr. ed. James Q. Wilson. Read by Nadia May. 8 cass. (Running Time: 11 hrs.). 2001. 56.95 (978-0-7861-1987-5(X), 2757); audio compact disk 80.00 (978-0-7861-9737-8(4), 2757) Blckstn Audio.

Moral Virtue. Leonard Peikoff. Read by Leonard Peikoff. 7 cass. (Running Time: 6 hrs. 30 min.). 1989. 79.00 (978-1-56114-014-5(7), LP09D) Second Renaissance.
This series features three lectures, each of which includes a question-&-answer period, plus a fourth session devoted entirely to a Q&A on general topics in Objectivism. The third talk, on independence. Dr. Peikoff first describes in detail how he initially presented the concept of independence his forthcoming book - & then explains why it was fundamentally mistaken, what misguided methodology he was employing & how he finally came to rewrite the sequence correctly.

Morality: Life or Death for a Nation. 7.00 (CLD) J Van Impe.
Features messages of love & hope, reconciliation & restoration.

Morality & Ethics. SERCON Panel. 1 cass. (Running Time: 1 hr.). 9.00 (A0120-87) Sound Photosyn.
A discussion at the Science Fiction writers convention featuring Donald Kingsbury, Randall, Dutcher, Winston & Lupoff.

Morality for Beautiful Girls. Alexander McCall Smith. 7 CDs. (Running Time: 8 hrs. 15 mins.). (No. 1 Ladies' Detective Agency Ser.: No. 3). 2004. audio compact disk 29.99 (978-1-4025-4368-5(9), 01112) Recorded Bks.

Morality for Beautiful Girls. unabr. ed. Alexander McCall Smith. 6 cass. (Running Time: 8 hrs. 15 min.). (No. 1 Ladies' Detective Agency Ser.: No. 3). 2003. 59.00 (978-1-4025-4743-0(9)) Recorded Bks.

Morality for Beautiful Girls. unabr. ed. Alexander McCall Smith. 5 cass. (Running Time: 8 hrs. 15 mins.). (No. 1 Ladies' Detective Agency Ser.: No. 3). 2004. 24.99 (978-1-4025-4179-7(1), 02984) Recorded Bks.

Morality Universe & the Light-Streams: Debts Past & Present. Jonathan Murro & Ann Ree Colton. 1 cass. 7.95 A R Colton Fnd.
Discusses the goal of God-Realization.

Morals & Dogma of the Ancient & Accepted Scottish Rite. Albert Pike. 2008. 124.95 (978-0-548-83705-4(8)) Kessinger Pub.

Morals in America: Homosexuality. Brad Harrub. (ENG.). 2008. audio compact disk 5.00 (978-0-9821815-0-8(7)) Focus Pr.

Morals in America: Medical Ethics. Brad Harrub. (ENG.). 2008. audio compact disk 5.00 (978-0-9821815-1-5(5)) Focus Pr.

Moratorium on Brains. Ayn Rand. Read by Ayn Rand. 2 cass. (Running Time: 1 hr. 83 min.). Incl. Moratorium on Brains: Questions & Answers. (Running Time: 60 min.). (AR04D); 24.95 (978-1-56114-018-3(X), AR04D) Second Renaissance.
A comprehensive indictment of Richard Nixon's imposition of a wage-price freeze to combat inflation. The range-of-the-moment pragmatism that makes Nixon regard economic totalitarianism as "free enterprise." The grotesque spectacle of trying to revive a nation's productivity -by-strait-jacketing the very people necessary to do it: the men of ability. An extensive question period covers such issues as: capital punishment; the definition of a human being with respect to abortion; the possibility of a philosophical reversal in America.

Moratorium on Brains. Comment by Ayn Rand. 2 cass. (Running Time: 1 hr. 50 min.). (Ford Hall Forum Ser.). 1971. 24.95 (AR04D) Second Renaissance.
Pt. 1: Comprehensive indictment of Nixon's wage-price freeze. Why business supported it, while labor unions, courageously, did not. Pt. 2: Q&A topics include: is capital punishment justified?; what is the definition of a human being, with respect to the issue of abortion?; is homosexuality immoral?; can America undergo a fundamental philosophic reversal.

Moratorium on Brains: Questions & Answers see Moratorium on Brains

Morbid Taste for Bones. Ellis Peters, pseud. Read by Patrick Tull. 5 Cass. (Running Time: 8.75 Hrs). 24.95 (978-1-4025-2356-4(4)) Recorded Bks.

Morbid Taste for Bones. unabr. ed. Ellis Peters. Read by Johanna Ward. 5 cass. (Running Time: 19800 sec.). (Chronicles of Brother Cadfael Ser.: Vol. 1). 1997. 39.95 (978-0-7861-1099-5(6), 1863) Blckstn Audio.
Soon after his arrival at the Benedictine monastery of Shrewsbury, Brother Cadfael finds himself on a mission to his Welsh homeland. Acting as translator, he must help his prior obtain the bones of Saint Winifred, which now rest in a small village grave. The Welsh villagers are loath to part with the relics of a martyr said to have miraculous powers, but before an agreement can be reached, the one villager most outspoken in his dissent is found murdered.

Morbid Taste for Bones. unabr. ed. Ellis Peters, pseud. Read by Patrick Tull. 8 CDs. (Running Time: 8.75 Hrs). audio compact disk 39.95 (978-1-4025-2379-3(3)) Recorded Bks.

Morbid Taste for Bones. unabr. ed. Ellis Peters, pseud. Narrated by Patrick Tull. 6 cass. (Running Time: 9 hrs.). (Chronicles of Brother Cadfael Ser.: Vol. 1). 1991. 51.00 (978-1-55690-349-6(9), 91206E7) Recorded Bks.
Cadfael's return to his Welsh homeland for a visit proves a rather discomfiting homecoming when an honorable nobleman turns up in a patch of forest with an arrow imbedded in his chest.

***Morbid Taste for Bones: The First Chronicle of Brother Cadfael.** unabr. ed. Ellis Peters. Read by Johanna Ward. (Running Time: 7 hrs.). 2010. 29.95 (978-1-4332-5826-8(9)); audio compact disk 69.00 (978-1-4332-5823-7(4)) Blckstn Audio.

Morcai Battalion. unabr. ed. Diana Palmer. Read by Todd McLaren. (YA). 2008. 59.99 (978-1-60514-964-6(0)) Find a World.

Morcai Battalion. unabr. ed. Diana Palmer. Narrated by Todd McLaren. (Running Time: 9 hrs. 30 mins. 0 sec.). (ENG.). 2007. audio compact disk 34.99 (978-1-4001-0583-0(8)); audio compact disk 69.99 (978-1-4001-3583-7(4)); audio compact disk 24.99 (978-1-4001-5583-5(5)) Pub: Tantor Media. Dist(s): IngramPubServ

Morceaux Choisis de la Litterature Francaise. Read by Jeanne Provost. 1 cass. (FRE.). 1987. 11.95 (SAC 985) Spoken Arts.

Morceaux Choisis de la Litterature Francaise. unabr. ed. 1 cass. (FRE.). 15.95 (CFR459) J Norton Pubs.

Mordechai Mouse & Other Tails for the Jewish Holidays. unabr. ed. Short Stories. Perf. by Naomi Leithold. 1 cass. (Running Time: 45 mins.). (J). 1995. 10.00 (978-0-9701891-1-0(7)) Simply Storytelling.

More about Codependence. Pia Mellody. Read by Pia Mellody. 6 cass. 50.00 (A12) Featuka Enter Inc.
Concentrates more on recovery & provides a more intellectual approach in order to teach about childhood trauma & focuses more on the path to recovery.

More about Henry. A. J. Goddard. 1 cass. (Running Time: 1 hr. 30 mins.). 2005. audio compact disk 12.95 (978-0-660-18679-5(9)) Pub: Canadian Broadcasting CAN. Dist(s): Georgetown Term
Billy goats and bulls. Square dances and harmonicas. Mechanization. Artificial insemination. Henry Haws' stories from a long life of farming were recorded by his grandson Adam Goddard and used to make this unusual and entertaining musical documentary.

More about Karmic Twenty-Ninth Degree. Susan Aiu. 1 cass. 8.95 (488) Am Fed Astrologers.
Natal, prog., trans., relocation, SR.

More about Paddington. unabr. ed. Michael Bond. Read by Stephen Fry. (Running Time: 9000 sec.). (J). (ps-3). 2007. 17.95 (978-0-06-076337-4(X), HarperChildAud) HarperCollins Pubs.

***More about Paddington.** unabr. ed. Michael Bond. Read by Stephen Fry. (ENG.). 2007. (978-0-06-147586-3(6)); (978-0-06-147587-0(4)) HarperCollins Pubs.

More Adventures of Gilly, the Guitar, Bk. 3. Cathy Ellis. 1 cass. (J). (ps-2). 1993. pap. bk. 17.95 (978-1-879542-09-9(9)) Ellis Family Mus.

More Adventures of Sherlock Holmes see Mas Aventuras de Sherlock Holmes

More Adventures of Sherlock Holmes. Arthur Conan Doyle. Read by Carlos Zambrano. (Running Time: 3 hrs.). 2002. 16.95 (978-1-60083-193-5(1), Audiofy Corp) Iofy Corp.

More Adventures of the Great Brain. John D. Fitzgerald. Read by Ron McLarty. 3 cass. (Running Time: 3 hrs. 24 mins.). (Great Brain Ser.). (J). (gr. 3-7). 2004. 30.00 (978-0-8072-0746-8(2), Listening Lib); pap. bk. & tchr.'s training gde. ed. 36.00 (978-0-8072-0860-1(4), Listening Lib) Random Audio Pubg.
J. D. idolizes his older brother Tom, a.k.a. The Great Brian, a silver-tongued con artist with a genius for making a profit.

More Adventures of the Superkids: CD #1. (J). 2005. audio compact disk (978-1-59833-970-3(2)) Rowland Reading.

More Adventures of the Superkids: CD #2. (J). 2005. audio compact disk (978-1-59833-971-0(0)) Rowland Reading.

More Adventures with Basie, The Electric Bass Guitar. Cathy Ellis. Perf. by Eric Bradley. Interview with Patricia Moya. 1 cass. (Complete Guide for the Guitar Ser.: Bk. 3). (J). (ps-2). 1993. 18.95 (978-1-879542-35-8(8), EFMBS3TP) Ellis Family Mus.
Can be used in conjunction with "The Adventures of Gilly, the Guitar." Continue with "Basie" learning to sight read basic music on the staff & on the electric bass. Pieces include: "School Days," "Oh Susanna," & "When the Saints Go Marching in".

More Adventures with Basie, the Electric Bass Guitar, Bk. 2. Cathy Ellis. Perf. by Eric Bradley. Interview with Patricia Moya. 1 cass. (Complete Guide for the Guitar Ser.). (J). (ps-2). 1993. 16.95 (978-1-879542-34-1(X), EFMBS2TP) Ellis Family Mus.
Can be used in conjunction with "The Adventures of Gilly, the Guitar." Continue learning with "Basie".

More Affairs of the Heart. unabr. ed. Virginia Woolf et al. Read by Jennifer Wiltsie & J. P. Linton. 1 cass. (Running Time: 1 hr. 30 min.). (Love Story Classics Ser.). (J). (gr. 8 up). 1994. 11.95 (978-0-9637488-2-9(3)) Love Story Class.
The second volume of an unabridged anthology of short stories on the theme of love, all stories written by famous authors.

More Alive Fitness & Companionship for Mature Adults. Joanne B. Murphy. 1 cass. (Running Time: 1 hr.). 1988. 12.95 (978-0-9623498-1-2(X)) Joanne L Murphy.
Designed to increase flexibility, strength & endurance, plus improve physical, mental & emotional health.

More All-of-a-Kind Family. Sydney Taylor. Read by Suzanne Toren. (Running Time: 4 hrs.). 2005. 21.95 (978-1-60083-557-5(0)) Iofy Corp.

More All-of-A-Kind Family. Sydney Taylor. Read by Suzanne Toren. (Running Time: 14400 sec.). (J). (gr. 4-7). 2006. audio compact disk 27.95 (978-1-59316-088-3(7)) Listen & Live.

More All-of-a-Kind Family. unabr. ed. Sydney Taylor. Narrated by Suzanne Toren. 3 cass. (Running Time: 4 hrs.). (Sydney Taylor Ser.). (J). (gr. 4 up). 2001. 21.95 (978-1-885408-64-8(1), LL054) Listen & Live.
Ella finds a boyfriend & Henny disagrees with Papa over her curfew. Thus, continues the tale of a Jewish family of five sisters - Ella, Henny, Sarah, Charlotte & Gertie - living at the turn of the century in New York's Lower East Side.

More All-of-A-Kind Family. unabr. ed. Sydney Taylor. Read by Suzanne Toren. (J). 2007. 34.99 (978-1-60252-487-3(4)) Find a World.

More American Heroes. Jonathon Sprout. 1 cass. (Running Time: 42 mins.). (J). 2000. 9.98 (978-0-9677954-1-6(9)) Sprout Recordings.
The songs provide good resource material for American history projects & units on historical figures such as Tecumseh, Neil Armstrong, Susan B. Anthony & Helen Keller & more.

More American Heroes. Jonathon Sprout. 1 CD. (Running Time: 42 mins.). (J). (gr. 4-8). 2000. audio compact disk 14.98 (978-0-9677954-0-9(0)) Sprout Recordings.

More American West in Fiction. unabr. ed. Bret Harte. Read by Eddie Rabbitt & J. Newton. 4 cass. (Running Time: 6 hrs.). 2001. 25.00 (978-1-59040-176-7(X), Phoenix Audio) Pub: Amer Intl Pub. Dist(s): PerseuPGW

More Arabian Tales see Mas Cuentos de las 1001 Noches

More Arabian Tales. Read by Laura García. (Running Time: 3 hrs.). 2001. 16.95 (978-1-60083-149-2(4), Audiofy Corp) Iofy Corp.

More Baby Songs. 1 cass. (J). 10.98 (226) MFLP CA.
Contains "Walking," "Tickly Toddle," "Sittin' in a High Chair," "Daddy be a Horsie," "Family Harmony" & 5 more.

More Baby Songs. Perf. by Hap Palmer. 1 cass. (J). (ps). 11.95 (EA 597C); 11.95 LP. (EA 597) Kimbo Educ.
Preschool songs for listening, singing & moving fun. Little Baby, Shout & Whisper, Sleepy Time Sea & more.

More Baby's First Fairy Tales. Penton. 1 cass. (Running Time: 1 hr. 30 min.). (Baby's First Ser.). (J). (ps). 2000. 8.95 (978-1-56015-742-7(9), Penton Kids) Penton Overseas.

More Basic Course. unabr. ed. Foreign Service Institute Staff. 18 cass. (Running Time: 18 hrs.). (YA). (gr. 10-12). 1994. pap. bk. 295.00 (978-0-88432-379-2(X), AFMR10) J Norton Pubs.
The principal language of Burkina Faso, formerly known as Upper Volta, in West Africa. Includes dialogs, basic sentences, extensive drills & practice.

More Bert & I. Narrated by Marshall Dodge & Robert Bryan. (Running Time: 33 min.). 8.95 (978-0-9607546-4-9(4), 5) Bert and I Inc.
Humorous tales from DownEast.

More Birding by Ear Eastern & Central North America: A Guide to Bird-Song Identification. unabr. ed. Richard K. Walton & Robert W. Lawson. Ed. by Roger Tory Peterson. 3 CDs. (Running Time: 3 hrs.). (Peterson Field Guide Audio Ser.). (ENG., 2000. audio compact disk 30.00 (978-0-618-22592-7(7)) HM Harcourt.

More Blues Jam Trax for Guitar. Ralph Agresta. 1997. audio compact disk 12.95 (978-0-8256-1602-0(6)) Pub: Music Sales. Dist(s): H Leonard

More Brains Than Bullets; The Road to Casa Piedras; West of Dodge. abr. ed. Louis L'Amour. (Running Time: 3 hrs.). (ENG.). 2009. audio compact disk 14.99 (978-0-7393-8316-2(7), Random AudioBks) Pub: Random Audio Pubg. Dist(s): Random

More Brazilian Music Acoustic Guitar. Carlos Barbosa-Lima. 1993. bk. 18.95 (978-0-7866-1194-2(4), 95073P) Mel Bay.

More Brazilian Music Acoustic Guitar. Carlos Barbosa-Lima. 1993. 10.98 (978-1-56222-901-6(X), 95073C) Mel Bay.

More Brazilian Music for Acoustic Guitar. Carlos Barbosa-Lima. 1993. pap. bk. 23.95 (978-0-7866-1193-5(6), 95073CDP) Mel Bay.

***More Cds & Book.** Foreign Service Institute. (ENG & MIS.). 2005. pap. bk. 296.00 (978-1-57970-318-9(6), Audio-For) J Norton Pubs.

More Charles Kuralt's American Moments. Read by Charles Kuralt. 2004. 7.95 (978-0-7435-1998-4(1)) Pub: S&S Audio. Dist(s): S and S Inc

More Cheers & Chants. Lynda Haller. (J). (gr. 3-12). 1988. 9.95 (978-0-9614174-5-1(5)) Cheertime USA.

More Classic American Short Stories. unabr. abr. ed. Ambrose Bierce et al. Read by Garrick Hagon & Liza Ross. 2 CDs. (Running Time: 9235 sec.). 2007. audio compact disk 17.98 (978-962-634-441-5(5), Naxos AudioBooks) Naxos.

More Complete Audio Writing (Nineteen Eighty-Seven) Richard Kostelanetz. 5 cass. (Running Time: 30 hrs.). 125.00 ea. Archae Edns.
Tape one includes many short pieces; two includes: New York City, The Gospels & Die Evangelien, all originally commissioned by European radio; three includes all six versions of Invocations in sequence; four includes four hours of Epiphanies in English, followed by German, Chinese & then Vietnamese.

More Complete Audio Writing (Nineteen Eighty-Seven) Richard Kostelanetz. Ed. by Richard Kostelanetz. 5 cass. (Running Time: 30 hrs.). bk. 500.00 (978-0-932360-84-7(X)) Archae Edns.

More Concentration see Mas Concentracion

More Content Words. Alana Trisler. (More Content Words Ser.). (gr. k-3). 2005. stu. ed. 2.30 (978-0-8388-6330-5(2)) Ed Pub Serv.

More Early Horror Works. H. P. Lovecraft. Narrated by Erik Sellin. 2008. audio compact disk 11.99 (978-0-9764805-6-3(5)) C CD Bks.

More Effective Prayer Life: Spanish Version. 2004. (978-1-59024-178-3(9)) B Hinn Min.

More Energy - Hypnosis. 1 CD . (Running Time: 50 mins.). (LBR Relaxation Ser.: No. 3). 1999. audio compact disk (978-0-9749845-2-0(3)) L Rubinstein.
Hypnosis CD. Track 1 is to be used as a power nap which will wake you up at the end. Track 2 is to be used to fall asleep to.

More English with a Smile. Barbara Zaffran & David Krulik. (English with a Smile Ser.: Bk. 3). 1995. 20.00 (978-0-8442-0576-2(1)) M-H Contemporary.

More Especially for Missionaries, Vol. 1. Ed J. Pinegar. Read by Ed J. Pinegar. 1 cass. (Running Time: 1 hr.). 1993. 4.98 (978-1-55503-591-4(4), 06004784) Covenant Comms.
How to have a great day on your mission.

More Especially for Missionaries, Vol. 2. Ed J. Pinegar. Read by Ed J. Pinegar. 1 cass. (Running Time: 1 hr.). 1993. 4.98 (978-1-55503-592-1(2), 06004776) Covenant Comms.
The purpose of missionary work.

More Excellent Way. Speeches. Chuck Missler & Nancy Missler. 2 CDs. (Running Time: 8100 sec.). (King's High Way Ser.). 2007. audio compact disk 14.95 (978-0-9795136-1-9(8)) Kings High Way.

More Excellent Way. Chuck Missler & Nancy Missler. 2 cass., notes. (Running Time: 3 hrs.). 1999. 14.95 (978-1-880532-43-0(3)) Koinonia Hse.
Is your marriage relationship all that you want it to be? Is it all God wants it to be? Just because we are Christians doesn't mean that we automatically have God's love flowing from our lives. Chuck & Nancy each relate their own story of how God turned their marriage around. Contains notes for further study.

More Excellent Way: The Marriage Turnaround of Chuck & Nancy Missler. Speeches. 1 MP3. (Running Time: 8100 sec.). (ENG.). 2007. audio compact disk 10.95 (978-0-9795136-0-2(X)) Kings High Way.

More Excellent Way: The Marriage Turnaround of Chuck & Nancy Missler. Chuck Missler & Nancy Missler. 2 cass. (Running Time: 3 hr. 30 mins.). (King's High Way Ser.). 1991. vinyl bd. 14.95 (978-1-880532-92-8(1)) Koinonia Hse.
Biblical basis for healing personal relationships. Include Notes.

More FabulousTales Told from My Front Room!, No. 6. Melea J. Brock. Illus. by Melea J. Brock. 1. (Running Time: 1 Hr.). Dramatization. 1997. 10.98 (978-0-9667455-6-6(6)) Right-Side-Up.

More Famous Composers, Vol. 2. abr. ed. Darren Henley. Read by Marin Alsop. (Running Time: 8212 sec.). (Junior Classics Ser.). 2007. audio compact disk 17.98 (978-962-634-422-4(9), Naxos AudioBooks) Naxos.

More Favorite Stories of Christmas Past. unabr. ed. Henry Van Dyke et al. (Running Time: 5 hrs. 0 mins. 0 sec.). (ENG.). 2008. audio compact disk 39.99 (978-1-4001-3822-7(1)) Pub: Tantor Media. Dist(s): IngramPubServ

More Favorite Stories of Christmas Past, Vol. 2. unabr. ed. Henry Van Dyke et al. Narrated by Joyce Bean & Simon Prebble. (Running Time: 5 hrs. 0 mins. 0 sec.). 2008. audio compact disk 19.99 (978-1-4001-5822-5(2)) Pub: Tantor Media. Dist(s): IngramPubServ

More Favorite Stories of Christmas Past, Vol. 2. unabr. ed. Henry Van Dyke et al. Narrated by Simon Prebble & Joyce Bean. (Running Time: 5 hrs. 0 mins. 0 sec.). 2008. audio compact disk 19.99 (978-1-4001-0822-0(5)) Pub: Tantor Media. Dist(s): IngramPubServ

More Fiedler's Favorites for Children. Perf. by Boston Pops Orchestra & Arthur Fiedler. 1 cass. (J). (ps up). 7.98 (262) MFLP CA.

Includes "Flight of the Bumblebee," "Song of India," "In the Hall of the Mountain King," "Bugler's Holiday," "Persian Market," "Carnival of the Animals," "Elephant," "Dance of the Sugar Plum Fairy," "Norwegian Rustic March," "The Arkansas Traveler," & "Sleigh Ride,".

More French - English. 1 cass. (Lyric Language Ser.). (FRE & ENG.). (J). 7.98 Blisterpack. (POI 513) NewSound.

More Funny Stuff You Can Do on the Piano. Duane Shinn. 1 cass. 19.95 (NS-9) Duane Shinn.

Presents 14 different things to do to create a laugh whenever the occasion calls for it.

More Games for the Road. unabr. ed. 1 cass. bk. 14.95 (S23953) J Norton Pubs.

Games designed to strengthen skills in language arts, math, social studies & science, range in difficulty so that pre-schoolers can enjoy some, older children will be challenged by others.

More German - English. 1 cass. (Lyric Language Ser.). (GER & ENG.). (J). 7.98 Blisterpack. (POI 515) NewSound.

More Good Boats. unabr. collector's ed. Roger C. Taylor. Read by Bob Erickson. 8 cass. (Running Time: 8 hrs.). 1984. 48.00 (978-0-7366-0525-0(8), 1499) Books on Tape.

More Gospel Truth. Contrib. by Gospel Truth Singers & Tom Fettke. (ENG.). 1997. audio compact disk 12.00 (978-0-00-520092-6(X)) Lillenas.

More Great Hymns Cd: More Great Hymns CD. Cd. audio compact disk 18.00 (978-0-89869-287-7(3)) Church Pub Inc.

More guided meditations from tony D'souza: 2 CD Set. Tony D'Souza. Voice by Tony D'Souza. 2009. audio compact disk 19.95 (978-0-9790304-4-4(7)) Broadband.

More Guitar Workshop. Composed by Jim Kelly. 1999. audio compact disk 14.95 (978-0-7935-9454-2(5), 00695306, Berklee Pr) H Leonard.

More Horror Movie Madness. 1 cass. (Running Time: 1 hr.). 1999. (4253-4); audio compact disk (4253-2) Audioscope.

Movie themes include: "Texas Chainsaw Massacre," "Night of the Living Dead," "Friday the 13th," "The Shining," "Nightmare on Elm Street," "Theme from Dracula," "Children of the Corn," "Jaws," "Rosemary's Baby," "Amityville Horror" & more. Includes 3-D graphics.

More hot Sex. Tracey Cox. Read by Marie-Louise Walker. (Running Time: 9 hrs. 45 mins.). 2009. 79.99 (978-1-74214-174-9(9), 9781742141749) Pub: Bolinda Pubng AUS. Dist(s): Bolinda Pub Inc

More Hot Sex. unabr. ed. Tracey Cox. Read by Marie-Louise Walker. 8 CDs. (Running Time: 9 hrs. 45 mins.). 2008. audio compact disk 87.95 (978-1-921415-39-5(8), 9781921415395) Pub: Bolinda Pubng AUS. Dist(s): Bolinda Pub Inc

More hot Sex. unabr. ed. Tracey Cox. Read by Marie-Louise Walker. (Running Time: 9 hrs. 45 mins.). 2009. 43.95 (978-1-74214-015-5(7), 9781742140155) Pub: Bolinda Pubng AUS. Dist(s): Bolinda Pub Inc

More I Praise You. Contrib. by Johnathan Crumpton & Luke Gambill. Prod. by Luke Gambill. (Worship Choir Ser.). (ENG.). 2008. audio compact disk 90.00 (978-5-557-46974-6(5), Brentwood-Benson Music) Brentwood Music.

More I Praise You: Alto. Contrib. by Johnathan Crumpton & Luke Gambill. Prod. by Russell Mauldin. (ENG.). 2008. audio compact disk 5.00 (978-5-557-46544-1(8), Brentwood-Benson Music) Brentwood Music.

More I Praise You: Bass. Contrib. by Johnathan Crumpton & Luke Gambill. Prod. by Russell Mauldin. (ENG.). 2008. audio compact disk 5.00 (978-5-557-46542-7(1), Brentwood-Benson Music) Brentwood Music.

More I Praise You: Passionate Songs for Passionate Worship. Contrib. by Ronnie Freeman & Luke Gambill. (Worship Choir Ser.). (ENG.). 2008. audio compact disk 16.99 (978-5-557-47017-9(4), Brentwood-Benson Music) Brentwood Music.

More I Praise You: Soprano. Contrib. by Johnathan Crumpton & Russell Mauldin. Prod. by Russell Mauldin. (ENG.). 2008. audio compact disk 5.00 (978-5-557-46545-8(6), Brentwood-Benson Music) Brentwood Music.

More I Praise You: Tenor. Contrib. by Johnathan Crumpton & Luke Gambill. Prod. by Russell Mauldin. (ENG.). 2008. audio compact disk 5.00 (978-5-557-46543-4(X), Brentwood-Benson Music) Brentwood Music.

More I See You. Perf. by Oscar Peterson et al. 1 cass., 1 CD. 7.98 (TA 33370); audio compact disk 12.78 CD Jewel box. (TA 83370) NewSound.

More Information Than You Require. John Hodgman. (ENG.). (YA). (gr. 8). 2008. audio compact disk 29.95 (978-0-14-314352-9(2), PengAudBks) Penguin Grp USA.

More Information Than You Require. unabr. ed. John Hodgman. Read by John Hodgman. (Running Time: 11 hrs.). (ENG.). (gr. 12 up). 2009. audio compact disk 34.95 (978-0-14-314513-4(4), PengAudBks) Penguin Grp USA.

More Irish Folktales for Children. Sharon Kennedy. 1 cass. (Running Time: 70 min.). (J). (gr. k-5). 2001. 8.99 (Round8110); audio compact disk 12.99 (Round8110) Rounder Records.

Captures the magic and adventure of Irish folklore with four tales. In "Annie O'Reilly and the Magic Dancing Pig," a selfish king meets his match in a clever girl whose pig possesses a special secret even more extraordinary than its ability to dance. Pegeen's dream in "Bannogue Bridge" yields a golden treasure for her impoverished family. In "Finn McCool," the legendary Irish giant finds himself needing the help of his tiny but tricky wife. "Tommy O'Rourke Visits the Moon" suggests the Irish folktale tradition as a small boy's ability to tell mesmerizing stories becomes more important than his lack of athletic prowess.

More Irish Stories for Christmas. John B. Keane. 1 cass. 1996. 11.95 (978-1-57098-108-1(6)) Robs Rinehart.

More Italian - English. 1 cass. (Lyric Language Ser.). (ITA & ENG.). (J). 7.98 Blisterpack. (POI 516) NewSound.

More Legends of the Great Lakes. Perf. by Carl Behrend. 2001. audio compact disk 14.99 (978-0-9728212-3-0(6)) Old Country Bks.

More Lessons in Leadership: Mac Hammond Speaks to Business Professionals about Growing in Influence. Mac Hammond. 4 cass. (Best of the Winner's Luncheons Ser.: Vol. 2). 1998. 24.00 (978-1-57399-075-2(2)) Mac Hammond.

More Lessons in Leadership: The Best of the Winner's Luncheons Vol 2. Mac Hammond. 4 CDs. (Running Time: 3 hours). 2002. audio compact disk 20.00 (978-1-57399-148-3(1)) Mac Hammond.

Mac Hammond speaks to business professionals about growing in influence.

More! Level 1 Class Audio CDs. Herbert Puchta et al. (Running Time: 2 hrs. 38 mins.). (ENG., 2008. audio compact disk 41.00 (978-0-521-71297-2(1)) Cambridge U Pr.

More! Level 1 Workbook with Audio CD Czech Edition. Herbert Puchta et al. (More! Ser.). 2009. pap. bk. 17.00 (978-0-521-18358-1(8)) Cambridge U Pr.

More! Level 2 Class Audio CDs. Herbert Puchta et al. (Running Time: 2 hrs. 17 mins.). (ENG., 2008. audio compact disk 43.05 (978-0-521-71304-7(8)) Cambridge U Pr.

More! Level 2 Workbook with Audio CD Czech Edition. Herbert Puchta et al. (More! Ser.). 2009. pap. bk. 17.00 (978-0-521-17214-1(4)) Cambridge U Pr.

More! Level 3 Class Audio CDs. Herbert Puchta et al. (Running Time: 2 hrs. 38 mins.). (ENG., 2008. audio compact disk 43.05 (978-0-521-71311-5(0)) Cambridge U Pr.

More! Level 3 Workbook with Audio CD Czech Edition. Herbert Puchta et al. (More! Ser.). 2009. pap. bk. 17.00 (978-0-521-18278-2(6)) Cambridge U Pr.

More! Level 4 Class Audio CDs (2) Herbert Puchta et al. (Running Time: 2 hrs. 10 mins.). (ENG., 2009. audio compact disk 43.05 (978-0-521-71320-7(X)) Cambridge U Pr.

More! Level 4 Workbook with Audio CD Czech Editon. Herbert Puchta et al. (More! Ser.). 2009. pap. bk. 17.00 (978-0-521-17295-0(0)) Cambridge U Pr.

More Love: Tender Moments. Stuart Wilde. 2 cass. (Running Time: 1 hr. per cass.). pap. bk. waves. (978-0-930603-45-8(1)); (978-0-930603-21-2(4)) White Dove NM.

This subliminal tape is especially designed to assist in opening yourself to receive & give more love. The subliminal affirmations are to help you pull that "special" person into your life or develop a greater sense of love & caring for those who are already around you.

More Love in the Western see Assorted Prose

More Love, More Joy! Meditations. Perf. by Jennifer Martin. Created by Jennifer Martin. Prod. by Ryan West. 2007. audio compact disk 14.95 (978-1-934681-23-7(7)) Discovery Bay.

More Love Tactics: How to Win That Special Someone. unabr. ed. Thomas W. McKnight & Robert H. Phillips. Narrated by Franette Liebow. 2 cass. (Running Time: 3 hrs.). 2001. 16.95 Set. (978-1-882071-85-2(9)) B-B Audio.

More Love Tactics picks up where the best seller Love Tactics leaves off. It provides a host of new and effective strategies to help you win the one you want, while also addressing many important areas not covered in the first book.The four parts of M.

More Lynn Stanford Music for Ballet Class. 1 cass. 15.00 (BOD8301C); audio compact disk 18.00 (BOD8301CD) Kimbo Educ.

This breathtaking evolution in class music includes music for barre & center.

More... Magical Relationships, unabr. ed. Ariel Kane & Shya Kane. Contrib. by Helene DeLillo. 2 cass. (Running Time: 2 hrs. 2 min.). (Being in the Moment Ser.). 1995. (978-1-888043-09-9(1)) ASK Prodns.

More of the Kanes' magical relationships technology, bringing home the keys for having relationships be exciting, alive, fresh & satisfying.

More Mastery: Vocabulary for Academic Reading. Linda Wells & Gladys Valcourt. (C). 1999. 15.00 (978-0-472-00282-5(1)) U of Mich Pr.

More Mastery: Vocabulary for Academic Reading. Linda Wells & Gladys Valcourt. (C). 2001. 15.00 (978-0-472-00301-3(1), 00301) U of Mich Pr.

More Max Michael Jackson. Ben Graham. (Running Time: 60 mins). 2005. audio compact disk (978-1-84240-313-6(3)) Chrome Dreams GBR.

The self proclaimed 'King Of Pop' is currently at the helm of a media frenzyso intense that even he, one of the most famous men in the world, has notpreviously seen its like. With possibly the most controversial, highprofile, court case the world has ever seen, about to begin, Jackson is onour screens nightly and is likely to be so for many months to come.This outcome of this trial will determine not only the future direction ofhis career but also dictate whether or not he still has one. With this inmind More Maximum Michael Jackson brings his story up to date to include theevents that led to the current litigation.More Maximum Michael Jackson is a continuation of the earlier Maximumrelease and completes his story to date; this unauthorised biographyincludes additional interview material and comments from this extraordinaryicon, delving deeper to discover what events and experiences have mouldedhim into the man he is today.An ideal purchase for fans everywhere.

More Maximum Eminem: The Unauthorized Biography of Eminem. Martin Roach. (Maximum Ser.). (ENG., 2003. audio compact disk 14.95 (978-1-84240-195-8(5)) Pub: Chrome Dreams GBR. Dist(s): IPG Chicago

More Maximum Oasis. Tim Footman. As told by Jones Sian. 1 CD. (Maximum Ser.). 2005. audio compact disk (978-1-84240-317-4(6)) Chrome Dreams GBR.

Undoubtedly the biggest UK bands of the 90?s, Oasis are back next month with their first new album in three years. Don't Believe The Truth is rumoured to be their best since Morning Glory, with some classic songs from Liam complementing Noel?s normal but extraordinary fare. Live appearances are scheduled across the world for later in the year, all-ensuring that the Oasis publicity wagon is back in top gear after such a long hiatus. The Gallagher brothers will be hogging the limelight once again like only they know how!?More Maximum Oasis? is a continuation of Chrome Dreams? earlier Maximum release and completes their story to date. This unauthorised biography includes additional interview material and comments from one of the most popular and critically acclaimed bands of our time. This CD is another must for Oasis? long-term fans as well as those recently converted to the faith.

More Maximum Tupac. Keith Rodway. As told by Jones Sian. 1 CD. (Maximum Ser.). 2005. audio compact disk (978-1-84240-315-0(X)) Chrome Dreams GBR.

One of hip-hop's most controversial icons, Tupac Shakur is to Rap music whatJohn Lennon was to Rock. Remembered both as a multi-platinum sellingrecording artist and a critically acclaimed actor, Tupac remains a hero tomillions At the end of last year the Eminem produced Tupac album 'Loyal ToThe Game' was released, once again pushing him back to the top of the HipHop music tree.As the fascination of this gangster rapper goes from strength to strength,this CD continues where Maximum 2Pac left off, bringing the story up-to-datewith the legacy that lives on. This compelling tale illustrates the triumphsand tragedies associated with the often-controversial lives of thoseinvolved in America's most influential art form - Rap. Essential listeningfor all Tupac and Hip Hop fans.

More Miracles. (Dovetales Ser.: Tape 14). pap. bk. 6.95; 4.95 (978-0-944391-29-7(X)) DonWise Prodns.

More, More, More: How to get more of anything you really want & less of what you Don't. Robert Imbriale. (ENG.). 2008. audio compact disk 19.95 (978-0-9777500-5-4(1), Ultimate Pub CA) Ultimate Wealth.

More Music & the Mind, Michael Ballam. 2 cass. 2004. 14.95 (978-1-57734-595-4(9), 3111474) Covenant Comms.

Additional information & research proving music's beneficial effects on the mind.

More Music from Braveheart. Perf. by James Horner. 1 cass., 1 CD. (J). audio compact disk 14.38 CD Jewel box. (LON 458287) NewSound.

More Music That Teaches Spanish. 1996. spiral bd. 31.95 (978-0-9650980-1-4(X)) Dolo Publns.

More Napalm & Silly Putty. abr. ed. George Carlin. 2 CDs. (Running Time: 2 hrs. 30 mins.). (ENG.). 2002. audio compact disk 22.95 (978-1-56511-530-9(9), 1565115309) Pub: HighBridge. Dist(s): Workman Pub

More Nature in Art. unabr. ed. Aldous Huxley. 1 cass. (Running Time: 56 min.). (Human Situation Ser.). 1959. 11.00 (01108) Big Sur Tapes.

More Naughty Little Sister Stories. Dorothy Edwards. Read by Jan Francis. (Running Time: 5280 sec.). (J). 2001. audio compact disk 21.95 (978-0-7540-6765-8(3)) AudioGo GBR.

More New Adventures of Sherlock Holmes, Vol. 17. abr. ed. Perf. by John Stanley & Alfred Shirley. 1 cass. (Running Time: 1 hr.). 9.95 Digitally Re-Mastered. (978-1-56100-948-0(2), Nova Audio Bks) Brilliance Audio.

Includes "The Dog Who Changed His Mind" (originally broadcast Sep 28, 1947), & "The Missing Heiress" (originally broadcast Oct 5, 1947).

More New Adventures of Sherlock Holmes, Vol. 19. abr. ed. Perf. by John Stanley & Alfred Shirlely. 1 cass. (Running Time: 1 hr.). 9.95 Digitally Re-Mastered. (978-1-56100-975-6(X), Nova Audio Bks) Brilliance Audio.

Includes: "The Laughing Lemur of the Hightower Heath" (originally broadcast Oct 26, 1947), & "The Adventure of the Cooper Beeches" (originally broadcast Nov 2, 1947).

More New Adventures of Sherlock Holmes, Vol. 20. abr. ed. Perf. by John Stanley & Alfred Shirley. 1 cass. (Running Time: 1 hr.). 9.95 Digitally Re-Mastered. (978-1-56100-976-3(8), Nova Audio Bks) Brilliance Audio.

Includes: "The Cadaver in the Roman Toga" (originally broadcast Nov 9, 1947), & "The Well Staged Murder" (Originally broadcast Nov 16, 1947).

More News from Lake Wobegon. abr. unabr. ed. Garrison Keillor. 4 CDs. (Running Time: 5 hrs.). (ENG.). 1990. audio compact disk 36.95 (978-0-942110-37-1(4), 0942110374) Pub: HighBridge. Dist(s): Workman Pub

More News from Lake Wobegon: Humor. abr. unabr. ed. Garrison Keillor. Contrib. by Garrison Keillor. 1 CD. (Running Time: 1 hr. 6 mins.). 2003. audio compact disk 13.95 (978-1-56511-275-9(X), 156511275X) Pub: HighBridge. Dist(s): Workman Pub

More News From Lake Wobegon: Love. abr. unabr. ed. Garrison Keillor. 4 CDs. (Running Time: 1 hr. 6 mins.). (ENG.). 1998. audio compact disk 13.95 (978-1-56511-295-7(4), 1565112954) Pub: HighBridge. Dist(s): Workman Pub

***More of Paul's Letters.** unabr. ed. Zondervan. (Running Time: 0 hr. 15 mins. 54 sec.). (Best-Loved Stories of the Bible, NIrV Ser.). (ENG.). (J). 2010. 1.99 (978-0-310-86540-7(9)) Pub: Zondkidz. Dist(s): Zondervan

More or Less? Sundance/Newbridge, LLC Staff. (Early Math Ser.). (gr. k-1). 2000. 12.00 (978-1-58273-305-0(8)) Sund Newbrdge.

More Perfect Than the Moon. unabr. ed. Patricia MacLachlan. Read by Glenn Close. (J). 2008. 34.99 (978-1-60514-598-3(X)) Find a World.

***More Perfect Than the Moon.** unabr. ed. Patricia Maclachlan. Read by Glenn Close. (ENG.). 2004. (978-0-06-081832-6(8), KTegenBooks); (978-0-06-081831-9(X), KTegenBooks) HarperCollins Pubs.

More Perfect Union. unabr. ed. J. A. Jance. Read by Gene Engene. 6 cass. (Running Time: 8 hrs. 6 min.). Dramatization. (J. P. Beaumont Mystery Ser.). 1993. 39.95 (978-1-55686-466-7(3), 752467) Books in Motion.

A young woman ironworker plunges from a skeletal skyscraper. An accident? Suicide? Detective Beaumont didn't think so, especially when the body count started climbing, eventually leading him to the headquarters of the ironworkers' local.

More Perfect Union. unabr. collector's ed. J. A. Jance. Read by Connor O'Brien. 6 cass. (Running Time: 9 hrs.). (J. P. Beaumont Mystery Ser.). 1997. 48.00 (978-0-7366-3822-7(9), 4490) Books on Tape.

A young women plunges from a skeletal skyscraper with sheer horror frozen on her beautiful face. Is it an accident or a suicide?.

More Perfect Union: The Story of Our Constitution. unabr. ed. Betsy Maestro & Giulio Maestro. 1 cass. (Running Time: 15 min.). (J). (gr. 2-5). 1993. pap. bk. 18.90 (978-0-8045-6665-0(8), 6665) Spoken Arts.

The men who met in Philadelphia to create our nation's most precious document lived through a very human drama.

More Phonics Songs. 1 cass. (Running Time: 1 hr.). (J). 2001. pap. bk. 10.95 (THR 104C) Kimbo Educ.

12 long vowel rhyming word families along with consonants & blends are taught through snappy songs with amusing lyrics. Reproducible workbook & lyrics included.

More Popular Piano Solos. Phillip Keveren. 2002. audio compact disk 10.95 (978-0-634-04536-3(9), 0634045369) H Leonard.

More Popular Piano Solos, Level 1. Phillip Keveren. 2002. audio compact disk 10.95 (978-0-634-04438-0(9), 0634044389) H Leonard.

More Popular Piano Solos, Level 2. Phillip Keveren. 2002. audio compact disk 10.95 (978-0-634-04439-7(7), 0634044397) H Leonard.

More Popular Piano Solos, Level 3. Phillip Keveren. 2002. audio compact disk 10.95 (978-0-634-04440-3(0), 0634044400) H Leonard.

More Popular Piano Solos - Level 5. 2003. audio compact disk 10.95 (978-0-634-04537-0(7)) H Leonard.

More Power to You. 5 cass. 11.95 (978-0-943026-19-0(9), A8) Carothers.

Includes album.

More Power to You. abr. ed. Jack L. Canfield. Read by Jack L. Canfield. 1 cass. (Self-Help Ser.). 1986. 7.95 HarperCollins Pubs.

More Precious Than Gold. abr. ed. Elaine Barbieri. Read by Sofia Noelle. 1 cass. (Running Time: 1 hr. 30 min.). 1995. 5.99 (978-1-57096-012-3(7), RAZ 913) Romance Alive Audio.

In the Black Hills of South Dakota, Carolina is left to die after an Indian attack on her wagon train. Stricken with amnesia, she struggles to unlock the secrets of her forgotten past, not realizing that she is also healing the invisible wounds of her reluctant rescuer, Drake McNeil.

More Precious Than Jewels: Proverbs 31: The Godly Wife & Mother. Kimberly Hahn. Read by Kimberly Hahn. 12 cass. 49.95 (5228-C) Ignatius Pr.

Discussion on woman's unique roles & special vocations. Kimberly's stories of struggling to balance her life as a wife, mom & teacher.

More Questions & Answers about Demons. Jack Deere. 1 cass. (Running Time: 1 hr. 30 min.). (Demonic Inroads Ser.: Vol. 5). 2000. 5.00 (JD02-005) Morning NC.
First laying a foundation of insight into Satan's overall strategy, Jack then builds upon it with practical knowledge of the Christian's authority over demonic forces.

More Ralph Twigger Stories, No. 4. Melea J. Brock. Illus. by Melea J. Brock. 1. (Running Time: 45 mins,). Dramatization. 1996. 10.00 (978-0-9667455-4-2(X)) Right-Side-Up.

More Random Acts of Kindness. unabr. ed. Read by Edward Asner et al. Ed. by Conari Press Staff. 2 cass. (Running Time: 2 hrs. 30 mins.). 1996. 17.95 (978-1-57453-059-9(3)) Audio Lit.
True stories of people who have been the givers or recipients of caring & compassionate acts.

***More Ready Than You Realize: Evangelism as Dance in the Postmodern Matrix.** Brian D. McLaren. (Running Time: 4 hrs. 13 mins. 0 sec.). (ENG.). 2008. 14.99 (978-0-310-30482-1(2)) Zondervan.

More Ready to Sing. Contrib. by Russell Mauldin. 1994. 11.98 (978-1-55897-394-7(X), 75602258) Pub: Brentwood Music. Dist(s): H Leonard

More Reggae for Kids. 1 cass. (Running Time: 49 min.). (J). (gr. 5 up). 1997. 9.00; audio compact disk 13.00 RAS Records.

More Rhyme Than Reason. David Novak. 2002. audio compact disk 15.00 (978-0-9714059-2-9(1)) A Telling Exp Inc.

More Sales. Voice by Judith Wright. 2002. audio compact disk (978-0-9719100-3-4(0)) Evia Pr.

More Scary Stories to Tell in the Dark. abr. unabr. ed. Alvin Schwartz & Stephen Gammell. Perf. by George S. Irving. 1 cass. (Running Time: 1 hr. 15 min.). (J). (gr. 3-5). 1990. 11.95 (978-1-55994-284-3(3), CPN 1869, Harper Audio) HarperCollins Pubs.

More Scary Stories to Tell in the Dark. unabr. ed. Ed. by Alvin Schwartz. 1 read-along cass. (Running Time: 1 hr.). (Middle Grade Cliffhangers Ser.). (J). (gr. 4-6). 1986. 15.98 incl. bk. & guide. (978-0-8072-1152-6(4), SWR57SP, Listening Lib) Random Audio Pubg.
Stories of ghosts & skeletons, corpses & their murderers, death & unexplained phenomena.

More Science Projects for All Students. Ed. by Judith A. Bazler. (gr. 4-9). 2005. audio compact disk 149.95 (978-0-8160-5001-7(5)) Facts On File.

More, Sex, Lies & Superspeedways, Vol. 2. 2nd ed. Excerpts. Henry Smokey Yunick. Read by Dick Berggren et al. 7 CDs. (Running Time: 8 hrs. 40 mins.). 2003. audio compact disk 29.95 (978-0-9724378-4-4(3), Carbon Pr) Carb Pr.
Another Collection of Stories from Smokey Yunick?s autobiography: Best Damn Garage in TownSmokey Yunick, the world?s most famous mechanic, accomplished more in one life than most people could in five. He flew 50 missions as a B-17 pilot in WWII. He was an integral part of the birth of stock car racing and ran open wheel cars during the glory days of the Indy 500. He spent years in the jungles of Ecuador and held 10 U.S. patents. Smokey was concerned for the future, so he developed more efficient and powerful engines for passenger cars and safer crash barriers for race tracks. These are the real stories of racing and everything automotive in America ? told by someone who was there every step of the way!To add to the fun we had people from all around racing read Smokey?s stories. And while they were at it, we asked them to give you their thoughts on Smokey ? you won?t believe what they had to say!.

More Short & Shivery: Thirty Terrifying Tales, unabr. ed. Short Stories. Retold by Robert D. San Souci. Narrated by Mark Hammer. 4 pieces. (Running Time: 5 hrs.). (gr. 5 up). 1995. 35.00 (978-0-7887-0210-5(6), 94435E7) Recorded Bks.
Thirty spooky stories drawn from the folklore of cultures around the world.

More Silly Songs. 1 cass. (Disney Ser.). (J). 6.38 (DISN 60632); audio compact disk 11.18 (DISN 60632) NewSound.
Includes: "On Top of Spaghetti," "I Scream, You Scream, We All Scream for Ice Cream," "Pop, Goes the Weasel" & many more.

More Silly Songs: Twenty More Simply Super Singable Silly Songs. Prod. by Walt Disney Records Staff. 1 CD. (Running Time: 35 min.). (J). 1998. pap. bk. 12.98 (978-0-7634-0437-6(3)); 7.98 (978-0-7634-0436-9(5)) W Disney Records.

More Singable Songs. Perf. by Raffi. 1 cass . (Running Time: 35 min.). (J). 2001. 10.95 (KSR 8104C); lp 10.95 (KSR 8104); audio compact disk 16.95 (KSR 8104CD) Kimbo Educ.
Six Little Ducks - You Gotta Sing - Sambalele - Shake My Sillies Out & more.

More Singable Songs. Perf. by Raffi. (Running Time: 27 mins.). (J). 1999. (978-1-886767-33-1(5)); (978-1-886767-59-1(9)); audio compact disk (978-1-886767-32-4(7)); audio compact disk (978-1-886767-58-4(0)) Rounder Records.
Old & new children's favorites receive the special Raffi treatment. Sing, shake, dance & quack along to Raffi's sequel to the original classic.

More Singable Songs for the Very Young. Perf. by Raffi. 1 cass. (Running Time: 35 min.). (J). (ps). 10.98 (263); audio compact disk 17.98 (D263) MFLP CA.
Incredible music of the pied piper of children's music. Songs include: "Six Little Ducks," "You Gotta Sing," "New River Train," "Les Petites Marionettes," "Who Built the Ark" & many more.

More Singable Songs for the Very Young. Perf. by Raffi. 1 cass. (Running Time: 35 min.). (J). 7.98 (RDR 8052); audio compact disk 12.78 (RDR 8052) NewSound.

More... Sit down & Tone Up: Strength Training from the Comfort of Your Chair. Perf. by Jodi Stolove. Prod. by Jodi Stolove. Composed by Michael Silversher. 1 cass. (Running Time: 25 min.). 2002. 9.95 (978-0-9630939-7-4(5)) Chair Dancing.

More Songs about Me. Perf. by William Janiak. 1 LP. (Running Time: 35 min.). (J). pupil's gde. ed. 11.95 (KIM 70234); 10.95 incl. guide. (KIM 70234C) Kimbo Educ.
We Are All Nodding Our Heads, Go 'Round & 'Round the Chairs, My Kind of Day, Laugh & Cry Song, If You Have This On - Stand up Sit Down, I Like to Move to the Left & Right, What Is Today?, Clap & Stop & more.

More Songs from Pooh Corner. Perf. by Kenny Loggins. Composed by Richard M. Sherman & Robert B. Sherman. 1 cass. (Running Time: 35 min.). (J). 2000. 9.98 (Sony Wonder); audio compact disk 16.98 (Sony Wonder) Sony Music Ent.
Includes: "Your Heart Will Lead You Home," "You'll Be in My Heart," "Always, in All Ways," "Flying Dreams" (duet with Olivia Newton-John), "That'll Do," "Turn Around," "Beauty & the Beast," "Baby Mine," "The Inchworm," "Hana Aluna Lullabye" & "Goodnight.".

More Speech Improvement CDs & Booklet. Phyllis Rooder Weiss. 3 CDs. (Running Time: 2 hrs.). 2005. audio compact disk 39.50 (978-1-57970-154-3(X), S23725D) J Norton Pubs.

More Stories & Songs of Jesus. Christopher C. Walker & Paule Freeburg, Sr. Read by Christopher C. Walker & Paule Freeburg, Sr. 1 cass. (Running Time: 1 hr.). (J). (gr. k-3). 1999. 12.95 (10418); audio compact disk 24.95 (10420) OR Catholic.
24 stories from the life of Jesus with a song for each story.

***More Stories Behind the Best-Loved Songs of Christmas.** Ace Collins. (Running Time: 5 hrs. 30 mins. 0 sec.). (ENG.). 2008. 15.99 (978-0-310-30483-8(0)) Zondervan.

More Stories of the Old Duck Hunters, Vol. 2. abr. ed. Gordon MacQuarrie. Read by Karl Schmidt. 2 cass. (Running Time: 2 hrs. 30 min.). (Gordon MacQuarrie Trilogy). 1994. 16.95 (978-1-57223-015-6(0), 150) Willow Creek Pr.
Entertaining stories from the pages of the Gordon MacQuarrie trilogy. Classic hunting & fishing yarns from a master storyteller. Winner of the 1995 Ben Franklin award - Best Audio.

More Styles of Christmas: Intermediate Level Instrumental Play-along Packs - Alto Sax. James L. Hosay. 2006. pap. bk. 14.95 (978-90-431-2304-4(8), 9043123048) H Leonard.

***More Styles of Christmas: Intermediate Level Instrumental Play-along Packs - Bassoon/Trombone/Euphonium TC/BC.** James L. Hosay. (ENG.). 2006. pap. bk. 14.95 (978-90-431-2307-5(2), 9043123072) H Leonard.

More Styles of Christmas: Intermediate Level Instrumental Play-along Packs - Bb Clarinet. James L. Hosay. 2006. pap. bk. 14.95 (978-90-431-2303-7(X), 904312303X) H Leonard.

More Styles of Christmas: Intermediate Level Instrumental Play-along Packs - Bb Trumpet. James L. Hosay. 2006. pap. bk. 14.95 (978-90-431-2305-1(6), 9043123056) H Leonard.

More Styles of Christmas: Intermediate Level Instrumental Play-along Packs - Flute. James L. Hosay. 2006. pap. bk. 14.95 (978-90-431-2302-0(1), 9043123021) H Leonard.

More Styles of Christmas: Intermediate Level Instrumental Play-along Packs - Horn. James L. Hosay. 2006. pap. bk. 14.95 (978-90-431-2306-8(4), 9043123064) H Leonard.

More Styles of Christmas: Intermediate Level Instrumental Play-along Packs - Soprano/Tenor Sax. James L. Hosay. 2006. pap. bk. 14.95 (978-90-431-2308-2(0), 9043123080) H Leonard.

More Sublime Chant: The Art of Gregorian, Ambrosian, Gallican & Sarum Chant. Perf. by Cathedral Singers. 1 cass. (Running Time: 1 hr.). 1999. 10.95 (CS-459); audio compact disk 15.95 (CD-459) GIA Pubns.

More Tales from the Dugout: More of the Greatest True Baseball Stories of All Time. abr. ed. Mike Shannon. 3 cass. (Running Time: 4 hrs. 30 mins.). 2004. 24.00 (978-1-932378-50-4(2)) Pub: A Media Intl. Dist(s): Natl Bk Netwk

More Tales from the Dugout: More of the Greatest True Baseball Stories of All Time. abr. ed. Mike Shannon. 4 CDs. (Running Time: 4 hrs. 30 mins.). 2004. audio compact disk 28.00 (978-1-932378-51-1(0)) Pub: A Media Intl. Dist(s): Natl Bk Netwk

More Tales from the Greek Legends. Edward Ferrie. Read by Benjamin Soames. (J). 2006. audio compact disk 17.98 (978-962-634-412-5(1), Naxos AudioBooks) Naxos.

More Tales of Christmas. Richard M. Siddoway. 1 cass. 1994. 7.95 (978-1-57008-091-3(7), Bkcraft Inc) Deseret Bk.

More Tales of Fiction & Suspense. Max Brand. 1 cass. 1995. 5.99 (978-1-57375-023-3(9)) Audioscope.

More Tales of Oliver Pig. unabr. ed. Jean Van Leeuwen. Read by Suzanne Toren. Illus. by Arnold Lobel. 1 cass. (Running Time: 25 mins.). (Follow the Reader Ser.). (J). (gr. k-3). 1984. pap. bk. 17.00 (978-0-8072-0050-6(6), FTR 80 SP, Listening Lib) Random Audio Pubg.
More fun with the Pig family, baking mud pies with raisins, singing about crocodiles & pigs in wigs. Includes book & guide.

***More Tales of the City.** abr. ed. Armistead Maupin. Read by Armistead Maupin. (ENG.). 2009. (978-0-06-197736-7(5), Harper Audio); (978-0-06-197740-4(3), Harper Audio) HarperCollins Pubs.

More Tales of the City. unabr. ed. Armistead Maupin. Narrated by Barbara Rosenblat. 7 cass. (Running Time: 9 hrs. 45 mins.). (Tales of the City Ser.: Vol. 2). 1995. 60.00 (978-0-7887-0219-8(X), 94444E7) Recorded Bks.
Continues to eavesdrop on the tenants at 28 Barbary Lane.

More Tales of Uncle Remus: Further Adventures of Brer Rabbit, His Friends, Enemies, & Others. unabr. ed. Julius Lester. Narrated by Julius Lester. 3 pieces. (Running Time: 3 hrs. 15 mins.). (gr. 3 up). 2002. 28.00 (978-0-7887-9047-8(1)) Recorded Bks.

More Than a Carpenter. abr. ed. Josh D. McDowell. (Running Time: 1 hr. 14 mins. 0 sec.). (ENG.). 2009. audio compact disk 6.99 (978-1-4143-2479-1(0), Tyndale Audio) Tyndale Hse.

More Than a Carpenter Today. abr. ed. Josh McDowell. Narrated by Josh McDowell. (ENG.). 2006. 9.09 (978-1-60814-312-2(0)); audio compact disk 12.99 (978-1-59859-124-8(X)) Oasis Audio.

More Than a Carpenter Today: An Oasis Audio Production. Josh McDowell. Read by Josh McDowell. (Running Time: 9000 sec.). 2006. audio compact disk 24.00 (978-0-7861-7048-7(4)) Blckstn Audio.

More Than a Hobby. abr. ed. David Green. Narrated by Mark Warner. (ENG.). 2005. 13.99 (978-1-60814-313-9(9)) Oasis Audio.

More Than a Hobby: How a $600 Start-up Became America's Home & Craft Superstore. abr. ed. David Green. Told to Dean Merrill. (Running Time: 12600 sec.). 2005. audio compact disk 19.99 (978-1-59859-010-4(3)) Oasis Audio.

More Than a Job: A Curriculum on Work & Society, Reading Level 3 & Above. 1993. 18.00 (978-0-88336-862-6(5)) New Readers.

More Than a Mistress. Mary Balogh. Narrated by Jenny Sterlin. 10 cass. (Running Time: 14 hrs. 30 mins.). 88.00 (978-0-7887-5977-2(9)) Recorded Bks.

More Than a Mistress. unabr. ed. Mary Balogh. 2001. 88.00 (L1002L8) Recorded Bks.
A witty & sensual tale of a Regency-era duke who does the unthinkable by falling in love with his mistress.

More Than a Pink Cadillac: Mary Kay Inc. 's 9 Leadership Keys to Success. unabr. ed. Jim Underwood. Narrated by Joel Leffert. 5 cass. (Running Time: 7 hrs. 30 mins.). 2003. 59.75 (978-1-4025-7526-6(2), 97654MC, Griot Aud) Recorded Bks.

More than a Pink Cadillac: Mary Kay Inc's. 9 Leadership Keys to Success. Jim Underwood. Read by Jim Underwood. 2004. 24.00 (978-1-932378-14-6(6)) Pub: A Media Intl. Dist(s): Natl Bk Netwk
Reveals how extraordinary leadership and a value-based mindset made Mary Kay Inc. an icon.

More Than a Pink Cadillac: Mary Kay Inc's. 9 Leadership Keys to Success. abr. ed. Jim Underwood. Read by Jim Underwood. 6 cass. (Running Time: 6 hrs.). 2004. audio compact disk 28.00 (978-1-932378-15-3(4)) Pub: A Media Intl. Dist(s): Natl Bk Netwk

More Than a Promise. Janet Woods. Read by Caroline Lennon. 7 cass. 2007. 61.95 (978-1-84559-568-5(8)) Pub: ISIS Audio GBR. Dist(s): Ulverscroft US

More Than a Skeleton: Shattering Deception or Ultimate Truth? abr. ed. Paul L. Maier. Read by J. Charles. 3 CDs. (Running Time: 3 hrs.). 2003. audio compact disk 19.95 (978-1-59355-266-4(1), 1593552661); audio compact disk 62.25 (978-1-59355-267-1(X), 159355267X) Brilliance Audio.
"The man who saved Christianity" - grateful words spoken by millions after Dr. Jonathan Weber revealed the truth about an archaeological dig two years ago. But Jon isn't interested in the hype. He's far more concerned with how people are being misled by prophecy enthusiasts and their bizarre end-times scenarios, particularly the wrong-headed predictions of his nemesis, Melvin Morris Merton. Still, Jon is a professor, not a crusader. He's happy with his life of teaching (Harvard and Hebrew University), writing (a best-selling "biography" of Jesus), and research (Near East studies). He's also a newlywed, deeply in love with his brilliant and beautiful wife, Shannon. Not even an annoying lawsuit from Merton can shake his world. But Joshua Ben-Yosef can. This Israeli speaks a dozen languages - fluently and without accent. His words ripple with wisdom and authority, and crowds follow him, enthralled. He heals the sick, gives sight to the blind, casts out demons, and even raises the dead. Once again, Jon is drawn into a hot pursuit of the truth that at times casts him into the very lonely, very dangerous role of one man against the world. Review the evidence, join the dig near Nazareth that uncovers a first-century mosaic, and find out if three lines of Hebrew could change the course of history.

More Than a Skeleton: Shattering Deception or Ultimate Truth? abr. ed. Paul L. Maier. Read by J. Charles. (Running Time: 3 hrs.). 2006. 39.25 (978-1-4233-0340-4(7), 9781423303404, BADLE); 24.95 (978-1-4233-0339-8(3), 9781423303398, BAD); 39.25 (978-1-4233-0338-1(5), 9781423303381, Brinc Audio MP3 Lib); audio compact disk 24.95 (978-1-4233-0337-4(7), 9781423303374, Brilliance MP3) Brilliance Audio.
"The man who saved Christianity" - grateful words spoken by millions after Dr. Jonathan Weber revealed the truth about an archaeological dig two years ago. But Jon isn't interested in the hype. He's far more concerned with how people are being misled by prophecy enthusiasts and their bizarre end-times scenarios, particularly the wrong-headed predictions of his nemesis, Melvin Morris Merton. Still, Jon is a professor, not a crusader. He's happy with his life of teaching (Harvard and Hebrew University), writing (a best-selling "biography" of Jesus), and research (Near East studies). He's also a newlywed, deeply in love with his brilliant and beautiful wife, Shannon. Not even an annoying lawsuit from Merton can shake his world. But Joshua Ben-Yosef can. This Israeli speaks a dozen languages - fluently and without accent. His words ripple with wisdom and authority, and crowds follow him, enthralled. He heals the sick, gives sight to the blind, casts out demons, and even raises the dead. Once again, Jon is drawn into a hot pursuit of the truth that at times casts him into the very lonely, very dangerous role of one man against the world. Review the evidence, join the dig near Nazareth that uncovers a first-century mosaic, and find out if three lines of Hebrew could change the course of history.

More Than a Song. Contrib. by Tom Fettke. (ENG.). 1986. 12.00 (978-0-00-503173-5(7)) Lillenas.

More Than Amazing Grace: Judges 16:22-31. Ed Young. 1998. 4.95 (978-0-7417-2175-4(9), A1175) Win Walk.

More Than Friends. Barbara Delinsky. Read by Jennifer Wiltsie. 2006. 15.95 (978-0-7435-5251-6(2)) Pub: S&S Audio. Dist(s): S and S Inc

More Than Friends. abr. ed. Barbara Delinsky. Read by Jennifer Wiltsie. 3 cass. (Running Time: 43 hrs. 0 mins. 0 sec.). (ENG.). 2006. 25.00 (978-0-7435-0882-7(3)) Pub: S&S Audio. Dist(s): S and S Inc

More Than Friends. abr. ed. Barbara Delinsky. Read by Jennifer Wiltsie. (Running Time: 43 hrs. 0 mins. 0 sec.). (ENG.). 2009. audio compact disk 14.99 (978-0-7435-7615-4(2)) Pub: S&S Audio. Dist(s): S and S Inc

More Than Friends. unabr. ed. Barbara Delinsky. Read by Barbara Rosenblat. 12 CDs. (Running Time: 14 hrs. 50 mins). 2007. 98.75 (978-1-4193-7761-7(2)) Recorded Bks.

***More than Human.** unabr. ed. Theodore Sturgeon. Read by Harlan, Stefan and Ellison Rudnicki. (Running Time: 8 hrs. 30 mins.). 2010. 29.95 (978-1-4332-7514-2(7)); 54.95 (978-1-4332-7510-4(4)); audio compact disk 76.00 (978-1-4332-7511-1(2)) Blckstn Audio.

More Than Memory. unabr. ed. Dorothy Garlock. Read by Kate Forbes. 8 vols. (Running Time: 12 hrs.). 2001. bk. 69.95 (978-0-7927-2487-2(9), CSL 376, Chivers Sound Lib); audio compact disk 94.95 (978-0-7927-9919-1(4), SLD 070, Chivers Sound Lib) AudioGO.
Nelda Hanson, a successful young designer in Chicago, has come home to sell the family farm. Here, just eight years ago, she was a pregnant teenage bride, torn from the arms of her new husband minutes after the ceremony. Nelda won't see him again, not even after she bore his child. Now suddenly, & dangerously, Lute Hanson is back in her life. Nelda hates her weakness in loving him, as if she could have ever stopped, as if all the hurt over so much time could not return to consume them both.

More Than Money: Questions Every MBA Needs to Answer. unabr. ed. Mark Albion. Read by Jim Manchester. 4 CDs. (ENG.). 2008. audio compact disk 24.95 (978-1-60283-537-5(3)) Pub: AudioGO. Dist(s): Perseus Dist

More Than Music: Images from the Rock. 1 cass. (Running Time: 62 mins.). 9.95 (978-0-921788-45-4(2)) Kindred Prods.

More Than Riches. unabr. ed. Josephine Cox. Read by Maggie Ollerenshaw. 10 cass. (Running Time: 10 hrs.). 1995. 84.95 (978-0-7451-6519-6(2), CAB 1135) AudioGO.
With Adam away in the army, Rosie is desperately lonely awaiting his letters which never come. Meanwhile, Adam's best friend, Doug, is studiously charming & attentive & the confused Rosie falls for him. Soon she's carrying Doug's baby & feeling that there is no choice but to marry him. Then a letter arrives from Adam, telling her he's on his way home.

More than You Know. Beth Gutcheon. Narrated by Alexandra O'Karma. 8 CDs. (Running Time: 9 hrs.). audio compact disk 78.00 (978-1-4025-1568-2(5)) Recorded Bks.

More Than You Know: A Novel. unabr. ed. Beth Gutcheon. Narrated by Alexandra O'Karma. 6 cass. (Running Time: 9 hrs.). 2001. 54.00 (978-0-7887-9045-4(5)) Recorded Bks.
Reminiscing about her past, the aged Hannah remembers the joy, astonishment, frustration and most of all, the terror of her first love.

More Than 50 Most Loved Hymns. Contrib. by Billy Ray Hearn. 2005. audio compact disk 21.98 (978-5-559-05595-4(6)) Pt of Grace Ent.

More Than 85 Broads: Women Making Career Choices, Taking Risks, & Defining Success on Their Own Terms. abr. ed. Janet Hanson. Narrated by Kate Reading. (Running Time: 16200 sec.). 2008. audio compact disk 28.00 (978-1-933309-56-9(3)) Pub: A Media Intl. Dist(s): Natl Bk Netwk

More Tickets... 16 Solostucke Mit Begleitstimme/16 Solo Pieces with Accompaniment. Peter Morscheck & Chris Burgmann. 2007. pap. bk. 19.95 (978-3-89922-065-0(X)) AMA Verlag DEU.

More to It Than Meets the Ear. 1 cass. 1993. 12.00 Am Assoc Med.
Challenging dictation that demonstrates the reality of medical transcription. (Not intended for use as a practice tape).

More True Stories: A High-Beginning Reader. 2nd ed. Sandra Heyer. 2002. 24.30 (978-0-201-69528-1(6)) AddisonWesley.

More True Tales from the Times of Ancient Civilizations & the Bible. 2001. 8.95 (978-1-930514-17-1(4), MTTAC) Diana Waring.

More True Tales from the Times of Romans, Reformers, Revolutionaries. 2001. 8.95 (978-1-930514-18-8(2), MTTRRR) Diana Waring.

More True Tales from the Times of World Empires, World Missions, World Wars. Short Stories. 1 cass. (Running Time: 80 mins.). 2001. 8.95 (978-1-930514-19-5(0), MTTRRR) Diana Waring.

More Twisted, Vol. 2. unabr. ed. Jeffery Deaver. Read by Boyd Gaines et al. 2006. 17.95 (978-0-7435-6187-7(2)) Pub: S&S Audio. Dist(s): S and S Inc

More Whootie Owl's Stories to Grow By. Short Stories. Created by Elaine L. Lindy. 1. (Running Time: 44 mins.). Dramatization. (J). 1999. 9.95 (978-0-9672831-1-1(6)) Whootie Owl LLC.

More William. Richmal Crompton. Read by Martin Jarvis. 4 CDs. (J). 2004. audio compact disk 34.95 (978-0-7540-6637-8(1), Chivers Child Audio) AudioGO.

More Worship Songs for Children: A Collection of 22 Scripture Songs. June Fischer Armstrong. (Children's Music Ser.). 12.95 (978-1-56212-642-1(3), 001840); audio compact disk 12.95 (978-1-56212-643-8(1), 001845) FaithAliveChr.

Morecambe & Wise: Bring Me Sunshine, Vol. 1. Eddie Braben. 2004. audio compact disk 29.95 (978-0-563-52493-9(6)) AudioGO.

Morehouse. J Parker.

Moreta: Dragonlady of Pern. unabr. ed. Anne McCaffrey. Read by Sheila Hart. (Running Time: 11 hrs.). (Dragonriders of Pern Ser.). 2005. 39.25 (978-1-59737-026-4(6), 9781597370264, BADLE); 24.95 (978-1-59737-025-7(8), 9781597370257, BAD); audio compact disk 102.25 (978-1-59737-022-6(3), 9781597370226, BriAudCD Unabrid) Brilliance Audio.

An air of pleasant anticipation hung so thickly over the Halls, Holds, and Weyrs of Pern that it had affected even the businesslike ways of Moreta, the Weyrwoman of Fort Weyr. Her dragon, Queen Orlith, would soon clutch; spring had made a glorious debut; the Gather at Ruatha Hold was extremely merry; and Moreta was enjoying the attentions of Alessan, the new Lord Holder of Ruatha Hold. With only eight Turns remaining before the deadly Thread would cease to Fall, all seemed well on Pern. Then, without warning, a runnerbeast fell ill. Soon myriads of holders, craftsmen, and dragonriders were dying; and the mysterious ailment had spread to all but the most inaccessible holds. Pern was in mortal danger. For, if dragonriders did not rise to char Thread, the parasite would devour any and all organic life it encountered. The future of the planet rested in the hands of Moreta and the other dedicated, selfless Pern leaders. But of all their problems, the most difficult to overcome was time . .

Moreta No. 4: Dragonlady of Pern. unabr. ed. Anne McCaffrey. Read by Sheila Hart. (Running Time: 39600 sec.). (Dragonriders of Pern Ser.). 2005. audio compact disk 39.25 (978-1-59737-024-0(X), 9781597370240, Brinc Audio MP3 Lib); audio compact disk 24.95 (978-1-59737-023-3(1), 9781597370233, Brilliance MP3); audio compact disk 37.95 (978-1-59737-021-9(5), 9781597370219, Bril Audio CD Unabri) Brilliance Audio.

Morgan: American Financier. unabr. ed. Jean Strouse. Narrated by Nelson Runger. 29 cass. (Running Time: 42 hrs. 15 mins.). 1999. 186.00 (978-0-7887-3534-9(9), 95222E7) Recorded Bks.

Contemporaries described J. Pierpoint Morgan as a "financial Moses..." He was also called a "bully, drunk with wealth & power..." To separate the legend from the man, Jean Strouse uses a wealth of uncataloged biographical documents from the Pierpoint Morgan Library. Her work sheds light on the life of a remarkable man & his impact on today's international finance. Includes an interview with the author.

Morgan Stanley Dean Witter Guide to Personal Investing, Robert M. Gardiner. Read by Richard Beebe. 2 cass. 1997. 17.95 (978-1-55935-255-0(8)) Soundelux.

Morgan's Passing. unabr. ed. Anne Tyler. Read by Mary Woods. 7 cass. (Running Time: 10 hrs. 30 min.). 1987. 56.00 (978-0-7366-1162-6(2), 2087) Books on Tape.

Halfway through a puppet show, Cinderella flops over. The Prince's voice asks if there is a doctor in the house. Remarkably there is: Morgan appears & on cue delivers "Cinderella's" baby in the back seat of a car. Then he disappears. But soon, Cinderella, The Prince & the golden baby become his obsession.

Morgan's Run. unabr. ed. Colleen McCullough. Read by William Gaminara. 18 vols. (Running Time: 27 hrs.). 2001. bk. 127.95 (978-0-7927-2445-2(3), CSL 334, Chivers Sound Lib) AudioGO.

One of the greatest human experiments ever undertaken: to populate an unknown land with the criminal, the unloved & the unwanted of English society. Amid conditions of brutality, "The First Fleet" was sent to a place that no European but the legendary Captain Cook had ever seen.

Morgan's Run. unabr. ed. Colleen McCullough. Read by William Gaminara. 3 CDs. (Running Time: 15 hrs.). 2002. audio compact disk 69.95 (978-0-7927-2668-5(5), CMP 334, Chivers Sound Lib) AudioGO.

It was one of the greatest human experiments ever undertaken. To populate an unknown land with the criminal, the unsolved and the unwanted of English society. amid conditions of brutality, "The First Fleet" was sent to a place that no European except the legendary Captain Cook had ever seen. Left to live or die on the hostile Australian continent, these convicts and their guards occupy the center of this epic story. And Richard Morgan, convicted felon, makes hi mark upon the new frontier.

Morgette & the Shadow Bomber. unabr. ed. Glenn G. Boyer. Read by Raymond Todd. (Running Time: 7.5 hrs. 0 mins.). (ENG.). 2009. 29.95 (978-1-4332-1681-7(7)); 54.95 (978-1-4332-1677-0(9)); audio compact disk 69.00 (978-1-4332-1678-7(7)) Blckstn Audio.

***Morir en el Intento.** abr. ed. Jorge Ramos. Read by Jorge Ramos. (ENG.). 2005. (978-0-06-084280-2(6), Harper Audio); (978-0-06-084281-9(4), Harper Audio) HarperCollins Pubs.

Morir en el Intento: La Peor Tragedia de Immigrantes en la Historia de los Estados Unidos. abr. ed. Jorge Ramos. 5 CDs. (Running Time: 5 Hrs). (SPA.). 2005. audio compact disk 29.95 (978-0-06-079230-5(2)) HarperCollins Pubs.

Moriturus see Poetry of Edna St. Vincent Millay

Mormom in the White House? 10 Things Every American Should Know about Mitt Romney. unabr. ed. Hugh Hewitt. Read by Lloyd James. (Running Time: 36000 sec.). 2007. 59.95 (978-0-7861-6820-0(X)); audio compact disk 29.95 (978-0-7861-6965-8(6)); audio compact disk 72.00 (978-0-7861-6819-4(6)) Blckstn Audio.

Mormon Heritage, Vol. 1. D's. 1 cass. 7.98 (1000128) Covenant Comms.

Music & narration from the Mormon epoch performed by this outstanding duo.

Mormon Heritage, Vol. 2. D's. 1 cass. 7.98 (10001018) Covenant Comms.

Enjoy the expansion of the Church through music & word.

Mormon in the White House? Ten Things Every Conservative Should Know about Mitt Romney. unabr. ed. Hugh Hewitt. Read by Lloyd James. (Running Time: 36000 sec.). 2007. audio compact disk 29.95 (978-0-7861-5794-5(1)) Blckstn Audio.

Mormon in the White House? 10 Things Every Conservative Should Know about Mitt Romney. unabr. ed. Hugh Hewitt. Read by Lloyd James. (Running Time: 36000 sec.). 2007. 29.95 (978-0-7861-4971-1(X)) Blckstn Audio.

***Mormon Mirage: A Former Member Looks at the Mormon Church Today.** ed. Latayne C. Scott. (Running Time: 14 hrs. 52 mins. 19 sec.). (ENG.). 2009. 16.99 (978-0-310-32592-5(7)) Zondervan.

Mormon Way of Doing Business: How Eight Western Boys Reached the Top of Corporate America. abr. ed. Jeff Benedict. (Running Time: 3 hrs. 30 mins.). (ENG.). 2008. 14.98 (978-1-60024-107-9(7)) Pub: Hachet Audio. Dist(s): HachBkGrp

Mormonism, The Truth about. Dan Corner. 1 cass. 3.00 (59) Evang Outreach.

Mormons at Your Door. Walter Ralston Martin. 2 cass. 1997. 11.99 Gospel Lght.

Evangelism.

Mormons, Muslims & JW's: Logos Feburary 8, 1998. Ben Young. 1998. 4.95 (978-0-7417-6072-2(X), B0072) Win Walk.

Mormyridae & Other Osteoglossomorpha. W. Harder. (World Biodiversity Database Ser.). 2000. audio compact disk 129.00 (978-3-540-14811-1(6)) Spri.

Morning - Evening Meditation One: Cultivate Conscious Living & Self-Awareness. Mark Bancroft. Read by Mark Bancroft. 1 cass., bklet. (Running Time: 1 hr.). (Spirituality & Consciousness Ser.). 1998. 12.95 (978-1-58522-000-7(0), 705) EnSpire Pr.

Two complete sessions plus printed instructionmanual/guidebook. With healing music soundtrack.

Morning - Evening Meditation One: Cultivate Conscious Living & Self-Awareness. Mark Bancroft. Read by Mark Bancroft. 1 CD, bklet. (Running Time: 1 hr.). (Spirituality & Consciousness Ser.). 2006. audio compact disk 20.00 (978-1-58522-001-4(9)) EnSpire Pr.

***Morning & Evening.** unabr. ed. C. H. Spurgeon. Narrated by James Adams. (ENG.). 2007. 24.98 (978-1-59644-474-6(6), Hovel Audio) christianaud.

Morning & Evening. unabr. ed. Charles H. Spurgeon. 10 CDs. (Running Time: 5 hrs. 45 mins. 0 sec.). (ENG.). 2007. audio compact disk 49.98 (978-1-59644-473-7(8), Hovel Audio) christianaud.

Morning & Evening. unabr. ed. Charles H. Spurgeon. Narrated by James Adams. (Running Time: 5 hrs. 45 mins. 0 sec.). (ENG.). 2007. lp 29.98 (978-1-59644-525-3(4)) christianaud.

Morning & Evening: Music, Meditation, & Prayer. Marianne Williamson. 1 cass. (Running Time: 45 min.). (ENG.). 1997. 10.95 (978-1-56170-429-3(6), M818) Hay House.

Beautiful meditations & prayers to heal the body, mind & soul. A wonderful way to begin & end your day.

Morning & Evening Meditations. Louise L. Hay. Read by Louise L. Hay. 1 cass. (Running Time: 54 min.). 1983. 18.00 CD, 132 mins., incl. Self-Healing: Creating Your Health. (978-1-56170-081-3(9), 801) Hay House.

Ms. Hay leads you through a meditation to start your day & another to end it before bed.

Morning & Evening Meditations. Louise L. Hay. 1 CD. 2003. audio compact disk 10.95 (978-1-4019-0140-0(9), 1409) Hay House.

Morning & Evening Meditations. Rhegina Sinozich. (ENG.). 2008. audio compact disk 14.95 (978-0-9706297-5-3(3)) Abrezia Pr.

Morning & Evening Meditations. abr. ed. Louise L. Hay. Read by Louise L. Hay. 1 cass. (Running Time: 1 hr.). 1999. (978-1-84032-112-8(1), HoddrStoughton) Hodder General GBR.

Motivation to begin your day with positive affirmation & close your day with gratitude.

Morning Commute. Elizabeth Grant. Created by Elizabeth Grant. (ENG.). 2007. audio compact disk 11.95 (978-0-9801754-0-0(2)) Liz Grant.

Morning Cup of Balance: One 15-Minute Routine for a Lifetime of Strength & Stability. Kim Bright-Fey. 2005. bk. 12.95 (978-1-58173-531-4(6)) Sweetwtr Pr AL.

Morning Cup of Massage: One 15-Minute Routine for a Lifetime of Energy & Harmony. Kim Bright-Fey. 2005. bk. 12.95 (978-1-58173-532-1(4)) Sweetwtr Pr AL.

Morning Cup of Pilates: One 15-Minute Routine to Invigorate the Body, Mind & Spirit. Marsha K. Dorman. 2004. bk. 12.95 (978-1-58173-246-7(5)) Sweetwtr Pr AL.

Morning Cup of Strengthening: One 15-Minute Routine for a Stronger Mind & Body. Beth Pierpoint. 2004. bk. 12.95 (978-1-58173-247-4(3)) Sweetwtr Pr AL.

Morning Cup of Stretching: One 15-Minute Routine to Wake up Your Mind & Body. Beth Pierpoint. 2003. bk. 12.95 (978-1-58173-261-0(9)) Sweetwtr Pr AL.

Morning Cup of Tai Chi: One 15-Minute Routine to Nurture Your Body, Mind, & Spirit. John A. Bright-Fey. 2004. bk. 12.95 (978-1-58173-248-1(1)) Sweetwtr Pr AL.

Morning Cup of Yoga: One 15-Minute Routine for a Lifetime of Health & Wellness. Jane Goad Trechsel. Frwd. by Rodney Yee. 2002. bk. 12.95 (978-1-58173-202-3(3)) Sweetwtr Pr AL.

Morning Exercise. abr. ed. Robert A. Monroe. Read by Robert A. Monroe. (Mind Food Ser.). 1984. 14.95 (978-1-56102-410-0(4)) Inter Indus.

The daily planner for the day's activities.

Morning for Flamingos. James Lee Burke. (Dave Robicheaux Ser.). 2004. 10.95 (978-0-7435-4145-9(6)) Pub: S&S Audio. Dist(s): S and S Inc

Morning for Flamingos. unabr. ed. James Lee Burke. Narrated by Mark Hammer. 9 cass. (Running Time: 12 hrs. 15 mins.). (Dave Robicheaux Ser.). 1993. 78.00 (978-1-55690-940-5(3), 93436) Recorded Bks.

Louisiana policeman Dave Robicheaux goes undercover for the DEA.

Morning Girl. unabr. ed. 1 cass. (Running Time: 1:30 hrs.). (YA). 2005. 17.95 (978-0-9741711-5-9(8)) Audio Bkshelf.

Morning Girl. unabr. ed. Michael Dorris. Read by Eliza Duggan & Riley Duggan. 2 CDs. (Running Time: 1 hr. 30 mins.). (YA). 2005. audio compact disk 24.95 (978-0-9741711-6-6(6)) Audio Bkshelf.

A story about a boy and a girl growing up on a Bahamian island in 1492. A story of coming-of-age.

Morning Glory. LaVyrle Spencer. Narrated by Kate Forbes. 12 cass. (Running Time: 17 hrs. 15 mins.). 1989. 98.00 (978-1-4025-2252-9(5)) Recorded Bks.

Morning Glory. Perf. by Elizabeth Taylor. 1946. (DD-8850) Natl Recrd Co.

Morning Glory. abr. ed. LaVyrle Spencer. Read by Loryn Locklin. 2 cass. (Running Time: 3 hrs.). 2001. 18.00 (978-1-59040-152-1(2), Phoenix Audio) Pub: Amer Intl Pub. Dist(s): PerseuPGW

Morning Glory: Times of Wonderful Teaching, Spirit-Inspired Prayer, & Worshipful Music. 6 cass. (Running Time: 3 hrs). 2002. 24.00 (978-1-57399-156-8(2)) Mac Hammond.

How do you learn to pray from the depths of your heart? In these live morning prayer sessions with prayer leader and teacher Lynne Hammond, you'll experience wonderful teaching, heart-felt prayer, worshipful music and even holy moments of silence. Lynne also shares insightful and challenging excerpts from a book written in the 17th century by one of the best-known women in church history. Discover the Morning Glory that's experienced in these live prayer sessions and learn how to pray effectively from the depths of your heart.

Morning Glory: Times of Wonderful Teaching, Spirit-Inspired Prayer, & Worshipful Music. Lynne Hammond. (ENG.). 2002. audio compact disk 24.00 (978-1-57399-157-5(0)) Mac Hammond.

Morning Glory Afternoon. unabr. ed. Irene Bennett Brown. Read by Stephanie Brush. 6 cass. (Running Time: 7 hrs. 30 min.). 2001. 39.95 (978-1-55686-910-5(X)) Books in Motion.

When a teen-aged switchboard operator in a 1924 Kansas town learns of the Klan's treacherous plans, the young woman is challenged to confront both the evil doers, and to face her own past.

Morning Has Broken. Jose Hobday. 11 cass. (Running Time: 9 hrs. 16 min.). 69.95 Set. (AA2384) Credence Commun.

A retreat which rejoices in being a Christian.

Morning Is a Long Time Coming: Sequel to Summer of My German Soldier. unabr. ed. Bette Greene. Narrated by Dale Dickey. 6 pieces. (Running Time: 8 hrs. 30 mins.). (gr. 8 up). 1997. 51.00 (978-0-7887-0372-0(2), 94563E7) Recorded Bks.

This sequel to "Summer of My German Soldier" reveals what happens when eighteen-year-old Patty Bergen leaves her Southern Bible-belt town for Paris. As she begins a tender love affair with a Frenchman, she begins to overcome the abuse that ruined her childhood.

Morning Joy-Music. 2007. audio compact disk 16.95 (978-1-56136-425-1(8)) Master Your Mind.

Morning Light. 2004. audio compact disk 16.99 (978-7-5124-0030-6(6)) Destiny Image Pubs.

Morning Magic. Read by Joanie Bartels. Prod. by David Wohlstadter et al. 1 cass. (Running Time: 50 min.). (Magic Ser.). (J). (ps). 1986. 9.95 (DM2) Discov Music.

Traditional & contemporary songs.

Morning Magic. Read by Joanie Bartels. Prod. by David Wohstadter et al. 1 cass. (Running Time: 33 min.). (Magic Ser.). (J). 1986. pap. bk. 8.95 incl. lyric bk. (978-1-881225-02-7(X)) Discov Music.

New packaging includes full length audio cassette & complete full color lyric book with words to "wake-up songs" & photos of Joanie & kids.

Morning Meditation/Peaceful Sleep: Guided Meditation. Concept by Vicky Thurlow. Voice by Vicky Thurlow. (ENG.). 2008. audio compact disk 14.95 (978-0-9817055-8-3(8)) DVT Invest.

Morning Mist-Music. 2007. audio compact disk 16.95 (978-1-56136-417-6(7)) Master Your Mind.

Morning, Noon & Night in Japanese. Akemi Tanahashi. 2001. audio compact disk 27.60 (978-4-7574-0345-1(3)) Pub: ALC JPN. Dist(s): Cheng Tsui

Morning of the Monkey. unabr. ed. Robert H. Van Gulik. Narrated by Frank Muller. 2 cass. (Running Time: 2 hrs.). (Judge Dee Mysteries Ser.). 1984. 18.00 (978-1-55690-350-2(2), 84910E7) Recorded Bks.

Judge Dee finds a unique gold ring with minute bloodstains, then a fingerless corpse. The only explanation for its discovery can be murder.

Morning of the World. Bob Hartman & Michael McGuire. 1 cass. (J). (ps-3). 1994. bk. 11.99 (3-1212) David C Cook.

Children's Bible story.

Morning Power Affirmations. Read by Mary Richards. 1 cass. (Running Time: 50 min.). (Power Words of Affirmation Ser.). 2007. audio compact disk 19.95 (978-1-56136-196-0(8)) Master Your Mind.

Morning Prayer - Evening Prayer II: Chants, Songs & Prayers. Gregory Norbet. 1 cass. (Running Time: 1 hr. 30 min.). 1998. 10.95; audio compact disk 16.95 (10639) OR Catholic.

More settings of morning & evening prayer with original songs & readings from scripture.

Morning Prayer Evening Prayer Vol. 2: Chants, Songs & Prayers. Gregory Norbet. 1998. pap. bk. 8.95 (978-0-915531-91-2(7), 10637) OR Catholic.

Morning Prayer Evening Prayer Vol. 2: Chants, Songs & Prayers. Gregory Norbet. Read by Gregory Norbet. 1 cass. (Running Time: 1 hr. 30 min.). 1996. 10.95 (10119); audio compact disk 16.95 (10120) OR Catholic.

Includes songs, scripture readings & original inspirational readings.

Morning Ragas. Music by Padma Talwalkar. 1 cass. (Running Time: 1 hr.). (From Dawn to Midnight Ser.: Vol. 3). 1990. (A90003); audio compact disk (CD A92074) Multi-Cultural Bks.

Morning Ragas, Vol. 1. Music by Rajan Mishra et al. 1 cass. (Running Time: 1 hr.). (From Dawn to Midnight Ser.). 1990. (A90001); audio compact disk (CD A92072) Multi-Cultural Bks.

Morning Ragas, Vol. 2. Music by Amjad A. Khan et al. 1 cass. (Running Time: 1 hr.). (From Dawn to Midnight Ser.). 1990. (A90002); audio compact disk (CD A92073) Multi-Cultural Bks.

Morning Ragas, Vol. 4. Music by Mallikarjun Mansur. 1 cass. (Running Time: 1 hr.). (From Dawn to Midnight Ser.). 1990. (A90004); audio compact disk (CD A92075) Multi-Cultural Bks.

Morning Recitation. audio compact disk 10.00 (978-0-88139-705-5(9)) Buddhist Text.

Morning Reflections: A Collection of Bible Verses, Prayers, & Inspirational Poetry for Daily Reflection. Karen Jean Matsko Hood. (ENG.). 2010. audio compact disk 24.95 (978-1-59210-158-0(5)); audio compact disk 13.95 (978-1-59808-661-4(8)) Whsprng Pine.

***Morning Reflections, Catholic Edition: A Collection of Bible Verses, Prayers, & Inspirational Poetry for Daily Reflection.** Karen Jean Matsko Hood. (ENG.). 2011. audio compact disk 24.95 (978-1-59434-552-4(X)) Whsprng Pine.

Morning Reflections, Catholic Edition: A Collection of Inspirational Poetry, Prayers, & Bible Verses for Daily Reflection. Karen Jean Matsko Hood. (ENG.). 2011. audio compact disk 13.95 (978-1-59649-236-3(8)) Whsprng Pine.

Morning Show Murders. unabr. ed. Al Roker & Dick Lochte. Read by Al Roker. (ENG.). 2009. audio compact disk 35.00 (978-0-307-57737-5(6), Random AudioBks) Pub: Random Audio Pubg. Dist(s): Random

Morning Sickness: Myths, Miseries, & Management. Miriam Erick. Read by Miriam Erick. Read by Richard Fleming. Ed. by D. Friend. 1 cass. (Running Time: 45 min.). 1992. 8.00 (978-0-9613063-7-3(8)) Grinnen-Barrett Pub Co.

Covers 10 common myths associated with morning sickness. Offers quick, common sense & effective solutions to help reduce misery & disability. Written by a national expert/researcher in the field.

***Morning Song.** unabr. ed. Renaissance Books. (ENG.). 2011. audio compact disk 14.99 (978-1-4272-1276-4(7)) Pub: Macmill Audio. Dist(s): Macmillan

Morning Spy, Evening Spy. unabr. ed. Colin MacKinnon. Read by Dick Hill. (Running Time: 39600 sec.). 2006. 65.95 (978-0-7861-4872-1(1)); audio compact disk 29.95 (978-0-7861-6848-4(X)); audio compact disk 29.95 (978-0-7861-7457-7(9)); audio compact disk 81.00 (978-0-7861-6036-5(5)) Blckstn Audio.

Morning Spy, Evening Spy: Simultaneous Release with the Hardcover, Print Run 100,000. unabr. ed. Colin MacKinnon. 9 cass. (Running Time: 12 hrs. 30 mins.). 2006. 29.95 (978-0-7861-4616-1(8)) Blckstn Audio.

Morning Star. Neville Goddard. 1 cass. (Running Time: 1 hr. 2 min.). 1970. 8.00 (24) J & L Pubns.
Neville taught Imagination Creates Reality. He was a powerfully influential teacher of God as Consciousness.

Morning Star of the Reformation. unabr. ed. Andy Thomson. Read by Lynn Taccogna. (Running Time: 3 hrs. 30 mins.). 2009. 19.95 (978-1-4332-1633-6(7)); 24.95 (978-1-4332-1629-9(9)); audio compact disk 30.00 (978-1-4332-1630-5(2)) Blckstn Audio.

Morning's Gone. Jon Cleary & Stan Pretty. 2007. 69.95 (978-1-84652-149-2(1)); audio compact disk 84.95 (978-1-84652-150-8(5)) Pub: Magna Story GBR. Dist(s): Ulverscroft US

Mornings on Horseback: The Story of an Extraordinary Faimly, a Vanished Way of Life & the Unique Child Who Became Theodore Roosevelt. abr. ed. David McCullough. Read by Edward Herrmann. 5 CDs. (Running Time: 0 hrs. 0 mins. 0 sec.). (ENG.). 2003. audio compact disk 39.95 (978-0-7435-3346-1(1), Audioworks) Pub: S&S Audio. Dist(s): S and S Inc

Mornings on Horseback: The Story of an Extraordinary Faimly, a Vanished Way of Life & the Unique Child Who Became Theodore Roosevelt. abr. ed. David McCullough. Read by Edward Herrmann. 2004. 20.95 (978-0-7435-3919-7(2)) Pub: S&S Audio. Dist(s): S and S Inc

Mornings on Horseback: The Story of an Extraordinary Faimly, a Vanished Way of Life & the Unique Child Who Became Theodore Roosevelt. unabr. ed. David McCullough. Read by Grover Gardner. 10 cass. (Running Time: 15 hrs.). 1990. 80.00 (978-0-7366-1799-4(X), 2636) Books on Tape.
Winner of the Los Angeles Times Book Prize for biography, Mornings on Horseback is the story of young Theodore Roosevelt, a singular child who, though handicapped by asthma & pathetically weak eyes, advocated the strenuous life. A remarkable metamorphosis, particularly given the patrician circumstances in which he was born & raised. After all, the Roosevelts had been established for generations & expected to smooth the way for family members. TR's father enjoyed vigorous good health; we can imagine the effect on his small, frail namesake. His mother, a celebrated Southern beauty, matched her attractiveness with style & intelligence. She set the standard for TR's first love, Alice Lee, whose death in tragic circumstances tempered the steel in his character.

Morning's Refrain. abr. ed. Tracie Peterson. Narrated by Sherri Berger. (Running Time: 7 hrs. 12 mins. 20 sec.). (Song of Alaska Ser.). (ENG.). 2010. 18.19 (978-1-60814-613-0(8)); audio compact disk 25.99 (978-1-59859-667-0(5)) Oasis Audio.

Morningstar Worship & Warfare. Contrib. by Various Artists & Rick Joyner. Prod. by Leonard Jones. (ENG.). 2008. audio compact disk 16.99 (978-7-5124-0275-1(9)) EagleStar.

Morningtown Ride. Perf. by Mike Anderson. 1 cass. (Running Time: 40 min.). (J). (gr. 2-6). 1987. 10.00 (978-1-929050-03-1(8)) MW Prods.
Children's music.

Moroccan Arabic: Advanced. Ernest T. Abdel-Massih. 4 cass. 1982. 46.64 U MI Lang Res.

Moroccan Arabic: Introduction To. Ernest T. Abdel-Massih. 3 cass. 1982. 40.78 U MI Lang Res.

Moroccan Sufi Music. unabr. ed. 1 cass. 12.95 (7238) J Norton Pubs.

Morocco: Crossroads of Time. Randall Barnwell & Bill Lawrence. 1 CD. (Running Time: 1 hr.). audio compact disk 19.95 (978-1-55961-289-0(4), Ellipsis Arts) Relaxtn Co.

Morphic Resonance: Formative Causation. unabr. ed. Rupert Sheldrake. 1 cass. (Running Time: 1 hr. 26 min.). 1982. 11.00 (02301) Big Sur Tapes.

Morphic Resonance & Memory. Rupert Sheldrake. 1 cass. (Running Time: 1 hr. 30 min.). 1985. 11.00 Big Sur Tapes.
Discusses formative causation, morphogenetic fields, heredity & evolutionary process, organismic behavior, memory & habits of nature.

Morphic Resonance & the Collective Unconscious. Rupert Sheldrake. 2 cass. 18.00 (A0656-90) Sound Photosyn.
Proposing that memory is inherent in nature, & that nature is not governed by changeless laws, but rather by habits, Rupert Sheldrake points toward a new & truly evolutionary understanding of ourselves & of the world. Dr. Sheldrake discusses some of the implications of morphic resonance for individual & collective memory, for ritual & in archetypal patterns which pervade the religious, cultural, economic & political realms.

Morrie: In His Own Words. collector's ed. Morris S. Schwartz. Read by Jonathan Marosz. 2 cass. (Running Time: 3 hrs.). 1999. 17.95 (978-0-7366-5168-4(3), 4913) Books on Tape.
Presents the author's philosophies by which he triumphantly lived, even as he faced the end of his life. Diagnosed at age 77 with Lou Gehrig's Disease, instead of withdrawing & becoming fearful as people with degenerative or terminal illnesses often do, embraced his illness, choosing to live as fully as possible in the time left. He also embarked on his greatest teaching adventure: sharing his evolving knowledge of living & dying.

Morrie: In His Own Words, unabr. ed. Morris S. Schwartz. Read by Jonathan Marosz. 2 cass. (Running Time: 3 hrs.). 1999. 17.95 (978-0-7366-4473-0(3), 4913) Books on Tape.
Presents the philosophies by which Morrie Schwartz triumphantly lived, even as he faced the end of his life.

Morrie: In His Own Words, unabr. ed. Morris S. Schwartz. Read by Jonathan Marosz. 2 CDs. (Running Time: 3 hrs.). 1999. audio compact disk 19.95 (978-0-7366-4482-2(2), 4913-CDR) Books on Tape.

Morrie: In His Own Words. unabr. collector's ed. Morris S. Schwartz. Read by Jonathan Marosz. 2 cass. (Running Time: 3 hrs.). 1999. 17.95 (978-0-7366-4470-9(9), 4913) Books on Tape.
Presents the author's philosophies by which he triumphantly lived, even as he faced the end of his life. Diagnosed at age 77 with Lou Gehrig's Disease, instead of withdrawing & becoming fearful as people with degenerative or terminal illnesses often do, embraced his illness, choosing to live as fully as possible in the time left. He also embarked on his greatest teaching adventure: sharing his evolving knowledge of living & dying.

Morrigan's Cross. Nora Roberts. Read by Dick Hill. (Circle Trilogy: Bk. 1). 2009. 74.99 (978-1-60775-694-1(3)) Find a World.

Morrigan's Cross. abr. ed. Nora Roberts. Read by Dick Hill. (Running Time: 21600 sec.). (Circle Trilogy: Bk. 1). 2007. audio compact disk 14.99 (978-1-4233-0907-9(3), 9781423309079, BCD Value Price) Brilliance Audio.

Morrigan's Cross. unabr. ed. Nora Roberts. Read by Dick Hill. (Running Time: 11 hrs.). (Circle Trilogy: Bk. 1). 2006. 24.95 (978-1-4233-0904-8(9), 9781423309048, BAD); 87.25 (978-1-4233-0899-7(9), 9781423308997, BrilAudUnabridg); audio compact disk 102.25 (978-1-4233-0901-7(4), 9781423309017, BriAudCD Unabrid); audio compact disk 39.25 (978-1-4233-0903-1(0), 9781423309031, Brinc Audio MP3 Lib); audio compact disk 24.95 (978-1-4233-0902-4(2), 9781423309024, Brilliance MP3); audio compact disk 36.95 (978-1-4233-0900-0(6), 9781423309000, Bril Audio CD Unabri) Brilliance Audio.
Please enter a Synopsis.

Morrigan's Cross. unabr. ed. Nora Roberts. Read by Dick Hill. (Running Time: 11 hrs.). (Circle Trilogy: Bk. 2). 2006. 39.25 (978-1-4233-0905-5(7), 9781423309055, BADLE) Brilliance Audio.

Morris Dictionary of Word & Phrase. unabr. ed. Read by Heywood Hale Broun & William Morris. 1 cass. (Running Time: 56 min.). (Broun Radio Ser.). 12.95 (40320) J Norton Pubs.
On this tape, Broun & William Morris tell you who was the "Real McCoy," why some cowboys "dally" & others "tie fast," what a "martini" means to a scuba diver & more.

Morris Dictionary of Word & Phrase Origins (audio CD) William Morris. Interview with Heywood Hale Broun, Jr. (ENG.). 2007. audio compact disk 12.95 (978-1-57970-469-8(7), Audio-For) J Norton Pubs.

Morris' Disappearing Bag. 2004. pap. bk. 32.75 (978-1-55592-276-4(7)); pap. bk. 32.75 (978-1-55592-277-1(5)) Weston Woods.

***Morris Goes to School.** unabr. ed. B. Wiseman. (ENG.). 2007. (978-0-06-143493-8(0)) HarperCollins Pubs.

Morris Goes to School. unabr. ed. Bernard Wiseman. Illus. by Bernard Wiseman. 1 cass. (Running Time: 15 min.). (I Can Read Bks.). (J). (gr. k-3). 1991. 8.99 (978-1-55994-495-3(1), TBC 4951) HarperCollins Pubs.

***Morris the Moose.** abr. ed. B. Wiseman. (ENG.). 2007. (978-0-06-134018-5(9)) HarperCollins Pubs.

Morris the Moose. abr. ed. Bernard Wiseman. Illus. by Bernard Wiseman. Read by Michael Danek. 1 cass. (Running Time: 10 min.). (I Can Read Bks.). (J). (ps-3). 1996. 8.99 (978-0-694-70005-9(3)) HarperCollins Pubs.

Morris's Disappearing Bag see Saco Invisible de Morris

Morris's Disappearing Bag. 2004. bk. 24.95 (978-0-89719-782-3(8)); 8.95 (978-1-56008-376-4(X)); cass. & flmstrp 30.00 (978-0-89719-541-6(8)) Weston Woods.

Morris's Disappearing Bag. Rosemary Wells. 1 cass., 5 bks. (Running Time: 15 min.). (J). pap. bk. 32.75 Weston Woods.
It was Christmas morning & Morris got the most wonderful gift of all.

Morris's Disappearing Bag. Rosemary Wells. 1 cass. (Running Time: 15 min.). (J). (gr. k-5). 2000. bk. 24.95 Weston Woods.

Morris's Disappearing Bag. Rosemary Wells. 1 cass. (J). (gr. k-5). 2004. pap. bk. 14.95 (978-0-89719-783-0(6), PRA230); 8.95 (978-0-89719-979-7(0), 230) Weston Woods.

Morrow. HarperCollins Pubs.

Morse Code 0-5 Teacher. 2nd ed. Gordon West. 2 CDs. (Running Time: 2 hrs. 25 mins.). 2003. audio compact disk 14.95 (978-0-945053-37-8(1)) Pub: Master Pub Inc. Dist(s): W5YI Group
2 Audio CD set recorded by Gordon West teaches Morse Code from 0 to 5 words-per-minute.

Morse the Horse Gets His Chance. Todd Shipman. (Running Time: 300 sec.). (J). 2007. audio compact disk 14.99 (978-1-59886-960-6(4)) Tate Pubng.

Morse's Greatest Mystery & Other Stories. unabr. ed. Colin Dexter. Read by Frederick Davidson. 5 cass. (Running Time: 7 hrs.). 1996. 39.95 (978-0-7861-0957-9(2), 1734) Blckstn Audio.
Colin Dexter tantalizes us with six new Inspector Morse adventures, ranging from bite-size morsels of intrigue to longer stories for listeners to sink their teeth into. Then, for added variety, Dexter shows his range with five mysteries featuring new characters, & some familiar ones; one story features that other great English detective, Sherlock Holmes, in a tale that rivals those of Conan Doyle himself.

Morse's Greatest Mystery & Other Stories. unabr. ed. Colin Dexter. Read by Terrence Hardiman. 6 cass. (Running Time: 9 hrs.). (Inspector Morse Mystery Ser.: Bk. 12). 2000. 49.95 (978-0-7451-4368-2(7), CAB 1051) Pub: Chivers Audio Bks GBR. Dist(s): AudioGO
How can the discovery of a short story by an Oxford graduate lead Morse to a murderer? What happens when Morse himself becomes the victim of a crime? And why does a theft at Christmas lead Morse to look upon the festive season with uncharacteristic good will?.

Morse's Greatest Mystery & Other Stories. unabr. ed. Colin Dexter. Narrated by Patrick Tull. 6 cass. (Running Time: 8 hrs.). 1996. 51.00 (978-0-7887-0481-9(8), 94674E7) Recorded Bks.
Collection filled with charismatic characters, unexpected plot twists, & rich touches of dark humor.

Mort. Terry Pratchett. Read by Nigel Planer. (Running Time: 27000 sec.). (Death Ser.). (ENG.). 2008. audio compact disk 71.95 (978-0-7531-4027-7(6)) Isis Pubng Ltd GBR.

Mort. unabr. ed. Terry Pratchett. Read by Nigel Planer. 6 cass. (Running Time: 7 hrs. 45 min.). (Discworld Ser.). (J). 2001. 54.95 (978-1-85695-845-5(0), 950901) Pub: ISIS Lrg Prnt GBR. Dist(s): Ulverscroft US

Mort. unabr. ed. Terry Pratchett. 7 CDs. (Discworld Ser.). (J). 2006. audio compact disk 71.95 (978-0-7531-1746-0(0)) Pub: ISIS Lrg Prnt GBR. Dist(s): Ulverscroft US

Mort a Venise, Thomas Mann. Read by G. Bejean. 3 cass. 31.95 (1582-VSL) Olivia & Hill.
Gustave von Aschenbach, a highly respected German author, arrives in Venice where he finds himself attracted to Tadzio, a 14-year old Polish boy. Although Aschenbach learns there is a cholera epidemic in the city, he chooses to remain.

Mort Crim's Second Thoughts: One Hundred Upbeat Messages for Beat up Americans. unabr. ed. Mort Crim. 2 cass. (Running Time: 3 hrs.). 1997. 14.95 (978-1-55874-570-4(X)) Health Comm.
1999 Audie Award Winner, collection of essays from his daily radio series.

Mort de Judas. Paul Claudel. 1 cass. (Running Time: 1 hrs.). (FRE.). 1996. pap. bk. 19.50 (978-1-58085-365-1(X)) Interlingua VA.

Mort de Twenty-One Cyclistes. 1 cass. (Running Time: 1 hr.). Dramatization. (Maitres du Mystere Ser.). (FRE.). 1996. 11.95 (1378-MA) Olivia & Hill.
Popular radio thriller, interpreted by France's best actors.

Mort D'Ivan Ilitch, Leo Tolstoy. Read by Christophe Lemee. 2 cass. (FRE.). 1995. 28.95 (1768-TH) Olivia & Hill.
Ivan Ilich on his death bed is surrounded by the various members of his family. The most famous agony in literature.

Mortal: Godspeed 1991-1997. 1 CD. 1999. audio compact disk 16.98 (KMGD8646) Provident Mus Dist.

Mortal Allies. Brian Haig. 17 CDs. (Running Time: 21 hrs.). 2002. audio compact disk 136.00 (978-0-7366-8687-7(8)) Books on Tape.
Two opposites, a conservative Navy lawyer and a flamboyantly liberal one, lead to intrigue as they mount a defense case in South Korea.

Mortal Allies. abr. ed. Brian Haig. Read by John Rubenstein. 4 cass. (Running Time: 6 hrs.). 2003. 25.98 (978-1-58621-338-1(5)) Hachet Audio.

Mortal Allies. abr. ed. Brian Haig. Read by John Rubinstein. (ENG.). 2005. 14.98 (978-1-59483-374-8(5)) Pub: Hachet Audio. Dist(s): HachBkGrp

Mortal Allies. unabr. ed. Brian Haig. 14 cass. (Running Time: 21 hrs.). 2002. 112.00 (978-0-7366-8626-6(6)) Books on Tape.

Mortal Bane. Roberta Gellis. Narrated by Nadia May. (Running Time: 12 hrs.). 2002. 34.95 (978-1-59912-395-0(9)) Iofy Corp.

Mortal Bane. unabr. ed. Roberta Gellis. Read by Nadia May. 8 cass. (Running Time: 11 hrs. 30 mins.). 2002. 56.95 (978-0-7861-2356-8(7), 3015); audio compact disk 72.00 (978-0-7861-9396-7(4), 3015) Blckstn Audio.
Magdalene la Batarde is the madam of the Old Priory Guesthouse in Southwark. She and her women are expected to engage in a number of sinful activities, but bloody murder isn't one of them-until Baldassare, the messenger, dies. Though Baldassare isn't a regular client of the Old Priory Guesthouse, Magdalene and her women refuse to allow his death to go unavenged. Chances are if they don't find the killer, they will be assumed guilty, because they are whores, and will be gutted and hanged.

Mortal Causes: An Inspector Rebus Novel. unabr. ed. Ian Rankin. Read by David Rintoul. 8 cass. (Running Time: 8 hrs.). 1996. 69.95 (CAB1265) AudioGO.
A brutally tortured body is discovered in Edinburgh & it seems as if a sinister echo of the city's plague-ridden past has resurfaced. But the Inspector believes a more modern evil, sectarian terrorism, is behind the gruesome discovery.

Mortal Christ. Jack R. Christianson. 2004. 9.95 (978-1-57734-797-2(8)); audio compact disk 10.95 (978-1-57734-798-9(6)) Covenant Comms.

Mortal Danger: How Misconceptions about Russia Imperil America. unabr. ed. Aleksandr Solzhenitsyn. Narrated by Frank Muller. 2 cass. (Running Time: 3 hrs.). 1982. 18.00 (978-1-55690-351-9(0), 82012E7) Recorded Bks.
The Soviet Union's best-known dissident makes a plea for better East-West understanding.

Mortal Error. abr. ed. Bonar Menninger. Read by John Hockenberry. 2 cass. (Running Time: 3 hrs.). 17.00 Set. S&S Audio.

Mortal Fear. Greg Iles. 2 cass. 1997. 23.95 Penguin Grp USA.

Mortal Fear. abr. ed. Greg Iles. Read by Jay O. Sanders. 4 cass. Library ed. (Running Time: 6 hrs.). 2002. 62.25 (978-1-59086-128-8(0), 1590861280, CD Lib Edit) Brilliance Audio.
By day, Harper Cole trades commodities over the internet from his isolated Mississippi farmhouse. At night, he is systems operator of E.R.O.S., an exclusive, sexually explicit on-line service that guarantees total anonymity to its rich and famous clientele. But now someone has penetrated E.R.O.S.'s state-of-the-art security...someone who has brutally murdered six celebrated women. Each time, the weapon and the city are different. And each time, the killer has claimed the same horrifying trophy. For Harper Cole, who has suddenly become the prime suspect, there is only one way to lure the elusive madman into the open. But Harper Cole has dangerous sexual secrets of his own. His daring plan will place everything and everyone he loves in the path of a brilliant, unstoppable killer.

Mortal Fear. abr. ed. Greg Iles. Read by Jay O. Sanders. (Running Time: 6 hrs.). 2006. 24.95 (978-1-4233-0143-1(9), 9781423301431, BAD) Brilliance Audio.

Mortal Fear. abr. ed. Greg Iles. Read by Jay O. Sanders. (Running Time: 6 hrs.). 2007. audio compact disk 14.99 (978-1-4233-3183-4(4), 9781423331834, BCD Value Price) Brilliance Audio.

Mortal Fear. unabr. ed. Robin Cook. Read by Donada Peters. 8 cass. (Running Time: 8 hrs.). 1992. 64.00 (978-0-7366-2294-3(2), 3079) Books on Tape.

Mortal Fear. unabr. ed. Greg Iles. Read by Dan John Miller & Eric G. Dove. (Running Time: 21 hrs.). 2010. 29.99 (978-1-4418-1148-6(6), 9781441811486, Brilliance MP3); 29.99 (978-1-4418-1150-9(8), 9781441811509, BAD); 44.97 (978-1-4418-1149-3(4), 9781441811493, Brinc Audio MP3 Lib); 44.97 (978-1-4418-1151-6(6), 9781441811516, BADLE); audio compact disk 39.99 (978-1-4418-1146-2(X), 9781441811462, Bril Audio CD Unabri); audio compact disk 99.97 (978-1-4418-1147-9(8), 9781441811479, BriAudCD Unabrid) Brilliance Audio.

Mortal Fear, unabr. ed. Greg Iles. Narrated by Richard Ferrone. 15 cass. (Running Time: 22 hrs. 30 mins.). 1997. 125.00 (978-0-7887-0911-1(9), 95051E7) Recorded Bks.
The internet serves as the playing ground for this chilling psychosexual thriller as women drop out of an exclusive on-line server only to be found brutally murdered.

Mortal Friends. unabr. ed. James Carroll. Read by Dana Craig. 18 cass. 107.10 Audio Bk.
A rich novel sweeping from the bloodstained Irish Rebellion of the early twenties to the tumultuous Boston of the Kennedys.

Mortal Friends. unabr. ed. Jane Stanton Hitchcock. (Running Time: 11 hrs. 50 mins.). 2009. 29.95 (978-1-4332-9225-5(4)); 65.95 (978-1-4332-9221-7(1)) Blckstn Audio.

Mortal Friends. unabr. ed. Jane Stanton Hitchcock. Narrated by Jennifer Van Dyck. 10 CDs. (Running Time: 11 hrs. 50 mins.). 2009. audio compact disk 100.00 (978-1-4332-9222-4(X)) Blckstn Audio.

***Mortal Friends.** unabr. ed. Jane Stanton Hitchcock. Read by Jennifer Van Dyck. (ENG.). 2009. (978-0-06-177655-7(6), Harper Audio); (978-0-06-190237-6(3), Harper Audio) HarperCollins Pubs.

Mortal Immortal see Desiree's Baby

Mortal Instruments: City of Bones; City or Ashes; City of Glass. unabr. ed. Cassandra Clare. Read by Ari Graynor & Natalie Moore. (Running Time: 42 hrs. 0 mins. 0 sec.). (Mortal Instruments Ser.). (ENG.). (YA). 2009. 49.99 (978-1-4423-0377-5(8)) Pub: S&S Audio. Dist(s): S and S Inc

Mortal Lessons: Notes on the Art of Surgery. Richard Selzer. Read by Christopher Hurt. 7 cass. (Running Time: 7 hrs.). 1983. 42.00 (978-0-7366-0614-1(9), 1576) Books on Tape.
An inquiry into the meaning behind medicine. Beautiful & poetic essays on the practive of surgery.

Mortal Prey. collector's ed. John Sandford, pseud. Narrated by Richard Ferrone. 8 cass. (Running Time: 9 hrs. 30 mins.). (Prey Ser.). 2002. 39.95 (978-1-4025-1855-3(2), 97052) Recorded Bks.
Years ago, Lucas Davenport almost died at the hands of Clara Rinker, a pleasant, soft-spoken, low-key Southerner, and the best hitwoman in the business. Now retired and living in Mexico, she nearly dies herself when a sniper kills her boyfriend, the son of a local druglord, and while the boy's father vows vengeance, Rinker knows something he doesn't ... the boy wasn't the target - she was - and now she's going to have to disappear to find the killer herself.

Mortal Prey. unabr. ed. John Sandford, pseud. Narrated by Richard Ferrone. 8 cass. (Running Time: 11 hrs. 30 mins.). (Prey Ser.). 2002. 72.00 (978-1-4025-1823-2(4)); audio compact disk 97.00 (978-1-4025-2070-9(0)) Recorded Bks.

Mortal Sins. Penn Williamson. 2001. (978-1-58621-016-8(5)) Hachet Audio.

Mortal Sins. abr. ed. Penelope Williamson. Read by Theodore Bikel. (ENG.). 2005. 14.98 (978-1-59483-461-5(X)) Pub: Hachet Audio. Dist(s): HachBkGrp

Mortal Sins, abr. ed. Penn Williamson. 4 cass. (Running Time: 6 hrs.). 2000. 24.98 Hachet Audio.
In 1927 Louisiana, Chief Investigator Daman Rourke investigates the murder of a Creole aristocrat. The chief suspect is the victim's wife & Rourke's old flame. As the evidence mounts against her, three murders rock the city & Rourke is torn between old loyalties & his pursuit of the truth.

Mortal Sins. unabr. ed. Penn Williamson. Narrated by Jack Garrett. 11 cass. (Running Time: 16 hrs.). 2000. 94.00 (978-0-7887-4947-6(1), 96455E7) Recorded Bks.
The year is 1927 & the Big Easy is abuzz at the gruesome death of Charles St. Claire. The evidence points to St. Claire's widow glamorous movie actress Remy Lelourie. Handsome police detective Damon Rourke is as ready to believe her guilt as everyone else even if she is his former lover. The only trouble is that Rourke has an obsession with finding the truth & the truth in this case is tangled up in family ties that go back generations.

Mortal Stakes. unabr. collector's ed. Robert B. Parker. Read by Michael Prichard. 6 cass. (Running Time: 6 hrs.). (Spenser Ser.). 1989. 48.00 (978-0-7366-1530-3(X), 2400) Books on Tape.
Everybody loves a winner & the Rabbs are major league. Marty is the Red Sox star pitcher, Linda the loving wife. She loves everyone except the blackmailer out to wreck her life. America's favorite pastime has suddenly become a very dangerous sport & one wrong move means strike three, with Spencer out for good.

Morte D'Arthur see Cambridge Treasy Malory

Morte D'Arthur. abr. ed. Thomas Malory. Read by Derek Jacobi. Contrib. by Derek Jacobi. 8 CDs. (Running Time: 9 hrs.). (ENG.). 2005. audio compact disk 34.95 (978-1-56511-938-3(X), 156511938X) Pub: HighBridge. Dist(s): Workman Pub

Morte D'Arthur, Vol. 1. Read by Frederick Davidson. Photos by Thomas Malory. 11 cass. (Running Time: 16 hrs. 30 min.). 1999. 76.95 (2293) Blckstn Audio.
This monumental work made the Arthurian cycle available for the first time in English. Took a body of legends, which had gone from the folklore to Celtic Britain into French literature by way of Brittany, gave the tales an English perspective & produced a work which ever since has had tremendous influence upon literature.

Morte D'Arthur, Vol. 6. unabr. ed. Read by Frederick Davidson. Photos by Thomas Malory. 7 cass. (Running Time: 10 hrs.). 1998. 49.95 (978-0-7861-1444-3(4), 2307) Blckstn Audio.
Malory took a body of legends, gave the tales an English perspective & produced a monumental work which ever since has had tremendous influence upon literature.

Morte d'Arthur: Lancelot & Guinevere. Perf. by Thomas Malory et al. Contrib. by Allegro Ensemble. Music by Allegro Ensemble. 2 cass. 15.95 (SCN 127) J Norton Pubs.
It is the final, tragic years of Arthur's reign & the story is concerned with the love affair between Lancelot & Queen Guinevere, Arthur's last battles & his departure to Avalon.

Morte D'Arthur: Volume I. unabr. ed. Thomas Malory. Read by Frederick Davidson. (Running Time: 1 hr. 0 mins.). (ENG.). 2009. 29.95 (978-1-4417-0051-3(X)); audio compact disk 118.00 (978-1-4417-0048-3(X)) Blckstn Audio.

Morte D'Arthur: Volume II. unabr. ed. Thomas Malory. Read by Frederick Davidson. (Running Time: 2 hrs. 0 mins.). (ENG.). 2009. 44.95 (978-1-4417-0057-5(9)); audio compact disk 123.00 (978-1-4417-0054-4(4)) Blckstn Audio.

Morte d'Arthur, Vol. 1. unabr. ed. Thomas Malory. Read by Frederick Davidson. (Running Time: 15 hrs. 30 mins.). 1998. 76.95 (978-0-7861-1417-7(7)) Blckstn Audio.

Mortgage Delinquency & Foreclosure Relief: Learn about the Options That Can Save Your Home & Credit Without Filing for Bankruptcy. Scripts. Directed By Michael M. Meiser. 1 CD. (Running Time: 50 mins.). 2003. cd-rom & audio compact disk 29.95 (978-0-9745732-0-5(5)) Concept Guides.
Program includes: Audio CD* Practical Workbook with forms & Letters* CD-Rom with full-size digital files of Workbook.*

Mortgage Foreclosure & Alternatives. 3rd ed. Jacalyn N. Kolk et al. Contrib. by Florida Bar Staff. (Florida Bar's FasTrain Ser.). 2003. pap. bk. 68.00 (978-0-8205-9964-9(6)) Pub: FL Bar Legal Ed. Dist(s): LEXIS Pub

Mortgage Foreclosures. 1987. bk. 85.00 incl. book.; 50.00 cass. only.; 35.00 book only. PA Bar Inst.

Mortgage Foreclosures: 1991. 1991. 65.00 (AC-640) PA Bar Inst.

Mortgage Lending Loan Officer Basic Training. S. K. Kenney. 2008. per. 199.99 (978-1-933039-29-9(9)) Eiram Pubng.

Mortgages. 2nd abr. ed. Eric Tyson & Ray Brown. Read by Brett Barry. (Running Time: 12600 sec.). (For Dummies Ser.). 2007. audio compact disk 14.95 (978-0-06-117593-0(5)) HarperCollins Pubs.

***Mortgages for Dummies 2nd Ed.** abr. ed. Eric Tyson & Ray Brown. Read by Brett Barry. (ENG.). 2006. (978-0-06-128727-5(X), Harper Audio); (978-0-06-128728-2(8), Harper Audio) HarperCollins Pubs.

Mortification: Blood World. 1 CD. 1999. audio compact disk 16.98 (KMGD9788) Provident Mus Dist.

Mortification: Primitive Rhythm Machine. 1 CD. 1999. audio compact disk 16.98 (KMGD9526) Provident Mus Dist.

Mortification: The Best of Five Years. 1 CD. 1999. audio compact disk 16.98 (KMGD9547) Provident Mus Dist.

Mortimer: The Very Rich Mouse. 2nd rev. ed. Dixon DeVore, II. Prod. by Cricket Power Records and Tapes Staff. 1 stereo cass. (J). (gr. k-5). 1987. pap. bk. (978-0-9614998-1-5(8), CP3109-A) Cricket Power.

Mortimer's Cross. unabr. ed. Joan Aiken. Read by Judy Bennett. 2 cass. (Running Time: 2 hrs.). (J). 1997. 16.98 (LL 3047) AudioGO.

Mortimer's Cross. unabr. ed. Joan Aiken. 2 cass. (Running Time: 2 hrs. 55 min.). (Middle Grade Cassette Library). (YA). (gr. 3-5). 1987. 16.98 (978-0-8072-7208-4(6), YA 804 CX, Listening Lib) Random Audio Pubg.
Arabel Jones & her cantankerous pet raven Mortimer, the greatest problem-solving pair since Holmes & Watson, tackle new brain teasers in three stories. When Mortimer is not quoting Poe, he is engaged in feats of derring-do, helping Arabel to unravel mysteries. When will this duo find a case they can't crack? Nevermore.

Mortmain see Robert Penn Warren Reads Selected Poems

***Mosaic.** Diane Armstrong. Read by Deidre Rubenstein. (Running Time: 20 hrs.). 2010. 119.99 (978-1-74214-633-1(3), 9781742146331) Pub: Bolinda Pubng AUS. Dist(s): Bolinda Pub Inc

Mosaic. Jeri Taylor. (Star Trek Voyager Ser.). 2004. 10.95 (978-0-7435-4630-0(X)) Pub: S&S Audio. Dist(s): S and S Inc

Mosaic. unabr. ed. Diane Armstrong. Read by Deidre Rubenstein. 14 cass. (Running Time: 20 hrs.). 2001. 112.00 (978-1-74030-460-3(8)) Pub: Bolinda Pubng AUS. Dist(s): Bolinda Pub Inc

Mosaic. unabr. ed. Diane Armstrong. Read by Deidre Rubenstein. (Running Time: 20 hrs.). 2009. audio compact disk 123.95 (978-1-74214-419-1(5), 9781742144191) Pub: Bolinda Pubng AUS. Dist(s): Bolinda Pub Inc

Mosaic. unabr. ed. Michael Holroyd. 6 cass. (Running Time: 7 hrs. 42 mins.). (Isis Cassettes Ser.). (J). 2005. 54.95 (978-0-7531-2027-9(5)) Pub: ISIS Lrg Prnt GBR. Dist(s): Ulverscroft US

Mosaic. unabr. ed. John R. Maxim. Read by Dick Hill. (Running Time: 12 hrs.). 2008. 39.25 (978-1-4233-5456-7(7), 9781423354567, Brlnc Audio MP3 Lib); 39.25 (978-1-4233-5458-1(3), 9781423354581, BADLE); 24.95 (978-1-4233-5455-0(9), 9781423354550, Brilliance MP3); 24.95 (978-1-4233-5457-4(5), 9781423354574, BAD) Brilliance Audio.

Mosaic, Set. abr. ed. John R. Maxim. Read by Dick Hill. 2 cass. 1999. 17.95 (FS9-43400) Highsmith.

Mosaic: Pieces of My Life So Far. abr. unabr. ed. Amy Grant. Read by Amy Grant. (Running Time: 4 hrs.). 2007. 39.25 (978-1-4233-4312-7(3), 9781423343127, BADLE); 24.95 (978-1-4233-4311-0(5), 9781423343110, BAD); audio compact disk 26.95 (978-1-4233-4307-3(7), 9781423343073, Bril Audio CD Unabri); audio compact disk 24.95 (978-1-4233-4309-7(3), 9781423343097, Brilliance MP3) Brilliance Audio.

Mosaic: Pieces of My Life So Far. unabr. ed. Amy Grant. Read by Amy Grant. 3 cass. (Running Time: 14400 sec.). 2007. 62.25 (978-1-4233-4306-6(9), 9781423343066, BrilAudUnabridg); audio compact disk 39.25 (978-1-4233-4310-3(7), 9781423343103, Brlnc Audio MP3 Lib); audio compact disk 69.25 (978-1-4233-4308-0(5), 9781423343080, BriAudCD Unabrid) Brilliance Audio.

Mosaic: Poems of an Ancient Order. Lester Hirsh. (Running Time: 30mins). 2003. 15.00 (978-1-930149-23-6(9), Writ Pub Coop) Pub: Beech River. Dist(s): Enfield Pubs NH

Mosaic 1 Listening/Speaking. 4th rev. ed. Created by McGraw-Hill Contemporary Staff. 2001. 23.13 (978-0-07-255614-8(5), 9780072556148, ESL/ELT) Pub: McGrw-H Hghr Educ. Dist(s): McGraw

Mosaic 2 Listening/Speaking. 4th rev. ed. Created by McGraw-Hill Contemporary Staff. 2001. 23.13 (978-0-07-255615-5(3), 9780072556155, ESL/ELT) Pub: McGrw-H Hghr Educ. Dist(s): McGraw

Mosaicos: Spanish as a World Language. 4th ed. Castells et al. 2005. audio compact disk 22.60 (978-0-13-196979-7(X)) Pearson Educ CAN CAN.

Mosaicos: Spanish as a World Language. 4th ed. Created by Pearson/Prentice Hall. 2005. audio compact disk 15.20 (978-0-13-196984-1(6)) Pearson Educ CAN CAN.

Mosaicos: Spanish as a World Language. 4th ed. Created by Pearson/Prentice Hall. 2005. audio compact disk 61.20 (978-0-13-154642-4(2)) Pearson Educ CAN CAN.

Mosby Soundbytes: Psychiatry. Mosby Staff. 1996. 36.00 (978-0-8151-3712-2(5), MosElsHlth) Elsevier HthSci.

Mosby's Memoirs & Other Stories. unabr. collector's ed. Saul Bellow. Read by Wolfram Kandinsky. 7 cass. (Running Time: 10 hrs. 30 mins.). 1986. 56.00 (978-0-7366-1038-4(3), 1968) Books on Tape.
A collection of stories, including "Leaving the Yellow House," "The Old System," "Looking for Mr. Green," "The Gonzaga Manuscripts," "A Father-to-Be" & "Mosby's Memoirs".

Mosby's Men. unabr. ed. John H. Alexander. Narrated by Norman Dietz. 3 cass. (Running Time: 4 hrs. 45 mins.). 1988. 26.00 (978-1-55690-352-6(9), 88500E7) Recorded Bks.
John Alexander rode with the Confederate guerrillas in 1864. His account tells how he joined Colonel Mosby & his infamous rough riders, how they managed their ventures behind enemy lines & how they evaded capture by the Union troops.

Mosby's Rangers. unabr. ed. Jeffrey D. Wert. Read by Dick Estell. 9 cass. (Running Time: 13 hrs. 30 min.). 1992. 72.00 (978-0-7366-2111-3(3), 2915) Books on Tape.
The tale of Lieutenant John Singleton Mosby, who led a guerrilla battalion for the Confederacy during the last two years of the Civil War.

***Moscow Club.** abr. ed. Joseph Finder. (Running Time: 6 hrs. 0 mins. 0 sec.). (ENG.). 2010. audio compact disk 14.99 (978-1-4272-1172-9(8)) Pub: Macmill Audio. Dist(s): Macmillan

Moscow Rules. Daniel Silva. Read by Phil Gigante. (Gabriel Allon Ser.: No. 8). 2009. 69.99 (978-1-60812-682-8(X)) Find a World.

Moscow Rules. abr. ed. Daniel Silva. Read by Phil Gigante. (Running Time: 6 hrs.). (Gabriel Allon Ser.: No. 8). 2008. audio compact disk 14.99 (978-1-4233-0659-7(7), 9781423306597, BCD Value Price) Brilliance Audio.

Moscow Rules. abr. ed. Daniel Silva. Read by Phil Gigante. 5 CDs. (Running Time: 6 hrs.). (Gabriel Allon Ser.: No. 8). 2008. audio compact disk 26.95 (978-1-4233-2803-2(5), 9781423328032, BACD) Brilliance Audio.

Moscow Rules. abr. ed. Daniel Silva. Read by Phil Gigante. (Running Time: 6 hrs.). (Gabriel Allon Ser.: No. 8). 2009. audio compact disk 14.99 (978-1-4233-2804-9(3), 9781423328049, BCD Value Price) Brilliance Audio.

Moscow Rules. unabr. ed. Daniel Silva. Read by Phil Gigante. 1 MP3-CD. (Running Time: 12 hrs.). (Gabriel Allon Ser.: No. 8). 2007. 24.95 (978-1-59335-769-6(9), 9781593357696, Brilliance MP3); 39.25 (978-1-59710-936-9(3), 9781597109369, BADLE); 24.95 (978-1-59710-937-6(1), 9781597109376, BAD); 39.25 (978-1-59335-787-0(7), 9781593357870, Brlnc Audio MP3 Lib); 92.25 (978-1-59600-033-9(3), 9781596000339, BrilAudUnabridg); audio compact disk 107.25 (978-1-59600-036-0(8), 9781596000360, BriAudCD Unabrid) Brilliance Audio.
Please enter a Synopsis.

Moscow Rules. unabr. ed. Daniel Silva. Read by Phil Gigante. 1 MP3-CD. (Running Time: 10 hrs.). (Gabriel Allon Ser.: No. 8). 2008. 24.95 (978-1-4233-2799-8(3), 9781423327998, Brilliance MP3); 39.25 (978-1-4233-2802-5(7), 9781423328025, BADLE); 39.25 (978-1-4233-2800-1(0), 9781423328001, Brlnc Audio MP3 Lib); 24.95 (978-1-4233-2801-8(9), 9781423328018, BAD); audio compact disk 36.95 (978-1-4233-2797-4(7), 9781423327974, Bril Audio CD Unabri); audio compact disk 97.25 (978-1-4233-2798-1(5), 9781423327981, BriAudCD Unabrid) Brilliance Audio.

Moscow Rules. unabr. ed. Daniel Silva. Read by Phil Gigante. (Gabriel Allon Ser.: No. 8). (YA). 2008. 89.99 (978-1-60514-820-5(2)) Find a World.

***Moscow Sting.** unabr. ed. Alex Dryden. (Running Time: 13 hrs. 0 mins.). 2010. 18.99 (978-1-4001-8627-3(7)); 24.99 (978-1-4001-6627-5(6)); 37.99 (978-1-4001-9627-2(2)) Tantor Media.

***Moscow Sting.** unabr. ed. Alex Dryden. Narrated by Anne Flosnik & Simon Vance. 9 CDs. (Running Time: 10 hrs. 30 mins. 0 sec.). 2010. audio compact disk 34.99 (978-1-4001-1627-0(9)); audio compact disk 69.99 (978-1-4001-4627-7(5)) Pub: Tantor Media. Dist(s): IngramPubServ

Moscow Vector. Patrick Larkin. Read by Erik Bergmann. Characters created by Robert Ludlum. (Covert-One Ser.). 2005. 23.95 (978-1-59397-710-8(7)) Pub: Macmill Audio. Dist(s): Macmillan

Moscow Vector. abr. ed. Patrick Larkin. Read by Erik Bergmann. Characters created by Robert Ludlum. (Covert-One Ser.). 2005. 17.95 (978-1-59397-709-2(3)) Pub: Macmill Audio. Dist(s): Macmillan

Moscow Vector. abr. ed. Robert Ludlum & Patrick Larkin. Read by Erik Bergmann. Created by Robert Ludlum. 5 CDs. (Running Time: 6 hrs. 0 mins. 0 sec.). (Covert-One Ser.). (ENG.). 2005. audio compact disk 29.95 (978-1-59397-675-0(5)) Pub: Macmill Audio. Dist(s): Macmillan

Moscow Vector. abr. unabr. ed. Patrick Larkin & Robert Ludlum. Read by Erik Bergmann. (Running Time: 6 hrs. 0 mins. 0 sec.). (Covert-One Ser.). (ENG.). 2007. audio compact disk 14.95 (978-1-4272-0313-7(X)) Pub: Macmill Audio. Dist(s): Macmillan

Moscow Vector. unabr. ed. Patrick Larkin. Characters created by Robert Ludlum. 2 pieces. (Covert-One Ser.). 2005. 49.95 (978-0-7927-3677-6(X), CMP 817); 69.95 (978-0-7927-3675-2(3), CSL 817); audio compact disk 110.95 (978-0-7927-3676-9(1), SLD 817) AudioGO.

Moscow Vector. unabr. ed. Robert Ludlum & Patrick Larkin. Read by Erik Bergmann. Created by Robert Ludlum. 12 CDs. (Running Time: 14 hrs. 30 mins. 0 sec.). (Covert-One Ser.). (ENG.). 2005. audio compact disk 49.95 (978-1-59397-677-4(1)) Pub: Macmill Audio. Dist(s): Macmillan

Moscow 1941: A City & Its People at War. unabr. ed. Rodric Braithwaite. Narrated by Simon Vance. (Running Time: 14 hrs. 0 mins. 0 sec.). (ENG.). 2006. audio compact disk 39.99 (978-1-4001-0319-5(3)); audio compact disk 29.99 (978-1-4001-5319-0(0)); audio compact disk 79.99 (978-1-4001-3319-2(X)) Pub: Tantor Media. Dist(s): IngramPubServ

Mose the Fireman/Stormalong. unabr. ed. Rabbit Ears Books Staff. Read by Michael Keaton & John Candy. 2 CDs. (Running Time: 2700 sec.). (Rabbit Ears Treasury of American Tall Tales Ser.: Vol. 2). (J). (gr. 1). 2007. audio compact disk 11.95 (978-0-7393-5062-1(5), Listening Lib) Pub: Random Audio Pubg. Dist(s): Random

Moses: A Life. Jonathan Kirsch. Read by Geoffrey Howard. 2000. 88.00 (978-0-7366-4923-0(9)) Books on Tape.

Moses: A Man of Selfless Dedication. Charles R. Swindoll. (ENG.). 2007. audio compact disk 58.00 (978-1-57972-753-6(0)) Insight Living.

Moses: Prophet & Political Radical. Richard Rohr. Read by Richard Rohr. 1 cass. (Running Time: 65 min.). 1992. 9.95 (978-7-900782-08-3(7), AA2533) Credence Commun.
Rohr shows us how the prophetic gift leads us to criticize our political situation.

Moses Set: A Life. abr. ed. Jonathan Kirsch. Read by Michael Gross. 4 cass. (Running Time: 6 hrs.). 1999. 24.95 (978-1-57453-318-7(5)) Audio Lit.
Moses is a mysterious & complex figure, at once good shepherd & ruthless warrior, spiritual leader & renegade, lawmaker & lawbreaker. Beyond the images of Sunday school & movies, Kirsch offers a fresh look at the life & work of the liberator & prophet.

Moses & Other Stories from the Old Testament. abr. ed. David Angus. Read by Kerry Shale. 2 CDs. (Junior Classics Ser.). (J). 2005. audio compact disk 17.98 (978-962-634-367-8(2)) Naxos UK GBR.

Moses Baby in the Bulrushes. Dalmatian Press Staff. (J). (ps-3). 2000. pap. bk. 4.97 (978-1-888567-36-6(8)) Dalmatian Pr.

Moses Called by God. 1 cass. (Running Time: 1 hr.). (Mother Angelica Live Ser.). 1987. 10.00 (978-1-55794-094-0(0), T45) Eternal Wrd TV.

Moses Code Frequency Meditation: Includes 7 Songs from the Movie the Moses Code. James F. Twyman. 2008. audio compact disk 15.00 (978-1-4019-2314-3(3)) Hay House.

Moses in Esoteric Tradition. Zalman Sch[illegible]ter. 1 cass. 9.00 (A0619-90) Sound Photosyn.
At the San Francisco Jewish Communi[illegible]nter.

Moses Successor: Numbers 27:12-23. Ed Young. 1985. 4.95 (978-0-7417-1443-5(4), 443) Win Walk.

Moses Znaimer - Dalton Camp Lecture. Speeches. Moses Znaimer. 1 CD. (Running Time: 1 hr.). 2006. audio compact disk 15.95 (978-0-660-19552-0(6), CBC Audio) Canadian Broadcasting CAN.

Moshe Dor. unabr. ed. Moshe Dor. Read by Moshe Dor. 1 cass. (Running Time: 29 min.). 1990. 10.00 (060890) New Letters.
Dor is an Israeli poet who has won Israel's equivalent of the Pulitzer prize, called the Bialik prize. In this interview Dor reads poems, talks about his unusual political beliefs & his songs are performed by an Israeli folksinger.

Moshi Moshi. 1 cass. (Running Time: 1 hr.). (Yoroshiku Ser.: Stages 1 and 2). (YA). (gr. 6-8). EducServs AUS.

Moshino's Works for Girl Studio. Katsura Moshino. (ENG & JPN., 1999. bk. 19.95 (978-4-309-90290-6(1)) Pub: Edtns Treville JPN. Dist(s): RAM Publications

Mosquito, Pt. 1. unabr. collector's ed. Gayl Jones. Read by Rebecca Nicholas. 8 cass. (Running Time: 12 hrs.). 1999. 64.00 (978-0-7366-4830-1(5), 5176-A) Books on Tape.
Mosquito is an African-American truck driver. Set in a south Texas border town, this is a story of her accidental & yet growing involvement in "the new underground railroad", a sanctuary movement for Mexican immigrants. Mosquito's journey begins when she discovers Maria, a stowaway who nearly gives birth in the back of the truck. Along the road, Mosquito introduces us to Delgadina, a Chicana bartender who fries cactus, writes haunting stories & studies to become a detective. We also meet Monkey Bread, a childhood pal who is, improbably, assistant to a blonde star in Hollywood & then there's her song & even a complete play. This is an unforgettable journey.

Mosquito, Pt. 2. unabr. collector's ed. Gayl Jones. Read by Rebecca Nicholas. 9 cass. (Running Time: 13 hrs. 30 min.). 1999. 72.00 (978-0-7366-4899-8(2), 5176-B) Books on Tape.
Mosquito is an African-American truck driver. Set in a south Texas border town, this is a story of her accidental & yet growing involvement in "the new underground railroad", a sanctuary movement for Mexican immigrants. Mosquito's journey begins when she discovers Maria, a stowaway who nearly gives birth in the back of the truck. Along the road, Mosquito introduces us to Delgadina, a Chicana bartender who fries cactus, writes haunting stories & studies to become a detective. We also meet Monkey Bread, a childhood pal who is, improbably, assistant to a blonde star in Hollywood & then there's her song & even a complete play. This is an unforgettable journey.

Mosquitoes. unabr. collector's ed. William Faulkner. Read by Michael Prichard. 7 cass. (Running Time: 10 hrs. 30 mins.). 1992. 56.00 (978-0-7366-2110-6(5), 2914) Books on Tape.
An unusual assortment of people have been summoned to a society matron's yacht. No one knows why.

Mosquitoes & Mountains. Elbert Willis. 1 cass. (Faithfulness Through Love Ser.). 4.00; 4.00 Fill the Gap.

***Mosquitoes Are Running My Summer! & Other Silly Dilly Camp Songs.** unabr. ed. Alan Katz. (Running Time: 2 hrs.). 2010. 4.99 (978-1-4418-5945-7(4), 9781441859457, BAD); 19.97 (978-1-4418-5946-4(2), 9781441859464, BADLE); audio compact disk 9.99 (978-1-4418-5943-3(8), 9781441859433, Bril Audio CD Unabri); audio compact disk 19.97 (978-1-4418-5944-0(6), 9781441859440, BriAudCD Unabrid) Brilliance Audio.

Moss-Green Princess see Black Fairy Tales

An Asterisk (*) at the beginning of an entry indicates that the title is appearing for the first time.

Mossflower. Brian Jacques. Narrated by Brian Jacques. 10 CDs. (Running Time: 11 hrs. 45 mins.). (Redwall Ser.). audio compact disk 111.00 (978-1-4025-2322-9(X)) Recorded Bks.

Mossflower. Brian Jacques. Narrated by Brian Jacques. 9 pieces. (Running Time: 11 hrs. 45 mins.). (Redwall Ser.). (gr. 3 up). 1988. 87.00 (978-1-4025-0652-9(X), 96884) Recorded Bks.
When the peaceful land of Mossflower is conquered by an evil wildcat queen, it is up to a heroic mouse, Martin, to save his homeland and drive her away. The spell of this animal fantasy is irresistible.

Mossflower. Brian Jacques & Brian Jacques. 7 cass. (Running Time: 11 hrs. 45 mins.). (Redwall Ser.). 2004. 29.99 (978-1-4025-0529-4(9), 00934) Recorded Bks.

Mossflower. unabr. ed. Brian Jacques. Narrated by Ron Keith. 10 cass. (Running Time: 14 hrs. 30 mins.). (Redwall Ser.). (J). (gr. 4-8). 1997. 87.00 (978-0-7887-0538-0(5), 94733E7) Recorded Bks.
Return to the magical animal world in this prequel to "Redwall." Long before the abbey of Redwall is built, the land is know simply as Mossflower, a cruel wildcat queen who demands obedience & offers the castle's dungeon to those who defy her, comes along.

Most Agreeable Man: Lyman Foster Brackett, Performer, Composer & Hymnal Editor for the Church of Christ, Scientist. Peter J. Hodgson. 2003. pap. bk. (978-0-9740548-0-3(1)) Longyear.

Most Amazing Dinosaur Songs. 1 cass. (Running Time: 37:06 min.). 2004. 3.98 (978-1-56628-406-6(6)); audio compact disk 6.98 (978-1-56628-405-9(8)) M-H Contemporary.

Most Beautiful Gift. abr. ed. Jonathan Snow. (ENG.). 2006. 5.98 (978-1-59483-691-6(4)) Pub: Hachet Audio. Dist(s): HachBkGrp

Most Beautiful House in the World. unabr. ed. Witold Rybczynski. Read by Nadia May. 4 cass. (Running Time: 5 hrs. 30 mins.). 1992. 32.95 (978-0-7861-0353-9(1), 1310) Blckstn Audio.
Witold Rybczyski takes us on an extraordinary odyssey as he tells the story of the designing & building of his own house. Rybczynski's project began as a workshed; through a series of "happy accidents," however, the structure gradually evolved into a full-fledged house.

Most Beautiful Word: Psalms 130:4. Ed Young. 1980. 4.95 (978-0-7417-1139-7(7), A0139) Win Walk.

Most Dangerous Game. Richard Connell. 10.00 (LSS1117) Esstee Audios.

Most Dangerous Game. Richard Connell. Adapted by Bob E. Flick. Des. by Adam Mayefsky. 1 CD. (Running Time: 52 mins.). Dramatization. 2002. audio compact disk 15.00 (978-1-884214-24-0(X)) Ziggurat Prods.
Employs multiple voices to tell this haunting classic short story about a hunter becoming the hunted. Accomplished big-game hunter Sanger Rainsford is washed ashore on a South American island owned by General Zaroff, a maniacal sportsman whose quarry is the two-legged kind. When Rainsford finds himself the prey of the madman, he must kill or be killed.

Most Dangerous Game Part I: America's Nuclear Strategy. 1 cass. (Running Time: 1 hr.). 10.95 (K090AB090, HarperThor) HarpC GBR.

Most Dangerous Game Part II: Soviet Perspectives on Nuclear War. 1 cass. (Running Time: 1 hr.). 10.95 (K090BB090, HarperThor) HarpC GBR.

Most Dangerous Game Part III: Nuclear Faceoffs in Europe. 1 cass. (Running Time: 1 hr.). 10.95 (K090CB090, HarperThor) HarpC GBR.

Most Dangerous Game Part IV: International Roundtable. 1 cass. (Running Time: 1 hr.). 10.95 (K090DB090, HarperThor) HarpC GBR.

***Most Dangerous Man in America: Rush Limbaugh's Assault on Reason.** unabr. ed. John K. Wilson. Read by Lois Betterton. (Running Time: 11 hrs. 5 mins.). (ENG.). 2011. 29.95 (978-1-4417-7928-1(0)); 72.95 (978-1-4417-7925-0(6)); audio compact disk 32.95 (978-1-4417-7927-4(2)); audio compact disk 105.00 (978-1-4417-7926-7(4)) Blckstn Audio.

Most Dangerous Man in America: Scenes from the Life of Benjamin Franklin. unabr. ed. Catherine Drinker Bowen. Read by Lois Betterton. 7 cass. (Running Time: 10 hrs.). 1990. 49.95 (978-0-7861-0169-6(5), 1151) Blckstn Audio.
In this, the last book in Catherine Drinker Bowen's brilliant career, she focuses on specific scenes in Franklin's colorful life, including his early discoveries with electricity, activity in the Albany Congress, nine years in London & of course, his part in America's revolutionary plans.

***Most Dangerous Place: Pakistan's Lawless Frontier.** unabr. ed. Imtiaz Gul. Narrated by Kevin Foley. (Running Time: 10 hrs. 0 mins. 0 sec.). (ENG.). 2010. 24.99 (978-1-4001-6797-5(3)); 16.99 (978-1-4001-8797-3(4)); audio compact disk 83.99 (978-1-4001-4797-2(7)); audio compact disk 34.99 (978-1-4001-1797-0(6)) Pub: Tantor Media. Dist(s): IngramPubServ

Most Dangerous Word: Proverbs 27:1. Ed Young. (J). 1980. 4.95 (978-0-7417-1121-2(4), A0121) Win Walk.

Most Determined Woman. unabr. ed. Emma Blair. 15 cass. 1998. 116.95 (978-1-85903-206-0(0)) Pub: Magna Story GBR. Dist(s): Ulverscroft US

Most Evil. unabr. ed. Steve Hodel & Ralph Pezzullo. Read by Malcolm Hillgartner. 1 MP3-CD. (Running Time: 7 hrs.). 2009. 39.97 (978-1-4418-0048-0(4), 9781441800480, Brlnc Audio MP3 Lib); 24.99 (978-1-4418-0049-7(2), 9781441800497, BAD); audio compact disk 36.99 (978-1-4418-0045-9(X), 9781441800459) Brilliance Audio.

Most Evil. unabr. ed. Ralph Pezullo. Read by Steve Hodel & Malcolm Hillgartner. Ed. by Steve Hodel. 1 MP3-CD. (Running Time: 7 hrs.). 2009. 24.99 (978-1-4418-0047-3(6), 9781441800473, Brilliance MP3); audio compact disk 87.97 (978-1-4418-0046-6(8), 9781441800466, BriAudCD Unabrid) Brilliance Audio.

Most Evil. unabr. ed. Ralph Pezzullo. Read by Steve Hodel & Malcolm Hillgartner. Ed. by Steve Hodel. (Running Time: 7 hrs.). 2009. 39.97 (978-1-4418-0050-3(6), 9781441800503, BADLE) Brilliance Audio.

Most Heartwarming Christmas Collection Ever! 10 vols. (Running Time: 10 hrs.). bk. 39.98 (978-1-57019-627-0(3), OTR47122) Pub: Radio Spirits. Dist(s): AudioGO

Most Heartwarming Christmas Collection Ever! 10 vols. (Running Time: 10 hrs.). 2003. bk. 34.98 (978-1-57019-628-7(1), OTR47124) Pub: Radio Spirits. Dist(s): AudioGO

Most Important Fish in the Sea. H. Bruce Franklin. (ENG.). 2007. audio compact disk 25.00 (978-1-59726-164-7(5)) Pub: Island Pr. Dist(s): Chicago Distribution Ctr

Most Important Place on Earth: What a Christian Home Looks Like & How to Build One. abr. ed. Robert Wolgemuth. (Running Time: 3 hrs. 30 mins.). 2004. audio compact disk 24.99 (978-0-7852-0921-8(2)) Nelson.
Many people did not grow up in a Christian home, and many more do not consider their childhood experience a good model. Robert Wolgemuth presents this inspiring, practical aduiobook for people who want to have a Christian home. So, what's so great about a Christian home? There's redemption. There's forgiveness. There's hope. Laughter and genuine happiness. There's discipline and purpose there. And there's grace . . . lots of grace. The Most Important Place on Earth, read by the author, covers eight answers to the question "What does a Christian home look like?" It's filled with stories and practical ideas that will convince any reader that a Christian home is not an illusive stereotype. It's something that really can be achieved. And it's something worth having. You'll see.

Most Important Provision. Mac Hammond. 1 CD. (Running Time: 1 hr). 2005. audio compact disk 5.00 (978-1-57399-265-7(8)) Mac Hammond.

***Most Important Year in a Woman's Life/the Most Important Year in a Man's Life: What Every Bride Needs to Know / What Every Groom Needs to Know.** Robert Wolgemuth et al. (Running Time: 9 hrs. 29 mins. 0 sec.). (ENG.). 2008. 19.99 (978-0-310-30484-5(9)) Zondervan.

Most Miraculous Thing in the World: Proverbs 4:23. Ed Young. (J). 1982. 4.95 (978-0-7417-1254-7(7), 254) Win Walk.

Most Mysterious Word: Judges 6:13. Ed Young. (J). 1980. 4.95 (978-0-7417-1123-6(0), A0123) Win Walk.

Most of It see Twentieth-Century Poetry in English, No. 6, Recordings of Poets Reading Their Own Poetry

***Most Powerful Idea in the World: A Story of Steam, Industry, & Invention.** unabr. ed. William Rosen. (Running Time: 12 hrs. 30 mins.). 2010. 18.99 (978-1-4001-8709-6(5)) Tantor Media.

***Most Powerful Idea in the World: A Story of Steam, Industry, & Invention.** unabr. ed. William Rosen. Narrated by Michael Prichard. (Running Time: 13 hrs. 30 mins. 0 sec.). 2010. 24.99 (978-1-4001-6709-8(4)); audio compact disk 69.99 (978-1-4001-4709-0(3)); audio compact disk 34.99 (978-1-4001-1709-3(7)) Pub: Tantor Media. Dist(s): IngramPubServ

Most Powerful Information on Land Patents ever Recorded. Johnson David. 2 CDs. (Running Time: 148 mins). 2004. audio compact disk 34.95 (978-0-9758865-1-9(7)) Law Rsrch Grp.

Most powerful interview series for wealth, health, happiness, love & Success: Discover how to simply & easily tap into the power you already Posses. Interview with Mark Morrison. 2008. audio compact disk 49.97 (978-1-4276-3271-5(5)) AardGP.

Most Precious Gift. Neville Goddard. 1 cass. (Running Time: 62 min.). 1970. 8.00 (85) J & L Pubns.
Neville taught Imagination Creates Reality. He was a powerfully influential teacher of God as Consciousness.

Most Reluctant Convert. David C. Downing & Patrick Cullen. 4 cass. (Running Time: 5 hrs. 30 mins.). 2002. 32.95 (978-0-7861-2608-8(6), 3173) Blckstn Audio.

Most Reluctant Convert. unabr. ed. David C. Downing. Read by Patrick Cullen. (Running Time: 5 hrs. 30 mins.). 2003. 24.95 (978-0-7861-8761-4(1), 3173); audio compact disk 40.00 (978-0-7861-8930-4(4), 3173) Blckstn Audio.

Most Requested: Music for the Spirit. Joe Wise. 1994. 10.95 (328); audio compact disk 15.95 (328) GIA Pubns.

Most Requested Messages Of 2006. 2006. audio compact disk 24.00 (978-1-57972-741-3(7)) Insight Living.

Most Requested Messages Of 2007. Charles R. Swindoll. (ENG.). 2007. audio compact disk 24.00 (978-1-57972-799-4(9)) Insight Living.

Most Successful Small Business in the World: The First Ten Principles. unabr. ed. Michael Gerber. Read by Michael Gerber. (Running Time: 8 hrs. 30 mins.). 2010. 29.95 (978-1-4417-1079-6(5)); audio compact disk 34.95 (978-1-4417-1078-9(7)) Blckstn Audio.

Most Successful Small Business in the World: The First Ten Principles. unabr. ed. Michael E. Gerber. Read by Michael E. Gerber. (Running Time: 8 hrs. 30 mins.). 2010. 54.95 (978-1-4417-1075-8(2)); audio compact disk 76.00 (978-1-4417-1076-5(0)) Blckstn Audio.

Most Successful Solutions to Price Inflation. unabr. ed. Hans F. Sennholz et al. 1 cass. (Running Time: 1 hr. 40 min.). 12.95 (289) J Norton Pubs.

Most Surprising Return. AIO Team Staff. Prod. by Focus on the Family Staff. 2 CDs. (Running Time: 2 hrs.). (Adventures in Odyssey Ser.). (ENG.). (J). 2005. audio compact disk 14.99 (978-1-58997-185-1(X)) Pub: Focus Family. Dist(s): Tyndale Hse

Most They Ever Had. unabr. ed. Rick Bragg. (Running Time: 8.5 hrs. 0 mins.). 2009. 54.95 (978-1-4417-0781-9(6)); audio compact disk 76.00 (978-1-4417-0782-6(4)) Blckstn Audio.

Most They Ever Had. unabr. ed. Rick Bragg. Read by Rick Bragg. (Running Time: 8 hrs. 30 mins.). 2009. 29.95 (978-1-4417-0785-7(9)); audio compact disk 32.95 (978-1-4417-0784-0(0)) Blckstn Audio.

***Most Unusual Camera.** 2010. audio compact disk (978-1-59171-176-6(2)) Falcon Picture.

Most Useful Phrases for Courting see Ingles Callejero: Las Frases Mas Utiles para ENAMORAR

Most Useful Phrases for Finding a Job see Ingles Callejero: Las Frases Mas Utiles para SOLICITAR TRABAJO

***Most Wanted.** abr. ed. Michele Martinez. Read by Anne Twomey. (ENG.). 2005. (978-0-06-083901-7(5), Harper Audio); (978-0-06-083899-7(X), Harper Audio) HarperCollins Pubs.

Most Wanted. abr. ed. Michele Martinez. Read by Anne Twomey. 2005. audio compact disk 29.95 (978-0-06-075969-8(0)) HarperCollins Pubs.

Most Wanted. unabr. ed. Michele Martinez. 2005. 29.95 (978-0-7927-3492-5(0), CMP 761); 59.95 (978-0-7927-3490-1(4), CSL 761); audio compact disk 89.95 (978-0-7927-3491-8(2), SLD 761) AudioGO.

Most Wanted. unabr. ed. Jacquelyn Mitchard. Read by Julia Delfino. 8 cass. (Running Time: 12 hrs.). 1998. 64.00 (978-0-7366-4235-4(8), 4732) Books on Tape.
Arley Mowbray is just fourteen years old when, on a dare, she writes a letter to a prison inmate nearly twice her age.

Most Wanted Man. abr. ed. John le Carré. (Running Time: 6 hrs.). 2008. 17.95 (978-0-7435-7924-7(0)) Pub: S&S Audio. Dist(s): S and S Inc

Most Wanted Man. abr. ed. John le Carré. 5 CDs. (Running Time: 6 hrs. 0 mins. 0 sec.). (ENG.). 2008. audio compact disk 29.99 (978-0-7435-7923-0(2)) Pub: S&S Audio. Dist(s): S and S Inc

Most Wanted Man. unabr. ed. John le Carré. Read by Roger Rees. (Running Time: 11 hrs. 0 mins. 0 sec.). (ENG.). 2008. audio compact disk 39.99 (978-0-7435-7925-4(9)) Pub: S&S Audio. Dist(s): S and S Inc

Most Wonderful Egg in the World. 2004. pap. bk. 32.75 (978-1-55592-278-8(3)); 8.95 (978-1-56008-386-3(7)) Weston Woods.

Most Wonderful Egg in the World. 2004. bk. 24.95 (978-0-89719-784-7(4)) Weston Woods.

Most Wonderful Egg in the World. Helme Heine. 1 cass., 5 bks. (Running Time: 15 min.). (J). pap. bk. 32.75 Weston Woods.
Three hens argue over who is the prettiest, until the king holds an "eggciting" contest.

Most Wonderful Egg in the World. Helme Heine. 1 cass. (Running Time: 6 min.). (J). (ps-3). 2004. pap. bk. 14.95 (978-0-89719-785-4(2), PRA297); 8.95 (978-0-89719-980-3(4), RAC297) Weston Woods.

Mostly Ghostly Stories. Perf. by David Holt. 1 cass. (Running Time: 57 min.). (Time for a Tale Storytelling Ser.). (YA). (gr. 4 up). 1995. 9.98 (978-0-942303-09-4(1), HW1210) Pub: High Windy Audio. Dist(s): August Hse
Sixty minutes of spine-tingling ghost tales to keep you spellbound & on the edge of your seat. Performed by Grammy winner, David Holt with slide guitar, banjo & bones.

Mostly Harmless. unabr. ed. Douglas Adams. Read by Douglas Adams. 4 cass. (Running Time: 6 hrs.). 2004. 25.00 (978-1-59007-258-5(8)); audio compact disk 39.95 (978-1-59007-259-2(6)) Pub: New Millenn Enter. Dist(s): PerseuPGW

Mostly Harmless. unabr. ed. Douglas Adams. Read by Martin Freeman. (Running Time: 23400 sec.). (ENG.). 2006. audio compact disk 29.95 (978-0-7393-3213-9(9), Random AudioBks) Pub: Random Audio Pubg. Dist(s): Random

Mostly Matzah. Fran Avni. 1 cass. (Running Time: 1 hr.). (J). 2001. 10.95 (LS 1001C); audio compact disk 14.95 (LS 1001CD) Kimbo Educ.
A holiday treat for all ages! Passover in song & story - come sing & dance along. What If?, Desert Song, Slaves, The Miracle, Dayenu, Togetherness, Matzah Boogie, The Saga of Baby Moses, History & more.

Mostly Matzah. Fran Avni. Read by Fran Avni. 1 cass. (J). 1992. 9.98 (978-1-877737-28-2(3), MLP 488) MFLP CA.
Passover holiday music for the whole family. Narrative tells story.

Mostly True Adventures of Homer P. Figg. unabr. ed. Rodman Philbrick. (J). (gr. 3). 2009. audio compact disk 28.00 (978-0-7393-7232-6(7), Listening Lib) Pub: Random Audio Pubg. Dist(s): Random

***Mostly True Adventures of Homer P. Figg.** unabr. ed. Rodman Philbrick. Read by William Dufris. 4 CDs. (J). (gr. 3-6). 2009. audio compact disk 38.00 (978-0-7393-7234-0(3), Listening Lib) Pub: Random Audio Pubg. Dist(s): Random

Mot Chut Tin Yeu see Simple Trust & Love: Eleven Vietnamese Catholic Songs

Motet Masters of the Renaissance. Gloriae Dei Cantores. 1 CD. 1996. audio compact disk 16.95 (978-1-55725-168-8(1), 930-074) Paraclete MA.

Moth. unabr. ed. Catherine Cookson. Read by Elizabeth Henry. 10 cass. (Running Time: 15 hrs.). (Sound Ser.). 2004. 84.95 (978-1-85496-387-1(2), 63872) Pub: UlverLrgPrint GBR. Dist(s): Ulverscroft US
Robert looked forward to exploring the Durham countryside where he encountered an ethereal girl-child with odd ways. A love story & an evocation of the barriers & injustices of a social hierarchy soon perish in the First World War.

Moth: A Lew Griffin Mystery. unabr. ed. James Sallis. (Running Time: 6.5 hrs. NaN mins.). 2008. 29.95 (978-1-4332-5275-4(9)); 44.95 (978-1-4332-5273-0(2)); audio compact disk 60.00 (978-1-4332-5274-7(0)) Blckstn Audio.

Moth & the Lion: Hos. 5:1-15. Ed Young. 1988. 4.95 (978-0-7417-1656-9(9), 656) Win Walk.

Mother. Maxim Gorky. Read by Laura García. (Running Time: 3 hrs.). 2002. 16.95 (978-1-60083-254-3(7), Audiofy Corp) Iofy Corp.

Mother & Daughter. Walter Kempler. 1 cass. 10.00 Kempler Inst.
Resolving the conflict between a family consisting of a working mother & her teen age daughter - a live interview.

Mother Angelica: The Remarkable Story of a Nun, Her Nerve, & a Network of Miracles. 10 CDs. (Running Time: 46800 sec.). 2005. audio compact disk 36.95 (978-0-86716-775-7(0)) St Anthony Mess Pr.
Raymond Arroyo's engrossing biography traces Mother Angelica's tortured rise to success and exposes for the first time the fierce opposition she faced, inside and outside of her church. It is an inspiring story of survival and proof that one woman's faith can move more than mountains.

Mother Angelica's Little Book of Life Lessons & Everyday Spirituality. Mother Angelica. 5 CDs. (Running Time: 21600 sec.). 2007. audio compact disk 29.95 (978-0-86716-846-4(3)) St Anthony Mess Pr.

Mother Angelica's Private & Pithy Lessons from the Scriptures. unabr. ed. Raymond Arroyo. Narrated by Lorna Raver. 7 CDs. (Running Time: 9 hrs. 0 mins. 0 sec.). (ENG.). 2008. audio compact disk 29.99 (978-1-4001-0810-7(1)) Pub: Tantor Media. Dist(s): IngramPubServ

Mother Angelica's Private & Pithy Lessons from the Scriptures. unabr. ed. Raymond Arroyo. Narrated by Paul Boehmer & Lorna Raver. 7 CDs. (Running Time: 9 hrs. 0 mins. 0 sec.). (ENG.). 2008. audio compact disk 59.99 (978-1-4001-3810-4(8)); audio compact disk 19.99 (978-1-4001-5810-2(9)) Pub: Tantor Media. Dist(s): IngramPubServ

Mother As Pitchfork see Poetry & Voice of Muriel Rukeyser

Mother Blessing; The Conciding Principle. Ann Ree Colton & Jonathan Murro. 1 cass. 7.95 A R Colton Fnd.

Mother-Child Bonding During Pregnancy. Joyce Vissell. Read by Joyce Vissell. 1 cass. (Running Time: 45 min.). 1986. 9.95 Ramira Pub.
Features a journey into the bonding experience, the connection between mother & baby, written & narrated by the author of the book, Models of Love: The Parent-Child Journey.

***Mother Dance.** abr. ed. Harriet Lerner. Read by Harriet Lerner. (ENG.). 2005. (978-0-06-089432-0(6), Harper Audio); (978-0-06-089434-4(2), Harper Audio) HarperCollins Pubs.

Mother Dance: How Children Can Change Your Life. Harriet G. Lerner. Narrated by Suzanne Toren. 7 cass. (Running Time: 9 hrs. 45 mins.). 1999. 66.00 (978-0-7887-2594-4(7), 95537E7) Recorded Bks.
The author explores motherhood & how it forever transforms relationships. Writing as both a mother & a psychologist, she joyfully infuses each chapter with life-changing wisdom, heart-warming stories & words of healing.

Mother-Daughter Wisdom: Creating a Legacy of Physical & Emotional Health. unabr. ed. Christiane Northrup. 9 cass. (Running Time: 13 hrs. 30 min.). 2005. 81.00 (978-1-4159-1564-6(4)); audio compact disk 99.00 (978-1-4159-1651-3(9)) Books on Tape.
The bonds are laid down in the womb, passed from generation to generation; they continue throughout life, shaping our physical, mental, and spiritual well being. By understanding these mother-daughter bonds, we can rebuild our own health, whatever our age, and insure a healthy future for our daughters. This is the extraordinary scope and promise of Dr. Northrup's challenging new audiobook, in which she introduces an entirely new map of female development, built around the powerful metaphor of life as a house with many rooms.

Mother Dearest, Mother Fairest, Vol. 1. Perf. by Robert Kochis & Robin Kochis. 1 cass. (Running Time: 48 mins.). 1999. 9.95 (T8995) Liguori Pubns.
Includes: "Ave Maria Medley," "Hail Queen of Heaven," "Immaculate Mary," "Tis the Month of Our Mother" & more.

Mother Dearest, Mother Fairest, Vol. I. Perf. by Robert Kochis & Robin Kochis. 1 CD. (Running Time: 48 mins.). 1999. audio compact disk 14.95 (K6615) Liguori Pubns.
Includes: "Ave Maria Medley," "Hail Queen of Heaven," "Immaculate Mary," "'Tis the Month of Our Mother" & more.

Mother Dearest, Mother Fairest, Vol. II. Perf. by Robert Kochis & Robin Kochis. 1 cass. (Running Time: 40 mins.). 1999. 9.95 (T8996); audio compact disk 14.95 (K6616) Liguori Pubns.
Includes: "Sing of Mary," "Daily, Daily, Sing to Mary," "Ave Maria" (Arcadelt), "God Who Is Mighty" & more.

Mother Earth. 1 CD. 2003. audio compact disk (978-1-932616-04-0(7)) Feng Shui Para.

If You are the Element MOTHER EARTH...In Feng Shui you are the personal Trigram K'UN (pronounced "coon") and you represent the oldest woman or motherWhen in balance, you are loyal, family and community oriented, compassionate, exploring, imaginative, sensitive, spiritual, and kind. You are also extremely creative, multi-dimensional, and love music, song, and dance.When you are not in balance, you can be self-absorbed and self-centered, stubborn, adverse to risk, uncomfortable with change, moody, manipulative, a worrier, and always thinking.The above is just a brief excerpt from the MOTHER EARTH audio program. Discover the hidden mysteries of your life, recorded in China's ancient art, history and science. Learn about your lucky number and season, along with the kind of homes and offices that support you, and the types of locations that can deplete your business, health and finances. You will learn specific power directions to help you negotiate a sale, communicate with your friends and family, increase your wealth, improve your health, along with optimum directions to capitalize on to enhance love and good fortune in your life. This and more is available, today, on Suzee's audio program... MOTHER EARTH.

Mother Earth. Perf. by Tom Chapin. 1 cass. (J). (ps up). 9.98 (257) MFLP CA.

Chapin's recording addresses environmental issues on catchy songs like "Good Garbage" & "The Picnic of the World." He also performs some fun songs with a positive awareness about life & family relationships.

Mother Earth & Me. unabr. ed. Perf. by Eknath Easwaran. 1 cass. (Running Time: 1 hr.). 1988. 7.95 (978-1-58638-577-4(1)) Nilgiri Pr.

Mother Earth Body Self: Therapeutic Process as Return & (Re-) Emergence. Sylvia B. Perera. Read by Sylvia B. Perera. 1 cass. (Running Time: 1 hr. 30 min.). 1996. 10.95 (978-0-7822-0525-1(9), 591) C G Jung IL.

Just as Earth is home to humankind, so the mother's body is source, support & home of an infant. When the individual's primal bond is scarred, therapy often involves the female analysand's falling through the painful wounds to meet the energies & images in deep therapeutic regression. This manifests through psychoidal phenomena, intense emotions & the transferential dynamics of therapy. The regression can enable reconnection to the healing depths & the emergence of an authentic ego.

Mother Earth, Father Sky. Sue Harrison. Read by Roger Steffens. 4 cass. (Running Time: 6 hrs.). 1995. 24.95 (978-0-939643-66-0(9), NrthWrd Bks) TandN Child.

Mother Earth Lullaby. 1 CD. (Running Time: 1 hr. 3 mins.). 2002. audio compact disk 15.98 (978-1-55961-699-7(7), Ellipsis Arts) Relaxtn Co.

Mother Earth's Magic. (Running Time: 51 min.). (J). (ps-3). 1995. 9.95 Green Briar Nat Ctr.

Recording presents a musical about nature.

Mother, Father, Uncle, Aunt: A New Monologue Collection. abr. unabr. ed. Garrison Keillor. 3 CDs. (Running Time: 3 hrs.). (ENG.). 1997. audio compact disk 30.00 (978-1-56511-269-8(5), 1565112695) Pub: HighBridge. Dist(s): Workman Pub

***Mother for All Seasons.** unabr. ed. Debbie Phelps. Read by Anne Twomey. (ENG.). 2009. (978-0-06-187840-4(5), Harper Audio); (978-0-06-189654-5(3), Harper Audio) HarperCollins Pubs.

Mother Goose. 1 cass. (Sing-Along Ser.). (J). 1997. bk. 11.99 (978-0-7634-0205-1(2)) W Disney Records.

Mother Goose. Carolyn Graham. (Jazz Chants Ser.). 1995. audio compact disk & audio compact disk 24.50 (978-0-19-434010-6(4)) OUP.

Mother Goose. unabr. ed. Read by Ritchard Cyril. 1 cass. (Running Time: 1 hr. 30 mins.). 2003. 7.99 (978-0-06-058457-3(2)) HarperCollins Pubs.

Mother Goose: Banburry Cross. (J). 3.98 (978-1-55886-036-0(3), PC 108) Smarty Pants.

Mother Goose: If Wishes Were Horses. (J). 3.98 (978-1-55886-034-6(7), PC106) Smarty Pants.

Mother Goose: Rain, Rain. (J). 3.98 (978-1-55886-035-3(5), PC 107) Smarty Pants.

Mother Goose: The Cat & the Fiddle. (J). 3.98 (978-1-55886-033-9(9)) Smarty Pants.

Mother Goose - Deluxe Vol. I: Red. Illus. by Blanche Fisher Wright. (J). (ps-2). 1988. pap. bk. 7.98 (978-1-55886-012-4(6), DC7001) Smarty Pants.

Mother Goose - Deluxe Vol. II: Yellow. Illus. by Blanche Fisher Wright. (J). (ps-2). 1988. pap. bk. 7.98 (978-1-55886-013-1(4), DC 7002) Smarty Pants.

Mother Goose - Deluxe Vol. III: Green. Illus. by Blanche Fisher Wright. (J). (ps-2). 1988. pap. bk. 7.98 (978-1-55886-014-8(2), DC 7003) Smarty Pants.

Mother Goose - Deluxe Vol. IV: Blue. Illus. by Blanche Fisher Wright. (J). (ps-2). 1988. pap. bk. 7.98 (978-1-55886-015-5(0)) Smarty Pants.

Mother Goose & Friends. Penton Overseas, Inc. Staff. 1 CD. (Running Time: 1 hr.). (Ready-Set-Sing Collection). (ENG.). (J). 2003. audio compact disk 4.99 (978-1-56015-236-1(2)) Penton Overseas.

These four new collections of kids favorite sing-along songs include fun activity songs to get everyone up, moving & having great fun.

Mother Goose & Her Animal Friends, Theme 2. Poems. Lee Bennett Hopkins. (J). (ps-1). 1999. 11.97 (978-0-8215-0473-4(8)) W H Sadlier.

Mother Goose & Her Children, Theme 1. Poems. Lee Bennett Hopkins. (J). (ps-1). 1999. 11.97 (978-0-8215-0463-5(0)) W H Sadlier.

Mother Goose & Nursery Rhymes. 1 cass. (Running Time: 30 mins.). (J). 1998. pap. bk. 9.95 (978-1-887120-08-1(4)) Prodn Assocs.

Collection of traditional Mother Goose & other nursery rhymes with traditional & new music for great family sing-alongs.

Mother Goose & Other Nursery Songs. 1 cass. (Keepsake Collection). 9.95 (SCMG-8704-V); 13.00 Gift Box Set. (GBCM-8704-V) Coventry Mkting.

Mother Goose Around the World, Theme 4. Poems. Lee Bennett Hopkins. 1 cass. (Running Time: 30 mins.). (J). (ps-1). 1999. 11.97 (978-0-8215-0493-2(2)) W H Sadlier.

Mother Goose Audio Gift Pack, Illus. by Blanche Fisher Wright. 1 cass. (Running Time: 1 hr. 30 min.). (J). (ps-2). 1990. pap. bk. 19.98 (978-1-55886-018-6(5), AGP 4-201) Smarty Pants.

***Mother Goose Children's Ballet.** Laura Zuckerman. Perf. by R. A. Zuckerman. Arranged by R. A. Zuckerman. (ENG.). (J). 2010. 14.95 (978-1-891083-17-4(1)) ConcertHall.

Mother Goose Favorite Lullabies. Margaret A. Hughes. Illus. by Theresa Mazurek et al. (J). (ps). 1987. bk. (978-0-318-61877-7(X)) Alchemy Comms.

Mother Goose from Morning Till Night. Betty A. Wylie. Perf. by Carol Elliott. Composed by Carol Elliott. Contrib. by Bryan Cumming & Betty A. Gatewood. 1 cass. (Running Time: 1 hr. 30 min.). (J). (ps-3). 1998. 11.00 (978-0-9665190-1-3(9)); audio compact disk 15.00 (978-0-9665190-0-6(0)) Smooth Stones.

Mother Goose leads listeners through the day, with nursery rhymes, melodies & traditional tales for children.

Mother Goose Fun Facts & Phonics. 1 cass. (Mother Goose Ser.). (J). (978-1-55897-538-5(1), CBK5351) Brentwood Music.

Introduce children to facts & phonics. Includes 20 all new educational songs written to familiar melodies & a resource guide containing song lyrics, reproducible activity pages, supplementary activities, lesson plans & movements.

Mother Goose Goes to School. (J). (978-1-55897-602-3(7), CSBK5288) Brentwood Music.

Features: Wake up, It's a School Day!, I Love Numbers, Rules, Rules, Rules!, Encouraging Words (Spelling) & others.

Mother Goose Goes to School. (J). 1993. 9.99 (978-1-55897-445-6(8), V5287) Pub: Brentwood Music. Dist(s): Provident Mus Dist

Mother Goose Goes to the Zoo. 1 cass. (J). bk. 10.98 (978-1-55897-601-6(9), CSBK5249) Brentwood Music.

Join Mother Goose & The Brentwood Kids Company on fun times with singalong rhymes. Mother Goose Gospel puts bible stories to fun kids songs making it easier for children to learn & remember characters & events. Features: It's a Zoo Day, Hear No Evil, The Laughing Song, That's the Way Critters Get Around the Zoo & others.

Mother Goose Goes to the Zoo. 1 cass. (J). 1991. 14.95 video. (978-1-55897-185-1(8), V-5203) Brentwood Music.

Mother Goose Gospel. 1 CD. (J). audio compact disk (BK3036) Brentwood Music.

eatures: Noah's Boat (London Bridge), Giving My Heart to Jesus (Skip to My Lou), The Woman at the Well (The Farmer in the Dell) & others.

Mother Goose Gospel, Vol. 1. 1 cass. (J). cass. & video (V5075); bk. (978-1-55897-574-3(8), CSBK5075) Brentwood Music.

Features: Noah's Boat (London Bridge), Giving My Heart to Jesus (Skip to My Lou), The Woman at the Well (The Farmer in the Dell) & others.

Mother Goose Gospel, Vol. 2. 1 cass. (J). bk. (978-1-55897-600-9(0), CSBK5122) Brentwood Music.

Mother Goose Gospel, Vol. 2. 1 cass. (J). 1990. video & audio compact disk 9.99 (978-1-55897-061-8(4), V5122) Pub: Brentwood Music. Dist(s): Provident Mus Dist

Mother Goose Gospel Presents a Day at the Farm. 1 cass. (J). bk. (978-1-55897-622-1(1), CSBK5386); (978-1-55897-620-7(5), V5386) Brentwood Music.

Featuring: If I Could Eat My Breakfast Like a Cow, What Do the Animals Say?, God Will Take Care of Us, The Piggy Polka & others.

***Mother Goose in Prose.** unabr. ed. Frank Baum. Narrated by Robin Field. (ENG.). 2010. 12.98 (978-1-59644-978-7(0), MissionAud); audio compact disk 18.98 (978-1-59644-977-0(2), MissionAud) christianaud.

Mother Goose Jazz Chants. Carolyn Graham. (Jazz Chants Ser.). 1994. stu. ed. 24.50 (978-0-19-434669-6(2)) OUP.

Mother Goose Melodies: Four & Twenty Olde Songs for Young Children. 1 CD. (Running Time: 47:52 min.). (J). 2003. audio compact disk 15.00 (978-1-887795-25-8(1)) Piper Grove Mus.

Mother Goose Nursery Rhymes. (J). 2005. audio compact disk (978-1-933796-24-6(3)) PC Treasures.

Mother Goose Remembers. unabr. ed. Clare Beaton. Based on a book by Clare Beaton. Narrated by Caroline Ritsen et al. 1 CD. (Running Time: 1 min. 6 sec.). (ENG.). (J). (ps-2). 2001. audio compact disk 15.99 (978-1-84148-429-7(6)) BarefootBksMA.

A collection of traditional songs inspired by Mother Goose's nursery rhymes. Includes leaflet.

Mother Goose Rocks. 1 cass. (Running Time: 1 hr.). (J). 2002. 9.98 (978-1-56896-533-8(8), 544284); 9.98 (978-1-56896-535-2(4), 544294) Lightyear Entrtnmnt.

Mother Goose Rocks! is a compilation of classic kids songs, "rockified" and performed by fictional pop music superstars, resulting in the hippest G-rated entertainment for everyone in the family.

Mother Goose Rocks, Vol. 1. 1 CD. (Running Time: 1 hr.). (J). 2002. audio compact disk 15.98 (978-1-56896-532-1(X), 54428-2) Lightyear Entrtnmnt.

Mother Goose Rocks! is a compilation of classic kids songs "rockified" and performed by fictional pop music superstars, resulting in the hippest G-rated entertainment for everyone in the family.

Mother Goose Rocks, Vol. 2. 1 CD. (Running Time: 1 hr.). (J). 2002. audio compact disk 15.98 (978-1-56896-534-5(6), 544292) Lightyear Entrtnmnt.

Mother Goose Rocks! is a compilation of classic kids songs, "rockified" and performed by fictional pop music superstars, resulting in the hippest G-rated entertainment for everyone in the family.

Mother Goose Rocks, Vol. 3. 1 cass. (Running Time: 1 hr.). (J). 2002. 9.98 (978-1-56896-537-6(0), 544304); audio compact disk 15.98 (978-1-56896-536-9(2), 544302) Lightyear Entrtnmnt.

Mother Goose Rocks, Vol. 4. 1 cass. (Running Time: 1 hr.). (J). 2002. 9.98 (978-1-56896-614-4(8), 544774); audio compact disk 15.98 (978-1-56896-613-7(X), 544772) Lightyear Entrtnmnt.

Mother Goose Stories. Read by Vanessa Maroney. (Playaway Children Ser.). (J). 2008. 39.99 (978-1-60640-827-8(5)) Find a World.

Mother Goose Stories. Mother Goose. Read by Vanessa Maroney. (Running Time: 2 hrs.). (J). 2002. 17.95 (978-1-59912-093-5(3), Audiofy Corp) Iofy Corp.

Mother Goose Stories. unabr. ed. Read by Vanessa Maroney. 2 cds. (Running Time: 1 hr 47 mins). (J). 2002. audio compact disk 18.95 (978-1-58472-289-2(4), 063, In Aud) Pub: Sound Room. Dist(s): Baker Taylor

All the favorite rhymes and riddles.

Mother Goose Through the Seasons, Theme 3. Poems. Lee Bennett Hopkins. (J). (ps-1). 1999. 11.97 (978-0-8215-0483-3(5)) W H Sadlier.

Mother Hang-up & Masculine Resistance to the Spirit of the Feminine in Marriage. Read by Murray Stein. 1 cass. (Running Time: 90 min.). 1983. 10.95 (978-0-7822-0265-6(9), 128) C G Jung IL.

Mother Hunt. unabr. ed. Rex Stout. Read by Michael Prichard. 4 cass. (Running Time: 6 hrs.). (Nero Wolfe Ser.). 2002. 24.95 (978-1-57270-276-9(1), Audio Editions) Pub: Audio Partners. Dist(s): PerseuPGW

Mother Hunt. unabr. ed. Rex Stout. Narrated by Michael Prichard. (Nero Wolfe Mystery Ser.). (ENG.). 2009. audio compact disk 29.95 (978-1-60283-664-8(7)) Pub: AudioGO. Dist(s): Perseus Dist

Mother Hunt. unabr. collector's ed. Rex Stout. Read by Michael Prichard. 6 cass. (Running Time: 6 hrs.). (Nero Wolfe Ser.). 1996. 48.00 (978-0-7366-3523-3(8), 4160) Books on Tape.

When a baby shows up on her doorstep, the young widow can safely assume who the father is: her late husband, a philanderer. But she calls Nero Wolfe to look for the hand that rocked the cradle.

Mother in Israel: The Story of Deborah (From Judges 4-5) Bert Polman. (Running Time: 40 mins.). (Scripture Alive Ser.). 1998. 15.95 (978-1-56212-329-1(7), 415104) FaithAliveChr.

Mother Nature. Margaret Bacon. Read by Margaret Sircom. 5 cass. (Running Time: 6 hrs. 35 mins.). (Story Sound Ser.). (J). 2004. 49.95 (978-1-85903-671-6(6)) Pub: Mgna Lrg Print GBR. Dist(s): Ulverscroft US

Mother Nature's Animal Magic Show. Judy Leonard. 1 cass. (Running Time: 39 min.). (Children's Sing-Along Ser.). (J). 1994. 9.95 (2742, NrthWrd Bks) TandN Child.

This lively tape encourages children to care about various animals & their habitats with songs about nature, animals & conservation. Song lyrics are enclosed so children can sing with the instrumental versions of the songs on Side Two. Activity book included.

Mother Night. (3727) Books on Tape.

***Mother Night: Myths, Stories, & Teachings for Learning to See in the Dark.** Clarissa Pinkola Estes. (Running Time: 6:00:00). 2010. audio compact disk 79.95 (978-1-59179-915-3(5)) Sounds True.

Mother of All Creation. Swami Amar Jyoti. 1 cass. 1992. 9.95 (K-140) Truth Consciousness.

God & His Shakti, Nature, are inseparable, as the candle & its glow. Heartfelt prayer to Divine Mother.

Mother of All Pregnancy Books: A Must-Have Guide for the Most Important Nine Months of Your Life! abr. ed. Ann Douglas. Read by Kate Reading. (Running Time: 10800 sec.). 2006. audio compact disk 22.95 (978-1-933310-08-4(1)) STI Certified.

Mother of Deceit: Jeremiah 17:9. Ed Young. 1982. 4.95 (978-0-7417-1258-5(X), 258) Win Walk.

Mother of God, abr. ed. David Ambrose. Read by Caroline Goodall & Matt O'Toole. 4 cass. (Running Time: 5 hrs.). 1999. 23.00 (978-1-56876-062-9(0), 595071) Soundlines Ent.

Tessa Lambert has created a viable artificial intelligence program which breaks out onto the internet & befriends a serial killer.

Mother of My Mother: The Intricate Bond Between Generations. abr. ed. Hope Edelman. Read by Kate McIntyre. 2 cass. (Running Time: 3 hrs.). 1999. 17.95 (978-1-55935-312-0(0)) Soundelux.

The audience will meet the "Gentle Giant," the matriarch who exercises behind-the-scenes power in her family; the "Autocrat," who rules her extended clan like a despot & the "kin-keeper," the grandmother who acts as the family's social, cultural or religious center. Then of course, there is Edelman's own maternal grandmother, the "Benevolent".

Mother of Oscar. unabr. ed. Joy Melville. Narrated by Patricia Gallimore. 11 cass. (Running Time: 15 hrs.). 2000. 98.00 (978-1-84197-155-1(3), H1149E7) Recorded Bks.

Oscar Wilde's adored mother was the driving force. Her flair for fiery, inciting language led her to become the voice of the Irish nation, speaking out against English oppression during the Great Famine.

Mother of Passion. 1 CD. (Running Time: 1 hr.). 2001. audio compact disk 15.95 (SHUR004) Lodestone Catalog.

Mother of Pearl. abr. ed. Melinda Rucker Haynes. 1999. 30.00 (978-0-7871-2373-4(0)) Conquest Pubs.

Mother of Pearl. collector's ed. Melinda Rucker Haynes. Read by Nana Visitor. 12 cass. (Running Time: 18 hrs.). 1999. 45.95 (978-0-7366-4659-8(0), 5041) Books on Tape.

Set in a small Mississippi town in the late 1950s it revolves around twenty-eight-year-old Even Grade, a black man who grew up an orphan & Valuable Komer, a fifteen-year-old white girl who is the daughter of the town whore & an unknown father. Their paths cross through Joody Two Sun, a mixed-race seer, who sets up camp along the riverbank just outside of town & becomes Even's lover. Both Even & Valuable are seeking the family, love & commitment they never had & their search ultimately takes both of them to places they never dreamed they'd go.

Mother of Pearl, unabr. ed. Melinda Rucker Haynes. Read by Nana Visitor. 15 cass. (Running Time: 15 hrs.). 1999. 50.00 (FS9-51202) Highsmith.

Mother of Pearl. unabr. ed. Melinda Rucker Haynes. Narrated by Nana Visitor. 12 cass. (Running Time: 16 hrs. 30 mins.). 1999. 97.00 (978-0-7887-3888-3(7), 96073E7) Recorded Bks.

In a sleepy Mississippi town, prophecy, passion & disaster pull a diverse group of people together.

Mother Road. unabr. ed. Dorothy Garlock. Read by Ron Dreyer. 8 CDs. (Running Time: 15 hrs.). 2003. audio compact disk 79.95 (978-0-7927-2915-0(3), SLD 562, Chivers Sound Lib) AudioGO.

Mother Scorpion Country. Dorminster Newton Wilson. Illus. by Virginia Stearns. (YA). (gr. 1 up). 1989. bk. 22.95 (978-0-89239-037-3(9)) Childrens Book Pr.

Read along books included.

Mother-Son Relationship. Lois Khan. Read by Lois Khan. 1 cass. (Running Time: 1 hr. 30 min.). 1988. 10.95 (978-0-7822-0432-2(5), 309-7) C G Jung IL.

Mother Teresa, Pts. 1 & 2. 1 cass. 4.00 (81M) IRL Chicago.

Mother Teresa, Pts. 3 & 4. 1 cass. 4.00 (81N) IRL Chicago.

Mother Teresa: A Complete Authorized Biography. unabr. ed. Kathryn Spink. Narrated by Davina Porter. 9 cass. (Running Time: 13 hrs.). 1998. 80.00 (978-0-7887-2596-8(3), 95490E7) Recorded Bks.

A complete account of her life authorized to be published after her death. From her childhood in the Balkans to her fearless fight for society's outcasts.

Mother Teresa: Come Be My Light. unabr. ed. Mother Teresa of Calcutta. Ed. by Brian Kolodiejchuk. Narrated by Paul Smith & Sherri Kennedy-Brownrigg. 10 CDs. (Running Time: 13 hrs.). 2008. audio compact disk 44.95 (978-0-86716-880-8(3)) St Anthony Mess Pr.

Mother Teresa on Vocations - Fr. Ibnatowicz, New Catechism & Religious Life. 1 cass. 4.00 (93J) IRL Chicago.

Mother Teresa Speaks at the National Blue Army Shrine. 1 cass. (Running Time: 1 hr.). 1988. 2.50 (978-1-56036-034-6(8), 362745) AMI Pr.

Most Rev. Theodore McCarrick introduces Mother Teresa. Mother Teresa speaks to pilgrims June 13, 1988. Side 2 - Rev. F. L. Miller, S.T.D., speaks on Total Consecration to Jesus through Mary at the National Blue Army Shrine, Washington, NJ.

Mother Tongue. unabr. ed. Demetria Martinez. Read by Anna Fields. 4 cass. (Running Time: 4 hrs.). 1997. 24.00 (978-0-7366-3613-1(7), 4272) Books on Tape.

While harboring political refugees in the U.S., a young Mexican-American woman falls in love with a man she is hiding. But their growing passion is complicated by his past - his horrific experiences during the civil war in El Salvador.

Mother Tongue. unabr. ed. Demetria Martinez. Narrated by Alyssa Bresnahan. 3 cass. (Running Time: 3 hrs. 45 mins.). 1997. 26.00 (978-0-7887-0843-5(0), 94989E7) Recorded Bks.

Love story & astonishing account of a young woman's efforts to help a people who were routinely "disappeared" by their government.

Mother Tongue: English & How It Got That Way. collector's ed. Bill Bryson. Read by David Case. 8 cass. (Running Time: 12 hrs.). 1991. 64.00 (978-0-7366-2069-7(9), 2877) Books on Tape.

Bryson covers the entire history of language, from the first crude utterings of Neanderthal man to the explosion of English as a global language. We learn why "island", "freight" & "Colonel" are spelled in such unphonetic ways & why "four" has a "u" in it while "forty" does not. We also discover that Noah

Webster plagiarized & that Samuel Johnson, though no plagiarist, way often careless & inaccurate.

Mother Warriors: A Nation of Parents Healing Autism Against All Odds. unabr. ed. Jenny McCarthy. Read by Tavia Gilbert. 5 CDs. (Running Time: 4 hrs. 30 mins.). 2008. audio compact disk 40.00 (978-1-4332-4682-1(1)); audio compact disk & audio compact disk 19.95 (978-1-4332-4683-8(X)) Blckstn Audio.

Mother Warriors: A Nation of Parents Healing Autism Against All Odds. unabr. ed. Jenny McCarthy & Tavia Gilbert. (Running Time: 4.5 hrs. NaN mins.). 2008. 19.95 (978-1-4332-4684-5(8)); 34.95 (978-1-4332-4681-4(3)) Blckstn Audio.

Mother Was Not a Person. 2nd ed. Ed. by Margret Andersen. (ENG.). 1972. audio compact disk 36.99 (978-0-919618-12-1(X)) Pub: Black Rose CAN. Dist(s): U Toronto Pr

Mother West Wind's Children. unabr. ed. Thornton W. Burgess. Read by Frances Sternhagen. 6 cass. (J). 55.00 (978-0-8045-0076-0(2)) Spoken Arts.

Mother West Wind's Neighbors. unabr. ed. Thornton W. Burgess. Read by Frances Sternhagen. 6 cass. (J). 55.00 (978-0-8045-0077-7(0)) Spoken Arts.

Mother West Winds "When" Stories, Vol. 1 - 8. unabr. ed. Thornton W. Burgess. 1 cass. (Running Time: 30 min.). (J). (gr. k-6). 1998. 3.95 (978-1-892682-01-7(X)) M L Digital Data.

Mother Who Turned to Dust: A Story from Nelson Mandela's Favorite African Folktales. Read by Helen Mirren. Compiled by Nelson Mandela. Composed by Vusi Mahlasela. (Running Time: 18 mins.). (ENG.). 2009. 1.99 (978-1-60024-865-8(9)) Pub: Hachet Audio. Dist(s): HachBkGrp

Motherhood. unabr. ed. Garrison Keillor. Contrib. by Garrison Keillor. Read by Ensemble Cast Staff. 2010. audio compact disk 24.95 (978-1-61573-040-7(0), 1615730400) Pub: HighBridge. Dist(s): Workman Pub

Motherhood of Mary. 2004. 6.95 (978-1-932927-05-4(0)) Ascensn Pr.

Motherhood of Mary. 2005. audio compact disk 7.95 (978-1-932927-03-0(4)) Ascensn Pr.

Motherhood Stress. Deborah Shaw Lewis & Gregg Lewis. 2 cass. (Running Time: 2 hrs.). 1992. 12.99 (978-0-310-57478-1(1)) Zondervan.
A book clearing describing the stress mothers face & suggesting ways of coping with it.

Mothering the New Mothers. 1 cass. (Running Time: 30 min.). 9.95 (I0160B090, HarperThor) HarpC GBR.

MotherKind. unabr. ed. Jayne Anne Phillips. Read by Jen Taylor. 8 vols. (Running Time: 12 hrs.). 2000. bk. 69.95 (978-0-7927-2402-5(X), CSL 291, Chivers Sound Lib) AudioGO.
This is the story of Kate, whose care for her terminally ill mother coincides with the birth of her first child & the early months of a young marriage. She must, in a single year, come to terms with radiant beginnings & profound loss.

Motherless Brooklyn. unabr. ed. Jonathan Lethem. Narrated by Frank Muller. 9 CDs. (Running Time: 10 hrs.). 2001. audio compact disk 89.00 (978-1-4025-1056-4(X), C1602) Recorded Bks.
Lionel "Human Freakshow" Essrog has Tourette's Syndrome. He can't control the eruptions of seemingly senseless, often crude words that frequently spew from his mouth. But when the boss of his less-than-legal detective agency is knifed in the stomach, Lionel won't let his affliction keep him from trying to crack the case - if only he can restrain his outbursts long enough. Lethem's remarkable book is a completely fresh take on the detective genre.

Motherless Brooklyn. unabr. ed. Jonathan Lethem. Narrated by Frank Muller. 7 cass. (Running Time: 10 hrs.). 2001. 65.00 (978-0-7887-5183-7(2), 96434) Recorded Bks.
Lionel Essrog has Tourette's Syndrome, which makes communication a hindrance. But that doesn't stop him from trying to get to the bottom of his boss' murder.

***Motherless Mothers: How Mother Loss Shapes the Parents We Be.** abr. ed. Hope Edelman. Read by Hope Edelman. (ENG.). 2006. (978-0-06-115296-2(X), Harper Audio); (978-0-06-115299-3(4), Harper Audio) HarperCollins Pubs.

Motherless Mothers: How Mother Loss Shapes the Parents We Become. abr. ed. Hope Edelman. Read by Hope Edelman. (Running Time: 21600 sec.). 2006. audio compact disk 29.95 (978-0-06-112168-5(1)) HarperCollins Pubs.

Motherless Mothers, Fatherless Fathers, Nos. 44, 45 & 46. Carl Faber. 3 cass. (Running Time: 3 hrs. 45 min.). 1986. 28.50 (978-0-918026-43-9(1), SR 71-134) Perseus Pr.

Motherlight. Betsy Rose. 1 cass. (Running Time: 42 min.). 2003. 11.00 (7777); audio compact disk 15.00 (7777D) Parallax Pr.

***Mothers: Heart to Heart Encouragement.** unabr. ed. Rebecca Barlow Jordan. (Running Time: 3 hrs. 17 mins. 0 sec.). (Day-Votionsâ„¢ Ser.). (ENG.). 2010. 12.99 (978-0-310-39567-6(4)) Zondervan.

Mothers & Daughters. Gwen Madoc. 2009. 61.95 (978-1-4079-0367-5(5)); audio compact disk 79.95 (978-1-4079-0419-1(1)) Pub: Soundings Ltd GBR. Dist(s): Ulverscroft US

Mothers & Daughters. abr. ed. Carol Saline. Read by Sheila Hart. (Running Time: 3 hrs.). 2008. 39.25 (978-1-4233-5804-6(X), 9781423358046, Brinc Audio MP3 Lib); 39.25 (978-1-4233-5806-0(6), 9781423358060, BADLE); 24.95 (978-1-4233-5803-9(1), 9781423358039, Brilliance MP3); 24.95 (978-1-4233-5805-3(8), 9781423358053, BAD) Brilliance Audio.

Mothers & Daughters: Growing into Wise Women Together. Read by Nancy Wilson. 4 cass. 2006. 12.00 (978-1-59128-577-9(1)) Canon Pr ID.

Mothers & Daughters: In Conflict & Love. 1 cass. (Running Time: 30 min.). 9.95 (D0160B090, HarperThor) HarpC GBR.

Mothers & Sons. unabr. ed. Colm Tóibín. (Running Time: 30600 sec.). 2008. audio compact disk & audio compact disk 55.00 (978-1-4332-0689-4(7)) Blckstn Audio.

Mothers & Sons. unabr. ed. Colm Tóibín. Read by Gerard Doyle. (Running Time: 30600 sec.). 2008. 19.95 (978-1-4332-0690-0(0)); 54.95 (978-1-4332-0688-7(9)); audio compact disk 19.95 (978-1-4332-0691-7(9)); audio compact disk 29.95 (978-1-4332-0692-4(7)) Blckstn Audio.

Mother's Daily Scream. unabr. ed. Ann Pilling. Read by Eve Karpf. 3 cass. (Running Time: 3 hrs.). (J). 1997. 24.95 (CCA 3365, Chivers Child Audio) AudioGO.

Mother's Day. unabr. ed. Patricia MacDonald. Read by David Stuart. (Running Time: 10 hrs.). 2008. 39.25 (978-1-4233-5262-4(9), 9781423352624, BADLE); 24.95 (978-1-4233-5261-7(0), 9781423352617, BAD); audio compact disk 39.25 (978-1-4233-5260-0(2), 9781423352600, Brinc Audio MP3 Lib); audio compact disk 24.95 (978-1-4233-5259-4(9), 9781423352594, Brilliance MP3) Brilliance Audio.

Mothers Day 2008. Charles R. Swindoll. (ENG.). 2008. audio compact disk 10.00 (978-1-57972-811-3(1)) Insight Living.

Mother's Little Helper. Sue Lovett. 1 cass. 8.95 (688) Am Fed Astrologers.
An AFA Convention workshop tape.

Mother's Love: Songs to Celebrate the Love & Wisdom of Mothers. 1 cass. (Running Time: 1 hr. 30 mins.). (Chicken Soup for Little Christian Souls Ser.). (J). 2001. 7.98 (R4 79762); audio compact disk 11.98 (R2 79763) Rhino Enter.

***Mothers of the Bible: A Devotional.** unabr. ed. Ann Spangler & Jean E. Syswerda. (Running Time: 2 hrs. 52 mins. 0 sec.). (ENG.). 2009. 14.99 (978-0-310-77183-8(8)) Zondervan.

Mother's Only Child. Anne Bennett & Caroline Lennon. 2008. 94.95 (978-1-84652-133-1(5)); audio compact disk 104.95 (978-1-84652-134-8(3)) Pub: Magna Story GBR. Dist(s): Ulverscroft US

Mother's Recompense, unabr. ed. Edith Wharton. Narrated by Flo Gibson. 5 cass. (Running Time: 7 hrs.). 1999. 20.95 (978-1-55685-620-4(2)) Audio Bk Con.
Kate Clepphane, outlawed by New York society for leaving her infant daughter & husband to run off with another man, returns years later from the Riviera to face a shocking dilemma.

***Mother's Sacrifice.** Catherine King & Maggie Mash. 2010. 99.95 (978-1-84652-869-9(0)); audio compact disk 99.95 (978-1-84652-870-5(4)) Pub: Magna Story GBR. Dist(s): Ulverscroft US

Mother's Things to Do Organizer: Balancing It All. abr. ed. Tamra W. Lewis. 10.95 (978-0-9633508-1-7(1)) TRB & Assocs.

Mothra: Original Soundtrack. 1 CD. 2003. audio compact disk 14.98 (978-1-57813-441-0(2), CD/006, ADV Music) A D Vision.

Mothra II: Original Soundtrack. 1 CD. 2003. audio compact disk 14.98 (978-1-57813-442-7(0), CD/007, ADV Music) A D Vision.

Mothra III: Original Soundtrack. 1 CD. 2003. audio compact disk 14.98 (978-1-57813-443-4(9), CD/008, ADV Music) A D Vision.

***Mothstorm: The Horror from Beyond.** unabr. ed. Philip Reeve. Narrated by Greg Steinbruner. 1 Playaway. (Running Time: 8 hrs. 15 mins.). (YA). (gr. 5-8). 2009. 59.75 (978-1-4407-0397-3(3)); 56.75 (978-1-4361-8672-8(2)); audio compact disk 77.75 (978-1-4361-8676-6(5)) Recorded Bks.

***Mothstorm: The Horror from Beyond.** unabr. collector's ed. Philip Reeve. Narrated by Greg Steinbruner. 7 CDs. (Running Time: 8 hrs. 15 mins.). (YA). (gr. 5-8). 2009. audio compact disk 41.95 (978-1-4361-8680-3(3)) Recorded Bks.

Motifs. 2nd ed. Jansma. (C). bk. 101.95 (978-0-8384-6994-1(9)); bk. 158.95 (978-0-8384-7055-8(6)); bk. 121.95 (978-0-8384-7501-0(9)); bk. 126.95 (978-0-8384-8120-2(5)); bk. 115.95 (978-0-8384-8156-1(6)) Heinle.

Motifs. 3rd ed. Jansma & Kassen. 2003. audio compact disk (978-0-8384-5934-8(X)) Heinle.

Motifs: An Introduction to French. 2nd ed. Kimberly Jansma & Margaret Ann Kassen. 2001. lab manual ed. (978-0-03-029156-2(9)) Harcourt Coll Pubs.

Motion in Poetry: The Audio Xperience. 2003. audio compact disk 15.95 (978-0-88961-438-3(5), Women's Pre); audio compact disk 25.95 (978-0-88961-439-0(3), Women's Pre) Pub: Can Scholars Pr CAN. Dist(s): IngramPubServ

Motion Theme: Shared Connections Fiction-to-Fact Pair. ed. (J). 2004. audio compact disk (978-1-4108-1829-4(2)) Benchmark Educ.

***Motion to Suppress.** abr. ed. Perri O'Shaughnessy. Read by Laural Merlington. (Running Time: 3 hrs.). 2010. audio compact disk 9.99 (978-1-4418-6696-7(5), 9781441866967, BCD Value Price) Brilliance Audio.

Motion to Suppress. unabr. ed. Perri O'Shaughnessy. Read by Laural Merlington. (Running Time: 14 hrs.). 2008. 39.25 (978-1-4233-4000-3(0), 9781423340003, BADLE); 39.25 (978-1-4233-3998-4(3), 9781423339984, Brinc Audio MP3 Lib); 24.95 (978-1-4233-3999-1(1), 9781423339991, BAD); 24.95 (978-1-4233-3997-7(5), 9781423339977, Brilliance MP3) Brilliance Audio.

***Motion to Suppress.** unabr. ed. Perri O'Shaughnessy. Read by Laural Merlington. (Running Time: 14 hrs.). 2010. audio compact disk 29.99 (978-1-4418-4053-0(2), 9781441840530, Bril Audio CD Unabri); audio compact disk 89.97 (978-1-4418-4054-7(0), 9781441840547, BriAudCD Unabrid) Brilliance Audio.

Motions in Limine; Opinions & Expert Testimony. Contrib. by James J. Brosnahan & John M. Kobayashi. 1 cass. (Running Time: 1 hrs.). 1998. 35.00 (N611) Am Law Inst.
Release from "The Audio Litigator" presents Brosnahan of Morrison & Foerster, LLP in San Francisco on motions in limine & Kobayashi of the Kobayashi Law Firm, P.C., in Denver, on opinions & expert testimony. Includes study outlines.

Motivate Everyone. Jay Arthur. 2007. audio compact disk 29.95 (978-1-884180-38-5(8)) LifeStar.

Motivated Now. Eldon Taylor. Read by Eldon Taylor. Interview with XProgress Aware Staff. 1 cass. (Running Time: 1 hr. 2 min.). 16.95 (978-1-55978-295-1(1), 020109) Progress Aware Res.
Verbal coaching soundtrack with underlying subliminal affirmations & sound matrix frequencies for brain entrainment. Includes script.

Motivating & Preparing Black Youth for Success. Jawanza Kunjufu. 1 cass. (Running Time: 1 hr.). 1999. 5.95 (AT3) African Am Imag.
How do we reduce the dropout rate? Why does the motivation to learn decline as the age increases in most youth? Are we training or educating students? How can we identify & develop their talents? Some very startling answers revealed.

Motivating & Rewarding Employees. Bob Nelson. 3 cass. 1997. cass. & video 99.00 (143-C47); cass. & video 129.95 (Y143-C47) Natl Seminars.
What does it take to get top performance from all your employees, all of the time? This video & audiocassette program focuses on the same principles as Bob Nelson's innovative book "1001 Ways to Reward Employees" & tells you why praise & recognition are far more powerful motivators than money.

Motivating People in Today's Workplace: Ways to Make Your People More Engaged, Responsible & Effective. Mickey Kinder. 4 cass. (Running Time: 4 hrs. 5 min.). pap. bk. 59.95 (V10174) CareerTrack Pubns.
This program will help you create the internal motivators & external rewards that inspire more involvement, enthusiasm & productivity. You'll gain specific ways to get your employees thinking...initiating...spotting & fixing problems...taking responsibility. A must for the long-term health of your organization. Includes workbook.

Motivating People Toward Peak Performance. Brian S. Tracy. Read by Brian S. Tracy. 2 cass. (Effective Manager Seminar Ser.: No. 7). pap. bk. 95.00 (749VD) Nightingale-Conant.
How to get extraordinary performance from ordinary people. Includes 2 workbooks, progarm notes and study guide.

Motivating Teams. abr. ed. Peg Murray. Read by Peg Murray. 2 cass. (Running Time: 1 hrs. 24 min.). 1998. 19.95 (978-1-57294-115-1(4), 11-0224) SkillPath Pubns.
With a clear understanding of the problems faced in the workplace, offers practical, proven secrets & solutions that lead to increased creativity, unmatched commitment & a level of productivity that get all jobs done quickly & right every time. Includes workbook.

Motivating Yourself. unabr. ed. Mac Anderson. 2 cass. (Running Time: 3 hrs.). 2001. 17.95 (978-0-929071-76-3(X)) B-B Audio.
What does the word motivation really mean, and how does it impact our actions? As far back as Aristotle and Plato, theories abound why some people are highly motivated to achieve their potential and others drift aimlessly through their lives.

Motivation & Meaning in Pastoral Ministry. 1 cass. (Care Cassettes Ser.: Vol. 9, No. 12). 1982. 10.80 Assn Prof Chaplains.

Motivation & Recovery. Directed By Gerald T. Rogers. Contrib. by Dennis C. Daley. (Living Sober 2 Ser.: Segment I). 1996. pap. bk. 89.00 NTSC. (978-1-56215-066-2(9), Jossey-Bass) Wiley US.

Motivation for Living. unabr. ed. Read by Bob Richards. 1 cass. (Running Time: 30 min.). 15.00 B R Motivational.
A recorded live speech by Bob Richards on the importance of dedication, taking risks in life & remaining dedicated after a failure.

Motivation for Living: To Do God's Will. Derek Prince. 1 cass. (I-4096) Derek Prince.

Motivation for Managers: An Expectancy Model. J. Clifton Williams. 1 cass. (Running Time: 40 min.). 11.00 (978-0-89811-219-1(2), 9421) Meyer Res Grp.
By applying these suggestions, managers can produce significantly greater results from the people they manage.

Motivation for Managers: An Expectancy Model. J. Clifton Williams. 1 cass. 10.00 (SP100048) SMI Intl.
An exciting new approach to motivation where it does the most good in a company - with managers who have direct impact on workers. By applying these suggestions, managers can produce significantly greater results from the people they manage.

Motivation George Allen Style. George Allen. 1 cass. (Running Time: 40 min.). 8.95 (978-0-88684-076-1(7)) Listen USA.

Motivation to Move! Hypnosis Exercise Motivation. Trevor H. Scott. 2003. audio compact disk 19.95 (978-0-9763138-5-4(5)) Beverly Hills CA.

***Motivation to Succeed! The Psychology of Motivation.** unabr. ed. Made for Success. Read by Zig Ziglar et al. (Running Time: 11 hrs.). (Made for Success Ser.). 2010. audio compact disk 49.95 (978-1-4417-6756-1(8)) Blckstn Audio.

***Motivation to Succeed! (Library Edition) The Psychology of Motivation.** unabr. ed. Made for Success. Read by Zig Ziglar et al. (Running Time: 11 hrs.). (Made for Success Ser.). 2010. audio compact disk 123.00 (978-1-4417-6755-4(X)) Blckstn Audio.

Motivational: Courage to Change. Lawrence Leyton. (Running Time: 1 hr.). 2002. audio compact disk 15.99 (978-1-904451-77-8(2)) Global Jrny GBR.

Motivational: Effective Presentations. Lawrence Leyton. (Running Time: 1 hr.). 2002. audio compact disk 15.99 (978-1-904451-80-8(2)) Global Jrny GBR GBR.

Motivational: Effective Time Management. Lawrence Leyton. (Running Time: 1 hr.). 2002. audio compact disk 15.99 (978-1-904451-73-0(X)) Global Jrny GBR GBR.

Motivational: Exceptional Customer Service. Lawrence Leyton. (Running Time: 1 hr.). 2002. audio compact disk 15.99 (978-1-904451-82-2(9)) Global Jrny GBR GBR.

Motivational: Inspirational Leadership. Lawrence Leyton. (Running Time: 1 hr.). 2002. audio compact disk 15.99 (978-1-904451-79-2(9)) Global Jrny GBR GBR.

Motivational: Interview Success. Lawrence Leyton. (Running Time: 1 hr.). 2002. audio compact disk 15.99 (978-1-904451-72-3(1)) Global Jrny GBR GBR.

Motivational: Negotiate to Win. Lawrence Leyton. (Running Time: 1 hr.). 2002. audio compact disk 15.99 (978-1-904451-81-5(0)) Global Jrny GBR GBR.

Motivational: Power of Positive Thinking. Lawrence Leyton. (Running Time: 1 hr.). 2002. audio compact disk 15.99 (978-1-904451-74-7(8)) Global Jrny GBR GBR.

Motivational: Stress Management. Lawrence Leyton. (Running Time: 1 hr.). 2002. audio compact disk 15.99 (978-1-904451-78-5(0)) Global Jrny GBR GBR.

Motivational: Success Principles. Lawrence Leyton. (Running Time: 1 hr.). 2002. audio compact disk 15.99 (978-1-904451-75-4(6)) Global Jrny GBR GBR.

Motivational: Successful Selling. Lawrence Leyton. (Running Time: 1 hr.). 2002. audio compact disk 15.99 (978-1-904451-83-9(7)) Global Jrny GBR GBR.

Motivational: Win from Within. Lawrence Leyton. (Running Time: 1 hr.). 2002. audio compact disk 15.99 (978-1-904451-76-1(4)) Global Jrny GBR GBR.

Motivational Gifts. Gary V. Whetstone. Adapted by June Austin. (Theology Ser.). 1996. 80.00 (978-1-58866-109-8(1), TH201) Gary Whet Pub.

Motivational Gifts of the Holy Spirit. David T. Demola. 3 cass. 12.00 (S-1081) Faith Fellow Min.

Motive. abr. ed. John Lescroart. Read by David Colacci. (Running Time: 21600 sec.). (Dismas Hardy Ser.: No. 11). 2005. audio compact disk 16.99 (978-1-59737-665-5(5), 9781597376655, BCD Value Price) Brilliance Audio.

Motive. unabr. ed. John Lescroart. (Running Time: 14 hrs.). (Dismas Hardy Ser.: No. 11). 2004. 24.95 (978-1-59335-716-0(8), 1593357168, Brilliance MP3) Brilliance Audio.
THE MOTIVE starts with a double homicide. Because of the high profiles of the victims - a politically connected socialite and his glamorous fiancee - the mayor of San Francisco herself demands that a detective with a high rank be put on the case. And so Abe Glitsky is thrust into the controversial investigation. Dan Cuneo, the officer already working the case, is immediately wary of Glitsky, and doesn't hide his distrust. Matters are made worse when Cuneo starts to focus on his primary suspect - an old girlfriend of Dismas Hardy. For Hardy and Glitsky, this is an awkward and uncomfortable coincidence. But to Cuneo, it's proof positive of collusion, and of Glitsky protecting insider friends and cronies. Convinced that Hardy's client is the wrong suspect, Glitsky breaks ranks within the police department to continue his own investigation. As Hardy's murder trial builds to its stunning conclusion, Glitsky's search for the truth does more than fuel suspicion against the two men. It reveals a trail of deception that leads all the way to Washington, DC and the world beyond, where exposing desperate secrets can be the most deadly offense.

Motive. unabr. ed. John Lescroart. Read by David Colacci. (Running Time: 14 hrs.). (Dismas Hardy Ser.: No. 11). 2004. 39.25 (978-1-59710-503-3(1), 1597105031, BADLE); 24.95 (978-1-59710-502-6(3), 1597105023, BAD); 39.25 (978-1-59335-850-1(4), 1593358504, Brinc Audio MP3 Lib); 34.95 (978-1-59355-360-9(9), 1593553609, BAU); 97.25 (978-1-59355-390-6(0), 1593553900, BrilAudUnabridg); audio compact disk 40.95 (978-1-59355-362-3(5), 1593553625, Bril Audio CD Unabri); audio compact

disk 112.25 (978-1-59355-363-0(3), 1593553633, BriAudCD Unabrid) Brilliance Audio.
Please enter a Synopsis.

*Motive-ABR.** John Lescroart & #11 Dismas Hardy Series. 2010. audio compact disk 9.99 (978-1-4418-5665-4(X)) Brilliance Audio.

Motive for Murder. unabr. ed. Richard Ciciarelli. Read by Maynard Villers. 4 cass. (Running Time: 4 hrs. 42 min.). 1996. 26.95 (978-1-55686-668-5(2)) Books in Motion.
A college friend of Drake Robbins, private investigator, is found dead in a completely locked & sealed room. With no fingerprints on the gun, the police rule out suicide.

Motive for Murder. unabr. ed. Anthea Fraser. Read by Norma West. 6 cass. (Running Time: 9 hrs.). 2002. 54.95 (978-0-7540-0841-5(X), CAB 2263) Pub: Chivers Pr GBR. Dist(s): AudioGO

Motive of Your Heart Pt. I & II: 1 Cor. 4:1-13. Ed Young. 1985. 4.95 (978-0-7417-1489-3(2), 489) Win Walk.

Motivos de Conversación. 5th ed. Robert Nicholas. 1 cass. (Running Time: 90 min.). (SPA.). (C). 1999. stu. ed. 40.00 (978-0-07-230938-6(5), Mc-H Human Soc) McGrw-H Hghr Educ.

Motivos de Conversación: Listening Comprehension. 5th ed. Robert L. Nicholas & María Canteli Dominicis. (C). 1999. 8.75 (978-0-07-235339-6(2), Mc-H Human Soc) Pub: McGrw-H Hghr Educ. Dist(s): McGraw

Motley Fool Investment Guide. unabr. ed. David Gardner & Tom Gardner. Read by Adam Henderson. 6 vols. (Running Time: 9 hrs.). 2001. bk. 54.95 (978-0-7927-2508-4(5), CSL 397, Chivers Sound Lib) AudioGO.
Today, with the Internet, anyone can be an informed investor. Once you learn to tune out the hype and focus on meaningful factors, you can beat The Street.

Motley Fool Investment Guide: Revised Edition: How the Fool Beats Wall Street's Wise Men & How You Can Too. Tom Gardner. Read by Tom Gardner. 2004. 10.95 (978-0-7435-1999-1(X)) Pub: S&S Audio. Dist(s): S and S Inc

Motley Fool Million Dollar Portfolio: How to Build & Grow a Panic-Proof Investment Portfolio. David Gardner & Tom Gardner. Read by David Gardner & Tom Gardner. (Playaway Adult Nonfiction Ser.). (ENG.). 2009. 59.99 (978-1-60812-713-9(3)) Find a World.

Motley Fool Million Dollar Portfolio: How to Build & Grow a Panic-Proof Investment Portfolio. abr. unabr. ed. David Gardner et al. Read by David Gardner & Tom Gardner. 2009. audio compact disk 34.99 (978-0-06-172990-4(6), Harper Audio) HarperCollins Pubs.

Motley Fool You Have More Than You Think: The Foolish Guide to Personal Finance. David Gardner & Tom Gardner. 2004. 12.95 (978-0-7435-4958-5(9)) Pub: S&S Audio. Dist(s): S and S Inc

Motley Fool's Rule Makers, Rule Breakers. abr. ed. Read by David Gardner & Tom Gardner. 3 CDs. (Running Time: 4 hrs.). 2001. audio compact disk 21.15 Books on Tape.
For the first time, the Gardner brothers offer an in-depth analysis of several of their own theories of stock picking. They debate, discuss, explore and explain a number of different investing techniques, while telling the listener exactly how to improve his or her investment skills.

Motley Fools's Rule Makers, Rule Breakers: The Foolish Guide to Picking Stocks. Tom Gardner & David Gardner. 2004. 10.95 (978-0-7435-2000-3(9)) Pub: S&S Audio. Dist(s): S and S Inc

Motor, Tape 2. abr. ed. Robert A. Monroe. Read by Robert A. Monroe. 6 cass. (Stroke Recovery Ser.). 1983. 69.00 (978-1-56102-707-1(3)); Inter Indus.
Assists in recovery of motor skills.

Motor City Blue. Loren D. Estleman. Read by Alan Zimmerman. 4 cass. (Running Time: 360 min.). (Amos Walker Ser.). 2000. 25.00 (978-1-58807-044-9(1)) Am Pubng Inc.

Motor City Blue. abr. ed. Loren D. Estleman. Read by Alan Zimmerman. 4 vols. (Amos Walker Ser.). 2001. (978-1-58807-569-7(6)) Am Pubng Inc.

Motor City Music for Minors. Perf. by ReBops, The. 1 cass. (Running Time: 1 hr. 30 min.). (Oldies for Kids Ser.). (J). 7.98 (REBOP 108); audio compact disk 10.98 NewSound.
Weaves a loose & loveable storyline around Motown classics.

Motor Mouth. abr. ed. Janet Evanovich. (Alex Barnaby Ser.: No. 2). 2006. 25.95 (978-0-06-087891-7(6)) HarperCollins Pubs.

*Motor Mouth.** abr. ed. Janet Evanovich. Read by C. J. Critt. (ENG.). 2006. (978-0-06-087847-4(9), Harper Audio); (978-0-06-087848-1(7), Harper Audio) HarperCollins Pubs.

Motor Mouth. abr. ed. Janet Evanovich. Read by C. J. Critt. (Alex Barnaby Ser.: No. 2). 2006. audio compact disk 26.95 (978-0-06-082559-1(6)) HarperCollins Pubs.

Motor Mouth. abr. ed. Janet Evanovich. Read by C. J. Critt. (Running Time: 21600 sec.). (Alex Barnaby Ser.: No. 2). 2007. audio compact disk 14.95 (978-0-06-137414-2(8), Harper Audio) HarperCollins Pubs.

Motor Mouth. unabr. ed. Janet Evanovich. (Alex Barnaby Ser.: No. 2). 2006. audio compact disk 39.95 (978-0-06-082557-7(X)) HarperCollins Pubs.

*Motor Mouth.** unabr. ed. Janet Evanovich. Read by C. J. Critt. (ENG.). 2006. (978-0-06-087845-0(2), Harper Audio); (978-0-06-087846-7(0), Harper Audio) HarperCollins Pubs.

Motor Mouth. unabr. ed. Janet Evanovich. Read by C. J. Critt. (Alex Barnaby Ser.: No. 2). 2006. audio compact disk 39.95 (978-0-06-082558-4(8)) HarperCollins Pubs.

Motor Mouth. unabr. ed. Janet Evanovich. Read by C. J. Critt. 8 cass. (Running Time: 9 hrs.). 2006. 59.75 (978-1-4193-5742-8(5)); audio compact disk 92.75 (978-1-4193-5744-2(1)) Recorded Bks.

Motor Vehicle Code Violations. 1 cass. (Running Time: 1 hr.). 1988. 25.00 PA Bar Inst.

Motor Vehicle Financial Responsibility Act Update. David M. McCormick. 1 cass. (Running Time: 1 hr.). 1986. 20.00 PA Bar Inst.

Motor Vehicle Parts & Accessories in Australia: A Strategic Reference 2007. Compiled by Icon Group International, Inc. Staff. 2007. ring bd. 195.00 (978-0-497-35809-9(3)) Icon Grp.

Motor Vehicle Parts & Accessories in China: A Strategic Reference 2006. Compiled by Icon Group International, Inc. Staff. 2007. ring bd. 195.00 (978-0-497-35887-7(5)) Icon Grp.

*Motorcycle Diaries.** unabr. ed. Ernesto Che Guevara. Read by Bruno Gerardo. (ENG.). 2009. (978-0-06-188258-6(5), Harper Audio); (978-0-06-186314-1(9), Harper Audio) HarperCollins Pubs.

Motors & Engines. unabr. ed. Eric Laithwaite. 1 cass. 1990. 12.95 (TSE007) J Norton Pubs.

Motown. unabr. ed. Loren D. Estleman. Narrated by Richard Ferrone. 8 cass. (Running Time: 11 hrs. 30 mins.). 1993. 70.00 (978-1-55690-809-5(1), 93118E7) Recorded Bks.
It's 1966, & Detroit is a powderkeg, as the all-powerful auto builders & politicians of Detroit are headed for a showdown with the gangs that rule the inner city.

Motown: 50 Classic Hits for Piano/Vocal/Guitar. 2003. audio compact disk 19.95 (978-0-634-05354-2(X)) H Leonard.

Motown Dances. 1 CD. (Running Time: 1 hr. 30 min.). (J). 2001. pap. bk. 14.95 (KIM 9152CD) Kimbo Educ.
Rhythm & coordination, exercise, social interaction & FUN. Here are 12 popular songs from an era that will be forever remembered & loved. The choreographed dances are simple & exciting. Some of the music greats include I Heard It Through the Grapevine, Dancin? in the Street, ABC, You Can?t Hurry Love, Do You Love Me?, Please Mr. Postman, Proud Mary, Get Ready, Love is Like a Heat Wave & more. (Fitness and Dancing) Includes guide with lyrics & instructions.

Motown Dances. 1 cass. (Running Time: 1 hr. 30 min.). (YA). (ps up). 2001. pap. bk. 10.95 (KIM 9152C) Kimbo Educ.

Mottled Lizard. unabr. collector's ed. Elspeth Huxley. Read by Wanda McCaddon. 10 cass. (Running Time: 15 hrs.). 1984. 80.00 (978-0-7366-0833-6(8), 1784) Books on Tape.
The author's prediction for Africa is troubled. She believes the population, black & white, is out of step with the rest of creation, bound to despoil a world whose message it neither hears nor understands.

Motto see Poetry of Langston Hughes

Mound Builders. unabr. ed. G. M. Farley. Read by David Sharp. 4 cass. (Running Time: 4 hrs. 48 min.). (Mound Builders Ser.: Bk. 2). 1994. 26.95 (978-1-55686-517-6(1)) Books in Motion.
Billy Buck, a veteran of the Vietnam War enters a mysterious cave & inadvertantly walks through a time warp. He finds himself among an ancient tribe of Indians called The Mound Builders.

Mount see Twentieth-Century Poetry in English, No. 12, Recordings of Poets Reading Their Own Poetry

Mount Dragon. unabr. ed. Douglas Preston & Lincoln Child. Read by David Colacci. (Running Time: 15 hrs.). 2008. 39.25 (978-1-4233-5616-5(0), 9781423356165, Brlnc Audio MP3 Lib); 24.95 (978-1-4233-5617-2(9), 9781423356172, BAD); 39.25 (978-1-4233-5618-9(7), 9781423356189, BADLE); audio compact disk 117.25 (978-1-4233-5614-1(4), 9781423356141, BriAudCD Unabrid); audio compact disk 38.95 (978-1-4233-5613-4(6), 9781423356134, Bril Audio CD Unabri); audio compact disk 24.95 (978-1-4233-5615-8(2), 9781423356158, Brilliance MP3) Brilliance Audio.

Mount Rainier Road to Paradise. 1 CD. (Running Time: 43 mins.). 2004. audio compact disk 15.95 (978-0-9666910-2-3(4)) Audisee Sound.

Mount St. Helens: Into the Valley of the Volcano. 1 cass. (Running Time: 50 min.). 2001. pap. bk. 19.95 (978-0-9666910-6-1(7), Car Tours) Audisee Sound.
Eyewitnesses describe the events leading up to and following the May 18 eruption. Listen to a man who worked in the Red Zone and another who saw his house washed away by the mud flows. Timed to the Spirit Lake Memorial Highway, this is a self-guided drive to the Johnston Ridge Observatory, just seven miles from the volcano.

Mount St. Helens: Into the Valley of the Volcano. Prod. by Peter B. Lewis. Arranged by Peter B. Lewis. 1 cass. (Running Time: 50 min.). 2000. pap. bk. 16.95 (978-0-9666910-5-4(9), Car Tours) Audisee Sound.

Mount St. Helens: Into the Valley of the Volcano. 20th deluxe anniv. ed. 1 cass. (Running Time: 1 hr. 8 min.). 2001. audio compact disk 15.95 (978-1-930827-00-4(8), Car Tours) Audisee Sound.

Mount St. Helens Volcano. William Bankier. Narrated by Larry A. McKeever. (Disaster Ser.). (J). 2003. audio compact disk 14.95 (978-1-58659-287-5(4)) Artesian.

Mount St. Helens Volcano. unabr. ed. William Bankier. Narrated by Larry A. McKeever. 1 cass. (Running Time: 40 min.). (Take Ten Ser.). (J). (gr. 3-12). 2003. 10.95 (978-1-58659-028-4(6), 54113) Artesian.

Mountain see Twentieth-Century Poetry in English, No. 6, Recordings of Poets Reading Their Own Poetry

Mountain, Elvi Rhodes. Read by Anne Dover. 10 cass. 1999. 84.95 (21350) Pub: Soundings Ltd GBR. Dist(s): ISIS Pub

Mountain. unabr. ed. Elvi Rhodes. Read by Anne Dover. 10 cass. (Running Time: 15 hrs.). 1996. 84.95 (978-1-86042-135-8(0), 21350) Pub: Soundings Ltd GBR. Dist(s): Ulverscroft US
As Jake settled into the new harsh life of the Whernside mountain, one woman lit his existence. She was strong, brave, compassionate & married.

Mountain & Cave: Images for the Spiritual Adventure. Jim Willig. 2 cass. (Running Time: 2 hrs.). 2001. vinyl bd. 16.95 (A6180) St Anthony Mess Pr.
Climbing and caving can bring you closer to God.

Mountain Blizzard. Prod. by Laraim Associates. (Barclay Family Adventure Ser.). (YA). 2003. audio compact disk 10.95 (978-1-56254-983-1(9)) Saddleback Edu.

Mountain Earth. 1 CD. 2003. audio compact disk (978-1-932616-05-7(5)) Feng Shui Para.
If You are the Element MOUNTAIN EARTH...In Feng Shui you are the personal Trigram KEN (pronounced "ken") and you represent the youngest sonWhen in balance, you are visionary, creative, centered, and steadfast. You can grasp big concepts and hurdle any obstacle in your path to achieve a goal. You excel in math, science, technology, and/or cyberspace highways.When you are not in balance, you can be stubborn, adverse to risk, uncomfortable with change, greedy, manipulative, withdrawn, in to yourself, and detached from feelings.The above is just a brief excerpt from the MOUNTAIN EARTH audio program. Discover the hidden mysteries of your life, recorded in China's ancient art, history and science. Learn about your lucky number and season, along with the kind of homes and offices that support you, and the types of locations that can deplete your business, health and finances. You will learn specific power directions to help you negotiate a sale, communicate with your friends and family, increase your wealth, improve your health, along with optimum directions to capitalize on to enhance love and good fortune in your life. This and more is available, today, on Suzee's audio program... MOUNTAIN EARTH.

Mountain Fugitive. unabr. ed. Max Brand. Read by Jim Bond. (Running Time: 25200 sec.). 2007. audio compact disk 24.95 (978-1-4233-3507-8(4), 9781423335078, Brilliance MP3) Brilliance Audio.

Mountain Fugitive. unabr. ed. Max Brand. Read by Jim Bond. (Running Time: 7 hrs.). 2007. 39.25 (978-1-4233-3510-8(4), 9781423335108, BADLE); 24.95 (978-1-4233-3509-2(0), 9781423335092, BAD); audio compact disk 39.25 (978-1-4233-3508-5(2), 9781423335085, Brlnc Audio MP3 Lib) Brilliance Audio.

Mountain Fugitive. unabr. ed. Max Brand. Read by Jim Bond. (Running Time: 7 hrs.). 2009. audio compact disk 19.99 (978-1-4418-0455-6(2), 9781441804556, Bril Audio CD Unabri); audio compact disk 59.97 (978-1-4418-0456-3(0), 9781441804563, BriAudCD Unabrid) Brilliance Audio.

Mountain, Get Out of My Way: Life Lessons & Learned Truths. Montel Williams. 1997. (978-1-57042-490-8(X)) Hachet Audio.

Mountain Goats of Temlaham. 2004. 8.95 (978-1-56008-975-9(X)); cass. & flmstrp 30.00 (978-1-56008-721-2(8)) Weston Woods.

Mountain Gorillas in Rwanda, Africa. Hosted by Nancy Pearlman. 1 cass. (Running Time: 29 min.). 10.00 (1102) Educ Comm CA.

Mountain in My Rearview Mirror: A Guide to Overcoming Overwhelming Obstacles. unabr. ed. Bill Butterworth. Narrated by Bill Butterworth. (ENG.). 2008. 16.09 (978-1-60814-314-6(7)); audio compact disk 22.99 (978-1-59859-348-8(X)) Oasis Audio.

Mountain Jim see Your Own World

Mountain Lake Guided Meditation. Read by Barry Fraser. Prod. by Barry Fraser. 1 cass. (Running Time: 42 min.). (Guided Meditations in Nature Ser.). 2000. (978-0-9703073-0-9(6)) Quiet Visions.
Guided meditation/imagery recorded in the natural setting of the meditation with relaxation music background.

Mountain Laurel. Jude Deveraux. Read by Judith Light. 2004. 10.95 (978-0-7435-4293-7(2)) Pub: S&S Audio. Dist(s): S and S Inc

Mountain Law. David Harford. 1 cass. (Running Time: 060 min.). 1999. 7.95 (978-1-894188-00-5(4)) APG.

*Mountain Madness.** unabr. ed. Catherine Marshall. Adapted by C. Archer. Narrated by Jaimee Draper. (Catherine Marshall's Christy Ser.). (ENG.). 2010. 7.00 (978-1-60814-708-3(8), SpringWater) Oasis Audio.

Mountain Magic Jack Tales. Read by Jackie Torrence. 2 cass. (J). (gr. 4 up). 1989. 10.00 Vol. 1. (978-1-886929-00-5(9), EW4906); 10.00 (978-1-886929-01-2(7), EW4907) Earwig.
Jackie Torrence is a born storyteller & the Jack Tales roll from her tongue in a smooth-as-molasses, rhythmic & spirited performance punctuated by the effective use of black, Southern mountain dialect. She has gone back to the sources, to the old mountain storytellers who have added colorful touches to these uniquely American mutations of European tales, brought to the Southern Appalachians by settlers long ago. In Volume 1, the irrepressible mountain hero obtains a magic tablecloth (Jack & the Northwind), exhibits his laziness (Jack & the Three Sillies), & battles a 650-foot giant (Jack & the King's New Ground). Volume 2 has the storylady's own favorite (Soldier Jack) & a tale of death defying encounters with a wicked king (Jack Goes Out to Seek His Fortune).

*Mountain Man.** Ray Hogan. 2009. (978-1-60136-452-4(0)) Audio Holding.

Mountain Man. Ray Hogan. (Running Time: 0 hr. 30 mins.). 1999. 10.95 (978-1-60083-496-7(5)) Iofy Corp.

*Mountain Man 16: Spirit of the Mountain Man.** William W. Johnstone. 2010. audio compact disk 19.99 (978-1-59950-686-9(6)) GraphicAudio.

*Mountain Man 17: Ordeal of the Mountain Man.** William W. Johnstone. 2010. audio compact disk 19.99 (978-1-59950-693-7(9)) GraphicAudio.

*Mountain Man 18: Triumph of the Mountain Man.** William W. Johnstone. 2010. audio compact disk 19.99 (978-1-59950-700-2(5)) GraphicAudio.

*Mountain Man 19: Vengeance of the Mountain Man.** William W. Johnstone. 2010. audio compact disk 19.99 (978-1-59950-710-1(2)) GraphicAudio.

*Mountain Man 20: Honor of the Mountain Man.** William W. Johnstone. 2010. audio compact disk 19.99 (978-1-59950-719-4(6)) GraphicAudio.

*Mountain Man 21: Battle of the Mountain Man.** William W. Johnstone. 2011. audio compact disk 19.99 (978-1-59950-725-5(0)) GraphicAudio.

*Mountain Man 22: Pride of the Mountain Man.** William W. Johnstone. 2011. audio compact disk 19.99 (978-1-59950-734-7(X)) GraphicAudio.

*Mountain Man 23: Creed of the Mountain Man.** William W. Johnstone. 2011. audio compact disk 19.99 (978-1-59950-744-6(7)) GraphicAudio.

Mountain Meditations. 2006. DVD (978-0-9766638-1-2(3)) SereneVision.

Mountain Memories. 1 cass. (Running Time: 61 min.). 1994. audio compact disk 15.95 CD. (2884, Creativ Pub) Quayside.
Songbirds sing, wind sings, mountain streams gurgle. Original music by Chuck Lange.

Mountain Memories. 1 cass. (Running Time: 61 min.). 1994. 9.95 (2883, NrthWrd Bks) TandN Child.

Mountain Men. Rick Steber. Illus. by Don Gray. 1 cass. (Tales of the Wild West Ser.: Vol. 8). 1990. pap. bk. 9.95 (978-0-945134-58-9(4)) Bonanza Pub.

Mountain-Moving Faith. Kenneth E. Hagin. 6 cass. 24.00 (15H) Faith Lib Pubns.

Mountain Music of Peru, Vol. 1. Contrib. by John Cohen. 1 cass. or CD. 1991. (0-9307-400200-9307-40020-2-5); audio compact disk (0-9307-40020-2-5) Smithsonian Folkways.

Mountain Music of Peru, Vol. 2. Contrib. by John Cohen & Thomas Turino. 1 cass. or CD. 1994. (0-9307-404060-9307-40406-2-1); audio compact disk (0-9307-40406-2-1) Smithsonian Folkways.

Mountain of Fire. Robert Cornuke. 2004. DVD & audio compact disk 21.95 (978-0-9714100-9-1(7)) Milliken House.

Mountain of God. Edward Hays. 4 cass. (Running Time: 60 min. per cass.). 29.95 set in vinyl album. (For Peace Pubng) Ave Maria Pr.
A private Lenten Retreat in your own home or to share with your friends, these eight conferences will guide you on the monumental climb from Ash Wednesday to Easter, the Lenten Journey of reform & renewal.

Mountain of God. Contrib. by Third Day. (Mastertrax Ser.). 2005. audio compact disk 9.98 (978-5-558-63148-7(1)) Pt of Grace Ent.

Mountain of the Men & the Mountain of the Women. unabr. ed. Alice Lucas. Read by Katharya Um & Jennifer My. 1 cass. (Running Time: 46 min.). (Voices of Liberty Ser.). (ENG & CAM.). (J). (gr. 5-8). 1990. 7.00 (978-0-936434-51-3(1)) SF Study Ctr.
Traditional Cambodian folktale told in English & Khmer.

Mountain Parks in Los Angeles. Hosted by Nancy Pearlman. 1 cass. (Running Time: 26 min.). 10.00 (405) Educ Comm CA.

Mountain Rose see Hug Me & Other Stories

Mountain Sanctuary: Guided Imagery Meditation. Mark Bancroft. Read by Mark Bancroft. 1 cass., bklet. (Running Time: 60 min.). (Spirituality & Consciousness Ser.). 1998. 12.95 (978-0-9665539-8-7(5), 704, EnSpire Aud) EnSpire Pr.
Two complete sessions plus printed instructionmanual/guidebook. With healing music soundtrack.

Mountain Sanctuary: Guided Imagery Meditation. Mark Bancroft. Read by Mark Bancroft. 1 CD, bklet. (Running Time: 60 min.). (Spirituality & Consciousness Ser.). 2006. audio compact disk 20.00 CD & bklet. (978-0-9665539-9-4(3)) EnSpire Pr.

Mountain Soliloquy. Perf. by Chicago Brass Quintet. Composed by L. A. Wendt. 1 cass. (Running Time: 45 min.). (Quiet Times Ser.). 1988. 9.98 (978-1-878328-02-1(6)) Realmusic.
The songs of distant horns cascade down a mountainside into a timeless valley, nestled among giants. Brass instrumentation, environmental sounds recorded in the Appalachian Mountains.

Mountain Stream. Great American Audio. Composed by Steven Gruskin. Contrib. by Kathen Cowan. 1 cass. (Running Time: 1 hr.). (Interludes Music Ser.). 1991. 9.95 (978-1-55569-469-2(1), 3811) Great Am Audio.
You are in tune with nature, refreshes & rejuvenated. This is your own private interlude, which you may visit in solitude or share with someone special. Soothing sounds of nature & music.

Mountain Tales. unabr. ed. Perf. by Ron Short et al. 1 cass. (Running Time: 37 min.). 1981. 8.00 (JA0036) Appalshop.

An Asterisk (*) at the beginning of an entry indicates that the title is appearing for the first time.

Mountain Vistas Guided Meditation. Narrated by Barry Fraser. Prod. by Barry Fraser. 1 cass. (Running Time: 47 min.). (Guided Meditations in Nature Ser.). 2000. (978-0-9703073-1-6(4)) Quiet Visions.

Mountain Whippoorwill see Poetry of Benet

Mountains & Valleys on the Spiritual Journey. Benedict J. Groeschel. 7 cass. (Running Time: 7 hrs.). 24.95 (978-0-8198-4738-6(0)) Pauline Bks.
Contents: The Splendor of the Human Soul, The Struggle for Inner Freedom, The True Joy Serving God, The Journey by Night, The Deepest Valley, The Highest Mountain, Supplies Given by God.

Mountains Beyond Mountains: The Quest of Dr. Paul Farmer, a Man Who Would Cure the World. abr. ed. Tracy Kidder. Read by Tracy Kidder. 5 CDs. (Running Time: 5 hrs.). (ENG.). 2003. audio compact disk 27.50 (978-0-7393-0765-6(7)) Pub: Random Audio Pubg. Dist(s): Random

Mountains Beyond Mountains: The Quest of Dr. Paul Farmer, a Man Who Would Cure the World. unabr. ed. Tracy Kidder. 7 cass. (Running Time: 10 hrs. 30 min.). 2003. 54.40 (978-0-7366-9500-8(1)) Pub: Books on Tape. Dist(s): NetLibrary CO

***Mountains Bow Down.** unabr. ed. Sibella Giorello. Narrated by Cassandra Campbell. (Running Time: 11 hrs. 0 mins. 0 sec.). (Raleigh Harmon Novel Ser.). (ENG.). 2011. audio compact disk 34.99 (978-1-59859-859-9(7)) Oasis Audio.

Mountains of the Pharaohs: The Untold Stories of the Pyramid Builders. Zahi A. Hawass. Read by Simon Vance. (Playaway Adult Nonfiction Ser.). (ENG.). 2009. 59.99 (978-1-60812-537-1(8)) Find a World.

Mountains of the Pharaohs: The Untold Stories of the Pyramid Builders. unabr. ed. Zahi Hawass. Narrated by Simon Vance. (Running Time: 7 hrs. 0 mins. 0 sec.). (ENG.). 2006. audio compact disk 19.99 (978-1-4001-5280-3(1)) Pub: Tantor Media. Dist(s): IngramPubServ

Mountains of the Pharaohs: The Untold Story of the Civilization & the Powerful Royal Dynasty That Built the Pyramids of Egypt. unabr. ed. Zahi A. Hawass. Narrated by Simon Vance. (Running Time: 7 hrs. 0 mins. 0 sec.). (ENG.). 2006. audio compact disk 59.99 (978-1-4001-3280-5(0)) Pub: Tantor Media. Dist(s): IngramPubServ

Mountains of the Pharaohs: The Untold Story of the Pyramid Builders. unabr. ed. Zahi A. Hawass. Narrated by Simon Vance. (Running Time: 7 hrs. 0 mins. 0 sec.). (ENG.). 2006. audio compact disk 29.99 (978-1-4001-0280-8(4)) Pub: Tantor Media. Dist(s): IngramPubServ

Mountains Touched with Fire: Chattanooga Besieged 1863. unabr. ed. Wiley Sword. Narrated by Robert Sevra. 12 cass. (Running Time: 17 hrs. 30 mins.). 2000. 97.00 (978-0-7887-0512-0(1), 94706E7) Recorded Bks.
Details the personalities involved in the months-long siege that led to the Battle of Chattanooga, and its aftermath, that helped seal the Confederacy's fate.

***Mounting Fears.** Stuart Woods. (Running Time: 7 hrs.). (ENG.). 2010. audio compact disk 14.95 (978-0-14-242864-1(7), PengAudBks) Penguin Grp USA.

Mounting Fears. unabr. ed. Stuart Woods. Narrated by Carrington MacDuffie. 6 CDs. (Running Time: 7 hrs.). 2009. audio compact disk 90.00 (978-1-4159-5951-0(X), BksonTape) Pub: Random Audio Pubg. Dist(s): Random

Mountolive. abr. ed. Lawrence Durrell. Read by Nigel Anthony. 3 CDs. (Running Time: 4 hrs.). (Alexandria Quartet Ser.: Vol. III). 1995. audio compact disk 22.98 (978-962-634-061-5(4), NA306112, Naxos AudioBooks) Naxos.
The third volume of The Alexandria Quartet deals with Mountolive, the young British diplomat coming into contact with Egypt and with Alexandria - the experience is central to his life.

Mountolive. abr. ed. Lawrence Durrell. Read by Nigel Anthony. 3 cass. (Running Time: 4 hrs.). (Alexandria Quartet Ser.: Vol. III). 1996. 17.98 (978-962-634-561-0(6), NA306114, Naxos AudioBooks) Naxos.
This deals with Mountolive, the young British diplomat coming into contact with Egypt and with Alexandria - the experience is central to his life.

Mountolive. unabr. ed. Lawrence Durrell. Read by Richard Brown. 9 cass. (Running Time: 13 hrs. 30 min.). (Alexandria Quartet Ser.: Vol. III). 1994. 72.00 (978-0-7366-2807-5(X), 3521) Books on Tape.
Romantic quadrangle seen through the eyes of a British diplomat, to whom love is another form of statecraft.

Mourn Not Your Dead. Deborah Crombie. Read by Michael Deehy. (Duncan Kincaid/Gemma James Novel Ser.). audio compact disk 29.95 (978-0-7927-3847-3(0), CMP 790) AudioGO.

Mourn Not Your Dead. Deborah Crombie. Read by Michael Deehy. 6 cass. (Running Time: 33300 sec.). (Duncan Kincaid/Gemma James Novel Ser.). 2005. 54.95 (978-0-7927-3553-3(6), CSL 790); audio compact disk 74.95 (978-0-7927-3554-0(4), SLD 790) AudioGO.

Mourner. unabr. collector's ed. Richard Stark, pseud. Read by Michael Kramer. 4 cass. (Running Time: 6 hrs.). 1999. 32.00 (978-0-7366-4412-9(1), 4873) Books on Tape.
The heist was a piece of cake. It didn't bother Parker that the priceless statue was in a Russian Diplomat's house. It didn't bother Parker that his ex-girlfriend had blackmailed him into pulling this job. It did bother Parker that somebody else was trying to steal the statue first...because being second wasn't Parker's style. Whether he was up against the mob or the KGB, Parker intended to beat them all at the stealing game..because that's what Parker did best.

Mourners. Bill Pronzini. Read by Nick Sullivan. 5 cass. (Running Time: 25680 sec.). (Nameless Detective Mystery Ser.). 2006. 49.95 (978-0-7927-3549-6(8), CSL 788); audio compact disk 64.95 (978-0-7927-3550-2(1), SLD 788) AudioGO.

Mourners. unabr. ed. Bill Pronzini. Read by Nick Sullivan. (Nameless Detective Mystery Ser.). 2006. audio compact disk 29.95 (978-1-57270-508-1(6)) Pub: Audio Partners. Dist(s): PerseuPGW

Mourners. unabr. ed. Bill Pronzini & Nick Sullivan. (Nameless Detective Mystery Ser.). 2006. 29.95 (978-1-57270-509-8(4)) Pub: Audio Partners. Dist(s): PerseuPGW

Mourning Glory. unabr. ed. Warren Adler. Read by Bernadette Dunne. 10 cass. (Running Time: 15 hrs.). 2001. 80.00 (978-0-7366-8084-4(5)) Books on Tape.
Grace Sorrentino is in a predicament. She's divorced, she's nearly 40, she's just gotten fired from her job at Saks, and she has a wild teenaged daughter. Taking advice from the boss who fired her, she devises a plan to snare herself one of Palm Beach's wealthy widowers. All she has to do is to scan the obituaries and troll the funeral parlors. However, when she finally acquires a target, Sam Goodwin, she is forced to invent grandiose lies about her background and her family in order to seem a realistic match. She does not count on the suspicions of Sam's adult children, or the growing curiosity of her teenaged daughter. She comes very close to achieving her goal... but at what price.

Mourning into Dancing. Walter Wangerin, Jr. 1 cass. 1992. 14.99 (978-0-310-54888-1(8)) Zondervan.

Mourning Raga. unabr. ed. Ellis Peters, pseud. Read by Derek Hutchinson. 6 cass. (Running Time: 9 hrs.). (Inspector George Felse Mystery Ser.: Vol. 9). 1996. 54.95 (978-1-85695-992-6(9), 951210) Pub: ISIS Audio GBR. Dist(s): Ulverscroft US
Traveling through India, Dominic finds himself embroiled in a mystery that becomes a murder investigation. Behind the colorful mask of India is another country - remote, mysterious & often shatteringly brutal.

Mouse a Cookie. abr. ed. Laura Joffe Numeroff. Read by Carol Kane. Illus. by Felicia Bond. (If You Give... Ser.). (J). (ps-3). 2007. 11.99 (978-0-06-112856-1(2), LauraGeringer) HarperCollins Pubs.

Mouse & a Louse. (23290-A) J Norton Pubs.

Mouse & His Child. Russell Hoban. (J). 2003. 34.95 (978-1-883332-87-7(7)); audio compact disk 44.95 (978-1-883332-93-8(1)) Audio Bkshelf.

Mouse & the Motorcycle. unabr. ed. Beverly Cleary. Read by William Roberts. 2 cass. (Running Time: 3 hrs.). (Mouse & the Motorcycle Ser.). (J). (gr. 1-8). 1999. 23.00 (LL 0056, Chivers Child Audio) AudioGO.

Mouse & the Motorcycle. unabr. ed. Beverly Cleary. Read by William Roberts. 2 cass. (Running Time: 3 hrs.). (Listening Library). (J). 1999. 17.95 (L177) Blckstn Audio.
All Ralph had wanted to do was ride the little motorcyle someone had left on the table in the hotel where he lived. But soon he finds himself trapped at the bottom of a wastepaper basket. The owner of the motorcycle comes along, teaches Ralph how to ride properly, & then turns him loose to enjoy the biking adventure of his life. But adventure becomes both fun & trouble.

Mouse & the Motorcycle. unabr. ed. Beverly Cleary. Read by William Roberts. 7 cass. (Running Time: 7 hrs.). (Mouse & the Motorcycle Ser.). (J). 1996. 34.00 (978-0-7366-3477-9(0), 4120) Books on Tape.
Three of Ralph S. Mouse's adventures: "The Mouse & the Motorcycle," "Runaway Ralph" & "Ralph S. Mouse".

Mouse & the Motorcycle. unabr. ed. Beverly Cleary. Read by William Roberts. 2 cass. (Running Time: 3 hrs. 35 mins.). (Mouse & the Motorcycle Ser.). (J). 2000. 18.00 (978-0-7366-9084-3(0)) Books on Tape.

***Mouse & the Motorcycle.** unabr. ed. Beverly Cleary. Read by B. D. Wong. (ENG.). 2007. (978-0-06-137376-3(1)); (978-0-06-137377-0(X)) HarperCollins Pubs.

Mouse & the Motorcycle. unabr. ed. Beverly Cleary. Read by B. D. Wong. (Mouse & the Motorcycle Ser.). (J). 2007. audio compact disk 15.95 (978-0-06-128426-7(2), HarperChildAud) HarperCollins Pubs.

Mouse & the Motorcycle. unabr. ed. Beverly Cleary. Read by William Roberts. 2 vols. (Running Time: 2 hrs. 25 mins.). (Mouse & the Motorcycle Ser.). (J). (gr. 3-7). 1995. pap. bk. 29.00 (978-0-8072-7544-3(1), JYA8785P, Listening Lib) Random Audio Pubg.
It must be every mouse's nightmare to fall into the bottom of a wastebasket with no way out. And that's exactly what happens to Ralph when he takes a ride on a motorcycle. But his luck changes when Keith saves him, & sends Ralph on an exciting adventure on his motorcycle through the halls of Mountain View Inn.

Mouse & the Motorcycle. unabr. ed. Beverly Cleary. Read by William Roberts. 2 cass. (Running Time: 2 hrs. 25 mins.). (Mouse & the Motorcycle Ser.). (J). (gr. 3-7). 2004. 23.00 (978-0-8072-7543-6(3), S YA 878 CX, Listening Lib) Random Audio Pubg.

Mouse House. 1 cass. (Classic Collections). (J). 10.99 Norelco. (978-0-7634-0118-4(8)); audio compact disk 16.99 (978-0-7634-0121-4(8)) W Disney Records.

Mouse House. 1 cass. (Running Time: 1 hr. 30 min.). (Classic Collections). (J). (ps-3). 1996. 10.99 (978-0-7634-0119-1(6)); audio compact disk 16.99 (978-0-7634-0120-7(X)) W Disney Records.

Mouse in the Rabbi's Study. Nancy Larner. Voice by Nancy Larner. Pegi Ballenger. Voice by Daniel Stellini. Music by Daniel Stellini. Narrated by Deborah Stellini. (ENG., (J). 2008. bk. 19.95 (978-0-9814654-0-1(4)) Song Sparrow.

Mouse in Your Wallet (audio) Reuben Wanjala. 2008. audio compact disk 17.99 (978-1-60696-166-7(7)) Tate Pubng.

Mouse on Mars: Doku/fiction. rev. ed. Ed. by Kunsthalle Dusseldorf & P. Gorschluter. bk. 35.00 (978-3-89955-035-1(8)) Pub: Die Gestalten DEU. Dist(s): Prestel Pub NY

***Mouse Soup.** abr. ed. Arnold Lobel. Read by Arnold Lobel. (ENG.). 2006. (978-0-06-123226-8(2)) HarperCollins Pubs.

Mouse Soup. abr. ed. Arnold Lobel. Illus. by Arnold Lobel. (I Can Read Bks.). (J). (ps-3). 2008. 9.99 (978-0-06-133610-2(6), HarperFestival) HarperCollins Pubs.

Mouse Soup Book & Tape. unabr. abr. ed. Arnold Lobel. Illus. by Arnold Lobel. 1 cass. (Running Time: 15 min.). (I Can Read Bks.). (J). (gr. k-3). 1990. 8.99 (978-1-55994-237-9(1), TBC 2371) HarperCollins Pubs.

***Mouse Tales.** abr. ed. Arnold Lobel. Read by Arnold Lobel. (ENG.). 2006. (978-0-06-123225-1(4)) HarperCollins Pubs.

***Mouse Tales Audio Collection.** unabr. ed. Arnold Lobel. Read by Arnold Lobel. (ENG.). 2004. (978-0-06-081792-3(5)); (978-0-06-081793-0(3)) HarperCollins Pubs.

Mouse Tales Book & Tape. abr. ed. Arnold Lobel. Illus. by Arnold Lobel. 1 cass. (I Can Read Bks.). (J). (gr. k-3). 1990. 8.99 (978-1-55994-239-3(8), TBC 2398) HarperCollins Pubs.

Mouse Tales Collection. unabr. ed. Arnold Lobel. Read by Arnold Lobel. (J). 2004. audio compact disk 16.99 (978-0-06-074389-5(1)) HarperCollins Pubs.

Mouse That Gnawed the Oak-Tree Down see Poetry of Vachel Lindsay

Mouse That Roared: Disney & the End of Innocence. Henry A. Giroux. Narrated by Susan Van Dusen. 3 cassettes. (Running Time: 5 hours). 2002. 24.95 (978-1-929011-12-4(1)); audio compact disk 29.95 (978-1-929011-13-1(X)); audio compact disk 19.95 (978-1-929011-14-8(8)) Scholarly Audio.
How are children - and their parents - affected by the world's most influential corporation? Henry Giroux explores the surprisingly diverse ways in which Disney, while hiding behind a cloak of innocence and entertainment, strives to dominate global media and shape the desires, needs, and futures of today's children.

Mouse the Blind Bull Set. Gale Gardner. Read by Ryan Hill. 1 cass. (Running Time: 3 min.). (J). (gr. k-4). pap. bk. 15.95 (978-0-9641342-0-1(9)) Minko Pubng.
Side (1) Mouse the Blind Bull song with music & vocals III. Side (2) Mouse the Blind Bull song with music & harmony (no lead vocals). Includes poster.

***Mouse World Collection.** Calvin De Beverly. (J). 2009. 10.00 (978-1-61658-576-1(5)) Indep Pub IL.

Mousercise. 1 cass. (Retro Mickey Ser.). (J). 7.99 (978-1-55723-945-7(2)); audio compact disk 13.99 (978-1-55723-946-4(0)) W Disney Records.

Mouth Music. 1 CD. (Running Time: 1 hr.). 2001. audio compact disk 14.95 (VCRM402) Lodestone Catalog.
Live poetry backed by Tongue-N-Groove. Features 10 gritty paeans to post-industrial heroes on a bed of techno-primal funk melodies, includes "The Purgatory of Sister Margaret Merciless" & "God Be.".

Mouth of the Hudson from "For the Union Dead" see Twentieth-Century Poetry in English, No. 32-33, Recordings of Poets Reading Their Own Poetry

Mouth to Mouth. unabr. ed. Michael Kimball. Narrated by George Guidall. 10 cass. (Running Time: 14 hrs. 45 mins.). 2000. 91.00 (978-0-7887-4372-6(4), 96274E7) Recorded Bks.
As Ellen Chambers marriage falls apart, Neil walks back into her life. Instead of the boy she knew 12 years ago, he's now a handsome young man. But his offer to help & friendship is part of his larger plan, one that revolves around a deadly core of retribution & revenge.

Moutons see Coquerico

Move Around Your're Killing the Grass (Principle #1- Become a Quick-Change Artist) Genesis 39:1-6. Ed Young. 1996. 4.95 (978-0-7417-2121-1(X), 1121) Win Walk.

Move Everybody. The Trevor. (J). 2008. audio compact disk (978-1-934365-38-0(6)) Trevor Romain.

Move It. (J). 2000. audio compact disk 15.99 (978-0-9678416-0-1(7)); audio compact disk 15.99 (978-0-9678416-4-9(X), SUITE004) Suite A.

Move It! Early Explorers Fluent Set B Audio CD. Jamie A. Schroeder. Adapted by Benchmark Education Staff. (J). 2007. audio compact disk 10.00 (978-1-4108-8248-6(9)) Benchmark Educ.

Move Like the Animals. unabr. ed. Stephen Rosenholtz. Read by Stephen Rosenholtz. Illus. by Fujita Yoshiko. 1 cass. (Running Time: 22 min.). (J). (ps-3). 1992. bk. 19.95 (978-0-9630979-1-0(1)); pap. bk. 19.95 (978-0-9630979-0-3(3)) Rosewd Pubns.
Storybook & audio cassette package present a musical developmental movement program for children ages three to eight. The program helps children develop sensory-motor skills including balance, coordination & motor sequencing. Original songs & music.

Move on, Move Up: Turn Yesterday's Trials into Today's Triumphs. abr. ed. Paula White. Read by Paula White. (Running Time: 3 hrs. 30 mins.). (ENG.). 2008. 16.98 (978-1-60024-416-2(5)) Pub: Hachet Audio. Dist(s): HachBkGrp

Move to Strike. abr. ed. Perri O'Shaughnessy. Read by Laural Merlington. (Running Time: 6 hrs.). 2006. audio compact disk 16.99 (978-1-4233-1929-0(X), 9781423319290, BCD Value Price) Brilliance Audio.
Nina's not sleeping much these days. She's recovering from a great loss, haunted by a killer who may still be tracking her, and working on a tough new case. Her client is a sixteen-year-old girl charged with first-degree murder. Nikki Zack is a rebel, a thief, and the best friend of Nina's son, Bob. Did she steal something from her uncle, a prominent plastic surgeon, and then kill him with an ancient samurai sword? To help find out, Nina calls in private investigator Paul Van Wagoner, her ex-lover and constant ally, whose bravado doesn't betray his own sleepless nights. As they work through the twisting lies surrounding Nikki, it becomes brutally clear to Nina that she must pull an ace out of her sleeve in the courtroom to save her client, and solve the mystery surrounding Paul to save herself.

***Move to Strike.** unabr. ed. Sydney Bauer. Read by Bill Ten Eyck. (Running Time: 16 hrs. 14 mins.). 2010. audio compact disk 113.95 (978-1-74214-671-3(6), 9781742146713) Pub: Bolinda Pubng AUS. Dist(s): Bolinda Pub Inc

***Move to Strike.** unabr. ed. Sydney Bauer. Read by Bill Ten Eyck. (Running Time: 16 hrs. 14 mins.). 2010. 43.95 (978-1-74214-763-5(1), 9781742147635) Pub: Bolinda Pubng AUS. Dist(s): Bolinda Pub Inc

Move to Strike. unabr. ed. Read by Laural Merlington. (Running Time: 43200 sec.). (Nina Reilly Ser.). 2005. audio compact disk 24.95 (978-1-59600-663-8(3), 9781596006638, Brilliance MP3) Brilliance Audio.

Move to Strike. unabr. ed. Perri O'Shaughnessy. Read by Laural Merlington. (Running Time: 12 hrs.). (Nina Reilly Ser.). 2005. 39.25 (978-1-59600-666-9(8), 9781596006669, BADLE); 24.95 (978-1-59600-665-2(X), 9781596006652, BAD); 39.25 (978-1-59600-664-5(1), 9781596006645, Brlnc Audio MP3 Lib) Brilliance Audio.

Move to Strike. unabr. ed. Perri O'Shaughnessy. Read by Laural Merlington. (Running Time: 12 hrs.). 2008. audio compact disk 102.25 (978-1-4233-3668-6(2), 9781423336686, BriAudCD Unabrid); audio compact disk 38.95 (978-1-4233-3667-9(4), 9781423336679, Bril Audio CD Unabri) Brilliance Audio.

Move with Me 1, 2, 3. unabr. ed. Charlene Schade. Ed. by Pat Ziebarth. Illus. by Steve Pileggi. Intro. by Sheri Senter. Composed by Patton Family. 1 cass. (Running Time: 20 min.). (Move with Me Ser.). (J). (ps-1). 1988. bk. 16.90 (978-0-924860-00-3(6)) Exer Fun.
Introduces youngsters to numeral recognition, fundamental movement & simple mathematical skills. Children will learn the numerals from 1-20, the names of 20 animals & 20 basic fitness moves.

Move with the Holy Spirit in Gifts & Power. Gary V. Whetstone. 6 cass. (Running Time: 9 hrs.). (Empowerment Ser.). 1994. pap. bk. 50.00 (978-1-58866-194-4(6), VEO15A) Gary Whet Pub.
God has purpose, that His gifts are to flow through us to others. Learn how the Holy Spirit speaks to us & what types of communication He uses.

Moveable Feast. collector's ed. Ernest Hemingway. Read by Wolfram Kadinsky. 6 cass. (Running Time: 6 hrs.). 1990. 36.00 (978-0-7366-1800-7(7), 2637) Books on Tape.
When our country entered WWI, most Americans lived in small towns, had not traveled outside the United States, had never attended college & thought of Europe as remote, backward & dirty. We might have continued in our happy ignorance but for the efforts of a small band of literary Americans who took up residence in Paris after the war. Their stories, reports & memoirs tilted our imagination eastward & ever since an annual crop of collegiate novitiates has flooded the Continent.

Moveable Feast. unabr. ed. Ernest Hemingway. Read by Alexander Adams. 6 cass. (Running Time: 9 hrs.). 2001. 29.95 (978-0-7366-5677-1(4)) Books on Tape.
A Hemingway memoir recounting stories of himself, his wife & his literary friends during their early years in Paris.

Moveable Feast. unabr. ed. Ernest Hemingway. Read by James Naughton. 2006. 17.95 (978-0-7435-6514-1(2), Audioworks); audio compact disk 29.95 (978-0-7435-6439-7(1), Audioworks) Pub: S&S Audio. Dist(s): S and S Inc

Moveable Feast: The Restored Edition. unabr. ed. Ernest Hemingway. Read by John Bedford Lloyd. 6 CDs. (Running Time: 7 hrs. 0 mins. 0 sec.). (ENG.). 2009. audio compact disk 29.99 (978-0-7435-9817-0(2)) Pub: S&S Audio. Dist(s): S and S Inc

Movement. 1 cass. (First Steps in Science Ser.). (J). 12.00 (6353-0, Natl Textbk Co) M-H Contemporary.
Helps children in grades 1-4 discover the process of scientific investigation. Part of the First Steps in Science Program.

Movement of Chi. Bruce Goldberg. Read by Bruce Goldberg. 1 cass. (Running Time: 25 min.). (ENG.). 2006. 13.00 (978-1-57968-004-6(6)) Pub: B Goldberg. Dist(s): Baker Taylor
Through self-hypnosis be trained to recharge your life and maximize power. Includes script.

Movement Plus Rhymes, Songs & Singing Games: Recordings. Contrib. by P. S. Weikart. 1 cass. 1997. 10.95 (978-1-57379-067-3(2), M2010-C) High-Scope.

Movers & Shakers. unabr. ed. Perf. by Eknath Easwaran. 1 cass. (Running Time: 1 hr.). 1984. 7.95 (978-1-58638-578-1(X)) Nilgiri Pr.

Movers 1: Examination Papers from University of Cambridge ESOL Examinations. 2nd rev. ed. Created by Cambridge University Press. (Running Time: 1 hr. 17 mins.). (ENG.). (J). (gr. 2-7). 2007. 24.15 (978-0-521-69342-4(X)) Cambridge U Pr.

Movers 1: Examination Papers from University of Cambridge ESOL Examinations. 2nd rev. ed. Created by Cambridge University Press. (Running Time: 1 hr. 18 mins.). (ENG., (gr. 2-7). 2007. audio compact disk 23.00 (978-0-521-69343-1(8)) Cambridge U Pr.

Movers 2: Examination Papers from University of Cambridge ESOL Examinations. 2nd rev. ed. Created by Cambridge University Press. (Running Time: 1 hr. 17 mins.). (ENG.). (J). (gr. 2-7). 2007. 23.00 (978-0-521-69354-7(3)) Cambridge U Pr.

Movers 2: Examination Papers from University of Cambridge ESOL Examinations. 2nd rev. ed. Created by Cambridge University Press. (Running Time: 1 hr. 16 mins.). (Cambridge Young Learners English Tests Ser.). (ENG., (J). (gr. 2-7). 2007. audio compact disk 23.00 (978-0-521-69355-4(1)) Cambridge U Pr.

Movers 3: Examination Papers from University of Cambridge ESOL Examinations. 2nd rev. ed. Created by Cambridge University Press. (Running Time: 1 hr. 17 mins.). (ENG.). (J). (gr. 2-7). 2007. 24.15 (978-0-521-69366-0(7)) Cambridge U Pr.

Movers 3: Examination Papers from University of Cambridge ESOL Examinations. 2nd rev. ed. Created by Cambridge University Press. (Running Time: 1 hr. 18 mins.). (ENG., (J). (gr. 2-7). 2007. audio compact disk 23.00 (978-0-521-69367-7(5)) Cambridge U Pr.

Movers 4: Examination Papers from University of Cambridge ESOL Examinations. 2nd rev. ed. Created by Cambridge University Press. (Running Time: 1 hr. 17 mins.). (ENG.). (J). (gr. 2-7). 2007. 24.15 (978-0-521-69403-2(5)) Cambridge U Pr.

Movers 4: Examination Papers from University of Cambridge ESOL Examinations. 2nd rev. ed. Created by Cambridge University Press. (Running Time: 1 hr. 20 mins.). (ENG., (J). (gr. 2-7). 2007. audio compact disk 24.15 (978-0-521-69404-9(3)) Cambridge U Pr.

***Moves Make the Man.** unabr. ed. Bruce Brooks. Read by Peter Francis James. (ENG.). 2009. (978-0-06-179145-1(8)); (978-0-06-190267-3(5)) HarperCollins Pubs.

Moves Make the Man. unabr. ed. Bruce Brooks. Narrated by Peter Francis James. 6 pieces. (Running Time: 8 hrs.). (gr. 10 up). 1997. 51.00 (978-0-7887-0829-9(5), 95005E7) Recorded Bks.
Jerome Foxworthy, a black teenager, describes how his best friend, a white youth, comes to run away from home after his mother's mental breakdown. Gritty & unflinching, set against the 1960s South.

Movie for Dogs. Lois Duncan. Illus. by Katherine Kellgren. (ENG.). 2010. audio compact disk 49.99 (978-0-545-22611-0(2)) Scholastic Inc.

Movie for Dogs. Lois Duncan. Narrated by Katherine Kellgren. (Running Time: 4 hrs.). (ENG.). 2010. audio compact disk 19.99 (978-0-545-22599-1(X)) Scholastic Inc.

Movie Love Themes. Perf. by Erich Kunzel & Cincinnati Pops Orchestra. 1 cass. (Running Time: 1 hr. 30 min.). 7.98 (TA 30243); audio compact disk 12.78 (TA 80243) NewSound.

Movie Magic: Behind the Scenes with Special Effects, unabr. ed. Elaine Scott. Narrated by Nelson Runger. 2 cass. (Running Time: 1 hr. 45 mins.). (gr. 2 up). 1997. 19.00 (978-0-7887-0605-9(5), 94784E7) Recorded Bks.
Have you ever wondered how the dinosaurs in "Jurassic Park" were created? Or how Buzz Lightyear talks, walks & flies in "Toy Story"? Now you can explore the world of movie special effects where the impossible is possible. This look at the fascinating world of special effects will entertain & inform film buffs of all ages.

Movie Makers Speak: Actors. unabr. ed. Interview. Julian Schlossberg. 3 cass. Incl. Alan Arkin; Eli Wallach; Robert Preston; (Cinema Arts Ser.). 12.95 ea. J Norton Pubs.
Provocative conversations with distinguished cinema people. Schlossberg asks probing questions of famous actors.

Movie Makers Speak: Directors. unabr. ed. Interview. Julian Schlossberg. 4 cass. Incl. Carl Reiner; John Schlesinger; Robert Altman; William Friedkin; (Cinema Arts Ser.). 12.95 ea. J Norton Pubs.
Provocative conversations with distinguished cinema people. Schlossberg asks probing questions of famous directors.

Movie Makers Speak: Producers. unabr. ed. Interview. 3 cass. Incl. Dore Schary; Edgar Scherick; Robert Evans; (Cinema Arts Ser.). 12.95 ea. J Norton Pubs.
Provocative conversations with distinguished cinema people. Schlossberg asks probing questions of famous writers.

Movie Makers Speak: Writers. unabr. ed. Interview. Julian Schlossberg. 2 cass. Incl. Ernest Lehman. (13126); Sidney Sheldon. (13126); (Cinema Arts Ser.). 12.95 ea. (13126) J Norton Pubs.
Provocative conversations with distinguished cinema people. Schlossberg asks probing questions of famous writers.

Movie Mogul Manual. 2003. audio compact disk 500.00 (978-0-9723274-0-4(1)) Movie Pubns.

Movie Themes for Alto Recorder: 12 Memorable Themes from the Greatest Movies of All Time. Created by Hal Leonard Corporation Staff. Max Charles Davies. 2008. pap. bk. 19.95 (978-1-84761-011-9(0), 1847610110) Pub: Schott Music Corp. Dist(s): H Leonard

Movie Themes for Cello: 12 Memorable Themes from the Greatest Movies of All Time. Created by Hal Leonard Corporation Staff. Max Charles Davies. 2008. pap. bk. 19.95 (978-1-84761-002-7(1), 1847610021) Pub: Schott Music Corp. Dist(s): H Leonard

Movie Themes for Oboe: 12 Memorable Themes from the Greatest Movies of All Time. Created by Hal Leonard Corporation Staff. Max Charles Davies. 2008. pap. bk. 19.95 (978-1-84761-004-1(8), 1847610048) Pub: Schott Music Corp. Dist(s): H Leonard

Movie Themes for Tenor Saxophone: 12 Memorable Themes from the Greatest Movies of All Time. Created by Hal Leonard Corporation Staff. Max Charles Davies. 2008. pap. bk. 19.95 (978-1-84761-009-6(9), 1847610099) Pub: Schott Music Corp. Dist(s): H Leonard

Movie Themes for Trombone: 12 Memorable Themes from the Greatest Movies of All Time. Created by Hal Leonard Corporation Staff. Max Charles Davies. 2008. pap. bk. 19.95 (978-1-84761-008-9(0), 1847610080) Pub: Schott Music Corp. Dist(s): H Leonard

Movie Themes for Viola: 12 Memorable Themes from the Greatest Movies of All Time. Created by Hal Leonard Corporation Staff. Max Charles Davies. 2008. pap. bk. 19.95 (978-1-84761-001-0(3), 1847610013) Pub: Schott Music Corp. Dist(s): H Leonard

Movie Themes for Violin: 12 Memorable Themes from the Greatest Movies of All Time. Created by Hal Leonard Corporation Staff. Max Charles Davies. 2008. pap. bk. 19.95 (978-1-84761-000-3(5), 1847610005) Pub: Schott Music Corp. Dist(s): H Leonard

Movie Title Hits. 2000. bk. 13.95 (978-1-85909-704-5(9), Warner Bro) Alfred Pub.

Moviegoer. Ed. by Walker Percy. Prod. by New Letters on the Air Staff. 1 cass. (Running Time: 30 min.). 8.00 (NL 45) Am Audio Prose.
Walker Percy reads from his National Book Award-winning novel "The Moviegoer" & talks about his fascination with language.

Moviegoer. unabr. ed. Read by Christopher Hurt. Ed. by Walker Percy. 5 cass. (Running Time: 7 hrs.). 1993. 39.95 (978-0-7861-0391-1(4), 1343) Blckstn Audio.
Binx Bolling, a small-time stockbroker who lives quietly in suburban New Orleans, pursues an interest in the movies, affairs with his secretaries & living out his days. But soon he is on a "search" for some spiritual truth to anchor him.

Moviegoer. unabr. ed. Read by Christopher Hurt. Ed. by Walker Percy. 6 CDs. (Running Time: 7 hrs.). 2000. audio compact disk 48.00 (978-0-7861-9925-9(3), 1343) Blckstn Audio.

Moviegoer. unabr. ed. Read by Christopher Hurt. Ed. by Walker Percy. 1 CD. (Running Time: 6 hrs. 30 mins.). 2001. audio compact disk 19.95 (zm1343) Blckstn Audio.

Moviegoer. unabr. ed. Walker Percy. Read by Christopher Hurt. (Running Time: 7 hrs.). 2003. 24.95 (978-0-7861-9662-3(9), 1343) Blckstn Audio.

***Moviegoer.** unabr. ed. Walker Percy. Read by Christopher Hurt. (Running Time: 6 hrs. 45 mins.). 2010. audio compact disk 19.95 (978-1-4417-4009-0(0)) Blckstn Audio.

Movies Go Baroque. 1 cass., 1 CD. 7.98 (TA 30336); audio compact disk 12.78 CD Jewel box. (TA 80336) NewSound.

Movies in My Mind: Audio Adventures for Children. Mark Cooper & Carl Johnson. Prod. by Imagination Development Group Staff. (J). 2001. audio compact disk 19.95 (978-1-931184-00-7(3)) Imagination Dev.

Movies in My Mind Vol. 2: Audio Adventures for Children. (Running Time: 60 mins.). (YA). 2002. pap. bk. 19.95 (978-1-931184-04-5(6)) Pub: Imagination Dev. Dist(s): Penton Overseas

Movies in My Mind Vol. 3: Audio Adventures for Children. (Running Time: 60 mins.). (YA). 2002. pap. bk. 19.95 (978-1-931184-05-2(4)) Pub: Imagination Dev. Dist(s): Penton Overseas

Movies, Movies, Movies. unabr. ed. Read by Heywood Hale Broun et al. 1 cass. (Heywood Hale Broun Ser.). 12.95 (40034) J Norton Pubs.
Broun talks with Penelope Gilliatt, Herman Weinberg & Howard Koch.

Movimientos. 1 cass. (Primeros Pasos en Ciencia Ser.). (SPA.). (J). 12.00 (7453-0, Natl Textbk Co) M-H Contemporary.
Helps children in grades 1-4 discover the process of scientific investigation. Part of the First Steps in Science Program.

Movin' Perf. by Hap Palmer. 1 cass. (J). 11.95 (EA 546C); 11.95 LP. (EA 546) Kimbo Educ.
Funky Penguin - Jamaican Holiday - Midnight Moon - Enter Sunlight & more.

Movin' & Shakin' for Youngsters. Prod. by Angela Russ. Lyrics by Angela Russ. Arranged by Bill Burchell. Composed by Bill Burchell. 1 CD. (Running Time: 34 mins). (J). 2001. audio compact disk 13.99 (978-0-9660122-6-2(7)) Russ Invis.
Children sing and dance to this captivating music with easy, instructional, active lyrics that keep them stretching, swaying, clapping, marching, tapping, wiggling, and laughing to kid's favorite songs and lullabies. Some songs are even sung with a bilingual twist. Before long, youngsters are singing original lyrics to familiar tunes. They are having so much fun, they don't even know they're learning about their body parts, following simple commands, identifying colors, counting, or scaling their ABCs.

Movin' in, Building a Town: The Story of Naperville. unabr. ed. Amy Lowe. 1 CD. (Running Time: 59 mins.). (J). (gr. 3-6). 2006. audio compact disk 15.98 (978-1-893967-30-4(1)) Emphasis Ent.

Movin' in the Right Direction! (A Program or Songbook to Build Character & Integrity in Young People for Unison & 2-Part Voices) A Program or Songbook to Build Character & Integrity in Young People for Unison & 2-Part Voices. Composed by Sally K. Albrecht & Jay Althouse. (ENG.). 2008. audio compact disk 39.95 (978-0-7390-5242-6(X)) Alfred Pub.

Moving: Program from the Award Winning Public Radio Series. Interview. Hosted by Fred Goodwin. Comment by John Hockenberry. 1 CD. (Running Time: 1 hr). 2001. audio compact disk 21.95 (978-1-932479-67-6(8), LCM 179) Lichtenstein Creat.
Take your whole life, wrap it in bubble wrap, stuff it in a box, and watch four big guys load it onto a van and drive away. Stressful? You bet, and Americans do it, on the average, every five years.Dr. Thomas T. Olkowski, PhD. and Ms. Audrey McCollum, MSW, on the psychological stresses of moving and what parents can do to make a move easier on their children. Cultural psychologist Dr. David Matsumoto on culture shock and how to defuse it. Singer-Songwriter Loudon Wainwright III talks about the joys of putting down roots at last, and takes us along for one of his moves in a performance of his song "Cardboard Boxes." Social historian Dr. Kenneth T. Jackson comments on the American propensity for pulling up stakes, while author Dr. Scott Sanders makes the case for staying put.We also hear from a few recent relocators, and a family on the eve of their first night in their new home. Plus commentator John Hockenberry on rooting through cardboard boxes in search of extention cords and a can opener.

Moving Ahead with Math, Level 5. Ann Edson & Allan A. Schwartz. 8 cass. 10.95 (978-0-89525-087-2(X), AC 64) Ed Activities.
Includes: rounding whole numbers-10's, 100's; common multiples of numbers; adding & subtracting fractions & decimals; multiplying fractions & decimals; using millions; finding the area of a rectangle & triangle; finding the volume of a rectangular prism. Includes activity books and guide.

Moving at the Speed of Love. Sai Maa Lakshmi Devi. 2004. audio compact disk 16.00 (978-1-933488-10-3(7)) HIU Pr.
In this powerful meditation from an intensive in San Rafael, CA, September 2003, Sai Maa teaches us how to unite mind and heart. We journey into pure space to experience ourselves as creators, co-creating with the angels and cosmic beings, while anchored fully in our physical bodies. We are here, we are there, each cell vibrating at the speed of love.

Moving Beyond ADHD & Perfectionism: Realities, Myths, Strategies & Tools. Twila L. Gates. Perf. by Twila L. Gates. Prod. by Molly O'Neill & PowerSystems. (ENG.). 2008. audio compact disk 19.99 (978-1-935277-10-1(3)) PowerSystems.

Moving Bodies. Arthur Giron. Read by Emily Bergl et al. (Running Time: 7020 sec.). 2008. audio compact disk 25.95 (978-1-58081-392-1(5)) Pub: L A Theatre. Dist(s): NetLibrary CO

Moving Day. unabr. ed. Meg Cabot. Read by Tara Sands. (Allie Finkle's Rules for Girls Ser.: Bk. 1). (J). 2008. 44.99 (978-1-60514-624-9(2)) Find a World.

Moving Day. unabr. ed. Meg Cabot. Narrated by Tara Sands. 4 CDs. (Running Time: 4 hrs. 13 mins.). (Allie Finkle's Rules for Girls Ser.: Bk. 1). (ENG.). (J). (gr. 4-7). 2008. audio compact disk 54.95 (978-0-545-03966-6(5)) Scholastic Inc.
When nine-year-old Allie Finkle's parents announce that they are moving her and her brothers from their suburban split-level into an ancient Victorian town, Allie's sure her life is over.

Moving Day. unabr. ed. Meg Cabot. Read by Tara Sands. 4 CDs. (Running Time: 4 hrs. 13 mins.). (Allie Finkle's Rules for Girls Ser.: Bk. 1). (ENG.). (J). (gr. 4-7). 2008. audio compact disk 19.95 (978-0-545-03948-2(7), Scholastic) Scholastic Inc.

Moving Day: 11 Cor.5:1-9. Ed Young. 1990. 4.95 (978-0-7417-1783-2(2), 783) Win Walk.

***Moving Finger: A BBC Full-Cast Radio Drama.** Agatha Christie. Narrated by June Whitfield. (Running Time: 1 hr. 30 mins. 0 sec.). (ENG.). 2010. audio compact disk 24.95 (978-0-563-52414-4(6)) Pub: AudioGO. Dist(s): Perseus Dist

Moving Finger: A BBC Full-Cast Radio Drama. unabr. ed. Agatha Christie. Read by Joan Hickson. 4 cass. (Running Time: 5 hrs. 30 min.). (Miss Marple Ser.: No. 4). 1999. 24.95 (978-1-57270-123-6(4), N41123u) Pub: Audio Partners. Dist(s): PerseuPGW
Burton & his sister are staying in a quiet English village where a number of residents, including themselves, are receiving a series of vile anonymous letters. But could these letters have triggered a suicide? When a murder soon follows, Burton steps in to help Inspector Nash find the culprit. Just as the case looks like it's solved, Miss Marple conveniently visits the quaint town & reopens the investigation, dazzling the villagers with her untangling of the murderous events.

Moving Finger: A BBC Full-Cast Radio Drama. unabr. ed. Agatha Christie. Narrated by Martin Jarvis. (Running Time: 22200 sec.). (Miss Marple Ser.: No. 4). (ENG.). 2007. audio compact disk 29.95 (978-1-57270-851-8(4)) Pub: AudioGO. Dist(s): Perseus Dist

Moving Forward. Betty L. Randolph. Read by Betty L. Randolph. Read by Leonard Baron. Ed. by Success Education Institute International Staff. 1 cass. (Success Ser.). 1989. bk. 9.98 (978-1-55909-123-7(1), 99S) Randolph Tapes.
Features male-female voice tracks with the right-left brain.

Moving Forward: Taking the Lead in Your Life. abr. unabr. ed. Dave Pelzer. Read by L. J. Ganser. (Running Time: 5 hrs. 30 mins.). (ENG.). 2008. 24.98 (978-1-60024-229-8(4)) Pub: Hachet Audio. Dist(s): HachBkGrp

Moving Forward into the Past: The Dissolution of Traditional Gender Constructions. Helen Fisher. Read by Helen Fisher. 1 cass. (Running Time: 1 hr. 26 min.). 1993. 10.95 (978-0-7822-0449-0(X), 527) C G Jung IL.
Anthropologist Helen Fisher traces the evolution of human sexuality & disentangles those sexual differences that evolved millenia ago from those gender differences that were socially constructed during our more recent adaptation to farm-living. She then offers a provocative interpretation of recent trends in gender roles & explores where men & women might go from here. Part of the conference set Who Do We Think We Are?: The Mystery & Muddle of Gender.

Moving from Contact to Client: Networking Follow-up Strategies. Speeches. Michael J. Hughes. 1 CD. (Running Time: 29 mins). 2005. audio compact disk 18.47 (978-1-895186-35-2(8)) Multi-Media ON CAN.
Research has confirmed that follow up is the single biggest opportunity area for sales and business professionals. An effective follow up program sets you apart from your competitors and offers you the advantage you need to get more business faster! In this third installment from the Four Cornerstones of Networking Success, author Michael J. Hughes, known as Canada?s Networking Guru, shares with you how to develop and manage a fail-safe networking contact follow up program. This recording will share with you a step-by-step follow up plan that will drive results and help you develop meaningful relationships. Guaranteed.

Moving from Pain into Pleasure: Fibromyalgia & Chronic Pain. Frank Wildman. 1 cass. (Running Time: 1 hr. 17 min.). (Intelligent Body Ser.). 1996. 15.00 (978-1-889618-55-5(1)) Feldenkrais Move.
Feldenkrais awareness through movement lessons.

Moving from Third to Fourth Dimension. Swami Amar Jyoti. 1 cass. 1976. 9.95 (R-4) Truth Consciousness.
Seeing this world from the fourth dimension. "Go forward. Follow the sun." Intimacy with God. On the path to the Pathless.

Moving House Plus Three More. unabr. ed. Rosemary Hayes. Read by Stig Wemyss. 2 cass. (Running Time: 2 hrs. 30 mins.). (Aussie Bites Ser.). (J). 2001. lib. bdg. 24.00 (978-1-74030-367-5(9)) Pub: Bolinda Pubng AUS. Dist(s): Bolinda Pub Inc

Moving House Plus Three More. unabr. ed. Read by Stig Wemyss. 2 cass. (Running Time: 2 hrs. 15 mins.). (Aussie Bites Ser.). (J). 1999. lib. bdg. 24.00 (978-1-74030-074-2(2)) Pub: Bolinda Pubng AUS. Dist(s): Bolinda Pub Inc

Moving House Plus Three More. unabr. ed. Read by Stig Wemyss. 2 cass. (Running Time: 2 hrs. 15 mins.). (Aussie Bites Ser.). (J). 2001. lib. bdg. 24.00 (978-1-74030-341-5(5)) Pub: Bolinda Pubng AUS. Dist(s): Bolinda Pub Inc

Moving House Plus Three More. unabr. ed. Narrated by Stig Wemyss. 2 cass. (Running Time: 2 hrs. 17 mins.). (J). 2001. lib. bdg. 24.00 (978-1-74030-528-0(0)) Pub: Bolinda Pubng AUS. Dist(s): Bolinda Pub Inc

Moving House Plus Three More. unabr. ed. Read by Stig Wemyss. 2 cass. (Running Time: 2 hrs. 45 mins.). (Aussie Bites Ser.). (J). 2001. 24.00 (978-1-74030-573-0(6)) Pub: Bolinda Pubng AUS. Dist(s): Bolinda Pub Inc

Moving House Plus Three More. unabr. ed. Read by Stig Wemyss. 2 cass. (Aussie Bites Ser.). (J). 2002. lib. bdg. 24.00 (978-1-74030-879-3(4)) Pub: Bolinda Pubng AUS. Dist(s): Bolinda Pub Inc

Moving in the Gifts of the Holy Spirit. Speeches. Tim N. Enloe. 2 CDs. 2000. audio compact disk 17.99 (978-0-9749739-4-4(7)) E M Pubns.
Practical teaching on how to move in the nine manifestation gifts of the Holy Spirit (1 Cor 12:8-11). Disc one contains, "Misconceptions About the Gifts." Disc two contains, "Practical Helps.".

Moving Landscape with Falling Rain see Twentieth-Century Poetry in English, No. 24, Recordings of Poets Reading Their Own Poetry

Moving Life's Mountains Series, Elbert Willis. 4 cass. 13.00 Fill the Gap.

Moving Mama to Town. unabr. ed. Ronder Thomas Young. Narrated by Jeff Woodman. 5 pieces. (Running Time: 6 hrs. 30 mins.). (gr. 5 up). 1998. 46.00 (978-0-7887-1908-0(4), 95329E7) Recorded Bks.
Thirteen-year-old Freddy James Johnson is taking charge of his family after their father abandons the family. He is packing up the farm & moving everyone into town. Can Freddy do enough to hold the bewildered family together.

Moving Mama to Town: Class Set. unabr. ed. Ronder Thomas Young. Read by Jeff Woodman. 5 cass. (Running Time: 6 hrs. 30 min.). (J). 1998. pap. bk. 106.70 (978-0-7887-2560-9(2), 46730) Recorded Bks.
Thirteen-year-old Freddy James Johnson is taking charge of his family after their father abandons the family. He is packing up the farm & moving everyone into town. Includes 10 books.

Moving Mama to Town: Homework Set. unabr. ed. Ronder Thomas Young. Read by Jeff Woodman. 5 cass. (Running Time: 6 hrs. 30 min.). (J). 1998. bk. 58.24 (978-0-7887-1936-3(X), 40643) Recorded Bks.
Thirteen-year-old Freddy James Johnson is taking charge of his family after their father abandons the family. He is packing up the farm & moving everyone into town.

Moving Mars. unabr. ed. Greg Bear. Read by Sharon Williams. (Running Time: 15 hrs.). 2008. 39.25 (978-1-4233-5314-0(5), 9781423353140, BADLE); 39.25 (978-1-4233-5312-6(9), 9781423353126, Brlnc Audio MP3 Lib); 24.95 (978-1-4233-5313-3(7), 9781423353133, BAD); audio compact disk 24.95 (978-1-4233-5311-9(0), 9781423353119, Brilliance MP3) Brilliance Audio.

Moving Moment, 1985. Read by Jack Schwarz. Contrib. by Will Noffke. 1985. 15.00 Aletheia Psycho.

Moving On. Jane Coleman. Read by Sherry Edelman. (Running Time: 0 hr. 36 mins.). 1999. 10.95 (978-1-60083-499-8(X)) Iofy Corp.

***Moving On.** Jane Candia Coleman. 2009. (978-1-60136-453-1(9)) Audio Holding.

Moving On. T. Forest & J. Huizenga. 1989. 41.91 (978-0-8013-0120-9(3), 75784) Longman.

Moving On. unabr. ed. Simon Weston. Read by Gareth Armstrong. 7 cass. (Running Time: 7 hrs. 47 mins.). (Isis Cassettes Ser.). (J). 2004. 61.95 (978-0-7531-1901-3(3)) Pub: ISIS Lrg Prnt GBR. Dist(s): Ulverscroft US

Moving On, Pt. 1. unabr. collector's ed. Larry McMurtry. Read by Michael Prichard. 10 cass. (Running Time: 15 hrs.). 1992. 80.00 (978-0-7366-2185-4(7), 2981-A) Books on Tape.
Patsy & Jim drift through the West, from one rodeo & honky-tonk to another. Each is looking for something, neither knows exactly what. Life always seems to be around the next bend.

Moving On, Pt. 2. collector's ed. Larry McMurtry. Read by Michael Prichard. 10 cass. (Running Time: 15 hrs.). 1992. 80.00 (978-0-7366-2186-1(5), 2981-B) Books on Tape.

Moving On: Two Healing Trances for Resolving Sexual Abuse Issues. Short Stories. Bill O'Hanlon. Narrated by Bill O'Hanlon. 1 CD. (Running Time: 60 mins). 2009. audio compact disk 16.95 (978-0-9823573-5-4(4)) Crown Hse GBR.

Moving On Vol. 1: A Program for Resolving Sexual Abuse. 1 CD. 2004. audio compact disk 15.00 (978-0-9764498-4-3(6)) O'H O'H Inc.
A healing hypnotic program for sexual abuse survivors. This 30 minute audio program is empowering and permissive and designed to help listeners reclaim their lives and move on to vibrant futures.

Moving On Vol. 2: A Program for Resolving Sexual Abuse. 1 CD. (Running Time: 30 mins.). 2004. audio compact disk 15.00 (978-0-9764498-5-0(4)) O'H O'H Inc.
A healing hypnotic program for sexual abuse survivors. This 30 minute audio program is empowering and permissive and designed to help listeners reclaim their lives and move on to vibrant futures.(More of the same, only better. Moving On 1 was so popular, Bill recorded a second 30 minute hypnotic program with all new material.).

Moving on in the Freedom of the Spirit. Françoise Darcy-Bérubé. 1 cass. (Running Time: 1 hr.). 2001. 8.95 (A6801) St Anthony Mess Pr.
Describes tensions in our Christian identity, the impact they have on our ministry and the need we have to receive nourishment feom the Bible. Challenges religious educators to move on in the Spirit in spite of the defensive dispositions of some to sojourn in the past.

Moving on the Waters - Mari Gayatri: Movement Out of Meditation. Mari Gayatri. 1 cass. (Running Time: 1 hr. 30 min.). 1991. 12.00 Gypsy Dog.
Definitive yoga tape. Movement Out of Meditation designed to suit quiet or active student - also original devotional music (Kirtan). Grows with the student. Every session new & alive. Promotes mindfulness, innerpeace, equanimity.

Moving Out of the Master's House: A Mental You Haul. 2004. audio compact disk 15.00 (978-0-9657332-2-9(X)) DeVonne Prod.

Moving Pictures. Terry Pratchett. Read by Tony Robinson. 2 cass. (Running Time: 3 hrs.). (Discworld Ser.). 2000. 16.99 (978-0-552-14010-2(4)) Pub: Transworld GBR. Dist(s): Trafalgar

Moving Pictures. unabr. ed. Terry Pratchett. Read by Nigel Planer. 8 cass. (Running Time: 8 hrs.). (Discworld Ser.). (J). 2001. 69.95 (978-0-7531-0139-1(4), 970601) Pub: ISIS Lrg Prnt GBR. Dist(s): Ulverscroft US
Cameras roll - which means the imps inside have to paint really fast - on the fantastic Discworld when the alchemists discover the magic of the silver screen. Victor Tugelbend & Theda Withel battle the forces of evil & cinema advertising...Gaspode the Wonder Dog nearly saves the day...watch the filming of "Blown Away," the oddest Civil War picture ever made.

Moving Pictures. unabr. ed. Terry Pratchett. Read by Nigel Planer. 10 CDs. (Running Time: 10 hrs. 12 mins.). (Discworld Ser.). (J). 2002. audio compact disk 89.95 (978-0-7531-1477-3(1)) Pub: ISIS Lrg Prnt GBR. Dist(s): Ulverscroft US

Moving Target. Elizabeth Lowell. Narrated by Alyssa Bresnahan. 12 CDs. (Running Time: 14 hrs. 15 mins.). audio compact disk 116.00 (978-1-4025-1530-9(8)) Recorded Bks.

Moving Target. Elizabeth Lowell. Narrated by Alyssa Bresnahan. 10 cass. (Running Time: 14 hrs. 15 mins.). 2001. 93.00 (978-0-7887-8859-8(0), 96636) Recorded Bks.
In this work, the author propels listeners to electrifying its tow mysteriuos treasures: a finely woven ancient scarf and four beautifully illustrated pages from a priceless medieval manuscripts.

***Moving Target.** abr. ed. Elizabeth Lowell. Read by Maria Tucci. (ENG.). 2004. (978-0-06-081408-3(X), Harper Audio); (978-0-06-078327-3(3), Harper Audio) HarperCollins Pubs.

Moving Target. unabr. ed. Ross MacDonald, pseud. Read by Tom Parker. 5 cass. (Running Time: 7 hrs.). 2001. 39.95 (978-0-7861-2073-4(8), 2834); audio compact disk 48.00 (978-0-7861-9694-4(7), 2834) Blckstn Audio.
Like many Southern California millionaires, Ralph Sampson keeps odd company. There's the sun-worshipping holy man to who Sampson once gave his very own mountain and the fading actress with sidelines in astrology and S&M. Now one of Sampson's friends may have arranged his kidnapping. And as Lew Archer follows the clues from the canyon sanctuaries of the mega-rich to jazz joints where you can get beaten up between sets.

***Moving Through Transitions.** Ira Progoff. 2010. audio compact disk 15.00 (978-1-935859-09-3(9)) Dialogue Assoc.

Moving Toward Enlightenment. Lorraine M. Coburn. 2006. 14.99 (978-0-9786516-7-1(7)); audio compact disk 14.99 (978-0-9786516-2-6(6)) Miracles Media.

Moving Toward God with Our Fears. Carole Riley. 4 cass. (Running Time: 3 hrs. 9 min.). 1994. 34.95 (TAH323) Alba Hse Comns.
This liberating audio-cassette program is excellent for anyone shackled by paralyzing fears of any type. Good for spiritual & mental health groups.

Moving Toyshop. Edmund Crispin. 2008. 54.95 (978-0-7531-3052-0(1)); audio compact disk 71.95 (978-0-7531-3053-7(X)) Pub: ISIS Audio GBR. Dist(s): Ulverscroft US

Moving West Songs: With Historical Narration. Keith McNeil & Rusty McNeil. Read by Keith McNeil & Rusty McNeil. 1 CD. (Running Time: 1 hr. 30 min.). (American History Through Folksong Ser.). (YA). (gr. 4 up). 1996. audio compact disk 22.95 (978-1-878360-10-6(8)) WEM Records.

Moving West Songs: With Historical Narration, Set. Keith McNeil & Rusty McNeil. Read by Keith McNeil & Rusty McNeil. 2 cass. (Running Time: 2 hrs.). (American History Through Folksong Ser.). (YA). (gr. 4 up). 1989. 19.95 (978-1-878360-02-1(7), 505C) WEM Records.
Forty-four of the songs which Americans sang as their nation expanded westward across the entire continent during the short period between the War of 1812 & the Civil War.

Moving with Machines: Early Explorers Fluent Set B Audio CD. Michelle Schaub. Adapted by Benchmark Education Staff. (J). 2007. audio compact disk 10.00 (978-1-4108-8247-9(0)) Benchmark Educ.

Moving with Mozart. 1 cass. (Running Time: 40 mins.). (J). (ps-2). 1999. 10.95 (978-1-56346-092-0(0)) Kimbo Educ.
This project places an emphasis on directed movement activities while a variety of Mozart compositions play in the background.

Moving with Mozart. Music by Wolfgang Amadeus Mozart. 1 CD. (Running Time: 1 hr.). (J). 2001. pap. bk. 14.95 (KIM 9154CD) Kimbo Educ.
Introduce young children to the timeless beauty of classical music. This unique approach involves children in activities & movement fun! You'll love this new way to introduce little ones to soothing music & increase brain power. Includes vocal instructions & instrumentals for extended activities & quiet time.

Moving with Mozart. Music by Wolfgang Amadeus Mozart. 1 cass. (Running Time: 1 hr.). (J). (gr. k-2). 2001. pap. bk. 10.95 (KIM 9154C) Kimbo Educ.

Moving with the Spirit. Greg Skipper & Gail Skipper. 1999. 40.00 (978-0-7673-9727-8(4)); 8.00 (978-0-7673-9648-6(0)); audio compact disk 16.98 (978-0-7673-9707-0(X)); audio compact disk 45.00 (978-0-7673-9700-1(2)) LifeWay Christian.

Moving with the Spirit Senior Adult. Greg Skipper & Gail Skipper. 1999. 11.98 (978-0-7673-9716-2(9)) LifeWay Christian.

Moving Within the Circle. unabr. ed. 1 cass. bk. 34.95 (S11370) J Norton Pubs.
Contemporary Native American music & dance.

Moving Without Madness: A Guide to Handle the Stress, Vol. 1. abr. ed. 1 cass. (978-1-891076-06-0(X)) Gemini Press.

Moviola Man. unabr. ed. Bill Mahan & Colleen Mahan. Read by Marvin Miller. 7 cass. (Running Time: 7 hrs.). 47.60 (B-119) Audio Bk.
A novel about the Hollywood TV film industry.

Mowgli's Brothers. unabr. ed. Rudyard Kipling. Read by Cindy Hardin & Walter Zimmerman. 1 cass. (Running Time: 56 min.). (J). 1979. 7.95 (N-28) Jimcin Record.
Best-Loved episodes from The Jungle Book.

Mowgli's Brothers. unabr. ed. Rudyard Kipling. Read by Ralph Cosham. 2 cass. (Running Time: 3 hrs.). (J). 1994. bk. 16.95 (978-1-883049-09-6(1), 391214, Commuters Library); lib. bdg. 18.95 (978-1-883049-28-7(8)) Sound Room.
A collection of stories from "The Jungle Books": "Mowgli's Brothers", "Kaa's Hunting", "Tiger-Tiger!", & "Letting in the Jungle". Includes vinyl case with notes, author's picture and biography.

***Mowgli's Brothers: A Story from the Jungle Books.** Rudyard Kipling. 2009. (978-1-60136-510-1(1)) Audio Holding.

Mowing see Robert Frost Reads

Mowing see Twentieth-Century Poetry in English, No. 6, Recordings of Poets Reading Their Own Poetry

Moxie: The American Challenge. unabr. ed. Philip S. Weld. Read by Christopher Hurt. 8 cass. (Running Time: 8 hrs.). 1984. 48.00 (978-0-7366-0622-6(X), 1584) Books on Tape.
The account of Philip Weld's great sailing victory in the 1980 Observer Single-Handed Transatlantic Race. On a course which spanned 2,810 miles from Plymouth, England to Newport, Rhode Island, Weld won in the record-breaking time of 17 days, 23 hours & 12 minutes. Not only did this make Weld the first American to win but at a lean 65 years the oldest as well.

Moxon's Master see Eyes of the Panther & Other Stories

Moxy Maxwell Collection: Moxy Maxwell Does Not Love Stuart Little, Moxy Maxwell Does Not Love Writing Thank You Notes. unabr. ed. Peggy Gifford. Read by Clea Lewis. (ENG.). (J). (gr. 2-6). 2008. audio compact disk 19.95 (978-0-7393-6344-7(1), Listening Lib) Pub: Random Audio Pubg. Dist(s): Random

Moxy Maxwell Collection: Moxy Maxwell Does Not Love Stuart Little, Moxy Maxwell Does Not Love Writing Thank You Notes. unabr. ed. Peggy Gifford. Read by Clea Lewis. 3 CDs. (Running Time: 2 hrs. 43 mins.). (J). (gr. 3-5). 2008. audio compact disk 24.00 (978-0-7393-6347-8(6), Listening Lib) Pub: Random Audio Pubg. Dist(s): Random

***Moxy Maxwell Does Not Love Practicing the Piano: But She Does Love Being in Recitals.** unabr. ed. Peggy Gifford. Narrated by Clea Lewis. 2 CDs. (Running Time: 1 hr. 48 mins.). (J). (gr. 3-5). 2009. audio compact disk 24.00 (978-0-307-58193-8(4), Listening Lib) Pub: Random Audio Pubg. Dist(s): Random

Mozart. Prod. by A&E Television Network Staff. 1 cass. 1998. 9.95 (978-0-7670-0735-1(2)) A & E Home.
Composers & Musicians.

Mozart. Julie Koerner. (Musicbooks Ser.). 1997. bk. 13.50 (978-1-56799-543-5(8), Friedman-Fairfax) M Friedman Pub Grp Inc.

Mozart. Contrib. by Wolfgang Amadeus Mozart. 1 CD. (Running Time: 1 hr. 30 mins.). (Baby's First Ser.). (ENG.). (J). 2003. audio compact disk 7.95 (978-1-59125-328-0(4)) Penton Overseas.

Mozart. unabr. ed. Marcia Davenport. Read by Nadia May. 8 cass. (Running Time: 11 hrs. 30 mins.). 1991. 56.95 (978-0-7861-0264-8(0), 1231) Blckstn Audio.
This biography of the 18th century composer recreates Mozart - the man & his music - against the background of the world he lived in. Davenport builds from his infancy toward the climactic meeting in 1787 of Mozart, Lorenzo Da Ponte & Casanova in Prague, when "Don Giovanni" was written, to Mozart's early death.

Mozart: A Life. Peter Gay. Read by Alexander Adams. 2000. audio compact disk 32.00 (978-0-7366-5211-7(6)) Books on Tape.

Mozart: A Life. Peter Gay. Read by Alexander Adams. 4 cass. (Running Time: 6 hrs.). 2000. 24.95 (978-0-7366-4944-5(1)) Books on Tape.
The archetypal child prodigy whose genius triumphed over early precociousness & who later broke away from a loving but tyrannical father to pursue his vision unhampered.

Mozart: A Life. unabr. ed. Peter Gay. Read by Alexander Adams. 2001. audio compact disk Books on Tape.

Mozart: A Life. unabr. ed. Maynard Soloman. Read by Edward Lewis. 14 cass. (Running Time: 21 hrs.). 1996. 112.00 (978-0-7366-3524-0(6), 4161) Books on Tape.
The brief existence of one of history's true prodigies remains filled with puzzles. But one key to explaining them, says Maynard Solomon, is the behavior of Mozart's controlling father, Leopold, who envied, manipulated & ultimately disinherited his son.

Mozart: A Life. unabr. collector's ed. Peter Gay. Read by Alexander Adams. 4 cass. (Running Time: 6 hrs.). 1999. 32.00 (978-0-7366-4823-3(2), 5168) Books on Tape.
Peter Gay's passionate & painstaking research of Mozart traces the legendary development of the man whose life was a whirlwind of achievement & the composer who pushed every instrument to its limit & every genre - especially opera - into new realms. More than an engrossing biography, this is a meditation on the nature of genius & for any music lover, a fascinating myth that have long shrouded the maestro's life.

Mozart: A Musical Picture Book. Ernst A. Ekker. Illus. by Doris Eisenburger. (ENG.). (J). 2006. audio compact disk 20.00 (978-0-7358-2056-2(2)) Pub: North-South Bks NYC. Dist(s): IngramPubServ

Mozart: Alla Turca. Ed. by Peter Pickow. 1 CD. (Running Time: 1 hr.). (Concert Performer Ser.). 2004. audio compact disk 6.95 (978-0-8256-1749-2(9), AM949828) Pub: Music Sales. Dist(s): H Leonard

Mozart: Rare Choral Works. Directed By Vox Caeli Sinfonia & Gloriae Dei Cantores. 2 CDs. 2006. audio compact disk 29.95 (978-1-55725-479-5(6)) Paraclete MA.

Mozart: Sonata K. 545. Ed. by Peter Pickow. (Concert Performer Ser.). 2004. audio compact disk 6.95 (978-0-8256-1750-8(2), AM949837) Pub: Music Sales. Dist(s): H Leonard

Mozart: The Golden Touch. abr. ed. Lister Sinclair. 5 CDs. (Running Time: 18000 sec.). Dramatization. 2006. audio compact disk 39.95 (978-0-660-19566-7(6), CBC Audio) Canadian Broadcasting CAN.

Mozart: The Greatest Hits. 1 CD. (Running Time: 1 hr. 30 min.). audio compact disk 10.98 (978-1-57908-157-7(6), 3603) Platinm Enter.

Mozart - Beethoven. Perf. by Gordon Jeffries. 1 cass. (Running Time: 52 min.). (Soothing Classics Ser.). 1991. (978-1-55961-134-3(0)); 9.95 (978-1-55961-107-7(3)) Relaxtn Co.

Mozart - Before You Were Born? Executive Producer Kim Mitzo Thompson & Karen Mitzo Hilderbrand. Arranged by Hal Wright. 2000. audio compact disk 12.99 (978-1-57583-224-1(0)) Twin Sisters.

Mozart & Baroque Music to Empower Learning & Performance, Vol. 1. Ivan Barzakov. Music by Wolfgang Amadeus Mozart et al. 1 cass. (Running Time: 1 hr. 30 min.). 1998. 9.95 (OLC601); audio compact disk 17.95 (CD-OL601) OptimaLearning.
Mozart piano sonatas on Side A to stimulate mental performance such as planning, analysis, math or computer work. Uniquely sequenced Baroque music on Side B empowers studying, test-taking, writing, calming & healing (replaces OLC304). Includes written instructions.

Mozart & Friends. unabr. abr. ed. Jeffrey Siegel. (Running Time: 3600 sec.). (Keyboard Conversations Ser.). (ENG.). 2006. audio compact disk 14.95 (978-0-7393-3263-4(5), Random AudioBks) Pub: Random Audio Pubg. Dist(s): Random

Mozart As Healer. Don Campbell. Music by Wolfgang Amadeus Mozart. 2 cass. (Running Time: 3 hrs.). 1999. 18.95 (83-0072) Explorations.
The author of the "The Mozart Effect" further delves into many of Mozart's compositions to find the music's exciting potential to spark creativity, soothe emotions & heal the human body. Includes self-healing exercises & the latest research on sound, learning & healing.

Mozart Effect. abr. ed. Don Campbell. Read by Don Campbell. (Running Time: 3 hrs.). 2009. 39.97 (978-1-4233-7170-0(4), 9781423371700, BADLE); 39.97 (978-1-4233-7168-7(2), 9781423371687, Brlnc Audio MP3 Lib); 24.99 (978-1-4233-7167-0(4), 9781423371670, Brilliance MP3); 24.99 (978-1-4233-7169-4(0), 9781423371694, BAD) Brilliance Audio.

Mozart Effect: Music for Children. Compiled by Don Campbell. 3 CDs. (Running Time: 1 hr. 35 mins.). (ps-12). 2001. audio compact disk 54.00 (7682, ZephPr) Chicago Review.

Mozart Effect: Music for Children. Read by Don Campbell. 3 cass. (Running Time: 4 hrs. 30 min.). (J). 1999. 29.98 (40341); audio compact disk 52.98 (40339) Courage-to-Change.
Compilation of Mozart's most powerful, playful & affecting compositions, selected to enhance IQ, inspire creativity or explore body movement & motion.

Mozart Effect Vol. 1: Tune Up Your Mind. 1 cass. (Running Time: 1 hr. 30 min.). 7.18 (CG 84301); audio compact disk 12.78 (CG 84301) NewSound.

Mozart Effect Vol. 2: Relax, Daydream & Draw. 1 cass. (Running Time: 1 hr. 30 min.). 7.18 (CG 84302); audio compact disk 12.78 (CG 84302) NewSound.

Mozart Effect Vol. 3: Mozart in Motion. 1 cass. (Running Time: 1 hr. 30 min.). 7.18 (CG 84303); audio compact disk 12.78 (CG 84303) NewSound.

Mozart Effect for Babies: From Playtime to Sleepytime. 1 cass. (Running Time: 1 hr. 30 min.). (J). 1999. 10.98 (40227); audio compact disk 18.95 (40226) Courage-to-Change.
Studies have shown that listening to classical music increases spatial & temporal reasoning ability in preschoolers.

Mozart for a Mother's Soul. Teresa B. Kindred. Illus. by Beth O'Bryant. (BookNotes Ser.). 2000. bk. 13.99 (978-0-88088-413-6(4)) Peter Pauper.

Mozart for Accelerated Learning: Unleash Your Potential Through the Genuis of Mozart! abr. ed. Roland Roberts. 2 cass. (Running Time: 2 hrs.). 2000. 24.95 (978-1-899836-62-8(4)) Crown Hse GBR.

Mozart for Flute. Mizzy McCaskill & Dona Gilliam. 2003. bk. 19.95 (978-0-7866-7101-4(7), 97063BCD) Mel Bay.

Mozart for Monday Mornings: Jumpstart Your Week on a Winning Streak. 1 cass. (Running Time: 1 hr. 30 min.). (Set Your Life to Music Ser.). 5.58 (PHI 462433); audio compact disk 10.38 (PHI 462433) NewSound.

Mozart for Toddlers. Jimmie Haskell & Norman Weinberger. 1 cass. (Running Time: 1 hr. 30 min.). (J). (gr. 1-4). 1999. (978-0-9677360-5-1(6), 2321); audio compact disk 12.95 (978-0-9677360-2-0(1), 2301) Munchkin Inc.
This recording joins a bevy of other recent releases claiming to provide "nourishment for the mind." However, this CD is unique in that it tailors the music to its target audience of toddlers by providing bite-sized chunks of classical pieces, designed to fit the young child's attention span. The music is divided into three sections. "Wake Up" features sprightly tunes such as "Country Dance" and "Overture to Magic Flute." "Play Time" consists of livelier tunes such as "March" from The Marriage of Figaro. The last section,

"Sleepy Time," focuses on lovely arrangements of somnolent melodies such as "Serenade".

Mozart in Motion. Don Campbell. 1 cass. (Running Time: 1 hr. 30 min.). (Mozart Effect Ser.: Vol. 3). (J). 7.18 (CG 84293); audio compact disk 12.78 (CG 84293) NewSound.

Mozart Naturally. 1 CD. (Running Time: 1 hr.). 1994. audio compact disk 15.95 (2622, Creativ Pub) Quayside.
Piano orchestrations of Mozart. Pure sounds from nature, from songbirds to flowing brooks.

Mozart Naturally. 1 cass. (Running Time: 1 hr.). 1994. 9.95 (2621, NrthWrd Bks) TandN Child.

Mozart Nino Prodigio. unabr. ed. Abuelo Historias Del. (SPA.). 2007. audio compact disk 13.00 (978-958-8318-05-9(X)) Pub: Yoyo Music COL. Dist(s): YoYoMusic

Mozart WombSong Collection. Jimmie Haskell & Norman Weinberger. 1 CD. (J). (gr. k-2). 1999. audio compact disk (978-0-9677360-1-3(3), 2201); audio compact disk (978-0-9677360-9-9(9), 2211) Munchkin Inc.

Mozart WombSong Collections. Jimmie Haskell & Norman Weinberger. 1 cass. (J). (gr. k-2). 1999. (978-0-9677360-4-4(8), 2221) Munchkin Inc.

Mozart:for Mother & Baby. (Running Time: 60 mins.). 2002. audio compact disk 15.99 (978-1-904972-39-6(X)) Global Jrny GBR GBR.

Mozart's Magic Fantasy. 1 cass. (Running Time: 1 hr.). (J). (gr. 1 up). 9.98 (2226); audio compact disk 16.98 (D2226) MFLP CA.
Mozart's last opera was "The Magic Flute," an ingenious musical feast containing some of the composer's most beloved melodies. Along the way we hear many of the opera's memorable arias, sung in English to make this delightful music more accessible to children.

Mozart's Magic Fantasy. Susan Hammond. 1 cass. (Running Time: 1 hr.). (J). 1993. 10.98; audio compact disk 18.98 Consort Bk Sales.

Mozart's Magic Flute: An Exploration of the Life of the Psyche. Josip Pasic. Read by Josip Pasic. 2 cass. (Running Time: 2 hrs. 20 min.). 1991. 18.95 set. (978-0-7822-0344-8(2), 456) C G Jung IL.
The most fundamental of psychological tenents - that the psyche goes through a developmental process of becoming - is both depicted & challenged in Mozart's masterpiece, The Magic Flute. Jungian analyst Josip Pasic leads a seminar exploring the work as an allegory for analysis or individuation.

Mozart's Magnificent Voyage: Tales of the Dream Children. Susan Hammond. Perf. by Classical Kids. 1 CD. (Running Time: 1 hr. 30 min.). (J). 1998. audio compact disk 12.78 (CG 84297) NewSound.
Karl, Mozart's son goes back in time to Mozart's childhood & far ahead into the future. Along the way Karl learns much about his father & comes to understand the great composer's legacy of timeless music.

Mozart's Magnificent Voyage: Tales of the Dream Children. Susan Hazen-Hammond. (J). 1993. (978-1-896449-66-1(2)) CBSD CAN.

Mozart's Wife. Juliet Waldron. Read by Celeste Lawson. 10 cass. (Running Time: 14 hrs. 30 mins.). 2003. 69.95 (978-0-7861-2384-1(2), 3061) Blckstn Audio.
Mozart's wife aroused strong feelings among her contemporaries. Maturing from child to wife to hard headed widow, Konstnaze paid her husband's debts, provided for their children, and relentlessly mythologized her brilliant husband. Yet she never marked his grave.

Mozart's Wife. Juliet Waldron. Read by Celeste Lawson. (Running Time: 17 hrs. 30 mins.). 2002. 41.95 (978-1-59912-549-7(8)) Iofy Corp.

Mozart's Wife. unabr. ed. Juliet Waldron. Read by Celeste Lawson. 12 CDs. (Running Time: 14 hrs. 30 mins.). 2003. audio compact disk 96.00 (978-0-7861-9338-7(7), 3061) Blckstn Audio.
Was she a giddy sugarplum or calculating shrew? Mozart's wife aroused strong feelings among her contemporaries. Her in-laws loathed her. Mozart's friends, more than forty years after his death, remained eager to gossip about her "failures" as wife to the world's first superstar. Maturing from child to wife to hard-headed widow, Konstanze paid her husband's debts, provided for their children, and relentlessly marketed and mythologized her brilliant husband.

Mpipidi & the Motlopi Tree: A Story from Nelson Mandela's Favorite African Folktales. Read by Matt Damon. Compiled by Nelson Mandela. Composed by Vusi Mahlasela. (Running Time: 9 mins.). (ENG.). 2009. 1.99 (978-1-60024-788-0(1)) Pub: Hachet Audio. Dist(s): HachBkGrp

MP3 AMER Creation. Joseph Ellis. 2007. audio compact disk 39.99 (978-1-60252-222-0(7)) Find a World.

MP3 Bible-KJV. Narrated by Alexander Scourby. (Running Time: 259200 sec.). 2006. audio compact disk 29.95 (978-1-59856-074-9(3)); audio compact disk 16.97 (978-1-59856-075-6(1)) Hendrickson MA.

MP3 Bible-NVI. Created by Zondervan Publishing Staff. (SPA.). 2006. audio compact disk 39.99 (978-0-8297-4979-3(9)) Pub: Vida Pubs. Dist(s): Zondervan

MP3 Boom. Tom Brokaw. 2007. audio compact disk 39.99 (978-1-60252-323-4(1)) Find a World.

Mp3 Everyday Basic Spanish. (SPA & ENG.). 2008. pap. bk. 49.95 (978-0-9769266-7-2(9)) Weapons of Mass.

MP3 Giving: How Each Can Change World. Bill Clinton. 2007. audio compact disk 34.99 (978-1-60252-226-8(X)) Find a World.

MP3 Our Dumb World. The Onion. 2007. audio compact disk 34.99 (978-1-60252-229-9(4)) Find a World.

Mp3 spanish Language. Henry Raymond. 2006. cd-rom 44.99 (978-1-59895-468-5(7)) Find a World.

MP3 the War: An Intimate HIST. Geoffrey Ward. 2007. audio compact disk 34.99 (978-1-60252-234-3(0)) Find a World.

Mr. AL - Bop Til You Drop. Perf. by Mr. AL. 1 cass. 10.95; audio compact disk 13.95 Child Like.

Mr. AL - Kids Wanna Rock. Perf. by Mr. AL. 1 cass. (J). 10.95; audio compact disk 13.95 Child Like.

Mr. AL - Sing Me Some Sanity. Perf. by Mr. AL. 1 cass. (J). 10.95 (MHC-95) Child Like.
Designed specifically with teachers in mind, will help through the routines of the day. Transition songs will help classroom management. Half of the songs are instrumental music designed for quiet time. Who can get along without Mr. AL's famous song, "Clean Up Time." Includes activity ideas.

Mr. AL a carte: Favorite Selections from Mr. Al's Collection. Perf. by Mr. AL. 1 cass. (J). (ps up). 10.95 (CRP-C01) Child Like.
Selections from the first eight albums. Includes "Bop Till You Drop," "Let's Get Started," "The Back to School Bop," "Clean Up Time," "Hello everybody," & more, plus two new songs, "The Train" & "Pizza Rules!".

Mr. AL a carte: Favorite Selections from Mr. Al's Collection. Perf. by Mr. AL. 1 CD. (YA). (ps up). audio compact disk 13.95 (CRP-D01) Child Like.
Selections from the first eight albums. Includes "Bop Til You Drop," "Let's Get Started," "The Back to School Bop," "Clean Up Time," "Hello Everybody," & more, plus two new songs, "The Train" & "Pizza Rules!".

Mr. AL Sings & Moves. Perf. by Mr. AL. 1 cass. (J). (ps-5). 10.95 (MHC-94); audio compact disk 13.95 (MHD-94) Child Like.
Children will shake those sillies out & have a great time becoming more aware of their body parts with songs like: "Wiggle Your Knees Boogie," "Rock & Roll Body Parts," "Shake everything," "Hop on One Foot Bop," "Creepy Crawlin'," & "Galloping Country Style." Includes activity ideas.

Mr. AL Sings Colors & Shapes. Perf. by Mr. AL. 1 cass. (J). (ps-3). 10.95 (MHC-92) Child Like.
Songs for seven colors & the common shapes to make it easier for children to learn the concepts. Includes activity ideas. Songs include: "I Like the Color Red," "Orange, Orange, Orange," "Brown Is the Coolest Color Around," "Do the Circle," "The Square shuffle" & many more.

Mr. AL Sings Friends & Feelings. Perf. by Mr. AL. 1 cass. (J). (ps-5). 10.95 (MHC-93) Child Like.
Designed to help kids verbalize their feelings & emotions & develop their social & emotional skills. Includes activity ideas. Songs include: "I'm Happy," " I Get So Mad," "What Do You Worry About?," "You Gotta Have Hugs," & a teacher favorite, "We Hold the Future.".

Mr. AL's Collection. Perf. by Mr. AL. 12 cass. (J). (ps). 109.95 (CLC-020) Child Like.
All twelve of Mr. AL's releases.

Mr. AL's Collection. Perf. by Mr. AL. 8 CDs & 4cass. (J). (ps-3). audio compact disk 129.95 (CLD-021) Child Like.

Mr. American, Pt. 1. unabr. ed. George MacDonald Fraser. Read by David Case. 9 cass. (Running Time: 13 hrs. 30 mins.). 2000. 72.00 (978-0-7366-5492-0(5), 5313-A) Books on Tape.
Mark Franklin American tourist, goes unnoticed when he disembarks in Liverpool in 1909. Soon, he moves to a small village, restores an ancient home, becomes a squire, and marries into high society. But, his new position is threatened when an old associate from the Butch Cassidy-Sundance Kid gang appears with an appalling demand and threat.

Mr. American, Pt. 2. unabr. ed. George MacDonald Fraser. Read by David Case. 9 cass. (Running Time: 13 hrs. 30 mins.). 2000. 72.00 (978-0-7366-5493-7(3), 5313-B) Books on Tape.
Mark Franklin American tourist, goes unnoticed when he disembarks i n Liverpool in 1909. Soon, he moves to a small village, restores an ancient home, becomes a squire, and marries into high society. But, his new position is threatened when an old associate from the Butch Cassidy-Sundance Kid gang appears with an appalling demand and threat.

Mr. & Miss Anonymous. abr. ed. Fern Michaels. Read by Laural Merlington. (Running Time: 5 hrs.). 2010. audio compact disk 14.99 (978-1-4233-4475-9(8), 9781423344759, BCD Value Price) Brilliance Audio.

Mr. & Miss Anonymous. unabr. ed. Fern Michaels. Read by Laural Merlington. (Running Time: 10 hrs.). 2009. 39.97 (978-1-4233-4473-5(1), 9781423344735, BADLE); 24.99 (978-1-4233-4472-8(3), 9781423344728, BAD); 24.99 (978-1-4233-4470-4(7), 9781423344704, Brilliance MP3); 39.97 (978-1-4233-4471-1(5), 9781423344711, Brinc Audio MP3 Lib); audio compact disk 36.99 (978-1-4233-4468-1(5), 9781423344681, Bril Audio CD Unabri); audio compact disk 97.97 (978-1-4233-4469-8(3), 9781423344698, BriAudCD Unabrid) Brilliance Audio.

Mr. & Mrs. Bridge. unabr. abr. ed. Evan S. Connell. Read by Paul Newman & Joanne Woodward. (Running Time: 21600 sec.). 2007. audio compact disk 36.00 (978-1-4332-0551-4(3)) Blckstn Audio.

Mr. & Mrs. Bridge. unabr. abr. ed. Evan S. Connell. Read by Paul Newman & Joanne Woodward. (Running Time: 21600 sec.). 2007. audio compact disk 19.95 (978-1-4332-0552-1(1)) Blckstn Audio.

***Mr. & Mrs. Happy Handbook.** abr. ed. Steve Doocy. Read by Steve Doocy. (ENG.). 2006. (978-0-06-123001-1(4), Harper Audio); (978-0-06-123002-8(2), Harper Audio) HarperCollins Pubs.

Mr. & Mrs. Happy Handbook: Everything I Know about Love & Marriage. abr. ed. Steve Doocy. Read by Steve Doocy. Read by Kathy Doocy. Told to Kathy Doocy. (Running Time: 12600 sec.). 2007. audio compact disk 14.95 (978-0-06-137409-8(1), Harper Audio) HarperCollins Pubs.

Mr. & Mrs. North. Contrib. by Richard Denning & Barbara Britton. (Running Time: 10800 sec.). 2004. 9.98 (978-1-57019-559-4(5)) Radio Spirits.

Mr. & Mrs. North: Bet on Death. Perf. by Joseph Curtin & Alice Frost. 2008. audio compact disk 18.95 (978-1-57019-862-5(4)) Radio Spirits.

Mr. & Mrs. North: Case of the Missing Sparkler. 1 cass. (CM8497) Natl Recrd Co.

Mr & Mrs Pig's Evening Out. 2004. bk. 24.95 (978-0-7882-0654-2(0)); 8.95 (978-1-56008-976-6(8)); cass. & flmstrp 30.00 (978-1-56008-722-9(6)) Weston Woods.

Mr. Bach Comes to Call. Susan Hammond. 1 cass. 1993. 10.98 (978-1-895404-42-5(8)) Consort Bk Sales.

Mr. Bach Comes to Call. Susan Hammond. 1 cass. (J). 1993. 18.98 Consort Bk Sales.

Mr. Bach Comes to Call. Perf. by Toronto Boys Choir & Studio Arts Orchestra. 1 cass. (Running Time: 1 hr.). (J). (gr. 1 up). 9.98 (2214); audio compact disk 16.98 compact disc. (D2214) MFLP CA.
If you love the genius of Bach, share the joy with your kids & fledgling musicians by playing this exquisite blending of music, drama, history & humor!.

Mr. Barrett's Secret & Other Stories. unabr. collector's ed. Kingsley Amis. Read by Richard Green. 6 cass. (Running Time: 6 hrs.). 1995. 36.00 (978-0-7366-3179-2(8), 3848) Books on Tape.
In this volume of short stories, Amis also uses variety to entertain us. We discover why Mr. Barrett worries about his daughter's association with the poet Browning & we share a bizarre incident with a timid literary agent who becomes a hostage. In another, more eerie story, a parson meets an identical twin he didn't know he had, with unnerving results.

***Mr. Bevis.** 2010. audio compact disk (978-1-59171-216-9(5)) Falcon Picture.

Mr. Blandings Builds His Dream House. Perf. by Cary Grant. 1 cass. (Running Time: 1 hr.). 1949. 7.95 (CC-5060) Natl Recrd Co.
Cary Grant in a comedy about an advertising V.P. who buys a house for $10,000... then must tear it apart; it ends up being a $45,000 dream house. William Powell plays Senator Ashton, a stumbling, idiotic harmless man who wishes to become President. He is known as Senator Ashcan & he comes close to realizing his incompetent goal, but an indiscretion does him in.

Mr. Blue. Myles Connolly. Read by Paul Rogers. 4 cass. (Running Time: 4 hrs.). 1987. 18.95 (318) Ignatius Pr.

Mr. Bridge. unabr. ed. Evan S. Connell. Narrated by George Guidall. 9 cass. (Running Time: 12 hrs. 15 mins.). 1991. 78.00 (978-1-55690-353-3(7), 91214E7) Recorded Bks.
In this novel & its companion, "Mrs. Bridge," Connell has brilliantly realized the lives of upper-middle-class Americans living in the years just before & during World War II.

Mr. Bridge. unabr. collector's ed. Evan S. Connell. Read by Christopher Hurt. 7 cass. (Running Time: 10 hrs. 30 mins.). 1989. 56.00 (978-0-7366-1506-8(7), 2378) Books on Tape.
Mr. Bridge is the companion volume to Connell's Mrs. Bridge. It is made up of fragments of experience from the life of a middle-aged suburban couple between the two wars. Brief episodes are juxtaposed to reveal the stereotyped values & emotional & spiritual aridity of the prosperous & ever-so-proper Bridges.

Mr. Brightly's Evening Off. unabr. ed. Kathleen Rowntree. Narrated by Diana Bishop. 7 cass. (Running Time: 9 hrs. 30 mins.). 2000. 62.00 (978-1-84197-063-9(8), H1060E7) Recorded Bks.
Mr. Brightly is an exemplary man. A lay reader & church treasurer, he brightens the lives of the local people, churchgoers or not. To his wife, he's indulgent. To Mrs. Parminter, he's welcome company on Wednesdays. To Cressida, he's a veritable godsend on Friday's. Brightly is also known as a financial guru, so everyone wants to entrust money to him. Everyone but the new vicar, that is, whose scrutiny of the church funds yields alarming results. An explanation is possible, or a massive case of fraud. The true Mr. Brightly stands to be revealed.

Mr. Bug's Phonics, No. 1. Richmond Hsieh & Catherine Yang Eisele. 1997. 39.95 (978-0-19-435251-2(X)) OUP.

Mr. Bug's Phonics, No. 2. Richmond Hsieh. 1998. 39.95 (978-0-19-435258-1(7)) OUP.

***Mr. Chartwell: A Novel.** unabr. ed. Rebecca Hunt. (ENG.). 2011. audio compact disk 32.00 (978-0-307-87993-6(3), Random AudioBks) Pub: Random Audio Pubg. Dist(s): Random

Mr. Chickee's Messy Mission. Christopher Paul Curtis. Read by Joe Holt. 5. (Running Time: 5 hrs. 15 mins.). 2006. audio compact disk 36.00 (978-0-7393-4848-2(5)) Books on Tape.

Mr Clarinet. Nick Stone. Read by Jeff Harding. 13 cass. (Running Time: 17 hrs. 20 mins.). (Isis Cassettes Ser.). 2006. 99.95 (978-0-7531-3623-2(6)) Pub: ISIS Lrg Prnt GBR. Dist(s): Ulverscroft US

Mr Clarinet. Nick Stone. Read by Jeff Harding. 15 CDs. (Running Time: 59700 sec.). (Isis (CDs) Ser.). 2006. audio compact disk 104.95 (978-0-7531-2595-3(1)) Pub: ISIS Lrg Prnt GBR. Dist(s): Ulverscroft US

Mr. Darcy, Vampyre. unabr. ed. Amanda Grange. Read by Elizabeth Jasicki. (Running Time: 11 hrs.). 2010. audio compact disk 29.99 (978-1-4418-3653-3(5), 9781441836533, Bril Audio CD Unabri); audio compact disk 99.97 (978-1-4418-3654-0(3), 9781441836540, BriAudCD Unabrid) Brilliance Audio.

***Mr. Darcy, Vampyre.** unabr. ed. Amanda Grange. Read by Elizabeth Jasicki. (Running Time: 10 hrs.). 2010. 24.99 (978-1-4418-3655-7(1), 9781441836557, Brilliance MP3); 39.97 (978-1-4418-3656-4(X), 9781441836564, Brinc Audio MP3 Lib) Brilliance Audio.

Mr. Death & Bobo. abr. ed. Anne Moody. Perf. by Anne Moody. 1 cass. 1984. 12.95 (SWC 1642) HarperCollins Pubs.

Mr. Deeds Goes to Town. Perf. by Gary Cooper & Jean Arthur. Based on a story by Clarence Kelland. 1 cass. (Running Time: 1 hr.). 1937. 7.95 (DD-5100) Natl Recrd Co.
This is the story of Longfellow Deeds, who lives in the town of Mandrake Falls, population 600. He inherits $20,000,000 from a long lost uncle & goes to New York where he runs into all kinds of trouble with the press. He avoids newspaper reporters, but one tricks him to get a story & dubs him the Cinderella Man. When he decides to give his fortune away he is declared incompetent.

***Mr. Denton on Doomsday.** 2010. audio compact disk (978-1-59171-206-0(8)) Falcon Picture.

Mr. Dickens Goes to the Play. unabr. ed. Alexander Woollcott. Read by Flo Gibson. 5 cass. (Running Time: 6 hrs.). 2000. 35.95 Audio Bk Con.

Mr. Dickens Goes to the Play. unabr. ed. Alexander Woollcott. Narrated by Flo Gibson. 5 cass. (Running Time: 9 hrs. 28 mins.). (YA). (gr. 10 up). 2000. 37.95 (978-1-55685-645-7(8)) Audio Bk Con.
Dickens' interest in the theater is told with relish with dramatizations of such plays as "Nicholas Nickleby" & "David Copperfield" & in letters to Macready & Forster, to name a few.

***Mr. Dingle, the Strong.** 2010. audio compact disk (978-1-59171-156-8(8)) Falcon Picture.

Mr. District Attorney. unabr. ed. 2 cass. (Running Time: 2 hrs.). 10.95 (978-1-57816-003-7(0), DA2401) Audio File.
Mr. District Attorney solves crimes & defends the rights of citizens on four old time radio broadcasts.

Mr. Dog's Report on the Farm. (J). 2005. audio compact disk (978-1-933796-02-4(2)) PC Treasures.

Mr. Dogwood Goes to Washington. Leigh Anne Florence. Read by Scott Johnson & Kat Johnson. Illus. by James Asher. (J). 2008. audio compact disk 8.00 (978-0-9741417-6-3(3)) HotDigg Pr.

Mr. Funfiddle's Christmas. Lyrics by Dennis Allen & Nan Allen. 10 cass. (Running Time: 10 hrs.). (J). 1995. bk. 54.99 (TA-9184PK); 12.99 (TA-9184C) Lillenas.
Who can explain why we celebrate Christmas? Mr. Funfiddle, that's who! Along with his friends Peace, Joy, Love & Hope, Mr. Funfiddle guides us through the glitter & excitement to the true meaning of the Christmas season. Your children will love the colorful characters & the fun, contemporary songs. Invite the fun & merriment of Mr. Funfiddle's Christmas into your church. Accompaniment cassette with Side 1, stereo trax & Side 2 split-channel.

***Mr. Funny Pants.** unabr. ed. Michael Showalter. (Running Time: 8 hrs. 30 mins.). (ENG.). 2011. 24.98 (978-1-60024-808-5(X)) Pub: Hachet Audio. Dist(s): HachBkGrp

***Mr. Garrity & the Graves.** 2010. audio compact disk (978-1-59171-166-7(5)) Falcon Picture.

Mr. Gatling's Terrible Marvel: The Gun That Changed Everything & the Misunderstood Genius Who Invented It. Julia Keller. Read by Norman Dietz. (Playaway Adult Fiction Ser.). 2008. 59.99 (978-1-60640-861-2(5)) Find a World.

Mr. Gatling's Terrible Marvel: The Gun That Changed Everything & the Misunderstood Genius Who Invented It. unabr. ed. Julia Keller. Narrated by Norman Dietz. (Running Time: 10 hrs. 0 mins. 0 sec.). (ENG.). 2008. audio compact disk 19.99 (978-1-4001-5644-3(0)) Pub: Tantor Media. Dist(s): IngramPubServ

Mr. Gatling's Terrible Marvel: The Gun That Changed Everything & the Misunderstood Genius Who Invented It. unabr. ed. Julia Keller. Read by Norman Dietz. (Running Time: 10 hrs. 0 mins. 0 sec.). (ENG.). 2008. audio compact disk 59.99 (978-1-4001-3644-5(X)); audio compact disk 29.99 (978-1-4001-0644-8(3)) Pub: Tantor Media. Dist(s): IngramPubServ

Mr. Gonopolis & His 12 Holsteins: The Whimsical Moosical. Uncle Higgly & George Maurer. (J). (gr. 3-6). 1987. 8.95 (978-0-935583-04-5(1)) Wounded Coot.
Story by a rural Minnesota humorist original music includes "The Gonopolis Rag", "Hitch Your Wagon to a Cow" & others.

Mr Gumpy's Motor Car. 2004. bk. 24.95 (978-0-7882-0580-4(3)); pap. bk. 14.95 (978-0-7882-0641-2(9)); 8.95 (978-0-89719-912-4(X)); cass. & flmstrp 30.00 (978-0-89719-512-6(4)) Weston Woods.

Mr Gumpy's Outing. 2004. bk. 24.95 (978-0-7882-0561-3(7)); pap. bk. 14.95 (978-0-7882-0628-3(1)); 8.95 (978-1-56008-977-3(6)); cass. & flmstrp 30.00 (978-1-56008-723-6(4)) Weston Woods.

Mr. Harold Colbert see Osbert Sitwell Reading His Poetry

Mr. Higginbotham's Catastrophe see Great American Short Stories, Vol. III, A Collection

Mr. Higginbotham's Catastrophe. Nathaniel Hawthorne. Perf. by Walter Covell. 1 cass. (Running Time: 1 hr. 10 min.). Dramatization. 7.95 (S-63) Jimcin Record.
A scientist tries to make a perfect woman by removing her one imperfection.

Mr. Justice Harbottle see Classic Ghost Stories, Vol. 3, A Collection

Mr. Keen, Tracer of Lost Persons. Created by Radio Spirits. (Running Time: 10800 sec.). 2004. 9.98 (978-1-57019-711-6(3)) Radio Spirits.

Mr. Keen, Tracer of Lost Persons, collector's ed. Perf. by Bennett Kilpack & Jim Kelly. 6 cass. (Running Time: 9 hrs.). 1998. bk. 34.98 (4143) Radio Spirits.
Mr. Keen, the charming & kindly old tracer of missing persons with his assistant, Mike Clancy, in 18 exciting episodes from radio's golden age.

Mr. Keen, Tracer of Lost Persons: Case of Girl Who Flirted & Case of Woman Who Married a Murderer. 1 cass. (Running Time: 1 hr.). 2001. 6.98 (2063) Radio Spirits.

Mr. Keen, Tracer of Lost Persons: Quicksand Murder & Photograph Album Murder. 1 cass. (Running Time: 1 hr.). 2001. 6.98 (1933) Radio Spirits.

Mr. Keen, Tracer of Lost Persons: The Abandoned Well Murder Case & The Poisoned Sandwich Murder Case. 1 cass. (Running Time: 1 hr.). 2001. 6.98 (2146) Radio Spirits.

Mr. Kipling's Army. unabr. ed. Byron Farwell. Read by Bill Kelsey. 6 cass. (Running Time: 9 hrs.). 1994. 48.00 (978-0-7366-2662-0(X), 3399) Books on Tape.
Witty, informative account of officers & men in British army during Empire's heyday.

Mr. Lincoln: The Life of Abraham Lincoln. Instructed by Allen Guelzo. 6 cass. (Running Time: 6 hrs.). bk. 29.95 (978-1-56585-998-2(7), 8561) Teaching Co.

Mr. Lincoln: The Life of Abraham Lincoln. Instructed by Allen Guelzo. 6 CDs. (Running Time: 6 hrs.). 2005. bk. 39.95 (978-1-59803-009-9(4), 8561) Teaching Co.

Mr. MacGregor. Alan Titchmarsh. Read by Alan Titchmarsh. 2 cass. (Running Time: 3 hrs.). 1999. 16.85 (978-0-671-03346-0(8)) S and S Inc.
His life is complicated by a jealous co-presenter, an affair with one of the TV stations newsreader.

Mr Macgregor. Alan Titchmarsh. 8 CDs. (Isis (CDs) Ser.). (J). 2005. audio compact disk 79.95 (978-0-7531-2403-1(3)) Pub: ISIS Lrg Prnt GBR. Dist(s): Ulverscroft US

Mr. MacGregor. unabr. ed. Alan Titchmarsh. Read by Alan Titchmarsh. 8 cass. (Running Time: 12 hrs.). (Isis Ser.). (J). 1999. 69.95 (978-0-7531-0717-1(1), 991206) Pub: ISIS Lrg Prnt GBR. Dist(s): Ulverscroft US

***Mr. Majestyk.** Elmore Leonard. Read by Frank Muller. (ENG.). 2010. (978-0-06-205970-3(X), Harper Audio) HarperCollins Pubs.

***Mr. Majestyk.** unabr. ed. Elmore Leonard. Read by Frank Muller. (ENG.). 2010. (978-0-06-199470-8(7), Harper Audio) HarperCollins Pubs.

Mr. Majestyk. unabr. ed. Elmore Leonard. Narrated by Frank Muller. 3 cass. (Running Time: 4 hrs. 30 mins.). 26.00 (978-0-7887-0258-7(0), 94467E7) Recorded Bks.
On the battlefields of Laos, Army ranger Vince Majestyk decides he's seen too much violence. He turns in his gun & heads for the peaceful melon fields of Arizona. But local thugs are pushing him too far & he's ready for war again. Available to libraries only.

Mr. Majestyk. unabr. collector's ed. Elmore Leonard. Read by Alexander Adams. 5 cass. (Running Time: 5 hrs.). 1995. 30.00 (978-0-7366-3151-8(8), 3825) Books on Tape.
Bullies love the smell of fear because they can seize power over the weak. And most of us don't fight back. Who wants confrontation? Certainly not Vincent Majestyk, a peaceful farmer. But mobsters push him to his limit, demanding that he hire their people. A cop on a power trip also gets his goat. And a beautiful woman tells him to run & hide. None of them knows his past, but they'll soon find out how an ex-combat soldier - trained to kill - goes to war when he's had enough.

Mr. Maybe. unabr. ed. Jane Green. 8 cass. (Running Time: 12 hrs.). 2002. 64.00 (978-0-7366-8718-8(1)) Books on Tape.
Twenty-seven-year-old publicist Libby Mason has found the almost-perfect guy: Nick is "gorgeous," fun to talk to, and great in bed - but he's perpetually strapped for cash and allergic to commitment. Along comes Ed, he of the Big Fat Bank Account and a longing for stability, who is nonetheless stodgy, awkward, and lousy in the sack. What to do? Can Libby join the class of ladies who lunch yet still have her dream lover?.

Mr Mcdoodle & His Scooter. (Sails Literacy Ser.). (gr. 2 up). 10.00 (978-0-7578-6823-8(1)) Rigby Educ.

Mr. Midshipman Easy. unabr. collector's ed. Frederick Marryat. Read by Bill Kelsey. 11 cass. (Running Time: 16 hrs. 30 min.). 1996. 88.00 (978-0-7366-3499-1(1), 4139) Books on Tape.
As the 18th century gives way to the 19th, an eccentric young man joins Britain's navy to see the world & to practice his own odd brand of philosophy.

Mr. Midshipman Fury. G. S. Beard. 2007. 61.95 (978-1-84559-728-3(1)); audio compact disk 79.95 (978-1-84559-729-0(X)) Pub: Soundings Ltd GBR. Dist(s): Ulverscroft US

Mr. Midshipman Hornblower. C. S. Forester. Read by Geoffrey Howard. 2001. 48.00 (978-0-7366-7160-6(9)); audio compact disk 56.00 (978-0-7366-9125-3(1)) Books on Tape.

Mr. Midshipman Hornblower. C. S. Forester. Read by Ioan Gruffudd. 2 cass. (Running Time: 2 hrs. 2 mins.). (Hornblower Ser.: No. 1). 1998. 16.99 (978-1-85998-975-3(6)) Trafalgar.
Mr. Midshipman Hornblower chronicles the beginning of seventeen year-old Horatio Hornblower's beginnings in the British Navy during the Napoleonic War in the late 1700's. This book is the 'introduction' to the rest of the Hornblower series of books. It takes you through young Horatio's first seamanship experiences such as his first command of a ship, becoming a leiutenant, & many other adventures.

Mr. Midshipman Hornblower. unabr. ed. C. S. Forester. Read by Christian Rodska. 8 cass. (Running Time: 8 hrs. 19 min.). (Hornblower Ser.: No. 1). 1992. 69.95 (978-0-7451-5940-9(0), CAB 654) AudioGO.
Shaking off the label of "the midshipman who was seasick in Spithead," a shy & lonely seventeen-year-old Horatio Hornblower embarks on a memorable career in Nelson's navy on H.M.S. Justinian. In action, adventure & battle he is forged into one of the most formidable junior officers in the service.

Mr. Midshipman Hornblower. unabr. ed. C. S. Forester. Read by Bill Kelsey. 8 cass. (Running Time: 12 hrs.). (Hornblower Ser.). 2001. 29.95 (978-0-7366-6757-9(1)) Books on Tape.
Hornblower goes to sea at age seventeen.

Mr. Midshipman Hornblower. unabr. collector's ed. C. S. Forester. Read by Bill Kelsey. 8 cass. (Running Time: 8 hrs.). (Hornblower Ser.: No. 1). 1983. 64.00 (978-0-7366-0650-9(5), 1611) Books on Tape.
Get a glimmer of just how much Bonaparte was hated & why. Like other great continental despots, Napoleon was ruthless. His own fortune a product of the terrible revolution, he employed terror without hesitation. He & all he was for were an anathema to solid, conservative, royal, Protestant England.

***Mr. Monster.** unabr. ed. Dan Wells. (Running Time: 8 hrs. 0 mins.). (John Cleaver Ser.). 2010. 15.99 (978-1-4001-8832-1(6)); 29.99 (978-1-4001-9832-0(1)) Tantor Media.

***Mr. Monster.** unabr. ed. Dan Wells. Narrated by Kirby Heyborne. (Running Time: 9 hrs. 0 mins. 0 sec.). (John Cleaver Ser.). 2010. 19.99 (978-1-4001-6832-3(5)); audio compact disk 29.99 (978-1-4001-1832-8(8)); audio compact disk 71.99 (978-1-4001-4832-5(4)) Pub: Tantor Media. Dist(s): IngramPubServ

Mr. Moto Is So Sorry. John P. Marquand. 4 cass. (Running Time: 6 hrs.). 2001. 32.00 (978-0-7366-6189-8(1)) Books on Tape.
Times were turbulent in the Orient. Japan, China & Russia were willing to go to any lengths to obtain their goals. The Japanese had their top secret agent, the super-polite, but super-deadly Mr. I.A. Moto, working night and day.

Mr. Murder. unabr. ed. Dean Koontz. 10 cass. 24.95 Set. (88119) Books on Tape.
A psychotic killer will stop at nothing to eliminate Marty Stillwater & recapture the family & life he believes is his.

Mr. Murder. unabr. ed. Dean Koontz. 2004. 21.95 (978-0-7435-1986-1(8)) Pub: S&S Audio. Dist(s): S and S Inc

Mr. Nutch see Osbert Sitwell Reading His Poetry

Mr. Ouchy's First Day. B. G. Hennessy. Intro. by B. G. Hennessy. Illus. by Paul Meisel. 1 cass. (Running Time: 12 mins.). (J). (gr. k-3). 2007. bk. 27.95 (978-0-8045-6946-0(0)); bk. 29.95 (978-0-8045-4160-2(4)) Spoken Arts.

Mr. Paradise. unabr. ed. Elmore Leonard. Read by Robert Forster. 6 cass. (Running Time: 9 hrs.). 2004. 29.95 (978-0-06-058626-3(5)) HarperCollins Pubs.

***Mr. Paradise.** unabr. ed. Elmore Leonard. Read by Robert Forster. 2004. (978-0-06-074603-2(3), Harper Audio); (978-0-06-079963-2(3), Harper Audio) HarperCollins Pubs.

Mr. Paradise. unabr. ed. Elmore Leonard. Read by Robert Forster. 2005. audio compact disk 14.95 (978-0-06-087463-6(5)) HarperCollins Pubs.

Mr. Perfect. unabr. ed. Linda Howard. Read by Laura Hicks. 8 vols. (Running Time: 12 hrs.). 2001. bk. 69.95 (978-0-7927-2461-2(5), CSL 350, Chivers Sound Lib) AudioGO.
What would make the perfect man? That's the topic of conversation at a table of professional women at their favorite restaurant. They write down a tongue-in-cheek checklist that's both funny & racy. A list as it has come to be called, spreads like wildfire throughout their company. And the joke turns deadly serious.

Mr. Perfect. unabr. ed. Linda Howard. Read by Laura Hicks. 10 CDs. (Running Time: 15 hrs.). 2002. audio compact disk 94.95 (978-0-7927-9861-3(9), SLD 112, Chivers Sound Lib) AudioGO.
What would make the perfect man? That's the topic of conversation at a table of professional women in their favorite restaurant. Would he be tall, dark and handsome? As the conversation picks up momentum, so do their requirements for Mr. Perfect. They write up a checklist that's both funny a racy and the next thing they know, what started out as a joke turns deadly serious when one of the four women is murdered.

Mr. Phillips. John Lanchester. Read by Tim Curry. 2004. 15.95 (978-0-7435-4294-4(0)) Pub: S&S Audio. Dist(s): S and S Inc

Mr. Phillips. unabr. ed. John Lanchester. Narrated by Simon Prebble. 5 cass. (Running Time: 6 hrs. 45 mins.). 2001. 45.00 (978-0-7887-5470-8(X), 96605x7) Recorded Bks.
Although Mr. Phillips was sacked on Friday, he is unable to break the news to his wife. So on Monday morning he dresses for the office, packs his briefcase & begins aimlessly wandering the London streets. This is a humorous, touching insightful look at personal priorities & the possibilities are open to everyone.

Mr. Pim Passes By. unabr. ed. A. A. Milne. Read by Flo Gibson. 2 cass. (Running Time: 2 hrs.). 1998. bk. 14.95 (978-1-55685-536-8(2)) Audio Bk Con.
When this dear old gentleman passes by he causes quite a stir & turmoil. Is it really a case of bigamy.

Mr. Playboy: Hugh Hefner & the American Dream. unabr. ed. Steven Watts. (Running Time: 21 hrs. NaN mins.). 2008. 44.95 (978-1-4332-4925-9(1)); 105.95 (978-1-4332-4922-8(7)); audio compact disk 120.00 (978-1-4332-4923-5(5)) Blckstn Audio.

Mr. Playboy: Hugh Hefner & the American Dream. unabr. ed. Steven Watts. Read by Ray Porter. 15 CDs. (Running Time: 18 hrs. 30 mins.). 2008. audio compact disk 39.95 (978-1-4332-4924-2(3)) Blckstn Audio.

Mr. Policeman & the Cook see Classic Detective Stories, Vol. II, A Collection

Mr. Popper's Penguins. Richard Atwater & Florence Atwater. Narrated by Paul Hecht. 2 CDs. (Running Time: 2 hrs.). (gr. 3 up). 2001. audio compact disk 22.00 (978-0-7887-5216-2(2), C1364E7) Recorded Bks.

Mr. Popper's Penguins. unabr. ed. Richard Atwater & Florence Atwater. Narrated by Paul Hecht. 2 cass. (Running Time: 2 hrs.). (J). 2001. pap. bk. & stu. ed. 40.20 Recorded Bks.
When Mr. Popper reads about Antarctica, he is so fascinated that he writes to Admiral Drake there. Instead of answering the letter, the Admiral sends him a full grown penguin. From then on, his life is filled with adventure.

Mr. Popper's Penguins. unabr. ed. Richard Atwater & Florence Atwater. Narrated by Paul Hecht. 2 pieces. (Running Time: 2 hrs.). (gr. 3 up). 2001. 26.00 (978-0-7887-2724-5(9), 95664E7) Recorded Bks.

Mr. Popper's Penguins. unabr. ed. Richard Atwater & Florence Atwater. Read by Nick Sullivan. (Running Time: 2 hrs.). (ENG.). 2009. 9.98 (978-1-60024-676-0(1)); audio compact disk 13.98 (978-1-60024-675-3(3)) Pub: Hachet Audio. Dist(s): HachBkGrp

Mr. Preble Gets Rid of His Wife see Middle-Aged Man on the Flying Trapeze

Mr. President. Steck-Vaughn Staff. (J). 2002. 9.00 (978-0-7398-6212-4(X)) SteckVau.

Mr. President. unabr. ed. 2 cass. (Running Time: 2 hrs.). 10.95 (978-1-57816-067-9(7), MP2401) Audio File.
Four radio shows based on stories about four presidents & the listener is invited to guess their identity.

***Mr. President, Volume 1.** RadioArchives.com. (Running Time: 600). (ENG.). 2002. audio compact disk 29.98 (978-1-61081-002-9(3)) Radio Arch.

Mr. Putter & Tabby Bake the Cake. Cynthia Rylant. Read by John McDonough. 1 cass. (Running Time: 15 mins.). (Mr. Putter & Tabby Ser.). (J). (gr. 1 up). 2000. pap. bk. & stu. ed. 30.00 (978-0-7887-4342-9(2), 41136) Recorded Bks.
Christmas is Mr. Putter's favorite time of the year. But he has to think very hard about a gift for his neighbor, Mrs. Teaberry. She likes strange things, like coconuts that look like monkey heads & tiny dresses that fit her teapots. She even likes fruitcake! Among the delightful creations of this popular Newbery Medal honoree, Mr. Putter is perhaps the most comical & endearing.

Mr. Putter & Tabby Bake the Cake. unabr. ed. Cynthia Rylant. Narrated by John McDonough. 1 cass. (Running Time: 15 mins.). (Mr. Putter & Tabby Ser.). (gr. 1 up). 2000. 11.00 (978-0-7887-4230-9(2), 96206E7) Recorded Bks.

Mr. Putter & Tabby Bake the Cake, Class set. Cynthia Rylant. Read by John McDonough. 1 cass. (Running Time: 15 mins.). (Mr. Putter & Tabby Ser.). (J). (gr. 1 up). 2000. stu. ed. 139.30 (978-0-7887-4442-6(9), 47133) Recorded Bks.

Mr. Putter & Tabby Feed the Fish. Cynthia Rylant. Narrated by John McDonough. 1 cass. (Running Time: 15 mins.). (Mr. Putter & Tabby Ser.). (gr. 1 up). 2002. 10.00 (978-0-7887-9011-9(0)) Recorded Bks.
Putter buys some fish at the store. Tabby is happy. But soon Tabby is so twitchy that Mr. Putter calls Mrs. Teaberry who has a very relaxing solution to Tabby's problem.

Mr. Putter & Tabby Fly the Plane. unabr. ed. Cynthia Rylant. Narrated by John McDonough. 1 cass. (Running Time: 15 mins.). (Mr. Putter & Tabby Ser.). (gr. 1 up). 2002. 10.00 (978-1-4025-1420-3(4)) Recorded Bks.
Ever since he was a boy, Mr. Putter has always loved planes. And he still loves playing with toys - even though he is pretty old. While visiting the toy store with his fine cat, Tabby, he decides to buy a brand new, red and white, remote-controlled biplane! Remembering when he was young, how he stayed awake at night wishing for such a toy, Mr. Putter thinks about the boy he met earlier that day. The boy was a little shy, clumsy and forgetful - just like Mr. Putter was when he was that age! Being the great guy he is, Mr. Putter does something very special for the boy.

Mr. Putter & Tabby Paint the Porch. Cynthia Rylant. Narrated by John McDonough. (Running Time: 15 mins.). (Mr. Putter & Tabby Ser.). (gr. 1 up). 10.00 (978-0-7887-9015-7(3)) Recorded Bks.

Mr. Putter & Tabby Pick the Pears. unabr. ed. Cynthia Rylant. Narrated by John McDonough. 1 cass. (Running Time: 15 mins.). (Mr. Putter & Tabby Ser.). (gr. 1 up). 1995. 10.00 (978-0-7887-9017-1(X), 96759) Recorded Bks.
Fall is Mr. Putter and Tabby's favorite time of year - a time to harvest juicy fruits and feast on baked goodies. But this year it's not going to be so easy. Old age is making Mr. Putter's legs, knees, and feet ... cranky. Even his cat Tabby suffers from a cranky tail. But that won't stop them! Mr. Putter comes up with a zingy way to pick the pears. And thanks to Mrs. Teaberry and her good dog Zeke, he and Tabby are showered with loads of yummy apple treats, but no pears - so no pear jelly. Can Mr. Putter will find a way to get pear jelly after all?.

Mr. Putter & Tabby Pour the Tea. Cynthia Rylant. Narrated by John McDonough. (Running Time: 15 mins.). (Mr. Putter & Tabby Ser.). (gr. 1 up). 10.00 (978-0-7887-9013-3(7)) Recorded Bks.

Mr. Putter & Tabby Row the Boat. Cynthia Rylant. Narrated by John McDonough. (Running Time: 15 mins.). (Mr. Putter & Tabby Ser.). (gr. 1 up). 10.00 (978-0-7887-8839-0(6)) Recorded Bks.

Mr. Putter & Tabby Take the Train. Cynthia Rylant. Read by John McDonough. 1 cass. (Running Time: 15 mins.). (Mr. Putter & Tabby Ser.). (J). (gr. 1 up). 1999. pap. bk. & stu. ed. 30.00 (978-0-7887-2988-1(8), 40870) Recorded Bks.
When Mrs. Teaberry telephones Mr. Putter to share her brilliant idea, he gets a little nervous. Sometimes her ideas involve "running fast or wearing feathers." But this time Mrs. Teaberry wants to ride the train with Mr. Putter & their pets. When they get to the train station, though, they meet with a big surprise.

Mr. Putter & Tabby Take the Train, Cynthia Rylant. Read by John McDonough. 1 cass. (Running Time: 15 mins.). (Mr. Putter & Tabby Ser.). (J). (gr. 1 up). 1999. stu. ed. 148.30 (978-0-7887-3018-4(5), 46835) Recorded Bks.

Mr. Putter & Tabby Take the Train. unabr. ed. Cynthia Rylant. Narrated by John McDonough. 1 cass. (Running Time: 15 mins.). (Mr. Putter & Tabby Ser.). (gr. 1 up). 1999. 10.00 (978-0-7887-2958-4(6), 95732E7) Recorded Bks.

Mr. Putter & Tabby Toot the Horn. unabr. ed. Cynthia Rylant. Narrated by John McDonough. 1 cass. (Running Time: 15 mins.). (Mr. Putter & Tabby Ser.). (gr. 1 up). 2001. 10.00 (978-0-7887-4396-2(1), 96323E7) Recorded Bks.
Mr. Putter & Mrs. Teaberry both like music & decided to form their own band. Mr Putter was a good sport but decides that everyone will be happier if he uses the horn to hold up his tomato plant.

Mr. Putter & Tabby Toot the Horn. unabr. ed. Cynthia Rylant. Narrated by John McDonough. 1 cass. (Running Time: 15 mins.). (Mr. Putter & Tabby Ser.). (J). 2001. pap. bk. & stu. ed. Recorded Bks.

Mr. Putter & Tabby Walk the Dog. unabr. ed. Cynthia Rylant. Narrated by John McDonough. 1 cass. (Running Time: 15 mins.). (Mr. Putter & Tabby Ser.). (gr. 1 up). 2001. 10.00 (978-0-7887-2619-4(6), 95623E7) Recorded Bks.
When old Mr. Putter & his cat, Tabby, offer to walk old Mrs. Teaberry's dog, they have no idea how much trouble he will be.

Mr Rabbit & the Lovely Present. 2004. bk. 24.95 (978-0-89719-897-4(2)); pap. bk. 32.75 (978-1-55592-279-5(1)); pap. bk. 14.95 (978-1-56008-067-1(1)); 8.95 (978-0-7882-0276-6(6)); 8.95 (978-1-56008-418-1(9)) Weston Woods.

Mr. Rabbit & the Lovely Present. Charlotte Zolotow. Read by Peter Fernandez. Illus. by Maurice Sendak. 1 cass. (Running Time: 1 hr. 30 min.). (J). 2000. pap. bk. 19.97 (978-0-7366-9195-6(2)) Books on Tape.
Unsure of what to give her mother for a birthday present, a young girl seeks advice form a friendly rabbit who translates the mother's love of color into an imaginative yet quite practical gift.

Mr. Rabbit & the Lovely Present. Charlotte Zolotow. 1 read-along cass. (Running Time: 10 min.). (J). 1987. 9.95 Live Oak Media.
Unsure of what to give her mother for a birthday present, a young girl seeks advice from a friendly rabbit who translate the mother's love of color into an imaginative yet practical gift.

Mr. Rabbit & the Lovely Present. Charlotte Zolotow. Illus. by Maurice Sendak. 11 vols. (Running Time: 10 mins.). 1987. bk. 28.95 (978-1-59519-064-2(3)); pap. bk. 18.95 (978-1-59519-062-8(7)); pap. bk. 35.95 (978-1-59519-063-5(5)); 9.95 (978-1-59112-094-0(2)); audio compact disk 12.92 (978-1-59519-061-1(9)) Live Oak Media.

Mr. Rabbit & the Lovely Present. Charlotte Zolotow. Read by Peter Fernandez. Illus. by Maurice Sendak. 11 vols. (Running Time: 10 mins.). (J). (gr. k-3). 1987. bk. 25.95 (978-0-87499-047-8(5)) Live Oak Media.

Mr. Rabbit & the Lovely Present. Charlotte Zolotow. 1 cass., 5 bks. (Running Time: 7 min.). (J). pap. bk. 32.75 Weston Woods.
A little girl wants to give her mother something special for her birthday & asks Mr. Rabbit for help. Caldecott Honor Book.

Mr. Rabbit & the Lovely Present. Charlotte Zolotow. 1 cass. (Running Time: 7 min.). (J). (ps-4). 12.95 (RAC082A) Weston Woods.

Mr. Rabbit & the Lovely Present. Charlotte Zolotow. Illus. by Maurice Sendak. 1 cass. (Running Time: 7 min.). (J). (ps-4). bk. 24.95; pap. bk. 12.95 (PRA082A) Weston Woods.

Mr. Rabbit & the Lovely Present. unabr. ed. Charlotte Zolotow. Read by Peter Fernandez. Illus. by Maurice Sendak. 11 vols. (Running Time: 10 mins.). (J). (gr. k-3). 1987. pap. bk. 16.95 (978-0-87499-046-1(7)); pap. bk. & tchr. ed. 33.95 (978-0-87499-048-5(3)) Live Oak Media.
Unsure of what to give her mother for a birthday present, a young girl seeks advice from a friendly rabbit who translate the mother's love of color into an imaginative yet practical gift.

Mr Rabbit & the Lovely Present; Charlotte & the White Horse. 2004. 8.95 (978-1-56008-867-7(2)); cass. & flmstrp 30.00 (978-0-89719-544-7(2)) Weston Woods.

Mr Revere & I: Being an Account of Certain Episodes in the Career of Paul Revere, Esq. as Revealed by his Horse. Robert Lawson. Narrated by Davina Porter. 3 CDs. (Running Time: 3 hrs. 30 mins.). (gr. 2 up). audio compact disk 29.00 (978-1-4025-2323-6(8)) Recorded Bks.

Mr. Revere & I: Being an Account of Certain Episodes in the Career of Paul Revere, Esq. as Revealed by his Horse. unabr. ed. Robert Lawson. Narrated by Davina Porter. 3 pieces. (Running Time: 3 hrs. 30 mins.). (gr. 2 up). 1995. 27.00 (978-0-7887-0212-9(2), 94437E7) Recorded Bks.
The events leading up to & including the midnight ride of Paul Revere as told by his horse, Scheherezade, the brave, beautiful mare who carried him that fateful night.

Mr. Rickey Calls a Meeting. unabr. ed. Ed Schmidt. Perf. by Edward Asner et al. 1 cass. (Running Time: 1 hr. 39min.). 1996. 25.95 (978-1-58081-038-8(1), TPT72) Pub: L A Theatre. Dist(s): NetLibrary CO
On a spring day in 1947, Mr. Rickey, the wily & powerful manager of the Brooklyn Dodgers, Summons heavyweight champion Joe Louis, tap star Bill "Bojangles" Robinson, & actor Paul Robeson to his hotel room in midtown Manhattan. Rickey wants their support when he taps Jackie Robinson to be the Major Leagues' first black ballplayer. But a power struggle ensues when the eloquent Robeson raises questions about Rickey's plan to integrate white baseball.

***Mr. Rosenblum Dreams in English.** unabr. ed. Natasha Solomons. Read by James Adams. 2010. audio compact disk 34.95 (978-1-61573-110-7(5), 1615731105) Pub: HighBridge. Dist(s): Workman Pub

Mr. Sammler's Planet. unabr. ed. Saul Bellow. Read by Wolfram Kandinsky. 8 cass. (Running Time: 11 hrs. 30 mins.). 1993. 56.95 (978-0-7861-0346-1(9), 1303) Blckstn Audio.
Is it time to go? Sammler asks dispassionately. Are we to blow this great blue, white, green planet or be blown from it? Under the comedy & sadness, the shocking force of much of the action, & the superb character-drawing of this brilliantly written novel runs a strain of speculation, both daring & serene, on the future of life on this planet, Mr. Sammler's planet & any other planets for which we may be destined.

Mr. Sammler's Planet. unabr. ed. Saul Bellow. (Running Time: 41400 sec.). 2008. audio compact disk & audio compact disk 81.00 (978-0-7861-6257-4(0)) Blckstn Audio.

Mr. Sammler's Planet. unabr. ed. Saul Bellow. Read by Wolfram Kandinsky. (Running Time: 41400 sec.). 2008. audio compact disk 29.95 (978-0-7861-6258-1(9)) Blckstn Audio.

Mr. Scarborough's Family. unabr. ed. Anthony Trollope. Read by Flo Gibson. 12 cass. (Running Time: 18 hrs.). 1998. bk. 39.95 (978-1-55685-454-5(4)) Audio Bk Con.
Darkly ironic, as it takes a cynical look at the law & its codes relating to marriage & inheritance.

Mr. Sebastian & the Negro Magician. Daniel Wallace. Narrated by Tom Stechschulte et al. (Running Time: 36900 sec.). 2007. audio compact disk 34.99 (978-1-4281-3733-2(5)) Recorded Bks.

Mr. Sebastian & the Negro Magician. unabr. ed. Daniel Wallace. 9 CDs. (Running Time: 10 hrs. 15 mins.). 2007. audio compact disk 102.75 (978-1-4281-3736-3(X)) Recorded Bks.

Mr. Smith & Other Nonsense see Twentieth-Century Poetry in English, No. 30, Recordings of Poets Reading Their Own Poetry

Mr. Standfast. unabr. ed. John Buchan. Read by Frederick Davidson. 9 cass. (Running Time: 13 hrs. 30 min.). 1999. 62.95 (2417) Blckstn Audio.
Reluctantly posing as a pacifist, Richard Hannay infiltrates an anti-war league to capture an unimpeachable German spy. The second in the series of five novels following Hannay's exploits, picks up after Hannay has returned home from the Somme & is working for the War Office under an assumed name. Takes readers along with him for the twists & turns of espionage during the turbulent years of World War I.

Mr. Standfast. unabr. ed. John Buchan. Read by Edmund Dehn. 10 cass. (Running Time: 12 hrs. 30 min.). 2001. 84.95 (978-1-85695-450-1(1), 93084) Pub: ISIS Audio GBR. Dist(s): Ulverscroft US
Richard Hannay is taken from active service to take part in the mysterious secret service. A group of pacifists is working against the war effort & in this seemingly sincere movement Hannay detects something more sinister.

Mr Standfast. unabr. ed. John Buchan. Read by Frederick Davidson. 9 cass. (Running Time: 13 hrs.). 2006. 62.95 (978-0-7861-1588-4(2), 2417) Blckstn Audio.

Mr. Standfast. unabr. collector's ed. John Buchan. Read by David Case. 9 cass. (Running Time: 13 hrs. 30 min.). 1994. 72.00 (978-0-7366-2883-9(5), 3585) Books on Tape.
Can WW I hero Richard Hannay give the British Intelligence Service what it needs: Germany's plans for the Second Battle of the Somme?.

Mr. Sugar Came to Town. Read by Harriet Rohmer & Anna Olivarez. Adapted by Harriet Rohmer & Cruz Gomez. 1 cass. (Running Time: 30 min.). (Tales of the Americas Ser.).Tr. of Visita del Senor Azucar. (SPA & ENG.). (J). (ps-3). 1997. 9.95 (978-0-89239-060-1(3)) Pub: Childrens Book Pr. Dist(s): PerseuPGW
Mr. Sugar comes to town & seduces the children away from Grandma Lupe's tasty & nutritious tamales in this cautionary tale about the hazards of substance abuse.

Mr. Sugar Came to Town: La Visita del Sr. Azucar. Cruz Gomez. Ed. by Harriet Rohmer. Contrib. by Anna Olivarez. (ENG & SPA.). (J). (ps-7). 1990. bk. 22.95 (978-0-89239-062-5(X)) Childrens Book Pr.

Mr. Tall Cactus & His Shorter, Prickly Neighbors. unabr. ed. Daniel Lonsberry. Read by Daniel Lonsberry. Perf. by Persephone Dimson. 1 cass. (Running Time: 30 min.). (J). (ps-4). 1997. (978-0-9658255-0-4(7)) Magic Carpet Rides.
Side 1 consists of four songs that emphasize the values taught in the story. Side 2 consists of the audio version of the story from the book as read by the author with piano accompaniment.

***Mr. Toppit.** unabr. ed. Charles Elton. (Running Time: 12 hrs.). 2010. 29.95 (978-1-4417-5963-4(8)); 72.95 (978-1-4417-5959-7(X)); audio compact disk 105.00 (978-1-4417-5960-3(3)); audio compact disk 32.95 (978-1-4417-5962-7(X)) Blckstn Audio.

Mr. Tucket. unabr. ed. Gary Paulsen. Narrated by John Randolph Jones. 3 pieces. (Running Time: 3 hrs. 30 mins.). (Tucket Adventures Ser.: Bk. 1). (gr. 6 up). 1994. 27.00 (978-0-7887-0010-1(3), 94209E7) Recorded Bks.
It is 1848 & 14-year-old Francis is captured from a wagon train by Pawnee Indians. Saved by a one-armed mountain man, Mr. Grimes, Francis takes off with his rescuer on a wild adventure peopled by actual historical characters, including Jim Bowie & set against an historically accurate background.

Mr. White's Confession: A Novel. unabr. ed. Robert Clark. Narrated by George Guidall. 8 cass. (Running Time: 11 hrs.). 70.00 (978-0-7887-2498-5(3), 95573E7) Recorded Bks.
Traces the haunting connection between a police detective working in St. Paul, Minnesota during the late 1930s & a reclusive, damaged amateur photographer. Their paths, intersected by two murders, twist into a dark pattern that lingers in the heart long after the last chapter. Available to libraries only.

Mr Wolf's Pancakes. Jan Fearnley. Read by Sophie Aldred. (Running Time: 72000 sec.). (J). (ps-k). 2005. DVD, audio compact disk, audio compact disk 9.95 (978-0-7540-6675-0(4), Chivers Child Audio) AudioGO.

Mr. Wrong. unabr. ed. Terry Campbell. Read by Lynda Evans. 4 cass. (Running Time: 5 hrs.). 2001. 26.95 (978-1-55686-930-3(4)) Books in Motion.
Rourke Hawthorne considers it his duty to assist his widowed employee, Kat Snow, in re-entering the dating game. But in a matter of days, Hawthorne shifts from helpful friend to disagreeable male protecting his territory.

Mr. Wrong. unabr. ed. Elizabeth Jane Howard. Read by Prunella Scales. 6 cass. (Running Time: 22500 sec.). (Superintendent Daiziel & Sergeant Pascoe Mysteries Ser.). 2001. 54.95 (978-0-7540-0611-4(5), CAB2034) AudioGO.
Nine short stories from a family Christmas, a picnic, a house party in France to the subtle tensions of relationships, flat sharing & adultery, comes a haunting journey into the macabre.

Mr. X. Perf. by Herbie Mann et al. Prod. by Jason Miles. 1 CD. (Running Time: 1 hr. 2 min.). 1996. audio compact disk 15.98 (978-1-56896-140-8(5), 54170-2) Lightyear Entrtnmnt.
Contemporary music, vocal and instrumental styles, jazz-based with elements of soul, funk, and international rhythms in a delicious melange of indelible melodies.

Mr. X. Peter Straub. Read by Keith Szarabajka. 2004. 15.95 (978-0-7435-4295-1(9)) Pub: S&S Audio. Dist(s): S and S Inc

Mr. X. unabr. ed. Peter Straub. Read by Adam Henderson. 14 vols. (Running Time: 21 Hrs.). 2000. bk. 110.95 (978-0-7927-2409-4(7), CSL 298, Chivers Sound Lib) AudioGO.
Every year on his birthday, Ned Dunston is cursed with visions of horrors committed by a savage figure he calls Mr. X. A dreadful premonition brings him home to find his mother on her deathbed.

Mr. X. unabr. ed. Peter Straub. Read by Adam Henderson. 2 CDs. (Running Time: 10 hrs.). 2002. audio compact disk 49.95 (978-0-7927-2665-4(0), CMP 298, Chivers Sound Lib) AudioGO.

MRI, Arthroscopy & Surgical Anatomy of the Joints. David W. Stoller. (ENG.). 1998. audio compact disk 299.00 (978-0-7817-1580-5(6)) Lppncott W W.

***Mrs. Adams in Winter: A Journey in the Last Days of Napoleon.** unabr. ed. Michael O'Brien. Narrated by Cassandra Campbell. (Running Time: 11 hrs. 0 mins.). 2010. 17.99 (978-1-4001-8631-0(5)); 24.99 (978-1-4001-6631-2(4)); 34.99 (978-1-4001-9631-9(0)); audio compact disk 34.99 (978-1-4001-1631-7(7)); audio compact disk 69.99 (978-1-4001-4631-4(3)) Pub: Tantor Media. Dist(s): IngramPubServ

Mrs. Astor Regrets: The Hidden Betrayals of a Family Beyond Reproach. unabr. ed. Meryl Gordon. Narrated by Lorna Raver. 2 MP3-CDs. (Running Time: 14 hrs. 0 mins. 0 sec.). (ENG.). 2009. 24.99 (978-1-4001-6061-7(8)); audio compact disk 34.99 (978-1-4001-1061-2(0)); audio compact disk 69.99 (978-1-4001-4061-9(7)) Pub: Tantor Media. Dist(s): IngramPubServ

Mrs. Bridge: A Novel. unabr. ed. Evan S. Connell. Narrated by Sally Darling. 7 cass. (Running Time: 9 hrs. 15 mins.). 1991. 60.00 (978-1-55690-356-4(1), 91201E7) Recorded Bks.
An unflinching portrait of an identity submerged. India Bridge's life is a collection of redundancies. When India tries to reach beyond the limitations around her, she begins to realize the scattered truths that hide themselves in fear & solitude.

Mrs. Bridge: A Novel. unabr. collector's ed. Evan S. Connell. Read by Christopher Hurt. 5 cass. (Running Time: 7 hrs. 30 mins.). 1989. 40.00 (978-0-7366-1485-6(0), 2361) Books on Tape.
Mrs. Bridge, wife of a Kansas City Lawyer. Discusses the everyday incidents of marriage; the gradual achievements of a workable adjustment, visits with friends, the bringing-up of two daughters & a son & later the unsuccessful attempts to alleviate the loneliness & boredom of middle age.

Mrs. Busk see Osbert Sitwell Reading His Poetry

Mrs Caldicot's Cabbage War. unabr. ed. Vernon Coleman. Read by Anne Dover. 5 cass. (Soundings Ser.). 2006. 49.95 (978-1-84559-387-2(1)) Pub: ISIS Lrg Prnt GBR. Dist(s): Ulverscroft US

Mrs Caldicot's Knickerbocker Glory. unabr. ed. Vernon Coleman. Read by Anne Dover. 8 cass. (Soundings Ser.). 2007. 69.95 (978-1-84559-388-9(X)) Pub: ISIS Lrg Prnt GBR. Dist(s): Ulverscroft US

Mrs. Chippy's Last Expedition: The Remarkable Journal of Shakleton's Polar-Bound Cat. unabr. ed. Caroline Alexander. Narrated by Steven Crossley. 3 cass. (Running Time: 4 hrs.). 1998. 26.00 (978-0-7887-2003-1(1), 95390E7) Recorded Bks.
A marvelous diary of Sir Shackleton's 1914 expedition to Antarctica, as written by the shipwright's world-weary cat.

Mrs. Craddock. W. Somerset Maugham. Read by Flo Gibson. 7 cass. (Running Time: 10 hrs.). 1990. 25.95 (978-1-55685-179-7(0)) Audio Bk Con.
When this edition appeared in 1902, it shocked the literati. With a passionate nature & her heart in her hand, Bertha's life & loves are explored with deep sensitivity.

Mrs. Craddock. unabr. collector's ed. W. Somerset Maugham. Read by Jill Masters. 8 cass. (Running Time: 12 hrs.). 1986. 64.00 (978-0-7366-0792-6(7), 1744) Books on Tape.
Bertha Ley is mistress of Court Ley, a great spread of land. She marries Edward Craddock, a man beneath her station. A gentleman farmer, he is steady & a doer who turns Court Ley into an efficient farm. But Bertha wants passion & ardor; she gets reality.

Mrs. Craggs: Crimes Cleaned Up. unabr. ed. H. R. F. Keating. Read by Joe Dunlop. 6 cass. (Running Time: 7 hrs. 15 min.). 2001. 54.95 (978-1-85089-842-9(1), 90061) Pub: ISIS Audio GBR. Dist(s): Ulverscroft US
Mrs. Craggs is a cleaning lady who solves crimes with an ease & swiftness that can reduce the police to embarrassment. She misses nothing, & thinks faster than most of them.

Mrs. Dalloway. Virginia Woolf. Narrated by Flo Gibson. (ENG.). 2007. audio compact disk 27.95 (978-1-55685-945-8(7)) Audio Bk Con.

Mrs. Dalloway. Virginia Woolf. Read by Sophie Chauveau. 4 cass. 1995. 39.95 (1771-TH) Olivia & Hill.
Follow Mrs. Dalloway as she walks through London on a clear June morning, observing the people around her & reflecting on her life past & present.

Mrs. Dalloway. Virginia Woolf. Narrated by Virginia Leishman. 6 cass. (Running Time: 7 hrs. 45 mins.). 54.00 (978-1-4025-2242-0(8)) Recorded Bks.

Mrs. Dalloway. Virginia Woolf. 5 cass. (Running Time: 7 hrs. 45 mins.). 2004. 24.99 (978-1-4025-5756-9(6), 03254) Recorded Bks.

Mrs. Dalloway. unabr. ed. Virginia Woolf. Read by Flo Gibson. 5 cass. (Running Time: 6 hrs. 30 min.). 1999. 20.95 (978-1-55685-517-7(6)) Audio Bk Con.
A day in Clarissa Dalloway's life is explored through her thoughts, actions & reminiscences & by the flashbacks of those about her.

Mrs. Dalloway. unabr. ed. Virginia Woolf. Read by Phyllida Law. 6 cass. (Running Time: 7 hrs. 27 min.). 2001. 54.95 (978-0-7540-0615-2(8), CAB2038) AudioGO.
Exploring the hidden springs of thought & action in one day of a woman's life.

Mrs. Dalloway. unabr. ed. Virginia Woolf. Read by Phyllida Law. 12 cass. (Running Time: 18 hrs.). 2003. audio compact disk 64.95 (978-0-7540-5586-0(8), CCD 277) AudioGO.

Mrs. Dalloway. unabr. ed. Virginia Woolf. Read by Wanda McCaddon. 4 cass. (Running Time: 6 hrs.). 2001. 29.95 (978-0-7366-6808-8(X)) Books on Tape.
Mrs. Dolloway's day is refracted in the lives of others in this early stream of consciousness novel.

Mrs. Dalloway. unabr. collector's ed. Virginia Woolf. Read by Wanda McCaddon. 6 cass. (Running Time: 6 hrs.). 1984. 48.00 (978-0-7366-0835-0(4), 1786) Books on Tape.
Clarissa Dalloway, in her 50's, wife of an English MP, emerges from her house in Westminster one fine June morning to buy flowers for her party & by that simple act she entwines her life with the lives of others who will hear with her. Big Ben tolls away the hours of their destinies that day.

Mrs. De Winter. unabr. ed. Susan Hill. Read by Lisanne Cole. 8 cass. (Running Time: 12 hrs.). 64.00 (978-0-7366-2884-6(3), 3586) Books on Tape.
By ending "Rebecca" with Manderley in ruins, Daphne du Maurier left millions of readers wondering what happened to the de Winters. Did Maxim & his young wife finally exorcise Rebecca's haunting spirit? In a sequel to the classic tale of romantic suspense, Susan Hill re-creates the hauntingly beautiful world of "Rebecca".

Mrs. Frisby & the Rats of NIMH. unabr. ed. Robert C. O'Brien. Narrated by Barbara Caruso. 5 pieces. (Running Time: 7 hrs. 15 mins.). (Rats of NIMH Ser.). (gr. 5 up). 1993. 44.00 (978-1-55690-954-2(3), 93446E7a) Recorded Bks.
Mrs. Frisby, a field mouse, who lives in a garden, must move her family before the farmer begins plowing. Will the rats of NIMH, a group of highly intelligent laboratory rats, help her find a solution to her dilemma.

Mrs. Frisby & the Rats of NIMH. unabr. ed. Robert C. O'Brien. Narrated by Barbara Caruso. 6 CDs. (Running Time: 7 hrs. 15 mins.). (gr. 5 up). 2000. audio compact disk 56.00 (978-0-7887-3452-6(0), 93446E5) Recorded Bks.
Mrs. Frisby, a field mouse who lives in a garden, must move her family before the farmer begins plowing. Will the rats of NIMH, a group of highly intelligent laboratory rats, help her find a solution to her dilemma.

Mrs. Fytton's Country Life. Mavis Cheek. Read by Phyllida Nash. 2003. audio compact disk 94.95 (978-0-7540-8763-2(8)) Pub: Chivers Audio Bks GBR. Dist(s): AudioGO

Mrs. Fytton's Country Life. unabr. ed. Mavis Cheek. Read by Phyllida Nash. 10 cass. (Running Time: 15 hrs.). 2001. 84.95 (978-0-7540-0589-6(5), CAB2012) Pub: Chivers Audio Bks GBR. Dist(s): AudioGO
Angela Fytton, wonder-wife, supermother, bedroom vamp & business partner has been unceremoniously dumped. Like many a good wife before her, her husband has decided to swap her for a younger model. Now, divorced but determined, she moves to the country, where she waits.

Mrs. God. Peter Straub. 2004. 10.95 (978-0-7435-4296-8(7)) Pub: S&S Audio. Dist(s): S and S Inc

Mrs. Jordan's Profession: The Actress & the Prince. collector's ed. Claire Tomalin. Read by Donada Peters. 8 cass. (Running Time: 12 hrs.). 2000. 64.00 (978-0-7366-5566-8(2)) Books on Tape.
On the London stage in the late eighteenth century, Dora Jordan was a star. In 1791, she attracted the attention of Prince William, third son of King George III, who eventually prevailed upon her to live with him. For more than twenty years, she was a loyal & loving mate, bearing him ten children, helping to pay his debts out of her earnings & acting for all intents & purposes as his wife. Eventually, under pressure from the royal family & moved by his own ambitions, William abandoned her. Dora was to die in poverty & loneliness in 1816. William became King William IV in 1830.

***Mrs. Katz & Tush.** unabr. ed. Patricia Polacco. Read by Patricia Polacco. 1 CD. (Running Time: 13 mins.). (J). (ps-3). 2009. bk. 29.95 (978-0-8045-4214-2(7)) Spoken Arts.

Mrs. Keith's Crime. unabr. ed. Lucy Clifford. Read by Flo Gibson. 6 cass. (Running Time: 8 hrs. 30 min.). (gr. 8 up). 1999. 24.95 (978-1-55685-603-7(2)) Audio Bk Con.
A tragic story that prompted Robert Browning to say that he wished he had written it.

Mrs. Kimble. Jennifer Haigh. Read by Martha Plimpton. 6 cass. (Running Time: 39120 sec.). 2006. 54.95 (978-0-7927-3540-3(4), CSL 781); audio compact disk 79.95 (978-0-7927-3859-6(4), SLD 781) AudioGO.

***Mrs. Kimble.** unabr. ed. Jennifer Haigh. Read by Martha Plimpton. (ENG.). 2004. (978-0-06-079848-2(3), Harper Audio); (978-0-06-081403-8(9), Harper Audio) HarperCollins Pubs.

Mrs. Kimble: A Novel. Jennifer Haigh. Read by Martha Plimpton. 1975. 14.95 (978-0-06-074348-2(4)) HarperCollins Pubs.

Mrs. Klein. Nicholas Wright. 2 CDs. (Running Time: 5460 sec.). 1994. audio compact disk 25.95 (978-1-58081-291-7(0), CDTPT196) L A Theatre.

Mrs. Klein. Nicholas Wright. Contrib. by Julie Harris et al. 2 CDs. (Running Time: 5460 sec.). 2000. audio compact disk 25.95 (978-1-58081-292-4(9), CDTPT197) Pub: L A Theatre. Dist(s): NetLibrary CO

Mrs. Klein. unabr. ed. Nicholas Wright. Perf. by Lindsay Crouse et al. 1 cass. (Running Time: 1 hr. 32 min.). 1994. 19.95 (978-1-58081-009-8(8)) L A Theatre.
The air is thick with Freud & sex as eminent psychoanalyst Melanie Klein comes roaring to life in a 1930's English drawing room. London offers the witty, overbearing Mrs. Klein refuge from rising European fascism. But perhaps her children are still in need of refuge from her. Was Klein a devoted mother, or a monster who used her psychoanalytic skills to drive her son to suicide.

Mrs. Liversedge see Osbert Sitwell Reading His Poetry

Mrs. Mack. unabr. ed. Patricia Polacco. Narrated by Kate Forbes. 1 cass. (Running Time: 45 mins.). (gr. 4 up). 2001. 10.00 (978-0-7887-4399-3(6), 96235E7) Recorded Bks.
In the summer of Patricia's tenth year, her father decides she's old enough to learn to ride horses. But when he takes her to a stable in Dogpatch, the roughest part of town, she thinks it must be a terrible mistake. Dressed in a fancy riding outfit, she immediately feels out of place.

Mrs. Mack. unabr. ed. Patricia Polacco. Narrated by Kate Forbes. 1 cass. (Running Time: 45 mins.). (J). 2001. pap. bk. & stu. ed. 34.99 Recorded Bks.

Mrs. Mcginty's Dead. Agatha Christie. Read by Hugh Fraser. (Running Time: 22080 sec.). (Hercule Poirot Mystery Ser.). 2007. 27.95 (978-1-57270-732-0(1)) Pub: Audio Partners. Dist(s): PerseuPGW

Mrs. Mcginty's Dead. unabr. ed. Agatha Christie. Narrated by Hugh Fraser. 5 CDs. (Running Time: 22080 sec.). (Hercule Poirot Mystery Ser.). (ENG.). 2007. audio compact disk 27.95 (978-1-57270-731-3(3)) Pub: AudioGO. Dist(s): Perseus Dist

Mrs. McGinty's Dead: A BBC Full-Cast Radio Drama. Agatha Christie. 2006. audio compact disk (978-0-563-51021-5(8)) AudioGo GBR.

Mrs. McGinty's Dead: A BBC Full-Cast Radio Drama. unabr. ed. Agatha Christie. Narrated by Full Cast. (Running Time: 2 hrs. 0 mins. 0 sec.). (ENG.). 2010. audio compact disk 24.95 (978-1-60283-813-0(5)) Pub: AudioGO. Dist(s): Perseus Dist

Mrs. McWilliams & the Lighting see Great American Short Stories, Vol. II, A Collection

Mrs. McWilliams & the Lightning see Californian's Tale

Mrs. Mike. unabr. ed. Benedict Freedman & Nancy. Read by Cassandra Campbell. (Running Time: 1 hr. 0 mins.). (ENG.). 2009. 29.95 (978-1-4332-9478-5(8)); 65.95 (978-1-4332-9474-7(5)); audio compact disk 100.00 (978-1-4332-9475-4(3)) Blckstn Audio.

Mrs. Miniver. Jan Struther. Read by Brigit Forsyth. 4 cass. (Running Time: 6 hrs.). 2001. 44.95 (20391) Pub: ISIS Audio GBR. Dist(s): Ulverscroft US

Mrs. Miniver. unabr. ed. Jan Struther. Read by Brigit Forsyth. 4 cass. (Running Time: 4 hrs. 34 min.). (Isis Ser.). (J). 1991. 44.95 (978-1-85089-642-5(9), 20391) Pub: ISIS Lrg Prnt GBR. Dist(s): Ulverscroft US

Mrs. Miracle. unabr. ed. Debbie Macomber. Read by Jennifer Van Dyck. (Running Time: 7 hrs.). 2009. 24.99 (978-1-4418-0775-5(6), 9781441807755, Brilliance MP3); 24.99 (978-1-4418-0777-9(2), 9781441807779, BAD); 39.97 (978-1-4418-0776-2(4), 9781441807762, Brlnc Audio MP3 Lib); 39.97 (978-1-4418-0778-6(0), 9781441807786, BADLE); audio compact disk 26.99 (978-1-4418-0773-1(X), 9781441807731, Bril Audio CD Unabri); audio compact disk 97.97 (978-1-4418-0774-8(8), 9781441807748, BriAudCD Unabrid) Brilliance Audio.

Mrs. Murgatroyd's Pumpkins. (J). 2008. audio compact disk 15.95 (978-0-9820885-2-4(3)) TBell.

Mrs. Nutch see Osbert Sitwell Reading His Poetry

Mrs. Ockleton's Rainbow Kite & Other Tales: Thinking Through Literature. Garry Burnett. Contrib. by Gordon Giltrap. (Running Time: 60 min.). (J). (gr. 4-7). 2006. audio compact disk 15.95 (978-1-84590-026-7(X)) Crown Hse GBR.

Mrs O'Malley in Alligator Alley. (Sails Literacy Ser.). (gr. 1 up). 10.00 (978-0-7578-2662-7(8)) Rigby Educ.

Mrs. Pargeter's Package, unabr. ed. Simon Brett. Read by Simon Brett. 5 CDs. (Running Time: 6 hrs. 30 mins.). 1999. audio compact disk 59.95 (978-0-7531-0711-9(2), 107112) Pub: ISIS Audio GBR. Dist(s): Ulverscroft US

Mrs. Pargeter's Package. unabr. ed. Simon Brett. Read by Simon Brett. 6 cass. (Running Time: 6 hrs. 30 min.). (Isis Ser.). (J). 2001. 54.95 (978-1-85089-648-7(8), 91061) Pub: ISIS Lrg Prnt GBR. Dist(s): Ulverscroft US

Mrs. Pargeter's Plot. unabr. ed. Simon Brett. Read by Simon Brett. 5 CDs. (Running Time: 5 hrs. 45 mins.). (Isis Ser.). (J). 2000. audio compact disk 59.95 (978-0-7531-0904-5(2), 109042) Pub: ISIS Lrg Prnt GBR. Dist(s): Ulverscroft US
The indomitable Melita Pargeter had decided to build her dream house on the plot left to her by her husband, the much loved, much missed "businessman", Mr. Pargeter & there is only one person she could possibly trust to make this dream come true, her talented builder, Concrete Jacket. Her plans go awry, however, as there is a dead body found lying in the new wine cellar & Concrete's been arrested for his murder. The builder isn't an angel, but he also isn't the killer. Mrs. Pargeter sets out to unmask the real killer with the help of her former husband's "associates".

Mrs. Pargeter's Plot, unabr. ed. Simon Brett. Read by Simon Brett. 5 cass. (Running Time: 7 hrs. 30 min.). (Isis Ser.). (J). 2001. 49.95 (978-0-7531-0103-2(3), 961001) Pub: ISIS Lrg Prnt GBR. Dist(s): Ulverscroft US
Melita decides to build her dream house on the plot left to her by her husband. Her plans go awry when there is a dead body found lying in the new wine cellar. She sets out to unmask the real killer with the help of her former husbands "associates.".

Mrs. Pargeter's Point of Honour. unabr. ed. Simon Brett. Read by Simon Brett. 6 CDs. (Running Time: 9 hrs.). (Isis (CDs) Ser.). 2001. audio compact disk 64.95 (978-0-7531-1119-2(5), 111195) Pub: ISIS Audio GBR. Dist(s): Ulverscroft US
When Mrs Pargeter is asked by an elderly widow to return a large number of stolen paintings to their rightful owners, she doesn?t hesitate for it?s a point of honour to complete any of her late husband?s unfinished business. But all does not run smoothly. For a start, Detective Inspector Craig Wilkinson, still embittered by his failure to arrest Mr Pargeter when he was alive, starts to show an unhealthy interest in his widow.

Mrs. Pargeter's Point of Honour, unabr. ed. Simon Brett. Read by Simon Brett. 6 cass. (Running Time: 6 hrs.). (Isis Ser.). (J). 2001. 54.95 (978-0-7531-0466-8(0), 981201) Pub: ISIS Lrg Prnt GBR. Dist(s): Ulverscroft US
When Mrs. Pargeter is asked by an elderly widow to return a large number of stolen paintings to their owners, she doesn't hesitate to complete any of her late husband's unfinished business. so she contacts Truffler Mason, Hedgeclipper Clinton & others of the Mr. Pargeter's associates to sort out the operation but all does not run smoothly. For a start, Detective Inspector Craig Wilkinson, still embittered by his failure to arrest Mr. Pargeter while he was alive, starts to show an unhealthy interest in the man's widow.

Mrs. Pargeter's Pound of Flesh. unabr. ed. Simon Brett. Read by Simon Brett. 6 cass. (Running Time: 6 hrs. 30 mins.). (Isis Ser.). (J). 2004. 54.95 (978-1-85695-571-3(0), 93051) Pub: ISIS Lrg Prnt GBR. Dist(s): Ulverscroft US

Mrs. Piggle-Wiggle. Betty Bard MacDonald. Read by Marion Ross. 2 CDs. (Running Time: 3 hrs.). (J). 2000. audio compact disk 20.00 Pub Mills.
An old woman has a knack for making children behave like angels.

Mrs. Piggle-Wiggle. Betty Bard MacDonald. Read by John McDonough. 2 cass. (Running Time: 2 hrs. 45 mins.). (J). (gr. 1 up). 1999. stu. ed. 89.30 (978-0-7887-3877-7(1), 47043) Recorded Bks.
Mrs. Piggle-Wiggle knows all there is to know about children. If a boy won't share his peppermint sticks, she brings out her "Selfishness Kit." If a girl refuses to take a bath, she applies the never-fail "Radish Cure".

Mrs. Piggle-Wiggle. unabr. ed. Betty MacDonald. Read by Karen White. (Running Time: 9660 sec.). (ENG.). (J). (gr. 3). 2005. audio compact disk 27.00 (978-0-307-28248-4(1), Listening Lib) Pub: Random Audio Pubg. Dist(s): Random

Mrs. Piggle-Wiggle. unabr. ed. Betty Bard MacDonald. Read by Marion Ross. 2 cass. (Running Time: 3 hrs.). (J). (gr. k up). 2000. 18.00 (978-1-57511-071-4(7)) Pub Mills.
An old woman has a knack for making children behave like angels.

Mrs. Piggle-Wiggle. unabr. ed. Betty Bard MacDonald. Read by Marion Ross. 2 CDs. (Running Time: 180 mins.). (J). (gr. k up). 2001. audio compact disk 20.00 (978-1-57511-078-3(4)) Pub: Pub Mills. Dist(s): TransVend

Mrs. Piggle-Wiggle. unabr. ed. Betty Bard MacDonald. 2 vols. (Running Time: 2 hrs. 57 mins.). (J). (gr. 2-5). 2004. pap. bk. 29.00 (978-0-8072-1180-9(X), S YA 1022 SP, Listening Lib) Random Audio Pubg.

Mrs. Piggle-Wiggle. unabr. ed. Betty Bard MacDonald. Narrated by John McDonough. 2 cass. (Running Time: 2 hrs. 45 mins.). (J). (gr. 1 up). 1999. pap. bk. & stu. ed. 32.20 (978-0-7887-3851-7(8), 41049X4) Recorded Bks.
Mrs. Piggle-Wiggle knows all there is to know about children. If a boy won't share his peppermint sticks, she brings out her "Selfishness Kit." If a girl refuses to take a bath, she applies the never-fail "Radish Cure".

Mrs. Piggle-Wiggle, unabr. ed. Betty Bard MacDonald. Narrated by John McDonough. 2 pieces. (Running Time: 2 hrs. 45 mins.). (gr. 1 up). 2000. 19.00 (978-0-7887-3816-6(X), 96060E7) Recorded Bks.

Mrs. Piggle-Wiggle. unabr. ed. Betty Bard MacDonald. 2 cass. (Running Time: 2 hrs. 57 mins.). (J). (gr. 2-5). 2004. 23.00 (978-0-8072-1178-6(8), S YA 1022 CX, Listening Lib) Random Audio Pubg.

Mrs. Piggle-Wiggle's Farm. unabr. ed. Betty Bard MacDonald. Narrated by John McDonough. 3 cass. (Running Time: 3 hrs. 30 mins.). (J). 2001. pap. bk. & stu. ed. 43.20 Recorded Bks.
Whenever youngsters have troublesome habits, their parents send them to the farm. This is a whimsical approach to childhood troubles that keep youngsters laughing out loud.

Mrs. Piggle-Wiggle's Farm. unabr. ed. Betty Bard MacDonald. Narrated by John McDonough. 3 pieces. (Running Time: 3 hrs. 30 mins.). (gr. 1 up). 2001. 29.00 (978-0-7887-4550-8(6), 96097E7) Recorded Bks.

Mrs. Piggle-Wiggle's Magic. Betty Bard MacDonald. 2 vols. (Running Time: 3 hrs. 30 mins.). (J). (gr. 2-5). 2004. pap. bk. 29.00 (978-1-4000-9001-3(6), Listening Lib) Random Audio Pubg.

Mrs. Piggle-Wiggle's Magic. Betty Bard MacDonald. Read by John McDonough. 3 cass. (Running Time: 4 hrs.). (J). 2000. pap. bk. & stu. ed. 51.95 (978-0-7887-4343-6(0), 41137) Recorded Bks.
All the children in town love Mrs. Piggle-Wiggle & so do their parents. She applies fun-filled treatment to a host of childhood troubles including Tattle-tale-itis & Not-Want-To-Go-to-Schoolers.

Mrs. Piggle-Wiggle's Magic, Betty Bard MacDonald. Read by John McDonough. 3 cass. (Running Time: 4 hrs.). (J). (gr. 1 up). 2000. stu. ed. 196.80 (978-0-7887-4443-3(7), 47134) Recorded Bks.

Mrs. Piggle-Wiggle's Magic. unabr. ed. Betty Bard MacDonald. 2 cass. (Running Time: 3 hrs. 30 mins.). (J). (gr. 2-5). 2004. 23.00 (978-0-8072-1186-1(9), Listening Lib) Random Audio Pubg.

Mrs. Piggle-Wiggle's Magic. unabr. ed. Betty Bard MacDonald. Narrated by John McDonough. 3 pieces. (Running Time: 4 hrs.). (gr. 1 up). 2000. 29.00 (978-0-7887-4224-8(8), 96098E7) Recorded Bks.

Mrs. Pollifax & the Golden Triangle. unabr. ed. Dorothy Gilman. Narrated by Barbara Rosenblat. 5 cass. (Running Time: 7 hrs. 15 mins.). (Mrs. Pollifax Mystery Ser.: Vol. 8). 1993. 44.00 (978-1-55690-823-1(7), 93124E7) Recorded Bks.
Mrs. Pollifax, secret agent for the CIA, must work overtime when her new husband Cyrus is kidnapped while they are vacationing in Thailand.

Mrs. Pollifax & the Hong Kong Buddha. unabr. ed. Dorothy Gilman. Narrated by Barbara Rosenblat. 5 cass. (Running Time: 6 hrs. 45 mins.). (Mrs. Pollifax Mystery Ser.: Vol. 7). 1991. 44.00 (978-1-55690-354-0(5), 91103E7) Recorded Bks.
Mrs. Pollifax's unusually bright skies turn dark as she faces international terrorists in the Far East.

Mrs. Pollifax & the Lion Killer. abr. ed. Dorothy Gilman. Read by J. Charles. 2 cass. (Running Time: 3 hrs.). 2000. 7.95 (978-1-57815-175-2(9), 1118, Media Bks Audio) Media Bks NJ.
The intrepid charmer Mrs. Pollifax is at it again, this time in an adventure with a young friend through the African country of Ubangiba.

Mrs. Pollifax & the Lion Killer. abr. ed. Dorothy Gilman. Read by J. Charles. 3 CDs. (Running Time: 3 hrs.). (YA). 2000. audio compact disk 11.99 (978-1-57815-509-5(6), 1118 CD3, Media Bks Audio) Media Bks NJ.
Mrs. Pollifax is at it again, this time in an adventure with a your friend through the African country of Ubangiba.

Mrs. Pollifax & the Lion Killer. unabr. ed. Dorothy Gilman. Read by J. Charles. (Running Time: 6 hrs.). 2008. 39.25 (978-1-4233-5778-0(7), 9781423357780, BADLE); 39.25 (978-1-4233-5776-6(0), 9781423357766, Brlnc Audio MP3 Lib); 24.95 (978-1-4233-5775-9(2), 9781423357759, Brilliance MP3); 24.95 (978-1-4233-5777-3(9), 9781423357773, BAD) Brilliance Audio.

Mrs. Pollifax & the Lion Killer. unabr. ed. Dorothy Gilman. Narrated by Barbara Rosenblat. 6 CDs. (Running Time: 6 hrs. 15 mins.). (Mrs. Pollifax Mystery Ser.: Vol. 12). 1999. audio compact disk 48.00 (978-0-7887-3407-6(5), C1013E7) Recorded Bks.
Mrs. Pollifax must begin a perilous investigation. Fortunately for all, staunch determination & polished karate skills are on her side.

Mrs. Pollifax & the Lion Killer. unabr. ed. Dorothy Gilman. Narrated by Barbara Rosenblat. 5 cass. (Running Time: 6 hrs. 15 mins.). (Mrs. Pollifax Mystery Ser.: Vol. 12). 1997. 44.00 (978-0-7887-0459-8(1), 94652E7) Recorded Bks.

Mrs. Pollifax & the Second Thief. abr. ed. Dorothy Gilman. Read by J. Charles. 2 cass. (Running Time: 3 hrs.). 2000. 7.95 (978-1-57815-020-5(5), 1005, Media Bks Audio) Media Bks NJ.
A CIA operative & full-time grandmother is off to the Sicilian countryside to rescue a former CIA comrade.

Mrs. Pollifax & the Second Thief. unabr. ed. Dorothy Gilman. Read by Multivoice Production Staff. (Running Time: 5 hrs.). 2008. 24.95 (978-1-4233-5451-2(6), 9781423354512, Brilliance MP3); 24.95 (978-1-4233-5453-6(2), 9781423354536, BAD); 39.25 (978-1-4233-5452-9(4), 9781423354529, Brlnc Audio MP3 Lib); 39.25 (978-1-4233-5454-3(0), 9781423354543, BADLE) Brilliance Audio.

Mrs. Pollifax & the Second Thief. unabr. ed. Dorothy Gilman. Narrated by Barbara Rosenblat. 5 cass. (Running Time: 6 hrs. 15 mins.). (Mrs. Pollifax Mystery Ser.: Vol. 10). 1993. 44.00 (978-1-55690-911-5(X), 93407E7) Recorded Bks.
Mrs. Pollifax goes to Italy to help track down an assassin.

Mrs. Pollifax & the Whirling Dervish. unabr. ed. Dorothy Gilman. Narrated by Barbara Rosenblat. 5 cass. (Running Time: 7 hrs. 15 mins.). (Mrs. Pollifax Mystery Ser.: Vol. 9). 1995. 44.00 (978-0-7887-0350-8(1), 94542E7) Recorded Bks.
Mrs. Pollifax has to help a bumbling CIA agent confirm the identities of seven undercover informants in Morocco. A simple assignment, but right away, things go wrong.

Mrs. Pollifax, Innocent Tourist. unabr. ed. Dorothy Gilman. Narrated by Barbara Rosenblat. 6 CDs. (Running Time: 6 hrs. 15 mins.). (Mrs. Pollifax Mystery Ser.: Vol. 13). 1999. audio compact disk 48.00 (978-0-7887-3422-9(9), C1028E7) Recorded Bks.
When genteel Mrs. Pollifax is assigned to smuggle an inflammatory manuscript out of Jordan, she finds herself up against a cunning, dagger-carrying Arab who is not what he seems.

Mrs. Pollifax, Innocent Tourist. unabr. ed. Dorothy Gilman. Narrated by Barbara Rosenblat. 5 cass. (Running Time: 6 hrs. 15 mins.). (Mrs. Pollifax Mystery Ser.: Vol. 13). 2000. 44.00 (978-0-7887-1758-1(8), 95236E7) Recorded Bks.

Mrs. Pollifax on Safari. unabr. ed. Dorothy Gilman. Narrated by Barbara Rosenblat. 5 cass. (Running Time: 6 hrs. 45 mins.). (Mrs. Pollifax Mystery Ser.: Vol. 5). 1992. 44.00 (978-1-55690-699-2(4), 92217E7) Recorded Bks.
Mrs. Pollifax accompanies a photo safari in Africa while she tracks a professional killer.

Mrs. Pollifax on the China Station. unabr. ed. Dorothy Gilman. Narrated by Barbara Rosenblat. 5 cass. (Running Time: 7 hrs. 15 mins.). (Mrs. Pollifax Mystery Ser.: Vol. 6). 1990. 44.00 (978-1-55690-355-7(3), 90101E7) Recorded Bks.
Mrs. Pollifax on a rescue mission to China, must get an agent out. That's where the trouble begins.

Mrs. Pollifax Pursued. unabr. ed. Dorothy Gilman. Read by Multivoice Production Staff. (Running Time: 5 hrs.). 2008. 39.25 (978-1-4233-5436-9(2), 9781423354369, Brlnc Audio MP3 Lib); 39.25 (978-1-4233-5438-3(9), 9781423354383, BADLE); 24.95 (978-1-4233-5437-6(0), 9781423354376, BAD); 24.95 (978-1-4233-5435-2(4), 9781423354352, Brilliance MP3) Brilliance Audio.

Mrs. Pollifax Pursued. unabr. ed. Dorothy Gilman. Narrated by Barbara Rosenblat. 4 cass. (Running Time: 6 hrs.). (Mrs. Pollifax Mystery Ser.: Vol. 11). 1996. 35.00 (978-0-7887-0227-3(0), 94452E7) Recorded Bks.
A missing salami leads to the discovery that a woman is hiding in the house. Even more unsettling is the revelation that ever since the young woman had a chance encounter with the heir to the throne of Ubangiba, she has been followed by deadly hit-men. What do these men want?.

Mrs. Pollifax Pursued. unabr. ed. Dorothy Gilman. Read by Barbara Rosenblat. 4 cass. (Running Time: 6 hrs.). 1996. Rental 11.50 (94452) Recorded Bks.

Mrs. Pollifax Unveiled. Dorothy Gilman. Narrated by Barbara Rosenblat. 6 CDs. (Running Time: 6 hrs.). (Mrs. Pollifax Mystery Ser.: Vol. 13). 2000. audio compact disk 48.00 (978-0-7887-4901-8(3), C1276E7) Recorded Bks.
After harrowing experiences all over the world, America's most endearing & unlikely CIA agent is bored with gardening. When headquarters calls with a deadly mission in Syria, she's on her way.

Mrs. Pollifax Unveiled. abr. ed. Dorothy Gilman. Narrated by Barbara Rosenblat. 5 cass. (Running Time: 6 hrs.). (Mrs. Pollifax Mystery Ser.: Vol. 13). 2000. 37.00 (978-0-7887-4308-5(2), 96223E7) Recorded Bks.

Mrs. Pollifax Unveiled. unabr. ed. Dorothy Gilman. Read by Sharon Williams. (Running Time: 5 hrs.). 2007. 39.25 (978-1-4233-3147-6(8), 9781423331476, BADLE) Brilliance Audio.

Mrs. Pollifax Unveiled. unabr. ed. Dorothy Gilman. Read by Laural Merlington. (Running Time: 5 hrs.). 2007. 39.25 (978-1-4233-3145-2(1), 9781423331452, Brlnc Audio MP3 Lib); 24.95 (978-1-4233-3144-5(3), 9781423331445, Brilliance MP3) Brilliance Audio.

Mrs. Pollifax Unveiled. unabr. ed. Dorothy Gilman. Read by Sharon Williams. (Running Time: 5 hrs.). 2007. 24.95 (978-1-4233-3146-9(X), 9781423331469, BAD) Brilliance Audio.

Mrs., Presumed Dead. unabr. ed. Simon Brett. Read by Simon Brett. 6 cass. (Running Time: 6 hrs. 15 min.). (Isis Ser.). (J). 2004. 54.95 (978-1-85695-429-7(3), 89042) Pub: ISIS Lrg Prnt GBR. Dist(s): Ulverscroft US

Mrs. Protheroe see Monsieur Beaucaire & Other Stories

***Mrs. Rosey Posey & the Baby Bird.** Robin Jones Gunn. (Running Time: 0 hr. 5 mins. 0 sec.). (I Can Read! Ser.). (ENG.). (J). 2009. 3.99 (978-0-310-77273-6(7)) Pub: Zondkidz. Dist(s): Zondervan

***Mrs. Rosey Posey & the Fine China Plate.** Robin Jones Gunn. (Running Time: 0 hr. 5 mins. 30 sec.). (I Can Read! Ser.). (ENG.). (J). 2009. 3.99 (978-0-310-77275-0(3)) Pub: Zondkidz. Dist(s): Zondervan

***Mrs. Rosey Posey & the Hidden Treasure.** Robin Jones Gunn. (Running Time: 0 hr. 5 mins. 49 sec.). (I Can Read! Ser.). (ENG.). (J). 2009. 3.99 (978-0-310-77274-3(5)) Pub: Zondkidz. Dist(s): Zondervan

***Mrs. Rosey Posey & the Yum-Yummy Birthday Cake.** Robin Jones Gunn. (Running Time: 0 hr. 5 mins. 0 sec.). (I Can Read! Ser.). (ENG.). (J). 2009. 3.99 (978-0-310-77276-7(1)) Pub: Zondkidz. Dist(s): Zondervan

Mrs. Southern's Enemy see Osbert Sitwell Reading His Poetry

Mrs. Ted Bliss. unabr. ed. Stanley Elkin. Narrated by George Guidall. 9 cass. (Running Time: 12 hrs. 45 mins.). 1997. 78.00 (978-0-7887-1073-5(7), 95086E7) Recorded Bks.
Why are so many men interested in Mrs. Ted Bliss, newly widowed from a Chicago butcher? Is it her smile, her flawless Buick Le Sabre or her late husband's business connections.

Mrs. Tiggy-Winkle. unabr. ed. Beatrix Potter. 1 cass. (Running Time: 20 min.). Dramatization. (Magic Looking Glass Ser.). (J). (gr. 2-6). 1989. 9.95 (978-0-7810-0054-3(8), NIM-CW-131-5-C) NIMCO.
An English folk tale.

Mrs. Warren's Profession. unabr. ed. George Bernard Shaw. Read by Flo Gibson. 2 cass. (Running Time: 2 hrs. 30 min.). 1993. 14.95 (978-1-55685-281-7(9)) Audio Bk Con.
When Vivie learns that her mother's harlotry is the origin of her financial support, nothing in her world can ever be the same. There are serious consequences for her suitor, her mother, & herself.

Mrs. Warren's Profession. unabr. ed. George Bernard Shaw. Perf. by Kaitlin Hopkins et al. 1 cass. (Running Time: 1 hr. 42 min.). 1996. 19.95 (978-1-58081-029-6(2), TPT70) L A Theatre.
Modern parallels abound in the plight of Cambridge educated mathematics whiz Vivie Warren, who discovers that her comfortable upbringing was financed in unspeakable ways. Shaw pits his clever heroine against a memorable gallery of rouges in this superbly intelligent & still-shocking comedy.

Mrs. Warren's Profession. unabr. ed. George Bernard Shaw. Perf. by Shirley Knight et al. 2 CDs. (Running Time: 1 hr. 39 mins.). Dramatization. 2001. audio compact disk 25.95 (978-1-58081-217-7(1), CDTPT70) Pub: L A Theatre. Dist(s): NetLibrary CO

Mrs. Watson Wants Your Teeth. Alison McGhee. Read by Rachael Lillis. Illus. by Harry Bliss. (J). (ps-2). 2006. 9.95 (978-1-59519-896-9(2)) Live Oak Media.

Mrs. Watson Wants Your Teeth. unabr. ed. Alison McGhee. Read by Rachael Lillis. Illus. by Harry Bliss. 1 CD. (Running Time: 12 mins.). (Picture Book Readalong Ser.). (J). (ps-2). 2007. bk. 28.95 (978-1-59519-902-7(0)); bk. 25.95 (978-1-59519-898-3(9)) Live Oak Media.

Mrs. Wiggs of the Cabbage Patch. unabr. ed. Alice Caldwell Hegan Rice. Narrated by Flo Gibson. 3 cass. (Running Time: 4 hrs. 30 min.). (J). 1984. 16.95 (978-1-55685-062-2(X)) Audio Bk Con.
Mrs. Wiggs copes with poverty & problems with a vaiant spirit & a loving heart, as does "Lovey Mary" in the companion piece.

Mrs. Wishy-Washy. Joy Cowley. 1 read-along cass. (J). 1986. 5.95 (978-0-86867-044-7(8)) Wright Group.
The Cow, the pig & the duck all love the mud. Mrs. Wishy Washy scrubs them all clean. Includes book.

Mrs. Zant & the Ghost see Classic Ghost Stories, Vol. 1, A Collection

Mrs. Zant & the Ghost. unabr. ed. Wilkie Collins. Read by Walter Zimmerman. 1 cass. (Running Time: 1 hr. 59 min.). Dramatization. 1981. 7.95 (S-2) Jimcin Record.
A ghost that haunts in the daylight.

MRTW Acting for Radio. MRTW Staff. Prod. by Brian Price. 1 cass. 12.95 (978-1-57677-027-6(3), TAP002) Lodestone Catalog.

MRTW Directing: Working with Actors. MRTW Staff. Prod. by Brian Price. 1 cass. 12.95 (978-1-57677-029-0(X), TAP004) Lodestone Catalog.

MRTW Live Vol. 1: Heaven As Usual; The Odyssey of Runyon Jones. John A. Kirchner & Norman Corwin. Directed By David Ossman. 1 cass. 12.95 (978-1-57677-033-7(8), MRTW001) Lodestone Catalog.

MRTW Live Vol. 2: Cow Tipping; The Reign of Doug. Joel Pierson & Brian Price. Directed By David Ossman & Sarah Montague. 1 cass. (YA). 12.95 (978-1-57677-034-4(6), MRTW002) Lodestone Catalog.

MRTW Live Vol. 3: Our Lady Shoes; Wally Melon Leaves Slumberland. Bebe Moore Campbell & Nathaniel Lachenmeyer. Directed By Vanessa Whitburn & Norman Jayo. 1 cass. Dramatization. 12.95 (978-1-57677-035-1(4), MRTW003) Lodestone Catalog.
Ethnic drama.

MRTW Live Vol. 4: Vince Washburn, New Age Detective. Jerry Stearns & David Ossman. Directed By Skip Pizzi & Meredith Ludwig. 1 cass. 12.95 (978-1-57677-036-8(2), MRTW003) Lodestone Catalog.

MRTW Live Vol. 5: Elevator Pirates; A Night's Work. Michael Heflin & Matt Mayerchak. Directed By David Ossman & Norman Jayo. 1 cass. 12.95 (978-1-57677-037-5(0), MRTW005) Lodestone Catalog.
Wild sci-fi.

MRTW Live Performance. 5 cass. (Running Time: 5 hrs.). 39.95 (978-1-57677-038-2(9), MRTW125) Lodestone Catalog.

MRTW Musical Integration. MRTW Staff. Prod. by Brian Price. 1 cass. 12.95 (978-1-57677-031-3(1), TAP006) Lodestone Catalog.

MRTW Performance Tapes. 5 cass. (Running Time: 5 hrs.). 2001. 35.95 (MRTW125) Lodestone Catalog.
The best live plays from 16 years of the famed audio workshop includes: fantasy, drama, comedy & youth, ethnic drama, mystery & wild sci-fi.

MRTW Teaching Tapes. MRTW Staff. Prod. by Brian Price. 6 cass. (Running Time: 6 hrs.). 39.95 (978-1-57677-032-0(X), TAP126) Lodestone Catalog.

MRTW Writing for Radio. MRTW Staff. Prod. by Brian Price. 1 cass. 12.95 (978-1-57677-026-9(5), TAP001) Lodestone Catalog.

Ms. Adventures of Ms. Wiz. unabr. ed. Terence Blacker. Read by Helen Lederer. 2 cass. (Running Time: 2 hrs.). (J). 1993. bk. 18.95 (978-0-7451-8456-2(1), CCA3180, Chivers Child Audio) AudioGO.

MS Found in a Bottle see Great American Short Stories

MS Found in a Bottle see Flying Dutchman

MS Found in a Bottle, Hop-Frog, The Shadow. Edgar Allan Poe. 1 cass. 1989. 7.95 (S-10) Jimcin Record.
Tales of the grotesque.

Ms. Hempel Chronicles. unabr. ed. Bynum, Sarah Shun-lien Bynum. Read by Tavia Gilbert. (Running Time: 1 hr. 0 mins.). (ENG.). 2009. 29.95 (978-1-4417-0044-5(7)); 44.95 (978-1-4417-0040-7(4)); audio compact disk 69.00 (978-1-4417-0041-4(2)) Blckstn Audio.

Ms. Murder. unabr. ed. Read by Juliet Mills. 4 cass. (Running Time: 5 hrs.). 1994. 24.95 (978-1-879371-70-5(7)) Pub Mills.
A unique collection of mystery stories featuring women detectives by some of the world's best fiction writers, including: Agatha Christie, Mignon G. Eberhart, Dorothy L. Sayers, Gladys Mitchell, & Phylis Bentley.

MSM Music Super Memory. Byron Duckwall. Read by Byron Duckwall. 1 cass. (Running Time: 1 hr. 25 min.). 1991. pap. bk. 22.00 (978-1-883617-00-4(6)) Evergreen Music.
A new music technique or system for memorizing music.

Much Ado about Nothin. unabr. ed. William Shakespeare. Read by Mary Woods. 2 cass. (Running Time: 3 hrs.). 1993. 14.95 (978-1-55685-305-0(X)) Audio Bk Con.
By clever scheming, friends encourage Beatrice & Benedick's love affair, whereas Don John plots to ruin Hero & Claudio's chances of happiness together.

Much Ado about Nothing. William Shakespeare. Narrated by Full Cast Production Staff. (Running Time: 2 hrs.). 2006. 14.95 (978-1-59912-990-7(6)) Iofy Corp.

Much Ado about Nothing. abr. ed. William Shakespeare. 3 CDs. (Running Time: 3 hrs.). 2005. audio compact disk 19.95 (978-0-660-18962-8(3)) Pub: Canadian Broadcasting CAN. Dist(s): Georgetown Term

***Much Ado about Nothing.** abr. ed. William Shakespeare. Read by Rex Harrison. (ENG.). 2003. (978-0-06-074317-8(4), Caedmon) HarperCollins Pubs.

***Much Ado about Nothing.** abr. ed. William Shakespeare. Read by Rex Harrison. (ENG.). 2004. (978-0-06-081329-1(6), Caedmon) HarperCollins Pubs.

Much Ado about Nothing. unabr. ed. William Shakespeare. Read by Samuel West et al. Contrib. by Arkangel Productions. (Running Time: 7920 sec.). (Arkangel Shakespeare Ser.). (ENG.). 2005. audio compact disk 19.95 (978-1-932219-25-8(0)) Pub: AudioGO. Dist(s): Perseus Dist
This sparkling comedy of manners revolves around the amorous adventures of two couples, gentle Claudio and Hero, who want to marry, and the warring Beatrice and Benedick, who think they don't. This witty romp is one of Shakespeare's best-loved comedies. Performed by Samuel West, Amanda Root, and the Arkangel cast.

Much Ado about Nothing. unabr. ed. William Shakespeare. Perf. by Rex Harrison & Rachel Roberts. 2 cass. (Running Time: 1 hr. 48 mins.). Dramatization. 17.95 (H150) Blckstn Audio.
This playful, sophisticated comedy on the subject of marriage & marital bondage raised the English language to new heights of wit & lighthearted ribaldry. At once a sobering examination of dishonesty & deception & a boisterous celebration of that overwhelming natural phenomenon we call love.

Much Ado about Nothing. unabr. ed. William Shakespeare. Read by Full Ensemble Cast. (YA). 2006. 34.99 (978-1-59895-509-5(8)) Find a World.

Much Ado about Nothing. unabr. ed. William Shakespeare. Read by Audio Partners Staff. 2 cass. (Running Time: 2 hrs. 12 mins.). (Arkangel Shakespeare Ser.). 2004. 17.95 (978-1-932219-65-4(X), Atlntc Mnthly) Pub: Grove-Atltic. Dist(s): PerseuPGW
This sparkling comedy of manners revolves around the amorous adventures of two couples, gentle Claudio and Hero, who want to marry, and the warring Beatrice and Benedick, who think they don't. This witty romp is one of Shakespeare's best-loved comedies. Performed by Samuel West, Amanda Root, and the Arkangel cast.

Much Ado about Nothing. unabr. ed. William Shakespeare. Perf. by Rex Harrison & Rachel Roberts. 2 cass. (Running Time: 1 hr. 48 min.). 2000. pap. bk. 17.95 (40995E5); audio compact disk 25.00 (21617E5) Recorded Bks.
Filled with witticisms & innuendoes, this play is both a sobering look at dishonesty & a celebration of love.

Much Ado about Nothing. unabr. abr. ed. William Shakespeare. Read by Rex Harrison. 2 CDs. (Caedmon Shakespeare Ser.: Vol. 2). (gr. 9-12). 1996. audio compact disk 25.00 (978-0-694-51664-3(3)) HarperCollins Pubs.

Much Afraid. Perf. by Jars of Clay. Prod. by Stephen Lipson. 1 cass. 1997. 10.98 (978-0-7601-1489-6(7), C70017) Pub: Brentwood Music. Dist(s): Provident Mus Dist
Christian rock music. Includes: "Overjoyed," "Crazy Times," "Fade to Grey," "Tea & Sympathy," "Five Candles (Your Were There)," "No One Loves Me Like You," "Frail," "Weighed Down," "Portrait of an Apology," "Truce" & "Much Afraid".

Much Depends on Dinner: The Extraordinary History & Mythology, Allure & Obsessions, Perils & Taboos of an Ordinary Meal. unabr. ed. Margaret Visser. Narrated by Suzanne Toren. 11 cass. (Running Time: 15 hrs.). 2000. 97.00 (978-0-7887-4317-7(1), 96198E7) Recorded Bks.
Using the frame-work of a simple meal, Dr. Visser shows us how our food has defined who we are & how we live.

Much Too Promised Land: America's Elusive Search for Arab-Israeli Peace. unabr. ed. Aaron David Miller. Read by William Hughes. (Running Time: 48600 sec.). 2008. 29.95 (978-1-4332-1024-2(X)); 65.95 (978-1-4332-1022-8(3)); audio compact disk 29.95 (978-1-4332-1025-9(8)); audio compact disk 29.95 (978-1-4332-1026-6(6)); audio compact disk & audio compact disk 90.00 (978-1-4332-1023-5(1)) Blckstn Audio.

***Muchacho: A Novel.** unabr. ed. LouAnne Johnson. Narrated by Ozzie Rodriguez. 4 CDs. (Running Time: 4 hrs. 48 mins.). (YA). (gr. 9 up). 2009. audio compact disk 45.00 (978-0-7393-8599-9(2), Listening Lib) Pub: Random Audio Pubg. Dist(s): Random

Muchacho: A Novel. unabr. ed. LouAnne Johnson. Read by Ozzie Rodriguez. (ENG.). (J). (gr. 7). 2009. audio compact disk 28.00 (978-0-7393-8597-5(6), Listening Lib) Pub: Random Audio Pubg. Dist(s): Random

Muchacho Ponga. Phil Lebherz & Phillip Reed. (SPA.). (YA). 2008. audio compact disk 29.95 (978-0-615-21386-6(3)) Epic CA.

Muchacho Que Bateaba Solo Jonrones. unabr. ed. Matt Christopher. 2 cass. (Running Time: 3 hrs.).Tr. of Kid Who Only Hit Homers. (J). (gr. 1-8). 1999. 23.00 (LL 0046, Chivers Child Audio) AudioGO.

Muchacho Que Bateaba Solo Jonrones. unabr. ed. Matt Christopher. 2 vols. (Running Time: 1 hr. 40 mins.). Dramatization.Tr. of Kid Who Only Hit Homers. (J). (gr. 3-5). 1994. pap. bk. 29.00 (978-0-8072-7447-7(X), YA862SP, Listening Lib); 23.00 (978-0-8072-7446-0(1), YA862CX, Listening Lib) Random Audio Pubg.
When Sylvester meets George Baruth, he goes from being a terrible hitter to the boy who only hit homers! But how will he answer some of the difficult questions that go with his new talent?.

Muchacho Que Bateaba Solo Jonrones, Set. unabr. ed. Matt Christopher. 2 cass.Tr. of Kid Who Only Hit Homers. (YA). 1999. 16.98 (FS9-25223) Highsmith.

Mucho Mojo. unabr. ed. Joe R. Lansdale. Read by Phil Gigante. (Running Time: 8 hrs.). (Hap & Leonard Ser.). 2009. 24.99 (978-1-4233-8392-5(3), 9781423383925, Brilliance MP3); 39.97 (978-1-4233-8393-2(1), 9781423383932, Brinc Audio MP3 Lib) Brilliance Audio.

Mucho Mojo. unabr. ed. Joe R. Lansdale. Read by Philippe Gigantes. (Running Time: 8 hrs.). (Hap & Leonard Ser.). 2009. 39.97 (978-1-4233-8395-6(8), 9781423383956, BADLE) Brilliance Audio.

Mucho Mojo. unabr. ed. Joe R. Lansdale. Read by Phil Gigante. (Running Time: 8 hrs.). (Hap & Leonard Ser.). 2009. 24.99 (978-1-4233-8394-9(X), 9781423383949, BAD); audio compact disk 29.99 (978-1-4233-8390-1(7), 9781423383901); audio compact disk 87.97 (978-1-4233-8391-8(5), 9781423383918, BriAudCD Unabrid) Brilliance Audio.

***Mud City.** Deborah Ellis. Narrated by Meera Simhan. 3 CDs. (Running Time: 3 hrs. 5 mins.). (J). (gr. 5-7). 2009. audio compact disk 30.00 (978-0-7393-8583-8(6), Listening Lib) Pub: Random Audio Pubg. Dist(s): Random

Mud Flat Mystery. unabr. ed. James Stevenson. Narrated by John McDonough. 1 cass. (Running Time: 30 mins.). (gr. 1 up). 1998. 10.00 (978-0-7887-2057-4(0), 95410E7) Recorded Bks.
A large cardboard box is delivered to Duncan's house, but he is on vacation. The other residents of Mud Flat are itching to know what's inside & the ensuing mischief is the result of their curiosity.

***Mud Mess.** Melinda Melton Crow. Illus. by Ronnie Rooney. (Truck Buddies Ser.). (ENG.). 2010. audio compact disk 14.60 (978-1-4342-2585-6(2)) CapstoneDig.

Muddle Earth, Book 3, Vol. 3. Paul Stewart & Chris Riddell. Read by Clive Mantle. 3 CDs. (Running Time: 13080 sec.). (J). (gr. 4-7). 2005. audio compact disk 29.95 (978-0-7540-6700-9(9)) AudioGo GBR.

***Muddy Boots & Silk Stockings.** Julia Stoneham. 2010. 61.95 (978-1-4079-0703-1(4)); audio compact disk 79.95 (978-1-4079-0704-8(2)) Pub: Soundings Ltd GBR. Dist(s): Ulverscroft US

Muddy River Playhouse. Jay O'Callahan. Perf. by Jay O'Callahan. 1 CD. (Running Time: 50 mins.). Dramatization. (YA). 2006. audio compact disk 15.00 (978-1-877954-52-8(7)) Pub: Artana Prodns. Dist(s): High Windy Audio
Jay O?Callahan grew up in a neighborhood near Boston called Pill Hill. His creaky old house, a tree that was seven realms high, and an aunt who directed amateur plays with a sherry flask in hand inspired these stories.

Muddy Shoes Candy Heart. Sasa Vazic. Ed. by Anita Virgil. 2005. audio compact disk (978-0-9628567-2-3(X)) Peaks Pr.

Muddy Waters. Judy Astley. 2007. 61.95 (978-0-7531-3826-7(3)); audio compact disk 79.95 (978-0-7531-2809-1(8)) Pub: ISIS Audio GBR. Dist(s): Ulverscroft US

Muddy Waters Story. Keith Rodway. (ENG.). 2001. audio compact disk 24.95 (978-1-84240-079-1(7)) Pub: Chrome Dreams GBR. Dist(s): IPG Chicago

***Mudhouse Sabbath.** unabr. ed. Lauren Winner. Narrated by Kate Reading. (ENG.). 2006. 10.98 (978-1-59644-341-9(3), Hovel Audio) christianaud.

Mudhouse Sabbath. unabr. ed. Lauren F. Winner. 3 CDs. (Running Time: 2 hrs. 48 mins. 0 sec.). (ENG.). 2006. audio compact disk 18.98 (978-1-59644-340-2(5), Hovel Audio) christianaud.
Lauren Winner shares the spiritual practices she has adopted in her quest to reconcile Judaism and Christianity.Despite her conversion from Orthodox Judaism to Christianity, Lauren Winner finds that her life is still shaped by the spiritual essences of Judaism - rich traditions and religious practices that she can't leave behind. In Mudhouse Sabbath, Winner illuminates eleven spiritual practices that can transform the way we view the world, and God. Whether discussing her own prayer life, the spirituality of candle-lighting, or the differences between the Jewish Sabbath and a Sunday spent at the Mudhouse, her favorite coffee shop, Winner writes with appealing honesty and rare insight.

Muenke Syndrome - A Bibliography & Dictionary for Physicians, Patients, & Genome Researchers. Compiled by Icon Group International, Inc. Staff. 2007. ring bd. 28.95 (978-0-497-11377-3(5)) Icon Grp.

Muerto de Amor see Poesia y Drama de Garcia Lorca

Muestra y Cuentra Entre Dinosaurios. Steck-Vaughn Staff. 1 cass. (Running Time: 1 hr. 30 min.). (SPA.). 1999. (978-0-7398-0751-4(X)) SteckVau.

Muezzin's Call & Islamic Chants audio CD. 1 CD. (ARA.). 2005. audio compact disk 18.95 (978-1-57970-235-9(X), C11122D) J Norton Pubs.

Mufari's Beautiful Daughters. 2004. pap. bk. 14.95 (978-1-55592-052-4(7)) Weston Woods.

Mufaro's Beautiful Daughters. 1 Read-Along cass. (J). (gr. k-5). 1990. 8.95 (978-0-89719-985-8(5), 08#24.95) Weston Woods.
Two daughters are tested to see who is worthy to marry the king.

Mufaro's Beautiful Daughters. 2004. pap. bk. 32.75 (978-1-55592-280-1(5)); 8.95 (978-0-7882-0056-4(9)); cass. & flmstrp 30.00 (978-0-89719-592-8(2)) Weston Woods.

Mufaro's Beautiful Daughters. John Steptoe. Illus. by John Steptoe. 22 vols. (Running Time: 37 mins.).Tr. of Las Bellas Hijas De Mufaro. 2001. pap. bk. 33.95 (978-1-59112-132-9(9)); 9.95 (978-0-87499-654-8(6)); audio compact disk 12.95 (978-1-59112-317-0(8)) Live Oak Media.

Mufaro's Beautiful Daughters. John Steptoe. Illus. by John Steptoe. 11 vols. (Running Time: 17 mins.).Tr. of Las Bellas Hijas De Mufaro. (J). (ps-3). 2001. bk. 25.95 (978-0-87499-656-2(2)); pap. bk. 33.95 (978-0-87499-657-9(0)) Live Oak Media.

Mufaro's Beautiful Daughters. John L. Steptoe. Read by Robin Miles. 11 vols. (Running Time: 17 mins.). (Live Oak Readalong Ser.). (J). (ps-4). 2001. pap. bk. 16.95 (978-0-87499-655-5(4)) Pub: Live Oak Media. Dist(s): AudioGO
Modern fable of pride going before a fall when two sisters, one spiteful, one considerate, vie to be the young king's bride.

Mufaro's Beautiful Daughters. John L. Steptoe. 1 cass., 5 bks. (Running Time: 15 min.). (J). pap. bk. 32.75 Weston Woods.
Two daughters are tested to see who is worthy to marry the king.

Mufaro's Beautiful Daughters. John L. Steptoe. 1 cass. (Running Time: 15 min.). (J). (gr. k-5). pap. bk. 12.95 Weston Woods.

Mufaro's Beautiful Daughters. John L. Steptoe. 1 Read-Along cass. (Running Time: 14 min.). (J). (gr. k-5). 1990. bk. 24.95 (978-1-56008-002-2(7), HRA334) Weston Woods.

Mufaro's Beautiful Daughters: An African Tale see Bellas Hijas de Mufaro

Mugged Pug. unabr. ed. Darrel and Sally Odgers. Read by Alan King. (Running Time: 50 mins.). (Jack Russell: Dog Detective Ser.). (J). 2007. audio compact disk 39.95 (978-1-74093-826-6(7)) Pub: Bolinda Pubng AUS. Dist(s): Bolinda Pub Inc

Mugger. unabr. ed. Ed McBain, pseud. Read by Paul Shay. 6 cass. (Running Time: 6 hrs.). (87th Precinct Ser.: Bk. 2). 1990. 36.00 (978-0-7366-1721-5(3), 2562) Books on Tape.
This mugger was special. He preyed on women. He waited in the darkness, then clubbed his victims. As the reeled with pain & fear, he bowed & said, "Clifford thanks you, madam." The cops in the 87th Precinct were not amused. They wanted the mugger badly. Especially after he put one victim in the hospital...& the next one in the morgue. Patrolman Bert Kling has a personal reason to go after her murderer...a reason that became a burning obsession & an easy way for a cop to get killed.

Muggie Maggie. Beverly Cleary. Read by Kate Forbes. 1 cass. (Running Time: 45 mins.). (J). 2000. pap. bk. & stu. ed. 24.24 (978-0-7887-4344-3(9), 41138) Recorded Bks.
Maggie is worried. In her first week of third grade, her class is already learning to write cursive with all those difficult loops & lines. Maybe she will just refuse to learn it.

Muggie Maggie. Beverly Cleary. Read by Kate Forbes. 1 cass. (Running Time: 45 mins.). (J). 2000. stu. ed. 81.70 (978-0-7887-4444-0(5), 47135) Recorded Bks.

***Muggie Maggie.** unabr. ed. Beverly Cleary. Read by Kathleen Mcinerney. (ENG.). 2009. (978-0-06-180571-4(8)); (978-0-06-174469-3(7)) HarperCollins Pubs.

Muggie Maggie. unabr. ed. Beverly Cleary. Narrated by Kate Forbes. 1 cass. (Running Time: 45 mins.). (gr. 2 up). 2000. 11.00 (978-0-7887-4234-7(5), 96013E7) Recorded Bks.

Muhammad: A Prophet for Our Time. Karen Armstrong. 2007. audio compact disk 29.99 (978-1-4281-3639-7(8)) Recorded Bks.

Muhammad: A Prophet for Our Time. unabr. ed. Karen Armstrong. 6 CDs. (Running Time: 7 hrs. 15 mins.). 2007. audio compact disk 72.75 (978-1-4281-3642-7(8)); 51.75 (978-1-4281-3640-3(1)) Recorded Bks.
A former Roman Catholic nun and winner of a Muslim Public Affairs Council Media Award, Karen Armstrong shows how Muhammad's life can teach us a great deal about our world.More is known about Muhammad than any other major religion founder, yet he remains mysterious. Born in 570 CE, he spent six decades spreading his message of peace and compassion. Yet for many people today, their knowledge of Muhammad is rife with misconceptions and

misinformation, often fueled by bigotry. Armstrong sets the record straight, shattering the myth that Islam is a religion of cruelty and violence. One of the world's leading religious experts, Armstrong is a deeply respected voice in the continuous struggle for interfaith understanding. Her cogent assessment of Muhammad's genius and insightful summary of his authentic beliefs are priceless in this modern world troubled by religious extremism and intolerance.

***Muhammad: A Story of the Last Prophet.** unabr. ed. Deepak Chopra. 6 CDs. (Running Time: 7 hrs. 0 mins. 0 sec.). (ENG.). 2010. audio compact disk 29.95 (978-1-60283-925-0(5)) Pub: AudioGO. Dist(s): Perseus Dist

Muhammad: The Truth Exposed: the Prophet of Islam. adpt. ed. Voice by Wajahat Sayeed. Orig. Title: Islam & Modern Science. 2006. audio compact disk 19.99 (978-0-9773009-1-4(9)) Book of Sings.

Muhammad Ali: Beyond the Myth. Created by Soundworks. 1 CD. (Running Time: 2689 sec.). 1999. audio compact disk 15.95 (978-1-885959-57-7(5)) Jerden Recs.
Hear Ali, Joe Frazier & many more speak about Ali.

Muhammad Ali: His Life & Times. unabr. ed. Thomas Hauser. Read by Michael Prichard. 14 cass. (Running Time: 21 hrs.). 1992. 112.00 (978-0-7366-2187-8(3), 2982) Books on Tape.
Ali created his own image - he worked the media better than Barnam. Behind the mask is the man revealed here in the words of more than 200 people who have known him best.

Muhammad & His Heirs; The Rise & Fall of the Caliphate. unabr. ed. Julian C. Hollick. 1 cass. (Running Time: 1 hr.). (World of Islam Ser.). 1985. 15.00 (978-1-56709-054-3(0), 1027) Indep Broadcast.
Side A: This program examines the life & character of Muhammad, the founder of Islam, as well as the immediate succession & the origins of the Sunni-Shi's split within the Islamic world. Side B: This program explores the extraordinary rise of the Islamic Caliphate empire & its decay, ending in the abolition of the Caliphate by Kemal Ataturk in 1924.

Mujeres dificiles, hombres Complicados. Cesar Lozano.Tr. of Difficult woman, complicated Woman. (SPA.). 2009. audio compact disk 17.00 (978-1-935405-45-0(4)) Hombre Nuevo.

Mujeres en Conquista. Carlos Cuauhtemoc Sanchez. audio compact disk 15.95 (978-968-7277-65-3(3)) Pub: EdSelect MEX. Dist(s): Giron Bks

Mukiwa: A White Boy in Africa. unabr. collector's ed. Peter Godwin. Read by David Case. 10 cass. (Running Time: 15 hrs.). 1998. 80.00 (978-0-7366-4038-1(X), 4537) Books on Tape.
A white Rhodesian recounts his experience growing up in the country that became Zimbabwe.

Mulan. 1 cass. (Running Time: 1 hr. 30 min.). (Disney Ser.). (J). 9.58 Soundtrack. (DISN 60631); audio compact disk 14.38 (JEWEL BOX, SOUNDTRACK) NewSound.
A young Chinese girl disguises herself as a warrior to save her aged father from going to war against the invading Huns.

Mulan. 1 cass. (Running Time: 1 hr.). (Read & Sing Alongs Ser.). (J). bk. 12.99 (978-0-7634-0407-9(1)); 13.99 Norelco. (978-0-7634-0410-9(1)); audio compact disk 22.99 (978-0-7634-0413-0(6)) W Disney Records.

Mulan. 1 cass. (Running Time: 1 hr.). (J). (ps-3). 1998. 13.99 (978-0-7634-0411-6(X)); audio compact disk 22.99 (978-0-7634-0412-3(8)) W Disney Records.

Mulan. Disney Staff. 1 cass. (Read-Along Ser.). (J). (ps-3). 1998. bk. 7.99 (978-0-7634-0406-2(3)) W Disney Records.

Mulan. Retold by Janet Hardy-Gould. (Dominoes Ser.). 2004. 12.95 (978-0-19-424370-4(2)) OUP.

Mulan (Read-Along) 1 cass. (Disney Ser.). (J). bk. 6.38 Blisterpack. (DISN 60306) NewSound.

Mulatto see Poetry & Reflections

Mulberry Lane. Elvi Rhodes. 12 CDs. (Sound Ser.). 2003. audio compact disk 99.95 (978-1-84283-180-9(1)) Pub: UlverLrgPrint GBR. Dist(s): Ulverscroft US

Mulberry Lane. unabr. ed. Elvi Rhodes. Read by Gordon Griffin. 12 cass. (Running Time: 13 hrs.). (Sound Ser.). 2002. 94.95 (978-1-84283-103-8(8)) Pub: UlverLrgPrint GBR. Dist(s): Ulverscroft US
The inhabitants of quiet, tree-lined Mulberry Lane take a keen interest in their neighborhood. So when number fifteen comes onto the market, they naturally hope for a pleasant family which will fit in nicely. Instead they get a half-way house for young offenders - or, as some of the locals call them, "a gang of ex-convicts". Brian, the warden of this house, faces an uphill struggle as he tries to persuade his new neighbors to accept the scheme. He wants to be part of the community - in particular, he wants to get to know Karen, a single mother struggling to bring up her two young children. Yet however friendly Karen may become, there are others who will scupper the scheme at all costs.

Mulberry Tree. abr. ed. Jude Deveraux. Read by Karen Ziemba. 2004. 15.95 (978-0-7435-4297-5(5)) Pub: S&S Audio. Dist(s): S and S Inc

Mulberry Tree. unabr. ed. Jude Deveraux. Read by Melissa Hughes. 9 vols. (Running Time: 13 hrs. 30 min.). 2002. bk. 79.95 (978-0-7927-2702-6(9), CSL 488, Chivers Sound Lib); audio compact disk 94.95 (978-0-7927-2727-9(4), SLD 488, Chivers Sound Lib) AudioGO.
Lillian Manville, the devoted wife of business titan Jimmie Manville, had always taken her life's blessings for granted - until Jimmie's death turned everything upside down. She is bewildered to learn that Jimmie has willed her nothing but a rundown farmhouse of his childhood and left his fortune to his greedy siblings. All she has now is a house she's never seen - and a cryptic note about a mysterious scandal that had haunted Jimmie ever since boyhood.

Mulch. unabr. ed. Ann Ripley. Read by Lynda Evans. 6 cass. (Running Time: 8 hrs.). (Gardening Mystery Ser.: Bk. 1). 2001. 39.95 (978-1-55686-871-9(5)) Books in Motion.
Organic gardener Louise Eldridge is filling in the low spots of her garden with grass collected from her neighborhood. Body parts start turning up in the grass bags. Louise investigates.

Mule: 11 Samuel 18:9, 705. Ed Young. 1989. 4.95 (978-0-7417-1705-4(0), 705) Win Walk.

***Mules & Men.** abr. ed. Zora Neale Hurston. Read by Ruby Dee. (ENG.). 2005. (978-0-06-088669-1(2), Harper Audio); (978-0-06-088670-7(6), Harper Audio) HarperCollins Pubs.

Muletrain to Maggody. Joan Hess. Narrated by C. J. Critt. 8 cass. (Running Time: 11 hrs.). (Arly Hanks Mystery Ser.). 2004. 79.75 (978-0-7887-9494-0(9)); audio compact disk 99.75 (978-1-4025-7539-6(4)) Recorded Bks.

Mulga Bill's Bicycle. 2004. 8.95 (978-1-56008-978-0(4)); 8.95 (978-0-7882-0297-1(9)); cass. & flmstrp 30.00 (978-1-56008-724-3(2)) Weston Woods.

Mulholland Falls. abr. ed. Robert Tine. Read by Kyle Chandler. 2 cass. (Running Time: 3 hrs.). 1996. 17.00 (978-1-56876-056-8(6)) Soundlines Ent.
A powerful crime drama about four cops who formed an elite unit on the Los Angeles Police Force in the 1950's.

Muliebrity: Qualities of a Woman. Read by Joni Arredia. 3 cass. (Running Time: 3 hr. 30 mins.). 17.95 (978-0-9653203-4-4(0)) Perc Pub.

***Mullah's Storm.** unabr. ed. Thomas W. Young. Read by Scott Brick. 7 CDs. (Running Time: 8 hrs.). 2010. audio compact disk 29.95 (978-0-14-242884-9(1), PengAudBks) Penguin Grp USA.

***Mulligan: A Parable of Second Chances.** Wally Armstrong & Ken Blanchard. (Running Time: 2 hrs. 52 mins. 49 sec.). (ENG.). 2010. 16.99 (978-0-310-59884-8(2)) Zondervan.

Multi-ethnic Stories. Short Stories. Based on a story by Linda Umberg. 1. (Running Time: 35). Orig. Title: CHOCOLATE & other Multicultural Stories. (SPA.). (J). 2004. audio compact disk 10.95 (978-1-892306-07-4(7)) Cantemos-bilingual.
Book and CD contains in both Spanish and English:The Origin of the Chinese Zodiac, Anative American Tale The Origin of Death, African Tale The Distant Fire, Indian Blind Men and the Elephant, a listening game and a Mexican song including the Origin of Chocolate.

Multi-Platinum Marriage: Going from Surviving to Thriving. Elia Gourgouris. 2008. audio compact disk 16.95 (978-1-59038-938-6(7)) Deseret Bk.

***Multi-Site Church Revolution: Being One Church in Many Locations.** unabr. ed. Zondervan. (Running Time: 6 hrs. 10 mins. 0 sec.). (Leadership Network Innovation Ser.). (ENG.). 2009. 16.99 (978-0-310-30471-5(7)) Zondervan.

Multi-Site Church Roadtrip: Exploring the New Normal. unabr. ed. Geoff Surratt et al. (Running Time: 7 hrs. 12 mins. 0 sec.). (Leadership Network Innovation Ser.). (ENG.). 2009. 18.99 (978-0-310-32337-2(1)) Zondervan.

Multi-Tasking: Program from the Award Winning Public Radio Series. Interview. Hosted by Peter Kramer. Comment by Howard Bloom. 1 CD. (Running Time: 1hr). 2005. audio compact disk 21.95 (978-1-932479-68-3(6), LCM 372) Lichtenstein Creat.
"To do two things at once - is to do neither," Roman philosopher Publilius Syrus wrote in 100 A.D., and modern science may just be proving him right. Turns out that our capacity to multitask is far more limited than most of us think, and that in some situations, this misunderstanding can be downright dangerous. We?ll also visit the control tower of a busy airport and talk to air traffic controllers who say that they?re not really multitasking at all, and talk to orchestral conductors about the challenge of directing the polymetric compositions of Charles Ives. With commentary by sociobiologist Howard Bloom.

Multi-Trauma Victim. unabr. ed. Instructed by JoAnn C. Tess-Piburn & Stephen Murphy. 4 cass. (Running Time: 7 hrs.). 1990. pap. bk. 79.00 (HT64) Ctr Hlth Educ.
Saving lives is the heart of nursing. If you are of the critical care breed, you know that it takes skills that you can recall! Learn the subtle signs of shock, head, spine, chest & abdominal trauma. Soft bound book included.

Multi-Voice Testimony. National Shorthand Reporters Association. 9.00 T-1. (CT-44) Natl Ct Report.
Side one, six five-minute selections of three-& four-voice testimony, 170 wpm; side two, six five-minute selections of three-& four-voice testimony, 180 wpm.

Multicultura; Lullabies Around the World: 10 Different Languages with English Translations. Prod. by Sara Jordan. Arranged by Sara Jordan. Illus. by Glen Wyand. 1 cass. (Running Time: 57 min. 38 secs.). (GER, RUS, SPA, YID & FRE.). (J). (ps-2). 1996. pap. bk. 14.95 (978-1-895523-80-5(X), JMP115K) Jordan Music.
Award winner of both a Parents' Choice Silver Award and Directors' Choice Award. Eleven lullabies sung by singers, each in his/her native tongue and then sung in English. Includes Italian, Spanish, French, Russian, Polish, Mandarin and Yiddish lullabies. Multicultural activities are also included in the accompanying lyrics book.

Multicultural Children's Songs. Perf. by Ella Jenkins. 1 cass. (Running Time: 46 min.). (J). (ps-4). 1995. (0-9307-45050-9307-45045-2-9); audio compact disk (0-9307-45045-2-9) Smithsonian Folkways.
Includes "In Trinidad," "Dance Tunes from Many Lands," "Thank You in Many Languages" & more.

Multicultural Collection. G. Soto et al. Illus. by S. Byrd. 66 vols. (Running Time: 57 mins.). 2003. pap. bk. 91.95 (978-0-87499-673-9(2)) Live Oak Media.

Multicultural Folk Dance Treasure Chest, 1. Lane. 2007. DVD 54.95 (978-0-7360-7143-7(1)) HumanKinUSA.

Multicultural Folk Dance Treasure Chest, 2. Lane. 2007. DVD 54.95 (978-0-7360-7144-4(X)) HumanKinUSA.

***Multicultural Ministry: Finding Your Church's Unique Rhythm.** Zondervan. (Running Time: 5 hrs. 27 mins. 47 sec.). (ENG.). 2010. 9.99 (978-0-310-86935-1(8)) Zondervan.

Multicultural Organ Donation. 1 cass. (Care Cassettes Ser.: Vol. 19, No. 7). 1993. 10.80 Assn Prof Chaplains.

Multicultural Rhythm Stick Fun. Georgiana Stewart. 1 CD. (Running Time: 1 hr.). (J). 2001. pap. bk. 14.95 (KIM9128CD) Kimbo Educ.
Children won't be able to resist tapping their rhythm sticks to this colorful rainbow of rhythms. Title selections are: Ambos a Dos (Puerto Rico), Calypso (Caribbean), Piper Piper (Ireland), Zum Gali Gali (Israel), Children's Song (Greece), Kourilengay (West Africa), La Cucaracha (Mexico), Show Ha Mo (China), Haru Ga Kita (Japan), Tarantella (Italy) & much more! Includes guide.

Multicultural Rhythm Stick Fun. Georgiana Stewart. 1 cass. (Running Time: 1 hr.). (J). (ps-2). 2001. pap. bk. 11.95 (KIM 9128) Kimbo Educ.

Multicultural Song Collection, 4 Pack. (Metro Reading Program Ser.). (J). (gr. k). 1999. 29.95 (978-1-58120-087-4(0)) Metro Teaching.

Multicultural Tales to Tell, Set. Pleasant DeSpain. 2 pieces. (Running Time: 1 hr. 44 mins.). (American Storytelling Ser.). 1997. 18.00 (978-0-87483-345-4(0), AH3450) Pub: August Hse. Dist(s): Natl Bk Netwk
These brief tales come from cultures the world over & emphasize our interconnectedness - not our differences with other peoples. They come from Africa, Korea, Denmark, Guatemala, Mexico, Holland, Fiji, China, Germany, Tibet, & from native Americans.

Multicultural Writers Guide. Greta Huttanus & Mechelle Avey. 1 cass. (Running Time: 45 mins.). (Academe Presents Ser.). 2008. 10.00 (978-1-930758-00-1(6)) Yeva Corp.
Quarterly newsletter for business executives.

Multiculturalism & the Anti-Conceptual Mentality. Peter Schwartz. 1 cass. (Running Time: 1 hr. 30 min.). 1995. 12.95 (978-1-56114-502-7(5), HS13C) Second Renaissance.
Multiculturalism as a return to primitivism; politically & epistemologically.

Multidimensional Aspects of the Self. unabr. ed. Robert A. Monroe. Read by Robert A. Monroe. (Running Time: 45 min.). (Explorer Ser.). 1983. 12.95 (978-1-56113-003-0(6), 4) Monroe Institute.
How thought forms limit us.

Multidimensional Interpretation. Constance Mayer. 1 cass. 8.95 (225) Am Fed Astrologers.
Improve diagnostic skills & synthesis of chart components.

Multidimensional Model of Consciousness. Willard Johnson. 1 cass. 9.00 (A0199-87) Sound Photosyn.
ICSS '87, Ruth Inge Heinze & Jeurgen Kremer on tape.

Multidrug Resistant Tuberculosis Manual: Introductory but Comprehensive OSHA (Occupational Safety & Health) Training for the Managers & Employees in a Worker Safety Program, Particularly for Infection Control & Infectious Disease Training in Healthcare Organizations & Hospitals & Those Working with TB (Tuberculosis) & AIDS, Including Doctors, Nurses, & Allied Health Personnel. Daniel Farb. 2003. audio compact disk 59.95 (978-1-932634-85-3(1)) Pub: UnivofHealth. Dist(s): AtlasBooks

Multiemployer Pension Plans. 1987. bk. 125.00; 65.00 PA Bar Inst.

Multimedia Stereo Speakers with volume Control. (J). 2007. 29.95 (978-1-56911-340-0(8)) Lming Res.

Multiple & Opposing Theories of the Self As Seen Through Analytical Psychology: Toward a Unified Field Theory. Read by Diane Martin. 3 cass. (Running Time: 4 hrs.). 1990. 24.95 Set. (978-0-7822-0160-4(1), 420) C G Jung IL.

***Multiple Blessings: Surviving to Thriving with Twins & Sextuplets.** unabr. ed. Jon and Kate Gosselin & Beth Carson. (Running Time: 4 hrs. 54 mins. 0 sec.). (ENG.). 2009. 19.99 (978-0-310-32226-9(X)) Zondervan.

Multiple Blessings: Surviving to Thriving with Twins & Sextuplets. unabr. ed. Jon Gosselin et al. Read by Jon Gosselin & Kate Gosselin. (Running Time: 5 hrs. 0 mins. 0 sec.). (ENG.). 2009. audio compact disk 32.99 (978-0-310-32225-2(1)) Zondervan.

Multiple Cat. unabr. ed. Marian Babson. Read by Diana Bishop. 6 cass. (Running Time: 9 hrs.). 2000. 54.95 (978-0-7540-0432-5(5), CAB 1855) Pub: Chivers Audio Bks GBR. Dist(s): AudioGO
Annabel is mistaken for a top interior designer & invited to redecorate a reclusive millionaire's London flat. Hoping that her entry into Arthur Arbuthnot's home will provide her with tidbits for the gossip columns, Annabel finds out that the only thing he cares about is Sally, a stray cat! When Arthur is found dead, all hell breaks out, especially since the main beneficiary of his will is Sally.

Multiple Choice. unabr. ed. Claire Cook. (Running Time: 23400 sec.). 2007. audio compact disk 45.00 (978-1-4332-0728-0(1)) Blckstn Audio.

Multiple Choice. unabr. ed. Claire Cook. Read by Carrington MacDuffie. (Running Time: 23400 sec.). 2007. 44.95 (978-1-4332-0727-3(3)); audio compact disk 29.95 (978-1-4332-0729-7(X)) Blckstn Audio.

Multiple Endocrine Neoplasia - A Bibliography & Dictionary for Physicians, Patients, & Genome Researchers. Compiled by Icon Group International, Inc. Staff. 2007. ring bd. 28.95 (978-0-497-11378-0(3)) Icon Grp.

Multiple Percussion Book: Concepts for a Musical Performance. Nick Petrella. Contrib. by John Allemeier. 2004. audio compact disk 24.95 (978-0-8258-4169-9(0)) Fischer Inc NY.

Multiple Personality Disorder: Program from the Award Winning Public Radio Series. Hosted by Fred Goodwin. Comment by John Hockenberry. Contrib. by Frank Putnam et al. 1 cass. (Running Time: 1 hr.). (Infinite Mind Ser.). 1998. audio compact disk 21.95 (978-1-888064-41-4(2), LCM 14) Lichtenstein Creat.
A controversial diagnosis which some doctors do not believe exists. But other experts say this disorder may give us clues about the ability of the brain to rewire itself after injury. We talk to top researchers and also hear from people diagnosed with MPD about the fascinating details of their "reintegration.".

Multiple Sclerosis. Steven Gurgevich. (ENG.). 2005. audio compact disk 19.95 (978-1-932170-34-4(0), HWH) Tranceformation.

Multiple Sclerosis: A Positive Approach. Matthew Manning. Music by Paul Fitzgerald & Mark Flanagan. 1 cass. 11.95 (MM-118) White Dove NM.
This tape does not claim to cure MS. By developing positive attitudes, generating a positive self-image, relaxing & focusing on what can be achieved, you may make the disease easier to live with, & may alleviate some of the symptoms. The tape looks at the diets of cultures that do not have MS. Side Two is a relaxation & visualization exercise to help face fears of MS & change them to hope.

Multiple Sclerosis: Is Water Its Cure? Interview with F. Batmanghelidj & Bob Butts. 1 cass. (Running Time: 1 hr. 8 min.). 10.00 Global Hlth.
Hear from an MS sufferer who used Dr. Batmanghelidj's program to put an end to his debilitating symptoms.

Multiple Sclerosis: Program from the Award Winning Public Radio Series. Interview. Hosted by Fred Goodwin. 1 CD. (Running Time: 1 hr). (Infinite Mind Ser.). 2002. audio compact disk 21.95 (978-1-888064-86-5(2), LCM 212) Lichtenstein Creat.
In this hour, we explore the chronic neurological disease Multiple Sclerosis. Guests include Dr. Randall Schapiro, founder and director of the Fairview Multiple Sclerosis Center and Minneapolis Clinic Multiple Sclerosis Program; Dr. Patricia O'Looney, director of biomedical research programs at the National Multiple Sclerosis Society; Barbara Paley-Israel, a writer who was diagnosed with MS in 1986 and has become an advocate for people with the disease; social worker Deborah Miller, Director of Comprehensive Care at the Mellen Center for MS Treatment and Research, part of The Cleveland Clinic; TONY award-winning director and playwright Emily Mann; and special commentator Zoe Koplowitz, author of Winning Spirit: Life Lessons Learned in Last Place. We also include an update on developments with the MS drug Tysabri.

Multiple Streams of Income: How to Generate a Lifetime of Unlimited Wealth. Robert G. Allen. 6 cass. (Running Time: 6 hrs.). 1996. bk. 59.95 (13760AC) Nightingale-Conant.
This remarkable program will enable you to easily double, triple, even quadruple your income. It will also help you achieve financial independence & peace of mind.

Multiple Streams of Income: How to Generate a Lifetime of Unlimited Wealth. unabr. abr. ed. Robert G. Allen. Read by Robert G. Allen. 8 CDs. (Running Time: 90 hrs. 0 mins. 0 sec.). (ENG., 2002. audio compact disk 39.95 (978-0-7435-2040-9(8), Nightgale) Pub: S&S Audio. Dist(s): S and S Inc
When you create multiple streams of income, you are forming a powerful tide of prosperity that can provide a lifetime of fortune and freedom. You won't only be helping yourself - friends and family will also prosper from your good fortune.

Multiple Tasks - Split Ear. 1 cass. (Running Time: 1 hr.). 2000. 15.95 Prof Pride.
Most popular, info from directions. Extremely difficult. Used in hiring. Specify Adam boy Practice or Alpha Bravo (International).

Multiple Uses: Positive Solutions, Problem Solutions, Relaxation & Goal Achievements. Russell E. Mason. 1 cass. 1975. pap. bk. 60.00 (978-0-89533-008-6(3)) F I Comm.

work with the MPC, how have these revisions worked in practice? Have they provided an orderly process for zoning & land development administration & review or a sometimes confusing maze of requirements & omissions, resulting in excessive cost & delay.

Municipalities Planning Code. 1989. 45.00 (AC-492) PA Bar Inst.

Muppet Hits: Take Two. 1 cass. (J). Norelco incl. lyric bk. (978-1-884676-00-0(6)); Blister with CD incl. lyric bk. (978-1-884676-03-1(0)); (978-1-884676-01-7(4)) J Henson Recs. *Includes lyric book.*

Muppets from Space. Perf. by Special Sauce et al. Music by George Clinton. 1 cass. (Running Time: 35 min.). (J). 1999. 9.98 (Sony Wonder); audio compact disk 13.98 (Sony Wonder) Sony Music Ent. *The Dust Brothers team up with Seal's younger brother Jeymes to give Earth, Wind & Fire's "Shining Star" a whole new groove while George Clinton joins up & coming Muppet Pepe for a new twist on his Parliament classic "Flashlight" called "Spaceflight".*

Muqtada Al-Sadr, the Shia Revival, & the Struggle for Iraq. unabr. ed. Patrick Cockburn. Read by John Lee. (Running Time: 9 hrs. 0 mins. 0 sec.). (ENG.). 2008. audio compact disk 24.99 (978-1-4001-5658-0(0)); audio compact disk 34.99 (978-1-4001-0658-5(3)) Pub: Tantor Media. Dist(s): IngramPubServ

Muqtada: Muqtada-Al-Sadr, the Shia Revival, & the Struggle for Iraq. unabr. ed. Patrick Cockburn. (Running Time: 9 hrs. 0 mins. 0 sec.). (ENG.). 2008. audio compact disk 69.99 (978-1-4001-3658-2(X)) Pub: Tantor Media. Dist(s): IngramPubServ

mural de Frutas. (Saludos Ser.: Vol. 1). (SPA.). (gr. 3-5). 10.00 (978-0-7635-1800-4(X)) Rigby Educ.

Mural of Fruit. (Greetings Ser.: Vol. 1). (gr. 3-5). 10.00 (978-0-7635-1793-9(3)) Rigby Educ.

Murder, a Mystery, & a Marriage. unabr. abr. ed. Mark Twain & Garrison Keillor. Read by Roy Blount, Jr. & Garrison Keillor. Intro. by Roy Blount, Jr. 2 CDs. (Running Time: 2 hrs.). 2001. audio compact disk 22.95 (978-1-56511-506-4(6), 1565115066) Pub: HighBridge. Dist(s): Workman Pub

Murder among Us: A Mitchell & Markby Mystery. Ann Granger. Narrated by Judith Boyd. 7 cass. (Running Time: 9 hrs. 45 mins.). 63.00 (978-1-84197-290-9(8)); audio compact disk 93.00 (978-1-4025-1543-9(X)) Recorded Bks.

Murder & Madness. unabr. collector's ed. Donald T. Lunde. Read by Michael Prichard. 7 cass. (Running Time: 7 hrs.). (Portable Stanford Ser.). 1984. 42.00 (978-0-7366-0971-5(7), 1913) Books on Tape. *An examination of causes behind murder in the U.S. with comparative looks at violence in other countries.*

Murder & Mint Tea. unabr. ed. Janet Lane Walters. Read by Christine Clayburg. 4 cass. (Running Time: 5 hrs. 30 min.). 2001. 26.95 (978-1-58116-040-6(2)) Books in Motion. *Retired Nurse Katherine Miller shares the top floor of her home with her cat, and rents out the bottom floor. But trouble arises when bold, manipulative, and beautiful Rachel moves in, upsetting household after household.*

Murder & Obsession: New Original Stories. collector's unabr. ed. Read by Geoffrey Howard. Ed. by Otto Penzler. 11 CDs. (Running Time: 11 hrs.). 1999. 72.00 (978-0-7366-5183-7(7), 4978) Books on Tape. *From lethal spikes to fatal kisses, from mad dogs to battle crazed Englishmen, here indeed is Murder & Obsession, a star-studded collection of previously unpublished short mysteries.*

Murder & Obsession: New Original Stories. collector's unabr. ed. Otto Penzler. Read by Geoffrey Howard. 9 cass. (Running Time: 13 hrs. 30 min.). 1999. 36.00 (978-0-7366-4571-3(3), 4978) Books on Tape.

Murder & Obsession: New Original Stories. unabr. ed. Read by Geoffrey Howard. Ed. by Otto Penzler. 5 CDs. (Running Time: 6 hrs.). 2001. audio compact disk 19.95 (978-0-7366-5737-2(1)) Books on Tape. *A star-studded collection of previously unpublished short mysteries on the compelling subject of obsessions from 15 bestselling authors.*

Murder & Obsession: New Original Stories. unabr. ed. Ed. by Otto Penzler. 5 CDs. (Running Time: 6 hrs.). 2001. audio compact disk 19.95 Books on Tape. *From lethal spikes to fatal kisses, from mad dogs to battle crazed Englishmen, here indeed is Murder & Obsession, a star-studded collection of previously unpublished short mysteries.*

Murder & Obsession Vol. 1: New Original Stories. unabr. ed. Read by Geoffrey Howard. Ed. by Otto Penzler. 4 cass. (Running Time: 6 hrs.). 2001. 17.95 (978-0-7366-5733-4(9)); audio compact disk 19.95 (978-0-7366-5736-5(3)) Books on Tape.

Murder & Obsession Vol. 2: New Original Stories. unabr. ed. Read by Geoffrey Howard. Ed. by Otto Penzler. 4 cass. (Running Time: 6 hrs.). 2001. 17.95 (978-0-7366-5734-1(7)) Books on Tape. *A star-studded collection of previously unpublished short mysteries on the compelling subject of obsessions from 15 bestselling authors.*

Murder & Obsession Vol. 2: New Original Stories. unabr. ed. Read by Geoffrey Howard. Ed. by Otto Penzler. 4 cass. (Running Time: 6 hrs.). 2000. 24.95 (978-0-7366-4938-4(7)) Books on Tape.

Murder & Obsession Vol. 2: New Original Stories. unabr. ed. Read by Geoffrey Howard. Ed. by Otto Penzler. 4 cass. (Running Time: 6 hrs.). 2000. 24.95 (978-0-7366-4939-1(5)) Books on Tape.

Murder & the First Lady, unabr. ed. Elliott Roosevelt. Narrated by Frank Muller. 4 cass. (Running Time: 5 hrs. 30 mins.). (Eleanor Roosevelt Mystery Ser.: No. 1). 1986. 35.00 (978-1-55690-357-1(X), 86130E7) Recorded Bks. *While FDR mixes martinis for Missy LeHand & Harry Hopkins worries about the war that summer of '39, Mrs. Roosevelt has more pressing problems on hand: how to catch a murderer. The victim is the son of a congressman & the accused, the First Lady's own secretary.*

Murder & the Golden Goblet. Amy Myers. 2008. 61.95 (978-1-84559-924-9(1)); audio compact disk 79.95 (978-1-84559-925-6(X)) Pub: Soundings Ltd GBR. Dist(s): Ulverscroft US

Murder & the Monalet Ruby. unabr. ed. Loretta Jackson & Vickie Britton. Read by Stephanie Brush. 8 cass. (Running Time: 9 hrs. 27 min.). (Ardis Cole Ser.). 2001. 49.95 (978-1-55686-952-5(5)) Books in Motion. *While handling a bequest of pioneer and Sioux artifacts in South Dakota, Ardis Cole inherits a load of trouble she hadn't expected - such as a stolen ruby, an heir who has disappeared, and a skeleton in the cellar!.*

Murder Artist. abr. ed. John Case. Read by Dick Hill. (Running Time: 6 hrs.). 2004. audio compact disk 74.25 (978-1-59355-446-0(X), 159355446X, BACDLib Ed) Brilliance Audio.

Murder Artist. unabr. ed. John Case. Read by Dick Hill. (Running Time: 14 hrs.). 2004. 39.25 (978-1-59710-505-7(8), 1597105058, BADLE); 24.95 (978-1-59710-504-0(X), 159710504X, BAD); 24.95 (978-1-59335-722-1(2), 1593357222, Brilliance MP3); 39.25 (978-1-59335-856-3(3), 1593358563, Brinc Audio MP3 Lib); 97.25 (978-1-59355-443-9(5), 1593554435, BrilAudUnabridg); 34.95 (978-1-59355-442-2(7), 1593554427, BAU) Brilliance Audio. *As a television news correspondent, Alex Callahan has traveled to some of the most dangerous corners of the globe, covering famine, plague, and war. He's seen more than his share of blood and death, and knows what it means to be afraid. But what he's never known is the terror that grabs him when, on a tranquil summer afternoon, he ceases to be an observer of the dark side and, to his shock, becomes enmeshed in it. Separated from his wife, and struggling not to become a stranger to his six-year-old twin sons, Alex is logging some all-too-rare quality time with the boys when they vanish without a trace amid the hurly-burly of a countryside Renaissance Fair. Then the phone call comes. A chilling silence, slow, steady breathing, and the familiar, plaintive voice of a child - "Daddy?" - complete the nightmare and set in motion a juggernaut of frenzy and agony. The longer the police search, exhausting leads without success, the deeper Alex's certainty grows that time is running out. And when, at last, telltale signs reveal a hidden pattern of bizarre and ghoulish abductions, Alex vows to use his own relentless investigative skills to rescue his children from the shadowy figure dubbed The Piper. Whoever this elusive stranger is, the profile that slowly emerges - from previous crimes involving twins, from the zealously secret world of professional magicians, and from the eerie culture of voodoo - suggests that The Piper is a predator unlike any other. A twisted soul hell-bent on fulfilling an unspeakably dark dream. A fiend with a terrifying true calling. What Alex Callahan is closing in on is a monster with a mission.*

Murder at Ebbets Field. unabr. ed. Troy Soos. Narrated by Johnny Heller. 6 cass. (Running Time: 8 hrs. 15 mins.). (Mickey Rawlings Baseball Ser.: Vol. 2). 1997. 51.00 (978-0-7887-0817-6(1), 94967E7) Recorded Bks. *The 1914 race for the pennant is heating up. But when Giant's rookie Mickey Rawlings discovers the body of the new owner at Coney Island, bad luck stalks him.*

Murder at Fenway Park. unabr. ed. Troy Soos. Narrated by Johnny Heller. 7 CDs. (Running Time: 7 hrs. 30 mins.). (Mickey Rawlings Baseball Ser.: Vol. 1). 1999. audio compact disk 58.00 (978-0-7887-3418-2(0), C1024E7) Recorded Bks. *Reporting for his first day as a Red Sox player, young rookie, Mickey Rawlings discovers a faceless body in the stadium. When he tries to clear his name after police name him their only suspect, nameless foes attempt to silence him.*

Murder at Fenway Park, unabr. ed. Troy Soos. Narrated by Johnny Heller. 6 cass. (Running Time: 7 hrs. 30 mins.). (Mickey Rawlings Baseball Ser.: Vol. 1). 1997. 51.00 (978-0-7887-0874-9(0), 95009E7) Recorded Bks.

Murder at Five Finger Light. unabr. ed. Sue Henry. Read by Staci Snell. 5 cass. (Running Time: 7 hrs.). (Jessie Arnold Mystery Ser.). 2005. 63.00 (978-1-4159-0822-8(2)); audio compact disk 81.00 (978-1-4159-0823-5(0)) Books on Tape.

Murder at Ford's Theater. unabr. ed. Margaret Truman. Read by Richard Allen. 6 cass. (Running Time: 9 hrs.). (Capital Crimes Ser.: Vol. 19). 2002. 74.25 (978-1-59086-348-0(8), 1590863488, Unabridge Lib Edns) Brilliance Audio.

Murder at Ford's Theater. unabr. ed. Margaret Truman. Read by Richard Allen. (Running Time: 9 hrs.). (Capital Crimes Ser.: Vol. 19). 2004. 39.25 (978-1-59335-590-6(4), 1593355904, Brinc Audio MP3 Lib) Brilliance Audio. *The body of Nadia Zarinski, an attractive young woman who worked for Senator Bruce Lerner - and who volunteered at Ford's - is discovered in the alley behind the theatre. Soon a pair of mismatched cops - young, studious Rick Klayman and gregarious veteran Moses "Mo" Johnson - start digging into the victim's life, and find themselves confronting an increasing cast of suspects. There's Virginia Senator Lerner himself, rumored to have had a sexual relationship with Nadia - and half the women in D.C. under ninety...Clarice Emerson, producer/director of Ford's Theatre and ex-wife of the senator, whose nomination to the head of the National Endowment for the Arts (NEA) is now threatened by the scandal...Jeremiah Lerner, her aimless, hot-tempered son, said to have been sleeping with Nadia when his famous father wasn't... Bernard Crowley, the theatre's controller, whose emotions overflow at the mention of the crime... faded British stage star Sydney Bancroft, desperate for recognition and a comeback, and armed with damning information about Clarise Emerson...and other complex characters from both sides of the footlights.*

Murder at Ford's Theater. unabr. ed. Margaret Truman. Read by Richard Allen. (Running Time: 9 hrs.). (Capital Crimes Ser.: Vol. 19). 2004. 24.95 (978-1-59335-132-8(1), 1593351321) Soulmate Audio Bks.

Murder at Ford's Theatre. unabr. ed. Margaret Truman. Read by Richard Allen. (Running Time: 9 hrs.). (Capital Crimes Ser.: Vol. 19). 2004. 39.25 (978-1-59710-506-4(6), 1597105066, BADLE) Brilliance Audio.

Murder at Ford's Theatre. unabr. ed. Margaret Truman. Read by Richard Allen. (Running Time: 9 hrs.). (Capital Crimes Ser.). 2004. 24.95 (978-1-59710-507-1(4), 1597105074, BAD) Brilliance Audio.

Murder at Gettysburg. Jim Walker. Narrated by Ed Sala. 9 cass. (Running Time: 12 hrs. 30 mins.). (Mysteries in Time Ser.). 54.00 (978-1-4025-0966-7(9)); audio compact disk 112.00 (978-1-4025-2906-1(6)) Recorded Bks.

Murder at Government House. unabr. ed. Elspeth Huxley. Narrated by Jill Tanner. 6 cass. (Running Time: 9 hrs.). 1989. 51.00 (978-1-55690-359-5(6), 89830E7) Recorded Bks. *Trouble is brewing in the African colony of Chania in the 1930s. With the murder of the Governor, it boils over.*

Murder at Government House. unabr. collector's ed. Elspeth Huxley. Read by Donada Peters. 6 cass. (Running Time: 9 hrs.). 1989. 48.00 (978-0-7366-1647-8(0), 2499) Books on Tape. *Life at Government House in the African colony of Chania seems relaxed & booming though Olivia Brandeis, a young anthropologist, senses trouble brewing. And when the Governor, Sir Malcolm McLeod, is found strangled at his desk, her intuition is proven sound. Enter Superintendent Vachell. His interrogation removes the crust of calm from the local community. But it is not until Olivia relates her encounter with a tribal witchdoctor that the riddle surrounding the murder is solved.*

Murder at Hobcaw Barony, unabr. ed. Elliott Roosevelt. Narrated by Nelson Runger. 6 cass. (Running Time: 6 hrs. 45 mins.). (Eleanor Roosevelt Mystery Ser.: No. 3). 1986. 51.00 (978-1-55690-360-1(X), 86680E7) Recorded Bks. *The supporting cast included Tallulah Bankhead, Joan Crawford & Humphrey Bogart, but the star of the mystery, Mrs. Roosevelt, outshone them all.*

Murder at Midnight. 6 cass. 24.98 Moonbeam Pubns.

Murder at Midnight. Avi. (ENG.). (J). (gr. 3-7). 2010. audio compact disk 49.95 (978-0-545-16090-2(1)) Scholastic Inc.

Murder at Midnight. Avi. Narrated by Jeff Woodman. (Running Time: 4 hrs.). (J). (gr. 3-7). 2010. audio compact disk 25.95 (978-0-545-20208-4(6)) Scholastic Inc.

Murder at Midnight: Island of the Dead & Black Swan. 1 cass. (Running Time: 1 hr.). 2001. 6.98 (2379) Radio Spirits.

Murder at Midnight: Murder Out of Mind & Death Worshippers. 1 cass. (Running Time: 1 hr.). 2001. 6.98 (1856) Radio Spirits.

Murder at Midnight: The Cabala & The Ace of Death. 1 cass. (Running Time: 1 hr.). 2001. 6.98 (1555) Radio Spirits.

Murder at Midnight: The House Where Death Lived & Death Across the Board. 1 cass. (Running Time: 1 hr.). 2001. 6.98 (1688) Radio Spirits.

Murder at Monticello: A Homer Kelly Mystery. Jane Langton. 5 cass. (Running Time: 7 hrs. 30 mins.). 2001. 40.00 (978-0-7366-6205-5(7)) Books on Tape. *Invited to the Virginia bicentennial celebration of Jefferson's presidency, Homer is excited to join the festivities. But more than fireworks are about to explode at Monticello. A scholar is working on a book exonerating the founding father from latter-day criticism & scandal. Camped in the dark woods behind Monticello is a young trespasser, Tom Dean, who swears that the only Jeffersonian good deed was his sponsorship of the Lewis & Clark expedition & somewhere a vicious murderer of local women is on the prowl. When Tom is arrested as a prime suspect, Homer is drawn into the lives of the two troubled Toms.*

Murder at Monticello: A Homer Kelly Mystery. unabr. ed. Jane Langton. Read by Michael Prichard. 5 cass. (Running Time: 7 hrs.). 2001. 29.95 (978-0-7366-5694-8(4)) Books on Tape.

Murder at Moot Point. unabr. ed. Marlys Millhiser. Read by Lynda Evans. 8 cass. (Running Time: 9 hrs.). (Charlie Greene Mystery Ser.: Bk. 1). 2001. 49.95 (978-1-55686-762-0(X)) Books in Motion. *While traveling to secure a book deal for a client, literary agent Charlie Greene is accused of murder and must prove her innocence against impressive evidence.*

Murder at Pearl Harbor. Jim Walker. Narrated by Richard Ferrone. 8 cass. (Running Time: 11 hrs.). (Mysteries in Time Ser.). 74.00 (978-1-4025-0964-3(2)) Recorded Bks.

Murder at the ABA. unabr. ed. Isaac Asimov. Read by Daniel Grace. 8 cass. (Running Time: 8 hrs.). 1977. 48.00 (978-0-7366-0043-9(4), 1054) Books on Tape. *Set at a recent meeting of the American Booksellers Association, the characters are so realistic that the author was compelled to write a disclaimer about names & events.*

Murder at the FBI. Margaret Truman. Read by Allison Green. 5 cass. (Running Time: 6 hrs. 30 min.). (Capital Crimes Ser.: Vol. 6). 1993. 43.40 (978-1-56544-026-5(9), 250026); Rental 7.80 30 day rental Set. (250026) Literate Ear. *The FBI is in grave danger. One of its special agents is found dead on the FBI firing range in front of hundreds of tourists. Two agents assigned to the case pursue the investigation & their own illegal love affair.*

***Murder at the Foul Line: Original Tales of Hoop Dreams & Deaths from Today's Great Writers.** unabr. ed. Otto Penzler. (Running Time: 11 hrs.). (Sports Mystery Ser.). 2010. 24.99 (978-1-4418-8022-2(4), 9781441880222, BAD); 39.97 (978-1-4418-8023-9(2), 9781441880239, BADLE) Brilliance Audio.

***Murder at the Foul Line: Original Tales of Hoop Dreams & Deaths from Today's Great Writers.** unabr. ed. Otto Penzler. Read by Angela Dawe. (Running Time: 11 hrs.). (Sports Mystery Ser.). 2010. 24.99 (978-1-4418-8020-8(8), 9781441880208, Brilliance MP3) Brilliance Audio.

***Murder at the Foul Line: Original Tales of Hoop Dreams & Deaths from Today's Great Writers.** unabr. ed. Otto Penzler. Read by Dick Hill & Angela Dawe. (Running Time: 11 hrs.). (Sports Mystery Ser.). 2010. 39.97 (978-1-4418-8021-5(6), 9781441880215, Brinc Audio MP3 Lib) Brilliance Audio.

***Murder at the Foul Line: Original Tales of Hoop Dreams & Deaths from Today's Great Writers.** unabr. ed. Otto Penzler. Read by Dick Hill Dawe & Angela Dawe. (Running Time: 11 hrs.). (Sports Mystery Ser.). 2010. audio compact disk 29.99 (978-1-4418-8018-5(6), 9781441880185, Bril Audio CD Unabri); audio compact disk 79.97 (978-1-4418-8019-2(4), 9781441880192, BriAudCD Unabrid) Brilliance Audio.

Murder at the Gardner. unabr. collector's ed. Jane Langton. Read by Ruth Stokesberry. 7 cass. (Running Time: 10 hrs. 30 min.). 1990. 56.00 (978-0-7366-1741-3(8), 2581) Books on Tape. *After a series of seemingly harmless pranks at Boston's Isabella Stewart Gardner Museum, the trustees call in ex-detective & Harvard lecturer Homer Kelly to investigate. But when art patron Madeline Hepplewhite is murdered after surprising the prankster, Homer has to answer questions a bit more pressing than "Who tied a balloon to the Cellini?".*

Murder at the Kennedy Center. Margaret Truman. Read by Allison Green. 6 cass. (Running Time: 9 hrs.). (Capital Crimes Ser.: Vol. 9). 1993. 48.00 (978-1-56544-014-2(5), 250029); Rental 8.40 30 day rental Set. (250029) Literate Ear. *A revolver shot destroyed the beautiful young woman's angry threat. Is the next President of the United States involved.*

Murder at the Kennedy Center, unabr. ed. Margaret Truman. Narrated by Richard Poe. 8 cass. (Running Time: 11 hrs. 30 mins.). (Capital Crimes Ser.: Vol. 9). 1990. 70.00 (978-1-55690-363-2(4), 90103E7) Recorded Bks. *A presidential candidate suddenly finds he has a running mate he didn't expect - a corpse. He knows only one man capable of solving the crime, clearing his son, putting his campaign back on track & catching the killer. His best friend Mac Smith. Oddly enough, it was Mac & his dog Rufus who found the body in the first place.*

***Murder at the Laurels.** Lesley Cookman. 2010. 69.95 (978-1-4079-0746-8(8)); audio compact disk 84.95 (978-1-4079-0747-5(6)) Pub: Soundings Ltd GBR. Dist(s): Ulverscroft US

Murder at the Library of Congress, abr. ed. Margaret Truman. 2 cass. (Capital Crimes Ser.: Vol. 16). 1999. 18.00 (FS9-51094) Highsmith.

Murder at the Library of Congress. unabr. ed. Margaret Truman. Narrated by Richard Poe. 8 CDs Library ed. (Running Time: 8 hrs. 30 min.). (Capital Crimes Ser.: Vol. 16). 2003. audio compact disk 89.75 (978-1-4025-7039-1(2)) Recorded Bks.

Murder at the Library of Congress. unabr. ed. Margaret Truman. Narrated by Richard Poe. 6 cass. Library ed. (Running Time: 8 hrs. 30 mins.). (Capital Crimes Ser.: Vol. 16). 2003. 58.00 (978-1-4025-2561-2(3), 96179) Recorded Bks. *Journalist Annabel Reed-Smith is at the Library of Congress researching a diary of Christopher Columbus¿ voyage. When a scholar studying the same subject is killed in the stacks nearby, Annabel begins to suspect that the library may contain information someone would do anything to keep secret. Library Edition.*

Murder at the Library of Congress. unabr. collector's ed. Margaret Truman. Narrated by Richard Poe. 6 cass. (Running Time: 8 hrs. 30 min.). (Capital Crimes Ser.: Vol. 16). 2003. 34.95 (978-1-4025-2562-9(1), RG132) Recorded Bks.

Murder at the National Gallery. Margaret Truman. Narrated by Richard Poe. 11 CDs. (Running Time: 13 hrs.). (Capital Crimes Ser.: Vol. 13). audio compact disk 111.00 (978-0-7887-4910-0(2), C1291E7) Recorded Bks.
The National Gallery is making lavish plans to display some of Italy's most treasured masterpieces by Caravaggio. When the White House asks local gallery owner Annabel Reed to help smooth the negotiations with the Italian government, she jumps at the chance but the prestigious assignment soon pits Annabel & her law professor husband against a cast of unscrupulous characters, from Washington's colorful art community to Italy's smoldering underworld. Available to libraries only.

Murder at the National Gallery. Margaret Truman. Read by Richard Poe. (Capital Crimes Ser.: Vol. 13). 2000. audio compact disk 111.00 Recorded Bks.

Murder at the National Gallery. unabr. ed. Margaret Truman. Narrated by Richard Poe. 9 cass. (Running Time: 13 hrs.). (Capital Crimes Ser.: Vol. 13). 2000. 81.00 (978-0-7887-4416-7(X), 95958E7) Recorded Bks.
While the National Gallery makes preparations to display Italian masterpieces, the White House asks local gallery owner Annabel Reed-Smith to help smooth negotiations with Italy. But the prestigious assignment soon pits Annabel against unscrupulous characters from Washington's art community & Italy's smoldering underworld.

Murder at the Opera. abr. ed. Margaret Truman. Read by Phil Gigante. (Running Time: 21600 sec.). (Capital Crimes Ser.: Vol. 22). 2007. audio compact disk 14.99 (978-1-4233-1834-7(X), 9781423318347, BCD Value Price) Brilliance Audio.

Murder at the Opera. unabr. ed. Margaret Truman. Read by Phil Gigante. (Running Time: 10 hrs.). (Capital Crimes Ser.: Vol. 22). 2006. 39.25 (978-1-4233-1833-0(1), 9781423318330, BADLE); 82.25 (978-1-4233-1829-3(3), 9781423318293, BrilAudUnabridg); audio compact disk 39.25 (978-1-4233-1831-6(5), 9781423318316, Brlnc Audio MP3 Lib); audio compact disk 92.25 (978-1-4233-1827-9(7), 9781423318279, BriAudCD Unabrid); audio compact disk 34.95 (978-1-4233-1826-2(9), 9781423318262, Bril Audio CD Unabri); audio compact disk 24.95 (978-1-4233-1830-9(7), 9781423318309, Brilliance MP3) Brilliance Audio.
Truman offers what no other mystery novelist can: unparalleled knowledge of Washington, D.C., a city whose institutions she exposes brick by brick, and whose secrets she reveals clue by clue. The subterfuge we suspect each day in the morning newspapers plays itself out page by page in Truman's novels, and Murder at the Opera is one of her most thrilling efforts to date. The heart-stopping story includes an attempt on the President's life, undertaken on opening night at the Kennedy Center - a venue where it's hard to tell if the greatest actors are on stage or sitting in the best seats.

Murder at the Opera: A Capital Crimes Novel. unabr. ed. Margaret Truman. Read by Phil Gigante. (Running Time: 10 hrs.). (Capital Crimes Ser.). 2006. 24.95 (978-1-4233-1832-3(3), 9781423318323, BAD) Brilliance Audio.

Murder at the Palace. unabr. ed. Elliott Roosevelt. Narrated by Nelson Runger. 5 cass. (Running Time: 7 hrs.). (Eleanor Roosevelt Mystery Ser.: No. 5). 1988. 44.00 (978-1-55690-358-8(8), 88882E7) Recorded Bks.
In the fall of 1942, Eleanor journeys to London as her husband's personal emissary. Her agenda is a full one, but the murder of Sir Anthony Brooke-Harding provides a mystery too intriguing to ignore.

Murder at the Pottawatomie Light. Scripts. Narrated by William H. Olson. 3 cass. (Running Time: 3.5 hrs.). 2002. 10.95 (978-1-890352-18-9(7)) Jackson Harbor.
This post Civil War story will keep the reader guessing as to who the culprit is while showing the life of a 19th Century lighthouse keeper and his family.

***Murder at the Racetrack: Original Tales of Mystery & Mayhem down the Final Stretch from Today's Great Writers.** unabr. ed. Otto Penzler. (Running Time: 10 hrs.). (Sports Mystery Ser.). 2010. audio compact disk 29.99 (978-1-4418-8030-7(5), 9781441880307, Bril Audio CD Unabri) Brilliance Audio.

***Murder at the Racetrack: Original Tales of Mystery & Mayhem down the Final Stretch from Today's Great Writers.** unabr. ed. Otto Penzler. Read by Natalie Ross & Phil Gigante. (Running Time: 10 hrs.). (Sports Mystery Ser.). 2010. 24.99 (978-1-4418-8032-1(1), 9781441880321, Brilliance MP3) Brilliance Audio.

***Murder at the Racetrack: Original Tales of Mystery & Mayhem down the Final Stretch from Today's Great Writers.** unabr. ed. Otto Penzler. Read by Phil Gigante & Natalie Ross. (Running Time: 10 hrs.). (Sports Mystery Ser.). 2010. 39.97 (978-1-4418-8033-8(X), 9781441880338, Brlnc Audio MP3 Lib) Brilliance Audio.

***Murder at the Racetrack: Original Tales of Mystery & Mayhem down the Final Stretch from Today's Great Writers.** unabr. ed. Otto Penzler. Read by Natalie Ross & Phil Gigante. (Running Time: 11 hrs.). (Sports Mystery Ser.). 2010. 24.99 (978-1-4418-8034-5(8), 9781441880345, BAD) Brilliance Audio.

***Murder at the Racetrack: Original Tales of Mystery & Mayhem down the Final Stretch from Today's Great Writers.** unabr. ed. Otto Penzler. Read by Natalie Ross and Phil Gigante. (Running Time: 11 hrs.). (Sports Mystery Ser.). 2010. 39.97 (978-1-4418-8035-2(6), 9781441880352, BADLE); audio compact disk 79.97 (978-1-4418-8031-4(3), 9781441880314, BriAudCD Unabrid) Brilliance Audio.

Murder at the Savoy. unabr. ed. Maj Sjöwall & Per Wahlöö. Read by Tom Weiner. (Running Time: 7.5 hrs. 0 mins.). (ENG.). 2009. 29.95 (978-1-4332-6336-1(X)); 54.95 (978-1-4332-6332-3(7)); audio compact disk 69.00 (978-1-4332-6333-0(5)) Blckstn Audio.

Murder at the Vicarage. Agatha Christie. Read by James Saxon. 6 CDs. (Running Time: 7 hrs. 30 mins.). (ENG.). 2009. audio compact disk 29.95 (978-1-60283-578-8(0)) Pub: AudioGO. Dist(s): Perseus Dist

Murder at the Vicarage. unabr. ed. Agatha Christie. Read by James Saxon. 6 cass. (Running Time: 8 hrs. 15 min.). (Miss Marple Ser.: No. 1). 2001. 29.95 (978-1-57270-208-0(7), N61208u) Pub: Audio Partners. Dist(s): PerseuPGW
Everyone said the death of Colonel Protheroe would be a service to the world. So when he is found shot, no one is terribly surprised, and nearly everyone in the town of St. Mary Mead is a suspect. Amidst this uproar, the famed Miss Marple attempts carefully and shrewdly to trap the murderer.

Murder at the Vicarage. unabr. ed. Agatha Christie. 2 vols. (Running Time: 3 hrs.). Dramatization. (Miss Marple Ser.: No. 1). 2003. audio compact disk 29.95 (978-0-563-49686-1(X), BBCD 033) BBC Worldwide.
In the sleepy little English country village of St. Mary Mead, all is not as it seems. Colonel Protheroe, local magistrate and overbearing landowner, is the most detested man in the village. Everyone, even the vicar, wishes he were dead. And very soon he is shot in the head in the vicar's own study. Faced with a surfeit of suspects, only the inscrutable Miss Marple can unravel the tangled web of clues.

Murder at the Washington Tribune. abr. ed. Margaret Truman. Read by Dick Hill. (Running Time: 14400 sec.). (Capital Crimes Ser.: Vol. 21). 2006. audio compact disk 14.99 (978-1-59737-441-5(5), 9781597374415, BCD Value Price) Brilliance Audio.
Please enter a Synopsis.

Murder at the Washington Tribune. abr. unabr. ed. Margaret Truman. Read by Dick Hill. (Running Time: 36000 sec.). (Capital Crimes Ser.: Vol. 21). 2005. audio compact disk 97.25 (978-1-59737-440-8(7), 9781597374408, BACDLib Ed) Brilliance Audio.
From senators to summer interns, from all the president's men to all-powerful women, Margaret Truman captures the fascinating, high-wire drama of Washington, D.C., like no other writer. Now this master of mystery fiction takes us into the capital's chaotic fourth estate. At the big, aggressive newspaper The Washington Tribune, a young woman has been murdered. And the hunt for her killer is making sensational and lethal headlines. The victim, fresh out of journalism school, hoped to make a splash at the Trib - and then a maintenance man found her in a supply closet, brutally strangled to death. The Trib's journalists are at once horrified and anxious to solve the crime before the cops do, and put this scandal to rest. But the Metropolitan Police Department isn't going to let byline-hungry reporters get in the way of its investigation, and soon enough the journalists and the cops have established warring task forces. Then a second woman is killed, in Franklin Square. Like the first, she was young, attractive, and worked in the media. For veteran Trib reporter Joe Wilcox, whose career is mired in frustration and disappointment, the case strikes close to home. His daughter is a beautiful rising TV news star. As his relationship with a female MPD detective grows more intimate, Joe sees a chance to renew himself as a reporter and as a man. Spearheading the Trib's investigation, he baits a trap for the killer with a secret from his own past. Suddenly Joe is risking his career, his marriage, and even his daughter's life by playing a dangerous game with a possible serial killer, while a police detective is bending rules for the reporter she likes and trusts but may not know as well as she thinks she does. As Joe's daughter finds herself trapped at the heart of a frantic manhunt, the walls come down between family, friendship, ethics, and ambition - and a killer hides in plain sight..

Murder at the Washington Tribune. unabr. ed. Margaret Truman. Read by Dick Hill. (Running Time: 10 hrs.). (Capital Crimes Ser.: Vol. 21). 2005. 39.25 (978-1-59737-445-3(8), 9781597374453, BADLE); 82.25 (978-1-59737-438-5(5), 9781597374385, BrilAudUnabridg); audio compact disk 39.25 (978-1-59737-443-9(1), 9781597374439, Brlnc Audio MP3 Lib); audio compact disk 24.95 (978-1-59737-442-2(3), 9781597374422, Brilliance MP3); audio compact disk 36.95 (978-1-4233-0614-6(7), 9781423306146, Bril Audio CD Unabri) Brilliance Audio.

Murder at the Washington Tribune. unabr. ed. Margaret Truman. Read by Dick Hill. (Running Time: 10 hrs.). (Capital Crimes Ser.). 2005. 24.95 (978-1-59737-444-6(X), 9781597374446, BAD) Brilliance Audio.

Murder at the Watergate. unabr. ed. Margaret Truman. Narrated by Richard Poe. 7 cass. (Running Time: 9 hrs. 30 mins.). (Capital Crimes Ser.: Vol. 15). 1999. 69.75 (978-1-4025-6163-4(6), 96009MC, Griot Aud) Recorded Bks.

Murder at Troyte's Hill. Catherine L. Pirkis. 1981. (N-80) Jimcin Record.

Murder at Union Station. abr. ed. Margaret Truman. Read by Guerin Barry. (Running Time: 4 hrs.). (Capital Crimes Ser.: Vol. 20). 2004. audio compact disk 69.25 (978-1-59355-935-9(6), 1593559356, BACDLib Ed) Brilliance Audio.
Historic Union Station means nothing to the elderly man speeding south on the last lap of what will turn out to be a one-way journey from Tel Aviv to D.C. - on a train that will soon land him at Gate A-8 and, moments later, at St. Peter's Gate. This weary traveler, whose terminal destination is probably hell, is Louis Russo, former mob hit man and government informer. Two men are at the station to meet him. One is Richard Marienthal, a young writer whose forthcoming book is based on Russo's life. The other is the man who'll kill him. Russo has returned to help promote Marienthal's book, which, although no one has been allowed to read it, already has some people shaking in their Gucci boots. Those in power fear that the contents will expose not only organized crime's nefarious business but also a top-secret assignment abroad that Russo once masterminded for a very-high-profile Capitol Hill client. As news of Russo's murder rockets from the MPD to the FBI and the CIA, from Congress to the West Wing, the final chapter of the story begins its rapid-fire unfolding. In addition to the bewildered Marienthal and his worried girlfriend, Murder at Union Station features an array of memorable characters: rock-ribbed right-wing Senator Karl Widmer; ruthless New York publisher Pamela Warren; boozy MPD Detective Bret Mullin; shoe-shine virtuoso Joe Jenks; dedicated presidential political adviser Chet Fletcher; and President Adam Parmele himself - not to mention freelance snoops, blow-dried climbers, and a killer or two. There's no place like the nation's capital, and as her myriad fans know, Margaret Truman always gets it right. Murder at Union Station is a luxury express, nonstop delight.

Murder at Union Station. unabr. ed. Margaret Truman. Read by Guerin Barry. (Running Time: 8 hrs.). (Capital Crimes Ser.: Vol. 20). 2004. 24.95 (978-1-59335-772-6(9), 1593357729, Brilliance MP3); 39.25 (978-1-59335-906-5(3), 1593359063, Brlnc Audio MP3 Lib); 39.25 (978-1-59710-508-8(2), 1597105082, BADLE); 29.95 (978-1-59355-932-8(1), 1593559321, BAU); 74.25 (978-1-59355-933-5(X), 159355933X, BrilAudUnabridg) Brilliance Audio.

Murder at Union Station. unabr. ed. Margaret Truman. Read by Guerin Barry. (Running Time: 8 hrs.). (Capital Crimes Ser.). 2004. 24.95 (978-1-59710-509-5(0), 1597105090, BAD) Brilliance Audio.

Murder at Wrigley Field. unabr. ed. Troy Soos. Narrated by Johnny Heller. 6 cass. (Running Time: 8 hrs. 15 mins.). (Mickey Rawlings Baseball Ser.: Vol. 3). 1998. 53.00 (978-0-7887-2282-0(4), 95533E7) Recorded Bks.
While doughboys are fighting the Kaiser "over there," Mickey Rawlings is in the midst of a battle on the homefront. Major League baseball may be suspended for the duration of the war & Mickey's best friend, a rookie named Willie Kaiser, has just been murdered.

Murder Being Once Done. unabr. ed. Ruth Rendell. Read by Robin Bailey. 6 cass. (Running Time: 9 hrs.). (Inspector Wexford Mystery Ser.: Bk. 7). 2000. 49.95 (978-0-7451-4041-4(6), CAB 738) Pub: Chivers Audio Bks GBR. Dist(s): AudioGO
In a gloomy London cemetery, a girl is found murdered: a girl with a fraudulent name, no friends, no possessions and no past. Her mystery proves to be one of the most gruesome and challenging investigations of Inspector Wexford's career.

Murder Book. abr. ed. Jonathan Kellerman. Read by John Rubinstein. 5 CDs. (Running Time: 6 hrs.). (Alex Delaware Ser.: No. 16). (ENG.). 2002. audio compact disk 29.95 (978-0-553-71380-0(9)) Pub: Random Audio Pubg. Dist(s): Random

Murder Book. unabr. ed. Jonathan Kellerman. 10 cass. (Running Time: 15 hrs.). (Alex Delaware Ser.: No. 16). 2002. 64.00 (978-0-7366-8824-6(2)) Books on Tape.

***Murder by Experts.** Perf. by John Dickson Carr & Bret Halliday. 2010. audio compact disk 24.95 (978-1-57019-924-0(8)) Radio Spirits.

Murder by Experts. Created by Radio Spirits. (Running Time: 10800 sec.). 2004. 9.98 (978-1-57019-565-5(X)) Radio Spirits.

Murder by Impulse. abr. ed. Doris R. Meredith. Ed. by Steve Holland. 4 cass. (Running Time: 6 hrs.). 1993. 24.95 (978-1-883268-05-3(2)) Spellbinders.
Eccentric attorney John Lloyd Brauson & his beautiful assistant, Lydia Fairchild, are challenged by a crime they must solve before more violence erupts.

Murder by Masquerade. abr. ed. Doris R. Meredith. Read by Bernard Bridges. Ed. by Stephen Holland. 4 cass. 1994. 24.95 set. (978-1-883268-11-4(7)) Spellbinders.
Texas lawyer John Lloyd Branson with the assistance of his lovely legal clerk, traps a killer preying on Amarillo prostitutes.

Murder by Mind. abr. ed. Paul Wynes. 1 cass. 1997. 17.00 (978-1-883268-48-0(6)) Spellbinders.

Murder by Moonlight see Sherlock Holmes No. 2

Murder by Moonlight & Other Mysteries: New Adventures of Sherlock Holmes Volumes 19-24. abr. ed. Anthony Boucher & Denis Green. Read by Basil Rathbone & Nigel Bruce. 6 CDs. (Running Time: 21600 sec.). (ENG.). 2006. audio compact disk 29.95 (978-0-7435-6467-0(7), Audioworks) Pub: S&S Audio. Dist(s): S and S Inc

Murder by Reference. abr. ed. Doris R. Meredith. 1 cass. 1997. 25.00 (978-1-883268-28-2(1)) Spellbinders.

Murder by the Book. unabr. ed. Rex Stout. Read by Michael Prichard. 6 cass. (Running Time: 8 hrs.). (Nero Wolfe Ser.). 2000. 29.95 (978-1-57270-168-7(4), N61168u) Pub: Audio Partners. Dist(s): PerseuPGW
Nero Wolfe must solve the suspicious death of a law office clerk. His probable homicide-causing offense? Submitting a manuscript for publication.

Murder by the Book. unabr. ed. Rex Stout. Narrated by Michael Prichard. (Running Time: 25800 sec.). (Nero Wolfe Ser.). (ENG.). 2006. audio compact disk 29.95 (978-1-57270-536-4(1)) Pub: AudioGO. Dist(s): Perseus Dist
Manhattan Police Inspector Cramer asks for Wolfe's help in solving the suspicious death of a law office clerk who has been fished out of the Hudson River. His probable homicide-causing offense? Submitting a manuscript for publication! With the manuscript missing and the only two to read it dead, the only clues are a cryptic quotation from the Bible and a list of names in the dead man's pocket.

Murder by the Book. unabr. collector's ed. Rex Stout. Read by Michael Prichard. 8 cass. (Running Time: 8 hrs.). (Nero Wolfe Ser.). 1995. 64.00 (978-0-7366-3103-7(8), 3779) Books on Tape.
Leonard Dyke's writing style didn't offend. But all of his work featured unhappy endings - murder. When four people die, including the author, police finally call on Nero Wolfe.

Murder by the Numbers. unabr. ed. Max Allan Collins. Read by Paul Regina. 4 cass. (Running Time: 6 hrs.). 1998. 19.95 (978-1-882071-47-0(6)) B-B Audio.
The legendary real-life lawman Eliot Ness is deservedly famous through the TV series and the film THE UNTOUCHABLES as the scourge of criminals in 1930s Chicago. Less well known are his exploits in Cleveland, where he continued his crime busting career.

Murder by the Tale. unabr. ed. Dell Shannon. Read by Alan Sklar. 6 vols. (Running Time: 9 hrs.). 2000. bk. 54.95 (978-0-7927-2227-4(2), CSL 116, Chivers Sound Lib) AudioGO.
Includes eight stories featuring the popular Lieutenant Luis Mendoza of the Los Angeles Police Department.

Murder Can Spoil Your Appetite. unabr. ed. Selma Eichler. Read by Barbara Rosenblat. 7 cass. (Running Time: 8 hrs.). (Desiree Shapiro Mystery Ser.: Bk. 7). 2001. 49.95 (978-0-7861-2070-3(3), 2831); audio compact disk 64.00 (978-0-7861-9697-5(1), 2831) Blckstn Audio.
Normally, pudgy private eye Desiree Shapiro would no more turn down a job than she would pass up a second helping of chocolate mousse. But this case is decidedly unappetizing. Her new client is powerful crime boss Vito da Silva and he wants her to find out who murdered his protege, political up-and-comer Frankie Vincent. It's an offer Desiree can't refuse. Venturing into New Jersey, Dez teams up with a local police detective and starts digging. It turns out Vincent's squeaky-clean image hid the kind of character flaws that would make any number of people delighted to attend his funeral, including his wife.

Murder Carries a Torch. unabr. ed. Anne George. Narrated by Ruth Ann Phimister. 6 cass. (Running Time: 8 hrs. 30 mins.). (Southern Sisters Mystery Ser.). 2002. 54.00 (978-1-4025-2567-4(2)) Recorded Bks.
The Southern sisters have just returned from a trip to Europe, but they barely have time to get over jet lag before they are involved in another mystery. An anguished cousin has lost his wife to a snake-handling preacher, and when the sisters travel to a remote mountain settlement to find her, they discover a corpse instead.

Murder Clinic: Gulf Stream Green & Death in the Dressing Room. 1 cass. (Running Time: 1 hr.). 2001. 6.98 (1689) Radio Spirits.

Murder for Revenge. collector's unabr. ed. Short Stories. Ed. by Otto Penzler. 9 cass. (Running Time: 13 hrs. 30 min.). 1999. 36.00 (978-0-7366-4798-4(8), 5146) Books on Tape.
This collection of original works was born of a deliciously wicked idea: ask twelve of America's best writers to explore a single subject - people willing, often gleefully so, to kill for revenge.

Murder for Revenge. collector's unabr. ed. Ed. by Otto Penzler. 11 CDs. (Running Time: 11 hrs.). 2000. audio compact disk 32.95 (978-0-7366-5208-7(6)) Books on Tape.

Murder for Revenge. unabr. ed. Ed. by Otto Penzler. 8 cass. (Running Time: 11 hrs.). 2001. 17.95 (978-0-7366-5732-7(0)) Books on Tape.

Murder for Revenge. unabr. ed. Ed. by Otto Penzler. 11 CDs. (Running Time: 12 hrs.). 2001. audio compact disk 49.50 (978-0-7366-5735-8(5)) Books on Tape.
Exploration of sweet, cold-blooded revenge. A collection of original works by twelve of America's best writers to explore a single subject - people willing, often gleefully so, to kill for revenge.

Murder for Revenge, Vol. 1 unabr. ed. Ed. by Otto Penzler. 4 cass. (Running Time: 6 hrs.). 2000. 24.95 (978-0-7366-4764-9(3)) Books on Tape.
This collection of original works was born of a deliciously wicked idea: ask twelve of America's best writers to explore a single subject - people willing, often gleefully so, to kill for revenge.

Murder for Revenge, Vol. 2. unabr. ed. Ed. by Otto Penzler. 4 cass. (Running Time: 6 hrs.). 2000. 24.95 (978-0-7366-4765-6(1)) Books on Tape.

Murder Game. unabr. ed. Christine Feehan. Narrated by Tom Stechschulte. 12 CDs. (Running Time: 14 hrs. 15 mins.). 2009. audio compact disk 110.95 (978-0-7927-6026-9(3), Chivers Sound Lib) AudioGO.

Murder Games. abr. ed. Lionel Davidson. Read by Emile Jalbert. 6 cass. 35.70 (B-133) Audio Bk.

Murder Gets a Life. unabr. ed. Anne George. Narrated by Ruth Ann Phimister. 6 cass. (Running Time: 8 hrs. 30 mins.). (Southern Sisters Mystery Ser.). 2001. 57.00 (978-0-7887-8869-7(8)) Recorded Bks.
Mary Alice has hardly had time to meet Sunshine, her new daughter-in-law, when her attention is diverted by Sunshine's spirit-channeling grandmother and a well-dressed corpse. Soon she and her sister are sleuthing their way through a mystery.

Murder in a Cathedral. unabr. ed. Ruth Dudley Edwards. Read by Bill Wallis. 6 cass. (Running Time: 9 hrs.). 1998. 49.95 (978-0-7540-0067-9(2), CAB1490) Pub: Chivers Audio Bks GBR. Dist(s): AudioGO
For many years Westonbury Cathedral has been dominated by a clique of High-Church gays. But when Norm Cooper, a strict evangelist, is appointed dean, there is outrage & fear. David Elworthy, the new bishop, is distraught at the prospect of warfare between the factions. But the bishop's problems worsen when a corpse is found in the cathedral. Was it murder & who is likely to be next.

Murder in a Good Cause. unabr. ed. Medora Sale. Read by Lynda Evans. 8 cass. (Running Time: 8 hrs. 54 min.). (Inspector John Sanders Mystery Ser.). 2001. 49.95 (978-1-55686-841-2(3)) Books in Motion.
The death of a wealthy actress at a party in her honor leads Sanders into sinister operations of a terrorist group. Meeting Harriet Jeffries, Sanders is pleasantly distracted from the case.

Murder in a Hot Flash. unabr. ed. Marlys Millhiser. Read by Lynda Evans. 6 cass. (Running Time: 8 hrs.). (Charlie Greene Mystery Ser.: Bk. 3). 2001. 39.95 (978-1-55686-782-8(4)) Books in Motion.
Charlie's mother Edwina, pulls her headlong into murder on a Utah movie set, when Mrs. Greene is accused of "doing in" the director.

Murder in Advent. unabr. ed. David Williams. Read by Christopher Kay. 6 vols. (Running Time: 8 hrs.). (Storysound Ser.). (J). 2002. 54.95 (978-1-85903-534-4(5)) Pub: Mgna Lrg Print GBR. Dist(s): Ulverscroft US

Murder in Arizona. Tom McCloud. 2 cass. 1995. 17.00 (978-1-883268-22-0(2)) Spellbinders.

***Murder in Bare Feet.** Roger Silverwood. 2010. 59.95 (978-1-4079-1111-3(2)); audio compact disk 64.95 (978-1-4079-1112-0(0)) Pub: Soundings Ltd GBR. Dist(s): Ulverscroft US

Murder in Brentwood, unabr. ed. Mark Fuhrman. Read by Jeff Riggenbach. 8 cass. (Running Time: 11 hrs. 30 mins.). 1997. 56.95 (978-0-7861-1208-1(5), 1990) Blckstn Audio.
Outrage about the scapegoating of Mark Fuhrman. Now the former LAPD detective tells his side of the story in a damning expose. The veteran detective gives the inside story of why & how Simpson's interrogation was bungled; how police criminalists made previously unrevealed errors that torpedoed the prosecution's case.

Murder in Cabin A-13 see Asesinato en el Camarote A-13

Murder in Cabin A-13. 1 cass. (Running Time: 1 hr. 30 mins.). (SmartReader Ser.). (J). 1999. pap. bk. & tchr. ed. 19.95 (978-0-7887-0116-0(9), 79304T3) Recorded Bks.
A honeymoon voyage turns into a nightmare when a groom is found stabbed in his cabin. The door is locked from the inside & the bride is hysterical. Help put the clues together to expose the criminal.

Murder in Chicago. abr. ed. Tom McCloud. Read by Bernard Bridges. 2 cass. (Running Time: 3 hrs.). 17.00 (978-1-883268-31-2(1)) Spellbinders.
An old Nam buddy asks Clint McCord to move his parents to Chicago. Clint soon learns this isn't a milk run. Somebody wants his cargo of furniture, antiques & rare jewelry...& will do anything to get it. McCord is attacked & ends up in the hospital. Clair Devoe, a beautiful physician, provides plenty of TLC to get Clint onto the trail of the hijackers.

Murder in Chinatown. unabr. ed. Victoria Thompson. Narrated by Suzanne Toren. 8 CDs. (Running Time: 9 hrs. 30 mins.). (Gaslight Mystery Ser.: Bk. 9). 2008. audio compact disk 92.75 (978-1-4281-8848-8(7)); 72.75 (978-1-4281-8846-4(0)) Recorded Bks.
Edgar Award finalist Victoria Thompson colorfully portrays the prejudices and hardships of turn-of-the-century New York City. Called to Chinatown to deliver a baby, midwife Sarah Brandt soon helps search for a missing girl. But nobody seems to know where she is. Has she been sold to a brothel, or has she run off with a secret love?.

Murder in Congress. abr. ed. 1 cass. 1997. 17.00 (978-1-883268-41-1(9)) Spellbinders.

Murder in Cow Town. unabr. ed. Tom McCloud. Read by Bernard Bridges. Ed. by Richard Haywood. 2 cass. (Running Time: 3 hrs.). 1995. 17.00 (978-1-883268-18-3(4)) Spellbinders.
Clint & Jeff McCord are hired by a wealthy Texas rancher to deliver a valuable "herd" of ostriches to his ranch near Fort Worth. Masked ostrich rustlers & a big-bird "stampede" force the brothers into a low-profile criminal investigation that takes them through the back streets of Fort Worth's worst areas.

Murder in Focus. unabr. ed. Medora Sale. Read by Lynda Evans. 8 cass. (Running Time: 9 hrs. 12 min.). (Inspector John Sanders Mystery Ser.). 2001. 49.95 (978-1-55686-806-1(5)) Books in Motion.
Toronto Homicide detective John Sanders' week of Ottawa training plunges him into a murder investigation and internal police chaos, with the help of a lovely, professional photographer.

Murder in Foggy Bottom. abr. ed. Margaret Truman. Read by Alan Sklar. 3 CDs, Library ed. (Running Time: 3 hrs.). (Capital Crimes Ser.: Vol. 17). 2003. audio compact disk 62.25 (978-1-59086-557-6(X), 159086557X) Brilliance Audio.
Once it was a swamp. Now Foggy Bottom is swimming with real-estate sharks. When a man is found stabbed to death in this trendy D.C. neighborhood, it is major news. But within forty-eight hours the nation is gripped by a fear that leaves this comparatively small crime in the dark. Three passenger planes are shot out of the sky. Everywhere - in law enforcement, in the media, and in the most secret realms of government - men and women scramble to find out who shot hand-held missiles at the planes, and why. It is a search that reaches from Moscow to the Pacific Northwest, putting some people's lives in jeopardy and turning others' lives inside out. But no one can guess the truth: that the epicenter of the terrorist outbreak is Washington D.C.... and a dead man behind a park bench in a place called Foggy Bottom. Praise for Margaret Truman "A first-rate mystery writer," said Charles Champlin in the Los Angeles Times Book Review, "drawing on an I-was-there expertise that makes the Washington scene clang with credibility." "She can write suspense with the best of them," says Larry King. Her work is "the most satisfying sort of popular fiction, a thoughtful thriller," adds The Atlanta Journal-Constitution.

Murder in Foggy Bottom. unabr. ed. Margaret Truman. Read by Alan Sklar. 6 cass. (Running Time: 8 hrs.). (Capital Crimes Ser.: Vol. 17). 2000. 29.95 (978-1-56740-393-0(X), 156740393X, BAU) Brilliance Audio.
In Margaret Truman's latest mystery, the scene opens with an obscure death in Washington's Foggy Bottom, home of the State Department, shifts to mass murder in the downing of aircraft, and then moves on to mayhem in the streets of the new Moscow. Leaving an airport near New York, a D.C.-bound commuter plane falls to earth. At almost the same time, another crash occurs. And then... Firmly ruling out coincidence, investigators seek means and motive. The means are soon apparent: small-scale weaponry with large-scale impact. Their country of origin? A place where nearly everything - hardware, information, love - can be found for a price. Max Pauling, a State Department investigator, seductive, good-looking, and hard to fool, quickly takes off on a trail still as warm as the smoking wreckage. A host of vivid characters people the narrative, including a lovely State Department analyst who finds herself attracted to undercover types; a militia leader in Idaho who leads his people into gunfire; a reporter at odds with his boss but not with a good story; and a secretary of state who loves baseball slightly more than her job. Fast-paced and informative about flying, food, statecraft, and the violent "wetwork" under the dryly elegant exterior of diplomacy, Margaret Truman's Murder in Foggy Bottom is another winner in the Capital Crimes series. Praise for Margaret Truman "A first-rate mystery writer, said Charles Champlin in the Los Angeles Times Book Review, "drawing on an I-was-there expertise that makes the Washington scene clang with credibility." "She can write suspense with the best of them," says Larry King. Her work is "the most satisfying sort of popular fiction, a thoughtful thriller," adds The Atlanta Journal-Constitution.

Murder in Foggy Bottom. unabr. ed. Margaret Truman. Read by Alan Sklar. 7 CDs. (Running Time: 8 hrs.). (Capital Crimes Ser.: Vol. 17). 2005. 39.25 (978-1-59600-672-0(2), 9781596006720, Brinc Audio MP3 Lib); 39.25 (978-1-59600-674-4(9), 9781596006744, BADLE); 24.95 (978-1-59600-671-3(4), 9781596006713, Brilliance MP3) Brilliance Audio.

Murder in Foggy Bottom. unabr. ed. Margaret Truman. Read by Alan Sklar. (Running Time: 8 hrs.). 2005. 24.95 (978-1-59600-673-7(0), 9781596006737, BAD) Brilliance Audio.

Murder in Friday Street. unabr. ed. Amy Myers. Read by Julia Franklin. 7 cass. 2009. 61.95 (978-1-84559-506-7(8)) Pub: Soundings Ltd GBR. Dist(s): Ulverscroft US

***Murder in Greenwich.** abr. ed. Mark Fuhrman. Read by Len Cariou. (ENG.). 2006. (978-0-06-113541-5(0), Harper Audio); (978-0-06-113540-8(2), Harper Audio) HarperCollins Pubs.

Murder in Grub Street. unabr. ed. Bruce Alexander. Read by Stuart Langton. 7 cass. (Running Time: 10 hrs. 30 min.). (Sir John Fielding Mystery Ser.: Vol. 2). 1998. 56.00 (978-0-7366-3998-9(5), 4498) Books on Tape.
Sir John Fielding, a blind magistrate, comes across a crime that shocks even eighteenth-century London. A bookseller-publisher, his wife & two sons are found murdered in their living quarters above his shop in Grub Street. On the scene, ranting & brandishing an axe, stands John Clayton, identified by the broadsheets as a "mad poet." Clearly, the culprit has been caught & justice in Fielding's court will be swift. But Fielding himself is not so sure. To satisfy both his curiosity & his conscience, he decides to dig a little deeper with the help of his "eyes," young Jeremy Proctor.

Murder in Havana. unabr. ed. Margaret Truman. Narrated by Richard Poe. 8 cass. (Running Time: 11 hrs.). (Capital Crimes Ser.: Vol. 18). 2004. 79.75 (978-1-4025-3342-6(X)) Recorded Bks.
In this adventure, former secret agent Max Pauling is offered a chance to do investigative work in Cuba. Although not anticipating danger, one of his sources is killed and he is assaulted. Max realizes that someone doesn?t want him to uncover certain secrets of the isla bonita.

Murder in Hell's Corner. Amy Myers. 2007. 69.95 (978-1-84559-623-1(4)) Pub: ISIS Audio GBR. Dist(s): Ulverscroft US

Murder in Hell's Corner. Amy Myers. 2007. audio compact disk 84.95 (978-1-84559-683-5(8)) Pub: Soundings Ltd GBR. Dist(s): Ulverscroft US

***Murder in Knoxville.** Wayne Zurl. Read by David Colacci. (ENG.). 2010. 2.99 (978-1-61114-018-7(8)) Mind Wings Aud.

***Murder in Knoxville: A Sam Jenkins Mystery.** Wayne Zurl. Read by David Colacci. (ENG.). 2010. 2.99 (978-0-9825278-8-7(8)) Mind Wings Aud.

Murder-in-Law. abr. ed. Brent Kroetch. Read by Alan Zimmerman. 4 cass. (Running Time: 6 hrs.). 2000. 25.00 (978-1-58807-018-0(2)) Am Pubng Inc.

Murder in Mesopatamia. Agatha Christie. Read by Anna Massey. 4 cass. (Running Time: 7 hrs.). 1999. 16.85 (978-0-00-105571-1(2)) Ulvrscrft Audio.
Nurse Amy Leatheran had a most unusual patient. Who or what did she fear? At the site of the Iraqi desert, surely she was safe from danger. Most of the expedition were old colleagues & friends. Yet they seemed an unnaturally formative group - there was tension, uneasiness even in the air. Something very sinister was going on & it involved murder.

Murder in Mesopotamia. unabr. ed. Agatha Christie. Read by Anna Massey. 6 CDs. (Running Time: 7 hrs.). (Hercule Poirot Mystery Ser.). 2001. audio compact disk 39.95 (978-1-57270-214-1(1), N65214u) Pub: Audio Partners. Dist(s): PerseuPGW
In this classic Poirot story, the diminutive Belgian digs for clues to a triple murder at an archaeological site.

Murder in Mesopotamia. unabr. ed. Agatha Christie. Read by Anna Massey. 6 cass. (Running Time: 7 hrs.). (Hercule Poirot Mystery Ser.). 2001. 29.95 (978-1-57270-213-4(3), N61213u) Pub: Audio Partners. Dist(s): PerseuPGW

Murder in Mesopotamia. unabr. ed. Agatha Christie. Narrated by Anna Massey. (Running Time: 25380 sec.). (Hercule Poirot Mystery Ser.). (ENG.). 2005. audio compact disk 29.95 (978-1-57270-478-7(0)) Pub: AudioGO. Dist(s): Perseus Dist

***Murder in Midwinter.** Lesley Cookman. 2010. 76.95 (978-1-4079-0749-9(2)); audio compact disk 84.95 (978-1-4079-0750-5(6)) Pub: Soundings Ltd GBR. Dist(s): Ulverscroft US

Murder in Montparnasse. Kerry Greenwood. Read by Stephanie Daniel. (Running Time: 8 hrs. 10 mins.). (Phryne Fisher Mystery: Ser.). 2009. 74.99 (978-1-74214-236-4(2), 9781742142364) Pub: Bolinda Pubng AUS. Dist(s): Bolinda Pub Inc

Murder in Montparnasse. unabr. ed. Kerry Greenwood. 7 cass. (Running Time: 8 hrs. 10 mins.). (Phryne Fisher Ser.). 2005. 40.00 (978-1-74030-813-7(1)); audio compact disk 83.95 (978-1-74093-096-3(7)) Pub: Bolinda Pubng AUS. Dist(s): Bolinda Pub Inc

Murder in Montparnasse: A Mystery of Literary Paris. unabr. ed. Howard Engel. Read by Geoffrey Howard. 6 cass. (Running Time: 8 hrs. 30 mins.). 2002. 44.95 (978-0-7861-2373-5(7), 3031); audio compact disk 56.00 (978-0-7861-9383-7(2), 3031) Blckstn Audio.
It's autumn 1925, and a killer uncannily like England's Jack the Ripper is stalking the streets of Paris and preying on young women.

Murder in Musicland. unabr. ed. Diana Kirk. Read by Juanita Parker. 4 cass. (Running Time: 5 hrs.). 1999. 26.95 (978-1-55686-885-6(5)) Books in Motion.
Private investigator Phyllis McPhee is hired by Biff Newton to track down his young wife. Phyllis discovers that the woman has shady past & the search becomes more than she expected when her possible leads begin showing up in the morgue. Things are complicated even further when sheriff Sam Malone becomes involved & the two form a tense relationship.

Murder in My Back Yard. unabr. ed. Ann Cleeves. Read by Gordon Griffin. 8 cass. (Running Time: 12 hrs.). 2001. 69.95 (978-1-86042-864-7(9), 2-864-9) Pub: Soundings Ltd GBR. Dist(s): Ulverscroft US
Inspector Ramsay faces a murder investigation on his own doorstep following his impulsive decision to buy a cottage in the quiet Northumberland village of Hepplebum. When local uproar over a proposed housing development ends in murder, the pressure is on Ramsay to act from within & interrogate every possible suspect. But then tragedy strikes a second time & Ramsay must test his true measure as a detective working against the clock.

Murder in Oklahoma. unabr. ed. Tom McCloud. Read by Bernard Bridges. Ed. by Richard Haywood. 2 cass. (Running Time: 3 hrs.). 17.00 (978-1-883268-17-6(6)) Spellbinders.
Those brother truckers, Clint & Jeff McCord stop in Chicago at a local art gallery to pick up a load bound for exhibition at the Dallas Museum of Art. But first they have to convince the police they had nothing to do with murdering the gallery owner.

***Murder in Paradise.** Alanna Knight. 2010. 54.95 (978-1-4079-0955-4(X)); audio compact disk 71.95 (978-1-4079-0956-1(8)) Pub: Soundings Ltd GBR. Dist(s): Ulverscroft US

Murder in Steeple Martin. Lesley Cookman. 2008. 69.95 (978-1-4079-0089-6(7)); audio compact disk 84.95 (978-1-4079-0090-2(0)) Pub: Soundings Ltd GBR. Dist(s): Ulverscroft US

Murder in Store, unabr. ed. Pamela Smith Hill. Read by Patricia Gallimore. 6 cass. (Running Time: 8 hrs.). (Isis Ser.). (J). 1997. 54.95 (978-0-7531-0185-8(8), 970403) Pub: ISIS Lrg Prnt GBR. Dist(s): Ulverscroft US
Sally, aged eighteen & anxious to experience life, evades her schoolteacher in Scotland & takes a job in the cosmetics department of an old-established & prestigious London store. Dry rot in the attic leads to the discovery of old bloodstains connected with a murder hushed up more than a hundred years earlier. Sally becomes more involved than she expected with Sigismondo, the sinister chauffeur to her departmental manager. The store, now owned by millionaire Oscar J. Schussler, is the scene of both modern drug-running & ancient murder.

Murder in the Casbah & Other Mysteries. abr. ed. Anthony Boucher & Denis Green. Read by Basil Rathbone & Nigel Bruce. 2005. 17.95 (978-0-7435-5526-5(0)) Pub: S&S Audio. Dist(s): S and S Inc

Murder in the CIA. Margaret Truman. Read by Allison Green. 6 cass. (Running Time: 8 hrs. 30 min.). (Capital Crimes Ser.: Vol. 8). 1993. 49.00 (978-1-56544-013-5(7), 250030); Rental 8.40 30 day rental Set. (250030) Literate Ear.
Two beautiful women, best friends, move in fast international circles. Their interests with government agencies gets one of them killed.

Murder in the CIA, unabr. ed. Margaret Truman. Narrated by Richard Poe. 8 cass. (Running Time: 10 hrs. 45 mins.). (Capital Crimes Ser.: Vol. 8). 1991. 70.00 (978-1-55690-364-9(2), 91219E7) Recorded Bks.
According to the autopsy report, Barrie Mayer died of a heart attack while standing in line at London's Heathrow airport. The fact that Barrie was young & in superb health was enough to raise suspicions in her best friend Collette Cahill's mind. But the added fact that Barrie was also a part-time courier for the CIA & held a less-than-professional attitude towards her little "side-line" profession pushed Cahill over the edge from suspicion to downright fear.

Murder in the Dark. Kerry Greenwood. Read by Stephanie Daniel. (Running Time: 8 hrs. 25 mins.). (Phryne Fisher Ser.). 2009. 74.99 (978-1-74214-237-1(0), 9781742142371) Pub: Bolinda Pubng AUS. Dist(s): Bolinda Pub Inc

Murder in the Dark. unabr. ed. Kerry Greenwood. Read by Stephanie Daniel. (Running Time: 30180 sec.). (Phryne Fisher Ser.). 2007. audio compact disk 83.95 (978-1-74093-976-8(X), 9781740939768) Pub: Bolinda Pubng AUS. Dist(s): Bolinda Pub Inc

Murder in the First. unabr. ed. Dan Gordon. Perf. by Edward Asner et al. 1 cass. (Running Time: 1 hr. 41 min.). 1995. 19.95 (978-1-58081-039-5(X), TPT61) L A Theatre.
Courtroom drama based on a true incident that exposed the shocking conditions on Alcatraz & led to the closure of the notorious prison. The tale begins when eighteen year old Willie Moore makes the biggest mistake of his life: stealing five dollars from a rural store that happens to contain a post office, & ends up on the dread island of Alcatraz.

Murder in the Heartland. unabr. ed. M. William Phelps. Read by J. Charles. (Running Time: 11 hrs.). 2009. 39.97 (978-1-4233-4965-5(2), 9781423349655, BADLE); 39.97 (978-1-4233-4963-1(6), 9781423349631, Brinc Audio MP3 Lib); 24.99 (978-1-4233-4964-8(4), 9781423349648, BAD); 24.99 (978-1-4233-4962-4(8), 9781423349624, Brilliance MP3); audio compact disk 89.97 (978-1-4233-4961-7(X), 9781423349617, BriAudCD Unabrid); audio compact disk 29.99 (978-1-4233-4960-0(1), 9781423349600, Bril Audio CD Unabri) Brilliance Audio.

***Murder in the High Himalaya: Loyalty, Tragedy, & Escape from Tibet.** unabr. ed. Jonathan Green. (Running Time: 11 hrs. 30 mins.). 2010. 29.95 (978-1-4417-4783-9(4)); 65.95 (978-1-4417-4779-2(6)); audio compact disk 32.95 (978-1-4417-4782-2(6)); audio compact disk 100.00 (978-1-4417-4780-8(X)) Blckstn Audio.

Murder in the Mews: Three Perplexing Cases for Poirot. unabr. ed. Agatha Christie. Read by Nigel Hawthorne & Hugh Fraser. 4 cass. (Running Time: 5 hrs.). (Mystery Masters Ser.). 2002. 25.95 (978-1-57270-283-7(4), Audio Editions) Pub: Audio Partners. Dist(s): PerseuPGW

Murder in the Mews: Three Perplexing Cases for Poirot. unabr. ed. Agatha Christie. Narrated by Nigel Hawthorne & Hugh Fraser. 4 CDs. (Running Time: 5 hrs.). (Mystery Masters Ser.). (ENG.). 2002. audio compact disk 26.95 (978-1-57270-284-4(2)) Pub: AudioGO. Dist(s): Perseus Dist

Murder in the Middle Pasture. John R. Erickson. 2 cass. (Running Time: 3 hrs.). (Hank the Cowdog Ser.: No. 4). (J). (gr. 2-5). 2001. (978-0-7366-6138-6(7)) Books on Tape.

Murder in the Middle Pasture. John R. Erickson. 2 cass. (Running Time: 2 hrs.). (Hank the Cowdog Ser.: No. 4). (J). (gr. 2-5). 1989. 16.95 (978-0-87719-135-3(2)) Lone Star Bks.

Murder in the Middle Pasture. unabr. ed. John R. Erickson. Read by John R. Erickson. 2 cass. (Running Time: 3 hrs.). (Hank the Cowdog Ser.: No. 4). (J). (gr. 2-5). 2001. 16.95 (978-0-7366-6893-4(4)) Books on Tape.
A killer coyote attacks the ranch but Hank comes to the rescue & saves the gang's Christmas Eve.

Murder in the Middle Pasture. unabr. ed. John R. Erickson. Read by John R. Erickson. Illus. by Gerald L. Holmes. 2 cass. (Hank the Cowdog Ser.: No. 4). (J). (gr. 2-5). 1985. bk. 13.95 (978-0-916941-09-3(4)) Maverick Bks.

Murder in the Middle Pasture. unabr. ed. John R. Erickson. Read by John R. Erickson. 2 cassettes. (Running Time: approx. 3 hrs.). (Hank the Cowdog Ser.: No. 4). (J). 2002. 17.99 (978-1-59188-304-3(0)) Maverick Bks.

Murder in the Middle Pasture. unabr. ed. John R. Erickson. Read by John R. Erickson. 3 CDs. (Running Time: Approx. 3 hours). (Hank the Cowdog Ser.:

Vol. 4). (J). 2002. audio compact disk 19.99 (978-1-59188-604-4(X)) Maverick Bks.

Murder in the Middle Pasture. unabr. ed. John R. Erickson. 2 cass. (Running Time: 3 hrs.). (Hank the Cowdog Ser.: No. 4). (J). (gr. 2-5). 2000. 18.00 (978-0-8072-8271-7(5), Listening Lib) Random Audio Pubg.

Murder in the Middle Pasture. unabr. ed. John R. Erickson. 2 cass. (Hank the Cowdog Ser.: No. 4). (J). (gr. 2-5). 1998. 17.00 (21646) Recorded Bks.

Murder in the Middle Pasture. unabr. collector's ed. John R. Erickson. 3 CDs. (Running Time: 4 hrs. 30 mins.). (Hank the Cowdog Ser.: No. 4). (J). (gr. 2-5). 2001. audio compact disk 28.00 Books on Tape.
Hank faces a baffling new mystery which begins with the death of a calf on the ranch. Hank goes on a very dangerous mission to spy on the coyote village and arrest the murderer. A pack of wild dogs also complicates the plot. It takes all of Hank's deductive powers and keen insight to solve this one!.

***Murder in the Mist.** Amy Myers. 2010. 61.95 (978-1-4079-0647-8(X)); audio compact disk 79.95 (978-1-4079-0648-5(8)) Pub: Soundings Ltd GBR. Dist(s): Ulverscroft US

Murder in the Museum. Simon Brett. Read by Geoffrey Howard. 6 cass. (Running Time: 8 hrs. 30 mins.). 2002. 44.95 (978-0-7861-2692-7(2), 3267) Blckstn Audio.

Murder in the Museum. unabr. ed. Simon Brett. Read by Geoffrey Howard. 7 pieces. (Running Time: 8 hrs. 30 mins.). 2006. audio compact disk 56.00 (978-0-7861-8684-6(4), 3267); audio compact disk 24.95 (978-0-7861-8609-9(7), 3267) Blckstn Audio.

Murder in the Museum. unabr. ed. Simon Brett. Read by Simon Brett. 7 cass. (Running Time: 8 hrs. 28 mins.). (Isis Cassettes Ser.). (J). 2004. 61.95 (978-0-7531-1923-5(4)); audio compact disk 79.95 (978-0-7531-2295-2(2)) Pub: ISIS Lrg Prnt GBR. Dist(s): Ulverscroft US

Murder in the Napa Valley. unabr. ed. David Osborn. Read by Donada Peters. 5 cass. (Running Time: 5 hrs.). 1993. 40.00 (978-0-7366-2534-0(8), 3286) Books on Tape.
Margaret Barlow stumbles into winery's evil web of family greed, dark secrets...& cold-blooded murder.

Murder in the Oval Office, unabr. ed. Elliott Roosevelt. Narrated by Nelson Runger. 5 cass. (Running Time: 7 hrs. 45 mins.). (Eleanor Roosevelt Mystery Ser.: No. 6). 1989. 44.00 (978-1-55690-365-6(0), 89940E7) Recorded Bks.
The cast of villains is suitably unsavory, the cast of luminaries as stellar as ever: Sally Rand; J. Edgar Hoover; Bob Hope; & a young & ambitious Texan with a lust for power, Lyndon Baines Johnson. Eleanor Roosevelt faces a "locked-room" mystery when Congressman Colmer is found dead in the Oval Office.

***Murder in the Rough: Original Tales of Bad Shots, Terrible Lies, & Other Deadly Handicaps from Today's Great Writers.** unabr. ed. Otto Penzler. (Running Time: 12 hrs.). (Sports Mystery Ser.). 2010. 24.99 (978-1-4418-8028-4(3), 9781441880284, BAD); 39.97 (978-1-4418-8029-1(1), 9781441880291, BADLE) Brilliance Audio.

***Murder in the Rough: Original Tales of Bad Shots, Terrible Lies, & Other Deadly Handicaps from Today's Great Writers.** unabr. ed. Otto Penzler. Read by Jeffrey Cummings. (Running Time: 12 hrs.). (Sports Mystery Ser.). 2010. 24.99 (978-1-4418-8026-0(7), 9781441880260, Brilliance MP3); 39.97 (978-1-4418-8027-7(5), 9781441880277, Brlnc Audio MP3 Lib); audio compact disk 29.99 (978-1-4418-8024-6(0), 9781441880246, Bril Audio CD Unabri); audio compact disk 79.97 (978-1-4418-8025-3(9), 9781441880253, BriAudCD Unabrid) Brilliance Audio.

Murder in the Rue de Paradis. unabr. ed. Cara Black. Narrated by Carine Montbertrand. (Running Time: 11 hrs. 45 mins.). (Aimée Leduc Investigation Ser.: No. 8). 2008. 56.75 (978-1-4361-7702-3(2)); audio compact disk 123.75 (978-1-4361-5431-4(6)) Pub: Recorded Bks. Dist(s): NetLibrary CO

Murder in the Smithsonian. Margaret Truman. Read by Betsy Hershberg. 5 cass. (Running Time: 7 hrs. 30 min.). (Capital Crimes Ser.: Vol. 4). 1993. 44.20 (978-1-56544-035-7(8), 250024); Rental 7.80 30 day rental Set. (250024) Literate Ear.
Blood dripped to the vestibule floor of the National Museum of American History. A body fell to the edge of the famed Foucault pendulum. Dr. Lewis Tunney lay slain by Thomas Jefferson's sword. A brilliant historian & personal friend to the Vice President, Tunney had just stumbled onto an international art scandal.

Murder in the Smokies: A Clint McCord Trucking Adventure. unabr. ed. Tom McCloud. Read by Bernard Bridges. Ed. by Richard Haywood. 2 cass. (Running Time: 3 hrs.). 1994. 17.00 (978-1-883268-14-5(1)) Spellbinders.
Long haul trucker Clint McCord uncovers the ring leader of a cult responsible for ritual sacrifice & kidnapping.

Murder in the Sunshine State: A Clint McCord Trucking Adventure. unabr. ed. Tom McCloud. Read by Bernard Bridges. Ed. by Richard Haywood. 2 cass. 1994. 17.00 (978-1-883268-13-8(3)) Spellbinders.
Clint McCord & his brother Jeff reluctantly get involved in a police sting to trap notorious drug smugglers.

Murder in the Supreme Court. Margaret Truman. Read by Betsy Hershberg. 5 cass. (Running Time: 6 hrs. 30 min.). (Capital Crimes Ser.: Vol. 3). 1993. 44.20 (978-1-56544-038-8(2), 250028); Rental 7.80 30 day rental Set. (250028) Literate Ear.
Chief Supreme Court Clerk Clarence Sutherland handed a book to Chief Justice Jonathan Poulson, emphasizing a particular page's relevance to the matter before the court. The case was Nidel v. Illinois, an abortion rights question. This would be one of his last official acts.

Murder in the Title. unabr. ed. Simon Brett. Narrated by Simon Prebble. 5 cass. (Running Time: 6 hrs. 30 mins.). (Charles Paris Mystery Ser.). 2000. 49.75 (978-0-7887-4496-9(8), H1088E7) Recorded Bks.
Charles Paris, charming but hard-drinking middle-aged actor is on stage again. This time he's playing a corpse. Charles has a bit part in "The Message Is Murder." The play is outdated, the cast is temperamental & soon strange accidents occur. It seems this production is developing a deadly plot of its own & so Charles must put his sleuthing skills to work in order to survive.

Murder in the White House. Margaret Truman. Read by Betsy Hershberg. 5 cass. (Running Time: 7 hrs.). (Capital Crimes Ser.: Vol. 1). 1993. 44.20 (978-1-56544-046-3(3), 250031); Rental 8.80 30 day rental Set. (250031) Literate Ear.
The Lincoln Sitting Room. Woodward & Bernstein said that President Nixon & Secretary of State Henry Kissinger knelt & prayed on the floor of this room the night before Nixon's resignation. Years later, Secretary of State Lansard Blaine's blood pours from the gash in his neck, soaking into the thick carpeting.

Murder in the Wings. unabr. ed. Tom McCloud. Read by Bernard Bridges. Ed. by Richard Haywood. 2 cass. (Running Time: 3 hrs.). (Clint McCord Adventure Ser.). 1995. 17.00 (978-1-883268-21-3(4)) Spellbinders.
Clint McCord is hired to haul theatrical props & gets caught up in the murder of a young actor.

***Murder in Vegas: New Crime Tales of Gambling & Desperation.** unabr. ed. Michael Connelly. Read by Natalie Ross & Phil Gigante. (Running Time: 15 hrs.). 2010. 24.99 (978-1-4418-3698-4(5), 9781441836984, Brilliance MP3); 39.97 (978-1-4418-3699-1(3), 9781441836991, Brlnc Audio MP3 Lib) Brilliance Audio.

***Murder in Vegas: New Crime Tales of Gambling & Desperation.** unabr. ed. Michael Connelly. Read by Phil Gigante & Joyce Bean. (Running Time: 15 hrs.). 2010. 24.99 (978-1-4418-3700-4(0), 9781441837004, BAD); 39.97 (978-1-4418-3701-1(9), 9781441837011, BADLE); audio compact disk 79.97 (978-1-4418-3697-7(7), 9781441836977, BriAudCD Unabrid) Brilliance Audio.

***Murder in Vegas: New Crime Tales of Gambling & Desperation.** unabr. ed. Michael Connelly. Read by Natalie Ross et al. (Running Time: 15 hrs.). 2010. audio compact disk 29.99 (978-1-4418-3696-0(9), 9781441836960, Bril Audio CD Unabri) Brilliance Audio.

Murder Inside the Beltway. Margaret Truman. Read by Patrick G. Lawlor. (Playaway Adult Fiction Ser.). (ENG.). 2009. 64.99 (978-1-60812-666-8(8)) Find a World.

Murder Inside the Beltway. unabr. ed. Margaret Truman. Read by Patrick G. Lawlor. (Running Time: 10 hrs.). (Capital Crimes Ser.). 2008. 39.25 (978-1-4233-6720-8(0), 9781423367208, BADLE); 39.25 (978-1-4233-6718-5(9), 9781423367185, Brlnc Audio MP3 Lib); 24.95 (978-1-4233-6719-2(7), 9781423367192, BAD); 24.95 (978-1-4233-6717-8(0), 9781423367178, Brilliance MP3); audio compact disk 92.25 (978-1-4233-6716-1(2), 9781423367161, BriAudCD Unabrid); audio compact disk 32.99 (978-1-4233-6715-4(4), 9781423367154, Bril Audio CD Unabri) Brilliance Audio.

Murder Is Announced. unabr. ed. Agatha Christie. Read by Rosemary Leach. 6 cass. (Running Time: 8 hrs. 36 mins.). (Miss Marple Ser.: No. 5). 2002. 29.95 (978-1-57270-258-5(3)) Pub: Audio Partners. Dist(s): PerseuPGW
A notice in the Gazette reads: "A murder is announced and will take place on Friday, October 29, at Little Paddocks." The guests arrive, thinking they have come to a mystery party. When death and chaos ensure, the indomitable Miss Marple sorts it out.

Murder Is Announced: A Miss Marple Mystery. unabr. ed. Agatha Christie. Narrated by Rosemary Leach. 7 CDs. (Running Time: 8 hrs. 42 mins. 0 sec.). (Miss Marple Ser.). (ENG.). 2010. audio compact disk 29.95 (978-1-60283-903-8(4)) Pub: AudioGO. Dist(s): Perseus Dist

Murder Is Easy. rev. ed. Agatha Christie. Read by Sean Barrett. (Running Time: 3 hrs.). (ENG., 2007. audio compact disk 24.00 (978-0-230-01580-7(8)) Pub: Macmillan UK GBR. Dist(s): IPG Chicago

Murder Is Easy. unabr. ed. Agatha Christie. Read by Hugh Fraser. (Running Time: 22140 sec.). (Audio Editions Mystery Masters Ser.). 2005. 27.95 (978-1-57270-489-3(6)) Pub: Audio Partners. Dist(s): PerseuPGW
Retired police officer and occasional sleuth Luke Fitzwilliam wasn't thrilled to be stuck next to dotty old Miss Fullerton on the London-bound train. But at least she was amusing, regaling him with tall tales of "perfect murders" in the quaint village of Wychwood. When Miss Fullerton turns up dead, Luke becomes seriously worried and takes on the case. A visit to isolated Wychwood confirms his fears: There's a dark and dangerous secret that is dispatching the locals. Actor Hugh Fraser gives a captivating reading of this elaborate, engaging whodunit.

Murder Is Easy. unabr. ed. Agatha Christie. Narrated by Hugh Fraser. (Running Time: 22140 sec.). (Audio Editions Mystery Masters Ser.). (ENG.). 2005. audio compact disk 27.95 (978-1-57270-490-9(X)) Pub: AudioGO. Dist(s): Perseus Dist

***Murder Is my Racquet: Fourteen Original Tales of Love, Death, & Tennis by Today's Great Writers.** unabr. ed. Otto Penzler. Read by Dan John Miller. (Running Time: 9 hrs.). (Sports Mystery Ser.). 2010. 24.99 (978-1-4418-8014-7(3), 9781441880147, Brilliance MP3) Brilliance Audio.

***Murder Is my Racquet: Fourteen Original Tales of Love, Death, & Tennis by Today's Great Writers.** unabr. ed. Otto Penzler. Read by Dan john Miller. (Running Time: 9 hrs.). (Sports Mystery Ser.). 2010. 39.97 (978-1-4418-8015-4(1), 9781441880154, Brlnc Audio MP3 Lib) Brilliance Audio.

***Murder Is my Racquet: Fourteen Original Tales of Love, Death, & Tennis by Today's Great Writers.** unabr. ed. Otto Penzler. Read by Dan John Miller. (Running Time: 9 hrs.). (Sports Mystery Ser.). 2010. 24.99 (978-1-4418-8016-1(X), 9781441880161, BAD); 39.97 (978-1-4418-8017-8(8), 9781441880178, BADLE); audio compact disk 29.99 (978-1-4418-8002-4(X), 9781441880024, Bril Audio CD Unabri); audio compact disk 79.97 (978-1-4418-8013-0(5), 9781441880130, BriAudCD Unabrid) Brilliance Audio.

Murder List. abr. ed. Julie Garwood. Read by Joyce Bean. (Running Time: 21600 sec.). 2006. audio compact disk 16.99 (978-1-4233-1940-5(0), 9781423319405, BCD Value Price) Brilliance Audio.
When Chicago detective Alec Buchanan is offered a prime position with the FBI, he takes it as the perfect opportunity to leave the Windy City and follow in his brothers' footsteps to the top echelons of law enforcement. But first he must complete one last assignment: acting as a glorified bodyguard to hotel heiress Regan Hamilton Madison. The gorgeous exec has become entangled in some potentially deadly business: Someone has e-mailed her a graphic crime-scene photo - and the victim is no stranger. Regan suspects that the trouble started when she agreed to help a journalist friend expose a shady self-help guru who preys on lonely, vulnerable women. In fact, the smooth-as-an-oil-slick Dr. Lawrence Shields may have been responsible for the death of one of his devotees. Hoping to find some damning evidence, Regan attends a Shields seminar. At the gathering, the doctor persuades his guests to partake in an innocent little "cleansing" exercise. He asks them to make a list of the people who have hurt or deceived them over the years, and poses the question: Would your world be a better place if these people ceased to exist? Treating the exercise as a game, Regan plays along. The experience is all but forgotten - until the first person on Regan's list turns up dead. Shock turns to horror when other names from the list start to surface as corpses, and a harrowing tango of desire and death is set into motion. Now brutal murders seem to stalk Regan's every move - and a growing attraction to Alec may compromise her safety, while stirring up tender emotions she thought she could no longer feel. Yet as the danger intensifies and a serial killer circles ever closer, Regan must discover who has turned her private revenge fantasies into grisly reality.

Murder List. unabr. ed. Julie Garwood. Read by Joyce Bean. (Running Time: 12 hrs.). 2004. 24.95 (978-1-59335-683-5(8), 1593356838, Brilliance MP3); 39.25 (978-1-59335-817-4(2), 1593358172, Brlnc Audio MP3 Lib); 87.25 (978-1-59086-246-9(5), 1590862465, BAudLibEd); 32.95 (978-1-59086-245-2(7), 1590862457, BAU); audio compact disk 102.25 (978-1-59086-249-0(X), 159086249X, Bril Audio CD Unabri); audio compact disk 36.95 (978-1-59086-248-3(1), 1590862481, Bril Audio CD Unabri) Brilliance Audio.
It begins with a favor - and leads to a nightmare beyond imagining. Regan Hamilton Madison agrees to attend a seminar given by Dr. Lawrence Shields, a psychologist with a shady reputation. Regan's friend is a reporter, and hopes she can find some evidence to prove that Shields is a fraud. During the welcome reception, the charismatic doctor persuades his guests to participate in an innocent little "cleansing" exercise. He asks them to make a list of the people who have hurt or deceived them over the years, posing the question: Would your world be a better place if these people ceased to exist? Despite initial skepticism, Regan embraces the idea, calling her rogues' gallery of names her "wish list." At the end of the exercise, Shields instructs each participant to bring the sheet of paper to the fireplace and throw it into the flames. Opting to get a jump on the crowd, Regan decides to leave instead. Soon after, one by one, the people whose names appeared on Regan's wish list begin to disappear. Shock turns to horror when the bodies start to surface. Regan immediately tells her story to the Chicago Police Department - but her desire to clear her name is met with startling disbelief. With a noose of suspicion coiling around her neck, and with brutal murders seeming to stalk her every move, Regan must discover the deadly motive behind this chilling game of psychological torment- and more urgent, who has turned her private revenge fantasies into chilling reality.

Murder List. unabr. ed. Julie Garwood. Read by Joyce Bean. (Running Time: 12 hrs.). 2004. 39.25 (978-1-59710-510-1(4), 1597105104, BADLE); 24.95 (978-1-59710-511-8(2), 1597105112, BAD) Brilliance Audio.

Murder Made Absolute, Michael Underwood. Read by Graham Roberts. 5 cass. (Running Time: 7 hrs. 30 min.). 1999. 49.95 (67975) Pub: Soundings Ltd GBR. Dist(s): Ulverscroft US

Murder Makes a Pilgrimage: A Sister Mary Helen Mystery, unabr. ed. Carol Anne O'Marie. Read by Vera Rosewalker. 8 vols. (Running Time: 12 hrs.). 2000. bk. 69.95 (978-0-7927-2325-7(2), CSL 214, Chivers Sound Lib) AudioGO.
Sister Mary Hellen & her friend Eileen join a ten-person tour to the shrine of St. James in Santiago, Spain. But on the way the two good sisters promptly run straight into murder! Sister Mary Helen finds a body behind the saint's silver casket: a beautiful American woman strangled to death. Certain that one of her fellow pilgrims is the girl's murderer, Sister Mary Helen begins to gather clues that will lead to a cold-blooded killer.

Murder Makes Waves. unabr. ed. Anne George. Narrated by Ruth Ann Phimister. 8 CDs. (Running Time: 9 hrs.). (Southern Sisters Mystery Ser.). 2001. audio compact disk 78.00 (978-1-4025-0495-2(0), C1551) Recorded Bks.
Sixty-something sisters Mary Alice and Patricia Anne head to Florida to relax at a beachfront condo. But when a body washes up on the waves, the sisters find themselves awash in a sea of dirty real estate dealings and evidence of murders.

Murder Makes Waves. unabr. ed. Anne George. Narrated by Ruth Ann Phimister. 6 cass. (Running Time: 9 hrs.). (Southern Sisters Mystery Ser.). 2001. 57.00 (978-0-7887-5457-9(2), 96284x7) Recorded Bks.
Sixty-something sisters Mary Alice & Patricia Anne head to Florida to relax at a beachfront condo. But when a body washes up on the waves, the sisters find themselves awash in a sea of dirty real estate dealings & evidence of murder.

Murder Manual. unabr. ed. Steven Womack. Read by Ron Varela. 8 cass. (Running Time: 10 hrs. 30 min.). (Harry Denton Ser.). 2001. 49.95 (978-1-58116-051-2(8)) Books in Motion.
Hired to tail the noted author of Life's Little Maintenance Manual, Harry Denton finds the writer strangled and drowned in his own hot tub.

Murder Manual. unabr. ed. Steven Womack. Narrated by L. J. Ganser. 8 cass. (Running Time: 11 hrs.). 1998. 74.00 (978-0-7887-4390-0(2), 95943E7) Recorded Bks.
Detective Harry Denton is just about to close down his private investigation business when he finally gets an assignment: photograph a famous self-help author with his mistress. When Harry finds him, however, the creator of "Life's Little Maintenance Manual" is very alone & very dead. Now, instead of a detective, Harry is a murder suspect.

Murder Most Foul: The Collection. unabr. ed. Arthur Conan Doyle. Read by Derek Jacobi & Edward Hardwicke. 4 CDs. (Running Time: 5 hrs.). 2009. audio compact disk 26.95 (978-1-934997-42-0(0)) Pub: CSAWord. Dist(s): PerseuPGW

Murder Most Foul, the Collection. Algernon Blackwood et al. Read by Brian Cox et al. (CSA Word Recording Ser.). (ENG.). 2009. 59.99 (978-1-60775-708-5(7)) Find a World.

Murder Most Foul: the Collection 1: The Collection 1. (Running Time: 1 hr. 30 mins.). 2003. 21.95 (978-1-59912-967-9(1)) Iofy Corp.

Murder Most Foul: the Collection 2: The Collection 2. (Running Time: 3 hrs.). 2003. 21.95 (978-1-60083-066-2(8)) Iofy Corp.

Murder Moves In. unabr. ed. E. X. Ferrars. Read by Frances Jeater. 6 cass. (Running Time: 6 hrs.). 1998. 54.95 (978-0-7540-0110-2(5), CAB1533) Pub: Chivers Audio Bks GBR. Dist(s): AudioGO
Burnham Priors was a quaint English village, not a place where one would expect to find a murder. But murder was exactly what confronted Robina Mellanby when she arrived at Burnham Priors. Robina was a young widow with two children when she married Sam Mellanby. She had no idea that the tiny village where Sam lived was filled with terrible events that would now threaten her own life.

***Murder Must Advertise.** Dorothy L. Sayers. Narrated by Ian Carmichael & Full Cast Production Staff. (Running Time: 2 hrs. 20 mins. 0 sec.). (ENG., 2010. audio compact disk 24.95 (978-1-84607-147-8(X)) Pub: AudioGO. Dist(s): Perseus Dist

Murder Must Advertise. Dorothy L. Sayers. Narrated by John Franklyn-Robbins. 7 cas. (Running Time: 12.25 hrs.). (Lord Peter Wimsey Mystery Ser.). 29.95 (978-1-4025-2800-2(0)) Recorded Bks.

Murder Must Advertise. unabr. ed. Dorothy L. Sayers. Read by Ian Carmichael. 6 cass. (Running Time: 10 hrs. 18 mins.). (Lord Peter Wimsey Mystery Ser.). 2003. 29.95 (978-1-57270-300-1(8)) Pub: Audio Partners. Dist(s): PerseuPGW
When ad man Victor Dean falls down the stairs in the offices of Pym?s Publicity, a respectable London advertising agency, it looks like an accident. When Lord Peter Wimsey is called in he soon discovers there?s more to copywriting than meets the eye cocaine, blackmail, and wanton women can be read between the lines.

Murder Must Advertise. unabr. ed. Dorothy L. Sayers. 2 CDs. (Running Time: 2 hrs. 20 mins.). (Lord Peter Wimsey Mystery Ser.). 2008. audio compact disk 29.95 (978-0-7927-5411-4(5)) AudioGO.
The elegant, intelligent amateur sleuth Lord Peter Wimsey is one of detective literature's most popular creations. Ian Carmichael is the personification of Dorothy L. Sayers's charming investigator in this BBC Radio 4 full-cast dramatization. When copywriter Victor Dean falls to his death on the stairs of Pym's Advertising Agency, no one seems to mind. That is, until Lord Peter joins the firm incognito as Dean's replacement and starts asking questions which lead him into a network of blackmailers, drug pushers and one of the most deadly plots of crime fiction. However, before the crimes can be solved and the truth revealed, five more people must die.

Murder Must Advertise. unabr. ed. Dorothy L. Sayers. Read by Ian Carmichael. 10 cass. (Running Time: 15 hrs.). (Lord Peter Wimsey Mystery

Ser.). 2000. 69.95 (978-0-7451-6862-3(0), CAB 331) Pub: Chivers Audio Bks GBR. Dist(s): AudioGO
When Victor Dean fell to his death on the stairs at Pym's Advertising Agency, nobody was sorry. For nobody had really liked him. But when Lord Peter Wimsey, alias Death Bredon, joins the firm and asks some awkward questions, it appears that Dean's death was no accident. Soon, Lord Peter has uncovered a network of blackmailer and dope dealers who are prepared to kill again.

Murder Must Advertise. unabr. ed. Dorothy L. Sayers. Narrated by John Franklyn-Robbins. 10 CDs. (Running Time: 12 hrs.). (Lord Peter Wimsey Mystery Ser.). audio compact disk 44.95 (978-1-4025-2832-3(9)) Recorded Bks.

Murder Must Advertise. unabr. ed. Dorothy L. Sayers. Narrated by John Franklyn-Robbins. 9 cass. (Running Time: 12 hrs.). (Lord Peter Wimsey Mystery Ser.). 1997. 78.00 (978-0-7887-1289-0(6), 95145E7) Recorded Bks.
Lord Wimsey is in a case that begins as the investigation of an accident, but soon leads to an advertising agency that is selling some very unusual services.

Murder of a Suicide. unabr. ed. E. X. Ferrars. Read by Garard Green. 6 cass. (Running Time: 7 hrs. 30 min.). 2001. 54.95 (970104) Pub: ISIS Audio GBR. Dist(s): Ulverscroft US
When Toby & his round-faced companion, George get caught in torrential rain one night, they are surprised to find that they are not the only ones out in such a fierce storm. It seems that Edgar Prees, an aging botanist of prestige & reputation, is attempting to commit suicide by jumping off a cliff-top. The two men drive Edgar home, collapsed & shaken. When he is found the next morning - shot to death with his own revolver - it seems that his attempt at suicide has succeeded. But as Toby & George are thrust into the case, it becomes apparent that suicide is not always as simple as it would seem.

Murder of a Suicide. unabr. ed. E. X. Ferrars. Read by Garard Green. 6 cass. (Isis Ser.). (J). 2004. 54.95 (978-0-7531-0129-2(7)) Pub: ISIS Lrg Prnt GBR. Dist(s): Ulverscroft US

Murder of Crows. Jack Bates. Read by Dave Giorgio. (ENG.). 2009. audio compact disk 5.49 (978-0-9821192-8-0(3)) Mind Wings Aud.

***Murder of Crows.** Jack Bates. Read by Dave Giorgio. (Running Time: 55). (ENG.). 2009. 2.99 (978-1-61114-008-8(0)) Mind Wings Aud.

***Murder of Crows: A Sir Robert Carey Mystery.** unabr. ed. P. F. Chisholm. (Running Time: 8 hrs. 30 mins.). 2010. 29.95 (978-1-4417-4284-1(0)); 54.95 (978-1-4417-4280-3(8)); audio compact disk 76.00 (978-1-4417-4281-0(6)) Blckstn Audio.

Murder of Helen Jewett: The Life & Death of a Prostitute in 19th Century New York. unabr. collector's ed. Patricia Cline Cohen. Read by Kate Reading. 12 cass. (Running Time: 18 hrs.). 1999. 96.00 (978-0-7366-4420-4(2), 4881) Books on Tape.
In 1836, the murder of a young New York City prostitute & the ensuing trial captivated the nation. From her beginnings as a servant in Maine, Jewett refashioned herself into a highly paid courtesan. She captivated her customers through her seductive letters, which mixed traditional feminine demureness with sexual boldness. But she was to meet her match in an arrogant 17-year-old clerk named Richard Robinson. The scion of an established Connecticut family, he became Jewett's lover in a tempestuous affair & ten months later killed her. Despite overwhelming evidence of his guilt, Robinson was acquitted.

Murder of Honor. unabr. ed. Robert Andrews. Read by David Jones & David Daoust. 5 cass. (Running Time: 7 hrs.). 2001. 27.95 (978-1-58788-201-2(9), 1587882019, BAU) Brilliance Audio.
In the world of cops, drive-by killings don't rank high on the popularity charts. They're usually random, and barring credible witnesses, they largely go unsolved. So when Father Robert O'Brien, a popular Washington priest with a high public profile, is murdered in a drive-by shooting, D.C. police aren't beating down doors to get the case. Homicide detectives Frank Kearney and José Phelps have been members of the force for twenty-five years, partners from the start. They're smart cops - smart enough to know they've been played for patsies when the O'Brien murder lands in their laps. This is payback time for two cops who've been a little too brash, a little too independent. But what appears to be a motiveless drive-by in a city with one of the nation's highest homicide rates soon turns into a dirtier, far more complex case involving corrupt politicians, self-serving media, warring drug lords, millions of dollars in questionable cash - and more murder. As Frank and José dig deeper, fending off the police bureaucracy and meddling politicos, it becomes increasingly clear that this case might cost them more than their careers. It might cost them their lives.

Murder of Honor. unabr. ed. Robert Andrews. Read by David Daoust. 5 cass. (Running Time: 7 hrs.). 2001. 57.25 (978-1-58788-202-9(7), 1587882027); audio compact disk 24.95 (978-1-59600-748-2(6), 9781596007482, Brilliance MP3) Brilliance Audio.

Murder of Honor. unabr. ed. Robert Andrews. Read by David Daoust. (Running Time: 7 hrs.). 2005. 39.25 (978-1-59600-751-2(6), 9781596007512, BADLE); 24.95 (978-1-59600-750-5(8), 9781596007505, BAD); audio compact disk 39.25 (978-1-59600-749-9(4), 9781596007499, Brlnc Audio MP3 Lib) Brilliance Audio.

Murder of Jesus. 2 cass. 7.95 (22-4, HarperThor) HarpC GBR.

Murder of King Tut: The Plot to Kill the Child King. unabr. ed. James Patterson & Martin Dugard. Read by Joe Barrett. (Running Time: 6 hrs.). (ENG.). 2009. 14.98 (978-1-60024-636-4(2)) Pub: Hachet Audio. Dist(s): HachBkGrp

***Murder of King Tut: The Plot to Kill the Child King.** unabr. ed. James Patterson & Martin Dugard. Read by Joe Barrett. (Running Time: 6 hrs.). (ENG.). 2010. audio compact disk 14.98 (978-1-60788-654-9(5)) Pub: Hachet Audio. Dist(s): HachBkGrp

Murder of Promise. unabr. ed. Robert Andrews. Read by David Daoust. 6 cass. (Running Time: 8 hrs.). 2002. 29.95 (978-1-58788-993-6(5), 1587889935, BAU); 69.25 (978-1-58788-994-3(3), 1587889943, Unabridge Lib Edns) Brilliance Audio.
When legendary Washington Post reporter Mary Keegan is found murdered, homicide detectives Frank Kearney and Jose Phelps pull up the file on another open case. There as here, the victim was a female who had been hacked to death in a public park. And there is one other link: each was missing a little finger, a grisly souvenir - perhaps the calling card of a serial killer. When, a week later, a third woman is found in similar circumstances, they're sure of it. Kearney and Phelps are certain the killer will strike again and know they're working against time. Using the best evidence modern forensics and computer science can supply and the good guesswork twenty-five years of homicide investigations have sharpened, they begin to see some patterns, but not enough to connect up the dots. Then the finger of one of the victims is found sealed inside a plastic baggie in a raided crack house. Cutting corners, pulling in favors, they track the evidence back to what they believe will be the killer, only to find he is one step ahead of them. In a climactic nightmare chase, Kearney races to save the person dearest to him as he faces off against a cunning homicidal maniac.

Murder of Promise. unabr. ed. Robert Andrews. Read by David Daoust. (Running Time: 8 hrs.). 2004. 39.25 (978-1-59335-555-5(6), 1593355556, Brlnc Audio MP3 Lib) Brilliance Audio.

Murder of Promise. unabr. ed. Robert Andrews. Read by David Daoust. (Running Time: 8 hrs.). 2004. 39.25 (978-1-59710-512-5(0), 1597105120, BADLE); 24.95 (978-1-59710-513-2(9), 1597105139, BAD) Brilliance Audio.

Murder of Promise. unabr. ed. Robert Andrews. Read by David Daoust. (Running Time: 8 hrs.). 2004. 24.95 (978-1-59335-135-9(6), 1593351356) Soulmate Audio Bks.

Murder of Quality. John le Carré. Read by John le Carré. 2 cass. (Running Time: 3 hrs.). (George Smiley Ser.). 1999. (978-1-84032-103-6(2), HoddrStoughton) Hodder General GBR.
Miss Brimley had received a letter from a worried woman reader: "I'm not mad. And I know my husband is trying to kill me".

Murder of Quality. unabr. ed. John le Carré. Read by Frederick Davidson. 4 cass. (Running Time: 5 hrs. 30 mins.). (George Smiley Ser.). 1991. 32.95 (978-0-7861-0272-3(1), 1238) Blckstn Audio.
Undercover agent George Smiley emerges from retirement to solve a baffling, bloody crime. He becomes entangled with a woman as dangerous as she is charming...& a tottering, brilliant man haunted by a perverse secret of his past. Smiley pursues the murderer amid the hollow pomp & ceremony of the Establishment, where a man's fate is decided over tea & a sentence of death can be passed out with biscuits & sherry.

***Murder of Quality.** unabr. ed. John le Carré. (Running Time: 5 hrs. 15 mins.). 2010. audio compact disk 29.95 (978-1-4417-3580-5(1)) Blckstn Audio.

***Murder of Quality.** unabr. ed. John le Carré. Read by Ralph Cosham. (Running Time: 4 hrs. 30 mins.). 2010. 29.95 (978-1-4417-4246-9(8)); 34.95 (978-1-4417-4244-5(1)); audio compact disk 49.00 (978-1-4417-4245-2(X)) Blckstn Audio.

Murder of Quality. unabr. ed. John le Carré. Read by Rupert Keenlyside. 6 cass. (Running Time: 6 hrs.). (George Smiley Novels Ser.). 1986. 36.00 (978-0-7366-0456-7(1), 1428) Books on Tape.
George Smiley steps in to solve a baffling, bloody crime. One key to the puzzle is a woman as dangerous as she is charming. Another is a tottering but brilliant operative haunted by a perverse secret buried deep in his past. Through them & beyond, Smiley trails his man to the heart of the Establishment where one's fate is decided over tea & a sentence of death can be passed out with biscuits & sherry.

Murder of Quality. unabr. ed. John le Carré. Narrated by Keith Lloyd. 4 cass. (Running Time: 5 hrs. 15 mins.). (George Smiley Novels Ser.). 1990. 35.00 (978-1-55690-361-8(8), 90063E7) Recorded Bks.
A murder at an exclusive boarding school involved George Smiley as investigator.

Murder of Quality: A BBC Radio Drama. John le Carré. Narrated by Simon Russell Beale. (Running Time: 1 hr. 30 mins. 0 sec.). (ENG.). 2010. audio compact disk 19.95 (978-1-60283-636-5(1)) Pub: AudioGO. Dist(s): Perseus Dist

Murder of Roger Ackroyd. Agatha Christie. Narrated by Flo Gibson. 2008. audio compact disk 27.95 (978-1-55685-987-8(2)) Audio Bk Con.

Murder of Roger Ackroyd. Agatha Christie. Read by Robin Bailey. (Running Time: 7 hrs.). 2005. 27.95 (978-1-59912-387-5(8)) Iofy Corp.

Murder of Roger Ackroyd, unabr. ed. Agatha Christie. Narrated by Flo Gibson. 5 cass. (Running Time: 7 hrs. 30 min.). (gr. 10 up). 2000. 20.95 (978-1-55685-638-9(5)) Audio Bk Con.
Blackmail & murder point to several suspects. Only Master sleuth Hercule Poirot can come up with the surprising answer.

Murder of Roger Ackroyd. unabr. ed. Agatha Christie. Read by Robin Bailey. 6 cass. (Running Time: 7 hrs. 3 mins.). (Hercule Poirot Mystery Ser.). 2001. 29.95 (978-1-57270-209-7(5), N61209u) Pub: Audio Partners. Dist(s): PerseuPGW
Village rumor hints that Mrs. Ferrars poisoned her husband, but no one is sure. When the killer strikes again, master sleuth Hercule Poirot takes over the investigation.

Murder of Roger Ackroyd. unabr. ed. Agatha Christie. Narrated by Robin Bailey. (Running Time: 25380 sec.). (Audio Editions Mystery Masters Ser.). (ENG.). 2006. audio compact disk 29.95 (978-1-57270-516-6(7)) Pub: AudioGO. Dist(s): Perseus Dist

Murder of Roger Ackroyd: A BBC Radio Full-Cast Dramatization. Agatha Christie. (Running Time: 1 hr. 30 mins. 0 sec.). (ENG.). 2009. audio compact disk 24.95 (978-1-60283-732-4(5)) Pub: AudioGO. Dist(s): Perseus Dist

Murder of the Maharajah. unabr. ed. H. R. F. Keating. Read by Frederick Davidson. 8 cass. (Running Time: 11 hrs. 30 mins.). (Inspector Ghote Mystery Ser.: No. 12). 1995. 56.95 (978-0-7861-0800-8(2), 1624) Blckstn Audio.
A princely state in India, 1930, under the British Raj. To Bhopore & its opulent Summer Palace comes a handful of Western visitors to meet the outrageous Maharajah & his entourage. There they meet the Maharajah's heir, the sensual Porgy, & his English chorus-girl mistress. They meet the enigmatic chief minister - & the aloof British Resident, with his dignified little nine-year-old son. And before long they also meet sudden death...various people in the Palace become suspects, & an imperturbable District Superintendent of Police is called in. But who will he find guilty of the murder of the Maharajah?.

Murder Offshore. abr. ed. Paul Wynes. 1 cass. 1997. 17.00 (978-1-883268-50-3(8)) Spellbinders.

Murder Olympic Style. unabr. ed. Tom McCloud. Read by Bernard Bridges. Ed. by Richard Haywood. 2 cass. (Running Time: 3 hrs.). 1996. 17.00 (978-1-883268-37-4(0)) Spellbinders.
Clint McCord is hired to haul a load of high fashion clothing from Los Angeles to Atlanta. A routine D.O.T. inspection turns up two dead bodies & a comatose child in his trailer. It soon becomes apparent someone wants this child dead, as well as an oriental gold medal prospect.

Murder on a Bad Hair Day. unabr. ed. Anne George. Narrated by Ruth Ann Phimister. 6 cass. (Running Time: 8 hrs. 30 mins.). (Southern Sisters Mystery Ser.). 2000. 57.00 (978-0-7887-4882-0(3), 96282E7) Recorded Bks.
A delightful mystery combining humor & suspense with a Southern flair. Patricia Anne & Mary Allice are sisters who, after years of sibling rivalry, have discovered a mutual interest in folk art. However, Patricia Anne never dreamed that attending a gallery opening would land them in the middle of a murder investigation.

Murder on a Girls' Night Out. Anne George. Narrated by Ruth Ann Phimister. 7 CDs. (Running Time: 7 hrs. 30 mins.). (Southern Sisters Mystery Ser.). 2001. audio compact disk 69.00 (978-0-7887-5170-7(0), C1332E7) Recorded Bks.
When impulsive Mary Alice buys a country western club, her cautious younger sister Patricia Ann thinks she has lost her mind, especially after the precious owner turns up dead in a gangland-style execution.

Murder on a Girls' Night Out. unabr. ed. Anne George. Narrated by Ruth Ann Phimister. 6 cass. (Running Time: 7 hrs. 30 mins.). (Southern Sisters Mystery Ser.). 1996. 57.00 (978-0-7887-4367-2(8), 96280E7) Recorded Bks.
Tale of two "60 something" sisters reveals the deadly consequences of a hasty real estate purchase. When impulsive Mary Alice buys a country western club, her cautious younger sister Patricia Ann thinks she has lost her mind, especially after the previous owner turns up dead in a gangland-style execution.

Murder on a midsummer Night. Kerry Greenwood. Read by Stephanie Daniel. (Running Time: 9 hrs. 10 mins.). (Phryne Fisher Mystery: Ser.). 2009. 79.99 (978-1-74214-177-0(3), 9781742141770) Pub: Bolinda Pubng AUS. Dist(s): Bolinda Pub Inc

Murder on a Midsummer Night. unabr. ed. Kerry Greenwood. Read by Stephanie Daniel. (Running Time: 9 hrs. 10 mins.). (Phryne Fisher Ser.). 2008. audio compact disk 87.95 (978-1-74214-067-4(X), 9781742140674) Pub: Bolinda Pubng AUS. Dist(s): Bolinda Pub Inc

Murder on Campus. Hazel Holt & Hazel Holt. Read by Patricia Gallimore. 5 cass. (Sheila Malory Mystery Ser.: No. 5). 2007. 49.95 (978-1-84559-490-9(8)) Pub: ISIS Lrg Prnt GBR. Dist(s): Ulverscroft US

Murder on Campus. Hazel Holt & Hazel Holt. Read by Patricia Gallimore. (Running Time: 21600 sec.). (Sheila Malory Mystery Ser.: No. 5). 2007. audio compact disk 64.95 (978-1-84559-595-1(5)) Pub: ISIS Lrg Prnt GBR. Dist(s): Ulverscroft US

Murder on Capitol Hill. Margaret Truman. Read by Betsy Hershberg. 5 cass. (Running Time: 6 hrs. 45 min.). (Capital Crimes Ser.: Vol. 2). 1993. 43.40 (978-1-56544-053-1(6), 250025); Rental 8.80 30 day rental Set. (250025) Literate Ear.
The guest of honor, Senate Majority Leader Cale Caldwell, makes a dramatic appearance at his party...with an ice pick implanted in his chest. Almost anyone at the gala could have killed him.

Murder on Embassy Row. Margaret Truman. Read by Betsy Hershberg. 6 cass. (Running Time: 9 hrs.). (Capital Crimes Ser.: Vol. 5). 1993. 49.00 (978-1-56544-042-5(0), 250027); Rental 8.50 30 day rental Set. (250027) Literate Ear.
Sal Manzio & Connie Lake, officers in Washington's special consular police force, are foiled in their attempts to uncover the truth behind the murder of the British Ambassador to the United States. That is, until a second grisly murder propels them into an international chase through London, Denmark & back to Embassy Row.

Murder on Her Mind. unabr. ed. Sierra Adare. Read by Juanita Parker. 8 cass. (Running Time: 8 hrs. 48 min.). 2001. 49.95 (978-1-58116-030-7(5)) Books in Motion.

Murder on K Street. Margaret Truman. Read by Phil Gigante. (Playaway Adult Fiction Ser.). 2008. 64.99 (978-1-60640-792-9(9)) Find a World.

Murder on K Street: A Capital Crimes Novel. abr. ed. Margaret Truman. Read by Phil Gigante. (Running Time: 6 hrs.). (Capital Crimes Ser.). 2008. audio compact disk 14.99 (978-1-4233-4055-3(8), 9781423340553, BCD Value Price) Brilliance Audio.

Murder on K Street: A Capital Crimes Novel. unabr. ed. Margaret Truman. (Running Time: 10 hrs.). (Capital Crimes Ser.: Vol. 23). 2007. 39.25 (978-1-4233-4053-9(1), 9781423340539, BADLE); 24.95 (978-1-4233-4052-2(3), 9781423340522, BAD); audio compact disk 34.95 (978-1-4233-4048-5(5), 9781423340485, Bril Audio CD Unabri) Brilliance Audio.

Murder on K Street: A Capital Crimes Novel. unabr. ed. Margaret Truman. Read by Phil Gigante. 8 cass. (Running Time: 10 hrs.). (Capital Crimes Ser.: Vol. 23). 2007. 87.25 (978-1-4233-4047-8(7), 9781423340478, BrilAudUnabridg); audio compact disk 92.25 (978-1-4233-4049-2(3), 9781423340492, BriAudCD Unabrid); audio compact disk 39.25 (978-1-4233-4051-5(5), 9781423340515, Brlnc Audio MP3 Lib); audio compact disk 24.95 (978-1-4233-4050-8(7), 9781423340508, Brilliance MP3) Brilliance Audio.

Murder on Mad Mountain. unabr. ed. Nicholas Carter. 1 cass. (Running Time: 58 min.). 12.95 (496) J Norton Pubs.
The "Murder on Mad Mountain" is about the murder of an opera singer & her domestics during a blizzard. In "Webs of Murder" a valuable cargo of spider webs has been stolen & the store owner is killed.

Murder on Martha's Vineyard. unabr. ed. David Osborn. Read by Donada Peters. 7 cass. (Running Time: 7 hrs.). 1992. 56.00 (978-0-7366-2188-5(1), 2983) Books on Tape.
Margaret has come to Martha's vineyard for a quiet vacation with her grandchildren. But it's not to be. A Boston socialite shows up floating in a neighbor's pond & Margaret is the prime suspect.

Murder on Nob Hill. unabr. ed. Shirley Tallman. Read by Anna Fields. 6 cass. (Running Time: 8 hrs. 30 mins.). (Sarah Woolson Mystery Ser.: Bk. 1). 2004. 44.95 (978-0-7861-2812-9(7), 3256); audio compact disk 39.95 (978-0-7861-8698-3(4)); audio compact disk 24.95 (978-0-7861-8468-2(X), 3256); audio compact disk 56.00 (978-0-7861-8493-4(0), 3256); reel tape 32.95 (978-0-7861-2677-4(9)) Blckstn Audio.
Sarah Woolson dreamed of being a lawyer, but in 1880 everyone believes a woman's place is in the home. Yet Sarah finagles her way into a prestigious law firm and acquires her first client, a society matron accused of murder. Sarah is sure of her client's innocence but finds it nearly impossible to prove. When more victims fall prey to the killer, Sarah becomes involved with shady legal maneuvers, a daring raid, and the most powerful and dangerous tong lord in the city's Chinese District.

Murder on Perdido Key. 2000. 19.95 (978-0-9707199-0-4(6)) Dogwd Hill.

Murder on Safari. unabr. ed. Elspeth Huxley. Narrated by Jill Tanner. 6 cass. (Running Time: 8 hrs. 15 mins.). 1989. 51.00 (978-1-55690-362-5(6), 89820E7) Recorded Bks.
Big cats are not the only game in the hunter's sights. Lady Baradale is dead & a killer stalks.

Murder on Safari. unabr. collector's ed. Elspeth Huxley. Read by Donada Peters. 8 cass. (Running Time: 8 hrs.). 1989. 48.00 (978-0-7366-1599-0(7), 2460) Books on Tape.
Lord & Lady Baradale, on a posh safari in Kenya, anticipate splendid photo trophies for their luxurious labors. But rather than collecting trophies, they give some up. When Lady Baradale's jewels are stolen, a young Canadian policeman, Vachell, is called in. He sets to work on the theft, but is interrupted by murder. Lady Baradale's body is discovered with a bullet hole in the skull. Every member of the hunting party is suspect.

Murder on the Appian Way. unabr. ed. Steven Saylor. Read by Scott Harrison. 12 cass. (Running Time: 17 hrs. 30 mins.). 1996. 83.95 (978-0-7861-0983-8(1), 1760) Blckstn Audio.
Rome has been in a state of turmoil as the rival gangs of Publius Clodius, a high-born, populist politician & his arch-enemy Titus Milo have fought to control the consular elections. When Clodius is murdered on the famed Appian Way & Milo is accused of the crime, the city explodes with riots & arson & even the near sacrosanct Senate House is burned to the ground.

***Murder on the Ballarat Train.** Kerry Greenwood. Read by Stephanie Daniel. (Running Time: 4 hrs. 47 mins.). (Phryne Fisher Mystery: Ser.). 2010. 59.99

(978-1-74214-603-4(1), 9781742146034) Pub: Bolinda Pubng AUS. Dist(s): Bolinda Pub Inc

Murder on the Ballarat Train. unabr. ed. Kerry Greenwood. Read by Stephanie Daniel. (Running Time: 4 hrs. 47 mins.). (Phryne Fisher Mystery: Ser.). 2009. audio compact disk 57.95 (978-1-74214-585-3(X), 9781742145853) Pub: Bolinda Pubng AUS. Dist(s): Bolinda Pub Inc

***Murder on the Brighton Express.** unabr. ed. Edward Marston. Narrated by Sam Dastor. 7 CDs. (Running Time: 8 hrs. 10 mins.). 2010. audio compact disk 89.95 (978-0-7927-7231-6(8)) AudioGO.

Murder on the Cape. unabr. ed. Tom McCloud. Read by Bernard Bridges. Ed. by Richard Haywood. 2 cass. (Running Time: 3 hrs.). 1995. 17.00 (978-1-883268-15-2(X)) Spellbinders.
Clint McCord is hired to haul a sensitive, high-tech, space computer to Cape Canaveral. Before he can unload the ultra high speed computer at the NASA dock, a dead body is found in his new soft ride trailer. McCord is enlisted by his old military commander to help solve the crime.

Murder on the Chesapeake. unabr. ed. David Osborn. Read by Donada Peters. 6 cass. (Running Time: 6 hrs.). 1993. 48.00 (978-0-7366-2437-4(6), 3202) Books on Tape.
Margaret Barlow investigates murder at her alma mater, an exclusive girls' prep school.

Murder on the Dance Floor. Susan B. Kelly & Susan Kelly. 2008. 54.95 (978-1-84559-734-4(6)); audio compact disk 64.95 (978-1-84559-735-1(4)) Pub: Soundings Ltd GBR. Dist(s): Ulverscroft US

Murder on the Gravy Train. unabr. ed. Phyllis C. Richman. Read by Susan O'Malley. 6 cass. (Running Time: 8 hrs. 30 mins.). (Chas Wheatley Mystery Ser.). 2001. 44.95 (978-0-7861-1969-1(1), 2739); audio compact disk 56.00 (978-0-7861-9756-9(0), 2739) Blckstn Audio.
Chas Wheatley, a food writer with a taste for sleuthing, takes on the scandalous world of Washington tongue waggers & the deep-throated secrets of the restaurant business.

Murder on the Iditarod Trail. Sue Henry. (Jessie Arnold Mystery Ser.). audio compact disk 17.99 (978-0-7366-7810-0(7)) Books on Tape.

Murder on the Iditarod Trail. Sue Henry. Read by Mary Peiffer. 6 cass. (Running Time: 9 hrs.). (Jessie Arnold Mystery Ser.). 1999. 29.95 (978-0-7366-4592-8(6)) Books on Tape.
The Iditarod brings thousands of competitors & their teams to Anchorage each year. During the two weeks it takes to complete the grueling course, participants battle frostbite & overpowering fatigue. It's an arduous sport but not a deadly one - until now. Someone is systematically killing the top "mushers" & Sergeant Alex Jensen has been called in to find the murderer. This is also the first time that Jessie Arnold has a shot at winning. But as her position in the race improves, so do her chances of being the killer's next target.

Murder on the Iditarod Trail. collector's unabr. ed. Sue Henry. Read by Mary Pfeiffer. 7 cass. (Running Time: 10 hrs. 30 min.). (Jessie Arnold Mystery Ser.). 2000. audio compact disk 56.00 (978-0-7366-5159-2(4)) Books on Tape.

Murder on the Iditarod Trail. unabr. collector's ed. Sue Henry. Read by Mary Peiffer. 7 CDs. (Running Time: 8 hrs. 12 mins.). (Jessie Arnold Mystery Ser.). 2001. audio compact disk 56.00 Books on Tape.
This collection of original works was born of a deliciously wicked idea: ask twelve of America's best writers to explore a single subject - people willing, often gleefully so, to kill for revenge.

Murder on the Iditarod Trail. unabr. collector's ed. Sue Henry. Read by Mary Peiffer. 6 cass. (Running Time: 9 hrs.). (Jessie Arnold Mystery Ser.). 1999. 48.00 (978-0-7366-4413-6(X), 4874) Books on Tape.
The Iditarod brings thousands of competitors & their teams to Anchorage each year. During the two weeks it takes to complete the grueling course, participants battle frostbite & overpowering fatigue. It's an arduous sport but not a deadly one - until now. Someone is systematically killing the top "mushers" & Sergeant Alex Jensen has been called in to find the murderer. This is also the first time that Jessie Arnold has a shot at winning. But as her position in the race improves, so do her chances of being the killer's next target.

Murder on the Internet. Ron Ellis. 5 cass. (Running Time: 6 hrs. 30 mins.). (Soundings Ser.). (J). 2005. 49.95 (978-1-84559-055-0(4)) Pub: ISIS Lrg Prnt GBR. Dist(s): Ulverscroft US

Murder on the Leviathan. unabr. ed. Boris Akunin. Read by Michael Kramer. 6 cass. (Running Time: 9 hrs.). 2004. 54.00 (978-0-7366-9744-6(6)) Books on Tape.
Detective Erast Fandorin must link a Paris massacre to a shipboard murderer.

***Murder on the Links.** Agatha Christie. Narrated by Full Cast Production Staff & John Moffatt. 2 CDs. (Running Time: 1 hr. 30 mins. 0 sec.). (ENG., 2010. audio compact disk 24.95 (978-0-563-51011-6(0)) Pub: AudioGO. Dist(s): Perseus Dist

Murder on the Links. collector's ed. Agatha Christie. Read by Roe Kendall. 6 cass. (Running Time: 9 hrs.). 2000. 48.00 (978-0-7366-4911-7(5)) Books on Tape.
Monsieur Renauld dies on a golf course just days after sending a plea for help to Detective Hercule Poirot. Since Renauld possessed a plundered fortune, a scorned wife, a mistress & an estranged son, there is no lack of suspects. It's up to Poirot to put the police onto the culprit before more murders occur. His insistence that the police arrested the wrong man in their investigation into the killing is proven correct when a second murder takes place.

Murder on the Links, unabr. ed. Agatha Christie. Read by Flo Gibson. 5 cass. (Running Time: 6 hrs. 30 min.). 1998. bk. 20.95 (978-1-55685-504-7(4)) Audio Bk Con.
Two murders mystify the police in a small French town. Renauld's wife, mistress & estranged son are suspects, but brilliant Hercule Poirot comes up with a different solution.

Murder on the Links. unabr. ed. Agatha Christie. 2 CDs. 2008. audio compact disk 19.95 (978-1-60283-518-4(7)) AudioGO.

Murder on the Links. unabr. ed. Agatha Christie. Read by Hugh Fraser. (ENG.). 2008. audio compact disk 27.95 (978-1-60283-557-3(8)) Pub: AudioGO. Dist(s): Perseus Dist

Murder on the Nile Soundtrack. Prod. by Myattic Studio. (YA). 2000. audio compact disk 89.95 (978-0-7365-3278-5(1)) Films Media Grp.

Murder on the Orient Express. Agatha Christie. Contrib. by John Moffatt. 2 CDs. (Running Time: 2 hrs. 20 mins.). 2006. audio compact disk 29.95 (978-0-7927-3986-9(8), BBCD 137) AudioGO.

Murder on the Orient Express. Agatha Christie. Read by David Suchet. (Running Time: 7 hrs.). 2005. 27.95 (978-1-59912-383-7(5)) Iofy Corp.

Murder on the Orient Express. abr. ed. Agatha Christie. Contrib. by John Moffatt et al. (Running Time: 7800 sec.). (BBC Radio Ser.). (ENG.). 2007. audio compact disk 19.95 (978-1-60283-043-1(6)) Pub: AudioGO. Dist(s): Perseus Dist

Murder on the Orient Express. unabr. ed. Agatha Christie. Read by David Suchet. 6 cass. (Running Time: 6 hrs. 30 mins.). (Hercule Poirot Mystery Ser.). 2001. 29.95 (978-1-57270-211-0(7), N61211u) Pub: Audio Partners. Dist(s): PerseuPGW
A Russian princess, a Hungarian count, a Swedish beauty, and an assortment of Americans, English and French are brought together on the elegant Orient Express. A brutal murder and an unexpected blizzard bring in the vacationing Hercule Poirot.

Murder on the Orient Express: A Hercule Poirot Mystery. unabr. ed. Agatha Christie. Narrated by David Suchet. (Mystery Masters Ser.). (ENG.). 2005. audio compact disk 29.95 (978-1-57270-467-1(5)) Pub: AudioGO. Dist(s): Perseus Dist
On the elegant, plush Orient Express - the famous train from Istanbul to Paris - Ratchett, an imperious millionaire gangster, killer, kidnapper, and child abuser, confronts Inspector Hercule Poirot and offers the little Belgian $20,000 if he will help him stay alive. Poirot declines, adding, ""I do not like your face, Monsieur." Later that evening, as the train sits halted and snowbound, Ratchett is found dead inside a room locked from the inside, a victim of multiple stab wounds. Clearly, the clever, ruthless killer is still on board the train. Detective Poirot must find the killer of the much-hated millionaire among thirteen suspects, each with a compelling reason to kill Ratchett. Can Poirot solve this baffling crime by the time the train reaches Paris? Read by David Suchet.

Murder on the Oval Track. abr. ed. 1 cass. 1997. 17.00 (978-1-883268-39-8(7)) Spellbinders.

Murder on the Potomac. unabr. ed. Margaret Truman. Narrated by Richard Poe. 6 cass. (Running Time: 9 hrs.). (Capital Crimes Ser.: Vol. 12). 1994. 53.00 (978-0-7887-3759-6(7), 95957E7) Recorded Bks.
Offers a glimpse of chilling, behind-the-scenes power struggles in the nation's capital. When an old friend is suspected of foul play, law professor Mackensie Smith finds himself pulled into a murder investigation that places his wife in deadly peril.

Murder on the Potomac. unabr. ed. Margaret Truman. Narrated by Richard Poe. 8 CDs. (Running Time: 9 hrs.). (Capital Crimes Ser.: Vol. 12). 2000. audio compact disk 78.00 (978-0-7887-4482-2(8), C1184E7) Recorded Bks.

Murder on the Prowl. unabr. ed. Rita Mae Brown & Sneaky Pie Brown. 7 cass. (Running Time: 9 hrs. 15 min.). (Mrs. Murphy Mystery Ser.). 2003. 68.00 (978-1-4025-6248-8(9)) Recorded Bks.
A fake obituary is printed in the local newspaper, and the people of Crozet, Virginia are quite dismayed. But when another fake obituary appears, quickly followed by a murder, Mrs. Murphy the sleuthing cat and her human friend Harry Haristeen find themselves on a dangerous path.

Murder on the Ropes Vol. 1: Original Boxing Mysteries. unabr. ed. Read by Ed Begley, Jr. et al. Ed. by Otto Penzler. 4 cass. (Running Time: 6 hrs.). (Sports Mysteries Ser.). 2004. 25.00 (978-1-931056-98-4(6), N Millennium Audio) Pub: New Millenn Enter. Dist(s): PerseuPGW
The second installment of New Millennium's Sports Mysteries anthology. This second round, set within the arena of the world of boxing, is an involving collection from some of the most interesting voices of mystery. See how, set within a common context, each author takes the reader in so many interesting directions.

Murder on the Ropes Vol. 2: Original Boxing Mysteries. unabr. abr. ed. Read by Ed Begley, Jr. et al. Ed. by Otto Penzler. 4 cass. (Running Time: 6 hrs.). (Sports Mysteries Ser.). 2004. 25.00 (978-1-931056-99-1(4), N Millennium Audio) Pub: New Millenn Enter. Dist(s): PerseuPGW

Murder on the Run. unabr. ed. Medora Sale. Read by Lynda Evans. 6 cass. (Running Time: 6 hrs. 18 min.). (Inspector John Sanders Mystery Ser.). 1998. 39.95 (978-1-55686-825-2(1)) Books in Motion.
A series of copycat murders & attempted murder, has Inspector Sanders & his friend Eleanor baffled.

Murder on the Run. unabr. ed. Gloria White. (Running Time: 25200 sec.). (Ronnie Ventana Mystery Ser.). 2007. 44.95 (978-1-4332-0705-1(2)); audio compact disk 55.00 (978-1-4332-0706-8(0)); audio compact disk 29.95 (978-1-4332-0707-5(9)) Blckstn Audio.

Murder on the Run. unabr. ed. Gloria White. Read by Carol Cowan. 5 cass. (Running Time: 6 hrs. 43 min.). (Ronnie Ventana Mystery Ser.). 1993. 30.00 (978-0-9624010-4-6(8)) Readers Chair.
This is the first Ronnie Ventana mystery. Ronnie believes she has witnessed a prominent political figure commit murder. Her investigation leads through the barrios & ritziest neighborhoods of San Francisco to an unexpected discovery.

Murder on the Titanic. Jim Walker. Narrated by Jeff Woodman. 11 cass. (Running Time: 15 hrs. 45 mins.). (Mysteries in Time Ser.). 94.00 (978-1-4025-0968-1(5)) Recorded Bks.

Murder on the Trans-Siberian Express. unabr. ed. Stuart M. Kaminsky. 6 cass. (Running Time: 8 hrs. 30 mins.). (Inspector Porfiry Rostnikov Mystery Ser.: No. 14). 2005. 59.75 (978-1-4025-3874-2(X)) Recorded Bks.
Chief Inspector Porfiry Rostnikov rides into the frigid east on the legendary Trans-Siberian Express. Six thousand miles long and built at a cost of more than a trillion czarist rubles and thousands of lives, the line from Moscow to Vladivostok carries the one-legged inspector in his pursuit of a treasured historical document, as well as a greater find with even more explosive consequences. For behind the quest and many miles away back in Moscow looms the figure of Rostnikov¿s superior, Director of the Office of Special Investigation Igor Yaklovev, whose long-nurtured designs for power await their moment of fruition... while the entire Russian government faces a hard and unsuspected fall.

Murder on the Yellow Brick Road. Stuart M. Kaminsky. Read by Christopher Lane. 4 CDs. (Running Time: 4 hrs.). (Toby Peters Mystery Ser.: No. 2). 2000. audio compact disk 32.00 (978-0-7861-9826-9(5), 1511) Blckstn Audio.
Toby Peters is summoned to the scene of the crime by a very young & frightened starlet named Judy Garland. He begins to put together the scanty clues. Within an hour, he is hired by Lewis B. Meyer himself to keep the name of Judy Garland & MGM clean of the scandal & to hold off the police & the newspapers. But before long, Peters realized that he is on to nothing less than a plot threatening the life of Judy Garland. Enlisting the aid of Judy, Clark Gable & Raymond Chandler, Peters uncovers clue after clue but the odds are heavily stacked against him.

Murder on the Yellow Brick Road. unabr. ed. Stuart M. Kaminsky. Read by Christopher Lane. 3 cass. (Running Time: 4 hrs.). (Toby Peters Mystery Ser.: No. 2). 1994. 23.95 (978-0-7861-0785-8(5), 1511) Blckstn Audio.
It is November 1st, 1940. In the famous sound stage of "The Wizard of Oz" on the MGM lot, a little man is lying face-up on the yellow brick road. Someone has murdered a Munchkin. Toby Peters is summoned to the scene. He begins to put scant clues together.

Murder on the Yukon Quest. collector's unabr. ed. Sue Henry. Read by Mary Pfeiffer. 7 cass. (Running Time: 10 hrs. 30 min.). (Jessie Arnold Mystery Ser.). 1999. 56.00 (978-0-7366-4664-2(7)) Books on Tape.
The contest of a lifetime & Jessie Arnold & her team of dogs are ready for the competition. After it starts & well along the trail, Jessie is stunned to learn that a young novice racer has been kidnapped. The girl's father has been warned that no one but Jessie is to be told, especially not the police. Unable to ignore the plight of the missing girl, Jessie is in a life & death battle against an unknown murderer who will kill anyone who gets in his way.

Murder on the Yukon Quest. unabr. ed. Sue Henry. Read by Mary Peiffer. 8 CDs. (Running Time: 9 hrs. 25 mins.). (Jessie Arnold Mystery Ser.). 2001. audio compact disk 64.00 Books on Tape.

Murder on the Yukon Quest. unabr. ed. Sue Henry. Read by Mary Peiffer. 7 cass. (Running Time: 10 hrs.). (Jessie Arnold Mystery Ser.). 2000. 29.95 (978-0-7366-4697-0(3)) Books on Tape.
Jessie Arnold finds herself in a life and death battle against a desperate, unknown kidnapper who will stop at nothing.

Murder on Trial, Michael Underwood. Read by John Hendry. 4 cass. (Running Time: 6 hrs.). 1999. 44.95 (68335) Pub: Soundings Ltd GBR. Dist(s): Ulverscroft US

Murder Past Due. D. R. Meredith. 5 cass. (Running Time: 7 hrs.). 45.00 (978-1-4025-2947-4(3)) Recorded Bks.

Murder Room. unabr. ed. P. D. James. (Adam Dalgliesh Mystery Ser.). 2003. audio compact disk 81.60 (978-0-7366-9606-7(7)) Pub: Books on Tape. Dist(s): NetLibrary CO

Murder Room. unabr. ed. P. D. James. Read by Charles Keating. 10 cass. (Running Time: 15 hrs.). (Adam Dalgliesh Mystery Ser.). 2003. 80.00 (978-0-7366-9445-2(5)) Books on Tape.

Murder Room. unabr. ed. P. D. James. Read by Charles Keating. 12 CDs. (Running Time: 15 hrs.). (Adam Dalgliesh Mystery Ser.). (ENG.). 2003. audio compact disk 44.95 (978-0-7393-0756-4(8)) Pub: Random Audio Pubg. Dist(s): Random

Murder Room: The Heirs of Sherlock Holmes Gather to Solve the World's Most Perplexing Cold Cases. unabr. ed. Michael Capuzzo. Read by Adam Grupper. 12 CDs. (Running Time: 14 hrs.). 2010. audio compact disk 39.99 (978-0-7435-3264-8(3)) Pub: S&S Audio. Dist(s): S and S Inc

Murder Runs in the Family. Anne George. Narrated by Ruth Ann Phimister. 7 CDs. (Running Time: 8 hrs. 15 mins.). (Southern Sisters Mystery Ser.). audio compact disk 69.00 (978-0-7887-9890-0(1)) Recorded Bks.

Murder Runs in the Family. unabr. ed. Anne George. Narrated by Ruth Ann Phimister. 6 cass. (Running Time: 8 hrs. 15 mins.). (Southern Sisters Mystery Ser.). 2001. 58.00 (978-0-7887-4999-5(4), 96283E7) Recorded Bks.
Two feisty sisters do some amateur sleuthing into the death of a visiting genealogist.

Murder, She Meowed. unabr. ed. Rita Mae Brown & Sneaky Pie Brown. Narrated by Kate Forbes. 6 cass. (Running Time: 8 hrs. 15 mins.). (Mrs. Murphy Mystery Ser.). 2002. 56.00 (978-1-4025-3398-3(5), RG257) Recorded Bks.
What do steeplechase, playing cards and daggers have in common? They all play vital roles in the intricately woven plot of Sneaky Pie and her human cohort Rita Mae Brown in this delightful mystery. While Mary "Harry" Haristeen and her cat, Mrs. Murphy attend the annual steeplechase at Montpelier, Mrs. Murphy discovers something amiss. During the celebration following the race, one of the jockeys is found dead in the barn, a dagger through his heart and the queen of clubs impaled by the dagger. Hot on the killer's trail, Mrs. Murphy is joined by a wistful band of barn mice when the killer strikes again. But can she make her human p[partner understand before yet another life is lost.

Murder Shoots the Bull. Anne George. Narrated by Ruth Ann Phimister. 6 cass. (Running Time: 8 hrs. 30 mins.). (Southern Sisters Mystery Ser.). 1999. 57.00 (978-1-4025-0999-5(5), 96285) Recorded Bks.
Patricia Anne has been good friends with her neighbor Mitzi for 40 years. So when Mitzi's husband is accused of murder, Patricia Anne knows she has to do something to help the poor man. That means enlisting the aid of her sister for a little spirited detective work.

Murder Story. unabr. ed. John William Wainwright. Narrated by Christopher Kay. 4 cass. (Running Time: 6 hrs.). 2000. 40.00 (978-1-84197-103-2(0), H1085E7) Recorded Bks.
Private Eye Harry Thompson's had a good day. He got a case through the laxity of the local police & he solved it quickly & efficiently. All that's left is the long drive home to Rogate-on-Sands. Until Harry stops at the Services, that is. He automatically helps a woman in trouble & saves her life.

Murder Suicide: A Novel. abr. ed. Keith Ablow. Read by Kevin O'Rourke. 2004. 17.95 (978-1-59397-465-7(5)) Pub: Macmill Audio. Dist(s): Macmillan

Murder to Go. unabr. ed. Sara Paretsky & Marcia Muller. Read by Barbara Bain. 4 cass. (Running Time: 6 hrs.). 2001. 25.00 (978-1-59040-174-3(3), Phoenix Audio) Pub: Amer Intl Pub. Dist(s): PerseuPGW

Murder Too Many. unabr. ed. Elizabeth Ferrars. Read by Nigel Graham. 6 cass. (Running Time: 6 hrs 58 min.). 2001. 54.95 (978-1-85089-773-6(5), 90103) Pub: ISIS Audio GBR. Dist(s): Ulverscroft US
Andrew has returned to Knotlington for a conference & also to help an old friend. Two years ago a member of the Fine Arts Dept. was murdered & Stephen is serving a life sentence for the crime, but many people think he's innocent.

Murder under Palms. unabr. ed. Stefanie Matteson. Read by Susan O'Malley. 6 cass. (Running Time: 8 hrs. 30 mins.). 2003. 44.95 (978-0-7861-1653-9(6), 2481) Blckstn Audio.
Charlotte's at a reunion & everything seems perfect until a world-renowned jewelry designer is found stabbed to death at the party. Charlotte knows that almost any guest could be the murderer. And she is determined to find the killer - before he or she claims another victim.

***Murder under the Midnight Sun.** Nicholas Rhea & Terry Molloy. 2010. 61.95 (978-1-84652-558-2(6)); audio compact disk 79.95 (978-1-84652-559-9(4)) Pub: Magna Story GBR. Dist(s): Ulverscroft US

Murder Unprompted. unabr. ed. Simon Brett. Read by Geoffrey Howard. 4 cass. (Running Time: 5 hrs. 30 mins.). 1997. 32.95 (978-0-7861-1081-0(3), 1851) Blckstn Audio.
"I want you all out - gone - dead - exterminated!" high strung Alex Household cried out, when, after a lifetime of struggle, he lost the starring role in a new play called "The Hooded Owl" - to an actor who couldn't remember his lines. But did that mean that it was Alex who had shot the leading man during his climactic speech?.

Murder Unprompted. unabr. ed. Simon Brett. Narrated by Simon Prebble. 4 cass. (Running Time: 6 hrs.). (Charles Paris Mystery Ser.). 1999. 38.00 (978-0-7887-4081-7(4), H1075E7) Recorded Bks.
Charles Paris, seasoned actor & part-time sleuth has taken the part of understudy to the lead in a West End play. It's not an easy position, however. Rivalry on the set is straining everyone's nerves. It started when Alex Household, high-strung & egotistical, lost the starring role to an actor who keeps dropping his lines. In anger, Alex screams, "I want you all out! Gone! Dead! Exterminated!" Now, on opening night, someone has murdered leading man on stage during his climactic speech. Was it Alex, in an act of revenge or is it some other villain at work behind the scenes.

An Asterisk (*) at the beginning of an entry indicates that the title is appearing for the first time.

Murder Unprompted. unabr. ed. Simon Brett. Narrated by Simon Prebble. 5 CDs. (Running Time: 6 hrs.). 2001. audio compact disk 49.00 (978-0-7887-3982-8(4), C1145E7) Recorded Bks.
Charles Paris, seasoned actor & part-time sleuth, has taken the part of understudy to the lead in a West End play. It's not an easy position, however, rivalry on the set is straining everyone's nerves.

Murder Walks the Plank. unabr. ed. Carolyn G. Hart. 7 cass. (Running Time: 10 hrs. 30 min.). (Death on Demand Mystery Ser.: No. 15). 2004. 79.75 (978-0-7366-9769-9(1)) Recorded Bks.

Murder Wears a Cowl: A Medieval Mystery Featuring Hugh Corbett. unabr. ed. Paul C. Doherty. 6 cass. (Running Time: 9 hrs.). 1998. 69.95 (978-1-85903-142-1(0)) Pub: Magna Story GBR. Dist(s): Ulverscroft US

Murderer Next Door: Why the Mind Is Designed to Kill. David Buss. Read by Michael Prichard. (Playaway Adult Nonfiction Ser.). (ENG.). 2009. 65.00 (978-1-60775-642-2(0)) Find a World.

Murderer Next Door: Why the Mind Is Designed to Kill. unabr. ed. David Buss. Read by Michael Prichard. (Running Time: 11 hrs. 0 mins. 0 sec.). (ENG.). 2005. audio compact disk 69.99 (978-1-4001-3172-3(3)); audio compact disk 34.99 (978-1-4001-0172-6(7)); audio compact disk 22.99 (978-1-4001-5172-1(4)) Pub: Tantor Media. Dist(s): IngramPubServ

Murderers. abr. ed. W. E. B. Griffin. Read by Dick Hill. 2 cass. (Running Time: 3 hrs.). (Badge of Honor Ser.: Vol. 6). 2000. 7.95 (978-1-57815-001-4(9), 1017, Media Bks Audio) Media Bks NJ.
It's up to Special Operations Division detectives to quickly piece together three seemingly unrelated murders in a fierce.

Murderers. abr. ed. W. E. B. Griffin. Read by Dick Hill. 3 CDs. (Running Time: 3 hrs.). (Badge of Honor Ser.: Vol. 6). 2000. audio compact disk 11.99 (978-1-57815-500-2(2), 1017 CD3, Media Bks Audio) Media Bks NJ.
A policeman is found dead in his home - is it connected to corruption in the narcotics division? A beautiful young woman dies of a drug overdose in her parents' mansion - was it accidental? Special Operations Division must put together the pieces & do it quickly.

Murderers. unabr. ed. W. E. B. Griffin. Read by Michael Russotto. 12 cass. (Running Time: 18 hrs.). (Badge of Honor Ser.: Vol. 6). 1995. 96.00 (978-0-7366-2949-2(1), 3643) Books on Tape.
The Special Operations Division sweats three increasingly complex killings. A fourth looks imminent.

Murderers & Other Friends: Another Part of Life. unabr. ed. John Mortimer. Read by John Mortimer. 7 cass. (Running Time: 9 hrs. 45 min.). 1996. 61.95 (978-1-85695-953-7(8), 950703) Pub: ISIS Audio GBR. Dist(s): Ulverscroft US
Details the life & times of John Mortimer through the eyes of his friends.

Murderers' Row Vol. 1: Original Baseball Mysteries. abr. unabr. ed. Nelson DeMille et al. Read by Dan Cashman et al. Perf. by Jim Grey & Mike Lupica. 4 cass. (Running Time: 6 hrs.). (Sports Mysteries Ser.). 2004. 25.00 (978-1-931056-30-4(7), N Millennium Audio) New Millenn Enter.
A collection of short stories in the country will set bones to chilling and become page turners to sports buffs and mystery buffs alike. Some stories mix fact with fiction creating a bone-chilling reality and plausibility that one finds immediately captivating. Some stories create characters so interesting and so embody the soul of the sport of baseball, that one cannot stop until the story-line has been completely told. Whatever one's take on the sport or whatever one's taste in reading, there is something for everyone in this masterwork of sports and mystery combined.

Murderers' Row Vol. 2: Original Baseball Mysteries. abr. unabr. ed. Nelson DeMille et al. Read by Lee Horsley. Perf. by Jim Grey & Mike Lupica. Ed. by Otto Penzler. 4 cass. (Running Time: 6 hrs.). (Sports Mysteries Ser.). 2004. 25.00 (978-1-931056-31-1(5), N Millennium Audio) New Millenn Enter.

Murdering America Incorporated. unabr. ed. Craig Fraley. Read by Kevin Foley. 8 cass. (Running Time: 8 hrs. 48 min.). (Kiahawk Ser.). 2001. 49.95 (978-1-55686-818-4(9)) Books in Motion.
Why did the investigative reporter kill his own story on the freeway collapse that caused the death of nineteen people? Twenty years later, two journalism students uncover the real story.

Murdering Dickens: Silas & Nancy, the Murder from Oliver Twist. unabr. ed. Charles Dickens & Steven Thomas Oney. Photos by George Harland. 1 CD. (Running Time: 1 hr. 8 min.). (Cape Cod Mystery Radio Theater Ser.: 24). (YA). 1996. audio compact disk 12.50 (978-0-9745668-0-1(2)) Cape Cod Radio.
Re-creation of the original stage reading.

Murdering Mr. Lincoln: A New Detection of the 19th Century's Most Famous Crime. unabr. ed. Charles Higham. Read by Dan Cashman. 2004. 32.95 (978-1-59007-550-0(1)) Pub: New Millenn Enter. Dist(s): PerseuPGW

Murdering Mr. Lincoln: A New Detection of the 19th Century's Most Famous Crime. unabr. ed. Charles Higham. 9 CDs. (Running Time: 10 hrs. 30 mins.). 2004. audio compact disk 34.95 (978-1-59007-551-7(X)) Pub: New Millenn Enter. Dist(s): PerseuPGW

Murder@Maggody.com. unabr. ed. Joan Hess. Narrated by C. J. Critt. 8 CDs. (Running Time: 9 hrs. 30 mins.). (Arly Hanks Mystery Ser.). 2001. audio compact disk 89.00 (978-1-4025-0512-6(4), C1568) Recorded Bks.
Beleaguered chief of police Arly Hanks has her hands full when modern technology moves into small town Maggody, bringing with it controversy and murder. Maggody's high school has a new computer lab. Folks are calling the internet the Devil's workshop, but the adult computer class is filling up. Soon friends are exchanging E-mail, and the preacher is posting sermon notes. But when some mighty unusual images flash across monitors - and a pretty computer student is found dead in an abandoned shack - the town demands Arly find the answers. With tempers flaring and rumors raging, it will take all of Arly's low-tech resourcefulness to find the cold-blooded killer.

Murder@Maggody.com. unabr. ed. Joan Hess. Narrated by C. J. Critt. 7 cass. (Running Time: 9 hrs. 30 mins.). (Arly Hanks Mystery Ser.). 2001. 65.00 (978-0-7887-4874-5(2), 96266E7) Recorded Bks.
The police chief Arly Hanks has her hands full with the high school's new computer lab when some unusual images flash across the monitors.

Murders at Impasse Louvain. unabr. ed. Richard Grayson. Read by Gordon Griffin. 4 cass. (Running Time: 6 hrs.). (Sound Ser.). 2004. 44.95 (978-1-85496-704-6(5), 67045) Pub: UlverLrgPrint GBR. Dist(s): Ulverscroft US
Fashionable painter Felix Hassler is found strangled to death with his wife bound & gagged at his side. Madame Hassler had also been found with the President of France when he died two years before - in bed. Inspector Gautier tries to resolve the case without reviving old scandal, but soon discovers that Madame Hassler has something to hide & that someone high-up is protecting her.

Murders in the Rue Morgue see Classic Detective Stories, Vol. II, A Collection

Murders in the Rue Morgue see Tales of Terror

Murders in the Rue Morgue see Three Tales of Mystery

Murders in the Rue Morgue. Ed. by Oxford University Press Staff. 2008. audio compact disk 11.95 (978-0-19-479001-7(0)) OUP.

Murders in the Rue Morgue. Edgar Allan Poe. (Reading & Training, Intermediate Ser.). (J). (gr. 4-7). 2005. pap. bk. 21.95 (978-88-7754-779-8(0)) Cideb ITA.

Murders in the Rue Morgue. unabr. ed. Edgar Allan Poe. 1 cass. Dramatization. 1977. 7.95 (D-2) Jimcin Record.
Bizarre murders solved by C. Auguste Dupin.

Murders in the Rue Morgue & Other Stories. Edgar Allan Poe. Read by David Case. (Playaway Adult Fiction Ser.). (ENG.). 2009. 49.99 (978-1-60775-763-4(X)) Find a World.

Murders in the Rue Morgue & Other Stories. Edgar Allan Poe. Read by David Case. (ENG.). 2005. audio compact disk 24.99 (978-1-4001-0117-7(4)); audio compact disk 19.99 (978-1-4001-5117-2(1)) Pub: Tantor Media. Dist(s): IngramPubServ

Murders in the Rue Morgue & Other Stories. unabr. ed. Edgar Allan Poe. Narrated by David Case. (Running Time: 4 hrs. 30 mins. 0 sec.). (ENG.). 2009. 19.99 (978-1-4001-6124-9(X)); audio compact disk 39.99 (978-1-4001-4124-1(9)) Pub: Tantor Media. Dist(s): IngramPubServ

Murders in the Rue Morgue & Other Stories. unabr. ed. Edgar Allan Poe. Narrated by David Case. (Running Time: 4 hrs. 30 mins. 0 sec.). (ENG.). 2009. audio compact disk 19.99 (978-1-4001-1124-4(2)) Pub: Tantor Media. Dist(s): IngramPubServ

Murders in the Rue Morgue & Other Stories. unabr. collector's ed. Edgar Allan Poe. Read by David Case. 5 cass. (Running Time: 5 hrs.). 1992. 30.00 (978-0-7366-2189-2(X), 2984) Books on Tape.
This tale is a literary landmark: the first modern detective story. There are no clues for C. August Dupin - only a locked room mystery. Other stories include "The Purloined Letter" & "The Raven".

Murders in the Rue Morgue, The Mystery of Marie Roget & The Purloined Letter: The Dupin Stories. Edgar Allan Poe. Read by Kerry Shale. 4 cass. (Running Time: 4 hrs. 15 min.). 2002. 22.98 (978-962-634-776-8(7), nA427614, Naxos AudioBooks); audio compact disk 28.98 (978-962-634-276-3(5), NA427612, Naxos AudioBooks) Naxos.
Three classic crime novels.

Murders in Volume Two: A Henry Gamadge Mystery. Elizabeth Daly. Read by Ray Verna. 4 cass. (Running Time: 6 hrs.). 1993. Rental 8.30 30 day rental Set. (250016) Literate Ear.
One hundred years have passed since the beautiful young governess strolled into the Vauregard estate's arbor. She carried with her Volume Two from a set of Byron's poems & was never seen again.

Murders in Volume Two: A Henry Gamadge Mystery. Elizabeth Daly. Read by Ray Verna. 4 cass. (Running Time: 6 hrs.). 1993. 41.00 (978-1-56544-054-8(4), 250016) Literate Ear.

Murders of Richard III. Elizabeth Peters, pseud. Read by Liza Ross. 7 CDs. (Running Time: 10 hrs. 30 min.). 2001. audio compact disk 69.95 (978-0-7531-1059-1(8), 110598) Pub: ISIS Audio GBR. Dist(s): Ulverscroft US

Murders of Richard III, unabr. ed. Elizabeth Peters, pseud. Read by Grace Conlin. 5 cass. (Running Time: 7 hrs.). 1995. 39.95 (978-0-7861-0869-5(X), 1667) Blckstn Audio.
When attractive American Jacqueline Kirby is invited to an English country mansion for a weekend costume affair, she expects only one mystery. Since the hosts & guests are all fanatic devotees of King Richard III, they hope to clear his name of the 500-year-old accusation that he killed the little princes in the Tower of London. Jacqueline is amused at the group's eccentricities until history begins to repeat itself. A dangerous practical joker recreates famous fifteenth-century murder methods - beheading, poisoning, smothering & even drowning in a butt of malmsey. As the jokes become more & more macabre, one at last proves fatal. Jacqueline puts all her observations together for a dazzling solution that will surprise even the most attentive listener.

Murders of Richard III. unabr. ed. Elizabeth Peters, pseud. Read by Grace Conlin. (Running Time: 25200 sec.). (Jacqueline Kirby Mystery Ser.). 2007. audio compact disk 55.00 (978-0-7861-6000-6(4)) Blckstn Audio.

Murders of Richard III: A Jacqueline Kirby Mystery. unabr. ed. Elizabeth Peters, pseud. Read by Grace Conlin. (Running Time: 25200 sec.). 2007. audio compact disk 29.95 (978-0-7861-6001-3(2)) Blckstn Audio.

Murders of the Heart see Murders of the HeART!

Murders of the HeART! 2nd ed. Short Stories. Jody Wright. 2 CDs. (Running Time: 2 hrs. 10 mins.). Orig. Title: Murders of the Heart. 2003. audio compact disk 19.95 (978-0-9722299-3-7(0)) WSG Gallery.
Fascinated by art and artists? Don't miss these short stories by author Jody Wright. She weaves eight tales of murder set within the world of art!This collection of short stories takes you on a wide range of adventures from the perfect crime to synesthesia.Potters, sculptors, painters, writers, and art critiques join in the line of characters who are snared into the web of murder.Jody and Carl Wright are the readers of these tales and take upon the many characters, male and female, young and old - in an entertaining, lively look at art, deception and resolution. Sound effects are included for more dramatic presentation.

Muriel Anderson: Hometown Live! Muriel Anderson. 1995. bk. 22.95 (978-0-7866-1447-9(1), MB95664BCD) Mel Bay.

Muriel Rukeyser. unabr. ed. Muriel Rukeyser. 1 cass. (Running Time: 1 hr. 30 min.). (Author Speaks Ser.). 1991. 14.95 J Norton Pubs.
Archival recordings of 20th-century authors.

Muriel Rukeyser Memorial. unabr. ed. Muriel Rukeyser. 1 cass. (Running Time: 29 min.). 1991. 10.00 (010783) New Letters.

Murmel Murmel Munsch! unabr. ed. 1 CD. (Running Time: 49 mins.). 2006. audio compact disk 15.99 (978-1-897166-27-7(3)) Pub: Child Group CAN. Dist(s): KOCH Enter

Murmuring the Judges. unabr. ed. Quintin Jardine. Read by James Bryce. 10 cass. (Running Time: 11 hrs. 50 min.). (Isis Ser.). (J). 2001. 84.95 (978-0-7531-1113-0(6)) Pub: ISIS Lrg Prnt GBR. Dist(s): Ulverscroft US

Murmuring the Judges. unabr. ed. Quintin Jardine. Read by James Bryce. 10 CDs. (Running Time: 11 hrs. 28 min.). (Isis Ser.). (J). 2003. audio compact disk 89.95 (978-0-7531-2243-3(X)) Pub: ISIS Lrg Prnt GBR. Dist(s): Ulverscroft US

Muros Caen. unabr. ed. Zondervan Publishing Staff. 1998. 5.99 (978-0-8297-2685-5(3)) Pub: Vida Pubs. Dist(s): Zondervan

Muros Caen. unabr. ed. Zondervan Publishing Staff. 1998. audio compact disk 7.99 (978-0-8297-2686-2(1)) Zondervan.

Murphy the Mistletoe: Adventures from the Garden of Eden to the Garden of Nede. Frieda Carrol. Read by Frieda Carrol. 1 cass. (Running Time: 9 min.). (J). (gr. 3-9). 1989. 10.95 (978-0-913597-64-4(3), Alpha Pyramis Pub) Prosperity & Profits.
Rhyming story about a mistletoe and its journey.

Murphy the Mistletoe: Adventures from the Garden of Eden to the Garden of Nede. Frieda Carrol. Read by Frieda Carrol. (Running Time: 9 min.). 6.95 (37 SOR 21CT) Sell Out Recordings.
Features a story that tells in poetry form about a mistletoe and his adventures.

Murphy's Ambush. unabr. ed. Gary Paulsen & Brian Burks. Narrated by Norman Dietz. 3 cass. (Running Time: 4 hrs.). 1999. 26.00 (978-0-7887-0485-7(0), 94678E7) Recorded Bks.
Life in Turrett, New Mexico was quiet until Travis Price rode into town bleeding & gravely wounded by an arrow. Paulsen & Burks serve up a vast & heroic vision of the Old West.

Murphy's Law: Exodus 5-6. Ed Young. 1984. 4.95 (978-0-7417-1420-6(5), 420) Win Walk.

Murray Adaskin. Murray Adaskin. 2004. audio compact disk 15.95 (978-0-662-33321-0(7)) Pub: Canadian Broadcasting CAN. Dist(s): Georgetown Term

Murray Kempton: Bobby Kennedy see Buckley's Firing Line

Murray Schafer. Murray Schafer. 2004. audio compact disk 15.95 (978-0-662-33318-0(7)) Pub: Canadian Broadcasting CAN. Dist(s): Georgetown Term

Murray's Nightmare. Created by Saddleback Educational Publishing. 1 cass. (Running Time: 4200 sec.). (PageTurner Science Fiction Ser.). (J). 2002. audio compact disk 10.95 (978-1-56254-488-1(8), SP 4888) Saddleback Edu.
Word-for-word read-along of Murray's Nightmare.

Murther & Walking Spirits. unabr. ed. Robertson Davies. Narrated by George Guidall. 10 cass. (Running Time: 14 hrs.). 1991. 85.00 (978-1-55690-632-9(3), 91422E7) Recorded Bks.
Connor Gilmartin's inauspicious, but much beloved, mortal life comes to an untimely end when he discovers his wife in bed with one of his more ludicrous associates. Enraged at being so unceremoniously cut down, Gilmartin avenges himself against his now panic-stricken murderer.

Muruga. Perf. by Muruga. 1 cass. 10.00 (A0708-90) Sound Photosyn.
Multifaceted drumming to "realize unity of the cosmic self".

***Musashi Flex.** unabr. ed. Steve Perry. Read by Joe Barrett. (Running Time: 10 hrs. 0 mins.). 2010. 29.95 (978-1-4332-5169-6(8)); 59.95 (978-1-4332-5166-5(3)); audio compact disk 90.00 (978-1-4332-5167-2(1)) Blckstn Audio.

Muscian Approaching Sleep. Jan Morris. (ENG.). 2006. 4.00 (978-1-933675-16-9(0)) Dos Madres Pr.

Muscles by Juliana: The Audio Study Aid, Juliana Luecking. Read by Juliana Luecking. Perf. by Steve Elson. Music by Steve Elson. 3 cass. (Running Time: 2 hrs. 30 min.). 1998. 35.00 (978-0-9672970-0-2(1)) J Luecking.
Reviews 124 pairs of human muscles, listing locations, joints, origins & insertions & actions. For students of human anatomy & physiology.

Muse in the Body: Love Poems by Women. unabr. ed. Poems. Read by Eleni Sikeliands et al. Ed. by Catherine Bartlett. 1 cass. (Running Time: 1 hr. 30 min.). 1996. 12.95 (978-1-57453-020-9(8)) Audio Lit.
Explores the poetry of both physical & spiritual longing & fulfillment from ancient Greece to New York's East Village. Sappho, Mirabai, H.D., Emily Dickinson & twenty other women poets express all the facets of desire in 50 poems.

Muse in the Machine: American Fiction & Mass Publicity. Mark Conroy. 2004. audio compact disk 9.95 (978-0-8142-9028-6(0)) Pub: Ohio St U Pr. Dist(s): Chicago Distribution Ctr

Musee des Beaux Arts see Twentieth-Century Poetry in English, No. 1, Recordings of Poets Reading Their Own Poetry

Museum Cafes & Arts: Inspired Recipes from Favorite Museum Cafes; Chamber Music by the Rossetti String Quartet; Art from America's Great Museums. Sharon O'Connor. (Sharon O'Connor's Menus & Music Ser.: 17). 2002. pap. bk. 27.95 (978-1-883914-34-9(5)) Menus & Music.

Museum of Dr. Moses: Tales of Mystery & Suspense. unabr. ed. Joyce Carol Oates. Read by Robert Fass & Laura Hicks. 1 MP3-CD. (Running Time: 7 hrs. 45 mins.). 2007. 39.95 (978-0-7927-4920-2(0)); audio compact disk 64.95 (978-0-7927-4890-8(5)); 54.95 (978-0-7927-4937-0(5)) AudioGO.
In "The Man Who Fought Roland LaStarza" a woman's world is upended when she learns the brutal truth about a family friend's death - and what her father is capable of. Meanwhile, a businessman desperate to find his missing two-year-old grandson in "Suicide Watch" must determine whether the horrifying tale his junkie son tells him about the boy's whereabouts is a confession or a sick test. In "Valentine, July Heat Wave" a man prepares a gruesome surprise for the wife determined to leave him. And the children of a BTK-style serial killer struggle to decode the patterns behind their father's seemingly random bad acts, as well as their own, in "Bad Habits." In these and other stories, Joyce Carol Oates explores with bloodcurdling insight the ties that bind - or worse.

Museum of Innocence. unabr. ed. Orhan Pamuk. Read by John Lee. Tr. by Maureen Freely. (ENG.). 2009. audio compact disk 45.00 (978-0-7393-6926-5(1), Random AudioBks) Pub: Random Audio Pubg. Dist(s): Random

Museum of the Open Road - I-480/80 East - Cleveland to Youngstown, Ohio. Bruce T. Marshall. Narrated by Bruce T. Marshall. 1 CD. (Running Time: 52 mins.). 2002. audio compact disk 9.95 (978-0-9763188-4-2(9)) Museum Open Road.
A timed commentary of history, geography, people, and stories along the Ohio Turnpike (I-480/80) east from Cleveland to Youngstown, Ohio-to be played while traveling this route.

Museum of the Open Road - I-70 East - Columbus, Ohio to Wheeling, West Virginia. Bruce T. Marshall. Narrated by Bruce T. Marshall. 1 CD. (Running Time: 1 hr., 13 mins.). 2003. audio compact disk 9.95 (978-0-9763188-9-7(X)) Museum Open Road.
A timed commentary of history, geography, people, and stories along I-70 West from Columbus, Ohio to Wheeling, West Virginia-to be played while traveling this route.

Museum of the Open Road - I-70 West - Columbus, Ohio to Richmond, Indiana. Bruce T. Marshall. Narrated by Bruce T. Marshall. 1 CD. (Running Time: 1 hr., 8 mins.). 2003. audio compact disk 9.95 (978-0-9763188-8-0(1)) Museum Open Road.
A timed commentary of history, geography, people, and stories along I-70 West from Columbus, Ohio to Richmond, Indiana-to be played while traveling this route.

Museum of the Open Road - I-71 North - Columbus to Cleveland, Ohio. Bruce T. Marshall. Narrated by Bruce T. Marshall. 1 CD. (Running Time: 1 hr., 15 mins.). 2004. audio compact disk 9.95 (978-0-9763188-7-3(3)) Museum Open Road.
A timed commentary of history, geography, people, and stories along I-71 North from Columbus to Cleveland, Ohio-to be played while traveling this route.

Museum of the Open Road - I-71 South - Cleveland to Columbus, Ohio. Bruce T. Marshall. Narrated by Bruce T. Marshall. 1 CD. (Running Time: 1 hr., 15 mins.). 2004. audio compact disk 9.95 (978-0-9763188-5-9(7)) Museum Open Road.
A timed commentary of history, geography, people, and stories along I-71 South from Cleveland to Columbus, Ohio-to be played while traveling this route.

Museum of the Open Road - I-71 South - Columbus to Cincinnati, Ohio. Bruce T. Marshall. Narrated by Bruce T. Marshall. 1 CD. (Running Time: 1 hr., 10 mins.). 2004. audio compact disk 9.95 (978-0-9763188-6-6(5)) Museum Open Road.
A timed commentary of history, geography, people, and stories along I-71 South from Columbus to Cincinnati, Ohio-to be played while traveling this route.

Museum of the Open Road - I-77 South - Cleveland to New Philadelphia, Ohio. Bruce T. Marshall. Narrated by Bruce T. Marshall. 1 CD. (Running Time: 50 mins.). 2002. audio compact disk 9.95 (978-0-9763188-2-8(2)) Museum Open Road.
A timed commentary of history, geography, people, and stories along I-77 South from Cleveland to New Philadelphia, Ohio-to be played while traveling this route.

Museum of the Open Road - I-80/90 West - Cleveland to Toledo, Ohio. Bruce T. Marshall. Narrated by Bruce T. Marshall. 1 CD. (Running Time: 55 mins.). 2002. audio compact disk 9.95 (978-0-9763188-3-5(0)) Museum Open Road.
A timed commentary of history, geography, people, and stories along the Ohio Turnpike (I-80/90) west from Cleveland to Toledo, Ohio-to be played while traveling this route.

Museum of the Open Road - I-90 East - Cleveland, Ohio to Erie, Pennsylvania. Bruce T. Marshall. Narrated by Bruce T. Marshall. 1 CD. (Running Time: 1 hr., 19 min.). 2002. audio compact disk 9.95 (978-0-9763188-0-4(6)) Museum Open Road.
A timed commentary of history, geography, people, and stories about Interstate 90 East from Cleveland, Ohio to Erie, Pennsylvania.

Museum of the Open Road - I-90 West - Erie, Pennsylvania to Cleveland, Ohio. Bruce T. Marshall. Narrated by Bruce T. Marshall. 1 CD. (Running Time: 1 hr., 3 mins.). 2002. audio compact disk 9.95 (978-0-9763188-1-1(4)) Museum Open Road.
A timed commentary of the history, geography, people, and stories along I-90 West from Erie, Pennsylvania to Cleveland, Ohio-to be played while traveling this route.

***Museum of Thieves.** unabr. ed. Lian Tanner. Read by Claudia Black. (Keepers Ser.). (ENG.). (J). 2010. audio compact disk 34.00 (978-0-307-71081-9(5), Listening Lib) Pub: Random Audio Pubg. Dist(s): Random

Musgrave Ritual see Memoirs of Sherlock Holmes

Musgrave Ritual see Sherlock Holmes: Selected Stories

Musgrave Ritual see Famous Cases of Sherlock Holmes

Mushroom Forest. Phil Baron. Ed. by Ken Forsse & Mary Becker. Illus. by Allyn Conley-Gorniak et al. (J). (ps). 1986. bk. (978-0-318-60968-3(1)) Alchemy Comms.

Mushroom in the Rain. 2004. bk. 24.95 (978-1-56008-012-1(4)); pap. bk. 18.95 (978-1-55592-444-7(1)); pap. bk. 38.75 (978-1-55592-446-1(8)); pap. bk. 32.75 (978-1-55592-281-8(3)); pap. bk. 14.95 (978-0-7882-0593-4(5)); 8.95 (978-0-7882-0062-5(3)); cass. & flmstrp 30.00 (978-0-89719-600-0(7)); audio compact disk 12.95 (978-1-55592-917-6(6)) Weston Woods.

Mushroom in the Rain. Mirra Ginsburg. Illus. by Jose Dewey & Ariane Dewey. 1 cass., 5 bks. (Running Time: 7 min.). (J). pap. bk. 32.75 Weston Woods.
When it starts to rain, an ant, a butterfly, a mouse, a sparrow & a rabbit take shelter under a tiny mushroom.

Mushroom in the Rain. Mirra Ginsburg. 1 cass. (Running Time: 7 min.). (J). (ps-4). 1989. 8.95 (978-0-89719-994-0(4), 340) Weston Woods.

Mushroom in the Rain. Mirra Ginsburg. Illus. by Jose Aruego et al. 1 cass. (Running Time: 7 min.). (J). (ps-1). 1989. pap. bk. 12.95 (PRA340) Weston Woods.

Mushroom Man. Stuart Pawson & Andrew Wincott. 2009. 61.95 (978-1-84652-377-9(X)); audio compact disk 79.95 (978-1-84652-378-6(8)) Pub: Magna Story GBR. Dist(s): Ulverscroft US

Mushrooms & Culture. unabr. ed. Henry Munn. 1 cass. (Running Time: 1 hr. 28 min.). 1977. 11.00 (01702) Big Sur Tapes.

Mushrooms & Evolution: Speech at Sunshine Gardens. Dennis J. McKenna. 2 cass. 18.00 (A0194-84) Sound Photosyn.

Mushrooms & Nine Other Stories. unabr. ed. Story Time Staff. Read by Alfreda C. Doyle. 2 cass. (Running Time: 1 hr. 30 min.). (J). (gr. 4-8). 1992. 9.95 (SRC 0069PLUS9) Sell Out Recordings.
A group of stories about nature & other topics. Mushrooms in varieties start this tape off with a meeting attended by many mushrooms.

Mushrooms & other Fungi: Interactive Guide. G. J. Keizer. 2003. bk. 68.50 (978-92-3-188801-4(3)) Pub: UNESCO FRA. Dist(s): Renouf Publ

Musi: Making a Difference. Richard G. Boehm et al. (Harcourt Brace Social Studies). (gr. k-7). 2003. 48.00 (978-0-15-310375-9(2)) Harcourt Schl Pubs.

Music see Poetry of Ralph Waldo Emerson

Music. Deborah Dunleavy. Illus. by Louise Phillips. (Jumbo Bks.). (ENG.). (J). (gr. 4-6). 2001. audio compact disk 14.95 (978-1-55337-067-3(8)) Pub: Kids Can Pr CAN. Dist(s): U Toronto Pr

Music. unabr. ed. Running Press Staff. 1 cass. (Berkeley University Weekly Broadcasts Ser.). 12.95 (23706) J Norton Pubs.
Contains: "Life Set to Music" on the significance of tribal African music; "Musical East Meets West," in which U.S. students perform Balinese & Japanese music; "Music Ad Lib," about improvisation in classical music form; "The New Look in Jazz," with examples of different jazz periods up to the present West Coast style.

Music. 4th ed. Daniel T. Politoske. (C). 1988. bk. (978-0-318-62496-9(6)) P-H.

Music: A Child's Place. Richard G. Boehm et al. (Harcourt Brace Social Studies). (gr. k-7). 2003. 48.00 (978-0-15-310371-1(X)) Harcourt Schl Pubs.

Music: A Jungian Insight into the Listening Experience. Read by Kenneth Phillips. 1 cass. (Running Time: 1 hr. 30 min.). 1979. 10.95 (978-0-7822-0227-4(6), 058) C G Jung IL.

Music: A Living Language. 4th ed. Tom Manoff. 2000. audio compact disk (978-0-393-10274-1(2)) Norton.

Music: An Appreciation. unabr. ed. Roger Kamien. 10 cass. (Running Time: 15 hrs.). 1999. 55.75 (978-0-07-913114-0(X), Mc-H Human Soc) McGrw-H Hghr Educ.

Music: An Appreciation. unabr. ed. Roger Kamien. 10 CDs. (Running Time: 15 hrs.). 1999. audio compact disk 54.35 (978-0-07-913115-7(8), Mc-H Human Soc) McGrw-H Hghr Educ.

Music: An Appreciation. 5th ed. Roger Kamien. (C). 1992. 16.50 (978-0-07-911476-1(8)) McGraw.

Music: An Appreciation. 7th ed. Kamien. 1 cass. (Running Time: 1 hr. 30 mins.). (C). 1999. stu. ed. 91.25 (978-0-07-290203-7(5)) Pub: Glencoe. Dist(s): McGraw

Music: An Appreciation. 8th ed. Roger Kamien. 4 CDs. 2003. audio compact disk 53.13 (978-0-07-284489-4(2), 9780072844894) Pub: Glencoe. Dist(s): McGraw

Music: An Appreciation, Set. 4th ed. Roger Kamien. 4 CDs. (C). 2001. audio compact disk 43.12 (978-0-07-242640-3(3)) Pub: Glencoe. Dist(s): McGraw

Music? An Appreciation -Cd Set. Kamien & Kamein. audio compact disk (978-0-07-836365-8(9)) McGraw Legal.

Music: Apples or Onions. Jack R. Christianson. 1 cass. 7.98 (978-1-55503-216-6(8), 06003958) Covenant Comms.
The good & bad effects of the music we listen to.

Music: Communities. Richard G. Boehm et al. (Harcourt Brace Social Studies). (gr. k-7). 2003. 48.00 (978-0-15-310379-7(5)) Harcourt Schl Pubs.

Music: Original Soundtracks of the Creation Museum. 2007. audio compact disk 14.99 (978-0-9760405-8-3(1)) Angelhse Media.

Music: Serious & Otherwise. 10.00 (HT402) Esstee Audios.

Music: The Art of Listening. 5th ed. Jean Ferris. 2 CDs. (Running Time: 2 hrs.). 1998. audio compact disk 38.75 (978-0-697-34385-7(5), Mc-H Human Soc) Pub: McGrw-H Hghr Educ. Dist(s): McGraw
For use with the book "Music: The Art of Listening".

Music: United States. Richard G. Boehm et al. (Harcourt Brace Social Studies). (gr. k-7). 2003. 75.70 (978-0-15-312198-2(X)) Harcourt Schl Pubs.

Music & Dyslexia: Opening New Doors. Read by Christopher Aruffo. Ed. by T. R. Miles & John Westcombe. 4 CDs. (Running Time: 4 hrs. 57 mins.). 2004. audio compact disk 34.95 (978-0-9761435-0-5(X)) Acoustic Learn.
It is now recognized that dyslexia affects people's lives in all sorts of different ways. This book shows how some dyslexics can be highly gifted musicians. It is important, however, that they should not be put off from studying music just because, at least in the early stages, many of them find it difficult to read and remember the symbols of musical notation. The foreword is by Baroness Mary Warnock. 10 of the 21 contributors to the book are themselves dyslexic. Each relates their personal experiences (whether as amateurs or professionals) and in most cases of their eventual success. The other contributors are teachers or researchers who have wide experiences of dyslexic musicians of all ages. The book's message is one of optimism. Dyslexic musicians can succeed provided only that they are given sufficient encouragement and understanding.

Music & Me. 1999. audio compact disk 7.98 (978-0-633-04550-0(0)) LifeWay Christian.

Music & Silence. abr. ed. Rose Tremain. Read by Michael Praed et al. 6 CDs. (Running Time: 7 hrs. 54 mins.). 2009. audio compact disk 34.98 (978-962-634-975-5(1)) Pub: HNH Intl HKG. Dist(s): Naxos

Music & Silence. unabr. ed. Rose Tremain. Read by Jenny Agutter. 14 cass. (Running Time: 21 hrs.). 2002. 89.95 (CAB 2139) AudioGO.
In the year 1629, a young English lutenist named Peter Claire arrives at the Danish Court to join King Christian IV's Royal Orchestra. From the moment when he realizes that the musicians perform in a freezing cellar underneath the royal apartments, Peter Claire understands that he's come to a place where the opposing states of light and dark, good and evil, are waging war to the death.

Music & the Land: The American Indian Tradition. 1 cass. (Running Time: 30 min.). 9.95 (G0220B090, HarperThor) HarpC GBR.

Music & the Mind, Michael Ballam. 2 cass. (Running Time: 3 hrs.). 2004. 14.95 (978-1-57734-594-7(0), 3111466) Covenant Comms.
How music can lift & heal the mind & body.

Music & the Mind: Program from the Award Winning Public Radio Series. Interview. Hosted by Fred Goodwin. Comment by John Hockenberry. 1 CD. (Running Time: 1hr.). (Infinite Mind Ser.). 2002. audio compact disk 21.95 (978-1-888064-73-5(0), LCM 211) Lichtenstein Creat.
Music can get us "amped up" or "mellowed out;" it can soothe, arrouse, amuse, irritate, and delight us. Why? Why should mere sequences of musical sounds have such power over how we feel? And how do good musicians orchestrate that power? "Music and the Mind" includes a round table discussion on music and emotion, featuring composer and performance artist Laurie Anderson; musicologist Dr. David Huron, Professor of Music and Director of the Cognitive and Systematic Musicology Laboratory at Ohio State University; and neuroscientist Dr. Mark Jude Tramo, Assistant Professor of Neurology, Harvard Unversity. In a special report on "Muzak and the Mind," the Infinite Mind's Devorah Klahr hears from Alvin Collis, Vice President of Audio Architecture at the Muzak Corporation. Reporter Eva Neuberg looks into the so-called "Mozart effect" with Dr. Lawrence Parsons, National Science Foundation; Dr. William Thompson, Professor of Music, York University; Dr. Lori Custadero, Teachers College, Columbia University; and Dr. Frances Rauscher, Professor of Psychology, University of Wisconsin, Oshkosh. Pianist Emanuel Ax compares the joys of Mozart to the joys of procreation. Plus commentator John Hockenberry talks about Hendrix, Beethoven, and N'Sync, and plays the flute (not at the same time).

Music & Worship: A Variety of Spiritual Experiences. 5 cass. Incl. Music & Worship: Incline Your Ear & Come Unto Me: Overview of the Series. Jacqueline Coren. 1981.; Music & Worship: O for a Thousand Tongues to Sing: The Basic Function of Music in the Mennonite Church. Martin Ressler. 1981.; Music & Worship: Psallite Domino - Sing Praise to the Lord: The Role of Chant in the Catholic Monastic Life. Marilyn Meeker. 1981.; Music & Worship: Sing Unto the Lord a New Song: Music in the Hasidic Tradition. Zalman Schachter-Shalomi. 1981.; Music & Worship: Worship in Spirit & Truth: Friends & Music. Ruth Pitman. 1981.; 1981. 17.50 Set. Pendle Hill.

Music & Worship: Incline Your Ear & Come Unto Me: Overview of the Series see Music & Worship: A Variety of Spiritual Experiences

Music & Worship: O for a Thousand Tongues to Sing: The Basic Function of Music in the Mennonite Church see Music & Worship: A Variety of Spiritual Experiences

Music & Worship: Psallite Domino - Sing Praise to the Lord: The Role of Chant in the Catholic Monastic Life see Music & Worship: A Variety of Spiritual Experiences

Music & Worship: Sing Unto the Lord a New Song: Music in the Hasidic Tradition see Music & Worship: A Variety of Spiritual Experiences

Music & Worship: Worship in Spirit & Truth: Friends & Music see Music & Worship: A Variety of Spiritual Experiences

Music Appreciation, Vol. 1. 1 cass. 1992. (A92017); audio compact disk (CD A92017) Multi-Cultural Bks.
Silence, sound & musical sound, voice & instruments.

Music Appreciation, Vol. 2. 1 cass. 1992. (A92018); audio compact disk (CD A92018) Multi-Cultural Bks.
Articulation of Raga, Raga in performance, Laya, Tala & Badhat.

Music Appreciation, Vol. 3. 1 cass. 1992. (A92019); audio compact disk (CD A92019) Multi-Cultural Bks.
Forms of music (Dhrupad, Khayal, Thumri,) Gharanas & styles, music & nature, listening to music.

Music as Medicine. Perf. by Kay Gardner. 6 cass. (Running Time: 8 hrs. 30 min.). 1999. pap. bk. 59.95 (83-0067) Explorations.
Twelve-session curriculum teaches the major elements & techniques within the science of sound healing, the mysteries of music's therapeutic role through the ages & techniques for creating melodies, rhythms & harmonies with the power to heal. Includes booklet.

Music as Medicine. Music by Nawang Khechog. 1 CD. (Running Time: 1 hr. 8 mins.). 2006. audio compact disk 16.98 (978-1-59179-206-2(1), M855D) Sounds True.
Ancient Tibetan teachings tell us that merely seeing an image of the Medicine Buddha - or even hearing his name - holds the power to heal. Now, acclaimed musician and former Buddhist monk Nawang Khechog joins premier Native American flutist, R. Carlos Nakai to invoke the blessings of this potent deity on their new recording, Music as Medicine. This recording contains: Tibetan flute, long horn, overtone chanting, Native American flute and drum, universal horn, and calming chants to restore balance and health to listeners everywhere.

Music Baby-O. unabr. ed. 1 CD. (Running Time: 45 mins.). (J). 2005. audio compact disk 15.00 (978-1-887795-27-2(8)) Piper Grove Mus.

Music Behind the Magic. Contrib. by Alan Menken et al. 1994. pap. bk. 59.98 (978-1-55723-619-7(4)) W Disney Records.

Music Behind the Magic. Contrib. by Alan Menken et al. 1 cass. (J). 1994. pap. bk. 41.40 Boxed set. (978-1-55723-620-3(8)) W Disney Records.

Music Box Hymns. 1 Cass. . (Running Time: 1 hr. 30 min.). 7.99 (978-0-7601-1151-2(0)); audio compact disk 11.99 CD. Provident Mus Dist.

Music Box Murders. unabr. ed. Larry Karp. Read by Cameron Beierle. 12 cass. (Running Time: 12 hrs. 12 min.). 2001. 64.95 (978-1-58116-144-1(1)) Books in Motion.
Dr. Thomas Perdue, a collector of rare and unique music boxes, has his latest acquisitions stolen from a repair shop with the restorer found dead. Thomas is determined to find his music box, and the killer.

Music Business Contract Library. Greg Forest. 2008. pap. bk. 24.95 (978-1-4234-5458-8(8), 1423454588) H Leonard.

Music by Dr. Escudero see Musica del Dr. Escudero

***Music CD for Punto y Aparte.** 4th ed. Sharon Foerster & Anne Lambright. (ENG.). (C). 2010. audio compact disk 20.31 (978-0-07-740457-4(2), 0077404572, Mc-H Human Soc) Pub: McGrw-H Hghr Educ. Dist(s): McGraw

***Music CD for the Western Humanities.** 7th ed. Roy Matthews & Dewitt Platt. (ENG.). (C). 2010. audio compact disk 30.94 (978-0-07-741641-6(4), 0077416414, Mc-H Human Soc) Pub: McGrw-H Hghr Educ. Dist(s): McGraw

Music Education Teacher. unabr. ed. Interview with Grace Eilert. 1 cass. (Running Time: 21 min.). 12.95 (15044) J Norton Pubs.
In this vocational interview Grace Eilert, music education supervisor, says that the demand for school music educators has never been stronger. The recognition of music as a part of the total education program provides students with exciting musical experiences.

Music, Enneagram Types of Transcedence. Claudio Naranjo. 2 cass. (Running Time: 3 hrs.). 1997. 18.00 (34204) Big Sur Tapes.
Multi-talented Naranjo is a classical pianist as well as a pschotherapist & enneagram pioneer. In this presentation he performs excerpts from works of various composers to illustrate the development of their personalities, as defined by the enneagram types. The music eloquently shows us how the composers could & did rise beyond the limits of their particular types.

Music Explosion. 1994. ring bd. 39.95 (978-1-889163-12-3(0)) Panda Bear Pub.

Music Expressions Grade 1: Lesson. Ed. by Alfred Publishing. (Expressions Music Curriculum Ser.). (ENG.). 2003. audio compact disk 450.00 (978-0-7579-1499-7(3)) Alfred Pub.

Music Expressions Grade 2: Lesson. Ed. by Alfred Publishing. (Expressions Music Curriculum Ser.). (ENG.). 2003. audio compact disk 475.00 (978-0-7579-1501-7(9)) Alfred Pub.

Music Expressions Grade 3: Lesson. Ed. by Alfred Publishing. (Expressions Music Curriculum Ser.). (ENG.). 2003. audio compact disk 500.00 (978-0-7579-1503-1(5)) Alfred Pub.

Music Expressions Grade 4: Lesson. Ed. by Alfred Publishing. (Expressions Music Curriculum Ser.). (ENG.). 2003. audio compact disk 525.00 (978-0-7579-1505-5(1)) Alfred Pub.

Music Expressions Grade 5: Lesson. Ed. by Alfred Publishing. (Expressions Music Curriculum Ser.). (ENG.). 2003. audio compact disk 525.00 (978-0-7579-1507-9(8)) Alfred Pub.

Music Expressions Grade 6 (Middle School 1) Lesson. Ed. by Alfred Publishing. (Expressions Music Curriculum Ser.). (ENG.). 2004. audio compact disk 500.00 (978-0-7579-2106-3(X)) Alfred Pub.

Music Expressions Grades 7-8 (Middle School 2) Lesson. Ed. by Alfred Publishing. (ENG.). 2006. audio compact disk 500.00 (978-0-7579-2117-9(5)) Alfred Pub.

Music Expressions Kindergarten: Lesson. Susan L. Smith & Robert W. Smith. (Expressions Music Curriculum Ser.). (ENG.). 2003. audio compact disk 340.00 (978-0-7579-0156-0(5)) Alfred Pub.

Music for a Pipedream. Garry Kvistad & Vinnie Martucci. 1 cass. (Running Time: 50 min.). 9.95 (978-1-55961-210-4(X)) Relaxtn Co.

Music for Abraham Lincoln: Campaign Songs, Civil War Tunes, Laments for a President. Anne Enslow & Ridley Enslow. 1 CD. (Running Time: 1 hr.). (Music for Abraham Lincoln Ser.). (YA). (gr. 5 up). 2009. audio compact disk 23.93 (978-0-7660-3635-2(9)) Enslow Pubs.

Music for Advent. Directed By J. Michael Thompson. 2005. 3.24 (978-0-8146-7845-9(9)) Liturgical Pr.

Music for Ayurveda. Janetta Petkus. 3 cass. (Running Time: 3 hrs.). 24.95 (978-1-55961-528-0(1)) Relaxtn Co.

Music for Ayurveda. Janetta Petkus. 3 CDs. (Running Time: 4 hrs. 30 mins.). 1999. audio compact disk 29.95 (978-1-55961-527-3(3)) Relaxtn Co.

Music for Ballet: Dance Class & Performance. Richard Rogers. Perf. by Cole Porter & Irving Berlin. 1 cass. 15.00 incl. guide. (KIM 3003C) Kimbo Educ.
Popular music.

Music for Birth: Soothing the Mother & Infant - Before, During & after Birth. Howard Richman. 1 cass. (Running Time: 9 min.). (Entrainment Music Ser.). 1988. 15.95 (978-0-929060-63-7(6)) Sound Feelings.
Features music which aims at soothing the mother & infant before, during & after birth.

Music for Brain Wave Vibration. Prod. by BEST Life Media. 2008. audio compact disk 17.95 (978-1-935127-01-7(2)) Pub: BEST Life. Dist(s): SCB Distributors

Music for Brainwave Massage. abr. ed. Jeffrey Thompson. (Running Time: 2:00:-00). 2006. audio compact disk 19.98 (978-1-55961-779-6(9)) Sounds True.

***Music for Brass Ensemble: For Trombone.** Keith O'Quinn. 2009. pap. bk. 24.98 (978-1-59615-463-6(2), 1596154632) Pub: Music Minus. Dist(s): H Leonard

Music for Children: Inspiring Creativity Through Sound Imagery. Howard Richman. 1 cass. (Running Time: 30 min.). (Stress Entrainment Music Ser.). (J). 15.95 (978-0-929060-62-0(8)) Sound Feelings.
To Encourage Creativity, Emotional Expression and Relaxation in Children of All Ages, by Using the Musical Entrainment Process. Five

Specially-Composed Piano Pieces Entitled "Mad," "Scared," "Stress," "Sad" & "Happy".

Music for Deep Relaxation. unabr. ed. Twin Sisters. Read by Twin Sisters. (YA). 2008. 44.99 (978-1-59922-319-3(8)) Find a World.

Music for Easter. abr. ed. J. Michael Thompson. 1 cass. (Running Time: 1 hr. 18 mins.). 2005. 16.95 (978-0-8146-7875-6(0)) Liturgical Pr.

Music for Fitness Walkers: Classical Walking, unabr. ed. 3 cass. (Running Time: 3 hrs.). 1994. 38.50 (S01630) J Norton Pubs.

Music for Fitness Walkers: Latin Walking, unabr. ed. 3 cass. (Running Time: 3 hrs.). 1994. 38.50 (S01655) J Norton Pubs.

Music for Fitness Walkers: Sixties Walking, unabr. ed. 3 cass. (Running Time: 3 hrs.). 1994. 13.95 (S01635) J Norton Pubs.

Music for Fitness Walkers: Walk to the Marches, unabr. ed. 3 cass. 1994. 38.50 (S01645) J Norton Pubs.

Music for Flute/Piano. 1995. cass. & audio compact disk 12.95 (978-0-7692-4916-2(7), Warner Bro) Alfred Pub.

Music for Forgiveness-Music. 2007. audio compact disk 16.95 (978-1-56136-426-8(6)) Master Your Mind.

Music for Healing: Experience Vitality, Relaxation & Wholeness. 2003. audio compact disk 29.95 (978-1-56589-186-9(4)) Pub: Crystal Clarity. Dist(s): Natl Bk Netwk

Music for Healing & Unwinding: Two Pioneers in the Emerging Field of Sound Healing. unabr. ed. Steven Halpern & Joseph Nagler. (Running Time: 2 hrs. 0 mins. 0 sec.). 2006. audio compact disk 19.98 (978-1-55961-727-7(6)) Sounds True.

Music for Health & Balance. Russill Paul. 4 cass. (Running Time: 4 hrs.). 1999. 29.95 (978-1-55961-511-2(7)) Relaxtn Co.

Music for Health & Balance. Russill Paul et al. 4 CDs. (Running Time: 4 hrs.). (Healing Music Ser.). 1999. audio compact disk 34.95 (978-1-55961-510-5(9)) Relaxtn Co.

Music for Imagination & Creativity, Vol. 1. Ivan Barzakov. Music by Richard Wagner et al. 1 cass. (Running Time: 1 hr.). 9.95 (OLC501) OptimaLearning.
Stimulates creativity, imagination & intuition. Develops visualization abilities, as well as problem solving & decision making skills. Excellent for writing & other artistic endeavors; to gain inspiration & to lift the spirit. Very beneficial when used to overcome grief & loss. Includes written instructions.

Music for Imagination & Creativity, Vol. 2. Ivan Barzakov. Music by Richard Wagner et al. 1 cass. (Running Time: 1 hr.). 9.95 (OLC502) OptimaLearning.
Includes written instructions.

Music for Intimacy: Relationships. Howard Richman. 1 cass. (Running Time: 23 min.). (Entrainment Music Ser.). 1988. 15.95 (978-0-929060-64-4(4)) Sound Feelings.
Features music, which aims at resolving conflict among groups, couples & individuals.

Music for Lent. abr. ed. J. Michael Thompson. 1 cass. (Running Time: 54 mins.). 2003. 14.95 (978-0-8146-7844-2(0)) Liturgical Pr.

Music for Little Mozarts, Bk. 1. E. L. Lancaster et al. 1 CD. (Running Time: 1 hr. 30 min.). (Music for Little Mozarts Ser.). (ENG.). (J). 1999. audio compact disk 14.95 (978-0-7390-0375-6(5), 14578) Alfred Pub.

Music for Little Mozarts, Bk. 1. E. L. Lancaster et al. 1 CD. (Running Time: 1 hr.). 1999. audio compact disk 14.95 (978-0-7390-0376-3(3), 14658) Alfred Pub.
General Midi, requires sytheizer.

Music for Little Mozarts, Bk. 2. E. L. Lancaster et al. 1 CD. (Running Time: 1 hr. 30 mins.). (Music for Little Mozarts Ser.). (ENG.). (J). 1999. audio compact disk 14.95 (978-0-7390-0591-0(X), 14582) Alfred Pub.

Music for Little Mozarts Bk. 3: Lesson Book & Discovery Book. E. L. Lancaster et al. 1 CD. (Running Time: 1 hr. 30 min.). 2000. audio compact disk MIDI. (978-0-7390-0648-1(7), 17185) Alfred Pub.

Music for Little Mozarts Bk. 3: Lesson Book & Discovery Book. E. L. Lancaster et al. 1 CD. (Running Time: 1 hr. 30 min.). (Music for Little Mozarts Ser.). (ENG.). (J). (ps-1). 2000. audio compact disk 14.95 (978-0-7390-0647-4(9), 17184) Alfred Pub.

Music for Little Mozarts Bk. 3: Lesson Book & Discovery Book. E. L. Lancaster et al. 1 CD. (Running Time: 1 hr. 30 min.). 2001. audio compact disk 14.95 MIDI. (978-0-7390-0655-9(X), 17191) Alfred Pub.

Music for Little Mozarts Bk. 3: Lesson Book & Discovery Book. E. L. Lancaster et al. 1 CD. (Running Time: 1 hr. 30 min.). (Music for Little Mozarts Ser.). (ENG.). (J). (ps-1). 2001. audio compact disk 14.95 (978-0-7390-0654-2(1), 17190) Alfred Pub.

Music for Little People. John M. Feierabend. Music by Luann Saunders. 1 cass. (Running Time: 45 min.). (J). (gr. 3). 1989. pap. bk. 14.95; 5.00 (978-0-913932-47-6(7)) Leonard Bernstein.
Folk songs, nursery rhymes, & lullabies.

Music for Little People. John M. Feierabend. (J). 1989. 14.95 (978-0-913932-07-0(8)) Leonard Bernstein.

Music for Little People: CD Only. Composed by John M. Feierabend. 2004. audio compact disk 19.95 (978-1-4234-0781-2(4), 1423407814) H Leonard.

Music for Lovers. Read by Steven Halpern. 1 cass., 1 CD. (Running Time: 1 hr.). 7.98 (HAL 7869); audio compact disk 12.78 (HAL 7869) NewSound.

Music for Meditation. Composed by Vanraj Bhatia. 1 cass. (Running Time: 1 hr.). 1993. (M93026); audio compact disk (CD M93026) Multi-Cultural Bks.

Music for Meditation: Experience Calmness, Joy & Inner Freedom. 2003. audio compact disk 29.95 (978-1-56589-187-6(2)) Pub: Crystal Clarity. Dist(s): Natl Bk Netwk

Music for Mellow Minds. Janalea Hoffman. 1 cass. (Running Time: 45 min.). 1982. 11.95 (978-1-886051-06-5(2)) Rhythmic Med.
Music written at exactly 60-beats-a-minute for deep relaxation & sleep control.

Music for Modern Dance Class. L. Stanford & David Hochoy. 2 cass. (Running Time: 3 hrs.). 27.00 (BOD9019C) Kimbo Educ.
Ten unrepeated selections of improvisational music designed for use in contemporary dance class using the Graham, Limon, Ailey, Horton & Lyric techniques. Includes Dark Nine, Walks on Ten, Jump on Five & more.

Music for Oboe & Strings. 2006. audio compact disk 15.00 (978-1-931569-11-8(8)) Pub: U of Wis Pr. Dist(s): Chicago Distribution Ctr

Music for Optimal Performance, Vol. 1. Ivan Barzakov. Music by Vivaldi et al. 1 cass. (Running Time: 1 hr.). pap. bk. 9.95 (OLC401) OptimaLearning.
Optimizes both mental & physical performance. Generates ideas in writing, exam preparation, homework or organizing. Energizes physical exercise, routine work or daily tasks. Includes written instructions.

Music for Optimal Performance, Vol. 2. Ivan Barsakov. Music by Vivaldi et al. 1 cass. (Running Time: 1 hr.). pap. bk. 9.95 (OLC402) OptimaLearning.
Includes written instructions.

Music for Organ, Brass & Percussion. Perf. by Empire Brass Quintet. 1 cass. (Running Time: 1 hr.). 7.98 (TA 30218); audio compact disk 12.78 (TA 80218) NewSound.

Music for Out-of-Body Experiences. Bruce Goldberg. (ENG.). 2005. audio compact disk 17.00 (978-1-57968-073-2(9)) Pub: B Goldberg. Dist(s): Baker Taylor

Music for Out-of-Body Experiences/COBE. Bruce Goldberg. (ENG.). 2005. 13.00 (978-1-57968-117-3(4)) Pub: B Goldberg. Dist(s): Baker Taylor

Music for Regression & Progression. Bruce Goldberg. (ENG.). 2005. 13.00 (978-1-57968-115-9(8)); audio compact disk 17.00 (978-1-57968-071-8(2)) Pub: B Goldberg. Dist(s): Baker Taylor

Music for Relaxation. Composed by Vishwa Mohan Bhatt. 1 cass. (Running Time: 1 hr.). 1994. (M94014); audio compact disk (CD M94014) Multi-Cultural Bks.

Music for Relaxation: Sound Therapy from an Emmy-Winning Artist. Jim Oliver. 1 cass. (Running Time: 1 hr.). 1990. 9.95 (978-1-55961-063-6(8)) Relaxtn Co.

Music for Romance. Composed by Louis Banks. 1 cass. (Running Time: 1 hr.). 1994. (M94013); audio compact disk (CD M94013) Multi-Cultural Bks.

Music for Sight Singing. 6th ed. Contrib. by Robert W. Ottman. 2003. audio compact disk 19.60 (978-0-13-184709-5(0), P-H) Pearson Educ CAN CAN.

Music for Sleep. audio compact disk (978-1-55961-668-3(7)) Relaxtn Co.

Music for Sleep: Clinically Proven Audio System to Help You Fall Asleep, Stay Asleep, & Wake up Rejuvenated. abr. ed. Jeffrey Thompson. (Running Time: 1:00:00). 2003. audio compact disk 29.98 (978-1-55961-790-1(X)) Sounds True.

Music for Sleep CD. 2004. audio compact disk (978-1-59250-212-7(1)) Gaiam Intl.

Music for Soul Plane Ascension. Bruce Goldberg. (ENG.). 2005. 13.00 (978-1-57968-118-0(2)); audio compact disk 17.00 (978-1-57968-074-9(7)) Pub: B Goldberg. Dist(s): Baker Taylor

Music for Superconscious Mind Tap. Bruce Goldberg. (ENG.). 2005. 13.00 (978-1-57968-116-6(6)); audio compact disk 17.00 (978-1-57968-072-5(0)) Pub: B Goldberg. Dist(s): Baker Taylor

Music for Superlearning. Ormond McGill. 2 cass. 2000. (978-1-933332-08-6(5)) Hypnotherapy Train.

Music for Tap & Jazz Class. 1 cass. (Running Time: 1 hr.). (J). 15.00 (KIM 9103C); lp 15.00 (KIM 9103) Kimbo Educ.
17 dynamic new selections for tap & jazz, ideal for class work or recitals. Features several standards with a variety of tempos, big band numbers & lengthy selections for workouts. Four Leaf Clover, Zippidy-Doo-Da, Come Follow the Band, The Heat Is On, Tuxedo Junction, I Love My Piano & more.

Music for the Heart. 2002. audio compact disk 14.98 (978-1-893967-18-2(2)) Emphasis Ent.

Music for the Inner Muse-Music. 2007. audio compact disk 16.95 (978-1-56136-428-2(2)) Master Your Mind.

Music for the Mozart Effect Vol. 1: Strengthen the Mind. Perf. by Don Campbell. 1 cass. (Running Time: 1 hr.). 7.98 (SHM 6501); audio compact disk 12.78 (SHM 6501) NewSound.
Includes selections from Mozart's "Violin Concertos Nos. 3 & 4," "Piano Concertos Nos. 1 & 3," "Symphony No. 14," "Divertimento in D Major" & "Eine Kleine Nachtmusik".

Music for the Mozart Effect Vol. 1: Strengthen the Mind. Prod. by Don Campbell. 1 CD. (Running Time: 50 min.). 1997. (978-1-891319-01-3(9)); audio compact disk (978-1-891319-00-6(0)) Spring Hill CO.

Music for the Mozart Effect Vol. 2: Heal the Body. Perf. by Don Campbell. 1 cass. (Running Time: 1 hr.). 7.98 (SHM 6502); audio compact disk 12.78 (SHM 6502) NewSound.

Music for the Mozart Effect Vol. 2: Heal the Body. Prod. by Don Campbell. 1 cass. (Running Time: 1 hr. 09 min.). 1997. (978-1-891319-02-0(7)) Spring Hill CO.

Music for the Mozart Effect Vol. 2: Heal the Body, Prod. by Don Campbell. 1 CD. (Running Time: 1 hr. 09 min.). 1997. audio compact disk (978-1-891319-03-7(5)) Spring Hill CO.

Music for the Mozart Effect Vol. 3: Unlock the Creative Spirit. Perf. by Don Campbell. 1 cass. (Running Time: 1 hr.). 7.98 (SHM 6503); audio compact disk 12.78 (SHM 6503) NewSound.

Music for the Mozart Effect Vol. 3: Unlock the Creative Spirit. Prod. by Don Campbell. 1 CD. (Running Time: 1 hr. 09 min.). 1997. (978-1-891319-04-4(3)) Spring Hill CO.

Music for the Mozart Effect Vol. 3: Unlock the Creative Spirit, Prod. by Don Campbell. 1 CD. (Running Time: 1 hr. 09 min.). 1997. audio compact disk (978-1-891319-05-1(1)) Spring Hill CO.

Music for the Paschal Triduum. abr. ed. The Schola Cantorum of St. Peter the Apostle. Directed By J. Michael Thompson. 1 CD. (Running Time: 1 hr. 8 mins.). 2005. audio compact disk 16.95 (978-0-8146-7900-5(5)) Liturgical Pr.

Music for the Spiritual Tourist. Compiled by Mick Brown. 1 CD. (Running Time: 59 min..). 1999. bk. (978-1-891319-17-4(5)) Spring Hill CO.

Music for the Spiritual Tourist. Prod. by Mick Brown. 1 cass. (Running Time: 57 min.). 1999. 10.98 (978-1-891319-22-8(1)) Spring Hill CO.

Music for the Twelve Days of Christmas. The Schola Cantorum of St. Peter the Apostle. Directed By J. Michael Thompson. 1 CD. (Running Time: 59 mins.). 2005. audio compact disk 16.95 (978-0-8146-7902-9(1)) Liturgical Pr.
Continues the celebration of the Christmas season by rejoicing in the birth of the Savior. Many of the chant selections are assigned to a specific feat in the twelve days of Christmas (from December 25 through the Epiphany); others are "liturgical folk chant," used in processions or as devotions at the Creche.

Music for the Whole Child. Dennis Westphall & Lorraine Bayes. 1 cass. (Running Time: 1 hr. 5 min.). (J). (ps-5). 1995. pap. bk. 19.95 (978-0-945337-10-2(8), TTT 009) Tickle Tune Typhoon.
Incorporates music in the classroom & presents Dr. Howard Gardner's theory of the Multiple Intelligences using music as the teaching tool. Includes workbook.

Music for the Year of Luke: Hymns, Chant, & Anthems for Ordinary Time, Cycle C. abr. ed. Schola Cantorum of St. Peter the Apostle Staff & J. Michael Thompson. 1 CD. (Running Time: 1 hr.). 2005. audio compact disk 16.95 (978-0-8146-7955-5(2)) Liturgical Pr.

Music for the Year of Mark: Hymns, Chant, & Anthems for Ordinary Time. unabr. ed. F. Michael Thompson. 1 CD. (Running Time: 1 hr. 1 min.). 2005. audio compact disk 16.95 (978-0-8146-7954-8(4)) Liturgical Pr.

Music for the Year of Matthew: Hymns, Chant & Anthems for Ordinary Time, Cycle A. abr. ed. 1 cass. (Running Time: 1 hr. 30 mins.). 2001. 16.95 (978-0-8146-7934-0(X)) Liturgical Pr.

Music for Very Little People. Composed by John M. Feierabend. (ENG.). 2004. audio compact disk 14.95 (978-1-4234-0780-5(6), 1423407806) H Leonard.

Music for Yoga. 3 CDs. 2003. audio compact disk 29.95 (978-1-56589-188-3(0)) Pub: Crystal Clarity. Dist(s): Natl Bk Netwk

Music for Yoga & Other Joys. Jai Uttal. 1 CD. (Running Time: 1 hr. 16 mins.). 2006. audio compact disk 16.98 (978-1-59179-133-1(2), M768D) Sounds True.

Music for Young Masters: Secrets of the Heart. Bunny Hull. 1 CD. (Running Time: 41 mins.). (J). (ps-3). 2007. audio compact disk 13.95 (978-0-9721478-5-9(3)) BrassHeart.

Music for Your Baby's Brain. 1 CD. (Running Time: 1 hr.). 1999. audio compact disk (978-0-9665815-3-9(9)) Brllnt Begnngs.

Music Four Fun Pack. 4 cass. (Running Time: 2 hrs. 10 mins.). (J). 1998. pap. bk. 24.95 (978-1-887120-09-8(2)) Prodn Assocs.
Collection of songs & stories for sing-along & listening pleasure. Includes "American Cowboy Songs," "Mother Goose & Nursery Rhymes," "The Halloween Party," & "Camp Sing-Along".

Music from "Conversations with God" & other Selections. Michael Mish. 1 cass. 1997. 12.00 (978-0-9622465-9-3(X), MMM2010) Mish Mash Music.

Music from Health Journeys. Perf. by Steven Mark Kohn. Composed by Steven Mark Kohn. 1 CD. (Running Time: 55 minutes). (Health Journeys Ser.: 2131). 1991. audio compact disk 17.98 (978-1-881405-19-1(2)) Hlth Jrnys.
Steven Mark Kohn's first music CD includes both the calming meditative background music featured on the General Wellness and Stress imagery programs and the more powerful and complex music that accompanies our programs for Weight Loss, Alcohol & Drugs and Smoking.

Music from Spiritwalker. abr. ed. Perf. by Tim Gennert. Composed by Tim Gennert. 1 cass. (Running Time: 58 mins.). 1995. 8.99 (978-1-57453-041-4(0)) Audio Lit.
Soundtrack from the audio program "Spiritwalker: Messages from the Future." The music captures the emotions & moods of the book.

Music from the Coffee Lands: A Putumayo Blend. 1 cass. (Running Time: 1 hr.). 7.98 (PWM 135); audio compact disk 12.78 (PWM 135) NewSound.

Music from the Complete Book of Rhymes, Songs, Poems, Fingerplays & Chants. Jackie Silberg. Contrib. by Michael Oshiver. 2006. audio compact disk 19.95 (978-0-87659-052-2(0)) Pub: Gryphon Hse. Dist(s): Consort Bk Sales

Music from the Forests of Riau & Mentawai. Anno. by Philip Yampolsky et al. 1 CD. (Running Time: 1 hr. 10 min.). (Music of Indonesia Ser.: Vol. 7). 1995. pap. bk. (0-9307-40423-2-8) Smithsonian Folkways.
Focuses on the music of three indigenous forest societies of western Indonesia. Features songs & drumming for shamanic curing rituals & private singing & instrumental music (played on xylophones or a gong-row).

Music from the Outskirts of Jakarta: Gambang Kromong. Anno. by Philip Yampolsky. 1 cass. (Running Time: 1 hr. 8 min.). (Music of Indonesia Ser.: Vol. 3). 1991. (0-9307-400570-9307-40057-2-9); audio compact disk (0-9307-40057-2-9) Smithsonian Folkways.
Combines Indonesian, Chinese & sometimes European-derived instruments in musical styles at times reminiscent of gamelan music & at other times of small-group jazz of the 1920s & 1930s.

Music from the Park. 1 cass. (Running Time: 1 hr.). (Classic Collections). (J). 11.99 (978-0-7634-0123-8(4)); 11.99 (978-0-7634-0122-1(6)); audio compact disk 19.99 (978-0-7634-0125-2(0)) W Disney Records.

Music from the Park. 1 CD. (Running Time: 1 hr.). (Classic Collections). (J). (ps-3). 1996. audio compact disk 19.99 (978-0-7634-0124-5(2)) W Disney Records.

Music from the Sacramentary. 1 cass. (Running Time: 1 hr.). (ENG & LAT.). 1998. (978-0-937690-63-5(5), 2396); audio compact disk (978-0-937690-62-8(7), 2394) Wrld Lib Pubns.
Tool for teaching priests how to chant.

Music Game: How 2 Play 2 Win! Leroy Mcmath. 2007. audio compact disk 16.95 (978-0-9793721-1-7(9)) Pub: L McMath. Dist(s): Bookworld

Music Games. Ed. by Alfred Publishing. (ENG.). 2003. audio compact disk 9.95 (978-0-7390-3461-3(8)) Alfred Pub.

Music, Imagery & Parkinson's. Janalea Hoffman. 1 cass. (Running Time: 45 min.). 1993. 11.95 (978-1-886051-13-3(5)) Rhythmic Med.
A cassette written specifically for people who have Parkinson's Disease. Therapeutic music with verbal exercises to help ease the symptoms of the disease.

Music in a New World. 1 cass. (Running Time: 1 hr.). Incl. Pt. 1. Music in a New World: Afro-Cuban. (C056AB090); Pt. 2. Music in a New World: Laotian. (C056AB090); 9.00 (C056AB090, HarperThor); 9.00 (C056BB090, HarperThor); 9.00 (C056CB090, HarperThor); 9.00 (C056EB090, HarperThor); 9.00 (C056DB090, HarperThor) HarpC GBR.

Music in a New World: Afro-Cuban see Music in a New World

Music in a New World: Hmong see Music in a New World

Music in a New World: Laotian see Music in a New World

Music in a New World: Russian see Music in a New World

Music in a New World: Samoan see Music in a New World

Music in a New World: Southern Slavic see Music in a New World

Music in a New World: Soviet Central Asian see Music in a New World

Music in a New World: Tai Dam see Music in a New World

Music in a New World: Turkish see Music in a New World

Music in a New World: Vietnamese see Music in a New World

Music in Dreams Vol. 1: The Hawaiian Edition. Eliasar Simon. 2007. audio compact disk 19.95 (978-0-9769480-2-5(8)) Salidona Publng.

Music in Every Room: Around the World in a Bad Mood. unabr. collector's ed. John Krich. Read by Richard Brown. 8 cass. (Running Time: 12 hrs.). 1987. 64.00 (978-0-7366-1163-3(0), 2088) Books on Tape.
Charts the third world journey of John Krich, dreamer but doer & his traveling partner Iris, once a happy college cheerleader, now feminist & hopeful mystic.

Music in Shakespeare's Plays. unabr. ed. John H. Long. 1 cass. (Running Time: 1 hr. 30 min.). 1977. 12.95 (23500) J Norton Pubs.
Provides an in-depth analysis of Renaissance musical theory & a performance on the musical instruments of the time.

Music in the Air. Perf. by Dixie Hummingbirds, The. 1 CD. audio compact disk 16.98 (978-1-57908-482-0(6), 1461) Platinm Enter.

Music in the Air, unabr. ed. Perf. by Dixie Hummingbirds, The. 1 cass. (Running Time: 1 hr.). 10.98 (978-1-57908-483-7(4), 1461) Platinm Enter.

Music in the Family. Donna R. Carter. Illus. by Cortrell J. Harris. 1 cass. (J). 1995. bk. 19.95 (978-1-885242-02-0(6)) Lindsey Pubng.
Performing arts.

Music in Theory & Practice, Vol. II. 6th ed. Bruce Benward & Gary C. White. 1 cass. (Running Time: 1 hr. 30 mins.). (C). 1997. 26.25 (978-0-697-36591-0(3), 9780697365910, Mc-H Human Soc) Pub: McGrw-H Hghr Educ. Dist(s): McGraw

Music Inspired by Great Lakes Legends. 2005. audio compact disk 15.00 (978-0-9728212-4-7(4)) Old Country Bks.

Music Inspired by No Suitable Mate. JESJEN Staff. 2004. audio compact disk 14.99 (978-2-901005-01-8(2)) Pub: Whitaker Hse. Dist(s): Anchor Distributors

Music Inspired by the Chronicles of Narnia: The Lion, the Witch & the Wardrobe. Prod. by Peter York. Contrib. by Andrew Adamson. 2005. audio compact disk 17.98 (978-5-558-86744-2(2)) Pt of Grace Ent.

Music Is for Everyone: Collection for Special Learners. Faith Johnson & Laurie Farnan. 1988. 14.95 (978-0-634-05333-7(7)) H Leonard.

Music Is Magic: A Musical Learning Experience for Children. Peggy Pascal et al. 1 cass. (Running Time: 1 hr.). (J). 9.95 (978-0-9649682-0-2(7)) Sweet Punkin.
Discusses opposites, feelings, rhymes, body parts, rhythm instruments, zoo, colors, wiggles. Includes teachers book and song book.

Music Is You. Rosita Perez. 3 cass. (Running Time: 3 hrs.). 1994. 29.95 (978-0-9611354-2-3(5)) T Knox Pub.
Motivational talks set to music advocating the necessity for thinking less & feeling more.

Music K5 CD Set. 45.00 (978-1-59166-244-0(3)) BJUPr.

Music K5 Porgram Accompaniment Cassette. (J). 1987. 15.50 (978-1-59166-023-1(8)) BJUPr.

Music K5 Teacher's Help Cassette. (J). 1987. 15.50 (978-1-59166-022-4(X)) BJUPr.

***Music Lesson: A Spiritual Search for Growth Through Music.** unabr. ed. Victor L. Wooten. (Running Time: 7 hrs. 30 mins.). 2010. 14.99 (978-1-4001-8817-8(2)); 19.99 (978-1-4001-6817-0(1)); audio compact disk 71.99 (978-1-4001-4817-2(0)); audio compact disk 29.99 (978-1-4001-1817-5(4)) Pub: Tantor Media. Dist(s): IngramPubServ

***Music Listening CD 1 for the Humanistic Tradition.** 6th ed. Gloria K. Fiero. (ENG.). (C). 2010. audio compact disk 24.06 (978-0-07-734621-8(1), 0077346211, Mc-H Human Soc) Pub: McGrw-H Hghr Educ. Dist(s): McGraw

***Music Listening CD 1 for the Humanistic Tradition (for use with Volume I or Books 1-3)** 6th ed. Gloria Fiero. (ENG.). (C). 2010. audio compact disk 25.94 (978-0-07-742920-1(6), 0077429206, Mc-H Human Soc) Pub: McGrw-H Hghr Educ. Dist(s): McGraw

Music Listening CD 1 THT 5e. 5th ed. Gloria K. Fiero. (C). 2006. audio compact disk 25.63 (978-0-07-291013-1(5), 9780072910131, Mc-H Human Soc) Pub: McGrw-H Hghr Educ. Dist(s): McGraw

***Music Listening CD 2 for Humanistic Tradition (for use with Volume II or Books 4-6)** 6th ed. Gloria Fiero. (ENG.). (C). 2010. audio compact disk 25.94 (978-0-07-742921-8(4), 0077429214, Mc-H Human Soc) Pub: McGrw-H Hghr Educ. Dist(s): McGraw

Music Machine Series: All About Love. 1 cass. (Running Time: 1 hr.). (J). 2000. 6.99 HARK Ent.
Will fill your home with fun-filled praise of the Lord. Provides wholesome messages that are sure to last a lifetime.

Music Machine Series: Fruit of the Spirit. 1 cass. (Running Time: 1 hr.). 2000. 6.99 HARK Ent.

Music Machine Series: Majesty of God. 1 cass. (Running Time: 1 hr.). (J). 2000. 6.99 HARK Ent.

Music Made Easy: Guitar. Morton Manus. (ENG.). 2005. audio compact disk 19.95 (978-0-7390-3734-8(X)) Alfred Pub.

Music Made Easy: Guitar. Ron Manus. (ENG.). 2004. audio compact disk 19.95 (978-0-7390-3366-1(2)) Alfred Pub.

Music Maestro Parade. unabr. ed. Aristoplay, Ltd. Staff. Perf. by Amy Kullenberg et al. Narrated by John Osenmacher. 1 cass. (Running Time: 47 min.). (Play, Listen & Learn Ser.). (J). (gr. 4). 1993. pap. bk. 15.00 (978-1-57057-011-7(6), 4011) Talicor.
Recording 32 instrument sounds & history with 4 lotto games on side 2.

Music Makers. 1999. audio compact disk 7.98 (978-0-633-04552-4(7)) LifeWay Christian.

Music Makers. 2003. audio compact disk 7.98 (978-0-633-07637-5(6)) LifeWay Christian.

Music Makers. 2004. audio compact disk 7.98 (978-0-633-08010-5(1)) LifeWay Christian.

Music Makers. 2004. audio compact disk 7.98 (978-0-633-08512-4(X)) LifeWay Christian.

Music Makers. 2004. audio compact disk 7.98 (978-0-633-17339-5(8)) LifeWay Christian.

Music Makers. 2005. audio compact disk 7.98 (978-0-633-17533-7(1)) LifeWay Christian.

Music Makers. 2005. audio compact disk 7.98 (978-0-633-17731-7(8)) LifeWay Christian.

Music Man (Choral Highlights) - Showtrax. Perf. by Meredith Willson. Arranged by Mac Huff. 1 CD. (Running Time: 7 mins.). 2000. audio compact disk 35.00 H Leonard.
Medley of songs. Includes "Gary," "Indiana," "Goodnight My Someone," "Seventy Six Trombones," "The Wells Fargo Wagon".

Music Mania. Stephanie K. Burton. 1994. pap. bk. & tchr. ed. 29.95 (978-1-889163-00-0(7)) Panda Bear Pub.

Music Mania. Stephanie K. Burton. 1994. 9.95 (978-1-889163-11-6(2)); audio compact disk 13.95 (978-1-889163-10-9(4)) Panda Bear Pub.

Music Moves for Piano Keyboard Games for Beginners Book A. Composed by Marilyn Lowe. Contrib. by Edwin E. Gordon. (J). 2006. spiral bd. 19.95 (978-1-57999-698-7(1)) GIA Pubns.

***Music, Music for Everyone.** unabr. ed. Vera B. Williams. Read by Martha Plimpton.Tr. of iMusica para todo el mundo!. (ENG.). 2009. (978-0-06-180598-1(X), GreenwillowBks); (978-0-06-176242-0(3), GreenwillowBks) HarperCollins Pubs.

Music of Biak, Irian Jaya: Wor, Church Songs, Yospan. Anno. by Philip Yampolsky. 1 CD. (Running Time: 1 hr. 13 min.). (Music of Indonesia Ser.: Vol. 10). 1996. audio compact disk (0-9307-40426-2-5) Smithsonian Folkways.
Presents music for celebrations & church services on Biak, sung in both the formal manner & in a relaxed, hand-clapping, party mood; & "yospan," string-band music for dance parties.

Music of Biak, Irian Jaya: Wor, Church Songs, Yospan. Anno. by Philip Yampolsky. 1 CD. (Running Time: 1 hr. 13 min.). (Music of Indonesia Ser.: Vol. 12). 1996. audio compact disk (0-9307-40428-2-3) Smithsonian Folkways.
Melodic gong ensembles & male singing with percussion are found throughout Sumatra. Two of each are heard here: West Sumatran talempong, kulintang, the choral didong songs & Salawat dulang, competitive duet singing.

Music of Bob Dylan Arranged for Fingerstyle Guitar. Fred Sokolow. 2001. per. 24.95 (978-0-7866-5974-6(2)) Mel Bay.

***Music of Brain Art Festival 2009 Cd: Featuring Brain Wave Vibration.** (Running Time: 55 mins.). 2009. audio compact disk 19.95 (978-1-935127-34-5(9)) Pub: BEST Life. Dist(s): SCB Distributors

Music of Christmas. Dennis Allen & Nan Allen. 1996. 75.00 (978-0-7673-0695-9(3)) LifeWay Christian.

Music of Christmas. Dennis Allen & Nan Allen. 1996. audio compact disk 85.00 (978-0-7673-0726-0(7)) LifeWay Christian.

Music of Christmas. Mormon Youth Chorus and Symphony. 1 cass. 8.98 (1000594) Covenant Comms.
Eleven selected Christmas songs.

Music of Disney's Cinderella. 1 cass. (Classic Collections). (J). 11.99 (978-1-55723-878-8(2)); 11.99 (978-1-55723-877-1(4)); audio compact disk 19.99 (978-1-55723-879-5(0)); audio compact disk 19.99 (978-1-55723-880-1(4)) W Disney Records.

Music of Disney's One Saturday Morning. Prod. by Disney Staff. 1 cass. (Running Time: 1 hr.). (J). (gr. 4-7). 1998. 12.98 (978-0-7634-0501-4(9)) W Disney Records.

Music of Dolphins. Karen Hesse. Read by Michele McHall. 2 cass. (Running Time: 2 hrs. 50 mins.). (J). 2000. 18.00 (978-0-7366-5010-6(5)) Books on Tape.
When the U.S. Coast Guard finds a girl lost at sea off he coast of Florida, they think she is a mermaid, but later realize she is a human who has been raised by dolphins since the age of four. At first, Mila rejoices in the new skills she can learn as a human, but when scientists begin demanding behavior that Mila is uncomfortable with, she backs away. Now she must try to adapt in a foreign culture.

Music of Dolphins. unabr. ed. Karen Hesse. Read by Michele McHall. 2 cass. (Running Time: 3 hrs.). (J). (gr. 1-8). 1999. 23.00 (LL 0154, Chivers Child Audio) AudioGO.

Music of Dolphins, unabr. ed. Karen Hesse. Read by Michele McHall. 2 cass. (Running Time: 3 hrs.). (YA). 1999. 16.98 (FS9-50965) Highsmith.

Music of Dolphins. unabr. ed. Karen Hesse. Read by Michele McHall. 2 vols. (Running Time: 2 hrs. 48 mins.). (J). (gr. 5-9). 2004. pap. bk. 29.00 (978-0-8072-8135-2(2), YA113SP, Listening Lib); 23.00 (978-0-8072-8134-5(4), BWYA113CX, Listening Lib) Random Audio Pubg.
When the U.S. Coast Guard finds a girl lost at sea off the coast of Florida, they think she is a mermaid. They later realize she is a human who has been raised by dolphins since the age of four. Library album package.

Music of Espionage. Perf. by Spies. 1 cass. (Running Time: 1 hr.). 7.98 (TA 35503); audio compact disk 12.78 (TA 85503) NewSound.

Music of Everyday Ecstasy. Prod. by Margot Anand. 1 cass. (Running Time: 1 hr. 2 min.). 1998. 9.98 (978-1-891319-14-3(0)); audio compact disk 15.98 (978-1-891319-13-6(2)) Spring Hill CO.

Music of First City, Leavenworth, Kansas. Perf. by Bob Spear & Tim Daniels. Composed by Bob Spear. 2005. audio compact disk 14.95 (978-1-933117-03-4(6)) Sharp Spr.

Music of General Hospital. Prod. by Walt Disney Records Staff. 1 cass. (Running Time: 1 hr.). 1998. 12.98 (978-0-7634-0415-4(2)); audio compact disk 22.50 (978-0-7634-0416-1(0)) W Disney Records.

Music of General Hospital Album. 1 cass. (Running Time: 1 hr.). (Classic Collections). (J). 13.99 (978-0-7634-0390-4(3)); audio compact disk 22.99 (978-0-7634-0391-1(1)) W Disney Records.

Music of Indonesia: Indonesian Guitars. Philip Yampolsky. 1 CD. (Running Time: 1 hr. 14 min.). (YA). 1999. audio compact disk 14.00 Smithsonian Folkways.

Music of Indonesia Vol. 18: Sulawesi - Festivals, Funerals & Work. Philip Yampolsky. 1 CD. (Running Time: 74 min.). (YA). 1999. audio compact disk 14.00 Smithsonian Folkways.

Music of Kevin Keegan. Kevin Keegan. (ENG.). 2004. audio compact disk 23.95 (978-0-8023-8156-9(1)) Dufour.

Music of Love. unabr. ed. Kay Gregory. Read by Lynda Evans. 4 cass. (Running Time: 5 hrs. 30 min.). 2001. 26.95 (978-1-55686-940-2(1)) Books in Motion.
When patronly neighbor Joe McLane urges Belinda Ballantine to get her bike fixed, she comes in contact with Bike Shop owner, Hal Blake, that handsome jogger she noticed on the running path.

Music of Mexico for Acoustic Guitar, Vol. 2. Ruben Delgado. 1998. pap. bk. 19.95 (978-0-7866-4504-6(0), 95347BCD) Mel Bay.

Music of Mexico for Acoustic Guitar, Vol. 3. Ruben Delgado. 1997. pap. bk. 17.95 (978-0-7866-2666-3(6), 96517BCD) Mel Bay.

Music of New Mexico: Hispanic Traditions. James K. Leger. Prod. by Howard Bass. 1 cass. (Running Time: 1 hr.). 1992. (0-9307-404090-9307-40409-2-8); audio compact disk (0-9307-40409-2-8) Smithsonian Folkways.
Sacred hymns, serenades, narrative ballads & lyric folk songs give a glimpse of the diverse & captivating cultural landscape of Hispanic New Mexico. Spanish lyrics have English translations.

Music of New Mexico: Native American Traditions. Anno. by Edward W. Wahpeconiah. Prod. by Howard Bass. 1 cass. (Running Time: 1 hr. 8 min.). 1992. (0-9307-404080-9307-40408-2-9); audio compact disk (0-9307-40408-2-9) Smithsonian Folkways.
Portrait of Pueblo, Navajo & Mescalero Apache music from New Mexico. Ranges from San Juan Pueblo Cloud Dance song to modern Navajo songs.

Music of Nias & North Sumatra: Hoho, Gendang Karo, Gondang Toba. Anno. by Philip Yampolsky. 1 cass. (Running Time: 1 hr. 12 min.). (Music of Indonesia Ser.: Vol. 4). 1992. Incl. notes. (0-9307-404200-9307-40420-2-1); audio compact disk (0-9307-40420-2-1) Smithsonian Folkways.
The Toba, one of the few societies to use tuned drums to carry a melody, combine them with gongs & oboe-like instruments, creating dynamic melodies & rhythms. The Karo ensemble features expert drumming full of snaps & pops. The Ono niha people from the island of Nias perform ornate songs call ed "hoho" which use only four tones to embody their oral tradition.

Music of Our World: Multicultural Festivals, Songs & Activities. 2003. audio compact disk 29.95 (978-0-634-06321-3(9)) H Leonard.

***Music of Our World - Ireland: Songs & Activities for Classroom & Community.** Composed by Mark Brymer & Brad Shank. (ENG.). 2005. pap. bk. 29.95 (978-1-4234-9545-1(4), 1423495454) H Leonard.

Music of Pakistan. unabr. ed. Rough Guides Staff. (Rough Guide World Music Cds Ser.). 2004. audio compact disk 14.95 (978-1-84353-168-5(2)) Pub: Rough Guides GBR. Dist(s): DK Pub Inc

Music of Paul Simon Arranged for Fingerstyle Guitar. Fred Sokolow. 2001. per. 24.95 (978-0-7866-5973-9(4)) Mel Bay.

Music of Robert W.Smith. 1997. bk. 19.95 (978-0-7692-1622-5(6), Warner Bro) Alfred Pub.

***Music of Tea: Soundtrack from the Meaning of Tea.** Composed by Joel Douek & Eric Czar. Loreena McKennitt. (ENG.). 2008. audio compact disk 19.95 (978-0-615-20443-7(0)) TalkLeaves.

Music of the American Colonies. Perf. by Anne Enslow & Ridley Enslow. 1 CD. (Running Time: 61 mins.). (YA). (gr. 5-12). 2000. pap. bk. & tchr. ed. 31.93 (978-0-7660-1614-9(5)) Enslow Pubs.
Selections reflecting the cultural & musical diversity of Colonial America, with songs in French & Dutch, readings from a Native American & an African slave & a Spanish fandango tune. The accompanying booklet has instructions for dances & the lyrics to each selection & more related information.

Music of the American Colonies. Perf. by Anne Enslow & Ridley Enslow. (YA). 2002. audio compact disk 23.93 (978-0-7660-2239-3(0)) Enslow Pubs.
This CD is perfect for young listeners who are studying the American colonial period. It consists of 22 songs and two primary source readings. The CD comes inside a jewel case.

Music of the Americas, 1492-1992. Gloriae Dei Cantores. 1 CD. (Running Time: 90 mins.). 1992. audio compact disk 33.95 (978-1-55725-085-8(5)) Paraclete MA.

Music of the Andes. Perf. by Chaskinakuy. 1 cass. (Running Time: 1 hr.). (J). (ps up). 9.98 (2590) MFLP CA.
Take an exotic trip on winding trails through the mountains of South America with these Andean folklore melodies played on pan pipes, charango flutes & more.

Music of the Angels. Gerald J. Markoe. 1 cass. 10.95 (LA112); audio compact disk 15.95 (LA112D) Lghtwrks Aud & Vid.
This soothing music for harp, strings, winds, bells, angel voices & celestial sounds relaxes the body, clears the mind & opens the heart. It transports you to an experience of floating on a cloud, being surrounded by love.

Music of the Angels II. Gerald J. Markoe. 1 cass. (Running Time: 1 hr.). 10.95 (LA113); audio compact disk 15.95 (LA113D) Lghtwrks Aud & Vid.
Gerald Jay Markoe's sequel to his popular best-selling original album features soothing instrumental harp, strings, winds, bells, angel voices & celestial sounds to relax the body, clear the mind & open the heart.

Music of the British Isles for Banjo. Kyle Datesman. (ENG.). 2009. pap. bk. 17.95 (978-0-7866-2783-7(2)) Mel Bay.

Music of the Bukharan Jewish Ensemble. Perf. by Fatima Kuinova & Shashmaqam. Anno. by Ted Levin. Prod. by Ted Levin et al. 1 cass. (Running Time: 58 min.). 1991. (0-9307-400540-9307-40054-2-2); audio compact disk (0-9307-40054-2-2) Smithsonian Folkways.
Music reflects the many diverse cultures of Uzbekistan & Tadzhikistan.

Music of the Comte de St. Germain: A Performance of L'Incostanza Delusa Suite. Instructed by Manly P. Hall. bk. 8.95 (978-0-89314-188-2(7), C800107) Philos Res.

Music of the Dance: Stravinsky. Prod. by Zobeida Perez. (YA). 1994. 17.00 (978-0-89898-799-7(7), BMR05084, Warner Bro) Alfred Pub.

Music of the Desert Bedouins. 1 CD. (ARA.). 2005. audio compact disk 18.95 (978-1-57970-234-2(1), C11121D) J Norton Pubs.

Music of the Deserts. Music by Zakir Hussain. 1 cass. (Running Time: 1 hr.). (Soundscapes: Vol. 4). 1993. (M93030); audio compact disk (CD M93030) Multi-Cultural Bks.
Sandstorm, The Great Indian Desert, Ladakh, The Ice Desert, Desert Heartbeat, Where Deserts Meet, Nomads.

Music of the Infinite Mind 2002: Program from the Award Winning Public Radio Series. Excerpts. Hosted by Fred Goodwin. 1 CD. (Running Time: 1 hr). 2002. audio compact disk 21.95 (978-1-932479-69-0(4), LCM 221) Lichtenstein Creat.
In this hour, a special presentation:The Music of The Infinite Mind. From the very beginning, The Infinite Mind has set out to explore the science AND art of the human mind. As you'll hear today, in our four years, a number of extraordinary musicians - and a few moonlighting scientists - have joined us to offer their artistic perspective on a range of topics - from autism to parenting to moving.We thought it would be fun to take the tapes off the shelf, dust them off, and take a listen to some of these magical performances. Guests include Suzanne Vega; Dr. Jill Bolte Taylor, the singing scientist; Jessye Norman; psychiatrist and pianist Dr. Richard Kogan; Laurie Berkner; Louden Wainwright III; Dar Williams; and Judy Collins.

Music of the Infinite Mind 2003: Program from the Award Winning Public Radio Series. Excerpts. Hosted by Fred Goodwin. 1 CD. (Running Time: 1hr). 2003. audio compact disk 24.95 (978-1-932479-70-6(8), LCM 274) Lichtenstein Creat.
In this second annual presentation of musical performers who have visited The Infinite Mind's studios, we talk with and hear performances from Aimee Mann, Janice Ian, the Cowboy Junkies, the Roches, Dar Williams and Suzanne Vega.

Music of the Infinite Mind 2006: Program from the Award-Winning Public Radio Series, 433. Interview. Hosted by Peter Kramer. 1 CD. (Running Time: 59 minutes). 2006. audio compact disk 21.95 (978-1-933644-32-5(X)) Lichtenstein Creat.
Our annual collection of performances and conversations with some of the top artists who've joined us in our studios!We begin with Louden Wainwright III who says that with age, comes wisdom, and he performs the world premiere of his song about aging: Doin' the Math.Next, writer's block is something all creative people dread; A[illegible] Mann talks about her own experiences with it and how she wrote [illegible]g it Quits about it.For our show on Shoplifting, comedienne and singer [illegible]eLaria has appropriated the Jane's Addiction song Been Caught Stealin' and given it a jazz beat. She also confesses her own reasons for shoplifting as a child. ("Something about nuns" she says)Christopher Louviere played lead guitar for legendary cajun folk singer Clint West for seven years, now he's struck out on his own with an album titled the same as our show: Hypomania. Louviere himself is diagnosed with bipolar disorder; he talks about his experiences and plays the song Benzo Train from the album.After a short break, we come to the Black Eyed Peas, who joined us for our show on Religion to talk about how religion, spirituality...and the 9/11 attacks...affected their rap spiritual, and number one hit, Where is the Love?The Infinite Mind's Jackson Braider introduces us to the Multitasking genius of Charles Ives, a composer who wrote extraordinary symphonies of multitasking. And did it while inventing life insurance for the common man, no less.Finally, the ladies of Menopause: The Musical say their minds go void, and they get annoyed, but they're still smiling and singing through it all.

Music of the Mountains. Music by Shiv K. Sharma. 1 cass. (Running Time: 1 hr.). (Soundscapes: Vol. 2). 1993. (M93028); audio compact disk (CD M93028) Multi-Cultural Bks.
Himalayan Dawn, Sunrise on the Peaks, Spirit of Kashmir, Echoes from the Valley, Mountain Love Song, Evening Prayer, Ballad, Twilight Shadows, Springtime, Shikara by Moonlight.

Music of the Nez Perce. Bernie Krause. 1 cass. (Running Time: 39 min.). (Music & Word Ser.). 1994. 9.95 (2307, NrthWrd Bks) TandN Child.
Three surviving members of a group of 26 Nez Perce men who first performed in the 1920s, these drummers & singers share the traditional music of their tribe.

Music of the Nile Valley. unabr. ed. 1 cass. (Running Time: 1 hr.). 12.95 (7355) J Norton Pubs.

Music of the North American Indians for Acoustic Guitar. Steven Zdenek Eckels. 2000. pap. bk. 17.95 (978-0-7866-2146-0(X), 96015BCD) Mel Bay.

Music of the Rivers. Music by Hari P. Chaurasia. 1 cass. (Running Time: 1 hr.). (Soundscapes: Vol. 1). 1993. (M93027); audio compact disk (CD M93027) Multi-Cultural Bks.
Water, Poems, Song of the River, Delta-Journey to the Sea.

Music of the Sea & Sky. 1994. 17.00 (978-0-89898-796-6(2), BMR05085, Warner Bro) Alfred Pub.

Music of the Seas. Music by Bhaskar Chandavarkar. 1 cass. (Running Time: 1 hr.). (Soundscapes: Vol. 3). 1993. (M93029); audio compact disk (CD M93029) Multi-Cultural Bks.
Deep Blue, Coastal Garba, Goa Polka, Southern Lighthouse, Seascapes, Palms in Moonlight, Fisherman's Dawn, Surging Seas, Beach Dance, Against the Tide, Easter Thunder.

Music of the Season. Contrib. by Janet Walters. Prod. by Paul A. Tatge. 2006. audio compact disk 12.98 (978-5-558-16089-5(6)) APAB CAN.

Music of the Spheres. Mark Earlix. 1 cass. (Running Time: 1 hr. 30 min.). 2000. 12.95 (978-0-9678058-2-5(1)) Art of Healing.

Music of the Spheres. Elizabeth Redfern. 2004. 15.95 (978-0-7435-1987-8(6)) Pub: S&S Audio. Dist(s): S and S Inc

Music of the Spheres. unabr. ed. Dane Rudhyar. 1 cass. (Running Time: 1 hr. 22 min.). 1970. 11.00 (10107) Big Sur Tapes.
Music expresses the order & structure of the cosmos, which was dealt with in great detail by Pythagoras. Rudhyar discusses his study of this ancient insight & his own use of it as a composer.

Music of the Twentieth Century: Style & Structure. Bryan R. Simms. 1996. 60.00 (978-0-02-864603-9(7), Macmillan Ref) Gale.

Music of the Western World, A History of (1100 AD-1980 AD) unabr. ed. 12 cass. (Running Time: 12 hrs.). 59.50 (978-0-88432-391-4(9), S11100) J Norton Pubs.
Commentary by various authors with musical examples.

Music of the Work & the Glory, Vol. 1. Lynn S. Lund & Gerald N. Lund. 1 cass. (Running Time: 1 hr.). 1995. 10.95 (978-1-57008-190-3(5), Bkcraft Inc); audio compact disk 15.95 (978-1-57008-189-7(1), Bkcraft Inc) Deseret Bk.

***Music of the 1930s, Volume 1.** RadioArchives.com. (Running Time: 600). (ENG.). 2010. audio compact disk 29.98 (978-1-61081-175-0(5)) Radio Arch.

Music of Tibet. Perf. by Gyuto Multiphonic Choir. 1 cass. (Running Time: 1 hr.). 10.50 (A0031-86) Sound Photosyn.
Compiled by Huston Smith & benefitting the Tibetan Relief Fund this is the original on location recording of the monks harmonic chanting.

Music Only Cassettes for Hypnosis Album. Bruce Goldberg. (ENG.). 2005. 65.00 (978-1-885577-83-2(4)) Pub: B Goldberg. Dist(s): Baker Taylor

Music Only CD Album for Hypnosis. Bruce Goldberg. (ENG.). 2005. audio compact disk 75.00 (978-1-57968-028-2(3)) Pub: B Goldberg. Dist(s): Baker Taylor

Music Performance Success. Steven Gurgevich. (ENG.). 2002. audio compact disk 19.95 (978-1-932170-15-3(4), HWH) Tranceformation.

Music Play. Wendy H. Valerio et al. 1 cass. (Running Time: 1 hr.). 1998. 10.95 (CS-426); audio compact disk 15.95 (CD-426) GIA Pubns.

Music Resounds see Classical Russian Poetry

Music Resources for Multicultural Perspectives. Selected by William M. Anderson. 2 CDs. (Running Time: 1 hr. 40 mins.). 1998. bk. 32.00 (978-1-56545-112-4(0)) MENC.
A two-CD sampler of the world's musical riches, including music from North America, Latin America and the Caribbean, Europe, Sub-Saharan Africa, the Middle East, South Asia, East Asia and Southeast Asia. These can be used with the MENC book publication.

Music Rough Guides: Ultimate Musical Adventures. Compiled by Phil Stanton. 2008. audio compact disk 2.95 (978-1-906063-26-9(5)) Pub: Rough Guides GBR. Dist(s): PerseuPGW

Music Suggestions for Children's Liturgies. Voice by Christopher C. Walker. 1 cass. (Running Time: 1 hr.). 1994. 7.95 (9912) OR Catholic.
The importance of song texts, what kind of melodies work well, types of music for different moments in liturgy, etc.

Music That Changed the World. Compiled by Michael Enright & Robert Harris. (ENG.). 2009. audio compact disk Rental 39.95 (978-0-660-19919-1(X), CBC Audio) Canadian Broadcasting CAN.

Music That Teaches French. 1999. spiral bd. 31.95 (978-0-9650980-8-3(7)) Dolo Publns.

Music That Was Really Different. 1 cass. (Running Time: 30 min.). 1985. (0288) Evang Sisterhood Mary.
Views a Christian perspective about rock & beat music & the song of the overcomers in the end of times.

Music, the Divine Art. Michael Ballam. 2 cass. (Running Time: 2 hrs.). 13.98 (16003152) Covenant Comms.
An inspiring seminar to lift the soul. Includes some of his best songs.

Music, the Divine Art, Michael Ballam. 2 cass. (Running Time: 2 hrs.). 14.98 (978-1-55503-245-6(1), 16003152) Covenant Comms.

Music Theory for the Rock Guitarist. Ben Bolt. 1996. bk. 9.95 (978-0-7866-2720-2(4), 94525BCD) Mel Bay.

Music Time Activity. 1999. audio compact disk 7.98 (978-0-633-04551-7(9)) LifeWay Christian.

Music Time Activity. 2003. audio compact disk 7.98 (978-0-633-07636-8(8)) LifeWay Christian.

Music Time Activity. 2004. audio compact disk 7.98 (978-0-633-08009-9(8)) LifeWay Christian.

Music Time Activity. 2004. audio compact disk 7.98 (978-0-633-08262-8(7)) LifeWay Christian.

Music Time Activity. 2004. audio compact disk 7.98 (978-0-633-08511-7(1)) LifeWay Christian.

Music Time Activity. 2004. audio compact disk 7.98 (978-0-633-17338-8(X)) LifeWay Christian.

Music Time Activity. 2005. audio compact disk 7.98 (978-0-633-17532-0(3)) LifeWay Christian.

Music Time Activity. 2005. audio compact disk 7.98 (978-0-633-17730-0(X)) LifeWay Christian.

Music to Awaken Superconscious. J. Donald Walters. 2003. audio compact disk 15.95 (978-1-56589-770-0(6)) Pub: Crystal Clarity. Dist(s): Natl Bk Netwk

Music to Awaken Superconsciousness Spoken Word. J. Donald Walters. 2003. audio compact disk 10.95 (978-1-56589-203-3(8)) Pub: Crystal Clarity. Dist(s): Natl Bk Netwk

Music to Celebrate Christmas. Prod. by Sheldon Cohen. 2008. audio compact disk 14.95 (978-0-87946-375-5(9)) ACTA Pubns.

Music to Develop Your Chakras, Vol. 4: Astral Journeys: Astral Journeys, Vol 4. Prod. by Clairvoyance Foundation LLC. (ENG.). 2008. audio compact disk 16.88 (978-0-9818876-4-7(3)) Clairvoyance.

Music to Develop Your Chakras, Volume 1: Spiritual & Evocative, Vol. 1. Prod. by Clairvoyance Foundation LLC. Compiled by Mary Kirby. (ENG.). 2008. audio compact disk 16.88 (978-0-9818876-2-3(7)) Clairvoyance.

Music to Develop Your Chakras, Volume 2: Creative Sensual Energy, Vol. 2. Compiled by Clairvoyance Foundation LLC. Prod. by Clairvoyance Foundation LLC. Mary A. Kirby. (ENG.). 2008. audio compact disk 16.88 (978-0-9818876-3-0(5)) Clairvoyance.

Music to Develop Your Chakras, Volume 3: Healing & Energizing the Rebirth. Compiled by Clairvoyance Foundation LLC. Prod. by Clairvoyance Foundation LLC. (ENG.). 2008. audio compact disk 16.88 (978-0-9818876-1-6(9)) Clairvoyance.

Music to Facilitate Imagery. Janalea Hoffman. 1 cass. (Running Time: 45 min.). 1984. 9.95 (978-1-886051-02-7(X)) Rhythmic Med.
Music & guided imagery to use for meditation.

Music to Heal the Body & the Soul. Prod. by Sheldon Cohen. 2 CDs. (Running Time: 2 hrs.). 2005. audio compact disk 14.95 (978-0-87946-301-4(5), 417) ACTA Pubns.
Does music heal? You know from your own experience that it does. Enjoy this double compact disc set, arranged and conducted by Sheldon Cohen, producer of the bestselling CD The Rosary Including the Mysteries of Light, and performed by several members of the Pacific Pops Orchestra. Whether from classical or religious traditions, these instrumental pieces create an atmosphere in which the music itself can help heal both the body and the soul. Music includes:Canon in D?..PachelbelClaire de Lune?..DebussySongs My Mother Taught Me?..DvorakWere You There?Amazing GraceNearer My God to Thee.

Music to Soothe the Spirit. Created by ACTA Publications. (Running Time: 3755 sec.). 2008. audio compact disk 14.95 (978-0-87946-345-8(7)) ACTA Pubns.

Music Tree, Pt. 2A. Frances Clark. (ENG.). 2000. audio compact disk 12.95 (978-0-87487-969-8(8), Warner Bro) Alfred Pub.

Music Tree, Pt. 2B. Frances Clark. (ENG.). 2000. audio compact disk 12.95 (978-0-87487-970-4(1), Warner Bro) Alfred Pub.

Music Tree Pt. 1: Midi Disk. Louise Goss & Frances Clark. 2000. 12.95 (978-0-87487-962-9(0), Warner Bro) Alfred Pub.

Music Tree Keyboard Literature: Part 3, CD & GM Disk. Frances Clark et al. (ENG.). 2004. audio compact disk 19.95 (978-1-58951-013-5(5)) Alfred Pub.

Music Tree Keyboard Technic: Part 3, 2 CDs & 2 GM Disks. Frances Clark et al. (ENG.). 2004. audio compact disk 24.95 (978-1-58951-014-2(3)) Alfred Pub.

Music Tree Student's Book: Part 3, 2 CDs & 2 GM Disks. Frances Clark et al. (ENG.). 2004. audio compact disk 24.95 (978-1-58951-012-8(7)) Alfred Pub.

Music Tree Students' Choice: Part 3, CD & GM Disk. Frances Clark et al. (ENG.). 2004. audio compact disk 19.95 (978-1-58951-015-9(1)) Alfred Pub.

Music Tree Time to Begin. Frances Clark. (ENG.). 2000. audio compact disk 12.95 (978-0-87487-967-4(1), Warner Bro) Alfred Pub.

Music Tree Time to Begin Midi. Frances Clark. 12.95 (978-0-87487-961-2(2), Warner Bro) Alfred Pub.

Music U. S. A. Prod. by Zobeida Perez. (YA). 1994. 17.00 (978-0-89898-790-4(3), BMR05078, Warner Bro) Alfred Pub.

Music, When Soft Voices Die see Poetry of Shelley

Music! Words! Opera! Level 1 Lower Elementary, Grades K-2 Level 1: Teacher's Manual. Excerpts. Sandra Purrington et al. Ed. by Marthalie P. Furber. Illus. by Johanna Vogelsang & Roger Roth. Frwd. by Charles Fowler. 1 cass. 1990. tchr. ed. & ring bd. 69.95 (978-0-918812-65-0(8), SE0694) MMB Music.

Music! Words! Opera! Level 2 Upper Elementary/Junior High, Grades 3-5 Level 2: Teacher's Manual. Excerpts. Clifford Brooks et al. Ed. by Karen Rice & Marthalie Furber. Illus. by Johanna Vogelsang. Frwd. by Charles Fowler. 1 cass. 1991. tchr. ed. & ring bd. 79.95 (978-0-918812-66-7(6), SE0706) MMB Music.

Music Worldwide. Elizabeth Sharma. (Running Time: 1 hr. 10 mins.). (Cambridge Assignments in Music Ser.). (ENG.). (gr. 9-11). 1998. audio compact disk 69.00 (978-0-521-37481-1(2)) Cambridge U Pr.

Music You Can Believe in, Vol. 1. Perf. by Michael W. Smith et al. 1 cass. (Running Time: 1 hr.). 1995. audio compact disk Brentwood Music.
This specially priced collection features some of the biggest songs & artists of 1995 in Christian music.

Music You Can Believe in, Vol. 2. Perf. by Michael W. Smith et al. 1 CD. (Running Time: 1 hr.). 1996. audio compact disk Brentwood Music.
This specially priced album features 12 of the best songs of 1996.

Music 1 CD Set. audio compact disk 60.00 (978-1-59166-245-7(1)) BJUPr.

Music 1 Program Accompaniment Cassette. (J). 1987. 15.50 (978-1-59166-025-5(4)) BJUPr.

Music 1 Teacher's Help Cassette. (J). 1987. 15.50 (978-1-59166-024-8(6)) BJUPr.

Music 2 CD Set. audio compact disk 45.00 (978-1-59166-360-7(1)) BJUPr.

Music 2 Program Accompaniment Cassette. (J). 1987. 15.50 (978-1-59166-027-9(0)) BJUPr.

Music 2 Teacher's Help Cassette. (J). 1987. 15.50 (978-1-59166-026-2(2)) BJUPr.

Music 2005: Program from the Award Winning Public Radio series: Best of the Infinite Mind. Interview. Hosted by Peter Kramer. 1 CD. (Running Time: 1 Hour). 2005. audio compact disk 21.95 (978-1-932479-26-3(0), LCM 378) Lichtenstein Creat.
In our third annual presentation of musical artists who have visited the studios of The Infinite Mind to perform and discuss their songs, we travel from Bernstein to Broadway, Nashville to the West Village ... and to the East Village as well. The program begins with Linda Muggleston singing "100 Easy Ways to Lose a Man" from Leonard Bernstein's first Broadway show, the Tony-award winning Wonderful Town. Muggleston performed the song before a live audience of 3,500 at our State of Mind: America 2004 presentation at Radio City Music Hall in May 2004. Carrie Newcomer shares two songs, both of them for our show on dreams: "Sparrow" and "Moon Over Tucson." Longtime New York singer/songwriter Suzanne Vega explains the inspirations and meaning behind her ballad "The Queen and The Soldier," while the Nashville group BR5-49 takes us back to the 1950s with a performance of Hank Williams' great hit, "Your Cheatin' Heart." Next, we return to Radio City Music Hall and our live State of Mind: America 2004 production and a visit from the cast of the surprising Broadway musical hit, Avenue Q. In the Tony Award-winning play, a crew of puppets living in New York's East Village offer up a kind of Sesame Street for adults as they explore the word of the day, "Schadenfreude," German for those who gain pleasure in the misery of others. Nora York is a singer, composer, and vocal teacher in New York. She joins us to perform one of her signature pieces, "What I Want," from The Infinite Mind program on "Satisfaction." Dublin-born Susan McKeown uses the music of tradition to explore her desire to be a mother in "Mother of Mine," from The Infinite Mind program "Pregnancy and the Mind." From the Tony award-winning musical Wicked (the story of Oz told from the standpoint of the witch), Eden Espinosa performs the show-stopping "The Wizard and I" at our State of Mind live broadcast at Radio City Music Hall. Finally, longtime The Infinite Mind commentator John Hockenberry ruminates on the true measure of fame, as he pictures his own life as TV biography (guitar and all!).

Music 3 CD Set. audio compact disk 60.00 (978-1-59166-361-4(X)) BJUPr.

Music 3 Program Accompaniment Cassette. (J). 1988. 15.50 (978-1-59166-031-6(9)) BJUPr.

Music 3 Teacher's Help Cassette. (J). 1988. 15.50 (978-1-59166-030-9(0)) BJUPr.

Music 4 Cassettes I-V. (J). 1989. 74.50 (978-1-59166-044-6(0)) BJUPr.

Music 4 Program Accopaniment Cassette. (J). 1989. 15.50 (978-1-59166-046-0(7)) BJUPr.

Music 4 Teacher's Help Cassette. (J). 1989. 15.50 (978-1-59166-045-3(9)) BJUPr.

Music 5 Cassettes I-V. (J). 1990. 74.50 (978-1-59166-048-4(3)) BJUPr.

Music 5 Program Songs. 15.50 (978-1-59166-050-7(5)) BJUPr.

Music 5 Teacher's Help. 15.50 (978-1-59166-049-1(1)) BJUPr.

Music 6 Cassettes I-V. 74.50 (978-1-59166-052-1(1)) BJUPr.

Music 6 Program Songs. 15.50 (978-1-59166-054-5(8)) BJUPr.

Music 6 Songs for Success. 12.00 (978-1-59166-055-2(6)) BJUPr.

Music 6 Teacher's Help. 15.50 (978-1-59166-053-8(X)) BJUPr.

Música Cristiana. Zondervan Publishing Staff. 1 CD. (Running Time: 30 min.). (SPA.). 2003. audio compact disk 3.99 (978-0-8297-3852-0(5)) Pub: Vida Pubs. Dist(s): Zondervan

Música Cristiana. unabr. ed. 2003. 2.99 (978-0-8297-3854-4(1)) Zondervan.

Musica Cristiana Grupera. unabr. ed. 2003. 9.99 (978-0-8297-4214-5(X)) Zondervan.

Musica Cristiana Tropical, Vol. 1. unabr. ed. Doris Machin. (SPA.). 2000. 9.99 (978-0-8297-2770-8(1)) Pub: Vida Pubs. Dist(s): Zondervan

Musica Cristiana Tropical, Vol. 2. unabr. ed. Zondervan Publishing Staff. (SPA.). 2001. 9.99 (978-0-8297-3169-9(5)) Pub: Vida Pubs. Dist(s): Zondervan

Musica Cristiano Volumen 2. (SPA.). 2008. audio compact disk 3.99 (978-0-8297-6112-2(8)) Pub: Vida Pubs. Dist(s): Zondervan

Música Cubana: Cuba. Isabelle Leymarie. (SPA., 2003. bk. 49.80 (978-84-494-2409-0(7), 1150) Oceano Grupo ESP.

Musica Cubana: Los últimos 50 Años. Tony Évora. (SPA., 2003. audio compact disk 65.00 (978-84-206-2024-4(6)) Pub: Alianza Editorial ESP. Dist(s): Lectorum Pubns

Musica de Alabanza para Ninos. unabr. ed. Charles F. Stanley. (SPA.). 2002. 3.99 (978-0-8297-3684-7(0)) Pub: Vida Pubs. Dist(s): Zondervan

Musica de Alabanza Para Niqos. unabr. ed. Claudio Freidzon. Serie Vida para Niños. (SPA.). (J). 2002. audio compact disk 4.99 (978-0-8297-3682-3(4)) Pub: Vida Pubs. Dist(s): Zondervan

Musica de la Estampida para Cantar y Jugar: Sing & Play Stampede Music. Created by Group Publishing. (Power Lab Ser.). 2008. audio compact disk 4.99 (978-5-557-52137-6(2)) Group Pub.

Musica de la Estampida para Cantar y Jugar: Version para Lideres. Created by Group Publishing. (Power Lab Ser.). 2008. audio compact disk 8.99 (978-5-557-52138-3(0)) Group Pub.

Musica del Dr. Escudero. Angel Escudero. 1 cass. (Running Time: 1 hr. 30 mins.).Tr. of Music by Dr. Escudero. (SPA.). 2001. Astran.

Música Mesiánica para Niños. unabr. ed. Gregory Boyd. Serie Vida para Niños. (SPA.). (J). 2002. audio compact disk 4.99 (978-0-8297-3692-2(1)) Pub: Vida Pubs. Dist(s): Zondervan

Música Mesiánica para Niños. unabr. ed. Juan Jose Churruarin. (SPA.). 2002. 3.99 (978-0-8297-3694-6(8)) Pub: Vida Pubs. Dist(s): Zondervan

Musica para una Fiesta. Perf. by Jenny W. Vincent et al. 1 cass. (Running Time: 25 min.). (SPA & ENG.). 1990. 9.95 Cantemos Recs.
Thirteen folk dances & songs of New Mexico & one South American song.

Musica para una Vida con Proposito. (SPA.). 2004. (978-0-8297-4494-1(0)) Vida Pubs.

Música para una Vida con Propósito. unabr. ed. Zondervan Publishing Staff. (SPA.). 2003. audio compact disk 14.99 (978-0-8297-4492-7(4)) Pub: Vida Pubs. Dist(s): Zondervan

Musical Abilities. 1 cass. (Running Time: 1 hr.). 10.95 (038) Psych Res Inst.
Unleash potentials & talents for musical performance or composition.

Musical Acupuncture. Janalea Hoffman. 1 cass. (Running Time: 45 min.). 1993. 12.95 (978-1-886051-11-9(9)) Rhythmic Med.
Therapeutic music written specifically for the listener to experience how music can conduct & move energy in the body very similar to acupuncture treatments.

Musical Adventures: Activity Fun Pack. Sally A. Bonkrude. Ed. by Steve Bonkrude & Karla Lange. Illus. by Terri Bahn. 1 cass. (Running Time: 1 hr.). Dramatization. (J). (ps-3). 1988. bk. 24.95 (978-0-924829-06-2(0)); 6.95 (978-0-924829-14-7(1)) Musical Imag.
Teacher tips, reproducible activity pages, songs and a cassette tape put together to explore the voice, sound, high and low, beat, dynamics and pre-reading skills.

Musical Biofeedback. Janalea Hoffman. 1 cass. (Running Time: 45 min.). 1993. 12.95 (978-1-886051-10-2(0)) Rhythmic Med.
Therapeutic music written specifically to lower heart rate & blood pressure as you match your heart rate & breathing rate with the slow, steady beat of the music.

Musical Body. abr. unabr. ed. David Ison. Read by David Ison. (Running Time: 2:00:00). 2009. audio compact disk 19.98 (978-1-55961-988-2(0)) Sounds True.

Musical Body: Chakra Meditations for Spiritual Exploration. unabr. ed. David Ison. (Running Time: 9:00:00). 2009. audio compact disk 39.98 (978-1-60297-005-2(X)) Sounds True.

Musical Depreciation Revue: The Spike Jones Anthology. 2 CDs. (Running Time: 3 hrs.). 2001. audio compact disk 31.98 (R2 71574) Rhino Enter.

Musical Donkey. Saeed Jaffrey. 1 cass. (Running Time: 22 min.). (Karadi Tales Ser.). (YA). (gr. 1 up). 1998. bk. 9.99 (978-81-86838-37-2(6)) APG.
Fairy tales & folklore.

Musical Evening with Jane Austen & Emily Bronte. unabr. ed. Robert K. Wallace. 12.95 (23649) J Norton Pubs.
Recital-lecture based on selections from the works of the two authors with musical accompaniment.

Musical Hypnosis. Janalea Hoffman. 1 cass. (Running Time: 45 min.). 1993. 12.95 (978-1-886051-07-2(0)) Rhythmic Med.
Music written specifically to use for deep relaxation. One side composed from 80-beats-a-minute down to 50-beats-a-minute. One side composed at 65-beats-a-minute down to 50-beats-a-minute.

Musical Journey in the Footsteps of Lewis & Clark. Anne Enslow & Ridley Enslow. 1 CD. (Running Time: 1 hr. 12 mins.). (Musical Journey in the Footsteps of Lewis & Clark Ser.). (J). (gr. k-5). 2008. audio compact disk 31.93 (978-0-7660-3288-0(4)) Enslow Pubs.

Musical Journey in the Footsteps of Lewis & Clark. Anne Enslow & Ridley Enslow. (Musical Journey in the Footsteps of Lewis & Clark Ser.). (J). (gr. k-5). 2008. audio compact disk 23.93 (978-0-7660-3287-3(6)) Enslow Pubs.

Musical Life of Gustav Mole. unabr. ed. Kathryn Meyrick. Read by Patrick Macnee & Andrew Belling. 1 cass. (Running Time: 40 min.). (J). (ps-5). 1990. 6.99 (978-0-85953-376-8(X)) Childs Play GBR.
Lucky the mole born into a musical family! Patrick Macnee narrates Gustav's life against a background of musical delights. An irresistable introduction to instruments, performing groups - types of music.

Musical Massage. Prod. by Janalea Hoffman. 1 cass. (Running Time: 45 min.). 14.95 Aquarius Prods.
Written with healing & nurturing in mind. Janalea Hoffman suggests that listeners experience it with their entire body, feeling the vibrations of the beautiful music as though it was a musical massage.

Musical Massage. Janalea Hoffman. 1 cass. (Running Time: 45 min.). 1993. 12.95 (978-1-886051-08-9(9)) Rhythmic Med.
Music written to achieve deep relaxation. Feel the musical tones massaging the body.

Musical Massage, Vols. I, II, III. 3 CDs. (Running Time: 3 hrs.). audio compact disk 26.95 (978-1-55961-321-7(1)) Relaxtn Co.

Musical Massage, Vols. I, II, III. 3 cass. (Running Time: 2 hrs. 38 mins.). 1992. 19.95 (978-1-55961-127-5(8)) Relaxtn Co.

Musical Massage: Resonance. Jorge Alfano. 1 box cass. bk. 9.95 (978-1-55961-588-4(5)); 9.95 (978-1-55961-582-2(6)) Relaxtn Co.

Musical Massage: Synergy. Jorge Alfano. 1 box cass. bk. 9.95 (978-1-55961-587-7(7)); 9.95 (978-1-55961-580-8(X)) Relaxtn Co.

Musical Massage Vol. I: Harp, Flute, Cello, Piano & Nature Sounds. 4 cass. (Running Time: 4 hrs.). 1992. 9.95 (978-1-55961-162-6(6)) Relaxtn Co.

Musical Massage Vol. II: Guitar, Piano, Bamboo, Flute & Nature Sounds. 1 cass. (Running Time: 1 hr.). 1992. 9.95 (978-1-55961-163-3(4)) Relaxtn Co.

Musical Massage Vol. III: Piano, Flutes, Harp, Cello & Nature Sounds. 4 cass. (Running Time: 4 hrs.). 1988. 9.95 (978-0-931245-68-8(0)) Relaxtn Co.

Musical Massage Vol. IV: Piano, Flute, Guitar, Bells & Nature Sounds. 4 cass. (Running Time: 4 hrs.). 1988. 9.95 (978-0-931245-69-5(9)) Relaxtn Co.

Musical Massage Collection. Perf. by David Darling et al. 1 CD. (Running Time: 1 hr.). 2000. audio compact disk 29.95 (978-1-55961-585-3(0)) Relaxtn Co.

Musical Massage Collection 2. audio compact disk (978-1-55961-643-0(1)) Relaxtn Co.

Musical Massages: Balance. David Darling. 1 cass. (Running Time: 1 hr.). 9.95 (978-1-55961-589-1(3)) Relaxtn Co.

***Musical Math.** Created by Heidi Butkus. Lyrics by Heidi Butkus. Arranged by Mike Cravens. (ENG.). (J). 2007. audio compact disk 15.00 (978-0-9845641-2-5(8)) HeidiSongs.

Musical Math: Grades Preschool-First. Kimberly Jordano & Trisha Callella. Ed. by Kim Cernek. Illus. by Ann W. Iosa & Rick Grayson. Des. by Moonhee Pak et al. (J). 2001. pap. bk. & tchr. ed. 16.98 (978-1-57471-772-3(3), 2589) Creat Teach Pr.

Musical Max. 2004. bk. 24.95 (978-1-56008-092-3(2)); pap. bk. 14.95 (978-1-56008-068-8(X)); 8.95 (978-1-56008-979-7(2)); 8.95 (978-1-56008-113-5(9)); cass. & flmstrp 30.00 (978-1-56008-725-0(0)) Weston Woods.

Musical Memories of Laura Ingalls Wilder. William T. Anderson. Photos by Leslie A. Kelly. 2001. pap. bk. 19.99 (978-1-931343-20-6(9)) Hibbard Pubns.
The well-loved stories of Laura Ingalls Wilder will come to life all over again as you listen to the songs and read the stories behind the songs. These were the songs that were a part of life for the Ingalls family and thousands of other pioneering families. Includes full-color photos throughout.

Musical Neurons. Connie K. Anderson. 1 cass. (Running Time: 1 hr.). (J). (ps-4). 1998. (978-0-9649986-4-3(5)) Iguana Prodns.
A collection of original songs that make children more attentive, smarter & happier.

Musical Openings: Using Music in the Language Classroom. D. Cranmer & C. Laroy. 1995. bk. 28.00 (978-0-582-07503-0(3), 79846) Longman.

Musical Physiology. Joel Alter & Cheri Quincy. 1 cass. (Running Time: 20 min.). 9.00 (A0240-87) Sound Photosyn.
With Sound Photosynthesis: a 20 minute compilation of shamanistic music.

Musical Pictures: Mussorgsky. (YA). 1994. 17.00 (978-0-89898-793-5(8), BMR05097, Warner Bro) Alfred Pub.

Musical Playtime Fun. Carol Hammett. 1 LP. (Running Time: 35 min.). (J). (ps-2). 1990. pap. bk. & pupil's gde. ed. 11.95 (KIM 9120); 10.95 (978-0-937124-41-3(9), KIM 9120C) Kimbo Educ.
Preschoolers love activity time at home & at school! Fuzzy Wizzy Caterpillar, Circle the Moon, Animal Parade, Mexican Jumping Beans, Snappy Turtle, Tying Shoes, Circle Time Action, Welcome & more. Includes activity guide.

Musical Roadsigns: Accents, Dynamics, & All That Jazz. Duane Shinn. 1 cass. (Running Time: 1 hr.). 19.95 (HAR-5) Duane Shinn.
How to use accents, staccato, sforzando, crescendo, diminuendo, 8va, fermata, ritard & other "road signs" that make music interesting.

Musical Scarves & Activities. 1 cass. (Running Time: 35 mins.). (J). (gr. k-2). 2002. 14.95 (978-1-56346-113-2(7)) Kimbo Educ.
Rhythmic activities such as stretching, group lay, partner play, marching, juggling, creative expression, toss and catch and more done with scarves to popular and classic songs.

Musical Score see Inner Sanctum

Musical Stories. 1 cass. (Running Time: 46 min.). (Picture Book Parade Ser.). (J). (ps-4). 1981. 8.95 (978-0-89719-944-5(8), WW714C) Weston Woods.
Anthology includes "The Star-Spangled Banner," "She'll Be Comin' 'Round the Mountain," "Yankee Doodle," "Clementine," "The Fox Went Out on a Chilly Night," "London Bridge Is Falling Down," "I Know an Old Lady," "The Erie Canal," "Waltzing Matilda" & "Over in the Meadow".

Musical Times Tables. (J). (ps-3). 2000. 2.99 (978-1-85781-201-5(8)) Cimino Pub Grp.

Musical Traditions of St. Lucia, West Indies: Dances & Songs from a Caribbean Island. Contrib. by Jocelyne Gulibault & Embert Charles. 1 cass. or CD. 1993. (0-9307-404160-9307-40416-2-8); audio compact disk (0-9307-40416-2-8) Smithsonian Folkways.

Musical World of Halim El-Dabh. Denise A. Seachrist. 2003. pap. bk. 29.00 (978-0-87338-752-1(X)) Kent St U Pr.

Musicality & Personality. unabr. ed. Paul R. Farnsworth. 1 cass. (Running Time: 16 min). 1960. 12.95 (11007) J Norton Pubs.
A discussion of musical creativity, with emphasis on personality characteristics.

Musician's Guide Through the Legal Jungle: Answers to Frequently Asked Questions about Music Law. unabr. ed. Joy R. Butler. Read by James Chatelain & Lynne Reynolds. 2 cass. (Running Time: 3 hrs.). (Guide Through the Legal Jungle Audiobook Ser.). 2000. pap. bk. 29.95 (978-0-9672940-0-1(2)) Sashay Commns.
Listen in on a conversation between a musician & a legal expert as they address the legal issues of greatest interest to performing artists & songwriters. Booklet included.

Musician's Handbook. M. Carlyle Hume. 1 CD. (Running Time: 1 hr.). 1998. pap. bk. 64.67 (978-0-13-996034-5(1), Prentice Hall) P-H.

Musicians of Bremen see Cinderella & Other Fairy Tales

Musicians of Bremen. 2004. bk. 24.95 (978-0-7882-0572-9(2)); 8.95 (978-1-56008-980-3(6)); cass. & flmstrp 30.00 (978-1-56008-726-7(9)) Weston Woods.

Musicophilia: Tales of Music & the Brain. abr. ed. Oliver Sacks. Read by Simon Prebble. (Running Time: 21600 sec.). (ENG.). 2007. audio compact disk 29.95 (978-0-7393-5739-2(5), Random AudioBks) Pub: Random Audio Pubg. Dist(s): Random

Musics of the Soviet Union. Anno. by Margarita Mazo et al. 1 cass. (Running Time: 40 min.). 1989. (0-9307-400020-9307-40002-2-9); audio compact disk (0-9307-40002-2-9) Smithsonian Folkways.
Begins with passionate Lithuanian lullabies & proceeds through ancient seasonal & ceremonial village songs from southern & northern Russia & the asymmetrical dance rhythms performed by Estonian bagpipers. From the distant Mongolian frontier, the amazing art of Tuvan multiphonic "throat singing" can be heard, as well as the richly harmonic male choral singing still practiced in Georgia.

Musik hinter Stacheldraht: Tagebuchblatter aus dem Sommer 1940 Herausgegeben von Eva Fox-Gal Mit Beitragen von Eva Fox-Gal und Richard Dove. Hans Gal. Contrib. by Deborah J. Vietor-Englander. (Exil-Dokumente - Verboten, Verbrannt, Vergessen Ser.: Vol. 3). (GER., 2003. bk. 52.95 (978-3-906764-87-0(7)) Pub: P Lang CHE. Dist(s): P Lang Pubng

Musique. Jacques Prevert. Read by Jacques Prevert. Perf. by Juliette Greco et al. 1 cass. (Running Time: 1 hr.). (FRE.). 1995. 16.95 (1666-RF) Olivia & Hill.
It is with his songs that Prevert first became known to the general public.

Mussolini. unabr. ed. Jasper Ridley. Read by Nadia May. 11 cass. (Running Time: 16 hrs.). 1999. 76.95 (978-0-7861-1632-4(3), 2460) Blckstn Audio.
Describes his upbringing in the violent society of nineteenth-century Italy & the revolutionary traditions of Italian Socialism; his suspension from school for attacking other boys with knives; his imprisonment in Switzerland as an Anarchist tramp. He developed into a brilliant orator & journalist. He founded the Fascist Party, became Prime Minister & dictator & showed his true colors as an empire-builder & eventually a racist & persecutor of the Jews. His one great mistake was to enter the Second World War on the losing side. He was executed by Communist partisans in 1945.

Mussolini: His Part in My Downfall. unabr. ed. Spike Milligan. Read by Spike Milligan. 8 cass. (Running Time: 8 hrs. 30 min.). (Isis Ser.). (J). 1994. 69.95 (978-1-85089-839-9(1), 88091) Pub: ISIS Lrg Prnt GBR. Dist(s): Ulverscroft US

Mussolini & The Rise of Fascism. 10.00 (HE808) Esstee Audios.
His dictatorship first took root after World War I. What was its appeal & how did it work.

Must Catholics Believe in Fatima? Eamon R. Carroll. 1 cass. 1989. 2.50 (978-1-56036-066-7(6)) AMI Pr.

Must History Repeat the Great Conflicts of This Century? Instructed by Joseph S. Nye. 4 cass. (Running Time: 6 hrs.). 1991. 39.95 (978-1-56585-244-0(3)) Teaching Co.

Must Love Dogs. Claire Cook. Narrated by Carrington MacDuffie. (Running Time: 7 hrs.). 2005. 27.95 (978-1-59912-551-0(X)) Iofy Corp.

Must Love Dogs. Claire Cook. (Running Time: 25200 sec.). 2005. DVD, audio compact disk, audio compact disk 55.00 (978-0-7861-7697-7(0)) Blckstn Audio.

Must Love Dogs. Claire Cook. Read by Carrington Mac Duffie. (Running Time: 7 mins.). 2005. 44.95 (978-0-7861-3670-4(7)) Blckstn Audio.

Must Love Dogs. movie tie-in unabr. ed. Claire Cook. Read by Carrington MacDuffie. 7 CDs. (Running Time: 25200 sec.). 2005. audio compact disk 29.95 (978-0-7861-7777-6(2), ZE3517); audio compact disk 29.95 (978-0-7861-8000-4(5), ZM3517) Blckstn Audio.

Must Love Dogs. movie tie-in unabr. ed. Claire Cook & Carrington MacDuffie. 6 cass. (Running Time: 9 hrs.). 2005. 29.95 (978-0-7861-3547-9(6), E3517) Blckstn Audio.

***Must See Inside.** Mario Jannatpour. Narrated by Dave Giorgio. (ENG.). 2010. audio compact disk 29.95 (978-1-60031-073-7(7)) Spoken Books.

***Mustaine.** unabr. ed. Dave Mustaine & Joe Layden. Read by Tom Wayland. (ENG.). 2010. (978-0-06-199759-4(5), Harper Audio) HarperCollins Pubs.

***Mustaine: A Heavy Metal Memoir.** unabr. ed. Dave Mustaine & Joe Layden. Read by Tom Wayland. (ENG.). 2010. (978-0-06-198884-4(7), Harper Audio) HarperCollins Pubs.

Mustang Fever. unabr. ed. Gary McCarthy. Read by Gene Engene. 6 cass. (Running Time: 7 hrs.). (Derby Man Ser.: Bk. 3). 1994. 39.95 (978-1-55686-551-0(1)) Books in Motion.
Darby Buckingham decided it was time to end a vicious cattle baron's control of the Nevada range...time to end the murder of the mustangs.

Mustang Herder. unabr. ed. Max Brand. Read by Will Osborne. 6 vols. (Running Time: 9 hrs.). 1996. bk. 54.95 (978-0-7927-2204-5(3), CSL 093, Chivers Sound Lib) AudioGO.
Sammy came out West to make lots of money. He decided the best money could be made buying horses cheap in Texas & selling them for a profit up North. All he had to do was herd his mustangs safely through some of the roughest territory in the West.

Mustang Man. unabr. ed. Louis L'Amour. Read by Terrence Mann. (Running Time: 18000 sec.). (Sacketts Ser.). (ENG.). 2006. audio compact disk 25.95 (978-0-7393-2116-4(1), Random AudioBks) Pub: Random Audio Pubg. Dist(s): Random

***Mustanger.** Frank Bonham. 2009. (978-1-60136-410-4(5)) Audio Holding.

Mustanger. Frank Bonham. (Running Time: 2 hrs. 6 mins.). 1999. 10.95 (978-1-60083-492-9(2)) Iofy Corp.

Mustangers. unabr. ed. Gary McCarthy. Read by Maynard Villers. 4 cass. (Running Time: 5 hrs. 12 min.). 1996. 26.95 (978-1-55686-676-0(3)) Books in Motion.
Pete Sills, a young mustanger & Jack Kendall, a wise & rugged veteran, pit all their knowledge & strength against a fabulous, wild, palomino stallion called Sun Dancer.

Mustard Pancakes. (YA). 2005. 13.98 (978-0-9773429-0-7(5)) Arrow Dist Co.

Mutant Message Down Under. unabr. ed. Marlo Morgan. Narrated by Roslyn Alexander. 4 cass. (Running Time: 5 hrs. 45 mins.). 1995. 40.00 (978-0-7887-0193-1(2), 94417E7) Recorded Bks.
A woman recounts her experiences while on a spiritual walkabout with an Australian aboriginal tribe.

Mutant Message from Forever. unabr. ed. Marlo Morgan. Read by Donada Peters. 6 cass. (Running Time: 9 hrs.). 1999. 48.00 (978-0-7366-4398-6(2), 4859) Books on Tape.
This follows the lives of Australian aboriginal twins taken from their young mother shortly after their birth by Christian missionaries. The boy, named Geoff, is ultimately adopted by an American minister & raised in New England with little sense of who he is or of his cultural heritage. Beatrice, given only a first name, is placed in a Catholic orphanage, where she encounters continual racism & experiences shattering losses for the first eighteen years of her life. Upon adulthood, Beatrice, hungering to know more about her ancestral roots, walks away from city life & heads for the outback. Meanwhile Geoff, after years of addiction, finds himself on Death Row accused of a double murder. After many decades, Beatrice leaves her nomadic life & becomes a "runner between both worlds." Her work will bring her into contact with her brother to whom she gives the "mutant message from forever," although neither is aware of the relationship.

Mutant Message from Forever: A Novel of Aboriginal Wisdom. unabr. ed. Marlo Morgan. Narrated by Patricia Conolly. 7 cass. (Running Time: 8 hrs. 15 mins.). 1999. 60.00 (978-0-7887-2923-2(3), 95713E7) Recorded Bks.
This story of Australian aboriginal twins separated at birth will carry you from outrage to elation.

Mutation. unabr. ed. Robin Cook. Read by Donada Peters. 6 cass. (Running Time: 9 hrs.). 1992. 48.00 (978-0-7366-2258-5(6), 3047) Books on Tape.
Brilliant doctor seeks to create the son of his dreams & produces instead a living nightmare.

***Mutation of Time.** unabr. ed. John Peel. Narrated by Jean Marsh & Peter Purves. (Running Time: 5 hrs. 0 mins. 0 sec.). (Doctor Who Ser.). (ENG.). 2010. audio compact disk 39.95 (978-1-4084-0999-2(2)) Pub: AudioGO. Dist(s): Perseus Dist

***Mute.** 2010. audio compact disk (978-1-59171-244-2(0)) Falcon Picture.

Mute Witness. Charles O'Brien. Narrated by Jenny Sterlin. 10 cass. (Running Time: 14 hrs. 30 mins.). 91.00 (978-1-4025-0935-3(9)) Recorded Bks.

Mutha Is Half a Word. Perf. by La Wanda Page. 2000. audio compact disk 16.98 (978-1-929243-26-6(X)) Uproar Ent.

Mutiny at Fort Jackson: The Untold Story of the Fall of New Orleans. Michael D. Pierson. (Civil War America Ser.). (ENG., 2009. 15.00 (978-0-8078-8706-6(4)); audio compact disk 15.00 (978-0-8078-8708-0(0)) U of NC Pr.

Mutiny of the Elisnore. unabr. ed. Jack London. Narrated by John Bolen. 1 CD (MP3). (Running Time: 11 hrs. 12 mins.). (ENG.). 2001. audio compact disk 23.00 (978-1-4001-5015-1(9)) Pub: Tantor Media. Dist(s): IngramPubServ

Mutiny of the Elisnore. unabr. ed. Jack London. Narrated by John Bolen. 10 CDs. (Running Time: 11 hrs. 12 mins.). (ENG.). 2001. audio compact disk 48.00 (978-1-4001-0015-6(1)) Pub: Tantor Media. Dist(s): IngramPubServ

Mutiny of the Elsinore. Jack London. Read by John Bolen. (Running Time: 11 hrs. 15 mins.). 2001. 29.95 (978-1-60083-588-9(0), Audiofy Corp) Iofy Corp.

Mutiny of the Elsinore. Jack London. Read by John Bolen. (ENG.). 2005. audio compact disk 96.00 (978-1-4001-3015-3(8)) Pub: Tantor Media. Dist(s): IngramPubServ

Mutiny of the Elsinore. unabr. ed. Jack London. Narrated by John Bolen. (Running Time: 11 hrs. 0 mins. 0 sec.). (Tantor Unabridged Classics Ser.). (ENG.). 2009. audio compact disk 65.99 (978-1-4001-4084-8(6)); audio compact disk 32.99 (978-1-4001-1084-1(X)); audio compact disk 22.99 (978-1-4001-6084-6(7)) Pub: Tantor Media. Dist(s): IngramPubServ

Mutiny on Board H. M. S. Bounty. William Bligh. Read by Jonathan Reese. (ENG.). 2005. audio compact disk 19.99 (978-1-4001-5121-9(X)) Pub: Tantor Media. Dist(s): IngramPubServ

Mutiny on Board H. M. S. Bounty. unabr. ed. William Bligh. Read by Jonathan Reese. (Running Time: 8 hrs. 30 mins. 0 sec.). (Tantor Unabridged Classics Ser.). (ENG.). 2009. 19.99 (978-1-4001-6125-6(8)); audio compact disk 27.99 (978-1-4001-1125-1(0)); audio compact disk 55.99 (978-1-4001-4125-8(7)) Pub: Tantor Media. Dist(s): IngramPubServ

Mutiny on Board H. M. S. Bounty. unabr. ed. William Bligh. Read by Bernard Mayes. 6 cass. (Running Time: 8 hrs. 30 mins.). 1994. 44.95 (978-0-7861-0831-2(2), 1530) Blckstn Audio.
The narrative - deeply personal yet objective - documents the voyage & Bligh's relationships to his men & thereby exposes the oft debated question of what manner of man he really was.

Mutiny on Board H. M. S. Bounty. unabr. ed. William Bligh. Read by Jonathan Reese. (YA). 2008. 54.99 (978-1-60514-600-3(5)) Find a World.

Mutiny on Board H. M. S. Bounty. unabr. collector's ed. William Bligh. Read by Jonathan Reese. 6 cass. (Running Time: 9 hrs.). 1996. 48.00 (978-0-7366-3327-7(8), 3979) Books on Tape.
Bligh, a stern skipper, stood between his crew & paradise, so they mutinied & set him adrift. How did he survive to tell about it.

Mutiny on Board H. M. S. Bounty: A Voyage to the South Sea & the Terrible Mutiny on Board. unabr. ed. William Bligh. Narrated by Norman Dietz. 6 cass. (Running Time: 8 hrs.). 1986. 51.00 (978-1-55690-366-3(9), 86910E7) Recorded Bks.
A first-hand account of the infamous mutiny & subsequent escape of the survivors. Records the events of the most celebrated mutiny in the annals of the sea: the 1789 revolt against Captain William Bligh in the West Indies. Was Bligh a sadistic disciplinarian who terrorized his crew? Or a superb & misunderstood seaman? Over 200 years later, the controversy surrounding this legendary captain still rages. The truth may lie in this.

Mutiny on Board H. M. S. Bounty (Library) William Bligh. Read by Jonathan Reese. (ENG.). 2005. audio compact disk 59.99 (978-1-4001-3121-1(9)) Pub: Tantor Media. Dist(s): IngramPubServ

Mutiny on Mars: A David Foster Starman Adventure. Michael D. Cooper. Abr. by Michael D. Cooper. Read by Charlie O'Dowd. 2 cass. (Running Time: 180 mins.). No. 1. 2004. (978-1-58807-791-2(8)); 18.00 (978-1-58807-474-4(9)) Am Pubng Inc.
By the middle of the 21st Century, a severe, global depression set in, unprecedented in scope. Governments fell and the infrastructure of the Earth decayed, initiating the worst period in human history. The age became known as the Collapse, and was characterized by worldwide violence, terrorism, and unrestrained criminal opportunism. But the century ended with a glimmer of hope. The concepts of stewardship, accountability, and mutual responsibility revived. Starlight Enterprise was founded in 2089, committed to rebuilding the Earth and its culture. It quickly became known for high ideals, philanthropy, and interplanetary ventures. In the early 22nd Century, Starlight Enterprise produced its first Starmen. The Starmen were the gifted and highly trained venturers of Starlight Enterprise. With their exploits, a new age of exploration and discovery began. Earth had not seen such a time for more than six centuries. In the course of their adventures, the Starmen gradually learned the amazing history of the Solar System - a history is far different from what Earth had long believed. Finally, they discovered the opportunity and responsibility of the people of Earth to defend and preserve their home ? now understood not to be a country or even a planet, but the entire system of worlds circling our star. The Starman series follows the adventures of three new Starmen and chronicles the saga of the Solar System in the glorious middle years of the 22nd Century.Mutiny On Mars: Starman #1.The Starmen were Starlight Enterprise's top explorers. They were dispatched to discover and explore the corners of the Solar System, no matter how remote or hostile. Their assignments often carried a high level of risk, but were also where the greatest discoveries could be made. Clothed in the coveted red uniform both in space and in

port, the Starmen were respected, honored, and revered by all - and they were rare. Since the founding of Starlight Academy in 2103, only 110 people had ever become Starmen. By 2150, the Solar System held only 56 of them. In this first book in the Starman series, new Starmen David Foster, Joe Taylor, and Mark Seaton, the class of 2151, find themselves on Mars when pirates take over the Martian settlements. Can these three young men repulse the pirates?.

Mutiny on the Bounty. 8 cass. (Running Time: 4 hrs.). 1989. 35.00 (A0030B090, HarperThor); 95.60 (HarperThor) HarpC GBR.

Mutiny on the Bounty. unabr. ed. Charles Nordhoff & James Norman Hall. Read by Jonathan Reese. 8 cass. (Running Time: 12 hrs.). (Bounty Ser.). 1978. 64.00 (1149-A) Books on Tape.
The "Bounty" existed, as did Captain Bligh & Fletcher Christian. The story comes to life in this novel of the famous incident.

Mutiny on the Bounty: The Story of Captain William Bligh. Godwin Chu & Jerry Stemach. (Classic Adventures Ser.). 2001. audio compact disk 18.95 (978-1-4105-0173-8(6)) D Johnston Inc.

Mutiny on the Bounty Vol. 7: The Story of Captain William Bligh. Jerry Stemach & Godwin Chu. Ed. by Jerry Stemach et al. Illus. by Jeff Ham & Susan Baptist. Contrib. by Ted S. Hasselbring. (Start-to-Finish Books). (J). (gr. 2-3). 2001. 35.00 (978-1-58702-756-7(9)) D Johnston Inc.

Mutiny on the Bounty Vol. 7: The Story of Captain William Bligh. abr. ed. Jerry Stemach & Godwin Chu. Ed. by Jerry Stemach et al. Illus. by Jeff Ham & Susan Baptist. Narrated by Nick Sandys. Contrib. by Ted S. Hasselbring. 1 cass. (Running Time: 1 hr.). (Start-to-Finish Books). (J). (gr. 2-3). 2001. (978-1-58702-741-3(0), F46) D Johnston Inc.
This story about the British Admiral, William Bligh, takes place in 1789 when Bligh is captain of the Bounty. While returning from a voyage to Tahiti to transport Breadfruit trees, some of his sailors mutiny. Bligh and a few loyal men are placed in a rowboat and set adrift to navigate more than 3,000 miles of ocean. Although Bligh survives the mutiny experience and builds a memorable career, he is remembered most for his difficult temper in dealing.

Mutiny Run. unabr. ed. Frank Eccles. Read by Peter Wickham. 8 cass. 2007. 69.95 (978-1-84559-334-6(0)) Pub: Soundings Ltd GBR. Dist(s): Ulverscroft US

Mutual Fund Investing for Everyone. unabr. ed. David K. Luhman. Read by David K. Luhman. 1 cass. (Running Time: 1 hr. 30 min.). (Personal Finance for Everyone Ser.: Vol. 3). 1996. 9.00 (978-1-889297-13-2(5)) Numen Lumen.
Mutual funds vs. other investments, mutual fund basics, types of funds, selecting funds, building your portfolio, the efficient market, mutual fund strategies, mutual fund providers, getting information about funds, mutual fund taxation.

Mutual Funds: Business Week's Guide. Jeffrey M. Laderman. 6 cass. bk. 159.00 (CPE4570) Bisk Educ.
Learn everything you need to know about mutual funds to invest in them safely & successfully. Discover the questions you should ask yourself before you invest, get step-by-step instructions on how to setup & monitor a portfolio, how to balance risk against reward & how your mutual fund investments affect your tax liability.

Mutual Reception in Transits. Sophia Mason. 1 cass. 8.95 (561) Am Fed Astrologers.

Muy Caliente! Afro-Cuban Play-Along CD & Book. Chuck Sher. (SPA.). 2000. pap. bk. 22.00 (978-1-883217-08-2(3), 00242134) Pub: Sher Music. Dist(s): H Leonard

Muzzling an Ox: 1 Cor.9:1-19. Ed Young. 1986. 4.95 (978-0-7417-1500-5(7), 500) Win Walk.

Muzzy Readers. unabr. ed. 6 cass. (J). pap. bk. 59.95 (SEN300) J Norton Pubs.
Includes books.

Mxpx: the Ultimate Collection. Contrib. by MXPX & Brandon Ebel. (Ultimate Collection). 2008. audio compact disk 18.99 (978-5-557-48831-0(6)) Tooth & Nail.

My Abandonment. unabr. ed. Peter Rock. (Running Time: 7.5 hrs. NaN mins.). 2009. 29.95 (978-1-4332-6418-4(8)); audio compact disk 24.95 (978-1-4332-6417-7(X)); audio compact disk 60.00 (978-1-4332-6415-3(3)); audio compact disk 54.95 (978-1-4332-6414-6(5)) Blckstn Audio.

My ABCs on CD: (A fun audio version of the Book) Excerpts. Michelle Spray. Perf. by Michelle Spray. Perf. by Dawn Costantiello. Music by Keith Spray. 1. (Running Time: 30 mins). (ENG.). (J). 2006. audio compact disk 8.95 (978-0-9714160-6-2(0)) Bk Shelf CT.
Children will love this interactive audio CD as they will quickly learn and sing along to the songs about using their imagination, BIG WORDS, and try to guess the cool sound effects that go along with each letter of the alphabet. Parents will find themselves guessing the sounds also! Perfect for that half hour car ride!.

My Africa see Poems from Black Africa

My African Journey. unabr. collector's ed. Winston L. S. Churchill. Read by David Case. 5 cass. (Running Time: 5 hrs.). 1992. 30.00 (978-0-7366-2150-2(4), 2949) Books on Tape.
Churchill's 1908 journey to Kenya & Uganda. He describes a land & people that have all but disappeared.

My Alexandria. Mark Doty. 1995. 10.95 (978-0-252-02249-4(1)) Pub: U of Ill Pr. Dist(s): Chicago Distribution Ctr

My Almost Epic Summer. unabr. ed. Adele Griffin. Read by Jessica Almasy. 4 CDs. (Running Time: 4 hrs. 30 mins.). (YA). 2006. audio compact disk 44.75 (978-1-4193-9460-7(6), C3732); 29.75 (978-1-4193-9455-3(X)) Recorded Bks.
Irene has always dreamed of owning a beauty salon in sunny Los Angeles where she will re-create the hairstyles of Great Women of Literature. But she's just been fired from her own mother's salon for shampooing techniques that left patrons in tears. Now, forced to babysit while everyone else spends a glamorous summer at the beach, Irene wonders when real life will begin. Then she meets beautiful lifeguard Starla - and one of Starla's admirers starts noticing Irene. Things are getting complicated. Maybe its time Irene becomes the heroine of her own literary drama!.

My American Journey: An Autobiography. abr. ed. Colin L. Powell. 4 cass. (Running Time: 4 hrs.). 20.95 (44556) Books on Tape.
He rose from the streets of Harlem to the highest position in the U.S. military. Learn how he did it & why he believes in the American dream.

My American Journey: An Autobiography. abr. ed. Colin Powell & Joseph E. Persico. Read by Colin Powell. (Running Time: 14400 sec.). (ENG.). 2006. audio compact disk 14.99 (978-0-7393-4108-7(1), Random AudioBks) Pub: Random Audio Pubg. Dist(s): Random

My Anecdotal Life: A Memoir. unabr. ed. Carl Reiner. Read by Carl Reiner. 6 CDs. (Running Time: 6 hrs.). 2004. audio compact disk 39.95 (978-1-59007-505-0(6)) Pub: New Millenn Enter. Dist(s): PerseuPGW
More than once, Carl Reiner has had friends say, "Hey, Reiner, you ought to write those things down." And at eighty, he finally has. In this funny and engaging memoir, one of the best raconteurs on the planet recalls his life in show business in short comic takes. Reiner tells of how, after answering an ad for free acting classes on his brother Charlie's advice, he forsakes a budding career as a machinist for an acting career.

My Anecdotal Life: A Memoir. unabr. abr. ed. Carl Reiner. Read by Carl Reiner. 4 cass. (Running Time: 6 hrs.). 2004. 24.95 (978-1-59007-504-3(8)) Pub: New Millenn Enter. Dist(s): PerseuPGW

My Antonia. 7 CDs. (Running Time: 7 hours, 45 minutes). 2004. audio compact disk 29.95 (978-1-59678-000-2(2), Super AudioBks) RU Creative.
Super Audiobooks(tm) presents My Antonia, by Willa Cather. Recorded in all digital unabridged audio CD format. Using state of the art digital speech synthesis, Super Audiobooks are recorded clearly and at a natural pace, are easy to understand, and great fun to listen to! Plays great in your home or car stereo and home computer, or download to your iPod or mp3 player for the ultimate portable audiobook. 7 discs: 7 hours, 45 minutes running time.

My Antonia. Willa Cather. Narrated by Grover Gardner. (ENG.). 2007. audio compact disk 29.95 (978-1-55685-941-0(4)) Audio Bk Con.

My Antonia. Willa Cather. Narrated by Cindy Hardin Killavey. (Running Time: 8 hrs. 30 mins.). 1987. 26.95 (978-1-59912-862-7(4)) Iofy Corp.

My Antonia. Willa Cather. Read by Patrick G. Lawlor. (Running Time: 8 hrs.). 2020. 27.95 (978-1-60083-642-8(9), Audiofy Corp) Iofy Corp.

My Antonia. Based on a story by Willa Cather. (ENG.). 2007. 5.00 (978-1-60339-083-5(9)); audio compact disk 5.00 (978-1-60339-084-2(7)) Listenr Digest.

My Antonia. Willa Cather. Narrated by George Guidall. 8 CDs. (Running Time: 8 hrs. 30 mins.). audio compact disk 78.00 (978-1-4025-2927-6(9)) Recorded Bks.

My Antonia. Willa Cather. Read by Patrick G. Lawlor. (ENG.). 2003. audio compact disk 78.00 (978-1-4001-3074-0(3)) Pub: Tantor Media. Dist(s): IngramPubServ

My Antonia. abr. ed. Willa Cather. Read by Joan Allen. 4 cass. (Running Time: 3 hrs.). 2004. 25.00 (978-1-59007-129-8(8)) Pub: New Millenn Enter. Dist(s): PerseuPGW
A masterful story of primitive themes told with elegance and affection, this novel depicts the violent yet inspiring existence of the foreign and native-born settlers to Nebraska in the early years of this century.

My Antonia, unabr. ed. Willa Cather. Read by Grover Gardner. 6 cass. (Running Time: 8 hrs. 30 min.). 1993. 2.95 (978-1-55685-282-4(7)) Audio Bk Con.
After the death of her father, Antonio Shimerda, a Bohemian immigrant, works as a servant for neighbors in the farmlands of Nebraska. She leaves for an unfortunate love affair with an Irish railway conductor, but returns home, eventually marries Anton Cuzak & raises a large family in the style of a true pioneer. As Willa Cather said, "She was a rich mine of life, like the founders of early races".

My Antonia. unabr. ed. Willa Cather. Read by Kathryn Yarman. 7 cass. (Running Time: 10 hrs. 30 mins.). 1994. 49.95 (978-0-7861-0495-6(3), 892570) Blckstn Audio.
Cather's finest novel deals with the life of Bohemian immigrants & native American settlers in the vast frontier farmlands of Nebraska. It is a work which is particularly noted for its lucid & moving depiction of the prairie & the lives of those who live close beside it.

My Antonia. unabr. ed. Willa Cather. Read by Jeff Cummings. (Running Time: 27000 sec.). 2007. 59.95 (978-0-7861-0107-8(5)); 19.95 (978-0-7861-4939-1(6)); audio compact disk 29.95 (978-0-7861-7014-2(X)); audio compact disk 72.00 (978-0-7861-6854-5(4)); audio compact disk 19.95 (978-0-7861-5883-6(2)) Blckstn Audio.

My Antonia. unabr. ed. Willa Cather. Read by Stephanie Brush. 8 cass. (Running Time: 9 hrs. 24 min.). 1999. 49.95 (978-1-55686-945-7(2)) Books in Motion.
Portray's the life of pioneering Bohemian farmers & the courageous heroine, Antonia.

My Antonia. unabr. ed. Willa Cather. Read by David Colacci. 6 cass. (Running Time: 8 hrs.). 2002. 29.95 (978-1-59086-292-6(9), 1590862929, BAU) Brilliance Audio.
My Ántonia chronicles the life of Ántonia, a Bohemian immigrant woman, as seen through the eyes of Jim, the man unable to forget her. Jim, now a successful New York lawyer, recollects his upbringing on a Nebraska farm. Even after twenty years, Ántonia continues to live a romantic life in his imagination. When he returns to Nebraska, he finds Ántonia has lived a battered life. Although the man to whom she dedicated her life abandons her, she remains strong and full of courage.

My Antonia. unabr. ed. Willa Cather. Read by David Colacci. (Running Time: 32400 sec.). (Classic Collection (Brilliance Audio) Ser.). 2005. audio compact disk 97.25 (978-1-59737-140-7(8), 9781597371407, BriAudCD Unabrid); audio compact disk 32.95 (978-1-59737-139-1(4), 9781597371391, Bril Audio CD Unabri) Brilliance Audio.

My Antonia. unabr. ed. Willa Cather. Read by Patrick G. Lawlor. (YA). 2007. 64.99 (978-1-59895-800-3(3)) Find a World.

My Antonia, unabr. ed. Willa Cather. Read by Kathryn Yarman. 7 cass. (Running Time: 11 hrs. 30 min.). 1999. 49.95 (FS9-24915) Highsmith.

My Antonia, unabr. ed. Willa Cather. Read by Jim Killavey & Cindy Killavey. 7 cass. (Running Time: 11 hrs. 30 min.). 1994. 35.00 (C-254) Jimcin Record.
My Antonia captures in lyrical & compassionate prose the people, places & times of the Nebraskan wilderness of the last century. Cather's masterpiece. In vinyl album.

My Antonia, unabr. ed. Willa Cather. Narrated by George Guidall. 6 cass. (Running Time: 8 hrs. 30 mins.). 1994. 51.00 (978-1-55690-976-4(4), 94115E7) Recorded Bks.
Antonia Shimerdas moves to the harsh Nebraska heartland with her impoverished Bohemian family when she is still a girl. For young Jim Burden, who lives with his grandparents on a homestead nearby, Antonia is an embodiment of the female pioneer. When Jim grows up, his memories return to Antonia. In his effort to understand what she meant to him, he creates an enduring picture of the American frontier & of a woman of unusual spirit.

My Antonia. unabr. ed. Willa Cather. Read by David Colacci. (Running Time: 8 hrs.). 2004. 24.95 (978-1-59335-160-1(7), 1593351607) Soulmate Audio Bks.
My Ántonia chronicles the life of Ántonia, a Bohemian immigrant woman, as seen through the eyes of Jim, the man unable to forget her. Jim, now a successful New York lawyer, recollects his upbringing on a Nebraska farm. Even after twenty years, Ántonia continues to live a romantic life in his imagination. When he returns to Nebraska, he finds Ántonia has lived a battered life. Although the man to whom she dedicated her life abandons her, she remains strong and full of courage.

My Antonia. unabr. ed. Willa Cather. Narrated by Patrick G. Lawlor. (Running Time: 8 hrs. 0 mins. 0 sec.). (ENG.). 2008. audio compact disk 27.99 (978-1-4001-0845-9(4)); audio compact disk 19.99 (978-1-4001-5845-4(1)); audio compact disk 55.99 (978-1-4001-3845-6(0)) Pub: Tantor Media. Dist(s): IngramPubServ

My Ántonia. unabr. ed. Willa Cather. Read by David Colacci. (Running Time: 8 hrs.). 2004. 39.25 (978-1-59335-366-6(8), 1593353928, Brlnc Audio MP3 Lib) Brilliance Audio.

My Ántonia. unabr. ed. Willa Cather. Read by David Colacci. (Running Time: 8 hrs.). 2004. 39.25 (978-1-59710-517-0(1), 1597105171, BADLE); 24.95 (978-1-59710-516-3(3), 1597105163, BAD) Brilliance Audio.

My Aunt Otilia's Spirits. Richard Garcia. (J). 1992. 13.95 (978-0-89239-034-2(4)) Childrens Book Pr.

My Autobiography, Pegboard Five: Women I Have Loved. Jack Mothershed. Read by Jack Mothershed. 2 CDs. (Running Time: 2 hrs.). (I Was Thinking about Writing an Autobiography Ser.). 2000. audio compact disk 15.95 (978-1-893359-70-3(0)) Winward Ways.

My Autobiography, Pegboard Four: Word Discoveries That Have Blown My Hair Back. Jack Mothershed. 2 CDs. (Running Time: 2 hrs.). (I Was Thinking about Writing an Autobiography Ser.). 2000. audio compact disk 15.95 (978-1-893359-65-9(4)) Winward Ways.

My Autobiography, Pegboard 1: The Incidents That Might Have Caused My Bad Back. Jack Mothershed. 2 CDs. (Running Time: 2 hrs.). (I Was Thinking about Writing an Autobiography Ser.). 2000. audio compact disk 15.95 (978-1-893359-50-5(6)) Winward Ways.

My Autobiography, Pegboard 2: Writers Who Changed My Life. Jack Mothershed. 2 CDs. (Running Time: 2 hrs.). (I Was Thinking about Writing an Autobiography Ser.). 2000. audio compact disk 15.95 (978-1-893359-55-0(7)) Winward Ways.

My Autobiography, Pegboard 3: Languages I Have Learned & People Who Spoke Them. Jack Mothershed. 2 CDs. (Running Time: 2 hrs.). (I Was Thinking about Writing an Autobiography Ser.). 2000. audio compact disk 15.95 (978-1-893359-60-4(3)) Winward Ways.

My Autobiography, Pegboard 6: Women Who Have Loved Me. Jack Mothershed. 2 CDs. (Running Time: 2 hrs.). (I Was Thinking About Writing an Autobiography Ser.). 2000. audio compact disk 15.95 (978-1-893359-75-8(1)) Winward Ways.

My Baby: From Birth to Six Months. 1 cass. (Running Time: 1 hr. 30 mins.). (SmartReader Ser.). (J). 1999. pap. bk. & tchr. ed. 19.95 (978-0-7887-0126-9(6), 79314T3) Recorded Bks.
Caring for a new baby is a full-time job. This simple guide outlines how you can give your baby a good start in life.

My Beach Bag: Early Explorers Emergent Set B Audio CD. Katherine Scraper. Adapted by Benchmark Education Staff. (J). 2007. audio compact disk 10.00 (978-1-4108-8194-6(6)) Benchmark Educ.

My Bear Gruff. Perf. by Charlotte Diamond. 1 cass. (Running Time: 1 hr. 30 min.). (J). (C0322) NewSound.

***My Beautiful Idol.** unabr. ed. Pete Gall. (Running Time: 6 hrs. 54 mins. 0 sec.). (ENG.). 2009. 12.99 (978-0-310-30930-7(1)) Zondervan.

My Beautiful Wooden Leader see Poetry & Voice of Margaret Atwood

My Beloved Son. unabr. ed. Catherine Cookson. Read by Elizabeth Henry. 10 cass. (Running Time: 15 hrs.). (Sound Ser.). 1991. 84.95 (978-1-85496-458-8(5), 64585) Pub: UlverLrgPrint GBR. Dist(s): Ulverscroft US
Patricia Ellen Jebeau had never been a dreamer - but she had married one, & despite being left a widow with nothing she was not bitter. After all, she had five-year-old Joseph for whom she would do anything. Helped by her brother-in-law, Ellen was installed in the old family seat & soon realized that Screehaugh lacked a mistress. But her ruthless ambition left Joseph with a traumatic heritage - would he ever emerge as his own true self.

My Best Friend. Lisa Monet. Read by Lisa Monet. Perf. by Redwood Children's Chorus. 1 cass. (J). (ps-2). 1992. 9.98 (978-1-877737-00-8(3), MLP 2300) MFLP CA.
Sing & play along songs for young children.

My Best Friend. unabr. ed. Laura Wilson. 7 cass. (Running Time: 9 hrs. 35 mins.). (Isis Ser.). (J). 2004. 61.95 (978-0-7531-1368-4(6)) Pub: ISIS Lrg Prnt GBR. Dist(s): Ulverscroft US

My Best Friend. unabr. ed. Laura Wilson. Read by Anna Bentinck. 9 CDs. (Running Time: 34500 sec.). (Isis (CDs) Ser.). 2004. audio compact disk 84.95 (978-0-7531-1711-8(8)) Pub: ISIS Lrg Prnt GBR. Dist(s): Ulverscroft US

My Best Friend Is a Salamander. Peter Himmelman. 1 cass. (Running Time: 44 min.). (J). (ps-5). 1997. 10.98 (3008-4); audio compact disk 15.98 (3008-2) Baby Music.
Fresh-sounding children's album featuring salamander neighbors with mud-covered furniture, aliens who speak gibberish & boys who turn into sunflowers.

My Best Friend Thinks I'm a Genius. George Ivanoff & Toby Quarmby. (Rigby Focus Forward Ser.). (J). (gr. 4-7). 2008. pap. bk. 13.20 (978-1-4190-3849-5(4), Rigby PEA) Pearson EdAUS AUS.

My Bible Stories: The Hop-Aboard Handbook & Sing-along. Carol Greene. 1 cass. (J). (ps up). 1993. pap. bk. 13.99 (978-0-570-04752-0(8), 56-1771) Concordia.

My Bible Teaches Me about God. (Junior Kids Church Ser.: Vol. 5). (J). (ps). 1998. bk. 134.99 (978-1-57405-436-1(8)) CharismaLife Pub.

My Big Fat Greek Diet. abr. ed. Yphantides Nick. 4 cass. (Running Time: 6 hrs.). 2004. 25.99 (978-1-58926-717-6(6), 6717) Oasis Audio.

My Big Fat Greek Diet: How a 467 Pound Physician Hit His Ideal Weight & You Can Too. abr. ed. M.D., Nick Yphantides. Narrated by Tim Lundeen. (ENG.). 2004. 19.59 (978-1-60814-315-3(5)) Oasis Audio.

My Big Fat Greek Diet: How a 467 Pound Physician Hit His Ideal Weight & You Can Too. abr. ed. Nick Yphantides. Narrated by Tim Lundeen. 5 CDs. (Running Time: 6 hrs.). (ENG.). 2004. audio compact disk 27.99 (978-1-58926-718-3(4), 6718) Oasis Audio.

***My Big Fat Supernatural Honeymoon.** unabr. ed. P. N. Elrod. (Running Time: 12 hrs.). 2010. 39.97 (978-1-4418-3474-4(5), 9781441834744, Brlnc Audio MP3 Lib); 39.97 (978-1-4418-3475-1(3), 9781441834751, BADLE); 24.99 (978-1-4418-3473-7(7), 9781441834737, Brilliance MP3); audio compact disk 79.97 (978-1-4418-3472-0(9), 9781441834720, BriAudCD Unabrid); audio compact disk 29.99 (978-1-4418-3471-3(0), 9781441834713, Bril Audio CD Unabri) Brilliance Audio.

***My Big Fat Supernatural Wedding.** unabr. ed. P. N. Elrod. (Running Time: 11 hrs.). 2010. 24.99 (978-1-4418-3468-3(0), 9781441834683, Brilliance MP3); 39.97 (978-1-4418-3469-0(9), 9781441834690, Brlnc Audio MP3 Lib); 39.97 (978-1-4418-3470-6(2), 9781441834706, BADLE); audio compact disk 29.99 (978-1-4418-3466-9(4), 9781441834669, Bril Audio CD Unabri); audio compact disk 79.97 (978-1-4418-3467-6(2), 9781441834676, BriAudCD Unabrid) Brilliance Audio.

My Birthday Tape. unabr. ed. Cake and Candle Cassettes, Inc. Staff. Read by Ron Triglio. 1 cass. (Running Time: 3 min.). (J). (gr. k-5). 1983. 6.95 (978-0-9649745-1-7(7)) Cake & Candle.
Features a child's first name narrated throughout the arrangement. Two verses of "Happy Birthday to You" are sung to the child by name.

My Blindy Girl: A Mother's journey through Achromatopsia. Ellen Tomaszewski. (ENG., 2008. pap. bk. & pap. bk. 16.99 (978-0-9785160-3-1(6)) Etcetera USA.

My Blindy Girl CD: A Quest for Wholeness. l.t. ed. Ellen Tomaszewski. Read by Ellen Tomaszewski. Read by Kathryn Mack. (ENG.). 2008. 29.99 (978-0-9785160-4-8(4)) Etcetera USA.

My Blue Blanket. Joyce Landorf Heatherley. 1 cass. (Running Time: 1 hr.). 1988. 7.95 (978-0-929488-20-2(2)) Balcony Pub Inc.
Choosing to set aside those blue blankets of security that numb us from genuine & lasting recovery from painful experiences.

My Blue Ontario's Shores see Twentieth-Century Poetry in English, No. 17, Walt Whitman Speaks for Himself

My Blue Violets. Sara Rose. (Running Time: 15960 sec.). 2008. audio compact disk 24.99 (978-1-60462-773-2(5)) Tate Pubng.

My Body Machine. Janeen Brady. Illus. by Evan Twede. (J). (ps-6). 1989. stu. ed. 11.95 (978-0-944803-66-0(0)) Brite Music.

My Body/Mi Cuerpo. abr. ed. Created by Mark Wesley & Gladys Rosa-Mendoza. (English Spanish Foundations Ser.). (J). 2008. audio compact disk 9.95 (978-1-931398-60-2(7)) Me Mi Pubng.

My Bodyworks: Songs about Your Bones, Muscles, Heart, & More! Jane Schoenberg. Music by Steven Schoenberg. Illus. by Cynthia Fisher. (J). 2004. bk. 16.95 (978-1-56656-583-7(9)) Interlink Pub.

My Bonny Light Horseman: Being an Account of the Further Adventures of Jacky Faber, in Love & War. L. A. Meyer. Read by Katherine Kellgren. 10 CDs. (Running Time: 12 hrs.). (Bloody Jack Adventures Ser.: Bk. 6). (YA). (gr. 7 up). 2009. audio compact disk 29.95 (978-1-59316-446-1(7)) Listen & Live.

My Booky Wook: A Memoir of Sex, Drugs, & Stand-Up. Russell Brand. (Running Time: 2 hrs.). 2008. audio compact disk 32.95 (978-1-84456-483-5(5), HoddrStoughton) Pub: Hodder General GBR. Dist(s): IPG Chicago

***My Booky Wook 2: This Time It's Personal.** unabr. ed. Russell Brand. (ENG.). 2010. (978-0-06-202717-7(4), Harper Audio) HarperCollins Pubs.

My Boyfriend's Back: True Stories of Rediscovering Love with a Long-Lost Sweetheart. Donna Hanover. Narrated by Donna Hanover. 4 CDs. (Running Time: 5 hrs.). 2005. audio compact disk 27.95 (978-1-59316-048-7(8), LL140) Listen & Live.
Ed and Donna were each other?s first loves, as high school seniors, as freshman at Stanford. Now their 30th reunion at Stanford was approaching, they were both divorced... My Boyfriend?s Back: Second Chance Love is the story of Donna and Ed?s rekindled love, their second chance, which culminated in their joyous marriage on August 3, 2003. It is also the story of other couples who have shared the phenomena of re-finding their first loves and building committed lives together, which therapists have identified as part of the new relationship movement of the 21st century, and which Donna investigated to better understand what she and Ed were expecting and why it triggered such an outpouring of emotion from everyone who learned of it.My Boyfriend?s Back: Second Chance Love is Donna and Ed?s romance; it is also a primer of practical sources, experiences and anecdotal information to help other women, and men, reconnect with their past loves, and it uses expert and authoritative voices to explain the risks and rewards.While Donna and Ed?s wedding has been written about in InStyle, People, etc., and reported on the nightly news shows, Donna has no given any in-depth personal interviews. She has a stack of requests that start with Barbara Walters, Diane Sawyer, Katie Couric, and Larry King, and will be pleased to talk with such media figures about that book and its contents at the time of publication.

My Brilliant Career. Miles Franklin. Read by Anais 9000. 2009. 27.95 (978-1-60112-207-0(1)) Babblebooks.

***My brilliant Career.** Miles Franklin. Read by Megan Rees. (Running Time: 10 hrs. 30 mins.). 2010. 89.99 (978-1-74214-605-8(8), 9781742146058) Pub: Bolinda Pubng AUS. Dist(s): Bolinda Pub Inc

My Brilliant Career. unabr. ed. Miles Franklin. Read by Megan E. Rees. 8 cass. (Running Time: 10 hrs. 30 mins.). 1998. (978-1-86340-705-2(7), 571028) Bolinda Pubng AUS.
Sybylla confesses to her rich & handsome suitor that she is given to writing stories & bound, therefore, on a brilliant career. The story of growing up passionate & rebellious in rural New South Wales, where the most that girls could hope for was to marry or to teach. Sybylla will do neither, but that doesn't stop her from falling in love & it doesn't make the choices any easier.

My brilliant career - Re-release. unabr. ed. Miles Franklin. Read by Megan Rees. (Running Time: 10 hrs. 30 mins.). 2009. audio compact disk 93.95 (978-1-921415-87-6(8), 9781921415876) Pub: Bolinda Pubng AUS. Dist(s): Bolinda Pub Inc

My Brother. unabr. ed. Jamaica Kincaid. Read by Jamaica Kincaid. 4 cass. (Running Time: 6 hrs.). 1998. 24.95 (PengAudBks) Penguin Grp USA.

My Brother, Ant. Betsy Byars. Read by Bonnie Kelly-Young. Illus. by Marc Simont. 1 cass. (Running Time: 30 mins.). (J). 2000. pap. bk. 19.97 (978-0-7366-9214-4(2)) Books on Tape.
Four stories.

My Brother, Ant. Betsy Byars. 1 cass. (Running Time: 35 min.). (J). 2001. pap. bk. 15.95 (VX-92C) Kimbo Educ.
Ant is the little brother who's big on laughs. These four upbeat stories are funny & endearing.

My Brother, Ant. Betsy Byars. 9.95 (978-1-59112-287-6(2)) Live Oak Media.

My Brother, Ant. Betsy Byars. Illus. by Marc Simont. 11 vols. (Running Time: 11 mins.). 1999. bk. 28.95 (978-1-59112-627-0(4)); pap. bk. 31.95 (978-1-59112-628-7(2)); audio compact disk 12.95 (978-1-59112-625-6(8)) Live Oak Media.

My Brother, Ant. Betsy Byars. Illus. by Marc Simont. (Running Time: 11 mins.). (J). (gr. k-4). 1999. 9.95 (978-0-87499-519-0(1)) Live Oak Media.

My Brother, Ant. unabr. ed. Betsy Byars. Read by Bonnie Kelly-Young. Illus. by Marc Simont. 11 vols. (Running Time: 11 mins.). (Ant Ser.). (J). (gr. k-3). 1999. bk. 25.95 (978-0-87499-517-6(5)); pap. bk. 16.95 (978-0-87499-516-9(7)); pap. bk. & tchr. ed. 29.95 (978-0-87499-518-3(3)) Live Oak Media.
Ant is the little brother who's big on laughs. Includes reading chest.

My Brother, Ant. unabr. ed. Betsy Byars. Narrated by Jeff Woodman. 1 cass. (Running Time: 15 mins.). (gr. 1 up). 1998. 10.00 (978-0-7887-1903-5(3), 95324E7) Recorded Bks.
Laugh out loud when Anthony hears monsters under his bed, decorates his big brother's homework & writes to Santa in July. Traces the unique relationship between young brothers.

My Brother, Ant. unabr. ed. Betsy Byars. Read by Jeff Woodman. 1cass. (Running Time: 15 min.). (J). (gr. 2). 1998. 22.24 (978-0-7887-1931-8(9), 40638) Recorded Bks.
Anthony's adventures include hearing monsters under his bed, decorating his big brother's homework & writing to Santa in July. This is a unique relationship between Ant & his brother. Homework set.

My Brother Dan's Delicous: Love the Baby. Steven Layne. Narrated by Steven Layne. (ENG.). (J). 2009. audio compact disk 15.95 (978-1-58980-741-9(3)) Pelican.

My Brother Michael. unabr. ed. Mary Stewart. Read by Jane Asher. 8 cass. (Running Time: 8 hrs.). 1993. 69.95 (978-0-7451-6304-8(1), CAB 432) AudioGO.

My Brother Sam Is Dead. unabr. ed. James Lincoln Collier & Christopher Collier. Read by John C. Brown. 4 CDs. (Running Time: 4 hrs. 30 min.). (YA). 1996. audio compact disk 39.95 (978-1-883332-55-6(9)) Audio Bkshelf.

My Brother Sam Is Dead. unabr. ed. James Lincoln Collier & Christopher Collier. Read by John C. Brown. 4 cass. (Running Time: 4 hrs. 30 min.). (YA). (gr. 5 up). 1996. 24.95 (978-1-883332-19-8(2), 494110) Audio Bkshelf.
15 year old Tim Meeker watches as his older brother goes off to fight in the Revolutionary War - a War with no clearcut loyalties - dividing families, friends & towns. A stirring historical tale full of action & suspense.

My Brother Sam Is Dead. unabr. ed. James Lincoln Collier & Christopher Collier. Read by John C. Brown. (J). 2008. 59.99 (978-1-60514-902-8(0)) Find a World.

My Brother Thinks He's a Banana & Other Provocative Songs for Children. Perf. by Barry Louis Polisar. 1 cass. (Running Time: 1 hr.). (J). 1977. 9.95 (978-0-9615696-4-8(6)) Rainbow Morn.

My Brother Threw up on My Stuffed Toy Bunny: And Other Songs for Older Children. Perf. by Barry Louis Polisar. (J). (ps-6). 1988. 19.95 (978-0-938663-04-1(6)) Pub: Rainbow Morn. Dist(s): IPG Chicago

My Brother's Keeper. unabr. ed. Angela Kamper & Charles Miranda. Read by Humphrey Bower. (Running Time: 24000 sec.). 2008. audio compact disk 83.95 (978-1-921334-05-4(3), 9781921334054) Pub: Bolinda Pubng AUS. Dist(s): Bolinda Pub Inc

My Business 2004 Conference: Conference Proceedings. Ed. by Bharat Rao et al. 2004. audio compact disk 15.00 (978-0-918902-54-2(1)) Polytechnic Pr.

My Business 2004 Conference: Conference Program. Ed. by Mel Horwitch. 2004. audio compact disk 15.00 (978-0-918902-56-6(8)) Polytechnic Pr.

My CD Xpress: the New Century Handbook. 3rd ed. Christine A. Hult & Thomas N. Huckin. 2005. audio compact disk 43.00 (978-0-321-29220-9(0)) Longman.

My Child Is Pregnant: What Are My Rights? Hosted by Mardie Caldwell. Featuring Felice Webster. (ENG.). 2008. audio compact disk 12.95 (978-0-9705734-3-8(X)) Pub: Am Carrage Hse Pubng. Dist(s): STL Dist NA

My Christmas Is Best: Traditional Songs for the Season from Around the World. unabr. ed. Oscar Brand. Perf. by Oscar Brand. 1 cass. (Running Time: 1 hr.). (J). 1985. 8.98 (978-0-89845-413-0(1), CP 1776) HarperCollins Pubs.
Describes the many different ways Christmas is celebrated around the world with stories & songs.

My Christmas Tape. unabr. ed. Cake and Candle Cassettes, Inc. Staff. Read by Ron Trigilio. 1 cass. (Running Time: 5 min.). (J). (gr. k-5). 1991. 6.95 (978-0-9649745-3-1(3)) Cake & Candle.
Personalized audio cassette tape which mentions a child's first name eighteen times. Narrations talk to young listeners about the value & spirit of Christmas.

My Church: Developing Congregational Ownership. Sanford G. Kulkin. 8 cass. (Running Time: 4 hrs.). 1992. ring bd. 195.00 (978-1-58034-008-3(3)) IML Pubns.
Shows how to develop & enhance congregational ownership of the pastor's or church leader's vision; so that more than the usual twenty percent of a congregation are enlisted in the church's ministry.

My Conquest: News 4 New York TV Interview. Marco A. V. Bitetto. Read by Marco A. V. Bitetto. 1 cass. (Running Time: 1 hr.). 2000. (978-1-58578-322-9(6)) Inst of Cybernetics.

My Conversion. Charles H. Spurgeon. Read by Charlie T. Jones. (Laws of Leadership Ser.). (ENG.). 2007. audio compact disk 19.95 (978-1-933715-60-5(X)) Executive Bks.

My Country Versus Me: The First-Hand Account by the Los Alamos Scientist Who Was Falsely Accused of Being a Spy. abr. ed. Wen Ho Lee & Helen Zia. Read by Fred Stella. 5 CDs. (Running Time: 6 hrs.). 2002. audio compact disk 29.95 (978-1-58788-788-6(6), 1587887886, CD); audio compact disk 69.25 (978-1-58788-789-5(4), 1587887894, CD Lib Edit) Brilliance Audio.
Wen Ho Lee, a patriotic American scientist born in Taiwan, had devoted almost his entire life to science and to helping improve U.S. defense capabilities. He loved his job at Los Alamos National Laboratory and spent his leisure time fishing, cooking, gardening, and with his family. Then, suddenly, everything changed and he found himself in the spotlight, accused of espionage by members of Congress and the national media and portrayed as the most dangerous traitor since the Rosenbergs. He was even told that their fate - execution - might well be his own. Although Dr. Lee was horrified by these words, he knew he was innocent and believed that this was all a big mistake that would be cleared up quickly. But in December 1999, his worst fears were confirmed when he was manacled, shackled, brought to jail, and put in a tiny, solitary-confinement cell, where he would remain for the next nine months. His arrest sparked controversy throughout the country; it triggered concern for national security, debate about racial profiling and media distortion, and outrage over a return to McCarthy-era paranoia. Throughout the ordeal, Dr. Lee steadfastly maintained his innocence. Now, at last, he is free to tell his story. In this compelling narrative, Dr. Lee chronicles his experience before, during, and after his imprisonment. He takes readers inside Los Alamos and discusses how violations of national security occur in many government agencies. He describes how the FBI infiltrated his private life - lying to him and spying on him for nearly two decades. He relates his own anti-Communist stance, the result of tragic events from his past, and tells how he assisted the FBI to help protect nuclear secrets. He explains the role that the New York Times and unsourced "leaks" played in the country's rush to judgment. He details his harsh treatment in jail and how citizens can be incarcerated solely on government allegations and without factual justification. Finally, Dr. Lee accounts for why he downloaded codes, demonstrating once and for all that he is innocent of every charge leveled against him except for one, a security violation that many others had committed. A riveting story about prejudice, fear, suspicion - and courage - My Country Versus Me offers a revelatory first-hand account of one of the major abuses of our government's power in our time.

My Country Versus Me: The First-Hand Account by the Los Alamos Scientist Who Was Falsely Accused of Being a Spy. unabr. ed. Wen Ho Lee & Helen Zia. Read by Fred Stella. 8 cass. (Running Time: 11 hrs.). 2002. 34.95 (978-1-58788-765-9(7), 1587887657, BAU); 87.25 (978-1-58788-766-6(5), 1587887665, Unabridge Lib Edns) Brilliance Audio.

My Country Versus Me: The First-Hand Account by the Los Alamos Scientist Who Was Falsely Accused of Being a Spy. unabr. ed. Wen Ho Lee & Helen Zia. Read by Fred Stella. (Running Time: 11 hrs.). 2004. 39.25 (978-1-59335-354-4(5), 1593353545, Brinc Audio MP3 Lib) Brilliance Audio.

My Country Versus Me: The First-Hand Account by the Los Alamos Scientist Who Was Falsely Accused of Being a Spy. unabr. ed. Wen Ho Lee & Helen Zia. Read by Fred Stella. (Running Time: 11 hrs.). 2004. 39.25 (978-1-59710-519-4(8), 1597105198, BADLE); 24.95 (978-1-59710-518-7(X), 159710518X, BAD) Brilliance Audio.

My Country Versus Me: The First-Hand Account by the Los Alamos Scientist Who Was Falsely Accused of Being a Spy. unabr. ed. Wen Ho Lee & Helen Zia. Read by Fred Stella. (Running Time: 11 hrs.). 2004. 24.95 (978-1-59335-024-6(4), 1593350244) Soulmate Audio Bks.

My Cousin. Short Stories. (5121) Am Audio Prose.

My Cousin Rachel. unabr. ed. Daphne Du Maurier. Read by Richard Green. 8 cass. (Running Time: 12 hrs.). 64.00 (978-0-7366-0140-5(6), 1143) Books on Tape.
Philip Ashley & his Uncle Ambrose share a happy bachelor existence on the family estate in Cornwall until ill health sends Ambrose to Italy. There he meets & marries a distant cousin, Rachel. After his death Rachel journeys to Cornwall where Philip's initial reluctance to meet her is dispelled by her charm. But rumors concerning Rachel's conduct in Italy persist & soon Phillip is desperate to know if the woman he is falling in love with could really be the poisoner of his beloved Uncle Ambrose.

My Cousin Rachel. unabr. ed. Daphne Du Maurier. Read by Jonathan Pryce. 8 cass. (Running Time: 12 hrs.). 2000. 59.95 (978-0-7451-6151-8(0), CAB 378) Pub: Chivers Audio Bks GBR. Dist(s): AudioGO
Ambrose married Rachel, Countess Sangallettie in Italy, and never returned home. His letters to his cousin Philip hinted that he was being poisoned, and when Philip arrived in Italy, Ambrose was dead. Rachel travels to England, and soon Philip is torn between love and suspicion. Is she the angel she seems to be, or a scheming murderess?.

My Cozy Dry Bed: For Bedwetting & Nighttime Toilet Training. rev. ed. Robert B. Speigel. 2 cass. (Audio-Suggestion Bedtime Story Tapes Ser.). (ENG., (J). (gr. k-6). 1993. cass. & cd-rom 49.95 (978-0-937977-00-2(4), 97700) Speigel&Assoc.
Therapeutic audio-cassette program to treat bedwetting problems in children. Includes parent's information tape.

My Crazy Christmas Catastrophe Cat. Kristen Twedt. (J). 2003. audio compact disk 5.95 (978-0-9744751-2-7(2)) Timothy Lane.

My Credit Suck! Please Help Me! Jeanette McCarter. 2007. audio compact disk 25.00 (978-1-4276-2903-6(X)) AardGP.

My Cup Runneth Over. Harold Kushner. 2005. audio compact disk 15.95 (978-0-660-19292-5(6)) Canadian Broadcasting CAN.

My Cup Runneth Over: Setting Goals for Single Parents & Working Couples. unabr. ed. Daryl D. Green. Perf. by Gabriel Dennis. Contrib. by Roslyn Robinson. Narrated by Estraletta Green. 1 cass. (Running Time: 1 hr.). 1999. 9.95 (978-1-889745-05-3(7)) Triangle Publctns.
Uses modern management techniques to help families develop objectives. It is essential for families in search of purpose.

***My Dad's a Birdman.** unabr. ed. David Almond. (Running Time: 1 hr.). 2010. 39.97 (978-1-4418-9011-5(4), 9781441890115, Candlewick Bril); 14.99 (978-1-4418-9010-8(6), 9781441890108, Candlewick Bril) Brilliance Audio.

***My Dad's a Birdman.** unabr. ed. David Almond. Read by Sarah Coomes. (Running Time: 2 hrs.). 2010. audio compact disk 19.99 (978-1-4418-9006-1(8), 9781441890061, Candlewick Bril); audio compact disk 14.99 (978-1-4418-9008-5(4), 9781441890085, Candlewick Bril); audio compact disk 39.97 (978-1-4418-9007-8(6), 9781441890078, Candlewick Bril); audio compact disk 39.97 (978-1-4418-9009-2(2), 9781441890092, Candlewick Bril) Brilliance Audio.

My Daniel, unabr. ed. Pam Conrad. Narrated by Barbara Caruso. 3 pieces. (Running Time: 4 hrs.). (gr. 4 up). 1997. 27.00 (978-0-7887-0489-5(3), 94644E7) Recorded Bks.
When Julia Creath Summerwaite takes her granchildren to the Natural History Museum, she once again becomes the young tomboy who helped her brother Daniel look for dinosaur bones on the Nebraska prairie.

My Dark Places: An L. A. Crime Memoir. unabr. collector's ed. James Ellroy. Read by Michael Prichard. 10 cass. (Running Time: 15 hrs.). 1997. 80.00 (978-0-913369-69-2(1), 4320) Books on Tape.

***My Darling Jackass.** Adapted by Siren Audio Studios. Prod. by Siren Audio Studios. Created by Alexia Drew. (ENG.). 2011. audio compact disk (978-0-9844180-8-4(3)) Siiren Audio.

My Daughters Thought I Could Coach Basketball. 1996. 9.95 (978-0-9621127-2-0(0)) Daly Consulting.

My Dead Body. unabr. ed. Charlie Huston. Read by Scott Brick. (Running Time: 11 hrs. 0 mins.). 2009. 29.95 (978-1-4417-2253-9(X)); 65.95 (978-1-4417-2249-2(1)); audio compact disk 100.00 (978-1-4417-2250-8(5)) Blckstn Audio.

My Dear Young Friends: Pope John Paul II Speaks to Youth on Life, Love, & Courage. John Paul II, pseud. Ed. by John Vitek. (YA). 2003. pap. bk. & pap. bk. 9.95 (978-0-88489-748-4(6)) St Marys.

My Detachment: A Memoir. unabr. ed. Tracy Kidder. Read by Tracy Kidder. 5 CDs. (Running Time: 6 hrs.). 2005. audio compact disk 38.25 (978-1-4159-2424-2(4)); 36.00 (978-1-4159-2423-5(6)) Books on Tape.
With remarkable clarity and with great detachment, Kidder looks back at himself from across three and a half decades, confessing how, as a young lieutenant, he sought to borrow from the tragedy around him and to imagine himself a romantic hero. Unrelentingly honest, rueful, and revealing, My Detachment gives us war without heroism, while preserving those rare moments of redeeming grace in the midst of lunacy and danger. The officers and men of My Detachment are not the sort of people who appear in war movies - they are the ones who appear only in war, and they are unforgettable.

My Dinner of Herbs. Efrem Zimbalist, Jr.. Read by Efrem Zimbalist, Jr. (Running Time: 19800 sec.). 2007. 34.95 (978-1-4332-0125-7(9)); audio compact disk 45.00 (978-1-4332-0126-4(7)); audio compact disk 29.95 (978-1-4332-0127-1(5)) Blckstn Audio.

My Doctor, My Friend. Bennett L. Gemson. 1985. 11.95 Ed Activities.

My Dog May Be a Genius. abr. ed. Jack Prelutsky. Read by Jack Prelutsky. 1 CD. (Running Time: 1 hrs. 10 mins.). (J). (gr. k-5). 2008. 14.95 (978-0-06-145145-4(2), HarperChildAud) HarperCollins Pubs.

***My Dog May Be a Genius.** unabr. ed. Jack Prelutsky. Read by Jack Prelutsky. (ENG.). 2008. (978-0-06-162958-7(8)); (978-0-06-162959-4(6)) HarperCollins Pubs.

My Dog Skip, unabr. ed. Willie Morris. Narrated by Frank Muller. 3 cass. (Running Time: 3 hrs. 15 mins.). 26.00 (978-0-7887-0494-9(X), 94686E7) Recorded Bks.
The classic tale of a boy & his dog is told with refreshing new charm & innocence by a man who, 40 years later, still clearly recalls the magic of those golden days spent with his irrepressible four-legged companion. Available to libraries only.

My Double & How He Undid Me see Man Without a Country

My Double & How He Undid Me. Based on a story by Edward Everett Hale. (ENG.). 2007. 5.00 (978-1-60339-099-6(5)); audio compact disk 5.00 (978-1-60339-100-9(2)) Listenr Digest.

My Dream of You. Read by Dearbhla Molloy. 16 CDs. (Running Time: 60360 sec.). (Rumpole Crime Ser.). 2002. audio compact disk 119.95 (978-0-7927-2670-8(7), SLD 370, Chivers Sound Lib) AudioGO.

My Dream of You. Nuala O'Faolain. Read by Dearbhla Molloy. 2004. 15.95 (978-0-7435-1988-5(4)) Pub: S&S Audio. Dist(s): S and S Inc

My Early Life. unabr. ed. Winston L. S. Churchill. 10 cass. (Running Time: 12 hrs. 52 mins.). (Isis Cassettes Ser.). (J). 2005. 84.95 (978-0-7531-2187-0(5)) Pub: ISIS Lrg Prnt GBR. Dist(s): Ulverscroft US

My Early Life: A Roving Commission. unabr. ed. Winston Churchill. Read by Michael Tudor Barnes. 12 CDs. (Running Time: 49500 sec.). (Isis (CDs) Ser.). 2005. audio compact disk 99.95 (978-0-7531-2469-7(6)) Pub: ISIS Lrg Prnt GBR. Dist(s): Ulverscroft US

My Early Life: A Roving Commission. unabr. ed. Winston L. S. Churchill. Read by Frederick Davidson. 9 cass. (Running Time: 13 hrs.). 1994. 62.95 (978-0-7861-0733-9(2), 1488) Blckstn Audio.
This is the story of the first twenty-five years of Mr. Churchill's life, up to the point where his unique parliamentary career was just beginning. From childhood & his apprentice days at Harrow & Sandhurst we follow him on active service to Cuba, the North West Frontier, Omdurman & the Boer War (including the historic story of his escape from captivity), whilst in the background are his early adventures in politics & literature.

My Early Life: A Roving Commission. unabr. collector's ed. Winston L. S. Churchill. Read by Rupert Keenlyside. 9 cass. (Running Time: 13 hrs. 30 min.). 1985. 72.00 (978-0-7366-0911-1(3), 1854) Books on Tape.
Churchill was never quite his own man. His actions were always a little larger than life & his escapades, mainly fighting, were wild & reckless. He loved the glory of war & after every campaign wrote a book. Learn first hand what it means to be driven by destiny.

My Enemy, My Brother: Men & Days of Gettysburg. unabr. ed. Joseph E. Persico. Narrated by Richard M. Davidson. 9 cass. (Running Time: 12 hrs. 30 mins.). 1998. 80.00 (978-0-7887-2183-0(6), 95479E7) Recorded Bks.
Takes a fresh look at the pivotal Civil War battle that lasted for three horrible days in the small Pennsylvania town, drawing on diaries, letters & memoirs.

My Enemy, the Queen. unabr. collector's ed. Victoria Holt. Read by Donada Peters. 9 cass. (Running Time: 13 hrs. 30 min.). 1994. 72.00 (978-0-7366-2741-2(3), 3467) Books on Tape.
Was Queen Elizabeteh I afraid or too wily to marry? Or was the beautiful Lettice Devereaux the spoiler in royal romances.

My Enemy's Enemy. unabr. collector's ed. Kingsley Amis. Read by Richard Green. 6 cass. (Running Time: 6 hrs.). 1978. 36.00 (978-0-7366-0129-0(5), 1135) Books on Tape.
A selection of seven short stories centered on the disillusionment of the post-World War II era.

My England Years. abr. ed. Bobby Charlton. Read by Christian Rodska. (Running Time: 2 hrs. 24 mins. 0 sec.). (ENG.). 2008. audio compact disk 19.95 (978-1-4055-0544-4(3)) Pub: Little BrownUK GBR. Dist(s): IPG Chicago

My Experiments with Truth. abr. ed. Mohandas Gandhi. Read by Frederick Davidson. 3 CDs. (Running Time: 3 hrs.). (ENG.). 2001. audio compact disk 24.95 (978-1-56511-518-7(X), 156511518X) Pub: HighBridge. Dist(s): Workman Pub

My Eyes Have Seen Holy. Contrib. by Bebo Norman. (Mastertrax Ser.). 2006. audio compact disk 9.98 (978-5-558-20093-5(6)) Pt of Grace Ent.

My Eyes See Thee. Neville Goddard. 1 cass. (Running Time: 1 hr. 2 min.). 1964. 8.00 (72) J & L Pubns.
Neville taught Imagination Creates Reality. He was a powerfully influential teacher of God as Consciousness.

My Fair Lazy: One Reality Television Addict's Attempt to Discover If Not Being a Dumb Ass Is the New Black, or, a Culture-Up Manifesto. unabr. ed. Jen Lancaster. (Running Time: 9 hrs.). 2010. audio compact disk 29.95 (978-0-14-314579-0(7), PengAudBks) Penguin Grp USA.

My Fair Temptress. Christina Dodd. (Governess Brides Ser.: Bk. 7). 2005. audio compact disk 29.95 (978-0-06-079078-3(4)) HarperCollins Pubs.

My Faith Still Holds: An Easter Worship Celebration. Contrib. by Mosie Lister. (ENG.). 1993. 12.00 (978-0-00-500538-5(8)) Lillenas.

My Family & I/Mi Familia y Yo. abr. ed. Created by Mark Wesley & Gladys Rosa-Mendoza. (English Spanish Foundations Ser.). (J). 2008. audio compact disk 9.95 (978-1-931398-58-9(5)) Me Mi Pubng.

My Family Has Jobs: Early Explorers Early Set B Audio CD. Jeanne Baca Schulte. Adapted by Benchmark Education Staff. (J). 2007. audio compact disk 10.00 (978-1-4108-8225-7(X)) Benchmark Educ.

My Family Is All I Have. Helen-Alice Dear. 2009. 61.95 (978-1-4079-0335-4(7)); audio compact disk 79.95 (978-1-4079-0336-1(5)) Pub: Soundings Ltd GBR. Dist(s): Ulverscroft US

My Family Tree: A Recorded History. unabr. ed. Robin Moore. Read by Robin Moore. 1 cass. (Running Time: 30 min.). 1993. 8.95 (978-1-55994-805-0(1)) HarperCollins Pubs.

My Father: Solo Track. Martha Gushee. Perf. by Christine Wyrtzen. 1 cass. (Running Time: 30 min.). (50-Day Spiritual Adventure Ser.). 1993. 9.99 (978-1-879050-28-0(5)) Chapel of Air.
Accompaniment track for solo singer.

My Father As I Recall Him. Mamie Dickens. Narrated by Flo Gibson. 2 cass. (Running Time: 2 hrs. 7 mins.). 2006. 14.95 (978-1-55685-858-1(2)) Audio Bk Con.

***My Father At 100.** unabr. ed. Ron Reagan. Read by Ron Reagan. (Running Time: 12 hrs.). 2011. 29.95 (978-1-4417-7186-5(7)); audio compact disk 32.95 (978-1-4417-7185-8(9)) Blckstn Audio.

***My Father at 100 (Library Edition)** unabr. ed. Ron Reagan. Read by Ron Reagan. (Running Time: 12 hrs.). 2011. 72.95 (978-1-4417-7183-4(2)); audio compact disk 105.00 (978-1-4417-7184-1(0)) Blckstn Audio.

My Father, Frank Lloyd Wright. unabr. ed. John L. Wright. Read by Robin Lawson. 4 cass. (Running Time: 5 hrs. 30 mins.). Orig. Title: My Father Who Is on Earth. 1997. 32.95 (978-0-7861-1079-7(1), 1849) Blckstn Audio.
Frank Lloyd Wright is widely regarded as the 20th century's greatest architect - an unconventional genius who transformed both residential & commercial building design with his concept of "organic" architecture. In this charming memoir, Wright the architect & father comes to life through the vivid recollections & firsthand knowledge of his son.

***My Father, Maker of the Trees: How I Survived Rwandan Genocide.** unabr. ed. Eric Irivuzumugabe & Tracey Lawrence. Narrated by Dion Graham. (ENG.). 2009. 12.98 (978-1-59644-752-3(4), Hovel Audio) christianaud.

My Father, Maker of the Trees: How I Survived Rwandan Genocide. unabr. ed. Eric Irivuzumugabe & Tracy Lawrence. 5 CDs. (Running Time: 4 hrs. 45 mins. 0 sec.). (ENG.). 2009. audio compact disk 21.98 (978-1-59644-751-6(6), Hovel Audio) christianaud.

My father moved through dooms of love see Twentieth-Century Poetry in English, No. 5, Recordings of Poets Reading Their Own Poetry

My Father, My President: A Personal Account of the Life of George H. W. Bush. abr. ed. Doro Bush Koch. (Running Time: 6 hrs.). (ENG.). 2006. 14.98 (978-1-59483-594-0(2)) Pub: Hachet Audio. Dist(s): HachBkGrp

My Father, My President: A Personal Account of the Life of George H. W. Bush. abr. ed. Doro Bush Koch. (Running Time: 6 hrs.). (ENG.). 2009. 44.98 (978-1-60788-269-5(8)) Pub: Hachet Audio. Dist(s): HachBkGrp

My Father, My Son. unabr. collector's ed. Elmo Zumwalt, Jr. & Elmo Zumwalt, III. Read by Dick Estell. 8 cass. (Running Time: 8 hrs.). 1987. 48.00 (978-0-7366-1245-6(9), 2160) Books on Tape.
True story from Vietnam. Admiral (father) orders defoliation; Lt. (son) develops cancer from Agent Orange.

My Father Was a Hero. Cole Moreton. 6 cass. (Soundings Ser.). (J). 2005. 54.95 (978-1-84283-990-4(X)) Pub: ISIS Lrg Prnt GBR. Dist(s): Ulverscroft US

My Father Was Mad at My Brother. Short Stories. (5122) Am Audio Prose.

My Father Who Is on Earth see My Father, Frank Lloyd Wright

My Father's Daughter: How to Make It As a Hollywood Assistant. abr. ed. Tina Sinatra. Read by Tina Sinatra. 3 cass. (Running Time: 4 hrs. 30 mins.). 2000. 25.00 (978-0-7435-0672-4(3), Audioworks) S&S Audio.
As a singer & actor, Frank Sinatra captured the hearts & the imagination of the public as few others have. During his lifetime he was alternately adored & vilified; he was viewed as a great lover but accused of abusing the women in his life; he was seen as a compassionate, generous man, while at the same time he was linked to some of the nation's most calculating & corrupt criminals. Sorting through these many contradictions & separating fact from fiction as only someone close to him could, Tina Sinatra comes forward with a full biography of her father that provides a clear-eyed look behind the scenes at a life that was full of incongruity, but always lived to the fullest. The world may remember Frank Sinatra as one of show business's greatest, but in this eagerly awaited biography, Tina remembers him as something more: a father & a man.

***My Father's Fortune.** Michael Frayn. (Running Time: 8 hrs. 0 mins. 0 sec.). (ENG.). 2011. audio compact disk 29.95 (978-1-60998-153-2(7)) Pub: AudioGO. Dist(s): Perseus Dist

My Fathers Love. Russell Mauldin. 1998. 8.00 (978-0-7673-9221-1(3)); 75.00 (978-0-7673-9194-8(2)); audio compact disk 12.00 (978-0-7673-9224-2(8)); audio compact disk 85.00 (978-0-7673-9210-5(8)); audio compact disk 16.98 (978-0-7673-9205-1(1)) LifeWay Christian.

My Father's Love. Russell Mauldin. 1998. 11.98 (978-0-7673-9190-0(X)) LifeWay Christian.

***My Father's Mask.** unabr. ed. Joe Hill. (ENG.). 2007. (978-0-06-155230-4(5)); (978-0-06-155232-8(1)) HarperCollins Pubs.

***My Father's Names.** Elmer L. Towns. (ENG.). audio compact disk 21.95 (978-0-578-02558-2(2)) Sapphire Dig.

My Father's Secret War. Lucinda Franks. Read by Joyce Bean. (Playaway Adult Nonfiction Ser.). (ENG.). 2009. 69.99 (978-1-60812-555-5(6)) Find a World.

My Father's Secret War: A Memoir. unabr. ed. Lucinda Franks. Read by Joyce Bean. (Running Time: 12 hrs. 30 mins. 0 sec.). (ENG.). 2007. audio compact disk 37.99 (978-1-4001-0381-2(9)); audio compact disk 24.99 (978-1-4001-5381-7(6)); audio compact disk 75.99 (978-1-4001-3381-9(5)) Pub: Tantor Media. Dist(s): IngramPubServ

My Father's Tears & Other Stories. unabr. ed. John Updike. Read by Luke Daniels. (Running Time: 9 hrs.). 2009. 39.97 (978-1-4233-9795-3(9), 9781423397953, Brlnc Audio MP3 Lib); 39.97 (978-1-4233-9797-7(5), 9781423397977, BADLE); 24.99 (978-1-4233-9796-0(7), 9781423397960, BAD); 24.99 (978-1-4233-9794-6(0), 9781423397946, Brilliance MP3); audio compact disk 92.97 (978-1-4233-9793-9(2), 9781423397939, BriAudCD Unabrid); audio compact disk 29.99 (978-1-4233-9792-2(4), 9781423397922, Bril Audio CD Unabri) Brilliance Audio.

My Favorite Homeschooling Ideas. Debi Pearl. 1 cassette. (ENG.). 1997. audio compact disk 6.95 (978-1-892112-57-6(4)) Pub: No Greater Joy. Dist(s): STL Dist NA

My Favorite Husband. unabr. ed. Jess Oppenheimer. Perf. by Madelyn Pugh et al. 1 CD. (Running Time: 53 mins.). 2000. audio compact disk 25.95 (978-1-58081-184-2(1), CDRDP30) Pub: L A Theatre. Dist(s): NetLibrary CO

My Favorite Husband. unabr. ed. Jess Oppenheimer et al. Perf. by Marilu Henner & Jeff Conaway. 1 cass. (Running Time: 53 mins.). 2000. 20.95 (978-1-58081-165-1(5), RDP30) L A Theatre.

My Favorite Husband, Vol. 1. collector's ed. Perf. by Lucille Ball & Richard Denning. Prod. by Jess Oppenheimer. 6 cass. (Running Time: 9 hrs.). 1998. bk. 34.98 (4053) Radio Spirits.
Great comedy! Lucille Ball stars as Liz, the zany housewife, and Richard Denning portrays the typical screwy husband, sometimes forgetful, sometimes lovable. The show that spawned TV's famous "I Love Lucy". 18 episodes.

My Favorite Husband, Vol. 2. collector's ed. Perf. by Lucille Ball & Richard Denning. 6 cass. (Running Time: 9 hrs.). 2000. bk. 34.98 (4552) Radio Spirits.
The lives of Liz, the zany housewife and George Cooper, the stereotypical husband, who lived "in a little white two-story house" at 321 Bundy Lane "in the bustling little suburb of Sheridan Falls." 18 broadcasts. The show that spawned TV's famous "I Love Lucy.".

My Favorite Husband: A Night of Dancing. Featuring Lucille Ball. 6 cass. (Running Time: 6 hrs.). 1999. 19.98 (AB169) Radio Spirits.

My Favorite Husband: Be a Pal & Husbands are Sloppy Dressers. Perf. by Lucille Ball & Richard Denning. 1 cass. (Running Time: 1 hr.). 2001. 6.98 (2202) Radio Spirits.

My Favorite Husband: Christmas Card Dilemma & The Girls Sneak up on Their Husbands. Perf. by Lucille Ball & Richard Denning. 1 cass. (Running Time: 1 hr.). 2001. 6.98 (2229) Radio Spirits.

My Favorite Husband: George's Mother Visits & Liz & George Reminisce. Perf. by Lucille Ball & Richard Denning. 1 cass. (Running Time: 1 hr.). 2001. 6.98 (2425) Radio Spirits.

My Favorite Husband: Learning to Drive & Is There a Baby in the House? Perf. by Lucille Ball & Richard Denning. 1 cass. (Running Time: 1 hr.). 2001. 6.98 (2265) Radio Spirits.

My Favorite Husband: Liz & Iris with the Same Original Dress & Spring House Cleaning. Perf. by Lucille Ball & Richard Denning. 1 cass. (Running Time: 1 hr.). 2001. 6.98 Radio Spirits.

My Favorite Husband: Liz Has a Portrait Painted & The Kissing Booth. Perf. by Lucille Ball & Richard Denning. 1 cass. (Running Time: 1 hr.). 2001. 6.98 (2043) Radio Spirits.

My Favorite Husband: Liz Sells Dresses & Quiz Show. Perf. by Lucille Ball & Richard Denning. 1 cass. (Running Time: 1 hr.). 2001. 6.98 (2248) Radio Spirits.

My Favorite Husband: Liz Takes up Sculpting & Liz Cooks Dinner for Twelve. Perf. by Lucille Ball & Richard Denning. 1 cass. (Running Time: 1 hr.). 2001. 6.98 (2064) Radio Spirits.

My Favorite Husband: Trying to Cash the Prize Check & Liz has the Flimjabs. Perf. by Lucille Ball & Richard Denning. 1 cass. (Running Time: 1 hr.). 2001. 6.98 (2440) Radio Spirits.

My Favorite Husband Pt. 1 & Pt. 2: Women's Rights. Perf. by Lucille Ball & Richard Denning. 1 cass. (Running Time: 1 hr.). 2001. 6.98 (2466) Radio Spirits.

My Favorite Musical Numbers. Mandy Manley Little. 2001. 15.98 (978-0-9677763-2-3(5)) MVO Records.

My Favorite Songs: Maria Von Trapp's Childhood Folk Songs. Maria Von Trapp. Tr. by Maria Von Trapp. 2009. bk. 19.95 (978-1-932168-73-0(7)) Veritas Pr PA.

My Favorite Stories. Narrated by Dale Bulla. 1 cass. (Running Time: 49 min.). (J). (gr. 3 up). 1992. 9.95 (978-1-884197-03-1(5)) N Horizon Educ.
Three folktales told by Dale Bulla, storyteller. No. 1 The Peddler, No. 2 The Tailor, No. 3 Jack & the Giants.

My Favorite Summer 1956. Mickey Mantle & Phil Pepe. Read by Phil Pepe. 2 cass. (Running Time: 3 hrs.). 1991. 15.95 (978-1-879371-09-5(X), 20130) Pub Mills.
It was 1956, a time of peace & prosperity, of the baby boom & the exodus to suburbia. America liked Ike, but Loved Lucy. And at venerable Yankee Stadium, a young man named Mickey Mantle was having the season of his life. In MY FAVORITE SUMMER, the Mick chronicles that amazing season as only he can. He had as great a season as any professional athlete ever had, anytime, anywhere - in 1956. Mickey Mantle's favorite summer.

My Favourite Goodbye. unabr. ed. Sheila O'Flanagan. Read by Frances Tomelty. 12 cass. (Running Time: 18 hrs.). 2002. 96.95 (978-0-7540-0803-3(7), CAB 2225) AudioGO.

My FBI: Bringing down the Mafia, Investigating Bill Clinton & Fighting the War on Terror. abr. ed. Louis J. Freeh. Narrated by Adam Grupper. 2005. 17.95 (978-1-59397-804-4(9)) Pub: Macmill Audio. Dist(s): Macmillan

My Fears Relieved: 11 Cor.12:8-9; Gal. 6:14. Ed Young. 1988. 4.95 (978-0-7417-1669-9(0), 669) Win Walk.

My Fertility Success. Laurie Morse. 2005. audio compact disk 15.99 (978-0-9767262-1-0(1)) L Morse.

My Fifty Years in the Navy. unabr. collector's ed. Charles C. Clark. Read by John MacDonald. 8 cass. (Running Time: 8 hrs.). 1986. 48.00 (978-0-7366-1005-6(7), 1938) Books on Tape.
Rear Admiral Charles C. Clark commanded the battleship Oregon when she raced from San Francisco to the Caribbean via Cape Horn to join the battle of Santiago in 1898. The voyage was a tremendous achievement. It captured the imagination of the American people & made Clark a hero.

My First Bible in Songs. Kenneth N. Taylor. Illus. by Richard Hook. 1 cass. (J). (ps-1). 1994. Tyndale Hse.

My First Bible Songs. Contrib. by Jean Anne Shafferman & Anna Laura Page. (ENG.). (ps-3). 2003. audio compact disk 29.95 (978-0-7390-3208-4(9)) Alfred Pub.

***My First Bluegrass Guitar Picking Songs Book/CD Set.** Steve Kaufman. (ENG.). 2010. pap. bk. 17.99 (978-0-7866-8213-3(2)) Mel Bay.

My First Book about Jesus. Walter Wangerin, Jr. Read by Joe Ochman. 1 cass. (Running Time: 27 min.). 1987. bk. 9.95 Checkerboard.

My First Day. abr. ed. Music by Eric Hester. 1 CD. (Running Time: 30 mins.). (J). 2002. audio compact disk 12.95 (978-0-9716828-1-8(X)) Pub: My Frst Day Product. Dist(s): Penton Overseas
Buddy Bear comes to life in this CD. Designed to help preschoolers prepare for their first day of preschool and introduce them to the preschool environment.

My First Hymns: Amazing Grace. (J). audio compact disk Provident Mus Dist.

***My First Lullabies.** Created by Twin Sisters. (Wholesome Music for Wholesome Kids Ser.). (ENG.). (J). 2009. audio compact disk (978-1-59922-409-1(7)) Twin Sisters.

***My First Mandolin Picking Songs Book/CD Set.** Steve Kaufman. 2010. pap. bk. 15.99 (978-0-7866-8253-9(1)) Mel Bay.

My First Praise & Worship: Praise Him, Praise Him. (J). audio compact disk Provident Mus Dist.

My First Praise Songs. Contrib. by Anna Laura Page & Jean Anne Shafferman. (ENG.). (ps-3). 2006. audio compact disk 29.95 (978-0-7390-4052-2(9)) Alfred Pub.

My First Sing-Along: Silly Old Bear Songs. 1 cass. (Running Time: 27 min.). (J). pap. bk. 6.38 (DISN 60629) NewSound.
Featuring the songs "Winnie the Pooh," & "Little Rain Cloud". Includes board book.

My First Sing-Along: Tiggerfic Songs. 1 cass. (Running Time: 27 min.). (J). 6.38 (DISN 60630) NewSound.
Features the songs "The Wonderful Thing about Tiggers," & "Up, Down, Touch the Ground". Includes board book.

My First Songs in English see Mis Primeras Canciones en Ingles

My First Spirituals. Contrib. by Jean Anne Shafferman & Anna Laura Page. (ENG.). (ps-3). 2004. audio compact disk 29.95 (978-0-7390-3501-6(0)) Alfred Pub.

***My First Story Reader Sesame Street.** Ed. by Publications International Staff. (J). 2010. 31.98 (978-1-4127-1941-4(0)) Pubns Intl Ltd.

My First 100 Years: A Look Back from the Finish Line. R. Waldo McBurney. Read by R. Waldo McBurney. (ENG.). 2007. audio compact disk 19.00 (978-0-9794672-0-2(9)) AudioBookMan.

My First 46 Years in Television. Betty White. 1 cass. (Running Time: 54 mins.). 2001. 12.95 Smithson Assocs.

My Footprint: Carrying the Weight of the World. abr. unabr. ed. Jeff Garlin. Read by Jeff Garlin. (Running Time: 6 hrs. 30 mins. 0 sec.). (ENG.). 2010. audio compact disk 29.99 (978-0-7435-9736-4(2)) Pub: S&S Audio. Dist(s): S and S Inc

My Foot's in the Stirrup... My Pony Won't Stand. abr. ed. Stephen A. Bly. 2 cass. (Running Time: 3 hrs.). (Code of the West Ser.: No. 5). 2001. 17.99 (978-1-58926-015-3(5)) Oasis Audio.
All Tap & Pepper want is to settle down on a small ranch, get a few cattle and raise a family. But nothing is easy for an ex-convict and former dance-hall girl trying to break with their pasts.

My Foot's in the Stirrup... My Pony Won't Stand. unabr. ed. Stephen A. Bly. Read by Jerry Sciarrio. 6 CDs. (Running Time: 6 hrs. 30 min.). 2001. audio compact disk 39.00 (978-1-58116-123-6(9)) Books in Motion.
Tap's new job as brand inspector places him smack dab in the middle of the worst kind of trouble. But what Tap and Pepper don't realize is that the past and present are about to collide in a strange and powerful way.

My Foot's in the Stirrup... My Pony Won't Stand. unabr. ed. Stephen A. Bly. Read by Jerry Sciarrio. 6 cass. (Running Time: 6 hrs. 30 min.). (Code of the West Ser.: Bk. 5). 2001. 39.95 (978-1-58116-098-7(4)) Books in Motion.

My Freedom. Contrib. by Krystal Meyers. (Mastertrax Ser.). 2008. audio compact disk 9.98 (978-5-557-36650-2(4)) Pt of Grace Ent.

My Friend. Perf. by Jerry Bernard. 1 cass. 10.98 (978-1-57908-430-1(3)); audio compact disk 16.98 (978-1-57908-429-5(X)) Platinm Enter.

My Friend Flicka. unabr. ed. Dave Blossom. Read by Mary Woods. 7 cass. (Running Time: 10 hrs. 30 mins.). (J). 1988. 56.00 (978-0-7366-1427-6(3), 2313) Books on Tape.
Ken, a young daydreamer, baffles his brusque, practical father. His mother tries to bring the two together. What finally closes the gap is Flicka, Ken's beloved filly, his first lesson in the responsibility of growing up.

My Friend Flicka. unabr. ed. Mary O'Hara. Read by Dave Blossom & Michael Louis Wells. (Running Time: 36000 sec.). (J). (gr. 4-7). 2006. audio compact disk 34.95 (978-0-06-089931-8(X), HarperChildAud) HarperCollins Pubs.

***My Friend Flicka.** unabr. ed. Mary O'hara. Read by Michael Louis Wells. (ENG.). 2005. (978-0-06-113057-1(5)); (978-0-06-113058-8(3)) HarperCollins Pubs.

My Friend Fritz see Amigo Fritz

My Friend Fritz. Chatrian Erickman. Read by Yadira Sánchez. (Running Time: 3 hrs.). 2002. 16.95 (978-1-60083-211-6(3), Audiofy Corp) Iofy Corp.

My Friend Irma. Perf. by Marie Wilson. 2 cass. (Running Time: 2 hrs.). 10.95 (978-1-57816-066-2(9), MF2401) Audio File.
Includes: "April 11, 1947" The first program in the series tells how Irma first met her roommate. "February 3, 1952" Irma is writing a column with choice bits of neighborhood gossip. "February 24, 1952" Irma loses Al's friendship ring down the bathroom drain. "April 27, 1954" Irma decides to save her bosses' marriage when she learns that his wife wants a divorce. Set in vinyl album.

My Friend Irma. Perf. by Marie Wilson & Cathy Lewis. (CC4313) Natl Recrd Co.

My Friend Irma. collector's ed. Perf. by Marie Wilson et al. 2001. bk. 34.98 (4430) Radio Spirits.
18 comedy classics.

My Friend Irma: Cub Scout Speech & Psychological Tests. Perf. by Marie Wilson. 1 cass. (Running Time: 1 hr.). 2001. 6.98 (1934) Radio Spirits.

My Friend Irma: Dancing Fools & Double Surprise. Perf. by Marie Wilson. 1 cass. (Running Time: 1 hr.). 2001. 6.98 (2444) Radio Spirits.

My Friend Irma: Dictation System & Jane Quits Her Job. Perf. by Marie Wilson. 1 cass. (Running Time: 1 hr.). 2001. 6.98 (1915) Radio Spirits.

My Friend Irma: Doubles Troubles. Perf. by Marie Wilson. 6 cass. (Running Time: 6 hrs.). 1999. 19.98 (AB257) Radio Spirits.

My Friend Irma: The Reward & The Eyes Have It. Perf. by Marie Wilson. 1 cass. (Running Time: 1 hr.). 2001. 6.98 (2484) Radio Spirits.

My Friend Irma: Women's Club & The Baby. Perf. by Marie Wilson. 1 cass. (Running Time: 1 hr.). 2001. 6.98 (2380) Radio Spirits.

My Friend Justin. unabr. ed. Jennifer A. Conroy. Read by Maynard Villers. 6 cass. (Running Time: 6 hrs. 30 min.). 1996. 39.95 (978-1-55686-731-6(X)) Books in Motion.
Comical fantasy. Danny, a twelve year-old introverted boy, is helped out of his shell by a new adult neighbor, Justin, who becomes Danny's protector. One problem - Justin is a vampire.

My Friend the Professor. Lucilla Andrews. 2 cass. 1985. 24.95 (978-1-85496-016-0(4), 60164) Pub: ISIS Audio GBR. Dist(s): Ulverscroft US

My Friendly Snowman see Grandma Jasmine: The Gifts of Musical Stories

***My Friends.** unabr. ed. Kurt Johnston & Mark Oestreicher. (Running Time: 3 hrs. 24 mins. 0 sec.). (Middle School Survival Ser.). (ENG.). (YA). 2009. 9.99 (978-0-310-77222-4(2)) Zondervan.

My Friends, Audiocassette. Taro Gomi. (Metro Reading Ser.). (J). (gr. k). 2000. 8.46 (978-1-58120-983-9(5)) Metro Teaching.

My Friends Call Me Monster. R. L. Stine. Read by Vinnie Penna. (Running Time: 2 hrs. 33 mins.). (Goosebumps HorrorLand Ser.: No. 7). (J). (gr. 4-7). 2009. 35.00 (978-1-60775-488-6(6)) Find a World.

My Friends Call Me Monster. R. L. Stine. (Goosebumps HorrorLand Ser.: No. 7). (J). (gr. 4-7). 2009. audio compact disk 9.95 (978-0-545-11160-7(9)) Scholastic Inc.

My Friends Call Me Monster. R. L. Stine. Narrated by Vinnie Penna. 2 CDs. (Running Time: 2 hrs. 33 mins.). (Goosebumps HorrorLand Ser.: No. 7). (ENG.). (J). (gr. 4-7). 2009. audio compact disk 29.95 (978-0-545-11941-2(3)) Scholastic Inc.

My Gal Sunday. Mary Higgins Clark. 2004. 15.95 (978-0-7435-4056-8(5)) Pub: S&S Audio. Dist(s): S and S Inc

My Gal Sunday. abr. ed. Mary Higgins Clark. 2 cass. (Running Time: 4 hrs.). 1997. 17.60 (978-0-671-57733-9(6), 908765, Audioworks) S&S Audio.

My Gal Sunday. unabr. ed. Mary Higgins Clark. Read by Mary Peiffer. 6 cass. (Running Time: 6 hrs.). 1997. 36.00 (978-0-913369-55-5(1), 4273) Books on Tape.
The reigning queen of suspense introduces us to her second duo of amateur detectives. This time the formidable couple is none other than Henry Britland IV, a wealthy & worldy ex-President of the United States & his beautiful wife Sunday, a dynamic Congresswoman.

My God & My All. Elizabeth Goudge. 9 cass. (Running Time: 13 hrs. 30 min.). 36.95 (703) Ignatius Pr.
The life of St. Francis of Assisi.

***My god Is so big CD.** Kingsway. (ENG.). 2006. audio compact disk 15.99 (978-92-823-0402-0(7)) Pub: Kingsway Pubns GBR. Dist(s): STL Dist NA

My God, My Country, My Heritage. Mary Galvano. 2007. audio compact disk 15.00 (978-0-9800820-1-2(3)) Galvano Ma.

***My God, My God, Why?** Featuring Arun Andrews. 2009. audio compact disk 6.00 (978-1-61256-004-5(0)) Ravi Zach.

My God Will Hear Me. Elbert Willis. 1 cass. (Running Time: 1 hr.). (Secret to Believing Prayer Ser.). 4.00 Fill the Gap.

My Good Night Christmas: With Read & Sing-along CD. Susan L. Lingo. Illus. by Kathy Parks. (J). 2001. bk. 17.99 (978-0-7847-1205-4(0)) Standard Pub.

My Grandfather, the Cubist. Contrib. by Joy Electric. Prod. by Ronnie Martin. 2008. audio compact disk 13.99 (978-5-557-42226-0(9)) Tooth & Nail.

My Grandfather's Blessing: Stories of Stregth, Refuge, & Belonging. abr. ed. Rachel Naomi Remen. 2004. 10.95 (978-0-7435-4298-2(3)) Pub: S&S Audio. Dist(s): S and S Inc

My Grandfather's House: A Genealogy of Doubt & Faith. unabr. ed. Robert Clark. Narrated by Brian Keeler. 8 cass. (Running Time: 11 hrs. 30 mins.). 2001. 74.00 (978-0-7887-4046-6(6), 96155E7) Recorded Bks.
The author explores mysteries of a different nature in this powerful history of doubt, faith & religious belief.

My Grandfather's Son: A Memoir. unabr. ed. Clarence Thomas. Read by Clarence Thomas. (Running Time: 43200 sec.). 2007. audio compact disk 39.95 (978-0-06-137345-9(1), Harper Audio) HarperCollins Pubs.

My Grandmother's Ghost see Poetry & Voice of James Wright

My Grandmother's Love Letters (poem) see Poetry of Hart Crane

My Guardian Angel. Sylvie Weil. Read by Vanessa Benjamin. (Running Time: 16200 sec.). (J). 2007. 34.95 (978-1-4332-0079-3(1)) Blckstn Audio.

My Guardian Angel. Sylvie Weil. Read by Banessa Benjamin. (Running Time: 16200 sec.). (J). 2007. audio compact disk 36.00 (978-1-4332-0080-9(5)) Blckstn Audio.

My Guardian Angel. Sylvie Weil. Read by Vanessa Benjamin. (Running Time: 16200 sec.). (J). 2007. audio compact disk 19.95 (978-1-4332-0081-6(3)) Blckstn Audio.

My Gun Is Quick. unabr. ed. Mickey Spillane. Read by Larry McKeever. 8 cass. (Running Time: 8 hrs.). (Mike Hammer Ser.). 1991. 48.00 (978-0-7366-2016-1(8), 2832) Books on Tape.
Mike Hammer met her on the wrong side of the tracks. She was young, beautiful & not too far gone - yet. She still had a chance. Mike thought if she just had a little extra money & a caring shoulder she could make it. That night he gave her both. He never even knew her name. The next day, staring up at him from the front page of the newspaper was her face. She was dead, victim of a hit-&-run. But Mike knows better. Someone didn't want her to go straight, to leave "the life." Mike vows to find out who.

***My Halloween Fun Songbook & CD.** Compiled by Elizabeth C. Axford. Des. by Elizabeth C. Axford. (ENG., (J). 2010. spiral bd. 29.95 (978-1-931844-14-7(3)) Pub: Piano Pr. Dist(s): BkWhole

My Haunted House. unabr. ed. Angie Sage. Read by Katherine Kellgren. 6 CDs. (Running Time: 7 hrs.). (Araminta Spookie Ser.: Bk. 1). (J). (gr. 4-6). 2006. audio compact disk 64.75 (978-1-4281-1817-1(9)); 49.75 (978-1-4281-1812-6(8)) Recorded Bks.
Araminta Spookie (or "Minty," if you prefer) lives in a strange ol' house. It's haunted, in fact. You see, Minty's parents went vampire hunting and never came back. And now she lives with her aunt Tabby and uncle Drac (who sleeps hanging upside down). Haunted or not, Minty loves the creepy place. Trouble is, her aunt wants to pull up stakes and move. Aunt Tabby thinks the house is cold and dusty and full of spiders. True enough, but Minty won't give up her home without a fight. All she needs is a little help from a haunted suit of armor and a ghost named Edmund. Then she can carry out the Awful Ambush - and scare away any potential buyers!.

***My Heart-Christ's Home.** Robert Boyd Munger. (Running Time: 1 hr. 42 mins. 0 sec.). (ENG.). 2010. audio compact disk 5.98 (978-1-61045-042-3(6)) christianaud.

My Heart Leaps up When I Behold see Selected Poetry of William Wordsworth

My Heart Rejoices. Randy Smith. 1997. 8.00 (978-0-7673-3172-2(9)); 11.98 (978-0-7673-3169-2(9)); audio compact disk 85.00 (978-0-7673-3171-5(0)) LifeWay Christian.

My Heart Will Go On, Level 1. (Yamaha Clavinova Connection Ser.). 2004. disk 1.04 (978-0-634-09585-6(4)) H Leonard.

My Heartbeat. unabr. ed. Garret Freymann-Weyr. Read by Christy Carlson Romano. 3 cass. (Running Time: 3 hrs. 15 mins.). (J). (gr. 7 up). 2004. 30.00 (978-0-8072-1243-1(1), Listening Lib); audio compact disk 30.00 (978-0-8072-1599-9(6), Listening Lib) Random Audio Pubg.

My Hero: Extraordinary People on the Heroes Who Inspire Them. unabr. ed. My Hero Project Staff. Narrated by Alan Sklar & Ellen Archer. Intro. by Earvin "Magic" Johnson, Jr. (Running Time: 5 hrs. 30 mins. 0 sec.). (ENG.). 2005. audio compact disk 24.99 (978-1-4001-0198-6(0)) Pub: Tantor Media. Dist(s): IngramPubServ

My Hero: Extraordinary People on the Heroes Who Inspire Them. unabr. ed. The My Hero Project. Narrated by Alan Sklar & Ellen Archer. Intro. by Earvin "Magic" Johnson, Jr. (Running Time: 5 hrs. 30 mins. 0 sec.). (ENG.). 2005. audio compact disk 19.99 (978-1-4001-5198-1(8)); audio compact disk 49.99 (978-1-4001-3198-3(7)) Pub: Tantor Media. Dist(s): IngramPubServ

My Hero/Good Friends. Steck-Vaughn Staff. 2002. (978-0-7398-5906-3(4)) SteckVau.

My Horizontal Life: A Collection of One-Night Stands. Chelsea Handler. Read by Cassandra Campbell. (Playaway Adult Nonfiction Ser.). 2009. 49.99 (978-1-60812-533-3(5)) Find a World.

My Horizontal Life: A Collection of One-Night Stands. unabr. ed. Chelsea Handler. Narrated by Cassandra Campbell. 5 CDs. (Running Time: 6 hrs. 30 mins. 0 sec.). (ENG.). 2008. audio compact disk 49.99 (978-1-4001-3826-5(4)); audio compact disk 19.99 (978-1-4001-5826-3(5)); audio compact disk 24.99 (978-1-4001-0826-8(8)) Pub: Tantor Media. Dist(s): IngramPubServ

My Husband. Neville Goddard. 1 cass. (Running Time: 62 min.). 1965. 8.00 (8) J & L Pubns.
Neville taught Imagination Creates Reality. He was a powerfully influential teacher of God as Consciousness.

My Husband's Sweethearts. unabr. ed. Bridget Asher. Read by Carrington MacDuffie. (Running Time: 9 hrs. NaN mins.). 2008. 29.95 (978-1-4332-5525-0(1)) Blckstn Audio.

My Husband's Sweethearts. unabr. ed. Bridget Asher. (Running Time: 9 hrs. 0 mins.). 2009. audio compact disk 24.95 (978-1-4332-5524-3(3)) Blckstn Audio.

My Husband's Sweethearts: A Novel. unabr. ed. Bridget Asher. Read by Carrington MacDuffie. (Running Time: 9 hrs. NaN mins.). 2008. 59.95 (978-1-4332-5522-9(7)); audio compact disk 70.00 (978-1-4332-5523-6(5)) Blckstn Audio.

My Husband's Wife Is Always Right & Spiritual A. D. D. Joni Hilton. 1 cass. 9.98 (978-1-57734-157-4(0), 06005594) Covenant Comms.
Putting the marriage first makes a marriage.

My Invented Country: A Nostalgic Journey Through Chile. unabr. ed. Isabel Allende. Read by Blair Brown.Tr. of Mi Pais Inventado: Un Paseo Nostalgico por Chile. 2003. audio compact disk 29.95 (978-0-06-055927-4(6)) HarperCollins Pubs.

My Island Home. unabr. collector's ed. James Norman Hall. Read by Larry McKeever. 8 cass. (Running Time: 12 hrs.). 1984. 64.00 (978-0-7366-0460-4(X), 1432) Books on Tape.
"My Island Home" is a candid recounting of James Norman Hall's adventures.

My Jewish Discovery. Craig Taubman. 1 cass. (Running Time: 36 min.). (Jewish Discovery Ser.). (J). 1995. 9.98 (UPC 04791000UPC 0479100125); audio compact disk 14.98 (UPC 0479100125) Craig n Co.
Parents Choice Gold Award 1995. Educational & whimsical journey through Jewish culture. Creates an ideal opportunity for families to share & experience the beauty & spirit of Jewish people.

My Journey: From an Iowa Farm to a Cathedral of Dreams. abr. ed. Robert H. Schuller. Read by Tim Jerome. 2001. 25.95 (978-0-694-52647-5(9)) HarperCollins Pubs.

My Journey to Purpose. unabr. ed. Dianthus. 4 cass. (Running Time: 5 hrs. 16 min.). (ENG.). 1998. 19.95 (978-0-9622160-5-3(4)) Dianthus.
Purpose is a choice of direction in living. During an experience at Lourdes, I heard Mary's words, "You will be working with the sick & dying. You will make time for them when you see them." This is my story. Includes album.

***My Journey with Farrah.** unabr. ed. Alana Stewart. Read by Deanna Hurst. (ENG.). 2009. (978-0-06-197406-9(4), Harper Audio); (978-0-06-197737-4(3), Harper Audio) HarperCollins Pubs.

My Kid Is Acting Out & I'm about to Shout! Effective Parenting Made Easy. Rossi Davis. Narrated by Sharon Eisenhour. (ENG.). 2008. audio compact disk 17.95 (978-1-60031-033-1(8)) Spoken Books.

My Kid Is My Guru: Christopher's Wisdom. Short Stories. Mariann Aalda. 1cass. (Running Time: 45 mins.). 2004. audio compact disk 18.95 (978-0-9711867-0-5(7)) PeopleLikeUs.
A Teaching Tale to "warm your heart, nourish your soul, and change your life," written and narrated by actress, author and certified clinical hypnotherapist, Mariann Aalda. This "through the eyes of a child" view of adult self-help, is the first in a series of "relaxation and transformation" CD's intended to have a soothing, yet energizing, affect on the lives of today's modern woman. The stories in the series are all true, and in some way illustrate how the author's son, Christopher, faced dispiriting challenges and disheartening circumstances as a little boy, an adolescent and a young man. They are also a testament to the alchemy of mindful parenting; his mother was his guide, but Christopher was her teacher, and together they grew in wisdom and enlightenment. Tracks include a stress-busting progressive relaxation; a confidence and esteem-building guided imagery, and a study-guide for the enhancement and enrichment of your listening pleasure. This first installmentis is on finding and building...TRUST.

My Kingdom & My Pot of Gold: The Guided Imagery CDs. Pamela M. Goldberg. Illus. by Jimmy Boring. (J). 2008. pap. bk. (978-0-9778941-7-8(7)) Camp MakeBelieve.

My Kinsman, Major Molineux see Great American Short Stories, Vol. II, A Collection

My Kinsman, Major Molineux. unabr. ed. Nathaniel Hawthorne. Read by Walter Covell. 1 cass. (Running Time: 50 min.). 1983. 7.95 (S-50) Jimcin Record.
A man goes to visit his kinsman & encounters some very strange goings-on.

My Kooky Family. (J). 2005. audio compact disk (978-1-933796-14-7(6)) PC Treasures.

***My Korean Deli: Risking It All for a Convenience Store.** unabr. ed. Ben Ryder Howe. (Running Time: 10 hrs. 5 mins.). (ENG.). 2011. 29.95 (978-1-4417-7935-9(3)); audio compact disk 29.95 (978-1-4417-7934-2(5)) Blckstn Audio.

***My Korean Deli: Risking It All for a Convenience Store.** unabr. ed. Ben Ryder Howe. Read by To be Announced. (Running Time: 10 hrs. 5 mins.). (ENG.). 2011. 65.95 (978-1-4417-7932-8(9)); audio compact disk 100.00 (978-1-4417-7933-5(7)) Blckstn Audio.

My Lady Judge. Cora Harrison. 2008. 84.95 (978-1-4079-0092-6(7)); audio compact disk 89.95 (978-1-4079-0093-3(5)) Pub: Soundings Ltd GBR. Dist(s): Ulverscroft US

My Lady Ludlow. Elizabeth Gaskell. Read by Flo Gibson. 5 cass. (Running Time: 7 hrs. 30 min.). 1990. 20.95 (978-1-55685-180-3(4)) Audio Bk Con.
We meet a lady of high principles & prejudice whose kind heart wars & wins over a seemingly unrelenting nature.

My Lady's Money. Wilkie Collins. Read by Jim Killavey. 4 cass. (Running Time: 6 hrs.). 1989. 28.00 (C-70) Jimcin Record.
Victorian mystery novel. Includes album.

My Lady's Money. unabr. collector's ed. Wilkie Collins. Read by Jim Roberts. 6 cass. (Running Time: 6 hrs.). 1982. 36.00 (978-0-7366-3863-0(6), 9070) Books on Tape.
"My Lady's Money" was published in the mid 1800's & is a perfect vignette of its time. The regularity of the era, the sense of place & time & the comfortable circumstances are captured in this reading.

My Last Duchess see Treasury of Robert Browning

My Last Duchess see Classics of English Poetry for the Elementary Curriculum

My Last Duchess see Famous Story Poems

My Latest Grievance. Elinor Lipman. (Running Time: 29100 sec.). (Sound Library). 2006. audio compact disk & audio compact disk 29.95 (978-0-7927-4228-9(1), CMP 959) AudioGO.

My Latest Grievance. unabr. ed. Elinor Lipman. 6 cass. (Running Time: 29100 sec.). (Sound Library). 2006. 54.95 (978-0-7927-4227-2(3), CSL 959); audio compact disk 74.95 (978-0-7927-4053-7(X), SLD 959) AudioGO.

My Lenten Walk with Jesus, Grades 1-3. Francine M. O'Connor. 1 cass. (Running Time: 24 min.). (J). 1991. bk. & tchr. ed. 9.95 (978-0-89243-666-8(2), 80112) Liguori Pubns.
Lectionary-based packets aid primary-grade religious educators in teaching the true meaning of the Lenten season. Text, games & activities. Student Packet includes: Hand-out lessons; activity component. Teacher's Packet includes: Leader's guide; sample set of student hand-out lessons; sample of activity component; audiocassette with guided meditations.

My Lenten Walk with Jesus, Grades 1-3, Cycle C. Francine M. O'Connor. 1 cass. (Running Time: 24 min.). (Cycle C Ser.). (J). 1993. bk. & tchr. ed. 9.95 (978-0-89243-420-6(1), 80110) Liguori Pubns.

My Lenten Walk with Jesus, Grades 1-3, Cycle C. Francine M. O'Connor. 1 cass. (Running Time: 24 min.). (Cycle C Ser.). (J). (gr. 1-3). 1993. bk. & stu. ed. 2.50 (978-0-89243-421-3(X), 80031) Liguori Pubns.

My Lenten Walk with Jesus, Grades 1-3, Cycle A. Francine M. O'Connor. 1 cass. (Cycle A Ser.). (J). (gr. 1-3). 1993. bk. & tchr. ed. 9.95 (978-0-89243-454-1(6), 80113); bk. & stu. ed. 2.50 packet. (978-0-89243-453-4(8), 80034) Liguori Pubns.
Lectionary-based program will help children discover that the Lenten Sunday gospels have a special message just for them. Ideal for Lenten parish & school religion classes. The teacher's packet includes 8-four-page lessons. Audiotape has special guided meditations for the class.

My Lenten Walk with Jesus, Grades 1-3, Cycle B. Francine M. O'Connor. 1 cass. (Running Time: 24 min.). (J). (gr. 1-3). 1991. bk. & stu. ed. 2.50 (978-0-89243-665-1(4), 80033) Liguori Pubns.
Lectionary-based packets aid primary-grade religious educators in teaching the true meaning of the Lenten season. Text, games & activities. Student Packet includes: Hand-out lessons; activity component. Teacher's Packet includes: Leader's guide; sample set of student hand-out lessons; sample of activity component; audiocassette with guided meditations.

My Life. abr. ed. Bill Clinton. Read by Bill Clinton. 4 cass. (Running Time: 6 hrs. 30 mins.). 2004. 45.00 (978-1-4159-0528-9(2)); audio compact disk 45.00 (978-1-4159-0527-2(4)) Books on Tape.
The life of a great national and international figure is told openly, directly, in President Clinton's signature style.

My Life. abr. ed. Bill Clinton. Read by Bill Clinton. 6 CDs. (Running Time: 6 hrs. 30 mins.). (ENG.). 2004. audio compact disk 35.00 (978-0-7393-1706-8(7)) Pub: Random Audio Pubg. Dist(s): Random

My Life. abr. ed. Burt Reynolds. Read by Burt Reynolds. Prod. by Brad Fregger. 4 cass. (Running Time: 5 hrs. 15 min.). 1994. 24.00 (978-1-886392-00-7(5), Parrot Bks) Walberg Pubng.
Burt Reynolds' autobiography recounted with remarkable candor, poignancy & humor, "My Life" is an unforgettable joyride through one of the most exceptional movie careers ever.

My Life, Pt. 1. unabr. collector's ed. Leon Trotsky. Read by Wolfram Kandinsky. 13 cass. (Running Time: 19 hrs. 30 min.). 1994. 104.00 (978-0-7366-2786-3(3)) Books on Tape.
First authoritative account of the rise of the counterrevolutionary Soviet bureaucracy led by Joseph Stalin.

My Life, Pt. 2. collector's ed. Leon Trotsky. Read by Wolfram Kandinsky. 9 cass. (Running Time: 13 hrs. 30 min.). 1994. 72.00 (978-0-7366-2787-0(1)) Books on Tape.

***My Life among the Serial Killers.** abr. ed. Helen Morrison. Read by Helen Morrison. (ENG.). 2004. (978-0-06-081354-3(7), Harper Audio) HarperCollins Pubs.

***My Life among the Serial Killers: Inside the Minds of the World's Most Notorious Murderers.** abr. ed. Helen Morrison. Read by Helen Morrison. (ENG.). 2004. (978-0-06-076415-9(5), Harper Audio) HarperCollins Pubs.

My Life among the Serial Killers: Inside the Minds of the World's Most Notorious Murderers. abr. ed. Helen Morrison. Read by Helen Morrison. Ed. by Allessi. 2004. audio compact disk 29.95 (978-0-06-058683-6(4)) HarperCollins Pubs.

My Life an Offering. Elisabeth Elliot. Read by Elisabeth Elliot. 4 cass. (Running Time: 4 hrs.). 1989. 18.95 (978-0-8474-2009-4(4)) Back to Bible.
Features talks on areas of prayer.

My Life & Creativity. unabr. ed. Frank Barron. 1 cass. 1987. 9.00 (978-1-56964-751-6(8), A0010-87) Sound Photosyn.
The creative Frank Barron gives us an example of his consistent, thorough research that has been developing the definitive body of work in this subject area.

My Life & Death: A Past-Life Interview with Titanic's Designer. Interview. William Barnes & Frank Baranowski. Interview with Linda Nathanson. 4 CDs. (Running Time: 4 hours). 2005. audio compact disk 28.00 (978-1-887010-14-6(9)) Edin Bks.
Regression therapist, Dr. Frank Baranowski, uncovers within William Barnes, the persona of an Irish shipbuilder, Thomas Andrews, who died during one of the most dramatic events of the 20th century and captures one of the most convincing cases of reincarnation ever recorded.

My Life & Hard Times see Thurber Carnival

My Life & Hard Times. unabr. collector's ed. James Thurber. Read by Wolfram Kandinsky. 3 cass. (Running Time: 3 hrs.). 1998. 18.00 (978-0-7366-0231-0(3), 1227) Books on Tape.
James Thurber tells the story of his early life.

My Life & Ministry. Kenneth E. Hagin. 6 cass. 24.00 (36H) Faith Lib Pubns.

***MY LIFE & 1,000 HOUSES: Failing Forward to Financial Freedom, vol. 1.** Independence Day. 2008. 29.99 (978-0-615-30556-1(3)) HomesTwoGo.

My Life as a Fake. Peter Carey. 6 cass. (Running Time: 9 hrs. 45 mins.). 2004. 29.99 (978-1-4025-5600-5(4), 03224) Recorded Bks.

My Life As a Fifth-Grade Comedian. Elizabeth Levy. Read by Johnny Heller. 3 cass. (Running Time: 3 hrs. 45 mins.). (J). 1999. pap. bk. & stu. ed. 41.20 (978-0-7887-3180-8(7), 40915) Recorded Bks.
Class clown Bobby Garrick laughs through every school day. But when he makes a bet not to do homework, the principal threatens to expel him. The only way he can stay is to study & take on an additional assignment: organize a school-wide "laugh-off." Will Bobby be able to get his act together.

My Life As a Fifth-Grade Comedian, Elizabeth Levy. Read by Johnny Heller. 3 cass. (Running Time: 3 hrs. 45 mins.). (J). 1999. stu. ed. 98.30 (978-0-7887-3226-3(9), 46882) Recorded Bks.

My Life As a Fifth-Grade Comedian. unabr. ed. Elizabeth Levy. Narrated by Johnny Heller. 3 pieces. (Running Time: 3 hrs. 45 mins.). (gr. 4 up). 1999. 28.00 (978-0-7887-3135-8(1), 95801E7) Recorded Bks.

My Life as a Man. unabr. ed. Philip Roth. Read by Dan John Miller. (Running Time: 12 hrs.). 2010. 39.97 (978-1-4418-0542-3(7), 9781441805423, Brlnc Audio MP3 Lib); 39.97 (978-1-4418-0544-7(3), 9781441805447, BADLE); 24.99 (978-1-4418-0541-6(9), 9781441805416, Brilliance MP3); 24.99 (978-1-4418-0543-0(5), 9781441805430, BAD); audio compact disk 29.99 (978-1-4418-0539-3(7), 9781441805393, Bril Audio CD Unabri); audio compact disk 92.97 (978-1-4418-0540-9(0), 9781441805409, BriAudCD Unabrid) Brilliance Audio.

***My Life as a Russian Novel: A Memoir.** unabr. ed. Emmanuel Carrere. (Running Time: 9 hrs. 30 mins.). 2010. 16.99 (978-1-4001-8848-2(2)) Tantor Media.

***My Life as a Russian Novel: A Memoir.** unabr. ed. Emmanuel Carrere. Narrated by Simon Vance. (Running Time: 8 hrs. 0 mins. 0 sec.). 2010. 24.99 (978-1-4001-6848-4(1)); audio compact disk 34.99 (978-1-4001-1848-9(4)); audio compact disk 83.99 (978-1-4001-4848-6(0)) Pub: Tantor Media. Dist(s): IngramPubServ

My Life As a Seer: The Lost Memoirs, abr. ed. Edgar Cayce. 2 cass. (Running Time: 3 hrs.). 1999. 17.95 (978-1-55935-304-5(X)) Soundelux.
When Cayce's longtime secretary died three years ago, an amazing discovery was found among her records. Edgar Cayce had, many years ago, worked on a memoir of his life. Now, Cayce tells his story - in his own words.

My Life As a Seer: The Lost Memoirs. unabr. ed. Edgar Cayce. Read by Edward Lewis. 10 cass. (Running Time: 15 hrs.). 2000. 60.00 (5167) Books on Tape.
A recent discovered memoir of the world-renowned psychic healer. Here he speaks once more & gives us his ultimate message to humanity.

My Life As A Traitor. unabr. ed. Zarah Ghahramani & Robert Hillman. Read by Marjanne Doree. (YA). 2008. 64.99 (978-1-60514-903-5(9)) Find a World.

My Life as a Traitor: A Story of Courage & Survival in Tehran's Brutal Evin Prison. unabr. ed. Zarah Ghahramani. 7 CDs. (Running Time: 8 hrs.). 2008. audio compact disk 74.95 (978-0-7927-5264-6(3)) AudioGO.
Zarah Ghahramani was born in Tehran in 1981, two years after Ayatollah Khomeini returned to Iran to establish the Islamic Republic. Her life changed suddenly in 2001 when, after having taken part in student demonstrations, she was arrested (literally snatched off the street by secret police) and charged with "inciting crimes against the people of the Islamic Republic of Iran." While imprisoned in Tehran's notorious Evin Prison she faced brutal interrogation: her head was shaved, and she was beaten. After being released, she was forbidden to return to university, and soon realized that she had no future in her native land. Robert Hillman, an Australian writer, met and befriended Zarah in Iran in 2003, and helped her to escape to Australia, where she now has permanent residency. My Life As a Traitor is a beautifully written memoir of Zarah's life in Iran, revealing the human face behind the turmoil of the modern Middle East.

My Life as a 10-Year-Old Boy! Nancy Cartwright. Read by Nancy Cartwright. (Running Time: 6 hrs.). 2004. 26.95 (978-1-59912-552-7(8)) Iofy Corp.

My Life As a 10-Year-Old Boy. unabr. ed. Nancy Cartwright. Read by Nancy Cartwright. 20 cass. (Running Time: 6 hrs.). 2004. reel tape 27.95 (978-0-7861-2830-3(5), E3355); audio compact disk 29.95 (978-0-7861-8383-8(7), ZE3355); audio compact disk 24.95 (978-0-7861-8409-5(4), 3355) Blckstn Audio.

My Life As a 10yr Old Boy. Nancy Cartwright. 5 cass. (Running Time: 6 hrs.). 2002. 39.95 (978-0-7861-2864-8(X), 3355) Blckstn Audio.

My Life as an Experiment: One Man's Humble Quest to Improve Himself. unabr. ed. A. J. Jacobs. Read by A. J. Jacobs. 6 CDs. (Running Time: 6 hrs. 30 mins. 0 sec.). (ENG.). 2009. audio compact disk 29.99 (978-0-7435-9874-3(1)) Pub: S&S Audio. Dist(s): S and S Inc

My Life Closed Twice Before Its Close see Poems & Letters of Emily Dickinson

My Life Flows On: Sounds of Comfort & Hope. Contrib. by Rob Glover & Elliot Wimbush. 2008. audio compact disk 17.00 (978-1-58459-405-5(5)) Wrld Lib Pubns.

***My Life in Dog Years.** unabr. ed. Gary Paulsen. (Running Time: 3 hrs.). 2011. 12.99 (978-1-4558-0174-9(7), 9781455801749, BAD); 39.97 (978-1-4558-0175-6(5), 9781455801756, BADLE); 12.99 (978-1-4558-0172-5(0), 9781455801725, Brilliance MP3); 39.97 (978-1-4558-0173-2(9), 9781455801732, Brlnc Audio MP3 Lib); audio compact disk 12.99 (978-1-4558-0170-1(4), 9781455801701, Bril Audio CD Unabri); audio compact disk 39.97 (978-1-4558-0171-8(2), 9781455801718, BriAudCD Unabrid) Brilliance Audio.

My Life in France. abr. ed. Julia Child & Alex Prud'homme. Read by Flo Salant Greenberg. 4 CDs. (Running Time: 18000 sec.). (ENG.). 2006. audio compact disk 28.00 (978-0-7393-2526-1(4), Random AudioBks) Pub: Random Audio Pubg. Dist(s): Random

***My Life in the Middle Ages: A Survivor's Tale.** abr. ed. James Atlas. Read by James Atlas. (ENG.). 2005. (978-0-06-083935-2(X), Harper Audio); (978-0-06-083934-5(1), Harper Audio) HarperCollins Pubs.

My Life in the Middle Ages: A Survivor's Tale. unabr. ed. James Atlas. Read by James Atlas. 2005. audio compact disk 29.95 (978-0-06-076334-3(5)) HarperCollins Pubs.

***My Life, My Way.** abr. ed. Cliff Richard. (Running Time: 2 hrs. 24 mins.). (ENG.). 2009. audio compact disk 26.95 (978-1-4055-0537-6(0)) Pub: Little BrownUK GBR. Dist(s): IPG Chicago

My Life on a Hillside Allotment. Terry Walton. 2008. 61.95 (978-1-84559-883-9(0)); audio compact disk 79.95 (978-1-84559-884-6(9)) Pub: Soundings Ltd GBR. Dist(s): Ulverscroft US

My Life on a Plate. India Knight. Narrated by Jill Tanner. 7 CDs. (Running Time: 8 hrs. 30 mins.). 2000. audio compact disk 74.75 (978-1-4025-4048-6(5)) Recorded Bks.

My Life on a Plate. unabr. ed. India Knight. Narrated by Jill Tanner. 6 cass. (Running Time: 8 hrs. 30 mins.). 2002. 59.75 (978-1-4025-3190-3(7)) Recorded Bks.
Skewers the myths of marriage and happiness with gleeful accuracy. Written by a colunmist for London's Sunday Times, it is the story of 33-year-old wife and mother Clara Hutt. Her search for fulfillment in a les than- perfect life is filled with sharp wit and brilliant insight.

My Life on a Plate. unabr. ed. India Knight. Narrated by Jill Tanner. 6 cass. (Running Time: 8 hrs. 30 mins.). 2002. 34.95 (978-1-4025-3191-0(5), RG203) Recorded Bks.
This hilarious novel skewers the myths of marriage and happiness with gleeful accuracy. Written by a colunmist for London's Sunday Times, it is the story of 33-year-old wife and mother Clara Hutt. Her search for fulfillment in a lessthan- perfect life is filled with sharp wit and brilliant insight.

My Life on the Rock. Jeff Cavins. 6 CDs. (Running Time: 6 hrs.). 2001. audio compact disk 34.95 (978-1-57058-507-4(5), rc11-cd) St Joseph Communs.
?Jeff Cavins? spiritual pilgrimage is quickly becoming one of the most well known and inspiring stories of our time. We are all searching for meaning in our lives. Where did we come from, who are we, and what is the goal of life? In short, we are all in search for the narrative thread of our lives. My Life On The Rock is the story of one man?s quest for that narrative thread. How Jeff found it will not only inspire you, but also help equip you to be a better witness to others.?Bishop Robert Carlson (Diocese of Sioux Falls, SD)?I have been asked manny times to recommend a book or tape to give to a loved one who has left the Catholic Church. My Life On The Rock is definitely on my recommendation list. What makes Jeff?s story so appealing is that it deals with both the theological and emotional issues related to returning to the Catholic Church.?Bishop Paul V. Dudley (Retired, Diocese of Sioux Falls, SD)?Jeff?s conversion story is an inspiration for any Christian who longs to be faithful to God?s Word. Read how Jeff re-discovered the Catholic Church as the only context in which the Bible truly comes to life... You?ll be glad you did!?Scott Hahn, Ph. D.

My Life So Far. unabr. ed. Jane Fonda. Read by Jane Fonda. 18 CDs. (Running Time: 22 hrs.). 2005. audio compact disk 144.00 (978-1-4159-2129-6(6)); 120.00 (978-1-4159-1999-6(2)) Books on Tape.
Actress and activist Fonda has been on the Hollywood comeback trail in the past year, but her autobiography is about so much more than her recent or most infamous achievements. Broken into three parts, or acts, the book recounts her tumultuous childhood with her distant and judgmental father, Henry Fonda, and the brief amount of time she spent with her troubled mother, who committed suicide when Jane was 12 years old. In the midst of this, there was a possible molestation, a series of stepmothers, crosscountry moves, and a laundry list of physical ailments. In act two, Fonda details her marriages, her Vietnam activism, her career, her children, and her decades-long struggle with eating disorders. Moving in to act three, her sixties and beyond, the author describes the contentment, self-awareness, and healing that have come with age and wisdom.

My Life So Far: An Evening with Andy Andrews. As told by Andy Andrews. 2003. audio compact disk 16.95 (978-0-9776246-5-2(X)) Lightning Crown Pub.

My Life Story - Australian Version. Bridget Betts & Afshan Ahmad. Information Plus. (YA). 2007. cass. & cd-rom 59.00 (978-1-933848-05-1(7)) NW Media.

My Life Story- North American Version. Bridget Betts & Afshan Ahman. Prod. by Northwest Media. (YA). 2006. audio compact disk 59.00 (978-1-933848-04-4(9)) NW Media.
A major task of life story work is preparing the child for new relationships and to minimise the trauma of transitions. Until a child has made some sense of their past, they may not be able to make sense of their future. My Life Story provides a framework for recording information. Children can take some control, and choose where to start, and it is a tool that can be easily used by both teachers and caregivers.This animated CD-Rom goes beyond just recording facts of a child's life. It includes more than 40 interactive activities aimed at helping young people think and talk about what has happened to them in their life journey, how they see themselves now, and what their hopes, fears, wishes and dreams are for the future.

My Life, the Story of Robert E. Harrill-the Fort Fisher Hermit. Scripts. Michael Edwards. 1. (Running Time: 45 min.). Dramatization. 1995. audio compact disk 12.95 (978-0-9720952-3-5(3)) Michael Edwards.
Based on the life and death of one of North Carolina's most notorious and controversial individuals. Robert Harrill had been a failure most of his life, then at age 62, he started over on the shores of the Cape Fear (Fort Fisher) and became a huge success as a "hermit".

My Life with the Chimpanzees. abr. ed. Jane Goodall. 2 cass. (Running Time: 3 hrs.). 2001. 17.98 (978-1-57042-707-7(0)) Hachet Audio.

My Life with the Chimpanzees. abr. ed. Jane Goodall. (ENG.). 2005. 14.98 (978-1-59483-438-7(5)) Pub: Hachet Audio. Dist(s): HachBkGrp

***My Life with the Lincolns.** unabr. ed. Gayle Brandeis. Narrated by Emily Janice Card. 6 CDs. (Running Time: 6 hrs. 36 mins.). (YA). (gr. 5-8). 2010. audio compact disk 50.00 (978-0-307-71038-3(6), Listening Lib) Pub: Random Audio Pubg. Dist(s): Random

My Life with the Lincolns. unabr. ed. Gayle Brandeis. Read by Emily Janice Card. (J). (gr. 5). 2010. audio compact disk 34.00 (978-0-307-71036-9(X), Listening Lib) Pub: Random Audio Pubg. Dist(s): Random

***My Life with the Saints.** James Martin. Read by James Martin. 2010. audio compact disk 39.95 (978-0-86716-953-9(2)) St Anthony Mess Pr.

My Life with the Wave. unabr. ed. Catherine Cowan. Narrated by Johnny Heller. Based on a story by Octavio Paz. 1 cass. (Running Time: 15 mins.). (gr. k up). 1998. 10.00 (978-0-7887-1956-1(4), 95351E7) Recorded Bks.
On his first trip to the seashore, a shimmering wave pleads to go home with him. But her moods are changeable as the foaming tide. What's a boy to do with a naughty wave.

My Life with the Wave. unabr. ed. Catherine Cowan. Read by Johnny Heller. 1 cass. (Running Time: 15 min.). (J). (gr. 2). 1998. 32.75 (978-0-7887-1960-8(2), 40661); 189.50 (978-0-7887-2763-4(X), 46362) Recorded Bks.
On his first trip to the seashore, a young boy makes friends with a shimmering wave. Class set.

My Lips Will Praise You. 2000. 75.00 (978-0-633-00535-1(5)); 11.98 (978-0-633-00531-3(2)); audio compact disk 85.00 (978-0-633-00527-6(4)); audio compact disk 16.98 (978-0-633-00523-8(1)) LifeWay Christian.

My Little House Songbook & Tape. Perf. by Rosemary Killen. Adapted by Laura Ingalls Wilder. Illus. by Holly Jones. (Running Time: 15 min.). (J). 12.95 (HarperChildAud) HarperCollins Pubs.

My Little Sister & Other Poems. unabr. ed. Abba Kovner. Read by Abba Kover. 1 cass. (Running Time: 59 min.). (Watershed Tapes of Contemporary Poetry). 1980. 12.95 (23644) J Norton Pubs.
Israeli poet reads his work in Hewbrew & his colleague Shirley Kaufman reads her translations of the same poems in English.

My Lobotomy: A Memoir. unabr. ed. Howard Dully & Charles Fleming. Read by Johnny Heller. (YA). 2008. 59.99 (978-1-60514-965-3(9)) Find a World.

My Lobotomy: A Memoir. unabr. ed. Howard Dully & Charles Fleming. Narrated by Johnny Heller. 7 CDs. (Running Time: 9 hrs. 0 mins. 0 sec.). (ENG.). 2007. audio compact disk 34.99 (978-1-4001-0536-6(6)) Pub: Tantor Media. Dist(s): IngramPubServ

My Lobotomy: A Memoir. unabr. ed. Howard Dully & Charles Fleming. Read by Johnny Heller. (Running Time: 9 hrs. 0 mins. 0 sec.). (ENG.). 2007. audio compact disk 69.99 (978-1-4001-3536-3(2)); audio compact disk 24.99 (978-1-4001-5536-1(3)) Pub: Tantor Media. Dist(s): IngramPubServ

My Lord & My God: Thomas Meets the Risen Christ (From the Gospel of John & the Psalms) Bert Polman. (Running Time: 30 mins.). (Scripture Alive Ser.). 1998. 15.95 (978-1-56212-336-9(X), 415102) FaithAliveChr.

My Lord John, unabr. ed. Georgette Heyer. Read by Edmund Dehn. 12 cass. (Running Time: 18 hrs.). 1999. 94.95 (978-0-7531-0477-4(6), 981003) Pub: ISIS Audio GBR. Dist(s): Ulverscroft US
Deposed by Henry Bolingbrooke, Richard II has died mysteriously. Bolingbroke has become Henry IV & must now consolidate his hold on the throne & country, threatened by a host of enemies - the french, Welsh rebels, Scottish raiders & most dangerously by his own vassals.

My Losing Season: A Memoir. Pat Conroy. Read by Chuck Montgomery. 2002. audio compact disk 112.00 (978-0-7366-8834-5(X)) Books on Tape.

My Losing Season: A Memoir. unabr. ed. Pat Conroy. Read by O. Sanders. 9 cass. (Running Time: 13 hrs. 30 mins.). 2002. 88.00 (978-0-7366-8833-8(1)) Books on Tape.
Pat Conroy's true story of his college basketball team, and the way he learned from its defeats.

***My Lost Daughter.** unabr. ed. Nancy Taylor Rosenberg. Narrated by Coleen Marlo. (Running Time: 15 hrs. 30 mins. 0 sec.). 2010. 29.99 (978-1-4001-6970-2(4)); 20.99 (978-1-4001-8970-0(5)); audio compact disk 39.99 (978-1-4001-1970-7(7)) Pub: Tantor Media. Dist(s): IngramPubServ

***My Lost Daughter (Library Edition)** unabr. ed. Nancy Taylor Rosenberg. Narrated by Coleen Marlo. (Running Time: 15 hrs. 30 mins. 0 sec.). 2010. audio compact disk 95.99 (978-1-4001-4970-4(3)) Pub: Tantor Media. Dist(s): IngramPubServ

My Louisiana Sky. Kimberly Willis Holt. Read by Judith Ivey. 3 cass. (Running Time: 4 hrs. 10 mins.). (J). 2000. 24.00 (978-0-7366-9009-6(3)) Books on Tape.
Set in Louisiana in the 1950s this explores a 12-year-old girl's struggle to accept her grandmother's death & the changing world around her.

My Louisiana Sky. unabr. ed. Kimberly Willis Holt. Read by Judith Ivey. 3 vols. (Running Time: 4 hrs. 6 mins.). (J). (gr. 5-9). 2004. pap. bk. 36.00 (978-0-8072-8290-8(1), YA152SP, Listening Lib); 30.00 (978-0-8072-8289-2(8), LL0184, Listening Lib) Random Audio Pubg.
Set in Louisiana in the 1950s, this tender novel explores a 12-year-old girl's struggle to accept her grandmother's death & the changing world around her.

My Love for Layne. A. J. Spencer, 1st. (ENG.). 2008. audio compact disk 12.99 (978-0-9755851-0-8(X)) A Eanes.

My Love Is Wandering. Barrie Konicov. 1 cass. 11.98 (978-0-87082-363-3(9), 087) Potentials.
The author has designed this program with the impact of the situation, to heal the separation & transform the relationship of the listener.

My Lucky Day. Keiko Kasza. (J). (gr. k-3). 2006. bk. 29.95 (978-0-8045-4136-7(1), SACD4136); bk. (978-0-8045-6937-8(1), SAC6937) Spoken Arts.
When a delicious-looking piglet knocks on Mr. Fox's door by mistake, the fox can hardly believe his good luck. It's not everyday that dinner just shows up on your doorstep. Or is it? Could it be that "dinner" is a whole lot smarter than it looks?.

***My Lucky Life in & Out of Show Business: A Memoir.** unabr. ed. Dick Van Dyke. (ENG.). 2011. audio compact disk 35.00 (978-0-307-91429-3(1), Random AudioBks) Pub: Random Audio Pubg. Dist(s): Random

My Mama Had a Dancing Heart. Libba Moore Gray. Illus. by Raúl Colón. 41 vols. (Running Time: 8 mins.). 2001. pap. bk. 35.95 (978-1-59112-543-3(X)); 9.95 (978-0-87499-738-5(0)); audio compact disk 12.95 (978-1-59112-319-4(4)) Live Oak Media.

My Mama Had a Dancing Heart. abr. ed. Libba Moore Gray. 1 cass. (Running Time: 8 mins.). (J). (ps-2). 2001. bk. 25.95 (978-0-87499-740-8(2)); pap. bk. 33.95 (978-0-87499-741-5(0)) Live Oak Media.
My mama had a dancing heart / and she shared that heart with me." So begins a picture book whose beauty is both in the words, stitched together like an heirloom quilt, and in the art, a magical collection of paintings that captures the love found in the best mother-daughter relationships.

My Mama Had a Dancing Heart. abr. ed. Libba Moore Gray. Read by Bonnie Kelly-Young. Illus. by Raúl Colón. 11 vols. (Running Time: 8 mins.). (J). (ps-2). 2001. pap. bk. 16.95 (978-0-87499-739-2(9)) Pub: Live Oak Media. Dist(s): AudioGO
The love between a mother and daughter, recalled in memories of the joy they shared for dance and for life - and the magic it brought them.

My Mama Says There Aren't Any Zombies, Ghosts, Vampires, Creatures, Demons, Monsters, Fiends, Goblins, or Things see Alexander & the Terrible, Horrible, No Good, Very Bad Day

My Mama Was a Train. Perf. by James Coffey. 1 cass. 2002. 9.95; audio compact disk 14.95 Blue Vision Music.

My Man Jeeves. Short Stories. P. G. Wodehouse. Narrated by P. G. Wodehouse. Narrated by David Thorn. Engineer David Thorn & Bobbie Frohman. Music by Hans Bisner. 4 CDs. (Running Time: 5 hrs.). (Jeeves & Wooster Ser.). 2007. audio compact disk (978-0-9787553-8-6(3)) Alcazar AudioWorks.

My Man Jeeves. P. G. Wodehouse. Read by Simon Prebble. (Running Time: 18000 sec.). (Jeeves & Wooster Ser.). 2006. 34.95 (978-0-7861-4507-2(2)); audio compact disk 36.00 (978-0-7861-7197-2(9)) Blckstn Audio.

My Man Jeeves. unabr. ed. P. G. Wodehouse. Read by Martin Jarvis. 3 cass. (Running Time: 3 hrs. 30 min.). (Jeeves & Wooster Ser.). 2002. 21.95 (978-1-57270-286-8(9), Audio Editions) Pub: Audio Partners. Dist(s): PerseuPGW
This hilarious collection featuring the inimitable manservent Jeeves and his twit of an employer, Bertie Wooster.

My Man Jeeves. unabr. ed. P. G. Wodehouse. Read by Martin Jarvis. 4 CDs. (Running Time: 3 hrs. 30 min.). (Jeeves & Wooster Ser.). (ENG.). 2002. audio compact disk 25.95 (978-1-57270-287-5(7)) Pub: AudioGO. Dist(s): Perseus Dist

My Man Jeeves. unabr. ed. P. G. Wodehouse. Read by Simon Prebble. (Running Time: 18000 sec.). (Jeeves & Wooster Ser.). 2006. audio compact disk 19.95 (978-0-7861-7656-4(3)) Blckstn Audio.

My Mom Travels a Lot. Caroline Feller Bauer. 1 read-along cass. (Running Time: 5 min.). (J). 1982. 9.95 Live Oak Media.
This zeroes in on the "problem" of a working mom who travels a lot.

***My Mommy Hung the Moon: A Love Story.** unabr. ed. Jamie Lee Curtis. Read by Jamie Lee Curtis. Illus. by Laura Cornell. 2010. (978-0-06-204190-6(8)); (978-0-06-199675-7(0)) HarperCollins Pubs.

My Mommy's an Angel! l.t. ed. Amy H. Tan. Narrated by Amy H. Tan. Illus. by Mariam Tan. (Angel Ser.). (J). 2002. bk. 18.95 (978-0-9717299-0-2(5)) JeaMei Pubng.

My Mommy's Having a Baby. Gloria Shelley. Perf. by Trisha Shelley & Joey Shelley. 1 cass. (Running Time: 23 min.). Dramatization. (J). (ps-3). 1997. pap. bk. 12.95 (978-0-9659094-0-2(9)) Growing Up Great.
Molly & Joey are good friends both waiting for their moms to have a baby. Together they sing their way into your child's heart as they explore the changes that occur while preparing and then adjusting to the addition of a new baby into the family. Ten original songs plus activity book containing words to the songs. Packaging is designed to become a crib decoration with the proud new sibling's picture.

My Mother Is. Byron Katie. 1 CD. (Running Time: 66 mins). 2004. audio compact disk 15.00 (978-1-890246-16-7(6)); 12.00 (978-1-890246-19-8(0)) B Katie Int Inc.
What part of your body do you feel frustrated by or want to change? On this program, a woman investigates the size of her breasts and how it affects her relationship; a man does The Work on his penis's sexual performance, and a woman confronts her belief that her body is damaged.

My Mother My Child. Susie Kinslow Adams. 2006. audio compact disk 19.99 (978-1-59886-667-4(2)) Tate Pubng.

My Mother's Betrothal. Shih Hu. Ed. by Mary Rouse. 1 cass. (Running Time: 1 hr.). 1946. 8.95 (978-0-88710-051-2(1)) Yale Far Eastern Pubns.
Includes materials.

My Mother's House see Chateau de Ma Mere

My Name & I see Robert Graves Reads from His Poetry & the White Goddess

My Name Is Asher Lev. Chaim Potok. 2003. audio compact disk 30.95 (978-1-893079-31-1(7)) Jewish Contempry Classics.

My Name Is Cheech, the School Bus Driver. Cheech Marin. 1 cass. (Running Time: 1 hr.). (J). 6.38 (SME 63452); audio compact disk 9.58 (SME 63452) NewSound.
A collection of rhythms & sounds based upon the South American cumbia, which sounds like Southern California Samba meets Tex-Mex Reggae.

My Name Is Cheech, the School Bus Driver. Perf. by Cheech Marin. 1 cass. (Running Time: 40 min.). (J). 1997. 11.98 (Sony Wonder) Sony Music Ent.

My Name Is Cheech, the School Bus Driver. Perf. by Cheech Marin. 1 cass. (Running Time: 1 hr.). (J). (ps up). 1997. 7.98 (Sony Wonder); audio compact disk 11.98 Sony Music Ent.
Takes a turn at making the kids laugh, Teaches how to mix & use colors, shows how math can be fun & gives a quick lesson in language with Latin inspired songs that speak directly to kids in an intelligent way that is upbeat & educational at the same time. Spanish version.

My Name Is John, Thomas Eno. 2 cass. 2004. 11.98 (978-1-55503-779-6(8), 07001096) Covenant Comms.
A New Testament novel for our time.

My Name Is Legion. Mark Chironna. 4 cass. 1992. 25.00 (978-1-56043-917-2(3)) Destiny Image Pubs.

My Name is Lyle. 1 cass. (Running Time: 35 min.). (J). (gr. 4-7). 1997. 9.95; audio compact disk 14.95 Rounder Kids Mus Dist.
Includes lyrics.

***My Name Is Mary Sutter.** Robin Oliveira. Contrib. by Kimberly Farr. (Running Time: 15 hrs.). (ENG.). 2010. audio compact disk 39.95 (978-0-14-242813-9(2), PengAudBks) Penguin Grp USA.

My Name Is Memory. unabr. ed. Ann Brashares. 9 CDs. (Running Time: 11 hrs.). (ENG.). 2010. audio compact disk 39.95 (978-0-14-242782-8(9), PengAudBks) Penguin Grp USA.

My Name Is Red. unabr. ed. Orhan Pamuk. Read by John Lee. Tr. by Erdag M. Göknar. 16 CDs. (Running Time: 20 hrs. 30 mins.). 2008. audio compact disk 39.95 (978-0-7393-6924-1(5), Random AudioBks) Pub: Random Audio Pubg. Dist(s): Random

***My Name Is Russell Fink.** unabr. ed. Michael Snyder. (Running Time: 9 hrs. 29 mins. 0 sec.). (ENG.). 2009. 12.99 (978-0-310-77216-3(8)) Zondervan.

My Name Is Will: A Novel of Sex, Drugs, & Shakespeare. unabr. ed. Jess Winfield. Read by Jess Winfield. (Running Time: 8 hrs.). (ENG.). 2009. 19.98 (978-1-60024-934-1(5)) Pub: Hachet Audio. Dist(s): HachBkGrp

My Neck of the Woods: The Lewis Families of Southeastern North Carolina & Northeastern South Carolina. J. D. Lewis. 2005. pap. bk. 59.95 (978-0-8063-5145-2(4), 9739) Pub: Clearfield Co. Dist(s): Genealog Pub

***My Nest Isn't Empty, It Just Has More Closet Space: The Amazing Adventures of an Ordinary Woman.** unabr. ed. Lisa Scottoline & Francesca Scottoline Serritella. 5 CDs. (Running Time: 6 hrs.). (ENG.). 2010. audio compact disk 24.99 (978-1-4272-1089-0(6)) Pub: Macmill Audio. Dist(s): Macmillan

My New Friend. Patricia D. Martin. (J). 2009. pap. bk. 8.99 (978-1-60799-182-3(9)) Tate Pubng.

My New York. unabr. ed. Kathy Jakobsen. 1 cass. (Running Time: 8 min.). (J). (gr. k-4). 1994. bk. 27.90 (978-0-8045-6830-2(8), 6830) Spoken Arts.
Travel to the Central Park Zoo, Chinatown and the Museum of Natural History. Ride the ferry to the Statue of Liberty and Ellis Island. New York City comes to life through the richly detailed art.

My Newish Jewish Discovery. Craig Taubman. Read by Ed Asner. 1 cass. (Running Time: 40 min.). (Jewish Discovery Ser.). (J). (ps-2). 1997. 9.98; audio compact disk 14.98 Craig n Co.
Received Parent's Choice Gold Award 1998.

***My Next Promotion Comes with Honor, vol. 1.** Mason Betha. (ENG.). 2005. audio compact disk 24.00 (978-1-60989-005-6(1)) Born To Succee.

My Nine Lives by Clio. Marjorie Priceman. 1 cass. (Running Time: 15 min.). (J). 2001. bk. 26.95 (978-0-8045-6866-1(9), 6866) Spoken Arts.
This is the authentic journal of Clio, a cat. She's lived through critical points in history and shaped its course. Study guide included.

My November Guest see Robert Frost Reads

My Old Man & the Sea, unabr. ed. David Hays & Daniel Hays. Narrated by George Guidall & Jeff Woodman. 6 cass. (Running Time: 7 hrs. 45 mins.). 51.00 (978-0-7887-0464-2(8), 94657E7) Recorded Bks.
In this classic tale of true-life adventure, a father & son sail 17,000-miles from Connecticut to Cape Horn & back. It is also the story of conquering inner struggles as well as great distances. Available to libraries only.

My Old School Teacher. Short Stories. (5122) Am Audio Prose.

My One Hundred Adventures. unabr. ed. Polly Horvath. Read by Tai Alexandra Ricci. (ENG.). (J). (gr. 1). 2008. audio compact disk 30.00 (978-0-7393-7162-6(2), Listening Lib) Pub: Random Audio Pubg. Dist(s): Random

My One Hundred Adventures. unabr. ed. Polly Horvath. Read by Tai Alexandra Ricci. 5 CDs. (Running Time: 5 hrs. 29 mins.). (J). (ps-3). 2008. audio compact disk 45.00 (978-0-7393-7164-0(9), Listening Lib) Pub: Random Audio Pubg. Dist(s): Random

My Own Business. (YA). 2009. cd-rom (978-0-9818766-1-0(7)) My Business.

My Own Ten Rules for a Happy Marriage see Thurber Country

My Papa's Waltz see Twentieth-Century Poetry in English, No. 29, Recordings of Poets Reading Their Own Poetry

My Parent's Bedroom (A Story from Say You're One of Them) unabr. ed. Uwem Akpan. Read by Robin Miles. (Running Time: 1 hr.). (ENG.). 2008. 3.98 (978-1-60024-303-5(7)) Pub: Hachet Audio. Dist(s): HachBkGrp

***My Parents Give My Bedroom to a Biker: A Story from Guys Read: Funny Business.** unabr. ed. Paul Feig. (ENG.). 2010. (978-0-06-202769-6(7)); (978-0-06-206249-9(2)) HarperCollins Pubs.

My Parents Kept Me from Children Who Were Rough. Poems. Stephen Spender. (J). (CDL5 1237) HarperCollins Pubs.

My Parents, Myself. Barrie Konicov. 1 cass. (Running Time: 1 hr.). 11.98 (978-0-87082-348-0(5), 088) Potentials.
The author talks about animosity between parents & their children, why some parents either cannot or will not let go of their children & why some children just will not break free of their parents. He then explains that unless you are not free of your parents, your life will never be your own.

My Payoffs for Feeling Inadequate & Great Expectations. 1 cass. (Overcoming Roadblocks in Recovery Ser.). 1984. 8.95 (1527G) Hazelden.

My Personal Journey & Professional Career. Carol O'Connell. 1 cass. (Running Time: 1 hr.). 9.00 (A0208-87) Sound Photosyn.
From the ICSS, this tape includes Marks & Swan.

My Pet Tyrannosaurus. Jane Murphy. 1 cass. (Running Time: 35 min.). (J). 2001. pap. bk. 19.95 (KIM 11SC) Kimbo Educ.
In Justin's dream, his new pet, Tee-Rex, had the best day in his 65 million years. Includes a read along book & dinosaur guide.

My Pet Tyrannosaurus. Jane Murphy. 1 read-along cass. (J). (ps-2). 2001. bk. 8.95 (978-0-937124-17-8(6), KIM 11C) Kimbo Educ.
Justin's dream came true. One night a special pet appeared - a dinosaur! Includes read along book & dinosaur guide.

My Philosophy & How It Grew. unabr. ed. Carl Ransom Rogers. 1 cass. (Running Time: 1 hr. 12 min.). 1972. 11.00 (02201) Big Sur Tapes.
At the 1972 annual meeting of the Association for Humanistic Psychology, which took place in Honolulu, Hawaii, Dr. Rogers speaks on the subject of this tape's title.

My Philosophy of Life. Instructed by Manly P. Hall. 8.95 (978-0-89314-189-9(5), C800102) Philos Res.

My Pilgrimage with Diabetes. Harold Nelson. 1986. 10.80 (0404) Assn Prof Chaplains.

My Place is With You. Perf. by Clay Crosse. 1 cass. 1994. audio compact disk Brentwood Music.
This stunning debut garnered 2 No. 1 singles & the Dove Award for New Artist of the Year. Features: I Surrender All, I Call Your Name & Midnight Cry.

My Play a Tune Book: Mother Goose Songs. J. Ellis. (J). 1990. bk. 15.95 (978-0-938971-44-3(1)) JTG Nashville.

My Pocket Doctor: Diabetes Reference Guide & Journal. Prod. by Bonnie Schachter. Based on a work by Gerald A. Levine. As told by Sylvia Hernandez RD. Based on a work by Sylvia Hernandez RD & Emile Barchichat MS. (ENG.). 2007. audio compact disk 12.50 (978-0-9791329-2-6(4)) Pocket Refer.

My Prairie Summer/Laura Ingalls. Steck-Vaughn Staff. 1997. (978-0-8172-7382-8(4)) SteckVau.

My Prayer - ShowTrax. Perf. by Platters, The. Arranged by Ed Lojeski. 1 CD. (Running Time: 5 mins.). 2000. audio compact disk 19.95 (08201153) H Leonard.
This 1956 #1 pop hit, with its 12/8 ballad feel, will provide a tender moment in your program.

***My Princess Boy.** Cheryl Kilodavis. Illus. by Cheryl Kilodavis. (J). 2010. pap. bk. 9.99 (978-0-615-39594-4(5)) KD Talent.

My Principal Lives Next Door. unabr. ed. Sanibel Elementary School Staff. 1 cass. (Running Time: 8 min.). (J). (ps-3). 1991. pap. bk. 14.45 (978-0-8045-6752-7(2), 6752) Spoken Arts.

My Professor's Study: Audio CD. C. J. Powers. Adapted by C. J. Powers. (ENG.). (J). 2007. audio compact disk 9.99 (978-0-9799294-0-3(7)) Powers Prod.

My Queer Life. unabr. ed. Michael Thomas Ford. Read by Michael Thomas Ford. 2 cass. (Running Time: 3 hrs.). 2000. 18.00 (978-0-9702152-0-8(7)) Fluid Wds.
Collection of selected humorous essays from each of his bestselling humor books. Includes "Alec Baldwin Doesn't Love Me," "That's Mr. Faggot to You.".

***My Reading Life.** unabr. ed. Pat Conroy. Read by Pat Conroy. (Running Time: 8 hrs.). (ENG.). 2010. audio compact disk 30.00 (978-0-307-74920-8(7), Random AudioBks) Pub: Random Audio Pubg. Dist(s): Random

My Recollections, Countess of Cardigan. Read by Flo Gibson. 2 cass. (Running Time: 3 hrs.). 1987. 14.95 (978-1-55685-098-1(0)) Audio Bk Con.
The much pursued Adeline Horsey shares her life, loves & Victorian scandal.

My Red Hat Grandma & Me: Book 1. Hilda Principe. (Running Time: 180 sec.). (J). 2007. audio compact disk 9.99 (978-1-60247-219-8(X)) Tate Pubng.

My Red Umbrella see Mi Paraguas Rojo

My Red Umbrella. 2004. 8.95 (978-1-56008-981-0(4)); cass. & flmstrp 30.00 (978-1-56008-727-4(7)) Weston Woods.

My Red Umbrella; Man Who Didn't Wash His Dishes, the; One Fine Day; Cat & the Collector. 2004. (978-0-89719-835-6(2)); cass. & flmstrp (978-0-89719-743-4(7)) Weston Woods.

My Redeemer Lives. 2004. audio compact disk (978-1-931713-35-1(9)) Word For Today.

My Redeemer Lives. Chuck Smith. 8 cass. (Running Time: 10 hrs. 30 mins.). 2001. 24.99 (978-0-936728-91-9(4)) Word For Today.
A collection of teachings on the crucifixion. Basically a chronology of the events that occurred preceding the crucifixion of Jesus.

My Redeemer Lives MP3. 2004. audio compact disk (978-1-931713-36-8(7)) Word For Today.

My Relatives Say. Mary Louise Wilson. 1 CD. (Running Time: 59 mins.). (YA). (gr. 4 up). 2001. audio compact disk 14.98 (978-0-9650872-7-8(1)) Scoria.
Shows the natural forces that shaped these wisdom tales of Dakotah Sioux. In the opening story "The World Never Ends,' she reflects on the importance of storytelling as each generation passes along its knowledge. Included among the eight stories are transformation myths such as "The Dakotah Have Had Horses for a Long Time," "How Snake Creek Came to Be", and "Why the fawn Has Spots. The value of a caring community is emphasized in stories such as "Earth Beans and ("The Blue Heron Who Stayed for the Winter.

My Religion. Helen Keller. Narrated by Lillian Gish. 2010. 19.95 (978-0-87785-463-0(7)) Swedenborg.

***My Remarkable Journey.** Larry King. Read by Larry King. (Playaway Adult Nonfiction Ser.). (ENG.). 2009. 59.99 (978-1-61574-530-2(0)) Find a World.

My Revolutions. unabr. ed. Hari Kunzru. Read by Simon Prebble. (YA). 2008. 54.99 (978-1-60514-692-8(7)) Find a World.

My Revolutions. unabr. ed. Hari Kunzru. Read by Simon Prebble. 8 CDs. (Running Time: 9 hrs. 30 mins.). (ENG., 2008. audio compact disk 34.95 (978-1-59887-585-0(X), 159887585X) Pub: HighBridge. Dist(s): Workman Pub

My Rhinoceros & Other Friends. Guy Carawan. 1 cass. (Running Time: 33 min.). (J). (gr. k-7). 1983. 9.95 (978-0-939065-19-6(3), GW 1023) Gentle Wind.
Includes the anti-pollution anthem "Garbage" & several children's songs by Woody Guthrie.

My River Chronicles: Rediscovering America on the Hudson. unabr. ed. Jessica DuLong. Read by Jessica DuLong. 1 MP3-CD. (Running Time: 10 hrs. 0 mins. 0 sec.). 2009. 24.99 (978-1-4001-6413-4(3)); audio compact disk 69.99 (978-1-4001-4413-6(2)); audio compact disk 34.99 (978-1-4001-1413-9(6)) Pub: Tantor Media. Dist(s): IngramPubServ

***My River Chronicles: Rediscovering the Work That Built America - A Personal & Historical Journey.** unabr. ed. Jessica DuLong. Narrated by Jessica Dulong. (Running Time: 10 hrs. 0 mins.). 2009. 16.99 (978-1-4001-8413-2(4)) Tantor Media.

My River Runs to Thee see Poems & Letters of Emily Dickinson

My Romantic Favorites. David Glen Hatch. 1 cass. (Running Time: 1 hr.). 9.95 (1000926); audio compact disk 14.95 (2800578) Covenant Comms.
Classic love songs.

My Romantic Favorites, Vol. 2. David Glen Hatch. 1 cass. (Running Time: 1 hr.). 9.95 (10001093); audio compact disk 14.95 (2800748) Covenant Comms.

My Romantic Favorites, Vol. 3. David Glen Hatch. 1 cass. (Running Time: 1 hr.). 9.95 (10001220) Covenant Comms.
An exquisite collection of romantic melodies to warm the heart & soul.

My Rotten Life. unabr. ed. David Lubar. Read by Matthew Brown & Kathleen H. McInerney. 3 CDs. (Running Time: 3 hrs. 0 mins. 0 sec.). (Nathan Abercrombie, Accidental Zombie Ser.). (ENG.). (J). (gr. 3-7). 2009. audio compact disk 19.99 (978-1-4272-0696-1(1), Rena Bks) Pub: St Martin. Dist(s): Macmillan

***My Rotten Redheaded Older Brother.** unabr. ed. Patricia Polacco. Read by Patricia Polacco. 1 CD. (Running Time: 11 mins.). (J). (ps-3). 2009. audio compact disk 29.95 (978-0-8045-4215-9(5)) Spoken Arts.

My Savior Lives. Ed. by Josh Hudnall. Directed By Andy Catarisano. Contrib. by New Life Worship. Prod. by Jon Egan. 2007. 12.99 (978-5-557-93521-0(5)) Integrity Music.

My Savior Lives. Contrib. by New Life Worship. 2006. audio compact disk 13.99 (978-5-558-03606-0(0)) Integrity Music.

My Savior's Love. Bruce Greer. 1995. 11.98 (978-0-7673-0669-0(4)) LifeWay Christian.

My Savior's Love. Bruce Greer. 1995. 75.00 (978-0-7673-0705-5(4)) LifeWay Christian.

My Saviors Love. Bruce Greer. 1995. audio compact disk 85.00 (978-0-7673-0725-3(9)); audio compact disk 16.98 (978-0-7673-0683-6(X)) LifeWay Christian.

***My School.** unabr. ed. Kurt Johnston & Mark Oestreicher. (Running Time: 3 hrs. 46 mins. 0 sec.). (Middle School Survival Ser.). (ENG.). (YA). 2009. 9.99 (978-0-310-77223-1(0)) Zondervan.

My Second Saturn Return. John H. Goode. 1 cass. (Running Time: 1 hr.). 8.95 (409) Am Fed Astrologers.

My Secret War: The World War II Diary of Madeline Beck, Long Island, New York 1941. Mary Pope Osborne. Read by Barbara Rosenblat & Claire Slemmer. Directed By Robin Miles. (Dear America Ser.). (J). (gr. 3-7). 2008. bk. 39.95 (978-1-4301-0359-2(0)); audio compact disk 28.95 (978-1-4301-0357-8(4)) Live Oak Media.

***My Senator & Me: A Dog's Eye View of Washington, D. C.** Edward Kennedy. Illus. by David Small. Narrated by David De Vries. (J). 2010. audio compact disk 9.99 (978-0-545-24952-2(X)) Scholastic Inc.

My Senator & Me: A Dog's-Eye View of Washington, D. C. Edward M. Kennedy. Illus. by David Small. Narrated by David DeVries. 1 cass. (Running Time: 24 mins.). (J). (gr. 2-5). 2007. bk. 24.95 (978-0-545-04380-9(8)); bk. 29.95 (978-0-545-04379-3(4)) Weston Woods.

My Sergei: A Love Story. abr. ed. Ekaterina Gordeeva. Read by Irina Lechova. (ENG.). 2006. 9.99 (978-1-59483-837-8(2)) Pub: Hachet Audio. Dist(s): HachBkGrp

My Sergei: A Love Story, unabr. ed. Ekaterina Gordeeva. Read by Kate Reading. 8 cass. (Running Time: 8 hrs.). 1996. 48.00 (978-0-7366-3575-2(0), 755074) Books on Tape.
This drama begins when the Soviet ice-skating hierarchy commanded a serious 11 year-old girl, Katia, to skate with a fun-loving 15 year-old boy, Sergei. The pairing not only generated four World Championships & two Olympic gold medals, but also spawned a romance that ended when Sergei died of a heart attack at age 28.

My Shakespeare. Perf. by Edward Atienza et al. Concept by David William. Directed By David William. Music by Ann Monyious & Bruce Ubukata. 1 cass. (Running Time: 1 hr.). (Stratford Festival Ser.). 2005. audio compact disk 12.95 (978-0-660-17969-8(5)) Pub: Canadian Broadcasting CAN. Dist(s): Georgetown Term

My Ship, My Navy & Me. unabr. ed. Edward L. White. 2 cass. (Running Time: 3 hrs.). 15.95 (S1517) J Norton Pubs.
This is a salty story full of personal reminiscence, peppered at times with the healthy vulgarity of men without women - yet without intent to offend. It's also the story of all six Enterprises from the tiny sloop of 1776 to today's nuclear-powered carrier.

My Side of the Mountain. Jean Craighead George. Narrated by Jeff Woodman. 4 CDs. (Running Time: 4 hrs.). (gr. 3 up). audio compact disk 39.00 (978-0-7887-9522-0(8)) Recorded Bks.

My Side of the Mountain, unabr. ed. Jean Craighead George. Narrated by Jeff Woodman. 3 pieces. (Running Time: 4 hrs.). (gr. 3 up). 1994. 27.00 (978-0-7887-0144-3(4), 94369E7) Recorded Bks.
Tired of living in a crowded New York City apartment, young Sam Gribley runs away from home & learns to live on his own in the wilderness of the Catskill Mountains; eating wild plants, building his own treehouse & surviving by resourcefulness & courage.

My Side of the Mountain, unabr. ed. Jean Craighead George. Read by Jeff Woodman. 3 cass. (Running Time: 4 hrs.). (J). 1994. Rental 9.50 (94369) Recorded Bks.

My Sister, My Love: The Intimate Story of Skyler Rampike. unabr. ed. Joyce Carol Oates. Read by Mike Chamberlain. 18 CDs. (Running Time: 22 hrs. 30 mins.). 2008. audio compact disk 120.00 (978-1-4159-5530-7(1), BksonTape) Pub: Random Audio Pubg. Dist(s): Random
"Dysfunctional families are all alike. Ditto 'survivors.'" So begins the unexpurgated first-person narrative of nineteen-year-old Skyler Rampike, the only surviving child of an "infamous" American family. A decade ago the Rampikes were destroyed by the murder of Skyler's six-year-old ice-skating champion sister, Bliss, and the media scrutiny that followed. Part investigation into the unsolved murder; part elegy for the lost Bliss and for Skyler's own lost childhood; and part corrosively funny exposé of the pretensions of upper-middle-class American suburbia, this captivating novel explores with unex-pected sympathy and subtlety the intimate lives of those who dwell in Tabloid Hell. Likely to be Joyce Carol Oates's most controversial novel to date, as well as her most boldly satirical, this unconventional work of fiction is sure to be recognized as a classic exploration of the tragic interface between private life and the perilous life of "celebrity." In MY SISTER, MY LOVE: THE INTIMATE STORY OF SKYLER RAMPIKE, the incomparable Oates once again mines the depths of the sinister yet comic malaise at the heart of our con-temporary culture.

My Sister Sarah. Victor Pemberton. (Story Sound CD Ser.). (J). 2002. audio compact disk 99.95 (978-1-85903-583-2(3)) Pub: Mgna Lrg Print GBR. Dist(s): Ulverscroft US

My Sister's Child. unabr. ed. Lyn Andrews. Read by Julia Franklin. 10 cass. (Running Time: 11 hrs. 45 mins.). (Sound Ser.). 2002. 84.95 (978-1-86042-966-8(1)) Pub: UlverLrgPrint GBR. Dist(s): Ulverscroft US
The Ryan family have barely grown accustomed to having a steady income and a safe roof over their heads when a fire destroys the modest coal haulage business their father, Jack, has built, leaving his family wondering how they will survive. It's not long before they're forced to turn to Conor, Jack's brother from Ireland, a man whose noisy joviality hides a mean viciousness. With her mother sick and her half-sister, annie, becoming increasingly feckless, it's down to Ellen to fight Conor's drunken tyranny.

My Sister's Keeper. Jodi Picoult. 10 cassettes. (Running Time: 13.75 hrs). 2005. 89.75 (978-1-4025-7322-4(7)); audio compact disk 109.75 (978-1-4025-8640-8(X)) Recorded Bks.

My Sister's Keeper. Jodi Picoult. 8 cass. (Running Time: 13 hrs. 45 mins.). 2004. 34.99 (978-1-4025-7321-7(9), 03984) Recorded Bks.

My Sister's Keeper. Jodi Picoult. (Running Time: 49500 sec.). 2005. audio compact disk 29.99 (978-1-4193-6437-2(5)) Recorded Bks.

My Sisters, O My Sisters. unabr. ed. Poems. May Sarton. Read by May Sarton. 1 cass. (Running Time: 58 min.). 1984. 12.95 (23657) J Norton Pubs.
This poet's dramatic voice echos with a feminist consciousness that has been thriving for decades.

My Small Country Living. unabr. collector's ed. Jeanine McMullen. Read by Jill Masters. 7 cass. (Running Time: 10 hrs. 30 min.). 1986. 56.00 (978-0-7366-0782-7(X), 1736) Books on Tape.
McMullen a BBC producer fell in love with Wales & the farm that she bought on impulse. Here we meet the people who helped her: "Mrs. P," her eccentric Australian mother; "the artist," her less-than-steadfast boyfriend; the vet Bertie Ellis; her animals.

My Son . . . My Son: A Guide to Healing after Death, Loss or Suicide. Iris Bolton & Curtis Mitchell. 4 cass. (Running Time: 5 hrs.). 1995. 24.00 (978-0-9616326-3-2(1)) Bolton Pr.

My Son . . . My Son: A Guide to Healing after Death, Loss or Suicide. rev. ed. Iris Bolton & Curtis Mitchell. 4 cass. (Running Time: 5 hrs.). 1995. bk. 39.00 (978-0-9616326-5-6(8)) Bolton Pr.

My Son Jimi. James A. Hendrix. Read by James A. Hendrix. 2 CDs. (Running Time: 2 hrs. 30 min.). 2002. audio compact disk 24.95 (978-1-57511-116-2(0), Audio Sel) Pub Mills.
In this initimate biography, Hendrix's father shares stories and letters, many previously unknown, about this remarkable musician and man.

My Son... My Son: A Guide to Healing after Death, Loss or Suicide. rev. ed. Iris Bolton & Curtis Mitchell. 4 cass. (Running Time: 5 hrs.). 1995. pap. bk. 32.50 (978-0-9616326-4-9(X)) Bolton Pr.

My Son, the Greatest: The Best of Allan Sherman. Allan Sherman. 1 CD. (Running Time: 1 hr. 30 mins.). 2001. audio compact disk 11.98 (R2 75771) Rhino Enter.

My Soul Is an Enchanted Boat see Poetry of Shelley

My Soul Magnifies the Lord: A Rosary Meditation. 1 cass. (Running Time: 1 hr. 15 min.). 1999. 9.95 (T9045) Liguori Pubns.
Guides through the complete rosary.

My Soul to Keep. Tananarive Due. Narrated by Peter Francis James. 13 CDs. (Running Time: 17 hrs. 30 min. hrs.). 2004. audio compact disk 142.00 (978-1-4025-3073-9(0)) Recorded Bks.

My Soul to Keep. unabr. ed. Tananarive Due. 12 cass. (Running Time: 17 hrs. 30 min.). 2004. 53.95 (978-1-4025-0532-4(9)) Recorded Bks.
Five hundred years ago, Dawit was inducted into The Immortals, an elite group of humans who never age and never get sick. Now living in Miami with his wife and daughter, "David" will have to break ancient codes in order to remain with the family he loves.

My Soul to Keep. unabr. ed. Tananarive Due. Narrated by Peter Francis James. 11 cass. (Running Time: 13 hrs.). 2004. 102.00 (978-1-4025-0530-0(2)) Recorded Bks.

My Spirit Shall Live On: The Final Days of Paramahansa Yogananda. Daya Mata. 1 cass. (Running Time: 1 hr.). 1995. 6.50 (2130) Self Realization.
Sri Daya Mata, one of Paramahansa Yogananda's foremost disciples & the president of Self-Realization Fellowship, recalls the great Master's final days & hours, including his prediction of his earthly departure, the dramatic moment of its fulfillment & the passing of his spiritual mantle.

My Story. 2000. 6.50 (978-0-9702183-9-1(7)) Aslans Pl.

My Story - Wrinkles & All. unabr. ed. Kathy Staff. Read by Kathy Staff. 5 cass. (Running Time: 6 hrs. 35 min.). 1999. 63.95 (978-1-85903-306-7(7)) Pub: Magna Story GBR. Dist(s): Ulverscroft US
The part of Nora Batty in "Last of the Summer Wine" has made the author a household name. But what lies behind this character with her curlers & wrinkled stockings? This autobiography reveals the fascinating life & faith of Britain's most unlikely sex symbol. The author has played many varied parts on television, including several roles in "Coronation Street" & "Crossroads," making her one of the most popular characters in TV soap opera. However, beneath the larger than life characters she so often portrays, is a thoughtful & deeply spiritual person.

My Street Begins at My House. Perf. by Ella Jenkins. 1 cass. (Running Time: 36 min.). (J). (ps-4). 1989. (0-9307-450050-9307-45005-2-1); audio compact disk (0-9307-45005-2-1) Smithsonian Folkways.
Salute to a child's own neighborhood experience. Songs & rhythmic activities.

My Stroke of Insight: A Brain Scientist's Personal Journey. unabr. ed. Jill Bolte Taylor. Read by Jill Bolte Taylor. 5 CDs. (Running Time: 6 hrs.). (ENG.). (gr. 12 up). 2008. audio compact disk 29.95 (978-0-14-314400-7(6), PengAudBks) Penguin Grp USA.

***My Stroke of Luck.** abr. ed. Kirk Douglas. Read by Kirk Douglas. Read by Michael Douglas. (ENG.). 2006. (978-0-06-117433-9(5), Harper Audio); (978-0-06-117432-2(7), Harper Audio) HarperCollins Pubs.

My Sweet Audrina. unabr. ed. V. C. Andrews. Read by Donada Peters. 11 cass. (Running Time: 16 hrs. 30 mins.). 1989. 88.00 (978-0-7366-1616-4(0), 2476) Books on Tape.
V. C. Andrews, author of the Dollanganger series, has created a fascinating new cast of characters in this haunting story of love & deceit, innocence & betrayal & the suffocating power of parental love. Audrina Adare wanted to be as good as her sister. She knew her father could not love her as he loved her sister. Her sister was so special, so perfect & dead. Now she will come face to face with the dangerous, terrifying secret that everyone knows except sweet Audrina.

My Talks with Dean Spanley, unabr. ed. Lord Dunsany. Narrated by Flo Gibson. 3 cass. (Running Time: 2 hrs. 30 min.). (gr. 10 up). 1999. 14.95 (978-1-55685-574-0(5)) Audio Bk Con.
Over several glasses of Port Dean Spanley reminisces about his days as a dog.

My Tank Is Fight! Deranged Inventions of WWII. unabr. ed. Zack Parsons. (Running Time: 8 hrs. 0 mins. 0 sec.). (ENG., 2001. audio compact disk 19.99 (978-1-4001-5347-3(6)) Pub: Tantor Media. Dist(s): IngramPubServ

My Tank Is Fight! Deranged Inventions of WWII. unabr. ed. Zack Parsons. Read by Patrick G. Lawlor. (Running Time: 8 hrs. 0 mins. 0 sec.). (ENG.). 2007. audio compact disk 29.99 (978-1-4001-0347-8(9)) Pub: Tantor Media. Dist(s): IngramPubServ

My Tank Is Fight! Deranged Inventions of WWII. unabr. ed. Zack Parsons. Read by Patrick G. Lawlor. Illus. by Josh Hass. (Running Time: 8 hrs. 0 mins. 0 sec.). (ENG.). 2007. audio compact disk 59.99 (978-1-4001-3347-5(5)) Pub: Tantor Media. Dist(s): IngramPubServ

My Tapestried Chamber see Classic Ghost Stories, Vol. 3, A Collection

My Teacher Is an Alien. Bruce Coville. Read by Liza Ross. 2 cass. (Running Time: 2 hrs. 25 mins.). (My Teacher Is an Alien Ser.: Bk. 1). (J). (gr. 4-7). 2000. 18.00 (978-0-7366-9087-4(5)) Books on Tape.
Susan & Peter find out that teacher "Mr. Smith" is an alien, so they must save the sixth grade from a fate worse than math tests!.

My Teacher Is an Alien. unabr. ed. Bruce Coville. Read by Liza Ross. 2 cass. (Running Time: 3 hrs.). (My Teacher Is an Alien Ser.: Bk. 1). (J). (gr. 4-7). 1999. 23.00 (LL 0123, Chivers Child Audio) AudioGO.

My Teacher Is an Alien, unabr. ed. Bruce Coville. Read by Liza Ross. 2 cass. (Running Time: 3 hrs.). (My Teacher Is an Alien Ser.: Bk. 1). (J). (gr. 4-7). 1999. 16.98 (FS9-43233) Highsmith.

My Teacher Is an Alien. unabr. ed. Bruce Coville. Read by Liza Ross. 2 cass. (Running Time: 2 hrs. 24 mins.). (My Teacher Is an Alien Ser.: Bk. 1). (J). (gr. 3-6). 1998. 23.00 (978-0-8072-8028-7(3), YA971CX, Listening Lib) Random Audio Pubg.
Susan knows that her substitute teacher is weird. But she doesn't realize how weird until she catches him peeling off his face.

My Teacher Is an Alien. unabr. ed. Bruce Coville. Read by Liza Ross. 2 vols. (Running Time: 2 hrs. 24 mins.). (My Teacher Is an Alien Ser.: Bk. 1). (J). (gr. 3-6). 2004. pap. bk. 29.00 (978-0-8072-8029-4(1), S YA 971 SP, Listening Lib) Random Audio Pubg.

My Teddy Bear & Me: Musical Play Activities for Infants & Toddlers. 1 cass. (Running Time: 1 hr.). (J). (ps). 2001. pap. bk. 10.95 (KIM 7039C) Kimbo Educ.
Children enjoy hours of fun & music with their all time favorite - the Teddy Bear. Ideal for use with parents, siblings, baby-sitters, preschools, day care settings & more. Tickle, Tickle, Teddy, Nosey Bear, Tiptoe Teddy Bear, Teddy Leads the Band & more. Includes guide.

My Teddy Freddy: Activity Fun Pack. Sally A. Bonkrude. Ed. by Karla Lange & Steve Bonkrude. Intro. by Steve Bonkrude. Illus. by Terri Bahn. 1 cass. Dramatization. (J). (ps). 1988. bk. 12.95 (978-0-924829-01-7(X)); 5.95 (978-0-924829-09-3(5)) Musical Imag.
Covers a wide variety of emotions & ways to deal with them.

My Theodosia. unabr. ed. Anya Seton. Read by Wanda McCaddon. 10 cass. (Running Time: 15 hrs.). 1982. 80.00 (978-0-7366-0251-8(8), 1245) Books on Tape.
Aaron Burr's daughter, Theodosia, was dedicated to him with single-mindedness. Better than anyone else in the world, she understood her father. It was to her he unburdened himself & in this reconstruction of Theodosia's life we see him clearly mirrored. Theodosia Burr emerges as a strong & loyal individual, one who never flinched in the face of what she believed to be her duty.

My Thirty Years with Ayn Rand: An Intellectual Memoir. Leonard Peikoff. Read by Leonard Peikoff. 1 cass. (Running Time: 1 hr. 25 min.). 1987. 12.95 (LP10C) Second Renaissance.
Who was Ayn Rand? - is the question to which this talk provides a luminous answer. What was the most distinctive feature of Ayn Rand's method of thinking? By what remarkable process did she arrive at her revolutionary theory of concept-formation? Why did second-raters so often attach themselves to her? These are some of the topics addressed in this vivid portrait of the woman who challenged every fundamental philosophical premise dominating today's culture.

***My Thoughts Be Bloody: The Bitter Rivalry Between Edwin & John Wilkes Booth That Led to an American Tragedy.** unabr. ed. Nora Titone. (Running Time: 19 hrs. 0 mins. 0 sec.). (ENG.). 2010. audio compact disk 49.99 (978-1-4423-3749-7(4)) Pub: S&S Audio. Dist(s): S and S Inc

My Three Years in a Chinese Prison. Lyons/Watt. (ENG.). 2008. audio compact disk 12.95 (978-1-57970-495-7(6), Audio-For) J Norton Pubs.

My Three Years in a Chinese Prison. unabr. ed. Daniel Lyons & George Watt. 1 cass. (Running Time: 43 min.). 12.95 (140) J Norton Pubs.

My Trio Book (Mein Trio-Buch) (Suzuki Violin Volumes 1-2 arranged for three Violins) Composed by Kerstin Wartberg. (ENG.). 2002. audio compact disk 12.95 (978-1-58951-199-6(9)) Alfred Pub.

My Trip to Alpha One. unabr. ed. Alfred Slote. 1 cass. (Running Time: 41 min.). (Children's Cliffhangers Ser.). (J). (gr. 3-5). 1987. 3.99 (SWR30P, Listening Lib); 4.50 (Listening Lib) Random Audio Pubg.

My Trip to Alpha One. unabr. ed. Alfred Slote. 1 cass. (Running Time: 41 min.). (Children's Cliffhangers Ser.). (J). (gr. 4-7). 1987. bk. 15.98 incl. guide. (978-0-8072-1098-7(6), SWR30SP, Listening Lib) Random Audio Pubg.

My Turn: Caring for Aging Parents & Other Elderly Loved Ones. Sandra W. Haymon. 6 cass. (Running Time: 6 hrs.). 1996. pap. bk. 29.95 (978-0-9652965-1-9(2)) Magnolia Prods.
A "how to guide" for caregivers of aging loved ones. Topics include: CPR, hospitalization, feeding tubes, Living Wills, durable power of attorney, surrogate caregiver, living arrangements, emotional issues, death & grief.

My Turn at Bat: The Story of my Life. unabr. ed. Ted Williams & John Underwood. Narrated by Tom Stechschulte. 6 cass. (Running Time: 8 hrs.). 2000. 55.00 (978-0-7887-4383-2(X), 96320X5) Recorded Bks.
He won six batting titles & two MVP awards. But there was also plenty of controversy, including a thrown bat that hit a woman in the stands & countless snipes at the media & "gutless" politicians. This is his autobiography.

My Turn at the Bully Pulpit: Straight Talk about the Things That Drive Me Nuts. unabr. ed. Greta Van Susteren & Elaine Lafferty. 3 cass. (Running Time: 4 hrs. 30 min.). 2003. 32.00 (978-0-7366-9427-8(7)) Books on Tape.
Greta Van Susteren offers a collection of rants and opinions on America's major issues.

My Uncle Sosthenes see De Maupassant Short Stories

My Uncle's Death see Assorted Prose

***My Utmost for His Highest: An Updated Edition in Today's Language.** unabr. ed. Oswald Chambers. Narrated by Michael Card. (ENG.). 2007. 16.98 (978-1-59644-499-7(1), Hovel Audio) christianaud.

My Utmost for His Highest: An Updated Edition in Today's Language. unabr. ed. Oswald Chambers. Narrated by Michael Card. 8 CDs. (Running Time: 14 hrs. 0 mins. 0 sec.). (ENG.). 2007. audio compact disk 24.98 (978-1-59644-498-0(3), Hovel Audio) christianaud.

My Utmost for His Highest: An Updated Edition in Today's Language. unabr. ed. Oswald Chambers. 1 MP3CD. (Running Time: 14 hrs. 0 mins. 0 sec.). (ENG.). 2007. lp 19.98 (978-1-59644-500-0(9), Hovel Audio) christianaud.

My Very Best Christmas, Violin Edition. Notes by Karen Khanagov. 2001. audio compact disk 19.95 (978-0-7866-4060-7(X)) Mel Bay.

My Very Own Cookbook: Refills. 2000. audio compact disk 16.00 (978-0-00-000000-2(0)) Pub: Wings Pr. Dist(s): IPG Chicago

My Very Own Space. Chaitania Hein. Read by Chaitania Hein. Read by Bob Kechley. 1 cass. (Running Time: 1 hr.). (Dance Impulse with Chaitania Ser.). (J). (ps-2). 1986. 9.99 (978-0-929676-00-5(9)) Alim Azim Prodns.
Storytelling with music & creative dance instruction.

My Vicksburg. unabr. ed. Ann Rinaldi. Narrated by Kathy Garver. (Running Time: 3 hrs. 45 mins. 48 sec.). (ENG.). (J). 2009. 13.99 (978-1-60814-557-7(3), SpringWater); audio compact disk 19.99 (978-1-59859-548-2(2), SpringWater) Oasis Audio.

My View of Shakespeare. unabr. ed. A. L. Rowse. Read by Bill Kelsey. 4 cass. (Running Time: 4 hrs.). 1998. 24.00 (978-0-7366-4009-1(6), 4507) Books on Tape.
Shakespeare's life has been shrouded in mystery & obscurity. A major scholar clears up persistent difficulties in this biography.

***My Virginia.** Darci Picoult. Read by Darci Picoult. (Running Time: 4740 sec.). (L. A. Theatre Works Audio Theatre Collections). (ENG.). 2010. audio compact disk (978-1-58081-717-2(3)) L A Theatre.

My Visit to the Dinosaurs Book & Tape. abr. ed. Aliki. Illus. by Aliki. (Let's-Read-And-Find-Out-Science Ser.). (J). (gr. k-4). 1990. 8.99 (978-1-55994-247-8(9)) HarperCollins Pubs.

My Visit with MGM. unabr. ed. Edit Villareal. 1993. 19.95 (978-1-58081-151-4(5)) L A Theatre.

My War Gone by, I Miss It So. Anthony Lloyd. Narrated by Steven Crossley. 10 CDs. (Running Time: 12 hrs.). 2000. audio compact disk 97.00 (978-0-7887-4915-5(3), C1296E7) Recorded Bks.
A harrowing account of Bosnia in 1993. The author exposes the unspeakable terror, visceral thrill of combat & countless lives laid waste in Europe's bloodiest conflict since World War II.

My War Gone by, I Miss It So. unabr. ed. Anthony Loyd. Narrated by Steven Crossley. 8 cass. (Running Time: 12 hrs.). 2000. 72.00 (978-0-7887-4040-4(7), 96124E7) Recorded Bks.

My Watch see $30,000 Bequest & Other Stories

My Way or Yahweh: Genesis 16. Ed Young. 1994. 4.95 (978-0-7417-2030-6(2), 1030) Win Walk.

My Weird School. unabr. ed. Dan Gutman. Read by John Beach. 2 cass. (Running Time: 2 hrs. 44 mins.). (My Weird School Ser.: Nos. 1-4). (J). 2004. 19.55 (978-1-4000-9143-0(8)) Pub: Books on Tape. Dist(s): NetLibrary CO

My Wicked Earl. Linda Needham. Narrated by Linda Maroney. 7 cass. (Running Time: 9 hrs. 45 mins.). 61.00 (978-0-7887-9546-6(5)) Recorded Bks.

My Wicked, Wicked Ways. unabr. collector's ed. Errol Flynn. Read by Dan Lazar. 12 cass. (Running Time: 18 hrs.). 1979. 96.00 (978-0-7366-0170-2(8), 1172) Books on Tape.
Flynn's life story begins with his wild youth in New Guinea & the South Seas. He tells of circling the globe, pursuing an acting career in London & Hollywood & spending 20 years as a screen idol & symbol of masculine virility.

***My Wife's Affair: A Novel.** unabr. ed. Nancy Woodruff. Narrated by Johnny Heller. (Running Time: 6 hrs. 30 mins. 0 sec.). (ENG.). 2010. 19.99 (978-1-4001-6734-0(5)); 14.99 (978-1-4001-8734-8(6)); audio compact disk 71.99 (978-1-4001-4734-2(4)); audio compact disk 29.99 (978-1-4001-1734-5(8)) Pub: Tantor Media. Dist(s): IngramPubServ

My Witness... to the Ends of the Earth. Eugene LaVerdiere. 4 cass. (Running Time: 3 hrs. 35 min.). 1993. 33.95 (TAH291) Alba Hse Comns.
A very original & exciting vision & interpretation of Luke/Acts starting from the statement made in Luke 1, 8: "You will receive power when the Holy Spirit comes upon you & you will be my witnesses in Jerusalem, throughout Judea & Samaria to the ends of the earth".

My Witness... to the Ends of the Earth. unabr. ed. Eugene LaVerdiere. 4 cass. (Running Time: 3 hrs. 7 min.). 1993. 33.95 (TAH291) Alba Hse Comns.
Four cassette program with a very original & exciting vision & interpretation of Luke/Acts.

My Work As a Novelist: A. J. Byatt. Interview with A. J. Byatt. Prod. by David Gerard. 50.00 St Mut.
Designed for high school, college & university students engaged in the study of the contemporary novel & for the general reader with an interest in the living English novel. Features a conversation with the novelist.

My Work As a Novelist: Alan Sillitoe. Interview with Alan Sillitoe. Prod. by David Gerard. 50.00 St Mut.

My Work As a Novelist: Brigid Brophy. Interview with Brigid Brophy. Prod. by David Gerard. 5.00 St Mut.

My Work As a Novelist: David Lodge. Interview with David Lodge. Prod. by David Gerard. 50.00 St Mut.

My Work As a Novelist: Hugh MacDiarmid. Interview with Hugh MacDiarmid. Prod. by David Gerard. 50.00 St Mut.
Designed for high school, college & university students engaged in the study of the contemporary novel & for the general reader with an interest in the living English novel. Features a conversation with the novelist.

My Work As a Novelist: Iris Murdoch. Interview with Iris Murdoch. Prod. by David Gerard. 50.00 St Mut.
Designed for high school, college & university students engaged in the study of the contemporary novel & for the general reader with an interest in the living English novel. Features a conversation with the novelist.

My Work As a Novelist: John Braine. Interview with John Braine. Prod. by David Gerard. 50.00 St Mut.
Designed for high school, college & university students engaged in the study of the contemporary novel & for the general reader with an interest in the living English novel. Featuring a conversation with the novelist.

My Work As a Novelist: John Wain. Interview with John Wain. Prod. by David Gerard. 50.00 St Mut.
Designed for high school, college & university students engaged in the study of the contemporary novel & for the general reader with an interst in the living English novel. Features a conversation with the novelist.

My Work As a Novelist: Sir Angus Wilson. Interview with Angus Wilson. Prod. by David Gerard. 50.00 St Mut.
Designed for high school, college & contemporary students engaged in the study of the contemporary novel & for the general reader with an interest in the living English novel. Features a conversation with the novelist.

My Work As a Novelist: Stan Barstow. Interview with Stan Barstow. Prod. by David Gerard. 50.00 St Mut.
Designed for high school, college & university students engaged in the study of the contemporary novel & for the general reader with an interest in the living English novel. Features a converstation with the novelist.

My Work As a Novelist: Stanley Middleton. Interview with Stanley Middleton. Prod. by David Gerard. 50.00 St Mut.
Designed for high school, college & university students engaged in the study of the contemporary novel & for the general reader with an interest in the living novel. Features a conversation with the novelist.

My World & Welcome to It see Thurber Carnival

My World & Welcome to It. unabr. ed. Short Stories. James Thurber. Read by John Cullum. 4 cass. (Running Time: 6 hrs.). (gr. 9-12). 2004. 24.95 (978-1-57270-076-5(9), C41076u) Pub: Audio Partners. Dist(s): PerseuPGW
Here are 22 Thurber stories, including "The Secret Life of Walter Mitty".

My World & Welcome to It. unabr. ed. James Thurber. 7 cass. (Running Time: 10 hrs.). 2001. 29.95 (978-0-7366-6779-1(2)) Books on Tape.
More whimsical & funny stories from Thurber including "The Secret Life of Walter Mitty" & "You Know How the French Are".

My World & Welcome to It. unabr. collector's ed. James Thurber. Read by Wolfram Kandinsky. 7 cass. (Running Time: 7 hrs.). Incl. Courtship Through the Ages. (1636); Interview with a Lemming. (1636); Secret Life of Walter Mitty. (1636); You Know How the French Are. (1636); 1983. 42.00 (978-0-7366-0677-6(7), 1636) Books on Tape.

***My Worst Best Friend.** unabr. ed. Dyan Sheldon. (Running Time: 7 hrs.). 2010. 19.99 (978-1-4418-8914-0(0), 9781441889140, Candlewick Bril); 39.97 (978-1-4418-8915-7(9), 9781441889157, Candlewick Bril); audio compact disk 19.99 (978-1-4418-8912-6(4), 9781441889126, Candlewick Bril); audio compact disk 39.97 (978-1-4418-8913-3(2), 9781441889133, Candlewick Bril) Brilliance Audio.

***My Worst Best Friend.** unabr. ed. Dyan Sheldon. Read by Jeannie Stith. (Running Time: 7 hrs.). 2010. audio compact disk 24.99 (978-1-4418-8910-2(8), 9781441889102, Candlewick Bril); audio compact disk 54.97 (978-1-4418-8911-9(6), 9781441889119, Candlewick Bril) Brilliance Audio.

My Year in Iraq: The Struggle to Build a Future of Hope. abr. ed. Read by Boyd Gaines. Ed. by Paul Bremer. Told to Malcolm McConnell. 2006. 17.95 (978-0-7435-5568-5(6)) Pub: S&S Audio. Dist(s): S and S Inc

My Year of Meats. abr. ed. Ruth L. Ozeki. 2 cass. (Running Time: 3 hrs.). 1998. bk. 17.95 (978-1-57453-289-0(8)) Audio Lit.
Two women on opposite sides of the world, an American documentary filmmaker & the long-suffering wife of her Japanese boss - find their lives inextricably linked in a struggle against the determination of the meat industry to make the world safe for hormone-laced American beef. While doing a Japanese TV series, Jane investigate the truth about beef industry practies & decides to sabotage the series by airing controversial footage.

My Year of Meats. unabr. ed. Ruth Ozeki. Read by Anna Fields. 9 CDs. 2004. audio compact disk 44.95 (978-0-7861-9198-7(8)) Blckstn Audio.

My Year of Meats. unabr. ed. Ruth Ozeki. Read by Anna Fields. 2006. reel tape 39.95 (978-0-7861-2486-2(5)) Blckstn Audio.

My Year of Meats. unabr. ed. Ruth L. Ozeki. Read by Anna Fields. 9 CDs. (Running Time: 11 hrs. 30 mins.). 2003. audio compact disk 72.00 (978-0-7861-9183-3(X), 3131); audio compact disk 24.95 (978-0-7861-8918-2(5), 3131); 56.95 (978-0-7861-2478-7(4), 3131) Blckstn Audio.
Jane, a struggling filmmaker in New York, is given her big break, a chance to travel through the United States to produce a Japanese television program sponsored by American meat exporters. Meanwhile, Akiko, a painfully thin Japanese woman struggling with bulimia, is being pressured by her child-craving husband to put some meat on her bones, literally.

My Year Off: Rediscovering Life after a Stroke. abr. ed. Robert McCrum. 2001. (978-0-333-76665-1(2)) Macmillan UK GBR.

My Years with Churchill. N. McGowan. Read by John Middleton. 5 cass. (Running Time: 5 hrs.). 1999. 49.95 (68750) Pub: Soundings Ltd GBR. Dist(s): ISIS Pub

My Years with Churchill. unabr. ed. Norman McGowan. 5 cass. (Running Time: 5 hrs. 30 min.). 1995. 49.95 (68750) Eye Ear.

My Years with Churchill. unabr. ed. Norman McGowan. Read by John Middleton. 5 cass. (Running Time: 7 hrs. 30 mins.). (Sound Ser.). 1994. 49.95 (978-1-85496-875-3(0), 68750) Pub: UlverLrgPrint GBR. Dist(s): Ulverscroft US

My 1st Encyclopedia. 27.50 (978-1-56997-102-4(1)) Knowldge Adv.

Myanmar Newspaper Reader, Luzor. 5 cass. (Running Time: 7 hrs. 30 min.). (MIS.). 1996. 34.00 (3165) Dunwoody Pr.
Intended for the student who has mastered the alphabet primer. Fifty-two selections are included from two dailies in Yangon, "The New Light of Myanmar" & "The Mirror," issued during May to October 1995. English translation included.

Myelodysplastic Syndromes. Read by Jane F. Desforges. 1 cass. (Running Time: 1 hr. 30 min.). 1986. 12.00 (C8616) Amer Coll Phys.

Myocardial & Pericardial Disease. Read by J. Michael Criley. 1 cass. (Running Time: 1 hr. 30 min.). 1985. 12.00 (C8549) Amer Coll Phys.

Myotonic Dystrophy - A Bibliography & Dictionary for Physicians, Patients, & Genome Researchers. Compiled by Icon Group International, Inc. Staff. 2007. ring bd. 28.95 (978-0-497-11259-2(0)) Icon Grp.

MyPhoto Calendare Software: Create customized Photo Calendars. 2004. spiral bd. 29.95 (978-0-9754991-0-8(6)) Digilabs.

Myriad-Minded Poet: Rabindranath Tagore. unabr. ed. Julian C. Hollick & Marilyn Turkovich. 1 cass. (Running Time: 1 hr.). (ENG & BEN.). 1985. pap. bk. 30.00 (978-1-56709-023-9(0), 1032) Indep Broadcast.
Tagore, the first Asian to win the Nobel Prize for Literature, is one of the world's intellectual giants. He was a prolific writer of poetry, short stories, novels, musical dramas, essays & songs. The tape introduces high school & college students to Tagore's poetry in its original Bengali & the English translation. It includes reminiscences by the film-maker Satyajit Ray. The curriculum booklet contains a wide selection of Tagore's writing, poetry & a short story.

Myrtle Smyth Audiotape Series: Myrtle Smyth, C.S., of Belfast, Northern Ireland. unabr. ed. Myrtle Smith. Prod. by David Keyston. 26 CDs. (Running Time: 29 hrs. 6 min.). 1999. audio compact disk (978-1-893107-00-7(0), MS) Healing Unltd.
Lectures on 26 topics.

Myself: A Case of Mistaken Identity. Alan Watts. 2 CDs. (Running Time: 1 hr 30 mins). Orig. Title: The Tao of Philosophy, Vol. II. 2005. audio compact disk 19.95 (978-1-59179-377-9(7), AB00131D) Sounds True.
"If we're honest with ourselves," asserts Alan Watts, "the most fascinating question in the world is clearly 'Who am I?'" In Myself: A Case of Mistaken Identity, you will join one of the West's most celebrated teachers of Eastern thought in pursuit of this eternal riddle of the self. In four archival recordings - captured here at the height of his career as a lecturer and author - Alan Watts explodes some of our most deeply held beliefs about our sense of self and how we perceive the world around us. With striking and often hilarious examples, he demonstrates the profound effect of words and symbols on these so-called "common sense" perceptions. The Wisdom of Alan Watts series offers Watts at his best, bringing one of the century's most lucid and entertaining teachers of Asian philosophy to a new generation of listeners. Talks include: "Myth of Myself," "Man in Nature," "Symbols and Meaning," and "Limits of Language.".

Myself, My Enemy. unabr. ed. Jean Plaidy. Read by Rosalind Shanks. 14 cass. (Running Time: 16 hrs. 30 min.). (Isis Ser.). (J). 1997. 99.95 (978-1-85695-298-9(3), 970513) Pub: ISIS Lrg Prnt GBR. Dist(s): Ulverscroft US

Myself, My Enemy. unabr. ed. Jean Plaidy. Read by Rosalind Shanks. 15 CDs. (Running Time: 16 hrs. 27 mins.). (Isis Ser.). (J). 2002. audio compact disk 104.95 (978-0-7531-1495-7(X)) Pub: ISIS Lrg Prnt GBR. Dist(s): Ulverscroft US

Myself When I Am Real. Bebo Norman. Contrib. by Jordyn Thomas & Robert Beeson. Prod. by Ed Cash. 2002. audio compact disk 11.99 (978-5-552-64749-1(1)) Essential Recs.

Myself When I Am Real. Perf. by Bebo Norman. 2002. audio compact disk Provident Mus Dist.

Myserious Traveler. (Running Time: 3 hrs.). 2004. 9.98 (978-1-57019-695-9(8)) Radio Spirits.

***MySpace for Moms & Dads: A Guide to Understanding the Risks & the Rewards.** Connie Neal. (Running Time: 5 hrs. 49 mins. 0 sec.). (ENG.). 2009. 14.99 (978-0-310-30485-2(7)) Zondervan.

Mystere de la Chambre Jaune, Gaston Leroux. Read by Jacques Roland. 6 cass. (Running Time: 6 hrs.). (FRE.). 1996. 52.95 (1845-LQP) Olivia & Hill.
A brilliant example of the perfect crime committed in a closed environment.

Mysteres Au Grand Hotel. audio compact disk 12.95 (978-0-8219-3779-2(0)) EMC-Paradigm.

Mysteres Dans le Showbiz. Boutegege & Longo. audio compact disk 12.95 (978-0-8219-3771-6(5)) EMC-Paradigm.

Mysteries & Thrillers. 8 cass. (Running Time: 12 hrs.). 2002. 39.98 (978-1-57019-542-6(0), 4469) Radio Spirits.

Mysteries & Thrillers. unabr. ed. Radio Spirits Staff. 12 CDs. (Running Time: 12 hrs.). 2005. audio compact disk 39.98 (978-1-57019-541-9(2), 4470) Radio Spirits.
Lock the doors, close the blinds and pull up the covers. This 40-episode collection of radio's masterpieces of horror and suspense will send chills down your spine. Return to radio's glorious "theater of the imagination" with Orson Welles and Bill Johnstone in The Shadow, Vincent Price and William Conrad in Escape and Peter Lorre and Agnes Moorehead in tales well calculated to keep you in Suspense.

Mysteries of Atlantis Revisited. Edgar Cayce et al. 1 cass. (Running Time: 60 min.). 1989. 9.95 HarperCollins Pubs.

Mysteries of Death's Ancient Practices. Marty Kent. 1 cass. (Running Time: 1 hr.). 9.00 (A0716-90) Sound Photosyn.
A strong & moving statement from Death: The Last Taboo Symposium.

Mysteries of God Vol. 1: Unveiling the Hidden Principles of the Kingdom of God. Mac Hammond. 8 CDs. (Annointing Ser.). 2006. audio compact disk 40.00 (978-1-57399-322-7(0)) Mac Hammond.

Mysteries of God Vol. 2: Unveiling Hidden Truths about Your Family, Future, & Faith. 6 CDs. 2006. audio compact disk 30.00 (978-1-57399-324-1(7)) Mac Hammond.

Mysteries of God Vol. 3: Unveiling Hidden Truths about Worthiness, Worldliness, & Wickedness. Mac Hammond. 3 CDs. 2006. audio compact disk 15.00 (978-1-57399-350-0(6)) Mac Hammond.

Mysteries of God Vol. 4: Unveiling Hidden Truths about Our Desires, Deeds, & Destiny. Mac Hammond. 5 CDs. 2007. audio compact disk 25.00 (978-1-57399-366-1(2)) Mac Hammond.

Mysteries of God, Vol. 5: Unveiling Hidden Truths about Casual Christianity. Mac Hammond. 5 CDs. 2007. audio compact disk 25.00 (978-1-57399-373-9(5)) Mac Hammond.

Mysteries of God, Vol. 6: Unveiling Hidden Truths about Discipleship & Due Seasons. Mac Hammond. 5 CDs. 2007. audio compact disk 25.00 (978-1-57399-374-6(3)) Mac Hammond.

Mysteries of History: The Missing Talmud - The Missing Vessels of the Temple. unabr. ed. Shmuel Irons. Read by Shmuel Irons. 2 cass. (Running Time: 3 hrs.). 19.95 (978-1-889648-17-0(5)) Jwish Her Fdtn.
A clear view of ancient history based on the Bible & Talmud & other ancient primary sources. A new way of looking at the past.

Mysteries of Human Consciousness. Colin Wilson. 2 cass. 18.00 (A0238-90) Sound Photosyn.
An optimistic vision of human consciousness, presented with humorous & insightful anecdotes taken from the lives of occult figures, literary artists, & from his own life experiences, conversations & prodigious research.

Mysteries of Motion. (4031) Am Audio Prose.

Mysteries of Motion. unabr. ed. Hortense Calisher. Read by Donada Peters. 16 cass. (Running Time: 24 hrs.). 128.00 (1922A/B) Books on Tape.
In Cabin Six the half-dozen men & women - & one stowaway - who are passengers on the first American space shuttle for civilians are entering the space age as we all are. Tom Gilpin, social reformer & cult hero; Veronica, the sexual explorer; Mulenberg, the businessman; William Wert, the diplomat who will be head man on arrival; Soraya, survivor of Iran's revolution; Lievering, possible survivor of the death camps - by the time they arrive at the first orbiting habitat, you know all their secret histories.

Mysteries of Motion, Pt. 1. unabr. collector's ed. Hortense Calisher. Read by Donada Peters. 7 cass. (Running Time: 10 hrs. 30 mins.). 1985. 56.00 (978-0-7366-0981-4(4), 1922-A) Books on Tape.
Aboard America's first civilian space shuttle.

Mysteries of Motion, Pt. 2. collector's ed. Hortense Calisher. Read by Donada Peters. 9 cass. (Running Time: 13 hrs. 30 min.). 1985. 72.00 (978-0-7366-0982-1(2), 1922-B) Books on Tape.

***Mysteries of Paris & London.** Richard Maxwell. (Victorian Literature & Culture Ser.). (ENG.). 27.50 (978-0-8139-2939-2(3)) U Pr of Va.

Mysteries of the Astral Light. Instructed by Manly P. Hall. 8.95 (978-0-89314-190-5(9), C860914) Philos Res.

Mysteries of the Cabala. Instructed by Manly P. Hall. 5 cass. 8.50 ea. o.p. Pt. 1: Ancient of Days - Nature of the Godhead. (800158-A) Philos Res.

Mysteries of the Cabala. Instructed by Manly P. Hall. 5 cass. (Running Time: 2 hrs. 30 min.). 1999. 40.00 Set. incl. album. (978-0-89314-192-9(5), S800158) Philos Res.

Mysteries of the Kingdom of God. Featuring Bill Winston. 3. 2004. 15.00 (978-1-59544-009-9(7)) Pub: B Winston Min. Dist(s): Anchor Distributors
Thereis a better way to live in this earth; where all of your needs are met and you have all of the solutions to every problem at your disposal. The key is in understanding the Kingdom of God.

Mysteries of the Kingdom of God. Featuring Bill Winston. 3. 2004. audio compact disk 24.00 (978-1-59544-010-5(0)) Pub: B Winston Min. Dist(s): Anchor Distributors
There is a better way to live in this earth; where all of your needs are met and you have all of the solutions to every problem at your disposal. The key is in understanding the Kingdom of God.

Mysteries of the Middle Ages: The Rise of Feminism, Science, & Art from the Cults of Catholic Europe. abr. ed. Thomas Cahill. Read by Thomas Cahill. 5 CDs. (Running Time: 6 hrs.). (ENG.). 2006. audio compact disk 29.95 (978-0-7393-3431-7(X), Random AudioBks) Pub: Random Audio Pubg. Dist(s): Random

Mysteries of the Middle Ages: The Rise of Feminism, Science, & Art from the Cults of Catholic Europe. unabr. ed. Thomas Cahill. 10 CDs. (Running Time: 12 hrs.). 2006. audio compact disk 76.50 (978-1-4159-3283-4(2)) Pub: Books on Tape. Dist(s): NetLibrary CO

Mysteries of the Planet Mars. Chuck Missler. 2 CD's. (Running Time: 120 mins.). (Briefing Packages by Chuck Missler). 1996. audio compact disk 19.95 (978-1-57821-298-9(7)) Koinonia Hse.
Is there life on the Planet Mars?Are there monuments on Mars? What about the mile-wide "Face" on Mars?Has the Earth received "visitors" from the Planet Mars? Why did the ancient cultures worship the wandering planet?Recent news releases by NASA have claimed provocative conclusions from studies of alleged Martian meteorites. The question of life on other planets has been raised again, not by Hollywood but by the scientific community.This briefing examines the startling discoveries regarding this fascinating member of our solar system and their impact on our understanding of the Scriptures.

Mysteries of the Rosary. 1 cass. (Running Time: 1 hr.). 2001. bk. 8.95 (A7081) St Anthony Mess Pr.
Dwell on the special life events of Christ and of his mother, Mary, as related in Scripture and reflected in the liturgical year. All fifteen decades are on each side of the cassette.

Mysteries of the Unknown: Dreams & Dreaming. abr. ed. Art Insana. Read by Full Cast Production Staff. (ENG.). 2006. 5.98 (978-1-59483-844-6(5)) Pub: Hachet Audio. Dist(s): HachBkGrp

Mysteries of the Unknown: Mystic Places. abr. ed. Art Insana. (ENG.). 2006. 5.98 (978-1-59483-692-3(2)) Pub: Hachet Audio. Dist(s): HachBkGrp

Mysteries of the Unknown: Powers of Healing. abr. ed. Read by Full Cast. (ENG.). 2006. 5.98 (978-1-59483-834-7(8)) Pub: Hachet Audio. Dist(s): HachBkGrp

Mysteries of Udolpho. Ann Radcliffe. Read by Kerri Harris. 2007. 19.95 (978-0-9729683-1-7(8)) Bkworm Audio.

Mysteries of Udolpho, Pt. 2 Ann Radcliffe. 10 cass. (Running Time: 15 hrs.). 65.95 Audio Bk Con.
This is considered to be the mother of the Gothic novel & it has all the right ingredients of terror, horror, violence & supernatural effects played out in the gloomy, medieval castle of Udolpho. However, there are a lot of tears to wade through & innumerable fainting spells, before the plot begins to thicken.

Mysteries of Udolpho (Part 1), Vol. 1. unabr. ed. Ann Radcliffe. Read by Flo Gibson. 10 cass. (Running Time: 14 hrs. 30 min.). 1993. 29.95 (978-1-55685-301-2(7)) Audio Bk Con.
This is considered to be the mother of the Gothic novel & it has all the right ingredients of terror, horror, violence & supernatural effects played out in the gloomy, medieval castle of Udolpho. However, there a lot of tears to wade through & innumerable fainting spells, before the plot begins to thicken.

Mysteries of Udolpho (Part 2), Vol. 2. unabr. ed. Ann Radcliffe. Narrated by Flo Gibson. (Running Time: 14 hrs. 15 mins.). 1993. 29.95 (978-1-55685-820-8(5)) Audio Bk Con.

Mysteries of Udolpho (Parts 1 And 2) A Romance. unabr. ed. Ann Radcliffe. Narrated by Flo Gibson. (Running Time: 28 hrs. 8 mins.). 1993. 57.95 (978-1-55685-821-5(3)) Audio Bk Con.

Mysteries of Winterthurn. Joyce Carol Oates. Read by Joyce Carol Oates. 1 cass. (Running Time: 30 min.). 8.95 (AMF-24) Am Audio Prose.
The author reads from her novel & discusses Gothic genres & the detective novel.

Mysteries to Die For: A Collection. unabr. ed. 9 cass. (Running Time: 13 hrs. 30 min.). 1996. 72.00 (3616); Rental 17.50 (3616) Books on Tape.
An anthology of 23 of some of the best mystery & crime stories. From tales of danger & darkness, probings of the darkest depths of the human psyche, passports to deadly adventures & scavenging dirty little Hollywood secrets, 19 of the genre's best practitioners present these mystery gems. Authors include Robert Barnard, Lawrence Block, Mary Higgins Clark, Stanley Ellin, Ralph McInerny, Ruth Rendell, Robert Twohy & Donald E. Westlake.

Mysteries Within: Superstition, Religion & Medicine, abr. ed. Sherwin B. Nuland. 4 CDs. (Running Time: 60 hrs. 0 mins. 0 sec.). (ENG.). 2000. 25.00 (978-0-7435-0009-8(1), Audioworks) Pub: S&S Audio. Dist(s): S and S Inc

Mysteriious Flame of Queen Loana. unabr. ed. Umberto Eco. 13 CDs. (Running Time: 15 hrs.). 2005. audio compact disk 119.75 (978-1-4193-4470-1(6)) Recorded Bks.

Mysteriose Konzert. 3 cass. (Running Time: 3 hrs.). (Mystery Thrillers in German Ser.). (GER.). 2001. pap. bk. 49.95 (SGE119) J Norton Pubs.
Recorded by native professional actors in a radio-play format, these short-episode thrillers on an intermediate level were especially created to develop listening comprehension skills. Book provides a transcripts of the recording, exercises & vocabulary.

Mysteriose Konzert. Hans J. Konig. 59.95 (978-0-8219-3632-0(8)) EMC-Paradigm.

Mysteriose Konzert. unabr. ed. Hans J. Konig. 3 cass. (GER.). 39.95 (SGE119); J Norton Pubs.

Mysterious Affair at Styles. Agatha Christie. 6 cdS. (Running Time: 5 3/4 hRS.). 2007. audio compact disk (978-0-9787553-9-3(1)) Alcazar AudioWorks.

Mysterious Affair at Styles, Agatha Christie. Read by Flo Gibson. 4 cass. (Running Time: 6 hrs.). 1995. 19.95 (978-1-55685-373-9(4)) Audio Bk Con.
The brilliant detective, Hercule Poirot, makes his debut in a small English village where he solves the baffling murder of the mistress of Styles Court.

***Mysterious Affair at Styles.** Agatha Christie. Narrated by John Moffatt & Full Cast Production Staff. (Running Time: 2 hrs. 0 mins. 0 sec.). (ENG., 2010. audio compact disk 24.95 (978-0-563-51031-4(5)) Pub: AudioGO. Dist(s): Perseus Dist

Mysterious Affair at Styles. Agatha Christie. 3 cass. (Running Time: 3 hrs.). (Hercule Poirot Mystery Ser.). 1992. bk. 19.95 Set. (978-1-882071-21-0(2)) B-B Audio.
Mystery & detective story.

Mysterious Affair at Styles. Agatha Christie. 4 cass. (Running Time: 6 hrs. 40 min.). 26.95 (978-1-885546-07-4(6)) Big Ben Audio.
Enter Hercule Poirot. The cerebral & eccentric Belgian detective who has escorted millions through Agatha Christie's legendary novels, was first introduced here. Styles Court is a magnificent English manor house owned by a rich, strong-willed matron who, to the dismay of her stepson, has recently married a fortune hunter. Death by violence of the mistress of Styles Court is so cleverly plotted, & baffling, that it challenges even the skill of Hercule Poirot.

Mysterious Affair at Styles. Agatha Christie. Read by Ralph Cosham. (Running Time: 6 hrs. 30 mins.). 2003. 22.95 (978-1-59912-094-2(1), Audiofy Corp) Iofy Corp.

Mysterious Affair at Styles. Agatha Christie. Read by David Suchet. (Running Time: 6 hrs.). 2005. 27.95 (978-1-59912-384-4(3)) Iofy Corp.

Mysterious Affair at Styles. Agatha Christie. Narrated by Ralph Cosham. (Running Time: 22800 sec.). (Unabridged Classics in MP3 Ser.). (ENG.). 2008. audio compact disk 14.95 (978-1-58472-575-6(3), In Aud); audio compact disk 24.00 (978-1-58472-576-3(1), In Aud) Sound Room.

Mysterious Affair at Styles. Agatha Christie. Read by Penelope Dellaporta. (Running Time: 30600 sec.). (Hercule Poirot Mystery Ser.). (ENG.). 2006. audio compact disk 59.99 (978-1-4001-3271-3(1)); audio compact disk 19.99 (978-1-4001-5271-1(2)); audio compact disk 29.99 (978-1-4001-0271-6(5)) Pub: Tantor Media. Dist(s): IngramPubServ

Mysterious Affair at Styles. abr. ed. Agatha Christie. Read by Stan Winiarski. 3 cass. (Running Time: 4 hrs. 30 min.). 1998. 19.95 (978-1-882071-59-3(X), 023) B-B Audio.
Join the famous Hercule Poirot in the mystery mode that Christie does best. Match wits with the master detective to unravel the complexity of clues and point a fateful finger at the real murderer, from among a stunning, cunning cast of candidates.

Mysterious Affair at Styles. unabr. ed. Agatha Christie. Read by David Suchet. 5 cass. (Running Time: 6 hrs. 15 mins.). (Hercule Poirot Mystery Ser.). 2004. 22.95 (978-1-57270-017-8(3), N51017u) Pub: Audio Partners. Dist(s): PerseuPGW
Published in 1920, this is the first mystery written by Christie, introducing Poirot, the Belgian Detective Par Excellence.

Mysterious Affair at Styles. unabr. ed. Agatha Christie. Read by David Suchet. (Mystery Masters Ser.). (ENG.). 2003. audio compact disk 29.95 (978-1-57270-297-4(4)) Pub: AudioGO. Dist(s): Perseus Dist

Mysterious Affair at Styles. unabr. ed. Agatha Christie. Read by Nadia May. 5 cass. (Running Time: 7 hrs.). 1996. 39.95 (978-0-7861-0410-9(4), 1362) Blckstn Audio.
Cerebral & eccentric Belgian detective steps out of retirement & into the limelight of a classic mystery. Styles Court is a magnificent English manor house owned by a rich, strong-willed matron who, to the dismay of her stepson, has recently married a fortune hunter. The scene is set for death by violence. The murder of the mistress of Styles Court is so baffling, so cleverly plotted, that it challenges even the skill of Hercule Poirot.

Mysterious Affair at Styles. unabr. ed. Agatha Christie. Read by Nadia May. 6 CDs. (Running Time: 7 hrs.). 2000. audio compact disk 48.00 (978-0-7861-9928-0(8), 1362) Blckstn Audio.
The cerebral & eccentric Belgian detective steps out of retirement & into the limelight of a classic mystery. Styles Court is a magnificent English manor house owned by a rich, strong-willed matron who, to the dismay of her stepson, has recently married a fortune hunter. The scene is set for death by violence. The murder of the mistress of Styles Court is so baffling, so cleverly plotted, that it challenges even the skill of Hercule Poirot.

Mysterious Affair at Styles, unabr. ed. Agatha Christie. Read by Nadia May. 5 cass. (Running Time: 5 hrs.). 1999. 39.95 (FS9-34274) Highsmith.

Mysterious Affair at Styles. unabr. ed. Agatha Christie. Narrated by Penelope Dellaporta. (Running Time: 8 hrs. 30 mins. 0 sec.). (Hercule Poirot Mysteries Ser.). (ENG.). 2009. lab manual ed. 55.99 (978-1-4001-3919-4(8)); audio compact disk 27.99 (978-1-4001-0919-7(1)) Pub: Tantor Media. Dist(s): IngramPubServ

Mysterious Affair at Styles. unabr. ed. Agatha Christie. Narrated by Penelope Dellaporta. (Running Time: 8 hrs. 30 mins. 0 sec.). (Hercule Poirot Mysteries Ser.). (ENG.). 2009. 19.99 (978-1-4001-5919-2(9)) Pub: Tantor Media. Dist(s): IngramPubServ

Mysterious Affair at Styles. unabr. collector's ed. Agatha Christie. Read by Penelope Dellaporta. 6 cass. (Running Time: 9 hrs.). 1996. 48.00 (978-0-7366-3226-3(3), 3887) Books on Tape.
This famous first case introduces Hercule Poirot, Christie's long-lived protagonist, who's called to an English estate after its heiress is murdered. The victim had inherited the estate - Styles Court - & then, oddly, married a fortune hunter, now a prime suspect. But a jealous stepson has motive, as does a scheming servant. You're invited to find the ingenious solution before the final page.

Mysterious Affair at Styles: A Hercule Poirot Mystery. unabr. ed. Agatha Christie. Read by David Suchet. 6 CDs. (Running Time: 6 hrs. 15 mins.). 2008. audio compact disk 64.95 (978-0-7927-5270-7(8)) AudioGO.

Mysterious Affair at the Styles. unabr. ed. Agatha Christie. Read by Ralph Cosham. (YA). 2006. 54.99 (978-1-59895-191-2(2)) Find a World.

Mysterious & Macabre. Read by Peter Joyce. 4 cass. 1997. 44.95 (978-1-86015-444-7(1)) Ulverscroft US.

Mysterious & Macabre. unabr. ed. Short Stories. Edgar Allan Poe et al. Read by Peter Joyce. 4 cass. 1998. 39.95 T T Beeler.
A top notch collection of spine-tingling tales.

Mysterious Benedict Society. unabr. ed. Trenton Lee Stewart. Read by Del Roy. 11 CDs. (Running Time: 13 hrs. 17 mins.). (Mysterious Benedict Society Ser.: Bk. 1). (J). (gr. 4-8). 2006. audio compact disk 60.00 (978-0-7393-4859-8(0)) Books on Tape.

Mysterious Benedict Society. unabr. ed. Trenton Lee Stewart. Read by Del Roy. 11 CDs. (Running Time: 47820 sec.). (Mysterious Benedict Society Ser.: Bk. 1). (ENG.). (J). (gr. 5-7). 2007. audio compact disk 51.00 (978-0-307-28439-6(5), Listening Lib) Pub: Random Audio Pubg. Dist(s): Random

Mysterious Benedict Society & the Perilous Journey. unabr. ed. Trenton Lee Stewart. Read by Del Roy. 11 CDs. (Running Time: 12 hrs. 59 mins.). (Mysterious Benedict Society Ser.: Bk. 2). (J). (gr. 5-7). 2008. audio compact disk 75.00 (978-0-7393-7342-2(0), Listening Lib) Pub: Random Audio Pubg. Dist(s): Random

Mysterious Benedict Society & the Perilous Journey. unabr. ed. Trenton Lee Stewart. Read by Del Roy. (Running Time: 46740 sec.). (Mysterious Benedict Society Ser.: Bk. 2). (J). (gr. 3-7). 2008. audio compact disk 50.00 (978-0-7393-7340-8(4), Listening Lib) Pub: Random Audio Pubg. Dist(s): Random

***Mysterious Benedict Society & the Prisoner's Dilemma.** unabr. ed. Trenton Lee Stewart. Read by Del Roy. 9 CDs. (Running Time: 10 hrs. 47 mins.). (Mysterious Benedict Society Ser.: Bk. 3). (J). (gr. 4-7). 2009. audio compact disk 75.00 (978-0-307-58241-6(8), BksonTape) Pub: Random Audio Pubg. Dist(s): Random

Mysterious Benedict Society & the Prisoner's Dilemma. unabr. ed. Trenton Lee Stewart. (Mysterious Benedict Society Ser.: Bk. 3). (J). (gr. 3). 2009. audio compact disk 44.00 (978-0-307-58239-3(6), Listening Lib) Pub: Random Audio Pubg. Dist(s): Random

Mysterious Bible Codes. Grant R. Jeffrey. 2 vols. 1997. (978-0-921714-33-0(5)) Fon3tier Res CAN.

Mysterious Biography **see Carl Sandburg's Poems for Children**

Mysterious Cases of Mr. Pin. unabr. ed. Mary Elise Monsell. Narrated by John McDonough. 1 cass. (Running Time: 1 hr.). (gr. 2 up). 1997. 10.00 (978-0-7887-0900-5(3), 95038E7) Recorded Bks.
When Mr. Pin moves to chilly Chicago, he soon is up to his beak in mysterious problems & clues. But with the help of his new young friend, Maggie, he finds clever, tasty solutions to three troublesome cases.

Mysterious Disappearances **see Eyes of the Panther & Other Stories**

Mysterious Edge of the Heroic World. E. L. Konigsburg. Read by Edward Herrmann. 4. (Running Time: 5 hrs. 25 mins.). 2007. 33.75 (978-1-4281-7176-3(2)) Recorded Bks.

Mysterious Edge of the Heroic World. unabr. ed. E. L. Konigsburg. Read by Edward Herrmann. 4 cass. (Running Time: 4 hrs. 30 mins.). (YA). (gr. 5-8). 2007. 30.95 (978-1-4281-7177-0(0)); audio compact disk 46.75 (978-1-4281-7181-7(9)) Recorded Bks.

Mysterious Edge of the Heroic World. unabr. ed. E. L. Konigsburg. Read by E. L. Konigsburg. Read by Edward Herrmann. (Running Time: 4 hrs. 30 mins. 0 sec.). (ENG.). (J). (gr. 5-9). 2007. audio compact disk 24.95 (978-0-7435-6908-8(3)) Pub: S&S Audio. Dist(s): S and S Inc

Mysterious Flame of Queen Loana. Umberto Eco. Read by George Guidall. 13 CDs. (Running Time: 15.5). 2005. audio compact disk 39.99 (978-1-4193-4389-6(0)) Recorded Bks.

Mysterious Flame of Queen Loana. unabr. ed. Umberto Eco. 11 cass. (Running Time: 15 hrs.). 2005. 94.75 (978-1-4193-4468-8(4)) Recorded Bks.

Mysterious Giant of Barletta. Tomie dePaola. (J). 1984. bk. 40.74 (978-0-676-30992-8(5)) SRA McGraw.

Mysterious Gurdjieff. unabr. ed. Stephan Hoeller. 1 cass. (Running Time: 1 hr. 30 min.). 1981. 11.00 (40001) Big Sur Tapes.
An historical overview of Gurdjieff's life & his unique trickster manner of teaching & facilitating transformation.

Mysterious Island. unabr. ed. Jules Verne. Read by Gene Engene. 16 cass. (Running Time: 21 hrs.). 69.95 (978-1-55686-121-5(4), 121) Books in Motion.
During the Civil war, five men & a dog quietly escape from Richmond & the clutches of the Confederate army. Their means of escape is a hot air balloon. While aloft, they are caught in a terrible hurricane which blows them thousands of miles out to sea. The balloon springs a leak & slowly falls from the sky. The escapees fortunately reach an island ... a mysterious island.

Mysterious Journey: Amelia Earhart's Last Flight. Martha Wickham. Illus. by David Lund. 1 cass. (Running Time: 13 min.). Dramatization. (Smithsonian Odyssey Ser.). (ENG.). (J). (gr. 2-5). 1997. 7.95 (978-1-56899-414-7(1), C6006) Soundprints.
Lucy stands in awe before the big red Lockheed Vega airplane in the Amelia Earhart exhibit at the National Air & Space Museum. Suddenly, she finds herself airborne in the cockpit of a twin engine airplane, the Lockheed Electra, which Amelia Earhart flew on her ill fated 1937 flight.

Mysterious Journey: Amelia Earhart's Last Flight, Incl. toy. Martha Wickham. Illus. by David Lund. (Smithsonian Odyssey Ser.). (J). (gr. 2-5). 1997. bk. 35.95 (978-1-56899-413-0(3)); pap. bk. 25.95 (978-1-56899-411-6(7)) Soundprints.

Mysterious Lands. Ann Zwinger. Read by Ann Zwinger. 2 cass. (Running Time: 2 hrs. 30 min.). 1994. 16.95 (978-0-939643-44-8(8), 3508, NrthWrd Bks) TandN Child.
Explores the four great American deserts - where time stands still and where humankind survives only with great effort. Shows abundance & tenacity of desert life forms.

Mysterious Lights & other Cases. Seymour Simon. Narrated by Johnny Heller. (Running Time: 1 hr.). (Einstein Anderson Ser.). (gr. 3 up). 10.00 (978-0-7887-9365-3(9)) Recorded Bks.

Mysterious Mansion **see Great French & Russian Stories, Vol. 1, A Collection**

Mysterious Mansion. unabr. ed. Honoré de Balzac. (Running Time: 56 min.). Dramatization. 1979. 8.95 (N-29) Jimcin Record.
A story of horror & one of faith.

Mysterious Miss Marie Corelli: Queen of Victorian Bestsellers. unabr. ed. Teresa Ransom. Narrated by Judith Boyd. 9 cass. (Running Time: 12 hrs.). 2000. 79.00 (978-1-84197-071-4(9), H1069) Recorded Bks.
Marie Corelli was the most popular author of her time, enjoyed by Queen Victoria as well as the newly literate poor, but she is now practically unknown. Her books were loved by the public but loathed by the critics, to whom she refused to sell copies. Upon her death in 1924, it became glaringly apparent that no one knew the real Marie. She had deliberately confused the facts, so her age & parentage were a mystery. Her acclaimed imagination made her Scottish, American, Italian & 17 when her career began. No one discovered her actual illegitimacy, or that she was a good 10 years older than she claimed. By creating a new persona, Marie entered her own idealized fictional world.

Mysterious Montague: A True Tale of Hollywood, Golf, & Armed Robbery. abr. ed. Leigh Montville. Read by Scott Brick. (Running Time: 21600 sec.). (ENG.). 2008. audio compact disk 29.95 (978-0-7393-6677-6(7), Random AudioBks) Pub: Random Audio Pubg. Dist(s): Random

Mysterious Mr. Blot & Other Stories: In Which We Discover Him. unabr. ed. Pere Butter. Read by Pere Butter. Read by Apple Butter. Illus. by Barbara Robinson. 1 CD. (Running Time: 22 mins.). (Mr. Blot Ser.: Vol. B-1). (YA). (gr. 5 up). 2002. audio compact disk 6.00 (978-0-915090-90-7(2)) Firefall.
The introductory book to the Mr. Blot series of whimsey for word-aware children and adults: in which we discover him.Mr. Blot tampers with the weather in a series of surprises.

Mysterious Mr. Quin: Twelve Complete Mysteries. unabr. ed. Agatha Christie. Read by Hugh Fraser. (Running Time: 31800 sec.). 2006. 31.95 (978-1-57270-530-2(2)) Pub: Audio Partners. Dist(s): PerseuPGW

Mysterious Mr. Quin: Twelve Complete Mysteries. unabr. ed. Agatha Christie. Read by Hugh Fraser. 7 CDs. (Running Time: 31800 sec.). (Audio Editons Mystery Masters Ser.). (ENG.). 2006. audio compact disk 31.95 (978-1-57270-529-6(9)) Pub: AudioGO. Dist(s): Perseus Dist

Mysterious Rider, unabr. ed. Zane Grey. Read by Pat Bottino. 9 cass. (Running Time: 13 hrs.). 1999. 62.95 (978-0-7861-1560-0(2), 2390) Blckstn Audio.
No one knows where he came from, but he is such a terrible gun fighter that they call him "Hell Bent." Then the tragedy comes & out of the shadow comes into the sun shine of love.

Mysterious Rider. unabr. ed. Zane Grey. Read by Jack Sondericker. 8 cass. (Running Time: 11 hrs. 12 min.). 2001. 49.95 (978-1-58116-170-0(0)); audio compact disk 65.00 (978-1-58116-171-7(9)) Books in Motion.
No one knows why the mysterious rider showed up at the ranch, or where he came from. He seems gentle and kindly, but fire smolders behind those eyes which can ignite in a sudden blaze of gunfire. Tragedy lurks around the corner, and someone must make the ultimate sacrifice so others can live, and the mysterious stranger holds the trump card.

Mysterious Rider, unabr. ed. Zane Grey. Read by Pat Bottino. 9 cass. 1999. 62.95 (FS9-50954) Highsmith.

Mysterious Skin. abr. ed. Scott Heim. Read by Michael Ciccolini. 2 cass. (Running Time: 3 hrs.). 1996. 17.95 (978-1-57453-009-4(7), 330045) Audio Lit.

Mysterious Stranger. unabr. ed. Mark Twain. Narrated by Don Randall. 4 CDs. (Running Time: 3 hrs. 54 mins.). 2006. audio compact disk 29.95 (978-0-9790364-2-2(9)) A Audiobooks.
Considered one of Twain's most important short works, The Mysterious Stranger tells the story of the devil coming to a medieval village in the persona of a beautiful, lovable, yet exasperatingly amoral young man. Befriending a small group of boys, Satan exhibits strange charm, compassion and indifference as the tale comes to a surprising conclusion.

Mysterious Stranger. unabr. ed. Mark Twain. Read by Tom Beyer. 4 cass. (Running Time: 4 hrs. 30 min.). Dramatization. 1991. 26.95 (978-1-55686-383-7(7), 383) Books in Motion.
Three young boys, in medieval Austria, experience a visit by a strange and enchanted boy who reveals himself as an angel of a god named Satan.

Mysterious Stranger: And Other Stories. Mark Twain. Read by Jonathan Kent. (Running Time: 25200 sec.). (Unabridged Classics in Audio Ser.). (ENG.). 2005. audio compact disk 59.00 (978-1-4001-3167-9(7)) Pub: Tantor Media. Dist(s): IngramPubServ

Mysterious Stranger: And Other Stories. Mark Twain. Read by Jonathan Kent. (Running Time: 25200 sec.). (Unabridged Classics in Audio Ser.). (ENG.). 2005. audio compact disk 29.99 (978-1-4001-0167-2(0)) Pub: Tantor Media. Dist(s): IngramPubServ

Mysterious Stranger & Other Stories. Mark Twain. Read by Jonathan Kent. (Playaway Young Adult Ser.). (ENG.). 2009. 60.00 (978-1-60775-634-7(X)) Find a World.

Mysterious Stranger & Other Stories. unabr. ed. Mark Twain. Narrated by Jonathan Kent. (Running Time: 7 hrs. 0 mins. 0 sec.). (ENG.). 2009. 19.99 (978-1-4001-5922-2(9)); lab manual ed. 55.99 (978-1-4001-3922-4(8)); audio compact disk 27.99 (978-1-4001-0922-7(1)) Pub: Tantor Media. Dist(s): IngramPubServ

Mysterious Stranger & Other Stories. unabr. collector's ed. Mark Twain. Read by Jonathan Kent. 7 cass. (Running Time: 7 hrs.). (J). 1997. 42.00 (978-0-7366-3649-0(8), 4314) Books on Tape.
Includes: "The Mysterious Stranger," "The Story of the Bad Little Boy," "The Celebrated Jumping Frog of Calaveras County," "The Diary of Adam & Eve," "The Joke That Made Ed's Fortune," "The Man That Corrupted Hadleyburg," "Edward Mills & George Benton: A Tale" & "A Fable".

Mysterious Tadpole. 2004. bk. 24.95 (978-0-89719-676-5(7)); pap. bk. 32.75 (978-1-55592-282-5(1)); pap. bk. 14.95 (978-1-56008-069-5(8)); 8.95 (978-0-89719-904-9(9)); 8.95 (978-1-56008-419-8(7)); cass. & flmstrp 30.00 (978-0-89719-504-1(3)) Weston Woods.

Mysterious Tadpole. Steven Kellogg. audio compact disk (978-1-4025-4619-8(X)) Recorded Bks.

Mysterious Tadpole. Steven Kellogg. 1 cass., 5 bks. (Running Time: 9 min.). (J). pap. bk. 32.75 Weston Woods.
A birthday gift from Uncle McAllister appears to be a tadpole, but it turns out to be much, much more.

Mysterious Tadpole. Steven Kellogg. 1 cass. (Running Time: 9 min.). (J). (ps-4). 1999. pap. bk. 12.95 (QRAC251) Weston Woods.

Mysterious Tadpole, the; Salmon for Simon, A; Fire Stealer, the; Clown of God. 2004. (978-0-89719-848-6(4)); cass. & flmstrp (978-0-89719-704-5(6)) Weston Woods.

Mysterious Thelonious. Chris Raschka. Illus. by Chris Raschka. 11 vols. (Running Time: 7 mins.). pap. bk. 18.95 (978-1-59112-421-4(2)) Live Oak Media.

Mysterious Thelonious. Chris Raschka. Read by Charles Turner. 11 vols. (Running Time: 7 mins.). (Music Makers Ser.). (J). (gr. k-6). 2000. bk. 25.95 (978-0-87499-674-6(0)) Live Oak Media.
This book makes music even for readers who don't know who jazz great Thelonious Monk was. The words slither all over the page. Each spread contains Monk and his piano in various guises on a background that comes as close to synesthesia as possible. Raschka matches the 12 musical notes of the chromatic scale to the 12 values of the color wheel and makes harmonies of watercolor washes, its message of "no wrong notes" is loud and clear.

Mysterious Thelonious. Chris Raschka. Illus. by Chris Raschka. (Running Time: 7 mins.). 2000. 9.95 (978-0-87499-672-2(4)); audio compact disk 12.95 (978-1-59112-420-7(4)) Live Oak Media.

Mysterious Traveler. Radio Spirits Staff. Read by Maurice Tarpiln. 2007. audio compact disk 39.98 (978-1-57019-831-1(4)) Pub: Radio Spirits. Dist(s): AudioGO

Mysterious Traveler. collector's ed. Perf. by Maurice Tarplin. 6 cass. (Running Time: 9 hrs.). Dramatization. 1998. bk. 34.98 (4048) Radio Spirits.
18 scary episodes.

Mysterious Traveler: Dark Density. Perf. by Maurice Tarplin. 6 cass. (Running Time: 6 hrs.). 1999. 19.98 (AB109) Radio Spirits.

Mysterious Traveler: Journey into the Strange. Perf. by Maurice Tarplin. (ENG.). 2008. audio compact disk 18.95 (978-1-57019-865-6(9)) Radio Spirits.

Mysterious Traveler: No One on the Line & Fire in the Sky. Perf. by Maurice Tarplin. 1 cass. (Running Time: 1 hr.). 2001. 6.98 (1517) Radio Spirits.

Mysterious Traveler: Queen of the Cats. 6 cass. (Running Time: 6 hrs.). 1999. 19.98 (AB193) Radio Spirits.

Mysterious Traveler: The Devil & the Deep Blue Sea & I Won't Die Alone. Perf. by Maurice Tarplin. 1 cass. (Running Time: 1 hr.). 2001. 6.98 (1551) Radio Spirits.

Mysterious Traveler: The Good Die Young & The Accusing Corpse. Perf. by Maurice Tarplin. 1 cass. (Running Time: 1 hr.). 2001. 6.98 (2502) Radio Spirits.

Mysterious Traveler: The Most Famous Man in the World & No Grave Can Hold Me. Perf. by Maurice Tarplin. 1 cass. (Running Time: 1 hr.). 2001. 6.98 (2203) Radio Spirits.

Mysterious Traveller see Extraordinary Adventures of Arsene Lupin

Mystery. Peter Straub. 2004. 10.95 (978-0-7435-4299-9(1)) Pub: S&S Audio. Dist(s): S and S Inc

Mystery, Volume 1. (Running Time: 6 hrs.). 2004. audio compact disk 29.95 (978-1-57816-199-7(1)) Audio File.

***Mystery: An Alex Delaware Novel.** abr. ed. Jonathan Kellerman. (ENG.). 2011. audio compact disk 32.00 (978-0-7393-6906-7(7), Random AudioBks) Pub: Random Audio Pubg. Dist(s): Random

***Mystery: An Alex Delaware Novel.** unabr. ed. Jonathan Kellerman. (ENG.). 2011. audio compact disk 45.00 (978-0-7393-6908-1(3), Random AudioBks) Pub: Random Audio Pubg. Dist(s): Random

Mystery - A Ransom Nation. Reuven Doron. 1 cass. (Running Time: 1 hr. 30 min.). (Mystery of Israel & the Church Ser.: Vol. 2). 2000. 5.00 (RD01-002) Morning NC.
Reuven offers insight into the proper relationship between Israel & the church.

Mystery-Adventure, Vol. 1. 6 cass. (Running Time: 6 hrs.). 24.95 Set in bookshelf album. (978-1-57816-028-0(6), MA1012) Audio File.
Includes: "Big Town" (9-23-42); "Counterspy" (5-2-50); "Crime Club" (6-19-47); "Crime Doctor" (4-29-45); "Dragnet" (1-25-51); "Gangbusters" (10-9-48); "Inner Sanctum" (4-17-50); "Lights Out" (6-8-43); "Mr. District Attorney" (4-11-51); "Mysterious Traveler" (7-27-47); "Suspense" (1-6-49); "The Whistler" (4-4-46).

Mystery-Adventure, Vol. 2. 6 cass. (Running Time: 6 hrs.). 24.95 Set in bookshelf album. (978-1-57816-029-7(4), MA2022) Audio File.
Includes: "The Big Story" (12-15-47); "Escape" (6-30-50); "Green Hornet" (10-31-39); "Inner Sanctum" (6-5-45); "A Life in Your Hands" (9-13-49); "Lights Out" (4-6-38); "Molle Mystery Theatre" (1940s); "Mystery House" (1944); "Mystery in the Air" (8-14-47); "Murder at Midnight" (1946); "Suspense" (5-1-47); "The Whistler" (6-2-48).

Mystery & Adventure. abr. ed. 4 cass. (Running Time: 6 hrs.). 10.95 (4005) Audio Bk.
Recordings of original programs from the golden days of radio: "The Shadow," "Sherlock Holmes," "Jack Armstrong" & "Flash Gordon".

Mystery & Meaning of the Ancient Rituals. Manly P. Hall. 5 cass. (Running Time: 2 hrs. 30 min.). 1999. 40.00 set incl. album. (978-0-89314-193-6(3), S620523) Philos Res.

Mystery & Mirth for Anyone Stuck in Traffic. collector's ed. Jonathan Lowe. 1 cass. (Running Time: 1 hr. 30 min.). 2000. 9.95 (978-0-7366-4924-7(7)) Books on Tape.
Tired of fighting traffic? Here's a 90 minute production of original horror & humor to take your mind away from the aggravation. It's the perfect gift, too, for anyone getting old while waiting for those lights to change. Professionally mixed, these ear-catching audio dramas utilize the talents of a dozen actors, with a portion of the proceeds to benefit Sun Sounds Reading Service for the Visually Impaired.

Mystery at Bear Lake. Prod. by Laraim Associates. (Barclay Family Adventure Ser.). (J). 2005. audio compact disk (978-1-56254-995-4(2)) Saddleback Edu.

Mystery at Blackbeard's Cove: Audio. Audrey Penn. 2008. audio compact disk 29.95 (978-1-933718-17-0(X)) Pub: Tanglewood Pr IN. Dist(s): Natl Bk Netwk

Mystery at Lilac Inn. unabr. ed. Carolyn Keene. Read by Laura Linney. (Running Time: 11760 sec.). (Nancy Drew Ser.). (ENG.). (J). (gr. 3-7). 2007. audio compact disk 14.95 (978-0-7393-5060-7(9), Listening Lib) Pub: Random Audio Pubg. Dist(s): Random

Mystery at Lilac Inn 4, Vol. 4. unabr. ed. Carolyn Keene. Read by Laura Linney. 2 cass. (Running Time: 3 hrs. 16 mins.). (Nancy Drew Mystery Stories). (J). (gr. 4-7). 2004. 19.55 (978-0-8072-0764-2(0), S YA 410 CX, Listening Lib) Pub: Random Audio Pubg. Dist(s): NetLibrary CO

Mystery at Marin Marsh. abr. ed. Denise M. Jordan. Illus. by Carol Stutz. (Rigby Literacy Ser.). 2001. audio compact disk 10.40 (978-0-7578-2051-9(4), Rigby PEA) Pearson EdAUS AUS.

Mystery at Salvage Rock. E. A. Olsen. (Oceanography Ser.). (J). (gr. 3 up). 1970. pap. bk. 10.60 (978-0-87783-195-2(5)) Oddo.

Mystery at the Gym. unabr. ed. Roni S. Denholtz. 1 cass. (Running Time: 20 min.). (Adventure Abounds Ser.). (J). (gr. 3-6). 1984. bk. 16.99 (978-0-934898-65-2(0)); pap. bk. 9.95 (978-0-934898-78-2(2)) Jan Prods.
Linda & her brother Brian often play racquetball at the "Y" where their father works. One day they find jewlery hidden there, & that night the place is broken into. They set out to investigate.

Mystery at the Haunted House. David A. Adler. Narrated by Christina Moore. 1 cass., 1 bk. (Running Time: 30 mins.). (J). (gr. 2-9). 2001. bk. & stu. ed. 23.24 (41152B7) Recorded Bks.

Mystery at the Haunted House. unabr. ed. David A. Adler. Narrated by Christina Moore. 1 cass. (Running Time: 30 mins.). (Cam Jansen Ser.: No. 13). (gr. 2 up). 2001. 10.00 (978-0-7887-4395-5(3), 96289E7) Recorded Bks.
Cam Jansen, her aunt & uncle & friend Eric go through the scary haunted house at the amusement park. Everyone enjoyed the wonderful time until her aunt tries to buy some snacks. Her wallet is missing! Will Cam be able to solve the mystery of the missing money with her amazing photographic memory?.

Mystery Atlanta Style, Contrib. by Ruth Birmingham et al. 6 cass. (Running Time: 9 hrs.). 2000. 18.95 (978-1-889409-10-8(3)) LadybugPr CA.

Mystery Club, 12 cass. (Running Time: 12 hrs.). 1999. 29.98 (AB129) Radio Spirits.

Mystery Club Solves a Murder. unabr. ed. Harley L. Sachs. 7 cass. (Running Time: 7 hrs.). 2000. 35.00 (978-0-9705390-2-1(9)) I D E V C O.
Six elderly women in a Portland, Oregon retirement building set out to solve the murder of a resident one of them has found dead on the roof.

Mystery Dogs. Fred Grove. (Running Time: 0 hr. 18 mins.). 2000. 10.95 (978-1-60083-541-4(4)) Iofy Corp.

***Mystery House.** RadioArchives.com. (Running Time: 600). (ENG.). 2009. audio compact disk 29.98 (978-1-61081-085-2(6)) Radio Arch.

Mystery House: Prowler of the Cumberland & Spearfinger. Esther Luttrell. Read by Esther Luttrell. 1 cass. (Running Time: 30 min.). (Mystery House: Vol. 1). (J). (gr. 1-6). 1999. 7.95 (978-0-9667485-7-4(3)) Oak Shadow Pr.

Mystery in the Air: Beyond Good & Evil & Crime & Punishment. Peter Lorre. 1 cass. (Running Time: 1 hr.). 2001. 6.98 (2607) Radio Spirits.

Mystery in the Computer Game. Read by Aimee Lilly. Characters created by Gertrude Chandler Warner. (Boxcar Children Ser.: No. 78). (J). 2004. audio compact disk 19.99 (978-1-58926-281-2(6)) Oasis Audio.

Mystery in the Computer Game. Gertrude Chandler Warner. (Running Time: 5400 sec.). (Boxcar Children Ser.: No. 78). (J). 2005. audio compact disk 14.95 (978-0-7861-7490-4(0)) Blckstn Audio.

Mystery in the Computer Game. unabr. ed. Gertrude Chandler Warner. Read by Aimee Lilly. 2 cass. (Running Time: 2 hrs.). (Boxcar Children Ser.: No. 78). (J). 2003. 12.99 (978-1-58926-120-4(8), A65L-0110, Oasis Kids) Oasis Audio.
The Boxcar Children have become experts at Ringmaster, a computer game, and the creators ask them to help test the new game, Ringmaster II. But when they do, clues about situations and people in the game are surprisingly familiar. Is there something wrong? The children are determined to find out!.

Mystery in the Computer Game. unabr. ed. Gertrude Chandler Warner. Narrated by Aimee Lilly. (Boxcar Children Ser.). (ENG.). 2003. 10.49 (978-1-60814-095-4(4)) Oasis Audio.

Mystery in the Fortune Cookie. Gertrude Chandler Warner. (Running Time: 5400 sec.). (Boxcar Children Ser.: No. 96). (J). 2005. audio compact disk 14.95 (978-0-7861-7480-5(3)) Blckstn Audio.

Mystery in the Fortune Cookie. unabr. ed. Gertrude Chandler Warner. 2 cass. (Running Time: 1 hr. 50 min.). (Boxcar Children Ser.: No. 96). (J). 2003. 12.99 (978-1-58926-286-7(7), Oasis Kids) Oasis Audio.

Mystery in the Fortune Cookie. unabr. ed. Gertrude Chandler Warner. Narrated by Aimee Lilly. (Boxcar Children Ser.). (ENG.). (J). 2003. 10.49 (978-1-60814-093-0(8)) Oasis Audio.

Mystery in the Fortune Cookie. unabr. ed. Gertrude Chandler Warner. Narrated by Aimee Lilly. 2 CDs. (Running Time: 1 hr. 50 min.). (Boxcar Children Ser.: No. 96). (ENG.). (J). 2003. audio compact disk 14.99 (978-1-58926-287-4(5), Oasis Kids) Oasis Audio.

Mystery Is My Hobby: Deadly Boxing Match & the Wife Abuser. Perf. by Glen G. Langdon. 1 cass. (Running Time: 1 hr.). 2001. 6.98 (1518) Radio Spirits.

Mystery Is My Hobby: Kenneth Pringer-Polo Player & Waynewright Murder Case. Perf. by Lon Clark. 1 cass. (Running Time: 1 hr.). 2001. 6.98 (1552) Radio Spirits.

Mystery Lady. Perf. by Etta James. 1 cass. . (Running Time: 1 hr.).; 9.98; audio compact disk 16.98 Lifedance.
Vocals with piano, saxophone, trumpet, bass & percussion. Grammy Award winner James' low-key voice performs Billie Holiday classics. Includes "Body & Soul," "Don't Explain," "Embraceable You," "How Deep Is the Ocean," "I Don't Stand a Ghost of a Chance (With You)," "I'll Be Seeing You," "(I'm Afraid) The Masquerade Is Over," "Lover Man (Oh Where Can You Be)," "The Man I Love," "The Very Thought of You" & "You've Changed." Demo CD or cassette available.

Mystery Method: How to Get Beautiful Women into Bed. Mystery. Read by Alan Sklar. Frwd. by Neil Strauss. (Playaway Adult Nonfiction Ser.). (ENG.). 2009. 59.99 (978-1-60812-538-8(6)) Find a World.

Mystery Method: How to Get Beautiful Women into Bed. unabr. ed. Mystery & Chris D. Odom. Narrated by Neil Strauss & Alan Sklar. (Running Time: 7 hrs. 0 mins. 0 sec.). (ENG.). 2007. audio compact disk 29.99 (978-1-4001-0411-6(4)) Pub: Tantor Media. Dist(s): IngramPubServ

Mystery Method: How to Get Beautiful Women into Bed. unabr. ed. Mystery & Chris D. Odom. Narrated by Alan Sklar. Frwd. by Neil Strauss. (Running Time: 7 hrs. 0 mins. 0 sec.). (ENG.). 2007. audio compact disk 19.99 (978-1-4001-5411-1(1)); audio compact disk 59.99 (978-1-4001-3411-3(0)) Pub: Tantor Media. Dist(s): IngramPubServ

Mystery Mile. unabr. ed. Margery Allingham. Read by Francis Matthews. 6 cass. (Running Time: 8 hrs.). (Albert Campion Ser.). 2000. 29.95 (978-1-57270-137-3(4), N61137u) Pub: Audio Partners. Dist(s): PerseuPGW
Upper class amateur sleuth, Albert Campion is on the case to discover who is trying to murder Judge Crowdy Lobbett & four others have already died in his place. Can Campion solve the case without becoming another victim.

Mystery Mile. unabr. ed. Margery Allingham. Read by Francis Matthews. 8 CDs. (Running Time: 12 hrs.). (Albert Campion Ser.). 2000. audio compact disk 79.95 (978-0-7540-5336-1(9), CCD 027) Pub: Chivers Audio Bks GBR. Dist(s): AudioGO
Judge Crowdy Lobbett knew too much about the Simister Gang. So Simister had him followed & tried to kill him. He followed him through the United States & across the heart of England, all the way to the Mystery Mile. And there he encountered Albert Campion.

Mystery! Mystery! Read by Jim Weiss. 1 cass. (Running Time: 1 hr.). (J). (GHP13) NewSound.

Mystery! Mystery! for Children. Short Stories. As told by Jim Weiss. 1 cass. (Running Time: 1 hr.). Dramatization. (Storyteller's Version Ser.). (J). (gr. 2 up). 1993. 10.95 (978-1-882513-13-0(4), 1124-13); audio compact disk 14.95 (978-1-882513-38-3(X), 1124-013) Greathall Prods.
Three of the most popular mysteries of all time in one volume. Edgar Allan Poe's "The Purloined Letter", G.K. Chesterton's beloved Father Brown in "The Blue Cross" and a favorite Sherlock Holmes case - "The Red Headed League".

Mystery of a Hansom Cab. Fergus Hume. Read by Anais 9000. 2008. 27.95 (978-1-60112-182-0(2)) Babblebooks.

Mystery of a Hansom Cab. Fergus W. Hume. Read by Walter Covell. 7 cass. (Running Time: 10 hrs. 30 min.). 1989. 42.00 (C-153) Jimcin Record.
Australian murder mystery. Includes album.

Mystery of a Hansom Cab. unabr. ed. Fergus W. Hume. Read by Flo Gibson. 6 cass. (Running Time: 8 hrs.). 1995. 24.95 (978-1-55685-609-9(1)) Audio Bk Con.
In this 19th century best seller there is a labyrinth of dark secrets, missing papers, blackmail & a cladestine marriage when a drunk man is chloroformed in a hansom cab in Melbourne.

Mystery of a Hansom Cab. unabr. ed. Fergus W. Hume. Read by Walter Covell. 7 cass. (Running Time: 10 hrs.). 1986. 49.95 (978-0-7861-0552-6(6), 2046) Blckstn Audio.
One lonely night, a cabbie discovers that his intoxicated passenger has been suffocated with a handkerchief saturated in chloroform. The murderer, the victim & the motive are all unknown.

Mystery of a Hansom Cab. unabr. collector's ed. Fergus W. Hume. Read by Walter Covell. 7 cass. (Running Time: 10 hrs. 30 min.). 1986. 56.00 (978-0-7366-3915-6(2), 9153) Books on Tape.

Mystery of Babylon. Chuck Missler. 2 cass. (Running Time: 3 hrs.). (Briefing Packages by Chuck Missler). 1994. vinyl bd. 14.95 (978-1-880532-97-3(2)) Koinonia Hse.
The most important city in Iraq is not Baghdad and you have probably never heard it mentioned on the 10 o'clock news.It is mentioned over 300 times in the Bible (and it is even mentioned three times in the family tree of our Lord Jesus Christ!) This is, of course, the fabled Babylon.It was founded by the first world dictator, Nimrod, and it may well be destined to be the capital of the final world dictator,commonly called the Antichrist! And this may all be emerging on our near horizon.

Mystery of Babylon: An Alternate View. Chuck Missler. 2 CD's. (Running Time: 2 hours). (Briefing Packages by Chuck Missler). 2004. audio compact disk 19.95 (978-1-57821-249-1(9)) Koinonia Hse.

Mystery of Commitment. Vilma Seelaus. 1 cass. (Running Time: 1 hr. 24 min.). 7.95 (TAH092) Alba Hse Comns.
The complex concept of commitment & how it relates to one as a person, priest or religious is examined. Side A: Introduction, Commitment & the Mystery of Person, Who We are & Who God is, Commitment & Mission Side B: Commitment & Religious Life, Imperfection in Relation to Perfectionism, Mystery of Call, Conclusion.

Mystery of Death. Adrienne Von Speyr. Tr. by Graham Harrison from GER. 5 cass. 1988. pap. bk. 9.95 (978-0-89870-204-0(6), 945) Ignatius Pr.
Stirring and provocative look at death and its many meanings.

Mystery of Edwin Drood. Charles Dickens. Read by David Thorn. (Running Time: 36000 sec.). 2006. 59.95 (978-0-7861-4527-0(7)); audio compact disk 72.00 (978-0-7861-7177-4(4)) Blckstn Audio.

Mystery of Edwin Drood. Charles Dickens. Read by Walter Covell. 8 cass. (Running Time: 11 hrs.). 1989. 39.00 (C-157) Jimcin Record.
Famous unsolved mystery. Includes album.

Mystery of Edwin Drood. Charles Dickens. 1 cass. (Running Time: 1 hr.). (Radiobook Ser.). 1987. 4.98 (978-0-929541-26-6(X)) Radiola Co.

Mystery of Edwin Drood. abr. ed. Charles Dickens. Perf. by Paul Scofield. 2 cass. (Running Time: 3 hrs.). (Ultimate Classics Ser.). 2004. 18.00 (978-1-931056-67-0(6), N Millennium Audio) New Millenn Enter.
When young Edwin Drood mysteriously diasappears from the quiet cathedral town of Cloisterhaur, foul play seems certain. The prime suspect is John Jasper, Edwin's uncle who frequents the dark opium underworld beneath his church choir.

Mystery of Edwin Drood. abr. ed. Charles Dickens. Read by Paul Scofield. 3 CDs. (Running Time: 3 hrs.). 2004. audio compact disk 24.95 (978-1-59007-576-0(5)) Pub: New Millenn Enter. Dist(s): PerseuPGW

Mystery of Edwin Drood, unabr. ed. Charles Dickens. Read by Flo Gibson. 7 cass. (Running Time: 10 hrs 30 min.). (gr. 7 up). 1991. 25.95 (978-1-55685-214-5(2)) Audio Bk Con.
An opium den, a graveyard, a cathedral tower, a young ladies' school, dark London streets & a turbulent river are part of the backdrop of this mystery. Hilariously funny & horribly grim, once again Dickens peoples this novel with unforgettable characters. It is up to you to solve the mystery in this unfinished novel.

Mystery of Edwin Drood. unabr. ed. Charles Dickens. Read by Walter Covell. 8 cass. (Running Time: 11 hrs. 30 mins.). 1986. 56.95 (978-0-7861-0550-2(X), 2044) Blckstn Audio.
Who killed Edwin Drood? Was it his opium-addict uncle, John Jasper, or the quarrelsome Neville Landless? Or was Drood actually dead? Taking us from the calm cathedral town of Cloisterharn to London's filthy opium dens, Dickens creates a haunting atmosphere & slowly unravels the threads of revelations, twisted though they may be.

Mystery of Edwin Drood. unabr. ed. Charles Dickens. Read by David Thorn. (Running Time: 36000 sec.). 2006. audio compact disk 29.95 (978-0-7861-7608-3(3)) Blckstn Audio.

Mystery of Edwin Drood. unabr. ed. Charles Dickens. Read by Walter Covell. 8 cass. (Running Time: 12 hrs.). 2001. 29.95 (978-0-7366-6764-7(4)) Books on Tape.
Dicken's contribution to the field of crime & detection. Against a background of opium dens & nocturnal graveyard visits to the moldering monastic crypts, the author weaves a plot centered on the ominous disappearance of young Edwin Drood.

Mystery of Edwin Drood, unabr. ed. Charles Dickens. Read by Walter Covell. 8 cass. (Running Time: 12 hrs.). 1999. 56.95 (FS9-34228) Highsmith.

Mystery of Edwin Drood. unabr. collector's ed. Charles Dickens. Read by Walter Covell. 8 cass. (Running Time: 12 hrs.). 1986. 64.00 (978-0-7366-3918-7(7), 9157) Books on Tape.

Mystery of Edwin Drood & Tolkien & Time Fiction (audio CD) Gilbert Highet. (ENG.). 2007. audio compact disk 12.95 (978-1-57970-483-4(2), Audio-For) J Norton Pubs.

***Mystery of Evil & the Miracle of Life.** Featuring Ravi Zacharias. 1995. audio compact disk 9.00 (978-1-61256-050-2(4)) Ravi Zach.

Mystery of Grace. unabr. ed. Charles de Lint. Read by Paul Michael Garcia & Tai Sammons. (Running Time: 10 hrs. 0 mins.). (ENG.). 2009. 29.95 (978-1-4332-9470-9(2)); 59.95 (978-1-4332-9466-2(4)); audio compact disk 90.00 (978-1-4332-9467-9(2)) Blckstn Audio.

Mystery of Heroism see Great American Short Stories, Vol. II, A Collection

Mystery of Heroism see Red Badge of Courage & Other Stories

Mystery of Heroism. 1983. (S-47) Jimcin Record.

***Mystery of History Volume I Second Edition Audio Book, vol. One.** 2nd ed. Linda Hobar. (Running Time: 674). 1. (ENG.). 2010. stu. ed. 42.95 (978-0-615-37566-3(9)) Mystery of Hist.

***Mystery of History Volume II Audio Book: The Early Church adn the Middle Ages, vol. II.** The Mystery of History. (Running Time: 838). 2008. 48.95 (978-0-615-39226-4(1)) Mystery of Hist.

Mystery of Israel & the Church Series. unabr. ed. Reuven Doron. 4 cass. (Running Time: 6 hrs.). 2000. 20.00 (RD01-000) Morning NC.
Includes: "One New Man," "The Mystery - A Ransom Nation," "The Appointed Time" & "The Womb of Intercession." Reuven offers insight into the proper relationship between Israel & the church.

Mystery of Jaguar Reef. Thomas M. Lopez. 2 cass. (Running Time: 2 hrs.). 2001. 16.95 (ZBSF021); audio compact disk 22.95 (ZBSF022) Lodestone Catalog.
Jack Flanders travels to Belize to investigate a strange case of altered personality & as usual, he finds more than meets the ear. Scuba diving, a mysterious pirate wreck, spirits of the dead & sultry tropical nights are all to be expected.

Mystery of Jaguar Reef, unabr. ed. Thomas M. Lopez. 2 cass. (Running Time: 2 hr.). 1996. 16.95 (978-1-881137-46-7(5), ZBSF021); audio compact disk 22.95 (978-1-881137-45-0(7), ZBSF022) ZBS Found.
Jack uncovers a mystery of mixed-up identities while scuba-diving in the Great Barrier Reef off the coast of Belize, Central America.

Mystery of Love, Divine & Human. Instructed by Manly P. Hall. 8.95 (978-0-89314-191-2(7), C831120) Philos Res.

Mystery of Magnets. Sundance/Newbridge, LLC Staff. (Early Science Ser.). (gr. k-3). 2007. audio compact disk 12.00 (978-1-4007-6325-2(8)); audio compact disk 12.00 (978-1-4007-6327-6(4)); audio compact disk 12.00 (978-1-4007-6326-9(6)) Sund Newbrdge.

Mystery of Mary & the Immaculate Conception. Frederick L. Miller. 1 cass. (Running Time: 1 hr.). 1990. 2.50 (978-1-56036-057-5(7)) AMI Pr.

Mystery of Mary's Perpetual Virginity. Frederick L. Miller. 1 cass. (Running Time: 1 hr.). 1990. 2.50 (978-1-56036-058-2(5)) AMI Pr.

Mystery of Missing Big Wig: Audiocassette. Jill Eggleton. (Sails Literacy Ser.). (gr. 3 up). 10.00 (978-0-7578-6994-5(7)) Rigby Educ.

Mystery of Mr. Nice. unabr. ed. Bruce Hale. Read by Jon Cryer. 1 cass. (Running Time: 1 hr. 24 mins.). (Chet Gecko Mystery Ser.: No. 2). (J). (gr. 3-6). 2004. pap. bk. 17.00 (978-0-8072-0343-9(2), Listening Lib) Random Audio Pubg.

Mystery of Mrs. Dickenson see Classic Detective Stories, Vol. II, A Collection

Mystery of Mrs. Dickenson. abr. ed. Nicholas Carter. 1 cass. (Running Time: 50 min.). Dramatization. 1977. pap. bk. 9.95; 8.95 (D-1) Jimcin Record.
Nick Carter & Auguste Duplin track down missing valuables.

Mystery of My Being: John of the Cross & Transformation in God. Margaret Dorgan. 1 cass. (Running Time: 43 min.). 1991. 7.95 (TAH252) Alba Hse Comns.
Sister Dorgan explores the questions "Why did God call me into existence?" & "What is the divine purpose for my life".

Mystery of Old Dan. Howard W. Gabriel, III. (J). (gr. k-12). 1987. 4.95 (978-0-936997-13-1(3), T87-11) M & H Enter.
Grani always wanted to become a detective. She gets a chance at solving part of the greatest mysteries of the 20th century.

Mystery of Red Mountain. Howard W. Gabriel, III. (J). (gr. k-12). 1987. 4.95 (T87-10) M & H Enter.
A youngster who wants to surpass mediocrity finally gets his chance.. Johnnie must risk his life & that of his pal Matt to save his dad's important job as prison warden.

Mystery of Robert E. Lee: A Light & Enlightening Lecture, Featuring Elliot Engel. 2000. bk. 15.00 (978-1-890123-25-3(0)) Media Cnslts.

Mystery of Swordfish Reef. unabr. ed. Arthur W. Upfield. Read by Peter Hosking. 5 cass. (Running Time: 4 hrs. 28 mins.). (Inspector Napoleon Bonaparte Mysteries). 2000. 40.00 (978-1-74030-170-1(6)) Pub: Bolinda Pubng AUS. Dist(s): Bolinda Pub Inc

mystery of Swordfish Reef. unabr. ed. Arthur W. Upfield. Read by Peter Hosking. (Running Time: 7 hrs. 25 mins.). (Inspector Napoleon Bonaparte Mysteries). 2009. audio compact disk 77.95 (978-1-74214-125-1(0), 9781742141251) Pub: Bolinda Pubng AUS. Dist(s): Bolinda Pub Inc

Mystery of the Babe Ruth Baseball. unabr. ed. David A. Adler. 1 read-along cass. (Running Time: 43 mins.). (Follow the Reader Ser.). (J). (gr. 2-4). 1987. pap. bk. & tchr.'s training gde. ed. 3.99 (FTR89P, Listening Lib) Random Audio Pubg.
When a prized baseball-autographed by Babe Ruth-is stolen, Cam's amazing mental camera is put to the test in another of her zestful mysteries.

Mystery of the Babe Ruth Baseball. unabr. ed. David A. Adler. Read by Susan Sandler. 1 cass. (Running Time: 43 mins.). (Cam Jansen Ser.: No. 6). (J). (gr. 2-4). 1985. pap. bk. 17.00 (978-0-8072-0068-1(9), FTR89SP, Listening Lib) Random Audio Pubg.

Mystery of the Blue Ring. unabr. ed. Patricia Reilly Giff. 1 read-along cass. (Running Time: 51 min.). (Polka Dot Private Eye Ser.). (J). (gr. 1-2). 1989. pap. bk. 15.98 (978-0-8072-0163-3(4), FTR 134 SP, Listening Lib) Random Audio Pubg.
When a blue ring is missing, the whole class thinks it was Dawn Bosco who stole it. With the detective kit her grandmother gave her - a polka dot hat & fake glasses, Dawn sets out to track down the thief. Includes book and guide.

***Mystery of the Blue Train: A BBC Full-Cast Radio Drama.** Agatha Christie. Narrated by Maurice Denham & Full Cast Production Staff. (Running Time: 2 hrs. 35 mins. 0 sec.). (ENG.). 2010. audio compact disk 24.95 (978-1-84607-035-8(X)) Pub: AudioGO. Dist(s): Perseus Dist

Mystery of the Blue Train: A BBC Full-Cast Radio Drama. unabr. ed. Agatha Christie. Read by John Moffatt. 6 cass. (Running Time: 8 hrs. 26 mins.). 2003. 29.95 (978-1-57270-355-1(5)) Pub: Audio Partners. Dist(s): PerseuPGW

Mystery of the Blue Train: A BBC Full-Cast Radio Drama. unabr. ed. Agatha Christie. Read by John Moffatt. 7 CDs. (Running Time: 8 hrs. 26 mins.). (Mystery Masters Ser.). (ENG.). 2003. audio compact disk 32.95 (978-1-57270-356-8(3)) Pub: AudioGO. Dist(s): Perseus Dist
On her way to meet her lover, Ruth Kettering is found strangled to death on the train. Missing is the valuable Heart of Fire rubies, which her father gave her. Poirot delves into the case, sorting through the stories of the passengers on the train, Ruth's lover, and her husband Derek Kettering. The eccentric and fastidious Hercule Poirot must untangle the web of lies, love, and changing affections to find Ruth's true murderer.

Mystery of the Box in the Attic. 1 cass. (Running Time: 1 hr. 30 mins.). 2001. 11.99 (HEL 1046) VAI Audio.
Tales with music for young people. Tchaikovsky's beloved ballets that creates a delightful & enriching learning experience & a wonderful introduction to the world of ballet.

Mystery of the Carnival Prize. David A. Adler. Narrated by Christina Moore. (Running Time: 45 mins.). (Cam Jansen Ser.: No. 9). (J). 1999. 10.75 (978-1-4193-1595-4(1)) Recorded Bks.

Mystery of the Cupboard. unabr. ed. Lynne Reid Banks. 4 cass. (Running Time: 6 hrs.). 14.95 (71880) Books on Tape.
The startling mystery of the magic cupboard is finally revealed! When Omri's mother inherits a house in the country from an unknown cousin, Omri happens upon an old journal & a sealed cashbox. His mind races...can it be...are these family artifacts related to the magic in the cupboard? Omri is fascinated by the story in the journal. It reveals long kept family secrets & precious links between past & present. The adventure unfolds when he slowly pieces together the clues that hold the key to the astonishing mystery.

Mystery of the Cupboard. unabr. ed. Lynne Reid Banks. Read by Lynne Reid Banks. 3 vols. (Running Time: 4 hrs. 35 mins.). (Indian in the Cupboard Ser.: No. 4). (J). (gr. 3-7). 1993. pap. bk. 36.00 (978-0-8072-7416-3(X), YA852SP, Listening Lib) Random Audio Pubg.
A faded journal reveals how the cupboard & its magic were created - & changed the destiny of Omri's family.

Mystery of the Dinosaur Bones. unabr. ed. David A. Adler. Read by Susan Sandler. 1 cass. (Running Time: 45 mins.). (Cam Jansen Ser.: No. 3). (J). (gr. 2-4). 1984. pap. bk. & tchr.'s training gde. ed. 17.00 (978-0-8072-0056-8(5), FTR 83SP, Listening Lib) Random Audio Pubg.
Only Cam, with her photographic memory, realizes that someone is stealing dinosaur bones from the museum. But no one except her friend, Eric, will believe her. They dig up plenty of clues to uncover the culprit.

Mystery of the Dinosaur Bones. unabr. ed. David A. Adler. Narrated by Barbara Caruso. 1 cass. (Running Time: 45 mins.). (Cam Jansen Ser.: No. 3). (gr. 2 up). 1997. 10.00 (978-0-7887-0673-8(X), 94813E7) Recorded Bks.
A lively, funny tale of Cam Jansen's search for dinosaur bones missing from a museum exhibit.

Mystery of the Fire Spirits. Ted Andrews. Read by Ted Andrews. 1 cass. (Running Time: 45 min.). 1994. 10.00 (978-1-888767-01-8(4)) Life Magic Ent.
Music & meditation to guide listener to experience the spirit & creative energies of fire to awaken sexuality, psychic ability & artistic energies.

Mystery of the Jelly Bean Trail. unabr. ed. Roni S. Denholtz. 1 cass. (Running Time: 20 min.). (Fun to Read Ser.). (J). (gr. 3-6). 1983. bk. 16.99 (978-0-934898-41-6(3)); pap. bk. 9.95 (978-0-934898-29-4(4)) Jan Prods.
This story about two friends who explore the woods near their homes includes a sub-theme about the need to be careful with prescription drugs.

Mystery of the Lost Ark. Chuck Missler. 2 cass. (Running Time: 3 hrs.). (Briefing Packages by Chuck Missler). 1993. vinyl bd. 14.95 (978-1-880532-82-9(4)) Koinonia Hse.
** What ever happened to the fabled Ark of the Covenant? * Why are so many searching for it? * Does it really have magical powers?* What does it have to do with the planned rebuilding of the Temple in Jerusalem?Join Chuck as he examines the history of the Ark of the Covenant, in light of the numerous searches and legends surrounding this elusive artifact. Included is a detailed look at the Tabernacle and the Camp of Israel, describing the Levitical symbolism of God's plan of redemption.This briefing pack reviews the origin, role, history, and possible destiny, of this mysterious element of Israel's heritage.*

Mystery of the Missing Cookies: Early Explorers Fluent Set A Audio CD. Benchmark Education Staff. (J). 2006. audio compact disk 10.00 (978-1-4108-7642-3(X)) Benchmark Educ.

Mystery of the Missing Leopard/Wild Cat. Steck-Vaughn Staff. (J). 1999. (978-0-7398-0933-4(4)) SteckVau.

Mystery of the Mummy's Curse. Read by Aimee Lilly. Characters created by Gertrude Chandler Warner. (Boxcar Children Ser.: No. 88). 2004. audio compact disk 19.99 (978-1-58926-280-5(8)) Oasis Audio.

Mystery of the Mummy's Curse. Gertrude Chandler Warner. (Running Time: 5400 sec.). (Boxcar Children Ser.: No. 88). (J). 2005. audio compact disk 14.95 (978-0-7861-7481-2(1)) Blckstn Audio.

Mystery of the Mummy's Curse. unabr. ed. Created by Gertrude Chandler Warner. 2 cass. (Running Time: 1 hr. 50 min.). (Boxcar Children Ser.: No. 88). (J). 2003. 12.99 (978-1-58926-124-2(0), A65L-0150, Oasis Kids) Oasis Audio.
Henry, Jessie, Violet and Benny are helping the Greenfield Museum set up an exhibit about ancient Egypt, when all sorts of strange things begin to go wrong! Is the spooky sarcophagus really cursed, or is someone trying to make sure the exhibit isn?t successful? The children are sure to find out, whether they?re ready or not!.

Mystery of the Mummy's Curse. unabr. ed. Gertrude Chandler Warner. Narrated by Aimee Lilly. (Boxcar Children Ser.). (ENG.). (J). 2003. 10.49 (978-1-60814-096-1(2)) Oasis Audio.

Mystery of the Red Mountain. Howard W. Gabriel, III. 1 cass. (Running Time: 1 hr.). (J). 1987. 4.95 (978-0-936997-12-4(5)) M & H Enter.
A youngster who wants to surpass mediocrity finally gets his chance. Johnnie must risk his life & that of his pal Matt to save his dad's important job as prison warden.

Mystery of the Ring. unabr. ed. Short Stories. Marion Lillie. Read by Marilyn Langbehn. 2 cass. (Running Time: 2 hrs.). Dramatization. 1992. 16.95 (978-1-55686-404-9(3), 404) Books in Motion.
A young woman's curiosity about the original owner of a 1929 class ring, with the initials VE inscribed inside, leads to an intensive search & surprising ending.

Mystery of the Shot Tower. unabr. ed. Marion Lillie. Read by Laurie Klein. 2 cass. (Running Time: 2 hrs. 36 min.). Dramatization. 1993. 16.95 (978-1-55686-471-1(X), 471) Books in Motion.
Summer 1925. 12 year old Digger & his brother discover the seeds of true courage when they are trapped in the shot tower of an aging fort.

Mystery of the Sphinx. Composed by Fritz Heede. 2002. audio compact disk 14.95 (978-1-893792-84-5(6)) Terra Entmnt.

Mystery of the Spider's Clue. Gertrude Chandler Warner. (Running Time: 5400 sec.). (Boxcar Children Ser.: No. 87). (J). 2005. audio compact disk 14.95 (978-0-7861-7479-9(X)) Blckstn Audio.

***Mystery of the Spider's Clue.** unabr. ed. Gertrude Chandler Warner. Narrated by Aimee Lilly. (Running Time: 2 hrs. 0 mins. 13 sec.). (Boxcar Children Ser.). (ENG.). 2003. 10.49 (978-1-60814-722-9(3)) Oasis Audio.

Mystery of the Spider's Clue. unabr. ed. Gertrude Chandler Warner. Read by Aimee Lilly. 2 cass. (Boxcar Children Ser.: No. 87). (J). 2004. 12.99 (978-1-58926-294-2(8), Oasis Kids); audio compact disk 14.99 (978-1-58926-295-9(6), Oasis Kids) Oasis Audio.

Mystery of the Star Ruby. Gertrude Chandler Warner. (Running Time: 5400 sec.). (Boxcar Children Ser.: No. 89). (J). 2005. audio compact disk 14.95 (978-0-7861-7482-9(X)) Blckstn Audio.

Mystery of the Star Ruby. unabr. ed. Created by Gertrude Chandler Warner. 2 cass. (Running Time: 1 hr. 50 min.). (Boxcar Children Ser.: No. 89). (J). 2003. 12.99 (978-1-58926-125-9(9), A65L-0160, Oasis Kids) Oasis Audio.
Jessie finds a stunning ruby in the annual Ruby Hollow Gem Mine competition, but before she can enter it in the competition, it disappears! Has she lost it, or did someone take it? Now, instead of digging for gems, the children dig for clues. Who wants to win so much that they?d steal from the children? They?re determined to find out!.

Mystery of the Star Ruby. unabr. ed. Gertrude Chandler Warner. Narrated by Aimee Lilly. (Boxcar Children Ser.). (ENG.). (J). 2003. 10.49 (978-1-60814-097-8(0)) Oasis Audio.

Mystery of the Stolen Bike. unabr. ed. Marc Brown. Read by Mark Linn-Baker. Text by Stephen Krensky. 1 cass. (Running Time: 38 mins.). (Arthur Chapter Bks.: Bk. 8). (J). (gr. 2-4). 1999. pap. bk. 17.00 (978-0-8072-0401-6(3), EFTR199SP, Listening Lib) Random Audio Pubg.

Mystery of the Third Lucretia. unabr. ed. Susan Runholt. Read by Krista Sutton. 5 CDs. (Running Time: 6 hrs. 10 mins.). (YA). (gr. 5-8). 2008. audio compact disk 45.00 (978-0-7393-6749-0(8), Listening Lib) Pub: Random Audio Pubg. Dist(s): Random
"Go a-way," the painter snarled when Kari tried to see what was on his canvas. She and Lucas were at the Minneapolis Institute of Arts, and the guy's easel was set up in front of one of Rembrandt's famous Lucretia paintings. Something in this guy's voice gave Kari the creeps. She had no problem following his instruction; she never wanted to see him again. But a year later, she did see him in London. Walking through the National Gallery, Kari heard a familiar snarl. It was the same guy, and he was copying from another Rembrandt. Was it just a coincidence? If so, why was he in disguise? Using the kind of ingenuity and determination that only two teenage girls could come up with, Kari and Lucas embark on an international adventure to figure out who this mystery man is and what he's up to. But neither is prepared for what they find. Suddenly what began as a madcap pursuit becomes deadly serious. Will they risk their lives in the name of art?.

Mystery of the Third Lucretia. unabr. ed. Susan Runholt. Read by Krista Sutton. (Running Time: 22200 sec.). (J). (gr. 7-12). 2008. audio compact disk 35.00 (978-0-7393-6747-6(1), Listening Lib) Pub: Random Audio Pubg. Dist(s): Random

Mystery of the Third Oak, Janna Goodman. 2 cass. 2004. 9.98 (978-1-55503-781-9(X), 07001118) Covenant Comms.
A young Beehive unravels an intriguing plot.

Mystery of the Yellow Room. collector's ed. Gaston Leroux. Read by John Richmond. 8 cass. (Running Time: 8 hrs.). (J). 1999. 48.00 (978-0-7366-4894-3(1)) Books on Tape.
An attacker makes his way through locked doors & barred windows.

Mystery of the Yellow Room. unabr. ed. Gaston Leroux. Read by Walter Covell. 8 cass. (Running Time: 8 hrs.). 1984. 48.00 (978-0-7366-3889-0(X), 9118) Books on Tape.
Mademoiselle Stangerson retires to bed in The Yellow Room. Suddenly revolver shots echo through the house & she screams for help. Her father & a servant run to the locked room where they find the wounded girl-alone. The only other exit, a window-barred. How had the assailant escaped.

Mystery of the Yellow Room. unabr. ed. Gaston Leroux. Read by Walter Covell. 6 cass. (Running Time: 8 hrs.). 1984. 36.00 Jimcin Record.
Mademoiselle Stragerson retires to bed in the Yellow Room. Suddenly revolver shots echo through the house & she screams for help. Her father & a servant run to the locked room where they find the wounded girl alone. The only other exit, a window, barred. How had the assailant escaped.

Mystery of the Yellow Room. unabr. ed. Gaston Leroux. Read by Flo Gibson. 5 cass. (Running Time: 7 hrs.). 1999. 20.95 (978-1-55685-594-8(X)) Audio Bk Con.
Rouletabille, a young newspaper reporter, turns into a master sleuth when murder is attempted in the yellow room.

Mystery of the Yellow Room. unabr. ed. Gaston Leroux. Narrated by Simon Vance. (Running Time: 7 hrs. 0 mins. 0 sec.). (Tantor Unabridged Classics Ser.). (ENG.). 2008. audio compact disk 19.99 (978-1-4001-5799-0(4)); audio compact disk 55.99 (978-1-4001-3799-2(3)) Pub: Tantor Media. Dist(s): IngramPubServ

Mystery of the Yellow Room. unabr. ed. Gaston Leroux. Narrated by Simon Vance. (Running Time: 7 hrs. 0 mins. 0 sec.). (Tantor Unabridged Classics Ser.). (ENG.). 2008. audio compact disk 27.99 (978-1-4001-0799-5(7)) Pub: Tantor Media. Dist(s): IngramPubServ

Mystery of Time. unabr. ed. Perf. by Eknath Easwaran. 1 cass. (Running Time: 1 hr.). 1979. 7.95 (978-1-58638-579-8(8)) Nilgiri Pr.

mystery of Wolves. Isobelle Carmody. Read by Isobelle Carmody. (Running Time: 3 hrs. 30 mins.). (Legend of Little Fur Ser.). (J). 2009. 54.99 (978-1-74214-369-9(5), 9781742143699) Pub: Bolinda Pubng AUS. Dist(s): Bolinda Pub Inc

Mystery of Wolves: The Legend of Little Fur. unabr. ed. Isobelle Carmody. Read by Isobelle Carmody. (Running Time: 12600 sec.). (Legend of Little Fur Ser.). (J). (gr. 3-7). 2007. audio compact disk 54.95 (978-1-921334-55-9(X), 9781921334559) Pub: Bolinda Pubng AUS. Dist(s): Bolinda Pub Inc

Mystery of Zen. unabr. ed. Gilbert Highet. Read by Gilbert Highet. 1 cass. (Running Time: 30 min.). 9.95 (23316-A,B) J Norton Pubs.
Describes the experiences of a German who studied Zen through the art of archery & then goes into the mysticism which Zen embodies.

Mystery of 2012: Predictions, Prophecies, & Possibilities. unabr. ed. John Major Jenkins et al. (Running Time: 5:07:03). 2009. audio compact disk 29.95 (978-1-59179-722-7(5)) Sounds True.

Mystery on Blizzard Mountain. Gertrude Chandler Warner. (Running Time: 5400 sec.). (Boxcar Children Ser.: No. 86). (J). 2005. audio compact disk 14.95 (978-0-7861-7487-4(0)) Blckstn Audio.

***Mystery on Blizzard Mountain.** unabr. ed. Gertrude Chandler Warner. Narrated by Aimee Lilly. (Boxcar Children Ser.). (ENG.). 2003. 10.49 (978-1-60814-657-4(X)) Oasis Audio.

Mystery on Blizzard Mountain. unabr. ed. Gertrude Chandler Warner. Read by Aimee Lilly. 2 cass. (Running Time: 1 hr. 50 min.). (Boxcar Children Ser.: No. 86). (J). 2003. 12.99 (978-1-58926-123-5(2), A65L-0140, Oasis Kids) Oasis Audio.
The Boxcar Children are helping map out a new trail on Blizzard Mountain. But as they do so, they discover that there is a treasure hidden somewhere nearby, and someone is determined to find it before the children do! Will they find the treasure and finish blazing the trail, or will they be chased from the mountain?.

Mystery on Blizzard Mountain. unabr. ed. Created by Gertrude Chandler Warner. Narrated by Aimee Lilly. 2 CDs. (Running Time: 1 hr. 50 min.). (Boxcar Children Ser.: No. 86). (ENG.). (YA). 2003. audio compact disk 14.99 (978-1-58926-129-7(1), A65L-014D, Oasis Kids) Oasis Audio.

Mystery on the Docks. Thacher Hurd. Illus. by Thacher Hurd. 41 vols. (Running Time: 11 mins.). 2001. pap. bk. 39.95 (978-1-59112-529-7(4)); 9.95 (978-0-87499-750-7(X)); audio compact disk 12.95 (978-1-59112-321-7(6)) Live Oak Media.

Mystery on the Docks. Thacher Hurd. Illus. by Thacher Hurd. (Running Time: 11 mins.). (J). (ps-3). 2001. pap. bk. 37.95 (978-0-87499-752-1(6)) Live Oak Media.

Mystery on the Docks. Thacher Hurd. Illus. by Thacher Hurd. 11 vols. (Running Time: 11 mins.). (J). (ps-4). 2001. pap. bk. 16.95 (978-0-87499-751-4(8)) Pub: Live Oak Media. Dist(s): AudioGO
Melodrama about Ralph, the short order cook who helps save his favorite opera singer from the rat kidnappers.

Mystery Ranch. Gertrude Chandler Warner. Read by Phyllis Newman. 2 cass. (Running Time: 1 hr. 42 min.). (Boxcar Children Ser.: No. 4). (J). (gr. 2-5). 2000. 18.00 (978-0-7366-5011-3(3)) Books on Tape.

Mystery Ranch. unabr. ed. Gertrude Chandler Warner. Read by Phyllis Newman. 2 cass. (Running Time: 2 hrs.). (Boxcar Children Ser.: No. 4). (J). (gr. 2-5). 1997. 23.00 (LL 0012, Chivers Child Audio) AudioGO.
Grandpa Alden's sister Jane is all alone on her ranch out west & the Alden girls have gone to care for her. When Henry & Benny Alden come to join the girls, the four children find themselves unraveling an intriguing mystery with some amazing results!.

Mystery Ranch. unabr. ed. Gertrude Chandler Warner. Read by Phyllis Newman. 2 vols. (Running Time: 1 hr. 41 mins.). (Boxcar Children Ser.: No. 4). (J). (gr. 3-7). 1993. pap. bk. 29.00 (978-0-8072-7344-9(9), YA 833 SP, Listening Lib) Random Audio Pubg.
The Alden children find an exciting new adventure out west when the girls go to care for their Aunt Jane, who's not so much sick as lonely & unhappy. After the boys come out to join them, they explore the huge ranch & uncover some unexpected surprises.

Mystery School. Gay Luce. 2 cass. (Running Time: 3 hrs.). 14.00 Set. (A0077-87) Sound Photosyn.

Mystery Stories of Violet Strange. Anna Katharine Green. Read by Shelly Frasier. (Running Time: 9 hrs. 30 mins.). 2002. 27.95 (978-1-60083-608-4(9), Audiofy Corp) Iofy Corp.

Mystery Stories of Violet Strange. Anna Katharine Green. Read by Shelly Frasier. (ENG.). 2005. audio compact disk 84.00 (978-1-4001-3037-5(9)) Pub: Tantor Media. Dist(s): IngramPubServ

Mystery Stories of Violet Strange. unabr. ed. Anna Katharine Green. Narrated by Shelly Frasier. 8 CDs. (Running Time: 9 hrs. 35 mins.). (ENG.). 2002. audio compact disk 42.00 (978-1-4001-0037-8(2)); audio compact disk 20.00 (978-1-4001-5037-3(X)) Pub: Tantor Media. Dist(s): IngramPubServ

Mystery Stories of Violet Strange. unabr. ed. Anna Katharine Green. Narrated by Shelly Frasier. (Running Time: 9 hrs. 30 mins. 0 sec.). (ENG.). 2009. audio compact disk 32.99 (978-1-4001-1105-3(6)); audio compact disk 65.99 (978-1-4001-4105-0(2)); audio compact disk 22.99 (978-1-4001-6105-8(3)) Pub: Tantor Media. Dist(s): IngramPubServ

Mystery Teachings on Health Potential. 1 cass. (Running Time: 1 hr.). 1990. 8.95 (978-0-8356-1933-2(8)) Theos Pub Hse.
Examines the inner side of health.

Mystery Theatre Vol. 1: The Tell Tale Heart, Kitchen Table, Sight Unseen, Adventures of the Noble Bachelor. abr. ed. Based on a book by Edgar Allan Poe et al. Adapted by Len Peterson. Prod. by Esse Ljungh. Based on a book by Alan King et al. Prod. by Don Mowatt. Based on a book by Arthur Conan Doyle et al. 2 cass. (Running Time: 2 hrs.). (Mystery Theatre Ser.: Vol. 1). 2004. 18.99 (978-1-894003-05-6(5)) Pub: Scenario Prods CAN. Dist(s): PerseuPGW
Radio plays originally produced by the Canadian Broadcasting Corporation in the 1960's.

Mystery Theatre Vol. 2: The Hitch Hiker, Perfectly Happy Life, the Signal Man, the Duel. abr. ed. Based on a book by Allan King & Ted Ferguson. Prod. by Earl Pennington. Based on a book by Charles Dickens. Adapted by George Salverson. Prod. by George Salverson. 2 cass. (Running Time: 2 hrs.). (Mystery Theatre Ser.: Vol. 2). 2004. 18.99 (978-1-894003-06-3(3)) Pub: Scenario Prods CAN. Dist(s): PerseuPGW

Mystery Theatre Vol. 3: The Monkeys Paw, the Minds of Falun, the Sandman, Double Strip. abr. ed. Based on a book by W. W. Jacobs et al. Adapted by John Bethune. Prod. by Jean Bartels et al. Based on a book by E. T. A. Hoffmann et al. Adapted by Gavin Douglas. Prod. by Peter Donkin et al. 2 cass. (Running Time: 2 hrs.). (Mystery Theatre Ser.: Vol. 3). 2004. 18.99 (978-1-894003-07-0(1)) Pub: Scenario Prods CAN. Dist(s): PerseuPGW
Radio plays originally produced by the Canadian Broadcasting Corporation in the 1960's.

Mystery Theatre Vol. 4: Dr Heidegger's Experiment, Mr. Higginbottom's Catastrophe, the Secret History. abr. ed. Based on a book by Nathaniel Hawthorne. Adapted by Roger Crowther. Prod. by Peter Donkin. Based on a book by Frederick Spoerly. 2 cass. (Running Time: 2 hrs.). (Mystery Theatre Ser.: Vol. 4). 2004. 18.99 (978-1-894003-09-4(8)) Pub: Scenario Prods CAN. Dist(s): PerseuPGW

Mystery Traveler. 6 cass. (Running Time: 9 hrs.). 2002. 34.98 (4048) Radio Spirits.
You are invited to join the narrator on another journey into the strange and terrifying. I hope that you will enjoy the trip. Go along for the ride with Maurice Tarplin, the Mysterious Traveler, as he thrills you a little and chills you a little through 18 scary stories, including I died Last Night, The Man Who Tried to Save Lincoln, Death is the Visitor and 15 more. "So settle back, get a good grip on your nerves, and be comfortable, if you can".

Mystery Writer. Jessica Mann. (Isis (CDs) Ser.). 2006. audio compact disk 79.95 (978-0-7531-2610-3(9)) Pub: ISIS Lrg Prnt GBR. Dist(s): Ulverscroft US

Mystery Writer. Jessica Mann. Read by Anna Bentinck. 7 cass. (Running Time: 9 hrs.). (Isis Cassettes Ser.). 2006. 61.95 (978-0-7531-3584-6(1)) Pub: ISIS Lrg Prnt GBR. Dist(s): Ulverscroft US

Mystery Writer at Work: Tony Hillerman. unabr. ed. Billie Judy & Jonathan T. Stratman. Read by Tony Hillerman. Featuring Tony Hillerman. 1 cass. (Running Time: 1 hr.). (Writer at Work Ser.). cass. & video 19.95 (978-1-884016-04-2(9), 141) Reel Life Prods.
Popular writer of Navajo mystery novels at his home in Albuquerque, NM, talks about his work. Also scenes of local area where his characters "live".

Mystery Writers of America Presents Death Do Us Part: New Stories about Love, Lust, & Murder. unabr. ed. Harlan Coben. Narrated by John Lee et al. 1 MP3-CD. (Running Time: 11 hrs. 0 mins. 0 sec.). (ENG.). 2008. 24.99 (978-1-4001-5720-4(X)); audio compact disk 69.99 (978-1-4001-3720-6(9)) Pub: Tantor Media. Dist(s): IngramPubServ

Mystery Writers of America Presents Death Do Us Part: New Stories about Love, Lust, & Murder. unabr. ed. Harlan Coben & Mystery Writers of America Staff. Narrated by John Lee et al. Contrib. by Jeff Abbott. 9 CDs. (Running Time: 11 hrs. 0 mins. 0 sec.). (ENG.). 2008. audio compact disk 34.99 (978-1-4001-0720-9(2)) Pub: Tantor Media. Dist(s): IngramPubServ

Mystery Writers of America Presents the Prosecution Rests: New Stories about Courtrooms, Criminals, & the Law. unabr. ed. Linda Fairstein. (Running Time: 14 hrs. 0 mins. 0 sec.). (ENG.). 2009. audio compact disk 29.99 (978-1-4001-6189-8(4)) Pub: Tantor Media. Dist(s): IngramPubServ

Mystery Writers of America Presents the Prosecution Rests: New Stories about Courtrooms, Criminals, & the Law. unabr. ed. Linda Fairstein. Narrated by Paul Boehmer & Cassandra Campbell. (Running Time: 14 hrs. 0 mins. 0 sec.). (ENG.). 2009. audio compact disk 39.99 (978-1-4001-1189-3(7)); audio compact disk 79.99 (978-1-4001-4189-0(3)) Pub: Tantor Media. Dist(s): IngramPubServ

***Mystery 12-copy CD Pre-Pack.** Jonathan Kellerman. (ENG.). 2011. audio compact disk 384.00 (978-0-7393-5281-6(4), Random AudioBks) Pub: Random Audio Pubg. Dist(s): Random

Mystic Art of God-Realization. Swami Jyotirmayananda. 1 cass. (Running Time: 45 min.). 1990. 10.00 Yoga Res Foun.

Mystic Art of Prayer, No. 1. Swami Jyotirmayananda. 1 cass. (Running Time: 1 hr.). 1990. 12.99 Yoga Res Foun.

Mystic Art of Prayer, No. 2. Swami Jyotirmayananda. Read by Swami Jyotirmayananda. 1 cass. (Running Time: 1 hr.). 12.99 (726) Yoga Res Foun.

Mystic Art of Prayer, No. 3. Swami Jyotirmayananda. 1 cass. (Running Time: 1 hr.). 1990. 12.99 Yoga Res Foun.

Mystic Arts of Erasing All Signs of Death. unabr. ed. Charlie Huston. (Running Time: 7 hrs. NaN mins.). 2009. 29.95 (978-1-4332-5754-4(8)); audio compact disk 19.95 (978-1-4332-5753-7(X)); audio compact disk 44.95 (978-1-4332-5750-6(5)) Blckstn Audio.

Mystic Arts of Erasing All Signs of Death. unabr. ed. Charlie Huston. Read by Paul Michael Garcia. 8 CDs. (Running Time: 10 hrs.). 2009. audio compact disk 60.00 (978-1-4332-5751-3(3)) Blckstn Audio.

Mystic Empire. unabr. ed. Tracy Hickman & Laura Hickman. Read by Lloyd James. (Running Time: 48600 sec.). (Bronze Canticles Ser.: Bk. 3). 2007. 85.95 (978-0-7861-4884-4(5)); audio compact disk 99.00 (978-0-7861-5996-3(0)); audio compact disk 29.95 (978-0-7861-7116-3(2)) Blckstn Audio.

Mystic Harp. 1 cass. (Running Time: 1 hr.). (Interludes Music Ser.). 1989. 9.95 (978-1-55569-285-8(0), MOD-3906) Great Am Audio.

Mystic Harp: Performed by Derek Bell of the Chieftains. Derek Bell. 2002. audio compact disk 15.95 (978-1-56589-072-5(8)) Pub: Crystal Clarity. Dist(s): Natl Bk Netwk

Mystic Harp 2. Derek Bell. 2003. audio compact disk 15.95 (978-1-56589-768-7(4)) Pub: Crystal Clarity. Dist(s): Natl Bk Netwk

Mystic Life. unabr. ed. Thomas Merton. Read by Thomas Merton. 11 cass. (Running Time: 10 hrs. 23 min.). 1976. 119.95 Elec Paperback.
In these 22 talks made shortly before his death in 1968, the author uses the wisdom of Islamic mysticism, practiced by the Surfi masters, as the focus for a wide-ranging exploration of the deeper aspects of spirituality, not simply as esoteric knowledge for a few, but as the practical basis of a more meaningful spiritual life for everyone.

Mystic Light. Joseph Michael Levry. 2004. 19.00 (978-1-885562-06-7(3)) Root Light.

Mystic Light: Healing Beyond Medicine. Perf. by Joseph Michael Levry. 2003. audio compact disk 19.00 Root Light.

Mystic Memory Power. unabr. ed. Gary Arnold. 1 cass. (Running Time: 1 hr.). (C). 1997. pap. bk. 12.95 (978-1-57867-163-2(9)) Windhorse Corp.
Learn the three ancient secrets of developing the power of concentration.

Mystic Quest. Tracy Hickman & Laura Hickman. Read by Lloyd James. (Running Time: 61200 sec.). (Bronze Canticles Ser.: Bk. 2). 2006. 89.95 (978-0-7861-4508-9(0)); audio compact disk 120.00 (978-0-7861-7196-5(0)) Blckstn Audio.

Mystic Quest. unabr. ed. Laura Hickman & Tracy Hickman. Read by Lloyd James. (Running Time: 61200 sec.). (Bronze Canticles Ser.: Bk. 2). 2006. audio compact disk 44.95 (978-0-7861-7655-7(5)) Blckstn Audio.

Mystic Rites & Mystic Art. Theosophical Society Staff. 1 cass. (Running Time: 1 hr.). 1990. 8.95 (978-0-8356-1934-9(6)) Theos Pub Hse.
The arts, world religion & ritual.

Mystic River. Dennis Lehane. 11 cass. (Running Time: 16 hrs. 30 mins.). 2001. 88.00 (978-0-7366-6197-3(2)) Books on Tape.
When Jimmy Marcus' daughter is found murdered, his childhood friend Sean Devine is assigned to the case. His personal life unraveling, the investigation takes Sean back into a world of violence & pain he thought he'd left behind. It also puts him on a collision course with Jimmy Marcus.

Mystic River. Dennis Lehane. Read by David Strathairn. 1975. 9.99 (978-0-06-074361-1(1)) HarperCollins Pubs.

Mystic River. Dennis Lehane. Read by Scott Brick. 1975. 14.95 (978-0-06-074439-7(1)) HarperCollins Pubs.

***Mystic River.** abr. ed. Dennis Lehane. Read by David Strathairn. (ENG.). 2008. (978-0-06-084858-3(8), Harper Audio); (978-0-06-180504-2(1), Harper Audio) HarperCollins Pubs.

***Mystic River.** unabr. ed. Dennis Lehane. Read by Scott Brick. (ENG.). 2008. (978-0-06-180507-3(6), Harper Audio); (978-0-06-180505-9(X), Harper Audio) HarperCollins Pubs.

Mystic River. unabr. abr. ed. Dennis Lehane. Read by David Strathairn. 5 CDs. (Running Time: 6 hrs. 30 mins.). 2001. audio compact disk 29.95 (978-0-694-52464-8(6)) HarperCollins Pubs.

Mystic Vision. unabr. ed. Gary Arnold. 1 cass. (Running Time: 1 hr.). 1997. pap. bk. 12.95 (978-1-57867-115-1(9)) Windhorse Corp.
Shows how to conquer beliefs of fear, guilt & suffering.

Mystic Vista. Robert M. Hutmacher. Perf. by Denise La Giglia. 1 cass. (Running Time: 1 hr. 30 min.). 1998. 10.95 (CS-435); audio compact disk 15.95 (CD-435) GIA Pubns.

Mystic Warrior. Tracy Hickman & Laura Hickman. Read by James Lloyd. 12 CDs. (Running Time: 17 hrs. 30 mins.). (Bronze Canticles Ser.: Bk. 1). 2004. audio compact disk 96.00 (978-0-7861-8686-0(0)) Blckstn Audio.

Mystic Warrior. Tracy Hickman & Laura Hickman. Read by James Lloyd. 11 cass. (Running Time: 17 hrs. 30 mins.). (Bronze Canticles Ser.: Bk.. 1). 2004. 76.95 (978-0-7861-2690-3(6)) Blckstn Audio.

Mystic Warrior. Tracy Hickman & Laura Hickman. Read by Lloyd James. (Running Time: 15 hrs.). (Bronze Canticles Ser.: Bk. 1). 2004. 44.95 (978-1-59912-554-1(4)) Iofy Corp.

Mystic Warrior. unabr. ed. Tracy Hickman & Laura Hickman. Read by James Lloyd. 2 CDs. (Running Time: 17 hrs. 30 mins.). (Bronze Canticles Ser.: Bk. 1). 2004. audio compact disk 24.95 (978-0-7861-8611-2(9)) Blckstn Audio.

Mystic Warrior. unabr. ed. Tracy Hickman & Laura Hickman. Read by Lloyd James. 12 pieces. (Running Time: 17 hrs. 30 mins.). (Bronze Canticles Ser.: Bk. 1). 2004. reel tape 34.95 (978-0-7861-2647-7(7)); audio compact disk 49.95 (978-0-7861-8727-0(1)) Blckstn Audio.

Mystic Waters. 1 CD. (Running Time: 43 min.). (Elements of Nature Ser.). 1994. audio compact disk 15.95 (2834, Creativ Pub) Quayside.
Voices of surf, sea, river & stream merge with the inspired melodies of Bruce Kurnow's harp, harmonica & keyboard.

Mystic Waters. 1 cass. (Running Time: 43 min.). (Elements of Nature Ser.). 1994. 9.95 (2832, NrthWrd Bks) TandN Child.

Mystic Yoga Breathing. George King. 2007. (978-0-937249-49-9(1)) Aetherius Soc.

Mystical Approach to Religious Experience. John Yungblut. 5 cass. (Running Time: 5 hrs.). Incl. Mystical Approach to Religious Experience: Jesus, the Jewish Mystic. 1975.; Mystical Approach to Religious Experience: The Cultivation of the Mystical Faculty. 1975.; Mystical Approach to Religious Experience: The Meaning of Mysticism. 1975.; Mystical Approach to Religious Experience: The Point of Departure. 1975.; Mystical Approach to Religious Experience: Vagaries & Aberrations of the Mystical Way. 1975.; 1975. 17.50; 4.50 ea. Pendle Hill.

Mystical Approach to Religious Experience: Jesus, the Jewish Mystic see Mystical Approach to Religious Experience

Mystical Approach to Religious Experience: The Cultivation of the Mystical Faculty see Mystical Approach to Religious Experience

Mystical Approach to Religious Experience: The Meaning of Mysticism see Mystical Approach to Religious Experience

Mystical Approach to Religious Experience: The Point of Departure see Mystical Approach to Religious Experience

Mystical Approach to Religious Experience: Vagaries & Aberrations of the Mystical Way see Mystical Approach to Religious Experience

Mystical Attunement: Awaken Your Spiritual Power. abr. ed. Darrin Owens. (Running Time: 1 hr.). (ENG.). 2005. audio compact disk 17.99 (978-1-84409-047-1(7)) Pub: Findhorn Pr GBR. Dist(s): IPG Chicago

Mystical Ireland. Noirin Ni Riain. 2003. audio compact disk 39.95 (978-1-59179-122-5(7)) Sounds True.

Mystical Kabbalah. Perf. by David A. Cooper. 5 cass. (Running Time: 7 hrs.). 1999. 49.95 (83-0003) Explorations.
Access the profound path of inner knowing with Rabbi Cooper, a master practitioner who makes the concepts & practices extremely accessible & surprisingly applicable to daily life. Includes teaching stories & guided meditations.

Mystical Kabbalah. David A. Cooper. 6 CDs. (Running Time: 7 Hrs). 2005. audio compact disk 29.95 (978-1-59179-395-3(5), AW00448D) Sounds True.
Kabbalah, it is said, was brought down from heaven by angels. The great mystics of Judaism originally passed its teachings by word of mouth only, believing that the secrets of the kabbalah transcend the written word. In this great oral tradition, The Mystical Kabbalah will immerse listeners in this traditional school of sacred wisdom for reaching peace through union with God. On this unparalleled five-cassette study course, Rabbi David Cooper ? who has been acclaimed as ?one of today?s leading teachers of Jewish meditation? ? synthesizes this uniquely preserved wisdom with elegant meditations he developed during his years of study and research in the Old City of Jerusalem. Here are original teachings on the sephirot, ?the mystical structures that underpin all reality? ? the ohr ain sof ? the original light of creation ... the magid ? our inner guide to mystical insights, and much more. Both practical and inspirational, The Mystical Kabbalah is the perfect introduction to Judaism?s most time-honored system for spiritual growth.

Mystical Keys to Ascended Mastery. unabr. ed. Almine. 2006. audio compact disk 13.95 (978-0-9724331-9-8(8), 397-010) SpiritJrnys.

Mystical Keys to Manifestation. unabr. ed. Almine. 2006. audio compact disk 13.95 (978-0-9724331-8-1(X), 397-009) SpiritJrnys.

Mystical Life. Thomas Merton. 1 cass. (Running Time: 1 hr.). 8.95 (AA2264) Credence Commun.

Mystical Life of Jesus: An Uncommon Perspective on the Life of Christ. unabr. ed. Sylvia Browne. Read by Jeannie Hackett. 5. (Running Time: 20700 sec.). (ENG.). 2006. audio compact disk 29.95 (978-1-59887-068-8(8), 1598870688) Pub: HighBridge. Dist(s): Workman Pub

Mystical Life Way of the American Indians. Instructed by Manly P. Hall. 8.95 (978-0-89314-194-3(1), C850616) Philos Res.

Mystical Marriage of Your Thinking & Feeling. Jack Boland. 1 cass. (Running Time: 1 hr.). 8.00 (BW04) Master Mind.

Mystical Meanings of Playing Cards. Instructed by Manly P. Hall. 8.95 (978-0-89314-195-0(X), C801109) Philos Res.

Mystical Mind. Eldon Taylor. 12 cass. (Running Time: 12 hrs.). bk. 199.95 (978-1-55978-784-0(8), A111) Progress Aware Res.

Mystical Paths. unabr. ed. Susan Howatch. Read by Roe Kendall. 15 cass. (Running Time: 22 hrs.). 2002. 95.95 (978-0-7861-2177-9(7), 2928) Blckstn Audio.
Nicholas Darrow is a strong-willed and independent young man who has grown up in the shadow of the Church of England and the loving but watchful eye of his father, an Anglican priest. And like his father, he has both a gift and a burden in the form of psychic abilities. Although his father warns him to nurture his special powers with care, Nicholas can see no harm in the occasional dazzling "psychic flourish" ... until one results in a friend's attempted suicide. Now, staggering under the weight of remorse, horrified by the dangerous edge of his powers, watching the paths his life has followed converge in "crisis, chaos, and the Devil on the loose," Nicholas moves toward the brink of emotional collapse. When a terrifying vision suggests to him that he might be (literally) possessed, he must begin, at last, to face the truth of his past - and, in particular, of his relationship with his father to find the one path that may lead him out of the seemingly impenetrable darkness that engulfs him.

Mystical Power: Talks on Spirituality & Modern Life. Marianne Williamson. 4 CDs. 2005. audio compact disk 23.95 (978-1-4019-0659-7(1)) Hay House.

Mystical Process of Grace/Prayer Medium of Miracles. Marianne Williamson. Read by Marianne Williamson. 1 cass. (Running Time: 1 hr. 30 min.). (Lectures on a Course in Miracles). 1999. 10.00 (978-1-56170-752-2(X), M877) Hay House.

Mystical Side of Reality. Joy Mills. 1 cass. (Running Time: 1 hr.). 1994. 9.95 (978-0-9671280-1-6(3)) J Mills & Assocs.
Lecture series on spirituality & self-healing.

Mystical Stream-Music. 2007. audio compact disk 16.95 (978-1-56136-424-4(X)) Master Your Mind.

Mystical Theology of the Limbic Fissure. O'Leary Peter. (ENG.). 2005. 4.00 (978-1-933675-07-7(1)) Dos Madres Pr.

Mystical Tradition: Judaism, Christianity, & Islam. Instructed by Luke Timothy Johnson. 2008. 199.95 (978-1-59803-464-6(2)); audio compact disk 99.95 (978-1-59803-465-3(0)) Teaching Co.

Mystical Traveler: How to Advance to a Higher Level of Spirituality. Sylvia Browne. 2 CDs. 2008. audio compact disk 19.95 (978-1-4019-1863-7(8)) Hay House.

Mysticism As a Frontier Experience. David Steindl-Rast. 4 cass. (Running Time: 4 hrs.12 min.). 1985. 36.00 (05107) Big Sur Tapes.

Mysticism of Devi Puja. Swami Jyotirmayananda. 1 cass. (Running Time: 45 min.). 1990. 10.00 Yoga Res Foun.

Mystics & the Development of Consciousness. John Welch. 1 cass. (Running Time: 1 hr.). (Voices of John & Teresa). 1987. 7.95 (TAH172) Alba Hse Comns.
Develops consciousness through interiorizing language & symbols.

Mystic's View of Life & Death. 1 cass. (Running Time: 1 hr.). 1989. 8.95 (978-0-8356-1913-4(3), 1913, Quest) Theos Pub Hse.
Explores the "Mystic Center," Asceticism, includes author interviews.

An Asterisk (*) at the beginning of an entry indicates that the title is appearing for the first time.

Mystique. unabr. ed. Amanda Quick, pseud. Narrated by Barbara Rosenblat. 9 cass. (Running Time: 12 hrs. 15 mins.). 1999. 78.00 (978-0-7887-0415-4(X), 94607E7) Recorded Bks.
A tale of a legendary knight, a headstrong lady & a quest for an ancient crystal. To find the mystical Stone of Scarcliffe, Sir Hugh needs the assistance of Lady Alice of Lingwood, a flame-haired beauty with a dazzling intellect. Together, Hugh & Alice begin a dangerous adventure that brings them more than they expect: murder, deception & the possibility of lasting love.

Myth Analysis from Self Psychology: Ovid's Narcissus. Read by Lionel Corbett & Cathy Rives. 1 cass. (Running Time: 1 hr. 30 min.). 1989. 10.95 (978-0-7822-0047-8(8), 382-8) C G Jung IL.

Myth & Culture. Michael Meade. 2 cass. (Running Time: 3 hrs.). 1993. 18.00 (OC342-72) Sound Horizons AV.

Myth & History. William Thompson. 4 cass. (Running Time: 6 hrs.). 36.00 (OC17W) Sound Horizons AV.

Myth & Magic of Publishing. Betty Lundsted. 1 cass. (Running Time: 1 hr.). 8.95 (219) Am Fed Astrologers.
Technical inside information from publisher's viewpoint.

Myth & Meaning of Monopoly Capitalism. Read by G Edward Griffin. 1 cass. (Running Time: 1 hr.). 10.00 (AC14) Am Media.
A refutation of the popular myth that portrays monpoly as an outgrowth of capitalism. Monopoly is not based on free-enterprise competition, but the escape from it.

Myth & Metaphor in Society: A Conversation with Joseph Campbell & Jamake Highwater. Joseph Campbell & Jamake Highwater. 1 cass. (Running Time: 1 hr.). 12.95 (978-1-56176-941-4(X), MYS-76941) Mystic Fire.
Challenges many conceptions of religion, mythology & art.

Myth & Psyche: An Introduction to Jungian Perspectives on Human Mythology. Robert Moore. Read by Robert Moore. 12 cass. (Running Time: 10 hrs.). 1993. 64.95 (978-0-7822-0407-0(4), 501S) C G Jung IL.
According to Jung, mythmaking is a natural & impersonal potential present in the collective unconscious of all peoples throughout all times. Drawing on the contributions of Jung, Campbell & Eliade, this course explores the role of myth in human life. Five of the major mythological themes prominent in world mythology are examined in terms of their contemporary psychological & cultural significance: Creation, the Divine Child, the Hero, the Shaman & the Apocalypse.

Myth & Ritual Approach to Shakespearean Tragedy. unabr. ed. Herbert Weisinger. 1 cass. (Running Time: 55 min.). 1969. 12.95 (23093) J Norton Pubs.
An attempt to get at the patterns of thought & feeling underlying Shakespearean tragedy.

Myth Conceptions. unabr. ed. Robert Asprin. Narrated by Jeff Woodman. 5 cass. (Running Time: 6 hrs. 15 mins.). (Myth Ser.: Vol. 2). 1998. 44.00 (978-0-7887-1894-6(0), 95316E7) Recorded Bks.
Mixes comedy & otherwordly adventure in a stunning universe of magic & interdimensional travel.

Myth Directions. unabr. ed. Robert Asprin. Narrated by Jeff Woodman. 5 cass. (Running Time: 6 hrs.). (Myth Ser.: Vol. 3). 1998. 46.00 (978-0-7887-2187-8(9), 95483E7) Recorded Bks.
A wild interdimensional ride with incorrigible young magician, Skeeve. Tanda, the demon of Skeeve's dreams, wants him to travel with her to another dimension to steal a national trophy & he'd do anything to win her affection.

***Myth in Human History.** Instructed by Grant L. Voth. 2010. audio compact disk 269.95 (978-1-59803-669-5(6)) Teaching Co.

Myth, Magic & Mystery. unabr. ed. Theodore Roszak et al. 2 cass. (Running Time: 2 hrs. 30 min.). 19.95 (29360-29361) J Norton Pubs.
Now that our faith in science is under attack, adventerous minds explore old & new religious & esoteric disciplines in search of a different image of man.

Myth, Magic & Reality. 1 CD. 2003. audio compact disk (978-1-932616-09-5(8)) Feng Shui Para.
Take Control of Your Environment and Achieve Your Dreams!!In this audio program, Suzee shares the true myth, magic and reality of Feng Shui and explores the connection of the Universe (TAO), with balance (YIN/YANG) and vitality (CH'I), expressing itself via the FIVE CHINESE ELEMENTS. Unlike most books on the subject, Suzee actually teaches you how to increase the prospects for health, wealth, love and good fortune in your life by recognizing, regulating and integrating these natural forces in your work and home environments.

Myth Makers. Doctor Who. 2 CDs. 2001. cd-rom 13.99 (978-0-563-47777-8(6)) London Brdge.

Myth, Music, & Dance of the American Indian. Ruth De Cesare. (ENG.). 1997. audio compact disk 11.95 (978-0-7390-2908-4(8)) Alfred Pub.

Myth, Music & Dance of the American Indian. unabr. ed. 1 cass. (Running Time: 1 hr.). 16.95 (S11365) J Norton Pubs.
Includes songbook.

Myth of a Christian Nation: How the Quest for Political Power Is Destroying the Church. unabr. ed. Greg Boyd. (Running Time: 7 hrs. 5 mins. 0 sec.). (ENG.). 2008. 14.99 (978-0-310-27818-4(X)) Zondervan.

***Myth of a Christian Religion: How Believers Must Rebel to Advance the Kingdom of God.** Gregory A. Boyd. (Running Time: 5 hrs. 39 mins. 0 sec.). (ENG.). 2009. 19.99 (978-0-310-30267-4(6)) Zondervan.

Myth of Absolute Time; Cocteau Rodeo. 1 CD. 1998. audio compact disk 15.95 (978-1-57677-112-9(1), HEAD001) Lodestone Catalog.

Myth of Alzheimer's: What You Aren't Being Told about Today's Most Dreaded Diagnosis. Peter J. Whitehouse. Read by Raymond Todd. Told to Daniel George. (Playaway Adult Nonfiction Ser.). 2008. 54.99 (978-1-60640-765-3(1)) Find a World.

Myth of Alzheimer's: What You Aren't Being Told about Today's Most Dreaded Diagnosis. unabr. ed. Peter J. Whitehouse. Read by Raymond Todd. Told to Daniel George. (Running Time: 32400 sec.). 2008. 24.95 (978-1-4332-0416-6(9)); audio compact disk 24.95 (978-1-4332-0417-3(7)); audio compact disk 29.95 (978-1-4332-0418-0(5)); audio compact disk & audio compact disk 55.00 (978-1-4332-0415-9(0)) Blckstn Audio.

Myth of Alzheimer's: What You Aren't Being Told about Today's Most Dreaded Diagnosis. unabr. ed. Peter J. Whitehouse & Daniel George. Read by Raymond Todd. (Running Time: 32400 sec.). 2008. 44.95 (978-1-4332-0414-2(2)) Blckstn Audio.

Myth of Disarmament. unabr. ed. Salvador De Madariaga. 1 cass. (Running Time: 24 min.). 12.95 (27010) J Norton Pubs.
An exposition of the fallacies which underlie the concept of disarmament & a demonstration that the problem is tackled at the wrong end.

Myth of Freedom. Vajracarya. 1 cass. 1976. 10.00 Vajradhatu.
A seminar by the scholar & meditation master trained in the philosophical & meditative traditions of Buddhism in Tibet.

Myth of Freedom & the Way of Meditation. Osel Tendzin. 3 cass. (Running Time: 4 hrs. 30 min.). 1976. 34.00 Vajradhatu.
Includes: Does Freedom Exist? The Development of Ego, Entering the Buddhist Path.

Myth of Laziness: America's Top Learning Expert Shows How Kids - and Parents - Can Become more Productive. abr. ed. Mel Levine. 2004. 15.95 (978-0-7435-4300-2(9)) Pub: S&S Audio. Dist(s): S and S Inc

Myth of Mental Illness. unabr. ed. Thomas Szasz. 1 cass. (Running Time: 39 min.). 12.95 (29031) J Norton Pubs.
Szasz views mental illness as a disguise for moral & psychosocial problems of living.

Myth of Monolopy Power. unabr. ed. Jarret B. Wollstein. 1 cass. (Running Time: 32 min.). 12.95 (264) J Norton Pubs.

Myth of Otherworldliness. Swami Amar Jyoti. 1 cass. 1980. 9.95 (R-29) Truth Consciousness.
Egolessness is for this world. Light should shine wherever we are, here & now. Divine manifestation into the material plane. Life Divine on earth.

Myth of Psychotherapy. unabr. ed. Thomas Szasz. Read by Robin Lawson. 6 cass. (Running Time: 9 hrs.). 1999. 44.95 Blckstn Audio.
Moral & religious perspective has been clearly replaced by medical & therapeutic rhetoric. It is little wonder that the world is plagued by legions of rapists, drug users, murderers, thieves, child abusers, you name it, all of whom are now referred to as having one form or another of "addiction," & are thus either "sick" or suffering from "mental illness." Accordingly, modern psychotherapists claim that these are in need of specialized "therapy" or "treatment" to help them "cope with their disease." Moral relativism, bolstered by psychotherapy, has prevailed over the traditional ideas of self-control, individual responsibility & moral culpability.

Myth of Psychotherapy. unabr. ed. Thomas Szasz. Read by Robin Lawson. 6 cass. (Running Time: 8 hrs. 30 mins.). 1993. 44.95 (978-0-7861-0348-5(5), 1305) Blckstn Audio.
Until recent years, "bad" & "immoral" were terms used to describe people who are now referred to as "sick" & "in need of treatment." Moral & religious perspective has been clearly replaced by medical & therapeutic rhetoric. It is little wonder why the world is plagued by legions of rapists, drug users, murderers, thieves, child abusers - you name it, all of whom are now referred to as having one form or another of "addiction," & are thus either "sick" or suffering from "mental illness." Accordingly, modern psychotherapists claim that these are in need of specialized "therapy" or "treatment," to help them "cope with their disease." Moral relativism - bolstered by psychotherapy - has prevailed over the traditional ideas of self-control, individual responsibility & moral culpability.

***Myth of Stress: Where Stress Really Comes from & How to Live a Happier & Healthier Life.** unabr. ed. Andrew Bernstein. Read by Andrew Bernstein. (Running Time: 8 hrs. 0 mins. 0 sec.). (ENG.). 2010. audio compact disk 29.99 (978-1-4423-3469-4(X)) Pub: S&S Audio. Dist(s): S and S Inc

Myth of the Innocent Civilian. Harold Thomas. Narrated by Harold Thomas. 1 cass. (Running Time: 2 hrs.). 2002. 5.00 (978-0-9728261-2-9(2)) AIR.

Myth of the Natural: Practice, Passion, & the Good News about Great Performance. unabr. ed. Geoff Colvin. Narrated by David Drummond. (Running Time: 7 hrs. 30 mins. 0 sec.). (ENG.). 2008. audio compact disk 59.99 (978-1-4001-3871-5(X)) Pub: Tantor Media. Dist(s): IngramPubServ

Myth of the Natural: Practice, Passion, & the Good News about Great Performance. unabr. ed. Geoff Colvin. Read by David Drummond. (Running Time: 7 hrs. 30 mins. 0 sec.). (ENG.). 2008. audio compact disk 29.99 (978-1-4001-0871-8(3)) Pub: Tantor Media. Dist(s): IngramPubServ

***Myth of the Rational Market.** unabr. ed. Justin Fox. Read by Alan Sklar. (ENG.). 2010. (978-0-06-199293-3(3), Harper Audio) HarperCollins Pubs.

***Myth of the Rational Market: A History of Risk, Reward, & Delusion on Wall Street.** unabr. ed. Justin Fox. Read by Alan Sklar. (ENG.). 2010. (978-0-06-199089-2(2), Harper Audio) HarperCollins Pubs.

Myth of the Shadow & the Shadow of Myth. Nathan Schwartz-Salant. Read by Nathan Schwartz-Salant. 1 cass. (Running Time: 1 hr. 30 min.). 1991. 10.95 (978-0-7822-0364-6(7), 462) C G Jung IL.
Mythology can help us to understand & integrate the shadow, but this endeavor can also be undermined by the use of mythology. In particular, the limiting madness of the shadow can be denied & with this denial one can lose a sense of soul & embodied life. Schwartz-Salant examines the nature of madness & evil & the means of coming to terms with these powerful elements of the shadow. The keynote lecture of the conference Gold in Dark Places: Shadow Work in the Struggle for Selfhood.

Myth of the Shared Dream. Read by Wendy Doniger. 1 cass. (Running Time: 1 hr.). 1985. 9.95 (978-0-7822-0222-9(5), 159) C G Jung IL.

Myth of Wholeness: Self Development, Self Deception, & the Scapegoating Process. Read by Arthur Colman. 1 cass. (Running Time: 1 hr. 30 min.). 1988. 10.95 (978-0-7822-0037-9(0), 354) C G Jung IL.

Myth, Pathos & the Possible Human. Read by Jean Houston. 1 cass. (Running Time: 2 hrs.). 1979. 12.95 (978-0-7822-0093-5(1), 048) C G Jung IL.

Myth We Call Perfection. John Lund. 2004. 9.95 (978-1-59156-287-0(2)); audio compact disk 11.95 (978-1-59156-288-7(0)) Covenant Comms.

Mythic Dreamer. Perf. by R. Carlos Nakai. 1 cass. (Running Time: 1 hr.). 7.98 (CANR 608); audio compact disk 12.78 (CANR 608) NewSound.

Mythic Journey. Interview with Laurens Van der Post & Michael Toms. 2 cass. (Running Time: 1 hr. 30 min.). 1997. 16.95 (978-1-56170-445-3(8), 994) Hay House.
An adventurer, soldier, statesman, writer & philosopher, addresses major issues of our time including - the election of Nelson Mandela & the future of South Africa, the Christ within & the mythic origins of Nazism.

Mythic Realm: Myth, Mania & Depression. Daniel Lindley, Jr. 1 cass. (Running Time: 1 hr. 30 min.). (Language & Life of Symbols Ser.). 1995. 10.95 (978-0-7822-0493-3(7), 569) C G Jung IL.

Mythic Wheel of Life: Finding Your Place in the World. Charles Faulkner. 3 CDs. 2005. audio compact disk 39.95 (978-1-884605-16-1(8)) Genesis II.
Only 25 years ago, stories were thought to be only for children and old people. ?Serious? people studied science?for the facts. As it turns out, we don?t live in a world of facts. We live in worlds of meaning, in worlds of myth and metaphor, made by our imaginations.Through a lively mix of lecture, demonstration, exercises and lots of metaphors and stories, Charles will guide you through these worlds and around The Mythic Wheel of Life. You?ll learn how your personal Living Metaphors? are part of a deeper and natural order in the very structure of your unconscious mind. You?ll learn how this structure shapes your dreads and desires, and how it combines with time to create the seasons of your life. With a conscious appreciation of this deep structure found in everyone?s imagination, you?ll see how myths and metaphors are being expressed all around you, and gain new and exciting ways to create living change for yourself and others.CD 1: Metaphors, Time and ImaginationHow the world we really live in is in our imagination. The meta-metaphors of life. How our unconscious metaphors determine our dreads and desires. How to elicit a person?s or organization?s Living Metaphors?.CD 2: Changing Your Time and SeasonHow Living Metaphors? exist in time and the seasons of the year and how to use this to naturally create profound personal transformation.CD 3: The Mythic Wheel of LifeAn introduction to the unconscious structure of stories. The history of the world as story and metaphor. How to determine the themes of your life and significant characters in it to find your place and enrich it.

Mythic Wheel of Life: Finding Your Place in the World. Charles Faulkner. 3 cass. 1991. set in binder. (978-1-884605-00-0(1)) Genesis II.
Personal & professional development.

Mythological Dynamics of Evolutionary Process. Frank Barr. 2 cass. (Running Time: 3 hrs.). 14.00 (A0003-87) Sound Photosyn.
Absorbing material if you can hang in there & pay attention. The rough video helps with the many diagrams.

Mythology. abr. ed. Thomas Bulfinch. Narrated by Barry Cooper. 2 cass. (Running Time: 2 hrs. 7 min.). 12.95 (978-0-89926-173-7(6), 855) Audio Bk.
Includes the stories of Pandora, Psyche, Cupid, Apollo, Atlas, Venus & Hercules.

Mythology & Clinical Practice. Read by Nathan Schwartz-Salant. 4 cass. (Running Time: 4 hrs. 45 min.). 1991. 31.95 (978-0-7822-0251-9(9), 435) C G Jung IL.
Noted Jungian analyst & author Schwartz-Salant explores the importance of mythology for understanding & containing psychic life within the analytic process. The myths of Pan, Dionysus, Gilgamesh & Egyptian images of creation are examined in the context of transference/countertransference dynamics & the creation of the containing environment.

Mythology & Psychology: A Jungian Perspective. Robert Moore. Read by Robert Moore. 2 cass. (Running Time: 1 hr. 40 min.). 1992. 16.95 (978-0-7822-0410-0(4), 501-1) C G Jung IL.
Part of the set "Myth & Psyche: An Introduction to Jungian Perspective on Human Mythology".

Mythology, Astrology & Dreams. Sara A. Keller. 1 cass. (Running Time: 1 hr. 30 min.). 1988. 8.95 (623) Am Fed Astrologers.

Mythology of Creation. Robert Moore. Read by Robert Moore. 2 cass. (Running Time: 1 hr. 40 min.). 1992. 16.95 (978-0-7822-0411-7(2), 501-2) C G Jung IL.

Mythology of Gender: Conflicts, Truces & Harmonies Between Men & Women. Michael Meade. Read by Michael Meade. Ed. by Richard Chelew. 2 cass. (Running Time: 2 hrs.). 1994. bk. 17.00 (978-1-880155-13-4(3)) Oral Trad Arch.
Storyteller, drummer, mythologist Meade explores the conflicts between men & women. He reveals some possible resolutions found in stories & myths of ancient cultures. Includes bookpack.

Mythology of the Apocalypse. Robert Moore. Read by Robert Moore. 2 cass. (Running Time: 1 hr. 40 min.). 1992. 16.95 (978-0-7822-0415-5(5), 501-6) C G Jung IL.
Part of the set "Myth & Psyche: An Introduction to Jungian Perspective on Human Mythology".

Mythology of the Divine Child. Robert Moore. Read by Robert Moore. 2 cass. (Running Time: 1 hr. 40 min.). 1992. 16.95 (978-0-7822-0412-4(0), 501-3) C G Jung IL.

Mythology of the Great Self Within. Robert Moore. Read by Robert Moore. 6 cass. (Running Time: 7 hrs.). 1993. 45.95 (978-0-7822-0418-6(X), 505) C G Jung IL.
World mythological traditions present many images of a Great Self that dwells within each human individual. This course examines a number of these images from mythological & spiritual traditions & then turns to a discussion of the psychological basis for this phenomenon. Special attention is given to the implications for our experience of both pathological grandiosity & creative visioning.

Mythology of the Hero. Robert Moore. Read by Robert Moore. 2 cass. (Running Time: 1 hr. 40 min.). 1992. 16.95 (978-0-7822-0413-1(9), 501-4) C G Jung IL.
Part of the set "Myth & Psyche: An Introduction to Jungian Perspective on Human Mythology".

Mythology of the Shaman. Robert Moore. Read by Robert Moore. 2 cass. (Running Time: 1 hr. 40 min.). 1992. 16.95 (978-0-7822-0414-8(7), 501-5) C G Jung IL.
Part of the set "Myth & Psyche: An Introduction to Jungian Perspectives on Human Mythology".

Myths about Marriage: Barriers to Intimacy. unabr. ed. Lynne Logan. Read by Lynne Logan. 1 cass. (Running Time: 1 hrs.). 1995. 11.00 (978-1-890907-00-6(6), 0001) Heaven Only.
Marriage principals, barriers to intimacy & how to increase communication.

Myths about Sexual Abuse, Pt. 8. (D035DB090) Natl Public Radio.

Myths & Realities. Elizabeth A. Einstein. Read by Elizabeth A. Einstein. 1 cass. (Running Time: 1 hr.). (Stepfamily Living Ser.: No. 1). 1989. 9.95 (978-1-884944-07-9(8)) E Einstein.
Making a stepfamily is complicated so people need to understand how misperceptions & misunderstandings can delay the normal developmental process.

Myths Collection 1: A Short History of Myth, the Penelopiad, & Weight. unabr. ed. Karen Armstrong et al. Read by Sandra Burr. (Running Time: 28800 sec.). (Myths Ser.). 2006. audio compact disk & audio compact disk 29.95 (978-1-4233-0791-4(7), 9781423307914) Brilliance Audio.
A Short History of Myth: What are myths? How have they evolved? And why do we still so desperately need them? Heralding a major series of retellings of international myths by authors from around the world, Karen Armstrong's characteristically insightful and eloquent book serves as a brilliant and thought-provoking introduction to myth in the broadest sense - and why we dismiss it only at our peril. The Penelopiad: In a splendid contemporary twist to the ancient story of Penelope and Odysseus, Margaret Atwood has chosen to give the telling of it to Penelope and to her twelve hanged Maids, asking: "What led to the hanging of the maids, and what was Penelope really up to?" In Atwood's dazzling, playful retelling, the story becomes as wise and compassionate as it is haunting, and as wildly entertaining as it is disturbing. Weight: In ancient Greek mythology, the victorious Olympians force Atlas, guardian of the Garden of Hesperides and its golden apples of life, to bear the weight of the earth and the heavens for eternity. With her typical wit and verve, Jeanette Winterson brings Atlas into the twenty-first century. Simultaneously, she asks her own difficult questions about the nature of choice and coercion, and how we forge our own destiny.

Myths, Lies, & Downright Stupidity: Get Out the Shovel - Why Everything You Know Is Wrong. abr. ed. John Stossel. Read by John Stossel. (Running Time: 10800 sec.). 2007. audio compact disk 14.98 (978-1-4013-8740-2(3), Hyperion Audio) Pub: Hyperion. Dist(s): HarperCollins Pubs

Myths Lies & Maple Leafs. Colin Mochrie et al. (Running Time: 3600 sec.). 2005. audio compact disk 16.95 (978-0-660-19463-9(5)) Canadian Broadcasting CAN.

Myths of Human Sexuality. 1 cass. (Running Time: 1 hr.). 10.95 (I0650B090, HarperThor) HarpC GBR.

Myths of Native Americans. Rick Steele. Read by Rick Steele. Read by Terry Jacobs & Larry Branson. 1 cass. (Running Time: 44 min.). Dramatization. 1994. 9.95 (978-1-885656-00-1(9)) Steele Prods.
Four myths from Native American culture dealing with the beginning of the world.

Myths of the Family. James Hillman. 4 cass. (Running Time: 6 hrs.). 1997. 29.95 (978-1-879323-55-1(9)) Sound Horizons AV.

Myths of the Family, Pt. 1. James Hillman. 2 cass. (Running Time: 3 hrs.). 16.95 (978-1-879323-01-8(X)) Sound Horizons AV.

Myths of the Family, Pt. 2. James Hillman. 2 cass. (Running Time: 3 hrs.). 19.95 (978-1-879323-07-0(9)) Sound Horizons AV.

Myths to Grow By. Thomas P. Lavin. 4 cass. (Running Time: 6 hrs. 30 min.). 1995. 31.95 (978-0-7822-0508-4(9), 582) C G Jung IL.
This course addresses the personal development aspects of mythological systems, using the writings of Joseph Campbell & others as a guide. Seen in their developmental function, myths are blueprints or road maps to personal growth. This course explores mythological images & patterns as maps to personal & cultural development.

Mz Goose & Her Wonderful Rhymes: They Make You Happy All of the Time. Elyse F. Aronson. Illus. by Olivia Korringa & Kathy Jakobsen. Music by Liam Carolan. 1 cass. (Running Time: 36 mins.). (ENG.). (J). (ps-3). 2000. 12.95 (978-0-9669510-1-1(8)) Pub: Good Things. Dist(s): Penton Overseas
A collection of 51 new, non-violent nursery rhymes for today's world. With music, sound effects & children's voices.

M1028. 2004. DVD & audio compact disk 19.99 (978-0-01-223325-2(0)) D Christiano Films.

N

N-Acetylglutamate Synthase Deficiency - A Bibliography & Dictionary for Physicians, Patients, & Genome Researchers. Compiled by Icon Group International, Inc. Staff. 2007. ring bd. 28.95 (978-0-497-11260-8(4)) Icon Grp.

N Is for Noose. abr. ed. Sue Grafton. Read by Judy Kaye. 4 CDs . (Running Time: 4 hrs.). (Kinsey Millhone Mystery Ser.). (ENG.). 2002. audio compact disk 26.00 (978-0-553-71339-8(6)) Pub: Random Audio Pubg. Dist(s): Random

N Is for Noose. unabr. ed. Sue Grafton. Read by Mary Peiffer. 7 cass. (Running Time: 10 hrs. 30 min.). (Kinsey Millhone Mystery Ser.). 1998. 56.00 (978-0-7366-4141-8(6), 4645) Books on Tape.
Private investigator Kinsey Millhone is back, sassy & self-reliant as ever. Visiting a small town in the Sierras, Kinsey aids a recent widow, Selma Newquist, who believes that her detective husband did not die of a heart attack, as reported, but from foul play. Kinsey sifts through the paper trail Tom Newquist left behind, trying to discover what he was investigating before he died. Kinsey is about to call it quits when she is severely beaten in her motel room. Spurred to probe further she soon unearths clues regarding a long-unsolved murder that may or may not implicate the colleagues of Tom Newquist. Wry & intelligent, Kinsey Millhone solves the case.

N Is for Noose, unabr. ed. Sue Grafton. Read by Mary Peiffer. 6 cass. (Running Time: 9 hrs.). (Kinsey Millhone Mystery Ser.). 1999. 39.95 (FS9-34536) Highsmith.

N or M? unabr. ed. Agatha Christie. Read by James Warwick. 4 cass. (Running Time: 6 hrs.). 2001. 24.95 (978-1-57270-210-3(9), N41210u, Audio Edits Mystry) Pub: Audio Partners. Dist(s): PerseuPGW
When a dying man's final words provide the only clue to the identities of Hitler's most dangerous agents, Tommy & Tuppence Beresford go undercover at a fashionable seaside resort, where they set an elaborate trap.

***N or M? A Tommy & Tuppence Mystery.** Agatha Christie. Narrated by James Warwick. 5 CDs. (Running Time: 6 hrs. 18 mins. 0 sec.). (ENG.). 2010. audio compact disk 29.95 (978-1-60283-337-1(0)) Pub: AudioGO. Dist(s): Perseus Dist

N. Ravikiran: Chitraveena. 1 cass. (Running Time: 1 hr.). (Dikshitar Masterpieces Ser.: Vol. 2). 1992. (C92049) Multi-Cultural Bks.
Karnatic classical music.

N. Scott Momaday. Interview with N. Scott Momaday. 1 cass. (Running Time: 45 min.). 1970. 13.95 (L054) TFR.
Momaday talks about winning a Pulitzer prize for his first novel, "House Made of Dawn." He traces his Indian background & credits his mother with making him a storyteller. He also discusses some of the Kiowa legends he used in "The Way to Rainy Mountain".

N. Scott Momaday. Interview. Interview with N. Scott Momaday & Kay Bonetti. 1 cass. (Running Time: 1 hr. 09 min.). 1983. 13.95 (978-1-55644-078-6(2), 3092) Am Audio Prose.
Interview focuses on matters pertinent to Momaday's Indian identity & heritage & its relationship to his craft & vision of Native American writing & its place in the larger tradition.

N. Scott Momaday Interview. 20.97 (978-0-13-090325-9(6)) P-H.

N. Scott Momaday Reading. 20.97 (978-0-13-030388-2(7)) P-H.

N Shakespeare Workshop. Stephen Greenblatt. (C). 1997. audio compact disk 25.00 (978-0-393-10157-7(6)) Norton.

N-Space & Wormholes. Ed. by Marco A. V. Bitetto. 1 cass. 2000. (978-1-58578-302-1(1)) Inst of Cybernetics.

N-Sync: The Unauthorized Biography of N-Sync. Harry Drysdale-Wood. (Maximum Ser.). (ENG.). 2001. audio compact disk 14.95 (978-1-84240-025-8(8)) Pub: Chrome Dreams GBR. Dist(s): IPG Chicago

N Word: Who Can Say It, Who Shouldn't, & Why. unabr. ed. Jabari Asim. Read by Mirron Willis. (Running Time: 34200 sec.). 2007. 54.95 (978-0-7861-6851-4(X)); 24.95 (978-0-7861-4953-7(1)); audio compact disk 63.00 (978-0-7861-6850-7(1)); audio compact disk 29.95 (978-0-7861-7002-9(6)) Blckstn Audio.

N Word: Who Can Say It, Who Shouldnt, & Why. unabr. ed. Jabari Asim. Read by Mirron Willis. (Running Time: 34200 sec.). 2007. audio compact disk 27.95 (978-0-7861-5840-9(9)) Blckstn Audio.

Na Bregovite na Xadson see On the Edge of the Hudson

***Na Damhsai Ceili.** Johnny Connolly. (ENG.). 1997. 32.95 (978-0-8023-7121-8(3)) Pub: Clo Iar-Chonnachta IRL. Dist(s): Dufour

***Na Fonnadoiri.** Risteard Macaodha. (ENG.). 1996. 25.95 (978-0-8023-7119-5(1)) Pub: Clo Iar-Chonnachta IRL. Dist(s): Dufour

Na Hana a Ka La'i. Hokulani Cleeland. Illus. by Brook Parker. 1 cass. (HAW.). (J). 1999. pap. bk. 5.95 (978-1-58191-050-6(9)) Aha Punana Leo.

Na Keiki 'Elima. William H. Wilson. Illus. by Lilinoe Andrews. (HAW.). (J). (gr. k-3). 1992. pap. bk. 6.95 (978-1-890270-25-4(3)) Aha Punana Leo.

Na Klar! An Introductory German Course. 4th ed. Donato et al. (GER.). (C). (gr. 6-12). 2003. stu. ed. 14.68 (978-0-07-284984-4(3)) Pub: Glencoe. Dist(s): McGraw

Na Koko O Keia Keiki Hawai'i. William H. Wilson. Illus. by Brook Parker. 1 cass. (HAW.). (J). (gr. k-2). 1999. pap. bk. 5.95 (978-1-58191-060-5(6)) Aha Punana Leo.

Na Mele Hula: A Collection of Hawaiian Hula Chants. Nona Beamer. 1987. pap. bk. 25.00 (978-0-939154-58-6(7)) Pub: Inst Polynesian. Dist(s): UH Pr

Na Mele Hula Vol. 2: A Collection of Hawaiian Hula Chants. Nona Beamer. 2002. pap. bk. 27.00 (978-0-939154-57-9(9)) Pub: Inst Polynesian. Dist(s): UH Pr

Nā Mele O Tūtū & Me: The Songs of Tūtū & Me. 1 CD. (HAW.). (J). 2004. audio compact disk (978-1-933835-03-7(6)) Part Dev.

Na Moku Kaulana. Keiki C. Kawai'ae'a. Illus. by Umi Kahalio'umi. 1 cass. (HAW.). (J). 1999. pap. bk. 5.95 (978-1-58191-078-0(9)) Aha Punana Leo.

***Naamah's Blessing.** unabr. ed. Jacqueline Carey. (Running Time: 28 hrs. 0 mins.). (Naamah Ser.). 2011. 29.99 (978-1-4001-8376-0(6)); 44.99 (978-1-4001-6376-2(5)); audio compact disk 59.99 (978-1-4001-1376-7(8)) Pub: Tantor Media. Dist(s): IngramPubServ

***Naamah's Blessing (Library Edition)** unabr. ed. Jacqueline Carey. (Running Time: 28 hrs. 0 mins.). (Naamah Ser.). 2011. 59.99 (978-1-4001-9376-9(1)); audio compact disk 143.99 (978-1-4001-4376-4(4)) Pub: Tantor Media. Dist(s): IngramPubServ

***Naamah's Curse.** unabr. ed. Jacqueline Carey. (Running Time: 25 hrs. 0 mins.). (Naamah Ser.). 2010. 27.99 (978-1-4001-8375-3(8)) Tantor Media.

***Naamah's Curse.** unabr. ed. Jacqueline Carey. Narrated by Anne Flosnik. (Running Time: 21 hrs. 30 mins. 0 sec.). (Naamah Ser.). (ENG.). 2010. 39.99 (978-1-4001-6375-5(7)); audio compact disk 109.99 (978-1-4001-4375-7(6)); audio compact disk 54.99 (978-1-4001-1375-0(X)) Pub: Tantor Media. Dist(s): IngramPubServ

Naamah's Kiss. unabr. ed. Jacqueline Carey. Narrated by Anne Flosnik. (Running Time: 27 hrs. 30 mins. 0 sec.). (Naamah Ser.). (ENG.). 2009. 39.99 (978-1-4001-6251-2(3)); audio compact disk 54.99 (978-1-4001-1251-7(6)); audio compact disk 109.99 (978-1-4001-4251-4(2)) Pub: Tantor Media. Dist(s): IngramPubServ

Nab Bible on Cass Catholic. 2004. 79.95 (978-0-529-11172-2(1)) Nelson.

Nab New Testament on. 2004. lthr. 49.95 (978-0-529-11492-1(5)) Nelson.

Nachalo. abr. ed. Sophia Lubensky. 4 cass. (Running Time: 6 hrs.). 1996. 23.80 (978-0-07-911282-8(X), Mc-H Human Soc) McGrw-H Hghr Educ.

Nachalo Bk. 2: When in Russia. Sophia Lubensky. (C). 1997. 8.75 (978-0-07-039045-4(2), Mc-H Human Soc) Pub: McGrw-H Hghr Educ. Dist(s): McGraw

Nachalo Bk. 2: When in Russia. unabr. ed. Sophia Lubensky. 4 cass. (Running Time: 6 hrs.). 1997. 21.30 (978-0-07-912204-9(3), Mc-H Human Soc) McGrw-H Hghr Educ.

Nachalo Vol. 1, Bk. 1: When in Russia, Sophia Lubensky. (C). 1995. 8.75 (978-0-07-039038-6(X), Mc-H Human Soc) Pub: McGrw-H Hghr Educ. Dist(s): McGraw

Nachbarn. Cinza Medaglia. pap. bk. 20.95 (978-88-7754-965-5(3)) Pub: Cideb ITA. Dist(s): Distribks Inc

Nacht des Schwarzen Zaubers. Heinz G. Konsalik. 2001. audio compact disk 12.50 (978-3-453-00540-2(6)) Pub: Verlag Wilhelm Heyne DEU. Dist(s): Distribks Inc

Naciketas: Readings from the Upanishads on Death. Dean Brown. 1 cass. 9.00 (A0715-90) Sound Photosyn.
From Death: The Lasy Taboo symposium, a scholarly perspective.

Nacimiento de una Vision Emocionante. Charles R. Swindoll.Tr. of Birth of an Exciting Vision. (SPA.). 2007. audio compact disk 46.00 (978-1-57972-749-9(2)) Insight Living.

Nada Es Imposible. unabr. ed. René Gonzaléz. (SPA.). 2002. 9.99 (978-0-8297-3524-6(0)) Zondervan.

Nada Es Imposible. unabr. ed. Rene Gonzalez. 2002. audio compact disk 14.99 (978-0-8297-3522-2(4)) Zondervan.

Nada Especial. unabr. ed. Marcos Vidal. 1998. audio compact disk 14.99 (978-0-8297-2650-3(0)) Zondervan.

Nadia of the Nightwatch Squadron. unabr. ed. Tom Townsend. Read by Lynda Evans. 4 cass. (Running Time: 5 hrs.). 1999. 26.95 (978-1-55686-881-8(2)) Books in Motion.
This work of historical fiction is based on the true experiences of female soviet pilots in WWII.

Nadia, Secret of Blue Water: Motion Picture Soundtrack. 1 disc. 2003. audio compact disk 14.98 (978-1-57813-341-3(6), CNS/004, ADV Music) A D Vision.

Nadia, Secret of Blue Water: TV Soundtrack 1. 1 disc. 2003. audio compact disk 14.98 (978-1-57813-373-4(4), CNS/001, ADV Music) A D Vision.

Nadia, Secret of Blue Water: TV Soundtrack 2. 1 disc. 2003. audio compact disk 14.98 (978-1-57813-374-1(2), CNS/002, ADV Music) A D Vision.

Nadia, Secret of Blue Water: TV Soundtrack 3. 1 disc. 2003. audio compact disk 14.98 (978-1-57813-375-8(0), CNS/003, ADV Music) A D Vision.

Nadine Gordimer. unabr. ed. Read by Nadine Godimer & Rebekah Presson. Ed. by James McKinley. 1 cass. (Running Time: 29 min.). (New Letters on the Air Ser.). 1994. 10.00 (111494); 18.00 2-sided cass. New Letters.
Gordimer is interviewed by Rebekah Presson & reads from None to Accompany Me.

Nadja, Andre Breton. Read by Sophie Chauveau. 2 cass. 1992. 28.95 (1527-TH) Olivia & Hill.
A chance encounter with a mysterious woman in the streets of Paris haunts the writer in this autobiographical surrealist novel.

***Nadya.** unabr. ed. Pat Murphy. Read by Kirsten Potter. (Running Time: 16 hrs. 0 mins.). (Wolf Chronicles Ser.). 2010. 29.95 (978-1-4417-3386-3(8)); 89.95 (978-1-4417-3382-5(5)); audio compact disk 118.00 (978-1-4417-3383-2(3)) Blckstn Audio.

Nahid Rachlin. unabr. ed. Nahid Rachlin. 1 cass. (Running Time: 29 min.). (New Letters on the Air Ser.). 1992. 10.00 (032792) New Letters.
The Iranian-born author reads from a new collection of short stories, "Veil" & talks about her conflict as a Middle-Eastern woman who loves her culture & yet insists upon being liberated.

***Nahum.** abr. ed. J. J. Benitez. (SPA.). 2009. 59.99 (978-1-61574-783-2(4)) Find a World.

Nail: Volume 3. 2006. 5.99 (978-5-558-24564-6(6)) Tooth & Nail.

Nail & Its Disorders. Milady Publishing Company Staff. 1 cass. (Standard Ser.: Chapter 17). 1995. 6.95 (978-1-56253-289-5(8), Milady) Delmar.

Nail Biter. Sarah Graves. Read by Lindsay Ellison. 6 cass. (Running Time: 32100 sec.). (Home Repair Is Homicide Mystery Ser.). 2006. 54.95 (978-0-7927-3864-0(0), CSL 882); audio compact disk 79.95 (978-0-7927-3865-7(9), SLD 882) AudioGO.

Nail Biter. unabr. ed. Sarah Graves. Read by Lindsay Ellison. 8 CDs. (Running Time: 32040 sec.). (Home Repair Is Homicide Mystery Ser.). 2005. audio compact disk 34.95 (978-1-57270-503-6(5), Audio Edits Mystry) Pub: Audio Partners. Dist(s): PerseuPGW
The ninth title in Sarah Graves's bestselling Home Repair is Homicide series, Nail Biter opens with a group of self-styled "witches" that has taken over an Eastport, Maine waterfront resort for Halloween. Jacobia "Jake" Tiptree is called on to answer his new tenants' multiple demands-many dealing with supernatural moaning-but she would rather be excavating an unusual discovery she made in the foundation of her 1823 Federal-style home. Instead, when a fundamentalist preacher turns up dead and all eyes turn to the witches, Jake's soon up to her eyeballs in trouble.

Nail Biter. unabr. ed. Sarah Graves. Read by Lindsay Ellison. 6 cass. (Running Time: 32040 sec.). (Home Repair Is Homicide Mystery Ser.). 2005. 31.95 (978-1-57270-505-0(1), Audio Edits Mystry) Pub: Audio Partners. Dist(s): PerseuPGW

Nail Biting. Bruce Goldberg. 1 cass. (Running Time: 20 min.). (ENG.). 2006. 13.00 (978-1-885577-15-3(X)) Pub: B Goldberg. Dist(s): Baker Taylor
This self hypnosis program trains the listener to eliminate the need for biting their nails.

Nail DVD. 2005. 9.98 (978-5-559-05589-3(1)) Tooth & Nail.

Nail Scarred Hands. Greg Skipper. 1998. 8.00 (978-0-7673-9974-6(9)); 40.00 (978-0-7673-9958-6(7)); audio compact disk 12.00 (978-0-7673-9968-5(4)) LifeWay Christian.

Nail Scarred Hands Cassette Kit. Greg Skipper. 1998. 54.95 (978-0-7673-9970-8(6)) LifeWay Christian.

Nail Scarred Hands Listening Cd You Can Series. Greg Skipper. 1998. audio compact disk 16.98 (978-0-7673-9931-9(5)) LifeWay Christian.

Nail Scarred Hands Series. Greg Skipper. 1998. 11.98 (978-0-7673-9940-1(4)) LifeWay Christian.

Nail Scarred Hands Split Acc. Greg Skipper. 1998. audio compact disk 45.00 (978-0-7673-9930-2(7)) LifeWay Christian.

Nail the Job Interview. Caryl Rae Krannich. Read by Kimberly Schraf. (Running Time: 2 hrs. 30 mins.). 2005. 19.95 (978-1-59912-901-3(9)) Iofy Corp.

Nail the Job Interview. abr. ed. Caryl Krannich & Ronald Krannich. 2 CDs. (Running Time: 2 hrs. 30 mins.). (What's New Ser.). 2004. audio compact disk 19.95 (978-1-59316-023-4(2), LL115) Listen & Live.
Landing a good job is a competitive process and often the final decision is based on your performance at the interview. By following the advice of prominent career and human resources experts, Caryl and Ron Krannich, you'll know you have the right answers at your job interview.

Nailbiting. 1 cass. (Running Time: 1 hr.). 10.95 (047) Psych Res Inst.
Subliminal biofeedback to eliminate the habit of nailbiting.

Nailing It. Norman Dietz. Read by Norman Dietz. (Running Time: 3 mins.). 2005. 22.95 (978-0-7861-3691-9(X)) Blckstn Audio.

Nailing It. Norman Dietz. Read by Norman Dietz. (Running Time: 10800 sec.). 2005. DVD, audio compact disk, audio compact disk 27.00 (978-0-7861-7678-6(4)) Blckstn Audio.

Nailing It. unabr. ed. Norman Dietz. Read by Norman Dietz. (Running Time: 3 mins.). 2005. 29.95 (978-0-7861-7916-9(3)) Blckstn Audio.

Nailing the Flesh. Ben Young. 2000. 4.95 (978-0-7417-6187-3(4), B0187) Win Walk.

Nailing the Job Interview Freeway Guide: Prepare & Get Hired! Created by Playaway. (Playaway Adult Nonfiction Ser.). (ENG.). 2009. 34.99 (978-1-60812-708-5(7)) Find a World.

Naive & Sentimental Lover. unabr. ed. John le Carré. Read by Rupert Keenlyside. 12 cass. (Running Time: 18 hrs.). (George Smiley Novels Ser.). 1986. 96.00 (978-0-7366-0965-4(2), 1907) Books on Tape.
Aldo Cassidy is the naive & sentimental lover, a tycoon caught between two loves. Trapped with him are Shamus, a wild artist who carouses by day or night & Helen, the artist's nakedly alluring wife. The question of who will wind up with whom is only one of the mysteries in a world founded upon spontaneity & feeling.

Naive Male. Robert Bly. Read by Robert Bly. Ed. by William Booth. 1 cass. (Running Time: 1 hr. 30 min.). 1988. 10.00 Ally Pr.
Women as well as men will respond to this high-spirited, good-humored critique of the naively sensitive male.

Naja Kwako. Prod. by Good News Productions Int'l.Tr. of I am Coming to You. (KIN.). (YA). 2007. audio compact disk 5.00 (978-1-59305-167-9(0)) Good News Prod Intl.

Nakama 2 Student Audio CD. Seiichi Makino. (YA). 1999. cass. & cd-rom 3.56 (978-0-618-01815-4(8), 322673) CENGAGE Learn.

Naked. David Sedaris. 1999. (978-1-57042-745-9(3)) Hachet Audio.

Naked. abr. ed. David Sedaris. Read by David Sedaris. Read by Amy Sedaris. (Running Time: 3 hrs.). (ENG.). 2009. 39.98 (978-1-60024-941-9(8)) Pub: Hachet Audio. Dist(s): HachBkGrp

Naked. abr. ed. David Sedaris & Amy Sedaris. Read by David Sedaris & Amy Sedaris. 3 CDs. (Running Time: 3 hrs.). (ENG.). 2001. audio compact disk 24.98 (978-1-58621-223-0(0)) Pub: Hachet Audio. Dist(s): HachBkGrp

Naked. unabr. abr. ed. David Sedaris. Read by David Sedaris. Read by Amy Sedaris. (ENG.). 2005. 14.98 (978-1-59483-179-9(3)) Pub: Hachet Audio. Dist(s): HachBkGrp

Naked Accountant Asks: Who's Standing on Your Financial Hose? Jean Backus. 2cds. 2008. audio compact disk 12.95 (978-1-932226-69-0(9)) Wizard Acdmy.

Naked Blade, Naked Gun. Axel Kilgore. Read by Carol Eason. 2 vols. No. 13. 2004. 18.00 (978-1-58807-169-9(3)); (978-1-58807-660-1(1)) Am Pubng Inc.

naked Buddha: A practical guide to the Buddha's life & Teachings. Adrienne Howley. Read by Deidre Rubenstein. (Running Time: 5 hrs. 30 mins.). 2009. 64.99 (978-1-74214-247-0(8), 9781742142470) Pub: Bolinda Pubng AUS. Dist(s): Bolinda Pub Inc

Naked Buddha: A Practical Guide to the Buddha's Life & Teachings. unabr. ed. Adrienne Howley. Read by Deidre Rubenstein. (Running Time: 19800 sec.). 2006. audio compact disk 63.95 (978-1-74093-669-9(8)) Pub: Bolinda Pubng AUS. Dist(s): Bolinda Pub Inc

naked Buddha: A practical guide to the Buddha's life & Teachings. unabr. ed. Adrienne Howley. Read by Deidre Rubenstein. (Running Time: 5 hrs. 30 mins.). 2008. 43.95 (978-1-74214-016-2(5), 9781742140162) Pub: Bolinda Pubng AUS. Dist(s): Bolinda Pub Inc

Naked Came the Phoenix. unabr. ed. Nevada Barr et al. Read by Susan Ericksen. Ed. by Marcia Talley. 5 cass. (Running Time: 7 hrs.). 2001. 27.95 (978-1-58788-573-0(5), 1587885735, BAU); 61.25 (978-1-58788-574-7(3), 1587885743, Unabridge Lib Edns) Brilliance Audio.
The promise of discretion and pampering - and a longer overdue reconciliation with her mother - draws Caroline Blessing, the young wife of a newly elected congressman, to the fancy Phoenix Spa. But after her first night in the beautiful Blue Ridge Mountains, Caroline wakes to find the rich and famous guests in turmoil and under suspicion: the spa's flamboyant and ambitious owner has been murdered. As the secrets come out - and the body count rises - can Caroline keep herself from becoming the next victim?

In the tradition of such collaborative classics as NAKED CAME THE MANATEE and THE FLOATING ADMIRAL, each chapter in this serial novel is written by one of today's most talented mystery novelists. NEVADA BARR's ninth and latest in her Anna Pigeon series is BLOOD LURE. J.D. ROBB is the New York Times bestselling author of the futuristic romantic suspense series featuring Lieutenant Eve Dallas. Her most recent titles include BETRAYAL IN DEATH and JUDGMENT IN DEATH. NANCY PICKARD is the author of the popular Jenny Cain mystery series. LISA SCOTTOLINE is a New York Times bestselling author of legal thrillers, most recently THE VENDETTA DEFENSE and MOMENT OF TRUTH. Author of five New York Times bestselling novels, PERRI O'SHAUGHNESSY is really two sisters, Pamela and Mary, who collaborate on a series of legal thrillers and short stories. J.A. JANCE writes two police procedural series: twelve books featuring Detective J.P. Beaumont and nine with Sheriff Joanna Brady. FAYE KELLERMAN is the New York Times bestselling author of the Peter Decker/Rina Lazarus mystery series. Her most recent novel is THE FORGOTTEN. MARY JANE CLARK is a producer and writer at CBS News and the author of three media thrillers, including LET ME WHISPER IN YOUR EAR. MARCIA TALLEY is the author of UNBREATHED MEMORIES and the award-winning SING IT TO HER BONES. She is also the editor of NAKED CAME THE PHOENIX. ANNE PERRY, author of the acclaimed Victorian Series starring William Monk and Thomas and Charlotte Pitt, has written over thirty novels, including THE ONE THING MORE. DIANA GABALDON's THE FIERY CROSS, fifth in the Outlander series, is due to be published late this year. VAL McDERMID has published fifteen novels and one work of non-fiction and has won the Gold Dagger and the Grand Prix des Romans d'Aventures. Her most recent novel is A PLACE OF EXECUTION. LAURIE R. KING writes two crime fiction series as well as stand-alone novels, most recently FOLLY.

Naked Came the Phoenix. unabr. ed. Read by Susan Ericksen. Ed. by Marcia Talley. (Running Time: 7 hrs.). 2004. 24.95 (978-1-59710-523-1(6), 1597105236, BAD) Brilliance Audio.

Naked Came the Phoenix. unabr. ed. Marcia Talley. Read by Susan Ericksen. (Running Time: 7 hrs.). 2004. 39.25 (978-1-59710-522-4(8), 1597105228, BADLE) Brilliance Audio.

Naked Came the Phoenix. unabr. ed. Marcia Talley et al. Read by Susan Ericksen. Ed. by Marcia Talley. (Running Time: 7 hrs.). 2004. 39.25 (978-1-59335-375-9(8), 1593353758, Brlnc Audio MP3 Lib) Brilliance Audio.

Naked Came the Phoenix. unabr. ed. Marcia Talley et al. Read by Susan Ericksen. Ed. by Marcia Talley. (Running Time: 7 hrs.). 2004. 24.95 (978-1-59335-112-0(7), 1593351127) Soulmate Audio Bks.

***Naked Cruelty: A Carmine Delmonico Novel.** Colleen McCullough. Narrated by Charles Leggett. (Running Time: 14 hrs. 0 mins. 0 sec.). (ENG.). 2010. audio compact disk 29.95 (978-1-60998-107-5(3)) Pub: AudioGO. Dist(s): Perseus Dist

Naked Detective. unabr. ed. Laurence Shames. Narrated by Ron McLarty. 5 cass. (Running Time: 7 hrs. 15 mins.). 2001. 45.00 (978-0-7887-4362-7(7), 96243E7) Recorded Bks.

Pete Amsterdam isn't really a private investigator. But he has a licence, a gun & a phone book listing - all so he can write-off his wine cellar as an office. Reluctantly pulled from his first case, Pete feels trapped by the conventions of detective stories. Stumbling through the Key West crime scene, he hardly realizes the danger he's in.

Naked Empire. unabr. ed. Terry Goodkind. Read by Jim Bond. 14 cass. (Running Time: 23 hrs.). (Sword of Truth Ser.: Bk. 8). 2003. 117.25 (978-1-59086-302-2(X), 159086302X, CD Unabrid Lib Ed); 39.95 (978-1-59086-301-5(1), 1590863011, BAU); audio compact disk 49.95 (978-1-59086-303-9(8), 1590863038, CD); audio compact disk 142.25 (978-1-59086-304-6(6), 1590863046, Unabridge Lib Edns) Brilliance Audio.

NAKED EMPIRE. It begins . . . "You knew they were there, didn't you?" Kahlan asked in a hushed tone as she leaned closer. Against the darkening sky, she could just make out the shapes of three black-tipped races taking to wing, beginning their nightly hunt. That was why he'd stopped. That was what he'd been watching as the rest of them waited in uneasy silence. "Yes," Richard said. He gestured over his shoulder without turning to look. "There are two more, back there." Kahlan briefly scanned the dark jumble of rock, but she didn't see any others. Lightly grasping the silver pommel with two fingers, Richard lifted his sword a few inches, checking that it was clear in its scabbard. A last fleeting glimmer of amber light played across his golden cape as he let the sword drop back, in place. In the gathering gloom of dusk, his familiar tall, powerful contour seemed as if it were no more than an apparition made of shadows. Just then, two more of the huge birds shot by right overhead. One, wings stretched wide, let out a piercing scream as it banked into a tight gliding turn, circling, once in assessment of the five people below before stroking its powerful wings to catch its departing comrades in their swift journey west. This night they would find ample food.

Naked Empire. unabr. ed. Terry Goodkind. Read by Jim Bond. (Running Time: 23 hrs.). (Sword of Truth Ser.: Bk. 8). 2004. 44.25 (978-1-59335-623-1(4), 1593356234, Brlnc Audio MP3 Lib) Brilliance Audio.

Naked Empire. unabr. ed. Terry Goodkind. Read by Jim Bond. (Running Time: 23 hrs.). (Sword of Truth Ser.). 2004. 44.25 (978-1-59710-525-5(2), 1597105252, BADLE); 29.95 (978-1-59710-524-8(4), 1597105244, BAD) Brilliance Audio.

Naked Empire. unabr. ed. Terry Goodkind. Read by Jim Bond. (Running Time: 23 hrs.). (Sword of Truth Ser.: Bk. 8). 2004. 29.95 (978-1-59335-216-5(6), 1593352166) Soulmate Audio Bks.

***Naked Gospel: The Truth You May Never Hear in Church.** unabr. ed. Andrew Farley. (Running Time: 5 hrs. 23 mins. 0 sec.). (ENG.). 2009. 14.99 (978-0-310-77356-6(3)) Zondervan.

***Naked Heat.** unabr. ed. Richard Castle. 2010. 34.99 (978-1-4013-9613-8(5)) Hyperion.

***Naked Heat WMA.** Richard Castle. (ENG.). 2010. 21.99 (978-1-4013-9614-5(3)) Pub: Hyperion. Dist(s): HarperCollins Pubs

naked Husband. unabr. ed. Mark D'Arbanville. Read by Humphrey Bower. (Running Time: 6 hrs.). 2007. audio compact disk 63.95 (978-1-74093-863-1(1)) Pub: Bolinda Pubng AUS. Dist(s): Bolinda Pub Inc

Naked in Baghdad: The Iraq War as Seen by National Public Radio's Correspondent Anne Garrels. unabr. rev. ed. Anne Garrels. Read by Anne Garrels. Read by Vint Lawrence. 7 CDs. (Running Time: 8 hrs. 0 mins. 0 sec.). (ENG.). 2003. audio compact disk 36.95 (978-1-59397-358-2(6)) Pub: Macmill Audio. Dist(s): Macmillan

Naked in Borneo see May Swenson

Naked in Death. abr. ed. J. D. Robb, pseud. Read by Susan Ericksen. (Running Time: 21600 sec.). (In Death Ser.). 2007. audio compact disk 14.99 (978-1-4233-3657-0(7), 9781423336570, BCD Value Price) Brilliance Audio.

Naked in Death. unabr. ed. J. D. Robb, pseud. Read by Susan Ericksen. 6 cass. (Running Time: 9 hrs.). (In Death Ser.). 2004. 29.95 (978-1-59355-825-3(2), 1593558252, BAU); 74.25 (978-1-59355-826-0(0), 1593558260, BAudLibEd); audio compact disk 33.95 (978-1-59355-827-7(9), 1593558279, BriAudCD Unabrid); audio compact disk 82.25 (978-1-59355-828-4(7), 1593558287, BriAudCD Unabrid) Brilliance Audio.

Eve Dallas is a New York police lieutenant hunting for a ruthless killer. In over ten years on the force, she's seen it all - and knows that her survival depends on her instincts. And she's going against every warning telling her not to get involved with Roarke, an Irish billionaire - and suspect in Eve's murder investigation. But passion and seduction have rules of their own, and it's up to Eve to take a chance in the arms of a man she knows nothing about - except the addictive hunger of needing his touch.

Naked in Death. unabr. ed. J. D. Robb, pseud. Read by Susan Ericksen. (Running Time: 9 hrs.). (In Death Ser.). 2004. 39.25 (978-1-59335-538-8(6), 1593355386, Brlnc Audio MP3 Lib); 24.95 (978-1-59335-277-6(8), 1593352778, Brilliance MP3) Brilliance Audio.

Naked in Death. unabr. ed. J. D. Robb, pseud. Read by Susan Ericksen. (Running Time: 9 hrs.). (In Death Ser.). 2004. 39.25 (978-1-59710-526-2(0), 1597105260, BADLE); 24.95 (978-1-59710-527-9(9), 1597105279, BAD) Brilliance Audio.

Naked in Death, unabr. ed. J. D. Robb, pseud. Narrated by Cristine McMurdo-Wallis. 8 cass. (Running Time: 11 hrs.). (In Death Ser.). 2000. 70.00 (978-0-7887-4049-7(0), 96125E7) Recorded Bks.

Meet Eve Dallas, a policewoman walking the thin line between seduction & danger. After 10 years on the force, she should know better than to fall in love with the prime suspect in her murder investigation.

Naked in Death-ABR. J. D. Robb, pseud & #1 In Death Series. 2010. audio compact disk 9.99 (978-1-4418-4185-8(7)) Brilliance Audio.

Naked Is the Best Disguise: Sherlock Holmes Revisited. unabr. ed. Read by Heywood Hale Broun & Samuel Rosenberg. 1 cass. (Running Time: 56 min.). (Broun Radio Ser.). 11.95 (40075) J Norton Pubs.

A Conversation with the author of "Naked is the Best Disguise".

Naked Justice. unabr. ed. William Bernhardt. Read by Jonathan Marosz. 11 cass. (Running Time: 16 hrs. 30 min.). (Ben Kincaid Ser.: No. 6). 1997. 88.00 (978-0-7366-3789-3(3), 4463) Books on Tape.

Wallace Barrett was a college football hero who went on to become mayor of Tulsa, the city's first black mayor, in fact. But when Barrett's wife & two young daughters are gruesomely murdered, no one doubts he's guilty. The evidence is stacked against him: He was seen splattered with blood, fleeing the scene of the crime. lawyer Ben Kincaid takes the case in the teeth of a media frenzy. With expert witnesses standing in line to testify against his client, Kincaid needs a miracle.

***Naked Lady Who Stood on Her Head: A Psychiatrist's Stories of His Most Bizarre Cases.** unabr. ed. Gary Small & Gigi Vorgan. Read by Jim Meskimen. (ENG.). 2010. (978-0-06-206240-6(9), Harper Audio); (978-0-06-202754-2(9), Harper Audio) HarperCollins Pubs.

Naked Land. unabr. collector's ed. Hammond Innes. Read by Christopher Hurt. 7 cass. (Running Time: 10 hrs. 30 mins.). 1984. 56.00 (978-0-7366-0852-7(4), 1803) Books on Tape.

Innes sets his story in French Morocco, land of the Berbers, where murderous tribesman compete for an arid & inaccessible piece of land known as Kasbah Foum.

Naked Lunch, abr. ed. William S. Burroughs. Read by William S. Burroughs. 2 cass. (Running Time: 3 hrs.). 1995. 17.00 (978-1-57042-220-1(6), 4-522206) Hachet Audio.

The unnerving tale of a monumental descent into the hellish world of a narcotics addict. He travels from New York to Tangiers, then into The Interzone, a nightmarish modern urban wasteland in which the forces of good & evil vie for control of the individual & all of humanity.

Naked Lunch: Modern Classic Collection (the Restored Text) unabr. ed. William S. Burroughs. Read by Mark Bramhall. 9 CDs. (Running Time: 10 hrs. 30 mins.). 2009. audio compact disk 19.95 (978-1-4332-5967-8(2)) Blckstn Audio.

Naked Lunch: Modern Classic Collection (the Restored Text) unabr. ed. William S. Burroughs. Read by Mark Bramhall. Ed. by James Grauerholz & Barry Miles. (Running Time: 8 hrs. NaN mins.). 2009. 29.95 (978-1-4332-5968-5(0)) Blckstn Audio.

Naked Lunch: The Restored Text. unabr. ed. William S. Burroughs. Read by Mark Bramhall. Ed. by James Grauerholz & Barry Miles. (Running Time: 8 hrs. NaN mins.). 2009. audio compact disk 54.95 (978-1-4332-5964-7(8)); audio compact disk 70.00 (978-1-4332-5965-4(6)) Blckstn Audio.

Naked Once More. unabr. ed. Elizabeth Peters, pseud. Read by Grace Conlin. 9 cass. (Running Time: 13 hrs.). 1995. 62.95 (978-0-7861-0809-1(6), 1632) Blckstn Audio.

Bestselling author, ex-librarian Jacqueline Kirby is thinking of retiring until her agent convinces her to write a sequel to "Naked in the Ice," a seven year old blockbuster that skyrocketed Kathleen Darcy to instant fame. Now the author's heirs are looking for a writer to pen the sequel. No one doubts her sanity until Jacqueline starts digging through the missing woman's papers & her past, until she gets mixed up with Kathleen's enigmatic lover & until a series of nasty accidents convince her much too late that someone wants to bring her story & her life to a premature end.

Naked Once More. unabr. ed. Elizabeth Peters, pseud. Narrated by Barbara Rosenblat. 10 cass. (Running Time: 13 hrs. 30 mins.). 1997. 85.00 (978-0-7887-0928-9(3), 95068E7) Recorded Bks.

Join Jacqueline Kirby, a popular author & outspoken ex-librarian while she untangles a perilous plot while penning the sequel to a best-selling novel.

Naked Once More: A Jacqueline Kirby Mystery. unabr. ed. Elizabeth Peters, pseud. Read by Grace Conlin. (Running Time: 13 hrs. 0 mins.). 2008. 29.95 (978-1-4332-5849-7(8)); audio compact disk 99.00 (978-1-4332-5846-6(3)) Blckstn Audio.

Naked Prey. unabr. ed. John Sandford, pseud. 8 cass. (Running Time: 11 hrs. 30 min.). (Prey Ser.). 2003. 78.00 (978-1-4025-4396-8(4)) Recorded Bks.

Naked Public Square. unabr. ed. Richard J. Neuhaus. Read by Christopher Hurt. 9 cass. (Running Time: 13 hrs.). 1989. 62.95 (978-0-7861-0068-2(0), 1064) Blckstn Audio.

Neuhaus uses his central metaphor, the naked public square, to describe the empty & uncomely condition of today's political doctrine, which has been developed without consideration of religion & religious values.

Naked She Lay: An Anthology of Classic Erotic Verse. Read by Edward De Souza et al. Ed. by Anthony Anderson. 2 cass. (Running Time: 2 hrs. 30 mins.). 1999. 13.98 (978-962-634-668-6(X), NA216814, Naxos AudioBooks) Naxos.

Naked She Lay: Classic Erotic Verse: Classic Erotic Verse. (Running Time: 2 hrs. 30 mins.). 2003. 22.95 (978-1-60083-853-8(7)) Iofy Corp.

Naked Sun. unabr. ed. Isaac Asimov. Read by William Dufris. (Running Time: 7 hrs. 30 mins. 0 sec.). (Robot Ser.). (ENG.). 2007. audio compact disk 29.99 (978-1-4001-0422-2(X)); audio compact disk 19.99 (978-1-4001-5422-7(7)); audio compact disk 59.99 (978-1-4001-3422-9(6)) Pub: Tantor Media. Dist(s): IngramPubServ

Naked Sun. unabr. ed. Ted Willis. 7 cass. 1998. 76.95 (978-1-85903-077-6(7)) Pub: Magna Story GBR. Dist(s): Ulverscroft US

Naked Truth. Leslie Nielsen. 2004. 7.95 (978-0-7435-4943-1(0)) Pub: S&S Audio. Dist(s): S and S Inc

Naked Without Shame. 2003. 14.95 (978-1-932631-16-6(X)); audio compact disk 14.95 (978-1-932631-17-3(8)) Ascensn Pr.

Naktergalen Vol. 3: The Nightingale. 3rd unabr. ed. Ed. by Ingrid Lang. Tr. by Sweden Elex. Illus. by Scott Zins. Prod. by Scott Zins. 1 cass. (Running Time: 13 min.). (Listen & Learn Language Audio Ser.: Vol. LL0399). (ENG & SWE.). 1999. pap. bk. 15.95 (978-1-892623-04-1(8)) Intl Book.

English & Swedish bilingual text with the Swedish narration.

Namaste Jii: Reading Writing & Conversation. Arun Prakash. (YA). 2007. audio compact disk 25.00 (978-1-4276-2625-7(1)) AardGP.

Namath: A Biography. unabr. ed. Mark Kriegel. Read by Scott Brick. 14 cass. (Running Time: 21 hrs.). 2004. 112.00 (978-1-4159-0370-4(0)) Books on Tape.

The first major biography of the sports hero who changed the face of football.

Name. Neville Goddard. 1 cass. (Running Time: 1 hr. 2 min.). 1965. 8.00 (50) J & L Pubns.

Neville taught Imagination Creates Reality. He was a powerfully influential teacher of God as Consciousness.

Name. abr. ed. Franklin Graham. Read by Jim Bond. (Running Time: 3 hrs.). 2006. audio compact disk 39.25 (978-1-4233-0406-7(3), 9781423304067, Brlnc Audio MP3 Lib) Brilliance Audio.

Name. abr. ed. Franklin Graham & Bruce Nygren. Read by Jim Bond. 3 CDs. (Running Time: 3 hrs.). 2002. audio compact disk 24.95 (978-1-59086-673-3(8), 1590866738); audio compact disk 62.25 (978-1-59086-674-0(6), 1590866746) Brilliance Audio.

Why does the name of Jesus stir both awe and animosity? Franklin Graham faced that question himself in April of 1999, just days after the tragic killing of students at Columbine High School shocked America and the world. Colorado's governor had asked Franklin to speak at the memorial service for families and friends. As a chilling drizzle soaked the crowd of 70,000, Franklin boldly urged all mourners to seek comfort, hope and salvation through the Lord Jesus Christ. Later he received both congratulations and criticism for his remarks. To Franklin's surprise, even clergymen complained that the emphasis on Jesus was offensive. Later Franklin reflected,"Why is it when people curse using His Name, hardly anyone complains? But if you speak about Him with respect or pray in His Name, some people call it 'foul'?" The Name is Franklin's response to those questions. The Name explains, reveals, and honors the most important Person who ever lived. It is an articulate, passionate, motivating, and moving tribute to the One who bears the Name above all names and before whom some day "every knee will bow.".

Name. abr. ed. Franklin Graham & Bruce Nygren. Read by Jim Bond. (Running Time: 3 hrs.). 2006. 24.95 (978-1-4233-0405-0(5), 9781423304050, Brilliance MP3); 49.97 (978-1-4233-0408-1(X), 9781423304081, BADLE); 24.95 (978-1-4233-0407-4(1), 9781423304074, BAD) Brilliance Audio.

Name above All Names. Contrib. by Mosie Lister. 1989. 10.99 (978-0-685-68464-1(4), TA-9116C) Lillenas.

Name Above All Names: Isaiah 9:6. Dan Hayden. 2004. audio compact disk 24.95 (978-1-932691-05-4(7)) Pub: Sola Scriptura. Dist(s): STL Dist NA

Name All the Animals: A Memoir. abr. ed. Alison Smith. 2004. 15.95 (978-0-7435-3928-9(1)) Pub: S&S Audio. Dist(s): S and S Inc

Name Analysis. Mary E. Korpan-Roy. Read by Mary E. Korpan-Roy. 1 cass. (Running Time: 1 hr. 30 min.). 1994. 8.95 (1154) Am Fed Astrologers.

Name Dropping. unabr. ed. Barnaby Conrad. Read by Barnaby Conrad. 5 cass. (Running Time: 7 hrs.). 2000. 39.95 (978-0-7861-2674-3(4), 3232); audio compact disk 48.00 (978-0-7861-8745-4(X), 3232) Blckstn Audio.

Name into Word. unabr. ed. Gilbert Highet. 1 cass. (Running Time: 1 hr.). (Gilbert Highet Ser.). 11.95 (23324) J Norton Pubs.

A tawdry piece of jewelry was named after St. Audrey & a rough tough hooligan was named after an Irish family named Hoolihan: How words have changed & how they go on changing.

Name into Word & Changing Words. Gilbert Highet. (ENG.). 2006. audio compact disk 9.95 (978-1-57970-442-1(5), Audio-For) J Norton Pubs.

Name Is Empty Brown. unabr. ed. Orville D. Johnson. Read by Maynard Villers. 4 cass. (Running Time: 5 hrs. 30 min.). 1996. 26.95 (978-1-55686-673-9(9)) Books in Motion.

M. T. Brown was a legend in his own time - the keenest shot with pistol or rifle as anyone who ever gambled or travelled on the Mississippi riverboats.

Name of Her Own. abr. ed. Jane Kirkpatrick. Read by Barbara Rosenblat. 6 cass. (Running Time: 7 hrs.). 2003. 25.99 (978-1-58926-112-9(7), W64L-0110) Oasis Audio.

Name of Her Own. unabr. ed. Jane Kirkpatrick. Read by Barbara Rosenblat. 8 CDs. (Running Time: 7 hrs.). 2003. audio compact disk 29.99 (978-1-58926-113-6(5), W64L-011D) Oasis Audio.

Set in the fur trapping era of 1811 history suggests was a man's world, but women walked there, too. They worked and loved and wept. They changed. One of those women was Marie Dorion, a passionate mother who crossed the United States with her husband, two sons and 68 men as part of the first grand fur expedition.

Name of Jesus. Dan Comer. 1 cass. 3.00 (60) Evang Outreach.

Name of Jesus, Vols. 1 & 2. Kenneth E. Hagin. 12 cass. 48.00 (44H, 45H) Faith Lib Pubns.

Name of the Beast see Suspense

Name of the Enemy: Jihadi Salafis. Quintan Wiktorowicz. Narrated by Grover Gardner. (Running Time: 7560 sec.). 2004. audio compact disk 24.00 (978-1-58472-805-4(1)) Sound Room.

Name of the Enemy: Jihadi Salafis: Jihadi Salafis. Quintan Wiktorowicz. Read by Grover Gardner. (Running Time: 2 hrs.). 2004. 16.95 (978-1-59912-095-9(X), Audiofy Corp) Iofy Corp.

Name of the Rose. unabr. ed. Umberto Eco. Read by Alexander Adams. 14 cass. (Running Time: 21 hrs.). 1996. 112.00 (978-0-7366-3259-1(X), 3916) Books on Tape.

The year is 1327. The place is a wealthy abbey in Italy. In seven days, someone kills seven monks. It's up to English Brother William of Baskerville to decipher secret symbols & dig into the eerie labyrinth of abbey life to solve the crimes. His tools: intelligence, wit & a ferocious curiosity. His enemy: a killer with the awesome features of the Antichrist.

Name of the Wind. unabr. ed. Patrick Rothfuss. Read by Nick Podehl. (Running Time: 28 hrs.). (Kingkiller Chronicle Ser.). 2009. 44.97 (978-1-4233-8929-3(8), 9781423389293, Brlnc Audio MP3 Lib); 44.97 (978-1-4233-8931-6(X), 9781423389316, BADLE); 29.99 (978-1-4233-8928-6(X), 9781423389286, Brilliance MP3); 29.99 (978-1-4233-8930-9(1), 9781423389309, BAD); audio compact disk 99.97 (978-1-4233-8927-9(1), 9781423389279, BriAudCD Unabrid); audio compact disk 44.99 (978-1-4233-8926-2(3), 9781423389262, Bril Audio CD Unabri) Brilliance Audio.

Name of This Book Is Secret. unabr. ed. Pseudonymous Bosch. Read by David Pittu. (J). 2008. 54.99 (978-1-60252-983-0(3)) Find a World.

Name of This Book Is Secret. unabr. ed. Pseudonymous Bosch. Read by David Pittu. 5 CDs. (Running Time: 6 hrs. 22 mins.). (ENG.). (J). (gr. 3-7). 2008. audio compact disk 29.95 (978-0-545-05340-2(4)) Scholastic Inc.

Name of This Book Is Secret. unabr. ed. Pseudonymous Bosch. Read by David Pittu. (Running Time: 22920 sec.). (J). (gr. 4-7). 2008. audio compact disk 54.95 (978-0-545-05341-9(2)) Scholastic Inc.

Name That Matters Most. Chris Heimerdinger. 1 cass. 1999. 9.95 (978-1-57734-481-0(2), 06005993) Covenant Comms.
Becoming a true follower of Christ.

Name That Pet/Animal Senses & Defenses. Steck-Vaughn Staff. 2002. (978-0-7398-5986-5(2)) SteckVau.

Name Withheld. collector's ed. J. A. Jance. Read by Jonathan Marosz. 6 cass. (Running Time: 9 hrs.). (J. P. Beaumont Mystery Ser.). 2000. 48.00 (978-0-7366-5636-8(7)) Books on Tape.
This case draws Beaumont into the cutting edge of biotechnology, where business as usual means ruthless betrayal of personal & trade secrets. The more Beau uncovers about the unsavory life of the corpse, the more he's convinced that justice has already been served.

Name Withheld. unabr. ed. J. A. Jance. Read by Gene Engene. 8 cass. (Running Time: 10 hrs. 48 min.). (J. P. Beaumont Mystery Ser.). 1996. 46.95 (978-1-55686-651-7(8), 893938) Books in Motion.

Names see House Made of Dawn

Names & Character of God. Marcia Greenwood. Read by Marcia Greenwood. 1999. 5.00 (978-1-930761-00-1(7)) TGMinist.

Names & Faces of Heroes see Long & Happy Life

Names & Nature of God. 2003. (978-1-59024-097-7(9)); audio compact disk (978-1-59024-096-0(0)) B Hinn Min.

Names in Monterchi: To Rachel see Poetry & Voice of James Wright

Names of God. Lester Sumrall. 5 cass. (Running Time: 7 hrs. 30 mins.). 1999. 20.00 (978-1-58568-094-8(X)) Sumrall Pubng.

Names of Jesus. Elmer Towns. 2008. audio compact disk 21.95 (978-1-4276-3139-8(5)) AardGP.

Names of the Holy Spirit. Elmer Towns. 2008. audio compact disk 23.95 (978-0-578-00186-9(1)) Sapphire Dig.

Names Who Make Theater. unabr. ed. Read by Heywood Hale Broun et al. 1 cass. (Running Time: 1 hr. 30 min.). (Heywood Hale Broun Ser.). 11.95 (40085) J Norton Pubs.
A Talk with Harold Clurman & Jerome Lawrence.

Namesake: A Novel. unabr. ed. Jhumpa Lahiri. 6 cass. (Running Time: 9 hrs.). 2003. 48.00 (978-0-7366-9426-1(9)) Books on Tape.
When an Indian family immigrates to America, their son must come to terms with his unusual name, American culture and family heritage.

Namesake: A Novel. unabr. ed. Jhumpa Lahiri. Read by Jhumpa Lahiri. (Running Time: 39600 sec.). (ENG.). 2006. audio compact disk 34.95 (978-0-7393-4136-0(7), Random AudioBks) Pub: Random Audio Pubg. Dist(s): Random

***Naming: The First Book of Pellinor.** unabr. ed. Alison Croggon. (Running Time: 15 hrs.). (Pellinor Ser.). 2011. 39.97 (978-1-4418-6279-2(X), 9781441862792, Candlewick Bril); 39.97 (978-1-4418-6277-8(3), 9781441862778, Candlewick Bril); 19.99 (978-1-4418-6276-1(5), 9781441862761, Candlewick Bril); audio compact disk 29.99 (978-1-4418-6274-7(9), 9781441862747, Candlewick Bril); audio compact disk 69.97 (978-1-4418-6275-4(7), 9781441862754, Candlewick Bril) Brilliance Audio.

Naming Evil. Based on a book by Joan Chittister. 1 cass. (Running Time: 60 mins). 2004. 7.00 (978-1-890890-39-1(1)) Benetvision.

Naming Evil. Joan Chittister. CD. (Running Time: 60 mins). 2004. 10.00 (978-1-890890-40-7(5)) Benetvision.

Naming of Olga da Polga. unabr. ed. Michael Bond. Read by Tammy Grimes. 1 cass. (Running Time: 45 mins.). (J). (ps-3). 1986. 8.98 (978-0-89845-643-1(6), CP 1798) HarperCollins Pubs.
Stories about the delightful, irrepressible guinea-pig Olga da Polga.

Naming of Parts see Dylan Thomas Reading

Naming of the Dead. abr. ed. Ian Rankin. Read by James Gale. (Running Time: 7 hrs.). (ENG.). 2007. 14.98 (978-1-59483-879-8(8)) Pub: Hachet Audio. Dist(s): HachBkGrp

Naming the Place, Placing the Name. Perf. by Jennifer Reifsneider. Created by Jennifer Reifsneider. Intro. by Wes Mills. 1 33rpm. (Running Time: 3 mins. 52 secs). 2000. (978-0-9726562-0-7(0)) J Reifsneider.
Sound Art, 2 tracks on 33 rpm vinyl record:"Basic English": a simutaneous reading of the 850 most essential words in the English language, as compiled by CK Ogden for international communication."Contents (The Myth of Sisyphus)": sound accompanies illustrated installation. Jacket includes 2 color illustrations, comments by Wes Mills. Created for an exhibition of contemporary sculpture and installation by publisher/performer Jennifer Reifsneider.

Nana. Emile Zola. Read by Rosangela López. (Running Time: 3 hrs.). 2002. 16.95 (978-1-60083-202-4(4), Audiofy Corp) Iofy Corp.

Nana. abr. ed. Emile Zola. 3 CDs. (SPA.). 2002. audio compact disk 17.00 (978-958-8161-01-3(0)) YoYoMusic.

Nana. unabr. ed. Emile Zola. Read by Walter Zimmerman. 14 cass. (Running Time: 20 hrs. 30 mins.). 1988. 89.95 (978-0-7861-0602-8(6), 2092) Blckstn Audio.
Living among the pleasure-loving society of Napoleon III's France was a beautiful, capricious, good-natured yet noxious prostitute named Nana. For her, rich men gave up their fortunes & honor; poor men gave up their mates & even their lives. Yet Zola's heroine squanders fortunes & her life ends in squalor.

Nana. unabr. ed. Emile Zola. Read by Walter Zimmerman. 14 cass. (Running Time: 20 hrs. 45 min.). 1989. 69.00 (C-195) Jimcin Record.
Realistic novel of the life of a courtesan.

Nana, Pt. 1. unabr. collector's ed. Emile Zola. Read by Jill Masters. 7 cass. (Running Time: 10 hrs. 30 min.). 1989. 56.00 (978-0-7366-1617-1(9), 2477-A) Books on Tape.
This young & glamorous prostitute symbolized all that was seductive & fatal about the France of her era.

Nana, Pt. 2. unabr. collector's ed. Emile Zola. Read by Jill Masters. 7 cass. (Running Time: 10 hrs. 30 min.). 1989. 56.00 (978-0-7366-1618-8(7), 2477-B) Books on Tape.
This young and glamorous prostitute symbolized all that was seductive & fatal about the France of her era.

Nana Upstairs & Nana Downstairs. unabr. ed. Tomie dePaola. Read by Tomie dePaola. 1 CD. (Running Time: 7 mins.). (J). (gr. k-3). 2006. pap. bk. 19.95 (978-0-8045-4157-2(4)); pap. bk. 17.95 (978-0-8045-6943-9(6)) Spoken Arts.
For year old Tommy loves visiting the house where his grandmother, Nana Downstairs, and his great-grandmother, Nana Upstairs live. Every Sunday, Tommy and Nana Upstairs share candy and tell stories - until one day Tommy's mother tells him Nana Upstairs won't be there anymore. Tommy must struggle to understand what it means to lose someone he loves.

Nana's Kitchen - You Can Cook. Steck-Vaughn Staff. 1 cass. (Running Time: 90 min.). (J). 1999. (978-0-7398-2444-3(9)) SteckVau.

***Nancy.** unabr. ed. Michael Deaver. Read by Michael Deaver. (ENG.). 2004. (978-0-06-081301-7(6), Harper Audio); (978-0-06-075229-3(7), Harper Audio) HarperCollins Pubs.

Nancy & Plum. unabr. ed. Betty Bard MacDonald. Narrated by Kate Forbes. 4 cass. (Running Time: 5 hrs. 30 mins.). (J). 2001. pap. bk. & stu. ed. Recorded Bks.
When Nancy & Plum lose their parents, Uncle John sends the girls to Mrs. Monday's boarding house. Their Uncle thinks they are enjoying tender loving care. Instead, Mrs. Monday feeds them burnt oatmeal & dresses them in raggedy clothes.

Nancy & Plum. unabr. ed. Betty Bard MacDonald. Narrated by Kate Forbes. 4 pieces. (Running Time: 5 hrs. 30 mins.). (gr. 2 up). 2001. 38.00 (978-0-7887-4725-0(8), 96399B7) Recorded Bks.

***Nancy Bhan.** Beairtle O. Domhnaill. (ENG.). 2008. audio compact disk 28.95 (978-0-8023-8169-9(3)) Pub: Clo Iar-Chonnachta IRL. Dist(s): Dufour

Nancy Caroline's Emergency Care in the Streets. 6th ed. American Academy of Orthopaedic Surgeons (AAOS) et al. 2007. 80.95 (978-0-7637-4058-0(6)) Jones Bartlett.

Nancy CD: A Portrait of My Years with Nancy Reagan. unabr. ed. Michael K. Deaver. Read by Michael K. Deaver. 6 cass. (Running Time: 9 hrs.). 2004. audio compact disk 29.95 (978-0-06-058530-3(7)) HarperCollins Pubs.

Nancy Drew Vol. 1: The Secret of the Old Clock. unabr. ed. Carolyn Keene. 2 cass. (Running Time: 3 hrs. 14 mins.). (ENG.). (J). 2002. 8.95 (978-0-8072-0756-7(X), Listening Lib) Pub: Random Audio Pubg. Dist(s): Random
Nance Drew's keen mind is tested when she searches for a missing will.

Nancy Drew Girl Detective: Dressed to Steal. unabr. ed. Carolyn Keene. (Running Time: 3 hrs. 30 mins.). (J). 2007. 19.95 (978-1-4332-0037-3(6)) Blckstn Audio.

Nancy Drew Girl Detective: Framed. unabr. ed. Carolyn Keene. Read by Rebecca Rogers. (J). 2008. 39.99 (978-1-60514-904-2(7)) Find a World.

Nancy Drew Girl Detective: Framed. unabr. ed. Carolyn Keene. Read by Rebecca Rogers. (Running Time: 10800 sec.). (Nancy Drew: Girl Detective Ser.). (J). (gr. 3-7). 2007. 19.95 (978-1-4332-0032-8(5)) Blckstn Audio.

Nancy Drew Girl Detective: Framed: Framed. unabr. ed. Carolyn Keene. Read by Rebecca Rogers. 3 CDs. (Running Time: 10800 sec.). (Nancy Drew: Girl Detective Ser.). (J). (gr. 3-7). 2007. audio compact disk 19.95 (978-1-4332-0033-5(3)) Blckstn Audio.

Nancy Du Plessis. Nancy Du Plessis. Read by Nancy Du Plessis. 1 cass. (Running Time: 29 min.). 1986. 10.00 New Letters.
A performance piece from "Notes from the Moroccan Journals" which dramatizes the story of a passport marriage between an American woman & a Moroccan musician.

Nancy Lopez. 1 cass. (Reading With Winners: Ser. 2). 1984. 32.95 (978-0-89811-189-7(7), 9902D); Lets Talk Assocs.

Nancy Lopez: A Winner. Read by Nancy Lopez. 1 cass. 9.95 (978-0-89811-097-5(1), 7148) Lets Talk Assocs.
Nancy Lopez talks about the people & events which influenced his career & her own approach to her speciality.

Nancy Raven Sings Her Favorites, Vol. 1. Perf. by Nancy Raven. 1 CD. (Running Time: 1 hr. 10 min.). (J). (gr. k-6). 1999. audio compact disk (CD-001) Lizards Rock.
Songs from around the world with instrumentation of those countries. Some Spanish - all good for families, singing along.

Nancy reagan the unauthorized Biography. Kitty Kelly. 2004. 10.95 (978-0-7435-4444-3(7)) Pub: S&S Audio. Dist(s): S and S Inc

Nancy Taylor Rosenberg Sullivan CD Collection: Sullivan's Law, Sullivan's Justice, Sullivan's Evidence. abr. ed. Nancy Taylor Rosenberg. Read by Sandra Burr. (Running Time: 18 hrs.). 2009. audio compact disk 34.99 (978-1-4233-7969-0(1), 9781423379690, BACD) Brilliance Audio.

***Nancy Wake.** unabr. ed. Peter FitzSimons. Read by Stephanie Daniel. (Running Time: 11 hrs. 27 mins.). 2010. audio compact disk 93.95 (978-1-74214-483-2(7), 9781742144832) Pub: Bolinda Pubng AUS. Dist(s): Bolinda Pub Inc

Nanny Claus - the North Pole Nanny: A Magical Christmas Musical for Unison & 2-Part Voices (Listening) Composed by Andy Beck et al. (ENG.). 2009. audio compact disk 16.95 (978-0-7390-5847-3(9)) Alfred Pub.

Nanny Claus - the North Pole Nanny: A Magical Christmas Musical for Unison & 2-Part Voices (SoundTrax) Composed by Andy Beck et al. (ENG.). 2009. audio compact disk 59.95 (978-0-7390-5848-0(7)) Alfred Pub.

***Nanny Diaries.** abr. ed. Emma McLaughlin & Nicola Kraus. (Running Time: 5 hrs. 15 mins.). (ENG.). 2002. 12.50 (978-0-553-75536-7(6), Random AudioBks) Pub: Random Audio Pubg. Dist(s): Random

Nanny Diaries. abr. ed. Emma McLaughlin & Nicola Kraus. Read by Julia Roberts. 4 CDs. (Running Time: 4 hrs. 40 mins.). (ENG.). 2004. audio compact disk 14.99 (978-0-7393-1773-0(3)) Pub: Random Audio Pubg. Dist(s): Random

Nanny Diaries. unabr. ed. Emma McLaughlin & Nicola Kraus. Read by Kathe Mazur. 7 cass. (Running Time: 10 hrs. 30 mins.). 2002. 63.00 (978-0-7366-8746-1(7)); audio compact disk 68.85 (978-0-7366-8747-8(5)) Pub: Books on Tape. Dist(s): NetLibrary CO
What do you do when you are a nanny to an obscenely rich Park Avenue matron named X? Mrs. X refuses to do anything for herself, including cook, clean, or take care of her four-year-old son. You are expected to do everything, including maintaining the mental health of said four-year-old, even while Mrs. X decides that it is time for a divorce. You'll have to bear up under the strain with wit and panache, even as the boundaries between your working life and your so-called private life blur, merge, and disappear.

***Nanny Mcphee Returns.** unabr. ed. Emma Thompson. 4 CDs. (Running Time: 5 hrs.). (J). 2010. audio compact disk 16.99 (978-1-4272-1116-3(7)) Pub: Macmill Audio. Dist(s): Macmillan

Nanny Murders. Merry Bloch Jones. Read by Marguerite Gavin. (Running Time: 30600 sec.). 2005. cass., cass., DVD 54.95 (978-0-7861-3031-3(8)); DVD, audio compact disk, audio compact disk 63.00 (978-0-7861-7934-3(1)) Blckstn Audio.

Nanny Murders. unabr. ed. Merry Bloch Jones. Read by Marguerite Gavin. 7 cass. (Running Time: 30600 sec.). 2005. 29.95 (978-0-7861-3047-4(4)); DVD & audio compact disk 29.95 (978-0-7861-8150-6(8)); audio compact disk 29.95 (978-0-7861-7999-2(6)) Blckstn Audio.

Nanny Returns. unabr. ed. Emma McLaughlin & Nicola Kraus. Read by Susan Bennett. 10 CDs. (Running Time: 12 hrs.). 2009. audio compact disk 39.99 (978-1-4423-0403-1(0)) Pub: S&S Audio. Dist(s): S and S Inc

Nansi Richards: Queen of the Triple Harp. unabr. ed. 1 cass. 10.95 (C11057) J Norton Pubs.
Nansi Richards performs traditional Welsh music & her own compositions on the Welsh triple harp.

***Naomi & Her Daughters: A Novel.** Walter Wangerin, Jr. (Running Time: 6 hrs. 31 mins. 42 sec.). (ENG.). 2010. 24.99 (978-0-310-59043-9(4)) Zondervan.

Naomi James: An Amazing Lone Journey. Interview with Naomi James. 1 cass. (Running Time: 30 min.). 8.00 (B0030B090, HarperThor) HarpC GBR.

Naomi's Guide to Aging Gratefully: Facts, Myths, & Good News for Boomers. Naomi Judd. Read by Renée Raudman. (Playaway Adult Nonfiction Ser.). (ENG.). 2009. 60.00 (978-1-60775-635-4(8)) Find a World.

Naomi's Guide to Aging Gratefully: Facts, Myths, & Good News for Boomers. unabr. ed. Naomi Judd. Read by Renée Raudman. 6 CDs. (Running Time: 7 hrs. 30 mins. 0 sec.). (ENG.). 2007. audio compact disk 59.99 (978-1-4001-3329-1(7)) Pub: Tantor Media. Dist(s): IngramPubServ
In Naomi's Guide to Aging Gratefully, Judd debunks society's myth s about aging. She helps us define ourselves from within, find our real beauty, and enjoy the benefits that come with growing older. With fifteen important life choices, she shows how to find freedom and simplicity in the latter half of life. Each chapter offers vital, proactive suggestions for developing a healthier body, mind, and spirit at every age.

Naomi's Special Gift. Yoriko Tsutsui. Illus. by Akiko Hayashi. 1913. bk. 12.95 (978-1-74126-024-3(8)) Pub: RICPub AUS. Dist(s): SCB Distributors

Napa Jack's First Flight. Robert G. Kresko et al. Read by Robert G. Kresko & Richard Lawrence. 1 cass. (Running Time: 20 min.). Dramatization. (J). (gr. k-4). 1995. bk. 20.00; 6.00 NVMC.
Children's fiction with music.

Napa Sonoma Uncorked. Read by David Hy Pierce. 2004. bk. 34.95 (978-1-891267-86-4(8), 828) Wine Appreciation.

Napa Uncorked. David Hyde Pierce. (Running Time: 2 hrs.). 2004. audio compact disk 19.95 (978-1-891267-59-8(0), 812) Wine Appreciation.

Napalm & Silly Putty. abr. ed. George Carlin. Perf. by George Carlin. 2 CDs. (Running Time: 2 hrs. 30 mins.). (ENG.). 2001. audio compact disk 24.95 (978-1-56511-451-7(5), 1565114515) Pub: HighBridge. Dist(s): Workman Pub

Naperville, IL: Powerful Speaking for Managers. unabr. ed. Innovation Groups Staff. 1 cass. (Running Time: 1 hrs. 30 min.). (Transforming Local Government Ser.: Vol. 16). 1999. 10.00 (978-1-882403-72-1(X), IG9916) Alliance Innov.

Napkin Notes: On the Art of Living. G. Michael Durst. Read by G. Michael Durst. 4 cass. (Running Time: 2 hrs. 45 min.). 1988. 36.00 Train Sys.

Naples '44. unabr. collector's ed. Norman Lewis. Read by Richard Brown. 5 cass. (Running Time: 7 hrs. 30 min.). 1990. 40.00 (978-0-7366-1692-8(6), 2539) Books on Tape.
A diary of the Allied occupation of Naples during WWII.

Napolean of the Crime: The Life & Times of Adam Worth, the Real Moriarty. unabr. ed. Ben Macintyre. Narrated by Simon Prebble. 8 cass. (Running Time: 11 hrs. 15 mins.). 1998. 70.00 (978-0-7887-1986-8(6), 95373E7) Recorded Bks.
The model for the evil genius in Sherlock Holmes mysteries.

Napoleon. unabr. ed. Paul Johnson. 4 cass. (Running Time: 6 hrs.). 2002. 32.00 (978-0-7366-8622-8(3)) Books on Tape.
Napoleon truly was the Great Man of his age, a towering and terrible genius who managed to conquer the Continent. In Napoleon's insatiable hunger for power, Johnson sees a pragmatist constrained neither by patriotism nor by ideology, a brilliant opportunist who fulfilled his ambition in the aftermath of the French Revolution. Johnson puts Napoleon in the context of his times, but his effort seems to underline even more profoundly how Napoleon stood out above them.

Napoleon. unabr. ed. Felix Markham. Narrated by Alexander Spencer. 8 cass. (Running Time: 10 hrs. 45 mins.). 1988. 70.00 (978-1-55690-367-0(7), 88240E7) Recorded Bks.
The life of Napoleon Bonaparte. Bases on newly discovered documents, including personal letters of Empress Marie-Louise & the decoded diaries of General Bertrand, who accompanied Napoleon to his exile on St. Helena.

Napoleon, Pt. 1. unabr. ed. Emil Ludwig. Read by Frederick Davidson. 10 cass. (Running Time: 27 hrs. 30 mins.). 1993. 69.95 (978-0-7861-0379-9(5), 1334A, B) Blckstn Audio.
The story of Napoleon, the great empire builder, is surely one of the most thrilling subjects in all history. Ludwig's portrait covers it all: Napoleon's intrigues & love affairs, the horror of the French Revolution, the great battles of the Nile, of Moscow, Austerlitz, Waterloo.

Napoleon, Pt. 2. unabr. ed. Emil Ludwig. Read by Frederick Davidson. 9 cass. (Running Time: 27 hrs. 30 mins.). 1993. 62.95 (978-0-7861-0380-5(9), 1334A, B) Blckstn Audio.

Napoleon: 1812. unabr. collector's ed. Nigel Nicolson. Read by Grover Gardner. 8 cass. (Running Time: 8 hrs.). 1986. 48.00 (978-0-7366-0962-3(8), 1904) Books on Tape.
Napoleon entered Russia with 500,000 men, lost 95% of them in 6 months.

Napoleon Vol. 1: From Brumaire to Tilsit, 1799-1807. unabr. ed. Georges Lefebvre. Read by David Case. 9 cass. (Running Time: 1 hr. 30 min. per cass.). 1992. 72.00 set. (2950); Rental 17.50 set. (2950) Books on Tape.
An important study of the French during the time of Napoleon.

Napoleon Vol. I: From 18 Brumaire to Tilsit 1799-1807. unabr. collector's ed. Georges Lefebvre. Read by David Case. 9 cass. (Running Time: 13 hrs. 30 min.). 1992. 72.00 (978-0-7366-2151-9(2), 2950) Books on Tape.
Study of the French during the time of Napoleon.

Napoleon Vol. II: From Tilsit to Waterloo 1807-1815. unabr. collector's ed. Georges Lefebvre. Read by David Case. 12 cass. (Running Time: 18 hrs.). 1992. 96.00 (978-0-7366-2295-0(0), 3080) Books on Tape.
History of a France dominated by Napoleon Bonaparte.

Napoleon & Hitler. unabr. ed. Desmond Seward. Read by Frederick Davidson. 8 cass. (Running Time: 12 hrs.). 1990. 56.95 (978-0-7861-0187-0(3), 1164) Blckstn Audio.
Desmond Seward examines the lives of these remarkable men (Napoleon & Hitler) & demonstrates the numerous striking parallels between their careers & their roles in shaping the destiny of modern Europe.

Napoleon & Hitler: A Comparative Biography. collector's ed. Desmond Seward. Read by John Richmond. 7 cass. (Running Time: 10 hrs. 30 min.). 2000. 56.00 (978-0-7366-5507-1(7)) Books on Tape.

Napoleon & Josephine: An Improbable Marriage, Evangeline Bruce. Read by Flo Gibson. 14 cass. (Running Time: 20 hrs. 30 min.). 1995. 42.95 (978-1-55685-400-2(5)) Audio Bk Con.
This impeccably researched book gives remarkable insight into one of history's most fascinating love stories. The Reign of Terror, post-revolutionary France & Napoleon's extensive military campaigns are vividly described as these two magnetic personalities are brought to life.

Napoleon Bonaparte, Pt. 1. unabr. ed. Alan Schom. Read by Geoffrey Howard. 12 cass. (Running Time: 18 hrs. 30 mins.). 1999. 96.00 (4770-A) Books on Tape.
The author follows Napoleon's career from his childhood in Corsica to his death in exile on the island of St. Helena.

Napoleon Bonaparte, Pt. 2. unabr. ed. Alan Schom. Read by Geoffrey Howard. 12 cass. (Running Time: 18 hrs.). 1999. 96.00 (4770-B) Books on Tape.

Napoleon Bonaparte: A Life. unabr. ed. Alan Schom. Read by Geoffrey Howard. 24 cass. (Running Time: 36 hrs.). 1999. 192.00 (978-0-7366-4313-9(3), 4770-A/B) Books on Tape.
Napoleon's career from his childhood in Corsica to his death in exile on the island of St. Helena.

***Napoleon Bonaparte: England's Prisoner.** unabr. ed. Frank Giles. Read by John Lee. (Running Time: 10 hrs. 30 mins.). 2010. 29.95 (978-1-4417-2373-4(0)); 65.95 (978-1-4417-2369-7(2)); audio compact disk 100.00 (978-1-4417-2370-3(6)) Blckstn Audio.

***Napoleon Hill - The Road to Riches: 13 Keys to Success.** unabr. ed. Greg S. Reid. 1 MP3-CD. (Running Time: 4 hrs.). 2011. 24.99 (978-1-4418-7819-9(X), 9781441878199, Brilliance MP3); 39.97 (978-1-4418-7820-5(3), 9781441878205, Brlnc Audio MP3 Lib); audio compact disk 24.99 (978-1-4418-7817-5(3), 9781441878175, Bril Audio CD Unabri) Brilliance Audio.

***Napoleon Hill - The Road to Riches: 13 Keys to Success.** unabr. ed. Greg S. Reid & Napoleon Hill. 3 CDs. (Running Time: 4 hrs.). 2011. audio compact disk 79.97 (978-1-4418-7818-2(1), 9781441878182, BriAudCD Unabrid) Brilliance Audio.

Napoleon Hill's Golden Rules: The Lost Writings. unabr. ed. Napoleon Hill. Read by Oliver Wyman. 6 CDs. (Running Time: 6 hrs. 55 mins.). (ENG.). 2009. audio compact disk 29.95 (978-1-60283-548-1(9)) Pub: AudioGO. Dist(s): Perseus Dist

Napoleon Hill's Grow Rich Now! abr. ed. Napoleon Hill. Read by Napoleon Hill. 1 cass. 1999. 17.95 (978-1-55935-330-4(9)) Soundelux.
Leader in the field of motivational literature, shows how applying his three-foundation principles of success can lead to wealth.

Napoleon Hill's Keys to Positive Thinking, abr. ed. Michael J. Ritt. Read by Richard Beebe. 2 cass. 1998. 17.95 (978-1-55935-271-0(X)) Soundelux.
Ten steps to health, wealth & success.

Napoleon Hill's Keys to Success: The 17 Principles of Personal Achievement. abr. ed. Napoleon Hill. Read by Joe Slattery. (Running Time: 3 hrs. 0 mins. 0 sec.). (ENG.). 2003. audio compact disk 26.95 (978-1-932429-17-6(4)) Pub: Highroads Media. Dist(s): Macmillan

Napoleon Hill's Keys to Success: The 17 Principles of Personal Achievement. unabr. ed. Napoleon Hill. Read by Joe Slattery. (Running Time: 6 hrs. 0 mins. 0 sec.). (ENG.). 2003. audio compact disk 44.95 (978-1-932429-16-9(6)) Pub: Highroads Media. Dist(s): Macmillan

Napoleon Hill¿s Power System 36 CD Set: (Original, Unabridged Editions of Law of Success & Think & Grow Rich) Napoleon Hill. Narrated by R. C. Ossenbach. Prod. by Alfred Eaton. (ENG.). 2008. audio compact disk 159.00 (978-0-9820053-0-9(X)) Wirgo.

Napoleon Hill's "The Master-Key to Riches" & "Grow Rich! with Peace of Mind", abr. ed. Napoleon Hill. Read by Rob Actis. 4 cass. (Running Time: 5 hrs.). 1999. 24.95 (978-1-55935-296-3(5)) Soundelux.
Includes rare selections of Napoleon Hill imparting his motivational wisdom in his own voice.

Napoleon of Notting Hill. G. K. Chesterton. 2008. audio compact disk 37.39 (978-1-906147-33-4(7)) CSA Telltapes GBR.

Napoleon of Notting Hill. unabr. ed. G. K. Chesterton. Read by Frederick Davidson. 4 cass. (Running Time: 6 hrs.). 1988. 32.95 (978-0-7861-0036-1(2), 1035) Blckstn Audio.
Auberon Quinn, a common man who looks like a cross between a baby & an owl & is often seen in public places standing on his head & tossing his silk hat into the air, is one day told that he's been selected to be His Majesty the King.

Napoleon of Notting Hill. unabr. collector's ed. G. K. Chesterton. Read by Stuart Courtney. 8 cass. (Running Time: 8 hrs.). 1983. 48.00 (978-0-7366-0469-7(3), 1444) Books on Tape.
Examines the question "What if the Crown of England devolved upon a common man?.

Napoleon XIV: The Second Coming. 1 CD. (Running Time: 1 hr. 30 mins.). 2001. audio compact disk 16.98 (R2 72402) Rhino Enter.

Napoleon, 1812: To Moscow & Back. unabr. ed. Nigel Nicolson. Narrated by Patrick Tull. 5 cass. (Running Time: 7 hrs. 30 mins.). 1987. 44.00 (978-1-55690-368-7(5), 87420E7) Recorded Bks.
An account of Napoleon's disastrous invasion of Russia & retreat from Moscow.

Napoleon's Egypt: Invading the Middle East. unabr. ed. Juan Cole. (Running Time: 41400 sec.). 2007. 79.95 (978-1-4332-0292-6(1)); audio compact disk 99.00 (978-1-4332-0293-3(X)) Blckstn Audio.

Napoleon's Egypt: Invading the Middle East. unabr. ed. Juan Cole. Read by Grover Gardner. (Running Time: 41400 sec.). 2007. 29.95 (978-1-4332-0183-7(6)); audio compact disk 29.95 (978-1-4332-0184-4(4)); audio compact disk 29.95 (978-1-4332-0185-1(2)) Blckstn Audio.

Napoleon's Marshals. unabr. collector's ed. R. P. Dunn-Pattison. Read by Bill Kelsey. 10 cass. (Running Time: 15 hrs.). 1996. 80.00 (978-0-7366-3500-4(9), 4140) Books on Tape.
Napoleon richly rewarded the men who pledged their lives to him. They were the secret to his success.

Napoleon's Wars: An International History, 1803-1815. unabr. ed. Charles Esdaile. (Running Time: 25 hrs. 0 mins. 0 sec.). (ENG.). 2008. audio compact disk 119.99 (978-1-4001-3964-4(3)); audio compact disk 39.99 (978-1-4001-5964-2(4)) Pub: Tantor Media. Dist(s): IngramPubServ

Napoleon's Wars: An International History, 1803-1815. unabr. ed. Charles Esdaile. Read by Simon Prebble. (Running Time: 25 hrs. 0 mins. 0 sec.). (ENG.). 2008. audio compact disk 59.99 (978-1-4001-0964-7(7)) Pub: Tantor Media. Dist(s): IngramPubServ

Nappily Ever After: A Novel. unabr. ed. Trisha R. Thomas. Read by Lisa Renee Pitts. (Running Time: 9 hrs. NaN mins.). 2009. 29.95 (978-1-4332-2977-0(3)); audio compact disk 59.95 (978-1-4332-2973-2(0)); audio compact disk 70.00 (978-1-4332-2974-9(9)) Blckstn Audio.

Napping House. 2004. bk. 24.95 (978-0-89719-786-1(0)); cass. & flmstrp 30.00 (978-0-89719-566-9(3)) Weston Woods.

Napping House. Audrey Wood. Illus. by Don Wood. 1 cass. (Running Time: 4 min.). (J). (ps-3). 2000. bk. 24.95 Weston Woods.
The repetitive text invites young viewers to join in describing the wakeful flea on a slumbering mouse on a snoozing cat on a dozing dog on a dreaming child on a snoring grandma. All is calm until a fateful itch throws the pyramid into an eruptive reverie.

Napping House. Audrey Wood. Illus. by Don Wood. 1 cass. (J). (ps-3). 2004. 8.95 (978-0-89719-954-4(5), 307) Weston Woods.

Napping House & Other Storybook Classics. Audrey Wood et al. Narrated by Melissa Leebaert & David DeVries. (Playaway Children Ser.). (ENG.). (J). (ps-4). 2009. 44.99 (978-1-60812-565-4(3)) Find a World.

Naptime with Mozart. Composed by Wolfgang Amadeus Mozart. 1 cass. (Running Time: 1 hr.). (Classical Babies Ser.). (J). 2002. 7.99 (978-1-894677-19-6(6)); audio compact disk 9.99 (978-1-894677-18-9(8)) Pub: Kidzup CAN. Dist(s): Penton Overseas
Combines soothing ageless classics and best loved favorites from composer Wolfgang Amadeus Mozart.

Narada Bhakti Sutras - MP3 CD. Speeches. Swami Prabhavananda. 1 CD. Orig. Title: Narada Bhakti Sutras MP3 CD. 2007. 59.95 (978-0-87481-975-5(X)) Vedanta Pr.

Narada Bhakti Sutras MP3 CD see Narada Bhakti Sutras - MP3 CD

Narada's Way of Divine Love: The Bhakti Sutras. Tr. by Swami Prabhavananda. 15 cass. (Running Time: 21 hrs. 15 mins.). 2000. 125.00 (978-0-87481-375-3(1)) Vedanta Pr.
A complete set of 30 lectures of Swami Prabhavananda on the Hindu scripture "The Narada Bhakti Sutras.".

Narada's Way of Divine Love Vol. 1: The Bhakti Sutras. Tr. by Swami Prabhavananda. 1 cass. (Running Time: 1 hr. 30 mins.). 2000. 10.95 (978-0-87481-376-0(X)) Vedanta Pr.
Lectures 1 & 2 on the Narada Bhakti Sutras, a scripture of Hinduism.

Narada's Way of Divine Love Vol. 2: The Bhakti Sutras. Tr. by Swami Prabhavananda. 1 cass. (Running Time: 1 hr. 30 mins.). 2000. 10.95 (978-0-87481-377-7(8)) Vedanta Pr.
Lectures 3 & 4 on the Narada Bhakti Sutras, a scripture of Hinduism.

Narada's Way of Divine Love Vol. 3: The Bhakti Sutras. Tr. by Swami Prabhavananda. 1 cass. (Running Time: 1 hr. 30 mins.). 2000. 10.95 (978-0-87481-378-4(6)) Vedanta Pr.
Lectures 5 & 6 on the Narada Bhakti Sutras, a scripture of Hinduism.

Narada's Way of Divine Love Vol. 4: The Bhakti Sutras. Tr. by Swami Prabhavananda. 1 cass. (Running Time: 1 hr. 30 mins.). 2000. 10.95 (978-0-87481-379-1(4)) Vedanta Pr.
Lectures 7 & 8 on the Narada Bhakti Sutras, a scripture of Hinduism.

Narada's Way of Divine Love Vol. 5: The Bhakti Sutras. Tr. by Swami Prabhavananda. 1 cass. (Running Time: 1 hr. 30 mins.). 2000. 10.95 (978-0-87481-380-7(8)) Vedanta Pr.
Lectures 9 & 10 on the Narada Bhakti Sutras, a scripture of Hinduism.

Narada's Way of Divine Love Vol. 6: The Bhakti Sutras. Tr. by Swami Prabhavananda. 1 cass. (Running Time: 1 hr. 30 mins.). 2000. 10.95 (978-0-87481-381-4(6)) Vedanta Pr.
Lectures 11 & 12 on the Narada Bhakti Sutras, a scripture of Hinduism.

Narada's Way of Divine Love Vol. 7: The Bhakti Sutras. Tr. by Swami Prabhavananda. 1 cass. (Running Time: 1 hr. 30 mins.). 2000. 10.95 (978-0-87481-382-1(4)) Vedanta Pr.
Lectures 13 & 14 on the Narada Bhakti Sutras, a scripture on devotion to God.

Narada's Way of Divine Love Vol. 8: The Bhakti Sutras. Tr. by Swami Prabhavananda. 1 cass. (Running Time: 1 hr. 30 mins.). 2000. 10.95 (978-0-87481-383-8(2)) Vedanta Pr.
Lectures 15 & 16 on the Narada Bhakti Sutras, a scripture on devotion to God.

Narada's Way of Divine Love Vol. 9: The Bhakti Sutras. Tr. by Swami Prabhavananda. 1 cass. (Running Time: 1 hr. 30 mins.). 2000. 12.95 Vedanta Pr.
Lectures 17 & 18 on the Narada Bhakti Sutras, a scripture on devotion to God.

Narada's Way of Divine Love Vol. 10: The Bhakti Sutras. Tr. by Swami Prabhavananda. 2000. 10.95 (978-0-87481-385-2(9)) Vedanta Pr.
Lectures 19 & 20 on the Narada Bhakti Sutras, a scripture on devotion to God.

Narada's Way of Divine Love Vol. 11: The Bhakti Sutras. Tr. by Swami Prabhavananda. 1 cass. (Running Time: 1 hr. 30 mins.). 2000. 10.95 (978-0-87481-386-9(7)) Vedanta Pr.
Lectures 21 & 22 on the Narada Bhakti Sutras, a scripture on devotion to God.

Narada's Way of Divine Love Vol. 12: The Bhakti Sutras. Tr. by Swami Prabhavananda. 1 cass. (Running Time: 1 hr. 30 mins.). 2000. 10.95 (978-0-87481-387-6(5)) Vedanta Pr.
Lectures 24 & 25 on the Narada Bhakti Sutras, a scripture on devotion to God.

Narada's Way of Divine Love Vol. 13: The Bhakti Sutras. Tr. by Swami Prabhavananda. 1 cass. (Running Time: 1 hr. 30 mins.). 2000. 10.95 (978-0-87481-388-3(3)) Vedanta Pr.
Lectures 25 & 26 on the Narada Bhakti Sutras, a scripture on devotion to God.

Narada's Way of Divine Love Vol. 14: The Bhakti Sutras. Tr. by Swami Prabhavananda. 1 cass. (Running Time: 1 hr. 30 mins.). 2000. 10.95 (978-0-87481-389-0(1)) Vedanta Pr.
Lectures 27 & 28 on the Narada Bhakti Sutras, a scripture on devotion to God.

Narada's Way of Divine Love Vol. 15: The Bhakti Sutras. Tr. by Swami Prabhavananda. 1 cass. (Running Time: 1 hr. 30 mins.). 2000. 10.95 (978-0-87481-390-6(5)) Vedanta Pr.
Lectures 29 & 30 on the Narada Bhakti Sutras, a scripture on devotion to God.

Narciso see Poesia y Drama de Garcia Lorca

Narcissism: Program from the Award Winning Public Radio Series. Interview. Hosted by Fred Goodwin. 1 CD. (Running Time: 1 hr). 2003. audio compact disk 21.95 (978-1-932479-71-3(6), LCM 290) Lichtenstein Creat.
Narcissists can be arrogant, self-aggrandizing, and manipulative. But what's it like to have narcissistic personality disorder? And how can it be treated? Guests include Dr. Jeffrey Young, the founder and director of the Schema Therapy Institute of New York and the Cognitive Therapy Centers of New York and Connecticut and co-author of Reinventing Your Life; Sandy Hotchkiss, a licensed clinical social worker and the author of Why is it Always About You? The Seven Deadly Sins of Narcissism; Dr. Corinne Pache, an assistant professor of classics at Yale University and a fellow at Harvard University's Center for Hellenic Studies in Washington D.C., who talks about the myth of Narcissus and Echo; poet Tony Hoagland, whose latest collection is called What Narcissism Means to Me; and Samuel Vaknin, who has been diagnosed with narcissistic personality disorder and has written extensively about the topic.

Narcissism & Human Evil. Read by Robert Moore. 1 cass. (Running Time: 1 hr.). 1988. 9.95 (978-0-7822-0180-2(6), 323) C G Jung IL.
An analysis of contemporary Jungian understandings of evil (Jung, von Franz, Sanford) & the personal & archetypal dimensions of the shadow.

Narcissism & Its Transformation in Psychotherapy. Read by Donald Kalsched. 2 cass. (Running Time: 3 hrs. 30 min.). 1987. 21.95 (978-0-7822-0106-2(7), 257) C G Jung IL.

Narcissism & the Fragmenting Self. Read by Jeffrey Burke Satinover. 1 cass. (Running Time: 1 hr. 30 min.). 1980. 10.95 (978-0-7822-0245-8(4), 060) C G Jung IL.

Narcissist's Daughter: A Novel. unabr. ed. Craig Holden. Read by Erik Steele. 4 cass. 2005. 39.95 (978-0-7927-3493-2(9), CSL 762); audio compact disk 64.95 (978-0-7927-3494-9(7), SLD 762) AudioGO.

Narcocorrido: Un Viaje al Mundo de la Musica de las Drogas, Armas y Guerrilleros. unabr. ed. Elijah Wald. Narrated by Francisco Rivela. 9 cass. (Running Time: 12 hrs. 30 mins.). (SPA.). 82.00 (978-0-7887-8936-6(8)) Recorded Bks.
Available to libraries only.

Narcolepsy: Please Don't Tickle My Funny Bone. Sherrye H. Gibbs. Read by Neva Duyndam. 1 cass. 1990. 9.95 (978-1-878159-15-1(1)) Duvall Media.
How can something so desirable & important as sleep also be a serious health problem? What is a "sleep attack" or cataplexy? What happens during a hypnagogic Hallucination? These & many other questions are answered in this sensitive tape written by a daughter about her mother who has narcolepsy.

Nariz y Otro Cuentos. unabr. ed. Nicolai Gogol. Read by Laura García. 3 CDs.Tr. of Nose & Other Tales. (SPA.). 2001. audio compact disk 17.00 (978-958-9494-39-4(0)) YoYoMusic.

***Narnian: The Life & Imagination of C. S. Lewis.** abr. ed. Alan Jacobs. Read by Alan Jacobs. (ENG.). 2005. (978-0-06-089452-8(0), Harper Audio); (978-0-06-089453-5(9), Harper Audio) HarperCollins Pubs.

Narnian: The Life & Imagination of C. S. Lewis. unabr. abr. ed. Alan Jacobs. Read by Alan Jacobs. 2005. audio compact disk 39.95 (978-0-06-083125-7(1)) HarperCollins Pubs.

Naropa, Pt. 1. Read by Chogyam Trungpa. 7 cass. (Running Time: 10 hrs. 30 min.). 1972. 72.00 (A034) Vajradhatu.
Seven talks: 1) The Ground, Path, & Fruition of Tantra; 2) Tantric Practice; 3) Discovery of Pain; 4) Suffering as a Means of Realization; 5) Naropa's Approach to Pain; 6) Six Doctrines of Naropa; 7) Yoga from a Mahamudra Point of View.

Naropa, Pt. 2. Read by Chogyam Trungpa. 6 cass. 1973. 61.00 (A035) Vajradhatu.
Six talks: 1) Pain & Hopelessness in Relation to Tantra; 2) Prajna & Intellect; 3) Relationship of Prajna & Shunyata; 4) Beyond Shunyata; 5) Mahamudra & Vajrayana.

Naropa: His Life & Teachings. Read by Chogyam Trungpa. 6 cass. 1976. 56.50 (A036) Vajradhatu.
Seven talks: 1) Arrogance & Suffering; 2) Words & Sense; 3) First Thought, Best Thought; 4) Arrogance & Aggression in Searching for the Guru; 5) The Freak Show; 6) Meeting Tilopa; 7) The Kingdom of Dharma.

Naropa I. Vajracarya. 7 cass. (Running Time: 10 hrs. 30 min.). 1972. 72.00 Vajradhatu.
Topics Include: The Ground, Path, & Fruition of Tantra, Tantric Practice, Suffering as a Means of Realization, Naropa's Approach to Pain, Six Doctrines of Naropa.

Naropa II. Vajracarya. 6 cass. (Running Time: 9 hrs.). 1973. 61.00 Vajradhatu.
Deals with: Pain & Hopelessness in Relation to Tantra, Prajna & Intellect, Relationship of Prajna & Shunyata, Beyond Shunyata, Mahamudra & Vajrayana.

Narrated Life History of Central Europe: George Bizet, Edvard Grieg, Johann Strauss II: Part IV: Modern. Marcia Dangerfield. Narrated by William Sargent. 1 CD. (Running Time: 3761 sec.). (Classical Genius Composer Ser.). 2007. audio compact disk 14.95 (978-1-934488-15-7(1)) L England.

Narrated Life History of Felix Mendelssohn: Part III: Romantic. Marcia Dangerfield. Narrated by William Sargent. 1 CD. (Running Time: 3808 sec.). (Classical Genius Composer Ser.). 2007. audio compact disk 14.95 (978-1-934488-07-2(0)) L England.

Narrated Life History of Franz Schubert: Part II: Classical. Marcia Dangerfield. Narrated by William Sargent. 1 CD. (Running Time: 3647 sec.). (Classical Genius Composer Ser.). 2007. audio compact disk 14.95 (978-1-934488-05-8(4)) L England.

Narrated Life History of Frederic Chopin: Part III: Romantic. Marcia Dangerfield. Narrated by William Sargent. 1 CD. (Running Time: 3645 sec.). (Classical Genius Composer Ser.). 2007. audio compact disk 14.95 (978-1-934488-08-9(9)) L England.

Narrated Life History of George Frideric Handel, Antonio Lucio Vivaldi: Part I: Baroque. Marcia Dangerfield. Narrated by William Sargent. 1 CD. (Running Time: 3964 sec.). (Classical Genius Composer Ser.). 2007. audio compact disk 14.95 (978-1-934488-01-0(1)) L England.

Narrated Life History of Italian Opera: Gioacchino Rossini, Giuseppe Verdi, Giacomo Puccini: Part III: Romantic. Marcia Dangerfield. Narrated by William Sargent. 1 CD. (Running Time: 4074 sec.). (Classical Genius Composer Ser.). 2007. audio compact disk 14.95 (978-1-934488-11-9(9)) L England.

Narrated Life History of Johann Sebastian Bach: Part I: Baroque. Marcia Dangerfield. Narrated by William Sargent. 1 CD. (Running Time: 3593 sec.). (Classical Genius Composer Ser.). 2007. audio compact disk 14.95 (978-1-934488-00-3(3)) L England.

Narrated Life History of Johannes Brahms: Part IV: Modern. Marcia Dangerfield. Narrated by William Sargent. 1 CD. (Running Time: 3738 sec.). (Classical Genius Composer Ser.). 2007. audio compact disk 14.95 (978-1-934488-12-6(7)) L England.

Narrated Life History of Joseph Haydn: Part II: Classical. Marcia Dangerfield. Narrated by William Sargent. 1 CD. (Running Time: 3694 sec.). (Classical Genius Composer Ser.). 2007. audio compact disk 14.95 (978-1-934488-03-4(8)) L England.

Narrated Life History of Ludwig Van Beethoven: Part II: Classical. Marcia Dangerfield. Narrated by William Sargent. 1 CD. (Running Time: 3778 sec.). (Classical Genius Composer Ser.). 2007. audio compact disk 14.95 (978-1-934488-04-1(6)) L England.

Narrated Life History of Mid-Twentieth Century: Arnold Schoenberg, Edward Elgar, Alexander Nikolayevich Scriabin, Paul Hindemith, Olivier Messiaen, Benjamin Britten, Sir Malcolm Arnold, Henryk Mikolaj Gorecki, John Milton Cage, & Micheal Nyman: Part V: 20th Century. Marcia Dangerfield. Narrated by William Sargent. 1 CD. (Running Time: 4416 sec.). (Classical Genius Composer Ser.). 2007. audio compact disk 14.95 (978-1-934488-23-2(2)) L England.

Narrated Life History of Peter Tchaikovsky: Part IV: Modern. Marcia Dangerfield. Narrated by William Sargent. 1 CD. (Running Time: 3834 sec.). (Classical Genius Composer Ser.). 2007. audio compact disk 14.95 (978-1-934488-13-3(5)) L England.

Narrated Life History of Robert Schumann: Part III: Romantic. Marcia Dangerfield. Narrated by William Sargent. 1 CD. (Running Time: 3665 sec.). (Classical Genius Composer Ser.). 2007. audio compact disk 14.95 (978-1-934488-09-6(7)) L England.

Narrated Life History of Soviet Russia: Segei Rachmaninoff, Sergei Prokofiev, Dmitri Shostakovich: Part V: 20th Century. Marcia Dangerfield. Narrated by William Sargent. 1 CD. (Running Time: 3673 sec.).

(Classical Genius Composer Ser.). 2007. audio compact disk 14.95 (978-1-934488-22-5(4)) L England.

Narrated Life History of the Americans: John Philip Sousa, George Gershwin, Aaron Copland, Samuel Barber: Part V: 20th Century. Marcia Dangerfield. Narrated by William Sargent. 1 CD. (Running Time: 3688 sec.). (Classical Genius Composer Ser.). 2007. audio compact disk 14.95 (978-1-934488-18-8(6)) L England.

Narrated Life History of the Czechs in Prague: Bedrich Smetana, Antonin Dvorak: Part IV: Modern. Marcia Dangerfield. Narrated by William Sargent. 1 CD. (Running Time: 3752 sec.). (Classical Genius Composer Ser.). 2007. audio compact disk 14.95 (978-1-934488-16-4(X)) L England.

Narrated Life History of the Expressionists: Charles Camille Saint-Saens, Ottorino Respighi, Jean Sibelius, Paul Dukas: Part IV: Modern. Marcia Dangerfield. Narrated by William Sargent. 1 CD. (Running Time: 3597 sec.). (Classical Genius Composer Ser.). 2007. audio compact disk 14.95 (978-1-934488-17-1(8)) L England.

Narrated Life History of the First Romantics: Franz Liszt, Hector Berlioz, Niccolo Paganini: Part III: Romantic. Marcia Dangerfield. Narrated by William Sargent. (Running Time: 3794 sec.). (Classical Genius Composer Ser.). 2007. audio compact disk 14.95 (978-1-934488-06-5(2)) L England.

Narrated Life History of the Futurists: Igor Stravinsky, Bela Bartok, Erik Satie: Part V: 20th Century. Marcia Dangerfield. Narrated by William Sargent. 1 CD. (Running Time: 3665 sec.). (Classical Genius Composer Ser.). 2007. audio compact disk 14.95 (978-1-934488-21-8(6)) L England.

Narrated Life History of the Impressionists: Achille-Claude Debussy, Joseph-Maurice Ravel: Part V: 20th Century. Marcia Dangerfield. Narrated by William Sargent. 1 CD. (Running Time: 3737 sec.). (Classical Genius Composer Ser.). 2007. audio compact disk 14.95 (978-1-934488-20-1(8)) L England.

Narrated Life History of the Russian Kuchka: Alexander Borodin, Modest Mussorgsky, & Nikolai Rimsky-Korsakov: Part IV: Modern. Marcia Dangerfield. Narrated by William Sargent. 1 CD. (Running Time: 3710 sec.). (Classical Genius Composer Ser.). 2007. audio compact disk 14.95 (978-1-934488-14-0(3)) L England.

Narrated Life History of the Symphonists: Anton Bruckner, Gustav Mahler, Richard Strauss: Part V: 20th Century. Marcia Dangerfield. Narrated by William Sargent. 1 CD. (Running Time: 3617 sec.). (Classical Genius Composer Ser.). 2007. audio compact disk 14.95 (978-1-934488-19-5(4)) L England.

Narrated Life History of Wilhelm Richard Wagner: Part III. Marcia Dangerfield. Narrated by William Sargent. 1 CD. (Running Time: 3711 sec.). (Classical Genius Composer Ser.). 2007. audio compact disk 14.95 (978-1-934488-10-2(0)) L England.

Narrated Life History of Wolfgang Amadeus Mozart: January 27, 1756 - December 5 1791. abr. ed. Marcia Dangerfield. Narrated by William Sargent. 1 CD. (Running Time: 3818 sec.). (Classical Genius Composer Ser.). 2007. audio compact disk 14.95 (978-1-934488-02-7(X)) L England.

Narrative see Twentieth-Century Poetry in English, No. 5, Recordings of Poets Reading Their Own Poetry

Narrative Causalities. Emma Kafalenos. (Theory interpretation Narrativ Ser.). 2006. audio compact disk 9.95 (978-0-8142-9102-3(3)) Pub: Ohio St U Pr. Dist(s): Chicago Distribution Ctr

Narrative of Arthur Gordon Pym. Edgar Allan Poe. Read by John Chatty. 6 cass. (Running Time: 9 hrs.). 1989. 34.00 (C-168) Jimcin Record.
Strange adventure story. Includes album.

Narrative of Arthur Gordon Pym, unabr. ed. Edgar Allan Poe. Narrated by Jamie Hanes. 5 cass. (Running Time: 6 hrs. 30 mins.). 1988. 44.00 (978-1-55690-369-4(3), 88390E7) Recorded Bks.
A mutiny at sea & subsequent events told in documentary style.

Narrative of Arthur Gordon Pym of Nantucket. Edgar Allan Poe. Narrated by Christopher Plummer. (Running Time: 3 hrs.). 2006. 14.95 (978-1-60083-036-5(6)) Iofy Corp.

Narrative of Arthur Gordon Pym of Nantucket. unabr. ed. Edgar Allan Poe. Read by John Chatty. 6 cass. (Running Time: 8 hrs. 30 mins.). 1994. 44.95 (978-0-7861-0625-7(5), 2115) Blckstn Audio.
Set in 1827, this is an exciting blend of science, romance, adventure, realism & supernaturalism. It is based on the actual experiences of J. N. Reynolds, whose book Poe consulted. The narrative comprises the details of a mutiny on board the American brig "Grampus," on her way to the South Seas. The young hero, Pym, aided by Augustus, the captain's son, becomes a stowaway. Poe incorporates it all: butchery, shipwreck, famine, massacre & deliverance. But it is Pym's friendship & friction with Augustus that form the major part of the book's aesthetic design.

Narrative of Arthur Gordon Pym of Nantucket. unabr. collector's ed. Edgar Allan Poe. Read by John Chatty. 6 cass. (Running Time: 9 hrs.). 1988. 48.00 (978-0-7366-3928-6(4), 9166) Books on Tape.
Poe's story is based on the actual experience of J. N. Reynolds, whose book Poe had reviewed. The narrative is about a mutiny aboard the American brig Grampus, bound for the South seas. It has everything - butchery, shipwreck, famine & vengeance.

Narrative of Arthur Gordon Pym (U) unabr. ed. Edgar Allan Poe. (Running Time: 8 hrs.). 2009. audio compact disk 34.98 (978-962-634-953-3(0), Naxos AudioBooks) Naxos.

Narrative of Faith Sojourner. Olive Gilbert. Narrated by Bobbie Frohman. Engineer Scott Weiser. Music by David Thorn. (ENG.). 2009. audio compact disk 24.95i (978-0-9821853-6-0(7)) Alcazar AudioWorks.

Narrative of the Life of Davy Crockett by Himself. unabr. ed. Davy Crockett. Read by Jim Roberts. 4 cass. (Running Time: 6 hrs.). (J). (gr. 5-8). 1994. 24.00 (C-261) Jimcin Record.
"Born on a mountain-top in Tennessee" to die a hero's death at the Alamo. Davy Crockett continues to be a legendary American hero. This is history in his own words. Set in vinyl album.

Narrative of the Life of Frederick Douglass. Frederick Douglass. Read by Anais 9000. 2009. 27.95 (978-1-60112-227-8(6)) Babblebooks.

Narrative of the Life of Frederick Douglass: An American Slave. Frederick Douglass. Narrated by Pete Papageorge. (Running Time: 16800 sec.). (Unabridged Classics in MP3 Ser.). (ENG.). 2008. audio compact disk 14.95 (978-1-58472-606-7(7), In Aud); audio compact disk 24.00 (978-1-58472-599-2(0), In Aud) Sound Room.

Narrative of the Life of Frederick Douglass: An American Slave. unabr. ed. Frederick Douglass. Read by Walter Covell. 3 cass. (Running Time: 4 hrs.). 1993. 23.95 (978-0-7861-0634-9(4), 2124) Blckstn Audio.
Frederick Douglass was born into slavery in Maryland in February, 1818. Douglass was taken from his grandmother's cabin when he was about seven. He was sold numerous times in the slave markets of the South. Remarkably, however, he was able to secretly teach himself to read & write a crime punishable by death & thus was able to pass on to us this fascinating & eloquent indictment of America's pre-Civil War record of cruelty, ignorance & callousness & of the most heinous of institutions.

Narrative of the Life of Frederick Douglass: An American Slave. unabr. ed. Frederick Douglass. Narrated by Charles Turner. 3 cass. (Running Time: 4 hrs. 45 mins.). 1991. 26.00 (978-1-55690-633-6(1), 91424E7) Recorded Bks.
Douglass came into the world with one surety: he was born a slave & would die a slave. But early learning, a natural precociousness & a passion to rise above his circumstances finally won Douglass his freedom. The life story of an American slave.

Narrative of the Life of Frederick Douglass: An American Slave. unabr. ed. Frederick Douglass. Read by Pete Papageorge. 4 CDs. (Running Time: 4 hrs 40 mins). 2002. pap. bk. (978-1-58472-293-9(2), In Aud) Sound Room.
The powerful story of a slave who became one of the most effective African-American leaders.

Narrative of the Life of Frederick Douglass: An American Slave. unabr. ed. Frederick Douglass. Read by Pete Papageorge. 4 CDs. (Running Time: 4 hrs 39 mins). 2002. audio compact disk 26.95 (978-1-58472-291-5(6), 082, In Aud) Pub: Sound Room. Dist(s): Baker Taylor
The powerful story of a slave who became one of America's most effective African-American leaders.

Narrative of the Life of Frederick Douglass: An American Slave. unabr. collector's ed. Frederick Douglass. Read by Jonathan Reese. 4 cass. (Running Time: 4 hrs.). 1995. 24.00 (978-0-7366-3104-4(6), 3780) Books on Tape.
Frederick Douglass, one-time slave, knew that education meant freedom.

Narrative of the Life of Frederick Douglass: An American Slave Written by Himself. unabr. ed. Frederick Douglass. Read by Walter Covell. 3 cass. (Running Time: 4 hrs.). 1993. 21.00 Jimcin Record.
Frederick Douglass first spoke in public after his escape from slavery at the Antheneum on Nantucket Island. This fascinating book is the result of the encouragement & support to have his story told by the people present at that historic meeting.

Narrative of the Life of Frederick Douglass - an American. Frederick Douglass. Read by Pete Papageorge. (Running Time: 5 hrs.). 2002. 23.95 (978-1-59912-096-6(8), Audiofy Corp) Iofy Corp.

Narrative of the Life of Frederick Douglass, an American Slave. unabr. ed. 4 CDs. (Running Time: 4 hrs. 40 mins.). (YA). (gr. 9 up). 2002. audio compact disk 43.00 (978-1-58472-165-9(0), Commuters Library) Sound Room.

Narrative of the Life of Frederick Douglass, an American Slave. unabr. ed. Frederick Douglas. Read by Jonathan Reese. (YA). 2008. 44.99 (978-1-60514-905-9(5)) Find a World.

Narrative of the Life of Frederick Douglass, an American Slave, with EBook. unabr. ed. Frederick Douglass. Narrated by Jonathan Reese. (Running Time: 4 hrs. 30 mins. 0 sec.). (ENG.). 2009. 19.99 (978-1-4001-6111-9(8)); 6.08 (978-1-4001-8111-7(9)); audio compact disk 19.99 (978-1-4001-1111-4(0)) Pub: Tantor Media. Dist(s): IngramPubServ

Narrative of the Life of Frederick Douglass, an American Slave, with eBook. unabr. ed. Frederick Douglass. Narrated by Jonathan Reese. (Running Time: 4 hrs. 30 mins.). 2009. 19.99 (978-1-4001-9111-6(4)); audio compact disk 39.99 (978-1-4001-4111-7(7)) Pub: Tantor Media. Dist(s): IngramPubServ

Narratore Italian Anthology Full Sec: Multilingual Books Literature. Excerpts. Ed. by Maurizio Falyhera & Christina Grocometti. 13 CD's. (Running Time: 19 hrs.). (Audio Anthology of Italian Literature Ser.). (ITA.). 1999. per. 229.00 (978-1-58214-134-3(7)) Language Assocs.

Narrow Corner. unabr. collector's ed. W. Somerset Maugham. Read by Erik Bauersfeld. 8 cass. (Running Time: 8 hrs.). 1980. 48.00 (978-0-7366-0218-1(6), 1216) Books on Tape.
Three men voyaging together in a small vessel: An exiled doctor, a disreputable sea captain & a young man fleeing from justice, are driven to take shelter on a small island in the Malay Archipelago.

Narrow Dog to Carcassonne. Terry Darlington. Read by Steve Hodson. (Running Time: 40800 sec.). 2007. audio compact disk 89.95 (978-0-7531-2684-4(2)) Pub: ISIS Audio GBR. Dist(s): Ulverscroft US

Narrow Dog to Carcassonne. unabr. ed. Terry Darlington. Read by Steve Hodson. 9 cass. (Running Time: 39600 sec.). 2006. 76.95 (978-0-7531-3562-4(0)) Pub: ISIS Audio GBR. Dist(s): Ulverscroft US

Narrow Fellow in the Grass see Classic American Poetry

Narrow Fellow in the Grass see Poems & Letters of Emily Dickinson

Narrow Gate: The Way to the City of God. Read by Basilea Schlink. 1985. (0205); (0205) Evang Sisterhood Mary.
Signposts on the way to heaven & how to find the love of Jesus.

Narrow Road to the Interior & Hojoki. unabr. ed. Matsuo Basho & Kamono Chomei. Read by Togo Igawa & Takashi Sudo. 2 CDs. (Running Time: 2 hrs. 30 mins.). 2008. audio compact disk 17.98 (978-962-634-879-6(8)) Naxos.

Narrowboat Girl: An Absorbing Tale of Advneture & True Love. Annie Murray. Read by Annie Aldington. 12 cass. (Running Time: 14 hrs. 30 mins.). (Soundings Ser.). (J). 2004. 94.95 (978-1-84283-147-2(X)) Pub: ISIS Lrg Prnt GBR. Dist(s): Ulverscroft US

Narrowboat Girl: An Absorbing Tale of Advneture & True Love. Annie Murray. 2009. audio compact disk 99.95 (978-1-4079-0920-2(7)) Pub: Soundings Ltd GBR. Dist(s): Ulverscroft US

Narrows. Michael Connelly. Read by Len Cariou. (Harry Bosch Ser.: No. 10). 2004. audio compact disk 81.00 (978-1-4159-0010-9(8)) Books on Tape.

Narrows. abr. ed. Michael Connelly. 4 cass. (Running Time: 6 hrs.). (Harry Bosch Ser.: No. 10). 2004. 26.98 (978-1-58621-634-4(1)) Hachet Audio.

Narrows. unabr. ed. Michael Connelly. Read by Len Cariou. (Harry Bosch Ser.: No. 10). (ENG.). 2005. 14.98 (978-1-59483-174-4(2)) Pub: Hachet Audio. Dist(s): HachBkGrp

Narrows. unabr. ed. Michael Connelly. Read by Len Cariou. (Running Time: 11 hrs.). (Harry Bosch Ser.: No. 10). (ENG.). 2009. 70.98 (978-1-60024-594-7(3)) Pub: Hachet Audio. Dist(s): HachBkGrp

NAS Complete Bible on Supersaver. Narrated by Steven Stevens. 2004. bk. 35.88 (978-0-529-11790-8(8)) Nelson.

NASA Case Studies. Ed. by Marco A. V. Bitetto. 1 cass. (Running Time: 1 hr. 30 min.). 2000. (978-1-58578-083-9(9)) Inst of Cybernetics.

Nasal Reconstruction after Tumor Surgery: Interdisciplinary Panel Discussion. Moderated by William R. Panje. 2 cass. (Running Time: 3 hrs.). (Otorhinolaryngology Ser.: OT-1). 1986. 19.00 (6854) Am Coll Surgeons.

NASDAQ Level II Trading Strategies. Instructed by Mike McMahon. 2000. 19.95 (978-1-883272-94-4(7)) Marketplace Bks.
Trade like the real pros using Nasdaq Level II quotes! Learn to maximize each trade by reading a Level II quote, selecting the right routing system, and spotting hot trading opportunities by watching the actions of the market makers.

Nash, the American People: TestGen EQ CTB. 6th rev. ed. Nash. audio compact disk 49.97 (978-0-321-18640-9(0)) Addson-Wesley Educ.

Nashville Sound. 2006. audio compact disk 6.00 (978-1-59987-520-0(9)) Braun Media.

Nasreddin Hodja: Stories to Read & Retell. 2nd ed. Compiled by Raymond C. Clark. 1 CD. (gr. 8-12). 2005. pap. bk. & stu. ed. 28.00 (978-0-86647-216-6(9)); audio compact disk 18.00 (978-0-86647-215-9(0)) Pro Lingua.

Nasser. 10.00 (RME115) Esstee Audios.

Nasty. Contrib. by Jewel Well. 2009. 34.00 (978-0-9743601-8-8(X)) Jewel W.

Nasty Breaks. unabr. ed. Charlotte Elkins & Aaron Elkins. Read by Susan O'Malley. 5 cass. (Running Time: 7 hrs. 30 min.). 2000. 27.95 (978-0-7861-1384-2(7)) Blckstn Audio.
After a bizarre, botched kidnapping of the sexy wife, the owner of a salvage company turns up dead on the beach. Lee Ofsted discovers that nearly every manager at the company has a motive for murder. Lee has to size up her competition for she knows too much for the killer to let her live.

Nasty Breaks. unabr. ed. Charlotte Elkins & Aaron Elkins. Narrated by Barbara Rosenblat. 5 cass. (Running Time: 7 hrs.). 1998. 44.00 (978-0-7887-2001-7(5), 95388E7) Recorded Bks.
Nobody proves that golf is a killer of a game like pro golfer & amateur sleuth, Lee Ofsted.

Nasty, but Necessary; "On Top" C. S. Lovett. 1 cass. 6.95 (7021) Prsnl Christianity.
Expands on teaching of the book, "Dynamic Truths".

Nasty Habits. unabr. ed. Gillian White. Read by Jilly Bond. 7 cass. (Running Time: 8 hrs. 35 mins.). (Isis Cassettes Ser.). (J). 2004. 61.95 (978-0-7531-1926-6(9)); audio compact disk 79.95 (978-0-7531-2284-6(7)) Pub: ISIS Lrg Prnt GBR. Dist(s): Ulverscroft US

***NASTYbook.** unabr. ed. Barry Yourgrau. Read by Barry Yourgrau. (ENG.). 2005. (978-0-06-084560-5(0)); (978-0-06-084561-2(9)) HarperCollins Pubs.

Natal Retrograde Planets. Carol Ruth. 1 cass. (Running Time: 1 hr. 30 min.). 1984. 8.95 (299) Am Fed Astrologers.

Natalie Grant. Perf. by Natalie Grant. 1 CD. (Running Time: 1 hr. 30 min.). 1999. audio compact disk Brentwood Music.

Natalie Grant. Perf. by Natalie Grant. 1 CD. (Running Time: 1 hr. 30 min.). 1998. audio compact disk 16.98 CD. Provident Mus Dist.

Natalie Grant. Perf. by Natalie Grant. 1 cass. (Running Time: 1 hr. 30 min.). 1998. 10.98 (978-0-7601-2126-9(5)) Provident Music.

Natalie Grant. Perf. by Natalie Grant. 1 CD. (Running Time: 1 hr. 30 min.). 1999. audio compact disk 16.98 (978-0-7601-2127-6(3)) Provident Music.

Natalie Petesch & Sonia Scott-Fleming. unabr. ed. Natalie Petesch & Sonia Scott-Fleming. Read by Natalie Petesch & Sonia Scott-Fleming. 1 cass. (Running Time: 29 min.). 1991. 10.00 (032480) New Letters.
Natalie reads "End of the World" & Sonia reads "Steps." Both short stories.

Natalie Petesch I: "Journal for The New Year" unabr. ed. Short Stories. Natalie Petesch. Read by Natalie Petesch. 1 cass. (Running Time: 29 min.). 1985. 10.00 New Letters.
Reading of a short story called "Journal for The New Year" & an excerpt from "The Long Hot Summers of Yasha K." which deals with the beginning of the Civil Rights movement.

Natalie Petesch II: "The Long Hot Summer of Yasha K" Read by Natalie Petesch. 1 cass. (Running Time: 29 min.). 1986. 10.00 New Letters.
An excerpt from a story which deals with the beginning of the Civil Rights Movement.

Natalie Petesch II: "The Long Hot Summers of Yasha K." New Letters.

Natalie Wood: A Life. Gavin Lambert. Read by Robert Blumenfeld. 9 cass. (Running Time: 12 hrs.). 2004. 79.95 (978-0-7927-3117-7(4), CSL 623, Chivers Sound Lib) AudioGO.

Natalie Wood: A Life. unabr. ed. Gavin Lambert. Read by Robert Blumenfeld. 11 CDs. (Running Time: 16 hrs.). 2004. audio compact disk 99.95 (978-0-7927-3118-4(2), SLD 623, Chivers Sound Lib) AudioGO.

Nataraj-Nadabrahma. 1 cass. (Running Time: 2 hrs. 5 mins.). (Meditations from Osho Ser.). 10.95 (TR-0002) Oshos.
Nataraj is a dancing meditation, Nadabrahma is a modern version of an ancient Tibetan humming technique.

Nataraja: A New Collection of Electronic & World Music, from Yogini Shiva Rea. Compiled by Shiva Rea. (Running Time: 1 hr. 14 mins.). 2006. audio compact disk 17.98 (978-1-59179-466-0(8), M1045D) Sounds True.

Natasha: The Biography of Natalie Wood. unabr. ed. Suzanne Finstad. Read by Lana Wood. 7 cass. (Running Time: 9 hrs.). 2001. 69.25 (978-1-58788-461-0(5), 1587884615, Lib Edit); 29.95 (978-1-58788-462-7(3), 1587884623, Nova Audio Bks); audio compact disk 35.95 (978-1-58788-463-4(1), 1587884631, CD); audio compact disk 87.25 (978-1-58788-464-1(X), 158788464X, CD Lib Edit) Brilliance Audio.
After twenty years, the story of Natalie Wood's extraordinary life and mysterious death is revealed in a riveting new biography We watched her mature on the movie screen before our eyes in Miracle on 34th Street, Rebel Without a Cause, West Side Story, Splendor in the Grass, and on and on. She has been hailed, along with Marilyn Monroe and Elizabeth Taylor, as one of the top three movie actresses in film history, a legend in her own lifetime and beyond. But the story of what she endured, of what her life was like when the doors of the soundstages slid closed, has long been obscured. Natasha is based on years of exhaustive research into Natalie's turbulent life and mysterious death. Suzanne Finstad conducted more than four hundred interviews with Natalie's family, close friends, legendary costars, lovers, film crews, attorneys, police officials, and Dr. Thomas Noguchi, the coroner who investigated her strange death by drowning. Finstad has reconstructed a life of emotional abuse and exploitation, of almost unprecedented fame, great loneliness, and loss. Finstad tells this tragic beauty's story with sensitivity and grace, revealing a complex and conflicting mix of fragility and strength in a woman who was swept away by forces she could not control. Natasha is the definitive biography of Natalie Wood.

Natasha: The Biography of Natalie Wood. abr. ed. Suzanne Finstad. Read by Lana Wood. (Running Time: 9 hrs.). 2006. 39.25 (978-1-4233-0152-3(8), 9781423301523, BADLE); 24.95 (978-1-4233-0151-6(X), 9781423301516, BAD); audio compact disk 39.25 (978-1-4233-0150-9(1), 9781423301509, Brlnc Audio MP3 Lib); audio compact disk 24.95 (978-1-4233-0149-3(8), 9781423301493, Brilliance MP3) Brilliance Audio.

Natchez Trace Parkway: A Road Through the Wilderness. Eddie Thomas & Frank Thomas. 6 cass. (Running Time: 8 hrs. 30 min.). 1994. pap. bk. 39.95 (978-1-885154-47-7(X)) Thomasfilms.
Complete, award winning, self-guided driving tour along the Natchez Trace Parkway, for travel in either North or South direction - Queued to mileposts, with map & reminder cards. Original Road Music (background & featured) along with brief written instructions on how to use tape series.

***Nate Donovan: Revolutionary Spy.** unabr. ed. Peter Marshall et al. Narrated by Marc Cashman. (Running Time: 7 hrs. 32 mins. 47 sec.). (Crimson Cross Ser.). (ENG.). 2010. 18.19 (978-1-60814-761-8(4)); audio compact disk 25.99 (978-1-59859-779-0(5)) Oasis Audio.

Nate the Great. Marjorie Weinman Sharmat. (J). 2003. 17.00 (978-0-8072-1933-1(9), Listening Lib) Pub: Random Audio Pubg. Dist(s): Random
Shortly after a breakfast generously supplied with pancakes, Natethe Great got an urgent call from Annie. "I lost a picture," said Annie. "Can you help me find it?" "Of course," said Nate. "I have found lost balloons, books, slippers, chickens. Even a lost goldfish. Now I, Nate the Great, will find a lost picture." "Oh, good," Annie said. Nate, with the cool detachment of a Sam Spade, immediately plunges into his new and baffling case. Getting all the facts, asking the right questions, narrowing down the suspects. Nate, the boy detective who "likes to work alone," solves the mystery and tracks down the culprit. In the process he also discovers the whereabouts of Super Hex, the missing cat. From the Trade Paperback edition.

Nate the Great & the Crunchy Christmas. Marjorie Weinman Sharmat. (Running Time: 18 mins.). (Nate the Great Ser.). (J). (gr. 1-3). 2003. 17.00 (978-0-8072-1939-3(8), Listening Lib) Pub: Random Audio Pubg. Dist(s): Random

Nate the Great & the Halloween Hunt. Marjorie Weinman Sharmat. (Nate the Great Ser.). (J). 2003. 17.00 (978-0-8072-1935-5(5), Listening Lib) Pub: Random Audio Pubg. Dist(s): Random
It is Halloween night and all the kids are dressed in scary and funny costumes.nbsp;nbsp;Their Trick or Treat bags are getting heavier. Nate's good friend Rosamond needs his help.nbsp;nbsp;Her cat, Little Hex, is missing.nbsp;nbsp;Little Hex hates Halloween, so maybe he's hiding.nbsp;nbsp;Or is he lost?nbsp;nbsp;Nate and his trusty dog Sludge take the case and hunt in the night for Little Hex.nbsp;nbsp;They pass robots, pirates, and witches.nbsp;nbsp;But where will they find Little Hex? From the Trade Paperback edition.

Nate the Great & the Halloween Hunt. unabr. ed. Marjorie Weinman Sharmat. Read by Lionel Wilson. 1 cass. (Running Time: 16 mins.). (Nate the Great Ser.). (J). (gr. 1-3). 1994. pap. bk. 17.00 (978-0-8072-0198-5(7), FTR170SP, Listening Lib) Random Audio Pubg.

Nate the Great & the Missing Key. Marjorie Weinman Sharmat. (Nate the Great Ser.). (J). 2003. 17.00 (978-0-8072-1936-2(3), Listening Lib) Pub: Random Audio Pubg. Dist(s): Random

Nate the Great & the Missing Key. unabr. ed. Marjorie Weinman Sharmat. 1 read-along cass. (Running Time: 18 min.). (Nate the Great Ser.). (J). (gr. 1-4). 1984. (Listening Lib) Random Audio Pubg.
Nate the Great doesn't want to go to a birthday party for Annie's ferocious dog, Fang. But he can't resist a mystery. When Annie loses her house key & can't get inside to set up the party, Nate & his trusty dog, Sludge, are hot on the trail.

Nate the Great & the Missing Key. unabr. ed. Marjorie Weinman Sharmat. Read by Lionel Wilson. 1 cass. (Running Time: 14 mins.). (Nate the Great Ser.). (J). (gr. 1-3). 1984. pap. bk. 17.00 (978-0-8072-0040-7(9), FTR 75 SP, Listening Lib) Random Audio Pubg.

Nate the Great & the Monster Mess. Marjorie Weinman Sharmat. (Running Time: 18 mins.). (Nate the Great Ser.). (J). (gr. 1-3). 2003. 17.00 (978-0-8072-1938-6(X), Listening Lib) Pub: Random Audio Pubg. Dist(s): Random

Nate the Great & the Phony Clue. Marjorie Weinman Sharmat. (Running Time: 13 mins.). (Nate the Great Ser.). (J). (gr. 1-3). 2003. 17.00 (978-0-8072-1940-9(1), Listening Lib) Pub: Random Audio Pubg. Dist(s): Random

Nate the Great & the Snowy Trail. Marjorie Weinman Sharmat. (Running Time: 15 mins.). (Nate the Great Ser.). (J). (gr. 1-3). 2003. 17.00 (978-0-8072-1937-9(1), Listening Lib) Pub: Random Audio Pubg. Dist(s): Random

Nate the Great Collected Stories, Vols. 1 & 2. unabr. ed. Prod. by Listening Library Staff. 2 cass. (Running Time: 1 hr. 42 mins.). (J). (gr. 1-4). 2004. 23.00 (978-0-8072-1666-8(6), Listening Lib) Pub: Random Audio Pubg. Dist(s): Random

Nate the Great Collected Stories Vol. 1: Nate the Great; Nate the Great Goes Undercover; Nate the Great & the Halloween Hunt; Nate the Great & the Monster Mess. unabr. ed. Marjorie Weinman Sharmat. Read by John Lavelle. (Running Time: 3300 sec.). (ENG.). (J). (gr. 1-4). 2008. audio compact disk 14.99 (978-0-8072-1665-1(8), ImaginStudio) Pub: Random Audio Pubg. Dist(s): Random

Nate the Great Collected Stories Vol. 2: Nate the Great & the Phony Clue; Nate the Great & the Missing Key; Nate the Great & the Snowy Trail; Nate the Great & the Crunchy Christmas. unabr. ed. Marjorie Weinman Sharmat. Read by John Lavelle. (ENG.). (J). (gr. 1). 2009. audio compact disk 14.99 (978-0-307-58287-4(6), Listening Lib) Pub: Random Audio Pubg. Dist(s): Random

***Nate the Great Collected Stories: Volume 3: Lost List; Sticky Case; Fishy Prize; Boring Beach Bag; Stolen Base; Mushy Valentine; Talks Turkey; Hungry Book Club.** unabr. ed. Marjorie Weinman Sharmat. (ENG.). (J). 2011. audio compact disk 22.00 (978-0-307-91669-3(3), Listening Lib) Pub: Random Audio Pubg. Dist(s): Random

Nate the Great Goes Undercover. Marjorie Weinman Sharmat. (Nate the Great Ser.). (J). 2003. 17.00 (978-0-8072-1934-8(7), Listening Lib) Pub: Random Audio Pubg. Dist(s): Random

Nate the Great Goes Undercover. unabr. ed. Marjorie Weinman Sharmat. 1 cass. (Running Time: 14 mins.). (Nate the Great Ser.). (J). (gr. 1-3). 1985. pap. bk. 17.00 (978-0-8072-0076-6(X), FTR93SP, Listening Lib) Random Audio Pubg.
Neighborhood detective Nate investigates the disappearance of his friend Annie's favorite painting. Includes book and guide.

Nate the Great Goes Undercover. unabr. ed. Marjorie Weinman Sharmat. Read by Lionel Wilson. Illus. by Marc Simont. 1 cass. (Running Time: 14 mins.). (Nate the Great Ser.). (J). (gr. 1-3). 2004. pap. bk. 17.00 (978-0-8072-0201-2(0), FTR172SP, Listening Lib) Random Audio Pubg.

Nate the Great Goes Undercover. unabr. ed. Marjorie Weinman Sharmat & Ruth Stiles Gannett. Read by Robert Sevra. 1 cass. (Running Time: 47 mins.). (Nate the Great Ser.). (J). (gr. 2-5). 1997. pap. bk. 17.00 (978-0-8072-0229-6(0), FTR176SP, Listening Lib) Random Audio Pubg.
Nate the Great has his first night case! Somebody is raiding Oliver's garbage can each night, but who? The list of suspects is long but when Nate goes undercover of the garbage-can lid, he narrows the suspects down to one.

Nathan & the Ice Rockets. unabr. ed. Debra Oswald. (Aussie Bites Ser.). (J). 2002. audio compact disk 39.95 (978-1-74030-841-0(7)) Pub: Bolinda Pubng AUS. Dist(s): Bolinda Pub Inc

Nathan Bedford Forrest. unabr. ed. Jack Hurst. Read by Jeff Riggenbach. 12 cass. (Running Time: 17 hrs. 30 mins.). 1995. 83.95 (978-0-7861-0666-0(2), 1568) Blckstn Audio.
In this detailed & fascinating account of the legend of the "Wizard of the Saddle," we see a man whose strengths & flaws were both of towering proportions. A man possessed of physical valor perhaps unprecedented among his countrymen. And ironically, Forrest, the first grand wizard of the Ku Klux Klan, was a man whose social attitudes changed over the span of his lifetime than those of most American historical figures.

Nathan Bedford Forrest: A Biography. unabr. ed. Jack Hurst. Read by Jeff Riggenbach. (Running Time: 17 hrs. 0 mins.). 2010. 44.95 (978-1-4417-1396-4(4)); audio compact disk 123.00 (978-1-4417-1393-3(X)) Blckstn Audio.

Nathan Coulter. unabr. ed. Wendell Berry. (Running Time: 4 hrs. 15 mins. 0 sec.). (ENG.). 2009. audio compact disk 21.98 (978-1-59644-747-9(8), christaudio) christianaud.

***Nathan Coulter.** unabr. ed. Wendell Berry. Narrated by Paul Michael. (ENG.). 2009. 12.98 (978-1-59644-748-6(6), christaudio) christianaud.

Nathan Hale. unabr. ed. Robert Hogrogian. 1 cass. (Running Time: 16 min.). (People to Remember Ser.: Set I). (J). (gr. 4-7). 1979. bk. 16.99 (978-0-934898-35-5(9)); pap. bk. 9.95 (978-0-934898-02-7(2)) Jan Prods.
The inspiring saga of Nathan Hale, who was willing to give his life for his country.

Nathan Hale: The Life & Death of America's First Spy. unabr. ed. M. William Phelps. Read by Phil Gigante. 1 MP3-CD. (Running Time: 8 hrs.). 2008. 39.25 (978-1-4233-7406-0(1), 9781423374060, Brilnc Audio MP3 Lib); 39.25 (978-1-4233-7408-4(8), 9781423374084, BADLE); 24.95 (978-1-4233-7407-7(X), 9781423374077, BAD); 24.95 (978-1-4233-7405-3(3), 9781423374053, Brilliance MP3); audio compact disk 34.99 (978-1-4233-7403-9(7), 9781423374039, Bril Audio CD Unabri); audio compact disk 102.25 (978-1-4233-7404-6(5), 9781423374046, BriAudCD Unabrid) Brilliance Audio.

***Nathaniel.** John Saul. 2010. audio compact disk 9.99 (978-1-4418-5694-4(3)) Brilliance Audio.

Nathaniel. abr. ed. John Saul. Read by Laural Merlington. 4 cass. (Running Time: 6 hrs.). 2003. 62.25 (978-1-59086-885-0(4), 1590868854, BAudLibEd); audio compact disk 74.25 (978-1-59086-887-4(0), 1590868870, BACDLib Ed) Brilliance Audio.
From the blood of the past, evil rises to seek undying vengeance... Prairie Bend. Brilliant summers amid golden fields. Killing winters of razorlike cold. A peaceful, neighborly village, darkened by legends of death? Who is Nathaniel? For a hundred years, the people of Prairie Bend have whispered the name in wonder and fear. Some say he is simply a folk tale - a legend created to frighten children on cold winter nights. Some swear he is a terrifying spirit returned to avenge the past. And soon...very soon...some will come to believe that Nathaniel lives still-darkly, horrifyingly real. Nathaniel. For young Michael Hall, newly arrived in isolated Prairie Bend after having lost his father to a sudden tragic accident, Nathaniel is the voice that calls him across the prairie night...the voice that draws him into the shadowy depths of the old, crumbling barn where he has been forbidden to go...the voice-chanting, compelling -he will follow faithfully beyond the edge of terror...Nathaniel.

Nathaniel. abr. ed. John Saul. Read by Laural Merlington. (Running Time: 6 hrs.). 2006. audio compact disk 16.99 (978-1-4233-1568-1(5), 9781423315681, BCD Value Price) Brilliance Audio.

Nathaniel. abr. ed. John Saul. Read by Laural Merlington. (Running Time: 6 hrs.). 2006. 39.25 (978-1-4233-0156-1(0), 9781423301561, BADLE); 24.95 (978-1-4233-0155-4(2), 9781423301554, BAD); 39.25 (978-1-4233-0154-7(4), 9781423301547, Brinc Audio MP3 Lib); audio compact disk 24.95 (978-1-4233-0153-0(6), 9781423301530, Brilliance MP3) Brilliance Audio.

Nathaniel Hawthorne: The Haunted Chamber. unabr. ed. Joseph Schiffman. 1 cass. (Running Time: 26 min.). (Six American Authors Ser.). 1969. 11.95 (23034) J Norton Pubs.
The life, thought, art & relevance of Hawthorne.

Nathaniel Hawthorne Audio Collection. unabr. ed. Nathaniel Hawthorne. Read by Paul Auster & James Naughton. 2003. audio compact disk 29.95 (978-0-06-055568-9(8)) HarperCollins Pubs.

***Nathaniel Hawthorne Audio Collection.** unabr. ed. Nathaniel Hawthorne. Read by Paul Auster & James Naughton. (ENG.). 2004. (978-0-06-075572-0(5), Harper Audio); (978-0-06-081341-3(5), Harper Audio) HarperCollins Pubs.

Nathaniel the Grublet. 1 cass. (Running Time: 1 hr.). (J). 2000. 6.99 HARK Ent.
Will fill your home with fun-filled praise of the Lord. Provides wholesome messages that are sure to last a lifetime.

Nathaniel the Grublet. Bridgestone Staff. 2004. audio compact disk 7.98 (978-1-56371-030-8(7)) Brdgstn Multimed Grp.

Nathaniel the Grublet. Narrated by Dean Jones. 1 cass. (J). 9.95 (ANTG) Brdgstn Multimed Grp.
Lessons about honesty & peer pressure.

Nathaniel's Nutmeg: How One Man's Courage Changed the Course of History. unabr. ed. Giles Milton. Read by Stephen Thorne. 10 cass. (Running Time: 15 hrs.). (Isis Ser.). (J). 2001. 84.95 (978-0-7531-0952-6(2), 000708) Pub: ISIS Lrg Prnt GBR. Dist(s): Ulverscroft US

Nathaniel's Nutmeg: How One Man's Courage Changed the Course of History. unabr. ed. Giles Milton. Read by Stephen Thorne. 10 CDs. (Running Time: 15 hrs.). (Isis Ser.). (J). 2002. audio compact disk 89.95 (978-0-7531-1147-5(0), 111470) Pub: ISIS Lrg Prnt GBR. Dist(s): Ulverscroft US

Nathan's Run. unabr. ed. John Gilstrap. Narrated by George Guidall. 8 cass. (Running Time: 10 hrs. 45 mins.). 70.00 (978-0-7887-0526-7(1), 94721E7) Recorded Bks.
Nathan Bailey is a 12-year-old juvenile hall orphan with a problem. Covered in blood, he is caught on videotape fleeing from a murder scene. Will the boy evade the police long enough to tell the truth, or will a hit man kill him before he gets the chance. Available to libraries only.

Natiki: A Story from Nelson Mandela's Favorite African Folktales. Read by Parminder Nagra. Compiled by Nelson Mandela. (Running Time: 5 mins.). (ENG.). 2009. 1.99 (978-1-60024-792-7(X)) Pub: Hachet Audio. Dist(s): HachBkGrp

Nation. Terry Pratchett. Contrib. by Stephen Briggs. (Playaway Children Ser.). (ENG.). (J). 2009. 59.99 (978-1-61545-576-8(0)) Find a World.

***Nation.** unabr. ed. Terry Pratchett. Read by Stephen Briggs. (ENG.). 2008. (978-0-06-170744-5(9)); (978-0-06-170743-8(0)) HarperCollins Pubs.

Nation. unabr. ed. Terry Pratchett. Read by Stephen Briggs. 8 CDs. (Running Time: 9 hrs. 30 mins.). (J). 2008. audio compact disk 29.95 (978-0-06-165821-1(9)) HarperCollins Pubs.

Nation: My Favorite Stories from the First 50 Years of the Award Winning News Broadcast. Schieffer Bob. 5 CDs. (Running Time: 6 hrs.). 2004. audio compact disk 29.99 (978-1-4193-0719-5(3)) Recorded Bks.

***Nation in Decay.** Featuring Ravi Zacharias. 2006. audio compact disk 9.00 (978-1-61256-008-3(3)) Ravi Zach.

Nation Rising: Untold Tales of Flawed Founders, Fallen Heroes, & Forgotten Fighters from America's Hidden History. unabr. ed. Kenneth C. Davis. Read by Robertson Dean. (ENG.). 2010. audio compact disk 32.00 (978-0-7393-3451-5(4), Random AudioBks) Pub: Random Audio Pubg. Dist(s): Random

Nation Without a Conscience. abr. ed. Beverly LaHaye & Tim LaHaye. 2 cass. (Running Time: 3 hrs.). 1994. 14.99 (978-0-8423-7435-4(3)) Tyndale Hse.
This revealing look at American society is strong evidence of our nation's decaying moral base.

National Barn Dance. 2 cass. (Running Time: 2 hrs.). (YA). 1985. 10.95 (978-1-57816-044-0(8), BD2401) Audio File.
Includes: "April 1, 1939" April Fool's Day show from the Eighth Street Theatre in Chicago. With emcee Joe Kelly. Uncle Ezra, Hoosier Hot Shots, The Bass Family & Maple City Four. "October 2, 1943" The program's 10th Anniversary. With Joe Kelly, Arkie, The Arkansas Woodchopper, Lulu Belle & Scooty & others. "April 15, 1944" Celebrating the 20th Anniversary of radio station WLS are Joe Kelly, Arkie, Pat Buttram, Dinning Sisters, Hoosier Hot Shots & Cindy Walker. "September 22, 1945" Theme is the Policemen's Ball with emcee Jack Holden, Lulu Belle, Scotty, Arkie, Pat Buttram & others. Set in vinyl album.

National Caregiver Training Program. Marion Karpinski. 2000. ring bd. 1999.95 (978-0-9653873-8-5(0)) Medifecta Hlth.

National Catholic Bible Conference CD Set. Compiled by Ascension Press. 2007. audio compact disk 199.95 (978-1-934217-23-8(9)) Ascensn Pr.

National Commission on Terrorist Attacks Upon the United States: The 9/11 Commission Report. unabr. ed. 18 cass. (Running Time: 23 hrs.). 2004. 149.00 (978-1-58472-808-5(6), Pocket Univ) Sound Room.

National Conference on Products Liability Law, 1989 - Panel. 1989. 175.00 (978-1-55917-596-8(6)) Natl Prac Inst.

National Day of Prayer 2007. Charles R. Swindoll. (ENG.). 2007. audio compact disk 10.00 (978-1-57972-767-3(0)) Insight Living.

National Directory for the Formation, Life, & Ministry of Permanent Deacons. Compiled by Usccb. 2006. audio compact disk 12.95 (978-1-57455-916-3(8)) US Conference.

National Environmental Policy Act (NEPA), Ecosystem Analysis & Environmental Impact Assessment. 10 cass. (Running Time: 13 hrs.). 1995. pap. bk. 172.50 (MA45) Am Law Inst.
Covers the present state of the law & practice. Includes study guide.

National Fruits & Nuts Quiz. unabr. ed. Interview with Paula Poundstone et al. 1 cass. (Running Time: 1 hr.). 1997. 10.95 (978-1-886373-09-9(4)) Human Media.
Fun-filled way for listeners to test & increase knowledge of nutrition & health.

National Gallery Complete Illustrated Catalogue. exp. ed. National Gallery Staff. (National Gallery London Publications). (ENG., 2002. audio compact disk 125.00 (978-0-300-09183-0(4)) Yale U Pr.

National Lampoon Live Un-Leashed. abr. ed. Frank Caliendo. Told to Rob Cantrell et al. (ENG.). 2009. audio compact disk 18.98 (978-1-929243-82-2(0)) Uproar Ent.

National Lampoon That's Not Funny, That's Sick! Perf. by Bill Murray et al. 1 CD. (Running Time: 1 hr.). 2003. audio compact disk 16.95 (978-1-929243-54-9(5)) Uproar Ent.
Originally recorded in 1977 (but to the best of our knowledge never released commercially) "That's Not Funny, That's Sick!" is as fresh today as it was when it was first performed. The writers/performers include such comic legends as Bill Murray, Brian Doyle-Murray, Christopher Guest, Larraine Newman, Paul Schaffer, Harold Ramis and Richard Belzer.

National Lampoon's Loaded Weapon 1, unabr. ed. Gene Quintano. Read by Tim Curry. 2 cass. (Running Time: 3 hrs.). 1993. 16.95 (978-1-56876-001-8(9)) Soundlines Ent.
This zany presentation, is a comedy filled with action, adventure & a murderous plot. A suicidal-gun-happy cop is on the trail of General Mortars who has lost the microfilm with the secret recipe for putting drugs in Wilderness Girls cookies. What ensues is a comical side-splitting comedy of spoofs.

National Lampoon's Rules of the Road: Greatest Truckers' Dongs of All Time. Perf. by National Lampoon Staff. 1 CD. (Running Time: 1 hr.). 2003. audio compact disk 16.95 (978-1-929243-53-2(7)) Uproar Ent.
Greatest truckers' songs of all time! "I've always felt that long distance truck drivers are as open and free as the road itself. If Lyndon hadn't decided to become President, I would have wanted him to be a trucker." - Lady Bird Johnson.

National Library of Medicine Update. 1 cass. (Running Time: 1 hr.). (Medical Library Association 1998 Annual Meeting & Exhibit Ser.). 1998. 12.00 (GS4) Med Lib Assn.

National Meeting of the Institute, 1990 Series. 7 cass. (Running Time: 7 hrs.). 28.00 (90N1-7) IRL Chicago.

National Meeting of the Institute, 1992 Series. 8 cass. (Running Time: 8 hrs.). 32.00 (92N1-8) IRL Chicago.

National Meeting of the Institute, 1993 Series. 6 cass. (Running Time: 6 hrs.). 24.00 (93N1-6) IRL Chicago.

National Meeting of the Institute, 1994 Series. 9 cass. (Running Time: 9 hrs.). 36.00 (94N1-9) IRL Chicago.

National Meeting of the Institute, 1995 Series. 8 cass. (Running Time: 8 hrs.). 32.00 (95N1-8) IRL Chicago.

National Military Parks: Battle of Fredericksburg (VA) 1 cass. (Running Time: 1 hr.). 11.95 (CENP303) Comp Comms Inc.
On December 13, 1862, General Ambrose E. Burnside ordered two attacks against Lee's forces. The tour of this battlefield takes the visitor to the scenes of the heaviest fighting at both ends of Lee's line as well as command posts for each army.

National Military Parks: Chancellorsville (VA) 1 cass. (Running Time: 1 hr.). 11.95 (CENP304) Comp Comms Inc.
April 1863 - General Joseph Hooker, new commander of the Union Army, moved his forces to Chancellorsville, thus threatening Lee's position in Fredericksburg. Prepared in cooperation with the National Park Services to help you more fully understand the tactics & strategies used by each General during the battle. Comes with its own map.

National Military Parks: Shiloh (TN) 1 cass. (Running Time: 1 hr.). 11.95 (CENP301) Comp Comms Inc.
The Battle of Shiloh (April 6-7, 1862) prepared in cooperation with the National Park Service to help you more fully understand the tactics & strategies used by each General during the battles. Each comes with its own map.

National Panic: God's Answer: Samuel 16:1-13. Ed Young. 1982. 4.95 (978-0-7417-1228-8(8)) Win Walk.

National Park: Grand Canyon - A Family's Adventure. 1 cass. (Running Time: 1 hr.). 12.95 (CC331) Comp Comms Inc.
Explains the early history associated with the Canyon, both human & geological, how it was formed, where to go & what to see from trails, museums, to the Phantom Ranch.

National Park Adventures: Stories That Take You Away. unabr. ed. Read by Noah Adams. Contrib. by N.P.R.-National Public Radio Staff. 1 CD. (Running Time: 1 hr.). (ENG.). 2009. audio compact disk 14.95

(978-1-59887-856-1(5), 1598878565) Pub: HighBridge. Dist(s): Workman Pub

National Parks: America's Best Idea. abr. ed. Dayton Duncan & Ken Burns. Read by Ken Burns. (ENG.). 2009. audio compact disk 30.00 (978-0-7393-6632-5(7), Random AudioBks) Pub: Random Audio Pubg. Dist(s): Random

***National Parks: America's Best Idea.** unabr. ed. Dayton Duncan & Ken Burns. Read by Danny Campbell. 13 CDs. (Running Time: 15 hrs. 30 mins.). 2009. audio compact disk 100.00 (978-1-4159-6555-9(2), BksonTape) Pub: Random Audio Pubg. Dist(s): Random

National Parks: Banff National Park. 1 cass. (Running Time: 1 hr. 30 min.). 12.95 (CCI-325); 11.95 (CCI-325A) Comp Comms Inc.
Hear about the park's ancient geological history, wildlife, mountain ranges & its hot springs, also hear about the "Lake of the Little Fishes" - Lake Louise & more.

National Parks: Bryce, Zion, Lake Powell, So. Utah. 1 cass. (Running Time: 1 hr.). 12.95 (CC335) Comp Comms Inc.
Tells you where to go, what to see & gives you valuable information for camping & hiking. Visit the North Rim of the Grand Canyon, Bryce Canyon National park, Zion National Park, Glen Canyon Dam, Lake Powell & more.

National Parks: Detailed History of the Grand Canyon. 1 cass. (Running Time: 1 hr.). 12.95 (CC330) Comp Comms Inc.
Traces the development of the canyon from its geological beginnings some 2 billion years ago to the present day.

National Party No More: The Conscience of a Conservative Democrat. unabr. ed. Zell Miller. Narrated by Ed Sala. 8 CDs. (Running Time: 9 hrs.). 2004. audio compact disk 29.99 (978-1-4025-7988-2(8), 01572) Recorded Bks.
A longtime Democrat who steadfastly refuses to join the Republicans, Senator Zell Miller nevertheless believes his party has lost touch with the majority of Americans. Tackling such combustible issues as tax cuts, gun control, the environment and the war on terrorism, Miller shows why he believes Democrats no longer understand what most Americans value. The solution? According to Miller, the Democratic Party can either shape up or ship out. Written by a man with a long and distinguished career of loyalty to his party, A National Party No More is a sobering, timely and thoroughly brave work of modern political thought.

National Road: A Ride Through Time. Scripts. Sylvia Miller. 2 cass. (Running Time: 2 hrs. 40 mins.). 2000. 15.99 (978-0-9727481-0-0(5)) Syl Miller.
History, stories, songs, and places of interest on the National Road through Ohio (starting in Wheeling, WV.).

National Road: A Ride Through Time. Scripts. Sylvia Miller. 2 CDs. (Running Time: 2 hrs. 40 mins.). 2000. audio compact disk 17.99 (978-0-9727481-1-7(3)) Syl Miller.
The history, stories, songs, and places of interest on the National Road in Ohio (starting in Wheeling, WV.).

National Security & the Public's Right to Know. unabr. ed. Friends of the FBI. 1 cass. (Running Time: 1 hr. 53 min.). 12.50 (179) J Norton Pubs.

National Soul. Bill Moyers. Read by Bill Moyers. 1 cass. (Running Time: 1 hr. 32 min.). (World of Ideas Ser.: Vol. 1). 1990. 10.95 (978-1-56176-145-6(1)) Mystic Fire.
Myth, morality & ethics in American consciousness.

National Taxpayers Union '78 Awards Dinner. unabr. ed. Byrd et al. 1 cass. (Running Time: 1 hr. 7 min.). 10.95 (944) J Norton Pubs.

National Velvet. Perf. by Elizabeth Taylor et al. 1 cass. (Running Time: 1 hr.). 1947. 7.95 (DD-8800) Natl Recrd Co.

National Velvet. abr. ed. Hollywood. 1999. pap. bk. 13.10 (978-1-900912-71-6(6)) Pub: Mr Punch Prodns GBR. Dist(s): Ulverscroft US
Velvet Brown, the English farm girl with a passion for horses, wins the spirited steed Pie in the local town lottery. With the help of young Mi Taylor they train the horse & win the Grand National.

Nationale Varietaten im Unterricht Deutsch als Fremdsprache. Sara Hagi et al. Vol. 64. (GER., 2006. bk. 48.95 (978-3-631-54796-0(X)) P Lang Pubng.

Nation's Favorite Comic Poems. John Betjeman. 2 cass. (Running Time: 2 hrs.). 1998. 16.85 (978-0-563-55850-7(4)) BBC WrldWd GBR.
Contains Griff Rhys Jones' personal selection of his favorite comic poems. Poets featured include Spike Milligan, Ogden Nash, Jonathan Swift & John Betjeman.

Nation's Unity. Ayn Rand. Read by Ayn Rand. 2 cass. (Running Time: 1 hr. 55 min.). 24.95 (978-1-56114-019-0(8), AR05D) Second Renaissance.
What is the true meaning of the cries for "national unity?" In this probing examination of the 1972 McGovern-Nixon presidential campaign, Ayn Rand demonstrates how "unity" rests upon the inviolability of individual rights & how McGovern's egalitarian ideology makes the unity he claims to seek unachievable. The live question period covers: the definition of a moral sanction; the feasibility of political action to bring about social change; re-writing the Declaration of Independence; how to evaluate hypocritical, self-contradictory political candidates; Objectivism vs. conservatism.

Nation's Unity. Comment by Ayn Rand. 2 cass. (Running Time: 1 hr. 55 min.). (Ford Hall Forum Ser.). 1972. 24.95 (AR05D) Second Renaissance.
Pt. 1: How genuine unity rests upon the inviolability of individual rights. Pt. 2: Q&A topics include: the definition of a moral sanction; the feasibility of political action to bring about social change; re-writing the Declaration of Independence.

Native AMER of the Eastern Woodlands: The Iroquois. Compiled by Benchmark Education Staff. 2006. audio compact disk 10.00 (978-1-4108-6632-5(7)) Benchmark Educ.

Native AMER of the Plains: The Lakota. Compiled by Benchmark Education Staff. 2006. audio compact disk 10.00 (978-1-4108-6631-8(9)) Benchmark Educ.

Native AMER of the Southwest: The Navajo CD - EE. Compiled by Benchmark Education Staff. 2006. audio compact disk 10.00 (978-1-4108-6630-1(0)) Benchmark Educ.

Native American: Stargazer Edition. unabr. ed. 1 cass. (Running Time: 1 hr.). 11.95 (C11315) J Norton Pubs.
An inquiry into extra-terrestrial phenomena.

Native American: Tribal Songs Edition. unabr. ed. 1 cass. 11.95 (C11156) J Norton Pubs.
Ceremonial & social songs & dances of eight Native American Indians.

Native American Coyote Stories. Michael Lacapa. Read by Michael Lacapa. 1 cass. (Running Time: 1 hr. 07 min.). Dramatization. 1996. bk. 12.00 (978-0-9666415-0-9(7), SBP001) Sage Prod AZ.
Stories used in Southwest Indian cultures to teach values & life's lessons.

Native American Filmmakers. 1 cass. (Running Time: 30 min.). 9.95 (G0310B090, HarperThor) HarpC GBR.

Native American Flute: Myth, History, & Craft. C. S. Fuqua. 2007. audio compact disk 22.95 (978-1-58749-636-3(4)) Awe-Struck.

***Native American Flute: Understanding the Gift.** 3rd ed. John Vames. (ENG., 2005. pap. bk. 29.95 (978-0-9740486-2-8(3)) Molly Moon.

Native American Footwear, Jewelry, & Giftware in Germany: A Strategic Reference 2007. Compiled by Icon Group International, Inc. Staff. 2007. ring bd. 195.00 (978-0-497-35978-2(2)) Icon Grp.

Native American Poetry. Perf. by Medicine Story. 1 cass. (Running Time: 1 hr. 30 min.). 6.00 Story Stone.
A collection of Native American poetry recited by Medicine Story on WFCR radio.

Native American Poetry. unabr. ed. Ed. by James McKinley. 1 cass. (Running Time: 29 min.). (New Letters on the Air Ser.). 1983. 10.00 (021183); 18.00 2-sided cass. New Letters.
A celebration of Native American writers & orators featuring ancient stories & speeches as well as work by contemporary poets.

Native American Songs for Piano Solo. Gail Smith. 1997. pap. bk. 21.95 (978-0-7866-2847-6(2), 95451CDP) Mel Bay.

Native American Stories - Sounds from the Heart. Michael Lacapa. Read by Michael Lacapa. Perf. by Tom McMillan. 1 cass. (Running Time: 48 min.). Dramatization. 1997. bk. 12.00 (978-0-9666415-1-6(5), SBP002) Sage Prod AZ.
Memories of growing up on the Apache Reservation.

Native American Wisdom: Black Elk Speaks, Shadowcatchers & Wisdomkeepers, unabr. ed. Steve Wall. Read by Fred Contreras et al. Told to John G. Neihardt. 6 cass. (Running Time: 9 hrs.). (Native American Wisdom Ser.). 1998. bk. 49.95 (978-1-57453-227-2(8)) Audio Lit.
Includes: "Black Elk Speaks" & Shadowcatchers & "Wisdomkeepers".

Native American Women: Keepers of the Tradition. 1 cass. (Running Time: 30 min.). 9.95 (HO-84-12-19, HarperThor) HarpC GBR.

Native American Writing Series. unabr. ed. 16 cass. (Running Time: 29 min. per cass.). 1985. 10.00 ea. New Letters.
A collection of weekly half-hour radio programs with Native American authors talking & presenting their own works.

Native American Youth: The New Warriors. 1 cass. (Running Time: 30 min.). 9.95 (G0560B090, HarperThor) HarpC GBR.

Native Americans & Suicide: Program from the Award Winning Public Radio Series. Interview. Hosted by Fred Goodwin. Comment by John Hockenberry. 1 CD. (Running Time: 1hr.). (Infinite Mind Ser.). 2001. audio compact disk 21.95 (978-1-888064-72-8(2), LCM 194) Lichtenstein Creat.
In this hour, we explore the high rate of suicide among American Indians and Alaska Natives. Throughout the United States, American Indians and Alaska Natives are one and a half times more likely to commit suicide than the general population.Guests include Sharon Watson, of Minnesota's Chippewa White Earth Reservation, whose son died of suicide; Dr. Spero Manson, division head at the National Center for American Indian and Alaska Native Mental Health Research; Dr. James Thompson, deputy medical director at the American Psychiatric Association; Medicine Dream an Anchorage-based band who lost a Cheyenne friend to suicide; Diana Weber, a social worker who assists the people of the Louden Tribal Council, in Alaska; Regine Attla, a tribal administrator on preparation for a funeral; Dr. Denise Middlebrook, a public health advisor for the Substance Abuse and Mental Health Service Administration; and Theda New Breast, who runs wellness workshops in Montana for American Indians and Alaska Natives.

Native Americans Audio CD Theme Set: Set of 6 Set B. Adapted by Benchmark Education Staff. (English Explorers Ser.). (J). (gr. 3-6). 2007. audio compact disk 60.00 (978-1-4108-9828-9(8)) Benchmark Educ.

Native Angels: Musical Miracles from the New World. 1 cass. (Running Time: 47 mins.). 1999. 9.95 (T9050); audio compact disk 14.95 (K6720) Liguori Pubns.
Songs include: "Oh Senora," "Sa qui turo Zente Plete," "Victoria Victoria" & more.

Native Forest Network Issues - Mexico's Sierra Madre, Idaho's Cove - Mallard Campaign & Canada's Hydro Quebec. Hosted by Nancy Pearlman. 1 cass. (Running Time: 30 min.). 10.00 (1201) Educ Comm CA.

Native Ground: Southern Mountain Tunes. abr. ed. Perf. by Wayne Erbsen. 1 cass. (Running Time: 34 min.). 1988. 9.95 (978-0-9629327-3-1(6), NG001) Native Ground.
Vintage American tunes from the rural South during the mid-19th century.

Native Ground - Southern Mountain Tunes. 1 cass. (Running Time: 34 min.). Native Ground.
Fourteen vintage American tunes take the listener back to the rural South during the mid 19th-Century with sparse but lively arrangements on old-time clawhammer banjo, fiddle & guitar. Includes: "Polly Put the Kettle on," "Train 45," "Grandfather's Clock," "Jack of Diamonds," "Ducks on the Pond," "Hangman's Reel," "Bonepart's Retreat," "Going Across the Sea," "Tator Patch," Ook Pick Waltz," "Liza Jane," "Last Chance".

Native Joy for Real. Poems. Joy Harjo. Perf. by Joy Harjo. 1 CD. (Running Time: 50 min). 2005. audio compact disk 16.00 (978-0-916727-23-9(8)) Wings Pr.
Native Joy for Real marks Joy Harjo's debut as a singer/songwriter, an album so strong, so brimming with soul and beauty that even long time fans will be astonished by the power of its poetic vision. Harjo has created ten singular invocations of contemporary life, on and off the reservation, that deal with the joys and tribulations of everyday existence. The music blends traditional Native rhythms and singing with jazz, rock, blues and a touch of hip hop. Harjo's trademark intensity is still inspiring. The songs feature memorable refrains, smoky sax work, subtle powwow based beats, and uplifting lyrics. The unifying factor is Harjo's poetic and political vision. Harjo (Muskogee Creek) is a successful and critically acclaimed poet, children's author and professor at UCLA. With Native Joy for Real, she makes a giant step towards mainstream credibility.

Native Nation Building: Radio Series. Prod. by Ian Record & Jay Stauss. 5 CDs. 2006. audio compact disk 20.00 (978-1-931143-28-8(5)) Univ AZ Udall Ctr.

Native of the Mind: The Roots of Psychological Disorder; Psychological Suffering; The Need for Security; What Is a Healthy Mind? & The Self (ANOM 82), Nos. 1-5. unabr. ed. J. Krishnamurti. Read by J. Krishnamurti. Ed. by Krishnamurti Foundation of America Staff. 5 cass. (Running Time: 5 hrs.). 1982. 42.50 Krishnamurti.

Native Religion of the Americas. unabr. ed. Ake Hultkrantz. Read by Ben Kingsley. (Running Time: 10800 sec.). (Religion, Scriptures, & Spirituality Ser.). 2006. audio compact disk 25.95 (978-0-7861-6477-6(8)) Pub: Blckstn Audio. Dist(s): NetLibrary CO

Native Religions of the Americas. unabr. ed. Ake Hultkrantz. Read by Ben Kingsley. Ed. by Walter Harrelson & Mike Hassell. 2 cass. (Running Time: 3 hrs.). Dramatization. (Religion, Scriptures & Spirituality Ser.). 1994. 17.95 (978-1-56823-019-1(2), 10462) Knowledge Prod.
North, Central & South American Indians have a rich religious heritage, though much has been lost as these peoples were conquered by Europeans. Here we describe the distinctive religious cultures of the native American peoples.

Native Son. Richard Wright. 2 cass. (Running Time: 2 hrs. 9 min.). 19.95 (8121Q) Filmic Archives.
The searing account of Bigger Thomas, a black youth whose tragic life was drawn from Richard Wright's own memories of the Chicago ghetto. Vivid, unforgettable & heartbreaking. Wright's best-selling masterpiece forces us to witness the inhumanity of our society.

***Native Son.** unabr. ed. Richard Wright. Read by Peter Francis James. (ENG.). 2009. (978-0-06-163251-8(1)) HarperCollins Pubs.

Native Son. unabr. ed. Richard Wright. Read by Peter Francis James. 12 cass. (Running Time: 18 hrs.). 1998. 102.00 Recorded Bks.

Native Son. unabr. ed. Richard Wright. Narrated by Peter Francis James. 15 CDs. (Running Time: 17 hrs. 45 mins.). 2004. audio compact disk 142.00 (978-1-4025-1558-3(8)) Recorded Bks.
Since its publication in 1940, Native Son has become a classic of African-American literature and one of the most important books of this century. A stark and troubling account of murder, guilt, and racial hatred, it was among the first works to sound the alarm for the impending social violence that would explode during the 1960s. Bigger Thomas, a 20-year-old black man, is uneducated, unsophisticated, and unemployed. When a wealthy family offers him a chauffeur¿s position, Bigger is torn between gratitude for the job and anger over his subservient status. On his first evening, the family¿s daughter orders Bigger to spend a drunken night on the town with her and a gentleman friend. But events spin out of control and, by morning, the young woman is dead.

Native Son, unabr. ed. Richard Wright. Narrated by Peter Francis James. 12 cass. (Running Time: 17 hrs. 45 mins.). 1998. 102.00 (978-0-7887-2112-0(7), 95437E7) Recorded Bks.
The account of murder, guilt & racial hatred.

***Native Son.** unabr. ed. Richard Wright. Read by Peter Francis James. (ENG.). 2009. (978-0-06-088639-4(0), Harper Audio) HarperCollins Pubs.

Native Son. unabr. ed. Richard Wright et al. Read by Peter Francis James. 15 CDs. (Running Time: 17 hrs. 30 mins.). 2008. audio compact disk 39.95 (978-0-06-145783-8(3), Caedmon) HarperCollins Pubs.

Native Son: Fear Is the Devil's Fire. Music by Lee Kweller. Text by Joshua Brown & John Esposito. 1 cass. (Running Time: 10 min.). (Educational Song Ser.: Vol. 4). (YA). (gr. 7-12). 1998. pap. bk. 19.98 (978-1-57649-004-4(1), 76004) Arkadia Ent.
Based on Richard Wright's classic novel about social injustice & racial strife. Includes study guide.

Native Speaker. unabr. ed. Chang-Rae Lee. Read by David Colacci. (Running Time: 11 hrs.). 2009. 24.99 (978-1-4233-9146-3(2), 9781423391463, Brilliance MP3); 24.99 (978-1-4233-9148-7(9), 9781423391487, BAD); 39.97 (978-1-4233-9147-0(0), 9781423391470, Brinc Audio MP3 Lib); 39.97 (978-1-4233-9149-4(7), 9781423391494, BADLE) Brilliance Audio.

Native Tongue, unabr. ed. Carl Hiaasen. Narrated by George Wilson. 11 cass. (Running Time: 15 hrs. 45 mins.). 1992. 91.00 (978-1-55690-761-6(3), 92421E7) Recorded Bks.
Joe Winder, ex-reporter presently working as press writer for "The Amazing Kingdom of Thrills," is trying not to get involved in the disappearance of the last two blue-tongued mango voles on earth & the bizarre death of Orky, the killer whale. But not getting involved turns out to be almost as hard as staying alive.

Native Wisdom. Ken Cohen. 2003. audio compact disk 16.95 (978-1-59179-099-0(9)) Sounds True.

***Nativity Giant Floor Puzzle.** Created by Twin Sisters. (Giant Floor Puzzles Ser.). (ENG.). (J). 2009. audio compact disk (978-1-59922-444-2(5)) Twin Sisters.

Nativity Story. Angela Hunt. Read by Renée Raudman. (Playaway Adult Nonfiction Ser.). 2008. 44.99 (978-1-60640-559-8(4)) Find a World.

Nativity Story. unabr. ed. Angela Hunt. Read by Renée Raudman. Contrib. by Mike Rich. (Running Time: 6 hrs. 0 mins. 0 sec.). (ENG.). 2006. audio compact disk 24.99 (978-1-4001-0339-3(8)); audio compact disk 19.99 (978-1-4001-5339-8(5)); audio compact disk 49.99 (978-1-4001-3339-0(4)) Pub: Tantor Media. Dist(s): IngramPubServ

Nattergalen see Nightingale

Nattergalen Vol. 103: The Nightingale. 3rd unabr. ed. Ed. by Janne Lillestol. Tr. by Janne Lillestol. Illus. by Scott Zins. Prod. by Scott Zins. 1 cass. (Running Time: 18 min.). (Listen & Learn Language Ser.: Vol. LL0399). (ENG & NOR.). 1999. pap. bk. 15.95 (978-1-892623-10-2(2)) Intl Book.
English & Norwegian bilingual text with the Norwegian narration.

Natural. Joe Klein. Narrated by George Wilson. 6 CDs. (Running Time: 7 hrs. 30 mins.). audio compact disk 58.00 (978-1-4025-3480-5(9)) Recorded Bks.

Natural. Bernard Malamud. 2009. (978-1-60136-162-2(9)) Audio Holding.

Natural. unabr. ed. Bernard Malamud. Read by Christopher Hurt. 5 cass. (Running Time: 7 hrs.). 1993. 39.95 (978-0-7861-0454-3(6), 1406) Blckstn Audio.
Bernard Malamud has raised all the passion & craziness & fanaticism of baseball to its ordained place in mythology. This is one of the few American novels that uses popular folk material in the interest of serious fiction & the reverberations of the book carry far beyond the baseball park. This novel, first published in 1952, has since become a new American classic.

Natural. unabr. ed. Bernard Malamud. Read by Christopher Hurt. (Running Time: 23400 sec.). 2007. audio compact disk 55.00 (978-0-7861-5919-2(7)); audio compact disk 29.95 (978-0-7861-7301-3(7)) Blckstn Audio.

Natural. unabr. ed. Bernard Malamud. Read by Michael Kramer. 5 cass. (Running Time: 7 hrs. 30 min.). 1996. 40.00 (978-0-7366-3227-0(1), 3888) Books on Tape.
America's national pastime has come a long way since 1839, when Abner Doubleday, a West Point cadet, first laid out a diamond at Cooperstown, NY, site of today's Baseball Hall of Fame. But it took Bernard Malamud to make the game mythology, which he did in this classic parable of mankind's quest.

Natural: The Misunderstood Presidency of Bill Clinton. Joe Klein. 4 cass. (Running Time: 7 hrs. 30 mins.). 2004. 19.99 (978-1-4025-0878-3(6), 01134) Recorded Bks.

Natural: The Misunderstood Presidency of Bill Clinton. unabr. ed. Joe Klein. Narrated by George Wilson. 5 cass. (Running Time: 7 hrs. 30 mins.). 2002. 52.00 (978-1-4025-1275-9(9)) Recorded Bks.
Go behind the scenes of Bill Clinton's presidency.

Natural Acts: A Sidelong View of Science & Nature. David Quammen. Read by David Quammen. 2 cass. (Running Time: 3 hrs.). 1990. 16.95 (978-0-939643-28-8(6), NrthWrd Bks) TandN Child.
Essays from Natural Acts & Flight of the Iguana.

Natural Advantages of Women: How We Are Hard-Wired for Personal Greatness. Michelle Miller. 1 CD. (Running Time: 3585 sec.). 2003. audio compact disk 12.95 (978-1-932226-12-6(5)) Wizard Acdmy.
The Natural Advantages of Women explains why women do what they do, exploring female traits like emotion, passion, intuition, and nurturing.Based on the scientific findings of recent brain studies worldwide, this book explains physical manifestations in the female brain that help to explain these traits. It offers proof that women are not only "hard-wired" differently

from men, but that they have the ability to use this "wiring" to great advantage in their personal and professional lives.Whether you?re a man or a woman, at the beginning or in the middle of your career, this book will touch your life in a profound way. Listen in as author Michele Miller gives us a fascinating peek behind the curtain of the female mind.Includes:59min 45sec Audio CD52 page booklet.

Natural Alternatives to the Drugs We've Been Taking: Prevent Pain, Disease & Sickness with Vitamins. Illus. by Angela Brown. Voice by Earl Mindell. Prod. by Les Lingle. 1 cass. (Running Time: 30 mins.). (Words of Wellness - Your Show for Simple Solutions Ser.: 322). 2000. 12.95 (978-1-930995-15-4(6), LLP322) Life Long Pubg.
What you should know about health care prevention costs less than a soda, consumed in seconds, available in any grocery store & could save your life.

Natural Blues & Country Western Harmonica. unabr. ed. 3 cass. (Running Time: 4 hrs. 30 min.). pap. bk. 35.00 (S23950); 19.95 (S23944); 17.95 (S23945) J Norton Pubs.
Volume I gives slow-motion examples & step-by-step instruction on playing the harmonica. Volume II provides games & exercises that loosen your mouth & tongue & explains & illustrates the 26 songs notated in the Natural Blues & Country Western Harmonica book.

Natural Bone & Bone Substitutes. Moderated by Gary E. Friedlaender. 2 cass. (Orthopaedic Surgery Ser.: OR-2). 1986. 19.00 (8652) Am Coll Surgeons.

***Natural Born Charmer.** unabr. ed. Susan Elizabeth Phillips. Read by Anna Fields. (ENG.). 2007. (978-0-06-126241-8(2), Harper Audio); (978-0-06-126242-5(0), Harper Audio) HarperCollins Pubs.

Natural Born Charmer. unabr. ed. Susan Elizabeth Phillips & Susan E. Phillips. Read by Anna Fields. 10 CDs. (Running Time: 12 hrs.). (Chicago Stars Bks.: No. 7). 2007. audio compact disk 39.95 (978-0-06-122719-6(6)) HarperCollins Pubs.

Natural Breast Enlargement: Ocean. Eldon Taylor. Read by Eldon Taylor. Ed. by Leslie Brice. 1 cass. (Running Time: 1 hr.). 1992. 16.95 (978-1-56705-335-7(1)) Gateways Inst.
Self improvement.

Natural Breathing. Dennis Lewis. 3 CDs. (Running Time: 3 hrs). 2005. audio compact disk 24.95 (978-1-59179-316-8(5), AW00400D) Sounds True.

Natural Bridge. Contrib. by Ben Lennon. (ENG.). 1999. 13.95 (978-0-8023-7139-3(6)); audio compact disk 21.95 (978-0-8023-8139-2(1)) Pub: Clo Iar-Chonnachta IRL. Dist(s): Dufour

Natural Brilliance Personal Learning Course: Move from Feeling Stuck to Achieving Success. Paul R. Scheele. Read by Paul R. Scheele. 6 cass. (Running Time: 3 hrs.). 1997. pap. bk. 149.95 (978-0-925480-62-0(2), 9NLC) Learn Strategies.
Self-study course to break through limitations for more success in life. Includes manual.

Natural Causes. unabr. ed. Michael Palmer. Narrated by Alyssa Bresnahan. 11 cass. (Running Time: 16 hrs.). 1994. 91.00 (978-0-7887-0085-9(5), 94325E7) Recorded Bks.
If it weren't for Dr. Sarah Baldwin's expert use of the acupuncture needles, Lisa Summer would have lost her life during the sudden bleeding that complicated her labor. But after saving the girl's life, Sarah finds herself the subject of an intensive medical investigation - one that questions her holistic methods & threatens her career.

Natural Causes. unabr. ed. Michael Palmer. Read by Alyssa Bresnahan. 11 cass. (Running Time: 16 hrs.). 1994. Rental 18.50 (94325) Recorded Bks.
A young OB/GYN who combines a traditional training with a background in holistic healing is implicated in the mysterious deaths of patients at a Boston hospital.

Natural Cello. 1 cass. (Running Time: 1 hr.). 1994. audio compact disk 15.95 (2628, Creativ Pub) Quayside.
Cello, solo selections & flute & string accompaniment. Original music by Thomas Smith mixes beautifully with serene sounds from the natural world.

Natural Cello. 1 cass. (Running Time: 1 hr.). 1994. 9.95 (2627, NrthWrd Bks) TandN Child.

Natural Child: Parenting from the Heart. Jan Hunt. Contrib. by Keaton Simons. 2008. audio compact disk 29.95 (978-0-9685754-6-8(3)) Pub: Nat5 Child CAN. Dist(s): Consort Bk Sales

Natural Christmas. 1 CD. (Running Time: 1 hr.). 1994. audio compact disk 15.95 (2214, Creativ Pub) Quayside.
Traditional Christmas music blended with natural sounds.

Natural Christmas. 1 cass. (Running Time: 1 hr.). 1994. 9.95 (2212, NrthWrd Bks) TandN Child.

Natural Contemplation. Thomas Merton. 1 cass. (Running Time: 1 hr.). (Rilke - Poet of Inwardness Ser.). 8.95 (AA2077) Credence Commun.
How the experience of inwardness in the poet is what the contemplative seeks.

Natural Cures "They" Don't Want You to Know About. unabr. ed. Kevin Trudeau. Read by Kevin Trudeau. (YA). 2008. 54.99 (978-1-60514-842-7(3)) Find a World.

Natural Curiosity. Margaret Drabble. Read by Margaret Drabble. Prod. by Moveable Feast Staff. 1 cass. (Running Time: 30 mins.). 8.95 (AMF-218) Am Audio Prose.
Margaret Drabble reads from her novel "A Natural Curiosity" & talks about Great Britain's industrial north, sociological novels & modern man's atavistic impulse.

Natural Curiosity. unabr. ed. Margaret Drabble. Read by Frances Jeater. 8 cass. (Running Time: 12 hrs.). 2001. 69.95 (93018) Pub: ISIS Audio GBR. Dist(s): Ulverscroft US

Natural Curiosity. unabr. ed. Margaret Drabble. Read by Frances Jeater. 8 cass. (Running Time: 11 hrs. 30 min.). (Isis Ser.). (J). 2001. 69.95 (978-1-85695-501-0(X), 93018); audio compact disk 89.95 (978-0-7531-1053-9(9)) Pub: ISIS Lrg Prnt GBR. Dist(s): Ulverscroft US

Natural Disasters. Dorling Kindersley Publishing Staff. (Eyewitness Videos Ser.). (ENG.). (J). (gr. 3). 2009. 12.99 (978-0-7566-5545-7(5)) DK Pub Inc.

Natural Drumming: Lessons 3 And 4. Contrib. by Joe Morello & Danny Gottlieb. (Running Time: 1 hr. 38 mins.). 2006. 24.95 (978-5-558-09183-0(5)) Mel Bay.

Natural Ease for Daily Living. Osa Jackson-Wyatt. 2 cass. (Running Time: 3 hrs.). (Natural Ease Ser.: Vol. I). (978-0-9643200-1-7(0)) Phys Therapy.
Health & fitness. Includes manual.

Natural Effects II (at the Blue Dragon). Jazz, Poetry & Kats, December 8th 2001. Choreography by Eddy Todd. Prod. by Tim Nuzum. Compiled by David Wilde. (Wildemuse Ser.). (C). 2002. audio compact disk 10.00 (978-1-882204-43-4(3)) Wilde Pub.

Natural Enemy. unabr. collector's ed. Jane Langton. Read by Mary Peiffer. 6 cass. (Running Time: 9 hrs.). 1992. 48.00 (978-0-7366-2231-8(4), 3021) Books on Tape.
The poor man died gasping for breath, yellow-jackets swarming. Had his asthma finally killed him, or is it a more sinister demise? Homer Kelly is determined to find out.

Natural Forces. Swami Amar Jyoti. 2 cass. (Running Time: 3 hrs.). 1979. 12.95 (K-24) Truth Consciousness.
Not harnessing the natural forces, but allowing them to work through us. On individuality & freedom. The meaning of awakened living by the Principle.

Natural Gardening: How to Create Your Own Garden Paradise. Donald W. Trotter. Read by Donald W. Trotter. 2 cass. (Running Time: 2 hrs.). 2000. 18.95 (978-1-56170-768-3(6), 4067) Hay House.

Natural Gas Meter Reading Handbook. Virgil Johnson. 2007. audio compact disk 149.99 (978-0-9755301-7-7(8)) V Johnson Tech.

Natural Gas Transmission & Distribution in Sweden: A Strategic Reference 2006. Compiled by Icon Group International, Inc. Staff. 2007. ring bd. 195.00 (978-0-497-82423-5(X)) Icon Grp.

Natural Guitar. Perf. by Chuck Lange. 1 cass. (Running Time: 1 hr.). 1994. audio compact disk 15.95 (2218, Creativ Pub) Quayside.
Chuck Lange's acoustic guitar mixes with the sounds of woods & water.

Natural Guitar. Perf. by Chuck Lange. 1 cass. (Running Time: 1 hr.). 1994. 9.95 (2216, NrthWrd Bks) TandN Child.

Natural Harp. Perf. by Leticia Schmidt. 1 cass. (Running Time: 1 hr.). 1994. audio compact disk 15.95 (2222, Creativ Pub) Quayside.
Classic & new age music played by Leticia Schmidt on the elegant acoustic harp - all blended with sounds of nature.

Natural Harp. Perf. by Leticia Schmidt. 1 cass. (Running Time: 1 hr.). 1994. 9.95 (2220, NrthWrd Bks) TandN Child.

Natural Healing for Anxiety & Depression: A Dialogue Between Harold H. Bloomfield, M. D. & Deepak Chopra, M. D. unabr. ed. Harold H. Bloomfield & Deepak Chopra. Read by Harold H. Bloomfield & Deepak Chopra. 1 cass. (Running Time: 1 hr. 30 min.). 2000. 10.95 Hay House.

Natural Healing for Dogs & Cats. Cheryl Schwartz. Read by Cheryl Schwartz. 2 cass. (Running Time: 2 hrs.). 2000. 18.95 (978-1-56170-773-7(2), 4072) Hay House.

Natural High Without Drugs. 1 cass. 10.00 (978-1-58506-018-4(6), 45) New Life Inst OR.
Evaluate your awareness to a higher, happier level without using illegal drugs.

Natural History of Love. abr. ed. Diane Ackerman. Read by Diane Ackerman. 2 cass. (Running Time: 3 hrs.). 1994. 16.95 (978-1-879371-73-6(1), 391252) Pub Mills.
Ackerman draws on a variety of sources: classical, contemporary, cultural, religious & biological, revealing a lyrical "tour d'horizon" of love's many forms & faces.

Natural History of Love. unabr. ed. Diane Ackerman. Narrated by Barbara Caruso. 11 cass. (Running Time: 15 hrs. 45 mins.). 1995. 91.00 (978-0-7887-0153-5(3), 94375E7) Recorded Bks.
Explores the elusive, eternal, endlessly fascinating matter of love. From Cleopatra's sex appeal to medieval kisses, from the aphrodisiac qualities of radishes to a cuddle chemical called oxytocin, Ackerman leads us on a "tour d'horizon" of love's many faces & forms.

Natural History of Southwestern Ontario. Contrib. by Christopher Dewdney & Steve Venright. (Running Time: 2 hrs. 30 mins.). 2004. audio compact disk 16.95 (978-1-55245-147-2(X)) Pub: Coach Hse Bks CAN. Dist(s): Chicago Distribution Ctr

Natural History of the Senses. unabr. ed. Diane Ackerman. Narrated by Davina Porter. 10 cass. (Running Time: 13 hrs. 45 mins.). 1995. 85.00 (978-0-7887-0313-3(7), 94505E7) Recorded Bks.
Combines biology & anthropology, art & science as she leads us on a grand tour of the realm of the senses that includes the evolution of the kiss, the sadistic cuisine of 18th-century England, the chemistry of pain & the melodies of the planets.

Natural History of the Senses, Set. abr. ed. Diane Ackerman. Read by Diane Ackerman. 4 cass. (Running Time: 6 hrs.). 1995. 24.95 (978-1-879371-72-9(3), 693229) Pub Mills.
A vibrant celebration of our ability to smell, taste, hear, touch & see. A startling & entertaining account of how human beings experience & savor the world.

Natural History of Visions. unabr. ed. Aldous Huxley. 1 cass. (Running Time: 1 hr. 15 min.). (Human Situation Ser.). 1959. 11.00 (01121) Big Sur Tapes.

Natural Landmarks: Early Explorers Early Set B Audio CD. Christina Riska. Adapted by Benchmark Education Staff. (J). 2007. audio compact disk 10.00 (978-1-4108-8224-0(1)) Benchmark Educ.

Natural Law & Human Nature, Pts. I-II. Instructed by Joseph Koterski. 12 CDs. (Running Time: 12 hrs.). 2002. audio compact disk 69.95 (978-1-56585-351-5(2)) Teaching Co.

Natural Law & Human Nature, Vol. 2. Instructed by Joseph Koterski. 6 cass. (Running Time: 6 hrs.). 2002. 129.95 (978-1-56585-109-2(9)) Teaching Co.

Natural Law & Human Nature: Parts I-II. Instructed by Joseph Koterski. 12 cass. (Running Time: 12 hrs.). 54.95 (978-1-56585-108-5(0)) Teaching Co.

Natural Lifestyle Learning: Clear alternatives to full Inclusion. David Feldman. 2003. spiral bd. 59.00 (978-1-57861-480-6(5), IEP Res) Attainment.

Natural Lifestyle Learning Applications. David Feldman. 2003. spiral bd. 39.00 (978-1-57861-176-8(8), IEP Res) Attainment.

Natural Man. unabr. collector's ed. Ed McClanahan. Read by Walter Zimmerman. 6 cass. (Running Time: 6 hrs.). 1989. 36.00 (978-0-7366-1548-8(2), 2417) Books on Tape.
The Natural Man is a comedy about coming of age in the late 1940s in an out-of-the-way corner of America call Needmore, Kentucky. At the center is Harry Eastep, a high school senior, bookish, bespectacled & filled with vague yearnings after the considerable person of Oodles Ockerman.

Natural Music for Sleep. Jeffrey Thompson & Joseph Nagler. (Running Time: 1:00:00). 2003. audio compact disk 11.95 (978-1-55961-671-3(7)) Sounds True.

Natural Nisciene; The Mighty Law of Attraction. Ann Ree Colton & Jonathan Murro. 1 cass. (Running Time: 1 hr.). 7.95 A R Colton Fnd.

Natural Pain Relief. Eldon Taylor. 1 cass. (Running Time: 1 hr. 2 min.). (Inner Talk Ser.). 16.95 (978-1-55978-051-3(7), 5313A) Progress Aware Res.
Soundtrack - Tropical Lagoon with underlying subliminal affirmations.

Natural Pain Relief: Babbling Brook. Eldon Taylor. 1 cass. 16.95 (978-1-55978-462-7(8), 5313F) Progress Aware Res.

Natural Pain Relief: Classic. Eldon Taylor. Read by Eldon Taylor. Ed. by Leslie Brice. 1 cass. (Running Time: 1 hr.). 1992. 16.95 (978-1-56705-082-0(4)) Gateways Inst.
Self improvement.

Natural Pain Relief: Harmonies. Eldon Taylor. Read by Eldon Taylor. Ed. by Leslie Brice. 1 cass. (Running Time: 1 hr.). 1992. 16.95 (978-1-56705-083-7(2)) Gateways Inst.

***Natural Pain Relief: How to Soothe & Dissolve Physical Pain with Mindfulness.** Shinzen Young. 2011. pap. bk. & pap. bk. 14.95 (978-1-60407-088-0(9)) Sounds True.

Natural Pain Relief: Music Theme. Eldon Taylor. 1 cass. 16.95 (978-1-55978-053-7(3), 5313C) Progress Aware Res.

Natural Pain Relief: Ocean. Eldon Taylor. Read by Eldon Taylor. Ed. by Leslie Brice. 1 cass. (Running Time: 1 hr.). 1992. 16.95 (978-1-56705-084-4(0)) Gateways Inst.

Natural Pain Relief: Stream. Eldon Taylor. Read by Eldon Taylor. Ed. by Leslie Brice. 1 cass. (Running Time: 1 hr.). 1992. 16.95 (978-1-56705-085-1(9)) Gateways Inst.

Natural Piano. Perf. by Ken Johnson. 1 cass. (Running Time: 1 hr.). 1994. audio compact disk 15.95 (2226, Creativ Pub) Quayside.
George Winston-style keyboard performed by Ken Johnson on grand piano. Variety of wild creatures & other stirring natural sounds.

Natural Piano. Perf. by Ken Johnson. 1 cass. (Running Time: 1 hr.). 1994. 9.95 (2224, NrthWrd Bks) TandN Child.

Natural Process for Opening the Heart. Doris Jeanette. 3 cass. (Running Time: 3 hrs.). 2002. 39.95 (978-0-9742218-0-9(5)); audio compact disk 39.95 (978-0-9742218-1-6(3)) Ctr New Psych.
A Natural Process for Opening the Heart authored by Dr. Doris Jeanette, a licensed Philadelphia psychologist. They are available as CD's or audiotapes. Unconditionally guaranteed, they can provide comfort through the holidays. A Natural Process for Opening the Heart offers guidance toward a more rewarding inner life with the self as well as with others. These tapes help each person find, access and use their own inner emotional, physical and spiritual strengths. Chockfull of new ways for reducing depression and anxiety attacks, they explain how to give up guilt and self-pity and free one's spirit for more love.Description of: A Natural Process for Opening the Heart:3 audiocassettes guide the listener toward discovering and using their emotional, physical and spiritual strengths. The first tape, Feelings. the source of authentic love. Helps individuals locate and love the emotional self. Tape 2, Fear. the pathway to freedom and joy. Explains the difference between fear and anxiety and offers ways to face both so that energy is freed up for creative living. 3- When You're Hurting... Explains how we repeat painful patterns from the past. Offers comfort and ways to resolve these conditioned responses so that our heart opens to more love.

Natural Procreation Alternatives: For Men with Low Sperm Counts in Childbearing Efforts. Howard W. Gabriel, III. 1987. bk. 14.95 (978-0-936997-14-8(1), T87-12) M & H Enter.
A Primary Factor in Male Infertility Is Low or Borderline Sperm Count. A Seven Step, Thirty-Day Action Program Is Presented to Help Such Men Improve Their Sperm Concentration, Sperm Motility & Sperm Morphology. Contains Research Findings & Case Reviews.

Natural Products in Philippines: A Strategic Reference 2007. Compiled by Icon Group International, Inc. Staff. 2007. ring bd. 195.00 (978-0-497-82391-7(8)) Icon Grp.

Natural Progesterone: The Amazing Hormone. Rachel Lee. Read by Rachel Lee. 1 cass. (Running Time: 1 hr. 30 min.). 1998. (978-0-912986-25-8(5)) Am Media.

Natural Reserve System of the University of California. Hosted by Nancy Pearlman. 1 cass. (Running Time: 28 min.). 10.00 (216) Educ Comm CA.

Natural Rights. unabr. ed. Eric Mack. 1 cass. (Running Time: 44 min.). 10.95 (738) J Norton Pubs.

Natural Science & the Planet Earth. unabr. ed. Jack Sommer. Read by Edwin Newman. (Running Time: 10800 sec.). (Audio Classics: Science & Discovery Ser.). 2006. audio compact disk 25.95 (978-0-7861-6432-5(8)) Pub: Blckstn Audio. Dist(s): NetLibrary CO

Natural Science & the Planet Earth. unabr. ed. Jack Sommer. Read by Edwin Newman. Ed. by Mike Hassell. 2 cass. (Running Time: 2 hrs. 45 min.). Dramatization. (Science & Discovery Ser.). (YA). (gr. 11 up). 1993. 17.95 (978-0-938935-73-5(9), 10408) Knowledge Prod.
Alexander von Humboldt & others sparked a centuries-long debate about natural history & geological destiny by discussing what today we call the environment. Some now believe the earth cannot safely accomodate its growing burdens; others say longer life spans & more people are signs of progress. Are humans destroying the earth or building a better world? Will the future bring despair & destruction or hope & improvement.

Natural Selection. abr. unabr. ed. Dave Freedman. Read by Brian Emerson. 9 cass. (Running Time: 46800 sec.). 2006. 27.95 (978-0-7861-4482-2(3)); audio compact disk 27.95 (978-0-7861-7247-4(9)); audio compact disk 29.95 (978-0-7861-7674-8(1)) Blckstn Audio.

Natural Selection. unabr. ed. Dave Freedman. Read by Brian Emerson. (Running Time: 46800 sec.). 2006. 79.95 (978-0-7861-4660-4(5)); audio compact disk 99.00 (978-0-7861-6749-4(1)) Blckstn Audio.

Natural Self Confidence. 1 cass. 12.95 (978-1-884305-61-0(X)) Changeworks.
A beautiful inspiring tape that offers a natural setting where you can experience the depths of confidence within your unconscious mind.

Natural Self-Healing: Classic. Eldon Taylor. Read by Eldon Taylor. Ed. by Leslie Brice. 1 cass. (Running Time: 1 hr.). 1992. 16.95 (978-1-56705-061-5(1)) Gateways Inst.
Self improvement.

Natural Self-Healing: Easy. Eldon Taylor. Read by Eldon Taylor. Ed. by Leslie Brice. 1 cass. (Running Time: 1 hr.). 1992. 16.95 (978-1-56705-062-2(X)) Gateways Inst.

Natural Self-Healing: Harmonies. Eldon Taylor. Read by Eldon Taylor. Ed. by Leslie Brice. 1 cass. (Running Time: 1 hr.). 1992. 16.95 (978-1-56705-063-9(8)) Gateways Inst.

Natural Self-Healing: Ocean. Eldon Taylor. Read by Eldon Taylor. Ed. by Leslie Brice. 1 cass. (Running Time: 1 hr.). 1992. 16.95 (978-1-56705-064-6(6)) Gateways Inst.

Natural Self-Healing: Stream. Eldon Taylor. Read by Eldon Taylor. Ed. by Leslie Brice. 1 cass. (Running Time: 1 hr.). 1992. 16.95 (978-1-56705-065-3(4)) Gateways Inst.

Natural Selling Concepts: How to Be Your Best, Tough Sales Questions Answered by Carl Bromer. Interview. 4 CDs. (Running Time: 4 hrs.). 2004. audio compact disk 59.95 (978-0-9745736-2-5(0)) B-Elite Pubng.

Natural Shame, Sexuality & Spirituality. John Bradshaw. (Running Time: 16200 sec.). 2008. audio compact disk 120.00 (978-1-57388-187-6(2)) J B Media.

Natural Suspect. unabr. ed. William Bernhardt. 5 cass. (Running Time: 7 hrs. 30 mins.). 2002. 48.00 (978-0-7366-8751-5(3)) Books on Tape.
When the volatile tycoon Arthur Hightower decides to disinherit his spoiled children and cheating wife, he makes the biggest mistake of his life. He turns up on Thanksgiving Day, clubbed to death and stuffed in a meat locker, and his wife Julia stands charged with murdering him for his millions. The sensational New York trial galvanizes a curious cast of suspects: a small-time lawyer about to hit the big-time, an assistant D.A. who keeps a huge pet rabbit, a wannabe reporter sitting on a scoop that could get him killed, and a mystery woman everyone seems to know. Who is the murderer and who wrote each chapter.

Natural Tranquilizers. D.A. Tubesing. 1 cass. (Running Time: 59 min.). (Stressbreaks Ser.: No. 2). 11.95 (978-0-938586-85-2(8), NT) Whole Person.
Most of us occasionally reach for a tranquilizer - alcohol, medication, cigarettes - when we're uptight or overwrought. The six brief relaxation routines on this unusual tape provide a healthy substitute. Halpern sounds in the background. Clear the Deck sweeps away the mental clutter that causes tension. Body Scan takes a tour of the body, seeking & releasing tension. 99 Countdown prepares the listener for sleep by evoking a deep relaxation response. Calm Down sends a gift of peace through positive phrases. Soothing colors looses the "knots" that bind, so the listener can relax. Breathe Ten turns simple deep breathing into an effective exercise to use anywhere.

Natural Vision. unabr. ed. Jack Heggle. 1 cass. (Running Time: 6 hrs.). 1998. 79.95 (978-1-884605-10-9(9)) Genesis II.
Twelve lessons help to improve vision naturally. Includes kit (eye patch, eye chart and booklet).

Natural Vision Improvement Kit. Meir Schneider. 2 CDs. (Running Time: 2 hrs. 30 mins.). 2006. stu. ed. 26.95 (978-1-59179-256-7(8), W905D) Sounds True.

Naturalism & the American Novel. unabr. ed. Erskine Caldwell. 1 cass. (Running Time: 24 min.). 1953. 11.95 (23054) J Norton Pubs.
The author of God's Little Acre & Tobacco Road reacts to being catalogued as a member of the naturalistic school of writing.

Naturalist. unabr. collector's ed. Edward O. Wilson. Read by Michael Prichard. 9 cass. (Running Time: 13 hrs. 30 mins.). 1995. 72.00 (978-0-7366-3136-5(4), 3811) Books on Tape.
Edward O. Wilson loves ants. And he knows more about them than any man alive. How does he explain this? "Most children have a bug period," he says. "I never grew out of mine." In all other respects, he grew up & became a professor at Harvard & a winner of two Pulitzer prizes for his writings on ants & on human nature. He founded the controversial field of sociobiology, the study of how social behavior in animals has evolved. Wilson says his "brilliant enemies" have only encouraged him & he shows how in this gracious, entertaining autobiography.

Naturalists. abr. ed. Terry Tempest Williams et al. 1 cass. (Running Time: 1 hr. 12 min.). 1999. 11.95 (978-1-57453-140-4(9)) Audio Lit.
Collection of nine audio essays by naturalists that explores the diversity, beauty & fragility of our planet.

Nature see Ralph Waldo Emerson: Poems and Essays

Nature & Defense of Private Property. Read by James D. Gwartney. 1 cass. 3.00 (134) ISI Books.

Nature Baby Vol, 1: Water Baby. 1 cass. (Running Time: 35 min.). (J). 4.78 (KID 72952) NewSound.

Nature Baby Vol.1: Water Baby. 1 CD. (Running Time: 35 min.). (J). audio compact disk 7.98 (KID 72952) NewSound.

Nature, Depth & Beauty of Death. J. Krishnamurti. 1 cass. (Running Time: 1 hr. 15min.). (Brockwood Park Talks 1984 Ser.: No. 4). 8.50 (ABT844) Krishnamurti.
Is there time in the very action of thought? Beauty is truth as love is truth. Is beauty when the observer is not? Death means you hold on to nothing.

Nature Girl. abr. ed. Carl Hiaasen. Read by Jane Curtin. 5 CDs. (Running Time: 18000 sec.). (ENG.). 2007. audio compact disk 14.99 (978-0-7393-5868-9(5), Random AudioBks) Pub: Random Audio Pubg. Dist(s): Random

Nature Girl. unabr. ed. Carl Hiaasen. 9 cass. (Running Time: 13 hrs.). 2006. 81.00 (978-1-4159-3474-6(6)); audio compact disk 84.15 (978-1-4159-3475-3(4)) Pub: Books on Tape. Dist(s): NetLibrary CO

Nature Heals from Within. Humbart Smokey Santillo. 1 cass. (Running Time: 60 mins.). 1995. cass. & audio compact disk 8.95 (978-0-934252-66-9(1)) Hohm Pr.
Provides all the inspiration you need to take the next step in improving your life & health through nutrition.

Nature Is the Center of the Mandala. unabr. ed. Terence McKenna. 1 cass. 1987. 9.00 (978-1-56964-811-7(5), A0173-87) Sound Photosyn.
Our winged hearts, accelerated, beating around the generative bush.

Nature, Magic & Community. Malidoma P. Some. Read by Malidoma P. Some. Ed. by Richard Chelew. 1 cass. (Running Time: 1 hr. 30 min.). (Wisdom of Africa Ser.). 1993. 10.95 (978-1-880155-09-7(5), OTA9302) Oral Trad Arch.
Malidoma Some, PhD, an initiated Dagara tribesman & graduate of the Sorbonne & Brandeis University, entertains, dazzles & confounds as he eloquently describes birth, death, love & marriage in the Dagara village, where every aspect of life is inseparable with community, nature & what we might call magic. Malidoma uniquely bridges two cultures, the Western academic tradition & the ancient wisdom of Africa.

Nature Meditation: Ambient Music for Quiet Times. 1 cass. (Running Time: 1 hr.). 1992. 9.95 (978-1-55961-167-1(7)) Relaxtn Co.

Nature Notes For 1906. 2006. 22.95 (978-0-7861-4439-6(4)); audio compact disk 27.00 (978-0-7861-7346-4(7)) Blckstn Audio.

Nature Notes for 1906. unabr. ed. Edith Holden. Read by Vanessa Benjamin. 2006. 19.95 (978-0-7861-7721-9(7)) Blckstn Audio.

Nature Nuts. Mary Miche. 1 cass. (Running Time: 1 hr. 30 min.). (J). (ps-6). 1990. 11.50 (978-1-883505-07-3(0)) Song Trek Music.
Selection of 18 educational songs about the environment, ecology & recycling garbage for children.

Nature of a Religious Spirit. Rick Joyner. 1 cass. (Running Time: 1 hr. 30 min.). (Combating the Religious Spirit Ser.: Vol. 1). 2000. 5.00 (RJ12-001) Morning NC.
"The Nature of a Religious Spirit," "Combating the Spirit of Jezebel" & "Warning Signs of a Religious Spirit." Exposing a deadly enemy of Christianity, this series assaults one of the enemy's most powerful strongholds.

Nature of Alexander. unabr. ed. Mary Renault. Read by Peter MacDonald. 7 cass. (Running Time: 10 hrs. 30 min.). 1983. 56.00 (978-0-7366-0522-9(3), 1496) Books on Tape.
As an eager pupil of Aristotle, Alexander was imbued with a great love of literature & a keen interest in other countries. Between the ages of 20 when he suceeded his murdered father & 33 when he died, Alexander became master of almost all the then-known world & spread Greek culture to an extent which lasted for centuries.

Nature of Alexander. unabr. ed. Mary Renault. Narrated by Nelson Runger. 6 cass. (Running Time: 9 hrs. 30 mins.). 1988. 51.00 (978-1-55690-370-0(7), 88540E7) Recorded Bks.
An account of the life of Alexander the Great.

Nature of Anxiety. unabr. ed. Kurt Goldstein. 1 cass. (Running Time: 18 min.). 10.95 (29022) J Norton Pubs.
A lecture on the fundamental nature of anxiety, the relation of fear to anxiety & the importance of the catastrophic reaction.

Nature of Consciousness. 4 cass. (Running Time: 6 hrs.). 45.00 (311) MEA A Watts Cass.

Nature of Devotion. unabr. ed. Perf. by Eknath Easwaran. 1 cass. (Running Time: 1 hr.). 1990. 7.95 (978-1-58638-580-4(1)) Nilgiri Pr.

Nature of Drug Dependency & Addiction to the Addicted. 1 cass. (Running Time: 1 hr.). (Introduction to Chemical Dependency Ser.). 1974. 8.95 (1471G) Hazelden.

Nature of Evil. unabr. ed. Nathaniel Branden. 1 cass. (Running Time: 1 hr. 2 min.). (Basic Principles of Objectivism Ser.). 11.95 (579) J Norton Pubs.
Covers why evil is impotent; what makes the victory of evil possible; & the sanction of the victim.

Nature of Evil, Nos. 31, 32 & 33. Carl Faber. 3 cass. (Running Time: 3 hrs. 30 min.). 1985. 28.50 (978-0-918026-44-6(X), SR 64-284) Perseus Pr.

Nature of Friendship. Nathaniel Branden. 1 CD. (Running Time: 44 mins.). 2005. audio compact disk 10.95 (978-1-57970-248-9(1), AF0837D, Audio-For) J Norton Pubs.
A discussion of friendship and other relationships, the differentiation between friends and acquaintances, and the involvement of intimacy and sex with friends.

Nature of Gnostic Knowledge: What do the Knowers Know? Stephan Hoeller. 1 cass. (Running Time: 1 hr. 30 min.). 1999. 11.00 (40026) Big Sur Tapes.
1991 Los Angeles.

Nature of Human Intelligence. Edwin Locke. 2 cass. (Running Time: 3 hrs.). 1991. 24.95 (978-1-56114-164-7(X), IL07D) Second Renaissance.

Nature of Human Nature. unabr. ed. Ashley Montagu. 1 cass. (Running Time: 48 min.). 10.95 (35119) J Norton Pubs.
An examination & criticism of the traditional conceptions of human nature & the presentation of modem social & biological science.

Nature of Human Nature CD. Ashley M. F. Montagu. 1 CD. (Running Time: 48 mins.). 2006. audio compact disk 12.95 (978-1-57970-363-9(1), C35119D, Audio-For) J Norton Pubs.
An examination of the traditions concerning the nature of human nature, a criticism of the traditional conceptions of human nature, and the presentation of a point of view designed to meed the requirements of social and biological science.

Nature of Humanness. unabr. ed. Wilson Van Dusen. 1 cass. (Running Time: 1 hr. 30 min.). 1969. 11.00 (05402) Big Sur Tapes.
A discussion about the personal humanness to archetypal drama. Is it possible for an actor to examine & understand his role, the play & the whole theater, find balance & come into accord with what is? He movingly relates his own role in the human drama to his own experiences of satori.

Nature of Hurt. J. Krishnamurti. 1 cass. (Running Time: 1 hr.). (Krishnamurti with Dr. Allan W. Anderson Ser.: No. 11). 8.50 (APA7411) Krishnamurti.
These 1974 dialogues cover the entire spectrum of Krishnamurti's teaching in a series highly regarded for its depth of inquiry into each particular subject.

Nature of Illusion. Swami Amar Jyoti. 1 cass. (Running Time: 1 hr. 30 min.). 1989. 9.95 (R-94) Truth Consciousness.
Why we create all these illusions. Nearness to the Lord; what causes distance & separation.

Nature of Illusion: A Weekend Inquiry with Adyashanti. Featuring Adyashanti. (ENG.). 2007. audio compact disk 65.00 (978-1-933986-26-5(3)) Open Gate Pub.

Nature of Intelligence. unabr. ed. Nathaniel Branden. 1 cass. (Running Time: 45 min.). 10.95 (824) J Norton Pubs.
A discussion about how most people sabotage their own personal development by not operating at their full abstract capacity & function with only part of their intelligence.

Nature of Jade. unabr. ed. Deb Caletti. Read by Julia Whelan. (Running Time: 8 hrs.). 2010. 39.97 (978-1-4233-9656-7(1), 9781423396567, Brlnc Audio MP3 Lib); 19.99 (978-1-4233-9655-0(3), 9781423396550, Brilliance MP3); 39.97 (978-1-4233-9658-1(8), 9781423396581, BADLE); 19.99 (978-1-4233-9657-4(X), 9781423396574, BAD); audio compact disk 19.99 (978-1-4233-9653-6(7), 9781423396536, Bril Audio CD Unabri) Brilliance Audio.

Nature of Jade. unabr. ed. Deb Caletti. Read by Julia Whelan. (Running Time: 9 hrs.). (YA). 2010. audio compact disk 54.97 (978-1-4233-9654-3(5), 9781423396543, BriAudCD Unabrid) Brilliance Audio.

Nature of Jesus, Pt. 1. unabr. ed. Read by Gayle D. Erwin. 1 cass. (Running Time: 1 hr.). 1992. 4.95 (978-1-56599-501-7(5), C-1) Yahshua Pub.
The Gospels.

Nature of Jesus, Pt. 2. unabr. ed. Read by Gayle D. Erwin. 1 cass. (Running Time: 1 hr.). 1992. 4.95 (978-1-56599-502-4(3), C-2) Yahshua Pub.

Nature of Jesus, Pt. 3. unabr. ed. Read by Gayle D. Erwin. 1 cass. (Running Time: 1 hr.). 1992. 4.95 (978-1-56599-503-1(1), C-3) Yahshua Pub.
Philippians 2.

Nature of Jesus, Pt. 4. unabr. ed. Read by Gayle D. Erwin. 1 cass. (Running Time: 1 hr.). 1992. 4.95 (978-1-56599-504-8(X), C-4) Yahshua Pub.

Nature of Justice. Read by Murray Newton Rothbard & Robert LeFevre. (Running Time: 1 hr. 30 min.). (Long Beach City College Ser.). 1983. 9.00 (F149) Freeland Pr.
Each speaker presents a view-point backed by years of experience & research. Panel discussion.

Nature of Liberty. unabr. ed. Salvador De Madariaga. 1 cass. (Running Time: 20 min.). 10.95 (25008) J Norton Pubs.
A free man is identified as that person who knows how to retain the power to choose his part in life & who lives in a society that does not prevent him from actually exercising that power.

Nature of Liberty CD. Salvador De Madariaga. 1 CD. (Running Time: 20 mins.). (Sound Seminars Ser.). 2006. audio compact disk 12.95 (978-1-57970-404-9(2), C25008D, Audio-For) J Norton Pubs.

Nature of Love. unabr. ed. Nathaniel Branden. 1 cass. (Running Time: 1 hr. 19 min.). 11.95 (602) J Norton Pubs.
Covers the attacks on romantic love by psychologists; the crisis in marriage; psychological visibility; & love as self-discovery.

Nature of Man & the Nature of Social Justice. Read by James Schall. 1 cass. (Running Time: 1 hr.). 3.00 (132) ISI Books.

Nature of Marxism. John Ridpath. 4 cass. (Running Time: 4 hrs.). 1994. 39.95 (978-1-56114-271-2(9), CR12D) Second Renaissance.
Analysis of the significance of Marxism.

Nature of Monsters. unabr. ed. Clare Clark. Read by Julia Barrie. 14 CDs. (Running Time: 15 hrs.). 2007. audio compact disk 123.75 (978-1-4281-4257-2(6)) Recorded Bks.

Nature of Monsters. unabr. ed. Clare Clark. Read by Julia Barrie. 11 cass. (Running Time: 15 hrs.). 2007. 92.75 (978-1-84632-944-9(2), Clipper Audio) Recorded Bks.

Nature of Music. 6 cass. (Running Time: 6 hrs.). 65.00 (C051SB090, HarperThor); 10.95 ea. (HarperThor) HarpC GBR.

Nature of Music. Maureen McCarthy Draper. 1 CD. (Running Time: 50 mins. 11 sec.). audio compact disk (978-1-891319-59-4(0)); audio compact disk (978-1-891319-57-0(4)) Spring Hill CO.

Nature of Music. unabr. ed. Karl Signell. 6 cass. (Running Time: 6 hrs.). 1993. pap. bk. 44.50 (978-0-88432-643-4(8), S11300) J Norton Pubs.
A new multicultural, interdisciplinary approach to music on six cassettes featuring lively discussion & 168 musical examples. Twelve award-winning audio programs, originally broadcast on National Public Radio & produced by Karl Signell & Deborah Jane Lamberton. Typical Guests: Ethnomusicologists McAllester, Roseman, Feld, Nattlez, scholars Deutsch, Gardner, Barzun; musicians Menuhin, Zappa, Balfa. Includes listener's guide.

Nature of Poetry. unabr. ed. Frank C. Baxter. 1 cass. (Running Time: 1 hr.). 10.95 (SAC 7021) Spoken Arts.
Baxter, a teacher of our day, discusses his perspective on poetry.

Nature of Reality. unabr. ed. Huston Smith. 1 cass. (Running Time: 1 hr. 30 min.). 1979. 11.00 (04204) Big Sur Tapes.

Nature of Rights. Ayn Rand. 1 cass. (Running Time: 25 min.). 1993. 12.95 (978-1-56114-340-5(5), AR51C) Second Renaissance.

Nature of Sacred Space. Read by Robert Moore. 1 cass. (Running Time: 1 hr. 30 min.). 1984. 9.95 (978-0-7822-0170-3(9), 150) C G Jung IL.

Nature of Sexual Interaction. Nathaniel Branden. 1 cass. (Running Time: 1 hr. 3 min.). 11.95 (614) J Norton Pubs.
The importance of understanding oneself sexually.

Nature of Shame. John Bradshaw. (Running Time: 7200 sec.). 2008. audio compact disk 85.00 (978-1-57388-165-4(1)) J B Media.

Nature of the Beast. unabr. ed. Frances Fyfield. Read by Rula Lenska. 10 CDs. (Running Time: 15 hrs.). 2002. audio compact disk 94.95 (978-0-7540-5510-5(8)) AudioGO.

Nature of the Beast. unabr. ed. Frances Fyfield. Read by Rula Lenska. 8 cass. (Running Time: 12 hrs.). 2002. 69.95 (978-0-7540-0826-2(6), CAB 2248) Pub: Chivers Pr GBR. Dist(s): AudioGO

Nature of the Brain That Lives Religiously. J. Krishnamurti. 1 cass. (Running Time: 1 hr. 15 min.). (Brockwood Park Talks, 1985 Ser.: No. 4). 8.50 (ABT854) Krishnamurti.
Subjects examined: Do we realize that we are the world & the world is us? Can we together understand the world, ourselves & our relationship to the world? Can we inquire together into why we want continuity & what is ending? How are time & thought involved in this process? And what is death? If we realize the immense significance of living with that ending - that is called death in our daily life - there is real transformation, real mutation, even in the brain cells. Can the brain ever understand that which is limitless? Can the brain be quiet? Is there a mind which is not the brain to understand that immensity.

Nature of the Church: Logos Feburary 15, 1998. Ben Young. 1998. 4.95 (978-0-7417-6073-9(8), B0073) Win Walk.

Nature of the Creative Process. Jon Klimo. 3 cass. (Running Time: 3 hrs.). 27.00 (A0781-90) Sound Photosyn.
Doing what he's talking about by talking about what he's doing.

Nature of the Father, Pt. 1. unabr. ed. Read by Gayle D. Erwin. 1 cass. (Running Time: 1 hr.). 1992. 4.95 (978-1-56599-508-6(2), C-8) Yahshua Pub.

Nature of the Father, Pt. 2. unabr. ed. Read by Gayle D. Erwin. 1 cass. (Running Time: 1 hr.). 1992. 4.95 (978-1-56599-509-3(0), C-9) Yahshua Pub.

Nature of the Flesh, Pt. 1. Lee Lefebre. 1 cass. (Running Time: 1 hr. 03 min.). (GraceLife Conference Ser.: Vol. 2). 1993. 6.00 (978-1-57838-107-4(X)) CrossLife Express.
Christian living.

Nature of the Flesh, Pt. 1. Read by Lee Lefebre. 1 cass. (Running Time: 1 hr. 03 min.). (Exchanged Life Conference Ser.: Vol. 2). 1993. 6.00 (978-1-57838-006-0(5)) CrossLife Express.

Nature of the Flesh, Pt. 2. Lee Lefebre. 1 cass. (Running Time: 46 min.). (GraceLife Conference Ser.: Vol. 3). 1993. 6.00 (978-1-57838-108-1(8)) CrossLife Express.

Nature of the Flesh, Pt. 2. Read by Lee Lefebre. 1 cass. (Running Time: 46 min.). (Exchanged Life Conference Ser.: Vol. 3). 1993. 6.00 (978-1-57838-007-7(3)) CrossLife Express.

Nature of the Minister's Stress: The Minister's Management of Stress. Wayne Oates. 1986. 10.80 (0503) Assn Prof Chaplains.

Nature of the Sacred. Read by Thomas Molnar. 1 cass. (Running Time: 47 min.). 3.00 (138) ISI Books.

Nature of the Spiritual. Don Nori. 1 cass. (Running Time: 46 min.). 1992. 7.00 (978-0-938612-45-2(X)) Destiny Image Pubs.

Nature of Utopianism. Read by Thomas Molnar. 1 cass. 3.00 (128) ISI Books.

Nature of Water & Air. Regina McBride. Narrated by Terry Donnelly. 9 cass. (Running Time: 12 hrs. 15 mins.). 2001. 81.00 (978-1-4025-1000-7(4), 96958) Recorded Bks.
A moody coming-of-age tale filled with Irish folklore. From a rundown estate on the sea-sprayed Western coast of Ireland, young Clodagh begins a harsh journey into adulthood that will take her from the grip of tragedy into the arms of love.

Nature of Water & Air. Regina McBride. 7 cass. (Running Time: 12 hrs. 15 mins.). 2004. 29.99 (978-1-4025-0863-9(8), 00994) Recorded Bks.

Nature Projects on File. Diagram Group. (YA). (gr. 4-9). 2002. audio compact disk 149.95 (978-0-8160-4972-1(6)) Facts On File.

Nature Recordings: Babbling Brook. Jordan Peters. (Running Time: 1 hr.). 2002. audio compact disk 15.99 (978-1-904972-48-8(9)) Global Jrny GBR GBR.

Nature Recordings: Birdsong. Jordan Peters. (Running Time: 1 hr.). 2002. audio compact disk 15.99 (978-1-904972-47-1(0)) Global Jrny GBR GBR.

Nature Recordings: Rainforest. Jordan Peters. (Running Time: 1 hr.). 2002. audio compact disk 15.99 (978-1-904972-24-2(1)) Global Jrny GBR GBR.

Nature Recordings: the Sea. Jordan Pet[illegible] Running Time: 1 hr.). 2002. audio compact disk 15.99 (978-1-9049[illegible]4(9)) Global Jrny GBR GBR.

Nature Recordings: Thunderstorm. Jorda[illegible]eters. (Running Time: 1 hr.). 2002. audio compact disk 15.99 (978-1-904972-34-1(9)) Global Jrny GBR GBR.

Nature Renewing Naturally: Thunder, Rain, & Birds; Rebalancing, Rejuvenating, & Rejoicing. Created by Thomas W. Gustin. 1 CD. (Running Time: 1 hr, 19 mins, 00 secs). 2004. audio compact disk 8.00 (978-0-9761848-6-7(9), EC6) Gustech.
Features 2 extremely high quality recordings made 17 Jun 04 & 20 Mar 04 here at the Emerald Cave. As with all Emerald Cave Nature recordings, this CD is Nature as "heard" with no loops, no mixing, no enhancements. When surrounded by the thunder, rain & birds, you will rekindle the magic in your life with this natural escape that rebalances, rejuvenates, & rejoices all of life.

Nature Smarts by Dancing Beetle. Eugene Ely et al. 1 cass. (Running Time: 1 hr. 14 min.). (J). 1994. 10.00 Erthviibz.
Nature's amazing facts & ecology come together when Ms. Mud Dauber & the spunky musical humans read & sing with Dancing Beetle.

Nature Sounds. 1 cass. (Running Time: 1 hr.). (Lullaby Ser.). (J). (TWIN 160); audio compact disk (TWIN 160) NewSound.

Nature Sounds. Twin Sisters Productions Staff. 1 CD. (Running Time: 1 hr.). (Growing Minds with Music Ser.). (J). 1998. audio compact disk 12.99 (978-1-57583-062-9(0)) Twin Sisters.
Original musical arrangements are coupled with the gentle waves of ocean, the soft sounds of rain & the authentic sounds of a mother's heartbeat. Relaxing & softly pleasing to the ear.

Nature Sounds. Twin Sisters Productions Staff. 1 cass. (Running Time: 1 hr.). (Growing Minds with Music Ser.). (J). 1998. 8.99 (978-1-57583-063-6(9)) Twin Sisters.
Original musical arrangements are coupled with the gentle waves of ocean, the soft sounds of rain, & the authentic sounds of a mother's heartbeat. Relaxing & softly pleasing to the ear.

Nature's Chant. 1 CD. (Running Time: 1 hr.). 1994. audio compact disk 15.95 (2626, Creativ Pub) Quayside.
Featuring the voices of the renowned Oratorio Singers from St. Paul, Minnesota, these mystic chants blend with pure sounds of nature - songbird melodies, breezy wind & light rain.

Nature's Chant. 1 cass. (Running Time: 1 hr.). 1994. 9.95 (2625, NrthWrd Bks) TandN Child.

Nature's Classroom. Hosted by Nancy Pearlman. 1 cass. (Running Time: 28 min.). 10.00 (236) Educ Comm CA.

Nature's Fury. Radio Spirits Publishing Staff. Read by William Conrad. 9 CDs. (Running Time: 9 hrs.). 2006. bk. 39.98 (978-1-57019-813-7(6), OTR 40122) Pub: Radio Spirits. Dist(s): AudioGO

Nature's Game of Hide & Seek. Hosted by Nancy Pearlman. 1 cass. (Running Time: 29 min.). 10.00 (225) Educ Comm CA.

Nature's Heartland. Boon, Groe and Seeger. 2003. audio compact disk 69.95 (978-0-9727157-0-6(3)) NaturesPub.

Nature's Lullabyes Series. Bernie Krause. 1 cass. (Running Time: 1 hr.). (J). 1994. 17.95 (2665, NrthWrd Bks) TandN Child.
Includes Starry Sea, Sleepytime Showers & Twilight Brook.

Nature's Noel. 1 CD. (Running Time: 1 hr.). 1994. audio compact disk 15.95 (2324, Creativ Pub) Quayside.
Bruce Kumow - musician, composer & master of the harp, keyboard & harmonica - beautiful holiday music. Nature's creatures add their festive voices.

Nature's Noel. 1 cass. (Running Time: 1 hr.). 1994. 9.95 (2322, NrthWrd Bks) TandN Child.
Bruce Kumow - musician, composer, & master of the harp, keyboard, & harmonica - beautiful holiday music. Nature's creatures add their festive voices.

Nature's Quest. (Running Time: 60 mins.). 2002. audio compact disk 15.99 (978-1-904972-67-9(5)) Global Jrny GBR GBR.

NatureScapes: Naturescapes. unabr. ed. Twin Sisters Productions. Read by Twin Sisters. (YA). 2007. 44.99 (978-1-60252-771-3(7)) Find a World.

Naufrages. unabr. ed. Dan Dastier. Read by Sebastian Lazennec. 2007. 69.99 (978-2-35569-053-2(7)) Find a World.

Naufragios: Advanced Level. de Vaca Cabeza. (Leer y Aprender Ser.). (SPA.). pap. bk. 20.95 (978-88-7754-437-7(6), CID4376) Pub: Cideb ITA. Dist(s): Distribks Inc

Naufragos. Nunez. audio compact disk 12.95 (978-0-8219-3753-2(7)) EMC-Paradigm.

Naughty Marietta. Perf. by Nelson Eddy & Jeanette MacDonald. Hosted by Cecil B. DeMille. 1 cass. (Running Time: 1 hr.). (Old Time Radio Classic Singles Ser.). 4.95 (NM125) Audio File.
A classic musical with great performances.

Naughty Marietta. Perf. by Nelson Eddy & Jeanette MacDonald. 1 cass. (Running Time: 1 hr.). 1955. 7.95 (DD-8435) Natl Recrd Co.
Jeanette, a French countess, is being forced to marry a man she does not love & so she escapes to New Orleans on a ship loaded with women that have been sent to America with a wish to get married.

Naughty Nautical Neighbors, Vol. 2. Annie Auerbach. Read by Denis Lawrence. (Running Time: 28 mins.). (J). (gr. 2-5). 2004. pap. bk. 17.00 (978-0-8072-1987-4(8), Listening Lib) Random Audio Pubg.

***Naughty Neighbor.** unabr. ed. Janet Evanovich. Read by C. J. Critt. (ENG.). 2008. (978-0-06-162956-3(1)); (978-0-06-162957-0(X)) HarperCollins Pubs.

Naughty Neighbor. unabr. ed. Janet Evanovich. Read by C. J. Critt. (Running Time: 18000 sec.). 2008. audio compact disk 14.95 (978-0-06-073712-2(3), Harper Audio) HarperCollins Pubs.

Naughty Songs for Boys & Girls. Barry Louis Polisar. 1 CD. (Running Time: 0 hr. 45 mins. 0 sec.). (ENG.). (J). (gr. k-6). 1978. audio compact disk 14.95 (978-0-938663-45-4(3), 4878 CD) Pub: Rainbow Morn. Dist(s): IPG Chicago

Naughty Songs for Boys & Girls. Barry Louis Polisar. Perf. by Barry Louis Polisar. 1 cass. (Running Time: 1 hr.). (J). 1993. 9.95 (978-0-9615696-5-5(4), 4878 Cass) Pub: Rainbow Morn. Dist(s): IPG Chicago

Nautical Chart. unabr. ed. Arturo Pérez-Reverte. Tr. by Margaret Sayers Peden. Narrated by George Guidall. 13 cass. (Running Time: 18 hrs.). 2002. 101.00 (978-1-4025-1279-7(1), 96969) Recorded Bks.
At a maritime auction in Barcelona, Merchant Marine officer Manuel Coy sees an intense bidding war erupt over a seemingly innocuous 18th-century atlas. The auction winner is the beautiful Tanger Soto, who is obsessed with a Jesuit ship sunk by pirates in the 17th century. Joining forces, Tanger and Manuel hit the seas in search of Dei Gloria and its precious, yet unidentified, cargo. Their quest sends them not only into dangerous waters, but also into the perilous recesses of the human heart.

Nauvoo Brass Bands. Mormon Youth Chorus and Symphony. 1 cass. (Running Time: 1 hr.). 9.95 (10001212); audio compact disk 14.95 (2800853) Covenant Comms.
Experience the music that inspired Joseph & the early Saints.

Navajo: Songs from Canyon de Chelly Edition. unabr. ed. 1 cass. (Running Time: 1 hr.). 11.95 (C11154) J Norton Pubs.

Navajo, Breakthrough: An Introductory Course. unabr. ed. Alan Wilson. 2 cass. (Running Time: 3 hrs.). 1992. pap. bk. 49.00 (978-0-88432-447-8(8), AFNV10) J Norton Pubs.
Parts of the recording were done in the field rather than in a studio. Suitable for those who wish to learn to read & write the language.

Navajo Healing in Life Crisis. unabr. ed. Donald Sandner. 1 cass. (Running Time: 1 hr. 30 min.). 1973. 11.00 (10201) Big Sur Tapes.
The Navajos consider physical or mental distress to result from the individual's disharmony with the cosmos & they have developed a rich tradition of artistic ritual for healing. The medicine man leads the patient through various rites of purification & invocation & finally to identification with the beauty of the universe.

Navajo Laughter: The Navajo Way. unabr. ed. Alan Wilson. 1 cass. (Running Time: 1 hr. 20 min.). (J). (gr. 10-12). 1992. pap. bk. 39.00 (978-0-88432-452-2(4), AFNV30) J Norton Pubs.
Foreign Language Instruction. Humorous stories of the Navajo. Presented in Navajo with an English translation & cultural notes in English.

Navajo Nights. unabr. ed. 1 cass. (Running Time: 50 min.). 12.95 (C11314) J Norton Pubs.
Compilation of Navajo healing stories.

Navajo Place Names CD & Book: An Observer's Guide. Alan Wilson. 1 CD. (Running Time: 54 mins.). (NAV.). 2005. audio compact disk 19.95 (978-1-57970-240-3(6), AFNV50D) J Norton Pubs.

Navajo Songs. Contrib. by Laura Boulton et al. 1 cass. (Running Time: 47 min.). 1992. (0-9307-404030-9307-40403-2-4); audio compact disk (0-9307-40403-2-4) Smithsonian Folkways.
Lifestyles, philosophies & traditions of the Navajo nation are represented by songs for herding, planting, harvesting, hunting, blessing hogans & soothing children. 1933 & 1940 field recordings from settlements in New Mexico & Arizona.

Navajo Songs, Traditional. unabr. ed. 1 cass. (Running Time: 47 min.). 11.95 (C11153) J Norton Pubs.

Navajo Speak: Intermediate. unabr. ed. Alan Wilson. 2 cass. (Running Time: 2 hrs.). (YA). (gr. 10-12). 1992. pap. bk. 49.00 (978-0-88432-451-5(6), AFNV20) J Norton Pubs.
Parts of the recording were done in the field rather than in a studio. Suitable for those who wish to learn to read & write the language.

Navajo Symbols of Healing. Donald Sander. 1 cass. 7.00 (A0113-86) Sound Photosyn.
Fron International Conference Study of Shamanism 1986, with slides.

Naval Institute Guide to Combat Fleets of the World 2002-2003: Their Ships, Aircraft, & Systems. A. D. Baker, III. 2002. audio compact disk 159.95 (978-1-55750-207-0(2)) Naval Inst Pr.

Naval Institute Guide to Combat Fleets of the World, 2004-2006: Their Ships, Aircraft, & Systems. Eric Wertheim. 2005. audio compact disk 200.00 (978-1-59114-935-4(5)) Naval Inst Pr.

Naval Treaty see Memoirs of Sherlock Holmes

Naval Treaty. unabr. ed. Arthur Conan Doyle. Read by Walter Covell. 1 cass. (Running Time: 1 hr. 22 min.). 1982. 7.95 (N-72) Jimcin Record.
Stolen plans endanger England. It's up to Sherlock Holmes to find them.

Navegamos. Alma Flor Ada. 1 cass. (Running Time: 25 min.). (SPA.). (J). 1987. pap. bk. 3.28 (978-0-201-16874-7(X)) Pearson ESL.
Includes script.

Navegando 1A: Audio CD Program. James F. Funston & Alejandro Vargas Bonilla. (Middle School Program Ser.). (SPA.). 2006. audio compact disk 268.00 (978-0-8219-2816-5(3)) EMC-Paradigm.

Navegando 1A: Audio CD Program Manual. James F. Funston & Alejandro Vargas Bonilla. (Middle School Program Ser.). (SPA.). 2006. audio compact disk (978-0-8219-2817-2(1)) EMC-Paradigm.

Navegando 1A: Listening Activities. James F. Funston & Alejandro Vargas Bonilla. (Middle School Program Ser.). (SPA.). 2006. audio compact disk 128.00 (978-0-8219-2808-0(2)) EMC-Paradigm.

Navegando 1A: Test Generator CD, IBM/Mac. James F. Funston & Alejandro Vargas Bonilla. (Middle School Program Ser.). (SPA.). 2006. audio compact disk 92.00 (978-0-8219-2814-1(7)) EMC-Paradigm.

Navegando 1A: Testing/Assessment Program. James F. Funston & Alejandro Vargas Bonilla. (Middle School Program Ser.). (SPA.). 2006. audio compact disk 149.00 (978-0-8219-2810-3(4)) EMC-Paradigm.

Navegando 2: Audio CD Program. James F. Funston & Alejandro Vargas Bonilla. (High School Program Ser.). (SPA.). 2006. audio compact disk 278.00 (978-0-8219-2856-1(2)) EMC-Paradigm.

Navegando 2: Audio CD Program Manual. James F. Funston & Alejandro Vargas Bonilla. (High School Program Ser.). (SPA.). 2006. audio compact disk (978-0-8219-2857-8(0)) EMC-Paradigm.

Navegando 2: Listening Activities. James F. Funston & Alejandro Vargas Bonilla. (High School Program Ser.). (SPA.). 2006. audio compact disk 138.00 (978-0-8219-2848-6(1)) EMC-Paradigm.

Navegando 2: Test Generator CD, IBM/Mac. James F. Funston & Alejandro Vargas Bonilla. (High School Program Ser.). (SPA.). 2006. audio compact disk 95.00 (978-0-8219-2854-7(6)) EMC-Paradigm.

Navegando 2: Testing/Assessment Program. James F. Funston & Alejandro Vargas Bonilla. (High School Program Ser.). (SPA.). 2006. audio compact disk 155.00 (978-0-8219-2850-9(3)) EMC-Paradigm.

Navegando 3: Audio CD Program. James F. Funston & Alejandro Vargas Bonilla. (High School Program Ser.). (SPA.). 2006. audio compact disk 288.00 (978-0-8219-2880-6(5)) EMC-Paradigm.

Navegando 3: Audio CD Program Manual. James F. Funston & Alejandro Vargas Bonilla. (High School Program Ser.). (SPA.). 2006. audio compact disk (978-0-8219-2881-3(3)) EMC-Paradigm.

Navegando 3: Listening Activities. James F. Funston & Alejandro Vargas Bonilla. (High School Program Ser.). (SPA.). 2006. audio compact disk 138.00 (978-0-8219-2873-8(2)) EMC-Paradigm.

Navegando 3: Test Generator CD, IBM/Mac. James F. Funston & Alejandro Vargas Bonilla. (High School Program Ser.). (SPA.). 2006. audio compact disk 95.00 (978-0-8219-2879-0(1)) EMC-Paradigm.

Navegando 3: Testing/Assessment Program. James F. Funston & Alejandro Vargas Bonilla. (High School Program Ser.). (SPA.). 2006. audio compact disk 159.00 (978-0-8219-2875-2(9)) EMC-Paradigm.

Navidad Con Vida. unabr. ed. Zondervan Publishing Staff. (SPA.). 1997. 7.99 (978-0-8297-2271-0(8)) Pub: Vida Pubs. Dist(s): Zondervan

Navidad con Vida. unabr. ed. Zondervan Publishing Staff. (SPA.). 1997. audio compact disk 9.99 (978-0-8297-2272-7(6)) Pub: Vida Pubs. Dist(s): Zondervan

Navidades. Contrib. by Lulu Delacre. (SPA.). (J). (ps-3). 1992. 4.95 (978-0-590-60920-3(3)) Pub: Scholastic Inc. Dist(s): HarperCollins Pubs

Navigating Hope: How to Turn Life's Challenges into a Journey of Transformation. Caroline Myss. (Running Time: 2:00:00). 2010. audio compact disk 19.95 (978-1-59179-768-5(3)) Sounds True.

Navigating Life Transitions: When Life Changes Threaten You or Your Relationship. David Grudermeyer & Rebecca Grudermeyer. 2 cass. (Running Time: 3 hrs.). pap. bk. 18.95 (T-52) Willingness Wrks.
Includes handout.

***Navigating the Seven Planes of Consciousness: Advanced Skills.** John Friedlander. (Psychic Psychology Ser.). (ENG.). 2011. audio compact disk 49.95 (978-1-58394-278-9(5)) Pub: North Atlantic. Dist(s): Random

Navigation by Stars. 1 cass. (Running Time: 29 min.). 14.95 (23331) MMI Corp.
Using the constellations to find your way, history of navigation, development of chronometer & more.

Navigator. Clive Cussler & Paul Kemprecos. No. 7. (ENG.). (gr. 8). 2008. audio compact disk 14.95 (978-0-14-314342-0(5), PengAudBks) Penguin Grp USA.

Navigator. unabr. ed. Clive Cussler. Read by Paul Kemprecos. 9 cass. (Running Time: 13 hrs. 30 mins.). (NUMA Files Ser.: No. 7). 2007. 110.00 (978-1-4159-3518-7(1)) Books on Tape.

Navigator. unabr. ed. Clive Cussler & Paul Kemprecos. 12 CDs. (Running Time: 13 hrs. 30 mins.). (NUMA Files Ser.: No. 7). 2007. audio compact disk 110.00 (978-1-4159-3519-4(X)) Books on Tape.

Navigator. unabr. ed. Clive Cussler & Paul Kemprecos. Read by Scott Brick. 12 CDs. (Running Time: 15 hrs.). No. 7. (ENG.). (gr. 8). 2007. audio compact disk 39.95 (978-0-14-314202-7(X), PengAudBks) Penguin Grp USA.

Navigator. unabr. ed. Eoin McNamee. Read by Kirby Heyborne. 7 CDs. (Running Time: 9 hrs.). (Navigator Trilogy: No. 1). (YA). (gr. 5-8). 2006. audio compact disk 55.00 (978-0-7393-4852-9(3)) Pub: Random Audio Pubg. Dist(s): Random

Navigator. unabr. ed. Eoin McNamee. Read by Kirby Heyborne. 7 CDs. (Running Time: 31860 sec.). (Navigator Trilogy: No. 1). (ENG.). (J). (gr. 5-7). 2007. audio compact disk 37.00 (978-0-7393-3887-2(0), Listening Lib) Pub: Random Audio Pubg. Dist(s): Random

Navigators see Poetry & Voice of Marilyn Hacker

Navy Brat. Kimberly Willis Holt. Read by Emily Janice Card. (Piper Reed Ser.: No. 1). (J). 2009. 35.00 (978-1-60775-599-9(8)) Find a World.

Navy Brat. unabr. ed. Kimberly Willis Holt. Read by Emily Janie Card. 2 CDs. (Running Time: 7140 sec.). (Piper Reed Ser.: No. 1). (J). (gr. 3 up). 2007. audio compact disk 22.00 (978-0-7393-5958-7(4), Listening Lib) Pub: Random Audio Pubg. Dist(s): Random

Navy Brat. unabr. ed. Kimberly Willis Holt. Narrated by Emily Janice Card. 2 CDs. (Running Time: 2 hrs.). (Piper Reed Ser.: No. 1). (J). (gr. 3-5). 2007. audio compact disk 24.00 (978-0-7393-6128-3(7)) Pub: Random Audio Pubg. Dist(s): Random

Navy Seals: Blacklight. abr. ed. Mike Murray. 2 cass. (Running Time: 3 hrs.). 2002. 9.95 (978-1-931953-16-0(3)) Listen & Live.
Across the globe, a merciless terrorist known as Conrad is wreaking havoc. After leaving his calling card with a group of murdered students and teachers, he resurfaces to blow an American passenger jet out of the sky. He makes no demands, and cannot be appeased. For his only mission is violent retribution against the United States-with no end in sight.

Navy Seals: Green Solitaire. abr. ed. Mike Murray. 2 cass. (Running Time: 3 hrs.). 2002. 9.95 (978-1-931953-17-7(1)) Listen & Live.
The Blacklight Team is called to arms to rescue a group of international hostages held by a terrorist force that will stop at nothing to achieve their aims.

Navy Seals: Insurrection Red. abr. ed. Mike Murray. 2 cass. (Running Time: 3 hrs.). 2002. 9.95 (978-1-931953-15-3(5)) Listen & Live.

Navy Wife's Log. unabr. ed. Phyllis Thompson Wright. Narrated by Flo Gibson. (Running Time: 7 hrs. 31 mins.). 1999. 24.95 (978-1-55685-464-4(1)) Audio Bk Con.

Naya Nuki: Girl Who Ran. Kenneth Thomasma. 3 cass. (Running Time: 3 hrs.). (J). 1996. 19.95 (978-1-880114-11-7(9)) Grandview.

Nazareno: Vida, Pasion y Muerte de Jesus de Nazaret. abr. ed. Felipe Silva. (Running Time: 7200 sec.). (SPA.). 2007. audio compact disk 16.95 (978-1-933499-06-2(0)) Fonolibro Inc.

Nazca, Land of the Incas. Medwyn Goodall. 1 CD. (Running Time: 1 hr.). 1996. audio compact disk Mystic Fire.

Nazi Aims & Methods. Ernest Yaniger. Read by Tim O'Connor. 1 cass. (Running Time: 31 min.). 1980. 10.00 (HE827) Esstee Audios.
A monologue probing deep into German life under the Nazi heel.

Nazi-American Biomedical Biowarfare Connection: Rockefeller, Kissinger, Bush & the Rise of the Fourth Reich. unabr. ed. Leonard G. Horowitz. Contrib. by Dave Emory. 2 cass. (Running Time: 3 hrs.). 1997. 19.95 Set. (978-0-923550-22-6(4)) Tetrahedron Pub.
A stirring expose linking the Rockefeller & Bush families to "racial hygiene" genetic research & population reduction agendas. Powerful revelations linking vaccine industrialists to epidemics of cancer & other current & coming plagues.

Nazi Eyes on Canada. Alan King. 2 pieces. (Running Time: 2 hrs. 30 mins.). 2004. reel tape 21.99 (978-1-894003-13-1(6)) Pub: Scenario Prods CAN. Dist(s): PerseuPGW

Nazi Legacy. unabr. ed. Richard Bamberg & Joy Bamberg. Read by Stephanie Brush. 6 cass. (Running Time: 8 hrs. 30 min.). 1996. 39.95 (978-1-55686-694-4(1)) Books in Motion.
A former Nazi officer who has subverted southern politics for forty years & his son are set to renew Nazi power in America by funding radical militias' efforts to incite revolution.

Nazi Officer's Wife. Edith Hahn Beer. Narrated by Barbara Rosenblat. 6 cassettes. (Running Time: 9 hours). 2003. 29.95 (978-1-893079-25-0(2), JCCAUDIOBOOKS) Pub: Jewish Contempry Classics. Dist(s): Baker Taylor
Brilliantly narrated by Barbara Rosenblat, this true story reveals the remarkable survival of a young Jewish woman in the Third Reich.

Nazi Officer's Wife. Edith Hahn Beer. Narrated by Barbara Rosenblat. Directed By Susan Dworkin. 7 CDs. (Running Time: 9 hours). 2003. audio compact disk 79.95 (978-1-893079-26-7(0), JCCAUDIOBOOKS) Pub: Jewish Contempry Classics. Dist(s): Baker Taylor
Barbara Rosenblat narrates Edith's extraordinary tale of survival. Edith, a brilliant young Jewish law student from Vienna at the time of the Nazi triumph in Austria, adopted the identity of a Christian friend to become a "U-Boat", a Jewish fugitive hiding in the hear of the Third Reich.

Nazi Terror: The Gestapo, Jews & Ordinary Germans. Eric A. Johnson. Read by Edward Lewis. 13 cass. (Running Time: 19 hrs.). 2000. 85.95 (978-0-7861-1859-5(8), 2658) Blckstn Audio.
Questions about Nazi Terror answered based on years of research in Gestapo archives, on more than 1,100 Gestapo & special court case files & on surveys & interviews with German perpetrators, Jewish victims & ordinary Germans who experienced the Third Reich firsthand. This settles many nagging questions about who, exactly, was responsible for what, who knew what & when they knew it.

***Nazi Terror: The Gestapo, Jews, & Ordinary Germans.** unabr. ed. Eric A. Johnson. Read by Edward Lewis. (Running Time: 19 hrs. NaN mins.). (ENG.). 2011. 44.95 (978-1-4417-8468-1(3)); audio compact disk 123.00 (978-1-4417-8466-7(7)) Blckstn Audio.

NC Civics & Economy 2003. Holt, Rinehart and Winston Staff. 2003. audio compact disk 73.53 (978-0-03-050958-2(0)) Holt McDoug.

Nclex Excel! Drexel University Audio Prep Course. 21 CDs. (Running Time: 30 Hrs). (C). 2005. DVD 199.00 (978-0-9773273-1-7(0)) Drexek NCKEX.
Drexel University's NCLEX EXCEL Audio Prep Course is for nursing students preparing to take their NCLEX Exam. With more than 25 years of NCLEX preparation experience, Drexel University's NCLEX EXCEL program is widely recognized for its high-quality curriculum.

NCLEX Excel: Drexel University's Audio NCLEX Prep Course. 18 Cassettes. (Running Time: 30 Hours). (C). 2005. bk. 199.00 (978-0-9773273-2-4(9)) Drexek NCKEX.

NCLEX Hot Topics. Scripts. Sig Nubla. Read by Sig Nubla. 1 CD. (Running Time: 60 mins). 2003. audio compact disk 25.00 (978-0-9747794-0-9(7)) Nursetudor.com.
Study material for nursing.

NCLEX Hot Topics 2. Scripts. Sig Nubla. Read by Sig Nubla. 1 CD. (Running Time: 60 mins). 2003. audio compact disk 25.00 (978-0-9747794-1-6(5)) Nursetudor.com.
Question and Answer format of the most information to prepare for the nursing board exams.

NCLEX HOT Topics 3. Scripts. Sig Nubla. Read by Sig Nubla. 1 CD. (Running Time: 50 mins). 2003. audio compact disk 25.00 (978-0-9747794-2-3(3)) Nursetudor.com.

NCLEX-RN AudioLearn. 12 Disks. (Running Time: 14.6 hours). (C). 2008. audio compact disk 199.00 (978-1-59262-009-8(4)) Pub: AudioLearn. Dist(s): Rittenhouse

NCLEX Vocabulary. Scripts. Sig Nubla. 1' CD. (Running Time: 1 hr 10 mins). 2003. audio compact disk 25.00 (978-0-9747794-3-0(1)) Nursetudor.com.
Essential termnology for nursing board exam candidates.

Ne Vous Noyez Pas dans un Verre d'Eau. Richard Carlson.Tr. of Don't Sweat the Small Stuff. pap. bk. 18.95 (978-2-89558-034-8(0)) Pub: Coffragants CAN. Dist(s): Penton Overseas

Ne Vous Noyez Pas dans une Verre D'Eau. Audio. 1 cass. (Running Time: 1 hr. 30 min.).Tr. of Don't Sweat the Small Stuff. (FRE.). (J). bk. 14.95 (978-2-89517-018-1(5)) Pub: Coffragants CAN. Dist(s): Penton Overseas
Recorded completely in international French language by well-known actors or speakers.

Neal Amid. 1 CD. (Running Time: 39 mins.). 2001. audio compact disk 15.95 (CAT1001) Lodestone Catalog.

Neal Bowers. unabr. ed. Neal Bowers. Read by Neal Bowers. 1 cass. (Running Time: 29 min.). 1989. 10.00 New Letters.
Bowers reads poetry from the Golf Ball Diver & is interviewed.

***Neal Pollack Anthology of American Literature.** unabr. ed. Neal Pollack. Read by Neal Pollack. (ENG.). 2006. (978-0-06-114297-0(2), Harper Audio); (978-0-06-114296-3(4), Harper Audio) HarperCollins Pubs.

Neal Pollack Anthology of American Literature: The Complete Neal Pollack Recordings. Neal Pollack. Read by Neal Pollack. 3 CDS. (Running Time: 3 hrs.). 2001. audio compact disk (978-0-06-001407-0(5)) HarperCollins Pubs.
CD sampler.

Neal Pollack Anthology of American Literature: The Complete Neal Pollack Recordings. unabr. ed. Neal Pollack. Read by Neal Pollack. 3 CDs. (Running Time: 3 hrs.). 2002. audio compact disk 21.95 (978-0-06-001168-0(8)) HarperCollins Pubs.

Neal-Schuman Directory of Public Library Job Descriptions. Rebecca Brumley. 2005. audio compact disk 125.00 (978-1-55570-523-7(5)) Neal-Schuman.

Neale Donald Walsch on Abundance. unabr. ed. Neale Donald Walsch. Read by Neale Donald Walsch. 1 cass. (Running Time: 1 hr. 30 mins.). 1999. 11.95 (978-1-57731-116-4(7)) Pub: New Wrld Lib. Dist(s): PerseuPGW
Shows how true abundance has nothing to do with what we have & everything to do with what we are being.

Neale Donald Walsch on Holistic Living. unabr. ed. Neale Donald Walsch. Read by Neale Donald Walsch. 1 cass. (Running Time: 1 hr. 30 mins.). 1999. 11.95 (978-1-57731-115-7(9)) Pub: New Wrld Lib. Dist(s): PerseuPGW
A wide range of issues including health, illness, spirituality, life, death & more.

Neale Donald Walsch on Relationships. unabr. ed. Neale Donald Walsch. Read by Neale Donald Walsch. 1 cass. (Running Time: 1 hr. 30 mins.). 1999. 11.95 (978-1-57731-114-0(0)) Pub: New Wrld Lib. Dist(s): PerseuPGW
Discusses the purpose of relationships in our lives.

Neanderthal. John Darnton. Narrated by George Guidall. 11 CDs. (Running Time: 13 hrs.). 2000. audio compact disk 111.00 (978-0-7887-4903-2(X), C1278E7) Recorded Bks.
When archaeologists find a 25-year-old Neanderthal skull, they are eager to study creatures thought to be extinct some 40,000 years. But nothing can prepare them for the danger involved or for the impact their discovery could have on modern civilization.

Neanderthal. abr. ed. John Darnton. Narrated by George Guidall. 9 cass. (Running Time: 13 hrs.). 2000. 83.00 (978-0-7887-4403-7(8), 96133E7) Recorded Bks.

Neap Tide. unabr. ed. Dorothy Hewett. Read by Natalie Bate. 5 cass. (Running Time: 7 hrs. 33 mins.). 2001. (978-1-74030-156-5(0), 500740) Bolinda Pubng AUS.

Near & Dear. unabr. ed. Pamela Evans. Narrated by Juanita McMahon. 10 cass. (Running Time: 13 hrs.). 2000. 92.00 (978-1-84197-150-6(2), H1144E7) Recorded Bks.
Compared with most 60's housewives, Jane Parker has it all. Her husband Mick has his own business & a lot of good luck that achieved Mick's success, but that luck changes. Mick disappears & with no money, Jane is left to support her family alone.

Near & Far: Early Explorers Emergent Set B Audio CD. Katherine Scraper. Adapted by Benchmark Education Staff. (J). 2007. audio compact disk 10.00 (978-1-4108-8200-4(4)) Benchmark Educ.

Near-Death Experiences. unabr. ed. Kenneth Ring. 2 cass. (Running Time: 1 hr. 58 min.). 1985. 18.00 (02101) Big Sur Tapes.
Presents a documentation of many cases of "out-of-body" experiences & return.

Near Myths. unabr. ed. John Ebdon. Read by John Ebdon. 4 cass. (Running Time: 6 hrs.). 1997. 44.95 (940510) Eye Ear.
John Ebdon returns to Crete, Simi & Rhodes, introducing a gallery of the people who live & work there, as well as a cross-section of their visitors. He then sets sail on an island-hopping boat with a host of interesting & outrageous, yet familiar, characters. His affection for the Greeks is without stint & his curiosity about them & their beautiful surroundings is boundless.

Near Myths: A Love Affair with Greece, unabr. ed. John Ebdon. Read by John Ebdon. 4 cass. (Running Time: 5 hrs. 15 min.). (Isis Ser.). (J). 1994. 44.95 (978-1-85695-805-9(1), 940510) Pub: ISIS Lrg Prnt GBR. Dist(s): Ulverscroft US

Near Reaches. Robert A. Monroe. Read by Robert A. Monroe. (Running Time: 45 min.). (Gateway Experience - Prospecting Ser.). 1984. 14.95 (978-1-56113-290-4(X)) Monroe Institute.
Discover the treasures of time & space.

Near to the Fire. Kenneth G. Mills. 1 cass. (Running Time: 1 hr.). 1979. 5.45 (978-0-919842-04-5(6), KGOC11) Ken Mills Found.
"We are not destined to be limits," the author declares in this 1979 Tucson lecture. "We are destined to be witnesses to the experience of the Infinite.".

***Nearest Exit.** unabr. ed. Olen Steinhauer. Read by David Pittu. 10 CDs. (Running Time: 12 hrs.). 2010. audio compact disk 39.99 (978-1-4272-0973-3(1)) Pub: Macmill Audio. Dist(s): Macmillan

Nearest Far Away Place. abr. ed. Timothy White. Read by William Schallert. 2 cass. (Running Time: 3 hrs.). 1998. 16.95 (978-1-882071-55-5(7)) B-B Audio.
The long awaited study of the seminal California surfin band and the culture that produced it. Timothy Whites book is simultaneously a social history of the era and an intimate portrait of the group. Intertwined with personal details of the bands mem.

Nearness of Jesus. Read by Basilea Schlink. 1 cass. (Running Time: 30 min.). 1985. (0248) Evang Sisterhood Mary.
Discusses how we can experience this today & the stepping stones that mark His path.

Neat. Charlayne Woodard. Read by Charlayne Woodard. 1 cass. (Running Time: 1 hr. 30 min.). 2000. 19.95 L A Theatre.

Neat. unabr. ed. Charlayne Woodard. Read by Charlayne Woodard. 2 CDs. (Running Time: 1 hr. 42 mins.). 2000. audio compact disk 25.95 (978-1-58081-193-4(0), CDTPT147) Pub: L A Theatre. Dist(s): NetLibrary CO
This autobiographical drama focuses on the relationship between the author & her brain-damaged aunt Beneatha.

Neat. unabr. ed. Charlayne Woodard. Read by Charlayne Woodard. 2 cass. (Running Time: 1 hr. 42 mins.). 2000. 23.95 (978-1-58081-171-2(X), TPT147) L A Theatre.

Neat & Clean: Ocean. Eldon Taylor. Read by Eldon Taylor. Ed. by Leslie Brice. 1 cass. (Running Time: 1 hr.). 1992. 16.95 (978-1-56705-336-4(X)) Gateways Inst.
Self improvement.

Neat & Tidy. Eldon Taylor. 1 cass. (Running Time: 1 hr. 2 min.). (Inner Talk Ser.). 16.95 incl. script. (978-1-55978-156-5(4), 5382C) Progress Aware Res.
Soundtrack - Musical Themes with underlying subliminal affirmations.

Neat & Tidy: Babbling Brook. Eldon Taylor. 1 cass. (Running Time: 1 hr.). 16.95 (978-1-55978-501-3(2), 5382F) Progress Aware Res.

Nebraska! abr. ed. Read by Sambrook Erickson. Ed. by Dana Fuller Ross. 4 cass. (Running Time: 6 hrs.). (Wagon West Ser.: No. 2). 2002. 25.00 (978-1-58807-007-4(7)) Am Pubng Inc.
NEBRASKA! This is a story of fearless devotion to a hard-won ideal, of betrayal from within, and of sabotage that reaches as far as Britain's and imperial Russia's shores. And, above all, it is the story of "Whip" Holt, the ruggedly quiet leader of this leg of the perilous migration, and of Cathy Van Ayl, who leaves her family behind in Missouri to continue on with Whip Holt's train...perhaps, to win his heart.

Nebraska! abr. ed. Read by Sambrook Erikson. Ed. by Dana Fuller Ross. 2 vols. (Wagons West Ser.: No. 2). 2002. (978-1-58807-504-8(4)) Am Pubng Inc.

Nebraska! abr. ed. Read by Sambrook Erikson. Ed. by Dana Fuller Ross. 5 vols. (Wagons West Ser.: No. 2). 2003. audio compact disk 30.00 (978-1-58807-344-0(0)); audio compact disk (978-1-58807-822-3(1)) Am Pubng Inc.

Nebraska! abr. ed. Dana Fuller Ross, pseud. Read by Phil Gigante. (Running Time: 5 hrs.). (Wagons West Ser.: No. 2). 2009. audio compact disk 14.99 (978-1-4418-1673-3(9), 9781441816733, BACD) Brilliance Audio.

Nebraska! unabr. ed. Dana Fuller Ross, pseud. Read by Phil Gigante. (Running Time: 14 hrs.). (Wagons West Ser.: No. 2). 2009. 39.97 (978-1-4418-1670-2(4), 9781441816702, Brlnc Audio MP3 Lib); 24.99 (978-1-4418-1669-6(0), 9781441816696, Brilliance MP3); 24.99 (978-1-4418-1671-9(2), 9781441816719, BAD); 39.97 (978-1-4418-1672-6(0), 9781441816726, BADLE); audio compact disk 29.99 (978-1-4418-1667-2(4), 9781441816672, Bril Audio CD Unabri); audio compact disk 82.97 (978-1-4418-1668-9(2), 9781441816689, BriAudCD Unabrid) Brilliance Audio.

***Necessary End.** unabr. ed. Peter Robinson. Narrated by James Langton. (Running Time: 11 hrs. 30 mins.). (Inspector Banks Mystery Ser.). 2010. 17.99 (978-1-4001-8271-8(9)); 24.99 (978-1-4001-6271-0(8)); audio compact disk 34.99 (978-1-4001-1271-5(0)); audio compact disk 83.99 (978-1-4001-4271-2(7)) Pub: Tantor Media. Dist(s): IngramPubServ

***Necessary Endings: The Employees, Businesses, & Relationships That All of Us Have to Give up in Order to Move Forward.** unabr. ed. Henry Cloud. (ENG.). 2011. (978-0-06-200704-9(1), Harper Audio) HarperCollins Pubs.

Necessary Ends. unabr. ed. Stanley Middleton. Narrated by Christopher Kay. 7 cass. (Running Time: 9 hrs. 15 mins.). 2000. 62.00 (978-1-84197-059-2(X), H1057E7) Recorded Bks.
Sam Martin's an observer. At 81, he looks 60 & he's healthy. In business, he helped his company to international fame. Yet he missed something. Age allows him time to realize that his success didn't really matter. Left by his wife & a stranger to his kids, his solitude only increases. Now he focuses on the daily crises of his little community. Moving to Norfolk is a welcome change. Aiding a lost child leads to friendship with her family, whose needs become integral to Sam's life; a small kindness introduces the intriguing Alice, who proves he needn't only live his life through other people.

Necessary Ends. unabr. ed. Stanley Middleton. Narrated by Christopher Kay. 8 CDs. (Running Time: 9 hrs. 15 mins.). 2000. audio compact disk 82.00 (978-1-84197-089-9(1), C1181E7) Recorded Bks.

Necessary Evil. Sharon Gosling. 2009. audio compact disk 15.95 (978-1-84435-345-3(1)) Pub: Big Finish GBR. Dist(s): Natl Bk Netwk

Necessary Evil. Alex Kava. Read by Deborah Hazlett. 2 CDs. (Maggie O'Dell Ser.: Bk. 5). 2006. audio compact disk 49.95 (978-0-7927-3961-6(2), CMP 897) AudioGO.

Necessary Evil. Alex Kava. Read by Deborah Hazlett. 9 cass. (Running Time: 39240 sec.). (Maggie O'Dell Ser.: Bk. 5). 2006. 79.95 (978-0-7927-3890-9(X), CSL 897); audio compact disk 99.95 (978-0-7927-3891-6(8), SLD 897) AudioGO.

Necessary Evil. abr. ed. Alex Kava. (Maggie O'Dell Ser.: Bk. 5). 2006. 14.95 (978-1-59397-445-9(0)) Pub: Macmill Audio. Dist(s): Macmillan

Necessary Illusions: Thought Control in Democratic Societies. Noam Chompsky. Read by Noam Chompsky. 5 vols. (Running Time: 18000 sec.). (Massey Lecture Ser.). 2005. audio compact disk 39.95 (978-0-660-19387-8(6)) Canadian Broadcasting CAN.

Necessary Indulgence Relaxation Kit. abr. ed. Created by Relaxation Company Staff. 1 CD. (Running Time: 1 hr. 0 mins. 0 sec.). (ENG.). 2007. audio compact disk 19.98 (978-1-55961-848-9(5)) Pub: Relaxtn Co. Dist(s): S and S Inc

Necessary Madness. unabr. ed. Jenn Crowell. Read by Kathleen O'Malley. 6 cass. (Running Time: 6 hrs.). 1997. 36.00 (978-0-7366-3662-9(5), 4336) Books on Tape.
After eight years of marriage, Gloria's beloved husband succumbs to leukemia, leaving her alone to raise a son.

Necessary Madness. unabr. ed. Jenn Crowell. Read by Sheila Hart. (Running Time: 6 hrs.). 2009. 39.97 (978-1-4233-8595-0(0), 9781423385950, Brlnc Audio MP3 Lib); 24.99 (978-1-4233-8594-3(2), 9781423385943, Brilliance MP3); 39.97 (978-1-4233-8597-4(7), 9781423385974, BADLE); 24.99 (978-1-4233-8596-7(9), 9781423385967, BAD) Brilliance Audio.

Necessary Other: Gender, Power & Love in Contemporary Relationships. Read by Caroline Stevens. 1 cass. (Running Time: 1 hr. 30 min.). 1987. 10.95 (978-0-7822-0303-5(5), 245) C G Jung IL.

Necessary Treason: The Poet & the Translator. unabr. ed. George Steiner. 1 cass. (Running Time: 58 min.). 1970. 11.95 (23148) J Norton Pubs.
A thorough discussion of language translation, the recreation of a work with another way of life imposed.

Necessity of Being Absolutely Modern. unabr. ed. Stephen Spender. 1 cass. (Running Time: 50 min.). 1953. 11.95 (23128) J Norton Pubs.
A discussion of the life, work, & influence of Rimbaud.

Necessity of Guru. Swami Jyotirmayananda. 1 cass. (Running Time: 1 hr.). 1990. 12.99 Yoga Res Foun.

Necessity of Joy. unabr. ed. Pat Wagner. Read by Pat Wagner. Read by Alan Dumas. Ed. by Judy Byers. 1 cass. (Running Time: 55 min.). 1997. 12.95 (978-0-9642678-5-5(3)) Pattern Res.
Practical application of joy in the workplace.

Necessity of Prayer. unabr. ed. E. M. Bounds. Narrated by Veronica Murphy. 4 CDs. (Running Time: 4 hrs. 0 mins. 0 sec.). (Devotional Classics Ser.). (ENG.). 2004. audio compact disk 21.98 (978-1-59644-006-7(6), Hovel Audio) christianaud.
"Prayer is simple faith, claiming its natural, yet marvelous prerogatives - faith taking possession of its illimitable inheritance." Edward M. Bounds practice of prayer and writings on the topic are like a hearty furnace, stoked and glowing brightly red. Now, others may gather around the luminance of that fire and warm themselves in the glow.

Necessity of Prayer - Delete. E. M. Bounds. Narrated by Veronica Murphy. CD (#). 2004. 29.98 (978-1-59644-007-4(4)) christianaud.

Necessity of Prayer - Delete. unabr. ed. E. M. Bounds. Narrated by Veronica Murphy. Download. (ENG.). 2004. 14.98 (978-1-59644-005-0(8)) christianaud.

Neck Healing & Comfort. Steven Gurgevich. (ENG.). 2002. audio compact disk 19.95 (978-1-932170-20-7(0), HWH) Tranceformation.

Necklace see Great French & Russian Stories, Vol. 1, A Collection

Necklace see Maupassant's Best Known Stories

Necklace see Favorite Stories by Guy de Maupassant

Necklace: Thirteen Women & the Experiment That Transformed Their Lives. unabr. ed. Cheryl Jarvis. (Running Time: 6 hrs. NaN mins.). 2008. 29.95 (978-1-4332-4654-8(6)); 44.95 (978-1-4332-4651-7(1)); audio compact disk & audio compact disk 19.95 (978-1-4332-4653-1(8)) Blckstn Audio.

Necklace: Thirteen Women & the Experiment That Transformed Their Lives. unabr. ed. Cheryl Jarvis. Read by Pam Ward. 5 CDs. (Running Time: 6 hrs.). 2008. audio compact disk 50.00 (978-1-4332-4652-4(X)) Blckstn Audio.

Necklace of Raindrops & Other Stories. unabr. ed. Short Stories. Joan Aiken. Perf. by Joan Aiken. 1 cass. (Running Time: 1 hr. 30 min.). Incl. Baker's Cat. (J). (CP 1690); Bed for the Night. (J). (CP 1690); Cat Sat on the Mat. (J). (CP 1690); Elves in the Shelves. (J). (CP 1690); There's Some Sky in This Pie. (J). (CP 1690); (J). 1984. 9.95 (978-1-55994-044-3(1), CP 1690) HarperCollins Pubs.

N'ecoutez Pas Mesdames. Sacha Guitry. 1 cass. (Running Time: 1 hr. 30 min.). (FRE.). 1995. 21.95 (1723-Q) Olivia & Hill.
Another of Guitry's short plays on the theme of fidelity & adultery. Brilliantly acted by Guitry & a cast.

Necromancer. unabr. ed. Michael Scott. Read by Paul Boehmer. (Running Time: 11 hrs. 14 mins.). (Secrets of the Immortal Nicholas Flamel Ser.). (ENG.). (J). 2010. audio compact disk 44.00 (978-0-307-71077-2(7), Listening Lib) Pub: Random Audio Pubg. Dist(s): Random

Necronomicon. Illus. by Joseph Vargo. Composed by Joseph Vargo. Composed by William Piotrowski. Engineer William Piotrowski. Nox Arcana. 1. (Running Time: 50 mins). 2004. audio compact disk 13.99 (978-0-9675756-5-0(6), MG 1002-CD) Monolith.
Delve into the Necronomicon, a dark symphony based upon H.P. Lovecraft's forbidden tome of unspeakable horrors.

***Necropolis.** unabr. ed. Anthony Horowitz. Narrated by Simon Prebble. 1 Playaway. (Running Time: 10 hrs. 30 mins.). (YA). (gr. 7 up). 2009. 59.75 (978-1-4407-0437-6(6)) Recorded Bks.

***Necropolis.** unabr. ed. Anthony Horowitz. Narrated by Simon Prebble. 9 cass. (Running Time: 10 hrs. 30 mins.). (Gatekeepers Ser.: Bk. 4). (YA). (gr. 7 up). 2009. 67.75 (978-1-4407-0429-1(5)); audio compact disk 97.75 (978-1-4407-0433-8(3)) Recorded Bks.

***Necropolis.** unabr. collector's ed. Anthony Horowitz. Narrated by Simon Prebble. 9 CDs. (Running Time: 10 hrs. 30 mins.). (Gatekeepers Ser.: Bk. 4). (YA). (gr. 7 up). 2009. audio compact disk 51.95 (978-1-4407-2560-9(8)) Recorded Bks.

Necropsy of Love. Al Purdy. 1 CD. (Running Time: 1 hr. 10 mins.). 2004. audio compact disk 12.95 (978-1-894177-01-6(0)) Pub: Cyclops Pr CAN. Dist(s): Literary Pr Gp
A stunning audio collection of poems written and read by Canada's greatest lyric poet. When Purdy passed away in April, 2000 he left behind not only the huge gift of his writing, but literally of his own voice captured on this recording.

Nectar of Devotion. 15 cass. (Running Time: 23 hrs. 30 min.). 39.95 Bhaktivedanta.
The most intimate study of Bhakti-yoga given at the Samadhi of Srila Rupa Gosvami in the holy dhama of Vrndavana in 1972. Includes 1 folder.

Nectar of Devotion: The Complete Science of Bhakti-Yoga. 16 cass. (Running Time: 24 hrs.). 60.00 Bhaktivedanta.
A summary study of Bhakti-rasamrta-sindhu by Srila Rupa Gosvami. Includes 1 vinyl album.

Nectar of Immortality. unabr. ed. Rama Berch. 1 cass. (Running Time: 1 hr. 30 min.). (Chants of Awakening Ser.: Vol. 3). 1999. (978-1-930559-13-4(5)); audio compact disk (978-1-930559-14-1(3)) STC Inc.
Sanskrit chants for use during meditation, relaxation, or yoga.

Nectar of Instruction. Srila Rupa Gosvami. Tr. by Srila Prabhupada. 3 cass. (Running Time: 4 hrs. 30 min.). 15.00 Bhaktivedanta.
The text book on how to control the senses & become a Gosvami. Overcome the obstacles to devotional service, improve your personal qualities & habits, practice the regulative devotional principles, develop living & meaningful relationships with devotees, disindentify yourself with your material body, increase your taste for chanting the Holy Names. Includes 1 vinyl album.

Ned Kelly: A Short Life. unabr. ed. Ian Jones. Read by Paul English. 12 cass. (Running Time: 18 hrs.). 1998. 96.00 (978-1-86340-794-6(4), 580335) Pub: Bolinda Pubng AUS. Dist(s): Lndmrk Audiobks
Australia's immortal outlaw emerges as a man who hated conflict, yet never escaped it. A private man incapable of being ordinary & unnoticed, who was seen as what he represented rather than what he was, & whose enemies helped to make him a legend.

Ned Kelly: A short life - Re-release. unabr. ed. Ian Jones. Read by Paul English. (Running Time: 18 hrs. 15 mins.). (Classic Ser.). 2009. audio compact disk 123.95 (978-1-74214-029-2(7), 9781742140292) Pub: Bolinda Pubng AUS. Dist(s): Bolinda Pub Inc

Neddiad: How Neddie Took the Train, Went to Hollywood, & Saved Civilization. unabr. ed. Daniel M. Pinkwater. Read by Daniel M. Pinkwater. 4 cass. (Running Time: 4 hrs. 30 mins.). (YA). (gr. 5-9). 2007. 33.75 (978-1-4281-4864-2(7)); audio compact disk 46.75 (978-1-4281-4869-7(8)) Recorded Bks.

Need. unabr. ed. Carrie Jones. Read by Julia Whelan. (Running Time: 8 hrs.). 2009. 24.99 (978-1-4233-9927-8(7), 9781423399278, Brilliance MP3); 24.99 (978-1-4233-9929-2(3), 9781423399292, BAD); 39.97 (978-1-4233-9930-8(7), 9781423399308, BADLE); audio compact disk 29.99 (978-1-4233-9925-4(0), 9781423399254) Brilliance Audio.

Need. unabr. ed. Carrie Jones. Read by Julia Whelan. 1 MP3-CD. (Running Time: 8 hrs.). (YA). 2009. 39.97 (978-1-4233-9928-5(5), 9781423399285, Brinc Audio MP3 Lib); audio compact disk 87.97 (978-1-4233-9926-1(9), 9781423399261, BriAudCD Unabrid) Brilliance Audio.

Need Do Nothing/Living in the Now. Marianne Williamson. Read by Marianne Williamson. 1 cass. (Running Time: 90 mins.). (Lectures on a Course in Miracles). 1999. 10.00 (978-1-56170-232-9(3), M735) Hay House.

Need for Authority & the Need for Revolt: Ouranos & Kronos. Read by Mario Jacoby. 1 cass. (Running Time: 2 hrs.). 1984. 12.95 (978-0-7822-0097-3(4), ND7312) C G Jung IL.

Need for Change & Why Human Beings Do Not Change. J. Krishnamurti. 1 cass. (Running Time: 1 hr.). (Transformation of Man Ser.: No. 2). 8.50 (ATOM762) Krishnamurti.
This well-liked series between J. Krishnamurti, Professor David Bohm, & psychiatrist, Dr. David Shainberg, explores the conditions of human life & the need to bring about a deep, radical, fundamental change in human consciousness if mankind is to emerge from its misery & conflict.

Need for Free Market & Less Government Authority. unabr. ed. Leonard E. Read & Dean Russell. 1 cass. (Running Time: 1 hr. 5 min.). 11.95 (105) J Norton Pubs.

Need of Being Versed in Country Things see Robert Frost in Recital

Needed: Small Groups. 1 cass. (Running Time: 1 hr. 30 min.). (Care Cassettes Ser.: Vol. 14, No. 7). 1987. 10.80 Assn Prof Chaplains.

Needful Things. unabr. ed. Stephen King. Read by Stephen King. Read by Tim Sample. (ENG., 2008. audio compact disk 59.95 (978-1-59887-754-0(2), 1598877542) Pub: HighBridge. Dist(s): Workman Pub

Needle & Thread. Ann M. Martin. Read by Ann M. Martin. (Running Time: 17880 sec.). (Main Street Ser.: No. 2). (ENG.). (J). (gr. 4-7). 2007. audio compact disk 25.95 (978-0-545-00526-5(4)) Scholastic Inc.

Needle & Thread. unabr. ed. Ann M. Martin. Read by Ariadne Meyers. (Main Street Ser.: No. 2). (J). 2007. 44.99 (978-1-60252-689-1(3)) Find a World.

Needle & Thread. unabr. ed. Ann M. Martin. Read by Ann M. Martin. 4 CDs. (Running Time: 4 hrs. 58 mins.). (Main Street Ser.: Bk. 2). (ENG.). (J). (gr. 4-6). 2007. audio compact disk 49.95 (978-0-545-00530-2(2)) Scholastic Inc.

Needle in the Right Hand of God: The Norman Conquest of 1066 & the Making & Meaning of the Bayeux Tapestry. R. Howard Bloch. Read by Stephen Hoye. (Playaway Adult Nonfiction Ser.). 2008. 59.99 (978-1-60640-984-8(0)) Find a World.

Needle in the Right Hand of God: The Norman Conquest of 1066 & the Making & Meaning of the Bayeux Tapestry. unabr. ed. R. Howard Bloch. Read by Stephen Hoye. (Running Time: 7 hrs. 0 mins. 0 sec.). (ENG.). 2007. audio compact disk 29.99 (978-1-4001-0371-3(1)); audio compact disk 19.99 (978-1-4001-5371-8(9)); audio compact disk 59.99 (978-1-4001-3371-0(8)) Pub: Tantor Media. Dist(s): IngramPubServ

Needle's Eye. unabr. ed. Margaret Drabble. 14 cass. (Isis Ser.). (J). 2002. 99.95 (978-0-7531-1376-9(7)) Pub: ISIS Lrg Prnt GBR. Dist(s): Ulverscroft US

Needless Casualties of War Audio Book. John Paul Jackson. Read by Carol Cavazos. 3 CDs. 2000. audio compact disk 22.00 (978-1-58483-066-5(2)) Streams PubHse.
In this audio book, John Paul Jackson reveals some startling insights that will uncover spiritual strategies of the dark side. Find out how you can protect yourself from Satan's onslaught and escape his unforseen and unperceived attacks.

Needs & Wants Past & Present Audio CD. Adapted by Benchmark Education Company Staff. Based on a work by Margaret McNamara. (Content Connections Ser.). (J). (gr. k-2). 2008. audio compact disk 10.00 (978-1-60634-908-3(2)) Benchmark Educ.

Needs of Your Mate: Genesis 2:1-25. Ed Young. 1986. 4.95 (978-0-7417-1539-5(2), 539) Win Walk.

Ne'er-Do-Well. unabr. ed. Rex Ellingwood Beach. Read by Flo Gibson. 8 cass. (Running Time: 11 hrs. 50 mins.). 2001. 26.95 (978-1-55685-662-4(8)) Audio Bk Con.
After a drunken spree, a playboy is shipped off to Central America without a penny in his pocket. Politics & intrigue regarding the building of the Panama Canal, passionate love, jealousy & suspected murder add to the plot. Warning: contains some racism.

Neerihiinjik: We Traveled from Place to Place: Johnny Sarah Haa Googwandak: The Gwich'in Stories of Johnny & Sarah Frank. Ed. by Craig Mishler. 1995. 29.00 (978-1-55500-054-7(1)) Pub: Alaska Native. Dist(s): Chicago Distribution Ctr

Nefer the Silent. Christian Jacq. Read by Ezra Knight. 2004. 15.95 (978-0-7435-4445-0(5)) Pub: S&S Audio. Dist(s): S and S Inc

Negaholics: How to Handle Negativity in the Workplace. Cherie Carter-Scott. 6 cass. (Running Time: 9 hrs.). 59.95 Set. (141-C47) Natl Seminars.
Learn to deal with Negaholics positively & powerfully, & experience less stress & more personal success - your job satisfaction & productivity will soar.

Negative, Set. abr. ed. Michael Covino. Read by Elliott Gould et al. 2 cass. (Running Time: 3 hrs.). 1994. 16.95 (978-1-56876-022-3(1)) Soundlines Ent.
An amazing first novel from a great writer, about an eccentric director, who is forced to send his film to the negative cutter, when he feels the film is undone. A looney professor, & a Cornell educated mobster's son kidnap the film & hold it for ransom. This wonderful novel is filled with more spins than a rollercoaster.

Negative Beliefs & Loss of Control. 1 cass. (Running Time: 1 hr. 30 min.). (Recovery - The New Life Ser.). 1979. 8.95 (1592G) Hazelden.

Negative Body Image. Harley Meyer. 1986. 10.80 (0902) Assn Prof Chaplains.

Negative Calorie Effect: How It Works. Neal D. Barnard. 2 cass. (Running Time: 1 hr.). (C). 1995. Set. (978-1-882330-50-8(1)) Magni Co.

***Negative Image: A Constable Molly Smith Novel.** unabr. ed. Vicki Delany. (Running Time: 8 hrs. 30 mins.). (Constable Molly Smith Ser.). 2010. 29.95 (978-1-4417-6481-2(X)); 54.95 (978-1-4417-6478-2(X)); audio compact disk 76.00 (978-1-4417-6479-9(8)) Blckstn Audio.

Neglected American. (23302) J Norton Pubs.

Neglected Friends. Ormerod Greenwood. 5 cass. (Running Time: 7 hrs. 30 min.). Incl. Neglected Friends: Daniel Wheeler (1771-1840) 1979.; Neglected Friends: Hannah Kilham (1774-1832) 1979.; Neglected Friends: Hilda Clark (1881-1955) 1979.; Neglected Friends: Pierre Ceresole (1879-1945) 1979.; Neglected Friends: William Allen (1770-1843) 1979.; 1979. 17.50; 4.50 ea. Pendle Hill.

Neglected Friends: Daniel Wheeler (1771-1840) see Neglected Friends

Neglected Friends: Hannah Kilham (1774-1832) see Neglected Friends

Neglected Friends: Hilda Clark (1881-1955) see Neglected Friends

Neglected Friends: Pierre Ceresole (1879-1945) see Neglected Friends

Neglected Friends: William Allen (1770-1843) see Neglected Friends

Neglected Masterpieces of World Drama. unabr. ed. John Simon. 5 cass. (Running Time: 5 hrs. 20 min.). 54.00 (S105) J Norton Pubs.

Neglected Masterpieces of World Drama, Vol. 1. unabr. ed. 1 cass. (Running Time: 1 hr. 13 min.). 1969. 11.95 (23129) J Norton Pubs.
Analyzes Thomas Lovell Beddoes' masterpiece, the Gothic-romance, poetic drama, Death's Jest Book. Sketches life of Beddoes & suggests possible source of his attitudes towards death & his ultimate suicide.

Neglected Masterpieces of World Drama, Vol. 2. unabr. ed. 1 cass. (Running Time: 48 min.). 1970. 11.95 (23130) J Norton Pubs.
Analyzes Alfred Jarry's masterwork Uba Roe & the Uba cycle. Sketches life of Jarry & suggests possible source of Jarry's attitude that "anything can be its opposite".

Neglected Masterpieces of World Drama, Vol. 3. unabr. ed. 1 cass. (Running Time: 1 hr. 1 min.). 1970. 11.95 (23131) J Norton Pubs.
Briefly sketches Buechner's life. Examines thoroughly Woyzzeck, delving into images & themes.

Neglected Masterpieces of World Drama, Vol. 4. unabr. ed. 1 cass. (Running Time: 1 hr. 11 min.). 1970. 11.95 (23132) J Norton Pubs.
Briefly sketches life of Heinrich von Kleist. Develops growth of "doubleness" trait. Analyzes Penthesilea & underlying "love is war" theme.

Neglected Masterpieces of World Drama, Vol. 5. 1 cass. (Running Time: 1 hr. 7 min.). 1970. 11.95 (23133); 54.00 Set. J Norton Pubs.
Analyzes E. E. cummings' HIM, i.e., relative value at its first presentation. Also includes a thorough discussion of Durrematt's "An Angel Comes to Babylon," with selected readings from the manuscript.

Neglected Mother. Elbert Willis. 1 cass. (Running Time: 1 hr. 30 min.). (Tribute to Mothers Ser.). 4.00 Fill the Gap.

Negotiate Anything, Anywhere with Anyone. abr. ed. Frank L. Acuff. Read by Frank L. Acuff. Ed. by Vera Derr. 2 cass. (Running Time: 3 hrs.). 1995. 15.95 Set. (978-0-85013-244-1(4)) Dartnell Corp.
Learn how to get what you want - no matter who, what or where you are negotiating. The time-tested tactics & strategies in this program prepare you for success - so you can negotiate better deals & greater profits.

Negotiate Like the Pros. John P. Dolan. 6 cass. (Running Time: 4 hrs. 56 min.). 79.95 Set. (Q10037) CareerTrack Pubns.
In this program, you'll learn the skills necessary to make winning deals. Negotiation doesn't mean using intimidation or dirty tricks. It means getting what you want in a way that is fair & respectful to the other party. In other words, both sides benefit.

Negotiate Like the Pros. John P. Dolan. 2 cass. (Running Time: 3 hrs.). 1997. 15.95 (978-1-55977-672-1(2)) CareerTrack Pubns.

Negotiate This! By Caring, but Not T-H-A-T Much. unabr. ed. Herb Cohen. Read by Herb Cohen. 7 cass. (Running Time: 9 hrs.). 2004. 32.95 (978-1-59007-457-2(2)); audio compact disk 55.00 (978-1-59007-458-9(0)) Pub: New Millenn Enter. Dist(s): PerseuPGW

Negotiate Your Way to Riches: How to Convince Others to Give You What You Want. unabr. ed. Read by Peter Wink. Peter Wink. (Running Time: 6 hrs.). (ENG.). 2009. 24.98 (978-1-59659-401-2(2), GildAudio) Pub: Gildan Media. Dist(s): HachBkGrp

Negotiating a Good Old Age: Challenges of Residential Living in Late Life. Mary G. Schmidt. (Jossey-Bass Social & Behavioral Science Ser.). 1990. bk. 43.50 (978-1-55542-293-6(4), Jossey-Bass) Wiley US.

Negotiating & Drafting Commercial Real Estate Finance Documents. (Running Time: 6 hrs.). 1999. bk. 99.00 (ACS-2242) PA Bar Inst.
Takes a look at sophisticated commercial real estate finance documents in negotiating & drafting techniques.

Negotiating & Drafting Mortgage Documents. 1989. 75.00 (AC-505) PA Bar Inst.

Negotiating & Litigating Computer Contracts. Richard Raysman & Joseph P. Zammit. (Running Time: 11 hrs.). 1992. pap. bk. 295.00 NY Law Pub.
Simulated negotiations, a mock trial & individual presentations explore copyright ownership of data; software copyright infringement; protection of intellectual property; control of the product; warranties; pricing; performance obligations; & acceptance procedures. Includes course book.

Negotiating Computer Hardware & Software Contracts. Franklin A. Miles, Jr. 1 cass. (Running Time: 1 hr.). 1988. 20.00 PA Bar Inst.

Negotiating Contracts in the Entertainment Industry. Moderated by Michael I. Rudell. (Running Time: 16 hrs. 30 min.). 1992. pap. bk. 295.00 NY Law Pub.
Book publishing, television, film, theatre & music - emphasis on key clauses & issues needed to negotiate successfully on behalf of your client or company, explored through background explanations, analysis & simulated negotiations. Includes course book.

Negotiating for Business Results. Contrib. by Judith E. Fisher. 1 cass. (Running Time: 39 mins.). pap. bk. 99.95 (1028AV); cass. & video 99.95 (1028AV) J Wilson & Assocs.

Negotiating Repayment Plans. Jane K. Cleland. 1 cass. (Running Time: 60 min.). (Improving Accounts Receivable Collections: Tape 6). 1991. 39.50 (978-1-877680-12-0(5)) Tiger Pr.
Tape 6 deals with the nitty-gritty of setting up, confirming & following up effective repayment plans.

Negotiating Settlements with Insurance Adjusters. Read by James R. Ronca & Gerald Goodling. 1 cass. (Running Time: 1 hr. 30 min.). 20.00 (AL-56) PA Bar Inst.

Negotiating Skills in the Workplace, 4 cass. (Running Time: 6 hrs.). (Essential Business Skills Ser.). 1999. bk. & wbk. ed. 129.00 INCL. MULTIPLE CHOICE TESTS . (978-0-7612-0829-7(1), 80210CHDG) AMACOM.
Make every negotiation session a "win-win" proposition. The Institute for Certification, a department of Professional Secretaries International, will grant points toward CPS recertification to qualified individuals who successfully compete this course. 1 CEU.

Negotiating Strategies & Tactics. Brian S. Tracy. Read by Brian S. Tracy. 2 cass. (Running Time: 3 hrs.). (Effective Manager Seminar Ser.: No. 9). 95.00 (751VD) Nightingale-Conant.
How to negotiate successfully...& leave the "other guy" feeling good. Includes video & 2 workbooks.

Negotiating Strategies for the Real World. William L. Ury. 6 cass. (Running Time: 9 hrs.). 199.00 (CPE1060) Bisk Educ.
Explains techniques to make one smoother, more self confident & consistently successful in everything one negotiates. Includes textbook and quizzer.

Negotiating the Commercial Lease. 1997. bk. 99.00 (ACS-1253) PA Bar Inst.
This is intended for attorneys & other real estate professionals who represent owners, tenants & others involved in negotiating retail, office, warehouse & other commercial leases. Each author has extensive experience with all types of real estate leases. This was developed against a background of current practice with the applicable law, as it exists & continues to develop along with the inter-relationship of business & legal issues.

Negotiating the Game: The Win-Win Negotiating Strategy. abr. ed. Herb Cohen. Read by Herb Cohen. 1993. 12.00 (978-1-55994-823-4(X)) HarperCollins Pubs.

Negotiation & Conflict Resolution. rev. ed. Gerald R. Williams. Read by Gerald R. Williams. 6 cass. (Running Time: 5 hrs. 30 min.). 1998. pap. bk. 185.00 Set. (978-0-943380-35-3(9)) PEG MN.
Negotiation techniques & strategies.

Negotiation Boot Camp: How to Resolving Conflict, Satisfy Customers, & Make Better Deals. abr. ed. Ed Brodow. Read by Ed Brodow. (Running Time: 10800 sec.). (ENG.). 2006. audio compact disk 21.95 (978-0-7393-3435-5(2), Random AudioBks) Pub: Random Audio Pubg. Dist(s): Random

Negotiation Genius: How to Overcome Obstacles & Achieve Brilliant Results at the Bargaining Table & Beyond. unabr. ed. Deepak Malhotra & Max H. Bazerman. Read by Norman Dietz. (Running Time: 14 hrs. 0 mins. 0 sec.). (ENG.). 2007. audio compact disk 34.99 (978-1-4001-0540-3(4)); audio compact disk 69.99 (978-1-4001-3540-0(0)); audio compact disk 24.99 (978-1-4001-5540-8(1)) Pub: Tantor Media. Dist(s): IngramPubServ

Negotiation in Dietetic Practice. Darlene Dougherty. 1 cass. (Running Time: 60 min.). (Audio Cassette Ser.). 1990. bk. & stu. ed. 25.00 incl. bklt., 10p. (978-0-88091-081-1(X), 1213) Am Dietetic Assn.
This audiotape program explains the principles of negotiation & illustrates, in a workplace setting, how to engineer a successful negotiation process.

Negotiator. unabr. ed. Frederick Forsyth. Read by Richard Brown. 13 cass. (Running Time: 19 hrs. 30 min.). 1989. 104.00 (978-0-7366-2844-0(4), 3552) Books on Tape.
One man's conviction that in a world running out of fuel, the U. S. can survive only by gaining absolute control of one of the Mideast's richest-oil producing states is the match that flares into this deadly game. The newly-elected American president, John Cormack, is about to sign the most sweeping U. S.-Soviet disarmament treaty ever envisioned. A man such as Cormack, committed to peace, would never countenance the takeover of another government. So the president must be stopped. The kidnapping of a man on a country road in Oxfordshire is the first step, seemingly unrelated, in a plan to engineer Cormack's slow destruction. Only one man can stop it...that man is Quinn - the Negotiator. He is the only man who stands between a leader too shattered to govern & the faceless kidnappers. Quinn finally realizes that ransom never was the objective & that he has been lured into a tightening web.

Negro President: Jefferson & the Slave Power. Garry Wills. 5 cass. (Running Time: 8 hrs. 45 mins.). 2004. 24.99 (978-1-4025-5771-2(X), 03264) Recorded Bks.

Negro Servant see Poetry of Langston Hughes

Negro Speaks of Rivers see Classic American Poetry

Negro Speaks of Rivers see Poetry of Langston Hughes

Negro Speaks of Rivers see Poetry & Reflections

Negro Writer in America. unabr. ed. Pacifica, WBAI Staff. Read by James Baldwin et al. 1 cass. (Running Time: 46 min.). 1961. 11.95 (23062) J Norton Pubs.
A discussion on black writing in America.

***Neighbor.** abr. ed. Lisa Gardner. Read by Emily Janice Card et al. (ENG.). 2010. audio compact disk 14.99 (978-0-307-75093-8(0), Random AudioBks) Pub: Random Audio Pubg. Dist(s): Random

***Neighbor.** unabr. ed. Lisa Gardner. 11 CDs. (Running Time: 13 hrs. 30 mins.). 2009. audio compact disk 90.00 (978-1-4159-6317-3(7), BksonTape) Pub: Random Audio Pubg. Dist(s): Random

Neighbor. unabr. ed. Lisa Gardner. Read by Emily Janice Card et al. (ENG.). 2009. audio compact disk 39.95 (978-0-7393-6662-2(9), Random AudioBks) Pub: Random Audio Pubg. Dist(s): Random

Neighborhood. Paulette Bourgeois. Read by Paulette Bourgeois. Illus. by Brenda Clark. Music by Bruce Cockburn. (Franklin Ser.). (ENG.). (J). (ps-3). 1999. 9.95 (978-1-55074-752-2(5)) Kids Can Pr CAN.

***Neighborhood Watch: A Novel.** unabr. ed. Cammie McGovern. (Running Time: 10 hrs. 0 mins.). 2010. 34.99 (978-1-4001-9762-0(7)); 16.99 (978-1-4001-8762-1(1)) Tantor Media.

***Neighborhood Watch: A Novel.** unabr. ed. Cammie McGovern. Narrated by Coleen Marlo. 1 MP3-CD. (Running Time: 8 hrs. 0 mins. 0 sec.). 2010. 24.99 (978-1-4001-6762-3(0)); audio compact disk 83.99 (978-1-4001-4762-5(X)); audio compact disk 34.99 (978-1-4001-1762-8(3)) Pub: Tantor Media. Dist(s): IngramPubServ

Neighbors & Friends. University of Iowa, CEEDE Staff. 2 cass. (ENG & SPA.). (YA). (gr. 7-12). 1988. 87.00 (978-0-7836-1146-4(3), 8081); 87.00 (978-0-7836-1144-0(7), 8079) Triumph Learn.
Stories about everyday problems & situations. Complete set in Lao includes: teachers' guide, activity masters, English for home language activity masters, 2 student texts, 2 cassette tapes & 2 English for home language texts.

Neighbors & Friends. University of Iowa, CEEDE Staff. 2 cass. (Running Time: 3 hrs.). (ENG & SPA.). (YA). (gr. 9-12). 1988. 87.00 (978-0-7836-1145-7(5), 8080); 87.00 (978-0-7836-1142-6(0), 8078) Triumph Learn.
Stories about everyday problems & situations. Complete set in Cambodian includes: teachers' guide, activity masters, English for home language activity masters, 2 student texts, 2 cassette tapes & 2 English for home language texts.

Neighbor's Big Fat Cat. (J). 2005. audio compact disk (978-1-933796-21-5(9)) PC Treasures.

Neil Armstrong Is My Uncle & Other Lies Muscle Man McGinty Told Me. unabr. ed. Nan Marino. Read by Emily Bauer. 1 MP3-CD. (Running Time: 4 hrs.). 2009. 19.99 (978-1-4233-9334-4(1), 9781423393344, Brilliance MP3);

An Asterisk (*) at the beginning of an entry indicates that the title is appearing for the first time.

Networking Essentials: All the Prep U Need for MCSE, Vol. 1 unabr. ed. Global Education Research Institute Staff. 3 cass. (Running Time: 1 hr., 20 min.). (MCSE Prep Ser.: Vol. 2000). 1999. 9.99 Global Educ Rsrch.
Question bank for MCSE Examination, so the computer professionals can review the most important questions while driving or while resting their eyes.

Networking with Millionaires. abr. ed. Thomas J. Stanley & Thomas Stanley. Read by Thomas J. Stanley & Thomas Stanley. 4 cass. (Running Time: 43 hrs. 0 mins. 0 sec.). (ENG.). 2001. audio compact disk 30.00 (978-0-7435-0794-3(0), Sound Ideas) Pub: S&S Audio. Dist(s): S and S Inc
Dollar to dollar, the most productive way to penetrate the affluent market is to network with its members, advisors & key members of its affinity groups.

Networking with Millionnaires. abr. ed. Thomas Stanley. Read by Thomas Stanley. 2006. 17.95 (978-0-7435-6116-7(3)) Pub: S&S Audio. Dist(s): S and S Inc

Neue Horizonte: A First Course in German Language & Culture. 2nd ed. David B. Dollenmayer. (ENG & GER.). (C). 1988. 32.76 (978-0-669-13922-8(X)) HM Harcourt.

Neugriechisch Ohne Muhe. 1 cass. (Running Time: 1 hr. 30 min.). (GER & GRE.). 2000. bk. 75.00 (978-2-7005-1003-4(8)) Pub: Assimil FRA. Dist(s): Distribks Inc

***Neurobiology: An Audio Seminar for Clinicians.** Cardwell C. Nuckols. Ed. by Charles Hodge. Prod. by Dennis S. Miller. (ENG.). 2010. audio compact disk (978-1-55982-028-8(4)) Grt Lks Training.

Neurobiology of We. Daniel Siegel. (Running Time: 28800 sec.). 2008. audio compact disk 69.95 (978-1-59179-949-8(X)) Sounds True.

Neuroethics: Program from the Award Winning Public Radio Series. Interview. Hosted by Fred Goodwin. 1 CD. (Running Time: 1 hr). 2003. audio compact disk 21.95 (978-1-932479-72-0(4), LCM 287) Lichtenstein Creat.
In this hour, we explore Neuroethics. As we gain greater and greater understanding of the brain and how to manipulate it, where do we set boundaries? Guests include Dr. Arthur Caplan, director of the Center for Bioethics at the University of Pennsylvania and chair of the school's department of medical ethics; Dr. Michael Gazzaniga, professor of cognitive neuroscience and director of the Center for Cognitive Neuroscience at Dartmouth College and a member of the President's Council on Bioethics; Hank Greely, professor of law at Stanford University; Dr. Turhan Canli, a psychologist at Stony Brook University; and Brian Alexander, author of Rapture: How Biotech Became the New Religion. Commentary by John Hockenberry.

Neurofibromatosis Type 1 - A Bibliography & Dictionary for Physicians, Patients, & Genome Researchers. Compiled by Icon Group International, Inc. Staff. 2007. ring bd. 28.95 (978-0-497-11261-5(2)) Icon Grp.

Neurofibromatosis Type 2 - A Bibliography & Dictionary for Physicians, Patients, & Genome Researchers. Compiled by Icon Group International, Inc. Staff. 2007. ring bd. 28.95 (978-0-497-11379-7(1)) Icon Grp.

Neurolinguistics & Therapeutic Change. Stephanie Clement. 1 cass. (Running Time: 1 hr.). 8.95 (499) Am Fed Astrologers.
Combine with astrology for powerful counseling tool.

Neurological Complications of HTLV-III. Justin McArthur. (AIDS: The National Conference for Practitioners Ser.). 1986. 9.00 (978-0-932491-59-6(6)) Res Appl Inc.

Neurological Surgery: Newer Considerations in Imaging & Surgery of the Lumbar Spine. (Postgraduate Programs Ser.: C84-PG18). 1984. 45.00 (8498) Am Coll Surgeons.
Details imaging techniques, highlighted by CT & NMR to surgical diseases of the Lumbar spine, including stabilization techniques.

Neurological Surgery: Update in Cerebrovascular. Moderated by Russell H. Patterson, Jr. (Postgraduate Courses Ser.: C86-PG18). 1986. 57.00 (8628) Am Coll Surgeons.
Provides current opinion in subjects in cerebrovascular surgery.

Neurological Surgery: What Other Specialists Think Neurosurgeons Should Know about Their Specilties. (Postgraduate Programs Ser.: C85-PG13). 45.00 Am Coll Surgeons.
Demonstrates understanding & communication between neurosurgeons & other surgical specialities. 6 hours CME category 5 credits.

Neurology for the Psychiatry Specialty Board Review. 2nd ed. Leon A. Weisberg. (Continuing Education in Psychiatry & Psychology Ser.: Vol. 7). 1998. audio compact disk 95.00 (978-0-87630-869-1(8)) Pub: Brunner-Routledge. Dist(s): Taylor and Fran

Neuromancer, abr. ed. William Gibson. Read by William Gibson. 4 cass. (Running Time: 6 hrs.). 1994. 23.00 (978-1-57042-059-7(9), 4-520599) Hachet Audio.
Silicon-quick, street-smart, hot-wired to the leading edges of art & technology, NEUROMANCER upped the ante on an entire genre. Includes music by Agrabright, Barg, Black Rain & U2.

Neuromancer. unabr. collector's ed. William Gibson. Read by Arthur Addison. 6 cass. (Running Time: 9 hrs.). 1997. 48.00 (978-0-7366-3836-4(9), 4556) Books on Tape.
Case is a cyberspy, the best in the business, but he plays his games close to the edge & double-crosses the wrong people.

Neuromuscular Training Bowling. Marshall Holman & Johnny Petraglia. 4 cass. (Running Time: 6 hrs.). 39.95 (1312) SyberVision.
Includes video training guide.

Neuromuscular Training Golf. Al Geiberger. 4 cass. 49.95 (1012) SyberVision.
Includes video & training guide.

Neuromuscular Training Racquetball. Dave Peck. 4 cass. (Running Time: 6 hrs.). 39.95 (1118) SyberVision.
Includes video training guide.

Neuromuscular Training Skiing. Jean Claude Killy. 4 cass. (Running Time: 6 hrs.). 49.95 (1212) SyberVision.
Includes video & training guide.

Neuromuscular Training Tennis. Stan Smith. 4 cass. (Running Time: 6 hrs.). 49.95 (1112) SyberVision.
Includes video & trianing guide.

NeuroPep Talk. unabr. ed. Robert A. Wilson. 1 cass. (Running Time: 1 hr. 30 min.). 1988. 9.00 (978-1-56964-773-8(9), A0284-88) Sound Photosyn.
Dealing with Brian Machines & assorted hardware.

Neurophysiology of Tradition: Psyche, Synapse & Jungian Psychology. Jeffrey B. Satinover. Read by Jeffrey Burke Satinover. 5 cass. (Running Time: 7 hrs.). 1994. 39.95 (978-0-7822-0463-6(5), 540) C G Jung IL.

Neuroprosthetics: Program from the Award-Winning Public Radio Series, 410. Interview. Hosted by Peter Kramer. 1 CD. (Running Time: 59 minutes). 2006. audio compact disk 21.95 (978-1-933644-30-1(3)) Lichtenstein Creat.
his week on The Infinite Mind we devote the hour to Dr. John Donoghue and his ground-breaking work in an emerging field that scientists are calling neuroprosthetics. Donoghue is head of the neuroscience department at Brown University and co-founder of Cyberkinetics Neurotechnology Systems, based in Foxborough, MA. Donoghue and his team of colleagues invented a brain-interface technology that enabled a paralyzed person to operate a computer and robotic arm by thought alone. In this program we visit Donoghue's laboratory at Brown University and ask him to describe the efforts that led to his breakthrough. We'll talk about ethics, science, commerce and the future of this exciting new field. We'll also hear from Richard Martin, a journalist who interviewed Matthew Nagle, the first human subject in Donoghue's trial. Martin will talk with us about other possible medical and military applications for Donoghue's work and the ethical implications of the innovations. With commentary from John Hockenberry.

Neuropsychology of Achievement. Steven DeVore. Read by Richard Gebhart. 8 cass. (Running Time: 12 hrs.). 39.95 (978-1-56275-006-0(2), 3037) SyberVision.
Learn the 21 essential characteristics to achieve your dreams.

Neuropsychology of Creativity. William C. Miller. 8 cass. 39.95 (3031) SyberVision.
Includes study guide, plus book The Creative Edge.

Neuropsychology of Executive Health. Kenneth R. Pelletier. 8 cass. (Running Time: 12 hrs.). 1988. 39.95 (2012) SyberVision.
Provides the strategies for reaching the top while maintaining good health & quality personal relationships.

Neuropsychology of Memory Power. Arthur Bornstein. Read by Richard Gebhart. 8 cass. (Running Time: 12 hrs.). 1989. 69.95 (3029) SyberVision.
Teaches the three principles of memory training: How to create visual pictures that link the information you need to retain, exaggerate & amplify those pictures so they are more stimulating to the memory & supplement the pictures with sounds.

Neuropsychology of Self-Discipline. 8 cass. (Running Time: 12 hrs.). 1986. cass. & video 49.95 (3017) SyberVision.
Topics include: Self-Discipline; Your Master Key to Achievement; The Fire That Burns Deep Within: Seven Steps to Developing Iron Will Discipline; The Power of Purpose: Determining What You Really Want to Achieve; The Magic of Mentors: How to Turn Your Vision Into a Step-by-Step Blueprint of Achievement; Mega Learning: How to Master the Knowledge & Skills You Need to Achieve Your Goals; Vision Quest: Winning Through Persistence & Perserverance.

Neuropsychology of Self-Discipline: The Master Key to Success, Sybervision Staff. 8 cass. (Running Time: 12 hrs.). 69.95 (628AX) Nightingale-Conant.
Your future success depends on your amount of self-discipline. Utilizing Stanford University's research on achievement, this high-intensity program isolates the ten primary characteristics of self-disciplined people. With this revolutionary learning technique, you'll banish unwanted habits & achieve goals that have been burning in your mind for years! Includes study guide.

Neuropsychology of Smoking Cessation: How to Quit Smoking. Tom Ferguson & Karl Pribram. Read by Richard Gebhart. 8 cass. (Running Time: 12 hrs.). 1988. cass. & video 49.95 (2080) SyberVision.
Describes 10 characteristics of people who quit smoking for life.

Neuropsychology of Staying Young. 8 cass. (Running Time: 12 hrs.). 49.95 (2011) SyberVision.
Provides advice on controlling the aging process through proper eating habits, exercise, skin care & a positive attitude. Includes study guide.

Neuropsychology of Successful Marriage. Brent Barlow. 8 cass. (Running Time: 12 hrs.). 29.95 (5010) SyberVision.
Designed to help you practice your new skills together as you listen. This interactive course can teach you to deepen your commitment, handle conflict, money & change constructively, increase trust & cooperation & much more. Includes study guide.

Neuropsychology of Successful Parenting. Katharine Kersey. 1986. 29.95 (5011) SyberVision.
Shows you how to take the right kinds of action in every child-rearing situation- from disciplining toddlers to dealing with rebellious teenagers. Discusses how to encourage a child who's having problems in school; how to stop bad behavior without punishment; find out why being "firm but fair" is so important. The program includes: Roots & Wings: The Power of Successful Parenting; The Positive Parent: The 10 Characteristics of Parents with Confident, Competent & Independent Children; The Magic of Respect: How to Increase Your Child's Feelings of Self-Worth; The Power of Encouragement: How to Help Your Child Develop the Habits of Success; The Independent Child: Teaching Children to Solve Their Own Problems; The Child Unique: How to Recognize & Develop Your Child's Individuality; The Joy of Parenting: How to Enjoy Your Children.

Neuropsychology of Weight Control. Sybervision Staff. 8 cass. (Running Time: 12 hrs.). cass. & video 79.95 (6271PAVB) Nightingale-Conant.
Your mind has a natural "fat thermostat" that controls the rate at which you process food. Learn to think scientifically about your diet & self-image by developing the 12 characteristics of a lean person. Includes study guide.

Neuroscience Reprints. Ed. by Marco A. V. Bitetto. 1 cass. (Running Time: 1 hr. 30 min.). 2000. (978-1-58578-053-2(7)) Inst of Cybernetics.

Neuroses. Robert Stone. 1 cass. (Running Time: 1 hr. 30 min.). 1983. 10.00 (978-0-938137-08-5(5)) Listen & Learn.
Anxiety Neurosis, Phobic Neurosis, Obsessive-Compulsive Neurosis, Hysterical Neurosis: Dissociative Type, Hypochondriacal Neurosis, Neurasthenic Neurosis, Depressive Neurosis.

Neurosis, Psychosis, & Dreams. Frederick Perls. 2 cass. (Running Time: 1 hr. 58 min.). 1978. 18.00 (04401) Big Sur Tapes.

Neurotic Aspects of Mind. Read by Chogyam Trungpa. 1 cass. (Running Time: 1 hr. 30 min.). 1971. 12.50 (A003) Vajradhatu.
Four talks: 1) Neurosis of the Centralized Watcher; 2) Occupational Misery & Open Space; 3) Meditation; Cutting Through the Red Tape of Mind; 4) The Heart of the Emotions; Shunyata.

Neurotic Aspects of Mind, NYC. Vajracarya. 1 cass. (Running Time: 1 hr. 30 min.). 1971. 9.00 Vajradhatu.
Four talks given in NYC: 1) Neurosis of the Centralized Watcher. 2)Occupational Misery & Open Space. 3) Meditation. 4) The Heart of the Emotions.

Neurotic Styles. Scripts. David Shapiro. Read by Rene Weideman. Compiled by Audio-VideoGraphics. Music by Kaloyan Tanev. Des. by Keith Kavanaugh. 9 Cass. (Running Time: 60 mins. per cass.). (C). 2003. 74.95 (978-0-9719511-0-5(1)) Essent of Behavior.
About the Classic Works in Human Behavior Audio Series: The series presents some classic texts on human behavior in audio format. When producing an audio book, we are mindful of the fact that not every good book makes for a good listening experience. Some books use language that is too complicated for audio, others are too theoretical. We only choose books that, in our opinion, are a pleasure to listen to in audio. We chose the audio format for the series to make it easy for the busy professional to continuously learn and stay updated - at home, work, in the car, while exercising, etc. This series is part of our effort to create an audio library of the most important works in the areas of psychiatry and psychology. For more information, questions or suggestions, please visit us on our website: www.essentialsofbehavior.com.

***Neurotic Styles: Audio Book.** David Shapiro. Read by Rene Weideman. Prod. by Essentials of Behavior. (Running Time: 502). 2010. 59.95 (978-0-9719511-2-9(8)) Essent of Behavior.

Neurotica. 1 cass. (Running Time: 1 hr.). 10.95 (I0760B090, HarperThor) HarpC GBR.

Neutral Corner. unabr. ed. A. J. Liebling. Read by Wolfram Kandinsky. 8 cass. (Running Time: 12 hrs.). 1992. 64.00 (978-0-7366-2259-2(4), 3048) Books on Tape.
Whether reliving the high drama of the Patterson-Johansson 1959 championship fight or reveling in Cassius Clay's style as a boxer & as a poet, Liebling always finds the human story that makes these 15 essays, all originally published in The New Yorker between 1952 & 1963, universally appealing.

Neutralizing Karma; The Four Aspects of Healing. Ann Ree Colton. 1 cass. (Running Time: 1 hr. 30 min.). 7.95 A R Colton Fnd.
Discusses the goal of God-Realization.

Nevada! abr. ed. Dana Fuller Ross, pseud. Read by Sambrook Erikson. 4 vols. (Wagons West Ser.: No. 8). 2003. (978-1-58807-528-4(1)) Am Pubng Inc.

Nevada! abr. ed. Dana Fuller Ross, pseud. Read by Sambrook Erickson. 4 cass. (Running Time: 6 hrs.). (Wagon West Ser.: No. 8). 2003. 25.00 (978-1-58807-013-5(1)) Am Pubng Inc.
In the midst of an ever-mounting Civil War, major General Lee Blake is summoned to spear-head a mission of utmost importance to the Union causethe transport of an invaluable shipment of silver from the Comstock. Aided by his long time friend and wagonmaster Whip Holt, Whip's courageous son, a beautiful sharp-shooting newswoman, and a seductive courtesan, the journey begins. However, the task is fraught with danger and adventure as Confederate saboteurs and cunning British agents will stop at nothing to prevent the "silver train" from reaching its destination.

Nevada! abr. ed. Dana Fuller Ross, pseud. Read by Sambrook Erikson. 5 vols. (Wagons West Ser.: No. 8). 2004. audio compact disk (978-1-58807-854-4(X)) Am Pubng Inc.

Nevada! abr. ed. Dana Fuller Ross, pseud. Read by Sambrook Erickson. 5 vols. (Wagons West Ser.: No. 8). 2004. audio compact disk 30.00 (978-1-58807-375-4(0)) Am Pubng Inc.

Nevada! unabr. ed. Dana Fuller Ross, pseud. (Running Time: 12 hrs.). (Wagons West Ser.: No. 8). 2011. audio compact disk 29.99 (978-1-4418-2474-5(X), 9781441824745, Bril Audio CD Unabri) Brilliance Audio.

Nevada Barr CD Collection: Blood Lure; Hunting Season; Flashback. abr. ed. Nevada Barr. Read by Joyce Bean. (Running Time: 64800 sec.). (Anna Pigeon Ser.). 2005. audio compact disk 34.95 (978-1-59737-709-6(0), 9781597377096, BACD) Brilliance Audio.

Nevada Barr CD Collection 2: High Country; Hard Truth; Winter Study. abr. ed. Nevada Barr. Read by Joyce Bean. (Running Time: 18 hrs.). 2009. audio compact disk 34.99 (978-1-4233-9197-5(7), 9781423391975) Brilliance Audio.

Nevada Barr Collection: Blood Lure; Hunting Season; Flashback. abr. ed. Nevada Barr. Read by Joyce Bean. 12 cass. (Running Time: 18 hrs.). (Anna Pigeon Ser.). 2004. 29.95 (978-1-59355-636-5(5), 1593556365) Brilliance Audio.
Blood Lure (Bill Weideman, Melissa Coates): In Blood Lure, Anna returns to the West, where she is sent on a training assignment to study grizzly bears in Waterton/Glacier National Peace Park. But back in her beloved mountains, where the air is pure and cool, Anna fails to find the spiritual renewal she expected. Instead, nature seems to have become twisted, carrying a malevolence almost human in its focus. Hunting Season (Ruth Bloomquist, Melissa Coates): When Anna answers a call to historic Mt. Locust, the last thing she expects to encounter is murder. But the man Anna finds in the stand's old bedroom is no tourist in distress. He's nearly naked, and very dead, his body bearing marks consistent with an S & M ritual gone awry. When hidden agendas and old allegiances are revealed, it's suddenly Anna's life on the line. Flashback (Ruth Bloomquist, Mikael Naramore): Running from a proposal of marriage from Sheriff Paul Davidson, Anna Pigeon takes a post as a temporary supervisory ranger on remote Garden Key in Dry Tortugas National Park. This island paradise served as a prison for the Lincoln conspirators during and after the Civil War. When a mysterious boat explosion - and the discovery of unidentifiable body parts - keeps her anchored to the present, Anna finds crimes of past and present closing in on her. A tangled web that was woven before she arrived begins to threaten her sanity and her life.

Nevada Dawn. abr. ed. Georgina Gentry. Read by Erin Leigh. 1 cass. (Running Time: 1 hr. 30 min.). 1995. 5.99 (978-1-57096-032-1(1), RAZ 932) Romance Alive Audio.
Beautiful, spoiled socialite Cherish Blasingame is swept from her private railroad car in the middle of the undiscovered West...straight into the arms of the half-naked outlaw known only as Nevada. Yet even as she struggles in her virile captor's arms, she knows that his sizzling touch has forever changed her future.

Nevada Weather History: Heroes & Victims. Mark McLaughlin. Read by Mark McLaughlin. 1 cass. (Running Time: 1 hrs. 16 min.). 1995. (978-0-9657202-0-5(9)) Mic Mac Pub.
True accounts of 125 years of Nevada weather events - tragedy, bravery, survival. Contains music & sound effects.

Never: A Book of Daily Don'ts for Personal Happiness & Success. unabr. ed. Michael K. Levine. Read by Pam Ward et al. (Running Time: 1800 sec.). 2007. 15.95 (978-1-4332-1358-8(3)); audio compact disk 19.95 (978-1-4332-1360-1(5)); audio compact disk & audio compact disk 17.00 (978-1-4332-1359-5(1)) Blckstn Audio.

Never Again. Earl Ravenal. 1 cass. (Running Time: 1 hr.). 1986. 9.95 (978-0-945999-21-8(6)) Independent Inst.
Criticle Reassessment of U. S. Intervention in Vietnam; Sets Forth Policy of Non-Intervention in Other Countries & a Defense-Only Policy for America.

Never Again: Securing America & Restoring Justice. abr. ed. John Ashcroft. (Running Time: 6 hrs.). (ENG.). 2006. 14.98 (978-1-59483-618-3(3)) Pub: Hachet Audio. Dist(s): HachBkGrp

Never Again: Securing America & Restoring Justice. abr. ed. John Ashcroft. (Running Time: 6 hrs.). (ENG.). 2009. 44.98 (978-1-60788-267-1(1)) Pub: Hachet Audio. Dist(s): HachBkGrp

***Never Again Good-Bye.** Terri Blackstock. (Running Time: 6 hrs. 57 mins. 0 sec.). (Second Chances Ser.). (ENG.). 2008. 14.99 (978-0-310-30513-2(6)) Zondervan.

Never Again Once More. Mary B. Morrison. Narrated by Indigo Brown. 6 cass. (Running Time: 9 hrs.). 2002. 58.00 (978-1-4025-3955-8(X)) Recorded Bks.

Never Alone. Perf. by Ernie Haase & Greater Vision. Prod. by Wayne Haun. 1 cass. (Running Time: 1 hr. 30 min.). 2000. (DAY 1195); audio compact disk (DAY 1195 D) Daywind Mus.
Includes new uplifting songs, old favorites such as "Oh What a Savior," as well as a special guest appearance by Greater Vision on "I Won't Look at the Lions," written by member Rodney Griffin. Each track offers something a little different...from the big band sounds of "The Big Parade" to

straightahead Southern Gospel such as "When Jesus Comes in the Clouds".

Never Alone: Daniel 3:19-30. Ed Young. 1995. 4.95 (978-0-7417-2070-2(1), 1070) Win Walk.

Never Be Lied to Again. abr. ed. David J. Lieberman. Read by David J. Lieberman. 2 CDs. (Running Time: 13 hrs. 0 mins. 0 sec.). (ENG.). 1998. audio compact disk 19.95 (978-0-7435-2286-1(9), Sound Ideas) Pub: S&S Audio. Dist(s): S and S Inc
Use these groundbreaking techniques to take control of every personal and business situation...and never be lied to again.

Never Be Lied to Again, unabr. ed. David J. Lieberman. Narrated by Richard M. Davidson. 4 cass. (Running Time: 5 hrs. 15 mins.). 1999. 37.00 (978-0-7887-2925-6(X), 95714E7) Recorded Bks.
A renowned psychologist shows you how to stop the lies & uncover the truth in any conversation or situation. Easy-to-use tools let you determine, with uncanny accuracy, if you are being lied to. Based on new developments in hypnosis & psycholinguistics, shows you how to influence anyone to tell the truth.

Never be Lied to Again: How to Get the Truth in Five Minutes or Less in Any Conversation or Situation. David J. Lieberman. 2004. 7.95 (978-0-7435-1989-2(2)) Pub: S&S Audio. Dist(s): S and S Inc

Never be nervous Again. Dorothy Sarnoff. 2004. 5.95 (978-0-7435-4147-3(2)) Pub: S&S Audio. Dist(s): S and S Inc

Never Be Nervous Again, Dorothy Sarnoff & Gaylen Moore. 6 cass. (Running Time: 9 hrs.). 59.95 (651AX) Nightingale-Conant.
Join the 70,000 who have conquered their fear of public speaking through this program. Learn to hold audiences spellbound. Make humor & personal style your tools for banishing fear & taking total command of your audience. Includes portfolio case & listener's guide.

Never Be Nervous Again. Dorothy Sarnoff & Gaylen Moore. Read by Dorothy Sarnoff. 6 cass. (Running Time: 4 hrs.). 1989. 59.95 (978-0-671-67568-4(0)) S&S Audio.
Includes listener's guide.

Never Been Out of His Care: Solo Track. Phil Johnson. Perf. by Christine Wyrtzen. 1 cass. (Running Time: 1 hr.). (50-Day Spiritual Adventure Ser.). 1993. 9.99 (978-1-879050-26-6(9)) Chapel of Air.
Accompaniment track for solo singer.

Never Call Retreat. unabr. ed. Bruce Catton. Narrated by Nelson Runger. 14 cass. (Running Time: 20 hrs.). (Centennial History of the Civil War Ser.: Vol. 3). 1990. 112.00 (978-1-55690-371-7(5), 90019E7) Recorded Bks.
Part 3 of the Centennial - History of the Civil War - from Dec. 1862 through Gettysburg, Appomattox & the assassination of Lincoln.

Never Call Retreat. unabr. ed. Read by Michael Prichard. 13 cass. (Running Time: 19 hrs. 30 min.). (Centennial History of the Civil War Ser.: Pt. III). 98.00 (1202-C); Rental 11.95 (1202-C) Books on Tape.
The war ends, the stage is set for reconstruction.

Never Call Retreat: Lee & Grant - The Final Victory. unabr. ed. Newt Gingrich & William R. Forstchen. Read by Boyd Gaines. 13 CDs. 2005. audio compact disk 112.95 (978-0-7927-3661-5(3), SLD 810) AudioGO.

Never Call Retreat: Lee & Grant - The Final Victory. unabr. ed. Newt Gingrich & William R. Forstchen. Read by Boyd Gaines. Albert S. Hanser. 15 CDs. (Running Time: 19 hrs. 0 mins. 0 sec.). (ENG.). 2005. audio compact disk 49.95 (978-1-59397-717-7(4)) Pub: Macmill Audio. Dist(s): Macmillan

Never Change. Elizabeth Berg. Narrated by Suzanne Toren. 6 CDs. (Running Time: 7 hrs. 15 mins.). audio compact disk 58.00 (978-1-4025-3477-5(9)) Recorded Bks.

Never Change. Elizabeth Berg. 2004. 15.95 (978-0-7435-1880-2(2)) Pub: S&S Audio. Dist(s): S and S Inc

Never Come Morning. Nelson Algren. Read by Barrett Whitener. 2001. 72.00 (978-0-7366-5915-4(3)) Books on Tape.

Never Come Morning. unabr. ed. Nelson Algren. (Running Time: 11 hrs. 50 mins.). 2009. 65.95 (978-1-4417-0247-0(4)); audio compact disk 100.00 (978-1-4417-0248-7(2)) Blckstn Audio.

Never Come Morning. unabr. ed. Nelson Algren. (Running Time: 10 hrs. 30 mins.). 2010. 29.95 (978-1-4417-0251-7(2)) Blckstn Audio.

Never Come Morning. unabr. ed. Nelson Algren. Read by Stefan Rudnicki. (Running Time: 10 hrs. 30 mins.). 2010. audio compact disk 39.95 (978-1-4417-0250-0(4)) Blckstn Audio.

Never Come Morning. unabr. ed. Nelson Algren. Perf. by Kurt Brocker et al. 1 cass. (Running Time: 1 hr. 18 min.). 1995. 19.95 (978-1-58081-081-4(0)) L A Theatre.
Traces the gritty lives of Polish youths in the Chicago slums during the 1940's. A "noir" tale that evokes the dark colors & tormented emotions of the great Ashcan School artists, in portraits tainted with words.

Never Cross a Vampire. Stuart M. Kaminsky. Narrated by Tom Parker. (Running Time: 6 hrs.). (Toby Peters Mystery Ser.: No. 5). 1997. 24.95 (978-1-59912-555-8(2)) Iofy Corp.

Never Cross a Vampire, unabr. ed. Stuart M. Kaminsky. Read by Tom Parker. 4 cass. (Running Time: 6 hrs.). (Toby Peters Mystery Ser.: No. 5). 1999. 32.95 (FS9-43271) Highsmith.

Never Cry Wolf. unabr. ed. Farley Mowat. Read by Wolfram Kandinsky. 6 cass. (Running Time: 6 hrs.). 1994. 36.00 (978-0-7366-2847-1(9), 3555) Books on Tape.
Story of Mowat's mission to study Canadian wolves.

Never Die Easy: The Autobiography of Walter Payton. unabr. ed. Walter Payton & Don Yaeger. 7 cass. (Running Time: 10 hrs. 15 mins.). 2001. 66.00 (978-0-7887-5465-4(3)) Recorded Bks.
Written in the final months of Payton's life, the autobiography includes extensive comments from his friends and family that fully illuminate a man who inspired anyone who met.

Never Dream of Dying. Raymond Benson. Ed. by Simon Vance. 7 cass. (Running Time: 10 hrs.). 2004. 49.95 (978-0-7861-2840-2(2), 3396); audio compact disk 64.00 (978-0-7861-8335-7(7), 3396) Blckstn Audio.

Never Eat Alone: And Other Secrets to Success, One Relationship at a Time. Keith Ferrazzi. Narrated by Richard Harris. Told to Tahl Raz. (Running Time: 40500 sec.). 2005. audio compact disk 39.99 (978-1-4193-5982-8(7)) Recorded Bks.

Never Enough. unabr. ed. Joe McGinniss. Narrated by Michael McConnohie. 1 MP3-CD. (Running Time: 9 hrs. 30 mins.). 2008. 49.95 (978-0-7927-5322-3(4)) AudioGO.

Never Enough. unabr. ed. Joe McGinniss. Narrated by Michael McConnohie. 8 CDs. (Running Time: 10 hrs.). 2008. audio compact disk 79.95 (978-0-7927-5233-2(3)) AudioGO.
At thirty-nine, Nancy Kissel had it all: the royal lifestyle of the expatriate wife, three young children and what a friend described as "the best marriage in the universe." That marriage - to investment banker Robert Kissel - ended one November night in 2003 in their luxury apartment high above Hong Kong's glittering Victoria Harbour when Robert was murdered and Nancy became the prime suspect. Her 2005 trial captivated Hong Kong's expatriate community and attracted global attention. Less than a year after the jury returned its unexpected verdict, Rob's brother, Andrew, was also found dead: stabbed in the back at his multimillion-dollar Greenwich mansion. Never Enough is the harrowing true story of two brothers who grew up wanting to own the world but instead wound up murdered half a world apart; and of Nancy Kissel, a modern American woman for whom having it all might not have been enough.

Never Enough. unabr. ed. Joe McGinniss. Read by Michael McConnohie. (YA). 2008. 64.99 (978-1-60514-906-6(3)) Find a World.

Never Fear. unabr. ed. Scott Frost. Read by Shelly Frasier. 1 MP3-CD. (Running Time: 8 hrs. 30 mins. 0 sec.). (ENG.). 2006. audio compact disk 24.99 (978-1-4001-5246-9(1)); audio compact disk 34.99 (978-1-4001-0246-4(4)); audio compact disk 69.99 (978-1-4001-3246-1(0)) Pub: Tantor Media. Dist(s): IngramPubServ
Seventeen years ago, three women were killed, their bodies dumped in the wasteland of the L.A. River. The serial killer was never found, and the case was mysteriously closed. Now, all these years later, Detective Alex Delillo reopens the River Killer case to help solve her own brother's murder. Alex never knew she had a brother until she went to identify his body. He was found next to the river near Griffith Park, a single gunshot wound in his head. LAPD is calling it suicide, but when Alex reconstructs her brother's final hours she stumbles across his research on an old LAPD case-the River Killings. The prime suspect was none other than their own father. As Alex gets closer to the truth, her father's past comes into focus, and alarming flashbacks from her childhood start to plague her. A journeyman actor who disappeared when she was a child, he had a history of violence against women, but was he capable of murder? Meanwhile, the schizophrenic son of the killer's third victim is out for his own revenge, and someone in the shadows is stalking Alex's every move and leaving a body count. In a chilling turn, Alex finds that the truth is as murky and as empty as the L.A. River itself.

Never Give In! Winston Churchill's Greatest Speeches. Winston Churchill. Intro. by Winston S. Churchill. Selected by Winston S. Churchill. 2 CDs. (Running Time: 2 hrs. 30 mins.). 2005. audio compact disk 29.95 (978-0-7927-3733-9(4), BBCD 125) AudioGO.

Never Give Up: My Stroke, My Recovery, & My Return to the NFL. unabr. ed. Tedy Bruschi. Read by Mark Adams. Told to Michael Holley. (Running Time: 7 hrs.). (ENG.). 2008. 24.98 (978-1-59659-236-0(2), GildAudio) Pub: Gildan Media. Dist(s): HachBkGrp

Never Give Up! Relentless Determination to Overcome Life's Challenges. abr. ed. Joyce Meyer. Read by Sandra McCollom. (Running Time: 6 hrs.). (ENG.). 2009. 19.98 (978-1-60024-414-8(9)); audio compact disk 29.98 (978-1-60024-413-1(0)) Pub: Hachet Audio. Dist(s): HachBkGrp

Never Going Back to Ok. Contrib. by Afters. Prod. by Dan Muckala. 2008. audio compact disk 13.99 (978-5-557-51414-9(7)) INO Rec.

Never Grow Up. Music by Anne Hills & Cindy Mangsen. 1 CD. (Running Time: 1 hr. 30 min.). 1998. audio compact disk 14.98 Rounder Records.
Great traditional folk songs are reminiscent of the entertainment families enjoyed in days gone by. The lively instrumentation on guitar, harmonica & piano makes this a treasure for music lovers.

Never Grow Up. Music by Anne Hills & Cindy Mangsen. 1 cass. (Running Time: 1 hr. 30 min.). (J). 1998. 9.98 Rounder Records.

Never Have Your Dog Stuffed: And Other Things I've Learned. abr. ed. Alan Alda. Read by Alan Alda. 4 cds. (Running Time: 18000 sec.). (ENG.). 2005. audio compact disk 27.50 (978-0-7393-2277-2(X), Random AudioBks) Pub: Random Audio Pubg. Dist(s): Random
*He’s one of America’s most recognizable and acclaimed actors–a star on Broadway, an Oscar nominee for The Aviator, and the only person to ever win Emmys for acting, writing, and directing, during his eleven years on M*A*S*H. Now Alan Alda has written a memoir as elegant, funny, and affecting as his greatest performances. “My mother didn’t try to stab my father until I was six,” begins Alda’s irresistible story. The son of a popular actor and a loving but mentally ill mother, he spent his early childhood backstage in the erotic and comic world of burlesque and went on, after early struggles, to achieve extraordinary success in his profession. Yet Never Have Your Dog Stuffed is not a memoir of show-business ups and downs. It is a moving and funny story of a boy growing into a man who then realizes he has only just begun to grow. It is the story of turning points in Alda’s life, events that would make him what he is–if only he could survive them. From the moment as a boy when his dead dog is returned from the taxidermist’s shop with a hideous expression on his face, and he learns that death can’t be undone, to the decades-long effort to find compassion for the mother he lived with but never knew, to his acceptance of his father, both personally and professionally, Alda learns the hard way that change, uncertainty, and transformation are what life is made of, and true happiness is found in embracing them. Never Have Your Dog Stuffed, filled with curiosity about nature, good humor, and honesty, is the crowning achievement of an actor, author, and director, but surprisingly, it is the story of a life more filled with turbulence and laughter than any Alda has ever played on the stage or screen. From the Hardcover edition.*

Never Have Your Dog Stuffed: And Other Things I've Learned. unabr. ed. Alan Alda. Read by Marc Cashman. 8 CDs. (Running Time: 9 hrs.). 2005. audio compact disk 72.00 (978-1-4159-2432-7(5)); 54.00 (978-1-4159-2431-0(7)) Books on Tape.
*He's one of America's most recognizable and acclaimed actors - a star on Broadway, an Oscar nominee for The Aviator, and the only person to ever win Emmys for acting, writing, and directing, during his eleven years on M*A*S*H. Now Alan Alda has written a memoir as elegant, funny, and affecting as his greatest performances. "My mother didn't try to stab my father until I was six," begins Alda's irresistible story. The son of a popular actor and a loving but mentally ill mother, he spent his early childhood backstage in the erotic and comic world of burlesque and went on, after early struggles, to achieve extraordinary success in his profession. Yet Never Have Your Dog Stuffed is not a memoir of show-business ups and downs. It is a moving and funny story of a boy growing into a man who then realizes he has only just begun to grow. It is the story of turning points in Alda's life, events that would make him what he is - if only he could survive them. From the moment as a boy when his dead dog is returned from the taxidermist's shop with a hideous expression on his face, and he learns that death can't be undone, to the decades-long effort to find compassion for the mother he lived with but never knew, to his acceptance of his father, both personally and professionally, Alda learns the hard way that change, uncertainty, and transformation are what life is made of, and true happiness is found in embracing them. Never Have Your Dog Stuffed, filled with curiosity about nature, good humor, and honesty, is the crowning achievement of an actor, author, and director, but surprisingly, it is the story of a life more filled with turbulence and laughter than any Alda has ever played on the stage or screen.*

Never Hit a Jellyfish with a Spade: How to Survive Life's Smaller Challenges. unabr. ed. Guy Browning. Narrated by Simon Vance. (Running Time: 6 hrs. 0 mins. 0 sec.). (ENG.). 2005. audio compact disk 24.99 (978-1-4001-0176-4(X)); audio compact disk 49.99 (978-1-4001-3176-1(6)) Pub: Tantor Media. Dist(s): IngramPubServ

Never Hit a Jellyfish with a Spade: How to Survive Life's Smaller Challenges. unabr. ed. Guy Browning. Read by Simon Vance. (Running Time: 6 hrs. 0 mins. 0 sec.). (ENG.). 2005. audio compact disk 19.99 (978-1-4001-5176-9(7)) Pub: Tantor Media. Dist(s): IngramPubServ

Never Let Me Go. unabr. ed. Kazuo Ishiguro. Read by Rosalyn Landor. 6 cass. (Running Time: 10 hrs.). 2005. 54.00 (978-1-4159-1558-5(X)) Books on Tape.
Hailsham seems like a pleasant English boarding school, far from the influences of the city. Its students are well tended and supported, trained in art and literature, and become just the sort of people the world wants them to be. But, curiously, they are taught nothing of the outside world and are allowed little contact with it. Within the grounds of Hailsham, Kathy grows from schoolgirl to young woman, but it's only when she and her friends Ruth and Tommy leave the safe grounds of the school (as they always knew they would) that they realize the full truth of what Hailsham is. Never Let Me Go breaks through the boundaries of the literary novel. It is a gripping mystery, a beautiful love story, and also a scathing critique of human arrogance and a moral examination of how we treat the vulnerable and different in our society. In exploring the themes of memory and the impact of the past, Ishiguro takes on the idea of a possible future to create his most moving and powerful book to date.

Never Let Me Go. unabr. ed. Kazuo Ishiguro. Read by Rosalyn Landor. 8 CDs. (Running Time: 10 hrs.). 2005. audio compact disk 61.20 (978-1-4159-1629-2(2)) Pub: Books on Tape. Dist(s): NetLibrary CO

Never Let Me Go. unabr. ed. Kazuo Ishiguro. Read by Rosalyn Landor. (Running Time: 9 hrs.). (ENG.). 2005. audio compact disk 40.00 (978-0-7393-1798-3(9), Random AudioBks) Pub: Random Audio Pubg. Dist(s): Random

***Never Let Me Go.** unabr. ed. Kazuo Ishiguro. Read by Rosalyn Landor. (ENG.). 2010. audio compact disk 19.99 (978-0-307-91307-4(4), Random AudioBks) Pub: Random Audio Pubg. Dist(s): Random

Never Let the Past Ruin the Future. Instructed by Manly P. Hall. 1 cass. (Running Time: 1 hr.). 8.95 (978-0-89314-197-4(6), C861214) Philos Res.

Never Let Them See You Cry: More from Miami, America's Hottest Beat. unabr. collector's ed. Edna Buchanan. Read by Donada Peters. 7 cass. (Running Time: 10 hrs. 30 min.). 1993. 56.00 (978-0-7366-2342-1(6), 3121) Books on Tape.
Breathtaking, bizarre & unforgettable stories that make up life in Miami, America's hottest crime beat.

Never Let You Go: Audio Book on CD. unabr. ed. Erin Healy. 2010. audio compact disk 29.99 (978-1-4003-1627-4(8)) Nelson.

Never Look Away. unabr. ed. Linwood Barclay. Read by Jeffrey Cummings. (Running Time: 13 hrs.). 2010. audio compact disk 29.99 (978-1-4418-0421-1(8), 9781441804211, Bril Audio CD Unabri) Brilliance Audio.

***Never Look Away.** unabr. ed. Linwood Barclay. Read by Jeffrey Cummings. (Running Time: 13 hrs.). 2010. 24.99 (978-1-4418-0423-5(4), 9781441804235, Brilliance MP3); 39.97 (978-1-4418-0424-2(2), 9781441804242, Brinc Audio MP3 Lib); 39.97 (978-1-4418-0426-6(9), 9781441804266, BADLE); 24.99 (978-1-4418-0425-9(0), 9781441804259, BAD); audio compact disk 92.97 (978-1-4418-0422-8(6), 9781441804228, BriAudCD Unabrid) Brilliance Audio.

Never Look Back. Betsy Brannon Green. 3 cass. 2004. 14.95 (978-1-57734-983-9(0)) Covenant Comms.

***Never Lose Again: Become a Top Negotiator by Asking the Right Questions.** unabr. ed. Steven Babitsky & James J. Mangraviti. (Running Time: 8 hrs. 0 mins. 0 sec.). (ENG.). 2011. audio compact disk 34.99 (978-1-4272-1138-5(8)) Pub: Macmill Audio. Dist(s): Macmillan

Never Lose Your Hope. Speeches. Joel Osteen. 1 Cass. (Running Time: 30 Mins.). (J). 1999. 6.00 (978-1-59349-031-7(3), JA0030) J Osteen.

Never Make the First Offer: And Other Wisdom No Dealmaker Should Be Without. unabr. ed. Donald Dell & John Boswell. Read by Sean Pratt. (Running Time: 5 hrs. 30 mins.). (ENG.). 2009. 27.98 (978-1-59659-473-9(X), GildAudio) Pub: Gildan Media. Dist(s): HachBkGrp

Never Make the First Offer: And Other Wisdom No Dealmaker Should Be Without. unabr. ed. Donald Dell & John Boswell. Read by Sean Pratt. (Running Time: 6 hrs.). (ENG.). 2010. audio compact disk 29.98 (978-1-59659-377-0(6), GildAudio) Pub: Gildan Media. Dist(s): HachBkGrp

Never Quit: Peter 4:19. Ed Young. 1989. 4.95 (978-0-7417-1706-1(9), 706) Win Walk.

***Never Say Die: The Myth & Marketing of the New Old Age.** unabr. ed. Susan Jacoby. (Running Time: 15 hrs. 0 mins.). 2011. 20.99 (978-1-4526-7037-9(4)); 29.99 (978-1-4526-5037-1(3)); audio compact disk 39.99 (978-1-4526-0037-6(6)) Pub: Tantor Media. Dist(s): IngramPubServ

***Never Say Die (Library Edition) The Myth & Marketing of the New Old Age.** unabr. ed. Susan Jacoby. (Running Time: 15 hrs. 0 mins.). 2011. 39.99 (978-1-4526-2037-4(7)); audio compact disk 95.99 (978-1-4526-3037-3(2)) Pub: Tantor Media. Dist(s): IngramPubServ

Never Say Diet: Make Five Decisions & Break the Fat Habit for Good. unabr. ed. Chantel Hobbs. Narrated by Chantel Hobbs. (Running Time: 5 hrs. 5 mins. 0 sec.). (ENG.). 2008. 16.09 (978-1-60814-000-8(8)) Oasis Audio.

Never Say Diet: Make Five Decisions & Break the Fat Habit for Good. unabr. ed. Chantel Hobbs. Narrated by Chantel Hobbs. (Running Time: 5 hrs. 5 mins. 0 sec.). (ENG.). 2009. audio compact disk 22.99 (978-1-59859-478-2(8)) Oasis Audio.

Never Say Goodbye. unabr. ed. Hilary Green. 9 CDs. (Soundings (CDs) Ser.). 2007. audio compact disk 84.95 (978-1-84559-516-6(5)) Pub: ISIS Lrg Prnt GBR. Dist(s): Ulverscroft US

Never Say Goodbye. unabr. ed. Hilary Green. Read by Julia Franklin. 8 cass. (Soundings Ser.). 2007. 69.95 (978-1-84559-431-2(2)) Pub: ISIS Lrg Prnt GBR. Dist(s): Ulverscroft US

Never Seduce a Scoundrel. unabr. ed. Sabrina Jeffries. Read by Justine Eyre. (Running Time: 9 hrs.). (School for Heiresses Ser.). 2010. audio compact disk 19.99 (978-1-4418-3913-8(5), 9781441839138, Bril Audio CD Unabri) Brilliance Audio.

***Never Seduce a Scoundrel.** unabr. ed. Sabrina Jeffries. (Running Time: 10 hrs.). (School for Heiresses Ser.). 2010. 19.99 (978-1-4418-3917-6(8), 9781441839176, BAD); 39.97 (978-1-4418-3918-3(6), 9781441839183, BADLE) Brilliance Audio.

***Never Seduce a Scoundrel.** unabr. ed. Sabrina Jeffries. Read by Justine Eyre. (Running Time: 9 hrs.). (School for Heiresses Ser.). 2010. 39.97 (978-1-4418-3916-9(X), 9781441839169, Brinc Audio MP3 Lib); 19.99 (978-1-4418-3915-2(1), 9781441839152, Brilliance MP3); audio compact disk 79.97 (978-1-4418-3914-5(3), 9781441839145, BriAudCD Unabrid) Brilliance Audio.

Never Shall Forget: Victory in Praise Music & Arts Seminar Mass Choir. Perf. by John P. Kee & Victory in Praise Music and Arts Seminar Mass Choir. 1 cass. (Running Time: 1 hr. 30 min.). Provident Mus Dist.

Never Sniff a Gift Fish. unabr. ed. Patrick F. McManus. Narrated by Norman Dietz. 5 cass. (Running Time: 6 hrs. 30 mins.). 1983. 46.00 (978-0-7887-4065-7(2), 96035E7) Recorded Bks.
Whether he's poking fun at fly fishing & hunting, or taking on some other sportsman's icon, Patrick F. McManus is sure to have you laughing aloud.

Never Stand Alone. unabr. ed. Janet MacLeod Trotter. Read by Lin Sagovsky. 12 cass. (Running Time: 12 hrs.). 1998. 96.95 (978-0-7540-0230-7(6), CAB 1653) AudioGO.
During the year of the miner's strike, two families are divided. When Carol Shannon & Mick Todd became lovers, all hell breaks loose. The consequences they face now is nothing compared to those they will have to face in the years to come.

Never Stand Behind a Sneezing Cow: And Other Tales from Foggy Crossing. Michael Perry. 1 cass. (Running Time: 1 hr. 30 min.). 1996. 9.95 (978-0-9631695-4-9(8)) Whist & Jugg.
Live audience recording of humorist reading stores from "Foggy Crossing" stories.

Never Stand Behind a Sneezing Cow: And Other Tales from Foggy Crossing. Michael Perry. Perf. by Michael Perry. 1 CD. (Running Time: 68 mins.). 2002. audio compact disk 10.00 (978-0-9631695-7-0(2), SCOWCD) Whist & Jugg.
Live audience recording of humorist Michael Perry telling stories about the people of Foggy Crossing, Wisconsin...as heard on Minnesota and Wisconsin public radio. Subjects addressed include parade disasters, what you should never say on an ambulance, coon dog etiquette, Foggy Crossing Football, and of course, the business about the cow. More info at www.sneezingcow.com.

Never Take No for an Answer: One Women, One Life & the Money Mystique. abr. ed. Karen Sheridan. Read by Karen Sheridan. 1 cass. (Running Time: 1 hr.). 1997. 14.95 (978-0-9660337-0-0(1)) K Sheridan.
Life story with lessons for women about money management.

Never Tell Me Never, unabr. ed. Janine Shepherd. Read by Marie-Louise Walker. 8 cass. (Running Time: 9 hrs. 30 mins.). 1999. (978-1-876584-03-0(3), 590584) Bolinda Pubng AUS.
On an afternoon bike ride in the Blue Mountains Janine Shepherd's life was altered irrevocably. When the champion cross country skier in training for the Winter Olympics was hit by a truck, doctors warned her parents that she was not expected to survive her ordeal. Even if by some small chance she recovered, she would never walk again. Coming to terms with her shattered Olympic dreams, refusing to believe what expert medical staff were telling her about her chances of any kind of recovery, Janine focused every sinew of her being on healing her broken body & crushed moral.

***Never Tell Our Business to Strangers: A Memoir.** unabr. ed. Jennifer Mascia. (Running Time: 13 hrs. 30 mins.). 2010. 29.95 (978-1-4417-5150-8(5)); audio compact disk 32.95 (978-1-4417-5149-2(1)) Blckstn Audio.

Never to Be Forgotten Vol. 1: A Year-by-Year Look at York County's Past: 250th Chronicles Set. 3rd ed. Ed. by James McClure. 1996. bk. 95.00 (978-1-929348-03-9(7)) York County Comm.

Never to Be Forgotten, Patterns, Builders & Heroes: 250th Chronicles Set. 2000. audio compact disk 15.00 (978-1-929348-08-4(8)) York County Comm.

Never to Be Forgotten, Patterns, Builders & Heroes Set: 250th Chronicles. 2000. bk. 95.00 (978-1-929348-07-7(X)) York County Comm.

Never Too Late. Nancy Cratty. 3 cass. 2004. 14.95 (978-1-59156-269-6(4)); audio compact disk 15.95 (978-1-59156-385-3(2)) Covenant Comms.

Never War. D. J. MacHale. Read by William Dufris. (Pendragon Ser.: Bk. 3). (J). (gr. k). 2009. 59.99 (978-1-60775-865-5(2)) Find a World.

Never War. unabr. ed. Read by William Dufris. (Running Time: 36000 sec.). (Pendragon Ser.: Bk. 3). (J). (ps-7). 2005. audio compact disk 24.95 (978-1-59737-255-8(2), 9781597372558, Brilliance MP3); 82.25 (978-1-59737-252-7(8), 9781597372527, BrilAudUnabridg); 29.95 (978-1-59737-251-0(X), 9781597372510, BAU); DVD & audio compact disk 39.25 (978-1-59737-256-5(0), 9781597372565, Brlnc Audio MP3 Lib) Brilliance Audio.
Fifteen-year-old Bobby Pendragon is a loyal friend, sports star, devoted pet owner - and Traveler. Along with his uncle Press, Bobby has visited the alternate dimension of Denduron and participated in a civil war. He's also waded through the endangered underwater territory of Cloral. Now Bobby once again finds himself thrust beyond the boundaries of time and space into a place that seems somewhat familiar: First Earth. Bobby and the Traveler from Cloral - Spader - have flumed to New York City, 1937. Against a backdrop of gangsters, swing music, and the distant sound of a brewing war, the two must uncover the evil Saint Dane's newest plot. But is Bobby ready for the difficult choices ahead?.

Never War. unabr. ed. D. J. MacHale. Read by William Dufris. (Running Time: 10 hrs.). (Pendragon Ser.: Bk. 3). 2005. 39.25 (978-1-59737-258-9(7), 9781597372589, BADLE); 24.95 (978-1-59737-257-2(9), 9781597372572, BAD) Brilliance Audio.

Never War. unabr. ed. D. J. MacHale. Read by William Dufris. (Running Time: 10 hrs.). (Pendragon Ser.: Bk. 3). 2009. audio compact disk 19.99 (978-1-4233-9899-8(8), 9781423398998); audio compact disk 49.97 (978-1-4233-9900-1(5), 9781423399001, BriAudCD Unabrid) Brilliance Audio.

***Never Wave Goodbye: A Novel of Suspense.** unabr. ed. Doug Magee. Narrated by Tavia Gilbert. (Running Time: 9 hrs. 30 mins. 0 sec.). (ENG.). 2010. 24.99 (978-1-4001-6785-2(X)); 34.99 (978-1-4001-9785-9(6)); 17.99 (978-1-4001-8785-0(0)); audio compact disk 83.99 (978-1-4001-4785-4(9)); audio compact disk 34.99 (978-1-4001-1785-7(2)) Pub: Tantor Media. Dist(s): IngramPubServ

Neverwhere. Neil Gaiman. (ENG.). 2006. audio compact disk 36.95 (978-1-59887-036-7(X)) Pub: Penguin-HghBrdg. Dist(s): Penguin Grp USA

***Neverwhere.** unabr. ed. Neil Gaiman. Read by Neil Gaiman. (ENG.). 2007. (978-0-06-154911-3(8)); (978-0-06-155525-1(8)) HarperCollins Pubs.

Neverwhere. unabr. ed. Neil Gaiman. Read by Neil Gaiman. 2007. audio compact disk 39.95 (978-0-06-137387-9(7), Harper Audio) HarperCollins Pubs.

Nevesta. Anton Chekhov. 1 cass. (Running Time: 1 hr. 30 min.). (RUS.). 1996. pap. bk. 24.50 (978-1-58085-565-5(2)) Interlingua VA.
Includes Russian text. The combination of written text & clarity & pace of diction will open the door for intermediate & advanced students to genuine comprehension & the use of literary texts for advancement in rapid understanding of written & oral language materials. The audio text plus written text concept makes foreign languages accessible to a much wider range of students than books alone.

Neveu de Rameau. Denis Diderot. Perf. by Pierre Fresnay & Julien Bertheau. 1 CD. (FRE.). 1991. 29.95 (1414-LV) Olivia & Hill.
A sparkling dialogue between Moi, a French philosopher & Lui, Rameau's nephew, a wild, unkempt & dissolute musician.

New Acoustics. 1 cass. (Running Time: 1 hr. 30 min.). 1998. 16.98 (978-1-56826-935-1(8)) Rhino Enter.

***New Adventures Vol. 1: Two Exclusive Audio Adventures Starring the Eleventh Doctor.** Matt Smith et al. Narrated by Karen Gillan et al. (Running Time: 3 hrs. 0 mins. 0 sec.). (ENG.). 2010. audio compact disk 19.95 (978-1-60283-933-5(6)) Pub: AudioGO. Dist(s): Perseus Dist

New Adventures of Harry Nile Volume 1. Jim French. (ENG.). 2008. audio compact disk 9.95 (978-1-60245-158-2(3)) GDL Multimedia.

New Adventures of Harry Nile Volume 2. Jim French. (ENG.). 2008. audio compact disk 9.95 (978-1-60245-159-9(1)) GDL Multimedia.

New Adventures of Mickey Spillane's Mike Hammer. unabr. ed. M. J. Elliot & JoBe Cerny. Read by Stacy Keach. 3 CDs. (Running Time: 3 hrs.). 2009. audio compact disk & audio compact disk 19.95 (978-1-4332-5139-9(6)) Blckstn Audio.

New Adventures of Mickey Spillane's Mike Hammer. unabr. ed. Stacey Keach. (Running Time: 3 hrs. NaN mins.). 2008. 19.95 (978-1-4332-5260-0(0)); 24.95 (978-1-4332-5258-7(9)); audio compact disk 33.00 (978-1-4332-5259-4(7)) Blckstn Audio.

New Adventures of Mickey Spillane's Mike Hammer Vol. 2: A Little Death. unabr. ed. Max Allan Collins & Mickey Spillane. (Running Time: 3 hrs. 0 mins.). 2009. 19.95 (978-1-4417-1259-2(3)) Blckstn Audio.

New Adventures of Mickey Spillane's Mike Hammer Vol. 2: The Little Death. unabr. ed. Mickey Spillane. Read by Stacy Keach. (Running Time: 3 hrs. 0 mins.). 2009. 24.95 (978-1-4417-1255-4(0)) Blckstn Audio.

New Adventures of Mickey Spillane's Mike Hammer Vol. 2: The Little Death. unabr. ed. Mickey Spillane & Max Allan Collins. Read by Stacy Keach. 2 CDs. (Running Time: 3 hrs.). 2009. audio compact disk 30.00 (978-1-4417-1256-1(9)) Blckstn Audio.

New Adventures of Mickey Spillane's Mike Hammer, Vol. 2: A Little Death. unabr. ed. Mickey, Max Allan and Spillane Collins. Read by Stacy and A. full cast Keach. (Running Time: 2 hrs. 30 mins.). 2009. audio compact disk 24.95 (978-1-4417-1258-5(5)) Blckstn Audio.

***New Adventures of Mickey Spillane's Mike Hammer, Vol. 3: Encore for Murder.** Max Allan Collins. Read by Stacy Keach. (Running Time: 2.5 hrs. NaN mins.). (ENG.). 2011. 22.95 (978-1-4417-3215-6(2)); audio compact disk 28.00 (978-1-4417-3216-3(0)) Blckstn Audio.

***New Adventures of Mickey Spillane's Mike Hammer, Vol. 3: Encore for Murder.** unabr. ed. Max Allan Collins. Read by Stacy Keach. (Running Time: 2.5 hrs. NaN mins.). (ENG.). 2011. 19.95 (978-1-4417-3219-4(5)); audio compact disk 19.95 (978-1-4417-3218-7(7)) Blckstn Audio.

New Adventures of Nero Wolfe: The Case of the Midnight Ride & Other Tales. Perf. by Sydney Greenstreet. 4 CDs. (Running Time: 4 hrs). Dramatization. 2005. audio compact disk 15.95 (978-0-9770819-1-2(5)) Choice Vent.
Based on the famous detective created by Rex Stout, THE NEW ADVENTURES OF NERO WOLFE stars Sydney Greenstreet as "the balkiest, bulkiest, smartest, and most unpredictible detetective in the world... that brilliant eccentric private detective, orchid fancier and gargantuan gourmet. Nero Wolfe, armchair detective in the classic tradition, and Archie Goodwin, wise-cracking hard-boiled invetigator, shine in eight radio tales from this classic detective series first broadcast in 1950-1951. Co-stars include Howard McNear, Gerald Mohr, Bill Johnstone, Harry Bartell, Larry Dobkin and Lamont Johnson. This four CD digitally remastered audio collection includes a Program Guide with photographs and an essay by noted radio historian Anthony Tollin.

New Adventures of Paul Bunyan. (J). 1993. 6.98 (978-1-884159-01-5(X)) Carousel Classics.

***New Adventures of Sherlock Holmes.** RadioArchives.com. (Running Time: 600). (ENG.). 2009. audio compact disk 29.98 (978-1-61081-091-3(0)) Radio Arch.

New Adventures of Sherlock Holmes. Perf. by John Stanley & Alfred Shirley. 10 cass. (Running Time: 10 hrs.). 2001. 34.98 (4483); audio compact disk 39.98 (4484) Radio Spirits.
Twenty of Sherlock Holmes' greatest radio adventures digitally remastered including Adventure of the Serpent God, Case of the Avenging Blade, Case of the Sanguinary Spectre, and Adventure of the Wooden Claw.

New Adventures of Sherlock Holmes. unabr. ed. Perf. by John Stanley et al. 10 vols. (Running Time: 10 hrs.). (10-Hour Collections). 2002. bk. 39.98 (978-1-57019-418-4(1), OTR4484) Pub: Radio Spirits. Dist(s): AudioGO

New Adventures of Sherlock Holmes. unabr. ed. Perf. by John Stanley et al. 10 vols. (Running Time: 10 hrs.). (10-Hour Collections). 2002. bk. 34.98 (978-1-57019-417-7(3), OTR4483) Pub: Radio Spirits. Dist(s): AudioGO

New Adventures of Sherlock Holmes, Set. gif. ed. Anthony Boucher & Denis Green. (ENG.). 2001. 49.95 (978-0-7435-2045-4(9), Audioworks) Pub: S&S Audio. Dist(s): S and S Inc
This Special Edition includes 26 original episodes on 13 cassettes. WELCOME... to the Golden Age of Radio and the Best in Classic Mystery From 1939 to 1946 Americans gathered around their radio to listen to The New Adventures of Sherlock Holmes - featuring Basil Rathbone as the high strung crime solver and Nigel Bruce as his phlegmatic assistant, Dr. Watson. Witty, fast-paced and always surprising, these great radio plays, written by the prolific writing team of Anthony Bouchere and Denis Green, are as fresh today as they were then. The latest audio technology was employed to bring the best audio quality and fidelity to the original performances, which feature nostalgic war-time announcements, original commercials and radio narration.

New Adventures of Sherlock Holmes, Vol. 1. abr. ed. Anthony Boucher & Denis Green. Read by Basil Rathbone & Nigel Bruce. 6 CDs. (Running Time: 60 hrs. 0 mins. 0 sec.). (Sherlock Holmes Ser.). (ENG.). 2009. audio compact disk 14.99 (978-1-4423-0019-4(1)) Pub: S&S Audio. Dist(s): S and S Inc

New Adventures of Sherlock Holmes, Vol. 1 Perf. by Basil Rathbone & Nigel Bruce. 4 cass. (Running Time: 4 hrs.). 1998. bk. 24.98 (4331) Radio Spirits.
Includes: "The Unfortunate Tobacconist," "The Paradol Chamber," "The Viennese Strangler," "The Notorious Canary Trainer," "The April Fool's Day Adventure," "The Strange Adventure of the Uneasy Easy Chair," "The Strange Case of the Demon Barber" & "The Mystery of the Headless Monk".

New Adventures of Sherlock Holmes, Vol. 2 Perf. by Basil Rathbone & Nigel Bruce. 4 cass. (Running Time: 4 hrs.). 1998. bk. 24.98 (4332) Radio Spirits.
Includes: "The Amateur Mendicant Society," "The Mystery of the Vanishing White Elephant," "The Case of the Limping Ghost," "The Girl with the Gazelle," "The Case of the Out of Date Murder," "The Waltz of Death," "Colonel Warburton's Madness" & "The Iron Box".

New Adventures of Sherlock Holmes, Vol. 3 Perf. by Basil Rathbone & Nigel Bruce. 4 cass. (Running Time: 4 hrs.). 1998. bk. 24.98 (4333) Radio Spirits.
Includes: "A Scandal in Bohemia," "The Second Generation," "In Flanders Field," "The Eyes of Mr. Leyton," "The Tell Tale Pigeon Feathers," "The Indiscretion of Mr. Edwards," "The Problem of Thor Bridge," & "The Double Zero.".

New Adventures of Sherlock Holmes, Vol. 4. Perf. by Basil Rathbone & Nigel Bruce. 4 cass. (Running Time: 4 hrs.). 1998. bk. 24.98 (4334) Radio Spirits.
Includes: "Murder in the Casbah," "The Tankerville Club," "The Strange Case of the Murderer in Wax," "The Man with the Twisted Lip," "The Guileless Gypsy," "The Camberwell Poiseners," "The Terrifying Cats" & "The Submarine Caves".

New Adventures of Sherlock Holmes, Vol. 5. 2 cass. (Running Time: 3 hrs.). 2000. audio compact disk 15.99 (978-0-7435-0550-5(6), Audioworks) S&S Audio.

New Adventures of Sherlock Holmes, Vol. 5. Perf. by Basil Rathbone & Nigel Bruce. 4 cass. (Running Time: 4 hrs.). 1998. bk. 24.98 (4335) Radio Spirits.
"The Living Doll," "The Disappearing Scientists," "The Adventure of the Speckled Band," "The Purloined Ruby," "The Book of Tobit," "Murder Beyond the Mountains," "The Manor House Case" & "The Adventure of the Stuttering Ghost".

New Adventures of Sherlock Holmes, Vol. 6. Perf. by Basil Rathbone & Nigel Bruce. 4 cass. (Running Time: 4 hrs.). 1998. bk. 24.98 (4336) Radio Spirits.
Includes: "The Great Gandolfo," "The Adventure of the Original Hamlet," "Murder by Moonlight," "The Singular Affair of the Coptic Compass," "The Gunpowder Plot," "The Babbling Butler," "The Accidental Murderess" & "The Adventure of the Blarney Stone".

New Adventures of Sherlock Holmes: Colonel Warburton's Madness & Other Mysteries, Vol. 7-12. unabr. ed. Denis Green & Anthony Boucher. Read by Nigel Bruce & Basil Rathbone. 6 CDs. (Running Time: 6 hrs.). (Sherlock Holmes Ser.). (ENG.). 2004. audio compact disk 29.95 (978-0-7435-3856-5(0)) Pub: S&S Audio. Dist(s): S and S Inc
Welcome to the Golden Age of Radio and the best in classic mystery. From 1939-1946 Americans gathered around their radio to listen to The New Adventures of Sherlock Holmes - featuring Basil Rathbone as the high strung crime solver and Nigel Bruce as his phlegmatic assistant, Dr. Watson. Witty, fast-paced and always surprising, these great radio plays - written by the prolific writing team of Anthony Boucher and Denis Green - are as fresh today as they were then. The latest audio technology was employed to bring the best audio quality and fidelity to the original performances, which feature nostalgic war-time announcements, original commercials and radio narrations. This special CD edition includes 12 of the series' best episodes: • The Unfortunate Tobacconist and The Paradol Chamber • The Viennese Strangler and The Notorious Canary Trainer • The April Fool's Day Adventure and The Strange Adventure of the Uneasy Easy Chair • The Strange Case of the Demon Barber and The Mystery of the Headless Monk • The Amateur Mendicant Society and The Case of the Vanishing White Elephant • The Case of the Limping Ghost and The Girl with the Gazelle.

New Adventures of Sherlock Holmes: The Case of the Bleeding Chandelier & The Adventure of the Veiled Lodger. 1 CD. (Running Time: 1 hr.). (Old-Time Radio Blockbusters Ser.). 2001. audio compact disk 4.98 (7710) Radio Spirits.

New Adventures of Sherlock Holmes Vol. 6: The Case of the Limping Ghost & the Girl with the Gazelle. abr. ed. Anthony Boucher. Read by Basil Rathbone & Nigel Bruce. 1 cass. (Running Time: 1 hr.). 1998. 5.98 S&S Audio.

New Adventures of Sherlock Holmes Vol. 17: The Living Doll & the Disappearing Scientists. abr. ed. Anthony Boucher. Read by Basil Rathbone & Nigel Bruce. 1 cass. (Running Time: 1 hr.). 1999. Rental 5.98 (978-0-671-04357-5(9), Audioworks) S&S Audio.

New Adventures of Sherlock Holmes Collection, Vol. 2. abr. ed. Anthony Boucher & Denis Green. Read by Basil Rathbone & Nigel Bruce. (Running Time: 60 hrs. 0 mins. 0 sec.). (Sherlock Holmes Ser.). (ENG.). 2009. audio compact disk 14.99 (978-1-4423-0020-0(5)) Pub: S&S Audio. Dist(s): S and S Inc

New Adventures of Sherlock Holmes Slip Case, Vols. 1-13. unabr. ed. Anthony Boucher & Denis Greene. Perf. by Basil Rathbone & Nigel Bruce. 13 cass. 129.35 set. S&S Audio.

New Age. Neville Goddard. 1 cass. (Running Time: 1 hr. 2 min.). 1962. 8.00 (35) J & L Pubns.
Neville taught Imagination Creates Reality. He was a powerfully influential teacher of God as Consciousness.

***New Age.** Featuring Ravi Zacharias. 1990. audio compact disk 9.00 (978-1-61256-041-0(5)) Ravi Zach.

New Age Astrology. Loretta Tucker. 1 cass. (Running Time: 1 hr.). 8.95 (720) Am Fed Astrologers.
An AFA Convention workshop tape.

New Age Awareness. Swami Amar Jyoti. 1 cass. (Running Time: 1 hr.). 1982. 9.95 (O-20) Truth Consciousness.
Being open to receive from the cosmos. The right to evolve. Changing our central identification, living consciously.

New Age Consciousness. Swami Amar Jyoti. 1 cass. (Running Time: 1 hr.). 1982. 9.95 (M-30) Truth Consciousness.
Full awakening as Conscious Beings. Not merely betterment but extending consciousness to the Ultimate Destination.

New Age Facts & Prophecies. Jean Munzer. 2 cass. (Running Time: 2 hrs. 30 min.). 1994. 19.95 (978-1-57124-015-6(2)) Creat Seminars.
What is the meaning of "The New Age".

New Age Gawain & the Green Knight. unabr. ed. Diane Edgecomb. Perf. by Diane Edgecomb. Music by Margot Chamberlain. 1 cass. (Running Time: 46 min.). (YA). 1996. 10.00 (978-0-9651669-1-1(0)) Living Myth Audio.
A fanciful modernization of the medieval classic, "Sir Gawain & the Green Knight". It takes Gawain from the bosom of Arthur's men's group to a legendary castle where an unusual triple goddess tries his patience & assails his new age virtue.

New Age Kind of Love: John 2:18-29, B0012. Ben Young. 1996. 4.95 (978-0-7417-6012-8(6), B0012) Win Walk.

New Age Loon. 1 cass. (Running Time: 1 hr.). 1994. audio compact disk 15.95 (0291, Creativ Pub) Quayside.
Fusion of New Age music with the unique sounds of the loon.

New Age Loon. 1 cass. (Running Time: 1 hr.). 1994. 9.95 (0290, NrthWrd Bks) TandN Child.

New Age Loon Two. 1 cass. (Running Time: 1 hr.). 1994. audio compact disk 15.95 (2234, Creativ Pub) Quayside.
Songs of the loon blend & merge with pieces of New Age music. Serene & uplifting.

New Age Loon Two. 1 cass. (Running Time: 1 hr.). 1994. 9.95 (2232, NrthWrd Bks) TandN Child.

New Age Movement. Voddie Baucham, Jr. (YA). 2002. audio compact disk 25.00 (978-0-633-09037-1(9)) LifeWay Christian.

New Age Movement. Mother Angelica & Father Michael. 1 cass. (Running Time: 1 hr.). (Mother Angelica Live Ser.). 1988. 10.00 (978-1-55794-106-0(8), T57) Eternal Wrd TV.
Describes the dangers of the New Age Movement.

New Age of Mind & Consciousness see Futureshaping

New Age Spirits from the Underworld. Jack Van Impe. Read by Jack Van Impe. 1 cass. (Running Time: 1 hr. 18 min.). 7.00 J V I Minist.
Biblical analysis of the New Age Movement.

New Age Spirits from the Underworld. Jack Van Impe. 1 cass. (Running Time: 1 hr. 18 min.). 7.00 J Van Impe.
Exposes some shocking truths about the New Age movement which undoubtedly fulfill major end-time prophecies.

New Age Spiritual Values: Simplicity, Moderation, Cooperation. Asha Praver. (Introduction to the Spiritual Life Ser.). 9.95 (AT-63) Crystal Clarity.
Topics include: The meaning of simplicity; discipline as the route to moderation; times when you should be "excessive"; cooperation as perfect discipleship; opening up to God's love; how to live in a temporary world.

New Age Wolf. 1 cass. (Running Time: 1 hr.). 1994. audio compact disk 15.95 (2254, Creativ Pub) Quayside.
Wolf vocalizations play upon a background of modern New Age compositions.

New Age Wolf. 1 cass. (Running Time: 1 hr.). 1994. 9.95 (2252, NrthWrd Bks) TandN Child.

New America: Reaching Out to a 21st Century Renaissance. Dott Clarke Koch. 2006. bk. 12.95 (978-0-9789043-1-9(1)) Wildot.

New American Bible. Narrated by Stephen Johnston. (ENG.). 2007. 24.95 (978-0-9801087-5-0(6)) Alpha DVD.

New American Bible. unabr. rev. ed. Narrated by Buck Ford. (ENG.). 2005. 19.99 (978-1-60814-001-5(6)) Oasis Audio.

New American Bible. unabr. rev. ed. Created by Oasis Audio Staff. Narrated by Buck Ford. (Running Time: 20 hrs. 52 mins. 0 sec.). (ENG.). 2005. audio compact disk 39.99 (978-1-59859-003-6(0)) Oasis Audio.

New American Bible: New Testament. rev. ed. 16 cass. (Running Time: 16 hrs.). 1997. 43.95 (978-0-89942-618-1(2), 618/00) Cathlic Bk Pub.

New American Standard Bible: Old & New Testament Entire Bible on CD MP3 Format. Read by Steven B. Stevens. Prod. by TAW~Global. 2 CDs (MP3). (Running Time:). 2005. audio compact disk 34.99 (978-0-9726363-6-0(6), Promises for Life) Brite Bks.

New American Standard Bible (NASB) Narrated by E. W. Red Jeffries. 48 cass. - 4 albums. 1996. vinyl bd. 99.99 (978-1-58968-022-7(7), 1851A); vinyl bd. 99.99 Set, incl. carrying case with handle. (978-1-58968-023-4(5), 1852H) Chrstn Dup Intl.
The complete version of the New American Standard Bible.

New American Standard Bible (NASB) deluxe ed. Read by E. W. Jeffries. 1997. vinyl bd. 199.99 (978-1-58968-031-9(6)) Chrstn Dup Intl.

New American Standard Bible (NASB) New Testament. Narrated by E. W. Jeffries. 6 cass. - sleeve. (Running Time: 9 hrs.). 1996. 29.97 Set, twin-pak with full-color sleeves. (978-1-58968-028-9(6), 1842S) Chrstn Dup Intl.
The New American Standard Bible of the New Testament & Psalms.

New American Standard Bible (NASB) New Testament. Narrated by E. W. Red Jeffries. 12 cass. - album. 1996. vinyl bd. 29.99 (978-1-58968-021-0(9), 1850A) Chrstn Dup Intl.

New American Standard Bible (NASB) New Testament (Spoken Word) Narrated by E. W. Jeffries. 12 cass. 1996. 24.97 (978-1-58968-025-8(1), 1840S) Chrstn Dup Intl.

New American Standard Bible (NASB) Old Testament. Narrated by E. W. Jeffries. 36 cass. - 3 sleeves. 1996. 69.97 (978-1-58968-024-1(3), 1839S) Chrstn Dup Intl.

New American Standard Bible (NASB) Old Testament. Narrated by E. W. Red Jeffries. 36 cass. 3 albums. 1996. vinyl bd. 79.99 (978-1-58968-020-3(0), 1849A) Chrstn Dup Intl.

New American Standard Bible (NASB) Old Testament. deluxe ed. Read by E. W. Jeffries. 1997. vinyl bd. 169.99 (978-1-58968-029-6(4)) Chrstn Dup Intl.

New American Standard Bible (NASB) Psalms & Proverbs. Read by E. W. Jeffries. 6 cass. - album. (Running Time: 9 hrs.). 2000. vinyl bd. 14.97 (978-1-58968-149-1(5)) Chrstn Dup Intl.

New American Standard Bible (NASB) Psalms (Spoken Word) Narrated by E. W. Jeffries. 4 cass. - sleeve. 1996. 9.97 (978-1-58968-027-2(8), 1856S) Chrstn Dup Intl.

New American Standard Bible (NASB) (Spoken Word) Narrated by E. W. Jeffries. 48 cass. - 4 sleeves. 1996. 84.97 (978-1-58968-026-5(X), 1841S) Chrstn Dup Intl.

New American Standard Bible New Testament. Read by Steven B. Stevens. (ENG.). 2007. audio compact disk 39.99 (978-1-930034-46-4(6)) Casscomm.

New American Standard Bible Psalms & Proverbs on CD - 1859. 1 CD. (Running Time: 1 hr. 30 min.). 1998. audio compact disk 15.39 Chrstn Dup Intl.

New American Story. unabr. ed. Bill Bradley. Narrated by Michael Prichard. (Running Time: 14 hrs. 30 mins. 0 sec.). (ENG.). 2007. audio compact disk 39.99 (978-1-4001-0448-2(3)); audio compact disk 29.99 (978-1-4001-5448-7(0)); audio compact disk 79.99 (978-1-4001-3448-9(X)) Pub: Tantor Media. Dist(s): IngramPubServ

New American Streamline: Connections. Bernard Hartley & Peter Viney. 1995. 39.95 (978-0-19-434832-4(6)) OUP.

New American Streamline: Connections. Bernard Hartley & Peter Viney. 1995. audio compact disk 39.95 (978-0-19-434848-5(2)) OUP.

New American Streamline: Departures. Bernard Hartley. 1995. audio compact disk 39.95 (978-0-19-434847-8(4)) OUP.

New American Streamline: Departures. Robert Maidment. 1995. 39.95 (978-0-19-434828-7(8)) OUP.

New American Streamline Destinations. Bernard Hartley & Peter Viney. 1995. 55.50 (978-0-19-434836-2(9)); audio compact disk 55.50 (978-0-19-434849-2(0)) OUP.

New American Workplace. abr. unabr. ed. Edward E. Lawler, III. Read by Patrick Cullen. 5 cass. (Running Time: 36000 sec.). 2006. 25.95 (978-0-7861-4547-8(1)); audio compact disk 25.95 (978-0-7861-7131-6(6)); audio compact disk 29.95 (978-0-7861-7606-9(7)) Blckstn Audio.

New American Workplace. unabr. ed. Edward E. Lawler, III. Read by Patrick Cullen. (Running Time: 36000 sec.). 2006. 59.95 (978-0-7861-4635-2(4)); audio compact disk 72.00 (978-0-7861-6831-6(5)) Blckstn Audio.

New & Evolving Trends in Diabetes & Diabetic Ketoacidosis. Contrib. by David E. Goldstein et al. 1 cass. (Running Time: 1 hr. 30 min.). (American Academy of Pediatrics UPDATE: Vol. 17, No. 4). 1998. 20.00 Am Acad Pediat.

New & Not Bad Pretty Good Jokes. unabr. ed. Garrison Keillor. Contrib. by Garrison Keillor. Contrib. by Paula Poundstone. (Running Time: 1 hr.). (ENG.). 2005. audio compact disk 9.95 (978-1-56511-996-3(7), 1565119967) Pub: Penguin-HghBrdg. Dist(s): Workman Pub

New Appelman's Insurance Coverage Teleconference: Confidentiality in Bad Faith Actions, Other Insurance Clauses, & Overlapping Coverage Issues Audio CD (December 2007) 2007. 149.00 (978-1-59579-793-3(9)) Pub: LexisNexis Mealey. Dist(s): LEXIS Pub

New Appleman's Insurance Teleconference: The Impact of Mass Catastrophes on Insurance Coverage Audio CD (October 2007) 2007. 149.00 (978-1-59579-749-0(1)) Pub: LexisNexis Mealey. Dist(s): LEXIS Pub

New Approach to Medicine. Interview with Andrew Weil & Michael Toms. 2 cass. (Running Time: 1 hr. 30 min.). (New Dimensions Ser.). 1997. 15.95 (978-1-56170-417-0(2)) Hay House.
Discusses the challenging face of healing in our western culture & explores how we as patients can help improve the care we receive.

New Approach to Spirituality; Authority of the Church & Freedom of the Spirit. Joseph F. Girzone. Read by Joseph F. Girzone. 1 cass. (Running Time: 1 hr. 30 min.). 1992. 7.95 (978-0-911519-12-9(2)) Richelieu Court.
Girzone's public talk on these topics.

New Approaches to Imaging in Trauma Care. 3 cass. (Running Time: 4 hrs. 30 min.). (General Sessions Ser.: C84-SP6). 1984. 22.50 (8421) Am Coll Surgeons.

New Arabian Nights, unabr. ed. Robert Louis Stevenson. Read by Mary Woods. 2 cass. (Running Time: 3 hrs.). (YA). 1990. 14.95 (978-1-55685-162-9(6)) Audio Bk Con.
Like Sheherazade, Stevenson, the consummate storyteller, is at the peak of his craft.

New Arrival English. Jane Yeldin & Caroline T. Linse. (J). 1992. 28.75 (978-0-8384-2255-7(1)) Heinle.

New Art of Negotiating: How to Close Any Deal. unabr. ed. Gerard I. Nierenberg & Henry H. Calero. Read by Scott Peterson. (Running Time: 5 hrs. 55 mins.). (ENG.). 2009. 24.98 (978-1-59659-361-9(X), GildAudio) Pub: Gildan Media. Dist(s): HachBkGrp

New Atlantis, abr. ed. Francis Bacon. 2 cass. (Running Time: 3 hrs.). 2000. 16.00 (978-0-7661-0844-8(9)) Kessinger Pub.

New Atlantis. unabr. ed. Francis Bacon. 1 cass. (Running Time: 1 hr. 30 mins.). 2000. 16.00 (978-0-7661-0843-1(0)) Kessinger Pub.
Refers to the philosophy of the Rosicrucians & Freemasons. Mystery.

New Attitude Audio Experience. Joshua Harris. Featuring Joshua Harris. 2 cass. 1995. 14.95 (978-1-56857-026-6(0)) Noble Pub Assocs.

New Ballgame: 1 Peter 2:18-25. Ed Young. 1983. 4.95 (978-0-7417-1277-6(6), 277) Win Walk.

New Beginning. Perf. by Allen and Allen. 1 cass. (Running Time: 1 hr. 30 min.). 10.98 (978-1-57908-265-9(3), 1325); audio compact disk 15.98 (978-1-57908-264-2(5)) Platinm Enter.

New Beginning. Perf. by Allen and Allen. 1 cass. (Running Time: 1 hr. 30 min.). 1998. 9.98; audio compact disk 15.98 Platinum Chrst Dist.

New Beginning. Derek Prince. 3 cass. (Running Time: 4 hrs.). 17.85 (098-099-100) Derek Prince.
God has made the full & perfect provision for each of us to have the new beginning that we all need.

New Beginning - ShowTrax. Music by John Jacobson. Arranged by Roger Emerson. 1 CD. (Running Time: 5 mins.). 2000. audio compact disk 19.95 (08711269) H Leonard.
Inspired by the words of Maya Angelou, this contemporary original is a joyful welcome to the new century.

New Beginnings. unabr. ed. Wanda E. Brunstetter. Read by Ellen Grafton. (Running Time: 4 hrs.). (Rachel Yoder - Always Trouble Somewhere Ser.). 2010. audio compact disk 14.99 (978-1-4418-1176-9(1), 9781441811769) Brilliance Audio.

***New Beginnings.** unabr. ed. Wanda E. Brunstetter. Read by Ellen Grafton. (Running Time: 4 hrs.). (Rachel Yoder - Always Trouble Somewhere Ser.). 2010. 14.99 (978-1-4418-1178-3(8), 9781441811783, Brilliance MP3); 39.97 (978-1-4418-1179-0(6), 9781441811790, Brlnc Audio MP3 Lib); 14.99 (978-1-4418-1180-6(X), 9781441811806, BAD); 39.97 (978-1-4418-1181-3(8), 9781441811813, BADLE); audio compact disk 44.97 (978-1-4418-1177-6(X), 9781441811776, BriAudCD Unabrid) Brilliance Audio.

New Beginnings. unabr. ed. Warren W. Wiersbe. Read by Warren W. Wiersbe. 1 cass. (Running Time: 1 hr. 15 min.). 1989. 4.95 (978-0-8474-2362-0(X)) Back to Bible.
Messages that cover the doctrines of salvation & "real" righteousness.

New Beginnings: Finding the Real You & Blossoming after Divorce. Dale Huffaker. 2 cass. (Running Time: 1 hr. 30 min.). 1997. 16.95 (978-0-9654153-0-9(9)) D Huffaker.
One individual's divorce & journey to healing & understanding.

New Beginnings: Panel of Superiors of New Communities: Br. James Curran, Fr. Jonathan Robinson, Mother Agnes Mary Donovan, Mother Peter Marie Duffy. 1 cass. (National Meeting of the Institute, 1995 Ser.). 4.00 (95N4) IRL Chicago.

New Behavior Generator. Paul R. Scheele. 1 cass. (Paraliminal Tapes Ser.). 1988. 34.95 (978-0-925480-00-2(2)) Learn Strategies.
Move past behaviors which are blocking you & acquire new behaviors.

New Being. Yamil Ledesma. (SPA.). 2006. audio compact disk 14.99 (978-0-8297-5058-4(4)) Zondervan.

New Believer's Bible: Book of John: More Than a Carpenter Today. unabr. ed. Greg Laurie. Narrated by Stephen Baldwin. (ENG.). 2005. 6.99 (978-1-60814-317-7(1)) Oasis Audio.

New Believer's Bible: Gospel of John. Stephen Baldwin. (Running Time: 016200 sec.). 2005. 19.99 (978-1-58926-911-8(X)) Oasis Audio.

New Believer's Bible: Gospel of John. unabr. ed. Narrated by Stephen Baldwin. (ENG.). 2005. 13.99 (978-1-60814-316-0(3)) Oasis Audio.

New Believer's Bible - Gospel of John. unabr. ed. Read by Stephen Baldwin. 3 CDs. audio compact disk 21.99 (978-1-58926-910-1(1)) Oasis Audio.

New Believer's Bible Handbook: First Steps for New Christians. Greg Laurie. (Running Time: 16200 sec.). 2004. audio compact disk 17.99 (978-1-59859-081-4(2)) Oasis Audio.

New Beverly Hills Diet Slim Kit, unabr. ed. Judy Mazel. Read by Judy Mazel. 4 cass. (Running Time: 5 hrs.). 1998. bk. 24.95 (978-1-55874-650-3(1)) Health Comm.

***New Bible Cure for Cancer.** unabr. ed. Don Colbert. Narrated by Tim Lundeen. (Running Time: 2 hrs. 0 mins. 0 sec.). (Bible Cure Ser.). (ENG.). 2010. 9.09 (978-1-60814-691-8(X)); audio compact disk 12.99 (978-1-59859-740-0(X)) Oasis Audio.

***New Bible Cure for Depression & Anxiety.** unabr. ed. Don Colbert. Narrated by Tim Lundeen. (Running Time: 2 hrs. 54 mins. 30 sec.). (Bible Cure Ser.). (ENG.). 2010. 9.09 (978-1-60814-686-4(3)); audio compact disk 12.99 (978-1-59859-735-6(3)) Oasis Audio.

***New Bible Cure for Diabetes.** unabr. ed. Don Colbert. Narrated by Tim Lundeen. (Running Time: 2 hrs. 16 mins. 23 sec.). (Bible Cure Ser.). (ENG.). 2010. 9.09 (978-1-60814-687-1(1)); audio compact disk 12.99 (978-1-59859-736-3(1)) Oasis Audio.

***New Bible Cure for Heart Disease.** unabr. ed. Don Colbert. Narrated by Tim Lundeen. (Running Time: 3 hrs. 6 mins. 0 sec.). (Bible Cure Ser.). (ENG.). 2010. 9.09 (978-1-60814-690-1(1)); audio compact disk 12.99 (978-1-59859-739-4(6)) Oasis Audio.

***New Bible Cure for Osteoporosis.** unabr. ed. Don Colbert. Narrated by Tim Lundeen. (Running Time: 2 hrs. 23 mins. 27 sec.). (Bible Cure Ser.). (ENG.). 2010. 9.09 (978-1-60814-689-5(8)); audio compact disk 12.99 (978-1-59859-738-7(8)) Oasis Audio.

***New Bible Cure for Sleep Disorders.** unabr. ed. Don Colbert. Narrated by Tim Lundeen. (Running Time: 2 hrs. 34 mins. 30 sec.). (Bible Cure Ser.). (ENG.). 2010. 9.09 (978-1-60814-688-8(X)); audio compact disk 12.99 (978-1-59859-737-0(X)) Oasis Audio.

New Biology of Suicide: Week of March 9, 1998. Perf. by Suzanne Vega. Hosted by Fred Goodwin. Comment by John Hockenberry. Contrib. by Jan Fawcett et al. 1 cass. (Running Time: 1 hr.). (Infinite Mind Ser.). audio compact disk 15.00 (978-1-888064-53-7(6)) Lichtenstein Creat.
Leading researchers explain how breakthroughs in biochemistry help predict the risk of suicide. Also discussions with those who have come back from the brink of suicide.

New Birth. Kenneth E. Hagin. 2 cass. (Running Time: 3 hrs.). 1992. 8.00 (67H) Faith Lib Pubns.

New Birth. Derek Prince. 1 cass. (Running Time: 1 hr. 30 min.). (B-2013) Derek Prince.

New Birth. unabr. ed. Myrtle Smyth. Prod. by David Keyston. 1 cass. (Running Time: 1 hr. 11 min.). 2000. 8.95 (978-1-893107-36-6(1), M28) Healing Unltd.
Lecture of the metaphysical content on the subject.

***New Birth or Rebirth: Jesus Talks with Krishna.** unabr. ed. Ravi Zacharias. Narrated by Simon Vance. (ENG.). 2008. 9.98 (978-1-59644-584-0(X), Hovel Audio) christianaud.

New Birth or Rebirth: Jesus Talks with Krishna. unabr. ed. Ravi Zacharias. Read by Simon Vance. (Running Time: 2 hrs. 0 mins. 0 sec.). (ENG.). 2008. audio compact disk 15.98 (978-1-59644-583-3(1), Hovel Audio) christianaud.

New Body: Awakening Your Motivational Power to Shape a Perfect Body. unabr. ed. Forrest R. Tower. 3 cass. (Running Time: 3 hrs.). 1991. pap. bk. 45.00 (978-0-9627597-1-0(6)) F Tower Enter.
Designed to empower you with consistent drive to exercise. The reader/listener will become motivated to shape & tone their body.

New Body Guided Imagery. Forrest R. Tower. 1 cass. (Running Time: 1 hr.). 1991. 12.95 F Tower Enter.
This tape brings you to a deep hypnotic state of relaxation, then verbally walks you through either an aerobic or weightlifting workout. The process motivates the listener to exercise.

New Body Motivational Implants. Forrest R. Tower. 1 cass. (Running Time: 1 hr.). 1991. 12.95 (978-0-9627597-2-7(4)) F Tower Enter.
Positive affirmations with a musical background. This "self-talk" tape is designed to motivate the listener to exercise on a regular basis to shape a perfect body.

New Body Subliminal Motivation. unabr. ed. Forrest R. Tower. 1 cass. (Running Time: 1 hr.). 1991. 12.95 (978-0-9627597-4-1(0)) F Tower Enter.
Subliminal affirmation in a musical background. This tape motivates the listener to exercise on a regular basis to shape and tone their body.

New Boy, unabr. ed. R. L. Stine. Narrated by C. J. Critt. 3 pieces. (Running Time: 3 hrs. 45 mins.). (Fear Street Ser.). (gr. 5 up). 1997. 27.00 (978-0-7887-0275-4(0), 94483E7) Recorded Bks.
In this devilishly clever tale, teenaged Janie suspects the new hunk at Shadyside High School is the mastermind behind a series of shocking murders.

New Boy Is Lost! 2nd ed. Elizabeth Claire. 1 CD. Orig. Title: Where Is Taro? Teacher's Kit. (gr. 2-7). 2004. pap. bk. & tchr. ed. 39.00 (978-0-86647-194-7(4)) Pro Lingua.

New Boy Is Lost! Audio Cassette. Scripts. Elizabeth Claire. Read by Elizabeth Claire. Marilyn Rosenthal. 1. (Running Time: 1 hr.). Orig. Title: Where Is Taro? Audio Cassette. 2000. (978-0-937630-17-4(9)) Eardley Pubns.

New Breed. unabr. ed. W. E. B. Griffin. Read by Michael Russotto. 11 cass. (Running Time: 16 hrs. 30 mins.r cass.). (Brotherhood of War Ser.: No. 7). 1996. 88.00 (3823); Rental 14.95 (3823) Books on Tape.
A new breed of courageous fighting men carry on the traditions of their fathers in strange, faraway battlefields.

New Breed. unabr. collector's ed. W. E. B. Griffin. Read by Michael Russotto. 11 cass. (Running Time: 16 hrs. 30 mins.). (Brotherhood of War Ser.: Bk. 7). 1995. 88.00 (978-0-7366-3149-5(6), 3823) Books on Tape.

New Breed of Ministry. P. Cain. 1 cass. (Running Time: 1 hr.). 1990. 10.00 (978-0-00-147087-3(6)) BJUPr.

New Breed of Royalty: The Repairman: Jeremiah 18:4. Ed Young. (J). 1979. 4.95 (978-0-7417-1072-7(2), A0072) Win Walk.

New Buffettology: How Warren Buffett Got & Stayed Rich in Markets Like This & How You Can Too! abr. ed. Mary Buffett & David Clark. Read by Mary Buffett. 2006. 14.95 (978-0-7435-6273-7(9)) Pub: S&S Audio. Dist(s): S and S Inc

New Business: Finding & Keeping It. Emmet L. Robinson & Ed Eisen. Read by Emmet L. Robinson & Ed Eisen. 1 cass. (Running Time: 1 hr.). 1995. 14.95 King Street.
How to get new business without spending a dime on paid advertising.

New Business Corporation Law. 1 cass. (Running Time: 1 hr.). 1989. 45.00 (AC-478) PA Bar Inst.

***New Business Matters: Business English with a Lexical Approach.** 2nd ed. Mark Powell. (ENG.). (C). 2003. 75.95 (978-0-7593-9854-2(2)) Pub: Heinle. Dist(s): CENGAGE Learn

New Cambridge Advanced English, Set. 2nd rev. ed. Leo Jones. (Running Time: hrs. mins.). (ENG.). 1998. 42.00 (978-0-521-62940-9(3)) Cambridge U Pr.

***New Cambridge Advanced English Audio CDs (4)** 2nd ed. Leo Jones. (Running Time: 4 hrs. 36 mins.). (ENG.). 2010. audio compact disk 40.00 (978-0-521-18349-9(9)) Cambridge U Pr.

***New Cambridge English Course Level 1 Class Audio CDs (3)** Michael Swan & Catherine Walter. (Running Time: 3 hrs. 17 mins.). (New Cambridge English Course Ser.). (ENG.). 2010. audio compact disk 50.00 (978-0-521-13523-8(0)) Cambridge U Pr.

***New Cambridge English Course Level 2 Class Audio CDs (3)** Michael Swan & Catherine Walter. (Running Time: 2 hrs. 49 mins.). (New Cambridge English Course Ser.). (ENG.). 2010. audio compact disk 40.00 (978-0-521-14824-5(3)) Cambridge U Pr.

***New Cambridge English Course Level 3 Class Audio CDs (2)** Michael Swan et al. (Running Time: 2 hrs. 26 mins.). (New Cambridge English Course Ser.). (ENG.). 2010. audio compact disk 41.00 (978-0-521-17186-1(5)) Cambridge U Pr.

***New Cambridge English Course Level 4 Class Audio CDs (3)** Michael Swan et al. (Running Time: 3 hrs.). (New Cambridge English Course Ser.). (ENG.). 2010. audio compact disk 48.00 (978-0-521-14928-0(2)) Cambridge U Pr.

New Cambridge English Course 1, Set. Michael Swan & Catherine Walter. 4 cass. (Running Time: 3 hrs. 31 mins.). (New Cambridge English Course Ser.). (ENG.). 1990. 52.50 (978-0-521-37502-3(9)) Cambridge U Pr.

New Cambridge English Course 2. Michael Swan & Catherine Walter. 3 cass. (Running Time: 2 hrs. 53 mins.). (New Cambridge English Course Ser.). (ENG.). 1990. 42.00 (978-0-521-37503-0(7)) Cambridge U Pr.

New Cambridge English Course 3, Set. Michael Swan et al. 3 cass. (Running Time: 2 hrs. 31 mins.). (New Cambridge English Course Ser.). (ENG., 1992. 42.00 (978-0-521-37504-7(5)) Cambridge U Pr.

New Cambridge English Course 3, Set. Michael Swan et al. 3 cass. (Running Time: hrs. mins.). (New Cambridge English Course Ser.). (ENG., 1992. stu. ed. 14.70 (978-0-521-37508-5(8)) Cambridge U Pr.

New Cambridge English Course 4. Michael Swan et al. (Running Time: 1 hr. 2 mins.). (New Cambridge English Course Ser.). (ENG.). 1993. stu. ed. 14.70 (978-0-521-37509-2(6)) Cambridge U Pr.

New Cambridge English Course 4, Set. Michael Swan et al. 3 cass. (Running Time: hrs. mins.). (New Cambridge English Course Ser.). (ENG.). 1993. 42.00 (978-0-521-37505-4(3)) Cambridge U Pr.

New Catechism. Fr. Barbour. 2 cass. (Running Time: 3 hrs.). 8.00 Set. (93B) IRL Chicago.

New Catechism. Alfred McBride. 5 cass. (Running Time: 4 hrs. 46 min.). 1994. 40.95 (TAH310) Alba Hse Comns.
Fr. McBride's talks are filled with numerous useful & concrete suggestions for teaching the catechism, as well as abundant background information for understanding & appreciating it.

New Catechism & Religious Life: Mother Theresa on Vocations. Fr. Ibnatowicz. 1 cass. (Running Time: 1 hr.). 4.00 (93J) IRL Chicago.

New Catholic Catechism. Fr. Hardon. 9 cass. (Running Time: 13 hrs. 30 min.). 36.00 (94H) IRL Chicago.

New Celtic Worship. Contrib. by Edens Bridge. Prod. by Richard Lacy & Barrie Gledden. 2006. audio compact disk 13.98 (978-5-558-61248-6(7)) Maranatha Music.

New Centurions. unabr. ed. Joseph Wambaugh. Read by Alec Murdock. 10 cass. (Running Time: 15 hrs.). 59.50 (137) Audio Bk.
Serge Duran is a tough ex-marine who learns everything fast except how to escape his Chicano identity. Gus Pelbesly is a baby faced youth, tops at entrapping prostitutes & painfully unsure of his manhood, Roy Fehler is a thinking man, a self-proclaimed liberal until he faces his own true feelings about Blacks. These are men with all kinds of troubles. They are also a new breed of cop, dealing daily with a world coming apart around them.

New Century Handbook. 3rd ed. Christine A. Hult & Thomas N. Huckin. 2006. audio compact disk 43.00 (978-0-321-36541-5(0)); audio compact disk 43.00 (978-0-321-36542-2(9)) Longman.

New Century of Light. unabr. ed. Swami Amar Jyoti. 1 cass. (Running Time: 1 hr.). (Satsangs of Swami Amar Jyoti Ser.). 2000. 9.95 (978-0-933572-52-2(2), K-168) Truth Consciousness.
The message for the new century. Every thought and deed contribute to world energy. The raising of mass scale consciousness.

New Chastity & Other Arguments Against Women's Liberation. unabr. ed. Midge Decter. Read by Lois Betterton. 5 cass. (Running Time: 7 hrs.). 1990. 39.95 (978-0-7861-0226-6(8), 1199) Blckstn Audio.
Women's Lib, its errors & excesses & the impassioned, not always accurate, rhetoric of its prophetesses from Betty Friedan & Simone de Beauvoir to Kate Millett, Germaine Greer & Gloria Steinem are brilliantly dissected in this bold & slashing broadside by one of the country's leading social critics.

New Chazarah Techniques. Elimelech Gottlieb. 1 cass. (Running Time: 1 hr. 30 min.). 1999. 6.00 (Q60SD) Torah Umesorah.

New "Check-the-Box" & S Corporation Rules. 1997. bk. 99.00 (ACS-1278) PA Bar Inst.
Offers an overview & analysis.

New Chinese Three Hundred: A Beginning Language Course. Beijing Language Institute Staff. 12 cass. (Running Time: 12 hrs.). 1992. 125.00 (NCT12) Cheng Tsui.

New Chinese 300: A Beginning Language Course. abr. ed. Beijing Language Institute Staff. 3 cass. (Running Time: 1 hr.). (CHI & ENG.). (gr. 13 up). 1992. pap. bk. 45.95 (978-0-88727-121-2(9)) Cheng Tsui.

New Chinese 300: A Beginning Language Course. unabr. ed. Beijing Language Institute Staff. 12 cass. (Running Time: 1 hr.). (CHI & ENG.). (gr. 13 up). 1992. 119.95 (978-0-88727-003-1(4)) Cheng Tsui.

New Chinese 300 Set: A Beginning Language Course. unabr. ed. Bejing Language Institute Staff. 3 vols. (Running Time: 1 hr.). (C & T Asian Language Ser.). (gr. 13 up). 1992. pap. bk. 68.95 (978-0-88727-002-4(6)) Cheng Tsui.
Ideal for: Beginning. A bestselling spoken Chinese text for the beginner using 500-plus vocabulary items. S and P.

New Coach Blues. Steck-Vaughn Staff. 2003. (978-0-7398-8418-8(2)) SteckVau.

New Codependency: Help & Guidance for Today's Generation. unabr. ed. Melody Beattie. Narrated by Lorna Raver. (Running Time: 10 hrs. 30 mins. 0 sec.). (ENG.). 2009. audio compact disk 34.99 (978-1-4001-1164-0(1)); audio compact disk 69.99 (978-1-4001-4164-7(8)) Pub: Tantor Media. Dist(s): IngramPubServ

New Codependency: Help & Guidance for Today's Generation. unabr. ed. Melody Beattie. Read by Lorna Raver. (Running Time: 10 hrs. 30 mins. 0 sec.). (ENG.). 2009. audio compact disk 24.99 (978-1-4001-6164-5(9)) Pub: Tantor Media. Dist(s): IngramPubServ

New Colossus see Classic American Poetry

New Commandment: Love Thine Enemies. Instructed by Manly P. Hall. 8.95 (978-0-89314-198-1(4), C830403) Philos Res.

New Common Denominator of Success. Albert E. N. Gray. Read by Charlie Tremendous Jones. (Laws of Leadership Ser.). (ENG.). 2008. audio compact disk 19.95 (978-1-933715-79-7(0)) Executive Bks.

New Commonwealth Procurement Code. 1998. bk. 99.00 (ACS-2161) PA Bar Inst.
Act 57 of 1998, represents a watershed in the way billions of dollars in goods, services & construction are purchased each year. For the first time, most procurement law & regulations are gathered in one place, greatly simplifying the process for Commonwealth agencies, contractors, vendors, design professionals, political subdivisions & other falling within its scope.

New Concepts & New Approaches to the Management of Peptic Ulcer Disease. Moderated by Marvin H. Sleisenger. Contrib. by Jon I. Isenberg & Walter L. Peterson. 1 cass. (Running Time: 1 hr. 30 min.). 1986. 12.00 (A8650) Amer Coll Phys.
This topic is discussed by a moderator & experts who offer differing opinions.

New Concepts in Solar Homes. Hosted by Nancy Pearlman. 1 cass. (Running Time: 29 min.). 10.00 (214) Educ Comm CA.

New Concepts of Mechanisms & Treatment of Heart Failure. Moderated by Jay N. Cohn. Contrib. by William W. Parmley & Edmund H. Sonnenblick. 1 cass. (Running Time: 90 min.). 1986. 12.00 (A8645) Amer Coll Phys.
This topic is dicussed by a moderator & experts who offer differing opinions.

New Conceptual Selling: The Face-To-Face Sales Formula That Helps Leading Companies. abr. ed. Stephen E. Heiman & Diane Sanchez. Read by Stephen E. Heiman & Diane Sanchez. 2 cass. (Running Time: 1 hrs. 32 min.). 1998. (978-1-889888-07-1(9)) Miller Heiman.
In a casual interview format, Diane Sanchez, President & CEO & Stephen E. Heiman, co-founder of Miller Heiman, discuss the basic concepts behind the New Conceptual Selling, revised & updated for the 20th century.

New Conga Joy. Created by Bill Matthews. 1995. audio compact disk 15.00 (978-0-9718861-2-4(1)) Fremont Drum.

New Conga Joy, No. 2. Created by Bill Matthews. 1998. audio compact disk 15.00 (978-0-9718861-3-1(X)) Fremont Drum.
24 drum rhythms in full ensemble.

New Consciousness. Swami Amar Jyoti. 1 cass. (Running Time: 1 hr. 30 min.). 1980. 9.95 (P-35) Truth Consciousness.
Steps for letting go to reach the melting point for transformation. Touching the root causes of karmas so a new consciousness can be born. The meaning of interference with others.

New Consciousness in a New Society. unabr. ed. Willis Harman. 1 cass. (Running Time: 1 hr. 30 min.). 1972. 11.00 (00901) Big Sur Tapes.

New Consecration Sunday. Herb Miller. 2004. bk. 10.75 (978-0-687-06396-3(5)) Abingdon.

New Covenant. Contrib. by Johnathan Crumpton et al. Prod. by Ed Kee. (ENG.). 2008. audio compact disk 24.99 (978-5-557-48379-7(9), Brentwood-Benson Music) Brentwood Music.

New Covenant. Read by Wayne Monbleau. 6 cass. (Running Time: 8 hrs.). 1985. 45.00 Set. (978-0-944648-21-6(5), 301) Loving Grace Pubns.
Religious.

New Creation. Kenneth Copeland. Perf. by Kenneth Copeland. 1 cass. (Spiritual Death of Jesus: The Great Plan Ser.: Tape 3). 1995. cass. & video 5.00 (978-1-57562-024-4(3)) K Copeland Pubns.
Biblical teaching on spiritual death of Jesus.

New Creation. Derek Prince. 2 cass. (Running Time: 1 hr. per cass.). 1991. 5.95 ea. Derek Prince.
Do you have unsaved friends or relatives? Show them how the "New Creation" brings life that is divine, eternal, incorruptible, undefeatable & indestructible.

New Creation Realities. E. W. Kenyon. Read by Stephen Sobozenski. 6 cass. (Running Time: 353 mins.). 2003. 28.00 (978-1-57770-034-0(1)) Kenyons Gospel.
The rights and privileges of the new creation in the Light of the Pauline Revelation. Makes the Bible a living reality!.

New Crusades. Avi Lipkin. 2 CD's plus MP3. (Running Time: 2 hours). (Briefing Packages by Chuck Missler). 2004. audio compact disk 19.95 (978-1-57821-266-8(9)) Koinonia Hse.
Avi Lipkin lays out the groundwork for the coming era in history he dubs "The Neo Crusades". A time of coming religious warfare that will inflame the Middle-East, Europe and the World.Avi Lipkin has spoken to numerous churches, synagogues and civic groups (including radio and TV appearances). He offers compelling proof that fanatic Islam is the number one threat to world peace today.Contains two (2) one-hour casssette tapes.

New Dawn Rising. Maria Illo & William Brizendine. 1 cass. (Running Time: 1 hr.). 1994. 9.95 (978-0-9613159-3-1(8)) Emerald Forest.
Original songs with two guitars.

New Day see Philip Levine

New Day: Meditations for Personal & Spiritual Growth. John Frederick. Read by Dick Van Dyke & Julie Harris. 2 cass. (Running Time: 3 hrs.). 17.95 (978-1-56135-182-4(2)) FMS Prodns.

New Day Coming. Steve Grace. 1 CD. (Running Time: 45 min.). 2004. audio compact disk 14.95 (978-1-59601-005-5(3)) STL Dist NA.

New Day, New You: 366 Devotions for Enjoying Everyday Life. abr. ed. Joyce Meyer. Read by Sandra McCollom. (Running Time: 6 hrs.). (ENG.). 2007. 24.98 (978-1-60024-035-5(6)) Pub: Hachet Audio. Dist(s): HachBkGrp

New Day's Promise. Read by Mary Richards. 1 cass. (Running Time: 45 min.). (Energy Break Ser.). 2007. audio compact disk 19.95 (978-1-56136-151-9(8)) Master Your Mind.

New Deal. 10.00 (HD414) Esstee Audios.

New Deal & Political Reform CD. Franklin D. Roosevelt. 1 CD. (Running Time: 48 mins.). 2006. audio compact disk 12.95 (978-1-57970-394-3(1), AF0495D, Audio-For) J Norton Pubs.
Two "Fireside Chats" originally broadcast in 1935.

New Deal & Post War International Monetary System. unabr. ed. Murray Newton Rothbard. 1 cass. (Running Time: 1 hr. 25 min.). 11.95 (215) J Norton Pubs.
Examines the blunders in the monetary field made by FDR & those that followed him.

New Deal & the Postwar Money System CD Set. ed. Murray N. Rothbard. 2 CDs. (Running Time: 88 mins.). 2006. audio compact disk 14.95 (978-1-57970-396-7(8), AF0215D, Audio-For) J Norton Pubs.
Dr. Rothbard examines the blunders in the monetary field made by Franklin Roosevelt and those who followed him. (From the series "Cornell Lectures on 20th-Century Economic History.").

New Deal or Raw Deal? How FDR's Economic Legacy Has Damaged America. unabr. ed. Burton W. Folsom, Jr. & Jr Folsom. Narrated by Alan Sklar. (Running Time: 12 hrs. 0 mins. 0 sec.). (ENG.). 2009. audio compact disk 69.99 (978-1-4001-4264-4(4)); audio compact disk 24.99 (978-1-4001-6264-2(5)); audio compact disk 34.99 (978-1-4001-1264-7(8)) Pub: Tantor Media. Dist(s): IngramPubServ

New Developments in Employment Discrimination Litigation. 1986. 35.00; bk. 70.00 PA Bar Inst.
Includes book.

New Developments in Infectious Diseases. Read by Joseph E. Johnson, III. 1 cass. (Running Time: 1 hr. 30 min.). 1985. 12.00 (C8533) Amer Coll Phys.

New Developments in the Federal Law of Habeas Corpus: A Satellite Teleconference Presented by the Federal Judicial Center, Thursday, September 12, 1996, 60 Plus Cities Nationwide in Cooperation with the ALI-ABA Video Law Review. American Law Institute-American Bar Association, Committee on Continuing Professional Education Staff. 3 cass. (Running Time: 3 hrs. 50 min.). 1996. 75.00 (D255) Am Law Inst.
National experts on federal habeas corpus come together to update judges, staff attorneys, prosecutors, defense counsel & law clerks on the far-reaching effects of the new law. Includes study materials.

New Developments in the Management & Treatment of Diabetes. Moderated by Arthur H. Rubenstein. Contrib. by Jonathan B. Jaspan & Jay S. Skyler. 1 cass. (Running Time: 1 hr. 30 min.). 1986. 12.00 (A8664) Amer Coll Phys.
This topic is discussed by a moderator & experts who offer differing opinions.

New Dimensions. unabr. ed. Terence McKenna. 1 cass. (Running Time: 1 hr. 30 min.). 1983. 9.00 (978-1-56964-707-3(0), A0082-83) Sound Photosyn.
An artistic confluence of Terence's words & Faustin Bray & Brian Wallace's music. The precurser to "True Hallucinations".

New Dimensions in Stewardship. Bill Winston. 3 cass. (C). 1998. 15.00 (978-1-931289-80-1(8)) Pub: B Winston Min. Dist(s): Anchor Distributors

New Dimensions Interview with Krishnamurti - 1983. 1 cass. (Running Time: 35 min.). 8.50 (AND83) Krishnamurti.

New Dimensions Interview with Krishnamurti - 1984. 1 cass. (Running Time: 35 min.). 8.50 (AND84) Krishnamurti.

New Dimensions of Being. unabr. ed. Nathaniel Branden. 1 cass. (Running Time: 1 hr. 22 min.). 10.95 (845) J Norton Pubs.
Branden discusses romantic love, barriers in communication, the importance of complementary differences in partners, open relationships, self-esteem & honesty & integrity.

New Directions in Ericksonian Psychotherapy. Stephen G. Gilligan. 11 cass. (Running Time: 16 hrs. 30 min.). 1991. set in binder. (978-1-884605-03-1(6)) Genesis II.
Professional development psychotherapy.

New Discoveries in Natural Cancer Therapies. unabr. ed. Betty L. Morales. 1 cass. (Running Time: 20 min.). 10.95 (941) J Norton Pubs.

New Dispensation: As Presented by the Spirit World, Through the Automatic-Writings of Frances Bird. Frances Bird. Read by Kenneth Carey. 6 cass. (Running Time: 9 hrs. 10 min.). (Automatic Writings Ser.). 1988. pap. bk. 53.95 (978-1-55768-703-6(X)) LC Pub.
Gives insight into the nature of life awaiting in the spirit world, with explanations of what takes place following the transition, called death.

New Dynamics of Goal Setting: How to Use Flextactics to Shape Your Life & Thrive on Challenge. Denis Waitley. 6 cass. (Running Time: 6 hrs.). 1990. 59.95 incl. Flex Planner. (978-1-55525-074-4(2), 6081AB) Nightingale-Conant.
How can you stay focused on your goals in today's unpredictable world? With this indispensable guide, you'll get the newest, most effective tactics for setting & achieving goals & thriving in these rapidly changing times.

New Dynamics of Winning: Gaining the Mind-Set of a Champion. Denis Waitley. Read by Denis Waitley. 6 cass. (Running Time: 9 hrs.). 59.95 (708AD) Nightingale-Conant.
"The New Dynamics of Winning" brings together for the first time everything that science now knows about peak performance. With this powerful program, you'll gain what Denis Waitley calls the "superstar's edge." For example: Suppose you're faced with a difficult problem at work. You've got to make a decision fast. With the mental focus you'll acquire through "The New Dynamics of Winning," you'll respond forcefully & with absolute confidence. Includes Personal Success Survey & poster.

New Earth: Awakening to Your Life's Purpose. Eckhart Tolle. 2005. 39.99 (978-1-59895-022-9(3)) Find a World.

New Earth: Awakening to Your Life's Purpose. unabr. ed. Eckhart Tolle. Read by Eckhart Tolle. 8 CDs. (Running Time: 9 hrs.). (gr. 8 up). 2008. audio compact disk 29.95 (978-0-14-314349-9(2)) Penguin Grp USA.

New Elite: Inside the Minds of the Truly Wealthy. abr. ed. Doug Harrison & Jim Taylor. Read by Jim Bond & Kraus Stephen. 6 CDs. (Running Time: 7 hrs.). 2008. audio compact disk 29.95 (978-1-4233-6435-1(X), 9781423364351, Bril Audio CD Unabri) Brilliance Audio.

New Elite: Inside the Minds of the Truly Wealthy. abr. ed. Doug Harrison et al. Read by Jim Bond. 1 MP3-CD. (Running Time: 7 hrs.). 2008. 39.25 (978-1-4233-6438-2(4), 9781423364382, Brinc Audio MP3 Lib); 24.95 (978-1-4233-6437-5(6), 9781423364375, Brilliance MP3); audio compact disk 82.25 (978-1-4233-6436-8(8), 9781423364368, BriAudCD Unabrid) Brilliance Audio.

New Elite: Inside the Minds of the Truly Wealthy. unabr. abr. ed. Doug Harrison et al. Read by Jim Bond. (Running Time: 7 hrs.). 2008. 39.25 (978-1-4233-6440-5(6), 9781423364405, BADLE); 24.95 (978-1-4233-6439-9(2), 9781423364399, BAD) Brilliance Audio.

***New Empire of Debt: The Rise & Fall of an Epic Financial Bubble.** unabr. ed. William Bonner & Addison Wiggin. Read by Sean Pratt. (Running Time: 15 hrs. 30 mins.). (ENG.). 2009. 39.98 (978-1-59659-485-2(3), GildAudio) Pub: Gildan Media. Dist(s): HachBkGrp

New England. National Textbook Company Staff. 1 cass. (Running Time: 1 hr.). (Discover America Ser.). 15.00 (978-0-8442-7494-2(1), Natl Textbk Co) M-H Contemporary.
Offers a fascinating introduction to key locations in the country. Especially designed for intermediate ESL students, combines language learning with American culture study.

New England Almanac: A Kingdom of Ice see New England Almanac: Portraits in Sound of New England Life and Landscape

New England Almanac: Heartbeats in a Frozen Land see New England Almanac: Portraits in Sound of New England Life and Landscape

New England Almanac: In Search of the White Village see New England Almanac: Portraits in Sound of New England Life and Landscape

New England Almanac: Living History see New England Almanac: Portraits in Sound of New England Life and Landscape

New England Almanac: New England Pastoral see New England Almanac: Portraits in Sound of New England Life and Landscape

New England Almanac: On the Edge of the Sea see New England Almanac: Portraits in Sound of New England Life and Landscape

New England Almanac: Portraits in Sound of New England Life & Landscape. 1 cass. (Running Time: 1 hr.). Incl. Pt. 1. New England Almanac: The People of the Lake. (G036AB090); Pt. 2. New England Almanac: A Kingdom of Ice. (G036AB090); 10.95 (G036AB090, HarperThor); 10.95 (G036BB090, HarperThor); 10.95 (G036CB090, HarperThor); 10.95 (G036DB090, HarperThor); 10.95 (G036EB090, HarperThor); 10.95 (G036FB090, HarperThor); 9.95 (G036GB090, HarperThor) HarpC GBR.

New England Almanac: Snowdrifts see New England Almanac: Portraits in Sound of New England Life and Landscape

New England Almanac: Stories from the New England Hearth see New England Almanac: Portraits in Sound of New England Life and Landscape

New England Almanac: Summer People see New England Almanac: Portraits in Sound of New England Life and Landscape

New England Almanac: The Harvest see New England Almanac: Portraits in Sound of New England Life and Landscape

New England Almanac: The People of the Lake see New England Almanac: Portraits in Sound of New England Life and Landscape

New England Almanac: The Thaw see New England Almanac: Portraits in Sound of New England Life and Landscape

New England Almanac: The Woodsmen see New England Almanac: Portraits in Sound of New England Life and Landscape

New England Autumn. Mimi Lupin. 1988. bk. 9.95 (978-0-07-039163-5(7)) McGraw.

New England Bachelor see Richard Eberhart Reading His Poetry

New England Candlelight Tales. 1 cass. 12.95 (978-1-929244-03-4(7), CORA006) Colonial Radio.

New England Candlelight Tales. Perf. by Colonial Radio Theatre Staff. 1 cass. (Running Time: 1 hr. 6 mins.). 2001. 12.95 (COLR006) Lodestone Catalog.
Creepy Boston ghost stories will give you the shivers, but not too scary for the younger kids.

New England Days. Sarah Orne Jewett. Narrated by Tana Hicken. (Running Time: 18000 sec.). (Unabridged Classics in MP3 Ser.). (ENG.). 2008. audio compact disk 24.00 (978-1-58472-462-9(5), In Aud); audio compact disk 14.95 (978-1-58472-611-1(3), In Aud) Sound Room.

New England Nun: And Other Stories. Mary E. Wilkins Freeman. 1977. (D-5) Jimcin Record.

New England Nun & Other Stories, unabr. ed. Mary E. Wilkins Freeman. Read by Mary Woods et al. 2 cass. (Running Time: 3 hrs.). 1990. 14.95 (978-1-55685-181-0(2)) Audio Bk Con.
The title story & "The Scent of Roses", "A Gentle Ghost", "A Stolen Christmas" & "Pot of Gold" are pungent with country air & stalwart characters of New England.

New England Spring, 1942 see Poetry of Edna St. Vincent Millay

New England Stories. unabr. ed. Short Stories. Sarah Orne Jewett. Read by Tana Hicken. 2 cds. (Running Time: 2 hrs 14 mins). 2002. audio compact disk 18.95 (978-1-58472-294-6(0), 005, In Aud) Pub: Sound Room. Dist(s): Baker Taylor
Four of Jewett's best stories. Miss Tempy's Watchers, The Only Rose, Miss Esther's Guest, Martha's Lady.

New England White. abr. ed. Stephen L. Carter. Read by Bahni Turpin. 6 CDs. (Running Time: 25200 sec.). (ENG.). 2007. audio compact disk 31.95 (978-0-7393-4338-8(6), Random AudioBks) Pub: Random Audio Pubg. Dist(s): Random

New England White. unabr. ed. Stephen L. Carter. Read by Bahni Turpin. 18 CDs. (Running Time: 21 hrs.). 2007. audio compact disk 129.00 (978-1-4159-3902-4(0)); 129.00 (978-1-4159-4200-0(5)) Books on Tape.
With the powers of observation and richness of plot and character, the author of The Emperor of Ocean Park returns to the New England university town of Elm Harbor, where a murder begins to crack the veneer that has hidden the racial complications of the town's past, the secrets of a prominent family, and the most hidden bastions of African-American political influence. And at the center: Lemaster Carlyle, the university president, and his wife, Julia Carlyle, a deputy dean at the divinity school - African Americans living in "the heart of whiteness." Lemaster is an old friend of the president of the United States. Julia was the murdered man's lover years ago. The meeting point of these connections forms the core of a mystery that deepens even as Julia closes in on the politically earth-shattering motive behind the murder.

New English Course, No. 2. 1 cass. (Running Time: 1 hr. 30 mins.). 1.75 (978-0-89285-114-0(7), 1046) ELS Educ Servs.

New Enlightenment: A Complete Vision for Living a Spiritual Life in an Evolving World. unabr. ed. Andrew Cohen. 7 CDs. (Running Time: 7 hrs.). 2005. audio compact disk 79.95 (978-1-883929-45-9(8)) Moksha Pr.
Over the course of nearly two decades, Andrew Cohen an internationally recognized spiritual teacher and the creative force behind What Is Enlightenment? magazine has redefined the meaning and significance of enlightenment for the modern age. Now, for the first time, this CD collection presents Cohen's revolutionary teaching, which he calls Evolutionary Enlightenment, in its entirety.

New Entrepreneurs: Making a Living, Making a Life Through Network Marketing. Rene Reid Yarnell. 2000. 15.95 (978-1-883599-16-4(4)) Quantum NV.

New Estate Planning Techniques for the Changing Tax Environment. Instructed by Lynne Stebbins. 2 CDs. (Running Time: 120 mins.). 2004. audio compact disk 19.95 (978-1-59280-122-0(6)) Marketplace Bks.
Staying in-step with the ever-changing tax climate is critical for financial professionals. Now, specialist Lynne Stebbins provides an in-depth overview of the Bush-era tax changes and their impact on retirement planning strategies, in this thorough new workshop.Highlighting a wide range of cutting-edge tools for estate, retirement and business planning - from dividend giveaways with C-corps to buy-sell agreements - Stebbins thoroughly explains how to apply each tool to address specific client needs.

New Europe. abr. ed. Michael Palin. Narrated by Michael Palin. (Running Time: 27000 sec.). (ENG.). 2008. audio compact disk 29.95 (978-1-60283-354-8(0)) Pub: AudioGO. Dist(s): Perseus Dist

New Europe: An Economic Necessity. (Running Time: 46 min.). 1989. 12.95 (C0080B090, HarperThor) HarpC GBR.

New Every Morning, unabr. ed. Ann Purser. Read by Lynne Verrall. 8 cass. (Running Time: 12 hrs.). (Isis Ser.). (J). 2004. 69.95 (978-0-7531-0456-9(3), 981106) Pub: ISIS Lrg Prnt GBR. Dist(s): Ulverscroft US
At Ringford Church of England School, Sarah Drinkwater replaces the headteacher, coming in like March wind, blowing out cobwebs & oblivious to traditional village opposition. Her charms have an uncomfortable effect on John Barnett, confirmed bachelor & local farmer. Her brave fight to save the school from closure changes many minds, though not that of Ivy Beasley, whose dreams & schemes have a powerful effect on events. Future lives depend on the final decision. Will it be heartbreak or celebration.

***New Exhibit.** 2010. audio compact disk (978-1-59171-278-7(5)) Falcon Picture.

New Fascism: Rule by Consensus. Comment by Ayn Rand. 1 cass. (Running Time: 55 min.). (Ford Hall Forum Ser.). 1965. 12.95 (AR03C) Second Renaissance.
How the "cult of compromise" is moving America toward a fascist form of statism.

New Fascism: Rule by Consensus. Ayn Rand. Read by Ayn Rand. 1 cass. (Running Time: 55 min.). 1965. 12.95 (978-1-56114-066-4(X), AR03C) Second Renaissance.

New Flatlanders: A Seeker's Guide to the Theory of Everything. Eric Middleton. (gr. 13). 2008. audio compact disk 24.95 (978-1-59947-139-6(6)) Pub: Templeton Pr. Dist(s): Chicago Distribution Ctr

New Flava. 1 cass. (Running Time: 1 hr.). 10.98 (978-1-57908-311-3(0), 1390); audio compact disk 15.98 CD. (978-1-57908-310-6(2), 1390) Platinm Enter.

New French with Ease. 4 cass. (Running Time: 6 hrs.). (FRE.). 1998. 59.95 Assimil USA.

New Friends. D. F. Pearce & S. Miloslavskaya. 2 cass. (Running Time: 3 hrs.). (C). 1991. bk. 90.00 (978-0-569-09297-5(3)) St Mut.
Language: Russian Level 3 recorded by native speakers.

New Frontier. Peter David. (Star Trek Ser.). 2004. 13.95 (978-0-7435-4807-6(8)) Pub: S&S Audio. Dist(s): S and S Inc

New Frontiers in the Prevention of Post-Surgical Sepsis. 2 cass. (Running Time: 3 hrs.). (General Sessions Ser.: C84-SP2). 1984. 15.00 (8417) Am Coll Surgeons.

New Frontiers in Ultrasonic & Traditional Liposuction. Elliott Lavey. 1 cass. (Running Time: 40 min.). 1998. bk. 15.00 (978-1-58111-075-3(8)) Contemporary Medical.

New Frugality: How to Consume Less, Save More, & Live Better. unabr. ed. Chris Farrell. Read by Chris Farrell. 6 CDs. (Running Time: 7 hrs.). (ENG.). 2009. audio compact disk 26.95 (978-1-61573-034-6(6), 1615730346) Pub: HighBridge. Dist(s): Workman Pub

New Girl. Meg Cabot. Read by Tara Sands. (Allie Finkle's Rules for Girls Ser.: Bk. 2). (J). 2008. 44.99 (978-1-60640-546-8(2)) Find a World.

New Girl. Meg Cabot. Narrated by Tara Sands. (Allie Finkle's Rules for Girls Ser.: Bk. 2). (ENG.). (J). 2008. audio compact disk 49.95 (978-0-545-03967-3(3)) Scholastic Inc.

New Girl. Meg Cabot. Narrated by Tara Sands. (Allie Finkle's Rules for Girls Ser.: Bk. 2). (ENG.). (J). (gr. 4-7). 2008. audio compact disk 19.95 (978-0-545-03949-9(5)) Scholastic Inc.

New Girl. unabr. ed. Meg Cabot. Narrated by Tara Sands. 4 CDs. (Running Time: 4 hrs. 10 mins.). (Allie Finkle's Rules for Girls Ser.: Bk. 2). (J). (gr. 3-5). 2008. audio compact disk 49.95 (978-0-545-14281-6(4)) Scholastic Inc.

New Golden Age: The Coming Revolution Against Political Corruption & Economic Chaos. unabr. ed. Ravi Batra. Read by Brian Emerson. (Running Time: 37800 sec.). 2007. 29.95 (978-0-7861-4809-7(8)); 59.95 (978-0-7861-4810-3(1)); audio compact disk 29.95 (978-0-7861-6191-1(4)); audio compact disk 29.95 (978-0-7861-7173-6(1)); audio compact disk 72.00 (978-0-7861-6192-8(2)) Blckstn Audio.

New Golden Ring Vol. 1: Five Days Singing. 1 cass. (Running Time: 1 hr.). 9.98 (C-41); audio compact disk 14.98 CD. (CD-41) Folk-Legacy.
Songs from an even larger gathering of friends.

New Golden Ring Vol. 2: Five Days Singing. 1 cass. (Running Time: 1 hr.). 9.98 (C-42); audio compact disk 14.98 CD. (CD-42) Folk-Legacy.
Great songs, great harmonies & great fun.

***New Good Life: Living Better Than Ever in an Age of Less.** unabr. ed. John Robbins. (Running Time: 10 hrs. 0 mins.). 2010. 16.99 (978-1-4001-8697-6(8)) Tantor Media.

***New Good Life: Living Better Than Ever in an Age of Less.** unabr. ed. John Robbins. Narrated by Paul Boehmer. (Running Time: 12 hrs. 0 mins. 0 sec.). (ENG.). 2010. 24.99 (978-1-4001-6697-6(7)); audio compact disk 34.99 (978-1-4001-1697-3(X)); audio compact disk 69.99 (978-1-4001-4697-0(6)) Pub: Tantor Media. Dist(s): IngramPubServ

New Gospel Legends: The Best of Thomas Whitfield. Perf. by Thomas Whitfield. 1 cass. (Running Time: 1 hr.). 1998. 10.98 (978-0-7601-2839-8(1)); audio compact disk 16.98 (978-0-7601-2838-1(3)) Provident Mus Dist.

New Grammar in Action 1: Collaborations Begginers 1. Barbara H. Foley & Elizabeth Neblett. 2000. pap. bk. 90.95 (978-0-8384-8672-6(X)) Heinle.
A streamlined, fun-filled course in English that immediately gets students speaking, reading and writing in the language.

New Great Themes of Scripture. Richard Rohr. 10 cass. (Running Time: 13 hrs.). 2001. 49.95 (A7090) St Anthony Mess Pr.
Instead of treating the Bible as a collection of isolated books, Rohr explores the Bible as one inspired anthology.

New Grub Street, unabr. ed. George R. Gissing. Narrated by Flo Gibson. 11 cass. (Running Time: 16 hrs. 38 min.). (gr. 10 up). 1999. 34.95 (978-1-55685-619-8(9)) Audio Bk Con.
A semi-autobiographical novel about a group of novelists & journalists striving to earn a living & dealing with poverty, stress & marital problems.

New Hampshire Criminal Code. Lexis Editorial Staff. pap. bk. 48.00 (978-0-8205-8111-8(9)) LEXIS Pub.

New Hampshire Criminal Code with CD-ROM & New Hampshire Selected Motor Vehicle, Boating & Related Laws Annotated with CD-ROM 2004-2005 Combo. pap. bk. 89.50 (978-0-8205-8131-6(3)) LEXIS Pub.

New Hampshire, February see Richard Eberhart Reading His Poetry

New Handbook for Third World Journalists, Illus. by Albert L. Hester. 4 cass. (Running Time: 6 hrs.). 1999. 49.95 (978-0-9673027-0-6(6)) Green Berry Pr.

New Headway English Course. Liz Soars & John Soars. 2003. 31.95 (978-0-19-436668-7(5)) OUP.

New Headway English Course: Intermediate. Liz Soars & John Soars. 1999. 17.50 (978-0-19-435750-0(3)) OUP.

New Headway English Course: Intermediate Class. 2nd ed. Liz Soars & John Soars. 1999. 31.95 (978-0-19-470227-0(8)) OUP.

New Headway English Course: Pre-Intermediate Class. John Soars & Liz Soars. 2005. 31.95 (978-0-19-436674-8(X)) OUP.

New Headway English Course: Upper-Intermediate. John Soars & Liz Soars. 1999. stu. ed. 17.50 (978-0-19-436175-0(6)) OUP.

New Headway English Course: Upper-Intermediate. Liz Soars & John Soars. 1999. 31.95 (978-0-19-435804-0(0)) OUP.

New Heaven & the New Earth: Rev. 21:1-8. Ed Young. 1987. 4.95 (978-0-7417-1584-5(8), 584) Win Walk.

New Heliocentric Astrology. ACT Staff. 1 cass. (Running Time: 1 hr.). 8.95 (014) Am Fed Astrologers.

New History Generator. Paul R. Scheele. Read by Paul R. Scheele. 1 cass. (Running Time: 50 min.). (Paraliminal Tapes Ser.). 1989. 34.95 (978-0-925480-11-8(8)) Learn Strategies.
Helps free listener from the limitations of past negative events.

New Hope for Alzheimer's Disease. Read by H. Richard Casdorph. 1 cass. (Running Time: 45 min.). 10.00 (AC17) Am Media.
Alzheimer's, characterized by a loss of memory, is caused by aluminum deposits in the brain. Casdorph identifies the consumer products that are probable sources & also describes treatment.

New Hope for Healing Fibromyalgia. 2003. audio compact disk 14.95 (978-0-9743448-6-7(9)) NMA Media Pr.

New Hope for Life's Challenges. 2002. audio compact disk 25.00 (978-1-57972-392-7(6)) Insight Living.

New Hope for Life's Challenges. 2002. 16.95 (978-1-57972-369-9(1)) Insight Living.

New Horizons in English, Level 1. 3rd ed. Michael Walker. 18 cass. (Running Time: 11 hrs. 49 min.). 1991. 75.10 (978-0-201-53503-7(3)) AddisonWesley.

New Horizons in English, Level 2. 3rd ed. Michael Walker. 18 cass. (Running Time: 11 hrs. 49 min.). 75.10 (978-0-201-53507-5(6)) AddisonWesley.
Exercises to help the ESL student learn English. (accompanying New Horizons in English ESL book program). 6 sets of cassettes.

New Horizons in English, Level 3. Michael Walker. 18 cass. (Running Time: 11 hrs. 49 min.). 75.10 (978-0-201-53511-2(4)) AddisonWesley.
Exercises to help the ESL student learn English. (accompanying New Horizons ESL book program).

New Horizons in English, Level 4. Michael Walker. 18 cass. (Running Time: 11 hrs. 49 min.). 75.10 (978-0-201-53515-0(7)) Longman.
Exercises to help the ESL student learn English. (accompanying New Horizons in English ESL book program). 6 sets of cassettes.

New Horizons in English, Level 5. Michael Walker. 18 cass/. (Running Time: 11 hrs. 49 min.). 75.10 (978-0-201-53519-8(X)) Longman.

New Horizons in English, Level 6. Michael Walker. 18 cass. (Running Time: 11 hrs. 49 min.). 80.00 (978-0-201-53523-5(8)) AddisonWesley.

New Ideas from Translations of Ancient Greeks. Susan Horton. 1 cass. (Running Time: 1 hr.). 8.95 (677) Am Fed Astrologers.
An AFA Convention workshop tape.

New Image. C. S. Lovett. Read by C. S. Lovett. 1 cass. (Running Time: 1 hr. 10 min.). 6.95 (547) Prsnl Christianity.
Here's the "New Image" the Holy Spirit uses to transform your body. To be used with the "Help Lord" book.

New Immigration Laws: Dividing Families. 1 cass. (Running Time: 30 min.). 9.95 (G0610B090, HarperThor) HarpC GBR.

New Industrial State. unabr. ed. Read by Ken Carberry. 10 cass. (Running Time: 15 hrs.). 1989. 100.00 (978-0-942563-03-0(4)); Rental 22.00 (978-0-942563-12-2(3)) CareerTapes.
Focuses on the world of advanced technology, highly specialized manpower & the five or six hundred giant corporations that bring the technology & manpower into use. Shows how these firms supply themselves with capital, how the men who comprise them are motivated & how organized intelligence has replaced ownership as the source of power in the modern enterprise. Includes outline.

New Insight into IELTS Student's Book Audio CD. Vanessa Jakeman & Clare McDowell. (Running Time: 1 hr. 13 mins.). (ENG.). 2008. audio compact disk 25.00 (978-0-521-68092-9(1)) Cambridge U Pr.

New Insight into IELTS Workbook Audio CD. Vanessa Jakeman & Clare McDowell. (Running Time: 1 hr. 20 mins.). (ENG.). 2008. audio compact disk 25.00 (978-0-521-68094-3(8)) Cambridge U Pr.

New Insights into Astrology. Nona G. Press. 1 cass. (Running Time: 1 hr. 30 min.). 1992. 8.95 (1086) Am Fed Astrologers.

New Interchange: Audio Sampler 1-3. Jack C. Richards. (978-0-521-95019-0(8)) Cambridge U Pr.

New Interchange No. 3A: English for International Communication. Jack C. Richards. 3 cass. (Running Time: 4 hrs. 34 mins.). (ENG.). 2002. lab manual ed. 67.00 (978-0-521-77380-5(6)) Cambridge U Pr.

New Interchange No. 3A: English for International Communication. 2nd ed. Jack C. Richards et al. 2 cass. (Running Time: 1 hr. 10 mins.). (ENG.). 1997. 41.00 (978-0-521-62873-0(3)) Cambridge U Pr.

New Interchange No. 3A: English for International Communication. 2nd rev. ed. Jack C. Richards et al. 2 cass. (Running Time: hrs. mins.). (ENG.). 1998. 56.00 (978-0-521-62854-9(7)) Cambridge U Pr.

New Interchange Vol. 1A,Bk. 2: English for International Communication. Jack C. Richards. 3 cass. (Running Time: 3 hrs. 31 mins.). (ENG.). 2002. lab manual ed. 67.00 (978-0-521-77376-8(8)); lab manual ed. 67.00 (978-0-521-77378-2(4)) Cambridge U Pr.

New Interchange Vol. 1A,Bk. 2: English for International Communication. 2nd ed. Jack C. Richards et al. 1 cass. (Running Time: hrs. mins.). (ENG.). 1997. stu. ed. 15.00 (978-0-521-62871-6(7)) Cambridge U Pr.

New Interchange Vol. 1B: English for International Communication. 2nd ed. Jack C. Richards et al. 1 cass. (Running Time: hrs. mins.). (ENG.). 1997. stu. ed. 15.00 (978-0-521-62869-3(5)) Cambridge U Pr.

New Interchange Vol. 2A: English for International Communication. 2nd ed. Jack C. Richards et al. 1 cass. (Running Time: hrs. mins.). (ENG.). 1998. stu. ed. 15.00 (978-0-521-62852-5(0)) Cambridge U Pr.

New Interchange Vol. 2B: English for International Communication. 2nd ed. Jack C. Richards et al. 1 cass. (Running Time: hrs. mins.). (ENG.). 1998. stu. ed. 15.00 (978-0-521-62652-1(8)) Cambridge U Pr.

New Interchange Vol. 3A: English for International Communication. Jack C. Richards et al. 1 cass. (Running Time: hrs. mins.). (ENG.). 1998. stu. ed. 15.00 (978-0-521-62834-1(2)) Cambridge U Pr.

New Interchange Vol. 3B: English for International Communication. Jack C. Richards et al. 1 cass. (Running Time: hrs. mins.). (ENG.). 1998. stu. ed. 15.00 (978-0-521-62832-7(6)) Cambridge U Pr.

New Interchange Intro. Jack C. Richards. (New Interchange English for International Communication Ser.). 2002. (978-0-521-65913-0(2)) Cambridge U Pr.

New Interchange Intro A: English for International Communication. Jack C. Richards. (Running Time: hrs. mins.). (ENG.). 2000. stu. ed. 15.00 (978-0-521-77385-0(7)) Cambridge U Pr.

New Interchange Intro B: English for International Communication. Jack C. Richards. (Running Time: hrs. mins.). (ENG.). 2000. stu. ed. 16.00 (978-0-521-77373-7(3)) Cambridge U Pr.

New Interchange Intro B Bk. A, Vol. B: English for International Communication. Jack C. Richards. (Running Time: hrs. mins.). (ENG.). 2000. stu. ed. 15.00 (978-0-521-77384-3(9)) Cambridge U Pr.

New Interchange Intro Class CDs: English for International Communication. Jack C. Richards. (Running Time: hrs. mins.). (ENG.). 2000. stu. ed. 56.00 (978-0-521-77375-1(X)) Cambridge U Pr.

New Interchange Introduction: English for International Communication. Jack C. Richards. (Running Time: hrs. mins.). (ENG.). 2000. stu. ed. 56.00 (978-0-521-77386-7(5)); stu. ed. 16.00 (978-0-521-77374-4(1)) Cambridge U Pr.

New Interchange Introduction: English for International Communication. Jack C. Richards. 2 cass. (Running Time: 4 hrs. 10 mins.). (ENG.). 2002. lab manual ed. 67.00 (978-0-521-77382-9(2)) Cambridge U Pr.

New Interchange Resource Pack. Jack C. Richards et al. (ENG.). 2004. audio compact disk 5.00 (978-0-521-54241-8(3)) Cambridge U Pr.

New Interchange 3: English for International Communication. Jack C. Richards et al. 2 cass. (Running Time: hrs. mins.). (ENG.). 1998. 56.00 (978-0-521-62836-5(9)) Cambridge U Pr.

New International Version Bible: Old & New Testament entire Bible. Read by Steven B. Stevens. Prod. by TAW~Global. 2 CDs (MP3). (Running Time:). 2005. 34.99 (978-0-9726363-5-3(8), Promises for Life) Brite Bks.

New Interpreters Bible, Vol. 3. bk. 110.00 (978-0-687-01971-7(0)) Abingdon.

New Jersey Law Enforcement Handbook CD-ROM, 2007 Edition. 1905. audio compact disk 129.95 (978-1-4224-1547-4(3)) Pub: Gould. Dist(s): LEXIS Pub

New Jersey No-Fault: Handling Automobile Negligence Claims. Contrib. by Gerald H. Baker. (Running Time: 4 hrs.). 1984. 70.00 NJ Inst CLE.
Highlights the Automobile Reparation Reform Act of 1972, personal injury protection coverage, medical expense deductibles, tort exemption options, dealing with insurance companies. Includes program handbook.

New Jersey Shore: From Atlantic City to Long Beach Island via Long Beach Island. unabr. ed. Bill McCoy. 1 CD. (Running Time: 1 hr.). (Travelog Recorded Driving Tours Ser.). 2002. audio compact disk 19.95 (978-1-931739-11-5(0)) Travelog Corp.
Recorded car tour of the New Jersey Shore. Every tour includes a detailed map, turn-by-turn directions and a tour and save card for discounts along the route. A companion website, www.travelog.com provides tour planning resources. All tours are written by leading travel writers. Package includes both a CD and a Cass.

New Jersey Song. Perf. by Hunter Hayes. Created by Hunter Hayes. Selected by Alan H. Peterson. (New Jersey Song). 1998. audio compact disk 19.95 (978-1-877858-49-9(8)) Amer Focus Pub.

New Jersey's Skylands: From Morristown to Stokes State Forest & the Delaware Water Gap. Bill McCoy. (Travelog Recorded Driving Tour Ser.). 2001. audio compact disk 19.95 (978-1-931739-03-0(X)) Travelog Corp.

New Jerusalem & Council at Adam-ondi-Ahman. unabr. ed. Duane S. Crowther. Read by Duane S. Crowther. 1 cass. (Running Time: 1 hr. 30 min.). 1989. 13.98 (978-0-88290-355-2(1), 1829) Horizon Utah.
The author describes the return of the Saints to Jackson County, Missouri & the return of the Ten Tribes. The world scene is described as the New Jerusalem becomes a world center & the rest of the earth is engaged in the global conflict of a Fourth World War.

New Jewish Tunes: Ruach 5761 & 5763 Songbook. Transcontinental Music Publications Staff. Created by Hal Leonard Corporation Staff. 2 vols. 2003. pap. bk. 29.95 (978-0-8074-0887-2(5), 993221) Pub: URJ Pr. Dist(s): H Leonard

New Kid at School. Kate McMullan. Narrated by L. J. Ganser. (Running Time: 1 hr. 30 mins.). (Dragon Slayers' Academy Ser.: No. 1). (J). 2003. 10.75 (978-1-4193-1608-1(7)) Recorded Bks.

New Kid on the Block. unabr. ed. Jack Prelutsky. Read by Jack Prelutsky. 1 CD. (Running Time: 1 hr. 12 mins.). (J). 2001. audio compact disk 18.00 Books on Tape.
Buddy Stebbins follows directions to the mysterious 13th floor of the old & run down Zachary building. When he stumbles upon the 13th floor, he unknowingly climbs aboard a leaking pirate ship in a howling storm, 300 years in the past. He meets the dashing pirate, Captain Crackstone, an ancestor of his. When he was growing up, Buddy had heard stories about this Captain, a ghost his great-grandfather had hoped to contact & coax into revealing the location of buried treasure. Could this be Buddy's chance to obtain the clues his great-grandfather never discovered? If so, how will Buddy return home to find the hidden treasure?.

New Kid on the Block. unabr. ed. Jack Prelutsky. Read by Jack Prelutsky. 1 cass. (Running Time: 1 hr.). (J). 2000. 15.00 (978-0-7366-5482-1(8)) Books on Tape.
Twelve year old Buddy Stebbins follows directions to the mysterious 13th floor of the old & run down Zachary building. When he stumbles upon the 13th floor, he unknowingly climbs aboard a leaking pirate ship in a howling storm, 300 years in the past. He meets the dashing pirate, Captain Crackstone, an ancestor of his. When he was growing up, Buddy had heard stories about this Captain, a ghost his great grandfather had hoped to contact & coax into revealing the location of buried treasure. Could this be Buddy's chance to obtain the clues his great-grandfather never discovered? if so, how will Buddy return home to find the hidden treasure.

***New Kid on the Block.** unabr. ed. Jack Prelutsky. Read by Jack Prelutsky. (ENG.). 2007. (978-0-06-144897-3(4), GreenwillowBks); (978-0-06-144896-6(6), GreenwillowBks) HarperCollins Pubs.

New Kid on the Block. unabr. ed. Jack Prelutsky. Read by Jack Prelutsky. 1 cass. (Running Time: 40 mins.). (J). (ps-3). 1986. 11.00 (978-0-8072-0115-2(4), FTR115CXR, Listening Lib) Random Audio Pubg.
The ordinary becomes extraordinary when he reads & sings favorites from this collection of zany poems & verses.

New Kid on the Block. unabr. ed. Poems. Jack Prelutsky. Read by Jack Prelutsky. 1 CD. (Running Time: 53 mins.). (Middle Grade Cassette Librariestm Ser.). (J). (gr. 3-6). 2004. audio compact disk 18.00 (978-0-8072-0246-3(0), S FTR 115 CD, Listening Lib) Random Audio Pubg.
"Hilarious poems about strange creatures and people-from jellyfish stew to a bouncing mouse, and a boneless chicken.".

New Kid on the Block. unabr. abr. ed. Jack Prelutsky. Read by Jack Prelutsky. (Running Time: 3600 sec.). (J). (ps-3). 2007. 14.95 (978-0-06-135943-9(2), HarperChildAud) HarperCollins Pubs.

New Kids of the Polk Street School. unabr. ed. Patricia Reilly Giff. 6 cass. (Running Time: 5 hrs. 15 min.). (J). (gr. 1). 1990. pap. bk. 89.98 (978-0-8072-0195-4(2), FTR 150 S, Listening Lib) Random Audio Pubg.

***New Kind of Christian: A Tale of Two Friends on a Spiritual Journey.** unabr. ed. Brian McLaren. Narrated by Paul Michael. (ENG.). 2006. 14.98 (978-1-59644-317-4(0), Hovel Audio) christianaud.

New Kind of Christian: A Tale of Two Friends on a Spiritual Journey. unabr. ed. Brian D. McLaren. 6 CDs. (Running Time: 8 hrs. 0 mins. 0 sec.). (ENG.). 2006. audio compact disk 24.98 (978-1-59644-316-7(2), Hovel Audio) christianaud.
A New Kind of Christian's conversation between a pastor and his daughter's high school science teacher reveals that wisdom for life's most pressing spiritual questions can come from the most unlikely sources. This stirring fable captures a new spirit of Christianity - where personal, daily interaction with God is more important than institutional church structures, where faith is more about a way of life than a system of belief, where being authentically good is more important than being doctrinally "right," and where one's direction is more important than one's present location. Brian McLaren's delightful account offers a wise and wondrous approach for revitalizing Christian spiritual life and Christian congregations.

New Kind of Christian: A Tale of Two Friends on a Spiritual Journey. unabr. ed. Brian D. McLaren. Narrated by Paul Michael. 1 MP3CD. (Running Time: 8 hrs. 0 mins. 0 sec.). (ENG.). 2006. lp 19.98 (978-1-59644-315-0(4), Hovel Audio) christianaud.

New Kind of Leader. P. Cain. 1 cass. (Running Time: 1 hr. 30 min.). 1990. 12.00 (978-0-00-147084-2(1)) BJUPr.

New Kind of Leader Series. Paul Cain. 2 cass. (Running Time: 3 hrs.). 2000. 10.00 (PC03-000) Morning NC.
"Restoring Apostolic Leadership" & "World Evangelization." This series addresses the characteristics of the coming apostolic leadership.

New Kind of Love. E. W. Kenyon. Read by Stephen Sobozenski. 2 Cass. (Running Time: 174 mins.). 2002. 13.00 (978-1-57770-032-6(5)) Kenyons Gospel.
The Message to answer the heart cry of millions. If you follow the Law of Love, you cannot fail.

***New Kind of Youth Ministry.** Zondervan. (Running Time: 4 hrs. 19 mins. 12 sec.). (ENG.). 2010. 14.99 (978-0-310-86991-7(9)) Zondervan.

New King James Version New Testament. Narrated by Eric R. Martin. (ENG.). 2003. audio compact disk 29.99 (978-1-930034-19-8(9)) Casscomm.

New Knowledge, Framework For. unabr. ed. Read by Idries Shah. 1 cass. (Running Time: 44 min.). 10.95 J Norton Pubs.

New Lead the Field. Earl Nightingale. Read by Earl Nightingale. 6 cass. (Running Time: 9 hrs.). 59.95 (116-2A) Nightingale-Conant.
Your map to happiness, wealth & success.

New Lease of Death. unabr. ed. Ruth Rendell. Read by Nigel Anthony. 6 cass. (Running Time: 9 hrs.). (Inspector Wexford Mystery Ser.: Bk. 2). 2000. 49.95 (978-0-7451-6758-9(6), CAB 1374) Pub: Chivers Audio Bks GBR. Dist(s): AudioGO
Inspector Wexford had remembered ther Painter Case, it was his very first murder case. There was no mystery, Painter had done it and was hanged for it. There had been no doubt, until now. Someone wants the case re-examined, someone who wants history changed, and Wexford proved wrong.

New Lectures in the Psychology of Self-Esteem CD Set. Nathaniel Branden. 30 CDs. (Running Time: 26 hrs.). 2005. audio compact disk 188.95 (978-1-57970-251-9(1), AFNB01D, Audio-For) J Norton Pubs.
Nathaniel Branden, Ph.D., created a series of lectures which substantially expand upon his books "The Psychology of Self-Esteem," "Breaking Free," and "The Disowned Self." Here are some highlights from this comprehensive presentation of biocentric psychology: the need, the motivating power of self-esteem, its relationship to love, work, and personal relationships, man-woman relationships, emotions, disowning the self, alienation, anxiety, depression, and more.

New Lectures on the Psychology of Self-Esteem. unabr. ed. Nathaniel Branden. 20 cass. (Running Time: 26 hrs.). 188.95 (AFNB01) J Norton Pubs.
Dr. Branden has created a series of lectures which substantially updates & expands upon the materials in The Psychology of Self-Esteem, Breaking Free & The Disowned Self. Here are some of the highlights of this comprehensive presentation of Biocentric Psychology: The need, the motivating power of self-esteem, its relationship to love, work & personal relationships, man-woman relationships, emotions, disowning the self, alienation, anxiety, depression & more. Described in detail below, sold individually or as a complete set.

New Life: Live in Harvey, Il. Ed. by Brent Hufnagel. Contrib. by Canton Spirituals. Prod. by Carla Reed. (Running Time: 1 hr. 48 mins.). 2004. 19.98 (978-5-559-51698-1(8), Verity) Brentwood Music.

New Life Affirmation: For Childbirth, Baby & Mother to Be. Lea Blumberg. 1 CD. 2003. audio compact disk 19.95 (978-0-9747487-2-6(2)) L Blumberg.
Affirmations for childbirth, baby, and the life changes for mother to be.

New Life Styles. unabr. ed. Milton Diamond. 1 cass. (Running Time: 1 hr.). (Human Sexuality Ser.). 11.95 (34026) J Norton Pubs.
Vignettes provide a look at new practices, with their attendant sexual advantages & problems.

New Light from Old Scrolls: Dead Sea Scrolls & Nag Hammadi. Stephan Hoeller. 1 cass. (Running Time: hr. 30 min.). 1999. 11.00 (40032) Big Sur Tapes.
1991 Los Angeles.

New Limited Liability Company & Limited Liability Partnership Law. (Running Time: 5 hrs.). 1994. 92.00 (20424) NYS Bar.
This most important piece of legislation affecting business law practice in many years has recently gone into effect in New York State & this recording covers some of the most important issues that practitioners will face in counseling clients & organizing their own practices regarding taxation, formation of entities & drafting of operating agreements & choice of entity, among others.

New Lives for Old: 11 Cor. 5:12-19. Ed Young. 1990. 4.95 (978-0-7417-1786-3(7), 786) Win Walk.

New Lobbying & Ethics Reform Bill - Honest Leadership & Open Government Act Of 2007 (HLOGA) Capitol Learning Audio Course. Cleta Mitchell. Prod. by TheCapitol.Net. (ENG.). 2007. 47.00 (978-1-58733-051-3(2)) TheCapitol.

New Look at an Old Friend. Louise Fimlaid. 1 cass. (Running Time: 1 hr. 30 min.). 1992. 8.95 (1030) Am Fed Astrologers.

New Look at Astrology. Serafin Lanot. 1 cass. (Running Time: 1 hr. 30 min.). 8.95 (436) Am Fed Astrologers.
Filipino view - new techniques.

New Look at Christian Origins. unabr. ed. James Pike. 1 cass. (Running Time: 1 hr. 30 min.). 1971. 11.00 (04502) Big Sur Tapes.
Bishop Pike examines the discoveries & research since the Dead Sea scrolls, leading to new interpretations of events surrounding the birth of Christianity. he reassesses the historical Jesus, the role of his brother & family, & the influence of Paul.

New Look at Prayer. abr. ed. William Huebsch. Read by William Huebsch. 2 cass. (Running Time: 1 hr. 35 min.). 1992. 7.95 pap. bk. (978-0-89622-754-5(5)) Twenty-Third.
For adults. Through descriptions of everyday life, author leads listeners to discover the presence of God in our own experiences to an exciting renewal of spiritual life.

***New Love Story.** Sinead Murray. (ENG.). 11.95 (978-0-8023-7064-8(0)) Pub: Clo Iar-Chonnachta IRL. Dist(s): Dufour

New Madrid Run. unabr. ed. Michael Reisig. Read by Cameron Beierle. 8 cass. (Running Time: 11 hrs.). 2001. 49.95 (978-1-55686-992-1(4)) Books in Motion.
Within a few terrifying hours, the Earth's poles shift, and modern civilization is shattered. But Travis Christian, owner of Island Air Charters in the Florida Keys, has miraculously survived nature's initial onslaught. As he faces the terrible new elements of a changed world and the baser ambitions of his fellow man, he attempts to navigate a battered sailboat through high seas, pirates and fierce storms toward hope of a safe harbor.

New Man. Neville Goddard. 1 cass. (Running Time: 1 hr. 2 min.). 1967. 8.00 (37) J & L Pubns.
Neville taught Imagination Creates Reality. He was a powerfully influential teacher of God as Consciousness.

New Man. Osho Oshos. Read by Osho Oshos. 1 cass. (Running Time: 1 hr. 30 min.). 10.95 (DBB-5021) Oshos.
"The coming twenty years are going to be the most dangerous in the whole history of humanity," says Osho. "Only more consciousness, more alertness, can save it".

New Man New Tongue. John MacArthur, Jr. 4 cass. (Running Time: 6 hrs.). 15.95 (20162, HarperThor) HarpC GBR.

New Manchester Girl: The True Story of Scynthia Catherine Stewart, 1865-1867. Scripts. 1 CD. (Running Time: 45 minutes). Dramatization. 2003. audio compact disk 15.00 (978-0-9714236-1-9(X)) Gaare Busn Serv.
The true story of Scynthia Catherine Stewart of New Manchester, GA, from 1851-1867. Father Walter Washington Stewart was a bossman at the New Manchester Mill, which was taken over by the Confederate government at the beginning of the Civil War to make goods for the Confederate Army. Gen. William Tecumseh Sherman, in his effort to conduct total warfare and bring the South to its knees, ordered the mills in Georgia burned and the workers charged with treason. Father Walter was off fighting in the Rebel Army, but Scyntia, her siblings, and her mother were taken to Louisville, KY, as prisoners of war. This story tells of an incredible family reunion in Louisville, and subsequent return home, finding strawberry manna from heaven growing in their yard, to help them make it through the hard first year after the war.

New Map of the World. Perf. by Paul Coleman. 2002. audio compact disk 16.98 Provident Mus Dist.

New Market Leaders: Who's Winning & How in the Battle for Customers. Fred Wiersema. Read by Fred Wiersema. 2006. 14.95 (978-0-7435-6213-3(5)) Pub: S&S Audio. Dist(s): S and S Inc

New Masters of Excellence. Tom Peters. Read by Tom Peters. 6 cass. (Running Time: 9 hrs.). 69.95 (179A) Nightingale-Conant.

New Meditation Handbook: Meditations to Make Our Life Happy & Meaningful. 4th unabr. ed. Geshe Kelsang Gyatso. Read by Kelsang Dekyi. 4 CDs. (Running Time: 5 hrs. 0 mins. 0 sec.). (ENG., 2005. audio compact disk 24.95 (978-0-9548790-0-6(7)) Pub: Tharpa Pubns GBR. Dist(s): IPG Chicago

New Men. unabr. ed. C. P. Snow. Read by Ian Whitcomb. 7 cass. (Running Time: 10 hrs. 30 mins.). (Strangers & Brothers Ser.). 1996. 56.00 (978-0-7366-3439-7(8), 4083) Books on Tape.
Focuses with great realism on a group of nuclear scientists & high government officials working together in England during the war.

New Mexico! Dana Fuller Ross, pseud. Read by Lloyd James. 4 vols. (Wagons West Ser.: No. 22). 2004. (978-1-58807-623-6(7)) Am Pubng Inc.

New Mexico! abr. ed. Dana Fuller Ross, pseud. Read by Lloyd James. 4 vols. (Running Time: 6 hrs.). (Wagons West Ser.: No. 22). 2004. 25.00 (978-1-58807-154-5(5)) Am Pubng Inc.

New Mexico: An Audio Tour of Northern & Southern New Mexico. 1 cass. (Running Time: 1 hr. 30 min.). 1990. 13.95 (CC270) Comp Comms Inc.
A crossroad of rich cultures, fascinating history & dramatic landscape.

New Mexico: An Audio Tour of the Land of Enchantment. Roadrunner Audio Staff. Intro. by Tony Hillerman. 1 cass. (Running Time: 1 hr. 30 min.). (Roadrunner Audio Tours Ser.). 1988. 12.95 (978-0-944857-01-4(9)) Matthew Media.

New Mexico: Santa Fe - Taos. 1 cass. (Running Time: 1 hr. 30 min.). 1990. 13.95 (CC271) Comp Comms Inc.
Discover historic Spanish Villages in the Sangre de Cristo Mountains, lava-ribbed Rio Grande Gorge, ancient Indian pueblos & early Spanish settlements along the Rio Grande Valley.

New Mexico: The Turquoise Trails & the Rio Grande Valley. 1 cass. (Running Time: 1 hr. 30 min.). 1990. 13.95 (CC272) Comp Comms Inc.
Explore ghost towns & powerful landscapes as you follow the old mining trail from Albuquerque to Santa Fe. Discover the early Spanish settlements & Indian pueblos along the original route of the Camino Real beside the Rio Grande.

New Military Humanism: Lessons from Kosovo. unabr. ed. Noam Chomsky. Read by Bob Harris. 6 cass. (Running Time: 9 hrs.). 1999. 20.00 (978-1-56751-178-9(3)) Common Courage.
Chomsky demolishes the lies & obfuscation that have characterized reporting from Kosovo from day one. Provides a clear-eyed look at this conflict.

New Millennium. Interview with Jean Houston & Michael Toms. 2 cass. (Running Time: 1 hr. 30 min.). 1997. 15.95 (978-1-56170-418-7(0), 337) Hay House.
A philosopher, psychologist & author, describes why she thinks we are living in the most exciting time of human history.

New Millennium Herbal Anthology: An Illustrated Guide into the Medicinal & Magikal Worlds of the Herbal Kingdom. Keath Eben Brasken. 2004. bk. & pap. bk. 37.77 (978-0-9728650-6-7(3)) Seed Sprinkler.

New Model of Psychological Types. Read by John Beebe. 4 cass. (Running Time: 7 hrs.). 1988. 35.95 (978-0-7822-0014-0(1), 317) C G Jung IL.

New Moon. unabr. ed. Stephenie Meyer. Read by Ilyana Kadushin. 12 CDs. (Running Time: 14 hrs. 51 mins.). (Twilight Saga: No. 2). (YA). (gr. 9 up). 2006. audio compact disk 80.00 (978-0-7393-3779-0(3), Listening Lib) Pub: Random Audio Pubg. Dist(s): Random

New Moon. unabr. ed. Stephenie Meyer. Read by Ilyana Kadushin. 12 CDs. (Running Time: 53460 sec.). (Twilight Saga: No. 2). (ENG.). (J). (gr. 7-12). 2006. audio compact disk 54.00 (978-0-7393-3720-2(3), Listening Lib) Pub: Random Audio Pubg. Dist(s): Random

New Moon People. Dorothy Santangelo. 1 cass. (Running Time: 1 hr.). 8.95 (302) Am Fed Astrologers.
Energies applied to people with Sun & Moon in same sign.

New Morality. 10.00 (HT406) Esstee Audios.

New Myth of Meaning. Read by Edward Edinger. 1 cass. (Running Time: 1 hr. 30 min.). 1984. 10.95 (978-0-7822-0061-4(3), ND7707) C G Jung IL.

***New Name.** John Eldredge & Craig McConnell. (ENG.). 2011. audio compact disk 28.99 (978-1-933207-44-5(2)) Ransomed Heart.

New Neuropsychology of Weight Control. Sybervision Staff. 8 cass. (Running Time: 8 hrs.). 1996. 69.95 Set, incl. wkbk. & journal. (6271PAY) Nightingale-Conant.
This program is a 12-week eating plan that provides daily menus, meal plans, tasty recipes, cooking instructions & shopping lists. It also identifies the 12 key characteristics of lean, high-energy people.

New Neuropsychology of Weight Control. unabr. ed. Garth Fisher et al. Read by Richard Gebhart. 8 cass. (Health Ser.). 1991. 79.95 (2114); cass. & video 99.95 (2117) SyberVision.
How to lose weight eating more of the foods that will burn up excess fuel. Includes video.

New New Thing: A Silicon Valley Story. abr. ed. Michael Lewis. Read by Bruce Reizen. 2 cass. (Running Time: 3 hrs.). 1999. 17.95 (FS9-51080) Highsmith.

New New Thing: A Silicon Valley Story. unabr. ed. Michael Lewis. Read by Bruce Reizen. (Running Time: 10 hrs.). 2008. 24.95 (978-1-4233-7139-7(9), 9781423371397, Brilliance MP3); 24.95 (978-1-4233-7141-0(0), 9781423371410, BAD); 39.25 (978-1-4233-7140-3(2), 9781423371403, Brlnc Audio MP3 Lib); 39.25 (978-1-4233-7142-7(9), 9781423371427, BADLE) Brilliance Audio.

New News from Pluto. Robert Donath. 1 cass. (Running Time: 1 hr.). 8.95 (520) Am Fed Astrologers.

New Non-Discrimination Rules. Moderated by James P. Klein. 1 cass. (Running Time: 1 hr. 30 min.). 20.00 (T7-9301) PLI.

New Normal? Program from the Award Winning Public Radio Show. Hosted by Fred Goodwin. Contrib. by John Hockenberry. 1 cd. (Running Time: 1 Hour). (Infinite Mind Ser.). 2001. audio compact disk 21.95 (978-1-932479-18-8(X), LCM #192) Lichtenstein Creat.
Living with the threat of terrorist attacks, we wonder: is fear, anxiety and disorientation our new way of life? We talk about "getting back to normal," but perhaps this is it. This special program explores what we all can do to cope with our inner uncertainty, and, perhaps, strike a blow against terrorism in the process. The program also looks at how the nation's mental health system is coping with this national crisis. Guests include: Mary Guardino, of Freedom From Fear; Dr. Robert Ursano, expert in the psychological effects of crisis and disaster; Cynthia Folcarelli, executive vice president of the National Mental Health Association; Giselle Stolper, executive director of the Mental Health Association of New York; Dr. Russ Newman, executive

director for professional practice for the American Psychological Association; and Avner Tavori, an Israeli-born television and radio journalist. With commentary by John Hockenberry.

New Nutrition for the Whole Person. Andrew Weil. 2 cass. (Running Time: 3 hrs.). 18.00 (A0489-89) Sound Photosyn.
Andy does it again! A healthy amusing political statement.

New Option Generator. Paul R. Scheele. Read by Paul R. Scheele. 1 cass. (Running Time: 35 min.). (Paraliminal Tapes Ser.). 1991. 34.95 (978-0-925480-17-0(7)) Learn Strategies.
Helps listener gain freedom from paradoxes & doublebinds.

New Order in Europe. 10.00 (HE833) Esstee Audios.
Hitler's attempt to change the thinking of Europe.

New Orleans: The Lure of the French Quarter. unabr. ed. Andrew Flack. Read by Barbara Duff & Denis J. Sullivan. 1 cass. (Running Time: 1 hr.). (Day Ranger Walking Adventures on Audio Cassette Ser.). 1990. 19.95 (978-1-877894-03-9(6)) Day Ranger.
Scripted dialogue & music to accompany an original walking route through the French Quarter of New Orleans. Uses first hand accounts, eyewitness stories & brief excerpts of identified literature. Detailed maps included.

New Orleans Classics: For Double Bass. Created by Hal Leonard Corporation Staff. Matt Perrine. 2006. pap. bk. 24.98 (978-1-59615-113-0(7), 1596151137) Pub: Music Minus. Dist(s): H Leonard

New Orleans Classics: For Trombone. Created by Hal Leonard Corporation Staff. 2006. pap. bk. 24.98 (978-1-59615-111-6(0), 1596151110) Pub: Music Minus. Dist(s): H Leonard

New Orleans Mourning. unabr. ed. Julie Smith. Narrated by Cristine McMurdo-Wallis. 10 cass. (Running Time: 14 hrs.). (Skip Langdon Mystery Ser.: Bk. 1). 1999. 87.00 (978-0-7887-3480-9(6), 95775E7) Recorded Bks.
A revealing glimpse into the hidden world of New Orleans high society, introducing Skip Langdon. Skip is a rookie cop assigned to investigate a Mardi Gras murder because of her own upper-crust background. A menagerie of exotic characters in an intricately plotted mystery.

New Orleans Mourning. unabr. ed. Julie Smith. Narrated by Cristine McMurdo-Wallis. 12 CDs. (Running Time: 14 hrs.). (Skip Langdon Mystery Ser.: Bk. 1). 2000. audio compact disk 116.00 (978-0-7887-4635-2(9), C1210E7) Recorded Bks.

New Owner. unabr. ed. Iris Bromige. 6 cass. (Isis Ser.). (J). 2002. 54.95 (978-0-7531-1303-5(1)) Pub: ISIS Lrg Prnt GBR. Dist(s): Ulverscroft US

New Oxford Picture Dictionary, Set. E. C. Parnwell. 4 cass. (Running Time: 6 hrs.). (New Oxford Picture Dictionary (1988 Ed.) Ser.). 1988. 54.95 (978-0-19-434329-9(4)) OUP.

New Parade: Level Starter. 2nd ed. Mario Herrera Salazar & Theresa Zanatta. (C). 1999. stu. ed. 24.13 (978-0-201-63140-1(7)) Longman.

New Paradigm for Psychotherapy. unabr. ed. Stanislav Grof. 1 cass. (Running Time: 1 hr. 26 min.). 1980. 11.00 (00802) Big Sur Tapes.

New Paradigm in Science & Theology. David Steindl-Rast et al. 1 cass. (Running Time: 1 hr.). 9.00 (A0407-89) Sound Photosyn.
Fritjof & David intellectualize while Joanna heartfully overviews. The personalities expressed their points classically & eloquently.

New Paradigms: The Exact Formula for Success. 4th rev. ed. Michele Blood. Read by Bob Proctor. Illus. by Musivation International Staff. 6 cass. (Running Time: 3 hrs.). 1995. bk. 69.95 (978-1-890679-06-4(2), M117) Micheles.
Motivational program to improve ones life to the positive & towards success.

New Patches for Old. 2004. 8.95 (978-1-56008-982-7(2)); cass. & flmstrp 30.00 (978-1-56008-728-1(5)) Weston Woods.

New Pennsylvania Mortgage Lien Law - What Every General Petitioner Should Know. Read by Leonard A. Bernstein. 1 cass. (Running Time: 1 hr.). 1991. 20.00 (AL-117) PA Bar Inst.

New Pennsylvania Takeover Legislation. 1 cass,. (Running Time: 1 hr. 30 min.). 1988. 45.00; bk. 95.00 PA Bar Inst.
Inlcudes book.

New Person to Person 2 cass. 1 Communicative Speaking & Listening Skills. Jack C. Richards. 1995. 31.95 (978-0-19-434680-1(3)) OUP.

New Person to Person 2 cass. 1 Communicative Speaking & Listening Skills. Jack C. Richards. 1997. 0.00 (978-0-19-470075-7(5)) OUP.

New Person to Person 2 cass. 2 Communicative Speaking & Listening Skills. Jack C. Richards. 1996. 31.95 (978-0-19-434683-2(8)) OUP.

New Person to Person 2 cds. 1 Communicative Speaking & Listening Skills. Jack C. Richards. 1995. audio compact disk 35.95 (978-0-19-434684-9(6)) OUP.

New Person to Person 2 cds. 2 Communicative Speaking & Listening Skills. Jack C. Richards et al. 1996. audio compact disk 35.95 (978-0-19-434685-6(4)) OUP.

New Pet. Dan Yaccarino. Narrated by L. J. Ganser. 1 cass. (Running Time: 25 mins.). (gr. k up). 2004. 10.00 (978-0-7887-9529-9(5)) Recorded Bks.
An exchange student on the planet Meep, Blast Off Boy misses his dog, Scooter. To cheer him up, the Glorp family brings home a schloppo for a new pet. But Blast Off Boy isn¿t happy about having a schloppo. Who really wants a big, green monster that likes to put people¿s heads in its mouth?.

New Physical Education: Strengthening Your Physical Education Program with the Best, Current Practices & Activities. Hosted by Elaine Lindsay. 4 CDs. (Running Time: 3 hrs 59 mins). (YA). (gr. 6-12). 2008. audio compact disk 95.00 (978-1-886397-89-7(9)) Bureau of Educ.

New Physics in Mind & Body. Fred A. Wolf. 7 cass. (Running Time: 10 hrs. 30 min.). 63.00 (OC62) Sound Horizons AV.

New Physics of Healing. unabr. ed. Deepak Chopra. 2001. audio compact disk 24.95 (978-1-56455-919-7(X)) Sounds True.
Is it possible to access this river of intelligent energy, first described in India?s ayurvedic medical tradition more than 5,000 years ago? How do specific emotions influence your biochemistry and your health? Can your imagination affect the course of an illness? How do you break through the ingrained belief patterns to discover your true healing potential? This updated edition offers a fascinating exploration of these and many other questions.

New Plantation South: Land, Labor, & Federal Favor in Twentieth-Century Arkansas. Jeannie Whayne. (Carter G. Woodson Institute Ser.). (ENG.). 1996. 22.50 (978-0-8139-2594-3(0)) U Pr of Va.

New Policeman. unabr. ed. Kate Thompson. Read by Marcella Rhiordan. 6 cass. (Running Time: 6 hrs. 30 mins.). (YA). (gr. 7-10). 2007. 51.75 (978-1-4281-4754-6(3)); audio compact disk 66.75 (978-1-4281-4759-1(4)) Recorded Bks.

New Portable MBA. abr. ed. Eliza G. C. Collins & Mary Anne Devanna. Read by Mario Machado. 4 cass. (Running Time: 6 hrs.). 2001. 25.00 (978-1-59040-018-0(6), Phoenix Audio) Pub: Amer Intl Pub. Dist(s): PerseuPGW
This comprehensive program features the top wisdom from the best university programs, from managing people to setting strategy.

New Positioning. Jack Trout & Steve Rivkin. Read by Jack Trout. 2 cass. (Running Time: 3 hrs.). 1995. 16.95 (978-1-55935-193-5(4)) Soundelux.
The latest on the world's #1 business strategy.

New Practical Chinese Reader. Ed. by Beijing Language and Culture Press Staff. 2002. audio compact disk 11.95 (978-7-88703-197-6(4)) China Lang Univ CHN.

New Practical Chinese Reader. Ed. by Xun Liu. 2 vols. (CHI & ENG.). 2004. pap. bk. & wbk. ed. 16.95 (978-7-88703-196-9(6), NPCRWC1) China Bks.

New Practical Chinese Reader. Ed. by Xun Liu. (CHI & ENG.). 2004. tchr. ed. 9.95 (978-7-88703-089-4(7), NPCRIT1); wbk. ed. 17.95 (978-7-88703-082-5(X), NPCRWT1) China Bks.

New Practical Chinese Reader, Vol. 2. Ed. by Xun Liu. 2 vols. (CHI & ENG.). 2004. pap. bk. & wbk. ed. 16.95 (978-7-88703-199-0(0), NPCRWC2) China Bks.

New Practical Chinese Reader, Vol. 2. Ed. by Xun Liu. 2 pieces. (CHI & ENG.). 2004. wbk. ed. 17.95 (978-7-88703-115-0(X), NPCRWT2) China Bks.

New Practical Chinese Reader, Vol. 3. Ed. by Xun Liu. 3 vols. (CHI & ENG.). 2004. pap. bk. & wbk. ed. 21.95 (978-7-88703-201-0(6), NPCRWC3) China Bks.

New Practical Chinese Reader, Vol. 3. Ed. by Xun Liu. 3 pieces. (CHI & ENG.). 2004. wbk. ed. 26.95 (978-7-88703-146-4(X), NPCRWT3) China Bks.

New Practical Chinese Reader, Vol. 4. Ed. by Xun Liu. 2 CDs. (CHI & ENG.). 2004. wbk. ed. 19.95 (978-7-88703-177-8(X), NPCRWCD4) China Bks.

New Practical Chinese Reader: Textbook. Ed. by Liu Xun. 4 vols. (CHI & ENG.). 2004. pap. bk. 29.95 (978-7-88703-195-2(8), NPCRC1) China Bks.

New Practical Chinese Reader: Textbook, Vol. 2. Ed. by Liu Xun. 4 vols. (CHI & ENG.). 2004. pap. bk. 29.95 (978-7-88703-198-3(2), NPCRC2) China Bks.

New Practical Chinese Reader: Textbook, Vol. 3. Ed. by Liu Xun. 4 vols. (CHI & ENG.). 2004. pap. bk. 29.95 (978-7-88703-200-3(8), NPCRC3) China Bks.

New Practical Chinese Reader: Textbook, Vol. 4. Ed. by Liu Xun. 5 vols. (CHI & ENG.). 2004. pap. bk. 34.95 (978-7-88703-192-1(3), NPCRC4) China Bks.

New Practical Chinese Reader 1: Text Book. Ed. by Liu Xun. 4 pieces. (CHI & ENG.). 2004. reel tape 34.95 (978-7-88703-081-8(1), NPCRT1) China Bks.

New Practical Chinese Reader 2: Text Book. Ed. by Liu Xun. 4 pieces. (CHI & ENG.). 2004. reel tape 34.95 (978-7-88703-111-2(7), NPCRT2) China Bks.

New Practical Chinese Reader 3: Text Book. Ed. by Liu Xun. 4 pieces. (CHI & ENG.). 2004. reel tape 34.95 (978-7-88703-145-7(1), NPCRT3) China Bks.

New Practical Chinese Reader 4: Text Book. Ed. by Liu Xun. 5 pieces. (CHI & ENG.). 2004. reel tape 43.95 (978-7-88703-176-1(1), NPCRT4) Pub: China Lang Univ CHN. Dist(s): China Bks

New Practice Readers. Donald G. Anderson. 2006. audio compact disk 99.00 (978-0-7915-2135-9(4)) Phoenix Lrn.

New Practice Readers: Book B. Donald G. Anderson. 2006. audio compact disk 99.00 (978-0-7915-2136-6(2)) Phoenix Lrn.

New Practice Readers: Book C. Donald G. Anderson. 2006. audio compact disk 99.00 (978-0-7915-2137-3(0)) Phoenix Lrn.

New Practice Readers: Book D. Donald G. Anderson. 2006. audio compact disk 99.00 (978-0-7915-2138-0(9)) Phoenix Lrn.

New Predictive Techniques. Charles Hannan & Louis Hannan. 1 cass. (Running Time: 1 hr.). 8.95 (533) Am Fed Astrologers.

New Principle of Control: Romans 8:1-4. Ben Young. 1996. 4.95 (978-0-7417-6005-0(3), B0005) Win Walk.

New Principle of Control: Romans 8:1-4. Ed Young. 1984. 4.95 (978-0-7417-1375-9(6), 375) Win Walk.

New Priorities for the University: Meeting Society's Needs for Applied Knowledge & Competent Individuals. Ernest A. Lynton & Sandra E. Elman. (Higher & Adult Education Ser.). 1987. bk. 32.95 (978-1-55542-029-1(X), Jossey-Bass) Wiley US.

New Product Development: Moving from Research to Commercialization. Instructed by Carl R. Pacifico & Robert J. Polacek. 7 cass. (Running Time: 7 hrs. 6 min.). pap. bk. 205.00 (64) Am Chemical.
Provides a treatment for managing aspects of development of new products. Includes manual.

New Progress to Proficiency, Set. 2nd rev. ed. Leo Jones. (Running Time: hrs. mins.). (ENG.). 2002. 58.80 (978-0-521-63551-6(9)) Cambridge U Pr.

***New Progress to Proficiency Audio CDs (3)** 3rd rev. ed. Leo Jones. (Running Time: 3 hrs. 25 mins.). (ENG.). 2010. audio compact disk 56.00 (978-0-521-18361-1(8)) Cambridge U Pr.

New Psalms. Ernest Lee. (Running Time: 60 min.). 2003. 11.98 (978-5-550-13058-2(0)) Pub: Pt of Grace Ent. Dist(s): STL Dist NA

New Psycho-Cybernetics: A Mind Technology for Living Your Life Without Limits. Maxwell Maltz & Dan Kennedy. 6 cass. (Running Time: 6 hrs.). 1998. cass. & video 79.95 (978-1-55525-075-1(0), 18470AV) Nightingale-Conant.
Tap into the power of the new psycho-cybernetics.

New Psychology of Achievement. abr. ed. Brian Tracy. Read by Brian Tracy. (Running Time: 2 hrs. 0 mins. 0 sec.). (ENG.). 2009. audio compact disk 19.99 (978-0-7435-8344-2(2), Nightgale) Pub: S&S Audio. Dist(s): S and S Inc

***New Reagan Revolution: How Ronald Reagan's Principles Can Restore America's Greatness.** unabr. ed. Michael Reagan. (Running Time: 10 hrs. 5 mins.). (ENG.). 2011. 29.95 (978-1-4417-7893-2(4)); audio compact disk 29.95 (978-1-4417-7892-5(6)) Blckstn Audio.

***New Reagan Revolution: How Ronald Reagan's Principles Can Restore America's Greatness.** unabr. ed. Michael Reagan. Read by To be Announced. (Running Time: 10 hrs. 5 mins.). (ENG.). 2011. 65.95 (978-1-4417-7890-1(X)); audio compact disk 100.00 (978-1-4417-7891-8(8)) Blckstn Audio.

New Reality: How to Make Change Your Competitive Advantage. Karl G. Schoemer. Read by Gary Applegate. 1 cass. (Running Time: 44 mins.). 1998. (978-1-929037-05-6(8)) KGS Inc.
Helps change your competitive advantage.

New Reconstructive Concepts in the Management of Lower Leg Trauma: Interdisciplinary Panel Discussion. Moderated by Stephen J. Mathes. 2 cass. (Running Time: 3 hrs.). (Plastic & Maxillofacial Surgery Ser.: PL-2). 1986. 19.00 (8661) Am Coll Surgeons.

New Referees' Rules! 1 cass. (Running Time: 1 hr. 20 min.). 1991. 45.00 (AL-120) PA Bar Inst.
Includes copy of the new rules.

New Relocation Method. Bill Hansen. 1 cass. (Running Time: 1 hr.). 8.95 (144) Am Fed Astrologers.
R. A. Plotter - -understand difficult areas of the world.

New Revelations: A Conversation with God. abr. ed. Neale Donald Walsch. Read by Edward Asner & Ellen Burstyn. 2004. 15.95 (978-0-7435-4446-7(3)) Pub: S&S Audio. Dist(s): S and S Inc

New Revised Standard Bible. Marquis Laughlin. 2006. 24.99 (978-1-59859-096-8(0)) Oasis Audio.

New Road. Gerry Harrington. Contrib. by Charlie Piggott. (ENG.). 2000. 13.95 (978-0-8023-7142-3(6)) Pub: Clo Iar-Chonnachta IRL. Dist(s): Dufour

New Road: Traditional Music on Fiddle & Accordian. Gerry Harrington. Contrib. by Charlie Piggott. (ENG.). 2000. audio compact disk 21.95 (978-0-8023-8142-2(1)) Pub: Clo Iar-Chonnachta IRL. Dist(s): Dufour

***New Road to Serfdom: A Letter of Warning to America.** Daniel Hannan. 2011. audio compact disk 44.99 (978-1-61120-015-7(6)) Dreamscap OH.

New Rules of College Admissions: Ten Former Admission Officers Reveal What It Takes to Get into College Today. unabr. ed. Read by Geoffrey Blaisdell. Ed. by Stephen Kramer & Michael London. 6 CDs. (Running Time: 28800 sec.). 2006. audio compact disk 19.95 (978-0-7861-6899-6(4)) Blckstn Audio.

New Rules of College Admissions: Ten Former Admission Officers Reveal What It Takes to Get into College Today. unabr. ed. Read by Geoffrey Blaisdell & Laura Derocher. Ed. by Stephen Kramer & Michael London. 5 cass. (Running Time: 28800 sec.). 2006. 19.95 (978-0-7861-4601-7(X)) Blckstn Audio.

New Rules of College Admissions: Ten Former Admissions Officers Reveal What It Takes to Get into College Today. unabr. ed. Read by Geoffrey Blaisdell. (Running Time: 28800 sec.). 2006. 65.95 (978-0-7861-4767-0(9)) Blckstn Audio.

New Rules of College Admissions: Ten Former Admissions Officers Reveal What It Takes to Get into College Today. unabr. ed. Read by Geoffrey Blaisdell & Laura Derocher. (Running Time: 28800 sec.). 2006. audio compact disk 81.00 (978-0-7861-6377-9(1)) Blckstn Audio.

New Rules of College Admissions: Ten Former Admissions Officers Reveal What It Takes to Get into College Today. unabr. ed. Read by Geoffrey Blaisdell & Laura Derocher. Ed. by Stephen Kramer & Michael London. (Running Time: 28800 sec.). 2006. audio compact disk 29.95 (978-0-7861-7504-8(4)) Blckstn Audio.

New Rules of Marketing & PR: How to Use News Releases, Blogs, Podcasting, Viral Marketing, & Online Media to Reach Buyers Directly. unabr. ed. David Meerman Scott. Read by Walter Dixon. (Running Time: 10 hrs.). (ENG.). 2008. 29.98 (978-1-59659-311-4(3), GildAudio) Pub: Gildan Media. Dist(s): HachBkGrp

New Rules of Marketing & PR: How to Use News Releases, Blogs, Podcasting, Viral Marketing, & Online Media to Reach Buyers Directly. unabr. ed. David Meerman Scott. Read by Walter Dixon. (Running Time: 7 hrs.). (ENG.). 2009. audio compact disk 29.98 (978-1-59659-290-2(7), GildAudio) Pub: Gildan Media. Dist(s): HachBkGrp

***New Rules of Marketing & PR 2. 0: How to Use News Releases, Blogs, Podcasting, Viral Marketing & Online Media to Reach Buyers Directly.** unabr. ed. David Meerman Scott. Read by Sean Pratt. (Running Time: 11 hrs. 30 mins.). (ENG.). 2010. 34.98 (978-1-59659-563-7(9), GildAudio) Pub: Gildan Media. Dist(s): HachBkGrp

New Rules of Marriage: A Breakthrough Program for 21st-Century Relationships - What You Need to Know to Make Love Work. abr. ed. Terrence Real. Read by Terrence Real. (Running Time: 21600 sec.). 2007. audio compact disk 29.95 (978-0-7393-4195-7(2), Random AudioBks) Pub: Random Audio Pubg. Dist(s): Random

***New Rules of Money.** abr. ed. Ric Edelman. Read by Ric Edelman. (ENG.). 2005. (978-0-06-088109-2(7), Harper Audio); (978-0-06-088108-5(9), Harper Audio) HarperCollins Pubs.

New Rules of Professional Conduct. 1988. bk. 40.00; 25.00 PA Bar Inst.

New Russians, Pt. 1. unabr. ed. Hedrick Smith. Read by Nadia May. 10 cass. (Running Time: 32 hrs.). 1991. 69.95 (978-0-7861-0132-0(6), 1118A,B) Blckstn Audio.
The story of the second Russian Revolution. Hedrick Smith exposes the roots of reform developing during the late seventies & early eighties, but which were hidden from view. He shows how they came together under the leadership of Mikhail Gorbachev, & how Gorbachev rose through the system, gathering allies & ideas.

New Russians, Pt. 2. unabr. ed. Hedrick Smith. Read by Nadia May. 12 cass. (Running Time: 32 hrs.). 1991. 83.95 (978-0-7861-0133-7(4), 1118A,B) Blckstn Audio.

New Sanctuary: Hebrews. Ed Young. 1992. 4.95 (978-0-7417-1906-5(1), 906) Win Walk.

New Science of Life - Lecture. Rupert Sheldrake. 2 cass. (Running Time: 3 hrs.). 18.00 (OC41L) Sound Horizons AV.

New Science of Life - Workshop. Rupert Sheldrake. 6 cass. (Running Time: 9 hrs.). 54.00 (OC41W) Sound Horizons AV.

New Science of Persuasion... for Men Only. Patrick Wanis. As told by Patrick Wanis. (ENG.). 2008. 39.95 (978-0-9779192-8-4(5)) WOW Prods.

New Scripture & Myths: Morality & the Jesus Ethic. Ann Ree Colton. 1 cass. (Running Time: 1 hr.). 7.95 (978-0-917189-14-2(0)) A R Colton Fnd.

New Sense of Jesus. Joseph F. Girzone. Read by Joseph F. Girzone. 1 cass. (Running Time: 1 hr.). 1992. 7.95 (978-0-911519-11-2(4)) Richelieu Court.
Girzone's personal reflections on Jesus' messages in the gospels. This is one of Girzone's public talks.

New Situational English Books 1 & 2 CD: English Language Teaching. 2006. audio compact disk (978-0-7428-1662-6(1)) CCLS Pubg Hse.

New Situational English Books 3 & 4 CD: English Language Teaching. 2006. audio compact disk (978-0-7428-1532-2(3)) CCLS Pubg Hse.

New Song, abr. ed. Jan Karon. Read by Jan Karon. 4 cass. (Running Time: 6 hrs.). (Mitford Ser.: Bk. 5). 1999. 24.95 (FS9-50892) Highsmith.

New Song, unabr. ed. Jan Karon. Read by John McDonough. 12 cass. (Running Time: 18 hrs.). (Mitford Ser.: Bk. 5). 1999. 55.95 (FS9-50951) Highsmith.

New Song. unabr. ed. Jan Karon. (Running Time: 17 hrs.). (Mitford Ser.: Bk. 5). (gr. 12 up). 2007. audio compact disk 39.95 (978-0-14-314226-3(7), PengAudBks) Penguin Grp USA.

New Song. unabr. ed. Jan Karon. Narrated by John McDonough. 15 CDs. (Running Time: 17 hrs. 30 mins.). (Mitford Ser.: Bk. 5). 2001. audio compact disk 142.00 (978-1-4025-0496-9(9), C1552) Recorded Bks.
In A New Song, just as Father Tim Kavanagh is reveling in his retirement from the pulpit, he finds himself preparing to face new challenges, far from his beloved North Carolina mountain village. When the small Episcopal church across the sound on Whitecap Isl[illegible] asks for an interim priest, Father Tim and his wife Cynthia agree to ans[illegible] call. Taking over the oceanside parish should be almost lik[illegible]tended vacation for them. But soon a host of problems threatens Fathe[illegible]m's new congregation and his own peace of mind.

New Song. unabr. ed. Jan Karon. Narrated by John McDonough. 12 cass. (Running Time: 17 hrs. 30 mins.). (Mitford Ser.: Bk. 5). 1999. 102.00 (978-0-7887-3098-6(3), 95809E7) Recorded Bks.
Just as Episcopal priest Father Tim Kavanagh is reveling in his retirement from the pulpit, he finds himself called to take over as interim priest of the troubled Whitecap Island church. You will greet old friends from Mitford & meet new ones from Whitecap.

New Song for Indiana Ophelias see Carl Sandburg's Poems for Children

New Song from Old Hymns Cassette. Arranged by Alice Parker. 1998. 10.95 (978-1-56854-280-5(1), NSONG) Liturgy Tr Pubns.

New Songs for New Singers Bk. 1: Piano Accompaniment Only, 30 Settings of Classic & New Texts. Henry Wadsworth Longfellow et al. Composed by Jack C. Goode et al. (YA). 2001. audio compact disk 14.95 (978-1-889079-30-1(8)) Darcey Pr.

New Songs for New Singers Bk. 1: 30 Settings of Classic & New Texts. Kim Lewelling et al. Composed by Jack C. Goode et al. (YA). 2001. bk. 25.95 (978-1-889079-35-6(9)) Darcey Pr.

New Songs for New Singers Bk. 2: Piano Accompaniment Only, 26 Settings of Classic & New Texts. Kris Matters et al. Composed by Jack C. Goode et al. (YA). 2001. audio compact disk 14.95 (978-1-889079-33-2(2)) Darcey Pr.

New Songs for New Singers Bk. 2: 26 Settings of Classic & New Texts. Kris Matters et al. Composed by Jack C. Goode et al. 2001. bk. 25.95 (978-1-889079-36-3(7)) Darcey Pr.

New Southern Favorites Vol. 2. Contrib. by Johnathan Crumpton et al. Prod. by Craig Adams. (ENG.). 2003. audio compact disk 5.00 (978-5-552-26503-9(3), Brentwood-Benson Music) Brentwood Music.

New Spanish Poetry. Andrew P. Debicki. 1 cass. (Running Time: 1 hr.). (669) Natl Humanities.

New Species for the 21st Century: Exploring the Sacredness of Your Humanity. Jim Rosemergy. 2 cass. (Running Time: 3 hrs.). 2000. 17.95 (978-0-87159-834-9(5)) Unity Schl Christ.

New Spirit Within: Heb 12:3; Psalms 51:10. Ed Young. (J). 1980. 4.95 (978-0-7417-1113-7(3), A0113) Win Walk.

New Spirituality for the Twenty-First Century. David Spangler. 2 cass. (Running Time: 3 hrs.). 1992. 18.00 (OC303-66) Sound Horizons AV.

New Spring. unabr. rev. ed. Robert Jordan. Read by Michael Kramer & Kate Reading. 11 CDs. (Running Time: 13 hrs. 0 mins. 0 sec.). (Wheel of Time Ser.). (ENG.). 2004. audio compact disk 39.95 (978-1-55927-954-3(0)) Pub: Macmill Audio. Dist(s): Macmillan

New Statewide Support Guidelines. 1989. 50.00 (AC-539) PA Bar Inst.

New Steps in English CD: English Language Teaching. 2005. audio compact disk (978-0-7428-1481-3(5)) CCLS Pubg Hse.

New Stories from the South: The Year's Best 2004. unabr. ed. Ed. by Shannon Ravenel. 10 cass. (Running Time: 12 hrs. 45 mins.). 2004. 89.75 (978-1-4193-0513-9(1), SV017MC); audio compact disk 109.75 (978-1-4193-0515-3(8), CV019MC) Recorded Bks.

New Story. Thomas Berry. 1 CD. (Running Time: 1 hr. 30 mins.). 2005. audio compact disk 12.95 (978-0-660-18972-7(0)) Pub: Canadian Broadcasting CAN. Dist(s): Georgetown Term

New Strategic Selling: The Unique Sales System Proven Successful by the World's Best Companies Revised & Updated for the 21st Century. abr. ed. Stephen E. Heiman & Diane Sanchez. Read by Stephen E. Heiman & Diane Sanchez. 2 cass. (Running Time: 2 hrs. 9 min.). 1998. (978-1-889888-05-7(2)) Miller Heiman.

New Strong-Willed Child: Birth Through Adolescence. unabr. ed. James C. Dobson. 6 CDs. (Running Time: 6 mins. 45 sec.). (ENG.). 2004. audio compact disk 26.99 (978-0-8423-8799-6(4)) Tyndale Hse.

New Sun Dance Ritual. Sarah Dubin-Vaughn. 1 cass. (Running Time: 1 hr.). 9.00 (A0356-88) Sound Photosyn.
ICSS '88, with Suzanne Palmer & Shafer.

New Supervisor: Skills for Success. Contrib. by Bruce B. Tepper. 1 cass. (Running Time: 48 mins.). pap. bk. 99.95 (1026AV); pap. bk. 99.95 (1026AV) J Wilson & Assocs.

New Tax Practitioner-Client Privilege that Protects Tax Advice from Disclosure: What CPAs, Enrolled Actuaries, & Lawyers Need to Know. 2 cass. (Running Time: 2 hrs.). 1998. 129.00 Set; incl. study guide. (D288) Am Law Inst.
Explains the attorney-client privilege that now extends to tax advice communicated on or after July 22, 1998, between taxpayers & federally authorized tax practitioners.

New Tax Saving Ideas: Using the New Tax Law. Michael A. Rome et al. 2 cass. (Running Time: 3 hrs. 30 min.). (RPL Audio Books Ser.). 1998. 18.00 (978-1-879755-03-1(3), 503) Recorded Pubns.
Understand new tax planning opportunities available for families, investors & business owners.

New Terrorism: Fanaticism & the Arms of Mass Destruction. Walter Laqueur. Read by Edward Holland. 2002. 88.00 (978-0-7366-8579-5(0)) Books on Tape.

New Testament. 12 cass. (Running Time: 18 hrs.). 1994. 29.98; 39.98 Set. (978-7-902033-29-9(4)) Chrstn Dup Intl.
Bible.

New Testament. Read by E. W. Jeffries. 12 cass. (Running Time: 18 hrs.). 1993. 29.98 (978-7-902031-26-4(7)) Chrstn Dup Intl.
New American Standard Bible.

New Testament. Contrib. by E. W. Jeffries. 12 cass. (Running Time: 18 hrs.). 1995. 26.50 (978-7-902030-23-6(6)) Chrstn Dup Intl.

New Testament. Contrib. by E. W. Jeffries. 1 cass. (Running Time: 1 hr. 30 min.). 1997. 89.98 (978-7-902031-07-3(0)) Chrstn Dup Intl.

New Testament. Read by E. W. Jeffries. 1 cass. 1997. 62.99 Chrstn Dup Intl.

New Testament. Stephen Johnston. 12 cass. 2004. 29.95 (978-1-56563-771-9(2)); 29.95 (978-1-56563-773-3(9)); 29.95 (978-1-56563-786-3(0)); audio compact disk 39.95 (978-1-56563-751-1(8)); audio compact disk 39.95 (978-1-56563-749-8(6)); audio compact disk 39.95 (978-1-56563-753-5(4)) Hendrickson MA.

New Testament. Read by James Earl Jones. 16 cass. (Running Time: 24 hrs.). 79.95 (978-1-888909-00-5(5), 10201) Locke Grp.

New Testament. Contrib. by P. Kumar. 12 cass. (Running Time: 18 hrs.). (TEL.). 1994. 29.98 (978-7-902030-29-8(5)) Chrstn Dup Intl.
Bible.

New Testament. Eric Martin. 12 cass. 2004. 21.99 (978-0-88368-833-5(6)) Whitaker Hse.

New Testament. Read by Max E. McLean. 12 cass. (Running Time: 19 hrs.). (46322); audio compact disk (47049) Fellow Perform Arts.

New Testament. Contrib. by Paul Mims. 12 cass. (Running Time: 18 hrs.). 1994. 24.50 (978-7-902030-70-0(8)) Chrstn Dup Intl.
King James Bible.

New Testament. Contrib. by Paul Mims. 12 cass. (Running Time: 18 hrs.). 1994. 29.98 (978-7-902030-35-9(X)) Chrstn Dup Intl.

New Testament. Paul Mims. 1 cass. (Running Time: 1 hr. 30 min.). 1997. 79.98 (978-7-902031-00-4(3)) Chrstn Dup Intl.

New Testament. Narrated by Paul Mims. 16 cass. (Running Time: 24 hrs.). 1997. 39.99 (978-7-902030-14-4(7)) Chrstn Dup Intl.

New Testament. Narrated by Samuel Montoya. 16 cass. (Running Time: 24 hrs.). (SPA.). 1994. 39.98 (978-7-902031-89-9(5)) Chrstn Dup Intl.

New Testament. Read by Samuel Montoya. (SPA.). 49.95 Trinity Tapes.

New Testament. Read by Alexander Scourby. 15 CDs. 2004. audio compact disk 39.95 (978-1-56563-757-3(7)); audio compact disk 39.95 (978-1-56563-761-0(5)) Hendrickson MA.

New Testament. unabr. ed. Bible Adventures Staff. Read by Michael Tudor Barnes et al. 14 cass. (Running Time: 16 hrs.). (Isis Ser.). (J). 1994. 104.95 (978-1-85695-809-7(4), 940911) Pub: ISIS Lrg Prnt GBR. Dist(s): Ulverscroft US

New Testament. unabr. ed. Read by Lael Woodbury. 12 cass. (Running Time: 12 hrs.). (Scriptures on Cassette Ser.). 1990. 23.95 (978-1-887938-01-3(X)) Snd Concepts.
LDS standard works on cassette.

New Testament, Pts. I-II. Instructed by Bart D. Ehrman. 12 CDs. (Running Time: 12 hrs.). (C). 2000. bk. 69.95 (978-1-56585-366-9(0), 656) Teaching Co.

New Testament, Set. Narrated by Rex Cambell. 14 CDs. 2004. bk. 29.95 (978-1-59156-349-5(6)) Covenant Comms.

New Testament, Vol. 1 & 2. Instructed by Bart D. Ehrman. 12 pieces. (Running Time: 12 hrs.). (C). 2000. bk. 54.95 (978-1-56585-181-8(1), 656) Teaching Co.

New Testament, Vol. 2. Instructed by Bart D. Ehrman. 6 cass. (Running Time: 6 hrs.). 2000. 129.95 (978-1-56585-182-5(X)) Teaching Co.

New Testament: An Introduction, Course No. 316. Elizabeth McNamer. 8 lectures. 44.91 Teaching Co.
The New Testament is our context; what was its context? Elizabeth McNamer makes this text accessible to the novice & more rewarding for the experienced reader. The 27 books in the canon of the New Testament were written between 50 & 14 c.e. (common era). This course describes how these books came to be written, where & when they were written, why & to whom they were written, & why they & not others found their way into the canon.

New Testament: Arabic. 16 cass. (Running Time: 24 hrs.). (ARA.). 1994. 39.98 (978-7-902030-01-4(5)) Chrstn Dup Intl.
Bible.

New Testament: King James Version, Narrated by Rex Campbell. 14 CDs. (Running Time: 21 hrs.). audio compact disk 49.95 (978-1-57734-413-1(8), 0200557) Covenant Comms.

New Testament: King James Version, Narrated by Rex Campbell. 11 cass. (Running Time: 16 hrs. 30 min.). 2004. 22.95 (978-1-55503-208-1(7), 050033) Covenant Comms.

New Testament: King James Version. Read by Marvin Miller. 16 cass. (Running Time: 20 hrs.). 45.95 (TC-901) Audio Bk.

New Testament: King James Version. Read by George W. Sarris. 15 cass. (Running Time: 2 hrs. 30 mins.). 1985. 95.95 (978-0-7861-0173-3(3), 1154) Blckstn Audio.
Nearly 2000 years after the Crucifixion & more pertinent & vital than ever, the Bible has proven itself to be, "living & active & sharper than any two-edged sword & piercing as far as the division of soul & spirit of both joints & marrow & able to judge the thoughts & intentions of the heart." (Heb. 4:12).

New Testament: King James Version. Read by Alexander Scourby. 39.95 Trinity Tapes.

New Testament: King James Version. unabr. ed. Read by Gregory Peck. Ed. by Stephen Peck. 16 cass. (Running Time: 21 hrs. 30 min.). 1985. 59.95 (NT-C-GP) Trinity Tapes.

New Testament: Living Bible. Dramatization. 27.97 Trinity Tapes.

New Testament: New American Standard Version. Read by Jeffries & Al Sanders. 39.95 Trinity Tapes.

New Testament: Selections from the Bible (The Authorized Version) Read by Hugh Dickinson et al. 6 cass. (Running Time: 8 hrs.). 1997. 32.98 (978-962-634-613-6(2), NA611314, Naxos AudioBooks); audio compact disk 41.98 (978-962-634-113-1(0), NA611312, Naxos AudioBooks) Naxos.
Contains the best-known and most important sections from The New Testament including selections from the Gospels, using Matthew as the main text, the Epistles of Paul, the Acts of the Apostles and Revelations.

New Testament: Selections from the Bible (the Authorized Version) Read by Hugh Dickinson et al. (Playaway Adult Nonfiction Ser.). (ENG.). 2009. 69.99 (978-1-60812-760-3(5)) Find a World.

New Testament - CD Box Set. Read by Lael J. Woodbury. 16 CDs. 1984. audio compact disk 29.95 (978-1-887938-19-8(2)) Snd Concepts.

New Testament - English Standard Version. Read by Marquis Laughlin. 21 CDs. (Running Time: 21 hrs. 28 min.). 2002. audio compact disk 29.95 (978-0-9726331-0-9(3)) Sola Scriptura.
Audio New Testamend on CD (English Standard Version) as read by Marquis Laughlin.

New Testament-Am. Created by Whitaker House. 2006. audio compact disk 39.77 (978-7-901006-89-8(7)) Whitaker Hse.

New Testament as Told by Max McLean: Experience the Power, Max E. McLean. 12 cass. (Running Time: 18 hrs.). 1998. 49.95 (978-1-886463-22-6(0)) Oasis Audio.

New Testament Bible. Narrated by Stephen Johnston. 10 cass. (Running Time: 15 hrs.). 2000. 15.99 (978-0-9659197-3-9(0)) Am Bible.

New Testament Bible Stories for Little People. Ruth J. Jay. 8.75 incl. bk. (978-0-8474-1253-2(9)) Back to Bible.

New Testament Bible Stories for Little People. Ruth J. Jay. 1 cass. (Running Time: 20 min.). (J). 4.95 (978-0-8474-1902-9(9)) Back to Bible.

New Testament-Cev. Narrated by Stephen Johnston. 2005. 14.99 (978-0-89957-958-0(2)) AMG Pubs.

New Testament-ESV. 2007. audio compact disk 29.99 (978-0-89957-712-8(1)) AMG Pubs.

New Testament Evangelist. Derek Prince. 1 cass. (Running Time: 1 hr.). (I-5021) Derek Prince.

New Testament for Today: Commentary. Joseph A. Grassi et al. 63 cass. Incl. New Testament for Today: Letters to the Corinthians. 3 cass. 18.95 incl. study guide & outline. (TAH053); New Testament for Today: The Acts of the Apostles. 4 cass. 24.95 incl. study guide & outline. (TAH051); New Testament for Today: The Book of Revelation (The Apocalypse) 4 cass. 24.95 incl. study guide & outline. (TAH061); New Testament for Today: The Gospel of John. 9 cass. 57.95 incl. study guide & outline. (TAH047); New Testament for Today: The Gospel of Luke. 9 cass. 57.95 incl. study guide & outline. (TAH048); New Testament for Today: The Gospel of Mark. 7 cass. 44.95 incl. study guide & outline. (TAH50); New Testament for Today: The Gospel of Matthew. 7 cass. 44.95 incl. study guide & outline. (TAH049); New Testament for Today: The Letter to the Galatians. 2 cass. 12.95 incl. study guide & outline. (TAH054); New Testament for Today: The Letter to the Hebrews. 3 cass. 18.95 incl. study guide & outline. (TAH059); New Testament for Today: The Letter to the Philippians. 2 cass. 12.95 incl. study guide & outline. (TAH055); New Testament for Today: The Letters of James, Peter, John, Jude. 3 cass. 18.95 incl. study guide & outline. (TAH060); New Testament for Today: The Letters of the Romans. 3 cass. 18.95 incl. study guide & outline. (TAH052); New Testament for Today: The Letters to the Collosians & Ephesians. 3 cass. 17.95 incl. study guide & outline. (TAH056); New Testament for Today: The Letters to the Thessalonians. 2 cass. 12.95 incl. study guide & outline. (TAH057); New Testament for Today: The Pastoral Letters. 2 cass. 12.95 incl. study guide & outline. (TAH058); 352.95 incl. study guide & outline. (TAH046) Alba Hse Comns.
A popular series of commentaries based on modern ecumenical scholarship prepared by Protestant & Catholic authors.

New Testament for Today: Letters to the Corinthians see New Testament for Today: Commentary

New Testament for Today: The Acts of the Apostles see New Testament for Today: Commentary

New Testament for Today: The Book of Revelation (The Apocalypse) see New Testament for Today: Commentary

New Testament for Today: The Gospel of John see New Testament for Today: Commentary

New Testament for Today: The Gospel of Luke see New Testament for Today: Commentary

New Testament for Today: The Gospel of Mark see New Testament for Today: Commentary

New Testament for Today: The Gospel of Matthew see New Testament for Today: Commentary

New Testament for Today: The Letter to the Galatians see New Testament for Today: Commentary

New Testament for Today: The Letter to the Hebrews see New Testament for Today: Commentary

New Testament for Today: The Letter to the Philippians see New Testament for Today: Commentary

New Testament for Today: The Letters of James, Peter, John, Jude see New Testament for Today: Commentary

New Testament for Today: The Letters of the Romans see New Testament for Today: Commentary

New Testament for Today: The Letters to the Collosians & Ephesians see New Testament for Today: Commentary

New Testament for Today: The Letters to the Thessalonians see New Testament for Today: Commentary

New Testament for Today: The Pastoral Letters see New Testament for Today: Commentary

New Testament, Greece, & Rome History. Marlin Detweiler & Laurie Detweiler. Perf. by Meshell Watt. 1998. 6.95 (978-1-930710-06-1(2)) Veritas Pr PA.

New Testament Greek Vocabulary: Learn on the Go. unabr. ed. Jonathan T. Pennington. (Running Time: 2 hrs. 0 mins. 0 sec.). (ENG.). 2003. 13.99 (978-0-310-26164-3(3)) Zondervan.

New Testament Greek Vocabulary Set: Words That Occur Ten Times or More, unabr. ed. Jonathan T. Pennington. Read by Jonathan T. Pennington. 2 cass. (Running Time: 2 hrs., 15 min.). 1999. pap. bk. 21.99 (978-0-9676911-0-7(9)) Pennington Ink.
Each word is first read in Greek, followed by an English definition. 40-pg. booklet contains all of the words and their definitions.

New Testament (Ignatius Bible) Revised Standard Version. Read by Mark Taheny. 12 cass. (Running Time: 18 hrs.). 46.95 (954-C) Ignatius Pr.
Regarded by many Bible scholars as the most beautiful, accurate & clearest modern translation of the Bible in English.

New Testament in Amharic (FSI) 16 cass. (Running Time: 24 hrs.). 1988. 69.95 (S50270) J Norton Pubs.
1988 Common Version.

New Testament in Arabic. unabr. ed. 16 cass. (Running Time: 16 hrs.). 69.95 (S50030) J Norton Pubs.
Van Dyke edition.

New Testament in Armenian. 8 cass. (Running Time: 8 hrs.). (ARM.). 2001. (S50180) J Norton Pubs.
Gospels only.

New Testament in Bulgarian, rev. ed. 16 cass. (Running Time: 24 hrs.). 1994. 69.95 (S50190) J Norton Pubs.
1924 revised edition.

New Testament in Cantonese. 18 cass. (Running Time: 18 hrs.). 74.95 J Norton Pubs.
Union version.

New Testament in English. 16 cass. (Running Time: 16 hrs.). 64.95 (S50080) J Norton Pubs.

New Testament in French. Read by Charles Guillot. 16 cass. (Running Time: 16 hrs.). 69.95 (S50020) J Norton Pubs.
The Segond version.

New Testament in German. Read by Edwin Auchenbach. 24 cass. (Running Time: 24 hrs.). 79.95 (S50060) J Norton Pubs.
Luther Version.

New Testament in Greek. 12 cass. (Running Time: 12 hrs.). (GEC.). 2001. 59.50 (S50300) J Norton Pubs.
1967 Vellas version Modern Greek.

New Testament in Haitian. 18 cass. (Running Time: 27 hrs.). 2001. 74.95 (S50220) J Norton Pubs.
Alliance Bilingue Universelle Version.

New Testament in Hebrew, 16 cass. (Running Time: 24 hrs.). 1994. 69.50 (S50260) J Norton Pubs.
Modern Language BSI Version.

New Testament in Hindi. 16 cass. (Running Time: 16 hrs.). 79.95 (S50100) J Norton Pubs.

New Testament in Hungarian, 16 cass. (Running Time: 36 hrs.). 1994. 69.95 (S50160) J Norton Pubs.
Karoly version.

New Testament in Italian. Read by Elio Milazzo. 16 cass. (Running Time: 16 hrs.). (ITA.). 69.95 (S50040) J Norton Pubs.
Riveduta version.

New Testament in Japanese. 24 cass. (Running Time: 24 hrs.). 2001. 79.95 (S50350) J Norton Pubs.
Colloquial version JBS.

New Testament in Khmer. 16 cass. (Running Time: 16 hrs.). 69.95 (S50310) J Norton Pubs.

New Testament in Korean. 24 cass. (Running Time: 24 hrs.). 89.95 (S50070) J Norton Pubs.

New Testament in Latvian, 16 cass. (Running Time: 24 hrs.). 1994. 69.95 (S50230) J Norton Pubs.
Lat ev. Lut. Baznica Amerika Version.

New Testament in Lithuanian, 16 cass. (Running Time: 24 hrs.). 1994. 69.95 (S50240) J Norton Pubs.
1988 Kannas Version.

New Testament in Mandarin. Tang Ding Kuo. 16 cass. (Running Time: 16 hrs.). 69.95 (S50090) J Norton Pubs.
Union version.

New Testament in Navajo. 24 cass. (Running Time: 38 hrs.). (NAV.). 2001. 79.95 (S50320) J Norton Pubs.
1975 American Bible Society version.

New Testament in Portuguese. Read by Davi Nunes. 16 cass. (Running Time: 16 hrs.). (POR.). 69.95 (S50050) J Norton Pubs.
Almeida version.

New Testament in Russian. 12 cass. (Running Time: 18 hrs.). 1994. 59.95 (S50150) J Norton Pubs.
Authorized Version.

New Testament in Spanish. abr. ed. Read by Samuel Montoya. 16 cass. (Running Time: 16 hrs.). vinyl bd. 69.95 (S50010) J Norton Pubs.
1960 Reina-Valera version.

New Testament in Swahili: Kenya Bible Society Translation. 17 cass. (Running Time: 25 hrs. 30 min.). 69.95 (S50120) J Norton Pubs.

New Testament in Tagalog, 16 cass. (Running Time: 24 hrs.). 1994. 69.95 (S50140) J Norton Pubs.

New Testament in Telugu, 12 cass. (Running Time: 12 hrs.). 1994. 69.95 (S50130) J Norton Pubs.

New Testament in Ukrainian, 16 cass. (Running Time: 24 hrs.). 1994. 69.95 (S50250) J Norton Pubs.
1963 Basillian Fathers Version.

New Testament in Urdu. 16 cass. (Running Time: 16 hrs.). 69.95 (S50110) J Norton Pubs.

New Testament-NASB-Voice Only. Narrated by Stephen Johnston. 2007. audio compact disk 39.95 (978-1-59856-117-3(0)) Hendrickson MA.

New Testament-NASB-Voice Only. Narrated by Stephen Johnston. 2007. audio compact disk 24.97 (978-1-59856-132-6(4)) Hendrickson MA.

New Testament-Nylon Zipper. Eric Martin. 14 CDs. 2004. audio compact disk 24.99 (978-0-88368-831-1(X)) Whitaker Hse.

New Testament-Nylon Zipper. Alexander Scourby. 14 CDs. 2004. audio compact disk 24.99 (978-0-88368-827-4(1)) Whitaker Hse.

New Testament-Nylon Zipper. Steven Stevens. 14 CDs. 2004. audio compact disk 24.99 (978-0-88368-820-5(4)) Whitaker Hse.

New Testament on Audio. Narrated by Alexander Scouby. 12 cass. (Running Time: 18 hrs.). 19.95 (QA2429CS) Questar CA.
Classic King James version.

New Testament on Cassette. Read by Frederick Ryan. 16 cass. (Running Time: 24 hrs.). 37.95 (978-0-8198-5110-9(8)) Pauline Bks.

***New Testament on Women.** Gaye Strathearn. 2010. audio compact disk 14.99 (978-1-60641-638-9(3)) Deseret Bk.

New Testament Package, Bks. 9-16, Tapes 9-16. 8 cass. (Running Time: 12h rs.). (J). DonWise Prodns.
Presents Biblical stories & fables for children, including "God's Glory, Discoveries, Parables, Miracles, Friends, More Miracles, The Greatest Love & Followers".

New Testament Package, Tape 3 & 4. 2 cass. (Running Time: 3 hrs.). (J). (978-0-944391-55-6(9)) DonWise Prodns.
Presents New Testament stories "Dreams" & "The Song Trip", especially designed for children.

New Testament Package, Tape 5 & 6. 2 cass. (Running Time: 3 hrs.). (J). (978-0-944391-56-3(7)) DonWise Prodns.
Presents New Testament stories "Mighty Men" & "Kings" especially designed for children.

New Testament Package, Tape 7 & 8. 2 cass. (Running Time: 3 hrs.). (J). (978-0-944391-57-0(5)) DonWise Prodns.
Presents New Testament stories "Men of God" & "Adventures" especially designed for children.

New Testament Package, Tape 9 & 10. 2 cass. (Running Time: 3 hrs.). (J). (978-0-944391-58-7(3)) DonWise Prodns.
Presents New Testament stories "God's Glory" & "Discoveries" especially designed for children.

New Testament Package, Tape 11 & 12. 2 cass. (Running Time: 3 hrs.). (J). (978-0-944391-59-4(1)) DonWise Prodns.
Presents New Testament stories "Parables" & "Miracles" especially designed for children.

New Testament Package, Tape 13 & 14. 2 cass. (Running Time: 3 hrs.). (J). (978-0-944391-60-0(5)) DonWise Prodns.
Presents New Testament stories "Friends" & "More Miracles" especially designed for children.

New Testament Package, Tape 15 & 16. 2 cass. (Running Time: 3 hrs.). (J). (978-0-944391-61-7(3)) DonWise Prodns.
Presents New Testament stories "The Greatest Love" & "Followers" especially designed for children.

New Testament Postcards: A Study of Philemon, 2 John, 3 John & Jude Series, Charles R. Swindoll. 3 cass. (Running Time: 6 hrs.). 1997. 16.95 (978-1-57972-022-3(6)) Insight Living.
Christian living in a hostile culture.

New Testament Scholarship as We End One Century & Open Another. Raymond E. Brown. 2004. 26.50 (978-1-904756-04-0(2)) STL Dist NA.

New Testament Study Today. Patrick Henry. 10 cass. Incl. New Testament Study Today: Far Out: Apocalyptic, Esoteric, & Other Intriguing Interpretations. 1975.; New Testament Study Today: Here We Have No Lasting City (Hebrews 13: 14) - But Here We Are Nevertheless. 1975.; New Testament Study Today: Ignorance or Sin? The Gnostic Challenge. 1975.; New Testament Study Today: Jesus - Traditions & History. 1975.; New Testament Study Today: New Questions? Or New Answers to Old Questions? 1975.; New Testament Study Today: Paul: Translator or Reviser? 1975.; New Testament Study Today: Present Quandaries, Future Prospects. 1975.; New Testament Study Today: Salvation Is From the Jews (John 4: 22)-But Which Ones? 1975.; New Testament Study Today: The Apostolic Book & the Apostolic See. 1975.; New Testament Study Today: Water, Bread, Wine: Patterns in Religion. 1975.; 1975. 30.00 Set.; 4.50 ea. Pendle Hill.

New Testament Study Today: Far Out: Apocalyptic, Esoteric, & Other Intriguing Interpretations see New Testament Study Today

New Testament Study Today: Here We Have No Lasting City (Hebrews 13: 14) - But Here We Are Nevertheless see New Testament Study Today

New Testament Study Today: Ignorance or Sin? The Gnostic Challenge see New Testament Study Today

New Testament Study Today: Jesus - Traditions & History see New Testament Study Today

New Testament Study Today: New Questions? Or New Answers to Old Questions? see New Testament Study Today

New Testament Study Today: Paul: Translator or Reviser? see New Testament Study Today

New Testament Study Today: Present Quandaries, Future Prospects see New Testament Study Today

New Testament Study Today: Salvation Is From the Jews (John 4: 22)-But Which Ones? see New Testament Study Today

New Testament Study Today: The Apostolic Book & the Apostolic See see New Testament Study Today

New Testament Study Today: Water, Bread, Wine: Patterns in Religion see New Testament Study Today

New Testament Survey, W. Stanley Outlaw et al. Contrib. by Sound Impressions Staff. 12 cass. (Running Time: 18 hrs.). 1992. 49.95 (978-0-89265-658-5(1), 28038) Randall Hse.
Contains an overview.

New Testament Survey I. Gary V. Whetstone. Instructed by June Austin. 11 cass. (Running Time: 16 hrs. 30 mins.). (New Testament Ser.: NT101). 1997. pap. bk. 220.00 (978-1-928774-63-1(6), BN 101 A00) Gary Whet Pub.
A survey of the Gospels, with a concentrated biblical study of the life of the Lord Jesus Christ & practical applications of biblical principles for our day-to-day life.

New Testament Survey II. Gary V. Wetstone. Instructed by June Austin. 11 cass. (Running Time: 16 hrs. 30 mins.). (New Testament Ser.: Vol. NT102). 1996. 220.00 (978-1-928774-68-6(7), BN 102 A00) Gary Whet Pub.
A further survey of the New Testament books, with a concentrated biblical study of the lives of the apostles & the beginning of the church.

New Testament Truths from Ezekiel. Dan Corner. 1 cass. (Running Time: 1 hr.). 3.00 (112) Evang Outreach.

New Testament Warnings. Dan Corner. 1 cass. 3.00 (61) Evang Outreach.

New Testament with Psalms. Narrated by E. W. Jeffries. 16 cass. (Running Time: 90 mins. per cass.). 2000. 32.50 (978-7-902030-79-3(1)) Chrstn Dup Intl.

New Testament with Psalms. Narrated by Paul Mims. 16 cass. (Running Time: 24 hrs.). 2000. 29.50 (978-7-902030-72-4(4)) Chrstn Dup Intl.

New Testament Witnesses of Christ. Peter et al. 6 cass. 2004. 24.95 (978-1-59156-119-4(1)); audio compact disk 24.95 (978-1-59156-120-0(5)) Covenant Comms.

New Text for a Modern China. Irene Liu & Xiaoqi Liu. 2 cass. (Running Time: 60 mins.). (CHI & ENG.). (gr. k up). 2002. 35.95 (978-0-88727-383-4(1)) Cheng Tsui.

New Therapy in Esophageal Disorders. Read by Donald O. Castell. 1 cass. (Running Time: 1 hr. 30 min.). 1985. 12.00 (C8540) Amer Coll Phys.

New Thinking for the New Millenium. abr. ed. Edward De Bono. Read by David Ackroyd. 4 cass. (Running Time: 6 hrs.). 2004. 25.00 (978-1-931056-37-3(4), New Millenn Pr) New Millenn Enter.
Demonstrates tried-and-true methods for creative thinking to help bring about: the creative problem-solving necessary for success, the ability to design the future, the skills to create values to live by, and the development of new ideas.

New Thought for a New Millennium: Twelve Powers for the 21st Century. Michael A. Maday. Read by Susan Kavanaugh & Michael Moran. 4 cass. (Running Time: 6 hrs.). 1998. (978-0-87159-837-0(X)) Unity Schl Christ.

New Time Management. Merrill E. Douglass & Larry Baker. Read by Merrill E. Douglass & Larry Baker. 6 cass. (Running Time: 9 hrs.). 69.95 (880A) Nightingale-Conant.

New Tomorrow: God's Wonderful Way to a Fresh, Clean Start. Mac Hammond. 5 cass. (Running Time: 5 hrs.). 1997. 30.00 Set. (978-1-57399-055-4(8)) Mac Hammond.
Making a fresh start in life.

New Treasure Seekers, unabr. ed. E. Nesbit. Read by Flo Gibson. 5 cass. (Running Time: 6 hrs. 30 min.). (J). (gr. 2-4). 1992. 20.95 (978-1-55685-262-6(2)) Audio Bk Con.
In their continued zeal to do good, the Bastable children have a series of riotous adventures with mixed results.

New Treasury of Great Humorists. abr. ed. Winters & Peter Barry. 4 cass. (Running Time: 6 hrs.). 2001. 25.00 (978-1-59040-124-8(7), Phoenix Audio) Pub: Amer Intl Pub. Dist(s): PerseuPGW

New Treatment Paradigms in Colorectal Cancer: A Monograph. Ed. by John Marshall. 2006. pap. bk. 24.95 (978-1-891483-40-0(4)) PRR.

New Treatment Paradigms in Lung Cancer: A Monograph. Ed. by Alan B. Sandler. 2006. pap. bk. 24.95 (978-1-891483-44-8(7)) PRR.

New Tricks. David Rosenfelt. 2009. audio compact disk 29.95 (978-1-59316-424-9(6)) Listen & Live.

New Twists for the 5-String Banjo: A Guide to the Use of Keith Turners. Vincent Sadovsky. 1 CD. 2002. bk. 17.95 (978-0-7866-6120-6(8), 99793BCD) Mel Bay.

New U. S. Trusteee Program: Effect on Bankruptcy Practice. John J. Grauer. 1 cass. (Running Time: 1 hr.). 1987. 20.00 PA Bar Inst.

New Underground Railroad. (YA). 2003. audio compact disk 20.00 (978-0-9702762-2-3(2)) New Underground.

New Understanding of the Atom. unabr. ed. John T. Sanders. Read by Edwin Newman. (Running Time: 10800 sec.). (Audio Classics: Science & Discovery Ser.). 2006. audio compact disk 25.95 (978-0-7861-6430-1(1)) Pub: Blckstn Audio. Dist(s): NetLibrary CO

New Understanding of the Atom. unabr. ed. John T. Sanders. Read by Edwin Newman. Ed. by Jack Sommer & Mike Hassell. 2 cass. (Running Time: 2 hrs. 45 min.). Dramatization. (Science & Discovery Ser.). (YA). (gr. 11 up). 1993. 17.95 (978-1-56823-002-3(8), 10412) Knowledge Prod.
Einstein overthrew Newtonian physics, but like Newton he still believed that physical events have definite causes. Then Niels Bohr, a Danish physicist, joined others in describing a strange new world of uncertainty & mystery. Quantum mechanics has intrigued & confounded many by joining keen insights with apparent contractions & indeterminacy. Quantum theory also was later used to create semiconductors, the technology of the computer revolution.

New Version of Sandy Beach. Ormond McGill. 2000. (978-1-933332-12-3(3)) Hypnotherapy Train.

New Version of Sandy Beach. Ormond McGill. 2004. audio compact disk (978-1-933332-30-7(1)) Hypnotherapy Train.

New Vision. Perf. by Imani Project Staff. 1 cass. (Running Time: 1 hr.). 10.98 (978-1-57908-230-7(0), 1303); audio compact disk 15.98 (978-1-57908-229-1(7)) Platinm Enter.

New Vision of Living & Dying. Sogyal Rinpoche. 1 cass. (Running Time: 1 hr. 30 min.). 1994. 10.99 (978-0-9624884-4-3(5)); 10.99 (978-0-9624884-2-9(9)) Rigpa Pubns.
Sogyal Rinpoche invites us to turn our attention within & to look deeply into our lives. Reflecting with him on impermanence, we come to see that life is nothing but a continuing dance of birth & death, a dance of change. Rinpoche shows us what hope there is in death & how we can go beyond our fears to discover what it is in us that survives death & is changeless.

New War on Terrorism: Fact & Fiction. Noam Chomsky. (AK Press Audio Ser.). (ENG.). 2002. audio compact disk 14.98 (978-1-902593-62-3(6)) Pub: AK Pr GBR. Dist(s): Consort Bk Sales

New Way of Thinking. 10.00 (HD416) Esstee Audios.

New Ways to Go. Penny Ur et al. CD. 1. (SPA.). 2002. audio compact disk (978-84-8323-268-2(5)) Cambridge U Pr.

New Ways to Go, No. 2. Penny Ur et al. 2 CDs. (Running Time: 2 hrs. 3 mins.). (SPA.). 2003. audio compact disk & audio compact disk (978-84-8323-281-1(2)) Cambridge U Pr.

New Ways to Go, No. 3. Penny Ur & Mark Hancock. (SPA.). 2002. audio compact disk (978-84-8323-289-7(8)) Cambridge U Pr.

New Ways to Go, No. 4. Penny Ur & Mark Hancock. 4 CDs. (SPA.). 2007. audio compact disk (978-84-8323-296-5(0)) Cambridge U Pr.

New Ways to Go, Set. Penny Ur et al. 2002. cass. & cass. (978-84-8323-266-8(9)) Cambridge U Pr.

New Ways to Go, Set 2. Penny Ur et al. 2 cass. (Running Time: 2 hrs. 22 mins.). (SPA.). 2003. cass. & cass. (978-84-8323-279-8(0)) Cambridge U Pr.

New Ways to Go, Set 4. Penny Ur & Mark Hancock. 4 cass. (Running Time: 2 hrs. 41 mins.). (SPA.). 2003. cass. & cass. (978-84-8323-295-8(2)) Cambridge U Pr.

New Ways to Go Class Cassette 3. Penny Ur & Mark Hancock. (SPA.). 2002. (978-84-8323-288-0(X)) Cambridge U Pr.

New Ways to Save Your Garden, Farm, & Planet. Chris Bird. 2 cass. (Running Time: 3 hrs.). 18.00 (A0433-89) Sound Photosyn.
The author of "The Secret Life of Plants" has a convincing tone.

New Ways to Take Control of Your Life - How to Be Happy. Robert E. Griswold. Read by Robert E. Griswold. 1 cass. (Running Time: 1 hr.). (Super Strength Ser.). 1994. 10.95 (978-1-55848-315-6(2)) EffectiveMN.
Two complete programs to help relax, take control & make posititive changes to make your life happier & more fulfilling.

New Wine or Old Deception. Roger Oakland. 2 cass. (Running Time: 1 hr.). 1995. Set. (978-0-9637797-2-4(9)) Understand Times.
A biblical perspective of experience based Christianity.

New Wineskin. Larry Randolph. 1 cass. (Running Time: 1 hr. 30 min.). (Church in Transition Ser.: Vol. 1). 2000. 5.00 (LR01-001) Morning NC.
Larry prepares us for the needed changes we must accept in order to receive our bridegroom.

New Wineskins for Future Churches. Ralph W. Neighbour, Jr. 2 cass. (Running Time: 3 hrs.). 2001. 10.00 (CDC18) Touch Pubns.
Teaches the basic principles of the cell church & casts visions for a New Testament model in four sessions. Ideal for sharing the vision with your elders, pastoral team & small group/cell leaders.

New Woman & the Empire. Iveta Jusová. 2005. audio compact disk 9.95 (978-0-8142-9083-5(3)) Pub: Ohio St U Pr. Dist(s): Chicago Distribution Ctr

New Woman in Psychotherapy. Read by June Singer. 1 cass. (Running Time: 1 hr. 30 min.). 1984. 10.95 (978-0-7822-0255-7(1), ND7305) C G Jung IL.

New World. Frank French. 1 cass. (Running Time: 1 hr. 30 min.). 1991. 9.98 (DPC 101) Humanics Pub Grp.
Artist & entrepreneur Frank French wrote, recorded & produced this provacative & detailed arrangement of New Age Music. Meditative music that inspires, uplifts & empowers.

***New World.** unabr. ed. Tom Rob Smith. (Running Time: 13 hrs.). (ENG.). 2011. 24.98 (978-1-60788-684-6(7)); audio compact disk 34.98 (978-1-60788-683-9(9)) Pub: Hachet Audio. Dist(s): HachBkGrp

New World Coming. Nathan Miller. Read by Lloyd James. (Running Time: 18 hrs. 30 mins.). 2003. 50.95 (978-1-59912-556-5(0)) Iofy Corp.

New World Coming. unabr. ed. Nathan Miller. Read by Patrick Cullen. 15 CDs. (Running Time: 19 hrs.). 2003. audio compact disk 120.00 (978-0-7861-9130-7(9), 3156); 85.95 (978-0-7861-2523-4(3), 3156) Blckstn Audio.
Vividly portrays the 1920s, focusing on the men and women who shaped this extraordinary time, including three of America's most conservative presidents.

New World, New Love. Rosalind Laker, pseud. Read by Laurence Bouvard. 8 cass. (Running Time: 10 hrs.). (Soundings Ser.). (J). 2004. 69.95 (978-1-84283-567-8(X)) Pub: ISIS Lrg Prnt GBR. Dist(s): Ulverscroft US

New World Order. Chuck Missler & Dennis Cuddy. 2 CDs. (Running Time: 120 mins.). (Briefing Packages by Chuck Missler). 1997. audio compact disk 19.95 (978-1-57821-310-8(X)) Koinonia Hse.
Is the New World Order the product of "conspiracy kooks"? Is there really a major movement toward global government? Is the sovereign nation-state obsolete?There have been literally hundreds of quotes by advocates for global government. This is not the figment of some conspiracy theorist's imagination. The fact that there has been a concerted, coordinated push toward global government becomes undeniable when one spends time reading the articles, speeches, proposed laws, and treaties that the globalist groups have been pushing onto the American public.Chuck Missler and Dr. Dennis Cuddy, moderated by John Loeffler, explore the realities being thrust upon us by the current agenda of the global socialists.What are the implications for the Biblical believer?.

New World Order: Program for Global Governance. Chuck Missler & Dennis Cuddy. 2 cass. (Running Time: 3 hrs.). (Briefing Packages by Chuck Missler). 1995. vinyl bd. 14.95 (978-1-880532-53-9(0)) Koinonia Hse.

New Year's Day with Mr. Pepys. (23287-A) J Norton Pubs.

New Years Eve Service: December 1997/January 1998. Ben Young. 1997. Rental 4.95 (978-0-7417-6064-7(9), B0064) Win Walk.

New Year's Quilt. Jennifer Chiaverini. Narrated by Christina Moore. (Running Time: 22500 sec.). (Elm Creek Quilts Ser.: No. 11). 2007. audio compact disk 29.99 (978-1-4281-7002-5(2)) Recorded Bks.

New York see Acting with an Accent

New York. National Textbook Company Staff. 1 cass. (Running Time: 1 hr. 30 min.). (Discover America Ser.). 15.00 (978-0-8442-7490-4(9), Natl Textbk Co) M-H Contemporary.
Offers a fascinating introduction to key locations in the country. Especially designed for intermediate ESL students, combines language learning with American culture study.

New York. abr. ed. Edward Rutherfurd. Read by Mark Bramhall. (ENG.). 2009. audio compact disk 38.00 (978-0-7393-8287-5(X), Random AudioBks) Pub: Random Audio Pubg. Dist(s): Random

New York Appellate Practice: (Fourth Department Version) (Running Time: 5 hrs.). 1995. 92.00 (20755) NYS Bar.
Covers the "nuts-&-bolts" requirements, recommended tactics & necessary legal theory behind the successful taking & perfecting of a civil appeal in New York State's appellate courts. Although designed primarily for practitioner's who have not had extensive New York appellate experience, the program also serves seasoned appellate lawyers as a useful, up-to-date review of the numerous details one must know & master to handle a civil appeal in New York. Includes 300 page coursebook.

New York Appellate Practice: (Third Department Version) 3 cass. (Running Time: 5 hrs. 30 min.). 1995. 92.00 (20751) NYS Bar.
Covers the "nuts-&-bolts" requirements, recommended tactics, & necessary legal theory behind the successful taking & perfecting of a civil appeal in New York State's appellate courts. Although designed primarily for practitioner's who have not had extensive New York appellate experience, the program also serves seasoned appellate lawyers as a useful, up-to-date review of the numerous details one must know & master to handle a civil appeal in New York. Includes 300 page cousebook.

New York As Sacred City. Thomas Berry. 3 cass. (Running Time: 4 hrs. 30 min.). 24.00 (OC16W) Sound Horizons AV.

New York City: A Walk Across the Brooklyn Bridge. 1 cass. (Running Time: 1 hr.). 1990. 12.95 (CC219) Comp Comms Inc.
A walk across the Brooklyn Bridge, its history & impact on the development of the area. Wonderful views of important sights in New York & Brooklyn from a new perspective.

New York City: Chinatown, Little Italy, Soho (Walking Tour) 1 cass. (Running Time: 1 hr. 30 min.). 12.95 (CC214) Comp Comms Inc.
Look at the ethnic & artistic sides of New York City, the Soho district. The tour begins at Canal St. & Mott St. & ends in SoHo at West Broadway & Spring St.

New York City: Fifth Avenue (Walking Tour) 1 cass. (Running Time: 1 hr. 30 min.). 12.95 (CC211) Comp Comms Inc.
Stroll the shopping district including Saks Fifth Avenue, Bergman Goodman's & Tiffany's. Explore Rockefeller Center, 47th Street Diamond District, the New York Public Library, Music Hall & more.

New York City: Greenwich Village (Walking Tour) 1 cass. (Running Time: 1 hr. 30 min.). 12.95 (CC213) Comp Comms Inc.
The walking tour will take you through the windig streets, past historic houses of the 18th, 19th & 20th centuries, past the coffeehouses, bistros & boutiques, to Sheridan Square & Washington Square.

New York City: Millionaire's Mile (Upper 5th Ave) (Walking Tour) 1 cass. (Running Time: 1 hr. 30 min.). 12.95 (CC214) Comp Comms Inc.
Your tour takes you past turn-of-the-century residences, major art galleries & New York's best museums including the Metropolitan Museum of Art, the Whitney & the Guggenheim. Begins at the Frick Museum at Fifth Ave. & 71st St. & runs north to Otto Kahn Museum at Fifth & 91st St.

New York City: Wall St. & Olde New York (Walking Tour) 1 cass. (Running Time: 1 hr. 30 min.). 12.95 (CC212) Comp Comms Inc.
The New York & American Stock Exchanges & Wall Street Buildings. Included on your walking excursion: Bowling Green, St. Paul's Church, Nevelson Sculpture Park & Dutch New York.

New York City Audio Guided Walking Tour on CD: NYC/NY Travel Guide with Map(s) Narrated by Brian Turcina. 1 CD. (Running Time: 3 hours 10 mins). 2003. audio compact disk 19.95 (978-0-9748420-2-8(8)) Decision Strat.
With our Walking Tour Tapes/CDs, Our Expert Tour Guides Will show you everything you've ever wanted to see in New York City. Our Tapes/CDs provide step-by-step directions, highlighting:-important sites & monuments -historical locations -Interesting places and sites -great restaurants and hot spots We give you an insider's tour of Manhattan, making sure that you bring home memories that will last a lifetime.Our Tour Guides know all of the hidden, secret and unknown sites in New York. So, you won't miss a beat.Here's What's Included:-An Audio Walking Tour of Historic Harlem -An Audio Walking Tour of Central Park -An Audio Walking Tour of Exciting Greenwich Village -An Audio Walking Tour of Rockefeller Center and Midtown Plus:-Pocket-Sized Companion Maps of each Walking Tour -Coupons worth over $100.00, for food, travel and entertainment in New York It's like having your own personal tour guide, showing you the ins and outs of The Big Apple!.

New York Dead. abr. ed. Stuart Woods. Read by Efrem Zimbalist, Jr. 4 cass. (Running Time: 6 hrs.). (Stone Barrington Ser.: No. 1). 2002. 25.00 (978-1-59040-240-5(5), Phoenix Audio) Pub: Amer Intl Pub. Dist(s): PerseuPGW
New York cop Stone Barrington witnesses a horrifying event. Suddenly, he's on the cover of every New York paper. And before long he's hopelessly entwined with Sasha Nijinsky, tv's hottest anchorwoman. Stone finds himself caught in a perilous web of unspeakable crimes, dangerous friends, and sexual depravity. All of which have one thing in common - Sasha.

New York Dead, abr. ed. Stuart Woods. Read by Efrem Zimbalist, Jr. 4 cass. (Running Time: 6 hrs.). (Stone Barrington Ser.: No. 1). 1999. 25.00 (FS9-51018) Highsmith.

New York Dead. unabr. ed. Stuart Woods. Read by Robert Lawrence. 5 cass. (Running Time: 8 hrs.). (Stone Barrington Ser.: No. 1). 2001. 61.25 (978-1-58788-149-7(7), 1587881497, Unabridge Lib Edns); 29.95 (978-1-58788-148-0(9), 1587881489, BAU) Brilliance Audio.
It Was Just Luck Everyone is always telling Stone Barrington that he's too smart to be a cop, but it's pure luck that places him on the streets in the dead of night, just in time to witness the horrifying incident that turns his life inside out. Suddenly he is on the front page of every New York newspaper, and his life is hopelessly entwined in the increasingly shocking life (and death) of Sasha Nijinsky, the country's hottest and most beautiful television anchorwoman. No matter where he turns, the case is waiting for him, haunting his nights and turning his days into a living hell. Stone finds himself caught in a perilous web of unspeakable crimes, dangerous friends, and sexual depravity that has throughout it one common thread: Sasha. "Suspenseful and surprising." Atlanta Journal-Constitution "Hollywood slick and fast-moving." Los Angeles Daily News.

New York Dead. unabr. ed. Stuart Woods. Read by Robert Lawrence. (Running Time: 8 hrs.). (Stone Barrington Ser.: No. 1). 2004. 39.25 (978-1-59335-399-5(5), 1593353995, Brlnc Audio MP3 Lib) Brilliance Audio.

New York Dead. unabr. ed. Stuart Woods. Read by Robert Lawrence. (Running Time: 8 hrs.). (Stone Barrington Ser.: No. 1). 2004. 39.25 (978-1-59710-529-3(5), 1597105295, BADLE); 24.95 (978-1-59710-528-6(7), 1597105287, BAD) Brilliance Audio.

New York Dead. unabr. ed. Stuart Woods. Read by Robert Lawrence. (Running Time: 28800 sec.). (Stone Barrington Ser.: No. 1). 2007. audio compact disk 87.25 (978-1-4233-3414-9(0), 9781423334149, BriAudCD Unabrid); audio compact disk 34.95 (978-1-4233-3413-2(2), 9781423334132, Bril Audio CD Unabri) Brilliance Audio.

New York Dead. unabr. ed. Stuart Woods. Read by Robert Lawrence. (Running Time: 8 hrs.). (Stone Barrington Ser.: No. 1). 2004. 24.95 (978-1-59335-142-7(9), 1593351429) Soulmate Audio Bks.

New York Diary: 1999 - 2004. Based on a book by Pamela Peeters. (FLE.). 2004. audio compact disk 35.00 (978-0-9778185-2-5(7)) P Peeters Prod.

New York Jew. unabr. collector's ed. Alfred Kazin. Read by Michael Prichard. 11 cass. (Running Time: 16 hrs. 30 mins.). 1987. 88.00 (978-0-7366-1161-9(4), 2086) Books on Tape.
Illustrates Kazin's private spiritual & intellectual self. It is a wellspring of creativity.

New York State & City Tax Institute. (Running Time: 12 hrs.). 1995. 92.00 (2089) NYS Bar.
Case law developments, policy issues, new legislation & procedural changes in the governmental agencies, of relevance & interest to practitioners, CPAs & business executives, are examined in depth. Includes 275 page coursebook.

New York State Codes: 2007 Edition Complete Collection CD (5 User) ICC. 2007. audio compact disk 1551.00 (978-1-58001-629-2(4)) Int Code Counc.

***New York State Codes, 2007 Edition Complete Collection.** ICC/New York. 2010. audio compact disk 1185.00 (978-1-60983-010-6(5)) Int Code Counc.

***New York State Codes, 2010 Edition Complete Collection.** ICC/New York. 2010. audio compact disk 658.00 (978-1-60983-009-0(1)) Int Code Counc.

New York State Tax Practice & Procedure. (Running Time: 5 hrs. 30 min.). 1994. 92.00 Incl. 183p. coursebk. (20451) NYS Bar.
This recording focuses on all phases of practice in this specialized area of law, from audits to litigation & appeals, including negotiations, settlements & compromises. The experienced lecturers include private practitioners as well as personnel from the Division of Tax Appeals & the Department of Taxation & Finance.

New York Stories. unabr. ed. Edith Wharton. 4 cass. (Running Time: 6 hrs.). 2001. 30.00; audio compact disk 30.00 Airplay.

New York Times Pocket MBA Series: Analyzing Financial Statements. Eric Press. Read by Jeff Woodman. (Running Time: 3 hrs.). 2005. 19.95 (978-1-59912-891-7(8)) Iofy Corp.

New York Times Pocket MBA Series: Sales & Marketing. Michael A. Kamins. Read by Grover Gardner. (Running Time: 2 hrs. 30 mins.). 2005. 19.95 (978-1-59912-890-0(X)) Iofy Corp.

New York Times Pocket MBA Series: Business Planning: Business Planning. Edward E. Williams et al. Read by Eric Conger. (Running Time: 2 hrs. 30 mins.). 2005. 19.95 (978-1-59912-892-4(6)) Iofy Corp.

New York Times Pocket MBA Series: Leadership & Vision: Leadership & Vision. Ramon J. Aldag & Buck Joseph. Read by Jeff Woodman. (Running Time: 3 hrs.). 2005. 19.95 (978-1-59912-912-9(4)) Iofy Corp.

New York Trilogy. unabr. ed. Paul Auster. Read by Joe Barrett. (Running Time: 12 hrs.). 2010. 24.99 (978-1-4233-9580-5(8), 9781423395805, Brilliance MP3); 39.97 (978-1-4233-9581-2(6), 9781423395812, Brlnc Audio MP3 Lib); 39.97 (978-1-4233-9582-9(4), 9781423395829, BADLE); audio compact disk 29.99 (978-1-4233-9578-2(6), 9781423395782, Bril Audio CD Unabri); audio compact disk 82.97 (978-1-4233-9579-9(4), 9781423395799, BriAudCD Unabrid) Brilliance Audio.

New York Weekends - More or Less. Ralph Stern. Read by Dell Wade. 1 cass. (Running Time: 1 hr. 10 min.). Dramatization. (North Country & Thousand Islands Ser.). 1991. 9.95 (978-1-879677-01-2(6)); 9.95 (978-1-879677-00-5(8)); 9.95 (978-1-879677-02-9(4)) Spector Audio.
Audio travel guide with engaging narrative, background music, & sound effects. Describes places to go & things to do, ranging from unusual museums, innovative workshops, festivals, rafting trips, musical events, & adventures for people of all ages & interests.

New Yorker. 1 cass. (Running Time: 1 hr.). 1975. 12.95 (L060) TFR.
A documentary on the 50th birthday of the magazine. Hear from editors Roger Angell, Lee Lorenz & Brenden Gill & some assessments of the book & magazine come from Nora Ephron, David Halberstam, John Leonard & Calvin Trillen. Includes brief discussions from cartoonist Saul Steinberg & writers Donald Barthelme & Woody Allen.

New Yorker Out Loud, Vol. 1. John Updike. Perf. by Gabriel Byrne & Frances McDormand. 2 cass. (Running Time: 2 hrs. 37 min.). 1997. (978-0-9662042-1-6(2)) Mouth Almighty.
Readings of stories from "The New Yorker" magazine.

New Yorker Out Loud, Vol. 1. John Updike et al. 1 cass. (Running Time: 1 hr.). 15.98 (MERC 536608) NewSound.

New Yorkers. unabr. ed. Cathleen Schine. Read by Nicole Roberts. (YA). 2007. 54.99 (978-1-60252-772-0(5)) Find a World.

New Yorkers. unabr. ed. Cathleen Schine. Read by Nicole Roberts. 7 CDs. (Running Time: 29700 sec.). 2007. audio compact disk 32.95 (978-1-59887-090-9(4), 1598870904) Pub: HighBridge. Dist(s): Workman Pub

New Yorkers at Work: Oral Histories of Life, Labor & Industry. Ed. by Debra E. Bernhardt. Narrated by Martha Greenhouse & Frederick O'Neal. Composed by Oscar Brand & Bobbies McGee. 4 cass. (Running Time: 4 hrs.). (YA). 27.00 set. R F Wagner Labor Archives.
Presents oral history interviews with 150 New Yorkers whose work & union experiences span the century.

New York's Westchester County: From Tarrytown to Croton-on-Hudson via Chappaqua & Bedford. unabr. ed. 1 cass. (Running Time: 1 hr. 30 mins.). 2002. 19.95 (978-1-931739-08-5(0)) Travelog Corp.

New You. 2003. 10.00 (978-1-881541-82-0(7)) A Wommack.

New You. 2. 2004. audio compact disk 14.00 (978-1-881541-95-0(9)) A Wommack.

Newberry: The Life & Times of a Maine Clam. unabr. ed. Vincent G. Dethier. Read by David Skigen. 2 cass. (Running Time: 1 hr. 30 min.). (YA). (gr. k up). 1995. reel tape 14.95 (978-1-883332-15-0(X)) Audio Bkshelf.
Let this tape tickle your funnybone as the entire crew of Maine shorelife come alive! Laugh (& learn) along with Newberry.

Newberry Award & Honor, abr. ed. Elizabeth J. Gray et al. 7 cass. (Running Time: 10 hrs. 30 mins.). (J). (gr. 4-7). 1999. 55.95 (978-0-87499-578-7(7)) Live Oak Media.
Includes: "Adam of the Road," "Blue Willow," "Journey Outside," "Miss Hickory," "Rabbit Hill," "The Summer of the Swans" & "Twenty-One Balloons.".

Newberry Award & Honor, abr. ed. Robert Lawson et al. 7 vols. (Running Time: 7 hrs.). (J). (gr. 4-7). 2000. pap. bk. 99.95 (978-0-87499-491-9(8)) Live Oak Media.

Newbery Award Series, Sharon Creech et al. 10 cass. (Running Time: 15 hrs.). (J). 2000. 64.00 (5116) Books on Tape.
Includes: "Walk Two Moons," "The View from Saturday" & "Shadow of a Bull.".

Newborn King: Based on the Gospel of Matthew. Cindy Holtrop & Shirley Cooman. (Running Time: 1 hr. 10 mins.). (Noel Ser.). 1998. 15.95 (978-1-56212-371-0(8), 416101) FaithAliveChr.

Newcomer Phonics. Kaye Wiley. audio compact disk 24.50 (978-0-201-60413-9(2)) Longman.

Newcomes, Pt. II. William Makepeace Thackeray. 10 cass. (Running Time: 14 hrs. 30 min.). 65.95 Audio Bk Con.
The complex relationships between three generations of newcomes, involving unhappy marriages, a domineering mother-in-law & bankruptcy, are played against the backdrops of Paris, Baden, London & the English countryside Loveable old Colonel Newcome & his charming son, Clive, the artist, are the heroes.

Newcomes (Part 1), Vol. 1. unabr. ed. William Makepeace Thackeray. Read by Flo Gibson. 12 cass. (Running Time: 18 hrs.). 1998. 39.95 (978-1-55685-527-6(3)) Audio Bk Con.
The Complex relationships between three generations, involving unhappy marriages, a domineering mother-in-law & bankruptcy, are played against the backdrops of Paris, Baden, London & the English countryside. Loveable old Colonel Newcome & his charming, Clive, the artist, are the heroes.

Newcomes (Part 2), Vol. 2. unabr. ed. William Makepeace Thackeray. Narrated by Flo Gibson. (Running Time: 14 hrs. 27 mins.). 1998. 29.95 (978-1-55685-822-2(1)) Audio Bk Con.

Newcomes (Parts 1 And 2) unabr. ed. William Makepeace Thackeray. Narrated by Flo Gibson. (Running Time: 32 hrs. 20 mins.). 1998. 61.95 (978-1-55685-823-9(X)) Audio Bk Con.

Newer Drugs in Heart Failure. Read by Kanu Chatterjee. 1 cass. (Running Time: 1 hr. 30 min.). 1985. 12.00 ((C8535)) Amer Coll Phys.

Newer Treatments in Gynecologic Cancer. Contrib. by David H. Moore et al. 1 cass. (Running Time: 1 hr. 30 min.). (American College of Obstetrics & Gynecologists UPDATE: Vol. 21, No. 9). 1998. 20.00 Am Coll Obstetric.

Newes from the Dead. unabr. ed. Mary Hooper. Read by Rosalyn Landor & Michael Page. 1 MP3-CD. (Running Time: 7 hrs.). 2009. 24.99 (978-1-4233-9231-6(0), 9781423392316, Brilliance MP3); 24.99 (978-1-4233-9233-0(7), 9781423392330, BAD); 39.97 (978-1-4233-9232-3(9), 9781423392323, Brlnc Audio MP3 Lib); 39.97 (978-1-4233-9234-7(5), 9781423392347, BADLE) Brilliance Audio.

Newes from the Dead. unabr. ed. Mary Hooper. Read by Michael Page & Rosalyn Landor. 7 CDs. (Running Time: 7 hrs.). 2009. audio compact disk 29.99 (978-1-4233-9229-3(9), 9781423392293, Bril Audio CD Unabri) Brilliance Audio.

Newes from the Dead. unabr. ed. Mary Hooper. Read by Rosalyn Landor & Michael Page. 7 CDs. (Running Time: 7 hrs.). 2009. audio compact disk 87.97 (978-1-4233-9230-9(2), 9781423392309, BriAudCD Unabrid) Brilliance Audio.

Newest Nicktoons. (J). 2002. 9.98 (978-0-7379-0211-2(6), 74355) Rhino Enter.
Kids can listen to over 50 songs from 12 of their favorite Nickelodeon shows, such as SpongeBob SquarePants, Rugrats, Rocket Power, Hey Arnold, CatDog, The Wild Thornberry's, Invader Zim, As Told By Ginger and more.

Newest P & W Favorites. 1 cass. (Running Time: 1 hr. 30 min.). 1999. 10.98 (978-0-7601-2689-9(5)) Provident Music.

Newest P&W Favorites. 1 CD. (Running Time: 1 hr. 30 min.). 1999. audio compact disk 16.98 (978-0-7601-2690-5(9)) Provident Music.

Newjack: Guarding Sing Sing. unabr. ed. Read by Ted Conover. 8 cass. (Running Time: 12 hrs.). 2000. 35.95 (978-1-56740-371-8(9), 1567403719, BAU) Brilliance Audio.
NEWJACK: Guarding Sing Sing is the story of Conover's rookie year as a guard at Sing Sing. It is a nerve-jangling account of his passage into the storied prison and the culture of its guards - both fresh-faced "newjacks" like Conover and brutally hardened veterans. As he struggles to be a good officer, Conover angers inmates, dodges blows, works to balance decency with toughness, and participates in prison rituals - strip frisks, cell searches, cell "extractions" - that exact a toll on inmates and officers alike. The tale begins with the corrections academy and ends with the flames and smoke of New Year's Eve on Conover's floor of the notorious B-Block. Along the way, Conover also recounts the history of Sing Sing, from draconian early punishment, to fame as the citadel of capital punishment, to its present status as New York State's "bottom of the barrel" prison. This book will become a landmark of American journalism - the definitive presentation of the impasse between the need to imprison criminals and the dehumanization of inmates and guards - that almost inevitably takes place behind bars. "Newjack is an astonishing work by a gifted - and dedicated - journalist. Ted Conover takes us into the dangerous, sad, amusing and instructive soul of one of America's best known prisons." - Tom Brokaw.

Newjack: Guarding Sing Sing. unabr. ed. Ted Conover. Read by Ted Conover. (Running Time: 12 hrs.). 2005. 39.25 (978-1-59600-634-8(X), 9781596006348, BADLE); 24.95 (978-1-59600-633-1(1), 9781596006331, BAD); 24.95 (978-1-59600-631-7(5), 9781596006317, Brilliance MP3); 39.25 (978-1-59600-632-4(3), 9781596006324, Brlnc Audio MP3 Lib) Brilliance Audio.

Newlyweds Legal Guide. Daniel Blume. 1 cass. (Running Time: 45 min.). 1996. 19.95 (978-0-912349-01-5(8)) Continent Media.

Newman: His Life & Spirituality. Louis Bouyer. 12 cass. (Running Time: 18 hrs.). 47.95 (311) Ignatius Pr.
The great English convert, writer & preacher, John Henry Newman.

Newness of the Unchanging. Kenneth G. Mills. 1 cass. pap. bk. 10.95 (978-0-919842-02-1(X), KGOM5) Ken Mills Found.
"What is it that is unchanging in our experience?" This question forms the central theme in this spontaneous lecture given by the author in 1977 in Tucson, Arizona. Includes transcript booklet.

Newport-Astoria. Dan Heller. 1 cass. (Running Time: 1 hr. 30 min.). 1995. 9.95 (978-1-885433-04-6(2)) Takilma East.

Newport, R. I. Circle Tour. 1 cass. (Running Time: 90 min.). 12.95 (CCI-206) Comp Comms Inc.
Tours through "The Golden Age when bold Newport merchants & brave Newport sea captains made Newport one of the biggest seaports in colonial America.

News at Ten, abr. ed. Stan Chambers. Read by Stan Chambers. 2 cass. (Running Time: 3 hr.). 2000. 18.00 (978-1-57511-032-5(6)) Pub Mills.
The author has been a fixture in news reporting since 1948. A fascinating first hand overview of many of the major stories covered by one of broadcast journalism's most respected field reporters.

News for Dogs. Lois Duncan & Katherine Kellgren. (J). (gr. 3-7). 2009. audio compact disk 19.95 (978-0-545-14294-6(6)) Scholastic Inc.

News for Now 1 Audio CD. Karen Blanchard & Christine Root. 2003. audio compact disk 10.95 (978-1-887744-27-0(4), DeltPubng) Delta Systems.

News for Now 2 Audio CD. Karen Blanchard & Christine Root. 2003. audio compact disk 10.95 (978-1-887744-30-0(4), DeltPubng) Delta Systems.

News for Now 3 Audio CD. Karen Blanchard & Christine Root. 2003. audio compact disk 10.95 (978-1-887744-33-1(9), DeltPubng) Delta Systems.

News for the Delphic Oracle see Poetry of William Butler Yeats

News from Lake Wobegon. abr. unabr. ed. Garrison Keillor. Read by Garrison Keillor. 4 CDs. (Running Time: 4 hrs.). (ENG.). 1990. audio compact disk

36.95 (978-0-942110-38-8(2), 0942110382) Pub: HighBridge. Dist(s): Workman Pub

News from Tartary. unabr. collector's ed. Peter Fleming. Read by David Case. 9 cass. (Running Time: 13 hrs. 30 mins.). 1988. 72.00 (978-0-7366-1332-3(3), 2235) Books on Tape.
In 1935 the author set out from Peking for Kashmir. It was a 3500 mile journey across the roof of the world. He chose as his traveling companion Ella Maillart, Swedish journalist.

News from Thrush Green. unabr. ed. Miss Read. Read by Gwen Watford. 4 cass. (Running Time: 6 hrs. 10 mins.). (Thrush Green Chronicles Ser.: Vol. 3). 2000. 24.95 (978-1-57270-189-2(7), M41189u) Pub: Audio Partners. Dist(s): PerseuPGW
The Thrush Green cottage known as Tullivers has remainedcuriously unoccupied for many years. When Phil, an attractive young woman & her young son move in after being deserted by husband & father, the village takes them under its wing. Harold Shoosmith arrives unannounced at their door with advice & help when Phil starts working in her wild garden, help that includes hooking her up with his best friend, a successful London publisher who prints her stories. When Phil's estranged husband dies in a car accident her new freedom brings more changes to her life as well as a new love to the village.

News Jog. Hosted by Leonard Peikoff. 1 cass. (Running Time: 1 hr.). (Philosophy: Who Needs It? Ser.). 1998. 12.95 (LPXXC57); 12.95 (LPXXC59) Second Renaissance.
Goldwater & Intel.

News Jog. Leonard Peikoff. 1 cass. (Running Time: 1 hr.). (Philosophy: Who Needs It? Ser.). 1998. 12.95 (LPXXC60) Second Renaissance.
Assisted Suicide, et al.

News Jog. Hosted by Leonard Peikoff. 1 cass. (Running Time: 1 hr.). (Philosophy: Who Needs It? Ser.). 1998. 12.95 (LPXXC68) Second Renaissance.
African Bombings, et al.

News Jog. Hosted by Leonard Peikoff. 1 cass. (Philosophy: Who Needs It? Ser.). 1998. 12.95 (LPXXC70); 12.95 (LPXXC72); 12.95 (LPXXC74) Second Renaissance.
Clinton, Rushdie Killers & Environmentalists vs. Baseball Heroes.

News Jog. Leonard Peikoff. 1998. 12.95 (LPXXC76) Second Renaissance.
Topics include Clinton, Foreign Socialism, "Rounders," Gene Autry, et al.

News Jog: Election Results, Gingrich, Science vs. "Morality" Leonard Peikoff. 1 cass. (Running Time: 1 hr.). 1998. 12.95 (LPXXC81) Second Renaissance.

News Jog: Kevorkian, et al. Leonard Peikoff. 1 cass. (Running Time: 1 hr.). 1998. 12.95 (LPXXC84) Second Renaissance.

News Jog: Terrorism everywhere: Buffalo, Colorado, Iran & Washington. Leonard Peikoff. 1 cass. (Running Time: 1 hr.). 1998. 12.95 (LPXXC80) Second Renaissance.

News Media & Politics. F. Clifton White. 1 cass. (Running Time: 1 hr. 18 min.). 11.95 (330) J Norton Pubs.

News of the Universe: Poems of Twofold Consciousness. unabr. ed. Poems. Read by Robert Bly. Selected by Robert Bly. 2 cass. (Running Time: 3 hrs.). 1995. 15.95 (978-0-944993-49-1(4)) Audio Lit.
Some of the world's finest poetry including: Rilke, Kabir, William Blake, Walt Whitman, Emily Dickinson & Gary Snyder.

News of the World see Dylan Thomas Reads the Poetry of W. B. Yeats & Others

News Quiz - The First 25 Years. Simon Littlefield et al. 2 vols. (Radio Collection). 2003. 29.95 (978-0-563-52430-4(8)) BBC Worldwide.

News Radio. (Stereo Boom Box Ser.: Vol. 1). (J). (gr. 1-6). 1998. ring bd. 164.99 (978-1-57405-048-6(6)) CharismaLife Pub.

News Twisters. Edith Efron. 1 cass. (Running Time: 1 hr. 25 min.). 11.95 (187) J Norton Pubs.

***News Where You Are.** unabr. ed. Catherine O'Flynn. (Running Time: 8 hrs. 0 mins.). 2010. 29.95 (978-1-4417-4823-2(7)); 54.95 (978-1-4417-4819-5(9)); audio compact disk 29.95 (978-1-4417-4822-5(9)); audio compact disk 76.00 (978-1-4417-4820-1(2)) Blckstn Audio.

Newspaper Chinese ABC: An Introductory Reader. Zhenjie Li & Shixum Wang. 1 cass. (CHI & ENG.). (C). (gr. k up). 1994. 49.95 (978-0-88727-167-0(7)) Cheng Tsui.

Newspaper Days. unabr. collector's ed. H. L. Mencken. Read by Daniel Grace. 8 cass. (Running Time: 8 hrs.). 1976. 48.00 (978-0-7366-0015-6(9), 1025) Books on Tape.
"Newspaper Days" records the 7 years Mencken spent as reporter, drama critic & editor of the "Baltimore Herald".

Newspaper Taxi's. Keith Rodway & Chrome Dreams Staff. Read by Robin Clifford. (ENG., 2000. audio compact disk 15.95 (978-1-84240-001-2(0)) Pub: Chrome Dreams GBR. Dist(s): IPG Chicago

Newt Gingrich: The Romance of Self-Government. 1 cass. (Running Time: 1 hr.). 1989. 11.95 (K0720B090, HarperThor) HarpC GBR.

Newton & His Laws. Compiled by Benchmark Education Staff. 2005. audio compact disk 10.00 (978-1-4108-5499-5(X)) Benchmark Educ.

Newtonian Universe. 1 cass. (Running Time: 1 hr.). 14.95 (CBC579) MMI Corp.
A look at the cosmology of the 18th century focusing on Newton's influence on literature, philosophy & politics.

***Next.** abr. ed. Michael Crichton. Read by Erik Singer. (ENG.). 2006. (978-0-06-133626-3(2), Harper Audio); (978-0-06-133627-0(0), Harper Audio) HarperCollins Pubs.

Next. abr. ed. Michael Crichton. Read by Erik Singer. 2008. audio compact disk 14.99 (978-0-06-167353-5(6), Harper Audio) HarperCollins Pubs.

***Next.** unabr. ed. Michael Crichton. Read by Dylan Baker. (ENG.). 2006. (978-0-06-133871-7(0), Harper Audio); (978-0-06-133872-4(9), Harper Audio) HarperCollins Pubs.

Next. unabr. ed. Michael Crichton. Read by Dylan Baker. 11 CDs. (Running Time: 43200 sec.). 2006. audio compact disk 49.95 (978-0-06-087309-7(4), Harper Audio) HarperCollins Pubs.

Next Accident. Lisa Gardner. Read by Anna Fields. 2001. 64.00 (978-0-7366-7635-9(X)) Books on Tape.

Next Better Place. unabr. ed. Michael Keith. Read by Oliver Wyman. (YA). 2006. 39.99 (978-1-59895-640-5(X)) Find a World.

***Next Big Story: My Journey Through the Land of Possibilities.** unabr. ed. Soledad O'Brien & Rose Arce. Narrated by Coleen Marlo. (Running Time: 10 hrs. 0 mins.). 2010. 16.99 (978-1-4526-7027-0(7)); 24.99 (978-1-4526-5027-2(6)); audio compact disk 34.99 (978-1-4526-0027-7(9)) Pub: Tantor Media. Dist(s): IngramPubServ

***Next Big Story (Library Edition) My Journey Through the Land of Possibilities.** unabr. ed. Soledad O'Brien & Rose Arce. Narrated by Coleen Marlo. (Running Time: 10 hrs. 0 mins.). 2010. 34.99 (978-1-4526-2027-5(X)); audio compact disk 83.99 (978-1-4526-3027-4(5)) Pub: Tantor Media. Dist(s): IngramPubServ

Next Big Thing. unabr. ed. Anita Brookner. Read by Stephen Thorne. 6 cass. (Running Time: 9 hrs.). 2003. 54.95 (978-0-7540-0909-2(2), CAB 2331); audio compact disk 79.95 (978-0-7540-5552-5(3), CCD 243) AudioGO.

***Next Christians: The Good News about the End of Christian America.** unabr. ed. Gabe Lyons. (Running Time: 6 hrs. 30 mins. 0 sec.). (ENG.). 2010. audio compact disk 21.98 (978-1-61045-004-1(3)) christianaud.

***Next Decade: What the World Will Look Like.** unabr. ed. George Friedman. (ENG.). 2011. audio compact disk 45.00 (978-0-307-88106-9(7), Random AudioBks) Pub: Random Audio Pubg. Dist(s): Random

Next Dimension of Faith: Developing Confidence in God & His Word. Creflo A. Dollar. (ENG.). 2006. 15.00 (978-1-59944-082-8(2)); audio compact disk 21.00 (978-1-59944-083-5(0)) Creflo Dollar.

Next Door to Love, Level 1. Margaret Johnson. Contrib. by Philip Prowse. (Running Time: 50 mins.). (Cambridge English Readers Ser.). (ENG., 2005. 9.45 (978-0-521-60563-2(6)) Cambridge U Pr.

Next Episode. unabr. abr. ed. Hubert Aquin. Tr. by Sheila Fischman. Narrated by Carl Marrotte. 2 CD. (Running Time: 1 1/2 hr.). (ENG.). 2004. audio compact disk 19.95 (978-0-86492-390-5(2)) Pub: BTC Audiobks CAN. Dist(s): U Toronto Pr
A young FLQ revolutionary, whiling away his solitary confinement in a psychiatric institution, pens a political thriller in which a Quebecois terrorist re-discovers his long-lost lover. K, a personification of the province of Quebec, convinces him to embark on a mission to capture the elusive RCMP informer known as H. de Heutz. An international spy novel, a love story, and a separatist polemic all in one, this classic of contemporary Quebec literature was written in 1965 when Aquin was being held in a Montreal psychiatric hospital for possession of a stolen automobile and an automatic firearm. Well-known actor Carl Marotte captures the passion and urgency of Aquin's intellectual tour de force.

***Next Evolution of Marketing: Connect with Your Customers by Marketing with Meaning.** Bob Gilbreath. Contrib. by Bruce Reizen. (ENG.). 2009. 69.99 (978-1-4418-2811-8(7)) Find a World.

Next Evolution of Marketing: Connect with Your Customers by Marketing with Meaning. unabr. ed. Bob Gilbreath. Read by Bruce Reizen. (Running Time: 10 hrs.). 2009. 24.99 (978-1-4418-1683-2(6), 9781441816832, Brilliance MP3); 39.97 (978-1-4418-1684-9(4), 9781441816849, Brlnc Audio MP3 Lib); 24.99 (978-1-4418-1685-6(2), 9781441816856, BAD); 39.97 (978-1-4418-1686-3(0), 9781441816863, BADLE); audio compact disk 29.99 (978-1-4418-1681-8(X), 9781441816818, Bril Audio CD Unabri); audio compact disk 97.97 (978-1-4418-1682-5(8), 9781441816825, BriAudCD Unabrid) Brilliance Audio.

Next Generation. Peter David. (Star Trek Ser.). 2004. 10.95 (978-0-7435-4631-7(8)) Pub: S&S Audio. Dist(s): S and S Inc

Next Generation Gulliver's Fugitives. Keith Sharee. (Star Trek Ser.). 2004. 7.95 (978-0-7435-4231-9(2)) Pub: S&S Audio. Dist(s): S and S Inc

Next Generation Imzadi. Peter David. (Star Trek Ser.). 2004. 10.95 (978-0-7435-4627-0(X)) Pub: S&S Audio. Dist(s): S and S Inc

Next Generation of Health Care Implications for Spiritual Care. 1 cass. (Running Time: 1 hr.). (Care Cassettes Ser.: Vol. 21, No. 1). 1994. 10.80 Assn Prof Chaplains.

Next Generation q In-law. Peter David. (Star Trek Ser.). 2004. 7.95 (978-0-7435-4230-2(4)) Pub: S&S Audio. Dist(s): S and S Inc

Next Generation Q-Squared. Peter David. (Star Trek Ser.). 2004. 10.95 (978-0-7435-4632-4(6)) Pub: S&S Audio. Dist(s): S and S Inc

Next Great Bubble Boom. Harry S. Dent, Jr. 2004. 17.95 (978-0-7435-4303-3(3)) Pub: S&S Audio. Dist(s): S and S Inc

Next Holocaust. Chuck Missler. 2 cass. (Running Time: 3 hrs.). (Briefing Packages by Chuck Missler). 1996. vinyl bd. 14.95 (978-1-880532-37-9(9)) Koinonia Hse.
** What is the purpose of the Great Tribulation? * What is the prophetic role of Ammon, Moab, and Edom (now known as Jordan)?* Where does Jesus return? On the Mount of Olives or in Bozrah?While there are a number of passages that deal with this area, the most provocative aspect is that it appears this is one of the few areas that escape the rule of the coming world leader (commonly known as the "Antichrist"):Many [countries] shall be overthrown; but these shall escape out of his hand, [even] Edom, and Moab, and the chief of the children of Ammon. - Dan 11:41Thus, it seems this will be a refuge for the remnant that flees to Jerusalem when under attack during the Great Tribulation. Perhaps the current arrangements between Israel and Jordan are a prelude to this refuge.This study is an exploration of some of the less familiar prophecies of the end-times, the Tribulation, and the Second Coming of Jesus Christ. The recent peace agreement between Jordan and Israel may be much more prophetically significant than the current "Peace Process" between Israel and the PLO.Chuck also reviews the "Time of Jacob's Trouble" and the campaign of Armageddon.*

Next Holocaust: And the Refuge in Edom. Chuck Missler. 2 CD's. (Running Time: 2 hrs.). (Briefing Packages by Chuck Missler). 2006. audio compact disk 19.95 (978-1-57821-355-9(X)) Koinonia Hse.
What is the purpose of the Great Tribulation? What is the prophetic role of Ammon, Moab, and Edom (now known as Jordan)? Where does Jesus return? On the Mount of Olives or in Bozrah? Jesus warns the dwellers in Judea that when they see the "Abomination of Desolation" - a desecrating idol installed in the Holy of Holies of the Temple - to flee to the mountains. The remnant of Israel will find refuge there for three and a half years while God protects them and provides for them. In this study, Chuck explores some of the less familiar prophecies of the End Times, the Tribulation, and the Second Coming of Jesus Christ.

Next Level: A Parable of Finding Your Place in Life. unabr. ed. David Gregory. Narrated by Chris Fabry. (Running Time: 2 hrs. 30 mins. 0 sec.). (ENG.). 2008. audio compact disk 14.99 (978-1-59859-329-7(3)) Oasis Audio.

Next Level: Finding Your Place in Life. unabr. ed. David Gregory. Narrated by Chris Fabry. (ENG.). 2008. 10.49 (978-1-60814-319-1(8)) Oasis Audio.

Next Master Is Coming. George King. 2006. audio compact disk (978-0-937249-32-1(7)) Aetherius Soc.

Next Move of God. Paul Cain. 2 cass. (Running Time: 3 hrs.). 2000. 10.00 (PC01-000) Morning NC.
"The Face of the Next Move of God" & "Standards of Leadership." The requirements to be part of the next move of God are examined in these powerful messages.

Next of Kin. unabr. ed. Joanna Trollope. Read by Eleanor Bron. 8 cass. (Running Time: 12 hrs.). 2000. 59.95 (978-0-7451-6723-7(3), CAB 1339) Pub: Chivers Audio Bks GBR. Dist(s): AudioGO
British Dairy farmer Robin Meredith has just buried his Californian wife Caro. Although Caro was a central figure of the farm for more than 20 years, she had remained a mystery to the family. With Caro gone, her adopted daughter Judy is lost. into their midst comes Judy's friend Zoe, whose disturbing directness becomes a catalyst for change.

***Next of Kin: L-Book.** Jae. (ENG.). 2008. 21.95 (978-1-934889-46-6(6)) Lbook Pub.

Next of Kin: What Chimpanzees Tell Us about Who We Are. Roger Fouts. Jane Goodall. Told to Stephen Tukel Mills. 2004. 15.95 (978-0-7435-4448-1(X)) Pub: S&S Audio. Dist(s): S and S Inc

***Next Queen of Heaven.** unabr. ed. Gregory Maguire. 2010. (978-0-06-206243-7(3), Harper Audio); (978-0-06-200711-7(4), Harper Audio) HarperCollins Pubs.

Next Rung. unabr. ed. Zalman Schachter-Shalomi. Read by Zalman Schachter-Shalomi. 5 cass. (Running Time: 6 hrs.15 min.). 1994. 46.00 (31005) Big Sur Tapes.
This workshop explores historic sources & commentaries of Kabbalah.

Next Sampler. 1 cass. (Running Time: 30 min.). (J). 1986. 9.95 (978-0-939065-26-4(6), GW 1030) Gentle Wind.
Songs & stories for children.

***Next Step for Kids Curriculum.** (ENG.). 2007. audio compact disk 29.95 (978-1-932778-40-3(3)) Harv Chris.

Next Ten Years - Astrological Forecasts. Edward Kluska. 1 cass. 8.95 (199) Am Fed Astrologers.
An AFA Convention workshop tape.

Next Twenty Years. ACT Staff. 1 cass. (Running Time: 1 hr.). (Workshop Ser.). 8.95 (015) Am Fed Astrologers.

Next 100 Years: A Forecast for the 21st Century. unabr. ed. George Friedman. (Running Time: 9 hrs. NaN mins.). 2009. 29.95 (978-1-4332-1546-9(2)); 29.95 (978-1-4332-1544-5(6)); audio compact disk 29.95 (978-1-4332-1545-2(4)); audio compact disk 59.95 (978-1-4332-1542-1(X)); audio compact disk 80.00 (978-1-4332-1543-8(8)) Blckstn Audio.

Next 200 Years. unabr. collector's ed. Herman Kahn et al. Read by Michael Prichard. 6 cass. (Running Time: 9 hrs.). 1977. 48.00 (978-0-7366-3051-1(1), 3733) Books on Tape.
In a closely reasoned & carefully documented study, Herman Kahn & his associates at the Hudson Institute give us their expectations for what the next 200 years will bring.

Nez Perce Stories. Bernie Krause. 1 cass. (Running Time: 47 min.). (Music & Word Ser.). 1994. 9.95 (2305, NrthWrd Bks) TandN Child.
91-year-old Elizabeth Wilson recalled the stories & songs of her childhood, a time when she even knew Chief Joseph.

NGJ Sword Searcher Software. Des. by Brandon Staggs. 2008. cd-rom & audio compact disk 49.95 (978-1-934794-41-8(4)) No Greater Joy.

NHK's Let's Learn Japanese Bk. II: A Practical Conversation Guide. NHK Overseas Broadcasting Department Staff & Nobuko Mizutani. Ed. by Jun Maeda. (JPN & ENG., 1993. 40.00 (978-4-7700-1785-7(5)) Kodansha.

NHK's Let's Learn Japanese Bk. IV: A Practical Conversation Guide. NHK Overseas Broadcasting Department Staff & Nobuko Mizutani. Ed. by Jun Maeda. 1994. 40.00 (978-4-7700-1789-5(8)) Kodansha.

NHK's Let's Learn Japanese Vol. 1: A Practical Conversation Guide, Nobuko Mizutani. Ed. by Pocknell et al. 1993. pap. bk. (978-4-7700-1711-6(1)) Kodansha Intl JPN.

Ni Hao. rev. ed. Paul Fredlein & Shumang Fredlein. 2 cass. (Running Time: 3 hrs.). (CHI & ENG.). (gr. 5-9). 2005. pap. bk. 49.95 (978-1-876739-10-2(X)) Pub: ChinasoftAus AUS. Dist(s): Cheng Tsui

Ni Hao, 2. rev. ed. Paul Fredlein & Shumang Fredlein. 2 cass. (Running Time: 3 hrs.). (CHI & ENG.). (gr. 6-10). 2005. pap. bk. 71.50 (978-1-876739-16-4(9)) Pub: ChinasoftAus AUS. Dist(s): Cheng Tsui

Ni Hao, 3. rev. ed. Paul Fredlein & Shumang Fredlein. 2 cass. (Running Time: 3 hrs.). (CHI & ENG.). (gr. 7-11). 2005. pap. bk. 71.50 (978-1-876739-22-5(3)) Pub: ChinasoftAus AUS. Dist(s): Cheng Tsui

Ni Hao, 4. Paul Fredlein & Shumang Fredlein. 4 vols. (CHI & ENG.). (gr. 8-12). 2005. pap. bk. 75.95 (978-1-876739-04-1(5)) Pub: ChinasoftAus AUS. Dist(s): Cheng Tsui

Ni Hao, Vol. 3. Paul Fredlein & Shumang Fredlein. 3 vols. 2004. pap. bk. 59.95 (978-1-876739-21-8(5)) Pub: ChinasoftAus AUS. Dist(s): Cheng Tsui

Ni Hao, Vol. 4. Paul Fredlein & Shumang Fredlein. 4 vols. 2005. pap. bk. 64.95 (978-1-876739-03-4(7)) Pub: ChinasoftAus AUS. Dist(s): Cheng Tsui

Ni Hao Vol. 1: Audio Products. rev. ed. Shumang Fredlein & Paul Fredlein. 2 vols. (CHI.). 2005. pap. bk. 39.95 (978-1-876739-09-6(6)) Pub: ChinasoftAus AUS. Dist(s): Cheng Tsui

Ni Hao Vol. 2: Simplified Character Edition, rev. ed. Shumang Fredlein & Paul Fredlein. 4 vols. (CHI.). 2004. pap. bk. 55.00 (978-1-876739-15-7(0)) Pub: ChinasoftAus AUS. Dist(s): Cheng Tsui

Niagara see Best of Mark Twain

Niagara Falls All over Again. unabr. ed. Elizabeth McCracken. Narrated by George Guidall. 9 cass. (Running Time: 13 hrs.). 2002. 83.00 (978-1-4025-1515-6(4), 96995) Recorded Bks.
A graceful, moving tale of an unlikely pairing of two men and their lifelong partnership in show business.

Niagara Falls, or Does It? Henry Winkler & Lin Oliver. Read by Henry Winkler. 2 vols. (Running Time: 2 hrs. 16 mins.). (Hank Zipzer Ser.: No. 1). (J). (gr. 2-6). 2004. pap. bk. 29.00 (978-1-4000-9006-8(7), Listening Lib); audio compact disk 24.00 (978-1-4000-8613-9(2), Listening Lib) Random Audio Pubg.

Niagara Falls, or Does It? unabr. ed. Henry Winkler & Lin Oliver. Prod. by Listening Library Staff. 2 cass. (Running Time: 2 hrs. 16 mins.). (Hank Zipzer Ser.: No. 1). (J). (gr. 2-6). 2004. 23.00 (978-0-8072-1942-3(8), Listening Lib) Pub: Random Audio Pubg. Dist(s): Random
follows the mishaps of "the world's best underachiever." Hank Zipzer is a fourth-grader, and on the first day of school he's already in the principal's office. Hank has always had to deal with the problems of tardiness, an inability to sit still, and being easily distracted. Also, he has never been good at putting words on paper, which is why he decides to turn a five-paragraph essay on his summer vacation into a good-sized, working mock-up of Niagara Falls.

Niagara Falls, the Gorge & Glen. 1 cass. (Solitudes Ser.). 9.95 (C11204) J Norton Pubs.
This tape tunes in the sounds & experiences of the natural environment.

Niagara... More Than the Falls: A Self-Guided Audio Driving Tour of Canada's Niagara. 2 CDs. 2006. audio compact disk 24.95 (978-0-9778873-0-9(8)) CrowMark Assoc.
Niagara...More Than the Falls is a self-guided audio driving tour on 2 CDs. This tour lets you explore Canada's beautiful Niagara Gorge Region. The easy to follow directions lead you to Niagara-on-the-Lake where you will want to visit shops and boutiques or enjoy the wines and restaurant of the area. Formation of the Falls, the Great Gorge, gardens, War of 1812, wine, the story of hydroelectric power and tales of adventure seekers are a few of the themes you will explore along with the magnificent scenery. Whether you desire some serious hiking or a leisurely view of the natural beauty, you set the pace. We provide the informative background to enhance the enjoyment of each featured site. You choose the ones you want to visit. A detailed map and written directions are included. As a bonus, there is a free wine and culinary experience included as well as coupons for some of the attractions along the route. We Guide. You Decide.

Nibbled to Death by Ducks. unabr. ed. Robert Campbell. Narrated by Peter Waldren. 5 cass. (Running Time: 6 hrs. 30 mins.). (Jimmy Flannery Mystery Ser.: Vol. 6). 1992. 44.00 (978-1-55690-703-6(6), 92105E7) Recorded Bks.
Jimmy Flannery, Chicago precinct captain, investigates a suspicious nursing home.

Nibbles & Bites: Spice Series. Short Stories. 1 CD. (Running Time: 72 mins.). Dramatization. 2004. audio compact disk 15.95 (978-0-9759671-1-9(8)) Sounds Pubng Inc.
SoundsErotic original erotic, audio short stories are sensual stories for lovers. These short stories are written by award winning authors and read by professional voice talent.

Nibelungen. Archim Seiffarth. pap. bk. 21.95 (978-88-7754-754-5(5)) Pub: Cideb ITA. Dist(s): Distribks Inc

Nic at Night. Kathie Hill. 1996. 75.00 (978-0-7673-0824-3(7)); audio compact disk 85.00 (978-0-7673-0825-0(5)) LifeWay Christian.

***Nican Mopohua. leído A Cuatro Voces.** Miguel León-Portilla. (Entre Voces Ser.). 2009. audio compact disk 18.95 (978-607-16-0058-5(8)) Pub: Fondo MEX. Dist(s): Fondo CA

Niccolo Rising. unabr. ed. Dorothy Dunnett. Read by Steven Pacey. 16 cass. (Running Time: 24 hrs.). (House of Niccolo Ser.: Bk. 1). 2000. 99.95 (978-0-7451-6478-6(1), CAB 1094) Pub: Chivers Audio Bks GBR. Dist(s): AudioGO
The town folk of Bruges had gathered to witness the arrival of the ships from Venice. Their cargo was nothing less than marvelous: myrrh, emeralds, sapphires, ivory, and much more. Trade and war lie at the core of this magnificent chronicle of 15th century Europe. Adventure, romance and danger embrace lovers and enemies of the House of Niccolo.

Nice Change. unabr. ed. Ruth Hamilton & Nina Bawden. Read by Carole Boyd. 5 cass. (Running Time: 6 hrs.). (Isis Ser.). (J). 2004. 49.95 (978-0-7531-0212-1(9), 970706) Pub: ISIS Lrg Prnt GBR. Dist(s): Ulverscroft US
The Hotel Parthenon in Greece is the setting for a holiday of sorts for this memorable cast of British abroad where the most unlikely people fall in & out of love & where everyone harbors a secret desire.

Nice Class of Corpse. unabr. ed. Simon Brett. Read by Simon Brett. 6 cass. (Running Time: 6 hrs. 30 min.). 2001. 54.95 (978-1-85089-755-2(7), 87122) Pub: ISIS Audio GBR. Dist(s): Ulverscroft US
The sudden death of a frail resident disturbs the tranquility of the Deveraux Hotel. Mrs. Pargeter suspects murder.

Nice Couples Do: How to Turn Your Secret Dreams into Sensational Sex. abr. ed. Joan Elizabeth Lloyd. (Running Time: 3 hrs.). (ENG.). 2007. 9.98 (978-1-59483-646-6(9)) Pub: Hachet Audio. Dist(s): HachBkGrp

Nice Couples Do: How to Turn Your Secret Dreams into Sensational Sex. abr. ed. Joan Elizabeth Lloyd. Read by Maggie Albright. (Running Time: 1 hr. 30 mins.). (ENG.). 2009. 16.98 (978-1-60788-295-4(7)) Pub: Hachet Audio. Dist(s): HachBkGrp

Nice Cup of Tea. Created by Elaine Vail. 1. (Running Time: 60 mins). 2004. audio compact disk 15.95 (978-0-9764153-9-8(9)) R James TV.
A Nice Cup is a musical companion to a Nice Cup of Tea. Enjoy a wonderful Poem and some very relaxing music.

Nice Derangement of Epitaphs. unabr. ed. Ellis Peters, pseud. Narrated by Simon Prebble. 5 cass. (Running Time: 7 hrs. 15 mins.). (Inspector George Felse Mystery Ser.: Vol. 4). 1991. 44.00 (978-1-55690-374-8(X), 91226E7) Recorded Bks.
A vacation in Cornwall embroils the Felse family in the beguiling 18th-century legend of Jan Treverra & his beloved Morwena. When Felse assists a famous scholar in exhuming their bodies, he pulls away the stone on an even greater mystery.

***Nice Girls Don't Change the World.** Lynne Hybels. (Running Time: 0 hr. 44 mins. 0 sec.). (ENG.). 2009. 14.99 (978-0-310-30495-1(4)) Zondervan.

Nice Girls Don't Get... Nice Girls Don't Get the Corner Office & Nice Girls Don't Get Rich. abr. ed. Lois P. Frankel. (ENG.). 2005. 14.98 (978-1-59483-167-6(X)) Pub: Hachet Audio. Dist(s): HachBkGrp

Nice Girls Don't Get... Nice Girls Don't Get the Corner Office & Nice Girls Don't Get Rich. abr. ed. Lois P. Frankel. (Running Time: 4 hrs.). (ENG.). 2009. 39.98 (978-1-60788-042-4(3)) Pub: Hachet Audio. Dist(s): HachBkGrp

Nice Guys Can Get the Corner Office: Eight Strategies for Winning in Business Without Being a Jerk. Russ C. Edelman et al. Read by Patrick G. Lawlor. (Playaway Adult Nonfiction Ser.). (ENG.). 2009. 59.99 (978-1-60812-795-5(8)) Find a World.

Nice Guys Can Get the Corner Office: Eight Strategies for Winning in Business Without Being a Jerk. unabr. ed. Russ C. Edelman et al. Narrated by Patrick G. Lawlor. (Running Time: 8 hrs. 0 mins. 0 sec.). (ENG.). 2008. audio compact disk 29.99 (978-1-4001-0837-4(3)); audio compact disk 19.99 (978-1-4001-5837-9(0)); audio compact disk 59.99 (978-1-4001-3837-1(X)) Pub: Tantor Media. Dist(s): IngramPubServ

Nice Guys Finish Rich: The Secrets of a Supersalesman. Jim Hansberger. Read by Jim Hansberger. 6 cass. 59.95 (443AD) Nightingale-Conant.

***Nice Place to Visit.** 2010. audio compact disk (978-1-59171-248-0(3)) Falcon Picture.

Nice to Come Home To. unabr. ed. Rebecca Flowers. Read by Carrington MacDuffie. 8 CDs. (Running Time: 10 hrs.). 2008. audio compact disk 29.95 (978-1-59316-129-3(8)) Listen & Live.

Nice To Meet Ya! 1 CD. (Running Time: 1 hr. 30 min.). 1994. audio compact disk 16.99 MegaGrace.

Nicholas & Alexandra. unabr. ed. Robert K. Massie. Read by Robert K. Massie. Adapted by Lindsay Crouse. Illus. by Pamlyn Smith Design Inc Staff. 5 cass. (Running Time: 5 hrs. 30 mins.). 1998. 35.00 (978-1-885608-21-5(7)) Airplay.
A sympathetic portrait of Russia's last czar & his family has enjoyed renewed interest since the fall of Communism.

Nicholas & Alexandra, Pt. 1. unabr. collector's ed. Robert K. Massie. Read by Wolfram Kandinsky. 9 cass. (Running Time: 13 hrs. 30 min.). 1984. 72.00 (978-0-7366-0901-2(6), 1845-A) Books on Tape.
In his comprehensive history of the last of the Romanovs, Robert Massie explores the contention that the birth of the Tsarevich Alexis on August 12, 1904 more than anything else, determined the entire later course of Russian history.

Nicholas & Alexandra, Pt. 2. collector's ed. Robert K. Massie. Read by Wolfram Kandinsky. 9 cass. (Running Time: 13 hrs. 30 mins.). 1984. 72.00 (978-0-7366-0902-9(4), 1845-B) Books on Tape.

Nicholas & Alexandra, Vol. 1. unabr. ed. Robert K. Massie. Read by Frederick Davidson. 9 cass. (Running Time: 13 hrs. 30 min.). 1994. 62.95 (978-0-7861-0791-9(X), 1548-A) Blckstn Audio.
History offers few eras richer in drama than the last years of Imperial Russia. Dominating the story is the Russian Imperial family: the gentle, charming Nicholas & the beautiful, tormented Alexandra; their four unspoiled daughters, including the one who was to become most famous - Anastasia; & the youthful Alexis, whose suffering never dimmed his gay & lively intelligence. Their fall from the pinnacle of earthly power to imprisonment & death is the most moving of tragedies.

Nicholas & Alexandra, Vol. 2. unabr. ed. Robert K. Massie. Read by Frederick Davidson. 8 cass. (Running Time: 12 hrs.). 1994. 56.95 (978-0-7861-0846-6(0), 1548-B) Blckstn Audio.
A rich account of an imperial family & its struggle with disease & with the disintegration of a dynasty & empire that was to have momentous consequences for the world. Dominating the story is the Russian Imperial family: the gentle, charming Nicholas & the beautiful, tormented Alexandra, who fell under the sway of the mystic Rasputin; their four unspoiled daughters, including the one who was to become most famous, Anastasia & the youthful Alexis, whose hemophilia never dimmed his gay & lively intelligence. Their fall from the pinnacle of earthyly power to imprisonment & death is the most moving tragedies.

Nicholas & Alexandra: Abridged. (ENG.). 2007. (978-1-60339-015-6(4)); cd-rom & audio compact disk (978-1-60339-016-3(2)) Listenr Digest.

Nicholas & Alexandra: The Last Tsars of Imperial Russia. abr. ed. Robert K. Massie. Read by Lindsay Crouse. 6 cass. (Running Time: 8 hrs.). 1997. bk. 35.00; 79.95 Airplay.

Nicholas & the Moon Eggs. 2004. 8.95 (978-1-56008-983-4(0)); cass. & flmstrp 30.00 (978-1-56008-729-8(3)) Weston Woods.

Nicholas Language Series (Italian) Nssea Bundle. (Adventures with Nicholas Ser.). 2008. audio compact disk 8.95 (978-0-8416-0389-9(8)) Pub: Berlitz Pubng. Dist(s): Langenscheidt

Nicholas Nickelby. abr. ed. Charles Dickens. Read by Tom Courtenay. 2 cass. (Running Time: 3 hrs.). 2000. 7.95 (978-1-57815-122-6(8), 1084, Media Bks Audio) Media Bks NJ.
Nicholas has problems in school & then he leaves to seek his rightful inheritance.

Nicholas Nickleby. Charles Dickens. Narrated by Martin Jarvis. 1999. 13.00 (978-1-84032-133-3(4), HoddrStoughton) Pub: Hodder General GBR. Dist(s): Trafalgar

Nicholas Nickleby. Charles Dickens. Read by Anton Lesser. (Running Time: 7 hrs. 45 mins.). 2005. 38.95 (978-1-60083-855-2(3)) Iofy Corp.

Nicholas Nickleby. Charles Dickens. 2 cass. (Running Time: 3 hrs.). 1994. 8.95 (978-1-85695-523-2(0)) Multilingua.

Nicholas Nickleby. abr. ed. Charles Dickens. Read by Roger Rees. 1 cass. (Running Time: 1 hr. 30 min.). 1985. 12.95 (978-0-89845-061-3(6), SWC 1702) HarperCollins Pubs.

Nicholas Nickleby. abr. ed. Charles Dickens. Read by Martin Jarvis. 2 cass. (Running Time: 3 hrs.). 2001. (978-1-84032-403-7(1), HoddrStoughton) Hodder General GBR.

Nicholas Nickleby. abr. ed. Charles Dickens. Read by Anton Lesser. 6 CDs. (Running Time: 7 hrs. 40 min.). audio compact disk 41.98 (978-962-634-326-5(5), Naxos AudioBooks) Naxos.

Nicholas Nickleby. abr. ed. Charles Dickens. Perf. by Paul Scofield. 2 cass. (Running Time: 3 hrs.). (Ultimate Classics Ser.). 2004. 18.00 (978-1-931056-60-1(9), N Millennium Audio) New Millenn Enter.
The welfare of children, a theme that ennable many of the novels of Charles Dickens, captures the sympathy of our century as profoundly as it did that of the author's own contemporaries. Following the history of a fatherless young man, his mother and sister as they find themselves at the mercy of a greedy and unscrupulous uncle, Nicholas Nickleby is both a vivid indictment of the exploitive, brutal boarding schools of the late nineteenth century and a celebration of the little family's resilient generosity of spirit.

Nicholas Nickleby. abr. ed. Charles Dickens. Read by Paul Scofield. 3 CDs. (Running Time: 3 hrs.). 2004. audio compact disk 24.95 (978-1-59007-577-7(3)) Pub: New Millenn Enter. Dist(s): PerseuPGW

Nicholas Nickleby. unabr. ed. Charles Dickens. Read by Robert Whitfield. (Running Time: 113400 sec.). 2007. audio compact disk 39.95 (978-0-7861-6144-7(2)) Blckstn Audio.

Nicholas Nickleby. unabr. ed. Charles Dickens. Read by Robert Whitfield. (Running Time: 113400 sec.). 2007. audio compact disk 59.95 (978-0-7861-5904-8(9)) Blckstn Audio.

Nicholas Nickleby. unabr. ed. Charles Dickens. Read by Robert Whitfield. (YA). 2008. 184.99 (978-1-60514-907-3(1)) Find a World.

Nicholas Nickleby, Pt. I. Charles Dickens. Read by Robert Whitfield. 14 cass. (Running Time: 33 hrs. 30 mins.). 2001. 89.95 (978-0-7861-1877-9(6), 2676A,B) Blckstn Audio.
Nicholas, the hearty young hero, takes us on a journey through nineteenth-century England accompanied by some of Dicken's best swaggering scoundrels & most forgettable eccentrics.

Nicholas Nickleby, Pt. 2. Charles Dickens. Read by Flo Gibson. 9 cass. (Running Time: 13 hrs. 30 mins.). 59.95 Audio Bk Con.
Nicholas Nickleby serves as usher to the tyrannical schoolmaster Mr. Squeers, joins Mr. Crummles' theatrical company & clerks for the Brothers Cheeryble, always with the faithful Smike in tow. He falls in love with Madeline Bray & becomes a successful merchant.

Nicholas Nickleby, Pt. II. Charles Dickens. Read by Robert Whitfield. 9 cass. (Running Time: 33 hrs. 30 mins.). 2001. 62.95 (978-0-7861-1895-3(4), 2676A,B) Blckstn Audio.
Nicholas, the hearty young hero, takes us on a journey through nineteenth-century England accompanied by some of Dicken's best swaggering scoundrels & most forgettable eccentrics.

Nicholas Nickleby, Pt. C. collector's unabr. ed. Charles Dickens. Read by Wanda McCaddon. 8 cass. (Running Time: 12 hrs.). (J). 1982. 64.00 (978-0-7366-0248-8(8), 1242-C) Books on Tape.
An unlikely young man makes good in the theatre despite his years at the hands of a cruel schoolmaster. Dickens displays his comic genius.

Nicholas Nickleby, Pt. A. unabr. collector's ed. Charles Dickens. Read by Wanda McCaddon. 8 cass. (Running Time: 12 hrs.). (J). 1982. 64.00 (978-0-7366-0246-4(1), 1242-A) Books on Tape.

Nicholas Nickleby, Pt. B. collector's unabr. ed. Charles Dickens. Read by Wanda McCaddon. 9 cass. (Running Time: 13 hrs. 30 min.). (J). 1982. 72.00 (978-0-7366-0247-1(X), 1242-B) Books on Tape.

Nicholas Nickleby: Part 1. unabr. ed. Charles Dickens. Read by Robert Whitfield. (Running Time: 73800 sec.). 2007. audio compact disk 120.00 (978-0-7861-6951-1(6)) Blckstn Audio.

Nicholas Nickleby: Part 2. unabr. ed. Charles Dickens. Read by Robert Whitfield. (Running Time: 39600 sec.). 2007. audio compact disk 81.00 (978-0-7861-5903-1(0)) Blckstn Audio.

Nicholas Nickleby (Part 1), Vol. 1. Charles Dickens. Read by Flo Gibson. 12 cass. (Running Time: 18 hrs.). 1996. 39.95 (978-1-55685-393-7(9)) Audio Bk Con.
Nicholas Nickleby serves as usher to the tyrannical schoolmaster Mr. Squeers, joins Mr. Crummles' theatrical company & clerks for the Brothers Cheeryble, always with the faithful Smike in tow. He falls in love with Madeline Bray & becomes a successful merchant.

Nicholas Nickleby (Part 2), Vol. 2. unabr. ed. Charles Dickens. Narrated by Flo Gibson. (Running Time: 13 hrs. 10 mins.). 1996. 28.95 (978-1-55685-824-6(8)) Audio Bk Con.

Nicholas Nickleby (Parts 1 And 2) unabr. ed. Charles Dickens. Narrated by Flo Gibson. (Running Time: 32 hrs. 17 mins.). 1996. 59.95 (978-1-55685-825-3(6)) Audio Bk Con.

Nicholas Sparks Pak: Message in a Bottle & The Notebook. abr. ed. Read by Kathleen Quinlan et al. 2 cass. (Running Time: 6 hrs.). 2001. 34.95 (978-0-929071-57-2(3)) B-B Audio.
Plugn Play Travelpaks contain everything your customers will need for many hours of audiobook listening. 2 Fantastic Audiobooks with1 Portable Cassette Player plus1 Comfortable Headset plus 2 Batteriers NICHOLAS SPARKS PAK 6 HoursMESSAGE IN A BOTTLE.

Nichtov M'Aleph V'ad Tav: Spirit Duplicating Writing Primer. Avivia Langsam. (HEB.). 1997. tchr. ed. 18.00 (978-0-915152-03-2(7), A041) Pub: Langsam Publishing Co. Dist(s): Torah Umesorah

Nick Adams Stories. unabr. ed. Ernest Hemingway. Read by Stacy Keach. (Running Time: 7 hrs. 0 mins. 0 sec.). (ENG.). 2007. audio compact disk 29.95 (978-0-7435-6965-1(2)) Pub: S&S Audio. Dist(s): S and S Inc

Nick Carter: Master Detective. Perf. by Lon Clark & Helen Choate. 2009. audio compact disk 35.95 (978-1-57019-895-3(0)) Radio Spirits.

Nick Carter: Murder on mad mountain/webs of Murder. (ENG.). 2008. audio compact disk 12.95 (978-1-57970-516-9(2), Audio-For) J Norton Pubs.

Nick Carter, Master Detectiive: Case of the Policy Maker & Case of the Missing Street. Perf. by Lon Clark. 1 cass. (Running Time: 1 hr.). 2001. 6.98 (2445) Radio Spirits.

Nick Carter Master Detective. Perf. by Lon Clark et al. 2008. audio compact disk 35.95 (978-1-57019-874-8(8)) Radio Spirits.

Nick Carter, Master Detective, Vol. 1. collector's ed. Perf. by Lon Clark. 6 cass. (Running Time: 9 hrs..). 1998. bk. 34.98 (4010) Radio Spirits.
18 episodes including Angle of Murder, Body on a Slab, The Bull and Bear, Candidate's Corpse, Sunken Dollar, Corpse in the Cab, Death by Ricochet, Murder in a Decanter, Double Disguise, Eye for and Eye, Flying Duck Murders, Forgetful Killer, Death after Dark, Missing Harold Ascourt, Monkey Sees Murder, Murder by Fire, Murder Goes to College and Webs of Murder.

Nick Carter, Master Detective, Vol. 2. collector's ed. Perf. by Lon Clark. 6 cass. (Running Time: 9 hrs.). 2001. bk. 34.98 (4431) Radio Spirits.
18 episodes including, Unwilling Accomplice, Dead Witnesses, A Cat Brings Death, The Numbers Murders, Slingshot Murder, Death in the Pool, Murder in the Night, Death Plays the Lead, Ready for Murder, Mind Over Murder, Funeral Wreath, Death Goes to the Post, Death Behind the Scenes, Case of the Vanishing Lady, The Mystery of the Hangman's Wood, The Man Who Lived Too Long, Legend of Shakespeare's Ghost and The Witness Saw Nothing.

Nick Carter, Master Detective: Demented Daughter & Dictaphone Murder. Perf. by Lon Clark. 1 cass. (Running Time: 1 hr.). 2001. 6.98 (2187) Radio Spirits.

Nick Carter, Master Detective: Eight Records of Death & The Case of the Disappearing Corpse. Perf. by Lon Clark. 1 cass. (Running Time: 1 hr.). 2001. 6.98 (2286) Radio Spirits.

Nick Carter, Master Detective: The Barefoot Banker & Jeweled Queen. Perf. by Lon Clark. 1 cass. (Running Time: 1 hr.). 2001. 6.98 (2204) Radio Spirits.

Nick Carter, Master Detective: The Case of the Wrong Mr. Wright & The Case of the Perfect Alibi. Perf. by Lon Clark. 1 cass. (Running Time: 1 hr.). 2001. 6.98 (2621) Radio Spirits.

Nick Carter, Master Detective: The Drug Ring Murder & The Substitute Bride. Perf. by Lon Clark. 1 cass. (Running Time: 1 hr.). 2001. 6.98 (2543) Radio Spirits.

Nick Carter, Master Detective: The Echo of Death & Haunted Rocking Chair. Perf. by Lon Clark. 1 cass. (Running Time: 1 hr.). 2001. 6.98 (2561) Radio Spirits.

Nick Carter, Master Detective: The Glass Coffin & State's Prison Evidence. Perf. by Lon Clark. 1 cass. (Running Time: 1 hr.). 2001. 6.98 (2524) Radio Spirits.

Nick Carter, Master Detective: The Unexpected Corpse & the Flowery Farewell. Perf. by Lon Clark. 1 cass. (Running Time: 1 hr.). 2001. 6.98 (2065) Radio Spirits.

Nick Carter, Master Detective: Witch of Donderburg Mountain & Case of the Phantom Shoplifters. Perf. by Lon Clark. 1 cass. (Running Time: 1 hr.). 2001. 6.98 (2585) Radio Spirits.

Nick Carter, Mater Detective: Case of the Lost Old-Timer & Case of the Magic Rope. Perf. by Lon Clark. 1 cass. (Running Time: 1 hr.). 2001. 6.98 (1690) Radio Spirits.

Nick Danger: The Daily Feed Tapes. Perf. by Firesign Theatre Firesign Theatre Staff. 2 CDs. (Running Time: 3 hrs.). audio compact disk 24.95 (978-1-57677-147-1(4), MSUG013) Lodestone Catalog.
Detective Nick Danger is called to save America's poorest family from Rocky Roccoco's evil Happy Schemes.

***Nick of Time.** (ENG.). 2010. audio compact disk (978-1-59171-268-8(8)) Falcon Picture.

Nick of Time. unabr. ed. Ted Bell. Read by John Shea. 12 CDs. (Running Time: 11 hrs. 30 mins. 0 sec.). Vol. 1. (ENG.). (J). (gr. 4-7). 2008. audio compact disk 29.95 (978-1-4272-0466-0(7)) Pub: Macmill Audio. Dist(s): Macmillan

Nick Takes a Bet. unabr. ed. Michele Sobel Spirn. 1 cass. (Running Time: 20 min.). (Fun to Read Ser.). (J). (gr. 3-6). 1983. bk. 16.99 (978-0-934898-43-0(X)); pap. bk. 9.95 (978-0-934898-31-7(6)) Jan Prods.
Nick complains about his sister's cooking once too often. Knowing full well he can't even boil water, she challenges him to a bet that he can't prepare an edible dinner for the family. Readers will enjoy finding out how Nick plans to win the bet.

Nick the Knife **see Ellery Queen**

Nickel & Dimed: On (Not) Getting by in America. Barbara Ehrenreich. 2004. audio compact disk 29.99 (978-1-4193-0507-8(7)) Recorded Bks.

Nickel & Dimed: On (Not) Getting by in America. unabr. ed. Barbara Ehrenreich. Narrated by Cristine McMurdo-Wallis. 6 cass. (Running Time: 8 hrs. 15 mins.). 2001. 59.75 (978-1-4193-0780-5(0), 97874MC) Recorded Bks.

Nickel Mountain. unabr. ed. John Gardner. Read by Dan Lazar. 8 cass. (Running Time: 8 hrs.). 48.00 (978-0-913369-95-1(0), 1005) Books on Tape.
Henry Soames is a fat, gentle, middle-aged man who runs a diner deep in the forests of the Catskills. He is assisted by a young girl who has become pregnant by a rich man's errant son. Henry Soames marries her out of kindness. Together they experience the universal rituals of courtship, marriage, birth, loss of innocence & the acceptance of death.

Nickel on the Grass. Dick Jonas. 1 cass. (Running Time: 1 hr.). 15.00 EROSONIC.
Includes: "Throw a Nickel on the Grass," "Lady in Red," "Ain't No Fighter Pilots Down in Hell," "Little Brown Mouse," "It's a Lie," "Give Me Operations,"

"Marauder," "Air Corps Lament," "I Wanted Wings," "Bronco," "Ultra Hog," "Viet Vet," "Be-No," & "30-Plus Month Tour".

***Nickum.** Doris Davidson. 2010. 69.95 (978-1-4079-0734-5(4)); audio compact disk 84.95 (978-1-4079-0735-2(2)) Pub: Soundings Ltd GBR. Dist(s): Ulverscroft US

Nicky & Friends, Vol. 1. Terry Franklin & Barbi Franklin. 2002. 9.95 (978-7-901440-15-9(5)) Pub: Tylis Music. Dist(s): STL Dist NA

Nicky & Friends, Vol. 2. Terry Franklin & Barbi Franklin. (Running Time: 30 min.). 2002. 9.95 (978-7-901444-06-5(1)); audio compact disk 14.95 (978-7-901444-13-3(4)) Pub: Tylis Music. Dist(s): STL Dist NA

Nicky Deuce: Welcome to the Family. unabr. ed. Steven R. Schirripa & Charles Fleming. Read by Joe Grifasi. 3 CDs. (Running Time: 3 hrs. 15 mins.). 2005. audio compact disk 30.00 (978-0-307-28274-3(0), Listening Lib); 23.00 (978-0-307-28275-0(9), Listening Lib) Pub: Random Audio Pubg. Dist(s): Random

It's July, and Nicholas Borelli II's parents are scheduled to spend two weeks on a cruise. Nicholas will spend those two weeks, as he does every summer, at Camp Wannameka. The night before he's to leave, however, there's a phone call: thanks to an explosion in the septic system, camp is canceled. The only place for Nicholas to go instead is to his grandmother's house in Bensonhurst, Brooklyn, New York.Nicholas's father grew up in Brooklyn, but you'd hardly know it. An Italian dinner at Nicholas's house in the suburbs is whole wheat pasta, organic tomato sauce, and, if he's lucky, a tofu meatball. And Brooklyn? Well, Brooklyn is the place his father left and never talks about. Nicholas has never been there, and he doesn't want to go now. But when Nicholas tastes his grandma Tutti's meatballs for the first time, gets a nickname from his uncle Frankie, and makes a friend in the neighborhood, his feelings about Brooklyn - and family - begin to change.

Nicobar Bullion Case see Classic Detective Stories, Vol. II, A Collection

Nicodemus Initiation; From Meditation to Meditation. Ann Ree Colton & Jonathan Murro. 1 cass. 7.95 A R Colton Fnd.

Discusses the goal of God-Realization.

Nicolae: An Experience in Sound & Drama. unabr. ed. Tim LaHaye & Jerry B. Jenkins. Read by Jack Sondericker. 10 CDs. (Running Time: 11 hrs. 30 min.). (Left Behind Ser.: Bk. 3). 2001. audio compact disk 65.00 (978-1-58116-127-4(1)) Books in Motion.

As Nicolae Carpathia's forces face the opposition, Captain Rayford Steele enters service as Nicolae's pilot, just when catastrophic events take place.

Nicolae: The Rise of Antichrist. Tim LaHaye & Jerry B. Jenkins. Read by Richard Ferrone. 10 CDs. (Running Time: 11 hrs.). (Left Behind Ser.: Bk. 3). 2004. audio compact disk 39.95 (978-0-7887-5134-9(4), 00052) Recorded Bks.

Nicolae: The Rise of Antichrist. Tim LaHaye & Jerry B. Jenkins. Read by Richard Ferrone. 6 cass. (Running Time: 11 hrs.). (Left Behind Ser.: Bk. 3). 2004. 29.95 (978-0-7887-5125-7(5), 00054) Recorded Bks.

Nicolae: The Rise of Antichrist. unabr. ed. Tim LaHaye & Jerry B. Jenkins. Read by Jack Sondericker. 12 cass. (Running Time: 11 hrs. 30 min.). (Left Behind Ser.: Bk. 3). 1999. 64.95 (978-1-55686-889-4(8)) Books in Motion.

Nicolae: The Rise of Antichrist. unabr. ed. Tim LaHaye & Jerry B. Jenkins. Narrated by Richard Ferrone. 8 cass. (Running Time: 11 hrs.). (Left Behind Ser.: Bk. 3). 1997. 72.00 (978-0-7887-3478-6(4), 95694E7) Recorded Bks.

In the third novel of this apocalyptic saga, World War III has begun, orchestrated by the evil & powerful Nicolae Carpathia. As a small band of believers in Christ, the Tribulation Force, strive to gather the faithful together, they must outwit this antichrist & his demonic plans for all mankind.

Nicolae: The Rise of Antichrist. unabr. ed. Tim LaHaye & Jerry B. Jenkins. Narrated by Richard Ferrone. 10 CDs. (Running Time: 11 hrs.). (Left Behind Ser.: Bk. 3). 2000. audio compact disk 97.00 (978-0-7887-4638-3(3), C1213E7) Recorded Bks.

Nicomachean Ethics. Aristotle. Read by Nadia May. 8 CDs. (Running Time: 8 hrs. 30 mins.). 2000. audio compact disk 64.00 (978-0-7861-9861-0(3), 2592) Blckstn Audio.

Aristotle sets out to discover the good life for man: the life of happiness or eudaimonia. This is the famous doctrine of the golden mean: courage, for example, is a mean between cowardice & rashness & justice between a man's getting more or less than his due.

Nicomachean Ethics. unabr. ed. Aristotle. Read by Nadia May. 6 cass. (Running Time: 8 hrs. 30 mins.). 2000. 44.95 (978-0-7861-1793-2(1), 2592) Blckstn Audio.

He sets out to discover the good life for man: the life of happiness or eudaimonia. This is the famous doctrine of the golden mean: courage, for example, is a mean between cowardice & rashness & justice between a man's getting more or less than his due.

Nicomachean Ethics. unabr. ed. Aristotle. Read by Nadia May. (YA). 2008. 59.99 (978-1-60514-737-6(0)) Find a World.

Nicomede. Corneille. Perf. by Jacques Toja & Sylvia Monfort. 2 cass. (Running Time: 3 hrs.). 44.95 (1644-H) Olivia & Hill.

One of Corneille's most remarkable tragedies. Nicomede returns victorious from battle to encounter the hostility of his father the king & of his stepmother. But he meets all intrigues of prudence & cool irony & comes out victorious on the homefront as well.

Nicomede. Corneille. Perf. by Jacques Toja & Sylvia Monfort. 2 CDs. (Running Time: 3 hrs.). 1992. audio compact disk 44.95 (1643-H) Olivia & Hill.

Niederlandisch Ohne Muhe. 1 cass. (Running Time: 1 hr. 30 min.). (DUT & GER.). 2000. bk. 75.00 (978-2-7005-1006-5(2)) Pub: Assimil FRA. Dist(s): Distribks Inc

Niels Bukh DVD: A Visual Documentation of Gymnastics & Politics, 1912-52. Hans Bonde. 36.00 (978-87-635-0604-5(1)) Pub: Mus Tusculanum DNK. Dist(s): Intl Spec Bk

Niemann-Pick Disease - A Bibliography & Dictionary for Physicians, Patients, & Genome Researchers. Compiled by Icon Group International, Inc. Staff. 2007. ring bd. 28.95 (978-0-497-11380-3(5)) Icon Grp.

Nierenberg on Negotiating. Gerard I. Nierenberg. 1 cass. (Running Time: 1 hr.). 10.00 (SP100051) SMI Intl.

Ever notice how some people always seem to get their way, a more favorable agreement, or more money? That's because they know how to negotiate. Learn the fine points of negotiating & never again find yourself holding the short end of the stick.

Nietzsche & Individualism. John Ridpath. Read by John Ridpath. 2 cass. (Running Time: 3 hrs.). 1985. 24.95 (978-1-56114-040-4(6), CR01D) Second Renaissance.

These two lectures destroy once & for all the myth that Nietzsche was an advocate of individualism. By analyzing his metaphysics, epistemology & ethics, Dr. Ridpath explains the real significance & implications of the Nietzschean "Superman." He unmasks Nietzsche as an arch-enemy of genuine individualism.

Nietzsche in Turin: An Intimate Biography. collector's ed. Lesley Chamberlain. Read by Donada Peters. 6 cass. (Running Time: 9 hrs.). 1999. 40.00 (978-0-7366-4892-9(5)) Books on Tape.

A portrait of the majestic baroque city in which Nietzsche spent the last rational year of his life before his tragic breakdown & subsequent death.

Nietzsche in 90 Minutes. Paul Strathern. Narrated by Robert Whitfield. (Running Time: 1 hr. 30 mins.). 2003. 17.95 (978-1-59912-557-2(9)) Iofy Corp.

Nietzsche in 90 Minutes. unabr. ed. Paul Strathern. Read by Robert Whitfield. (Running Time: 1 hr. 30 mins.). 2006. 14.95 (978-0-7861-2434-3(2), 3113); reel tape 14.95 (978-0-7861-2530-2(6)); audio compact disk 14.95 (978-0-7861-9045-4(0)) Blckstn Audio.

Nietzsche in 90 Minutes. unabr. ed. Read by Paul Strathern & Robert Whitfield. Ed. by Paul Strathern. 2 CDs. (Running Time: 1 hr. 30 mins.). 2000. audio compact disk 16.00 (978-0-7861-9092-8(2), 3113) Blckstn Audio.

Nietzsche, Wittgenstein, Rawls & Foucault. unabr. ed. Michael Sugrue & Darren Stalloff. Read by Michael Sugrue & Darren Stalloff. Ed. by Teaching Company Staff. 2 cass. (Running Time: 3 hrs.). (Great Minds of the Western Intellectual Tradition Ser.). 1995. 19.95 (978-1-56585-113-9(7)) Teaching Co.

The lecture on Nietzsche is a philosophical discourse on the critique of Christianity. Wittgenstein's outlook on twentieth century philosophy. Rawls theory & principals of justice & Foucault's analysis of power through his studies of the origins of hospitals, prisons & institutions.

Nigeria & West Africa. unabr. ed. Wendy McElroy. Read by Richard C. Hottelet. (Running Time: 9000 sec.). (World's Political Hot Spots Ser.). 2006. audio compact disk 25.95 (978-0-7861-6446-2(8)) Pub: Blckstn Audio. Dist(s): NetLibrary CO

Nigeria & West Africa. unabr. ed. Wendy McElroy. Read by Richard C. Hottlet. Ed. by Mike Hassell. 2 cass. (Running Time: 3 hrs.). Dramatization. (World's Political Hot Spots Ser.). (YA). (gr. 11 up). 1992. 17.95 (978-0-938935-98-8(4), 10364) Knowledge Prod.

With early Nigerian culture dating back to at least 700 B.C., Nigeria has a long & rich history. British influence after the 16th century & especially in the 18th century, changed Nigeria's course.

Nigger of the Narcissus. unabr. collector's ed. Joseph Conrad. Read by Wolfram Kandinsky. 7 cass. (Running Time: 10 hrs. 30 min.). 1978. 56.00 (1098) Books on Tape.

Story of a voyage from an eastern port, but at another level the voyage becomes a symbol & is merely the stage on which Waite, a dying Negro, plays out the drama of his demise. "Heart of Darkness" is centered around the death of the powerful white trader Kurtz aboard a river steamer in the Belgian Congo.

Night see Poetry of Robinson Jeffers

Night. Elie Wiesel. Narrated by George Guidall. 4 CDs. (Running Time: 3 hrs. 45 mins.). audio compact disk 39.00 (978-1-4025-2324-3(6)) Recorded Bks.

Night. Elie Wiesel. 2004. pap. bk. 12.95 (978-1-4025-9423-6(2)) Recorded Bks.

Night. Elie Wiesel. 2 cass. (Running Time: 3 hrs. 45 mins.). 2004. 14.99 (978-1-4025-2031-0(X), 01394) Recorded Bks.

Night. Elie Wiesel. 2005. audio compact disk 14.99 (978-1-4193-9069-2(4)) Recorded Bks.

Night. unabr. ed. Elie Wiesel. Read by Jeffrey Rosenblatt. 4 cass. (Running Time: 4 hrs.). 2000. 24.95 (978-1-883332-40-2(0)) Audio Bkshelf.

The horrifying memoir of the Nobel Peace Prize winner tells of his experiences as a teenager in concentration camps during the Holocaust. From his family's deportation from their home in Hungary through the tortuous months he was imprisoned in the death camps at Birkenau, Auschwitz, Buna & Buchenwald, he documents the erosion of his health, his innocence & his faith.

Night. unabr. ed. Elie Wiesel. Read by Jeffrey Rosenblatt. 4 CDs. (Running Time: 4 hrs.). (YA). (gr. 7 up). 2000. audio compact disk 39.95 (978-1-883332-50-1(8)) Audio Bkshelf.

Night. unabr. ed. Elie Wiesel. Narrated by George Guidall. 3 cass. (Running Time: 3 hrs. 45 mins.). 1999. 26.00 (978-0-7887-3585-1(3), 95917E7) Recorded Bks.

Powerful fictional memoir lets you share in a Jewish boy's horrific experience in Nazi death camps. Offers a personal & unforgettable account of Hitler's reign of terror.

Night: Four Songs see Poetry of Langston Hughes

Night & Day. unabr. ed. Robert B. Parker. Read by James Naughton. (Jesse Stone Ser.: No. 8). (ENG.). 2009. audio compact disk 29.95 (978-0-7393-5745-3(X), Random AudioBks) Pub: Random Audio Pubg. Dist(s): Random

Night & Day. unabr. ed. Virginia Woolf. Read by Flo Gibson. 11 cass. (Running Time: 16 hrs.). 1994. 34.95 (978-1-55685-314-2(9)) Audio Bk Con.

Oh, what a tangled web these lovers weave as they seek to understand each others feelings or strike out for intellectual freedom! We enter the minds of five young people in London before World War I.

***Night at the Old Bergen County Racetrack.** Gordon Grand. 2009. (978-1-60136-525-5(X)) Audio Holding.

Night at the Radio. Perf. by Garry Papers et al. 4 cass. (Running Time: 4 hrs. 20 min.). 1997. 28.00 (978-1-891913-01-3(8)) Night At The Radio.

Twenty minutes of history & prices of 1942, plus various programs & episodes from 1940-1956, including "Search for Professor Loring Begins" (Jack Armstrong), "Captain Midnight's Origins" (Captain Midnight), "The Bakerville Gazette" (The Lone Ranger), "McGees Give a Party" (Fibber McGee & Molly), "H&R Blockhead" (Burns & Allen), "Crowbait Bob" (Gunsmoke), "A Pail of Air" (X Minus One), & "Mrs. Miniver" (Lux Radio Theater).

Night at the Radio. Perf. by Garry Papers et al. 4 cass. (Running Time: 4 hrs. 20 min.). 1998. 28.00 (978-1-891913-04-4(2)) Night At The Radio.

Twenty minutes of history & prices of 1945, plus various programs & episodes from 1939-1954, including "The Stolen Letter" (Jack Armstrong), "The Black Plane" (Captain Midnight), "Tara" (Sgt. Preston of the Yukon), "Molly's Birthday Cake" (Fibber McGee & Molly), "The Red Skelton Show", "Sorry, Wrong Number" (Suspense), "The Big Help" (Dragnet), "Lifeboat" (Screen Directors' Playhouse Playhouse).

Night at the Radio. Perf. by Garry Papers & Fibber McGee and Molly. 4 cass. (Running Time: 4 hrs. 20 min.). 1997. 28.00 (978-1-891913-02-0(6)) Night At The Radio.

Twenty minutes of history & prices of 1950, plus various programs & episodes from 1938-1954, including "Uncle Jim's Lab" (Jack Armstrong), "Parada Comes To" (Captain Midnight), "Origins of the Lone Ranger, Tonto, Silver" (The Lone Ranger), "Measles Quarantined" (Fibber McGee & Molly), "Community Chest" (Life of Riley), "Crisis at Easter Creek" (The Six Shooter), "On a Country Road" (Suspense) & "The Pride of the Yankees" (Lux Radio Theater).

Night at the Radio. Perf. by Garry Papers & Fibber McGee and Molly. 4 cass. (Running Time: 4 hrs. 20 min.). 1998. 28.00 (978-1-891913-03-7(4)) Night At The Radio.

Twenty minutes of history & prices of 1936, plus various programs & episodes from 1939-1956, including "Mysterious Stranger" (Jack Armstrong), "Surrounded" (Captain Midnight), "Not One Cent for Tribute" (The Green Hornet), "7th War Bond Drive" (Fibber McGee & Molly), "Arrival" (Life with Luigi), "With Folded Hands" (Dimension X), "What Makes a Murderer" (The Whistler), & "Brave New World" (CBS Radio Workshop).

Night at the Radio, Vol. 1 4 cass. (Running Time: 1 hr.). 1998. bk. 24.98 Boxed Set. (4160) Radio Spirits.

Night at the Radio, Vol. 2 4 cass. (Running Time: 4 hrs.). 1998. bk. 24.98 (4164) Radio Spirits.

Night at the Radio, Vol. 3 4 cass. (Running Time: 1 hr.). 1998. bk. 24.98 Boxed set. (4169) Radio Spirits.

Includes: "Jack Armstrong," "The Green Hornet," "Fibber McGee & Molly," "Life with Luigi," "The Whistler" & "CBS Radio Workshop.".

Night at the Vulcan. unabr. ed. Ngaio Marsh. Read by James Saxon. 6 cass. (Running Time: 7 hrs. 42 mins.). 2001. 29.95 (978-1-57270-165-6(X), N61165u, Audio Edits Mystry) Pub: Audio Partners. Dist(s): PerseuPGW

A successful opening night is marred by the death of the leading man after the show. No one knows if it is suicide or homicide. Inspector Roderick Alleyn takes the starring role in the investigation of the actor's dramatic demise.

Night Battles. unabr. ed. M. F. Bloxam. (Running Time: 6.5 hrs. NaN mins.). 2009. 29.95 (978-1-4332-6291-3(6)); audio compact disk 60.00 (978-1-4332-6288-3(6)); audio compact disk 44.95 (978-1-4332-6287-6(8)) Blckstn Audio.

Night Beat. Perf. by Frank Lovejoy. 6 cass. (Running Time: 9 hrs.). 2002. 34.98 (4013) Radio Spirits.

Randy Stone was a top reporter for the Chicago Star newspaper. Join him for 18 exciting stories, including Zero (the premier episode).

***Night Beat: Nightside Is Different.** Perf. by Frank Lovejoy. 2009. audio compact disk 31.95 (978-1-57019-914-1(0)) Radio Spirits.

Night Beat: Stories Start in Many Different Ways. Perf. by Frank Lovejoy. (ENG.). 2008. audio compact disk 18.95 (978-1-57019-857-1(8)) Radio Spirits.

Night Beat Stories Start in Many Different Ways. unabr. ed. Frank Lovejoy. 4 CDs. (Running Time: 4 hrs.). 2006. audio compact disk 15.95 (978-0-9770819-8-1(2), 8198) Choice Vent.

Night Before Christmas see Great Christmas Comedy: Selected Sketches

Night Before Christmas. 2007. audio compact disk 32.98 (978-5-557-58300-8(9)) Madacy Ent Grp CAN.

Night Before Christmas. Clement C. Moore. Read by Larry Robinson. (Live Oak Readalong Ser.). pap. bk. 18.95 (978-1-59519-331-5(6)) Pub: Live Oak Media. Dist(s): AudioGO

Night Before Christmas. Clement C. Moore. Illus. by Tomie dePaola. (Running Time: 6 mins.). 1984. 9.95 (978-1-59112-095-7(0)) Live Oak Media.

Night Before Christmas. Ed. by Clement C. Moore. Illus. by Clement C. Moore. Illus. by James Marshall. (J). (ps-6). 1988. bk. 5.95 Scholastic Inc.

Night Before Christmas. Clement C. Moore. Illus. by John Steven Gurney. (J). (ps-3). 2006. pap. bk. 18.95 (978-0-439-89843-0(9)) Scholastic Inc.

Night Before Christmas. Ed. by Clement C. Moore. Illus. by Clement C. Moore. Illus. by Jan Brett. 1 cass. (Running Time: 15 min.). (J). 2001. bk. 27.95 (978-0-8045-6859-3(6)) Spoken Arts.

As St. Nick and eight tiny reindeer descend through a brilliant night, the famous Christmas poem begins.

Night Before Christmas. Read by Larry Robinson. Ed. by Clement C. Moore. Illus. by Clement C. Moore & Tomie dePaola. 14 vols. (Running Time: 6 mins.). (J). (gr. k-3). 1984. pap. bk. & tchr. ed. 37.95 (978-0-941078-38-2(8)) Live Oak Media.

A classic edition of the ever popular poem set in mid-nineteenth century New England. Includes a reading chest.

Night Before Christmas. unabr. ed. C. Carlisimo et al. Read by Meryl Streep. (ENG.). (J). (gr. 1). 2007. audio compact disk 15.95 (978-0-7393-3504-8(9), Listening Lib) Pub: Random Audio Pubg. Dist(s): Random

Night Before Christmas. unabr. ed. Ed. by Clement C. Moore. Illus. by Clement C. Moore. 1 cass. (Running Time: 6 mins.). (J). (ps-3). 1997. 8.95 (978-1-56008-820-2(6), RAC373) Weston Woods.

One of the most beloved Christmas traditions, the story of Santa's visit on Christmas Eve.

Night Before Christmas. unabr. ed. Ed. by Clement C. Moore. Illus. by Clement C. Moore. Illus. by Ruth Sanderson. Narrated by Anthony Edwards. 1 cass. (Running Time: 6 mins.). (J). (ps-3). 1997. bk. 24.95 (978-0-7882-0668-9(0), PHRA373) Weston Woods.

Night Before Christmas. unabr. ed. Read by Larry Robinson. Ed. by Clement C. Moore. Illus. by Clement C. Moore & Tomie dePaola. 11 vols. (Running Time: 6 mins.). (J). (gr. k-3). 1984. bk. 25.95 (978-0-941078-39-9(6)); pap. bk. 16.95 (978-0-941078-37-5(X)) Live Oak Media.

A classic edition of the ever popular poem set in mid-nineteenth century New England.

Night Before Christmas & Other Favorite Holiday Stories: The Night Before Christmas; Giving Thanks; One Zillion Valentine's; Merry Christmas, Space Case; Sam & the Lucky Money. unabr. ed. Clement C. Moore et al. Read by Anthony Edwards et al. (J). 2008. 44.99 (978-1-60514-947-9(0)) Find a World.

Night Before Easter: A Resurrection Musical. Mosie Lister. (ENG.). 2008. audio compact disk 12.00 (978-5-557-37031-8(5)) Lillenas.

Night Bells see Gathering of Great Poetry for Children

Night Bells see Carl Sandburg's Poems for Children

***Night Call.** 2010. audio compact disk (978-1-59171-280-0(7)) Falcon Picture.

Night Caller. unabr. ed. John Lutz. Read by Scott Brick. 8 cass. (Running Time: 12 hrs.). 2001. 54.40 (978-0-7366-8480-4(8)) Pub: Books on Tape. Dist(s): NetLibrary CO

Ezekiel "Coop" Cooper is lonely. He's no longer with the NYPD due to cancer that's in remission. His daughter Bette is in New Jersey, and he doesn't talk with her about anything personal, but he loves her. He's looking forward to seeing her at the family bungalow, but when he gets there, he finds her dead, curled up in a way that suggests a ritual murder. He investigates the death, eventually joining forces with a mystery writer who believes a serial killer has murdered Bette. By the time they put all the pieces together, they realize that the killer is extremely dangerous, and could be headed to kill more people they know.

Night Christ Was Born. Contrib. by Dale Mathews & Michael Frazier. 1997. 11.98 (978-0-7601-1495-7(1), 75602089); 85.00 (978-0-7601-1782-8(9), 75606449) Pub: Brentwood Music. Dist(s): H Leonard

Night Christ Was Born. Contrib. by Dale Mathews & Michael Frazier. 1997. 85.00 (978-0-7601-1408-7(0), 75606312) Pub: Brentwood Music. Dist(s): H Leonard

Night Christ Was Born. Contrib. by Dale Mathews & Michael Frazier. 1997. 4.00 (978-0-7601-1413-1(7), 75602090); 4.00 (978-0-7601-1869-6(8), 75602087); 4.00 (978-0-7601-1870-2(1), 75602092); 4.00 (978-0-7601-1871-9(X), 75602088) Pub: Brentwood Music. Dist(s): H Leonard

Night Connections. Short Stories. 1 CD. (Running Time: 45 mins.). Dramatization. 2003. audio compact disk (978-0-9723923-4-1(3)) D Summer Commns.
Connections between late night people.

Night Country: A Novel. unabr. ed. Stewart O'Nan. Read by John Tye. (Running Time: 7 hrs.). 2004. 39.25 (978-1-59335-511-1(4), 1593355114, Brlnc Audio MP3 Lib) Brilliance Audio.
At midnight on Halloween in a cloistered New England suburb, a car carrying five teenagers leaves a winding road and slams into a tree, killing three of them. One escapes unharmed, another suffers severe brain damage. A year later, summoned by the memories of those closest to them, the three who died come back on a last chilling mission among the living. A strange and unsettling ghost story in the tradition of Ray Bradbury and Shirley Jackson, The Night Country creeps through the leaf-strewn streets and quiet cul-de-sacs of one bedroom community, reaching into the desperately connected yet isolated lives of three people changed forever by the accident: Tim, who survived yet lost everything; Brooks, the cop whose guilty secret has destroyed his life; and Kyle's mom, trying to love the new son the doctors returned to her. As the day wanes and darkness falls, one of them puts a terrible plan into effect, and they find themselves caught in a collision of need and desire, watched over by the knowing ghosts. Macabre and moving, The Night Country elevates every small town's bad high school crash into myth, finding the deeper human truth beneath a shared and very American tragedy.

Night Country: A Novel. unabr. ed. Stewart O'Nan. Read by John Tye. (Running Time: 7 hrs.). 2004. 39.25 (978-1-59710-531-6(7), 1597105317, BADLE); 24.95 (978-1-59710-530-9(9), 1597105309, BAD) Brilliance Audio.

Night Country: Or, the Darkness on the Edge of Town. unabr. ed. Stewart O'Nan. Read by John Tye. (Running Time: 7 hrs.). 2003. 69.25 (978-1-59355-233-6(5), 1593552335, BrilAudUnabridg); 27.95 (978-1-59355-232-9(7), 1593552327, BAU) Brilliance Audio.

Night Country: Or, the Darkness on the Edge of Town. unabr. ed. Stewart O'Nan. Read by John Tye. (Running Time: 7 hrs.). 2004. 24.95 (978-1-59335-242-4(5), 1593352425) Soulmate Audio Bks.

Night Crew. unabr. ed. John Sandford, pseud. Narrated by Richard Ferrone. 7 cass. (Running Time: 10 hrs. 15 mins.). 1997. 66.00 (978-0-7887-0913-5(5), 95053E7) Recorded Bks.
When a night crew of video free-lancers films a suicide in progress on the streets of Los Angeles, their foreman suddenly finds herself the target of a deadly stalker.

Night Drifter. unabr. ed. Susan Carroll. Narrated by Barbara Rosenblat. 11 cass. (Running Time: 15 hrs. 30 mins.). 2000. 97.00 (978-0-7887-4419-8(4), 95910E7) Recorded Bks.
Lance Leger is heir to the family castle on the Cornish coast. Gifted with supernatural powers, he can separate his soul from his body to go "night drifting." One night, he meets the beautiful Rosalind, but she's convinced he's merely a ghost.

Night Fall. abr. ed. Nelson DeMille. Read by Scott Brick. (ENG.). 2005. 14.98 (978-1-59483-140-9(8)) Pub: Hachet Audio. Dist(s): HachBkGrp

Night Fall. abr. ed. Nelson DeMille. Read by Scott Brick. (Running Time: 6 hrs.). (Replay Edition Ser.). (ENG.). 2007. audio compact disk 14.98 (978-1-60024-094-2(1)) Pub: Hachet Audio. Dist(s): HachBkGrp

Night Fall. unabr. ed. Cherry Adair. (Running Time: 7 hrs. NaN mins.). 2008. 44.95 (978-1-4332-5372-0(0)); audio compact disk 60.00 (978-1-4332-5373-7(9)) Blckstn Audio.

Night Fall. unabr. ed. Cherry Adair. (Running Time: 7 hrs. NaN mins.). 2008. 29.95 (978-1-4332-5374-4(7)); audio compact disk 19.95 (978-1-4332-5528-1(6)) Blckstn Audio.

Night Fall. unabr. ed. Nelson DeMille. 13 CDs. (Running Time: 13 hrs. 30 min.). 2004. audio compact disk 120.00 (978-1-4159-0494-7(4)); 96.00 (978-1-4159-0493-0(6)) Books on Tape.
On a Long Island beach at dusk, Bob Mitchell and Janet Whitney are videotaping themselves making love. When a terrible explosion lights up the sky, the couple flees, taking their camera with them. Five years later, the crash of Flight 800 is attributed to a mechanical malfunction. Suspecting a cover-up at the highest levels, John Corey and Kate Mayfield, members of the Elite Anti-terrorist Task Force, disobey orders by trying to find the one piece of evidence that will tell the truth about what really happened: the video tape of the couple making love on the beach followed by the last moments of Flight 800.

Night Fall. unabr. ed. Nelson DeMille. Read by Scott Brick. (ENG.). 2005. 16.98 (978-1-59483-139-3(4)) Pub: Hachet Audio. Dist(s): HachBkGrp

Night Fall. unabr. ed. Nelson DeMille. Read by Scott Brick. (Running Time: 15 hrs.). (ENG.). 2009. 59.98 (978-1-60024-900-6(0)) Pub: Hachet Audio. Dist(s): HachBkGrp

Night Feeding see Poetry & Voice of Muriel Rukeyser

Night Ferry. Michael Robotham. Narrated by Clare Corbett. (Running Time: 44100 sec.). 2007. audio compact disk 34.99 (978-1-4281-4782-9(9)) Recorded Bks.

Night Fever (from Saturday Night Fever) - ShowTrax. Arranged by Mac Huff. 1 CD. (Running Time: 1 hr. 30 min.). 2000. audio compact disk 19.95 (08621182) H Leonard.
The hottest ticket on Broadway! This feature number is electrifying.

Night Flyers. unabr. ed. Elizabeth McDavid Jones. Narrated by Stina Neilsen. 3 pieces. (Running Time: 3 hrs. 30 mins.). (American Girl Ser.). 1999. 28.00 (978-1-4025-4155-1(4)) Recorded Bks.

Night Flying. Rita Murphy. Narrated by Alexandra O'Karma. 4 CDs. (Running Time: 3 hrs. 45 mins.). (gr. 9 up). audio compact disk 39.00 (978-1-4025-0468-6(3)) Recorded Bks.

Night Flying. Rita Murphy. Narrated by Alexandra O'Karma. 3 pieces. (Running Time: 3 hrs. 45 mins.). (gr. 9 up). 2001. 28.00 (978-0-7887-5501-9(3)) Recorded Bks.
All the women in Georgia Hansen's family can fly. But flying, like everything else in Georgia's life, is strictly regulated by her grandmother. Georgia breaks her grandmother's most important rule, and must decide if she will admit her mistake or stand up to her grandmother and take control of her own life.

Night Following. Morag Joss. 2009. 69.95 (978-0-7531-4223-3(6)); audio compact disk 89.95 (978-0-7531-4224-0(4)) Pub: Isis Pubng Ltd GBR. Dist(s): Ulverscroft US

Night Frost. unabr. ed. R. D. Wingfield. Read by Stephen Thorne. 12 CDs. (Running Time: 18 hrs.). (Jack Frost Ser.: Bk. 3). 2001. audio compact disk 99.95 (978-0-7531-0964-9(6), 0964-6) Pub: ISIS Audio GBR. Dist(s): ISIS Pub
Denton is in the grip of a crime wave. A serial killer is terrorizing the senior citizens of the town & the local police are succumbing to a flu epidemic. Tired & demoralized, the force also has to contend with a seemingly perfect young couple suffering arson attacks & death threats; a suspicious suicide; burglaries; pornographic videos & poison-pen letters. In uncertain charge of the investigations is Detective Inspector Jack Frost, crumpled, slapdash & foul-mouthed as ever. He tries to cope despite inadequate back-up, but there is never enough time; the unsolved crimes pile up & the killings go on. Frost has to cut corners & take risks, knowing that his superiors will throw him to the wolves if anything goes wrong. For Frost, things always go wrong.

Night Gardener. abr. ed. George P. Pelecanos. (Running Time: 6 hrs.). (ENG.). 2006. 14.98 (978-1-59483-533-9(0)) Pub: Hachet Audio. Dist(s): HachBkGrp

Night Gardener. abr. ed. George P. Pelecanos. (Running Time: 6 hrs.). (ENG.). 2009. 44.98 (978-1-60024-980-8(9)) Pub: Hachet Audio. Dist(s): HachBkGrp

Night Gardener. unabr. ed. George P. Pelecanos. Narrated by Richard Davidson. 7 cass. 2006. 64.95 (978-0-7927-4531-0(0), CSL 1012) AudioGO.

Night Gardener. unabr. ed. George P. Pelecanos. Narrated by Richard Davidson. 9 CDs. (Running Time: 41520 sec.). 2006. audio compact disk 89.95 (978-0-7927-4482-5(9), SLD 1012); audio compact disk 54.95 (978-0-7927-4554-9(X), CMP 1012) AudioGO.

Night Gardening. unabr. ed. E. L. Swann. Read by Dick Hill. (Running Time: 6 hrs.). 2008. 39.25 (978-1-4233-5830-5(9), 9781423358305, BADLE); 39.25 (978-1-4233-5828-2(7), 9781423358282, Brlnc Audio MP3 Lib); 24.95 (978-1-4233-5827-5(9), 9781423358275, Brilliance MP3); 24.95 (978-1-4233-5829-9(5), 9781423358299, BAD) Brilliance Audio.

***Night Horseman.** Max Brand. Read by Alfred von Lecteur. 2010. 27.95 (978-1-60112-957-4(2)) Babblebooks.

Night Horseman. unabr. collector's ed. Max Brand. Read by Jonathan Marosz. 6 cass. (Running Time: 9 hrs.). 1994. 48.00 (978-0-7366-2742-9(1), 3468) Books on Tape.
Dan Barry fights his enemies during a long trek across the lonely desert.

Night Huntress. unabr. ed. Yasmine Galenorn. Narrated by Cassandra Campbell. (Running Time: 11 hrs. 0 mins.). (Sisters of the Moon Ser.). 2009. 17.99 (978-1-4001-8446-0(0)); 34.99 (978-1-4001-9446-9(6)) Tantor Media.

Night Huntress. unabr. ed. Yasmine Galenorn. Narrated by Cassandra Campbell. (Running Time: 11 hrs. 0 mins. 0 sec.). (Sisters of the Moon Ser.). (ENG.). 2010. 24.99 (978-1-4001-6446-2(X)); audio compact disk 69.99 (978-1-4001-4446-4(9)); audio compact disk 34.99 (978-1-4001-1446-7(2)) Pub: Tantor Media. Dist(s): IngramPubServ

Night in Bethlehem Music. Created by Group Publishing. 2007. audio compact disk 3.99 (978-5-557-59754-8(9)) Group Pub.

***Night Is for Hunting.** John Marsden. Read by Suzi Dougherty. (Running Time: 6 hrs. 30 mins.). (Tomorrow Ser.). (YA). 2009. 49.99 (978-1-74214-338-5(5), 9781742143385) Pub: Bolinda Pubng AUS. Dist(s): Bolinda Pub Inc

Night Is for Hunting. unabr. ed. John Marsden. 6 CDs. (Running Time: 6 hrs. 30 mins.). (Tomorrow Ser.). (YA). 2001. audio compact disk 77.95 (978-1-74030-401-6(2)) Pub: Bolinda Pubng AUS. Dist(s): Bolinda Pub Inc

Night Is for Hunting. unabr. ed. John Marsden. Read by Suzi Dougherty. 4 cass. (Running Time: 6 hrs. 30 mins.). (Tomorrow Ser.). (YA). 2004. 32.00 (978-1-876584-63-4(7), 591113) Bolinda Pubng AUS.
John Marsden has sold over two million books world-wide. John has won every major writing award in Australia for young people's fiction, as well as numerous awards both in the USA and Europe. John has three titles in the top ten list of all Australian books sold.

Night Is for Hunting. unabr. ed. John Marsden. Read by Suzi Dougherty. (Running Time: 23400 sec.). (Tomorrow Ser.). 2008. audio compact disk 43.95 (978-1-921415-29-6(0), 9781921415296) Pub: Bolinda Pubng AUS. Dist(s): Bolinda Pub Inc

Night Journey. abr. ed. Stephen King. Read by Frank Muller. 2 cass. (Running Time: 3 hrs.). (Green Mile Ser.: Vol. 5). 7.95 (PengAudBks) Penguin Grp USA.

Night Journeys. unabr. ed. Avi. Narrated by Jeff Woodman. 3 pieces. (Running Time: 3 hrs. 15 mins.). (gr. 6 up). 1997. 27.00 (978-0-7887-1795-6(2), 95267E7) Recorded Bks.
Eager for adventure & a hefty reward, 12-year-old Peter York volunteers to join a search for runaway indentured servants.

Night Journeys. unabr. ed. Avi. Read by Jeff Woodman. 3 cass. (Running Time: 3 hrs. 15 min.). (YA). 1997. bk. 40.20 (978-0-7887-1838-0(X), 40618) Recorded Bks.

Night Kill. unabr. ed. Anne Littlewood. (Running Time: 9 hrs. NaN mins.). 2008. 29.95 (978-1-4332-5196-2(5)); 59.95 (978-1-4332-5194-8(9)); audio compact disk 80.00 (978-1-4332-5195-5(7)) Blckstn Audio.

Night Kitchen Radio Theater Vol. 1: The Emperor's New Clothes & Pinocchio. unabr. ed. Tnk Workshop, Inc. Staff. 2 CDs. (Running Time: 2 hrs. 22 mins.). (J). (gr. k-3). 2006. audio compact disk 20.40 (978-0-7393-3798-1(X), Listening Lib); 23.00 (978-0-7393-3826-1(9), Listening Lib) Pub: Random Audio Pubg. Dist(s): Random
The Night Kitchen Radio Theater performances are based on the classic stories. THE EMPEROR'S NEW CLOTHES: The Emperor himself, his court, and his clothes - or lack of them - are ridiculous as only the master storyteller Hans Christian Andersen can make them. PINOCCHIO: The adventures of a talking wooden puppet who yearns to become a real boy.

Night Kitchen Radio Theater: Volume 1: The Emperor's New Clothes & Pinocchio. unabr. ed. Hans Christian Andersen et al. Read by Full Cast Production Staff. (Running Time: 8820 sec.). (ENG.). (J). (gr. 1). 2006. audio compact disk 19.95 (978-0-7393-3664-9(9), Listening Lib) Pub: Random Audio Pubg. Dist(s): Random

Night Light. unabr. ed. Terri Blackstock. (Running Time: 13 hrs. 0 mins. 0 sec.). (Restoration Ser.: No. 2). (ENG.). 2006. 14.99 (978-0-310-26947-2(4)) Zondervan.

Night Light. unabr. ed. Terri Blackstock. (Running Time: 13 hrs. 0 mins. 0 sec.). (Restoration Ser.: No. 2). (ENG.). (ps). 2006. audio compact disk 29.99 (978-0-310-26921-2(0)) Zondervan.

Night Listener. movie tie-in unabr. ed. Armistead Maupin. Read by Armistead Maupin. (Running Time: 34200 sec.). 2006. audio compact disk 39.95 (978-0-06-123891-8(0)) HarperCollins Pubs.

Night Magic. Tom Tryon. 2004. 10.95 (978-0-7435-4449-8(8)) Pub: S&S Audio. Dist(s): S and S Inc

Night Magic. unabr. ed. Karen Robards. Read by Renee Maxwell. 8 vols. (Running Time: 12 hrs.). 2000. bk. 69.95 (978-0-7927-2200-7(0), CSL 089, Chivers Sound Lib) AudioGO.
Clara Winston writes sizzling romance novels, always including a courageous new hero; the kind of man she hopes to meet someday. Then she meets CIA agent Jack McCain, a man running for his life! Suddenly Clara is swept into his troubled world, ready to break every rule in the book to win his heart.

Night Magic. unabr. ed. Karen Robards. Read by Renee Maxwell. 8 CDs. (Running Time: 12 hrs.). 2004. audio compact disk 79.95 (978-0-7927-3227-3(8), SLD 404, Chivers Sound Lib) AudioGO.
Clara Winston writes sizzling romance novels, always including a courageous hero, the kind of man she hopes to meet someday. Then she encounters CIA agent Jack McCain, a man in danger and running for his life. Suddenly Clara is swept into his troubled world, and ready to break every rule in the book to win his heart.

Night Manager. unabr. collector's ed. John le Carré. Read by David Case. 13 cass. (Running Time: 19 hrs. 30 min.). (George Smiley Novels Ser.). 1994. 104.00 (978-0-7366-2789-4(8), 3505) Books on Tape.
Set in today's world of espionage: the international cartel of illegal arms dealers & drug smugglers.

Night Ministry. Ann Ree Colton. 1 cass. (Running Time: 1 hr.). 7.95 A R Colton Fnd.

Night Mother. Marsha Norman. Contrib. by Sharon Gless & Katherine Helmond. 2 CDs. (Running Time: 3900 sec.). 2003. audio compact disk 25.95 (978-1-58081-294-8(5), CDRDP18) Pub: L A Theatre. Dist(s): NetLibrary CO

Night Mother. unabr. ed. Marsha Norman. Perf. by Sharon Gless & Katherine Helmond. 1 cass. (Running Time: 1 hr. 05 min.). 1993. 19.95 (978-1-58081-010-4(1), RDP18) L A Theatre.
Sad & searingly powerful story of an epileptic woman in her early forties. Jessie feels she has nothing to live for. And tonight, she plans to do something about it. Thus begins the nerve wracking duel between a woman systematically preparing for her own death & the frantic, comic & touching efforts of her mother to stop her.

Night Moves. Janelle Taylor. Narrated by Richard Poe. 7 cass. (Running Time: 9 hrs. 15 mins.). 2002. 65.00 (978-1-4025-3435-5(3)) Recorded Bks.

Night Moves. abr. ed. Tom Clancy & Netco Partners Staff. Read by Edward Herrmann. 1 CD. (Running Time: 1 hr. 30 mins.). 2004. audio compact disk 14.95 (978-0-06-074695-7(5)) HarperCollins Pubs.

Night Moves. unabr. ed. Alan Scholefield. Read by Terry Wale. 6 cass. (Running Time: 9 hrs.). 2001. 54.95 (978-1-86042-654-4(9), 26549) Pub: Soundings Ltd GBR. Dist(s): Ulverscroft US

Night Music of West Sumatra: Saluang, Rabab Pariaman, Dendang Pauah. Anno. by Philip Yampolsky. 1 cass. (Running Time: 1 hr. 13 min.). (Music of Indonesia Ser.: Vol. 6). 1994. (0-9307-40422O-9307-40422-2-9); audio compact disk (0-9307-40422-2-9) Smithsonian Folkways.
Chamber music performed with only one or two singers & a single accompanying flute or bowed lute.

***Night Myst.** unabr. ed. Yasmine Galenorn. (Running Time: 11 hrs. 0 mins.). (Indigo Court Ser.). 2010. 17.99 (978-1-4001-8764-5(8)) Tantor Media.

***Night Myst.** unabr. ed. Yasmine Galenorn. Narrated by Cassandra Campbell. (Running Time: 11 hrs. 0 mins. 0 sec.). (Indigo Court Ser.). (ENG.). 2010. 24.99 (978-1-4001-6764-7(7)); audio compact disk 34.99 (978-1-4001-1764-2(X)); audio compact disk 83.99 (978-1-4001-4764-9(6)) Pub: Tantor Media. Dist(s): IngramPubServ

Night, Night: 12 Lullaby Favorites for Your Bee-Autiful Baby. Created by Word Records. 2008. audio compact disk 3.99 (978-5-557-47086-5(7), Word Records) Word Enter.

Night Night Lullabies. Perf. by Cream Factory Cream Factory. 1 cass. (Running Time: 50 min.). (J). (ps). 10.98 (3009-4); audio compact disk 15.98 CD. (3009-4) Baby Music.
A mix of original & traditional lullabies.

Night-Night Lullabies. Perf. by Dream Factory. 1 cass. (Running Time: 50 min.). (J). 7.98 (BBO 3009); audio compact disk 12.78 (BBO 3009) NewSound.

Night Night/Sleep Tight: 12 Lullaby Favorites for Your Bee-Autiful Baby. Created by Word Records. 2008. audio compact disk 6.99 (978-5-557-47084-1(0), Word Records) Word Enter.

Night of Fire. Barbara Samuel. Narrated by Jill Tanner. 7 cass. (Running Time: 10 hrs. 15 mins.). 56.00 (978-1-4025-0370-2(9)); audio compact disk 89.00 (978-1-4025-2090-7(5)) Recorded Bks.

Night of Four Hundred Rabbits. unabr. ed. Elizabeth Peters, pseud. Read by Grace Conlin. 6 cass. (Running Time: 8 hrs. 30 mins.). 1997. 44.95 (978-0-7861-1098-8(8), 1862) Blckstn Audio.
The pyramids of Mexico City's Walk of the Dead towered above & around Carol Farley, their beauty shrouded in the terror they suddenly held for the young American. It began as Carol's Christmas vacation ended: an envelope waiting for her in her room, an anonymously-sent piece of mail with a newspaper clipping in it. Blurred, but still recognizable, was a picture of her father. It was the first time in years that Carol could be certain he was alive. And because he was, Carol Farley went to Mexico.

Night of Four Hundred Rabbits. unabr. ed. Elizabeth Peters, pseud. Read by Grace Conlin. (Running Time: 8 hrs. NaN mins.). 2009. 29.95 (978-1-4332-6489-4(7)); audio compact disk 70.00 (978-1-4332-6486-3(2)) Blckstn Audio.

Night of Long Knives. unabr. ed. Max Gallo. Read by Wolfram Kandinsky. 8 cass. (Running Time: 12 hrs.). 1976. 64.00 (978-0-7366-0017-0(5), 1027) Books on Tape.
Hitler authored many infamous atrocities but none more coldblooded or less understood than his early roundup & massacre of political dissidents. Max Gallo tells us the story of that bygone event in such a way that the years roll back & pose once again the question that plagues us to this day: what shall the western democracies do in the face of tyranny in a neighboring state.

Night of Many Dreams. unabr. ed. Gail Tsukiyama. Read by Anna Fields. 6 cass. (Running Time: 8 hrs. 30 mins.). 1999. pap. bk. 44.95 (978-0-7861-1335-4(9), 2229) Blckstn Audio.
Two sisters follow a different path from what their family expects. The sisters learn that their close-knit family is a source of strength as they pursue their separate dreams.

Night of Many Dreams. unabr. ed. Gail Tsukiyama. Read by Anna Fields. 6 cass. (Running Time: 9 hrs.). 1999. 29.95 (978-0-7861-1546-4(7)) Blckstn Audio.
Sisters, Joan & Emma escape Hong Kong to spend the war years in Macao. Returning home, they pursue separate dreams but each finds the same truths on the paths of their different interests & experience; that family & loved ones offer a real source of strength.

***Night of Many Dreams.** unabr. ed. Gail Tsukiyama. Read by Anna Fields. (Running Time: 8 hrs. 30 mins.). 2010. 29.95 (978-1-4417-5625-1(6)); audio compact disk 90.00 (978-1-4417-5622-0(1)) Blckstn Audio.

Night of Terror. 1 CD. (Running Time: 30 min.). (Halloween Party Ser.). (J). (gr. k-5). 2001. pap. bk. 5.98 (9684-2) Peter Pan.
Spooky songs, sounds and stories with holiday spirit. Includes Halloween Party Tip Guide.

Night of the Child. abr. ed. Robert Benson. Read by Carol McClure. 1 CD. (Running Time: 1 hr. 30 mins.). 2001. audio compact disk 13.99 (978-0-8358-0966-5(8)) Upper Room Bks.

Night of the Comanche Moon. abr. ed. T. T. Flynn. Read by Buck Schimer. (Running Time: 3 hrs.). (Five Star Westerns Ser.). 2007. 39.25 (978-1-4233-3562-7(7), 9781423335627, BADLE); 24.95 (978-1-4233-3561-0(9), 9781423335610, BAD) Brilliance Audio.

Night of the Comanche Moon. abr. ed. Read by Buck Schimer. (Running Time: 10800 sec.). (Five Star Westerns Ser.). 2007. audio compact disk 24.95 (978-1-4233-3559-7(7), 9781423335597, Brilliance MP3); audio compact disk 39.25 (978-1-4233-3560-3(0), 9781423335603, Brlnc Audio MP3 Lib) Brilliance Audio.

Night of the Comanche Moon. unabr. ed. T. T. Flynn. Read by Edward Lewis. 7 cass. (Running Time: 7 hrs.). 1995. 42.00 (978-0-7366-3294-2(8), 3949) Books on Tape.

Ann Carruthers, a young Englishwoman, trades tea & crumpers for the dust & violence of New Mexico to find her brother, who vanished there. She gets a rude introduction to frontier custom when a Comanche offers 100 horses for her. To buy time, she pretends to be with John Hardisty. He can ride, shoot & fight & he's her only hope in a lawless land.

***Night of the Fox.** unabr. ed. Jack Higgins. Read by Michael Page. (Running Time: 9 hrs.). (Dougal Munro/Jack Carter Ser.). 2010. 24.99 (978-1-4418-4409-5(0), 9781441844095, BAD); 24.99 (978-1-4418-4407-1(4), 9781441844071, Brilliance MP3); 39.97 (978-1-4418-4410-1(4), 9781441844101, BADLE); 39.97 (978-1-4418-4408-8(2), 9781441844088, Brlnc Audio MP3 Lib); audio compact disk 29.99 (978-1-4418-4405-7(8), 9781441844057, Bril Audio CD Unabri); audio compact disk 87.97 (978-1-4418-4406-4(6), 9781441844064, BriAudCD Unabrid) Brilliance Audio.

Night of the Fox. unabr. ed. Scripts. Jack Higgins. Read by Steven Pacey. 8 cass. (Running Time: 12 hrs.). 2004. 34.95 (978-1-59007-377-3(0)) Pub: New Millenn Enter. Dist(s): PerseuPGW

Night of the Generals. unabr. ed. Hans Hellmut Kirst. Read by Marvin Miller. 8 cass. (Running Time: 12 hrs.). 47.60 (B-106) Audio Bk.

Night of the Generals. unabr. ed. Hans Hellmut Kirst. Read by Daniel Grace. 7 cass. (Running Time: 10 hrs. 30 min.). 1976. 56.00 (978-0-7366-0029-3(9), 1041) Books on Tape.

Three slayings in three cities look remarkably like the work of the same man. Is it one of the German generals?.

Night of the Hawk. abr. ed. Dale Brown. Read by Joseph Campanella. 4 cass. (Running Time: 6 hrs.). 2001. 25.00 (978-1-59040-130-9(1), Phoenix Audio) Pub: Amer Intl Pub. Dist(s): PerseuPGW

Night of the Homework Zombies. Scott Nickel. (School Zombies Ser.). (J). (gr. 3-5). 2007. audio compact disk 14.60 (978-1-59889-385-4(8)) CapstoneDig.

Night of the Howling Dogs. unabr. ed. Graham Salisbury. Narrated by Robert Ramirez. 5 CDs. (Running Time: 5 hrs.). (YA). (gr. 5-9). 2008. audio compact disk 51.75 (978-1-4361-1586-5(8)); 41.75 (978-1-4361-1581-0(7)) Recorded Bks.

Graham Salisbury has received numerous high-profile accolades from the ALA, VOYA, and several parent organizations. A Junior Library Guild Premier election, Night of the Howling Dogs is a rousing adventure set in Hawaii. On a Boy Scout trip, Dylan is looking forward to camping out at the foot of the Pu'u Kapukapu volcano. But when an earthquake strikes, Dylan is forced to team up with a bully named Louie on a daring mission to rescue many of their scattered comrades.

Night of the Hunter. Davis Grubb. Read by Jeff Harding. 8 CDs. (Running Time: 12 hrs.). (Isis (CDs) Ser.). 2001. audio compact disk 79.95 (978-0-7531-1145-1(4)) Pub: ISIS Audio GBR. Dist(s): Ulverscroft US

Night of the Hunter. unabr. ed. Davis Grubb. Read by Jeff Harding. 6 cass. (Running Time: 9 hrs.). (Isis Ser.). (J). 2000. 54.95 (978-0-7531-0755-3(4), 000313) Pub: ISIS Lrg Prnt GBR. Dist(s): Ulverscroft US

When Ben Harper goes to the gallows for a bank robbery killing, he leaves his young children John & Pearl to hide the $10,000. Soon a strange preacher comes to town & claims to have known their daddy. He preaches the word of the Lord, but darkness lurks in his heart, a knife lies in his pocket & he wants that money.

Night of the Jaguar. unabr. ed. Michael Gruber. 1 MP3-CD. (Running Time: 15 hrs.). 2006. 49.95 (978-0-7927-3973-9(6), Chivers Sound Lib) AudioGO.

Night of the Jaguar. unabr. ed. Michael Gruber. Read by Jonathan Davis. 10 cass. (Running Time: 55140 sec.). (Sound Library). 2006. 84.95 (978-0-7927-3930-2(2), Chivers Sound Lib); audio compact disk 110.95 (978-0-7927-3931-9(0), Chivers Sound Lib) AudioGO.

Night of the Juggler. unabr. ed. William P. McGivern. (Running Time: 25200 sec.). 2007. 54.95 (978-1-4332-0754-9(0)); audio compact disk 29.95 (978-1-4332-0756-3(7)); audio compact disk 63.00 (978-1-4332-0755-6(9)) Blckstn Audio.

Night of the Letter. unabr. ed. Dorothy Eden. Read by Delia Corrie. 5 cass. (Running Time: 7 hrs. 30 min.). (Sound Ser.). 2004. 49.95 (978-1-85496-661-2(8)) Pub: UlverLrgPrint GBR. Dist(s): Ulverscroft US

The Templar curse was just a half-forgotten legend to everyone except Brigit Templar Gaye. She had met with a strange accident & now lay helpless in her bed in the oppressive old Templar mansion. Her husband had found a marvelous girl to look after the children, but why did she drift through the house at night as if she owned it.

Night of the Lighted Freedom Audio Book. Dana Marquess. (ENG.). (J). 2007. audio compact disk 9.95 (978-1-932278-50-7(8)) Pub: Mayhaven Pub. Dist(s): Baker Taylor

Night of the Lions. unabr. ed. Kuki Gallmann. Read by Nicolette McKenzie. 5 cass. (Running Time: 7 hrs. 30 mins.). (J). 2001. 49.95 (978-0-7531-0682-2(5)) Pub: ISIS Audio GBR. Dist(s): Ulverscroft US

Based on books 9-12 in the Left Behind: The Kids series, this third package of "Live-Action Audio" is gripping for young and old alike. Best for ages 10-14 but loved by all ages.

Night of the Lions. unabr. ed. Kuki Gallmann. Read by Helen Bourne. 6 CDs. (Running Time: 6 hrs.). (Isis Ser.). (J). 2002. audio compact disk 64.95 (978-0-7531-1578-7(6)) Pub: ISIS Lrg Prnt GBR. Dist(s): Ulverscroft US

Africa evokes in travellers a deep recognition and an inexplicable yearning to return. It is a place which retains what most of the world has lost: space, roots, traditions, awesome beauty, true wilderness, rare animals, extraordinary people. It will always attract those who can still dream.

Night of the Living Bed. unabr. ed. Denys Cazet. Illus. by Denys Cazet. Read by Barbara Caruso. 1 cass. (Running Time: 17 mins.). (Minnie & Moo Ser.). (J). (gr. k-4). 2005. bk. 25.95 (978-1-59519-389-6(8)); bk. 28.95 (978-1-59519-393-3(6)); pap. bk. 16.95 (978-1-59519-388-9(X)); pap. bk. 18.95 (978-1-59519-392-6(8)) Live Oak Media.

Halloween is frighteningly funny when Minnie and Moo are on the loose! After Minnie has a nightmare (a giant mouse eats the last bit of chocolate!), she and Moo awaken to find their bed rolling down the hill into town. What better "costumes" than two cows in pajamas - so the daffy duo join in the festivities and manage to snare a few treats of their own in this hilarious holiday romp.

Night of the Living Bed, Set. unabr. ed. Denys Cazet. Illus. by Denys Cazet. Read by Barbara Caruso. 1 CD. (Running Time: 17 mins.). (Minnie & Moo Ser.). (J). (gr. k-4). 2005. pap. bk. 31.95 (978-1-59519-394-0(4)) Live Oak Media.

Night of the Living Bed, Set. unabr. ed. Denys Cazet. Illus. by Denys Cazet. Read by Barbara Caruso. 1 cass. (Running Time: 17 mins.). (Minnie & Moo Ser.). (J). (gr. k-4). 2005. pap. bk. 29.95 (978-1-59519-390-2(1)) Live Oak Media.

Night of the Living Dead. abr. ed. John Russo & George Romero. 2004. 5.95 (978-0-7435-4148-0(0)) Pub: S&S Audio. Dist(s): S and S Inc

Night of the Loch Ness Monster. Jerry Stemach. (Nick Ford Mysteries Ser.). 2000. audio compact disk 18.95 (978-1-4105-0140-0(X)) D Johnston Inc.

Night of the Loch Ness Monster. Jerry Stemach. Ed. by Jerry Stemach. Ed. by Gail Portnuff Venable & Dorothy Tyack. Illus. by Jeff Ham. Narrated by Ed Smaron. Contrib. by Ted S. Hasselbring. (J). (gr. 2-3). 2000. 35.00 (978-1-58702-456-6(X)) D Johnston Inc.

Night of the Loch Ness Monster, Vol. 6. Jerry Stemach. Ed. by Jerry Stemach. Ed. by Gail Portnuff Venable & Dorothy Tyack. Illus. by Jeff Ham. Narrated by Ed Smaron. Contrib. by Ted S. Hasselbring. (Start-to-Finish Books). (J). (gr. 2-3). 2002. 100.00 (978-1-58702-982-0(0)) D Johnston Inc.

Night of the Lock Ness Monster, Vol. 6. unabr. ed. Jerry Stemach. Ed. by Jerry Stemach. Ed. by Gail Portnuff Venable & Dorothy Tyack. Illus. by Jeff Ham. Narrated by Ed Smaron. Contrib. by Ted S. Hasselbring. 1 cass. (Running Time: 1 hr.). (Start-to-Finish Books). (J). (gr. 2-3). 2000. (978-1-893376-52-6(4), F13K2) D Johnston Inc.

In this story, Nick has agreed to install a dinosaur exhibit at the Loch Ness Monster Visitors Center in Scotland. When Nick and the kids arrive at Loch Ness, they help save an elderly man who has had a heart attack after seeing the monster. Nick and the girls take the man to the hospital while Jeff and Ken "stake out" the Loch. Ken explores an old castle and is kidnapped. Nick and the director of the Visitor's Center use sonar to locate the mysterious monster.

***Night of the Meek.** 2010. audio compact disk (978-1-59171-154-4(1)) Falcon Picture.

Night of the Ninjas. unabr. ed. Mary Pope Osborne. 1 cass. (Running Time: 45 mins.). (Magic Tree House Ser.: No. 5). (J). (gr. k-3). 2004. pap. bk. 17.00 (978-0-8072-0338-5(6), Listening Lib) Random Audio Pubg.

Night of the Panther. unabr. collector's ed. E. C. Ayres. Read by Barrett Whitener. 8 cass. (Running Time: 8 hrs.). 1998. 48.00 (978-0-7366-4076-3(2), 4585) Books on Tape.

In this eco-mystery, P.I. Tony Lowell stumbles on murder & corruption in the Florida Everglades.

Night of the Party. unabr. ed. Iris Bromige. 6 cass. (Isis Ser.). (J). 2004. 54.95 (978-1-85695-544-7(3)) Pub: ISIS Lrg Prnt GBR. Dist(s): Ulverscroft US

Night of the Party. unabr. ed. Iris Bromige. Read by Helen Bourne. 6 cass. (Running Time: 9 hrs.). 2001. 54.95 (90035) Pub: ISIS Audio GBR. Dist(s): Ulverscroft US

Night of the Short Knives, unabr. ed. Burke Wilkinson. Narrated by Flo Gibson. 6 cass. (Running Time: 9 hrs.). 1985. 24.95 (978-1-55685-020-2(4)) Audio Bk Con.

A tale of international intrigue at S.H.A.P.E.

***Night of the Solstice.** unabr. ed. L. J. Smith. Read by Khristine Hvam. (Running Time: 7 hrs.). 2010. 39.97 (978-1-4418-7206-7(X), 9781441872067, Brlnc Audio MP3 Lib); audio compact disk 19.99 (978-1-4418-7203-6(5), 9781441872036, Bril Audio CD Unabri) Brilliance Audio.

***Night of the Solstice.** unabr. ed. L. J. Smith. Read by Khristine Hvam. (Running Time: 7 hrs.). 2010. 39.97 (978-1-4418-7207-4(8), 9781441872074, BADLE) Brilliance Audio.

***Night of the Solstice.** unabr. ed. Trish Telep Editors & L. J. Smith. Read by Khristine Hvam. (Running Time: 7 hrs.). 2010. 19.99 (978-1-4418-7205-0(1), 9781441872050, Brilliance MP3); audio compact disk 59.97 (978-1-4418-7204-3(3), 9781441872043, BriAudCD Unabrid) Brilliance Audio.

Night of the Soul Stealer. unabr. ed. Joseph Delaney. Read by Christopher Evan Welch. (Last Apprentice Ser.: Bk. 3). (J). 2007. audio compact disk 29.95 (978-0-06-135532-5(1), HarperChildAud) HarperCollins Pubs.

Night of the Soul Stealer. unabr. ed. Joseph Delaney. Read by Christopher Evan Welch. 6 CDs. (Running Time: 7 hrs. 30 mins.). (Last Apprentice Ser.: Bk. 3). (YA). (gr. 7-9). 2007. audio compact disk 51.75 (978-1-4281-7251-7(3)); 41.75 (978-1-4281-7246-3(7)) Recorded Bks.

Following Revenge of the Witch and Curse of the Bane, Night of the Soul Stealer is a pulse-quickening installment in best-selling author Joseph Delaney's popular series. With frighteningly vivid images of various grotesqueries, this teen chiller about a master monster hunter and his young student is sure to spark imaginations everywhere.

***Night of the Spear: The Last Watcher Episode 2.** D. B. Clifton. Read by Simon Prebble. (Running Time: 71). (ENG.). 2010. 2.99 (978-0-9827919-0-5(9)) Mind Wings Aud.

***Night of the Spear: The Last Watcher, Episode 2.** D. B. Clifton. (Running Time: 71). (ENG.). 2010. 2.99 (978-1-61114-020-0(X)) Mind Wings Aud.

Night of the Tiger. unabr. ed. Robert H. Van Gulik. Narrated by Frank Muller. 2 cass. (Running Time: 2 hrs.). (Judge Dee Mysteries Ser.). 1984. 18.00 (978-1-55690-375-5(8), 84160E7) Recorded Bks.

Judge Dee is trapped in an embattled fortress. Outside an enemy prepares a final assault. Within, a murderer is loose.

Night of the Triffids. unabr. ed. Simon Clark. Read by Steven Pacey. 10 cass. (Running Time: 15 hrs.). 2002. 84.95 (978-0-7540-0766-1(9), CAB 2188) AudioGO.

John Wyndham's extraordinary bestseller is one man's description of doomsday: almost the entire population has become blind, and the world has a new master, the monstrous triffid plant. Simon Clark takes up the story twenty-five years later, where David Masen, the grown son of Bill, wakes one morning to discover that the world has been plunged into darkness. The few sighted people in the island community have their artificial lights, but once more the triffid has the advantage.

Night of the Twisters: The Most Dangerous Night of Their Lives . Ruckman Ivy. Narrated by Duggan Riley. 3 CDs. (Running Time: 2 hrs. 45 mins.). (J). (gr. 4-7). 2009. audio compact disk 39.95 (978-0-9814890-6-3(0)) Audio Bkshelf.

Night of Thunder. Stephen Hunter. Read by Buck Schirner. (Bob Lee Swagger Ser.). 2009. 79.99 (978-1-60812-687-3(0)) Find a World.

Night of Thunder. abr. ed. Stephen Hunter. Read by Buck Schirner. (Running Time: 6 hrs.). (Bob Lee Swagger Ser.). 2009. audio compact disk 14.99 (978-1-4233-6963-9(7), 9781423369639, BCD Value Price) Brilliance Audio.

Night of Thunder. unabr. ed. Stephen Hunter. Read by Buck Schirner. (Running Time: 10 hrs.). (Bob Lee Swagger Ser.). 2008. 39.25 (978-1-4233-6961-5(0), 9781423369615, BADLE); 39.25 (978-1-4233-6959-2(9), 9781423369592, Brlnc Audio MP3 Lib); 24.95 (978-1-4233-6960-8(2), 9781423369608, BAD); 24.95 (978-1-4233-6958-5(0), 9781423369585, Brilliance MP3); audio compact disk 107.25 (978-1-4233-6957-8(2), 9781423369578, BriAudCD Unabrid); audio compact disk 36.99 (978-1-4233-6956-1(4), 9781423369561, Bril Audio CD Unabri) Brilliance Audio.

Night of Two Stars: Recorded Live at Carnegie Hall. unabr. ed. Featuring Wally Ballou et al. Contrib. by Kurt Vonnegut. 2 cass. (Running Time: 2 hr.). Dramatization. (978-1-892091-00-0(3), RAFO001, RadioArt); audio compact disk (978-1-892091-02-4(X), RAFO002, RadioArt) Radio Found.

Live stereo recording of Bob & Ray's 1984 Carnegie Hall Concert. Contains 37 routines, including all their classic bits: "The Slow Talkers of America," "Wally Ballou & the Cranberry Man in Times Square," "The McBeeBee Twins," "Wally Balou at the Paper Clip Factory," "Soap Opera Reminiscence including Mary Backstayge & "Mr. Trace, Keener Than Most Persons." With an appreciation by Kurt Vonnegut, Jr.

Night of Wenceslas. unabr. collector's ed. Lionel Davidson. Read by Rupert Keenlyside. 6 cass. (Running Time: 9 hrs.). 1982. 48.00 (978-0-7366-0340-9(9), 1326) Books on Tape.

A young man trapped behind the Iron Curtain struggles to get free. Tense, funny, excellent entertainment.

Night over Water. unabr. ed. Ken Follett. Read by David Case. 11 cass. (Running Time: 16 hrs. 30 mins.). 1991. 88.00 (978-0-7366-2017-8(6), 2833); Rental 18.50 Set. (2833) Books on Tape.

September, 1939. Two days after Britain declares war on Germany, a group gathers in Southampton to board a Pan American Clipper. It will fly them to safety in America. The passenger list includes an English aristocrat fleeing with his family & a fortune in jewels, a German scientist escaping from the Nazis, a murderer under F.B.I. escort & a charming thief. They will be in the air for 30 hours & once aloft there is no turning back. But one passenger has orders to see that the Clipper never reaches the U.S. at any cost.

Night over Water. unabr. ed. Ken Follett. Read by Tom Casaletto. (Running Time: 15 hrs.). 2004. 39.25 (978-1-59335-883-9(0), 1593358830, Brlnc Audio MP3 Lib); 39.25 (978-1-59710-533-0(3), 1597105333, BADLE); 24.95 (978-1-59710-532-3(5), 1597105325, BAD); 24.95 (978-1-59335-749-8(4), 1593357494, Brilliance MP3); 29.95 (978-1-59355-653-2(5), 1593556535, BAU) Brilliance Audio.

On a bright September morning in 1939, two days after Britain declares war on Germany, a group of privileged but desperate people gather in Southhampton to board the largest, most luxurious airliner ever built - the Pan American Clipper - bound for New York. The passengers include a fascist English aristocrat fleeing with his family and a fortune in jewels; a German scientist escaping from the Nazis; a murderer under FBI escort; a beautiful young woman heading for a new life; and a handsome, charming, unscrupulous thief. They will be in the air for thirty hours, soothed by the carpeted lounges, the curtained beds, the gourmet dining room, and the endless champagne. But once inside the flying palace there is no escape. Over the Atlantic, the Clipper's passengers are gripped by mounting fear and tension as their journey reaches the point of no return.

Night over Water. unabr. ed. Ken Follett. Read by Tom Casaletto. (Running Time: 15 hrs.). 2007. audio compact disk 38.95 (978-1-4233-2865-0(5), 9781423328650, Bril Audio CD Unabri); audio compact disk 112.25 (978-1-4233-2866-7(3), 9781423328667, BriAudCD Unabrid) Brilliance Audio.

Night Piece for Julia see Crimson Ramblers of the World, Farewell

Night Preacher. Louise Vernon. Narrated by Fern Ebersole. (ENG.). (YA). 2009. audio compact disk 15.95 (978-0-9801244-2-2(5)) IG Publish.

Night Prey. John Sandford, pseud. Read by Jay O. Sanders. (Running Time: 30 hrs. 0 mins. 0 sec.). (ENG.). 2003. audio compact disk 9.95 (978-0-7435-3280-8(5), S&S Encore) Pub: S&S Audio. Dist(s): S and S Inc

John Sandford's bestselling Lucas Davenport series continues with the fast-paced, compelling thriller, Night Prey. A series of deaths leads to the possibility of a brutal serial killer of unusual skill and savagery. And if Lucas is right, the killer is just getting warmed up.

Night Prey. John Sandford, pseud. Read by Jay O. Sanders. (Prey Ser.). 2004. 10.95 (978-0-7435-4301-9(7)) Pub: S&S Audio. Dist(s): S and S Inc

Night Prey. unabr. ed. John Sandford, pseud. Narrated by Richard Ferrone. 8 cass. (Running Time: 12 hrs.). (Prey Ser.). 1995. 70.00 (978-0-7887-0192-4(4), 94416E7) Recorded Bks.

A state investigator suspects the re-emergence of an uncaught serial killer & goes to Lucas Davenport for help in the investigation.

Night Probe! unabr. ed. Clive Cussler. Read by Michael Prichard. 9 cass. (Running Time: 13 hrs. 30 min.). (Dirk Pitt Ser.). 1993. 72.00 (978-0-7366-2343-8(4), 3122) Books on Tape.

A long-lost secret treaty between the U. S. & Britain becomes the prize in a contest between Dirk Pitt & England's top agent.

Night Ragas, Vol. 1. Music by Mallikarjun Mansur. 1 cass. (Running Time: 1 hr.). (From Dawn to Midnight Ser.). 1990. (A90013); audio compact disk (CD A92084) Multi-Cultural Bks.

Night Ragas, Vol. 2. Music by Pandit Jasraj. 1 cass. (Running Time: 1 hr.). (From Dawn to Midnight Ser.). 1990. (A90014); audio compact disk (CD A92085) Multi-Cultural Bks.

Night Ragas, Vol. 3. Music by Hariprasad Chaurasia. 1 cass. (Running Time: 1 hr.). (From Dawn to Midnight Ser.). 1990. (A90015); audio compact disk (CD A92086) Multi-Cultural Bks.

Night Ragas, Vol. 4. Music by Shruti Sadolikar. 1 cass. (Running Time: 1 hr.). (From Dawn to Midnight Ser.). 1990. (A90016); audio compact disk (CD A92087) Multi-Cultural Bks.

***Night Ride.** Peter Dawson. 2009. (978-1-60136-454-8(7)) Audio Holding.

Night Ride. Peter Dawson. (Running Time: 0 hr. 12 mins.). 2000. 10.95 (978-1-60083-542-1(2)) Iofy Corp.

***Night Road.** abr. ed. Kristin Hannah. (Running Time: 6 hrs.). 2011. 9.99 (978-1-4558-0194-7(1), 9781455801947, BAD) Brilliance Audio.

***Night Season.** unabr. ed. Chelsea Cain. (Running Time: 8 hrs. 30 mins. 0 sec.). (ENG.). 2011. audio compact disk 34.99 (978-1-4272-1150-7(7)) Pub: Macmill Audio. Dist(s): Macmillan

Night Secrets. unabr. ed. Cherry Adair. (Running Time: 10 hrs. 5 mins.). 2008. 29.95 (978-1-4332-5285-3(6)); audio compact disk 19.95 (978-1-4332-5529-8(4)) Blckstn Audio.

Night Secrets. unabr. ed. Thomas H. Cook. Narrated by George Guidall. 7 cass. (Running Time: 9 hrs. 30 mins.). (Frank Clemons Mystery Ser.: Vol. 3). 1994. 60.00 (978-0-7887-0031-6(6), 94230E7) Recorded Bks.

An exotic gypsy woman who stands accused of murder becomes the obsession of New York private eye Frank Clemons.

Night Secrets: A Novel. unabr. ed. Cherry Adair. (Running Time: 10 hrs. 5 mins.). 2008. 65.95 (978-1-4332-5283-9(X)); audio compact disk 90.00 (978-1-4332-5284-6(8)) Blckstn Audio.

Night Shadow. unabr. ed. Cherry Adair. Read by Carrington MacDuffie. (Running Time: 7.5 hrs. NaN mins.). 2008. 29.95 (978-1-4332-5445-1(X)) Blckstn Audio.

Night Shadow. unabr. ed. Cherry Adair. (Running Time: 7.5 hrs. 0 mins.). 2008. audio compact disk 19.95 (978-1-4332-5530-4(8)) Blckstn Audio.

Night Shadow: A Novel. unabr. ed. Cherry Adair. Read by Carrington MacDuffie. (Running Time: 7.5 hrs. NaN mins.). 2008. audio compact disk 60.00 (978-1-4332-5444-4(1)); audio compact disk 54.95 (978-1-4332-5443-7(3)) Blckstn Audio.

Night She Died. unabr. ed. Dorothy Simpson. Read by Bruce Montague. 8 cass. (Running Time: 7 hrs. 30 min.). (Isis Ser.). (J). 1991. 69.95

An Asterisk (*) at the beginning of an entry indicates that the title is appearing for the first time.

(978-1-85089-822-1(7), 91115) Pub: ISIS Lrg Prnt GBR. Dist(s): Ulverscroft US

Night Sins. abr. ed. Tami Hoag. Read by Joyce Bean. 4 cass. (Running Time: 6 hrs.). 2002. 53.25 (978-1-58788-638-6(3), 1587886383, Lib Edit) Brilliance Audio.
A peaceful Minnesota town, where crime is something that just doesn't happen, is about to face its worst nightmare. A young boy disappears. There are no witnesses, no clues - only a note, cleverly taunting, casually cruel. Has a cold-blooded kidnapper struck? Or is this a reawakening of a long-quiet serial killer? A tough-minded investigator on her first make-or-break case . . . A local cop who fears that big city evils have come to stalk his small town home . . . Together they are hunting for a madman who knows no bounds, to protect a town that may never feel safe again.

Night Sins. abr. ed. Tami Hoag. Read by Joyce Bean. (Running Time: 6 hrs.). 2006. 39.25 (978-1-4233-0160-8(9), 9781423301608, BADLE); 24.95 (978-1-4233-0159-2(5), 9781423301592, BAD); 24.95 (978-1-4233-0157-8(9), 9781423301578, Brilliance MP3); audio compact disk 39.25 (978-1-4233-0158-5(7), 9781423301585, Brlnc Audio MP3 Lib); audio compact disk 16.99 (978-1-4233-1931-3(1), 9781423319313, BCD Value Price) Brilliance Audio.

Night Sins. abr. ed. Tami Hoag. Read by Joyce Bean. (Running Time: 6 hrs.). 2009. audio compact disk 9.99 (978-1-4418-0839-4(6), 9781441808394, BCD Value Price) Brilliance Audio.

Night Sins, abr. ed. Tami Hoag. Read by Rosalind Allen. 2 cass. (Running Time: 3 hrs.). 1996. 17.00 (978-1-56876-058-2(2), 394501) Soundlines Ent.
This New York Times Bestseller is the prequel to Guilty As Sin, in this first novel, Deerlake Minnesota is rocked by the bizarre kidnapping of Josh Kirkwood. With very little leads & only the eery notes left by the kidnapper, Megan O'Malley, a field agent for the Minnesota Bureau of Criminal Apprehension & Mitch Holt the local chief of Police must go hunting for a madman who knows no bounds.

Night Sky. unabr. ed. Clare Francis. Read by Robert Powell. 18 cass. (Running Time: 24 hrs. 30 mins.). 2001. 127.95 (978-0-7540-0621-3(2), CAB 2044) Pub: Chivers Audio Bks GBR. Dist(s): AudioGO
Three people find their lives inextricably interwoven in a web of courage, betrayal & love: Julie Lescaux, a young Englishwoman caught up in dangerous operations of the French Resistance; Paul Vasson, the vicious Paris pimp turned Nazi collaborator & David Freymann, a German scientist caught up in unimaginable horror, destined to lose everything except his faith in his own discovery.

Night Soldiers. collector's ed. Alan Furst. Read by Stuart Langton. 11 cass. (Running Time: 16 hrs. 30 min.). 2000. 88.00 (978-0-7366-5572-9(7)) Books on Tape.
In Bulgaria in 1934, nineteen-year-old Khristo Stoianev sees his brother kicked to death by a gang of strutting thugs. Realizing a growing menace of fascism, he takes a risk on the promise of communism & flees to Moscow, where he is trained as an agent of the NKVD, precursor of the KGB. His first mission is to Catalonia, where he is soon caught up in the bloody horrors of the Spanish Civil War. Then he learns that he is to become the victim of one of Stalin's purges & is forced to flee once again, this time to Paris. He is a hunted man & before his silent war is over, every rule will be broken... & all loyalties discarded.

Night Sounds. Ed. by Kent Harrison. 1 cass. (Running Time: 1 hr.). (J). (ps up). 1989. 7.95 (978-0-9625388-1-0(7)) Ursa Major Corp.
A relaxing, soothing rendition of authentic nature sounds of crickets, Great Grey Owls, distant coyotes, & Great Horned Owls. Night Sounds brings inside the serenity of nature's symphony. Great for background music or as an aid to relaxation or sleep.

Night Stalker: The Life & Crime of Richard Ramirez. abr. ed. Philip Carlo. Read by Danny Aiello. 2 cass. (Running Time: 3 hrs.). 1998. 16.95 (978-1-882071-83-8(2), 634043) B-B Audio.
From out of the darkness he comes, silent and deadly. Cloaked all in black, he moves in shadows, blending and becoming one with them. No one ever sees him.....until it is too late.He is one of the most feared serial killers of all time. He is Richa.

Night Stalkers: Top Secret Missions of the U. S. Army's Special Operations. unabr. ed. Michael J. Durant & Steven Hartov. Read by Patrick G. Lawlor. Told to Robert L. Johnson. (Running Time: 11 hrs. 0 mins. 0 sec.). (ENG.). 2007. audio compact disk 75.99 (978-1-4001-3348-2(3)) Pub: Tantor Media. Dist(s): IngramPubServ

Night Stalkers: Top-Secret Missions of the U. S. Army's Special Operations Aviation Regiment. Michael J. Durant & Steven Hartov. Read by Patrick G. Lawlor. Told to Robert L. Johnson. (Playaway Adult Nonfiction Ser.). 2008. 69.99 (978-1-60640-710-3(4)) Find a World.

Night Stalkers: Top-Secret Missions of the U. S. Army's Special Operations Aviation Regiment. unabr. ed. Michael J. Durant & Steven Hartov. Read by Patrick G. Lawlor. Told to Robert L. Johnson. (Running Time: 11 hrs. 0 mins. 0 sec.). (ENG.). 2007. audio compact disk 24.99 (978-1-4001-5348-0(4)) Pub: Tantor Media. Dist(s): IngramPubServ

Night Stalkers: Top Secret Missions of the U. S. Army's Special Operations Aviation Regiment. unabr. ed. Steven Hartov & Michael J. Durant. Read by Patrick G. Lawlor. (Running Time: 11 hrs. 0 mins. 0 sec.). (ENG.). 2007. audio compact disk 37.99 (978-1-4001-0348-5(7)) Pub: Tantor Media. Dist(s): IngramPubServ

***Night Star.** unabr. ed. Alyson Noël. Read by Katie Schorr. 7 CDs. (Running Time: 8 hrs.). (ENG., (YA). 2010. audio compact disk 29.99 (978-1-4272-1065-4(9)) Pub: Macmill Audio. Dist(s): Macmillan

Night Stuff see Carl Sandburg Reading Cool Tombs & Other Poems

Night the Animals Talked (The Nativity) 1 cass. (Running Time: 1 hr.). (J). 3.98 Clamshell. (978-1-55886-146-6(7), BB/PT 453) Smarty Pants.

Night the Bear Ate Goombaw, unabr. ed. Patrick F. McManus. 34.00 (94759R4) Recorded Bks.

Night the Bear Ate Goombaw. unabr. ed. Patrick F. McManus. Narrated by Norman Dietz. 4 cass. (Running Time: 6 hrs.). 1996. 35.00 (978-0-7887-0754-4(X), 94759E7) Recorded Bks.
A collection of hilarious short pieces about fishing, its exotic equipment & activities like "gunkholing".

Night the Stars Fell. 1 cass. (Running Time: 25 min.). 14.95 (8366) MMI Corp.
Discussion of meteor astronomy. Covers meteors, asteroids, planetoids, comets, meteor showers, path of comets & more.

Night the White Deer Died, unabr. ed. Gary Paulsen. Narrated by Mark Hammer. 2 pieces. (Running Time: 2 hrs. 45 mins.). (gr. 7 up). 1994. 19.00 (978-0-7887-0069-9(3), 94302E7) Recorded Bks.
A lonely girl finds a friend in the alcoholic Indian who haunts the town square begging for money. Paulsen rips away the Hollywood stereotypes to reveal the reality of Native American life today.

Night They Murdered Chelsea. unabr. ed. Margaret Hinxman. Read by Graham Roberts. 5 cass. (Running Time: 7 hrs.). 2000. 49.95 (978-1-86042-002-3(8), 20028) Pub: Soundings Ltd GBR. Dist(s): Ulverscroft US
When the news was leaked that scriptwriters were planning a gruesome end for one of the major figures in the long-running TV serial "Wild Fortune," no one could have guessed that on the night they murdered Chelsea, Dame Charlotte Saint-Clair, who played her, would be found murdered in a manner that precisely paralleled her death on screen.

Night Time! 1 CD. (Running Time: 50 mins.). 2002. bds. 15.95 (MA442-CD) Big Kids Prods.

Night to Remember. unabr. ed. Walter Lord. Read by Fred Williams. 4 cass. (Running Time: 5 hrs. 30 mins.). 1998. 32.95 (978-0-7861-1289-0(1), 2190) Blckstn Audio.
This is the story of the "unsinkable" Titanic. She was four city blocks long, with the latest, most ingenious safety devices, a French "sidewalk cafe," private promenade decks - but only twenty lifeboats for the 2,207 passengers & crew on board. Gliding through a calm sea, disdainful of all obstacles, the Titanic brushed an iceberg. Two hours & forty minutes later, she upended & sank. Only 705 survivors were picked up from her half-filled boats. And she had been called "the ship that God Himself couldn't sink".

Night to Remember. unabr. ed. Walter Lord. Read by Martin Jarvis. 6 cass. (Running Time: 9 hrs.). 2000. 49.95 (978-0-7540-0185-0(7), CAB 1608) Pub: Chivers Audio Bks GBR. Dist(s): AudioGO
"God Himself could not sink this ship!" On April 10th, 1912, the unsinkable Titanic left Southampton on her maiden voyage to New York. At 11:40 p.m. on April 14th, the Titanic struck an iceberg and was lost. 1,500 people died at sea.

Night to Remember. unabr. ed. Walter Lord. Narrated by Richard M. Davidson. 4 cass. (Running Time: 5 hrs. 45 mins.). 1995. 35.00 (978-0-7887-0390-4(0), 94582E7) Recorded Bks.
Lord's classic account of the last hours of the "unsinkable" ship, the "Titanic" & the subsequent rescue of the survivors was originally published in 1955. Lord, working from survivors' published accounts, interviews with survivors & their relatives, & contemporary news coverage, constructs a picture of the collision with the iceberg, the subsequent events & the confluence of errors that likened the event to a classic Greek tragedy in which only 1500 of the total 2200 passengers & crew survived.

***Night to Remember.** unabr. ed. Walter Lord. Read by Fred Williams. (Running Time: 5 hrs. 30 mins.). 2010. 29.95 (978-1-4417-4394-7(4)); audio compact disk 55.00 (978-1-4417-4391-6(X)) Blckstn Audio.

Night to Remember & the Night Lives On. unabr. ed. Walter Lord. Read by Wolfram Kandinsky. 10 cass. (Running Time: 15 hrs.). 1990. 80.00 (978-0-7366-1742-0(6), 2582) Books on Tape.
A Night to Remember is the story of the "unsinkable" Titanic. "The ship that God himself couldn't sink" was built by the White Star Line & billed as the largest & most glamorous ship in the world. Her maiden voyage was an event attracting some of society's finest, including members of the Astor family. Gliding through a calm sea, disdainful of all obstacles, the Titanic brushed an iceberg in mid-Atlantic. Less than three hours later, early in the morning of April 15, 1912, she disappeared below the surface taking with her 1500 souls. It was a disaster that rocked the world. "All the drama, horror, tragedy of that grim heart-breaking night are here, never before presented in such superb narrative style". The Night Lives On was prompted by the 1985 discovery of the hulk on the ocean's floor. Walter Lord discusses the enduring public fascination with this tragedy. He examines the many questions asked at the time & the several that persist to this day.

Night Too Dark. unabr. ed. Dana Stabenow. Read by Marguerite Gavin. (Running Time: 10 hrs. 0 mins. 0 sec.). (Kate Shugak Novels Ser.). (ENG.). 2010. audio compact disk 39.99 (978-1-4272-0888-0(3)) Pub: Macmill Audio. Dist(s): Macmillan

Night Tourist. Katherine Marsh. Read by Andrew Rannels. (Running Time: 17160 sec.). (ENG.). (J). (gr. 4-7). 2007. audio compact disk 49.95 (978-0-545-02491-4(9)) Scholastic Inc.

Night Tourist. unabr. ed. Katherine Marsh. Read by Andrew Rannels. (YA). 2007. 49.99 (978-1-60252-851-2(9)) Find a World.

Night Tourist. unabr. ed. Katherine Marsh. Read by Andrew Rannels. 4 CDs. (Running Time: 4 hrs. 46 mins.). (ENG.). (J). (gr. 4-7). 2007. audio compact disk 29.95 (978-0-545-02465-5(X)) Scholastic Inc.

Night Train. Perf. by Rex Harrison. 1 cass. (Running Time: 1 hr.). 1946. 7.95 (DD-8445) Natl Recrd Co.
In "Night Train," Rex is a British agent who is in Germany trying to keep a secret formula from the hands of the Nazis. Two very British "blokes" help him when he is discovered by the Nazis to be a British spy. "Three Cheers for Miss Bishop" is a story of a school teacher who teaches Freshman English. The loves, disappointments, triumphs, happiness & feelings of accomplishment are all involved in this heart-warming story.

Night Train to Memphis. unabr. ed. Elizabeth Peters, pseud. Read by Kathleen Turner. 6 CDs. (Running Time: 6 hrs.). (Vicky Bliss Mystery Ser.). 2001. audio compact disk 30.00 (978-1-885608-46-8(2)) Airplay.
Here is her fifth caper. Vicky Bliss is Egypt bound to help solve a murder & uncover a thief.The thief turns out to be none other than Vicki's missing lover,the master of disguise "John Smythe!" Is Vicky up the Nile river & in over her beautiful blonde head?.

Night Train to Memphis. unabr. ed. Elizabeth Peters, pseud. Read by Kathleen Turner. 6 cass. (Running Time: 10 hrs.). (Vicky Bliss Mystery Ser.). 1997. 28.00 (978-1-885608-26-0(8)) Airplay.
Here is her fifth caper Vicky Bliss is Egypt bound to help solve a murder & uncover a thief. The thief turns out to be none other than Vicki's missing lover. The master of disguise "John Smythe!" Is Vicky up the Nile river & in over her beautiful blonde head.

Night Train to Memphis. unabr. ed. Elizabeth Peters, pseud. Read by Grace Conlin. 9 cass. (Running Time: 13 hrs.). (Vicky Bliss Mystery Ser.). 1996. 62.95 (978-0-7861-1065-0(1), 1836) Blckstn Audio.
An assistant curator of Munich's National Museum, Vicky is no expert on Egypt, but she does have a Ph.D. in solving crimes. So when an intelligence agency offers her a luxury Nile cruise if she'll help solve a murder & stop a heist of Egyptian antiquities, all 5'11" of her takes the plunge.

***Night Train to Memphis.** unabr. ed. Elizabeth Peters, pseud. Read by Grace Conlin. (Running Time: 13 hrs.). 2010. audio compact disk 29.95 (978-1-4417-3584-3(4)) Blckstn Audio.

Night Train to Memphis. unabr. ed. Elizabeth Peters, pseud. Narrated by Barbara Rosenblat. 10 cass. (Running Time: 13 hrs. 45 mins.). (Vicky Bliss Mystery Ser.). 1995. 85.00 (978-0-7887-0109-2(6), 94372E7) Recorded Bks.
Vicky Bliss goes in pursuit of a gang of art thieves on a luxury cruise down the Nile.

Night Train to Turkistan. unabr. collector's ed. Stuart Stevens. Read by Bill Whitaker. 5 cass. (Running Time: 7 hrs. 30 mins.). 1990. 40.00 (978-0-7366-1801-4(5), 2638) Books on Tape.
Night Train to Turkistan is high spirited & funny, but it is also much more. It is an encounter with a gifted young observer who shares his intimate experiences & reflections with us.

***Night Vision.** Randy Wayne White. (Doc Ford Ser.). (ENG.). 2011. audio compact disk 39.95 (978-0-14-242891-7(4), PengAudBks) Penguin Grp USA.

Night Visitor. unabr. ed. Gillian White. Read by Jilly Bond. 8 CDs. (Running Time: 9 hrs. 38 mins.). (Isis (CDs) Ser.). (J). 2004. audio compact disk 79.95 (978-0-7531-2267-9(7)) Pub: ISIS Lrg Prnt GBR. Dist(s): Ulverscroft US

Night Visitor: Nicodemus: John 3:1-8. Ed Young. (J). 1978. 4.95 (978-0-7417-1031-4(5), A0031) Win Walk.

Night Vistor. unabr. ed. Gillian White. Read by Jilly Bond. 8 cass. (Running Time: 9 hrs. 38 min.). (Isis Ser.). (J). 2001. 69.95 (978-0-7531-1138-3(1)) Pub: ISIS Lrg Prnt GBR. Dist(s): Ulverscroft US
Rose's early life was full of tragedy. Her father disappeared one night, presumed drowned, and her twin brother died when he was only ten, on a bike that had been his cherished birthday present. No wonder she depends on her husband, Michael. He is the only certainty in her life, and provides her with love and stability. All Rose asks of Michael is complete fidelity, and when she has cause to doubt him she devises a terrible revenge.

***Night Walk.** As told by Frances Rinaldi. (ENG.). (J). 2010. audio compact disk 9.97 (978-0-9826047-3-1(4)) Red FoxLLC FL.

Night Watch. unabr. ed. Terry Pratchett. Read by Stephen Briggs. 11 CDs. (Running Time: 42000 sec.). (Discworld Ser.). 2003. audio compact disk 99.95 (978-0-7531-1649-4(9)) Pub: ISIS Lrg Prnt GBR. Dist(s): Ulverscroft US

Night Watch. unabr. ed. Terry Pratchett. 9 cass. (Discworld Ser.). (J). 2003. 76.95 (978-0-7531-1568-8(9)) Pub: ISIS Lrg Prnt GBR. Dist(s): Ulverscroft US

Night Watch. unabr. ed. Sarah Waters. Read by Juanita McMahon. 16 CDs. (Running Time: 69300 sec.). 2006. audio compact disk 39.99 (978-1-4193-7535-4(0)) Recorded Bks.

Night Watch. unabr. collector's ed. David Atlee Phillips. Read by John MacDonald. 9 cass. (Running Time: 13 hrs. 30 min.). 1987. 72.00 (978-0-7366-1180-0(0), 2100) Books on Tape.
For 25 years David Atlee Phillips stood "the night watch" for the CIA. Phillips details his experiences in 18 countries. Along the way, we learn much about "The Company," certainly one of the least understood & most controversial pillars of our defense ever to have been invented.

Night Watcher. John Lutz. Read by Scott Brick. 2002. 80.00 (978-0-7366-8928-1(1)); audio compact disk 104.00 (978-0-7366-8937-3(0)) Books on Tape.

Night Winds. 1 cass. (Running Time: 1 hr.). (Interludes Music Ser.). 1989. 9.95 (978-1-55569-294-0(X), MOD-3907) Great Am Audio.

***Night Without Armor.** abr. ed. Jewel. (ENG.). 2006. (978-0-06-114195-9(X), Harper Audio); (978-0-06-114194-2(1), Harper Audio) HarperCollins Pubs.

Night Woman. unabr. ed. Nancy Price. Read by Donada Peters. 7 cass. (Running Time: 10 hrs. 30 min.). 1993. 56.00 (978-0-7366-2344-5(2), 3123) Books on Tape.
Mary Eliot wrote the books that made her husband famous. She thought his death would free the secret but it may cost her life.

Night Work. Laurie R. King. Narrated by Alyssa Bresnahan. 10 CDs. (Running Time: 11 hrs. 45 mins.). (Kate Martinelli Mystery Ser.: No. 4). audio compact disk 97.00 (978-0-7887-9863-4(4)) Recorded Bks.

Night Work. unabr. ed. Nelson George. Narrated by Mark Johnson. 4 cass. (Running Time: 6 hrs.). 2003. 39.75 (978-1-4025-6629-5(8), F0147MC, Griot Aud) Recorded Bks.

Night Work. unabr. ed. Steve Hamilton. Read by Dick Hill. (Running Time: 8 hrs.). 2007. 39.25 (978-1-4233-0726-6(7), 9781423307266, BADLE); 24.95 (978-1-4233-0725-9(9), 9781423307259, BAD); 74.25 (978-1-4233-0720-4(8), 9781423307204, BrilAudUnabridg); audio compact disk 29.95 (978-1-4233-0721-1(6), 9781423307211, Bril Audio CD Unabri); audio compact disk 24.95 (978-1-4233-0723-5(2), 9781423307235, Brilliance MP3); audio compact disk 87.25 (978-1-4233-0722-8(4), 9781423307228, BriAudCD Unabrid); audio compact disk 39.25 (978-1-4233-0724-2(0), 9781423307242, Brlnc Audio MP3 Lib) Brilliance Audio.

Night Work. unabr. ed. Laurie R. King. Narrated by Alyssa Bresnahan. 8 cass. (Running Time: 11 hrs. 45 mins.). (Kate Martinelli Mystery Ser.: No. 4). 2001. 74.00 (978-0-7887-4363-4(5), 96314E7) Recorded Bks.
Kate yearns for a period of routine assignments, instead a string of murders has San Francisco police baffled & her attempts to find a common thread will pull her far beyond her area.

Nightbeat, collector's ed. Perf. by Frank Lovejoy. 6 cass. (Running Time: 9 hrs.). 1998. bk. 17.49 (4013) Radio Spirits.
18 episodes from the 50s series about Randy Stone, a top reporter for The Chicago Star.

Nightbeat: The Black Cat & Big John McMasters. Perf. by Frank Lovejoy. 1 cass. (Running Time: 1 hr.). 2001. 6.98 (2622) Radio Spirits.

Nightbeat: Young Girl Framed for Murder & Is Showgirl a Pickpocket? Perf. by Frank Lovejoy. 1 cass. (Running Time: 1 hr.). 2001. 6.98 (1691) Radio Spirits.

Nightcrawlers. unabr. ed. Bill Pronzini. Read by Nick Sullivan. (Nameless Detective Mystery Ser.). 2005. 29.95 (978-0-7927-3499-4(8), CMP 764); 49.95 (978-0-7927-3497-0(1), CSL 764); audio compact disk 64.95 (978-0-7927-3498-7(X), SLD 764) AudioGO.

Nightfall see Best of Isaac Asimov

Nightfall. Bill Howell. 3 CDs. (Running Time: 4 hrs. 30 mins.). 2005. audio compact disk 19.95 (978-0-660-18960-4(7)) Pub: Canadian Broadcasting CAN. Dist(s): Georgetown Term

***Nightfall.** Stephen Leather. 2010. 61.95 (978-1-4450-0294-1(9)); audio compact disk 84.95 (978-1-4450-0295-8(7)) Pub: Isis Pubng Ltd GBR. Dist(s): Ulverscroft US

Nightfall. Silent Sound. 1 CD. (Running Time: 49 mins.). 2002. audio compact disk 16.98 (978-1-891319-67-9(1)) Spring Hill CO.

***Nightfall: After Sunset, Wind Chill, Dark Side of the Mind, Buried Alive, Vol. 2 Eerie.** Brian Taylor et al. 2009. (978-1-60136-549-1(7)) Audio Holding.

***Nightfall: Hands off, Assassin Game, the Repossession, the Book of Hell, Vol. 1 Terror.** John Graham et al. 2009. (978-1-60136-548-4(9)) Audio Holding.

***Nightfall: In the Eye of the Beholder, the Jogger, the Devil's Backbone, Camilla, Vol. 4 Chiller.** Burke Campbell et al. 2009. (978-1-60136-551-4(9)) Audio Holding.

***Nightfall: The Contract, Baby Doll, the Brides of Olivera, Future Fear, Vol. 5 Fear.** John Richard Wright et al. 2009. (978-1-60136-552-1(7)) Audio Holding.

***Nightfall: The Maid's Bell, the Thinking Room, Where Does the News Come from?, Wildcats, Vol. 3 Dread.** Edith Wharton et al. 2009. (978-1-60136-550-7(0)) Audio Holding.

***Nightfall: The Willoughby Obsession, the Old Post Road, Angel of Death, the Room, Vol. 6 Scream.** G. R. Robertson et al. 2009. (978-1-60136-553-8(5)) Audio Holding.

Nightfire: A Visit to Cleveland General. Sydney J. Van Scyoc. Dramatization. 1985. 9.95 Audio Saga.
Two science fiction tales that take place in the future. "Nightfire" takes place during the War of the Americas when non-combatants were sentenced to forty years of satellite and hoverpod confinement. "Cleveland General": A dark comedy about hospitals of the future.

Nightgown of the Sullen Moon. Nancy Willard. (J). 1986. 20.00 (978-0-676-31050-4(8)) SRA McGraw.

Nightingale see Palgrave's Golden Treasury of English Poetry

***Nightingale.** Anonymous. 2009. (978-1-60136-600-9(0)) Audio Holding.

Nightingale. unabr. ed. Hans Christian Andersen. Narrated by Aurora Wetzel. 1 cass. (Running Time: 1 hr. 30 min.).Tr. of Nattergalen. (J). (ps up). 1992. 9.95 (978-1-887393-02-7(1)) Aurora Audio.
True art vs. artificiality.

Nightingale & the Rose see Ruiseñor y la Rosa - El Cumpleaños de la Infanta

Nightingale & the Rose. Oscar Wilde. Read by Carlos Zambrano. (Running Time: 1 hr.). 2002. 14.95 (978-1-60083-146-1(X), Audiofy Corp) Iofy Corp.

Nightingale & the Rose: And The Selfish Giant. unabr. ed. Oscar Wilde. Narrated by Aurora Wetzel. 1 cass. (Running Time: 1 hr. 30 min.). (J). (ps up). 1994. 9.95 (978-1-887393-09-6(9)) Aurora Audio.
Two beautiful fairy tales.

Nightingale Collection. Narrated by Tom Bosley. (Running Time: 1 hr. 30 mins.). 2006. 14.95 (978-1-60083-008-2(0)) Iofy Corp.

Nightingale Legacy. abr. ed. Catherine Coulter. Read by Anne Flosnik. (Running Time: 5 hrs.). (Legacy Ser.: Vol. 2). 2010. audio compact disk 14.99 (978-1-4418-3524-6(5), 9781441835246, BACD) Brilliance Audio.

Nightingale Legacy. unabr. ed. Catherine Coulter. Read by Monica Buckley. 10 cass. (Running Time: 13 hrs.). (Legacy Ser.: Vol. 2). 2002. 29.95 (978-1-59086-575-0(8), 1590865758) Brilliance Audio.
On the eve of her nineteenth birthday, the vivacious Caroline Derwent-Jones looks forward to being free of her oafish guardian, Mr. Ffalkes. But Mr. Ffalkes has other plans for Caroline and her inheritance; Caroline must escape. In her flight, Caroline encounters Lord Chilton of Mount Hawke, Frederic North Nightingale, and finds herself tangled in mystery and romance. Amid murder, enigmatic secrets, and a long standing tradition of no women at Mount Hawke, Lord Chilton discovers his desire for Caroline.

Nightingale Legacy. unabr. ed. Catherine Coulter. Read by Monica Buckley. (Running Time: 13 hrs.). (Legacy Ser.: Vol. 2). 2004. 39.25 (978-1-59335-593-7(9), 1593355939, Brlnc Audio MP3 Lib) Brilliance Audio.

Nightingale Legacy. unabr. ed. Catherine Coulter. Read by Monica Buckley. (Running Time: 13 hrs.). (Legacy Ser.: Vol. 2). 2004. 39.25 (978-1-59710-534-7(1), 1597105341, BADLE); 24.95 (978-1-59710-535-4(X), 159710535X, BAD) Brilliance Audio.

Nightingale Legacy. unabr. ed. Catherine Coulter. Read by Monica Buckley. (Running Time: 13 hrs.). (Legacy Ser.: Vol. 2). 2010. audio compact disk 29.99 (978-1-4418-3525-3(3), 9781441835253, Bril Audio CD Unabri); audio compact disk 89.97 (978-1-4418-3526-0(1), 9781441835260, BriAudCD Unabrid) Brilliance Audio.

Nightingale Legacy. unabr. ed. Catherine Coulter. Read by Monica Buckley. (Running Time: 13 hrs.). (Legacy Ser.: Vol. 2). 2004. 24.95 (978-1-59335-143-4(7), 1593351437) Soulmate Audio Bks.

Nightingales: And Other Stories. Short Stories. Jon Manchip White. Read by Jon Manchip White. 1 cass. (Running Time: 72 mins.). 1997. 10.00 (978-0-916078-15-7(9), Iris) Iris Pub Group.
Jon Manchip White reads fantastic stories based on Welsh traditions and myths. Short stretches of Welsh folk music played on a harp puntuate the stories.

Nightingale's Song. unabr. ed. Robert Timberg. Read by Patrick G. Lawlor. (Running Time: 17 hrs. 50 mins.). 2008. 44.95 (978-1-4332-6040-7(9)); 95.95 (978-1-4332-6036-0(0)); audio compact disk 120.00 (978-1-4332-6037-7(9)); audio compact disk 29.95 (978-1-4332-6039-1(5)) Blckstn Audio.

Nightjohn. Gary Paulsen. Narrated by Michele-Denise Woods. 2 CDs. (Running Time: 1 hr. 30 mins.). (gr. 7 up). audio compact disk 22.00 (978-0-7887-9523-7(6)) Recorded Bks.

Nightjohn. unabr. ed. Gary Paulsen. Narrated by Michele-Denise Woods. 2 pieces. (Running Time: 1 hr. 30 mins.). (gr. 7 up). 2001. 19.00 (978-1-55690-854-5(7), 93222E7) Recorded Bks.
Twelve-year old Sarny's brutal life as a slave becomes even more dangerous when a newly arrived slave offers to teach her how to read.

Nightlife. unabr. ed. Thomas Perry. Narrated by Shelly Frasier. 13 CDs. (Running Time: 12 hrs. 30 mins. 0 sec.). (ENG.). 2006. audio compact disk 79.99 (978-1-4001-3241-6(X)); audio compact disk 29.99 (978-1-4001-5241-4(0)); audio compact disk 39.99 (978-1-4001-0241-9(3)) Pub: Tantor Media. Dist(s): IngramPubServ
When the cousin of Los Angeles underworld figure Hugo Poole is found shot to death in his Portland, Oregon, home, police find nothing at the scene of the crime except several long strands of blond hair hinting that a second victim may have been involved. Hotel security tapes from the victim's last vacation reveal an out-of-focus picture of a young blond woman entering and leaving his room. Could she also be a murder victim? Portland homicide detective Catherine Hobbes is determined to solve the case and locate the missing blonde, but her feelings, and the investigation, are complicated when Hugo hires private detective Joe Pitt to perform a parallel investigation. As Joe and Catherine form an uneasy alliance, the murder count rises-and both realize that the pretty young woman in the security tapes is not a victim at all. As Catherine follows the evidence, she finds herself in a deadly contest with an unpredictable adversary capable of changing her appearance and identity at will. Catherine must use everything she knows, as a homicide detective and as a woman, to stop a murderer who kills on impulse and with ease, and who becomes more efficient and elusive with each crime.

Nightmare Abbey. Thomas Peacock. Read by Flo Gibson. 2 cass. (Running Time: 3 hrs.). 1996. 14.95 (978-1-55685-413-2(7)) Audio Bk Con.
With Mr. Flosky perhaps representing a caricature of Coleridge, Scythrop Glowry as Shelley & Mr. Cypress as Byron, the author satirizes concepts of romanticism in England in the early 1800's.

***Nightmare Academy.** unabr. ed. Dean Lorey. Read by Oliver Wyman. (ENG.). 2007. (978-0-06-154637-2(2)); (978-0-06-154638-9(0)) HarperCollins Pubs.

Nightmare along Pennsylvania Avenue. unabr. ed. Perry Stone. Narrated by Tim Lundeen. (Running Time: 13 hrs. 0 mins. 0 sec.). (ENG.). 2009. 25.89 (978-1-60814-627-7(8)); audio compact disk 36.99 (978-1-59859-681-6(0)) Oasis Audio.

***Nightmare as a Child.** (ENG.). 2010. audio compact disk (978-1-59171-272-5(6)) Falcon Picture.

Nightmare at Noon see Poetry of Benet

***Nightmare at 2,000 Feet.** (ENG.). 2010. audio compact disk (978-1-59171-250-3(5)) Falcon Picture.

Nightmare at 20,000 Feet. unabr. ed. Richard Matheson. (Running Time: 10 hrs. 50 mins.). (ENG.). 2009. 29.95 (978-1-4332-7291-2(1)); 65.95 (978-1-4332-7287-5(3)); audio compact disk 100.00 (978-1-4332-7288-2(1)) Blckstn Audio.

Nightmare Begins. abr. ed. Jerry Ahern. Read by Charlie O'Dowd. 2 vols. No. 2. 2003. pap. bk. (978-1-58807-812-4(4)) Am Pubng Inc.

Nightmare Begins. abr. ed. Jerry Ahern. Read by Charlie O'Dowd. 2 cass. (Running Time: 3 hrs.). (Survivalist Ser.: No. 2). 2003. 18.00 (978-1-58807-303-7(3)) Am Pubng Inc.

Nightmare Flower, Bk. 1. Elizabeth Engstrom. Read by Marilyn Landbehn. 4 cass. (Running Time: 4 hrs. 30 min.). 1995. 26.95 (978-1-55686-568-8(6)) Books in Motion.
Quietly unnerving yet eloquent short tales about people, life & death that are both moving & thought provoking & in some cases spine-chilling.

Nightmare Flower, Bk. 2. unabr. ed. Elizabeth Engstrom. Read by Marilyn Langbehn. 4 cass. (Running Time: 5 hrs. 42 min.). 1995. 26.95 (978-1-55686-593-0(7)) Books in Motion.
Written in typical Engstrom style providing a slant on life both moving & thought-provoking, these novellas of dark fantasy will mystify & intrigue & nothing is as it appears.

Nightmare for Dr. Morelle. unabr. ed. Ernest Dudley. 4 cass. (Running Time: 6 hrs.). 1999. 39.95 (CAB 1705) AudioGO.

Nightmare for Future Reference see Poetry of Benet

Nightmare in Pink. unabr. ed. John D. MacDonald. Read by Michael Prichard. 6 cass. (Running Time: 9 hrs.). (Travis McGee Ser.: Vol. 2). 2001. 29.95 (978-0-7366-6787-6(3)) Books on Tape.
When a wartime buddy calls for help, McGee is there.

Nightmare in Pink. unabr. collector's ed. John D. MacDonald. Read by Michael Prichard. 6 cass. (Running Time: 6 hrs.). (Travis McGee Ser.: Vol. 2). 1983. 36.00 (978-0-7366-0700-1(5), 1663) Books on Tape.
McGee tackles a high-risk, freelance assignment as a favor to Mike, his old wartime Buddy. Mike's sister Nina needs help. Nina is dark-haired & delicately built, a self-possessed young woman with a flair for design who works in an advertising agency. Her fiance is dead, victim of murder & the rap laid on him doesn't stop there. McGee unearths a swindle so gigantic that an Army of accountants & attorneys are busy trying to keep it covered.

Nightmare Number Three see Poetry of Benet

Nightmare on Elm Street. abr. ed. New Line Cinema Staff. Read by Freddy Krueger. 1 cass. (Running Time: 1 hr.). 10.95 S&S Audio.

Nightmare Song (A Poem from the Poets' Corner) The One-and-Only Poetry Book for the Whole Family. unabr. ed. William S. Gilbert. Read by John Lithgow. John Lithgow. (Running Time: 10 mins.). (ENG.). 2008. 0.99 (978-1-60024-318-9(5)) Pub: Hachet Audio. Dist(s): HachBkGrp

Nightmare Stairs. unabr. ed. Robert Swindells. Read by Alison Reid. 3 CDs. (Running Time: 12000 sec.). (J). (gr. 4-6). 2006. audio compact disk 29.95 (978-1-4056-5575-0(5), Chivers Sound Lib) AudioGO.

Nightmare, with Angel see Poetry of Benet

Nightmares & Dreamscapes, Vol. 1. unabr. ed. Stephen King. Read by Stephen King. Read by Tim Curry et al. (Running Time: 9 hrs. 30 mins. 0 sec.). (ENG.). 2009. audio compact disk 39.99 (978-0-7435-8335-0(3)) Pub: S&S Audio. Dist(s): S and S Inc

Nightmares & Dreamscapes, Vol. 2. unabr. ed. Stephen King. Read by Stephen King. Read by Kathy Bates et al. (Running Time: 9 hrs. 30 mins. 0 sec.). (ENG.). 2009. audio compact disk 39.99 (978-0-7435-8337-4(X)) Pub: S&S Audio. Dist(s): S and S Inc

Nightmares & Dreamscapes, Vol. 3. unabr. ed. Stephen King. Read by Stephen King. Read by Gary Sinise et al. (Running Time: 8 hrs. 0 mins. 0 sec.). (ENG.). 2009. audio compact disk 39.99 (978-0-7435-8339-8(6)) Pub: S&S Audio. Dist(s): S and S Inc

***Nightmare's Edge.** Bryan Davis. (Running Time: 10 hrs. 40 mins. 0 sec.). (Echoes from the Edge Ser.). (ENG.). (YA). 2009. 12.99 (978-0-310-29427-6(4)) Zondervan.

Nightmares on Congress Street, Part IV. unabr. ed. Read by Full Cast Production Staff. Created by Rocky Coast Radio Theatre. (Running Time: 7200 sec.). (ENG.). 2005. audio compact disk 39.99 (978-1-4001-3191-4(X)) Pub: Tantor Media. Dist(s): IngramPubServ

Nightmares on Congress Street, Part IV. unabr. ed. W. W. Jacobs et al. (Running Time: 7200 sec.). (ENG.). 2005. audio compact disk 16.99 (978-1-4001-5191-2(0)) Pub: Tantor Media. Dist(s): IngramPubServ

Nightmares on Congress Street, Part IV. unabr. ed. Edgar Allan Poe et al. (Running Time: 7200 sec.). (ENG.). 2005. audio compact disk 19.99 (978-1-4001-0191-7(3)) Pub: Tantor Media. Dist(s): IngramPubServ

Nightmares on Congress Street, Part V. unabr. ed. Eileen Avery et al. Read by Full Cast Production Staff. (Running Time: 2 hrs. 0 mins. 0 sec.). (ENG.). 2006. audio compact disk 39.99 (978-1-4001-3263-8(0)) Pub: Tantor Media. Dist(s): IngramPubServ

Nightmares on Congress Street, Part V. unabr. ed. Rocky Coast Radio Theatre. Read by Full Cast Production Staff. (Running Time: 2 hrs. 0 mins. 0 sec.). (ENG.). 2006. audio compact disk 19.99 (978-1-4001-0263-1(4)) Pub: Tantor Media. Dist(s): IngramPubServ

Nightmares on Congress Street, Part 5. unabr. ed. Rocky Coast Radio Theatre. Read by Full Cast Production Staff. (Running Time: 2 hrs. 0 mins. 0 sec.). (ENG.). 2006. audio compact disk 16.99 (978-1-4001-5263-6(1)) Pub: Tantor Media. Dist(s): IngramPubServ

Nightriders: The Wells Fargo Trail. unabr. ed. Jim Walker. Narrated by Jack Garrett. 8 cass. (Running Time: 11 hrs.). 1994. 68.00 (978-0-7887-5479-1(3), K0063L8) Recorded Bks.
When a rash of gold robberies breaks out in California, Zac is dispatched to conduct an undercover investigation. He'll need to work fast, for an angered vigilante group is interpreting the law in its own way, & innocent people are being hanged. With his strong sense of moral justice & some help from a few honest friends, Zac will give the thieves more than they bargained for.

Nightrise. Anthony Horowitz. Read by Simon Prebble. 9. (Running Time: 10 hrs. 25 mins.). (Power of Five Ser.: Bk. 3). 2007. 67.75 (978-1-4281-5552-7(X)); audio compact disk 97.75 (978-1-4281-5557-2(0)) Recorded Bks.

Nightrose. abr. ed. Dorothy Garlock. Read by Jane Allen. 1 cass. (Running Time: 1 hr. 30 min.). 1994. 5.99 (978-1-57096-020-8(8), RAZ 917) Romance Alive Audio.
Fiercely independent, Katy Burns tries to protect her niece & her sister Mary, until rugged frontiersman Garrick Rowe's passionate attentions persuade her to surrender.

Nightrunners of Bengal. unabr. ed. John Masters. Narrated by Patrick Tull. 10 cass. (Running Time: 15 hrs. 30 mins.). 1990. 85.00 (978-1-55690-376-2(6), 90064E7) Recorded Bks.
Set during the Sepoy Mutiny of Indian soldiers in Bengal, India, in 1857, this historical novel focuses on British Capt. Rodney Savage of the 13th Rifles & his love for Sumitra, the Rani of Kishanpur (& widow of the murdered Rajah), as they race to uncover the mutinous conspirators & save an Empire.

Night's Black Agents. David Armstrong. 6 CDs. (Sound Ser.). (J). 2003. audio compact disk 64.95 (978-1-84283-517-3(3)) Pub: ISIS Lrg Prnt GBR. Dist(s): Ulverscroft US

Night's Black Agents. David Armstrong. Read by Michael Tudor Barnes. 5 cass. (Sound Ser.). (J). 2003. 49.95 (978-1-84283-245-5(X)) Pub: ISIS Lrg Prnt GBR. Dist(s): Ulverscroft US

Nights in Rodanthe. unabr. ed. Nicholas Sparks. Read by JoBeth Williams. (ENG.). 2005. 14.98 (978-1-59483-363-2(X)) Pub: Hachet Audio. Dist(s): HachBkGrp

Nights in Rodanthe. unabr. ed. Nicholas Sparks. Read by JoBeth Williams. 5 CDs. (Running Time: 5 hrs. 30 mins.). (ENG.). 2008. audio compact disk 17.98 (978-1-60024-291-5(X)) Pub: Hachet Audio. Dist(s): HachBkGrp

Nights in Rodanthe. unabr. ed. Nicholas Sparks. Read by JoBeth Williams. (Running Time: 5 hrs. 30 mins.). (ENG.). 2009. 49.98 (978-1-60788-084-4(9)) Pub: Hachet Audio. Dist(s): HachBkGrp

Nights in White Satin. unabr. ed. Michelle Spring. Read by Julia Sands. 8 cass. (Isis Ser.). (J). 2003. 69.95 (978-0-7531-0984-7(0)); audio compact disk 89.95 (978-0-7531-1725-5(8)) Pub: ISIS Lrg Prnt GBR. Dist(s): Ulverscroft US

Nights of Rain & Stars. unabr. ed. Maeve Binchy. Read by Terry Donnelly. 29.95 (978-0-7927-3327-0(4)); 54.95 (978-0-7927-3325-6(8)); audio compact disk 79.95 (978-0-7927-3326-3(6)) AudioGO.

***Nights of Villjamur.** unabr. ed. Mark Charan Newton. Narrated by Steven Crossley. (Running Time: 17 hrs. 0 mins. 0 sec.). (Legends of the Red Sun Ser.). (ENG.). 2010. 29.99 (978-1-4001-6760-9(4)); 21.99 (978-1-4001-8760-7(5)); audio compact disk 95.99 (978-1-4001-4760-1(3)); audio compact disk 39.99 (978-1-4001-1760-4(7)) Pub: Tantor Media. Dist(s): IngramPubServ

Nights on, Nights Off. Maggie Bennett & Margaret Sircom. 2007. 61.95 (978-1-84652-060-0(6)); audio compact disk 79.95 (978-1-84652-061-7(4)) Pub: Magna Story GBR. Dist(s): Ulverscroft US

***Nightshade.** unabr. ed. Andrea Cremer. Read by Rebecca Lowman. (Running Time: 11 hrs. 59 mins.). (ENG.). (J). 2010. audio compact disk 48.00 (978-0-307-74593-4(7), Listening Lib) Pub: Random Audio Pubg. Dist(s): Random

Nightshade. unabr. ed. John Saul. Read by Chet Green. 7 cass. (Running Time: 11 hrs.). 2000. 32.95 (978-1-56740-359-6(X), 156740359X, BAU) Brilliance Audio.

Nightshade. unabr. ed. John Saul. Read by Chet Green. (Running Time: 11 hrs.). 2005. 39.25 (978-1-59600-638-6(2), 9781596006386, BADLE); 24.95 (978-1-59600-637-9(4), 9781596006379, BAD); audio compact disk 24.95 (978-1-59600-635-5(8), 9781596006355, Brilliance MP3); audio compact disk 39.25 (978-1-59600-636-2(6), 9781596006362, Brlnc Audio MP3 Lib) Brilliance Audio.
A horrific shadow from the past . . . and a shocking tragedy in the present. Fifteen-year-old Matt Moore has a loving mother and a caring stepfather, a host of friends, and a growing relationship with the most beautiful girl in school. All signs point to a bright future, until fate intervenes. A sudden fire leave Matt's senile and troubled grandmother homeless. When she moves in with the family, her ceaseless demands cause unrelieved tension - and with her comes a shameful secret between her daughters that traps Matt between a dead aunt who haunts him and his own mother, who seeks redemption for her sister's sins - and her own.

Nightshade. unabr. ed. John Saul. Read by Chet Green. (Running Time: 10 hrs.). 2008. audio compact disk 97.25 (978-1-4233-3670-9(4), 9781423336709, BriAudCD Unabrid); audio compact disk 36.95 (978-1-4233-3669-3(0), 9781423336693, Bril Audio CD Unabri) Brilliance Audio.

Nightsong see Poetry & Voice of Marilyn Hacker

Nightsounds, Vol. I. Bill Shaugnessy et al. Ed. by Chelley Kitzmiller & Steven Sanders. 1 cass. (Running Time: 1 hr. 27 min.). (Nightsounds Audio Drama Ser.). 1988. 9.95 (978-0-929536-02-6(9)) Emb Cassettes.
Features short, dramatized, stories of horror & suspense designed for an adult listening audience.

Nighttime in the Desert & Other Desert Songs. unabr. ed. Perf. by Patty Horn & Butterfield Elementary School 'Bobcat Chorus'. 1 cass. (Running Time: 30 min.). (J). 1995. 8.95 (978-0-9644105-3-4(2)) Two Geckos Mus.
Desert songs for children set to guitar music & vocals.

Nighttime in the Desert & Other Desert Songs, Vol. 1. unabr. ed. Patty Horn. Perf. by Butterfield Elementary School 'Bobcat Chorus'. Illus. by Jason Keller. 1 cass. (Running Time: 30 min.). (J). (gr. k-5). 1995. pap. bk. 15.95 (978-0-9644105-5-8(9)) Two Geckos Mus.

Nighttime Is My Time. abr. ed. Mary Higgins Clark. Read by Jan Maxwell. (Running Time: 43 hrs. 0 mins. 0 sec.). (ENG.). 2009. audio compact disk 14.99 (978-0-7435-8332-9(9)) Pub: S&S Audio. Dist(s): S and S Inc

Nighttime Is My Time. unabr. ed. Mary Higgins Clark. Read by Jan Maxwell. 9 CDs. (Running Time: 80 hrs. 0 mins. 0 sec.). (ENG.). 2004. audio compact disk 39.95 (978-0-7435-3582-3(0), Audioworks) Pub: S&S Audio. Dist(s): S and S Inc

Nightwalker. unabr. ed. Heather Graham. Read by Tanya Eby Sirois & Tanya Fred Stella. (Running Time: 9 hrs.). 2009. 39.97 (978-1-4233-9129-6(2), 9781423391296, BADLE) Brilliance Audio.

Nightwalker. unabr. ed. Heather Graham. Read by Fred Stella & Tanya Eby Sirois. 1 MP3-CD. (Running Time: 9 hrs.). 2009. 24.99 (978-1-4233-9126-5(8), 9781423391265, Brilliance MP3) Brilliance Audio.

Nightwalker. unabr. ed. Heather Graham. Read by Tanya Eby Sirois & Fred Stella. 1 MP3-CD. (Running Time: 9 hrs.). 2009. 39.97 (978-1-4233-9127-2(6), 9781423391272, Brlnc Audio MP3 Lib) Brilliance Audio.

Nightwalker. unabr. ed. Heather Graham. Read by Fred Stella & Tanya Eby Sirois. 8 CDs. (Running Time: 9 hrs.). 2009. audio compact disk 34.99 (978-1-4233-9124-1(1), 9781423391241, Bril Audio CD Unabri) Brilliance Audio.

Nightwalker. unabr. ed. Heather Graham. Read by Tanya Eby Sirois & Fred Stella. 8 CDs. (Running Time: 9 hrs.). 2009. audio compact disk 97.97 (978-1-4233-9125-8(X), 9781423391258, BriAudCD Unabrid) Brilliance Audio.

Nightwalker. unabr. ed. Heather Graham. Read by Tanya Eby Sirois & Tanya Fred Stella. (Running Time: 9 hrs.). 2009. 24.99 (978-1-4233-9128-9(4), 9781423391289, BAD) Brilliance Audio.

Nightwalkers. abr. ed. Laura Simms. Read by Laura Simms. 2 cass. (Running Time: 1 hr. 45 min.). Dramatization. (Myth & the Natural World Ser.). 1993. 16.95 (978-0-939643-45-5(6), 3510, NrthWrd Bks) TandN Child.
A haunting collection of 12 contemporary & traditional ghost stories that explore the thin edge between the visible & invisible worlds.

Nightwalkers. unabr. ed. P. T. Deutermann. Read by Dick Hill. 1 MP3-CD. (Running Time: 12 hrs.). (Cam Richter Ser.). 2009. 24.99 (978-1-4233-3627-3(5), 9781423336273, Brilliance MP3); 39.97 (978-1-4233-3630-3(5), 9781423336303, BADLE); 24.99 (978-1-4233-3629-7(1), 9781423336297, BAD); 39.97 (978-1-4233-3628-0(3), 9781423336280, Brlnc Audio MP3 Lib); audio compact disk 36.99 (978-1-4233-3625-9(9), 9781423336259, Bril Audio CD Unabri); audio compact disk 97.97 (978-1-4233-3626-6(7), 9781423336266, BriAudCD Unabrid) Brilliance Audio.

Nightwatch. unabr. ed. Richard P. Henrick. Read by Michael Prichard. 8 cass. (Running Time: 12 hrs.). 2000. 48.00 (5177) Books on Tape.
When the President of the United States is assassinated on an isolated highway in the Crimea, & his Vice President's travel party is fired on by a Huey helicopter raining death, only the quick action of a Secret Service agent saved his life. Meanwhile, the mastermind of the coup attempt, the Chairman of the Joint Chiefs of Staff is ready to assume power. Who can save the country from a firestorm of treason, nuclear terror & death from within the nation's own halls of power.

Nightwing, unabr. ed. Martin Cruz Smith. Narrated by Richard Ferrone. 7 cass. (Running Time: 10 hrs.). 1991. 60.00 (978-1-55690-664-0(1), 91417E7) Recorded Bks.
An invasion of vampire bats threatens a south-western town & its inhabitants. The author of "Gorky Park" & "Polar Star," mixes Indian mythology with virology in this masterful thriller.

Nightwork. unabr. ed. Irwin Shaw. Read by Wolfram Kandinsky. 9 cass. (Running Time: 13 hrs. 30 min.). 1979. 72.00 (978-0-7366-0225-9(9), 1222) Books on Tape.
The narrative of two con men - one amateur (whose stolen bankroll sets the whole thing in motion) & one debonair professional, whose schemes are wild & hugely profitable.

Nighty-Nightmare. unabr. ed. James Howe. Read by Victor Garber. 2 vols. (Running Time: 1 hr. 49 mins.). (Bunnicula Ser.). (J). (gr. 3-7). 2004. pap. bk. 29.00 (978-0-8072-8397-4(5), YA201SP, Listening Lib); 23.00 (978-0-8072-8396-7(7), YA201CX, Listening Lib) Random Audio Pubg.
An overnight camping trip! Howie, the Monroe's faithful dog, is not excited & Chester the cat is worried. The woods, Chester informs Harold, are not only full of cockleburs & ticks, but of spirits, evil spirits who prey on the innocent. Harold is not taking Chester seriously. But when two strange men & their even stranger dog set up camp next to the Monroes, things begin to happen. Could Chester be right.

Nigun Anthology - Volume 1: A Collection of Soulful Jewish Melodies. Created by Hal Leonard Corporation Staff. 2004. pap. bk. 34.95 (978-0-8074-0907-7(3), 993265) Pub: URJ Pr. Dist(s): H Leonard

Niki Davies I'm Walking Down. Niki Davies. 2000. bk. 17.95 (978-1-85909-670-3(0), Warner Bro) Alfred Pub.

Nikki Giovanni. unabr. ed. Nikki Giovanni. Read by Nikki Giovanni. 1 cass. (Running Time: 1 hr.). 1988. 10.00 (021988) New Letters.
In an address given at Missouri Western State College during Black History Month in 1987, Giovanni mixes philosophy with a poetry reading.

Nikki Giovanni, Vol. II. unabr. ed. Ed. by Jim McKinley. Prod. by Rebekah Presson. 1 cass. (Running Time: 29 min.). (New Letters on the Air Ser.). 1994. 10.00 (013194) New Letters.
This is a studio recording featuring the outspoken & often outrageously opinionated "Black Princess of Poetry" Giovanni talks about her life, "I don't own an iron. The iron is the enemy of women" & her politics & reads poems from various books that she's published throughout the years. Giovanni has recently turned 50 & has many funny & insightful ideas about how to live & age gracefully.

Nikki Giovanni Poetry Collection. unabr. ed. Nikki Giovanni. Read by Nikki Giovanni. 4 CDs. (Running Time: 6 hrs.). 2002. audio compact disk 22.00 (978-0-06-051429-7(9)) HarperCollins Pubs.

Nikki the Invisible Girl: Nikki's Birthday Wish/Nikki & the Missing Jewels/Nikki & the Halloween Ghost. Ilona Bray. (Running Time: 3720 sec.). (J). (gr. k-6). 2007. audio compact disk 12.95 (978-1-933781-09-9(2)) TallTales Aud.

Niko Niko. 1 cass. (Running Time: 1 hr.). (Yoroshiku Ser.: Stages A and B). (JPN.). (J). (gr. k-5). EducServs AUS.

Nikolai Gogol: The Overcoat. unabr. ed. 2 cass., bklet. (Running Time: 2 hrs.). (RUS.). (YA). 1993. pap. bk. 39.50 (978-1-57970-012-6(8), SRU120) J Norton Pubs.

Nikolai Tolstoy I. unabr. ed. Leo Tolstoy. Read by Nikolai Tolstoy. 1 cass. (Running Time: 29 min.). 1989. 10.00 New Letters.
Tolstoy reads from The Coming of the King, a novel about Merlin & is interviewed.

Nikolai Tolstoy II: The Minister & the Massacres. unabr. ed. Leo Tolstoy. Read by Nikolai Tolstoy. Interview with Rebekah Presson. 1 cass. (Running Time: 29 min.). 1989. 10.00 (102089) New Letters.
In his book, "The Minister & the Massacre", Nikolai Tolstoy charges former British Prime Minister, Harold MacMillan, with responsibility in the forced repatriation of hundreds of thousands of White Russians & Royalist Yugoslavs.

Nimisha's Ship. unabr. ed. Anne McCaffrey. Read by Susan Ericksen. (Running Time: 11 hrs.). 2007. 39.25 (978-1-4233-3028-8(5), 9781423330288, BADLE); 24.95 (978-1-4233-3027-1(7), 9781423330271, BAD); audio compact disk 39.25 (978-1-4233-3026-4(9), 9781423330264, Brinc Audio MP3 Lib); audio compact disk 24.95 (978-1-4233-3025-7(0), 9781423330257, Brilliance MP3) Brilliance Audio.

Nimitz Class. unabr. ed. Patrick Robinson. Narrated by George Guidall. 13 CDs. (Running Time: 15 hrs. 45 mins.). 1999. audio compact disk 122.00 (978-0-7887-3434-2(2), C1040E7) Recorded Bks.
In 2002, the Nimitz-Class Carrier Thomas Jefferson, & her crew of 6,000 suddenly vanish from the radar screens. Did the mammoth ship actually self-destruct, or is there a more sinister cause of the catastrophe.

Nimitz Class, unabr. ed. Patrick Robinson. Narrated by George Guidall. 11 cass. (Running Time: 15 hrs. 45 mins.). 1997. 96.00 (978-0-7887-1296-8(9), 95130E7) Recorded Bks.
In 2002, the Nimitz-Class Carrier Thomas Jefferson & her crew of 6,000 suddenly vanish from the radar screens. Did the mammoth ship actually self-destruct, or is there a more sinister cause of the catastrophe.

***Nimitz Class Low Price.** abr. ed. Patrick Robinson. Read by Jay O. Sanders. (ENG.). 2004. (978-0-06-081839-5(5), Harper Audio); (978-0-06-081838-8(7), Harper Audio) HarperCollins Pubs.

Nim's Island. Wendy Orr. Read by Kate Reading. (Playaway Children Ser.). (J). 2008. 34.99 (978-1-60640-752-3(X)) Find a World.

Nim's Island. unabr. ed. Wendy Orr. (Running Time: 9000 sec.). (J). (gr. 3-7). 2008. audio compact disk & audio compact disk 19.95 (978-1-4332-0997-0(7)) Blckstn Audio.

Nim's Island. unabr. ed. Wendy Orr. Read by Kate Reading. (Running Time: 9000 sec.). (J). (gr. 3-7). 2008. 14.95 (978-1-4332-0995-6(0)); 22.95 (978-1-4332-0993-2(4)); audio compact disk 14.95 (978-1-4332-0996-3(9)); audio compact disk & audio compact disk 24.00 (978-1-4332-0994-9(2)) Blckstn Audio.

Nina: Adolescence. unabr. ed. Amy Hassinger. Read by Mia Barron. 6 cass. (Running Time: 9 hrs.). (YA). 2003. 32.95 (978-1-59316-012-8(7)) Listen & Live.
Fifteen year old Nina, along with her family, is struggling to hold things together in the wake of the accidental death of her brother years earlier.

Nina - Adolescence. unabr. ed. Amy Hassinger. Read by Mia Barron. (YA). 2007. 39.99 (978-1-60252-569-6(2)) Find a World.

Nina Balatka. Anthony Trollope. Read by Anais 9000. 1 CD. (Running Time: 6.9 hours). 2006. 27.95 (978-1-60112-005-2(2)) Babblebooks.

Nina Balatka. unabr. ed. Anthony Trollope. Narrated by Flo Gibson. (Running Time: 7 hrs. 4 mins.). 2006. 20.95 (978-1-55685-769-0(1)) Audio Bk Con.

Nina Fairy Ballerina: Daisy Shoes & New Girl. unabr. ed. Anna Wilson. Read by Jill Shilling. 2 CDs. (Running Time: 6060 sec.). (J). (gr. 1-4). 2007. audio compact disk 21.95 (978-1-4056-5606-1(9), Chivers Child Audio) AudioGO.

Nine: Inside the Secret World of the Supreme Court. abr. ed. Jeffrey Toobin. Read by Jeffrey Toobin. (Running Time: 23400 sec.). (ENG.). 2007. audio compact disk 31.95 (978-0-7393-5459-9(0), Random AudioBks) Pub: Random Audio Pubg. Dist(s): Random

Nine - Five Danger Zone: Occupational Hazards. (Running Time: 30 min.). 10.95 (G0690B090, HarperThor) HarpC GBR.

Nine Betts Lane. Eileen De Lisle. 8 cass. (Sound Ser.). (J). 2003. 69.95 (978-1-84283-427-5(4)) Pub: ISIS Lrg Prnt GBR. Dist(s): Ulverscroft US

Nine Coaches Waiting, unabr. ed. Mary Stewart. Narrated by Davina Porter. 9 cass. (Running Time: 13 hrs. 30 mins.). 1991. 78.00 (978-1-55690-377-9(4), 91314E7) Recorded Bks.
An English governess takes charge of the heir apparent to a French chateau & uncovers a dark terror.

Nine Dragons. abr. ed. Michael Connelly. Read by Len Cariou. (Running Time: 6 hrs. 30 mins.). (Harry Bosch Ser.: No. 14). 2009. 14.98 (978-1-60024-742-2(3)) Pub: Hachet Audio. Dist(s): HachBkGrp

Nine Dragons. abr. ed. Michael Connelly. Read by Len Cariou. (Running Time: 6 hrs. 30 mins.). 2010. audio compact disk 14.98 (978-1-60788-254-1(X)) Pub: Hachet Audio. Dist(s): HachBkGrp

Nine Dragons. unabr. ed. Michael Connelly. Read by Len Cariou. (Running Time: 11 hrs.). (Harry Bosch Ser.: No. 14). 2009. 26.98 (978-1-60024-744-6(X)); audio compact disk 39.98 (978-1-60024-743-9(1)) Pub: Hachet Audio. Dist(s): HachBkGrp

Nine Emotional Lives of Cats. Jeffrey Moussaieff Masson. Read by Michael Prichard. 2002. 48.00 (978-0-7366-8798-0(X)) Books on Tape.

Nine for California. unabr. ed. Sonia Levitin. Narrated by Kate Forbes. 1 cass. (Running Time: 15 mins.). (ps up). 1996. 10.00 (978-0-7887-9591-6(0), 96816) Recorded Bks.
"Come to California, my dears. What good is gold, without my family?" When Pa sends a letter and some money to Ma, she loudly exclaims "We're coming!" - and just like that, the great adventure of Nine For California begins! Mama, Baby Betsy, Billy, Joe, Ted, and Amanda board a Wells Fargo stagecoach bound for California - a cramped and dangerous twenty-one-day journey through mountains and desert wastes. Luckily, Mama brings a special sack filled with all kinds of useful things. Whenever Amanda gets bored, something unexpected happens - stampedes, storms, Indians, outlaws - but Mama's sack always has just the right thing for the job.

***Nine Freedoms Lecture Album.** George King. 2010. audio compact disk (978-0-937249-56-7(4)) Aetherius Soc.

***Nine Freedoms Transmission Album.** George King. 2010. audio compact disk (978-0-937249-57-4(2)) Aetherius Soc.

Nine Gifts of the Holy Spirit, Album 1: Gifts of Relevation & Power. Derek Prince. 6 cass. (Running Time: 9 hrs.). 29.95 (I-NG1) Derek Prince.

Nine Gifts of the Holy Spirit, Album 2: Vocal Gifts - Use & Abuse. Derek Prince. 6 cass. (Running Time: 9 hrs.). 29.95 (I-NG2) Derek Prince.

Nine Hundred Words of Wisdom: The Real Truth about 900. Sean Naughton. Ed. by Barbara DeMarco. 1993. 98.00 (978-0-9638246-2-2(7)) Future Freedom.

Nine Latin American Folk Songs for Solo Voice & Piano: Medium High Voice (Spanish, English Language Edition) Composed by Bruce Trinkley. (SPA.). 2004. audio compact disk 12.95 (978-0-7390-3376-0(X)) Alfred Pub.

Nine Latin American Folk Songs for Solo Voice & Piano: Medium Low Voice (Spanish, English Language Edition) Composed by Bruce Trinkley. (SPA.). 2004. audio compact disk 12.95 (978-0-7390-3379-1(4)) Alfred Pub.

Nine Lives. unabr. ed. Bernice Rubens. Read by Di Langford. 6 cass. (Running Time: 7 hrs.). (Isis Ser.). (J). 2002. 54.95 (978-0-7531-1554-1(9)) Pub: ISIS Lrg Prnt GBR. Dist(s): Ulverscroft US
The killer's modus operandi was the same in each instance: strangulation, always with a guitar string pulled tight from behind until life is exinct. And though the murders are taking place up and down the country, there is one other similarity that Inspector Wilkins can't help noticing: each and every victim is a psychotherapist. Donald Dorricks is on a mission. Nine psychotherapists to go and his crusade is over. Yet even after giving himself up and confessing to the killings, he still protests his innocence. And just as Inspector Wilkins struggles to catch the killer, Dorrick's wife Verine attempts to understand the reasoning behind the murders.

Nine Lives. unabr. ed. Bernice Rubens. Read by Di Langford. 7 CDs. (Running Time: 7 hrs. 30 mins.). (Isis Ser.). (J). 2003. audio compact disk 71.95 (978-0-7531-2244-0(8)) Pub: ISIS Lrg Prnt GBR. Dist(s): Ulverscroft US
Donald Dorricks is on a mission. Nine psychotherapists to go and his crusade is over. Yet even after giving himself up and confessing to the killings, he still protests his innocence. As inspector Wilkins struggles to catch the killer. Dorrick's wife Verine attempts to understand the reasoning behind the murders.

Nine Minutes, Twenty Seconds: The Tragedy & Triumph of ASA Flight 529. abr. ed. Gary M. Pomerantz. 2004. 15.95 (978-0-7435-4074-2(3)) Pub: S&S Audio. Dist(s): S and S Inc

Nine Minutes, Twenty Seconds: The Tragedy & Triumph of ASA Flight 529. unabr. ed. Gary M. Pomerantz. Read by Adam Henderson. 8 vols. (Running Time: 12 hrs.). 2002. bk. 69.95 (978-0-7927-2530-5(1), CSL 419, Chivers Sound Lib); audio compact disk 94.95 (978-0-7927-9856-9(2), SLD 107, Chivers Sound Lib) AudioGO.
In August 1995, twenty-six passengers and a crew of three board a commuter plane in Atlanta headed for Gulfport, Mississippi. Shortly after takeoff they hear an explosion and, looking out the windows on the left side, see a mangled engine lodged against the wing. From the moment, nine minutes and twenty seconds elapse until the crippled plane crashes in a west Georgia hayfield, nine minutes and twenty seconds in which Gary Pomerantz takes readers deep into the hearts and minds of the people aboard, each of whom prepares in his or her own way for what may come.

Nine Missing Men: Luke 17:11-19. Ed Young. (J). 1981. 4.95 (978-0-7417-1203-5(2), A0203) Win Walk.

Nine Optimal Days: With Optimal Thinking. unabr. ed. Rosalene Glickman. (Running Time: 1 hr. 35 mins.). (ENG.). 2009. 12.95 (978-1-59659-483-8(7), GildAudio) Pub: Gildan Media. Dist(s): HachBkGrp

Nine Points of View on Intuition. unabr. ed. Helen Palmer. 1 cass. (Running Time: 1 hr. 6 min.). 1990. 11.00 (HP007) Big Sur Tapes.
Describes internal attention practices that help uncover the intuitive predispositions of the Enneagram personality types.

***Nine Pound Hammer.** unabr. ed. John Claude Bemis. Read by John H. Mayer. 8 CDs. (Running Time: 10 hrs. 22 mins.). (Clockwork Dark Ser.: Bk. 1). (J). (gr. 4-7). 2009. audio compact disk 55.00 (978-0-7393-8078-9(8), Listening Lib) Pub: Random Audio Pubg. Dist(s): Random

Nine Pound Hammer. unabr. ed. John Claude Bemis. Read by John H. Mayer. (Clockwork Dark Ser.: Bk. 1). (ENG.). (J). (gr. 4). 2009. audio compact disk 40.00 (978-0-7393-8076-5(1), Listening Lib) Pub: Random Audio Pubg. Dist(s): Random

Nine Princes in Amber. Roger Zelazny. Read by Roger Zelazny. 2 vols. (Chronicles of Amber: Bk. 1). 2002. (978-1-58807-502-4(8)) Am Pubng Inc.

Nine Princes in Amber. Roger Zelazny. Read by Roger Zelazny. 4 vols. (Chronicles of Amber: Bk. 1). 2003. audio compact disk (978-1-58807-684-7(9)) Am Pubng Inc.

Nine Princes in Amber. abr. ed. Roger Zelazny. 2 vols. (Running Time: 3 hrs.). (Chronicles of Amber: Bk. 1). 2002. 18.00 (978-1-58807-126-2(X)) Am Pubng Inc.
Amber, the one real world, wherein all others, including our own Earth, are but Shadows. Amber bums in Corwin's blood. Exiled on Shadow Earth for centuries, the prince is about to return to Amber to make a mad and desperate rush upon the throne. From Arden to the blood-slippery Stairway into the Sea, the air is electrified with the powers of Eric, Random, Bleys, Caine, and all the princes of Amber whom Corwin must overcome. Yet, his savage path is blocked and guarded by eerie structures beyond imaging - impossible realities forged by demonic assassins and staggering horrors to challenge the might of Corwin's superhuman fury.

Nine Princes in Amber. abr. ed. Roger Zelazny. 3 vols. (Running Time: 3 hrs.). (Chronicles of Amber: Bk. 1). 2003. audio compact disk 25.00 (978-1-58807-253-5(3)) Am Pubng Inc.

***Nine Rooms of Happiness: Loving Yourself, Finding Your Purpose, & Getting over Life's Little Imperfections.** unabr. ed. Lucy Danziger & Catherine Birndorf. (Running Time: 11 hrs. 0 mins.). 2010. 17.99 (978-1-4001-8646-4(3)) Tantor Media.

***Nine Rooms of Happiness: Loving Yourself, Finding Your Purpose, & Getting over Life's Little Imperfections.** unabr. ed. Lucy Danziger & Catherine Birndorf. Narrated by Marguerite Gavin. (Running Time: 10 hrs. 0 mins. 0 sec.). 2010. 24.99 (978-1-4001-6646-6(2)); audio compact disk 69.99 (978-1-4001-4646-8(1)); audio compact disk 34.99 (978-1-4001-1646-1(5)) Pub: Tantor Media. Dist(s): IngramPubServ

Nine Tailors: A BBC Full-Cast Radio Drama. Dorothy L. Sayers. Narrated by Ian Carmichael & Full Cast Production Staff. 3 CDs. (Running Time: 3 hrs. 15 mins. 0 sec.). (ENG.). 2001. audio compact disk 29.95 (978-0-563-47835-5(7)) Pub: AudioGO. Dist(s): Perseus Dist

Nine Tailors: A BBC Full-Cast Radio Drama. unabr. ed. Dorothy L. Sayers. Read by Ian Carmichael. 8 cass. (Running Time: 10 hrs. 23 min.). (Lord Peter Wimsey Mystery Ser.). 2001. 34.95 (978-1-57270-220-2(6), N81220u) Pub: Audio Partners. Dist(s): PerseuPGW
Nine long chimes peal from an ancient church belfry, sounding the death of a stranger. Thus the famous Lord Peter Wimsey is summoned to the case by a plea from the rector. Against the quiet backdrop of a parish in the odd, flat fens of East Anglia, Lord Peter must puzzle out the clues to solving this murder in one of his most brilliant & complicated cases ever. As the mystery unfolds, Lord Peters uncovers an unexpected connection between a long-ago jewel theft & the present-day murder.

Nine Tailors: A BBC Full-Cast Radio Drama. unabr. ed. Dorothy L. Sayers. Read by Ian Carmichael. 8 cass. (Running Time: 12 hrs.). (Lord Peter Wimsey Mystery Ser.). 2000. 59.95 (978-0-7451-6260-7(6), CAB 203) Pub: Chivers Audio Bks GBR. Dist(s): AudioGO
Storm-bound over the New Year at a Fenland rectory, Lord Peter Wimsey helps out with the ringing of the New Years Eve church bells. Some months later, a handless, disfigured corpse is found in a fresh grave in the churchyard. Lord Peter receives a plea from the rector and embarks on one of his most complicated investigations. Could this crime be linked to the theft of the Wilbraham Emeralds that were stolen fifteen years ago?.

Nine Things You Simply Must Do to Succeed in Love & Life -Lib. (Running Time: 6 hrs. 0 mins.). 2005. audio compact disk 45.00 (978-0-7861-8083-7(8)) Blckstn Audio.

Nine Traits of Highly Successful Work Teams. Loren Ankarlo. 4 cass. (Running Time: 3 hrs. 23 min.). 59.95 (Q10195) CareerTrack Pubns.
Proven methods for building & maintaining teams that work. You'll find out how to keep your team motivated, on track & moving forward - no matter what gets thrown your way. Includes 72 page workbook.

Nine Ways to Deepen Devotion. unabr. ed. Perf. by Eknath Easwaran. 1 cass. (Running Time: 1 hr.). 1989. 7.95 (978-1-58638-581-1(X)) Nilgiri Pr.

Nine Ways to Raise the Planet's Vibration. Kryon. Read by Lee Carroll. 1 cass. (Running Time: 53 min.). 1996. 10.00 (978-1-888053-01-2(1)) Kryon Writings.
Recording of live event. Channeling of spiritual information.

Nine Years in the Saddle. unabr. ed. James V. Lee. Read by Rusty Garrett. 2 cass. (Running Time: 3 hrs. 5 mins.). 2001. 14.95 (978-0-9663870-2-5(3)) Salado Pr.
A true-story western about a young cowboy who herded cattle, hunted mountain lions & engaged in bootlegging in the Southwest in the early 19th century.

Nine Years Is the Exact Right Amount of Time to Be in a Bad Relationship (an Essay from Things I've Learned from Women Who've Dumped Me) abr. ed. Bob Odenkirk. Read by Bob Odenkirk. Ed. by Ben Karlin. (Running Time: 15 mins.). (ENG.). 2008. 1.98 (978-1-60024-341-7(X)) Pub: Hachet Audio. Dist(s): HachBkGrp

Nineteen Classic Short Stories. unabr. ed. Saki et al. Read by Patrick Malahide. 6 cass. (Running Time: 9 hrs.). (CSA TellTapes Ser.: Vol. 5). 1996. 54.95 (50548) Eye Ear.
Includes "Classic Tales of Horror," "Classic Tales of Humor," "Classic Ghost Stories #2," "Classic Crime Stories," "Classic Irish Stories," & "Classic Vampire Stories".

Nineteen Eighties & the Nineteen Nineties - A Time of Transformation. Steve Cozzi. 1 cass. (Running Time: 1 hr. 30 min.). 8.95 (067) Am Fed Astrologers.
Important charts, cycles and aspects of the next 20 years.

Nineteen Eighty-Four Consecration of Pope John Paul the Second. Frederick L. Miller. 1 cass. (Running Time: 1 hr. 30 min.). 1990. 2.50 (978-1-56036-054-4(2)) AMI Pr.

Nineteen Fifty-Five. Short Stories. Alice Walker. Read by Alice Walker. 1 cass. (Running Time: 36 min.). 1981. 13.95 (978-1-55644-029-8(4), 1161) Am Audio Prose.
The Pulitzer-Prize-winning author of "The Color Purple" reads this humane & compassionate story about the exploitation of black musicians by the white rock & roll industry.

Nineteen Minutes. unabr. ed. Jodi Picoult. Read by Carol Monda. 18 cass. (Running Time: 21 hrs. 25 mins.). 2007. 113.75 (978-1-4281-4434-7(X)); audio compact disk 123.75 (978-1-4281-4436-1(6)) Recorded Bks.

Nineteen Minutes. unabr. ed. Jodi Picoult. Narrated by Carol Monda. 18 cass. (Running Time: 21 hrs. 15 mins.). 2008. 72.95 (978-1-4281-4435-4(8)) Recorded Bks.

Nineteen Minutes. unabr. ed. Jodi Picoult. Read by Carol Monda. 18 CDs. (Running Time: 21 hrs.). 2007. audio compact disk 44.99 (978-1-4281-4433-0(1)) Recorded Bks.

Nineteen Ninety-Eight Dove Award Nominees: The Best in Christian Music. 1 cass. (Running Time: 1 hr. 30 min.). 1998. 10.98 (978-0-7601-2311-9(X)); audio compact disk 15.98 (978-0-7601-2312-6(8)) Provident Mus Dist.

Nineteen Ninety-Three Amendments to the Federal Rules of Civil Procedure. (Running Time: 5 hrs.). 1994. 92.00 Incl. 204p. coursebk. (2012) NYS Bar.
With the enactment in late 1993 of fundamental changes to the Federal Rules of Civil Procedure, this recording highlights areas where the revisions may have the most impact on practitioners: service of process, sanctions & discovery. Where appropriate, comparisons to practice in state courts are made by the panelists.

Nineteen Ninety-Three Tyler Prize for Environmental Achievement - Drs. Bormann & Likens on Watershed Conservation Models. Hosted by Nancy Pearlman. 1 cass. (Running Time: 29 min.). 10.00 (1122) Educ Comm CA.

Nineteen Seventy-Nine Swiss Money Seminar. Douglas Casey et al. 10 cass. (Running Time: 15 hrs.). 65.00 (1340-1342) J Norton Pubs.
This series includes a number of experts in economics, numismatics, real estate, gold & silver investments, & other fields, who talk about the many advantages of living in Switzerland & transacting business there. Swiss residency, annuities, tax havens, endowment plans & OPEC funds are discussed.

Nineteen Sixty-Four Convention Acceptance Speech. Barry Goldwater. 1 cass. (Running Time: 43 min.). 10.95 (119) J Norton Pubs.

Nineteen Sixty-Two: Le Massacre des Harkis. 1 cass. (Running Time: 1 hr. 30 min.). (FRE.). 1995. 16.95 (1739-RF) Olivia & Hill.
The fate of the "harkis," the Algerians who chose to fight on the French side during the Algerian War.

Nineteenth Annual Institute on Employment Law. 6 cass. (Running Time: 8 hrs.). bk. 85.00 incl. 1176-page course handbook. (T6-9158) PLI.

Nineteenth-Century Capitalism. Ayn Rand. 1 cass. (Running Time: 60 min.). 1993. 12.95 (978-1-56114-119-7(4), AR41C) Second Renaissance.

Nineteeth Century. 1 cass. (Golden Treasury of Poetry & Prose Ser.). 1991. 16.95 (1060-SA) Olivia & Hill.

Nineties Rock Sessions for Guitar. Ed. by Ed Lazano. Contrib. by Louis Rochman & Peter Marunzak. 1 CD. (Running Time: 1 hr.). 1998. pap. bk. 12.95 (978-0-8256-1629-7(8), AM945197) Music Sales.

Nineties' Startling End-Time Signs & Your Future. Jack Van Impe. 1 cass. (Running Time: 1 hr. 30 min.). 7.00 J Van Impe.
Discover the latest, documented facts about this decade of destiny & how it will affect your future.

Nineties, Startling Endtime Signs, & Your Future. Jack Van Impe. Read by Jack Van Impe. 1 cass. (Running Time: 62 min.). 7.00 J V I Minist.
Endtime Bible prophecies relating to the 1990s.

***Ninety Days.** Victoria S. Johnson. Read by Laural Merlington. (Running Time: 53). (ENG.). 2010. 2.99 (978-1-61114-016-3(1)); audio compact disk 2.99 (978-0-9825278-4-9(5)) Mind Wings Aud.

Ninety Percent of Everything. unabr. ed. Jonathan Lethem et al. 2 cass. (Running Time: 3 hrs.). 1999. 17.95 (978-0-9648539-3-5(0)) Wyrmhole.
Working from Ramsdel's headquarters in a Jolly Freeze ice cream truck & the floating mansion Laputa, Liz & her colleagues strive to discover what the 6500 pound, blue-furred aliens who arrived on Earth six years ago are up to.

Ninety-Three. unabr. ed. Victor Hugo. Read by Frederick Davidson. 10 cass. (Running Time: 15 hrs.). 2000. 69.95 (978-0-7861-1768-0(0), 2571) Blckstn Audio.
The author's last novel captures the moment that shapes the destiny not only of France but of all European monarchy. Originally published in French, 1874.

Ninety-Three. unabr. ed. Victor Hugo. Read by Frederick Davidson. Tr. by Frank Lee Benedict. (Running Time: 48600 sec.). 2007. audio compact disk 99.00 (978-0-7861-5850-8(6)); audio compact disk 29.95 (978-0-7861-5851-5(4)) Blckstn Audio.

***Ninety Years Without Slumbering.** 2010. audio compact disk (978-1-59171-219-0(X)) Falcon Picture.

Ninguneo. John M. Bennett. 1 cass. (Running Time: 30 min.). 1991. 4.00 (978-0-935350-39-5(X)) Luna Bisonte.

Ninjas, Pirahas & Galileo. unabr. ed. 3 cass. (Running Time: 3 hrs. 45 min.). (YA). (gr. 6-8). 2004. 28.00 (978-1-4025-7005-6(8)) Recorded Bks.
Seventh grade pals experience the uncomfortable growth from childhood to adolescence in this intelligent and humorous tale by Greg Leitich Smith. All three are from privileged backgrounds and attend a private school with exacting standards. The looming science fair sets in motion a number of events. Overachieving and sometimes judgmental Honoria finds herself developing feelings for longtime friend Shohei. He is a bit of a slacker, frustrated by his adopted parents' rather extreme predilections for forcing Japanese culture upon him at all times.

Nino Bilingue - The Bilingual Child. 1 cass. (Running Time: 45 min.). (ENG & SPA.). (J). 10.95 (KMS 7213C); lp 11.95 (KMS 7213) Kimbo Educ.
Four magic words, trains, animals, meals & time concepts & more.

Nino Canto - The Singing Child. 1 cass. (Running Time: 45 min.). (ENG & SPA.). (J). 10.95 (KMS 7211C); lp 11.95 (KMS 7211) Kimbo Educ.
Songs about family, home, safety & friends.

Nino Creador - The Creative Child. 1 cass. (Running Time: 45 min.). (ENG & SPA.). (J). 10.95 (KMS 7212C); lp 11.95 LP. (KMS 7212) Kimbo Educ.
Includes cleaning, toys, truth, body, doctor & five senses.

Nino de Belen. Greg Skipper & Gail Skipper. 2001. 10.00 (978-0-311-48299-3(6)) Casa Bautista.

Nino Del Tambor. Tr. of Little Drummer Boy, the. (SPA.). 2004. 8.95 (978-0-7882-0284-1(7)) Weston Woods.

Nino Sabio - The Knowing Child. 1 cass. (Running Time: 45 min.). (ENG & SPA.). (J). 10.95 (KMS 7214C); lp 11.95 (KMS 7214) Kimbo Educ.
Introduces Alphabet, Counting to Ten, Months & Musical Instruments.

Niños adorando Volumen 3. Ninos Adorando. 2008. audio compact disk 14.99 (978-0-8297-5429-2(6)) Pub: Vida Pubs. Dist(s): Zondervan

Ninos Cantan Alabanzas Vol. 1: (Kids Sing Praise, Spanish Only) 1 cass. (Running Time: 1 hr.). (Kids Sing Praise Ser.). (SPA.). (978-1-55897-060-1(6), V5162) Brentwood Music.

Ninos de Aqui y de Alla. (Coleccion Parvulitos). (SPA.). 2003. 8.95 (978-0-8136-8533-5(8)) Modern Curr.

niños pueden tener trabajos Audio CD: Emergent Set A. Benchmark Education Staff. Ed. by Katherine Scraper. (Early Explorers Ser.). (J). 2008. audio compact disk 10.00 (978-1-60437-248-9(6)) Benchmark Educ.

Ninth Directive. unabr. collector's ed. Adam Hall. Read by Victor Rumbellow. 8 cass. (Running Time: 8 hrs.). (Quiller Ser.). 1980. 48.00 (978-0-7366-0211-2(9), 1209) Books on Tape.
The setting is Thailand. A very important representative of the Queen is scheduled to visit Bangkok on a good-will tour. A threat has been made against this official's life, & somewhere amidst the golden spires waits a deadly assassin. The top-secret British espionage bureau feels ordinary security precautions are not sufficient, so they call in agent Quiller.

***Ninth Grade Slays.** unabr. ed. Heather Brewer. Read by Kevin Pariseau. (Running Time: 7 hrs.). (Chronicles of Vladimir Tod: Bk. 2). 2010. 39.97 (978-1-4418-6850-3(X), 9781441868503, Brinc Audio MP3 Lib); 19.99 (978-1-4418-6849-7(6), 9781441868497, Brilliance MP3); 39.97 (978-1-4418-6852-7(6), 9781441868527, BADLE); audio compact disk 54.97 (978-1-4418-6848-0(8), 9781441868480, BriAudCD Unabrid) Brilliance Audio.

***Ninth Grade Slays.** unabr. ed. Heather Brewer. Read by Kevin Pariseau. (Running Time: 7 hrs.). (Chronicles of Vladimir Tod: Bk. 2). (YA). 2010. audio compact disk 19.99 (978-1-4418-6847-3(X), 9781441868473, Bril Audio CD Unabri) Brilliance Audio.

Ninth Key. unabr. ed. Jenny Carroll, pseud. Narrated by Johanna Parker. 6 CDs. (Running Time: 6 hrs.). (Mediator Ser.: Bk. 2). 2005. audio compact disk 62.75 (978-1-4193-5602-5(X), C3414); 52.75 (978-1-4193-4148-9(0), 98046) Recorded Bks.
New York Times best-selling author Meg Cabot fills each adventure in the Mediator series with suspense and humor. Suze Simon is liaison between ghosts and the living. But this teenager is no hand-holder - she's tough on the spirits who need her help. When the ghost of a murdered woman wakes Suze up one night with an troublesome request, the 16-year-old just wants to get rid of her.

Ninth Life: Sequel to Stray Cat. unabr. ed. Don Matheson. Narrated by Peter Waldren. 6 cass. (Running Time: 8 hrs.). 1990. 51.00 (978-1-55690-378-6(2), 90065E7) Recorded Bks.
Charlie Gamble is a scam artist, but he believes in helping his friend Rosy. She is caught in an art swindle masterminded by Sams, an ex-con & enforced by Sams' slow-witted sidekick. When Charlie goes up against Sams & his enforcer, it's an alley-cat fight to the finish, with Rosy & survival the two prizes.

Ninth Life of Louis Drax. unabr. ed. Liz Jensen. 2005. audio compact disk 34.99 (978-1-4193-1638-8(9)) Recorded Bks.

Ninth Wave: For violoncello & computer generated Tape. Composed by Rober Scott Thompson. 2006. audio compact disk 50.00 (978-1-934174-00-5(9)) Aucourant.

Ninth Witness. unabr. ed. Bodie Thoene & Brock Thoene. Narrated by Sean Barrett. (Running Time: 6 hrs. 0 mins. 0 sec.). (A. D. Chronicles Ser.). (ENG.). 2009. 16.09 (978-1-60814-530-0(1)); audio compact disk 22.99 (978-1-59859-590-1(3)) Oasis Audio.

Niobe's Journey. unabr. ed. Jane McClain. Read by Candy Pettiford. 1 cass. (Running Time: 1 hr. 30 min.). 1999. 8.45 (978-0-9666632-1-1(7)) Turtle Hse Ink.
Niobe travels with her companion, Evan, to get water from a healing well for her mother. Raymond, a guide, takes them on the last three days journey. Niobe must choose between Her companion & the guide as she climbs the cliff to the well where she receives an unexpected healing.

Nip & Tuck. abr. ed. Robert McConnell. Read by Robert McConnell. Illus. by James Watling. (Picture Bks.). (J). (ps-2). 2005. cass., cass., audio compact disk 7.95 (978-0-929141-30-5(X)) Pub: Napoleon Co CAN. Dist(s): AtlasBooks

Nip N Tuck. unabr. ed. Kathy Lette. Read by Shirley Barthelmie. (Running Time: 25200 sec.). 2007. audio compact disk 77.95 (978-1-74093-736-8(8)) Pub: Bolinda Pubng AUS. Dist(s): Bolinda Pub Inc

Nipple Trauma, Module 3. Sally Page Goertz & Sarah McCamman. (Breastfeeding Management Ser.). (C). 2000. audio compact disk 29.95 (978-0-7637-1130-6(6), 0763711306) Jones Bartlett.

Nippy. unabr. ed. Elizabeth Waite. Read by Annie Aldington. 12 cass. (Running Time: 18 hrs.). 1999. 94.95 (978-1-86042-540-0(2), 25402) Pub: Soundings Ltd GBR. Dist(s): Ulverscroft US
Becky Russel & Eleanor James were girls who deserved the best in life. But in suburban New Malden in the summer of 1920, what is best for some may not be enough for others. When they leave school at fourteen, the girls have little choice but to take menial jobs in the town. Eleanor is more disposed to the toil of the laundry house & the simple charms of the local lads, but Becky wants something better. Taking a job as a "nippy," a waitress at one of the West End's most prestigious tea-shops, she enters a privileged & exciting world where men like Gerald Palmer will spare no expense to court her affections & where business success enables her to ease some of Eleanor's struggles. Becky's sure she has fulfilled her dreams, but in a rich mans world, the game of love is never simple.

Nirmal. 1 cass. (Running Time: 45 min.). 9.95 (M/N) Nada Prodns.
(Pure expressions of a 14 year old Boy Prodigy). By Maulik Zaveri Raguvar; Bhajo Re Bhaya; Radha Syam; Darshana Do; Vrindavan Kunj Bhavan; Nam Hari Ka; Jaya Ganesh; Hai Malik; Syam Sundara.

NIrV Little Kids Adventure Audio Bible, Vol. 1. unabr. ed. Zondervan Publishing Staff. (Running Time: 5 hrs. 21 mins. 0 sec.). (Adventure Bible Ser.). (ENG.). 2005. 14.99 (978-0-310-71088-2(X)) Zondervan.

NIrV Little Kids Adventure Audio Bible, Vol 2. unabr. ed. Zondervan Publishing Staff. (Running Time: 5 hrs. 3 mins. 0 sec.). (Adventure Bible Ser.). (ENG.). 2005. 14.99 (978-0-310-71089-9(8)) Zondervan.

NIrV Little Kids Adventure Audio Bible, Vol. 3. unabr. ed. Zondervan Publishing Staff. (Running Time: 5 hrs. 9 mins. 0 sec.). (Adventure Bible Ser.). (ENG.). 2005. 14.99 (978-0-310-71090-5(1)) Zondervan.

Nirvana. Gary N. Arnold. (ENG.). 2009. audio compact disk 24.95 (978-1-57867-018-5(7)) Windhorse Corp.

Nirvana Blues. (2091) Am Audio Prose.

Nisava. 1 cass. (Running Time: 1 hr. 30 min.). 1989. 9.98 (978-1-877737-36-7(4), EB 2565); audio compact disk 12.98 CD. (978-1-877737-53-4(4)) MFLP CA.
Women's folk choir & various instruments performing dance music from Scandinavia, Bulgaria, Macedonia & East.

Niscience. Ann Ree Colton. 1 cass. 7.95 A R Colton Fnd.

Nissim Ezekiel. unabr. ed. Read by Nissim Ezekiel. 1 cass. (Running Time: 29 min.). 1985. 10.00 New Letters.
Indian poet recorded in Bombay reads from Hymns of Darkness & Third.

Nitai Pada Kamala. 1 cass. (Running Time: 1 hr. 30 min.). 4.95 (CD-14); audio compact disk 14.95 Bhaktivedanta.

Nitrisyon pou Timoun. Maude Heurtelou. (CRP.). (YA). 2007. audio compact disk 19.00 (978-1-58432-309-9(4)) Educa Vision.

NIV & KJV Complete Bible: With 4 Bonus Praise Tapes. Read by Stephen Johnston. 52 cass. (Running Time: 78 hrs.). 99.99 Super Packs. (978-0-529-06974-0(1), WBC-1); 79.99 Attache. (978-0-529-07263-4(7), WBC-8) Nelson.

NIV Audio Bible. unabr. ed. Zondervan Publishing Staff. 64 CDs. (Running Time: 18 hrs. 0 mins. 0 sec.). Dramatization. (NIV Audio Bible Ser.). (ENG.). 2001. audio compact disk 49.99 (978-0-310-92028-1(0)) Zondervan.

NIV Audio Bible - Voice Only - Wal-Mart. Zondervan Publishing Staff. 2004. audio compact disk 79.99 (978-0-310-92393-0(X)) Zondervan.

NIV Audio Bible Book Assortment AMS. Zondervan Publishing Staff. 2002. 179.88 (978-0-310-60075-6(8)) Zondervan.

NIV Audio Bible Dramatized - the New Testament: New International Version. unabr. ed. New International Version. Read by Full Ensemble Cast. (YA). 2006. 59.99 (978-1-59895-664-1(7)) Find a World.

NIV Audio Bible Dramatized - the Old Testament: New International Version. unabr. ed. New International Version. Read by Full Ensemble Cast. (YA). 2006. 79.99 (978-1-59895-665-8(5)) Find a World.

NIV Audio Bible Dramatized Sams. Zondervan Publishing Staff. 2006. audio compact disk 99.99 (978-0-310-60753-3(1)) Zondervan.

Niv Bible Nt Cd Voice Only. unabr. ed. Zondervan Publishing Staff. 1 CD. (Running Time: 18 hrs. 0 mins. 0 sec.). (NIV Audio Bible Ser.). (ENG.). 2002. audio compact disk 29.99 (978-0-310-92052-6(3)) Zondervan.

***NIV Bible Voice Only / Genesis.** unabr. ed. Zondervan. (Running Time: 3 hrs. 32 mins. 0 sec.). (ENG.). 2009. 2.99 (978-0-310-58727-9(1)) Zondervan.

***NIV Bible Voice Only / New Testament.** unabr. ed. Zondervan. (Running Time: 18 hrs. 0 mins. 0 sec.). (ENG.). 2009. 29.99 (978-0-310-58647-0(X)) Zondervan.

***NIV Bible Voice Only / Old Testament.** unabr. ed. Zondervan. (Running Time: 59 hrs. 0 mins. 0 sec.). (ENG.). 2009. 39.99 (978-0-310-58663-0(1)) Zondervan.

***NIV Bible Voice Only COMPLETE.** unabr. ed. Zondervan. (Running Time: 77 hrs. 0 mins. 0 sec.). (ENG.). 2009. 44.99 (978-0-310-58662-3(3)) Zondervan.

***NIV Bible Voice Only Deuteronomy.** unabr. ed. Zondervan. (Running Time: 2 hrs. 25 mins. 0 sec.). (ENG.). 2009. 2.99 (978-0-310-58731-6(X)) Zondervan.

***NIV Bible Voice Only Hebrews & James.** unabr. ed. Zondervan. (Running Time: 1 hr. 3 mins. 0 sec.). (ENG.). 2009. 2.99 (978-0-310-58658-6(5)) Zondervan.

***NIV Bible Voice Only Revelation.** unabr. ed. Zondervan. (Running Time: 1 hr. 15 mins. 0 sec.). (ENG.). 2009. 2.99 (978-0-310-58660-9(7)) Zondervan.

***NIV Bible Voice Only 1 & 2 Peter/John 1,2,3/Jude.** unabr. ed. Zondervan. (Running Time: 0 hr. 56 mins. 0 sec.). (ENG.). 2009. 2.99 (978-0-310-58659-3(3)) Zondervan.

***NIV Bible Voice Only 1 & 2 Thessalonians/1 & 2 Timothy/Titus/Philemon.** unabr. ed. Zondervan. (Running Time: 1 hr. 3 mins. 0 sec.). (ENG.). 2009. 2.99 (978-0-310-58657-9(7)) Zondervan.

***NIV Bible Voice Only/Acts.** unabr. ed. Zondervan. (Running Time: 2 hrs. 25 mins. 0 sec.). (ENG.). 2009. 2.99 (978-0-310-58653-1(4)) Zondervan.

***NIV Bible Voice Only/Daniel.** unabr. ed. Zondervan. (Running Time: 1 hr. 8 mins. 0 sec.). (ENG.). 2009. 2.99 (978-0-310-58817-7(0)) Zondervan.

***NIV Bible Voice Only/Ecclesiastes/Song of Songs.** unabr. ed. Zondervan. (Running Time: 0 hr. 49 mins. 0 sec.). (ENG.). 2009. 2.99 (978-0-310-58813-9(8)) Zondervan.

***NIV Bible Voice Only/Esther.** unabr. ed. Zondervan. (Running Time: 0 hr. 31 mins. 0 sec.). (ENG.). 2009. 2.99 (978-0-310-58809-2(X)) Zondervan.

***NIV Bible Voice Only/Exodus.** unabr. ed. Zondervan. (Running Time: 2 hrs. 57 mins. 0 sec.). (ENG.). 2009. 2.99 (978-0-310-58728-6(X)) Zondervan.

***NIV Bible Voice Only/Ezekiel.** unabr. ed. Zondervan. (Running Time: 3 hrs. 30 mins. 0 sec.). (ENG.). 2009. 2.99 (978-0-310-58816-0(2)) Zondervan.

***NIV Bible Voice Only/Ezra.** unabr. ed. Zondervan. (Running Time: 0 hr. 41 mins. 0 sec.). (ENG.). 2009. 2.99 (978-0-310-58699-9(2)) Zondervan.

***NIV Bible Voice Only/Galations/Ephesians/Philippians/Colossians.** unabr. ed. Zondervan. (Running Time: 1 hr. 15 mins. 0 sec.). (ENG.). 2009. 2.99 (978-0-310-58656-2(9)) Zondervan.

***NIV Bible Voice Only/Hosea/Joel/Amos.** unabr. ed. Zondervan. (Running Time: 1 hr. 10 mins. 0 sec.). (ENG.). 2009. 2.99 (978-0-310-58818-4(9)) Zondervan.

***NIV Bible Voice Only/Isaiah.** unabr. ed. Zondervan. (Running Time: 3 hrs. 42 mins. 0 sec.). (ENG.). 2009. 2.99 (978-0-310-58814-6(6)) Zondervan.

***NIV Bible Voice Only/Jeremiah/Lamentations.** unabr. ed. Zondervan. (Running Time: 4 hrs. 11 mins. 0 sec.). (ENG.). 2009. 2.99 (978-0-310-58815-3(4)) Zondervan.

***NIV Bible Voice Only/Job.** unabr. ed. Zondervan. (Running Time: 1 hr. 49 mins. 0 sec.). (ENG.). 2009. 2.99 (978-0-310-58810-8(3)) Zondervan.

***NIV Bible Voice Only/John.** unabr. ed. Zondervan. (Running Time: 1 hr. 57 mins. 0 sec.). (ENG.). 2009. 2.99 (978-0-310-58652-4(6)) Zondervan.

***NIV Bible Voice Only/Joshua.** unabr. ed. Zondervan. (Running Time: 1 hr. 40 mins. 0 sec.). (ENG.). 2009. 2.99 (978-0-310-58732-3(8)) Zondervan.

***NIV Bible Voice Only/Judges/Ruth.** unabr. ed. Zondervan. (Running Time: 1 hr. 47 mins. 0 sec.). (ENG.). 2009. 2.99 (978-0-310-58733-0(6)) Zondervan.

***NIV Bible Voice Only/Leviticus.** unabr. ed. Zondervan. (Running Time: 2 hrs. 7 mins. 0 sec.). (ENG.). 2009. 2.99 (978-0-310-58729-3(8)) Zondervan.

***NIV Bible Voice Only/Luke.** unabr. ed. Zondervan. (Running Time: 2 hrs. 27 mins. 0 sec.). (ENG.). 2009. 2.99 (978-0-310-58650-0(X)) Zondervan.

***NIV Bible Voice Only/Mark.** unabr. ed. Zondervan. (Running Time: 1 hr. 26 mins. 0 sec.). (ENG.). 2009. 2.99 (978-0-310-58649-4(6)) Zondervan.

***NIV Bible Voice Only/Matthew.** unabr. ed. Zondervan. (Running Time: 2 hrs. 19 mins. 0 sec.). (ENG.). 2009. 2.99 (978-0-310-58648-7(8)) Zondervan.

***NIV Bible Voice Only/Nahum/Habakkuk/Zephaniah/Haggai.** unabr. ed. Zondervan. (Running Time: 0 hr. 38 mins. 0 sec.). (ENG.). 2009. 2.99 (978-0-310-58820-7(0)) Zondervan.

***NIV Bible Voice Only/Nehemiah.** unabr. ed. Zondervan. (Running Time: 1 hr. 1 mins. 0 sec.). (ENG.). 2009. 2.99 (978-0-310-58700-2(X)) Zondervan.

***NIV Bible Voice Only/Numbers.** unabr. ed. Zondervan. (Running Time: 2 hrs. 53 mins. 0 sec.). (ENG.). 2009. 2.99 (978-0-310-58730-9(1)) Zondervan.

***NIV Bible Voice Only/Obadiah/Jonah/Micah.** unabr. ed. Zondervan. (Running Time: 0 hr. 32 mins. 0 sec.). (ENG.). 2009. 2.99 (978-0-310-58819-1(7)) Zondervan.

***NIV Bible Voice Only/Proverbs.** unabr. ed. Zondervan. (Running Time: 1 hr. 31 mins. 0 sec.). (ENG.). 2009. 2.99 (978-0-310-58812-2(X)) Zondervan.

***NIV Bible Voice Only/Psalms.** unabr. ed. Zondervan. (Running Time: 4 hrs. 29 mins. 0 sec.). (ENG.). 2009. 2.99 (978-0-310-58811-5(1)) Zondervan.

***NIV Bible Voice Only/Romans.** unabr. ed. Zondervan. (Running Time: 1 hr. 5 mins. 0 sec.). (ENG.). 2009. 2.99 (978-0-310-58654-8(2)) Zondervan.

***NIV Bible Voice Only/Zechariah/Malachi.** unabr. ed. Zondervan. (Running Time: 0 hr. 49 mins. 0 sec.). (ENG.). 2009. 2.99 (978-0-310-58821-4(9)) Zondervan.

***NIV Bible Voice Only/1 & 2 Corinthians.** unabr. ed. Zondervan. (Running Time: 1 hr. 43 mins. 0 sec.). (ENG.). 2009. 2.99 (978-0-310-58655-5(0)) Zondervan.

***NIV Bible Voice Only/1 Chronicles.** unabr. ed. Zondervan. (Running Time: 2 hrs. 8 mins. 0 sec.). (ENG.). 2009. 2.99 (978-0-310-58738-5(7)) Zondervan.

***NIV Bible Voice Only/1 Kings.** unabr. ed. Zondervan. (Running Time: 2 hrs. 7 mins. 0 sec.). (ENG.). 2009. 2.99 (978-0-310-58736-1(0)) Zondervan.

***NIV Bible Voice Only/1 Samuel.** unabr. ed. Zondervan. (Running Time: 2 hrs. 9 mins. 0 sec.). (ENG.). 2009. 2.99 (978-0-310-58734-7(4)) Zondervan.

***NIV Bible Voice Only/2 Chronicles.** unabr. ed. Zondervan. (Running Time: 2 hrs. 23 mins. 0 sec.). (ENG.). 2009. 2.99 (978-0-310-58698-2(4)) Zondervan.

***NIV Bible Voice Only/2 Kings.** unabr. ed. Zondervan. (Running Time: 2 hrs. 7 mins. 0 sec.). (ENG.). 2009. 2.99 (978-0-310-58737-8(9)) Zondervan.

***NIV Bible Voice Only/2 Samuel.** unabr. ed. Zondervan. (Running Time: 1 hr. 53 mins. 0 sec.). (ENG.). 2009. 2.99 (978-0-310-58735-4(2)) Zondervan.

NIV Dramatized Audio Bible. unabr. ed. Zondervan Publishing Staff. (Running Time: 76 hrs. 0 mins. 0 sec.). (ENG.). 2004. 49.99 (978-0-310-92562-0(2)) Zondervan.

NIV Dramatized Audio New Testament. unabr. ed. Zondervan Publishing Staff. (Running Time: 18 hrs. 0 mins. 0 sec.). (ENG.). 2004. 22.99 (978-0-310-92563-7(0)) Zondervan.

NIV Dramatized Audio Old Testament. unabr. ed. Zondervan Publishing Staff. (Running Time: 58 hrs. 0 mins. 0 sec.). (ENG.). 2004. 32.99 (978-0-310-92564-4(9)) Zondervan.

NIV Easter Pink/Melon Gift Bible with Easter Audio CD- FCS. Zondervan Publishing Staff. 2006. lthr. 19.99 (978-0-310-60498-3(2)) Zondervan.

NIV Kids' Club Vol. 1: Fun from Proverbs. Prod. by Stan Blair. 1 cass. (Running Time: 30 min.). (J). 1994. 9.98 (978-1-57919-037-8(5)); 9.98 Split Track version. (978-1-57919-040-8(5)) Randolf Prod.
Scripture memorization sing-along album.

NIV Kids' Club Vol. 2: Fun from Colossians. Prod. by Stan Blair. 1 cass. (Running Time: 1 hr.). (J). 1995. 9.98 (978-1-57919-038-5(3)) Randolf Prod.

NIV Kids' Club Vol. 3: Fun from Psalms. Prod. by Stan Blair. 1 cass. (Running Time: 1 hr.). (J). 1995. 9.98 (978-1-57919-039-2(1)) Randolf Prod.

NIV New Covenant-Prophecy: New Testament. Read by Ben D'Aubry. 11 cass. (Running Time: 16 hrs. 30 min.). 14.97 (978-0-529-06999-3(7), WBC-5) Nelson.

NIV New Testament. Read by Stephen Johnston. 12 cass. 24.97 Power Pack. (978-0-529-06977-1(6), WBC-3); 29.99 (978-0-529-06976-4(8), WBC-2) Nelson.

NIV Study Bible Complete Library for Macintosh(r). unabr. ed. Helen Brown & Roy Brown. 2000. audio compact disk 129.99 (978-0-310-23312-1(7)) Zondervan.

NIV/TNIV Audio Bible Assortment GM. Zondervan Publishing Staff. 2005. audio compact disk 899.91 (978-0-310-60573-7(3)) Zondervan.

Nixie's Song. unabr. ed. Tony DiTerlizzi & Holly Black. Narrated by Andrew McCarthy. 2 CDs. (Running Time: 1 hr. 45 mins.). (Beyond the Spiderwick Chronicles: Bk. 1). (J). (gr. 3-6). 2008. audio compact disk 25.75 (978-1-4281-9643-8(9)); 25.75 (978-1-4281-9638-4(2)) Recorded Bks.
Tony DiTerlizzi and Holly Black's best-selling Spiderwick Chronicles are great fun for young listeners. With oldfashioned New England far behind, 11-year-old Nichoal Vargas is ready for some fun in the sun - Florida-style. But then a gargantuan, fire-breathing dragon crashes the party, causing Nick's respite to go up in smoke.

Nixie's Song. unabr. ed. Tony DiTerlizzi & Holly Black. Read by Andrew McCarthy. (Running Time: 2 hrs. 0 mins. 0 sec.). (Beyond the Spiderwick Chronicles: Bk. 1). (ENG., (J). (gr. 2-7). 2007. audio compact disk 17.99 (978-0-7435-6915-6(6)) Pub: S&S Audio. Dist(s): S and S Inc

Nixon: A Life. abr. ed. Jonathan Atkins. Read by Alan Rachins. 4 cass. (Running Time: 6 hrs.). 2001. 25.00 (978-1-59040-172-9(7), Phoenix Audio) Pub: Amer Intl Pub. Dist(s): PerseuPGW

Nixon: Oliver Stone's. unabr. ed. Harriet Greenberg. Perf. by J. T. Walsh. 2 cass. (Running Time: 3 hrs.). 1996. 17.00 (978-1-56876-054-4(X)) Soundlines Ent.
Based on Olvier Stone's controversial film, about the Nixon presidency, with its achievements & failures.

Nixon: Ruin & Recovery, 1973-1990. unabr. ed. Stephen E. Ambrose. Read by John McDonald. 19 cass. (Running Time: 28 hrs. 30 min.). 1992. 152.00 (978-0-7366-2296-7(9), 3081A&B) Books on Tape.
In Nixon: Ruin & Recovery, Stephen E. Ambrose completes his acclaimed three-part biography of the man many historians call the most fascinating politician in American history.

Nixon: Ruin & Recovery, 1973-1990, Pt. 1. unabr. ed. Stephen E. Ambrose. Read by John MacDonald. 9 cass. (Running Time: 13 hrs. 30 mins.). 1992. 72.00 (3081-A) Books on Tape.

Nixon: Ruin & Recovery, 1973-1990, Pt. 2. unabr. ed. Stephen E. Ambrose. Read by John MacDonald. 10 cass. (Running Time: 15 hrs.). 1992. 80.00 (3081-B) Books on Tape.

Nixon: The Education of a Politician, 1913-1962, Pt. 1. unabr. ed. Stephen E. Ambrose. Read by John MacDonald. 9 cass. (Running Time: 13 hrs. 30 mins.). 1990. 72.00 (2583-A) Books on Tape.
Think what you will of Richard Nixon personally, he remains one of the most elusive & intriguing political figures in American history. Thus this biography, with its keys to his complexity, is a welcome & long-awaited event.

Nixon Pt. 1: The Triumph of a Politician, 1962-1972, unabr. ed. Stephen E. Ambrose. Read by Michael Wells. 11 cass. (Running Time: 30 hrs. 30 mins.). 1990. 76.95 (978-0-7861-0164-1(4), 1147-A,B) Blckstn Audio.
This is a balanced, unflinching portrait of one of our most complex & puzzling chief executives at the apogee of his career - rebounding from defeat to an innovative, high-risk presidency, already sowing the seeds of his ruin.

Nixon Pt. 2: The Triumph of a Politician, 1962-1972, unabr. ed. Stephen E. Ambrose. Read by Michael Wells. 10 cass. (Running Time: 30 hrs. 30 mins.). 1990. 69.95 (978-0-7861-0165-8(2), 1147-A,B) Blckstn Audio.

Nixon Vol. 1: The Education of a Politician, 1913-1962. unabr. ed. Stephen E. Ambrose. Read by Jay Robertson. 18 cass. (Running Time: 27 hrs.). 1990. 144.00 (978-0-7366-1743-7(4), 2583-A/B) Books on Tape.
Think what you will of Richard Nixon personally, he remains one of the most elusive & intriguing political figures in American history. Thus this biography, with its keys to his complexity, is a welcome & long-awaited event.

Nixon Vol. 1: The Education of a Politician, 1913-1962, Pt. 2. unabr. ed. Stephen E. Ambrose. Read by John MacDonald. 9 cass. (Running Time: 13 hrs. 30 mins.). 1990. 72.00 (2583-B) Books on Tape.

Nixon Vol. 2: The Triumph of a Politician, 1962-1972. unabr. ed. Stephen E. Ambrose. Read by Jay Robertson. 19 cass. (Running Time: 28 hrs. 30 mins.). 1990. 152.00 (978-0-7366-1831-1(7), 2667-A/B) Books on Tape.
Nixon: The Triumph of a Politician 1962-1972 is the second volume of Stephen Ambrose's three-part biography of Richard Nixon. This volume covers a full decade beginning with the "last" press conference in 1962 & ending at Nixon's 1972 re- election. During his first term, Nixon accomplished an opening into China & began the reduction of arms with the USSR. He engineered the first Cold War arms control agreement - but he had not ended the war in Vietnam or achieved his goal of decentralizing the domestic government. He had achieved much in foreign policy, but he had already begun to step outside the law to launch an attack on his enemies.

Nixon Vol. 2: The Triumph of a Politician, 1962-1972, Pt. 1. unabr. ed. Stephen E. Ambrose. Read by John MacDonald. 9 cass. (Running Time: 13 hrs. 30 mins.). 1990. 72.00 (2667-A) Books on Tape.

Nixon Vol. 2: The Triumph of a Politician, 1962-1972, Pt. 2. unabr. ed. Stephen E. Ambrose. Read by John MacDonald. 10 cass. (Running Time: 15 hrs.). 1990. 80.00 (2667-B) Books on Tape.

Nixon - Kennedy Debate. 1 cass. (Running Time: 1 hr. 22 min.). 11.95 (467) J Norton Pubs.
From the campaign debates of 1960, this is a recording of the fourth debate which included the topics of Quemoy & Matsu & Cuba. A radio commentator discusses some of the interesting points about the debate series.

***Nixon & Kissinger.** abr. ed. Robert Dallek. Read by Eric Conger. (ENG.). 2007. (978-0-06-144980-2(6), Harper Audio); (978-0-06-144981-9(4), Harper Audio) HarperCollins Pubs.

Nixon & Kissinger: Partners in Power. unabr. ed. Robert Dallek. Read by Eric Conger. 10 CDs. (Running Time: 39600 sec.). 2007. audio compact disk 44.95 (978-0-06-125642-4(0), Harper Audio) HarperCollins Pubs.

Nixon & Mao: The Week That Changed the World. Margaret MacMillan. Narrated by Barbara Caruso. (Running Time: 54900 sec.). 2007. audio compact disk 34.99 (978-1-4281-2051-8(3)) Recorded Bks.

Nixon & Mao: The Week That Changed the World. unabr. ed. Margaret MacMillan. Read by Barbara Caruso. 13 cass. (Running Time: 15 hrs. 25 mins.). 2007. 94.75 (978-1-4025-6569-4(0)); audio compact disk 102.75 (978-1-4193-1666-1(4)) Recorded Bks.

Nixon Chronicles: Circa 1973: Hearts & Minds. Short Stories. Composed by Bill Holt. Music by Network Music Staff. 1 CD. (Running Time: 66 mins.). 2002. audio compact disk 14.99 (978-0-9727876-0-4(7)) Wilmington Studios.
DVD video art gallery. Enjoy the world of early America country antiques, primitives, textiles, artifacts, whimsy, and more as seen through the loving eye of folk art photographer Carole Holt. This DVD is a soothing blend of exquisite photography, video artistry, and music. Relaxing and mesmerizingly beautiful. Runtime 75 minutes. Widescreen with Dolby 5.1 surround sound makes for beautiful video wall art.

Nixon in Winter. unabr. ed. Monica Crowley. Read by Anna Fields. 13 cass. (Running Time: 19 hrs.). 1999. 85.95 (978-0-7861-1566-2(1), 2388) Blckstn Audio.
The final public & private years of the thirty-seventh president, based on full reconstructions of the conversations Crowley had with him at the time.

Nixon in Winter. unabr. ed. Monica Crowley. Read by Anna Fields. (Running Time: 18 hrs. 0 mins.). 2008. 44.95 (978-1-4332-4513-8(2)); audio compact disk & audio compact disk 120.00 (978-1-4332-4512-1(4)) Blckstn Audio.

Nixon-Kennedy Debate: Campaign debates Of 1960. 2008. audio compact disk 12.95 (978-1-57970-527-5(8), Audio-For) J Norton Pubs.

Nixon-Kennedy Debates. John F. Kennedy & Richard M. Nixon. Narrated by Sander Vanocur. 4 cass. (Running Time: 6 hrs.). 1996. 24.95 (978-1-57511-014-1(8), 636488) Pub Mills.

Nixon Presidency. John M. Ashbrook & William Rusher. 1 cass. (Running Time: 56 min.). 10.95 (244) J Norton Pubs.

Nixon's Nineteen Seventy-Four Resignation Speech. Read by Richard M. Nixon. (Running Time: 15 min.). 10.95 (469) J Norton Pubs.
Nixon explains that confidence in his administration had fallen so low that he could no longer lead the country effectively.

Nixon's Watergate Denial Speech. 2008. audio compact disk 12.95 (978-1-57970-524-4(3), Audio-For) J Norton Pubs.

Nixon's Watergate Denial Speech. Read by Richard M. Nixon. (Running Time: 24 min.). 10.95 (468) J Norton Pubs.
Most significant attempt by President Nixon to convince the public of his innocence. He announces the resignations of his aides & the appointment of Eliot Richardson as Attorney General in the wake of Richard Kleindienst's resignation.

Nizam's Daughters: Sequel to a Close Run Thing. Allan Mallinson. Narrated by Erick Graham. 13 CDs. (Running Time: 14 hrs. 30 mins.). 2000. audio compact disk 128.00 (978-1-84197-170-4(7), C1305E7) Recorded Bks.
Fresh from Waterloo, Matthew Hervey, aide-de-camp to the Duke of Wellington, leaves the scene of his triumph to travel to India. Chintal is Hervey's destination & his mission is to glean intelligence for the Duke, who expects to become Governor-General of India.

Nizam's Daughters: Sequel to a Close Run Thing. unabr. ed. Allan Mallinson. Narrated by Erick Graham. 12 cass. (Running Time: 14 hrs. 30 mins.). 2000. 102.00 (978-1-84197-118-6(9), H1115E7) Recorded Bks.

NKJV Story of Jesus. Narrated by Eric Martin. (ENG.). 2003. audio compact disk 14.99 (978-1-930034-24-2(5)) Casscomm.

***Nkjv word of promise new Testament.** Thomas Nelson. 2007. audio compact disk 49.99 (978-0-7180-2482-6(6)) Nelson.

NLP: The New Technology of Achievement. 6 cass. (Running Time: 6 hrs.). 1999. 59.95 (83-0011) Explorations.
Can science give us a shortcut to success? Yes, according to results achieved with a high-tech form of psychology called NLP, or Neurolinguistic Programming. Ideas & techniques to achieve happiness & success, delivered by six internationally recognized master trainers. Includes pocket guide.

NLP: The New Technology of Achievement. 6 cass. (Running Time: 6 hrs.). 59.95 incls. Pocket Guide. (978-1-55525-060-7(2), 894AD) Nightingale-Conant.
NLP or Neuro-Linguistic Programming is a practical method of changing the way you think & behave faster & more easily than ever before. Its power has undergone scientific scrutiny & has created practical successes for many Fortune 500 executives. It is based on a few simple but powerful ideas.

NLP: The New Technology of Achievement. abr. ed. Charles Faulkner et al. Read by Charles Faulkner et al. (Running Time: 20 hrs. 0 mins. 0 sec.). (ENG.). 2003. audio compact disk 19.95 (978-0-7435-2905-1(7), Nightgale) Pub: S&S Audio. Dist(s): S and S Inc

Nm How to Pass Appr Audio Cds. Ed. by Kaplan Publishing Staff. 2005. (978-1-4195-2891-0(2)) Dearborn Financial.

NMR Physical&Biological Scienc. Pochapsky & Peter Parham. 2004. audio compact disk 83.00 (978-0-8153-4094-2(X), Garland Sci) Taylor and Fran.

No Angel. unabr. ed. Penny Vincenzi. Read by Carrington MacDuffie. 20 cass. (Running Time: 30 hrs.). (Spoils of Time Trilogy: Vol. 1). 2004. 69.95 (978-1-59007-510-4(2)) Pub: New Millenn Enter. Dist(s): PerseuPGW

No Angel. unabr. ed. Penny Vincenzi. Read by Carrington McDuffie. 23 CDs. (Running Time: 30 hrs.). (Spoils of Time Trilogy: Vol. 1). 2004. audio compact disk 125.00 (978-1-59007-511-1(0)) Pub: New Millenn Enter. Dist(s): PerseuPGW

No Angel: My Harrowing Undercover Journey to the Inner Circle of the Hells Angels. unabr. ed. Jay Dobyns & Nils Johnson-Shelton. Narrated by Mel Foster. (Running Time: 12 hrs. 0 mins. 0 sec.). (ENG.). 2009. audio compact disk 24.99 (978-1-4001-6248-2(3)); audio compact disk 37.99 (978-1-4001-1248-7(6)); audio compact disk 75.99 (978-1-4001-4248-4(2)) Pub: Tantor Media. Dist(s): IngramPubServ

No Apology: The Case for American Greatness. unabr. ed. Mitt Romney. Read by Mitt Romney. (Running Time: 12 hrs. 30 mins. 0 sec.). (ENG.). 2010. audio compact disk 39.99 (978-1-4272-0920-7(0)) Pub: Macmill Audio. Dist(s): Macmillan

No Asshole Rule: Building a Civilized Workplace & Surviving One That Isn't. abr. ed. Robert I. Sutton. (Running Time: 3 hrs. 30 mins.). (ENG.). 2007. 14.98 (978-1-59483-868-2(2)) Pub: Hachet Audio. Dist(s): HachBkGrp

***No Asshole Rule: Building a Civilized Workplace & Surviving One That Isn't.** abr. ed. Robert I. Sutton. Read by Robert I. Sutton. (Running Time: 3 hrs. 30 mins.). (ENG.). 2010. audio compact disk 14.98 (978-1-60024-585-5(4)) Pub: Hachet Audio. Dist(s): HachBkGrp

No Balance Due: Tired of Being in Debt up to Your Eyeballs? Lenny Tumbarello. Ed. by Lana Davis. 2006. 19.95 (978-0-9769942-6-8(7)); audio compact disk 48.95 (978-0-9769942-5-1(9)) We Too Can Do.

No Balloons Today: A Day at the Zoo. Sandra Robbins. Illus. by Alfredo Garzon. Music by Jeff Olmsted. 1 CD. (Running Time: 36 mins). (See-More's Stories Ser.). (J). 2001. pap. bk. 16.95 (978-1-882601-36-3(X)) See-Mores Wrkshop.

No Balloons Today: A Zoo Story. unabr. ed. Sandra Robbins. (J). (ps-3). 2001. 5.50 (978-1-882601-33-2(5)) See-Mores Wrkshop.
A comic story that stars See-More, the Shadow Box Theatre's hallmark puppet.

No Bells to Believe. Richard Hugo. 1 cass. (Running Time: 1 hr. 4 min.). (Watershed Tapes of Contemporary Poetry). 1980. 11.95 (23641) J Norton Pubs.
This retrospective carries the whole range of Pulitzer Prize winner Hugo's work.

No Big Deal. unabr. ed. Jean E. Cooper. Read by Stephanie Brush. 12 cass. (Running Time: 15 hrs. 36 min.). 2001. 64.95 (978-1-58116-049-9(6)) Books in Motion.
Unemployed computer engineer Poplar Reuss has the power "to find things," a gift the local police want to press into action on the Catuto case. But finding the source of the money and drugs the dead man carried might just get our "gifted" computer hack in more trouble than any woman could ever handle.

No Boundaries. Peter Matthiessen. 1996. Gang of Seven.

No Boundaries. abr. ed. Peter Matthiessen. 1 cass. (Running Time: 1 hr. 12 min.). 1999. 11.95 (978-1-57453-141-1(7)) Audio Lit.
Internationally renowned naturalist & author Matthiessen recounts compelling stories from his travels in Nepal & Africa & his early days at The New Yorker.

No Boundaries: Moving Beyond Supply Chain Management. James A. Tompkins. 1 cass. (Running Time: 1 hr. 30 min.). 1999. 17.99 (978-1-930426-00-9(3)) Tompkins Pr.
Explains the need to integrate operations all the way from the producer of raw materials to the ultimate customer.

***No Boundaries / Gan Teorainn.** Gabriel Fitzmaurice. Donie Lyons. (ENG.). 1995. 11.95 (978-0-8023-7114-0(0)) Pub: Clo Iar-Chonnachta IRL. Dist(s): Dufour

No-Brainers: 5 Hard Decisions That the Gospel Makes Easy. John Bytheway. 2006. audio compact disk 12.95 (978-1-59038-554-8(3)) Deseret Bk.

No Bull Selling: Winning Sales Strategy from America's Super Salesman. Hank Trisler. Read by Hank Trisler. 6 cass. (Running Time: 9 hrs.). 59.95 (458AD) Nightingale-Conant.
Sell better because you're having fun.

NO BULL SELLING, Revisited. Hank Trisler. 4 discs. (Running Time: 4 hrs.). 2005. cd-rom 59.95 (978-0-9760765-0-6(0)) Trisler.

***No Castles Here.** unabr. ed. A. C. E. Bauer. Read by John H. Mayer. 5 CDs. (Running Time: 6 hrs. 21 mins.). (J). (gr. 4-8). 2009. audio compact disk 45.00 (978-0-7393-8013-0(3), Listening Lib) Pub: Random Audio Pubg. Dist(s): Random

No Choice but Seduction. abr. ed. Johanna Lindsey. Read by Laural Merlington. (Running Time: 5 hrs.). (Malory Ser.). 2009. audio compact disk 14.99 (978-1-4233-2795-0(0), 9781423327950, BCD Value Price) Brilliance Audio.

No Choice but Seduction. unabr. ed. Johanna Lindsey. Read by Laural Merlington. (Running Time: 10 hrs.). (Malory Ser.). 2008. 39.25 (978-1-4233-2793-6(4), 9781423327936, BADLE); 24.95 (978-1-4233-2792-9(6), 9781423327929, BAD); audio compact disk 36.95 (978-1-4233-2788-2(8), 9781423327882, Bril Audio CD Unabri); audio compact disk 97.25 (978-1-4233-2789-9(6), 9781423327899, BriAudCD Unabrid) Brilliance Audio.

No Choice but Seduction. unabr. ed. Johanna Lindsey. Read by Laural Merlington. Directed By Laurel Kelly Young. Contrib. by Martin Woessner. (Running Time: 10 hrs.). (Malory Ser.). 2008. audio compact disk 24.95 (978-1-4233-2790-5(X), 9781423327905, Brilliance MP3); audio compact disk 39.25 (978-1-4233-2791-2(8), 9781423327912, Brinc Audio MP3 Lib) Brilliance Audio.

No Colder Place: A Bill Smith & Lydia Chin Mystery. unabr. ed. S. J. Rozan. Read by Sky Vogel. 8 vols. (Running Time: 12 hrs.). (American Collection). 2000. bk. 69.95 (978-0-7927-2230-4(2), CSL 119, Chivers Sound Lib) AudioGO.
When a Manhattan construction site is plagued by an escalating series of thefts and misfortunes, the contractors hire P. I. Bill Smith to investigate. Smith goes undercover as a bricklayer to try and uncover the person behind the job-site trouble. With his sometimes-partner, P. I. Lydia Chin, the two find themselves on a much more serious case of fraud and murder that could reach through the layers of corruption, and into the depths of the underworld.

No Colder Place: A Bill Smith/Lydia Chin Mystery. S. J. Rozan. Read by Sky Vogel. 8 CDs. 2004. audio compact disk 39.95 (978-0-7927-3267-9(7), SLD 119, Chivers Sound Lib) AudioGO.

No Comebacks. unabr. ed. Short Stories. Frederick Forsyth. Narrated by Frank Muller. 3 cass. (Running Time: 4 hrs. 30 mins.). 1984. 26.00 (978-1-55690-379-3(0), 84061E7) Recorded Bks.
A tycoon hires a hit-man to eliminate an "annoying problem." His employee does his job too well. Plus these stories: "Money with Menaces"; "A Careful Man"; "There Are No Snakes in Ireland" & "There are Some Days"...(Part 2 of the collection is entitled "The Emperor" & includes five more stories).

No Comebacks; The Good Shepherd. Frederick Forsyth. Read by Richard Brown. 7 cass. (Running Time: 10 hrs. 30 min.). 1987. 56.00 (978-0-7366-1160-2(6), 2085) Books on Tape.
A collection of ten fine short stories, The Shepherd, about a young pilot's experience in the air.

No Complaining Rule: Positive Ways to Deal with Negativity at Work. unabr. ed. Jon Gordon. Read by Jon Gordon. 4 CDs. (Running Time: 2 hrs.). (ENG.). 2008. audio compact disk 19.98 (978-1-59659-210-0(9), GildAudio) Pub: Gildan Media. Dist(s): HachBkGrp

No Compromise. Rick Joyner. 1 cass. (Running Time: 90 mins.). (Walking in Truth Ser.: Vol. 3). 2000. 5.00 (RJ02-003) Morning NC.
Rick reinforces our calling to walk in truth & integrity while pursuing God's perfect will for our lives.

No Compromise. Perf. by No Innocent Victim. 1 cass. 1997. audio compact disk 15.99 CD. (D8860) Diamante Music Grp.
Hard-core music & lifestyle is about bringing people together & boldly standing up for what you believe in. No Innocent Victim (NIV) believes that a better life comes through the knowledge & saving grace of Jesus Christ.

***No Country for Old Men.** abr. ed. Cormac McCarthy. Read by Sean Barrett. 4 CDs. (Running Time: 4 hrs.). 2009. audio compact disk 28.98 (978-962-634-980-9(8), Naxos AudioBooks) Naxos.

No Country for Old Men. unabr. ed. Cormac McCarthy. Narrated by Tom Stechschulte. 1 Playaway. (Running Time: 7 hrs. 30 mins.). 2009. 56.75 (978-1-4281-4316-6(5)); 51.75 (978-1-4193-4449-7(8)); audio compact disk 77.75 (978-1-4193-4458-9(7)) Recorded Bks.

No Country for Old Men. unabr. ed. Cormac McCarthy. Narrated by Tom Stechschulte. 7 CDs. (Running Time: 7 hrs. 45 mins.). 2005. audio compact disk 34.99 (978-1-4193-2694-3(5)) Recorded Bks.

No Cross, No Crown. 1 cass. (Running Time: 1 hr. 30 min.). 10.98 (978-1-57908-353-3(6), 5307); audio compact disk 15.98 (978-1-57908-352-6(8)) Platinm Enter.

No Cross, No Crown: Exemplified in the Life of William Penn. Instructed by Stephen McDowell. 2000. 5.95 (978-1-887456-25-8(2)) Providence Found.

***No Debt No Sweat! Money Bootcamp Leader Kit.** Steve Diggs. (ENG.). 2004. audio compact disk 250.00 (978-0-9624293-4-7(1)) Boyd & Franklin.

***No Debt No Sweat! Money Bootcamp Student Kit.** Steve Diggs. (ENG.). 2004. audio compact disk 82.00 (978-0-9624293-3-0(3)) Boyd & Franklin.

No Defense. unabr. ed. Kate Wilhelm. Read by Marguerite Gavin. 9 cass. (Running Time: 13 hrs.). 2000. 62.95 (978-0-7861-1900-4(4), 2693); audio compact disk 80.00 (978-0-7861-9794-1(3), 2693) Blckstn Audio.
Barbara Holloway is a trial lawyer who tends to take on difficult cases. One involved a woman accused of killing her own child, another involved a mentally disabled man & her last one found her entangled in such a mess that it's a wonder she lived through it all.

No Desmayes! Como Mantenerte en el Nivel Donde Estas Hasta Ser Promovido. unabr. abr. ed. Rene Gonzalez. (SPA.). 2006. audio compact disk 14.99 (978-0-8297-4871-0(7)) Pub: Vida Pubs. Dist(s): Zondervan

No Disguise/Ceim Ar Cheim. Contrib. by Art O. Dufaigh. (ENG.). 1999. 13.95 (978-0-8023-7137-9(X)) Pub: Clo Iar-Chonnachta IRL. Dist(s): Dufour

No Disguise/Ceim ar Cheim. Contrib. by Art O. Dufaigh. (ENG.). 1999. audio compact disk 21.95 (978-0-8023-8137-8(5)) Pub: Clo Iar-Chonnachta IRL. Dist(s): Dufour

No Distance Too Far. abr. ed. Lauraine Snelling. Narrated by Renee Ertl. (Running Time: 6 hrs. 51 mins. 33 sec.). (Home to Blessing Ser.: No. 2). (ENG.). 2010. 19.59 (978-1-60814-614-7(6)); audio compact disk 27.99 (978-1-59859-668-7(3)) Oasis Audio.

No Dogs Allowed, unabr. ed. Short Stories. Jane Cutler. Narrated by Johnny Heller. 2 pieces. (Running Time: 1 hr. 45 mins.). (gr. 1 up). 1997. 19.00 (978-0-7887-0691-2(8), 94865E7) Recorded Bks.
A rollicking collection of stories. When five-year-old Edward Fraser & his older brother Jason find out they can't have a pet because of allergies, Edward finds his own solution to the problem: he becomes a dog.

No Dominion. unabr. ed. Charlie Huston & Scott Brick. (Running Time: 9 hrs. NaN mins.). 2008. 29.95 (978-1-4332-3589-4(7)); 59.95 (978-1-4332-3585-6(4)); audio compact disk 70.00 (978-1-4332-3586-3(2)) Blckstn Audio.

No Doubt. Darren Brooks. (Maximum Ser.). (ENG., 2003. audio compact disk 14.95 (978-1-84240-183-5(1)) Pub: Chrome Dreams GBR. Dist(s): IPG Chicago

No Doubt. Contrib. by Lesters. 2007. audio compact disk 13.99 (978-5-557-52342-4(1)) Not Available.

No Down Payment. Carleton Sheets. 10 cass. (Running Time: 15 hrs.). 159.95 (10930PAB) Nightingale-Conant.
A unique, multimedia approach to wealth-building that will work for anyone - offers a step-by-step guide to investing profitably in real estate. Inlcudes 3 workbooks & manuals.

No Dream Too Big Tele-Seminar. Speeches. Vic Johnson. 1 CD. (Running Time: 4 hrs.). 2003. audio compact disk 97.00 (978-0-9745717-0-6(9), AsAManThinketh) No Dream.
Interactive Tele-Seminar conducted with a live audience.

No Easy Answers: Short Stories about Teenagers Making Touch Choices, Set unabr. ed. Donald R. Gallo. 6 cass. (Running Time: 8 hr.). (YA). (gr. 2). 1998. 121.70 CLASS SET . (978-0-7887-3282-9(X), 46372) Recorded Bks.
This collection of 16 stories provide realistic & positive accounts of today's teens facing moral dilemmas.

No Easy Answers: Short Stories about Teenagers Making Tough Choices, unabr. ed. Donald R. Gallo. 6 cass. (Running Time: 8 hr.). (YA). (gr. 2). 1998. 64.24 HMWK SET. (978-0-7887-1943-1(2), 40650) Recorded Bks.

No Easy Answers: Short Stories about Teenagers Making Tough Choices, unabr. ed. Short Stories. M. E. Kerr, pseud et al. Narrated by Jeff Woodman & Johnny Heller. 6 pieces. (Running Time: 8 hrs.). (gr. 7 up). 1998. 51.00 (978-0-7887-1915-8(7), 95336E7) Recorded Bks.
Provides realistic & positive accounts of today's teens facing pregnancy, drug use, peer pressure & violence.

No Effort Weight Loss Meditation, Subliminals & Sleep Programming. Dick Sutphen. 2 cass. (Running Time: 3 hrs.). pap. bk. 24.98 (978-0-911842-48-7(9), C821) Valley Sun.
Contains three techniques to use alone or combine with any diet plan.

No Es Cuestión de Suerte. unabr. ed. Rescate VanPelt. 2002. 9.99 (978-0-8297-3824-7(X)) Pub: Vida Pubs. Dist(s): Zondervan

No es Justo: Audiocassette. (SPA.). (gr. k-1). 10.00 (978-0-7635-6262-5(9)) Rigby Educ.

No Es Solo un Sentimiento. unabr. ed. Carlos Cintrón. (SPA.). 2001. 9.99 (978-0-8297-2558-2(X)) Pub: Vida Pubs. Dist(s): Zondervan

No Es Solo un Sentimiento. unabr. ed. Carlos Cintrón. 2001. audio compact disk 14.99 (978-0-8297-2559-9(8)) Zondervan.

No Escape. Perf. by James Cagney. (DM-5115) Natl Recrd Co.

No Excuse Leadership: Lessons from the U. S. Army's Elite Rangers. abr. ed. Brace E. Barber. Read by Dick Hill. (YA). 2008. 54.99 (978-1-60252-984-7(1)) Find a World.

No Excuses, Pts. I-II. 3rd rev. ed. Instructed by Robert Solomon. 12 CDs. (Running Time: 12 hrs.). 2000. bk. 69.95 (978-1-56585-344-7(X), 437) Teaching Co.

No Excuses, Vol. 1, Pts. I-II. 3rd rev. ed. Instructed by Robert Solomon. 12 cass. (Running Time: 12 hrs.). 2000. 54.95 (978-1-56585-099-6(8), 437) Teaching Co.

No Excuses: Concessions of a Serial Campaigner. unabr. ed. Robert Shrum. Narrated by Michael Prichard. 18 CDs. (Running Time: 22 hrs. 30 mins. 0 sec.). (ENG.). 2007. audio compact disk 49.99 (978-1-4001-0498-7(X)); audio compact disk 34.99 (978-1-4001-5498-2(7)); audio compact disk 99.99 (978-1-4001-3498-4(6)) Pub: Tantor Media. Dist(s): IngramPubServ

No Excuses: Existentialism & the Meaning of Life, Course No. 437. Instructed by Robert Solomon. 2 cass. (Running Time: 12 hrs.). 84.91 Teaching Co.
Existentialism is one of the most exciting & enduring philosophies of the Twentieth Century. With its powerful emphasis on individual responsibility & the importance of passion in life, it provides a vision of life that is particularly appealing to contemporary American students of all ages. This course explores the religious existentialism of the Danish philosopher Soren Kierkegaard, the warrior rhetoric & often shocking attacks on morality & religion by Friedrich Nietzsche, the bold & profound approach to philosophy advocated by Martin Heidegger, the "absurd" view of life envisioned by French-Algerian novelist Albert Camus, & the radical, uncompromising notion of freedom defended by the late French existentialist Jean-Paul Sartre. Includes 16 lectures.

No Excuses: Existentialism & the Meaning of Life, Vol. 2. 3rd rev. ed. Instructed by Robert Solomon. 6 cass. (Running Time: 6 hrs.). 2000. 129.95 (978-1-56585-100-9(5)) Teaching Co.

***No Excuses! The Power of Self-Discipline; 21 Ways to Achieve Lasting Happiness & Success.** unabr. ed. Brian Tracy. Read by Brian Tracy. (Running Time: 7 hrs.). (ENG.). 2010. 27.98 (978-1-59659-572-9(8), GildAudio) Pub: Gildan Media. Dist(s): HachBkGrp

***No Excuses! The Power of Self-Discipline; 21 Ways to Achieve Lasting Happiness & Success.** unabr. ed. Brian Tracy. Read by Brian Tracy. (Running Time: 7 hrs.). (ENG.). 2010. audio compact disk 29.98 (978-1-59659-520-0(5), GildAudio) Pub: Gildan Media. Dist(s): HachBkGrp

No Excuses Vol. 2: Existentialism & the Meaning of Life, 3rd rev. ed. Instructed by Robert Solomon. 6 CDs. (Running Time: 6 hrs.). 2000. audio compact disk 179.95 (978-1-56585-345-4(8)) Teaching Co.

No Excuses! Increasing Minority Student Achievement - Elementary, Vol. 1503E. (Enabling Teachers & Students to Thrive Ser.: Vol. 1500). (C). 2006. video 645.00 (978-1-58740-155-8(X)) SchImprove.

No Excuses! Increasing Minority Student Achievement - Secondary, 1503S. (Enabling Teachers & Students to Thrive Ser.: 1500). (C). 2006. video 645.00 (978-1-58740-156-5(8)) SchImprove.

No Eye Can See. abr. ed. Jane Kirkpatrick. 4 cass. (Running Time: 7 hrs. 30 min.). 2003. 25.99 (978-1-58926-145-7(3), W68L-0130); audio compact disk 29.99 (978-1-58926-146-4(1), W68L-013D) Oasis Audio.

No Fear. Robert Farago. Read by Robert Farago. (Running Time: 1 hr.). 2001. 16.95 (978-1-59912-929-7(9)) Iofy Corp.

No Fences, No Walls. unabr. ed. Perf. by Eknath Easwaran. 1 cass. (Running Time: 1 hr.). 1986. 7.95 (978-1-58638-582-8(8)) Nilgiri Pr.

No Finish Line: My Life As I See It. abr. ed. Marla Runyan & Sally Jenkins. Read by Emily Schirner. 4 CDs. (Running Time: 4 hrs.). 2001. audio compact disk 27.95 (978-1-58788-760-4(6), 1587887606, CD); audio compact disk 61.25 (978-1-58788-761-1(4), 1587887614, CD Lib Edit) Brilliance Audio.
"Blind? I think there's no doubt that Marla Runyan can see things much clearer than most of us with 20/20 vision." - Lance Armstrong Marla Runyan was nine years old when she was diagnosed with Stargardt's disease, an irreversible form of macular degeneration. With the uneasy but unwavering support of her parents, she refused to let her diagnosis limit her dreams. Despite her severely impaired, ever-worsening vision, Marla rode horseback and learned to play the violin. And she found her true calling in sports. A gifted and natural athlete, Marla began to compete in the unlikeliest event of all: the heptathlon, the grueling women's equivalent of the decathlon, consisting of seven events: the 200-meter dash, high jump, shot put, 100-meter hurdles, long jump, javelin throw, and 800-meter run. In 1996, she astonished the sports world by qualifying for the U.S. Olympic Trials and, along the way, set the American record for heptathlon 800. It was then that she decided to concentrate on her running. Four years of intense effort paid off. In 2000, she qualified for the U.S. Olympic team by finishing third in the 1,500 meters. In Sydney, she placed eighth in the finals, the top American finisher - the highest women's placing for the United States in the event's history. With self-deprecation and surprising wit, Marla reveals what it's like to see the world through her eyes, how it feels to grow up "disabled" in a society where expectations are often based on perceived abilities, and what it means to compete at the world-class level despite the fact that - quite literally, for her - there is no finish line.

No Finish Line: My Life As I See It. unabr. ed. Marla Runyan & Sally Jenkins. Read by Emily Schirner. 6 cass. (Running Time: 9 hrs.). 2001. 29.95 (978-1-58788-757-4(6), 1587887576, BAU); 69.25 (978-1-58788-758-1(4), 1587887584, Unabridge Lib Edns) Brilliance Audio.

No Finish Line: My Life As I See It. unabr. ed. Marla Runyan & Sally Jenkins. Read by Emily Schirner. (Running Time: 9 hrs.). 2004. 39.25 (978-1-59335-373-5(1), 1593353731, Brlnc Audio MP3 Lib) Brilliance Audio.

No Finish Line: My Life As I See It. unabr. ed. Marla Runyan & Sally Jenkins. Read by Emily Schirner. (Running Time: 9 hrs.). 2004. 39.25 (978-1-59710-536-1(8), 1597105368, BADLE); 24.95 (978-1-59710-537-8(6), 1597105376, BAD) Brilliance Audio.

No Finish Line: My Life As I See It. unabr. ed. Marla Runyan & Sally Jenkins. Read by Emily Schirner. (Running Time: 9 hrs.). 2004. 24.95 (978-1-59335-102-1(X), 159335102X) Soulmate Audio Bks.

No Fui Yo. . Alma Flor Ada. (Cuentos Para Todo el Ano Ser.). (SPA., (J). (gr. k-3). 4.95 (978-1-58105-245-9(6)) Santillana.

No Girls Allowed. Trudi Trueit. (Secrets of A Lab Rat Ser.). (ENG.). (J). (gr. 3-7). 2009. audio compact disk 19.95 (978-0-545-13861-1(2)) Scholastic Inc.

No Girls Allowed (Dogs Okay) unabr. ed. Trudi Strain Trueit. Narrated by Oliver Wyman. 2 CDs. (Running Time: 1 hr. 55 mins.). (Secrets of A Lab Rat Ser.). (ENG.). (J). (gr. 3-7). 2009. audio compact disk 29.95 (978-0-545-13866-6(3)) Scholastic Inc.

No God but God. 1 CD. (Running Time: 50 minutes 26 seconds). (YA). 2004. audio compact disk 15.00 (978-0-9742778-1-3(9)) WorldView Intl.
Passionate worship music from WorldView Community Church in Olmsted Falls, Ohio.

No Gods, No Guilt: How to enjoy life with no guilt, no shame, no Blame. Stephen Frederick Uhl. (ENG.). 2008. 9.95 (978-0-9793169-2-0(8)) Golden Rule AZ.

No Good Deed. unabr. ed. Lynn S. Hightower. Read by Anna Fields. 6 cass. (Running Time: 8 hrs. 30 mins.). 1998. 44.95 (978-0-7861-1438-2(X), 2324) Blckstn Audio.
The young girl - only fifteen - had saddled up & gone for a ride, but no one saw her return to the horse farm that afternoon. There's blood on the trail, & a discarded riding boot. Cincinnati police detective Sonora Blair has a feeling this girl's not coming back.

***No Good Deed.** unabr. ed. Lynn S. Hightower. Read by Anna Fields. (Running Time: 8 hrs. 30 mins.). 2010. 29.95 (978-1-4417-1324-7(7)); audio compact disk 76.00 (978-1-4417-1321-6(2)) Blckstn Audio.

***No Good Deeds.** unabr. ed. Laura Lippman. Read by Linda Emond. (ENG.). 2006. (978-0-06-122905-3(9), Harper Audio); (978-0-06-122906-0(7), Harper Audio) HarperCollins Pubs.

No Good Deeds. unabr. ed. Laura Lippman. Read by Linda Emond. 8 CDs. (Running Time: 36000 sec.). (Tess Monaghan Ser.: No. 9). 2006. audio compact disk 39.95 (978-0-06-089793-2(7), Harper Audio) HarperCollins Pubs.

No Good Deeds. unabr. ed. Laura Lippman. Read by Linda Emond. 8 cass. (Running Time: 9 hrs. 45 mins.). (Tess Monaghan Ser.: No. 9). 2006. 69.75 (978-1-4281-0209-5(4)); audio compact disk 99.75 (978-1-4281-0211-8(6)) Recorded Bks.
When P.I. Tess Monaghan learns that a mysterious teenager has information about the murder of a U.S. Attorney, she leaks the information to the media. But then an associate of the teen is murdered, and the feds threaten Tess with jail time unless she reveals her source.

No, Gracias, No Para Mi. 1 cass. (Running Time: 1 hr. 30 mins.). (SmartReader Ser.).Tr. of No Thanks, Not for Me. (SPA & ENG.). (J). 1999. pap. bk. & tchr. ed. 19.95 (978-0-7887-0282-2(3), 79322T3) Recorded Bks.

No Graves as Yet. Anne Perry. Read by Michael Page. (Playaway Adult Fiction Ser.). 2008. 94.99 (978-1-60640-913-8(1)) Find a World.

No Graves as Yet. unabr. ed. Anne Perry. Read by Michael Page. (Running Time: 12 hrs.). (World War One Ser.). 2003. 87.25 (978-1-59355-046-2(4), 1593550464, BrilAudUnabridg); 32.95 (978-1-59355-045-5(6), 1593550456, BAU); audio compact disk 102.25 (978-1-59355-049-3(9), 1593550499, BriAudCD Unabrid); audio compact disk 36.95 (978-1-59355-048-6(0), 1593550480, Bril Audio CD Unabri) Brilliance Audio.
On a sunny afternoon in late June, Cambridge professor Joseph Reavley is summoned from a student cricket match to learn that his parents have died in an automobile crash. Joseph's brother, Matthew, an officer in the Intelligence Service, reveals that their father had been en route to London to turn over to him a mysterious secret document - allegedly with the power to disgrace England forever and destroy the civilized world. A paper so damning that Joseph and Matthew dared mention it only to their restless sister. Now it has vanished. What has happened to this explosive document, if indeed it ever existed? How had it fallen into the hands of their father, a quiet countryman? Not even Matthew, with his Intelligence connections, can answer these questions. And Joseph is soon burdened with a second tragedy: the shocking murder of his most gifted student, handsome Sebastian Allard, loved and admired by everyone. Or so it appeared. Meanwhile, England's seamless peace is cracking - as the distance between the murder of an Austrian archduke by a Serbian anarchist and the death of a brilliant university student by a bullet to the head becomes shorter with each day.

No Graves as Yet. unabr. ed. Anne Perry. Read by Michael Page. (Running Time: 12 hrs.). (World War One Ser.). 2004. 39.25 (978-1-59335-504-3(1), 1593355041, Brlnc Audio MP3 Lib) Brilliance Audio.

No Graves as Yet. unabr. ed. Anne Perry. Read by Michael Page. (Running Time: 12 hrs.). (World War One Ser.). 2004. 39.25 (978-1-59710-539-2(2), 1597105392, BADLE); 24.95 (978-1-59710-538-5(4), 1597105384, BAD) Brilliance Audio.

No Graves as Yet. unabr. ed. Anne Perry. Read by Michael Page. (Running Time: 12 hrs.). (World War One Ser.). 2004. 24.95 (978-1-59335-230-1(1), 1593352301) Soulmate Audio Bks.

No Grease on the Gump. Willard Gellis. 1 CD. (Running Time: 1 hr. 2 min.). audio compact disk 12.95 (978-0-917455-34-6(7)) Big Foot NY.

No Grease on the Gump. Poems. Willard Gellis. Perf. by Orpheophrenia Productions Staff. 1 CD. (Running Time: 1 hr. 2 min.). audio compact disk 15.95 (978-0-917455-35-3(5)) Big Foot NY.

No Greater Audience. Contrib. by Michael Neale. 2007. 19.95 (978-5-557-72184-4(3)) Integrity Music.

No Greater Audience: Live with Christ Fellowship. Contrib. by Michael Neale & Don Moen. Prod. by Brent Milligan. 2007. audio compact disk 13.99 (978-5-557-72621-4(7)); audio compact disk 29.98 (978-5-557-72620-7(9)) Integrity Music.

No Greater Glory: The Four Immortal Chaplains & the Sinking of the Dorchester in World War II. Dan Kurzman. Read by William Dufris. 6 vols. 2004. bk. 32.95 (978-0-7927-3245-7(6), SLD 665, Chivers Sound Lib) AudioGO.

No Greater Joy Volume Two. Michael Pearl. 3 cass. 1999. (978-1-892112-89-7(2)) No Greater Joy.

No Greater Joy Volume 1, Vol. 1. unabr. ed. Michael Pearl. 3 cass. (Running Time: 4 hrs.). 1997. (978-1-892112-04-0(3)) No Greater Joy.
Child training.

No Greater Joy Volume 3, Vol. 3. Michael Pearl & Debi Pearl. 3 cass. (Running Time: 4 hrs). 2002. (978-1-892112-13-2(2)) No Greater Joy.

No Greater Love. unabr. ed. William X. Kienzle. 7 cass. (Running Time: 10 hrs. 30 mins.). (Father Koesler Mystery Ser.: No. 21). 2001. 56.00 (978-0-7366-7640-3(6)) Books on Tape.
Father Koesler has retired from St. Joseph's parish. Upon his return from vacation, he finds a message from Patrick McNiff, now a bishop and rector of St. Joseph's Seminary. McNiff asks Koesler to reside in the seminary, possibly teach a class, and - most important - help McNiff smooth out the factionalism of the faculty. In his new residence, Fr. Koesler learns about the problems dividing the seminary as well as those dividing his old home parish.

No Greater Sacrifice. Ray Boltz. 1997. video & audio compact disk 24.95 (978-7-01-996360-1(9)) Word Enter.

No Hang-Ups Tapes Vol. I: General Messages Female Voice. John Carfi & Cliff Carle. 1 cass. (Running Time: 15 min.). 1986. 5.98 (978-0-918259-02-8(9)) CCC Pubns.
Twenty funny prerecorded messages for answering machines with hilarious sound effects!.

No Hang-Ups Tapes Vol. I: General Messages Male Voice. John Carfi & Cliff Carle. 1 cass. (Running Time: 1 hr. 30 min.). 1986. 5.98 (978-0-918259-14-1(2)) CCC Pubns.
Features 20 funny pre-recorded messages for answering machines with hilarious sound effects!.

No Hang-Ups Tapes Vol. II: Business Messages Female Voice. John Carfi & Cliff Carle. 1 cass. (Running Time: 15 min.). 1986. 5.98 (978-0-918259-06-6(1)) CCC Pubns.
Twenty funny prerecorded messages for business answering machines, with sound effects.

No Hang-Ups Tapes Vol. II: Business Messages Male Voice. John Carfi & Cliff Carle. 1 cass. (Running Time: 1 hr. 30 min.). 1986. 5.98 (978-0-918259-15-8(0)) CCC Pubns.
Features 20 funny pre-recorded messages for business answering machines with sound effects!.

No Hang-Ups Tapes Vol. III: R Rated Male Voice. John Carfi & Cliff Carle. 1 cass. (Running Time: 1 hr. 30 min.). 1986. 5.98 (978-0-918259-16-5(9)) CCC Pubns.
Features "soft core" messages for answering machines.

No Hang-Ups Tapes Vol. III: R-Rated Messages Female Voice. John Carfi & Cliff Carle. 1 cass. (Running Time: 15 min.). 1986. 5.98 (978-0-918259-07-3(X)) CCC Pubns.
Twenty suggestive - but - soft - core - answering machine messages, recorded by the nations top adult movie stars, including John Holmes. (With sound effects).

No Hang-Ups Tapes Vol. IV: Sound Effects Only. John Carfi & Cliff Carle. 1 cass. (Running Time: 1 hr. 30 min.). 1986. 5.98 (978-0-918259-17-2(7)) CCC Pubns.
Features sound effects for answering machines.

No Hang-Ups Tapes Vol. V: Celebri-Tease. John Carfi & Cliff Carle. (Running Time: 32 min.). 1990. 5.98 (978-0-918259-26-4(6)) CCC Pubns.
Sixteen funny celebrity impersonation answering machine messages (8 male & 8 female) with sound effects.

No Hard Feelings: Managing Anger & Conflict in Your Work, Family & Love Life. Dennis O'Grady. Read by Dennis O'Grady. 4 cass. (Running Time: 6 hrs.). 1997. 49.95 (978-0-9628476-1-5(5)) New Insights.
To teach you how to manage unhealthy anger & resentment that is stealing your happiness.

No Haunui Laua 'O Hauiki. William H. Wilson. Illus. by Brook Parker. 1 cass. (Running Time: 1 hr. 30 min.). (HAW.). (J). (gr. 1-3). 1999. pap. bk. 5.95 (978-1-58191-063-6(0)) Aha Punana Leo.

No Hay Que Conformarse con una Vida Insatisfactoria. Tr. of There Is No Need to Settle for an Unsatisfied Life. (SPA.). 2008. audio compact disk 21.00 (978-0-944129-15-9(3)) High Praise.

No Heaven, No Hell. unabr. ed. Jane Brindle. Read by Ric Jerrom. 10 cass. (Running Time: 10 hrs.). 2000. 84.95 (978-0-7540-0490-5(2), CAB1913) AudioGO.
Virginia is the living image of her great-grandmother. She has the same presence & outstanding beauty. But behind her smile lies a terrible secret. One by one people die, her grandmother, her aunt, her father & others. Only her loving sister Lianne is spared. It seems that Virginia has inherited not only her great-grandmother's name & good looks, but also the unspeakable evil that took her to the grave.

No Hiding Place. unabr. ed. Valerie Wilson Wesley. Read by Rebecca Nicholas. 5 cass. (Running Time: 7 hrs. 30 min.). 1998. 40.00 (978-0-7366-4214-9(5), 4712) Books on Tape.

No Humans Involved. unabr. ed. Kelley Armstrong. Read by Laural Merlington. 1 MP3-CD. (Running Time: 12 hrs. 0 mins. 0 sec.). (Women of the Otherworld Ser.: Bk. 7). (ENG.). 2007. 29.99 (978-1-4001-5441-8(3)); audio compact disk 39.99 (978-1-4001-0441-3(6)); audio compact disk 79.99 (978-1-4001-3441-0(2)) Pub: Tantor Media. Dist(s): IngramPubServ

No Idle Hands: The Social History of American Knitting. Anne L. Macdonald. (ENG.). 2007. audio compact disk 29.95 (978-0-9796073-3-2(7)) Knitting Out.

No Immunity. Susan Dunlap & C. M. HÜrbert. 6 cass. (Running Time: 8 hrs. 30 mins.). 2002. 44.95 (978-0-7861-1613-3(7), 2441) Blckstn Audio.

No Immunity. unabr. ed. Susan Dunlap. Read by C. M. Herbert. 6 cass. (Running Time: 9 hrs.). 2001. 29.95 (978-0-7861-1926-4(8)) Pub: Blckstn Audio. Dist(s): Penton Overseas
Bestselling mystery author Susan Dunlap, brings us a powerful new novel featuring private detective and former medical examiner, Kiernan O'Shaughnessy.

No Immunity. unabr. ed. Susan Dunlap. Read by C. M. Hebert. (Running Time: 30600 sec.). 2008. audio compact disk & audio compact disk 70.00 (978-1-4332-3436-1(X)); audio compact disk & audio compact disk 29.96 (978-1-4332-3437-8(8)) Blckstn Audio.

No Immunity: A Kiernan O'Shaughnessy Mystery. unabr. ed. Susan Dunlap. Read by Lorelei King. 8 vols. (Running Time: 12 hrs.). 2000. bk. 69.95 (978-0-7927-2270-0(1), CSL 159, Chivers Sound Lib) AudioGO.
Framed for a death caused by a deadly fever, Kiernan gets more than she bargained for when she responds to a call from an old friend. Meanwhile, her housekeeper, Brad Tchernak, decides to conduct his own investigation of a hotshot geologist who has just returned from a multi-million dollar oil find in Central America. As the seemingly disparate cases intertwine, it becomes clear to Kiernan that she and Tchernak had better find what they are looking for fast, before they, too, become bodies of evidence.

No Immunity: A Kiernan O'Shaughnessy Mystery. unabr. ed. Susan Dunlap. 6 cass. (Running Time: 9 hrs.). 1999. 44.95 (2441) Blckstn Audio.
Betrayed & set up to take the blame for a death caused by a deadly & highly contagious case of Lassa fever, Kiernan O'Shaughnessy gets more than she bargained for when she responds to a call from an old college friend. And the trail of clues she follows - from her base in San Diego to the Nevada desert - is agonizingly complex.

No Impact Man: The Adventures of a Guilty Liberal Who Attempts to Save the Planet & the Discoveries He Makes about Himself & Our Way of Life in the Process. unabr. ed. Colin Beavan. Read by Colin Beavan. (Running Time: 7 hrs. 30 mins. 0 sec.). (ENG.). 2009. audio compact disk 29.99 (978-1-4272-0801-9(8)) Pub: Macmill Audio. Dist(s): Macmillan

No Importa la Condicion. Zondervan Publishing Staff. 2006. audio compact disk 14.99 (978-0-8297-4921-2(7)) Pub: Vida Pubs. Dist(s): Zondervan

No Intermissions: The Life of Agnes De Mille. unabr. ed. Carol Easton. Read by Donada Peters. 12 cass. (Running Time: 18 hrs.). 1997. 96.00 (978-0-7366-3655-1(2), 4325) Books on Tape.
Shows the shaping influence of Agnes De Mille on American dance & how it would not be the vibrant form it is today.

No Justice. unabr. ed. Robin Bowles. Read by Susan Lyons. 9 cass. (Running Time: 10 hrs. 15 mins.). 2004. 72.00 (978-1-74030-568-6(X)) Pub: Bolinda Pubng AUS. Dist(s): Lndmrk Audiobks

***No Kiss for the Devil.** Adrian Magson. 2010. 71.95 (978-1-4079-1231-8(3)); audio compact disk 79.95 (978-1-4079-1232-5(1)) Pub: Soundings Ltd GBR. Dist(s): Ulverscroft US

No Laughing Allowed. 1 CD. (Running Time: 41 mins.). (Baby Growlers Ser.: Vol. 3). (J). 2004. audio compact disk 13.00 (978-1-893185-55-5(9), Growler Tapes) TNG Earth.

No Laughing Matter. Steck-Vaughn Staff. (J). 2003. (978-0-7398-8440-9(9)) SteckVau.

***No Legal Grounds.** James Scott Bell. (Running Time: 10 hrs. 15 mins. 0 sec.). (ENG.). 2009. 14.99 (978-0-310-30496-8(2)) Zondervan.

No Less Than Victory: A Novel of World War II. unabr. ed. Jeff Shaara. Read by Paul Michael. 2009. audio compact disk 45.00 (978-0-307-57665-1(5), Random AudioBks) Pub: Random Audio Pubg. Dist(s): Random

No Limit. Contrib. by West Angeles Church of God in Christ Mass Choir & Charles E. Blake. Prod. by Jason White & Judith Christie McAllister. 2007. audio compact disk 13.99 (978-5-557-56806-7(9)) Pt of Grace Ent.

No Limit: Praying in the Realm of the Spirit. Phillip Halverson & Fern Halverson. 1 cass. (Running Time: 1 hr. 30 min.). 1997. 12.00 (978-1-57399-039-4(6)) Mac Hammond.
Teaching on prayer.

No Limit: Praying in the Realm of the Spirit. Phillip Halverson & Fern Halverson. 2 CDs. 2006. audio compact disk 10.00 (978-1-57399-362-3(X)) Mac Hammond.
You can step into a realm of prayer where there are no limitations and God works dynamically through you. Discover the excitement of praying in the limitless realm of the Spirit. (Note: Phillip went home to be with the Lord in 1985 and Fern in 2003.).

No Limitations. unabr. ed. Brother Shen. Narrated by Wayne Shepherd. (Running Time: 4 hrs. 26 mins. 18 sec.). (ENG.). 2009. 13.99 (978-1-60814-553-9(0)); audio compact disk 19.99 (978-1-59859-609-0(8)) Oasis Audio.

No Limits. Olevia Williams & King David Records. 2005. audio compact disk 15.98 (978-5-558-94879-0(5)) Pub: Pt of Grace Ent. Dist(s): STL Dist NA

No Lion at All. (Choices & Decisions Ser.). (J). 1990. 7.92 (978-0-8123-6461-3(9)) Holt McDoug.

No Longer a Dilly Dally. Short Stories. Carl Sommer. Narrated by Carl Sommer. 1 cass. Dramatization. (Another Sommer-Time Story Ser.). (J). 2003. bk. 16.95 (978-1-57537-550-2(8)) Advance Pub.

***No Longer a Dilly Dally / ¡Nunca Más A Troche y Moche!** ed. Carl Sommer. Illus. by Kennon James. (Another Sommer-Time Story Bilingual Ser.). (ENG & SPA.). (J). 2009. bk. 26.95 (978-1-57537-187-0(1)) Advance Pub.

No Longer a Dilly Dally Read-Along. Carl Sommer. Narrated by Carl Sommer. 1 cass. Dramatization. (Another Sommer-Time Story Ser.). (J). 2003. lib. bdg. 23.95 (978-1-57537-751-3(9)) Advance Pub.
Character Education story with character song by Karacter Kidz.

No Longer under the Curse. Mark Crow. 2 cass. (Running Time: 2 hrs.). 2001. (978-1-931537-20-9(8)) Vision Comm Creat.

No Love Lost. Scripts. Text by Norman Corwin. Directed By Norman Corwin. 1 CD. (Running Time: 58 mins). Dramatization. 2005. audio compact disk 15.95 (978-1-59938-003-2(X)) Lode Cat.

No Love Lost. Norman Corwin. Perf. by Lloyd Bridges et al. Prod. by Mary Beth Kirchner. 1 cass. (Running Time: 1 hr.). 12.95 (978-1-57677-073-3(7), CORW008) Lodestone Catalog.
Original play about Hamilton, Jefferson & Burr. Production Script available.

No Love Lost. Norman Corwin. 1 CD. (Running Time: 1 hr.). 2001. audio compact disk 15.95 Production Script available. (CORW023) Lodestone Catalog.
A roundtable discussion that never happened, but might have: Corwin research into their own words lets our founding fathers shake off the dust of history. Production Script available.

No Lovelier Death. Graham Hurley. 2009. 99.95 (978-0-7531-4330-8(5)); audio compact disk 104.95 (978-0-7531-4331-5(3)) Pub: Isis Pubng Ltd GBR. Dist(s): Ulverscroft US

No Ma'ikoha A Me Ka Wauke. Kawika Napoleon & William H. Wilson. Illus. by Brook Parker. 1 cass. (Running Time: 1 hr. 30 min.). (HAW.). (J). (gr. 1-3). 1999. pap. bk. 5.95 (978-1-58191-062-9(2)) Aha Punana Leo.

No Man Is an Island. unabr. ed. Thomas Merton. Read by Jonathan Montaldo. (Running Time: 32400 sec.). 2007. audio compact disk 35.95 (978-0-86716-865-5(X)) St Anthony Mess Pr.

No Man Is an Island: Our Common Purpose. Kenneth Wapnick. 2007. 53.00 (978-1-59142-330-0(9)); audio compact disk 59.00 (978-1-59142-329-4(5)) Foun Miracles.

No Man's Island. unabr. ed. Susan Sallis. 11 CDs. (Soundings (CDs) Ser.). 2006. audio compact disk 99.95 (978-1-84559-520-3(3)) Pub: ISIS Lrg Prnt GBR. Dist(s): Ulverscroft US

No Man's Island. unabr. ed. Susan Sallis. Read by Nicolette McKenzie. 10 cass. (Soundings Ser.). 2006. 84.95 (978-1-84559-485-5(1)) Pub: ISIS Lrg Prnt GBR. Dist(s): Ulverscroft US

No Man's Land, Pt. 1. unabr. collector's ed. John Toland. Read by John MacDonald. 7 cass. (Running Time: 10 hrs. 30 min.). 1988. 56.00 (978-0-7366-1358-3(7), 2258-A) Books on Tape.
No Man's Land is the story of the war's final climatic year & the events that led up to it. The book gives a view from the trenches, both German & Allied & provides a tour of military staffs & foreign offices.

No Man's Land, Pt. 2. collector's ed. John Toland. Read by John MacDonald. 8 cass. (Running Time: 12 hrs.). 1988. 64.00 (978-0-7366-1359-0(5), 2258-B) Books on Tape.

No Man's Range. Giff Cheshire. (Running Time: 0 hr. 54 mins.). 1999. 10.95 (978-1-60083-510-0(4)) Iofy Corp.

***No Man's Range.** Gifford Cheshire. 2009. (978-1-60136-455-5(5)) Audio Holding.

No Matter What! 9 Steps to Living the Life You Love. unabr. ed. Lisa Nichols. Read by Lisa Nichols. (Running Time: 9 hrs.). (ENG.). 2009. 24.98 (978-1-60024-293-9(6)) Pub: Hachet Audio. Dist(s): HachBkGrp

No Me Critiques. unabr. ed. Zona. (SPA.). 2003. 9.99 (978-0-8297-3654-0(9)) Vida Pubs.

No me Pertenezco. Rodrigo Rodriguez. (SPA.). 2008. audio compact disk 14.99 (978-0-8297-5504-6(7)) Pub: Vida Pubs. Dist(s): Zondervan

No Mercy. unabr. ed. Lori Armstrong. Read by Kirsten Potter & Jennifer Van Dyck. (Running Time: 11 hrs.). (Mercy Gunderson Ser.). 2010. 24.99 (978-1-4233-7752-8(4), 9781423377528, Brilliance MP3) Brilliance Audio.

No Mercy. unabr. ed. Lori Armstrong. Read by Kirsten Potter. (Running Time: 11 hrs.). (Mercy Gunderson Ser.). 2010. 24.99 (978-1-4233-7754-2(0), 9781423377542, BAD) Brilliance Audio.

No Mercy. unabr. ed. Lori Armstrong. Read by Kirsten Potter & Jennifer Van Dyck. (Running Time: 11 hrs.). (Mercy Gunderson Ser.). 2010. 39.97 (978-1-4233-7753-5(2), 9781423377535, Brinc Audio MP3 Lib) Brilliance Audio.

No Mercy. unabr. ed. Lori Armstrong. Read by Kirsten Potter. (Running Time: 11 hrs.). (Mercy Gunderson Ser.). 2010. 39.97 (978-1-4233-7755-9(9), 9781423377559, BADLE) Brilliance Audio.

No Mercy. unabr. ed. Lori Armstrong. Read by Kirsten Potter & Jennifer Van Dyck. (Running Time: 11 hrs.). (Mercy Gunderson Ser.). 2010. audio compact disk 29.99 (978-1-4233-7750-4(8), 9781423377504, Bril Audio CD Unabri); audio compact disk 97.97 (978-1-4233-7751-1(6), 9781423377511, BriAudCD Unabrid) Brilliance Audio.

***No Mercy.** unabr. ed. Sherrilyn Kenyon. Read by Holter Graham. (Running Time: 9 hrs. 0 mins. 0 sec.). (Dark-Hunter Novels Ser.). (ENG.). 2010. audio compact disk 34.99 (978-1-4272-0969-6(3)) Pub: Macmill Audio. Dist(s): Macmillan

No Middle Ground. Megan McKenna. 2 cass. (Running Time: 2 hrs. 10 min.). 17.95 Set. Credence Commun.
These are stories of peace & hope that McKenna told Pax Christi members when they invited her to their national meeting. She told such favorites as The Non-Violent Snake, The Man Who Saved the Scorpion, How the Rabbi Got Holy - a dozen in all. McKenna is always entertaining but never merely entertaining. If you're not prepared for the gospel message, this must be your first set of her tapes.

No Money down Marketing: Discover How to Quickly & Easily Market Your Products Without Using a Dime of Your Own Money! abr. ed. Speeches. 2 CDs. (Running Time: 2hrs). 2006. audio compact disk 29.95 (978-0-9777500-1-6(9)) Ultimate Wealth.

No Moon Tonight. unabr. ed. Don Charlwood. Narrated by Peter Wickham. 6 cass. (Running Time: 9 hrs.). (Sound Ser.). (J). 2003. 54.95 (978-1-84283-313-1(8)) Pub: ISIS Lrg Prnt GBR. Dist(s): Ulverscroft US

No More Alcohol. Shelley L. Stockwell. 1 cass. (Running Time: 1 hr.). (Self-Hynosis Ser.). 1986. 10.00 Creativity Unltd Pr.
Subconsciously eliminates alcohol dependancy by using motivation, guided imagery & positive action.

No More Cocoons. Jello Biafra. 2 CDs. (Running Time: 3 hrs.). (AK Press Audio Ser.). (ENG.). 1999. audio compact disk 16.98 (978-1-902593-17-3(0)) Pub: AK Pr GBR. Dist(s): Consort Bk Sales

No More Cocoons. abr. ed. Jello Biafra. 2 cass. (Running Time: 2 hrs.). (AK Press Audio Ser.). 2001. 11.98 (978-1-902593-18-0(9), AK Pr San Fran) AK Pr Dist.

No More Dead Dogs. Gordon Korman. 4 CDs. (Running Time: 4 hrs. 30 mins.). Orig. Title: Touchdown Stage Left. (gr. 5 up). audio compact disk 39.00 (978-0-7887-6162-1(5)) Recorded Bks.

No More Dead Dogs. Gordon Korman. 3 pieces. (Running Time: 4 hrs. 30 mins.). Orig. Title: Touchdown Stage Left. (gr. 5 up). 2001. 28.00 (978-0-7887-5104-2(2), 96534E7) Recorded Bks.
Wallace Wallace hates the book, "Old Shep, My Pal," because it's yet another story where the dog dies. Forced into detention, Wallace watches rehearsals for the school play - which happens to be "Old Shep, My Pal." He can't help but make suggestions. All the play needs is a rollerblading dog catcher, a stuffed animal glued remote-controlled car, a moped disguised as a Harley & some choreographed dance numbers with live rock tunes.

No More Dead Dogs. unabr. ed. Gordon Korman. 3 CDs. (Running Time: 4 hrs. 30 min.). Orig. Title: Touchdown Stage Left. (YA). (gr. 5-8). 2001. audio compact disk 39.00 (C1386) Recorded Bks.
Wallace, Wallace hates the book "Old Shep, My Pal," because it's yet another story where the dog dies. Forced into detention, Wallace watches rehearsals for the school play - which happens to be "Old Shep, My Pal." He can't help but make suggestions. All the play needs is a rollerblading dog catcher, a stuffed animal glued remote-controlled car, a moped disguised as a Harley & some choreographed dance numbers with live rock tunes.

No More Depression. Michael P. Kelly. 1 cass. (Running Time: 1 hr. 30 min.). 1992. 14.95 (978-1-883700-10-2(8)) ThoughtForms.
Self help.

No More Diapers for Elvis! I.t. unabr. ed. Judith Cohen & Michael Cohen. Illus. by Darlene Anderson. (Potti Pets Ser.). (J). (ps). 1997. pap. bk. (978-0-9664396-1-8(9)) PPP Enterp.

No More Disposition to Do Evil. Rory C. Reid. 2008. audio compact disk 14.99 (978-1-59955-159-3(4)) CFI Dist.

No More Dying Then. unabr. ed. Ruth Rendell. Read by Robin Bailey. 6 cass. (Running Time: 9 hrs.). (Inspector Wexford Mystery Ser.: Bk. 6). 2000. 49.95 (978-0-7451-6563-9(X), CAB 1179) Pub: Chivers Audio Bks GBR. Dist(s): AudioGO
Inspectors Burden and Wexford visit a formerly majestic stone mansion, that is now run-down. At the foot of the driveway once stood the statues of a young boy and girl. Strangely, the statue of the boy has disappeared, while the statue of the girl has been toppled over. The disappearance of a young girl and a small boy in the same neighborhood has the two inspectors baffled. Is there a connection?.

No More Excuses: Be the Man God Made You to Be. 10th abr. ed. Tony Evans. Read by Tony Evans. (Running Time: 2 hrs. 37 mins.). 2007. audio compact disk 22.99 (978-1-58134-924-5(6)) CrosswayIL.

No More Guilt. 1 cass. (Running Time: 1 hr.). 10.95 (024) Psych Res Inst.
Designed to provide release of past guilt-producing feelings by replacement with positive feedback.

No More Guilt: Focusing on Innocence. Marianne Williamson. Read by Marianne Williamson. 1 cass. (Running Time: 1 hr. 30 min.). (Lectures on a Course in Miracles). 1999. 10.00 (978-1-56170-248-0(X), M751) Hay House.

No More Headaches. Michael P. Kelly. 1 cass. (Running Time: 1 hr. 30 min.). 1992. 14.95 (978-1-883700-08-9(6)) ThoughtForms.
Self help.

No More Misbehavin' 38 Bad Behaviors & How to Stop Them. Michelle Borba. 2 cass. (Running Time: 3 hrs.). 2003. 18.95 (978-1-59125-326-6(8)) Penton Overseas.
These focused, practical solutions to the 38 biggest problems are literally just what the doctor ordered for busy, harassed parents all over the world! With No More Misbehavin', Dr. Borba has concentrated her wisdom, experience and skills as both a parent and a teacher into an extraordinarily effective guide that will become the ultimate resource and constant companion for parents of children ages three to twelve.

No More Mondays: Fire Yourself - & Other Revolutionary Ways to Discover Your True Calling at Work. unabr. ed. Dan Miller. Narrated by Dan Miller. (ENG.). 2008. 19.59 (978-1-60814-320-7(1)) Oasis Audio.

No More Mondays: Fire Yourself - And Other Revolutionary Ways to Discover Your True Calling at Work. unabr. ed. Dan Miller. Narrated by Dan Miller. (Running Time: 32400 sec.). (ENG.). 2008. audio compact disk 27.99 (978-1-59859-334-1(X)) Oasis Audio.

No More Monsters for Me! abr. ed. Peggy Parish. Illus. by Marc Simont. 1 CD. (Running Time: 30 mins.). (I Can Read Bks.). (J). (gr. k-3). 2008. 9.99 (978-0-06-133614-0(9), HarperFestival) HarperCollins Pubs.

No More Monsters for Me! Book & Tape. abr. ed. Peggy Parish. Illus. by Marc Simont. 1 cass. (Running Time: 1 hr. 30 min.). (I Can Read Bks.). (J). (ps-3). 1991. bk. 8.99 (978-1-55994-353-6(X), TBC 353X) HarperCollins Pubs.

No More Nasty. unabr. ed. Amy MacDonald. 3 cass. (Running Time: 3 hrs. 45 min.). (J). (gr. 3-5). 2004. 28.00 (978-1-4025-7578-5(5)) Recorded Bks.
Simon's fifth grade teacher quits and is replaced with his Great Aunt Mattie in this novel by Amy MacDonald. Simon has few friends and is already considered a teacher's pet, and now he fears his peers' reactions if they find out that this wacky septuagenarian with unorthodox teaching methods and a vocabulary of unusual words is related to him. In this sequel to No More

Nice, Simon struggles with his love of Aunt Mattie and his fear of rejection by classmates.

No More Night: An Easter Musical for Every Choir: Satb. Narrated by Deborah Craig-Claar. Contrib. by Gary Rhodes et al. 2006. audio compact disk 90.00 (978-5-558-02222-3(1), Word Music) Word Enter.

No More Nightmares: "The Keeper of Dreams" unabr. ed. Trenna Daniells. Read by Trenna Daniells. 1 cass. (Running Time: 30 min.). (One to Grow On! Ser.). (J). (gr. k-6). 1991. 9.95 (978-0-918519-14-6(4), 12012) Trenna Prods.
After too many nightmares Michael tries to avoid the dragon of his dreams by staying awake all night. His best friend Jennifer joins Michael on a journey to the castle of the Keeper of the Dreams. The wizard shows Michael he has the power to control his dreams, using a concept taught by many psychologists.

No More Nightmares - the Keeper of the Dreams. Trenna Daniells. Narrated by Trenna Daniells. (ENG.). (J). 2009. (978-0-918519-25-2(X)) Trenna Prods.

No More... Not Tonight Dear. unabr. ed. Robert G. Ford & Kay T. Ford. 1 cass. (Running Time: 1 hr. 30 min.). 1994. 12.95 (978-0-9636292-6-5(3)) Intl Headache.
Consumer information on headaches.

No More Pencils, No More Books, No More Teacher's Dirty Looks! Diane deGroat. Read by Jason Harris & Peter Pamela Rose. 1 CD. (Running Time: 12 mins.). (Gilbert Ser.). (J). (ps-3). 2009. pap. bk. 18.95 (978-1-4301-0694-4(8)) Live Oak Media.

No More Procrastination. Eldon Taylor. 1 cass. (Running Time: 1 hr. 2 min.). (Inner Talk Ser.). 16.95 (978-1-55978-085-8(1), 5303A) Progress Aware Res.
Soundtrack - Tropical Lagoon with underlying subliminal affirmations.

No More Procrastination: Babbling Brook. Eldon Taylor. 1 cass. (Running Time: 1 hr. 30 min.). 16.95 (978-1-55978-453-5(9), 5303F) Progress Aware Res.

No More Procrastination: Classic. Eldon Taylor. Read by Eldon Taylor. Ed. by Leslie Brice. 1 cass. (Running Time: 1 hr.). 1992. 16.95 (978-1-56705-042-4(5)) Gateways Inst.
Self improvement.

No More Procrastination: Easy. Eldon Taylor. Read by Eldon Taylor. Ed. by Leslie Brice. 1 cass. (Running Time: 1 hr.). 1992. 16.95 (978-1-56705-043-1(3)) Gateways Inst.

No More Procrastination: Music Theme. Eldon Taylor. 1 cass. (Running Time: 1 hr. 30 min.). 16.95 (978-1-55978-087-2(8), 5303C) Progress Aware Res.

No More Procrastination: Ocean. Eldon Taylor. Read by Eldon Taylor. Ed. by Leslie Brice. 1 cass. (Running Time: 1 hr.). 1992. 16.95 (978-1-56705-044-8(1)) Gateways Inst.

No More Procrastination: Rhythm. Eldon Taylor. Read by Eldon Taylor. Ed. by Leslie Brice. 1 cass. (Running Time: 1 hr.). 1992. 16.95 (978-1-56705-045-5(X)) Gateways Inst.

No More Procrastination: Stream. Eldon Taylor. Read by Eldon Taylor. Ed. by Leslie Brice. 1 cass. (Running Time: 1 hr.). 1992. 16.95 (978-1-56705-046-2(8)) Gateways Inst.

No More Sleepless Nights. abr. ed. Peter Hauri & Shirley Linde. Narrated by Lloyd James. (Running Time: 10800 sec.). 2006. audio compact disk 22.95 (978-1-933310-14-5(6)) STI Certified.

No More Sticky Word Problems. 2008. audio compact disk 3.99 (978-0-9802359-6-8(0)) Abena Pub.

No More Stress: A Simple Relaxation/Meditation Program for Health & Happiness, Vol. V. unabr. ed. David Essel. 1 cass. (Running Time: 1 hrs.). (David Essel's Dynamic Living Ser.). 1992. 9.95 (978-1-893074-03-3(X)) D Essel Inc.
No more stress...The easy way; 1) Progressive relaxation, 2) The breath technique, 3) Mantra repetition, 4) Creative Release...All in just minutes a day.

No More Stress: Relaxation & Meditation Program for Your Health & Happiness. David Essel. (ENG.). 2006. audio compact disk 9.95 (978-1-893074-16-3(1)) D Essel Inc.

No More Sugar Junkie. Shelley L. Stockwell. 1 cass. (Running Time: 1 hr.). (Self Hypnosis Ser.). 1986. 10.00 (978-0-912559-03-2(9)) Creativity Unltd Pr.
Break sugar addiction using the power of your own deepest wisdom.

No More Tantrums: Anger Control Training. John F. Taylor. 1 cass. (Running Time: 39 min.). (Answers to ADD Ser.). 1993. 9.95 (978-1-883963-04-0(4)) ADD Plus.
Lecture tape.

No More Worry. 1 cass. (Running Time: 1 hr. 30 min.). 10.00 (978-1-58506-015-3(1), 42) New Life Inst OR.
Stop needless worrying that just wastes time & energy & watch your life improve.

No Name, Vol. II. Wilkie Collins. 5 cass. (Running Time: 7 hrs.). 35.95 Audio Bk Con.
Born out of wedlock & orphaned without an inheritance, Magdalen tries to recoup some of her losses, while Mrs. Le Count works against her. Humor, intrigue & mystery enhance the plot.

No Name (Part 1), Vol. 1. unabr. ed. Wilkie Collins. Read by Flo Gibson. 12 cass. (Running Time: 18 hrs.). 1998. 39.95 (978-1-55685-511-5(7)) Audio Bk Con.

No Name (Part 2), Vol. 2. unabr. ed. Wilkie Collins. Narrated by Flo Gibson. (Running Time: 6 hrs. 40 mins.). 1998. 20.95 (978-1-55685-826-0(4)) Audio Bk Con.

No Name (Parts 1 And 2), Vol. 12. unabr. ed. Wilkie Collins. Narrated by Flo Gibson. (Running Time: 23 hrs. 55 mins.). 1998. 49.95 (978-1-55685-827-7(2)) Audio Bk Con.

No Need to Fear. Contrib. by Marty Parks. 2007. audio compact disk 24.99 (978-5-557-54315-6(5)) Lillenas.

No Negativity: 70 Powerful Ways to Destroy the Success Killing Beast of Negativity & Change Your Life Now! Ray Prieba & T. J. Rohleder. 2005. audio compact disk 59.95 (978-1-933356-01-3(4)) MORE Inc.

No Neutrality. Derek Prince. 1 cass. (Running Time: 1 hr.). (B-140) Derek Prince.

No Night Is Too Long. abr. ed. Barbara Vine, pseud. Read by Alan Cumming. 2 cass. (Running Time: 3 hrs.). 1995. 16.95 (978-0-945353-97-3(9), N20397) Pub: Audio Partners. Dist(s): PerseuPGW
Tim Cornish's life had been going so well, that is, until he is abandoned one summer in Alaska by paleontologist Ivo Steadman. From this solitary existence, Tim flees to a ghostly house overlooking the North Sea, where he is sentenced to ceaseless, heartstopping hell.

No Night Is Too Long. abr. ed. Barbara Vine, pseud. Read by Alan Cumming. 2 cass. (Running Time: 3 hrs.). 2000. 7.95 (978-1-57815-184-4(8), 1124, Media Bks Audio) Media Bks NJ.

***No Nightingales, No Snakes: A Full-Cast BBC Radio Drama.** Maeve Binchy. Narrated by Full Cast Production Staff & Niamh Cusack. 1. (Running Time: 1 hr. 15 mins. 0 sec.). (ENG., 2010. audio compact disk 24.95 (978-1-4056-7745-5(7)) Pub: AudioGO. Dist(s): Perseus Dist

No-No & the Secret Touch: The Gentle Story of a Little Seal Who Learns to Stay Safe, Say "No" & Tell! unabr. ed. Sherri Patterson et al. Illus. by Marian N. Krupp. 1 cass. (Running Time: 1 hr.). Dramatization. (J). (gr. 1-6). pap. bk. 14.95 (978-0-9632276-2-1(9)) Natl Self Esteem.
A gentle story about a little seal who learns to stay safe, say "no" & tell! The book is a story-coloring book with parent & teacher guide. The audio tape brings the entire story to life with music & song.

No No Baby Story CD (Babytown Storybook) Short Stories. Created by Quebla Publishing. Illus. by Quebla Publishing. Voice by Jaina Lane. 1 CD. (Running Time: 22 mins.). Dramatization. (BABYTOWN Ser.: Bk. 1). (J). 2005. 10.00 (978-0-9772738-3-6(0)) Quebla.
Can you imagine what life would be like if you were born able to talk? Well, Baby can! Considered the town?s most ambitious under-one-nager, Baby is proud to be like-a-girl as she ventures through life dissecting the who, what, and whys of everything in sight. Baby is the littlest prodigy with the biggest imagination, always ready to save the day. Children of all ages will be delighted to see just how silly things can be through the eyes of an infant.Meet Baby as she learns what babies can and cannot do. Baby feels like a big girl, but in NO NO BABY she finds out that she can?t have everything she wants.

No-Nonsense Leadership. Dave Anderson. 8 cass. (Running Time: 8 hours). 2001. 39.95 (978-0-9700018-9-4(4)) D Anderson Corp.

No-Nonsense Leadership: Real World Strategies to Maximize Personal & Corporate Potential. Dave Anderson. 7 CDs. (Running Time: 8 hrs.). 2001. audio compact disk 49.95 (978-0-9700018-7-6(0)) D Anderson Corp.

No One. unabr. ed. Eleanor Nilsson. (Aussie Bites Ser.). (J). 2002. audio compact disk 39.95 (978-1-74030-840-3(9)) Pub: Bolinda Pubng AUS. Dist(s): Bolinda Pub Inc

No One Could Have Known. unabr. ed. Josef Pieper. Read by Al Covaia. 7 cass. (Running Time: 10 hrs. 30 min.). 28.95 set. (322) Ignatius Pr.
Autobiography from the lay philosopher who popularized St. Thomas Aquinas. Covering the years 1904-1945 this story gives insights into the life of a German Christian.

No One Ever Walking see Poetry & Voice of Muriel Rukeyser

No One Heard Her Scream. unabr. ed. Jordan Dane. Read by Marguerite Gavin. (Running Time: 30600 sec.). 2008. 72.95 (978-1-4332-4476-6(4)); audio compact disk & audio compact disk 90.00 (978-1-4332-4477-3(2)) Blckstn Audio.

No One Heard Her Scream. unabr. ed. Jordan Dane & Marguerite Gavin. (Running Time: 30600 sec.). 2008. audio compact disk 29.95 (978-1-4332-4478-0(0)) Blckstn Audio.

No One Here Gets Out Alive. abr. ed. Jerry Hopkins & Danny Sugarman. (ENG.). 2006. 14.98 (978-1-59483-336-6(2)) Pub: Hachet Audio. Dist(s): HachBkGrp

No One Left Behind: The Lt. Comdr. Michael Scott Speicher Story. abr. ed. Amy Waters Yarsinske. Narrated by Gary Telles. 3 cass. (Running Time: 4 hrs. 30 mins.). 2002. 22.95 (978-1-885408-86-0(2)); audio compact disk 27.95 (978-1-885408-87-7(0)) Listen & Live.

No One Left-Behind: The Lt. Comdr. Michael Scott Speicher Story. abr. ed. Amy Waters Yarsinske. Read by Gary Telles. (Playaway Adult Nonfiction Ser.). (ENG.). 2009. 59.99 (978-1-60812-755-9(9)) Find a World.

No One Left Behind: The Lt. Comdr. Michael Scott Speicher Story. unabr. ed. Amy Waters Yarsinske. Narrated by Terence Aselford. 6 cass. (Running Time: 9 hrs.). 2003. 32.95 (978-1-885408-88-4(9)) Listen & Live.
True story of Lt. Comdr. Michael Scott Speicher, the first American pilot shot down during the Gulf War, found alive in Iraqi custody eleven years after the US government left him for dead.

No One Left to Tell. unabr. ed. Jordan Dane. (Running Time: 13 hrs. 0 mins.). 2008. 24.95 (978-1-4332-1409-7(1)); cass. & audio compact disk 24.95 (978-1-4332-1410-3(5)) Blckstn Audio.

No One Left to Tell. unabr. ed. Jordan Dane. Read by Tavia Gilbert. (Running Time: 41400 sec.). 2008. 79.95 (978-1-4332-1407-3(5)); audio compact disk & audio compact disk 90.00 (978-1-4332-1408-0(3)) Blckstn Audio.

No One Left to Tell. unabr. ed. Jordan Dane & Tavia Gilbert. 1 CD. (Running Time: 41400 sec.). 2008. audio compact disk 29.95 (978-1-4332-1411-0(3)) Blckstn Audio.

No One Sees God: The Dark Night of Atheists & Believers. Michael Novak. 2009. 59.95 (978-0-86716-910-2(9)) St Anthony Mess Pr.

No One Will Ever Know. Short Stories. Carl Sommer. Narrated by Carl Sommer. 1 cass. Dramatization. (Another Sommer-Time Story Ser.). (J). (gr. 1-4). 2003. bk. 16.95 (978-1-57537-555-7(9)) Advance Pub.

***No One will Ever Know / Nadie Se Va A Enterar.** ed. Carl Sommer. Illus. by Dick Westbrook. (Another Sommer-Time Story Bilingual Ser.). (ENG & SPA.). (J). 2009. bk. 26.95 (978-1-57537-188-7(X)) Advance Pub.

No One Will Ever Know Read-Along. Carl Sommer. Narrated by Carl Sommer. 1 cass. Dramatization. (Another Sommer-Time Story Ser.). (J). 2003. lib. bdg. 23.95 (978-1-57537-756-8(X)) Advance Pub.
Character Education story with character song by Karacter Kidz.

***No One Would Listen: A True Financial Thriller.** unabr. ed. Harry Markopolos. Read by Scott Brick. (Running Time: 13 hrs.). 2010. 24.99 (978-1-4418-7048-3(2), 9781441870483, Brilliance MP3); 39.97 (978-1-4418-7050-6(4), 9781441870506, BADLE); 39.97 (978-1-4418-7049-0(0), 9781441870490, Brinc Audio MP3 Lib); audio compact disk 29.99 (978-1-4418-7046-9(6), 9781441870469, Bril Audio CD Unabri); audio compact disk 99.97 (978-1-4418-7047-6(4), 9781441870476, BriAudCD Unabrid) Brilliance Audio.

No One You Know. unabr. ed. Michelle Richmond. Read by Carrington MacDuffie. (Running Time: 9 hrs. 30 mins.). 2008. audio compact disk 90.00 (978-1-4332-5254-9(6)) Blckstn Audio.

***No One's the Bitch.** unabr. ed. Jennifer Newcomb Marine & Carol Marine. Read by Paula Christensen & Coleen Marlo. (ENG.). 2010. (978-0-06-200717-9(3), Harper Audio) HarperCollins Pubs.

***No One's the Bitch: A Ten-Step Plan for the Mother & Stepmother Relationship.** unabr. ed. Jennifer Newcomb Marine & Carol Marine. Read by Paula Christensen & Coleen Marlo. (ENG.). 2010. (978-0-06-200306-5(2), Harper Audio) HarperCollins Pubs.

***No Ordinary Joes: The Extraordinary True Story of Four Submariners in War & Love & Life.** unabr. ed. Larry Colton. (Running Time: 14 hrs. 0 mins.). 2010. 19.99 (978-1-4001-8799-7(0)); 29.99 (978-1-4001-6799-9(X)); audio compact disk 39.99 (978-1-4001-1799-4(2)); audio compact disk 95.99 (978-1-4001-4799-1(9)) Pub: Tantor Media. Dist(s): IngramPubServ

No Ordinary Men Audio Book: Having the Heart, Brain & Courage to live as Godly Men. 2008. 29.95 (978-0-9801973-4-1(1)) Newgate Inc.

No Ordinary Time: Franklin & Eleanor Roosevelt: The Home Front in World War II. Doris Kearns Goodwin. Narrated by Nelson Runger. 28 cass. (Running Time: 39 hrs. 45 mins.). 129.00 (978-1-4025-2689-3(X)) Recorded Bks.

No Ordinary Time: Franklin & Eleanor Roosevelt: The Home Front in World War II. Doris Kearns Goodwin. 2004. 15.95 (978-0-7435-1990-8(6)) Pub: S&S Audio. Dist(s): S and S Inc

No Ordinary Time: Franklin & Eleanor Roosevelt: The Home Front in World War II. abr. ed. Doris Keams Goodwin. Read by Edward Herrmann. 6 CDs. (Running Time: 6 hrs. 0 mins. 0 sec.). (ENG.). 2005. audio compact disk 29.95 (978-0-7435-3965-4(6)) Pub: S&S Audio. Dist(s): S and S Inc

No Ordinary Time Pt. 2: Franklin & Eleanor Roosevelt: The Home Front in World War II. unabr. ed. Doris Keams Goodwin. Read by Julia Delfino. 10 cass. (Running Time: 15 hrs.). 2000. 60.00 (5181-B) Books on Tape.
A detailed & intimate portrait of Franklin & Eleanor Roosevelt & the birth of modern America.

No Other Generation: Twelve Voices from the Nuclear Age. Contrib. by Helen Caldicott et al. (Running Time: 56 min.). 1987. Original Face.
Twelve leading thinkers provide the framework for a new mode of political consciousness. Speakers also include Theodore Roszak, Swami Satchidananda, Joanna Macy & Daniel Ellsberg.

No Other Name but Jesus. Contrib. by Camp Kirkland. 1997. 24.95 (978-0-7601-2176-4(1), 75700255) Pub: Brentwood Music. Dist(s): H Leonard

***No Passengers Beyond This Point.** unabr. ed. Gennifer Choldenko. (ENG.). (J). 2011. audio compact disk 30.00 (978-0-307-73787-8(X), Listening Lib) Pub: Random Audio Pubg. Dist(s): Random

No Pay, No Way, Level 1. (J). 2002. audio compact disk (978-0-7398-5316-0(3)) SteckVau.

No Pay, No Way Level 1. (J). 2002. (978-0-7398-5085-5(7)) SteckVau.

No Perfect People Allowed: Creating a Come as You Are Culture in the Church. unabr. ed. John Burke. (Running Time: 12 hrs. 5 mins. 0 sec.). (ENG.). 2008. 14.99 (978-0-310-27875-7(9)) Zondervan.

No Perfect People, Please! Poems & audio cd By. Jim Whiting. (J). 2007. bk. 16.95 (978-0-9759276-2-5(0)) Culture Link.

No Physical Evidence. unabr. ed. Gus Lee. Read by Dick Hill. (Running Time: 15 hrs.). 2008. 39.25 (978-1-4233-5808-4(2), 9781423358084, Brinc Audio MP3 Lib); 39.25 (978-1-4233-5810-7(4), 9781423358107, BADLE); 24.95 (978-1-4233-5809-1(0), 9781423358091, BAD); 24.95 (978-1-4233-5807-7(4), 9781423358077, Brilliance MP3) Brilliance Audio.

No Pipe Dreams for Father. unabr. ed. Winifred Foley. Read by Sarah Sherborne. 2 cass. (Running Time: 3 hrs.). (Forest Ser.: Pt. 2). (J). 2004. 24.95 (978-0-7531-0154-4(8), 970314) Pub: ISIS Lrg Prnt GBR. Dist(s): Ulverscroft US
Recounting time spent with her mother & Auntie doing the family laundry, 'the worst day of the week', happy summer days with her sister fetching water from the well in the early morning sun; & memories of Granny's treacle puddings! These were also difficult times. With her father earning a pittance as a miner, they ran up debts with the doctor, having to borrow money form their equally poor neighbors tro pay him back; & watching friend & neighbors die from what are now, common, treatable ailments.

No Place for a Man. unabr. ed. Judy Astley. Read by Marlene Sidaway. 8 cass. (Running Time: 8 hrs. 33 mins.). (Isis Ser.). (J). 2001. 69.95 (978-0-7531-1193-2(4)) Pub: ISIS Lrg Prnt GBR. Dist(s): Ulverscroft US
Jess has just waved goodbye to her darling son, who's off backpacking to Australia. She's left with two teenage daughters and husband Matt - all of whom are regularly featured in her popular, light-hearted newspaper column about the enviably cheery muddle of her family life. Things become less rosy when Matt is made redundant. Only Jess sees the potential calamity.

No Place for a Man. unabr. ed. Judy Astley. Read by Marlene Sidaway. 8 CDs. (Running Time: 8 hrs. 33 mins.). (Isis Ser.). (J). 2002. audio compact disk 79.95 (978-0-7531-1394-3(5)) Pub: ISIS Lrg Prnt GBR. Dist(s): Ulverscroft US

No Place for Magic: The Fourth Tale of the Frog Princess. unabr. ed. E. D. Baker. Read by Katherine Kellgren. 6 CDs. (Running Time: 6 hrs. 15 mins.). (J). (gr. 4-6). 2006. audio compact disk 64.75 (978-1-4281-2163-8(3)); 39.75 (978-1-4281-2158-4(7)) Recorded Bks.
When Trolls kidnap Eadric's little brother, his mother won't let Emma use magic - even to rescue him. Together with some offbeat friends, Eadric and Emma soon embark on a quest to free the endangered lad. As they traverse hostile terrain, fight off terrifying foes, and find unexpected allies, Emma begins to discover the true measure of Eadric's devotion and strength.

No Place Like Home. unabr. ed. Barbara Samuel. Read by Kristine Thatcher. 7 cass. (Running Time: 10 hrs.). 2002. 32.95 (978-1-58788-727-7(4), 1587887274, BAU); 78.25 (978-1-58788-728-4(2), 1587887282, Unabridge Lib Edns) Brilliance Audio.
No Place Like Home tells the unforgettable story of a family bound together by tradition - and the emotional journey of an estranged daughter risking everything for a second chance at life and love. Twenty-one years ago Jewel Sabatino left her childhood behind and never looked back. After a magical taste of fame, she found herself alone with a son to raise and not much else. She survived with the help of Michael, her one true friend. But now Michael is too sick to care for himself, and Jewel has run out of options. She leaves New York for the hills of Colorado, unsure if the family she ran from will welcome her back. For Jewel, coming home is falling back into a world that smells of Italian restaurants and home-baked pies. It is the laughter of sisters preparing for a summer wedding, and the peaceful haven for a treasured soul mate's last days. It also means facing the unforgiving eyes of a father betrayed by his favorite child - and letting go of a son who is ready to become a man. But most of all, it is the love she discovers in her own wary heart when Michael's brother Malachi unexpectedly arrives on her doorstep.

No Place Like Home. unabr. ed. Barbara Samuel. Read by Kristine Thatcher. (Running Time: 10 hrs.). 2004. 39.25 (978-1-59335-513-5(0), 1593355130, Brinc Audio MP3 Lib) Brilliance Audio.

No Place Like Home. unabr. ed. Barbara Samuel. Read by Kristine Thatcher. (Running Time: 10 hrs.). 2004. 39.25 (978-1-59710-541-5(4), 1597105414, BADLE); 24.95 (978-1-59710-540-8(6), 1597105406, BAD) Brilliance Audio.

No Place Like Home. unabr. ed. Barbara Samuel. Read by Kristine Thatcher. (Running Time: 10 hrs.). 2004. 24.95 (978-1-59335-245-5(X), 159335245X) Soulmate Audio Bks.

No Place Like Home: A Novel. abr. ed. Mary Higgins Clark. Read by Jan Maxwell. (Running Time: 43 hrs. 0 mins. 0 sec.). (ENG.). 2009. audio compact disk 14.99 (978-0-7435-8331-2(0)) Pub: S&S Audio. Dist(s): S and S Inc

No Place Like Home: A Novel. abr. unabr. ed. Mary Higgins Clark. Read by Jan Maxwell. 8 CDs. (Running Time: 100 hrs. 0 mins. 0 sec.). (ENG.). 2005. audio compact disk 39.95 (978-0-7435-4003-2(4), Audioworks) Pub: S&S Audio. Dist(s): S and S Inc
At the age of ten, Liza Barton shot her mother in their New Jersey home while trying to protect her from her violent stepfather. Despite her stepfather's claim that the shooting was a deliberate act, the Juvenile Court ruled the death an accident. Trying to erase every trace of Liza's past, her adoptive parents changed Liza's name to Celia. At the age of twenty-eight, she married a sixty-year-old widower, and they had a son. Before their

marriage, Celia confided the secret of her earlier life. On his deathbed, her husband made her swear never to reveal her past to anyone, so that their son would not carry the burden of this family tragedy. Happily remarried, Celia is shocked when her second husband presents her with a gift-the New Jersey house where she killed her mother. On the day they move in, the words BEWARE - LITTLE LIZZIE'S PLACE have been painted on the lawn. Determined to prove that she was the victim of her stepfather's psychotic behavior, Celia sets out to gather the evidence. When the real estate agent who sold the house is brutally murdered she is once again branded a killer. As Celia fights to prove her innocence, she is not aware that her life and the life of her son are in jeopardy.

No Place to Hide. unabr. ed. Gerry Carroll. Read by David Hilder. 10 cass. (Running Time: 14 hrs. 30 mins.). 1995. 69.95 (978-0-7861-0858-9(4), 1656) Blckstn Audio.
April, 1975: Two years after the United States pulled its last ground combat troops out of South Vietnam, a skeleton crew of American officers must evacuate all remaining personnel. Set against the background of Saigon's desperate last days, this extraordinary novel puts us inside the cockpit of a Huey on a split-second rooftop landing; let's us feel the scorching heat of the jet afterburners on the flight deck of an aircraft carrier & takes us deep into the jungle, where the eerie silence is shattered by the crack of AK-47 rifles. A remarkable story of heroism, friendship & sacrifice in the face of war.

No Place to Hide: A Novel of the Vietnam War. unabr. ed. Gerry Carroll. Read by David Hilder. (Running Time: 13 hrs. 0 mins.). 2010. 29.95 (978-1-4417-1317-9(4)); audio compact disk 109.00 (978-1-4417-1314-8(X)) Blckstn Audio.

No Price Too High. Annie Wilkinson & Trudy Harris. (Story Sound Ser.). 2007. 76.95 (978-1-84652-002-0(9)); audio compact disk 99.95 (978-1-84652-005-1(3)) Pub: Mgna Lrg Print GBR. Dist(s): Ulverscroft US

No Punia Me Ka Lua Ula. William H. Wilson. Illus. by Brook Parker. 1 cass. (Running Time: 35 min.). (HAW.). (J). (gr. 1-3). 1999. pap. bk. 5.95 (978-1-58191-061-2(4)) Aha Punana Leo.

***No Quarter: The Battle of the Crater 1864.** unabr. ed. Richard Slotkin. Read by Dion Graham. (Running Time: 16 hrs.). 2010. 24.99 (978-1-4418-8578-4(1), 9781441885784, Brilliance MP3); 39.97 (978-1-4418-8579-1(X), 9781441885791, Brinc Audio MP3 Lib); 39.97 (978-1-4418-8580-7(3), 9781441885807, BADLE); audio compact disk 29.99 (978-1-4418-8576-0(5), 9781441885760, Bril Audio CD Unabri); audio compact disk 69.97 (978-1-4418-8577-7(3), 9781441885777, BriAudCD Unabrid) Brilliance Audio.

No Queen Today! (Sails Literacy Ser.). (gr. 2 up). 10.00 (978-0-7578-2672-6(5)) Rigby Educ.

No Quiero Derretirme! Alma Flor Ada. (Cuentos Para Todo el Ano Ser.). (SPA., (J). (gr. k-3). 4.95 (978-1-58105-251-0(0)) Santillana.

No Relationship to Thought. Andrew Cohen. 2 cass. (Running Time: 3 hrs. 10 min.). (Bodhgaya Ser.: Vol. 2). 1996. 16.00 (978-1-883929-10-7(5)) Moksha Pr.
An exploration of what it would actually mean to perceive & respond to life directly. If taken seriously, this must lead to the realization of one's true nature beyound time & thought.

No Risk/No Fault Parenting. Created by Barry Neil Kaufman. 2 CDs. (Running Time: 55 mins., 38 mins.). 2005. audio compact disk 35.00 (978-1-887254-15-1(3)) Epic Century.
This landmark presentation presents a new vision that enables parents to approach the child-rearing experience with ease, comfort and clarity. So many people know the type of parents they don't want to be ... but have little guidance in helping them become the parents they DO want to be.Mixing insights with actual stories, Bears presents compelling and useful alternatives, demonstrating that parenting provides us with opportunities to find trust in ourselves and delight in our children.

No Roof but Heaven. unabr. ed. Jeanne Williams. Read by Stephanie Brush. 12 cass. (Running Time: 13 hrs.). 1996. 64.95 (978-1-55686-722-4(0)) Books in Motion.
In 1875 Susanna Alden moves from Ohio to Kansas to teach school. She discovers bitter divisions remain from the Civil War, so establishes her school in a soddy on the open prairie.

No Room: Luke 1:1-7. Ed Young. (J). 1978. 4.95 (978-0-7417-1029-1(3), A0029) Win Walk.

No Room for Error: The Covert Operations of America's Special Tactics Units from Iran to Afghanistan. abr. ed. John T. Carney, Jr. & Benjamin Schemmer. 3 cass. (Running Time: 4 hrs. 30 mins.). 2002. 22.95 (978-1-885408-92-1(7), LL084); audio compact disk 27.95 (978-1-885408-93-8(5), LL085) Listen & Live.
Part memoir and part history, all action and adventure as it describes the creation and harrowing missions performed by the US Air Forces? Special Tactics Unit as told by its first commanding officer. Benjamin F. Schemmer, a West Point graduate, Ranger and paratrooper, is uniquely qualified to write on military matters from several vantage points. His military service included three years in the Office of the Secretary of Defense, where became director if land-force weapons systems. Colonel John T. Carney was the first commanding officer of the USAF?s Special Tactics Unit.

No Room for Error: The Covert Operations of America's Special Tactics Units from Iran to Afghanistan. unabr. ed. John T. Carney, Jr. & Benjamin Schemmer. 7 cass. (Running Time: 10 hrs. 30 mins.). 2002. 34.95 (978-1-885408-94-5(3), LL086) Listen & Live.
Part memoir and part history, No Room For Error, is all action and adventure as it describes the creation and harrowing missions performed by the US Air Forces? Special Tactics Unit as told by its first commanding officer. Benjamin F. Schemmer, a West Point graduate, Ranger and paratrooper, is uniquely qualified to write on military matters from several vantage points. His military service included three years in the Office of the Secretary of Defense, where became director if land-force weapons systems. Colonel John T. Carney was the first commanding officer of the USAF?s Special Tactics Unit.

No Room for 'Me' Swami Amar Jyoti. 1 cass. (Running Time: 1 hr. 30 min.). 1979. 9.95 (G-10) Truth Consciousness.
Anything done for 'me' puts us in bondage. Accepting the principle with no 'but' or 'if'.

No Room in the Ark. unabr. ed. Alan Moorehead. Read by Victor Rumbellow. 8 cass. (Running Time: 8 hrs.). 1979. 48.00 (978-0-7366-0250-1(X), 1244) Books on Tape.
Describes Moorehead's journey from Johannesburg to Uganda, the Belgian Congo & Kenya.

No Roses for Harry. 2004. bk. 24.95 (978-1-55592-695-3(9)); pap. bk. 18.95 (978-1-55592-708-0(4)); pap. bk. 38.75 (978-1-55592-715-8(7)); pap. bk. 32.75 (978-1-55592-711-0(4)); pap. bk. 14.95 (978-1-55592-699-1(1)); 8.95 (978-1-55592-548-2(0)); audio compact disk 12.95 (978-1-55592-554-3(5)) Weston Woods.

No Safe Place, abr. ed. Richard North Patterson. Read by Patricia Kalember. 4 cass. (Running Time: 6 hrs.). 1999. 24.00 (FS9-43220) Highsmith.

No Safe Place. unabr. ed. Richard North Patterson. Read by Alexander Adams. 13 cass. (Running Time: 19 hrs. 30 min.). 1998. 104.00 (978-0-7366-4197-5(1), 4695) Books on Tape.
In the year 2000, Kerry Kilcannon surprises everyone with his strength in early presidential primaries. But california will be the mot important & most meaningful race, for twelve years earlier Kerry's older brother was assassinated there in his own run for the nomination. Now, albeit unwillingly, Kerry bears his brother's political legacy & he can't avoid the echoes of his brother's murder in the circumstances of his own life.

No Safe Place, unabr. ed. Richard North Patterson. Read by Alexander Adams. 11 cass. (Running Time: 16 hrs. 30 min.). 1999. 39.95 (FS9-43219) Highsmith.

***No Safety.** Susan Dunlap. 2009. (978-1-60136-542-2(X)) Audio Holding.

No Score. unabr. ed. Lawrence Block. Read by Gregory Gorton. 6 vols. (Running Time: 9 hrs.). (Chip Harrison Mystery Ser.). 2000. bk. 54.95 (978-0-7927-2262-5(0), CSL 151, Chivers Sound Lib) AudioGO.
It is a mystery why a street-smart young man like Chip Harrison has to resort to elaborate plans to attract a young woman like Francine. But someone turns Chip's dream into a nightmare of danger. Chip has to act fast and furiously in a sizzling and suspenseful adventure.

No Second Troy see Poetry of William Butler Yeats

No Shortcuts to the Top: Climbing the World's 14 Hightest Peaks. abr. ed. Ed Viesturs & David Roberts. Read by Ed Viesturs. (Running Time: 21600 sec.). (ENG.). 2006. audio compact disk 29.95 (978-0-7393-3989-3(3), Random AudioBks) Pub: Random Audio Pubg. Dist(s): Random

No Simple Victory: World War II in Europe 1939-1945. Norman Davies. Read by Simon Vance. (Playaway Adult Nonfiction Ser.). (ENG.). 2008. 99.99 (978-1-60640-718-9(X)) Find a World.

No Simple Victory: World War II in Europe, 1939-1945. unabr. ed. Norman Davies. Narrated by Simon Vance. (Running Time: 21 hrs. 0 mins. 0 sec.). (ENG.). 2007. audio compact disk 54.99 (978-1-4001-0468-0(8)) Pub: Tantor Media. Dist(s): IngramPubServ

No Simple Victory: World War II in Europe, 1939-1945. unabr. ed. Norman Davies. Read by Simon Vance. (Running Time: 21 hrs. 0 mins. 0 sec.). (ENG.). 2007. audio compact disk 109.99 (978-1-4001-3468-7(4)); audio compact disk 39.99 (978-1-4001-5468-5(5)) Pub: Tantor Media. Dist(s): IngramPubServ

***No Sin to Love.** Roberta Grieve. 2010. 79.95 (978-1-4079-1107-6(4)); audio compact disk 84.95 (978-1-4079-1108-3(2)) Pub: Soundings Ltd GBR. Dist(s): Ulverscroft US

No Sleep for the Dead. Adrian Magson. 2007. 61.95 (978-1-84559-738-2(9)); audio compact disk 79.95 (978-1-84559-739-9(7)) Pub: Soundings Ltd GBR. Dist(s): Ulverscroft US

***No Sleep till Wonderland.** Paul Tremblay. Narrated by Stephen Thorne. (Running Time: 7 hrs. 20 mins. 0 sec.). (ENG.). 2011. audio compact disk 29.95 (978-1-60998-157-0(X)) Pub: AudioGO. Dist(s): Perseus Dist

No Smoking. Narrated by Nancie M. Barwick. 1 CD. (Running Time: 20 mins). 2003. audio compact disk 10.00 (978-0-9663488-5-9(0)) Hypnotherapy Wrks.

***No Snow for Christmas.** Jill Kalz. Illus. by Sahin Erkocak. (Pfeffernut County Ser.). (ENG.). 2010. audio compact disk 11.93 (978-1-4048-6240-1(4)) CapstoneDig.

No Spin Zone: Confrontations with the Powerful & Famous in America. unabr. ed. Bill O'Reilly. Read by Bill O'Reilly. 3 cass. (Running Time: 4 hrs. 30 mins.). 2002. 28.00 (978-0-7366-8546-7(4)); audio compact disk 32.00 (978-0-7366-8557-3(X)) Books on Tape.
The Author no one he dislikes off the hook, whether it be the Clintons and their legacy of scandal, the Reverend Jesse Jackson, or Dan Rather. He claims to speak for millions of angry white males, disenfranchised by the changing economy, the depredations of figures in power, and the lack of simple answers to their problems. He buttresses his opinions of these figures with their own words about the issues he cares about - issues including Medicare, the death penalty, and crime. This book is a direct challenge to the elite, striking a blow for "real Americans".

No Standing Zone. unabr. ed. Margaret Clark. Narrated by Dino Marnika. 2 cass. (Running Time: 2 hrs. 35 mins.). 2002. (978-1-74030-869-4(7)) Bolinda Pubng AUS.
Three major stress factors a marriage break-up, moving house, loss of income for the family,, and a new school. Link James and his sister Claire get the lot! How does a boy from the wealthy side of town cope with the tough guys at Westlands? How does the bad boy tag his father gave him influence his life?.

No Substitutions. abr. ed. Engle & Barnes. (Running Time: 2 hrs.). (Strange Matter Ser.). 2006. 9.95 (978-1-4233-0856-0(5), 9781423308560, BAD) Brilliance Audio.

No Substitutions. abr. ed. Engle & Julian Barnes. Read by Multivoice Production Staff. (Running Time: 2 hrs.). (Strange Matter Ser.). 2006. 25.25 (978-1-4233-0857-7(3), 9781423308577, BADLE) Brilliance Audio.

No Substitutions. abr. ed. Marty M. Engle. (Running Time: 7200 sec.). (Strange Matter Ser.). (J). (gr. 4-7). 2006. audio compact disk 9.95 (978-1-4233-0854-6(9), 9781423308546, BACD) Brilliance Audio.
Your next class could be your last. Curtis Chatman and Shelly Miller didn't plan for trouble. They expected a quiet sixth period in the library reading their favorite supernatural tales after Mr. Mayfield's dull biology class. They didn't expect suspension. Fairfield Junior High welcomes Stacy Calhoun, the new substitute. He holds an unnatural power over his class. An appearance as unsettling as his lesson plan, his silvery eyes catch every movement, his pointy ears every whisper. After a terrifying encounter in the library, Curtis and Shelly discover a shocking secret about their temporary teacher, a secret that could cost them their lives. Now, after a lifetime of avoiding trouble, it howled outside their window, simply dying to get in.

No Substitutions. abr. ed. Marty M. Engle & Johnny Ray Barnes, Jr. (Running Time: 7200 sec.). (Strange Matter Ser.). (J). (gr. 4-7). 2006. audio compact disk 25.25 (978-1-4233-0855-3(7), 9781423308553, BACDLib Ed) Brilliance Audio.

No Such Thing as a Bad Day. Hamilton Jordan. Narrated by Tom Stechschulte. 4 cass. (Running Time: 6 hrs.). 2000. 40.00 (978-0-7887-4872-1(6)) Recorded Bks.
A survivor of Non-Hodgkins lymphoma, melanoma and prostate cancer, former White House Chief of Staff Hamilton JOrdan shares hi personal and political reflections. Always trying to do the right thing, Jordan serves as an inspiration, stressing the importance of becoming proactive and maintaining a positive attitude, in the face of potential terminal disease.

No such thing as a Bad Day. Hamilton Jordan. Narrated by Tom Stechschulte. 5 CDs. (Running Time: 6 hrs.). audio compact disk 48.00 (978-1-4025-1547-7(2)) Recorded Bks.

No Such Thing as a Bad Day. abr. ed. Hamilton Jordan. Read by Hamilton Jordan. 4 CDs. (Running Time: 5 hrs.). 2000. audio compact disk 29.95 HighBridge.

No Suitable Mate/NSM. George Bloomer. 2004. audio compact disk 14.99 (978-0-88368-444-3(6)) Whitaker Hse.

No Survivors. Jerry Ahern. Read by Alan Zimmerman. 3 cass. (Running Time: 270 min.). No. 12. 2000. 22.00 (978-1-58807-032-6(8)) Am Pubng Inc.

No Survivors. abr. unabr. ed. Jerry Ahern. Read by Alan Zimmerman. 4 vols. (Running Time: 6 hrs.). No. 12. 2004. audio compact disk 28.00 (978-1-58807-274-0(6)) Am Pubng Inc.

No Survivors. unabr. ed. Jerry Ahern. Read by Alan Zimmerman. 2 vols. No. 12. 2003. (978-1-58807-542-0(7)) Am Pubng Inc.

No Survivors. unabr. ed. Jerry Ahern. Read by Alan Zimmerman. 3 vols. No. 12. 2004. audio compact disk (978-1-58807-705-9(5)) Am Pubng Inc.

***No Survivors.** unabr. ed. Tom Cain. Read by John Lee. 9 CDs. (Running Time: 11 hrs.). 2009. audio compact disk 110.00 (978-1-4159-6113-1(1), BksonTape) Pub: Random Audio Pubg. Dist(s): Random

No Sweat Bee. Jon Von Seggen. 1 cass. (Running Time: 1 hr.). Dramatization. 1996. 10.00 (978-1-58302-133-0(7), KCM-44) One Way St.
Collection of nine religious musical performance pieces for use with puppets. Includes script.

No Sweat Cantonese: A Fun Guide to Speaking Correctly. Amy Leung. 2004. pap. bk. 18.00 (978-962-8783-29-8(7)) Pub: Asia HKG. Dist(s): Weatherhill

No Sweat Exercise Plan: Lose Weight, Get Healthy, & Live Longer. Harvey B. Simon. 2007. audio compact disk 22.95 (978-1-933310-20-6(0)) STI Certified.

No Tacos for Saddam. abr. ed. Andrei Codrescu. Read by Andrei Codrescu. 1 cass. (Running Time: 1 hr.). 1999. 11.95 (978-1-57453-143-5(3)) Audio Lit.
Sometime grouch & always perceptive commentator for NPR's "All Things Considered", Codrescu talks of many things: eternal life, the normal family, crab enchiladas, obscenity in search of art & his hometown of Sibu, Romania.

No Talking. unabr. ed. Andrew Clements. Read by Keith Nobbs. (Running Time: 3 hrs. 0 mins. 0 sec.). (ENG.). (J). (gr. 3-7). 2007. audio compact disk 19.95 (978-0-7435-6692-6(0)) Pub: S&S Audio. Dist(s): S and S Inc

No Talking after Lights. unabr. ed. Angela Lambert. Read by Gemma Jones. 6 cass. (Running Time: 8 hrs. 15 min.). (Isis Ser.). (J). 1994. 54.95 (978-1-85695-881-3(7), 940808) Pub: ISIS Lrg Prnt GBR. Dist(s): Ulverscroft US

***No te comas el Marshmallow... Todavia!** Joachim De Posada. Narrated by Joachim De Posada. Prod. by FonoLibro Inc. Narrated by Javier Coronel & Sergio Dore. (Running Time: 120).Tr. of Don't eat the marshmallow... Yet!. 2010. 17.95 (978-1-61154-007-9(0)) Fonolibro Inc.

No Te Comas el Marshmellow Todavia. Joachim de Posada. 2008. audio compact disk 24.95 (978-1-933499-80-2(X)) Fonolibro Inc.

No Tears for the Lost. Adrian Magson. 2008. 69.95 (978-1-4079-0207-4(5)); audio compact disk 79.95 (978-1-4079-0208-1(3)) Pub: Soundings Ltd GBR. Dist(s): Ulverscroft US

No Thanks, Not for Me see No, Gracias, No Para Mi

No Thanks, Not for Me, Level 1. 2 cass. (Running Time: 1 hr. 30 mins.). (SmartReader Ser.). (J). 1999. pap. bk. & tchr. ed. 19.95 (978-0-7887-1158-9(X), 79419T3) Recorded Bks.
Peer pressure has a dark side when teens are offered drugs & alcohol. Find out how one young man deals with this sensitive issue.

No Thanks, Not for Me, Level 2. 2 cass. (Running Time: 1 hr. 30 mins.). (SmartReader Ser.). (J). 1999. pap. bk. & tchr. ed. 19.95 (978-0-7887-0124-5(X), 79312T3) Recorded Bks.

No, Tim: Early Explorers Emergent Set A Audio CD. Benchmark Education Staff. (J). 2006. audio compact disk 10.00 (978-1-4108-7594-5(6)) Benchmark Educ.

No, Tim (Spanish) Audio CD: Emergent Set A. Benchmark Education Staff. Ed. by Cynthia Swain. (Early Explorers Ser.). (J). 2008. audio compact disk 10.00 (978-1-60437-243-4(5)) Benchmark Educ.

No-Time Dutch. 6 cass. (Running Time: 6 hrs.). (English As a Second Language Course Ser.). (DUT.). 1972. 135.00 (978-0-88432-157-6(6), AFN270) J Norton Pubs.
This unusual method uses no text or printed materials. You learn by listening to cassettes while driving, cooking, gardening, walking, or doing som oehter monotonous task. You give only time that you are already devoting to something else you are doing. Introductory level.

No-Time Dutch. unabr. ed. 6 cass. (Running Time: 6 hrs.). 115.00 (AFN270) J Norton Pubs.

No Time for Generals: Hebrews 11:32. Ed Young. 1992. 4.95 (978-0-7417-1927-0(4), 927) Win Walk.

No Time for Goodbye. abr. ed. Linwood Barclay. Read by Christopher Lane. (Running Time: 6 hrs.). 2008. audio compact disk 14.99 (978-1-4233-4115-4(5), 9781423341154, BCD Value Price) Brilliance Audio.

No Time for Goodbye. unabr. ed. Linwood Barclay. Read by Christopher Lane. (Running Time: 11 hrs.). 2007. 39.25 (978-1-4233-4113-0(9), 9781423341130, BADLE); 24.95 (978-1-4233-4112-3(0), 9781423341123, BAD); 87.25 (978-1-4233-4107-9(4), 9781423341079, BrilAudUnabridg); audio compact disk 39.25 (978-1-4233-4111-6(2), 9781423341116, Brinc Audio MP3 Lib); audio compact disk 102.25 (978-1-4233-4109-3(0), 9781423341093, BriAudCD Unabrid); audio compact disk 38.95 (978-1-4233-4108-6(2), 9781423341086, Bril Audio CD Unabri); audio compact disk 24.95 (978-1-4233-4110-9(4), 9781423341109, Brilliance MP3) Brilliance Audio.

No Time for Goodbyes - Death of a Daughter or Son. abr. ed. Janice H. Lord. Ed. by Eugene D. Wheeler. 2 cass. . (Running Time: 3 hrs.). 1991. 7.95 (978-0-934793-35-3(2)) Pathfinder AZ.

No Time for Goodbyes - Death of Mate or Lover. abr. ed. Janice H. Lord. Ed. by Eugene D. Wheeler. 2 cass. . (Running Time: 3 hrs.). 1991. 7.95 (978-0-934793-36-0(0)) Pathfinder AZ.

No-Time French I. unabr. ed. (Running Time: 8 hrs.). (No-Time Language Method Ser.). 110.00 (N140) Books on Tape.
Uses no text or other printed materials, courses are introductory-level & help master the basics of the language for business or travel; yet the grammar & sentences are contemporary & not simplistic.

No-Time French I. unabr. ed. 8 cass. (Running Time: 8 hrs.). 125.00 (AFN140) J Norton Pubs.

No-Time French II. unabr. ed. 6 cass. (Running Time: 6 hrs.). 115.00 (AFN141) J Norton Pubs.

No-Time German I. 6 cass. (Running Time: 6 hrs.). 115.00 (AFN130) J Norton Pubs.

No-Time German I. unabr. ed. (Running Time: 6 hrs.). (No-Time Language Method Ser.). 100.00 (N130) Books on Tape.

No-Time German II. 6 cass. (Running Time: 6 hrs.). 115.00 (AFN131) J Norton Pubs.

No-Time Greek. 6 cass. (Running Time: 6 hrs.). 115.00 (N210) J Norton Pubs.

No-Time Hungarian. 6 cass. (Running Time: 6 hrs.). 115.00 (AFN200) J Norton Pubs.

No-Time Italian. 8 cass. (Running Time: 8 hrs.). 125.00 (AFN170) J Norton Pubs.

No-Time Japanese. 6 cass. (Running Time: 6 hrs.). 115.00 (AFN160) J Norton Pubs.

No-Time Japanese CD Course. A. E. Van Vogt. 6 CDs. (Running Time: 6 hrs.). (Native American Documentary Ser.). (JPN.). 2006. audio compact disk 135.00 (978-1-57970-355-4(0), AFN160D, Audio-For) J Norton Pubs.
This unusual method uses no text or printed materials. You learn by listening to recordings while driving, cooking, gardening, walking, or doing some other monotonous task. You give only time that you are already devoting to something else you are doing. That's why it requires "No Time"! The course is introductory-level and helps you master the basic of the language for business or travel; yet the grammar and sentences are contemporary and not simplistic. There is extensive vocabulary and conversation practice, plus an explanation of the structure and grammar of Japanese. The course consists of 2 hours each of conversation, speaking, and vocabulary. In just 40 minutes a day for one month, you can learn a 2-hour segment.

No Time Like Show Time. unabr. ed. Michael Hoeye. Read by Campbell Scott. 4 cass. (Running Time: 5 hrs. 55 mins.). (YA). 2004. 29.75 (978-0-8072-0887-8(6), Listening Lib) Pub: Random Audio Pubg. Dist(s): NetLibrary CO

***No Time Like the Past.** 2010. audio compact disk (978-1-59171-181-0(9)) Falcon Picture.

No-Time Persian. 6 cass. (Running Time: 6 hrs.). 115.00 (AFN220) J Norton Pubs.

No-Time Persian. 6 cass. (Running Time: 6 hrs.). (PER.). 1970. 135.00 (978-0-88432-166-8(5), AFN220) J Norton Pubs.
This unusual method uses no text or printed materials. Introductory level, heling master the basic of the language for business or travel, yet the grammar and sentences are contemporary and not simplistic. Extensive vocabulary and conversation practice, plus an explanation of the language's structure and grammar. Two hours each of conversation, speaking, and vocabulary.

No-Time Russian. 8 cass. (Running Time: 8 hrs.). 125.00 (AFN180) J Norton Pubs.

No-Time Spanish I. 8 cass. (Running Time: 8 hrs.). 125.00 (AFN150) J Norton Pubs.

No-Time Spanish I. unabr. ed. (Running Time: 8 hrs.). (No-Time Language Method Ser.). 110.00 (N150) Books on Tape.
Uses no text or other printed materials, courses are introductory-level & help master the basics of the language for business or travel; yet the grammar & sentences are contempory & not simplistic.

No-Time Spanish II. 6 cass. (Running Time: 6 hrs.). 115.00 (AFN151) J Norton Pubs.

No-time spanish part 1 CD Set. 8 CDs. (Running Time: 8 HRS.). (SPA.). 2005. audio compact disk 155.00 (978-1-57970-231-1(7), AFN150D) J Norton Pubs.

No-Time Swahili. 6 cass. (Running Time: 6 hrs.). 115.00 (AFN230) J Norton Pubs.

No-Time Tagalog. 6 cass. (Running Time: 6 hrs.). 115.00 (AFN260) J Norton Pubs.

No Time to Die. abr. ed. Liz Tilberis. Read by Liz Tilberis. 2 cass. (Running Time: 3 hrs.). 1997. 17.98 Set. (978-1-57042-581-3(7)) Hachet Audio.
Liz Tilberis tells the remarkable story of how she ascended the heights of the magazine & fashion worlds, survived ovarian cancer & used her drive & optimism to deal with every stroke fate dealt her.

No Time to Die, unabr. ed. Liz Tilberis. Read by Kimberly Schraf. 8 cass. (Running Time: 12 hrs.). 1999. 64.00 (978-0-7366-4339-9(7), 4833) Books on Tape.
In 1993, the author had it all. Having risen to the editorship of British Vogue, she was hired as editor-in-chief of Harper's Bazaar, the Bible of U.S. fashion. Moving to America she instantly become one of the most prominent figures in international media & fashion. Tragically, she was then diagnosed with third-stage ovarian cancer. A story of both an extraordinary career & a remarkable battle with cancer.

No Time to Lose. Steck-Vaughn Staff. 2003. (978-0-7398-8442-3(5)) SteckVau.

No Time to Wave Goodbye. unabr. ed. Jacquelyn Mitchard. Read by Susan Denaker. (ENG.). 2009. audio compact disk 35.00 (978-0-307-70178-7(6), Random AudioBks) Pub: Random Audio Pubg. Dist(s): Random

No Title. Ed Young. (J). 1981. 4.95 (978-0-7417-1154-0(0)) Win Walk.

No Truce With Kings see Award Winning Science Fiction

No True Glory: A Frontline Account of the Battle for Fallujah. abr. ed. Bing West. Read by Dennis Boutsikaris. (Running Time: 21600 sec.). (ENG.). 2005. audio compact disk 29.95 (978-0-7393-2301-4(6), Random AudioBks) Pub: Random Audio Pubg. Dist(s): Random

No Turning Back: Acts 21:1-26. Ben Young. 2000. 4.95 (978-0-7417-6173-6(4), B0173) Win Walk.

No Victory Without Battle. Ruth Prince. 1 cass. (Running Time: 1 hr.). 1990. 5.95 (A-8008) Derek Prince.
Ruth Prince exposes Satan's tactics against Christians who are wounded & "downed" - & gives strategy for victory from the Scriptures & personal experience.

No Vision No Future. unabr. ed. MiChelle A. Butler. 1 cass. (Running Time: 1 hr. 30 mins.). 2001. 5.00 (A159) Word Faith Pubng.

No Wasted Journey. unabr. ed. Huston Smith. 1 cass. (Running Time: 1 hr. 26 min.). 1968. 11.00 (02401) Big Sur Tapes.

No Way Out. AIO Team Staff. Prod. by Focus on the Family Staff. 4 CDs. (Adventures in Odyssey Ser.). (ENG.). (J). 2004. audio compact disk 24.99 (978-1-58997-229-2(5)) Pub: Focus Family. Dist(s): Tyndale Hse

No Way Out. Prod. by Focus on the Family Staff. 6 cass. (Running Time: 6 hrs.). (Adventures in Odyssey Ser.). (J). 2004. cass., cass., DVD 24.99 (978-1-58997-230-8(9)) Pub: Focus Family. Dist(s): Tyndale Hse

No way Out. Andrea Kane. Narrated by Ed Sala. 9 cass. (Running Time: 13 hrs. 15 mins.). 84.00 (978-1-4025-1738-9(6)) Recorded Bks.

No Way to Say Goodbye. unabr. ed. Kay Gregory. Read by Lynda Evans. 4 cass. (Running Time: 6 hrs.). 1999. 26.95 (978-1-55686-860-3(X)) Books in Motion.
Roxane is strangely attracted to her shady boss.

No Way to Treat a First Lady: A Novel. unabr. ed. Christopher Buckley. Read by Tim Matheson. 6 cass. (Running Time: 9 hrs.). 2002. 72.00 (978-0-7366-8828-4(5)) Books on Tape.
the First Lady is accused of murdering the President for his peccadilloes.

No Witnesses. unabr. ed. Ridley Pearson. Read by Alexander Adams. 9 cass. (Running Time: 13 hrs. 30 min.). (Lou Boldt & Daphne Matthews Mystery Ser.). 1995. 72.00 (978-0-7366-2950-8(5), 3644) Books on Tape.
Detective Lou Boldt & police psychologist Daphne Matthews track a high-tech killer who's poisoning food in Seattle's supermarkets. But the criminal is hard to track, faxing extortion letters from his laptop & snatching ransoms through ATMs. detective Lou Boldt & police psychologist Daphne Matthews try to follow the trail through the abyss of computer networks.

No Wonder My Parents Drank: Tales from a Stand-up Dad. abr. unabr. ed. Jay Mohr. Read by Jay Mohr. (Running Time: 7 hrs. 30 mins. 0 sec.). (ENG.). 2010. audio compact disk 29.99 (978-1-4423-0412-3(X)) Pub: S&S Audio. Dist(s): S and S Inc

No You, No Me. Perf. by Ceili Rain. 2002. audio compact disk Provident Mus Dist.

No. 1 Ladies' Detective Agency: The Maid & Tears of the Giraffe. Alexander McCall Smith. Read by Full Cast Production Staff. 2009. audio compact disk 19.95 (978-1-60283-638-9(8)) AudioGO.

Noah & the Ark. Paul Guernsey. Illus. by Lori Lohstoeter. (Greatest Stories Ever Told Ser.). (J). (gr. k up). 1993. pap. bk. 19.95 (978-0-88708-293-1(9), SSChildren) SandS Childrens.

Noah & the Ark. Read by Kelly McGillis. 1 cass. (Running Time: 25 min.). (J). bk. 19.95 S&S Audio.
Noah's challenge to save his people fill the ark with animals. It is dramatically enhanced by the music of Paul Winter Consort.

Noah & the Ark: Sing, Color'n Say. Phillip Siadi & Lenore Paxton. Read by Phillip Siadi & Lenore Paxton. 1 cass. (Running Time: 45 min.). (World of Language Bible Story Ser.). (J). (ps-3). 1993. 5.95 (978-1-880449-31-8(5)) Wrldkids Pr.
Sing-along-song teaches story of Noah & the Ark, children learn to say "Noah & the Ark" in 10 languages, language lesson tape, narrative section expands on story in depth. Musical sound effects. Companion coloring book, quizzes & puzzles.

Noah & the Ark: Sing, Color'n Say. Lenore Paxton & Phillip Siadi. Read by Lenore Paxton & Phillip Siadi. 1 cass. (Running Time: 45 min.). (World of Language Bible Story Ser.). (J). (ps-4). 1994. pap. bk. 7.95 (978-1-880449-11-0(0)) Wrldkids Pr.

***Noah Barleywater Runs Away.** unabr. ed. John Boyne. (Running Time: 5 hrs. 30 mins.). (ENG.). (J). 2011. audio compact disk 30.00 (978-0-307-91648-8(0), Listening Lib) Pub: Random Audio Pubg. Dist(s): Random

Noah Webster: The Life & Times of an American Patriot. unabr. collector's ed. Harlow G. Unger. Read by John Edwardson. 13 cass. (Running Time: 19 hrs. 30 mins.). 1999. 104.00 (978-0-7366-4488-4(1), 4927) Books on Tape.
Noah Webster is known chiefly as the original standard-bearer of "American" English. His speller has sold hundreds of millions of copies over the years, his dictionary achieved nothing short of a complete transformation of the way Americans wrote the language, & his elementary school curriculum was for 100 years the foundation of American education. Now this biography of him, the first in over sixty years, brilliantly restores Webster's momumental legacy as a teacher, legislator, philosopher, lawyer, crusading editor, a tireless social reformer, & one of history's most profoundly influential lexicographers.

Noah's Ark. 1 cass. (Running Time: 1 hr. 30 min.). (J). (978-0-944391-70-9(2)) DonWise Prodns.
Narrates biblical story designed especially for children.

Noah's Ark. 4 cass. (Running Time: 4 hrs.). (Wood Cassettes Toys Ser.). (J). (gr. k-6). 1991. 19.95 (978-1-55569-486-9(1), 8325) Great Am Audio.
Contains fully dramatized bible stories from the old testament, King James Version.

Noah's Ark. (What's a Good Story? Ser.). (YA). 1990. pap. bk. & stu. ed. 99.00 (60793) Phoenix Films.
Teaches about the problems of living together on planet Earth today.

Noah's Ark. 2004. 8.95 (978-1-55592-531-4(6)); cass. & flmstrp 30.00 (978-1-56008-730-4(7)); audio compact disk 12.95 (978-1-55592-532-1(4)) Weston Woods.

Noah's Ark. Dalmatian Press Staff. (J). (ps-3). 2000. pap. bk. 4.97 (978-1-888567-37-3(6)) Dalmatian Pr.

Noah's Ark. James Earl Jones. 1 cass. (J). 1991. 9.98 BMG Distribution.

Noah's Ark. Read by James Earl Jones. 1 cass. (Running Time: 1 hr. 30 min.). 1991. 9.98 (978-5-553-25924-2(X)) BMG Distribution.

Noah's Ark. Jerry Pinkney. (J). (gr. k-3). 2004. bk. 24.95 (978-1-55592-530-7(8)) Weston Woods.

Noah's Ark. unabr. ed. Peter Spier. Narrated by James Earl Jones. Music by Stewart Copeland. 1 cass. (Running Time: 55 min.). (Stories to Remember Ser.). (J). (gr. 1-5). 1990. 8.98 (978-1-879496-03-3(8)); audio compact disk 13.48 (978-1-56896-033-3(6)) Lightyear Entrtnmnt.
Based on the Caldecott Award-winning picture book by artist Peter Spier, this is a powerful retelling of Noah's story with narration by James Earl Jones & score by Stewart Copeland.

Noah's Ark. unabr. ed. Peter Spier. Narrated by James Earl Jones. Music by Stewart Copeland. 1 cass. (Running Time: 55 min.). (Stories to Remember Ser.). (J). (gr. 1-5). 1993. pap. bk. 8.98 incl. long box. (978-1-879496-04-0(6)) Lightyear Entrtnmnt.

Noah's Ark & Other Stories from the Bible. unabr. ed. Alfreda C. Doyle. Read by Alfreda C. Doyle. 1 cass. (Running Time: 23 min.). (J). (gr. 3-12). 1993. 16.95 (978-1-56820-116-0(8)) Story Time.
Stories that rhyme based on stories from the Bible.

Noah's Ark Dramatized Stories on Cassette see Arca De Noe' Historias Dramatizadas En Casete

Noah's Ark Read Along. 1 cass. (Running Time: 35 min.). (Sunday Morning Ser.). (J). (ps-3). 1999. pap. bk. 6.98 (978-0-7634-0576-2(0)) W Disney Records.

Noah's Big Boat. 1 cass. (Running Time: 35 min.). (Wee Sing Ser.). (J). bk. 7.98 Blisterpack. (PSS 7967) NewSound.

Noah's Compass. unabr. ed. Anne Tyler. Read by Arthur Morey. (ENG.). 2010. audio compact disk 35.00 (978-0-7393-8477-0(5), Random AudioBks) Pub: Random Audio Pubg. Dist(s): Random

Noah's Journey. unabr. ed. Joe Loesch. Ed. by Cheryl J. Hutchinson. Illus. by Ott Denney. 1 cass. (Running Time: 1 hr. 30 min.). (Bible Stories for Kids Ser.). (J). (ps-3). 1995. pap. bk. 14.95 (978-1-887729-06-2(2)); pap. bk. 16.95 (978-1-887729-07-9(0)) Toy Box Prods.
Come join Corky kangaroo & all his friends as they tell the story of Noah's ark, the great flood, & why God put his rainbow in the sky.

Noahs Journey Through the Eyes of the Animals. Box Toy Box Productions Staff. 2000. (978-1-887729-29-1(1)) Toy Box Prods.

Noah's Two-by-Two Adventure/Jonah & the Very Big Fish. Narrated by Jeffrey E. Burkart & Melanie Bergmann. (Arch Bks.). (J). (ps-3). 2006. pap. bk. 7.99 (978-0-7586-1173-8(2)) Concordia.

Nobel Lectures in Economic Sciences: 1996-2000. Ed. by Torsten Persson. 2003. pap. bk. 28.00 (978-981-02-4961-8(6)) Pub: Imperial College GBR. Dist(s): World Scientific Pub

Nobel Prize Laureate Dr. C. Sherwood Rowland, Discoverer of Chlorofluorocarbons (CFCs) & Their Role in Depleting the Atmospheric Ozone Layer. Hosted by Nancy Pearlman. 1 cass. (Running Time: 29 min.). 10.00 (1511) Educ Comm CA.

Nobel Prize Winners: Biographical Sketches for Listening & Reading. Lisa F. DeWitt. (gr. 7-12). 1991. pap. bk. & stu. ed. 28.00 (978-0-86647-110-7(3)) Pro Lingua.

Nobel Prize Winners: Biographical Sketches for Listening & Reading. Lisa F. DeWitt. 3 CDs. (gr. 7-12). 2005. pap. bk. & stu. ed. 28.00 (978-0-86647-203-6(7)); audio compact disk 20.00 (978-0-86647-202-9(9)) Pro Lingua.

Nobel Voices for Disarmament (Audio CD) United Nations. (ENG.). 2007. audio compact disk 15.00 (978-92-1-142258-0(2)) Untd Nat Pubns.

Nobility of Women. Sai Maa Lakshmi Devi. 2004. audio compact disk 16.00 (978-1-933488-14-1(X)) HIU Pr.
*The Nobility of WomenExcerpted in part from the Varalakshmi writings of Chalanda Sai MaaRecorded in Barcelona, Spain - July 2004 by Chalanda Sai MaaThis timely and empowering CD by Sai Maa Lakshmi Devi catalyzes the emergence of the nobility and grace inherent within all women.Tracks:1. Divine Feminine Qualities Within2. The Womb of Creation3. The Breath of Love4. The Sacredness of Our Love5. Divine Mother in All Women6. Lakshmi Gayatri Mantra** This is a powerful mantra to bring forth the presence of the Divine Mother within.*

Noble Bachelor see Adventures of Sherlock Holmes

Noble Deeds, unabr. ed. Christine M. Fraser. Read by Vivien Heilbron. 8 cass. (Running Time: 12 hrs.). (Noble Ser.: Vol. 2). 1999. 69.95 (CAB 1432) AudioGO.

Noble Heart. Pema Chödrön. 12 CDs. 2004. audio compact disk 79.95 (978-1-59179-230-7(4), AF00877D) Sounds True.
From a leading voice in American Buddhism, a self-guided meditation retreat to befriend our obstacles and enrich our lives.

Noble House, Pt. 1. James Clavell. 2000. 104.00 (978-0-7366-4865-3(8)) Books on Tape.

Noble House, Pt. 2. James Clavell. 2000. 104.00 (978-0-7366-4866-0(6)) Books on Tape.

Noble House, Pt. 3. unabr. ed. James Clavell. 13 cass. (Running Time: 19 hrs. 30 mins.). 2000. 112.00 (978-0-7366-4867-7(4)) Books on Tape.
British and American businessmen maneuver for control of Hong Kong's oldest trading house amidst mystery, adventure and romance.

Noble Lies. unabr. ed. Charles Benoit. Read by Malcolm Hillgartner. (Running Time: 27000 sec.). 2007. 54.95 (978-1-4332-1090-7(8)) Blckstn Audio.

Noble Lies. unabr. ed. Charles Benoit. Read by Malcolm Hilgartner. (Running Time: 27000 sec.). 2007. audio compact disk 55.00 (978-1-4332-1091-4(6)) Blckstn Audio.

Noble Lies. unabr. ed. Charles Benoit & Malcolm Hilgartner. (Running Time: 27000 sec.). 2007. audio compact disk 29.95 (978-1-4332-1092-1(4)) Blckstn Audio.

Noble One. Denise Robins. Read by Judith Boyd. 7 cass. (Running Time: 10 hrs. 30 min.). 1999. 61.95 (69056) Pub: Soundings Ltd GBR. Dist(s): Ulverscroft US

Noble Purpose: The Joy of Living a Meaningful Life. William Damon. Intro. by David G. Myers. 2 CDs. (Running Time: 80 mins.). 2005. audio compact disk 12.95 (978-1-932031-78-2(2)) Pub: Templeton Pr. Dist(s): Chicago Distribution Ctr

Noble Radiance. unabr. ed. Donna Leon. Read by Anna Fields. 5 cass. (Running Time: 7 hrs.). (Commissario Guido Brunetti Mystery Ser.: Bk. 7). 2001. 39.95 (978-0-7861-1998-1(5), 2768); audio compact disk 48.00 (978-0-7861-9729-3(3), 2768) Blckstn Audio.
In a small village at the foot of the Italian Dolomites, the gardens of a deserted farmhouse have lain untouched for decades. But the new owner, keen for renovations to begin, is summoned urgently to the house when his workmen disturb a macabre grave.

Noble Radiance. unabr. ed. Donna Leon. Narrated by Samuel Gillespie. 6 cass. (Running Time: 8 hrs.). (Commissario Guido Brunetti Mystery Ser.: Bk. 7). 1998. 58.00 (978-1-84197-043-1(3)) Recorded Bks.

Noble Thoughts from All Sides. Swami Amar Jyoti. 2 cass. (Running Time: 3 hrs.). 1976. 12.95 (N-16) Truth Consciousness.
The meaning of Satsang. On Ragas (moods); romance & chivalry; Yoga in America; scientific inquiry & devotion; self confidence & ego trips; changing others. Blessings of the Sad-Guru.

***Nobodies.** unabr. ed. N. E. Bode. (ENG.). 2005. (978-0-06-088142-9(9)); (978-0-06-088141-2(0)) HarperCollins Pubs.

Nobodies Album. unabr. ed. Carolyn Parkhurst. Read by Kimberly Farr. 2010. 35.00 (978-0-307-71471-8(3), Random AudioBks) Pub: Random Audio Pubg. Dist(s): Random

Nobody Dies in a Casino. unabr. ed. Marlys Millhiser. Read by Lynda Evans. 6 cass. (Running Time: 8 hrs. 48 min.). (Charlie Greene Mystery Ser.: Bk. 5). 2001. 39.95 (978-1-58116-147-2(6)) Books in Motion.
While vacationing in Las Vegas, Charlie witnesses a murder. She decides to get involved when the cop who hears her eye witness account is killed by "accident".

Nobody Else Like Me: Celebrating the Diversity of Children. Perf. by Cathy Fink & Marcy Marxer. 1 CD. (Running Time: 1 hr.). (J). audio compact disk (978-1-57940-024-8(8)) Rounder Records.
A musical celebration of the diversity of children. The album celebrates different cultures, different languages & different physical abilities while at the same time emphasizing how special each individual child is. You'll hear everything from acoustic folk guitar to a full soca band, rock 'n' roll to rap, hammered dulcimer to African percussion. A top-notch children's chorus joins Cathy & Marcy on eight songs & two songs feature children as lead singers, "Walkin' On My Wheels" & the rap song, "A Kid Like Me". This recording is an inspiration to children, parents & teachers in sharing our world.

Nobody Else Like Me: Celebrating the Diversity of Children. Cathy Fink & Marcy Marxer. 1 cass. (Running Time: 1 hr.). (Family Ser.). (J). 1999. (978-1-57940-025-5(6)) Rounder Records.

Nobody Hates a Dead Man. unabr. ed. P. J. Tracy. Read by Buck Schirner. 6 cass. (Running Time: 10 hrs.). (Monkeewrench Ser.). 2004. 82.25 (978-1-59086-631-3(2), 1590866312, BrilAudUnabridg) Brilliance Audio.
Minneapolis detectives Leo Magozzi and Gino Rolseth are bored - ever since they solved the Monkeewrench case, the Twin Cities have been in a murder-free dry spell, as people no longer seem interested in killing one another. But when elderly Morey Gilbert is found dead in the plant nursery he runs with his wife, Lily, the crime drought ends - not with a trickle, but with a torrent. Who would kill Morey, a man without an enemy, a man who might as well have been a saint? His tiny, cranky little wife is no help, and may even be a suspect; his estranged son, Jack, an infamous ambulance-chasing lawyer, has his own enemies; and his son-in-law, former cop Marty Pullman, is so depressed over his wife's death a year earlier he's ready to kill himself, but not Morey. The number of victims - all elderly - grows, and the city is fearful once again. Can Grace McBride's cold case-solving software program somehow find the missing link?.

***Nobody Like You.** Perf. by Timothy Byler. 2009. audio compact disk (978-0-9822237-0-3(6)) Palm Tree.

Nobody Lives Forever. Perf. by Ronald Reagan et al. 1 cass. (Running Time: 1 hr.). 1947. 7.95 (DD-5095) Natl Recrd Co.
Nick Blake returns home after spending two years in the army overseas & eight weeks in the army hospital. He heads for California with $60,000 he had from his previous occupation as a con-artist, one of the best in the business. Doc sets himm up to swindle a wealthy & beautiful widow. Nick becomes an "executive" in a deep sea salvage business, for this con-games, but something goes wrong.

Nobody Lives Forever. unabr. ed. John E. Gardner. Read by David Rintoul. 6 cass. (Running Time: 9 hrs.). 2000. 49.95 (CAB 745) Pub: Chivers Audio Bks GBR. Dist(s): AudioGO
As Bond sets off to Austria for a well-earned vacation, M issues a warning: "Take care, 007. The continent is a hotbed of villainy these days." Bond disembarks at Ostend, and soon grasps M's meaning as a bewildering game of cat-and-mouse begins and 007 is the prey.

Nobody Lives in Apt. N-2. Anne Schraff. Narrated by Larry A. McKeever. (Mystery Ser.). (J). 2000. audio compact disk 14.95 (978-1-58659-275-2(0)) Artesian.

Nobody Lives in Apt. N. 2. unabr. ed. Anne Schraff. Narrated by Larry A. McKeever. 1 cass. (Running Time: 40 min.). (Mystery Ser.). (J). 2000. 10.95 (978-1-58659-006-2(5), 54101) Artesian.

Nobody Move. unabr. ed. Denis Johnson. Read by Will Patton. 4 CDs. (Running Time: 4 hrs. 30 mins. 0 sec.). (ENG.). 2009. audio compact disk 24.95 (978-1-4272-0689-3(9)) Pub: Macmill Audio. Dist(s): Macmillan

Nobody Nowhere. abr. ed. Donna Williams. Read by Debra Winger. 2 cass. (Running Time: 3 hrs.). 1995. 16.95 (978-0-944993-81-1(8)) Audio Lit.
Labeled from childhood as deaf, retarded and insane, Donna Williams lived in her own world until the age of twenty-five. An incredible story of courage & inspiration.

Nobody Nowhere, unabr. collector's ed. Donna Williams. Read by Kate Reading. 6 cass. (Running Time: 9 hrs.). 1993. 48.00 (978-0-7366-2535-7(6), 3287) Books on Tape.
Insider's view of the autistic world told by a woman who triumphed over the affliction.

Nobody Said Anything. Short Stories. Raymond Carver. Read by Raymond Carver. 1 cass. (Running Time: 52 min.). Incl. Fat. (3051); Serious Talk. (3051); 10.95 (978-1-55644-070-0(7), 3051) Am Audio Prose.

Nobody Said Anything & Other Stories. unabr. ed. Short Stories. Raymond Carver. Read by Tim Behrens. 2 cass. (Running Time: 2 hrs.). Dramatization. 1992. 16.95 (978-1-55686-426-1(4), 426) Books in Motion.
Included are: Bicycles, Muscles, Cigarettes, They're Not Your Husband, What's in Alaska, & Put Yourself in My Shoes.

Nobody True. unabr. ed. James Herbert. 13 CDs. (Running Time: 13 hrs. 35 mins.). (Isis (CDs) Ser.). (J). 2005. audio compact disk 99.95 (978-0-7531-2290-7(1)) Pub: ISIS Lrg Prnt GBR. Dist(s): Ulverscroft US

Nobody True. unabr. ed. James Herbert. Read by Robert Powell. 12 cass. (Running Time: 13 hrs. 35 mins.). (Isis Cassettes Ser.). (J). 2005. 94.95 (978-0-7531-1887-0(4)) Pub: ISIS Lrg Prnt GBR. Dist(s): Ulverscroft US

Nobody Walks Alone: Spiritual Direction in the Carmelite Tradition. Kevin Culligan & Mary J. Meadow. 12 cass. (Running Time: 12 hrs.). 79.95 Credence Commun.
Culligan & Meadow offer a polished theology of grace, time-honed practices of meditation & sophisticated contemporary psychology. All are necessary. If you intend serious prayer, you need a clear theology of grace. If you expect transformation, you need techniques & practices to open you to grace. And today, we all think in psychological terms, so we need the traditional wisdom handed down to us in terms we can understand.

Nobody's Baby but Mine. unabr. collector's ed. Susan Elizabeth Phillips. Read by Anna Fields. 8 cass. (Running Time: 12 hrs.). (Chicago Stars Bks.: No. 3). 1997. 64.00 (978-0-913369-77-7(2), 4338) Books on Tape.

Nobody's Child. Anne Baker. 2009. audio compact disk 99.95 (978-1-4079-0482-5(5)) Pub: Soundings Ltd GBR. Dist(s): Ulverscroft US

Nobody's Darling. unabr. ed. Josephine Cox. Read by Carole Boyd. 12 cass. (Running Time: 12 hrs.). 1994. 96.95 (978-0-7451-4337-8(7), CAB 1020) AudioGO.
Although Ruby came from a family with little money, she was determined to move into the upper classes. Introduced to society at a party for the gentry of Blackburn, she encounters Luke Arnold, a sly & evil man who hides his true self beneath a patina of charm. Little does Ruby know what troubles Luke will bring.

Nobody's Fool. unabr. ed. Richard Russo. 15 cass. (Running Time: 22 hrs. 30 min.). 2003. 112.00 (978-0-7366-9450-6(1)) Books on Tape.

Nobody's Perfect. unabr. collector's ed. Donald E. Westlake. Read by Michael Kramer. 7 cass. (Running Time: 7 hrs.). (Dortmunder Ser.). 1996. 56.00 (978-0-7366-3542-4(4), 4189) Books on Tape.
Too bad Dortmunder doesn't take the painting's message to heart. He gets stuck in an elevator & the painting vanishes. Now he's got a few more days to live, unless he comes up with the painting - or another foolproof plan.

Nobody's Safe. abr. ed. Richard Steinberg. Read by Dick Hill. 2 cass. (Running Time: 3 hrs.). 1999. 17.95 (FS9-43402) Highsmith.

Noces Barbares. Yann Queffelec. Read by Yann Queffelec. 5 cass. (Running Time: 7 hrs. 30 mins.). (FRE.). 1991. 47.95 (1106-KFP) Olivia & Hill.
Ludovic, the product of a brutal rape, is despised by both his young mother & grandparents. After keeping him locked up in the attic for the first years of his life, they place him in an institution for the mentally retarded although he is normal.

Noche Buena: Christmas Music of Colonial Latin America. abr. ed. Contrib. by Savae. 2006. audio compact disk 17.00 (978-1-58459-241-9(9)) Wrld Lib Pubns.

Noche de la Tortuga, EDL Level 16. (Fonolibros Ser.: Vol. 13). (SPA.). 2003. 11.50 (978-0-7652-1034-0(7)) Modern Curr.

Noche de Pax: Himnos Navideos Desde el Santuario Whitefield. Perf. by Foundations Bible College Ensemble. Prod. by Foundations Bible College Theological Seminary. (SPA.). 2001. 7.95 (978-1-882542-36-9(3), 1882542363) Fndtns NC.

Noches en Casa Patas: Guadiana Esencia. Created by Rgb. (Running Time: 50 mins.). 2006. 29.95 (978-5-558-08924-0(5), Rivergate Bks) Rutgers U Pr.

Noches Latinas: Latina Nights. 2000. 12.95 (978-0-9666484-6-1(3)) Dimby Co Inc.

Nocturnal see Love Poems of John Donne

Nocturne see Nocturne

Nocturne. abr. ed. Read by Ed McBain, pseud. 4 cass. (Running Time: 6 hrs.). (87th Precinct Ser.: Bk. 48).Tr. of Nocturne. 2000. 12.99 (978-1-57815-179-0(1), 4417, Media Bks Audio) Media Bks NJ.
Detectives Carella & Hawes, find out that no murder is ever routine & while this one looks at first like a robbery, the evidence doesn't add up.

Nocturne. abr. ed. Ed McBain, pseud. Read by Ed McBain, pseud. 5 vols. (87th Precinct Ser.: Bk. 48).Tr. of Nocturne. 2001. audio compact disk 14.99 (978-1-57815-533-0(9), Media Bks Audio) Media Bks NJ.

Nocturne. unabr. ed. Diane Armstrong. Read by Deidre Rubenstein. (Running Time: 17 hrs. 15 mins.). 2009. audio compact disk 118.95 (978-1-74214-119-0(6), 9781742141190) Pub: Bolinda Pubng AUS. Dist(s): Bolinda Pub Inc

Nocturne. unabr. ed. Ed McBain, pseud. Read by Jonathan Marosz. 6 cass. (Running Time: 9 hrs.). (87th Precinct Ser.: Bk. 48).Tr. of Nocturne. 1997. 48.00 (978-0-7366-3777-0(X), 4450) Books on Tape.
A long time ago Svetlana Dyalovich, world-famed concert pianist, filled the concert halls of Europe with music. Now this little old lady lay dead on the cold floor of a cold apartment. It might just be another homicide in the city. But for detectives Carella & Hawes, the evidence doesn't add up, especially after they talk to Svetlana's granddaughter.

Nocturne: And Other Unabridged Twisted Stories. unabr. ed. Jeffery Deaver. Read by Michele Pawk et al. 2004. 15.95 (978-0-7435-3933-3(8)) Pub: S&S Audio. Dist(s): S and S Inc

Nocturnes: Five Stories of Music & Nightfall. unabr. ed. Kazuo Ishiguro. Read by Mark Bramhall et al. (ENG.). 2009. audio compact disk 32.00 (978-0-7393-8176-2(8), Random AudioBks) Pub: Random Audio Pubg. Dist(s): Random

Noel. 1 cass. (Running Time: 1 hr. 30 mins.). audio compact disk 10.98 CD. (978-1-57908-385-4(4), 1549) Platinm Enter.

Noel. Perf. by Joan Baez. 1 cass. 8.98 (445); audio compact disk 12.98 (D445) MFLP CA.
Traditional Christmas songs with an elegant touch. Songs include: "Ave Maria," "Deck the Halls," "What Child Is This," "Little Drummer Boy" & more.

Noel Coward: A Biography, Pt. 1. unabr. collector's ed. Philip Hoare. Read by David Case. 9 cass. (Running Time: 13 hrs. 30 min.). 1997. 72.00 (978-0-7366-3842-5(3), 4562-A) Books on Tape.
The personification of wit, glamor & elegance, Noel Coward was an artist of international renown. He was the master playwright of Blithe Spirit, private Lives & Design for Living. His compositions & lyrics were all the rage. His films wee hits & his novels, well-reviewed. There seemed to be nothing he couldn't do & as Philip Hoare shows in this definitive biography, do with supreme style & class. In this meticulously researched book, Philip Hoare has touched on every aspect of Noel Coward's life, including his homosexuality. The overall effect is an intimate & wide ranged study, a record of the public profile & private life of one of the twentieth century's most celebrated figures.

Noel Coward Pt. 2: A Biography. collector's ed. Philip Hoare. Read by David Case. 8 cass. (Running Time: 12 hrs.). 1997. 64.00 (978-0-7366-3843-2(1), 4562 B) Books on Tape.
The personification of wit, glamor & elegance, Noel Coward was an artist of international renown. He was the master playwright of Blithe Spirit. Private Lives & Design for Living. His compositions & lyrics were all the rage. His films were hits & his novels, well-reviewed. There seemed to be nothing he couldn't do & as Philip Hoare shows in this definitive biography, do with supreme style & class. In this meticulously researched book, Philip Hoare has touched on every aspect of Noel Coward's life, including his homosexuality. The overall effect is an intimate & wide ranged study, a record of the public profile & private life of one of the twentieth century's most celebrated figures.

Noel Coward: an Audio Biography: A BBC Radio Production. Read by Sheridan Morley. (Running Time: 2 hrs. 0 mins. 0 sec.). (ENG.). 2009. audio compact disk 24.95 (978-1-60283-773-7(2)) Pub: AudioGO. Dist(s): Perseus Dist

***Noel Coward Audio Collection.** abr. ed. Noel Coward. Read by Simon Jones. (ENG.). 2005. (978-0-06-084297-0(0), Harper Audio); (978-0-06-084298-7(9), Harper Audio) HarperCollins Pubs.

Noel Coward Audio Collection. unabr. ed. Noel Coward. Read by Simon Jones. 2005. audio compact disk 29.95 (978-0-06-076456-2(2)) HarperCollins Pubs.

Noel Coward Package. Noel Coward. 4 cass. (Running Time: 6 hrs.). 75.00 L A Theatre.
Includes: "Blithe Spirit", "Fallen Angels", "Present Laughter", & "Private Lives".

***Noel Coward Reads his Collected Verse.** abr. ed. Noel Coward. Read by Simon Jones. (ENG.). 2006. (978-0-06-125293-8(X), Harper Audio) HarperCollins Pubs.

Noel Jesus Is Born. Contrib. by Don Marsh et al. 1988. 90.00 (978-0-00-154744-5(5), 75609224); 11.98 (978-0-00-490624-9(1), 75609258) Pub: Brentwood Music. Dist(s): H Leonard

Noel: Night of Everlasting Love. Contrib. by J. Daniel Smith & Derric Johnson. Created by Derric Johnson. 2008. audio compact disk 16.98 (978-5-557-40836-3(3), Brentwood-Benson Music) Brentwood Music.

Noel: Night of Everlasting Love: Alto. Contrib. by J. Daniel Smith & Derric Johnson. 2008. audio compact disk 5.00 (978-5-557-40832-5(0), Brentwood-Benson Music) Brentwood Music.

Noel: Night of Everlasting Love: Bass. Contrib. by Ed Kee. Prod. by Derric Johnson. 2008. audio compact disk 5.00 (978-5-557-40830-1(4), Brentwood-Benson Music) Brentwood Music.

Noel: Night of Everlasting Love: Satb. Contrib. by J. Daniel Smith & Derric Johnson. Created by Derric Johnson. 2008. audio compact disk 90.00 (978-5-557-40835-6(5), Brentwood-Benson Music); audio compact disk 10.00 (978-5-557-40834-9(7), Brentwood-Benson Music) Brentwood Music.

Noel: Night of Everlasting Love: Soprano. Contrib. by Ed Kee et al. Prod. by Derric Johnson. 2008. audio compact disk 5.00 (978-5-557-40833-2(9), Brentwood-Benson Music) Brentwood Music.

Noel: Night of Everlasting Love: Tenor. Contrib. by Ed Kee et al. Prod. by Derric Johnson. 2008. audio compact disk 5.00 (978-5-557-40831-8(2), Brentwood-Benson Music) Brentwood Music.

Noeud de Vipères, Set. Francois Mauriac. 4 cass. (FRE.). 1991. 38.95 (1369-LV) Olivia & Hill.
After fierce financial wrangling, Louis, a "mother's boy," marries Isa, a girl from a fashionable family. When he learns that she had been attracted to another man, he condemns her to forty years of silence & bitterness. A study in avarice & family discord.

Noise - Can You Hear the Problem? Hosted by Nancy Pearlman. 1 cass. (Running Time: 29 min.). 10.00 (308) Educ Comm CA.

Noise! Noise! Noise! Short Stories. Carl Sommer. Narrated by Carl Sommer. 1 cass. Dramatization. (Another Sommer-Time Story Ser.). (J). (gr. 1-4). 2003. bk. 16.95 (978-1-57537-568-7(0)) Advance Pub.

***Noise! Noise! Noise! / ¡Ruido! ¡Ruido! ¡Ruido!** ed. Carl Sommer. Illus. by Kennon James. (Another Sommer-Time Story Bilingual Ser.). (ENG & SPA.). (J). 2009. bk. 26.95 (978-1-57537-186-3(3)) Advance Pub.

Noise! Noise! Noise! Read-along. Carl Sommer. Narrated by Carl Sommer. 1 cass. Dramatization. (Another Sommer-Time Story Ser.). (J). 2003. lib. bdg. 23.95 (978-1-57537-769-8(1)) Advance Pub.
Character Education story with character song by Karacter Kidz.

Noise of War: Caesar, Pompey, Octavian & the Struggle for Rome. unabr. ed. A. J. Langguth. Narrated by Ed Blake. 9 cass. (Running Time: 13 hrs. 15 mins.). 1999. 78.00 (978-0-7887-0307-2(2), 94500E7) Recorded Bks.
Takes you behind the scenes of one of history's most seductive dramas: the battle for control of the Roman Empire in 81 B.C. Moves from Caesar's battlefields in Britannia to Cleopatra's bedroom in Alexandria, from Spartacus' slave revolt outside Rome's walls to Brutus' conspiracy within Rome's grandest houses.

Noise Pollution: The Silent Problem - Michel Bayan's Collage of Music & Natural Sound to Reduce Stresses. Hosted by Nancy Pearlman. 1 cass. (Running Time: 29 min.). 10.00 (1307) Educ Comm CA.

Noisy Nora. 2004. bk. 24.95 (978-1-56008-152-4(X)); pap. bk. 18.95 (978-1-55592-450-8(6)); pap. bk. 38.75 (978-1-55592-449-2(2)); pap. bk. 32.75 (978-1-55592-283-2(X)); pap. bk. 32.75 (978-1-55592-284-9(8)); pap. bk. 14.95 (978-1-55592-666-3(5)); 8.95 (978-1-56008-984-1(9)); cass. & flmstrp 30.00 (978-1-56008-731-1(5)); audio compact disk 12.95 (978-1-55592-447-8(6)); audio compact disk 12.95 (978-1-55592-918-3(4)) Weston Woods.

Noisy Nora. Rosemary Wells. 1 cass., 5 bks. (Running Time: 10 min.). (J). pap. bk. 32.75 Weston Woods.
Nora makes herself heard even though everyone in the house is too busy to listen.

Noisy Nora. Rosemary Wells. Narrated by Mary Beth Hurt. 1 cass. (Running Time: 10 min.). (J). (ps-1). pap. bk. 12.95 Weston Woods.

Noisy Nora. Rosemary Wells. Narrated by Mary Beth Hurt. 1 cass. (Running Time: 10 min.). (J). (ps-1). 1997. bk. 8.95 (978-1-56008-120-3(1), RAC175); pap. bk. 14.95 (978-1-56008-153-1(8)) Weston Woods.
From the book by Rosemary Wells. Nora makes herself heard even though everyone in the house is too busy to listen.

Noisy Nora: And Other Stories. Rosemary Wells. Read by Mary Beth Hurt & Jenny Agutter. (ENG.). (J). 2008. 44.99 (978-1-60514-946-2(2)) Find a World.

Nomad: From Islam to America: A Personal Journey Through the Clash of Civilizations. unabr. ed. Ayaan Hirsi Ali. Read by Ayaan Hirsi Ali. (Running Time: 11 hrs. 0 mins. 0 sec.). 2010. audio compact disk 39.99 (978-0-7435-9912-2(8)) Pub: S&S Audio. Dist(s): S and S Inc

Nomadband is Intuit! Perf. by Intuit Staff. 1 cass. (Running Time: 35 mins.). 1999. 7.00 (A0046-86) Sound Photosyn.
Eclectic, romantic, original music, with intriguing lyrics & melodies, performed by Faustin Bray & Brian Wallace, with Philip Porter on bass & guitar, Allen Biggs on drums & Geofree Lipner on bass & tablas. Compositions by Brian Wallace.

***Nomads of Gor.** unabr. ed. John Norman. (Running Time: 15 hrs.). (Gorean Saga Ser.). 2011. 24.99 (978-1-4418-4913-7(0), 9781441849137, BAD); 39.97 (978-1-4418-4914-4(9), 9781441849144, BADLE) Brilliance Audio.

***Nomads of Gor.** unabr. ed. John Norman. Read by Ralph Lister. (Running Time: 15 hrs.). (Gorean Saga Ser.). 2011. 24.99 (978-1-4418-4911-3(4), 9781441849113, Brilliance MP3); 39.97 (978-1-4418-4912-0(2), 9781441849120, Brlnc Audio MP3 Lib); audio compact disk 29.99 (978-1-4418-4909-0(2), 9781441849090, Bril Audio CD Unabri); audio compact disk 112.97 (978-1-4418-4910-6(6), 9781441849106, BriAudCD Unabrid) Brilliance Audio.

Nomads of the North. unabr. ed. James Oliver Curwood. Read by David Sharp. 6 cass. (Running Time: 7 hrs.). 1995. 39.95 (978-1-55686-597-8(X)) Books in Motion.
A Husky pup & a bear cub are thrown into a raging river when a canoe overturns. Separated from their owner & provider, the two are faced with survival on their own in the Northern Wilderness.

Nomads/Fanaithe. Contrib. by John Faulkner. (ENG.). 1992. 13.95 (978-0-8023-7071-6(3)); audio compact disk 20.95 (978-0-8023-8071-5(9)) Pub: Clo Iar-Chonnachta IRL. Dist(s): Dufour

Noman. unabr. ed. William Nicholson. Read by Anne Flosnik. (Running Time: 32400 sec.). (Noble Warriors Ser.). (J). 2008. audio compact disk 92.25 (978-1-4233-1858-3(7), 9781423318583, BriAudCD Unabrid) Brilliance Audio.

Noman. unabr. ed. William Nicholson. Read by Anne Flosnik. Directed By Laura Grafton. Contrib. by Kristopher Kessel. (Running Time: 32400 sec.). (Noble Warriors Ser.). (J). (gr. 4-7). 2008. audio compact disk 24.95 (978-1-4233-1854-5(4), 9781423318545, Brilliance MP3); audio compact disk 39.25 (978-1-4233-1859-0(5), 9781423318590, Brlnc Audio MP3 Lib) Brilliance Audio.

Noman: Book Three of the Noble Warriors. unabr. ed. William Nicholson. Read by Anne Flosnik. (Running Time: 9 hrs.). (Noble Warriors Ser.). 2008. 39.25 (978-1-4233-1861-3(7), 9781423318613, BADLE); 24.95 (978-1-4233-1860-6(9), 9781423318606, BAD); audio compact disk 29.95 (978-1-4233-1853-8(6), 9781423318538, Bril Audio CD Unabri) Brilliance Audio.

Nomansland. unabr. ed. Lesley Hauge. (ENG.). (J). 2010. audio compact disk 34.00 (978-0-307-73791-5(8), Listening Lib) Pub: Random Audio Pubg. Dist(s): Random

Non-A, Non-B Viral Hepatitis. Moderated by Eugene R. Schiff. Contrib. by F. Blaine Hollinger & Willis C. Maddrey. 1 cass. (Running Time: 1 hr. 30 mins.). 1986. 12.00 (A8624) Amer Coll Phys.
This topic is discussed by a moderator & experts who offer differing opinions.

Non-Aerobic Workout. Denise Astin. 1 cass. (Running Time: 1 hr..). 1989. 9.95 Peter Pan.

***Non-Analytical Ways of Growth.** Ira Progoff. 2010. audio compact disk 15.00 (978-1-935859-04-8(8)) Dialogue Assoc.

Non-Biological Intelligence. Mark Ephram. 1 cass. (Running Time: 1 hr.). 9.00 (S0027-86) Sound Photosyn.
A mushrooming of interest of an unexpected character.

Non-Christian Views. Gordon Clark. 1 cass. (Running Time: 1 hr.). (Lectures on the Holy Spirit: No. 5). 5.00 Trinity Found.

Non-Combatants. Alexander Fullerton. (Soundings (CDs) Ser.). 2006. audio compact disk 84.95 (978-1-84559-362-9(6)) Pub: ISIS Lrg Prnt GBR. Dist(s): Ulverscroft US

Non-Combatants. unabr. ed. Alexander Fullerton. Read by Peter Wickham. 8 cass. (Soundings Ser.). 2006. 69.95 (978-1-84559-289-9(1)) Pub: ISIS Lrg Prnt GBR. Dist(s): Ulverscroft US

Non-Compliance with Discovery. Read by Bernard J. Avellino. 1 cass. (Running Time: 1 hr.). 1989. 20.00 (AL-66) PA Bar Inst.

Non-Covetousness. (706) Yoga Res Foun.

Non-Covetousness. Swami Jyotirmayananda. 1 cass. (Running Time: 1 hr.). 1990. 12.99 Yoga Res Foun.

Non-Fiction Contests: A Helpful Guide. Karen Jean Matsko Hood. 2006. 29.95 (978-1-59808-693-5(6)); audio compact disk 24.95 (978-1-59808-692-8(8)) Whsprng Pine.

Non-Food Agro-Industrial Research, Issue 3. Ed. by J. Coombs & K. Hall. 1 CD. (Running Time: 1 hr. 30 mins.). 2000. audio compact disk 65.00 (978-1-872691-27-5(7), CPL Pr) CPL Sci Pub GBR.

Non-Food-Related Franchising in Greece: A Strategic Reference 2007. Compiled by Icon Group International, Inc. Staff. 2007. ring bd. 195.00 (978-0-497-35994-2(4)) Icon Grp.

Non-Interventional Foreign Policy. Earl C. Ravenal. 1 cass. (Running Time: 1 hr. 5 min.). 11.95 (737) J Norton Pubs.

Non-Manipulative Selling. Tony Alessandra & Philip S. Wexler. 1 cass. (Running Time: 51 min.). 11.00 (978-0-89811-223-8(0), 9423) Meyer Res Grp.
Prospects want to buy when you stop manipulating & start effectively communicating.

Non-Manipulative Selling. Tony Alessandra & Philip S. Wexler. Read by Tony Alessandra & Philip S. Wexler. 6 cass. (Running Time: 9 hrs.). 1999. 39.95 (121A) Nightingale-Conant.

Non-Manipulative Selling. Tony Alessandra & Phillip S. Wexler. 1 cass. (Running Time: 1 hr.). 10.00 (SP100049) SMI Intl.
If you've tried every selling trick in the book & still don't meet your quota, it's time to become a sales professional with "Non-Manipulative Selling". Prospects want to buy when you stop manipulating & start effectively communicating.

Non-Marrieds. Milton Diamond. 1 cass. (Running Time: 1 hr.). (Human Sexuality Ser.). 11.95 (34025) J Norton Pubs.

Non-Negotiables: Daniel 1:1-21. Ed Young. 1995. 4.95 (978-0-7417-2066-5(3), 1066) Win Walk.

Non-Ordinary Author Reading from His Book, "Ordinary Money" Louis Jones. Read by Louis Jones. 1 cass. (Running Time: 1 hr.). 9.00 (A0668-90) Sound Photosyn.
This successful writer is a funny guy with clever word pictures.

Non-Ordinary States of Reality Through Vision Plants. unabr. ed. Terence McKenna. 1 cass. (Running Time: 1 hr.). 1988. 9.00 (978-1-56964-709-7(7), A0413-88) Sound Photosyn.
From the International Transpersonal Psychology Association.

Non-Parametric Methods in Astrological Research. George Noonan. 1 cass. (Running Time: 1 hr.). 8.95 (456) Am Fed Astrologers.

Non-Smoker Now. Betty L. Randolph. Read by Betty L. Randolph. Read by Leonard Baron. Ed. by Success Education Institute International. 1 cass. (Running Time: 1 hr.). (Health Ser.). 1989. 9.98 (978-1-55909-190-9(8), 30S) Randolph Tapes.
Lose the desire to smoke. Subliminal messages are heard 3-5 minutes before becoming ocean sounds or music.

Non-Smoking. abr. ed. Roger W. Breternitz. 1 cass. (Running Time: 45 min.). 1985. pap. bk. 9.95 (978-1-893417-07-6(7)) Vector Studios.
Hypnosis: Break the habitual chains of smoking. Has steps necessary to quitting, gives new will power to quit, changes belief system to know it can be done.

Non-Stealing. 1 cass. (Running Time: 1 hr.). 12.99 (706) Yoga Res Foun.

Non-Toxic Alternatives in Cancer Treatment. Ralph W. Moss. 1 cass. (Running Time: 2 hrs.). 15.95 (978-1-881025-33-7(0)) Equinox Pr.

Non-Traditional Book Markets. unabr. ed. Dan Poynter. Read by Dan Poynter. 1 cass. (Running Time: 1 hr.). 1995. 9.95 (978-1-56860-002-4(X), P-105) Para Pub.
Dan Poynter changes your thinking about marketing books as he has you looking beyond the bookstores. You will learn all about premiums, compatible product sales, audio tapes, fund raisers, catalogs, the export market, selling the military & much more. This tape is for both new & seasoned publishers. Includes resources.

Non-Transplant Surgery of the Liver. 2 cass. (Running Time: 2 hrs.). (General Sessions Ser.: C85-GS1). 15.00 (8536) Am Coll Surgeons.

Non-Violence. 1 cass. (Running Time: 1 hr.). 12.99 (705) Yoga Res Foun.

Nondual & Egoless: Life without an Ego. Gary Arnold. (ENG.). 2009. audio compact disk 24.95 (978-1-57867-008-6(X)) Pub: Windhorse Corp. Dist(s): New Leaf Dist

Nondual Meditation. Richard Cushing Miller. 2 Cassettes. (Running Time: 135 Minutes). (ENG.). 1996. 19.95 (978-1-893099-05-0(9)) Anahata Pr.

Nondualism & Dualistic Play. Swami Amar Jyoti. 1 cass. (Running Time: 1 hr.). 1986. 9.95 (R-78) Truth Consciousness.
Putting nondualism in your pocket & living in the world with realism & discrimination. Why idols were created.

None Can Be Loved Like Jesus. Read by Basilea Schlink. 1 cass. (Running Time: 30 min.). 1985. (0225) Evang Sisterhood Mary.
The Love for Jesus the greatest treasure in our lives & reflecting the glory of our Lord.

None of Maigret's Business. unabr. ed. Georges Simenon. Read by Michael Prichard. 4 cass. (Running Time: 5 hrs.). 2001. 17.95 (978-0-7366-5728-0(2)) Books on Tape.
Maigret's famous method typically involves his totally immersing himself in the sordid ambience of the crime in question, but this time Simenon presents the delightful circumstance of Maigret, on a medically imposed leave of absence, having to follow a particularly baffling case in the newspapers just like any layman playing amateur detective.

None of Maigret's Business. unabr. collector's ed. Georges Simenon. Read by Michael Prichard. 5 cass. (Running Time: 5 hrs.). 1983. 30.00 (978-0-7366-0535-9(5), 1509) Books on Tape.

None of This Ever Really Happened. unabr. ed. Peter Ferry. (Running Time: 7.5 hrs. 0 mins.). 2008. cass. & cass. 29.95 (978-1-4332-4394-3(6)) Blckstn Audio.

None of This Ever Really Happened. unabr. ed. Peter Ferry. Read by Anthony Heald. 1 MP3-CD. (Running Time: 7 hrs. 30 mins.). 2008. 44.95 (978-1-4332-4392-9(X)); audio compact disk 29.95 (978-1-4332-4395-0(4)); audio compact disk 60.00 (978-1-4332-4393-6(8)) Blckstn Audio.

None of This Ever Really Happened. unabr. ed. Peter Ferry & Anthony Heald. (Running Time: 7.5 hrs. NaN mins.). 2008. 29.95 (978-1-4332-4396-7(2)) Blckstn Audio.

None to Accompany Me. unabr. ed. Nadine Gordimer. Read by Susan Ericksen. (Running Time: 9 hrs.). 2008. 39.25 (978-1-4233-5892-3(9), 9781423358923, Brlnc Audio MP3 Lib); 39.25 (978-1-4233-5894-7(5), 9781423358947, BADLE); 24.95 (978-1-4233-5893-0(7), 9781423358930, BAD); 24.95 (978-1-4233-5891-6(0), 9781423358916, Brilliance MP3) Brilliance Audio.

Nonesuch. unabr. ed. Georgette Heyer. Read by Eve Matheson. 8 cass. (Running Time: 8 hrs.). 1996. 69.95 (978-0-7451-6692-6(X), CAB1308) AudioGO.
A wealthy, handsome bachelor believes he is past the age of falling in love. But when he comes north to inspect his unusual inheritance at Broom Hall in West Riding, his arrival leads to the most entertaining of ramifications.

Nonfebrile Seizures. Contrib. by Eileen P. Vining et al. 1 cass. (Running Time: 1 hr. 30 mins.). (American Academy of Pediatrics UPDATE: Vol. 18, No. 1). 1998. 20.00 Am Acad Pediat.

Nonmalignant Vulva Disease. Contrib. by Raymond H. Kaufman et al. 1 cass. (American College of Obstetrics & Gynecologists UPDATE: Vol. 23, No. 1). 1998. 20.00 Am Coll Obstetric.

Nonpharmacological Headache Pain Control System. Steven Goren & Keith Levick. 6 cass. (Running Time: 9 hrs.). 1992. 69.95 set incl. interactive wkbk. (978-0-9639424-0-1(9)) Tensionenders.

Nonprofit Accounting & Auditing Update 1995-96. William A. Broadus, Jr. 10 cass. (Running Time: 10 hrs.). 1995. 129.00 (742020EZ) Am Inst CPA.
This annual course covers the most important accounting & auditing pronouncements for not-for-profit organizations issued in the past year. And on the basis of current exposure drafts, it also tells you about new pronouncements likely to come out in the near future. Includes a workbook.

Nonprofit Corporation Act. Contrib. by Philip L. Chapman et al. 4 cass. (Running Time: 4 hrs.). 1983. 70.00 incl. program handbook. NJ Inst CLE.
Designed to help you analyze the changes effected by Title 15A, master what must be done to form, to maintain & to dissolve a nonprofit corporation in New Jersey.

Nonprofit Drucker, Vols. 1-5. Peter F. Drucker. 1989. 279.80 Leadership Network.
Leadership & management of nonprofit human-services institutions.

Nonprofit Drucker Vol. 1: Mission & Leadership. Peter F. Drucker. 1989. 69.95 (978-0-922750-01-6(7)) Leadership Network.

Nonprofit Drucker Vol. 2: Strategies. Peter F. Drucker. 1989. 69.95 (978-0-922750-02-3(5)) Leadership Network.

Nonprofit Drucker Vol. 3: Performance & Results. Peter F. Drucker. 1989. 69.95 (978-0-922750-03-0(3)) Leadership Network.

Nonprofit Drucker Vol. 4: People & Relationships. Peter F. Drucker. 1989. 69.95 (978-0-922750-04-7(1)) Leadership Network.

Nonprofit Drucker Vol. 5: Managing & Developing Yourself. Peter F. Drucker. 1989. 69.95 (978-0-922750-05-4(X)) Leadership Network.

Nonprofit Organizations: Current Issues & Developments. 4 cass. (Running Time: 5 hrs. 30 min.). 1989. bk. 55.00 (T6-9162) PLI.

Nonsense Novels. Stephen Leacock. Read by Flo Gibson. 2 cass. (Running Time: 3 hrs.). 1996. 19.95 (978-1-55685-422-4(6)) Audio Bk Con.
"Maddened by Mystery of The Defective Detective," "Guido the Gimlet of Ghent: A Romance of Chivalry," "Soaked in Seaweed or Upset in the Ocean," "Carolina's Christmas or The Inexplicable Infant" & "The Man in Asbestos: An Allegory of the Future" are a few of the wacky, weird & often funny tales.

Nonsense of Edward Lear & Phantasmagoria. unabr. ed. Lewis Carroll, pseud. 3 cass. (Running Time: 4 hrs. 30 min.). (YA). (gr. 6-9). 1990. 16.95 (978-1-55685-183-4(9)) Audio Bk Con.
The whimsy, fantasy & absurb humor in Lear's limericks, poems, songs & stories are ageless in appeal. Lewis Carroll's "Phantasmagoria" adds to the fun.

Nonsense Songs. unabr. ed. Edward Lear. Read by Alan Bennett. 1 cass. (Running Time: 1 hr.). (J). 1995. 9.95 (978-1-85549-248-6(2), CTC 082) AudioGO.
Incl., The Owl & the Pussy-Cat, The Duck & the Kangaroo, The Jumblies, The Quangle Wangle's Hat, Mr & Mrs Discobbolos & many more.

Nonsyndromic Deafness - A Bibliography & Dictionary for Physicians, Patients, & Genome Researchers. Compiled by Icon Group International, Inc. Staff. 2007. ring bd. 28.95 (978-0-497-11381-0(3)) Icon Grp.

Nonverbal Communication: Fostering Social Competency. Kathryn McCarthy. 1 cass. (Running Time: 1 hr. 10 min.). 1998. bk. 20.00 (978-1-58111-055-5(3)) Contemporary Medical.
Describes six areas of nonverbal communication, explains social skills, provides techniques to improve social competency.

Nonviolence. Eldon Taylor. 1 cass. (Running Time: 1 hr. 2 mins.). (Inner Talk Ser.). 16.95 incl. script. (978-1-55978-617-1(5), 53870F) Progress Aware Res.
Soundtrack - Brook with underlying subliminal affirmations.

Nonviolence: How It Works. Eknath Easwaran. 1 cass. (Running Time: 56 min.). 1990. 7.95 (978-1-58638-583-5(6), NHI) Nilgiri Pr.
The ideal of nonviolence presented through the life & writings of Mahatma Gandhi. The practical uses of nonviolence in today's world.

Nonviolence: Twenty-Five Lessons from the History of a Dangerous Idea. unabr. ed. Mark Kurlansky. Frwd. by Dalai Lama XIV. 7 CDs. (Running Time: 27000 sec.). 2006. audio compact disk 29.99 (978-1-4281-1019-9(4)) Recorded Bks.

Nonviolent Communication. Marshall Rosenberg. 4 CDs. 2004. audio compact disk 29.95 (978-1-59179-170-6(7), AW00805D) Sounds True.
On Nonviolent Communication, renowned peacemaker Marshall Rosenberg presents his complete system for speaking and hearing our deepest truths, addressing our unrecognized needs and emotions, and honoring the same in others. This definitive audio training program will help you "resolve the irresolvable" by using empathy and compassion to safely confront fear and anger when they block our communications with others.

Nonviolent Communication Training Course. unabr. ed. Marshall Rosenberg. 9 CDs. (Running Time: 9 Hrs). 2006. bk. 149.95 (978-1-59179-443-1(9), HH01022D) Sounds True.
Marshall Rosenberg's remarkable process of Nonviolent Communication has gained worldwide recognition as a tool for turning even the most volatile situations into a natural interchange of compassion, generosity, and mutual enrichment. Modeled after this visionary peacemaker's 9-day international intensive retreats, The Nonviolent Communication Training Course presents the first ever self-guided curriculum for putting Rosenberg's transformative ideas into everyday practice - whether you're in the office, at the dinner table, in a parent-teacher conference - any situation where you want to honor "what is alive" in yourself and others.

Noonan Syndrome - A Bibliography & Dictionary for Physicians, Patients, & Genome Researchers. Compiled by Icon Group International, Inc. Staff. 2007. ring bd. 28.95 (978-0-497-11262-2(0)) Icon Grp.

Noonday Demon: An Atlas of Depression. abr. ed. Andrew Solomon. 2004. 15.95 (978-0-7435-4311-8(4)) Pub: S&S Audio. Dist(s): S and S Inc

Noonday Friends, unabr. ed. Mary Stolz. Narrated by Barbara Caruso. 4 pieces. (Running Time: 4 hrs. 45 mins.). (gr. 4 up). 1992. 35.00 (978-1-55690-644-2(7), 92351E7) Recorded Bks.
The story of two girls - one Puerto Rican, the other Irish - from a poor neighborhood in New York City celebrates ethnic diversity & family values. Franny & Simone are best friends until after-school responsibilities begin to pull them apart.

Nop's Hope. unabr. ed. Donald McCraig. Narrated by Frank Muller. 5 cass. (Running Time: 6 hrs. 45 mins.). 1994. 44.00 (978-0-7887-0059-0(6), 94258E7) Recorded Bks.
Numb & shellshocked by tragedy, Penny Burkeholder leaves home to follow the sheepdog circuit with Hope, the remarkable Border Collie sired by Nop. Only the special friendship & wisdom of this protective dog can teach a broken Penny how to heal her soul.

Nop's Trials. unabr. ed. Donald McCaig. Narrated by Nelson Runger. 7 cass. (Running Time: 9 hrs. 30 mins.). 1991. 60.00 (978-1-55690-634-3(X), 91412E7) Recorded Bks.
When Nop won the gold belt buckle at the Innisfree Trials, he was considered unbeatable, one of the top three stockdogs in America. His owner, Lewis, thought himself far richer without the $5,000 someone offered him for his prized dog. But before Christmas could be declared officially over for another year, Nop has disappeared.

Nop's Trials. unabr. collector's ed. Donald McCaig. Read by Ron Shoop. 6 cass. (Running Time: 9 hrs.). 1987. 48.00 (978-0-7366-1075-9(8), 2002) Books on Tape.
A story of a family & two remarkable individuals - Lewis Burkholder, a farmer in Virginia, and his young Border Collie, Nop. When the dog is stolen, Nop embarks on an ordeal of peril & hardship that he survives only through courage & love. Similar qualities in Lewis enable him to search relentlessly for Nop.

Nora. unabr. ed. Ingmar Bergman. Perf. by David Dukes et al. 1 cass. (Running Time: 1 hr. 26 min.). 1997. 19.95 (978-1-58081-051-7(9), TPT82) L A Theatre.
Master Swedish filmmaker Ingmar Bergman has streamlined & introduced modern stagecraft to Ibsen's A Doll's House, exposing the contemporary heart of this 19th Century masterpiece. Taut with suspense, this critically acclaimed adaptation focuses on Nora, a young wife & mother who exploits her childlike charm to survive in a man's world. But Nora has a secret that threatens her cozy existence. She is forced to begin a journey fraught with perils, including a secret admirer who lusts to be of service & the dark, icy Norwegian waters - which may offer the only way out.

Nora: The Real Life of Molly Bloom. unabr. collector's ed. Brenda Maddox. Read by Donada Peters. 14 cass. (Running Time: 21 hrs.). 1995. 112.00 (978-0-7366-3228-7(X), 3889) Books on Tape.
With the imaginative pen of James Joyce, Nora Barnacle came to be Molly Bloom, the most famous female character in twentieth-century literature. Nora was the voice of Ireland for Joyce, a sort of muse who awakened the sights, sounds & sensibilities of Dublin. But Nora was hardly the semi-literate, uncultured woman of Joycean legend. Witty & intelligent, strong & shrewd, she was the mainstay for the hard-drinking, hard-working genius. She shaped Joyce's life...& the women of his fiction.

Nora & the Trolls. (J). 2003. audio compact disk (978-1-930429-45-1(2)) Love Logic.

Nora Bheag. Contrib. by Sean Hernon. (ENG.). 1997. 13.95 (978-0-8023-7123-2(X)); audio compact disk 21.95 (978-0-8023-8123-1(5)) Pub: Clo Iar-Chonnachta IRL. Dist(s): Dufour

Nora, Nora. Anne Rivers Siddons. Narrated by Cristine McMurdo-Wallis & Suzanne Toren. 9 CDs. (Running Time: 10 hrs. 45 mins.). 2001. audio compact disk 89.00 (978-0-7887-5154-7(9), C1317E7) Recorded Bks.
Peyton McKenzie is a shy, gawky teenager, living with her widowed father, when her cousin Nora comes for a visit. With her elegant clothes & her pink Thunderbird convertible, Nora is nothing like the conservative, churchgoing relatives Peyton has known & is soon showing Peyton a new & exciting world. Set in the social turbulence of the 1960's.

***Nora, Nora.** abr. ed. Anne Rivers Siddons. Read by Debra Monk. (ENG.). 2005. (978-0-06-087931-0(9), Harper Audio); (978-0-06-087930-3(0), Harper Audio) HarperCollins Pubs.

Nora, Nora. unabr. ed. Anne Rivers Siddons. Read by Kate Reading. 7 cass. (Running Time: 10 hrs. 30 mins.). 2000. 56.00 (978-0-7366-5517-0(4), 5357) Books on Tape.
It is 1961 & Peyton McKenzie, motherless since birth & now 13, doesn't quite know what to make of Nora Findlay. When Nora takes a teaching job at the local high school, it seems she might stay on in Lytton forever, slowly, Peyton begins to realize that underneath Nora's feisty facade something from her past is troubling her.

***Nora, Nora.** unabr. ed. Anne Rivers Siddons. Read by Kate Reading. (ENG.). 2005. (978-0-06-087914-3(9), Harper Audio); (978-0-06-087915-0(7), Harper Audio) HarperCollins Pubs.

Nora, Nora. unabr. ed. Anne Rivers Siddons. Narrated by Cristine McMurdo-Wallis & Suzanne Toren. 8 cass. (Running Time: 10 hrs. 45 mins.). 2001. 71.00 (978-0-7887-4353-5(8), 96305E7) Recorded Bks.
Peyton McKenzie is a shy, gawky teenager, living with her widowed father, when her cousin Nora comes for a visit. With her elegant clothes & her pink Thunderbird convertible, Nora is nothing like the conservative, churchgoing relatives Peyton has known & is soon showing Peyton a new & exciting world. Set in the social turbulence of the 1960's.

Nora, Nora. unabr. collector's ed. Anne Rivers Siddons. Read by Kate Reading. 8 CDs. (Running Time: 9 hrs. 36 mins.). 2000. audio compact disk 64.00 (978-0-7366-6172-0(7)) Books on Tape.
A freethinking young woman turns the small town of Lytton, Georgia on its ear, forever changing a young girl's life.

Nora Roberts CD Collection: Birthright; Northern Lights; Blue Smoke. abr. ed. Nora Roberts. Read by Bernadette Quigley et al. (Running Time: 18 hrs.). 2007. audio compact disk 34.95 (978-1-4233-2312-9(2), 9781423323129, BACD) Brilliance Audio.

Nora Roberts CD Collection: Hidden Riches; True Betrayals; Homeport; The Reef. abr. ed. Nora Roberts. Read by Sandra Burr et al. (Running Time: 12 hrs.). 2006. audio compact disk 34.95 (978-1-59737-716-4(3), 9781597377164, BACD) Brilliance Audio.
Hidden Riches: When Dora Conroy purchases a curious selection of auction items she unknowingly becomes the deadly focus of an international smuggler. She seeks help from her intriguing upstairs tenant, former cop Jed Skimmerhorn. They discover a shadowy path leading across the continent to a man who will stop at nothing to recover his hidden riches. True Betrayals: Kelsey Byden grew up believing her mother had died when she was three. Now twenty-six, she receives a letter from her mother explaining that she is alive. But there are more secrets to be found out and Kelsey decides to stay at her mother's splendid horse farm, where she falls in love with handsome gambler Gabe Slater. Homeport: Dr. Miranda Jones welcomed the distraction offered by a summons to Italy to verify the authenticity of a Renaissance bronze. However, her professional judgment is called into question when the bronze is declared a hoax. Desperate to prove The Dark Lady is really a previously unknown work of Michelangelo, Miranda turns to Ryan Boldari, a seductive - and supposedly reformed - art thief. The Reef: The Reef is the story of Tate Beaumont, a beautiful young student of marine archeology - and of Matthew Lassiter, a sea-scarred young man who shares her dream of finding Anguelique's Curse, the jeweled amulet surrounded by legend. Tate soon learns that her arrogant but attractive fellow diver holds as many secrets as the sea itself.

Nora Roberts CD Collection: River's End; Remember When; Angels Fall. abr. ed. Nora Roberts. Read by Sandra Burr et al. (Running Time: 15 hrs.). 2007. audio compact disk 34.95 (978-1-4233-3203-9(2), 9781423332039, BACD) Brilliance Audio.

Nora Roberts CD Collection: The Villa; Midnight Bayou; Three Fates. abr. ed. Nora Roberts. (Running Time: 18 hrs.). 2005. audio compact disk 34.95 (978-1-59737-710-2(4), 9781597377102, BACD) Brilliance Audio.
The Villa: Sophia Giambelli has never worried about competition. For three generations, the Giambelli wines have been renowned for their quality - from Napa Valley to Italy, and throughout the world. But things are about to change at Villa Giambelli. Tereza, the matriarch, has announced a merger with the MacMillan family's winery - and Sophia will be assuming a new role, working with Tyler MacMillan. Midnight Bayou: Declan Fitzgerald had always been the family maverick, but even he couldn't understand his impulse to buy a dilapidated mansion on the outskirts of New Orleans. Determined to restore Manet Hall to its former splendor, Declan begins the daunting renovation room by room. Only the companionship of the alluring Angelina Simone can distract him from the mysterious happenings in the house, but Angelina too has her own surprising connection to Manet Hall - uncovering a secret that's been buried for a hundred years. Three Fates: When the Lusitania sank, more than one thousand people died. One passenger, however, survived to become a changed man, giving up his life as a petty thief but keeping a small silver statue that would become a family heirloom to future generations. Now, nearly a century later, that heirloom, one of a priceless, long-separated set of three, has been snatched away from the Sullivans. And Malachi, Gideon, and Rebecca Sullivan are determined to recover their great-great-grandfather's treasure, reunite the Three Fates, and make their fortune.

Nora Roberts CD Collection 5: Honest Illusions; Montana Sky; Carolina Moon. abr. ed. Nora Roberts. Read by Sandra Burr et al. (Running Time: 15 hrs.). 2008. audio compact disk 34.95 (978-1-4233-3205-3(9), 9781423332053, BACD) Brilliance Audio.

***Nora Roberts CD Collection 6: High Noon; Tribute.** abr. ed. Nora Roberts. (Running Time: 11 hrs.). 2010. audio compact disk 19.99 (978-1-4418-5052-2(X), 9781441850522, BACD) Brilliance Audio.

***Norah.** unabr. ed. Debbie Macomber. Read by Tanya Eby. (Running Time: 5 hrs.). (Orchard Valley Ser.: Bk. 3). 2010. 14.99 (978-1-4418-6320-1(6), 9781441863201, Brilliance MP3); 14.99 (978-1-4418-6321-8(4), 9781441863218, BAD); audio compact disk 14.99 (978-1-4418-6319-5(2), 9781441863195, Bril Audio CD Unabri) Brilliance Audio.

***Norah, Lone Star Lovin'** unabr. ed. Debbie Macomber. Read by Tanya Eby. (Running Time: 9 hrs.). (Orchard Valley Ser.). 2010. 39.97 (978-1-4418-1945-1(2), 9781441819451, Brlnc Audio MP3 Lib); audio compact disk 92.97 (978-1-4418-1943-7(6), 9781441819437, BriAudCD Unabrid) Brilliance Audio.

Nora's Place & Other Poems, 1965-1995. Poems. Tom Leonard. Read by Tom Leonard. 1 CD. (Running Time: 1 hr.). (AK Press Audio Ser.). (ENG.). 2001. audio compact disk 13.98 (978-1-873176-39-9(2)) Pub: AK Pr GBR. Dist(s): Consort Bk Sales

Nora's Room. Jessica Harper. 1 cass., 1 CD. (J). 7.98 (ALA 2005); audio compact disk 9.58 CD Jewel box. (ALA 2005); 7.98 (ALA 2005); audio compact disk 9.58 (ALA 2005) NewSound.
Lyrics set to a swaying Caribbean-influenced beat.

Norbert Nipkin. Robert McConnell. Illus. by Steve Pilcher. (J). 1994. cass. & audio compact disk 7.95 (978-0-929141-24-4(5)) Pub: Napoleon Co CAN. Dist(s): AtlasBooks

Norbert Nipkin & the Magic Riddle Stone. Robert McConnell. Illus. by Steve Pilcher. (J). 1995. 7.95 (978-0-929141-25-1(3)) Pub: Napoleon Co CAN. Dist(s): AtlasBooks

Nordic Tales. Bjornstjerne Bjornson. Narrated by Walter Zimmerman. (Running Time: 2 hrs. 30 mins.). 1980. 15.95 (978-1-59912-863-4(2)) Iofy Corp.

Norfolk-Tales. Read by Bobby Norfolk. 1 cass. (Running Time: 52 min.). (J). (gr. 2 up). 1990. 10.00 (978-1-886929-06-7(8), EW-C4917) Earwig.
Folktales from European, Southern US, & African traditions.

Norfolk Tales: Stories of Adventure, Humor & Suspense. Bobby Norfolk. 1 CD. (Running Time: 52 mins.). 2002. audio compact disk 14.95 (978-0-87483-693-6(X)) Pub: August Hse. Dist(s): Natl Bk Netwk

Norfolktales: Stories of Adventure, Humor & Suspense. unabr. ed. Bobbu Norfolk. Read by Bobby Norfolk. (J). 2007. 39.99 (978-1-60252-570-2(6)) Find a World.

Normal?, What Is. Milton Diamond. 1 cass. (Running Time: 1 hr.). (Human Sexuality Ser.). 11.95 (34009) J Norton Pubs.

Normal Christian Life. unabr. ed. Watchman Nee. 6 CDs. (Running Time: 7 hrs. 45 mins. 0 sec.). (ENG.). 2006. audio compact disk 24.98 (978-1-59644-280-1(8), Hovel Audio) christianaud.
The Normal Christian Life is Watchman Nee's great Christian classic unfolding the path of faith and presenting the eternal purposes of God in simple terms. It is a powerful meditation on God, Jesus, and the Bible that brings the daily reality of following Christ into sharp focus.

***Normal Christian Life.** unabr. ed. Watchman Nee. Narrated by Paul Michael. (ENG.). 2006. 14.98 (978-1-59644-281-8(6), Hovel Audio) christianaud.

Normal Christian Life. unabr. ed. Watchman Nee. Narrated by Paul Michael. 1 MP3CD. (Running Time: 7 hrs. 45 mins. 0 sec.). (ENG.). 2006. lp 19.98 (978-1-59644-279-5(4), Hovel Audio) christianaud.

Normal Christian Life Audio Book. unabr. collector's ed. Watchman Nee. 50.00 (978-0-7363-1340-7(0)); audio compact disk 62.50 (978-0-7363-1341-4(9)) Living Stream Ministry.

***Norman Conquests: A Trilogy.** unabr. ed. Alan Ayckbourn. Read by Rosalind Ayers et al. 6 CDs. (Running Time: 4 hrs.). 2009. audio compact disk 65.95 (978-1-58081-565-9(0)) L A Theatre.

***Norman Conquests: Classic Radio Theatre Series.** Alan Ayckbourn. Told to Robin Herford & Tessa Peake-Jones. (Running Time: 4 hrs. 5 mins. 0 sec.). (ENG.). 2010. audio compact disk 34.95 (978-1-4084-2692-0(7)) Pub: AudioGO. Dist(s): Perseus Dist

***Norman Corwin: Centennial.** Perf. by Norman Corwin. 2010. audio compact disk 39.98 (978-1-57019-928-8(0)) Radio Spirits.

Norman Corwin - the NPR Documentary: Norman Corwin - A Note of Triumph. Scripts. Text by Norman Corwin. Directed By Norman Corwin. 1 CD. (Running Time: 58 mins.). Dramatization. 2005. audio compact disk 15.95 (978-1-59938-008-7(0)) Lode Cat.

Norman Corwin's 'Holidays' Scripts. Text by Norman Corwin. Directed By Norman Corwin. 1 CD. (Running Time: 2 hrs.). Dramatization. 2005. audio compact disk 15.95 (978-1-59938-007-0(2)) Lode Cat.

Norman Corwin's Holidays. Perf. by Rod MacLeish et al. Prod. by Connie Goldman. 1 CD. (Running Time: 1 hr.). 2001. audio compact disk 15.95 Lodestone Catalog.
Examines the origins & the meaning of New Year's, Memorial Day, Independence Day, Labor Day & Thanksgiving. Corwin's genius will fascinate & inspire you; make you mad & make you cry.

Norman Corwin's Victory Programs: Masterpiece Radio Broadcasts Commemorating the End of the Second World War. 2 cass. (Running Time: 1 hr. 30 min.). 1996. 16.95 Set. (978-1-57677-046-7(X)) Lodestone Catalog.
Contains two of Corwin's greatest achievements. "On a Note of Triumph" is Corwin's magnificent special program of soaring words, fascinating use of sound, & a brilliant musical score, created to celebrate the end of World War II in Europe. "50 Years after 15 August" is a brand new production, written & directed by Norman Corwin in 1995.

Norman Horowitz: President, Columbia Pictures Distribution see Scene Behind the Screen: The Business Realities of the TV Industry

Norman Kennedy: Scottish Ballads. 1 cass. (Running Time: 1 hr. 30 mins.). 9.98 (C-34) Folk-Legacy.
A splendid program from a strong traditionalist.

Norman Maclean. Interview. Interview with Norman F. Maclean & Kay Bonetti. 1 cass. (Running Time: 38 min.). 1985. 13.95 (978-1-55644-127-1(4), 5032) Am Audio Prose.
Focuses on the life & times as well as the craft & vision of the author who after retiring in 1973 stunned the literary world with a "A River Runs Through It".

Norman Mailer. Norman Mailer. 1 cass. (Author Speaks Ser.). 1991. 14.95 J Norton Pubs.
Archival recordings of 20th-century authors.

Norman Mailer: Reading & Interview. Interview with Norman Mailer & Kay Bonetti. 1 cass. (Running Time: 1 hr. 4 mins.). 15.95 (978-1-55644-018-2(9), 1103) Am Audio Prose.
Reads from "Miami & the Siege of Chicago," "An American Dream," "Armies of the Night" & discusses his novel about Egypt, "Ancient Evenings".

Norman Rudy, M. D. Tennis Injuries. Read by Norman Rudy. 1 cass. 9.95 (978-0-89811-118-7(8), 7170) Lets Talk Assocs.

Norman the Doorman. 2004. bk. 24.95 (978-1-56008-025-1(6)); pap. bk. 18.95 (978-1-55592-452-2(2)); pap. bk. 38.75 (978-1-55592-453-9(0)); pap. bk. 32.75 (978-1-55592-285-6(6)); 8.95 (978-1-56008-985-8(7)); cass. & flmstrp 30.00 (978-1-56008-732-8(3)); audio compact disk 12.95 (978-1-55592-919-0(2)) Weston Woods.

Norman the Doorman. Don Freeman. 1 cass., 5 bks. (Running Time: 11 min.). (J). pap. bk. 32.75 Weston Woods.
Norman's ambition to become an artist leads him to enter his sculpture in the museum's art show - & win!.

Norman the Doorman. Don Freeman. 1 cass. (Running Time: 11 min.). (J). (ps-4). 1990. pap. bk. 14.95 (978-1-56008-026-8(4), PRA064); 8.95 (978-1-56008-103-6(1), RAC064) Weston Woods.

Norman Thomas: Vietnam see Buckley's Firing Line

Norman to the Rescue. Loren Spiotta-DiMare. Read by Tom Chapin. 1 cass. (Running Time: 12 min.). (Humane Society of the United States Animal Tales Ser.). (J). (gr. 1-4). 1998. pap. bk. 19.95 Incl. plush animal. (978-1-58021-057-7(0)) Benefactory.
When a young girl screams for help after being caught in a riptide, Norman is the only one who hears her cries. Can this blind yellow lab save her from drowning?.

Norman to the Rescue. Loren Spiotta-DiMare. Read by Tom Chapin. 1 cass. (Running Time: 12 min.). (Humane Society of the United States Animal Tales Ser.). (J). (gr. 1-4). 1999. pap. bk. 9.95 (978-1-58021-055-3(4)) Benefactory.
When a young girl screams for help after being caught in a riptide, Norman is the only one who hears her cries. Can this blind yellow lab save her from drowning.

Norman Tuttle on the Last Frontier. unabr. ed. Tom Bodett. Read by Tom Bodett. 3 cass. (Running Time: 4 hrs. 49 mins.). 2004. 30.00 (978-1-4000-9057-0(1), Listening Lib); audio compact disk 35.00 (978-1-4000-9495-0(X), Listening Lib) Random Audio Pubg.
In the episodic adventures of a young, bumbling Alaskan teenager, Tom Bodett writes and reads at his best. We first meet Norman as he falls off his father's fishing boat into the cold waters of a summer sea. The subsequent rescue, a waxing and waning relationship with his father, and a budding romance flesh out a story-by turns funny and poignant-that will resonate with young men in that 13-15 age range. When Bodett is on his game (and he definitely is here), no better reader for this work than the author himself exists.

Normandy Stories. Guy de Maupassant. Read by Oliver Montgomery. (Running Time: 2 hrs. 30 mins.). 2004. 20.95 (978-1-60083-856-9(1)) Iofy Corp.

Normandy Stories. unabr. ed. Guy de Maupassant. Read by Oliver Montgomery. 2 CDs. audio compact disk 17.98 (978-962-634-311-1(7), NA231112) Naxos.

Norms for Judging Apparitions & Private Revelations. Fred Jelly. 1 cass. (Running Time: 1 hr. 20 min.). 1994. 7.95 (TAH300) Alba Hse Comns.
In this program Fr. Jelly clarifies these very key concepts: apparitions; visionaries; charismatic & sanctifying Grace; corporeal, imaginary & intellectual apparitions; public & private revelations; & the supernatural as miraculous & holy.

Norrie Disease - A Bibliography & Dictionary for Physicians, Patients, & Genome Researchers. Compiled by Icon Group International, Inc. Staff. 2007. ring bd. 28.95 (978-0-497-11263-9(9)) Icon Grp.

Norsk fonetikk for Utlendinger see Norwegian Phonetics for Foreigners CDs & Text

Norsk Fonetikk for Utlendinger (Norwegian Phonetics) 4 cass. (Running Time: 3 hrs. 30 mins.). pap. bk. 75.00 J Norton Pubs.
Designed for the advanced student, presents & analyzes the speech sounds of Norwegian.

Norsk for Utlendinger see Norwegian for Foreigners CDs & Text

Norsk for Utlendinger see Norwegian for Foreigners Cassette/Book Course

North. Donna Jo Napoli. Narrated by Kevin R. Free. 6 cass. (Running Time: 7 hrs. 30 mins.). (J). 2004. 54.75 (978-1-4025-9927-9(7)) Recorded Bks.

North American Cambridge Latin Course, Unit 1. 4th rev. ed. Contrib. by North American Cambridge Classics Project Staff. 1 cass. (Running Time: 90 mins.). (North American Cambridge Latin Course Ser.). (ENG.). 2004. 28.00 (978-0-521-00504-3(3)); audio compact disk 28.00 (978-0-521-00502-9(7)) Cambridge U Pr.

North American Cambridge Latin Course, Unit 2. 4th rev. ed. Contrib. by North American Cambridge Classics Project Staff. 1 cass. (Running Time: 90 mins.). (North American Cambridge Latin Course Ser.). (ENG.). 2004. 28.00 (978-0-521-00509-8(4)); audio compact disk 28.00 (978-0-521-00507-4(8)) Cambridge U Pr.

North American Cambridge Latin Course, Unit 3. 4th rev. ed. Contrib. by North American Cambridge Classics Project Staff. (North American Cambridge Latin Course Ser.). 2004. 31.00 (978-0-521-52553-4(5)); audio compact disk 31.00 (978-0-521-52551-0(9)) Cambridge U Pr.

North American Cambridge Latin Course, Unit 4. 4th rev. ed. Contrib. by North American Cambridge Classics Project Staff. . (Running Time:). (North American Cambridge Latin Course Ser.). 2004. audio compact disk 33.00 (978-0-521-52552-7(7)) Cambridge U Pr.
This full-color, single-volume, hardcover version of Unit 3 of the ^ICambridge Latin Course^R continues the publication of the North American Third Edition. The formula is the same as that for Units 1 and 2, which are already published and proving to be very successful. Units IIIA and IIIB, together with the Language Information Sections, have been brought together into one volume to meet the needs of students in the North American market.

North American Cambridge Latin Course: Unit 4. 4th rev. ed. Contrib. by North American Cambridge Classics Project Staff. (North American Cambridge Latin Course Ser.). 2004. 33.00 (978-0-521-52554-1(3)) Cambridge U Pr.

North American Free Trade Agreement. 6 cass. (Running Time: 6 hrs.). 1994. 92.00 (20164) NYS Bar.
Addresses the key issues surrounding NAFTA. The panel of speakers includes members of the American, Canadian & Mexican bars whose professional activities focus on the various topics of discussion. The presentations offer a review & update on the NAFTA-related issues especially those affecting New York. Includes course book.

North & South. abr. ed. John Jakes. Read by George Grizzard. 2 cass. (Running Time: 3 hrs.). 2001. 18.00 (978-1-59040-117-0(4), Phoenix Audio) Pub: Amer Intl Pub. Dist(s): PerseuPGW

North & South. unabr. ed. Elizabeth Gaskell. Read by Flo Gibson. 11 cass. (Running Time: 16 hrs. 30 min.). 1997. 34.95 (978-1-55685-457-6(9), 457-9) Audio Bk Con.
In one of Gaskell's finest novels & against a background of industrial unrest, misery, suspicion & jealousy & deaths of family & dear friends mill owner John Thornton & Margaret Hale's love is put to the test.

North & South. unabr. ed. Elizabeth Gaskell. Read by Juliet Stevenson. 14 CDs. (Running Time: 21 hrs.). 2002. audio compact disk 115.95 (978-0-7540-5516-7(7), CCD 207) Pub: Chivers Pr GBR. Dist(s): AudioGO

North & South, Pt. 1. unabr. collector's ed. John Jakes. Read by Michael Kramer. 12 cass. (Running Time: 18 hrs.). (North & South Trilogy). 1994. 96.00 (978-0-7366-2743-6(X), 3469-A) Books on Tape.
Two great American dynasties are torn apart by the storm of events surrounding the Civil War.

North & South, Pt. 2. collector's ed. John Jakes. Read by Michael Kramer. 10 cass. (Running Time: 15 hrs.). (North & South Trilogy). 1994. 80.00 (978-0-7366-2744-3(8), 3569-B) Books on Tape.

North & the South. Compiled by Benchmark Education Staff. 2006. audio compact disk 10.00 (978-1-4108-6636-3(X)) Benchmark Educ.

North by Night: A Story of the Underground Railroad. Katherine Ayres. Narrated by Christina Moore. 4 pieces. (Running Time: 5 hrs. 15 mins.). (gr. 5 up). 38.00 (978-1-4025-3636-6(4)) Recorded Bks.

North by Northwestern: A Seafaring Family on Deadly Alaskan Waters. abr. ed. Sig Hansen & Mark Sundeen. (Running Time: 6 hrs. 0 mins. 0 sec.). (ENG & ITA.). 2010. audio compact disk 29.99 (978-1-4272-0903-0(0)) Pub: Macmill Audio. Dist(s): Macmillan

North Carolina Academy of Trial Lawyers Archival Materials CD-ROM, 2007 Edition. audio compact disk 150.00 (978-1-4224-4624-9(7)) LEXIS Pub.

North Cascades Highway-Eastbound: From Sedro Woolley to Washington Pass. Scripts. 1 CD. (Running Time: 79 Min.). 2004. audio compact disk 15.95 (978-1-930827-31-8(8), Car Tours) Audisee Sound.
While you drive, CarTours will be your pesonal guide. You'll discover the history, geology, ecology and Native American culture of the North Cascades. you's hear tribal members, professional narration, and authentic sounds. You'll learn about the early industries in this region, the role of Seattle City Light along the Skagit River, and how these lands are cared for. Take your family and friend on this entertaining tour through one the wildest areas in Washington state.

North Chase. unabr. ed. Gary McCarthy. Read by Gene Engene. 4 cass. (Running Time: 5 hrs. 12 min). (Derby Man Ser.: Bk. 7). 1995. 26.95 (978-1-55686-587-9(2)) Books in Motion.
Wesley Bryant, crime lord of San Francisco, flees to Alaska with Darby Buckingham in hot pursuit. The pursuit becomes more dangerous as they cross the brutal tundra in a wilderness blizzard.

North Country Memories. Don McCune. Read by Don McCune. 1 cass. (Don McCune Library). 4.95 (A103) Don McCune Library.
Includes: "Alaska Flag Song," "The Spirit of Alaska" & "The Shooting of Dan McGrew".

North Country Sketches. unabr. ed. Sigurd F. Olson. Read by Denny Olson. 2 cass. (Running Time: 3 hrs.). 1991. 16.95 (978-0-939643-36-3(7), NrthWrd Bks) TandN Child.
Essays about canoe country & the North Woods from five of Olson's books.

North from Rome. unabr. collector's ed. Helen MacInnes. Read by Wanda McCaddon. 9 cass. (Running Time: 13 hrs. 30 min.). 1982. 72.00 (978-0-7366-0394-2(8), 1371) Books on Tape.
Bill Lammiter, a young American playwright has lost his girl & is on the point of leaving Rome after a fruitless bid to win her back from a rebound engagement to a rogue noble, Count Luigi Pirotta. Then Lammiter intervenes to save a mysterious Italian girl from a night-time encounter with thugs & finds himself enmeshed in a web of espionage & drug trafficking.

North Lauderdale, FL: Charter Schools. unabr. ed. Innovation Groups Staff. 1 cass. (Running Time: 1 hrs. 15 min.). (Transforming Local Government Ser.: Vol. 25). 1999. 10.00 (978-1-882403-81-3(9), IG9927) Alliance Innov.

North of Naples, South of Rome. Paolo Tullio. Read by Frederick Davidson. 8 CDs. (Running Time: 12 hrs.). 1999. audio compact disk 64.00 (z2429) Blckstn Audio.
Wine competition, samples the Italian cantina, demonstrates how to roast a pig whole, instructs on market-day haggling & surreptitious truffle-hunting & investigates the charms & scams of Naples. Looks with disbelief at a tortuous bureaucracy, informs how to win a local election, observes the Catholic Church's role in daily life & reflects upon a recent earthquake that saved the valley. With fascinating tours on local buildings, history, folklore & fashion, tours a carousel of picnics, feasts & firework.

North of Naples, South of Rome. Paolo Tullio. Read by Frederick Davidson. 6 cass. (Running Time: 9 hrs.). 1999. 29.95 (978-0-7861-1706-2(0)) Blckstn Audio.
The book that inspired the six-part PBS series, describes the bliss of Italian country living as Tullio returns to his home town of Gallinari.

North of Naples, South of Rome. unabr. ed. Paolo Tullio. Read by Frederick Davidson. 6 cass. (Running Time: 8 hrs. 30 mins.). 1999. 44.95 (978-0-7861-1601-0(3), 2429) Blckstn Audio.
Wine competition, samples the Italian cantina, demonstrates how to roast a pig whole, instructs on market-day haggling & surreptitious truffle-hunting & investigates the charms & scams of Naples. Looks with disbelief at a tortuous bureaucracy, informs how to win a local election, observes the Catholic Church's role in daily life & reflects upon a recent earthquake that saved the valley. With fascinating tours on local buildings, history, folklore & fashion, tours a carousel of picnics, feasts & firework.

North of Naples, South of Rome. unabr. ed. Paolo Tullio. Read by Frederick Davidson. 7 CDs. (Running Time: 8 hrs. 30 mins.). 2000. audio compact disk 56.00 (978-0-7861-9443-8(X), 2429) Blckstn Audio.

***North of Nowhere.** unabr. ed. Steve Hamilton. Read by Dan John Miller. (Running Time: 8 hrs.). (Alex Mcknight Ser.). 2010. 24.99

(978-1-4418-3451-5(6), 9781441834515, Brilliance MP3); 39.97 (978-1-4418-3452-2(4), 9781441834522, Brlnc Audio MP3 Lib); 24.99 (978-1-4418-3453-9(2), 9781441834539, BAD); 39.97 (978-1-4418-3454-6(0), 9781441834546, BADLE); audio compact disk 29.99 (978-1-4418-3449-2(4), 9781441834492, Bril Audio CD Unabri); audio compact disk 87.97 (978-1-4418-3450-8(8), 9781441834508, BriAudCD Unabrid) Brilliance Audio.

North Pole. unabr. collector's ed. Robert E. Peary. Read by Jonathan Reese. 7 cass. (Running Time: 10 hrs. 30 mins.). 1997. 56.00 (978-0-7366-3684-1(6), 4363) Books on Tape.
This is Robert Peary's account of the expedition he made in 1909, becoming the first man to reach the North Pole.

North Pole: Its Discovery in 1909 under the Auspices of the Peary Arctic Club. unabr. ed. Robert Peary. Read by Jonathan Reese. (Running Time: 9 hrs. 30 mins. 0 sec.). (ENG.). 2008. audio compact disk 32.99 (978-1-4001-0792-6(X)) Pub: Tantor Media. Dist(s): IngramPubServ

North Pole: Its Discovery in 1909 under the Auspices of the Peary Arctic Club. unabr. ed. Robert E. Peary. Narrated by Jonathan Reese. (Running Time: 9 hrs. 30 mins. 0 sec.). (ENG.). 2008. audio compact disk 65.99 (978-1-4001-3792-3(6)); audio compact disk 22.99 (978-1-4001-5792-1(7)) Pub: Tantor Media. Dist(s): IngramPubServ

North Pole Project. Contrib. by Number One Gun. Prod. by Jeff Schneeweis. 2008. audio compact disk 13.99 (978-5-557-50591-8(1)) Tooth & Nail.

North River. unabr. ed. Peter V. Hamill. Narrated by Henry Strozier. 10 CDs. (Running Time: 12 hrs. 15 mins.). 2007. audio compact disk 123.75 (978-1-4281-5655-5(0)); 82.75 (978-1-4281-5653-1(4)) Recorded Bks.
In North River, critically acclaimed, best-selling author Pete Hamill whisks listeners back to 1934 - when the Great Depression held New York City in its relentless grip - for a story of one remarkable man's perseverance. Haunted by the horrors of World War I, Dr. James Delaney's personal life is a nightmare. But everything changes when he returns home one day to find his three-year-old grandson on his doorstep.

North River: A Novel. unabr. ed. Pete Hamill. Read by Henry Strozier. 10 CDs. (Running Time: 12 hrs. 30 mins.). 2007. audio compact disk 34.99 (978-1-4281-5652-4(6)) Recorded Bks.

North Shore Fish. unabr. ed. Israel Horovitz. Perf. by Kristin Ace et al. 1 cass. (Running Time: 1 hr. 30 min.). 1993. 19.95 (978-1-58081-089-0(6)) L A Theatre.
Set on the fishstick packing line in a plant in Gloucester, Massachusetts. Rumors of the plant closing, a foreman who can't keep his hands to himself & domestic troubles are among the problems faced by the third generation women fish packers.

North Star, unabr. ed. Hammond Innes. Narrated by Jack Hrkach. 7 cass. (Running Time: 10 hrs. 30 mins.). 1982. 60.00 (978-1-55690-380-9(4), 82019E7) Recorded Bks.
A renegade trawler captain braves high seas to save a North Sea rig & its crew from destruction.

North Star. unabr. collector's ed. Hammond Innes. Read by Charles Garst. 7 cass. (Running Time: 10 hr. 30 min.). 1984. 56.00 (978-0-7366-0859-6(1), 1810) Books on Tape.
Michael Randall is a man in a hurry. Desperate to succeed, he seeks his fortune in the oil sands far beneath the North Sea.

North to the Bitterroot: With a Winchester, a Wagon & a Bowie Knife, They Were the Men Who Opened the Wild Frontier, abr. ed. Ralph Compton. Read by Jim Gough. 4 cass. (Running Time: 6 hrs.). (Sundown Riders Ser.). 1999. Rental 24.95 (978-1-890990-24-4(8)) Otis Audio.
Betrayed by a woman & hunted by a desperate man, Dutch Siringo led a group of hard-fighting teamsters through the heart of the Sioux territory, into the murderous Bozeman Trail, & comes face to face with harsh blizzards, hungry wolves & a fierce enemy.

North to Yesterday. Robert Flynn. Narrated by Norman Dietz. 9 cass. (Running Time: 13 hrs.). 82.00 (978-1-4025-2536-0(2)) Recorded Bks.

North to Yesterday. unabr. ed. Robert Flynn. Read by Stephen A. Holland. Ed. by Richard Haywood. 7 cass. (Running Time: 10 hrs.). 1993. 59.95 (978-1-883268-00-8(1)) Spellbinders.
A tumbling saga of a trail drive up to Kansas from the south of Texas.

North U Cruising & Seamanship: North U Cruising & Seamanship Seminar on CD. 4th ed. Narrated by Bill Gladstone. 2004. audio compact disk 40.00 (978-0-9724361-8-2(9)) North U.

North U Cruising & Seamanship CD: North U Cruising & Seamanship Seminar on CD. 4th ed. Narrated by Bill Gladstone. 2005. audio compact disk 40.00 (978-0-9744676-2-7(6)) North U.

North U Tactics: North U Tactics Seminar. 3rd ed. Narrated by Bill Gladstone. 2004. audio compact disk 40.00 (978-0-9724361-6-8(2)) North U.

North U Trim CD: North U Trim Seminar. 2nd ed. Narrated by Bill Gladstone. 2003. audio compact disk 50.00 (978-0-9724361-3-7(8)) North U.

North U Trim CD: North U Trim Seminar on CD - 2 Disk Set. 3rd ed. Narrated by Bill Gladstone. 2005. audio compact disk 40.00 (978-0-9744676-3-4(4)) North U.

North U Weather for Sailors CD: North U Revised Weather for Sailors Seminar on CD. 2nd ed. Narrated by Bill Biewenga. 2005. audio compact disk 40.00 (978-0-9744676-1-0(8)) North U.

North U Weather for Sailors Seminar. Narrated by Bill Biewenga. 2004. audio compact disk 40.00 (978-0-9724361-5-1(4)) North U.

North U Weather Routing Wizard. Compiled by Lou Roberts. 2005. audio compact disk 40.00 (978-0-9744676-4-1(2)) North U.

North Wind an the Sun, the; Brian Wildsmith's Birds. 2004. cass. & flmstrp 30.00 (978-0-89719-658-1(9)) Weston Woods.

North Wind & the Sun. 2004. bk. 24.95 (978-0-7882-0556-9(0)); pap. bk. 14.95 (978-0-7882-0621-4(4)) Weston Woods.

North Wind & the Sun, the; Brian Wildsmith's Birds. 2004. 8.95 (978-1-56008-848-6(6)) Weston Woods.

North Wind Engima. unabr. ed. Gerry W. Gotro. Read by Rusty Nelson. 8 cass. (Running Time: 9 hrs. 30 min.). 2001. 49.95 (978-1-55686-842-9(1)) Books in Motion.
An unexpected event changes the whole fabric of Giiwedin - the village of The North Wind - and nearly tears it to pieces. The once Shangrila now experiences theft, rape, death and destruction. The people are powerless and now wait for the enigma to play itself out.

Northanger Abbey. Jane Austen. Read by Juliet Stevenson. (Running Time: 2 hrs. 30 mins.). 2000. 20.95 (978-1-60083-857-6(X)) Iofy Corp.

Northanger Abbey. Jane Austen. Read by Juliet Stevenson. 2 cass. (Running Time: 2 hrs. 30 mins.). (Works of Jane Austen). 1996. 13.98 (978-962-634-576-4(4), NA207614, Naxos AudioBooks) Naxos.

Northanger Abbey. Jane Austen. Read by Juliet Stevenson. 2006. audio compact disk 47.98 (978-962-634-427-9(X), Naxos AudioBooks) Naxos.

Northanger Abbey. Jane Austen. Read by Donada Peters. (ENG.). 2006. audio compact disk 59.99 (978-1-4001-3205-8(3)) Pub: Tantor Media. Dist(s): IngramPubServ

Northanger Abbey. abr. ed. Jane Austen. Read by Glenda Jackson. (Running Time: 28800 sec.). 2008. audio compact disk 19.95 (978-1-4332-0955-0(1)); audio compact disk 70.00 (978-1-4332-1354-0(0)) Blckstn Audio.

Northanger Abbey. abr. ed. Jane Austen. Read by Juliet Stevenson. Prod. by Nicolas Soames. 2 CDs. (Running Time: 9000 sec.). (Works of Jane Austen). 1996. audio compact disk 17.98 (978-962-634-076-9(2), NA207612, Naxos AudioBooks) Naxos.

Northanger Abbey. abr. ed. Jane Austen. Perf. by Glenda Jackson. 4 cass. (Running Time: 6 hrs.). 2004. 25.00 (978-1-59007-130-4(1)) Pub: New Millenn Enter. Dist(s): PerseuPGW
The novel is modeled after the day's popular romances and Gothic thrillers, which it then proceeds to ridicule. The heroine is Catherine Morland, who encounters upper-crust society at Bath, falls in love, and becomes targeted by misinformed fortune-seekers. After moving to Northanger Abbey, her imagination goes to work and dreams up mysteries that lead to various social disasters.

Northanger Abbey, unabr. ed. Jane Austen. Narrated by Flo Gibson. 6 cass. (Running Time: 9 hrs.). 1986. 24.95 (978-1-55685-021-9(2)) Audio Bk Con.
A delightful spoof on the Gothic novels as a young girl attempts to improve her real life with a vivid imagination.

Northanger Abbey. unabr. ed. Jane Austen. Read by Anna Massey. 6 cass. (Running Time: 7 hrs. 45 mins.). (gr. 9-12). 1999. 29.95 (978-1-57270-118-2(8), F61118u) Pub: Audio Partners. Dist(s): PerseuPGW
Austin's first novel, written in the early 20's, is a satire of the Gothic novels popular at this time. She pokes fun at the romantic follies of the genteel classes in their pursuit of love, marriage & money.

Northanger Abbey. unabr. ed. Jane Austen. Read by Nadia May. 6 cass. (Running Time: 8 hrs. 30 mins.). 1995. 44.95 (978-0-7861-0816-9(9), 1639) Blckstn Audio.
A parody of the popular literature of the time & a tale of the romantic folly of men & women in pursuit of love, marriage & money. The humorous adventures of young Catherine Morland, who encounters "the difficulties & dangers of a six weeks' residence in Bath," leads to some of Austen's most brilliant social satire.

Northanger Abbey. unabr. ed. Jane Austen. Read by Nadia May. (Running Time: 27000 sec.). 2007. audio compact disk 55.00 (978-0-7861-6112-6(4)); audio compact disk 29.95 (978-0-7861-6113-3(2)) Blckstn Audio.

Northanger Abbey. unabr. ed. Jane Austen. Read by Jean DeBarbieris. 6 cass. (Running Time: 8 hrs. 30 min.). 39.95 (978-1-55686-227-4(X), 227) Books in Motion.
Catherine is convinced the medieval mansion, Northanger Abbey, harbors a dark secret that involves Henry Tilney's eccentric father. An English classic.

Northanger Abbey. unabr. ed. Jane Austen. Read by Donada Peters. 7 cass. (Running Time: 10 hrs.). 2001. 29.95 (978-0-7366-6780-7(6)) Books on Tape.
A pretty, well-intentioned but unsophisticated girl of seventeen sets off for the pleasures of Bath only to find trouble.

Northanger Abbey. unabr. ed. Jane Austen. Read by Donada Peters. (YA). 2007. 44.99 (978-1-59895-801-0(1)) Find a World.

Northanger Abbey. unabr. ed. Jane Austen. Read by Nadia May. 6 cass. (Running Time: 9 hrs.). 1999. 44.95 (FS9-34247) Highsmith.

Northanger Abbey. unabr. ed. Jane Austen. Read by Nancy Dow. 5 cass. (Running Time: 7 hrs.). 1980. 35.00 (C-31) Jimcin Record.
Jane Austen's cool, ironic humor, stylish prose & beautifully constructed plot are evident in this classic gothic satire.

Northanger Abbey, unabr. ed. Jane Austen. Narrated by Flo Gibson. 6 cass. (Running Time: 7 hrs. 30 mins.). 1981. 51.00 (978-1-55690-381-6(2), 81220E7) Recorded Bks.
A young girl attempts to improve on real life by invention.

Northanger Abbey. unabr. ed. Jane Austen. Narrated by Donada Peters. (Running Time: 7 hrs. 0 mins. 0 sec.). (ENG.). 2009. audio compact disk 27.99 (978-1-4001-1078-0(5)); audio compact disk 19.99 (978-1-4001-6078-5(2)); audio compact disk 55.99 (978-1-4001-4078-7(1)) Pub: Tantor Media. Dist(s): IngramPubServ

Northanger Abbey. unabr. collector's ed. Jane Austen. Read by Donada Peters. 7 cass. (Running Time: 7 hrs.). (YA). 1982. 56.00 (978-0-7366-2164-9(4), 2963) Books on Tape.
A young woman falls desperately, foolishly, unhappily in love.

Northbound Collection: Music & Nature. 1 CD. (Running Time: 1 hr.). 1994. audio compact disk 15.95 CD. (2264, Creativ Pub) Quayside.
Features the best of the music plus nature offerings by NorthSound.

Northbound Collection: Music & Nature. 1 cass. (Running Time: 1 hr.). 1994. 9.95 (2263, NrthWrd Bks) TandN Child.

Northeast Indians. 1 cass. (Running Time: 1 hr.). Dramatization. (J). pap. bk. 6.95 (978-0-86545-090-5(0)) Spizzirri.
Interesting facts about how the Northeast Indians lived, worked & hunted.

Northeast Indians. Ed. by Linda Spizzirri. 1 cass. (Running Time: 1 hr.). Dramatization. (J). (gr. 1-8). pap. bk. 4.98 (978-0-86545-040-0(4)) Spizzirri.
Interesting facts about how the Northeast Indians lived, worked & hunted. Includes educational coloring book.

Northeast Local. unabr. ed. Tom Donaghy. Perf. by Rengin Altay et al. 1 cass. (Running Time: 1 hr. 25 min.). 1993. 19.95 (978-1-58081-087-6(X)) L A Theatre.
A touching play that follows a working class couple through four decades of life & love as it traces their bittersweet journey in a funny, sad & mystifying world. In a blue collar neighborhood, Gina & Mickey come of age, have a son & wrestle with racism, alcoholism & other diseases as they shape their lives together & apart.

Northeast Region. Compiled by Benchmark Education Staff. 2005. audio compact disk 10.00 (978-1-4108-5489-6(2)) Benchmark Educ.

Northern & Central Coast of British Columbia - A Look At: "Raincoast: Wild Salmon, Wild Spirit," "Watershed, Canada's Threatened Rainforest"; Texas' Guadalupe River Trout; Return of Horses to Texan Native Americans. Hosted by Nancy Pearlman. 1 cass. (Running Time: 29 min.). 10.00 (1422) Educ Comm CA.

Northern European Studies Project Texts. Ed. by Alfta Lothursdottir & Padráic I. M. MacUidhir. Transcribed by Northvegr Foundation. 2004. audio compact disk 29.99 (978-0-9762195-0-7(6)) Northvegr.
The NESP Texts CD is a huge collection of well over 120 full, unedited texts. The texts include English translations of period texts as well as scholarly analysises for the time period of the late Iron Age up to the Medieval Age in Northern Europe. Icelandic Sagas, multiple translations of the Poetic and Prose Eddas, Grimm's Teutonic Mythology, Grimm's Household Tales (unedited complete collection) and much more are included. All that is needed is a CD-ROM drive and an internet browser. For more information visit the web at: http://www.northvegr.org/vik/cdrom.php.

Northern Light. unabr. ed. Jennifer Donnelly. Read by Hope Davis. 6 cass. (Running Time: 9 hrs. 2 mins.). (J). (gr. 7 up). 2004. 40.00 (978-0-8072-0896-0(5), S YA 437 CX, Listening Lib); audio compact disk 51.00 (978-0-8072-1787-0(5), Listening Lib) Pub: Random Audio Pubg. Dist(s): NetLibrary CO

***Northern Light.** unabr. ed. Jennifer Donnelly. Read by Hope Davis. (ENG.). (J). 2010. audio compact disk 40.00 (978-0-307-74623-8(2), Listening Lib) Pub: Random Audio Pubg. Dist(s): Random

Northern Lights. abr. ed. Nora Roberts. Read by Gary Littman. (Running Time: 21600 sec.). 2004. audio compact disk 16.99 (978-1-59600-417-7(7), 9781596004177, BCD Value Price) Brilliance Audio.
Lunacy was Nate Burke's last chance. As a Baltimore cop, he'd watched his partner die on the street - and the guilt still haunts him. With nowhere else to go, he accepts the job as Chief of Police in this tiny, remote Alaskan town. Aside from sorting out a run-in between a couple of motor vehicles and a moose, he finds his first few weeks on the job are relatively quiet. But just as he wonders whether this has been all a big mistake, an unexpected kiss on New Year's Eve under the brilliant Northern Lights of the Alaska sky lifts his spirit and convinces him to stay just a little longer. Meg Galloway, born and raised in Lunacy, is used to being alone. She was a young girl when her father disappeared, and she has learned to be independent, flying her small plane, living on the outskirts of town with just her huskies for company. After her New Year's kiss with the Chief of Police, she allows herself to give in to passion - while remaining determined to keep things as simple as possible. But there's something about Nate's sad eyes that gets under her skin and warms her frozen heart. And now, things in Lunacy are heating up. Years ago, on one of the majestic mountains shadowing the town, a crime occurred that is unsolved to this day - and Nate suspects that a killer still walks the snowy streets. His investigation will unearth the secrets and suspicions that lurk beneath the placid surface, as well as bring out the big-city survival instincts that made him a cop in the first place. And his discovery will threaten the new life - and the new love - that he has finally found for himself.

Northern Lights. abr. ed. Nora Roberts. (Running Time: 6 hrs.). 2009. audio compact disk 9.99 (978-1-4418-2653-4(X), 9781441826534) Brilliance Audio.

Northern Lights. unabr. ed. Tim O'Brien. Read by John MacDonald. 8 cass. (Running Time: 12 hrs.). 1986. 64.00 (978-0-7366-0897-8(4), 1841) Books on Tape.
Set in the rugged Arrowhead country of Minnesota. "Northern Lights" is a novel of fundamentals: men at war with their own natures, their images of a good life, their memories & the elements.

Northern Lights. unabr. ed. Nora Roberts. Read by Gary Littman. (Running Time: 16 hrs.). 2004. 39.25 (978-1-59710-544-6(9), 1597105449, BADLE); 24.95 (978-1-59710-545-3(7), 1597105457, BAD); 24.95 (978-1-59335-708-5(7), 1593357087, Brilliance MP3); 39.25 (978-1-59335-842-6(3), 1593358423, Brlnc Audio MP3 Lib); 36.95 (978-1-59355-194-0(0), 1593551940, BAU); 102.25 (978-1-59355-195-7(9), 1593551959, BAudLibEd); audio compact disk 112.25 (978-1-59355-198-8(3), 1593551983, BACDLib Ed) Brilliance Audio.
Lunacy was Nate Burke's last chance. As a Baltimore cop, he'd watched his partner die on the street - and the guilt still haunts him. With nowhere else to go, he accepts the job as Chief of Police in this tiny, remote Alaskan town. Aside from sorting out a run-in between a couple of motor vehicles and a moose, he finds his first few weeks on the job are relatively quiet. But just as he wonders whether this has been all a big mistake, an unexpected kiss on New Year's Eve under the brilliant Northern Lights of the Alaska sky lifts his spirit and convinces him to stay just a little longer. Meg Galloway, born and raised in Lunacy, is used to being alone. She was a young girl when her father disappeared, and she has learned to be independent, flying her small plane, living on the outskirts of town with just her huskies for company. After her New Year's kiss with the Chief of Police, she allows herself to give in to passion - while remaining determined to keep things as simple as possible. But there's something about Nate's sad eyes that gets under her skin and warms her frozen heart. And now, things in Lunacy are heating up. Years ago, on one of the majestic mountains shadowing the town, a crime occurred that is unsolved to this day - and Nate suspects that a killer still walks the snowy streets. His investigation will unearth the secrets and suspicions that lurk beneath the placid surface, as well as bring out the big-city survival instincts that made him a cop in the first place. And his discovery will threaten the new life - and the new love - that he has finally found for himself.

Northern Lights. unabr. ed. Nora Roberts. Read by Gary Littman. 13 CDs. (Running Time: 16 hrs.). 2004. audio compact disk 39.95 (978-1-59355-197-1(5), 1593551975, Bril Audio CD Unabri) Brilliance Audio.

Northern Lights (Minus Drums) Northern Lights. 2006. pap. bk. 24.98 (978-1-59615-454-4(3), 1596154543) Pub: Music Minus. Dist(s): H Leonard

Northern Night Song. 1 CD. (Running Time: 1 hr.). 1994. audio compact disk 15.95 CD. (2608, Creativ Pub) Quayside.
Songs of thrushes & sparrows, night frogs, haunting calls of owls & loons mixed with original contemporary music.

Northern Night Song. 1 cass. (Running Time: 1 hr.). 1994. 9.95 (2607, NrthWrd Bks) TandN Child.

Northern Pike see Poetry & Voice of James Wright

Northern Securities Case. Kenneth Bruce. 1 cass. (Running Time: 1 hr.). Dramatization. (Excursions in History Ser.). 12.50 Alpha Tape.

Northern Sotho. Charles Berlitz. 2 cass. (Running Time: 1 hr. 30 mins.). (Language/30 Brief Course Ser.). 1980. pap. bk. 24.95 (978-0-88432-406-5(0), AF1054) J Norton Pubs.
Quick, highly condensed introduction to the words & phrases you'll need to communicate effectively in the country you're visiting. Cassettes & phrase guide book are in a vinyl album.

Northern Sotho Language/30 CDs & Booklet. 2 CDs. (Running Time: 1 hr. 30 mins.). (NSO.). 2005. audio compact disk 26.95 (978-1-57970-141-3(8), AF1054D) J Norton Pubs.

Northrop Hall. Margaret Bacon. (Story Sound Ser.). (J). 2005. 69.95 (978-1-85903-778-2(X)) Pub: Mgna Lrg Print GBR. Dist(s): Ulverscroft US

NorthSound Collection: The Sounds of Nature. 1 CD. (Running Time: 1 hr.). 1994. audio compact disk 15.95 CD. (2268, Creativ Pub) Quayside.
Best of pure natural sounds without music.

NorthSound Collection: The Sounds of Nature. 1 cass. (Running Time: 1 hr.). 1994. 9.95 (2266, NrthWrd Bks) TandN Child.

NorthStar: Focus on Listening & Speaking, Level 0. Polly Merdinger & Laurie Barton. 2 cass. 2001. 35.95 (978-0-13-018194-7(3)) Longman.

NorthStar: Focus on Listening & Speaking, Level 1. Laurie Leach Frazier & Robin Mills. 2 cass. (Running Time: 3 hrs.). 2001. 47.75 (978-0-201-34668-8(0)) AddisonWesley.

NorthStar: Focus on Listening & Speaking, Level 1. Laurie Frazier & Robin K. Mills. Ed. by France Armstrong Boyd & Carol Numrich. 1998. audio compact disk 47.75 (978-0-201-52068-2(0)) AddisonWesley.

NorthStar: Focus on Listening & Speaking, Level 2. Helen Solorzano & Jennifer P. L. Schmidt. 2001. audio compact disk 47.75 (978-0-201-45807-7(1)) AddisonWesley.

NorthStar: Focus on Listening & Speaking, Level 2. Helen Solorzano & Jennifer P. L. Schmidt. 2001. 47.75 (978-0-201-34669-5(9)) Longman.

NorthStar: Focus on Listening & Speaking, Level 3. Kim Sanabria & Tess Ferree. 2001. audio compact disk 47.75 (978-0-201-52069-9(9)) AddisonWesley.

NorthStar: Focus on Listening & Speaking, Level 3. Kim Sanabria & Tess Ferree. 2001. 47.75 (978-0-201-31698-8(6)) Longman.

NorthStar: Focus on Listening & Speaking, Level 4. Sherry Preiss. 2 cass. (Running Time: 3 hrs.). 2001. 47.75 (978-0-201-69525-0(1)); audio compact disk 47.75 (978-0-201-45809-1(8)) Longman.

NorthStar: Focus on Reading & Writing, Level 1. Beth Maher & Natasha Haugnes. 2001. 19.95 (978-0-13-040891-4(3)) Longman.

NorthStar: Focus on Reading & Writing, Level 3. Laura Monahon English & Andrew English. 2001. 19.95 (978-0-13-040892-1(1)) Longman.

NorthStar: Focus on Reading & Writing, Level 4. Robert Cohen & Judy Miller. 2001. 19.95 (978-0-13-040894-5(8)) Longman.

Northumberland Fusiliers. 25th ed. 1999. 12.50 (978-1-888728-13-2(2)) Clssic Spclties.

Northumberland Rant: Traditional Music from the Edge of England. Perf. by Billy Pigg & Jack Armstrong. 1 CD. (Running Time: 65 min.). 1999. audio compact disk 14.00 Smithsonian Folkways.

Northward to the Moon. unabr. ed. Polly Horvath. Read by Becca Battoe. (ENG.). (J). (gr. 5). 2010. audio compact disk 28.00 (978-0-307-70639-3(7), Listening Lib) Pub: Random Audio Pubg. Dist(s): Random

Northwest Indians. 1 cass. (Running Time: 1 hr. 30 mins.). Dramatization. (J). pap. bk. 6.95 (978-0-86545-091-2(9)) Spizzirri.
The hunting, fishing carving, homes, ceremonies & attire of The Northwest Indies.

Northwest Indians. Ed. by Linda Spizzirri. 1 cass. (Running Time: 1 hr. 30 mins.). Dramatization. (J). (gr. 1-8). pap. bk. 4.98 (978-0-86545-047-9(1)) Spizzirri.
The hunting, fishing carving, homes, ceremonies & attire of The Northwest Indies. Includes educational coloring book.

Northwest Passage. unabr. collector's ed. Willy De Roos. Read by John MacDonald. 8 cass. (Running Time: 8 hrs.). 1984. 48.00 (978-0-7366-0894-7(X), 1838) Books on Tape.
The search from Europe to the Far East via the ice-blocked waters of arctic Canada has beckoned explorers for centuries.

Northwest Themes & Authors: An Anthology of Short Stories about the Northwest & Stories from Northwest Authors. Ed. by Karen Jean Matsko Hood. 2003. 24.95 (978-1-59210-056-9(2)); audio compact disk 29.95 (978-1-59210-169-6(0)) Whsprng Pine.

Northwestern University Wildcat Marching Band, V1 OP. Northwestern University Staff. Contrib. by Matthew Ludwig & Stephen Peterson. 1995. audio compact disk 19.00 (978-0-8101-3700-4(3)) Pub: Northwestern U Pr. Dist(s): Chicago Distribution Ctr

Northwoods Night. 1 CD. (Running Time: 1 hr.). 1994. audio compact disk 15.95 (0249, Creativ Pub) Quayside.
As night unfolds, you hear the hoots, croaks, trills, & wails of 26 species of frogs, owls, loons, waterfowl, & night-active songbirds.

Northwoods Night. 1 cass. (Running Time: 1 hr.). 1994. 9.95 (0245, NrthWrd Bks) TandN Child.

Northwoods Wildlife. 1 CD. (Running Time: 1 hr.). 1994. audio compact disk 15.95 (2544, Creativ Pub) Quayside.
Ospreys, bull frogs, river otters, & the great homed owl are just a few of the creatures on this audio companion to the comprehensive book of the same title.

Northwoods Wildlife. 1 cass. (Running Time: 1 hr.). 1994. 9.95 (0254, NrthWrd Bks) TandN Child.

Norton Anthology of African American Literature, Set. 2nd ed. Ed. by Henry Louis Gates, Jr. & Nellie Y. McKay. 2 CDs. (YA). 2004. audio compact disk (978-0-393-10602-2(0)) Norton.

Norton Introduction to Literature. 8th ed. Jerome Beaty. Ed. by J. Paul Hunter et al. 2 vols. 2002. bk. (978-0-393-97687-8(4)) Norton.

Norton Recordings to Accompany the Norton Scores & the Enjoyment of Music, Vol. I. 8th ed. Ed. by Kristine Forney. 4 CDs. 1999. 41.00 (978-0-393-10250-5(5)) Norton.

Norton Recordings to Accompany the Norton Scores & the Enjoyment of Music, Vol. I. 8th ed. Ed. by Kristine Forney. 4 cass. 1999. 21.00 (978-0-393-10252-9(1)) Norton.

Norton Recordings to Accompany the Norton Scores & the Enjoyment of Music, Vol. II. 8th ed. Ed. by Kristine Forney. 4 CDs. 1999. 41.00 (978-0-393-10251-2(3)) Norton.

Norton Recordings to Accompany the Norton Scores & the Enjoyment of Music, Vol. II. 8th ed. Ed. by Kristine Forney. 4 cass. 1999. 21.00 (978-0-393-10253-6(X)) Norton.

Norton Recordings to Accompany the Norton Scores & the Enjoyment of Music: Shorter Version. 8th ed. David Hamilton & Irene Girton. 4 CDs. 1999. 45.00 (978-0-393-10254-3(8)); 27.00 (978-0-393-10270-3(X)) Norton.

Norvegien Sans Peine. Francoise Heide & Tom Holta Heide. 1 cass. (Running Time: 1 hr., 30 min.). (FRE & NOR.). 2000. bk. 75.00 (978-2-7005-1370-7(3)) Pub: Assimil FRA. Dist(s): Distribks Inc

Norway's Fascinating Folklore. Read by Astrid K. Scott & Bryce Walker. 1 cass. (Running Time: 1 hr. 30 mins.). 1997. (978-1-891096-00-6(1)) Nordic Advent.

Norwegian. 2 cass. (Running Time: 1 hr. 20 mins.). (Language - Thirty Library). bk. 16.95 Moonbeam Pubns.
Using the proven method based on the famous U.S. Military accelerated language learning program, Language/30 courses stress conversationally useful words & phrases.

Norwegian. Ed. by Charles Berlitz. 2 cass. (Running Time: 1 hr. 30 mins.). (Language/30 Brief Course Ser.). pap. bk. 21.95 (AF1037) J Norton Pubs.
Quick, highly condensed introduction to the words & phrases you'll need to communicate effectively in the country you're visiting. Cassettes & phrase guide book are in a vinyl album.

Norwegian. Ed. by Berlitz Publishing. (In 60 MINUTES Ser.). 2008. audio compact disk 9.95 (978-981-268-395-3(X)) Pub: APA Pubns Serv SGP. Dist(s): Langenscheidt

Norwegian. abr. ed. Created by Berlitz. (Berlitz Phrase Books & CD Ser.). (NOR & ENG., 2008. audio compact disk 14.95 (978-981-268-402-8(6)) Pub: Berlitz Pubng. Dist(s): Langenscheidt

Norwegian: Language. rev. ed. Educational Services Corporation Staff. Intro. by Charles Berlitz. 2 cass. (Running Time: 3 hrs.). (NOR.). 1993. pap. bk. 21.95 (978-0-910542-67-8(8)) Educ Svcs DC.
Norwegian self-teaching language course.

Norwegian: Learn to Speak & Understand Norwegian with Pimsleur Language Programs. Pimsleur Staff & Pimsleur. 5 cass. (Running Time: 500 hrs. 0 mins. NaN sec.). (Pimsleur Language Program Ser.). (ENG.). 1999. 95.00 (978-0-671-04398-8(6), Pimsleur) Pub: S&S Audio. Dist(s): S and S Inc
SPEAK NORWEGIAN TO LEARN NORWEGIAN The Pimsleur Method will have you speaking Norwegian in just a few short, easy-to-use lessons. Learn at your own pace, comfortably and conveniently. No books to study. No memorization drills. LEARN NORWEGIAN AS YOU LEARNED ENGLISH You learned English by listening. With Pimsleur, you listen to learn Norwegian. This Language Program was developed by renowned memory expert, Dr. Paul Pimsleur. His research led him to the realization that the most important use of memory is in language learning. Based on this, Dr. Pimsleur designed a learning program that works for any language. The Pimsleur Language Program is an integrated system which immerses you in the language, encouraging you to hear, understand and use the language all at the same time. Now you can take advantage of Dr. Pimsleur's research. At the completion of these eight lessons you will comfortably understand and speak at a beginner level.

Norwegian: Learn to Speak & Understand Norwegian with Pimsleur Language Programs. unabr. abr. ed. Pimsleur. Created by Pimsleur. (Running Time: 5 hrs. 0 mins. 0 sec.). (Basic Ser.). (ENG.). 2007. audio compact disk 24.95 (978-0-7435-6628-5(9), Pimsleur); audio compact disk 49.95 (978-0-7435-6629-2(7), Pimsleur) Pub: S&S Audio. Dist(s): S and S Inc

Norwegian: Learn to Speak & Understand Norwegian with Pimsleur Language Programs. unabr. abr. ed. Pimsleur Staff. (Running Time: 16 hrs. 0 mins. 0 sec.). (Comprehensive Ser.). (ENG.). 2007. audio compact disk 345.00 (978-0-7435-6630-8(0), Pimsleur) Pub: S&S Audio. Dist(s): S and S Inc

Norwegian-American Music from Minnesota: Old Time & Traditional Favorites. Philip Nusbaum. 1 cass. (Running Time: 40 min.). (Minnesota Musical Traditions Ser.). 1989. pap. bk. 9.95 (C-002) Minn Hist.
Collection of Norwegian-American music popular among the settlers & still played by their descendents today. Inlcudes booklet.

Norwegian for Foreigners Cassette/Book Course, Vol. 1. Ase-Berit Strandskogen & Rolf Strandskogen. 6 cass. (Running Time: 4 hrs. 30 mins.). Orig. Title: Norsk for Utlendinger. (NOR.). 1979. pap. bk. 165.00 (978-0-88432-147-7(9), AFNW01) J Norton Pubs.
While the basic text is in Norwegian, the extensive Learner's Guide is in English & contains: notes to the learner, answer key, Norwegian script & key vocabulary & alphabetical word lists translated into English.

Norwegian for Foreigners CDs & Text. 6 CDs. (Running Time: 4 hrs. 30 mins.). Orig. Title: Norsk for Utlendinger. (NOR.). 2005. audio compact disk 165.00 (978-1-57970-199-4(X), AFNW01D) J Norton Pubs.

Norwegian Norsk Fonetikk for Utlendinger (Norwegian Phonetics) Ase-Berit & Rolf Strandskogen. 4 cass. (Running Time: 3 hrs.). (Norwegian Phonetics Ser.). (NOR.). 1979. pap. bk. 95.00 (978-0-88432-148-4(7), AFNW98) J Norton Pubs.
Designed for the advanced student, presents & analyzes the speech sounds of Norwegian.

Norwegian Phonetics for Foreigners CDs & Text. 4 CDs. (Running Time: 3 hrs. 30 mins.). Orig. Title: Norsk fonetikk for Utlendinger. (NOR.). 2005. audio compact disk 95.00 (978-1-57970-200-7(7), AFNW98D) J Norton Pubs.

Norwood. unabr. ed. Charles Portis. Read by Barrett Whitener. 3 cass. (Running Time: 4 hrs.). 2001. 23.95 (978-0-7861-2012-3(6), 2800); audio compact disk 32.00 (978-0-7861-9721-7(8), 2800) Blckstn Audio.
Sent on a mission to New York by Grady Fring, the Kredit King, Norwood has visions of "speeding across the country in a late model car, seeing all the sights." Instead, he gets involved in a wild journey that takes him in and out of stolen cars, freight trains and buses. By the time he returns home to Ralph, Texas, Norwood has met his true love, Rita Lee, on a Trailways bus.

Norwood Builder see Return of Sherlock Holmes

Nory Ryan's Song. Patricia Reilly Giff. Read by Susan Lynch. 3 vols. (Running Time: 3 hrs. 30 mins.). (J). (gr. 4-7). 2004. pap. bk. 36.00 (978-0-8072-2093-1(0), Listening Lib) Random Audio Pubg.

Nory Ryan's Song. unabr. ed. Patricia Reilly Giff. Read by Susan Lynch. (Running Time: 12660 sec.). (ENG.). (J). (gr. 5-7). 2008. audio compact disk 25.00 (978-0-7393-6327-0(1), Listening Lib) Pub: Random Audio Pubg. Dist(s): Random

***Nos gustan las frutas Audio CD.** Cynthia Swain. Adapted by Benchmark Education Company, LLC. (My First Reader's Theater Ser.). (SPA.). (J). 2009. audio compact disk 10.00 (978-1-935470-65-6(5)) Benchmark Educ.

Nos traen Agua: Audiocassette. (Saludos Ser.: Vol. 3). (SPA.). (gr. 3-5). 10.00 (978-0-7635-1828-8(X)) Rigby Educ.

Nose & Other Tales see Nariz y Otro Cuentos

Nose & Other Tales. Nicolas Gogol. Read by Laura Garcia. (Running Time: 3 hrs.). 2001. 16.95 (978-1-60083-170-6(2), Audiofy Corp) Iofy Corp.

Nose down, Eyes Up. unabr. ed. Merrill Markoe. (Running Time: 8 hrs. 0 mins. 0 sec.). (ENG.). 2009. audio compact disk 59.99 (978-1-4001-4147-0(8)); audio compact disk 19.99 (978-1-4001-6147-8(9)); audio compact disk 29.99 (978-1-4001-1147-3(1)) Pub: Tantor Media. Dist(s): IngramPubServ

Nosotras Que Nos Queremos Tanto. Marcela Serrano. 7 cass. (Running Time: 9 hrs. 30 min.). 2004. 37.95 (978-1-4025-6677-6(8)) Recorded Bks.

Nosotros Trabajamos en la Costura. Ed. by Rina Benmayor et al. 1 cass. (Running Time: 1 hr. 30 mins.). 15.00 (978-1-878483-46-1(3)) CentroPr.
Bilingual documentary.

Nostalgia. Ed. by Robert A. Monroe. 1 cass. (Running Time: 30 min.). (Meta Music Ser.). 1985. 12.95 (978-1-56102-217-5(9)) Inter Indus.
A musical Hemi-Sync guidance into memory - not only of the life patterns you remember so easily, but quite possibly those of another lifetime, another place.

Nostalgia: Yearning for the Yesterday That Never Was, Vol. XI. unabr. ed. Lois F. Timmins. 11 cass. (Running Time: 16 hrs.). 1991. 109.00 11 cass. (978-0-931814-18-1(9)) Comn Studies.
Discusses nostalgia, what it is, how it helps us and how we can use it to change ourselves.

Nostalgie: The Saxophone Music of M. William Karlins. Music by Paul Bro & Salvatore Spina. 1 CD. (Running Time: 1 hr. 30 mins.). 1998. audio compact disk 19.00 (978-0-8101-3709-7(7)) Northwestern U Pr.

Nostradamus. Michael Morin. 1 cass. (Running Time: 1 hr. 30 mins.). 1990. 8.95 (736) Am Fed Astrologers.

Nostradamus: Prophet of Doom. Jack Perkins. 1 cass. (Running Time: 1 hr. 30 mins.). 1997. 9.95 (978-0-7670-0004-8(8)) A & E Home.

Nostradamus: The New Revelations. abr. ed. John Hogue. Read by John Hogue. 2 cass. (Running Time: 3 hrs.). 1998. 17.95 (978-1-57453-288-3(X)) Audio Lit.
The enigmatic prophecies of the 16th-century seer Nostradamus have provoked controversy for 400 years.This program examines the fascinating man & reviews his uncannily accurate predictions. The main focus of this work is on our own tie, with its social & ecological disasters, yet the prophecies also offer hope for peace.

Nostradamus Ate My Hamster. Robert Rankin. Narrated by Robert Rankin. 6 CDs. (Running Time: 6 hrs. 45 mins.). 1996. audio compact disk 62.00 (978-1-4025-4047-9(7)) Recorded Bks.

Nostradamus Ate my Hamster. Robert Rankin. Narrated by Robert Rankin. 5 cass. (Running Time: 6 hrs. 45 mins.). 47.00 (978-1-84197-368-5(8)) Recorded Bks.

Nostromo. Joseph Conrad. Narrated by Joss Ackland. 4 cass. (Running Time: 6 hrs.). (HarperCollinsAudioBooks Ser.). (ENG., 1995. 22.99 (978-0-00-104807-2(4), HarpColl UK) Pub: HarpC GBR. Dist(s): IPG Chicago
Conrad paints in shocking detail the insidious effects of greed and exploitation. When the silver mines of the South American republic of Costaguana are threatened by rebel forces, a brave captain, Nostromo, steps in and offers to bury the silver to ensure its safety. Conrad uses the violence of Latin American politics to focus his pessimistic vision on the tragic and brutal essence of human nature itself.

Nostromo. abr. ed. Joseph Conrad. Read by Nigel Anthony. (Running Time: 27306 sec.). (Classic Fiction Ser.). 2008. audio compact disk 34.98 (978-962-634-871-0(2), Naxos AudioBooks) Naxos.

Nostromo, unabr. ed. Joseph Conrad. Read by Flo Gibson. 11 cass. (Running Time: 16 hrs. 30 min.). 1996. 34.95 (978-1-55685-435-4(8)) Audio Bk Con.
Conrad called this exciting tale of capitalism, revolution & buried treasure in a South American country "an intense creative effort on what I suppose will remain my largest canvas." Charles Gould's silver mine corrupts & destroys some & enhances the strength of others.

***Nostromo.** unabr. ed. Joseph Conrad. Read by John Lee. (Running Time: 16 hrs. 30 mins.). 2010. 44.95 (978-1-4417-5054-9(1)); 89.95 (978-1-4417-5050-1(9)); audio compact disk 123.00 (978-1-4417-5051-8(7)) Blckstn Audio.

Nostromo, unabr. ed. Joseph Conrad. Narrated by Frank Muller. 11 cass. (Running Time: 15 hrs. 45 mins.). 1987. 91.00 (978-1-55690-382-3(0), 87930E7) Recorded Bks.
A revolution in a Central American Republic disrupts the community & leads to the disappearance of a quantity of silver.

***Nostromo.** unabr. ed. Joseph Conrad. Narrated by Antony Ferguson. (Running Time: 19 hrs. 30 mins.). 2010. 23.99 (978-1-4526-7029-4(3)); 29.99 (978-1-4526-5029-6(2)); audio compact disk 39.99 (978-1-4526-0029-1(5)) Pub: Tantor Media. Dist(s): IngramPubServ

Nostromo. unabr. collector's ed. Joseph Conrad. Read by Wolfram Kandinsky. 13 cass. (Running Time: 19 hrs. 30 min.). 1998. 104.00 (978-0-7366-0071-2(X), 1081A) Books on Tape.
Set in civil-war-torn Central American Republic of Costaguana, "Nostromo" is a complex of personal stories. It involves conflicts of heroic proportions & tragic consequences. Conrad's device is to pose a cast of characters, each person living his own illusions next to Nostromo, a "natural" man. Greed & cupidity cancel each other out, while fidelity & discipline brings one through.

Nostromo: Na649812. Joseph Conrad. Read by Nigel Anthony. 2008. audio compact disk 34.98 (978-962-634-498-9(9), Naxos AudioBooks) Naxos.

***Nostromo (Library Edition)** unabr. ed. Joseph Conrad. Narrated by Antony Ferguson. (Running Time: 19 hrs. 30 mins.). 2010. 39.99 (978-1-4526-2029-9(6)); audio compact disk 95.99 (978-1-4526-3029-8(1)) Pub: Tantor Media. Dist(s): IngramPubServ

Not a Bird Will Sing. unabr. ed. Audrey Howard. Read by Carole Boyd. 12 cass. (Running Time: 53580 sec.). (Superintendent Daiziel & Sergeant Pascoe Mysteries Ser.). 2000. 96.95 (978-0-7540-0484-4(8), CAB1907) AudioGO.
Poppy Appleton has grown up in poverty, but kindly Eliza Goodall rescues her from squalor & takes her to Long Reach Farm where she teaches Poppy all the skills a young lady needs to become the mistress of such a farm. And when the time comes for Eliza's son, Richard, to choose a wife, it seems only natural that he should choose Poppy.

Not a Creature Was Stirring: A Christmas Musical for Kids. Tom Fettke et al. 1 cass. (Running Time: 37 min.). (J). 1989. 12.99 (TA-9119C) Lillenas.
A delightful tale of cats (played by older kids) & mice (younger kids) who live together in peace in the storage room of a local church. The traditional Christmas story is told in a clear & meaningful way, with lots of humor & color woven in. A children's musical that is easy to sing, a joy to prepare & highly effective. Twelve songs are included, both traditional & new, unison/optional 2-part. Accompaniment cassette with side 1, stereo trax & side 2 split-channel with trax & vocals.

***Not A Fire Exit.** Read by Sarah McMaster. Prod. by Christopher Finlan. (ENG.). 2009. 12.95 (978-0-9842847-2-6(9)) Milverstead.

Not a Good Day to Die: The Untold Story of Operation Anaconda. unabr. ed. Sean Naylor. 2 CDs. 2005. 49.95 (978-0-7927-3483-3(1), Chivers Sound Lib); 96.95 (978-0-7927-3481-9(5), CSL 758); audio compact disk 117.95 (978-0-7927-3482-6(3), SLD 758) AudioGO.

Not a Movie see Poetry of Langston Hughes

Not a New Love: A New You. Speeches. Creflo A. Dollar. 4 cass. (Running Time: 4 hrs. 30 mins.). 2006. 20.00 (978-1-59944-000-2(8)); audio compact disk 28.00 (978-1-59944-001-9(6)) Creflo Dollar.

Not a Penny More, Not a Penny Less. Jeffrey Archer. 2 cass. (Running Time: 3 hrs.). 2001. 15.95 (978-0-00-105018-1(4)) Pub: HarpC GBR. Dist(s): Trafalgar
One million dollars, that's what Harvey Metcalfe, lifelong king of shady deals, has pulled off with empty promises of an oil bonanza and instant riches. Overnight, four men, the heir to an earldom, a Harley Street doctor, a Bond Street art dealer and an Oxford Don, find themselves penniless. But this time Harvey has swindled the wrong men. They band together and shadow him from the casinos of Monte Carlo to the high-stakes windows at Ascot and the hallowed lawns of Oxford.

Not a Penny More, Not a Penny Less. abr. rev. ed. Jeffrey Archer. Read by Martin Jarvis. 3 CDs. (Running Time: 3 hrs. 45 mins. 0 sec.). (ENG.). 2004. audio compact disk 14.95 (978-1-59397-411-4(6)) Pub: Macmill Audio. Dist(s): Macmillan

Not a Penny More, Not a Penny Less. unabr. ed. Jeffrey Archer. Read by Alex Jennings. 8 cass. (Running Time: 12 hrs.). 2001. 69.95 (978-0-7451-4334-7(2), CAB 1017) Pub: Chivers Audio Bks GBR. Dist(s): AudioGO
One million dollars! That's what Harvey Metcalfe, king of shady deals, has pulled off with empty promises of an oil bonanza. Overnight, four men: the heir to an earldom, a Harley Street doctor, a Bond Street art dealer, and an Oxford don; are left penniless! The four men unite and track Harvey from Monte Carlo to Oxford. They have a simple plan: to sting him for exactly what they lost, to the penny!.

Not a Sparrow Falls. Linda Nichols. Ed. by Marguerite Gavin. 8 cass. (Running Time: 11 hrs. 30 mins.). 2004. 56.95 (978-0-7861-2871-6(2), 3361); audio compact disk 72.00 (978-0-7861-8345-6(4), 3361) Blckstn Audio.

Not a Sparrow Falls. abr. ed. Linda Nichols. Read by Joyce Bean. (Running Time: 10800 sec.). 2002. audio compact disk 24.95 (978-1-4233-0409-8(8), 9781423304098, Brilliance MP3) Brilliance Audio.
If Mama were here, everything would still be right. Or at least not as bad wrong as it had become. But Mama was dead, and Papa was gone, her brother and sisters scattered. And she was here... Mary Bridget Washburn was tired of running, tired of being haunted by the empty shell her life had become. How in the world did the little girl she'd once been now become a woman on the wrong side of the law? Determined to make a new start, she escapes to the quaint city of Alexandria, Virginia, where she takes on her mother's identity and finds sanctuary in the shadow of a decades-old church. But a little girl's plea proves her undoing, and the Reverend...well, someone's got to open his eyes before disaster comes calling. Can Mary Bridget hide her tainted past long enough to bring hope to a family falling apart?.

Not a Sparrow Falls. abr. ed. Linda Nichols. Read by Joyce Bean. 2 cass. (Running Time: 3 hrs.). 2002. 17.95 (978-1-59086-727-3(0), 1590867270); audio compact disk 24.95 (978-1-59086-730-3(0), 1590867300); 44.25 (978-1-59086-729-7(7), 1590867297); audio compact disk 62.25 (978-1-59086-731-0(9), 1590867319) Brilliance Audio.

Not a Sparrow Falls. abr. ed. Linda Nichols. Read by Joyce Bean. (Running Time: 3 hrs.). 2006. 39.25 (978-1-4233-0412-8(8), 9781423304128, BADLE); 24.95 (978-1-4233-0411-1(X), 9781423304111, BAD); audio compact disk 39.25 (978-1-4233-0410-4(1), 9781423304104, Brlnc Audio MP3 Lib) Brilliance Audio.

Not Another Talk Show. Erik Villesvik & Dan Epstein. Perf. by Phil Proctor & David Ossman. 1 cass. (Running Time: 1 hr.). 12.95 (978-1-57677-069-6(9), VILL001) Lodestone Catalog.

Not Becoming My Mother: And Other Things She Taught Me along the Way. unabr. ed. Ruth Reichl. Read by Ruth Reichl. 2 CDs. (Running Time: 2 hrs.). (ENG.). (gr. 12 up). 2009. audio compact disk 24.95 (978-0-14-314481-6(2), PengAudBks) Penguin Grp USA.

Not Counting Women & Children. Megan McKenna. Read by Megan McKenna. 1 cass. (Running Time: 1 hr. 15 min.). 1993. 9.95 (978-7-900784-83-4(7), AA2654) Credence Commun.
A fresh handling of the parable of the feeding of the 5000 the way basic communities deal with it.

Not Dead, Only Resting. Simon Brett. 4 cass. (Running Time: 6 hrs.). 2001. 39.75 (978-0-7887-6103-4(X)) Recorded Bks.
"Resting" between performances, suave but rumpled stage actor Charles Paris is busier than ever after he stumbles across the bloodied body of a charming restaurateur. Suddenly he finds himself sifting through London's theatrical & sexual underside - in search of a very active killer.

Not Dead, Only Resting. unabr. ed. Simon Brett. Read by Simon Brett. 6 cass. (Running Time: 9 hrs.). (Charles Paris Mystery Ser.: Bk. 10). 2000. 49.95 (978-0-7451-6568-4(0), CAB 1184) Pub: Chivers Audio Bks GBR. Dist(s): AudioGO
Charles Paris is, as ever, waiting for a call from his agent for work. A rare evening out at a high-profile restaurant among stars of stage and screen seems promising. But when the restaurant's chef is brutally murdered, Charles is immediately drawn into the investigation. However, the case soon becomes a myriad of complexities.

Not Dead, Only Resting. unabr. ed. Simon Brett. Narrated by Simon Prebble. 4 cass. (Running Time: 6 hrs.). 2001. 40.00 (978-0-7887-5960-4(4), H1184E7) Recorded Bks.
"Resting" between performances, suave but rumpled stage actor Charles Paris is busier than ever after he stumbles across the bloodied body of a charming restaurateur. Suddenly he finds himself sifting through London's theatrical & sexual underside - in search of a very active killer.

Not Easily Broken. unabr. ed. Narrated by Tracey Leigh. 6 cass. (Running Time: 30300 sec.). 2006. 59.95 (978-0-7927-4544-0(2), CSL 1022); audio compact disk 74.95 (978-0-7927-4492-4(6), SLD 1022); audio compact disk 44.95 (978-0-7927-4567-9(1), CMP 1022) AudioGO.

Not Easily Broken: A Novel. abr. ed. T. D. Jakes. Read by Pamala Tyson. (Running Time: 5 hrs.). (ENG.). 2006. 14.98 (978-1-59483-632-9(9)) Pub: Hachet Audio. Dist(s): HachBkGrp

Not Easily Broken: A Novel. abr. ed. T. D. Jakes. Read by Pamala Tyson. (Running Time: 6 hrs.). (Replay Edition Ser.). (ENG.). 2009. 19.98 (978-1-60788-275-6(2)) Pub: Hachet Audio. Dist(s): HachBkGrp

Not Even for Love. unabr. ed. Erin St. Claire, pseud. Read by Karen Ziemba. (Running Time: 5 hrs. 0 mins. 0 sec.). (ENG.). 2008. audio compact disk 14.99 (978-0-7435-6946-0(6)) Pub: S&S Audio. Dist(s): S and S Inc

Not Everyone Who Says to Me, Lord, Lord. Dan Corner. 1 cass. (Running Time: 1 hr. 30 mins.). 3.00 (62) Evang Outreach.

Not Far from Wigan Pier. Ted Dakin. 2008. 49.95 (978-1-84559-743-6(5)); audio compact disk 59.95 (978-1-84559-744-3(3)) Pub: Soundings Ltd GBR. Dist(s): Ulverscroft US

Not for Newcomers Only, Vol. 1. 1 cass. (Running Time: 1 hr.). 1985. 6.50 (978-0-933685-01-7(7), TP-20) A A Grapevine.
Includes articles from the AA Grapevine magazine aimed at newcomers to Alcoholics Anonymous, descriptive of AA program & principles.

Not for Newcomers Only, Vol. 1 & 2. 1 CD. (Running Time: 1 hr. 30 mins.). 2002. audio compact disk 10.00 (978-0-933685-37-6(8)) A A Grapevine.
Selections from audio tapes, articles from our magazine read by different people.

Not for Newcomers Only, Vol. 2. 1 cass. (Running Time: 1 hr.). 1986. 6.50 (978-0-933685-06-2(8), TP-21) A A Grapevine.
Includes articles from the AA Grapevine magazine aimed at newcomers to Alcoholics Anonymous, descriptive of AA program & principles.

***Not for Ours Only.** Featuring Ravi Zacharias. 1989. audio compact disk 9.00 (978-1-61256-039-7(3)) Ravi Zach.

Not-for-Profit Audits under A-133. Rhett D. Harrell. 3 cass. (Running Time: 4 hrs.). 129.00 set, incl. textbk. & quizzer. (CPE3080) Bisk Educ.
Covers internal subsidies, insurance, direct loans & appropriations, loan guarantees, contracts, coop-agreements & grants.

Not for Revenge. Donald Vogel. 1991. 6.95 (978-1-879154-07-0(2)) Vlly Hse Gllry.

Not for Revenge. unabr. ed. Donald S. Vogel. Read by Nick Alexander. 4 cass. (Running Time: 6 hrs.). 1991. 22.00 Set. Vlly Hse Gllry.
Based on the Valley House Gallery book.

***Not for Sale.** unabr. ed. David Batstone. Read by Michael McIlhonnie. (ENG.). 2009. (978-0-06-189655-2(1), Harper Audio); (978-0-06-186699-9(7), Harper Audio) HarperCollins Pubs.

Not for Sale: The Return of the Global Slave Trade- & How We Can Fight It. David Batstone. Read by Lloyd James. (Playaway Adult Nonfiction Ser.). (ENG.). 2009. 59.99 (978-1-61545-554-6(X)) Find a World.

***Not for Sale: The Return of the Global Slave Trade & How We Can Fight It.** unabr. ed. David Batstone. Narrated by Lloyd James. (ENG.). 2008. 16.98 (978-1-59644-601-4(3), Hovel Audio) christianaud.

Not for Sale: The Return of the Global Slave Trade & How We Can Fight It. unabr. ed. David Batstone. Narrated by Lloyd James. (Running Time: 9 hrs. 45 mins. 0 sec.). (ENG.). 2008. audio compact disk 26.98 (978-1-59644-600-7(5), Hovel Audio) christianaud.

Not for You Alone. Robert Murphy. (ENG.). 2005. 4.00 (978-1-933675-00-8(4)) Dos Madres Pr.

Not George Washington. unabr. ed. P. G. Wodehouse & Herbert Westbrook. Read by Frederick Davidson. 4 cass. (Running Time: 5 hrs. 30 mins.). 1999. 32.95 (978-0-7861-1377-4(4), 2261) Blckstn Audio.
This early, autobiographical novel aptly describes the perils of a writer's world in London circa 1900. The protagonist - an author manque - attempts by any means necessary to establish himself in literary circles. A unique feature of the novel, which foreshadows the techniques of the mature Wodehouse, is his telling of the story from the perspective of many characters.

Not George Washington, Set. unabr. ed. P. G. Wodehouse. Read by Frederick Davidson. 4 cass. 1999. 32.95 (FS9-43268) Highsmith.

***Not George Washington: An Autobiographical Novel.** unabr. ed. P. G. Wodehouse. Read by Frederick Davidson. (Running Time: 5 hrs. 0 mins.). 2010. 19.95 (978-1-4417-1369-8(7)); audio compact disk 49.00 (978-1-4417-1366-7(2)) Blckstn Audio.

***Not Guilty: A Detective Story from the Strand.** Will Scott. 2009. (978-1-60136-496-8(2)) Audio Holding.

Not Guilty: the Experience. Directed By Hank Walker. Contrib. by John P Kee and the New Life Community Choir & John Kee. Prod. by John Kee. (Running Time: 1 hr. 18 mins.). 2007. 14.98 (978-5-557-92788-8(3), Verity) Brentwood Music.

Not Husband Material! unabr. ed. Caroline Anderson. Read by Judith Porter. 4 cass. (Running Time: 6 hrs.). 2001. 44.95 (978-1-84283-033-8(3)) Pub: Soundings Ltd GBR. Dist(s): Ulverscroft US

Not in My Family: Songs of Healing & Inspiration. Contrib. by Vicki Mack Lataillade et al. 2006. audio compact disk 17.98 (978-5-558-02863-8(7)) GospoCen.

Not in the Flesh. abr. ed. Ruth Rendell. Read by Tim Curry. 5 CDs. (Running Time: 6 hrs.). (Inspector Wexford Mystery Ser.: Bk. 21). (ENG.). 2008. audio compact disk 29.95 (978-0-7393-6637-0(8), Random AudioBks) Pub: Random Audio Pubg. Dist(s): Random

Not in This Chamber Only at My Birth see Poetry of Edna St. Vincent Millay

Not Just a Soldier's War. Betty Burton. Read by Nicolette McKenzie. 10 cass. (Soundings Ser.). (J). 2006. 84.95 (978-1-84559-210-3(7)) Pub: ISIS Lrg Prnt GBR. Dist(s): Ulverscroft US

Not-Just-Anybody Family. unabr. ed. Betsy Byars. Read by Blain Fairman. 3 cass. (Running Time: 4 hrs., 30 min.). (Blossom Family Ser.: Bk. 1). (J). (gr. 1-8). 1999. 30.00 (LL 3043, Chivers Child Audio) AudioGO.

Not-Just-Anybody Family. unabr. ed. Betsy Byars. Read by Blain Fairman. 3 cass. (Running Time: 3 hrs. 19 mins.). (Blossom Family Ser.: Bk. 1). (YA). (gr. 4-11). 1987. pap. bk. 29.00 (978-0-8072-7324-1(4), YA-805 SP, Listening Lib); 24.00 (978-0-8072-7231-2(0), YA 805 CX, Listening Lib) Random Audio Pubg.
That would be the Blossom family & what a week they're having! Junior tries to fly, Maggie helps Vern break into jail to be with their grandfather Pap, Pap's dog has a grueling trip home, while the children's mother rides in the rodeo. Even more remarkable than the fascinating story line is Byar's uncanny knack for believably portraying all the characters thoughts - even the dog's!.

Not-Just-Anybody Family. unabr. ed. Betsy Byars. Read by Fairman Blain. 3 CDs. (Running Time: 3 hrs. 16 mins.). (J). (gr. 3-6). 2008. audio compact disk 30.00 (978-0-7393-7391-0(9), Listening Lib) Pub: Random Audio Pubg. Dist(s): Random

Not-Just-Anybody Family, Set. unabr. ed. Betsy Byars. Read by Blain Fairman. 3 cass. (Blossom Family Ser.: Bk. 1). (YA). 1999. 23.98 (FS9-34171) Highsmith.

***Not Just Science: Questions Where Christian Faith & Natural Science Intersect.** Zondervan. (Running Time: 12 hrs. 59 mins. 18 sec.). (ENG.). 2010. 9.99 (978-0-310-86927-6(7)) Zondervan.

Not Love at First Sight: Stories from New England. Willem Lange. 1 cass. (Running Time: 1 hr. 30 mins.). 1998. 10.95 (978-0-87451-868-9(7)) U Pr of New Eng.

Not Married, Not Bothered. Carol Clewlow. (Isis (CDs) Ser.). 2006. audio compact disk 89.95 (978-0-7531-2571-7(4)) Pub: ISIS Lrg Prnt GBR. Dist(s): Ulverscroft US

Not Married, Not Bothered. unabr. ed. Carol Clewlow. Read by Clare Wille. 8 cass. (Running Time: 10 hrs. 40 mins.). (Isis Cassettes Ser.). 2006. 69.95 (978-0-7531-3543-3(4)) Pub: ISIS Lrg Prnt GBR. Dist(s): Ulverscroft US

***Not My Boy! A Father, a Son, & One Family's Journey with Autism.** unabr. ed. Rodney Peete. (Running Time: 7 hrs. 0 mins. 0 sec.). (ENG.). 2010. 19.99 (978-1-4001-6530-8(X)); 14.99 (978-1-4001-8530-6(0)); audio compact disk 29.99 (978-1-4001-1530-3(2)); audio compact disk 59.99 (978-1-4001-4530-0(9)) Pub: Tantor Media. Dist(s): IngramPubServ

Not My Daughter. abr. ed. Barbara Delinsky. Read by Cassandra Campbell. (ENG.). 2010. audio compact disk 30.00 (978-0-7393-6952-4(0), Random AudioBks) Pub: Random Audio Pubg. Dist(s): Random

***Not My Daughter.** unabr. ed. Barbara Delinsky. Read by Cassandra Campbell. 10 CDs. 2010. audio compact disk 90.00 (978-0-307-70472-6(6), BksonTape) Pub: Random Audio Pubg. Dist(s): Random

Not My Will, but Thine. Neal A. Maxwell. 4 cass. (Running Time: 6 hrs.). 1998. 24.95 (978-1-57008-544-4(7), Bkcraft Inc) Deseret Bk.

Not One. Contrib. by Johnathan Crumpton & Camp Kirkland. Prod. by Ed Kee. (ENG.). 2008. audio compact disk 24.99 (978-5-557-46520-5(0), Brentwood-Benson Music) Brentwood Music.

Not Only Angels Have Wings. Karen Blomgren & Clarence Thomson. Read by Karen Blomgren & Clarance Thomson. 1 cass. (Running Time: 40 min.). 1992. 9.95 (978-7-900780-75-1(0), AA2493) Credence Commun.
Nine enjoyable songs, each about one of the Enneagram types.

Not Quite Dead Enough. unabr. collector's ed. Rex Stout. Read by Michael Prichard. 6 cass. (Running Time: 6 hrs.). (Nero Wolfe Ser.). 1994. 48.00 (978-0-7366-2828-0(2), 3536) Books on Tape.
Nero Wolfe ignores the army's call to duty until an "accident" undermines national security. Then he moves...forcefully!.

Not Quite Dead Enough & Booby Trap: Two Nero Wolfe Mysteries. unabr. ed. Rex Stout. Read by Michael Prichard. 4 cass. (Running Time: 6 hrs.). (Nero Wolfe Ser.). 2004. 24.95 (978-1-57270-361-2(X)) Pub: Audio Partners. Dist(s): PerseuPGW
Here are two Rex Stout short stories for war buffs and Nero Wolfe fans alike. In "Not Quite Dead Enough," Archie Goodwin - Nero Wolfe's perennial legman - literally steals the limelight. Recently inducted into Army Intelligence, Archie goes to Wolfe's flat to see why he hasn't been answering his or the Army recruiter's calls. Wolfe could be dead, but Archie later finds out he's been "training" to join the Army. It takes the murder of a woman Archie goes dancing with to get Nero Wolfe to investigate crime again. The wartime theme continues in "Booby Trap" as Archie and Wolfe investigate the murder of Captain Albert Cross, killed only hours before he was to make a report about a prototype grenade theft to the group of intelligence people Wolfe works with. Listener favorite Michael Prichard, named by Smart Money magazine as one of the "Top Ten Golden Voices," precisely captures the characters' personalities and the story locations.

Not Quite Dead Enough & Booby Trap: Two Nero Wolfe Mysteries. unabr. ed. Rex Stout. Read by Michael Prichard. 5 CDs. (Running Time: 6 hrs.). (Nero Wolfe Ser.). (ENG.). 2004. audio compact disk 27.95 (978-1-57270-362-9(8)) Pub: AudioGO. Dist(s): Perseus Dist

Not Quite Social see Robert Frost in Recital

Not Safe, but Good. abr. ed. Bret Lott. Narrated by Jon Gauger. (ENG.). 2007. 9.09 (978-1-60814-322-1(8)) Oasis Audio.

Not Safe, but Good. abr. ed. Bret Lott. Read by Sherri Berger. Narrated by Jon Gauger. (Running Time: 2 hrs. 30 mins. 0 sec.). (ENG.). 2007. audio compact disk 12.99 (978-1-59859-310-5(2)) Oasis Audio.

Not Safe, but Good: Short Stories Sharpened by Faith. abr. ed. Bret Lott. Narrated by Jon Gauger. (ENG.). 2007. 9.09 (978-1-60814-321-4(X)) Oasis Audio.

Not Safe, but Good Vol. 1, Pt. 1: Short Stories Sharpened by Faith. abr. ed. Bret Lott. Read by Sherri Berger. Narrated by Jon Gauger. (Running Time: 9000 sec.). (ENG.). 2007. audio compact disk 12.99 (978-1-59859-251-1(3)) Oasis Audio.

Not So Big Life: Making Room for What Really Matters. abr. ed. Sarah Susanka. Read by Sarah Susanka. (Running Time: 21600 sec.). (ENG.). 2007. audio compact disk 29.95 (978-0-7393-4157-5(X), Random AudioBks) Pub: Random Audio Pubg. Dist(s): Random

Not So Big Life: Making Room for What Really Matters. unabr. ed. Sarah Susanka. Read by Kimberly Farr. 8 CDs. (Running Time: 9 hrs.). 2007. audio compact disk 80.00 (978-1-4159-3573-6(4)); 80.00 (978-1-4159-4048-8(7)) Books on Tape.
For many of us, our schedules are chaotic and overcommitted. Here, Susanka shows us that it is possible to take our finger off the fast-forward button. She reveals that form and function serve not only architectural aims but life goals as well. We quickly discover we have all the space and time we need for the things in our lives that really matter. But perhaps the greatest reward is the discovery that small changes can yield enormous results. In her elegant, clear style, Susanka convinces us that less truly is more - much more.

Not So Fast, Songololo. 2004. bk. 24.95 (978-0-89719-678-9(3)); pap. bk. 32.75 (978-1-55592-286-3(4)); pap. bk. 14.95 (978-1-56008-070-1(1)); 8.95 (978-1-56008-420-4(0)) Weston Woods.

Not So Fast Songololo. 2004. cass. & flmstrp 30.00 (978-0-89719-638-3(4)) Weston Woods.

Not So Fast, Songololo. Niki Daly. 1 cass., 5 bks. (Running Time: 11 min.). (J). pap. bk. 32.75 Weston Woods.
Malusi, a South African boy, spends a day shopping with his grandmother.

Not So Fast, Songololo. Niki Daly. 1 cass. (Running Time: 11 min.). (J). (ps-4). bk. 24.95; pap. bk. 12.95 (PRA351); 8.95 (RAC351) Weston Woods.

Not-So-Jolly Roger. unabr. ed. Jon Scieszka. Read by William Dufris. 1 cass. (Running Time: 51 mins.). (Time Warp Trio Ser.: No. 2). (J). (gr. 2-5). 1998. pap. bk. 17.00 (978-0-8072-0394-1(7), EFTR194SP, Listening Lib) Random Audio Pubg.
The Time Warp Trio find themselves on a magical journey to Camelot where they must escape death & destruction.

Not-So-Jolly Roger. unabr. ed. Jon Scieszka. 1 cass. (Running Time: 51 min.). (Time Warp Trio Ser.: No. 2). (J). (gr. 2-4). 1999. pap. bk. 29.98 (978-0-8072-1302-5(0), EFTR194MP, Listening Lib) Random Audio Pubg.

Not That Again! How to Stop Fighting about the Same Old Things, David Grudermeyer & Rebecca Grudermeyer. 2 cass. (Running Time: 3 hrs.). pap. bk. 18.95 (T-58) Willingness Wrks.

Not That Far from Bethlehem. Contrib. by Point of Grace. (Ultimate Tracks (Word Tracks) Ser.). 2006. audio compact disk 8.98 (978-5-558-26950-5(2), Word Music) Word Enter.

Not the End of the World. Kate Atkinson. Read by Geraldine James. 2005. 54.95 (978-0-7540-8444-0(2), Chivers Child Audio) AudioGO.

Not the End of the World. Geraldine McCaughrean. Read by Kate Sachs & Glen McCready. (Running Time: 17940 sec.). (J). 2001. audio compact disk 34.95 (978-0-7540-6790-0(4)) AudioGo GBR.

Not the End of the World. unabr. ed. Christopher Brookmyre. 12 cass. (Isis Cassettes Ser.). (J). 2006. 94.95 (978-0-7531-1977-8(3)); audio compact disk 99.95 (978-0-7531-2311-9(8)) Pub: ISIS Lrg Prnt GBR. Dist(s): Ulverscroft US

Not the Girl Next Door: Joan Crawford - A Personal Biography. unabr. ed. Charlotte Chandler. Read by Christine Williams. (Running Time: 37800 sec.). 2008. 29.95 (978-1-4332-0925-3(X)); 59.95 (978-1-4332-0923-9(3)); audio compact disk 29.95 (978-1-4332-0926-0(8)); audio compact disk & audio compact disk 29.95 (978-1-4332-0927-7(6)); audio compact disk & audio compact disk 63.00 (978-1-4332-0924-6(1)) Blckstn Audio.

Not the Piano, Mrs. Medley! Evan Levine. Read by Peter Fernandez. Illus. by S. D. Schindler. 1 cass. (Running Time: 9 mins.). (J). (gr. k-3). 1996. pap. bk. 15.95 (978-0-87499-373-8(3)) Live Oak Media.
Mrs. Medley & her grandson, Max, & her dog, Word, are headed for the beach. They are halfway down the block when Mrs. Medley looks up at the sky. Even though the sun is shining now, it might rain. So back they go for umbrellas & boots. Then it's chairs, pillows...Levine's point that less is more is clearly but hilariously made.

Not the Piano, Mrs. Medley! Evan Levine. Read by Peter Fernandez. Illus. by S. D. Schindler. 14 vols. (Running Time: 9 mins.). 1996. pap. bk. & tchr. ed. 33.95 (978-0-87499-375-2(X)) Live Oak Media.

Not the Piano, Mrs. Medley! unabr. ed. Evan Levine. Read by Peter Fernandez. Illus. by S. D. Schindler. 1 cass. (Running Time: 9 mins.). (J). (gr. k-3). 1996. bk. 24.95 (978-0-87499-374-5(1)) Live Oak Media.

Not the Time, Not the Place. Perf. by Marvin Sapp. 1 cass. (Running Time: 1 hr.). 1999. 7.98 (978-0-7601-2756-8(5)) Brentwood Music.

Not Thinking of Death. Alexander Fullerton. 12 cass. (Sound Ser.). (J). 2003. 94.95 (978-1-84283-392-6(8)) Pub: ISIS Lrg Prnt GBR. Dist(s): Ulverscroft US

Not Too Scary Vocabulary! For the SAT & Other Standardized Tests. 2nd ed. Renee E. Mazer. Ed. by Renee E. Mazer. 2002. pap. bk. 39.95 (978-0-9664845-1-9(7)) High Score.

Not Too Scary Vocabulary! For the SAT & Other Standardized Tests & Success in Life. 2nd ed. Renee E. Mazer. 7 CDs. (Running Time: 9 hrs.). 2003. pap. bk. 49.95 (978-0-9664845-2-6(5)) High Score.

Not Too Scary Vocabulary for SAT: And Other Standardized Tests. abr. ed. Renee E. Mazer. Read by Renee E. Mazer. 6 cass. (Running Time: 9 hrs.). (YA). (gr. 9 up). 1999. pap. bk. 34.95 (978-0-9664845-0-2(9)) Pub: High Score. Dist(s): Penton Overseas
Vocabulary tapes to help students prepared for the SAT. Includes booklet.

Not Untrue & Not Unkind. unabr. ed. Ed O'Loughlin. (Running Time: 9 hrs. 30 mins.). 2010. 29.95 (978-1-4417-2938-5(0)) Blckstn Audio.

***Not Untrue & Not Unkind.** unabr. ed. Ed O'Loughlin. (Running Time: 9 hrs. 30 mins.). 2010. 59.95 (978-1-4417-2934-7(8)); audio compact disk 90.00 (978-1-4417-2935-4(6)) Blckstn Audio.

Not Untrue & Not Unkind. unabr. ed. Ed O'Loughlin. (Running Time: 9 hrs. 30 mins.). 2010. audio compact disk 29.95 (978-1-4417-2937-8(2)) Blckstn Audio.

***Not Without Hope.** unabr. ed. Nick Schuyler & Jeré Longman. Read by Ramon De Ocampo. (ENG.). 2010. (978-0-06-199941-3(5), Harper Audio); (978-0-06-200855-8(2), Harper Audio) HarperCollins Pubs.

Not Without My Daughter. unabr. ed. Betty Mahmoody & William Hoffer. Read by Penelope Dellaporta. 12 cass. (Running Time: 18 hrs.). 1991. 96.00 (978-0-7366-2018-5(4), 2834) Books on Tape.
In August 1984 a Michigan housewife accompanied her husband to his native Iran for a two-week vacation. Once there she & her four-year-old daughter became virtual prisoners. Her husband, suddenly a fanatic, was the jailer. Betty Mahmoody knew she had to get away. But in a land where women are near-slaves & Americans despised, her chances were slim. Her only hope lay in a clandestine network that would not take her child & without her Betty would not leave.

***Not Without My Tivo.** Adapted by Siren Audio Studios. Prod. by Siren Audio Studios. Based on a book by Alexia Drew. (ENG.). 2011. audio compact disk 29.99 (978-0-9844180-9-1(1)) Siiren Audio.

***Not Without Parables: Stories of Yesterday, Today & Eternity.** Catherine Doherty. Read by Madonna House Staff. audio compact disk 24.95 (978-1-897145-53-1(5)) Madonna Hse CAN.

Not Without You. Janelle Taylor. Narrated by Richard Ferrone. 8 cass. (Running Time: 11 hrs.). 74.00 (978-1-4025-3268-9(7)) Recorded Bks.

Not Yet Titled. Perf. by L. G. Wise. 1 cass. 1997. audio compact disk 15.99 CD. (D7524) Diamante Music Grp.
The debut album by Wise combines his trademark lyrical delivery with action packed tales of ghetto tragedy & triumph. This album features prominent members of his "clique", & 12 dramatic tracks that will not disappoint.

Note Drills in Treble & Bass Clefs. Duane Shinn. 1 cass. 19.95 (HAR-8) Duane Shinn.
Presents a Magic Keyboard Chart which slips behind the keys & guides to each in both clefs.

Note Investors Super Earnings Cash Flow: How to Prosper in the Low Risk High Return Discounted Mortgage Business. Joel Cassway. 1 cass. (Running Time: 1 hr. 30 min.). 1999. 29.95 (978-0-9671564-1-5(6)) Note Investors Grp.
Get rich slow in the discounted mortgage note broker home based business. Note brokers make money brokering notes, build wealth flipping discounted mortgages & investing in Real Estate paper cash flows & discounted notes for financial independence & financial freedom.

Note Investors Superearnings Plus: The Ultimate Low-Risk, High Return Discounted Mortgage Wealth Building Strategy. Joel Cassway. 8 cass. (Running Time: 4 hrs.). 199.00 (978-0-9671564-0-8(8)) Note Investors Grp.
Money making investment ideas - how to increase income, retire rich, find financial security with discounted notes, invest in no money down discounted mortgages & create a high positive cash flow investing for retirement using real estate mortgage note investor paper formulas.

Notebook see Poetry of William Blake

Notebook. abr. ed. Nicholas Sparks. Read by Kate Nelligan & Campbell Scott. (Running Time: 4 hrs.). (ENG.). 1996. 9.98 (978-1-60024-006-5(2)) Pub: Hachet Audio. Dist(s): HachBkGrp

Notebook. unabr. ed. Nicholas Sparks. 2 cass. (Running Time: 3 hrs.). 1997. (978-1-57042-134-1(X)) Hachet Audio.
Set amid the austere beauty of coastal North Carolina in 1946, The Notebook begins with the story of Noah Calhoun, a rural Southerner returned home from World War II. Noah, thirty-one, is restoring a plantation home to its former glory, and he is haunted by images of the beautiful girl he met fourteen years earlier, a girl he loved like no other. Unable to find her, yet unwilling to forget the summer they spent together, Noah is content to live with only memories...until she unexpectedly returns to his town to see him once again.

Notebook. unabr. ed. Nicholas Sparks. Read by Barry Bostwick. (ENG.). 2005. 16.98 (978-1-59483-316-8(8)) Pub: Hachet Audio. Dist(s): HachBkGrp

Notebook. unabr. ed. Nicholas Sparks. Read by Barry Bostwick. (Running Time: 6 hrs.). (ENG.). 2007. audio compact disk 14.98 (978-1-60024-256-4(1)) Pub: Hachet Audio. Dist(s): HachBkGrp

Notebook. unabr. ed. Nicholas Sparks. Read by Barry Bostwick. (Running Time: 6 hrs.). (ENG.). 2009. 49.98 (978-1-60024-598-5(6)) Pub: Hachet Audio. Dist(s): HachBkGrp

Notebook. unabr. ed. Nicholas Sparks. Narrated by George Guidall. 5 CDs. (Running Time: 6 hrs.). 1999. audio compact disk 46.00 (978-0-7887-3841-8(0), C1066E7) Recorded Bks.
Traces the lives of Noah & Allie, who survived the tests of time & distance in their courtship & have remained close during a long & fruitful marriage.

Notebook. unabr. ed. Nicholas Sparks. Narrated by George Guidall. 5 cass. (Running Time: 6 hrs.). 1997. 49.00 (978-0-7887-1000-1(1), 95082E7) Recorded Bks.

Notebook - The Wedding, Set. unabr. ed. Nicholas Sparks. Read by Barry Bostwick & Tom Wopat. (Running Time: 13 hrs.). (ENG.). 2006. 34.98 (978-1-60024-188-8(3)) Pub: Hachet Audio. Dist(s): HachBkGrp

Notebook & the Wedding, Set. unabr. ed. Nicholas Sparks. Read by Barry Bostwick & Tom Wopat. (Running Time: 13 hrs.). (ENG.). 2009. 74.98 (978-1-60788-149-0(7)) Pub: Hachet Audio. Dist(s): HachBkGrp

Notebooks of Paul Brunton, Set. cd-rom & audio compact disk 99.95 (978-0-943914-92-3(2)) Pub: Larson Pubns. Dist(s): Red Wheel Weiser

Notes from a Big Country. Bill Bryson. 2 cass. (Running Time: 3 hrs.). 1998. (978-0-552-14648-7(X), Corgi RHG) Transworld GBR.

Notes from a Liar & Her Dog. Gennifer Choldenko. Read by Ariadne Meyers. 4 vols. (Running Time: 5 hrs. 25 mins.). (J). (gr. 4-7). 2004. pap. bk. 38.00 (978-0-8072-2097-9(3), Listening Lib) Random Audio Pubg.

Notes from a Liar & Her Dog. unabr. ed. Gennifer Choldenko. Read by Ariadne Meyers. 4 cass. (Running Time: 5 hrs. 25 mins.). (J). (gr. 4-7). 2004. 32.00 (978-0-8072-0499-3(4), Listening Lib) Random Audio Pubg.
Eleven-year-old Ant, stuck in a family that she does not like, copes by pretending that her "real" parents are coming to rescue her, by loving her dog Pistachio, by volunteering at the zoo, and by bending the truth and telling lies.

Notes from a Small Island. Bill Bryson. Read by David Case. 1999. audio compact disk 80.00 (978-0-7366-5157-8(8)) Books on Tape.

Notes from a Small Island. abr. ed. Bill Bryson. Read by Bill Bryson. 5 CDs. (Running Time: 6 hrs.). (ENG.). 1998. audio compact disk 29.95 (978-0-553-45593-9(1)) Pub: Random Audio Pubg. Dist(s): Random

Notes from a Small Island. unabr. ed. Bill Bryson. Read by David Case. 8 cass. (Running Time: 12 hrs.). 1999. 64.00 (978-0-7366-4376-4(1), 4840) Books on Tape.
Bill Bryson is an unabashed Anglophile who, through a mistake of history, happened to be born & bred in Iowa. Righting that error, he spent 20 years in England before deciding to repatriate. This was partly to let his wife & children experience life in Bryson's homeland & partly because he had read that 3.7 million Americans believed that they had been abducted by aliens at one time or an other. It was thus clear to him that his people needed him. But before leaving his much-loved home in North Yorkshire, Bryson insisted on taking one last trip around Britain.

Notes from a Small Island. unabr. ed. Bill Bryson. Read by David Case. 10 CDs. (Running Time: 11 hrs. 48 mins.). 2001. audio compact disk 80.00 Books on Tape.

Notes from a Small Island. unabr. ed. Bill Bryson. Read by William Roberts. 8 cass. (Running Time: 12 hrs.). 2000. 59.95 (978-0-7451-6662-9(8), CAB 1278) Pub: Chivers Audio Bks GBR. Dist(s): AudioGO
After almost two decades in Great Britain, Bill Bryson moves back to America. But before leaving, he embarks on a farewell tour of England. In this humorous and captivating journey, Bryson contemplates why the British always seem so happy, and what one actually does at Stonehenge! Great Britain will never seem the same again.

Notes from a Small Island. unabr. ed. Bill Bryson. Narrated by Ron McLarty. 10 CDs. (Running Time: 12 hrs.). 1999. audio compact disk 93.00 (978-0-7887-3720-6(1), C1077E7) Recorded Bks.
After nearly two decades on British soil, the author takes a final jaunt through the heartland of the United Kingdom. As he travels by foot, train & bus, he encounters quirky age-old customs, charming architecture & salt-of-the-earth inhabitants.

Notes from a Small Island. unabr. ed. Bill Bryson. Narrated by Ron McLarty. 9 cass. (Running Time: 12 hrs.). 2000. 78.00 (978-0-7887-2938-6(1), 95491E7) Recorded Bks.

Notes from China. unabr. ed. Barbara W. Tuchman. Read by Walter Zimmerman. 3 cass. (Running Time: 3 hrs.). 1987. 18.00 (978-0-7366-1210-4(6), 2128) Books on Tape.
Travel report from a six-week trip around China in 1972, at the time of Nixon's visit there.

Notes from the Black Piano: Selected Poems by Bill Holm. 2nd ed. Poems. Bill Holm. Read by Bill Holm. Prod. by Scott Beyers. Engineer Scott Beyers. 1. (Running Time: 35 mins.). (ENG.). 2004. audio compact disk 10.00 (978-0-9665212-0-7(X), BIGCD-0X) EssayAudio.
In "Notes From the Black Piano", poet Bill Holm confronts themes of aging, nature, friendship, and music, revealing an everyman sensibility that celebrates the beauty, truth, and evanescence of everyday life. Like a modern-day Walt Whitman, Bill Holm traverses contemporary America and the world. He revels in humanity's creativity and resourcefulness; he rails at its waste. Read by the author.

Notes from the Heart. Mick\Mulcahy & Mick\Mulcahy. (ENG.). 2005. audio compact disk 23.95 (978-0-8023-8160-6(X)) Pub: Clo Iar-Chonnachta IRL. Dist(s): Dufour

***Notes from the Midnight Driver.** unabr. ed. Jordan Sonnenblick. (Running Time: 5 hrs.). 2011. 19.99 (978-1-61106-157-4(1), 9781611061574, BAD); 39.97 (978-1-61106-158-1(X), 9781611061581, BADLE); 39.97 (978-1-61106-156-7(3), 9781611061567, Brinc Audio MP3 Lib); 19.99 (978-1-61106-155-0(5), 9781611061550, Brilliance MP3); audio compact disk 49.97 (978-1-61106-154-3(7), 9781611061543, BriAudCD Unabrid); audio compact disk 19.99 (978-1-61106-153-6(9), 9781611061536, Bril Audio CD Unabri) Brilliance Audio.

***Notes from the Underground.** unabr. ed. Fyodor Dostoyevsky. Narrated by Norman Dietz. (Running Time: 5 hrs. 0 mins.). 2010. 13.99 (978-1-4001-8806-2(7)); 19.99 (978-1-4001-6806-4(6)); audio compact disk 24.99 (978-1-4001-1806-9(9)); audio compact disk 59.99 (978-1-4001-4806-6(5)) Pub: Tantor Media. Dist(s): IngramPubServ

***Notes from the Underground.** unabr. ed. Fyodor Dostoyevsky. Narrated by Simon Vance. (ENG.). 2009. 12.98 (978-1-59644-792-9(3), Hovel Audio) christianaud.

Notes from the Underground. unabr. ed. Fyodor Dostoyevsky. Narrated by Simon Vance. 4 CDs. (Running Time: 4 hrs. 24 mins. 0 sec.). (ENG.). 2009. audio compact disk 21.98 (978-1-59644-791-2(5), christaudio) christianaud.

Notes from the Universe: New Perspectives from an Old Friend. unabr. ed. Mike Dooley. Read by Mike Dooley. (Running Time: 2 hrs. 0 mins. 0 sec.). (ENG., 2007. audio compact disk 19.95 (978-0-7435-7079-4(0)) Pub: S&S Audio. Dist(s): S and S Inc

Notes from the Wild. Bernie Krause. 1996. bk. 18.95 (978-1-55961-385-9(8), Ellipsis Arts) Relaxtn Co.

Notes from Underground. Fyodor Dostoyevsky. Read by George Guidall. 4 CDs. (Running Time: 5 Hrs). audio compact disk 34.95 (978-1-4025-3591-8(0)) Recorded Bks.

Notes from Underground. unabr. ed. Fyodor Dostoyevsky. Read by Walter Zimmerman. 4 cass. (Running Time: 5 hrs. 30 mins.). 1989. 32.95 (978-0-7861-0508-3(9), 2008) Blckstn Audio.
The book, published in 1864, marks a turning point in Dostoevsky's writing: it announces the moral, political & social ideas that he will further examine in "Crime & Punishment" & "The Brothers Karamazov." The book opens with a tormented soul crying out, "I am a sick man...I am a spiteful man." This is the cry of an alienated individual who has become one of the greatest antiheroes in all literature.

Notes from Underground. unabr. ed. Fyodor Dostoyevsky. Read by Walter Zimmerman. 4 cass. (Running Time: 5 hrs.). 1980. 26.00 (C-34) Jimcin Record.
The book relates the experiences of a singular young man who spurns the rule of God & man. The problem he faces is that of all nihilists, which is to deny authority while simultaneously explaining order.

Notes from Underground. unabr. ed. Fyodor Dostoyevsky. Read by George Guidall. 3 Cassettes. (Running Time: 5 Hrs.). 1995. 19.95 (978-1-4025-3648-9(8)) Recorded Bks.

Notes from Underground. unabr. ed. Fyodor Dostoyevsky. Tr. by Jessie Coulson. Narrated by George Guidall. 4 cass. (Running Time: 5 hrs.). 1995. 35.00 (978-0-7887-0221-1(1), 94446E7) Recorded Bks.
Dostoevsky masterpiece written in the early years of his career contains deep philosophical, political & psychological themes.

Notes from Underground. unabr. ed. Fyodor Dostoyevsky. Tr. by Jessie Coulson. Narrated by George Guidall. 4 CDs. (Running Time: 5 hrs.). 2000. audio compact disk 38.00 (978-0-7887-3730-5(9), C1087E7) Recorded Bks.

Notes from Underground. unabr. collector's ed. Fyodor Dostoyevsky. Read by Walter Zimmerman. 6 cass. (Running Time: 6 hrs.). 36.00 (978-0-7366-3851-7(2), 9034) Books on Tape.
The book relates the experiences of a singular young man who spurns the rule of God & man. The problem he faces is that of all nihilists, which is to deny authority while simultaneously explaining order.

***Notes Left Behind.** unabr. ed. Brooke Desserich & Keith Desserich. Read by T. Ryder Smith & Coleen Marlo. (ENG.). 2009. (978-0-06-196399-5(2), Harper Audio); (978-0-06-196718-4(1), Harper Audio) HarperCollins Pubs.

Notes Left Behind: 135 Days with Elena. unabr. ed. Brooke Desserich & Keith Desserich. Read by Keith Desserich et al. 2009. audio compact disk 29.99 (978-0-06-195282-1(6), Harper Audio) HarperCollins Pubs.

Notes of Praise. Todd Liebenow et al. 2001. audio compact disk 15.00 (978-1-58302-193-4(0)) One Way St.

Notes on Nursing: What it Is & what it Is Not. Florence Nightingale. Ed. by Michele G. Kunz. Frwd. by Michele G. Kunz. Prod. by Joseph C. Kunz Kunz, Jr. (ENG.). 2008. 17.95 (978-1-933230-16-0(9)) Dick Kean.

Notes on Nursing: What it Is & what it Is Not. Florence Nightingale. Ed. by Michele G. Kunz. Frwd. by Michele G. Kunz. Prod. by Joseph C. Kunz, Jr. (ENG.). 2008. 17.95 (978-1-933230-17-7(7)) Dick Kean.

Notes on the Child & Childhood in the Analysis of Adults. Read by Kathrin Asper. 1 cass. (Running Time: 1 hr. 30 mins.). 1990. 10.95 (978-0-7822-0009-6(5), 412) C G Jung IL.

Notes on the River Navigations of North Americ. Felix Thackeray Haig. 2009. bk. 39.95 (978-1-60785-195-0(4)) ScolPub Univ Mich Lib.

Notes to Be Left in a Cornerstone see Poetry of Benet

Notes Towards a Unified Theory of Dumping (an Essay from Things I've Learned from Women Who've Dumped Me) abr. ed. Sam Lipsyte. Read by Sam Lipsyte. Ed. by Ben Karlin. (Running Time: 15 mins.). (ENG.). 2008. 1.98 (978-1-60024-354-7(1)) Pub: Hachet Audio. Dist(s): HachBkGrp

Nothin' but Jazz: Alto Sax - Grade 3-4. Composed by James L. Hosay. Chuck Mangione & Chris Vadala. 2004. pap. bk. 14.95 (978-90-431-1883-5(4), 9043118834) H Leonard.

Nothin' but Jazz: Trumpet - Grade 3-4. Vincent DiMartino. (ENG.). 2004. pap. bk. 14.95 (978-90-431-1882-8(6), 9043118826) Pub: de Haske Pubns NLD. Dist(s): H Leonard

Nothing but Change see Richard Eberhart Reading His Poetry

Nothing but the Blood. Contrib. by Swift. (Mastertrax Ser.). 2006. audio compact disk 9.98 (978-5-558-02876-8(9)) Rocket.

Nothing but the Blues. Bert Konowitz. 1 CD. (ENG.). 2000. audio compact disk 10.00 (978-0-7390-0872-0(2), 14485) Alfred Pub.

Nothing but the Night, unabr. ed. Bill Pronzini. Read by Brian O'Neill. 6 vols. (Running Time: 8 hrs. 30 mins.). (Chivers Sound Library American Collections). 2000. bk. 54.95 (978-0-7927-2312-7(0), CSL 201, Chivers Sound Lib) AudioGO.
Nick Hendryx rides the night, comfortable & in control, searching for the man who lost control of his car & slammed Annalisa Hendryx into a coma. Cam Gallagher fears the night & the memories it brings, the sounds & images of the anger & death that followed it into his home in California. The lives of Gallagher & Hendryx have taken separate courses; their roads will cross & cross again, with increasing threat, in the nights they begin to share.

Nothing but the Truth. Voddie Baucham, Jr. (YA). 2002. audio compact disk 15.00 (978-0-633-09034-0(4)) LifeWay Christian.

Nothing but the Truth. abr. ed. John Lescroart. Read by David Colacci. (Running Time: 6 hrs.). (Dismas Hardy Ser.: No. 6). 2009. audio compact disk 24.99 (978-1-4418-2536-0(3), 9781441825360, BACD) Brilliance Audio.

Nothing but the Truth. abr. ed. John Lescroart. Read by David Colacci. (Running Time: 6 hrs.). (Dismas Hardy Ser.: No. 6). 2010. audio compact disk 14.99 (978-1-4418-2537-7(1), 9781441825377, BCD Value Price) Brilliance Audio.

Nothing but the Truth. unabr. ed. John Lescroart. Read by David Colacci. (Running Time: 16 hrs.). (Dismas Hardy Ser.: No. 6). 2009. 24.99 (978-1-4418-0035-0(2), 9781441800350, Brilliance MP3); 39.97 (978-1-4418-0036-7(0), 9781441800367, Brinc Audio MP3 Lib); 24.99 (978-1-4418-0037-4(9), 9781441800374, BAD); 39.97 (978-1-4418-0038-1(7), 9781441800381, BADLE); audio compact disk 34.99 (978-1-4418-0033-6(6), 9781441800336, Bril Audio CD Unabri); audio compact disk 99.97 (978-1-4418-0034-3(4), 9781441800343, BriAudCD Unabrid) Brilliance Audio.

Nothing but the Truth: Level 4. George Kershaw. Contrib. by Philip Prowse. (Running Time: 2 hrs. 15 mins.). (Cambridge English Readers Ser.). (ENG.). 1999. 15.75 (978-0-521-65622-1(2)) Cambridge U Pr.

Nothing but Worship. Contrib. by New Life Community Choir & John P. Kee. 2007. audio compact disk 17.98 (978-5-557-71744-1(7), Verity) Brentwood Music.

Nothing Down: How to Buy Real Estate with Little or No Money Down. Robert G. Allen. Intro. by A. E. Whyte. 1 cass. (Running Time: 47 min.). (Listen & Learn USA Ser.). 8.95 (978-0-88684-007-5(4)) Listen USA.
Explains how to successfully invest in real estate.

Nothing down for the 2000s: Dynamic New Wealth Strategies in Real Estate. abr. ed. Robert G. Allen. Read by John Dossett. 2004. 17.95 (978-0-7435-4320-0(3)) Pub: S&S Audio. Dist(s): S and S Inc

Nothing Else Matters. Swami Amar Jyoti. 2 cass. (Running Time: 3 hrs.). 1981. 12.95 (C-29) Truth Consciousness.
Devotion, dedication & love for God. Making our motives crystal clear. Instead of techniques, opening the heart, living by the Truth.

Nothing Gold Can Stay. Dana Stabenow. Read by Marguerite Gavin. (Liam Campbell Mystery Ser.: Bk. 3). 2000. audio compact disk 64.00 (978-0-7366-6301-4(0)) Books on Tape.

Nothing Gold Can Stay. collector's unabr. ed. Dana Stabenow. Read by Marguerite Gavin. 7 cass. (Running Time: 10 hrs. 30 min.). (Liam Campbell Mystery Ser.: No. 3). 2000. 56.00 (978-0-7366-5647-4(2)) Books on Tape.
A few years after losing his wife & young son in a tragic accident, Alaska state trooper Liam Campbell has finally begun to make a new life in Newenham, a remote fishing village of proud, independent natives where the currents of loyalty, fear & violence run deep. Campbell's latest investigation into a seemingly routine homicide a robbery gone bad becomes something else when the first murder is followed by a second ... then a third. Soon a chilling pattern begins to emerge a twisting path that leads him back through the years & into the sights of a diabolical killer whose hidden agenda could have fatal consequences for Campbell & those he loves.

Nothing Gold Can Stay. unabr. ed. Dana Stabenow. Read by Marguerite Gavin. 8 CDs. (Running Time: 12 hrs.). (Liam Campbell Mystery Ser.: No. 3). 2001. audio compact disk 64.00 Books on Tape.

Nothing Gold Can Stay. unabr. ed. Dana Stabenow. Read by Marguerite Gavin. 6 cass. (Running Time: 9 hrs.). (Liam Campbell Mystery Ser.: Bk. 3). 2001. 29.95 (978-0-7366-5695-5(2)) Books on Tape.
Alaskan state trooper Liam Campbell finds himself in the sights of a diabolical killer with a hidden agenda.

***Nothing Happens until It Happens to You: A Novel Without Pay, Perks, or Privileges.** unabr. ed. T. M. Shine. (Running Time: 13 hrs. 30 mins. 0 sec.). (ENG.). 2010. 19.99 (978-1-4001-6913-9(5)); 15.99 (978-1-4001-8913-7(6)); audio compact disk 29.99 (978-1-4001-1913-4(8)) Pub: Tantor Media. Dist(s): IngramPubServ

(978-0-9677017-1-4(6)); audio compact disk 19.95 (978-0-9677017-2-1(4)) Images Co.
Science Fiction short stories in CD format (various authors).

Novacom Saga: 10 Hours of Action-Packed Audio Drama. Created by Focus on the Family Staff & AIO Team Staff. (Adventures in Odyssey Ser.). (ENG.). (J). 2009. audio compact disk 49.99 (978-1-58997-541-5(3), Tyndale Ent) Tyndale Hse.

Novel. unabr. ed. James A. Michener. Read by Alexander Adams. 10 cass. (Running Time: 15 hrs.). 1991. 80.00 (978-0-7366-2019-2(2), 2835) Books on Tape.
"The Novel," while different, does not disappoint. Actually it is four novels (or novellas) each told by a different person: author, editor, critic & reader. Cumulatively it's the story of how a novel is created today, from inception to consumption. It's also an inside look at the publishing industry & what makes it tick.

Novel: New Realities, New Illusions. Daniel Stern. 1 cass. (Running Time: 39 min.). 1968. 11.95 (23217) J Norton Pubs.
Stern, the author of many books, maintains that the novel is in a fix today despite many fascinating writers. He also reads two of his short stories.

Novel Look at the Novel: A Light & Enlightening Lecture by Dr. Elliot Engel, Vol. 57. Featuring Elliot Engel. (Running Time: 57 minutes). 2001. bk. 15.00 (978-1-890123-50-5(1)) Media Cnslts.

Novel Predictions: Is Fiction Fact? Maria K. Simms. 1 cass. (Running Time: 1 hr. 30 mins.). 8.95 (427) Am Fed Astrologers.
90 degree wheel used in events from novels.

Novel Professions: Interested Disinterest & the Making of the Professional in the Victorian Novel. Jennifer Ruth. (Victorian Critical Interventions Ser.). 2006. audio compact disk 9.95 (978-0-8142-9092-7(2)) Pub: Ohio St U Pr. Dist(s): Chicago Distribution Ctr

Novel System. Ed. by Marco A. V. Bitetto. 1 cass. (Running Time: 1 hr.). 1999. (978-1-58578-089-1(8)) Inst of Cybernetics.

Novel Writers Toolkit CD Set: 6 1/2 Hour CD Collection. Bob Mayer. (ENG.). 2009. 25.00 (978-0-9842575-1-5(9)) Who Dares.

***Novelas de la Dinastia Ming.** abr. ed. Read by Santiago Munevar. (SPA.). 2009. audio compact disk 17.00 (978-958-8318-96-7(3)) Pub: Yoyo Music COL. Dist(s): YoYoMusic

Novelas Ejemplares. unabr. ed. Miguel de Cervantes. Read by Santiago Munevar. 3 CDs. (SPA.). 2003. audio compact disk 17.00 (978-958-8218-27-4(6)) YoYoMusic.

Novelette see Dylan Thomas Reads the Poetry of W. B. Yeats & Others

Novelists & Dramatists. Lawrence A. Williams. 1 cass. (Running Time: 1 hr.). 8.95 (600) Am Fed Astrologers.
The chart shows in the writing.

Novello-Stylistic Etudes: Piano. 1 cass. (Running Time: 1 hr. 30 mins.). 1995. 26.95 (978-0-89724-949-2(6), Warner Bro) Alfred Pub.

Novels Theme: Reader's Theater Classics Set A Read Aloud Think Aloud CD Rom. Compiled by Benchmark Education Staff. 2007. audio compact disk 10.00 (978-1-4108-8554-8(2)) Benchmark Educ.

Novelty Christmas Songs: Top Anthems from the Lighter Side of Christmas. Contrib. by Various Artists. (ENG.). 2008. audio compact disk 24.95 (978-5-557-38262-5(3), Brentwood-Benson Music) Brentwood Music.

***November Blues.** collector's unabr. ed. Sharon M. Draper. Narrated by J. D. Jackson. 8 CDs. (Running Time: 9 hrs.). (YA). (gr. 8 up). 2009. audio compact disk 41.95 (978-1-4361-4789-7(1)) Recorded Bks.

***November Blues.** unabr. ed. Sharon M. Draper. Narrated by J. D. Jackson. 8 cass. (Running Time: 9 hrs.). (YA). (gr. 8 up). 2009. 56.75 (978-1-4361-4780-4(8)); audio compact disk 87.75 (978-1-4361-4785-9(9)) Recorded Bks.

November of the Heart. abr. ed. LaVyrle Spencer. Read by Barbara Rush. 2 cass. (Running Time: 3 hrs.). 2001. 18.00 (978-1-59040-151-4(4), Phoenix Audio) Pub: Amer Intl Pub. Dist(s): PerseuPGW

November Surf see Poetry of Robinson Jeffers

Novenas with Music. Lawrence Lovasik & Sheldon Cohen. 1 cass. (Running Time: 1 hr.). 1990. 8.95 (978-0-914070-69-6(X), 313) ACTA Pubns.
Four of the most popular novenas with original music by Sheldon Cohen for congregational or individual use.

Novice. Trudi Canavan. Read by Richard Aspel. (Running Time: 18 hrs. 40 mins.). (Black Magician Trilogy). 2009. 114.99 (978-1-74214-198-5(6), 9781742141985) Pub: Bolinda Pubng AUS. Dist(s): Bolinda Pub Inc

Novice. unabr. ed. Trudi Canavan. Read by Richard Aspel. (Running Time: 18 hrs. 40 mins.). (Black Magician Trilogy). 2008. audio compact disk 54.95 (978-1-921415-68-5(1), 9781921415685) Pub: Bolinda Pubng AUS. Dist(s): Bolinda Pub Inc

Novio Robado. Fabiola Franco. 59.95 (978-0-8219-3634-4(4)) EMC-Paradigm.

Novio Robado. Fabiola Franco. 3 cass. (Running Time: 4 hrs. 30 mins.). (SPA.). pap. bk. 49.95 (SSP110) J Norton Pubs.
Recorded by native professional actors, this short-episode thriller on the intermediate level, in a radio-play format, is especially created to develop your listening comprehension skills. Accompanying book provides a transcript of the recording, exercises & vocabulary.

Novus Ordo Seclorum: The Intellectual Origins of the Constitution. unabr. ed. Forrest McDonald. Read by Daniel Laurence. 7 cass. (Running Time: 10 hrs.). 1989. 49.95 (978-0-7861-0030-9(3), 1029) Blckstn Audio.
Explains both how & why the events which occurred in Philadelphia in September 1787 ushered in "a new order" in human affairs.

***Now.** unabr. ed. Morris Gleitzman. Read by Mary-Anne Fahey. (Running Time: 3 hrs. 26 mins.). (J). 2010. audio compact disk 54.95 (978-1-74214-736-9(4), 9781742147369) Pub: Bolinda Pubng AUS. Dist(s): Bolinda Pub Inc

Now! unabr. ed. M. Raymond. Read by Al Covaia. 9 cass. 36.95 set. (939) Ignatius Pr.
Fr. Raymond's appeal to Christians asking that we take responsibility for our spiritual selves, now!.

Now - Loved. C. L. Productions Staff. 1 cass. (Running Time: 50 min.). 1995. (AA2900) Credence Commun.
This tape is deeply Christian, not only in the use of scripture, but in the underlying theological structure. It is also a superb meditation tape.

Now Am Found: Matt. 18:21-35. Ed Young. 1988. 4.95 (978-0-7417-1666-8(6), 666) Win Walk.

***Now & Always.** unabr. ed. Lori Copeland. (Running Time: 7 hrs. 35 mins. 0 sec.). (ENG.). 2009. 13.99 (978-0-310-77168-5(4)) Zondervan.

Now & Ben: The Modern Inventions of Benjamin Franklin. Gene Barretta. 1 CD. (Running Time: 13 mins.). (J). (gr. 2-5). 2007. bk. 29.95 (978-0-8045-4175-6(2)); bk. 27.95 (978-0-8045-6952-1(5)) Spoken Arts.
What would you do if you lived in a community without a library, hospital, or fire department? If you were Benjamin Franklin, you'd set up these organizations. He also designed the lightning rod, suggested the idea for daylight savings, and even invented bifocals - all inspired by his common sense and intelligence. in this informative book, Gene Barretta brings Mr. Franklin to life as one of the most influential figures in American history.

Now & Forever. Anita Stansfield. 2 cass. (Running Time: 3 hrs.). (First Love Ser.). 1996. 11.98 (978-1-55503-911-0(1), 07001304) Covenant Comms.
A romantic sequel to "First Love & Forever" & "First Love, Second Chances". Feel all the yearning, intensity, & searching for truth that this family experiences. Sometimes blessings come only after an exceptional trial of one's faith.

Now & Forevermore. Keith Christopher. 2000. 75.00 (978-0-633-00671-6(8)); 11.98 (978-0-633-00669-3(6)); audio compact disk 85.00 (978-0-633-00672-3(6)); audio compact disk 16.98 (978-0-633-00670-9(X)) LifeWay Christian.

Now & Then. Contrib. by Steven Curtis Chapman. 2006. audio compact disk 19.99 (978-5-558-10134-8(2)) Pt of Grace Ent.

Now & Then. unabr. ed. Robert B. Parker. Read by Joe Mantegna. 5 CDs. (Running Time: 19800 sec.). (Spenser Ser.). (ENG.). 2007. audio compact disk 29.95 (978-0-7393-3995-4(8), Random AudioBks); audio compact disk 50.00 (978-1-4159-4319-9(2), BksonTape) Pub: Random Audio Pubg. Dist(s): Random
Spenser knows something's amiss the moment Dennis Doherty walks into his office. The guy's aggressive yet wary, in the way men frightened for their marriages always are. So when Doherty asks Spenser to investigate his wife Jordan's abnormal behavior, Spenser agrees. A job's a job, after all. Not surprisingly, Spenser catches Jordan with another man, tells Dennis what he's found out, and considers the case closed. But a couple of days later, all hell breaks loose, and three people are dead. This isn't just a marital affair gone bad. Spenser is in the middle of a hornet's nest of trouble, and he has to get out of it without getting stung. With Hawk watching his back and gun-for-hire Vinnie Morris providing extra cover, Spenser delves into a complicated and far-reaching operation: Jordan's former lover Perry Alderson is the leader of a group that helps sponsor terrorists. The Boston P.I. will use all his connections - both above and below the law - to uncover the truth behind Alderson's antigovernment organization. Alderson doesn't like Spenser poking around his business, so he decides to get to him through Susan Silverman. But what Alderson doesn't realize is that Spenser will do anything to keep Susan out of harm's way; nothing will keep him from the woman he loves.

***Now & Then.** unabr. ed. Jacqueline Sheehan. (Running Time: 12 hrs.). 2011. audio compact disk 29.99 (978-1-4418-6630-1(2), 9781441866301, Bril Audio CD Unabri) Brilliance Audio.

Now & Then: From Coney Island to Here. unabr. collector's ed. Joseph Heller. Read by Michael Kramer. 6 cass. (Running Time: 9 hrs.). 1998. 48.00 (978-0-7366-4234-7(X), 4740) Books on Tape.
A glimpse into the creative process of a major American writer.

***Now Build A Great Business.** unabr. ed. Brian Tracy & Mark Thompson. Read by Brian Tracy. (Running Time: 5 hrs.). (ENG.). 2011. audio compact disk & audio compact disk 29.98 (978-1-59659-548-4(5), GildAudio) Pub: Gildan Media. Dist(s): HachBkGrp

Now by the Path I Climbed I Journey Back see Poetry of Edna St. Vincent Millay

Now, Discover Your Strengths: How to Develop Your Talents & Those of the People You Manage. Marcus Buckingham & Donald O. Clifton. Narrated by Rick Rohan. 5 cass. (Running Time: 7 hrs. 15 mins.). 45.00 (978-0-7887-9453-7(1)) Recorded Bks.

Now, Discover Your Strengths: How to Develop Your Talents & Those of the People You Manage. abr. ed. Marcus Buckingham & Donald O. Clifton. Read by Marcus Buckingham. 3 CDs. (Running Time: 30 hrs. 0 mins. 0 sec.). (ENG.). 2001. audio compact disk 25.00 (978-0-7435-1814-7(4), Sound Ideas) Pub: S&S Audio. Dist(s): S and S Inc
Based on a Gallup study of over two million people who have excelled in their careers, Now, Develop Your Strengths uses a revolutionary program to help readers discover their distinct talents & strengths. The product of a twenty-five year, multimillion-dollar effort to identify the most prevalent human talents, the Strength Finder program introduces thirty-four talents or "themes" & reveals how they can best be translated into personal & career success.

Now Face to Face. unabr. ed. Karleen Koen. Read by Donada Peters. 17 cass. (Running Time: 25 hrs. 30 min.). 1997. 136.00 (978-0-7366-3543-1(2), 4190A/B) Books on Tape.
In colonial Virginia, Barbara Devane, the headstrong heroine of "Through a Glass Darkly," is a widow at 20. Her husband's death, marked by scandal, leaves her in financial & emotional ruin.

Now God Be Thanked, Pt. 1. unabr. collector's ed. John Masters. Read by Walter Zimmerman. 9 cass. (Running Time: 13 hrs. 30 min.). 1985. 72.00 (978-0-7366-0755-1(2), 1714-A) Books on Tape.
This is the first volume in a trilogy, "Loss of Eden," which depicts the impact of W.W.I on British life. It is a saga of the mingled fortunes of four families: the aristocratic Durand-Beaulieus, the industrial Strattons & Rowlands, & the reprobate Gorses.

Now God Be Thanked, Pt. 2. collector's ed. John Masters. Read by Walter Zimmerman. 9 cass. (Running Time: 13 hrs. 30 min.). (Loss of Eden Ser.). 1985. 72.00 (978-0-7366-0756-8(0), 1714-B) Books on Tape.

Now Habit: A Strategic Program for Overcoming Procrastination & Enjoying Guilt-Free Play. unabr. rev. ed. Neil A. Fiore. Read by Neil A. Fiore. (Running Time: 7 hrs.). (ENG.). 2007. audio compact disk 29.98 (978-1-59659-076-2(9), GildAudio) Pub: Gildan Media. Dist(s): HachBkGrp

***Now Habit at Work: Perform Optimally, Maintain Focus, & Ignite Motivation in Yourself & Others.** unabr. ed. Neil Fiore. Read by Erik Synnestvedt. (Running Time: 4 hrs.). (ENG.). 2010. 24.98 (978-1-59659-623-8(6), GildAudio) Pub: Gildan Media. Dist(s): HachBkGrp

***Now Habit at Work: Perform Optimally, Maintain Focus, & Ignite Motivation in Yourself & Others.** unabr. ed. Neil Fiore. Read by Sean Pratt. (Running Time: 4 hrs.). (ENG.). 2010. audio compact disk 29.98 (978-1-59659-521-7(3), GildAudio) Pub: Gildan Media. Dist(s): HachBkGrp

Now Hear This. 2nd ed. Barbara H. Foley. 4 cass. (Running Time: 6 hrs.). (ENG.). (C). 1994. 178.95 (978-0-8384-5271-4(X), 6321913, Newbury) Pub: Heinle. Dist(s): CENGAGE Learn
Presents a program which emphasizes listening in context to improve functional comprehension skills at the beginning level.

Now I Can Read. (Running Time: 45 min.). (Success Ser.). 9.98 (978-1-55909-137-4(1), 112) Randolph Tapes.

Now I Know I Am Righteous. Creflo A. Dollar. 20.00 (978-1-59089-201-5(1)) Pub: Creflo Dollar. Dist(s): STL Dist NA

Now I Lay Me down to Sleep: A Helen Bradley Mystery. unabr. ed. Patricia H. Rushford. Narrated by Cristine McMurdo-Wallis. 6 cass. (Running Time: 7 hrs. 45 mins.). 2001. 58.00 (978-0-7887-5113-4(1), K0027E7) Recorded Bks.
When journalist Helen Bradley gets an urgent request for help, her investigation will lead to medical secrets so valuable their keepers would rather kill than give them up.

Now Is the Air Made of Chiming Balls see Twentieth-Century Poetry in English, No. 1, Recordings of Poets Reading Their Own Poetry

Now Is the Hour. Hilary Green. 2007. 69.95 (978-1-84559-798-6(2)); audio compact disk 84.95 (978-1-84559-799-3(0)) Pub: Soundings Ltd GBR. Dist(s): Ulverscroft US

Now Is the Time. Prod. by Percy Gray. Contrib. by Ken Harding. 2005. audio compact disk 16.98 (978-5-558-80690-8(7)) Pt of Grace Ent.

Now Is the Time. unabr. ed. Ruth Lee. Read by Ruth Lee. 4 cass. (Running Time: 4 hrs. 2 min.). 1996. 22.95 (978-1-888988-02-4(9)) LeeWay.
Exploration of the concept of time using many different facets of our personalities & belief systems to understand why time is the only thing that keeps us all bound to earth. Includes binder.

Now Is the Time: Live at Willow Creek. Contrib. by Delirious. 2007. 18.99 (978-5-557-63296-6(4)) Pt of Grace Ent.

Now Is the Time to Open Your Heart. unabr. ed. Alice Walker. Read by Alfre Woodard. 6 CDs. (Running Time: 9 hrs.). 2004. audio compact disk 45.90 (978-1-4159-9986-8(4)) Pub: Books on Tape. Dist(s): NetLibrary CO
For many years, Alice Walker has been known for her outspoken positions against racism, sexism, and colonialism. Now, she takes her crusade into the midst of her fiction, as her protagonist (greatly resembling herself) sheds the burdens and blessings of her past to come to terms with an actuality heightened by the transcendental images of magical realism. To be purified, she must go down two rivers. First, there's the Colorado, where she takes an all-female white-water rafting trip which makes her decide to pursue celibacy. Then, there's the Amazon, where she purges her past using yage, a hallucinogenic herb which brings her closer to the World-Grandmother-Spirit. At last, she reaches a place of love and wholeness.

Now It's My Turn: A Daughter's Chronicle of Political Life. abr. ed. Mary Cheney. Read by Mary Cheney. 2006. 17.95 (978-0-7435-5578-4(3), Audioworks) Pub: S&S Audio. Dist(s): S and S Inc

Now, Let Me Tell You What I Really Think. unabr. ed. Chris Matthews. 2004. 15.95 (978-0-7435-4313-2(0)) Pub: S&S Audio. Dist(s): S and S Inc

Now May You Weep. Deborah Crombie. Read by Michael Deehy. 8 cass. (Duncan Kincaid/Gemma James Novel Ser.). 69.95 (978-0-7927-3404-8(1), CSL 729); audio compact disk 94.95 (978-0-7927-3405-5(X), SLD 729); audio compact disk 29.95 (978-0-7927-3406-2(8), CMP 729) AudioGO.

Now More Than Ever. Contrib. by Russ Taff & Bill Gaither. Prod. by Bill Gaither et al. (Gaither Gospel Ser.). 2007. audio compact disk 17.99 (978-5-557-94923-1(2)) Gaither Music Co.

Now Mourn the Space Cadet. unabr. ed. J. R. Chabot. Read by Maynard Villers. 6 cass. (Running Time: 7 hrs.). 2001. 39.95 (978-1-55686-829-0(4)) Books in Motion.
Conner Beach Detective Mickie Wilder begins gathering a list of suspects when an attractive airhead is found murdered in ritualistic fashion on a California beach.

Now One Foot, Now the Other. unabr. ed. Tomie dePaola. Read by Tomie dePaola. 1 CD. (Running Time: 11 mins.). (J). (gr. k-3). 2006. bk. 29.95 (978-0-8045-4161-9(2)); bk. 27.95 (978-0-8045-6947-7(9)) Spoken Arts.
Bobby and his grandfather, Bob, did so many things together. Then Bob suffered a stroke, and Bobby was frightened and confused until ge realized that even though Bob couldn't move or talk, he knew what was happening around him. And it was Bobby who began to help Bob with some of the things his grandfather had helped him with as a little boy. ORiginally published in 1981, Now One Foot, Now the Other lovingly and perceptively explores the relationship between a child and his grandfather in a situation experienced by many.

Now or Never: Getting down to the Business of Saving Our American Dream. unabr. ed. Jack Cafferty. Read by Dick Hill. (Running Time: 12 hrs. 0 mins. 0 sec.). (ENG.). 2009. audio compact disk 34.99 (978-1-4001-1213-5(3)); audio compact disk 24.99 (978-1-4001-6213-0(0)); audio compact disk 69.99 (978-1-4001-4213-2(X)) Pub: Tantor Media. Dist(s): IngramPubServ

***Now or Never: Why We Must Act Now to End Climate Change & Create a Sustainable Future.** unabr. ed. Tim Flannery. Narrated by Michael Page. (Running Time: 3 hrs. 30 mins.). 2009. 11.99 (978-1-4001-8386-9(3)) Tantor Media.

Now or Never: Why We Must Act Now to End Climate Change & Create a Sustainable Future. unabr. ed. Tim Flannery. Narrated by Michael Page. (Running Time: 3 hrs. 30 mins. 0 sec.). (ENG.). 2009. 19.99 (978-1-4001-6386-1(2)); audio compact disk 39.99 (978-1-4001-4386-3(1)); audio compact disk 19.99 (978-1-4001-1386-6(5)) Pub: Tantor Media. Dist(s): IngramPubServ

Now Proclaim Messiah's Birth. Perf. by Matthew Schenning. (ENG.). 2008. audio compact disk 17.99 (978-0-9786948-4-5(8)) Old Line Pub.

Now Prosperity. Creflo A. Dollar. 15.00 (978-1-59089-100-1(7)) Pub: Creflo Dollar. Dist(s): STL Dist NA

Now That I Have Cancer . . . I Am Whole: Meditations for Cancer Patients & Those Who Love Them. abr. ed. 1997. 10.95 (978-0-9658625-3-0(4)) Nght Song.

Now That the Raven Has Gone. George Bloomer. audio compact disk Whitaker Hse.

Now That the Raven Has Gone. unabr. ed. George Bloomer. 1 CD. (Running Time: 1 hr. 30 mins.). 2004. audio compact disk 14.99 (978-0-88368-884-7(0)) Pub: Whitaker Hse. Dist(s): Anchor Distributors
This message entitled derives from a message of purpose and destiny, delivered by Bishop Bloomer from Genesis chapter eight.

Now That's Funny! Joni Hilton. 1 cass. (Running Time: 1 hr. 30 mins.). 2004. 9.95 (978-1-57734-452-0(9), 06005969) Covenant Comms.
Want to feel better? Laugh.

Now the Dead Will Dance the Mambo: The Poems of Martin Espada. Martin Espada. 2 CDs. (Running Time: 2 hrs.). 2004. audio compact disk 15.95 (978-0-9728984-3-0(3)) Pub: Leapfrog Pr. Dist(s): Consort Bk Sales

Now Then. Perf. by Sundays Child. 1 cass. 1997. audio compact disk 13.99 CD. (D3004) Diamante Music Grp.
Sundays Chil lands on the Christian music scene, intent on heralding the end of grungy musical sludge, repeatedly citing their musical influences from the '80s passion rock bands - U2, The Alarm, The Choir & others. The band's new album resonates with passion & hope, all the while admissive of man's fallen nature.

Now Then Lad. Mike Pannett & Jonathan Keeble. 2009. 54.95 (978-1-84652-449-3(0)); audio compact disk 71.95 (978-1-84652-450-9(4)) Pub: Magna Story GBR. Dist(s): Ulverscroft US

Now This War Has Two Sides. Derrick Jensen. (Running Time: 1 hr. 55 mins. 0 sec.). (PM Audio Ser.). (ENG.). 2008. audio compact disk 19.99 (978-1-60486-007-8(3)) Pub: Pm Pre. Dist(s): IPG Chicago

Now Today I Decide: Confession of Faith. Alicia Knox. 2004. audio compact disk 19.95 (978-0-9762204-0-4(7)) Speaking HIS.

Now We Are Six. Poems. A. A. Milne. Read by Charles Kuralt. 1 cass. (Running Time: 1 hr. 30 mins.). (J). 8.78 Blisterpack. (PEN 86680) NewSound.
A collection of poetry. Verses about King John & the King of Peru alongside more down-to-earth fare about playing with toy trains & walking in the morning. Verses about fanciful subjcts & everyday events alike.

Now We Are Six. unabr. ed. Contrib. by Peter Dennis. (Running Time: 3600 sec.). (Winnie-the-Pooh Ser.). (J). (ps-7). 2005. audio compact disk 9.95 (978-0-7861-8194-0(X)) Blckstn Audio.

Now We Are Six. unabr. ed. Poems. A. A. Milne. Read by Peter Dennis. Illus. by Ernest H. Shepard. 1 cass. (Winnie-the-Pooh Ser.). (J). (978-1-57375-466-8(8), 71304) Audioscope.
These 35 verses have a gentle humor & playful rhythms that appeal to purists as well as Pooh-lovers-come-lately unfamiliar with the "Classic Pooh.".

Now We Are Six. unabr. ed. A. A. Milne. Read by Peter Dennis. (Running Time: 1 hr. 30 mins.). (Winnie-the-Pooh Ser.). 2005. 9.95 (978-0-7861-2931-7(X)) Blckstn Audio.

Now We Will Either Sleep, Lie Still or Dress Again see Brian Patten Reading His Poetry

Now What? The Chapman Guide to Marriage after Children. unabr. ed. Gary Chapman. Narrated by Maurice England. (Marriage Savers Ser.). (ENG.). 2007. 9.79 (978-1-60814-323-8(6)) Oasis Audio.

***Now What Do I Do? The Surprising Solution When Things Go Wrong.** Zondervan. (Running Time: 2 hrs. 2 mins. 51 sec.). (ENG.). 2010. 14.99 (978-0-310-42698-1(7)) Zondervan.

***Now You Hear It, Now You Don't.** (ENG.). 2010. audio compact disk (978-1-59171-309-8(9)) Falcon Picture.

Now You MOMbo. Interview. Nanci Olesen. Compiled by Nanci Olesen. 4 vols. (Running Time: 4 hours). 2005. audio compact disk 29.95 (978-0-9767443-0-6(9)) MOMbo Inc.
Now You MOMbo is a 4-CD set of eight half-hour audio programs to nurture, humor, and enlighten moms. Programs include: interviews with leading authors about motherhood and children, real moms discussing a variety of topics, commentaries, book reviews, and eclectic music.

Now You See Her. Cecelia Tishy. Read by Anna Fields. 6 cass. (Running Time: 8 hrs. 30 mins.). 2005. lib. bdg. 54.95 (978-0-7861-2902-7(6), 3394); audio compact disk 63.00 (978-0-7861-8276-3(8), 3394) Blckstn Audio.

Now You See Her. Cecelia Tishy. Read by Anna Fields. (Running Time: 8 hrs. 30 mins.). 2005. 27.95 (978-1-59912-559-6(5)) Iofy Corp.

***Now You See Her.** abr. ed. Joy Fielding. (Running Time: 6 hrs.). 2011. audio compact disk 26.99 (978-1-4233-6283-8(7), 9781423362838, BACD) Brilliance Audio.

Now You See Her. abr. ed. Cecelia Tishy & Whitney Otto. (ENG.). 2006. 14.98 (978-1-59483-787-6(2)) Pub: Hachet Audio. Dist(s): HachBkGrp

***Now You See Her.** unabr. ed. Joy Fielding. (Running Time: 10 hrs.). 2011. 39.97 (978-1-4233-6282-1(9), 9781423362821, BADLE); 24.99 (978-1-4233-6281-4(0), 9781423362814, BAD); 39.97 (978-1-4233-6280-7(2), 9781423362807, Brinc Audio MP3 Lib); 24.99 (978-1-4233-6279-1(9), 9781423362791, Brilliance MP3); audio compact disk 97.97 (978-1-4233-6278-4(0), 9781423362784, BriAudCD Unabrid); audio compact disk 36.99 (978-1-4233-6277-7(2), 9781423362777, Bril Audio CD Unabri) Brilliance Audio.

Now You See Her. unabr. ed. Linda Howard. Read by Laurel Lefkow. 8 vols. (Running Time: 12 hrs.). 2001. bk. 69.95 (978-0-7927-2486-5(0), CSL 375, Chivers Sound Lib) AudioGO.
A talented painter in her early thirties, Paris Sweeney has achieved enviable success; her work sells at an exclusive New York City gallery, and her popularity is at an all-time high. Life is good, and Sweeney, as she prefers to be called, is content. But lately, her dreams seem to echo a growing restlessness that has taken hold of her. Suddenly, impulsively, she falls into a night of passion with millionaire Richard Worth. Now the true dangers of her all-consuming urges are about to be revealed where Sweeney least expects - in her paintings.

***Now You See Her.** unabr. ed. James Patterson & Michael Ledwidge. (Running Time: 8 hrs.). (ENG.). 2011. 26.98 (978-1-60788-686-0(3)); audio compact disk 34.98 (978-1-60788-685-3(5)) Pub: Hachet Audio. Dist(s): HachBkGrp

Now You See Her. unabr. ed. Cecelia Tishy. Read by Anna Fields. 6 cass. (Running Time: 8 hrs. 30 mins.). 2005. reel tape 27.95 (978-0-7861-2901-0(8), E3394); audio compact disk 29.95 (978-0-7861-8277-0(6), ZE3394); audio compact disk 29.95 (978-0-7861-8319-7(5), 3394) Blckstn Audio.

Now You See Her, Set. abr. ed. Whitney Otto. 2 cass. (Running Time: 3 hrs.). 1994. 17.00 (978-1-57042-027-6(0), 4-520270) Hachet Audio.
Whitney Otto illuminates brilliantly the lives of five seemingly ordinary women. She vividly draws their dreams, their disappointments & their passions until they are transformed into five remarkable heroines - not only to be seen clearly, but never forgotten.

Now You See Me. abr. ed. Rochelle Krich. Read by Rochelle Krich. (Running Time: 14400 sec.). (Molly Blume Ser.: No. 4). 2006. audio compact disk 14.99 (978-1-59737-352-4(4), 9781597373524, BCD Value Price) Brilliance Audio.
Please enter a Synopsis.

Now You See Me. abr. unabr. ed. Rochelle Krich. Read by Deanna Hurst. (Running Time: 32400 sec.). (Molly Blume Ser.: No. 4). 2005. audio compact disk 92.25 (978-1-59600-055-1(4), 9781596000551, BACDLib Ed) Brilliance Audio.

Now You See Me. unabr. ed. Rochelle Krich. Read by Deanna Hurst. (Running Time: 9 hrs.). (Molly Blume Ser.). 2005. 39.25 (978-1-59710-932-1(0), 9781597109321, BADLE); 24.95 (978-1-59710-933-8(9), 9781597109338, BAD) Brilliance Audio.

Now You See Me. unabr. ed. Rochelle Krich. Read by Rochelle Krich. (Running Time: 32400 sec.). (Molly Blume Ser.: No. 4). 2005. audio compact disk 24.95 (978-1-59335-727-6(3), 9781593357276, Brilliance MP3); audio compact disk 34.95 (978-1-4233-0615-3(5), 9781423306153, Bril Audio CD Unabri) Brilliance Audio.
For feisty Los Angeles crime reporter Molly Blume, life is good. She is newly married (to the adoring and adorable Rabbi Zack), and her latest true-crime book is a hot seller. When an overardent fan's attentions arouse Molly's suspicion, however, her thoughts turn uneasily to stalkers. But the fan, Reuben Jastrow, swears that he desperately needs Molly's help in finding his eighteen-year-old daughter, Hadassah, who has run away from home to be with a man she met on the Internet. Molly hesitantly agrees - and immediately has regrets. For Reuben hasn't told her the whole truth. The more Molly looks for clues to the missing girl's fate, the more she wonders: Is Hadassah a random victim of a predator, or is the girl a pawn in a scheme of revenge against her family? It's a long, deadly path that stretches before Molly, a path mined with hidden passions and festering secrets. And it ends with a final twist and an unnerving truth: What we don't see can lead to danger . . . and tragedy. "The Mystery Woman who can do it all . . . Krich knows how to make conflicts between good and evil juicy." - Los Angeles Times.

Now You See Me. unabr. ed. Rochelle Krich. Read by Deanna Hurst. (Running Time: 32400 sec.). (Molly Blume Ser.: No. 4). 2005. 82.25 (978-1-59355-477-4(X), 9781593554774, BrilAudUnabridg); audio compact disk 39.25 (978-1-59335-861-7(X), 9781593358617, Brinc Audio MP3 Lib) Brilliance Audio.
Please enter a Synopsis.

Now You're Speaking My Language: Honest Communication & Deeper Intimacy for a Stronger Marriage. unabr. ed. Gary Chapman. Narrated by Gary Chapman. (ENG.). 2007. 17.49 (978-1-60814-324-5(4)); audio compact disk 24.99 (978-1-59859-290-0(4)) Oasis Audio.

Now You're Talking. unabr. ed. Joan R. Keyes & Roger Salinas. 5 cass. (Running Time: 7 hrs.). (J). (gr. 5 up). 1987. cass. & video 189.00 (978-1-55737-554-4(2), VHS003) Ed Activities.
Live-action interactive video, audiocassettes & workbook focus on communication skills.

Now You're Talking: Arabic in No Time. 1 cass. (Running Time: 90 min.). (ENG & ARA.). 1986. pap. bk. 14.95 (978-0-8120-7428-4(9)) Barron.

Now You're Talking: German in No Time. 3rd ed. Henry Strutz. 1 cass. (Running Time: 90 min.). (GER.). 2003. pap. bk. 14.95 (978-0-7641-7354-7(5)) Barron.

Now You're Talking: Spanish in No Time. 2nd ed. Heywood Wald. 1 cass. (Running Time: 1 hr. 30 mins.). (SPA & ENG.). 1992. pap. bk. 13.95 (978-0-8120-7884-8(5)) Barron.
Lists over 1500 popular expressions & key words & features native speakers who emphasize practical everyday language travelers will need to get around in a foreign country.

Nowhere Girl. unabr. ed. Angela Huth. Read by Angela Huth. 6 cass. (Running Time: 6 hrs. 45 min.). (Isis Ser.). (J). 1996. 54.95 (978-0-7531-0072-1(X), 961205) Pub: ISIS Lrg Prnt GBR. Dist(s): Ulverscroft US
Estranged from Jonathon, her second husband, Clare Lyall is less sure than ever about the role men should play in her life. When she meets Joshua at a party, she is impressed when he stubs his cigarette out on his thumb, & swayed further by the advice of her new friend, Mrs. Fox. "Take a lover, she says, "it's better to have a lover when you're young than neurosis when you're old.

Nowhere Is a Place. Bernice L. McFadden. Read by Myra Lucretia Taylor. 6 cass. (Running Time: 32820 sec.). 2006. 54.95 (978-0-7927-3908-1(6), CSL 906); audio compact disk 74.95 (978-0-7927-3909-8(4), SLD 906) AudioGO.

Nowhere to Call Home. Cynthia C. DeFelice. Read by Alyssa Bresnahan. 4 cass. (Running Time: 5 hrs. 15 mins.). (YA). 2000. pap. bk. & stu. ed. 60.00 (978-0-7887-4179-1(9), 41113); stu. ed. 205.30 (978-0-7887-4180-7(2), 47106) Recorded Bks.
Twelve-year-old Frances loses her home when the stock market crashes & Father shoots himself. Refusing to live with her aunt, Frances hops a train with the hoboes. But she quickly discovers there is a high price to pay for her newfound independence.

Nowhere to Call Home. unabr. ed. Cynthia C. DeFelice. Narrated by Alyssa Bresnahan. 4 pieces. (Running Time: 5 hrs. 15 mins.). (gr. 6 up). 2000. 37.00 (978-0-7887-4025-1(3), 96146E7) Recorded Bks.

Nowhere to Hide, Level 1. 2 cass. (Running Time: 1 hr. 30 mins.). (SmartReader Ser.). (J). 1999. pap. bk. & tchr. ed. 19.95 (978-0-7887-0770-4(1), 79350T3) Recorded Bks.
Confined to a wheelchair, Susie Lewis feels helpless when a ruthless killer breaks into her apartment. Desperately, she looks for a way to keep away from him & call for help.

Nowhere to Hide, Level 2. 2 cass. (Running Time: 1 hr. 30 mins.). (SmartReader Ser.). (J). 1999. pap. bk. & tchr. ed. 19.95 (978-0-7887-0117-7(7), 79305T3) Recorded Bks.

Nowhere, TX. unabr. abr. ed. David L. Robbins & Ralph Compton. 4 CDs. (Running Time: 5 hrs.). (ENG.). 2004. audio compact disk 22.95 (978-1-56511-851-5(0), 1565118510) Pub: HighBridge. Dist(s): Workman Pub
In a lawless, godless territory known as No Man's Land, Black Jack Shelton and his gang have the run of the new town of Nowhere, until Chick Storm and his riders are called in to take a stand. Chick knows right from wrong well enough to understand that sometimes a man has to let his guns speak for themselves.

Nozze Di Figaro see Marriage of Figaro

***NPR: The First 40 Years.** unabr. ed. NPR Staff. (ENG.). 2010. audio compact disk 29.95 (978-1-61573-103-9(2), 1615731032) Pub: HighBridge. Dist(s): Workman Pub

NPR Classic Driveway Moments: Radio Stories that Won't Let You Go. unabr. ed. Contrib. by Michele Norris. 2010. audio compact disk 22.95 (978-1-61573-038-4(9), 161573038X) Pub: HighBridge. Dist(s): Workman Pub

NPR Driveway Moments All about Animals: Radio Stories That Won't Let You Go. abr. unabr. ed. Contrib. by Steve Inskeep. (Running Time: 5400 sec.). (ENG.). 2007. audio compact disk 22.95 (978-1-59887-511-9(6), 1598875116) Pub: HighBridge. Dist(s): Workman Pub

NPR Driveway Moments: Baseball: Radio Stories That Won't Let You Go. Contrib. by Neal Conan. (ENG.). (J). 2009. 39.99 (978-1-60775-724-5(9)) Find a World.

NPR Driveway Moments Baseball: Radio Stories That Won't Let You Go. unabr. ed. Told to Neal Conan. (Running Time: 4500 sec.). (ENG., 2008. audio compact disk 22.95 (978-1-59887-587-4(6), 1598875876) Pub: HighBridge. Dist(s): Workman Pub

NPR Driveway Moments for Dads: Radio Stories That Won't Let You Go. Created by Highbridge Audio Staff. Contrib. by Scott Simon. (Running Time: 6300 sec.). (Original radio broadcast; 1. 75 hours on 2 CDs Ser.). (ENG.). 2007. audio compact disk 22.95 (978-1-59887-100-5(5), 1598871005) Pub: HighBridge. Dist(s): Workman Pub

NPR Driveway Moments Moms: Radio Stories That Won't Let You Go. unabr. ed. Contrib. by Peter Sagal. (ENG., 2009. audio compact disk 22.95 (978-1-59887-730-4(5), 1598877305) Pub: HighBridge. Dist(s): Workman Pub

NPR Favorite Driveway Moments: Radio Stories That Won't Let You Go. Read by Ensemble cast. Contrib. by RenÃ(c)e Montagne & Renee Montagne. (ENG.). 2009. audio compact disk 22.95 (978-1-59887-894-3(8), 1598878948) Pub: HighBridge. Dist(s): Workman Pub

NPR Funniest Driveway Moments: Radio Stories That Won't Let You Go. Contrib. by Robert Krulwich. (Playaway Adult Fiction Ser.). (ENG.). 2009. 39.99 (978-1-60775-725-2(7)) Find a World.

NPR Funniest Driveway Moments: Radio Stories That Won't Let You Go. unabr. ed. Contrib. by Robert Krulwich. (Running Time: 8100 sec.). (ENG., 2008. audio compact disk 22.95 (978-1-59887-624-6(4), 1598876244) Pub: HighBridge. Dist(s): Workman Pub

NPR Holiday Favorites. David Sedaris et al. (ENG.). 2009. 39.99 (978-1-60812-718-4(4)) Find a World.

***NPR Holiday Favorites.** unabr. ed. NPR Staff. Contrib. by Susan Stamberg. (ENG.). 2010. audio compact disk 14.99 (978-1-61573-512-9(7), 1615735127) Pub: HighBridge. Dist(s): Workman Pub

NPR More Funniest Driveway Moments: Radio Stories that Won't Let You Go. unabr. ed. Contrib. by Robert Krulwich. (ENG.). 2010. audio compact disk 22.95 (978-1-61573-037-7(0), 1615730370) Pub: HighBridge. Dist(s): Workman Pub

NPR Road Trips: Family Vacations: Stories That Take You Away. unabr. ed. Intro. by Noah Adams. 1 CD. (Running Time: 1 hr.). 2010. audio compact disk 14.95 (978-1-61573-039-1(7), 1615730397) Pub: HighBridge. Dist(s): Workman Pub

NPR Sunday Puzzles. unabr. ed. Will Shortz & Liane Hansen. 1 CD. (Running Time: 1 hr. 15 mins.). (ENG.). 2009. audio compact disk 14.95 (978-1-59887-893-6(X), 159887893X) Pub: HighBridge. Dist(s): Workman Pub

NRB Issues for the Nineteen Nineties: National Association of Evangelicals, 47th Annual Convention, Columbus, Ohio, March 7-9, 1989. Richard Bott, Sr. 1 cass. (Workshops Ser.: No. 22-Wednesd). 1989. 4.25; 4.00 Nat Assn Evan.

NRSV New Testament. unabr. ed. Narrated by Marquis Laughlin. (Running Time: 68400 sec.). (ENG.). 2005. audio compact disk 49.99 (978-1-59859-095-1(2)) Oasis Audio.

***NSF Standards: As Referenced in the 2009 IPC(r)/IRC(r)/UPC.** ICC/NSF. 2009. audio compact disk 881.00 (978-1-58001-920-0(X)) Int Code Counc.

NSTI Nanotech: Cleantech 2007: Technical Proceedings: Nanotech 2007, Vol. 1-4: Santa Clara, May 20-24 2007. Created by CRC Press Staff. 2007. ring bd. 525.00 (978-1-4200-6349-3(9)) Pub: CRC Pr. Dist(s): Taylor and Fran

Nsync X-Posed. Chrome Dreams. (ENG., 2002. audio compact disk 14.95 (978-1-84240-156-9(4)) Pub: Chrome Dreams GBR. Dist(s): IPG Chicago

NTC's American Idioms Dictionary. Spears. audio compact disk 20.00 (978-0-658-00129-1(9)) M-H Contemporary.

NTE (New Technology English) Bk. 1: Handling Social Conventions, Set Edwin T. Cornelius. Illus. by John Odam. (New Technology English Ser.: Vol. 4). 1984. pap. bk. 25.00 (978-0-89209-113-3(4)) Pace Grp Intl.

NTE (New Technology English) Bk. 2: Interacting in Social & Business Settings, Set. Edwin T. Cornelius. Illus. by John Odam. (New Technology English Ser.: Vol. 5). 1984. pap. bk. 25.00 (978-0-89209-114-0(2)) Pace Grp Intl.

NTE (New Technology English) Bk. 3: Expressing & Finding Out Attitudes, Set. Edwin T. Cornelius. Illus. by John Odam. (New Technology English Ser.: Vol. 6). 1984. pap. bk. 25.00 (978-0-89209-115-7(0)) Pace Grp Intl.

NTE (New Technology English) Bk. 4: Extending Personal Abilities, Set. Edwin T. Cornelius. Illus. by John Odam. (New Technology English Ser.: Vol. 7). 1984. pap. bk. 25.00 (978-0-89209-116-4(9)) Pace Grp Intl.

NTE Progress & Performance, Set. Edwin T. Cornelius. Illus. by John Odam. (New Technology English Ser.: Vol. 10). 1984. 36.00 (978-0-89209-158-4(4)) Pace Grp Intl.

Nubs: The True Story of a Mutt, a Marine & a Miracle. unabr. ed. Brian Dennis et al. Read by Christian Rummel. (Running Time: 20 mins.). (ENG.). 2009. 17.98 (978-1-60024-871-9(3)) Pub: Hachet Audio. Dist(s): HachBkGrp

Nuclear Bomb & the Fate of God. Read by Wolfgang Giegerich. 1 cass. (Running Time: 1 hr. 30 mins.). 1985. 10.95 (978-0-7822-0079-9(6), 158) C G Jung IL.

Nuclear Disaster at Chernobyl. Robin Cruise. Narrated by Larry A. McKeever. (Disaster Ser.). (J). 2003. audio compact disk 14.95 (978-1-58659-286-8(6)) Artesian.

Nuclear Disaster at Chernobyl. unabr. ed. Robin Cruise. Narrated by Larry A. McKeever. 1 cass. (Running Time: 40 min.). (Take Ten Ser.). (J). (gr. 3-12). 2003. 10.95 (978-1-58659-027-7(8), 54112) Artesian.

Nuclear Holocaust. unabr. ed. Helen Caldicott. 1 cass. (Running Time: 1 hr.). 10.95 (978-0-8045-1155-1(1), SAC 1155) Spoken Arts.
This Pediatrician Presents the Dangers of Both the Nuclear Arms Race & the Use of Nuclear Power. Seen from the Perspective of an Expert on Human Life, She Presents the Possibilities for Human Survival.

***Nuclear Jellyfish.** unabr. ed. Tim Dorsey. Read by Oliver Wyman. (ENG.). 2009. (978-0-06-172978-2(7)); (978-0-06-172979-9(5)) HarperCollins Pubs.

Nuclear Jellyfish. unabr. ed. Tim Dorsey. Read by Oliver Wyman. (Serge Storms Ser.: Bk. 11). 2009. audio compact disk 34.99 (978-0-06-171263-0(9), Harper Audio) HarperCollins Pubs.

Nuclear Jellyfish. unabr. ed. Tim Dorsey. Narrated by Oliver Wyman. 8 cass. (Running Time: 9 hrs. 30 mins.). (Serge Storms Ser.: Bk. 11). 2009. 67.75 (978-1-4361-7471-8(6)); audio compact disk 39.95 (978-1-4361-7473-2(2)); audio compact disk 92.75 (978-1-4361-7472-5(4)) Recorded Bks.

Nuclear Jellyfish. unabr. ed. Tim Dorsey. Narrated by Oliver Wyman. (Running Time: 9 hrs. 30 mins.). (Serge Storms Ser.: Bk. 11). 2009. 56.75 (978-1-4361-9251-4(X)) Recorded Bks.

Nuclear Jihadist: The True Story of the Man Who Sold the World's Most Dangerous Secrets... & How We Could Have Stopped Him. unabr. ed. Douglas Frantz & Catherine Collins. Read by Bob Craig. (Running Time: 16 hrs.). (ENG.). 2007. 26.98 (978-1-60024-130-7(1), Twelve) Pub: GrandCentral. Dist(s): HachBkGrp

Nuclear Power in the Energy Crisis. Peter Beckmann. 1 cass. (Running Time: 1 hr. 1 min.). 11.95 (990) J Norton Pubs.
Beckmann defends nuclear power as the safest source of energy, claiming both critics & advocates are wrong in comparing risks to benefits, rather than risks to risks. All the major ways of producing electricity, he maintains, take a huge toll in human lives, with just the transportation of coal accounting for many deaths & injuries.

Nudge: Improving Decisions about Health, Wealth, & Happiness. unabr. ed. Richard H. Thaler & Cass R. Sunstein. Read by Sean Pratt. (Running Time: 10 hrs. 30 mins.). (ENG.). 2008. 24.98 (978-1-59659-254-4(0), GildAudio) Pub: Gildan Media. Dist(s): HachBkGrp

Nudge: Improving Decisions about Health, Wealth, & Happiness. unabr. ed. Richard H. Thaler & Cass R. Sunstein. Read by Sean Pratt. (Running Time: 11 hrs.). (ENG.). 2009. audio compact disk 39.98 (978-1-59659-270-4(2)) Pub: Gildan Media. Dist(s): HachBkGrp

Nudge: Improving Decisions about Health, Wealth, & Happiness. unabr. rev. ed. Richard H. Thaler & Cass R. Sunstein. Read by Sean Pratt. (Running Time: 10 hrs. 30 mins.). (ENG.). 2009. 29.98 (978-1-59659-367-1(9), GildAudio) Pub: Gildan Media. Dist(s): HachBkGrp

Nuestra casa de Adobe. (Saludos Ser.: Vol. 2). (SPA.). (gr. 2-3). 10.00 (978-0-7635-5885-7(0)) Rigby Educ.

Nuestro Mundo: Grades K-2. (Nuevos Horizontes Ser.). (SPA.). 16.00 (978-1-56014-498-4(X)) Santillana.

Nuestro Mundo: La Ciberedicion. 2003. audio compact disk (978-0-618-08639-9(0)) Holt McDoug.

Nueva Tierra: Un Despertar al Proposito de Su Vida. Eckhart Tolle. 2008. audio compact disk 24.95 (978-1-933499-77-2(X)) Fonolibro Inc.

Nueva Vida. unabr. ed. D'Novo & Jose Medero. (SPA.). 2000. 4.99 (978-0-8297-2778-4(7)) Pub: Vida Pubs. Dist(s): Zondervan

Nueva Vida. unabr. ed. Jose Medero. 2000. audio compact disk 14.99 (978-0-8297-2779-1(5)) Zondervan.

Nuevas Fronteras: Gramatica y Conversacion. 3rd ed. Nancy Levy-Konesky. (SPA.). (C). 1996. bk. 61.00 (978-0-03-013403-6(X)) Harcourt.

Nuevas Vistas, Course 1. Holt, Rinehart and Winston Staff. 2001. audio compact disk 103.00 (978-0-03-064394-1(5)) Holt McDoug.

Nuevas Vistas, Course 2. 3rd ed. Holt, Rinehart and Winston Staff. 2002. audio compact disk 103.00 (978-0-03-064404-7(6)) Holt McDoug.

Nuevas Vistas, Set. 6th ed. Holt, Rinehart and Winston Staff. (SPA.). 2004. audio compact disk 105.06 (978-0-03-074154-8(8)) Holt McDoug.

Nuevo Aleman sin Esfuerzo. 4 CDs. (Running Time: 4 hrs.).Tr. of German with Ease. (SPA.). 2000. pap. bk. 95.00 (978-2-7005-1067-6(4)) Pub: Assimil FRA. Dist(s): Distribks Inc

Nuevo Frances sin Esfuerzo. 1 cass. (Running Time: 1 hr.).Tr. of French with Ease. (FRE & SPA.). 2000. bk. 75.00 (978-2-7005-1300-4(2)); pap. bk. 95.00 (978-2-7005-1065-2(8)) Pub: Assimil FRA. Dist(s): Distribks Inc

Nuevo Frances Sin Esfuerzo, Set. Anthony Bulger & Jean L. Cherel. Tr. by Felix J. Martinez. (Sin Esfuerzo Ser.).Tr. of French with Ease. 1983. bk. 75.00 (978-2-7005-1146-8(8)) Pub: Assimil FRA. Dist(s): Distribks Inc

Nuevo Ingles sin Esfuerzo. 1 cass. (Running Time: 1 hr. 30 mins.). (SPA & ENG.). 1999. 75.00 Distribks Inc.

Nuevo Ingles sin Esfuerzo. Equipo de Expertos 2100 Staff. 4 cass. (Running Time: 4 hrs.).Tr. of English with Ease. (SPA.). 2000. 75.00 (978-2-7005-1301-1(0)) Pub: Assimil FRA. Dist(s): Distribks Inc

Nuevo Italiano sin Esfuerzo. 4 cass. (Running Time: 6 hrs.).Tr. of Italian with Ease. (SPA.). pap. bk. 75.00 (978-2-7005-1302-8(9)) Pub: Assimil FRA. Dist(s): Distribks Inc

Nuevo Italiano sin Esfuerzo. 4 CDs. (Running Time: 6 hrs.).Tr. of Italian with Ease. (SPA.). 2000. pap. bk. 95.00 (978-2-7005-1068-3(2)) Pub: Assimil FRA. Dist(s): Distribks Inc

Nuevo Pacto. Lucas Marquez. (SPA.). 2004. 25.00 (978-0-89985-431-1(1)) Christ for the Nations.

Nuevo Ruso sin Esfuerzo. 1 cass. (Running Time: 1 hr. 30 min.).Tr. of Russian with Ease. (RUS & SPA.). 2000. bk. 75.00 (978-2-7005-1383-7(5)); bk. 95.00 (978-2-7005-2029-3(7)) Pub: Assimil FRA. Dist(s): Distribks Inc

Nuevo Testament. unabr. ed. 2005. 29.99 (978-1-58926-858-6(X), 6858) Pub: Oasis Audio. Dist(s): TNT Media Grp

Nuevo Testamento. unabr. ed. 2005. audio compact disk 29.99 (978-1-58926-859-3(8), 6859) Pub: Oasis Audio. Dist(s): TNT Media Grp

Nuevo Testamento Completa-RV 2000. Read by Juan Alberto Ovalle. (SPA.). 2004. audio compact disk 29.99 (978-1-930034-62-4(8)) Casscomm.

Nuevo Testamento y Salmos: A Viva Vos. 2001. audio compact disk (978-1-930564-99-2(6), BLS320e colores) Untd Bible Amrcas Svce.

Nuevos Destinos. unabr. ed. Cynthia B. Medina. 4 cass. (Running Time: 6 hrs.). 1998. 29.50 (978-0-07-561953-6(9), Mc-H Human Soc) McGrw-H Hghr Educ.

Nuevos Destinos: Intermediate Grammar Review. 2nd ed. Cynthia B. Medina. (ENG.). (C). 2003. stu. ed. 63.75 (978-0-07-254801-3(0), 0072548010, Mc-H Human Soc) Pub: McGrw-H Hghr Educ. Dist(s): McGraw

Nuevos Horizontes. Graciela Ascarrunz Gilman. (SPA.). (C). 2005. lab manual ed. 29.95 (978-0-471-76893-7(6)) Wiley US.

Nuevos Sofistas. unabr. ed. Juan Jacobo-Doger. Narrated by Ivan Acosta. 5 cass. (Running Time: 7 hrs. 30 mins.). (SPA.). 2005. 29.95 (978-1-4025-8361-2(3)) Recorded Bks.
In the familiar style of Juan Jacobo-Doger, Los nuevos sofistas, opens the doors to the human mind, bringing attention to devasting limits and inefficiencies of the political systems of our society. The few who have already committed themselves to denounce these systems become our best weapons against apathy and ignorance.

Nuggets - Original Artyfacts from the First Psychedelic Era: 1965-1968, 4 cass. (Running Time: 6 hrs.). 1998. 59.98 (978-1-56826-804-0(1)) Rhino Enter.

Nuits. Poems. Alfred de Musset. Read by Marianne Valery. 1 cass. (Running Time: 1 hr. 30 mins.). (FRE.). 1995. 19.95 (1726-LQP) Olivia & Hill.
Collection of romantic poems.

Nuits Fauves. Cyril Collard. 5 cass. (Running Time: 5 hrs.). (FRE.). 1995. 40.95 (1746-LV) Olivia & Hill.
This book by a young musician-actor who dies of AIDS in 1993 elicited great controversy in France. The dramatic life of a young HIV-positive bisexual who does not reveal his illness to a 17-year-old girl who falls madly in love with him. Read by a cast of actors.

Nuke Zone. unabr. ed. Keith Douglass. Read by David Hilder. 6 cass. (Running Time: 9 hrs.). (Carrier Ser.: No. 11). 2001. 48.00 (978-0-7366-6014-3(3)) Books on Tape.
To the Ukraine, it was the perfect set-up... to make the U. S. think Turkey, their own ally - had launched the nuclear missile attack against the U. S. Sixth Fleet. After all, the U. S. needed to be reminded of who owned the waters they had entered. Now "Tombstone" Magruder & the new Sixth Fleet are out to stop the war before it starts.

Nukkin Ya. unabr. ed. Phillip Gwynne. Read by Christopher Pitman. 8 cass. (Running Time: 12 hrs.). 2002. (978-1-74086-036-9(5)) Bolinda Pubng AUS.
A unforgettable story about Blacky and Clarence falling for each other which the whole town seems to have a problem with. But then again the whole town's had a lot of problems since Clarence's brother died. Now her cousin, Lovely, wants to make sure that Blacky never sees Clarence again. And Lovely means business.

Nuku Nuku Soundphase 4. 1 CD. (JPN.). 2003. audio compact disk 14.98 (978-1-57813-437-3(4), CCN/001) A D Vision.

Null Point. unabr. ed. Robert A. Monroe. Read by Robert A. Monroe. 1 cass. (Running Time: 45 min.). (Gateway Experience - Prospecting Ser.). 1984. 14.95 (978-1-56113-288-1(8)) Monroe Institute.
Unearth the mine of your mind.

***Nullification: How to Resist Federal Tyranny in the 21st Century.** unabr. ed. Thomas E. Woods, Jr. (Running Time: 6 hrs. 30 mins.). 2010. 14.99 (978-1-4001-8761-4(3)) Tantor Media.

***Nullification: How to Resist Federal Tyranny in the 21st Century.** unabr. ed. Thomas E. Woods, Jr. Narrated by Alan Sklar. (Running Time: 9 hrs. 0 mins. 0 sec.). (ENG.). 2010. 19.99 (978-1-4001-6761-6(2)); audio compact disk 71.99 (978-1-4001-4761-8(1)); audio compact disk 29.99 (978-1-4001-1761-1(5)) Pub: Tantor Media. Dist(s): IngramPubServ

***Nullification (Library Edition) How to Resist Federal Tyranny in the 21st Century.** unabr. ed. Thomas E. Woods, Jr. (Running Time: 6 hrs. 30 mins.). 2010. 29.99 (978-1-4001-9761-3(9)) Tantor Media.

Number: A Completely Different Way to Think about the Rest of Your Life. abr. ed. Lee Eisenberg. Read by Lee Eisenberg. 2006. 17.95 (978-0-7435-5569-2(4)) Pub: S&S Audio. Dist(s): S and S Inc

Number Hunt. 1 cass. (Running Time: 1 hr. 30 mins.). (Pooh Learning Ser.). (J). (ps-3). 2000. pap. bk. 6.98 (978-0-7634-0473-4(X)) W Disney Records.

Number Man see Carl Sandburg's Poems for Children

Number Ten. unabr. ed. Sue Townsend. 6 cass. (Running Time: 8 hrs. 15 min.). 2003. 54.00 (978-1-4025-6145-0(8)) Recorded Bks.

Number the Stars. Lois Lowry. Read by Blair Brown. 2 vols. (Running Time: 2 hrs. 46 mins.). (J). (gr. 5-9). 2004. pap. bk. 29.00 (978-1-4000-8637-5(X), Listening Lib); 23.00 (978-0-8072-1971-3(1), Listening Lib); audio compact disk 25.50 (978-1-4000-8556-9(X), Listening Lib) Pub: Random Audio Pubg. Dist(s): NetLibrary CO

Number the Stars. unabr. ed. Lois Lowry. Read by Blair Brown. (J). 2006. 39.99 (978-0-7393-7513-6(X)) Find a World.

Number the Stars. unabr. ed. Lois Lowry. Read by Blair Brown. 3 CDs. (Running Time: 2 hrs. 46 mins.). (ENG.). (J). (gr. 5). 2004. audio compact disk 25.00 (978-1-4000-8555-2(1), Listening Lib) Pub: Random Audio Pubg. Dist(s): Random

Number the Stars, unabr. ed. Lois Lowry. Narrated by Christina Moore. 3 pieces. (Running Time: 3 hrs. 30 mins.). (gr. 5 up). 27.00 (978-1-55690-856-9(3), 93224E7) Recorded Bks.
A young Danish girl & her family join their neighbors in trying to smuggle Jewish families to the safety of Sweden during the Nazi occupation of Denmark. Available to libraries only.

Number the Stars. unabr. ed. Lois Lowry. Narrated by Christina Moore. 3 CDs. (Running Time: 3 hrs. 30 mins.). (gr. 5 up). 2000. audio compact disk 29.00 (978-0-7887-3454-0(7), C1060E) Recorded Bks.

***Number 12 Looks Just Like You.** 2010. audio compact disk (978-1-59171-285-5(8)) Falcon Picture.

Number 13. 1981. (S-16) Jimcin Record.

Number 8. unabr. ed. Anna Fienberg. Read by Rebecca Macauley & Stig Wemyss. (Running Time: 8 hrs. 40 mins.). (J). 2007. audio compact disk 87.95 (978-1-74093-924-9(7), 9781740939249) Pub: Bolinda Pubng AUS. Dist(s): Bolinda Pub Inc

Numbered Account. Christopher Reich. Narrated by George Guidall. 18 CDs. (Running Time: 21 hrs. 45 mins.). audio compact disk 166.00 (978-0-7887-9883-2(9)) Recorded Bks.

Numbered Account. abr. ed. Christopher Reich. Read by Stephen Lang. (Running Time: 21600 sec.). (ENG.). 2008. audio compact disk 14.99 (978-0-7393-2914-6(6), Random AudioBks) Pub: Random Audio Pubg. Dist(s): Random

Numbered Account, unabr. ed. Christopher Reich. Narrated by George Guidall. 15 cass. (Running Time: 21 hrs. 45 mins.). 1998. 125.00 (978-0-7887-1972-1(6), 95359E7) Recorded Bks.
Nicholas Neumann, a young man with exemplary business school record, wonderful fiancee & a fine future in financial management, leaves his bright future behind for a job with his father's former employer, a major swiss bank, to solve the murder of his father which occurred 17 years ago.

Numbers. 1 cass. (J). 1995. 9.98 (Sony Wonder); audio compact disk 13.98 CD. Sony Music Ent.
Features upbeat counting songs including "One & One Make Two," "Knock Three Times" & "Eight Beautiful Notes".

Numbers. unabr. ed. Rachel Ward. Read by Sarah Coomes. (Running Time: 9 hrs.). 2010. audio compact disk 24.99 (978-1-4233-9629-1(4), 9781423396291, Bril Audio CD Unabri) Brilliance Audio.

***Numbers.** unabr. ed. Rachel Ward. Read by Sarah Coomes. (Running Time: 9 hrs.). 2010. 24.99 (978-1-4233-9631-4(6), 9781423396314, Brilliance MP3); 39.97 (978-1-4233-9632-1(4), 9781423396321, Brinc Audio MP3 Lib); 39.97 (978-1-4233-9634-5(0), 9781423396345, BADLE); 24.99 (978-1-4233-9633-8(2), 9781423396338, BAD); audio compact disk 69.97 (978-1-4233-9630-7(8), 9781423396307, BriAudCD Unabrid) Brilliance Audio.

Numbers-a-Minute Timing Copy for Ten-Key Adding & Calculating Machines. George S. Rhodes. (YA). 1980. 19.25 (978-0-89420-226-1(X), 126004) Natl Book.

Numbers Big & Small: Early Explorers Fluent Set A Audio CD. Benchmark Education Staff. (J). 2006. audio compact disk 10.00 (978-1-4108-7641-6(1)) Benchmark Educ.

Numbers Book: Student Syllabus, Set. Sue C. Cook. (J). (gr. k-2). 1974. 19.95 (978-0-89420-208-7(1), 193000) Natl Book.

Numbers Commentary. Chuck Missler. 1 CD Rom. (Running Time: 8 hours aprox). (Chuck Missler Commentaries). 2006. cd-rom 29.95 (978-1-57821-325-2(8)); audio compact disk 44.95 (978-1-57821-324-5(X)) Koinonia Hse.
In Hebrew, B?midbar means "in the wilderness," which is the real name of this book. The Greek translators called it Arithmoi, and in Latin it was Numeri, because the translators focused on the two census takings at the beginning and the end of the wanderings. But it?s basically "the wilderness wanderings." Numbers is really a book about arrested progress. In a sense, it never should have happened. It took only 40 hours to get Israel out of Egypt - the Passover. But it took 40 years to get Egypt out of Israel.

Numbers Every Day. Sundance/Newbridge, LLC Staff. (Early Math Ser.). (gr. k-1). 2000. 12.00 (978-1-58273-304-3(X)) Sund Newbrdge.

Numbers in My Room Audio CD. Adapted by Benchmark Education Company Staff. Based on a work by Brooke Harris. (My First Reader's Theater Ser.). (J). (gr. k-1). 2008. audio compact disk 10.00 (978-1-60634-106-3(5)) Benchmark Educ.

Numbers of Tarot (Tarot Course) Robert Michael Place. Perf. by Robert Michael Place. Ed. by Leisa/Anne ReFalo. Prod. by Leisa/Anne ReFalo. (ENG.). 2010. 25.00 (978-1-935194-07-1(0), Hermes Pubns) Tarot Connect.

Numerati: How They'll Get My Number & Yours. Stephen Baker. 2008. audio compact disk 29.95 (978-1-4332-4930-3(8)) Blckstn Audio.

Numerati: How They'll Get My Number & Yours. unabr. ed. Stephen Baker. (Running Time: 7 hrs. NaN mins.). 2008. 29.95 (978-1-4332-4931-0(6)); 44.95 (978-1-4332-4928-0(6)); audio compact disk 60.00 (978-1-4332-4929-7(4)) Blckstn Audio.

Numerical Trigonometry: Syllabus. Carlton W. Bryson & Allan W. Gray. (J). 1973. 70.70 (978-0-89420-164-6(6), 355000) Natl Book.

***Números en me cuarto Audio CD.** Brooke Harris. Adapted by Benchmark Education Company, LLC. (My First Reader's Theater Ser.). (SPA.). (J). 2009. audio compact disk 10.00 (978-1-935470-67-0(1)) Benchmark Educ.

***Números hasta 100 Antes, despues, y entre Audio CD.** April Barth. Adapted by Benchmark Education Co., LLC. (Content Connections Ser.). (SPA.). (J). 2010. audio compact disk 10.00 (978-1-61672-203-6(7)) Benchmark Educ.

Nun in the Closet. unabr. ed. Dorothy Gilman. Narrated by Roslyn Alexander. 5 cass. (Running Time: 6 hrs. 45 mins.). 2000. 44.00 (978-0-7887-0276-1(9), 94482E7) Recorded Bks.

Nuni of Nunivak Island: A New Friend - Audio Book. P. J. Nickels. Narrated by Paul Mackenzie. Music by Maynard Williams. Featuring Jillian Llamas. Music by Jillian Llamas. (Running Time: 60). (ENG.). 2009. audio compact disk 9.95 (978-0-9824960-0-8(1)) Pennie Rich.

Nuns Fret Not at Their Convent's Narrow Room see Selected Poetry of William Wordsworth

Nun's Tale. unabr. ed. Candace Robb. Read by Stephen Thorne. 8 cass. (Running Time: 9 hrs.). 1997. 69.95 (961006) Pub: ISIS Audio GBR. Dist(s): Ulverscroft US
In this engrossing tale of 14th-century England, a runaway nun collapses & dies, no time is wasted burying her. But affairs take a strange turn when, a year later, a woman appears claiming to be the nun, saying she has risen from the dead. And when murder follows close on her heels, John Thoresby, Archbishop of York, asks his favorite sleuth, Owen Archer, to investigate.

Nun's Tale. unabr. ed. Candace Robb. Read by Stephen Thorne. 10 CDs. (Running Time: 15 hrs.). 2001. audio compact disk 89.95 (978-0-7531-1249-6(3), 1249-3) Pub: ISIS Audio GBR. Dist(s): ISIS Pub
When a young nun collapses & dies of a fever in the town of Beverley, no time is wasted in burying her. The year is 1365 A. D. & the plague is an ever present fear. But, a year later, a woman appears claiming to be the nun, saying she has risen from the dead. When murder follows close on her heels, John Thoresby, Archbishop of York, asks his favorite sleuth, Owen Archer, to investigate. Owen's wife, Lucie the apothecary, is the only person able to win the nun's confidence. Drawn in despite her reservations, concerned by the woman's deep unhappiness, Lucie tries to unravel the nun's troubled revelations to find a clue to the past. But the secrets which finally emerge & the violence they provoke - will shock the community to its core.

Nuovo Francese Senza Sforzo. 1 cass. (Running Time: 1 hr. 30 min.).Tr. of French with Ease. (FRE & ITA., 1997. pap. bk. 75.00 (978-2-7005-1330-1(4)) Pub: Assimil FRA. Dist(s): Distribks Inc

Nuovo Francese Senza Sforzo. 1 CD. (Running Time: 1 hr. 30 min.).Tr. of French with Ease. (FRE & ITA.). 2000. bk. 95.00 (978-2-7005-1071-3(2)) Pub: Assimil FRA. Dist(s): Distribks Inc

Nuovo Greco Senza Sforzo. Tr. of Greek with Ease. (GRE & ITA.). 2000. bk. 75.00 (978-2-7005-1390-5(8)) Pub: Assimil FRA. Dist(s): Distribks Inc

Nuovo Inglese Senza Sforzo. 1 cass. (Running Time: 1 hr. 30 min.).Tr. of English with Ease. (ENG & ITA.). pap. bk. 95.00 (978-2-7005-1072-0(0)); pap. bk. 75.00 (978-2-7005-1332-5(0)) Pub: Assimil FRA. Dist(s): Distribks Inc

Nuovo Spagnolo Senza Sforzo. 1 cass. (Running Time: 1 hr. 30 min.).Tr. of Spanish with Ease. (ITA & SPA., 1997. pap. bk. 75.00 (978-2-7005-1333-2(9)) Pub: Assimil FRA. Dist(s): Distribks Inc

Nuremberg: The Reckoning. unabr. ed. William F. Buckley, Jr. Read by Stuart Langston. 7 cass. (Running Time: 10 hrs.). 2006. 49.95 (978-0-7861-2548-7(9), 3180); audio compact disk 64.00 (978-0-7861-8998-4(3), 3180) Blckstn Audio.

Nureyev Pt. 1: His Life. collector's ed. Diane Solway. Read by Donada Peters. 10 cass. (Running Time: 15 hrs.). 2000. 80.00 (978-0-7366-5053-3(9)) Books on Tape.
Everyone knows the name Rudolf Nureyev, but does anyone know the man behind the myth? Diane Solway does; she spent over four years & conducted more than 200 interviews with his family, his friends & lovers, his colleagues & even his doctors to research Nureyev: His Life the first book to capture him as he was onstage & off a great artist whose talent was matched only by his steely will to succeed. Here is his professional career: his famed partnership with Margot Fonteyn, his personal transformation of the Royal Ballet & the Paris Opera Ballet, his impact on dance companies all over the world, his collaborations with Martha Graham & Paul Taylor & behind all his accomplishments, the athletic grace & profound understanding that was his gift of genius. Here, too, is the private Nureyev: his Soviet childhood, his inner demons, the men & women who were willing to devote their lives to him. Solway chronicles his flamboyant, extravagant lifestyle, his celebrity-studded circle of friends, Jacqueline Onassis, Andy Warhol & Marlene Dietrich, to name only three of his stormy love affairs, his homosexual promiscuity & his death from AIDS in 1993. Nureyev was his own masterpiece, a man always in the process of reinventing himself.

Nureyev Pt. 2: His Life. collector's ed. Diane Solway. Read by Donada Peters. 10 cass. (Running Time: 15 hrs.). 2000. 80.00 (978-0-7366-5054-0(7)) Books on Tape.
Everyone knows the name Rudolf Nureyev, but does anyone know the man behind the myth? Diane Solway does; she spent over four years & conducted more than 200 interviews with his family, his friends & lovers, his colleagues & even his doctors to research Nureyev: His Life the first book to capture him as he was onstage & off a great artist whose talent was matched only by his steely will to succeed. Here is his professional career: his famed partnership with Margot Fonteyn, his personal transformation of the Royal Ballet & the Paris Opera Ballet, his impact on dance companies all over the world, his collaborations with Martha Graham & Paul Taylor & behind all his accomplishments, the athletic grace & profound understanding that was his gift of genius. Here, too, is the private Nureyev: his Soviet childhood, his inner demons, the men & women who were willing to devote their lives to him. Solway chronicles his flamboyant, extravagant lifestyle, his celebrity-studded circle of friends - Jacqueline Onassis, Andy Warhol & Marlene Dietrich, to name only three - his stormy love affairs, his homosexual promiscuity & his death from AIDS in 1993. Nureyev was his own masterpiece, a man always in the process of reinventing himself.

Nurk: The Strange, Surprising Adventures of a (Somewhat) Brave Shrew. unabr. ed. Ursula Vernon. Read by Bill Knowlton. 3 CDs. (Running Time: 2 hrs. 30 mins.). (J). (gr. 3-6). 2009. audio compact disk 34.00 (978-1-934180-66-2(1)) Full Cast Audio.

Nurse in the Valley. Grace Goodwin. Read by Hazel Temperley. 4 cass. (Running Time: 6 hrs.). 1999. 44.95 (6299X) Pub: Soundings Ltd GBR. Dist(s): Ulverscroft US

Nurse Managers. Ed. by Andrew Crowther. Frwd. by Reta Creegan. 2 discs. (Running Time: 2 hours). (Guide to Practice Ser.). 2004. pap. bk. 59.95 (978-0-9751585-0-0(3)) Pub: Ausmed AUS. Dist(s): MPHC

Nurse Mary Audiocassette Library: "Does Colic Drive You Crazy?" Mary J. Pattison. Read by Mary J. Pattison. 1 cass. (Running Time: 15 min.). 1999. 9.95 (978-1-929838-08-0(5), AC50) Nurse Mary Baby.
"Don't let non-stop crying send you over the edge. There are steps you can take to help you & your baby".

Nurse Mary Library: "ABC's of Infant Care" Mary J. Pattison. Read by Mary J. Pattison. 1 cass. (Running Time: 19 min.). 1999. 9.95 (978-1-929838-10-3(7), AC60) Nurse Mary Baby.
"How you can & your baby can feel calm, warm & connected".

Nurse Mary Library: "Baby Needs Something to Eat-The Breast or Bottle Decision" Mary J. Pattison. Read by Mary J. Pattison. 1 cass. (Running Time: 13 min.). 1999. 9.95 (978-1-929838-03-5(4), AC25) Nurse Mary Baby.
"Only you can make this personal choice - information to help you make the right decision for you & your baby".

Nurse Mary Library: "Baby Needs to Play & Exercise" Mary J. Pattison. Read by Mary J. Pattison. 1 cass. (Running Time: 10 min.). 1999. 9.95 (978-1-929838-09-7(3), AC55) Nurse Mary Baby.
"Mom & Dad each play an important role".

Nurse Mary Library: "Baby's First Night at Home" Mary J. Pattison. Read by Mary J. Pattison. 1 cass. (Running Time: 10 min.). 1999. 9.95 (978-1-929838-01-1(8), AC15) Nurse Mary Baby.
Practical advice to make first steps for parents as exciting as first steps for baby.

Nurse Mary Library: "Childcare Expectations & Checklist" Mary J. Pattison. Read by Mary J. Pattison. 1 cass. (Running Time: 20 min.). 1999. 9.95 (978-1-929838-07-3(7), AC45) Nurse Mary Baby.
"Making childcare safer for your baby & less traumatic for both of you".

Nurse Mary Library: "Dealing with Diaper Rash" Mary J. Pattison. Read by Mary J. Pattison. 1 cass. (Running Time: 7 min.). 1999. 9.95 (978-1-929838-12-7(3), AC70) Nurse Mary Baby.
"Time tested tips & treatment".

Nurse Mary Library: "Germ Alert" Mary J. Pattison. Read by Mary J. Pattison. 1 cass. (Running Time: 10 min.). 1999. 9.95 (978-1-929838-11-0(5), AC65) Nurse Mary Baby.
"Nurses know: Fewer germs mean less illness".

Nurse Mary Library: How Do You & Your Husband Really Feel about Your Baby? Mary J. Pattison. Read by Mary J. Pattison. 1 cass. (Running Time: 12 min.). 1999. 9.95 (978-1-929838-00-4(X), AC10) Nurse Mary Baby.
Exploring Emotionally-charged issues with your spouse - making baby's home-sweet-home.

Nurse Mary Library: "How Safe Is Your Home?" Mary J. Pattison. Read by Mary J. Pattison. 1 cass. (Running Time: 11 min.). 1999. 9.95 (978-1-929838-04-2(2), AC30) Nurse Mary Baby.
"Making baby's home a safe haven, not a catastrophe waiting to happen".

Nurse Mary Library: "Introducing Baby to Other Members of the Family" Mary J. Pattison. Read by Mary J. Pattison. 1 cass. (Running Time: 14 min.). 1999. 9.95 (978-1-929838-02-8(6), AC20) Nurse Mary Baby.
"Getting to Know you - bonding quickly with brother, sister, Fluffy or Fido".

Nurse Mary Library: "Mommy Needs to Go Back to Work" Mary J. Pattison. Read by Mary J. Pattison. 1 cass. (Running Time: 13 min.). 1999. 9.95 (978-1-929838-06-6(9), AC40) Nurse Mary Baby.
"Perhaps a Mother's toughest decision - considerations to help you do what is truly right for you and your baby".

Nurse Mary Library: "Mother's Greatest Fears" Mary J. Pattison. Read by Mary J. Pattison. 1 cass. (Running Time: 14 min.). 1999. 9.95 (978-1-929838-05-9(0), AC35) Nurse Mary Baby.
"Your new baby should be a source of joy, not anxiety - let me help you face your fears".

Nurse Mary Library: SIDS - How to Reduce Your Baby's Risk. Mary J. Pattison. Read by Mary J. Pattison. 1 cass. (Running Time: 13 min.). 1999. 9.95 (978-1-929838-14-1(X), AC80) Nurse Mary Baby.

Nurse-Midwifery: The Birth of a New American Profession. Laura Ellizabeth Ettinger. (Women, Gender, & Health Ser.). 2006. audio compact disk 9.95 (978-0-8142-9100-9(7)) Pub: Ohio St U Pr. Dist(s): Chicago Distribution Ctr

Nursery Days. Woody Guthrie. Read by Woody Guthrie. 1 cass. (Running Time: 40 min.). (J). (ps). 1992. (0-9307-450360-9307-45036-2-1); audio compact disk (0-9307-45036-2-1) Smithsonian Folkways.
Fun songs which deal with universal events in the lives of young children are filled with whimsy & enthusiasm. Includes "Riding in My Car," "Put Your Finger in the Air" & "Howdido" & Guthrie's suggestions about how parents & children can use these songs.

Nursery Resources: Winter 99-2000. 1 cass. (Running Time: 1 hr. 30 mins.). (J). 1999. pap. bk. 10.99 (978-1-57405-606-8(9)) CharismaLife Pub.

***Nursery Rhyme Classics: Best Loved Rhymes for Little Ones.** unabr. ed. Mark MacLeod. (J). 2010. audio compact disk 39.95 (978-1-74214-712-3(7), 9781742147123) Pub: Bolinda Pubng AUS. Dist(s): Bolinda Pub Inc

Nursery Rhyme Time. Georgiana Stewart. 1 CD. (Running Time: 1 hr.). (J). 2001. pap. bk. 14.95 (KIM 9158CD); pap. bk. 10.95 (KIM 9158C) Kimbo Educ.
Here are rhymes & rhythms for learning & action. Each rhyme is sung once followed by an instrumental with finger plays or simple activities & then sung again to reinforce language. "Three Little Kittens", "Mary Had a Little Lamb", "Old King Cole", "Dance Thumbkin Dance", "Three Wishes", "30 Days Has September", "ABC Song" & more! Includes guide with lyrics & activities.

Nursery Rhymes. 1 cass. (Running Time: 1 hr.). (Early Learning Ser.). (J). bk. (TWIN 415) NewSound.

Nursery Rhymes. 1 cass. (My First Sing-Alongs Ser.). (J). bk. 7.99 (978-1-55723-603-6(8)) W Disney Records.

Nursery Rhymes. Perf. by Peter Pan Kids. 1 cass. (Running Time: 90 mins.). (J). 2000. 7.98; audio compact disk 9.98 Peter Pan.
Every parent wants kids to know these rhyming songs & the Peter Pan kids spin traditional & contemporary versions. Includes "Hush Little Baby," "This Old Man," "Lullabye & Good Night" & others. This one is sure to enchant the youngest listeners.

Nursery Rhymes. Created by Publications International Staff. (Take-along Songs Ser.). (J). (ps). 2007. bds. 9.98 (978-1-4127-7438-3(1)) Pubns Intl Ltd.

Nursery Rhymes. Kim Mitzo Thompson & Karen Mitzo Hilderbrand. Arranged by Hal Wright. (J). 1995. pap. bk. 13.99 (978-1-57583-329-3(8), Twin 415CD); audio compact disk 12.99 (978-1-57583-307-1(7), Twin 115CD) Twin Sisters.

Nursery Rhymes. unabr. ed. Rock and Learn, Inc. Staff. Illus. by Anthony Guerra. 1 cass. (Running Time: 40 min.). (Rock n' Learn Ser.). (J). (ps-k). 1995. pap. bk. 12.99 (978-1-878489-53-1(4), RL953) Rock N Learn.
Over 40 rhymes performed with fun, pop music style. Teaches safety, manners, & responsibility. Audiocassette & full-color illustrated book.

***Nursery Rhymes: A Treasure Chest of Rhymes.** unabr. ed. Mark MacLeod. (J). 2010. audio compact disk 39.95 (978-1-74214-716-1(X), 9781742147161) Pub: Bolinda Pubng AUS. Dist(s): Bolinda Pub Inc

***Nursery Rhymes: Clever Rhymes to Sing & Learn.** unabr. ed. Mark MacLeod. (J). 2010. audio compact disk 39.95 (978-1-74214-715-4(1), 9781742147154) Pub: Bolinda Pubng AUS. Dist(s): Bolinda Pub Inc

Nursery Rhymes: Rhyming & Remembering. Perf. by Ella Jenkins. 1 cass. (Running Time: 1 hr. 30 mins.). (J). (ps). 1990. (0-9307-450190-9307-45019-2-4); audio compact disk (0-9307-45019-2-4) Smithsonian Folkways.
Ella encourages group participation by suggesting lyrics & activities while she sings 22 favorite nursery rhymes. Includes "The Muffin Man," "Hey Diddle Diddle," "Sing a Song of Sixpence" & "Little Bo Peep".

Nursery Rhymes for Little People. 1 cass. (Running Time: 1 hr.). (J). 10.95 Incl. song sheet. (KIM 0820C) Kimbo Educ.
Twenty familiar nursery rhymes that are easy to sing along with. Old King Cole, Jack & Jill, Humpty Dumpty & more.

***Nursery Rhymes Giant Floor Puzzle.** Created by Twin Sisters. (Giant Floor Puzzles Ser.). (ENG.). (J). 2008. audio compact disk (978-1-59922-349-0(X)) Twin Sisters.

Nursery Songs & Lullabies. 1 cass. (Running Time: 1 hr.). (Keepsake Collection). 9.95 (SCNL-8401-V); 13.00 Gift Box Set. (GBCN-8401-V) Coventry Mkting.

Nursery Songs for Little Ones see Chansons de Tous le Jours pour les Petits

Nursery Tap Hip to Toe, Vol. 2. 2006. DVD & audio compact disk 19.95 Consumer Vision.

Nursing. Tony Grice. 2009. audio compact disk 22.50 (978-0-19-456981-1(0)) OUP.

Nursing Documentation in Aged Care: A Guide to Practice (Audiobook Package) Ed. by Christine Crofton & Gaye Witney. 2 vols. (Running Time: 2 hrs). (Ausmed Guide to Practice Ser.). 2004. pap. bk. 59.95 (978-0-9751585-4-8(6)) Pub: Ausmed AUS. Dist(s): MPHC

Nursing Fundamentals: Administration of Meds. . . 1992. Patricia Hoefler. 1993. (978-1-56533-091-7(9)) MEDS Pubng.

Nursing Fundamentals: Bedmaking. . . 1992. Patricia Hoefler. 1993. (978-1-56533-087-0(0)) MEDS Pubng.

Nursing Fundamentals: Care of Skin. . . 1992. Patricia Hoefler. 1993. (978-1-56533-089-4(7)) MEDS Pubng.

Nursing Fundamentals: Infection Control. . . 1992. Patricia Hoefler. 1993. (978-1-56533-090-0(0)) MEDS Pubng.

Nursing Fundamentals: Vital Signs. . . 1992. Patricia Hoefler. 1993. (978-1-56533-088-7(9)) MEDS Pubng.

Nursing Procedures Drill. 10 cass. (Running Time: 15 hrs.). 1996. 295.00; 295.00 T J Terry.

Nursing Procedures Drill. T. J. Terry. 8 cass. (Running Time: 7 hrs. 30 min.). 1998. 59.95 (978-1-887258-28-9(0)); audio compact disk 59.95 (978-1-887258-29-6(9)) T J Terry.
Comprehensive collection of 172 nursing procedures presented in drill fashion for fast learning. Each proceedure includes: background, description, purpose, key points & expected outcomes.

Nurture CD Series. Lisa Bevere. 2008. audio compact disk 25.00 (978-1-933185-43-9(0)) Messengr Intl.

Nurture Your Soul Auto-Matically. Robert E. Griswold & Deirdre Griswold. Read by Robert E. Griswold & Deirdre Griswold. 1 cass. (Running Time: 1 hr.). (While-U-Drive Ser.). 1997. 11.98 (978-1-55848-908-0(8)) EffectiveMN.
Internalize some of the most inspiring wisdom from great philosophers, scientists, physicians, poets & spiritual leaders who have helped shape & enrich so many lives.

***NurtureShock: New Thinking about Children.** Po Bronson & Ashley Merryman. Read by Po Bronson. (Playaway Adult Nonfiction Ser.). 2009. 79.99 (978-1-60788-399-9(6)) Find a World.

NurtureShock: New Thinking about Children. unabr. ed. Po Bronson & Ashley Merryman. Read by Po Bronson & Ashley Merryman. (Running Time: 8 hrs.). 2009. 24.98 (978-1-60024-841-2(1)); audio compact disk 34.98 (978-1-60024-840-5(3)) Pub: Hachet Audio. Dist(s): HachBkGrp

Nurturing Nuggets for Activity & Recreation Professionals CD: Renewing Your Spirit Guided Imagery. Created by Susan Lanza. Peri Gabriel. (ENG.). (YA). 2008. audio compact disk 12.95 (978-0-9768227-4-5(1)) Buttonberry Bks.

Nurturing Nuggets for Caregivers CD: Healing Your Spirit Guided Imagery. Created by Susan E. Lanza. Peri Gabriel. (ENG.). (YA). 2009. audio compact disk 12.95 (978-0-9768227-6-9(8)) Buttonberry Bks.

Nurturing Nuggets for Dementia Caregivers CD: Soothing Your Spirit Guided Imagery. Created by Susan Lanza. Peri Gabriel. (ENG.). (YA). 2008. audio compact disk 12.95 (978-0-9768227-3-8(3)) Buttonberry Bks.

Nurturing Nuggets for Nurses CD: Awakening Your Spirit Meditation. Created by Susan Lanza. Peri Gabriel. (ENG.). 2008. audio compact disk 12.95 (978-0-9768227-2-1(5)) Buttonberry Bks.

Nurturing Nuggets for Social Workers & Case Managers CD: Affirming Your Spirit Guided Imagery. Created by Susan E. Lanza. Illus. by Peri Gabriel. (ENG.). (YA). 2009. audio compact disk 12.95 (978-0-9768227-5-2(X)) Buttonberry Bks.

Nurturing Self Esteem in ADD-ADHD Children. John F. Taylor. 1 cass. (Running Time: 50 min.). (Answers to ADD Ser.). 1993. 9.95 (978-1-883963-07-1(9)) ADD Plus.
Lecture tape.

Nurturing Your Child: Alternative Approaches to A. D. D. (Attention Deficit Disorder - a Five Speaker Forum) Martha Benedict et al. 2 cass. (Running Time: 2 hrs.). (Way of Life Health Lecture Ser.). 1999. 11.95 (978-0-9657944-1-1(5)) Guinea Pig.
Wholistic approaches offer natural alternatives to drugs.

Nurturing Your Inner Child. Steven Halpern. 1 cass. (Running Time: 1 hr.). (Soundwave Two Thousand, the Audio Active Subliminal Ser.). 1990. (2020) Inner Peace Mus.
Beautiful new age music with subliminal affirmations.

Nurturing Your Inner Child: A Program for Healing & Self Love. William G. DeFoore. (ENG.). 2004. audio compact disk 14.99 (978-0-9785244-4-9(6)) Halcyon Life.

Nuruddin Farah. unabr. ed. Read by Nuruddin Farah & Rebekah Presson. Ed. by James McKinley. 1 cass. (Running Time: 29 min.). (New Letters on the Air Ser.). 1993. 10.00 (012293); 18.00 2-sided cass. New Letters.
Farah is interviewed by Rebekah Presson & reads from Variations on the Theme of an African Dictatorship.

Nut Bush Farm see Weird Stories

Nutcracker see Cascanueces

Nutcracker see Casse-Noisette

Nutcracker. 1 cass. (Running Time: 1 hr. 30 mins.). audio compact disk 10.98 (978-1-57908-382-3(X), 1546) Platinm Enter.

Nutcracker. Classics for Family staff. 1 cass., 2 CD. (J). 1996. bk. 39.98; 24.98 Incl. bk. Consort Bk Sales.

Nutcracker. Friedman. (CD Ser.). (J). 2001. bk. 16.98 (978-1-56799-362-2(1), Friedman-Fairfax) M Friedman Pub Grp Inc.

Nutcracker. Perf. by Eugene Ormandy & Philadelphia Orchestra Staff. Adapted by Virginia Unser. Illus. by Wendy Wallin Malinow. Based on a story by E. T. A. Hoffmann. (BookNotes Ser.). 1998. bk. 14.99 (978-0-88088-406-8(1)) Peter Pauper.

Nutcracker. Marina Orsini. 1 CD. (Running Time: 30 min.). (J). (ps up). 2001. pap. bk. 12.95 (978-2-89517-065-5(7)) Pub: Coffragants CAN. Dist(s): Penton Overseas

Nutcracker. l.t. ed. Short Stories. Illus. by Graham Percy. 1 CD. (Running Time: 10 mins). (J). (ps-3). 2001. bk. 8.99 (978-84-8214-089-6(2)) Pub: Peralt Mont ESP. Dist(s): imaJen

Nutcracker. rev. ed. Illus. by Anna Luraschi. (Young Reading CD Packs Ser.). (J). (ps-3). 2007. bk. 9.99 (978-0-7945-1628-4(9), UsborneU) EDC Pubng.

Nutcracker: The Story of the Ballet. Read by Ann Rachlin. 1 cass. (Running Time: 1 hr.). (Children's First Classic Ser.). (J). (ps-2). 5.98 (978-1-55886-027-8(4)) Smarty Pants.
Presents the Nutcracker to the music of Tchaikovsky's ballet.

Nutcracker: The Untold Story, unabr. ed. E. T. A. Hoffmann. Read by Christopher Plummer. 3 cass. (Running Time: 4 hrs. 30 mins.). (J). (gr. 4-6). 1985. 24.95 (978-0-89845-442-0(5), SBC 128) HarperCollins Pubs.
Relates the entire original story, Coupled with the complete Tchaikovsky ballet score, sugarplum fairies & toy wooden soldiers come alive.

Nutcracker - The Luck of the Gambler see Cascanueces y la Suerte del Jugador

Nutcracker - the Luck of the Gambler. E. T. A. Hoffmann. Read by Laura García. (Running Time: 3 hrs.). 2002. 16.95 (978-1-60083-228-4(8), Audiofy Corp) Iofy Corp.

Nutcracker & Swan Lake Suites. Perf. by Philadelphia Orchestra & Eugene Ormandy. Music by Peter Illich Tchaikovsky. 1 cass. (Running Time: 1 hr.). (J). 5.98 (2133); audio compact disk 14.98 (D2133) MFLP CA.
A wonderful instrumental performance of the most beloved Nutcracker dance pieces. Perfect for holiday background music or to set your little "Sugar Plum Fairies" on their toes.

Nutcracker Dreams. Music by Nancy Jensen. 1 cass. (Running Time: 60 min.). 1994. audio compact disk 15.95 CD. (2643, Creativ Pub) Quayside.
Piano & keyboard-based music blends perfectly with delicate sounds of nature.

Nutcracker Dreams. Music by Nancy Jensen. 1 cass. (Running Time: 60 min.). 1994. 9.95 (2642, NrthWrd Bks) TandN Child.

Nutcracker Music Game. (J). (gr. 2-8). 2004. bk. 24.95 (978-1-55592-175-0(2)) Weston Woods.

Nutcracker-no CD (Catalan) Chronicle Books Staff. (J). 2006. bk. 19.95 (978-92-0-692962-9(3)) Chronicle Bks.

Nutcracker-no CD (Spanish) Chronicle Books Staff. (J). 2006. bk. 19.95 (978-92-0-682962-2(9)) Chronicle Bks.

Nutcracker Suite see Christmas with Ogden Nash

Nutcracker Suite. 1 cass. 1995. 9.95 (1902-4); audio compact disk 16.95 CD. (1902-2) Kultur NJ.
Christmas story, set to the music of Tchaikovsky's beloved ballet suite. A treat for music lovers of all ages.

Nutcracker Suite. Composed by Peter Illich Tchaikovsky. Contrib. by Alan Billingsley & Sally Albrecht. (ENG.). 2007. audio compact disk 44.99 (978-0-7390-4540-4(7)) Alfred Pub.

Nutcraker Christmas. 1 CD. (Running Time: 1 hr.). audio compact disk 10.98 (978-1-57908-388-5(9), 1661) Platinm Enter.

Nutmeg of Consolation. Patrick O'Brian. Read by Richard Brown. (Aubrey-Maturin Ser.). 1993. audio compact disk 88.00 (978-0-7366-6165-2(4)) Books on Tape.

Nutmeg of Consolation. unabr. ed. Patrick O'Brian. Read by Simon Vance. (Running Time: 39600 sec.). (Aubrey-Maturin Ser.). 2007. 29.95 (978-0-7861-4862-2(4)); audio compact disk 29.95 (978-0-7861-6048-8(9)) Blckstn Audio.

Nutmeg of Consolation. unabr. ed. Patrick O'Brian. Read by Richard Brown. 9 cass. (Running Time: 13 hrs. 30 min.). (Aubrey-Maturin Ser.). 1993. 72.00 (978-0-7366-2483-1(X), 3245) Books on Tape.
Jack Aubrey & Stephen Maturin sail for Australia's penal colonies & find adventure. Fourteenth in series.

Nutmeg of Consolation. unabr. ed. Patrick O'Brian. Read by Richard Brown. 9 cass. (Running Time: 12 hrs.). (Aubrey-Maturin Ser.). 2000. 0.00 (978-0-7366-5714-3(2)) Books on Tape.
Jack Aubrey & Stephen Maturin sail for Australia's penal colonies & find adventure.

Nutmeg of Consolation. unabr. ed. Patrick O'Brian. Narrated by Patrick Tull. 9 cass. (Running Time: 12 hrs. 45 mins.). (Aubrey-Maturin Ser.). 1995. 78.00 (978-0-7887-0228-0(9), 94453E7) Recorded Bks.
Jack & Stephen escape a fiery attack by Malay pirates while shipwrecked on a desert island to dubious safety in a penal colony at New South Wales.

Nutmeg of Consolation. unabr. ed. Patrick O'Brian. Read by Patrick Tull. 11 CDs. (Running Time: 12.75 Hrs). (Aubrey-Maturin Ser.). 2005. audio compact disk 34.95 (978-1-4193-4321-6(1)) Recorded Bks.

Nutmeg of Consolation. unabr. ed. Read by Simon Vance. (Running Time: 39600 sec.). (Aubrey-Maturin Ser.). 2006. 65.95 (978-0-7861-4752-6(0)); audio compact disk 81.00 (978-0-7861-6336-6(4)) Blckstn Audio.

Nutmeg of Consolation. unabr. ed. Read by Simon Vance. (Running Time: 39600 sec.). (Aubrey-Maturin Ser.). 2007. audio compact disk 29.95 (978-0-7861-7255-9(X)) Blckstn Audio.

Nutria, Nutria. (Coleccion Parvulitos). (SPA.). 2003. 8.95 (978-0-8136-8528-1(1)) Modern Curr.

Nutricia. abr. ed. Robert A. Monroe. Read by Robert A. Monroe. (Mind Food Ser.). 1985. 14.95 (978-1-56102-411-7(2)) Inter Indus.
Designed to aid in conscious control of dietary needs.

Nutricia. abr. ed. Robert A. Monroe. Read by Robert A. Monroe. (Human Plus Ser.). 1989. 14.95 (978-1-56102-021-8(4)) Inter Indus.
Control caloric intake.

Nutrition: Science & Applications, Second Edition Media ActivePresentation CD-ROM for Mac/Windows with LectureActive User's Guide, Pack. 2nd rev. ed. Lori A. Smolin. (ENG., (C). 2002. audio compact disk 249.95 (978-0-470-00662-7(5), JWiley) Wiley US.

Nutrition & Your Health: A Doctor's View. Michael Klaper. 1 cass. (Running Time: 30 min.). (Help Yourself to Health Ser.). 7.00 (978-0-929274-00-3(8)) Gentle World.
One of a series of tapes discussing the relationship between a diet free of animal products & improving one's health or a particular disease.

Nutrition Breakthroughs: New Pathways to Health & Healing. Betty Kamen. 6 cass. (Running Time: 9 hrs.). 1998. 39.95 (978-0-944501-12-2(5)) Nutrition Encounter.
The newest & best alternative healing modalities. Cutting edge information on new therapies & nutrition. Includes: supplements, scaling down, heart health, immunity & common problems.

Nutrition Edition. (J). 1990. 9.95 (978-1-887028-24-0(2)) Slim Goodbody.

Nutrition, Food, & Fitness: Teaching Package. Dorothy F. West. (gr. 9-12). tchr. ed. 200.00 (978-1-56637-938-0(5)) Goodheart.

Nutrition for Your Arteries. Read by Kurt W. Donsbach. 1 cass. (Running Time: 45 min.). 10.00 (AC16) Am Media.
Discusses how chemicals called free radicals create lesions inside the artery. The body then produces fibrin, which, in turn, attracts calcium & cholesterol. The problem is not cholesterol but free radicals.

Nutrition for Your Body Mind & Spirit. Speeches. Sorai Stuart. 8 cassettes. (Running Time: 10 hrs. (aprox)). 2002. 129.95 (978-0-9763260-2-1(7)) Artust Nasus Pub.

Nutrition Image Bank. Jones and Bartlett Publishers. 2009. audio compact disk 157.95 (978-0-7637-8199-6(1)) Jones Bartlett.

Nutrition Instructor Toolkit. Paul M. Insel et al. (C). 2001. tchr. ed. 99.00 (978-0-7637-1593-9(X), 1593-X) Jones Bartlett.

***Nutrition Made Clear.** Instructed by Roberta H. Anding. 2009. 199.95 (978-1-59803-605-3(X)); audio compact disk 269.95 (978-1-59803-606-0(8)) Teaching Co.

Nutrition Science Animations. Jones and Bartlett Publishers. (C). 2006. audio compact disk 25.95 (978-0-7637-4497-7(2)) Jones Bartlett.

Nutritional Astrology. Ted Zagar. 1 cass. 8.95 (375) Am Fed Astrologers.
Natural foods that sustain health.

***Nutritional Excellence: Eating for Health & Longevity.** Prod. by Eat Right America. (ENG.). 2010. audio compact disk 19.95 (978-0-9825541-5-9(X)) NutritExcell.

Nutritional Issues in Clinical Practice. Contrib. by Stanley H. Zlotkin et al. 1 cass. (Running Time: 1 hr.). (American Academy of Pediatrics UPDATE: Vol. 18, No. 1). 1998. 20.00 Am Acad Pediat.

Nutritional Supplements & Natural Products in Saudi Arabia: A Strategic Reference 2006. Compiled by Icon Group International, Inc. Staff. 2007. ring bd. 195.00 (978-0-497-82407-5(8)) Icon Grp.

Nutritional Supplements in Australia: A Strategic Reference 2007. Compiled by Icon Group International, Inc. Staff. 2007. ring bd. 195.00 (978-0-497-35810-5(7)) Icon Grp.

Nutritional Supplements in Singapore: A Strategic Reference 2007. Compiled by Icon Group International, Inc. Staff. 2007. ring bd. 195.00 (978-0-497-82415-0(9)) Icon Grp.

Nuts & Bolts of Public Speaking Set: Practical Tools for Powerful Presentations. 2 CDs. (Running Time: 120 mins). 2005. audio compact disk 29.95 (978-0-9769825-1-7(X)) Comn Fact.

Nutshell Kids. (JPN.). 2004. 8.95 (978-1-56008-986-5(5)) Weston Woods.

NVC I. unabr. ed. Robert A. Monroe. Read by Robert A. Monroe. (Running Time: 45 min.). (Gateway Experience - Adventure Ser.). 1983. 14.95 (978-1-56113-271-3(3)) Monroe Institute.
Learn the language of intuitive thought.

NVC II. unabr. ed. Robert A. Monroe. Read by Robert A. Monroe. 1 cass. (Running Time: 45 min.). (Gateway Experience - Adventure Ser.). 1983. 14.95 (978-1-56113-272-0(1)) Monroe Institute.
Broaden your perception in all state of beings.

NVI Nuevo Testamento. unabr. ed. Zondervan Publishing Staff. (Running Time: 18 hrs. 0 mins. 0 sec.). (SPA.). 2004. audio compact disk 39.99 (978-0-8297-4237-4(9)) Pub: Vida Pubs. Dist(s): Zondervan

Ny Bd of Ed. 2004. 8.95 (978-1-55592-361-7(5)) Weston Woods.

NYC: Dumbo 2004. Interview. 1. (Running Time: 50 mins). Dramatization. 2003. audio compact disk 10.00 (978-0-9743204-3-4(9)) Oversampling.
Each SoundWalk CD is 50 minutes of walking discovery through neighborhoods, guided by a local personality, packed full of interviews and cinematic sound effects.

NYC: Ground Zero. 2004. audio compact disk 24.95 (978-0-9743204-8-9(X)) Oversampling.

NYC: Little Italy 2005. 2004. audio compact disk 19.95 (978-0-9743204-9-6(8)) Oversampling.

NYC: Lower East Side 2004. Interview. 1. (Running Time: 50 mins). Dramatization. 2003. audio compact disk 10.00 (978-0-9743204-1-0(2)) Oversampling.

NYC: Meat Packing District 2004. 2004. audio compact disk 12.95 (978-0-9743204-6-5(3)) Oversampling.

Nyc: The Bronx 2004. Interview. 3 CDs. (Running Time: 3*50mins). 2003. audio compact disk 18.95 (978-0-9743204-5-8(5)) Oversampling.
Each SoundWalk CD is 50 minutes of walking adventure through neighborhoods, guided by a local personality, packed full of interviews and cinematic sound effects.

NYC: Wall St 2005. 2004. audio compact disk 19.95 (978-0-9743204-7-2(1)) Oversampling.

Nyoka & the Flat Top Mountain. (J). 2008. audio compact disk 15.95 (978-0-9820885-6-2(6)) TBell.

***NYS Canal Reference.** Jean Taper. 2009. audio compact disk 26.99 (978-1-61623-689-2(2)) Indep Pub IL.

O

***O: A Presidential Novel.** unabr. ed. Anonymous. (Running Time: 13 hrs. 0 mins. 0 sec.). (ENG.). 2011. audio compact disk 39.99 (978-1-4423-4114-2(9)) Pub: S&S Audio. Dist(s): S and S Inc

O - Becoming Other: Survival Beyond Transformation, Set. Lisa Raphael. Read by Lisa Raphael. Read by Merle Murad-Sampson & Dick Budin. 2 cass. (Running Time: 2 hrs. 37 min.). 1999. 15.95 (978-0-9662582-8-8(2)) Cadence Pub.
Psycho-spiritual dialogue & information received from discarnate beings through channeling.

O Aird go HAird: Tomas & Seosamh O Ceannabhain. Contrib. by Seosamh O. Ceannabhain. (ENG.). 1990. 13.95 (978-0-8023-7044-0(6)) Pub: Clo Iar-Chonnachta IRL. Dist(s): Dufour

O Bed! O Breakfast! Robert Dalby. Read by Jonathan Marosz. 2001. audio compact disk 48.00 (978-0-7366-7077-7(7)) Books on Tape.

O Bed! O Breakfast! unabr. ed. Robert Dalby. Read by Jonathan Marosz. 5 cass. (Running Time: 7 hrs. 30 mins.). 2001. 40.00 (978-0-7366-6032-7(1)) Books on Tape.
A tabloid movie queen & her hunky boyfriend stir up a genteel Southern town during their three-month location shoot.

O Bed! O Breakfast! unabr. collector's ed. Robert Dalby. Read by Jonathan Marosz. 6 CDs. (Running Time: 9 hrs.). 2001. audio compact disk 48.00 Books on Tape.
A tabloid movie queen and her hunky boyfriend stir up a genteel Southern town during their three-month location shoot.

O Bheal go Beal. Contrib. by Marcas O. Murchu. (ENG.). 1997. 13.95 (978-0-8023-7126-3(4)); audio compact disk 20.95 (978-0-8023-8126-2(X)) Pub: Clo Iar-Chonnachta IRL. Dist(s): Dufour

O. C. Supertones: the Ultimate Collection. Contrib. by OC Supertones & Brandon Ebel. (Ultimate Collection). 2008. audio compact disk 18.99 (978-5-557-48830-3(8)) Tooth & Nail.

O Caminho Mais Fácil para Entender o Ho'oponopono: As Respostas Mais Esclarecedoras para Suas Perguntas Mais Frequentes-Volume I, Vol. 1. Mabel Katz. (POR.). 2009. 9.95 (978-0-9748820-9-3(7)) Your Business.

O Canada: Play-Along Solo for Alto Saxophone. 2000. bk. 6.95 (978-0-634-02260-9(1)) H Leonard.

O Captain! My Captain! see Treasury of Walt Whitman

O Captain! My Captain! see Classic American Poetry

O Carib Isle see Poetry of Hart Crane

***O Champion Leader.** Directed By Sergius Halvorsen. (ENG.). 2010. audio compact disk 18.00 (978-0-88141-064-8(0)) St Vladimirs.

O Chicago go Carrachan. Contrib. by Maidhc Dainin O. Se. (ENG.). 1998. 13.95 (978-0-8023-7136-2(1)); audio compact disk 21.95 (978-0-8023-8136-1(7)) Pub: Clo Iar-Chonnachta IRL. Dist(s): Dufour

***O Chorca Dhuibhne.** Sean De Hora. (ENG.). 1989. 11.95 (978-0-8023-7016-7(0)) Pub: Clo Iar-Chonnachta IRL. Dist(s): Dufour

***O City of Broken Dreams.** abr. ed. John Cheever. Read by Meryl Streep et al. (ENG.). 2009. (978-0-06-125296-9(4), Caedmon) HarperCollins Pubs.

***O City of Broken Dreams.** unabr. ed. John Cheever. Read by Meryl Streep et al. (ENG.). 2009. (978-0-06-196865-5(X), Caedmon) HarperCollins Pubs.

O Come, All Ye Faithful. Created by Lillenas Publishing. 2007. audio compact disk 24.99 (978-5-557-69954-9(6)) Lillenas.

O coração de floetic de Rene Reyes see Floetic Heart of Rene Reyes: USA english Release

O Divine Redeemer. 1 cass. (Running Time: 1 hr.). 7.98 (1000535); audio compact disk 14.95 (109112) Covenant Comms.
Favorite religious songs.

O for a Dozen Tongues to Sing. Abingdon. 2006. audio compact disk 11.95 (978-0-687-49378-4(1)) Abingdon.

O Gentle Death. Janet Neel. Read by David Thorpe. 8 vols. (Running Time: 12 hrs.). 2003. 69.95 (978-0-7540-0957-3(2)) Pub: Chivers Audio Bks GBR. Dist(s): AudioGO

***O Ghluin Go Gluin.** Conall O. Domhnaill. (ENG.). 1990. 11.95 (978-0-8023-7045-7(4)) Pub: Clo Iar-Chonnachta IRL. Dist(s): Dufour

O Gladsome Light. Perf. by Eikona. 1 cass. 10.95 (EIKCS); audio compact disk 15.95 (EIKCD) Conciliar Pr.
A beautiful blend of hymns of the Orthodox Church & contemporary Christian songs. This unique recording features three sisters' melodious & inspiring versions of "Psalm 57," "Crown Them," & "Thrice Holy Hymn." 18 selections in all.

O Great Spirit. Perf. by Robert Gass & On Wings of Song. 1 cass. (Running Time: 1 hr.). 9.98 (SA226) White Dove NM.
This well-known Native American inspired chant is blended with the nighttime song of crickets & cicadas.

'O Haloa, Ka Hawai'i Mua Loa. William H. Wilson. Illus. by Brook Parker. 1 cass. (Running Time: 1 hr.). (HAW.). (J). 1999. pap. bk. 5.95 (978-1-58191-084-1(3)) Aha Punana Leo.

O. Henry: A Celebration. Ed. by Gary Gabriel. 6 cass. (Running Time: 6 hrs.). (Audio-Drama Ser.: Vol. 1). 1998. 14.95 (978-1-892077-00-4(0)) Lend-A-Hand Soc.

O. Henry Favorites. unabr. ed. O. Henry. Read by Robert Donley & Jack Whitaker. 6 cass. (Running Time: 4 hrs. 44 min.). Incl. After Twenty Years. 1975. (CXL 513 CX); Blackjack Bargainer. 1975. (CXL 513 CX); Champion of the Weather. 1975. (CXL 513 CX); Cop & the Anthem. 1975. (CXL 513 CX); Duplicity of Hargraves. 1975. (CXL 513 CX); From the Cabbie's Seat. 1975. (CXL 513 CX); Furnished Room. 1975. (CXL 513 CX); Gift of the Magi. 1975. (CXL 513 CX); Last Leaf. 1975. (CXL 513 CX); Passing of Black Eagle. 1975. (CXL 513 CX); Ransom of Red Chief. 1975. (CXL 513 CX); Retrieved Reformation. 1975. (CXL 513 CX); Roads of Destiny. 1975. (CXL 513 CX); 1975. 44.98 Set, library ed. (978-0-8072-2956-9(3), CXL 513 CX, Listening Lib) Random Audio Pubg.
This collection features many of O. Henry's best-loved tales. These stories demonstrate O. Henry's vivid imagination, his sympathy for human weakness & his ingenious depiction of ironic circumstance.

O. Henry Favorites. unabr. ed. O. Henry. Read by Robert Donley & Jack Whitaker. 6 cass. (Running Time: 4 hrs 44 min.). 1999. 15.95 (978-0-8072-3409-9(5), CB 103 CXR, Listening Lib) Random Audio Pubg.

O. Henry Library. unabr. ed. O. Henry. Read by Marvin Miller. 6 cass. (Running Time: 9 hrs.). Incl. Champion of the Weather. (C-415); From the Cabbie's Seat. (C-415); Gift of the Magi. (C-415); Ransom of Red Chief. (C-415); 35.70 (C-415) Audio Bk.

O. Henry Short Stories. O. Henry. Read by Robert Donley & Jack Whitaker. 2 cass. (Running Time: 3 hrs.). 19.95 set. (8211Q) Filmic Archives.
Robert Donley reads "The Gift of the Magi"; "The Furnished Room"; & "Roads of Destiny". Jack Whitaker reads "The Ransom of Red Chief".

O. Henry's Christmas Stories. O. Henry. (ENG.). 2007. 5.99 (978-1-60339-169-6(X)); audio compact disk 5.99 (978-1-60339-170-2(3)) Listenr Digest.

O Holy Child: Christmas Carols for Contemporary Christians. Perf. by Sheldon Cohen et al. 1 cass. (Running Time: 40 min.). 1995. 9.95 (978-0-87946-124-9(1), 314); audio compact disk 14.95 (978-0-87946-129-4(2), 402) ACTA Pubns.
A glorious production of traditional & contemporary Christmas carols with full orchestra & choir including two new original Christmas songs: "O Holy Child" & "The Christmas Rose." Traditional songs include: "Adeste Fidelis," "What Child Is This," "Halleluia Chorus," "Joy to the World," "He Is Born," "Let There Be Peace on Earth," & four more, performed in an upbeat, enjoyable style.

O Holy Night. Robert Kochis & Robin Kochis. 1 cass. (Running Time: 39 mins.). 1999. 9.95; audio compact disk 14.95 (K6810) Liguori Pubns.
Songs include: "Silent Night," "What Child Is This?" "Song of the Stable," "Away in the Manger" & more.

O Holy Night. Mormon Youth Chorus and Symphony. 1 cass. (Running Time: 1 hr.). 8.98 (10001336); audio compact disk 12.98 (2800942) Covenant Comms.
Seventeen carols including some less often heard.

O Holy Night. Contrib. by Point of Grace. (Ultimate Tracks (Word Tracks) Ser.). 2006. audio compact disk 8.98 (978-5-558-26949-9(9), Word Music) Word Enter.

O Holy Night. Moderated by Michael John Poirier. 1993. 11.00 (978-1-58459-120-7(X), 002665) Wrld Lib Pubns.

O Holy Night. Music by Michael John Poirier. 1993. audio compact disk 16.00 (978-1-58459-121-4(8), 002664) Wrld Lib Pubns.

O Is for Outlaw. Sue Grafton. Read by Judy Kay. 7 cass. (Running Time: 10 hrs.). (Kinsey Millhone Mystery Ser.). 2000. 39.95 (N160) Blckstn Audio.
The Latin term "pro bono," as most attorneys will attest, roughly translated means "for boneheads" & applies to work done without charge. Thus begins propelling us into a complex case for Kinsey Millhone.

O Is for Outlaw. Sue Grafton. Read by Judy Kaye. (Kinsey Millhone Mystery Ser.). 1999. 56.00 (978-0-7366-4744-1(9)); 44.95 (5082) Books on Tape.
Husband number one, vice-cop Mickey Magruder, remained a mystery until now. The call came from a guy who scavenges defaulted storage units & came up with a box of documents about her. Amid childhood memorabilia she finds an old undelivered letter. The letter will. force Kinsey to reexamine her beliefs about the breakup of her first marriage, about the honor of that first husband, about an old unsolved murder & it will put her life in the gravest peril.

O Is for Outlaw. abr. ed. Sue Grafton. Read by Judy Kaye. 4 cass. (Kinsey Millhone Mystery Ser.). 1999. 25.95 (FS9-51076) Highsmith.

O Is for Outlaw. unabr. ed. Sue Grafton. 6 cass. (Running Time: 9 hrs.). (Kinsey Millhone Mystery Ser.). 1999. 39.95 (FS9-51206) Highsmith.

O Jerusalem!, abr. ed. Larry Collings & Dominique La Pierre. 6 cass. (Running Time: 9 hrs.). 2000. 29.95 (978-1-57511-048-6(2)) Pub Mills.
Charts the development & history of the state of Israel & the struggle for Jerusalem.

O Jerusalem! unabr. ed. Larry Collins. Read by Frederick Davidson. (Running Time: 24 hrs. 0 mins.). 2009. 44.95 (978-1-4417-1389-6(1)); audio compact disk 123.00 (978-1-4417-1386-5(7)) Blckstn Audio.

O Jerusalem! unabr. ed. Larry Collins & Dominique Lapierre. Read by Frederick Davidson. 16 cass. (Running Time: 23 hrs. 30 mins.). 1993. 99.95 (978-0-7861-0416-1(3), 1368) Blckstn Audio.
At the center of this massive & brilliant book is the most universal of man's cities: Jerusalem, the mystic heart of three great religions, condemned to pay for the passions it inspires by being, through forty centuries, the most bitterly disputed site in the world. Collins & Lapierre's story is the fruit of five years of intensive research & many thousands of interviews. It is the epic drama of 1948, in which the Arabs & the Jews, heirs to generations of bitter conflict in a land sacred to them both, fought each other for the city of Jerusalem & for the hopes of fulfillment it represented to each. Here is the account of that struggle which encompasses the full spectrum of its participants, whose experiences, emotions, & acts of bravery have been meticulously brought together & illumined in this monumental & dramatic work.

O Jerusalem. unabr. ed. Laurie R. King. Narrated by Jenny Sterlin. 13 CDs. (Running Time: 13 hrs. 30 mins.). (Mary Russell Mystery Ser.: Vol. 5). 2000. audio compact disk 109.00 (978-0-7887-4207-1(8), C1136E7) Recorded Bks.
In 1918, an aging Sherlock Holmes & his apprentice, Mary Russell, travel to Palestine on a dangerous mission. Suddenly Russell finds that she is the protector & Holmes the one who needs saving.

O Jerusalem. unabr. ed. Laurie R. King. Narrated by Jenny Sterlin. 10 cass. (Running Time: 13 hrs. 30 mins.). (Mary Russell Mystery Ser.: Vol. 5). 1999. 83.00 (978-0-7887-3746-6(5), 95781E7) Recorded Bks.
A flashback to a chapter in the "Beekeeper's Apprentice," in which Holmes & his young apprentice, Mary Russell, travel to Palestine in search of Microft, Holmes's older brother. When Holmes & Russell reach Palestine, they join Mahmoud & Ali, all four traveling in the garb of Bedouins. Their journey begins with the investigation of a murder & ends with preventing the destruction of Jerusalem.

O Jerusalem! Day by Day & Minute by Minute, the Historic Struggle for Jerusalem & the Birth of Israel. unabr. ed. Scripts. Larry Collins & Dominique Lapierre. Read by Theodore Bikel. 16 cass. (Running Time: 24 hrs.). 2004. 55.00 (978-1-59007-296-7(0)); audio compact disk 99.95 (978-1-59007-297-4(9)) New Millenn Enter.

'O Kelekolio Ka Manini Li'ili'i. Lilinoe Andrews. Illus. by Maile Ka'ai. 1 cass. (Running Time: 1 hr.). (HAW.). (J). 1999. pap. bk. 6.95 (978-1-58191-070-4(3)) Aha Punana Leo.

'O Lepeamoa. Kawika Napoleon. Illus. by Brook Parker. 1 cass. (Running Time: 1 hr.). (HAW.). (J). (gr. 2-3). 1999. pap. bk. 5.95 (978-1-58191-057-5(6)) Aha Punana Leo.

O Little Town. unabr. ed. Don Reid. Narrated by Don Reid. (Running Time: 4 hrs. 29 mins. 26 sec.). (ENG.). 2008. 16.09 (978-1-60814-327-6(9)); audio compact disk 22.99 (978-1-59859-437-9(0)) Oasis Audio.

O Lyubvi. Anton Chekhov. 1 cass. (Running Time: 1 hrs.). (RUS.). 1996. pap. bk. 19.50 (978-1-58085-570-9(9)) Interlingua VA.

O Magnify the Lord. Good News Singe Staff. 2004. 7.99 (978-0-8474-2581-5(9)); audio compact disk 9.99 (978-0-8474-1914-2(2)) Back to Bible.

'O Maile, Ka Pua'a. Aha Punana Leo Curriculum Development Committee. Illus. by Nelson Makua. 1 cass. (Running Time: 1 hr.). (HAW.). (J). (gr. k-1). 1989. pap. bk. 5.95 (978-1-890270-06-3(7)) Aha Punana Leo.

O Me of Little Faith. Jason Boyett. (Running Time: 4 hrs 26 mins. 0 sec.). (ENG.). 2010. 12.99 (978-0-310-77330-6(X)) Zondervan.

O Mistress Mine: From "Twelfth Night" see Palgrave's Golden Treasury of English Poetry

O Mother of God: Hymns to Mary. Perf. by Pacific Pops Orchestra. 1 CD. (Running Time: 45 min.). 1999. audio compact disk 14.95 (978-0-87946-198-0(5), 408) ACTA Pubns.

O Mother of God: Hymns to Mary. Perf. by Pacific Pops Orchestra. 1 cass. (Running Time: 45 mins.). 1999. 9.95 (978-0-87946-199-7(3), 308) ACTA Pubns.

'O Ni'i Ka Polewao. Na'ilima Gaison. Illus. by Brook Parker. 1 cass. (Running Time: 1 hr.). (HAW.). (J). 1999. pap. bk. 6.95 (978-1-58191-024-7(X)) Aha Punana Leo.

O Novo Alemao Sem Custo. 1 cass. (Running Time: 1 hr. 30 min.).Tr. of German with Ease. (POR & GER.). 2000. bk. 75.00 (978-2-7005-1021-8(6)); bk. 95.00 (978-2-7005-2006-4(8)) Pub: Assimil FRA. Dist(s): Distribks Inc

O Novo Ingles Sem Custo. 1 cass. (Running Time: 1 hr. 30 min.).Tr. of English with Ease. (ENG & POR.). pap. bk. 75.00 (978-2-7005-1329-5(0)) Pub: Assimil FRA. Dist(s): Distribks Inc

'O Pa'ao. Kekoa Roback. Illus. by Brook Parker. 1 cass. (Running Time: 35 mins.). (HAW.). (J). (gr. 3-4). 1999. pap. bk. 5.95 (978-1-58191-064-3(9)) Aha Punana Leo.

O Pioneers! Willa Cather. Narrated by Flo Gibson. 2009. audio compact disk 24.95 (978-1-60646-075-7(7)) Audio Bk Con.

O Pioneers! Based on a novel by Willa Cather. 18.95 (978-0-8224-7631-3(2)) Globe Fearon.

O Pioneers! Willa Cather. Narrated by Cindy Hardin. (Running Time: 6 hrs.). 1990. 18.95 (978-1-59912-810-8(1)) Iofy Corp.

O Pioneers! Willa Cather. Read by Cindy Hardin. 5 cass. (Running Time: 6 hrs. 30 min.). 29.00 (C-208) Jimcin Record.
Saga of pioneer days.

***O, Pioneers!** Willa Cather. Narrated by Alexis O'Donahue. (Running Time: 362). (ENG.). 2010. 9.95 (978-1-936455-04-1(8)) Open Bk Aud.

O Pioneers!, unabr. ed. Willa Cather. Read by Flo Gibson. 4 cass. (Running Time: 5 hrs. 30 min.). (gr. 8 up). 1989. 19.95 (978-1-55685-148-3(0)) Audio Bk Con.
A Swedish family of settlers in Nebraska overcomes drought & other disasters & due to the efforts of Alexandra, builds a prosperous farm.

O Pioneers! unabr. ed. Willa Cather. Read by Kathryn Yarman. 5 cass. (Running Time: 7 hrs. 30 min.). 1991. 39.95 (978-0-7861-0088-0(5), 752398) Blckstn Audio.
The central characters in the story are the Bergsons, strong-willed Swedish immigrants who came to America to make a living on the great prairie. The father dies, worn out by disease & debt. His eldest daughter, Alexandra, becomes the head of the family, & this is the story of her love affair with the land.

O Pioneers! unabr. ed. Willa Cather. Read by Stephanie Brush. 6 cass. (Running Time: 6 hrs.). 2001. 39.95 (978-1-58116-145-8(X)); audio compact disk 32.50 (978-1-58116-146-5(8)) Books in Motion.
A moving tale of the frontier. When her father dies and leaves her in charge of a farm and her younger brothers, Alexandra Bergeson accepts the challenge of the unyielding land and all that comes with it.

O Pioneers! unabr. ed. Willa Cather. Read by Kathryn Yarman. 5 cass. (Running Time: 7 hrs. 30 mins.). 1999. 39.95 (FS9-24905) Highsmith.

O Pioneers!, unabr. ed. Willa Cather. Narrated by Barbara McCulloh. 5 cass. (Running Time: 6 hrs.). 1989. 44.00 (978-1-55690-384-7(7), 89460E7) Recorded Bks.
Daughter of Swedish immigrant farmers on the Nebraska prairie struggles against hardship & suffering.

***O Pioneers!** unabr. ed. Willa Cather. Read by Kathryn Yarman. (Running Time: 7 hrs.). 2010. 29.95 (978-1-4417-4167-7(4)); audio compact disk 69.00 (978-1-4417-4164-6(X)) Blckstn Audio.

***O Pioneers!** unabr. ed. Willa Cather. Narrated by Kate Reading. (Running Time: 6 hrs. 0 mins. 0 sec.). (ENG.). 2010. 19.99 (978-1-4001-6940-5(2)); 13.99 (978-1-4001-8940-3(3)); audio compact disk 22.99 (978-1-4001-1940-0(5)) Pub: Tantor Media. Dist(s): IngramPubServ

***O Pioneers! (Library Edition)** unabr. ed. Willa Cather. Narrated by Kate Reading. (Running Time: 6 hrs. 0 mins. 0 sec.). (ENG.). 2010. audio compact disk 54.99 (978-1-4001-4940-7(1)) Pub: Tantor Media. Dist(s): IngramPubServ

O Suzanne, Ja Konjugier Fur Mich! Uwe Kind & Ursula Meyer. (J). (gr. 7-12). 1980. 25.00 (978-0-686-66262-4(8), 58690) Prentice ESL.

O That I Were an Angel. 1 cass. (Running Time: 1 hr.). 7.98 (16003071) Covenant Comms.
Original songs by Wanda West Palmer.

O That I Were an Angel. Michael Ballam. 1 cass. 9.95 (100985); audio compact disk 14.95 (2800624) Covenant Comms.
Majestic renditions of Wanda Palmer's songs.

O Think Not I Am Faithful to a Vow see Poetry of Edna St. Vincent Millay

'O Wau Kekahi I Ke Alualu Holoholona. Tr. by Aha Punana Leo Curriculum Development Committee. Illus. by Germaine Arnaktauyok. 1 cass. (Running Time: 1 hr. 30 mins.). (HAW.). (J). 1992. pap. bk. 3.95 (978-1-890270-08-7(3)) Aha Punana Leo.

O Worship the King. Jeffery Bennett. 1999. 11.98 (978-0-633-03881-6(4)); audio compact disk 16.98 (978-0-633-03880-9(6)) LifeWay Christian.

O Worship the King. Prod. by Twin Sisters Productions Staff. 1 CD. (Running Time: 51 mins). (J). 2005. audio compact disk 6.99 (978-1-57583-809-0(5)) Twin Sisters.
O Worship The King with 25 classic hymns sung by kids for kids. Includes favorite hymns of worship and songs of personal devotion and faith. The contemporary arrangements span the ages to create a collection for today's young worshippers - ideal for use at home, church and school. BONUS! The ENHANCED CD includes 104 pages of sheet music that can be printed from your own computer!.

O Yisrayl. 1 cass. (Running Time: 1 hr. 05 min.). 1993. 8.00 (978-1-890967-32-1(7)) Hse of Yahweh.
This collection of inspiring songs proclaims that the Name of Yahweh will not pass away, & by His Name He guides & protects those who obey His every word!.

***O Youth & Beauty!** abr. ed. John Cheever. Read by Meryl Streep et al. (ENG.). 2009. (978-0-06-125298-3(0), Caedmon) HarperCollins Pubs.

***O Youth & Beauty!** unabr. ed. John Cheever. Read by Meryl Streep et al. (ENG.). 2009. (978-0-06-196864-8(1), Caedmon) HarperCollins Pubs.

Oahu Beaches. Dan Martin & Nathalie Walker. 2004. audio compact disk 4.95 (978-1-57306-173-5(5)) Bess Pr.

Oak & the Calf: Sketches of Literary Life in the Soviet Union. unabr. ed. Aleksandr Solzhenitsyn. Read by Richard Brown. 14 cass. (Running Time: 20 hrs. 30 mins.). 1989. 89.95 (978-0-7861-0093-4(1), 1086) Blckstn Audio.
The great Russian novelist & historian here reveals his round-by-round personal account of what it was like to be a writer in a Communist regime. He tells of his ten-year war to outwit Russia's rulers & gets his works published in his own country.

Oak Inside the Acorn. unabr. ed. Max Lucado. Read by Nathan Larkin. (J). 2007. 34.99 (978-1-60252-773-7(3)) Find a World.

Oak Inside the Acorn. unabr. ed. Max Lucado. Narrated by Nathan Larkin. (ENG.). (J). 2006. 10.49 (978-1-60814-325-2(2)) Oasis Audio.

Oak Ridge Boys Collection. Perf. by Oak Ridge Boys, The. 2 cass. (Running Time: 3 hrs.). 1998. 16.99 Set. (978-0-7601-2367-6(5)); audio compact disk 19.99 CD. (978-0-7601-2368-3(3)) Provident Mus Dist.

Oak Tree Has a Life Cycle Audio CD. Adapted by Benchmark Education Company Staff. Based on a work by Margaret McNamara. (Content Connections Ser.). (J). (gr. k-2). 2008. audio compact disk 10.00 (978-1-60634-897-0(3)) Benchmark Educ.

Oak Tree Horror. Anne Schraff. Narrated by Larry A. McKeever. (Horror Ser.). (J). 2002. 10.95 (978-1-58659-078-9(2)); audio compact disk 14.95 (978-1-58659-337-7(4)) Artesian.

Oaken Heart. unabr. ed. Margery Allingham. Read by Tracey Lloyd. 8 cass. (Running Time: 12 hrs.). (Isis Ser.). (J). 2001. 69.95 (978-0-7531-0503-0(9), 990205) Pub: ISIS Lrg Prnt GBR. Dist(s): Ulverscroft US
In her autobiographical work Allingham tells the story of a small English village called Auburn & the lives of its people during the Second World war.

Oasis, Vol. 1. 1 CD. (Running Time: 1 hr.). audio compact disk 15.98 (978-1-57908-270-3(X), 1321) Platinm Enter.

Oasis, Vol. 2. 1 CD. audio compact disk 15.98 (1322) Platinm Enter.

Oasis: The Unauthorized Biography of Oasis. Tim Footman. (Maximum Ser.). (ENG.). 2001. audio compact disk 14.95 (978-1-84240-048-7(7)) Pub: Chrome Dreams GBR. Dist(s): IPG Chicago

Oasis Collector's Box. Tim Footman. As told by Nancy Mc Clean. 3. (Running Time: 165mins). 2005. audio compact disk (978-1-84240-340-2(0)) Chrome Dreams GBR.
ContentsMaximum Oasis1. THE STORY2. NOEL AND LIAM3. MUSICAL YOUTH4. ENTER CREATION5. DEFINITE SUCCESS6. NORTH Vs. SOUTH7. GLORY GLORY8. FIELDS OF DREAMS9. BACKLASH10. HOME COMFORTS11. ALL CHANGE12. AND FOR THEIR NEXT TRICK.More Maximum Oasis1.The Hangover Years2.A Potted History of Oasis in the 20th Century3.Isaac Newton Blues4.Two Gone Blondes5.Live and Not Terribly Dangerous6.Chemical Brothers7. Kettle, Cigarettes, Guitar, Television8. All Change At The Back9.The Return of Burnage10.Where Did It All Go Right?Xposed OasisInterview set.

OASIS in the Overwhelm on Audio CD: 60-second strategies for balance in a busy World - Audio CD. Excerpts. Mildred Grenough. 1. (Running Time: 1 hr. 15 mins.). Dramatization. 2007. audio compact disk 19.95 (978-0-9778411-0-3(3), 0-9778411-0-3) OASIS in Over.
Author Millie Grenough guides you through Step-by-Step instruction in the 4 key OASIS Strategies; How to use the strategies in different situations; Scientific background: re-wire your brain toward health and happiness; Tips: achieve calm in chaos - every minute - at home and at work.The OASIS Strategies are four proven "sanity" strategies to change your brain and your life, even in the midst of stress at home and at work. You can learn the 60-second Strategies in one hour. You will notice the difference immediately in your daily life.Author Millie Grenough created the OASIS Strategies during her recovery from a near-death accident in the midst of her own high-velocity lifestyle. "Suddenly, and for months," she says, "I was thrust into a slow, surreal pace of living. I knew that I needed to find some strategies to get myself back to heatlh-but not back to the fast lane." The OASIS Strategies helped to restore Millie to total health, and they have helped people from all walks of life find balance and enjoyment in day-to-day living.Millie Grenough, motivational speaker and executive coach, is Clinical Instructor in Social Work of Psychiatry at Yale University School of Medicine. Coach Grenough developed the OASIS Strategies after a near-death accident forced her to change her hectic lifestyle. The OASIS Strategies have helped people from all walks of life find balance and enjoyment. Try them for yourself. Don't wait till you have an accident.

Oasis in the Zone. unabr. ed. Marcia Reynolds. 2 CDs. (Smart Audio Ser.). 2003. audio compact disk 19.99 (978-1-58926-078-8(3), R22J-010D) Oasis Audio.

Oasis of Love Guidelines Series. Elbert Willis. 4 cass. (Running Time: 6 hrs.). 13.00 Fill the Gap.

Oasis Project New Source for Youth Worship. Tony Wood. 1998. 11.98 (978-0-7673-9093-4(8)); audio compact disk 16.98 (978-0-7673-9118-4(7)); audio compact disk 45.00 (978-0-7673-9094-1(6)) LifeWay Christian.

Oasis Project New Source Stereo/Split Acc Cassette. Tony Wood. 1998. 40.00 (978-0-7673-9250-1(7)) LifeWay Christian.

OAT Audiolearn. Shahrad Yazdani. (C). 2002. 109.00 (978-0-9704199-3-4(7)) AudioLearn.

Oath. Frank E. Peretti. Narrated by Richard Ferrone. 14 cass. (Running Time: 18 hrs. 30 mins.). 114.00 (978-0-7887-9363-9(2)) Recorded Bks.

Oath. abr. ed. John Lescroart. Read by Robert Lawrence. (Running Time: 6 hrs.). (Dismas Hardy Ser.: No. 8). 2008. audio compact disk 14.99 (978-1-4233-5161-0(4), 9781423351610, BCD Value Price) Brilliance Audio.

Oath. unabr. ed. John Lescroart. Read by Robert Lawrence. 9 cass. (Running Time: 13 hrs.). (Dismas Hardy Ser.: No. 8). 2002. 34.95 (978-1-58788-981-3(1), 1587889811, BAU); 87.25 (978-1-58788-982-0(X), 158788982X, Unabridge Lib Edns) Brilliance Audio.
When the head of San Francisco's largest HMO dies in his own hospital, no one doubts that it is anything but the result of massive injuries inflicted by a random hit-and-run accident. But the autopsy soon tells a different story - an overdose of potassium killed him, and the attending physician, Eric Kensing, becomes the prime suspect in a high-profile homicide. Homicide lieutenant Abe Glitsky, though hindered by the inept bunglings of two politically appointed cops assigned to the investigation, quickly sets his sights on Kensing. Desperate and in need of an attorney, Kensing turns to lawyer Dismas Hardy for his defense. But as the pressure mounts to indict Kensing, Hardy goes on the offensive, believing that the murder had little to do with his client, and everything to do with business. Hardy knows that all is not well with the HMO, and makes a terrifying discovery: too many patients have been dying, many of them victims of murder - and it looks like it is the hospital that is killing them. His own marriage tested and his family strained as he struggles to save his client, Hardy must uncover a twisting conspiracy of avarice and violence that takes the lives it is sworn to save. A timely and gripping novel that puts lives - and a long-standing friendship - at grave risk.

Oath. unabr. ed. John Lescroart. Read by Robert Lawrence. (Running Time: 13 hrs.). (Dismas Hardy Ser.: No. 8). 2004. 39.25 (978-1-59335-635-4(8), 1593356358, Brlnc Audio MP3 Lib) Brilliance Audio.

Oath. unabr. ed. John Lescroart. Read by Robert Lawrence. (Running Time: 13 hrs.). (Dismas Hardy Ser.: No. 8). 2004. 39.25 (978-1-59710-546-0(5), 1597105465, BADLE); 24.95 (978-1-59710-547-7(3), 1597105473, BAD) Brilliance Audio.

Oath. unabr. ed. John Lescroart. Read by Robert Lawrence. (Running Time: 46800 sec.). (Dismas Hardy Ser.: No. 8). 2007. audio compact disk 107.25 (978-1-4233-3388-3(8), 9781423333883, BriAudCD Unabrid); audio compact disk 38.95 (978-1-4233-3387-6(X), 9781423333876, Bril Audio CD Unabri) Brilliance Audio.

Oath. unabr. ed. John Lescroart. Read by Robert Lawrence. (Running Time: 13 hrs.). (Dismas Hardy Ser.: No. 8). 2004. 24.95 (978-1-59335-244-8(1), 1593352441) Soulmate Audio Bks.

Oath. unabr. ed. Frank E. Peretti. Narrated by Tom Stechschulte. 14 cass. (Running Time: 18 hrs. 30 min.). 2003. 59.95 (978-1-4025-2866-8(3)) Recorded Bks.
When a nature photographer is killed and mutilated while camping, common sense points to a rogue bear on the prowl. But the search for answers uncovers a century of sin-and a beast of ghastly power.

Oath. unabr. ed. Elie Wiesel. Read by Frederick Davidson. 7 cass. (Running Time: 10 hrs.). 1996. 49.95 (978-0-7861-0954-8(8), 1731) Blckstn Audio.
What would you say to a young stranger who wishes to die? What arguments would you use to restore his will to live? What ideas & ideals would you invoke to save him? Faced with that dilemma, the principal character of Elie Wiesel's magnificent novel - an old wanderer named Azriel - decides to tell a story: his own. The very one he was not supposed to tell, the one he had pledged to keep to himself. The story unfolds in two places & at two points in time. Kolvillag in the 1920s, & a modern metropolis in the 1970s. It is about Jews & their enemies, friendship & hate, bigotry & war, testimony & silence - silence above all.

Oath of Fealty. unabr. ed. Elizabeth Moon. Read by Jennifer Van Dyck. 15 CDs. (Running Time: 18 hrs.). 2010. audio compact disk 29.99 (978-1-4418-3901-5(1), 9781441839015, Bril Audio CD Unabri) Brilliance Audio.

***Oath of Fealty.** unabr. ed. Elizabeth Moon. Read by Jennifer Van Dyck. 2 MP3-CDs. (Running Time: 18 hrs.). 2010. 29.99 (978-1-4418-3903-9(8), 9781441839039, Brilliance MP3); 44.97 (978-1-4418-3904-6(6), 9781441839046, Brlnc Audio MP3 Lib); 44.97 (978-1-4418-3906-0(2), 9781441839060, BADLE); 29.99 (978-1-4418-3905-3(4), 9781441839053, BAD); audio compact disk 99.97 (978-1-4418-3902-2(X), 9781441839022, BriAudCD Unabrid) Brilliance Audio.

***Oath of Gold.** unabr. ed. Elizabeth Moon. Read by Jennifer Van Dyck. (Running Time: 17 hrs.). (Deed of Paksenarrion Ser.). 2010. 29.99 (978-1-4418-5129-1(1), 9781441851291, Brilliance MP3); 44.97 (978-1-4418-5131-4(3), 9781441851314, Brlnc Audio MP3 Lib); 44.97 (978-1-4418-5130-7(5), 9781441851307, BADLE); audio compact disk 92.97 (978-1-4418-5128-4(3), 9781441851284, BriAudCD Unabrid); audio compact disk 29.99 (978-1-4418-5127-7(5), 9781441851277, Bril Audio CD Unabri) Brilliance Audio.

Obama: From Promise to Power. unabr. ed. David Mendell. Read by Dion Graham. Created by HarperAudio Staff. (Running Time: 50400 sec.). 2007. audio compact disk 44.95 (978-0-06-145214-7(9), Harper Audio) HarperCollins Pubs.

***Obama: The Ascent of a Politician.** unabr. ed. David Mendell. Read by Dion Graham. (ENG.). 2007. (978-0-06-155424-7(3)); (978-0-06-155425-4(1)) HarperCollins Pubs.

***Obama Diaries.** unabr. ed. Laura Ingraham. Read by Laura Ingraham. (Running Time: 13 hrs. 0 mins. 0 sec.). 2010. audio compact disk 39.99 (978-1-4423-3645-2(5)) Pub: S&S Audio. Dist(s): S and S Inc

***Obama Zombies: How the Liberal Machine Brainwashed My Generation.** unabr. ed. Jason Mattera. Narrated by Kirby Heyborne. (Running Time: 10 hrs. 0 mins.). 2010. 34.99 (978-1-4001-9662-3(0)); 16.99 (978-1-4001-8662-4(5)) Tantor Media.

Obamanomics: How Barack Obama Is Bankrupting You & Enriching His Wall Street Friends, Corporate Lobbyists, & Union Bosses. unabr. ed. Timothy P. Carney. (Running Time: 8 hrs. 30 mins.). 2009. 29.95 (978-1-4417-3211-8(X)); 54.95 (978-1-4417-3207-1(1)); audio compact disk 29.95 (978-1-4417-3210-1(1)); audio compact disk 76.00 (978-1-4417-3208-8(X)) Blckstn Audio.

Obamanos! The Rise of a New Political Era. unabr. ed. Hendrik Hertzberg. Narrated by Kent Cassella & Dick Hill. (Running Time: 11 hrs. 30 mins. 0 sec.). (ENG.). 2009. 24.99 (978-1-4001-6428-8(1)); audio compact disk 34.99 (978-1-4001-1428-3(4)); audio compact disk 69.99 (978-1-4001-4428-0(0)) Pub: Tantor Media. Dist(s): IngramPubServ

***Obamanos! The Rise of a New Political Era.** unabr. ed. Hendrik Hertzberg. Narrated by Dick Hill. (Running Time: 11 hrs. 30 mins.). 2009. 17.99 (978-1-4001-8428-6(2)) Tantor Media.

***Obama's Wars.** abr. ed. Bob Woodward. Read by Boyd Gaines. (Running Time: 7 hrs. 0 mins. 0 sec.). 2010. audio compact disk 29.99 (978-1-4423-3526-4(2)) Pub: S&S Audio. Dist(s): S and S Inc

Obasan. abr. ed. Joy Kogawa & Joy Kogawa. Narrated by Joy Kogawa. Prod. by CBC Radio Staff. 3 cass. (Running Time: 3 hrs. 30 mins.). (Between the Covers Classics). (ENG.). 2005. 19.95 (978-0-86492-304-2(X)) Pub: BTC Audiobks CAN. Dist(s): U Toronto Pr

Obasan. unabr. collector's ed. Joy Kogawa. Read by Jill Masters. 7 cass. (Running Time: 10 hrs. 30 mins.). 1986. 56.00 (978-0-7366-1009-4(X), 1942) Books on Tape.

OBCD-03 Clinical Obstetrical Ultrasound Case Studies, Vol. 3. Instructed by William Ott. 2003. audio compact disk 150.00 (978-1-931999-82-3(1)) Gulfcoast Ultrasound.

OBD: Obsessive Branding Disorder - The Illusion of Business & the Business of Illusion. unabr. ed. Lucas Conley. Read by Walter Dixon. (Running Time: 5 hrs.). (ENG.). 2008. 24.98 (978-1-59659-303-9(2), GildAudio) Pub: Gildan Media. Dist(s): HachBkGrp

Obedience. 2004. 14.99 (978-1-58602-201-3(6)); audio compact disk 29.99 (978-1-58602-202-0(4)) E L Long.

Obedience. Kenneth W. Hagin, Jr. 6 cass. (Running Time: 9 hrs.). 24.00 (14J) Faith Lib Pubns.

Obedience: A Means of Letting Go. Thomas Merton. 1 cass. (Running Time: 48 min.). 1993. 8.95 (AA2616) Credence Commun.
Obedience enables us to face the real life experience of losing friends, possessions, positions - all the things that go against our own will.

Obedience: Your Path to Destiny. Speeches. Creflo A. Dollar. 3 cass. (Running Time: 4 hrs.). 2002. 15.00 (978-1-59089-492-7(8)) Creflo Dollar.

Obedience the Key to Prosperity. Tsea. 2005. audio compact disk (978-0-9797500-0-7(8)) TSEA.

***Obelisk.** unabr. ed. Howard Gordon. (Running Time: 11 hrs. 0 mins. 0 sec.). (ENG.). 2011. audio compact disk 39.99 (978-1-4423-3582-0(3)) Pub: S&S Audio. Dist(s): S and S Inc

Obento Deluxe. 2nd ed. Peter Williams et al. 2004. audio compact disk 226.95 (978-0-17-012006-7(6)) Cheng Tsui.

Obento Senior Teacher Audio CD. Peter Williams et al. 2005. audio compact disk 199.99 (978-0-17-012755-4(9)) Cheng Tsui.

Obentoo, Vol. 1. Peter Williams & Kyoko Kusumoto. 6 cass. (JPN & ENG.). (YA). (gr. 7-10). 1999. 180.00 (978-0-17-009010-0(8)) Pub: CengageAUS AUS. Dist(s): Cheng Tsui

Obentoo, Vol. 2. Anne Fisher et al. 4 CDs. (JPN & ENG.). (YA). (gr. 8-11). 1999. audio compact disk 180.00 (978-0-17-009014-8(0)) Pub: CengageAUS AUS. Dist(s): Cheng Tsui

Obentoo, Vol. 3. Anne Fisher et al. (JPN & ENG.). (YA). (gr. 9-12). 2000. audio compact disk 180.00 (978-0-17-009018-6(3)) Pub: CengageAUS AUS. Dist(s): Cheng Tsui

Obesity. Deanna S. K. Jepson & Yasmin Alibha Brown. 2009. audio compact disk 13.95 (978-1-873413-78-4(5)) Pub: Merit Pub Intl. Dist(s): Midpt Trade

Obesity: A Problem of Western Civilization. Read by Marion Woodman. 1 cass. (Running Time: 1 hr.). 1979. 9.95 (978-0-7822-0330-1(2), 059) C G Jung IL.

Obeying the Voice of the Holy Spirit. Gloria Copeland. 1 cass. (Running Time: 1 hr. 30 mins.). (Walk with God - Obedience Ser.: No. 5). 1984. 5.00 (978-0-88114-709-4(5)) K Copeland Pubns.
Biblical teaching on obedience to God.

Obeying Universal Laws Can Be a Pleasant Experience. Manly P. Hall. 8.95 (978-0-89314-201-8(8), C871018) Philos Res.
Beliefs of nature.

Obituary see Asimov's Mysteries

***Object of Beauty.** unabr. ed. Steve Martin. Read by Campbell Scott. (Running Time: 7 hrs. 30 mins.). (ENG.). 2010. 24.98 (978-1-60788-613-6(8)) Pub: Hachet Audio. Dist(s): HachBkGrp

***Object of Beauty.** unabr. ed. Steve Martin. Read by Campbell Scott. 7 CDs. (Running Time: 7 hrs. 30 mins.). (ENG., 2010. audio compact disk 34.98 (978-1-60788-612-9(X)) Pub: Hachet Audio. Dist(s): HachBkGrp

Object of the Game. 1 cass. (Running Time: 1 hr. 30 mins.). (SmartReader Ser.). (J). 1999. pap. bk. & tchr. ed. 19.95 (978-0-7887-0278-5(5), 79318T3) Recorded Bks.
Tim Park, a young Korean boy, has difficulty understanding his schoolmates in Los Angeles. But when he tries out for the baseball team, he discovers a universal language.

Objection! How High-Priced Attorneys, Celebrity Defendants, & 24/7 Media Have Hijacked Our Criminal Justice System. Nancy Grace. Read by Marguerite Gavin. Told to Diane Clehane. (Running Time: 36000 sec.). 2005. audio compact disk 72.00 (978-0-7861-7541-3(9)) Blckstn Audio.

Objection! How High-Priced Attorneys, Celebrity Defendants, & 24/7 Media Have Hijacked Our Criminal Justice System. unabr. ed. Nancy Grace. Read by Marguerite Gavin. (Running Time: 41400 sec.). 2005. audio compact disk 29.95 (978-0-7861-7904-6(X)) Blckstn Audio.

Objection! How High-Priced Defense Attorneys, Celebrity Defendants, & 24/7 Media Have Hijacked Our Criminal Justice System. Nancy Grace. Read by Marguerite Gavin. Told to Diane Clehane. (Running Time: 41400 sec.). 2005. 59.95 (978-0-7861-3798-5(3)) Blckstn Audio.

Objection: To Intellectual Hurdles: Matthew 23:27-28; Rev. 21:4. Ed Young. 1998. 4.95 (978-0-7417-2194-5(5), 1194) Win Walk.

Objection: To Needing Salvation: Luke 12:13-21. Ed Young. 1998. 4.95 (978-0-7417-2192-1(9), 1192) Win Walk.

Objection to the Bible: Logos September 5, 1999. Ben Young. 1999. 4.95 (978-0-7417-6147-7(5), B0147) Win Walk.

Objection: To the Bible: Psalm 119:105; 11 Tim. 3:16. Ed Young. 1998. 4.95 (978-0-7417-2191-4(0), A1191) Win Walk.

Objection: To The Exclusivity Of Jesus: 1 John 5:13; John 14:1-6. Ed Young. 1998. 4.95 (978-0-7417-2193-8(7), 1193) Win Walk.

Objections As Opportunities. Planned Marketing Staff. 1 cass. (Running Time: 1 hr. 30 mins.). 1994. 75.00 (978-1-882306-03-9(1)) Planned Mktg. *Training.*

Objections at Trial. Myron H. Bright. 1 cass. (Running Time: 1 hr.). 1995. 175.00 (31105) Natl Prac Inst.

Objections at Trial & How to Deal with the Difficult Lawyer. Myron H. Bright & Ronald Carlson. 1994. 39.95 state specific manual. Natl Prac Inst.

Objective Communication. Leonard Peikoff. Read by Leonard Peikoff. 20 cass. (Running Time: 25 hrs.). 1993. 195.00 (978-1-56114-082-4(1), LP19D) Second Renaissance.
The course identifies certain principles of intellectual communication, & applies them to three areas: writing, speaking & arguing. It is concerned not with style, but with substance, i.e., with the basic methods necessary to achieve a clear, absorbing presentation of one's viewpoint. The lectures are part theory, part practical application. Throughout the sessions, volunteers were given an opportunity to make brief presentations, which were evaluated - by the class & the instructor - in the light of the principles discussed. Since the subjects of these exercises are limited to aspects of the philosophy of Objectivism, the exercises may also serve to expand or refresh your knowledge of Objectivism.

Objective First Certificate Audio CD Set. 2nd ed. Annette Capel & Wendy Sharp. (Running Time: 3 hrs. 10 mins.). (ENG., 2008. audio compact disk 41.00 (978-0-521-70069-6(8)) Cambridge U Pr.

Objective for Living: To Do God's Will. Derek Prince. 1 cass. (Running Time: 1 hr. 30 mins.). 5.95 (096) Derek Prince.
Aimlessness is a tragic waste of any human life, but God has planned unique objectives for every person.

Objective IELTS Advanced. Annette Capel & Michael Black. (Running Time: 3 hrs. 10 mins.). (Objective Ser.). (ENG.). 2006. 44.00 (978-0-521-60876-3(7)); audio compact disk 44.00 (978-0-521-60877-0(5)) Cambridge U Pr.

Objective IELTS Intermediate. Michael Black & Wendy Sharp. (Running Time: 3 hrs. 8 mins.). (Objective Ser.). (ENG.). 2006. 42.00 (978-0-521-60881-7(3)); audio compact disk 44.00 (978-0-521-60880-0(5)) Cambridge U Pr.

Objective KET, Set. Annette Capel & Wendy Sharp. (Running Time: 2 hrs. 34 mins.). (Objective Ser.). (ENG.). 2005. 42.00 (978-0-521-54151-0(4)) Cambridge U Pr.

Objective KET, Set. Annette Capel & Wendy Sharp. (Running Time: 2 hrs. 34 mins.). (Objective Ser.). (ENG.). 2005. audio compact disk 44.00 (978-0-521-54152-7(2)) Cambridge U Pr.

Objective Law. Ayn Rand. 1 cass. (Running Time: 30 min.). 1990. 12.95 (978-1-56114-112-8(7), AR27C) Second Renaissance.

Objective PET, Set. Louise Hashemi & Barbara Thomas. 2 cass. (Running Time: 3 hrs. 6 mins.). (Objective Ser.). (ENG.). 2003. 42.00 (978-0-521-80581-0(3)) Cambridge U Pr.

Objective PET Audio CDs (3) 2nd ed. Louise Hashemi & Barbara Thomas. (Running Time: 3 hrs. 6 mins.). (Objective Ser.). (ENG.). 2009. audio compact disk 56.00 (978-0-521-73274-1(3)) Cambridge U Pr.

Objective Proficiency, Set. Annette Capel & Wendy Sharp. (Running Time: 2 hrs. 50 mins.). (Objective Ser.). (ENG.). 2006. audio compact disk 61.95 (978-0-521-67883-4(8)) Cambridge U Pr.

Objective Value vs. Modern Economics. Northrup Buechner. 6 cass. (Running Time: 7 hrs.). 1995. 69.95 (978-1-56114-369-6(3), DB01D) Second Renaissance.
How the concept of objective economic value changes the science of economics from the ground up.

Objectivism. unabr. ed. Leonard Peikoff. Read by Johanna Ward. 16 CDs. (Running Time: 20 hrs. 30 mins.). 2003. audio compact disk 128.00 (978-0-7861-9099-7(X), 3128); audio compact disk 39.95 (978-0-7861-8867-3(7), 3128) Blckstn Audio.

Objectivism. unabr. ed. Leonard Peikoff. Read by Johanna Ward. 14 pieces. 2004. reel tape 49.95 (978-0-7861-2495-4(4)) Blckstn Audio.

Objectivism: The Philosophy & the Movement. unabr. ed. David Kelley. Read by David Kelley. 1 cass. (Running Time: 1 hr.). 1996. 14.95 (978-1-57724-001-3(4), Prncpal Srce Audio) Objectivist Ctr.
An explanation of how a spirit of independent thought, open inquiry, rational discussion & debate is necessary to Objectivism to capitalize on the promise of Ayn Rand's ideas.

Objectivism: The State of the Art. Leonard Peikoff. Read by Leonard Peikoff. 8 cass. (Running Time: 12 hrs.). 1987. 99.00 (978-1-56114-053-4(8), LP08D) Second Renaissance.
These six lectures represent Dr. Peikoff's most recent insights into Ayn Rand's philosophy. Includes: The Logical Structure of Philosophy; The Logical Structure of Metaphysics; Objectivity & the Role of Logic; Moral Principles; Question Periods. Aside from the value of the new philosophic content contained in these talks, Dr. Peikoff offers the listener a brilliant demonstration of the proper method of philosophic thinking.

Objectivism Pt. 1: The Philosophy of Ayn Rand. Leonard Peikoff. 12 cass. (Running Time: 12 hrs.). 145.00 (LP32D) Second Renaissance.
Seminars includes: "Reality," "Sense Perception," "Volition" & "Concept-Formation".

Objectivism Pt. 2: The Philosophy of Ayn Rand. Leonard Peikoff. 12 cass. (Running Time: 15 hrs.). 175.00 (LP33D) Second Renaissance.
Seminars include: "Objectivity," "Reason," "Man," "The Good," "Virtue," "Happiness," "Government" & "Capitalism".

Objectivism Pts. 1 & 2: The Philosophy of Ayn Rand Series. Leonard Peikoff. 24 cass. (Running Time: 27 hrs.). 295.00 (LP34D) Second Renaissance.
Pt. 1: "Reality," "Sense Perception," "Volition," "Concept-Formation." Pt. 2: "Objectivity," "Reason," "Man," "The Good," "Virtue," "Happiness," "Government" & "Capitalism".

Objectivism - Questions & Answers. Leonard Peikoff. Read by Leonard Peikoff. 1 cass. (Running Time: 1 hr.). 1985. 12.95 (978-1-56114-094-7(5), LP14C) Second Renaissance.
Covers such topics as: Kant & evil, objectively defining happiness, the "rights" of animals & the question of a woman President.

Objectivism & Theism. James Keifer. 2 cass. (Running Time: 2 hrs. 49 min.). 19.95 (239) J Norton Pubs.

Objectivism & Theism. Leonard Peikoff. Read by Johanna Ward. 14 cass. (Running Time: 20 hrs. 30 mins.). 2003. 89.95 (978-0-7861-2449-7(0), 3128) Blckstn Audio.

Objectivism, Libertarianism & Religion. Peter Schwartz. 1 cass. (Running Time: 30 min.). 1993. 9.95 (978-1-56114-354-2(5), CS05C) Second Renaissance.

Objectivism: the Philosophy of Ayn Rand. unabr. ed. Leonard Peikoff. Read by Johanna Ward. (Running Time: 19 hrs. 30 mins.). 2003. 49.95 (978-0-7861-2494-7(6)) Blckstn Audio.

Objectivism Through Induction. Leonard Peikoff. 11 cass. (Running Time: 16 hrs. 30 min.). 275.00 (LP53D) Second Renaissance.
"OTI" is designed to enhance & solidify your understanding of Objectivism, whatever your level of knowledge is. Moves the student from the realm of words to the realm of factual data. Induction, in essence, is generalization from perceptual experience.

Objectivism Through Induction: Final Examination. Leonard Peikoff. (Running Time: 1 hr. 40 min.). 15.95 (LP54C) Second Renaissance.
A ten-question exam as well as several other questions.

Objectivism Today 1994. unabr. ed. Kirsti Minsaas et al. Read by Kirsti Minsaas et al. 4 cass. (Running Time: 6 hrs.). 1996. 14.00 (978-1-57724-009-9(X), Prncpal Srce Audio) Objectivist Ctr.
Four major lectures presented at the Institute for Objectivist Studies' Objectives Today 1994 conference celebrating the progress of the Institute & the effects of objectivism on our culture.

Objectivism's Man-Worship vs. Contemporary Man-Hatred. Andrew Bernstein. 5 cass. (Running Time: 6 hrs.). 59.95 (CB54D) Second Renaissance.
Modern intellectuals reject man's capacity for heroism.

Objectivist Ethics. Nathaniel Branden. 1 cass. (Running Time: 1 hr. 24 min.). (Basic Principles of Objectivism Ser.). 11.95 (569) J Norton Pubs.
Foundation of The Objectivist Ethics: Man's life as the standard of value; rationality as the foremost virtue; & happiness as the moral goal of life.

Objectivist Ethics. Ayn Rand. Read by Ayn Rand. 1 cass. (Running Time: 1 hr.). 1962. 12.95 (978-1-56114-017-6(1), AR19C) Second Renaissance.
What are values? Are they an objective, metaphysical necessity for man - or merely a dispensable social convention? These are the questions with which Ayn Rand begins the presentation of her revolutionary code of morality. She demonstrates the basic error of previous philosophers in dealing with the subject of ethics - & provides a rational alternative.

Objectivist Ethics - Q & A. Ayn Rand. 1 cass. (Running Time: 30 min.). 1994. 12.95 (978-1-56114-368-9(5), AR45C) Second Renaissance.

Objectivist Virtue of Selfishness. Peter Schwartz. Read by Peter Schwartz. 2 cass. (Running Time: 2 hrs. 8 min.). 1989. 19.95 (978-1-56114-089-3(9), CS01D) Second Renaissance.
An introductory overview, contrasting the morality of self-interest with the morality of altruism. The significance of Ayn Rand's intellectual achievement, no only in establishing a scientific ethics, but also in demonstrating how living selfishly requires the most demanding of moral principles. The extensive question period includes why dishonesty is not in one's self-interest; what obligations exist between parent & child; why the poor & handicapped should support a laiscez-faire society; taxation.

Objectivist Virtue of Selfishness: Questions & Answers. 1 cass. (Running Time: 1 hr. 20 mins.). 1989. (CS01D) Second Renaissance.

Objectivity in Journalism. Peter Schwartz. Read by Peter Schwartz. 1 cass. (Running Time: 1 hr. 30 mins.). 1988. 9.95 (978-1-56114-031-2(7), HS04C) Second Renaissance.
Deals with the question of what constitutes objective news reporting.

Objects in Motion. Compiled by Benchmark Education Staff. 2005. audio compact disk 10.00 (978-1-4108-5492-6(2)) Benchmark Educ.

Oblong Box see Great American Short Stories, Vol. II, A Collection

Oblong Box. 1986. (S-75) Jimcin Record.

Oblong Box. unabr. ed. Edgar Allan Poe. Read by David Ely. 1 cass. (Running Time: 59 min.). Dramatization. 1983. 7.95 (S-53) Jimcin Record.
Two horror stories from the master.

Oblong Box & The Premature Burial. Edgar Allan Poe. 1 cass. (Running Time: 1 hr.). 1989. 7.95 (S-53) Jimcin Record.
Horror stories from the master.

Oboe classics for the intermediate Player. Elaine Douvas. 1999. pap. bk. 34.98 (978-1-59615-359-2(8), 586-041) Pub: Music Minus. Dist(s): Bookworld

oboe Soloist: Classic solos for Oboe. Delia Montenegro. 1996. pap. bk. 34.98 (978-1-59615-351-6(2), 586-053) Pub: Music Minus. Dist(s): Bookworld

Obra Maestra de Dios Vol 1, Vol. 1. Charles R. Swindoll.Tr. of God's Masterwork Vol 1. (SPA.). 2005. audio compact disk 39.00 (978-1-57972-659-1(3)) Insight Living.

Obra Maestra de Dios Vol 2, Vol. 2. Charles R. Swindoll.Tr. of God's Masterwork Vol 2. 2005. audio compact disk 39.00 (978-1-57972-660-7(7)) Insight Living.

Obra Maestra de Dios Vol 3, Vol 3. Charles R. Swindoll.Tr. of God's Masterwork Vol 3. 2005. audio compact disk 34.00 (978-1-57972-661-4(5)) Insight Living.

Obra Maestra de Dios Vol 4, Vol. 4. Charles R. Swindoll.Tr. of God's Masterwork Vol 4. 2005. audio compact disk 37.00 (978-1-57972-662-1(3)) Insight Living.

Obra Maestra de Dios Vol 5, Vol. 5. Charles R. Swindoll.Tr. of God's Masterwork Vol 5. (SPA.). 2006. audio compact disk 40.80 (978-1-57972-663-8(1)) Insight Living.

Obscurity in Poetry, Pt. A. Gilbert Highet. 1 cass. (Running Time: 1 hr. 30 mins.). (Gilbert Highet Ser.). 11.95 (23321) J Norton Pubs.
Why some important & memorable poems are difficult to understand & funny poems & punning verses can be poetry as well as grave & solemn works.

Observations: Letters & Lectures of Idries Shah. unabr. ed. Idries Shah. Read by David Wade. 2 cass. (Running Time: 2 hrs.). (ISHK Audio Cassettes by Leading Thinkers Shah Ser.: Vol. 7). 1998. 17.00 Set. (978-1-883536-14-5(6), OBSE2, Hoopoe Books) ISHK.
A is a fine example of Shah's insight on how Sufis teach that one can transcend the barrier of limit senses & penetrate beyond apparent reality. Presents exchanges between Sufi teacher & student.

Observatory. Kevin Zepper. Read by Kevin Zepper. 1 cass. (Running Time: 1 hr.). 1988. 5.75 (978-0-932593-16-0(X)) Black Bear.
Original poetry & music.

Observatory. unabr. ed. Emily Grayson. Narrated by Linda Stephens. 4 cass. (Running Time: 5 hrs. 45 mins.). 2001. 48.00 (978-0-7887-8851-2(5)) Recorded Bks.
Twins Liz and Harper lead completely different lives until Harper's daughter suddenly dies. Liz must set aside any differences and support her sister as never before.

Observed Relationships Between Focus of Attention & Electromagnetic Frequencies. Jean Millay. 2 cass. (Running Time: 3 hrs.). 18.00 (A0090-86) Sound Photosyn.
Quincy, Alter, Adams & Rauscher join Jean from ICSS '86.

Observing Just This Moment: Live Mindfulness with Marsha M. Linehan, Ph. D. , ABPP, Seattle Intensive 2004-2005, Day 1. Executive Producer Shree A. Vigil. Prod. by Behavioral Tech. 4 CD's. (Running Time: 60 mins). 2005. audio compact disk 15.95 (978-0-9745002-5-6(9)) Behavioral Tech.

Obsessed. unabr. ed. Ted Dekker. Read by Rob Lamont. 8 pieces. 29.99 (978-1-58926-824-1(5)) Oasis Audio.

Obsessed. unabr. ed. Ted Dekker. Read by Rob Lamont. audio compact disk 21.99 (978-1-58926-903-3(9)) Oasis Audio.

Obsessed. unabr. ed. Ted Dekker. Narrated by Rob Lamont. (ENG.). 2005. 15.39 (978-1-60814-326-9(0)); audio compact disk 34.99 (978-1-58926-825-8(3)) Oasis Audio.

Obsessed by Her Beauty see Twentieth-Century Poetry in English, No. 29, Recordings of Poets Reading Their Own Poetry

Obsession. Ben Young. 2000. 4.95 (978-0-7417-6184-2(X), B0184) Win Walk.

Obsession. abr. ed. Jonathan Kellerman. Read by John Rubinstein. (Running Time: 21600 sec.). (Alex Delaware Ser.: No. 21). (ENG.). 2007. audio compact disk 29.95 (978-0-7393-0998-8(6)) Pub: Random Audio Pubg. Dist(s): Random

Obsession. abr. ed. Karen Robards. Read by Joyce Bean. (Running Time: 6 hrs.). 2008. audio compact disk 14.99 (978-1-4233-2831-5(0), 9781423328315, BCD Value Price) Brilliance Audio.

Obsession. unabr. ed. Catherine Cookson. Read by Susan Jameson. 8 cass. (Running Time: 8 hrs.). 1996. 69.95 (978-0-7451-6664-3(4), CAB 1280) AudioGO.
Dr. Falconer is invited to Pine Hurst to celebrate the 21st birthday of the local lord's eldest daughter, Beatrice. There, he meets her three sisters who inform him of Beatrice's over-possessiveness of Pine Hurst. And when their father dies, Beatrice begins planning to protect her position & take-over Pine Hurst for herself.

Obsession. unabr. ed. Jonathan Kellerman. Read by John Rubinstein. (Alex Delaware Ser.: No. 21). (YA). 2007. 64.99 (978-0-7393-7515-0(6)) Find a World.

Obsession. unabr. ed. Jonathan Kellerman. Read by John Rubinstein. 9 CDs. (Running Time: 43200 sec.). (Alex Delaware Ser.: No. 21). (ENG.). 2007. audio compact disk 44.95 (978-0-7393-3418-8(2), Random AudioBks) Pub: Random Audio Pubg. Dist(s): Random

Obsession. unabr. ed. Karen Robards. 1 MP3 CD. (Running Time: 12 hrs.). 2007. 39.25 (978-1-4233-2827-8(2), 9781423328278, Brlnc Audio MP3 Lib); 24.95 (978-1-4233-2826-1(4), 9781423328261, Brilliance MP3); 92.25 (978-1-4233-2823-0(X), 9781423328230, BrilAudUnabridg); audio compact disk 107.25 (978-1-4233-2825-4(6), 9781423328254, BriAudCD Unabrid); audio compact disk 38.95 (978-1-4233-2824-7(8), 9781423328247, Bril Audio CD Unabri) Brilliance Audio.

Obsession. unabr. ed. Karen Robards. Read by Joyce Bean. (Running Time: 12 hrs.). 2007. 39.25 (978-1-4233-2829-2(9), 9781423328292, BADLE); 24.95 (978-1-4233-2828-5(0), 9781423328285, BAD) Brilliance Audio.

***Obsession.** unabr. ed. Gloria Vanderbilt. Read by Gloria Vanderbilt. (ENG.). 2009. (978-0-06-190240-6(3), Harper Audio); (978-0-06-190241-3(1), Harper Audio) HarperCollins Pubs.

Obsession: An Erotic Tale. unabr. ed. Gloria Vanderbilt. Read by Gloria Vanderbilt. 2 CDs. (Running Time: 2 hrs.). 2009. audio compact disk 19.99 (978-0-06-178011-0(1), Harper Audio) HarperCollins Pubs.

Obsession: Hope & Truth for the Addiction Epedemic. Brandon Nutt. (ENG.). 2009. audio compact disk 8.00 (978-0-9821815-8-4(2)) Focus Pr.

Obsession: The FBI's Legendary Profiler Probes the Psyches of Killers, Rapists, & Stalkers & Their Victims & Tells How to Fight Back. John E. Douglas. Based on a work by Mark Olshaker. 2004. 10.95 (978-0-7435-4314-9(9)) Pub: S&S Audio. Dist(s): S and S Inc

***Obsession - Guilty.** abr. ed. Karen Robards. Read by Joyce Bean. (Running Time: 12 hrs.). 2010. audio compact disk 19.99 (978-1-4418-5040-9(6), 9781441850409, BACD) Brilliance Audio.

Obsessions. Concept by Kenneth Thomas. 2005. audio compact disk (978-0-9760535-6-9(X), AQM) Atomic Quill Pr.

Obsessions: The Empty Tyranny. Gerald May. 4 cass. (Running Time: 4 hrs. 23 min.). 34.95 (AA2351) Credence Commun.
Discussion of obsession as not only actions, but just of all thought revealed in prayer & guidance to inner freedom.

Obsessive Compulsive Anonymous: Twelve Step Workshop for OCD. 4 cass. (Running Time: 5 hrs. 30 min.). 1999. 35.00 (978-0-9628066-3-6(3)) OCA.
Recovery program for Obsessive Compulsive Disorder as experienced by members of Obsessive Compulsive Anonymous.

Obsessive Compulsive Disorder. Prod. by Michelle Trudeau. 1 cass. (Running Time: 20 min.). 9.95 (I0320B090, HarperThor) HarpC GBR.

Obsessive Compulsive Disorder: Program from the Award Winning Public Radio Series. Marc Summers et al. Hosted by Fred Goodwin. Comment by John Hockenberry. 1 cass. (Running Time: 1 hr.). (Infinite Mind Ser.). 1999. audio compact disk 21.95 (978-1-888064-25-4(0), LCM 45) Lichtenstein Creat.
Everyone has straightened a picture frame, wondered if they locked the door, or washed their hands after touching something dirty. For people with Obsessive-Compulsive Disorder, or OCD, everyday worries and actions like these become insistent, anxiety-producing thoughts, and rituals that must be performed to ease that anxiety. This week on The Infinite Mind, you'll hear what it's like to live with OCD; about successful new treatments for the condition; and about the surprising link between OCD in children and common strep throat. With commentary from John Hockenberry.

Obsessive Compulsive Disorder (OCD) Let Your Inner Therapist Ease the Burden. Diane Walker & Karen Levy. Prod. by Diane Walker. 2001. 12.95 (978-0-9710324-0-8(8)); audio compact disk 14.95 (978-0-9710324-1-5(6)) Yes Pro.

Obsessive-Compulsive Disorders. Bruce Goldberg. (ENG.). 2005. audio compact disk 17.00 (978-1-57968-079-4(8)) Pub: B Goldberg. Dist(s): Baker Taylor

Obsessive-Compulsive Disorders. Bruce Goldberg. Read by Bruce Goldberg. 1 cass. (Running Time: 25 min.). (ENG.). 2007. 13.00 (978-1-885577-46-7(X)) Pub: B Goldberg. Dist(s): Baker Taylor
Remove negative and persistent thoughts, and unwanted rituals from behavior through self-hypnosis.

Obsessive Relationships: I Need Do Nothing. Marianne Williamson. Read by Marianne Williamson. 1 cass. (Running Time: 1 hr. 30 mins.). (Lectures on a Course in Miracles). 1999. 10.00 (978-1-56170-249-7(8), M752) Hay House.

Obsidian Butterfly. abr. ed. Laurell K. Hamilton. (Running Time: 9 hrs.). (Anita Blake, Vampire Hunter Ser.: No. 9). (ENG.). 2010. audio compact disk 29.95 (978-0-14-314509-7(6), PengAudBks) Penguin Grp USA.

Obsidian Butterfly. unabr. ed. Laurell K. Hamilton. Read by Kimberly Alexis. 16 CDs. (Running Time: 20 hrs.). (Anita Blake, Vampire Hunter Ser.: No. 9). (ENG.). 2010. audio compact disk 39.95 (978-0-14-314409-0(X), PengAudBks) Penguin Grp USA.

Obsidian Prey. abr. ed. Jayne Castle, pseud. Read by Joyce Bean. (Running Time: 5 hrs.). (Harmony Ser.: No. 7). 2009. audio compact disk 14.99 (978-1-4233-6866-3(5), 9781423368663, BACD) Brilliance Audio.

Obsidian Prey. abr. ed. Jayne Castle, pseud. Read by Joyce Bean. (Running Time: 5 hrs.). (Harmony Ser.: No. 7). 2010. audio compact disk 9.99 (978-1-4233-6867-0(3), 9781423368670, BCD Value Price) Brilliance Audio.

Obsidian Prey. unabr. ed. Jayne Castle, pseud. Read by Joyce Bean. (Running Time: 9 hrs.). (Ghost Hunters Ser.). 2009. audio compact disk 34.99 (978-1-4233-6860-1(6), 9781423368601) Brilliance Audio.

Obsidian Prey. unabr. ed. Jayne Castle, pseud. Read by Joyce Bean. (Running Time: 8 hrs.). (Harmony Ser.: No. 7). 2009. 24.99 (978-1-4233-6862-5(2), 9781423368625, Brilliance MP3); 39.97 (978-1-4233-6863-2(0), 9781423368632, Brlnc Audio MP3 Lib); 24.99 (978-1-4233-6864-9(9), 9781423368649, BAD); 39.97 (978-1-4233-6865-6(7), 9781423368656, BADLE); audio compact disk 92.97 (978-1-4233-6861-8(4), 9781423368618, BriAudCD Unabrid) Brilliance Audio.

***Obsolete Man.** 2010. audio compact disk (978-1-59171-160-5(6)) Falcon Picture.

Obstacles on the Way. Swami Amar Jyoti. 1 cass. (Running Time: 1 hr. 30 mins.). 1976. 9.95 (M-59) Truth Consciousness.
The three major obstacles on the path to freedom & how to avoid them. Questions for immortality.

Obstacles to Freedom. unabr. ed. Perf. by Eknath Easwaran. 1 cass. (Running Time: 1 hr.). 1985. 7.95 (978-1-58638-584-2(4)) Nilgiri Pr.

Obstacles to Your Faith. Tim Greenwood. Read by Tim Greenwood. Ed. by Marcia Greenwood. 1999. 5.00 (978-1-930761-01-8(5)) TGMinist.

Obstetric Anesthesia. Contrib. by Louis Weinstein et al. 1 cass. (American College of Obstetrics & Gynecologists UPDATE: Vol. 22, No. 1). 1998. 20.00 Am Coll Obstetric.

Obstetrical Malpractice: Failure to Diagnose Fetal Distress. Moderated by Stephen H. Mackauf & Stanley Tessel. (Running Time: 11 hrs.). 1992. pap. bk. 295.00 NY Law Pub.
Failure to recognize & treat fetal distress promptly during labor is the most common claim in obstetrical malpractice cases. These cassettes will help you recognize which claims are meritorious by focusing on subjects including auscultation of the fetal heart rate; basics of the electronic fetal monitor; interpretation & storage of the tracings; meconium; & fetal blood sampling.

Obstetrics & Gynecology Review, Vol. A148. unabr. ed. 31 cass. (Running Time: 35 hrs.). 1994. 695.00 (978-1-57664-355-6(7)) CME Info Svcs.
Continuing medical education home-study. Complete package contains audiotapes, syllabus, self-assessment examination to earn CME Category 1 credit.

Obstinate Heart - Jane Austen: A Biography. unabr. collector's ed. Valerie Grosvenor Myer. Read by Donada Peters. 7 cass. (Running Time: 10 hrs. 30 mins.). 1997. 56.00 (978-0-7366-3664-3(1), 4339) Books on Tape.
Jane Austen declined to marry men she did not love & her books served as both her companions & children.

***Obstruction of Justice.** abr. ed. Perri O'Shaughnessy. Read by Laural Merlington. (Running Time: 3 hrs.). (Nina Reilly Ser.). 2010. audio compact disk 9.99 (978-1-4418-6703-2(1), 9781441867032, BCD Value Price) Brilliance Audio.

Obstruction of Justice. unabr. ed. Perri O'Shaughnessy. Read by Laural Merlington. (Running Time: 13 hrs.). 2007. 39.25 (978-1-4233-3068-4(4), 9781423330684, BADLE); 24.95 (978-1-4233-3067-7(6), 9781423330677, BAD) Brilliance Audio.

Obstruction of Justice. unabr. ed. Perri O'Shaughnessy. Read by Laural Merlington. (Running Time: 13 hrs.). 2007. 39.25 (978-1-4233-3066-0(8), 9781423330660, Brlnc Audio MP3 Lib); 24.95 (978-1-4233-3065-3(X), 9781423330653, Brilliance MP3) Brilliance Audio.

***Obstruction of Justice.** unabr. ed. Perri O'Shaughnessy. Read by Laural Merlington. (Running Time: 13 hrs.). (Nina Reilly Ser.). 2010. audio compact disk 29.99 (978-1-4418-4087-5(7), 9781441840875, Bril Audio CD Unabri); audio compact disk 89.97 (978-1-4418-4088-2(5), 9781441840882, BriAudCD Unabrid) Brilliance Audio.

Obstruction of Justice. unabr. ed. Perri O'Shaughnessy. Read by Laural Merlington. 10 cass. 1999. 89.25 (FS9-34302) Highsmith.

Obtaining Grants to Fund Your Adoption. Hosted by Mardie Caldwell. (ENG.). 2008. audio compact disk 12.95 (978-1-935176-07-7(2)) Pub: Am Carrage Hse Pubng. Dist(s): STL Dist NA

Obtaining Information, Goods & Services. Scripts. Natasha Cooper. Prod. by Phillip Richards. 4 cass. (Running Time: 6 hrs. 30 min.). Dramatization. (Speaking Problem-Solvers Ser.). 2001. 69.99 (978-0-9677755-7-9(4)); audio compact disk 79.99 (978-0-9677755-8-6(2)) Cooper Learn Syst.

Obtaining Information, Goods & Services: English That Gets You All You Need. Scripts. Natasha Cooper. 4 cass. (Running Time: 6 hrs. 15 mins.). Dramatization. 2003. pap. bk. 89.99 (978-1-932521-15-3(1)) Cooper Learn Syst.
Phrases, exercises, and dialogues for phone, catalog and in-store purchases; credit card and bank account management; choosing the right service; transportation: public - car-rentals - taxis; utility and phone services: ordering - changing -closing; hard-to-get information and more.

Obtaining Information, Goods & Services: English That Gets You What You Need. Scripts. Natasha Cooper. 6 CDs. (Running Time: 6 hrs. 15 mins.). Dramatization. 2003. pap. bk. 99.99 (978-1-932521-16-0(X)) Cooper Learn Syst.
Packaged in a multimedia vinyl album with an accompanying book.

Obtaining Information, Goods & Services: English That Gets You What You Want. Scripts. Natasha Cooper. 4 cass. (Running Time: 6 hrs. 15 mins.). Dramatization. (ENG & RUS.). 2001. pap. bk. 99.99 (978-1-932521-17-7(8)); pap. bk. 109.99 (978-1-932521-18-4(6)) Cooper Learn Syst.
Phrases and dialogues for phone, catalog and in-store purchases; credit card and bank account management; choosing the right service; transportation; utilities; hard-to-get information.

Obtaining Priesthood Power. Blaine Yorgason & Brenton Yorgason. Read by Marvin Payne. 1 cass. (Running Time: 1 hr. 30 mins.). (Gospel Power Ser.). 6.95 (978-0-929985-46-6(X)) Jackman Pubng.
A father's letter to his son regarding understanding the priesthood & obtaining optimum power.

Obvious: All You Need to Know in Business. Period. James Dale. Read by Alan Sklar. (Playaway Adult Nonfiction Ser.). (ENG.). 2009. 39.99 (978-1-60812-530-2(0)) Find a World.

Obvious: All You Need to Know in Business. Period. unabr. ed. James Dale. (Running Time: 3 hrs. 30 mins. 0 sec.). (ENG.). 2007. audio compact disk 19.99 (978-1-4001-0396-6(7)) Pub: Tantor Media. Dist(s): IngramPubServ

Obvious: All You Need to Know in Business. Period. unabr. ed. James Dale. Narrated by Alan Sklar. (Running Time: 3 hrs. 30 mins. 0 sec.). (ENG.). 2007. audio compact disk 39.99 (978-1-4001-3396-3(3)); audio compact disk 19.99 (978-1-4001-5396-1(4)) Pub: Tantor Media. Dist(s): IngramPubServ

Obvious Diet: Your Personal Way to Lose Weight Fast - Without Changing Your Lifestyle. unabr. ed. Read by Dan Cashman. Frwd. by Nigella Lawson & Larry King. 3 cass. (Running Time: 6 hrs.). 2004. 25.00 (978-1-59007-242-4(1)) Pub: New Millenn Enter. Dist(s): PerseuPGW
When you are one of London's most-invited dinner guests, you are tempted by a lot of wonderful food. Bon vivant Ed Victor, premier literary agent to some of the world's most popular authors, had gained 30 pounds after a little too much of the good life at banquets, parties, and fine restaurants. Reasoning that the best way to diet is to follow rules of your own making, he devised a plan, helped by tips from his friends, that allowed him to lose all the weight he had gained, and then some.

O'Carolan Harp Tunes Dlcmr. Shelley Stevens. 1993. bk. 15.95 (978-0-7866-1166-9(9), 94885P); 9.98 (978-1-56222-902-3(8), 94885C) Mel Bay.

O'Carolan Tunes for Harp. Mary Fitzgerald. (ENG.). 2009. pap. bk. 14.99 (978-0-7866-7250-9(1)) Mel Bay.

Occasional Suite. Deirdra Baldwin. Perf. by Deirdra Baldwin. 1 cass. (Running Time: 58 min.). (Watershed Tapes of Contemporary Poetry Ser.). 1980. 11.95 (23639) J Norton Pubs.
A collaboration between the young poet & the music band "Standard Appliance".

Occasions Arise When the Mind Hesitates-Concentrations: Volume 6, Vol. 6. Speeches. As told by Bhagat Singh Thind. Clark Walker. (Running Time: 60 mins.). (ENG.). 2003. audio compact disk 12.00 (978-1-932630-07-7(4)) Pub: Dr Bhagat Sin. Dist(s): Baker Taylor

Occasions Arise When the Mind Hesitates-Concentrations: Volume 6, Vol. 6. Speeches. As told by Bhagat Singh Thind. (Running Time: 60 mins.). (ENG., 2003. 6.50 (978-1-932630-30-5(9)) Pub: Dr Bhagat Sin. Dist(s): Baker Taylor

Occitan sans Peine. 1 cass. (Running Time: 1 hr., 30 min.). (FRE.). 2000. bk. 75.00 (978-2-7005-1348-6(7)) Pub: Assimil FRA. Dist(s): Distribks Inc

Occult America: The Secret History of How Mysticism Shaped Our Nation. unabr. ed. Mitch Horowitz. (Running Time: 10 hrs. 30 mins.). 2009. 29.95 (978-1-4417-1111-3(2)); 65.95 (978-1-4417-1107-6(4)); audio compact disk 32.95 (978-1-4417-1110-6(4)); audio compact disk 100.00 (978-1-4417-1108-3(2)) Blckstn Audio.

Occult & Roman Superstitions. Timothy Kauffman. 1 cass. (Running Time: 1 hr. 30 mins.). (Conference on Christianity & Roman Catholicism Ser.: No. 6). 5.00 Trinity Found.

Occult Phenomena: Arena of Synchronicity. unabr. ed. Stephan Hoeller. 1 cass. (Running Time: 1 hr. 30 min.). 1996. 11.00 (40019) Big Sur Tapes.
Hoeller expands his discussion of synchronicity by examining how our acceptance of meaning changes as we get older. He explores how we can sensibly discover personal meaning in the extraordinary.

Occult Truth & Misconceptions. 1 cass. (Running Time: 1 hr.). 1990. 8.95 (978-0-8356-1905-9(2)) Theos Pub Hse.
Examines channelers, mystic rites, & the true meaning of the word occult.

Occult Vision. Colin Wilson. 2 cass. (Running Time: 3 hrs.). 18.00 (A0438-88) Sound Photosyn.
The mind power of this man is awesome.

Occult Vision Workshop. Colin Wilson. 4 cass. (Running Time: 6 hrs.). 36.00 set. (A0439-88) Sound Photosyn.
Get it here...from a long term researcher.

Occult World. Jack Van Impe. 1 cass. 7.00 J Van Impe.
Dr. Van Impe explains the prophetic significance of today's increased demonic activity.

Occultic Tendencies in Rock Music. David Benoit. Read by David Benoit. 1 cass. (Running Time: 1 hr. 15 min.). (What's Behind the Rock Ser.). 1987. 6.00 (978-0-923105-02-0(6)) Glory Ministries.
Presents a seminar that exposes the involvement of today's rock stars directly or indirectly in the Satanist Church.

Occupation, Writer. unabr. collector's ed. Robert Graves. Read by Richard Brown. 10 cass. (Running Time: 15 hrs.). 1992. 80.00 (978-0-7366-2152-6(0), 2951) Books on Tape.
Is a collection of the author's short stories, plays & miscellaneous essays. Included are "Lars Porsena," "Interview With a Dead Man," "How Mad Are Hatters?", "Colonel Blimps Ancestors," "But It Still Goes On" & many others, spanning the early 1920s through the late '40's.

Occupational Health & Safety Principles & Nursing Certification Review. Moderated by Annette B. Haag. 2001. 189.95 (978-0-9712831-1-4(7)) A B Haag.

***Occupied City.** unabr. ed. David Peace. (Running Time: 9 hrs. 30 mins.). 2010. 29.95 (978-1-4417-5483-7(0)); 59.95 (978-1-4417-5479-0(2)); audio compact disk 29.95 (978-1-4417-5482-0(2)); audio compact disk 90.00 (978-1-4417-5480-6(6)) Blckstn Audio.

Occupying Power. unabr. ed. Gwyn Griffin. Read by Wolfram Kandinsky. 10 cass. (Running Time: 15 hrs.). 1984. 80.00 (978-0-7366-0616-5(5), 1578) Books on Tape.
The Island of Baressa, a modest, oval splotch of land, was one of Italy's earliest & most embarrassing colonial acquisitions. This reclusive parcel of land escaped Mussolini's military attention. But not the British. On an August afternoon in 1940, commanded by Major Lemonfield, an assault force secures the island. What follows is an occupation that marries high moral purpose with puritanical force & hypocrisy.

***Occurance at Owl Creek Bridge.** (ENG.). 2010. audio compact disk (978-1-59171-308-1(0)) Falcon Picture.

Occurrence at Owl Creek Bridge see Great American Short Stories

Occurrence at Owl Creek Bridge see Fourteen American Masterpieces

Occurrence at Owl Creek Bridge. 1977. (N-13) Jimcin Record.

Occurrence at Owl Creek Bridge. Ambrose Bierce. Read by Vincent Price. (497) J Norton Pubs.

Occurrence at Owl Creek Bridge. unabr. ed. Ambrose Bierce. Narrated by Mark Hammer. 2 cass. (Running Time: 3 hrs.). 1982. 18.00 (978-1-55690-385-4(5), 82041E7) Recorded Bks.
Stories of the macabre & supernatural.

Occurrence at Owl Creek Bridge. unabr. collector's ed. Ambrose Bierce. Read by Jonathan Reese. 6 cass. (Running Time: 6 hrs.). (J). 1997. 36.00 (978-0-7366-3646-9(3), 4311) Books on Tape.
The Owl Creek bridge story recounts the hanging of a young Civil War soldier.

Occurrence at Owl Creek Bridge & Other Stories. Ambrose Bierce. Read by Jonathan Resse. (Running Time: 5 hrs. 30 mins.). 2004. 24.95 (978-1-59912-412-4(2)) Iofy Corp.

Occurrence at Owl Creek Bridge & Other Stories. unabr. ed. Ambrose Bierce. Narrated by Jonathan Reese. (Running Time: 6 hrs. 0 mins. 0 sec.). (ENG.). 2008. audio compact disk 45.99 (978-1-4001-3797-8(7)); audio compact disk 19.99 (978-1-4001-5797-6(8)) Pub: Tantor Media. Dist(s): IngramPubServ

Occurrence at Owl Creek Bridge & Other Stories. unabr. ed. Ambrose Bierce. Narrated by Jonathan Reese. (Running Time: 6 hrs. 0 mins. 0 sec.). (Tantor Unabridged Classics Ser.). (ENG.). 2008. audio compact disk 22.99 (978-1-4001-0797-1(0)) Pub: Tantor Media. Dist(s): IngramPubServ

Occurrence at Owl Creek Bridge & The Middle Toe of the Right Foot. Ambrose Bierce. (Running Time: 1 hr.). (Radiobook Ser.). 1987. 4.98 (978-0-929541-11-2(1)) Radiola Co.
Two complete stories.

Ocean. Dorling Kindersley Publishing Staff. Contrib. by Andrew Sachs. (DK Eyewitness Bks.). (ENG.). (J). 2006. 12.99 (978-0-7566-2370-8(7)) DK Pub Inc.

Ocean Apart. unabr. ed. Robin Pilcher. Read by Samantha Eggars. 10 cass. (Running Time: 15 hrs.). 2002. 45.00 (978-1-59040-237-5(5), Phoenix Audio) Pub: Amer Intl Pub. Dist(s): PerseuPGW
David considered himself a lucky man. Lovely and full of spirit, his wife, Rachel was all he could hope to find in a woman. Now cancer has taken her from him. In search of solace, he returns with his children to Incheilich, his parent's home in the Scottish countryside where he spends his days knee-deep in the garden's mud trying to escape his pain. Soon he travels to the United States, where he finds comfort in being a stranger in a strange land. Soon, with the heat of the American sun on his back, he begins once again to feel alive.

Ocean Dreams. Short Stories. Steven Fletcher. 1 CD. (Running Time: 79 mins.). 2005. audio compact disk 14.95 (978-0-9749138-1-0(2)) Gent Place.

Ocean Dreams. Bernie Krause. 1 CD. (Running Time: 1 hr.). (Wild Sanctuary Ser.). 1994. audio compact disk 15.95 CD. (2370, Creativ Pub) Quayside.
Shoreline of the Big Sur coast in California. Relaxing sounds of rhythmic Pacific Ocean waves with the surrounding natural world of shore birds & sea breezes.

Ocean Dreams. Bernie Krause. 1 cass. (Running Time: 1 hr.). (Wild Sanctuary Ser.). 1994. 9.95 (2369, NrthWrd Bks) TandN Child.

Ocean Dreams. Executive Producer Twin Sisters Productions Staff. 1 CD. (Running Time: 55 mins). (Growing Minds with Music Ser.). (J). 2003. audio compact disk 12.99 (978-1-57583-644-7(0)) Twin Sisters.
Peaceful ocean waves are blended with original, soul-soothing instrumental music.

Ocean Echos. 1 cass. (Running Time: 1 hr.). (Interludes Music Ser.). 1989. 9.95 (978-1-55569-280-3(X), MOD-3901) Great Am Audio.

Ocean Encounter. 1 cass. (Running Time: 1 hr.). 1994. audio compact disk 15.95 (2284, Creativ Pub) Quayside.
Gentle lapping of ocean surf. Recorded for NorthSound on remote Hawaiian beaches. Perfect relaxation experience.

Ocean Encounter. 1 cass. (Running Time: 1 hr.). 1994. 9.95 (2282, NrthWrd Bks) TandN Child.

Ocean Is Salty: Ocean Life Creatures. Steck-Vaughn Staff. 1 cass. (Running Time: 90 min.). (J). 1999. (978-0-7398-0925-9(3)) SteckVau.

Ocean Music. 1 CD. (Running Time: 1 hr.). 1994. audio compact disk 15.95 CD. (2274, Creativ Pub) Quayside.
Natural melodies of the ocean & the land that touches the waves. Chuck Lange original, refreshing songs.

Ocean Music. 1 cass. (Running Time: 1 hr.). 1994. 9.95 (2272, NrthWrd Bks) TandN Child.

Ocean Oasis. (Running Time: 75 mins). (YA). (gr. 5 up). 2004. DVD 19.99 (978-1-58448-366-3(0)) Slingshot.

Ocean of Love. Ari Frankel. Illus. by Alona Frankel. 1 cass. (Running Time: 42 min.). (J). (ps-3). 1996. pap. bk. 12.98 (978-1-888509-00-7(7), BMR1001) Baby Matters.
Highly recommended collection of clever, catchy songs for kids in a remarkable range of adult musical styles.

Ocean of Love. Ari Frankel. Illus. by Alona Frankel. 1 cass. (Running Time: 42 min.). (ps-3). 1997. 9.98 (978-1-888509-02-1(3), BMR1001) Baby Matters.

Ocean of Love. Ari Frankel. Illus. by Alona Frankel. 1 CD. (Running Time: 42 min.). (ps-3). 1997. audio compact disk 14.98 (978-1-888509-01-4(5), BMR1001) Baby Matters.

Ocean of Mercy. Music by Michael John Poirier. 1992. 11.00 (978-1-58459-105-4(6)); audio compact disk 16.00 (978-1-58459-106-1(4)) Wrld Lib Pubns.

Ocean Pearl. unabr. ed. J. C. Burke. Read by Edwina Wren. (Running Time: 8 hrs. 40 mins.). (YA). 2009. audio compact disk 83.95 (978-1-74214-096-4(3), 9781742140964) Pub: Bolinda Pubng AUS. Dist(s): Bolinda Pub Inc

Ocean Pollution. Compiled by Benchmark Education Staff. 2005. audio compact disk 10.00 (978-1-4108-5507-7(4)) Benchmark Educ.

Ocean Prize. James Pattinson & James Pattinson. 2008. audio compact disk 64.95 (978-1-84559-582-1(3)) Pub: Soundings Ltd GBR. Dist(s): Ulverscroft US

Ocean Prize. James Pattinson & James Pattinson. Read by Terry Wale. 5 cass. 2008. 49.95 (978-1-84559-553-1(X)) Pub: Soundings Ltd GBR. Dist(s): Ulverscroft US

Ocean Rhapsody-Music. 2007. audio compact disk 16.95 (978-1-56136-418-3(5)) Master Your Mind.

Ocean Trash & Global Warming. Hosted by Nancy Pearlman. 1 cass. (Running Time: 29 min.). 10.00 (712) Educ Comm CA.

Ocean Waves. Great American Audio. Composed by Steven Gruskin. Contrib. by Vinnie Della-Rocca. 1 cass. (Running Time: 1 hr.). (Interludes Music Ser.). 1991. 9.95 (978-1-55569-464-7(0), 3806) Great Am Audio.
You are in tune with nature, refreshed & rejuvenated. This is your own private interlude, which you may visit in solitude or share with someone special. Soothing sounds of nature & music.

Ocean Waves & Progressive Oscillatory Waves: Syllabus. E. H. Sluyter & Ethel Raddon. (J). 1977. 39.30 (978-0-89420-165-3(4), 234000) Natl Book.

Ocean Wonders. Bernie Krause. 1 CD. (Running Time: 1 hr.). (Wild Sanctuary Ser.). 1994. audio compact disk 15.95 (2336, Creativ Pub) Quayside.
Salty breezes, gentle waves, crashing surf, shorebirds, sea lions, humpback & killer whales, trigger & drum fish, shrimp blend together into a natural ocean symphony.

Ocean Wonders. Bernie Krause. 1 cass. (Running Time: 1 hr.). (Wild Sanctuary Ser.). 1994. 9.95 (2335, NrthWrd Bks) TandN Child.

Oceans. Brad Caudle & Melissa Caudle. 1 cass. (Rock 'n Learn Ser.). (J). bk. 7.98 (RNL975) NewSound.
Songs teach about coral reefs, creatures & fish of coral reefs, sharks, rays, whales, dolphins, creatures of the deep, names & locations of the world's oceans & much more.

***Oceans: CD add-on Set.** Perf. by Millmark Education Staff. (ConceptLinks Ser.). 2009. audio compact disk 50.00 (978-1-61618-350-9(0)) Millmark Educ.

Oceans: Includes Cassette. unabr. ed. Brad Caudle & Melissa Caudle. Perf. by Brad Caudle. Illus. by Anthony Guerra. 1 cass. (Running Time: 40 min.).

(Rock 'N Learn Ser.). (J). (gr. 2 up). 1998. pap. bk. 12.99 (978-1-878489-75-3(5), RL975) Rock N Learn.
The fun way to become an ocean expert! With the help of cool songs, learn the names of the oceans & how they move in currents, tides & waves. Colorful illustrations of over 70 ocean creatures introduce you to the coral reef, its inhabitants, & many other ocean creatures.

Oceans Vol. 123: Get Kids Excited About Oceans! unabr. ed. Kim Mitzo Thompson & Karen Mitzo Hilderbrand. 1 CD. (Running Time: 36 min.). (Get Kids Excited about Ser.). (J). 1999. audio compact disk 12.99 (978-1-57583-203-6(8)) Twin Sisters.
Children will learn about whales, dolphins, sea turtles, manatees and other animals that live in the ocean.

Oceans Activity Book Set. 2004. audio compact disk 13.99 (978-1-57583-359-0(X)) Twin Sisters.

Oceans Apart. unabr. ed. Karen Kingsbury. (Running Time: 13 hrs. 0 mins. 0 sec.). (ENG.). 2004. audio compact disk 29.99 (978-0-310-25403-4(5)) Zondervan.

Oceans Apart. unabr. ed. Zondervan Publishing Staff & Karen Kingsbury. (Running Time: 13 hrs. 0 mins. 0 sec.). (ENG.). 2004. 14.99 (978-0-310-26165-0(1)) Zondervan.

***Oceans Audio CD.** Perf. by Millmark Education Staff. (ConceptLinks Ser.). 2008. audio compact disk 28.00 (978-1-4334-0175-6(4)) Millmark Educ.

Ocean's Bridge. unabr. ed. Karen Kingsbury. (Running Time: 13 hrs. 0 mins. 0 sec.). (ENG.). 2007. 14.99 (978-0-310-27013-3(8)) Zondervan.

***Oceans Giant Floor Puzzle.** Created by Twin Sisters. (Giant Floor Puzzles Ser.). (ENG.). (J). 2008. audio compact disk (978-1-59922-347-6(3)) Twin Sisters.

Oceans of the World: Syllabus. Robert E. Adam. (J). 1978. 70.85 (978-0-89420-166-0(2), 233000) Natl Book.

***Oceans SB1 Audio CD Properties & Living Things.** Perf. by Millmark Education Staff. (Content Literacy Libraries Ser.). 2008. audio compact disk (978-1-4334-0428-3(1)) Millmark Educ.

***Oceans SB2 Audio CD Different Depths & Zones.** Perf. by Millmark Education Staff. (Content Literacy Libraries Ser.). 2008. audio compact disk (978-1-4334-0429-0(X)) Millmark Educ.

***Oceans SB3 Audio CD Waves & Currents.** Perf. by Millmark Education Staff. (Content Literacy Libraries Ser.). 2008. audio compact disk (978-1-4334-0430-6(3)) Millmark Educ.

***Oceans SB4 Audio CD Exploring & Protecting.** Perf. by Millmark Education Staff. (Content Literacy Libraries Ser.). 2008. audio compact disk (978-1-4334-0431-3(1)) Millmark Educ.

Ocho Amigos en Total, EDL Level 4. (Fonolibros Ser.: Vol. 25). (SPA.). 2003. 11.50 (978-0-7652-1014-2(2)) Modern Curr.

Octavia. Beryl Kingston & Tanya Myers. 2009. 89.95 (978-1-84652-289-5(7)); audio compact disk 99.95 (978-1-84652-290-1(0)) Pub: Magna Story GBR. Dist(s): Ulverscroft US

***Octavia Boone's Big Questions about Life, the Universe & Everything.** unabr. ed. Rebecca Rupp. (Running Time: 3 hrs.). 2010. 39.97 (978-1-4418-8945-4(0), 9781441889454, Candlewick Bril); 19.99 (978-1-4418-8944-7(2), 9781441889447, Candlewick Bril); audio compact disk 19.99 (978-1-4418-8942-3(6), 9781441889423, Candlewick Bril); audio compact disk 39.97 (978-1-4418-8943-0(4), 9781441889430, Candlewick Bril) Brilliance Audio.

***Octavia Boone's Big Questions about Life, the Universe & Everything.** unabr. ed. Rebecca Rupp. Read by Ellen Grafton. (Running Time: 3 hrs.). 2010. audio compact disk 22.99 (978-1-4418-8940-9(X), 9781441889409, Candlewick Bril); audio compact disk 44.97 (978-1-4418-8941-6(8), 9781441889416, Candlewick Bril) Brilliance Audio.

***Octavia's War.** Beryl Kingston. Read by Tanya Myers. 2010. 99.95 (978-1-84652-848-4(8)); audio compact disk 104.95 (978-1-84652-849-1(6)) Pub: Magna Story GBR. Dist(s): Ulverscroft US

Octavo Habito. abr. ed. Stephen R. Covey. Narrated by Alejo Felipe. (Playaway Adult Nonfiction Ser.). (SPA.). 2009. 39.99 (978-1-60847-833-0(5)) Find a World.

October Blood. Francine Du Plessix Gray. Read by Francine Du Plessix Gray. 1 cass. (Running Time: 30 min.). 8.95 (AMF-20) Am Audio Prose.
Ms. Gray reads from her novel & talks about growing up in a publishing family & the psychological demands of individuals in the fashion industry.

October Country. unabr. collector's ed. Ray Bradbury. Read by Michael Prichard. 7 cass. (Running Time: 10 hrs. 30 min.). 1990. 56.00 (978-0-7366-1745-1(0), 2584) Books on Tape.
This collection of Ray Bradbury selections includes 14 of his early stories, along with "Homecoming" & "The Small Assassin," plus five more recent tales. Bizarre, terrifying, fantastic, Bradbury's parables always have something more than horror to impart. For the underlying theme is the distortion & disguises of love in a world that sorely needs the real thing.

October Light. unabr. ed. John Gardner. Read by Grover Gardner. 12 cass. (Running Time: 18 hrs.). 96.00 (978-0-7366-0795-7(1), 1746) Books on Tape.
James Page is a crusty old Vermonter. One day, mad at the world, he blasts his sister's television with a shotgun. She locks herself in her bedroom where she holds out with a box of apples from the attic & a trashy novel from under the bed. Their dilapidated farmhouse becomes a battleground, their anger strips away years of shame & guilt. Not only are the passions liberated, but a number of ghosts as well.

October Suite. unabr. ed. Maxine Clair. Narrated by Robin Miles. 9 cass. (Running Time: 11 hrs. 45 mins.). 2002. 74.00 (978-1-4025-0780-9(1), 96888) Recorded Bks.
October Brown, a young African-American woman, is just beginning her teaching career when she gets pregnant by a married man. When he abandons her, she gives the baby to her childless sister. But this sacrifice will haunt her as the boy grows up. To be part of her son's life, October must look beyond her desire to reclaim him and examine the truth of her family: her mother's murder, her father's disappearance, and the mysterious source of October's given name.

October Surprise. abr. ed. Gary G. Sick. Read by Joe Regalbuto. 2 cass. (Running Time: 3 hrs.). 1994. 15.95 (978-1-879371-25-5(1), 20220) Pub Mills.
The result of three years of research & hundreds of interviews, October Surprise is an account of how the 1980 Reagan-Bush presidential campaign, intent on delaying the release of the fifty-two American hostages in Teheran until after the election, made clandestine overtures to Iran & arranged illegal arms shipments through Israel.

October's Ghost. unabr. ed. Ryne Douglas Pearson. Narrated by George Guidall. 11 cass. (Running Time: 16 hrs. 15 mins.). 1995. 91.00 (978-0-7887-0101-6(0), 94342E7) Recorded Bks.
The year is 1992 & the United States is locked in diplomatic negotiations to build a secure relationship with a tenuous Russian government. In Cuba, a plan is in effect to topple the Western Hemisphere's last Communist dictator, Fidel Castro. But Castro is readying a 30-year-old nuclear-tipped missile. Locked in a game of global blind-man's buff, National Security Advisor Bud DiContino must prevent the Cuban situation from sparking an international incident.

Octopus. Denys Cazet. Illus. by Denys Cazet. Read by John Beach. 1 CD. (Running Time: 10 mins.). (Grandpa Spanielson's Chicken Pox Stories Ser.). (J). (ps-3). 2008. pap. bk. 18.95 (978-1-4301-0458-2(9)) Live Oak Media.

Octopus. Denys Cazet. Illus. by Denys Cazet. Read by John Beach. 1 cass. (Running Time: 10 mins.). (Grandpa Spanielson's Chicken Pox Stories Ser.). (J). (ps-3). 2008. pap. bk. 16.95 (978-1-4301-0455-1(4)) Live Oak Media.

Octopus. Frank Norris. Read by Anais 9000. 2008. 33.95 (978-1-60112-046-5(X)) Babblebooks.

Octopus, Set. Denys Cazet. Illus. by Denys Cazet. Narrated by John Beach. 1 cass. (Running Time: 10 mins.). (J). (ps-3). 2008. pap. bk. 29.95 (978-1-4301-0457-5(0)); pap. bk. 31.95 (978-1-4301-0460-5(0)) Live Oak Media.

Octopus: A Story of California. Frank Norris. Narrated by Flo Gibson. 13 cass. (Running Time: 18 hrs. 30 min.). 1997. 41.95 (978-1-55685-474-3(9)) Audio Bk Con.
Struggle for power & survival between wheat farmers & the Pacific & Southwestern Railroad involves the lives & deaths of many we learn to care about deeply. The contrast between scenes of starvation & desperation & descriptions of a tycoon's dinner party are devastating.

Octopus: A Story of California. unabr. ed. Frank Norris. Read by Jonathan Reese. 14 cass. (Running Time: 14 hrs.). 2001. 112.00 (978-0-7366-8380-7(1)) Books on Tape.
A novel of social consciousness set in the declining days of the Frontier West. It is the story of California wheat farmers who must struggle for survival in a world completely controlled by the railroad. The railroad has everyone and everything in its pocket: the law, the courts, and the state. Even when the farmers organize and seat one of their own on the board that sets prices for wheat, the railroad manages to suborn him as well. But if they do not beat the railroad, the railroad will take over their lands and their livelihood.

Octopus' Den. Deirdre Langeland. 1 cass. (Running Time: 35 min.). (J). (ps-2). 2001. bk. 19.95 (SP 4014C) Kimbo Educ.
Below the surface of the Mediterranean Sea, Octopus heads back to his den after a long night of hunting. Includes book.

Octopus' Den. Deirdre Langeland. Read by Peter Thomas. Illus. by Steven James Petruccio. 1 cass. (Running Time: 12 min.). (Smithsonian Oceanic Collection). (J). (ps-2). 1997. 5.00 (978-1-56899-476-5(1), C4014) Soundprints.
Octopus heads back to his den after a long night of hunting. A hungry moray eel attacks & Octopus shoots a cloud of ink into the water. Finally reaching his den, he finds another octopus there. He must find a new home.

Octopus Knows! Alexander Theodore Borgeas. 2009. spiral bd. 19.95i (978-0-9764475-0-4(9)) Cameltrotters.

Octopus Lady & Crow: And Other Animal People Stories of the Northwest Coast. unabr. ed. Read by Johnny Moses. 1 cass. (Running Time: 1 hr.). (Native American Storytime Ser.). (ps-8). 1995. 11.00 (978-0-930407-34-6(2)) Parabola Bks.
Both children and adults will enjoy these vivid and often hilarious traditional stories about what can happen to know-it-alls and to children who don't listen to their elders, why day and night come as they do, and why it is better to be kind, told with a humorous assortment of human and animal voices and sounds.

Octopussy: And the Living Daylights. unabr. ed. Ian Fleming. Read by Robert Whitfield. 2 cass. (Running Time: 2 hrs. 30 mins.). (ENG.). 2002. 17.95 (978-0-7861-2154-0(8), 2904); audio compact disk 24.00 (978-0-7861-9587-9(8), 2904) Blckstn Audio.
The legendary 007 is sent to Jamaica to deal with a rich, deranged major with a fondness for eight-legged creatures.

Octopussy: And the Living Daylights. unabr. ed. Ian Fleming. Read by Simon Vance. (Running Time: 2.5 hrs. 0 mins.). (James Bond Ser.: No. 14). 2009. audio compact disk 19.95 (978-1-4332-6137-4(5)) Blckstn Audio.

Octopussy & the Living Daylights: James Bond Series #14. unabr. ed. Ian Fleming. Read by Simon Vance. (Running Time: 1 hr. 0 mins.). (ENG.). 2009. 19.95 (978-1-4332-9041-1(3)) Blckstn Audio.

Octopussy, The Living Daylights & The Property of a Lady: Featuring James Bond. unabr. ed. Ian Fleming. Read by David Rintoul. 2 cass. (Running Time: 2 hrs.). 1996. 24.95 (978-0-7451-6717-6(9), CAB 1333) AudioGO.
It's Bond at his best in this spine-tingly collection of stories. In "Octopussy," a brilliant but twisted major who's worth his weight in gold pays a high price when his greedy past catches up with him. In "The Living Daylights," 007 has a rendezvous with a cold-blooded murderer in Berlin. In "The Property of a Lady," an auction at Southeby's heats up as the stakes are raised to the ultimate in terror!.

Oculocutaneous Albinism - A Bibliography & Dictionary for Physicians, Patients, & Genome Researchers. Compiled by Icon Group International, Inc. Staff. 2007. ring bd. 28.95 (978-0-497-11264-6(7)) Icon Grp.

Od Magic. unabr. ed. Patricia A. McKillip. (Running Time: 10 hrs. 0 mins.). 2009. 29.95 (978-1-4332-2401-0(1)); audio compact disk 80.00 (978-1-4332-2398-3(8)); audio compact disk 59.95 (978-1-4332-2397-6(X)) Blckstn Audio.

Oda a los Calcetines see Pablo Neruda Reading His Poetry

Oda a Walt Whitman see Poesia y Drama de Garcia Lorca

***Odalisque.** unabr. ed. Neal Stephenson. (Running Time: 13 hrs.). (Baroque Cycle Ser.). 2011. 39.97 (978-1-61106-229-8(2), 9781611062298, BADLE); 39.97 (978-1-61106-228-1(4), 9781611062281, Brlnc Audio MP3 Lib); 24.99 (978-1-61106-227-4(6), 9781611062274, Brilliance MP3); audio compact disk 79.97 (978-1-61106-226-7(8), 9781611062267, BriAudCD Unabrid); audio compact disk 29.99 (978-1-61106-225-0(X), 9781611062250, Bril Audio CD Unabri) Brilliance Audio.

Odasea: A Night Sea Journey. Jean-Vi Lenthe. Narrated by Jean-Vi Lenthe. Music by June Jean Millington et al. 6 CDs. (Running Time: 7 hrs. 15 mins.). Dramatization. 2003. audio compact disk 39.95 (978-0-9724703-0-8(1)) Wild Hare Pr.
A modern reimagining of Homer's epic journey, "The Odyssey," with an all-female crew struggling to sail home from the patriarchal wars of greed and addiction and reclaim their "Original Spirits." The author's lively narration is backed up by several women musicians and dramatic sound effects.

***Odd & the Frost Giants.** unabr. ed. Neil Gaiman. Read by Neil Gaiman. (ENG.). 2009. (978-0-06-196260-8(0)); (978-0-06-196262-2(7)) HarperCollins Pubs.

Odd & the Frost Giants. unabr. ed. Neil Gaiman. Read by Neil Gaiman. (J). (gr. 4-7). 2009. audio compact disk 17.99 (978-0-06-180831-9(8), HarperChildAud) HarperCollins Pubs.

Odd Couple. unabr. ed. Neil Simon. Read by Nathan Lane. (YA). 2008. 34.99 (978-1-60514-908-0(X)) Find a World.

Odd Couple. unabr. ed. Neil Simon. Perf. by Nathan Lane et al. 2 CDs. (Running Time: 1 hr. 32 mins.). (L. A. Theatre Works). 2001. audio compact disk 25.95 (978-1-58081-190-3(6), CDTPT124) Pub: L A Theatre. Dist(s): NetLibrary CO

Odd Couple. unabr. ed. Neil Simon. Perf. by David Paymer et al. 2 cass. (Running Time: 1 hr. 32 mins.). Dramatization. 2001. 23.95 (978-1-58081-130-9(2), TPT124) L A Theatre.
Poker buddies Felix Unger & Oscar Madison find themselves bachelors again.

Odd Girl Out. unabr. ed. Elizabeth Jane Howard. Read by Eleanor Bron. 8 cass. (Running Time: 12 hrs.). 1998. 69.95 (978-0-7540-0112-6(1), CAB1535) AudioGO.
Annie & Edmund Cornhill have a happy marriage. They are content & completely absorbed in their private idyll. Arabella, who comes to stay one lazy summer, is rich, ruthless & amoral. But as they come to know her, Arabella is also beautiful & loving. With elegant prose, the web of love that entangles these three very different people is traced.

Odd Girl Out: The Hidden Culture of Aggression in Girls. unabr. ed. Rachel Simmons. Narrated by Ruth Ann Phimister. 9 cass. (Running Time: 12 hrs. 15 mins.). 2002. 88.00 (978-1-4025-2875-0(2)) Recorded Bks.
Interviewed 300 girls and dozens of grown women to uncover a startling truth: girls manifest their aggression through subtle but devastating behaviors that parents and teachers fail to notice or feel helpless to stop.

Odd Girl Out: The Hidden Culture of Aggression in Girls. unabr. ed. Rachel Simmons. Narrated by Ruth A. Phimister. 7 cass. (Running Time: 12 hrs. 15 mins.). 2004. 29.99 (978-1-4025-2787-6(X), 01884) Recorded Bks.
The author interviewed 300 girls and dozens of grown women to uncover a startling truth: girls manifest their aggression through subtle but devastating behaviors that parents and teachers fail to notice or feel helpless to stop. Simmons examines the problem in this vitally important book.

Odd Hours. unabr. ed. Dean Koontz. Read by David Aaron Baker. (Running Time: 9 hrs.). (Odd Thomas Ser.: No. 4). 2008. 39.25 (978-1-4233-5684-4(5), 9781423356844, BADLE); 24.95 (978-1-4233-5683-7(7), 9781423356837, BAD); audio compact disk 92.25 (978-1-4233-5680-6(2), 9781423356806, BriAudCD Unabrid); audio compact disk 39.25 (978-1-4233-5682-0(9), 9781423356820, Brlnc Audio MP3 Lib); audio compact disk 44.95 (978-1-4233-5679-0(9), 9781423356790, Bril Audio CD Unabri); audio compact disk 24.95 (978-1-4233-5681-3(0), 9781423356813, Brilliance MP3) Brilliance Audio.

Odd Hours. unabr. ed. Dean Koontz. Read by David Aaron Baker. (Running Time: 9 hrs.). (Odd Thomas Ser.: No. 4). 2008. 84.99 (978-1-60640-922-0(0)) Find a World.

Odd Job. unabr. ed. Charlotte MacLeod. 6 cass. (Running Time: 6 hrs.). 2001. 48.00 (978-0-7366-6846-0(2)) Books on Tape.
Sarah Kelling must discover who killed a museum administrator before the murderer finds her.

Odd Jobs. 2005. audio compact disk (978-0-660-19477-6(5)) Canadian Broadcasting CAN.

***Odd Owls & Stout Pigs.** unabr. ed. Arnold Lobel. Read by Mark Linn-baker. Illus. by Adrianne Lobel. (ENG.). 2009. (978-0-06-196719-1(X)); (978-0-06-190165-2(2)) HarperCollins Pubs.

Odd Thomas. unabr. ed. Dean Koontz. 7 cass. (Running Time: 10 hrs. 30 min.). (Odd Thomas Ser.: No. 1). 2003. 72.00 (978-0-7366-9681-4(4)) Books on Tape.

Odd Thomas. unabr. ed. Dean Koontz. Read by David Aaron Baker. (Running Time: 37800 sec.). (Odd Thomas Ser.: No. 1). (ENG.). 2008. audio compact disk 19.99 (978-0-7393-6940-1(7), Random AudioBks) Pub: Random Audio Pubg. Dist(s): Random

Odd Women. George R. Gissing. Read by Anais 9000. 2008. 27.95 (978-1-60112-163-9(6)) Babblebooks.

Odd Women. unabr. ed. George R. Gissing. Narrated by Flo Gibson. 9 cass. (Running Time: 13 hrs.). (gr. 10 up). 1999. 28.95 (978-1-55685-628-0(8)) Audio Bk Con.
Two unmarried women suffering humiliation & poverty, their sister the victim of oppression in a loveless marriage & Rhoda Nunn, an ardent feminist, trying to educate spinsters to lead independent lives are a part of this novel which was far ahead of its time.

***Oddly Enough.** Bruce Coville. Read by Bruce Coville. (ENG.). (J). 2010. audio compact disk 34.00 (978-1-936223-35-0(X)) Full Cast Audio.

Odds Against. abr. ed. Dick Francis. Read by Ian McShane. (Sid Halley Adventure Ser.). 2008. audio compact disk 14.95 (978-0-06-149222-8(1), Harper Audio) HarperCollins Pubs.

Odds Against. unabr. ed. Dick Francis. Read by Tony Britton. 8 cass. (Running Time: 8 hrs.). (Sid Halley Adventure Ser.). 1998. 69.95 (978-0-7540-0086-0(9), CAB1509) AudioGO.
Sid Halley, champion jockey, had to give up racing when his hand was crushed. But his next job brings him a bullet in the chest. As he would soon discover, life as a private eye could get a lot worse, especially when a ruthless property dealer has plans for a racetrack. The plans have nothing to do with racing & everything to do with a conspiracy. Now a novice detective, Halley must fight to stay alive.

Odds Against. unabr. ed. Dick Francis. Read by Geoffrey Howard. 5 cass. (Running Time: 7 hrs. 30 min.). (Sid Halley Adventure Ser.). 1999. 39.95 (2343) Blckstn Audio.
Sadism & sabotage track an ex-jockey turned detective whose first case is a sure bet to be his last.

Odds Against. unabr. ed. Dick Francis. Read by Geoffrey Howard. 7 CDs. (Running Time: 7 hrs.). (Sid Halley Adventure Ser.). 2000. audio compact disk 56.00 (978-0-7861-8781-2(6), 2343) Blckstn Audio.

Odds Against. unabr. ed. Dick Francis. Read by Geoffrey Howard. 5 cass. (Running Time: 7 hrs.). (Sid Halley Adventure Ser.). 2004. 39.95 (978-0-7861-1492-4(4), 2343) Blckstn Audio.

Odds Against. unabr. ed. Dick Francis. Read by Tony Britton. 8 cass. (Running Time: 12 hrs.). (Sid Halley Adventure Ser.). 2000. 59.95 (CAB 1509) Pub: Chivers Audio Bks GBR. Dist(s): AudioGO
Sid Halley, champion jockey, had to give up racing when his hand was crushed. But his next job brings him a bullet in the chest. As he would soon discover, life as a private eye could get a lot worse, especially when a ruthless property dealer has plans for a racetrack. The plans have nothing to do with racing & everything to do with a conspiracy. Now a novice detective, Halley must fight to stay alive.

Odds Against. unabr. ed. Dick Francis. Read by Geoffrey Howard. 5 cass. (Running Time: 7 hrs. 30 mins.). (Sid Halley Adventure Ser.). 1999. 39.95 (FS9-50905) Highsmith.

Odds against Tomorrow. unabr. ed. William P. McGivern & Tom Weiner. (Running Time: 6.5 hrs. NaN mins.). 2008. 29.95 (978-1-4332-1673-2(6)); 44.95 (978-1-4332-1669-5(8)); audio compact disk 60.00 (978-1-4332-1670-1(1)) Blckstn Audio.

Ode see Poetry of Ralph Waldo Emerson

Ode: Intimations of Immortality from Recollections of Early Childhood see Selected Poetry of William Wordsworth

Ode Haus. Hoffmann. pap. bk. 21.95 (978-88-7754-792-7(8)) Pub: Cideb ITA. Dist(s): Distribks Inc

Ode on a Grecian Urn see Poetry of Keats

Ode on Melancholy see Poetry of Keats

Ode on Solitude. abr. ed. Alexander Pope. Perf. by Claire Bloom & Max Adrian. 1 cass. (Running Time: 1 hr. 30 mins.). 1984. 12.95 (SWC 1311) HarperCollins Pubs.

Ode to a Banker. Lindsey Davis. Narrated by Christopher Scott. 9 cass. (Running Time: 12 hrs.). (Marcus Didius Falco Ser.). 82.00 (978-1-84197-157-5(X)) Recorded Bks.

Ode to a Nightingale see Treasury of John Keats

Ode to a Nightingale see Poetry of Keats

Ode to Evening see Treasury of Oliver Goldsmith, Thomas Gray & William Collins

Ode to Grecian Urn see Treasury of John Keats

Ode to the Confederate Dead see Twentieth-Century Poetry in English, No. 2, Recordings of Poets Reading Their Own Poetry

Ode to the Sea see Twentieth-Century Poetry in English, No. 12, Recordings of Poets Reading Their Own Poetry

Ode to the West Wind see Treasury of Percy Bysshe Shelley

Ode to the West Wind see Poetry of Shelley

Ode to Walt Whitman see Poetry of Benet

Odes of Solomon. unabr. ed. Wayne Monbleau & Richard Tilton. Read by Wayne Monbleau & Richard Tilton. 1 cass. (Running Time: 42 min.). Dramatization. 1991. 10.00 (978-0-944648-06-3(1), SRU235180); audio compact disk 12.00 (978-0-944648-07-0(X), SKU235180) Loving Grace Pubns.
Twelve (12) First Century Christian Psalms narrated, with original sound recordings of music.

Odeskiye Rasskasy. Isaac Babel. 1 cass. (Running Time: 1 hrs.).Tr. of Tales of Odessa. (RUS.). 1997. pap. bk. 19.50 (978-1-58085-583-9(0)) Interlingua VA.

Odessa File. unabr. ed. Frederick Forsyth. Read by Frederick Davidson. 8 cass. (Running Time: 11 hrs. 30 mins.). 1991. 56.95 (978-0-7861-0303-4(5), 1267) Blckstn Audio.
The Odessa is an acronym for the secret organization which has protected the identities of former members of Hitler's dreaded SS. In 1964, a packet of dossiers arrives anonymously at the Ministry of Justice in Bonn. How & why this packet was sent is told in this story that takes one from reality into terror.

Odessa File. unabr. ed. Frederick Forsyth. Read by Frederick Davidson. (Running Time: 11 hrs. 5 mins.). 2009. 29.95 (978-1-4332-6496-2(X)); audio compact disk 90.00 (978-1-4332-6493-1(5)) Blckstn Audio.

Odessa File. unabr. ed. Frederick Forsyth. Read by Richard Green. 8 cass. (Running Time: 12 hrs.). 1986. 64.00 (978-0-7366-0886-2(9), 1830) Books on Tape.
The O.D.E.S.S.A. is a group of SS survivors still active many years after the fall of the Third Reich. Far from being harmless they are ready to launch a new offensive - codename: Werewolf. Its goal: carry out Hitler's "final solution" twenty years after his death.

Odile et Balivon. Kidzup Productions Staff. 1 cass. (Running Time: 1 hr. 30 mins.). (Kidzup Foreign Language Ser.). (FRE.). (J). 1999. 8.99 (978-1-894281-33-1(0)) Pub: Kidzup CAN. Dist(s): Penton Overseas
Brothe and sister team are here with their songs and stories. Features traditional & original music from jazz, rock & rap, to classical. Excellent for kids in a French immersion program or as a tutor for a second language.

Odisea. abr. ed. Homero. Read by Daniel Quintero. 3 CDs. (SPA.). 2003. audio compact disk 17.00 (978-958-8218-23-6(3)) YoYoMusic.

Odor of Death. Ted Knuckey. 8 discs. 2006. audio compact disk 30.95 (978-1-60031-012-6(5)) Spoken Books.

Odysseus. unabr. ed. Geraldine McCaughrean. Read by Cynthia Bishop. (J). 2008. 59.99 (978-1-60514-601-0(3)) Find a World.

Odysseus: A Life. unabr. ed. Charles Rowan Beye. Read by Mark Bramhall. 5 cass. (Running Time: 7 hrs.). 2005. 39.95 (978-0-7861-2673-6(6), 3231) Blckstn Audio.

Odysseus: A Life. unabr. ed. Charles Rowan Beye. Read by Mark Bramhall. 5 CDs. (Running Time: 7 hrs.). 2004. audio compact disk 40.00 (978-0-7861-8787-4(5), 3231) Blckstn Audio.

Odysseus: The Eternal Optimist & Searcher for Truth. Read by Poetry Center Staff. Narrated by Ralph Bates. 1 cass. (Running Time: 1 hr. 24 mins.). (Sound Seminars Lectures on the Classics). 1970. 14.95 (C23111) J Norton Pubs.
A study of the Greek myths as powerful symbols for the representation & analysis of contemporary religion, political & existential problems.

Odysseus: A Life: A Life. Charles Rowan Beye. Read by Mark Bramhall. (Running Time: 6 hrs.). 2004. 26.95 (978-1-59912-560-2(9)) Iofy Corp.

Odysseus & the Tale of Troy. unabr. ed. Padraic Colum. Read by Sean Pratt. 5 cds. (Running Time: 6 hrs 19 mins). (YA). 2002. audio compact disk 29.95 (978-1-58472-296-0(7), 072, In Aud) Pub: Sound Room. Dist(s): Baker Taylor
A retelling of Homer's epics.

Odysseus & the Tale of Troy. unabr. ed. Padraic Colum. Read by Sean Pratt. 1 cd. (Running Time: 6 hrs 19 mins). (YA). 2002. audio compact disk 18.95 (978-1-58472-391-2(2), In Aud) Pub: Sound Room. Dist(s): Baker Taylor
MP3 format.

Odysseus & the Tale of Troy. unabr. ed. Padraic Colum. Read by Sean Pratt. 5 CDs. (Running Time: 6 hrs 19 mins). (Classic Literature on CDs Ser.). (J). (gr. 4-8). 2002. pap. bk. (978-1-58472-298-4(3), In Aud) Sound Room.
A retelling of Homer's epics.

Odyssey. (Gateway Experience Ser.). 2000. 72.00 (978-1-56102-940-2(8)) Inter Indus.
Help with personal growth & self-exploration.

Odyssey. Narrated by Norman Dietz. 11 CDs. (Running Time: 12.5 hrs.). audio compact disk 34.95 (978-1-4025-2235-2(5)) Recorded Bks.

Odyssey. Homer. Read by Nadia May. Tr. by W. H. D. Rouse. 10 CDs. (Running Time: 15 hrs.). 1990. audio compact disk 80.00 (z1180) Blckstn Audio.

Odyssey. Homer. Read by Anton Lesser. (Running Time: 4 hrs.). 1999. 24.95 (978-1-60083-858-3(8)) Iofy Corp.

Odyssey. Homer. Read by Daniel Quintero. (Running Time: 3 hrs.). 2003. 16.95 (978-1-60083-286-4(5), Audiofy Corp) Iofy Corp.

Odyssey. Homer. Read by John Lescault. (Running Time: 12 hrs. 30 mins.). 2003. 34.95 (978-1-59912-099-7(2), Audiofy Corp) Iofy Corp.

Odyssey. Homer. Read by Anton Lesser. Tr. by William Cowper. 3 cass. (Running Time: 4 hrs.). 1995. 17.98 (978-962-634-531-3(4), NA303114, Naxos AudioBooks) Naxos.
The beauty of this classic, epic poem in a resonant & powerful 1791 translation, is perfectly complemented by the readers authoritative voice. The story of the adventures of Odysseus as he returns from the Trojan War to his kingdom of Ithaca.

Odyssey. Homer. Tr. by Stanley Lombardo. Narrated by Stanley Lombardo. 10 CDs. (Running Time: 44100 sec.). 2005. audio compact disk 42.00 (978-1-930972-06-3(7)) Pub: Parmenides Pub. Dist(s): Chicago Distribution Ctr
Elizabeth A. Kaye specializes in communications as part of her coaching and consulting practice. She has edited Requirements for Certification since the 2000-01 edition.

Odyssey. Homer. Tr. by George Herbert Palmer. Narrated by Norman Dietz. 11 CDs. (Running Time: 12 hrs. 30 mins.). audio compact disk 111.00 (978-1-4025-2325-0(4)) Recorded Bks.

Odyssey. Homer. Read by Norman Dietz. 11 CDs. (Running Time: 12.5 Hrs). 2005. audio compact disk 29.95 (978-1-4193-2354-6(7)) Recorded Bks.

Odyssey. Homer. Narrated by John Lescault. (Running Time: 44640 sec.). (Unabridged Classics in MP3 Ser.). 2008. audio compact disk 26.00 (978-1-58472-531-2(1), In Aud) Sound Room.

Odyssey. Homer & Stanley Lombardo. (ENG.). 2007. 29.40 (978-1-930972-23-0(7)) Parmenides Pub.

Odyssey. Tr. by Rodney Merrill. Intro. by Thomas R. Walsh. (ENG., 2002. 57.50 (978-0-472-00305-1(4), 00305) U of Mich Pr.

Odyssey. Read by Odds Bodkin Storytelling Library Staff. 4 cass. (Running Time: 4 hrs.). Dramatization. (Odds Bodkin Musical Story Collection). (gr. 4 up). 2003. bk. 34.95 (978-1-882412-17-4(6)) Pub: Rivertree. Dist(s): Penton Overseas
Epic storytelling in original language & music of Homer's Odyssey by Odds Bodkin, master talesman. Told as an adventure story, with thirty-seven character voices & musical leitmotifs. Includes poster & Odyssey Adventure Map!.

Odyssey. abr. ed. Homer. Read by Roger Rees. Tr. by Samuel Butler. 4 cass. (Running Time: 6 hrs.). 1999. 24.95 (978-1-57453-326-2(6)) Audio Lit.
Called the world's greatest adventure story, the Odyssey introduced a gallery of characters & events that have profoundly influenced western literature. Circe, Scylla & Charybdis, the Lotus Eaters, a visit with the dead & most resonant, Odysseus's determined search for home are all here in one of the classic translations.

Odyssey. abr. ed. Homer. Read by Anton Lesser. Tr. by William Cowper. 3 CDs. (Running Time: 4 hrs.). (J). (gr. 9-12). 1995. audio compact disk 22.98 (978-962-634-031-8(2), NA303112) Naxos.
The beauty of this classic, epic poem in a resonant & powerful 1791 translation, is perfectly complemented by the readers authoritative voice. The story of the adventures of Odysseus as he returns from the Trojan War to his kingdom of Ithaca.

Odyssey. abr. ed. Homer. Read by Roger Rees. 1 cass. (Running Time: 1.5 hrs.). 2004. 15.00 (978-1-59007-010-9(0)) Pub: New Millenn Enter. Dist(s): PerseuPGW
Scylla & Charybdis, Circe, the Lotus Eaters, a visit with the dead, & most resonant, Odysseus's determined search for home, are all here in one of the classic translations.

Odyssey. abr. ed. Homer & Lesser Anton. 4. 2007. audio compact disk 28.98 (978-962-634-473-6(3), Naxos AudioBooks) Naxos.

Odyssey. abr. ed. Monarch Notes Staff. 1 cass. (Running Time: 1 hr. 30 mins.). (Monarch Notes Ser.). 1985. 7.95 (978-0-671-54404-1(7)) S&S Audio.
Intended as a supplement to classroom study, offering plot summary, interpretive themes information on literary theme & style. The flashcards outline the author's life.

Odyssey. abr. unabr. ed. Homer. Read by Derek Jacobi. 8 CDs. (Running Time: 9 hrs.). (ENG.). 2000. audio compact disk 44.95 (978-1-56511-423-4(X), 156511423X) Pub: HighBridge. Dist(s): Workman Pub

Odyssey. rev. ed. Read by Odds Bodkin Storytelling Library Staff. 4 CDs. (Running Time: 4 hrs.). Dramatization. (Odds Bodkin Musical Story Collection). (gr. 4 up). 2003. bk. 49.95 (978-1-882412-18-1(4)) Pub: Rivertree. Dist(s): Penton Overseas
Epic storytelling in original language & music of Homer's Odyssey by Odds Bodkin, master talesman. Told as an adventure story, with thirty-seven character voices & musical leitmotifs. Includes poster & Odyssey Adventure Map!.

Odyssey. unabr. ed. Homer. Contrib. by Simon Armitage. 3 CDs. (Running Time: 3 hrs. 50 mins.). (ENG.). 2008. audio compact disk 24.95 (978-1-60283-483-5(0)) Pub: AudioGO. Dist(s): Perseus Dist

Odyssey. unabr. ed. Homer. Read by John Lescault. (YA). 2006. 49.99 (978-1-59895-172-1(6)) Find a World.

Odyssey. unabr. ed. Homer. Read by Nadia May. 8 cass. 1999. 56.95 (FS9-51112) Highsmith.

Odyssey. unabr. ed. Homer. Read by Anton Lesser. (Running Time: 45967 sec.). (Complete Classics Ser.). 2007. audio compact disk 62.98 (978-962-634-445-3(8), Naxos AudioBooks) Naxos.

Odyssey. unabr. ed. Homer. Read by Roger Rees. 4 cass. (Running Time: 6 hrs.). 2004. 25.00 (978-1-59007-001-7(1)) Pub: New Millenn Enter. Dist(s): PerseuPGW
Scylla & Charybdis, Circe, the Lotus Eaters, a visit with the dead, & most resonant, Odysseus's determined search for home, are all here in one of the classic translations.

Odyssey. unabr. ed. Homer. (Running Time: 13 hrs.). (ENG.). (gr. 12 up). 2005. audio compact disk 39.95 (978-0-14-305824-3(X), PengAudBks) Penguin Grp USA.

Odyssey. unabr. ed. Poems. Homer. Tr. by George H. Palmer. Narrated by Norman Dietz. 9 cass. (Running Time: 12 hrs. 30 mins.). 1999. 78.00 (978-1-55690-386-1(3), 89396E7) Recorded Bks.
The epic adventures of Odysseus on his return journey after the fall of Troy, to Ithaca & Penelope, his wife.

Odyssey. unabr. ed. Homer. Narrated by Simon Prebble. (Running Time: 11 hrs. 0 mins. 0 sec.). (ENG.). 2009. audio compact disk 24.99 (978-1-4001-6218-5(1)); audio compact disk 69.99 (978-1-4001-4218-7(0)); audio compact disk 34.99 (978-1-4001-1218-0(4)) Pub: Tantor Media. Dist(s): IngramPubServ

Odyssey, Vol. III, Bks. 13-18. Homer. Read by Stephen G. Daitz. 6 cass. (Running Time: 6 hrs.). (GEC & ENG.). 2001. pap. bk. 59.50 (S23870) J Norton Pubs.
Booklet contains the Greek text & English translation.

Odyssey, Vol. IV, Bks. 19-24. Homer. Ed. by Stephen G. Daitz. 6 cass. (Running Time: 5 hrs. 10 min.). (Living Voice of Greek & Latin Ser.). (GEC & ENG.). 1998. pap. bk. 59.50 (978-1-57970-030-0(6), S23880) J Norton Pubs.
Pertains to the last books in restored Ancient Greek pronunciation. Contains original Greek & English translation on facing pages.

Odyssey: Ain't Nothin' Odd about the Odyssey. Music by Lee Kweller. Text by Joshua Brown & John Esposito. 1 cass. (Running Time: 10 min.). (Educational Song Ser.: Vol. 1). (YA). (gr. 7-12). 1998. stu. ed. 19.98 (978-1-57649-001-3(7), 76001) Arkadia Ent.
Based on the poet Homer's tale on the cunning, fearless Odysseus, who overcame the unbelievable obstacles that stood between him & a happy reunion with his wife. The Odyssey was designed to be put to music & sung by travelling performers.

Odyssey: The Story of Odysseus. unabr. ed. Homer. Read by Anthony Heald. (Running Time: 11 hrs. 50 mins.). (ENG.). 2009. 29.95 (978-1-4332-8916-3(4)); 72.95 (978-1-4332-8912-5(1)); audio compact disk 100.00 (978-1-4332-8913-2(X)) Blckstn Audio.

Odyssey - An Epic Telling. Odds Bodkin. 4 cass. (Running Time: 6 hrs.). (J). bk. 27.98 Blisterpack. (RPI 707176); bk. 39.98 (RPI 70184) NewSound.

Odyssey Christmas. 3 cass. (Running Time: 3 hrs.). (Adventures in Odyssey Ser.). (J). 2004. 9.99 (978-1-56179-889-6(4)) Pub: Focus Family. Dist(s): Tommy Nelson

***Odyssey of Flight 33.** 2010. audio compact disk (978-1-59171-208-4(4)) Falcon Picture.

Odyssey of Homer. Homer. (Running Time: 11 hrs. 30 mins.). (C). 1998. 34.95 (978-1-59912-696-8(6)) Iofy Corp.

Odyssey of Homer. Instructed by Elizabeth Vandiver. 6 CDs. (Running Time: 6 hrs.). 1999. bk. 39.95 (978-1-56585-318-8(0), 302); 29.95 (978-1-56585-067-5(X), 302) Teaching Co.

Odyssey of Homer. unabr. ed. Yuri Rasovsky. 8 CDs. (Running Time: 7 hrs. 30 mins.). 2003. audio compact disk 64.00 (978-0-7861-9283-0(6), 3065); 56.95 (978-0-7861-2388-9(5), 3065) Blckstn Audio.
This is the story of a man, a hero, who inhabits three worlds: first the world of the myth in which gods and demigods sport and battle; and finally, the world of sorcerers and monsters, of magic and ghosts and unspeakable terrors.

Odyssey of Homer. unabr. ed. Read by Ennis Rees. 10.95 (978-0-8045-0849-0(6), SAC 849) Spoken Arts.

Odyssey of the North see Son of the Wolf

Odyssey of the North. unabr. ed. Jack London. Read by Jim Killavey. 1 cass. (Running Time: 1 hr. 15 mins.). Dramatization. 1981. 7.95 (S-11) Jimcin Record.
A story of cruel & remorseless revenge.

Odyssey (Translated into Prose by George Herbert Palmer) Homer. Tr. by George Herbert Palmer. Narrated by Flo Gibson. (ENG.). 2008. 39.95 (978-1-60646-046-7(3)) Audio Bk Con.

Oedipus at Colonus see Twentieth-Century Poetry in English, No. 10, Recordings of Poets Reading Their Own Poetry

Oedipus Rex. Narrated by Walter Kaufmann. 1 cass. (Running Time: 1 hr. 10 mins.). (Sound Seminars Lectures on the Classics). 1963. 14.95 (C23116) J Norton Pubs.
A comparison of the treatment of Oedipus by Aeschylus, Euripides, Sophocles & other earlier Greek writers. A discussion of Sophocles' Oedipus Tyrannus, Antigone & Oedipus at Colonus as three independent plays & not a trilogy.

Oedipus Rex: A play by Sophocles. Sophocles. Retold by Noe Venable. (Classic Literature Ser.). 2006. pap. bk. 69.00 (978-1-4105-0629-0(0)); audio compact disk 18.95 (978-1-4105-0627-6(4)) D Johnston Inc.

Oedipus Rising. Katherine De Jersey & Dale Richardson. 1 cass. (Running Time: 1 hr. 30 mins.). 8.95 (513) Am Fed Astrologers.
If psychology doesn't get you, Astrology will.

Oedipus the King. Sophocles. (Running Time: 1 hr. 45 mins.). 2003. 20.95 (978-1-60083-859-0(6)) Iofy Corp.

Oedipus the King. Sophocles. Tr. by Nicholas Rudall from GRE. Contrib. by Harry J. Lennix. 2 CDs. (Running Time: 4500 sec.). (L. A. Theatre Works Audio Theatre Collections). 2003. audio compact disk 25.95 (978-1-58081-285-6(6), CDTPT192) Pub: L A Theatre. Dist(s): NetLibrary CO

Oedipus the King. Sophocles. Perf. by Michael Sheen et al. Tr. by Duncan Steen from GRE. 2 cass. (Running Time: 2 Hrs.). Dramatization. (Classic Drama Ser.). 1999. 13.98 (978-962-634-677-8(9), NA217714, Naxos AudioBooks) Naxos.
The anguished tale of Oedipus, who having solved the riddle of the Sphinx and became King of Thebes, gradually realizes the crimes he unwittingly committed, remains a drama of unremitting power 2,500 years after it was written.

Oedipus the King. Sophocles. Perf. by Michael Sheen et al. Tr. by Duncan Steen from GRE. 2 CDs. (Running Time: 2 hrs.). Dramatization. (Classic Drama Ser.). (J). (gr. 9-12). 1999. audio compact disk 17.98 (978-962-634-177-3(7), NA217712) Naxos.

Oeuvres Choisies. Aimé Césaire. 1 cass., bklet. (FRE.). 1992. 22.95 (1531-HA) Olivia & Hill.
Some of the best known works of the poet from Martinique, including: "Cahier d'un retour au pays natal," "Inventaire de cayes," "Mot," "Dit d'errance," "Radordaille" & "Beau sang gicle.".

Of a Boy. unabr. ed. Sonya Hartnett. Read by Humphrey Bower. 4 CDs. (Running Time: 4 hrs. 40 mins.). 2004. audio compact disk 57.95 (978-1-74093-104-5(1)) Pub: Bolinda Pubng AUS. Dist(s): Bolinda Pub Inc

Of a Boy: 4 Cassettes (unabridged) unabr. ed. Sonya Hartnett. Read by Humphrey Bower. 4 cass. (Running Time: 4 hrs. 40 mins.). 2004. 32.00 (978-1-74030-832-8(8)) Pub: Bolinda Pubng AUS. Dist(s): Bolinda Pub Inc

Of a boy (What the birds See) Sonya Hartnett. Read by Humphrey Bower. (Running Time: 4 hrs. 40 mins.). 2009. 59.99 (978-1-74214-242-5(7), 9781742142425) Pub: Bolinda Pubng AUS. Dist(s): Bolinda Pub Inc

Of All Things. unabr. ed. Robert Benchley. Read by Flo Gibson. 3 cass. (Running Time: 4 hrs.). 2001. 16.95 (978-1-55685-647-1(4)) Audio Bk Con.
Almost a laugh per page under such titles as "The Social Life of a Newt," "The Tortures of a Weekend Visit" & "When Genius Remained Your Humble Servant".

Of Archetypes & Exetypes: A Whimsical Approach to the Potentiation of Energy. Read by Jean Houston. 1 cass. (Running Time: 1 hr. 30 mins.). 1976. 10.95 (978-0-7822-0092-8(3), 018) C G Jung IL.

Of Bees & Mist: A Novel. unabr. ed. Erick Setiawan. (Running Time: 14 hrs. 30 mins.). 2009. 29.95 (978-1-4417-1095-6(7)); 85.95 (978-1-4417-1091-8(4)); audio compact disk 34.95 (978-1-4417-1094-9(9)) Blckstn Audio.

Of Bees & Mist: A Novel. unabr. ed. Erick Setiawan. Read by Marguerite Gavin. 11 CDs. (Running Time: 14 hrs. 30 mins.). 2009. audio compact disk 118.00 (978-1-4417-1092-5(2)) Blckstn Audio.

Of Civil Government: Second Treatise. unabr. ed. John Locke. Read by Lois Betterton. 4 cass. (Running Time: 5 hrs. 30 mins.). 1990. 32.95 (978-0-7861-0195-5(4), 1171) Blckstn Audio.
His theories relating to the nature of the state & the manner in which governments can most effectively maintain a balance of power provided a vigorous incentive to American & French revolutionaries of the eighteenth century.

Of Commerce & Society see Poetry of Geoffrey

Of Course You're Angry. rev. ed. 1 cass. (Running Time: 1 hr.). (Discovery Ser.). 1987. 10.00 (978-0-89486-602-9(8), 5620G) Hazelden.

Of Dreams & Bedtime Stories. Contrib. by Oceania. 2001. 11.95; audio compact disk 16.95 Passion Press.

Of Fire & Night. abr. ed. Kevin J. Anderson. Read by David Colacci. (Running Time: 28800 sec.). (Saga of Seven Suns Ser.: Bk. 5). 2007. audio compact disk 14.99 (978-1-59737-220-6(X), 9781597372206, BCD Value Price) Brilliance Audio.
Please enter a Synopsis.

Of Fire & Night. unabr. ed. Kevin J. Anderson. Read by David Colacci. (Running Time: 19 hrs.). (Saga of Seven Suns Ser.: Bk. 5). 2006. 44.25 (978-1-59737-224-4(2), 9781597372244, BADLE); 107.25 (978-1-59737-216-9(1), 9781597372169, BrilAudUnabridg); audio compact disk 44.25 (978-1-59737-222-0(6), 9781597372220, Brinc Audio MP3 Lib); audio compact disk 127.25 (978-1-59737-218-3(8), 9781597372183, BriAudCD Unabrid); audio compact disk 29.95 (978-1-59737-221-3(8), 9781597372213, Brilliance MP3); audio compact disk 48.95 (978-1-59737-217-6(X), 9781597372176, Bril Audio CD Unabri) Brilliance Audio.

Of Fire & Night: The Saga of Seven Suns, Book 5. unabr. ed. Kevin J. Anderson. Read by David Colacci. (Running Time: 19 hrs.). (Saga of Seven Suns Ser.). 2006. 29.95 (978-1-59737-223-7(4), 9781597372237, BAD) Brilliance Audio.

Of Home & Heart. Anne Schraff. Narrated by Larry A. McKeever. (Standing Tall 3 Mystery Ser.). (J). 2003. 10.95 (978-1-58659-110-6(X)); audio compact disk 14.95 (978-1-58659-349-0(8)) Artesian.

Of Human Bondage see Servidumbre Humana

Of Human Bondage. W. Somerset Maugham. Read by Flo Gibson. 16 cass. (Running Time: 23 hrs. 30 min.). 1991. 46.95 (978-1-55685-189-6(8)) Audio Bk Con.
This frequently auto-biographical novel deals with Phillip Carey, an orphan & cripple, as he searches for love & the meaning of life. After a period of misery at school, he goes to Paris to study art, only to find that he lacks the needed talent. In London, after many misfortunes, including a tragic love affair with the petty, selfish Mildred, he decides to study medicine. His struggles to survive are poignant.

Of Human Bondage. W. Somerset Maugham. Narrated by Flo Gibson. (ENG.). 2008. audio compact disk 54.95 (978-1-55685-908-3(2)) Audio Bk Con.

Of Human Bondage. W. Somerset Maugham. Read by Fabio Camero. (Running Time: 3 hrs.). 2002. 16.95 (978-1-60083-244-4(X), Audiofy Corp) Iofy Corp.

***Of Human Bondage.** unabr. ed. W. Somerset Maugham. Narrated by Steven Crossley. (Running Time: 28 hrs. 0 mins. 0 sec.). 2010. 36.99 (978-1-4001-6976-4(3)); 29.99 (978-1-4001-8976-2(4)); audio compact disk 49.99 (978-1-4001-1976-9(6)) Pub: Tantor Media. Dist(s): IngramPubServ

***Of Human Bondage (Library Edition)** unabr. ed. W. Somerset Maugham. Narrated by Steven Crossley. (Running Time: 28 hrs. 0 mins.). 2010. 49.99 (978-1-4001-9976-1(X)); audio compact disk 119.99 (978-1-4001-4976-2(2)) Pub: Tantor Media. Dist(s): IngramPubServ

***Of Late I Think of Cliffordville.** 2010. audio compact disk (978-1-59171-159-9(2)) Falcon Picture.

Of Lions, Dragons, & Turkish Delights. Read by Michael Wilcox. 2008. audio compact disk 15.95 (978-1-59038-880-8(1)) Deseret Bk.

Of Living Death. Ayn Rand. Read by Ayn Rand. 1 cass. (Running Time: 1 hr.). 12.95 (978-1-56114-074-9(0), AR14C) Second Renaissance.
This devastating critique of the Pope's encyclical on birth control explains the philosophical meaning of the Catholic Church's hostility toward sexual enjoyment. It shows how the fundamental objective of the encyclical is to undercut man's self-esteem by inculcating in him a sense of guilt for enjoying sex & for daring to think that his own happiness is the purpose & justification of his life.

Of Living Death. Comment by Ayn Rand. 1 cass. (Running Time: 1 hr.). (Ford Hall Forum Ser.). 1968. 12.95 (AR14C) Second Renaissance.
How religion seeks to undercut man's self-esteem by inculcating guilt for enjoying sex & for daring to think that his own happiness is the purpose of his life.

Of Love & Dust. unabr. collector's ed. Ernest J. Gaines. Read by Dan Lazar. 7 cass. (Running Time: 7 hrs.). 1982. 42.00 (978-0-7366-0516-8(9), 1490) Books on Tape.
When young Marcus is bonded out of jail, he is sent to the Herbert Plantation to work in the fields. He treats Sidney Bonbon, the Cajun overseer, with contempt, & Bonbon retaliates by working him nearly to death. Marcus decides to take his revenge.

***Of Love & Evil.** unabr. ed. Anne Rice. Read by Paul Michael. (Anne Rice Ser.). (ENG.). 2010. audio compact disk 30.00 (978-0-7393-1613-9(3), Random AudioBks) Pub: Random Audio Pubg. Dist(s): Random

Of Love & Slaughter. Angela Huth. Read by Raymond Sawyer & G. Kruger. 11 CDs. (Running Time: 12 hrs. 29 mins.). (Isis (CDs) Ser.). (J). 2005. audio compact disk 99.95 (978-0-7531-2432-1(7)) Pub: ISIS Lrg Prnt GBR. Dist(s): Ulverscroft US

Of Love & Slaughter. unabr. ed. Angela Huth. 10 cass. (Isis Ser.). (J). 2003. 84.95 (978-0-7531-1550-3(6)) Pub: ISIS Lrg Prnt GBR. Dist(s): Ulverscroft US

Of Love & War. unabr. ed. Vanessa Alexander. 8 cass. (Running Time: 12 hrs.). 2001. 69.95 (978-1-84283-032-1(5)) Pub: Soundings Ltd GBR. Dist(s): Ulverscroft US

Of Man: The Island & the Continent. 7 cass. (Running Time: 6 hrs. 19 min.). 1996. 79.50 (978-1-889954-68-4(3)) J Cassidy Prodns.
Introductory lecture on Man; on Religion & Humanism. Then three lectures in Aesthetics, on Poetry & Music; on Human Feelings. Then three lectures in Ethics, the first two in Human Prejudice, the last one in Our Humanity.

Of Men & of Angels. abr. ed. Bodie Thoene & Brock Thoene. 2 cass. (Running Time: 3 hrs.). (Galway Chronicles: Bk. 2). 1998. 15.99 (978-0-7852-7477-3(4), 74774) Nelson.
Sequel to the bestselling "Only the River Runs Free" continues the story of the Irish village of Ballynockanor.

Of Mice & Men see Theatre Highlights

Of Mice & Men. John Steinbeck. Perf. by Burgess Meredith et al. 1 cass. (Running Time: 1 hr.). Dramatization. 7.95 (DD-6020) Natl Recrd Co.

Of Mice & Men. abr. ed. John Steinbeck. 1 cass. (Running Time: 1 hr.). 1998. 8.00 Hachet Audio.

Of Mice & Men. unabr. ed. John Steinbeck. Read by Gary Sinise. Contrib. by Gary Sinise. (Running Time: 3 hrs.). (ENG.). 2003. audio compact disk 24.95 (978-1-56511-770-9(0), 1565117700) Pub: Penguin-HghBrdg. Dist(s): Workman Pub

Of Mice & Men. unabr. ed. John Steinbeck. Narrated by Mark Hammer. 4 CDs. (Running Time: 4 hrs.). 1999. audio compact disk 31.00 (978-0-7887-3724-4(4), C1081E7) Recorded Bks.
Lenny & his good friend George have a dream of owning a farm together. When Lenny destroys their dream, George faces the most difficult decision of his life.

Of Mice & Men. unabr. ed. John Steinbeck. Narrated by Mark Hammer. 3 cass. (Running Time: 4 hrs.). 2000. 26.00 (978-0-7887-3118-1(1), 95788E7) Recorded Bks.
Lenny & his good friend George, have a dream of owning a farm together. When Lenny destroys their dream, George faces the most difficult decision of his life.

Of Murder & Madness: A True Story. unabr. ed. Gerry Spence. Read by John MacDonald. 14 cass. (Running Time: 21 hrs.). 1994. 112.00 (978-0-7366-2829-7(0), 3537) Books on Tape.
A true story about insanity & the law. "Not guilty by reason of insanity" got Joe Esquibel off, even though he killed his wife in a room full of witnesses.

Of One Blood. unabr. ed. Andrew White. Perf. by Lee Arenberg et al. 1 cass. (Running Time: 1 hr. 29 min.). 1993. 19.95 (978-1-58081-066-1(7)) L A Theatre.
A poignant & disturbing play about the infamous murder of three civil rights workers in Mississippi.

Of Stones & Spirits: Pursuing the Past of Antelope Hill. Ed. by Joan S. Schneider & Jeffrey H. Altschul. Vol. 76. 2000. per. 35.00 (978-1-879442-76-4(0)) Pub: Stats Res. Dist(s): U of Ariz Pr

Of the Christic Institute. Martha Honey. 1 cass. (Running Time: 1 hr. 30 mins.). (Roy Tuckman Interview Ser.). 9.00 (A0491-89) Sound Photosyn.
An important participant in the vital "Secret Team" investigation speaks on "Something's Happening".

Of the Chronicles of England see Cambridge Treasy Malory

Of the Farm. unabr. collector's ed. John Updike. Read by Jack Hrkach. 5 cass. (Running Time: 5 hrs.). 1984. 30.00 (978-0-7366-0693-6(9), 1656) Books on Tape.

Of Thee I Sing! (A Celebration of America's Music for 2-Part Choirs) Composed by Sally K. Albrecht & Jay Althouse. (ENG.). 2007. audio compact disk 44.99 (978-0-7390-4658-6(6)) Alfred Pub.

Of Time & Memory: A Mother's Story. unabr. ed. Don J. Snyder. Narrated by Brian Keeler. 8 CDs. (Running Time: 8 hrs. 30 mins.). 2001. audio compact disk 78.00 (978-1-4025-1055-7(1), C1601) Recorded Bks.
The death of Snyder's 19-year-old mother only two weeks after his birth was such a painful experience for his father and grandparents that they rarely spoke of her as he grew up. But as his father begins to fail in health and memory, Snyder feels compelled to give him a gift: the unremembered romance between a skinny soldier and the prettiest girl in town. By retracing the steps of her youth, Snyder slowly unveils the love story between his mother and father - as well as the stunning secret that made her death so unbearable.

Of Time & Memory: A Mother's Story. unabr. ed. Don J. Snyder. Narrated by Brian Keeler. 6 cass. (Running Time: 8 hrs. 30 mins.). 2001. 54.00 (978-0-7887-4992-6(7), 96086E7) Recorded Bks.
The author unveils the love story between his mother & father & the secret that made her death at age nineteen unbearable.

Of Time & the River Pt. 1: A Legend of Man's Hunger in His Youth. unabr. collector's ed. Thomas Wolfe. Read by John Edwardson. 14 cass. (Running Time: 21 hrs.). 1996. 112.00 (978-0-7366-3478-6(9), 4121-A) Books on Tape.
During his short life, he moved from his southern origins, but always returned there for his inspiration. His themes were encompassing & used the world as a backdrop.

Of Time & the River Pt. 2: A Legend of Man's Hunger in His Youth. collector's ed. Thomas Wolfe. Read by John Edwardson. 14 cass. (Running Time: 21 hrs.). 1996. 112.00 (978-0-7366-3479-3(7), 4121-B) Books on Tape.

Of Utmost Importance. 1 cass. (Running Time: 30 min.). 1985. (0255) Evang Sisterhood Mary.
Includes Christ of the World; Fascinated by Our Aim in Life; Overcoming the Future; What Really Counts.

Off Armageddon Reef. unabr. ed. David Weber. Read by Oliver Wyman. 25 CDs. (Running Time: 30 hrs. 0 mins. 0 sec.). Bk. 1. (ENG.). 2007. audio compact disk 59.95 (978-1-4272-0065-5(3)) Pub: Macmill Audio. Dist(s): Macmillan

Off Camera: Private Thoughts Made Public. Ted Koppel. Read by Ted Koppel. 3 cass. (Running Time: 5 hrs.). 2000. 25.00 (Random AudioBks) Random Audio Pubg.
Here, closely observed with an insider's eye, are all the significant matters of 1999 from the Clinton impeachment & the war in Kosovo to the transformation of the global economy & even the phenomenon of Viagra. Here, too, are the people (both on & off camera) who made the news from Slobodan Milosevic to Hillary Rodham Clinton to Michael Jordan to John F. Kennedy Jr.

Off Color Songs for Kids. Prod. by Barry Louis Polisar. 1 cass. (Running Time: 1 hr.). (J). (gr. 1-6). 1983. bk. 9.95 (978-0-9615696-8-6(9)) Pub: Rainbow Morn. Dist(s): IPG Chicago
A deep-voiced chorus sings about underwear in a Calypso style, & a rock & roll singer chants about being in love-with a giraffe!!! Other songs include are "Oh, no, I like my sister", "I forgot," & "What if a Zebra had spots".

Off-Loading. abr. ed. Robert A. Monroe. Read by Robert A. Monroe. (Running Time: 30 min.). (Human Plus Ser.). 1989. 14.95 (978-1-56102-022-5(2)) Inter Indus.
Release restrictive & destructive patterns.

Off Season. abr. ed. Anne Rivers Siddons. Read by Jane Alexander. (Running Time: 7 hrs.). (ENG.). 2008. 14.98 (978-1-60024-169-7(7)) Pub: Hachet Audio. Dist(s): HachBkGrp

Off Season. abr. ed. Anne Rivers Siddons. Read by Jane Alexander. (Running Time: 7 hrs.). (ENG.). 2009. audio compact disk 14.98 (978-1-60024-634-0(6)) Pub: Hachet Audio. Dist(s): HachBkGrp

Off Season. unabr. ed. Catherine Gilbert Murdock. Read by Natalie Moore. 5 CDs. (Running Time: 6 hrs.). (YA). (gr. 7-10). 2007. audio compact disk 45.00 (978-0-7393-5106-2(0), Listening Lib) Pub: Random Audio Pubg. Dist(s): Random

Off Season. unabr. ed. Anne Rivers Siddons. Read by Jane Alexander. (Running Time: 11 hrs.). (ENG.). 2008. 26.98 (978-1-60024-171-0(9)); audio compact disk 39.98 (978-1-60024-170-3(0)) Pub: Hachet Audio. Dist(s): HachBkGrp

Off Season. unabr. ed. Anne Rivers Siddons. Read by Jane Alexander. 10 CDs. 2008. audio compact disk 110.00 (978-1-4159-5885-8(8), BksonTape) Pub: Random Audio Pubg. Dist(s): Random

Off the Map. Richard Luftig. (ENG.). 2006. 4.00 (978-1-933675-19-0(5)) Dos Madres Pr.

***Off the Record.** unabr. ed. Elizabeth White. (Running Time: 9 hrs. 44 mins. 0 sec.). (ENG.). 2009. 13.99 (978-0-310-77190-6(0)) Zondervan.

Off the Record: The Press, the Government, & the War over Anonymous Sources. Norman Pearlstine. Read by Alan Sklar. (Playaway Adult Fiction Ser.). 2008. 64.99 (978-1-60514-972-1(1)) Find a World.

Off the Record: The Press, the Government, & the War over Anonymous Sources. unabr. ed. Norman Pearlstine. Narrated by Alan Sklar. 8 cds. (Running Time: 9 hrs. 30 mins. 0 sec.). (ENG.). 2007. 24.99 (978-1-4001-5481-4(2)) Pub: Tantor Media. Dist(s): IngramPubServ

Off the Record: The Press, the Government, & the War over Anonymous Sources. unabr. ed. Norman Pearlstine. Narrated by Alan Sklar. 8 CDs. (Running Time: 9 hrs. 30 mins. 0 sec). (ENG.). 2007. audio compact disk 34.99 (978-1-4001-0481-9(5)); audio compact disk 69.99 (978-1-4001-3481-6(1)) Pub: Tantor Media. Dist(s): IngramPubServ

Off the Road. unabr. ed. Nina Bawden. Read by Bernard Cribbins. 4 CDs. (Running Time: 6 hrs.). (J). 2002. audio compact disk 34.95 (978-0-7540-6538-8(3), CHCD 038) AudioGO.

Off the Track see Your Own World

Off with the Rat's Head: Tales of the Father, Son & King. Short Stories. Read by Michael Meade. 1 cass. (Running Time: 1 hr. 20 min.). 1990. 9.95 (978-0-938756-27-9(3)); 10.95 Boxed. (978-0-938756-47-7(8)) Yellow Moon.
Two African stories with discussion of their relevance to the male psyche. The stories are used to evoke the griefs & wounds of fathers & sons, to remind of the love & suffering between the two, & to make the first step in healing - looking at the wound.

Offer. unabr. ed. Catherine Coulter. Read by Denica Fairman. 10 vols. (Running Time: 15 min.). 2000. bk. 84.95 (978-0-7927-2243-4(4), CSL 132, Chivers Sound Lib) AudioGO.
Sabrina Eversleigh runs away from home after her brother-in-law tries to rape her. Caught in a blizzard, she is rescued by Phillip Mercerault. After nursing her back to health, Phillip learns that he is not a hero. Instead, he is a gentleman who has compromised a lady. Now there's only one thing to do: marry her! Sabrina, however, turns him down. But things don't turn out the way Sabrina has planned, and it is she who must now propose to Phillip.

Offer of Lowliness. 1 cass. (Running Time: 30 min.). 1985. (0223) Evang Sisterhood Mary.
Choosing Jesus' way in our everyday lives; For times when I can't get along with someone.

Offer You Can't Refuse. Jill Mansell. 2008. 76.95 (978-0-7531-3085-8(8)); audio compact disk 89.95 (978-0-7531-3086-5(6)) Pub: Isis Pubng Ltd GBR. Dist(s): Ulverscroft US

Offering. Perf. by Mary Youngblood. 1 cass. (Running Time: 1 hr.). 7.98 (SWR 917); audio compact disk 12.78 (SWR 917) NewSound.

Offerings of Praise. J. Daniel Smith. 2001. 75.00 (978-0-633-01388-2(9)); 11.98 (978-0-633-01342-4(0)); audio compact disk 85.00 (978-0-633-01389-9(7)); audio compact disk 16.98 (978-0-633-01343-1(9)) LifeWay Christian.

***Office for Outer Space Affairs.** United Nations. (ENG.). 2010. audio compact disk 15.00 (978-92-1-101219-4(8)) Untd Nat Pubns.

Office Furniture in Argentina: A Strategic Reference 2006. Compiled by Icon Group International, Inc. Staff. 2007. ring bd. 195.00 (978-0-497-35802-0(6)) Icon Grp.

Office Health Hazards. 1 cass. (Running Time: 41 min.). 10.95 (I0260B090, HarperThor) HarpC GBR.

Office of Desire. Martha Moody. Read by Renée Raudman & Todd McLaren. (Playaway Adult Fiction Ser.). 2008. 64.99 (978-1-60640-570-3(5)) Find a World.

Office of Desire. unabr. ed. Martha Moody. Read by Renée Raudman. Narrated by Todd McLaren. (Running Time: 9 hrs. 30 mins. 0 sec.). (ENG.). 2007. audio compact disk 34.99 (978-1-4001-0512-0(9)); audio compact disk 69.99 (978-1-4001-3512-7(5)); audio compact disk 24.99 (978-1-4001-5512-5(6)) Pub: Tantor Media. Dist(s): IngramPubServ

Office Politics: The Unspoken Strategies for Gaining Power & Getting Ahead. Marilyn M. Kennedy. Read by Marilyn M. Kennedy. 6 cass. (Running Time: 9 hrs.). 1991. 39.95 (882AD) Nightingale-Conant.
If you think office politics is for users, complainers or poor workers, you're wrong...& you're also denying yourself the very tools you need to advance in your career. Today an achievement-oriented man or woman simply must face the realities of personal power. So if you've been avoiding those realities, this unique program can show you how to face the facts of business life & to turn them decisively in your favor.

Office Psychiatry, Vol. A189: Mood Anxiety Disorders. unabr. ed. 12 cass. (Running Time: 12 hrs.). 1995. 550.00 (978-1-57664-358-7(1)) CME Info Svcs.
Continuing medical education home-study. Complete package contains audiotapes, syllabus, self-assessment examination to earn CME Category 1 credit.

Office Security Begins at the Front Desk. PUEI. 2007. audio compact disk 199.00 (978-1-934147-16-0(8), CareerTrack) P Univ E Inc.

Office Ultrasound in Gynecology. Contrib. by Steven R. Goldstein et al. 1 cass. (Running Time: 1 hr.). (American College of Obstetrics & Gynecologists UPDATE: Vol. 21, No. 1). 1998. 20.00 Am Coll Obstetric.

Officer Buckle & Gloria. 2004. pap. bk. 18.95 (978-0-7882-0313-8(4)); pap. bk. 32.75 (978-1-55592-287-0(2)); audio compact disk 12.95 (978-0-7882-0309-1(6)) Weston Woods.

Officer Buckle & Gloria. Peggy Rathmann. Narrated by John Lithgow. 1 cass., 5 bks. (Running Time: 12 min.). (J). pap. bk. 32.75 Weston Woods.
Officer Buckle knows more about safety than anyone in Napville, but nobody listens - until the Police Dept. buys a police dog named Gloria.

Officer Buckle & Gloria. Peggy Rathmann. Narrated by John Lithgow. 1 cass. (Running Time: 12 min.). (J). (ps-3). bk. 12.95 Weston Woods.

Officer Buckle & Gloria. unabr. ed. Based on a book by Peggy Rathmann. 1 cass. (Running Time: 12 mins.). (J). (ps-3). 1997. 8.95 (978-1-56008-815-8(X), RAC366) Weston Woods.

Officer Buckle & Gloria. unabr. ed. Based on a book by Peggy Rathmann. Narrated by John Lithgow. 1 cass. (Running Time: 12 mins.). (J). (ps-3). 1997. bk. 24.95 (978-0-7882-0669-6(9), HRA366) Weston Woods.

Officer of the Deck. unabr. ed. Herbert Kriloff. Narrated by Sean Mangan. 6 cass. (Running Time: 8 hrs. 30 mins.). 2004. 48.00 (978-1-74030-463-4(2)) Pub: Bolinda Pubng AUS. Dist(s): Lndmrk Audiobks

Officers & Gentlemen. unabr. ed. Evelyn Waugh. Read by Christian Rodska. 8 cass. (Running Time: 12 hrs.). (Sword of Honour Trilogy: Bk. 2). 2000. 59.95 (SAB 083) Pub: Chivers Audio Bks GBR. Dist(s): AudioGO
Guy Crouchback is now attached to a Commando unit on the Hebridean island of Mugg, where the whisky flows freely. But the comedy of Mugg is countered with the bitterness of Crete, and all the chaos and indignity of a total surrender.

Officers & Gentlemen. unabr. collector's ed. Evelyn Waugh. Read by David Case. 7 cass. (Running Time: 10 hrs. 30 min.). (World War II Trilogy). 1992. 56.00 (978-0-7366-2190-8(3), 2985) Books on Tape.
Second volume in WW II trilogy. Guy Crouchback returns as a commando trainee. He joins a special assault team in a Crete mission that never gets off the ground.

Officers' Wives, Pt. 1. unabr. collector's ed. Thomas J. Fleming. Read by Ruth Stokesberry. 10 cass. (Running Time: 15 hrs.). 1991. 80.00 (978-0-7366-1986-8(0), 2803A) Books on Tape.
On June 5, 1950, in the West Point chapel, three very different young women marry graduates of the U.S. Military Academy - three equally different men who have committed themselves to a lifetime of service in that mysterious monolith, the U.S. Army. Within weeks, Communist tanks roll into South Korea & the brides - & their husbands - begin a journey through the most turbulent 25 years in American history. Before it ends all of them, the wives & the officers, face heartbreaking choices as West Point's ideals of duty, honor, & country become raging conflicts in their lives. This is the first novel ever written about the U.S. Army from a woman's point of view.

Officers' Wives, Pt. 2. collector's ed. Thomas J. Fleming. Read by Ruth Stokesberry. 10 cass. (Running Time: 15 hrs.). 1991. 80.00 (978-0-7366-1987-5(9), 2803-B) Books on Tape.

Offices, Bks. I-III unabr. ed. Marcus Tullius Cicero. Read by Robert L. Halvorson. 4 cass. (Running Time: 6 hrs.). 28.95 (45) Halvorson Assocs.

Official Album of WDW. 1 cass. (Classic Collections). (J). 10.99 Norelco. (978-0-7634-0282-2(6)); 16.99 (978-0-7634-0285-3(0)) W Disney Records.

Official Album of WDW. 1 cass. (Running Time: 1 hr. 30 mins.). (Classic Collections). (J). (ps-3). 1997. 10.99 (978-0-7634-0283-9(4)); audio compact disk 16.99 (978-0-7634-0284-6(2)) W Disney Records.

Official Book Club Selection: A Memoir According to Kathy Griffin. abr. ed. Kathy Griffin. Read by Kathy Griffin. 2009. audio compact disk 32.00 (978-0-307-70190-9(5), Random AudioBks) Pub: Random Audio Pubg. Dist(s): Random

Official Chuck Norris Fact Book: 101 of Chuck's Favorite Facts & Stories. unabr. ed. Chuck Norris & Todd DuBord. (Running Time: 4 hrs. 18 mins. 0 sec.). (ENG.). 2009. audio compact disk 18.98 (978-1-59644-821-6(0)) christianaud.

OFFICIAL DICKSHUNARY of OCCONEECHEE NECK: Garysburg, north carolina (gazeburg, nor'f Care'lina) Maria Brazil. 2006. audio compact disk 9.99 (978-1-4276-2720-9(7)) AardGP.

Official Driving Tour of the Lewis & Clark Bicentennial Vol. 1: The Adventure Begins. 1 cass. (Running Time: 67 min.). 2003. 15.95 (978-1-930827-12-7(1), Car Tours) Audisee Sound.

Official Driving Tour of the Lewis & Clark Bicentennial Vol. 1: The Adventure Begins. 1 CD. (Running Time: 66 mins.). 2004. audio compact disk 15.95 (978-1-930827-32-5(6), Car Tours) Audisee Sound.

Official Driving Tour of the Lewis & Clark Bicentennial Vol. 9: The Mighty Columbia, Vol. 9. (Running Time: 66 minutes). 2002. 15.95 (978-1-930827-20-2(2), Car Tours) Audisee Sound.

Official Guide to Success. Tom Hopkins. bk. 75.00 (978-0-938636-16-8(2)) T Hopkins Intl.
Shows how to take control with positive attitude & motivational skills.

Official L Word Book. unabr. ed. Showtime Networks Staff. 2006. 39.95 (978-0-7435-5261-5(X), Fireside) Pub: S and S. Dist(s): S and S Inc

Official Privilege. unabr. ed. P. T. Deutermann. Read by J. Charles. 14 cass. (Running Time: 19 hrs.). 1995. 121.25 (978-1-56100-271-9(2), 1561002712, Unabridge Lib Edns) Brilliance Audio.
When the body of a young, black Navy lieutenant is found chained inside the boiler of a mothballed battleship in a Philadelphia shipyard, there is no question that it's murder. Stung by past scandals, the Navy moves to control the investigation by appointing one of their own, Commander Dan Collins, in charge of it. Dan's deputy investigator will be civilian Grace Ellen Snow from the NIS (Naval Investigative Service), the organization that should have been in control of the investigation. Dan and Grace make a connection between this murder, the death of the man's sister (also a Navy lieutenant), and a top Naval officer only to have the chain-of-command curtain come down around their investigation. Convinced they can uncover those responsible for the murders, they secretly continue their investigation - a search that brings them to the attention of a cunning, remorseless, and relentless man.

Official Privilege. unabr. ed. P. T. Deutermann. Read by J. Charles. (Running Time: 19 hrs.). 2007. 44.25 (978-1-4233-3056-1(0), 9781423330561, BADLE); 29.95 (978-1-4233-3055-4(2), 9781423330554, BAD); audio compact disk 44.25 (978-1-4233-3054-7(4), 9781423330547, Brinc Audio MP3 Lib); audio compact disk 29.95 (978-1-4233-3053-0(6), 9781423330530, Brilliance MP3) Brilliance Audio.

Official Privilege, unabr. ed. P. T. Deutermann. Read by J. Charles. 14 cass. (Running Time: 21 hrs.). 1999. 121.25 (FS9-43253) Highsmith.

Offrande Sauvage. l.t. ed. Jean-Pierre Milovanoff. (French Ser.). 2000. bk. 30.99 (978-2-84011-358-4(9)) Pub: UlverLrgPrint GBR. Dist(s): Ulverscroft US

Offspring: The Unauthorized Biography of Offspring. Keith Rodway. (Maximum Ser.). (ENG.). 2001. audio compact disk 14.95 (978-1-84240-022-7(3)) Pub: Chrome Dreams GBR. Dist(s): IPG Chicago

***Often Wrong, Never in Doubt.** abr. ed. Donny Deutsch. Read by Peter Knobler. (ENG.). 2005. (978-0-06-089417-7(2), Harper Audio); (978-0-06-089416-0(4), Harper Audio) HarperCollins Pubs.

Often Wrong, Never in Doubt: Unleash the Business Rebel Within. abr. ed. Donny Deutsch. Read by Peter Knobler. 2005. audio compact disk 29.95 (978-0-06-082364-1(X)) HarperCollins Pubs.

Og Mandino's Secrets of Success. Og Mandino. Intro. by A. E. Whyte. 1 cass. (Running Time: 45 min.). (Listen & Learn USA Ser.). 8.95 (978-0-88684-018-1(X)) Listen USA.
Offers the keys to unlocking the successful you.

Ogden Nash Reads Ogden Nash. abr. ed. Ogden Nash. 1 cass. (Running Time: 1 hr.). 1984. 12.95 (978-0-694-50011-6(9), SWC 1015) HarperCollins Pubs.

Ogden Nash's Parents Keep Out! abr. ed. Ogden Nash. Perf. by Ogden Nash. 1 cass. (Running Time: 1 hr. 30 mins.). (J). 1984. 9.95 (978-1-55994-049-8(2), CPN 1282) HarperCollins Pubs.

Oggi in Italia: A First Course in Italian. 2nd ed. Franca C. Merlonghi et al. 1982. reel tape 270.00 (978-0-685-42421-6(9)) HM.

Oggie Cooder. unabr. ed. Sarah Weeks. Read by William Dufris. (Running Time: 2 hrs.). 2009. 39.97 (978-1-4233-7279-0(4), 9781423372790, BADLE); 39.97 (978-1-4233-7277-6(8), 9781423372776, Brinc Audio MP3 Lib); 17.99 (978-1-4233-7278-3(6), 9781423372783, BAD); 17.99 (978-1-4233-7276-9(X), 9781423372769, Brilliance MP3); audio compact disk 17.99 (978-1-4233-7274-5(3), 9781423372745, Bril Audio CD Unabri) Brilliance Audio.

Oggie Cooder. unabr. ed. Sarah Weeks. Read by William Dufris. 2 CDs. (Running Time: 2 hrs.). (J). (gr. 3-5). 2009. audio compact disk 55.97 (978-1-4233-7275-2(1), 9781423372752, BriAudCD Unabrid) Brilliance Audio.

Oggie Cooder Party Animal. unabr. ed. Sarah Weeks. Read by William Dufris. (Running Time: 2 hrs.). 2009. 17.99 (978-1-4233-7282-0(4), 9781423372820, Brilliance MP3); 39.97 (978-1-4233-7283-7(2), 9781423372837, Brinc Audio MP3 Lib); 39.97 (978-1-4233-7285-1(9), 9781423372851, BADLE); 17.99 (978-1-4233-7284-4(0), 9781423372844, BAD); audio compact disk 17.99 (978-1-4233-7280-6(8), 9781423372806, Bril Audio CD Unabri) Brilliance Audio.

Oggie Cooder Party Animal. unabr. ed. Sarah Weeks. Read by William Dufris. 2 CDs. (Running Time: 2 hrs.). (J). (gr. 3-5). 2009. audio compact disk 55.97 (978-1-4233-7281-3(6), 9781423372813, BriAudCD Unabrid) Brilliance Audio.

Ogilvie & the Gold of the Raj. Philip Mccutchan. 2008. 54.95 (978-1-4079-0281-4(4)); audio compact disk 64.95 (978-1-4079-0282-1(2)) Pub: Soundings Ltd GBR. Dist(s): Ulverscroft US

Ogilvie & the Mullah. unabr. ed. Philip McCutchan & Philip Mccutchan. Read by Christopher Scott. 8 cass. 2007. 69.95 (978-1-84559-241-7(7)) Pub: ISIS Audio GBR. Dist(s): Ulverscroft US

Ogilvie & the Uprising. Philip Mccutchan. 2009. 54.95 (978-1-4079-0284-5(9)); audio compact disk 64.95 (978-1-4079-0285-2(7)) Pub: Soundings Ltd GBR. Dist(s): Ulverscroft US

Ogilvie's Act of Cowardice. Philip McCutchan. Read by Terry Wale. 6 cass. 2007. 54.95 (978-1-84559-463-3(0)) Pub: Soundings Ltd GBR. Dist(s): Ulverscroft US

Ogilvie's Dangerous Mission. Philip Mccutchan. 2008. 54.95 (978-1-84559-616-3(1)); audio compact disk 71.95 (978-1-84559-781-8(8)) Pub: Soundings Ltd GBR. Dist(s): Ulverscroft US

Ogonyok. 3 cass. (Running Time: 3 hrs.). (RUS.). pap. bk. 59.50 (SRU350) J Norton Pubs.

Ogre in a Toga. unabr. ed. Geoffrey McSkimming. Read by Geoffrey McSkimming. (Running Time: 1 hr.). (J). 2007. audio compact disk 39.95 (978-1-74093-932-4(8), 9781740939324) Pub: Bolinda Pubng AUS. Dist(s): Bolinda Pub Inc

Ogres & Pygmies see Robert Graves Reads from His Poetry & the White Goddess

Oh, Baby!; Girls Don't Have Cooties. unabr. ed. Nancy Krulik. Read by Anne Bobby. 2 cass. (Running Time: 1 hr. 52 mins.). (Katie Kazoo, Switcheroo Ser.: Nos. 3-4). (J). (ps-3). 2005. 23.00 (978-0-307-28179-1(5), Listening Lib); audio compact disk 20.40 (978-0-307-28180-7(9), Listening Lib) Pub: Random Audio Pubg. Dist(s): NetLibrary CO

Oh Blessed Hope. Perf. by Steve Brock. Prod. by Michael Sykes. 1 cass. (Running Time: 1 hr. 30 mins.). 1997. audio compact disk 15.99 (D2040) Diamante Music Grp.
An intriguing, diverse mix of Traditional Adult Contemporary & Inspirational Gospel songs.

Oh, Brother! Timothy Glass. Narrated by Allen Hite. (ENG.). (J). 2008. audio compact disk 14.95 (978-1-60031-032-4(X)) Spoken Books.

***Oh, Cats!** unabr. ed. Nola Buck. (ENG.). 2008. (978-0-06-179917-4(3)); (978-0-06-169482-0(7)) HarperCollins Pubs.

Oh Dear, Doctor! Robert Clifford. Read by Christopher Scott. 4 cass. (Running Time: 6 hrs.). 2001. 40.46 (978-1-86042-830-2(4)) Pub: Soundings Ltd GBR. Dist(s): Ulverscroft US

Oh God! Oh God! Oh God! Dr. Shultz on Sex & Spirituality. J. Kennedy Shultz. 1989. 18.95 (978-0-924687-03-7(7)) Rel Sci Vision Pr.
A common sense approach to sexuality in the '80s.

Oh Great! What Do I Do Now? 2 CD set. (Running Time: 100 mins). 2003. audio compact disk 15.95 (978-1-930429-30-7(4)) Pub: Love Logic. Dist(s): Penton Overseas

Oh Great! What Do I Do Now? Parenting Remedies for When Kids Cook-Up the Unexpected. unabr. ed. Charles Fay. Read by Charles Fay. Illus. by Bert Gurule Mizke. 1 cass. (Running Time: 1 hr. 40 mins.). 2000. 11.95 (978-1-930429-05-5(3)) Pub: Love Logic. Dist(s): Penton Overseas
Dr. Charles Fay brings you lots of giggles & plenty of easy-to-use strategies to help you handle the unexpected. Have a ready-made answer for that "classic" question. This new audio program is guaranteed to lower parents stress level & make life fun again. The great news is, it works on kids of all ages, toddler to teen.

Oh Great! What Do I Do Now? Parenting Remedies for When Kids Cook-Up the Unexpected. unabr. ed. Charles Fay. 2 cass. (Running Time: 1 hr. 30 mins.). 2001. 11.95 Penton Overseas.

Oh Had I Known It Once for All see Poetry of Pasternak

Oh How I Love Jesus. Perf. by Elisa Takage. 2006. audio compact disk 9.95 (978-1-59987-425-8(3)) Braun Media.

Oh I Want to Know You More. Contrib. by Russell Mauldin. 1996. 19.98 (978-0-7601-0766-9(1), 75605382) Pub: Brentwood Music. Dist(s): H Leonard

***Oh It Is Jesus.** Perf. by Tsea. 2010. audio compact disk 15.00 (978-0-9819971-6-2(3)) TSEA.

Oh, Kojo! How Could You! Verna Aardema. (J). 1987. bk. 44.88 (978-0-07-511624-0(3)) SRA McGraw.

Oh les Beaux Jours. Samuel Beckett. Perf. by Madeleine Renaud & Jean-Louis Barrault. 1 CD. (Running Time: 1 hr.). (FRE.). 1995. audio compact disk 29.95 (1315-AD) Olivia & Hill.
Recorded live at the Theatre de France in 1964. A woman, Winnie, is buried in the sand & talks about the irony of her life, while her husband, Willie, spends his time sleeping in a hole behind her, occasionally mumbling over the want ads & obituaries in his yellowing newspaper.

Oh, Lovely Rock see Twentieth-Century Poetry in English, No. 5, Recordings of Poets Reading Their Own Poetry

Oh Man Oh Mind. Yogi Hari. 1 cass. (Running Time: 45 min.). 9.95 (OM) Nada Prodns.
The teachings of the Saints & Sages distilled in the songs that address the mind, reminding it that it alone is responsible for its happiness or distress: Din Neekay Beetay Jatay Hai; Radhay Krishna Bol; Sacho Tayro Ram Nam; Samajjhay Mana; Ek Din Jana Ray Bhailyee; Ah Mana Mohan Murali Wala; Tarana.

Oh My God... She's Huge! (audio) Joan M. Landis. 2008. audio compact disk 27.99 (978-1-60696-087-5(3)) Tate Pubng.

Oh Play that Thing. unabr. ed. Read by Christian Conn. 2 pieces. 49.95 (978-0-7927-3365-2(7)); 79.95 (978-0-7927-3363-8(0)); audio compact disk 110.95 (978-0-7927-3364-5(9)) AudioGO.

Oh That I Were an Angel. Christina England Hale. (Running Time: 1 hr.). 2004. audio compact disk 16.98 (978-5-559-86644-4(X)) Pub: Pt of Grace Ent. Dist(s): STL Dist NA

Oh, the Places You'll Go! & the Lorax. unabr. ed. Dr. Seuss. Read by John Lithgow & Ted Danson. (Running Time: 1800 sec.). (ENG.). (J). (gr. 1). 2008. audio compact disk 9.99 (978-0-7393-6391-1(3), Listening Lib) Pub: Random Audio Pubg. Dist(s): Random

Oh to Be in England see Ship That Died of Shame

Oh, What a Beautiful Morning! (Easter) Luke 24:1-12. Told to Ed Young. 1992. 4.95 (978-0-7417-1917-1(7), 917) Win Walk.

Oh What a Moment. Contrib. by Camp Kirkland. 1992. 24.95 (978-0-00-508002-3(9), 75607924) Pub: Brentwood Music. Dist(s): H Leonard

Oh, What a Paradise It Seems. unabr. ed. John Cheever. Narrated by Henry Strozier. 2 cass. (Running Time: 3 hrs.). 1984. 18.00 (978-1-55690-387-8(1), 84022E7) Recorded Bks.
An aging man's desperate attempts to save a small lake from environmental destruction & his efforts to find love with a younger woman propel this quintessential Cheever story.

Oh What a Savior. Contrib. by Marty Hamby. 1996. 24.95 (978-0-7601-1109-3(X), 75600274) Pub: Brentwood Music. Dist(s): H Leonard

Oh What a Slaughter: Massacres in the American West: 1846-1890. unabr. ed. Larry McMurtry. Narrated by Michael Prichard. (Running Time: 4 hrs. 30 mins. 0 sec.). (ENG.). 2005. audio compact disk 24.99 (978-1-4001-0195-5(6)); audio compact disk 49.99 (978-1-4001-3195-2(2)); audio compact disk 19.99 (978-1-4001-5195-0(3)) Pub: Tantor Media. Dist(s): IngramPubServ

'Oh, Whistle, & I'll Come to You, My Lad' unabr. ed. M. R. James. Read by Walter Covell. 1 cass. (Running Time: 58 min.). Dramatization. 1981. 7.95 (S-16) Jimcin Record.
Terryifying tales of the supernatural.

Oh Yeah! John Farrell. 2003. audio compact disk 15.95 (978-1-59078-191-3(0)) Boyds Mills Pr.

Oh Yes see I Stand Here Ironing

***O'Hara's Choice.** abr. ed. Leon Uris. Read by John Bedford Lloyd. (ENG.). 2005. (978-0-06-085598-7(3), Harper Audio); (978-0-06-085597-0(5), Harper Audio) HarperCollins Pubs.

O'Hara's Choice. unabr. ed. Leon Uris. Read by Jack Garrett. 2003. 39.95 (978-0-06-056970-9(0)) HarperCollins Pubs.

O'Hara's Choice. unabr. ed. Leon Uris. 10 cass. (Running Time: 15 hrs.). 2003. 95.00 (978-1-4025-6741-4(3)) Recorded Bks.

***O'Hara's Choice.** unabr. ed. Leon Uris. Read by Jack Garrett. (ENG.). 2005. (978-0-06-085599-4(1), Harper Audio); (978-0-06-085600-7(9), Harper Audio) HarperCollins Pubs.

Ohio, A Sentimental Journey. Narrated by Michael Shaw & Janis Weber. Reviewed by Ohio Historical Society Staff. 1 CD. (Running Time: 70 mins.). (J). 2004. audio compact disk (978-0-9747666-2-1(3)) Amer Retro LLC.

Ohio Angels. unabr. ed. Harriet Scott Chessman. Read by Norma Lana. 3 cass. 2004. 29.95 (978-0-7927-3115-3(8), CSL 622, Chivers Sound Lib); audio compact disk 49.95 (978-0-7927-3116-0(6), SLD 622, Chivers Sound Lib) AudioGO.
In Harriet Scott Chessman's arresting first novel, Hallie Greaves comes home to Ohio one hot week in July. She hopes to help her mother who confines her life wholly to her bedroom. To enter her mother's room, however, is to face her own disappointments and yearnings. At an impasse in her painting and her marriage, Hallie confronts questions of love, memory, and sorrow. Ohio Angels is a moving portrait of the intricacies of marriage and friendship, and of the surprising possibilities for compassion and renewal.

***O'Hurley Born: The Last Honest Woman, Dance to the Piper.** unabr. ed. Nora Roberts. Read by Marie Caliendo. (Running Time: 14 hrs.). 2010. audio compact disk 29.99 (978-1-61106-126-0(1), 9781611061260, Bril Audio CD Unabri) Brilliance Audio.

***O'Hurley's Return: Skin Deep, Without a Trace.** unabr. ed. Nora Roberts. Read by Marie Caliendo. (Running Time: 14 hrs.). 2010. audio compact disk 29.99 (978-1-61106-125-3(3), 9781611061253, Bril Audio CD Unabri) Brilliance Audio.

***Oiche Chiun.** Maria Ni Chumhaill. (ENG.). 1993. 11.95 (978-0-8023-7095-2(0)) Pub: Clo Iar-Chonnachta IRL. Dist(s): Dufour

Oikos: Songs for the Living Earth. Jesse 'Wolf' Hardin. 1 cass. (Running Time: 1 hr. 12 mins.). 1999. 10.00 (978-1-893183-27-8(0), 522); audio compact disk 14.00 (978-1-893183-26-1(2), 521) Granite Pub.
19 haunting, enchanted lyrical songs performed by Jesse 'Wolf' Hardin, weaving together the traditions of Africa, Latin America, Russia, Native America & the Middle East.

Oil! abr. ed. Upton Sinclair. Read by Grover Gardner. (Running Time: 72000 sec.). 2008. audio compact disk 44.95 (978-1-4332-4446-9(2)); audio compact disk & audio compact disk 120.00 (978-1-4332-4444-5(6)) Blckstn Audio.

Oil! abr. ed. Upton Sinclair & Grover Gardner. (Running Time: 72000 sec.). 2008. 105.95 (978-1-4332-4443-8(8)) Blckstn Audio.

Oil! unabr. ed. Upton Sinclair. Read by Grover Gardner. 15 CDs. 2008. audio compact disk & audio compact disk 29.95 (978-1-4332-4445-2(4)) Blckstn Audio.

Oil & Gas Equipment & Services in Saudi Arabia: A Strategic Reference 2007. Compiled by Icon Group International, Inc. Staff. 2007. ring bd. 195.00 (978-0-497-82408-2(6)) Icon Grp.

Oil & Gas Equipment in Indonesia: A Strategic Reference 2006. Compiled by Icon Group International, Inc. Staff. 2007. ring bd. 195.00 (978-0-497-36030-6(6)) Icon Grp.

Oil & Gas Field Machinery in Colombia: A Strategic Reference 2006. Compiled by Icon Group International, Inc. Staff. 2007. ring bd. 195.00 (978-0-497-35899-0(9)) Icon Grp.

Oil & Gas Field Machinery in Denmark: A Strategic Reference 2007. Compiled by Icon Group International, Inc. Staff. 2007. ring bd. 195.00 (978-0-497-35912-6(X)) Icon Grp.

Oil & Gas Field Machinery in Singapore: A Strategic Reference 2006. Compiled by Icon Group International, Inc. Staff. 2007. ring bd. 195.00 (978-0-497-82416-7(7)) Icon Grp.

Oil & Gas Production in Brazil: A Strategic Reference 2007. Compiled by Icon Group International, Inc. Staff. 2007. ring bd. 195.00 (978-0-497-35841-9(7)) Icon Grp.

Oil & Marshes Along Our Coastline. Hosted by Nancy Pearlman. 1 cass. (Running Time: 29 min.). 10.00 (508) Educ Comm CA.

Oil & the Branch. Kelley Varner. 1 cass. (Running Time: 29 mins.). 7.00 (978-1-56043-974-5(2)) Destiny Image Pubs.

Oil & Water. unabr. ed. Edward Cowan. Read by Greg Shannon. 10 cass. (Running Time: 10 hrs.). 1975. 60.00 (978-0-913369-94-4(2), 1004) Books on Tape.
This is the story of the "Torrey Canyon", a globe-circling supertanker which made itself famous by driving fatally onto the Seven Stones Reef less than 20 miles from the Cornish coast of England. It was the first major supertanker disaster, & its reverberations echo still. Edward Cowan traces the voyage & its aftermath & tells a hair-raising story of petronomics in this interdependent age through which we are voyaging.

Oil Drilling in Coastal Waters. Hosted by Nancy Pearlman. 1 cass. (Running Time: 29 min.). 10.00 (232) Educ Comm CA.

Oil Notes. Rick Bass. Read by Rick Bass. 2 cass. (Running Time: 3 hrs.). 1990. 15.95 HarperCollins Pubs.

Oil Rig. unabr. ed. Frank Roderus. Read by Kevin Foley. 6 cass. (Running Time: 7 hrs. 42 min.). (Heller Ser.: Bk. 1). 1994. 39.95 (978-1-55686-569-5(4)) Books in Motion.
A simple oil & mineral sting by sharp Easterners against Westerners turns ugly. One man is dead, others face ruin until Carl Heller stings back.

Oil Spills. Compiled by Benchmark Education Staff. 2005. audio compact disk 10.00 (978-1-4108-5500-8(7)) Benchmark Educ.

OJ & Nicole Simpson: A Personal Retrospective. Larry Pines. Read by Larry Pines. 1 cass. (Running Time: 1 hr. 30 mins.). 1994. 8.95 (1104) Am Fed Astrologers.
A look at OJ & Nicole Simpson as a couple by their astrologer.

OJ Simpson: Who Dunnit? Albert Gaulden. Read by Albert Gaulden. 1 cass. (Running Time: 1 hr. 30 mins.). 1994. 8.95 (1138) Am Fed Astrologers.

Ojibwe, Set, study guide. Paul Pimsleur. 16 cass. (Pimsleur Language Learning Ser.). 1994. 345.00 Set, incl. study guide. (0671-57941-X) SyberVision.

Ojibwe: Learn to Speak & Understand Ojibwe with Pimsleur Language Programs. unabr. ed. Pimsleur Staff. (Running Time: 5 hrs. 0 mins. 0 sec.). (Basic Ser.). (ENG.). 2006. audio compact disk 24.95 (978-0-7435-6152-5(X), Pimsleur); audio compact disk 345.00 (978-0-7435-6180-8(5), Pimsleur) Pub: S&S Audio. Dist(s): S and S Inc

Ojibwe, for Speakers of English One. unabr. ed. 16 cass. (Running Time: 15 hrs.). (Pimsleur Tapes Ser.). (OJI.). 1994. 345.00 (18010) S&S Audio.
Spoken foreign-language proficiency training. Thirty, half-hour, intensive, spoken-language lesson units to be completed at the rate of one lesson per day for 30 days. By achieving eighty-percent correct answers to the questions in each unit, the Pimsleur Spoken Language Programmed Instructional Method will enable the learner to achieve the ACTFL Intermediate-Low Spoken Proficiency Level.

Okasan & Me: Japanese American Educational Program - CD for Kids. Cynthia Konda. 1 cass. (Running Time: 0.40). (JPN & ENG.). 2003. audio compact disk 19.99 (978-0-9743613-1-4(3)) Okasan Me.
Educational Program CD for everyone done in both English and Japanese.

***Okay for Now.** unabr. ed. Gary D. Schmidt. (ENG.). (J). 2011. audio compact disk 40.00 (978-0-307-91589-4(1), Listening Lib) Pub: Random Audio Pubg. Dist(s): Random

Okay Koala. unabr. ed. Margaret Clark. Read by Melissa Eccleston. 2 cass. (Running Time: 2 hrs.). 2002. (978-1-74030-369-9(5)) Bolinda Pubng AUS.

Oklahoma! Dana Fuller Ross, pseud. Read by Lloyd James. 4 vols. (Wagons West Ser.: No. 23). 2004. 25.00 (978-1-58807-155-2(3)); (978-1-58807-624-3(5)) Am Pubng Inc.

Oklahoma Pride. abr. ed. Dana Fuller Ross, pseud. Read by Tim Nelson. Abr. by Odin Westgaard. 4 cass. (Running Time: 6 hrs.). (Holts, an American Dynasty Ser.: Vol. 2). 2004. 25.00 (978-1-58807-451-5(X)) Am Pubng Inc.

Okropong. Perf. by Obo Addy. 1 cass. (Running Time: 35 min.). 9.98 (978-1-877737-66-4(6), EB 2500) MFLP CA.

Ol' Cactus Kapoor & Other Prickly Tales. unabr. ed. Thomas M. Lopez. 1 cass. (Running Time: 1 hr. 15 min.). (J). (gr. k-6). 1997. 9.95 (978-1-881137-79-5(1), RFK); audio compact disk 14.95 CD. (978-1-881137-78-8(3), RFKCD) ZBS Found.
Nine humorous short stories based on the sneaky but oddly beloved character from the "Ruby" series, Rodant Kapoor.

Ol' Man Adam an' His Chillun. abr. ed. Roark Bradford. Perf. by Mantan Moreland. 1 cass. (Running Time: 1 hr. 15 mins). 1984. 12.95 (SWC 1174) HarperCollins Pubs.

Ola. 2004. pap. bk. 14.95 (978-1-55592-088-3(8)); cass. & flmstrp 30.00 (978-1-56008-733-5(1)) Weston Woods.

Ola Gigante; El Primer Dia de Clases, Set. unabr. ed. (Coleccion Chiquilines - Imagen y Sonido). (SPA., (J). bk. 15.95 (978-950-11-0626-8(8), SGM268) Pub: Sigmar ARG. Dist(s): Continental Bk
Two well-known stories accompanied by a cassette. The themes chosen are very appropriate for elementary students, & the children who can not read will be able to listen, recognize the story & follow the action with the well illustrated books. The duration of each cassette is 10 to 12 minutes per side, with one story on each side of the cassette.

***Ola Latina.** abr. ed. Jorge Ramos. Read by Jorge Ramos. (ENG.). 2004. (978-0-06-081781-7(X), Harper Audio); (978-0-06-081780-0(1), Harper Audio) HarperCollins Pubs.

Ola; Letter Amy, A; Tikki Tikki Tembo, Holy Night. 2004. 8.95 (978-1-56008-987-2(3)) Weston Woods.

Ola; Letter to Amy, A; Tikki Tikki Tembo; Holy Night. 2004. cass. & flmstrp (978-0-89719-734-2(8)) Weston Woods.

Olam Shalem. unabr. ed. Edmond Lipsite. 3 cass. (Running Time: 3 hrs.). (HEB.). (YA). (gr. 10-12). 1985. pap. bk. 59.50 (978-0-88432-579-6(2), AFHE10) J Norton Pubs.
Beginner-level, uses modern Hebrew (Sephardic) for pronunciation in chanting basic prayers; teaches reading fluency; selections from the Siddur; prayers sung in traditional tune.

Olatunji Live at Starwood. Perf. by Babatunde Olatunji & Halim El-Dabh. 1. 2003. audio compact disk 12.95 (978-1-59157-026-4(3)) Assn for Cons.
A live performance of African music by Babatunde Olatunji and Drums of Passion, with special guest Halim El-Dabh, at the 1997 Starwood Festival.

Old Age: Journey into Simplicity. unabr. ed. Helen M. Luke. Read by Helen M. Luke. 2 cass. (Running Time: 3 hrs. 0 mins. 0 sec.). (ENG.). 1987. reel tape 16.95 (978-0-930407-26-1(1), 321-015) Pub: Morning Light Pr. Dist(s): PerseuPGW

Old Age - Journey to Simplicity. Read by Tesse Donnelly. 1 cass. (Running Time: 1 hr. 30 mins.). 1991. 10.95 (978-0-7822-0057-7(5), 433) C G Jung IL.

Old As the World. Read by Laura Simms. Music by Steve Gorn. 1 cass. (Running Time: 45 mins.). (J). 2000. 9.95 Yellow Moon.

Old Beggar. (J). 307. audio compact disk 10.00i (978-0-9675577-8-6(X)) Puddleduck Pubg.

Old Boys. unabr. ed. Charles McCarry. Read by Christopher Cazenove. 2004. 44.95 (978-1-59007-600-2(1)); audio compact disk 59.95 (978-1-59007-601-9(X)) Pub: New Millenn Enter. Dist(s): PerseuPGW

***Old Boys.** unabr. ed. Charles McCarry. Read by Stefan Rudnicki. (Running Time: 16 hrs. 30 mins.). (Paul Christopher Novels Ser.). 2010. 29.95 (978-1-4417-5873-6(9)); 89.95 (978-1-4417-5869-9(0)); audio compact disk 118.00 (978-1-4417-5870-5(4)) Blckstn Audio.

Old Business. Jason Sherman & Susan Coyne. 1 CD. (Running Time: 45 min.). 2005. audio compact disk 15.95 (978-0-660-19269-7(1)) Canadian Broadcasting CAN.

Old Chief Mshlanga. unabr. ed. Short Stories. Doris Lessing. Read by Doris Lessing. 1 cass. (Running Time: 29 min.). 1983. 10.95 (978-0-8045-1166-7(7), SAC 1166) Spoken Arts.
Encompasses all the complexities, agonies, joys & varied textures of African life & society from her book "African Stories".

Old Christmas & a scene from the Pickwick Papers. unabr. ed. Washington Irving & Charles Dickens. Read by Flo Gibson. 2 cass. (Running Time: 2 hrs. 30 min.). (YA). (gr. 6-12). 1989. 14.95 (978-1-55685-123-0(5)) Audio Bk Con.
Explores old traditions of the festive season & looks at a Dickensian skating party.

Old Contemptibles. unabr. ed. Martha Grimes. Read by Donada Peters. 7 cass. (Running Time: 10 hrs. 30 min.). (Richard Jury Novel Ser.). 1991. 56.00 (978-0-7366-1954-7(2), 2775) Books on Tape.
There are perhaps more restful retreats in the British Isles than The Old Contemptibles, a Lake District Inn, but Melrose Plant, a charming aristocrat, has come for duty rather than pleasure. Reason: Plant's friend Richard Jury is suspected of murdering a local woman, & Plant is there to prove him innocent. Contradictions blur the evidence & facts turn back in on themselves. All Plant can do is question...until it becomes clear where the questions lead. Then Plant faces a dreadful dilemma, to which any answer will cause pain, distress & damage.

Old Country. unabr. ed. Prod. by Listening Library Staff. 3 CDs. (Running Time: 3 hrs. 10 mins.). (J). (gr. 3-6). 2005. audio compact disk 30.00 (978-0-307-24544-1(6), Listening Lib); 23.00 (978-0-307-24543-4(8), Listening Lib) Random Audio Pubg.
The bulk of this tale takes place in the pseudo-mythical Old Country. At the present time, Great Grandmother Gisella tells her disbelieving young relative the story about how she had been both a girl and a fox. The complicated telling begins, intermingling rather gruesome civil war images, animal tales, Alice-in-Wonderland-esque style legal trials, and slapstick political characters and coups. When Gisella stares too long into Flame the Fox's eyes, they trade shapes. Gisella the fox spends much of the rest of the tale trying to find her family and Flame/Gisella so that she can return to her original form.

Old Country Advice to the American Traveler see Fourteen American Masterpieces

Old Curiosity Shop. Charles Dickens. Contrib. by Alex Jennings & Phil Daniels. 6 CDs. (Running Time: 6 hrs. 10 mins.). 2006. audio compact disk 64.95 (978-0-7927-4343-9(1), BBCD 170) AudioGO.

Old Curiosity Shop. Charles Dickens. (ENG.). 2009. audio compact disk 29.95 (978-1-60283-562-7(4)) Pub: AudioGO. Dist(s): Perseus Dist

Old Curiosity Shop. Charles Dickens. Narrated by Walter Covell. (Running Time: 23 hrs. 30 mins.). 1987. 58.95 (978-1-59912-871-9(3)) Iofy Corp.

Old Curiosity Shop. Charles Dickens. Read by Walter Covell. 1989. 63.00 Part I - 9 ninety minute cass. (C-177A); 68.00 Part I, incl. album.; 63.00 Part II - 9 ninety minute cass. (C-177B); 68.00 Part II, incl. album. Jimcin Record.
Episodic melodrama chronicles the adventures of Little Nell & the evil dwarf, Quilp.

Old Curiosity Shop. Charles Dickens. Narrated by Flo Gibson. (ENG.). 2009. audio compact disk 48.95 (978-1-60646-119-8(2)) Audio Bk Con.

Old Curiosity Shop. abr. ed. Charles Dickens. Perf. by Paul Scofield. 4 cass. (Running Time: 6 hrs.). (Ultimate Classics Ser.). 2004. 25.00 (978-1-931056-68-7(4), N Millennium Audio) New Millenn Enter.
The story of Little Nell. The story of the innocent Nell surrounded by surrealistic figures like Quiop and his gang and continuing onto a nightmarish journey through the industrial inferno with her half-crazed gambleholic grandfather. The death of Nell, based on the death of Mary Hogarth, caused a nation to weep.

Old Curiosity Shop. abr. ed. Charles Dickens. Read by Paul Scofield. 5 CDs. (Running Time: 6 hrs.). 2004. audio compact disk 34.95 (978-1-59007-578-4(1)) Pub: New Millenn Enter. Dist(s): PerseuPGW

Old Curiosity Shop. unabr. ed. Charles Dickens. Read by Flo Gibson. 14 cass. (Running Time: 21 hrs.). 2000. 42.95 (978-1-55685-656-3(3)) Audio Bk Con.
Little Nell & her grandfather are forced to leave the curiosity shop to live as beggars. Peopled with unforgettable characters such as Daniel Quilp, Dick Swiveller to name a few.

***Old Curiosity Shop.** unabr. ed. Charles Dickens. Narrated by Anton Lesser. 18 CDs. (Running Time: 22 hrs. 30 mins.). 2010. 107.98 (978-962-634-895-6(X)) Naxos.

Old Curiosity Shop, Pt. 1. unabr. ed. Charles Dickens. Read by Walter Covell. 9 cass. (Running Time: 26 hrs.). 1987. 62.95 (978-0-7861-0563-2(1), 2056A,B) Blckstn Audio.
The only novel in which Dickens allowed emotion to run away with both writer & reader. The heroine is little Nell Trent, whose grandfather keeps the Old Curiosity Shop but is tormented by his wicked creditors as he plunges farther into debt.

Old Curiosity Shop, Pt. 2. unabr. ed. Charles Dickens. Read by Walter Covell. 9 cass. (Running Time: 26 hrs.). 1987. 62.95 (978-0-7861-0564-9(X), 2056A,B) Blckstn Audio.

Old Curiosity Shop, Pt. A. unabr. collector's ed. Charles Dickens. Read by David Case. 9 cass. (Running Time: 13 hrs. 30 min.). 1993. 72.00 (978-0-7366-2345-2(0), 3124-A) Books on Tape.
Girl-child ripped from nest & thrown into world. Shows us Dickens' dark side.

Old Curiosity Shop, Pt. B. collector's unabr. ed. Charles Dickens. Read by David Case. 8 cass. (Running Time: 12 hrs.). 1993. 64.00 (978-0-7366-2346-9(9), 3124-B) Books on Tape.

***Old Dan Tucker.** Steve Kupferschmid. (Running Time: 2 mins.). (ENG.). 2010. audio compact disk 26.99 (978-1-4234-8605-3(6), 1423486056) Pub: Shawnee Pr. Dist(s): H Leonard

Old Devils. unabr. collector's ed. Kingsley Amis. Read by David Case. 8 cass. (Running Time: 12 hrs.). 1988. 64.00 (978-0-7366-1333-0(1), 2236) Books on Tape.
When Alun Weaver & his wife, Rhiannon, a famous beauty in her day, move into a quiet retirement community, they find it peopled by friends from former days. Suddenly all the ambitions & energies, overgrown like weeds with years, burst out afresh.

Old Dogs Can (& Must) Learn New Tricks: More Warren Bennis on Leadership & Change. Warren Bennis. 1 cass. (Running Time: 1 hr. 30 mins/). 1999. 12.95 (978-1-890009-35-9(0)) Exec Excell.

Old Dogs, New Tricks: Barry Louis Polisar Sings about Animals & Other Creatures. Barry Louis Polisar. 1 CD. (Running Time: 1 hr. 30 mins.). (ENG.). (J). (ps-4). 1993. audio compact disk 14.95 (978-0-938663-49-2(6), 5181 CD) Pub: Rainbow Morn. Dist(s): IPG Chicago
Thirteen prime picks enhance simply sung spoofs & silly antics, with richer accompaniments, subtle & tasteful embellishments. Includes bells, penny-whistles, fiddles, reverb & overdubbing, etc.

Old Dogs, New Tricks: Barry Louis Polisar Sings about Animals & Other Creatures. Perf. by Barry Louis Polisar. 1 cass. (Running Time: 1 hr. 30 mins.). (J). (gr. k-6). 1993. 9.95 (978-0-938663-17-1(8), 5181 CASS) Pub: Rainbow Morn. Dist(s): IPG Chicago

Old Elephant's Christmas. Brenda Baker. (J). 2002. audio compact disk 12.95 (978-1-55050-195-7(X)) Pub: Coteau CAN. Dist(s): Fitzhenry W Ltd

Old Enough to Know Better: The Worst of Barry Louis Polisar. unabr. abr. ed. Barry Louis Polisar. 2 CDs. (Running Time: 40 mins.). (ENG., (J). (gr. 2-4). 2006. audio compact disk 14.95 (978-0-938663-42-3(9)) Pub: Rainbow Morn. Dist(s): IPG Chicago
Barry's new CD is not what you might think from the title. The popular children's musician took a look back at his least favorite songs from his 1970s-era albums and reworked them into brand new songs. Barry's teen-aged children - once the subjects of some of his songs - contributed to the project. His daughter helped edit and re-shape many of the lyrics and his son joined him in the studio, playing saxophone and clarinet. The result is this two-CD compilation capping his groundbreaking efforts and provides two CDs for the cost of one.

Old Faith & the New. David Friedrich Strauss. Tr. by Mathilde Blind from GER. Intro. by G. A. Wells. Notes by G. A. Wells. (Westminster College-Oxford Classics in the Study of Religion Ser.). (ENG.). 1997. 37.98 (978-1-57392-118-3(1)) Prometheus Bks.

Old Family Movies: A Book of Poems. Robert Kirschten. 2008. pap. bk. 18.88 (978-0-9798401-0-4(4)) Pub: Vanity Human. Dist(s): AtlasBooks

Old Fashioned Christmas. Contrib. by Don Wyrtzen. 1983. 11.98 (978-0-00-498159-8(6), 75608799) Pub: Brentwood Music. Dist(s): H Leonard

Old Fashioned Christmas. Contrib. by Don Wyrtzen. 1983. 90.00 (978-0-00-640932-8(6), 75608821) Pub: Brentwood Music. Dist(s): H Leonard

Old-Fashioned Girl. Louisa May Alcott. (J). 1999. Audio Bk Con.

Old-Fashioned Girl. Louisa May Alcott. Read by Flo Gibson. 6 cass. (Running Time: 9 hrs.). (YA). (gr. 9-12). 1997. 24.95 (978-1-55685-501-6(X)) Audio Bk Con.
Polly, a young girl of modest means, comes to visit a wealthy, fashionable family who learn through her the true values of life.

Old-Fashioned Words. Kathryn Tucker Windham. (What Makes Us Southerners Ser.: Vol. 4). 2002. 12.00 (978-0-87483-659-2(X)); audio compact disk 16.95 (978-0-87483-660-8(3)) Pub: August Hse. Dist(s): Natl Bk Netwk

Old Fish Hawk. abr. ed. Mitch Jayne. Read by Mitch Jayne. 4 cass. (Running Time: 4 hrs. 50 min.). 1997. 19.95 (978-1-882467-05-1(1), Wldstone Audio) Wildstone Media.
He's the last of a vanishing breed, an Osage Indian, & ready to return to the land of his ancestors. Living on the fringes of the white man's world, he is weary of life & longs for the old ways.

Old Flame see Robert Lowell: A Reading

Old Flames. William Lashner. 2007. audio compact disk 39.95 (978-0-06-125645-5(5), Harper Audio) HarperCollins Pubs.

Old Folks. William H. Gass. Read by William H. Gass. 1 cass. (Running Time: 53 min.). 13.95 (978-1-55644-012-0(X), 1071) Am Audio Prose.
"The Tunnel," a work in progress, was previously published as a short story.

Old Friend from Far Away: How to Write a Memoir. unabr. ed. Natalie Goldberg. 2 CDs. (Running Time: 2 hrs. 30 min.). 2002. audio compact disk 24.95 (978-1-56455-959-3(9)) Sounds True.
Based on teachings from her highly acclaimed national workshops for writers of all levels, Goldberg explores: Techniques to connect with the senses and make memory vibrant: How to pull out the natural structure of the stories you carry within: How writing about the past can help free you from it, and much.

Old Friends. deluxe unabr. ed. Peter Steele Bixby. 5 cass. (Running Time: 6 hrs). 2000. lib. bdg. 25.00 (978-0-932079-02-2(4), 79024) TimeFare AudioBks.

Old Friends. unabr. ed. Tracy Kidder. Read by Alexander Adams. 6 cass. (Running Time: 9 hrs.). 1994. 48.00 (978-0-7366-2745-0(6), 3470) Books on Tape.
Two old men in a little room. Together they represent some 160 years of memories, of hope & achievement & sorrow - of life. They are strangers thrust together as roommates in a nursing home. On discovering that the problem of Linda Manor is "the universal problem of separateness," Lou Freed & Joe Torchio movingly set about solving it, with camaraderie & friendship & ultimately, love.

Old Friends. unabr. ed. Tracy Kidder. Read by Lowell George Seibel. (Running Time: 10 hrs.). 2008. 39.25 (978-1-4233-5812-1(0), 9781423358121, Brinc Audio MP3 Lib); 39.25 (978-1-4233-5814-5(7), 9781423358145, BADLE); 24.95 (978-1-4233-5811-4(2), 9781423358114, Brilliance MP3); 24.95 (978-1-4233-5813-8(9), 9781423358138, BAD) Brilliance Audio.

Old Friends. unabr. ed. Tracy Kidder. Narrated by Robert Sevra. 7 cass. (Running Time: 10 hrs. 30 mins.). 1993. 60.00 (978-1-55690-912-2(8), 93408E7) Recorded Bks.
A year in the lives of two old men, Lou Freed & Joe Torchio, nursing home residents in Northampton, Massachusetts. Kidder paints an intimate portrait of two strangers thrust together as roommates. They discover a shared need to make meaning of the past, while dealing with the feeling of separateness that comes with age.

Old Friends, Live at La Jolla. Perf. by Andre Previn et al. 1 cass. (Running Time: 1 hr. 30 mins.). 7.98 (TA 33309); audio compact disk 12.78 (TA 83309) NewSound.

Old Furniture see Poetry of Thomas Hardy

Old Glory. unabr. ed. Christopher Nicole. Read by Peter Joyce. 8 cass. (Running Time: 12 hrs.). 1999. 68.95 (978-1-86015-419-5(0)) T T Beeler.
Harry McGann is forced to flee his native Ireland & head to the new world. Fate leads him to join John Paul Jones in his fight for independence. Together, they experience danger on land & at sea.

Old Glory: An American Voyage. unabr. collector's ed. Jonathan Raban. Read by David Case. 12 cass. (Running Time: 18 hrs.). 1990. 96.00 (978-0-7366-1693-5(4), 2540) Books on Tape.
Jonathan Raban is an English author who fell in love with the Mississippi River when he was a boy (he was reading Huckleberry Finn). Over the years he dreamed about drifting its length. In 1979 he flew to Minneapolis, bought a 16' outboard launch, & set off for New Orleans. He takes us with him every step of the way.

***Old Gold Comedy Theatre, Volume 1.** RadioArchives.com. (Running Time: 300). (ENG.). 2004. audio compact disk 14.98 (978-1-61081-025-8(2)) Radio Arch.

***Old Gold Comedy Theatre, Volume 2.** RadioArchives.com. (Running Time: 600). (ENG.). 2004. audio compact disk 29.98 (978-1-61081-028-9(7)) Radio Arch.

***Old Goriot.** unabr. ed. Honoré de Balzac. Read by Frederick Davidson. (Running Time: 11 hrs. 5 mins.). (ENG.). 2011. 29.95 (978-1-4417-8462-9(4)); audio compact disk 100.00 (978-1-4417-8460-5(8)) Blckstn Audio.

***Old Harrys Game: The Award-Winning BBC Radio Comedy.** Created by Andy Hamilton. (Running Time: 21 hrs. 0 mins. 0 sec.). (ENG.). 2010. audio compact disk 139.95 (978-1-4084-1016-5(8)) Pub: AudioGO. Dist(s): Perseus Dist

Old House in Vauxhall Walk see Weird Stories

Old Indian Legends. unabr. ed. Zitkala-Sa. Read by Nancy Lee. (J). 2007. 34.99 (978-1-60252-774-4(1)) Find a World.

Old Ironsides see Classic American Poetry

Old Ironsides: Escape to the Wind. 1 cass. (Running Time: 60 mins.). Dramatization. 12.98 (978-1-929244-01-0(0)) Pub: Colonial Radio. Dist(s): Penton Overseas

Old Ironsides & the Barbary Pirates. 1 cass. (Running Time: 90 mins.). 12.95 (978-1-929244-02-7(9), COLR002) Colonial Radio.

Old Ironsides & the Barbary Pirates. Perf. by Colonial Radio Theatre Staff. 1 cass. (Running Time: 1 hr. 3 mins.). 2001. 12.95 (COLR002) Lodestone Catalog.

The U. S. S. Constitution leads us to the shores of Tripoli, battling savage & clever corsairs.

Old Ironsides' Escape to the Wind. 1 cass. (Running Time: 1 hr.). 12.95 (COLR003) Colonial Radio.

Old Ironsides' Escape to the Wind. Perf. by Colonial Radio Theatre Staff. 1 cass. (Running Time: 61 mins.). 2001. 12.95 (COLR003) Lodestone Catalog.

A famous encounter during the fledging U. S. Navy's struggle against Britain in the war of 1812.

***Old Jews Telling Jokes: 5,000 Years of Funny Bits & Not-So-Kosher Laughs.** unabr. ed. Sam Hoffman & Eric Spiegelman. 3 CDs. (Running Time: 3 hrs.). 2010. audio compact disk 24.95 (978-1-61573-513-6(5), 1615735135) Pub: HighBridge. Dist(s): Workman Pub

Old Kentucky Talk: A Collection of Words, Expressions & Folklore from the Old Days of the Commonwealth. unabr. ed. E. Clayton Gooden & David Gooden. 1 cass. (Running Time: 1 hr. 30 mins.). 1999. 9.95 Victoria Publishing.

Old Kentucky Talk No. 1: A Collection of Words, Expressions & Folklore from the Old Days of the Commonwealth. E. Clayton Gooden & David Gooden. 1 cass. (Running Time: 1 hr. 30 mins.). 1999. 9.95 (978-0-9674028-3-3(2)) Victoria Publishing.

A collection of regional speech.

Old Kentucky Talk No.1: A Collection of Words, Expressions & Folklore from the Old Days of the Commonwealth. unabr. ed. E. Clayton Gooden & David Gooden. 1 cass. (Running Time: 1 hr.). 1999. 9.95 (978-0-9674028-1-9(6)) Victoria Publishing.

Old Kentucky Talk Vol. 2: A Collection of Words, Expressions & Folklore from the Old Days of the Commonwealth. unabr. ed. Clayton E. Gooden & David Gooden. 1 cass. (Running Time: 1 hr.). 1999. 9.95 (978-0-9674028-4-0(0)) Victoria Publishing.

Old Landmark. 1 cass. (Running Time: 1 hr. 30 mins.). 10.98 (978-1-57908-343-4(9), 5302); audio compact disk 15.98 (978-1-57908-342-7(0)) Platinm Enter.

Old Love see Twentieth-Century Poetry in English, No. 12, Recordings of Poets Reading Their Own Poetry

Old Love's Domain. unabr. ed. Iris Bromige. Read by Robin Browne. 4 cass. (Running Time: 5 hrs. 15 min.). 2001. 44.95 (978-1-85695-575-1(3), 93015) Pub: ISIS Audio GBR. Dist(s): Ulverscroft US

A tragedy has left Laura unhappy & a job as custodian to Melloney Park, a gracious Jacobean mansion, seems ideal. Within days, however, the insistent presence of Ian threatens to break through her self-imposed barriers. Roger's proposal of marriage based on friendship is a welcome compromise. Too late, Laura realizes that marriage requires more than friendship.

Old MacDonald. (J). (ps-3). 2000. 2.99 (978-1-85781-202-2(6)) Cimino Pub Grp.

Old MacDonald & Other Sing Along Rhymes. Mother Goose. (ENG., (J). 2005. 15.95 (978-1-59249-526-9(5), 1D029) Soundprints.

Old Macdonald's. Composed by Peter Wastall. 2001. audio compact disk 26.95 (978-0-85162-306-1(9), 0851623069) H Leonard.

Old Macdonald's Farm. 2004. audio compact disk 7.95 (978-0-8256-2761-3(3)) Pub: Music Sales. Dist(s): H Leonard

Old MacDonald's Noisy Farm Audio CD. Adapted by Benchmark Education Company Staff. Based on a work by Jeffrey B. Fuerst. (Reader's Theater Nursery Rhymes & Songs Ser.). (J). (gr. k-1). 2008. audio compact disk 10.00 (978-1-60437-991-4(X)) Benchmark Educ.

Old Man & Mr. Smith. unabr. ed. Peter Ustinov. Read by John Sessions. 10 cass. (Running Time: 15 hrs.). 2000. 69.95 (CAB 790) Pub: Chivers Audio Bks GBR. Dist(s): AudioGO

The most surprising couple, God and Satan, meet in this hilarious tale. On a trip to Earth, they discover themselves to be out of touch with the developments in the modern world, especially when God's little trick of pulling new dollar bills out of thin air creates trouble with the FBI!.

Old Man & the Boy. unabr. collector's ed. Robert Ruark. Read by Dick Estell. 7 cass. (Running Time: 10 hrs. 30 mins.). 1990. 56.00 (978-0-7366-1864-9(3), 2695) Books on Tape.

The Old Man & the Boy is about the kind of boyhood every youngster dreams of, the kind of golden years every older man hopes for. It reads like fiction, but it's true. Robert Ruark grew up in North Carolina. His grandfather was his mentor, his companion in the field, his teacher at streamside & lake. Young Ruark thought he was learning to fish & hunt - really he was learning about life. Decades later, long after the old man was gone, Ruark realized how many of the lessons still sustained him. He paid his debt in this one-of-a-kind recollection.

Old Man & the Sea see Vieil Homme et la Mer

Old Man & the Sea. Ernest Hemingway. Read by Alexander Adams. 2 cass. (Running Time: 3 hrs.). 1999. 17.95 (978-0-7366-4430-3(X)) Books on Tape.

This is an outstanding collection of some of Ernest Hemingway's best short stories. "The Old Man & the Sea" is the triumphant yet tragic story of an aging Cuban fisherman & his supreme ordeal - a relentless battle with a giant marlin. It was given special recognition in the citation accompanying the author's Nobel Prize for Literature in 1954. Also included are "The Snows of Kilimanjaro," "The Short Happy Life of Francis Macomber," a volume of 14 stories published under the title of Winner Take Nothing, a full-length play The Fifth Column &, finally, four stories of the Spanish Civil War.

Old Man & the Sea. collector's ed. Ernest Hemingway. Read by Alexander Adams. 2 cass. (Running Time: 3 hrs.). 2000. audio compact disk 24.00 (978-0-7366-5177-6(2)) Books on Tape.

Old Man & the Sea. unabr. ed. Ernest Hemingway. Read by Charlton Heston. 2 cass. (Running Time: 2 hrs.). 17.95 (H131) Blckstn Audio.

An old Cuban fisherman triumphs over a giant marlin - only to have his prize catch literally eaten away by circling sharks.

Old Man & the Sea. unabr. ed. Ernest Hemingway. Read by Alexander Adams. 1 CD. (Running Time: 3 hrs.). 2001. audio compact disk; audio compact disk 19.95 Books on Tape.

An old fisherman triumphs over a giant marlin, only to have his prize catch eaten away by circling sharks.

Old Man & the Sea. unabr. ed. Ernest Hemingway. Read by Alexander Adams. 2 CDs. (Running Time: 3 hrs.). 2001. audio compact disk 19.95 Books on Tape.

This tale of an aged Cuban fisherman going head-to-head (or hand-to-fin) with a magnificent marlin encapsulates Hemingway's favorite motifs of physical & moral challenge.

Old Man & the Sea. unabr. ed. Ernest Hemingway. Read by Alexander Adams. 2 CDs. (Running Time: 3 hrs.). 2001. audio compact disk 19.95 (978-0-7366-5699-3(5)) Books on Tape.

An old fisherman triumphs over a giant marlin, only to have his prize catch eaten away by circling sharks.

Old Man & the Sea. unabr. ed. Ernest Hemingway. Read by Charlton Heston. 2 cass. (Running Time: 2 hrs. 35 mins.). 1992. 17.00 (978-1-55994-636-0(9), DCN 2084) HarperCollins Pubs.

An old fisherman triumphs over a giant marlin-only to have his prize catch eaten away by circling sharks.

Old Man & the Sea. unabr. ed. Ernest Hemingway. Narrated by Frank Muller. 3 CDs. (Running Time: 2 hrs. 45 mins.). 1999. audio compact disk 27.00 (978-0-7887-3412-0(1), C1018E7) Recorded Bks.

The tragic & timeless story of one man's extraordinary courage in the face of inevitable defeat.

Old Man & the Sea. unabr. ed. Ernest Hemingway. Read by Donald Sutherland. 3 cass. (Running Time: 2 hrs.). 2006. 25.75 (978-1-4281-1386-2(X), 98491); audio compact disk 28.75 (978-1-4281-1392-3(4), C3857) Recorded Bks.

Old Man & the Sea. unabr. ed. Ernest Hemingway. Narrated by Frank Muller. 2 cass. (Running Time: 2 hrs. 45 mins.). 1999. 18.00 (978-0-7887-0520-5(2), 94715E7) Recorded Bks.

Old Man & the Sea. unabr. ed. Ernest Hemingway. Read by Donald Sutherland. 2006. 12.95 (978-0-7435-6513-4(4), Audioworks); audio compact disk 20.00 (978-0-7435-6436-6(7)) Pub: S&S Audio. Dist(s): S and S Inc

Old Man & the Sea. unabr. collector's ed. Ernest Hemingway. Read by Alexander Adams. 2 cass. (Running Time: 3 hrs.). (J). 1999. 24.00 (978-0-7366-4524-9(1), 2585) Books on Tape.

This is an outstanding collection of some of Ernest Hemingway's best short stories. "The Old Man & the Sea" is the triumphant yet tragic story of an aging Cuban fisherman & his supreme ordeal - a relentless battle with a giant marlin. It was given special recognition in the citation accompanying the author's Nobel Prize for Literature in 1954. Also included are "The Snows of Kilimanjaro," "The Short Happy Life of Francis Macomber," a volume of 14 stories published under the title of Winner Take Nothing, a full-length play The Fifth Column &, finally, four stories of the Spanish Civil War.

Old Man Goriot. Honoré de Balzac. Read by Frederick Davidson. 8 cass. (Running Time: 11 hrs. 30 mins.). 2000. 56.95 (978-0-7861-1882-3(2), 2681) Blckstn Audio.

Betrayed by rapacious daughters, & Rastignac, an ambitious provincial youth alive to his opportunities, form the twin foci around which the grasping Parisian society of the 1820's revolves.

***Old Man in the Cave.** 2010. audio compact disk (978-1-59171-218-3(1)) Falcon Picture.

Old Man in the Corner. Emmuska Orczy. Read by Walter Covell. 6 cass. (Running Time: 9 hrs.). 1987. 36.00 (C-175) Jimcin Record.

The first "arm-chair detective" solves baffling cases.

Old Man Thunder: Father of the Bullet Train. unabr. ed. Bill Hosokawa. Read by Bill Wallace. 6 cass. (Running Time: 7 hrs. 25 min.). 1997. 35.00 Set; audio capsule avail. (978-0-9659580-1-1(9)) Sogo Way.

Biography of Shinji Sogo, the man who committed Japan to the massive, revolutionary Bullet Train Project.

Old Man's Love. Anthony Trollope. Read by Anais 9000. 2009. 27.95 (978-1-60112-228-5(4)) Babblebooks.

Old Man's Love. unabr. ed. Anthony Trollope. Read by Flo Gibson. 5 cass. (Running Time: 7 hrs.). (Classic Books on Cassettes Coll.). 1998. 20.95 (978-1-55685-500-9(1)) Audio Bk Con.

A middle-aged gentleman becomes engaged to his lovely ward & then struggles with his conscience when her young lover returns from the diamond fields of South Africa.

Old Man's Love. unabr. ed. Anthony Trollope. Read by Frederick Davidson. 5 cass. (Running Time: 7 hrs.). 2000. 39.95 (978-0-7861-1871-7(7), 2670) Blckstn Audio.

Old Man's Love. unabr. ed. Anthony Trollope. Read by Frederick Davidson. (Running Time: 7 hrs. NaN mins.). 2008. 29.95 (978-1-4332-6670-6(9)); audio compact disk 60.00 (978-1-4332-6667-6(9)) Blckstn Audio.

Old Man's Love. unabr. ed. Anthony Trollope. Read by Tony Britton. 8 cass. (Running Time: 12 hrs.). 2000. 59.95 (978-0-7540-0344-1(2), CAB 1767) Pub: Chivers Audio Bks GBR. Dist(s): AudioGO

William Whittlestaff is just 50 years old when he becomes guardian to Mary Lawrie, the orphaned and penniless daughter of an old friend. Whittlestaff gradually finds himself falling in love, but Mary has already given her heart to the young John Gordon. After three years absence, he returns on the very day of Whittlestaff's proposal.

Old Man's Winter Night see Robert Frost in Recital

Old Man's Winter Night see Twentieth-Century Poetry in English, No. 6, Recordings of Poets Reading Their Own Poetry

Old Mansion see Classic Ghost Stories, Vol. 2, A Collection

Old Me, New Me. unabr. ed. Mimi Lupin. 3 cass. (Running Time: 54 mins.). (J). 1997. 37.95 (978-0-945123-02-6(7)) Schoolhouse Ed Pub.

Old Me, New Me, Vol. 1 unabr. ed. Mimi Lupin. 3 cass. (Running Time: 54 mins.). (J). (gr. k-7). 1997. 37.95 (978-0-945123-00-2(0)) Schoolhouse Ed Pub.

Stories that help children learn impulse control, anger management & positive self talk.

Old Money. unabr. ed. Nicola Thorne. Read by Joanna David. 8 cass. (Running Time: 31380 sec.). (Mitchell Grant Adventures Ser.). 2000. 69.95 (978-0-7540-0501-8(1), CAB1924) AudioGO.

Nick & Giles are childhood friends, both seemingly born with silver spoons. Nick's father is a millionaire of Greek extraction: Giles's is a complacent, well bred lawyer. When worldly success goes the way that nature & England didn't intend, their families are shocked. But not as shocked as the boys are when, children of the rich & on the verge of manhood, they fall for the same girl.

Old Mother Hubbard & Her Dog. 2004. (978-0-89719-826-4(3)); cass. & fmstrp 30.00 (978-0-56008-734-2(X)) Weston Woods.

Old Mother Hubbard's Hungry Family Audio CD. Adapted by Benchmark Education Company Staff. Based on a work by Carrie Smith. (Reader's Theater Nursery Rhymes & Songs Ser.). (J). (gr. k-1). 2008. audio compact disk 10.00 (978-1-60437-983-9(9)) Benchmark Educ.

Old Mother West Wind & Three in Verse. unabr. ed. Thornton W. Burgess & Flo Gibson. Read by Flo Gibson. 2 cass. (Running Time: 2 hrs. 30 min.). (J). 1995. 14.95 (978-1-55685-356-2(4)) Audio Bk Con.

Old Mother West Wind & her Merry Little Breezes are joined by Reddy Fox, Sammy Jay & Many other woodland characters in Burgess' stories of pranks & rivalry. "Troll Talk," "The Tale of an Orchard" & "Clementina Quite Contrary" complete the collection.

Old Mrs. Jones see Classic Ghost Stories, Vol. 1, A Collection

Old Mrs. Jones. unabr. ed. Clara Riddell. Read by Walter Covell. 1 cass. (Running Time: 1 hr. 50 mins.). Dramatization. 1981. 7.95 (S-8) Jimcin Record.

A ghost returns to seek vengeance.

Old New York. unabr. ed. Edith Wharton. Read by Flo Gibson. 5 cass. (Running Time: 7 hrs. 30 min.). 1998. bk. 20.95 (978-1-55685-515-3(X)) Audio Bk Con.

Four novellas include: "False Dawn," "The Spark," "The Old Maid," & "New Year's Day".

Old Nickel & Dime Store. David Ray. Read by David Ray. 1 cass. (Running Time: 59 min). (Watershed Tapes of Contemporary Poetry Ser.). 1979. 11.95 (23648) J Norton Pubs.

Winner of the Whitman Awards reads selection from all five of his books.

Old No. 9 Travel Guide: Driving Trip in the Texas Hill Country by way of the Old No. 9 Highway. 2007. pap. bk. 20.00 (978-0-9676931-3-2(6)) Skyline Ranch.

Old Nurse's Story see Classic Ghost Stories, Vol. 2, A Collection

Old Nurse's Story see Great Ghost Stories, Volume II

Old Oaken Bucket see Favorite American Poems

Old, Old Tales from the Old, Old Book. unabr. ed. Nora A. Smith. Read by Flo Gibson. 9 cass. (Running Time: 13 hrs. 30 min.). (J). (gr. 4 up). 1994. 28.95 (978-1-55685-346-3(7)) Audio Bk Con.

Following the King James version closely, this story teller's Bible is written in simple language for young & old. Among these wonderful best-known stories are: "The Creation," "The Garden of Eden," "Cain & Abel," "The Story of the Flood," "Joseph the Dreamer," "Samson the Strong," "Baalam the Prophet," "Jotham's Fable," & "Joshua the General.".

Old Order Changeth. unabr. ed. Perf. by Eknath Easwaran. 1 cass. (Running Time: 1 hr.). 1984. 7.95 (978-1-58638-585-9(2)) Nilgiri Pr.

Old Patagonian Express: By Train Through the Americas. unabr. ed. Paul Theroux. Read by Michael Prichard. 12 cass. (Running Time: 18 hrs.). 1984. 96.00 (978-0-7366-0927-2(X), 1871) Books on Tape.

Old Patagonian Express: By Train Through the Americas. unabr. ed. Paul Theroux. Narrated by Norman Dietz. 12 cass. (Running Time: 17 hrs.). 1986. 97.00 (978-1-55690-388-5(X), 86640E7) Recorded Bks.

The author journeys from Bedford, Massachusetts to Patagonia, Argentina. He chronicles the life of border towns, custom officials, a vast variety of folks & even the mysteries of a small-town Central American soccer game.

Old Pipes & the Dryad. (J). (N-43) Jimcin Record.

Old Polish Traditions in the Kitchen & at the Table. Davidovic Mladen & Maria Lemnis. (Hippocrene International Cookbook Ser.). (ENG., 1997. audio compact disk 11.95 (978-0-7818-0488-2(4)) Hippocrene Bks.

Old Republic: Fatal Alliance. unabr. ed. Sean Williams. Read by Marc Thompson. (ENG.). 2010. audio compact disk 40.00 (978-0-307-73696-3(2), Random AudioBks) Pub: Random Audio Pubg. Dist(s): Random

Old Right & the New. Murray Newton Rothbard. 1 cass. (Running Time: 42 min.). 10.95 (157) J Norton Pubs.

In this address to the Organization of American Historians, Rothbard recounts the struggles of the isolationist Old Right of the 1930's with the interventionists before & shortly after World War II. He traces the transformation of conservatism by the interventionists as the Cold War arises.

Old Rookie. unabr. ed. Jim Morris & Joel Engel. 2002. 24.98 (978-1-58621-170-7(6)) Hachet Audio.

***Old Sam, Dakota Trotter.** Don Alonzo Taylor. Read by Randy Hawk. (J). 2010. audio compact disk 14.95 (978-1-883937-44-7(2)) Bethlehem ND.

Old Sanctuary: Hebrews 8:7-9;10. Ed Young. 1992. 4.95 (978-0-7417-1904-1(5), 904) Win Walk.

Old Scores. unabr. ed. Aaron Elkins. Narrated by Frank Muller. 6 cass. (Running Time: 7 hrs. 45 mins.). (Chris Norgren Mystery Ser.: Vol. 3). 1995. 51.00 (978-0-7887-0166-5(5), 94391E7) Recorded Bks.

The curator of Renaissance & Baroque art for the Seattle Art Museum goes to France in pursuit of answers about the mysteries surrounding a new acquisition.

Old Seal see Alte Siegel

Old Self & the New Self. Derek Prince. 1 cass. 5.95 (027) Derek Prince.

Two "persons" who are little understood, yet who occupy a position of unique importance in the New Testament revelation.

Old Silent. unabr. ed. Martha Grimes. Read by Donada Peters. 9 cass. (Running Time: 13 hrs. 30 min.). (Richard Jury Novel Ser.). 1990. 72.00 (978-0-7366-1833-5(3), 2668) Books on Tape.

During a winter's vacation meant to shake off melancholy, Richard Jury witnesses a murder at The Old Silent, a West Yorkshire Inn, & of course Jury, who is a Scotland Yard Superintendent, is on the case. Though witnessed, the killing remains a mystery. Did the victim's widow kill him? If so, why? No answer - Nell Healey remains as silent as the Yorkshire Moors.

Old Sins. unabr. ed. Penny Vincenzi. Read by Norma West. 24 cass. (Running Time: 36 hrs.). 2001. 109.95 (978-0-7531-0867-3(4), 000801) Pub: ISIS Audio GBR. Dist(s): Ulverscroft US

Old Soldiers Never Die. Douglas MacArthur. 1 cass. (Running Time: 35 min.). 10.95 (120) J Norton Pubs.

This is MacArthur's historic speech to a joint session of Congress in 1951 following his dismissal by President Truman from his command in Korea. The General captivated the American people with his interpretation of Asian & global affairs, his reminder that "there can be no substitute for victory," & his closing "old soldiers never die...".

Old Soldiers Never Die, Pt. 1. unabr. ed. Geoffrey Perret. Read by Jeff Riggenbach. 11 cass. (Running Time: 30 hrs. 30 mins.). 1998. 76.95 (978-0-7861-1370-5(7), 2288A,B) Blckstn Audio.

Groundbreaking biography reveals for the first time a complete & accurate account of MacArthur's tumultuous career.

Old Soldiers Never Die, Pt. 2. unabr. ed. Geoffrey Perret. Read by Jeff Riggenbach. 10 cass. (Running Time: 30 hrs. 30 mins.). 1998. 69.95 (978-0-7861-1412-2(6), 2288A,B) Blckstn Audio.

Always colorful, always controversial, Douglas MacArthur is one of the dominant characters in American military history. To his admirers he was the greatest American soldier; to his critics, he was a five star fake. With unprecedented access to official military records, reports, correspondence & diaries, this biography reveals for the first time a complete & accurate account of MacArthur's tumultuous career, including: The Pershing-MacArthur feud that cost MacArthur the Medal of Honor in World War I, President Truman's secret plan to fire MacArthur two years before the

Korean War & his failed presidential ambitions. Unmatched in its candor, authority & insight, this landmark biography charts the brilliant, if flawed, career of a unique American character.

Old Soldiers Never Die: Acts 20:17-35. Ed Young. 2000. 4.95 (978-0-7417-2248-5(8), 1248) Win Walk.

Old Soldiers Never Die: The Life of Douglas MacArthur. unabr. ed. Geoffrey Perret. Read by Jeff Riggenbach. (Running Time: 104400 sec.). 2008. audio compact disk & audio compact disk 160.00 (978-1-4332-3422-4(X)); audio compact disk & audio compact disk 44.95 (978-1-4332-3423-1(8)) Blckstn Audio.

***Old Southampton: Politics & Society in a Virginia County, 1834-1869.** Daniel W. Crofts. (ENG.). 45.00 (978-0-8139-2592-9(4)) U Pr of Va.

Old Spanish Trail. abr. ed. Ralph Compton. Read by Jim Gough. 4 cass. (Running Time: 6 hrs.). (Trail Drive Ser.: Vol. 2). 1999. Rental 24.95 (978-1-890990-22-0(1)) Otis Audio.
For the ranchers riding with Rand Hayes, things had gone from bad to worse. The Santa Fe man who'd contracted 5,000 head of cattle was dead, murdered by renegades. Now the Texans had a herd of longhorns & only one choice, cross two mountain ranges & the Mojave Desert to the market in Los Angeles on a trail blazed by ancient Spaniards.

Old Stag. unabr. collector's ed. Henry Williamson. Read by Donada Peters. 8 cass. (Running Time: 8 hrs.). 1986. 48.00 (978-0-7366-0906-7(7), 1849) Books on Tape.
In this collection of hunting stories, the quarry, through cunning & courage, gets clean away & moreover exacts a satisfying revenge on the hunters - animal or human. There is a fox who learns to climb trees, a wily baboon on the African veldt, a maverick wild dog, all portrayed with great fidelity.

Old Stonemason see **Poetry of Robinson Jeffers**

Old Story, with a Difference: Pickwick's Vision. Julian Wolfreys. (Victorian Critical Interventions Ser.). 2006. audio compact disk 9.95 (978-0-8142-9098-9(1)) Pub: Ohio St U Pr. Dist(s): Chicago Distribution Ctr

Old Tales for Tender Years. David Mitchell. Read by David Mitchell. (J). 1981. audio compact disk 14.95 (978-0-939065-96-7(7)) Gentle Wind.

Old Tales for Tender Years. Read by David Mitchell. 1 cass. (Running Time: 50 min.). (J). (gr. k-5). 1981. 9.95 (978-0-939065-03-5(7), GW 1003) Gentle Wind.
Includes: "The Story of the Three Bears", "The Old Woman Who lived in a Vinegar Bottle", "The Well of the World's End", stories by Frank Stockton, Carl Sandburg, Hans Christian Andersen & others.

Old Testament. 45 CDs. (Running Time: 67 hrs. 30 min.). 1999. audio compact disk 169.98 (978-7-902031-63-9(1)) Chrstn Dup Intl.

Old Testament. Contrib. by Christian Duplications International Staff. 48 cass. (Running Time: 72 hrs.). (SPA.). 1994. 89.98 Set. (978-7-902031-61-5(5)) Chrstn Dup Intl.
Bible.

Old Testament. Contrib. by E. W. Jeffries. 1 cass. (Running Time: 1 hr. 30 mins.). 1993. 79.98 (978-7-902031-19-6(4)) Chrstn Dup Intl.
New American Standard Bible.

Old Testament. Narrated by E. W. Jeffries. 1 cass. (Running Time: 1 hr. 30 mins.). 1995. 69.50 (978-7-902030-16-8(3)) Chrstn Dup Intl.

Old Testament. Narrated by E. W. Jeffries. 45 CDs. (Running Time: 67 hrs. 30 mins). 1999. audio compact disk 169.99 (978-7-902032-05-6(0)) Chrstn Dup Intl.

Old Testament. Narrated by Stephen Johnston. 1996. 59.99 (978-0-529-10640-7(X)) Nelson.

Old Testament. Contrib. by Paul Mims. 36 cass. (Running Time: 54 hrs.). 1994. 79.98 (978-7-902030-28-1(7)); 67.50 (978-7-902030-63-2(5)) Chrstn Dup Intl.
King James Bible.

Old Testament. Narrated by Samuel Montoya. 48 cass. (Running Time: 72 hrs. 30 mins.). (SPA.). 1994. 99.98 (978-7-902031-75-2(5)) Chrstn Dup Intl.

Old Testament. Read by Samuel Montoya. (SPA.). 159.95 Trinity Tapes.

Old Testament. deluxe ed. Contrib. by Paul Mims. 1 cass. (Running Time: 1 hr. 30 mins.). 1997. 99.98 (978-7-902030-00-7(7)) Chrstn Dup Intl.

Old Testament, Pt. 2. unabr. ed. Read by Michael Tudor Barnes et al. 16 cass. (Running Time: 23 hrs.). (Isis Ser.). 1994. 104.95 (978-1-85695-768-7(3), 940403) Eye Ear.
Joshua, Sides 1-4, Judges Sides 4-6, Ruth, Side 7, Samuel, Sides 7-14, Kings, Sides 15-22, Chronicles, Sides 23-30, Ezra, Side 30, Nehemiah, Sides 30-32, Esther, Side 32.

Old Testament, Pts. I-II. Instructed by Amy J. Levine. 12 pieces. (Running Time: 12 hrs.). (C). 2001. bk. 54.95 (978-1-56585-179-5(X), 653); bk. 69.95 (978-1-56585-365-2(2), 653) Teaching Co.

Old Testament, Set. Narrated by Charles Freed. 49 CDs. 2004. bk. 69.95 (978-1-59156-350-1(X)) Covenant Comms.

Old Testament, Vol. 2. Instructed by Amy J. Levine. 6 cass. (Running Time: 6 hrs.). 2001. 129.95 (978-1-56585-180-1(3)) Teaching Co.

Old Testament: An Introduction. 4 cass. (Running Time: 6 hrs.). 69.95 Set. (S31010) J Norton Pubs.

Old Testament: King James Version. 119.95 Trinity Tapes.

Old Testament: King James Version, Narrated by Charles Freed. 42 cass. (Running Time: 63 hrs.). 2004. 79.95 (978-1-57734-071-3(X), 0200549) Covenant Comms.

Old Testament: King James Version. abr. ed. Ed. by Marvin Miller. 12 cass. (Running Time: 18 hrs.). 35.95 (TC-902) Audio Bk.

Old Testament: King James Version. unabr. ed. 48 cass. (Running Time: 72 hrs.). 1984. 179.95 (OT-C_EZ) Trinity Tapes.

Old Testament: Selections from the Bible (The Authorized Version) Read by Philip Madoc et al. 6 cass. (Running Time: 7 hrs. 45 mins.). 1996. 32.98 (978-962-634-591-7(8), NA609114, Naxos AudioBooks) Naxos.

Old Testament: Selections from the Bible (the Authorized Version) abr. ed. Read by Philip Madoc et al. (Playaway Adult Nonfiction Ser.). (ENG.). 2009. 69.99 (978-1-60812-761-0(3)) Find a World.

Old Testament: Selections from the Bible (The Authorized Version) unabr. ed. Read by Philip Madoc et al. 6 CDs. (Running Time: 7 hrs. 45 mins.). 1996. audio compact disk 41.98 (978-962-634-091-2(6), NA609112, Naxos AudioBooks) Naxos.

Old Testament: The Histories. 16 cass. (Running Time: 24 hrs.). 2001. 104.95 (940403) Pub: ISIS Audio GBR. Dist(s): Ulverscroft US

Old Testament: The Pentateuch. 12 cass. (Running Time: 18 hrs.). 2001. 94.95 (940402) Pub: ISIS Audio GBR. Dist(s): Ulverscroft US

Old Testament: The Prophets. 14 cass. (Running Time: 21 hrs.). 2001. 99.95 (940405) Pub: ISIS Audio GBR. Dist(s): Ulverscroft US

Old Testament: The Songs & Widsoms. 8 cass. (Running Time: 12 hrs.). 2001. 69.95 (940404) Pub: ISIS Audio GBR. Dist(s): Ulverscroft US

Old Testament Pt. 1: The Pentateuch. unabr. ed. Read by Michael Tudor Barnes et al. 12 cass. (Running Time: 16 hrs. 45 min.). (Isis Ser.). 1994. 94.95 (940402) Eye Ear.
Genesis, Sides 1-6, Exodus, Sides 7-12, Leviticus, Sides 13-16, Numbers, Sides 16-20, Deuteronomy, Sides 20-24.

Old Testament Pt. 3: The Songs & Wisdoms. unabr. ed. Michael Tudor Barnes & Bible Adventures Staff. Read by Gretel Davis et al. 8 cass. (Running Time: 10 hrs. 15 min.). (Isis Ser.). (J). 1994. 69.95 (978-1-85695-788-5(8), 940404) Pub: ISIS Lrg Prnt GBR. Dist(s): Ulverscroft US

Old Testament Pt. 4: The Prophets. unabr. ed. Michael Tudor Barnes & Bible Baby Productions Staff. Read by Gretel Davis et al. 14 cass. (Running Time: 18 hrs. 45 min.). (Isis Ser.). (J). 1994. 99.95 (978-1-85695-793-9(4), 940405) Pub: ISIS Lrg Prnt GBR. Dist(s): Ulverscroft US

Old Testament & Ancient Egypt History. Marlin Detweiler & Laurie Detweiler. Perf. by Meshell Watt. 1998. 6.95 (978-1-930710-05-4(4)) Veritas Pr PA.

Old Testament & New Testament: Living Bible. Dramatization. 89.95 Trinity Tapes.

Old Testament & Other Bible Stories. D's. 1 cass. (Running Time: 1 hr.). 7.98 (1000896) Covenant Comms.
Humorous songs, drama & verse performed live.

Old Testament Bible Stories for Little People. Ruth J. Jay. 1 cass. (Running Time: 1 hr.). (J). 4.95 (978-0-8474-1901-2(0)); 8.75 incl. bk. (978-0-8474-1252-5(0)) Back to Bible.

Old Testament Challenge from Sickness & Disability. Carroll Stuhlmueller. 2 cass. (Running Time: 2 hrs. 6 min.). 1991. 18.95 (TAH237) Alba Hse Comns.
Carroll Stuhlmueller discusses the Torah (the five Books of Moses), the Neviim (Prophecy), & the Kethubim - the Writings (Wisdom & the Psalms) & their relationship to one another.

Old Testament Characters: Practical Life Lessons from the Lesser Known. 2004. 42.00 (978-1-57972-300-2(4)); 42.00 (978-1-57972-587-7(2)); audio compact disk 42.00 (978-1-57972-588-4(0)) Insight Living.

Old Testament (ESV) 47. (Running Time: 57 hrs). 2004. audio compact disk 119.95 (978-1-931047-46-3(4)) Fellow Perform Arts.

Old Testament Hebrew Vocabulary: Learn on the Go. unabr. ed. Jonathan T. Pennington. (Running Time: 2 hrs. 11 mins. 0 sec.). (ENG.). 2003. 13.99 (978-0-310-26166-7(X)) Zondervan.

Old Testament Response to Current Pastoral Questions. Carroll Stuhlmueller. 2 cass. (Running Time: 2 hrs. 17 min.). 1991. 18.95 (TAH236) Alba Hse Comns.
Assessment of current church happenings from a historical biblical perspective.

Old Testament Survey. W. Stanley Outlaw et al. Contrib. by Sound Impressions Staff. 12 cass. (Running Time: 18 hrs.). 1992. 49.95 (978-0-89265-657-8(3), 28037) Randall Hse.
Contains an overview.

Old Testament Survey I. Gary V. Whetstone. Instructed by June Austin. 13 cass. (Running Time: 19 hr. 30 mins.). (Old Testament Ser.: OT101). 1977. 260.00 (978-1-928774-98-3(9), BO 101 A00) Gary Whet Pub.
This course will familiarize the student with the people & events of the Old Testament from creation to the return of captivity.

Old Testament Survey II. Gary V. Whetstone. Instructed by June Austin. (Old Testament Ser.: Vol. OT 201). (C). 1997. 130.00 (978-1-58866-009-1(5)) Gary Whet Pub.

Old-Time Festival Tunes for Fiddle & Mandolin. Dan Levenson. (ENG.). 2009. spiral bd. 29.95 (978-0-7866-8023-8(7)) Mel Bay.

Old-Time Fiddle for the Complete Ignoramus! Wayne Erbsen. (For the Complete Ignoramus! Ser.). (ENG., 2005. pap. bk. 19.95 (978-1-883206-48-2(0)) Native Ground.

***Old-Time Fiddle Style Book/CD Set: A Collection of 35 Traditional Appalachian Tunes.** Ken Kolodner. 2010. pap. bk. 22.99 (978-0-7866-8157-0(8)) Mel Bay.

Old-Time Fiddling, Bk. 1. 2nd exp. ed. Compiled by Cindy Miles. 1 CD. (Running Time: 55 mins. 44 sec.). (J). 2005. audio compact disk 19.99 (978-0-9710446-7-8(8)) Miles Mus.
45 track split-track CD featuring fiddle in one channel and piano accompaniment in the other.

Old-Time Fiddling, Bk. 2. 2nd exp. ed. Compiled by Cindy Miles. 1 CD. (Running Time: 61 mins, 56 secs). (J). 2005. audio compact disk 19.99 (978-0-9710446-8-5(6)) Miles Mus.
35 track split-track CD featuring fiddle in one channel and piano accompaniment in the other.

Old-Time Fiddling, Bk. 3. 2nd exp. ed. Compiled by Cindy Miles. 1 CD. (Running Time: 60 mins, 52 secs). (J). 2005. audio compact disk 19.99 (978-0-9710446-3-0(5)) Miles Mus.

Old-Time Fiddling Across America. David Reiner & Peter Anick. 1989. 9.98 (978-1-56222-641-1(X), 94205C) Mel Bay.

Old-Time Fiddling Christmas Tunes. 2nd exp. ed. Compiled by Cindy Miles. 1 CD. (Running Time: 66 mins, 41 secs.). (J). 2005. audio compact disk 19.99 (978-0-9710446-9-2(4)) Miles Mus.
43 track split-track CD featuring fiddle in one channel and piano accompaniment in the other.

Old-Time Fiddling Gospel Favorites. Lucinda (Cindy) Miles. 1 CD. (Running Time: 78 mins, 34 sec). (YA). 2005. audio compact disk 19.99 (978-0-9710446-6-1(X)) Miles Mus.

Old-Time Gospel Banjo Solos. Jack Hatfield. 1998. bk. 32.95 (978-0-7866-3826-0(5), 96775CDP) Mel Bay.

Old-Time Gospel Favorites. Wayne Erbsen. 1997. audio compact disk 15.98 (978-0-7866-3232-9(1)) Mel Bay.

Old-Time Gospel Favorites: Fourteen Gospel Classics with Harmony & Old-Time Instruments. Perf. by Wayne Erbsen. 1 cass. (Running Time: 30 min.). 1994. 14.95 (978-1-883206-04-8(9), NG012) Native Ground.
Striking vocal arrangements of favorite Southern gospel songs using solos, duets, trios & quartets.

Old-Time Gospel Hour Coll. Robbie Hiner. 2000. 65.00 (978-0-633-00663-1(7)) LifeWay Christian.

Old-Time Gospel Instrumentals. Perf. by Wayne Erbsen. 1 cass. (Running Time: 30 min.). 1992. 9.95 (978-0-9629327-4-8(4), NG111) Native Ground.
Captures the spirit of old-time gospel & hymn music with haunting & lively renditions of many of the classic pieces of gospel music played on old-time instruments.

Old Time Gospel Piano. Tr. by Linda Cummings. Arranged by Stan Whitmire. 1996. bk. 15.98 (978-0-7866-2502-4(3), 96320) Mel Bay.

Old Time Gospel Songbook. Wayne Erbsen. 1997. pap. bk. 24.95 (978-0-7866-3233-6(X), 95033CDP) Mel Bay.

***Old-Time Hymns & Gospel Favorites for Mountain Dulcimer.** Anne Lough. 2010. lib. bdg. 19.99 (978-0-7866-7935-5(2)) Mel Bay.

Old Time Mysteries. Frwd. by David Kogan. 4 cass. (Running Time: 6 hrs.). 1999. 24.98 (5020) Radio Spirits.

Old Time Radio: The Best of Bogart. unabr. ed. Humphrey Bogart. 6 cass. (Running Time: 9 hrs.). 1998. 44.95 (Q101) Blckstn Audio.
Collection of radio shorts spanning a decade from the early '40s to '50s in which Bogart appears in character & out, with favorite leading ladies & fellow tough-guys.

Old Time Radio - American Icons: Old Time Radio Episodes. unabr. ed. Original Radio Episodes. Read by Original Radio Episodes. (YA). 2006. 39.99 (978-1-59895-340-4(0)) Find a World.

Old Time Radio - Best of the West & Gunsmoke: Old Time Radio. unabr. ed. Original Radio Episodes. Read by Original Radio Episodes. (YA). 2006. 39.99 (978-1-59895-427-2(X)) Find a World.

Old-Time Radio - Classic Favorites: Old Time Radio. unabr. ed. Original Radio Episodes. Read by Original Radio Episodes. (YA). 2006. 44.99 (978-1-59895-501-9(2)) Find a World.

Old Time Radio - Detectives & Crime Fighters: Old Time Radio. unabr. ed. Original Radio Episodes. Read by Original Radio Episodes. (YA). 2006. 44.99 (978-1-59895-502-6(0)) Find a World.

Old Time Radio - Superman on Radio. unabr. ed. Smithsonian. Read by Original Radio Episodes. (YA). 2006. 39.99 (978-1-59895-290-2(0)) Find a World.

Old-Time Radio Adventures Brick Pack. Perf. by Walter Pidgeon & Robert Taylor. 10 cass. (Running Time: 10 hrs.). Dramatization. 2001. 29.98 (7104) Radio Spirits.
21 episodes from "The Adventures of Frank Merriwell," "Bold Venture," "Box 13," "Dangerous Assignment," "The Green Hornet," "I Was a Communist for the FBI," "The Lone Ranger," "The Lux Radio Theatre," "Sergeant Preston of the Yukon" and "Tarzan".

Old Time Radio All-Time Favorites. collector's ed. Frwd. by George Burns. 4 vols. (Running Time: 5 hrs.). (Smithsonian Collection). 1995. bk. 24.98 (978-1-57019-000-1(3), OTR5002) Pub: Radio Spirits. Dist(s): AudioGO

Old-Time Radio Assortment Brick Pack. Perf. by George Burns et al. 10 cass. (Running Time: 10 hrs.). 2001. 29.98 (7102) Radio Spirits.

Old Time Radio Buys an Insurance Policy. unabr. ed. 2 cass. (Running Time: 2 hrs.). 10.95 (978-1-57816-161-4(4), OTR105) Audio File.
Broadcasts includes: "Amos 'N' Andy" (5/11/45); "Burns & Allen" (10/21/41); "A Day in the Life of Dennis Day" (10/22/47); & "Jack Benny" (5/24/53).

Old-Time Radio Classic Favorites. collector's ed. Featuring George Burns et al. 10 cass. (Running Time: 10 hrs.). 2001. bk. & pap. bk. 34.98 (4469) Radio Spirits.
Laugh with America's greatest comedians; track down public enemies with the Green Hornet and Dragnet's Sergeant Joe Friday; thrill to Inner Sanctum mysteries, tales of Escape, Suspense and The Whistler's strange stories; rocket into the future with X-Minus One and return to those thrilling days of yesteryear with The Lone Ranger. Includes booklet.

Old-Time Radio Classic Favorites. collector's ed. Featuring George Burns et al. 10 CDs. (Running Time: 10 hrs.). 2001. bk. & pap. bk. 39.98 (4470) Radio Spirits.

Old-Time Radio Classic Favorites. unabr. ed. Perf. by Jack Benny et al. 10 vols. (Running Time: 10 hrs.). (10-Hour Collections). 2002. bk. 34.98 (978-1-57019-366-8(5), OTR4469) Pub: Radio Spirits. Dist(s): AudioGO
This sampling of favorite shows features many of old-time radio's greatest stars including, Jack Benny, George Burns and Gracie Allen, Jack Webb, Lucille Ball and William Conrad.

Old-Time Radio Comedies. Perf. by Lou Costello et al. 10 cass. (Running Time: 10 hrs.). 2001. 29.98 (7100) Radio Spirits.
20 episodes including Abbott and Costello, Amos 'n' Andy, The Bickersons, Burns and Allen, The Charlie McCarthy Show, Fibber McGee and Molly, The Great Gildersleeve, The Jack Benny Program, The Life of Riley and My Favorite Husband.

Old Time Radio Comedy. unabr. ed. Minds Eye Staff. 4 cass. (Running Time: 6 hrs.). 1994. 18.95 (978-1-55935-186-7(1)) Soundelux.
Collection of some of the most memorable & hilarious examples of radio humor from the 'Golden Age of Radio' including Burns & Allen, Jack Benny, Groucho Marx, & Spike Jones & his City Slickers.

Old Time Radio Comedy Favorites. collector's ed. Perf. by George Burns et al. Frwd. by George Burns. Contrib. by Smithsonian Institution Staff. 4 vols. (Running Time: 5 hrs.). (Smithsonian Collection). 1995. bk. 24.98 (978-1-57019-010-0(0), OTR5000) Pub: Radio Spirits. Dist(s): AudioGO
Laugh along with the masters of classic radio comedy. The biggest names and greatest shows in comedy are featured on this collection of 12 original broadcasts. The accompanying 52-page historical booklet takes you behind the scenes of radio's funniest shows and features a foreword written by George Burns.

Old Time Radio Detectives & Crime Fighters. collector's ed. Frwd. by Stacy Keach, Sr. 4 vols. (Running Time: 5 hrs.). (Smithsonian Collection). 2002. bk. 24.98 (978-1-57019-020-9(8), OTR4030) Pub: Radio Spirits. Dist(s): AudioGO
Hear radio's most famous sleuths in action in 12 original episodes from radio's Golden Age. This collection also features a 52-page booklet filled with rare photographs and insightful commentary about the shows, performers and genre. The foreword was written by Stacy Keach, Sr., a renowned producer from the vintage radio detective genre.

Old-Time Radio Detectives Brick Pack. 10 cass. (Running Time: 10 hrs.). 2001. 29.98 (7101) Radio Spirits.

Old Time Radio Dramas. unabr. ed. Minds Eye Staff. 4 cass. (Running Time: 6 hrs.). 1994. 18.95 (978-1-55935-183-6(7)) Soundelux.

Old-Time Radio Dramas Brick Pack. 10 cass. (Running Time: 10 hrs.). 2001. 29.98 (7105) Radio Spirits.
19 episodes from "Academy Award Theatre," "Big Town," "The Black Museum," "Cavalcade of America," "The Columbia Workshop," "The Damon Runyon Theatre," "The First Nighter Program," "The Lux Radio Theatre," "Nightbeat," "The Third Man".

Old-Time Radio Famous Westerns. collector's ed. Featuring John Dehner et al. 10 cass. (Running Time: 10 hrs.). 2001. bk. & pap. bk. 29.98 (4472); bk. & pap. bk. 34.98 (4473) Radio Spirits.
Twenty broadcasts digitally restored and remastered and a booklet featuring rare photographs and historical commentary.

Old-Time Radio Famous Westerns. unabr. ed. Perf. by Brace Beemer et al. 10 vols. (Running Time: 10 hrs.). (10-Hour Collections). 2002. bk. 34.98 (978-1-57019-369-9(X), OTR4472) Pub: Radio Spirits. Dist(s): AudioGO
Return with us now to those thrilling days of yesteryear with radio's greatest cowboys, including Brace Beemer, John Dehner, Jimmy Stewart and William Conrad.

Old Time Radio Favorites. 1 cass. (Running Time: 1 hr.). (At the Sound of the Beep Ser.). 1989. 6.95 (978-1-55569-338-1(5), 6160) Great Am Audio.
Features Marshall Dillon, the Green Hornet or Jack Benny People on pre-recorded answering machine messages.

Old Time Radio for Dentists, Vol. 103. unabr. ed. Perf. by Jack Benny et al. 2 cass. (Running Time: 2 hrs.). Dramatization. 10.95 (978-1-57816-147-8(9)) Audio File.
Old time radio broadcasts with themes relating to dentists.

Old Time Radio for Doctors, Vol. 101. unabr. ed. Perf. by Basil Rathbone et al. 2 cass. (Running Time: 2 hrs.). Dramatization. 1997. 10.95 (978-1-57816-146-1(0)) Audio File.
Old time radio broadcasts with themes relating to doctors.

Old Time Radio for Golfers, Vol. 104. unabr. ed. Perf. by Jack Benny et al. 2 cass. (Running Time: 2 hrs.). Dramatization. 1997. 10.95 (978-1-57816-149-2(5)) Audio File.
Old time radio broadcasts with themes relating to golfers.

Old Time Radio for Teachers, Vol. 102. unabr. ed. Perf. by Eve Arden et al. 2 cass. (Running Time: 2 hrs.). Dramatization. 1997. 10.95 (978-1-57816-148-5(7)) Audio File.
Old time radio broadcasts with themes relating to teachers.

Old Time Radio Goes Car Shopping. unabr. ed. 2 cass. (Running Time: 2 hrs.). 10.95 Set. (978-1-57816-162-1(2), OTR106) Audio File.
Comedy gems include: "Amos 'N' Andy" (3/11/51); "Jack Benny" (4/24/49); "Fibber McGee & Molly" (10/9/45) & "Phil Harris & Alice Faye" (3/19/50).

Old Time Radio Goes Fishing. unabr. ed. 2 cass. (Running Time: 2 hrs.). 10.95 (978-1-57816-164-5(9), OTR108) Audio File.
Classic comedy includes: "Fibber McGee & Molly" (5/30/44 & 5/2/50); & "Great Gildersleeve" (5/5/48 & 5/17/50).

Old Time Radio Goes to the Old Ball Game. unabr. ed. 2 cass. (Running Time: 2 hrs.). 10.95 (OTR109) Audio File.
A World Series of Entertainment includes: "Jack Benny" (10/5/41); "Fibber McGee & Molly" (4/21/42); "Damon Runyon" (6/26/49); & "My Favorite Husband" (1940's).

Old-Time Radio Legends of Comedy. collector's ed. Featuring Freeman Gosden et al. 10 cass. (Running Time: 10 hrs.). 2001. bk. & pap. bk. 34.98 (4463) Radio Spirits.
Enjoy the greatest comedy in broadcast history with the shows and legendary stars who made old-time radio golden. All 20 broadcasts have been digitally restored and remastered for superb sound quality and a booklet is included featuring rare photographs and historical commentary.

Old-Time Radio Legends of Comedy. collector's ed. Featuring Freeman Gosden et al. 10 CDs. (Running Time: 10 hrs.). 2001. bk. & pap. bk. 39.98 (4464) Radio Spirits.

Old-Time Radio Master Detectives. collector's ed. Raymond Chandler & Dashiell Hammett. Perf. by Sydney Greenstreet et al. 10 cass. (Running Time: 10 hrs.). 2001. bk. & pap. bk. 34.98 (4466); bk. & pap. bk. 39.98 (4467) Radio Spirits.
Twenty-two broadcasts digitally restored and remastered and a booklet featuring rare photographs and historical commentary.

Old Time Radio Mysteries. collector's ed. Ray Bradbury. Perf. by Alice Frost et al. Frwd. by David Kogan. 6 CDs. (Running Time: 6 hrs.). Dramatization. (Smithsonian Collection). 1999. bk. & pap. bk. 39.98 (5021) Radio Spirits.
Collection of 12 episodes that have been digitally restored and remastered. The booklet is filled with rare photographs and insightful commentary about the shows, the performers, the medium and the genre.

Old Time Radio Mysteries. collector's ed. Ray Bradbury. Perf. by Alice Frost et al. Frwd. by David Kogan. 4 cass. (Running Time: 6 hrs.). Dramatization. (Smithsonian Collection). 2000. bk. & pap. bk. 24.98 (5020) Radio Spirits.

Old-Time Radio Mysteries Brick Pack. 10 cass. (Running Time: 10 hrs.). 2001. 29.98 (7107) Radio Spirits.
20 episodes from "The Clock," "Escape," "The Hall of Fantasy," "The Haunting Hour," "Inner Sanctum," "Lights Out," "The Mysterious Traveler," "The Shadow," "Suspense" and "The Whistler".

Old Time Radio Mystery Favorites. abr. ed. Smithsonian Institution Staff. 4 vols. (Running Time: 5 hrs.). (Smithsonian Institution Ser.). 2002. bk. 24.98 (978-1-57019-167-1(0), OTR5020) Pub: Radio Spirits. Dist(s): AudioGO
This incredible collection includes 12 of radio's most spellbinding tales of mystery and suspense. The accompanying 60-page booklet is filled with rare photographs and insightful commentary about the shows, performers and genre, and features a foreword written by David Kogan, the writer and creator of The Mysterious Traveler and Murder By Experts.

Old Time Radio Novels. unabr. ed. Minds Eye Staff. 4 cass. (Running Time: 6 hrs.). 1994. 18.95 (978-1-55935-184-3(5)) Soundelux.
Hollywood stars recreate their famous movie & stage roles, or act in dramatic adaptations of great novels, plays, & short stories. Includes "The Maltese Falcon," "The Grapes of Wrath," "The Scarlet Pimpernel," & "Rebecca".

Old Time Radio Pays Income Tax. unabr. ed. 2 cass. (Running Time: 2 hrs.). 10.95 (978-1-57816-163-8(0), OTR107) Audio File.
Hilarious broadcasts include: "Ozzie & Harriet" (3/13/49); "Fibber McGee & Molly" (1/11/44); "Great Gildersleeve" (1/16/44); & "Milton Berle Show" (3/9/48).

Old Time Radio Science Fiction, collector's ed. Perf. by Orson Welles & Arch Oboler. Frwd. by Ray Bradbury. 4 cass. (Running Time: 5 hrs.). (Smithsonian Collection). 1998. bk. & pap. bk. 24.98 (978-1-57019-021-6(6), 5006) Radio Spirits.
Ten digitally restored and remastered episodes of radio science fiction. Booklet describes each series and its place in the history of radio. Includes The Mercury Theatre on the Air's "The War of the Worlds," Suspense "Zero Hour," Lights Out "The Meteor Man," X Minus One "Mars is Heaven," The Mysterious Traveler "Operation Tomorrow," Escape "The Time Machine," "Rocket from Manhattan," Dimension X "The Martian Chronicles".

Old Time Radio Science Fiction, collector's ed. Perf. by Orson Welles & Arch Oboler. Frwd. by Ray Bradbury. 4 CDs. (Running Time: 5 hrs.). (Smithsonian Collection). 1996. bk. & pap. bk. 34.98 (978-1-57019-022-3(4), 5007) Radio Spirits.

Old-Time Radio Science Fiction Brick Pack. Perf. by Staats Cotsworth et al. 10 cass. (Running Time: 10 hrs.). 2001. 29.98 (7106) Radio Spirits.
20 episodes from "Beyond Tomorrow," "CBS Radio Workshop," "Dimension X," "Exploring the Unknown," "Tom Corbett, Space Cadet," "X-Minus One".

Old Time Radio Show Biz Teams. collector's ed. Smithsonian Institution Staff. Perf. by Jerry Lewis et al. Frwd. by Jerry Lewis. 4 cass. (Running Time: 5 hrs.). 1997. bk. & pap. bk. 24.98 (978-1-57019-055-1(0), 4032) Radio Spirits.
The Abbott and Costello Show, The Martin and Lewis Show, Bold Venture, The Adventures of Ozzie and Harriet, The Bickersons, Lum and Abner, Batman and Robin and more. Digitally restored and remastered. 12 episodes. Book is filled with rare photos and insightful commentary.

Old Time Radio Show Biz Teams. collector's ed. Smithsonian Institution Staff. Perf. by Jerry Lewis et al. Frwd. by Jerry Lewis. 4 CDs. (Running Time: 5 hrs.). (Smithsonian Collection). 1997. bk. & pap. bk. 34.98 (978-1-57019-060-5(7), 4033) Radio Spirits.

Old Time Radio Special Edition Favorites. 1998th ed. 1 cass. (Smithsonian Collection). 1998. 12.98 (5004); audio compact disk 12.98 CD. (5005) Radio Spirits.
"Bold Venture" - "Slate Shannon Accused of Murder" with Humphrey Bogart & Lauren Bacall; "The Lum & Abner Show" - Lum & Abner are given a baby to watch - the mother disappears, starring Chester Lauck & Norris Goff; "Escape!" - "The Drums of the Fore & Aft" starring Ben Wright & Hugh Thomas.

Old-Time Radio Thrilling Mysteries. 10 cass. (Running Time: 10 hrs.). 2001. 34.98 (4494); audio compact disk 39.98 (4495) Radio Spirits.
A creaking door, a sinister laugh, a scream in the night. These are the sounds from our collection of Thrilling Mysteries. Includes The Whister, Suspense's Man in Black, The Mysterious Traveler, The Keeper of the Sealed Book, the sinister host of Inner Sanctum, the Voice of Escape and many more. Their haunting tones invite listeners into thrilling worlds of mystery, suspense and horror.

Old Time Radio Westerns. collector's ed. Frwd. by Fred Foy. 4 vols. (Running Time: 5 hrs.). (Smithsonian Collection). 1996. bk. 24.98 (978-1-57019-038-4(0), OTR5008) Pub: Radio Spirits. Dist(s): AudioGO
Travel back to the Old West with this collection of 11 episodes of radio's greatest westerns. The 60-page historical booklet includes a foreword by legendary announcer Fred Foy, who immortalized the words, "Return with us now to those thrilling days of yesteryear... the Lone Ranger rides again!".

Old Time Radio Westerns. unabr. ed. Minds Eye Staff. 4 cass. (Running Time: 4 hrs.). 2000. 18.95 (978-1-55935-185-0(3), 492010) Soundelux.
Includes "The Lone Ranger," "The Six Shooter," "The Treasure of Sierra Madre" & "Shane".

Old-Time Radio Westerns Brick Pack. 10 cass. (Running Time: 10 hrs.). 2001. 29.98 (7103) Radio Spirits.
Includes episodes from "The Cisco Kid," "Fort Laramie," "Gunsmoke," "Have Gun, Will Travel," "Hopalong Cassidy," "The Lone Ranger," "The Six Shooter," "Tales of the Texas Rangers," "Wild Bill Hickock".

Old Time Radio's Greatest Detectives. Perf. by Barry Craig et al. 30 CDs. (Running Time: 30 hrs.). 2001. audio compact disk 69.98 (4559) Radio Spirits.
Blackie, Spade, Holmes, they're all here in this must-have collection of action packed detective thrillers.

Old Time Radio's Greatest Detectives, collector's ed. Perf. by Gerald Mohr et al. 20 cass. (Running Time: 30 hrs.). 1997. bk. & pap. bk. 59.98 (978-1-57019-063-6(1), 4395) Radio Spirits.
Sixty of radio's greatest dectiective eisodes from 20 of radio's most popular gumshoes. Digitally restored and remastered.

Old Time Radio's Greatest Mystery Shows. unabr. ed. Perf. by Orson Welles et al. 20 vols. (Running Time: 20 hrs.). (20 Hour Collections). 2002. bk. 69.98 (978-1-57019-494-8(7), OTR4213) Pub: Radio Spirits. Dist(s): AudioGO
Lock the doors, close the blinds and pull up the covers. This 40-episode collection of radio's masterpieces of horror and suspense will send chills down your spine. Return to radio's glorious "theater of the imagination" with Orson Welles and Bill Johnstone in The Shadow, Vincent Price and William Conrad in Escape and Peter Lorre and Agnes Moorehead in tales well calculated to keep you in Suspense.

Old-Time Radio's Greatest Shows. Perf. by George Burns. 20 cass. (Running Time: 30 hrs.). 1999. pap. bk. 69.98 (4418) Radio Spirits.
Features 60 programs from 60 different series, including; "Burns and Allen," "The Jack Benny Program," "The Jimmy Durante Show," "The Lone Ranger," "The Cisco Kid," "Hopalong Cassidy," "Dragnet," "Pat Novak for Hire," "Nightbeat," "Suspense," "Inner Sanctum Mysteries," "The Whistler," "The Milton Berle Show," "Gangbusters," "Tales of the Texas Rangers," "This Is Your F.B.I.," "Philip Marlowe," "Sam Spade, Detective," "Boston Blackie," "Escape," "The New Adventures of Nero Wolfe," "Ozzie & Harriet," "Baby Snooks and Daddy," "Philco Radio Time," "The Bickersons" and more. Includes 64 page booklet that details each show and it's history.

Old Time Radio's Greatest Shows, collector's ed. Perf. by George Burns et al. 20 cass. (Running Time: 30 hrs.). 1998. bk. & pap. bk. 59.98 (4018) Radio Spirits.

Old-Time Radio's Greatest Shows. unabr. ed. Perf. by George Burns et al. 20 vols. (Running Time: 20 hrs.). (20 Hour Collections). 2002. bk. 69.98 (978-1-57019-488-7(2), OTR4205) Pub: Radio Spirits. Dist(s): AudioGO
This 20-hour collection is a great introduction to the world of old-time radio. All the biggest names and most memorable programs are here. Whether you're in the mood for a good laugh, a chilling tale, a western adventure or a journey into the unknown, there's something for everyone.

Old-Time Radio's Greatest Shows. unabr. ed. Perf. by George Burns et al. 20 vols. (Running Time: 20 hrs.). (20 Hour Collections). 2002. bk. 59.98 (978-1-57019-487-0(4), OTR4204) Pub: Radio Spirits. Dist(s): AudioGO

Old Time Radio's Greatest Western Shows. unabr. ed. Perf. by Brace Beemer et al. 20 vols. (Running Time: 20 hrs.). (20 Hour Collections). 2002. bk. 59.98 (978-1-57019-495-5(5), OTR4216) Pub: Radio Spirits. Dist(s): AudioGO
The legendary gunslingers of the Old West ride again in this collection of 40 classic western stories. Hit the trail with 10 of the toughest heroes on horseback as they hand down justice to some of radio's meanest hombres.

Old Time Radio's Greatest Westerns. collector's ed. 20 cass. (Running Time: 30 hrs.). 2001. bk. & pap. bk. 59.98 (4410) Radio Spirits.
The legend and romance of the American West lives again. Cheer on the good guys as they pack their sixguns, sit tall in the saddle and ride off into the sunset when their work is finally complete and justice is served. Includes 3 episodes each from 20 series including, Cavalcade of America, Cisco Kid, Dr. Sixgun, Escape, Fort Laramie, Frontier Gentleman, Gunsmoke, Have Gun, Will Travel, Hawk Larabee, Hopalong Cassidy, Lone Ranger, Luke Slaughter, Red Ryder, Roy Rogers show, Screen Director's Playhouse, The Six Shooter, Straight Arrow, Suspense, Tales of the Texas Rangers and Wild Bill Hickok. Includes a 64 page booklet that details each show and it's history.

Old-Time Radio's Stars on Suspense. collector's ed. Perf. by Charlie Ruggles et al. 20 cass. (Running Time: 30 hrs.). 2000. bk. & pap. bk. 59.98 (4195) Radio Spirits.
60 episodes.

Old-Time Radio's 60 All-Time Favorites. collector's ed. 20 cass. (Running Time: 30 hrs.). 2001. bk. & pap. bk. 59.98 (4461); bk. & pap. bk. 69.98 (4462) Radio Spirits.
Laugh again with Jack Benny, Bob Hope, Fibber McGee and Molly, Red Skelton, Ozzie and Harriet, Fred Allen, Abbott and Costello, Lucille Ball and Burns and Allen. Thrill to the daring exploits of The Shadow, Sam Spade, Philip Marlowe, The Green Hornet, Dragnet's Joe Friday and Sergeant Preston of the Yukon. Also The Lone Ranger, Gunsmoke, The Cisco Kid and Have Gun, Will Travel. Sixty episodes. Includes booklet.

Old Time Religion: Matthew 5:21-30. Ed Young. (J). 1979. 4.95 (978-0-7417-1049-9(8), A0050) Win Walk.

Old-Timers Corner. Contrib. by Alcoholics Anonymous Members. 1 cass. (Running Time: 1 hr. 30 mins.). 1998. 6.50 (978-0-933685-29-1(7)) A A Grapevine.
Personal experience of AA members on the subject of long-term recovery from alcoholism/sobriety in the Fellowship of Alcoholics Anonymous.

***Old Times on the Mississippi.** Mark Twain. Read by Anais 9000. 2009. 27.95 (978-1-60112-234-6(9)) Babblebooks.

Old Turtle. Perf. by Douglas Wood. 1 cass. (Running Time: 38 min.). (J). 1995. 11.95 (978-1-57025-083-5(9)); audio compact disk 15.95 CD. (978-1-57025-190-0(8)) Pfeifer-Hamilton.
An audiotape that celebrates the spirit of Old Turtle! Douglas Wood beautifully narrates this special fable on side A, & performs his original songs on side B.

Old Way. unabr. ed. Elizabeth Marshall Thomas. Read by Elizabeth Marshall Thomas. (YA). 2007. 59.99 (978-1-60252-917-5(5)) Find a World.

Old Way: A Story of the First People. unabr. ed. Elizabeth Marshall Thomas. Read by Elizabeth Marshall Thomas. 9 CDs. (Running Time: 11 hrs. 30 mins. 0 sec.). (ENG.). 2006. audio compact disk 34.99 (978-1-4001-0307-2(X)); audio compact disk 24.99 (978-1-4001-5307-7(7)); audio compact disk 69.99 (978-1-4001-3307-9(6)) Pub: Tantor Media. Dist(s): IngramPubServ

Old West Collection. unabr. ed. Jimmy Gray. Read by Donnie Blanz. (YA). 2007. 34.99 (978-1-60252-918-2(3)) Find a World.

Old West: Stories & Legends. unabr. ed. Joe Loesch & Readio Theatre Staff. Read by Joe Loesch. (Running Time: 5 hrs. 0 mins. 0 sec.). (ENG.). 2009. audio compact disk 29.99 (978-1-59859-476-8(1), SpringWater) Oasis Audio.

Old West: Villains & Avengers. unabr. ed. Joe Loesch & Readio Theatre Staff. Read by Joe Loesch. (Running Time: 5 hrs. 0 mins. 0 sec.). (ENG.). 2009. audio compact disk 29.99 (978-1-59859-477-5(X), SpringWater) Oasis Audio.

Old Wild Wood. Short Stories. (2061) Am Audio Prose.

Old Willis Place: A Ghost Story. unabr. ed. Mary Downing Hahn. Read by Ellen Grafton. 1 MP3-CD. (Running Time: 5 hrs.). 2009. 39.97 (978-1-4233-8113-6(0), 9781423381136, Brinc Audio MP3 Lib); 39.97 (978-1-4233-8115-0(7), 9781423381150, BADLE); 24.99 (978-1-4233-8114-3(9), 9781423381143, BAD); 24.99 (978-1-4233-8112-9(2), 9781423381129, Brilliance MP3); audio compact disk 24.99 (978-1-4233-8110-5(6), 9781423381105, Bril Audio CD Unabri) Brilliance Audio.

Old Willis Place: A Ghost Story. unabr. ed. Mary Downing Hahn. Read by Ellen Grafton. 4 CDs. (Running Time: 5 hrs.). (YA). (gr. 5-8). 2009. audio compact disk 54.97 (978-1-4233-8111-2(4), 9781423381112, BriAudCD Unabrid) Brilliance Audio.

***Old Wives' Tale.** Arnold Bennett. Read by Alfred von Lecteur. 2010. 33.95 (978-1-60112-953-6(X)) Babblebooks.

Old Wives' Tale, Pt. 2. unabr. ed. Arnold Bennett. 8 cass. (Running Time: 12 hrs.). (Classic Books on Cassettes Ser.). 1988. 53.95 Audio Bk Con.
From the industrial midlands of Victorian England the lives of two sisters are traced from childhood to the grave. Contains memorable scenes of Paris under seige in 1870.

Old Wives' Tale, Vol. 2. unabr. ed. Arnold Bennett. Narrated by Flo Gibson. (Running Time: 11 hrs. 7 mins.). 1988. 26.95 (978-1-55685-828-4(0)) Audio Bk Con.

Old Wives' Tale - Part 1, Vol. 1. unabr. ed. Arnold Bennett. Narrated by Flo Gibson. 8 cass. (Running Time: 12 hrs.). (Classic Books on Cassettes Ser.). 1988. 26.95 (978-1-55685-111-7(1)) Audio Bk Con.

Old Wives' Tale (Parts 1 And 2) unabr. ed. Arnold Bennett. Narrated by Flo Gibson. (Running Time: 22 hrs. 6 mins.). 1988. 46.95 (978-1-55685-829-1(9)) Audio Bk Con.

Old Wizard. Gilbert Highet. Read by Gilbert Highet. 1 cass. (Running Time: 30 min.). 11.95 (23301-A) J Norton Pubs.

Old Woman see Gathering of Great Poetry for Children

Old Woman & Her Pig see Pony Engine & Other Stories for Children

Old Woman & Her Pig see Three Little Pigs & Other Fairy Tales

Old Woman & Her Pig. 2004. 8.95 (978-1-56008-988-9(1)); cass. & flmstrp 30.00 (978-1-56008-735-9(8)) Weston Woods.

Old Woman & the Eagle. Idries Shah. Illus. by Natasha Delmar. (J). 2005. pap. bk. 18.95 (978-1-883536-78-7(2), Hoopoe Books) ISHK.

Old Woman & the Eagle. Idries Shah. Read by Deb Bluford. Illus. by Natasha Delmar. (Sounds of Afghanistan Ser.). (J). (ps-3). 2005. bk. 28.95 (978-1-883536-77-0(4), Hoopoe Books) ISHK.

Old Woman in the Wood: A Tale of a Woman's Journey. Read by Caroline Stevens. 1 cass. (Running Time: 1 hr. 30 mins.). (Fairytales Ser.: No. 3). 1987. 10.95 (978-0-7822-0302-8(7), 229) C G Jung IL.

Old Yeller. unabr. ed. Fred Gipson. Read by Wolfram Kandinsky. 5 cass. (Running Time: 5 hrs.). (J). (gr. 4-7). 1989. 30.00 (978-0-7366-1648-5(9), 2500) Books on Tape.
Old Yeller is the eloquently simple story of a boy & his dog in the Texas hill country of the 1860s. It is an unforgettable & deeply moving experience. The big yellow dog showed up out of nowhere one night & stole a side of pork. When Travis went after him the next morning the dog started yelling like a baby & become Old Yeller. Travis soon found he couldn't get along without him. Old Yeller accompanies Travis on his road to adulthood & responsibility. Along the way he learns just how much he has come to love that big ugly dog & he learns something about the pain of life as well.

Old Yeller. unabr. ed. Fred Gipson. Read by Peter Francis James. 2010. audio compact disk 22.99 (978-0-06-196076-5(4), Caedmon) HarperCollins Pubs.

***Old Yeller.** unabr. ed. Fred Gipson. Read by Peter Francis James. (ENG.). 2010. (978-0-06-196762-7(9), Caedmon); (978-0-06-196761-0(0), Caedmon) HarperCollins Pubs.

Old Yeller, unabr. ed. Fred Gipson. Narrated by Norman Dietz. 3 pieces. (Running Time: 4 hrs.). (gr. 5 up). 1991. 27.00 (978-1-55690-389-2(8), 91104E7) Recorded Bks.
Travis had enough troubles of his own without an old, one-eared dog to worry about. He didn't know just how much he really needed him.

Old Yeller. unabr. ed. Fred Gipson. Narrated by Norman Dietz. 4 CDs. (Running Time: 4 hrs.). (gr. 5 up). 2000. audio compact disk 39.00 (978-0-7887-4652-9(9), C1201E7) Recorded Bks.

Olde Mother Goose. Perf. by Hubbards. 1 cass. (Running Time: 40 min.). (Little Star Collection). (ps-k). 1993. 12.95 (978-0-87483-213-6(6)) Pub: August Hse. Dist(s): Natl Bk Netwk
By weaving together an intriguing combination of traditional acoustic instruments & vocal arrangements, The Hubbards have produced a remarkably fresh version of the classic nursery rhymes that permeate our culture. Among the instruments played on this recording are the recorder, hurdy-gurdy, bagpipe, washboard, flute, harp, bassoon, pennywhistle, & melodeon. Includes booklet in blister pack.

Older the Fiddle, the Better the Tune: The Joys of Reaching a Certain Age. abr. rev. ed. Willard Scott. Read by Willard Scott. 2 cass. (Running Time: 3 hrs.). 2003. 18.98 (978-1-4013-9738-8(7)) Pub: Hyperion. Dist(s): HarperCollins Pubs

Oldest Americans: A Century of Living. 1 cass. (Running Time: 30 min.). 9.95 (I0570B090, HarperThor) HarpC GBR.

Oldest Living Confederate Widow Tells All. Allan Gurganus. Read by Allan Gurganus. (Running Time: 30 min.). 8.95 (AMF-221) Am Audio Prose.
Talks on the Civil War, North Carolina, and narrative voice.

Oldest Living Confederate Widow Tells All, Pt. 1. unabr. collector's ed. Allan Gurganus. Read by Donada Peters. 13 cass. (Running Time: 19 hrs. 30 mins.). 1992. 104.00 (978-0-7366-2113-7(X), 2917 A) Books on Tape.
History comes to life in the words of a 99-year-old Confederate war widow. Fascinating, poignant & beautifully written.

Oldest Living Confederate Widow Tells All, Pt. 2. Allan Gurganus. Read by Donada Peters. 13 cass. (Running Time: 19 hrs. 30 mins.). 1992. 104.00 (978-0-7366-2114-4(8), 2917-B) Books on Tape.

Oldest Rookie. unabr. ed. Jim Morris & Joel Engel. (ENG.). 2005. 14.98 (978-1-59483-425-7(3)) Pub: Hachet Audio. Dist(s): HachBkGrp

Ole Doc Methuselah. abr. ed. L. Ron Hubbard. Read by Roddy McDowall. 4 cass. (Running Time: 6 hrs.). (J). 1992. 24.95 (978-0-88404-654-7(0)) Bridge Pubns Inc.
The exciting interplanetary exploits of Solider of Light No. 77 & his alien pal Hippocrates in the late third Millenia.

Ole Doc Methuselah. abr. ed. L. Ron Hubbard. Read by Roddy McDowell. 4 cass. (Running Time: 6 hrs.). 1992. 24.95 (978-1-59212-033-8(4)) Gala Pr LLC.
A celebrated and enduring classic of space travel on a cosmic scale, Ole Doc Methuselah mixes equal parts of vivid action, spectacle and mystery - and a broad vein of humor - to chronicle the voyages and exploits of Ole Doc Methuselah and his unique alien companion, Hippocrates. Ole Doc journeys through the universe as a member of the elite Soldiers of Light - a heroic physician who fights the disease, corruption and social/political upheavals that have spread through mankind's lost planetary colonies.

Ole Lumpy Loved & Shared. Sheri Hauser. Music by John Jones. (J). 2008. 14.95 (978-1-60789-006-5(2)) Glory Bound.

Ole Paint Rocks. Janice Majorie McCament. (J). 2007. audio compact disk 9.99 (978-1-60247-233-4(5)) Tate Pubng.

Oleander, Jacaranda: A Childhood Perceived. unabr. ed. Penelope Lively. Read by Sheila Mitchell. 5 cass. (Running Time: 5 hrs. 15 min.). 1997. 49.95 (978-1-85695-833-2(7), 941105) Pub: ISIS Audio GBR. Dist(s): Ulverscroft US
Lively's interpretation of her childhood & of the subsequent trauma when she was sent to a "homeland" that she never regarded as home. Her snapshots of recollection of childhood in Egypt, during the 1930s build up a picture of her happy early years, under the ever-watchful eye of her nanny, Lucy. Even WWII did not disrupt her idyll, which was finally shattered by adolescence & her parent's divorce.

Olga Broumas. Olga Broumas. (Listener's Guide Ser.). (ENG.). 2000. audio compact disk 12.00 (978-1-55659-997-2(8)) Pub: Copper Canyon. Dist(s): Consort Bk Sales

Olga Meets Her Match. Michael Bond. Read by Lynda Bellingham. 2 CDs. (J). 2004. audio compact disk 21.95 (978-0-7540-6625-5(8), Chivers Child Audio) AudioGO.

Olga Sur, Kust Sireni (Olga Sur, The Lilac Bush) Alexander Kuprin. 1 cass. (Running Time: 1 hrs.). (RUS.). 1997. pap. bk. 19.50 (978-1-58085-581-5(4)) Interlingua VA.

Olimpiadas del Super Libro. Don Bowman. Tr. by Veronica Smith from ENG. Prod. by One Way Street Staff. Orig. Title: Super Book Olympics. (SPA.). (J). 2002. audio compact disk Rental 35.00 (978-1-58302-216-0(3)) One Way St.
Music to accompany Super Book Olympics Teaching Unit. (Spanish version).

Olive Delights Cookbook: A Collection of Olive Recipes. Karen Jean Matsko Hood. 2005. audio compact disk 13.95 (978-1-59649-985-0(0)) Whspmg Pine.

Olive Farm: A Love Story. Carol Drinkwater. Narrated by Carol Drinkwater. 10 CDs. (Running Time: 11 hrs.). audio compact disk 101.00 (978-1-4025-1544-6(8)) Recorded Bks.

Olive Farm: A Love Story. unabr. ed. Carol Drinkwater. Narrated by Carol Drinkwater. 8 cass. (Running Time: 11 hrs.). 2002. 72.00 (978-1-84197-322-7(X)) Recorded Bks.

Olive Harvest: A Memoir of Love, Old Trees, & Olive Oil. unabr. ed. Carol Drinkwater. Read by Carol Drinkwater. 8 cass. (Running Time: 11 hrs.). 2005. 79.75 (978-1-84505-376-5(1), H1859, Clipper Audio) Recorded Bks.
Returning to their home after an extended absence, Carol and her husband Michel are looking forward to summer together on the farm. Then a shocking blow leaves Carol alone and the future looks uncertain. The Olive Harvest takes us beyond the perimeters of her olive groves to where hunters, poets, bee-keepers, boars and gypsies abide. In search of the language of troubadours, the dark and sometimes barbarous heart of Provence is revealed. Nature and the generosity of the South of France's harvests offer a path to joy and an abundant resolution.

Olive Kitteridge. abr. ed. Elizabeth Strout. Read by Sandra Burr. (Running Time: 6 hrs.). 2008. audio compact disk 14.99 (978-1-4233-5010-1(3), 9781423350101, BCD Value Price) Brilliance Audio.

Olive Kitteridge. unabr. ed. Elizabeth Strout. Read by Sandra Burr. 1 MP3-CD. (Running Time: 10 hrs.). 2008. 24.95 (978-1-4233-5005-7(7), 9781423350057, Brilliance MP3); 24.95 (978-1-4233-5007-1(3), 9781423350071, BAD); 39.25 (978-1-4233-5008-8(1), 9781423350088, BADLE); audio compact disk 36.95 (978-1-4233-5003-3(0), 9781423350033, Bril Audio CD Unabri); audio compact disk 39.25 (978-1-4233-5006-4(5), 9781423350064, Brlnc Audio MP3 Lib); audio compact disk 97.25 (978-1-4233-5004-0(9), 9781423350040, BriAudCD Unabrid) Brilliance Audio.

Olive Route: A Personal Journey to the Heart of the Mediterranean. unabr. ed. Carol Drinkwater. Read by Carol Drinkwater. 14 CDs. (Running Time: 14 hrs.). 2007. audio compact disk 123.75 (978-1-4281-6682-0(3)) Recorded Bks.

Olive Season: Amour, a New Life & Olives Too. unabr. ed. Carol Drinkwater. 8 cass. (Running Time: 11 hrs. 15 min.). 2004. 105.95 (978-1-84197-803-1(5)) Recorded Bks.

Oliver. Syd Hoff. Illus. by Syd Hoff. Narrated by Russ T. Nailz. (Running Time: 11 mins.). (J). (gr. k-4). 2002. audio compact disk 12.95 (978-1-59112-659-1(2)) Live Oak Media.

Oliver. Syd Hoff. Illus. by Syd Hoff. 14 vols. (Running Time: 11 mins.). 2002. pap. bk. 31.95 (978-1-59112-661-4(4)); 9.95 (978-0-87499-901-3(4)); 9.95 (978-1-59112-289-0(9)) Live Oak Media.

Oliver. Syd Hoff. Illus. by Syd Hoff. 11 vols. (Running Time: 11 mins.). (J). (ps-2). 2002. pap. bk. 16.95 (978-0-87499-902-0(2)) Live Oak Media.
Oliver has always wanted to be a dancing elephant, but what will he do when he finds out the circus has enough elephants.

Oliver. unabr. ed. Syd Hoff. Illus. by Syd Hoff. Narrated by Russ T. Nailz. 1 cass. (Running Time: 8 min.). (J). (gr. k-3). 2002. 9.95 (978-0-87499-013-3(0)) Live Oak Media.
Story of the self-centered rabbit who decides to become the world's best cornet player, but who refuses to take lessons.

Oliver & Company. 1 cass. (Running Time: 35 mins.). (Read-Along Ser.). (J). bk. 7.99 (978-1-55723-024-9(2)); 11.99 (978-1-55723-965-5(7)); 11.99 (978-1-55723-964-8(9)); audio compact disk 19.99 (978-1-55723-966-2(5)); audio compact disk 19.99 (978-1-55723-967-9(3)) W Disney Records.

Oliver Goldsmith: She Stoops to Conquer or "The Mistakes of a Night" Peter Shaffer. Perf. by Michael Williams et al. Music by Mike Steer. 2 cass. 15.95 (SCN 072) J Norton Pubs.
Charles Marlow finds himself completely tongue-tied in the presence of eligible ladies, the only women with whom he is at ease are his social inferiors, so when he takes Kate Hardcastle for a serving-maid, he becomes a fluent & impudent lover.

***Oliver McCoy - the Boy Who Loved Onions.** Richard B. Joelson. (J). 2010. bk. 19.95 (978-0-9830039-0-8(4)) SLM Book.

Oliver Stone: America's Moral Amnesia. Narrated by Oliver Stone. 1 cass. (Running Time: 60 min.). 10.95 (K0320B090, HarperThor) HarpC GBR.

Oliver Twist see Oliverio Twist

Oliver Twist. Charles Dickens. Contrib. by Tim McInnerny et al. 3 CDs. (Running Time: 2 hrs. 35 mins.). 2006. audio compact disk 39.95 (978-0-7927-3996-8(5), BBCD 147) AudioGO.

Oliver Twist. Charles Dickens. Pam Ferris et al. (ENG.). 2009. audio compact disk 24.95 (978-1-60283-568-9(3)) Pub: AudioGO. Dist(s): Perseus Dist

Oliver Twist. Charles Dickens. (Running Time: 15 hrs. 30 mins. 0 sec.). (Cover to Cover Ser.). (ENG.). 2010. audio compact disk 29.95 (978-1-60283-876-5(3)) Pub: AudioGO. Dist(s): Perseus Dist

Oliver Twist. Charles Dickens. Read by John Lee. (Restoration Classics Audio Collection). 2003. audio compact disk 80.00 (978-0-7366-8789-8(0)); audio compact disk 112.00 (978-0-7366-8790-4(4)) Books on Tape.

Oliver Twist. Charles Dickens. Read by Simon Vance. (Playaway Young Adult Ser.). (YA). 2009. 69.99 (978-1-60812-556-2(4)) Find a World.

Oliver Twist. Charles Dickens. Read by Fabio Camero. (Running Time: 3 hrs.). 2001. 16.95 (978-1-60083-153-9(2), Audiofy Corp) Iofy Corp.

Oliver Twist. Charles Dickens. Narrated by Dick Cavett. (Running Time: 2 hrs. 30 mins.). 2006. 14.95 (978-1-59912-837-5(3)) Iofy Corp.

Oliver Twist. Charles Dickens. Read by Anton Lesser. (Running Time: 5 hrs.). 2006. 28.95 (978-1-60083-861-3(8)) Iofy Corp.

Oliver Twist. Charles Dickens. 2 cass. (Read-along Ser.). bk. 34.95 Set, incl. learner's guide & exercises. (S23938) J Norton Pubs.

Oliver Twist. Charles Dickens. Read by Anton Lesser. 4 cass. (Running Time: 5 hrs.). 2002. 22.98 (978-962-634-759-1(7), NA425914, Naxos AudioBooks) Naxos.
A thrilling study of childhood innocence thrust into the darkly comic world of Fagin, his apprentice the Artful Dodger, and their gang of child thieves. Who will help the orphaned Oliver escape from their clutches and discover his true history.

Oliver Twist. Charles Dickens. Read by Anton Lesser. 4 CDs. (Running Time: 5 hrs.). 2002. audio compact disk 28.98 (978-962-634-259-6(5), NA425912, Naxos AudioBooks) Naxos.

Oliver Twist. Charles Dickens. Narrated by Flo Gibson. (ENG.). 2008. audio compact disk 44.95 (978-1-55685-940-3(6)) Audio Bk Con.

Oliver Twist. abr. ed. Charles Dickens. (Classics Collection). 2001. 7.95 (978-1-57815-243-8(7), Media Bks Audio) Media Bks NJ.

Oliver Twist. abr. ed. Charles Dickens. Perf. by St. Charles Players. 2 cass. (Running Time: 1 hr. 55 mins.). Dramatization. (Story Theatre for Young Readers Ser.). 1999. 16.95 (978-1-56994-517-9(9), 336954, Monterey SoundWorks) Monterey Media Inc.
Orphaned & alone in turn-of-the-Century London, a boy falls in with a gang of young thieves. Befriending their leader, the colorful Artful Dodger, he goes to work for the villainous Fagin. Life on the street hurls Oliver into a danger-filled adventure, as he learns the way of the hard world, while clinging to the dream of a warm bed, a loving family & a home.

Oliver Twist. abr. ed. Charles Dickens. Perf. by Paul Scofield. 2 cass. (Running Time: 3 hrs.). (Ultimate Classics Ser.). 2004. 18.00 (978-1-931056-59-5(5), N Millennium Audio) New Millenn Enter.
A pauper's child reared in a workhouse, Oliver serves an apprenticeship in a loveless house. Despairing he runs away & is befriended by a gang of young pickpockets who offer him the only welcome home he has ever known.

Oliver Twist. abr. ed. Charles Dickens. Read by Paul Scofield. 3 CDs. (Running Time: 3 hrs.). 2004. audio compact disk 24.95 (978-1-59007-579-1(X)) Pub: New Millenn Enter. Dist(s): PerseuPGW

Oliver Twist. abr. ed. Charles Dickens & John Wells. 1999. (978-1-85998-482-6(7), HoddrStoughton) Hodder General GBR.
This abridged version of the trials of Oliver Twist makes the tale quite accessible to young listeners. Dick Cavett does an excellent job of moving from his familiar, level voice in the narrative passages to the true vibrancy of the dialogue. He handles British accents of the more lowly characters quite well, his characterization of Fagin being especially insidious and distinct. Mr. Brownlow and Monks are less developed, and their characterizations rely more on the text. The abridgment is quite a feat, having reduced a tumultuous tale into a tight storyline. However, some of the final sequences require more careful listening to absorb plot developments.

Oliver Twist. abr. adpt. ed. Charles Dickens. (Bring the Classics to Life: Level 3 Ser.). (ENG.). 2008. audio compact disk 12.95 (978-1-55576-478-4(9)) EDCON Pubng.

Oliver Twist. movie tie-in unabr. ed. Charles Dickens. Read by Nadia May. 13 CDs. (Running Time: 57600 sec.). 2005. audio compact disk 32.95 (978-0-7861-7789-9(6), ZE1659) Blckstn Audio.

Oliver Twist. unabr. ed. Charles Dickens. Read by Flo Gibson. 12 cass. (Running Time: 16 hrs. 30 min.). (gr. 8-10). 1986. 39.95 (978-1-55685-022-6(0)) Audio Bk Con.
An orphan, reared in a workhouse, is hired by an undertaker. He runs away to London where he is lured into a den of thieves & eventually escapes. The Master thief, Fagin, the artful dodger & the murderer, Bill Sikes, are part of the terror in this classic story.

Oliver Twist. unabr. ed. Charles Dickens. Read by Miriam Margolyes. 12 cass. (Running Time: 18 hrs.). (gr. 9-12). 2004. 44.95 (978-1-57270-074-1(2), F91074u) Pub: Audio Partners. Dist(s): PerseuPGW
Classic story of the poor orphan, Oliver.

Oliver Twist. unabr. ed. Charles Dickens. Read by Nadia May. 12 cass. (Running Time: 17 hrs. 30 mins.). 1995. 83.95 (978-0-7861-0861-9(4), 1659) Blckstn Audio.
Story of a work-house orphan captured & thrust into a den of thieves, where some of Dickens' most infernal villains preside: the Artful Dodger, Bill Sikes & Jew Fagin. Yet the unsullied goodness of the orphan Oliver presents allegorically Dickens' belief in "the principle of Good surviving in every adverse circumstance & triumphing at last".

Oliver Twist. unabr. ed. Charles Dickens. Read by Miriam Margolyes. (YA). 2007. 39.99 (978-1-60252-919-9(1)) Find a World.

Oliver Twist, unabr. ed. Charles Dickens. Narrated by Flo Gibson. 11 cass. (Running Time: 16 hrs. 30 mins.). 1987. 91.00 (978-1-55690-390-8(1), 87180E7) Recorded Bks.
A young orphan makes his way in the world.

Oliver Twist. unabr. ed. Charles Dickens. Read by Simon Vance. Narrated by Simon Vance. (Running Time: 16 hrs. 30 mins. 0 sec.). (Tantor Unabridged Classics Ser.). (ENG.). 2008. audio compact disk 35.99 (978-1-4001-0695-0(8)); audio compact disk 27.99 (978-1-4001-5695-5(5)); audio compact disk 72.99 (978-1-4001-3695-7(4)) Pub: Tantor Media. Dist(s): IngramPubServ

Oliver Twist. unabr. collector's ed. Charles Dickens. Read by Angela Cheyne. 10 cass. (Running Time: 15 hrs.). (YA). 1977. 80.00 (978-0-7366-0062-0(0), 1074) Books on Tape.
Though born in a workhouse & apprenticed to an undertaker, Oliver succeeds through pluck & purpose.

Oliver Twist, Set. Charles Dickens. Read by Charles Gonzales. 4 cass. (FRE.). 1995. 39.95 (1683-TH) Olivia & Hill.
This classic tale of the well known young lad, Oliver Twist.

Oliver Twist, Set. unabr. ed. Charles Dickens. Read by Nadia May. 12 cass. 1999. 83.95 (FS9-34213) Highsmith.

***Oliver Twist: Bring the Classics to Life.** adpt. ed. Charles Dickens. (Bring the Classics to Life Ser.). 2008. pap. bk. 21.95 (978-1-55576-508-8(4)) EDCON Pubng.

Oliver Twist: Movie Tie-in. movie tie-in unabr. ed. Charles Dickens & Nadia May. 12 cass. (Running Time: 17 hrs. 30 mins.). 2005. 29.95 (978-0-7861-3535-6(2), E1659) Blckstn Audio.

Oliver Twist: MP3 -Movie Tie-in. movie tie-in unabr. ed. Charles Dickens & Nadia May. 13 vols. (Running Time: 17 hrs. 30 mins.). 2005. audio compact disk 29.95 (978-0-7861-8010-3(2), ZM1659) Blckstn Audio.

Oliver Wendell Holmes: Destroyer of American Law. Thomas Bowden. 4 cass. (Running Time: 5 hrs.). pap. bk. 49.95 (PB53D) Second Renaissance.
Four classes (given at the 1998 Second Renaissance Conference) that examine Holmes' life & philosophy. Includes Q&A handout.

Oliverio Twist. abr. ed. Charles Dickens. Read by Fabio Camero. 3 CDs.Tr. of Oliver Twist. (SPA.). 2001. audio compact disk 17.00 (978-958-9494-24-0(2)) YoYoMusic.

Olive's Ocean. collector's unabr. ed. Kevin Henkes. Read by Blair Brown. 2 cass. (Running Time: 2 hrs. 30 mins.). (J). (gr. 4-7). 2005. 23.00 (978-0-307-20727-2(7), BksonTape) Random Audio Pubg.
Martha and Olive could have been friends. But they weren't - and now all that is left are eerie connections and secrets they both kept.

Olive's Ocean. unabr. ed. Kevin Henkes. Read by Blair Brown. 4 CDs. (Running Time: 6 hrs.). (J). 2004. audio compact disk 22.00 (978-0-06-074814-2(1), HarperChildAud) HarperCollins Pubs.

***Olive's Ocean.** unabr. ed. Kevin Henkes. Read by Blair Brown. (ENG.). 2005. (978-0-06-083494-4(3), GreenwillowBks); (978-0-06-083493-7(5), GreenwillowBks) HarperCollins Pubs.

Olive's Ocean. unabr. ed. Kevin Henkes. Read by Blair Brown. 3 CDs. (Running Time: 2 hrs. 30 mins.). (J). 2005. audio compact disk 30.00 (978-0-307-20728-9(5), BksonTape) Random Audio Pubg.

Olivia. unabr. ed. V. C. Andrews. Read by Laurel Lefkow. 8 cass. (Running Time: 12 hrs.). (Isis Ser.). (J). 2002. 69.95 (978-0-7531-0614-3(0)); audio compact disk 89.95 (978-0-7531-1402-5(X)) Pub: ISIS Lrg Prnt GBR. Dist(s): Ulverscroft US
Olivia Logan was always the responsible sister. Beautiful and flighty, belinda was lavished with attention from their parents, friends and boys at school. And as she matures into a young woman, her beauty becomes even more haunting. Then came the night, when Olivia was awakened by an unearthly wail from Belinda's bedroom. It was the tragic night that their father would forbid them to speak of ever again. The night would send generations of Logans down an unavoidable path of lies, deceit and heartbreak.

Olivia Audio Collection. unabr. ed. Ian Falconer. Read by Dame Edna Everage. (Running Time: 0 hr. 45 mins. 0 sec.). (ENG.). (J). 2009. audio compact disk 9.99 (978-0-7435-7959-9(3)) Pub: S&S Audio. Dist(s): S and S Inc

Olivia Joules & the Overactive Imagination. Helen Fielding. Read by Josephine Balley. 2004. audio compact disk 72.00 (978-1-4159-0276-9(3)) Books on Tape.

Olivia Kidney. unabr. ed. Ellen Potter. 2 cass. (Running Time: 3 hrs. 8 mins.). (J). (gr. 3-7). 2004. 23.00 (978-0-8072-1629-3(1), Listening Lib) Random Audio Pubg.

Olivia Kidney. unabr. ed. Ellen Potter. Read by Tara Sands. 3 CDs. (Running Time: 3 hrs. 8 mins.). (J). (gr. 3-7). 2004. audio compact disk 30.00 (978-0-8072-1771-9(9), Listening Lib) Random Audio Pubg.

Olivia Kidney & the Exit Academy. unabr. ed. Ellen Potter. 4 cass. (Running Time: 5 hrs. 25 mins.). (YA). (gr. 5-8). 2005. 35.00 (978-1-4000-9915-3(3), Listening Lib) Random Audio Pubg.
Feisty Olivia Kidney is back again in another zany, surreal, and ultimately satisfying adventure. After her well-meaning but inept father is fired from yet another handyman job, he is offered a position as a live-in superintendent at a mysterious brownstone on West 84th Street. The novel believably fuses realism and fantasy; while life appears to be somewhat normal outside of the building, inside, the first floor is a lagoon that must be maneuvered via boat, and the handsome owner, Ansel Plover, welcomes puzzling late-night guests. Olivia discovers that these visitors are all about to die and come in a dreamlike state to the "Exit Academy" to rehearse their deaths. This may all sound rather macabre, but Potter imbues the story with large doses of humor, so even the practice death scenes have a vaudeville air about them. Plot strands abound as Olivia befriends neighbors who attend a ridiculous finishing school, meets a champion skateboarder in Central Park, and encounters two colorful characters - Madame Brenda and the Princepessa - from Olivia Kidney (Philomel, 2003). The writing crackles with energy, and, beneath the bizarre happenings, themes emerge that are connected to Olivia's personal growth and acceptance of her brother's death.

Olivia's Luck. unabr. ed. Catherine Alliott. 14 cass. (Running Time: 21 hrs.). 2002. 110.95 (978-0-7540-0718-0(9), CAB 2140) AudioGO.

Olivia's Luck. unabr. ed. Catherine Alliott. Read by Suzy Aitchison. 14 cass. (Running Time: 21 hrs.). 2002. 89.95 (CAB 2140) AudioGO.
When Elizabeth's husband announces "I don't care what color you paint the hall, 'm leaving," Olivia is devastated. Left with an eccentric troop of builders camping out in her garden, a ten-year-old daughter with an attitude, and a very neurotic neighbor intent on foisting cast-off men in her direction. Olivia's dream home is suddenly less than dreamy.

Olivia's Touch. Peggy Stoks. Narrated by Christina Moore. 6 cass. (Running Time: 8 hrs. 30 mins.). (Abounding Love Ser.: Vol. 1). 54.00 (978-0-7887-9019-5(6)); audio compact disk 78.00 (978-1-4025-1561-3(8)) Recorded Bks.

***Olivion's Favorites.** unabr. ed. Troy Cle. Narrated by Laz Alonso. 7 CDs. (Running Time: 8 hrs. 33 mins.). (Marvelous World Ser.: Bk. 2). (YA). (gr. 5-8). 2009. audio compact disk 55.00 (978-0-7393-6779-7(X), Listening Lib) Pub: Random Audio Pubg. Dist(s): Random

Olly Spellmaker & the Sulky Smudge. Susan Price. Read by Glen McCready. 2 CDs. (Running Time: 7620 sec.). (J). 2005. DVD, audio compact disk, audio compact disk 21.95 (978-0-7540-6673-6(8), Chivers Child Audio) AudioGO.

Olsen Twins: Mary-Kate & Ashley's Cool Yule. Perf. by Mary-Kate Olsen & Ashley Olsen. 1 cass. (Running Time: 1 hr.). (J). 2002. 10.98 (978-0-7379-0070-5(9), 75928); audio compact disk 13.98 (978-0-7379-0073-6(3), 75929) Rhino Enter.
Join the olsen Twins for the coolest Christmas party, featuring Yuletide classics with a pop twist.

Oluolu Congrats. 5.00 (978-1-58513-070-2(2), 1-HE-C) Dance Fantasy.

Olympiad. Tom Holt. Narrated by Christopher Kay. 11 cass. (Running Time: 16 hrs.). 98.00 (978-1-84197-267-1(3)) Recorded Bks.

Olympic Corporation (Principle #3 - Speed Up) James 1:2-4. Ed Young. 1996. 4.95 (978-0-7417-2123-5(6), 1123) Win Walk.

Olympic Peninsula Loop: Heritage Corridor Tour. Interview. Text by Jens Lund. 1 cass. (Running Time: 110 mins). (Washington Heritage Tours Ser.: Vol. 4). (ENG., 1999. spiral bd. 17.95 (978-1-891466-02-1(X)) NW Heritage.

Olympics. Kristi McCracken. Narrated by Larry A. McKeever. (Ancient Greek Mystery Ser.). (J). 2007. 10.95 (978-1-58659-134-2(7)); audio compact disk 14.95 (978-1-58659-368-1(4)) Artesian.

***Om Guitar: Acoustic Meditation Music.** Contrib. by Stevin McNamara. (ENG.). 2008. audio compact disk 17.98 (978-5-557-58976-5(7)) Sounds True.

OM House: Healing Beyond Medicine Series. Joseph Michael Levry. 2002. 19.00 (978-1-885562-09-8(8)) Root Light.

OM MA NI PADME HUM: 100,000 subliminal Repetations. Woody Swartz. 1 cd. (Running Time: 54 min). (TIB.). 2004. audio compact disk Rental 24.95 (978-0-9729322-2-6(4)) Golden Skies.
OM MA NI PAD ME HUM Mantra with more than 100,000 thousands subliminal repetitions of the mantra.

Om Namah Shivaya. unabr. ed. Yogi Hari. (Mantra Ser.). 1999. audio compact disk 14.95 (978-1-57777-030-5(7), 407-004) Pub: Nada Prodns. Dist(s): Bookworld

Om Namah Sivaya. Voice by Sivananda Radha. 1 CD. (Running Time: 60 min.). 1997. audio compact disk 15.95 (978-0-931454-88-2(3)) Pub: Timeless Bks. Dist(s): Baker Taylor
Swami Radha chants traditional ancient mantras effective in keeping the mind centered whil working or for meditation.

Om Namo Bhagavate Vaasudevaaya: Mantra Series. unabr. ed. Yogi Hari. (Running Time: 5400 sec.). (Mantra Ser.). 2000. audio compact disk 14.95 (978-1-57777-032-9(3), 407-006) Pub: Nada Prodns. Dist(s): Bookworld

Om Namo Narayanaya. unabr. ed. Yogi Hari. (Mantra Ser.). 2001. audio compact disk 14.95 (978-1-57777-034-3(X), 407-005) Pub: Nada Prodns. Dist(s): Bookworld

Om Sri Ram Jai Ram Jai Jai Ram. unabr. ed. Yogi Hari. (Mantra Ser.). 2000. audio compact disk 14.95 (978-1-57777-033-6(1), 407-008) Pub: Nada Prodns. Dist(s): Bookworld

Om Upasana. (715) Yoga Res Foun.

Om Upasana. Swami Jyotirmayananda. 1 cass. (Running Time: 1 hr.). 1990. 12.99 Yoga Res Foun.

Omaha War Songs. 1 cass. (Running Time: 30 min.). 9.95 (C0730B090, HarperThor) HarpC GBR.

Omega. unabr. ed. Loren Robinson. Read by Cameron Beierle. (Hawk Adventure Ser.: Bk. 2). 2001. 49.95 (978-1-58116-020-8(8)) Books in Motion.
Lane Palmer is Hawk, a member of the anti-terrorist Counter Force of the FBI. Hawk is the target of world assassin Omega, who intends to capture Hawk for a rather large Libyan reward.

Omega Plan: The Medically Proven Diet That Gives You the Essential Nutrients You Need. abr. ed. Artemis Simopoulos. Read by Artemis Simopoulos. 2 cass. (Running Time: 3 hrs.). 1998. 18.00 HarperCollins Pubs.

Omega Rx Zone: The Miracle of the New High-Dose Fish Oil. abr. ed. Barry Sears. Read by Barry Sears. 2008. audio compact disk 14.95 (978-0-06-146772-1(3), Harper Audio) HarperCollins Pubs.

Omega Rx Zone: The Miracle of the New High-Dose Fish Oil. unabr. abr. ed. Barry Sears. Read by Barry Sears. 2 CDs. (Running Time: 3 hrs.). 2002. audio compact disk 22.00 (978-0-06-050163-1(4)) HarperCollins Pubs.

***Omega Rx Zone: The Power of the New High-Dose Fish Oil.** abr. ed. Barry Sears. Read by Barry Sears. (ENG.). 2005. (978-0-06-085688-5(2), Harper Audio); (978-0-06-085687-8(4), Harper Audio) HarperCollins Pubs.

***omega Scroll.** Adrian d'Hagé. Read by Jim Daly. (Running Time: 15 hrs. 10 mins.). 2009. 104.99 (978-1-74214-221-0(4), 9781742142210) Pub: Bolinda Pubng AUS. Dist(s): Bolinda Pub Inc

omega Scroll. unabr. ed. Adrian d'Hagé. Read by Jim Daly. (Running Time: 15 hrs. 10 mins.). 2007. audio compact disk 118.95 (978-1-74093-921-8(2), 9781740939218) Pub: Bolinda Pubng AUS. Dist(s): Bolinda Pub Inc

omega Scroll. unabr. ed. Adrian d'Hagé. Read by Jim Daly. (Running Time: 15 hrs. 10 mins.). 2008. 43.95 (978-1-74214-090-2(4), 9781742140902) Pub: Bolinda Pubng AUS. Dist(s): Bolinda Pub Inc

Omega Zone. unabr. ed. Barry Sears. 2 cass. (Running Time: 2 hrs.). 2004. 19.99 (978-1-58926-690-2(0), 6690) Oasis Audio.

Omen. unabr. ed. Christie Golden. Read by Marc Thompson. (Star Wars Ser.). (ENG.). 2009. audio compact disk 39.95 (978-0-7393-7663-8(2), Random AudioBks) Pub: Random Audio Pubg. Dist(s): Random

***Omen Machine: A Richard & Kahlan Novel.** unabr. ed. Terry Goodkind. Read by Sam Tsoutsouvas. (Running Time: 16 hrs.). (Sword of Truth Ser.). 2011. 29.99 (978-1-4418-8783-2(0), 9781441887832, Brilliance MP3); 44.97 (978-1-4418-8784-9(9), 9781441887849, Brlnc Audio MP3 Lib); audio compact disk 39.99 (978-1-4418-8781-8(4), 9781441887818, Bril Audio CD Unabri); audio compact disk 99.97 (978-1-4418-8782-5(2), 9781441887825, BriAudCD Unabrid) Brilliance Audio.

Omens of Death. unabr. ed. Nicholas Rhea. Read by Graham Padden. 7 cass. (Running Time: 9 hrs. 15 min.). 1999. 76.95 (978-1-85903-266-4(4)) Pub: Magna Story GBR. Dist(s): Ulverscroft US
When people die in suspicious circumstances, Detective Inspector Montague Pluke is at last able to put all his police training, together with his great knowledge of superstitions ancient & modern, to good use.

Omeros. unabr. ed. Derek Walcott. Read by Derek Walcott. Interview with Rebekah Presson. 1 cass. (Running Time: 29 min.). 1990. 10.00 (121490) New Letters.
Long the leading exponent of the written culture of the Carribean, Walcott now celebrates the island of his birth, Saint Lucia, in an epic poem, Omeros.

Omerta. unabr. ed. Mario Puzo. Read by Michael Imperioli. 6 cass. (Running Time: 9 hrs.). 2000. 48.00 (978-0-7366-5515-6(8), 5355) Books on Tape.
Don Raymonde Aprile is about to retire from organized crime. His adopted nephew, Astorre Viola, is set to take over the business. Though Aprile's retirement is seen as a business opportunity by his last rival, Timmona Portella, it is viewed with suspicion by Kurt Cilke, the FBI's special agent in charge of investigating organized crime. As Cilke mounts a campaign to wipe out the Mafia once and for all, Viola and Aprile find themselves in the midst of one last war.

Ominous Parallels: The End of Freedom in America. Leonard Peikoff. Read by Leonard Peikoff. 1 cass. (Running Time: 1 hr. 12 mins.). 1984. 12.95 (978-1-56114-059-6(7), LP01C) Second Renaissance.
The intellectual disease that rendered Germany vulnerable to Nazism & how to keep it from infecting America.

Omni Audio Experience, Vol. 1. Ray Bradbury. Interview with Ray Bradbury. 1 cass. (Running Time: 1 hr.). 9.95 (978-0-944305-00-3(8)) Bonneville Media.
Two stories from Ray Bradbury's "The Martian Chronicles" with sound effects and "new age" music. Includes interview with Ray Bradbury.

Omni Audio Experience, Vol. 2. Arthur C. Clarke. Read by Ken Nordine. 1 cass. (Running Time: 50 min.). 9.95 (978-0-944305-06-5(7)) Bonneville Media.

OMNI Audio Experience II. 1 cass. (Running Time: 1 hr.). Dramatization. 1989. 8.95 Bonneville Media.

Omniphonics: Powerful Esteem. 2 cass. (Running Time: 1 hr. 36 min.). 1999. 29.95 Set. (20405) Courage-to-Change.
Helps change negative thoughts into positive self-esteem. Inaudible positive affirmations run under music & soothing outer sounds.

Omnipotent Prayer: Spanish Version. 2004. (978-1-59024-179-0(7)) B Hinn Min.

Omnipresence Identification; Golden Glimpses. unabr. ed. Ann Ree Colton & Jonathan Murro. 1 cass. (Running Time: 45 min.). 1997. 7.95 (978-0-917189-23-4(X), 105) A R Colton Fnd.
Side 1: Discusses the awareness of God within one's self, within the affairs of one's life through the Law of Consequence, & in the 12 countenances of God or prototypers in the world. Side 2: Prophetic glimpses of the future. Reading the indicators of the future.

Omnipresence Timings: The Coinciding Principle; Preparation & Illumination. Jonathan Murro & Ann Ree Colton. 1 cass. (Running Time: 1 hr.). 7.95 A R Colton Fnd.
Discusses the goal of God-Realization.

***Omnitopia Dawn.** unabr. ed. Diane Duane. Narrated by Kirby Heyborne. (Running Time: 15 hrs. 30 mins. 0 sec.). (Omnitopia Ser.). (ENG.). 2010. 29.99 (978-1-4001-6846-0(5)); 20.99 (978-1-4001-8846-8(6)); audio compact disk 39.99 (978-1-4001-1846-5(8)) Pub: Tantor Media. Dist(s): IngramPubServ

***Omnitopia Dawn (Library Edition)** unabr. ed. Diane Duane. Narrated by Kirby Heyborne. (Running Time: 15 hrs. 30 mins. 0 sec.). (Omnitopia Ser.). (ENG.). 2010. audio compact disk 95.99 (978-1-4001-4846-2(4)) Pub: Tantor Media. Dist(s): IngramPubServ

Omnivore's Dilemma: A Natural History of Four Meals. unabr. ed. Michael Pollan. Read by Scott Brick. 13 CDs. (Running Time: 13 hrs.). (ENG.). (gr. 12 up). 2006. audio compact disk 39.95 (978-0-14-305841-0(X), PengAudBks) Penguin Grp USA.

On a Clear Day. unabr. ed. David Blunkett. Read by Stephen Thorne. 6 cass. (Running Time: 6 hrs.). 1996. 54.95 (978-0-7451-6643-8(1), CAB 1259) AudioGO.
At the age of four, David Blunkett boarded at a school for the blind where he began learning to read & write Braille. When he turned 16, he joined the Labour Party & soon became the first undergraduate in the neighborhood. Then, David chose to train with a guide dog & he was introduced to Ruby, who became the first dog allowed into the Palace of Westminster. Now a member of Parliament, his struggle to the top is made all the more remarkable, because he was born blind.

On a Clear Day... You Can See the Real You. Lucile Johnson. 1 cass. (Running Time: 1 hr.). 2004. 9.95 (978-1-55503-936-3(7), 06005241) Covenant Comms.
An uplifting & inspiring tape for women.

On a Coral Reef Audio CD. Adapted by Benchmark Education Company Staff. Based on a work by Cynthia Swain. (Early Explorers Set C Ser.). (J). (gr. k). 2008. audio compact disk 10.00 (978-1-60437-514-5(0)) Benchmark Educ.

On a Country Road see Suspense: Three Classic Stories

On a Day Like Today. Nicola Thorne. 2009. 76.95 (978-0-7531-3256-2(7)); audio compact disk 89.95 (978-0-7531-3257-9(5)) Pub: Isis Pubng Ltd GBR. Dist(s): Ulverscroft US

On a Diet: The Owner's Manual for Waist Management. abr. ed. Michael F. Roizen & Mehmet C. Oz. Read by Michael F. Roizen & Mehmet C. Oz. 2006. 17.95 (978-0-7435-6364-2(6)); audio compact disk 29.95 (978-0-7435-6363-5(8)) Pub: S&S Audio. Dist(s): S and S Inc

On a Favorite Cat see Anthology of Poetry for Children

On a Favorite Cat, Drowned in a Tub of Goldfishes see Palgrave's Golden Treasury of English Poetry

On a Flimmering Floom You Shall Ride see Carl Sandburg Reading Fog & Other Poems

On a Night Like This. unabr. ed. Ellen Sussman. Read by Michael Gough & Barbara Goodson. (ENG.). 2005. 14.98 (978-1-59483-341-0(9)) Pub: Hachet Audio. Dist(s): HachBkGrp

On a Note of Triumph. Text by Norman Corwin. Directed By Norman Corwin. 1 CD. (Running Time: 58 mins). Dramatization. 2005. audio compact disk 12.95 (978-1-59938-000-1(5)) Lode Cat.
V-E Day - This is Norman Corwin's original live broadcast which thrilled millions on May 8, 1945, and retains its vast power and its peircing relevance today. The origins, the horrors and the great lessons of World War II blaze forth in a vivid dramatic masterpiece, arguably the finest use of the radio medium ever achieved. Carl Sandburg called this radio drama "a vast announcement, a terrific interrogatory, one of the all-time great American poems." More than a historical tour-de-force, an inspiration for everyone with a magnificent score by Bernard Herrmann.

On a Note of Triumph. unabr. ed. Norman Corwin. Perf. by Martin Gabel. Composed by Bernard Herrmann. Conducted by Lud Gluskin. 1 cass. (Running Time: 1 hr.). 12.95 (978-1-57677-021-4(4), CORW001) Lodestone Catalog.
On V-E Day, May 8, 1945, this acclaimed special broadcast thrilled millions & retains all its power today. Here is Corwin's original masterpiece, arguably the finest use of the medium ever achieved. As the program reviews the causes & the course of the war against the Nazis, it brings home the vital lessons in a rivetting, amazing audio experience. The tremendous impact of this program, after more than half a century, can give only a partial idea of how hard it struck when it was broadcast live. Commemorative script available.

On a Note of Triumph. unabr. ed. Norman Corwin. 1 CD. (Running Time: 1 hr.). 2001. audio compact disk 15.95 (CORW26) Lodestone Catalog.

On a Pale Horse. Piers Anthony. Narrated by George Guidall. 11 CDs. (Running Time: 13 hrs.). (Incarnations of Immortality Ser.: Bk. 1). 2000. audio compact disk 111.00 (978-0-7887-4768-7(1), C1261E7) Recorded Bks.
Combines an examination of the meaning of life & death with a story of romance & loyalty set in a world of magic & wizardry.

On a Pale Horse. unabr. ed. Piers Anthony. Narrated by George Guidall. 9 cass. (Running Time: 13 hrs.). (Incarnations of Immortality Ser.: Bk. 1). 1996. 78.00 (978-0-7887-0513-7(X), 94707E7) Recorded Bks.
Combines a examination of the meaning of life & death with a story of romance & loyalty set in a world of magic & wizardry.

On a Scale of 1 To 10: Kyje 10L25-37. Ed Young. (J). 1982. 4.95 (978-0-7417-1215-8(6), A0215) Win Walk.

On a Search in America. Contrib. by Dizmas. Prod. by Brian Garcia. 2005. audio compact disk 13.99 (978-5-558-98204-6(7)) Sigma F RUS.

On a Squirrel Crossing the Road in Autumn see Richard Eberhart Reading His Poetry

On a Walk: Listen As You Walk for a Leaner, Healthier Life. adpt. unabr. ed. Michael F. Roizen & Mehmet C. Oz. Read by Michael F. Roizen & Mehmet C. Oz. 2 CDs. (Running Time: 2 hrs. 30 mins. 0 sec.). (ENG.). 2007. audio compact disk 19.95 (978-0-7435-6936-1(9)) Pub: S&S Audio. Dist(s): S and S Inc

On a Whim. Lisa McKendrick. 3 cass. 2004. 16.95 (978-1-57734-895-5(8)) Covenant Comms.

***On a Whim.** unabr. ed. Zondervan Publishing Staff. (Running Time: 8 hrs. 50 mins. 13 sec.). (Katie Weldon Ser.). 2010. 14.99 (978-0-310-86996-2(X)) Zondervan.

On Agate Hill. Lee Smith. Contrib. by Kate Forbes et al. (Running Time: 50400 sec.). 2006. audio compact disk 39.99 (978-1-4281-0004-6(0)) Recorded Bks.

On Agate Hill: A Novel. unabr. ed. Lee Smith. 12 cass. (Running Time: 14 hrs.). 2006. 94.75 (978-1-4281-0309-2(0)); audio compact disk 119.75 (978-1-4281-0311-5(2)) Recorded Bks.
On Agate Hill is set in North Carolina in the years from 1872 to 1927, and also in the present. The novel evokes the South in Reconstruction from an honest female perspective. It is the exuberantly romantic and episodic story of Molly Petree, an open-hearted and headstrong young Southern woman. The novel is framed with the letters and notes of a contemporary woman who seems almost a reincarnation of Molly herself.

On Aging. Hal Stone & Sidra Stone. 1 cass. (Running Time: 1 hr.). 1993. 10.95 (978-1-56557-018-4(9), T37) Delos Inc.
Hal Stone shows how to take an active & conscious approach to aging rather than to drift passively through the last years of life. From the earthiest & most practical suggestions about health care & money, to the divine realms of spiritual transformation, Hal explains his views on the aging process & shows how to continue to live a full & meaningful life during one's later years.

On Air: The Best of Tavis Smiley on the Tom Joyner Morning Show 2004 - 2008. Tavis Smiley. (ENG.). 2008. audio compact disk 23.95 (978-1-4019-2419-5(0)) Hay House.

On Aldous Huxley: Perennial Philosopher. Stephan Hoeller. 1 cass. (Running Time: 1 hr.). 1999. 11.00 (40027) Big Sur Tapes.
1996 Los Angeles.

On Aleister Crowley. unabr. ed. Robert W. Wilson. 1 cass. (Running Time: 1 hr.). 1988. 9.00 (978-1-56964-774-5(7), A0285-88) Sound Photosyn.

On All Hallows' Eve. unabr. ed. Grace Chetwin. Narrated by Grace Chetwin. 3 cass. (Running Time: 4 hrs.). (gr. 6). 1992. 27.00 (978-1-55690-606-0(4), 92211E7) Recorded Bks.
Meg & her sister Sue are ready for a few good scares when they go to the Halloween party at their new school on Long Island. But when they take shelter from Meg's arch-enemy, Kenny Stover, in a ruined cottage on Horse Hollow Road, they discover they have been scared right out of this world.

On an Old Woman Dying see Twentieth-Century Poetry in English, No. 12, Recordings of Poets Reading Their Own Poetry

On Anotha Level. Lannie Robertson & Led-Spirit. 1 cass. (Running Time: 1 hr.). 2000. 11.99 (978-0-9706112-0-8(X), Fifth Season Recs); audio compact disk 17.99 (978-0-9706112-1-5(8), Fifth Season Recs) Pt of Grace Ent.

On Apartheid. Interview with Alan Paton. 1 cass. (Running Time: 37 min.). 10.95 (27005) J Norton Pubs.
The author talks about the historical development & the current fear that infects many of his countrymen.

On Art & Sciences. abr. ed. Jean-Jacques Rousseau. Read by Robert L. Halvorson. 4 cass. (Running Time: 6 hrs.). 28.95 (15) Halvorson Assocs.

On Art & Spirit. Anais Nin. 1 cass. (Running Time: 1 hr. 30 mins.). 1999. 11.00 (04303) Big Sur Tapes.
1972 Berkeley.

On Art & Spirit. Tom Robbins. 1 cass. (Running Time: 1 hr. 30 mins.). 1999. 11.00 (13901) Big Sur Tapes.

On Assignment. Art Rascon. 1 cass. (Running Time: 1 hr. 30 mins.). 2004. 9.95 (978-1-57734-295-3(X), 07001835) Covenant Comms.
Inspiring stories from an LDS broadcast journalist.

On Baking: CostGenie Student Version. Sarah R. Labensky et al. 2006. audio compact disk 13.33 (978-0-13-158958-2(X)) Pearson Educ CAN CAN.

On Basilisk Station. unabr. ed. David Weber. Read by Allyson Johnson. 1 MP3-CD. (Running Time: 15 hrs.). (Honor Harrington Ser.: Bk. 1). 2009. 24.99 (978-1-4233-9340-5(6), 9781423393405, Brilliance MP3); 39.97 (978-1-4233-9341-2(4), 9781423393412, Brlnc Audio MP3 Lib); 39.97 (978-1-4233-9342-9(2), 9781423393429, BADLE); audio compact disk 29.99 (978-1-4233-9338-2(4), 9781423393382, Bril Audio CD Unabri); audio compact disk 99.97 (978-1-4233-9339-9(2), 9781423393399, BriAudCD Unabrid) Brilliance Audio.

On Bear Mountain. unabr. ed. Deborah Smith. Read by Dick Hill & Susie Breck. (Running Time: 13 hrs.). 2005. 39.25 (978-1-59600-755-0(9), 9781596007550, BADLE) Brilliance Audio.

On Beauty. Zadie Smith. Read by Peter Francis James. 16 CDs. (Running Time: 18 hrs.). (ENG.). (gr. 12 up). 2005. audio compact disk 44.95 (978-0-14-305800-7(2), PengAudBks) Penguin Grp USA.

On Beauty. unabr. ed. Zadie Smith. 2 CDs. 2005. 49.95 (978-0-7927-3840-4(3), Chivers Sound Lib); 89.95 (978-0-7927-3770-4(9), Chivers Sound Lib) AudioGO.

On Becoming a Leader. Warren Bennis & Robert Townsend. Read by Warren Bennis & Robert Townsend. 6 cass. (Running Time: 9 hrs.). 1991. 59.95 (793A) Nightingale-Conant.
The basic ingredients of leaders are identified & Bennis & Townsend share with you how to develop these characteristics.

On Becoming a Leader. abr. ed. Warren Bennis. 2 cass. (Running Time: 3 hrs.). 1996. 13.95 (52899) Books on Tape.
Bennis describes distinctive characteristics that great leaders share. Al Gore recommends this classic to all of his advisors.

***On Becoming a Leader: The Leadership Classic Revised & Updated.** unabr. ed. Warren Bennis. Read by Walter Dixon. (Running Time: 6 hrs. 30 mins.). (ENG.). 2010. 27.98 (978-1-59659-683-2(X), GildAudio) Pub: Gildan Media. Dist(s): HachBkGrp

On Becoming American. unabr. ed. Ted Morgan. Read by Donald Monat. 11 cass. (Running Time: 16 hrs. 30 min.). 1989. 88.00 (978-0-7366-1600-3(4), 2461) Books on Tape.
On Becoming American is an inquiry into American identity - what it is that sets Americans apart from the rest of the world. Ted Morgan discusses America through the prism of his own experience: he was a French aristocrat, Sanche de Gramont, who became Ted Morgan & an American citizen in 1977. A Pulitzer Prize-winning journalist, Morgan's experience illustrates why immigration is central to the American experience. He sees us with fresh eyes, & writes with humor about our passion for fast cars, fast food & the freedom we take for granted.

On Becoming Babywise: Giving Your Infant the Gift of Nighttime Sleep. Gary Ezzo & Robert Bucknam. Read by Anne Marie Ezzo. (Running Time: 24000 sec.). (ENG.). 2007. audio compact disk 26.99 (978-1-934384-01-5(1)) Pub: Treasure Pub. Dist(s): STL Dist NA

On Becoming Fearless... In Love, Work, & Life. abr. ed. Arianna S. Huffington. (Running Time: 3 hrs. 30 mins.). (ENG.). 2006. 14.98 (978-1-59483-631-2(0)) Pub: Hachet Audio. Dist(s): HachBkGrp

On Becoming Fearless... In Love, Work, & Life. abr. ed. Arianna S. Huffington. (Running Time: 3 hrs. 30 mins.). 2009. 39.98 (978-1-60788-141-4(1)) Pub: Hachet Audio. Dist(s): HachBkGrp

On Being a Psychic. Anne Armstrong. 1 cass. (Running Time: 58 min.). 1971. 11.00 Big Sur Tapes.
Describes the author's problems in learning to use her powers, how she first discovered them & their changing character as they continue to emerge.

On Being Excellent see Ser Excelente

On Being Swept Away: The Psychology of Courtship & Romantic Love. Judith Shaw. Read by Judith Shaw. 2 cass. (Running Time: 2 hrs.). 1992. 16.95 set. (978-0-7822-0401-8(5), 492) C G Jung IL.
Jungian analyst Judith Shaw examines the experience of "falling in love" & explores the process of projection in intimate relationships. Part of the set The Questions & Meanings of Intimate Relationship (catalog No. INTIMATE).

On Board the Titanic: What It Was Like When the Great Liner Sank. Shelley Tanaka. Read by Terry Bregy. (ENG.). (J). 2008. 34.99 (978-1-60514-792-5(3)) Find a World.

On Board the Titanic: What It Was Like When the Great Liner Sank. unabr. ed. Shelley Tanaka. Read by Terry Bregy. Illus. by Ken Marschall. 1 CDs. (Running Time: 50 mins.). (J). (gr. 4-7). 2008. audio compact disk 24.95 (978-0-9814890-1-8(X)) Audio Bkshelf.

On Bullshit. Harry G. Frankfurt. 2005. audio compact disk 9.99 (978-1-4193-4887-7(6)) Recorded Bks.

On Call in Hell: A Doctor's Iraq War Story. Richard Jadick. Read by Lloyd James. Told to Thomas Hayden. (Playaway Adult Nonfiction Ser.). 2008. 59.99 (978-1-60640-985-5(9)) Find a World.

On Call in Hell: A Doctor's Iraq War Story. unabr. ed. Richard Jadick & Thomas Hayden. (Running Time: 8 hrs. 0 mins. 0 sec.). (ENG.). 2007. audio compact disk 29.99 (978-1-4001-0360-7(6)) Pub: Tantor Media. Dist(s): IngramPubServ

On Call in Hell: A Doctor's Iraq War Story. unabr. ed. Richard Jadick & Thomas Hayden. (Running Time: 8 hrs. 0 mins. 0 sec.). (ENG.). 2007. audio compact disk 59.99 (978-1-4001-3360-4(2)); audio compact disk 19.99 (978-1-4001-5360-2(3)) Pub: Tantor Media. Dist(s): IngramPubServ

On Channeling. unabr. ed. Helen Palmer et al. 6 cass. (Running Time: 8 hrs. 18 min.). 1988. 56.00 Set. (08605) Big Sur Tapes.
The panel, all respected teachers & researchers on the many dimensions of psychic phenomena, are joined by two channelers who present themselves & their beings for questioning.

On Chesil Beach. unabr. ed. Ian McEwan. Read by Ian McEwan. 4 cass. (Running Time: 6 hrs.). 2007. 50.00 (978-1-4159-3879-9(2)); audio compact disk 50.00 (978-1-4159-3880-5(6)) Books on Tape.

On Chesil Beach. unabr. ed. Ian McEwan. Read by Ian McEwan. (YA). 2007. 54.99 (978-0-7393-7517-4(2)) Find a World.

On Chesil Beach. unabr. ed. Ian McEwan. Read by Ian McEwan. 4 CDs. (Running Time: 16200 sec.). (ENG.). 2007. audio compact disk 29.95 (978-0-7393-4371-5(8), Random AudioBks) Pub: Random Audio Pubg. Dist(s): Random

On Christian Doctrine. unabr. ed. Saint Augustine. Ed. by James H. Cain. Narrated by Simon Vance. 6. (Running Time: 6 hrs. 30 mins. 0 sec.). (ENG.). 2006. audio compact disk 23.98 (978-1-59644-002-9(3)) christianaud.
"There are certain rules for the interpretation of Scripture which I think might with great advantage be taught to earnest students of the word, that they may profit not only from reading the works of others who have laid open the secrets of the sacred writings, but also from themselves opening such secrets to others. These rules I propose to teach to those who are able and willing to learn." With these words Saint Augustine (354-430) began one of the finest theological treatments ever written on reading and interpreting Holy Scripture. Pastors, monks, and educated laypersons cherished De Doctrina Christiana from the time Augustine wrote it through the Middle Ages. Today if this wonderful little book is less well known, it nevertheless remains as insightful as ever.

On Christian Doctrine - Delete. unabr. ed. Saint Augustine. Ed. by James H. Cain. MP3CD (1). (ENG.). 2006. 14.98 (978-1-59644-003-6(1)) christianaud.
"There are certain rules for the interpretation of Scripture which I think might with great advantage be taught to earnest students of the word, that they may profit not only from reading the works of others who have laid open the secrets of the sacred writings, but also from themselves opening such secrets to others. These rules I propose to teach to those who are able and willing to learn..." With these words Saint Augustine (354-430) began one of the finest theological treatments ever written on reading and interpreting Holy Scripture. Pastors, monks, and educated laypersons cherished De Doctrina Christiana from the time Augustine wrote it through the Middle Ages. Today if this wonderful little book is less well known, it nevertheless remains as insightful as ever.

On Christian Doctrine - Delete. Saint Augustine. Ed. by James H. Cain. CD (#). 2004. 29.98 (978-1-59644-004-3(X)) christianaud.

On Christianity. Swami Amar Jyoti. 1 cass. (Running Time: 1 hr. 30 mins.). 1979. 9.95 (Q-10) Truth Consciousness.
Christianity & its relation to other religions. Paying attention to the principle within the outer shell. On sincere prayer.

On Christmas Day in the Morning. Perf. by Theresa Donohoo. 1 cass. (Running Time: 1 hr. 30 mins.). 1998. 10.95 (CS-432); audio compact disk 15.95 (CD-432) GIA Pubns.

On Christmas Eve. unabr. ed. Ann M. Martin. Read by Alison Fraser. 2 CDs. (Running Time: 8040 sec.). (ENG.). (J). (gr. 3). 2006. audio compact disk 22.00 (978-0-7393-3719-6(X), Listening Lib) Pub: Random Audio Pubg. Dist(s): Random

On Christmas Eve. unabr. ed. Jon J. Muth. Read by Alison Fraser. 2 cass. (J). 2006. 23.00 (978-0-7393-3808-7(0), Listening Lib) Pub: Random Audio Pubg. Dist(s): Random

On Christmas Eve. unabr. ed. Jon J. Muth. Read by Alison Fraser. 2 CDs. (J). 2006. audio compact disk 20.40 (978-0-7393-3776-9(9), Listening Lib) Pub: Random Audio Pubg. Dist(s): NetLibrary CO
Tess McAlister truly believes in magic, and is convinced that this is the year she will finally meet Santa Claus. Tess has many Christmas wishes, but her most fervent wish is not for herself, but for a friend. Her faith in the season results in a Christmas Eve so wondrous, so sparkling, that listeners won't be able to help but feel transformed. Like white Christmases and crackling fires in the hearth, On Christmas Eve portrays the magic and the spirit of hope that make the holidays merry.

On Coca & Other Natural Drugs. Andrew Weil. 1 cass. (Running Time: 1 hr.). 1976. 11.00 (3615) Big Sur Tapes.
Dr. Weil discusses the difference between coca, a beneficent natural stimulant which has been used by South American Indians for centuries without ill effects, & cocaine, a chemically refined derivative of the natural drug. Unlike coca, cocaine lends itself to abuse & psychological dependency.

On Communicating. Mark H. McCormack. Narrated by Mark H. McCormack. 4 cass. (Running Time: 4 hrs. 30 mins.). 45.00 (978-1-4025-0904-9(9)); audio compact disk 39.00 (978-1-4025-1155-4(8)) Recorded Bks.

On Communicating. abr. unabr. ed. Mark H. McCormack. Read by Mark H. McCormack. 4 cass. (Running Time: 6 hrs.). 2004. 25.00 (978-1-931056-12-0(9), N Millennium Audio) New Millenn Enter.
Avoiding trendy theories & shortsighted strategies, the author teaches verbal communication as art & science: how to explain anything to anyone; how to assert oneself without offending others; how to discern that the messenger means more than the message & more.

On Compromise. unabr. ed. John Morley. Read by Robert L. Halvorson. 4 cass. (Running Time: 6 hrs.). 28.95 (87) Halvorson Assocs.

On Course for Ielts. Darren Conway & Brent Shirreffs. 2004. 35.95 (978-0-19-457533-1(0)) OUP.

On Dangerous Ground. unabr. ed. Jack Higgins. Read by Patrick Macnee. 6 cass. (Running Time: 9 hrs.). (Sean Dillon Ser.). 2001. 32.00 (978-1-59040-138-5(7), Phoenix Audio) Pub: Amer Intl Pub. Dist(s): PerseuPGW

On Dangerous Ground. unabr. ed. Jack Higgins. Read by Michael Page. (Running Time: 8 hrs.). (Sean Dillon Ser.). 2010. 24.99 (978-1-4418-3895-7(3), 9781441838957, Brilliance MP3) Brilliance Audio.

***On Dangerous Ground.** unabr. ed. Jack Higgins. Read by Michael Page. (Running Time: 8 hrs.). (Sean Dillon Ser.). 2010. 39.97 (978-1-4418-3896-4(1), 9781441838964, Brinc Audio MP3 Lib); 39.97 (978-1-4418-3898-8(8), 9781441838988, BADLE); 24.99 (978-1-4418-3897-1(X), 9781441838971, BAD); audio compact disk 87.97 (978-1-4418-3894-0(5), 9781441838940, BriAudCD Unabrid); audio compact disk 29.99 (978-1-4418-3893-3(7), 9781441838933, Bril Audio CD Unabri) Brilliance Audio.

***On Dangerous Ground.** unabr. ed. Jack Higgins. (Running Time: 8 hrs.). (Sean Dillon Ser.). 2011. audio compact disk 14.99 (978-1-4418-3900-8(3), 9781441839008, BCD Value Price) Brilliance Audio.

On Dangerous Ground. unabr. ed. Jack Higgins. Read by Patrick Macnee. 6 cass. (Running Time: 9 hrs.). (Sean Dillon Ser.). 1999. 29.95 (FS9-34528) Highsmith.

On Dangerous Ground. unabr. ed. Jack Higgins. Perf. by Patrick Macnee. 6 cass. (Running Time: 9 hrs.). (Sean Dillon Ser.). 2004. 32.95 (978-1-59007-194-6(8)) Pub: New Millenn Enter. Dist(s): PerseuPGW
As 1997 approaches, England's prime minister learns of a secret document signed by Mao Tse-tung that could delay the Chinese takeover of Hong Kong for an additional 100 years. The British hire former terrorist Sean Dillon to keep the document from coming to light, before parties in Hong Kong retrieve it and destroy the balance of world power.

On Dangerous Ground. unabr. ed. Lesley Horton. Contrib. by Margaret Sircom. 10 cass. (Story Sound Ser.). (J). 2006. 84.95 (978-1-85903-974-8(X)) Pub: Mgna Lrg Print GBR. Dist(s): Ulverscroft US

On Dangerous Ground. unabr. ed. Lesley Horton & Margaret Sircom. Contrib. by Margaret Sircom. 12 vols. (Story Sound CD Ser.). (J). 2006. audio compact disk 99.95 (978-1-85903-988-5(X)) Pub: Mgna Lrg Print GBR. Dist(s): Ulverscroft US

On Deadly Ground. unabr. ed. Michael Norman. (Running Time: 13 hrs. 30 mins.). 2010. 29.95 (978-1-4417-2700-8(0)); 79.95 (978-1-4417-2696-4(9)); audio compact disk 109.00 (978-1-4417-2697-1(7)) Blckstn Audio.

On Death & Dying. abr. ed. Elisabeth Kübler-Ross et al. 4 CDs. (Running Time: 5 hrs. 0 mins. 0 sec.). (ENG.). 2005. audio compact disk 24.95 (978-1-59397-588-3(0)) Pub: Macmill Audio. Dist(s): Macmillan

***On Demand Display Prepack Borders.** (On Demand Ser.). 2007. bk. 359.40 (978-0-8416-0326-4(X)) Pub: Berlitz Pubng. Dist(s): Langenscheidt

On Divorce. 6 cass. (Running Time: 9 hrs.). 19.95 (2092, HarperThor) HarpC GBR.

On Eagle's Wings. Perf. by Michael Crawford. 1 cass., 1 CD. 8.78 (ALT 83076); audio compact disk 13.58 CD Jewel box. (ATL 83076) NewSound.

On Eagle's Wings. Perf. by Steve Hall. 1 cass. (Running Time: 1 hr.). 7.98 (BANK 8); audio compact disk 12.78 (BANK 8) NewSound.
Instrumentation other than grand piano include harp, guitar, flute, percussion & Irish & Scottish bagpipes.

On Early Trains see Poetry of Pasternak

On Earth As It Is in Heaven Vol. 17. Tommy Nelson & AIO Team Staff. Prod. by Focus on the Family Staff. 4 CDs. (Running Time: 6 hrs.). (Adventures in Odyssey Ser.: Vol. 17). (ENG.). (J). (gr. 3-7). 1994. audio compact disk 24.99 (978-1-56179-262-7(4)) Pub: Focus Family. Dist(s): Tyndale Hse

On Easter Knoll see Gathering of Great Poetry for Children

On Education. Read by Chogyam Trungpa. 1 cass. (Running Time: 1 hr.). 1985. 10.00 (A112) Vajradhatu.

On Education. Arthur Young. 1 cass. (Running Time: 1 hr. 30 mins.). 9.00 (A0667-90) Sound Photosyn.

On Eliot. Theodore Weiss. 1 cass. (Running Time: 58 min.). 1962. 11.95 (23231) J Norton Pubs.
Weiss discusses Eliot, the person & the fact that he was a full-blown poet, & wrote Prufrock at a very early age. He wrote about a man as a man ought to be.

On Faith & Devotion. Swami Amar Jyoti. 1 cass. (Running Time: 1 hr.). 1976. 9.95 (C-3) Truth Consciousness.
Why we cannot progress one inch on the spiritual path without faith & devotion. How to grow in faith.

On Fields of Fury, unabr. ed. Richard Wheeler. Read by Norman Dietz. 7 cass. (Running Time: 10 hrs.). 1991. 49.95 (978-0-7861-0281-5(0), 1247) Blckstn Audio.
A dramatic recreation, largely in the words of participants, of Grant's desperate attempt to end the Civil War from May through June of 1864. It began with an all-out-assault by Grant's Army of the Potomac against Lee in the wilderness in Virginia in May & ended before Petersburg in July in the Union defeat at the Crater.

On Fields of Fury. unabr. ed. Richard Wheeler. Read by Wolfram Kandinsky. 7 cass. (Running Time: 10 hrs. 30 min.). 1992. 56.00 (978-0-7366-2191-5(1), 2986) Books on Tape.
A dramatic recreation, largely in the words of participants, of General U.S. Grant's ambitious attempt to end the Civil War in 1864 - before Lincoln's reelection.

On Finnegans Wake. unabr. ed. Robert A. Wilson. 1 cass. (Running Time: 1 hr.). 1988. 9.00 (978-1-56964-801-8(8), A0273-88) Sound Photosyn.
Robert is a zealous Finnegans Wakeian which suits his massive associative memory, with Brian recording Faustin's interview.

On Fire. 1 cass. (Running Time: 1 hr.). 2000. 15.95 Prof Pride.
Track four simulated fire calls on a map. Basic information.

On Fire, unabr. ed. Larry Brown. Narrated by Ed Sala. 4 cass. (Running Time: 4 hrs. 45 mins.). 1996. 35.00 (978-0-7887-0501-4(6), 94694E7) Recorded Bks.
Account of the daily trauma firefighters face, from the blistering heat of burning homes to the crunch of broken glass at crash scenes.

On First Looking into Chapman's Homer see Poetry of Keats

On First Looking into the Arabian Nights. unabr. ed. Gilbert Highet. Read by Gilbert Highet. 1 cass. (Running Time: 30 mins.). 9.95 (23314-A) J Norton Pubs.

On Gay Wallpaper see William Carlos Williams Reads His Poetry

On Gerald Heard. John Cody. 2 cass. (Running Time: 3 hrs.). 1999. 18.00 (32009) Big Sur Tapes.
1992 Santa Cruz.

On God: An Uncommon Conversation. unabr. ed. Norman Mailer. Read by Kent Bateman & Malcolm Hillgartner. 4 cass. (Running Time: 5 hrs. 30 mins.). 2008. 54.95 (978-1-4332-1417-2(2)); audio compact disk 29.95 (978-1-4332-1419-6(9)); audio compact disk & audio compact disk 63.00 (978-1-4332-1418-9(0)) Blckstn Audio.

On-Going Healing of the Inner Child. Earnie Larsen. 1 cass. (Running Time: 1 hr.). 1993. 10.95 (978-1-56047-059-5(3), A125) E Larsen Enterprises.
Understanding the Inner Child; differences between Inner Child work & Family of Origin work; techniques for healing of the Inner Child; techniques for on-going healing of the Inner Child.

On Gold Mountain: The One-Hundred-Year Odyssey of My Chinese-American Family. unabr. collector's ed. Lisa See. Read by Kate Reading. 13 cass. (Running Time: 19 hrs. 30 mins.). 1996. 104.00 (978-0-7366-3295-9(6), 3950) Books on Tape.
Her heart is Chinese, despite the red hair she inherited from her Caucasian grandmother. This Lisa See declares in an absorbing, muli-generational saga of her Chinese-American family. In a sense, it is a portrait not only of her family, but also America, a country that welcomes its immigrants, but feels strong ambivalence about them.

On Green Dolphin Street. Sebastian Faulks. Narrated by Steven Crossley. 11 CDs. (Running Time: 13 hrs. 15 mins.). audio compact disk 120.00 (978-1-4025-3284-9(9)) Recorded Bks.

On Green Dolphin Street. unabr. ed. Sebastian Faulks. Narrated by Steven Crossley. 9 cass. (Running Time: 13 hrs. 15 mins.). 2002. 84.00 (978-1-84197-336-4(X)) Recorded Bks.
America 1959. Mary van der Linden, wife of a British diplomat, leads a carefree life among Washington's party-loving community. But the Eisenhower era is drawing to a close, and the battle for the White House between senators John Kennedy and Richard Nixon sets a new tone across the country. Against this backdrop, Mary's dramatic involvement with journalist Frank Renzo compels her to confront the cold war realities that lurk behind the blithe facade of cocktails and jazz.

***On Hallowed Ground: the Story of Arlington National Cemetery: The Story of Arlington National Cemetery.** unabr. ed. Robert M. Poole. Read by Robert M. Poole. (Running Time: 13 hrs.). 2010. 39.97 (978-1-4418-6825-1(9), 9781441868251, Brinc Audio MP3 Lib); 24.99 (978-1-4418-6824-4(0), 9781441868244, Brilliance MP3); 39.97 (978-1-4418-6826-8(7), 9781441868268, BADLE); audio compact disk 29.99 (978-1-4418-6822-0(4), 9781441868220, Bril Audio CD Unabri); audio compact disk 99.97 (978-1-4418-6823-7(2), 9781441868237, BriAudCD Unabrid) Brilliance Audio.

On Healing & Healers. unabr. ed. Perf. by Andrew Weil & Carl A. Hammerschlag. 4 cass. (Running Time: 4 hrs. 34 min.). Dramatization. 1997. bk. 39.95 Set. (978-1-889166-17-9(0)); (978-1-889166-18-6(9)); (978-1-889166-19-3(7)); (978-1-889166-20-9(0)); (978-1-889166-21-6(9)) Turtle Isl Pr.
Fact-filled review of complementary medicine to promote healthful changes in one's life. Includes cassettes 1, 2, 3, & 4.

On Her Majesty's Secret Service. unabr. ed. Ian Fleming. Read by David Rintoul. 6 cass. (Running Time: 6 hrs.). 1993. bk. 54.95 (978-0-7451-5932-4(X), CAB 291) AudioGO.

On Her Majesty's Secret Service. unabr. ed. Ian Fleming. Read by Robert Whitfield. 6 cass. (Running Time: 8 hrs. 30 mins.). 2002. 44.95 (978-0-7861-2198-4(X), 2945); audio compact disk 56.00 (978-0-7861-9531-2(2), 2945) Blckstn Audio.
Pits Secret Agent James Bond once more against SPECTRE's archfiend, Blofeld, architect of a nefarious scheme to destroy the free world... and finds 007 falling for the lovely Tracy, daughter of Marc-Ange Draco, head of the Corsican mafia.

On Her Majesty's Secret Service. unabr. ed. Ian Fleming. Read by Simon Vance. (Running Time: 7.5 hrs. 0 mins.). (James Bond Ser.: No. 11). 2009. audio compact disk 19.95 (978-1-4332-6134-3(0)) Blckstn Audio.

On Her Majesty's Secret Service: James Bond Series #11. unabr. ed. Ian Fleming. Read by Simon Vance. (Running Time: 1 hr. 0 mins.). (ENG.). 2009. 29.95 (978-1-4332-9038-1(3)) Blckstn Audio.

On His Blindness see Palgrave's Golden Treasury of English Poetry

On His Mistress see Treasury of John Donne

On Hitching Your Wagon to a Star: Col. 2:2-63. Ed Young. (J). 1982. 4.95 (978-0-7417-1255-4(5), 255) Win Walk.

On Holiday Again, Doctor? unabr. ed. Robert Clifford. Read by Christopher Scott. 4 cass. (Running Time: 5 hrs.). (Sound Ser.). (J). 2003. 44.95 (978-1-84283-341-4(3)) Pub: ISIS Lrg Prnt GBR. Dist(s): Ulverscroft US

On Honeymoon with Death. Quintin Jardine. (Soundings (CDs) Ser.). (J). 2005. audio compact disk 79.95 (978-1-84559-091-8(0)) Pub: ISIS Lrg Prnt GBR. Dist(s): Ulverscroft US

On Honeymoon with Death. unabr. ed. Quintin Jardine. Read by Joe Dunlop. 10 cass. (Running Time: 11 hrs. 30 mins.). (Sound Ser.). (J). 2002. 84.95 (978-1-84283-218-9(2)) Pub: ISIS Lrg Prnt GBR. Dist(s): Ulverscroft US

On Humility. Swami Amar Jyoti. 2 cass. (Running Time: 3 hrs.). 1978. 12.95 (K-21) Truth Consciousness.
Growing from the humility point, we find Oneness. Humble, pure, simple as a child, a true servant of God. Ending our movie.

On Investigating a Meditation Topic. Contrib. by Hua. (978-0-88139-604-1(4)) Buddhist Text.

On Isolation Tanks. unabr. ed. John Lilly. 1 cass. (Running Time: 1 hr. 30 mins.). 1988. 9.00 (978-1-56964-769-1(0), A0304-88) Sound Photosyn.
A fascinating compilation of the inventors varied approaches to the tank.

On Judicial Opinions. Irving Younger. (978-0-943380-56-8(1)) PEG MN.

On Judicial Opinions Considered as One of the Fine Arts. Irving Younger. 1 cass. (Running Time: 45 min.). 1988. 12.95 PEG MN.

On Killing: The Psychological Cost of Learning to Kill in War & Society. unabr. ed. Lt. Dave Grossman. Read by Lt. Dave Grossman. (Running Time: 13 hrs.). (ENG.). 2009. 18.98 (978-1-60024-595-4(1)); audio compact disk 26.98 (978-1-60024-593-0(5)) Pub: Hachet Audio. Dist(s): HachBkGrp

On KPFK with Roy Tuckman. Rolling Thunder Staff. 2 cass. (Running Time: 3 hrs.). (Roy Tuckman Interview Ser.). 18.00 (A0186-82) Sound Photosyn.

On Language. Aldous Huxley. 1 cass. (Running Time: 47 min.). (MIT Cambridge Centennial Lectures, 1961). 1961. 10.00 Big Sur Tapes.

On Leadership: Great Leaders, Great Teams, & Great Results. unabr. ed. Stephen R. Covey. (Running Time: 4 hrs. 0 mins. 0 sec.). (ENG.). 2007. audio compact disk 29.95 (978-1-933976-44-0(6)) Pub: Franklin Covey. Dist(s): S and S Inc

On Learning Golf. Percy Boomer. Read by Ian Esmo. 5 cass. (Running Time: 7 hrs.). 2000. 39.95 (978-0-7861-1567-9(X), 2398) Blckstn Audio.

On Liberty. unabr. ed. John Stuart Mill. Read by Robert L. Halvorson. 4 cass. (Running Time: 6 hrs.). 28.95 (9) Halvorson Assocs.

On Liberty - Vindication of the Rights of Women: John Stuart Mill, Mary Wollstonecraft. unabr. ed. George H. Smith & Wendy McElroy. Perf. by Don Jones & Jonathan Lutz. Narrated by Craig Deitschmann. 2 cass. (Running Time: 2 hrs. 50 mins.). Dramatization. (Giants of Political Thought Ser.: Vol. 5). 1986. 17.95 (978-0-938935-05-6(4), 390282) Knowledge Prod.
Both authors were ardent defenders of individual rights. "On Liberty," was a defense of individual rights against the state. "Vindication," is considered the first declaration of women's rights. This presentation includes the essential ideas of these classic works, with a narrative explanation of the author's character, his times, the controversies he faced & the opinions of critics & supporters.

On Liberty & Vindication of the Rights of Woman. David Gordon. Read by Craig Deitschman. (Running Time: 9000 sec.). 2006. audio compact disk 25.95 (978-0-7861-6984-9(2)) Pub: Blckstn Audio. Dist(s): NetLibrary CO

On-Line Spaceman & Other Cases. unabr. ed. Seymour Simon. Narrated by Johnny Heller. 1 cass. (Running Time: 1 hr. 30 mins.). (Einstein Anderson, Science Detective Ser.: No. 8). (gr. 3 up). 1997. 10.00 (978-1-4025-0705-2(4), 96900) Recorded Bks.
Twelve-year-old Adam "Einstein" Anderson is not your average kid. He enjoys baseball, telling bad jokes and puns, and - more than anything else - mysteries. With his amazing scientific knowledge, he solves all kinds of problems. Einstein's friends and family members love to challenge him with puzzling situations. Using basic scientific principles, he quickly disproves the mystery behind an alien sighting and a monster living in the town pond. And, he finds a way to keep the class bully from winning both a cooking competition and a snowball melting contest.

On Location. BYE. (C). 2005. 23.44 (978-0-07-288676-4(5), 0072886765, ESL/ELT) Pub: McGrw-H Hghr Educ. Dist(s): McGraw

On Location. BYE. 2005. audio compact disk 36.88 (978-0-07-319485-1(9), 0073194859, ESL/ELT) Pub: McGrw-H Hghr Educ. Dist(s): McGraw

On Location: Moments with God from Around the Globe. Kurt Johnston. (Super-Ser.). 2007. audio compact disk 39.00 (978-5-557-78141-1(2)) Group Pub.

On Location Phonics Audio Cassette Program. Thomas Bye. (New to English Ser.). (ENG.). (C). 2006. 25.94 (978-0-07-319478-3(6), 0073194786, ESL/ELT) Pub: McGrw-H Hghr Educ. Dist(s): McGraw

On Location Phonics Audio CD Program. BYE. (C). 2005. audio compact disk 23.44 (978-0-07-319482-0(4), 0073194824, ESL/ELT) Pub: McGrw-H Hghr Educ. Dist(s): McGraw

On Location Phonics Audio CD Program. BYE. 2005. audio compact disk 50.63 (978-0-07-319480-6(8), 0073194808, ESL/ELT) Pub: McGrw-H Hghr Educ. Dist(s): McGraw

On Location Phonics Audio CD Program. Thomas Bye. (ENG.). (C). 2006. audio compact disk 25.94 (978-0-07-319479-0(4), 0073194794, ESL/ELT) Pub: McGrw-H Hghr Educ. Dist(s): McGraw

On Looking East to the Sea with the Sunset Behind Me see Twentieth-Century Poetry in English, No. 27, Recordings of Poets Reading Their Own Poetry

On Looking Up by Chance at the Constellation see Twentieth-Century Poetry in English, No. 6, Recordings of Poets Reading Their Own Poetry

On Looking up by Chance at the Constellations see Robert Frost in Recital

On Love. unabr. ed. Franklin Merrell-Wolff. 1 cass. (Running Time: 1 hr. 30 mins.). 1970. 11.00 (08401) Big Sur Tapes.
Discussion of the many aspects of love; the author says love alone is not enough. It needs to be balanced with wisdom & power.

***On Loving God.** St. Bernard of Clairvaux. (ENG.). 2009. audio compact disk 15.95 (978-1-936231-11-9(5)) Cath Audio.

***On Loving God.** unabr. ed. Saint Bernard of Clairvaux. Narrated by John Polhamus. (ENG.). 2005. 9.98 (978-1-59644-066-1(X), Hovel Audio) christianaud.

On Loving God. unabr. ed. St. Bernard of Clairvaux. Narrated by John Polhamus. 2 CDs. (Running Time: 2 hrs. 30 mins. 0 sec.). (ENG.). 2005. audio compact disk 15.98 (978-1-59644-067-8(8), Hovel Audio) christianaud.

On Managing. Mark H. McCormack. Narrated by Mark H. McCormack. 6 CDs. (Running Time: 6 hrs. 30 mins.). audio compact disk 58.00 (978-1-4025-0907-0(3)) Recorded Bks.

On Managing. abr. unabr. ed. Mark H. McCormack. Read by Mark H. McCormack. 4 cass. (Running Time: 6 hrs.). 2004. 25.00 (978-1-931056-09-0(9), N Millennium Audio) New Millenn Enter.
Recognizing that every manager must have a set of core beliefs, the author shares his principles for success using a no-nonsense style & numerous anecdotes.

On Maturing & Maturity. Read by T. J. Kapacinskas. 1 cass. (Running Time: 1 hr.). 1976. 9.95 (978-0-7822-0107-9(5), 019) C G Jung IL.

On Meditation. Swami Amar Jyoti. 1 cass. (Running Time: 1 hr.). 9.95 (I-1) Truth Consciousness.
What is meditation, how to do it, what blocks it? Preparing the ground for meditation. The pathless path.

On Michael Jackson. unabr. ed. Margo Jefferson. 3 cass. (Running Time: 4 hrs. 30 mins.). 2006. 28.00 (978-1-4159-2950-6(5)); audio compact disk 36.00 (978-1-4159-2951-3(3)) Books on Tape.

On Mind & Mindlessness. Swami Amar Jyoti. 1 cass. (Running Time: 1 hr.). 1987. 9.95 (J-54) Truth Consciousness.
Mind is a 'drunken monkey bitten by scorpions.' The classical ways to stability, focus & peace. The final blueprint, conscious being in His drama.

On My Honor. Marion Dane Bauer. Read by Eric Conger. 2 cass. (Running Time: 1 hr. 57 mins.). (J). 2000. 18.00 (978-0-7366-5012-0(1)) Books on Tape.
Two boys whose friendship results in a drowning.

On My Honor. Marion Dane Bauer. Narrated by Johnny Heller. 2 CDs. (Running Time: 2 hrs.). (gr. 5 up). audio compact disk 22.00 (978-1-4025-0460-0(8)) Recorded Bks.

On My Honor. unabr. ed. Marion Dane Bauer. Read by Eric Conger. 2 vols. (Running Time: 1 hr. 56 mins.). Dramatization. (J). (gr. 5-9). 1992. pap. bk. 29.00 (978-0-8072-7370-8(8), YA 839 SP, Listening Lib); 23.00 (978-0-8072-7369-2(4), YA839CX, Listening Lib) Random Audio Pubg.
The riveting story of two boys whose friendship is abruptly cut short when one drowns swimming in a forbidden river. A Newbery Honor book.

On My Honor, unabr. ed. Marion Dane Bauer. Narrated by Johnny Heller. 2 pieces. (Running Time: 2 hrs.). (gr. 5 up). 1998. 19.00 (978-0-7887-2072-7(4), 95425E7) Recorded Bks.
On the way to Starved Rock State Park, 7th-graders Joel & his best friend decide to cool off in a raging river, which is a fatal mistake.

On My Honor. unabr. ed. Marion Dane Bauer. Narrated by Johnny Heller. 2005. 17.95 (978-0-7887-7145-3(0)) Recorded Bks.

On My Honor, Set. unabr. ed. Marion Dane Bauer. Read by Eric Conger. 2 cass. (YA). 1999. 16.98 (FS9-34154) Highsmith.

On My Own: The Journey Continues. unabr. ed. 3 cass. (Running Time: 4 hrs.). 2004. 28.00 (978-1-4025-1478-4(6)) Recorded Bks.
Sally Hobart Alexander continues the story of her journey into blindness in this uplifting tale of a life rebuilt and love renewed. Suzanne Toren¿s perceptive narration perfectly expresses the emotions of Sally¿s sometimes fun, often arduous, and always interesting journey.

On My Own at 107: Reflections on Life Without Bessie. Sarah L. Delany. Read by Gloria Foster. 2 cass. (Running Time: 2 hrs. 30 mins.). 2000. (978-0-694-51856-2(5), 395156) HarperCollins Pubs.
The Delany sisters told their remarkable story in "Having Our Say." Bessie Delany died in 1995 & here her sister shares her experience of living alone after their century-long relationship.

On My Way. unabr. ed. Tomie dePaola. 1 cass. (Running Time: 40 mins.). (Fairmount Avenue Ser.: Vol. 3). (J). (gr. 2-5). 2004. pap. bk. 17.00 (978-0-8072-0656-0(3), LFTR 247 SP, Listening Lib) Random Audio Pubg.
These writing and recollective skills are so fresh that kids will feel like he's sitting right next to them, telling his tales in and out of school with disarming charisma and not a hint of nostalgia.

On Mystic Lake. abr. ed. Kristin Hannah. Read by Susan Ericksen. (Running Time: 3 hrs.). 2010. audio compact disk 9.99 (978-1-4418-4514-6(3), 9781441845146, BCD Value Price) Brilliance Audio.

On Mystic Lake, abr. ed. Kristin Hannah. Read by Susan Ericksen. 2 cass. (Running Time: 3 hrs.). 1999. 17.95 (FS9-43371) Highsmith.

On Mystic Lake. unabr. ed. Kristin Hannah. Read by Susan Ericksen. (Running Time: 10 hrs.). 2010. 24.99 (978-1-4418-4495-8(3), 9781441844958, Brilliance MP3); 39.97 (978-1-4418-4497-2(X), 9781441844972, Brlnc Audio MP3 Lib); 39.97 (978-1-4418-4500-9(3), 9781441845009, BADLE); 24.99 (978-1-4418-4498-9(8), 9781441844989, BAD); audio compact disk 29.99 (978-1-4418-4492-7(9), 9781441844927, Bril Audio CD Unabri); audio compact disk 89.97 (978-1-4418-4493-4(7), 9781441844934, BriAudCD Unabrid) Brilliance Audio.

On Native Grounds Pt. 1: An Interpretation of Modern American Prose Literature. unabr. ed. Alfred Kazin. Read by Michael Prichard. 8 cass. (Running Time: 12 hrs.). 1987. 64.00 (978-0-7366-1178-7(9), 2099-A) Books on Tape.
Alfred Kazin is a gifted scholar, author & teacher. He made his reputation with literary criticism that upset tradition. His focus: American authors & their birthright.

On Native Grounds Pt. 2: An Interrpetation of Modern American Prose Literature. Alfred Kazin. Read by Michael Prichard. 8 cass. (Running Time: 12 hrs.). 1987. 64.00 (2099-B) Books on Tape.

On Navaha Shivaya. Perf. by Robert Gass. 1 cass. (Running Time: 1 hr. 30 min.). 1996. (978-1-891319-16-7(7)); audio compact disk 15.98 (978-1-891319-15-0(9)) Spring Hill CO.

On Ne Peut Pas Etre Heureux. l.t. ed. Francoise Giroud. (French Ser.). 2001. bk. 30.99 (978-2-84011-416-1(X)) Pub: UlverLrgPrint GBR. Dist(s): Ulverscroft US

On Negotiating. Mark H. McCormack. Narrated by Mark H. McCormack. 4 cass. (Running Time: 6 hrs.). 45.00 (978-1-4025-0905-6(7)); audio compact disk 54.00 (978-1-4025-1156-1(6)) Recorded Bks.

On Negotiating. abr. unabr. ed. Mark H. McCormack. Read by Mark H. McCormack. 4 cass. (Running Time: 6 hrs.). 2004. 25.00 (978-1-931056-10-6(2), N Millennium Audio) New Millenn Enter.
The author provides information that may be new even to a negotiator: features of win/win negotiation; the most effective negotiating tactics & how to reconcile different negotiating styles when they collide.

On Nineteen Eighty-Four. unabr. collector's ed. Peter Stansky. Read by Michael Prichard. 8 cass. (Running Time: 12 hrs.). (Portable Stanford Ser.). 1998. 64.00 (978-0-7366-0969-2(5), 1911) Books on Tape.
Appraisal of the book that defined our age.

***On Nuclear Terrorism.** unabr. ed. Michael Levi. (Running Time: 7.5 hrs. NaN mins.). (ENG.). 2010. 29.95 (978-1-4417-7851-2(9)); audio compact disk 24.95 (978-1-4417-7850-5(0)) Blckstn Audio.

***On Nuclear Terrorism.** unabr. ed. Michael Levi. Read by To be Announced. (Running Time: 7.5 hrs. NaN mins.). (ENG.). 2010. 54.95 (978-1-4417-7848-2(9)); audio compact disk 69.00 (978-1-4417-7849-9(7)) Blckstn Audio.

On Nutrition. Andrew Weil. 1 cass. (Running Time: 1 hr.). 1976. 11.00 (3614) Big Sur Tapes.
No two bodies are the same & even the same person may require different diets at different times in his life. Your own body will tell you what nutrients it needs if you pay attention to your food cravings. Nature has devised a complex feedback system in the foods we eat, so that the subtle mix of flavors found in a particular substance will only really taste good if we need those particular nutrients. Unfortunately, our civilized custom of separating out the most taste-gratifying part of the food (butter from milk, white sugar from sugar cane, etc.) overrides this natural feedback system & we end up getting too much of a good thing.

On, Off. unabr. ed. Colleen McCullough. Narrated by Lewis Grenville. 9 cass. (Running Time: 45420 sec.). (Carmine Delmonico Novel Ser.: No. 1). 2006. 79.95 (978-0-7927-4231-9(1), Chivers Sound Lib); audio compact disk 99.95 (978-0-7927-4054-4(8), Chivers Sound Lib); audio compact disk 49.95 (978-0-7927-4232-6(X), Chivers Sound Lib) AudioGO.

On Our Selection. unabr. ed. Steele Rudd. Read by Peter Hosking. 4 cass. (Running Time: 6 hrs.). 1999. (978-1-86442-321-1(8), 590481) Bolinda Pubng AUS.
About the selection on the Darling Downs in Queensland where Dad, Mother, Dave & the rest of the family nearly starve & eventually prosper. He meant them as a tribute to small selectors like his own family. In a broadcast late in his life he said he wanted "to tell faithfully all I knew of the life our family & neighboring families had lived.".

On Our Way to Somewhere. Scripts. Molly Larson Cook. Perf. by Molly Larson Cook. 1. (Running Time: 1 hour). Dramatization. 2002. audio compact disk 14.00 (978-0-9724468-1-5(8)) Blue Finch Pr.
Reading performance of one-woman comedy drama comprising four monologues in which contemporary women confront their changing roles as mothers, daughters, wives, and independent women. For each of them, the experience of moving becomes a metaphor for the often surprising detours on the highway of the heart.

On Possession. Ruth-Inge Heinze. 1 cass. (Running Time: 1 hr.). 9.00 (A0453-87) Sound Photosyn.
Address at the Psychical Research Society in Berkeley.

On Practical Spirituality. Read by Marianne Williamson. 5 cass. (Running Time: 5 hrs.). 1999. 59.95 (83-0039) Explorations.
Live seminar in which Williamson, author & lecturer on spirituality & new thought, covers the casual power of prayer, the magnetic theory of relationships, how your secret desires shape your existence & more.

On Purity. Swami Amar Jyoti. 1 cass. (Running Time: 1 hr.). 1978. 9.95 (P-19) Truth Consciousness.
The essential meaning of purity on its three levels. Leaving our limited space. The highest fulfillment of earth life.

On Re-Reading Bleak House. (23294-A) J Norton Pubs.

On Reading Poetry Aloud see Evening with Dylan Thomas

On Relationships. Ole Nydahl. 2 cass. (Running Time: 3 hrs.). 18.00 (A0271-88) Sound Photosyn.

On Relaxation. Swami Amar Jyoti. 1 cass. (Running Time: 1 hr.). 1978. 9.95 (P-23) Truth Consciousness.
What is true relaxation of the body, vital & mind? The principles & purpose of retreat. Exposing ourselves to ourselves.

On Returning to a Lake in Spring see Richard Eberhart Reading His Poetry

On Robinson Jeffers' Poetry. Robinson Jeffers. Read by Robert Brophy. 1 cass. (Running Time: 50 min.). 1969. 11.00 (06102) Big Sur Tapes.
Representing Jeffers as a philosopher-mystic, Brophy comments and reads from some of the themes which Jeffers developed. Among them are: Is there a God? Is there anything left after death other than worm's meat? How should men live.

***On Second Thought: Outsmarting Your Mind's Hard-Wired Habits.** unabr. ed. Wray Herbert. (Running Time: 11 hrs. 0 mins.). 2010. 17.99 (978-1-4001-8838-3(5)); 24.99 (978-1-4001-6838-5(4)) Pub: Tantor Media. Dist(s): IngramPubServ

***On Second Thought: Outsmarting Your Mind's Hard-Wired Habits.** unabr. ed. Wray Herbert. Narrated by Dan Miller. (Running Time: 8 hrs. 30 mins. 0 sec.). 2010. audio compact disk 34.99 (978-1-4001-1838-0(7)); audio compact disk 83.99 (978-1-4001-4838-7(3)) Pub: Tantor Media. Dist(s): IngramPubServ

***On Second Thought (Library Edition) Outsmarting Your Mind's Hard-Wired Habits.** unabr. ed. Wray Herbert. (Running Time: 11 hrs. 0 mins.). 2010. 34.99 (978-1-4001-9838-2(0)) Tantor Media.

On Secret Service. collector's unabr. ed. John Jakes. Read by Michael Kramer. 12 cass. (Running Time: 18 hrs.). 2000. 96.00 (978-0-7366-5516-3(6), 5356) Books on Tape.
Two great American dynasties are torn apart by the storm of events surrounding the Civil War.

On Secret Service. unabr. ed. John Jakes. 12 cass. (Running Time: 18 hrs.). 2000. 34.95 (978-0-7366-4931-5(X)) Books on Tape.
The story of a war within a war on various levels the North v. the South, the Union's Pinkerton Detective Agency v. the Confederacy's agent provocateurs, youthful idealism v. youthful lust - On Secret Service chronicles the lives & times of four young Americans.

On Secret Service. unabr. collector's ed. John Jakes. Read by Michael Kramer. 14 hrs. (Running Time: 16 hrs. 24 mins.). 2000. audio compact disk 112.00 (978-0-7366-6073-0(9)) Books on Tape.
Two great American dynasties are torn apart by the storm of events surrounding the Civil War.

On Secular Education AudioBook. R. L. Dabney. Read by Aaron Wells. Ed. by Douglas Wilson. (ENG.). 2007. audio compact disk 10.00 (978-1-59128-212-9(8)) Canon Pr ID.

On Self-Esteem. Gloria Steinem. 2 cass. (Running Time: 2 hrs.). 1995. 16.95 (978-1-879323-15-5(X)) Sound Horizons AV.
On this extraordinary audio program the bestselling author of Revolution from Within makes visible the interconnectedness between self-esteem, sexism, racism & politics.

On Selling. Mark H. McCormack. Narrated by Mark H. McCormack. 4 cass. (Running Time: 6 hrs.). 45.00 (978-1-4025-0906-3(5)); audio compact disk 54.00 (978-1-4025-1157-8(4)) Recorded Bks.

On Selling. abr. unabr. ed. Mark H. McCormack. Read by Mark H. McCormack. 4 cass. (Running Time: 6 hrs.). 2004. 25.00 (978-1-931056-11-3(0), N Millennium Audio) New Millenn Enter.
Drawing on his extraordinary success managing athletes & performers, the author spells out the basics of salesmanship & the steps every salesperson, from confused novice to seasoned professional, must master.

On Shakespeare see Poetry of John Milton

On Silence see Twentieth-Century Poetry in English, No. 28, Recordings of Poets Reading Their Own Poetry

On Solid Ground: Correct Foundations. 1 cass. (Running Time: 50 min.). Dramatization. (Adventures in Odyssey Ser.). (J). (gr. 3-7). 5.99 (CC111) Focus Family.
Whit & the gang at Kid's Radio give up-to-the-minute news reports about Abraham, Lot & a city called Sodom.

On Something's Happening! Faustin Bray & Brian Wallace. 1 cass. (Running Time: 1 hr. 30 mins.). (Roy Tuckman Interview Ser.). 9.00 (A0725-84) Sound Photosyn.
Roy meets F & B for the first time, launching a nefarious partnership.

On Something's Happening! Sufi T. Fernandez. 1 cass. (Running Time: 1 hr. 30 mins.). (Roy Tuckman Interview Ser.). 9.00 (A0455-89) Sound Photosyn.

On Something's Happening! Stephen Gaskin & Ina M. Gaskin. 1 cass. (Running Time: 1 hr. 30 mins.). (Roy Tuckman Interview Ser.). 9.00 (A0727-90) Sound Photosyn.
Stephen & Ina May talk about their experiences on The Farm & in their travels.

On Something's Happening! Oscar Janiger. 1 cass. (Running Time: 1 hr. 30 mins.). (Roy Tuckman Interview Ser.). 9.00 (A0448-86) Sound Photosyn.
The well known L.A. psychiatrist/experimentalist.

On Something's Happening! Jon Klimo. 3 cass. (Running Time: 1 hr. 30 mins.). (Roy Tuckman Interview Ser.). 27.00 Set. (A0417-89) Sound Photosyn.

On Something's Happening! Timothy Leary. 1 cass. (Running Time: 1 hr. 30 mins.). (Roy Tuckman Interview Ser.). 9.00 (A0283-87) Sound Photosyn.

On Something's Happening! Terence McKenna. 2 cass. (Running Time: 3 hrs.). (Roy Tuckman Interview Ser.). 18.00 Set. (A0281-88) Sound Photosyn.

On Something's Happening! Ole Nydahl. 2 cass. (Running Time: 3 hrs.). (Roy Tuckman Interview Ser.). 18.00 set. (A0632-90) Sound Photosyn.
Danish born Tibetan Buddhist Lama Ole Nydahl talks about his history from hippie smuggler to Tibetan Lama. He discusses Tibetan views of spirituality & practice, of interest to both beginners & advanced. The phones are opened to everyone, from Fundamental Xtians & advanced meditators, to an angry feminist who puts him to a stiff test.

On Something's Happening! Rupert Sheldrake & Terence McKenna. 2 cass. (Running Time: 3 hrs.). (Roy Tuckman Interview Ser.). 18.00 (A0131-87) Sound Photosyn.

On Something's Happening! Colin Wilson. 1 cass. (Roy Tuckman Interview Ser.). 9.00 (A0728-90) Sound Photosyn.
Subjects include Buddhism, panic attacks, raising consciousness, psychedelics, & a Laurel & Hardy model of consciousness & boredom.

On Something's Happening! Robert A. Wilson. 1 cass. (Running Time: 1 hr. 30 mins.). (Roy Tuckman Interview Ser.). 9.00 (A0280-88) Sound Photosyn.

On Something's Happening! World Research Foundation Staff. 2 cass. (Running Time: 3 hrs.). (Roy Tuckman Interview Ser.). 18.00 (A0483-89) Sound Photosyn.

On St. Theresa'a Difficulty in Keeping Her Feet On the Ground see Twentieth-Century Poetry in English, No. 28, Recordings of Poets Reading Their Own Poetry

***On Stranger Tides.** unabr. ed. Tim Powers. (Running Time: 13 hrs. 0 mins.). 2010. 29.95 (978-1-4417-5499-8(7)); 79.95 (978-1-4417-5495-0(4)); audio compact disk 32.95 (978-1-4417-5498-1(9)); audio compact disk 109.00 (978-1-4417-5496-7(2)) Blckstn Audio.

On Strategy. unabr. collector's ed. Harry G. Summers, Jr. Read by John MacDonald. 7 cass. (Running Time: 7 hrs.). 1987. 42.00 (978-0-7366-1099-5(5), 2025) Books on Tape.
What went wrong in Vietnam? Applying the principles of war to the way we fought there, the author illustrates why our effort was such a disaster. Some fatal errors: failure to learn form the Korean experience. Surrendering the initiative to the enemy. No comprehension of internal vietnamese problems. Failure to discern how North Vietnam cloaked its real objectives behind a much inflated insurgency.

On Strike! the Story of Cesar Chavez. Alan Venable. (Step into History Ser.). 2000. audio compact disk 18.95 (978-1-4105-0146-2(9)) D Johnston Inc.

On Strike! The Story of Cesar Chavez, Vol. 5. Alan Venable. Ed. by Jerry Stemach et al. Illus. by Bob Stotts. Narrated by Jos Saro Sol s. Contrib. by Ted S. Hasselbring. (Start-to-Finish Books). (J). (gr. 2-3). 2000. 35.00 (978-1-58702-474-0(8)) D Johnston Inc.

On Strike! The Story of Cesar Chavez, Vol. 5. unabr. ed. Alan Venable. Ed. by Jerry Stemach et al. Illus. by Bob Stotts. Narrated by Jos Saro Sol s. Contrib. by Ted S. Hasselbring. 1 cass. (Running Time: 1 hr.). (Start-to-Finish Books). (J). (gr. 2-3). 2000. (978-1-893376-97-7(4), F19K2) D Johnston Inc.

On Success. Earl Nightingale. 6 cass. (Running Time: 6 hrs.). 1995. 59.95 (8761A) Nightingale-Conant.

On Suffering. Swami Amar Jyoti. 1 cass. (Running Time: 1 hr. 30 mins.). 1977. 9.95 (K-7) Truth Consciousness.
Why is there suffering in God's creation? Getting attached to the relativity. The purification process.

On Sufism. Robert Ornstein. 2 cass. (Running Time: 3 hrs.). 1999. 18.00 (01803) Big Sur Tapes.

On Sundays We Wore White. unabr. ed. Eileen Elias. Read by Diana Bishop. 8 cass. (Running Time: 12 hrs.). 1995. 69.95 (978-1-85496-989-7(7), 29897) Pub: Soundings Ltd GBR. Dist(s): Ulverscroft US
Eileen Elias re-creates family life between the years 1910 & 1920, a life that today seems like a different world. It is a story of a home, bound by the convention of its time, when father knew best & on Sundays, little girls wore white; when people believed that there would be peace forever. Then the Great War changed everything, especially for a child.

On Taking the Fifth Amendment: Jeremiah 15:10. Ed Young. (J). 1981. 4.95 (978-0-7417-1164-9(8), A0164) Win Walk.

On Target for the TOEIC. Lin Lougheed. 2 cass. (Running Time: 1 hr. 20 mins.). (A-W Japan Ser.). 1990. 20.00 ea. AddisonWesley.

On Target: Spanish for Restaurant Owners & Managers. Frank Nuessel. (On Target Audio CD Packages Ser.). (SPA & ENG.). 2009. audio compact disk 10.99 (978-0-7641-9642-3(1)) Barron.

On That Day. Scott Soper. 1997. 10.95 (395); audio compact disk 15.95 (395) GIA Pubns.

On the Air Audio Sampler: Listening to Radio Talk. Catherine Sadow & Edgar Sather. 1 cass. (Running Time: 1 hr.). Cambridge U Pr.
Captures students' attention by using authentic and provocative radio programs from National Public Radio and WRKO, Boston. Topics range from an interview with astronaut Alan Shepard to a lively discussion of parking in Tokyo, to an interview with former president Jimmy Carter discussing his poetry.

On the Anvil: Being Shaped into God's Image. abr. ed. Max Lucado. Read by Mike Kellogg. 2 cass. (Running Time: 3 hrs.). 2004. 11.99 (978-1-58926-672-8(2)) Oasis Audio.
"In this collection of writings, well-loved author Max Lucado will take a tour of the "shop." We are all somewhere in the craftman's shop. Some are waiting to fulfill their purpose while others are on the anvil being melted down and changed into something useful through a painful process. Where are you in the shop? Are you available and ready to be used by the Master?".

On the Anvil: Being Shaped into God's Image. abr. ed. Max Lucado. Narrated by Mike Kellogg. (ENG.). 2004. 10.49 (978-1-60814-328-3(7)); audio compact disk 14.99 (978-1-58926-673-5(0)) Oasis Audio.

On the Banks of Plum Creek. abr. ed. Laura Ingalls Wilder. Read by Cherry Jones. 4. (Running Time: 3 Hours 30 minutes). (J). 2003. audio compact disk 25.99 (978-0-06-054400-3(7), Access) HarperCollins Pubs.

On the Banks of Plum Creek. unabr. abr. ed. Laura Ingalls Wilder. Read by Cherry Jones. 3 cass. (Running Time: 4 hrs. 30 mins.). (Little House Ser.). (J). 2003. 22.00 (978-0-06-001243-4(9)) HarperCollins Pubs.

On the Beach. unabr. ed. Nevil Shute. Read by James Smillie. 8 cass. (Running Time: 12 hrs.). 2000. 59.95 (978-0-7451-6281-2(9), CAB 376) Pub: Chivers Audio Bks GBR. Dist(s): AudioGO
The planet is dying. Massive nuclear exchanges in the northern hemisphere have created clouds of radioactive dust that are sweeping south. Soon they will reach Australia where the last civilized life awaits doomsday.

On the Beach. unabr. ed. Nevil Shute. Narrated by Simon Prebble. 7 cass. (Running Time: 9 hrs. 30 mins.). 1991. 60.00 (978-1-55690-391-5(X), 91127E7) Recorded Bks.
The unthinkable has occurred - nuclear war is devastating the planet. In Australia survivors face a limited future.

On the Beach. unabr. collector's ed. Nevil Shute. Read by Richard Green. 8 cass. (Running Time: 8 hrs.). 1979. 48.00 (978-0-7366-0181-8(3), 1183) Books on Tape.
The time is 1963. China & Russia have engaged in an all-out nuclear war against each other. The fighting actually begins in Albania, spreads to Tel Aviv, prompting Egypt to unleash a direct assault on London & Washington. The result of this military activity is the total destruction of all life in the northern hemisphere. This is the story of the last survivors.

On the Beach in Spanish Room. Janis Spence. Read by Janis Spence. (Running Time: 14400 sec.). 2003. audio compact disk 29.95 (978-0-9734223-0-6(0)) Rattling Bks CAN.

On the Big Blackfoot: Readings, Interviews & Reflections. Norman MacLean. Told to John MacLean. (Playaway Adult Nonfiction Ser.). (ENG.). 2009. 34.99 (978-1-60775-722-1(2)) Find a World.

On the Big Blackfoot: Readings, Interviews & Reflections. Norman F. Maclean. 1 cass. (Running Time: 1 hr.). 1996. 10.95 (978-0-939643-64-6(2)) Audio Pr.
Norman MacLean's profound understanding of the human experience and man's connectedness to nature was inspired by the Big Blackfoot River where he spent his formative years. This moving audio retrospective is a portrait of the river's influence on MacLean's life and his relationship with it. Through archival readings and interviews with MacLean, interwoven with recollections by his son, John, we are given insight into the man whose wisdom has left an indelible impression on our generation.

On the Black Hill. unabr. ed. Bruce Chatwin. Read by Justin Hecht. 6 cass. (Running Time: 9 hrs.). 48.00 (978-0-7366-1039-1(1), 1969) Books on Tape.
Lewis & Benjamin Jones, identical twins, farm the Vision, a property in the Welsh Borders, with the green fields of England on one side & the black hills of Wales on the other. This is the story of their intertwined double drama & how they sense the salvation that is theirs in the "abiding city on the hill".

***On the Blue Comet.** unabr. ed. Rosemary Wells. (Running Time: 6 hrs.). 2010. 39.97 (978-1-4418-8951-5(5), 9781441889515, Candlewick Bril); 19.99 (978-1-4418-8950-8(7), 9781441889508, Candlewick Bril) Brilliance Audio.

***On the Blue Comet.** unabr. ed. Rosemary Wells. Read by Malcolm Hillgartner. 1 MP3-CD. (Running Time: 6 hrs.). 2010. audio compact disk 19.99 (978-1-4418-8948-5(5), 9781441889485, Candlewick Bril); audio compact disk 24.99 (978-1-4418-8946-1(9), 9781441889461, Candlewick Bril); audio compact disk 39.97 (978-1-4418-8949-2(3), 9781441889492, Candlewick Bril); audio compact disk 54.97 (978-1-4418-8947-8(7), 9781441889478, Candlewick Bril) Brilliance Audio.

On the Bright Side, I'm Now the Girlfriend of a Sex God: Further Confessions of Georgia Nicolson. Louise Rennison. 3 cass. (Running Time: 3 hrs. 30 min.). (Confessions of Georgia Nicolson Ser.: No. 2). 2003. 22.00 (978-0-06-052622-1(X)) Pub: HarperCollins Pubs. Dist(s): HarpCollins

On the Bright Side, I'm Now the Girlfriend of a Sex God: Further Confessions of Georgia Nicolson. Louise Rennison. Narrated by Stina Nielsen. (Confessions of Georgia Nicolson Ser.: No. 2). (YA). 2001. 37.00 (978-1-4025-0709-0(7), 96931) Recorded Bks.
Intrepid 14-year-old heroine Georgia Nicolson finally snags herself a Sex God. Now everything is fabbity-fab-fab in Georgia's world, until she gets dumped. it's time to pull every trick out of the bag to win back her beloved Robbie.

On the Bright Side, I'm Now the Girlfriend of a Sex God: Further Confessions of Georgia Nicolson. Louise Rennison. Narrated by Stina Nielsen. 5 CDs. (Running Time: 5 hrs. 15 mins.). (Confessions of Georgia Nicolson Ser.: No. 2). (gr. 8 up). 2001. audio compact disk 48.00 (978-1-4025-1488-3(3), C1613) Recorded Bks.

On the Bright Side, I'm Now the Girlfriend of a Sex God: Further Confessions of Georgia Nicolson. Louise Rennison & Louise Rennison. 3 cass. (Running Time: 5 hrs. 15 mins.). (Confessions of Georgia Nicolson Ser.: No. 2). 2004. 14.99 (978-1-4025-0865-3(4), 70024) Recorded Bks.

On the Bright Side, I'm Now the Girlfriend of a Sex God: Further Confessions of Georgia Nicolson. unabr. ed. Louise Rennison. Narrated by Stina Nielsen. 4 pieces. (Running Time: 5 hrs. 15 mins.). (Confessions of Georgia Nicolson Ser.: No. 2). (gr. 8 up). 2001. 37.00 (978-0-7887-9496-4(5)) Recorded Bks.
Fourteen-year-old British schoolgirl Georgia Nicolson is now dating the Sex God - also known as Robbie - and things couldn't be any more fab. When they snog, life is marvy and gorgey and all that stuff. But then Georgia gets dumped because she's too young. Robbie admits she's a great kid, but thinks she might be more interested in his mate Dave, who is "a good laugh." To lure the Sex God back, Georgia decides to give Dave a go. She hopes that when Robbie sees her with another bloke, he'll go mad jealous and come running back to her.

On the Brink: Inside the Race to Stop the Collapse of the Global Financial System. unabr. ed. Read by Henry M. Paulson & Dan Woren. Created by Henry M. Paulson. (Running Time: 15 hrs.). (ENG.). 2010. 24.98 (978-1-60024-914-3(0)) Pub: Hachet Audio. Dist(s): HachBkGrp

On the Brink: Inside the Race to Stop the Collapse of the Global Financial System. unabr. ed. Read by Dan Woren. Illus. by Henry M. Paulson. 13 CDs. (Running Time: 15 hrs.). (ENG.). 2010. audio compact disk 34.98 (978-1-60024-912-9(4)) Pub: Hachet Audio. Dist(s): HachBkGrp

On the Brink of Divorce (Falling in Love Again) Mark 10:2-12, 729. Ed Young. 1989. 4.95 (978-0-7417-1729-0(8), 729) Win Walk.

On the Brink of Total Freedom: When You Are No Longer Willing to Postpone Your Own Happiness. abr. ed. Scott Morrison. 1 cass. (Running Time: 1 hr.). 1998. 7.50 (978-1-882496-23-5(X)) Twnty Frst Cntry Ren.
To be enlightened is to be unconditionally open & ready for what is.

On the Course with... Tiger Woods. unabr. ed. Matt Christopher. Narrated by J. D. Jackson. 2 pieces. (Running Time: 2 hrs. 45 mins.). (gr. 4 up). 2002. 19.00 (978-1-4025-0774-8(7)) Recorded Bks.

On the Court with... Andre Agassi. unabr. ed. Matt Christopher. Narrated by Richard M. Davidson. 2 cass. (Running Time: 2 hrs. 45 mins.). (gr. 4 up). 1997. 20.00 (978-0-7887-2220-2(4), 95519E7) Recorded Bks.
An inside look at one of the top tennis players in the world.

On the Court with... Grant Hill. unabr. ed. Matt Christopher. Read by Richard M. Davidson. 2 cass. (Running Time: 2 hr. 30 min.). (J). (gr. 4). 1998. 31.75 (978-0-7887-2012-3(0), 40667); 84.80 CLASS SET . (978-0-7887-2444-2(4), 46685) Recorded Bks.
In this exciting biography, the number one children's sports writer in America, puts listeners on the basketball court with the Detroit Pistons.

On the Court with... Grant Hill. unabr. ed. Matt Christopher & Richard M. Davidson. 2 pieces. (Running Time: 2 hrs. 30 mins.). (gr. 4 up). 1998. 19.00 (978-0-7887-1121-3(0), 95115E7) Recorded Bks.
Biography of one of the best role models in professional sports.

On the Court with... Kobe Bryant. unabr. ed. Matt Christopher. Narrated by Ramon de Ocampo. 2 pieces. (Running Time: 2 hrs. 15 mins.). (gr. 4 up). 2002. 19.00 (978-1-4025-0770-0(4)) Recorded Bks.
Basketball great Kobe Bryant may be the youngest player ever to start in an NBA game, but in terms of hard work and determination, few can match his experience. After leading his team to a state championship his senior year, he was voted the nation's best high school player. But even greater challenges awaited the phenomenal young star.

On the Court with... Michael Jordan. unabr. ed. Matt Christopher. Narrated by Richard M. Davidson. 3 pieces. (Running Time: 3 hrs.). (gr. 4 up). 1997. 27.00 (978-0-7887-0794-0(9), 94944E7) Recorded Bks.
Puts you on the basketball court with the Chicago Bulls superstar.

On the Day You Were Born. Debra Frasier. Contrib. by Matthew Smith. Music by Matthew Smith. 1 cass. (Running Time: 26 min.). (J). (ps). 1992. pap. bk. 20.00 (978-0-15-257996-8(6)) Harcourt CAN CAN.
Offering a story that puts a child's birth in universal perspective, this tape is one of the few in the small New Age-for-kids category that is well produced. Although it includes the text of Frasier's 1991 book, the tape is mostly music - an odd amalgam of space-age instrumentals & traditional round that incorporates bells, whistles & synthesizers with rhythms that can be used for clapping & singing along.

On the Day You Were Born. Debra Frasier. Music by Matthew Smith. 1 cass. (Running Time: 26 min.). (J). (ps-3). 1992. 8.00 (978-0-15-257997-5(4)) Harcourt CAN CAN.

On the Democratic Idea in America. unabr. ed. Irving Kristol. Read by Phillip J. Sawtelle. 4 cass. (Running Time: 5 hrs. 30 mins.). 1989. 32.95 (978-0-7861-0062-0(1), 1059) Blckstn Audio.
This is a collection of essays published in the 1970's. Although they were composed for different occasions, they all relate to one common concern: "the tendency of democratic republics to depart from - to progress away from one might say - their original animating principles & as a consequence, to precipitate grave crisis in the moral & political order.".

On the Democratic Idea in America. unabr. ed. Irving Kristol. Read by Michael Prichard. 5 cass. (Running Time: 5 hrs.). 1976. 30.00 (978-0-7366-0003-3(5), 1013) Books on Tape.
By calling for a return to ideas & policies more central to the American experience, Mr. Kristol became one of those who helped engineer the Reagan landslide of 1980. This explosion of his views is important, because it makes us consider which direction we want the country to travel & the best means of steering her through the murky future that lies ahead.

On the Divinity of Second Chances. unabr. ed. Kaya McLaren. Read by Kirsten Potter. Contrib. by Arthur Morey et al. (Running Time: 9 hrs.). (ENG.). (gr. 12 up). 2009. audio compact disk 29.95 (978-0-14-314471-7(5), PengAudBks) Penguin Grp USA.

On the Edge see Philip Levine

***On the Edge.** unabr. ed. Ilona Andrews. Narrated by Renée Raudman. (Running Time: 12 hrs. 0 mins. 0 sec.). (Edge Ser.). (ENG.). 2009. 24.99 (978-1-4001-6290-1(4)); 17.99 (978-1-4001-8290-9(5)); audio compact disk 34.99 (978-1-4001-1290-6(7)); audio compact disk 69.99 (978-1-4001-4290-3(3)) Pub: Tantor Media. Dist(s): IngramPubServ

On the Edge: In Your Dreams. Henry Billings. (ENG.). 2003. 24.27 (978-0-07-704353-7(7), 0077043537); 33.32 (978-0-07-704349-0(9), 0077043499) Pub: M-H Contemporary. Dist(s): McGraw

On the Edge: Out of the Blue. Henry Billings. (ENG.). 2003. 32.36 (978-0-07-704367-4(7), 0077043677) Pub: M-H Contemporary. Dist(s): McGraw

On the Edge: They Walk among Us. Henry Billings. (ENG.). 2003. 32.36 (978-0-07-704360-5(X), 007704360X); 33.32 (978-0-07-704356-8(1), 0077043561) Pub: M-H Contemporary. Dist(s): McGraw

On the Edge of Darkness. unabr. ed. Barbara Erskine. Read by Sally Armstrong. 16 cass. (Running Time: 24 hrs.). (Isis Ser.). (J). 1999. 104.95 (978-0-7531-0574-0(8), 990513) Pub: ISIS Lrg Prnt GBR. Dist(s): Ulverscroft US
A story of a woman trapped in the wrong time, & a deadly curse that haunts three generations.

***On the Edge of Survival.** unabr. ed. Spike Walker. (Running Time: 6 hrs. 30 mins.). 2010. 14.99 (978-1-4001-8905-2(5)); 19.99 (978-1-4001-6905-4(4)); audio compact disk 29.99 (978-1-4001-1905-9(7)) Pub: Tantor Media. Dist(s): IngramPubServ

***On the Edge of Survival (Library Edition) A Shipwreck, a Raging Storm, & the Harrowing Alaskan Rescue That Became a Legend.** unabr. ed. Spike Walker. (Running Time: 6 hrs. 30 mins.). 2010. 29.99 (978-1-4001-9905-1(0)); audio compact disk 71.99 (978-1-4001-4905-6(3)) Pub: Tantor Media. Dist(s): IngramPubServ

On the Edge of the Hudson. Laura Boss. Ed. by Stanley H. Barkan. (Review Women Writers Chapbook Ser.: No. 4).Tr. of Na Bregovite na Xadson. 1989. 10.00 (978-0-89304-419-0(9)) Cross-Cultrl NY.

On the Edge of the Sea of Darkness: Adventure. Peril. Lost Jewels. & the Fearsome Toothy Cows of Skree. unabr. ed. Andrew Peterson. Narrated by Peter Sandon. (Wingfeather Saga Ser.). (ENG.). 2008. 18.19 (978-1-60814-329-0(5)); audio compact disk 25.99 (978-1-59859-352-5(8)) Oasis Audio.

On the English Language see Fourteen American Masterpieces

On the Far Side of the Mountain. unabr. ed. Jean Craighead George. Narrated by Jeff Woodman. 3 pieces. (Running Time: 4 hrs. 15 mins.). (gr. 5 up). 1997. 27.00 (978-0-7887-0374-4(9), 94565E7) Recorded Bks.
The classic story of wilderness survival continues in this sequel to "My Side of the Mountain." Filled with authentic woodland lore & exciting adventure, it takes listeners back to Sam Gribley's treehouse in the Catskill Mountains, where he begins a dangerous fight for his pet falcon's freedom.

On the Far Side of Yesterday. unabr. ed. Catharine Sutherland. 3 cass. (Running Time: 6 hrs.). (Audio Books Ser.). 1992. 34.95 (978-1-85496-711-4(8)) Pub: UlverLrgPrint GBR. Dist(s): Ulverscroft US
Melinda Cameron's sleep is haunted by nightmares - & her waking hours are not much better. Does her new editor, Adam Copeland, have any real regard for her, & who is the woman whose name he murmurs in his sleep? Melinda embarks on a journey that brings her face to face with the past - & she is shaken by a shattering revelation that rocks the very foundation of her love for Adam. Can she come to terms with the shocking truth.

On the Farm with Ronno. 1 cass. (Running Time: 39 mins.). 1999. 10.95 (978-1-56346-093-7(9)) Kimbo Educ.
Ron Hiller, aka "Ronno," does most of the singing on this album celebrating farms & farm life.

On the Farm with Ronno. 1 cass. (Running Time: 38 min.). (J). (gr. k-3). 2001. pap. bk. 10.95 (KIM 9153C); pap. bk. 14.95 (KIM 9153CD) Kimbo Educ.
Lively learning songs about all kinds of farms, farm families, animals, work & machines, cultivation, growing cycles & harvesting. Ronno also includes silly songs for fun & laughter. Guide included.

On the Fly Guide to Balancing Work & Life. unabr. ed. Bill Butterworth. Read by Bill Butterworth. (YA). 2007. 34.99 (978-1-60252-775-1(X)) Find a World.

On the Fly Guide to Balancing Work & Life. unabr. ed. Bill Butterworth. Narrated by Bill Butterworth. (ENG.). 2007. 10.49 (978-1-60814-039-8(3)); audio compact disk 14.99 (978-1-59859-152-1(5)) Oasis Audio.

On the Fly Guide to Building Successful Teams. unabr. ed. Bill Butterworth. Narrated by Bill Butterworth. (ENG.). 2006. 10.49 (978-1-60814-102-9(0)); audio compact disk 14.99 (978-1-59859-153-8(3)) Oasis Audio.

On the Front Lines - CD: Stories of the Suffering & Their Families Embraced by Christ. Anne Sophie Meaney. Read by Anne Sophie Meaney. 2002. audio compact disk 14.95 (978-1-57918-230-4(5)) Queenship Pub.

On the Genealogy of Morals, Set. unabr. ed. Friedrich Nietzsche. Read by Robert L. Halvorson. 5 cass. (Running Time: 450 min.). 35.95 (67) Halvorson Assocs.

On the Good Ship Lollipop. 1 cass. (Running Time: 45 mins.). (J). 1999. 9.98 (978-1-56628-200-0(4)) MFLP CA.
Wide range collection of songs will give new generations an appreciation of the glories of group harmony. All performed with creativity & gusto by the Persuasions & some young guests.

On the Grind. abr. ed. Stephen J. Cannell. Read by Scott Brick. (Running Time: 6 hrs.). (Shane Scully Ser.: No. 8). 2009. audio compact disk 14.99 (978-1-4233-2677-9(6), 9781423326779, BCD Value Price) Brilliance Audio.

On the Grind. unabr. ed. Stephen J. Cannell. Read by Scott Brick. (Running Time: 7 hrs.). (Shane Scully Ser.: No. 8). 2009. 24.99 (978-1-4233-2672-4(5), 9781423326724, Brilliance MP3); 39.97 (978-1-4233-2675-5(X), 9781423326755, BADLE); 39.97 (978-1-4233-2673-1(3), 9781423326731, Brlnc Audio MP3 Lib); 24.99 (978-1-4233-2674-8(1), 9781423326748, BAD); audio compact disk 36.99 (978-1-4233-2670-0(9), 9781423326700); audio compact disk 97.97 (978-1-4233-2671-7(7), 9781423326717, BriAudCD Unabrid) Brilliance Audio.

On the Grind. unabr. ed. Stephen J. Cannell. Read by Scott Brick. (Running Time: 7 hrs.). (Shane Scully Ser.). 2009. audio compact disk 14.99 (978-1-4418-3639-7(X), 9781441836397, BCD Value Price) Brilliance Audio.

On the Gull's Road. (ENG.). 2007. (978-1-60339-075-0(8)); cd-rom & audio compact disk (978-1-60339-076-7(6)) Listenr Digest.

On the Halfpipe with... Tony Hawk. unabr. ed. Matt Christopher. Narrated by Ramon de Ocampo. 2 pieces. (Running Time: 1 hr. 30 mins.). (gr. 4 up). 2002. 19.00 (978-1-4025-0776-2(3)) Recorded Bks.

On the Harmfulness of Tobacco see Anton Chekhov

On the Horizon: NACADA Webinar Series 09: the Future of Academic Advising & Technology. Featuring Karen Thurmond et al. 2007. audio compact disk 140.00 (978-1-935140-51-1(5)) Nat Acad Adv.

On the Ice with... Wayne Gretzky. unabr. ed. Matt Christopher. Narrated by Richard M. Davidson. 3 pieces. (Running Time: 3 hrs.). (gr. 4 up). 1997. 27.00 (978-0-7887-1087-2(7), 95091E7) Recorded Bks.
He's been called "The Great One" ever since he laced up his first pair of skates. Puts you on the ice with the New York Rangers superstar center.

On the Jellicoe Road. Melina Marchetta. Read by Rebecca Macauley. (Running Time: 9 hrs. 5 mins.). (YA). 2009. 64.99 (978-1-74214-365-1(2), 9781742143651) Pub: Bolinda Pubng AUS. Dist(s): Bolinda Pub Inc

On the Jellicoe Road. unabr. ed. Melina Marchetta. Read by Rebecca Macauley. (Running Time: 9 hrs. 5 mins.). (YA). 2008. audio compact disk 87.95 (978-1-74093-856-3(9)) Pub: Bolinda Pubng AUS. Dist(s): Bolinda Pub Inc

On-the-Job English. 2003. 18.00 (978-1-56420-145-4(7)) New Readers.

On the Line. abr. ed. Larry King & Mark Stencel. Read by Larry King. 2 cass. (Running Time: 3 hrs.). 1993. 16.95 (978-1-879371-60-6(X)) Pub Mills.
On the Line examines how the 1992 presidential race became a "call-in campaign," The book details the discovery of talk shows by America's political candidates & explores how this permanently altered the rules of the political game.

On the Line. unabr. ed. Serena Williams. Read by Serena Williams. Told to Daniel Paisner. (Running Time: 10 hrs.). 2009. 24.98 (978-1-60024-858-0(6)); audio compact disk 34.98 (978-1-60024-857-3(8)) Pub: Hachet Audio. Dist(s): HachBkGrp

***On the Line: A Bill Smith/Lydia Chin Novel.** S. J. Rozan. Narrated by William Dufris. (Running Time: 9 hrs. 15 mins. 0 sec.). (ENG.). 2010. audio compact disk 29.95 (978-1-60998-101-3(4)) Pub: AudioGO. Dist(s): Perseus Dist

On the Marginal Way see Richard Wilbur Readings

On the Marriage of a Virgin see Dylan Thomas Reading On the Marriage of a Virgin, Over Sir John's Hill, In Country Sleep & Others

On the Marriage of a Virgin see Dylan Thomas Reading His Poetry

On the Mission Trail: In San Antonio, Texas. Pamela G. McBride. 1 cass. (Running Time: 45 min.). 1993. 9.95 (978-0-9640993-0-2(6)) Miles to Go.
Travel.

On the Morning of Christ's Nativity see Poetry of John Milton

On the Move. 1998. 14.99 (978-1-60689-170-4(7)) Pub: Youngheart Mus. Dist(s): Creat Teach Pr

On the Move. Greg Scelsa. 1 cass. (Running Time: 1 hr.). (J). 2001. pap. bk. 10.95 (YM5C); pap. bk. 14.95 (YM5CD) Kimbo Educ.
Rock to the Music, Scat Like That, Space Adventure, Friends, Sports Dance & more. Includes lyrics.

On the Move. Music by Greg Scelsa & Steve Millang. 1 LP. (Running Time: 35 mins.). (J). lp 10.95 (YM5) Kimbo Educ.
Rock to the Music, Scat Like That, Space Adventure, Friends, Sports Dance & more. Includes lyric sheet.

On the Move With Greg & Steve. Music by Greg Scelsa & Steve Millang. 1 cass. (Running Time: 35 mins.). (J). (ps-3). 1984. 10.98 (978-0-945267-00-3(2), YM 005-CN); audio compact disk 13.98 (YM-005-CD) Youngheart Mus.
Singing & movement activities.

On the Murder of Lieutenant Jose Del Castillo by the Falangist Bravo Martinez, July 12, 1936 see Philip Levine

On the Nature & Interpretation of Dreams. Read by John Van Eenwyk. 2 cass. (Running Time: 3 hrs.). 1987. 18.95 (978-0-7822-0314-1(0), 268) C G Jung IL.

On the Nature of Sufi Knowledge. unabr. ed. Idries Shah. Read by Idries Shah. Read by London College of Storytellers Staff. 2 vols. (Running Time: 3 hrs.). (Idries Shah Live on Tape Ser.). 1996. bk. 17.00 (978-1-883536-04-6(9), NASK1, Hoopoe Books) ISHK.
A lecture by Idries Shah, plus teaching stories & narratives selected from "Seeker after Truth" & "Wisdom of the Idiots".

On the Nature of Things. unabr. ed. Lucretius Carus. Read by Robert L. Halvorson. 6 cass. (Running Time: 9 hrs.). 42.95 (54) Halvorson Assocs.

On the Night of the Seventh Moon. unabr. ed. Victoria Holt. Read by Lin Sagovsky. 10 cass. (Running Time: 10 hrs.). 1999. 84.95 (978-0-7540-0255-0(1), CAB1678) AudioGO.
The night when, according to ancient Black Forest legend, Loke - the God of Mischief, was abroad in the world. Helena Trant was enchanted by the Black Forest: it's people, castles & legends. Then she started to live one of the legends & the enchantment turned into a terrifying nightmare.

On the Night of the Seventh Moon. unabr. ed. Victoria Holt. Narrated by Virginia Leishman. 8 cass. (Running Time: 11 hrs. 30 mins.). 1997. 70.00 (978-0-7887-1227-2(6), 95148E7) Recorded Bks.
Tale set in 1800s Europe. Beautiful Helena Trant becomes lost in the Black Forest on the legendary Night of the Seventh Moon, a time for drinking & love. When a handsome man rescues her from the swirling mist, she spends a bewitching night dining with him. It all seems a thrilling dream, but one day, that fateful night blurs the borders between reality & dreams.

On the Night of the Seventh Moon. unabr. collector's ed. Victoria Holt. Read by Donada Peters. 8 cass. (Running Time: 12 hrs.). 1994. 64.00 (978-0-7366-2830-3(4), 3538) Books on Tape.
The Black Forest hypnotizes Helena Trant, especially its legends of love. But one is a nightmare and it lies just ahead for Helena!.

On the Occasion of My Last Afternoon. Kaye Gibbons. 2000. audio compact disk 15.99 (978-0-7435-0561-1(1), Audioworks) S&S Audio.

On the Occasion of My Last Afternoon. abr. ed. Kaye Gibbons. Read by Polly Holliday. 4 cass. (Running Time: 6 hrs.). 1999. 23.00 (FS9-34643) Highsmith.

On the Occasion of My Last Afternoon. unabr. ed. Kaye Gibbons. Narrated by Sally Darling. 6 cass. (Running Time: 9 hrs.). 1999. 56.00 (978-0-7887-2499-2(1), 95574E7) Recorded Bks.
Growing up in a wealthy southern family has not protected Emma Tate Lowell from life's darker side. Now, at the end of her days, she considers the wisdom of her husband's advice to "face it all dry-eyed".

On the occasion of my last afternoon Cs. Kaye Gibbons. Read by Polly Holliday. 2004. 15.95 (978-0-7435-4315-6(7)) Pub: S&S Audio. Dist(s): S and S Inc

***On the Ocean Floor.** Joanna Cole. Illus. by Bruce Degen. (Magic School Bus Ser.). (ENG.). 2010. audio compact disk 18.99 (978-0-545-22759-9(3)) Scholastic Inc.

On the Oceans of Eternity. unabr. ed. S. M. Stirling. Read by Todd McLaren. Narrated by Todd McLaren. (Running Time: 29 hrs. 30 mins. 0 sec.). (Nantucket Ser.). (ENG.). 2009. audio compact disk 49.99 (978-1-4001-0681-3(8)); audio compact disk 99.99 (978-1-4001-3681-0(4)); audio compact disk 34.99 (978-1-4001-5681-8(5)) Pub: Tantor Media. Dist(s): IngramPubServ

On the Origin of Species. Charles Darwin. Read by David Case. (Running Time: 61200 sec.). (ENG.). 2006. audio compact disk 79.99 (978-1-4001-3215-7(0)) Pub: Tantor Media. Dist(s): IngramPubServ

On the Origin of Species. abr. ed. Charles Darwin. Adapted by Richard Dawkins. 5 CDs. (Running Time: 6 hrs. 30 mins. 0 sec.). (ENG.). 2008. audio compact disk 29.95 (978-1-934997-00-0(5)) Pub: CSAWord. Dist(s): PerseuPGW

On the Origin of Species. abr. ed. Charles Darwin. Read by Robert L. Halvorson. 2 cass. (Running Time: 3 hrs.). 14.95 (89) Halvorson Assocs.

On the Origin of Species. unabr. collector's ed. Charles Darwin. Read by David Case. 12 cass. (Running Time: 18 hrs.). 1992. 96.00 (978-0-7366-2232-5(2), 3022) Books on Tape.
Darwin transformed the way people thought about God & the world around them. His aim was to show the probability that every species is a development from previous species, implying man's evolution.

On the Paranormal. unabr. ed. Charles Tart. 1 cass. (Running Time: 1 hr. 24 min.). 1971. 11.00 (05202) Big Sur Tapes.

On the Path of God. Swami Amar Jyoti. 1 cass. (Running Time: 1 hr. 30 mins.). 1983. 9.95 (M-40) Truth Consciousness.
Treading on the one right way. How to know when we are on His path? Morality, a necessary step. The way to freedom.

On the Possession of Consciousness. Charles Ponce. 1 cass. (Running Time: 1 hr. 30 mins.). 9.00 (A0430-89) Sound Photosyn.
Charles has a captivating voice & agreeable concepts.

On the Psychology of Meditation. unabr. ed. Robert Ornstein. 1 cass. (Running Time: 1 hr. 20 min.). 1971. 11.00 (01802) Big Sur Tapes.

On the Pythagorean Philosophy of Numbers. Instructed by Manly P. Hall. 8.95 (978-0-89314-202-5(6), C820711) Philos Res.

On the Relation of the New Physics to Psychology. Read by Fritjof Capra. 1 cass. (Running Time: 1 hr.). 1983. 9.95 (978-0-7822-0032-4(X), 032) C G Jung IL.

On the Road. Jack Kerouac. Read by Alexander Adams. 1999. audio compact disk 72.00 (978-0-7366-5969-7(2)) Books on Tape.

On the Road. Jack Kerouac. Narrated by Frank Muller. 10 CDs. (Running Time: 11 hrs. 15 mins.). audio compact disk 97.00 (978-0-7887-9934-1(7)) Recorded Bks.

On the Road. unabr. ed. Jack Kerouac. Read by Tom Parker. 7 cass. (Running Time: 10 hrs.). 2003. 49.95 (978-0-7861-0894-7(0), 1700) Blckstn Audio.
Creates a sensation by chronicling a spontaneous and wandering way of life in a style that seems founded both on jazz and on drug-induced visions.

On the Road. unabr. ed. Jack Kerouac. Read by Tom Parker. 9 CDs. (Running Time: 10 hrs.). 2000. audio compact disk 72.00 (978-0-7861-9937-2(7), 1700) Blckstn Audio.

On the Road. unabr. ed. Jack Kerouac. Read by Tom Parker. 7 cass. (Running Time: 34200 sec.). 2005. 19.95 (978-0-7861-3466-3(6), E1700); DVD & audio compact disk 24.95 (978-0-7861-9666-1(1), 1700) Blckstn Audio.

On the Road. unabr. ed. Jack Kerouac. Read by Alexander Adams. 8 cass. (Running Time: 12 hrs.). 1999. 64.00 (4995); 64.00 (978-0-7366-4609-3(4), 4995) Books on Tape.
The soul of the Beat movement, but one of the most important novels of the century. Like nearly all of Kerouac's writings, this is thinly ficitionized autobiography, filled with a cast made of Kerouac's real life friends, lovers, and fellow travelers.

On the Road. unabr. ed. Jack Kerouac. Read by Alexander Adams. 9 CDs. (Running Time: 13 hrs. 30 mins.). 2001. audio compact disk 72.00 Books on Tape.
The counterculture escapades of members of the Beat generation.

On the Road. unabr. ed. Jack Kerouac. Read by Matt Dillon. 10 CDs. (Running Time: 10 hrs.). 2004. audio compact disk 19.95 (978-0-06-075533-1(4)) HarperCollins Pubs.

On the Road. unabr. ed. Jack Kerouac. Narrated by Frank Muller. 10 CDs. (Running Time: 11 hrs. 15 min.). 2001. audio compact disk 97.00 (C1433) Recorded Bks.
The only people for me are the mad ones, the ones who are mad to live, mad to talk, mad to be saved, desirous of everything at the same time, the ones who never yawn or say a commonplace thing, but burn, burn, burn like fabulous yellow roman candles exploding like spiders across the stars. This is the voice that defined a generation hip, poetic, restless with vitality. You will experience every intoxicating nuance. As he travels across 1950s America, aspiring writer Sal Paradise chronicles his escapades with the charismatic Dean Moriarty. Sal admires Dean's passion for experiencing as much as possible of life & his wild flights of poetic fancy.

On the Road. unabr. ed. Jack Kerouac. Narrated by Frank Muller. 8 cass. (Running Time: 11 hrs. 15 mins.). 1999. 70.00 (978-0-7887-2600-2(5), 95455E7) Recorded Bks.
As Sal Paradise chronicles his travels across 1950s America, outer & inner journeys merge & a legend is born.

On the Road. unabr. abr. ed. Jack Kerouac. Read by Matt Dillon. 7 cass. (Running Time: 11 hrs.). 2000. 39.95 (978-0-694-52361-0(5)) HarperCollins Pubs.

On the Road. 50th anniv. ed. Jack Kerouac. Contrib. by Will Patton. (Running Time: 11 hrs.). (ENG.). (gr. 12 up). 2007. audio compact disk 29.95 (978-0-14-314273-7(9), PengAudBks) Penguin Grp USA.

On the Road: The Original Scroll. unabr. ed. Jack Kerouac. Contrib. by John Ventimiglia. (Running Time: 13 hrs.). (ENG.). (gr. 12 up). 2008. audio compact disk 39.95 (978-0-14-314379-6(4), PengAudBks) Penguin Grp USA.

On the Road Again: Crosby & Hope. 6 vols. (Running Time: 6 hrs.). (Radio Spirits Historical Collections). bk. 34.98 (978-1-57019-686-7(9), OTR40062) Pub: Radio Spirits. Dist(s): AudioGO

On the Road Again: Crosby & Hope. Read by Bob Hope & Bing Crosby. 4 vols. (Running Time: 6 hrs.). (Radio Spirits Historical Collections). 2004. bk. 24.98 (978-1-57019-687-4(7), OTR40064) Pub: Radio Spirits. Dist(s): AudioGO

On the Road Again: More Car Songs. Contrib. by Dennis Buck. 1 cass. (Running Time: 1 hr.). (J). 2001. pap. bk. 10.95 (KIM 9129C) Kimbo Educ.
More miles of fun, giggles, smiles & happy times when you're on the road again with your favorite songs. This brand new collection of classic children's sing-alongs is sure to shorten any trip & add pleasure to every day. Some of the favorites include: On the Road Again, Witch Doctor, On Top of Spaghetti, Do Your Ears Hang Low?, The Wizard of Oz Medley, Octopus's Garden, Down by the Bay, Day O, Swinging on a Star, & more! Includes guide.

On the Road Audio CD. Adapted by Benchmark Education Company Staff. Based on a work by Francisco Blane. (My First Reader's Theater Ser.). (J). (gr. k-1). 2008. audio compact disk 10.00 (978-1-60634-092-9(1)) Benchmark Educ.

On the Road to Destiny. 2003. 30.00 (978-1-58602-153-5(2)) E L Long.

On the Road to Destiny. 2004. audio compact disk 50.00 (978-1-58602-154-2(0)) E L Long.

On the Road to Love. Leta N. Childers. Read by Leta N. Childers. 1 cass. (Running Time: 1 hr. 50 min.). 1999. bk. 6.50 (978-1-58495-026-4(9)) DiskUs Publishing.
Romantic comedy.

On the Road to Stalingrad. Cottam. (C). 2006. 14.95 (978-1-58510-158-0(3)) Focus Pub-R Pullins.

On the Road with Charles Kuralt. abr. ed. Charles Kuralt. Wallace Kuralt. 2004. 7.95 (978-0-7435-4450-4(1)) Pub: S&S Audio. Dist(s): S and S Inc

On the Road with Insight for Living. 2002. audio compact disk 14.99 (978-1-57972-451-1(5)) Insight Living.

On the Road with Lewis Grizzard. Lewis Grizzard. Read by Lewis Grizzard. 1 cass. (Running Time: 1 hr.). 1986. 9.98 (978-0-945258-00-1(3), STC-004); audio compact disk 9.98 (978-0-945258-04-9(6), STCD-004) Sthrn Tracks.
Southern humor.

On the Road with the Code Audio Version. Based on a book by Tony Burroughs. Based on a movie by Tony Burroughs. (ENG.). 2008. audio compact disk 18.95 (978-0-9819020-1-2(4)) High Light Hse.

On the Run. abr. ed. Iris Johansen. Read by Jennifer Van Dyck. 5 CDs. (Running Time: 21600 sec.). (ENG.). 2007. audio compact disk 14.99 (978-0-7393-4375-3(0), Random AudioBks) Pub: Random Audio Pubg. Dist(s): Random

On the Run. unabr. ed. Iris Johansen. Read by Jennifer Van Dyck. 10 CDs. 2005. audio compact disk 90.00 (978-1-4159-2607-9(7)); 72.00 (978-1-4159-2606-2(9)) Books on Tape.
For eight years, single mother Grace Archer has been living a picture-perfect life raising her daughter on a horse farm in the small town of Tallanville, Alabama. Watching Frankie grow into a talented and confident young girl has made Grace as happy as any mother could hope to be. Happy enough, even, to forget the past. But the past never quite goes away. Which is why a certain charismatic man also moved to Tallanville eight years ago to watch over her. But when violence threatens to shatter Grace and Frankie's idyllic home, the waiting is over. The ghosts of the past have returned. And they're hungry for blood. Now Grace must resume an identity she thought she had cast off forever, and match wits with an opponent as deadly as he is cunning. The prize: an extraordinary secret that only she can unfold. The forfeit: losing the thing more precious to her than life itself.

On the Run: An Angler's Journey down the Striper Coast. abr. ed. David Dibenedetto. Read by Christopher Lane. (Running Time: 16200 sec.). 2003. audio compact disk 28.00 (978-1-932378-76-4(6)) Pub: A Media Intl. Dist(s): Natl Bk Netwk

***On the Run Books 1-3: Chasing the Falconers, the Fugitive Factor, Now You See Them, Now You Don't.** unabr. ed. Gordon Korman. Read by Ben Rameaka. (Running Time: 9 hrs.). (On the Run Ser.). 2010. 29.97 (978-1-4418-7194-7(2), 9781441871947, BADLE) Brilliance Audio.

***On the Run Books 1-3: Chasing the Falconers, the Fugitive Factor, Now You See Them, Now You Don't.** unabr. ed. Gordon Korman. Read by Ben Rameaka. (Running Time: 9 hrs.). (On the Run Ser.). (YA). 2010. 29.97 (978-1-4418-7192-3(6), 9781441871923, Brilliance MP3); 29.97 (978-1-4418-7193-0(4), 9781441871930, Brlnc Audio MP3 Lib); audio compact disk 29.97 (978-1-4418-7191-6(8), 9781441871916, BriAudCD Unabrid) Brilliance Audio.

***On the Run Books 4-6: The Stowaway Solution, Public Enemies, Hunting the Hunter.** unabr. ed. Gordon Korman. Read by Ben Rameaka. (Running Time: 9 hrs.). (On the Run Ser.). 2010. 29.97 (978-1-4418-7198-5(5), 9781441871985, BADLE); 29.97 (978-1-4418-7196-1(9), 9781441871961, Brilliance MP3); 29.97 (978-1-4418-7197-8(7), 9781441871978, Brlnc Audio MP3 Lib) Brilliance Audio.

***On the Run Books 4-6: The Stowaway Solution, Public Enemies, Hunting the Hunter.** unabr. ed. Gordon Korman. Read by Ben Rameaka. (Running Time: 9 hrs.). (On the Run Ser.). (YA). 2010. audio compact disk 29.97 (978-1-4418-7195-4(0), 9781441871954, BriAudCD Unabrid) Brilliance Audio.

***On the Second Dynamic: Sex, Children & the Family.** L. Ron Hubbard. 2010. audio compact disk 15.00 (978-1-4031-6776-7(1)); audio compact disk 15.00 (978-1-4031-6765-1(6)); audio compact disk 15.00 (978-1-4031-6771-2(0)); audio compact disk 15.00 (978-1-4031-6777-4(X)); audio compact disk 15.00 (978-1-4031-6768-2(0)); audio compact disk 15.00 (978-1-4031-6779-8(6)); audio compact disk 15.00 (978-1-4031-6763-7(X)); audio compact disk 15.00 (978-1-4031-6773-6(7)); audio compact disk 15.00 (978-1-4031-6769-9(9)); audio compact disk 15.00 (978-1-4031-6764-4(8)); audio compact disk 15.00 (978-1-4031-6774-3(5)); audio compact disk 15.00 (978-1-4031-6778-1(8)); audio compact disk 15.00 (978-1-4031-6766-8(4)); audio compact disk

15.00 (978-1-4031-6775-0(3)); audio compact disk 15.00 (978-1-4031-6767-5(2)); audio compact disk 15.00 (978-1-4031-6772-9(9)); audio compact disk 15.00 (978-1-4031-6770-5(2)) Bridge Pubns Inc.

On the Shoulders of Giants. unabr. ed. Kareem Abdul-Jabbar. (Running Time: 10 hrs. 30 mins. 0 sec.). (ENG.). 2007. audio compact disk 34.99 (978-1-4001-0428-4(9)) Pub: Tantor Media. Dist(s): IngramPubServ

On the Shoulders of Giants: My Journey Through the Harlem Renaissance. unabr. ed. Kareem Abdul-Jabbar. (Running Time: 10 hrs. 30 mins. 0 sec.). (ENG.). 2007. audio compact disk 24.99 (978-1-4001-5428-9(6)); audio compact disk 69.99 (978-1-4001-3428-1(5)) Pub: Tantor Media. Dist(s): IngramPubServ

On the Side of Laughter: Formative Influences on Writers. Malcolm Muggeridge. 1 cass. (Running Time: 41 min.). 1969. 11.95 (23078) J Norton Pubs.
Interview with Malcolm Muggeridge highlighting the influences which shaped his fascinating career.

On the Sidewalk, Mr. Ex-Resident see Assorted Prose

On the Street Where You Live. abr. ed. Mary Higgins Clark. 2004. 15.95 (978-0-7435-4451-1(X)) Pub: S&S Audio. Dist(s): S and S Inc

On the Street Where You Live. unabr. ed. Mary Higgins Clark. Read by Jan Maxwell. 8 vols. (Running Time: 12 hrs.). 2001. bk. 69.95 (978-0-7927-2458-2(5), CSL 347, Chivers Sound Lib); audio compact disk 79.95 (978-0-7927-9912-2(7), SLD 063, Chivers Sound Lib) AudioGO.
Following the breakup of her marriage & the experience of being pursued by an obsessed stalker, Emily Graham accepts an offer to leave Albany & work in a major law firm in Manhattan. Emily buys a house her family had sold in 1892, after one of Emily's forebears, Madeline Shapley, then still a young girl, disappeared. Now, more than a century later, the skeleton of a young woman is found. Within her skeletal hand is the finger bone of another woman with a ring still on it, a Shapley family heirloom. In seeking to find a link between her family's past & the recent murder, Emily becomes a threat to a killer who has chosen her as the next victim.

On the Street Where You Live. unabr. ed. Mary Higgins Clark. Read by Mary Higgins Clark. 10 CDs. (Running Time: 90 hrs. 0 mins. 0 sec.). (ENG.). 2001. audio compact disk 39.95 (978-0-7435-0442-3(9), Audioworks) Pub: S&S Audio. Dist(s): S and S Inc

On the Street Where You Live. unabr. ed. Mary Higgins Clark. 2004. 23.95 (978-0-7435-5094-9(3)) Pub: S&S Audio. Dist(s): S and S Inc

On the Stroll. Alix Kates Shulman. Read by Alix Kates Shulman. 1 cass. (Running Time: 30 min.). 1984. 8.95 (AMF-12) Am Audio Prose.
Schulman talks about the novel.

On the Sunny Side. Perf. by Maria Muldaur. Prod. by Leib Ostrow. 1 cass. (Running Time: 38 min.). 1990. 9.98 (978-1-877737-56-5(9), MLP 2222); audio compact disk 12.98 (978-1-877737-57-2(7), MLP D2222) MFLP CA.
Twelve traditional & popular songs arranged for children & adults emphasizing "swing" & "folk" styles.

On the Three Metamorphoses: Nietzsche, A Course in Miracles, & the Stages of Spirituality. Kenneth Wapnick. 4 CDs. 2005. audio compact disk 20.00 (978-1-59142-175-7(6), CD105) Foun Miracles.

On the Town with the League of Gentlemen. Jeremy Dyson & Steve Pemberton. 2 cass. (Running Time: 2 hrs. 55 mins.). 1999. 15.00 (978-0-563-55739-5(7)) BBC WrldWd GBR.
A comedy group of three highly entertaining young men.

On the Trail. Perf. by Troubadour Staff. (J). 1999. audio compact disk 14.95 (978-0-939065-78-3(9)) Gentle Wind.

On the Trail. Troubadour Staff. 1 cass. (Running Time: 47 min.). (J). (gr. k-5). 1990. 9.95 (978-0-939065-50-9(9), GW1054) Gentle Wind.
Funny rock songs about chicken pox, loose teeth, & lost homework shine a humorous light on everyday family life.

On the Viability of Soul in Contemporary Organized Religion. Huston Smith. 1 cass. (Running Time: 1 hr. 25 min.). 1995. 10.95 (978-0-7822-0503-9(8), 578) C G Jung IL.
Renowned religion scholar Huston Smith explores the roots of soul in the numinous experience & examines the soul's viability in the soil of contemporary organized religion. He also discusses the role science has played in shaping Western concepts of soul.

On the Waterfront. Budd Schulberg. Contrib. by Bruce Davison et al. 2 CDs. (Running Time: 6720 sec.). (L. A. Theatre Works). 2003. audio compact disk 25.95 (978-1-58081-267-2(8), CDTPT181) Pub: L A Theatre. Dist(s): NetLibrary CO

On the Way to Somewhere. 1 cass. (Running Time: 1 hr. 30 mins.). (Musical Poems for Families Ser.: Vol. II). (J). (ps up). 9.98 (2210) MFLP CA.
Poems by William Blake, Walter de la Mare, Edna St. Vincent Millay, George MacDonald, Eleanor Farjeon, Rachel Field, John Drinkwater, Lord Houghton & others.

On the Way to the Wedding: Transforming the Love Relationship. Linda S. Leonard. 4 cass. (Running Time: 6 hrs.). 36.00 (OC116) Sound Horizons AV.

On the Wealth of Nations. unabr. ed. P. J. O'Rourke. Narrated by Michael Prichard. (Running Time: 5 hrs. 30 mins. 0 sec.). (Books That Changed the World Ser.). (ENG.). 2007. audio compact disk 24.99 (978-1-4001-0386-7(X)); audio compact disk 19.99 (978-1-4001-5386-2(7)) Pub: Tantor Media. Dist(s): IngramPubServ

On the Wealth of Nations. unabr. ed. P. J. O'Rourke. Read by Michael Prichard. (Running Time: 5 hrs. 30 mins. 0 sec.). (Books That Changed the World Ser.). (ENG.). 2007. audio compact disk 49.99 (978-1-4001-3386-4(6)) Pub: Tantor Media. Dist(s): IngramPubServ

On the Wing: To the Edge of the Earth with the Peregrine Falcon. abr. ed. Alan Tennant. 2004. 15.95 (978-0-7435-4304-0(1)) Pub: S&S Audio. Dist(s): S and S Inc

On the Wings of a Dragonfly. Terry Grosvenor. Perf. by Grosvenor Family and Friends. 1 cass. (Running Time: 44 min.). (J). (gr. k-7). 1995. 9.95 (978-0-9644433-1-0(7)) R&T Grosvenor.
This cassette contains 14 selections - all are based on classic children's poetry including works of Edward Lear, Henry Wadsworth Longfellow, Laura Richards, Mildred Meigs, Aileen Fisher, Lewis Carroll, Florence Jacques, Vachel Lindsey, Mathias Barr & Hillaire Belloc. All the music is composed, arranged & performed by Terry Grosvenor. The music has a contemporary style.

On the Wings of Heroes. unabr. ed. Richard Peck. Read by Lincoln Hoppe. (Running Time: 11640 sec.). (ENG.). (J). (gr. 5). 2007. audio compact disk 27.00 (978-0-7393-3883-4(8), Listening Lib) Pub: Random Audio Pubg. Dist(s): Random

On the Wings of Heroes. unabr. ed. Richard Peck. Read by Lincoln Hoppe. 3 CDs. (Running Time: 3 hrs. 14 mins.). (YA). (gr. 5-8). 2007. audio compact disk 38.00 (978-0-7393-4860-4(4), Listening Lib) Pub: Random Audio Pubg. Dist(s): Random

On the Wrong Track. unabr. ed. Steve Hockensmith. Read by William Dufris. (Holmes on the Range Ser.). (YA). 2008. 59.99 (978-1-60252-986-1(8)) Find a World.

On the Wrong Track. unabr. ed. Steve Hockensmith. Read by William Dufris. 8 CDs. (Running Time: 9 hrs. 30 mins. 0 sec.). (Holmes on the Range Ser.). (ENG.). 2007. audio compact disk 34.99 (978-1-4001-0355-3(X)); audio compact disk 69.99 (978-1-4001-3355-0(6)); audio compact disk 24.99 (978-1-4001-5355-8(7)) Pub: Tantor Media. Dist(s): IngramPubServ

On Thin Ice: Courageous Characters, Fabulous Friends. AIO Team Staff. Created by Focus on the Family Staff & Marshal Younger. 4 CDs. (Adventures in Odyssey Gold Ser.). (ENG.). (J). 2005. audio compact disk 24.99 (978-1-58997-234-6(1)) Pub: Focus Family. Dist(s): Tyndale Hse

On This Day I Complete My Thirty-Sixth Year see Poetry of Byron

On This Very Night: A Christmas Musical for Every Choir. Contrib. by Lari Goss. Created by Karla Worley. 2007. audio compact disk 16.98 (978-5-557-77125-2(5), Word Music) Word Enter.

***On Thursday We Leave for Home.** 2010. audio compact disk (978-1-59171-286-2(6)) Falcon Picture.

***on-Time, on-Target Manager.** unabr. ed. Ken Blanchard. Read by Brian Corrigan. (ENG.). 2005. (978-0-06-085012-8(4), Harper Audio); (978-0-06-085011-1(6), Harper Audio) HarperCollins Pubs.

On-Time, On-Target Manager: How a Last-Minute Manager Conquered Procrastination. unabr. ed. Ken Blanchard. Read by Brian Corrigan. 2 cass. (Running Time: 3 hrs.). 2004. 16.00 (978-0-06-058481-8(5)); audio compact disk 18.00 (978-0-06-058482-5(3)) HarperCollins Pubs.

On to Oregon!, unabr. ed. Honoré Morrow. Narrated by Norman Dietz. 4 pieces. (Running Time: 6 hrs.). (gr. 7 up). 1992. 35.00 (978-1-55690-585-8(8), 92122E7) Recorded Bks.
A thirteen-year-old pioneer boy leads his family along The Oregon Trail to safety. An unforgettable portrait of the bitter hardship & impossible odds of the 19th-century American frontier.

On Tolkien: Interviews, Reminiscences, & Other Essays. unabr. ed. Douglas A. Anderson. Narrated by Paul Boehmer. 2008. (978-1-4001-3648-3(2)); (978-1-4001-5648-1(3)); (978-1-4001-0648-6(6)) Tantor Media.

On Top of Old Smokey: A Collection of Songs & Stories from Appalachia. Illus. by Linda Anderson. 1992. bk. 14.95 (978-1-59093-053-3(3), Eager Minds) Warehse and Fulfillment.

On Transformation. J. Krishnamurti. Read by J. Krishnamurti. 1 cass. (Running Time: 1 hr. 30 mins.). 8.50 (AJQ794) Krishnamurti.

On Truth. Harry Frankfurt. 2006. audio compact disk 14.99 (978-1-4281-0545-4(X)) Recorded Bks.

On U. F. O.'s. Frank Stranges. 1 cass. (Roy Tuckman Interview Ser.). 9.00 (A0477-89) Sound Photosyn.
Definitely is, frankly, strange!.

On Vacation. Frank Cappelli. 1 cass. (Running Time: 1 hr.). (J). (ps-3). 8.98 (978-0-929304-02-1(0)) Peanut Heaven.
Music for children designed not only to entertain, but also to reinforce basic educational concepts & a sense of self-esteem.

On Vacation with the Family Circus. unabr. ed. Bil Keane. 1 cass. (Running Time: 30 min.). (Family Circus Sings! Ser.). (J). 1994. pap. bk. 5.95 Penton Overseas.
Here's a series that brings the whole family together to sing along & enjoy catchy, good-time tunes. Sure to capture the heart & imagination of any child.

On Viewing Fellini's "Eight & One-Half" Frank Barron. 1 cass. (Running Time: 1 hr.). 9.00 (A0278-88) Sound Photosyn.
Recorded at an Esalen workshop. Isabella Conti wrote her dissertation on Fellini's work & dialogued in this talk.

On War. abr. ed. Carl Von Clausewitz. Read by Nadia May. 8 cass. (Running Time: 11 hrs. 30 mins.). 1990. 56.95 (978-0-7861-0194-8(6), 1170) Blckstn Audio.
A Prussian soldier & writer, Clausewitz is said to have distilled Napoleon into theory. Best known among his numerous pronouncements is that war is a continuation of politics by other means. His theories & observations have been heeded by military strategists for nearly 200 years. This is considered to be "The Bible" of military strategy & tactics.

***On War.** unabr. ed. Carl von Clausewitz. Read by Nadia May. (Running Time: 11 hrs. 30 mins.). 2010. 29.95 (978-1-4417-4400-5(2)); audio compact disk 100.00 (978-1-4417-4397-8(9)) Blckstn Audio.

On We Go. 3 cass. (Running Time: 4 hrs. 30 mins.). 25.00 (SEN154) J Norton Pubs.

On Whale Island. unabr. ed. Daniel Hays. Read by Bruce Altman. (YA). 2006. 39.99 (978-1-59895-639-9(6)) Find a World.

On William Butler Yeats. Robert Pack. 1 cass. (Running Time: 1 hr.). 1962. 11.95 (23200) J Norton Pubs.
Discusses Yeats' rhetoric & his attempt to bring together time & eternity in his poetry. He demonstrates with "Sailing to Byzantium" & other works how Yeats is torn between holding onto life & wanting to walk out of it.

On Wings of Eagles. abr. ed. Ken Follett. 2 cass. (Running Time: 3 hrs.). 16.00 S&S Audio.

On Wings of Eagles. unabr. ed. Ken Follett. Read by Rupert Keenlyside. 11 cass. (Running Time: 16 hrs. 30 min.). 1983. 88.00 (978-0-7366-0950-0(4), 1893) Books on Tape.
They were all computer executives, employees of Ross Perot's Dallas-based EDS corporation. They were trained & led by former Green Beret Colonel Bull Simons. Their secret mission: to do what the U.S. government couldn't do. To rescue against staggering odds, two EDS colleagues locked up in an Iranian prison in 1978.

On Wings of Eagles. unabr. ed. Ken Follett. Read by Multivoice Production Staff. 8 cass. (Running Time: 11 hrs.). 2002. 29.95 (978-1-59086-155-4(8), 1590861558, BAU) Brilliance Audio.
A retired Green Beret colonel, computer executives and a Texas industrialist join forces to spring two Americans from an Iranian jail in "On Wings of Eagles," Ken Follett's nonfiction bestseller, here dramatized in Brilliance Audio's full-length, multiple-voice edition. Their real-life race against armed patrols and marauding tribesmen to bring Bill Gaylord and Paul Ciapparone home is described in the masterful style that Follett earlier employed in the best-selling thriller, "Eye of the Needle." A painstaking accurate account of modern heroes and international adventure, "On Wings of Eagles" is also a compelling picture of Iran in ferment just before the revolution that put Ayotollah Khomeini in power.

On Wings of Eagles. unabr. ed. Ken Follett. (Running Time: 11 hrs.). 2007. 24.95 (978-1-4233-2871-1(X), 9781423328711, BAD) Brilliance Audio.

On Wings of Eagles. unabr. ed. Ken Follett. Read by Multivoice Production Staff. (Running Time: 11 hrs.). 2007. 39.25 (978-1-4233-2872-8(8), 9781423328728, BADLE) Brilliance Audio.

On Wings of Eagles. unabr. ed. Ken Follett. Read by Multivoice Production Staff. (Running Time: 11 hrs.). 2007. 39.25 (978-1-4233-2870-4(1), 9781423328704, Brinc Audio MP3 Lib); 24.95 (978-1-4233-2869-8(8), 9781423328698, Brilliance MP3); audio compact disk 102.25 (978-1-4233-2868-1(X), 9781423328681, BriAudCD Unabrid); audio compact disk 38.95 (978-1-4233-2867-4(1), 9781423328674, Bril Audio CD Unabri) Brilliance Audio.

On Wings of Love. Brenton G. Yorgason. 2 cass. 9.98 (978-1-55503-854-0(9), 07001231) Covenant Comms.
A soaring novel of love & adventure.

On Wings of Peace. Daughters of St Paul. 1991. audio compact disk 14.95 (978-0-8198-5420-9(4), 332-262) Pauline Bks.

On Writing: A Memoir of the Craft. Stephen King. Narrated by Stephen King. 7 CDs. (Running Time: 8 hrs.). 2001. audio compact disk 69.00 (978-0-7887-5155-4(7), C1318E7) Recorded Bks.
Stephen King is responsible for more nightmares than the bogeyman & now provides insighted lessons for writers. His advice is friendly & to the point: acquire & hone the tools necessary for good writing, let your charactors reveal the story & dare to get started. He tells the story of his colorful childhood, his collection of rejection slips in adolescence & the struggling that led to his first major publishing success. Finally he talks about the accident that nearly killed him & the writing that helped him get his life back.

On Writing: A Memoir of the Craft. collector's ed. Stephen King. 6 cass. (Running Time: 8 hrs.). 2001. 34.95 Recorded Bks.

On Writing: A Memoir of the Craft. unabr. ed. Stephen King. Narrated by Stephen King. 6 cass. (Running Time: 8 hrs.). 2001. 54.00 (978-0-7887-5009-0(7), 96514E7) Recorded Bks.

On Writing: A Memoir of the Craft. unabr. ed. Stephen King. Read by Stephen King. 2006. 20.95 (978-0-7435-6337-6(9), Audioworks) Pub: S&S Audio. Dist(s): S and S Inc

On Writing Volume 1: Volume 1, Vol. 1. James Magnuson & Roberta Gellis. 4 CDs. (ENG.). 2005. audio compact disk 39.95 (978-1-880717-53-0(0), 829-036) Writers AudioShop.

On Writing Volume 2: Volume 2, Vol. 2. Carolyn Banks & Benjamin Alire Sáenz. 4 CDs. (ENG.). 2005. audio compact disk 39.95 (978-1-880717-54-7(9), 829-037) Writers AudioShop.

On Writing Well. abr. ed. William K. Zinsser. Read by William K. Zinsser. 2 CDs. (Running Time: 3 hrs.). 2004. audio compact disk 14.95 (978-0-06-058611-9(7)) HarperCollins Pubs.

***On Writing Well Audio Collection.** abr. ed. William Zinsser. Read by William Zinsser. (ENG.). 2004. (978-0-06-081805-0(0), Harper Audio); (978-0-06-081806-7(9), Harper Audio) HarperCollins Pubs.

On y Va!, Level 1, 2, 3. 2nd ed. Jeannette D. Bragger. (Secondary French Ser.). (FRE.). 1993. 18.95 (978-0-8384-4182-4(3)) Heinle.

On Your Mark. 3. (Running Time: 3 HRS.). 2000. 15.00 (978-1-57399-121-6(X)) Mac Hammond.
Forget those New Year's resolutions. Discover remarkable biblical principles for setting and achieving goals in this life-changing series. A powerfully practical tool for improving your life.

On Your Mark, Bk. 1. 2nd ed. Contrib. by Karen Davy. 3 cass. (Scott Foresman English Ser.). 2002. 47.70 (978-0-201-66391-4(0)); audio compact disk 47.70 (978-0-201-66393-8(7)) Longman.

On Your Mark, Bk. 2. 2nd ed. Contrib. by Karen Davy. 3 cass. 2002. 47.70 (978-0-201-66396-9(1)); audio compact disk 47.70 (978-0-201-66398-3(8)) Longman.

Once. Morris Gleitzman. Read by Morris Gleitzman. (Running Time: 3 hrs.). (J). 2009. 54.99 (978-1-74214-383-5(0), 9781742143835) Pub: Bolinda Pubng AUS. Dist(s): Bolinda Pub Inc

Once. unabr. ed. Morris Gleitzman. Read by Morris Gleitzman. 3 CDs. (Running Time: 10800 sec.). (J). (gr. 3-8). 2005. audio compact disk 54.95 (978-1-74093-691-0(4)) Pub: Bolinda Pubng AUS. Dist(s): Bolinda Pub Inc

***Once.** unabr. ed. Morris Gleitzman. Read by Morris Gleitzman. (J). 2010. audio compact disk 54.95 (978-1-74214-729-1(1), 9781742147291) Pub: Bolinda Pubng AUS. Dist(s): Bolinda Pub Inc

Once. unabr. ed. James Herbert. 14 cass. (Isis Ser.). (J). 2005. 99.95 (978-0-7531-1358-5(9)) Pub: ISIS Lrg Prnt GBR. Dist(s): Ulverscroft US

Once. unabr. ed. James Herbert. Read by Robert Powell. 15 CDs. (Isis (CDs) Ser.). (J). 2005. audio compact disk 104.95 (978-0-7531-1479-7(8)) Pub: ISIS Lrg Prnt GBR. Dist(s): Ulverscroft US

Once a Hero. Based on a book by Elizabeth Moon. (Serrano Legacy Ser.: Bk. 4). 2009. 12.99 (978-1-59950-549-7(5)) GraphicAudio.

Once a Hero. unabr. collector's ed. Katherine Sutcliffe. Read by Kate Reading. 6 cass. (Running Time: 9 hrs.). 1996. 48.00 (978-0-7366-3451-9(7), 4095) Books on Tape.
A war hero is branded a traitor, to the dismay of the aristocrat girl who loves him. Will she treat him like a traitor when they meet again.

Once a Hero Part 1. Elizabeth Moon. (Serrano Legacy Ser.: Bk. 4). 2008. audio compact disk 19.99 (978-1-59950-514-5(2)) GraphicAudio.

Once a Hero Part 2. Elizabeth Moon. (Serrano Legacy Ser.: Bk. 4). 2009. audio compact disk 19.99 (978-1-59950-518-3(5)) GraphicAudio.

Once a Runner. unabr. ed. John L. Parker, Jr. Read by Patrick G. Lawlor. (Running Time: 9 hrs.). 2009. 39.97 (978-1-4418-0090-9(5), 9781441800909, Brinc Audio MP3 Lib); 24.99 (978-1-4418-0091-6(3), 9781441800916, BAD) Brilliance Audio.

Once a Runner. unabr. ed. Read by John L. Parker, Jr. & Patrick G. Lawlor. (Running Time: 9 hrs.). 2009. audio compact disk 87.97 (978-1-4418-0088-6(3), 9781441800886, BriAudCD Unabrid) Brilliance Audio.

Once a Runner. unabr. ed. John L. Parker, Jr. & John L. Parker Jr. Read by Patrick G. Lawlor. (Running Time: 8 hrs.). 2009. 39.97 (978-1-4418-0092-3(1), 9781441800923, BADLE); 24.99 (978-1-4418-0089-3(1), 9781441800893, Brilliance MP3); audio compact disk 29.99 (978-1-4418-0087-9(5), 9781441800879, Bril Audio CD Unabri) Brilliance Audio.

Once a Spy. abr. ed. Keith Thomson. Read by Danny Campbell. (ENG.). 2010. audio compact disk 30.00 (978-0-307-70558-7(7), Random AudioBks) Pub: Random Audio Pubg. Dist(s): Random

Once & Future Church: Home Fellowships. Chuck Missler. 1 CD and 1CD-ROM. (Running Time: 2 hours). (Briefing Packages by Chuck Missler). 2003. audio compact disk 19.95 (978-1-57821-227-9(8)) Koinonia Hse.
Over the many decades that I have enjoyed my love affair with the Bible, I have had the marvelous benefit of many great teachers. But I also would like to let you in on a precious secret. The greatest personal growth I've ever witnessed occurred in a home Bible study. The fellowship of those intimate home groups, where people can interact, ask questions, and hold one another accountable, was the place of growth for all of us - teacher and student. This was, of course, the way it all started. A group of only a dozen - fisherman and others - along a seaside in Galilee. Even later as Paul traveled and planted, it was the intimacy of home fellowships that provided the earliest forums for the Gospel. The declarations in the synagogues and on Mars Hill were but an initiation. Their resulting questions were responded to in small groups in homes and on hillsides. Today, too many people get lost in church and are only getting a surface skimming of the Word of God. We encourage you to be intentional and get involved! If you are not presently in a small, weekly, Bible study group, we strongly encourage you to find one and give it a try. You may be in for a truly life-changing surprise.

Once & Future Spy: A Novel of Obsession. unabr. ed. Scripts. Robert Littell. Read by Scott Brick. 8 cass. (Running Time: 6 hrs.). 2004. 24.95 (978-1-59007-312-4(6)); 34.95 (978-1-59007-313-1(4)) Pub: New Millenn Enter. Dist(s): PerseuPGW

Once Around San Diego: The Essential Sights. F. Robert Richards & Lucy Richards. Read by F. Robert Richards. Contrib. by Rusty Dickson & Nathan Richards. 1 cass. (Running Time: 1 hr. 20 min.). 1997. pap. bk. 12.95 (978-0-9661311-0-9(X), 100) Comp Cir Tours.
A lighthearted romp around San Diego, California on this road trip sightseeing tour. A colorful 50 page souvenir booklet includes simple maps, photos & text.

Once Around the Wheel: Modern & Traditional Seasonal Songs. Ian Corrigan. Perf. by Ian Corrigan. Perf. by Moira Kyteler et al. 1986. 9.95 (978-1-59157-007-3(7)) Assn for Cons.

Once Around the Wheel: Modern & Traditional Seasonal Songs. Featuring Ian Corrigan. 2001. audio compact disk 12.95 (978-1-59157-006-6(9)) Assn for Cons.

Once by the Pacific see Robert Frost in Recital

***Once Dead, Twice Shy.** unabr. ed. Kim Harrison. Read by Mandy Siegfried. (ENG.). 2009. (978-0-06-179958-7(0)); (978-0-06-190203-1(9)) HarperCollins Pubs.

Once I Said Lightly see Poetry & Voice of Ted Hughes

Once in, Never Out. unabr. ed. Dan Mahoney. Read by Adams Morgan. 11 cass. (Running Time: 16 hrs.). 1999. 76.95 (978-0-7861-1509-9(2), 2359) Blckstn Audio.
Opens in Reykjavik, Iceland, when two bombs kill a British diplomat & his wife.

Once Is Enough. unabr. ed. Miles Smeeton. Read by Bill Kelsey. 8 cass. (Running Time: 8 hrs.). 1991. 48.00 (978-0-7366-1955-4(0), 2776) Books on Tape.
While attempting to round Cape Horn, the Tzu Hang was overwhelmed & dismasted...twice! But the Smeetons, Miles & Beryl, survived each disaster & sailed (limped) safely into port. The first time out Beryl was washed overboard & injured. She recovered & played a vital role in the repair work. Harboring in Chile, the Smeetons put Tzu Hang in even better condition for their second attempt. It proved more harrowing than their first.

Once Is Enough: Hebrews 7:20-28. Ed Young. 1992. 4.95 (978-0-7417-1900-3(2), 900) Win Walk.

Once More Around the Block: Familiar Essays. unabr. ed. Joseph Epstein. Read by Michael Russotto. 8 cass. (Running Time: 12 hrs.). 1990. 64.00 (978-0-7366-1802-1(3), 2639) Books on Tape.
There's no telling what will engage Joseph Epstein's attention, but one thing is certain; commonplace subjects take on a new appearance & meaning. Epstein queries a number of subjects, among them the pleasure of work, neighborhood, & keeping a journal; the comedy of Gluttony, lecturing & language snobbery; the mixed delights of issuing & receiving praise, friendship & growing into middle age. He writes with a humor that is at bottom serious & reveals a joy in being alive.

Once on a Time. A. A. Milne. Read by Flo Gibson. 4 cass. (Running Time: 5 hrs. 30 min.). (J). 1995. 19.95 (978-1-55685-370-8(X)) Audio Bk Con.
A battle between the kingdoms of Euralia & Borodia, royal romances, & magic spells are part of the fun of this rollicking yarn which Milne said he wrote for all ages.

Once Sang, from Act five see Twentieth-Century Poetry in English: Recordings of Poets Reading Their Own Poetry

Once, Twice, Three Times a Lady. Wanda Turner. 2004. 19.99 (978-0-7684-0203-2(4)) Destiny Image Pubs.

Once up on A Lilypad: Musical Adventures with Elizabeth Falconer Volume IV. Perf. by Elizabeth Falconer. 1 CD. (Running Time: 59:23). (J). 2003. audio compact disk 15.00 (978-0-9770499-5-0(7)) Koto World.
Jump to Japan with these fun-filled Japanese folktales. Adventure stories of old featuring inquisitive froggies, a mysterious "roofle" and even some of Pikachu's ancestors are accompanied with lively koto music and sounds.

Once upon a Bedtime Story. abr. ed. Jane Yolen. Read by Jane Yolen. Music by Adam Stemple. 1 cass. (Running Time: 1 hr. 11 min.). (J). (ps-4). 1999. 10.00 (978-0-9670427-0-1(4)); audio compact disk 15.00 (978-0-9670427-1-8(2)) Fabulous Records.
Eleven popular fairy tales from around the world.

Once upon a Crime. Anne Schraff. 1 cass. (Running Time: 61 mins 41 secs). (PageTurner Mystery Ser.). (YA). 2002. 10.95 (978-1-56254-476-8(4), SP 4764) Saddleback Edu.
Word-for-word read-along of Once Upon a Crime.

Once upon a Curse: The Sequel to the Frog Princess & Dragon's Breath. unabr. ed. E. D. Baker. Narrated by Katherine Kellgren. 5 cass. (Running Time: 6 hrs. 15 mins.). (J). 2005. 47.75 (978-1-4193-3926-4(5), 98030) Recorded Bks.
This entertaining sequel to The Frog Princess and Dragon's Breath will delight fantasy fans. Emma is about to turn 16 and is worried about an old family curse that has been passed down from generation to generation. Upon reaching their 16th birthday, the women of her family must not touch any flower or they will lose their kindness, beauty and youth. Emma saw it happen to her favorite aunt and is determined to find the cure before she too turns into an ugly witch.

Once upon a Day. Lisa Tucker. Read by Joyce Bean. (Playaway Adult Fiction Ser.). (ENG.). 2009. 74.99 (978-1-60775-883-9(0)) Find a World.

Once upon a Day. abr. ed. Lisa Tucker. Read by Joyce Bean. (Running Time: 6 hrs.). 2007. audio compact disk 14.99 (978-1-4233-1057-0(8), 9781423310570, BCD Value Price) Brilliance Audio.

Once upon a Day. unabr. ed. Lisa Tucker. Read by Joyce Bean. (Running Time: 11 hrs.). 2006. 24.95 (978-1-4233-1054-9(3), 9781423310549, BAD); 87.25 (978-1-4233-1049-5(7), 9781423310495, BrilAudUnabridg); audio compact disk 39.25 (978-1-4233-1053-2(5), 9781423310532, Brinc Audio MP3 Lib); audio compact disk 102.25 (978-1-4233-1051-8(9), 9781423310518, BriAudCD Unabrid); audio compact disk 24.95 (978-1-4233-1052-5(7), 9781423310525, Brilliance MP3); audio compact disk 38.95 (978-1-4233-1050-1(0), 9781423310501) Brilliance Audio.
Nineteen years ago, a famous man disappeared from Hollywood, taking his two children to a rocky, desolate corner of New Mexico where he raised them in complete isolation in a utopian "Sanctuary." Now, Dorothea, the man's twenty-three-year-old daughter, is leaving this place for the first time, in search of her missing brother. Dorothea's search will turn into an odyssey of discovery, leading to the shocking truth about her family's past and the terrifying events of that day that drove her father to flee Los Angeles in a desperate attempt to protect his children from a dangerous world. But Dorothea's journey will also introduce her to an unusual cast of characters, including a homeless girl from Missouri who becomes a jazz singer and a doctor turned cabdriver who has suffered his own losses. Together, they have a chance to make a discovery of a different kind: that though a heart can be broken by the tragic events of a day, a day can also bring a new chance at love and a deeper understanding of life's infinite possibilities. Lisa Tucker's The Song Reader and Shout Down the Moon were published to rapturous reviews all over the world. With Once Upon a Day, she confirms that she is a "brilliant new literary talent" (The Albuquerque Tribune).

Once upon a Day. unabr. ed. Lisa Tucker. Read by Joyce Bean. (Running Time: 11 hrs.). 2009. 39.97 (978-1-4418-5034-8(1), 9781441850348, BADLE) Brilliance Audio.

Once upon a Dinosaur. 1 cass. (Running Time: 1 hr.). (J). 2001. pap. bk. 10.95 (KIM 9083C); pap. bk. 14.95 (KIM 9083CD); pap. bk. & pupil's gde. ed. 11.95 (KIM 9083) Kimbo Educ.
Enhance your dinosaur theme units or story hours with songs & music that will stimulate your childrens imaginations. Give children the most important facts about those ever popular giant creatures of long ago & they'll learn effortlessly! Includes The Fossil Rock, The Reptile Rap, Meat Eater, Stegosaurus, Dinosaur Dance, Plant Eaters, My Pet Tyrannosaurus, Big Bad Al & much more. Includes song guide.

Once upon a Distant War. unabr. collector's ed. William Prochnau. Read by Michael Kramer. 14 cass. (Running Time: 21 hrs.). 1997. 112.00 (978-0-7366-3733-6(8), 4411) Books on Tape.
Documents the adventures of the war correspondents who introduced Vietnam to America.

Once upon a Holy Night. Ed. by Ellen Wood-Bryce. (Running Time: 25 mins.). (gr. 2-5). 2004. bk. 12.00 (978-0-687-09870-5(X)) Abingdon.

Once upon a Marigold. Jean Ferris & Carrington MacDuffie. 2007. audio compact disk 27.95 (978-1-59316-098-2(4)) Listen & Live.

Once upon A Marigold. unabr. ed. Jean Ferris. Read by Carrington MacDuffie. (J). 2007. 44.99 (978-1-60252-920-5(5)) Find a World.

Once upon a Midlife. Allan B. Chinen. Read by Dan Keding & Janice Del Negro. 1 cass. (Running Time: 1 hr. 5 mins.). (American Storytelling Ser.). 1997. 12.00 (978-0-87483-429-1(5)) August Hse.
These stories tell what happens in the "ever after," when the Prince goes bald & the Princess has a midlife crisis. They portray middle-aged men & women facing the issues of midlife: responsibility, the loss of ideals, gender differences, dealing with crisis, aging & mortality & the desire for renewal. Listeners will find that many midlife problems they thought were unique to our time are, in fact, timeless & universal & that the ultimate resolutions as described in these stories guide us through the peaks & valleys of midlife.

Once upon a Miracle: A Christmas Musical for Senior Adult Choir. Marty Parks. 2007. audio compact disk 90.00 (978-5-557-69919-8(8)); audio compact disk 90.00 (978-5-557-69918-1(X)) Lillenas.

Once upon a Miracle: A Christmas Musical for Senior Adult Choir. Marty Parks. 2007. audio compact disk 12.00 (978-5-557-69917-4(1)) Lillenas.

Once upon a More Enlightened Time: More Politically Correct Bedtime Stories. abr. ed. James Finn Garner. 1 cass. (Running Time: 1 hr.). 1996. 8.95 (53428) Books on Tape.
Sleeping Beauty becomes Sleeping Person of Better-Than-Average-Attractiveness. More classic tales, recast tongue-in-cheek for our times.

Once upon a more enlightened time more politically correct bedtime Stories: More Politically Correct Bedtime Stories. James Finn Garner. 2004. 5.95 (978-0-7435-4149-7(9)) Pub: S&S Audio. Dist(s): S and S Inc

Once upon a Night. Composed by Pepper Choplin. Contrib. by Brant Adams. 2007. audio compact disk 60.00 (978-5-557-80152-2(9), Glory Snd); audio compact disk 15.98 (978-5-557-80151-5(0), Glory Snd); audio compact disk 16.95 (978-5-557-80150-8(2), Glory Snd) Shawnee Pr.

Once upon a Noon Time: Fairy Tales & the Psychology of Men & Women at Midlife. Allan B. Chinen. Read by Allan B. Chinen. 3 cass. (Running Time: 3 hrs.). 1991. 22.95 (978-0-7822-0343-1(4), 455) C G Jung IL.
San Francisco analyst Allan Chinen leads a workshop exploring the archetypal tasks of midlife through the telling of stories from Germany, Persia, Italy & other countries.

***Once upon a Secret: The Story of My Affair with President John F. Kennedy & Its Aftermath.** unabr. ed. Mimi Alford. (ENG.). 2012. audio compact disk 30.00 (978-0-307-87779-6(5), Random AudioBks) Pub: Random Audio Pubg. Dist(s): Random

Once upon a Summer. Janette Oke. Read by Marguerite Gavin. 6 CDs. (Running Time: 7 hrs.). (Seasons of the Heart Ser.: Vol. 1). 2000. audio compact disk 48.00 (978-0-7861-9881-8(8), 2576) Blckstn Audio.
Sure, it's unusual to have an eighteen-year-old mother when you're twelve. But when you're an orphan & she's your aunt & the only mother you've ever had, well, as I explained, it had worked out real well. That's why I got so riled up when I heard Grandpa & Uncle Charlie talkin' about findin' a fella for Auntie Lou! You see, somethin' has to be done! I couldn't just sit back & watch our special family get broken up. But with Grandpa & Uncle Charlie workin' so hard to get Auntie Lou married off, I had a job cut out for me. Then, when that poor preacher came along & everything got really complicated.

Once upon a Summer. unabr. ed. Janette Oke. Read by Marguerite Gavin. 5 cass. (Running Time: 7 hrs.). (Seasons of the Heart Ser.: Vol. 1). 2000. 39.95 (978-0-7861-1773-4(7), 2576) Blckstn Audio.

Once upon a Tank in the Battle of the Bulge. 2008. audio compact disk 14.95 (978-0-9727330-4-5(3)) Chi Chi Pr.

Once upon a Time. bk. 13.00 (978-0-687-76220-0(0)) Abingdon.

***Once upon A Time.** (ENG.). 2010. audio compact disk (978-1-59171-310-4(2)) Falcon Picture.

Once upon a Time. Short Stories. Derek Burrows. 1 cass. (Running Time: 60 min.). (J). (gr. 3 up). 1990. 9.95 (978-0-938756-25-5(7), 005) Yellow Moon.
Stories from the Bahamas. Rich with African & European influence, there are several tales about B'Rabby, the trickster, & B'Boukee, the fool.

Once upon a Time: A True Story. unabr. collector's ed. Gloria Vanderbilt. Read by Mary Pfeiffer. 7 cass. (Running Time: 10 hrs. 30 mins.). 1990. 56.00 (978-0-7366-1865-6(1), 2696) Books on Tape.
Gloria Vanderbilt has written a memoir like no other - as engaging & unlikely as if a storybook figure were suddenly to speak, revealing at long last events of which we have only dreamed. The metaphor is appropriate, for Vanderbilt had indeed been a storybook figure, the object of intense curiosity & speculation since her birth. From Newport to Paris, Monte Carlo, Biarritz, London & New York, young Gloria traveled with her mother. It would seem to be the life of a fairytale princess. Then scandal & a bitter suit for her custody shattered the dream world in which she lived.

Once upon a Time: Behind the Fairy Tale of Princess Grace & Prince Rainier. abr. ed. J. Randy Taraborrelli. Read by Edward Herrmann. (ENG.). 2005. 14.98 (978-1-59483-345-8(1)) Pub: Hachet Audio. Dist(s): HachBkGrp

Once upon a Time in the North. unabr. ed. Philip Pullman. Read by Philip Pullman. 2 CDs. (Running Time: 2 hrs. 17 mins.). (YA). (gr. 7 up). 2008. audio compact disk 30.00 (978-0-7393-6700-1(5), Listening Lib) Pub: Random Audio Pubg. Dist(s): Random
Another mesmerizing episode from the universe of His Dark Materials set in the far frozen Arctic, including the very first meeting of those two legends and friends Lee Scoresby, the Texan balloonist, and Iorek Byrnison, the armored bear.

Once upon a Time in the North. unabr. ed. Philip Pullman. Read by Philip Pullman. Read by Full Cast Production Staff. (Running Time: 8220 sec.). (His Dark Materials Ser.). (ENG.). (J). (gr. 5). 2008. audio compact disk 25.00 (978-0-7393-6698-1(X)) Pub: Random Audio Pubg. Dist(s): Random

Once upon a Time Line: Collected Tales of Time & Space. Audio. 2 cass. (Running Time: 3 hrs.). 1998. 17.95 (978-0-9648539-1-1(4)) Wyrmhole.
Eight tales of magic & adventure, comedy & tragedy, taking place in the vast landscape of human history. Visions of today, yesterday & tomorrow are vividly brought to life. H.G. Wells set off from his living room at the turn of this century, starting a time travel craze that is more exciting & inventive today than ever. Listen as eight of science fiction's most popular author's create their own versions of travel through time & space.

Once upon a Time Series. Arlene Capriola & Rigmor Swenson. Ed. by Cherisse Mastry. Illus. by Kathy Burns. 10 cass. (Running Time: 10 hrs.). (J). (gr. k-2). 1998. (978-1-57022-157-6(X), ECS157X) ECS Lrn Systs.
Popular fairy tales.

Once upon a Time Series Book & Tape. Created by ECS Learning Systems. (J). 1998. (978-1-57022-168-2(5)) ECS Lrn Systs.

***Once upon a Time, There Was You: A Novel.** unabr. ed. Elizabeth Berg. Read by Elizabeth Berg. (ENG.). 2011. audio compact disk 35.00 (978-0-307-71378-0(4), Random Audio[illegible]) Pub: Random Audio Pubg. Dist(s): Random

Once upon a Time When We Were Colo[illegible] Clifton L. Taulbert. Read by Clifton L. Taulbert. 2 cass. (Running Time: 2 hrs. 20 min.). 1994. 16.95 (978-0-933031-57-9(2)) Coun Oak Bks.
A memoir of growing up in the Mississippi Delta. The author reads his story of a southern black community during racial segregation, telling the stories of those persons who inspired him to seek a better life beyond the segregated South. The tape includes black gospel & blues music from the era of segregation.

***Once upon a Town.** unabr. ed. Bob Greene. Read by Fritz Weaver. (ENG.). 2006. (978-0-06-117234-2(0), Harper Audio); (978-0-06-117231-1(6), Harper Audio) HarperCollins Pubs.

Once upon the River Love. Andreï Makine. Read by Geoffrey Howard. 5 cass. (Running Time: 7 hrs. 30 min.). 1999. 24.95 (978-0-7366-4595-9(0)) Books on Tape.
In the immense virgin pine forests of Siberia, where the snows of winter are vast & endless, sits the little village of Svetlaya, where men have gone away, never to return. Three young men, despite a harsh environment & meager resources, create their own special universe, in which they bond like brothers & dream of another life, in a world of passion & love.

Once upon the River Love. unabr. collector's ed. Andreï Makine. Read by Geoffrey Howard. 5 cass. (Running Time: 7 hrs. 30 mins.). 1998. 40.00 (978-0-7366-4255-2(2), 4754) Books on Tape.

***Once Was Lost.** unabr. ed. Sara Zarr. Read by Sara Zarr. 12 CDs. (YA). 2009. audio compact disk 45.00 (978-0-307-58233-1(7), BksonTape) Pub: Random Audio Pubg. Dist(s): Random

Once Was Lost. unabr. ed. Sara Zarr. (J). (gr. 7). 2009. audio compact disk 34.00 (978-0-307-58230-0(2), Listening Lib) Pub: Random Audio Pubg. Dist(s): Random

Once Were Warriors. abr. ed. Alan Duff. Read by Rawiri Paratene. 2 cass. (Running Time: 3 hrs.). 1996. 17.95 (978-1-57453-018-6(6), 330090) Audio Lit.
A young girl's death inspires the once proud Maori warriors to reclaim their history & their culture.

Once When I Was Weak, Emotional & Vulnerable: A Woman's Fury Rekindles Her Flame. Ricardo A. Scott. 1 cass. (Running Time: 1 hr.). (Ras Cardo Speaks to Women & Listens Ser.). 1999. pap. bk. (978-1-58470-022-7(X), RAS1949) Crnerstone GA.
Stories of women trying to empower their lives & how Ricardo has assisted them to do so.

Once When We Were Young. unabr. ed. Billy J. Brown. Read by Jim Gough. 13 cass. (Running Time: 19 hrs.). 2002. 85.95 (978-0-7861-2171-7(8), 2921) Blckstn Audio.
The stirring story of a young Texan and his two friends who become caught up in pre-Civil War excitement.

***Once, When We Were Young.** unabr. ed. Billy J. Brown. Read by Jim Gough. (Running Time: 11 hrs. 5 mins.). (ENG.). 2011. 29.95 (978-1-4417-8343-1(1)); audio compact disk 100.00 (978-1-4417-8341-7(5)) Blckstn Audio.

Oncology Nursing Review: J & B Version. 2nd ed. Ed. by Connie Henke Yarbro et al. (C). 1999. audio compact disk 37.50 (978-0-7637-1126-9(8), 1126-8) Jones Bartlett.

Oncomd: The Physician's Cancer Chemotherapy Drug Manual 2003. Edward Chu & Vincent T. Devita. (C). 2003. audio compact disk 69.95 (978-0-7637-2536-5(6)) Jones Bartlett.

One. 2001. audio compact disk 25.00 (978-0-9711240-1-1(9)) Blissen Pr.

***One.** Contrib. by Dave Williamson. Created by Dave Clark. (ENG.). 2007. audio compact disk 59.99 (978-5-557-43513-0(1)) Lillenas.

One: Discovering the Secrets of Soul Mate Love. Kathy Freston. Read by Kathy Freston. (Running Time: 6 hrs.). (ENG.). 2008. audio compact disk 29.98 (978-1-60286-028-5(9), WeinsteinBks) Perseus Bks Grp.

One: Discovering the Secrets of Soul Mate Love. unabr. ed. Kathy Freston. 2008. 24.98 (978-1-60286-072-8(6), WeinsteinBks) Pub: Perseus Bks Grp. Dist(s): PerseuPGW

***One: Songs Celebrating God's Call to Holiness.** Created by Lillenas Publishing Company. (ENG.). 2007. audio compact disk 10.00 (978-5-557-43512-3(3)) Lillenas.

***One: Songs Celebrating God's Call to Holiness.** Contrib. by Dave Williamson. Created by Dave Clark. (ENG.). 2007. audio compact disk 16.99 (978-5-557-43510-9(7)) Lillenas.

ONE - Divine - Audio CD. 2006. 29.95 (978-0-9789906-2-6(5)) One Unified.

ONE - Universal Version - Audio. 2006. 29.95 (978-0-9789906-5-7(X)) One Unified.

One- a Collection of Demos. 2002. audio compact disk 17.95 (978-0-9740939-1-8(2)) Tate Pubng.

One Across, Two Down. unabr. ed. Ruth Rendell. Read by Nicky Henson. 6 cass. (Running Time: 6 hrs. 30 min.). 1998. 49.95 (978-0-7540-0130-0(X), CAB1553) Pub: Chivers Audio Bks GBR. Dist(s): AudioGO
Stanley's interests in life include solving crossword puzzles & his mother-in-law's money. For 20 years, the puzzles have been his only pleasure, the money is only his dream. It has never occurred to Stanley that his mother-in-law would keep the money from him. Until now. Clever Stanley decides to construct a puzzle of his own that will give death a helping hand.

One Afternoon, Audiocassette. Yumi Heo. (Metro Reading Ser.). (J). (gr. k). 2000. 8.46 (978-1-58120-994-5(0)) Metro Teaching.

***One Amazing Thing.** unabr. ed. Chitra Banerjee Divakaruni. 1 Playaway. (Running Time: 8 hrs.). 2010. 59.75 (978-1-4407-7645-8(8)); 61.75 (978-1-4407-7642-7(3)); audio compact disk 77.75 (978-1-4407-7643-4(1)) Recorded Bks.

***One Amazing Thing.** unabr. collector's ed. Chitra Banerjee Divakaruni. 7 CDs. (Running Time: 8 hrs.). 2010. audio compact disk 44.95 (978-1-4407-7644-1(X)) Recorded Bks.

One & All: The Best of Cherish the Ladies. Perf. by Cherish the Ladies. 1 cass. (Running Time: 1 hr.). 8.78 (SIF 1187); audio compact disk 12.78 (SIF 1187) NewSound.

One & Last Love. unabr. ed. John Braine. Read by Richard Earthy. 7 cass. (Running Time: 8 hrs.). (Isis Cassettes Ser.). 2001. 61.95 (978-1-85089-707-1(7), 89105) Pub: ISIS Audio GBR. Dist(s): Ulverscroft US

One & Last Love. unabr. ed. John Braine & Peter Lovesey. 7 cass. (Isis Ser.). (J). 2004. 61.95 (978-1-85089-819-1(7)) Pub: ISIS Lrg Prnt GBR. Dist(s): Ulverscroft US

One & Only. Perf. by Big Daddy Weaver. 2002. audio compact disk Provident Mus Dist.

One & Only Me. Lisa Atkinson. Perf. by Lisa Atkinson. (J). 1999. audio compact disk 14.95 (978-0-939065-75-2(4)) Gentle Wind.

One & Only Me. Music by Lisa Atkinson. 1 cass. (Running Time: 43 min.). (J). (gr. k up). 1989. 9.95 (978-0-939065-47-9(9), GW1051) Gentle Wind.
Songs about monsters, bathtime & going to the grocery store.

One & Only Shrek: Plus 5 Other Stories. unabr. ed. William Steig. Illus. by William Steig. Read by Meryl Streep & Stanley Tucci. 1 CD. (Running Time: 1 hr. 30 mins. 0 sec.). (ENG.). (J). (ps-3). 2007. audio compact disk 14.95 (978-1-4272-0152-2(8)) Pub: Macmill Audio. Dist(s): Macmillan

One & the Same: My Life As an Identical Twin & What I've Learned about Everyone's Struggle to Be Singular. unabr. ed. Abigail Pogrebin. Narrated by Justine Eyre. (Running Time: 9 hrs. 0 mins. 0 sec.). (ENG.). 2009. 24.99 (978-1-4001-6484-4(2)); audio compact disk 34.99 (978-1-4001-1484-9(5)); audio compact disk 69.99 (978-1-4001-4484-6(1)) Pub: Tantor Media. Dist(s): IngramPubServ

***One & the Same: My Life As an Identical Twin & What I've Learned about Everyone's Struggle to Be Singular.** unabr. ed. Abigail Pogrebin. Narrated by Justine Eyre. (Running Time: 9 hrs. 0 mins.). 2009. 15.99 (978-1-4001-8484-2(3)) Tantor Media.

One & the Two: Gender, Identity & Relationship. Read by Robert Moore & Caroline Stevens. 8 cass. (Running Time: 12 hrs.). 1987. 62.95 (978-0-7822-0208-3(X), 253) C G Jung IL.

One Angry Broad: Assertive Living for Fearless Aging. Compiled by Sally Atman. 2006. audio compact disk 15.95 (978-1-928843-26-9(3)) Ad Lib Res.

One Bar Fill-Ins for the Rock Drummer. Rod Sims. 1995. pap. bk. 14.95 (978-1-57424-011-5(0), Centerbrook Publishing) Centerstream Pub.

One Beastly Beast. unabr. ed. Garth Nix. Read by Stig Wemyss. (Running Time: 2 hrs. 31 mins.). (J). 2009. audio compact disk 43.95 (978-1-74214-542-6(6), 9781742145426) Pub: Bolinda Pubng AUS. Dist(s): Bolinda Pub Inc

One Better. abr. ed. Rosalyn McMillan. (ENG.). 2006. 14.98 (978-1-59483-694-7(9)) Pub: Hachet Audio. Dist(s): HachBkGrp

One Blood: Inside Britain's New Street Gangs. 1 cass. (Running Time: 1 hr.). 12.99 (978-0-89051-286-9(8)) Master Bks.

One Blood - Audio. Narrated by Philip Fryer. 2005. audio compact disk 15.99 (978-0-89051-444-3(5)) Master Bks.
What does "race" really mean? Are there really multiple races of humans? Where did the concept of races originate? You may be surprised at the answers and appalled at the atrocities cited from history in this revealing audio.

One Breath at a Time: Spiritual Awakening & Serenity for People in Recovery. abr. ed. Scott Morrison. 1 cass. (Running Time: 1 hr.). 1998. 7.50 (978-1-882496-29-7(9)) Twnty Frst Cntry Ren.
Happiness, freedom, & joy on the road to spiritual awakening by way of rigorous honesty, humility, prayer, love, & meditation.

One Brief Shining Moment, unabr. collector's ed. William Manchester. Read by Arthur Addison. 7 cass. (Running Time: 10 hrs. 30 min.). 1999. 56.00 (978-0-7366-4453-2(9), 4898) Books on Tape.
This is a celebration of the life of John Fitzgerald Kennedy. The author writes that while JFK's death was a tragedy, his life was a triumph. Culling incidents from a friendship that spanned almost two decades, the author recalls family gatherings at Hyannisport, grueling campaign trips, & quiet evenings alone with the President in the White House family quarters. The resulting portrait provides us with myriad anecdotes & insights into a life that bristled with vigor, competitiveness, & an unflagging drive for excellence; a life that shone with elegance, intelligence, & compassion.

One Bullet Away: The Making of a Marine Officer. abr. ed. Nathaniel C. Fick. Read by Nathaniel C. Fick. 2005. 15.95 (978-0-7435-5244-8(X)) Pub: S&S Audio. Dist(s): S and S Inc

One Bullet Away: The Making of a Marine Officer. unabr. ed. Nathaniel C. Fick. Read by Andy Paris. 14 CDs. (Running Time: 16 hrs.). 2006. audio compact disk 119.75 (978-1-4193-7595-8(4), C3623); 109.75 (978-1-4193-7593-4(8), 98286) Recorded Bks.
Nathaniel Fick is a former captain in the First Reconnaissance Battalion of the United States Marine Corps. In this vividly told memoir, he recounts his training and years of service in Afghanistan and Iraq. From the classroom to the heat of combat, this contemplative account of one man's transformation from civilian to soldier abounds with action and intellect.

One Child. Perf. by Natalie Grant. 1 cass. (Running Time: 1 hr.). 1999. 7.98 (978-0-7601-2940-1(1)) Provident Music.

One Child. Perf. by Natalie Grant. 1 cass. (Running Time: 1 hr.). 1999. 8.98 (978-0-7601-3154-1(6)) Provident Music.

One Child's War. unabr. ed. Victoria Massey. Read by Diana Bishop. 4 cass. (Running Time: 4 hr. 30 min.). (Isis Ser.). (J). 2001. 44.95 (978-0-7531-0281-7(1), 970914) Pub: ISIS Lrg Prnt GBR. Dist(s): Ulverscroft US
Vicky Massey, was a bewildered seven-year-old when the threat of bombs wrenched her away from all that was familiar, friendly & comforting. The fact that Dick & Mary Williams welcomed her & did their very best to ease her homesickness made it worse. Anxious to protect her from worry they failed to realize that silence was the most terrifying of all.

One Christmas in Washington: Roosevelt & Churchill Forge the Grand Alliance. David J. Bercuson & Holger H. Herwig. (Running Time: 39600 sec.). 2005. audio compact disk 90.00 (978-0-7861-7546-8(X)) Blckstn Audio.

One Christmas in Washington: Roosevelt & Churchill Forge the Grand Alliance. David J. Bercuson & Holger H. Herwig. (Running Time: 39600 sec.). 2005. 65.95 (978-0-7861-3787-9(8)) Blckstn Audio.

One Christmas in Washington: Roosevelt & Churchill Forge the Grand Alliance. unabr. ed. David J. Bercuson & Holger H. Herwig. 10 CDs. (Running Time: 39600 sec.). 2005. audio compact disk 29.95 (978-0-7861-7628-1(8), ZE3557) Blckstn Audio.

One Christmas in Washington: Roosevelt & Churchill Forge the Grand Alliance. unabr. ed. David J. Bercuson & Holger H. Herwig. Read by Lloyd James. 1 MP3. (Running Time: 39600 sec.). 2005. audio compact disk 29.95 (978-0-7861-7869-8(8), ZM3557); 29.95 (978-0-7861-3763-3(0), E3557) Blckstn Audio.
One Christmas in Washington is the fascinating, in-depth look at one of the most crucial periods in modern history: the weeks between December 1941 and January 1942, when Churchill and Roosevelt - seemingly on the run after Dunkirk and Pearl Harbor - met at the White House, forging what turned out to be the Grand Alliance - while in the background, a gloomy and confused America went about their Christmas celebrations. This is the authoritative and emotional story of two proud and accomplished statesmen struggling to overcome biases, suspicion, and hubris to create what turned out to be the war-winning alliance. Bercuson and Herwig grippingly recreate the dramatic days of the Washington War conference of 1941, code-named ARCADIA using the diaries, meeting notes, personal letters, and detailed minutes that contain day-by-day, almost hour-by-hour accounts of these historic events.

One Clue Beyond: Tales of Supernatural Suspense, Psychic Puzzles & Occult Investigators. unabr. ed. Ed. by Otto Penzler. 8 cass. (Running Time: 12 hrs.). 2003. 34.95 (978-1-59007-065-9(8), N Millennium Audio) Pub: New Millenn Enter. Dist(s): PerseuPGW
A spine-tingling collection of supernatural suspense stories from the world's foremost writers. Featuring several new stories written especially for this anthology - including a new story from Harlan Ellison - this mesmerizing batch is a thrilling blend of new and classic tales sure to please fans of the supernatural, occult, mystery and suspense.

One Communion of Love. James V. Marchionda. 1 cass. (Running Time: 1 hr.). 2000. 11.00 (978-1-58459-063-7(7)); 16.00 (978-1-58459-064-4(5)) Wrld Lib Pubns.
Collection of text & music to enrich spiritual life.

One Corpse Too Many. Ellis Peters, pseud. Perf. by Derek Jacobi & Sean Pertwee. 1 cass. (Running Time: 1 hr. 20 min.). Dramatization. (Chronicles of Brother Cadfael Ser.: Vol. 2). 1999. 9.95 (978-1-56938-265-3(4), AMP-2654) Acorn Inc.
The calm of Cadfael's new life is disrupted when he unwittingly uncovers a brutal murder. He sets out on the trail of a killer in a city engulfed by war, where no one is above suspicion.

One Corpse Too Many. Ellis Peters, pseud. Read by Derek Jacobi. 2 cass. (Running Time: 3 hrs.). (Chronicles of Brother Cadfael Ser.: Vol. 2). 1998. (978-1-84032-150-0(4), HoddrStoughton) Hodder General GBR.
The official tally of the slain is 94 - but Brother Cadfael finds he has 95 to bury...In this matter of the "corpse too many," Brother Cadfael's extraordinary abilities are taxed to the limit. He has to track down a murdered & avenge a brutal death.

One Corpse Too Many. Ellis Peters, pseud. Read by Patrick Tull. 6. (Running Time: 11 Hours). 29.95 (978-1-4025-2809-5(4)) Recorded Bks.

One Corpse Too Many. unabr. ed. Ellis Peters. Read by Johanna Ward. 6 cass. (Running Time: 8 hrs. 30 mins.). 2000. 44.95 (978-0-7861-1126-8(7), 1891) Blckstn Audio.

***One Corpse Too Many.** unabr. ed. Ellis Peters. Read by Johanna Ward. (Running Time: 7 hrs. 30 mins.). 2010. 29.95 (978-1-4332-6473-3(0)); audio compact disk 69.00 (978-1-4332-6470-2(6)) Blckstn Audio.

One Corpse Too Many. unabr. ed. Ellis Peters, pseud. Read by Johanna Ward. 6 cass. (Running Time: 9 hrs.). (Chronicles of Brother Cadfael Ser.: Vol. 2). 1997. 44.95 (1891) Blckstn Audio.
In 1138, war between King Stephen & the Empress Maud takes Brother Cadfael from the quiet world of his abbey garden into a battlefield of passions, deceptions & death.

One Corpse Too Many. unabr. ed. Ellis Peters, pseud. Narrated by Patrick Tull. 7 cass. (Running Time: 9 hrs. 45 mins.). (Chronicles of Brother Cadfael Ser.: Vol. 2). 1991. 60.00 (978-1-55690-392-2(8), 91302E7) Recorded Bks.
When the castle of Shrewsbury is taken during the war between Empress Maud & King Stephen, 94 prisoners are taken, 94 are hanged. When Brother Cadfael arrives to perform the burial rites, he finds one corpse too many among the bodies stacked about the fortress.

One Dangerous Lady. Jane Stanton Hitchcock. Read by Barbara Rosenblat. (Running Time: 11 hrs. 30 mins.). 2005. reel tape 65.95 (978-0-7861-3039-9(3)); audio compact disk 81.00 (978-0-7861-7943-5(0)) Blckstn Audio.

One Dangerous Lady. unabr. ed. Jane Stanton Hitchcock. Read by Barbara Rosenblat. 9 CDs. (Running Time: 11 hrs. 30 mins.). 2005. audio compact disk 32.95 (978-0-7861-7985-5(6)); audio compact disk 29.95 (978-0-7861-8117-9(6)) Blckstn Audio.

One Dangerous Lady. unabr. ed. Jane Stanton Hitchcock. Read by Barbara Rosenblat. 8 cass. (Running Time: 46800 sec.). 2005. 29.95 (978-0-7861-3435-9(6)) Blckstn Audio.

***One Day.** unabr. ed. David Nicholls. Read by Anna Bentinck. (ENG.). 2010. audio compact disk 35.00 (978-0-307-91295-4(7), Random AudioBks) Pub: Random Audio Pubg. Dist(s): Random

One Day at a Time. Cristy Lane. 4 cass. (Running Time: 4 hrs.). 2001. 29.95 L S Records.
The greatest success and love story ever told. She came from the wrong side of the tracks, a family of 12. Two strikes against her - poverty and shyness. At fourteen her dreams were shattered. She vowed she would never sing again. She almost lost her life twice, and her strength and faith was tested again in 1982 when her husband was sent to prison for 3 years.

One Day at a Time. abr. ed. Danielle Steel. Read by Dan John Miller. (Running Time: 5 hrs.). 2010. audio compact disk 14.99 (978-1-4233-2087-6(5), 9781423320876, BCD Value Price) Brilliance Audio.

One Day at a Time. unabr. ed. Danielle Steel. Read by Dan John Miller. 1 MP3-CD. (Running Time: 9 hrs.). 2009. 24.99 (978-1-4233-2082-1(4), 9781423320821, Brilliance MP3); 39.97 (978-1-4233-2083-8(2), 9781423320838, Brinc Audio MP3 Lib); 39.97 (978-1-4233-2085-2(9), 9781423320852, BADLE); 24.99 (978-1-4233-2084-5(0), 9781423320845, BAD); audio compact disk 38.99 (978-1-4233-2080-7(8), 9781423320807, Bril Audio CD Unabri); audio compact disk 102.97 (978-1-4233-2081-4(6), 9781423320814, BriAudCD Unabrid) Brilliance Audio.

One Day at a Time: Affirmations for the First Ninety Days As a Nonsmoker. unabr. ed. David C. Jones. 1 cass. (Running Time: 1 hr.). 1996. 9.95 (978-1-878400-05-5(3)) Dolphin Pub.
Positive affirmations specifically relating to becoming a nonsmoker. This tape gives the new nonsmoker support for the first ninety days.

One Day At a Time: Christy Lane, Her Life Story. Lee Stoller & Pete Chaney. Perf. by Lee Stoller. Contrib. by Pete Chaney. 4 cass. (Running Time: 6 hrs.). 1984. cass. & video 25.00 (978-0-9614370-1-5(4)) L S Records.

One Day in the Life of Ivan Denisovich, unabr. ed. Aleksandr Solzhenitsyn. Read by Bernard Mayes. 4 cass. (Running Time: 5 hrs. 30 mins.). 1992. 32.95 (978-0-7861-0329-4(9), 1289) Blckstn Audio.
First published in the Soviet journal "Novy Mir" in 1962, this stands as a classic of contemporary literature. This is the story of labor camp inmate Ivan Denisovich Shukhov's struggle to maintain his dignity in the face of communist oppression. An unforgettable portrait of the world of Stalin's forced work camps, this is one of the most extraordinary literary documents to have emerged from the Soviet Union & confirms Solzhenitsyn's stature as a literary genius.

***One Day in the Life of Ivan Denisovich.** unabr. ed. Aleksandr Solzhenitsyn. Read by Richard Brown. (Running Time: 5 hrs. 30 mins.). 2010. 29.95 (978-1-4417-4160-8(7)); audio compact disk 55.00 (978-1-4417-4157-8(7)) Blckstn Audio.

One Day in the Life of Ivan Denisovich. unabr. ed. Aleksandr Solzhenitsyn. Read by Eli Wallach. 1 cass. (Running Time: 1 hr.). 1984. 12.95 (978-0-694-50262-2(6), SWC 1447) HarperCollins Pubs.

One Day in the Life of Ivan Denisovich, unabr. ed. Aleksandr Solzhenitsyn. Narrated by Frank Muller. 3 cass. (Running Time: 4 hrs. 30 mins.). 1999. 26.00 (978-1-55690-393-9(6), 82034E7) Recorded Bks.
A day in the life of a Soviet forced-labor camp by the country's best-known dissident.

One-Day MBA, Vol. 2. Aan Weiss. 12 CDs. 2005. audio compact disk 245.00 (978-1-928611-08-0(7), Las Bri) Summit Cons Grp.

One Day Mba, Vol. 4. Alan Weiss. Illus. by Alan Weiss. 2007. audio compact disk 295.00 (978-1-928611-12-7(5)) Summit Cons Grp.

One Day the Ice Will Reveal All Its Dead. unabr. ed. Clare Dudman. Read by Christopher Lane. 9 cass. (Running Time: 13 hrs.). 2004. 62.95 (978-0-7861-2642-2(6), 3248); audio compact disk 88.00 (978-0-7861-8739-3(5), 3248) Blckstn Audio.
In his lifetime Alfred Wegener was a German meteorologist who was better known for his offbeat scientific adventures than for his now famous theory of continental drift. In this lushly imagined and beautifully written novel, Clare Dudman charts his life from his 1880 birth to his last daring Arctic exploration in 1930. Dudman vividly chronicles the key episodes that punctuated his life.

One Day Will Be Your Last. Read by Mother Basilea Schlink. 1 cass. (Running Time: 30 min.). 1985. (0249) Evang Sisterhood Mary.
As seen from eternity; God's promises & their fulfilment.

One Day, Your Day. 1 cass. (Running Time: 1 hr.). 6.98 (978-1-57908-443-1(5)); audio compact disk 9.98 (978-1-57908-442-4(7)) Platinm Enter.

One Door Away from Heaven. Dean Koontz. 17 CDs. (Running Time: 21 hrs.). 2003. audio compact disk 160.00 (978-0-7366-9455-1(2)) Books on Tape.

One Door Away from Heaven. Dean Koontz. Read by Anne Twomey. 2001. 104.00 (978-0-7366-8319-7(4)) Books on Tape.

One Door Away from Heaven. unabr. ed. Dean Koontz. Read by Anne Twomey. (Running Time: 79200 sec.). (Dean Koontz Ser.). (ENG.). 2007. audio compact disk 39.95 (978-0-7393-4149-0(9), Random AudioBks) Pub: Random Audio Pubg. Dist(s): Random

One Drop of Blood. unabr. ed. Thomas Holland. Read by Patrick G. Lawlor. (Running Time: 12 hrs. 0 mins. 0 sec.). (ENG.). 2006. audio compact disk 75.99 (978-1-4001-3237-9(1)); audio compact disk 29.99 (978-1-4001-5237-7(2)); audio compact disk 37.99 (978-1-4001-0237-2(5)) Pub: Tantor Media. Dist(s): IngramPubServ
As the director of the U.S. Army's Central Identification Lab in Hawaii (CILHI), Robert Dean "Kel" McKelvey has made a career solving some of the country's most complex identification cases. Though fast approaching emotional meltdown, Kel now faces his thorniest case yet: the recovery of Jimmie Carl Trimble, a soldier from Arkansas who died a hero's death in Vietnam forty years ago. When a rare DNA sequence turns up at both the Army and FBI labs, it points to the unthinkable: a link between Trimble and a forty-year-old, unsolved racial killing in the Arkansas delta. Partnered uneasily with the volatile FBI Special Agent Michael Levine, Kel must peel back decades of silence to reveal a complex web of stolen identity, betrayal, patriotism, collusion, and lies.

One Dry Season: In the Footsteps of Mary Kingsley, unabr. ed. Caroline Alexander. Narrated by Lisette Lecat. 9 cass. (Running Time: 12 hrs. 15 mins.). 1998. 78.00 (978-0-7887-1924-0(6), 95345E7) Recorded Bks.
The story of the Victorian explorer & her travels in the French colony of Gabon, as she retraces the Kingsley's route through humid rain forests & up churning rivers.

One-Eye! Two-Eyes! Three-Eyes! A Very Grimm Fairy Tale. Aaron Shepard. Narrated by Anne Scobie. 1 cass. (Running Time: 13 mins.). (J). (ps-3). 2007. bk. 27.95 (978-0-8045-6954-5(1)) Spoken Arts.

One-Eye! Two-Eyes! Three-Eyes! A Very Grimm Fairy Tale. unabr. ed. Aaron Shepard. Narrated by Ann Scobie. 1 CD. (Running Time: 13 mins.). (J). (ps-3). 2007. bk. 29.95 (978-0-8045-4178-7(7)) Spoken Arts.

One False Move. Alex Kava. Read by Laura Hicks. 6 cass. 54.95 (978-0-7927-3302-7(9), CSL 687); audio compact disk 79.95 (978-0-7927-3303-4(7), SLD 687); audio compact disk 29.95 (978-0-7927-3304-1(5), CMP 687) AudioGO.

One False Move. unabr. ed. Harlan Coben. Read by Jonathan Marosz. 6 cass. (Running Time: 9 hrs.). (Myron Bolitar Ser.: No. 5). 2000. 48.00 (978-0-7366-4828-8(3), 5174) Books on Tape.
Sports agent Myron Bolitar is asked to keep an eye on the star of the new women's basketball league who's been receiving death threats on her life. As he moves headlong into the case, the odds are against his own better judgement, for in order to solve the case, win her heart & maybe to save his own, he must find the answer to the trail of lies, lust, & murder, where one false move can cost both of them their lives.

One False Move. unabr. ed. Harlan Coben. Read by Jonathan Marosz. (Running Time: 28800 sec.). (Myron Bolitar Ser.: No. 5). (ENG.). 2007. audio compact disk 19.99 (978-0-7393-4118-6(9), Random AudioBks) Pub: Random Audio Pubg. Dist(s): Random

One False Note. Gordon Korman. Read by David Pittu. (Running Time: 5 hrs.). (39 Clues Ser.: Bk. 2). (J). 2008. 49.99 (978-1-60775-486-2(X)) Find a World.

One False Note. Gordon Korman. Narrated by David Pittu. (ENG.). (J). (gr. 4-7). 2008. audio compact disk 19.95 (978-0-545-11157-7(9)) Scholastic Inc.

One False Note. unabr. ed. Gordon Korman. Narrated by David Pittu. 4 CDs. (Running Time: 5 hrs.). (39 Clues Ser.: No. 2). (ENG.). (J). (gr. 4-7). 2008. audio compact disk 49.95 (978-0-545-11939-9(1)) Scholastic Inc.

One Fat Englishman. unabr. collector's ed. Kingsley Amis. Read by David Case. 5 cass. (Running Time: 7 hrs. 30 mins.). 1989. 40.00 (978-0-7366-1486-3(9), 2362) Books on Tape.
Roger Micheldene, an English publisher, is on the loose in the U. S. He spends an October week shuttling between New York & Budweiser College in Pennsylvania. This exercises all his British appetites...snobbery, gluttony, anger, sloth & lust.

One Fearful Yellow Eye. unabr. collector's ed. John D. MacDonald. Read by Michael Prichard. 6 cass. (Running Time: 9 hrs.). (Travis McGee Ser.: Vol. 8). 1983. 48.00 (978-0-7366-0702-5(1), 1665) Books on Tape.
An urgent call for help from Gloria Geis involves Travis McGee in a bizarre plot. $600,000 in cash has mysteriously been extorted from her husband during the last painful year of his life . Geis' other heirs accuse her of stealing.

One Fell Soup. 1983. (3031) Am Audio Prose.

***One Fifth Avenue.** Candace Bushnell. (ENG.). 2008. 14.99 (978-1-4013-9028-0(5)); 14.99 (978-1-4013-9029-7(3)) Pub: Hyperion. Dist(s): HarperCollins Pubs

One Fifth Avenue. abr. ed. Candace Bushnell. Read by Donna Murphy. 7 CDs. (Running Time: 8 hrs.). 2009. 14.99 (978-1-4013-9314-4(4), Hyperion Audio) Pub: Hyperion. Dist(s): HarperCollins Pubs

One Fine Day. 2004. bk. 24.95 (978-1-56008-098-5(1)); pap. bk. 32.75 (978-1-55592-288-7(0)); pap. bk. 32.75 (978-1-55592-289-4(9)); 8.95 (978-1-56008-989-6(X)); cass. & flmstrp 30.00 (978-1-56008-736-6(6)) Weston Woods.

One Fine Day. Nonny Hogrogian. 1 cass., 5 bks. (Running Time: 3 min.). (J). pap. bk. 32.75 Weston Woods.
A fox needs to do some fast talking & walking before he can get his tail sewn on.

One Fine Day. Nonny Hogrogian. 1 cass. (Running Time: 3 min.). (J). (ps-3). bk. 24.95 Weston Woods.

One Fine Day. Nonny Hogrogian. 1 cass. (Running Time: 3 min.). (J). (ps-3). 1993. pap. bk. 14.95 (978-1-56008-099-2(X), PRA153); 8.95 (978-1-56008-118-0(X), RAC153) Weston Woods.
From the book by Nonny Hogrogian. A fox needs to do some fast talking & walking before he can get his tail sewn on.

One Fine Day in the Middle of the Night. unabr. ed. Christopher Brookmyre. 9 cass. (Isis Cassettes Ser.). (J). 2005. 76.95 (978-0-7531-1976-1(5)); audio compact disk 89.95 (978-0-7531-2335-5(5)) Pub: ISIS Lrg Prnt GBR. Dist(s): Ulverscroft US

One Fine Day the Rabbi Bought a Cross. unabr. ed. Harry Kemelman. Narrated by George Guidall. 5 cass. (Running Time: 6 hrs. 45 mins.). (Rabbi Small Mystery Ser.). 2000. 48.00 (978-0-7887-4324-5(4), 96230E7) Recorded Bks.
When vacationing in the Holy Land, Rabbi David Small finds himself involved in a challenging predicament. Jordan Goodman, a former resident of Barnard's Crossing, is the sole suspect in a murder case & the rabbi may be Jordan's only hope against a conviction.

One Fish, Two Fish, Red Fish, Blue Fish Book & CD. Dr. Seuss. (J). 1986. 18.66 SRA McGraw.

One Flew over the Cuckoo's Nest. Ken Kesey. Narrated by Mark Hammer. 12 CDs. (Running Time: 13 hrs. 15 mins.). audio compact disk 116.00 (978-1-4025-2102-7(2)) Recorded Bks.

One Flew over the Cuckoo's Nest. abr. ed. Ken Kesey & Ken Kesey. Read by Ken Kesey & Ken Kesey. 3. (Running Time: 12600 sec.). (ENG.). 2006. audio compact disk 24.95 (978-1-59887-052-7(1), 1598870521) Pub: HighBridge. Dist(s): Workman Pub

One Flew over the Cuckoo's Nest. unabr. ed. Ken Kesey. Read by Tom Parker. 7 cass. (Running Time: 10 hrs.). 2003. 49.95 (978-0-7861-1278-4(6), 2174) Blckstn Audio.
You've never met anyone like Randle Patrick McMurphy...the hero of "One Flew Over the Cuckoo's Nest." He's a boisterous, brawling, fun-loving rebel who swaggers into the ward of a mental hospital & takes over.... The contest starts as sport (with McMurphy taking bets on the outcome) but soon it develops into a grim struggle for the minds & hearts of the men, into an all-out war between two relentess opponents: Big Nurse, backed by the full power of authority...McMurphy, who has only his own indomitable will.

One Flew over the Cuckoo's Nest. unabr. ed. Ken Kesey. Read by Tom Parker. 9 CDs. (Running Time: 10 hrs.). 2000. audio compact disk 72.00 (978-0-7861-9893-1(1), 2174) Blckstn Audio.
You've never met anyone like Randle Patrick McMurphy... the hero of "One Flew over the Cuckoo's Nest." He's a boisterous, brawling, fun-loving rebel who swaggers into the ward of a mental hospital & takes over.... The contest starts as sport (with McMurphy taking bets on the outcome) but soon it develops into a grim struggle for the minds & hearts of the men, into an all-out war between two relentess opponents: Big Nurse, backed by the full power of authority... McMurphy, who has only his own indomitable will.

One Flew over the Cuckoo's Nest. unabr. ed. Ken Kesey. Read by Tom Parker. 7 pieces. (Running Time: 10 hrs. 30 min.). 2004. reel tape 35.95 (978-0-7861-2221-9(8)) Blckstn Audio.
You've never met anyone like Randle Patrick McMurphy... He's a boisterous, brawling, fun-loving rebel who swaggers into the ward of a mental hospital and takes over.

One Flew over the Cuckoo's Nest. unabr. ed. Ken Kesey. Read by Tom Parker. 7 cass. (Running Time: 10 hrs.). 2005. reel tape 29.95 (978-0-7861-3470-0(4), E2174) Blckstn Audio.

One Flew over the Cuckoo's Nest. unabr. ed. Ken Kesey. Read by Tom Parker. 13 vols. (Running Time: 36000 sec.). 2005. audio compact disk 24.95 (978-0-7861-9456-8(1), 2174); audio compact disk 29.95 (978-0-7861-8047-9(1), ZE2174) Blckstn Audio.

One Flew over the Cuckoo's Nest, unabr. ed. Ken Kesey. Read by Jonathan Marosz. 7 cass. (Running Time: 10 hrs. 30 mins.). 1999. 56.00 (978-0-7366-4499-0(7), 4935) Books on Tape.
The story of a mental ward & its inhabitants, especially the tyrannical Nurse Ratchett & Randle Patrick McMurphy, the brawling, life-loving new inmate who resolves to oppose her. We see the struggle through the eyes of Chief Bromden, the seemingly mute half-Indian patient, who witnesses & understands McMurphy's heroic attempt to do battle with the awesome power of The Combine.

One Flew over the Cuckoo's Nest. unabr. ed. Ken Kesey. Narrated by Mark Hammer. 9 cass. (Running Time: 13 hrs. 15 mins.). 1992. 78.00 (978-1-55690-707-4(9), 92327E7) Recorded Bks.
Randall McMurphy manages to get himself committed to an asylum in an attempt to escape the hard labor of jail. But he soon learns he might have made a mistake.

***One Flight Up: A Novel.** unabr. ed. Susan Fales-Hill. (Running Time: 12 hrs. 0 mins.). 2010. 17.99 (978-1-4001-8783-6(4)); audio compact disk 34.99 (978-1-4001-1783-3(6)) Pub: Tantor Media. Dist(s): IngramPubServ

***One Flight Up: A Novel.** unabr. ed. Susan Fales-Hill. Narrated by Cassandra Campbell. (Running Time: 12 hrs. 30 mins. 0 sec.). (ENG.). 2010. 24.99 (978-1-4001-6783-8(3)); audio compact disk 83.99 (978-1-4001-4783-0(2)) Pub: Tantor Media. Dist(s): IngramPubServ

One Foot in Eden see Twentieth-Century Poetry in English, No. 23, Recordings of Poets Reading Their Own Poetry

***One Foot in the Grave: A Night Huntress Novel, Book 2.** unabr. ed. Jeaniene Frost. Read by Tavia Gilbert. (Running Time: 13 hrs.). (Night Huntress Ser.). 2010. 29.95 (978-1-4417-4863-8(6)); audio compact disk 24.95 (978-1-4417-4862-1(8)) Blckstn Audio.

***One Foot in the Grave (Library Edition) A Night Huntress Novel, Book 2.** unabr. ed. Jeaniene Frost. Read by Tavia Gilbert. (Running Time: 13 hrs.). (Night Huntress Ser.). 2010. 59.95 (978-1-4417-4859-1(8)); audio compact disk 90.00 (978-1-4417-4860-7(1)) Blckstn Audio.

One for My Baby. unabr. ed. Tony Parsons. Narrated by Gerard Doyle. 8 cass. (Running Time: 11 hrs.). 2002. 75.00 (978-1-4025-3451-5(5)) Recorded Bks.

One for Sorrow: One for joy. Clive Woodall. 2005. audio compact disk 34.99 (978-1-4193-1709-5(1)) Recorded Bks.

One for Sorrow, Two for Joy. unabr. ed. Clive Woodall. Narrated by Ray Lonnen. 7 cass. (Running Time: 9 hrs. 30 mins.). (YA). 2005. 66.75 (978-1-84505-210-2(2), H1752) Recorded Bks.
In the land of Birddom, a terrible danger is spreading. Magpies and crows, led by the vicious Slyekin and his assassin Traska, have taken control by hunting down and exterminating one gentle species after another. But in the face of slaughter, a brave robin named Kirrick leads the charge against Slyekin. Flying to every corner of Birddom, Kirrick rallies eagles, owls and an assortment of other creatures to resist the menace. Before One for Sorrow, Two for Joy could even land on bookshelves, it was optioned by the Walt Disney Co. for a major motion picture. A classic epic of good versus evil, this rousing fable has been compared to Watership Down and The Lord of the Rings.

***One for the Angels.** 2010. audio compact disk (978-1-59171-173-5(8)) Falcon Picture.

One for the Mohave Kid. Louis L'Amour. 1 cass. (Running Time: 1 hr.). 2001. 10.95 (BMDD001) Lodestone Catalog.

***One for the Mohave Kid - Lonigan - War Party.** unabr. ed. Louis L'Amour. 2010. 14.99 (978-0-307-74880-5(4), Random AudioBks) Pub: Random Audio Pubg. Dist(s): Random

One for the Money. Janet Evanovich. (Stephanie Plum Ser.: No. 1). 2001. 12.95 (978-0-333-78015-2(9)) Pub: Macmillan UK GBR. Dist(s): Trafalgar

One for the Money. Janet Evanovich. (Stephanie Plum Ser.: No. 1). 2004. 10.95 (978-0-7435-4555-6(9)) Pub: S&S Audio. Dist(s): S and S Inc

One for the Money. abr. ed. Janet Evanovich. Read by Lori Petty. 3 CDs. (Running Time: 30 hrs. 0 mins. 0 sec.). No. 1. (ENG.). 2006. audio compact disk 9.95 (978-0-7435-5208-0(3), S&S Encore) Pub: S&S Audio. Dist(s): S and S Inc

One for the Money. unabr. ed. Janet Evanovich. Narrated by C. J. Critt. 6 cass. (Running Time: 8 hrs. 30 mins.). (Stephanie Plum Ser.: No. 1). 1995. 51.00 (978-0-7887-0449-9(4), 94639E7) Recorded Bks.
Stephanie Plum has lost her job, her car has been repossessed & most of her furniture has been sold off to pay her rent. Armed with an unregistered gun, she plunges headlong into her first case.

One for the Money. unabr. ed. Janet Evanovich. Narrated by C. J. Critt. 8 CDs. (Running Time: 8 hrs. 30 mins.). (Stephanie Plum Ser.: No. 1). 1999. audio compact disk 66.00 (978-0-7887-3406-9(7), C1012E7) Recorded Bks.
Stephanie Plum has lost her job as a New Jersey department store lingerie buyer, her Miata had been repossessed & most of her furniture has been sold off to pay last month's rent. Armed with an unregistered gun, Stephanie plunges headlong into her first case.

One for the Money. unabr. ed. Janet Evanovich. Narrated by C.J. Critt. (Stephanie Plum Ser.: No. 1). 2002. 24.95 (978-1-4025-3937-4(1)) Recorded Bks.

One Giant Leap: The First Moon Landing. Dana Meachen Rau. Illus. by Thomas Buchs. 1 cass. (Running Time: 1 hr.). Dramatization. (Smithsonian Odyssey Ser.). (J). (gr. 2-5). 1996. bk. 19.95 (978-1-56899-360-7(9), BC6001); 7.95 (978-1-56899-349-2(8), C6001) Soundprints.
Tomas & his friends have finally made it to the Smithsonian's National Air & Space Museum. Tomas has had his heart set on seeing the Moon Rock, but his friends keep dragging him to other exhibits. Frustrated, he decides to explore on his own & wanders over to the Lunar Module display. "Neil, Neil!" comes a voice & a tap on the shoulder. Confused, Tomas looks down & to his surprise he finds his clothing has been replaced by an astronaut suit with the name "Armstrong" stitched on its chest. And, Tomas is now sitting next to Buzz Aldrin & Mike Collins, leading the Apollo 11 crew to the first manned landing on the Moon!.

One Good Dog. unabr. ed. Susan Wilson. Read by Rick Adamson & Fred Berman. (Running Time: 8 hrs. 30 mins. 0 sec.). (ENG.). 2010. audio compact disk 34.99 (978-1-4272-0923-8(5)) Pub: Macmill Audio. Dist(s): Macmillan

One Good Turn. unabr. ed. Kate Atkinson. 10 cass. (Running Time: 51120 sec.). 2006. 89.95 (978-0-7927-4536-5(1), CSL 1042) AudioGO.

One Good Turn. unabr. ed. Kate Atkinson. Narrated by Steven Crossley. 2 CDs. (Running Time: 51120 sec.). 2006. audio compact disk 69.95 (978-0-7927-4560-0(4), CMP 1042) AudioGO.

One Good Turn. unabr. ed. Kate Atkinson. Read by Steven Crossley. 12 CDs. (Running Time: 51120 sec.). 2006. audio compact disk 110.95 (978-0-7927-4512-9(4), SLD 1042) AudioGO.

One Good Turn: A Novel. abr. ed. Kate Atkinson. Read by Robin Atkin Downes. (Running Time: 6 hrs.). (ENG.). 2006. 14.98 (978-1-59483-596-4(9)) Pub: Hachet Audio. Dist(s): HachBkGrp

One Good Turn: A Novel. abr. ed. Kate Atkinson. Read by Robin Atkin Downes. (Running Time: 6 hrs.). (ENG.). 2009. 44.98 (978-1-60788-276-3(0)) Pub: Hachet Audio. Dist(s): HachBkGrp

One Handed Catch. unabr. ed. M. J. Auch. Read by Ryan Sparkes. (J). 2008. 39.99 (978-1-60514-909-7(8)) Find a World.

One Heart. Rory Cooney. Perf. by Donna Pena & Pamela Warrick-Smith. 1 cass. (Running Time: 1 hr.). 1996. 10.95 (372); audio compact disk 15.95 (372) GIA Pubns.

One Heart. One Heart. 2000. (978-0-9814651-6-6(1)) ThunderVision.

One Heart, One Love. Perf. by Phil Perry. 1 cass., 1 CD. 8.78 (PM 82163); audio compact disk 13.58 CD Jewel box. (PM 82163) NewSound.

One Hello at a Time: Build Your Career with Networking. unabr. ed. Read by Pat Wagner & Alan Dumas. Ed. by Judy Byers. 1 cass. (Running Time: 55 min.). 1996. 12.95 (978-0-9642678-4-8(5)) Pattern Res.
A strategy for building mutually useful workplace relationships.

One-Hit Wonder. unabr. ed. Lisa Jewell. Narrated by Emma Powell. 10 cass. (Running Time: 12 hrs. 50 mins.). (Isis Ser.). (J). 2002. 84.95 (978-0-7531-1429-2(1)) Pub: ISIS Lrg Prnt GBR. Dist(s): Ulverscroft US
Bee Bearhorn had a number-one-hit single in 1985 - and was never heard of again. Fifteen years later she is found dead, and nobody seems to care. Ana Wills has always daydreamed about the exotic half-sister she hasn't seen for years. When she comes to London to clear her flat, Ana begins to unravel Bee's life: her missing cat, her secret country cottage and her mysterious weekends away.

One-Hit Wonder. unabr. ed. Lisa Jewell. Read by Emma Powell. 12 CDs. (Running Time: 13 hrs.). (Isis Ser.). (J). 2002. audio compact disk 99.95 (978-0-7531-1579-4(4)) Pub: ISIS Lrg Prnt GBR. Dist(s): Ulverscroft US

One Holy Fire: Let the Spirit Ignite Your Soul. abr. ed. Nicky Cruz. Narrated by Kelly Ryan Dolan. (Life of Glory Ser.). (ENG.). 2003. 16.79 (978-1-60814-330-6(9)) Oasis Audio.

One Holy Fire: Let the Spirit Ignite Your Soul. abr. ed. Nicky Cruz. 3 cass. (Running Time: 5 hrs.). (Life of Glory Ser.). 2004. 19.99 (978-1-58926-163-1(1)) Oasis Audio.

One Holy Fire: Let the Spirit Ignite Your Soul. abr. ed. Nicky Cruz & Kelly Ryan Dolan. 4 CDs. (Running Time: 5 hrs.). (Life of Glory Ser.). (ENG.). 2003. audio compact disk 23.99 (978-1-58926-164-8(X)) Oasis Audio.

One Hour from "Always Broke" Easy Money Solutions for the Perpetually Overdrawn. abr. ed. Sally Atman. Read by Sally Atman. 1 cass. (Running Time: 1 hr. 50 min.). 1999. bk. 10.95 (978-1-928843-07-8(7)) Ad Lib Res.
Addresses how to change one's concept of money in order to clean up credit, keep finances balanced & otherwise deal with the concept of money in a new light.

One Hour from "Huh?" The Top Ten Communication Methods from the "People Are from. abr. ed. 1 cass. (Running Time: 1 hr. 27 min.). 1999. (978-1-928843-03-0(4)) Ad Lib Res.

One-Hour Seminary. unabr. ed. Read by Gayle D. Erwin. 1 cass. (Running Time: 1 hr.). 1992. 4.95 (978-1-56599-521-5(X), C-21) Yahshua Pub.
Deuteronomy 10: 1-9.

One-Hour Survey of the Great Composers. Duane Shinn. 1 cass. (Running Time: 1 hr.). 19.95 (MU-3) Duane Shinn.
Presents 50 composers & looks at how they fit into the scheme of music as it developed.

One Hundred Children of Negativity. Swami Amar Jyoti. 1 cass. (Running Time: 1 hr.). 1975. 9.95 (B-2) Truth Consciousness.
Removing the blocks to release love & faith. Removing our negativities.

One Hundred Days (Plus One) Margaret McNamara. Illus. by Mike Gordon. Narrated by Emily Bauer. (J). (ps-2). 2008. audio compact disk 12.95 (978-1-4301-0615-9(8)) Live Oak Media.

One Hundred Fifty-One Activities to Increase Your Child's IQ. Simone Bibeau. 1986. 25.00 (978-0-318-60220-2(2)) Perception Pubns.

One Hundred Fifty-One Fun Activities to Increase Your Child's IQ: Will Your Children Be Successful? This Program Is for People Who Care! unabr. ed. Simone Bibeau. Read by Simone Bibeau. 2 cass. (Running Time: 2 hrs.). 1986. pap. bk. 25.00 (978-0-940406-15-5(2), 015) Perception Pubns.
Cassettes packed with games & activities to increase your child's ability to learn from his world. These tapes help parents to teach their child skills to increase his IQ through seeing, listening, movement, language, reading & math. All are based on games & other fun activities your child can enjoy alone or with the entire family. Learn how to turn the time spent with your child into quality learning time.

One Hundred Fifty Psalms of David: Arranged for One-Month's Daily Listening. unabr. ed. Perf. by Jane M. deVyver. 4 cass. (Running Time: 6 hrs.). 1994. 24.95 (978-1-881211-19-8(3)) Firebird Videos.
Chanted recording of complete Psalms. New King James Bible translation.

One Hundred Minutes to Better Photography. unabr. ed. Julian Padowicz. Read by Julian Padowicz. 2 cass. (Running Time: 2 hrs.). 1991. 19.95 (978-1-881288-00-8(5), BFI AudioBooks) BusnFilm Intl.
Explains principles & techniques of photography from both a technical & aesthetic aspect. Takes beginner to "advanced" level.

One Hundred One Dalmatians. 1 cass. (J). 11.99 (978-0-7634-0106-1(4)); 11.99 (978-0-7634-0105-4(6)); audio compact disk 19.99 (978-0-7634-0107-8(2)); audio compact disk 19.99 (978-0-7634-0108-5(0)) W Disney Records.

One Hundred One Dalmatians. 1 cass. (Running Time: 1 hr.). (Read-Along Ser.). (J). (ps-3). 1991. bk. 7.99 (978-1-55723-020-1(X)) W Disney Records.

One Hundred One Dalmatians. 1 cass. (Running Time: 1 hr.). (Sing-Along Ser.). (J). (ps-3). 1996. bk. 11.99 (978-0-7634-0103-0(X)) W Disney Records.

One Hundred One Dalmatians: Meet the Puppies. 1 cass. (My First Read Along Ser.). (J). bk. 7.99 (978-0-7634-0101-6(3)) W Disney Records.

One Hundred One Dalmations. 1 cass. (Running Time: 1 hr.). (Play Packs Ser.). (J). bk. 14.99 (978-0-7634-0104-7(8)) W Disney Records.

One Hundred One Dalmations Sing-a-Long. Prod. by Walt Disney Productions Staff. 1 cass. (Running Time: 35 mins.). (J). 1996. pap. bk. 22.50 (978-0-7634-0109-2(9)) W Disney Records.

One Hundred One Hot Licks Fingerstyle Guitar. Tommy Flint. 1982. bk. 15.95 (978-0-7866-2371-6(3), 93804BCD) Mel Bay.

One Hundred One Ideas to Organize Your Business Life: Eliminate the Little Hassles That Can Build up & Bury You. Paulette Ensign. 2 cass. (Running Time: 1 hr. 44 min.). 29.95 (V10142) CareerTrack Pubns.
You'll find that being organized isn't a personality characteristic. It's a skill & a state of mind you can achieve with a little help. Not to worry - these 101 ideas aren't complicated or gimmicky. They're subtle behavior shifts t hat easily become routine. They'll help save you time, money & aggravation. Plus, you'll gain the satisfaction (& rewards!) of being more productive.

One Hundred One Jazz Guitar Licks. Alan De Mause. 1996. bk. 17.95 (978-0-7866-2300-6(4), 93863BCD) Mel Bay.

One Hundred One Licks & Exercises for Electric Bass. Dan Gutt. 1996. bk. 17.95 (978-0-7866-2717-2(4), 93991BCD) Mel Bay.

One-Hundred One Ways to Organize Your Business Life. Paulette Ensign. 2 cass. (Running Time: 3 hrs.). 1995. 15.95 (978-1-55977-189-4(5)) CareerTrack Pubns.

One Hundred One Ways to Promote Yourself. unabr. abr. ed. Raleigh Pinskey. Read by Raleigh Pinskey. 2 cass. (Running Time: 3 hrs.). 1999. 17.95 (978-0-929071-55-8(7)) B-B Audio.
You may have the most outstanding business, product, ideas or talent in the world, but in order to be successful, you have to let the world know about it. Raleigh Pinskey offers you a crash course on how to get the attention you need. 101 Ways To Promote.

One Hundred Twenty-Five Most Important Metaphysical & Human Potential Concepts. Dick Sutphen. 2 cass. (Running Time: 3 hrs.). 1992. 14.95 Set. (978-0-87554-524-0(6)) Valley Sun.

One Hundred Words about My House. Richard Brown. Illus. by Richard Brown. 11 vols. (Running Time: 5 mins.). (J). (gr. k-2). 1990. pap. bk. 29.95 (978-0-87499-154-3(4)) Live Oak Media.
In this picture dictionary, one hundred words defining common household objects are introduced.

One Hundred Words about Transportation. Richard Brown. 1 readalong cass. (J). 1990. 9.95 Live Oak Media.
Introduces the beginning reader to one hundred different forms of transportation.

One Hundred Words about Working. Richard Brown. 1 readalong cass. (Running Time: 5 min.). (J). (ps-4). 1990. 9.95 Live Oak Media.
One hundred words introduce the beginning reader to various occupations.

One Hundred Years of Solitude. unabr. ed. Gabriel García Márquez. (Running Time: 30 mins.).Tr. of Cien Anos de Soledad. (ENG.). 2006. pupil's gde. ed. 5.98 (978-1-59483-713-5(9)) Pub: Hachet Audio. Dist(s): HachBkGrp

One I Do/Many I Don't: Gen. 24:12-14. Ed Young. 1989. 4.95 (978-0-7417-1739-9(5), 739) Win Walk.

One in a Million. unabr. ed. Kimberla Lawson Roby. 4 CDs. (Running Time: 4 hrs. 47 mins.). 2008. audio compact disk 49.95 (978-0-7927-5507-4(3)) AudioGO.
Ask Kennedi Mason and she'll say she and her husband, Blake, have a good marriage. That's why she can't wait to tell Blake the fabulous

news-that something he's always wanted has finally happened. But when Blake arrives home that evening, he has an announcement of his own, one that shocks Kennedi into silence. A poignant and witty story of hope and perception, expectation, and illusion, One in a Million beautifully shows us that sometimes what we think we have and what we think we want aren't real at all.

One in a Million. unabr. ed. Kimberla Lawson Roby. Narrated by Nehassaiu deGannes. (Running Time: 17220 sec.). (ENG.). 2008. audio compact disk 19.95 (978-1-60283-440-8(7)) Pub: AudioGO. Dist(s): Perseus Dist

One in a Million: From Rebel to Saint. Poems. Samuel Aubrey Wright. Narrated by Samuel Aubrey Wright. Music by UniqueTracks.com Staff & Shockwave-sound.com Staff. 1. (Running Time: 40mins). Dramatization. (YA). 2002. audio compact disk 11.95 (978-0-9722998-0-0(7)) wordofmouthpoetry.

One in a Million is the stirring testimony of one African American Poet who, upon coming to faith in God through Jesus Christ, was compelled to confront his own racial bigotry and deep seeded prejudice.Written and narrated by Word of Mouth's founding poet, Samuel Wright. This provocative composite of poetic works chronicles his miraculous transition, from Rebel to Saint. (Jazz, hip hop and Rhythm and Blues musical accompaniment.).

One in the Middle Is the Green Kangaroo. unabr. ed. Judy Blume. 1 read-along cass. (Running Time: 16 min.). (Follow the Reader Ser.). (J). (gr. k-3). 1983. (Listening Lib) Random Audio Pubg.

Freddy Dissel feels like the middle of a peanut butter sandwich, caught between his older brother & younger sister. But when his big chance comes to prove how special he is, Freddy jumps right onto center stage.

One in the Middle Is the Green Kangaroo. unabr. ed. Judy Blume. Read by Lionel Wilson. 1 cass. (Running Time: 16 mins.). (Follow the Reader Ser.). (J). (gr. k-3). 1983. 17.00 (978-0-8072-0044-5(1), FTR 77 SP, Listening Lib) Random Audio Pubg.

One Is a Positive Whole Number: Psalm 34:10; Col. 2:9-10. Ed Young. 1991. 4.95 (978-0-7417-1884-6(7), 884) Win Walk.

One Is the Sun. unabr. ed. Patricia Nell Warren. Read by Lorna Raver. (Running Time: 86400 sec.). 2008. 44.95 (978-1-4332-1213-0(7)); audio compact disk & audio compact disk 130.00 (978-1-4332-1210-9(2)) Blckstn Audio.

One Is the Sun. unabr. ed. Patricia Nell Warren. Read by Lorna Raver. 19 CDs. (Running Time: 24 hrs.). 2009. audio compact disk 34.95 (978-1-4332-1212-3(9)) Blckstn Audio.

One Is the Sun: Part One. unabr. ed. Patricia Nell Warren & Lorna Raver. (Running Time: 45000 sec.). 2008. 72.95 (978-1-4332-1209-3(9)) Blckstn Audio.

One Kind of Glory. Gilbert Highet. 1 cass. (Running Time: 30 min.). (Gilbert Highet Ser.). 11.95 (23327) J Norton Pubs.

This is a talk about the men & women who, although they themselves are forgotten, said & wrote things which have been remembered forever. Somerset Maugham said that a good story was one that could be told to strangers in a bar-car in a train & hold their attention.

One Kind of Glory & Tell Me a Story (audio CD) Gilbert Highet. (ENG.). 2006. audio compact disk 9.95 (978-1-57970-444-5(1), Audio-For) J Norton Pubs.

***One Kiss from You.** unabr. ed. Christina Dodd. Read by Justine Eyre. (Running Time: 8 hrs.). (Switching Places Ser.: No. 2). 2010. 24.99 (978-1-4418-2589-6(4), 9781441825896, Brilliance MP3); 24.99 (978-1-4418-2591-9(6), 9781441825919, BAD); 39.97 (978-1-4418-2590-2(8), 9781441825902, Brinc Audio MP3 Lib); 39.97 (978-1-4418-2592-6(4), 9781441825926, BADLE); audio compact disk 29.99 (978-1-4418-2588-9(6), 9781441825889, Bril Audio CD Unabri); audio compact disk 89.97 (978-1-4418-2593-3(2), 9781441825933, BriAudCD Unabrid) Brilliance Audio.

One L. Scott Turow. Read by Holter Graham. 2005. 23.95 (978-1-59397-708-5(5)) Pub: Macmill Audio. Dist(s): Macmillan

One L. unabr. ed. Scott Turow. 9 CDs. 2005. audio compact disk 89.95 (978-0-7927-3721-6(0), SLD 832) AudioGO.

One L. 30th unabr. ed. Scott Turow. Read by Holter Graham. 9 CDs. (Running Time: 11 hrs. 0 mins. 0 sec.). (ENG.). 2005. audio compact disk 39.95 (978-1-59397-673-6(9)) Pub: Macmill Audio. Dist(s): Macmillan

***One Lane Bridge.** unabr. ed. Don Reid. Narrated by Don Reid. (Running Time: 5 hrs. 5 mins. 43 sec.). (ENG.). 2010. 16.09 (978-1-60814-765-6(7)); audio compact disk 22.99 (978-1-59859-783-7(3)) Oasis Audio.

One Last Dance. abr. ed. Eileen Goudge. Read by Sandra Burr. 2 cass. (Running Time: 3 hrs.). 1999. 17.95 (FS9-43420) Highsmith.

One Last Dance. unabr. ed. Eileen Goudge. Read by Sandra Burr. (Running Time: 15 hrs.). 2008. 24.95 (978-1-4233-5919-7(4), 9781423359197, Brilliance MP3); 24.95 (978-1-4233-5921-0(6), 9781423359210, BAD); 39.25 (978-1-4233-5920-3(8), 9781423359203, Brinc Audio MP3 Lib); 39.25 (978-1-4233-5922-7(4), 9781423359227, BADLE) Brilliance Audio.

One Last Time: A Psychic Medium Speaks to Those We Have Loved & Lost. abr. ed. John J. Edward. Read by John J. Edward. 2 cass. (Running Time: 3 hrs.). 1998. 17.95 (978-1-55935-291-8(4)) Soundelux.

Includes author interview. Shares the messages of hope, solace, & love that have come from the hundreds of spirits he has contacted.

One Last Town. abr. ed. Matt Braun. Read by Jim Gough. 4 cass. (Running Time: 6 hrs.). 2002. 24.95 (978-1-890990-97-8(3), 99097) Otis Audio.

Western with sound effects.

One Less Thing to Worry About: Uncommon Wisdom for Coping with Common Anxieties. unabr. ed. Robin Cantor-Cooke & Jerilyn Ross. Read by Kirsten Potter. (ENG.). 2009. audio compact disk 31.95 (978-0-7393-8462-6(7), Random AudioBks) Pub: Random Audio Pubg. Dist(s): Random

***One. Life: Jesus Calls, We Follow.** Zondervan. (ENG.). 2010. 14.99 (978-0-310-41213-7(7)) Zondervan.

One-Life Solution: Reclaim Your Personal Life While Achieving Greater Professional Success. abr. ed. Henry Cloud. Read by Henry Cloud. 2008. audio compact disk 29.95 (978-0-06-157117-6(2), Harper Audio) HarperCollins Pubs.

One Life Versus Reincarnation. Paramhansa Yogananda. (Running Time: 43 mins.). 2007. audio compact disk 14.00 (978-0-87612-439-0(2)) Self Realization.

One Lifetime Is Not Enough. abr. ed. Zsa Zsa Gabor & Wendy Leigh. Read by Zsa Zsa Gabor. 2 cass. (Running Time: 3 hrs.). 1991. 16.00 S&S Audio.

Simultaneous release with the Delacorte hardcover.

One Light - One Sun. Raffi. 1 LP. (Running Time: 35 mins.). (J). 2001. lp 10.95 (KSR 8125) Kimbo Educ.

Includes Down on Grandpa's Farm, Take Me Out to the Ball Game, Octopus' Garden, Apples & Bananas, Des Colore, One Light, One Sun, Bowling Song & ten others.

One Light - One Sun. Perf. by Raffi. 1 cass. (Running Time: 1 hr.). (J). 1999. (978-1-886767-43-0(2)); audio compact disk (978-1-886767-42-3(4)) Rounder Records.

Raffi celebrates childhood with the moving "One Light, One Sun," the silly "Apples & Bananas" & "De Colores" - a beautiful ballad en espanol.

One Light, One Sun. Raffi. 1 cass . (Running Time: 35 mins.). (J). 2001. 10.95 (KSR8125C); audio compact disk 16.95 (KSR 8125CD) Kimbo Educ.

Includes Down on Grandpa's Farm, Take Me Out to the Ball Game, Octopus' Garden, Apples & Bananas, Des Colore, One Light, One Sun, Bowling Song & ten others.

One Light, One Sun. Perf. by Raffi. 1 cass. (J). (ps up). 10.98 (279); audio compact disk 17.98 (D279) MFLP CA.

Incredible music of the pied piper of children's music. Includes: "Tingalayo," "Fais Dodo," "De Colores," "Me & You," "Walk Outside," "Time to Sing," "Bowling Song," "Twinkle Twinkle, Little Star," "Apples & Bananas," "One Light, One Sun," "On Grandpa's Farm," "Octopus's Garden," & "In the World.".

One Light, One Sun. Perf. by Raffi. 1 cass. (Running Time: 35 mins.). (J). 7.98 (RDR 8057); audio compact disk 12.78 (RDR 8057) NewSound.

One Light, One Sun. Perf. by Raffi. 1 cass. (Running Time: 1 hr.). (J). 1999. (978-1-886767-69-0(6)); audio compact disk (978-1-886767-68-3(8)) Rounder Records.

Raffi celebrates childhood with the moving "One Light, One Sun," the silly "Apples & Bananas" & "De Colores" - a beautiful ballad en espanol.

One-Line Raps for Girls & Chaps: Rhythmic Self-Talk to Help Kids, & Adults Control Anger, Talk Respectfully, Stay Focused in School, & Build Self-Esteem. 2nd ed. No Bad Kid Band. Based on a work by Charlie Appelstein. 2006. audio compact disk 12.95 (978-0-9763694-7-9(8)) KidBridge Connect.

One Lonely Night. unabr. ed. Mickey Spillane. Read by Larry McKeever. 8 cass. (Running Time: 8 hrs.). (Mike Hammer Ser.). 1991. 48.00 (978-0-7366-2020-8(6), 2836) Books on Tape.

Someone is leaking military secrets to the Kremlin. It is up to Mike Hammer to find out who. His investigation points to Lee Deemer - man of the people - who looks like a sure winner in a state senate race. But to squeeze Deemer, Mike gets blood on his hands. Then there's no turning back - anything can happen.

One Magical Sunday: (but Winning Isn't Everything) unabr. ed. Phil Mickelson. Read by Phil Mickelson. Read by Amy Mickelson et al. (ENG.). 2005. 14.98 (978-1-59483-320-5(6)) Pub: Hachet Audio. Dist(s): HachBkGrp

One Magical Sunday: (but Winning Isn't Everything) unabr. ed. Phil Mickelson & Donald T. Phillips. Read by Phil Mickelson et al. (Running Time: 6 hrs.). (ENG.). 2009. 44.98 (978-1-60788-029-5(6)) Pub: Hachet Audio. Dist(s): HachBkGrp

One Man & His Bomb. unabr. ed. Narrated by Sheila Mitchell. 6 CDs. (Running Time: 23640 sec.). 2006. audio compact disk 64.95 (978-0-7927-4479-5(9), SLD 1009) AudioGO.

One Man & His Dog. Anthony Richardson. Read by Ray Dunbobbin. 4 cass. (Running Time: 6 hrs.). 1999. 44.95 (61845) Pub: Soundings Ltd GBR. Dist(s): ISIS Pub

One Man & His Dog. unabr. ed. Anthony Richardson. Read by Ray Dunbobbin. 4 cass. (Running Time: 6 hrs. 40 min.). (Sound Ser.). 2004. 44.95 (978-1-85496-184-6(5), 61845) Pub: UlverLrgPrint GBR. Dist(s): Ulverscroft US

Jan, a Czech refugee who joined the French Air Force in the war was shot down over Germany. Whilst sheltering in a farmhouse he found a motherless Alsation pup. Together they succeeded in getting back to the French lines.

One Man Army: 11 Kings 2:12. Ed Young. (J). 1981. 4.95 (978-0-7417-1157-1(5), A0157) Win Walk.

One-Man Band. Barbara Park. (Junie B., First Grader Ser.: No. 5). (J). (gr. k-3). 2004. 17.00 (978-0-8072-2350-5(6), ImaginStudio) Pub: Random Audio Pubg. Dist(s): Random

One Man Great Enough: Abraham Lincoln's Road to Civil War. unabr. ed. John C. Waugh. Read by David Drummond. (Running Time: 43200 sec.). 2007. audio compact disk 29.95 (978-1-4332-0530-9(0)); audio compact disk 72.00 (978-1-4332-0527-9(0)) Blckstn Audio.

One Man Great Enough: Abraham Lincoln's Road to Civil War. unabr. ed. John C. Waugh. Read by David Drummond. (Running Time: 43200 sec.). 2007. 29.95 (978-1-4332-0528-6(9)); audio compact disk 29.95 (978-1-4332-0529-3(7)) Blckstn Audio.

One Man Great Enough: Abraham Lincoln's Road to Civil War. unabr. ed. John C. Waugh & David Drummond. (Running Time: 43200 sec.). 2007. 59.95 (978-1-4332-0526-2(2)) Blckstn Audio.

One Man Running. Clive Egleton. Read by Christopher Kay. 10 CDs. (Running Time: 12 hrs. 40 mins.). (Soundings (CDs) Ser.). (J). 2004. audio compact disk 89.95 (978-1-84283-780-1(X)) Pub: ISIS Lrg Prnt GBR. Dist(s): Ulverscroft US

One Man Tango. abr. ed. Anthony Quinn & Daniel Paisner. Read by Anthony Quinn & Eric Conger. 2 cass,. (Running Time: 1 hr. 80 min.). 1995. 17.00 (978-0-694-51580-6(9)) HarperCollins Pubs.

One Man's America. unabr. collector's ed. Henry Grunwald. Read by Jonathan Reese. 9 cass. (Running Time: 13 hrs. 30 mins.). 1997. 72.00 (978-0-7366-3734-3(6), 4412-A); 64.00 (978-0-7366-3735-0(4), 4412-B) Books on Tape.

Henry Grunwald started as an immigrant copyboy & rose to become the Editor-in-Chief of Time magazine.

One Man's Empire. Geoffrey Bird & Graham Padden. 2009. 84.95 (978-1-84652-544-5(6)) Pub: Magna Story GBR. Dist(s): Ulverscroft US

One Man's Empire. Graham Padden & Geoffrey Bird. 2009. audio compact disk 99.95 (978-1-84652-545-2(4)) Pub: Magna Story GBR. Dist(s): Ulverscroft US

One Man's Family. unabr. ed. 3 cass. (Running Time: 3 hrs.). 15.95 (978-1-57816-084-6(7), OMF9002) Audio File.

A complete story presented in eighteen chapters from the popular series created by Carlton E. Morse.

One Man's Family, Bk. 71. 24 episodes on 6 ca. (Running Time: 60 min. per cass.). 1998. 24.98 Boxed set. (4341) Radio Spirits.

This portion covers the summer vacation of 1949 on Claudia & Nicky's "Sky Ranch." Finds nearly every member of the Barbour family relaxing by the pool, horseback riding, or dealing with the younger generation's difficulties.

One Man's Family, Bk. 78. 24 episodes on 6 ca. (Running Time: 60 min. per cass.). 1998. 24.98 Boxed set. (4301) Radio Spirits.

Longest running soap opera of all time is about the Barbour Family. This portion of the saga is the story of Teddy Barbour, adopted daughter of eldest son, Paul. For years, Teddy has been away from home serving as an Army nurse. Now in the fall of 1950, she returns home, where she is courted by a former Army dentist.

One Man's Family, Bk. 80. Carlton E. Morse. 3 cass. (Running Time: 3 hrs.). 1950. 23.85 (DD5712) Natl Recrd Co.

A complete story presented in 18 consecutive chapters about the Barbour family, Henry & Fanny, & their children Paul, Hazel, Clifford, Claudia & Jack. This segment involves Hazel's son, Pinky who flunks out of college, borrows money, & Grandfather Barbour has him work out his debt. Pinky's romance with a rich girl, Eunice, & how he handles the situation is a big part of the story.

One Man's Family, Vol. 1. 6 cass. (Running Time: 9 hrs.). 24.98 Set. Moonbeam Pubns.

One Man's Family, Vol. 2. 6 cass. (Running Time: 9 hrs.). 24.98 Set. Moonbeam Pubns.

***One Man's Family, Volume 1.** RadioArchives.com. (ENG.). 2002. audio compact disk 17.98 (978-1-61081-001-2(5)) Radio Arch.

***One Man's Family, Volume 2.** RadioArchives.com. (Running Time: 360). (ENG.). 2007. audio compact disk 17.98 (978-1-61081-064-7(3)) Radio Arch.

One Man's Journey to the East. Ram Dass. 2 cass. (Running Time: 2 hrs. 47 min.). 1969. 18.00 (00602) Big Sur Tapes.

Ram Dass, the former Richard Alpert, tells of his own journey from professor at Harvard, through psychedelia, to the finding of his guru in the East & the continuing changes in his own life.

One Man's Owl. unabr. collector's ed. Bernd Heinrich. Read by Walter Lawrence. 7 cass. (Running Time: 7 hrs.). 1990. 42.00 (978-0-7366-1866-3(X), 2697) Books on Tape.

One Man's Owl invites the reader to share in the experience of watching a great horned owl - not great horned owls in general but the particular "soggy, sorry-looking bundle of misery" that Bernd Heinrich adopted during a late spring snow when it was too young to fly or survive by itself. Combining reflections on natural history with a journal of the owl's development, the book is an engaging chronicle of how the author & "Bubo" came to know one another over three summers spent in the Maine woods, & how Bubo eventually grew into an independent hunter - & a personality that was "sometimes a clown, sometimes a terrorist." Bernd Heinrich is professor of zoology at the University of Vermont & the author of several books which include Bumblebee Economics & Ravens in Winter.

One Man's War. Tommy LaMore & Dan A. Baker. Read by Patrick G. Lawlor. (Running Time: 9 hrs. 30 mins.). 2003. 30.95 (978-1-59912-561-9(7)) Iofy Corp.

One Man's War. unabr. ed. Tommy LaMore & Dan Baker. Read by Patrick G. Lawlor. 8 CDs. (Running Time: 10 hrs.). 2003. audio compact disk 64.00 (978-0-7861-9142-0(2), 3148) Blckstn Audio.

One Man's War. unabr. ed. Tommy LaMore & Dan Baker. Read by Patrick Lawler. 7 cass. (Running Time: 10 hrs.). 2003. 49.95 (978-0-7861-2515-9(2), 3148) Blckstn Audio.

A compelling story not only for history aficionados and WWII scholars but also for those who are fascinated by the bittersweet nature of love in times of war.

One Man's War. unabr. ed. Tommy LaMore & Dan Baker. Read by Patrick G. Lawlor. 1 MP3. (Running Time: 10 hrs.). 2005. audio compact disk 24.95 (978-0-7861-8907-6(X), 3148) Blckstn Audio.

One Man's War: The WWII Saga of Tommy Lamore. unabr. ed. Tommy LaMore & Dan A. Baker. Read by Patrick G. Lawlor. 7 cass. (Running Time: 9 hrs. 30 mins.). 2005. reel tape 29.95 (978-0-7861-2745-0(7), E3148); audio compact disk 32.95 (978-0-7861-8546-7(5), 2E3148) Blckstn Audio.

Escaping certain death - not once but several times - lies at the core of this riveting, real-life story of an American soldier during World War II. In One Man's War: The WW II Saga of Tommy LaMore, a B-17 airman vividly details his experiences in war-ravaged Europe, from the horrific to the romantic and beyond. Intrigue, passion, and sacrifice imbue One Man's War in a compelling story not only for history aficionados and WWII scholars but also for those who are fascinated by the bittersweet nature of love in times of war.

One Man's West. unabr. collector's ed. David Lavender. Read by Michael Prichard. 8 cass. (Running Time: 12 hrs.). 1985. 64.00 (978-0-7366-0743-8(9), 1699) Books on Tape.

This is Lavender's effort to capture an era. The time when Colorado great ranches were breaking up, miners were being forced onto the dole, a whole way of life came grinding to a halt. Though few knew it, pioneers were passing into history.

***One Man's Wilderness: An Alaskan Odyssey.** unabr. ed. Sam Keith & Richard Proenneke. Narrated by Norman Dietz. (Running Time: 7 hrs. 0 mins. 0 sec.). 2010. 19.99 (978-1-4001-6953-5(4)); 14.99 (978-1-4001-8953-3(5)); audio compact disk 29.99 (978-1-4001-1953-0(7)); audio compact disk 71.99 (978-1-4001-4953-7(3)) Pub: Tantor Media. Dist(s): IngramPubServ

One Minute after You Die: A Preview of Your Final Destination. unabr. ed. Erwin W. Lutzer. 3 cass. (Running Time: 5 hrs.). 2003. 19.99 (978-1-58926-106-8(2), M64L-0100) Oasis Audio.

Opens up what the Bible has to say about death and the life after death, and explodes the lies about near-death experiences and reincarnation.

One Minute after You Die: A Preview of Your Final Destination. unabr. ed. Erwin W. Lutzer. Narrated by Erwin W. Lutzer. (Christian Perspective Ser.). (ENG.). 2003. 12.59 (978-1-60814-331-3(7)); audio compact disk 17.99 (978-1-58926-107-5(0), M68L-010D) Oasis Audio.

One Minute Apology: A Powerful Way to Make Things Better. unabr. ed. Ken Blanchard & Margret McBride. Read by Sam Tsoutsouvas. 2 cass. (Running Time: 3 hrs.). 2003. 16.00 (978-0-06-053824-8(4)); audio compact disk 18.00 (978-0-06-053823-1(6)) HarperCollins Pubs.

One Minute Audio Collection. Ken Blanchard et al. Read by Ken Blanchard et al. (ENG.). 2004. audio compact disk 39.95 (978-0-7435-3858-9(7), Nightgale) Pub: S&S Audio. Dist(s): S and S Inc

Three bestselling business audiobooks available for the first time in one extraordinary package. THE ONE MINUTE MANAGER By Ken Blanchard, Ph.D. and Spencer Johnson, M.D. With more than two million hardcover copies in print, The One Minute Manager ranks as one of the most successful management books ever published. Ken Blanchard and Spencer Johnson teach you the strategies of one-minute management to save time and increase your productivity whether it is in your business, your home, or even managing your children. PUTTING THE ONE MINUTE MANAGER TO WORK By Ken Blanchard, Ph.D and Robert Lorber, Ph.D. The bestselling team of Ken Blanchard and Robert Lorber bring you the ever-timely strategies of one-minute management in Putting the One Minute Manager to Work - an indispensable success tool for any manager striving to get the most from his or her people. THE ONE MINUTE MANAGER MEETS THE MONKEY By Ken Blanchard, Ph.D and William Oncken, Jr. In The One Minute Manager Meets the Monkey, authors Ken Blanchard and William Oncken, Jr. chastise executives who never have time for family or their own job enhancement because they accept too many responsibilities. They explain how to achieve a balance between supervision and delegation for reduced tension and improved productivity.

One Minute Can Change a Life. 2002. 16.95 (978-1-929664-05-4(2)) Life Support.

One Minute Entrepreneur: The Secret to Creating & Sustaining a Successful Business. unabr. ed. Don Hutson et al. Read by Don Hutson et al. (Running Time: 10800 sec.). (ENG.). 2008. audio compact disk 19.95 (978-0-7393-2905-4(7), Random AudioBks) Pub: Random Audio Pubg. Dist(s): Random

One-Minute Greek Myths. unabr. ed. Shari Lewis. Read by Shari Lewis. 1 cass. (Running Time: 1 hr.). 1989. 8.98 HarperCollins Pubs.

One Minute Manager. abr. ed. Spencer Johnson et al. 1 CD. (Running Time: 12 hrs. 0 mins. 0 sec.). (ENG., 2001. audio compact disk 19.95 (978-0-7435-0917-6(X), Sound Ideas) Pub: S&S Audio. Dist(s): S and S Inc

One Minute Manager. unabr. abr. ed. Ken Blanchard & Spencer Johnson. Read by Eric Conger. 2 CDs. (Running Time: 100 mins.). 2003. audio compact disk 18.00 (978-0-06-056750-7(3)) HarperCollins Pubs.

One Minute Manager Set. Ken Blanchard. Read by A. E. Whyte. 1 cass. (Running Time: 47 min.). (Listen & Learn USA! Ser.). 8.95 (978-0-88684-056-3(2)) Listen USA.
Reveals three secrets of management principles.

One Minute Manager Set. Ken Blanchard & Spencer Johnson. 2 cass. bk. 29.95 (OM0023) K Blanchard.
Discusses the number one motivator of people, how to praise & how & when to criticize; & how to create a situation where everybody wins.

One Minute Manager Set. Ken Blanchard & Spencer Johnson. 3 cass. (Running Time: 3 hrs.). 1996. 29.95 (2201AC) Nightingale-Conant.
Reveals step-by-step- how to instill a winning team spirit, ignite creativity, supercharge productivity & create a caring environment that taps the potential of every individual.

One Minute Manager Audio Collection. abr. ed. Kenneth Blanchard et al. Read by Kenneth Blanchard et al. (Running Time: 2 hrs. 30 mins. 0 sec.). (ENG.). 2009. audio compact disk 29.99 (978-0-7435-9651-0(X), Nightgale) Pub: S&S Audio. Dist(s): S and S Inc

One Minute Millionaire: The Enlightened Way to Wealth. abr. ed. Mark Victor Hansen & Robert G. Allen. Read by Mark Victor Hansen & Robert G. Allen. 3 CDs. (Running Time: 3 hrs. 20 mins.). (ENG.). 2002. audio compact disk 23.95 (978-0-553-71383-1(3), RHAA) Pub: Random Audio Pubg. Dist(s): Random

***One Minute Negotiator: Simple Steps to Reach Better Agreements.** unabr. ed. Don Hutson & George Lucas. (Running Time: 3 hrs. 0 mins. 0 sec.). (ENG.). 2010. audio compact disk 19.99 (978-1-4423-4100-5(9)) Pub: S&S Audio. Dist(s): S and S Inc

One Minute Salesperson. abr. ed. Spencer Johnson & Larry Wilson. Read by Spencer Johnson. 1 CD. (Running Time: 1 hr.). (ENG.). 2003. audio compact disk 15.00 (978-0-7393-0768-7(1), RHAA) Pub: Random Audio Pubg. Dist(s): Random

One Monday Morning. 2004. 8.95 (978-1-56008-990-2(3)); 8.95 (978-1-56008-991-9(1)); cass. & flmstrp 30.00 (978-0-89719-554-6(X)) Weston Woods.

One-Month Patterning. unabr. ed. Robert A. Monroe. Read by Robert A. Monroe. (Running Time: 45 min.). (Gateway Experience - Threshold Ser.). 1983. 14.95 (978-1-56113-258-4(6)) Monroe Institute.
Reshape your life with desired patterns.

One Month to Live: Thirty Days to a No-Regrets Life. abr. ed. Kerry Shook & Chris Shook. Read by Kerry Shook & Chris Shook. (Running Time: 14400 sec.). (ENG.). 2008. audio compact disk 21.95 (978-0-7393-5849-8(9), Random AudioBks) Pub: Random Audio Pubg. Dist(s): Random

One More Brevity see Robert Frost Reads

One More Encore. Perf. by Whitcross. 1 cass. (Running Time: 1 hr.). 1998. 10.98; audio compact disk 16.98 CD. Platinum Chrst Dist.
Includes "Say a Prayer," "No Second Chances," "Good Bye Cruel World," "Amazing Love," "Fallen," "Eye to Eye," "And of the Line," "Come Unto the Light," "Collide," "I Keep Prayin," "Far Away Places," "Home in Heaven," "Full Crucifixion," & "It's Already Done".

One More Encore. Perf. by White Cross. 1 cass. (Running Time: 1 hr.). 10.98 (978-1-57908-245-1(9)); audio compact disk 15.98 CD. (978-1-57908-244-4(0)) Platinm Enter.

***One More for the Road.** unabr. ed. Ray Bradbury. Read by Campbell Scott. (ENG.). 2005. (978-0-06-085503-1(7), Harper Audio); (978-0-06-085504-8(5), Harper Audio) HarperCollins Pubs.

***One More Pallbearer.** 2010. audio compact disk (978-1-59171-186-5(X)) Falcon Picture.

One More River. Bill Staines. 1 cass. (Running Time: 1 hr.). (J). 7.98 (RHR 111); audio compact disk 12.78 CD. (RHR 111) NewSound.

One More River. Perf. by Bill Staines. 1 cass., 1 CD. (J). 7.98 (RHR 111) NewSound.

One More River. unabr. ed. John Galsworthy. Read by David Case. (Running Time: 32400 sec.). (Forsyte Chronicles Ser.). 2007. 59.95 (978-1-4332-0565-1(3)); audio compact disk 72.00 (978-1-4332-0566-8(1)); audio compact disk 29.95 (978-1-4332-0567-5(X)) Blckstn Audio.

One More River, unabr. collector's ed. John Galsworthy. Read by David Case. 7 cass. (Running Time: 10 hrs. 30 min.). (Forsyte Saga Ser.). 1999. 56.00 (978-0-7366-4384-9(2), 4850) Books on Tape.
Detailed picture of the British propertied class, from the wealth & security of the mid-Victorian era through Edwardian high-noon to a post-WW I world of change, strikes & social malaise. By showing the Forsytes in all their strengths & weaknesses against a detailed background of English life.

One More River to Cross. unabr. ed. Will Henry. Narrated by Mark Hammer. 8 cass. (Running Time: 10 hrs. 30 mins.). 1996. 70.00 (978-0-7887-0720-9(5), 94897E7) Recorded Bks.
Follows an ex-slave in the wake of the Civil War as he searches for his promised land.

One More River to Cross. unabr. ed. Will Henry. Read by Mark Hammer. 8 cass. (Running Time: 10 hrs. 30 min.). 1996. Rental 16.50 (94897) Recorded Bks.

One More Sunday. unabr. collector's ed. John D. MacDonald. Read by Michael Prichard. 10 cass. (Running Time: 15 hrs.). 1984. 80.00 (978-0-7366-1015-5(4), 1946) Books on Tape.
MacDonald has no quarrel with religion, organized or not. But he is quick to label quackery for what it is.

One More Sunrise. abr. ed. Tracie Peterson & Michael Landon, Jr. Narrated by Aimee Lilly. (ENG.). 2008. 16.09 (978-1-60814-332-0(5)) Oasis Audio.

One More Sunrise. abr. ed. Tracie Peterson & Michael Landon. Narrated by Aimee Lilly. (Running Time: 6 hrs. 0 mins. 0 sec.). (ENG.). 2008. audio compact disk 22.99 (978-1-59859-242-9(4)) Oasis Audio.

One More Time: More Favorite Songs & One New Story. (J). 2005. audio compact disk 15.00 (978-1-878126-49-8(0)) Round Riv Prodns.

One Morning in Maine. unabr. ed. Robert McCloskey. Narrated by Christina Moore. 1 cass. (Running Time: 15 mins.). (ps up). 2001. 10.00 (978-0-7887-5031-1(3), 96484E7) Recorded Bks.
Today Sal & her father are crossing the bay to Buck's Harbor. Even more exciting, she discovers a loose tooth. When it falls out, she will make a very special wish. But after she digs for clams with her father, her tooth is gone! Now she must find another way to make her wish come true.

One Nation under God. 2001. 9.99 (978-1-58602-080-4(3)); audio compact disk 19.99 (978-1-58602-089-7(7)) E L Long.

One Nation under Therapy: How the Helping Culture Is Eroding Self-Reliance. unabr. ed. Christina Hoff Sommers & Sally Satel. (Running Time: 30600 sec.). 2007. 59.95 (978-1-4332-0742-6(7)); audio compact disk 81.00 (978-1-4332-0743-3(5)); audio compact disk 29.95 (978-1-4332-0744-0(3)) Blckstn Audio.

One New Man. Reuven Doron. 1 cass. (Running Time: 1 hr. 30 mins.). (Mystery of Israel & the Church Ser.: Vol. 1). 2000. 5.00 (RD01-001) Morning NC.
Reuven offers insight into the proper relationship between Israel & the church.

One Night in Frogtown. 2nd ed. Philip Pelletier. Music by Philip Pelletier. Illus. by Verne Lindner. (ENG.). (J). 2009. bk. 19.99 (978-0-9786176-3-9(0)) One World Mus.

One Night Stands & Lost Weekends. unabr. ed. Lawrence Block. Read by Scott Brick et al. 11 CDs. (Running Time: 13 hrs. 30 mins.). 2008. audio compact disk 100.00 (978-1-4159-5987-9(0), BksonTape) Pub: Random Audio Pubg. Dist(s): Random

***One Night that Changes Everything.** Lauren Barnholdt. (ENG.). (J). 2011. 39.99 (978-1-61120-008-9(3)) Dreamscap OH.

One of a Kind. Lisa M. Nelson. Perf. by Kevin-Anthony. 1 cass. (Running Time: 50 min.). (Positive Music for Today's Kids! Ser.). (J). 1992. 9.95 (978-0-9627863-5-8(7), BIP 005) Brght Ideas CA.
Seven songs of self-esteem. Instrumental sing-alongs on side 2.

One of a Kind: John 1:42. Ed Young. 1988. 4.95 (978-0-7417-1691-0(7), 691) Win Walk.

One of a Kind: The Story of Stuey the Kid Ungar, the World's Greatest Poker Palyer. unabr. ed. Nolan Dalla & Peter Alson. (Running Time: 10 hrs. 5 mins.). 2008. 29.95 (978-1-4332-2289-4(2)); audio compact disk 90.00 (978-1-4332-2286-3(8)) Blckstn Audio.

One of a Kind: The Story of Stuey the Kid Ungar, the World's Greatest Poker Player. unabr. ed. Nolan Dalla & Peter Alson. (Running Time: 10 hrs. 5 mins.). 2008. 65.95 (978-1-4332-2285-6(X)) Blckstn Audio.

One of A Kind -CD. Lyrics by The Trevor Romain Company. (J). 2006. audio compact disk (978-1-934365-69-4(6)) Trevor Romain.

One of Our Bombers Is Missing. unabr. ed. Dan Brennan. Read by Colin Bower. 6 cass. (Running Time: 8 hrs.). 1998. 69.95 Set. (978-1-85903-197-1(8)) Pub: Magna Story GBR. Dist(s): Ulverscroft US
A moving salute to the heroes who nightly endured the tension & terrors of bombing missions - bringing into tragic perspective the bald announcement "one of our bombers is missing".

One of Ours. unabr. ed. Willa Cather. Read by Flo Gibson. 8 cass. (Running Time: 11 hrs. 30 min.). 1997. 26.95 (978-1-55685-460-6(9)) Audio Bk Con.
Concerns sensitive & idealistic Claude Wheeler. Dissatisfied with his life as a Nebraskan farmer & with the ways of his family, he finds true meaning & beauty when he enters the army & goes to France in World War I.

One of Ours. unabr. ed. Willa Cather. Read by Kristen Underwood. 10 cass. (Running Time: 15 hrs.). 1998. 69.95 (978-0-7861-1360-6(X), 2269) Blckstn Audio.
Explores the destiny of a grandchild of the pioneers, a young Nebraskan whose yearnings impel him toward a frontier bloodier & more distant than the one that vanished before his birth. It is only when his country enters the First World War that Claude finds what he has been searching for all his life.

One of Ours, unabr. ed. Willa Cather. Read by Kristen Underwood. 10 cass. (Running Time: 15 hrs.). 1999. 69.95 (FS9-43269) Highsmith.

One of Us Works for Them. unabr. ed. Jack D. Hunter. Read by Kevin Patrick. 5 cass. (Running Time: 7 hrs. 30 min.). 1997. 39.95 (1898) Blckstn Audio.
Captain Carl Kraft is a man dancing on a dangerous tight-rope. By day he works as an Army Intelligence Officer, by night he secretly reports his department's strengths & weaknesses to a harsh & mysterious superior. Assigned the dirtiest job in his profession, he is ordered to set up a patsy - to frame a fellow officer a traitor.

One of Us Works for Them. unabr. ed. Jack D. Hunter. Read by Kevin Patrick. 5 cass. (Running Time: 7 hrs.). 2002. 39.95 (978-0-7861-1133-6(X), 1898) Blckstn Audio.

***One of Us Works for Them.** unabr. ed. Jack D. Hunter. Read by Kevin Patrick. (Running Time: 7 hrs.). 2010. 29.95 (978-1-4417-4541-5(6)); audio compact disk 69.00 (978-1-4417-4538-5(6)) Blckstn Audio.

One-on-One Discipleship: Ministry up Close & Personal. unabr. ed. Charles R. Swindoll. 6 cass. (Running Time: 4 hrs. 45 mins.). 1998. 30.95 (978-1-57972-284-5(9)) Insight Living.

One on One with Jack Welch. Mark Thompson & Richard Wilson. 1 CD. (Running Time: 1 hr.). 2002. audio compact disk 17.99 (978-0-9719341-9-1(3)) NPBI.
No one in corporate America has been more imitated, admired or quoted in the business press than Jack Welch. During his 20 years as Chairman and CEO of General Electric, he created the most valuable company in the world. In this unscripted, unrehearsed, intimate conversation, Jack Welch tells what makes him effective and how he built his billion dollar team.

One Past Midnight; The Langoliers. Stephen King. Read by Willem Dafoe. (Playaway Adult Fiction Ser.). 2009. 60.00 (978-1-60775-564-7(5)) Find a World.

One Percent Doctrine: Deep Inside America's Pursuit of Its Enemies since 9/11. abr. ed. Ron Suskind. Read by Edward Herrmann. 2006. 17.95 (978-0-7435-6173-0(2)) Pub: S&S Audio. Dist(s): S and S Inc

One Piece at a Time. Steck-Vaughn Staff. 2003. (978-0-7398-8420-1(4)) SteckVau.

One Pink Rose; One White Rose; One Red Rose, Vols. 2-4. Julie Garwood. Read by David Marshall Grant. (Clayborne Brides Ser.: Bk. 2-4). 2004. 10.95 (978-0-7435-4556-3(7)) Pub: S&S Audio. Dist(s): S and S Inc

One Plus One Equals One: Mark 8:34-38. Ed Young. 1986. 4.95 (978-0-7417-1530-2(9), 530) Win Walk.

One Poem at a Time. abr. unabr. ed. Samuel Hazo. Read by Samuel Hazo. (Running Time: 3 hrs.). 2008. 39.25 (978-1-4233-5338-6(2), 9781423353386, BADLE); 24.95 (978-1-4233-5337-9(4), 9781423353379, BAD); audio compact disk 39.25 (978-1-4233-5336-2(6), 9781423353362, Brlnc Audio MP3 Lib); audio compact disk 24.95 (978-1-4233-5335-5(8), 9781423353355, Brilliance MP3) Brilliance Audio.

One Poet Visits Another see Evening with Dylan Thomas

One-Pointed, Like an Arrow. Swami Amar Jyoti. 1 cass. (Running Time: 1 hr.). 1990. 9.95 (R-100) Truth Consciousness.
Emerging from the ocean of dreams into the sunshine of Reality requires one-pointed concentration without resistance to anything else.

One Police Plaza. unabr. ed. William J. Caunitz. Narrated by Richard Ferrone. 9 cass. (Running Time: 12 hrs. 45 mins.). 2001. 81.00 (978-0-7887-4994-0(3), 96298x7) Recorded Bks.
For Detective Lt. Dan Malone of New York's Fifth Precinct, the nude corpse of a travel agent found in a bathtub seems all in a day's work, until the little gold key she's holding leads to an after hours sex club & two of the numbers in her address book connect to the CIA. Suddenly, Malone is up to his neck in a mysterious conspiracy involving Israeli secret police, Muslim extremists, the U.S. Army & the NYPD.

One Potato, Two Potato: Program from the Award Winning Public Radio Series. Hosted by Fred Goodwin. 1 CD. (Running Time: 1 hr). (Infinite Mind Ser.). 2002. audio compact disk 21.95 (978-1-932479-13-3(9), LCM 244) Lichtenstein Creat.
Why are some people math whizzes while others are scared to do simple arithmetic without a calculator? This week we explore differences in math ability; new and old debates on math education (remember "The New Math?"); the link between autism and skills in rapid-fire calculation; and Hollywood's fascination with brilliant, troubled mathematicians. Plus a trip to AT&T's research labs and some of the best minds working in mathematics today. Guests include Brian Butterworth, Professor of Cognitive Neuropsychology in the Institute of Cognitive Neuroscience at University College in London; Keith Devlin, executive director of The Center for the Study of Language and Information at Stanford University; Jeremy Kilpatrick, professor of mathematics education at the University of Georgia; Gary Mesibov, professor of psychology at The University of North Carolina; Jerry Newport; and AT&T mathematics researchers David Applegate and Jeff Lagarius.

One Proven Method of Quitting Smoking - Hypnosis. Arlene V. Wayne. Read by Arlene V. Wayne. 2 cass. (Running Time: 1 hr. 30 min.). 1998. pap. bk. 27.99 Set. (978-1-892789-02-0(7)) Positive Changes.
Two seperate hypnosis sessions for smoking cessation.

One Quest. Claudio Naranjo. 1 cass. (Running Time: 1 hr.). 1999. 11.00 (04207) Big Sur Tapes.
1971 Esalen Institute.

One Raining, Pouring Morning Audio CD. Adapted by Benchmark Education Company Staff. Based on a work by Francisco Blane. (Reader's Theater Nursery Rhymes & Songs Ser.). (J). (gr. k-1). 2008. audio compact disk 10.00 (978-1-60634-001-1(8)) Benchmark Educ.

One Ranger: A Memior. David Marion Wilkinson & H. Joaquin Jackson. Read by Rex Linn. (Running Time: 41400 sec.). 2005. audio compact disk 81.00 (978-0-7861-7948-0(1)) Blckstn Audio.

One Ranger: A Memior. David Marion Wilkinson & H. Joaquin Jackson. (Running Time: 041400 sec.). 2005. cass. & DVD 65.95 (978-0-7861-3029-0(6)) Blckstn Audio.

One Ranger: A Memior. unabr. ed. David Marion Wilkinson & H. Joaquin Jackson. Read by Rex Linn. 8 cass. (Running Time: 41400 sec.). 2005. 29.95 (978-0-7861-3045-0(8)) Blckstn Audio.

One Ranger: A Memoir. unabr. ed. H. Joaquin Jackson & David Marion Wilkinson. Read by W. C. Jameson. 13 vols. (Running Time: 11 hrs. 30 mins.). 2005. audio compact disk 29.95 (978-0-7861-8152-0(4)) Blckstn Audio.

One Ranger: A Memoir. unabr. ed. H. Joaquin Jackson & David Marion Wilkinson. Contrib. by Rex Linn. 9 CDs. (Running Time: 041400 sec.). 2005. audio compact disk 32.95 (978-0-7861-7997-8(X)) Blckstn Audio.

One Ray of Light at Dawn. (ENG & CHI., 2001. bk. 50.00 (978-0-916393-13-7(5)) E G W International Corp.

One Ray of Light at Dawn. Short Stories. 2 CDs & booklet. (CHI., 2002. pap. bk. 20.00 (978-0-916393-15-1(1)) E G W International Corp.

One Rehearsal Wonders, Vol. 2. Created by Glorysound. 2007. audio compact disk 49.95 (978-5-557-49842-5(7), Glory Snd) Shawnee Pr.

One Rehearsal Wonders, Volume 2. Created by Glorysound. 2007. audio compact disk 16.95 (978-5-557-49843-2(5), Glory Snd); audio compact disk 15.98 (978-5-557-49819-7(2), Glory Snd) Shawnee Pr.

One River: Explorations & Discoveries in the Amazon Rain Forest. unabr. ed. Wade Davis. Read by David Case. 9 cass. (Running Time: 13 hrs. 30 mins.). 1998. 72.00 (4560-A); 64.00 (4560-B); 136.00 (4560-A/B) Books on Tape.
A naturalist discusses his exploration of the Amazon as well as his legendary teacher's, Richard Schultes.

One River More: A Celebration of Rivers & Fly Fishing. abr. ed. W. D. Wetherell. Narrated by Jeff Riggenbach. (Running Time: 16200 sec.). 2008. audio compact disk 28.00 (978-1-933309-43-9(1)) Pub: A Media Intl. Dist(s): Natl Bk Netwk

One Room & a Path. abr. ed. Virginia Maas. Read by M. J. Wilde. 4 cass. (Running Time: 6 hrs.). 2001. 25.00 (978-1-58807-066-1(2)) Am Pubng Inc.
It's the early days of World War II, and newly married Maudie Cameron feels left out of the war effort, so she decides to participate the only way she can. There is an extreme housing shortage in her small town of Tillicum, Washington, caused by the influx of soldiers to Fort Lewis, and workers to the shipyards nearby. In spite of her husband Charlie's misgivings, she becomes a landlady and rents out two one-room cabins and a trailer house located on the property that she and Charlie recently purchased. Her tenants are a succession of soldiers, their families, and shipyard workers. Her adventures as a landlady are sometimes sad, occasionally frightening, but mostly hilarious. This poignant, but light-hearted look at the effect of war on a typical cross-section of 'small town' Americans, shows how everyday people coped with problems on the home front. Author Virginia Maas describes how they dealt with everything from rationing and food shortages, to the loss of family members and friends in battle. The ever-present air raids and the convoys transporting troops to shipping out points made the war a constant presence in their lives. This is a story that will bring back memories to those who lived through World War II, and will show younger readers how "the greatest generation" coped with the major event of the last century.

One Room Sunday School Fall. bk. 9.99 (978-0-687-09137-9(3)) Abingdon.

One Room Sunday School Spring. bk. 7.95 (978-0-687-03415-4(9)) Abingdon.

One Room Sunday School Summer. bk. 7.95 (978-0-687-03416-1(7)) Abingdon.

One Room Sunday School Winter. bk. 9.99 (978-0-687-03413-0(2)) Abingdon.

One Scary Night: Thirty Haunting Halloween Tales. unabr. ed. Read by Paddi Edwards & Clive Revill. Ed. by Kathy Sjogren & Dave Field. 1 cass. (Running Time: 50 min.). (J). (gr. 3 up). 1993. pap. bk. 14.95 (978-1-883446-01-7(5)) Poet Tree CA.
This collection of 30 spine-tingling tales in verse will have young & old listeners screaming with delight. Selections include Lewis Carroll's

"Jabberwocky" & Edgar Allan Poe's "The Raven," set to frightful music & sound effects. The tales will create a haunting atmosphere for Halloween programs in libraries & schools.

***One Season of Sunshine.** unabr. ed. Julia London. Read by Natalie Ross. (Running Time: 12 hrs.). 2010. 19.99 (978-1-4418-4930-4(0), 9781441849304, Brilliance MP3); 19.99 (978-1-4418-4931-1(9), 9781441849311, BAD); 39.97 (978-1-4418-4933-5(5), 9781441849335, Brinc Audio MP3 Lib); 39.97 (978-1-4418-4932-8(7), 9781441849328, BADLE); audio compact disk 19.99 (978-1-4418-4928-1(9), 9781441849281, Bril Audio CD Unabri); audio compact disk 79.97 (978-1-4418-4929-8(7), 9781441849298, BriAudCD Unabrid) Brilliance Audio.

One Second After. unabr. ed. William R. Forstchen. (Running Time: 11 hrs. 50 mins.). 2009. audio compact disk 29.95 (978-1-4332-5699-8(1)) Blckstn Audio.

One Second After. unabr. ed. William R. Forstchen. (Running Time: 11 hrs. 50 mins.). (ENG.). 2009. 29.95 (978-1-4332-5700-1(9)); 65.95 (978-1-4332-5696-7(7)) Blckstn Audio.

One Second After. unabr. ed. William R. Forstchen. Narrated by Joe Barrett. 11 CDs. (Running Time: 13 hrs. 30 mins.). 2009. audio compact disk 90.00 (978-1-4332-5697-4(5)) Blckstn Audio.

One Shot. unabr. ed. Lee Child. Read by Dick Hill. (Running Time: 12 hrs.). (Jack Reacher Ser.). 2005. 39.25 (978-1-59710-548-4(1), 9781597105484, BADLE); 24.95 (978-1-59710-549-1(X), 9781597105491, BAD); 24.95 (978-1-59335-731-3(1), 9781593357313, Brilliance MP3); 39.25 (978-1-59335-865-5(2), 9781593358655, Brinc Audio MP3 Lib); 87.25 (978-1-59355-517-7(2), 9781593555177, BrilAudUnabridg); audio compact disk 38.95 (978-1-59355-519-1(9), 9781593555191, Bril Audio CD Unabri); audio compact disk 102.25 (978-1-59355-520-7(2), 9781593555207, BriAudCD Unabrid) Brilliance Audio.
Six shots. Five dead. One heartland city thrown into a state of terror. But within hours, the cops have it solved: a slam-dunk case. Except for one thing. The accused man says: You got the wrong guy. Then he says: Get Reacher for me. In Lee Child's astonishing new thriller, Reacher's arrival will change everything...about a case that isn't what it seems, about lives tangled in baffling ways, about a killer who missed one shot - and by doing so gives Jack Reacher one shot at the truth.

One Shot. 9th unabr. ed. Lee Child. Read by Dick Hill. (Running Time: 43200 sec.). (Jack Reacher Ser.). 2005. 34.95 (978-1-59355-516-0(4), 9781593555160, BAU) Brilliance Audio.

One Silly Hey Diddle Day Audio CD. Adapted by Benchmark Education Company Staff. Based on a work by Carrie Smith. (Reader's Theater Nursery Rhymes & Songs Ser.). (J). (gr. k-1). 2008. audio compact disk 10.00 (978-1-60437-987-7(1)) Benchmark Educ.

One Simple Act: Discovering the Power of Generosity. unabr. ed. Debbie Macomber. Read by Debbie Macomber. Read by Beth DeVries. (Running Time: 5 hrs. 30 mins. 0 sec.). (ENG.). 2009. audio compact disk 29.99 (978-0-7435-9744-9(3)) Pub: S&S Audio. Dist(s): S and S Inc

One Small Child. Composed by David Meece. Contrib. by Russell Mauldin & Tom Fettke. 2007. audio compact disk 24.98 (978-5-557-77091-0(7), Word Music) Word Enter.

One Small Dog. Johanna Hurwitz. Narrated by Johnny Heller. (Running Time: 1 hr. 30 mins.). (gr. 2 up). 10.00 (978-0-7887-9404-9(3)) Recorded Bks.

***One Soldier's Story.** abr. ed. Bob Dole. Read by Paul Hecht & Cynthia Darlowe. (ENG.). 2005. (978-0-06-084301-4(2), Harper Audio); (978-0-06-084302-1(0), Harper Audio) HarperCollins Pubs.

One Song. Marilyn Bergman & Alan Bergman. 1995. audio compact disk 22.95 (978-0-634-09557-3(9)) H Leonard.

One Sound: Traditional Buddhist Music from Tibet, China, Vietnam, Korea, Sri Lanka & Japan with Book. Ed. by Paul Morris. 1 CD. (Running Time: 1 hr.). 2000. 19.95 (978-1-55961-620-1(2)) Relaxtn Co.

One Step at a Time. unabr. ed. Marie Joseph. Read by Diana Bishop. 5 cass. (Running Time: 7 hrs. 30 mins.). 2001. 49.95 (978-1-86042-307-9(8), 23078) Pub: Soundings Ltd GBR. Dist(s): Ulverscroft US

One Step at a Time: 1 Kings 17:1-7. Ed Young. 1987. 4.95 (978-0-7417-1592-0(9), 592) Win Walk.

One Step Backward Taken see Robert Frost Reads

One Step Backward Taken see Twentieth-Century Poetry in English, No. 6, Recordings of Poets Reading Their Own Poetry

One Step Behind. unabr. ed. Henning Mankell. (Running Time: 57600 sec.). (Kurt Wallander Ser.). 2007. audio compact disk 99.00 (978-1-4332-0602-3(1)) Blckstn Audio.

One Step Behind. unabr. ed. Henning Mankell. Read by Dick Hill. (Running Time: 57600 sec.). (Kurt Wallander Ser.). 2007. 85.95 (978-1-4332-0601-6(3)); audio compact disk 29.95 (978-1-4332-0603-0(X)) Blckstn Audio.

One Step Behind. unabr. ed. Henning Mankell. Read by Dick Hill. (Running Time: 16 hrs. 0 mins.). (Kurt Wallander Ser.). 2009. audio compact disk 29.95 (978-1-4332-7075-8(7)) Blckstn Audio.

One Step from Wonderland. Jan McDaniel. Perf. by High Sierra Players Staff. Narrated by Steven Short. Score by Dave Fabrizio. Directed By Dave Fabrizio. Illus. by Katrina Kirkpatrick. 2 CDs. (Running Time: 1 hr. 30 mins.). Dramatization. (ENG.). 2004. audio compact disk 16.95 (978-1-58124-097-9(X)) Pub: Fiction Works. Dist(s): Brodart

One Step to Spanish, Vol. 1. 1 cass. (Running Time: 1 hr. 18 min.). (SPA.). (978-1-893746-10-7(0)) Visual Teaching.

One Step to Spanish, Vol. 2. 1 cass. (Running Time: 1 hr. 13 min.). (SPA.). (978-1-893746-11-4(9)) Visual Teaching.

One Step to Spanish, Vol. 3. 1 cass. (Running Time: 1 hr. 07 min.). (SPA.). (978-1-893746-12-1(7)) Visual Teaching.

One Step to Spanish, Vol. 4. 1 cass. (Running Time: 1 hr. 03 min.). (SPA.). (978-1-893746-13-8(5)) Visual Teaching.

One Step to Spanish, Vol. 5. 1 cass. (Running Time: 1 hr. 2 min.). (SPA.). (978-1-893746-14-5(3)) Visual Teaching.

***One Summer.** unabr. ed. David Baldacci. (Running Time: 8 hrs.). (ENG.). 2011. 26.98 (978-1-60941-300-2(8)); audio compact disk & audio compact disk 34.98 (978-1-60941-295-1(8)) Pub: Hachet Audio. Dist(s): HachBkGrp

One Summer. unabr. ed. Karen Robards. Read by Kate Fleming. 10 vols. (Running Time: 15 hrs.). 2000. bk. 84.95 (978-0-7927-2389-9(9), CSL 278, Chivers Sound Lib) AudioGO.
Johnny Harris is home again, his too-tight jeans & belligerent attitude honed to perfection by a ten-year stretch in prison for murder.

One Summer. unabr. ed. Nora Roberts. Read by Jill Apple. (Running Time: 6 hrs.). (Celebrity Magazine Ser.). 2009. 24.99 (978-1-4418-3011-1(1), 9781441830111, Brilliance MP3); 39.97 (978-1-4418-3012-8(X), 9781441830128, Brinc Audio MP3 Lib); 39.97 (978-1-4418-3013-5(8), 9781441830135, BADLE); audio compact disk 24.99 (978-1-4418-3009-8(X), 9781441830098, Bril Audio CD Unabri); audio compact disk 79.97 (978-1-4418-3010-4(3), 9781441830104, BriAudCD Unabrid) Brilliance Audio.

One Summer at Deer's Leap. unabr. ed. Elizabeth Elgin. Read by Anne Dover. 18 cass. (Running Time: 24 hrs.). (Isis Ser.). (J). 1999. 109.95 (978-0-7531-0657-0(4), 991111) Pub: ISIS Lrg Prnt GBR. Dist(s): Ulverscroft US
Cassie Johns is a lively young author on the brink of success. Driving through the beautiful Trough of Bowland to a fancy-dress party, she gives a lift to an attractive young man in a RAF uniform; ready for the party, Cassie assumes. But at the party there is no sign of the airman. Despite all warnings, Cassie becomes obsessed by the pilot: a man whose plane had crashed fifty years before, but whose long ago love affair with a girl at Deer's Leap makes him unable to rest in peace. His romantic story takes Cassie into a war torn past where old passion burns & becomes entwined with new.

One Sunday. unabr. ed. Joy Dettman. Read by Deidre Rubenstein. (Running Time: 13 hrs. 50 mins.). 2009. audio compact disk 108.95 (978-1-74093-944-7(1), 9781740939447) Pub: Bolinda Pubng AUS. Dist(s): Bolinda Pub Inc

One Terrific Thanksgiving. unabr. ed. Marjorie Weinman Sharmat. 1 cass. (Running Time: 10 min.). (J). (gr. k-4). 1992. bk. 24.90 (978-0-8045-6599-8(6), 6599) Spoken Arts.

One That Got Away: A Memoir. Howell Raines. Narrated by Tom Stechschulte. (Running Time: 36900 sec.). 2006. audio compact disk 34.99 (978-1-4193-8356-4(6)) Recorded Bks.

One Thing Holding You Back: Unleashing the Power of Emotional Connection. Raphael Cushnir. 2009. audio compact disk 29.95 (978-1-59179-684-8(9)) Sounds True.

One Thing I Have Asked. Read by Wayne Monbleau. 3 cass. (Running Time: 3 hrs.). 1993. 15.00 (978-0-944648-23-0(1), LGT-1200) Loving Grace Pubns.
Religious.

One Thing I Know. 1 cass. (Running Time: 1 hr.). 1999. Provident Music.

One Thing We All Need. Carolyn J. Rasmus. 2005. audio compact disk 12.95 (978-1-59038-466-4(0)) Deseret Bk.

One Thing You Need to Know: ...About Great Managing, Great Leading, & Sustained Individual Success. abr. ed. Marcus Buckingham. 2005. 17.95 (978-0-7435-5111-3(7)) Pub: S&S Audio. Dist(s): S and S Inc

One Thing You Need to Know: ...About Great Managing, Great Leading, & Sustained Individual Success. abr. ed. Marcus Buckingham. Read by Marcus Buckingham. 4 CDs. (Running Time: 40 hrs. 0 mins. 0 sec.). (ENG.). 2005. audio compact disk 29.95 (978-0-7435-4306-4(8)) Pub: S&S Audio. Dist(s): S and S Inc

One Thought Away: Syd Banks at Tampa Crossroads. rev. ed. Sydney Banks. 2003. audio compact disk (978-1-55105-399-8(3)) Lone Pine Publ CAN.

One Thousand French Words. unabr. ed. Conversa-Phone Institute Staff. 1 cass. (Running Time: 50 min.). (Round the World Basic Language Programs Ser.). 1988. 9.95 (978-1-56752-034-7(0), COCB-1366) Conversa-phone.
1000 French words on tape with translation manual.

One Thousand German Words. unabr. ed. Conversa-Phone Institute Staff. 1 cass. (Running Time: 50 min.). (Round the World Basic Language Programs Ser.). 1988. 9.95 (978-1-56752-035-4(9), COCB-1367) Conversa-phone.
1000 German words on tape with translation manual.

***One Thousand Gifts: A Dare to Live Fully Right Where You Are.** Zondervan. (ENG.). 2011. 16.99 (978-0-310-41236-6(6)) Zondervan.

One Thousand Ideas & Then Some. As told by Mary Hamilton. 1 cass. (Running Time: 43 min.). (J). (gr. 3 up). 1992. 10.00 (978-1-885556-02-8(0)) Hidden Spmg.
Six folktales from seven cultures! "1000 Ideas" - Russian & Ukranian, "None but Timothy Brennan" - Irish, "The Princess & the Dove" - Italian, "The Poor Man & the Rich Man's Purse" - Jewish, "Mr. Fox" - English, & "The King & His Advisor" from India.

One Thousand Italian Words. unabr. ed. Conversa-Phone Institute Staff. 1 cass. (Running Time: 50 min.). (Round the World Basic Language Programs Ser.). 1988. 9.95 (978-1-56752-036-1(7), COCB-1368) Conversa-phone.
1000 Italian words on tape with translation manual.

One Thousand Spanish Words. unabr. ed. Conversa-Phone Institute Staff. 1 cass. (Running Time: 50 min.). (Round the World Basic Language Programs Ser.). 1988. 9.95 (978-1-56752-033-0(2), COCB-1365) Conversa-phone.
1000 Spanish words on tape with translation manual.

One Thousand Useful Words in Mohawk. 1 cass. (Running Time: 1 hr.). 12.95 incl. bk., 158p. (AFMH94) J Norton Pubs.

One Thousand White Women: The Journals of May Dodd. Jim Fergus. Read by Laura Hicks. 10 cass. (Running Time: 53760 sec.). (Sound Library). 2006. 84.95 (978-0-7927-3724-7(5), CSL 834); audio compact disk 112.95 (978-0-7927-3694-3(X), SLD 834) AudioGO.

One Thousand White Women: The Journals of May Dodd. unabr. ed. Jim Fergus. Read by Laura Hicks. (Running Time: 54000 sec.). 2006. 39.95 (978-1-57270-526-5(4)) Pub: Audio Partners. Dist(s): PerseuPGW

One Thousand White Women: The Journals of May Dodd: A Novel. unabr. ed. Jim Fergus. Narrated by Laura Hicks. (Running Time: 54000 sec.). (ENG.). 2006. audio compact disk 44.95 (978-1-57270-525-8(6)) Pub: AudioGO. Dist(s): Perseus Dist

One Time Only Kid. unabr. ed. 1 CD. (Running Time: 40 mins.). 2002. audio compact disk 14.00 (978-0-9714115-1-7(4)) Seven Seals Pr.

One to a Million: Math Concepts. 2004. bk. 24.95 (978-0-7882-0558-3(7)) Weston Woods.

One to Count Cadence. unabr. ed. James Crumley. Read by Rob McQuay. 8 cass. (Running Time: 12 hrs.). 1997. 64.00 (978-0-7366-3816-6(4), 4484) Books on Tape.
Based on manhood, anger, war, & lies.

One to Grow on! Series - Blue Collection: Exploring the child's World of Dreams, Senses & Change. Trenna Daniells. Narrated by Trenna Daniells. (ENG.). (J). 2009. (978-0-918519-67-2(5)) Trenna Prods.

***One to Grow on! Series - Kids' Audio Story Sampler: Red, Blue, Green & Orange Collections.** Trenna Daniells. Narrated by Trenna Daniells. (ENG.). 2010. audio compact disk (978-0-918519-32-0(2)) Trenna Prods.

One to Grow on! Series - Orange Collection. Trenna Daniells. Narrated by Trenna Daniells. (ENG.). (J). 2009. (978-0-918519-20-7(9)) Trenna Prods.

One to Grow on! Series - Red Collection: Developing the Values of Self Knowledge. Trenna Daniells. Narrated by Trenna Daniells. (ENG.). (J). 2009. (978-0-918519-68-9(3)) Trenna Prods.

One to Grow on! the Orange Collection: A Child's relationship with the world, we all count & we can all make a difference. Seeing things creatively, positively, gaining confidence & the value of Honesty. Trenna Daniells. (ENG.). (J). 2009. (978-0-918519-30-6(6)) Trenna Prods.

One-to-One: Personal Counseling Tapes for Teens. unabr. ed. Val J. Peter et al. 3 cass. (Running Time: 1 hr. 36 mins.). (gr. 6-12). 1996. 14.99 (978-0-938510-78-9(9), 19-403) Boys Town Pr.
At one time or another, teens experience mixed-up emotions, insecurity, and self-doubt. Some know they have a problem but don't know quite how to express what's bothering them. And some long for advice but are afraid or confused about whom to trust. One to One is an innovative audiocassette that gives teens confidential, reliable information and advice. It contains conversations between teens seeking help and information and Boys Town professionals with extensive experience counseling troubled youth. Some conversations deal with issues of faith, others with highly personal issues such as suicide, sexuality, abuse, and addiction.

One to One Future: Building Relationships One Customer at a Time. abr. ed. Don Peppers & Martha Rogers. 2 cass. (Running Time: 3 hrs.). 1996. 14.95 (51699) Books on Tape.
The best description yet of life after mass marketing, from an advertising guru & a marketing scholar. Breakthrough one-to-one strategies.

***One Touch of Scandal.** unabr. ed. Liz Carlyle. Read by Nicola Barber. (ENG.). 2010. (978-0-06-206183-6(6), Harper Audio); (978-0-06-206182-9(8), Harper Audio) HarperCollins Pubs.

***One Touch of Topaz.** unabr. ed. Iris Johansen. Read by Angela Brazil. 1 Playaway. (Running Time: 4 hrs. 45 mins.). 2009. 64.95 (978-0-7927-6844-9(2)); audio compact disk 49.95 (978-0-7927-6843-2(4)) AudioGO.

***One True Love.** unabr. ed. Laura Lippman. Read by Linda Emond & Francois Battiste. (ENG.). 2008. (978-0-06-176315-1(2), Harper Audio); (978-0-06-176308-3(X), Harper Audio) HarperCollins Pubs.

***One True Theory of Love.** unabr. ed. Laura Fitzgerald. Read by Julia Whelan. (Running Time: 9 hrs.). 2010. 24.99 (978-1-4418-3965-7(8), 9781441839657, Brilliance MP3); 39.97 (978-1-4418-3966-4(6), 9781441839664, Brinc Audio MP3 Lib); 24.99 (978-1-4418-3967-1(4), 9781441839671, BAD); 39.97 (978-1-4418-3968-8(2), 9781441839688, BADLE); audio compact disk 29.99 (978-1-4418-3963-3(1), 9781441839633, Bril Audio CD Unabri); audio compact disk 79.97 (978-1-4418-3964-0(X), 9781441839640, BriAudCD Unabrid) Brilliance Audio.

One True Thing. Anna Quindlen. 2004. 10.95 (978-0-7435-4557-0(5)) Pub: S&S Audio. Dist(s): S and S Inc

One True Thing. Anna Quindlen. Read by Laura Linney. 2004. 10.95 (978-0-7435-4558-7(3)) Pub: S&S Audio. Dist(s): S and S Inc

One True Thing. unabr. ed. Anna Quindlen. Narrated by Christina Moore. 7 cass. (Running Time: 9 hrs. 45 mins.). 1995. 60.00 (978-0-7887-0198-6(3), 94422E7) Recorded Bks.
A young woman who returned home to nurse her dying mother finds herself arrested for murder upon her mother's death. She didn't do it, but she thinks she knows who did & why.

One Tuesday Morning. unabr. ed. Zondervan Publishing Staff & Karen Kingsbury. (Running Time: 14 hrs. 0 mins. 0 sec.). (9/11 Ser.). (ENG.). 2003. 14.99 (978-0-310-26167-4(8)) Zondervan.

One, Two, Buckle My Shoe. unabr. ed. Agatha Christie. Read by Hugh Fraser. 4 cass. (Running Time: 5 hrs. 19 mins.). 2004. 25.95 (978-1-57270-384-1(9)) Pub: Audio Partners. Dist(s): PerseuPGW

One, Two, Buckle My Shoe. unabr. ed. Agatha Christie. Narrated by Hugh Fraser. 5 CDs. (Mystery Masters Ser.). (ENG.). 2004. audio compact disk 27.95 (978-1-57270-385-8(7)) Pub: AudioGO. Dist(s): Perseus Dist

One, Two, Buckle My Shoe/One Potato, Two Potato. Created by Steck-Vaughn Staff. (Running Time: 295 sec.). (Primary Take-Me-Home Books Level K Ser.). 1998. 9.80 (978-0-8172-8655-2(1)) SteckVau.

One-Two-Three Magic: Effective Discipline for Children 2-12. unabr. ed. Thomas W. Phelan. 4 cass. (Running Time: 3 hrs 30 min.). 1997. bk. 24.95 ParentMagic.
One-Two-Three Magic, developed by Dr. Thomas D. Phelan, is a no-nonsense discipline program that enables parents to manage children ages 2-12 without arguing, yelling or spanking.

One Two Three of God. Ken Wilber. 3 CDs. (Running Time: 16200 sec.). 2006. audio compact disk 29.95 (978-1-59179-531-5(1), AW01087D) Sounds True.

One Under. Graham Hurley. 2007. 99.95 (978-0-7531-3729-1(1)); audio compact disk 104.95 (978-0-7531-2696-7(6)) Pub: ISIS Audio GBR. Dist(s): Ulverscroft US

One up on Wall Street: How to Use What You Already Know to Make Money in the Market. Peter Lynch. 2004. 10.95 (978-0-7435-4559-4(1)) Pub: S&S Audio. Dist(s): S and S Inc

One Voice Sampler. 1 cass. (Running Time: 1 hr.). (One Voice Worship Ser.). 1997. audio compact disk 1.49 (D0166) Diamante Music Grp.
Featuring nearly 40 excerpts from all four One Voice projects.

One Was Johnny. 2004. bk. 24.95 (978-0-7882-0567-5(6)); pap. bk. 14.95 (978-0-7882-0632-0(X)); cass. & flmstrp 30.00 (978-1-56008-737-3(4)) Weston Woods.

One Was Johnny: A Counting Book. Maurice Sendak. 1 cass. (Running Time: 3 min.). (J). (ps-3). 2000. pap. bk. 12.95 Weston Woods.
Designed to help children learn to count. Sendak's rhyming verse also introduces them to animals.

One Way Passage. Perf. by Ronald Reagan & Gloria Dixon. 1 cass. (Running Time: 1 hr.). 1938. 7.95 (DD-8120) Natl Recrd Co.
"One Way Passage" is the story of two lovers that meet on a ship returning to San Francisco, each knowing a secret about the other. "Magnificent Obsession" is the story of a wealthy playboy who is "in-a-way" responsible for the death of a famous doctor. He redeems himself, & also falls in love with the doctor's widow who hates him but.

One Way Praise. (J). 2003. audio compact disk 15.00 (978-1-58302-252-8(X)) One Way St.
This CD has praise music for children ages 8-13. There are twelve songs with children's voices and upbeat music or prayerful melodies. We know you'll enjoy using this CD in your children's service or even for puppets to present.

One Way Ticket see Poetry & Reflections

One-Way Trail. Max Brand. (Running Time: 2 hrs. 6 mins.). 2000. 10.95 (978-1-60083-518-6(X)) Iofy Corp.

***One-Way Trail.** Max Brand. 2009. (978-1-60136-411-1(3)) Audio Holding.

One Way Workout. Jon Von Seggen. 1 cass. (Running Time: 21 min.). 1994. 10.00 (978-1-58302-057-9(8), KPR-01) One Way St.
Performance exercises for the puppeteer.

One Went to Denver & the Other Went Wrong. abr. ed. Stephen A. Bly. 2 cass. (Running Time: 3 hrs.). (Code of the West Ser.: No. 2). 2001. 17.99 (978-1-58926-006-1(6)) Oasis Audio.
Bounty hunters who want him to return to Arizona for a crime he didn't commit pursue Tap Andrews. The chase brings Tap & his fiance head to head with their pasts.

One Went to Denver & the Other Went Wrong. unabr. ed. Stephen A. Bly. Read by Jerry Sciarrio. 4 cass. (Running Time: 5 hrs. 48 min.). (Code of the West Ser.: Bk. 2). 2001. 26.95 (978-1-58116-037-6(2)) Books in Motion.
Tap Andrews is tired of fighting off every guntoting bounty hunter that crosses his path, because he's innocent and he knows it. The truth lies in Denver, where another acquaintance is also facing her past.

One Wet Dog. unabr. ed. Gail Taylor. Read by Gail Taylor. Ed. by James B. Kirgan. 1 cass. (Running Time: 1 hr. 30 min.). (Essence of Nature Ser.: Vol. 14). (J). 1989. 12.99 stereo. (978-1-878362-14-8(3)) Emerald Ent.
On this tape Thumper, the adventure dog, explores the Tropical Rain Forest in the Pacific Coast Area of Olympic National Park, Washington. This tape includes actual sounds from this park.

One Who Sits on the Throne. Dan Corner. 1 cass. (Running Time: 1 hr.). 3.00 (63) Evang Outreach.

One Whole & Perfect Day. Judith Clarke. Read by Gretal Montgomery. (Playaway Young Adult Ser.). (ENG.). (YA). (gr. 7). 2009. 59.99 (978-1-60812-658-3(7)) Find a World.

One Whole & Perfect Day. unabr. ed. Judith Clarke. Read by Gretal Montgomery. 1 MP3-CD. (Running Time: 7 hrs.). 2008. 24.95 (978-1-4233-6666-9(2), 9781423366669, Brilliance MP3); 24.95 (978-1-4233-6668-3(9), 9781423366683, BAD); 39.25 (978-1-4233-6667-6(0), 9781423366676, Brinc Audio MP3 Lib); 39.25 (978-1-4233-6669-0(7), 9781423366690, BADLE); audio compact disk 29.99 (978-1-4233-6664-5(6), 9781423366645, Bril Audio CD Unabri); audio compact disk 82.25 (978-1-4233-6665-2(4), 9781423366652, BriAudCD Unabrid) Brilliance Audio.

One Wide River: Songs & Stories. Prod. by Phil Rosenthal. 1 cass. (Running Time: 40 min.). (J). (gr. 1-6). 1988. 9.98 (978-1-879305-04-5(6)) Am Melody.
A wonderfully varied collection of songs & stories featuring some of America's finest folk musicians & storytellers. Parent's Choice Award.

One Wintry Night: A David Phelps Christmas. Contrib. by David Phelps. 2007. audio compact disk 13.99 (978-5-557-59239-0(3), Word Records) Word Enter.

One Wobbly Wheelbarrow. (Language of Mathematics Ser.). 1989. 7.92 (978-0-8123-6411-8(2)) Holt McDoug.

One Woman Short. Nelson George. Narrated by Marc Johnson. 5 cass. (Running Time: 7 hrs. 30 mins.). 45.00 (978-1-4025-1334-3(8)); audio compact disk 58.00 (978-1-4025-2097-6(2)) Recorded Bks.

One Woman's Army: The Commanding General of Abu Ghraib Tells Her Story. unabr. ed. Janis Karpinski & Steven Strasser. Read by Bernadette Dunne. 5 cass. (Running Time: 7 hrs.). 2005. 45.00 (978-1-4159-2624-6(7)); audio compact disk 54.00 (978-1-4159-2625-3(5)) Books on Tape.

One World. Michael Twinn. Read by Diana Rigg. Music by Andrew Belling. 1 cass. (Running Time: 15 min.). (Citizenship, Life Skills & Responsibility - One World Ser.). (ENG., (J). 1991. 6.99 (978-0-85953-377-5(8)) Childs Play GBR.
"Half a World Away" concerns a group of children who, by going on a hunger strike, persuade their parents to help a less fortunate society that is "stricken by a mysterious purple cloud." "The Tower" tells of "a leader" who brings about death & destruction in the name of progress. Once ecological disaster occurs, he realizes that it's time for a new plan, but irreparable damage has already been done.

One World, Many Stories. Megan McKenna. 4 cass. (Running Time: 5 hrs.). 29.95 (AA2710) Credence Commun.
McKenena teaches a graduate theology class the essentials of liberation theology in the style of a liberation theologian. She uses scripture & story & discussion so the theology comes from within the students in reaction to the scripture & story. McKenna is brilliant in relating our theology to the theologies from around the world.

One World, One Light. Nelson Gill. 1 cass. (J). 2001. 10.95 (KNG 3103C); audio compact disk 14.95 (KNG 3103CD) Kimbo Educ.
Diverse rhythms promote friendship, perseverance & universal harmony. Come to Belize, Everybody Limbo, Raise Your Hand, Dance, Longest Journey & more.

One World, Ready or Not: The Manic Logic of Global Capitalism. William Greider. 2004. 15.95 (978-0-7435-4809-0(4)) Pub: S&S Audio. Dist(s): S and S Inc

One Writer's Beginnings. Eudora Welty. (William E. Massey Sr. Lectures in the History of American Civilization Ser.). 2004. audio compact disk 29.50 (978-0-674-01579-1(7)) HUP.

One Year Book of Psalms: 365 Inspirational Readings from One of the Best-Loved Books of the Bible. abr. ed. William Petersen & Randy Petersen. Read by William Petersen & Randy Petersen. 6 cass. (Running Time: 9 hrs.). 2002. 24.99 (978-1-58926-027-6(9), T09B-0110) Oasis Audio.
For millennia people have been singing, reading, praying and meditating on the Psalms. They have rejoiced in them, repented through them, and found immense comfort in them.

One Year Book of Psalms: 365 Inspirational Readings from One of the Best-Loved Books of the Bible. abr. unabr. ed. William Petersen & Randy Petersen. Read by William Petersen & Randy Petersen. Narrated by Mike Kellogg. 8 CDs. (Running Time: 12 hrs.). (ENG.). 2002. audio compact disk 29.99 (978-1-58926-028-3(7), T09B-011D) Oasis Audio.

One-Year Book of Psalms: 365 Inspirational Readings from One of the Best-Loved Books of the Bible: New Living Translation. unabr. abr. ed. William J. Petersen & Randy Petersen. Narrated by Mike Kellogg & Aimee Lilly. (ENG.). 2002. 20.99 (978-1-60814-333-7(3)) Oasis Audio.

One-Year Business Turnaround Audio Presentation. Mike Dandridge. 2008. audio compact disk 12.95 (978-1-932226-64-5(8)) Wizard Acdmy.

One Year Children's Bible. abr. ed. V. Gilbert Beers. Read by V. Gilbert Beers. 2 cass. (Running Time: 150 mins.). 2002. 17.99 (978-1-58926-029-0(5)) Oasis Audio.

***One Year for Leaders.** unabr. ed. Jim Seybert. Narrated by Jim Seybert. (Running Time: 9 hrs. 14 mins. 4 sec.). (ENG.). 2010. 14.99 (978-1-60814-786-1(X)) Oasis Audio.

One-Year Patterning. unabr. ed. Robert A. Monroe. Read by Robert A. Monroe. (Running Time: 45 min.). (Gateway Experience - Adventure Ser.). 1983. 14.95 (978-1-56113-268-3(3)) Monroe Institute.
Design your future for a year.

One You Really Want. unabr. ed. Jill Mansell. 10 cass. (Running Time: 12 hrs. 45 mins.). (Isis Cassettes Ser.). (J). 2005. 84.95 (978-0-7531-2167-2(0)) Pub: ISIS Lrg Prnt GBR. Dist(s): Ulverscroft US

One You Really Want. unabr. ed. Jill Mansell. Read by Trudy Harris. 13 CDs. (Running Time: 12 hrs. 45 mins.). (Isis (CDs) Ser.). (J). 2005. audio compact disk 99.95 (978-0-7531-2463-5(7)) Pub: ISIS Lrg Prnt GBR. Dist(s): Ulverscroft US

One Zillion Valentines. 2004. 8.95 (978-1-56008-992-6(X)) Weston Woods.

One Zillion Valentines. Frank Modell. 1 cass., 5 bks. (Running Time: 12 min.). (J). pap. bk. 32.75 Weston Woods.
Two enterprising friends prove valentines are for everyone by making, giving away & selling one zillion Valentines.

One Zillion Valentines. unabr. ed. Based on a book by Frank Modell. 1 cass. (Running Time: 12 mins.). (J). (ps-3). 1998. pap. bk. 14.95 (978-0-7882-0683-2(4), PRA378); 8.95 (978-0-7882-0087-8(9), RAC378) Weston Woods.

Onedin Line. unabr. ed. Cyril Abraham. Read by Ray Dunbobbin. 4 cass. (Running Time: 6 hrs.). 2001. 44.95 (60016) Pub: Soundings Ltd GBR. Dist(s): Ulverscroft US

O'Neill. Read by Heywood Hale Broun & Louis Shaffer. 1 cass. (Running Time: 20 mins.). (Heywood Hale Broun Ser.). 11.95 (40059) J Norton Pubs.
Discussion with the author of O'Neill: Son & Artist.

O'Neill, Son & Playwright. Louis Sheaffer. 1 cass. (Running Time: 19 min.). 1969. 11.95 (23058) J Norton Pubs.
A discussion of autobiographical dramatist Eugene O'Neill's all important family relations, & his ambivalent feelings toward each.

Oneman. Perf. by Oneman. 1 cass. (Running Time: 1 hr.). 1997. audio compact disk 15.99 (D7128) Diamante Music Grp.
A snapshot of one man's journey with Jesus Christ.

***Oneness.** Transcribed by Rasha. Orig. Title: Oneness: the Teachings. (ENG.). 2010. 0.00 (978-0-9659003-2-4(0)) Pub: Earthstar Pr. Dist(s): New Leaf Dist

Oneness & Unity of All. Swami Amar Jyoti. 1 cass. 1986. 9.95 (R 88) Truth Consciousness.
Science & spirituality of the New Age. Erasing the false distinction between individual self & the Unlimited. An inventory of where we stand.

Oneness: the Teachings see Oneness

One's Company. unabr. collector's ed. Peter Fleming. Read by David Case. 6 cass. (Running Time: 9 hrs.). 1989. 48.00 (978-0-7366-1507-5(5), 2379) Books on Tape.
In 1933 Peter Fleming, on assignment as a special correspondent for The Times of London, traveled through Russia & Manchuria & on to China where he spent seven months "investigating the Communist situation in South China" at a time when no previous journey had been made through this territory by a foreigner.

Onimusha. 1 CD. 2003. audio compact disk 14.98 (978-1-57813-403-8(X), CD/009) A D Vision.

Onimusha 3: Original Soundtrack. 1 CD. 2004. audio compact disk 14.98 (978-1-57813-388-8(2), CD/011, ADV Music) A D Vision.

Onion Field. unabr. ed. Joseph Wambaugh. Read by Daniel Grace. 10 cass. (Running Time: 15 hrs.). 1977. 80.00 (978-0-913369-97-5(7), 1007) Books on Tape.
The true story of the 1963 kidnapping of two Los Angeles policemen. The abduction ends in an abandoned onion field near Bakersfield. One of the officers is murdered & the other manages to escape only to undergo "psychological murder".

***Onion Field.** unabr. ed. Joseph Wambaugh. Read by Jonathan Davis. (Running Time: 18 hrs.). 2010. 29.99 (978-1-4418-7670-6(7), 9781441876706, Brilliance MP3); 44.97 (978-1-4418-7671-3(5), 9781441876713, Brinc Audio MP3 Lib); 44.97 (978-1-4418-7672-0(3), 9781441876720, BADLE); audio compact disk 34.99 (978-1-4418-7668-3(5), 9781441876683, Bril Audio CD Unabri); audio compact disk 84.97 (978-1-4418-7669-0(3), 9781441876690, BriAudCD Unabrid) Brilliance Audio.

Onion Girl. unabr. ed. Charles de Lint. Read by Kate Reading. (Running Time: 12 hrs. 0 mins.). (ENG.). 2008. 29.95 (978-1-4332-4771-2(2)); audio compact disk 72.95 (978-1-4332-4768-2(2)); audio compact disk 90.00 (978-1-4332-4769-9(0)) Blckstn Audio.

Onion's Finest Reporting. Onion Editors. 1 cass. (Running Time: 1 hr. 30 mins.). 2000. 13.00 (Random AudioBks) Random Audio Pubg.

Onion's Finest Reporting, Vol. 1. Scott Dikkers. 1 CD. (Running Time: 1 hr. 30 mins.). 2000. audio compact disk 15.50 (Random AudioBks) Random Audio Pubg.

Onions in the Stew: Tales of the Scots-Irish. Short Stories. As told by Donna Lively. 1 CD. (Running Time: 50 mins). Dramatization. 2004. audio compact disk 15.00 (978-0-9755290-3-4(X)) Green Lady.

Online Bible. 1998. audio compact disk 49.95 (978-0-311-48369-3(0)) Casa Bautista.

Online Copyright Manual for Everyone! Learn to Protect Yourself & Your Rights Before It's Too Late! Bob Hadley. 2 cds. (Running Time: 90 minutes). 2007. 19.95 (978-0-9792582-1-3(9)) Payday Pubng.

Online Instructor Resources to accompany Essentials of Rubin's Pathology. Emanuel Rubin & Howard M. Reisner. (ENG.). 2008. 595.00 (978-1-60547-166-2(6)) Lppncott W W.

***Only a Duke Will Do.** unabr. ed. Sabrina Jeffries. Read by Justine Eyre. (Running Time: 10 hrs.). (School for Heiresses Ser.). 2010. 19.99 (978-1-4418-4712-6(X), 9781441847126, BAD); 39.97 (978-1-4418-4711-9(1), 9781441847119, Brinc Audio MP3 Lib); 39.97 (978-1-4418-4713-3(8), 9781441847133, BADLE); 19.99 (978-1-4418-4710-2(3), 9781441847102, Brilliance MP3); audio compact disk 79.97 (978-1-4418-4709-6(X), 9781441847096, BriAudCD Unabrid); audio compact disk 19.99 (978-1-4418-4708-9(1), 9781441847089, Bril Audio CD Unabri) Brilliance Audio.

Only a Favor. unabr. ed. Christine Greenspan. Read by Stephanie Brush. 6 cass. (Running Time: 7 hrs. 48 min.). 2001. 39.95 (978-1-55686-963-1(0)) Books in Motion.
Murder doesn't bother the crooks who take young girls in trouble and convince them to give up their babies. Then they make a fortune selling the babies to people rich enough to buy anything. A smooth racket until one girl changes her mind.

***Only Answer to Cancer.** unabr. ed. Leonard Coldwell. Narrated by Wes Bleed. (Running Time: 9 hrs. 0 mins. 0 sec.). (ENG.). 2011. audio compact disk 29.99 (978-1-59859-796-7(5)) Oasis Audio.

***Only Answer to Stress, Anxiety & Depression.** unabr. ed. Leonard Coldwell. Narrated by Wes Bleed. (Running Time: 8 hrs. 0 mins. 0 sec.). (ENG.). 2011. audio compact disk 27.99 (978-1-59859-860-5(0)) Oasis Audio.

***Only Answer to Success: You Were Born to be a Champion.** unabr. ed. Leonard Coldwell & Wes Bleed. (Running Time: 9 hrs. 0 mins. 0 sec.). (ENG.). 2011. audio compact disk 29.99 (978-1-59859-861-2(9)) Oasis Audio.

Only at the Children's Table. Daria Baron-Hall. Illus. by Benton Mahan. (Publish-a-Book Ser.). (J). (gr. 1-6). 1995. lib. bdg. 22.83 (978-0-8172-2753-1(9)) Heinemann Rai.

Only Believe. 4.95 (C8) Carothers.

Only Child. unabr. ed. Andrew Vachss. (Running Time: 9 hrs.). (Burke Ser.). 2011. audio compact disk 29.99 (978-1-4418-2416-5(2), 9781441824165, Bril Audio CD Unabri) Brilliance Audio.

***Only Child.** unabr. ed. Andrew Vachss. Read by Phil Gigante. (Running Time: 9 hrs.). (Burke Ser.). 2011. 39.97 (978-1-4418-2421-9(9), 9781441824219, BADLE); 24.99 (978-1-4418-2420-2(0), 9781441824202, BAD); 39.97 (978-1-4418-2419-6(7), 9781441824196, Brinc Audio MP3 Lib); 24.99 (978-1-4418-2418-9(9), 9781441824189, Brilliance MP3); audio compact disk 79.97 (978-1-4418-2417-2(0), 9781441824172, BriAudCD Unabrid) Brilliance Audio.

Only Children. Alison Lurie. Read by Alison Lurie. 1 cass. (Running Time: 38 min.). 13.95 (978-1-55644-113-4(4), 4121) Am Audio Prose.
Satirical novelist of contemporary manners.

Only Clowns Passing Through see Your Own World

Only Dad. Alan Titchmarsh. pap. bk. (978-0-671-03372-9(7), Free Pr) S and S.

Only Dad. unabr. ed. Alan Titchmarsh. Narrated by Alan Titchmarsh. 7 cass. (Running Time: 8 hrs. 45 mins.). 2002. 56.00 (978-1-84197-334-0(3)) Recorded Bks.
Tom and Pippa Drummond have the perfect life. Tom is a partner in the successful restaurant The Pelican, Pippa grows and sells herbs whilst bringing up their lively daughter Tally. As they arrive in Tuscany on a much needed family holiday, it seems life couldn't be better. But overnight their whole world is turned upside down, and life will never be the same again. From being the perfect family and the envy of all their friends, they are thrust into a world that nobody would wish upon them.

Only Fools & Horses. Perf. by David Jason et al. 2 cass. (Running Time: 1 hr. 50 mins.). 1998. 16.85 (978-0-563-55704-3(4)) BBC WrldWd GBR.
Three men of three different generations, all without a woman in their life: Del Boy a wheeler-dealer with aspirations of great wealth, his not very bright younger 'Plonker' brother & Grandad, who, when he died was replaced by a new character, Uncle Albert.

Only His. Elizabeth Lowell. Narrated by Richard Ferrone. 9 cass. (Running Time: 12 hrs. 30 mins.). 78.00 (978-0-7887-5975-8(2)); audio compact disk 111.00 (978-1-4025-1553-8(7)) Recorded Bks.

Only His. unabr. ed. Elizabeth Lowell. 2001. 78.00 (L1010L8) Recorded Bks.

Only Human. Beryl Kingston. Read by Anne Dover. 10 cass. (Sound Ser.). (J). 2002. 84.95 (978-1-84283-203-5(4)) Pub: ISIS Lrg Prnt GBR. Dist(s): Ulverscroft US

Only in America. Dominic Holland. Read by Sophie Aldred. 6 vols. (Running Time: 23100 sec.). 2003. 54.95 (978-0-7540-8320-7(9)) Pub: Chivers Audio Bks GBR. Dist(s): AudioGO

Only in America: The Life & Crimes of Don King. unabr. collector's ed. Jack Newfield. Read by Edward Lewis. 8 cass. (Running Time: 12 hrs.). 1996. 64.00 (978-0-7366-3296-6(4), 3951) Books on Tape.
If Don King were a city, he'd be Las Vegas: flamboyant, money-driven, rooted in gambling. But King has an even seedier side. After he worked his way out of street crime, running numbers, & jail - for stomping a man to death - he became a powerhouse in the fight game. He did it by out-negotiating corporate giants, fleecing entire countries & ruining the lives of boxing's greatest champions, including Ali, Frazier, Holmes & Tyson. It's only fitting that biographer Jack Newfield, a columnist for the New York Post, takes the point of view of Don King's casualties - the fighters he cheated, exploited, betrayed & abandoned.

Only in Peace Can the Human Mind Be Free. J. Krishnamurti. 1 cass. (Running Time: 1 hr. 15 mins.). (Brockwood Park Talks, 1983 Ser.: No. 2). 8.50 (ABT832) Krishnamurti.
Subjects examined: Why is man incapable of living in peace? Are you individuals, struggling separate souls, each seeking his own fulfillment? Must human beings, thinking they are separate each seeking his own form of security, inevitably come into conflict with others? Even in a close relationship where there is a sense of affection, why is there conflict & turmoil? Can one live with another completely at peace? How do you observe your relationship with another? Can you look, observe, without any identity? Can you look at life not as a problem but with a mind that is free from problems?.

Only Integrity Is Going to Count. R. Buckminster Fuller. 5 CDs. 2004. audio compact disk 35.00 (978-0-9740605-2-1(6)) Pub: Critical Path Pub. Dist(s): Book Pub Co

Only Jealousy of Emer see Five One Act Plays

Only Jesus. Camp Kirkland. 1996. 75.00 (978-0-8054-9570-6(3)); 11.98 (978-0-8054-9563-8(0)); audio compact disk 85.00 (978-0-8054-9605-5(X)) BH Pubng Grp.

Only Love. Elizabeth Lowell. Narrated by Richard Ferrone. 8 cass. (Running Time: 11 hrs. 45 mins.). 71.00 (978-1-4025-1497-5(2)) Recorded Bks.

Only Love. abr. ed. Erich Segal. Read by John Rubinstein. 4 cass. (Running Time: 6 hrs.). 2001. 25.00 (978-1-59040-162-0(X), Phoenix Audio) Pub: Amer Intl Pub. Dist(s): PerseuPGW

Only Love Is Real: A Story of Soulmates Reunited. abr. ed. Brian L. Weiss. (ENG.). 2006. 14.98 (978-1-59483-695-4(7)) Pub: Hachet Audio. Dist(s): HachBkGrp

Only Men. Michael Pearl. 1 cd. (Running Time: 1 hr, 14 mins). 1998. audio compact disk (978-1-892112-92-7(2)) No Greater Joy.

Only Men. Michael Pearl. 1 cassette. 1998. (978-1-892112-56-9(6)) No Greater Joy.

Only Mine. Elizabeth Lowell. Narrated by Richard Ferrone. 9 cass. (Running Time: 12 hrs. 15 mins.). 84.00 (978-1-4025-0275-0(3)) Recorded Bks.

Only Mine. Elizabeth Lowell. Narrated by Richard Ferrone. 11 CDs. (Running Time: 12 hrs. 15 mins.). 1992. audio compact disk 111.00 (978-1-4025-3821-6(9)) Recorded Bks.

Only Negotiating Guide You'll Ever Need: 101 Ways to Win Every Time in Any Situation. abr. ed. Peter B. Stark & Jane Flaherty. Read by Peter B. Stark & Jane Flaherty. 3 CDs. (Running Time: 3 hrs.). (ENG.). 2004. audio compact disk 21.95 (978-0-7393-1036-6(4), RHAA) Pub: Random Audio Pubg. Dist(s): Random

Only One Time Around, Vol. 3. unabr. ed. William MacDonald. Read by William MacDonald. 2 cass. (Running Time: 2 hrs. 6 min.). (Upward Call Ser.). 1995. 10.95 (978-0-9629152-6-0(2)) Lumen Prodns.
A reflection on life's most important questions.

Only Passing Through: The Story of Sojourner Truth. Anne F. Rockwell. Read by Renee Joshua-Porter. Illus. by Gregory R. Christie. 1 cass. 2002. 13.95 Audio Bkshelf.

Only Passing Through: The Story of Sojourner Truth. Anne F. Rockwell. 1 CD. (Running Time: 41 mins.). (J). (gr. 3-6). 2002. audio compact disk 15.95 (978-1-883332-84-6(2), CD4-02) Audio Bkshelf.
Follows Sojourner Truth's life from slavery to emancipation, then shows her speaking out against the horrors of slavery. Her powerful words influenced a nation. Her famous "Ain't I a Woman?" speech is included, as well as a recounting of her visit with President Abraham Lincoln. The book clearly shows Sojourner's courage in standing up for what she believed in despite threats against her personal safety.

Only Passing Through: The Story of Sojourner Truth. Anne F. Rockwell. 1 CD. (Running Time: 41 mins.). (J). (gr. 2-7). 2002. audio compact disk 15.95 Audio Bkshelf.

Only Passing Through: The Story of Sojourner Truth. unabr. ed. Anne F. Rockwell. Read by Renee Joshua-Porter. Illus. by Gregory R. Christie. 1 cass. (Running Time: 41 mins.). (YA). (gr. 2 up). 2002. 13.95 (978-1-883332-80-8(X), 4-02) Audio Bkshelf.

Only Question. Swami Amar Jyoti. 1 cass. (Running Time: 1 hr.). 1979. 9.95 (J-27) Truth Consciousness.
Our questions symbolize our blocks; perfect simplified spirituality gives the right answers. Unsparing discrimination about ego.

Only Real Cure for Fear. unabr. ed. Swami Amar Jyoti. 1 cass. (Running Time: 1 hr.). (Satsangs of Swami Amar Jyoti Ser.). 2000. 9.95 (978-0-933572-56-0(5), K-169) Truth Consciousness.
The high price we pay for fear; the real causes and the only real remedy. Why do we fear God.

***Only Road North: 9,000 Miles of Dirt & Dreams.** unabr. ed. Erik Mirandette. (Running Time: 7 hrs. 21 mins. 0 sec.). (ENG.). 2009. 12.99 (978-0-310-77201-9(X)) Zondervan.

Only Rose. unabr. ed. Sarah Orne Jewett. Read by Tana Hicken. 2 cass. (Running Time: 2 hrs. 50 min.). 1994. lib. bdg. 18.95 (978-1-883049-49-2(0)) Sound Room.
Four of Jewett's best stories of New England including "The Only Rose," a touching story of loss & remembrance, "Martha's Lady," a story of the friendship of a young woman & a maid, "Aunt Cynthy Dallett," a story of caring, & "The Hilton's Holiday," Sarah Orne Jewett's favorite story.

Only Rose. unabr. ed. Short Stories. Sarah Orne Jewett. Read by Tana Hicken. 2 cass. (Running Time: 3 hrs.). (Jewett Ser.). 1994. bk. 16.95 (978-1-883049-43-0(1), 391319, Commuters Library) Sound Room.

Only Son: A Memoir. John Johnson. Narrated by Thomas Penny. 6 cass. (Running Time: 8 hrs. 15 mins.). 54.00 (978-1-4025-3270-2(9)) Recorded Bks.

Only the Best. unabr. ed. Una-Mary Parker. Read by Anita Wright. 15 CDs. (Isis Ser.). (J). 2003. audio compact disk 104.95 (978-0-7531-0969-4(7)) Pub: ISIS Lrg Prnt GBR. Dist(s): Ulverscroft US

Only the Best. unabr. ed. Una-Mary Parker & Anita Wright. 14 cass. (Running Time: 17 hrs. 12 mins.). (Isis Ser.). (J). 2002. 99.95 (978-0-7531-0909-0(3)) Pub: ISIS Lrg Prnt GBR. Dist(s): Ulverscroft US

Only the Dreamer Can Change the Dream. John Logan. Read by John Logan. 1 cass. (Running Time: 1 hr.). (Watershed Tapes of Contemporary Poetry Ser.). 1978. 11.95 (23631) J Norton Pubs.
Logan reads from five of his books.

Only the Fearless are Free. Guy Finley. 6 cass. (Running Time: 4 hrs.). 1998. 49.95 (978-1-929320-04-2(3)) Life of Learn.
The true cause & sure cure for every fear. Recorded live, shows how to rise above every loss & setback to find the fearless, free life.

Only the Going. Sister Ishpriya. 4 cass. (Running Time: 3 hrs.). 1995. Set. (AA2929) Credence Commun.
For the serious student. These are addresses of encouragement, support, & some enlightenment. Ishpriya has been living as a Christian presence among Hindu sannyasis. She shares with you what she considers most valuable from her experience.

***Only the Good Spy Young.** unabr. ed. Ally Carter. Read by Renée Raudman. (Running Time: 7 hrs.). (Gallagher Girls Ser.). 2010. 24.99 (978-1-4418-5959-4(4), 9781441859594, Brilliance MP3); 39.97 (978-1-4418-5960-0(8), 9781441859600, Brlnc Audio MP3 Lib); 24.99 (978-1-4418-5961-7(6), 9781441859617, BAD); 39.97 (978-1-4418-5962-4(4), 9781441859624, BADLE); audio compact disk 69.97 (978-1-4418-5958-7(6), 9781441859587, BriAudCD Unabrid) Brilliance Audio.

***Only the Good Spy Young.** unabr. ed. Ally Carter. Read by Renée Raudman. (Running Time: 7 hrs.). (Gallagher Girls Ser.). (YA). 2010. audio compact disk 24.99 (978-1-4418-5957-0(8), 9781441859570, Bril Audio CD Unabri) Brilliance Audio.

Only the Lonely: From the Files of Madison Finn. unabr. ed. Laura Dower. Narrated by Jessica Almasy. 4 CDs. (Running Time: 4 hrs.). (YA). (gr. 6-8). 2008. audio compact disk 46.75 (978-1-4281-8946-1(7)); 33.75 (978-1-4281-8941-6(6)) Recorded Bks.
Author Laura Dower debuts the fun-filled Madison Finn series. Everything is changing for Madison, or MadFinn as she is known online. Her parents are divorced and her best friends are away at summer camp - and the start of a new school year is creeping closer. So Madison starts a secret stash of files on her beloved laptop, chronicling life before seventh grade.

Only the Love Is Real: Transcending Negative Emotion. Marianne Williamson. Read by Marianne Williamson. 1 cass. (Running Time: 1 hr. 30 mins.). (Lectures on a Course in Miracles). 1999. 10.00 (978-1-56170-250-3(1), M753) Hay House.

Only the River Runs Free: A Novel. abr. ed. Bodie Thoene & Brock Thoene. 2 cass. (Running Time: 3 hrs.). (Galway Chronicles: Bk. 1). 1997. 16.99 (978-0-7852-7128-4(7), 71287) Nelson.
An intensely personal look at Ireland before the famine & the mass migrations.

Only the Truth Is Funny. abr. ed. Perf. by Rick Reynolds. 1 cass. (Running Time: 1 hr. 15 min.). 1996. 11.95 (978-1-57453-086-5(0)) Audio Lit.
Drawing from his successful one-man show & Showtime special, Reynolds recounts events in his bizarre childhood.

Only the World. Contrib. by Mandisa. (Soundtraks Ser.). 2007. audio compact disk 8.99 (978-5-557-56229-4(X)) Christian Wrld.

Only the World. Contrib. by Mandisa. Prod. by Shaun Shankel. 2007. audio compact disk 1.99 (978-5-557-70009-2(9)) Pt of Grace Ent.

Only the World. Contrib. by Mandisa. (Praise Hymn Soundtracks Ser.). 2007. audio compact disk 8.98 (978-5-557-60392-8(1)); audio compact disk 9.98 (978-5-557-60317-1(4)) Pt of Grace Ent.

Only Thing That's Beautiful in Me. Contrib. by Rush of Fools. (Mastertrax Ser.). 2008. audio compact disk 9.98 (978-5-557-36649-6(0)) Pt of Grace Ent.

Only Three Questions That Count: Investing by Knowing What Others Don't. Kenneth L. Fisher. Read by Erik Synnestvedt. Told to Jennifer Chou & Lara Hoffmans. (Playaway Adult Nonfiction Ser.). 2008. 74.99 (978-1-60640-505-5(5)) Find a World.

Only Three Questions That Count: Investing by Knowing What Others Don't. unabr. ed. Kenneth L. Fisher et al. Read by Erik Synnestvedt. (Running Time: 15 hrs.). (ENG.). 2007. 39.98 (978-1-59659-180-6(3), GildAudio) Pub: Gildan Media. Dist(s): HachBkGrp

Only Three Questions That Count: Investing by Knowing What Others Don't. unabr. ed. Kenneth L. Fisher et al. Read by Erik Synnestvedt. 13 CDs. (Running Time: 15 hrs.). (ENG.). 2008. audio compact disk 49.98 (978-1-59659-167-7(6), GildAudio) Pub: Gildan Media. Dist(s): HachBkGrp

***Only Uni.** unabr. ed. Camy Tang. (Running Time: 9 hrs. 52 mins. 0 sec.). (Sushi Ser.). (ENG.). 2008. 14.99 (978-0-310-30025-0(8)) Zondervan.

***Only Uni.** unabr. ed. Camy Tang. (Running Time: 9 hrs. 51 mins. 0 sec.). (Sushi Ser.). (ENG.). 2009. 12.99 (978-0-310-77198-2(6)) Zondervan.

Only Victor. unabr. ed. Alexander Kent, pseud. Read by Michael Jayston. 10 cass. (Running Time: 12 hrs. 30 min.). (Richard Bolitho Ser.: Bk. 18). 1991. 84.95 (978-0-7451-6092-4(1), CAB 586) AudioGO.
In February 1806 the frigate carrying Vice-Admiral Sir Richard Bolitho drops anchor off the shores of southern Africa. It is only four months since the resounding victory over the combined Franco-Spanish fleet at Trafalgar & the death of England's greatest naval hero. Bolitho's instructions are to assist in hastening the campaign in Africa where an expeditionary force is attempting to recapture Cape Town from the Dutch.

Only Way. Engineer Clint Grove. Music by Clint Grove. Executive Producer Neville McDonald. Featuring Healing Word Kids Choir Staff. Engineer Lloyd O'Connor. 1. (Running Time: 42min 29sec). (J). 2005. audio compact disk 9.99 (978-1-59971-064-8(1)) AardGP.
This CD is made with kids in mind, but any age will enjoy. The music is fun with a great message of Jesus.

Only Way I Know. unabr. ed. Mike Bryan & Cal Ripken, Jr. Read by Philip Franklin. 9 cass. (Running Time: 13 hrs. 30 mins.). 1997. 72.00 (978-0-7366-3736-7(2), 4413) Books on Tape.
A minor-league manager's son, rose from hot high school prospect to baseball legend.

Only Way to... Learn Astrology, Vol. I. unabr. ed. Marion D. March & Joan McEvers. Read by Marion D. March & Joan McEvers. 8 cass. (Running Time: 10 hrs.). 1993. 39.95 (978-1-883156-08-4(4)) Bulldog Audio.
Entry level astrology teaching.

Only Yesterday. unabr. collector's ed. Frederick L. Allen. Read by Larry McKeever. 9 cass. (Running Time: 13 hrs. 30 min.). 1987. 72.00 (978-0-7366-1119-0(3), 2042) Books on Tape.
The story of a distinct era in American history - the eleven years between the end of the war with Germany in 1918 & the stock market panic of 1929.

Only Yesterday: An Informal History of the 1920's. unabr. ed. Frederick L. Allen. Read by Grover Gardner. 8 cass. (Running Time: 11 hrs. 30 mins.). 1989. 56.95 (978-0-7861-0033-0(8), 1032) Blckstn Audio.
Included with the description of jazz, flappers, flasks, raccoon coats, marathon dancers, Red Grange, & Rudolph Valentino are narratives of several phenomena of import including the revolution in manners & morals, the Boston Police strike, the KKK, women's suffrage, Sigmund Freud, alcohol & Al Capone, Teapot Dome, & the crash.

Only You. John Devries. 1994. audio compact disk 85.00 (978-0-7673-9812-1(2)) LifeWay Christian.

Only You. John Devries. 1999. 8.00 (978-0-7673-9842-8(4)); 11.98 (978-0-7673-9833-6(5)); 75.00 (978-0-7673-9791-9(6)); audio compact disk 12.00 (978-0-7673-9844-2(0)) LifeWay Christian.

Only You! John Devries. 1999. audio compact disk 16.98 (978-0-7673-9814-5(9)) LifeWay Christian.

Only You. Elizabeth Lowell. Narrated by Richard Ferrone. 8 cass. (Running Time: 11 hrs.). 71.00 (978-1-4025-1229-2(5)) Recorded Bks.

Only You Can Be You: 21 Days to Making Your Life Count. unabr. ed. Erik Rees. (Running Time: 7 hrs. 47 mins. 51 sec.). (ENG.). 2009. 19.59 (978-1-60814-526-3(3)) Oasis Audio.

Only You Can Be You: 21 Days to Making Your Life Count. unabr. ed. Erik Rees. Narrated by Greg Whalen. 7 CDs. (Running Time: 7 hrs. 47 mins. 51 sec.). (ENG.). 2009. audio compact disk 27.99 (978-1-59859-586-4(5)) Oasis Audio.

OnMusic for Special Learners - Streaming. Eugenie Burkett & Alice Hammel. (ENG.). (C). 2009. 99.95 (978-0-9677747-1-8(3)) Cnnct Eductn.

OnMusic Fundamentals - Streaming. (C). 2009. 75.00 (978-0-9779276-8-5(7)) Cnnct Eductn.

Onstage & In-Control: Ten Easy Ways to Clobber Stage Fright. Stanley D. Munslow. 1 cd. (Running Time: 60 min). 2006. audio compact disk 18.95 (978-1-4276-0199-5(2)) AardGP.
For all musicians, vocalists, and entertainers. This one-hour "Learn & Affirm" program will give you the confidence you need to stay loose and play your best in front of any audience.

Onts. Dan Greenburg. Read by Dan Greenburg. 2 CDs. (Running Time: 1 hr. 40 mins.). (Secrets of Dripping Fang Ser.: Bk. 1). (J). (gr. 3-5). 2007. audio compact disk 24.00 (978-0-7393-5081-2(1)) Pub: Random Audio Pubg. Dist(s): Random

Onze Milles Verges. unabr. ed. Guillaume Apollinaire. Read by Michel Helgass. (YA). 2007. 79.99 (978-2-35569-079-2(0)) Find a World.

Oo-Pples/Boo-Noo-Noos. 2nd ed. Harcourt School Publishers Staff. (Trophies Ser.). (J). 2002. audio compact disk 32.10 (978-0-15-325788-9(1)) Harcourt Schl Pubs.

Oodles & Loads & Lots of Things. Lyrics by Janet Smith Post. Moderated by Jim Post. (J). 2000. audio compact disk 20.00 (978-0-9702826-3-7(X)) BTSBRBE.

Oodles of Animals. Nancy Stewart. 1 cass. (Running Time: 36 min.). (J). 1989. 9.95 (978-1-885430-04-5(3), FS1002) Frnds St Music.
Original children's songs.

OOGO the Caveboy: Audio Book. Christy Davis. (ENG.). (J). 2009. 6.39 (978-0-9840763-6-9(0)) CD Books ID.

***Oogy: The Dog Only a Family Could Love.** unabr. ed. Larry Levin. Read by Larry Levin. Read by Joe Barrett. (Running Time: 5 hrs.). (ENG.). 2010. 16.98 (978-1-60788-662-4(6)); audio compact disk 24.98 (978-1-60788-661-7(8)) Pub: Hachet Audio. Dist(s): HachBkGrp

Oon Criteek de Bernhardt see Sampler of American Humor

Oona: Living in the Shadows. unabr. ed. Jane Scovell. Read by Donada Peters. 7 cass. (Running Time: 10 hrs. 30 mins.). 1999. 56.00 (978-0-7366-4443-3(1), 4888) Books on Tape.
At age eighteen, Oona O'neill, a Manhattan debutante spurned by her neglectful, alcoholic father, Nobel Prize-winning playwright Eugene O'Neill, went to Hollywood to become an actress. Instead, a year later, in 1943, she married Charlie Chaplin, the world's adored King of Comedy. Thirty-six years her senior & thrice-divorced, Oona found in Chaplin the love & support that helped her escape the family curse of alcoholism & mental illness (both Oona's older half-brother & younger brother committed suicide at an early age). Oona & Chaplin moved to Switzerland in 1953 after Hollywood blacklisted the comic for leftist leanings. To the dismay of gossipmongers, theirs was a loving marriage blessed with eight children that lasted until Charlie's death in 1977. Then, overwhelmed by grief, Oona acted out the family addiction until cancer trumped alcohol in 1991.

Oona O' unabr. ed. Thomas Gallagher. Read by Dan Lazar. 6 cass. (Running Time: 6 hrs.). 36.00 (978-0-7366-0384-3(0), 1361) Books on Tape.
Oona O'Hagen is courageous, fanciful & witty; she has endless capacity for spontaneity & joy. She is, in short, what many people strive to become themselves, or to meet & marry: direct, honest & genuine. This is the story of this unlikely but wholly believable girl, her married lover, her baby & what happened to them.

Ooo. Read by Mary Richards. 1 cass. (Running Time: 45 min.). (Children's I Am Ser.). (J). 2007. audio compact disk 19.95 (978-1-56136-113-7(5)); audio compact disk 19.95 (978-1-56136-114-4(3)); audio compact disk 19.95 (978-1-56136-115-1(1)); audio compact disk 19.95 (978-1-56136-116-8(X)); audio compact disk 19.95 (978-1-56136-118-2(6)); audio compact disk 19.95 (978-1-56136-119-9(4)) Master Your Mind.

Ooo. Read by Mary Richards. Music by Wayne Musgrave. 1 cass. (Running Time: 45 min.). (Children's I Am Ser.). (J). 2007. audio compact disk 19.95 (978-1-56136-112-0(7)); audio compact disk 19.95 (978-1-56136-117-5(8)) Master Your Mind.

Ooo. Mary Richards & Mocho. Read by Mary Richards. 1 cass. (Running Time: 60 min.). (Subliminal Impact Ser.). 2007. audio compact disk 19.95 (978-1-56136-213-4(1)) Master Your Mind.
Excellent support for anyone recovering from addictions. My sobriety is more important than any fix.

Ooo. unabr. ed. Perf. by Charles Albert. Contrib. by Mary Richards. 1 cass. (Running Time: 50 min.). 2007. audio compact disk 19.95 (978-1-56136-201-1(8)) Master Your Mind.
A relaxing meditative journey through a magical musical realm, filled with rich woodwinds, joyful strings, gentle French Horn & the soothing sound of ethereal angelic voices.

Ooo. unabr. ed. Perf. by Charles Albert. Prod. by Mary Richards. 1 cass. (Running Time: 50 mins.). (Inner Peace Music Ser.). 2007. audio compact disk 19.95 (978-1-56136-211-0(5)) Master Your Mind.
Warm liquid sounds...transcendent inner peace.

Ooo. unabr. ed. Mary Richards. Read by Mary Richards. 1 cass. (Subliminal Impact Ser.). 2007. audio compact disk 19.95 (978-1-56136-210-3(7)) Master Your Mind.
Confidence begins with self esteem! You have a sense of purpose. You win with positive expectations. Powerful subliminal suggestions.

OOO-Moonbeams & Starlight-Music. 2007. audio compact disk 16.95 (978-1-56136-419-0(3)) Master Your Mind.

Oops! Perf. by Dan Crow. 1 CD. (Running Time: 1 hr. 30 mins.). (J). audio compact disk Rounder Records.
Educator, entertainer & songwriter Dan Crow is one of the most popular children's performers on the West Coast. His whimsical songs reveal a genuinely warm & funny person, sure to delight kids & adults of all ages. Here is a generous helping of songs about bugs, bananas, chickens, roosters, ham, gum & more.

Oops! Dan Crow. 1 cass. (Running Time: 36 min.). (J). (gr. k-4). 1988. 9.98 (8007) Rounder Records.

Oops! unabr. ed. John Lutz. Read by Edward Lewis. 5 cass. (Running Time: 7 hrs. 30 min.). 1998. 40.00 (978-0-7366-4221-7(8), 4721) Books on Tape.

Oops! I Forgot My Wife: A Story of Commitment As Marriage & Self-Centeredness Collide. Doyle Roth. 2004. bk. 19.99 (978-0-936083-18-6(2)) Pub: Lewis-Roth. Dist(s): Spring Arbor Dist

OOPS! I Forgot My Wife: A Story of Commitment as Marriage & Self-Centeredness Collide. Doyle Roth. 2007. audio compact disk 24.99 (978-0-936083-24-7(7)) Lewis-Roth.

Oops Ma! Judith Black. 2. (YA). 10.00 (978-0-9701073-8-1(2)) J Black Storyteller.

Oops! Wrong Family. Debi Toporoff. 2008. audio compact disk 17.99 (978-1-60462-399-4(3)) Tate Pubng.

Ooru naito rongu 3: Saishuu-shô see All Night Long

Ooze Slingers from Outer Space. Blake A. Hoena. Illus. by Steve Harpster. (Eek & Ack Ser.). (ENG.). (gr. 1-3). 2008. audio compact disk 14.60 (978-1-4342-0597-1(5)) CapstoneDig.

Op-Center. unabr. ed. Tom Clancy & Steve Pieczenik. 2002. 72.00 (978-0-7366-8434-7(4)) Books on Tape.
A beating heart of defense, intelligence, & crisis management technology. It is run by a crack team of operatives both within its won walls & out in the field. And when a job is too dirty, or too dangerous, Op-Center is the only place out government can turn.

Op-Center, Vol. 1. Tom Clancy & Steve Pieczenik. 8 CDs. (Running Time: 10 hrs. 30 min..). 2002. audio compact disk 64.00 (978-0-7366-8732-4(7)) Books on Tape.
Super-secret agency Op-Center must puzzle out who is to blame for an act of terrorism against South Korea.

Op-Center, Vol. 1. unabr. ed. Tom Clancy & Steve Pieczenik. Read by Michael Kramer. 7 cass. (Running Time: 10 hrs. 30 mins.). 2002. 56.00 (978-0-7366-8613-6(4)) Books on Tape.
A terrorist bomb explodes during a South Korean celebration of the anniversary of the election of its first president. Alarms are raised in Washington. No one is claiming responsibility. The first suspect is North Korea. Could it be making a power play against South Korea and unification? If so, how will the U.S. respond? Paul Hood, Director of the Op-Center, must answer these questions. The Op-Center, a largely autonomous new agency which takes on the government's toughest security problems, is only six months old, and has never been given a foreign crisis until now. Hood's team, which includes a general, a former ambassador, a psychologist, and a computer specialist, tries to find the solution, only to discover a factor that could change the new world order.

Op-Center, Vol. 2. Tom Clancy & Steve Pieczenik. 8 cass. (Running Time: 12 hrs.). 2002. 64.00 (978-0-7366-8628-0(2)); audio compact disk 72.00 (978-0-7366-8693-8(2)) Books on Tape.
Op-Center must keep Russia on a democratic course, but runs into its Russian mirror image - controlled by anti-democratic hardliners.

Op-Center, Vol. 3. unabr. ed. Tom Clancy & Steve Pieczenik. 9 cass. (Running Time: 13 hrs. 30 mins.c). 2002. 64.00 (978-0-7366-8714-0(9)) Books on Tape.
In the newly unified Germany, old horrors are reborn. It is the beginning of Chaos Days, a time when neo-Nazi groups gather to spread violence and resurrect dead dreams. But this year Germany isn't the only target. Plans are to destabilize Europe and cause turmoil throughout the United States. Paul Hood and his team, already in Germany to buy technology for the new Regional Op-Center, become entangled in the crisis. They uncover a shocking force behind the chaos - a group that uses cutting-edge technology to promote hate and to influence world events. A powerful profile of America's defense, intelligence, and crisis management technology.

Op-Center, Vol. 4. unabr. ed. Tom Clancy & Steve Pieczenik. 9 cass. (Running Time: 13 hrs. 30 mins.). 2002. 72.00 (978-0-7366-8759-1(9)); audio compact disk 96.00 (978-0-7366-8760-7(2)) Books on Tape.
Kurdish terrorists have attacked a dam inside the borders of Turkey, threatening the water supply of their very homeland. It is not insanity, but the first step in a simple plan: force all-out war in the Middle East, drawing in the major players in the new world order. What the terrorists don't know is that a new Regional Op-Center is now on-line in Turkey. A mobile version of the permanent crisis-management facility, the ROC is a cutting-edge surveillance and information mecca. And its team can see exactly what the Kurdish rebels are trying to do. But the terrorists are more resourceful than anyone thinks. They also have ways of obtaining classified information.

Op-Center, Vol. 6. Tom Clancy & Steve Peiczenik. 1 cass. (Running Time: 1 hr.). 2002. 56.00 (978-0-7366-8873-4(0)) Books on Tape.

Op-Center, Vol. 9. unabr. ed. Tom Clancy & Steve Pieczenik. 9 cass. (Running Time: 13 hrs. 30 mins.). 2002. 72.00 (978-0-7366-8638-9(X)) Books on Tape.
The crack team of operatives uses their defense, intelligence, and crisis management technology to bring down the opposition. When a job is too dirty or too dangerous, Op-Center is the only place the government can turn. Follow the circuitous path as the agents negotiate the most devious threats to the peace and prosperity of America - including those within.

Op-Center, Vol. 9. unabr. ed. Tom Clancy & Steve Pieczenik. 11 CDs. (Running Time: 13 hrs. 30 mins.). 2002. audio compact disk 88.00 (978-0-7366-8653-2(3)) Books on Tape.

Op-Center No. 3: Games of State. Jeff Rovin. Read by Michael Kramer. Created by Tom Clancy & Steve Pieczenik. 2002. audio compact disk 88.00 (978-0-7366-8715-7(7)) Books on Tape.

Op-Center No. 5: Balance of Power. Jeff Rovin. Read by Michael Kramer. Created by Tom Clancy & Steve Pieczenik. 2002. audio compact disk 88.00 (978-0-7366-8778-2(5)) Books on Tape.

Op-Center No. 6: State of Siege. Jeff Rovin. Read by Michael Kramer. Created by Tom Clancy & Steve Pieczenik. 2002. audio compact disk 64.00 (978-0-7366-8874-1(9)) Books on Tape.

Op-Center No. 7: Divide & Conquer. Jeff Rovin. Read by Michael Kramer. Created by Tom Clancy & Steve Pieczenik. 2002. 56.00 (978-0-7366-8843-7(9)); audio compact disk 72.00 (978-0-7366-8844-4(7)) Books on Tape.

Op-Center No. 8: Line of Control. Jeff Rovin. Read by Michael Kramer. Created by Tom Clancy & Steve Pieczenik. 2002. audio compact disk 72.00 (978-0-7366-8448-4(4)) Books on Tape.

Opal Deception. unabr. ed. Eoin Colfer. Read by Nathaniel Parker. 6 CDs. (Running Time: 7 hrs. 28 mins.). (Artemis Fowl Ser.: Bk. 4). (ENG.). (J). (gr. 5). 2005. audio compact disk 34.00 (978-0-307-24332-4(X), Listening Lib) Pub: Random Audio Pubg. Dist(s): Random

Opal Deception. unabr. collector's ed. Eoin Colfer. Read by Nathaniel Parker. 6 CDs. (Running Time: 7 hrs. 29 mins.). (Artemis Fowl Ser.: Bk. 4). (J). (gr. 4-7). 2005. audio compact disk 50.00 (978-0-307-24333-1(8), BksonTape) Random Audio Pubg.

Opal Deception, Vol. 4. unabr. collector's ed. Eoin Colfer. Read by Nathaniel Parker. 5 cass. (Running Time: 7 hrs. 20 mins.). (Artemis Fowl Ser.: Bk. 4). (J). (gr. 4-7). 2005. 40.00 (978-0-307-24331-7(1), BksonTape) Random Audio Pubg.
Twelve-year old Artemis Fowl, Internet fanatic and ingenious criminal mastermind, enters the world of fairies and gnomes to decode their secrets and steal their fortune.

Opal Seekers. unabr. ed. Patricia Shaw. Read by Stanley McGeagh. 13 cass. (Running Time: 19 hrs. 30 min.). 1998. (978-1-86340-704-5(9), 570220) Bolinda Pubng AUS.
Spanning half a century of dramatic change, a story of triumph & loss, & of the bravery & determination of those who carved out an existence for themselves in the beautiful but unforgiving land of Australia.

Opals & Outrage. Lynn Gardner. 6 cass. 2004. 24.95 (978-1-57734-800-9(1)) Covenant Comms.

OPEC Petrodollars & Canadian Gold. Norman Bailey & Ned E. Goodman. 1 cass. (Running Time: 46 min.). 11.95 (369) J Norton Pubs.

Open. unabr. ed. Lisa Moore. Read by Lisa Moore. Read by Mary Lewis & Holly Hogan. 1 CD. (Running Time: 21600 sec.). 2005. audio compact disk 24.95 (978-0-9734223-8-2(6)) Pub: Rattling Bks CAN. Dist(s): Hse Anansi

Open: An Autobiography. abr. ed. Andre Agassi. Read by Erik Davies. (ENG.). 2009. audio compact disk 32.00 (978-0-7393-5856-6(1), Random AudioBks) Pub: Random Audio Pubg. Dist(s): Random

***Open: An Autobiography.** unabr. ed. Andre Agassi. Narrated by Erik Davies. 15 CDs. (Running Time: 18 hrs.). 2009. audio compact disk 100.00 (978-1-4159-6543-6(9)) Random.

Open: Inside the Ropes at Bethpage Black. abr. ed. John Feinstein. (ENG.). 2005. 14.98 (978-1-59483-281-9(1)) Pub: Hachet Audio. Dist(s): HachBkGrp

Open & Receive: Guided Meditations. 1 cass. (Running Time: 38 mins.). 1991. 12.95 (978-1-886594-00-5(7), Inner Harmon) Inner Harmonics.
Guided meditations working with Light:Side A: Filling to Overflowing 19 minsSide B: Healing Yourself with Light 19 min.

Open & Shut. David Rosenfelt. Read by Grover Gardner. (Running Time: 28800 sec.). 2008. audio compact disk 29.95 (978-1-59316-126-2(3)) Listen & Live.

Open Boat see Great American Short Stories

Open Boat see Red Badge of Courage & Other Stories

Open Boat. (ENG.). 2007. (978-1-60339-053-8(7)); cd-rom & audio compact disk (978-1-60339-054-5(5)) Listenr Digest.

Open Boat. Stephen Crane. 10.00 (LSS1110) Esstee Audios.

Open Boat. unabr. ed. Stephen Crane. Read by Jim Killavey. 1 cass. (Running Time: 82 min.). Dramatization. 1981. 7.95 (S-1) Jimcin Record.
Struggle for life on the cruel sea.

Open Chord Cookbook. Dan Donnelly. 1 CD. (Running Time: 1 hr.). (ENG.). 2000. audio compact disk 10.00 (978-0-7390-0800-3(5), 19369) Alfred Pub.

Open Chord Rock: Essential Elements Guitar Songs. Created by Hal Leonard Corporation Staff. 2008. pap. bk. 12.99 (978-1-4234-3341-5(6), 1423433416) H Leonard.

Open Discovery: The Future of Family Law Practice. 1997. bk. 59.00 (ACS-1344) PA Bar Inst.
As of July 1, 1997, discovery was permitted without leave of court in certain family law cases. All family law practitioners, judges, & court personnel should include this in their possession in learning the effective use of discovery. Even if you are an experienced family lawyer who is familiar with the discovery process, this provides the perfect opportunity to review & sharpen your skills as a litigator.

Open Door see Classic Ghost Stories, Vol. 3, A Collection

Open Door see Weird Stories

Open Door to Spanish, Bk. 1. Margarita Madrigal. (C). (gr. 7-12). 1980. 45.00 (978-0-686-77563-8(5), 58471) Prentice ESL.

Open Door to Spanish, Bk. 2. Margarita Madrigal. (Open Door to Spanish Ser.). (J). (gr. 7-12). 1981. 45.00 (978-0-686-77684-0(4), 58472) Prentice ESL.

Open Doors: Identifying the Doors God Will Open in These Last Days. Lynne Hammond. (ENG.). 2007. audio compact disk 10.00 (978-1-57399-335-7(2)) Mac Hammond.

Open Doorways for Demons. Jack Deere. 1 cass. (Running Time: 1 hr. 30 mins.). (Demon Inroads Ser.: Vol. 2). 2000. 5.00 (JD02-002) Morning NC.
First laying a foundation of insight into Satan's overall strategy, Jack then builds upon it with practical knowledge of the Christian's authority over demonic forces.

Open Ended Relaxation-Guided. 2007. audio compact disk 19.95 (978-1-56136-044-4(9)) Master Your Mind.

Open Forum 1: Academic Listening & Speaking. Ed. by Oxford Staff. (Open Forum Ser.). 2006. 54.95 (978-0-19-441776-1(X)) OUP.

Open Heart. unabr. ed. Dalai Lama XIV. Read by Nicholas Vreeland & Richard Gere. (ENG.). 2005. 14.98 (978-1-59483-408-0(3)) Pub: Hachet Audio. Dist(s): HachBkGrp

Open Heart, Open Home: The Hospitable Way to Make Others Feel Welcome & Wanted. Karen Mains. 3 cass. (Running Time: 4 hrs.). 2002. 20.00 (978-0-8308-2301-7(8)) InterVarsity.

Open Heaven, Lord. 1999. 12.00 (978-0-9667124-8-3(X)); audio compact disk 17.99 (978-0-9667124-7-6(1)) Life Action Publishing.

Open House. Jill Mansell. (Isis (CDs) Ser.). 2006. audio compact disk 99.95 (978-0-7531-2609-7(5)) Pub: ISIS Lrg Prnt GBR. Dist(s): Ulverscroft US

Open House. unabr. ed. Elizabeth Berg. Read by Beth Fowler. 6 CDs. (Running Time: 9 hrs.). 2000. audio compact disk 64.95 (978-0-7927-9956-6(9), SLD 007, Chivers Sound Lib); bk. 54.95 (978-0-7927-2398-1(8), CSL 287, Chivers Sound Lib) AudioGO.
Samantha's husband has left her & after a spree of overcharging at Tiffany's she settles down to reconstruct a life for herself & her young son.

Open House. unabr. ed. Elizabeth Berg. Read by Becky Baker. (YA). 2006. 44.99 (978-1-59895-207-0(2)) Find a World.

Open House. unabr. ed. Jill Mansell. Read by Julia Franklin. 9 cass. (Running Time: 12 hrs.). (Isis Cassettes Ser.). 2006. 76.95 (978-0-7531-3478-8(0)) Pub: ISIS Lrg Prnt GBR. Dist(s): Ulverscroft US

Open House. unabr. abr. ed. Elizabeth Berg. Read by Becky Baker. 6 CDs. (Running Time: 6 hrs.). (ENG.). 2000. audio compact disk 34.95 (978-1-56511-467-8(1), 1565114671) Pub: HighBridge. Dist(s): Workman Pub

***Open Leadership: How Social Technology Can Transform the Way You Lead.** unabr. ed. Charlene Li. Read by Sean Pratt. (Running Time: 10 hrs.). (ENG.). 2010. 39.98 (978-1-59659-579-8(5), GildAudio) Pub: Gildan Media. Dist(s): HachBkGrp

Open Letter. Gretchen Chandler. Read by Neva Duyndam. 1 cass. (Running Time: 1 hr.). 1989. 9.95 (978-1-878159-06-9(2)) Duvall Media.
An open letter from a former mentally ill writer to parents & other caregivers.

Open MIC Karaoke, Volume 2. Contrib. by Newsboys. 2004. audio compact disk 7.99 (978-5-559-77845-7(1)) Pt of Grace Ent.

Open Mind. Dawna Markova. 6 cass. (Running Time: 8 hrs.). 1999. 59.95 Set. (83-0028) Explorations.
How to recognize how one learns in order to learn faster & communicate better. Focuses on unlocking the capacity to learn quickly, more deeply & more naturally.

Open Range. Lauran Paine. Read by Barrett Whitener. 5 cass. (Running Time: 7 hrs.). 2003. 39.95 (978-0-7861-2479-4(2), 3132) Blckstn Audio.
The open range men are free-grazing cattlemen, those who don't own land but drive their stock through the country to graze. Boss Spearman knows that times are changing. Local ranchers are staking claims to grazing areas and building up extensive cattle empires. Boss has no quarrel with that, but he won't be intimidated or scared off. So when Denton Baxter makes it clear, by killing one man and seriously wounding another, that he intends to drive Boss and his crew out, Boss must make a stand.

Open Range. unabr. ed. Lauran Paine. Read by Barrett Whitener. 6 CDs. (Running Time: 7 hrs.). 2003. audio compact disk 48.00 (978-0-7861-9132-1(5), 3132) Blckstn Audio.

Open Range. unabr. ed. Lauran Paine. Read by Barrett Whitener. 1 MP3. (Running Time: 7 hrs.). 2003. audio compact disk 24.95 (978-0-7861-8873-4(1), 3132) Blckstn Audio.

Open Range. unabr. ed. Lauran Paine. Read by Barrett Whitener. 6 CDs. (Running Time: 9 hrs.). 2004. audio compact disk 32.95 (978-0-7861-9093-5(0)); reel tape 29.95 (978-0-7861-2487-9(3)) Blckstn Audio.
A former gunslinger is forced to take up arms again when he and his cattle crew are threatened by a corrupt lawman.

Open Rhinoplasty: Indications, Techniques & Complications. Moderated by Eugene M. Tardy. 2 cass. (Running Time: 3 hrs.). (Otorhinolaryngology Ser.: OT-2). 1986. 19.00 (8655) Am Coll Surgeons.

Open Season. Archer Mayor. Perf. by Tom Stevens. (Joe Gunther Ser.). 2008. audio compact disk 42.95 (978-0-9798613-2-1(2)) Pub: Amp. Dist(s): Enfield Pubs NH

Open Season. unabr. ed. Linda Howard. Read by Deborah Hazlett. 8 vols. (Running Time: 12 hrs.). 2001. bk. 69.95 (978-0-7927-2516-9(6), CSL 405, Chivers Sound Lib); audio compact disk 94.95 (978-0-7927-9940-5(2), SLD 091, Chivers Sound Lib) AudioGO.
Daisy Minor, a small-town librarian, has a wardrobe as sexy as a dictionary and hasn't been on a date in years. One makeover later, she has transformed herself into a party girl extraordinaire and it's open season for man hunting. But on her way home late one night, Daisy sees something she's not supposed to see and is suddenly the target of a killer.

Open Secret. Jalal Al-Din Rumi. Read by Coleman Barks & Dorothy Fadiman. 1 cass. (Running Time: 1 hr.). (Insight Ser.). 1988. 9.95 (978-0-945093-18-3(7)) Enhanced Aud Systs.
Dramatic reading of Sufi mystic poetry accompanied by flute, violin, & tamboura music.

Open Secret. Vajracarya. Read by Chogyam Trungpa. 3 cass. (Running Time: 4 hrs. 30 mins.). 1978. 29.50 (A021) Vajradhatu.
Three talks. By practicing meditation our sanity can communicate clearly & naturally to others. Enlightenment becomes an "open secret" which proclaims itself fearlessly.

Open Secret: Work & Its Secret. unabr. ed. Vivekananda. Read by Bruce Robertson. 1 cass. (Running Time: 1 hr.). 1987. 7.95 (978-1-882915-04-0(6)) Vedanta Ctr Atlanta.
Methods of realizing one's own divinity through spiritual practice and or work.

Open Sesame: Ernie & Bert's Red Book. Maureen Harris & Jane Brauer. 1987. 39.95 (978-0-19-434175-2(5)) OUP.

Open Sesame Kit: Big Bird's Yellow Book. Jane S. Zion. 1984. 24.50 (978-0-19-434172-1(0)) OUP.

Open Sesame Multilevel Book. Carol Cellman. 1989. 24.50 (978-0-19-434265-0(4)) OUP.

Open source sex ed Audio: Pleasure zone Basics. Violet Blue. 2007. 5.00 (978-0-9799019-1-1(X)) Digita Pubns.

open Swimmer. unabr. ed. Tim Winton. Read by Humphrey Bower. (Running Time: 5 hrs.). 2007. audio compact disk 63.95 (978-1-74093-925-6(5), 9781740939256) Pub: Bolinda Pubng AUS. Dist(s): Bolinda Pub Inc

Open the Door: Celtic Stories & Songs. Short Stories. Perf. by Jennifer Armstrong. 1 cass. (Running Time: 75 mins.). (gr. 3 up). 2000. 9.95 (978-0-938756-56-9(7)) Yellow Moon.

Open the Door: Celtic Stories & Songs. Short Stories. Perf. by Jennifer Armstrong. 1 CD. (Running Time: 75 mins.). (YA). (gr. 3 up). 2000. audio compact disk 14.95 (978-0-938756-57-6(5)) Yellow Moon.
Four stories and three songs of traditional Celtic origin: W.B. Yeats' "The Lake Isle of Innisfree," "Wild Mountain Thyme," "Open the Door." Also includes "The Fishwife and the Changeling" and "The Marriage Basket".

Open the Eyes of My Heart: Ultimate Worship Anthems of the Christian Faith. Prod. by Jeff Moseley & Gene Zacharewicz. 2005. audio compact disk 19.98 (978-5-558-78760-3(0)) INO Rec.

Open the Window. Bob Livingston. 1 cass. (Running Time: 40 min.). 1991. 9.95 (978-0-939065-52-3(5)) Gentle Wind.
Humorous songs to open your imagination to life's possibilities.

Open the Window: Silly Songs Set to a Rockabilly Beat. Bob Livingston. Perf. by Bob Livingston. (J). 1999. audio compact disk 14.95 (978-1-58467-004-9(5)) Gentle Wind.

Open the Windows & Feel the Gentle Breeze of the Holy Spirit: A New Live Worship Experience. Perf. by Max Lucado. 1 cass. (Running Time: 1 hr.). 1998. 9.99 (978-1-878990-97-6(7)); audio compact disk 13.99 (978-1-878990-96-9(9)) Provident Mus Dist.
Songs of praise & words of inspiration.

Open Tomb, Open Hearts. Megan McKenna. Read by Megan McKenna. 1 cass. (Running Time: 1 hrs.). 1996. pap. bk. (AA2988) Credence Commun.
Story of Lazarus becomes a story of the freedom of faith, a rage against death in all its forms, & a longing for the fullness of life for everyone.

Open Tuning for Solo Guitar: 14 Songs, 9 Tuning. Dorian Michael. 1997. audio compact disk 19.95 (978-1-57424-050-4(1)) Centerstream Pub.

Open Water: No. 6 in the River Road Poetry Series. David Musgrave. Read by David Musgrave. Executive Producer Carol Jenkins. Carol Jenkins. (ENG.). 2008. audio compact disk 18.00 (978-0-9804148-5-1(7)) RivRoad AUS.

Open Way: The Path of the Bodhisattva. Osel Tendzin. Read by Osel Tendzin. 4 cass. (Running Time: 6 hrs.). 1977. 40.50 (A062) Vajradhatu.
Four talks: 1) The Motivation toward Openness; 2) Getting Sane & Getting Stuck; 3) Feeling the Transparency of Other; 4) Discriminating Awareness & Transcendent Action.

Open Wide: Tooth School Inside. unabr. ed. Laurie Keller. Illus. by Laurie Keller. Read by Michael McKean. 1 cass. (Running Time: 18 mins.). (J). (gr. k-5). 2006. bk. 24.95 (978-0-439-84917-3(9), WHRA650); bk. 29.95 (978-0-439-84918-0(7), WHCD650); pap. bk. 14.95 (978-0-439-84919-7(5), WPRA650); pap. bk. 18.95 (978-0-439-84920-3(9), WPCD650) Weston Woods.

Open Wide the Freedom Gates. unabr. ed. Dorothy Height. Narrated by Lizan Mitchell. 8 cass. (Running Time: 11 hrs. 45 mins.). 2003. 79.75 (978-1-4025-9449-6(6), F0189MC, Griot Aud) Recorded Bks.

Open Window see Selected European Short Stories

Open Window see Saki: Strange Tales

Open Windows. 2003. 13.15 (978-0-633-07716-7(X)) LifeWay Christian.

Open Windows. 2004. 13.65 (978-0-633-08088-4(8)) LifeWay Christian.

Open Windows. 2004. 13.65 (978-0-633-08340-3(2)) LifeWay Christian.

Open Windows. 2004. 13.65 (978-0-633-08590-2(1)) LifeWay Christian.

Open Windows. 2004. 13.65 (978-0-633-17404-0(1)) LifeWay Christian.

Open Windows. 2005. 13.65 (978-0-633-17598-6(6)) LifeWay Christian.

Open Windows. 2005. 13.65 (978-0-633-17796-6(2)) LifeWay Christian.

Open Windows Cassette. 13.00 (978-0-7673-4003-8(5)) LifeWay Christian.

Open Your Psychic Powers, Vol. 28. Jonathan Parker. 2 cass. (Running Time: 1 hr. 45 min.). 1992. 17.00 (978-1-58400-027-3(9)) QuantumQuests Intl.

Open Yourself to Change: An Inspirational Lecture on Empowerment. Scripts. Created by Joan Marie Ambrose. Narrated by Joan Marie Ambrose. 1 CD. (Running Time: 60 mins). 2002. audio compact disk 15.95 (978-0-9718654-0-2(X)) Ser Hse.
This CD lecure is an inspirational self-empowerment tool that encourages the audience to open themselves up to change. "When we change what we believe, we change what we do." Only by understanding can change occur.This lecture series will help you explore your options and teach you to take command of your life rather than allowing the outside forces to take control of your life.

Openers of the Doors to the Invisible. Instructed by Manly P. Hall. 8.95 (978-0-89314-203-2(4), C850602) Philos Res.

Opening & Aligning My Chakras: Discovering My Power Within. (ENG., 2009. audio compact disk 19.95 (978-0-9766735-6-9(8)) R Seals.

Opening & Closing Arguments. 1985. bk. 55.00 incl. book.; 30.00 cass. only.; 25.00 book only. PA Bar Inst.

Opening & Closing Arguments. 1989. 50.00 (AC-533) PA Bar Inst.

Opening Atlantis: A Novel of Alternate History. unabr. ed. Harry Turtledove. Narrated by Todd McLaren. (Running Time: 17 hrs. 0 mins. 0 sec.). (Atlantis Ser.). (ENG.). 2007. audio compact disk 39.99 (978-1-4001-0554-0(4)); audio compact disk 79.99 (978-1-4001-3554-7(0)); audio compact disk 29.99 (978-1-4001-5554-5(1)) Pub: Tantor Media. Dist(s): IngramPubServ

Opening Closed Minds. William J. Reilly. 1 cass. (Running Time: 1 hr.). 10.00 (SP100034) SMI Intl.
Don't just wait for people to believe you; learn the secrets of "Opening Closed Minds". Learn to earn & enjoy the trust & respect of other people from this condensation of Dr. Reilly's book, "Successful Human Relations", a classic in the field.

Opening Day: The Story of Jackie Robinson's First Season. unabr. ed. Jonathan Eig. Narrated by Richard Allen. 10 CDs. (Running Time: 12 hrs. 0 mins. 0 sec.). (ENG.). 2007. audio compact disk 34.99 (978-1-4001-0434-5(3)) Pub: Tantor Media. Dist(s): IngramPubServ

Opening Day: The Story of Jackie Robinson's First Season. unabr. ed. Jonathan Eig. Read by Richard Allen. (Running Time: 12 hrs. 0 mins. 0 sec.). (ENG.). 2007. audio compact disk 24.99 (978-1-4001-5434-0(0)); audio compact disk 69.99 (978-1-4001-3434-2(X)) Pub: Tantor Media. Dist(s): IngramPubServ

Opening Heaven's Windows: Recognizing the Key to Accessing Heaven¿s Blessing. Mac Hammond. 2009. audio compact disk 30.00 (978-1-57399-418-7(9)) Mac Hammond.

Opening Keynote Speaker. James Collins. (Transforming Local Government Ser.). Alliance Innov.

Opening MInds Audio Book: A Journey of Extraordinary Encounters, Crop Circles, & Resonance. Voice by Simeon Hein. (ENG.). 2007. 24.95i (978-0-9715863-3-8(0)) Mt Baldy Pr.

Opening New Doors. Frank Damazio. 2003. audio compact disk 14.99 (978-1-59383-010-6(6)) CityChristian.
Want to open up new doors God has set before you? Pastor Frank reveals how you can obtain the keys to open the doors of opportunity that God has prepared for you.

***Opening Night.** abr. ed. Ngaio Marsh. Read by Anton Lesser. (Running Time: 3 hrs. 45 mins. 0 sec.). (ENG.). 2009. audio compact disk 24.95 (978-1-4055-0745-5(4)) Pub: Little BrownUK GBR. Dist(s): IPG Chicago

Opening Night. unabr. ed. Ngaio Marsh. Read by James Saxon. 6 cass. (Running Time: 9 hrs.). (Inspector Alleyn Mystery Ser.). 2000. 49.95 (978-0-7451-6143-3(X), CAB 530) Pub: Chivers Audio Bks GBR. Dist(s): AudioGO
Dreams of stardom had lured Martyn Tame to the glittering lights of the West End. The Vulcan Theater had been her last hope, and now driven by sheer necessity, she was glad to accept the role of understudy. Then came the eagerly awaited opening night. To Martyn, the night brought a strange turn of events, and to one distinguished member of the cast, death: sudden and unforeseen.

Opening of Eyes: The Poetry of Intimacy & Imagination. Speeches. Featuring David Whyte. 1 CD. 2005. audio compact disk 15.00 (978-1-932887-07-5(0)) Pub: Many Rivers Pr. Dist(s): Partners-West

Opening of the Battle of Gettysburg see Poetry of Benet

Opening of the Battle of Gettysburg see Twentieth-Century Poetry in English, No. 23, Recordings of Poets Reading Their Own Poetry

Opening of the Divine Eye. Swami Amar Jyoti. 1 cass. (Running Time: 1 hr.). 1975. 9.95 (R-72) Truth Consciousness.
When the flower of Spirit totally blossoms, that is Divine Seeing.

Opening Our Hearts to Each Other. Susan Jeffers. Read by Susan Jeffers. 1 cass. (Running Time: 1 hr.). 1999. 13.10 (978-1-84032-127-2(X), HoddrStoughton) Hodder General GBR.
Specific techniques for overcoming the destructive mindsets that can thwart successful relationships.

Opening Our Hearts to Men. abr. ed. Susan Jeffers. Read by Susan Jeffers. 4 cass. (Running Time: 3 hrs.). 1999. (978-1-84032-117-3(2), HoddrStoughton) Hodder General GBR.
A completely new and self-affirming way for women to take charge of their lives.

Opening Our Hearts to Men. unabr. ed. Susan Jeffers. Read by Susan Jeffers. 4 cass. (Running Time: 8 hrs.). 1992. 25.00 (978-1-56170-041-7(X), 310) Hay House.
Susan Jeffers presents a completely new & self-affirming way for women to transform their lives & begin attracting a healthy kind of love. Especially good for those who wish to stregthen a relationship or start a healthy one.

Opening Session - Changing the Culture by Changing the Conversation. Innovation Groups Staff. Contrib. by Peter Block & Joel Henning. 1 cass. (Running Time: 1 hr.). (Transforming Local Government Ser.: Vol. 1). 1999. 10.00 (978-1-882403-57-8(6), IG9901) Alliance Innov.

Opening Shots: August 1914 - April 1915. Max Arthur. 3 CDs. (Running Time: 3 hrs. 0 mins. 0 sec.). (Forgotten Voices Ser.). (ENG., 2003. audio compact disk 22.00 (978-1-85686-800-6(1), Audiobks) Pub: Random GBR. Dist(s): IPG Chicago

Opening Statements: A Modern Approach. Sanford M. Brook. 1 cass. (Running Time: 1 hr. 09 min.). 1993. 55.00 Incl. supporting materials bklet. (AUDZ18OS) NITA.
How to make effective & persuasive opening statements that will make a lasting impression on jurors. Also addresses common mistakes made during openings & how to remedy them.

Opening Statements: A Modern Approach. Sanford M. Brook. 1 cass. (Running Time: 1 hr. 09 min.). 1993. 50.00 (FAZ180S) Natl Inst Trial Ad.
How to make effective & persuasive opening statements which make a lasting impression on jurors. Also addresses common mistakes made during openings & how to remedy them.

Opening the Chakras: Simple, Easy Guided Meditation for Opening the Chakras. Based on a book by Robert Morgen. 1. (Running Time: 1 hr, 21 mins, 27 secs). 2006. audio compact disk 59.95 (978-0-9773801-7-6(3)) MysticWolf.
Robert Morgen's ?Opening the Chakras? introduces intermediate meditators to their chakra system. With brief, simple explanations Morgen guides listeners through the process of working with and opening the chakras. The powerful guided meditations on this CD have been the highlight of Morgen?s Seminars and classes. The CD includes:1. Intro to the Chakras 1:302. Drawing Energy into the Chakras 10:583. Hugging the Tree 10:584. Opening the Chakras 14:305. Becoming the Universe 36:00.

Opening the Cornucopia. Marina Bokelman. Read by Marina Bokelman. (Running Time: 1 hr.). (Seasonal Medicine Wheel Ser.). 1992. 9.95 (978-1-886139-02-2(4), SMW-2) Sacred Paw.
Attunement with seasonal energy, Summer healing issues, transformational process work.

***Opening the door of your Heart.** Ajahn Brahm. Read by Francis Greenslade. (Running Time: 5 hrs. 45 mins.). 2009. 64.99 (978-1-74214-557-0(4), 9781742145570) Pub: Bolinda Pubng AUS. Dist(s): Bolinda Pub Inc

Opening the door of your Heart. unabr. ed. Ajahn Brahm. Read by Francis Greenslade. (Running Time: 5 hrs. 45 mins.). 2009. audio compact disk 63.95 (978-1-74214-078-0(5), 9781742140780) Pub: Bolinda Pubng AUS. Dist(s): Bolinda Pub Inc

***Opening the door of your Heart.** unabr. ed. Ajahn Brahm. Read by Francis Greenslade. (Running Time: 5 hrs. 45 mins.). 2010. 43.95 (978-1-74214-663-8(5), 9781742146638) Pub: Bolinda Pubng AUS. Dist(s): Bolinda Pub Inc

Opening the Door th Transcendence. unabr. ed. Swami Amar Jyoti. 1 cass. (Running Time: 1 hr.). (Satsangs of Swami Amar Jyoti). 1997. 9.95 (978-0-933572-26-3(3), M-106) Truth Consciousness.
Beyond paradoxes of the mind to the Absolute view. Honest, genuine aspiration. Will opens the door.

Opening the Doors of Creativity. Terence McKenna. 2 cass. (Running Time: 3 hrs.). 18.00 (A0718-90) Sound Photosyn.
At the Carnegie Art Museum in Southern California, this video captures a particularly fresh talk emphasizing the challenge of artistic creation - & the need for artists to again become mystical journeyers informing society by dissolving the conceptual boundary of ordinary expectation.

Opening the Gates of Light. unabr. ed. Swami Amar Jyoti. 1 cass. (Running Time: 1 hr.). (Satsangs of Swami Amar Jyoti Ser.). 2000. 9.95 (978-0-933572-55-3(7), R-122) Truth Consciousness.
Consciousness is already "expended" - we just have to open and see. Realizing: "Thou Art That.".

Opening the Heart. Swami Amar Jyoti. 1 cass. (Running Time: 1 hr.). 1981. 9.95 (J-39) Truth Consciousness.
Going beyond the walls of the mind. To seek is to open & expand. The holograms in the brain.

Opening the Heart Series. unabr. ed. 2 cass. (Running Time: 1 hr., 30 min.). 1996. 29.95 (978-1-56102-930-3(0)) Inter Indus.
Helps enable someone to deepen their emotional connections & open themselves to love.

Opening the Lotuses: The Manifesting Power of Logos. Ann Ree Colton. 1 cass. (Running Time: 1 hr.). 7.95 (978-0-917189-16-6(7)) A R Colton Fnd.

Opening to Angels. Perf. by Alma Daniel et al. Contrib. by Derek Partridge. 1 cass. (Running Time: 1 hr. 23 min.). 1999. 14.95 (978-1-56889-015-9(X), A5605); 29.90 Incl. public performance rights for schools & libraries. Lghtwrks Aud & Vid.
Learn how to contact your guardian angel & be more receptive to the angelic realm in your daily life. Interweaves inspirational passages, informative conversations, soaring music & guided meditations. Also features stephen Halpern, Philip Chapman, Aeoliah, Iasos, Erik Bergland & Steve Gaines.

Opening to Divine Love. Swami Amar Jyoti. 1 cass. (Running Time: 1 hr.). 1994. 9.95 (C-45) Truth Consciousness.
How does Divine Love manifest on earth? Allowing ourselves to express love, the great healer. "Instruction manual" for being human.

Opening to God: A Guide to Prayer. Thomas H. Green. Read by Paul Leingang. (Running Time: 12600 sec.). 1988. audio compact disk 4.95 (978-0-86716-869-3(2)) St Anthony Mess Pr.

Opening to Grief; The Threshold Task & Purification by Fire; The Passage Through Pain. Comment by Stephen Levine. (Running Time: 54 min.). 1987. Original Face.
Examines the healing nature of grief & the process of coping with loss.

Opening to Inner Light. Ralph Metzner. 1 cass. 9.00 (A0167-86) Sound Photosyn.

Opening to Learning Meditation. Margaret Paul. 1 cass. (Running Time: 26 min.). Dramatization. 1997. bk. 10.00 (978-0-912389-08-0(7)) Evolving Pubns.
Fifteen minute meditation to clear chakra system & open you to learning with core self, wounded self & higher guidance.

Opening to Prosperity. Mary Lee LaBay. (ENG.). 2006. audio compact disk 9.95 (978-1-934705-20-9(9)) Awareness Engin.

Opening to Receive Miracles. Lorraine M. Coburn. 2006. 14.99 (978-0-9786516-6-4(9)); audio compact disk 14.99 (978-0-9786516-1-9(8)) Miracles Media.

Opening to the Christ Consciousness. unabr. ed. Paul Ferrini. Read by Paul Ferrini. 2 cass. (Running Time: 1 hr. 54 min.). (Christ Mind Talks & Workshops Ser.). 1997. audio compact disk 16.95 (978-1-879159-31-0(7)) Heartways Pr.
A talk at Unity Church of Tustin in November 1997.

Opening to the Possibilities. Rhegina Sinozich. 2008. audio compact disk 14.95 (978-0-9706297-3-9(7)) Abrezia Pr.

Opening to True Guidance: How Spirit Talks to You Through Angelic Teachers & Other Messengers of God. unabr. ed. Meredith L. Young-Sowers. 2 cass. (Running Time: 2 hrs.). 1997. pap. bk. 25.00 (978-1-883478-09-4(X)) Stillpoint.
Learn the ways guidance is given & how to interpret it, as well as specific techniques for awakening soul guidance & experiencing God's essence as divine love & wisdom.

Opening up to a Higher Power. Eldon Taylor. 1 cass. (Running Time: 1 hr. 2 mins.). (Inner Talk Ser.). 16.95 (978-1-55978-201-2(3), 53796A) Progress Aware Res.
Soundtrack - Tropical Lagoon with underlying subliminal affirmations.

Opening up to a Higher Power: Environmental Theme. Eldon Taylor. 1 cass. (Running Time: 1 hr.). 16.95 (978-1-55978-547-1(0), 53796F) Progress Aware Res.

Opening up to a Higher Power: Music Theme. Eldon Taylor. 1 cass. (Running Time: 1 hr.). 16.95 (978-1-55978-203-6(X), 53796C) Progress Aware Res.

Opening up to a Higher Power: Ocean. Eldon Taylor. Read by Eldon Taylor. Ed. by Leslie Brice. 1 cass. (Running Time: 1 hr.). 1992. 16.95 (978-1-56705-338-8(6)) Gateways Inst.
Self improvement.

Opening up to Intuition. Thomas R. Condon. 1 cass. (Expanded Intuition Training Tape Ser.). 12.95 (978-1-884305-71-9(7)) Changeworks.
This tape uses Multi-Evocation in a lovely natural setting to help awaken & motivate your intuitive abilities. Designed to sensitize & gently evoke your intuitive part.

Opening up to Superconsciousness Series. 5 cass. (Running Time: 7 hrs. 30 mins.). 40.00 (SRW-84/LS-12) Crystal Clarity.
Discusses: The Conscious Mind; The Rhythm of superconciousness; The Limits of Intelligence; The Secret of Genius; The Wisdom of the Heart.

Openings & Closings. Richard Kostelanetz. Read by Richard Kostelanetz. 1 cass. (Running Time: 1 hr.). 1976. 10.00 (978-0-932360-73-1(4)) Archae Edns.
Contains single-sentence stories that are either the opening or closing of hypothetical fictions read by the author.

Openings & Closings in Criminal Trials. 1 cass. (Running Time: 1 hr. 30 min.). 1988. 15.00 PA Bar Inst.

Openings & Limitations. Robert Bly. Read by Robert Bly. Ed. by William Booth. 1 cass. (Running Time: 1 hr. 30 min.). 1990. 9.95 (C107) Ally Pr.
In this live reading, Robert Bly talks of limitations resisted & limitations welcomed. Four stages are laid out, with Rumi in the fourth.

Openness to the Truth. Swami Amar Jyoti. 1 cass. (Running Time: 1 hr. 30 mins.). 1981. 9.95 (K-43) Truth Consciousness.
Fresh thinking frees us from resistance to Truth. Horizontal & vertical growth. Unfoldment through corrected values. How to be new Beings at any age.

Opera Choruses: Recorded Pronunciation Guide. Ed. by John Rutter & Clifford Bartlett. 1 cass. (Oxford Choral Classics Ser.). 1995. 19.95 (978-0-19-343699-2(X)) OUP.

Opera Explained. Thomson Smillie. Read by David Timson. audio compact disk 8.99 (978-1-84379-068-6(8), 8.558143); audio compact disk 8.99 (978-1-84379-081-5(5), 8.558122); audio compact disk 8.99 (978-1-84379-084-6(X)) NaxMulti GBR.

Opera Explained: AIDA: Aida. Thomson Smillie. Read by David Timson. (Running Time: 1 hr.). 2005. 14.95 (978-1-60083-862-0(6)) Iofy Corp.

Opera Explained: CARMEN: Carmen. Thomson Smillie. Read by David Timson. (Running Time: 1 hr.). 2006. 14.95 (978-1-60083-863-7(4)) Iofy Corp.

Opera Explained: CAVALLERIA RUSTICANA: Cavalleria Rusticana. Thomson Smillie. Read by David Timson. (Running Time: 1 hr. 15 mins.). 2005. 14.95 (978-1-60083-864-4(2)) Iofy Corp.

Opera Explained: COSI FAN TUTTE: Cosi fan Tutte. Thomson Smillie. Read by David Timson. (Running Time: 1 hr. 15 mins.). 2005. 14.95 (978-1-60083-865-1(0)) Iofy Corp.

Opera Explained: DIE FLEDERMAUS: Die Fledermaus. Thomson Smillie. Read by David Timson. (Running Time: 1 hr.). 2005. 14.95 (978-1-60083-866-8(9)) Iofy Corp.

Opera Explained: DON GIOVANNI: Don Giovanni. Thomson Smillie. Read by David Timson. (Running Time: 1 hr. 15 mins.). 2005. 14.95 (978-1-60083-867-5(7)) Iofy Corp.

Opera Explained: FALSTAFF: Falstaff. Thomson Smillie. Read by David Timson. (Running Time: 1 hr. 15 mins.). 2005. 14.95 (978-1-60083-868-2(5)) Iofy Corp.

Opera Explained: FIDELIO: Fidelio. Thomson Smillie. Read by David Timson. (Running Time: 1 hr. 15 mins.). 2005. 14.95 (978-1-60083-869-9(3)) Iofy Corp.

Opera Explained: GILBERT & SULLIVAN: Gilbert & Sullivan. Thomson Smillie. Read by David Timson. (Running Time: 1 hr.). 2006. 14.95 (978-1-60083-870-5(7)) Iofy Corp.

Opera Explained: Il TROVATORE: Il Trovatore. Thomson Smillie. Read by David Timson. (Running Time: 1 hr. 15 mins.). 2005. 14.95 (978-1-60083-871-2(5)) Iofy Corp.

Opera Explained: la BOHEME: La Boheme. Thomson Smillie. Read by David Timson. (Running Time: 1 hr. 15 mins.). 2006. 14.95 (978-1-60083-872-9(3)) Iofy Corp.

Opera Explained: la TRAVIATA: La Traviata. Thomson Smillie. Read by David Timson. (Running Time: 1 hr. 15 mins.). 2005. 14.95 (978-1-60083-873-6(1)) Iofy Corp.

Opera Explained: MADAMA BUTTERFLY: Madama Butterfly. Thomson Smillie. Read by David Timson. (Running Time: 1 hr.). 2005. 14.95 (978-1-60083-875-0(8)) Iofy Corp.

Opera Explained: ORFEO ED EURIDICE: Orfeo ed Euridice. Thomson Smillie. Read by David Timson. (Running Time: 1 hr.). 2004. 14.95 (978-1-60083-876-7(6)) Iofy Corp.

Opera Explained: PAGLIACCI: Pagliacci. Thomson Smillie. Read by David Timson. (Running Time: 1 hr.). 2004. 14.95 (978-1-60083-877-4(4)) Iofy Corp.

Opera Explained: PELLEAS et MELISANDE: Pelleas et Melisande. Thomson Smillie. Read by David Timson. (Running Time: 1 hr. 15 mins.). 2004. 14.95 (978-1-60083-878-1(2)) Iofy Corp.

Opera Explained: RIGOLETTO: Rigoletto. Thomson Smillie. Read by David Timson. (Running Time: 1 hr. 15 mins.). 2006. 14.95 (978-1-60083-879-8(0)) Iofy Corp.

Opera Explained: TANCREDI: Tancredi. Thomson Smillie. Read by David Timson. (Running Time: 1 hr. 15 mins.). 2004. 14.95 (978-1-60083-880-4(4)) Iofy Corp.

Opera Explained: the BARBER of SEVILLE: The barber of Seville. Thomson Smillie. Read by David Timson. (Running Time: 1 hr. 15 mins.). 2005. 14.95 (978-1-60083-881-1(2)) Iofy Corp.

Opera Explained: the MAGIC FLUTE: The magic Flute. Thomson Smillie. Read by David Timson. (Running Time: 1 hr. 15 mins.). 2004. 14.95 (978-1-60083-883-5(9)) Iofy Corp.

Opera Explained: the MARRIAGE of FIGARO: The marriage of Figaro. Thomson Smillie. Read by David Timson. (Running Time: 1 hr. 15 mins.). 2004. 14.95 (978-1-60083-884-2(7)) Iofy Corp.

Opera Explained: TOSCA: Tosca. Thomson Smillie. Read by David Timson. (Running Time: 1 hr.). 2006. 14.95 (978-1-60083-885-9(5)) Iofy Corp.

Opera Explained: TURANDOT: Turandot. Thomson Smillie. Read by David Timson. (Running Time: 1 hr. 15 mins.). 2004. 14.95 (978-1-60083-886-6(3)) Iofy Corp.

Opera, Karate, & Bandits. Short Stories. (5121) Am Audio Prose.

Opera, Opera see Twentieth-Century Poetry in English, No. 8, Recordings of Poets Reading Their Own Poetry

Opera 101. Fred Plotkin. Read by Fred Plotkin. (Running Time: 18 hrs.). (C). 2004. 50.95 (978-1-59912-562-6(5)) Iofy Corp.

Opera 101: A Complete Guide to Learning & Loving Opera. Plotkin Fred. Read by Plotkin Fred. 15 CDs. (Running Time: 18 hrs.). 2004. audio compact disk 120.00 (978-0-7861-8649-5(6), 3269) Blckstn Audio.

Opera 101: A Complete Guide to Learning & Loving Opera. unabr. ed. Plotkin Fred. Read by Plotkin Fred. 13 cass. (Running Time: 18 hrs.). 2004. 85.95 (978-0-7861-2694-1(9), 3269) Blckstn Audio.
Opera 101 is recognized as the standard text in English for anyone who wants to become an opera lover. It is a clear, friendly, and truly complete handbook for learning how to listen to opera, whether on the radio, on recordings, or live at the opera house. Fred Plotkin, an internationally respected writer and teacher about opera who for many years was performance manager of the Metropolitan Opera, introduces listeners, whatever their level of musical knowledge, to all the elements that make up opera, including: The major part of Opera 101 is devoted to an almost minute-by-minute analysis of eleven key operas, ranging from Verdi?s thunderous masterpiece Rigoletto and Puccini?s electrifying Tosca through works by Mozart, Donizetti, Rossini, Offenbach, Tchaikovsky, and Wagner, to the psychological complexities of Richard Strauss?s Elektra.

Operas of Mozart, Pts. I-III. Instructed by Robert Greenberg. 12 cass. (Running Time: 18 hrs.). bk. 99.95 (978-1-56585-561-8(2), 780) Teaching Co.

Operas of Mozart, Pts. I-III. Instructed by Robert Greenberg. 24 CDs. (Running Time: 18 hrs.). 1995. bk. 129.95 (978-1-56585-563-2(9), 780) Teaching Co.

Operating in the Miraculous. Steve Hill. 2007. audio compact disk 25.00 (978-1-892853-76-9(0)) Togthr Hrvest.

Operating Room Environment Panel Discussion: Technology in the Operating Room - Benefits & Risks. 2 cass. (Running Time: 3 hrs.). (General Sessions Ser.: C85-SP2). 15.00 (8544) Am Coll Surgeons.

Operating Your Mental Software: Psycho-Epistemology/One. Harry Binswanger. 3 cass. (Running Time: 3 hrs. 30 min.). 32.95 (IB01D) Second Renaissance.
Observations on the role of the subconscious in thinking.

Operation see Twentieth-Century Poetry in English, No. 27, Recordings of Poets Reading Their Own Poetry

Operation: Before & After. Barrie Konicov. 1 cass. (Running Time: 1 hr. 30 mins.). 11.98 (978-0-87082-350-3(7), 091) Potentials.
Discusses how to help remove the fear of impending surgery & how to speed your recovery after the operation.

Operation: Greenhouse CD Series. 2004. audio compact disk 12.00 (978-1-59834-024-2(7)) Walk Thru the Bible.

Operation - Rescue in the Redwoods: Mini-Musical Production Guide. unabr. ed. Scripts. Sandy Ribar. Perf. by Elizabeth Treat & Gregory Treat. Engineer Rob Treat. 1 cass. (Running Time: 45 min.). Dramatization. (Kids on Assignment - The Adventures of Rex & Ruby Ser.: Vol. 1). (J). (ps-5). 1999. 15.90 (978-1-893401-09-9(X), KOARR) Pure & Simple.

Operation - Rescue in the Redwoods: Readalong - Singalong Pack. unabr. ed. Sandy Ribar. Perf. by Elizabeth Treat & Gregory Treat. Engineer Rob Treat. 1 cass. (Running Time: 45 min.). Dramatization. (Kids on Assignment - The Adventures of Rex & Ruby Ser.: Vol. 1). (J). (ps-5). 1999. pap. bk. 11.49 (978-1-893401-08-2(1), KOA000RR) Pure & Simple.

Operation - Rescue in the Redwoods: Storybook. unabr. ed. Sandy Ribar. Perf. by Elizabeth Treat & Gregory Treat. Engineer Rob Treat. 1 cass. (Running Time: 45 min.). Dramatization. (Kids on Assignment - The Adventures of Rex & Ruby Ser.: Vol. 1). (J). (ps-5). 1999. 7.95 (978-1-893401-03-7(0), KOA041) Pure & Simple.

Operation - Rescue in the Redwoods Vol. 3: Performance Tracks. unabr. ed. Sandy Ribar. Perf. by Elizabeth Treat & Gregory Treat. Engineer Rob Treat. 1 cass. (Running Time: 1 hr.). (Kids on Assignment - The Adventures of Rex & Ruby Ser.: Vol. 1). (J). 1999. 39.95 (978-1-893401-02-0(2), KOAO31RR) Pure & Simple.

Operation Crucible. unabr. ed. Frederick E. Smith. Read by Colin Bower. 6 cass. (Running Time: 8 hrs.). 1998. 69.95 (978-1-85903-223-7(0)) Pub: Magna Story GBR. Dist(s): Ulverscroft US
Autumn 1943: An angry American press has blamed the RAF for heavy US B-17 losses over Europe. 633 Squadron has been sent to give ground support to troops against overwhelming firepower & totally unforeseen odds.

Operation De-junk! Gladys Allen. 1 cass. (Running Time: 1 hr. 30 mins.). 2004. 3.95 (978-1-57734-369-1(7), 34441077) Covenant Comms.

Operation Fantasy Plan. abr. ed. Peter Gilboy. Read by Peter Gilboy. 2 cass. (Running Time: 3 hrs.). 1997. 17.00 (978-1-56876-069-8(8)) Soundlines Ent.
Peter Gaines has just been fired from the CIA, & he is determined to find out why. He back tracks to his last post "The Fantasy Store" a CIA run whorehouse in Thailand to find the answers.

Operation Homecoming: Iraq, Afghanistan, & the Home Front, in the Words of U. S. Troops & Their Families. unabr. ed. Full Cast Production Staff. Read by Joe Barrett et al. (Running Time: 1020 sec.). 2006. audio compact disk 29.95 (978-0-7861-7312-9(2)) Blckstn Audio.

Operation Homecoming: Iraq, Afghanistan, & the Home Front, in the Words of U. S. Troops & Their Families. unabr. ed. Read by Full Cast Production Staff. (Running Time: 61200 sec.). 2006. 89.95 (978-0-7861-4829-5(2)); audio compact disk 120.00 (978-0-7861-6393-9(3)) Blckstn Audio.

Operation Homecoming: Iraq, Afghanistan, & the Home Front, in the Words of U. S. Troops & Their Families. unabr. ed. Read by Full Cast Production Staff et al. (Running Time: 61200 sec.). 2006. 29.95 (978-0-7861-4729-8(6)); audio compact disk 32.95 (978-0-7861-6542-1(1)) Blckstn Audio.

***Operation Manual for the Mind.** L. Ron Hubbard. (DAN.). 2010. audio compact disk 15.00 (978-1-4031-7463-5(6)); audio compact disk 15.00 (978-1-4031-7474-1(1)); audio compact disk 15.00 (978-1-4031-7475-8(X)); audio compact disk 15.00 (978-1-4031-7476-5(8)); audio compact disk 15.00 (978-1-4031-7466-6(0)); audio compact disk 15.00 (978-1-4031-7478-9(4)); audio compact disk 15.00 (978-1-4031-7469-7(5)); audio compact disk 15.00 (978-1-4031-7464-2(4)); audio compact disk 15.00 (978-1-4031-7468-0(7)); audio compact disk 15.00 (978-1-4031-7467-3(9)); audio compact disk 15.00 (978-1-4031-7472-7(5)); audio compact disk 15.00 (978-1-4031-7470-3(9)); audio compact disk 15.00 (978-1-4031-1414-3(5)); audio compact disk 15.00 (978-1-4031-7477-2(6)); audio compact disk 15.00 (978-1-4031-7471-0(7)); audio compact disk 15.00 (978-1-4031-7473-4(3)); audio compact disk 15.00 (978-1-4031-7465-9(2)) Bridge Pubns Inc.

Operation Mincemeat: How a Dead Man & a Bizarre Plan Fooled the Nazis & Assured an Allied Victory. unabr. ed. Ben Macintyre. Read by John Lee. (ENG.). 2010. audio compact disk 35.00 (978-0-307-73569-0(9), Random AudioBks) Pub: Random Audio Pubg. Dist(s): Random

Operation Sea Lion. unabr. collector's ed. Peter Fleming. Read by Richard Brown. 9 cass. (Running Time: 13 hrs. 30 min.). 1987. 72.00 (978-0-7366-1125-1(8), 2048) Books on Tape.
In the summer of 1940 the Germans prepared to launch Operation Sea Lion, the invasion of England. The British, barely recovered from Dunkirk, rallied their defenses. But the operation never took place. This story was rescued from military archives & the memories of survivors who were involved.

Operation Sovereign. unabr. ed. Clive Egleton. Read by Gordon Griffin. 9 cass. (Running Time: 13 hrs.). 2000. 79.95 (978-1-86042-488-5(0), 24880) Pub: Soundings Ltd GBR. Dist(s): ISIS Pub
December 1941: With the threat of imminent Japanese invasion hanging over Hong Kong, the order goes out to smuggle 2.5 million in gold from the vaults of the Hong Kong & Shanghai Bank of Australia, via the SS Delphic Star. Codenamed Operation Sovereign, the mission seems doomed to failure as corrupt CID officials supervising the transfer intend to snatch the gold before it reaches the ship.

Operation Soveriegn. unabr. ed. Clive Egleton. Read by Gordon Griffin. 9 cass. (Running Time: 13 hrs. 30 mins.). 2001. 79.95 (24880) Pub: Soundings Ltd GBR. Dist(s): Ulverscroft US

Operation Sunshine. Jenny Colgan. 2008. 61.95 (978-0-7531-3016-2(5)); audio compact disk 79.95 (978-0-7531-3017-9(3)) Pub: ISIS Audio GBR. Dist(s): Ulverscroft US

Operation Valkyrie. unabr. ed. Frederick E. Smith. Read by Colin Bower. 8 cass. (Running Time: 10 hrs. 35 min.). 1999. 83.95 (978-1-85903-241-1(9)) Pub: Magna Story GBR. Dist(s): Ulverscroft US
July 1943, only a single mosquito made it back from the suicidal but successful Operation Vesuvius. Now barely a year later, the 633 Squadron was on another mission impossible.

***Operation Yes.** unabr. ed. Sara Lewis Holmes. Read by Jessica Almasy. (Running Time: 6 hrs.). 2011. 19.99 (978-1-61106-080-5(X), 9781611060805, Brilliance MP3); 39.97 (978-1-61106-082-9(6), 9781611060829, BADLE); 39.97 (978-1-61106-081-2(8), 9781611060812, Brinc Audio MP3 Lib); audio compact disk 19.99 (978-1-61106-078-2(8), 9781611060782, Bril Audio CD Unabri); audio compact disk 59.97 (978-1-61106-079-9(6), 9781611060799, BriAudCD Unabrid) Brilliance Audio.

Operational Necessity. unabr. ed. Gwyn Griffin. Read by Wolfram Kandinsky. 12 cass. (Running Time: 18 hrs.). 1977. 96.00 (978-0-7366-0082-8(5), 1092) Books on Tape.
Disheartened & desperate, a German U-boat crew machine guns the survivors of a torpedoed freighter. Captured as they near neutral sanctuary, the U-boat officers are returned to an Allied tribunal. During the trial the officers face their accuser, Gaston, lone survivor of the sinking. The German officers emerge as young & inexperienced, caught between their compassion for the survivors & the welfare of their own crew. The reader confronts the question of personal obedience vs. individual ethics until, in the conclusion, the court delivers its final verdict.

Operations Management: Contemporary Concepts & Cases. 3rd ed. Roger G. Schroeder. (McGraw-Hill/Irwin Series in Operations & Decision Sciences). 2007. tchr. ed. (978-0-07-313709-4(X)) McGraw.

Operations Management: Processes & Value Chains. 8th ed. Lee Krajewski et al. 2006. 26.67 (978-0-13-187304-9(0)) Pearson Educ CAN CAN.

Operatives, Spies & Sabateurs. Patrick K. O'Donnell & Christopher Lane. 7 cass. (Running Time: 10 hrs.). 2002. 49.95 (978-0-7861-2672-9(8), 3230) Blckstn Audio.

Operatives, Spies, & Saboteurs. Patrick K. O'Donnell. Read by Christopher Lane. (Running Time: 10 hrs.). 2004. 30.95 (978-1-59912-563-3(3)) Iofy Corp.

Operatives, Spies, & Saboteurs: The Unknown History of the Men & Women of World War II's OSS. unabr. ed. Patrick K. O'Donnell. Read by Christopher Lane. 8 CDs. (Running Time: 10 hrs.). 2000. audio compact disk 64.00 (978-0-7861-8747-8(6), 3230) Blckstn Audio.

Operator: David Geffen Builds Buys & Sells the New Hollywood. unabr. ed. Tom King. Read by Scott Brick. 12 cass. (Running Time: 18 hrs.). 2000. 96.00 (978-0-7366-5064-9(4), 5278) Books on Tape.
Complex, contentious, and blessed with the perfect-pitch ability to find the next big talent, Geffen has influenced American popular culture for the last three decades. Among other things, he discovered Jackson Brown and the Eagles, produced Risky Business, financed Cats, and co-founded Dream Works, the first new Hollywood studio in fifty-five years. In this book, the author captures the real Geffen and tells a great American story about success and the tradeoffs Geffen made to get it.

***Operators: The Wild & Terrifying Inside Story of America's War in Afghanistan.** unabr. ed. Michael Hastings. (Running Time: 9 hrs.). (ENG.). 2011. 26.98 (978-1-60941-424-5(1)) Pub: Hachet Audio. Dist(s): HachBkGrp

***Operators: The Wild & Terrifying Inside Story of America's War in Afghanistan.** unabr. ed. Michael Hastings. (Running Time: 9 hrs.). (ENG., 2011. audio compact disk & audio compact disk 34.98 (978-1-60941-419-1(5)) Pub: Hachet Audio. Dist(s): HachBkGrp

Ophie Out of Oz. unabr. ed. Kathleen O'Dell. Read by Ann Marie Lee. 3 CDs. (Running Time: 3 hrs. 42 mins.). (J). (gr. 4-7). 2006. audio compact disk 30.00 (978-0-307-28590-4(1), Listening Lib); 30.00 (978-0-307-28083-1(7), Listening Lib) Pub: Random Audio Pubg. Dist(s): Random
Ophie Peeler has always considered herself to be a Dorothy type, a girl destined for a glamorous adventure... someday... somehow... somewhere. And her life in fun and sunny California seemed to have an Oz-like magic. She was in every play, she sang "Over the Rainbow" to a packed school auditorium, and she had Lizzy, the best best friend ever. But now Ophie has moved to Oregon. No glamour, no magic, and no Lizzy. Just this weird girl, Brittany Borg, who seems to have stuck herself to Ophie (and who calls her "Hey, Peeler"!). Why oh why can't life ever be like it is in the movies?.

Ophthalmic Goods & Equipment in Brazil: A Strategic Reference 2006. Compiled by Icon Group International, Inc. Staff. 2007. ring bd. 195.00 (978-0-497-35842-6(5)) Icon Grp.

Ophthalmic Surgery: Current Concepts in Management of Head & Ocular Trauma. Moderated by Herbert E. Kaufman & Darrell E. Wolfley. (Postgraduate Courses Ser.: C86-PG15). 1986. 85.00 (8625) Am Coll Surgeons.
Provides an overview in the management of head trauma & its complications, facial fractures & associated complications with emphasis on ocular trauma. 9 hours CME credit.

Ophthalmology Review Criteria Guidelines. Margaret Bischel. Ed. by Margaret Bischel. 2004. ring bd. 49.00 (978-1-893826-63-2(5)) Apollo Managed.

Opiate Dependence Treatment Options: From Sober Recovery to Suboxone. Created by Jeffrey T. Junig. 2009. 19.99 (978-0-9840972-2-7(8)) Term Un Pub.

Opinion Letters. Read by John J. Soroko. 1 cass. 1990. 20.00 (AL-102) PA Bar Inst.

Opinions in SEC Transactions. unabr. ed. Contrib. by Richard H. Rowe. 4 cass. (Running Time: 5 hrs. 30 min.). 1989. pap. bk. 95.00 (T6-9104) PLI.

Opium Hunter. abr. ed. Axel Kilgore. Read by Charlton Griffin. 2 vols. No. 4. 2003. 18.00 (978-1-58807-160-6(X)); (978-1-58807-651-9(2)) Am Pubng Inc.

Opium Hunter. abr. ed. Axel Kilgore. Read by Carol Eason. 3 CDs. (Running Time: 3 hrs.). (Mercenary Ser.: No. 4). 2004. audio compact disk 25.00 (978-1-58807-328-0(9)) Am Pubng Inc.
Hank Frost, the one-eyed mercenary Captain with the over-used 9mm and a low-budget bank account, loses the commission on a multi-million-dollar deal. He's forced to agree to kill a Burmese drug warlord. With a mercenary commando team, Frost penetrates the steaming southeast Asian jungles to knock off the kingpin of the raw opium trade and avenge a savage murder. From New Orleans to upstate New York, Frost is duking it out with the billion-dollar drug business, a Cosa Nostra capo who wants to corner the market, and power-mad warlords at the head of the opium pipeline.

Opossum at Sycamore Road. Sally M. Walker. (J). (ps-2). 2001. bk. 19.95 (SP 7006C) Kimbo Educ.
A mother opossum & her babies search for food. Includes book.

Opportunies in Importing. Sam Komisar & Sydney Komisar. 1 cass. (Running Time: 57 min.). 10.95 (457) J Norton Pubs.
These importers show you how to make foreign contracts, secure exclusive U. S. rights, where to get paperwork assistance, get help from the Department of Commerce, sell your merchandise to retail chains, promote your business on TV, build a sales organization at absolutely no cost & other profitable ideas.

Opportunities. Stuart Wilde. 1 cass. (Running Time: 1 hr.). 11.95 (978-0-930603-09-0(5)) White Dove NM.
A subliminal tape. Relaxing musical background. Your conscious mind hears only the music while your subconscious mind, accepts the powerful affirmations.

Opportunities: Letting God Lead. Marianne Williamson. Read by Marianne Williamson. 1 cass. (Running Time: 1 hr. 30 mins.). (Lectures on a Course in Miracles). 1999. 10.00 (978-1-56170-251-0(X), M754) Hay House.

Opportunities: Survey of Administrators' Perspectives. 1 cass. (Running Time: 1 hr.). (Care Cassettes Ser.: Vol. 10, No. 1). 1983. 10.80 Assn Prof Chaplains.

Opportunity. unabr. ed. Poems. Sri Chinmoy Centre Staff. Read by Sri Chinmoy Centre Staff. 1 cass. (Running Time: 1 hr. 30 mins.). 1998. 9.95 (978-0-9664613-7-4(1)) Jharna Kala.

Opportunity & Reward: Matthew 25:14-30. Ed Young. (J). 1982. 4.95 (978-0-7417-1211-0(3), A0211) Win Walk.

Opportunity Cost; Subjective Value. John Robbins. 1 cass. (Introduction to Economics Ser.: No. 5). 5.00 Trinity Found.

Opportunity Recognition Audio Instructions: Recognizing Opportunity with Your Ears. Timothy /Bard Bard. Arranged by Timothy /Bard Bard. (ENG.). 2008. 14.95 (978-0-9793957-3-4(9)) T Bard Multi.

Opposite of Fate. abr. ed. Amy Tan. Read by Amy Tan. (Running Time: 9 hrs.). 2004. 39.25 (978-1-59710-550-7(3), 1597105503, BADLE); 24.95 (978-1-59710-551-4(1), 1597105511, BAD) Brilliance Audio.

Opposite of Fate. abr. ed. Amy Tan. Read by Amy Tan. (Running Time: 32400 sec.). 2005. audio compact disk 19.99 (978-1-59600-431-3(2), 9781596004313, BCD Value Price) Brilliance Audio.
Amy Tan was born into a family that believed in fate. In The Opposite of Fate: A Book of Musings, she explores this legacy, as well as American circumstances, and finds ways to honor the past while creating her own brand of destiny. She discovers answers in everyday actions and attitudes - from writing stories and decorating her house with charms, to dealing with three members of her family afflicted with brain disease and shaking off both family curses and the expectations that she should become a doctor and a concert pianist. With the same spirit, humor, and magic that characterize her beloved novels, Amy Tan presents a refreshing antidote to the world-weariness and uncertainties we face today, contemplating how things happen - in her own life and beyond - but always returning to the question of fate and its opposites: the choices, charms, influences, attitudes, and lucky accidents that shape us all.

Opposite of Fate: A Book of Musings. abr. ed. Amy Tan. Read by Amy Tan. (Running Time: 9 hrs.). 2004. 39.25 (978-1-59335-667-5(6), 1593356676, Brinc Audio MP3 Lib); 24.95 (978-1-59335-663-7(3), 1593356633, Brilliance MP3) Brilliance Audio.

Opposite of Fate: A Book of Musings. unabr. abr. ed. Amy Tan. Read by Amy Tan. (Running Time: 9 hrs.). 2003. audio compact disk 92.25 (978-1-59355-078-3(2), 1593550782, BriAudCD Unabrid); 29.95 (978-1-59355-075-2(8), 1593550758); 74.25 (978-1-59355-076-9(6), 1593550766, BrilAudUnabridg) Brilliance Audio.

Opposite of Invisible. unabr. ed. Liz Gallagher. Read by Lara Hirner. 3 CDs. (Running Time: 3 hrs. 31 mins.). (YA). (gr. 8 up). 2008. audio compact disk 45.00 (978-0-7393-6298-3(4), Listening Lib) Pub: Random Audio Pubg. Dist(s): Random
Alice and Jewel have been best friends since grade school. Together, they don't need anyone else, and together they blend into the background of high school. Invisible. To Alice, Jewel is the opposite of invisible. Jewel is her best friend who goes to Indie concerts and art shows with her. Jewel scoffs at school dances with her. Alice is so comfortable around Jewel that she can talk to him about almost anything. But she can't tell him that she likes the cool, popular Simon. And then Simon asks her to the school dance the same day that Jewel kisses her for the first time. Still, she can't say no to Simon. He seems like the easy choice, the one she's attracted to, the one she's ready for. But will it mean losing Jewel? In a bright debut novel set against the lively backdrop of Seattle, Alice must learn the difference between love and a crush, and what it means to be yourself when you're not sure who that is yet.

Opposite of Invisible. unabr. ed. Liz Gallagher. Read by Lara Hirner. (Running Time: 12660 sec.). (ENG.). (J). (gr. 9-12). 2008. audio compact disk 25.00 (978-0-7393-6296-9(8), Listening Lib) Pub: Random Audio Pubg. Dist(s): Random

Opposite of Love. unabr. ed. Julie Buxbaum. Read by Emily Janice Card. 8 CDs. (Running Time: 9 hrs.). 2008. audio compact disk 100.00 (978-1-4159-4686-2(8)) Random.

Opposite Way. Contrib. by Leeland & Jason McArthur. Prod. by Matt Bronlewee. 2008. audio compact disk 13.99 (978-5-557-48008-6(0)) Essential Recs.

Oppressive Society. Harvey Jackins. 1 cass. (Running Time: 1 hr. 30 mins.). 10.00 (978-1-893165-53-3(1)) Rational Isl.
Describes the oppressive nature of society & how it developed.

***Oprah: A Biography.** unabr. ed. Kitty Kelley. Read by Kitty Kelley. 16 CDs. (Running Time: 20 hrs.). 2010. audio compact disk 50.00 (978-0-307-74924-6(X), Random AudioBks); audio compact disk 100.00 (978-0-307-74926-0(6), BksonTape) Pub: Random Audio Pubg. Dist(s): Random

Oprah! Up Close & Down Home. unabr. collector's ed. Nellie Bly. Read by Maxine Robinson. 7 cass. (Running Time: 10 hrs. 30 min.). 1995. 56.00 (978-0-7366-3020-7(1), 3703) Books on Tape.
Oprah grew up in poverty & abuse. This no-holds-barred biography tells how she rose above it.

Oprah Winfrey: The Real Story. abr. ed. George Mair. Read by George Mair. 2 cass. (Running Time: 3 hrs.). 1996. 16.95 (978-1-882071-56-2(5)) B-B Audio.
Whatever her missteps and stumbles along the way, the journey of Oprah Gail Winfrey from Hattie Maes pig farm in Mississippi to the pinnacle of wealth, power, and success in American television is a journey we must all admire. In looking for the secre.

Oprah Winfrey Speaks: Insights from the World's Most Influential Voice. abr. ed. Janet C. Lowe. 2 cass. (Running Time: 3 hrs.). 1998. 17.95 (978-1-55935-286-4(8), 286-8BK) Soundelux.
Biography.

Opt for Vibrant Health. Read by Mary Richards & Dennis MacMillan. 1 cass. (Running Time: 1 hr. 23 mins.). (Series Two Thousand). 2007. audio compact disk 19.95 (978-1-56136-104-5(6)) Master Your Mind.

Opt for Vibrant Health... In This Age of AIDS. Read by Mary Richards. (Subliminal - Self Hypnosis Ser.). 12.95 (815) Master Your Mind.

Opti-Learning: A Powerful New System for Processing & Applying New Information at a Rapid Speed. 1 cass. (Running Time: 1 hr. 30 mins.). 2000. 119.95 (978-1-55525-096-6(3)) Nightingale-Conant.

Optical Communications & Networks(Cd-Rom) Ed. by Cambyse Guy Omidyar & Shum Ping. 2003. cd-rom & audio compact disk 58.00 (978-981-238-713-4(7)) World Scientific Pub.

Optical Storage End-User Trends: The Next Generation Image Disk System, Roundtable Discussion - Session Twelve. 1 cass. 1990. 8.50 Recorded Res.

Optical Translation Hardware & Software. 2 cass. (Running Time: 3 hrs.). 1990. 16.00 Recorded Res.

Optimal Affirmations: With Optimal Thinking. unabr. ed. Rosalene Glickman. (Running Time: 1 hr. 10 mins.). (ENG.). 2009. 8.95 (978-1-59659-482-1(9), GildAudio) Pub: Gildan Media. Dist(s): HachBkGrp

Optimal Health. Nick Hall et al. 6 cass. (Running Time: 6 hrs.). 1996. 59.95 Set, incl. wkbk. (13920A) Nightingale-Conant.

Optimal Level A1: Arbeitsbuch A1. M. Muller et al. 2005. pap. bk. 19.25 (978-3-468-47002-8(9)) Langenscheidt.

Optimal Level A1: Test Booklet A1. M. Muller et al. 2005. pap. bk. 27.50 (978-3-468-47011-0(8)) Langenscheidt.

Optimal Level A1: 2 Audio Cassettes (use with Lehrbuch) M. Muller et al. 2 cass. 2005. pap. bk. 36.50 (978-3-468-47004-2(5)) Langenscheidt.

Optimal Level A1: 2 Audio CDs (use with Lehrbuch) M. Muller et al. 2 CDs. 2005. pap. bk. 36.50 (978-3-468-47005-9(3)) Langenscheidt.

Optimal Level A2 (Spring 2005) Arbeitsbuch A2 (with CD) 2005. pap. bk. 19.25 (978-3-468-47032-5(0)) Langenscheidt.

Optimal Level A2 (Spring 2005) Test Booklet A2 (with CD) 2005. pap. bk. 27.50 (978-3-468-47039-4(8)) Langenscheidt.

Optimal Level A2 (Spring 2005) 2 Audio Cassettes (use with Lehrbuch) 2 cass. 2005. pap. bk. 36.50 (978-3-468-47034-9(7)) Langenscheidt.

Optimal Level A2 (Spring 2005) 2 Audio CDs (use with Lehrbuch) 2 CDs. 2005. pap. bk. 36.50 (978-3-468-47035-6(5)) Langenscheidt.

Optimal Performance. 1 cassette. (Running Time: 59:25 mins.). 1980. 12.95 (978-1-55841-054-1(6)) Emmett E Miller.
Achieve peak performance in any specific area of your life: athletic competition, stage performance, sales, etc. First, you carefully reconstruct an image of your personal best, then project an even higher level of performance into the future.

Optimal Performance. Read by Mary Richards. (Subliminal Impact Ser.). 12.95 (617) Master Your Mind.

Optimal Performance: Going for the Gold. 1 CD. 1983. audio compact disk 16.95 (978-1-55841-127-2(5)) Emmett E Miller.
Achieve peak performance in any specific area of your life; athletic competition, stage performance, sales, etc. First you carefully construct an image of your personal best, then project an even higher level of performance into the future.

Optimal Questions: With Optimal Thinking. unabr. ed. Rosalene Glickman. (Running Time: 1 hr. 10 mins.). (ENG.). 2009. 8.95 (978-1-59659-481-4(0), GildAudio) Pub: Gildan Media. Dist(s): HachBkGrp

Optimal Self-Trust: Absolute confidence when making Choices! Barry Neil Kaufman. (ENG.). 2007. audio compact disk 17.50 (978-0-9798105-1-0(5)) Option Inst.

Optimal Weight Loss. Eldon Taylor. 1 cass. (Running Time: 1 hr. 2 mins.). (Inner Talk Ser.). 16.95 (978-0-940699-95-3(8), 5300A) Progress Aware Res.
Soundtrack - Tropical Lagoon with underlying subliminal affirmations.

Optimal Weight Loss: Classic. Eldon Taylor. Read by Eldon Taylor. Ed. by Leslie Brice. 1 cass. (Running Time: 1 hr.). 1992. 16.95 (978-1-56705-027-1(1)) Gateways Inst.
Self improvement.

Optimal Weight Loss: Easy. Eldon Taylor. Read by Eldon Taylor. Ed. by Leslie Brice. 1 cass. (Running Time: 1 hr.). 1992. 16.95 (978-1-56705-028-8(X)) Gateways Inst.

Optimal Weight Loss: Environmental Theme. Eldon Taylor. 1 cass. (Running Time: 1 hr.). 1998. 16.95 (978-1-55978-450-4(4), 5300F) Progress Aware Res.

Optimal Weight Loss: Harmonies. Eldon Taylor. Read by Eldon Taylor. Ed. by Leslie Brice. 1 cass. (Running Time: 1 hr.). 1992. 16.95 (978-1-56705-029-5(8)) Gateways Inst.

Optimal Weight Loss: Ocean. Eldon Taylor. Read by Eldon Taylor. Ed. by Leslie Brice. 1 cass. (Running Time: 1 hr.). 1992. 16.95 (978-1-56705-030-1(1)) Gateways Inst.

Optimal Weight Loss: Power Imaging. Eldon Taylor. Read by Eldon Taylor. Ed. by Leslie Brice. 1 cass. (Running Time: 1 hr.). 1992. 12.95 (978-1-56705-019-6(0)) Gateways Inst.

Optimal Weight Loss: Rhythm. Eldon Taylor. Read by Eldon Taylor. Ed. by Leslie Brice. 1 cass. (Running Time: 1 hr.). 1992. 16.95 (978-1-56705-031-8(X)) Gateways Inst.

Optimal Weight Loss: Soundtrack: Leisure Listening. Eldon Taylor. 1 cass. (Running Time: 1 hr. 2 mins.). 16.95 (978-0-940699-02-1(8), 5300B) Progress Aware Res.
Musical soundtrack with underlying subliminal affirmations.

Optimal Weight Loss: Soundtrack: Musical Themes. Eldon Taylor. 1 cass. (Running Time: 1 hr. 2 mins.). 16.95 incl. script. (978-0-940699-03-8(6), 5300C) Progress Aware Res.

Optimal Weight Loss: Stream. Eldon Taylor. Read by Eldon Taylor. Ed. by Leslie Brice. 1 cass. (Running Time: 1 hr.). 1992. 16.95 (978-1-56705-032-5(8)) Gateways Inst.
Self improvement.

Optimal Weight Loss: Whisper. Eldon Taylor. Read by Eldon Taylor. Ed. by Leslie Brice. 1 cass. (Running Time: 1 hr.). 1992. 16.95 (978-1-56705-203-9(7)) Gateways Inst.

OptiMINDzation. Prod. by Stephen Pierce. 2006. audio compact disk 29.97 (978-1-932448-17-7(9)) Impulsive Prfts.

Optimism. Betty L. Randolph. Read by Betty L. Randolph. Read by Leonard Baron. Ed. by Success Education Institute International. 1 cass. (Success Ser.). 1989. bk. 14.98 Ocean Format. (978-1-55909-235-7(1), 210P); bk. 14.98 Music Format. (978-1-55909-236-4(X), 210PM) Randolph Tapes.
Includes 60,000 messages with the left-right brain.

Optimism: Program from the Award Winning Public Radio Series. Interview. Hosted by Fred Goodwin. Comment by John Hockenberry. 1 CD. (Running Time: 1 hr). 1999. audio compact disk 21.95 (978-1-932479-73-7(2), LCM 90) Lichtenstein Creat.
Optimism is more than just a perspective ... it's a scientifically quantifiable way to improve your chances of living a longer, healthier and even luckier life. This hour features the latest research in optimism, including a discussion with optimism expert Dr. Martin Seligman, a musical performance by rocker Heather Eatman, and, later in the show, a special report on the voting rights of psychiatric patients. With commentary by John Hockenberry.

Optimism Plus. Eldon Taylor. 1 cass. (Running Time: 1 hr. 2 mins.). (Inner Talk Ser.). 16.95 incl. script. (978-1-55978-764-2(3), 5416F) Progress Aware Res.
Soundtrack - Brook with underlying subliminal affirmations.

Optimism Plus: Pastoral Themes. Eldon Taylor. 1 cass. (Running Time: 1 hr.). 16.95 (978-1-55978-016-2(9), 5416M) Progress Aware Res.

Optimist in Spite of All: Helen Keller's Life Story. David Freudberg. Perf. by Annie Sullivan Macy et al. 1 cass. (Running Time: 1 hr.). 1993. 11.95 (978-0-9640914-2-9(9)) Human Media.
Short inspiring biography.

Optimists. unabr. ed. Andrew Miller. Read by Gordon Griffin. 7 cass. (Running Time: 9 hrs.). 2005. 69.75 (978-1-84505-450-2(4), H1840, Clipper Audio) Recorded Bks.

Optimize Your Thinking(r): How to Unlock Your Performance Potential. 2006. (978-0-9773129-5-5(X)) Opt Inc.

Optimizing Chemotherapy. 2008. audio compact disk 16.98 (978-1-55841-004-6(X)) Emmett E Miller.

Optimizing Radiation Therapy. (ENG.). 2009. audio compact disk 16.95 (978-1-55841-006-0(6)) Emmett E Miller.

Optimum Fitness. Scripts. Eldon Taylor. Read by Eldon Taylor. Interview with Progress Aware Staff. 1 cass. (Running Time: 1 hr. 2 mins.). 16.95 (978-1-55978-293-7(5), 02017) Progress Aware Res.
Verbal coaching soundtrack with underlying subliminal affirmations & sound matrix frequencies for brain entrainment.

Optimum Fitness: OZO. Eldon Taylor. Read by Eldon Taylor. Ed. by Leslie Brice. 1 cass. (Running Time: 1 hr.). 1992. 19.95 (978-1-56705-009-7(3)) Gateways Inst.
Self improvement.

Optimum Relaxation: Effective Techniques for Stress Reduction. 1 cass. 1998. 10.95 (978-0-938572-22-0(9)) Bunny Crocodile.
Deep breathing, stretching, muscle tension & relaxation, visualization. The exercises provide easy & effective techniques for stress reduction & optimum relaxation. Calming & uplifting piano music accompanies the guided exercises.

Optimum Weight: Achieve & Maintain Your Optimum Weight. Mark Bancroft. Read by Mark Bancroft. 1 cass., bklet. (Running Time: 1 hr.). (Health & Fitness Ser.). 1999. 12.95 (978-1-58522-020-5(5), 404) EnSpire Pr.
Two complete sessions plus printed instructionmanual/guidebook. With healing music soundtrack.

Optimum Weight: Achieve & Maintain Your Optimum Weight. Mark Bancroft. Read by Mark Bancroft. 1 CD, 1 bklet. (Running Time: 1 hr.). (Health & Fitness Ser.). 2006. audio compact disk 20.00 (978-1-58522-057-1(4)) EnSpire Pr.

Optimum Weight Loss: Echotech. Eldon Taylor. Read by Eldon Taylor. Ed. by Leslie Brice. 1 cass. (Running Time: 1 hr.). 1992. 19.95 (978-1-56705-006-6(9)) Gateways Inst.
Self improvement.

Optimum Weight Loss: OZO. Eldon Taylor. Read by Eldon Taylor. Ed. by Leslie Brice. 1 cass. (Running Time: 1 hr.). 1992. 19.95 (978-1-56705-018-9(2)) Gateways Inst.

Option Delta. abr. ed. Richard Marcinko & John Weisman. 2004. 10.95 (978-0-7435-4588-4(5)) Pub: S&S Audio. Dist(s): S and S Inc

Option Process 12 CD Lecture Series. Compiled by Barry Neil Kaufman. 12 CDs. (Running Time: 80 mins, 70 mins, 80 mins, 75 mins, 60 mins, 70 mi). 2005. audio compact disk 160.00 (978-1-887254-14-4(5)) Epic Century.
The definitive 12 Lecture Series by Barry Neil Kaufman, recorded liveduring training intensives at The Option Institute, has become a best-selling classic. For each area of discussion there is a comprehensive approach to uncovering beliefs which create unhappiness, helping you move toward a more loving, nonjudgmental attitude and lighting the path to new discoveries and new possibilities.

Option Spreads Made Easy. Instructed by George Fontanills. (Running Time: 90 mins.). 2005. audio compact disk 19.95 (978-1-59280-121-3(8)) Marketplace Bks.
Option Spreads Made Easy with George FontanillsThe popular author of Trade Options Online and The Options Course presents his proven techniques in a viewer-friendly, 90 min. video workshop that shows how to expand profit opportunities and manage risk with options. Using the basic bull call spread as his focus, Fontanills features simple strategies for structuring debit and credit spreads, the best market conditions for each, and how to achieve your trade goals by adjusting strike-price levels. George makes spreading strategies understandable and easy to implement. His thorough coverage includes an overview of equity options. Plus, he reveals ... Why the lowest-priced option isn't always the cheapest* How "in-the-money" spreads can be safer, even if they cost more * The "Sketch-pad" method of risk analysis - drawing a picture of your trade probabilities* Making time-value decay your ally, instead of your enemy* Understanding how volatility patterns impact your trading selectionIn his trademark, engaging style, Fontanills highlights the importance of planning your next move for when you're right - and wrong. Accompanied by online support materials, George's video primer is a great tool for traders of all levels, and the perfect companion to his bestselling books.*

Option Trading Tactics with Oliver Velez. Instructed by Oliver Velez. 1 cass. (Running Time: 90 min.). (Trade Secrets Audio Series). 2001. 19.95 (978-1-931611-41-1(6)) Marketplace Bks.
Learn to trade options the powerful, "Pristine.com way" in this new video presentation. With proper training, any investor can safely add options to their investment arsenal. Now, Pristine provides proven guidelines perfect for short & long-term players. Velez outlines 4 basic styles of option trading and specific methods for using charts to define price trends, recognize turning points and signal hot buy/sell opportunities.

Options. Robert A. Monroe. Read by Robert A. Monroe. (Running Time: 30 min.). (Human Plus Ser.). 1989. 14.95 (978-1-56102-023-2(0)) Inter Indus.
The ultimate problem-solving aid.

Options. unabr. ed. Robert A. Monroe. Read by Roland Simon. 1 cass. (Running Time: 30 min.). (Human Plus Ser.). (FRE.). 1993. 14.95 (978-1-56102-072-0(9)) Inter Indus.

Optomechanical Engineer Handbook: CRCnetBASE 1999. Ed. by Anees Ahmad. 1998. audio compact disk 199.95 (978-0-8493-9753-0(7), 9753) Pub: CRC Pr. Dist(s): Taylor and Fran

Or, Set. Blaise Cendrars. Read by Francois Berland. 2 cass. (FRE.). 1996. 26.95 (1815-LV) Olivia & Hill.
The exciting tale of the well-known adventurer, General Sutter, who left Europe penniless, pursued by the police, arrived in New York in 1834, crossed the United States & settled in California where, after becoming the richest man in the world, he was ruined by the discovery of gold on his land.

Or Mabinogi. Perf. by Ceredwin. 1 cass. or 1 CD. (Running Time: 00 hrs. 58 min.).; 9.98; audio compact disk 17.98 Lifedance.
This odd name is Celtic for "Legends of the Celts," & the music is rich with the haunting mystery that has become the trademark of neo-Celtic music, a la Enya. Particulary distinctive are the mellow, soft-feeling melodies wafting over the primal rhythms. Demo CD or cassette available.

Oración. Rodrigo Rodriguez. (SPA.). 2008. audio compact disk 14.99 (978-0-8297-5505-3(5)) Pub: Vida Pubs. Dist(s): Zondervan

Oracion Intercesora, Set. Kenneth Copeland. Tr. by Kenneth Copeland Publications Staff from ENG. 4 cass. (SPA.). 1984. pap. bk. & stu. ed. 20.00 (978-0-88114-318-8(9)) K Copeland Pubns.
Biblical study on intercessory prayer.

oración para el hombre de Hoy. P. Miguel Carmena. (SPA.). (YA). 2002. audio compact disk 18.95 (978-1-935405-88-7(8)) Hombre Nuevo.

***Oracle Night.** unabr. ed. Paul Auster. Read by Paul Auster. (ENG.). 2005. (978-0-06-087825-2(8), Harper Audio); (978-0-06-087826-9(6), Harper Audio) HarperCollins Pubs.

***Oracle of Stamboul: A Novel.** unabr. ed. Michael David Lukas. (ENG.). 2011. (978-0-06-206469-1(X), Harper Audio); (978-0-06-202737-5(9), Harper Audio) HarperCollins Pubs.

Oracles. Susannah Brin. Narrated by Larry A. McKeever. (Ancient Greek Mystery Ser.). (J). 2007. 10.95 (978-1-58659-135-9(5)); audio compact disk 14.95 (978-1-58659-369-8(2)) Artesian.

***Oracles of Delphi Keep.** unabr. ed. Victoria Laurie. Read by Susan Duerden. 13 CDs. (Running Time: 16 hrs. 45 mins.). (YA). (gr. 5-8). 2009. audio compact disk 75.00 (978-0-7393-8143-4(1), Listening Lib) Pub: Random Audio Pubg. Dist(s): Random

Oracles of Delphi Keep. unabr. ed. Victoria Laurie. Read by Susan Duerden. (ENG.). (J). (gr. 5). 2009. audio compact disk 60.00 (978-0-7393-8141-0(5), Listening Lib) Pub: Random Audio Pubg. Dist(s): Random

Orad por la Paz de Jerusalén. unabr. ed. Jonathan Settel. (SPA.). 1999. 7.99 (978-0-8297-2542-1(3)) Pub: Vida Pubs. Dist(s): Zondervan

Oral & Mental Starters for the Key Stage 3 Mathematics Framework Year 7. Mary Pardoe. 2005. audio compact disk 455.00 (978-0-340-88360-0(X), HodderMurray) Pub: Hodder Edu GBR. Dist(s): Trans-Atl Phila

Oral History: A Novel. unabr. ed. Lee Smith. 8 cass. (Running Time: 11 hrs. 30 mins.). 1998. 70.00 (978-0-7887-2609-5(9), 95619E7) Recorded Bks.
To research an assignment for an Oral History course, Jennifer drives to the Virginia hills where her father grew up.

Oral History Tapes. Edzia F. Milich. 10 cass. (Running Time: 15 mins.). 1993. 50.00 (978-0-9636347-1-9(2)) Rose Pub CA.
Holocaust.

Oral Language Development: Fifth Grade. (On Our Way to English Ser.). (gr. 5 up). audio compact disk 9.95 (978-0-7578-4496-6(0)) Rigby Educ.

Oral Language Development: First Grade. (On Our Way to English Ser.). (gr. 1 up). audio compact disk 9.95 (978-0-7578-1599-7(5)) Rigby Educ.

Oral Language Development: Fourth Grade. (On Our Way to English Ser.). (gr. 4 up). audio compact disk 9.95 (978-0-7578-4366-2(2)) Rigby Educ.

Oral Language Development: Kindergarten. (On Our Way to English Ser.). (gr. k up). audio compact disk 9.95 (978-0-7578-1612-3(6)) Rigby Educ.

Oral Language Development: Second Grade. (On Our Way to English Ser.). (gr. 2 up). audio compact disk 9.95 (978-0-7578-1411-2(5)) Rigby Educ.

Oral Language Development: Third Grade. (On Our Way to English Ser.). (gr. 3 up). audio compact disk 9.95 (978-0-7578-4236-8(4)) Rigby Educ.

Oral Motor Assessment & Treatment: Improving Syllable Production. Glyndon D. Riley & Jeanna Riley. 2 cass. (Running Time: 3 hrs.). 79.00 (W983) PRO-ED.
Improve articulation & fluency at the syllable level. Target in group ages four through eleven & older children & adults who exhibit oral motor discoordination. Part I trains the clinician to listen for syllable production problems. Part II of the manual describes the Oral Motor Assessment Scale, the numerical basis for assesing the level of severity of verbal oral motor problems. Part III presents an oral motor training program with fourteen levels of difficulty.

Oral Roberts's Prophetic Word for America. 2004. audio compact disk (978-1-59024-148-6(7)) B Hinn Min.

Oral Traditionals: Congolese: Paddling Song see Poems from Black Africa

Oral Traditionals: Ethiopian: Trousers of Wind see Poems from Black Africa

Oral Traditionals: Gabonese: The Little Bird see Poems from Black Africa

Oral Traditionals: Ghanian: Foolish Child see Poems from Black Africa

Oral Traditionals: Ghanian: Prayer for Every Day see Poems from Black Africa

Oral Traditionals: Liberian: Nana Kru see Poems from Black Africa

Oral Traditionals: Malagasy: Half Sigh see Poems from Black Africa

Oral Traditionals: Nigerian: O Lamb Give Me My Salt see Poems from Black Africa

Oral Traditionals: South African: Absent Lover see Poems from Black Africa

Oral Traditionals: South African: Keep It Dark see Poems from Black Africa

Oral Traditionals: South African: Pass Office Song see Poems from Black Africa

Oral Traditionals: South African: Shaka, King of the Zulus see Poems from Black Africa

Oral Traditionals: South African: Six to Six see Poems from Black Africa

Orange Code: How ING Direct Succeeded by Being a Rebel with a Cause. unabr. ed. Arkadi Kuhlmann & Bruce Philp. (Running Time: 11 hrs.). 2008. 39.25 (978-1-4233-7356-8(1), 9781423373568, BADLE) Brilliance Audio.

Orange Code: How ING Direct Succeeded by Being a Rebel with a Cause. unabr. ed. Arkadi Kuhlmann & Bruce Philp. Read by Bill Weideman & Jim Bond. 1 MP3-CD. (Running Time: 11 hrs.). 2008. 39.25 (978-1-4233-7354-4(5), 9781423373544, Brinc Audio MP3 Lib); 24.95 (978-1-4233-7353-7(7), 9781423373537, Brilliance MP3) Brilliance Audio.

Orange Code: How ING Direct Succeeded by Being a Rebel with a Cause. unabr. ed. Arkadi Kuhlmann & Bruce Philp. Read by Jim Bond & Bill Weideman. (Running Time: 11 hrs.). 2008. 24.95 (978-1-4233-7355-1(3), 9781423373551, BAD) Brilliance Audio.

Orange Code: How ING Direct Succeeded by Being a Rebel with a Cause. unabr. ed. Arkadi Kuhlmann & Bruce Philp. Read by Bill Weideman & Jim Bond. 9 CDs. (Running Time: 11 hrs.). 2008. audio compact disk 92.25 (978-1-4233-7352-0(9), 9781423373520, BriAudCD Unabrid); audio compact disk 34.99 (978-1-4233-7351-3(0), 9781423373513, Bril Audio CD Unabri) Brilliance Audio.

Orange County Choppers: The Tale of the Teutuls. unabr. ed. Paul Teutul, Sr. et al. Narrated by Todd McLaren. Told to Keith Zimmerman & Kent Zimmerman. 9 CDs. (Running Time: 6 hrs. 30 mins. 0 sec.). (ENG.). 2006. audio compact disk 34.99 (978-1-4001-0326-3(6)) Pub: Tantor Media. Dist(s): IngramPubServ

Orange County Choppers: The Tale of the Teutuls. unabr. ed. Paul Teutul, Sr. et al. Narrated by Todd McLaren. Told to Keith Zimmerman. (Running Time: 6 hrs. 30 mins. 0 sec.). (ENG.). 2006. audio compact disk 69.99 (978-1-4001-3326-0(2)) Pub: Tantor Media. Dist(s): IngramPubServ

Orange County Choppers: The Tale of the Teutuls. unabr. ed. Paul Teutul, Sr. et al. Narrated by Todd McLaren. Told to Keith Zimmerman & Kent Zimmerman. (Running Time: 6 hrs. 30 mins. 0 sec.). (ENG.). 2006. audio compact disk 24.99 (978-1-4001-5326-8(3)) Pub: Tantor Media. Dist(s): IngramPubServ

Orange Grove & Other Stories: Reading Level 2. 1993. 16.00 (978-0-88336-561-8(8)) New Readers.

***Orange Revolution: How One Great Team Can Transform an Entire Organization.** unabr. ed. Adrian Gostick & Chester Elton. (Running Time: 7 hrs. 0 mins.). 2010. 29.99 (978-1-4001-9732-3(5)); 14.99 (978-1-4001-8732-4(X)); 19.99 (978-1-4001-6732-6(9)); audio compact disk 71.99 (978-1-4001-4732-8(8)); audio compact disk 29.99 (978-1-4001-1732-1(1)) Pub: Tantor Media. Dist(s): IngramPubServ

Orange-Tree Plot. unabr. ed. Cynthia Harrod-Eagles. Read by Pippa Sparkes. 5 cass. (Running Time: 6 hr. 35 min.). 1998. 63.95 (978-1-85903-192-6(7)) Pub: Magna Story GBR. Dist(s): Ulverscroft US
At nineteen, Eugenie de Talcy flees revolutionary Paris in 1789 & finds herself destitute in England, forced to embark on the long & weary trek to London. To make matters worse, she is heartlessly drenched by an arrogant gentleman as he drives by. Arriving at the house of an old family friend, she learns that Lady Mary Berrington's adored nephew, the Earl of St. Osyth is the cause of her drenching. She finds herself a target of kidnappers, from whom St Osyth could save her, but she is too proud to ask him & must turn for help elsewhere, with potentially disastrous results.

Orange You Glad It's Halloween, Amber Brown? Paula Danziger. Read by Dana Lubotsky. Illus. by Tony Ross. 1 CD. (Running Time: 16 mins.). (J). (gr. 1-3). 2007. bk. 28.95 (978-1-4301-0082-9(6)); bk. 25.95 (978-1-4301-0079-9(6)); pap. bk. 18.95 (978-1-4301-0081-2(8)); pap. bk. 16.95 (978-1-4301-0078-2(8)) Live Oak Media.

Orange You Glad It's Halloween, Amber Brown?, Set. Paula Danziger. Read by Dana Lubotsky. Illus. by Tony Ross. 1 cass. (Running Time: 16 mins.). (J). (gr. 1-3). 2007. pap. bk. 29.95 (978-1-4301-0080-5(X)) Live Oak Media.

Orange You Glad It's Halloween, Amber Brown?, Set. unabr. ed. Paula Danziger. Read by Dana Lubotsky. Illus. by Tony Ross. 1 CD. (Running Time: 16 mins.). (J). (gr. 1-3). 2007. pap. bk. 31.95 (978-1-4301-0083-6(4)) Live Oak Media.

Oranges. unabr. ed. John McPhee. Read by Walter Zimmerman. 5 cass. (Running Time: 5 hrs.). 1988. 30.00 (978-0-7366-1456-6(7), 2337) Books on Tape.
Sketches of orange growers, discussions of the juice industry, a history of oranges & similar lore are combined in a lively, tart & amusing style.

Orbit. John J. Nance. Read by John J. Nance. (Playaway Adult Fiction Ser.). (ENG.). 2009. 64.99 (978-1-60775-682-8(X)) Find a World.

Orbit. abr. ed. John J. Nance. Read by John J. Nance. 5. (Running Time: 21600 sec.). 2007. audio compact disk 14.99 (978-1-59600-885-4(7), 9781596008854, BCD Value Price) Brilliance Audio.
Please enter a Synopsis.

Orbit. unabr. ed. John J. Nance. Read by John J. Nance. 7 cass. (Running Time: 32400 sec.). 2006. 74.25 (978-1-59086-766-2(1), 9781590867662, BrilAudUnabridg); audio compact disk 24.95 (978-1-59335-691-0(9),

9781593356910, Brilliance MP3); audio compact disk 92.25 (978-1-4233-1143-0(4), 9781423311430, BriAudCD Unabrid); audio compact disk 34.95 (978-1-4233-1142-3(6), 9781423311423, Bril Audio CD Unabri) Brilliance Audio.
Bestselling aviation expert and author John Nance returns with a riveting thriller set in the world of commercial spaceflight. The fact is that we are about to enter the era of publicly available space flight. And, as with any new technology in private hands, there will be accidents, which is where Orbit begins. The year is 2009, and the first commercial, passenger-carrying spaceflight operation, American Space Adventures, is making money and history with every launch. ASA decides to raffle off four seats on upcoming launches, and for Kip Dawson, it is a dream come true. But just as the pilot is pulling out the obligatory champagne after their successful launch, a micrometeorite punches through the wall of the spacecraft, killing him, and in the blink of an eye, Kip Dawson is truly alone. The world is horrified and stunned by the accident, and Kip begins to compose his own epitaph on a laptop on board, unaware that his message is being transmitted to earth. On earth, a massive struggle begins to attempt the impossible: launch a rescue mission. But Kip isn't aware that the world is hearing his cries and his heroism in the face of death may sabotage his own chance at survival.

Orbit. unabr. ed. John J. Nance. Read by John J. Nance. (Running Time: 9 hrs.). 2006. 39.25 (978-1-59710-915-4(0), 9781597109154, BADLE); audio compact disk 39.25 (978-1-59335-825-9(3), 9781593358259, Brlnc Audio MP3 Lib) Brilliance Audio.
Please enter a Synopsis.

Orbit. unabr. ed. John J. Nance. Read by John J. Nance. (Running Time: 9 hrs.). 2006. 24.95 (978-1-59710-914-7(2), 9781597109147, BAD) Brilliance Audio.

Orbita: Curso de Espanol para Extranjeros. Rafael Fente & Enrique Wulff. 1 cass. (Running Time: 1 hr. 30 mins.). (SPA.). (978-84-7143-656-6(6)) Sociedad General ESP.

Orbita: Curso de Espanol para Extranjeros, Level 1. Rafael Fente & Enrique Wulff. 1 cass. (Running Time: 1 hr. 30 mins.). (SPA.). (978-84-7143-655-9(8)) Sociedad General ESP.

Orbita X. unabr. ed. Zondervan Publishing Staff. (SPA.). 2001. 7.99 (978-0-8297-3394-5(9)) Pub: Vida Pubs. Dist(s): Zondervan

Orbital Symmetry Concepts in Organic Chemistry. unabr. ed. Read by Marye Anne Fox. 4 cass. (Running Time: 4 hrs. 6 min.). 435.00 (98) Am Chemical.

Orbiter 5 Shows How Earth Looks from the Moon see May Swenson

Orbiting Observatory, Pt. 1. 1 cass. (Running Time: 24 min.). 14.95 (23328) MMI Corp.
Discusses space telescope, function of OAO projects, what we can learn & more.

Orbiting Observatory, Pt. 2. 1 cass. (Running Time: 24 min.). 14.95 (23329) MMI Corp.
Discussion of machines in space, X-rays, Gamma rays, Can an astronaut compete with a machine?.

Orbitones, Spoonharps & Bellowphones: Experimental Musical Instruments. Bart Hopkin. 1 CD. (Running Time: 1 hr.). 1998. pap. bk. 19.95 (978-1-55961-481-8(1), Ellipsis Arts) Relaxtn Co.

Orca Song. (J). (ps-2). bk. 6.95 (978-1-59249-488-0(9), SC4004) Soundprints.

Orca Song. Michael C. Armour. (J). (ps-2). 2001. bk. 19.95 (SP 4004C) Kimbo Educ.
Orca & his whale pod hunt salmon circling within fishermen's nets. Includes book.

Orca Song. unabr. ed. Michael C. Armour. Read by Peter Thomas. Illus. by Katie Lee. Narrated by Peter Thomas. 1 cass. (Running Time: 9 min.). (Smithsonian Oceanic Collection). (J). (ps-2). 1994. 5.00 cass. (978-1-56899-074-3(X)) Soundprints.
Cassette is a dramatized readalong of the storybook, with authentic sound effects added. It consists of two sides - one with & one without page turning signals.

Orchard. Larry Watson. 5 cass. (Running Time: 8 hrs. 30 mins.). 2004. 29.99 (978-1-4025-6358-4(2), 03784) Recorded Bks.

Orchard. unabr. ed. Larry Watson. Narrated by George Guidall. 6 cass. (Running Time: 8 hrs. 30 min.). 2003. 59.00 (978-1-4025-6413-0(9)) Recorded Bks.
Portrait of obsession and betrayal. In Wisconsin during the 1950s, orchard keeper Henry is enraged when his wife Sonja poses nude for world-class painter Ned. As both men fight to possess Sonja, their jealousy threatens to explode in violence.

Orchard on Fire. Shena Mackay. Read by Rachel Atkins. 6 CDs. (Running Time: 9 hrs.). 2001. audio compact disk 64.95 (978-0-7531-1143-7(8), 111438) Pub: ISIS Audio GBR. Dist(s): Ulverscroft US

Orchard on Fire. unabr. ed. Shena Mackay. Read by Rachel Atkins. 6 cass. (Running Time: 7 hrs.). 2001. 25.00 (978-0-7531-0818-5(6), 000715) Pub: ISIS Audio GBR. Dist(s): Ulverscroft US

Orchard Valley Brides. unabr. ed. Debbie Macomber. Read by Tanya Eby. (Running Time: 9 hrs.). (Orchard Valley Ser.). 2010. 39.97 (978-1-4418-1947-5(9), 9781441819475, BADLE) Brilliance Audio.

***Orchard Valley Brides.** unabr. ed. Debbie Macomber. Read by Tanya Eby. (Running Time: 9 hrs.). (Orchard Valley Ser.). 2010. 24.99 (978-1-4418-1944-4(4), 9781441819444, Brilliance MP3); 24.99 (978-1-4418-1946-8(0), 9781441819468, BAD); audio compact disk 29.99 (978-1-4418-1942-0(8), 9781441819420, Bril Audio CD Unabri) Brilliance Audio.

Orchard Valley Grooms. unabr. ed. Debbie Macomber. Read by Tanya Eby. (Running Time: 9 hrs.). (Orchard Valley Ser.). 2010. audio compact disk 29.99 (978-1-4418-1935-2(5), 9781441819352, Bril Audio CD Unabri) Brilliance Audio.

***Orchard Valley Grooms.** unabr. ed. Debbie Macomber. Read by Tanya Eby. (Running Time: 9 hrs.). (Orchard Valley Ser.). 2010. 24.99 (978-1-4418-1937-6(1), 9781441819376, Brilliance MP3); 39.97 (978-1-4418-1938-3(X), 9781441819383, Brlnc Audio MP3 Lib); 24.99 (978-1-4418-1939-0(8), 9781441819390, BAD); 39.97 (978-1-4418-1940-6(1), 9781441819406, BADLE); audio compact disk 92.97 (978-1-4418-1936-9(3), 9781441819369, BriAudCD Unabrid) Brilliance Audio.

Orchestra see William Carlos Williams Reads His Poetry

Orchestra. Peter Ustinov. 1 cass. (J). (ps up). bk. 19.98 (6118); 9.98 (326); audio compact disk 15.98 (D326) MFLP CA.
Did you know there are more violins than any other instrument in an orchestra? This & many other interesting facts are presented in an informative explanation of orchestral music. From what makes sound to how instruments are created, from notes & melodies to intensities & feeling, this has it all!.

Orchestra. Peter Ustinov. 1 cass., 1 CD. (J). 7.98 (MRP 107); audio compact disk 11.98 CD Jewel box. (MRP 107) NewSound.

Orchestra Expressions: Student Edition. Kathleen DeBerry Brungard & Michael Alexander. (Expressions Music Curriculum Ser.). (ENG.). 2007. audio compact disk 150.00 (978-0-7390-4265-6(3)) Alfred Pub.

Orchestra Expressions, Book One Student Edition. Kathleen DeBerry Brungard & Michael Alexander. (Expressions Music Curriculum Ser.). (ENG.). 2004. audio compact disk 7.95 (978-0-7579-2344-9(5)) Alfred Pub.

Orchestra Expressions, Book One Student Edition. Kathleen DeBerry Brungard & Michael Alexander. (Expressions Music Curriculum Ser.). (ENG.). 2004. audio compact disk 150.00 (978-0-7579-2405-7(0)) Alfred Pub.

Orchestra Expressions, Book Two Student Edition. Kathleen DeBerry Brungard & Michael Alexander. (Expressions Music Curriculum Ser.). (ENG.). 2007. audio compact disk 8.95 (978-0-7390-4264-9(5)) Alfred Pub.

Orchestral Gems for Classical Guitar. Created by Hal Leonard Corporation Staff. 2006. pap. bk. 29.98 (978-1-59615-380-6(6), 1596153806) Pub: Music Minus. Dist(s): H Leonard

Orchestral Library Series, No. 1. Prod. by Zobeida Perez. (Bowmar Orchestral Library Ser.). (ENG.). 1994. audio compact disk 225.00 (978-0-89898-773-7(3), BMR05111, Warner Bro) Alfred Pub.

Orchestral Library Series, No. 2. Zobeida Perez. (Bowmar Orchestral Library Ser.). (ENG.). 1994. audio compact disk 189.00 (978-0-89898-774-4(1), Warner Bro) Alfred Pub.

Orchestral Spectaculars. Perf. by Erich Kunzel & Cincinnati Pops Orchestra. 1 cass. (Running Time: 1 hr.). 7.98 (TA 30115); audio compact disk 12.78 (TA 80115) NewSound.

Orchestrating Sales Success: The Art & Process of Appointment Generation. Charlie Van Hecke. Read by Charlie Van Hecke. 1 cass. (Running Time: 34 min.). 1998. bk.; 9.95 (978-0-9670965-1-3(0)); audio compact disk 12.95 (978-0-9670965-2-0(9)) Sales Support.
Helps sales professionals find new business by balancing technology with personal contacts.

Orchid, unabr. collector's ed. Jayne Castle, pseud. Read by Mary Peiffer. 7 cass. (Running Time: 10 hrs. 30 mins.). 1999. 56.00 (978-0-7366-4491-4(1), 4929) Books on Tape.
A top psychic on the space colony of St. Helens, Orchid Adams is far too exotic to settle for an ordinary man. It's just as well because she's got her hands full with her new client, Rafe Stonebraker. An unlicensed private eye with awesome psychic talents of his own, Rafe is trying to solve a strange theft & at the same time ward off a hostile takeover of the family shipping business. A wife would certainly go a long way towards salvaging his credibility. Orchid doesn't fit the profile he had in mind, but when opposites attract anything can happen.

***Orchid Affair.** Lauren Willig. (ENG.). 2011. audio compact disk 39.95 (978-0-14-242877-1(9), PengAudBks) Penguin Grp USA.

Orchid Beach. Stuart Woods. Read by Jonathan Marosz. (Holly Barker Ser.: No. 1). 1999. audio compact disk 56.00 (978-0-7366-5173-8(X)) Books on Tape.

***Orchid Beach.** abr. ed. Stuart Woods. Read by Debra Monk. (ENG.). 2005. (978-0-06-084205-5(9), Harper Audio); (978-0-06-084204-8(0), Harper Audio) HarperCollins Pubs.

Orchid Beach, unabr. ed. Stuart Woods. Read by Jonathan Marosz. 6 cass. (Running Time: 9 hrs.). (Holly Barker Ser.: No. 1). 1999. 48.00 (978-0-7366-4503-4(9), 4938) Books on Tape.
A former Army major, Holly Barker, has been pushed into early retirement at 37, the result of a scandalous sexual harassment case involving a high-profile colonel. Accepting a job as deputy chief of police in the sleepy backwater town of Orchid Beach, Florida, she now finds herself caught in a sinister game of cat-&-mouse, as friends & coworkers turn up dead, victims of vicious attacks. With the help of Daisy, a remarkable Doberman pinscher, Barker unravels the mystery, only to find herself in line to become the next victim.

Orchid Beach. unabr. ed. Stuart Woods. Read by Jonathan Marosz. 7 CDs. (Running Time: 8 hrs. 12 mins.). (Holly Barker Ser.: No. 1). 2001. audio compact disk 56.00 Books on Tape.

Orchid Beach, unabr. ed. Stuart Woods. Narrated by George Guidall. 6 cass. (Running Time: 9 hrs.). (Holly Barker Ser.: No. 1). 1999. 51.00 (978-0-7887-2915-7(2), 95505E7) Recorded Bks.
Retired early from the military police, Holly Barker arrives in Orchid Beach just in time to replace the brutally murdered police chief. She senses something sinister hiding in this sleepy Florida town.

Orchid Beach. unabr. ed. Stuart Woods. Narrated by George Guidall. 8 CDs. (Running Time: 9 hrs.). (Holly Barker Ser.: No. 1). 2000. audio compact disk 78.00 (978-0-7887-4465-5(8), C1162E7) Recorded Bks.

Orchid Fever: A Horticultural Tale of Love, Lust & Lunacy. unabr. ed. Eric Hansen. Read by Jeff Harding. 6 cass. (Running Time: 9 hrs.). (Isis Ser.). (J). 2001. 54.95 (978-0-7531-1003-4(2), 001208) Pub: ISIS Lrg Prnt GBR. Dist(s): Ulverscroft US

Orchid Thief: A True Story of Beauty & Obsession. abr. ed. Susan Orlean. Read by Anna Fields. 5 CDs. (Running Time: 5 hrs.). (ENG.). 2002. audio compact disk 29.95 (978-1-56511-690-0(9), 1565116909) Pub: HighBridge. Dist(s): Workman Pub

Orchidees pour Stepanich. 1 cass. (Running Time: 1 hr.). Dramatization. (Maitres du Mystere Ser.). (FRE.). 1996. 11.95 (1836-MA) Olivia & Hill.
Popular radio thriller, interpreted by France's best actors.

***Orcs.** unabr. ed. Stan Nicholls. Narrated by John Lee. (Running Time: 23 hrs. 30 mins. 0 sec.). (ENG.). 2010. 39.99 (978-1-4001-6685-5(3)); 28.99 (978-1-4001-8685-3(4)); 59.99 (978-1-4001-9685-2(X)); audio compact disk 143.99 (978-1-4001-4685-7(2)); audio compact disk 59.99 (978-1-4001-1685-0(6)) Pub: Tantor Media. Dist(s): IngramPubServ

***Orcs: Army of Shadows.** unabr. ed. Stan Nicholls. Narrated by John Lee. (Running Time: 8 hrs. 30 mins.). (Orcs Ser.). 2010. 19.99 (978-1-4001-6689-3(6)); 59.99 (978-1-4001-4689-5(5)); 29.99 (978-1-4001-8689-1(9)); 15.99 (978-1-4001-8689-1(7)) Tantor Media.

***Orcs: Army of Shadows (Library Edition)** unabr. ed. Stan Nicholls. Narrated by John Lee. (Running Time: 8 hrs. 30 mins.). (Orcs Ser.). 2010. 29.99 (978-1-4001-9689-0(2)) Tantor Media.

***Orcs: Bad Blood.** unabr. ed. Stan Nicholls. Narrated by John Lee. (Running Time: 11 hrs. 30 mins. 0 sec.). (Orcs Ser.). 2010. 24.99 (978-1-4001-6688-6(8)); 17.99 (978-1-4001-8688-4(9)); audio compact disk 34.99 (978-1-4001-1688-1(0)) Pub: Tantor Media. Dist(s): IngramPubServ

***Orcs: Bad Blood (Library Edition)** unabr. ed. Stan Nicholls. Narrated by John Lee. (Running Time: 11 hrs. 30 mins.). (Orcs Ser.). 2010. 34.99 (978-1-4001-9688-3(4)); audio compact disk 69.99 (978-1-4001-4688-8(7)) Pub: Tantor Media. Dist(s): IngramPubServ

Ordeal. unabr. ed. Nevil Shute. Narrated by Ian Stuart. 5 cass. (Running Time: 6 hrs. 30 mins.). 1989. 44.00 (978-1-55690-394-6(4), 89360E7) Recorded Bks.
A family struggles to survive after their house is bombed in the London "Blitz" of World War II.

Ordeal by Hunger, Set. unabr. ed. George R. Stewart. Read by Jeff Riggenbach. 9 cass. (Running Time: 13 hrs.). 1996. 62.95 (978-0-7861-0996-8(3), 1773) Blckstn Audio.
The tragedy of the Donner party constitutes one of the most amazing stories of the American West. In 1846 eighty-seven people - men, women, & children - set out for California, persuaded to attempt a new overland route. After struggling across the desert, losing many oxen, & nearly dying of thirst, they reached the very summit of the Sierras, only to be trapped by blinding snow & bitter storms. Many perished; some survived by resorting to cannibalism; all were subjected to unbearable suffering. Incorporating the diaries of the survivors & other contemporary documents, George Stewart wrote the definitive history of that ill-fated band of pioneers.

***Ordeal by Innocence.** Agatha Christie. Narrated by Robin Bailey. (Running Time: 7 hrs. 0 mins. 0 sec.). (ENG.). 2010. audio compact disk 29.95 (978-1-60283-912-0(3)) Pub: AudioGO. Dist(s): Perseus Dist

Ordeal by Innocence. unabr. ed. Agatha Christie. Read by Robin Bailey. 2003. 25.95 (978-1-57270-294-3(X)) Pub: Audio Partners. Dist(s): PerseuPGW

Ordeal of Andy Dean. unabr. ed. Douglas Hirt. Read by Rusty Nelson. 6 cass. (Running Time: 6 hrs. 24 min.). 2001. 39.95 (978-1-58116-059-8(3)) Books in Motion.
When a notorious gang robs one of the largest banks in the territory, little "Andy" Dean is found by the gang and adopted to their care. As the girl's father and the law make headway on the gang's trail, Andy is beginning to make a deep and lasting influence on one of the bankrobbers.

Ordeal of Gilbert Pinfold. unabr. ed. Evelyn Waugh. Narrated by Michael Cochrane. 4 CDs. (Running Time: 5 hrs. 0 mins. 0 sec.). (ENG.). 2010. audio compact disk 26.95 (978-1-934997-53-6(6)) Pub: CSAWord. Dist(s): PerseuPGW

Ordeal of Gilbert Pinfold: A Conversation Piece. unabr. collector's ed. Evelyn Waugh. Read by David Case. 5 cass. (Running Time: 5 hrs.). 1993. 30.00 (978-0-7366-2347-6(7), 3125) Bo[illegible]s on Tape.
Middle-aged novelist with a case of "b[illegible]ves" seeks rest on shipboard. Instead he hears voices talking about [illegible]

Ordeal of the Mountain Man. William W. J[illegible]stone. 4 cass. (Running Time: 6 hrs.). (Mountain Man Ser.: No. 17). 2001. 24.95 (978-1-890990-74-9(4)) Otis Audio.
After the marauding Grubbs gang cause an uprising in Muddy Gap, Wyoming, Smoke Jensen visits the town & then flees for his life, with the gang in hot pursuit, unwittingly leading them straight into Cheyenne territory.

Ordeal of the Woman Writer. Read by Heywood Hale Broun et al. 1 cass. (Running Time: 56 min.). (Broun Radio Ser.). 11.95 (40061) J Norton Pubs.
With Erica Jong ("Fear of Flying"), Toni Morrison ("Sula") & Marge Piercy ("Small Changes").

Orden del Temple. abr. ed. Raymond Khoury. 3. (Running Time: 12600 sec.). (SPA.). 2007. audio compact disk 24.95 (978-1-933499-08-6(7)) Fonolibro Inc.

Order. J. Krishnamurti. 1 cass. (Running Time: 1 hr.). (Krishnamurti with Dr. Allan W. Anderson Ser.: No. 5). 8.50 (APA745) Krishnamurti.
These 1974 dialogues cover the entire spectrum of Krishnamurti's teaching in a series highly regarded for its depth of inquiry into each particular subject.

Order in the School. unabr. ed. Daniel Greenberg. 1 cass. (Running Time: 1 hr.). 1991. 10.00 (978-1-888947-56-4(X)) Sudbury Valley.
On setting up a fair judicial system in a school.

Order... Order... Order. George Bloomer. audio compact disk Whitaker Hse.

Order... Order... Order. unabr. ed. George Bloomer. 1 cass. (Running Time: 90 mins.). 2004. audio compact disk 14.99 (978-0-88368-882-3(4)) Pub: Whitaker Hse. Dist(s): Anchor Distributors
Learn how to get in order, move the giants, and possess the land. God wants to bring order into your life to prepare you for the overflow of great things.

Ordering from the Cosmic Kitchen: The Essential Guide to Powerful, Nourishing Affirmations. Read by Patricia J. Craen. 5 CDs. 2004. audio compact disk 29.95 (978-1-893705-16-6(1), Cranes Nest) Hlth Horiz.
Audio book on CD.

Ordering Your Private World. Gordon MacDonald. 2 cass. (Running Time: 3 hrs.). 1989. 14.99 (978-2-01-053400-3(X)) Nelson.
Focuses on five areas: motivation, use of time, wisdom and knowledge, spiritual strength and restoration.

Orderly Affairs: Pathways to Financial Freedom for Everyone. Narrated by William M. Upson. 3 CDs. (ENG.). 2006. audio compact disk 24.99 (978-0-9678982-5-4(0)) St Bernie's Pr.

Orderly Man. unabr. collector's ed. Dirk Bogarde. Read by David Case. 8 cass. (Running Time: 12 hrs.). 1988. 64.00 (978-0-7366-1360-6(9), 2259) Books on Tape.
In 1970 the author retired from acting & turned towards a quieter, more contemplative, more settled way of life. He both dreaded & yearned for a change from the preceding 20 years of "continual motion." He sought "a place of my own" & found it in a dilapidated farmhouse in the south of France.

Orders for Cameron. unabr. ed. Philip McCutchan. Read by Christopher Scott. 4 cass. (Running Time: 6 hrs.). 1996. 49.95 (978-1-86042-123-5(7), 21237) Pub: Soundings Ltd GBR. Dist(s): Ulverscroft US
Oleander's task is to take part in the seaborne invasion of North Africa. Small & outmoded, Oleander nonetheless has a vital part in the operation, & Cameron is one of a group of volunteers put ashore to capture a germ warfare dump.

Orders Is Orders. unabr. ed. L. Ron Hubbard. Read by Brooke Bloom. 2 CDs. (Running Time: 2 hrs.). (Stories from the Golden Age Ser.). (ENG.). (gr. 6). 2009. audio compact disk 9.95 (978-1-59212-233-2(7)) Gala Pr LLC.

Orders of Change. Gregory Bateson. 2 cass. 1974. 12.50 Vajradhatu.
The author develops a scientific world view based entirely on the relationship between ideas & information.

Orders to Kill: The Truth Behind the Murder of Martin Luther King. William F. Pepper. Intro. by Dexter King. 2 cass. (Running Time: 3 hrs.). 1998. 17.00 (978-1-57042-564-6(7)) Hachet Audio.
An explosive account that debunks the myth & mystery surrounding Martin Luther King, Jr's assassination.

Ordinariness: Spirituality & Self-Esteem. Robert Wicks. 1 cass. (Running Time: 1 hr. 10 mins.). 1993. 8.95 (AA2643) Credence Commun.
You'll see a mood, a belief, a relationship in a different light. And you see how ordinary humility & holiness & self-esteem are united.

Ordinary Heroes. unabr. ed. Scott Turow. 12 CDs. (Running Time: 13 hrs. 30 mins.). 2005. audio compact disk 76.50 (978-1-4159-2482-2(1)); 104.00 (978-1-4159-2481-5(3)) Books on Tape.
Whilst mourning the death of his father, Stewart Dubin, a journalist covering the courtroom beat, decides to research the life of a man he had always respected, always admired, but possibly never quite loved.

Ordinary Lies: Selected Poems Read by the Poet. Robert J. Duffy. Read by Robert J. Duffy. 2003. audio compact disk 12.95 (978-1-882291-01-4(8)) Oyster River Pr.

Ordinary Life: Stories. unabr. ed. Elizabeth Berg. Read by Laura Hicks. 2002. 24.95 (978-1-57270-304-9(0)) Pub: Audio Partners. Dist(s): PerseuPGW

Ordinary Love & Good Will. Jane Smiley. Read by Jane Smiley. Prod. by Moveable Feast Staff. 1 cass. (Running Time: 30 min.). 8.95 (AMF-232) Am Audio Prose.
Smiley reads from two novellas & talks about the political implications of domestic dramas.

Ordinary Man. unabr. ed. JoAnne Lower. Read by JoAnne Lower. (Running Time: 1 hr.). 1994. (978-1-888940-05-3(0)) J Lower Ent.

Ordinary Parent's Guide to Teaching Reading: Audio Companion to Lessons 1-26. Jessie Wise & Sara Buffington. Read by Mike Russo. Contrib. by Mark Smith. (ENG.). 2007. audio compact disk 8.99 (978-1-933339-19-1(5)) Pub: Peace Hill. Dist(s): Norton

Ordinary People. unabr. ed. Judith Guest. Read by Roses Prichard. 6 cass. (Running Time: 9 hrs.). 1984. 48.00 (978-0-7366-0985-2(7), 1925) Books on Tape.
This is the story of the Jarrett family: Calvin, a determined, successful provider; Beth, his organized & efficient wife; & their two sons, Conrad & Buck. On a day much like any other, their sons were sailing. There was suddenly a squall, a boat in trouble...& only one son returns.

Ordinary People. unabr. ed. Judith Guest. Narrated by Aviva Skell. 5 cass. (Running Time: 7 hrs.). 1984. 44.00 (978-1-55690-395-3(2), 84110E7) Recorded Bks.
When a terrible accident takes the life of a couple's son, their lives begin to fall apart. This is the story of ordinary people in extraordinary circumstances & the lengths they will go to put their lives together again.

***Ordinary People, Extraordinary Power: How a Strong Apostolic Culture Releases Us to Do Transformational Things in the World.** unabr. ed. John Eckhardt. Narrated by Mirron Willis. (Running Time: 6 hrs. 53 mins. 0 sec.). (ENG.). 2010. audio compact disk 21.98 (978-1-61045-030-0(2)) christianaud.

***Ordinary People, Extraordinary Wealth.** abr. ed. Ric Edelman. Read by Ric Edelman. (ENG.). 2004. (978-0-06-081313-0(X), Harper Audio); (978-0-06-075230-9(0), Harper Audio) HarperCollins Pubs.

Ordinary Princess. unabr. ed. M. M. Kaye. Perf. by Carole Shelley. 1 cass. (Running Time: 1 hr. 30 mins.). (J). 1985. 8.98 (978-0-89845-411-6(5), CP 1774) HarperCollins Pubs.
Princess Amy (nee Amethyst) is blessed with wit, courage & ordinariness with a capital O. This is the story of her rather lengthy & ordinary apprenticeship before she meets her Prince Charming.

Ordinary Resurrections: Children in the Years of Hope. unabr. ed. Jonathan Kozol. Read by Dick Hill. 6 cass. (Running Time: 9 hrs.). 2000. 29.95 (978-1-56740-370-1(0), 1567403700, BAU) Brilliance Audio.
Jonathan Kozol's books have become touchstones of the American conscience. Unlike his previous books, however, Ordinary Resurrections is almost entirely narrative and takes us into the fascinating details of daily life as he has lived it with young children who befriended him over the course of several years. Like Amazing Grace, this book describes the children of New York's South Bronx, but it is a markedly different book in mood and vantage point. Here, we see life through the eyes of the children, not, as Kozol puts it, from the perspective of a grown-up man encumbered by a Harvard education. Here, too, we meet some dedicated and inspired teachers in an underfunded but upbeat public elementary school, and we return once more to St. Ann's Church and meet the parents and religious figures in the children's lives.

Ordinary Resurrections: Children in the Years of Hope. unabr. ed. Jonathan Kozol. Read by Dick Hill. (Running Time: 9 hrs.). 2005. 39.25 (978-1-59600-598-3(X), 9781596005983, BADLE); 24.95 (978-1-59600-597-6(1), 9781596005976, BAD); 24.95 (978-1-59600-595-2(5), 9781596005952, Brilliance MP3); audio compact disk 39.25 (978-1-59600-596-9(3), 9781596005969, Brinc Audio MP3 Lib) Brilliance Audio.

Ordinary Seaman. unabr. ed. Francisco Goldman. Narrated by Robert Ramirez. 11 cass. (Running Time: 16 hrs.). 1998. 93.00 (978-0-7887-2521-0(1), 95594E7) Recorded Bks.
The story of a young Nicaraguan seaman stranded on a rusty boat facing excruciating odds. It is also a fable of hope & perseverance.

***Ordinary Thunderstorms.** unabr. ed. William Boyd. Read by Gideon Emery. (ENG.). 2010. (978-0-06-200842-8(0), Harper Audio) HarperCollins Pubs.

***Ordinary Thunderstorms: A Novel.** unabr. ed. William Boyd. Read by Gideon Emery. (ENG.). 2010. (978-0-06-200756-8(4), Harper Audio) HarperCollins Pubs.

Ordinary Woman. Susan Sallis. Read by Anne Dover. 14 cass. (Running Time: 21 hrs.). 1999. 99.95 (20486) Pub: Soundings Ltd GBR. Dist(s): Ulverscroft US

Ordinary Women with Extraordinary Spirit! Perf. by Kathryn Beisner. 1 cass. (Running Time: 1 hr.). (J). (gr. 3 up). 1996. 9.95 (978-1-887577-01-4(7), OWCAS2750) KBS Prodns.
Stories of women aviators, baseball players & rodeo cowgirls of the early 1900's. Artfully highlighted with music & sound effects. Valuable bibliography inside each cassette.

Ordinary Work, Extraordinary Grace: My Spiritual Journey in Opus Dei. abr. ed. Scott Hahn. Read by Paul Smith. 4 CDs. (Running Time: 14400 sec.). 2007. audio compact disk 29.95 (978-0-86716-828-0(5)) St Anthony Mess Pr.

Ordination of Women: Romans 16:1. Ed Young. 1984. 4.95 (978-0-7417-1407-7(8), 407) Win Walk.

Oregon. Dan Heller. 1 cass. (Running Time: 1 hr.). 1996. 9.95 (978-1-885433-06-0(9)) Takilma East.

Oregon! abr. ed. Dana Fuller Ross, pseud. Read by Paul Ukena. 4 vols. (Wagons West Ser.: No. 4). 2002. (978-1-58807-512-3(5)) Am Pubng Inc.

Oregon! abr. ed. Dana Fuller Ross, pseud. Read by Paul Ukena. 4 cass. (Running Time: 6 hrs.). (Wagon West Ser.: No. 4). 2002. 27.00 (978-1-58807-009-8(3), 691098) Am Pubng Inc.
Valor and devotion ride side by side with intrigue and bitter rivalry. Wagon master, Whip Holt, is desired by two women - his wife and Cathy van Ayl Blake, who is married to the supreme commander of the American forces in the Oregon Territory.

Oregon! abr. ed. Dana Fuller Ross, pseud. Read by Paul Ukena. 5 vols. (Wagons West Ser.: No. 4). 2003. audio compact disk (978-1-58807-824-7(8)) Am Pubng Inc.

Oregon! abr. ed. Dana Fuller Ross, pseud. Read by Paul Ukena. 5 CDs. (Running Time: 6 hrs.). (Wagons West Ser.: No. 4). 2003. audio compact disk 32.00 (978-1-58807-346-4(7), 750749) Am Pubng Inc.

Oregon! unabr. ed. Dana Fuller Ross, pseud. Read by Phil Gigante. (Running Time: 12 hrs.). (Wagons West Ser.: No. 4). 2010. 39.97 (978-1-4418-2451-6(0), 9781441824516, BADLE) Brilliance Audio.

Oregon: Oregon Coast - Astoria to Lincoln City, Pt. I. (Running Time: 2 hrs.). 1990. 20.95 (CC285) Comp Comms Inc.
Treats you to the history, geology, stories & legends of the areas.

Oregon: Oregon Coast - Lincoln City to Brookings, Pt. II. (Running Time: 2 hrs.). 1990. 20.95 (CC286) Comp Comms Inc.
Takes you through the central & south coast of Oregon & treats you to Oregon Coast history, geology, museums, state parks, plant & animal communities & wildlife viewing sites.

Oregon Coast Reflections: A Collection of Poems with Oregon Coast Themes, Bible Verses & Prayers. Karen Jean Matsko Hood. 2006. 29.95 (978-1-59434-291-2(1)); audio compact disk 24.95 (978-1-59434-290-5(3)) Whspmg Pine.

Oregon Interview on the Believer's Security. Dan Corner. 1 cass. (Running Time: 1 hr. 30 mins.). 4.00 (OR) Evang Outreach.

Oregon Legacy. abr. ed. Dana Fuller Ross, pseud. Read by Tim Nelson. Abr. by Odin Westgaard. 4 cass. (Running Time: 6 hrs.). (Holts, an American Dynasty Ser.: Vol. 1). 2004. 25.00 (978-1-58807-450-8(1)) Am Pubng Inc.
The winter of 1887 will test the courage and will of the settlers in Oregon. Raging storms destroy farms, ranches and people. Toby Holt has his hands full trying to save his ranch, his son, and protect his wife. The betrayal and prejudice flung at the Holt family will make them stronger or destroy them forever.

Oregon Trail. Francis Parkman. Narrated by Jim Roberts. (Running Time: 13 hrs. NaN mins.). 2006. 29.95 (978-1-59912-839-9(X)) Iofy Corp.

Oregon Trail. Rick Steber. Illus. by Don Gray. 1 cass. (Running Time: 1 hr.). (Tales of the Wild West Ser.: Vol. 1). 1986. pap. bk. 9.95 (978-0-945134-51-0(7)) Bonanza Pub.

Oregon Trail. abr. ed. Ralph Compton. Read by Jim Gough. 4 cass. (Running Time: 6 hrs.). (Trail Drive Ser.: Bk. 9). 1999. 24.95 (978-1-890990-08-4(6).) Otis Audio.
Lou, Dill & 14 of their Texas cowhands have brought a herd to Independence, Missouri. After selling half the cattle to a wagon train heading West, the Texans decide to sign on to lead the pioneers across the Missouri River & the Nebraska Territory & into the wilds past Fort Laramie. With winter closing in, Lou's men are running out of time to reach the wide-open land of Oregon. And with a fortune in gold hidden in one of the pilgrims' wooden wagons & outlaws circling like wolves- there are miles of shooting & dying still ahead.

Oregon Trail. abr. ed. Francis Parkman. Read by Frank Muller. (YA). 2007. 34.99 (978-1-60252-921-2(3)) Find a World.

Oregon Trail. unabr. ed. Francis Parkman. Read by Robert Morris. 9 cass. (Running Time: 13 hrs.). 1994. 62.95 (978-0-7861-0738-4(3), 1495) Blckstn Audio.
This is the classic account of Francis Parkman's rugged trip over the eastern part of the Oregon Trail, with his cousin, Quincy Adams Shaw, which took place in the spring & summer of 1846. They left St. Louis by steamboat & arrived in Oregon on horseback, in company with guides & occasional other travelers. They encountered storms, buffalo hunts & meetings with Indians, soldiers, sportsmen & emigrants.

Oregon Trail. unabr. ed. Francis Parkman. Read by Jim Roberts. 8 cass. (Running Time: 11 hrs. 46 min.). (YA). (gr. 9-12). 1991. 59.00 (C-225) Jimcin Record.
An authentic look at the road Westward in 1846 that effectively captures the flavor of an era.

Oregon Trail. unabr. ed. Francis Parkman. Narrated by Adrian Cronauer. 8 cass. (Running Time: 11 hrs. 30 mins.). 1986. 70.00 (978-1-55690-396-0(0), 86570E7) Recorded Bks.
He traveled the Oregon Trail over a century ago. His account. In 1846, a young Harvard graduate, set out to explore life in the uncivilized West. With his friend Quincy Adams Shaw, he traveled up the Oregon Trail to the camps of the Pawnee & the Sioux.

Oregon Trail. unabr. collector's ed. Francis Parkman. Read by Dan Lazar. 8 cass. (Running Time: 12 hrs.). 1983. 64.00 (978-0-7366-0509-0(6), 1483) Books on Tape.
"The Oregon Trail" captures the flavor of an era with great authenticity & color, & makes it possible for us to journey into that land of long ago.

Oregon Trunk. unabr. ed. Wayne D. Overholser. Read by William Dufris. 5 cass. (Sagebrush Western Ser.). (J). 2005. 54.95 (978-1-57490-298-3(9)) Pub: ISIS Lrg Prnt GBR. Dist(s): Ulverscroft US

Oregon Wines, the South Willamette Region. 2nd ed. Prod. by Michael S. Dilley. Narrated by Bob Bosche. Comment by Kevin Chambers. 1 cass. (Running Time: 1 hr. 10 mins.). 1990. 9.95 (978-0-941429-02-3(4)) Producers Studio.
A colorful collection of interviews with the winemakers of the Southern Willamette valley in Oregon. Travel directions are given to each winery.

O'Reilly & the Age of Persuasion. Terry O'Reilly. 5 CDs. (Running Time: 5 Hours). 2007. audio compact disk 39.95 (978-0-660-19680-0(8), CBC Audio) Pub: Canadian Broadcasting CAN. Dist(s): Georgetown Term
This 5-CD set is Terry O'Reilly's second series helping us to understand the world of advertising. In this collection he concentrates on how ads affect us, where ads are placed and how they influence people. Find out how instructions on a shampoo bottle can be a potent marketing tool. Hear how market research used properly can work a miracle or if mishandled can spell disaster. Learn about the rise and fall of branded entertainment as he traces its roots back to the 1920?s.O?Reilly and the Age of Persuasion is an essential addition to marketing, business and media awareness classes.

***O'Reilly Factor for Kids: A Survival Guide for America's Families.** unabr. ed. Bill O'Reilly. Read by Rick Adamson. (ENG.). 2004. (978-0-06-079351-7(1), Harper Audio); (978-0-06-081436-6(5), Harper Audio) HarperCollins Pubs.

O'Reilly Factor for Kids: A Survival Guide for America's Families. unabr. ed. Bill O'Reilly & Charles Flowers. Read by Rick Adamson. 4 CDs. (Running Time: 6 hrs.). 2004. audio compact disk 29.95 (978-0-06-073844-0(8)) HarperCollins Pubs.

O'Reilly on Advertising. Interview. Terry O'Reilly. 5 CDs. (Running Time: 5 hrs.). (ENG.). 2006. audio compact disk 39.95 (978-0-660-19544-5(5), CBC Audio) Pub: Canadian Broadcasting CAN. Dist(s): Georgetown Term

Orenda. Gregory Greyhawk. 1 cass. (Running Time: 45 min.). 9.00 (978-1-882863-51-8(8)) Howling Dog.
Orenda includes work from his long awaited book "Wailing in Heaven, Whistling in Hell: New & Selected Poems." This audio cassette features: When You Give the Land Back; When We Take the Land Back; Wailing in Heaven; Money & Freedom, Freedom & Money; Interview at the Fib-Factory; When They Tell You; Triple Entendre; Diapers, Pablum, Ciggies & Bus Money; Rest-Period Journal Entry; Cover Letter, Sans Resume for Application to the Godhead; & much more.

Oresteia. unabr. ed. Aeschylus. (Running Time: 12600 sec.). 2007. 34.95 (978-0-7861-6909-2(5)) Blckstn Audio.

Oresteia. unabr. ed. Aeschylus. Contrib. by Hollywood Theater of the Ear. (Running Time: 12600 sec.). 2007. audio compact disk 36.00 (978-0-7861-6908-5(7)) Blckstn Audio.

Oresteia. unabr. ed. Aeschylus. Read by Yuri Rasovsky. (Running Time: 12600 sec.). 2007. 17.95 (978-0-7861-4912-4(4)); audio compact disk 19.95 (978-0-7861-7060-9(3)); audio compact disk 17.95 (978-0-7861-5934-5(0)) Blckstn Audio.

Organ Music of America Vol. I: Twentieth Century Romantics. Gloriae Dei Cantores. 1 CD. (Running Time: 1 hr.). 1991. audio compact disk 16.95 (978-1-55725-083-4(9)) Paraclete MA.

Organ Music of America Vol. II: Boston Classicists. Gloriae Dei Cantores. 1 CD. (Running Time: 1 hr. 30 mins.). 1993. audio compact disk 16.95 (978-1-55725-087-2(1)) Paraclete MA.

Organic & Natural Personal Care Products in South Korea: A Strategic Reference 2006. Compiled by Icon Group International, Inc. Staff. 2007. ring bd. 195.00 (978-0-497-35877-8(8)) Icon Grp.

Organic Chem: Lecture Success. 2nd ed. Marye Anne Fox & James Whitesell. (C). 1997. audio compact disk 101.00 (978-0-7637-0495-7(4), 0495-4) Jones Bartlett.

Organic Chemistry. 4th ed. Francis A. Carey. 2000. audio compact disk 113.75 (978-0-07-241099-0(X), McG-H Sci Eng) McGrw-H Hghr Educ.

Organic Church: Growing faith where life Happens. unabr. ed. Neil Cole. (Running Time: 8 hrs. 30 mins. 0 sec.). (ENG.). 2009. audio compact disk 26.98 (978-1-59644-729-5(X), christianSeed) christianaud.

***Organic Church: Growing faith where life Happens.** unabr. ed. Neil Cole. Narrated by Marc Cashman. (ENG.). 2009. 16.98 (978-1-59644-730-1(3), christianSeed) christianaud.

Organic Conceptualizations. Jon Klimo. 1 cass. 9.00 (A0362-88) Sound Photosyn.

Organic Foods. Jill Eisen. Contrib. by Paul Kennedy. Prod. by Liz Nagy & Patsy Stevens. 3. (Running Time: 10800 sec.). 2007. audio compact disk 24.95 (978-0-660-19678-7(6), CBC Audio) Canadian Broadcasting CAN.
After World War 2 organic farming had all but disappeared. In the 1960's and 70's thousands of young people went "back to the land" and helped reinvent organic farming and the whole food system. Food co-ops and sprang up across North America, looking nothing like your neighbourhood supermarket. Shoppers often shared the work of stacking shelves, bagging groceries - blurring the line between producer and consumer. Even the food was different. Whole wheat flour, brown rice, tamari, tofu and granola replaced the plastic foods of the 1960's. Today, organic food is a $14 billion-a-year industry in North America, and growing. Every major supermarket chain carries organic fruits and vegetables, frozen foods, dairy and packaged goods, and some have developed their own in-store organic brands. In this fascinating 3-CD set Jill Eisen explores just how organics made the leap from the 1960's to today.

Organic Gardening for the Pacific Northwest. Emma H. Gordon. 4 cass. (Running Time: 2 hrs. 1 min.). 1998. pap. bk. 29.95 Set. (978-0-9667900-0-9(6), OG-1C) Alpha Group Inc.
Consists of: soil preparation & natural control of pests & plant disease, native & unusual vegetables & how to grow them, herbs & their common uses. A reference guide to gardening books, seed catalogs, suppliers, media & websites is also included.

Organic Gardening for the Pacific Northwest. Emma H. Gordon. 4 cass. (Running Time: 2 hrs. 1 min.). 1998. audio compact disk 34.95 CD, incl. bklet. Set. (978-0-9667900-1-6(4)) Alpha Group Inc.

***Organic God.** Margaret Feinberg. (Running Time: 3 hrs. 39 mins. 0 sec.). (ENG.). 2008. 16.99 (978-0-310-30498-2(9)) Zondervan.

***Organic Outreach for Ordinary People: Sharing Good News Naturally.** Kevin G. Harney. (Running Time: 7 hrs. 2 mins. 0 sec.). (ENG.). 2009. 14.99 (978-0-310-30272-8(2)) Zondervan.

Organic Synthesis, Pt. II. Instructed by Barry M. Trost & Edwin Vedejs. 8 cass. (Running Time: 9 hrs. 12 min.). pap. bk. 270.00 (49) Am Chemical.
Covers a variety of synthetic techniques illustrating general principles of modern organic synthesis.

Organisms Audio CD Theme Set: Set of 6 Set B. Adapted by Benchmark Education Staff. (English Explorers Ser.). (J). (gr. 3-6). 2007. audio compact disk 60.00 (978-1-4108-9817-3(2)) Benchmark Educ.

Organisms: Past & Present Audio CD Theme Set: Set of 6 Set A. Adapted by Benchmark Education Staff. (English Explorers Ser.). (J). (gr. 3-6). 2007. audio compact disk 60.00 (978-1-4108-9832-6(6)) Benchmark Educ.

Organization & Time Management. Bill Winston. 6 cass. (C). 1991. 25.00 (978-1-931289-66-5(2)) Pub: B Winston Min. Dist(s): Anchor Distributors

Organizational Life As Spiritual Practice. Read by Murray Stein. 1 cass. (Running Time: 1 hr. 30 mins.). 1989. 10.95 (978-0-7822-0295-3(0), 395) C G Jung IL.

Organizations & Nation-States: New Perspectives on Conflict & Cooperation. Robert L. Kahn. Ed. by Mayer N. Zald. (Management-Social & Behavioral Science Ser.). 1990. bk. 46.95 (978-1-55542-291-2(8), Jossey-Bass) Wiley US.

Organize Your Vital Records: Do-It-Yourself Kit. Ed. by Socrates Media. 2005. audio compact disk 39.95 (978-1-59546-271-8(6)) Pub: Socrates Med LLC. Dist(s): Midpt Trade

Organized & Efficient. Eldon Taylor. 1 cass. (Running Time: 1 hr. 2 mins.). (Inner Talk Ser.). 16.95 (978-1-55978-097-1(5), 5311A) Progress Aware Res.
Soundtrack - Tropical Lagoon with underlying subliminal affirmations.

Organized & Efficient: Classic. Eldon Taylor. Read by Eldon Taylor. Ed. by Leslie Brice. 1 cass. (Running Time: 1 hr.). 1992. 16.95 (978-1-56705-075-2(1)) Gateways Inst.
Self improvement.

Organized & Efficient: Environmental Theme. Eldon Taylor. 1 cass. (Running Time: 1 hr.). 16.95 (978-1-55978-460-3(1), 5311F) Progress Aware Res.

Organized & Efficient: Music Theme. Eldon Taylor. 1 cass. (Running Time: 1 hr.). 16.95 (978-1-55978-099-5(1), 5311C) Progress Aware Res.

Organized & Efficient: Ocean. Eldon Taylor. Read by Eldon Taylor. Ed. by Leslie Brice. 1 cass. (Running Time: 1 hr.). 1992. 16.95 (978-1-56705-076-9(X)) Gateways Inst.

Organized & Efficient: Stream. Eldon Taylor. Read by Eldon Taylor. Ed. by Leslie Brice. 1 cass. (Running Time: 1 hr.). 1992. 16.95 (978-1-56705-077-6(8)) Gateways Inst.

Organized Executive: New Ways to Manage Time, Paper & People. Stephanie Winston. 1 cass. (Running Time: 4 hrs.). 1989. 59.95 (978-0-671-68168-5(0)) S&S Audio.

ORGANIZED EXECUTIVE: New Ways to Manage Time, Paper & People. Stephanie Winston. 2004. 7.95 (978-0-7435-4161-9(8)) Pub: S&S Audio. Dist(s): S and S Inc

Organized to Be the Best: New Timesaving Ways to Simplify & Improve How You Work, Set. Susan Silver. Read by Susan Silver. 12 cass. (Running Time: 12 hrs.). 1998. 99.95 (978-1-57294-146-5(4), 11-1201) SkillPath Pubns.
Learn powerful, practical tips & techniques you can use at work & at home to organize & prioritize your tasks, tools, time & space.

Organized You! unabr. ed. 2 cass. (Running Time: 1 hr. 12 min.). 1996. bk. 29.95 (978-0-9669831-0-4(6), 1201) S Pistone.
How to organize an office in a fast, simple, & logical method. Enjoy being proactive versus reactive, experience less stress & offer better customer service.

Organizer's Wife. Short Stories. Toni Cade Bambara. Read by Toni Cade Bambara. 1 cass. (Running Time: 52 min.). 1982. 13.95 (978-1-55644-036-6(7), 2021) Am Audio Prose.

Organizing a Company: 25 Keys to Choosing a Business Structure. unabr. ed. S. Jay Sklar & Joseph N. Bongiovanni. Read by Jeff Woodman. 2 cass. (Running Time: 2 hrs. 30 mins.). (New York Times Pocket MBA Ser.). 2001. 16.95 (978-1-885408-45-7(5), LL038) Listen & Live.
Learn the 25 keys to sole proprietorship, partnership, subchapter S & family ownership.

Organizing an AIDS Unit versus Scattering. Constance Wofsy. (AIDS: The National Conference for Practitioners). 1986. 9.00 (978-0-932491-54-1(5)) Res Appl Inc.

Organizing & Advising California Nonprofit Corporations. Read by Michael C. Hone et al. (Running Time: 2 hrs. 30 min.). 1990. pap. bk. 65.00 (BU-53124) Cont Ed Bar-CA.

Organizing & Advising Closely Held Corporations. Read by Bruce Maximov et al. cass. (Running Time: 5 hrs. 30 min.). 1992. 115.00 (BU-55237) Cont Ed Bar-CA.
Corporate, securities, & tax law experts explain the nuts & bolts of forming a closely held corporation &, through a series of lawyer-client skits, exemplify common operating problems & practical solutions.

Organizing & Advising Partnerships & Joint Ventures. Read by A. John Murphy, Jr. et al. (Running Time: 2 hrs. 45 min.). 1991. 70.00 Incl. 252p. tape materials. (BU-54173) Cont Ed Bar-CA.

Organizing & Conserving Personal Energy Resources. Instructed by Manly P. Hall. 8.95 (978-0-89314-204-9(2), C811122) Philos Res.

***Organizing for Life: Declutter Your Mind to Declutter Your World.** unabr. ed. Sandra Felton. Narrated by Melinda Schmidt. (ENG.). 2007. 9.09 (978-1-60814-659-8(6)) Oasis Audio.

Organizing for Life: Declutter Your Mind to Declutter Your World. unabr. ed. Sandra Felton. Narrated by Melinda Schmidt. (Running Time: 2 hrs. 37 mins. 0 sec.). (ENG.). 2007. audio compact disk 12.99 (978-1-59859-215-3(7)) Oasis Audio.

Organizing for Success: More Than 100 Tips, Tools, Ideas, & Strategies for Organizing & Prioritizing Work. abr. ed. Kenneth Zeigler. Read by Lawrence Bullock. (Running Time: 14400 sec.). 2006. audio compact disk 28.00 (978-1-933309-11-8(3)) Pub: A Media Intl. Dist(s): Natl Bk Netwk

Organizing from the Inside Out. Julie Morgenstern. Read by Julie Morgenstern. 2004. 10.95 (978-0-7435-1992-2(2)) Pub: S&S Audio. Dist(s): S and S Inc

Organizing from the Inside Out: The Foolproof System for Organizing Your Home Your Office & Your Life. abr. ed. Julie Morgenstern. Read by Julie Morgenstern. 2 CDs. (Running Time: 20 hrs. 0 mins. 0 sec.). (ENG.). 2000. audio compact disk 19.95 (978-0-7435-1778-2(4), Sound Ideas) Pub: S&S Audio. Dist(s): S and S Inc
Covers a new way of looking at the task of organizing effectively without labeling or blaming the person behind the lack of organization. Rather, she says, people who don't organize just never learned how to organize, through no fault of their own, after all, it's not a skill that's taught in school. That said, she gets down to work helping you figure out an organizing system that will really work for you, not a system based on cookie-cutter filing concepts or special storage units.

Organizing Your Home Office for Success. abr. ed. Lisa Kanarek. 2 cass. (Running Time: 1 hr. 20 min.). 1994. 14.00 (978-0-9643470-0-7(8)) Blakely Press.
Step-by-step guide to organizing your home office.

Organizing Your IEPs. 2005. pap. bk. 25.00 (978-1-57861-546-9(1), IEP Res) Attainment.

***Orginal Gangster: The Real Life Story of One of America's Most Notorious Drug Lords.** unabr. ed. Frank Lucas. (Running Time: 10 hrs. 45 mins.). 2010. audio compact disk 32.95 (978-1-4417-4040-3(6)) Blckstn Audio.

Orgullo y Perjurio. abr. ed. Jane Austen. 2. (Running Time: 7200 sec.).Tr. of Pride & Prejudice. (SPA.). 2007. audio compact disk 16.95 (978-1-933499-11-6(7)) Fonolibro Inc.

Orgullo y Prejuicio. abr. ed. Jane Austen. Read by Laura García. 3 CDs.Tr. of Pride & Prejudice. (SPA.). 2002. audio compact disk 17.00 (978-958-8161-11-2(8)) YoYoMusic.

Oriana Fallaci. Interview with Oriana Fallaci. 1 cass. (Running Time: 25 min.). 1973. 11.95 (L022) TFR.
Fallaci talks about her controversial interview technique & discusses her news coverage of violent events in Vietnam & Mexico.

Orient Express see Escape

Orient Express. unabr. collector's ed. John Dos Passos. Read by Erik Bauersfeld. 6 cass. (Running Time: 6 hrs.). 1982. 36.00 (978-0-7366-0355-3(7), 1341) Books on Tape.
Dos Passos treated himself to a trip through Russia & the Levant. He kept a journal & published it in 1927 as "Orient Express". Thus this book is a journey into the past & acquaints one with the way travel was & nations were not so very long ago.

Oriental Gardens. 1 cass. (Running Time: 1 hr.). (Interludes Music Ser.). 1989. 9.95 (978-1-55569-283-4(4), MOD-3904) Great Am Audio.

Orientation. unabr. ed. Robert A. Monroe. Read by Robert A. Monroe. (Running Time: 45 min.). (Gateway Experience - Discovery Ser.). 1981. 14.95 (978-1-56113-250-8(0)) Monroe Institute.
An introduction to Focus 3.

Orientation in American English, Level 1. unabr. ed. National Textbook Company Staff. 10 cass. (Running Time: 15 hrs.). 1989. 115.00 (978-0-8325-0551-5(X), Natl Textbk Co) M-H Contemporary.
From the first day of class students learn to speak & Listen in typical day-to-day situations.

Orientation in American English, Level 2. unabr. ed. National Textbook Company Staff. 5 cass. (Running Time: 7 hrs. 30 min.). 1989. 85.00 (978-0-8325-0579-9(X), Natl Textbk Co) M-H Contemporary.

Orientation in American English, Level 3. National Textbook Company Staff. 5 cass. (Running Time: 7 hrs. 30 mins.). 85.00 (978-0-8325-0582-9(X), Natl Textbk Co) M-H Contemporary.

Orientation in American English, Level 4. unabr. ed. National Textbook Company Staff. 5 cass. (Running Time: 7 hrs. 30 min.). 1989. 85.00 (978-0-8325-0565-2(X), Natl Textbk Co) M-H Contemporary.

Orientation to the Trance Experience. Ronald A. Havens & Catherine R. Walters. 1 cass. (Running Time: 31 min.). 2002. 24.95 (978-0-415-94441-0(4)) Pub: Routledge. Dist(s): Taylor and Fran
An instructive demonstration of neoEricksonian Hypnotherapy, highlighting the significance of timing, rhythm and pauses.

Origin. unabr. ed. Diana Abu-Jaber. Read by Elisabeth S. Rogers. 12 CDs. (Running Time: 14 hrs. 30 mins.). 2007. audio compact disk 110.95 (978-0-7927-4864-9(6), Chivers Sound Lib) AudioGO.
Lena is a fingerprint expert at a crime lab in the small city of Syracuse, New York, where winters are cold and deep. Suddenly, a series of crib deaths - indistinguishable from SIDS except for the fevered testimony of one distraught mother with connections in high places - draws the attention of the police and the national media and raises the possibility of the inconceivable: could there be a serial infant murderer on the loose? Orphaned as a child, out of place as an adult, gifted with delicate and terrifying powers of intuition, Lena finds herself playing a critical role in the case. But then there is the mystery of her own childhood to solve. Could the improbable deaths of a half-dozen babies be somehow connected to her own improbable survival?.

Origin: A Biographical Novel of Charles Darwin. unabr. ed. Irving Stone. Read by Dan Lazar. 20 cass. (Running Time: 30 hrs.). Incl. Pt. 1. Origin: A Biographical Novel of Charles Darwin. 9 cass. (Running Time: 13 hrs. 30 mins.). Irving Stone. Read by Dan Lazar. 1980. 72.00 (1547-A); Pt. 2. Origin: A Biographical Novel of Charles Darwin. 11 cass. (Running Time: 16 hrs. 30 mins.). Irving Stone. Read by Dan Lazar. 1980. 88.00 (1547-B); 1980. 160.00 (978-0-7366-0576-2(2), 1547- A & B) Books on Tape.
In "The Origin of the Species", Darwin found himself embroiled in controversy more bitter than any he had imagined. Yet his continuing scholarship & devoted family gave him the equilibrium he needed to complete his life work & defend his theories from their detractors. This is Stone's biographical fiction of Darwin.

Origin & Cause. unabr. ed. Shelly Reuben. Read by Adams Morgan. 8 cass. (Running Time: 11 hrs. 30 mins.). 2002. 56.95 (978-0-7861-2310-0(9), 2996); audio compact disk 80.00 (978-0-7861-9438-4(3), 2996) Blckstn Audio.
Cable-TV mogul Stanfield Standish wrote the book and broke the rules in the news and entertainment industry. When his charred body is found inside the burned-out remains of his classic 1930 Duesenberg sedan, his family files a $52-million damage suit. They blame the fatal "accident" on Courtland Motor Company, the firm that restored the antique. That's when Courtland's attorney, Max Bramble, suspicious, sharp, and inquisitive, takes over. His first move: hire private detective and ace arson investigator Wylie Nolan. If there's a flame, Nolan will discover the source. As Nolan brilliantly dissects the fascinating anatomy of a fire, Bramble digs deep into the Standish empire and discovers that the media tycoon scalded many on his way up the ladder. It's just possible that one of them paid him back with hot-blooded murder, cleverly plotted and fiery in its execution.

Origin & Cause. unabr. ed. Shelly Reuben. Read by Adams Morgan. (Running Time: 11 hrs. 50 mins.). (ENG.). 2009. 29.95 (978-1-4332-9753-3(1)) Blckstn Audio.

Origin & End of Unconsciousness. Swami Amar Jyoti. 1 cass. (Running Time: 1 hr.). 1981. 9.95 (R-33) Truth Consciousness.
Habit of identifying with the changeful, transitory phenomena. Inner mechanism of awakening is already in us.

Origin in Death. abr. ed. J. D. Robb, pseud. Read by Susan Ericksen. (Running Time: 21600 sec.). (In Death Ser.). 2006. audio compact disk 16.99 (978-1-59600-863-2(6), 9781596008632, BCD Value Price) Brilliance Audio.
Please enter a Synopsis.

Origin in Death. unabr. ed. J. D. Robb, pseud. Read by Susan Ericksen. (Running Time: 11 hrs.). (In Death Ser.). 2005. 39.25 (978-1-59710-633-7(X), 9781597106337, BADLE); 24.95 (978-1-59710-632-0(1), 9781597106320, BAD); 82.25 (978-1-59600-170-1(4), 9781596001701, BrilAudUnabridg); audio compact disk 97.25 (978-1-59600-173-2(9), 9781596001732, BriAudCD Unabrid); audio compact disk 36.95 (978-1-59600-172-5(0), 9781596001725, Bril Audio CD Unabri); audio compact disk 39.25 (978-1-59335-955-3(1), 9781593359553, Brinc Audio MP3 Lib); audio compact disk 24.95 (978-1-59335-954-6(3), 9781593359546, Brilliance MP3) Brilliance Audio.

Origin of All Things Pt. I: Lessons 1-8. 7 cass. (Running Time: 7 hrs.). 2000. 33.99 (978-1-55829-152-2(0)) Dake Publishing.
Covers the creation & testing of free moral agents, all about the Bible & how to interpret scripture, reality of God, Satan, angels, demons & other spiritual beings, rebellion & overthrow of the Pre-Adamite world, also the recreation & the second habitation of the earth.

Origin of Biblical Wealth. Taffi L. Dollar. (ENG.). 2006. audio compact disk 21.00 (978-1-59944-074-3(1)) Creflo Dollar.

Origin of Biblical Wealth. Taffi L. Dollar. (ENG.). 2006. 15.00 (978-1-59944-073-6(3)) Creflo Dollar.

***Origin of Civilization.** Instructed by Scott MacEachern. 2010. 249.95 (978-1-59803-627-5(0)); audio compact disk 359.95 (978-1-59803-628-2(9)) Teaching Co.

Origin of Conflict. J. Krishnamurti. 1 cass. (Running Time: 1 hr. 15 mins.). (Krishnamurti & Professor David Bohm - 1980 Ser.: No. 1). 8.50 (ABD801) Krishnamurti.
Krishnamurti & Prof. Bohm offer penetrating, in-depth dialogues which shed light on the fundamental issues of existence.

Origin of Consciousness. unabr. ed. Arthur Young. 1 cass. (Running Time: 1 hr.). 1986. 9.00 (978-1-56964-110-1(2), A0164-86) Sound Photosyn.

Origin of Evil. Chuck Missler. (ENG.). 2008. audio compact disk 19.95 (978-1-57821-419-8(X)) Koinonia Hse.

Origin of Life. Antonio Lazcana. 1 cass. (Running Time: 1 hr.). 9.00 (A0182-87) Sound Photosyn.
With Umberto Eco, at the Origins of Life Symposium, Stanford University.

Origin of Primal Energy. J. Krishnamurti. 1 cass. (Running Time: 1 hr. 15 mins.). (Madras - the Last Talks 1986 Ser.: No. 2). 8.50 (AMT1862) Krishnamurti.
Krishnamurti traveled to India in November, 1985, for the last time. These, his final public talks, were given a little over a month before his death. He addresses the fact that despite the amazing technological achievements of modern times, man has remained, psychologically, the barbarian he was when he first appeared on earth. Krishnamurti maintains that each of us is responsible for the brutality & divisiveness of the society in which we live, a society which is only a reflection of ourselves & as such, incapable of being saved from chaos except through a profound change in each human psyche. His lifelong work is the foundation for his insistence that such a change is possible.

Origin of Species. Charles Darwin. Read by David Case. 2007. 64.99 (978-1-60252-535-1(8)) Find a World.

Origin of Species. unabr. ed. Charles Darwin. Narrated by David Case. 2 MP3-CDs. (Running Time: 17 hrs. 0 mins. 0 sec.). (ENG.). 2008. 27.99 (978-1-4001-5864-5(8)) Pub: Tantor Media. Dist(s): IngramPubServ

Origin of Species. unabr. ed. Charles Darwin. Read by David Case. 14 CDs. (Running Time: 17 hrs. 0 mins. 0 sec.). (ENG.). 2008. audio compact disk 72.99 (978-1-4001-3864-7(7)) Pub: Tantor Media. Dist(s): IngramPubServ

Origin of Species. unabr. ed. Charles Darwin. Read by David Case. 14 CDs. (Running Time: 17 hrs. 0 mins. 0 sec.). (ENG.). 2008. audio compact disk 35.99 (978-1-4001-0864-0(0)) Pub: Tantor Media. Dist(s): IngramPubServ

Origin of Supernatural Increase. Creflo A. Dollar. 2008. audio compact disk 21.00 (978-1-59944-707-0(X)) Creflo Dollar.

Origin of the Milky Way & Other Living Stories of the Cherokee. Ed. by Barbara Duncan. Illus. by Shan Goshorn. (ENG.). 2008. 9.95 (978-0-8078-8674-8(2)); audio compact disk 9.95 (978-0-8078-8676-2(9)) U of NC Pr.

Origin of the World: Deerhead Records Long Poem Series #1. Poems. Lewis Warsh. Read by Lewis Warsh. Ed. by Elizabeth Reddin. Des. by Jeremy Mickel. Music by Sam Hillmer & Christopher Tignor. 2 CDs. (Running Time: 2 hrs.). 2. 2005. audio compact disk 12.00 (978-0-9727684-7-4(5), LP#1) Pub: Ugly Duckling Pr. Dist(s): SPD-Small Pr Dist
Recorded at the Parkside Lounge in New York City on March 26, 2002, as part of the Long Poem Project. This release is a co-production of Deerhead Records and Ugly Duckling Presse.

Original see Healing Pain & Grief: Releasing & Unloading Unnecessary Baggage, Allowing Room for Healing to Take Place

Original see Creating Protection: Protecting Yourself with the Power of Your Own Mind

Original see Harmonizing Your Chakras

Original see Finding Strength & Power Within: Regaining Power & Strength Through Creative Visualization

Original see Harmonizing Your Chakras

Original Adventures of Hank the Cowdog. John R. Erickson. Read by John R. Erickson. 2 cass. (Running Time: 2 hrs.). (Hank the Cowdog Ser.: No. 1). (J). (gr. 2-5). 1989. 16.95 (978-0-87719-132-2(8)) Lone Star Bks.

Original Adventures of Hank the Cowdog. unabr. ed. John R. Erickson. 2 cass. (Running Time: 2 hrs.). (Hank the Cowdog Ser.: No. 1). (J). (gr. 2-5). 2001. 24.00 (978-0-7366-6136-2(0)); 28.00 (978-0-7366-6868-2(3)) Books on Tape.
After being wrongly accused of murder, Hank reigns his position as Head of Ranch Security and joins the outlaw coyotes.

Original Adventures of Hank the Cowdog. unabr. ed. John R. Erickson. Read by John R. Erickson. 2 cass. (Running Time: 3 hrs.). (Hank the Cowdog Ser.: No. 1). (J). (gr. 2-5). 2001. 16.95 (978-0-7366-6260-4(X)) Books on Tape.
After being wrongly accused of murder, Hank resigns his position as Head of Ranch Security & joins the outlaw coyotes.

Original Adventures of Hank the Cowdog. unabr. ed. John R. Erickson. Read by John R. Erickson. Illus. by Gerald L. Holmes. 2 cass. (Running Time: 3 hrs.). (Hank the Cowdog Ser.: No. 1). (J). (gr. 2-5). 1983. bk. 13.95 (978-0-916941-01-7(9)) Maverick Bks.
Full text of Hank the Cowdog's first adventure.

Original Adventures of Hank the Cowdog. unabr. ed. John R. Erickson. Read by John R. Erickson. 2 cassettes. (Running Time: approx. 3 hours). (Hank the Cowdog Ser.: No. 1). (J). 2002. 17.99 (978-1-59188-301-2(6)) Maverick Bks.

Original Adventures of Hank the Cowdog. unabr. ed. John R. Erickson. Read by John R. Erickson. 3 CDs. (Running Time: Approx. 3 hours). (Hank the Cowdog Ser.: No. 1). (J). 2002. audio compact disk 19.99 (978-1-59188-601-3(5)) Maverick Bks.
Guts, glory, danger, and sacrifice are all in a day?s work for Hank the Cowdog, Head of Ranch Security. While investigating a vicious murder on his ranch, Hank finds himself the number one suspect. Resigning in a fit of despair, he heads for the hills to become an outlaw, and a band of ruthless coyotes is happy to teach him the trade. Or are they? They seem to be on his side?until they unveil their plan for a raid on Hank?s ranch! Hank knows he can?t beat them?will he be forced to join them?Hank sings ?How Do I Do It? And Rip and Snort sing ?Me Just A Worthless Coyote.?.

Original Adventures of Hank the Cowdog. unabr. ed. John R. Erickson. Read by John R. Erickson. 2 cass. (Running Time: 2 hrs. 30 mins.). (Hank the Cowdog Ser.: No. 1). (J). (gr. 2-5). 2000. 18.00 (978-0-8072-8238-0(3), Listening Lib) Random Audio Pubg.
Hank has been accused of murder! In a fit of despair, Hank resigns his position as Head of Ranch Security & decides to join the outlaw coyotes. There he's known as Hunk & Missy Coyote, sister to Scraunch - the meanest, roughest, toughest, most notorious coyote in the whole country. If Scraunch found Hank with his sister... well, look out for trouble.

Original Adventures of Hank the Cowdog. unabr. ed. John R. Erickson. 28 cass. (Running Time: 42 hrs.). (Hank the Cowdog Ser.: No. 1). (J). (gr. 2-5). 1998. 404.60 Recorded Bks.
Hank the Cowdog keeps the ranch safe from marauding coyotes, a vampire cat, & other freaky trespassers.

Original Adventures of Hank the Cowdog. unabr. ed. John R. Erickson. Read by John R. Erickson. (Hank the Cowdog Ser.: No. 1). (J). (gr. 2-5). 1998. 17.00 (21631B3) Recorded Bks.

Original Adventures of Hank the Cowdog. unabr. collector's ed. John R. Erickson. 3 CDs. (Running Time: 4 hrs. 30 mins.). (Hank the Cowdog Ser.: No. 1). (J). (gr. 2-5). 2001. audio compact disk 28.00 Books on Tape.
Guts, glory, danger and sacrifice are all in a day's work for Hank the Cowdog, Head of Ranch Security. While investigating a vicious murder on his ranch, Hank finds himself the number one suspect. Resigning in a fit of despair, he heads for the hills to become an outlaw, and a band of ruthless coyotes is happy to teach him the trade. Or are they? They seem to be on his side until they unveil their plan for a raid on Hank's ranch! Hank knows he can't beat them - will he be forced to join them?.

Original Adventures of Hank the Cowdog & the Further Adventures of Hank the Cowdog. unabr. ed. John R. Erickson. Read by John R. Erickson. 6 CDs. (Running Time: 6 hrs.). (Hank the Cowdog Ser.: Nos. 1-2). (J). 2002. audio compact disk 31.99 (978-0-916941-81-9(7)) Maverick Bks.
Guts, glory, danger, and sacrifice are all in a day's work for Hank the Cowdog, head of ranch security. While investigating a vicious murder on his ranch, Hank finds himself the number one suspect. Resigning in a fit of despair, he heads for the hills to become an outlaw, and a band of ruthless coyotes is happy to teach him the trade. Or are they? They seem to be on his side until they unveil their plan for a raid on Hank's ranch!.

Original Adventures of Hank the Cowdog & the Further Adventures of Hank the Cowdog. unabr. ed. John R. Erickson. Read by John R. Erickson. 4 cass. (Running Time: 6 hrs.). (Hank the Cowdog Ser.: Nos. 1-2). (J). 2002. 26.99 (978-0-916941-61-1(2)) Maverick Bks.

Original Black Sabbath. 1 cass. (Running Time: 1.3 hr. 0 mins.). 1987. pap. bk. 99.95 (978-0-8464-4960-7(9)) Beekman Bks.

Original Bluegrass Spectacular - Mandolin Edition. CMH Records Staff. Transcribed by Richard Kriehn. 1998. pap. bk. 29.95 (978-0-7866-4073-7(1), 97018CDP) Mel Bay.

Original Bluegrass Spectacular/Guitar Edition. CMH Records Staff. Transcribed by Flint. 1998. spiral bd. 32.95 (978-0-7866-4071-3(5), 96665CDP) Mel Bay.

Original Child Bomb. Thomas Merton. Read by Thomas Merton. 1 cass. (Running Time: 26 min.). 1962. 11.95 (23052) J Norton Pubs.
Prose reading by Merton.

Original Christianity & Original Yoga. 1 cass. (Yoga & Christianity Ser.). 9.95 (ST-51) Crystal Clarity.
Topics include: The delusion of worldly perfection; how to view beauty & "good works"; the value of orthodoxy; why Christ was a revolutionary; saints as the true custodians of spiritual traditions; the nature of the satanic force.

Original Complete Carnegie Hall Concert. Eddie Cantor. 1 cass. (Running Time: 1 hr.). 1990. (978-1-887958-01-1(0)) B Gari.
One man concert.

Original Cowboy Poets. CMH Records Staff. 1996. 11.98 (978-1-885505-11-8(6)) CMH Records.

Original Folkways Recordings, 1960-1962. Perf. by Doc Watson et al. Anno. by Ralph Rinzler. Contrib. by Matt Walters & Jeff Place. 2 cass. (Running Time: 3 hrs.). 1994. (0-9307-400290-9307-40029-2-6); audio compact disk (0-9307-40029-2-6) Smithsonian Folkways.
Includes 20 previously unreleased performances.

Original Freddie Ackerman. unabr. ed. Hadley Irwin. Narrated by John McDonough. 4 pieces. (Running Time: 5 hrs. 30 mins.). (gr. 5 up). 1997. 35.00 (978-0-7887-0738-4(8), 94915E7) Recorded Bks.
Refusing to spend another summer with his father & step-family, twelve-year-old Trevor Frederick Ackerman moves in with two eccentric great-aunts on an island in Maine, where a tantalizing mystery awaits him.

***Original Gangster: The Real Life Story of One of America's Most Notorious Drug Lords.** unabr. ed. Frank Lucas. (Running Time: 11 hrs. 0 mins.). 2010. 29.95 (978-1-4417-4041-0(4)); 65.95 (978-1-4417-4037-3(6)); audio compact disk 100.00 (978-1-4417-4038-0(4)) Blckstn Audio.

Original Gobible- New International Version: Narrated by Charles Taylor. Created by The GoBible LLC. 2009. audio compact disk 79.95 (978-1-4276-4208-0(7)) AardGP.

Original Man: The Life & Times of Elijah Muhammad. unabr. collector's ed. Claude Andrew Clegg, III. Read by Dick Estell. 11 cass. (Running Time: 16 hrs. 30 min.). 1998. 88.00 (978-0-7366-4372-6(9), 4837) Books on Tape.
The compelling biography of Elijah Muhammad, a man whose religious ideals & political actions have shaped African-American history.

***Original Meanings: Politics & Ideas in the Making of the Constitution.** unabr. ed. Jack N. Rakove. (Running Time: 15 hrs. 30 mins.). 2011. 29.95 (978-1-4417-7025-7(9)); 85.95 (978-1-4417-7022-6(4)); audio compact disk 34.95 (978-1-4417-7024-0(0)); audio compact disk 118.00 (978-1-4417-7023-3(2)) Blckstn Audio.

Original Music to Accompany Destinos. Created by McGraw-Hill Staff. 1999. audio compact disk 20.31 (978-0-07-234649-7(3), 9780072346497, Mc-H Human Soc) Pub: McGrw-H Hghr Educ. Dist(s): McGraw

Original Old-Time Radio Adaptations of the Classic Movies Directed by... Alfred Hitchcock: Notorious; Lifeboat. 2 cass. (Running Time: 2 hrs.). Dramatization. 2002. audio compact disk 11.98 (978-1-57019-480-1(7), 7052) Radio Spirits.

Original Old-Time Radio Adaptations of the Classic Movies Directed by Alfred Hitchcock: Notorious/Lifeboat. Perf. by Alfred Hitchcock. 2 cass. (Running Time: 2 hrs.). 2002. 9.98 (7002) Radio Spirits.
A U.S. spy convinces a woman to marry a Nazi and report on his activities. What will happen when her husband uncovers her betrayal/The survivors of a shipwreck confront the perils of the sea, and each other.

Original Old-Time Radio Adaptations of the Classic Movies Directed by Alfred Hitchcock: Notorious/Lifeboat. Perf. by Alfred Hitchcock & Ingrid Bergman. 2 CDs. (Running Time: 2 hrs.). 2002. audio compact disk 11.98 (7052) Radio Spirits.

Original Old-Time Radio Adaptations of the Classic Movies Directed by Alfred Hitchcock: Shadow of a Doubt/Suspicion. Perf. by Alfred Hitchcock & Cary Grant. 2 cass. (Running Time: 2 hrs.). 2002. 9.98 (7003) Radio Spirits.
A young girl's life is disrupted by the arrival of a favorite uncle, who just might be a serial killer/A bride who suspects her husband is trying to kill her.

Original Old-Time Radio Adaptations of the Classic Movies Directed by Alfred Hitchcock: The Paradine Case/Foreign Correspondent/The Lodger. Perf. by Alfred Hitchcock. 2 CDs. (Running Time: 2 hrs.). 2002. audio compact disk 11.98 (7051); 9.98 (7001) Radio Spirits.
A young widow is accused of killing her husband/American war correspondent finds himself entangled in a web of spies/The forecast episode of Suspense tells the story of the Buntings and their reclusive border. Is there a connection between a recent wave of murders and the Lodger.

Original Old-Time Radio Adaptations of the Classic Movies Directed by... Alfred Hitchcock: The 39 Steps; Spellbound. 2 cass. (Running Time: 2 hrs.). Dramatization. 2002. 9.98 (978-1-57019-405-4(X), 7004) Radio Spirits.

Original Pooh Treasury, Vol. 1 unabr. ed. A. A. Milne. Perf. by Peter Dennis. Illus. by Ernest H. Shepard. 3 cass. (Running Time: 4 hrs. 30 mins.). (J). 1996. bk. 17.00 (978-1-57375-456-9(0), 71294) Audioscope.
Ten stories including: "In Which a House Is Built at Pooh Corner for Eeyore," "In Which It is Shown that Tiggers Don't Climb Trees" & "In Which Tigger is Unbounced.".

Original Pooh Treasury Vol. 2: Eeyore Has a Birthday, Kanga & Baby Roo Come to the Forest, Christopher Robin Gives a Pooh Party. A. A. Milne. Prod. by Peter Dennis. Illus. by Ernest H. Shepard. (J). 1996. bk. 20.00 (978-1-57375-458-3(7)) Audioscope.

Original Prayer. Neil Douglas-Klotz. 8 CDs. (Running Time: 8 hrs 30 mins). 2005. audio compact disk 69.95 (978-1-59179-365-6(3), AF00972D) Sounds True.
Neil Douglas-Klotz has been praised by sources ranging from The Catholic Times to Creation Spirituality magazine as one of today's most visionary new voices in the revival of Christianity's mystical roots. With Original Prayer, this gifted author and translator offers a welcome new work: a meditative journey into one of the most enduring and beloved cornerstones of the Christian faith - the Lord's Prayer.Original Prayer begins by exploring the many rich layers of meaning enfolded within New Testament scriptures written in Aramaic, the language that Jesus and his disciples actually spoke. Through specific insights revealed within the Aramaic Lord's Prayer, listeners learn eight unique body prayers, an ancient Middle Eastern form of meditation that engages the entire body in the contemplation of scripture. This is the same devotional practice used by the early Christians to delve into the Gospels not as a scholarly exercise, but as a living, breathing experience of God.

Original Raps for the All Occasion Kid, Vols. I, II, and III. (J). 2003. pap. bk. (978-0-9745630-0-8(5)) F S Music.

Original Records. CMH Records Staff. 1996. 9.98 (978-1-885505-13-2(2)) CMH Records.

***Original Self.** unabr. ed. Thomas Moore. Read by Thomas Moore. (ENG.). 2005. (978-0-06-089369-9(9), Harper Audio); (978-0-06-089370-5(2), Harper Audio) HarperCollins Pubs.

Original "Shnoozles" Starring in "and Next Came a Roar" Scott Silletta. (ENG.). (J). 2005. 5.99 (978-0-9768852-1-4(2)) Pub: Shnoozles LLC. Dist(s): AtlasBooks

Original Sin. unabr. ed. P. D. James. Read by Penelope Dellaporta. 15 cass. (Running Time: 22 hrs. 30 min.). (Adam Dalgliesh Mystery Ser.). 1995. 120.00 (978-0-7366-3044-3(9), 3726) Books on Tape.
Adam Dalgliesh investigates the grisly murder of a publishing executive. Multiple suspects make maze of possiblities.

Original Sin. unabr. ed. P. D. James. Read by Michael Jayston. 12 cass. (Running Time: 18 hrs.). (Adam Dalgliesh Mystery Ser.). 2000. 79.95 (978-0-7451-6488-5(9), CAB 1104) Pub: Chivers Audio Bks GBR. Dist(s): AudioGO
The Peverell Press is ripe for change since the elder Chairman has just died and his partner has retired, leaving the latter's ruthless son, Gerard Etienne, as Chairman. Etienne has made many enemies, and when he is found dead on the premises, there's no shortage of suspects. Inspector Adam Dalgliesh is soon confronted with a murderer who is prepared to kill again.

Original Sin. unabr. ed. P. D. James. Read by Michael Jayston. 14 CDs. (Running Time: 14 hrs.). (Adam Dalgliesh Mystery Ser.). 2000. audio compact disk 115.95 (978-0-7540-5357-6(1), CCD 048) Pub: Chivers Audio Bks GBR. Dist(s): AudioGO
At the Peverell Press, the Chairman has just died & his partner has retired, leaving the latter's ruthless son, Gerard, as Chairman. Gerard has made many enemies & when he is found dead, there's no shortage of suspects for Adam Dalgliesh to question.

Original Sin. unabr. ed. P. D. James. Perf. by John Franklyn-Robbins. 12 cass. (Running Time: 17 hrs. 75 min.). (Adam Dalgliesh Mystery Ser.). Rental 18.50 (94484) Recorded Bks.

Original Sin. unabr. ed. P. D. James. Narrated by John Franklyn-Robbins. 12 cass. (Running Time: 17 hrs. 45 mins.). (Adam Dalgliesh Mystery Ser.). 2000. 97.00 (978-0-7887-0273-0(4), 94484E7) Recorded Bks.
Commander Adam Dagliesh and his investigative team are confronted with a murder at the offices of of the Peverell Press, one of the oldest of the London publishing houses. Now, they must pursue a killer prepared to strike and strike again.

Original Sinners: A New Interpretation of Genesis. unabr. ed. John R. Coats. Narrated by Richard Allen & Sean Runnette. (Running Time: 10 hrs. 0 mins.). 2009. 16.99 (978-1-4001-8525-2(4)) Tantor Media.

Original Sinners: A New Interpretation of Genesis. unabr. ed. John R. Coats. Narrated by Richard Allen & Sean Runnette. (Running Time: 10 hrs. 0 mins. 0 sec.). (ENG.). 2010. 24.99 (978-1-4001-6525-4(3)); audio compact disk 34.99 (978-1-4001-1525-9(6)); audio compact disk 69.99 (978-1-4001-4525-6(2)) Pub: Tantor Media. Dist(s): IngramPubServ

Original Story of Winnie the Pooh (Read-Along) John Baldry. 1 cass. (Running Time: 1 hr.). (J). 6.38 Blisterpack. (DISN 60279) NewSound.
How an orphaned bear cub from White River, Ontario, Canada was purchased in 1914 by Harry Colebourn, a young army officer en route to World War I, & named for his hometown of Winnipeg.

Original Top Ten. Perf. by Debby Boone et al. 1 cass. (Running Time: 43 min.). 1990. 10.99 (978-0-8499-1276-4(8)) Nelson.
Through their endearing songs, the Kingdom Chums help children learn about the values of love, courage, joy, loyalty & perseverance. The Original Top Ten provides fun for the whole family.

Origination of Something Glorious. 9 cass. 1998. 44.95 (978-1-57972-305-7(5)) Insight Living.

Originator. unabr. ed. Claire Carmichael. Read by Francis Greenslade. 3 cass. (Running Time: 5 hrs. 9 mins.). (gr. 9 up). 2002. (978-1-74030-205-0(2), 500744) Bolinda Pubng AUS.

Origins: The Ego Once- & Twice-Born. Read by Murray Stein. 1 cass. (Running Time: 1 hr. 30 mins.). (Psychological Approach to the Bible Ser.: Pt. I, No. 1). 1988. 10.00 (978-0-7822-0284-7(5), 359-1) C G Jung IL.

Origins & Character of Yiddish. Maurice Samuel. Read by Poetry Center Staff. 1 cass. (Running Time: 52 min.). (On Yiddish Ser.). 1967. 13.00 (23126) J Norton Pubs.
In-depth study of the Yiddish language as a "Frozen History" reflecting the experience of the Jewish people.

Origins & Future of Acupuncture. Ralph Alan Dale. Read by Ralph Alan Dale. 1 cass. (Running Time: 90 min.). 1981. bk. 14.00; 9.00 (16) Dialectic Pubng.
Why acupuncture originated in China & not in the West, the present status & the future of acupuncture.

Origins & Future of Massage. Ralph Alan Dale. Read by Ralph Alan Dale. 1 cass. (Running Time: 45 min.). 1980. 9.00 (8) Dialectic Pubng.
How & why massage began, how it developed, where it is now and where it is going.

Origins & Geographical Diffusion of World Inflation. Robert A. Mundell. 1 cass. (Running Time: 1 hr. 11 min.). (Symposium on the Geographical Aspects of Inflation Ser.: Tape 3 of 5). 10.95 (463) J Norton Pubs.

Origins & Ideologies of the American Revolution. Instructed by Peter C. Mancall. 24 cass. (Running Time: 24 hrs.). 99.95 (978-1-59803-233-8(X)) Teaching Co.

Origins & Ideologies of the American Revolution. Instructed by Peter C. Mancall. 24 CDs. (Running Time: 24 hrs.). 2006. audio compact disk 129.95 (978-1-59803-234-5(8)) Teaching Co.

Origins of Great Ancient Civilizations. Instructed by Kenneth W. Harl. 6 cass. (Running Time: 30 mins). 29.95 (978-1-59803-087-7(6)) Teaching Co.

Origins of Great Ancient Civilizations. Instructed by Kenneth W. Harl. 6 CDs. (Running Time: 60 mins). 2005. audio compact disk 39.95 (978-1-59803-106-5(6)) Teaching Co.

Origins of Life, I-II. Instructed by Robert M. Hazen. 12 cass. (Running Time: 12 hrs.). 2005. 129.95 (978-1-59803-099-0(X)); audio compact disk 69.95 (978-1-59803-101-0(5)) Teaching Co.

Origins of Man. unabr. ed. Robert A. Monroe. Read by Robert A. Monroe. (Running Time: 45 min.). (Explorer Ser.). 1985. 12.95 (978-1-56113-026-9(5), 27) Monroe Institute.
The account of the physical & nonphysical origins of man.

***Origins of the Human Mind.** Instructed by Stephen P. Hinshaw. 2010. 129.95 (978-1-59803-635-0(1)); audio compact disk 179.95 (978-1-59803-636-7(X)) Teaching Co.

Origins of the Human Mind. Edward O. Wilson et al. 2 cass. (Running Time: 2 hrs. 30 mins.). 1996. 17.95 (978-1-879557-35-2(5)) Pub: Audio Scholar. Dist(s): Penton Overseas
Selections from Harvard University Press. In clear, non-technical language, the mind's biological & behavioral roots are traced from their primitive beginnings in our ape-like ancestors to the explosive growth of our modern linguistic-based consciousness.

Origins of the Universe. unabr. ed. Jack Arnold. Read by Edwin Newman. (Running Time: 9000 sec.). (Audio Classics: Science & Discovery Ser.). 2006. audio compact disk 25.95 (978-0-7861-6429-5(8)) Pub: Blckstn Audio. Dist(s): NetLibrary CO

Origins of the Universe. unabr. ed. Jack Arnold. Read by Edwin Newman. Ed. by Jack Sommer & Mike Hassell. 2 cass. (Running Time: 2 hrs. 45 min.). Dramatization. (Science & Discovery Ser.). (YA). (gr. 11 up). 1993. 17.95 (978-1-56823-003-0(6), 10413) Knowledge Prod.
The story of the cosmos - its beginning & its changes through time - has been a topic of much speculation & myth. It also has attracted intense attention from scientists. There are many questions about the unverise's size, stability, growth, & its ultimate cause. This presentation also addresses such colorful cosmic topics as red shifts, white dwarfs, black holes, super strings, & the "big bang".

Origins of Totalitarianism. unabr. ed. Hanna Arendt. Read by Nadia May. (Running Time: 84600 sec.). 2007. 99.95 (978-1-4332-0662-7(5)); audio compact disk & audio compact disk 120.00 (978-1-4332-0663-4(3)) Blckstn Audio.

Origins of Totalitarianism. unabr. ed. Hannah Arendt. Read by Nadia May. (Running Time: 84600 sec.). 2007. 26.95 (978-1-4332-0664-1(1)); audio compact disk 26.95 (978-1-4332-0665-8(X)); audio compact disk 44.95 (978-1-4332-0666-5(8)) Blckstn Audio.

Orkney Murder. Alanna Knight. 2008. 54.95 (978-1-84559-919-5(5)); audio compact disk 71.95 (978-1-84559-920-1(9)) Pub: Soundings Ltd GBR. Dist(s): Ulverscroft US

Orlando. Virginia Woolf. Read by Clare Higgins. 8 vols. (Running Time: 12 hrs.). 2003. 69.95 (978-0-7540-8301-6(2)); audio compact disk 79.95 (978-0-7540-8744-1(1)) Pub: Chivers Audio Bks GBR. Dist(s): AudioGO

Orlando. Virginia Woolf. Read by Laura Paton. (Running Time: 2 hrs. 30 mins.). 1998. 20.95 (978-1-60083-887-3(1)) Iofy Corp.

Orlando. Virginia Woolf. Read by Laura Paton. 2 cass. (Running Time: 2 hrs. 30 mins.). (Modern Classics Ser.). 1994. 34.98 (978-962-634-504-7(7), NA200414, Naxos AudioBooks) Naxos.
Orlando emerges as a young man at the court of Queen Elizabeth I & progresses, with breath-taking ease, through three centuries until, by now, a woman, she arrives in the bustle & diversion of the 1920's.

Orlando. abr. ed. Virginia Wolff. Read by Laura Paton. 2 CDs. (Running Time: 2 hrs. 30 mins.). 1994. audio compact disk 17.98 (978-962-634-004-2(5), NA200412, Naxos AudioBooks) Naxos.
Orlando emerges as a young man at the court of Queen Elizabeth I & progresses, with breath-taking ease, through three centuries until, by now a woman, she arrives in the bustle & diversion of the 1920's.

Orlando. unabr. ed. Virginia Woolf. Narrated by Barbara Rosenblat. 7 cass. (Running Time: 9 hrs. 15 mins.). 1993. 60.00 (978-1-55690-907-8(1), 93403E7) Recorded Bks.
The saga of a character liberated from the restraints of time & sex. Orlando is born as a man in Elizabethan England & is transformed into a woman.

Orleanais ont la Parole. P. Biggs & C. Dalwood. 1977. 14.00 (978-0-582-37885-8(0)) Longman.

Orley Farm, Pt. 2. unabr. ed. Anthony Trollope. Read by Flo Gibson. 6 cass. (Running Time: 8 hrs. 30 min.). 1998. 41.95 Audio Bk Con.
Lady Mason's trial for forgery & for perjury shocks the neighborhood. A cast of unforgettable characters views her with disdain & a few with compassion & there are three love stories.

Orley Farm (Part 1), Vol. 1. unabr. ed. Anthony Trollope. Read by Flo Gibson. 12 cass. (Running Time: 18 hrs.). 1998. 39.95 (978-1-55685-606-8(7)) Audio Bk Con.
Lady Mason's trial for forgery & perjury shocks the neighborhood. A cast of unforgettable characters view her with disdain & a few with compassion.

Orley Farm (Part 2), Vol. 2. unabr. ed. Anthony Trollope. Narrated by Flo Gibson. (Running Time: 8 hrs. 14 mins.). 1999. 24.95 (978-1-55685-830-7(2)) Audio Bk Con.

Orley Farm (Parts 1 And 2) unabr. ed. Anthony Trollope. Narrated by Flo Gibson. (Running Time: 26 hrs. 12 mins.). 1993. 53.95 (978-1-55685-831-4(0)) Audio Bk Con.

Ormond's Favorite Background Music & Breath Control. Ormond McGill. 2 sided cassette. 2000. (978-1-933332-07-9(7)) Hypnotherapy Train.

Ornithine Transcarbamylase Deficiency - A Bibliography & Dictionary for Physicians, Patients, & Genome Researchers. Compiled by Icon Group International, Inc. Staff. 2007. ring bd. 28.95 (978-0-497-11265-3(5)) Icon Grp.

Oromo Newspaper Reader, Grammar Sketch & Lexicon. Yigazu Tucho et al. 1 cass. (Running Time: 1 hr. 30 min.). (MIS.). 1996. 12.00 (3126) Dunwoody Pr.
Thirty-two selections from several representatives of the Oromo in 1994 & 1995. Each selection includes the original text & translation & major sentence constructions are exemplified.

Oroonoko. Aphra Behn. Read by Anais 9000. 2008. 27.95 (978-1-60112-153-0(9)) Babblebooks.

Orphan of Ellis Island. unabr. ed. Elvira Woodruff. (Running Time: 12600 sec.). (Time Travel Adventures Ser.). (J). (gr. 4-7). 2007. 24.95 (978-1-4332-0715-0(X)); audio compact disk 27.00 (978-1-4332-0716-7(8)) Blckstn Audio.

Orphan of Ellis Island: A Time-Travel Adventure. unabr. ed. Elvira Woodruff. (Running Time: 12600 sec.). (J). (gr. 4-7). 2007. audio compact disk 29.95 (978-1-4332-0717-4(6)) Blckstn Audio.

Orphan Star. unabr. ed. Alan Dean Foster. Read by Stefan Rudnicki. (Running Time: 8 hrs.). (Pip & Flinx Ser.: No. 4). 2009. audio compact disk 87.97 (978-1-4233-9554-6(9), 9781423395546, BriAudCD Unabrid) Brilliance Audio.

Orphan Star. unabr. ed. Alan Dean Foster. Read by Stefan Rudnicki. (Running Time: 8 hrs.). (Pip & Flinx Ser.: No. 4). 2009. 39.97 (978-1-4233-9556-0(5), 9781423395560, Brlnc Audio MP3 Lib) Brilliance Audio.

Orphan Star. unabr. ed. Alan Dean Foster & Alan Dean Foster. Read by Stefan Rudnicki. (Running Time: 8 hrs.). (Pip & Flinx Ser.: No. 4). 2009. 24.99 (978-1-4233-9555-3(7), 9781423395553, Brilliance MP3); 39.97 (978-1-4233-9557-7(3), 9781423395577, BADLE); audio compact disk 29.99 (978-1-4233-9553-9(0), 9781423395539, Bril Audio CD Unabri) Brilliance Audio.

***Orphaned Swimming Pool: A Selection from the John Updike Audio Collection.** unabr. ed. John Updike. Read by John Updike. (ENG.). 2009. (978-0-06-196249-3(X), Caedmon); (978-0-06-196250-9(3), Caedmon) HarperCollins Pubs.

Orphans. unabr. ed. Lyle Kessler. Perf. by Kevin Anderson et al. 1 cass. (Running Time: 1 hr. 23 mins.). 1995. 19.95 (978-1-58081-011-1(X), CTA35) L A Theatre.
In a rundown house in Philadelphia live two orphan brothers: the reclusive, frightened Philip & the violent pickpocket thief, Treat. Into this savage & ferociously funny world enters Harold, a shadowy underworld figure of power & influence who irrevocably changes the precious balance between the two brothers. Transforming three lonely individuals into a constellation of needs & desires.

Orphans' Court Litigation. 1988. bk. 130.00 incl. book.; 65.00 cass. only.; 65.00 book only. PA Bar Inst.

Orphans of God. Contrib. by Avalon. (Ultimate Tracks (Word Tracks) Ser.). 2006. audio compact disk 8.98 (978-5-558-27134-8(5), Word Music) Word Enter.

Orphans of History. unabr. ed. Robert Holden. Read by Rhys McConnochie. Narrated by Stanley McGeagh. 3 cass. (Running Time: 6 hrs. 35 mins.). 2004. 28.00 (978-1-74030-564-8(7)) Pub: Bolinda Pubng AUS. Dist(s): Lndmrk Audiobks

Orphans of the Storm. Katie Flynn. (Soundings (CDs) Ser.). 2006. audio compact disk 99.95 (978-1-84559-458-9(4)) Pub: ISIS Lrg Prnt GBR. Dist(s): Ulverscroft US

Orphans of the Storm. unabr. ed. Katie Flynn. Read by Julia Franklin. 12 cass. (Soundings Ser.). 2006. 94.95 (978-1-84559-280-6(8)) Pub: ISIS Lrg Prnt GBR. Dist(s): Ulverscroft US

Orpheus see Poetry & Voice of Muriel Rukeyser

Orpheus, Nos. 54, 55, 56 & 57. Carl Faber. Read by Roy Tuckman. 4 cass. (Running Time: 4 hrs. 35 min.). 1986. 38.00 (978-0-918026-45-3(8), SR 77-717) Perseus Pr.

Orpheus & Eurydice see Poetry of Geoffrey

Orpheus & Eurydice: Journeys to the Underworld. Read by Christine Downing. 3 cass. (Running Time: 3 hrs. 45 min.). 1991. 24.95 (978-0-7822-0059-1(1), 447) C G Jung IL.
Christine Downing, author of "Psyche's Sisters" & "The Goddess: Mythological Images of the Feminine," explores in this workshop the myth of Orpheus & Eurydice & its suggestion that men & women respond differently to underworld experience.

Orpheus Deception. David Stone. Read by Erik Davies. (Running Time: 15 hrs.). (ENG.). (gr. 8). 2008. audio compact disk 39.95 (978-0-14-314302-4(6), PengAudBks) Penguin Grp USA.

Orpheus Emerged. unabr. ed. Jack Kerouac. Read by Grover Gardner. 2 cass. (Running Time: 3 hrs.). 2000. 17.95 (978-0-7366-5924-6(2)) Books on Tape.
Covers love & aesthetics, life versus art, the very ideas that defined the Beat Generation.

Orpheus Emerged. unabr. ed. Jack Kerouac. Read by Grover Gardner. 2 cass. (Running Time: 3 hrs.). 2000. Rental 17.95 (978-0-7366-5901-7(3)) Books on Tape.
Set in a large university, it follows the obsessions, passions, conflicts & dreams of a group of colorful, searching Bohemian intellectuals & liberties.

Orpheus Emerged. unabr. ed. Jack Kerouac. Read by Alexander Adams. 3 CDs. (Running Time: 3 hrs.). 2000. audio compact disk 19.95 (978-0-7366-5902-4(1)) Books on Tape.
In this book about love & aesthetics, life versus art, Kerouac is seen formulating the very ideas that defined the Beat Generation.

Orpheus Lost. Janette Turner Hospital. Read by Edwina Wren. (Running Time: 10 hrs. 15 mins.). 2009. 84.99 (978-1-74214-245-6(1), 9781742142456) Pub: Bolinda Pubng AUS. Dist(s): Bolinda Pub Inc

Orpheus Lost. unabr. ed. Janette Turner Hospital. Read by Edwina Wren. (Running Time: 10 hrs. 15 mins.). 2008. audio compact disk 93.95 (978-1-921334-75-7(4), 9781921334757) Pub: Bolinda Pubng AUS. Dist(s): Bolinda Pub Inc

Orson Welles. unabr. ed. Barbara Leaming. Read by Grace Conlin. 16 cass. (Running Time: 23 hrs. 30 mins.). 1996. 99.95 (978-0-7861-0951-7(3), 1728) Blckstn Audio.
Here is a remarkably detailed picture of the private Welles - from child prodigy & young lion in Dublin & New York, to the succes de scandale of his "War of the Worlds" broadcast & a directing career which began with the legendary "Citizen Kane," made when Welles was only in his twenties; from his affairs, carousing & stormy marriage to Rita Hayworth, to his association with Roosevelt & aspirations to the presidency.

Orson Welles Library. unabr. abr. ed. (Running Time: 14400 sec.). 2007. audio compact disk 19.95 (978-1-4332-0554-5(8)) Blckstn Audio.

Orson Welles Library. unabr. abr. ed. Orson Welles. Read by Orson Welles. (Running Time: 14400 sec.). 2007. audio compact disk 36.00 (978-1-4332-0553-8(X)) Blckstn Audio.

Orson Wells. Read by Orson Welles. 4 vols. (Running Time: 6 hrs.). (Smithsonian Legendary Performers Ser.). 2002. bk. 24.98 (978-1-57019-356-9(8), OTR5030) Pub: Radio Spirits. Dist(s): AudioGO

Orthodox & Roman Catholic Christianity. unabr. ed. Jean Porter. Read by Ben Kingsley. (Running Time: 9000 sec.). (Religion, Scriptures, & Spirituality Ser.). 2006. audio compact disk 25.95 (978-0-7861-6485-1(9)) Pub: Blckstn Audio. Dist(s): NetLibrary CO

Orthodox & Roman Catholic Christianity. unabr. ed. Jean Porter. Read by Ben Kingsley. Ed. by Walter Harrelson & Mike Hassell. 2 cass. (Running Time: 3 hrs.). Dramatization. (Religion, Scriptures & Spirituality Ser.). 1993. 17.95 (978-1-56823-008-5(7), 10451) Knowledge Prod.
These churches have their roots in first century Christianity; their basic doctrines were summarized in the great Councils of the Churches. Yet Orthodox & Catholic life have diverged through the centuries as each embraced different ideas about worship, ethics, & relations to politics & culture. Each faith remains a vital force among large bodies of followers.

Orthodoxy. G. K. Chesterton. 8 cass. 32.95 (312) Ignatius Pr.
Demonstration of the sanity of Christianity.

Orthodoxy. G. K. Chesterton. Narrated by John Franklyn-Robbins. 5 cass. (Running Time: 7 hrs. 15 mins.). 46.00 (978-1-4025-1253-7(8)) Recorded Bks.

***Orthodoxy.** Gilbert Keith Chesterton. (ENG.). 2009. audio compact disk 18.95 (978-1-936231-12-6(3)) Cath Audio.

Orthodoxy. unabr. ed. G. K. Chesterton. Read by Fred Williams. 5 cass. (Running Time: 7 hrs.). 1995. 39.95 (978-0-7861-0871-8(1), 1701) Blckstn Audio.
G. K. Chesterton was a journalist, playwright, poet, biographer, novelist, essayist, literary commentator, editor, orator, artist, & theologia. This is his great theological work, which amounts to an apology for the Christian faith heretofore unequalled, excepting perhaps by C. S. Lewis's "Mere Christianity".

***Orthodoxy.** unabr. ed. G. K. Chesterton. Read by Fred Williams. (Running Time: 7 hrs.). 2010. 29.95 (978-1-4417-4216-2(6)); audio compact disk 69.00 (978-1-4417-4213-1(1)) Blckstn Audio.

Orthodoxy. unabr. ed. G k Chesterton. Narrated by Simon Vance. 1 MP3 CD. (Running Time: 6 hrs. 30 mins. 0 sec.). (ENG.). 2006. lp 19.98 (978-1-59644-357-0(X), Hovel Audio) christianaud.
G.K. Chesterton was a journalist, playwright, poet, biographer, novelist, essayist, literary commentator, editor, orator, artist, and theologian. Orthodoxy is his great theological work, which amounts to an apology for the Christian faith heretofore unequalled, excepting perhaps by C.S. Lewis's Mere Christianity.A serious attack, in 1903, against Christianity by Robert Blatchford, well-known newspaper editor, impelled Chesterton to seize the gauntlet of refutation. His reply was immensely successful and was the early formation of his convincing credo that is so brilliantly and cogently argued in Orthodoxy, a masterwork that was published just five years later.

***Orthodoxy.** unabr. ed. G k Chesterton. Narrated by Simon Vance. (ENG.). 2006. 14.98 (978-1-59644-356-3(1), Hovel Audio) christianaud.

Orthodoxy. unabr. ed. G k Chesterton. Narrated by Simon Vance. 6 CDs. (Running Time: 6 hrs. 30 mins. 0 sec.). (ENG.). 2006. audio compact disk 24.98 (978-1-59644-355-6(3), Hovel Audio) christianaud.

Orthodoxy. unabr. collector's ed. G. K. Chesterton. Read by Bill Kelsey. 8 cass. (Running Time: 8 hrs.). 1996. 48.00 (978-0-7366-3440-3(1), 4084) Books on Tape.
"Orthodoxy" is a work of theology. Although raised in the Church of England, Chesterton converted to Roman Catholicism. Here he resolves the myriad paradoxes of his belief & constructs a convincing credo.

Orthodoxy: Read by Dale Ahlquist. G. K. Chesterton. 2008. audio compact disk 34.95 (978-1-58617-291-6(3)) Pub: Ignatius Pr. Dist(s): Midpt Trade

Orthopaedic Surgery: Multiply Injured Patient. (Postgraduate Programs Ser.: C85-PG7). 45.00 (8517) Am Coll Surgeons.
Presents the surgeon with an approach to the severely traumatized patient. 6 hours CME category 5 credits.

Orthopedic Medical Equipment & Supplies in Switzerland: A Strategic Reference 2006. Compiled by Icon Group International, Inc. Staff. 2007. ring bd. 195.00 (978-0-497-82426-6(4)) Icon Grp.

Orthopedic Surgery: Management of Complications on Spinal Cord Injury. Moderated by Frank J. Eismont. (Postgraduate Courses Ser.: C86-PG 7). 1986. 57.00 (8617) Am Coll Surgeons.
Reviews the most commonly seen complications following spinal cord injury & to present an update of the treatment of these problems. 6 hours CME credit.

Orthostatic Hypotension: Diagnosis & Management. Read by Irwin J. Schatz. 1 cass. (Running Time: 1 hr. 30 mins.). 1986. 12.00 (C8622) Amer Coll Phys.

Orwell. unabr. ed. Michael Shelden. Read by Frederick Davidson. 14 cass. (Running Time: 20 hrs. 30 mins.). 1993. 89.95 (978-0-7861-0393-5(0), 1345) Blckstn Audio.
Shelden's portrait of Orwell is illuminating & compelling. Orwell thrived on contradiction. He called himself a socialist, yet he was always pointing out the weaknesses in socialism. He devoted enormous efforts to writing his novels, yet admitted near the end of his life, "I am not a real novelist anyway." He was an intellectual who ran a small village shop & referred to himself as a "grocer"; he was an ex-policeman who lived among tramps.

Oryx & Crake. Margaret Atwood. 2003. 104.00 (978-0-7366-9388-2(2)) Books on Tape.

Oryx & Crake. unabr. ed. Margaret Atwood. 7 cass. (Running Time: 10 hrs. 30 min.). 2003. 80.00 (978-0-7366-9248-9(7)) Books on Tape.

Osage Dawn. unabr. ed. Darrel Sparkman. Read by Rusty Nelson. 6 cass. (Running Time: 6 hrs. 36 min.). 2001. 39.95 (978-1-58116-047-5(X)) Books in Motion.
Raised by the Osage after his parents were killed at the Battle of Cross Timbers, an adult Matt Crane is now a fur trapper with vengeance on his mind. Childhood rival Quick Killer has raided Crane's home and taken Crane's woman hostage.

Osama Bin Laden I Know: An Oral History of the Making of a Global Terrorist. Peter L. Bergen. Narrated by George Guidall. (Running Time: 60300 sec.). 2006. audio compact disk 34.99 (978-1-4193-7210-0(6)) Recorded Bks.

Osbert Sitwell Reading His Poetry. unabr. ed. Poems. Osbert Sitwell. 1 cass. (Running Time: 1 hr.). Incl. Danse Macabre. (SWC 1013); Elegy for Mr. Goodbeare. (SWC 1013); Fool's Song. (SWC 1013); Four Italian Poets. (SWC 1013); Fox Trot. (SWC 1013); Frieze of Doctors' Wives: Mrs. Humbleby, Mrs. Grandestin, Mrs. Frossart, Mrs. Chivers. (SWC 1013); Great Nemo. (SWC 1013); Journalist's Song. (SWC 1013); Local Press. (SWC 1013); Lousy Peter. (SWC 1013); Mary-Anne. (SWC 1013); Miss Lopez. (SWC 1013); Mr. Harold Colbert. (SWC 1013); Mr. Nutch. (SWC 1013); Mrs. Busk. (SWC 1013); Mrs. Liversedge. (SWC 1013); Mrs. Nutch. (SWC 1013); Mrs. Southern's Enemy. (SWC 1013); Municipal Idyll: A Dialogue. (SWC 1013); Osmund Toulmin. (SWC 1013); Out of the Flame. (SWC 1013); Preface. (SWC 1013); Three Miss Coltrums. (SWC 1013); Winter the Huntsman. (SWC 1013); Wrack at Tide's End. (SWC 1013); 1984. 12.95 (978-0-694-50009-3(7), SWC 1013) HarperCollins Pubs.

Oscar Asked Why? Jan Hulbert. (Metro Reading Ser.). (J). (gr. k). 2000. 8.46 (978-1-58120-995-2(9)) Metro Teaching.

Oscar Brand Celebrates the First Thanksgiving in Story & Song. unabr. ed. Oscar Brand. Perf. by Oscar Brand. 1 cass. (Running Time: 1 hr.). (J). 1984. 9.95 (978-0-89845-480-2(8), CDL5 1513) HarperCollins Pubs.
Oscar Brand presents in story & song real story of the Pilgrims, their origins in England, sailing to America, their encounters with the Indians, famine, & finally, the first Thanksgiving feast.

Oscar Hijuelos. unabr. ed. Óscar Hijuelos. Ed. by James McKinley. Prod. by Rebeah Presson. 1 cass. (Running Time: 29 min.). (On the Air Ser.). 1992. 10.00 New Letters.
Hijuelos reads from Pulitzer-Prize winning novel, The Mambo Kings Play Songs of Love & talks about its transformation into film.

***Oscar Otter.** unabr. ed. Nathaniel Benchley. (ENG.). 2008. (978-0-06-169483-7(5)); (978-0-06-172144-1(1)) HarperCollins Pubs.

Oscar Peterson: Note-for-Note Transcriptions of Classic Recordings! Oscar Peterson. 2000. pap. bk. 39.95 (978-0-9685120-0-5(3), 0968512003) Pub: PG Music CAN. Dist(s): H Leonard

Oscar Peterson with Roy Hargrave. Perf. by Oscar Peterson & Roy Hargrove. 1 cass. . (Running Time: 1 hr.). 7.98 (TA 33399); audio compact disk 12.78 NewSound.

Oscar Wilde. unabr. ed. Frank Harris. Read by Robert Whitfield. 8 cass. (Running Time: 11 hrs. 30 mins.). 1997. 56.95 (978-0-7861-1200-5(X), 1956) Blckstn Audio.
Harris, a journalist & editor, delighted in Wilde's genial wit & self-assurance. He was dazzled by Wilde's epigrams & ability to have "something surprising to say on almost every subject". Wilde's verbal charms evoked Harris' financial & emotional support when Victorian England disdained Wilde for his paganism & imprisoned him for homosexual offenses.

Oscar Wilde, Pt. 1. unabr. collector's ed. Richard Ellmann. Read by David Case. 11 cass. (Running Time: 16 hrs. 30 min.). 1998. 88.00 (978-0-7366-4199-9(8), 4697-A) Books on Tape.

Oscar Wilde, Pt. 2. unabr. collector's ed. Richard Ellmann. Read by David Case. 10 cass. (Running Time: 15 hrs.). 1998. 80.00 (978-0-7366-4200-2(5), 4697-B) Books on Tape.
Almost twenty years in work, Richard Ellmann's Oscar Wilde will stand as the definitive portrait of a conflicted & brilliant life.

Oscar Wilde: Collected Stories, unabr. ed. Short Stories. Oscar Wilde. Narrated by Frank Muller. 3 cass. (Running Time: 4 hrs. 30 mins.). 1986. 27.00 (978-1-55690-397-7(9), 86350E7) Recorded Bks.
Includes: "The Canterville Ghost," "Lord Arthur Savile's Crime," "The Model Millionaire," "The Devoted Friend," "The Happy Prince," "The Nightingale & the Rose," "The Sphinx Without a Secret" & "The Remarkable Rocket".

***Oscar Wilde Collection.** unabr. ed. Oscar Wilde. 2010. audio compact disk 69.95 (978-1-58081-753-0(X)) L A Theatre.

Oscar Wilde Fairy Tales. unabr. ed. Oscar Wilde. Read by Philippe De Montebello. 1 CD. (Running Time: 1 hr. 30 mins.). 2001. audio compact disk 14.00 (978-1-885608-25-3(X)) Airplay.
These classic tales & short stories are filled with spell binding imagery that will enchant adults & young adult listeners.

Oscar Wilde Fairy Tales. unabr. ed. Short Stories. Oscar Wilde. Read by Philippe De Montebello. 1 cass. (Running Time: 1 hr. 30 mins.). 1995. 14.95 (978-1-885608-02-4(0)) Airplay.

Oscar Wilde Fairy Tales: Volumes 1 And 2, Set. unabr. ed. Short Stories. Intro. by Christopher Plummer. 2 cass. (Running Time: 2 hrs.). (Family Classic Audio Books Ser.). 1999. 16.95 (978-1-892613-04-2(2)) NYS Theatre Inst.
Includes "Birthday of the Infanta," "The Happy Prince," "The Selfish Giant," "The Nightingale" & "The Rose.".

Oscar's Hijack. unabr. ed. David Ice & Scott Leslie. Read by Barrett Whitener. Prod. by Jonathan Lowe. Directed By Jonathan Lowe. 1 cass. (Running Time: 1 hr.). 2003. 14.95 (978-0-7861-2385-8(0), 3062); audio compact disk 15.00 (978-0-7861-9295-3(X), 3062) Blckstn Audio.
A truckload of awards destined for Hollywood is hijacked by an escaped convict. To pass their time on the road together, the hijacker and trucker play a tape of mystery stories, but the tape's three tales of revenge influence the driver to do one very crazy thing.

Oscar's Hijack. unabr. ed. Jonathan Lowe. Read by Barrett Whitener. 2004. audio compact disk 14.95 (978-0-7861-9290-8(9)); reel tape 14.95 (978-0-7861-2411-4(3)) Blckstn Audio.

Oscar's Trashy Songs. 1997. 9.98 (Sony Wonder); audio compact disk 13.98 Sony Music Ent.
Oscar the Grouch shares some of his trademark tunes, such as "I Love Trash" & "Grouchelot".

OSHA Bloodborne Pathogens 100 Users. Daniel Farb & Bruce Gordon. 2005. audio compact disk 899.95 (978-1-59491-211-5(4)) Pub: UnivofHealth. Dist(s): AtlasBooks

OSHA Bloodborne Pathogens 25 Users. Daniel Farb & Bruce Gordon. 2005. audio compact disk 299.95 (978-1-59491-209-2(2)) Pub: UnivofHealth. Dist(s): AtlasBooks

OSHA Bloodborne Pathogens 50 Users. Daniel Farb & Bruce Gordon. 2005. audio compact disk 499.95 (978-1-59491-210-8(6)) Pub: UnivofHealth. Dist(s): AtlasBooks

OSHA Compliance Guide, Vol. 9. rev. ed. H. Ray Kirk. Ed. by Jordan Suhrskdt. 2005. audio compact disk 174.50 (978-0-7355-5551-8(6), Aspen) WoltersKlu.

OSHA Compliance Guide CD, Ver 100. rev. ed. H. Ray Kirk. Ed. by Jordan Suhrstedt. 100 CDs. 2006. audio compact disk 174.50 (978-0-7355-5908-0(2), Aspen) WoltersKlu.

OSHA Compliance Guide Version 6.0. Ed. by Summers Press, Inc. Staff. 2002. audio compact disk 135.00 (978-0-7355-3406-3(3), Aspen) WoltersKlu.

OSHA Computer Related Illness. Created by University of Health Care. 2004. audio compact disk 49.95 (978-1-932634-14-3(2)) Pub: UnivofHealth. Dist(s): AtlasBooks

OSHA Control of Hazardous Energy 100 Users. Daniel Farb & Bruce Gordon. 2004. audio compact disk 599.95 (978-1-59491-220-7(3)) Pub: UnivofHealth. Dist(s): AtlasBooks

OSHA Control of Hazardous Energy 50 Users. Daniel Farb & Bruce Gordon. 2005. audio compact disk 329.95 (978-1-59491-219-1(X)) Pub: UnivofHealth. Dist(s): AtlasBooks

OSHA Eye Safety: Introductory but Comprehensive OSHA (Occupational Safety & Health) Training for the Managers & Employees in a Worker Safety Program & Injury Prevention & Vision Care. Daniel Farb. 2004. audio compact disk 49.95 (978-1-932634-27-3(4)) Pub: UnivofHealth. Dist(s): AtlasBooks

OSHA Fire Safety 100 Users. Daniel Farb & Bruce Gordon. 2005. audio compact disk 899.95 (978-1-59491-226-9(2)) Pub: UnivofHealth. Dist(s): AtlasBooks

OSHA Fire Safety 25 Users. Daniel Farb & Bruce Gordon. 2005. audio compact disk 299.95 (978-1-59491-224-5(6)) Pub: UnivofHealth. Dist(s): AtlasBooks

OSHA Fire Safety 50 Users. Daniel Farb & Bruce Gordon. 2005. audio compact disk 499.95 (978-1-59491-225-2(4)) Pub: UnivofHealth. Dist(s): AtlasBooks

OSHA Hazard Communications 100 Users. Daniel Farb & Bruce Gordon. 2005. audio compact disk 599.95 (978-1-59491-217-7(3)) Pub: UnivofHealth. Dist(s): AtlasBooks

OSHA Hazard Communications 50 Users. Daniel Farb & Bruce Gordon. 2005. audio compact disk 329.95 (978-1-59491-216-0(5)) Pub: UnivofHealth. Dist(s): AtlasBooks

OSHA Management Certificate Program: Introductory but Comprehensive OSHA (Occupational Safety & Health) Training for the Manager of an OSHA Program to Help the Administration of a Worker Safety Program, Covering Workplace Violence, Bloodborne Pathogense, Repetitive Strain Injury, Hazard Communications, Hazardous Energy, Medical Recordkeeping, Penalty Policies, & Surviving an OSHA Inspection. Daniel Farb & Bruce Gordon. 2004. audio compact disk 299.95 (978-0-9743674-2-2(7)) Pub: UnivofHealth. Dist(s): AtlasBooks

OSHA Recordkeeping Software: Version 8.0. Jordan Suhrstedt. 2006. audio compact disk 174.50 (978-0-7355-5552-5(4), Aspen) WoltersKlu.

Osha Recordkeeping Software: Version 9.1. 9th rev. ed. Jordan Suhrstedt. 2007. audio compact disk 174.50 (978-0-7355-7664-3(5), Aspen) WoltersKlu.

OSHA Regulatory Documents: A Reference of Federal Documents Pertaining to OSHA Workplace Safety Regulations for All Industries As an Aid to Compliance. Daniel Farb. 2004. audio compact disk 49.95 (978-1-59491-101-9(0)) Pub: UnivofHealth. Dist(s): AtlasBooks
This indispensable reference CD enables you to have the most important OSHA documents from the federal government available in one convenient CD ROM that installs on your hard drive.

OSHA Repetitive Strain Injury: Introductory but Comprehensive OSHA (Occupational Safety & Health) Training for the Managers & Employees in a Worker Safety Program, Covering Ergonomics in Industrial Settings & Computer Injuries among Office Workers. Daniel Farb & Bruce Gordon. 2004. audio compact disk 49.95 (978-1-932634-15-0(0)) Pub: UnivofHealth. Dist(s): AtlasBooks

OSHA Safe Lifting 100 Users. Daniel Farb & Bruce Gordon. 2005. audio compact disk 899.95 (978-1-59491-214-6(9)) Pub: UnivofHealth. Dist(s): AtlasBooks

OSHA Safe Lifting 25 Users. Daniel Farb & Bruce Gordon. 2005. audio compact disk 299.95 (978-1-59491-212-2(2)) Pub: UnivofHealth. Dist(s): AtlasBooks

OSHA Safe Lifting 50 Users. Daniel Farb & Bruce Gordon. 2005. audio compact disk 499.95 (978-1-59491-213-9(0)) Pub: UnivofHealth. Dist(s): AtlasBooks

OSHA Training Guide, Vol. 9. rev. ed. Ed. by Aspen Publishers Staff. 2005. audio compact disk 174.50 (978-0-7355-5553-2(2), Aspen) WoltersKlu.

Osha Training Guide Cd-Rom 7.0 2003. 5th rev. ed. H. Ray Kirk. 2003. audio compact disk 121.50 (978-0-7355-4407-9(7), Aspen) WoltersKlu.

OSHA Training Guide, Version 100. Ed. by Aspen Publishers Staff. 100 CDs. 2006. audio compact disk 174.50 (978-0-7355-5913-4(9), Aspen) WoltersKlu.

OSHA Training Guide, Version 11.0. Ed. by Aspen Publishers Staff. 2007. audio compact disk 197.50 (978-0-7355-6505-0(8), Aspen) WoltersKlu.

OSHA Training Guide Version 6.0. Summers Press, Inc. Staff. 2002. audio compact disk 121.50 (978-0-7355-3410-0(1), Aspen) WoltersKlu.

OSHA Workplace Violence: Introductory but Comprehensive OSHA (Occupational Safety & Health) Training for the Managers & Employees in a Worker Safety Program, Covering Workplace Security. Daniel Farb & Bruce Gordon. 2004. audio compact disk 49.95 (978-1-932634-20-4(7)) Pub: UnivofHealth. Dist(s): AtlasBooks

Oskar Morawetz. Oskar Morawetz. 2004. audio compact disk 15.95 (978-0-662-33315-9(2)) Pub: Canadian Broadcasting CAN. Dist(s): Georgetown Term

Osmund Toulmin see Osbert Sitwell Reading His Poetry

Ossian's Grave see Twentieth-Century Poetry in English, No. 5, Recordings of Poets Reading Their Own Poetry

Ossie Davis. Ossie Davis. 1 cass. (Running Time: 1 hr.). (Author Speaks Ser.). 1991. 14.95 J Norton Pubs.
Archival recordings of 20th-century authors.

Osteogenesis Imperfecta - A Bibliography & Dictionary for Physicians, Patients, & Genome Researchers. Compiled by Icon Group International, Inc. Staff. 2007. ring bd. 28.95 (978-0-497-11266-0(3)) Icon Grp.

Osteoporosis. 2003. audio compact disk 12.95 (978-0-9743448-4-3(2)) NMA Media Pr.

Osteoporosis: Current Trends in Management. Read by Boy Frame. 1 cass. (Running Time: 90 min.). 1986. 12.00 (C8602) Amer Coll Phys.

Osteporosis. Contrib. by Robert L. Barbieri et al. 1 cass. (Running Time: 1 hr.). (American College of Obstetrics & Gynecologists UPDATE: Vol. 23, No. 7). 1998. 20.00 Am Coll Obstetric.

Osterman Weekend. unabr. collector's ed. Robert Ludlum. Read by Michael Prichard. 6 cass. (Running Time: 9 hrs.). 1983. 48.00 (978-0-7366-0802-2(8), 1752) Books on Tape.
In a quiet suburban town a strange assortment of men & women gather for a momentous weekend. Meanwhile in Zurich, Moscow & Washington, the time machine is already ticking. But countermeasures are in motion. In Washington, D.C., John Tanner has already bet his life & the lives of his wife & children in a gamble to destroy the menacing conspiracy that hangs over us all.

Ostrich Boys. unabr. ed. Keith Gray. Read by Bruce Mann. (ENG.). (J). (gr. 7). 2010. audio compact disk 34.00 (978-0-7393-7914-1(3), Listening Lib) Pub: Random Audio Pubg. Dist(s): Random

Oswald. unabr. ed. Dan Yaccarino. Narrated by L. J. Ganser. 1 cass. (Running Time: 15 mins.). (ps up). 2001. 10.00 (978-1-4025-0707-6(0), 96929) Recorded Bks.
Oswald the Octopus is moving to Big City. His pet dog, Weenie, is coming too. All their things are packed in Oswald's big red car, even his piano. But when they get to their new home, they need lots of help moving the heavy piano. By the time Harry the penguin, Daisy the daisy, a snowman, and the Egg Twins help them, Oswald and Weenie have made many new friends. Now everyone is hungry. Can they find something yummy to eat?.

Oswald Bastable & Others. unabr. ed. E. Nesbit. Read by Flo Gibson. 5 cass. (Running Time: 7 hrs.). (J). (gr. 4 up). 1994. 20.95 (978-1-55685-332-6(7)) Audio Bk Con.
Oswald relates a series of adventures as the young Bastables harbour a supposed criminal, organize a bazaar & raffle with an unusual prize, & virtually convict themselves of arson. Other stories of fantasy include such delights as "Moll, the Measles & the Missing Will", "The Princess & the Cat", & "Sir Christopher Cockleshell".

Oswald Chambers: Abandoned to God: the Life Story of the Author of My Utmost for His Highest. unabr. ed. David McCasland. Read by Simon Vance. 8 CDs. (Running Time: 9 hrs. 30 mins. 0 sec.). (ENG.). 2007. audio compact disk 26.98 (978-1-59644-501-7(7), Hovel Audio) christianaud.

***Oswald Chambers: Abandoned to God: The Life Story of the Author of My Utmost for His Highest.** unabr. ed. David McCasland. Narrated by Simon Vance. (ENG.). 2007. 16.98 (978-1-59644-502-4(5), Hovel Audio) christianaud.

Oswald Reflection. unabr. ed. Larry D. Names. Read by Ron Varela. 8 cass. (Running Time: 10 hrs.). 2001. 49.95 (978-1-58116-097-0(6)) Books in Motion.
In 1958 someone stole photos taken by a young U.S. Marine stationed at a top secret U-2 spyplane airbase in Atsugi, Japan. Only they didn't take the film from his camera, including a photo of another Marine believed to be Lee Harvey Oswald. Journalist Tom Regan traces the elusive threads of a government cover-up and double identities while trying to find the missing man in the photo. If the documents Tom discovers are right, a horrific government conspiracy will be revealed.

Ot Hebrew Vocabulary: Learn on the Go. unabr. ed. Jonathan T. Pennington. (Running Time: 2 hrs. 11 mins. 24 sec.). (ENG.). 2003. audio compact disk 22.99 (978-0-310-25492-8(2)) Zondervan.

Ote. 2004. 8.95 (978-1-56008-993-3(8)); 8.95 (978-0-7882-0299-5(5)); cass. & flmstrp 30.00 (978-1-56008-738-0(2)) Weston Woods.

Othello. William Shakespeare. Ed. by Naxos Audiobooks Staff. (Running Time: 3 hrs. 1 min.). (New Shakespeare Audio Ser.). (ENG.). (C). 2000. 27.99 (978-0-521-79470-1(6)) Cambridge U Pr.

Othello. Prod. by William Shakespeare. Hosted by William Shakespeare. 2 CDs. (Running Time: 2 hrs.). 2005. audio compact disk 19.95 (978-0-660-19034-1(6)) Pub: Canadian Broadcasting CAN. Dist(s): Georgetown Term

Othello. William Shakespeare. (Running Time: 3 hrs.). (C). 2004. 23.95 (978-1-60083-888-0(X)) Iofy Corp.

Othello. William Shakespeare. Narrated by Full Cast Production Staff. (Running Time: 2 hrs.). (C). 2006. 14.95 (978-1-60083-048-8(X)) Iofy Corp.

Othello. William Shakespeare. Perf. by Anton Lesser et al. 3 cass. (Running Time: 3 hrs. 30 mins.). Dramatization. (Plays of William Shakespeare Ser.). (YA). (gr. 10 up). 2000. 17.98 (978-962-634-706-5(6), NA320614, Naxos AudioBooks); audio compact disk 22.98 (978-962-634-206-0(4), NA320612, Naxos AudioBooks) Naxos.
Although a swift-paced play, emotion-filled action is not lacking. From love and passion, nobility and purity to deception, tragedy and murder.

Othello. William Shakespeare. Perf. by Dublin Gate Theatre Staff. 1 cass. (Running Time: 1 hr.). Dramatization. 10.95 (978-0-8045-0783-7(X), SAC 7109) Spoken Arts.

Othello. abr. ed. William Shakespeare. Perf. by Cyril Cusack. 2 cass. (Running Time: 3 hrs.). (gr. 9-12). 1995. 18.00 (978-1-55994-730-5(6), CPN 225, Harper Audio) HarperCollins Pubs.

Othello. unabr. ed. William Shakespeare. Read by Anne-Marie Duff & Jasper Britton. Narrated by Don Warrington et al. (Running Time: 10860 sec.). (Arkangel Shakespeare Ser.). (ENG.). 2005. audio compact disk 24.95 (978-1-932219-26-5(9)) Pub: AudioGO. Dist(s): Perseus Dist

Othello. unabr. ed. William Shakespeare. Read by Cyril Cusack & Frank Silvera. 3 cass. (Running Time: 2 hrs. 48 mins.). Dramatization. 18.00 (H152) Blckstn Audio.
Moorish general Othello has earned the gratitude of the city of Venice, the love of Desdemona & the implacable hatred of lago, whose evil insinuations eventually drive Othello to murder & suicide.

Othello. unabr. ed. William Shakespeare. Read by Audio Partners Staff. 2 cass. (Running Time: 3 hrs. 1 min.). (Arkangel Shakespeare Ser.). 2004. 17.95 (978-1-932219-66-1(8), Atlntc Mnthly) Pub: Grove-Atltic. Dist(s): PerseuPGW
Othello's love for his beautiful wife Desdemona is doomed by his lethal jealousy, treacherously stoked by the malignant lago. This great tragedy confronts the mystery at the heart of evil and contains some of Shakespeare's most magnificent dramatic verse. Performed by Don Warrington, David Threlfall, and the Arkangel cast.

Othello. unabr. ed. William Shakespeare. Perf. by Frank Silvera & Cyril Cusack. 3 cass. (Running Time: 4 hrs. 30 mins.). Dramatization. 1984. 26.94 incl. text. (978-0-89845-233-4(3), CP 225) HarperCollins Pubs.
Cast includes: Celia Johnson, Anna Massey, Ernest Thesiger, Abraham Sofaer, James Hayter, David Dodimead, Alan Bates, Robert Stephens, Ronald Ibbs, Wallas Eaton, Donald Eccles, Laurence Hardy, Norman Mitchell, & Margaret Whiting.

Othello. unabr. ed. William Shakespeare. 3 cass. (Running Time: 4 hrs. 30 mins.). 1999. 18.00 (FS9-51074) Highsmith.

Othello. unabr. ed. William Shakespeare. Read by Chiwetel Ejiofor & Ewan McGregor. 2 CDs. (Running Time: 2 hrs. 30 mins.). 2008. audio compact disk 22.98 (978-962-634-929-8(8)) Naxos.

Othello. unabr. ed. William Shakespeare. 2 cass. (Running Time: 3 hrs.). (Arkangel Complete Shakespeare Ser.). 2001. 17.95 (PengAudBks) Penguin Grp USA.

Othello. unabr. ed. William Shakespeare. 2 cass. (Running Time: 2 hrs. 45 mins.). Dramatization. 2000. pap. bk. 34.20 (40744E5); 22.00 (21512E5) Recorded Bks.

Othello, Set. abr. ed. William Shakespeare. Ed. by Naxos Audiobooks Staff. 3 CDs. (Running Time: 3 hrs. 1 min.). (New Shakespeare Audio Ser.). (ENG.). (C). 2000. audio compact disk 29.99 (978-0-521-79471-8(4)) Cambridge U Pr.

Othello: A Full-Cast BBC Radio Drama. William Shakespeare. Read by Arthur Addison. 3 cass. (Running Time: 4 hrs. 30 min.). 2000. 16.95 (978-1-55685-392-0(0)) Audio Bk Con.
Othello, a Moor & commander of the Venetian army, elopes with Desdemona. Duped by lago into believing that she has been unfaithful, he murders her & after learning the truth, kills himself.

***Othello: A Full-Cast BBC Radio Drama.** William Shakespeare. Narrated by Lenny Henry & Full Cast Production Staff. 2. (Running Time: 2 hrs. 0 mins. 0 sec.). (ENG.). 2010. audio compact disk 24.95 (978-1-4084-6691-9(0)) Pub: AudioGO. Dist(s): Perseus Dist

***Othello: A Full-Cast BBC Radio Drama.** abr. ed. William Shakespeare. (ENG.). 2003. (978-0-06-074330-7(1), Caedmon); (978-0-06-079956-4(0), Caedmon) HarperCollins Pubs.

Othello: A Full-Cast BBC Radio Drama. unabr. ed. William Shakespeare. Read by Full Ensemble Cast. (YA). 2006. 34.99 (978-1-59895-627-6(2)) Find a World.

Othello: A Full-Cast BBC Radio Drama. unabr. ed. William Shakespeare. Read by Full Cast Production Staff. (YA). 2008. 54.99 (978-1-60514-834-2(2)) Find a World.

Othello: An A+ Audio Study Guide. unabr. ed. William Shakespeare. (Running Time: 30 mins.). (ENG.). 2006. 5.98 (978-1-59483-714-2(7)) Pub: Hachet Audio. Dist(s): HachBkGrp

Othello: The Audio BookNotes Guide. (Audio BookNotes Guide). (C). 2002. audio compact disk 9.95 (978-1-929011-06-3(7)) Scholarly Audio.

Othello, the Moor of Venice. William Shakespeare. Retold by Alan Venable. (Classic Literature Ser.). 2003. pap. bk. 69.00 (978-1-4105-0008-3(X)); audio compact disk 18.95 (978-1-4105-0196-7(5)) D Johnston Inc.

Other. unabr. ed. David Guterson. Read by Mark Bramhall. (Running Time: 39600 sec.). (ENG.). 2008. audio compact disk 39.95 (978-0-7393-2887-3(5), Random AudioBks) Pub: Random Audio Pubg. Dist(s): Random

Other Boleyn Girl. abr. ed. Philippa Gregory. Read by Ruthie Henshall. (Running Time: 6 hrs. 30 mins. 0 sec.). (ENG.). 2009. audio compact disk 14.99 (978-0-7435-8301-5(9)) Pub: S&S Audio. Dist(s): S and S Inc

Other Daughter. unabr. ed. Lisa Gardner. Read by Laurel Lefkow. 10 vols. (Running Time: 40620 sec.). (Chivers Sound Library). 2000. 84.95 (978-0-7927-2356-1(2), CSL 245, Chivers Sound Lib) AudioGO.
In Texas a serial killer is executed, taking to his grave the identity of his only child. In Boston, a nine-year-old girl is abandoned in a hospital, then adopted by a wealth young couple. Twenty years later, Melanie Stokes has no memory of her life before the adoption, but someone wants to give it back. Even if it includes the darkest nightmare the Stokes family ever faced: the murder of their first daughter in Texas. As Melanie pursues every lead in search of her real identity, it seems that the family she loves the most may be the people she should trust the least.

Other Day the Music Died (2000) 2000. 32.00 (978-1-59128-359-1(0)); 40.00 (978-1-59128-361-4(2)) Canon Pr ID.

Other Dog. Madeleine L'Engle. 1 cass. (Running Time: 12 mins.). (J). (gr. 3-7). 2002. bk. 26.90 (978-0-8045-6893-7(6)) Spoken Arts.
Touche L'Egnle-Franklin is a dog. His mistress went away for several days, and came back with another dog, or was it.

Other Eden. Sarah Bryant. Read by Tara Ward. 9 cass. 2007. 76.95 (978-1-84559-564-7(5)) Pub: ISIS Audio GBR. Dist(s): Ulverscroft US

Other End of Time. unabr. ed. Frederik Pohl. Narrated by George Guidall. 8 cass. (Running Time: 11 hrs.). 1997. 70.00 (978-0-7887-1301-9(9), 95136E7) Recorded Bks.
Depicts a futuristic Earth used as a pawn in a cloning experiment directed by the Beloved Leaders, aliens who are anything but lovable.

Other Eye. Jerry Kennealy. Read by Alan Zimmerman. 4 cass. (Running Time: 360 min.). 2000. 25.00 (978-1-58807-042-5(5)) Am Pubng Inc.

Other Eye. abr. ed. Jerry Kennealy. Read by Charlie O'Dowd. 4 vols. 2001. (978-1-58807-607-6(5)) Am Pubng Inc.

***Other Half of My Heart.** unabr. ed. Sundee T. Frazier. Read by Bahni Turpin. (Running Time: 8 hrs.). (J). 2011. audio compact disk 45.00 (978-0-307-87961-5(5), Listening Lib) Pub: Random Audio Pubg. Dist(s): Random

Other House. unabr. ed. Henry James. Narrated by Flo Gibson. 5 cass. (Running Time: 6 hr. 30 mins.). (gr. 10 up). 1999. 20.95 (978-1-55685-631-0(8)) Audio Bk Con.
About the love of three women for Tony Bream & the tragic death of his daughter is set in two stately homes in the British countryside.

Other House. unabr. ed. Henry James. Read by Frederick Davidson. 2001. 44.95 (978-0-7861-2108-3(4), P2375) Blckstn Audio.
Three women seek to secure the affections of one man, while he, in turn, tries to satisfy them all. But in the middle of this contest of wills stands his unwitting and vulnerable young daughter.

***Other House.** unabr. ed. Henry James. Read by Frederick Davidson. (Running Time: 8.5 hrs. NaN mins.). (ENG.). 2011. 29.95 (978-1-4417-8381-3(4)); audio compact disk 76.00 (978-1-4417-8379-0(2)) Blckstn Audio.

Other Kind of Smart: Simple Ways to Boost Your Emotional Intelligence for Greater Personal Effectiveness & Success. unabr. ed. Harvey Deutschendorf. Read by Fred Stella. (Running Time: 7 hrs.). 2010. 39.97 (978-1-4233-9119-7(5), 9781423391197, BADLE); 19.99 (978-1-4233-9118-0(7), 9781423391180, BAD); 19.99 (978-1-4233-9116-6(0), 9781423391166, Brilliance MP3); 39.97 (978-1-4233-9117-3(9), 9781423391173, Brinc Audio MP3 Lib); audio compact disk 19.99 (978-1-4233-9114-2(4), 9781423391142); audio compact disk 82.97 (978-1-4233-9115-9(2), 9781423391159, BriAudCD Unabrid) Brilliance Audio.

Other Kinds of Treason, Ted Allbeury. Read by Christopher Kay. 8 cass. (Running Time: 12 hrs.). 1999. 69.95 (65239) Pub: Soundings Ltd GBR. Dist(s): Ulverscroft US

***Other Kingdoms.** unabr. ed. Richard Matheson. (Running Time: 10 hrs. 5 mins.). (ENG.). 2011. 29.95 (978-1-4417-7311-1(8)); audio compact disk 29.95 (978-1-4417-7310-4(X)) Blckstn Audio.

***Other Kingdoms.** unabr. ed. Richard Matheson. Read by To be Announced. (Running Time: 10 hrs. 5 mins.). (ENG.). 2011. 65.95 (978-1-4417-7308-1(8)); audio compact disk 100.00 (978-1-4417-7309-8(6)) Blckstn Audio.

Other Lands. unabr. ed. David Anthony Durham. (Running Time: 24 hrs. 0 mins. 0 sec.). (Acacia Ser.: Bk. 2). (ENG.). 2009. audio compact disk 109.99 (978-1-4001-4351-1(9)) Pub: Tantor Media. Dist(s): IngramPubServ

Other Lands: Book Two of the Acacia Trilogy. unabr. ed. David Anthony Durham. (Running Time: 24 hrs. 0 mins. 0 sec.). (Acacia Ser.). (ENG.). 2009. audio compact disk 39.99 (978-1-4001-6351-9(X)); audio compact disk 54.99 (978-1-4001-1351-4(2)) Pub: Tantor Media. Dist(s): IngramPubServ

***Other Life: A Novel.** unabr. ed. Ellen Meister. (Running Time: 9 hrs. 0 mins.). 2011. 34.99 (978-1-4526-0028-4(7)); 15.99 (978-1-4526-7028-7(5)); 24.99 (978-1-4526-5028-9(4)) Tantor Media.

***Other Life (Library Edition) A Novel.** unabr. ed. Ellen Meister. (Running Time: 9 hrs. 0 mins.). 2011. 34.99 (978-1-4526-2028-2(8)); 83.99 (978-1-4526-3028-1(3)) Tantor Media.

Other Lives, Other Selves. Roger Woolger. 4 cass. (Running Time: 6 hrs.). 36.00 (OC107) Sound Horizons AV.

Other Paths to Glory. unabr. ed. Anthony Price. Read by Peter Joyce. 6 cass. 1997. 54.95 (978-1-86015-402-7(6)) T T Beeler.
In 1916, Paul Mitchell's Battalion was nearly wiped out. He is forced to relive the horrific battle when the few survivors begin to die mysteriously.

Other People. Sol Stein. Narrated by Marguerite Gavin. (Running Time: 10 hrs. 30 mins.). 2005. 30.95 (978-1-59912-564-0(1)) Iofy Corp.

Other People. Sol Stein. (Running Time: 10 hrs. 18 mins.). 2005. 65.95 (978-0-7861-3487-8(9)) Blckstn Audio.

Other People. Sol Stein & Marguerite Gavin. (Running Time: 10 hrs. 18 mins.). 2005. 29.95 (978-0-7861-8101-8(X)); audio compact disk 81.00 (978-0-7861-7893-3(0)) Blckstn Audio.

Other People's Children. unabr. ed. Joanna Trollope. Read by Clare Higgins. 8 cass. (Running Time: 12 hrs.). 1999. 59.95 (978-0-7540-0243-7(8), CAB1666) Pub: Chivers Audio Bks GBR. Dist(s): AudioGO
Examines the expanding unit of the step-family & explores the myths, truths & difficulties of trying to deal with present & past relations & other people's children.

Other People's Children. unabr. ed. Joanna Trollope. Read by Clare Higgins. 8 CDs. (Running Time: 8 hrs.). 1999. audio compact disk 84.95 (978-0-7540-5310-1(5), CCD 001) Pub: Chivers Audio Bks GBR. Dist(s): AudioGO
By 2010, there will be more stepfamilies than birth families in Britain, a fact which only emphasizes the importance of Joanna Trollope's intelligent scrutiny. Her new novel concerns that expanding unit, the stepfamily & explores the myths, the truths & the difficulties of trying to deal simultaneously with present relationships, past relationships & above all, other people's children.

Other People's Children. unabr. ed. Joanna Trollope. Narrated by Davina Porter. 7 cass. (Running Time: 10 hrs. 30 mins.). 1998. 66.00 (978-0-7887-3460-1(1), 95883E7) Recorded Bks.
When Josie remarries, she believes she can cope with anything - -until she discovers she is no match for an angry, displaced mother.

Other People's Children. unabr. ed. Joanna Trollope. Narrated by Davina Porter. 9 CDs. (Running Time: 10 hrs. 30 mins.). 2000. audio compact disk 81.00 (978-0-7887-3973-6(5), C1092E7) Recorded Bks.
When Josie remarries, she believes she can cope with anything, until she discovers she is no match for an angry, displaced mother.

Other People's Dirt: A Housecleaner's Curious Adventures. abr. ed. Louise Rafkin. Read by Louise Rafkin. 2 cass. (Running Time: 3 hrs.). 2000. pap. bk. 31.95 Listen & Live.
What started out as a quick way to earn a living became a curious preoccupation with all things clean & messy. An irreverent look at the untidy business of life.

Other People's Dirt: A Housecleaner's Curious Adventures. abr. ed. Louise Rafkin. Read by Louise Rafkin. 2 cass. (Running Time: 3 hrs.). 1997. 16.95 (978-1-885408-23-5(4), LL016) Listen & Live.

Other People's Dogs see Great American Essays: A Collection

Other People's Dreams. unabr. ed. Read by Anne Dover. Perf. by Tessa Barclay. 8 cass. (Running Time: 11 hrs.). 1999. 69.95 (978-1-86042-508-0(9), 25089) Pub: Soundings Ltd GBR. Dist(s): Ulverscroft US
Lindsay Dunforth has battled her way against sexual discrimination to become head of the Investment Portfolio Department of Oistrov Bank, an old & discriminating bank in the City. Against her will, William Tadiescki, a one-time Wall Street dealer, is employed as Research Analyst in her department, at a time when banking is unsettled due to Britain's possible entry into the European currency. Soon afterwards she receives a photo of

her daughter with the words 'Back Off.' She discovers that someone has accessed her personal file & that there have been several irregularities in two investment accounts. Then someone breaks into her house & leaves a more serious warning.

Other People's Habits Audiobook: How to use Positive Reinforcement to Bring Out the Best in People Around You. Aubrey C. Daniels. (ENG.). 2006. audio compact disk 29.95 (978-0-937100-15-8(3)) Perf Manage.

Other People's Husbands. Judy Astley. 2009. 61.95 (978-0-7531-3326-2(1)); audio compact disk 79.95 (978-0-7531-3327-9(X)) Pub: Isis Pubng Ltd GBR. Dist(s): Ulverscroft US

Other People's Marriages. unabr. ed. Rosie Thomas. Read by Rula Lenska. 12 cass. (Running Time: 12 hrs.). 1996. 96.95 (978-0-7451-6722-0(5), CAB 1338) AudioGO.

They were five families: the hospitable Frosts; the brash & sexy Cleggs; flirtatious Jimmy & aloof Star; the reliable Ransoms; & the perfect Wickhams. Old friends, their lives are interwoven through comfortable patterns of life. Then rich, sophisticated & newly widowed Nina Cort returns to her childhood city. In the course of a year, the five families & Nina discover you can never truly know the fabric of other people's marriages.

Other Places, Other Times: Late Nineteenth Century & Early Twentieth Century British & European Short Stories. Anton Chekhov et al. 6 cass. (Running Time: 6 hrs.). (AudioDrama 101 Ser.: Vol. 5). 2001. 14.95 (978-1-892077-04-2(3)) Lend A Hand.

Each story is introduced with a brief biographical sketch of the writer, and most are retold in thirty minutes or less. The way the stories are presented is reminiscent of old-time radio dramas. The twenty voices featured are varied and expressive. Background music is added.

Other Queen. abr. ed. Philippa Gregory. Read by Bianca Amato et al. (Running Time: 6 hrs.). 2008. 17.95 (978-0-7435-7107-4(X)) Pub: S&S Audio. Dist(s): S and S Inc

Other Queen. abr. ed. Philippa Gregory. Read by Bianca Amato et al. (Running Time: 6 hrs. 0 mins. 0 sec.). (ENG.). 2010. audio compact disk 14.99 (978-1-4423-0473-4(1)) Pub: S&S Audio. Dist(s): S and S Inc

Other Queen. unabr. ed. Philippa Gregory. Read by Stina Nielsen et al. (Running Time: 16 hrs.). 2008. 61.75 (978-1-4361-6486-3(9)); audio compact disk 123.75 (978-1-4361-2174-3(4)) Recorded Bks.

Other Side. Mary Gordon. Read by Mary Gordon. Prod. by Moveable Feast Staff. 1 cass. (Running Time: 30 min.). 8.95 (AMF-220) Am Audio Prose.

Gordon reads from her novel "The Other Side" & talks about the history of the American labor movement & the Irish immigrant experience.

Other Side. Jacqueline Woodson. Narrated by Susan Spain. (Running Time: 15 mins.). 2001. 10.00 (978-1-4025-4238-1(0)) Recorded Bks.

Other Side of "And" Series. Kenneth W. Hagin, Jr. 3 cass. 12.00 (15J) Faith Lib Pubns.

Other Side of Dark. Joan Lowery Nixon. Narrated by Christina Moore. 4 CDs. (Running Time: 4 hrs. 45 mins.). (gr. 9 up). audio compact disk 39.00 (978-0-7887-6159-1(5)) Recorded Bks.

Other Side of Dark. unabr. ed. Joan Lowery Nixon. Narrated by Christina Moore. 4 pieces. (Running Time: 4 hrs. 45 mins.). (gr. 9 up). 2001. 39.00 (978-0-7887-4714-4(2), 96362E7) Recorded Bks.

Suzy wakes up in a hospital bed to learn that she has spent the last four years in a catatonic state. She finds herself struggling to adjust & fighting to remember what happened to her. She is the only witness to a shooting that took her mother's life & left her injured.

Other Side of Dark. unabr. ed. Joan Lowery Nixon. Narrated by Christina Moore. 4 cass. (Running Time: 4 hrs. 45 mins.). (YA). (gr. 9-12). 2001. pap. bk. & stu. ed. 52.75 Recorded Bks.

Other Side of Dark. unabr. ed. Joan Lowery Nixon. Narrated by Christina Moore. 4 CDs. (Running Time: 4 hrs. 45 min.). (YA). (gr. 9-12). 2001. audio compact disk 39.00 (C1383) Recorded Bks.

Thirteen-year-old Stacy is sun-bathing in the back-yard when she hears a strange noise. Turning to look, she sees a man with a gun burst through the door; then everything goes black. She wakes up in a hospital bed to learn that she has spent the last four years in a catatonic state. Suddenly 17, she finds herself struggling to adjust & fighting to remember what happened to her. She is the only witness to the shooting that injured her & killed her mother. Slowly more details of that awful day come back. She knows that it was someone familiar to her, but she can?t quite see his face yet. Can Stacy remember in time to keep him from finishing what he started?.

Other Side of Darkness: Derek Jensen's Talks on His Published Works. Derrick Jensen. 3 vols. (Running Time: 2 hrs. 40 mins.). (Politics of the Living Book Ser.). (ENG.). 2005. audio compact disk 25.00 (978-1-931498-59-3(8)) Chelsea Green Pub.

Other Side of Dawn. John Marsden. Read by Suzi Dougherty. 5 cass. (Running Time: 7 hrs. 30 mins.). 2001. (500119) Bolinda Pubng AUS.

***Other Side of Dawn.** John Marsden. Read by Suzi Dougherty. (Running Time: 9 hrs. 30 mins.). (Tomorrow Ser.). (YA). 2009. 64.99 (978-1-74214-339-2(3), 9781742143392) Pub: Bolinda Pubng AUS. Dist(s): Bolinda Pub Inc

Other Side of Dawn. unabr. ed. John Marsden. Read by Suzi Dougherty. 5 cass. (Running Time: 9 hrs. 30 mins.). (Tomorow Ser.). 2000. 40.00 (978-1-74030-088-9(2)) Pub: Bolinda Pubng AUS. Dist(s): Bolinda Pub Inc

Other Side of Dawn. unabr. ed. John Marsden. Read by Suzi Dougherty. 8 CDs. (Running Time: 9 hrs. 30 mins.). (Tomorrow Ser.). 2001. audio compact disk 87.95 (978-1-74030-402-3(0)) Pub: Bolinda Pubng AUS. Dist(s): Bolinda Pub Inc

Other Side of Dawn. unabr. ed. John Marsden. Read by Suzi Dougherty. (Running Time: 34200 sec.). (Tomorrow Ser.). 2008. audio compact disk 43.95 (978-1-921415-35-7(5), 9781921415357) Pub: Bolinda Pubng AUS. Dist(s): Bolinda Pub Inc

Other Side of Life: A Discussion on Death, Dying & Graduation of the Soul. Sylvia Browne. 2 CDs. (Running Time: 3 hrs.). 1999. audio compact disk 16.95 (978-1-56170-746-1(5), 4054) Hay House.

Discusses many issues related to death, dying & the other side.

Other Side of Love: Handling Anger in a Godly Way. Gary Chapman. Ed. by Jim Vincent. Pref. by Andrew Bee. 2 cass. (Running Time: 3 hrs. 10 mins.). (ENG.). 1999. 14.99 (978-0-8024-6778-2(4)) Moody.

Anger is a universal human experience. For many of us, it is the single greatest challenge in every area of our lives. We have been taught that anger itself is a sin and should be avoided at all costs. However, anger is also understood to be 'nature's way' of preparing man to respond in times of danger. How then do we go about bringing this volatile emotion under the Lordship of Jesus Christ? Gary Chapman gives us the perfect tool to answer this and many other questions in The Other Side of Love. In this book, he takes a fresh look at the origin and purpose of anger. Asserting that anger is rooted in the holy nature of God, he reverently explains that anger flows from God's holiness and love. Gary Chapman draws on his extensive counseling experience to instruct us how to positively process our anger. This will help us to create and further cultivate healthy relationships. Helpful study questions for group or personal use conclude each chapter. Don't let anger get the best of you. Victory begins with understanding. Now is the time to make this critical investment in your walk with Christ.

Other Side of Me. abr. ed. Sidney Sheldon. (ENG.). 2005. 14.98 (978-1-59483-268-0(4)) Pub: Hachet Audio. Dist(s): HachBkGrp

Other Side of Midnight. unabr. ed. Scripts. Sidney Sheldon. Read by Steven Pacey. 10 cass. (Running Time: 15 hrs.). 2004. 37.95 (978-1-59007-383-4(5)) Pub: New Millenn Enter. Dist(s): PerseuPGW

Other Side of Silence. unabr. ed. Bill Pronzini. Read by Nick Sullivan. 6 CDs. (Running Time: 7 hrs. 30 mins.). 2008. audio compact disk 64.95 (978-0-7927-5648-4(7), Chivers Sound Lib) AudioGO.

Other Side of Sorrow. unabr. ed. Peter Corris. Read by Peter Hosking. 4 cass. (Running Time: 4 hrs. 35 mins.). 2001. (978-1-74030-139-8(0), 500530) Bolinda Pubng AUS.

Other Side of the Dale. unabr. ed. Gervase Phinn. Read by Gervase Phinn. 6 cass. (Running Time: 9 hrs.). 1999. 54.95 (978-0-7531-0438-5(5), 980805) Pub: ISIS Audio GBR. Dist(s): Ulverscroft US

Phinn is appointed a school inspector in North Yorkshire. His stories, full of warmth, wisdom & wit, are brought together in this collection set against the backdrop of the beautiful Yorkshire Dales.

Other Side of the Dale. unabr. ed. Gervase Phinn. 7 CDs. (Isis (CDs) Ser.). (J). 2005. audio compact disk 71.95 (978-0-7531-2346-1(0)) Pub: ISIS Lrg Prnt GBR. Dist(s): Ulverscroft US

***Other Side of the Door.** unabr. ed. Nicci French. Read by Anne Flosnik. (Running Time: 10 hrs.). 2010. 39.97 (978-1-4233-4381-3(6), 9781423343813, Brlnc Audio MP3 Lib); 24.99 (978-1-4233-4380-6(8), 9781423343806, Brilliance MP3); 24.99 (978-1-4233-4382-0(4), 9781423343820, BAD); 39.97 (978-1-4233-4383-7(2), 9781423343837, BADLE); audio compact disk 29.99 (978-1-4233-4378-3(6), 9781423343783, Bril Audio CD Unabri); audio compact disk 82.97 (978-1-4233-4379-0(4), 9781423343790, BriAudCD Unabrid) Brilliance Audio.

Other Side of the River. unabr. ed. Jessica Blair. Read by Marie McCarthy. 9 cass. (Running Time: 12 hr.). 1998. 90.95 (978-1-85903-201-5(X)) Ulvrscrft Audio.

A tale of courage triumphing over adversity.

***Other Side of the Story.** unabr. ed. Marian Keyes. Read by Terry Donnelley. (ENG.). 2004. (978-0-06-079797-3(5), Harper Audio); (978-0-06-081788-6(7), Harper Audio) HarperCollins Pubs.

Other Side of Things: No. 9 in the River Road Poetry Series. Vivian Smith. Read by Vivian Smith. Executive Producer Carol Jenkins. Judith Martinez. (ENG.). 2008. audio compact disk 18.00 (978-0-9804148-8-2(1)) RivRoad AUS.

Other Than Blue. unabr. ed. Read by Dave Kenney. Perf. by Dave Kenney. Ed. by Randy Beres & Charles Beres. 1 cass. (Running Time: 48 min.). 1994. 9.98 (978-1-883152-04-8(6)); audio compact disk 15.95 CD. (978-1-883152-05-5(4)) Amirra Pr.

Dolphin sounds laced with original instrumental compositions.

Other Times, Other Places. abr. ed. AIO Team Staff. Created by Focus on the Family Staff & Marshal Younger. 4 cass. (Adventures in Odyssey Gold Ser.). (ENG.). (J). (gr. 3-7). 2005. audio compact disk 24.99 (978-1-58997-286-5(4)) Pub: Focus Family. Dist(s): Tyndale Hse

Other Two see Women in Literature, the Short Story: A Collection

Other Two see White Heron

Other Two. unabr. ed. Edith Wharton. Read by Susan McInerney. 2 cass. (Running Time: 2 hrs. 28 min.). (Edith Wharton Ser.). 1994. bk. 16.95 (978-1-883049-12-6(1)); lib. bdg. 18.95 (978-1-883049-35-5(0)) Sound Room.

A collection of New York stories: "The Other Two", "The Dilettante", & "Autres Temps". Includes vinyl case with notes, author's picture and biography.

Other Vowel Sounds & Consonant Spellings, Level 4. (Laubach Way to Reading Ser.). 1993. 12.00 (978-0-88336-917-3(6)) New Readers.

Other Way to Listen. Byrd Baylor. 1 cass. (Running Time: 1 hr. 30 mins.). (J). (gr. k-6). 1988. 5.95 (978-0-929937-03-8(1)) SW Series.

A young boy & an old man walk in the hills. The boy learns to hear in a special way.

***Other Wes Moore: One Name, Two Fates.** unabr. ed. Wes Moore. Read by Wes Moore. Afterword by Tavis Smiley. 2010. audio compact disk 35.00 (978-0-307-87713-0(2), Random AudioBks) Pub: Random Audio Pubg. Dist(s): Random

Other Wise Man. Henry Van Dyke. 1 CD. (Running Time: 59min 1sec). 2004. pap. bk. 11.95 (978-1-932226-34-8(6)) Pub: Wizard Acdmy. Dist(s): Baker Taylor

Written by clergyman/poet Henry van Dyke in 1896, The Other Wise Man begins thusly:?You know the story of the Three Wise Men of the East, and how they traveled from far away to offer their gifts at the manger-cradle in Bethlehem. But have you ever heard the story of the Other Wise Man, who also saw the star in its rising, and set out to follow it, yet did not arrive with his brethren in the presence of the young child Jesus? Of the great desire of this fourth pilgrim, and how it was denied, yet accomplished in the denial; of his many wanderings and the probations of his soul; of the long way of his seeking and the strange way of his finding the One whom he sought - I would tell the tale as I have heard fragments of it in the Hall of Dreams, in the palace of the Heart of Man??This 1-hour audiobook contains the complete text of Henry van Dyke?s original story, artfully brought to life by a colorful cast of characters under the direction of David Nevland.Two roads diverged in a wood, and I?I took the one less traveled by,And that has made all the difference.- Robert Frost, The Road Not Taken, 1920?In choosing one path we ignore others. And wonder what might have been.? ? Binnesman, the Wise Man, (wise-ard, wisard, wizard) DATE UNKNOWN"Wisdom is the principal thing, therefore get wisdom. And with all thy getting, get understanding." ? Solomon, the first Wisard, 970 BC to 928 BCSee how from far, upon the eastern road,The star-led wizards haste with odours sweet:O run, prevent them with thy humble ode, And lay it lowly at His blessed feet.? John Milton, Ode On the Morning of Christ's Nativity, (Dec. 25, 1629) his seminal writing effort, 38 years before Paradise Lost, (1667)WizardFunction: nounEtymology: Middle English wysard, from wis, wys wise 1 archaic: a wise man, wise-ard, wis-ard: one who knows what ?that star' means.Includes:59min 1sec Audio CD54 page booklet.

Other Woman. abr. ed. Eric Jerome Dickey. Read by Kimberly Bailey. 2003. audio compact disk 29.95 (978-0-06-052464-7(2)) HarperCollins Pubs.

Other Woman: My Years with O. J. Simpson. abr. ed. Paula Barbieri. (ENG.). 2006. 9.99 (978-1-59483-839-2(9)) Pub: Hachet Audio. Dist(s): HachBkGrp

Other Women. unabr. ed. Margaret Bacon. 7 cass. 1998. 76.95 (978-1-85903-120-9(X)) Pub: Magna Story GBR. Dist(s): Ulverscroft US

Other Worlds. Elmer Green et al. 2 cass. (Running Time: 2 hrs. 30 min.). 19.95 (29366-29367) J Norton Pubs.

Aspects of consciousness previously ignored are coming under closer scrutiny. The rational, linear Western mind is opening itself to intuition & psychic perception.

***Other Worlds.** abr. ed. Barbara Michaels, pseud. Read by Barbara Rosenblat. (ENG.). 2005. (978-0-06-088896-1(2), Harper Audio); (978-0-06-088895-4(4), Harper Audio) HarperCollins Pubs.

Other Worlds. abr. ed. Barbara Michaels, pseud. Read by Barbara Rosenblat. 2 cass. (Running Time: 3 hrs.). 1999. 18.00 (FS9-43318) Highsmith.

Other Worlds. unabr. ed. Barbara Michaels, pseud. Narrated by Barbara Rosenblat. 5 cass. (Running Time: 7 hrs.). 1999. 49.00 (978-0-7887-3100-6(9), 95811E7) Recorded Bks.

Enter the sacrosanct territory of an exclusive men's club at the turn of the 20th century & join such illustrious guests as Harry Houdini & Sir Arthur Conan Doyle in their attempts to explain two unsolved ghost stories.

Other 1492: Ferdinand, Isabella, & the Making of an Empire. Instructed by Teofilo Ruiz. 6 cass. (Running Time: 6 hrs.). bk. 29.95 (978-1-56585-455-0(1), 899); bk. 39.95 (978-1-56585-509-0(4), 899) Teaching Co.

Other 90% How to Work Your Vast Untapped Potential for Leadership & Life. Robert K. Cooper. Narrated by Brian Keeler. 6 cass. (Running Time: 9 hrs.). 62.00 (978-1-4025-1857-7(9)) Recorded Bks.

Others. Read by Robert Powell. 2 cass. (Running Time: 3 hrs.). 2001. 16.99 (978-0-333-76586-9(9)) Pub: Macmillan UK GBR. Dist(s): Trafalgar

The book begins in the bowels of Hell. In this fiery underworld we meet a former Hollywood movie star, thrust there for a lifetime of depravity. But now this damned soul is given one more shot at redemption, a chance to live again as a human. Begging for a new judgment, he is sent back to earth, without memory of his past life or death. However, his new existence will be a wretched one, living in the body of Nicholas Dismas, a brilliant and tender-hearted private investigator sadly afflicted with horrendous physical deformities.

Others. unabr. ed. James Herbert. Read by Ric Jerrom. 14 cass. (Running Time: 21 hrs.). 2000. 110.95 (978-0-7540-0439-4(2), CAB 1862) Pub: Chivers Audio Bks GBR. Dist(s): AudioGO

Otherwise Engaged. abr. ed. Suzanne Finnamore. Read by Linda Hamilton. 2 cass. (Running Time: 3 hrs.). 1999. 18.00 (FS9-43424) Highsmith.

***Otherwise Engaged.** unabr. ed. Suzanne Brockmann. Narrated by Susan Boyce. 5 CDs. (Running Time: 6 hrs.). 2009. audio compact disk 59.95 (978-0-7927-6356-7(4)) AudioGO.

Otherwise Known As Sheila the Great. Judy Blume. Read by Judy Blume. 2 cass. (Running Time: 3 hrs. 10 mins.). (Fudge Ser.). (J). 2000. 18.00 (978-0-7366-9161-1(8)) Books on Tape.

Sheila Tubman the "Cootie Queen," spends the summer facing her worst fears.

Otherwise Known As Sheila the Great. unabr. ed. Judy Blume. Read by Judy Blume. 2 vols. (Running Time: 2 hrs. 45 mins.). (Fudge Ser.). (J). (gr. 3-7). 1997. pap. bk. 29.00 (978-0-8072-7646-4(4), YA912CX, Listening Lib) Random Audio Pubg.

Sheila wonders who she is: the capable Sheila the Great or the secret Sheila who will be spending the summer facing some of her worse fears.

Otherwise Known As Sheila the Great. unabr. ed. Read by Judy Blume. Ed. by Judy Blume. 2 cass. (Running Time: 2 hrs. 45 mins.). (Fudge Ser.). (J). 1997. pap. bk. 23.00 (978-0-8072-7647-1(2), YA912SP, Listening Lib) Random Audio Pubg.

During a summer in New York, Sheila learns a great deal about herself & how to overcome her feelings of inferiority.

Otherwise Known as Sheila the Great. unabr. ed. Judy Blume. Read by Judy Blume. (Running Time: 9900 sec.). (Fudge Ser.). (ENG.). (J). (gr. 3-7). 2007. audio compact disk 19.95 (978-0-7393-5625-8(9), Listening Lib) Pub: Random Audio Pubg. Dist(s): Random

Otis Spofford. Beverly Cleary. Read by Johnny Heller. 2 cass. (Running Time: 2 hrs. 30 mins.). (J). 2000. pap. bk. & stu. ed. 34.24 (978-0-7887-4181-4(0), 47089); stu. ed. 91.70 (978-0-7887-4182-1(9), 47089) Recorded Bks.

The only thing Otis loves more than stirring up a little excitement at school is teasing Ellen. Otis has been warned that one day he'll get his "come-uppance." He's not sure what that means but the day he plays "Indian" with Ellen he knows he is going to find out. Teaches that there is a fine line between good-natured fun & being a bully.

***Otis Spofford.** unabr. ed. Beverly Cleary. Read by Johnny Heller. (ENG.). 2009. (978-0-06-176243-7(1)); (978-0-06-180536-3(X)) HarperCollins Pubs.

Otis Spofford. unabr. ed. Beverly Cleary. Narrated by Johnny Heller. 2 pieces. (Running Time: 2 hrs.). (gr. 2 up). 2000. 21.00 (978-0-7887-4007-7(5), 94219E7) Recorded Bks.

Otorhinolaryngology: Base-of-Skull Tumors. Moderated by Sam E. Kinney. 6 cass. (Running Time: 6 hrs.). (Postgraduate Courses Ser.: C86-PG14). 1986. 57.00 (8624 (C86-PG14)) Am Coll Surgeons.

Presents surgical approaches to tumors involving the anterior & posterior skull base. 6 hours CME credit.

Otorhinolaryngology: Tumors of the Nasal Cavity & Sinuses. (Postgraduate Programs Ser.: C85-PG14). 45.00 (8524) Am Coll Surgeons.

Covers review of the benign & malignant nasal & paranasal sinus neoplasms, including their management by surgery, radiotherapy & chemotherapy. 6 hours CME category 5 credits.

Otorhinolaryngology: Vascular Tumors of the Head & Neck. (Postgraduate Programs Ser.: C84-PG14). 1984. 45.00 (8494) Am Coll Surgeons.

Provides a review of the contemporary methods of diagnosis & management of vascular tumors of the head & neck.

Otorom, Interactive Middle Ear Pathology & Surgical Procedures, No. 1. Vincent. 1996. pap. bk. 175.00 (978-0-7506-3063-4(9), Butter Sci Hein) Sci Tech Bks.

Otospondylomegaepiphyseal Dysplasia - A Bibliography & Dictionary for Physicians, Patients, & Genome Researchers. Compiled by Icon Group International, Inc. Staff. 2007. ring bd. 28.95 (978-0-497-11267-7(1)) Icon Grp.

OTR Goes Golfing. 2 CDs. (Running Time: 2 Hrs.). bk. 15.95 (978-1-57816-158-4(4), DFG906) Audio File.

For golfers, duffers, caddies, even golf widows, here's a selection of vintage programs from the Golden Age of Radio! Benny (03/22/42), Gildersleeve (09/06/42), Gangbusters (1940's), Boston Blackie (1940's).

Otra Onda. unabr. ed. 2000. audio compact disk 19.99 (978-0-8297-2564-3(4)) Zondervan.

Otra Onda. unabr. ed. Zondervan Publishing Staff. (SPA.). 2000. 9.99 (978-0-8297-2563-6(6)) Pub: Vida Pubs. Dist(s): Zondervan

***Ott on a Limb.** Susan Dunlap. 2009. (978-1-60136-544-6(6)) Audio Holding.

Otter see Poetry & Voice of Ted Hughes

Otter & Rabbit. Alice Damon. (YA). 1999. audio compact disk 10.00 (978-1-4276-1116-1(5)) AardGP.

Otter on His Own. 1 cass. (Running Time: 35 min.). (J). (gr. k-4). 2001. pap. bk. 19.95 (SP 4005C) Kimbo Educ.

Mom teaches her otter pup to dive, eat & play.

Otter on His Own: The Story of a Sea Otter. Doe Boyle. Illus. by Lisa Bonforte. Narrated by Peter Thomas. 1 cass. (Smithsonian Oceanic

Collection). (J). (ps-2). 1995. 5.00 (978-1-56899-134-4(7), C4005) Soundprints.
Boldly illustrated, this story introduces Sea Otter Pup, newly born & eager to learn. Mother teaches him to dive, eat, & play among the kelp of a sheltered Pacific cove. One day Pup swims past the rocky point. Danger lurks. Will Pup be prepared?.

Otterian Quartet. Richard John Friedlander. (ENG.). (J). 2008. pap. bk. 20.99 (978-1-59879-606-3(2), Livevst) Lifevest Pub.

Ottimista e Altre Storie. 1 cass. (Running Time: 35 mins.). (ITA.). pap. bk. 16.95 (SIT260) J Norton Pubs.

Otto of the Silver Hand. unabr. ed. Howard Pyle. Narrated by Edward Lewis. 2 cass. (Running Time: 2 hrs. 30 mins.). 2001. 17.95 (978-0-7861-2143-4(2), 2894) Blckstn Audio.
A rich and engrossing thread of romance runs through this tale of the motherless son of a valiant robber baron of Medieval Germany. Young Otto is born into a warring household in an age when lawless chiefs are constantly fighting each other or despoiling the caravans of the merchant burghers. Raised in a monastery, he returns to his family's domain only to become painfully involved in the blood feud between his father and the rival house of Trutz-Drachen.

Otto of the Silver Hand. unabr. ed. Howard Pyle & Geoffrey Howard. (Running Time: 9000 sec.). (J). (gr. 4-7). 2007. audio compact disk 19.95 (978-0-7861-6062-4(4)); audio compact disk 24.00 (978-0-7861-6061-7(6)) Blckstn Audio.

Otto Preminger: Censorship see Buckley's Firing Line

Otto Runs for President. Rosemary Wells. Illus. by Rosemary Wells. Narrated by Diana Canova. 1 CD. (Running Time: 12 mins.). (J). (ps-4). 2008. audio compact disk 12.95 (978-0-545-10686-3(9)) Weston Woods.

Otto Runs for President. Rosemary Wells. Illus. by Rosemary Wells. Narrated by Diana Canova. 1 CD. (Running Time: 12 mins.). (J). (ps-4). 2008. bk. 29.95 (978-0-545-10690-0(7)) Weston Woods.

Ouch! Natalie Babbitt. Illus. by Fred Marcellino. 11 vols. (Running Time: 14 mins.). pap. bk. 18.95 (978-1-59112-350-7(X)); pap. bk. (978-1-59112-558-7(8)) Live Oak Media.

Ouch! Natalie Babbitt. Illus. by Fred Marcellino. (Running Time: 14 mins.). 2000. audio compact disk 12.95 (978-1-59112-349-1(6)) Live Oak Media.

Ouch! unabr. ed. Read by Martin Jarvis. Retold by Natalie Babbitt. Music by Chris Kubie. 1 cass. (Running Time: 14 mins.). (J). 2000. 9.95 (978-0-87499-677-7(5)) Live Oak Media.
A delightful retelling of "The Giant with the Three Golden Hairs." When a baby boy's royal marriage is foretold, it's "happy news to a family that was nobody special, but not happy news to the King," who plots to prevent the inevitable.

Oud. 1 cass. 11.95 (7160) J Norton Pubs.

Our Adobe House: Audiocassette. (Greetings Ser.: Vol. 2). (gr. 2-3). 10.00 (978-0-7635-5873-4(7)) Rigby Educ.

Our African Winter. Arthur Conan Doyle. (Discoverers Ser.). 2001. 29.00 (978-0-7156-3084-6(9)) Pub: Duckworth Pub GBR. Dist(s): Intl Pubs Mktg

Our American Story. Rick Green & Kara Green. 2009. audio compact disk 34.95 (978-0-9769354-7-6(3)) Revolutionary Strat.

Our Asian Inheritance, No. 3. 1 cass. (Running Time: 1 hr.). 10.00 (978-1-893165-55-7(8)) Rational Isl.
Shared experiences of Asian Americans about being Asian & about Asians using re-evaluation counseling.

Our Asian Inheritance, No. 4. 4 cass. (Running Time: 6 hrs.). 40.00 (978-1-893165-56-4(6)) Rational Isl.

Our Asian Inheritance, Nos. 1 & 2. 1 cass. (Running Time: 1 hr. 30 mins.). 10.00 (978-1-893165-54-0(X)) Rational Isl.

Our Attitude Toward Christian Home Education. Michael J. McHugh. 1 CD. (Running Time: 1 hr.). 2002. audio compact disk 9.95 (CLP89535) Christian Liberty.
Designed to help parents perservere in their commitment to homeschooling. The message will enable parents to make their calling in the area of home education sure and steadfast.

Our Beautiful Day. Lois Duncan. Music by Robin Arquette. 1 cass. (Running Time: 30 min.). (J). (gr. k up). 1989. 9.95 RDA Enter.

Our Big Ego & Anger Is a Motivator. 1 cass. (Running Time: 1 hr. 30 mins.). (Recovery Is Forever Ser.). 1981. 8.95 (1536G) Hazelden.

Our Call to Holiness: Men's Retreat. John A. Hardon. 14 cass. (Running Time: 21 hrs.). 56.00 (95F) IRL Chicago.

Our Challenge: Our ABC of Transits. Milo Kovar. 1 cass. 8.95 (204) Am Fed Astrologers.
Sun's monthly transits: psychological growth value.

Our Chicago Audio Cassette. (Metro Reading Ser.). (J). (gr. 12). 1999. 1.12 (978-1-58120-426-1(4)) Metro Teaching.

Our Children's Eyes. Perf. by Lori Wilke. 1 cass. (Running Time: 4 min.). 1998. 9.98 Music sound track. (978-1-891916-38-0(6)) Spirit To Spirit.

Our Choice: A Plan to Solve the Climate Crisis. abr. ed. Al Gore. Read by Cynthia Nixon & John Slattery. 6 CDs. (Running Time: 6 hrs. 30 mins. 0 sec.). (ENG.). 2009. audio compact disk 29.99 (978-0-7435-7204-0(1)) Pub: S&S Audio. Dist(s): S and S Inc

***Our Civic Life: CD add-on Set.** Perf. by Millmark Education Staff. (ConceptLinks Ser.). 2009. audio compact disk 50.00 (978-1-61618-358-5(6)) Millmark Educ.

***Our Civic Life Audio CD.** Perf. by Millmark Education Staff. (ConceptLinks Ser.). 2009. audio compact disk 28.00 (978-1-4334-0696-6(9)) Millmark Educ.

***Our Civic Life Audio CD: Citizenship in a Democracy.** Perf. by Millmark Education Staff. (Content Literacy Libraries Ser.). 2009. audio compact disk (978-1-61618-141-3(9)) Millmark Educ.

***Our Civic Life Audio CD: Democracy & Decision-Making.** Perf. by Millmark Education Staff. (Content Literacy Libraries Ser.). 2009. audio compact disk (978-1-61618-145-1(1)) Millmark Educ.

***Our Civic Life Audio CD: Democratic Ideals.** Perf. by Millmark Education Staff. (Content Literacy Libraries Ser.). 2009. audio compact disk (978-1-61618-137-6(0)) Millmark Educ.

***Our Civic Life Audio CD: Rights & Responsibilities.** Perf. by Millmark Education Staff. (Content Literacy Libraries Ser.). 2009. audio compact disk (978-1-61618-133-8(8)) Millmark Educ.

Our Class Aim Is to Heal Not to Hurt. 2005. audio compact disk 11.95 (978-0-911203-94-3(X)) New Life.

Our Compromises. Swami Amar Jyoti. 1 cass. (Running Time: 1 hr.). 1979. 9.95 (J-18) Truth Consciousness.
What makes us compromise? Giving away the Higher for the lesser. Use & misuse of duty.

Our Confessions before the Angels. David T. Demola. 3 cass. (Running Time: 4 hrs. 30 mins.). 12.00 (S-1071A) Faith Fellow Min.

Our Country, Pt. 1. unabr. ed. Michael Barone. Read by William Lavelle. 14 cass. (Running Time: 41 hrs.). 1992. 89.95 (978-0-7861-0249-5(7), 1218-A,B) Blckstn Audio.
Barone draws from deep within the political & social record of modem America to tell the story of how the country of our forbears became our country.

Our Country, Pt. 2. unabr. ed. Michael Barone. Read by William Lavelle. 14 cass. (Running Time: 41 hrs.). 1992. 89.95 (978-0-7861-0250-1(0), 1218-A,B) Blckstn Audio.

Our Covenant Relationship. Speeches. Joel Osteen. 1 Cass. (Running Time: 30 Mins.). 2001. Rental 6.00 (978-1-59349-099-7(2), ja0099) J Osteen.

Our Covenant with God. Kenneth Copeland. 1 cass. (Running Time: 1 hr. 30 mins.). 1982. 5.00 (978-0-88114-048-4(1)) K Copeland Pubns.
Indepth biblical study on redemption.

Our Crowd: The Great Jewish Families of New York. unabr. collector's ed. Stephen Birmingham. Read by Jonathan Reese. 12 cass. (Running Time: 18 hrs.). 1992. 96.00 (978-0-7366-2298-1(5), 3082) Books on Tape.
For years, New York's great Jewish banking families have been aloof, mysterious, clannish & arrogant. Considering themselves an elite One Hundred, the families married only within "our crowd." Today their family trees interlace endlessly. Where they came from, how they made their money, how they spent it provides the plot for this fascinating narrative.

Our Cultural Value-Deprivation. Comment by Ayn Rand. 1 cass. (Running Time: 1 hr.). (Ford Hall Forum Ser.). 1966. 12.95 (AR06C) Second Renaissance.
Psychological & social consequences of the acute lack of values in modern-day culture.

Our Cultural Value-Deprivation. Ayn Rand. Read by Ayn Rand. 1 cass. (Running Time: 1 hr.). 1966. 12.95 (978-1-56114-069-5(4), AR06C) Second Renaissance.
The psychological & social consequences of the acute lack of values in today's culture.

Our Culture on the Couch: The Seven Steps to Global Healing. Contrib. by Kate Morgenstein. 2009. 20.00 (978-1-55841-000-8(7)) Emmett E Miller.

Our Daily Bread; Venerable Grandmothers. Ann Ree Colton & Jonathan Murro. 1 cass. (Running Time: 1 hr. 30 mins.). 7.95 A R Colton Fnd.

Our Dead Habits. Swami Amar Jyoti. 1 cass. 1979. 9.95 (J-23) Truth Consciousness.
Habits close off the treasure of fresh ideas within us, creating dullness & disease. Releasing the imprisoned mind.

Our Divine Companions: Encounter at Silver Springs, New York. Ann Ree Colton & Jonathan Murro. 1 cass. (Running Time: 1 hr. 30 mins.). 7.95 A R Colton Fnd.
Discusses the goal of God-Realization.

Our Divine Heritage. unabr. ed. Swami Amar Jyoti. 1 cass. (Running Time: 1 hr. 30 min.). (Satsangs of Swami Amar Jyoti Ser.). 1998. 12.95 (978-0-933572-33-1(6), M110) Truth Consciousness.
Earth consciousness reflects our true nature, which we all are seeking. Reclaiming our lost heritage.

Our Doctrine. Nathaniel Holcomb. 3 cass. (Running Time: 4 hrs. 30 mins.). 1999. (978-1-930918-26-9(7)) Its All About Him.

***Our Door Is Open: Creating Welcoming Cultures in Helping Organizations.** (ENG.). 2010. audio compact disk 18.00 (978-0-9773877-2-4(0)) Isld Press.

Our Dreams Transform Our Life. Pat Brockman. 4 cass. (Running Time: 5 hrs. 30 min.). 1993. 29.95 set. (AA2646) Credence Commun.
A highly imaginative & yet eminently practical workshop on dreams.

Our Dumb Century. abr. ed. Scott Dikkers. Read by Scott Dikkers. 1 cass. (Running Time: 1 hr. 50 min.). 1999. 13.00 (978-0-694-52199-9(X)) HarperCollins Pubs.

Our Dumb World: The Onion's Atlas of the Planet Earth. 73rd abr. ed. Onion Staff. (Running Time: 3 hrs. 30 mins.). (ENG.). 2007. 19.98 (978-1-60024-045-4(3)); audio compact disk 24.98 (978-1-60024-044-7(5)) Pub: Hachet Audio. Dist(s): HachBkGrp

Our Dumb World: The Onion's Atlas of the Planet Earth. 73rd abr. ed. The Onion. Read by Onion Editors. (YA). 2007. 39.99 (978-1-60252-729-4(6)) Find a World.

Our Earliest Memory. Kenneth Wapnick. 2008. 62.00 (978-1-59142-369-0(4)); audio compact disk 70.00 (978-1-59142-368-3(6)) Foun Miracles.

Our Endangered Values: America's Moral Crisis. unabr. ed. Jimmy Carter. Read by Jimmy Carter. 2005. 15.95 (978-0-7435-5371-1(3)) Pub: S&S Audio. Dist(s): S and S Inc

Our Enemy, the State. unabr. ed. Albert Jay Nock. Read by Phillip J. Sawtelle. 3 cass. (Running Time: 4 hrs.). 1989. 23.95 (978-0-7861-0087-3(7), 1080) Blckstn Audio.
This elegant essay on the nature of the state shows the important distinction between state power & social power.

Our Environment Theme Audio CD. ed. (J). 2004. audio compact disk (978-1-4108-1835-5(7)) Benchmark Educ.

Our Esthetic Vacuum. Ayn Rand. Read by Ayn Rand. 1 cass. (Running Time: 1 hr.). 12.95 (978-1-56114-010-7(4), AR25C) Second Renaissance.
Art is the sum & the barometer of a culture, Ayn Rand says. In this talk, she looks at the content of modern art & identifies what it reveals about today's culture. She describes the transformation of literature's view of man: from helpless puppet manipulated by forces beyond his control - to volitional being capable of choosing his goals & values - to depraved monster frantically seeking an escape from morality & from reality.

Our Esthetic Vacuum - Q & A. Ayn Rand. 1 cass. (Running Time: 40 min.). 1993. 12.95 (978-1-56114-323-8(5), AR49C) Second Renaissance.

Our Evolution on This Earth. Swami Amar Jyoti. 1 cass. (Running Time: 1 hr. 30 mins.). 1985. 9.95 (K-68) Truth Consciousness.
Dharma, the law governing our earthly existence. The virtues that carry us forward. We cannot hide from the Seer. Religious freedom. The dark tunnel, final test of faith.

Our Ewing Heritage with Related Families. rev. ed. Betty J. Durbin Carson & Doris M. Durbin Wooley. 2002. audio compact disk 16.00 (978-0-7884-2185-3(9)) Heritage Bk.

Our Experience Has Taught Us. 1 cass. (Running Time: 1 hr. 30 min.). 1989. 6.50 (978-0-933685-17-8(3), TP-35) A A Grapevine.
Features personal experiences of Alcoholics Anonymous members with the Twelve Traditions of AA.

Our Faces, Our Words. Lillian Smith. 1 cass. (Running Time: 1 hr. 30 mins.). 10.95 (978-0-8045-0916-9(6), SAC 44-5) Spoken Arts.

Our Faithful High Priest. Kenneth Copeland. 6 cass. (Running Time: 9 hrs.). 1991. 30.00 (978-0-88114-836-7(9)) K Copeland Pubns.
Biblical teaching on faith. Includes study guide.

Our Father. Clyde A. Bonar. 4 cass. (Running Time: 5 hrs. 35 min.). 1995. 34.95 (TAH335) Alba Hse Comns.
Through this audio-cassette you can learn to "hate what is evil, hold fast to what is good" as the words of St. Paul tell us. Discover the love of God working in your life as you uncover the deeper meaning of the great prayer, the Our Father.

Our Father. unabr. ed. Thomas Merton. Read by Thomas Merton. 2 cass. (Running Time: 1 hr. 14 min.). (Life & Prayer Ser.: No. 2). 1982. 19.95 Elec Paperback.
Discusses the various petitions of the fundamental Christian prayer.

Our Father: Perfect Prayer. Thomas Merton. 1 cass. (Running Time: 1 hr.). (Origins of Prayer Ser.). 8.95 (AA2070) Credence Commun.
Merton at his richest, sharing the best of monastic contemplation.

Our Father: The Heart of the Gospel. Albert Haase. 2 cass. (Running Time: 2 hrs.). 2001. vinyl bd. 16.95 (A6730) St Anthony Mess Pr.
In the early Church, candidates expecting to be community members prayed the Our Father three separate times each day.

Our Father: Unpacking the Lord's Prayer. (Running Time: 9900 sec.). 2008. audio compact disk 15.95 (978-0-87946-353-3(8)) ACTA Pubns.

Our Father & Prayer. Timothy O'Donnell. 1 cass. (National Meeting of the Institute, 1994 Ser.). 4.00 (94N8) IRL Chicago.

Our Fear of Psychic Abilities. Charles Tart. 1 cass. (Running Time: 55 min.). 1984. 11.00 (05201) Big Sur Tapes.
Lectures focusing on Parapsychology, Psi Phenomena & Altered States.

Our Federal Government. Cerebellum Academic Team. (Running Time: 30 mins.). (Just the Facts Ser.). 2001. 24.95 (978-1-59163-283-2(8)) Cerebellum.

Our First Revolution: The Remarkable British Upheaval That Inspired America's Founding Fathers. Michael Barone. Read by Stephen Hoye. (Playaway Adult Nonfiction Ser.). 2008. 64.99 (978-1-60640-571-0(3)) Find a World.

Our First Revolution: The Remarkable British Upheaval That Inspired America's Founding Fathers. unabr. ed. Michael Barone. Read by Stephen Hoye. (Running Time: 10 hrs. 0 mins. 0 sec.). (ENG.). 2007. audio compact disk 34.99 (978-1-4001-0477-2(7)) Pub: Tantor Media. Dist(s): IngramPubServ

Our First Revolution: The Remarkable British Upheaval That Inspired America's Founding Fathers. unabr. ed. Michael Barone. Read by Patrick G. Lawlor. (Running Time: 10 hrs. 0 mins. 0 sec.). (ENG.). 2007. audio compact disk 24.99 (978-1-4001-5477-7(4)) Pub: Tantor Media. Dist(s): IngramPubServ

Our First Revolution: The Remarkable British Upheaval That Inspired America's Founding Fathers. unabr. ed. Michael Barone. Read by Stephen Hoye. (Running Time: 10 hrs. 0 mins. 0 sec.). (ENG.). 2007. audio compact disk 69.99 (978-1-4001-3477-9(3)) Pub: Tantor Media. Dist(s): IngramPubServ

Our Five Basic Instincts. Swami Amar Jyoti. 1 cass. 1978. 9.95 (N-9) Truth Consciousness.
On anger, desire & the other basic instincts; tests on the spiritual path; nearness to Guru. Hearing the voice of God.

Our Founding Fathers. Cerebellum Academic Team. (Running Time: 30 mins.). (Just the Facts Ser.). 2001. 24.95 (978-1-59163-285-6(4)) Cerebellum.

Our Founding Mothers: Contributors to American Independence. 1 cass. (Running Time: 30 min.). 9.95 (H0110B090, HarperThor) HarpC GBR.

Our Friend Will be a Priest. Short Stories. (5122) Am Audio Prose.

Our Game. unabr. ed. John le Carré. Read by Frederick Davidson. (Running Time: 11 hrs. 50 mins.). 2009. audio compact disk 29.95 (978-1-4332-6210-4(X)) Blckstn Audio.

Our Game, unabr. ed. John le Carré. Narrated by John Franklyn-Robbins. 9 cass. (Running Time: 13 hrs. 15 mins.). (George Smiley Novels Ser.). 1997. 78.00 (978-0-7887-0809-1(0), RD802) Recorded Bks.
Takes you into the shadowy world of British spymasters where truth & lies intermingle.

Our Game. unabr. ed. John le Carré. Read by Frederick Davidson. 8 cass. (Running Time: 43200 sec.). (George Smiley Ser.). 1997. 56.95 (978-0-7861-1085-8(6), 1853) Blckstn Audio.
With the Cold War fought and won, British spymaster Tim Cranmer accepts early retirement to rural England and a new life with his alluring young mistress, Emma. But when both Emma and Cranmer's star double agent and lifelong rival, Larry Pettifer, disappear, Cranmer is suddenly on the run, searching for his brilliant protege, desperately eluding his former colleagues, in a frantic journey across Europe and into the lawless, battered landscapes of Moscow and southern Russia, to save whatever of his life he has left.

Our Game. unabr. ed. John le Carré. Read by Frederick Davidson. (Running Time: 41400 sec.). 2007. audio compact disk 29.95 (978-0-7861-5774-7(7)); audio compact disk 81.00 (978-0-7861-5773-0(9)) Blckstn Audio.

Our Game: An American Baseball Story. unabr. ed. Charles C. Alexander. Read by Tom Parker. 10 cass. (Running Time: 14 hrs. 30 mins.). 1998. 69.95 (978-0-7861-1366-8(9), 2274) Blckstn Audio.
Chronicles the first professional leagues, baseball's surge in the early twentieth century, the Golden Twenties and the Gray Thirties, the breaking of the color line in the late forties and the game's expansion to its current status as the premier team sport.

Our God Saves. Contrib. by Paul Baloche. 2007. audio compact disk 19.95 (978-5-557-60932-6(6)) Integrity Music.

Our God Saves. Contrib. by Paul Baloche & Don Moen. Prod. by Austin Deptula. 2007. audio compact disk 29.98 (978-5-557-60933-3(4)) Integrity Music.

Our Greatest Gift: A Meditation on Dying & Caring. abr. ed. Henri J. M. Nouwen. Read by Murray Bodo. 3 CDs. (Running Time: 10800 sec.). 2006. audio compact disk 24.95 (978-0-86716-795-5(5)) St Anthony Mess Pr.
In this best-seller the eminent spiritual guide Henri Nouwen describes three movements in our search for union with God.From loneliness to solitude explores our experience of our own selves and our longings.The second movement from hostility to hospitality focuses on our relationships with others. In the third movement the challenge is to progress from illusion to prayer. Nouwen?s plan leads us through good times and struggles, joys and sorrows, to joyful union with God. Nouwen says the journey is ?frightful as well as exhilarating because it is the great experience of being alone, alone in the world, alone before God.? As we are transformed in love, painful passages and tensions become signs of hope.

Our Greatest Gift: A Meditation on Dying & Caring. unabr. ed. Henri J. M. Nouwen. Read by Murray Bodo. 2 cass. (Running Time: 2 hrs.). 2000. 14.95 (978-0-86716-436-7(0), A4360) St Anthony Mess Pr.
A moving, personal look at human mortality. As Nouwen shares his own experiences with aging, loss, grief & fear, gently & eloquently reveals the gifts that the living & dying can give to one another. He challenges us to accept our death as part of our spiritual journey, not its end.

Our Hearts Were Young & Gay. unabr. ed. Cornelia Otis Skinner & Emily Kimbrough. Read by Celeste Lawson. (Running Time: 25200 sec.). (J). 2008. audio compact disk 29.95 (978-1-4332-1345-8(1)); audio compact disk & audio compact disk 55.00 (978-1-4332-1344-1(3)) Blckstn Audio.

Our Hearts Were Young & Gay. unabr. ed. Cornelia Otis Skinner & Emily Kimbrough. Read by Celeste Lawson. (Running Time: 25200 sec.). 2008. 54.95 (978-1-4332-1343-4(5)) Blckstn Audio.

Our High Priest Pt. 1: Hebrews 4:14-16. Ed Young. 1991. 4.95 (978-0-7417-1889-1(8), 889) Win Walk.

Our High Priest Pt. 2: Hebrews 5:1-10. Ed Young. 1991. 4.95 (978-0-7417-1890-7(1), 890) Win Walk.

Our Highest Goal. Read by Basilea Schlink. 1 cass. (Running Time: 30 min.). 1985. (0250) Evang Sisterhood Mary.
Discusses citizenship in heaven & victorious strength for your life.

Our Hills see Carl Sandburg's Poems for Children

Our House. Cathy Woodman. Read by Tanya Myers. 10 cass. (Running Time: 13 hrs. 15 mins.). (Story Sound Ser.). (J). 2005. 84.95 (978-1-85903-854-3(9)); audio compact disk 99.95 (978-1-85903-891-8(3)) Pub: Mgna Lrg Print GBR. Dist(s): Ulverscroft US

Our Husband. Stephanie Bond. Narrated by C. J. Critt. 8 cass. (Running Time: 12 hrs.). 72.00 (978-1-4025-0368-9(7)); audio compact disk 111.00 (978-1-4025-2912-2(0)) Recorded Bks.

Our Iceberg Is Melting: Changing & Succeeding under Any Conditions. unabr. ed. Holger Rathgeber et al. Read by Oliver Wyman. Frwd. by Spencer Johnson. 2 CDs. (Running Time: 3 hrs. 0 mins. 0 sec.). (ENG.). 2006. audio compact disk 19.95 (978-1-4272-0024-2(6)) Pub: Macmill Audio. Dist(s): Macmillan

Our Identity with Christ, Pt. I. Kenneth Copeland. Perf. by Kenneth Copeland. 1 cass. (Spiritual Death of Jesus: The Great Plan Ser.: Tape 2). 1995. cass. & video 5.00 (978-1-57562-023-7(5)) K Copeland Pubns.
Biblical teaching on spiritual death of Jesus.

Our Inner Ape: A Leading Primatologist Explains Why We Are Who We Are. unabr. ed. Frans B. M. De Waal. Narrated by Alan Sklar. (Running Time: 10 hrs. 30 mins. 0 sec.). (ENG.). 2005. audio compact disk 34.99 (978-1-4001-0192-4(1)); audio compact disk 69.99 (978-1-4001-3192-1(8)); audio compact disk 24.99 (978-1-4001-5192-9(9)) Pub: Tantor Media. Dist(s): IngramPubServ

***Our Island Story.** Henrietta E. Marshall. (ENG.). (J). 2006. audio compact disk 90.00 (978-0-9843490-2-9(2)) Alcazar AudioWorks.

Our Island Story: Volume 1 - from the Romans to Richard the Lionheart. H.E. Marshall. Read by Daniel Philpott & Anna Bentinck. (Running Time: 18450 sec.). (Junior Classics Ser.). (J). (gr. 1-7). 2006. audio compact disk 28.98 (978-962-634-395-1(8), Naxos AudioBooks) Naxos.

Our Island Story Volume 2: From the Magna Carta to Queen Elizabeth 1, Vol. 2. Read by Anna Bentinck & Daniel Philpott. 2006. audio compact disk 34.98 (978-962-634-410-1(5), Naxos AudioBooks) Naxos.

Our Island Story Volume 3: James I & Guy Fawkes to Queen Victoria. H.E. Marshall. Read by Anna Bentinck & Daniel Philpott. (J). 2006. audio compact disk 28.98 (978-962-634-411-8(3), Naxos AudioBooks) Naxos.

Our Kate. unabr. ed. Catherine Cookson. Read by Elizabeth Henry. 8 cass. (Running Time: 12 hrs.). 1999. 69.95 (6349X) Pub: Soundings Ltd GBR. Dist(s): Ulverscroft US

Our Kate. unabr. collector's ed. Catherine Cookson. Read by Penelope Dellaporta. 7 cass. (Running Time: 10 hrs. 30 mins.). 1986. 56.00 (978-0-7366-1074-2(X), 2001) Books on Tape.
Catherine Cookson novels are set in & around the North-East of England, past & present. This, her autobiography, makes plain how she knows her background & her characters so well.

Our Kind of People: Inside America's Black Upper Class. Lawrence Otis Graham. Narrated by Peter Francis James. 17 CDs. (Running Time: 20 hrs.). 1999. audio compact disk 160.00 (978-1-4025-3824-7(3)) Recorded Bks.

Our Kind of People: Inside America's Black Upper Class. unabr. ed. Lawrence Otis Graham. Narrated by Peter Francis James. 14 cass. (Running Time: 19 hrs. 30 mins.). 2001. 114.00 (978-0-7887-4837-0(8), F0005E7) Recorded Bks.
It takes you inside the world of the black upperclass: the society that lies somewhere between white America & mainstream black America.

***Our Kind of Traitor.** John le Carré. Contrib. by Robin Sachs. (Running Time: 12 hrs.). 2010. audio compact disk 29.95 (978-0-14-242842-9(6), PengAudBks) Penguin Grp USA.

Our Lady of Guadalupe. Megan McKenna. 1 cass. (Running Time: 1 hr.). 1995. (AA2920) Credence Commun.
After a thorough retelling of the lovely but bracing story of the apparition of Our Lady of Guadalupe, McKenna unpacks the theology inherent in the story - the clothing, the place & the symbols.

Our Lady of Guadalupe: Model of Evangelization. Virgilio Elizondo. 1 cass. (Running Time: 1 hr.). 2001. 8.95 (A6871) St Anthony Mess Pr.
Our Lady's vision and message to the Indian peasant Juan Diego in 1531 is a model of evangelization for the entire Church.

Our Lady of Guadalupe: Mother of the Civilization of Love. unabr. ed. Carl Anderson & Eduardo Chávez. Narrated by Kent Cassella & John Allen Nelson. 1 MP3-CD. (Running Time: 6 hrs. 30 mins. 0 sec.). (ENG.). 2009. 19.99 (978-1-4001-6403-5(6)); audio compact disk 29.99 (978-1-4001-1403-0(9)); audio compact disk 59.99 (978-1-4001-4403-7(5)) Pub: Tantor Media. Dist(s): IngramPubServ

***Our Lady of Guadalupe: Mother of the Civilization of Love.** unabr. ed. Carl Anderson & Eduardo Chavez. Narrated by John Allen Nelson. (Running Time: 6 hrs. 30 mins.). 2009. 14.99 (978-1-4001-8403-3(7)) Tantor Media.

***Our Lady of Immaculate Deception: A Mystery.** unabr. ed. Nancy Martin. Narrated by Karen White. 1 MP3-CD. (Running Time: 10 hrs. 30 mins. 0 sec.). 2010. 24.99 (978-1-4001-6656-5(X)); 16.99 (978-1-4001-8656-3(0)); 34.99 (978-1-4001-9656-2(6)); audio compact disk 34.99 (978-1-4001-1656-0(2)); audio compact disk 69.99 (978-1-4001-4656-7(9)) Pub: Tantor Media. Dist(s): IngramPubServ

Our Lady of Pain. Marion Chesney. 5 cass. (Running Time: 23640 sec.). (Edwardian Murder Mysteries Ser.). 2006. 49.95 (978-0-7927-3868-8(3), CSL 886); audio compact disk 64.95 (978-0-7927-3869-5(1), SLD 886) AudioGO.

Our lady of the Freedoms. Corwin Morman. 2004. 7.95 (978-0-7435-4164-0(2)) Pub: S&S Audio. Dist(s): S and S Inc

Our Lady of the Freedoms & Some of Her Friends. Norman Corwin. 1 CD. (Running Time: 1 hr.). 2001. audio compact disk 12.95 (CORW016) Lodestone Catalog.
A look at America, past & present, in the enthralling 1997 show that proved to be the final performance of Charles Kuralt. Production Script available.

Our Lady of the Lost & Found. Diane Schoemperlen. Narrated by Linda Stephens. 9 cass. (Running Time: 13 hrs.). 82.00 (978-1-4025-2181-2(2)) Recorded Bks.

Our Lady of the Lost & Found. Diane Schoemperlen. Narrated by Linda Stephens. 11 CDs. (Running Time: 13 hrs.). 2001. audio compact disk 116.00 (978-1-4025-3813-1(8)) Recorded Bks.

Our Lady of 121st Street. 2 CDs. (Running Time: 5160 sec.). 2005. audio compact disk 25.95 (978-1-58081-277-1(5), CDTPT190) Pub: L A Theatre. Dist(s): NetLibrary CO

***Our Last Best Chance: The Pursuit of Peace in a Time of Peril.** unabr. ed. King Abdullah, II. 8 CDs. (Running Time: 10 hrs.). (ENG.). 2011. audio compact disk 39.95 (978-0-14-242800-9(0), PengAudBks) Penguin Grp USA.

Our Liberty: Monument to a Dream. 1 cass. (Running Time: 30 min.). (J). 1986. 12.95 i. (978-0-930399-04-7(8)); 9.95 incl. minipack. BackPax Int.
Hear the stories of "Our Liberty" & her varied approaches (Ellis Island, Angel Island, over land & air). Know that all Americans have played a part with contributions big & small.

Our Lord & Our True Self. Swami Amar Jyoti. 1 cass. (Running Time: 1 hr.). 1987. 9.95 (M-70) Truth Consciousness.
If we know our True Self, we know our God. Our inner being, how much we live for Him, is what counts. Loosening the bonds of ego.

Our Lost Instinctual Heritage. Hal Stone & Sidra Stone. 1 cass. (Running Time: 1 hr.). (Mendocino Ser.). 1990. 10.95 (978-1-56557-005-4(7), T12) Delos Inc.
There is darkness & there is light. We cannot banish the darkness, but we can bring in the light. Drs. Hal & Sidra Stone focus the light of consciousness on the "darker" side of our human nature - showing how our disowned instinctual energies become daemonic & how we can reclaim these energies & bring them into our lives in a constructive fashion.

Our Man in Havana. Graham Greene. Read by Simon Prebble. 4 Cass. (Running Time: 7 Hours). 19.95 (978-1-4025-2367-0(X)) Recorded Bks.

Our Man in Havana. Graham Greene. 6 CDs. 2005. audio compact disk 39.75 (978-1-4193-2140-5(4)) Recorded Bks.

Our Man in Havana, unabr. ed. Graham Greene. Narrated by Simon Prebble. 5 cass. (Running Time: 6 hrs. 45 mins.). 1991. 49.75 (978-1-55690-398-4(7), 91123E7) Recorded Bks.
Wormold, high on incredulity, but low on cash, adds the occupation of spy to that of vacuum-cleaner salesman, thus becoming "The Man in Havana".

Our Man in Havana. unabr. ed. Graham Greene. Read by Jeremy Northam. 6 CDs. (Running Time: 7 hrs. 30 mins. 0 sec.). (ENG.). 2009. audio compact disk 31.95 (978-1-934997-26-0(9)) Pub: CSAWord. Dist(s): PerseuPGW

***Our Man in Tehran: The True Story behind the Secret Mission to Save Six Americans during the Iran Hostage Crisis & the Foreign Ambassador Who Worked with the CIA to Bring Them Home.** unabr. ed. Robert Wright. (Running Time: 14 hrs.). 2011. 29.95 (978-1-4417-7269-5(3)); 79.95 (978-1-4417-7266-4(9)); audio compact disk 32.95 (978-1-4417-7268-8(5)); audio compact disk 109.00 (978-1-4417-7267-1(7)) Blckstn Audio.

Our Maryland Heritage Bk. 16: White Families. William N. Hurley, Jr. 2002. audio compact disk 21.00 (978-0-7884-2138-9(7)) Heritage Bk.

Our Miss Brooks. 2 cass. (Running Time: 2 hrs.). 10.95 Set in vinyl album. (978-1-57816-071-6(5), OM2401) Audio File.
Includes: "October 31, 1948" Miss Brooks is scheduled to drive to the football game in Clay City with Mr. Boynton, but auto repairs cause a delay & she ends up driving the whole gang. "February 20, 1949" After Valentine's Day, biology teacher Mr. Boynton isn't paying enough attention to Miss Brooks. He's more interested in his frogs! "September 11, 1949" Miss Brooks' plans for a picnic before school resumes in the fall are cancelled when Principal Conklin orders all teachers to report earlier than usual. "March 11, 1950" Miss Brooks, awakened by a burglar in her house, discovers the crook is only after food, not money.

Our Miss Brooks. 2 CDs. (Running Time: 2 hrs.). 2004. audio compact disk 10.95 (978-1-57816-224-6(6)) Audio File.

Our Miss Brooks. Perf. by Eve Arden. 1 cass. (Running Time: 54 min.). 10.95 (752) J Norton Pubs.
In the first episode Miss Brooks is in a mixup concerning a speech to be delivered by the principal. The second episode finds Miss Brooks in a hilarious plot involving a moving van & the ladies' auxiliary.

Our Miss Brooks. Featuring Eve Arden. 1950. audio compact disk 12.95 (978-1-57970-506-0(5), Audio-For) J Norton Pubs.

Our Miss Brooks. Perf. by Eve Arden et al. (CC-3693) Natl Recrd Co.

Our Miss Brooks. Contrib. by Eve Arden. (Running Time: 10800 sec.). 2004. 9.98 (978-1-57019-640-9(0)) Radio Spirits.

Our Miss Brooks. Perf. by Eve Arden & Gale Gorden. 2008. audio compact disk 35.95 (978-1-57019-866-3(7)) Radio Spirits.

Our Miss Brooks. Perf. by Eve Arden & Gale Gordon. 1 cass. (Running Time: 1 hr.). 1949. 7.95 (CC-5040) Natl Recrd Co.
In the first part Miss Brooks is in charge of the students' money fund. She runs into trouble paying back $25.00, which Mrs. Davis took by mistake & spent. The second part finds Miss Brooks receiving a lesson in discipline.

Our Miss Brooks. Gwendolyn Brooks. Read by Gwendolyn Brooks. 2005. audio compact disk 22.95 (978-0-06-079077-6(6)) HarperCollins Pubs.

Our Miss Brooks. Perf. by Gale Gordon & Richard Crenna. 1 cass. (Running Time: 1 hr.). (Old Time Radio Classic Singles Ser.). 4.95 (978-1-57816-117-1(7), OM124) Audio File.
Includes: 1) "The Student's Money Fund" Miss Brooks is having a problem with missing funds (1/30/49). 2) "The Discipline Lesson" Miss Brooks learns about discipline (2/6/49).

Our Miss Brooks, Vol. 1. collector's ed. Perf. by Eve Arden et al. 6 cass. (Running Time: 9 hrs.). 1998. bk. 34.98 (4155) Radio Spirits.
Connie Brooks is Madison High's love-starved 10th grade English teacher. The object of her desire is Philip Boynton, a hopelessly shy biology teacher whom she's determined to teach about the birds and the bees. 18 episodes.

Our Miss Brooks, Vol. 2. Perf. by Eve Arden et al. 1 cass. (Running Time: 1 hr.). (Old Time Radio Classic Singles Ser.). 4.95 (978-1-57816-118-8(5), MB230) Audio File.
Includes: 1) "Mr. Conklin, the Alcoholic" (1/15/50). 2) "Saturday School Day" (1/29/50).

Our Miss Brooks, Vol. 2. collector's ed. Perf. by Eve Arden et al. 6 cass. (Running Time: 9 hrs.). 2001. bk. 34.98 (4433) Radio Spirits.
Connie Brooks, a love-starved high school English teacher is determined to teach bashful biology teacher Mr. Boynton about the birds and the bees. 18 classic programs.

Our Miss Brooks: April Fool's Day & Easter Egg Dye. Perf. by Eve Arden. 1 cass. (Running Time: 1 hr.). 2001. 6.98 (2188) Radio Spirits.

Our Miss Brooks: Connie is Chaperon & Christmas Letter Contest. Perf. by Eve Arden. 1 cass. (Running Time: 1 hr.). 2001. 6.98 (1692) Radio Spirits.

***Our Miss Brooks: Connie vs. Conklin.** Perf. by Eve Arden et al. 2010. audio compact disk 39.98 (978-1-57019-941-7(8)) Radio Spirits.

Our Miss Brooks: Europeans Visit Madison High & Trying to Sell the Trailer. Perf. by Eve Arden. 1 cass. (Running Time: 1 hr.). 2001. 6.98 (2022) Radio Spirits.

Our Miss Brooks: Fourth of July at Eagle Springs & The Conklin Carelessness Code. Perf. by Eve Arden. 1 cass. (Running Time: 1 hr.). 2001. 6.98 (1817) Radio Spirits.

Our Miss Brooks: Framing Mr. Boynton & a Note from Mr. LeBlanc. Perf. by Eve Arden. 1 cass. (Running Time: 1 hr.). 2001. 6.98 (1819) Radio Spirits.

Our Miss Brooks: Friday the 13th & Telegram for Mrs. Davis. Perf. by Eve Arden. 1 cass. (Running Time: 1 hr.). 2001. 6.98 (2266) Radio Spirits.

Our Miss Brooks: Madison High Auction & Mayor Rides by Madison High. Perf. by Eve Arden. 1 cass. (Running Time: 1 hr.). 2001. 6.98 (1520) Radio Spirits.

Our Miss Brooks: Magazine Article on Connie & New Year's Eve Party. Perf. by Eve Arden. 1 cass. (Running Time: 1hr.). 2001. 6.98 (1813) Radio Spirits.

Our Miss Brooks: Miss Brooks to Go to Clay High? & The Great Dane. Perf. by Eve Arden. 1 cass. (Running Time: 1 hr.). 2001. 6.98 (1815) Radio Spirits.

Our Miss Brooks: Mix-up Over an Elephant & Thanksgiving Mix-Up. Perf. by Eve Arden. 1 cass. (Running Time: 1 hr.). 2001. 6.98 (1821) Radio Spirits.

Our Miss Brooks: Mother's Day Presents & Mr. Boynton's Fire Rescue Practice. Perf. by Eve Arden. 1 cass. (Running Time: 1 hr.). 2001. 6.98 (1823) Radio Spirits.

Our Miss Brooks: Mr. Boynton Interviews at State U & Miss Brooks' Barbeque. Perf. by Eve Arden. 1 cass. (Running Time: 1 hr.). 2001. 6.98 (1895) Radio Spirits.

Our Miss Brooks: Mr. Conklin Fires the Football Coach & Measles. Perf. by Eve Arden. 1 cass. (Running Time: 1 hr.). 2001. 6.98 (1822) Radio Spirits.

Our Miss Brooks: Pensacola Popovers & Faculty Cheerleader. Perf. by Eve Arden. 1 cass.1 hr. 2001. 6.98 (1818) Radio Spirits.

Our Miss Brooks: Safety Week & Halloween Party. Perf. by Eve Arden. 1 cass. (Running Time: 1 hr.). 2001. 6.98 (1820) Radio Spirits.

Our Miss Brooks: Why Is Everybody Arguing? & Taxidermy. Perf. by Eve Arden. 1 cass. (Running Time: 1 hr.). 2001. 6.98 (1816) Radio Spirits.

Our Miss Brooks: Working in the Stockroom. Perf. by Eve Arden. 1 cass. (Running Time: 1 hr.). 2001. 6.98 (1814) Radio Spirits.

Our Miss Brooks, No. 2: Conklin, the Alcoholic & Saturday School Day. unabr. ed. 1 cass. (Running Time: 1 hr.). Dramatization. 1950. 7.95 (CC-9804) Natl Recrd Co.
Conklin, the Alcoholic: Eve Arden stars as schoolteacher Connie Brooks with Gale Gordon as school principal Osgood Conklin. On Friday the 13th, student Walter Denton (Richard Crenna) gives Conklin's name to an organization that helps alcoholics, & the results bring chaos at Madison High School. Colgate. Saturday School Day - Principal Osgood Conklin proclaims a "voluntary school day" for Saturday. Miss Brooks is elected spokesman for the student protest committee. Enter the school's superintendent & the fun begins. Jeff Chandler is biology teacher, Mr. Boynton. Colgate.

Our Miss Brooks Vol. 2. Perf. by Eve Arden et al. (ENG.). 2009. audio compact disk 35.95 (978-1-57019-883-0(7)) Radio Spirits.

Our Most Noble Victory: Poems on the Vietnam Experience. V. K. Inman. 2000. bk. & pap. bk. 12.00 (978-0-913551-02-8(3)) Arbuta Hse.

Our Mother of Perpetual Help Novena. 1 cass. (Running Time: 45 min.). pap. bk. 8.95 (978-0-87946-090-7(3), 309) ACTA Pubns.
Novena prayers, hymns & an inspiring message about devotion. Includes prayer booklet.

Our Musical Past. 2 cass. (YA). pap. bk. 16.95 (978-0-88432-403-4(6), S11020) J Norton Pubs.
Band & vocal music popular in America during the 1850's & 1860's. Includes 14 page booklet.

Our Musical World: Creative Insights into a Planet's Cultural Diversity. Léonie E/Michael L. Naylor. Léonie E/Michael L. Naylor. 2008. pap. bk. 70.00 (978-0-9816609-0-5(8)) Visions n Vib.

Our Mutal Friend. unabr. ed. Charles Dickens. Read by David Timson. (Running Time: 131637 sec.). (Complete Classics Ser.). 2007. audio compact disk 152.98 (978-962-634-442-2(3), Naxos AudioBooks) Naxos.

Our Mutual Friend. abr. ed. Charles Dickens. Read by David Timson. 9 CDs. (Running Time: 12 hrs.). 2008. audio compact disk 59.98 (978-962-634-857-4(7), Naxos AudioBooks) Naxos.

Our Mutual Friend. abr. ed. Charles Dickens. Perf. by Paul Scofield. 2 cass. (Running Time: 3 hrs.). (Ultimate Classics Ser.). 2004. 18.00 (978-1-931056-62-5(5), N Millennium Audio) New Millenn Enter.
A darkly dramatic picture of nineteenth century London, presenting a witty indictment of a society fallen prey to the dawning of commercialism.

Our Mutual Friend. abr. ed. Charles Dickens. Read by Paul Scofield. 3 CDs. (Running Time: 3 hrs.). 2004. audio compact disk 24.95 (978-1-59007-580-7(3)) Pub: New Millenn Enter. Dist(s): PerseuPGW

Our Mutual Friend. unabr. ed. Charles Dickens. Read by Robert Whitfield. (YA). 2008. 154.99 (978-1-60514-738-3(9)) Find a World.

Our Mutual Friend. unabr. ed. Charles Dickens. Read by Jim Killavey. 27 cass. (Running Time: 40 hrs.). 1989. 160.00 (X-194) Jimcin Record.
Full flowering of Dicken's genius.

Our Mutual Friend. unabr. ed. Charles Dickens & Robert Whitfield. (Running Time: 113400 sec.). 2007. audio compact disk 44.95 (978-0-7861-6071-6(3)) Blckstn Audio.

Our Mutual Friend, Pt. 1. unabr. ed. Charles Dickens. Read by Flo Gibson. 12 cass. (Running Time: 30 hrs. 5 mins.). (YA). (gr. 8 up). 1998. 77.95 Audio Bk Con.
Multiple characters & plots twist & turn through scenes that vary from grim to gay. Dust, as a symbol of money, deceit & death permeates this novel.

Our Mutual Friend, Pt. I. unabr. ed. Charles Dickens. Read by Robert Whitfield. 15 cass. (Running Time: 33 hrs. 30 mins.). 1999. 95.95 (978-0-7861-1665-2(X), 2493A,B) Blckstn Audio.
Vision of a dark, macabre London & the corrupting power of money. So begins the intrigue in a novel that is quintessentially Dickensian in flavor - in its grotesque caricatures, & its rich symbolism.

Our Mutual Friend, Pt. 2. unabr. ed. Charles Dickens. Read by Flo Gibson. 8 cass. (Running Time: 12 hrs.). (YA). (gr. 8 up). 1998. bk. 53.95 Audio Bk Con.
Multiple characters & plots twist & turn through scenes that vary from grim to gay. Dust, a symbol of money, deceit & death, permeats this novel which some consider Dickens' greatest.

Our Mutual Friend, Pt. II. unabr. ed. Charles Dickens. Read by Robert Whitfield. 8 cass. (Running Time: 33 hrs. 30 mins.). 1999. 56.95 (978-0-7861-1712-3(5), 2493A,B) Blckstn Audio.
Vision of a dark macabre London & the corrupting power of money. Quintessentially Dickensian in flavor - in its grotesque caricatures, & its rich symbolism.

Our Mutual Friend, Pt. A. unabr. collector's ed. Charles Dickens. Read by David Case. 12 cass. (Running Time: 18 hrs.). 1998. 96.00 (978-0-7366-4046-6(0), 4545-A) Books on Tape.
Concerns murder, unidentified corpses & the inheritance of a rich garbage collector.

Our Mutual Friend, Pt. B. unabr. collector's ed. Charles Dickens. Read by David Case. 12 cass. (Running Time: 18 hrs.). 1998. 96.00 (978-0-7366-4047-3(9), 4545-B) Books on Tape.

Our Mutual Friend: Radio Dramatization. unabr. ed. Charles Dickens. 7 CDs. (Running Time: 10 hrs. 30 mins.). 2003. audio compact disk 74.95 (978-0-563-49610-6(X), BBCD 015) BBC Worldwide.

Our Mutual Friend Part 1. unabr. ed. Charles Dickens. Read by Robert Whitfield. (Running Time: 61200 sec.). 2007. audio compact disk 108.00 (978-0-7861-6069-3(1)) Blckstn Audio.

Our Mutual Friend (Part 1) unabr. ed. Charles Dickens. Narrated by Flo Gibson. (Running Time: 18 hrs.). 1999. 39.95 (978-1-55685-604-4(0)) Audio Bk Con.

Our Mutual Friend Part 2. unabr. ed. Charles Dickens. Read by Robert Whitfield. (Running Time: 52200 sec.). 2007. audio compact disk 99.00 (978-0-7861-6070-9(5)) Blckstn Audio.

Our Mutual Friend (Part 2), Vol. 2. unabr. ed. Charles Dickens. Narrated by Flo Gibson. (Running Time: 12 hrs. 6 mins.). 1999. 26.95 (978-1-55685-832-1(9)) Audio Bk Con.

Our Mutual Friend (Parts 1 And 2) unabr. ed. Charles Dickens. Narrated by Flo Gibson. (Running Time: 30 hrs. 6 mins.). 1999. 57.95 (978-1-55685-833-8(7)) Audio Bk Con.

Our Mutual Friend (9CD) Na949612. Charles Dickens. Read by David Timson. 2008. audio compact disk 59.98 (978-962-634-496-5(2), Naxos AudioBooks) Naxos.

Our Nations Patriotic Songs: CD. Music by Raymond Montoya. (YA). 2003. audio compact disk 12.00 (978-0-9758596-8-1(4)) CommissionBel.

Our Need for Austerities. Swami Amar Jyoti. 1 cass. (Running Time: 1 hr. 30 mins.). 1980. 9.95 (P-39) Truth Consciousness.
Purpose & meaning of austerities & the guidance needed. Coming out of ego into freedom. Living & acting for Divine.

***Our Noise: The Story of Merge Records, the Indie Label That Got Big & Stayed Small.** unabr. ed. John Cook. Read by Ray Porter. (Running Time: 9 hrs. 0 mins.). 2010. 29.95 (978-1-4417-2800-5(7)); 59.95 (978-1-4417-2796-1(5)); audio compact disk 90.00 (978-1-4417-2797-8(3)) Blckstn Audio.

Our Only May Amelia. unabr. ed. Jennifer L. Holm. Read by Emmy Rossum. 3 vols. (Running Time: 4 hrs. 38 mins.). (J). (gr. 5-9). 2004. pap. bk. 36.00 (978-0-8072-8366-0(5), YA191SP, Listening Lib); 30.00 (978-0-8072-8365-3(7), YA191CX, Listening Lib) Random Audio Pubg.
With seven older brothers & a love of adventure, it is not easy for May Amelia Jackson being the only girl in her settlement in 1899 Washington. Now that Mama's going to have a baby, maybe there's hope for another girl along the banks of the Nasel River.

Our Only May Amelia. unabr. ed. Jennifer L. Holm. Read by Emmy Rossum. (Running Time: 16680 sec.). (ENG.). (J). (gr. 5-9). 2007. audio compact disk 28.00 (978-0-7393-5966-2(5), Listening Lib) Pub: Random Audio Pubg. Dist(s): Random

Our Oriental Heritage, Pt. 1. unabr. collector's ed. Will Durant & Ariel Durant. Read by Alexander Adams. 13 cass. (Running Time: 19 hrs. 30 min.). (Story of Civilization Ser.). 1994. 104.00 (978-0-7366-2692-7(1), 3427-A) Books on Tape.
First volume in The Story of Civilization, traces history of Egypt & Middle East, India, China & Japan.

Our Oriental Heritage, Pt. 2. collector's ed. Will Durant & Ariel Durant. Read by Alexander Adams. 13 cass. (Running Time: 19 hrs. 30 min.). (Story of Civilization Ser.). 1994. 104.00 (978-0-7366-2693-4(X)) Books on Tape.

Our Part of the Wall. Rick Joyner. 1 cass. (Running Time: 1 hr. 30 mins.). (Vision Series: Vol. 3). 2000. 5.00 (RJ16-003) Mrningstar Pubng.
This tape series will help to impart new vision or restore lost vision in the church.

***Our Patchwork Nation: The Surprising Truth about the Real America.** unabr. ed. Dante Chinni & James Gimpel. (Running Time: 8 hrs. 0 mins.). 2010. 29.99 (978-1-4001-9870-2(4)); 15.99 (978-1-4001-8870-3(9)); audio compact disk 29.99 (978-1-4001-1870-0(0)) Pub: Tantor Media. Dist(s): IngramPubServ

***Our Patchwork Nation: The Surprising Truth about the Real America.** unabr. ed. Dante Chinni & James Gimpel. Narrated by Peter Berkrot. (Running Time: 9 hrs. 0 mins. 0 sec.). (ENG.). 2010. 19.99 (978-1-4001-6870-5(8)); audio compact disk 71.99 (978-1-4001-4870-7(7)) Pub: Tantor Media. Dist(s): IngramPubServ

Our Personal Lives in 1988-89. Theresa Gurlacz. 1 cass. (Running Time: 1 hr. 30 mins.). 8.95 (613) Am Fed Astrologers.
An AFA Convention workshop tape.

Our Place in God's Play. unabr. ed. Swami Amar Jyoti. 1 cass. (Running Time: 1 hr. 30 min.). (Satsangs of Swami Amar Jyoti Ser.). 1998. 9.95 (978-0-933572-31-7(X), R111) Truth Consciousness.
All beings are interconnected in unity. Helping Earth to evolve. Environmental problems are symptoms of deeper malady. Playing by God's rules.

Our Polly. Anna Jacobs. Read by Julia Franklin. 12 cass. (Running Time: 14 hrs.). 2001. (978-1-84283-097-0(X)) Soundings Ltd GBR.
Little Billy is the light of Polly?s life it?s for her son?s sake that she puts up with an unkind mother-in-law and an isolated farm. Then Billy is knocked down by a car, his father killed attempting to save his life, and Polly, cast off by her husband?s family, is left with a child who may never walk again. Polly?s own family, the Kershaws, provide all the support they can, but they are unable to out manoeuvre the malicious Dr Browning-Baker. Forced to flee to the Fylde coast, Polly and Billy find that their future may lie with another damaged family and ex-Army captain whose First World War marriage was a terrible mistake, and his daughter, who has never recovered form the hostility of the mother she loves. But danger threatened their fragile happiness.

Our Power over Satan. C. S. Lovett. 1 cass. (Running Time: 1 hr.). 6.95 (7035) Prsnl Christianity.
Expands on truths of the "Dealing with the Devil" book.

Our Present President (Nineteen Eighty-Four) Gilbert Navarro. 1 cass. (Running Time: 1 hr.). 8.95 (251) Am Fed Astrologers.
An AFA Convention workshop tape.

Our Real Beliefs. Neville Goddard. 1 cass. (Running Time: 1 hr. 2 mins.). 1964. 8.00 (109) J & L Pubns.
Neville taught Imagination Creates Reality. He was a powerfully influential teacher of God as Consciousness.

Our Relation to the Higher. unabr. ed. Huston Smith. 2 cass. (Running Time: 3 hrs.). 1988. 18.00 (A0274-88) Sound Photosyn.
Arthur Young's "favorite philosopher" draws upon his definitive comparative religion knowledge to respond to a previous talk by Arthur, his "favorite scientist".

Our Relationship with Money. Iyanla Vanzant. 1 cass. (Running Time: 1 hr.). 2000. 12.00; audio compact disk 14.00 S&S Audio.

Our Relationship with the World. Iyanla Vanzant. 1 cass. (Running Time: 1 hrs.). 2000. 12.00; audio compact disk 14.00 S&S Audio.

Our Responsibility As Christians Today. 1985. (0247) Evang Sisterhood Mary.

Our Rights in Christ. Kenneth W. Hagin, Jr. 2 cass. 8.00 (03J) Faith Lib Pubns.

Our Risen Savior - the Promise Kept. 2005. 15.00 (978-1-933561-04-2(1)) BFM Books.

Our Rose, Set. unabr. ed. Victor Pemberton. Read by Marie McCarthy. 9 cass. (Running Time: 12 hrs.). 1999. 90.95 (978-1-85903-249-7(4)) Pub: Magna Story GBR. Dist(s): Ulverscroft US
Rose Humble is used to sorting out her family's problems. But as the war starts to cast its shadow, she realises there are some problems her quick wit & ready tongue cannot solve. People are not all they seem, including her sister, Queenie, & the man she loves, Michael Deveraux. As a volunteer ambulance-woman she witnesses great suffering on the streets of London, & she meets a young fire-fighter, Bill. Can she trust him? When Bill's secret is revealed & there is a devastating family tragedy, Rose is forced to re-think her world once more.

Our Sacred Honor: Stories Letters Songs Poems Speeches Hymns Birth Nation CST. William J. Bennett. 2004. 15.95 (978-0-7435-4810-6(8)) Pub: S&S Audio. Dist(s): S and S Inc

Our Savior Talks on CD. 2007. audio compact disk 39.95 (978-1-59038-818-1(6)) Deseret Bk.

Our School Community Audio CD. Adapted by Benchmark Education Company Staff. Based on a work by Cynthia Swain. (Early Explorers Set C Ser.). (J). (gr. k). 2008. audio compact disk 10.00 (978-1-60437-515-2(9)) Benchmark Educ.

Our Search for Bliss. Swami Amar Jyoti. 1 cass. 1991. 9.95 (M-82) Truth Consciousness.
On the five levels of Koshas (covers) of consciousness, symbolized by OM. The highest of these is Bliss.

Our Search for Happiness Book on CD: An Invitation of Understand the Church of Jesus Christ of Latter-day Saints. M. Russell Ballard. 2007. audio compact disk 19.95 (978-1-59038-823-5(2)) Deseret Bk.

Our Sixth-Grade Sugar Babies. Eve Bunting. Narrated by Christina Moore. 3 CDs. (Running Time: 3 hrs. 15 mins.). (gr. 4 up). audio compact disk 29.00 (978-1-4025-2326-7(2)) Recorded Bks.

Our Sixth-Grade Sugar Babies. unabr. ed. Eve Bunting. (J). 1998. bk. Set. (40817B3) Recorded Bks.

Our Sixth-Grade Sugar Babies, unabr. ed. Eve Bunting. Narrated by Christina Moore. 3 pieces. (Running Time: 3 hrs. 15 mins.). (gr. 4 up). 1998. 28.00 (978-0-7887-2628-6(5), 95632E7) Recorded Bks.
Eleven-year-old Vicki is out to prove she's mature enough to babysit her little stepsister. A new class project, where Vicki has to care for a five-pound bag of sugar like it's a baby, gives her the perfect opportunity, until a cute boy moves in across the street.

***Our Solar System: CD add-on Set.** Perf. by Millmark Education Staff. (ConceptLinks Ser.). 2009. audio compact disk 50.00 (978-1-61618-347-9(0)) Millmark Educ.

***Our Solar System Audio CD.** Perf. by Millmark Education Staff. (ConceptLinks Ser.). 2007. audio compact disk 28.00 (978-1-4334-0103-9(7)) Millmark Educ.

***Our Solar System SB1 Audio CD Earth in Space.** Perf. by Millmark Education Staff. (Content Literacy Libraries Ser.). 2008. audio compact disk (978-1-4334-0412-2(5)) Millmark Educ.

***Our Solar System SB2 Audio CD Neighbors in Space.** Perf. by Millmark Education Staff. (Content Literacy Libraries Ser.). 2008. audio compact disk (978-1-4334-0413-9(3)) Millmark Educ.

***Our Solar System SB3 Audio CD Exploring Other Worlds.** Perf. by Millmark Education Staff. (Content Literacy Libraries Ser.). 2008. audio compact disk (978-1-4334-0414-6(1)) Millmark Educ.

***Our Solar System SB4 Audio CD the Sun & Its Effects.** Perf. by Millmark Education Staff. (Content Literacy Libraries Ser.). 2008. audio compact disk (978-1-4334-0415-3(X)) Millmark Educ.

Our Solar System/along the Nature Trail. Created by Steck-Vaughn Staff. (Running Time: 1952 sec.). (Shutterbug Bks.). 2003. (978-0-7398-7790-6(9)) SteckVau.

Our Souls Have Grown Deep Like the Rivers: Black Poets Read Their Work. unabr. ed. Prod. by Rebekah Presson Mosby. 2 cass. (Running Time: 3 hrs.). 2000. 19.98 (R4 78012) Rhino Enter.

Our Souls Have Grown Deep Like the Rivers: Black Poets Read Their Work. unabr. ed. Prod. by Rebekah Presson Mosby & Ted Myers. 2 CDs. (Running Time: 3 hrs.). 2000. audio compact disk 29.98 (R2 78012) Rhino Enter.

Our Sovereign God. Elisabeth Elliot. Read by Elisabeth Elliot. 4 cass. (Running Time: 4 hrs.). 1989. 18.95 (978-0-8474-2007-0(8)) Back to Bible.
Discusses the sovereignty of God, teaching that all events in the believer's life have a purpose.

Our Story Begins: New & Selected Stories. unabr. ed. Tobias Wolff. Read by Anthony Heald. 10 cass. (Running Time: 46800 sec.). 2008. 29.95 (978-1-4332-0397-8(9)); 79.95 (978-1-4332-0395-4(2)); audio compact disk 29.95 (978-1-4332-0399-2(5)); audio compact disk 29.95 (978-1-4332-0398-5(7)); audio compact disk 99.00 (978-1-4332-0396-1(0)) Blckstn Audio.

Our Street. unabr. ed. Victor Pemberton. Read by Spencer Banks. 9 cass. (Running Time: 12 hrs.). 1999. 90.95 (978-1-85903-248-0(6)) Pub: Magna Story GBR. Dist(s): Ulverscroft US
The war is five years old & in bomb-torn North London, fifteen-year-old Frankie Lewis sometimes thinks it will go on forever. But one foggy night his life takes an extraordinary turn. Inveigled by his mates, "The Merton Street Gang," into playing yet another vindictive prank on the old German-Jewish widow who lives just off the Seven Sisters road, Frankie finds himself hauled unceremoniously across her doorstep & pulled into a world of books & culture he never knew existed.

Our Subjective Responsibility. Swami Amar Jyoti. 1 cass. 1988. 9.95 (K-106) Truth Consciousness.
When ego gets hurt: humility to learn the golden lessons. A code of right action, looking into our own face. Making sense out of our lives.

Our Sun, Our Weather. Sundance/Newbridge, LLC Staff. (Early Science Ser.). (gr. k-3). 2007. audio compact disk 12.00 (978-1-4007-6533-1(1)); audio compact disk 12.00 (978-1-4007-6534-8(X)); audio compact disk 12.00 (978-1-4007-6535-5(8)) Sund Newbrdge.

Our Sunshine. unabr. ed. Robert Drewe. Read by Michael Veitch. 2 cass. (Running Time: 3 hrs. 35 mins.). 2004. 24.00 (978-1-74030-969-1(3)); audio compact disk 57.95 (978-1-74093-031-4(2)) Pub: Bolinda Pubng AUS. Dist(s): Bolinda Pub Inc

Our Sweet Will. Swami Amar Jyoti. 1 cass. 1979. 9.95 (M-27) Truth Consciousness.
By sweet will avoiding self-delusion. Focusing on God, not 'dear self'. Hatha & Raja Yoga.

Our Tempestuous Day: A History of Regency England. unabr. ed. Carolly Erickson. Narrated by Simon Prebble. 7 cass. (Running Time: 9 hrs. 45 mins.). 1998. 60.00 (978-0-7887-1997-4(1), 95384E7) Recorded Bks.
With King George III suffering from dementia in 1811, Parliament appoints his son George IV to reign. For the next nine years, the substitute king scandalizes Europe with his drunkenness, his mistresses & his wanton spending.

Our Times: The Age of Elizabeth II. unabr. ed. A. N. Wilson. (Running Time: 17 hrs.). 2010. audio compact disk 39.95 (978-1-4417-1517-3(7)) Blckstn Audio.

Our Times: The Age of Elizabeth II. unabr. ed. A. N. Wilson. Read by Ralph Cosham. (Running Time: 17 hrs. 0 mins.). 2010. 44.95 (978-1-4417-1518-0(5)); 89.95 (978-1-4417-1514-2(2)); audio compact disk 123.00 (978-1-4417-1515-9(0)) Blckstn Audio.

***Our Tragic Universe.** Scarlett Thomas. Narrated by Sarah Le Fevre. (Running Time: 12 hrs. 10 mins. 0 sec.). 2010. audio compact disk 29.95 (978-1-60998-099-3(9)) Pub: AudioGO. Dist(s): Perseus Dist

Our True Environment: The Kingdom of Heaven. unabr. ed. Myrtle Smith. Prod. by David Keyston. 1 cass. (Running Time: 1 hrs. 10 min.). (Myrtle Smyth Audiotapes Ser.). 1998. , CD. (978-1-893107-01-4(9), M1, Cross & Crown) Healing Unltd.

Our True Sense of Seeing. Swami Amar Jyoti. 1 cass. 1984. 9.95 (R-59) Truth Consciousness.
A Wealth of examples of applying true seeing, being present in moment-to-moment living. The releasing factor; relaxation at the zero point.

Our Two Brains: Rational & Intuitive. Robert Ornstein & David Galin. 1 cass. (Running Time: 56 min.). 12.95 J Norton Pubs.

Our Two Brains: The Rational & the Intuitive (audio CD) Robert Ornstein & David Galin. (ENG.). 2007. audio compact disk 12.95 (978-1-57970-471-1(9), Audio-For) J Norton Pubs.

Our Village. unabr. ed. Mary Russell Mitford. Read by Rosemary Davis. 4 cass. (Running Time: 5 hrs.). (Isis Ser.). (J). 2004. 44.95 (978-1-85089-613-5(5), 89104) Pub: ISIS Lrg Prnt GBR. Dist(s): Ulverscroft US

Our Violent Universe, Pt. 1. 1 cass. (Running Time: 46 min.). 14.95 (31532) MMI Corp.
Covers various violent events, pulsars, quasars, solar flares, comets & more.

Our Violent Universe, Pt. 2. 1 cass. (Running Time: 42 min.). 14.95 (31532) MMI Corp.
Listening for echoes of creation-X-rays, quasars, "big bang" theory, solid state theory & more.

Our Wild & Crazy World. Judith H. Cohen & Roberta B. Wiener. 1 cass. (J). (gr. 4-5). 39.00 incl. 8 bks., 28 worksheets & guide. (978-0-89525-184-8(1), DC 330) Ed Activities.
Each human interest story in this program is taken from the pages of newspapers & magazines, & includes such topics as relaxing in a hot tub, taking a dog to an animal psychiatrist or losing weight to get a bonus. More mature students develop basic reading competency through such reading.

Our Word Is Our Weapon. Subcomandante Marcos. (Running Time: 45 mins.). (Open Media Ser.). (ENG.). 2004. audio compact disk 14.95 (978-1-58322-663-6(X)) Pub: Seven Stories. Dist(s): Consort Bk Sales

Our World Redeemed: The Sequel. Contrib. by Flame et al. 2008. audio compact disk 13.99 (978-5-557-63543-1(2)) C Mason Res.

Our 20th Century: The Events That Shaped Our Lives. 2000. 18.00 (978-0-9668567-5-0(9)); audio compact disk 22.00 (978-0-9668567-9-8(1)) MediaBay Audio.

Out. Natsuo Kirino. 13 cass. (Running Time: 67680 sec.). 2006. 99.95 (978-0-7927-3922-7(1), CSL 913); audio compact disk 119.95 (978-0-7927-3923-4(X), SLD 913) AudioGO.

Out. Natsuo Kirino. Read by Bernadette Dunne. 2 CDs. 2006. audio compact disk 49.95 (978-0-7927-3970-8(1), CMP 913) AudioGO.

***Out at Second.** unabr. ed. Matt Christopher. Read by Joshua Swanson. (Running Time: 4 hrs.). (ENG.). (J). 2011. 12.98 (978-1-60788-688-4(X)); audio compact disk 12.98 (978-1-60788-687-7(1)) Pub: Hachet Audio. Dist(s): HachBkGrp

Out in Space. Sundance/Newbridge, LLC Staff. (Early Science Ser.). (gr. k-3). 2007. audio compact disk 12.00 (978-1-4007-6424-2(6)); audio compact disk 12.00 (978-1-4007-6425-9(4)); audio compact disk 12.00 (978-1-4007-6426-6(2)) Sund Newbrdge.

Out in the Midday Sun. unabr. collector's ed. Elspeth Huxley. Read by Donada Peters. 8 cass. (Running Time: 12 hrs.). 1987. 64.00 (978-0-7366-1128-2(2), 2051) Books on Tape.
Huxley evokes the Africa of her adult life, in particular the legendary personalities of Kenya between the wars, the men & women who gave the country its character & helped to shape its destiny.

Out Loud: Playful Sound Poems. unabr. ed. Eve Merriam. 1 cass. (Running Time: 42 min.). (J). (gr. k-6). 1988. 9.95 (978-0-89845-764-3(5), CPN 1821) HarperCollins Pubs.

Out of Addictive Relationships - Into Healthy Love Relationships. Crystal Engleman-Lampe. 1 cass. 9.00 (A0346-88) Sound Photosyn.
From the California Association of Marriage & Family Counseling Convention.

Out of Africa. abr. ed. Isak Dinesen. Read by Julie Harris. 2 cass. (Running Time: 3 hrs.). 2004. 15.95 (978-0-88690-134-9(0), M20029) Pub: Audio Partners. Dist(s): PerseuPGW
The portrait of a strong, determined, sensitive woman on whom a rich, dramatic landscape & way of life made strong impressions.

Out of Africa. unabr. collector's ed. Isak Dinesen. Read by Wanda McCaddon. 9 cass. (Running Time: 13 hrs. 30 mins.). 1983. 72.00 (978-0-7366-0913-5(X), 1856) Books on Tape.
In 1921, the year that Baroness Karen Blixen found herself stranded by her divorce on a Kenyan mountain farm, most women in her circumstances would have fled to civilization. White women did not live alone in Black Africa, let alone manage 6000 acres of coffee plantation, native settlement, & virgin country. But instead of returning to her native Denmark, the 35-year-old Blixen stayed on & ran the farm. She learned Swahili & Arabic, doctored her Kikuyu squatters, shot marauding lions for the Masai, & along the way fell deeply in love with Africa & its people. In 1931 her farm fell victim to the collapse of world coffee markets & she was forced to leave. She returned to Denmark where she poured her memories into a passionate love letter to the life that would hold her in thrall till the end of her days.

Out of Body. unabr. ed. Thomas Baum. Read by Michael Prichard. 7 cass. (Running Time: 7 hrs.). 1997. 42.00 (978-0-7366-3768-8(0), 4441) Books on Tape.
Denton Hake has just been paroled from prison for a rape he has no memory of committing.

Out of Body. unabr. ed. Thomas Baum. Read by Fee Waybill. 4 cass. (Running Time: 6 hrs.). 1997. 24.95 Set. (978-1-57511-029-5(6)) Pub Mills.
When a man is paroled from prison for a rape he has no recollection of committing he begins experiencing bizarre mind lapses in which he seems to travel out of his body & witness things happening in other places & to other people. When he is accused of a murder he relies on his strange new found ability to attempt to clear his name & save himself from the death penalty.

Out-of-Body Experience. Bruce Goldberg. (ENG.). 2005. audio compact disk 17.00 (978-1-57968-034-3(8)) Pub: B Goldberg. Dist(s): Baker Taylor

Out-of-Body Experience. Bruce Goldberg. 1 cass. (Hypnotic Time Travel Ser.). (ENG.). 2006. 13.00 (978-1-885577-06-1(0)) Pub: B Goldberg. Dist(s): Baker Taylor
Self hypnosis program that takes you out of your body & directs you to travel & finally return to your present body.

Out of Body Experiences. unabr. ed. Charles Tart. 2 cass. (Running Time: 1 hr. 54 min.). 1970. 18.00 Set. (05205) Big Sur Tapes.
With entertaining case-studies & anecdotes, parapsychology researcher Tart brings to the topic depth & rigor as well as humor.

Out of Bounds. Perf. by Bobby Collins. 2000. audio compact disk 16.98 (978-1-929243-23-5(5)) Uproar Ent.

***Out of Captivity.** abr. ed. Marc Gonsalves et al. Read by Mark Deakins. (ENG.). 2009. (978-0-06-188260-9(7), Harper Audio) HarperCollins Pubs.

Out of Captivity: Surviving 1,967 Days in the Colombian Jungle. Marc Gonsalves & Keith Stansell. Read by Mark Deakins. Told to Gary Brozek. (Playaway Adult Nonfiction Ser.). 2009. 59.99 (978-1-61545-574-4(4)) Find a World.

***Out of Captivity: Surviving 1,967 Days in the Colombian Jungle.** abr. ed. Marc Gonsalves et al. Read by Mark Deakins. (ENG.). 2009. (978-0-06-187600-4(3), Harper Audio) HarperCollins Pubs.

Out of Control. unabr. ed. Jerry Ahern. Read by Alan Zimmerman. 4 vols. No. 3. 2002. (978-1-58807-509-3(5)) Am Pubng Inc.

Out of Control. unabr. ed. Jerry Ahern. Read by Alan Zimmerman. 3 vols. (Running Time: 4 hrs. 30 mins.). (Defender Ser.: No. 3). 2002. 22.00 (978-1-58807-023-4(9)) Am Pubng Inc.
As the race for Metro mayor heats up, the city explodes in a new wave of brutal violence. The radical FLNA has a simple strategy to insure their candidates victory: bombing, kidnapping, and cold-blooded murder. One way or another, the terrorists are heavily favored to make a killing. However, David Holden and his Patriots refuse to run scared. Outlawed and outcast, the Defender joins forces with a top-secret team of FBI special agents on a blood-soaked campaign to beat the enemy at his own savage game: to cast their vote for freedom with ballots and bullets.

Out of Control. unabr. ed. Jerry Ahern. Read by Alan Zimmerman. 3 vols. No. 3. 2003. audio compact disk (978-1-58807-696-0(2)) Am Pubng Inc.

Out of Control. unabr. ed. Jerry Ahern. Read by Alan Zimmerman. 4 CDs. (Running Time: 4 hrs. 30 mins.). No. 3. 2003. audio compact disk 29.00 (978-1-58807-265-8(7), 590369) Am Pubng Inc.

Out of Control. unabr. ed. Wanda E. Brunstetter. Read by Ellen Grafton. (Running Time: 4 hrs.). (Rachel Yoder - Always Trouble Somewhere Ser.). 2010. audio compact disk 14.99 (978-1-4418-1170-7(2), 9781441811707) Brilliance Audio.

***Out of Control.** unabr. ed. Wanda E. Brunstetter. Read by Ellen Grafton. (Running Time: 4 hrs.). (Rachel Yoder - Always Trouble Somewhere Ser.). 2010. 14.99 (978-1-4418-1172-1(9), 9781441811721, Brilliance MP3); 39.97 (978-1-4418-1173-8(7), 9781441811738, Brinc Audio MP3 Lib); 14.99 (978-1-4418-1174-5(5), 9781441811745, BAD); 39.97 (978-1-4418-1175-2(3), 9781441811752, BADLE); audio compact disk 44.97 (978-1-4418-1171-4(0), 9781441811714, BriAudCD Unabrid) Brilliance Audio.

Out of Control, Vol. 40. AIO Team Staff. Created by Focus on the Family Staff. 4 CDs. (Running Time: 3 hrs. 20 mins.). (Adventures in Odyssey Ser.: Vol. 40). (ENG.). (J). 2005. audio compact disk 24.99 (978-1-58997-208-7(2)) Pub: Focus Family. Dist(s): Tyndale Hse

Out of Darkness. Read by Colin Baker & Nicola Bryant. 2001. audio compact disk 13.99 (978-0-563-55848-4(2)) London Brdge.

Out of Darkness. Keith Terry. 3 CDs. 2004. audio compact disk 14.95 (978-1-59156-402-7(6)) Covenant Comms.

Out of Darkness, Set. Keith C. Terry. 2 cass. 11.98 (978-1-55503-867-0(0), 07001266) Covenant Comms.
A powerful novel of conversion, intrigue, & love.

Out of Darkness: The Story of Louis Braille. unabr. ed. Russell Freedman. Narrated by Nelson Runger. 1 cass. (Running Time: 1 hr. 30 mins.). (gr. 3 up). 1998. 10.00 (978-0-7887-1909-7(2), 95330E7) Recorded Bks.
Blind since the age of three, Louis desperately wanted to read & spent every spare moment punching holes in paper with a stylus, until by the age of 15 he had invented his own alphabet.

Out of Darkness: The Story of Louis Braille. unabr. ed. Russell Freedman. Read by Nelson Runger. 1 cass. (Running Time: 1 hr. 30 min.). (J). (gr. 6). 1998. 32.70 HMWK SET . (978-0-7887-1937-0(8), 40644); 189.00 CLASS SET . (978-0-7887-3613-1(2), 46389) Recorded Bks.
Blind since the age of three, young Louis Braille wanted to be able to read. By the age of 15, he had invented his own alphabet.

Out of Egypt. unabr. ed. Andre Aciman. Read by Geoffrey Howard. 7 cass. (Running Time: 10 hrs. 30 mins.). 1996. 56.00 (978-0-7366-3229-4(8), 3890) Books on Tape.
Before their exodus from Alexandria in 1956, three generations of a close-knit Jewish family had lived a prosperous life in Egypt's cosmopolitan second city. With perception, telling detail & elegant prose, Aciman relates the exploits & fortunes of his spirited relations: among others, his two grandmothers, who operated in a system of subtle courtesies & snobberies; his flamboyant uncle Vili, Italian patriot & British spy & his aunt Flora, the German refugee.

Out of Egypt into Your Promise. Voice by Eddie Long. 2005. audio compact disk 49.99 (978-1-58602-255-6(5)) E L Long.

Out of Gas. (J). 2005. audio compact disk (978-1-933796-13-0(8)) PC Treasures.

Out of Mao's Shadow: The Battle for China's Soul. unabr. ed. Philip P. Pan. Narrated by David Colacci. (Running Time: 13 hrs. 30 mins. 0 sec.). (ENG.). 2008. audio compact disk 79.99 (978-1-4001-3750-3(0)); audio compact disk 29.99 (978-1-4001-5750-1(1)) Pub: Tantor Media. Dist(s): IngramPubServ

Out of Mao's Shadow: The Battle for China's Soul. unabr. ed. Philip P. Pan. Read by David Colacci. (Running Time: 13 hrs. 30 mins. 0 sec.). (ENG.). 2008. audio compact disk 39.99 (978-1-4001-0750-6(4)) Pub: Tantor Media. Dist(s): IngramPubServ

Out of Mind. Catherine Sampson. Read by Kate Reading. (Running Time: 10 mins.). 2005. 59.95 (978-0-7861-3674-2(X)); audio compact disk 72.00 (978-0-7861-7688-5(1)) Blckstn Audio.

Out of Mind. unabr. ed. Catherine Sampson. Read by Kate Reading. 7 cass. (Running Time: 32400 sec.). 2005. 29.95 (978-0-7861-3543-1(3), E3513); audio compact disk 29.95 (978-0-7861-7781-3(0), ZE3513); audio compact disk 29.95 (978-0-7861-8004-2(8), ZM3513) Blckstn Audio.

***Out of My Head.** unabr. ed. Didier van Cauwelaert. Read by Bronson Pinchot. (Running Time: 5 hrs. 30 mins.). 2010. 29.95 (978-1-4417-5979-5(4)); audio compact disk 24.95 (978-1-4417-5978-8(6)) Blckstn Audio.

***Out of My Head (Library Edition)** unabr. ed. Didier van Cauwelaert. Read by Bronson Pinchot. (Running Time: 5 hrs. 30 mins.). 2010. 34.95 (978-1-4417-5975-7(1)); audio compact disk 55.00 (978-1-4417-5976-4(X)) Blckstn Audio.

Out of My Mind: Channeling Your Own Divinity. Barbara With. (ENG.). 1999. (978-0-9677458-2-4(9)) Mad Island Communs.

Out of My Mind: How to Talk to the Angels. 1998. 24.99 (978-0-9677458-1-7(0)) Mad Island Communs.

Out of My Mind: Manifestation. Barbara With. (ENG.). 2000. (978-0-9677458-3-1(7)) Mad Island Communs.

Out of My Mind: Personal Empowerment. Barbara With. (ENG.). 2000. (978-0-9677458-4-8(5)) Mad Island Communs.

Out of My Mind: Regeneration. Barbara With. (ENG.). 2000. (978-0-9677458-5-5(3)) Mad Island Communs.

Out of My Way Satan: Matt. 16:23. Ed Young. 1988. 4.95 (978-0-7417-1693-4(3), 693) Win Walk.

Out of Nowhere. Jeri Gilcrist. 3 cass. 2004. 14.95 (978-1-59156-223-8(6)) Covenant Comms.

Out of Nowhere. Doris Mortman. Read by Bernadette Dunne. 1999. audio compact disk 128.00 (978-0-7366-8042-4(X)) Books on Tape.

Out of Nowhere. unabr. ed. Doris Mortman. Read by Bernadette Dunne. 13 cass. (Running Time: 19 hrs. 30 min.). 1999. 104.00 (978-0-7366-4446-4(6), 4891) Books on Tape.
Life changed for Erica Baird when her mother was forced into the Witness Protection Program. Erica left everything behind, even her name. Overnight, Erica disappeared & Amanda Maxwell was born. The grownup Amanda has turned her photography hobby into a career as a forensic photographer with the NYC Police Department's Crime Scene Unit. Only one person in the world knows who she really is, her powerful father. When he is found dead at his desk, Amanda knows that her past has caught up with her. Amanda must be on her guard at every moment. Even so, her anonymity is threatened & somebody wants her dead.

Out of Range. unabr. ed. C. J. Box. Read by David Chandler. (Running Time: 9 hrs. 15 mins.). 2008. 56.75 (978-1-4361-6527-3(X)); 67.75 (978-1-4361-2379-2(8)); audio compact disk 92.75 (978-1-4361-2381-5(X)) Recorded Bks.

Out of Range. unabr. collector's ed. C. J. Box. Read by David Chandler. 8 CDs. (Running Time: 9 hrs. 15 mins.). (Joe Pickett Ser.). 2008. audio compact disk 44.95 (978-1-4361-2382-2(8)) Recorded Bks.

Out of Reach. unabr. ed. Patricia Lewin. Read by Laural Merlington. (Running Time: 8 hrs.). 2003. 29.95 (978-1-59355-402-6(8), 1593554028, BAU); 74.25 (978-1-59355-403-3(6), 1593554036, BrilAudUnabridg) Brilliance Audio.
A rising star in the CIA, Erin Baker is driven by tragedy from her past. When she was a child, her eight-year-old sister, Claire, was kidnapped. Though Claire was miraculously found, she was changed forever. As was Erin, who now just might get what she's always wanted: the chance to make a difference in someone's life. But she must be willing to risk everything she holds dear. When a child disappears near her home, Erin is certain there is a link to her sister's cold kidnapping case. She meets Alex Donovan, an FBI agent on the hunt to find the missing boy, whose record for locating missing children is unquestioned. Suddenly Alex and Erin find themselves on a desperate pursuit - from the streets of America's most peaceful neighborhoods to a horrifying underworld where children are stolen and trafficked. And as they get closer to the truth, they make their own lives, and the lives of everyone they love, into perfect targets for a killer.

Out of Reach. unabr. ed. Patricia Lewin. Read by Laural Merlington. (Running Time: 8 hrs.). 2004. 39.25 (978-1-59335-494-7(0), 1593354940, Brinc Audio MP3 Lib) Brilliance Audio.

Out of Reach. unabr. ed. Patricia Lewin. Read by Laural Merlington. (Running Time: 8 hrs.). 2004. 39.25 (978-1-59710-554-5(6), 1597105546, BADLE); 24.95 (978-1-59710-555-2(4), 1597105554, BAD) Brilliance Audio.

Out of Reach. unabr. ed. Patricia Lewin. Read by Laural Merlington. (Running Time: 8 hrs.). 2004. 24.95 (978-1-59335-263-9(8), 1593352638) Soulmate Audio Bks.

Out of Reach, Set unabr. ed. Elizabeth McGregor. Read by Cornelius Garrett. 8 cass. 1999. 69.95 (CAB 1478) AudioGO.

Out of School see Gathering of Great Poetry for Children

Out of Sight. unabr. ed. Elmore Leonard. Read by Alexander Adams. 7 cass. (Running Time: 7 hrs.). 1996. 42.00 (978-0-913369-32-6(2), 754876) Books on Tape.
A prison break in the Florida Everglades brings together federal marshal Karen Sisco, a knockout in high heels & Chanel suits & Jack Foley, the escapee, a criminal of legendary power & ability. Their acquaintance & later romance, begins while Karen & Foley share the trunk of the escape car.

***Out of Sight.** unabr. ed. Elmore Leonard. (ENG.). 2010. (978-0-06-199760-0(9), Harper Audio); (978-0-06-199383-1(2), Harper Audio) HarperCollins Pubs.

Out of Sight, unabr. ed. Elmore Leonard. Narrated by George Guidall. 5 cass. (Running Time: 7 hrs.). 1996. 44.00 (978-0-7887-0675-2(6), 94856E7) Recorded Bks.
When a Chanel-skirted federal marshall & a suave bank robber share a few hours together in the trunk of a car, their mutual chemistry doesn't lead to a predictable ending, especially in Elmore Leonard's world.

Out of Spain. Yvonne Behar. Ed. by Andree Aclion Brooks. 2000. bk. & pap. bk. 59.95 (978-0-9702700-7-8(0)) A A Brooks.

Out of Spain. Perf. by Joelle Partner. Prod. by Yvonne Behar. 1 CD. (Running Time: 1 hr.). 2000. audio compact disk 9.90 (978-0-9702700-6-1(2)) A A Brooks.

Out of Step. unabr. ed. Maggie Makepeace. Read by Diana Bishop. 8 cass. (Running Time: 10 hrs.). (Sound Ser.). 2001. 69.95 (978-1-86042-871-5(1)) Pub: UlverLrgPrint GBR. Dist(s): Ulverscroft US
Nell is content with her life, until she falls in love - with a cottage. From the moment she sees Bottom Cottage deep in a West Country valley, she knows she has to have it. But things become more complicated when she meets its owner, Rob, and falls for him as well. All her dreams seem to have come true, but Rob has two young children and an almost-ex-wife. Does he really want to be with her.

***Out of the Apple Orchard Audio CD.** Created by Yvonne David. 2010. audio compact disk 18.95 (978-0-615-35859-8(4)) Arbiter Pr.

Out of the Blue Set: Delight Comes into Our Lives. abr. ed. Mark Victor Hansen & Barbara Nichols. 2 cass. (Running Time: 3 hrs.). 1996. 18.00 (978-0-694-51633-9(3), CPN 2555) HarperCollins Pubs.
At a time when many of us are earnestly seeking an evolution of consciousness, delight is the next natural step toward soul awareness. The personal stories in this book demonstrate how ordinary people can contribute to the creation of a most desirable & entirely possible time - the new Age of Delight.

Out of the Corner of My Eye: Living with Vision Loss in Later Life. unabr. ed. Nicolette P. Ringgold. 2 cass. (Running Time: 2 hrs. 03 min.). 1991. 22.95 set. (978-0-89128-211-2(4)) Am Foun Blind.
A personal account of sudden vision loss & subsequent adjustment that is full of practical advice & cheerful encouragement, told by an 87-year-old retired college teacher who has maintained her independence & zest for life.

***Out of the Dark.** unabr. ed. David Weber. (Running Time: 18 hrs. 0 mins. 0 sec.). (ENG.). 2010. audio compact disk 49.99 (978-1-4272-1061-6(6)) Pub: Macmill Audio. Dist(s): Macmillan

Out of the Dark World. unabr. ed. Grace Chetwin. Narrated by Grace Chetwin. 3 cass. (Running Time: 4 hrs. 15 mins.). (gr. 6). 1991. 27.00 (978-1-55690-400-4(2), 91119E7) Recorded Bks.
Meg braves the terrors of her dream world to rescue a comatose boy from oblivion. Meg has nightmares, the same ugly dreams over & over again. She finds herself drawn irresistibly to the entrance of a sphere, an enormous black void while some strange voice in the corners of her mind, is asking her, begging her to help him.

Out of the Darkness. unabr. ed. Susan Kelly. Read by Pamela Klein. (Running Time: 8 hrs.). 2008. 24.95 (978-1-4233-7189-2(5), 9781423371892, BAD); 39.25 (978-1-4233-7188-5(7), 9781423371885, Brinc Audio MP3 Lib); 39.25 (978-1-4233-7190-8(9), 9781423371908, BADLE); 24.95 (978-1-4233-7187-8(9), 9781423371878, Brilliance MP3) Brilliance Audio.

Out of the Darkness: A Promising Future for Tourette Syndrome. Nancy Freeman. Read by Neva Duyndam. 1 cass. 1990. 9.95 (978-1-878159-13-7(5)) Duvall Media.
Blurting obscenities in church was only the beginning for Kevin. This narrative chronicles a young boy's thirteen year struggle with Tourette Syndrome, one of the most baffling disorders in medical history. With encouragement, he was finally able to overcome the symptoms that had once dominated his life.

Out of the Deep I Cry. Julia Spencer-Fleming. Read by Suzanne Toren. 10 vols. (Clare Fergusson/Russ Van Alstyne Mystery Ser.). 2004. 84.95 (978-0-7927-3220-4(0), CSL 656, Chivers Sound Lib); audio compact disk 99.95 (978-0-7927-3221-1(9), SLD 656, Chivers Sound Lib); audio compact disk 49.95 (978-0-7927-3222-8(7), CMP 656, Chivers Sound Lib) AudioGO.

Out of the Depths. Richard E. Lauersdorf. 2003. audio compact disk 59.95 (978-0-8100-1559-3(5)) Northwest Pub.

Out of the Depths. John Newton. Read by William Sutherland. 3 cass. (Running Time: 4 hrs.). 2000. 23.95 (978-0-7861-1579-2(3), 2408) Blckstn Audio.
The retelling of the events which led John Newton from sin & bondage to a life transformed by God'samazing grace.

Out of the Dust. Karen Hesse. Read by Marika Mashburn. 2 cass. (Running Time: 2 hrs. 10 mins.). (J). 2000. 18.00 (978-0-7366-9096-6(4)) Books on Tape.

Out of the Dust. unabr. ed. Karen Hesse. Read by Marika Mashburn. 2 cass. (Running Time: 3 hrs.). (J). (gr. 1-8). 1999. 23.00 (LL 0121, Chivers Child Audio) AudioGO.

Out of the Dust. unabr. ed. Karen Hesse. Read by Marika Mashburn. 2 vols. (Running Time: 2 hrs. 9 mins.). (J). (gr. 5-9). 1998. pap. bk. 29.00 (978-0-8072-8013-3(5), YA967SP, Listening Lib); 23.00 (978-0-8072-8012-6(7), YA967CX, Listening Lib) Random Audio Pubg.
Set in the Oklahoma dustbowl. this is a girl's story of her life during the Depression.

Out of the Dust. unabr. ed. Karen Hesse. Read by Marika Mashburn. 2 CDs. (Running Time: 7800 sec.). (ENG.). (J). (gr. 5-7). 2006. audio compact disk 13.00 (978-0-307-28403-7(4), Listening Lib) Pub: Random Audio Pubg. Dist(s): Random

Out of the Dust. unabr. ed. Karen Hesse. Narrated by Marika Mashburn. 2 cass. (Running Time: 2 hrs.). (J). pap. bk. 23.00 (LL1036AC) Weston Woods.

Out of the Dust, Set. unabr. ed. Karen Hesse. Read by Marika Mashburn. 2 cass. (YA). 1998. 18.00 (FS9-34630) Highsmith.

Out of the Flame see Osbert Sitwell Reading His Poetry

Out Of The Frying Pan Into The Fire: Acts 4:1-12. Ed Young. 1983. 4.95 (978-0-7417-1286-8(5), 286) Win Walk.

Out of the Madness: From the Projects to a Life of Hope. abr. ed. Jerrold Ladd. (ENG.). 2006. 14.98 (978-1-59483-741-8(4)) Pub: Hachet Audio. Dist(s): HachBkGrp

Out of the Night That Covers Me. Pat Cunningham Devoto. 2001. 24.98 (978-1-58621-126-4(9)) Hachet Audio.

Out of the Night That Covers Me. abr. ed. Pat Cunningham Devoto. (ENG.). 2005. 14.98 (978-1-59483-429-5(6)) Pub: Hachet Audio. Dist(s): HachBkGrp

Out of the Ordinary: Prayers, Poems, & Reflections for Every Season. Perf. by Bridget Pasker. Composed by Joyce Rupp. 1 CD. (Running Time: 54 mins.). 2000. audio compact disk 16.95 (978-0-87793-937-5(3)) Ave Maria Pr.
A companion recording to Out Of The Ordinary. Contains prayerful Taize-like chants composed by Joyce Rupp and performed by Bridget Pasker to enhance the many prayers and services in the book. The CD and Cassette provide a vocal rendering for all 16 chants found in the book's appendix.

Out of the Past. Perf. by Bing Crosby. (Running Time: 54 min.). 10.95 (#755) J Norton Pubs.
Side one is a potpourri of highlights from Bing's early career, including a show with Bob Hope. On side two Crosby sings some of his famous numbers, including "Alexander's Ragtime Band" & "Old Faithful.".

Out of the Past. Featuring Bing Crosby. 1950. audio compact disk 12.95 (978-1-57970-509-1(X), Audio-For) J Norton Pubs.

Out of the Past. unabr. ed. Christine Marion Fraser. Read by Lesley Mackie. 7 cass. (Running Time: 9 hrs., 30 min.). 1999. 61.95 (978-1-86042-408-3(2), 24082) Pub: Soundings Ltd GBR. Dist(s): Ulverscroft US
Devastated by the death of her mother & constant brutal treatment from the man she thought she loved, Andrea feels much older than her twenty-two years. Needing a complete change of scenery, she agrees to spend a month in the wild, remote Scottish highlands on Balgower farm where she grew up. Enveloped by her Aunt Nell's generous - albeit gossipy - hospitality, Rea slowly begins to thaw both in body & spirit. But her fragile peace of mind is rudely shattered by the reappearance of Leo Sinclair, local boy-made-good & now a debonair famous novelist.

Out of the Saltshaker: And into the World. abr. ed. Rebecca Manley Pippert. Narrated by Rebecca Manley Pippert. 3 CDs. (Running Time: 3 hrs. 48 mins. 0 sec.). (ENG.). 2005. audio compact disk 18.98 (978-1-59644-300-6(6), Hovel Audio) christianaud.

Out of the Saltshaker: Evangelism as a Way of Life. Rebecca Pippert. 2 cass. (Running Time: 120 min.). 1999. 15.00 (978-0-8308-2221-8(6)) InterVarsity.
Evangelism as a lifestyle. Stories, biblical insight & plain common sense, helps us feel relaxed & enthusiastic about sharing our faith.

***Out of the Saltshaker & into the World.** abr. ed. Rebecca Manley Pippert. (ENG.). 2005. 10.98 (978-1-59644-301-3(4), Hovel Audio) christianaud.

Out of the Sea, Early see May Swenson

Out of the Shadows. unabr. ed. Sue Hines. Read by Caroline Lee. 4 cass. (Running Time: 5 hrs. 30 mins.). (YA). 2001. 32.00 (978-1-74030-362-0(8)) Pub: Bolinda Pubng AUS. Dist(s): Bolinda Pub Inc

***Out of the Shadows.** unabr. ed. Sue Hines. Read by Caroline Lee. (Running Time: 5 hrs. 30 mins.). (YA). 2004. audio compact disk 40.00 (978-1-74093-461-9(X)) Pub: Bolinda Pubng AUS. Dist(s): Bolinda Pub Inc

Out of the Shadows. unabr. ed. Kay Hooper. Narrated by C. J. Critt. 11 CDs. (Running Time: 12 hrs. 30 mins.). 2001. audio compact disk 111.00 (978-1-4025-0511-9(6), C1567) Recorded Bks.
The small, friendly town of Gladstone, Tennessee seems the ideal place to raise a family - until two teenagers are found tortured to death. Sheriff Miranda Knight will do anything to catch the killer, including letting the FBI's psychic profiler tap into her own telepathic energy.

Out of the Shadows. unabr. ed. Kay Hooper. Read by C. J. Critt. 9 cass. (Running Time: 12 hrs. 30 mins.). 2001. 83.00 (978-0-7887-5985-7(X), 96601x7) Recorded Bks.

Out of the Shadows: Understanding Sexual Addiction, abr. ed. Patrick J. Carnes. Read by Janet Fontaine. 2 cass. (Running Time: 3 hrs.). 2000. 18.00 (978-1-57453-379-8(7)) Audio Lit.
This breakthrough work, the first to describe sexual addiction, is still the standard for recognizing & overcoming this destructive behavior. With insight & sensitivity, it outlines how to identify a sexual addict, recognize the way others may unwittingly become complicit or codenpendent & change the patterns that support the addiction.

Out of the Silent Planet. C. S. Lewis. Read by Geoffrey Howard. 2003. audio compact disk 19.95 (978-0-7861-9367-7(0)) Blckstn Audio.

Out of the Silent Planet. C. S. Lewis. Read by Geoffrey Howard. 4 cass. (Running Time: 6 hrs.). 2000. 32.95 (978-0-7861-1814-4(8), 2613); audio compact disk 49.99 (978-0-7861-9808-5(7), z2613) Blckstn Audio.
A planetary romance with elements of medieval mythology.

Out of the Silent Planet. unabr. collector's ed. C. S. Lewis. Read by Grover Gardner. 7 cass. (Running Time: 7 hrs.). 1983. 56.00 (978-0-7366-0843-5(5), 1794) Books on Tape.
Dr. Ransom, a noted philologist, is kidnapped & flown by spaceship to Malacandra (Mars) where he flees his human captors & establishes communication with the planet's extraordinary inhabitants. What he learns galvanizes his attempt to return to Earth with a message of great urgency.

Out of the Storm. abr. ed. Grace Livingston Hill. Read by Aimee Lilly. 2 cass. (Running Time: 1 hr. 30 mins. per cass.). (Grace Livingston Hill Romances Ser.). 2004. 8.99 (978-1-886463-56-1(5)) Oasis Audio.
Adrift on an angry ocean, lovely young Gail must struggle to save her life.... the life of a man she doesn't know.

Out of the Storm. unabr. ed. A. J. LaMontagne. Read by Jerry Sciarrio. 8 cass. (Running Time: 9 hrs. 48 min.). 2001. 49.95 (978-1-58116-026-0(7)) Books in Motion.
A young pilot is severely tested when the deadliest storm of the century imperils unsuspecting victims.

Out of the Sun. unabr. ed. Robert Goddard. Read by Paul Shelley. 10 cass. (Running Time: 15 hrs.). 2000. 69.95 (CAB 1394) Pub: Chivers Audio Bks GBR. Dist(s): AudioGO
When Harry Barnett is informed that his son is in the hospital in a diabetic coma, he's certain there must be some mistake, since he doesn't have a son. But he soon discovers that he does. David Venning was a brilliant mathematician & his tragic condition is the result of an accident or suicide attempt. But his notebooks are missing & two fellow employees have died under suspicious circumstances. Coincidence, or is David the victim of an attempted murder?.

Out of the Way! Socialism's Coming! Aziz Nesin. 2 cass. (Running Time: 2 hrs.). 2001. bk. 11.95 (978-1-84059-303-7(2)) Pub: Milet Pub. Dist(s): Tuttle Pubng

Out of the Way! Socialism's Coming! Aziz Nesin. 2 cass. (Running Time: 2 hrs.). (TUR & ENG.). (YA). 2001. bk. 11.95 (978-1-84059-302-0(4)) Pub: Milet Pub. Dist(s): Tuttle Pubng

Out of the Whirlwind. unabr. ed. Gilbert Morris. Read by Maynard Villers. 8 cass. (Running Time: 11 hrs. 6 min.). (Appomattox Ser.: Bk. 5). 1998. 49.95 (978-1-55686-839-9(1)) Books in Motion.
Burke Rocklin has one goal, to marry an heiress. Setting his sights on Belinda King, a spoiled young woman, his plans are waylaid by the Second Battle of Manassas, where he is critically wounded. Lying in a coma, his clothes & possesions stolen, he is mistakenly taken to the Union army hospital. There he finally awakens with no memory of his past.

Out of the Woods: Stories. unabr. ed. Chris Offutt. Narrated by Tom Stechschulte. 3 cass. (Running Time: 3 hrs.). 2001. 32.00 (978-0-7887-5508-8(0), 96192x7) Recorded Bks.
The author's gift for storytelling is striking in this short story collection featuring the fiercely independent Kentucky people whose heritage he shares. Grave diggers, truck drivers, drifters & gamblers assume flesh & bone under the spell of Tom Stechschulte's narration. Their concise, colorful language & hard-edged wisdom speak the enduring truths of which classics are made.

***Out of This Nettle.** Norah Lofts. 2010. 89.95 (978-1-4079-0991-2(6)); audio compact disk 99.95 (978-1-4079-0992-9(4)) Pub: Soundings Ltd GBR. Dist(s): Ulverscroft US

Out of Time. Carol Lynn Thomas. Read by Paul Michael Garcia. (Running Time: 9000 sec.). (J). (gr. 4-7). 2007. audio compact disk 24.00 (978-1-4332-0101-1(1)); audio compact disk 19.95 (978-1-4332-0102-8(X)) Blckstn Audio.

Out of Time. Carol Lynn Thomas & Paul Michael Garcia. (Running Time: 7200 sec.). (J). (gr. 4-7). 2007. 22.95 (978-1-4332-0100-4(3)) Blckstn Audio.

***Out of Time.** Zondervan Publishing Staff. (Running Time: 5 hrs. 64 mins. 8 sec.). (Time Thriller Trilogy). (YA). 2010. 9.99 (978-0-310-86971-9(4)) Zondervan.

Out of Time. unabr. ed. Carol Lynn Thomas. Read by Paul Michael Garcia. (J). 2007. 34.99 (978-1-60252-619-8(2)) Find a World.

Out of Times Abyss. Edgar Rice Burroughs. (Running Time: 4 mins.). 2009. audio compact disk 25.95 (978-1-897304-35-8(8)) Dorch Pub Co.

***Out of Time's Abyss.** Edgar Rice Burroughs. (Running Time: 4 mins.). 2009. 19.95 (978-1-897331-13-2(4), AudioRealms) Dorch Pub Co.

Out of Time's Abyss, unabr. ed. Edgar Rice Burroughs. Read by Brian Emerson. 3 cass. (Running Time: 4 hrs. 30 mins.). 1999. 23.95 (978-0-7861-1623-2(4), 2451) Blckstn Audio.
On Caprona, the Land That Time Forgot, all of the world's savage past still lived. Here were dinosaurs & flying reptiles, here were the most primitive of cavemen & the last of the Bronze Age Barbarians. But there was one more secret that the claws & fangs & sharp-edged spears guarded most of all. This is the story of the man who tried to find that final secret.

Out of Time's Abyss. unabr. ed. Edgar Rice Burroughs. Read by Brian Emerson. 1 CD. (Running Time: 3 hrs. 30 mins.). 2001. audio compact disk 19.95 (zm2451) Blckstn Audio.

Out of Time's Abyss. unabr. ed. Edgar Rice Burroughs. Read by Brian Emerson. (Running Time: 4 hrs.). 1999. 24.95 (978-0-7861-9574-9(6)) Blckstn Audio.

Out of Time's Abyss. unabr. ed. Edgar Rice Burroughs. Read by Brian Emerson. 3 CDs. (Running Time: 4 hrs.). 2000. audio compact disk 24.00 (978-0-7861-9913-6(X), z2451) Blckstn Audio.

Out of Work see Poetry & Reflections

Out of Work in America. unabr. ed. Read by Richard Vedder et al. 4 cass. (Running Time: 8 hrs.). (National Conference Program Ser.). 1993. bk. 75.95 (978-0-945999-37-9(2)); 58.95 set. (978-0-945999-36-2(4)) Independent Inst.
The conference re-evaluates Keynesian & other economic theories upon which current economic programs are based to determine their possible roles in generating joblessness. Based on The Institute's book "Out of Work", which presents evidence that government may be the major cause of unemployment," Out of Work in America" explores how real economic growth can be produced & the problem of unemployment can finally be ended.

Out of Your Mind. unabr. ed. Alan Watts. 12 CDs. (Running Time: 14 hrs. 25 min.). 2004. audio compact disk 99.95 (978-1-59179-165-2(0), AF00801D) Sounds True.
Since the publication of his first book, The Spirit of Zen in 1936, Alan Watts has brought the essential teachings of the East to generations of seekers, suggesting the need to "go out of your mind in order to come to your senses." Carefully distilled from hundreds of hours of never-before-released material, Out of Your Mind presents a philosophical tour de force from this legendary self-described "spiritual entertainer" - 12 lucid sessions sparking insights into the nature of reality; death and rebirth; the dilemma of polarity; the suspension of judgment; the art of contemplation; and much more.

Out on a Leash: Exploring the Nature of Reality & Love. unabr. ed. Shirley MacLaine. 2004. 15.95 (978-0-7435-4811-3(6)) Pub: S&S Audio. Dist(s): S and S Inc

Out on the Rim. unabr. ed. Ross Thomas. Narrated by Jerry Farden. 8 cass. (Running Time: 10 hrs. 30 mins.). (Durant & Wu Ser.). 1988. 70.00 (978-1-55690-399-1(5), 88883E7) Recorded Bks.
Hired to take care of five million dollars earmarked for rebels in the Philippine jungle, Durant & Wu are joined by terrorist expert, Booth Stallings; the tricky Otherguy Overby; & the sexy Georgia Blue.

Out Standing in Their Field 1963-1973, Vol. 2. Perf. by New Lost City Ramblers. Anno. by Jon Pankake. 1 cass. (Running Time: 72 min.). 1993. (0-9307-400400-9307-40040-2-9); audio compact disk (0-9307-40040-2-9) Smithsonian Folkways.
Twenty-seven tracks reflect the remarkable breadth of this trio's repertoire & underscore their richly deserved place in the folk song revival movement.

Out to Canaan. Jan Karon. Narrated by John McDonough. 12 CDs. (Running Time: 13 hrs. 15 mins.). (Mitford Ser.: Bk. 4). audio compact disk 116.00 (978-1-4025-3504-8(X)) Recorded Bks.

Out to Canaan. unabr. ed. Jan Karon. Read by John McDonough. (Running Time: 14 hrs.). (Mitford Ser.: Bk. 4). (gr. 12 up). 2006. audio compact disk 39.95 (978-0-14-305924-0(6), PengAudBks) Penguin Grp USA.

Out to Canaan. unabr. ed. Jan Karon. Narrated by John McDonough. 9 cass. (Running Time: 13 hrs. 15 mins.). (Mitford Ser.: Bk. 4). 1997. 83.00 (978-0-7887-0973-9(9), 95081E7) Recorded Bks.
The quiet town of Mitford is abuzz with change - a political candidate is pushing for aggressive development, real estate deals are threatening the familiar landscape & beloved Father Tim plans to retire.

Out to Pasture: But Not over the Hill. abr. ed. Effie Leland Wilder. Illus. by Laurie Allen Klein. 2 cass. (Running Time: 3 hrs.). 1996. 15.95 (978-1-56145-136-4(3)) Peachtree Pubs.

Out with the Old. Lynda Page. 10 cass. (Running Time: 13 hrs. 15 mins.). (Story Sound Ser.). (J). 2004. 84.95 (978-1-85903-719-5(4)) Pub: Mgna Lrg Print GBR. Dist(s): Ulverscroft US

Out with the Tide. Brian Cooper. Read by Gordon Griffin. 7 cass. 2007. 61.95 (978-1-84559-550-0(5)) Pub: Soundings Ltd GBR. Dist(s): Ulverscroft US

Outa Darkness Enta Lite. Arrow Records. 2008. audio compact disk 10.00 (978-1-59944-690-5(1)) Creflo Dollar.

Outback: A Journey to the Interior. unabr. ed. 2 CDs. (Running Time: 1 hr. 36 mins.). 2002. audio compact disk 19.95 (978-0-9709865-0-4(5)) Gifts Art.

Outback Heart. unabr. ed. Joanne van Os. Read by Joanne van Os. (Running Time: 13 hrs. 5 mins.). 2009. 43.95 (978-1-74214-440-5(3), 9781742144405) Pub: Bolinda Pubng AUS. Dist(s): Bolinda Pub Inc

Outback Murders. unabr. ed. Howard H. Hilton. Read by Kevin Foley. 8 cass. (Running Time: 10 hrs.). (Howard H. Hilton International Mystery Ser.). 1996. 49.95 (978-1-55686-663-0(1)) Books in Motion.
World water shortages spawn incidents of plague, drought & armed conflict. A highly efficient desalination system is developed in the Outback & followed by a power struggle.

Outbound Flight. abr. ed. Timothy Zahn. Read by Jonathan Davis. (Running Time: 21600 sec.). (Star Wars Ser.). (ENG.). 2006. audio compact disk 29.95 (978-0-7393-0324-5(4), Random AudioBks) Pub: Random Audio Pubg. Dist(s): Random

Outbound Travel Services in China: A Strategic Reference 2007. Compiled by Icon Group International, Inc. Staff. 2007. ring bd. 195.00 (978-0-497-35888-4(3)) Icon Grp.

Outbound Travel Services in Russia: A Strategic Reference 2007. Compiled by Icon Group International, Inc. Staff. 2007. ring bd. 195.00 (978-0-497-82403-7(5)) Icon Grp.

Outbreak. Chris Ryan. Read by Rupert Degas. (Running Time: 3 hrs. 7 mins. 0 sec.). (Code Red Ser.). (ENG., (YA). (gr. 7). 2008. audio compact disk 24.99 (978-1-84657-681-2(4)) Pub: Transworld GBR. Dist(s): IPG Chicago

Outbreak. unabr. ed. Robin Cook. Read by Donada Peters. 8 cass. (Running Time: 8 hrs.). 1993. 64.00 (978-0-7366-2348-3(5), 3126) Books on Tape.
Murder & mystery reach epidemic proportions when a devastating plague sweeps the country, killing all in its path.

Outbreak of World War Two. 10.00 (HE813) Esstee Audios.
Examines the events leading up to the start of the greatest conflict in human history.

Outcast. abr. ed. Paul Dengelegi. Read by Tim Nelson. Created by Barry Sadler. Abr. by Odin Westgaard. 2 cass. (Running Time: 3 hrs.). (Casca Ser.: No. 25). 2004. 18.00 (978-1-58807-125-5(1)) Am Pubng Inc.
The saga of the Eternal Mercenary, created by legendary Special Forces and Vietnam combat veteran Barry Sadler, continues. Casca - cursed by Christ on Golgotha, condemned to outlive the ages and wander the globe a constant soldier, forever fighting, surviving, waiting for Him to return. In Regency London, Casca makes a living as a bare-knuckles boxer until he wins one too many fights. He has offended Lord Banks - and cost his lordship a lot of money. Casca is attacked, but his curse keeps him alive to suffer the horrors of transportation to Botany Bay.

***Outcast.** unabr. ed. Aaron Allston. Read by Marc Thompson. 8 CDs. (Running Time: 10 hrs. 30 mins.). (Star Wars Ser.). 2009. audio compact disk 80.00 (978-1-4159-6007-3(0), BksonTape) Pub: Random Audio Pubg. Dist(s): Random

Outcast. unabr. ed. Aaron Allston. Read by Marc Thompson. (Star Wars Ser.). 2009. audio compact disk 39.95 (978-0-7393-7661-4(6), Random AudioBks) Pub: Random Audio Pubg. Dist(s): Random

Outcast. unabr. ed. Josephine Cox. Read by Maggie Ollerenshaw. 8 cass. (Running Time: 8 hrs.). 1993. 69.95 (978-0-7451-4112-1(9), CAB 795) AudioGO.
Thadius Grady has made a grave mistake by entrusting his entire fortune & his daughter, Emma, to his conniving brother-in-law, Caleb Crowther. Caleb refuses to let Thadius see Emma as his last dying wish. But, Caleb lives in fear of the past. How did Emma's mother mysteriously die? And why did they hate the river people so intensely? When Emma falls helplessly in love with a young barge operator, history seems likely to repeat itself.

Outcast. unabr. ed. Kathryn Lasky. (Running Time: 5 hrs. NaN mins.). (Guardians of Ga'Hoole Ser.: Bk. 8). 2009. audio compact disk 40.00 (978-1-4332-2630-4(8)); audio compact disk 34.95 (978-1-4332-2629-8(4)) Blckstn Audio.

Outcast. unabr. ed. Kathryn Lasky. Read by Pamela Garelick. (Running Time: 5 hrs.). (Guardians of Ga'Hoole Ser.: Bk. 8). 2010. 19.95 (978-1-4332-2633-5(2)) Blckstn Audio.

***Outcast.** unabr. ed. Kathryn Lasky. Read by Pamela Garelick. (Running Time: 5 hrs.). (Guardians of Ga'Hoole Ser.: Bk. 8). 2010. audio compact disk 19.95 (978-1-4332-2632-8(4)) Blckstn Audio.

Outcast. unabr. ed. Rosemary Sutcliff. Read by Johanna Ward. 6 cass. (Running Time: 8 hrs. 30 mins.). 2001. 44.95 (978-0-7861-1965-3(9), 2736); audio compact disk 56.00 (978-0-7861-9759-0(5), 2736) Blckstn Audio.
When a great storm comes, a Roman trading vessel is wrecked on the treacherous coast of southwest Britain & the infant son of a Roman soldier is the only survivor. Beric grows up with a Briton tribe, but to his foster people he remains an alien, one of the Red Crests. So when bad times come, the tribe holds him responsible & casts him out. Rejected by the only life he knows, the boy turns to his own people, but Rome too rejects him. Lost, bewildered, a captive in his father's land, he escapes from slavery, only to be captured again & condemned to labor for the rest of his life on the rowing benches of a galley of the Rhenus Fleet.

Outcast of Poker Flat see Luck of Roaring Camp & Other Stories

Outcast of the Islands. unabr. collector's ed. Joseph Conrad. Read by Wolfram Kandinsky. 8 cass. (Running Time: 12 hrs.). 1978. 64.00 (978-0-7366-0086-6(8), 1095) Books on Tape.
"An Outcast of the Islands" is the story of a self-deluded South Seas trader who, for reasons that are as false as his own self-assessment, marries a Malay woman. Ostracized by his own society, in time he earns the contempt of the natives. Hence, he truly becomes an "Outcast of the Islands".

Outcasts of Poker Flat see Great American Short Stories

Outcasts of Poker Flat see Fourteen American Masterpieces

Outcasts of Poker Flat. Bret Harte. 10.00 (LSS1126) Esstee Audios.

Outcasts of Poker Flat. abr. ed. Bret Harte. Read by Ed Begley. 1 cass. (J). 1984. 12.95 (978-0-694-50123-6(9), SWC 1166) HarperCollins Pubs.

Outcasts of Poker Flat. unabr. ed. Bret Harte. Read by Jack Benson. (Running Time: 52 min.). 1981. 8.95 (N-61) Jimcin Record.
Famous local color yarns of the old West.

Outcasts of 19 Schuyler Place. E. L. Konigsburg. Read by Molly Ringwald. 5 CDs. (Running Time: 5 hrs. 32 mins.). (J). (gr. 5-8). 2004. audio compact disk 38.25 (978-1-4000-8609-2(4), Listening Lib) Pub: Random Audio Pubg. Dist(s): NetLibrary CO

Outcasts of 19 Schuyler Place. unabr. ed. E. L. Konigsburg. Read by Molly Ringwald. 4 cass. (Running Time: 5 hrs 32 mins.). (J). (gr. 5-8). 2004. 32.00 (978-0-8072-2326-0(3), Listening Lib) Random Audio Pubg.
Twelve-year-old Margaret Rose Kane declares her independence when she politely, but firmly, refuses to "fit in" at summer camp. Fortunately, her great uncles Alex and Morris are happy to bring her to their home on Schuyler Place where she quickly learns about a dispute between the elderly men and a neighborhood group. The controversy centers on the uncle's colorful backyard towers that the neighbors believe lower their property values.

Outcasts United: A Refugee Team, an American Town. abr. ed. Warren St. John. Read by Lincoln Hoppe. (ENG.). 2009. audio compact disk 29.95 (978-0-7393-6617-2(3), Random AudioBks) Pub: Random Audio Pubg. Dist(s): Random

Outcome of Abiding in Jesus Series, Set. Elbert Willis. 4 cass. 13.00 Fill the Gap.

Outcry. unabr. ed. Henry James. Narrated by Flo Gibson. 2003. 19.95 (978-1-55685-733-1(0)) Audio Bk Con.
National pride and artistic considerations vie with greed and temptations over the possible sale of a great painting.

Outdoor Recreation & Hiking on Public Lands - River Etiquette; Prison Inmates Helping with Park Maintenance; Michael Hodgson's Wilderness Trip. Hosted by Nancy Pearlman. 1 cass. (Running Time: 30 min.). 10.00 (1212) Educ Comm CA.

Outdoor Schooling in Tulare County. Hosted by Nancy Pearlman. 1 cass. (Running Time: 30 min.). 10.00 (517) Educ Comm CA.

Outer Banks. abr. ed. Anne Rivers Siddons. Read by Kate Nelligan. 2 cass. (Running Time: 3 hrs.). 2000. 7.95 (978-1-57815-044-1(2), 1035, Media Bks Audio) Media Bks NJ.
A revealing story of one woman's struggle to face the dark truths about her golden past.

Outer Banks. unabr. ed. Anne Rivers Siddons. Narrated by C. J. Critt. 11 cass. (Running Time: 16 hrs. 15 mins.). 1994. 91.00 (978-1-55690-974-0(8), 94113E7) Recorded Bks.
When Katherine Stuart Lee is invited back for a reunion at the beachfront home on the outer banks of South Carolina, she is torn between the desire to forget or revive the memories. Does forgiveness come with maturity, or will reunion reignite the flames?.

***Outer Banks Low Price.** abr. ed. Anne Rivers Siddons. Read by Kate Nelligan. (ENG.). 2005. (978-0-06-087937-2(8), Harper Audio); (978-0-06-087936-5(X), Harper Audio) HarperCollins Pubs.

Outer Darkness. abr. ed. James Axler. 2 cass. (Running Time: 180 min.). (Outlanders Ser.: No. 10). 2000. 7.99 (978-1-55204-457-5(2)) DC Comics.

Outer Planet Colonization Technology. Ed. by Marco A. V. Bitetto. 1 cass. 2000. (978-1-58578-350-2(1)) Inst of Cybernetics.

Outer Planet Messages for the New Age. Ginger Chalford. 1 cass. (Running Time: 90 min.). 1988. 8.95 (641) Am Fed Astrologers.

Outer Space. Read by Peter Millman. 1 cass. (Running Time: 30 min.). 14.95 (CBC241) MMI Corp.
Talks about comets, meteorites, other phenomena.

Outer Space Inner Space. Todd Liebenow et al. Music by Mark Bradford. 2001. audio compact disk 15.00 (978-1-58302-191-0(4)) One Way St.

Outerbridge Reach. unabr. ed. Robert Stone. Read by Michael Shannon. 8 cass. (Running Time: 12 hrs.). 2000. Rental 11.50 (GKH 038) Chivers Audio Bks GBR.
Annapolis graduate and Vietnam veteran, Owen Browne started out as one of the golden boys of his generation. Now in his forties, Browne works for a yacht brokerage in Connecticut. When the owner of the company disappears, leaving his place unfilled in a round-the-world singlehanded sailing race, Browne offers to take it on impulse. But Browne has never been out on the high seas alone!.

Outermost House: A Year of Life on the Great Beach of Cape Cod. unabr. ed. Henry Beston. Narrated by Brett Barry. 5 CDs. (Running Time: 5 hrs.). 2007. audio compact disk 29.95 (978-0-9793115-0-5(0)) Silver Hollow.

Outfit. unabr. collector's ed. Richard Stark, pseud. Read by Michael Kramer. 4 cass. (Running Time: 6 hrs.). 1999. 32.00 (978-0-7366-4411-2(3), 4872) Books on Tape.
Ripping off the Outfit was the easy part of Parker's game. Going one-on-one with Bronson, the Outfit's Big Boss, was the hard part. Hard for anyone but Parker - because the entire underworld knew it was written in blood: whatever Parker did, he did deadly.

***Outfit: A Parker Novel.** Richard Stark. (Running Time: 5 hrs. 0 mins. 0 sec.). (ENG.). 2011. audio compact disk 19.95 (978-1-60998-147-1(2)) Pub: AudioGO. Dist(s): Perseus Dist

Outgrowing Parent-Child Roles: Relating to Each Other As Respectful Adults. unabr. ed. David Grudermeyer & Rebecca Grudermeyer. 2 cass. (Running Time: 3 hrs.). 1999. 18.95 (T-60) Willingness Wrks.

Outlander: With Bonus Content. Diana Gabaldon. Narrated by Davina Porter. (Running Time: 117000 sec.). (Outlander Ser.: Bk. 1). 2006. audio compact disk 49.99 (978-1-4193-8101-0(6)) Recorded Bks.

Outlander: With Bonus Content. unabr. ed. Diana Gabaldon. Narrated by Davina Porter. 23 cass. (Running Time: 32 hrs. 30 mins.). (Outlander Ser.: Bk. 1). 1997. 175.00 (978-0-7887-1298-2(5), 95132E7) Recorded Bks.
A landmark novel of Scottish lore in which one woman is torn between past & present, passion & love.

Outlanders 1: Exile to Hell. 2006. audio compact disk 19.99 (978-1-59950-089-8(2)) GraphicAudio.

Outlanders 10: Outer Darkness. Based on a novel by James Axler. 2007. audio compact disk 19.99 (978-1-59950-375-2(1)) GraphicAudio.

Outlanders 11: Armagaddon Axis. Based on a novel by James Axler. 2007. audio compact disk 19.99 (978-1-59950-388-2(3)) GraphicAudio.

Outlanders 12: Wreath of Fire. Directed By Terence Aselford. Contrib. by Nanette Savard et al. (Running Time: 21600 sec.). (Outlanders Ser.). 2008. audio compact disk 19.99 (978-1-59950-438-4(3)) GraphicAudio.

Outlanders 13: Shadow Scourge. Based on a novel by James Axler. 2008. audio compact disk 19.99 (978-1-59950-452-0(9)) GraphicAudio.

Outlanders 14: Hell Rising. James Axler. 2008. audio compact disk 19.99 (978-1-59950-503-9(7)) GraphicAudio.

Outlanders 15: Doom Dynasty. James Axler. 2009. audio compact disk 19.99 (978-1-59950-538-1(X)) GraphicAudio.

Outlanders 16: Tigers of Heaven. James Axler. 2004. audio compact disk 19.99 (978-1-933059-53-2(2)) GraphicAudio.

Outlanders 17: Purgatory Road. James Axler. 2004. audio compact disk 19.99 (978-1-933059-58-7(3)) GraphicAudio.

Outlanders 18: Sargasso Plunder. James Axler. 2004. audio compact disk 19.99 (978-1-933059-62-4(1)) GraphicAudio.

Outlanders 19: Tomb of Time. James Axler. 2005. audio compact disk 19.99 (978-1-933059-66-2(4)) GraphicAudio.

Outlanders 2: Destiny Run. James Axler. 2006. audio compact disk 19.99 (978-1-59950-124-6(4)) GraphicAudio.

Outlanders 20: Prodigal Chalice. James Axler. 2005. audio compact disk 19.99 (978-1-933059-70-9(2)) GraphicAudio.

Outlanders 21: Devil in the Moon. James Axler. 2005. audio compact disk 19.99 (978-1-933059-74-7(5)) GraphicAudio.

Outlanders 22: Dragoneye. James Axler. 2005. audio compact disk 19.99 (978-1-933059-78-5(8)) GraphicAudio.

Outlanders 23: Far Empire. James Axler. 2005. audio compact disk 19.99 (978-1-933059-82-2(6)) GraphicAudio.

Outlanders 24: Equinox Zero. James Axler. 2005. audio compact disk 19.99 (978-1-933059-86-0(9)) GraphicAudio.

Outlanders 25: Talon & Fang. James Axler. 2006. audio compact disk 19.99 (978-1-933059-90-7(7)) GraphicAudio.

Outlanders 26: Sea of Plague. James Axler. 2005. audio compact disk 19.99 (978-1-933059-94-5(X)) GraphicAudio.

Outlanders 27: Awakening. James Axler. 2005. audio compact disk 19.99 (978-1-933059-98-3(2)) GraphicAudio.

Outlanders 28: Mad God's Wrath. James Axler. 2005. audio compact disk 19.99 (978-1-59950-001-0(9)) GraphicAudio.

Outlanders 29: Sun Lord. 2005. audio compact disk 19.99 (978-1-59950-008-9(6)) GraphicAudio.

Outlanders 3: Savage Sun. 2006. audio compact disk 19.99 (978-1-59950-140-6(6)) GraphicAudio.

Outlanders 30: Mask of the Sphinx. 2005. audio compact disk 19.99 (978-1-59950-014-0(0)) GraphicAudio.

Outlanders 31: Uluru Destiny. 2006. audio compact disk 19.99 (978-1-59950-020-1(5)) GraphicAudio.

Outlanders 32: Evil Abyss. 2006. audio compact disk 19.99 (978-1-59950-026-3(4)) GraphicAudio.

Outlanders 33: Children of the Serpent. James Axler. (Running Time: 28800 sec.). (Outlanders Ser.). 2006. audio compact disk 19.99 (978-1-59950-031-7(0)) GraphicAudio.

Outlanders 34: Successors. 2005. audio compact disk 19.99 (978-1-59950-073-7(6)) GraphicAudio.

Outlanders 35: Cerberus Storm. 2006. audio compact disk 19.99 (978-1-59950-109-3(0)) GraphicAudio.

Outlanders 36: Refuge. 2006. audio compact disk 19.99 (978-1-59950-132-1(5)) GraphicAudio.

Outlanders 37: Rim of the World. 2006. audio compact disk 19.99 (978-1-59950-171-0(6)) GraphicAudio.

Outlanders 38: Lords of the Deep. 2006. audio compact disk 19.99 (978-1-59950-192-5(9)) GraphicAudio.

Outlanders 39: Hydra's Rising. 2007. audio compact disk 19.99 (978-1-59950-211-3(9)) GraphicAudio.

Outlanders 4: Omega Path. 2006. audio compact disk 19.99 (978-1-59950-182-6(1)) GraphicAudio.

Outlanders 40: Closing the Cosmic Eye. 2007. audio compact disk 19.99 (978-1-59950-322-6(0)) GraphicAudio.

Outlanders 41: Skull Throne. 2007. audio compact disk 19.99 (978-1-59950-339-4(5)) GraphicAudio.

Outlanders 42: Satan's Seed. 2007. audio compact disk 19.99 (978-1-59950-357-8(3)) GraphicAudio.

Outlanders 43: Dark Goddess. Based on a novel by James Axler. 2008. audio compact disk Rental 19.99 (978-1-59950-410-0(3)) GraphicAudio.

Outlanders 44: Grailstone Gambit. Based on a novel by James Axler. 2008. audio compact disk 19.99 (978-1-59950-477-3(4)) GraphicAudio.

Outlanders 45: Ghostwalk. James Axler. 2009. audio compact disk 19.99 (978-1-59950-522-0(3)) GraphicAudio.

Outlanders 46: Pantheon of Vengeance. James Axler. 2009. audio compact disk 19.99 (978-1-59950-561-9(4)) GraphicAudio.

Outlanders 47: Death Cry. James Axler. 2009. audio compact disk 19.99 (978-1-59950-585-5(1)) GraphicAudio.

Outlanders 48: Serpent's Tooth. Based on a novel by James Axler. 2009. audio compact disk 19.99 (978-1-59950-619-7(X)) GraphicAudio.

Outlanders 49: Shadow Box. Based on a novel by James Axler. 2010. audio compact disk 19.99 (978-1-59950-640-1(8)) GraphicAudio.

Outlanders 5: Parallax Red. 2007. audio compact disk 19.99 (978-1-59950-200-7(3)) GraphicAudio.

Outlanders 50: Janus Trap. Based on a novel by James Axler. 2010. audio compact disk 19.99 (978-1-59950-635-7(1)) GraphicAudio.

Outlanders 6: Doomstar Relic. 2007. audio compact disk 19.99 (978-1-59950-222-9(4)) GraphicAudio.

Outlanders 7: Iceblood. 2007. audio compact disk 19.99 (978-1-59950-313-4(1)) GraphicAudio.

Outlanders 8: Hellbound Fury. 2007. audio compact disk 19.99 (978-1-59950-330-1(1)) GraphicAudio.

Outlanders 9: Night Eternal. 2007. audio compact disk 19.99 (978-1-59950-348-6(4)) GraphicAudio.

Outlasting & Enduring Adversity. Speeches. Creflo A. Dollar. 2 cass. (Running Time: 3 hrs.). 2002. 10.00 (978-1-59089-222-0(4)) Creflo Dollar.

***Outlaw Demon Wails.** unabr. ed. Kim Harrison. Read by Gigi Bermingham. (ENG.). 2008. (978-0-06-162954-9(5)); (978-0-06-162955-6(3)) HarperCollins Pubs.

Outlaw Demon Wails. unabr. ed. Kim Harrison. Read by Gigi Bermingham. 14 CDs. (Running Time: 16 hrs. 30 mins.). (Hollows Ser.: Bk. 6). 2008. audio compact disk 44.95 (978-0-06-145298-7(X), Harper Audio) HarperCollins Pubs.

Outlaw Kingdom. abr. ed. Matt Braun. Read by Jim Gough. 4 cass. (Running Time: 6 hrs.). 2002. 24.95 (978-1-890990-89-3(2), 99089) Otis Audio.
Western with sound effects.

Outlaw Mountain. J. A. Jance. Contrib. by Yancy Butler. (Joanna Brady Mystery Ser.). 2008. 59.99 (978-1-60640-673-1(6)) Find a World.

Outlaw Mountain. unabr. ed. J. A. Jance. Read by Stephanie Brush. 12 cass. (Running Time: 11 hrs. 30 min.). (Joanna Brady Mystery Ser.). 1999. 64.95 (978-1-55686-928-0(2)) Books in Motion.
Sheriff Joanna Brady finds herself in a murky morass of graft and political corruption when investigating the death of the mayor's mother in the deadly Arizona sun.

***Outlaw Mountain.** unabr. ed. J. A. Jance. Read by C. J. Critt. (ENG.). 2010. (978-0-06-195389-7(X), Harper Audio); (978-0-06-196720-7(3), Harper Audio) HarperCollins Pubs.

Outlaw Mountain, Set. abr. ed. J. A. Jance. Read by Yancy Butler. 4 cass. (Joanna Brady Mystery Ser.). 1999. 25.00 (FS9-50995) Highsmith.

Outlaw Mountain, Set. unabr. ed. J. A. Jance. Read by Yancy Butler. 8 cass. (Joanna Brady Mystery Ser.). 1999. 36.00 (FS9-51010) Highsmith.

***Outlaw of Gor.** unabr. ed. John Norman. Read by Ralph Lister. (Running Time: 9 hrs.). (Gorean Saga Ser.). 2010. 24.99 (978-1-4418-4790-4(1), 9781441847904, Brilliance MP3); 39.97 (978-1-4418-4791-1(X), 9781441847911, Brlnc Audio MP3 Lib); 24.99 (978-1-4418-4792-8(8), 9781441847928, BAD); 39.97 (978-1-4418-4793-5(6), 9781441847935, BADLE); audio compact disk 29.99 (978-1-4418-4788-1(X), 9781441847881, Bril Audio CD Unabri); audio compact disk 87.97 (978-1-4418-4789-8(8), 9781441847898, BriAudCD Unabrid) Brilliance Audio.

Outlaw Princess of Sherwood. unabr. ed. Nancy Springer. 3 cass. (Running Time: 3 hrs. 15 min.). (Tales of Rowan Hood Ser.: No. 3). 2003. 29.00 (978-1-4025-6306-5(X)) Recorded Bks.

Outlaw Tamer. unabr. ed. Max Brand. Read by Brian O'Neill. 6 vols. (Running Time: 9 hrs.). 1999. bk. 54.95 (978-0-7927-2265-6(5), CSL 154, Chivers Sound Lib) AudioGO.
Even though young Sandy Sewyen could tame a killer horse or a wild bull, Peter Dunstan & his crew treated Sandy like a half-wit. Catalina Mirandos, exquisite belle of the range, promised to marry the man who captured & tamed her wild, white mare. Dunstan sent Sandy up into the mountains to find the horse. No one was more surprised than Dunstan when Sandy returned with the docile mare ready to claim his prize.

Outlaw Treasures. W. C. Jameson. (American Storytelling Ser.). (J). (gr. 3-7). 1997. 12.00 (978-0-87483-493-2(7)) Pub: August Hse. Dist(s): Natl Bk Netwk

Outlaw Valley. unabr. ed. Max Brand. Read by Kevin Foley. 6 cass. (Running Time: 6 hrs. 42 min.). 1994. 39.95 (978-1-55686-527-5(9)) Books in Motion.
Wild, young Terry Shawn meets a mysterious stranger & learns the real meaning of honesty & friendship. He also learns that adventure without regard for others could lead to disaster.

Outlaws. unabr. ed. Selma Lagerlöf. Read by Walter Zimmerman. 1 cass. (Running Time: 76 min.). Dramatization. 1980. 8.95 (N-49) Jimcin Record.
Best short stories of Nobel Prize winning author.

***Outlaws: A Presidential Agent Novel.** W. E. B. Griffin & William E. Butterworth, IV. (Running Time: 19 hrs.). (Presidential Agent Ser.). (ENG.). 2010. audio compact disk 44.95 (978-0-14-242883-2(3), PengAudBks) Penguin Grp USA.

***Outlaws All.** Max Brand. Contrib. by Jim Bond. (Playaway Adult Fiction Ser.). (ENG.). 2009. 44.99 (978-1-4418-2953-5(9)) Find a World.

Outlaws All. unabr. ed. Max Brand. Read by Richard Choate. 8 cass. (Running Time: 12 hrs.). 1997. 64.00 (4482) Books on Tape.
A trio of short novels from the legendary master of Westerns. . ALEC THE GREAT is set in Alaska during the gold rush & provides the background of the bitter enmity between Hugh Massey & Amie Calmont, once great friends & partners. RIDING INTO PERIL recounts the tale of Kantwell Irving Dangerfield, commonly known as the Kid - a man wronged by the law & bound for adventure & revenge. OUTLAWS ALL is a story in the tradition of Jack London: an encounter between a gentle giant of a man & a mighty wolf dog, known as The Ghos.

Outlaws All. unabr. ed. Max Brand. Read by Jim Bond. (Running Time: 9 hrs.). 2007. audio compact disk 24.95 (978-1-4233-3575-7(9), 9781423335757, Brilliance MP3); audio compact disk 39.25 (978-1-4233-3576-4(7), 9781423335764, Brlnc Audio MP3 Lib) Brilliance Audio.

Outlaws All. unabr. ed. Max Brand. Read by Jim Bond. (Running Time: 7 hrs.). 2007. 39.25 (978-1-4233-3578-8(3), 9781423335788, BADLE); 24.95 (978-1-4233-3577-1(5), 9781423335771, BAD) Brilliance Audio.

Outlaws All. unabr. ed. Max Brand. Read by Jim Bond. (Running Time: 9 hrs.). 2009. audio compact disk 19.99 (978-1-4418-0471-6(4), 9781441804716, Bril Audio CD Unabri); audio compact disk 59.97 (978-1-4418-0472-3(2), 9781441804723, BriAudCD Unabrid) Brilliance Audio.

Outlaws & Gunfighters of the Old West. Narrated by Phillip Steele & John D. LeVan. Music by John D. LeVan. 1 cass. (Running Time: 31 min.). (ENG.). 1997. 8.95 (978-1-56554-358-4(0)) Pelican.
Original songs are an entertaining view of the true history of these personalities and events.

Outlaw's Code. unabr. collector's ed. Max Brand. Read by Wolfram Kandinsky. 5 cass. (Running Time: 7 hrs. 30 min.). 1992. 40.00 (978-0-7366-2299-8(3), 3083) Books on Tape.
In the old days half the drifters & hard cases in the west ended up in El Paso. It had everything: easy money, easy women, easy laws. But then Marshal Neilan moved in to clean it up.

Outlaws of Poplar Creek; Bowdrie Follows a Cold Trail; His Brother's Debt. unabr. ed. Louis L'Amour. Read by Dramatization Staff. (Running Time: 10800 sec.). (ENG.). 2008. audio compact disk 14.99 (978-0-7393-5883-2(9), Random AudioBks) Pub: Random Audio Pubg. Dist(s): Random

Outliers: The Story of Success. unabr. ed. Malcolm Gladwell. Read by Malcolm Gladwell. (Running Time: 8 hrs.). (ENG.). 2008. 26.98 (978-1-60024-392-9(4)); audio compact disk 39.98 (978-1-60024-391-2(6)) Pub: Hachet Audio. Dist(s): HachBkGrp

Outline of History, Pt. 1. unabr. ed. H. G. Wells. Read by Bernard Mayes. 15 cass. (Running Time: 22 hrs. 30 mins.). 1993. 95.95 (1365-A) Blckstn Audio.
Disillusioned by the World War I peace settlement, convinced that humanity needed to awaken to the instability of the world order & remember lessons from the past. Wells hoped to remind mankind of its common past, provide it with a basis for international patriotism & guide it to renounce war.

Outline of History, Pt. 2. unabr. ed. H. G. Wells. Read by Bernard Mayes. 16 cass. (Running Time: 24 hrs.). 99.95 (1365-B) Blckstn Audio.
Wells hoped to remind mankind of its common past, provide it with a basis for international patriotism & guide it to renounce war.

Outline of History: The Whole Story of Man. unabr. ed. H. G. Wells. Read by Bernard Mayes. 16 cass. (Running Time: 45 hrs. 30 mins.). 2000. 99.95 (978-0-7861-0638-7(7), 1365A,B) Blckstn Audio.

Outline of History: The Whole Story of Man. unabr. ed. H. G. Wells. Read by Bernard Mayes. 15 cass. (Running Time: 45 hrs. 30 mins.). 2006. 95.95 (978-0-7861-0413-0(9), 1365A,B) Blckstn Audio.

***Outlive Your Life: You Were Made to Make a Difference.** unabr. ed. Max Lucado. 2010. audio compact disk 24.99 (978-0-8499-4613-4(1)) Nelson.

Outpatient Ministry: Creating a Partnership Between Hospital & Congregation. 1 cass. (Care Cassettes Ser.: Vol. 2, No. 5). 1994. 10.80 Assn Prof Chaplains.

Outpatient Surgery as Related to the G[illegible]ologist Obstetrician. 2 cass. (Gynecology & Obstetrics Ser.: C85-GC[illegible]5.00 (8562 (C85-GO4)) Am Coll Surgeons.

Outpost! abr. ed. Dana Fuller Ross, pseud. Read by Sambrook Erikson. 4 vols. (Wagons West: Bk. 3). 2003. 25.00 (978-1-58807-144-6(8)); (978-1-58807-644-1(X)) Am Pubng Inc.

Outpost! abr. ed. Dana Fuller Ross, pseud. Read by Sambrook Erikson. 5 vols. (Wagons West: Bk. 3). 2004. audio compact disk 30.00 (978-1-58807-400-3(5)); audio compact disk (978-1-58807-632-8(6)) Am Pubng Inc.

Outpost of Progress see Tales of Unrest

Outpost of Progress. (S-22) Jimcin Record.

***Outposts.** abr. ed. Simon Winchester. Read by Simon Winchester. (ENG.). 2005. (978-0-06-084557-5(0), Harper Audio); (978-0-06-084556-8(2), Harper Audio) HarperCollins Pubs.

Outposts: Journeys to the Surviving Relics of the British Empire. abr. ed. Simon Winchester. Read by Simon Winchester. 2005. audio compact disk 29.95 (978-0-06-079718-8(5)) HarperCollins Pubs.

Outpouring of the Spirit. Kenneth Copeland. 6 cass. 1993. mass mkt. 30.00 Set incl. study guide. (978-0-88114-288-4(3)) K Copeland Pubns.
Biblical study on Spirit-filled living.

Outpouring of the Spirit. Jack Deere. 1 cass. (Running Time: 90 mins.). (Intimacy with God & the End-Time Church Ser.: Vol. 4). 2000. 5.00 (JD09-004) Morning NC.
Oneness with the Father is essential for every believer in these last days & the teaching in this six-tape series will impart a heartfelt hunger for intimate fellowship with Him.

Outrageous Consulting. unabr. ed. Suzanne Bailey-Jones & Lara Ewing. 5 cass. (Running Time: 5 hrs. 9 mins.). 1997. 159.95 N L P Comp.
Broaden the range of capacities you use to create results in business. An incredibly valuable resource for consultants, trainers, coaches or any change agent in an organization.

***Outrageous Fortunes: The Twelve Surprising Trends That Will Reshape the Global Economy.** unabr. ed. Daniel Altman. (Running Time: 8 hrs. 30 mins.). 2011. 29.95 (978-1-4417-7228-2(6)); 59.95 (978-1-4417-7225-1(1)); audio compact disk 29.95 (978-1-4417-7227-5(8)); audio compact disk 76.00 (978-1-4417-7226-8(X)) Blckstn Audio.

Outrageous Joy. abr. ed. Patsy Clairmont. 2 cass. (Running Time: 3 hrs.). 1999. 16.99 (978-0-310-22660-4(0)) Zondervan.
Women of Faith equals joy! Triumphant joy, exuberant joy . . . outrageous joy! And no wonder, because as this sparkling, love-and-laughter-filled tape reveals, we serve an outrageously joyful God. With infectious good humor, authors and Women of Faith conference speakers Patsy Claimont, Barbara Johnson, Marilyn Meberg, Luci Swindoll, Sheila Walsh, and Thelma Wells offer irresistible reasons for rejoicing in every circumstance of life.

Outrageous Joy: The Life-Changing, Soul-Shaking Truth about God. abr. ed. Patsy Clairmont et al. (Running Time: 3 hrs. 0 mins. 0 sec.). (ENG.). 2003. 10.99 (978-0-310-26083-7(3)) Zondervan.

Outrageous Masquerade. Gillian Kaye. (Soundings Ser.). (J). 2006. 49.95 (978-1-84559-032-1(5)) Pub: ISIS Lrg Prnt GBR. Dist(s): Ulverscroft US

Outreach. Ed. by Robert A. Monroe. 1 cass. (Running Time: 30 min.). (Meta Music Ser.). 1985. 12.95 (978-1-56102-218-2(7)) Inter Indus.
A musical form organized around the Hemi-Sync process whereby one may - simply by listening quietly - expand one's awareness beyond the limits of time/space illusion.

Outreach: Technology in the Service of Public Library Patrons. 2 cass. 1990. 16.00 set. Recorded Res.

Outreach Spanish. William C. Harvey. 2 cass. (SPA.). 2001. 5.00 (978-0-7641-1412-0(3)) Barron.

Outreach to Visually Impaired & Special Patrons. 2 cass. 1990. 16.00 set. Recorded Res.

Outside Beauty. unabr. ed. Cynthia Kadohata. Read by Sue Jean Kim. (Running Time: 6 hrs. 0 mins. 0 sec.). (ENG.). (J). (gr. 7). 2008. audio compact disk 29.95 (978-0-7435-7210-1(6)) Pub: S&S Audio. Dist(s): S and S Inc

Outside Dog Book & Tape. abr. ed. Charlotte Pomerantz. Read by Becca Lish. Illus. by Jennifer Plecas. Contrib. by Becca Lish. (Running Time: 45

min.). (I Can Read Bks.). (J). (gr. k-3). 1996. 8.99 (978-0-694-70050-9(9)) HarperCollins Pubs.

Outside Looking In. unabr. ed. Kathleen Rowntree. Narrated by Diana Bishop. 7 cass. (Running Time: 9 hrs. 30 mins.). 2000. 63.00 (978-1-84197-134-6(0), H1132E7) Recorded Bks.
A quirky host of eye-opening characters inhabits the Best Kept Village, from lectures on litter, to revive a dwindling prestige, to making a mistake of trying to please everyone. To a peeping Tom that unites them all.

***Outside of a Horse.** unabr. ed. Ginny Rorby. Read by To be Announced. (Running Time: 8 hrs. NaN mins.). (ENG.). 2011. 29.95 (978-1-4417-7794-2(6)); 54.95 (978-1-4417-7791-1(1)); audio compact disk 76.00 (978-1-4417-7792-8(X)) Blckstn Audio.

Outside the Circle. rev. ed. Simon Firth. 2005. 59.95 (978-1-4129-1070-5(6)) Pub: P Chapman GBR. Dist(s): SAGE

Outside the Rules. unabr. ed. Dylan Jones. Read by Trudy Harris. 8 cass. (Running Time: 10 hrs. 35 mins.). (Storysound Ser.). (J). 2003. 69.95 (978-1-85903-656-3(2)) Pub: Mgna Lrg Print GBR. Dist(s): Ulverscroft US

Outsider see Extranjero

Outsider. (23299-A) J Norton Pubs.

Outsider. Albert Camus. Read by Hernando Iván Cano. (Running Time: 3 hrs.). 2002. 16.95 (978-1-60083-259-8(8), Audiofy Corp) Iofy Corp.

Outsider. unabr. ed. Ann Gabhart. Narrated by Renee Ertl. (Running Time: 10 hrs. 12 mins. 5 sec.). (ENG.). 2009. 24.49 (978-1-60814-528-7(X)); audio compact disk 34.99 (978-1-59859-588-8(1)) Oasis Audio.

Outsider & The Rats in the Walls. unabr. ed. H. P. Lovecraft. Read by Erik Bauersfeld. 1 cass. (Running Time: 1 hr.). (C). 1995. 7.95 (978-0-940884-78-6(X)) Necronomicon.
Two of Lovecraft's most-famous stories eerily read-performed by Bauersfeld, noted dramatic actor.

Outsider, the Mind Parasites, & Beyond. unabr. ed. Colin Wilson. 2 cass. 1987. 18.00 set. (978-1-56964-806-3(9), A0236-87) Sound Photosyn.
The author of these psychological stories reveals new conclusions.

Outsiders. S. E. Hinton. Read by Jim Fyfe. 4 cass. (Running Time: 5 hrs. 10 mins.). (J). 2000. 32.00 (978-0-7366-9154-3(5)) Books on Tape.
A moving credible view of the outsiders from the inside.

Outsiders. unabr. ed. S. E. Hinton. Read by Jim Fyfe. (J). 2006. 39.99 (978-0-7393-7519-8(9)) Find a World.

Outsiders. unabr. ed. S. E. Hinton. Read by Jim Fyfe. 4 cass. (Running Time: 6 hrs.). (YA). 1999. 29.98 (FS9-25210) Highsmith.

Outsiders. unabr. ed. S. E. Hinton. Read by Jim Fyfe. 4 vols. (Running Time: 5 hrs. 9 mins.). (Young Adult Cassette Library). (J). (gr. 7 up). 1988. pap. bk. 38.00 (978-0-8072-7302-9(3), YA806SP, Listening Lib); 32.00 (978-0-8072-7226-8(4), YA806CX, Listening Lib) Random Audio Pubg.
The war is on between the "greasers" & the "socs." Once you cross into enemy territory there are no rules, as fourteen-year-old Pony-boy & his friend Johnny discover when they overstep their boundaries. They pay with their innocence.

Outsiders. unabr. ed. S. E. Hinton. Read by Jim Fyfe. 5 CDs. (Running Time: 5 hrs. 9 mins.). (J). (gr. 7 up). 2004. audio compact disk 38.25 (978-0-8072-1606-4(2), S YA 349 CD, Listening Lib) Pub: Random Audio Pubg. Dist(s): NetLibrary CO

Outsiders, unabr. ed. S. E. Hinton. Narrated by Spike McClure. 4 pieces. (Running Time: 5 hrs. 30 mins.). (gr. 8 up). 35.00 (978-1-55690-775-3(3), 93133E7) Recorded Bks.
An orphaned young boy & his brothers come of age on the tough side of town. Available to libraries only.

Outsiders. unabr. ed. S. E. Hinton. Narrated by Spike McClure. 5 CDs. (Running Time: 5 hrs. 30 mins.). (gr. 8 up). 2000. audio compact disk 43.00 (978-0-7887-3738-1(4), C1109E7) Recorded Bks.
An orphaned young boy & his brothers come of age on the tough side of town.

Outsiders. unabr. ed. S. E. Hinton. Read by Jim Fyfe. (Running Time: 18540 sec.). (ENG.). (J). (gr. 7). 2006. audio compact disk 25.00 (978-0-7393-3901-5(X), Listening Lib) Pub: Random Audio Pubg. Dist(s): Random

outsider's Edge. unabr. ed. Brent D. Taylor. Read by Adrian Mulraney. (Running Time: 13 hrs. 40 mins.). 2009. 43.95 (978-1-74214-493-1(4), 9781742144931) Pub: Bolinda Pubng AUS. Dist(s): Bolinda Pub Inc

Outsiders' Edge. unabr. ed. Brent D. Taylor. Read by Adrian Mulraney. (Running Time: 49200 sec.). 2008. audio compact disk 108.95 (978-1-921415-17-3(7), 9781921415173) Pub: Bolinda Pubng AUS. Dist(s): Bolinda Pub Inc

***Outsmart Your Back Pain.** 2010. audio compact disk 19.95 (978-0-9845800-0-2(X)) D Vargas.

Outsmarting Goliath: How to Achieve Equal Footing with Companies That Are Bigger, Richer, Older & Better Known. unabr. ed. Debra Koontz Traverso. Read by Anna Fields. 6 cass. (Running Time: 8 hrs. 30 mins.). 2001. 44.95 (978-0-7861-1996-7(9), 2766); audio compact disk 56.00 (978-0-7861-9730-9(7), 2766) Blckstn Audio.
Many of today's consumers, potential customers, turn automatically to brand name products & services, forgetting that the well-advertised brontosauruses often deliver one-of-our-sizes-fits-all service & impersonal sales help. Yet a single phone call, a cleverly crafted letter, a stunning catalog, winning ad, or a well-prepared face-to-face presentation can change a customer's perception. In those crucial situations, the small up-starter can use the tips to capture more clients & give Goliath a headache.

Outsmarting the Female Fat Cell: The First Weight-Control Program Designed Specifically for Women. abr. ed. Debra Waterhouse. 2006. 14.98 (978-1-59483-852-1(6)) Pub: Hachet Audio. Dist(s): HachBkGrp

Outsourced. unabr. ed. R. Hillhouse. Read by Hillary Huber. (Running Time: 12 mins. 30 sec.). (J). 2007. 85.95 (978-0-7861-6805-7(6)) Blckstn Audio.

Outsourced. unabr. ed. R. J. Hillhouse. Read by Hillary Huber. (Running Time: 54000 sec.). 2007. 32.95 (978-0-7861-4980-3(9)); audio compact disk 29.95 (978-0-7861-6957-3(5)); audio compact disk 32.95 (978-0-7861-5784-6(4)); audio compact disk 99.00 (978-0-7861-6804-0(8)) Blckstn Audio.

Outsourcing: A Human Resources Alternative for Creating a Competitive Edge. 1 cass. (Running Time: 2 hrs.). (America's Supermarket Showcase '96 Ser.). 1996. 11.00 (NGA96-030) Sound Images.

Outspeaks: A Rhapsody. Poems. Albert Saijo. Read by Albert Saijo. 1 cass. (Running Time: 1 hr.). (Bamboo Ridge Ser.: Vol. 71). 1997. pap. bk. 18.00 (978-0-910043-52-6(3)); 8.00 (978-0-910043-51-9(5)) Bamboo Ridge Pr.
Beat poetry read by Asian American contemporary of (& co-author to) Jack Kerouac.

Outstanding! 47 Ways to Make Your Organization Exceptional. unabr. ed. John G. Miller. (Running Time: 4 hrs.). (ENG.). (gr. 12 up). 2010. audio compact disk 19.95 (978-0-14-314561-5(4), PengAudBks) Penguin Grp USA.

Outstanding Greek Modern Poetry. 4 cass. (Running Time: 6 hrs.). 42.50 (SGR401) J Norton Pubs.

***Outstretched Shadow.** unabr. ed. Mercedes Lackey & James Mallory. Narrated by Susan Ericksen. (Running Time: 32 hrs. 0 mins.). (Obsidian Ser.). 2010. 31.99 (978-1-4001-8382-1(0)); 44.99 (978-1-4001-6382-3(X)); audio compact disk 119.99 (978-1-4001-4382-5(9)); audio compact disk 59.99 (978-1-4001-1382-8(2)) Pub: Tantor Media. Dist(s): IngramPubServ

Outward Bound. unabr. ed. Sutton Vane. Read by Flo Gibson. 2 cass. (Running Time: 3 hrs.). 1998. bk. 14.95 (978-1-55685-542-9(7)) Audio Bk Con.
Seven passengers on a ship without a captain are bound for the unknown. Are they alive or dead.

Outwitting the Gestapo. unabr. ed. Lucie Aubrac. Read by Nadia May. 7 cass. (Running Time: 10 hrs.). 1996. 49.95 (978-0-7861-1002-5(3), 1779) Blckstn Audio.

Ouvertures: Cours in Termediaire de Francais: Testing Cassette Teacher's Assistant. 3rd ed. Siskin. (FRE.). 2001. pap. bk. & tchr. ed. 72.95 (978-0-470-00490-6(8), JWiley) Wiley US.

Ouvertures: Cours Intermediaire de Francais. 3rd ed. H. Jay Siskin et al. (FRE.). 2001. pap. bk. & lab manual ed. (978-0-03-028971-2(8)); pap. bk. & lab manual ed. (978-0-03-028984-2(X)) Harcourt Coll Pubs.

Ouvertures: Cours Intermediaire de Francais. 3rd ed. H. Jay Siskin et al. (ENG.). (C). 2000. lab manual ed. 61.95 (978-0-470-00381-7(2), JWiley) Wiley US.

Ouvertures: Cours Intermediaire de Francais, Instructor's Resource Manual. 3rd ed. Jay H. Siskin et al. (FRE.). 2001. pap. bk. & tchr. ed. (978-0-03-028918-7(X)) Harcourt Coll Pubs.

Ouvertures: Cours Intermediaire de Francais, Troisieme Edition. 3rd ed. Siskin. (FRE.). 1911. pap. bk. & tchr. ed. 66.95 (978-0-470-00269-8(7), JWiley) Wiley US.

Ouvertures: Cours Intermediaire de Francais, Troisieme Edition: Tapescript. 3rd ed. Siskin. (FRE.). 1911. pap. bk. 32.95 (978-0-470-00274-2(3), JWiley) Wiley US.

Ouvertures Set: Plus French Hits on the Web. 3rd ed. Siskin. 2002. bk., stu. ed., lab manual ed. 113.85 (978-0-470-00488-3(6), JWiley) Wiley US.

Ouvertures, Lab Audio CDs: Cours Intermediaire de Francais. H. Jay Siskin et al. (ENG.). (C). 2005. audio compact disk 21.95 (978-0-471-77415-0(4)) Wiley US.

Oval Portrait see Tales of Horror & Suspense

Oval Portrait. 1980. (N-47) Jimcin Record.

***Oval Portrait: A Tale of Terror.** Edgar Allan Poe. 2009. (978-1-60136-518-7(7)) Audio Holding.

Ovarian Carcinoma: Diagnosis, Treatment & Follow-up. Moderated by Leo D. Lagasse. 2 cass. (Running Time: 3 hrs.). (Gynecology & Obstetrics Ser.: GO-1). 1986. 19.00 (8640) Am Coll Surgeons.

Oven Bird see Robert Frost in Recital

Over & Underneath. Contrib. by Tenth Avenue North & Terry Hemmings. Prod. by Jason Ingram et al. 2008. audio compact disk 11.99 (978-5-557-43373-0(2)) Pt of Grace Ent.

Over Bethnal Green. Sally Worboyes. (Soundings (CDs) Ser.). 2006. audio compact disk 79.95 (978-1-84559-221-9(2)) Pub: ISIS Lrg Prnt GBR. Dist(s): Ulverscroft US

Over Bethnal Green. Sally Worboyes. Read by Annie Aldington. 8 cass. (Running Time: 9 hrs. 30 min.). (Sound Ser.). 2001. 69.95 (978-1-86042-997-2(1)) Pub: UlverLrgPrint GBR. Dist(s): Ulverscroft US
Jessie Smith had been looking forward to married life with Tom and baby Billy in their small terraced house in Bethnal Green. But Tom is called up as the horror of a new world war approaches. Jessie is left to cope with the baby alone as the bombs begin to fall on Bethnal Green. And when Tom does a runner and goes AWOL, things get rapidly worse. Jessie will need all her strength to survive.

Over Easy. Perf. by Parachute Express Staff. 1 cass. (Running Time: 1 hr. 30 mins.). (J). 7.98 (TLR 1009); audio compact disk 11.18 (TLR 1009) NewSound.

Over Her Dead Body. abr. ed. Kate White. Read by Lea Thompson. (ENG.). 2005. 14.98 (978-1-59483-244-4(7)) Pub: Hachet Audio. Dist(s): HachBkGrp

Over Her Dead Body. abr. ed. Kate White. Read by Lea Thompson. (Running Time: 6 hrs.). (ENG.). 2009. 49.98 (978-1-60788-052-3(0)) Pub: Hachet Audio. Dist(s): HachBkGrp

Over in the Meadow. 2004. bk. 24.95 (978-1-56008-213-2(5)); pap. bk. 18.95 (978-1-55592-809-4(9)); pap. bk. 38.75 (978-1-55592-759-2(9)); pap. bk. 32.75 (978-1-55592-290-0(2)); pap. bk. 14.95 (978-1-56008-088-6(4)); 8.95 (978-1-56008-994-0(6)); 8.95 (978-1-56008-438-9(3)); cass. & flmstrp 30.00 (978-0-89719-617-8(1)); audio compact disk 12.95 (978-1-55592-878-0(1)) Weston Woods.

Over in the Meadow. John Langstaff. 1 cass. (Running Time: 9 min.). (J). (ps-4). 8.95 (RAC057) Weston Woods.
From the book by John Langstaff.

Over in the Meadow. John Langstaff. Illus. by Feodor Rojankovsky. 1 cass., 5 bks. (Running Time: 9 min.). (J). pap. bk. 32.75 Weston Woods.
An old counting song for children is filled with the beauty & wonder of meadow life.

Over in the Meadow. John Langstaff. Illus. by Feodor Rojankovsky. 1 cass. (Running Time: 9 min.). (J). (ps-3). bk. 24.95; pap. bk. 12.95 (PRA057) Weston Woods.
From the book by John Langstaff.

Over in the Meadow. John Langstaff. (Running Time: 9 mins.). (Story Hour Collection). (J). 1998. pap. bk. 12.95 (JPRA057) Weston Woods.
An old counting song for children is filled with the beauty & wonder of meadow life.

Over in the Meadow. Music for Little People Band. 1 cass. (Running Time: 9 mins.). (J). (ps up). 1988. 6.98 (978-1-877737-03-9(8), MFLP #285) MFLP CA.
Sing-Along animal songs for children.

Over in the Meadow. Olive A. Wadsworth & Ezra Jack Keats. 1 cass. (Running Time: 9 mins.). (Blue-Ribbon Listen-and-Read Ser.). (J). (ps-2). 1985. 5.95 (978-0-590-63014-6(8)) Scholastic Inc.

Over in the Meadow: Sing-a-Story. Parachute Press. (J). 1987. 5.95 (978-0-553-45900-5(7), Random AudioBks) Random Audio Pubg.

Over in the Meadow; Fox Went Out on a Chilly Night, the; I Know an Old Lady; Complete Version of the Three Blind Mice. 2004. cass. & flmstrp (978-0-89719-722-9(4)) Weston Woods.

Over My Dead Body. Rex Stout. Narrated by Michael Prichard. (Running Time: 26700 sec.). (Nero Wolfe Ser.). (ENG.). 2007. audio compact disk 29.95 (978-1-57270-730-6(5)) Pub: AudioGO. Dist(s): Perseus Dist

Over My Dead Body. unabr. ed. Raymond Flynn. 8 cass. (Running Time: 12 hrs.). 2001. 69.95 (978-1-86042-867-8(3), 28673) Pub: Soundings Ltd GBR. Dist(s): Ulverscroft US

Over My Dead Body. unabr. ed. Rex Stout. Read by Michael Prichard. 6 cass. (Running Time: 8 hrs.). (Nero Wolfe Ser.). 2004. 29.95 (978-1-57270-062-8(9), N61062u) Pub: Audio Partners. Dist(s): PerseuPGW
When a fencing student ends up skewered through the heart, a Balkan beauty claiming to be Wolfe's daughter is accused of the crime. Nero Wolfe & his able assistant, Archie, thrust & parry into a tangle of identities & political intrigue. Is Wolfe's long-lost daughter a hot-blooded mistress of murder.

Over My Dead Body. unabr. collector's ed. Rex Stout. Read by Michael Prichard. 6 cass. (Running Time: 9 hrs.). (Nero Wolfe Ser.). 1994. 48.00 (978-0-7366-2747-4(2), 3472) Books on Tape.
Murder at a fencing studio engages detective Nero Wolfe & his assistant, Archie Goodwin, in a duel with death.

Over My Head. 1 cass. (Running Time: 60 min.). 1994. audio compact disk 15.95 CD. (2074, Creativ Pub) Quayside.
Northern bird calls & intriguing instrumentals.

Over My Head. 1 cass. (Running Time: 1 hr.). 1994. 9.95 (2072, NrthWrd Bks) TandN Child.

Over My Head: A Doctor's Own Story of Head Injury from the Inside Looking Out. 2000. audio compact disk 33.50 (978-0-9658750-1-1(6)) Peripatetic Pub.

Over Sea, under Stone. unabr. ed. Susan Cooper. Read by Alex Jennings. 6 cass. (Running Time: 7 hrs. 19 mins.). (Dark Is Rising Sequence Ser.). (J). (gr. 4-7). 2004. 40.00 (978-0-8072-0519-8(2), Listening Lib); 46.00 (978-0-8072-0668-3(7), S YA 316 SP, Listening Lib) Random Audio Pubg.

Over Sea, under Stone. unabr. ed. Susan Cooper & Susan Cooper. Read by Alex Jennings. (Running Time: 26400 sec.). (Dark Is Rising Sequence Ser.: Bk. 1). (ENG.). (J). (gr. 3-7). 2007. audio compact disk 34.00 (978-0-7393-6196-2(1), Listening Lib) Pub: Random Audio Pubg. Dist(s): Random

Over Sir John's Hill see Dylan Thomas Reading His Poetry

Over Sir John's Hill see Dylan Thomas

Over-the-Counter (OTC) Pharmaceuticals & Drugs in Japan: A Strategic Reference 2007. Compiled by Icon Group International, Inc. Staff. 2007. ring bd. 195.00 (978-0-497-82331-3(4)) Icon Grp.

Over the Course of a Lifetime. J. G. Woodward. Invincible Publishing. (ENG.). 2008. 19.95 (978-0-9822595-2-8(2)) Invincible Pub.

Over the Edge. Jonathan Kellerman. Read by Alexander Adams. (Alex Delaware Ser.: No. 3). 2000. audio compact disk 112.00 (978-0-7366-7135-4(8)) Books on Tape.

***Over the Edge.** Stuart Pawson. 2010. cass. & cass. 61.95 (978-1-84652-385-4(0)); audio compact disk & audio compact disk 79.95 (978-1-84652-386-1(9)) Pub: Magna Story GBR. Dist(s): Ulverscroft US

Over the Edge. abr. ed. Jonathan Kellerman. Read by John Rubinstein. 3 CDs. (Running Time: 10800 sec.). (Alex Delaware Ser.: No. 3). (ENG.). 2005. audio compact disk 14.99 (978-0-7393-2126-3(9), Random AudioBks) Pub: Random Audio Pubg. Dist(s): Random
When the phone rings in the middle of the night, child psychologist Alex Delaware does not hesitate. Driving through the dream-lit San Fernando Valley, Alex rushes to Jamey Cadmus, the patient he had failed five years before—and who now calls with a bizarre cry for help. But by the time Alex reaches Canyon Oaks Psychiatric Hospital, Jamey is gone, surfacing a day later in the hands of the police, who believe Jamey is the infamous Lavender Slasher, a psychotic serial killer. Wooed by a high-powered attorney to build a defense, Alex will get a chance to do what he couldn’t five years ago. And when he peers into a family’s troubled history and Jamey’s brilliant, tormented mind, the psychologist puts himself at the heart of a high-profile case. Because Alex knows that in a realm of money, loss, and madness, something terrible pushed Jamie over the edge—or else someone is getting away with murder. From the Paperback edition.

Over the Edge. collector's ed. Jonathan Kellerman. Read by Alexander Adams. 11 cass. (Running Time: 16 hrs. 30 min.). (Alex Delaware Ser.: No. 3). 2000. 88.00 (978-0-7366-5643-6(X)) Books on Tape.
The story of a teenage boy accused of 6 murders & the lawyer chosen to defend him.

Over the Edge. unabr. ed. Suzanne Brockmann. Read by Laura Hicks. 10 cass. (Running Time: 14 hrs.). (Troubleshooter Ser.: No. 3). 2004. 84.95 (978-0-7927-3177-1(8), CSL 639, Chivers Sound Lib); audio compact disk 110.95 (978-0-7927-3178-8(6), SLD 639, Chivers Sound Lib) AudioGO.
For Lieutenant Teri Howe, one of the best helicopter pilots in the naval reserves, nothing stands in the way of her passion for flying-until a past mistake surfaces, jeopardizing everything she's worked for. Senior Chief Stan Wolchonok has made a career of tackling difficult challenges, so it's no surprise when he comes to Teri's aid, knowing that his personal code of honor-and perhaps his heart-will be at risk.

***Over the Edge of the World.** abr. ed. Laurence Bergreen. (ENG.). 2004. (978-0-06-079992-2(7), Harper Audio) HarperCollins Pubs.

***Over the Edge of the World.** abr. ed. Laurence Bergreen. Read by Laurence Bergreen. (ENG.). 2004. (978-0-06-074778-7(1), Harper Audio) HarperCollins Pubs.

Over the Edge of the World: Magellan's Terrifying Circumnavigation of the Globe. abr. ed. Laurence Bergreen. 2003. 29.95 (978-0-06-057521-2(2)) HarperCollins Pubs.

Over the Edge of the World CD: Magellan's Terrifying Circumnavigation of the Globe. abr. ed. Laurence Bergreen. Read by Laurence Bergreen. 5 CDs. (Running Time: 6 hrs.). 2003. audio compact disk 29.95 (978-0-06-057730-8(4)) HarperCollins Pubs.

Over the End Line. unabr. ed. Alfred C. Martino. (YA). 2009. audio compact disk 29.95 (978-1-59316-431-7(9)) Listen & Live.

Over the Gate. unabr. ed. Miss Read. Read by Gwen Watford. 6 cass. (Running Time: 9 hrs.). (Fairacre Chronicles). 2000. 49.95 (978-0-7451-4127-5(7), CAB 810) Pub: Chivers Audio Bks GBR. Dist(s): AudioGO
Miss Read, the village teacher recalls odd incidents and excellent stories with characteristic grace and compassion. She recalls Mrs. Next-Door, the queen of copy-cats, who drives her neighbors crazy; the tragic tale of the ghost of Fairacre; as well as others.

Over the Hills & Far Away. Candida Lycett Green. Read by Mary Gardner. 5 cass. (Running Time: 8 hrs.). (Storysound Ser.). (J). 2003. 49.95 (978-1-85903-632-7(5)); audio compact disk 64.95 (978-1-85903-651-8(1)) Pub: Mgna Lrg Print GBR. Dist(s): Ulverscroft US

Over the Moon. Rachel Vail. Illus. by Scott Nash. 1 cass. (Running Time: 15 min.). (J). (gr. k-3). 1998. pap. bk. 16.90 (978-0-8045-6858-6(8), 6858) Spoken Arts.
In what is both a wildly comic take on a nursery classic and a lesson in prepositions, an endearing klutzy cow takes center stage.

Over the Moon. unabr. ed. Jean Ure. Read by Clare Corbett. 3 CDs. (Running Time: 2 hrs. 56 mins.). (J). (gr. 4-6). 2007. audio compact disk 29.95 (978-1-4056-5656-6(5), ChiversChildren) AudioGo GBR.

Over the Northern Border. unabr. ed. Max Brand. (Running Time: 2 hrs. 0 mins.). (ENG.). 2009. 19.95 (978-1-4332-2393-8(7)); 22.95

(978-1-4332-2389-1(9)); audio compact disk 28.00 (978-1-4332-2390-7(2)) Blckstn Audio.

Over the Top: Moving from Survival to Stability, from Stability to Success, from Success to Significance. abr. ed. Zig Ziglar. 1 cass. (Running Time: 1 hr. 30 mins.). 1994. 18.99 (978-0-7852-7973-0(3)) Nelson.
Drawing on his forty plus years as a world-class motivated speaker, Ziglar shows precisely how to achieve what people desire most from life - to be happy, healthy, reasonably prosperous and secure, and to have friends, peace of mind, good family relationships and hope.

Over the Wall. John H. Ritter. Narrated by Johnny Heller. 7 CDs. (Running Time: 7 hrs. 15 mins.). (gr. 7 up). audio compact disk 58.00 (978-0-7887-6155-3(2)) Recorded Bks.

Over the Wall. unabr. ed. John H. Ritter. Narrated by Johnny Heller. 6 pieces. (Running Time: 7 hrs. 15 mins.). (gr. 7 up). 2001. 48.00 (978-0-7887-4570-6(0), 96353E7) Recorded Bks.
Tyler is a great baseball player with hopes of becoming an All-Star. But he has a temper that is quicker than his swing. If he can't control it, he will lose his place on the team.

Over the Wall. unabr. ed. John H. Ritter. Narrated by Johnny Heller. 6 cass. (Running Time: 7 hrs. 15 mins.). (YA). 2001. pap. bk. & stu. ed. 72.99 Recorded Bks.

Over the Wall. unabr. ed. John H. Ritter. Narrated by Johnny Heller. 6 CDs. (Running Time: 6 hrs.). (YA). (gr. 5-8). 2001. audio compact disk 69.00 (C1379) Recorded Bks.
Thirteen-year-old Tyler loves spending the summer in New York with his cousin. Each day, they play baseball in a Central Park league. Tyler is a sharp hitter, so he hopes to become an All-Star. But he has a temper that is quicker than his swing. If he can't control it, he will lose his place on the team. There's trouble off the diamond, too. An awful accident has turned Tyler's dad into a distracted stranger. People tell Tyler that time will heal his father's wounds, but what about the hurt Tyler feels? He just wants to bat it away.

Over Thirty Ways to Make Easy Money at Home for under Twenty Dollars! unabr. ed. Carolyn Anderson. Read by Carolyn Anderson. 1 cass. (Running Time: 1 hr.). Dramatization. 1992. 6.00 (978-1-883778-01-9(8)) Starlite Prods.
Motivation tape to help others start homebased business.

Over to Candleford. unabr. ed. Flora Thompson. Read by Mollie Harris. 5 cass. (Running Time: 5 hrs. 45 min.). (Isis Ser.). (J). 1995. 49.95 (978-1-85695-802-8(7), 940802) Pub: ISIS Lrg Prnt GBR. Dist(s): Ulverscroft US

Over 40 & You're Hired! Secrets to Landing a Great Job. unabr. ed. Robin Ryan. (Running Time: 6 hrs. 30 mins.). 2010. audio compact disk 29.95 (978-1-4417-1557-9(6)) Blckstn Audio.

Over 40 & You're Hired! Secrets to Landing a Great Job. unabr. ed. Robin Ryan. Read by Robin Ryan. (Running Time: 6 hrs. 30 mins.). 2009. 54.95 (978-1-4417-1554-8(1)); audio compact disk 69.00 (978-1-4417-1555-5(X)) Blckstn Audio.

Over 40 & You¿re Hired! Secrets to Landing a Great Job. unabr. ed. Robin Ryan. Read by Robin Ryan. (Running Time: 6 hrs. 30 mins.). 2009. 29.95 (978-1-4417-1558-6(4)) Blckstn Audio.

Overboard see May Swenson

Overboard. unabr. collector's ed. Hank Searls. Read by Michael Prichard. 7 cass. (Running Time: 10 hrs. 30 mins.). 1985. 56.00 (978-0-7366-0663-9(7), 1625) Books on Tape.
Mitch Gordon awakens 70 miles from Tahiti to find himself alone in his 40-foot ketch. Sometime in the last dark hours his wife Lindy has been swept overboard into the giant Pacific swells. Lindy, buoyed by a flimsy life-jacket, struggles to survive until he can find her.

***Overboard! A True Bluewater Odyssey of Disaster & Survival.** unabr. ed. Michael Tougias. (Running Time: 11 hrs. 0 mins.). 2010. 29.95 (978-1-4417-4268-1(9)); audio compact disk 29.95 (978-1-4417-4267-4(0)) Blckstn Audio.

***Overboard! A True Bluewater Odyssey of Disaster & Survival.** unabr. ed. Michael J. Tougias. (Running Time: 11 hrs. 0 mins.). 2010. 65.95 (978-1-4417-4264-3(6)); audio compact disk 100.00 (978-1-4417-4265-0(4)) Blckstn Audio.

Overcame see Venció

Overcoat see Great French & Russian Stories, Vol. 1, A Collection

Overcoat see Shinyel

Overcoat. unabr. ed. Nikolai Gogol. Read by Walter Zimmerman. 1 cass. (Running Time: 1 hr. 22 mins.). 1981. 7.95 (N-81) Jimcin Record.

Overcome Addictions. Bruce Goldberg. Read by Bruce Goldberg. 1 cass. (Running Time: 25 min.). (ENG.). 2007. 13.00 (978-1-885577-41-2(9)) Pub: B Goldberg. Dist(s): Baker Taylor
Eliminate compulsive behavior by removing its cause through self-hypnosis.

Overcome Addictions. abr. ed. Glenn Harrold. 1 CD. (Running Time: 1980 sec.). 2005. audio compact disk 17.95 (978-1-901923-70-4(3), 247-041) Pub: Divinit Pubing GBR. Dist(s): Bookworld

Overcome Arthritis: I Did ~ You Can Too. Charles W. Snyder, III. 1 CD. (YA). 2003. audio compact disk 19.95 (978-0-9747089-0-4(9)) Servant Pubs.
How I overcame arthritis begining with how I developed this disease. What I learned that helped me overcome it. I explain what causes arthritis. When you remove the cause the arthritis goes away.

Overcome Breast Cancer Fears & Anxieties, Vol. 151. 2001. 24.95 (978-1-58557-040-9(0)) Dynamic Growth.

Overcome Destiny by Self Effort. 1 cass. (Running Time: 1 hr.). 12.99 (140) Yoga Res Foun.

Overcome Destiny by Self Effort, No. 2. Swami Jyotirmayananda. 1 cass. (Running Time: 1 hr.). 1990. 12.99 Yoga Res Foun.

Overcome Destiny by Self Effort II. (179) Yoga Res Foun.

Overcome Exam Nerves. Glenn Harrold. 2 CDs. (Running Time: 3 hrs.). 2002. audio compact disk 17.95 (978-1-901923-39-1(8)) Pub: Divinit Pubing GBR. Dist(s): Bookworld

Overcome Exam Nerves. Glenn Harrold. 1 cass. (Running Time: 1 hr. 30 mins.). 2003. 11.95 (978-1-901923-19-3(3)) Pub: Divinit Pubing GBR. Dist(s): Bookworld
Combining skilled hypnotherapy techniques with state of the art digital recording technology. From the UK's best selling self help audio series. Using post hypnotic suggestions, powerful echoed affirmations and visualisation techniques, this recording has been carefully designed to help the listener feel completely calm and composed when taking an examination or test of any kind.

Overcome Fear. 1 cass. (Health Ser.). 12.98 (101) Randolph Tapes.
Many of us have fears, even some from childhood. Some fears are associated with earthquakes, storms, flying, etc. This tape works.

Overcome Fears & Anxiety. 2004. audio compact disk 15.98 (978-1-55848-715-4(8)) EffectiveMN.

Overcome Fears & Phobias. Glenn Harrold. 2 CDs. (Running Time: 3 hrs.). 2002. audio compact disk 17.95 (978-1-901923-34-6(7)); 11.95 (978-1-901923-14-8(2)) Pub: Divinit Pubing GBR. Dist(s): Bookworld
This recording has been very carefully scripted and constructed with the sole aim of being as effective as possible. Glenn Harrold has drawn upon his wide experience as a clinical hypnotherapist having helped many clients overcome a wide range of common and obscure fears and phobias. Includes: A pleasant English voice guiding the listener into a completely relaxed state of mind & body.

Overcome Frigidity (Achieve Sexual Freedom) Norman J. Caldwell. Read by Norman J. Caldwell. Ed. by Achieve Now Institute Staff. 1 cass. (Running Time: 20 min.). (Health-Imaging Ser.). 1988. 9.97 (978-1-56273-074-1(6)) My Mothers Pub.
Feel the freedom of releasing your inner-mind.

Overcome Loneliness. 1 cass. (Running Time: 1 hr. 30 mins.). 10.00 (978-1-58506-019-1(4), 46) New Life Inst OR.
If you have ever felt the heartache of loneliness, try this program.

Overcome Maya, No. 1. Swami Jyotirmayananda. Read by Swami Jyotirmayananda. 1 cass. (Running Time: 1 hr.). 12.99 (733) Yoga Res Foun.

Overcome Maya, No. 2. Swami Jyotirmayananda. 1 cass. (Running Time: 1 hr.). 1990. 12.99 Yoga Res Foun.

Overcome Maya, No. 3. Swami Jyotirmayananda. 1 cass. (Running Time: 1 hr.). 1990. 12.99 Yoga Res Foun.

Overcome Maya, No. 4. Swami Jyotirmayananda. 1 cass. (Running Time: 1 hr.). 1990. 12.99 Yoga Res Foun.

Overcome Maya, No. 5. Swami Jyotirmayananda. Read by Swami Jyotirmayananda. 1 cass. (Running Time: 1 hr.). 12.99 (734) Yoga Res Foun.

Overcome Obstacles. 1 cass. (Running Time: 1 hr.). (Educational Ser.). 12.98 (88) Randolph Tapes.
Turn every obstacle into a challenge you can deal with effectively. With this dynamic tape you mentally rehearse & win within the INNER SPACE OF YOUR MIND.

Overcome Procrastination. 2002. audio compact disk 14.95 (978-0-9728185-4-4(5)) InGenius Inc.

Overcome Procrastination. Bruce Goldberg. (ENG.). 2005. audio compact disk 17.00 (978-1-57968-101-2(8)) Pub: B Goldberg. Dist(s): Baker Taylor

Overcome Procrastination. Bruce Goldberg. Read by Bruce Goldberg. 1 cass. (Running Time: 25 min.). (ENG.). 2007. 13.00 (978-1-885577-71-9(0)) Pub: B Goldberg. Dist(s): Baker Taylor
Through self-hypnosis remove once & for all the most important block to personal & professional fulfillment.

Overcome Procrastination. Speeches. Edward Strachar. 1 cass. (Running Time: 50 mins.). 2002. 14.95 (978-0-9719358-3-9(1)) InGenius Inc.

Overcome Shyness. 1 cass. (Running Time: 1 hr.). (Educational Ser.). 12.98 (89) Randolph Tapes.
I know how it feels. I used to be shy & blush easily. Now you can reach out & touch someone! Enjoy life!.

Overcome Smoking Forever. Created by Victoria Wizell. Voice by Victoria Wizell. 2 CDs. 2004. audio compact disk 39.00 (978-0-9679176-3-4(8)) Hyptalk.
Becoming a nonsmoker allows you to get healthy. To stay free of smoking forever, it is important that you have the support of your subconscious mind in maintaining your commitment as a nonsmoker.

Overcome Stress. Swami Jyotirmayananda. 1 cass. (Running Time: 45 min.). 1990. 10.00 Yoga Res Foun.

Overcome Tendency to Commit Suicide. (178) Yoga Res Foun.

Overcome Tendency to Commit Suicide. Swami Jyotirmayananda. 1 cass. (Running Time: 1 hr.). 1990. 12.99 Yoga Res Foun.

Overcome Test Anxiety. Mel Gilley. Ed. by Steven C. Eggleston. 1 cass. (Running Time: 1 hr.) (World of Hypnosis Ser.). 1987. 6.95 SCE Prod & List & Lrn.
Self-hypnosis to reduce anxiety over upcoming exams.

OVERCOME TEST ANXIETY & STUDY BETTER. Created by Anne H. Spencer-Beacham. 1. 2003. audio compact disk (978-1-932163-60-5(3)) Infinity Inst.

Overcome the Fear of Flying. Glenn Harrold. 2 CDs. (Running Time: 3 hrs.). 2002. audio compact disk 17.95 (978-1-901923-37-7(1)) Pub: Divinit Pubing GBR. Dist(s): Bookworld

Overcome the Fear of Flying. Glenn Harrold. 1 cass. (Running Time: 1 hr. 30 mins.). 2003. 11.95 (978-1-901923-17-9(7)) Pub: Divinit Pubing GBR. Dist(s): Bookworld

Overcome Worry, No. 1. Swami Jyotirmayananda. Read by Swami Jyotirmayananda. 1 cass. (Running Time: 45 min.). 10.00 (802) Yoga Res Foun.

Overcome Worry, No. 2. Swami Jyotirmayananda. 1 cass. (Running Time: 45 min.). 1990. 10.00 Yoga Res Foun.

Overcome Worry, No. 3. Swami Jyotirmayananda. Read by Swami Jyotirmayananda. 1 cass. (Running Time: 45 min.). 10.00 (803) Yoga Res Foun.

Overcome Worry, No. 4. Swami Jyotirmayananda. 1 cass. (Running Time: 45 min.). 1990. 10.00 Yoga Res Foun.

Overcome Your Disappointment. unabr. ed. Rosalene Glickman. (ENG.). 2007. 14.98 (978-1-59659-114-1(5), GildAudio) Pub: Gildan Media. Dist(s): HachBkGrp

Overcome Your Fear of Success. 1 cass. (Running Time: 1 hr. 30 mins.). (Super Ser.). 8.00 (BI05) Master Mind.

Overcome Your Foreign Accent & Speak English with Confidence. 3rd ed. Jeffrey Bedell. Read by Jeffrey Bedell. 8 cass. (Running Time: 4 hrs. 30 min.). 1987. 129.95 Am Spch Imprvmnt.
For the non-native speaker of English who want to improve English pronounciation & increase self-confidence in all English-Speaking situations. English level: high intermediate-advance.

Overcomer. Contrib. by Alvin Slaughter & Michael Coleman. Prod. by Aaron Lindsey. 2008. audio compact disk 13.99 (978-5-557-43330-3(9)) Integrity Music.

Overcomers Prayer. Veronica Winston. 3 cass. (Running Time: 3hr.21min.). (C). 1999. 15.00 (978-1-931289-67-2(0)) Pub: B Winston Min. Dist(s): Anchor Distributors

Overcomig Rejection Will Make You Rich (audio Book) 12 ways to turn rejection into unlimited abundance, success, & Freedom. Larry DiAngi. (ENG.). 2007. audio compact disk 49.95 (978-0-9762765-3-1(4)) Larry DiAngi.

Overcoming a Critical Spirit. Taffi L. Dollar. 2008. audio compact disk 14.00 (978-1-59944-738-4(X)) Creflo Dollar.

Overcoming a Dysfunctional Family: Gen. 25:27-29. Ed Young. 2000. 4.95 (978-0-7417-2262-1(3), 1262) Win Walk.

Overcoming Addictions, 2 cass. (Running Time: 2 hrs.). 2001. 24.95 (978-1-58557-034-8(6)) Dynamic Growth.

Overcoming Addictions. Eldon Taylor. Read by Eldon Taylor. Interview with XProgress Aware Staff. 1 cass. (Running Time: 1 hr. 2 mins.). 16.95 incl. script. (978-1-55978-296-8(X), 020110) Progress Aware Res.
Verbal coaching soundtrack with underlying subliminal affirmations & sound matrix frequencies for brain entrainment.

Overcoming Addictions: OZO. Eldon Taylor. Read by Eldon Taylor. Ed. by Leslie Brice. 1 cass. (Running Time: 1 hr.). 1992. 19.95 (978-1-56705-007-3(7)) Gateways Inst.
Self improvement.

Overcoming Allergies: How to Overcome Allergies. Sally Rockwell. 1986. 10.95 (978-0-916575-05-2(5)) Diet Design.
Relax as Dr. Sally discusses how to live with allergies. If you need a pep talk, hope and inspiration, listen to Dr. Sally.

Overcoming Anxiety. Brian Campbell. 1 cass. (Running Time: 1 hr.). 1997. 9.95 (978-1-57988-052-1(5)) Sanctuary Bks.

Overcoming Anxiety, 113. 1997. 24.95 (978-1-58557-006-5(0)) Dynamic Growth.

Overcoming Assumptions That Inhibit Spiritual Development. Narrated by Idries Shah. 2 vols. (Running Time: 2 hrs. 30 mins.). bk. 17.00 (978-1-883536-23-7(5), OVA11, Malor Bks) ISHK.
A lecture delivered before a live audience, plus teaching stories & narratives selected from "Tales of the Dervishes".

Overcoming Barriers. Jeff Davidson. 2005. audio compact disk 12.95 (978-1-60729-127-5(4)) Breath Space Inst.

Overcoming Barriers. Jeff Davidson. 2005. 11.95 (978-1-60729-357-6(9)) Breath Space Inst.

Overcoming Cosmological Dissociation. Jon Klimo. 2 cass. (Running Time: 3 hrs.). 18.00 (A0360-89) Sound Photosyn.
Once again, the navigator of whitewater stream of consciousness!.

Overcoming Crisis Video Book: The Secrets to Thriving in Challenging Times. Myles Munroe. 2009. audio compact disk 19.99 (978-0-7684-3053-0(4)) Destiny Image Pubs.

Overcoming Depression. Norman J. Caldwell. Read by Norman J. Caldwell. Ed. by Achieve Now Institute Staff. 1 cass. (Running Time: 20 min.). (Better Health Ser.). 1988. 9.97 (978-1-56273-047-5(9)) My Mothers Pub.
Lift yourself up - discover the importance of being you. Release good feelings - be happy now.

Overcoming Depression. Shad Helmstetter. 1 cass. (Running Time: 20 mins.). (Self-Talk Cassettes Ser.). 10.95 (978-0-937065-24-2(2)) Grindle Pr.

Overcoming Depression. Richard Jafolla & Mary-Alice Jafolla. Read by Richard Jafolla & Mary-Alice Jafolla. 1986. 12.95 Stppng Stones.
Motivational tape that works on the subconcious mind (subliminal) & concious mind to bring about self-improvement.

Overcoming Depression. Speeches. Paul Osteen & Billie Hunt. 1 tap. 2002. 6.00 (978-1-931877-04-6(1)) J Osteen.
"Overcoming Depression" offers assistance to those of us needing a helping hand when feeling depressed, 1 audio cassette.

Overcoming Depression. Betty L. Randolph. (Running Time: 45 min.). (Health Ser.). 1989. bk. 9.98 (978-1-55909-106-0(1), 87S) Randolph Tapes.

Overcoming Doubt. Swami Jyotirmayananda. 1 cass. (Running Time: 45 min.). 1990. 10.00 Yoga Res Foun.

Overcoming Doubt, Fear & Procrastination. Barbara W. Sykes. 1 cass. (Running Time: 45 mins.). 1998. 16.95 (978-0-9632857-9-9(3)) Collins Pubns.
Live seminar of Barbara Wright Sykes speaking on "Overcoming Doubt," "Fear & Procrastination".

Overcoming Dyslexia. Sally Shaywitz. Read by Anna Fields. 10 cass. (Running Time: 14 hrs. 30 mins.). 2004. 69.95 (978-0-7861-2653-8(1), 3217) Blckstn Audio.

Overcoming Dyslexia. unabr. ed. Sally Shaywitz. Read by Anna Fields. (Running Time: 14 hrs. 30 mins.). 2000. audio compact disk 24.95 (978-0-7861-8721-8(2), 3217) Blckstn Audio.

Overcoming Dyslexia. unabr. ed. Sally Shaywitz. Read by Anna Fields. 11 CDs. (Running Time: 14 hrs. 30 mins.). 2004. audio compact disk 88.00 (978-0-7861-8886-4(3), 3217) Blckstn Audio.

Overcoming Dyslexia. unabr. ed. Sally Shaywitz. Read by Anna Fields. 10 pieces. 2004. reel tape 39.95 (978-0-7861-2655-2(8)); audio compact disk 49.95 (978-0-7861-8881-9(2)) Blckstn Audio.

Overcoming Dyslexic Tendencies. Eldon Taylor. 1 cass. (Running Time: 1 hr. 2 mins.). (Inner Talk Ser.). 16.95 (978-1-55978-620-1(5), 53867F) Progress Aware Res.
Soundtrack - Brook with underlying subliminal affirmations.

Overcoming Emotions That Destroy CD Series. 2003. audio compact disk 17.00 (978-1-59834-028-0(X)) Walk Thru the Bible.

Overcoming Evil: Logos June 18, 2000. Ben Young. 2000. 4.95 (978-0-7417-6188-0(2), B0188) Win Walk.

Overcoming Evil with Good. Francis Frangipane. 1cass. (Running Time: 1 hr. 30 mins.). (Basics of Spiritual Warfare Ser.: Vol. 3). 2000. 5.00 (FF02-003) Morning NC.
Francis combines years of practical experience with a soundbiblical perspective in this popular & important series.

Overcoming Faith. Elbert Willis. 1 cass. (Running Time: 1 hr.). (Faith School Ser.: Vol. 2). 4.00 Fill the Gap.

Overcoming Fear. (Running Time: 45 min.). (Health Ser.). 9.98 (978-1-55909-124-4(X), 101) Randolph Tapes.

Overcoming Fear. Short Stories. Joel Osteen. 1 Cass. (Running Time: 30 Mins). 2001. Rental 6.00 (978-1-59349-116-1(6), JA0116) J Osteen.

Overcoming Fear of Failure. Shad Helmstetter. 1 cass. (Running Time: 1 hr.). (Self-Talk Ser.). 10.95 (978-0-937065-60-0(9)) Grindle Pr.
Companion Self-Talk Cassettes as mentioned in the book, "What To Say When You Talk To Your Self".

Overcoming Fears. Paul M. Lisnek. Read by Paul M. Lisnek. Ed. by Robert L. Sandidge. 1 cass. (Running Time: 1 hr.). 1994. 16.95 (978-1-57654-202-6(5)) Creat Core.
Guided imagery which helps overcome fears & achieve greater happiness.

Overcoming Fears: Creating Safety for You & Your World. Amy E. Dean. Read by Louise L. Hay. Ed. by Dan Olmos. 2 CDs. (Running Time: 2 hrs.). 1994. pap. bk. 18.00 (978-1-56170-079-0(7), 155) Hay House.
Louise guides you in releasing your fears & allowing yourself to live in peace & safety with these powerful affirmations & meditation.

Overcoming Fears: Creating Safety for You & Your World. Louise L. Hay. Read by Louise L. Hay. 1 cass. (Running Time: 1 hr.). 1992. 10.95 (978-1-56170-051-6(7), 266) Hay House.

Overcoming Fears: Creating Safety for You & Your World. Louise L. Hay. 1 CD. 2004. audio compact disk 10.95 (978-1-4019-0401-2(7)) Hay House.

Overcoming Fears & Anxiety Auto-Matically. Robert E. Griswold & Deirdre Griswold. Read by Robert E. Griswold & Deirdre Griswold. 1 cass. (Running

Time: 1 hr.). (While-U-Drive Ser.). 1997. 11.98 (978-1-55848-909-7(6)) EffectiveMN.
How to free oneself from false limitations & become more of what one was meant to be.

Overcoming Fears & Anxiety Auto-Matically. unabr. ed. Ray Levy & Joe Cates. 1 cass. (Running Time: 1 hr. 30 mins.). 2002. bk. 12.95 (978-0-9701173-5-9(3)) Cates Levy.
Strategies for parents and/or teachers who parent/teach children/youth who suffer from various fears or anxieties in life, school or relationships.

Overcoming Fingernail Biting. 1998. 24.95 (978-1-58557-010-2(9)) Dynamic Growth.

Overcoming Inertia. Swami Jyotirmayananda. Read by Swami Jyotirmayananda. 1 cass. (Running Time: 45 min.). 10.00 (825) Yoga Res Foun.

Overcoming Insecurity in Life, No. 1. Swami Jyotirmayananda. Read by Swami Jyotirmayananda. 1 cass. (Running Time: 45 min.). 10.00 (815) Yoga Res Foun.

Overcoming Insecurity in Life, No. 2. Swami Jyotirmayananda. 1 cass. (Running Time: 45 min.). 1990. 10.00 Yoga Res Foun.

Overcoming Intolerance. Swami Jyotirmayananda. 1 cass. (Running Time: 45 min.). 1990. 10.00 Yoga Res Foun.

Overcoming Jealousy. Eldon Taylor. 1 cass. (Running Time: 1 hr. 2 mins.). (Inner Talk Ser.). 16.95 incl. script. (978-1-55978-624-9(8), 53873F) Progress Aware Res.
Soundtrack - Brook with underlying subliminal affirmations.

Overcoming Life. Gloria Copeland. 2 cass. 1986. 10.00 Set. (978-0-88114-776-6(1)); (978-0-88114-781-0(8)) K Copeland Pubns.
Biblical teaching on victorious living.

Overcoming Life. Dwight Lyman Moody. (Pure Gold Classics Ser.). (ENG., 2007. pap. bk. 14.99 (978-0-88270-400-5(1)) Bridge-Logos.

Overcoming Life's Disappointments. abr. ed. Harold S. Kushner. Read by Harold S. Kushner. 4 CDs. (Running Time: 14400 sec.). (ENG.). 2006. audio compact disk 25.00 (978-0-7393-3319-8(4), Random AudioBks) Pub: Random Audio Pubg. Dist(s): Random

Overcoming Life's Disappointments. unabr. ed. Harold S. Kushner. Read by Arthur Morey. 4 cass. (Running Time: 6 hrs.). 2006. 36.00 (978-1-4159-3081-6(3)); audio compact disk 45.00 (978-1-4159-3082-3(1)) Books on Tape.
Kushner turns to the experience of Moses to find the requisite lessons of strength and faith. Moses towers over all others in the Old Testament: he is the man on the mountaintop to whom God speaks with unparalleled intimacy, and he leads his people out of bondage. But he is also deeply human, someone whose soaring triumphs are offset by frustration and longing: his people ignore his teachings, he is denied entrance to the Promised Land, his family suffers. But he overcomes. Through the example of Moses' remarkable resilience, we learn how to weather the disillusionment of dreams unfulfilled, the pain of a lost job or promotion, a child's failures, divorce or abandonment, and illness. We learn how to meet all disappointments with faith in ourselves and the future, and how to respond to heartbreak with understanding rather than bitterness and despair.

Overcoming Materialism. 5 cass. (Running Time: 7 hrs. 30 mins.). 16.95 (20130, HarperThor) HarpC GBR.

Overcoming Negativity in Others. Shad Helmstetter. 1 cass. (Running Time: 1 hr. 30 mins.). (Self-Talk Ser.). 10.95 (978-0-937065-58-7(7)) Grindle Pr.
Companion Self-Talk Cassettes as mentioned in the book, "What To Say When You Talk To Your Self".

Overcoming Negativity in Your Self. Shad Helmstetter. 1 cass. (Running Time: 1 hr. 30 mins.). (Self-Talk Ser.). 10.95 (978-0-937065-59-4(5)) Grindle Pr.

Overcoming Objections - Ask for It! Vol. 1: Discovering & Overcoming Objections with Winning Sales Closes. unabr. ed. Karl Walinskas. Perf. by Ted Ritsick & Beth Bloom-Wright. 1 cass. (Running Time: 50 min.). 1998. bk. 12.95 (978-0-9667084-5-5(8)) Speaking Connect.

Overcoming Obstacles. (Running Time: 45 min.). (Educational Ser.). 1989. bk. 9.98; 9.98 (978-1-55909-108-4(8), 88S) Randolph Tapes.
Turning every obstacle into a challenge you can deal with effectively.

Overcoming Obstacles. Shad Helmstetter. 1 cass. (Running Time: 45 mins.). (Self-Talk Cassettes Ser.). 10.95 (978-0-937065-10-5(2)) Grindle Pr.

Overcoming Obstacles. Swami Jyotirmayananda. Read by Swami Jyotirmayananda. 1 cass. (Running Time: 45 min.). 10.00 (826) Yoga Res Foun.

Overcoming Obstacles to Pursuing God. Francis Frangipane. 1 cass. (Running Time: 1 hr. 30 mins.). (Time to Seek God Ser.: Vol. 2). 2000. 5.00 (FF04-002) Morning NC.
This mini-series challenges believers with the important issue of intimacy with God.

Overcoming Offenses: N/a. Rick Joyner. 2005. audio compact disk 19.99 (978-1-929371-64-8(0)) Pub: Morning NC. Dist(s): Destiny Image Pubs

Overcoming Personal Limitations. Shad Helmstetter. 1 cass. (Running Time: 1 hr.). (Self-Talk Cassettes Ser.). 10.95 (978-0-937065-35-8(8)) Grindle Pr.

Overcoming Pessimism. Swami Jyotirmayananda. 1 cass. (Running Time: 45 min.). 1990. 10.00 Yoga Res Foun.

Overcoming Postpartum Depression: A Doctor's Own Story. unabr. ed. Lois V. Nightingale. 2 cass. (Running Time: 2 hrs.). 1998. 14.95 (978-1-889755-25-0(7)) Nightngale Rose.
Story & treatment of postpartum depression.

Overcoming Power of the Blood. Billye Brim. 6 cass. (Running Time: 6 hrs.). 1994. 30.00 (978-0-88114-960-9(8), TKC-11) K Copeland Pubns.
In-depth study of Jesus' blood.

Overcoming Procastination. William Knaus. 1 cass. (Running Time: 1 hr. 30 mins.). 9.95 (C018) A Ellis Institute.
Live from one of Dr. Bill Knaus' popular workshops. Discusses the causes of procrastination & offers a host of creative techniques to help you stop goofing & start living.

Overcoming Procrastination. Norman J. Caldwell. Read by Norman J. Caldwell. Ed. by Achieve Now Institute Staff. 1 cass. (Running Time: 20 min.). (Self-Directed Improvement Ser.). 1988. 9.97 (978-1-56273-057-4(6)) My Mothers Pub.
New-found enthusiasm & creative energy.

Overcoming Procrastination. Susan Fowler-Woodring. 2 cass. (Running Time: 3 hrs.). 1995. 15.95 (978-1-55977-020-0(1)) CareerTrack Pubns.

Overcoming Procrastination. Read by Robert E. Griswold. 1 cass. (Running Time: 1 hr.). 1992. 10.95 (978-1-55848-034-6(X)) EffectiveMN.
This program provides you with the best methods of doing things at the most appropriate time & achieving the success you desire.

Overcoming Procrastination. William Knaus. 1 cass. (Running Time: 90 min.). 1999. 9.95 (C018) A Ellis Institute.
Lists the causes of procrastination & offers a host of creative techniques to help you stop goofing & start living.

Overcoming Procrastination. William Knaus. 1 cass. (Running Time: 1 hr. 30 mins.). 9.95 (C018) Inst Rational-Emotive.
Live from one of Dr. Bill Knaus' popular workshops. Discusses the causes of procrastination & offers a host of creative techniques to help you stop goofing & start living.

Overcoming Procrastination. Barrie Konicov. Read by Barrie Konicov. 1 cass. (Running Time: 1 hr.). 16.98 (978-1-56001-311-2(7), SC-II 063) Potentials.

Overcoming Procrastination. Barrie Konicov. 1 CD. 2003. audio compact disk 16.98 (978-0-87082-967-3(X)) Potentials.
You keep putting it off, moving it aside, reassigning it to the bottom of the pile. You have put it off until the last minute and then find yourself having to do it anyway. It is completely up to you. Stop procrastinating and start doing. Don't put off purchasing this program. Do it now!You will find the self-hypnosis on track 1 and the subliminal on track 2. The easy-listening music of the subliminal, together with the self-hypnosis, is the original format which most people love and with which they are most familiar.

Overcoming Procrastination. Barrie Konicov. 2 CDs. 2003. audio compact disk 27.98 (978-1-56001-983-1(2)) Potentials.

Overcoming Procrastination: A Rhythmic Approach. Lloyd Glauberman. 2 cass. (Running Time: 3 hrs.). (Hypno-Peripheral Processing Tapes Ser.). 34.95 Set. (851PA-4M) Nightingale-Conant.
This breakthrough psychotechnology program combines the methods of hypnotherapy with the latest teachings of Neuro-Linguistic Programming. Each high-impact tape gently overloads your conscious mind with messages on two channels at once, creating a synergistic whole that unleashes both hemispheres of your brain.

Overcoming Procrastination: How to "Just Do It" Susan F. Woodring. 2 cass. (Running Time: 2 hrs. 36 min.). 29.95 Set. (Q10038) CareerTrack Pubns.
In this program you will learn how to develop "get-it-started-&-get-it-done" thinking. You'll gain time-proven strategies & psychological "tricks" that light your fire when all else fails. You'll learn how to begin (or restart) all your projects with new enthusiasm & the energy to see them through. This is ideal training for your entire staff.

Overcoming Procrastination: How to Make a Decision. Barrie Konicov. 1 cass. (Running Time: 1 hr.). 11.98 (978-0-87082-434-0(1), 063) Potentials.
Stop procrastinating & start doing! Deals with how not to set decisions aside & handle them now.

Overcoming Resistance. Swami Amar Jyoti. 1 cass. (Running Time: 1 hr. 30 mins.). 1978. 9.95 (K-20) Truth Consciousness.
What is resistance? Flowing in tune with changeful Nature. The science behind "resist no evil." The perfect lesson of suffering.

Overcoming Road Rage, Vol. 122. 2001. 24.95 (978-1-58557-025-6(7)) Dynamic Growth.

Overcoming Selfishness: The Little-Known Secret to a Happy (& Victorious) Life. Lynne Hammond. 1 cass. (Running Time: 1 hr. 30 mins.). 1996. 15.00 (978-1-57399-023-3(X)) Mac Hammond.
Teaching on the importance of overcoming the characteristic of selfishness.

Overcoming Selfishness: The Little-Known Secret to a Happy (and Victorious) Life. Lynne Hammond. 3 CDs. 2006. audio compact disk 15.00 (978-1-57399-308-1(5)) Mac Hammond.
This series is for all who've ever longed to possess the Christ-like quality of selfishness. You'll learn the four steps to increasing in love and how to walk by your heart instead of your head.

Overcoming Shyness. 1 cass. (Running Time: 45 min.). (Educational Ser.). 1989. 9.98 (978-1-55909-110-7(X), 89S) Randolph Tapes.

Overcoming Shyness. Eldon Taylor. 1 cass. (Running Time: 1 hr. 2 mins.). (Inner Talk Ser.). 16.95 incl. script. (978-1-55978-171-8(8), 5357C) Progress Aware Res.
Soundtrack - Musical Themes with underlying subliminal affirmations.

Overcoming Shyness. Philip G. Zimbardo. 2007. audio compact disk 12.95 (978-1-57970-481-0(6), Audio-For) J Norton Pubs.

Overcoming Shyness: Easy. Eldon Taylor. Read by Eldon Taylor. Ed. by Leslie Brice. 1 cass. (Running Time: 1 hr.). 1992. 16.95 (978-1-56705-340-1(8)) Gateways Inst.
Self improvement.

Overcoming Shyness: Ocean. Eldon Taylor. Read by Eldon Taylor. Ed. by Leslie Brice. 1 cass. (Running Time: 1 hr.). 1992. 16.95 (978-1-56705-341-8(6)) Gateways Inst.

Overcoming Shyness: Tropical Lagoon. Eldon Taylor. 1 cass. (Running Time: 1 hr.). 16.95 (978-1-55978-322-4(2), 5357A) Progress Aware Res.

Overcoming Stress in School. Eldon Taylor. 1 cass. (Running Time: 1 hr. 2 mins.). (Inner Talk Ser.). 16.95 incl. script. (978-1-55978-530-3(6), 53815F) Progress Aware Res.
Soundtrack - Babbling Brook with underlying subliminal affirmations.

Overcoming Stress in School: Contemporary Moments. Eldon Taylor. 1 cass. (Running Time: 1 hr.). 16.95 (978-1-55978-611-9(6), 53815N) Progress Aware Res.

Overcoming Stress, the Silent Killer. Earnie Larsen. 1 cass. (Running Time: 1 hr.). 1989. 10.95 (978-1-56047-008-3(9), A112) E Larsen Enterprises.
Explains how to break the stress cycle.

Overcoming Substance Abuse. Steven Halpern. Read by Steven Halpern. 1 cass. (Running Time: 1 hr.). (Soundwave 2000 AudioActive Subliminal Ser.). 1990. 9.98 (978-1-878625-13-7(6), SRXB 2023) Inner Peace Mus.
Relaxing, beautiful music with subliminal affirmations to support individuals in recovery.

Overcoming Temptation. Swami Amar Jyoti. 1 cass. (Running Time: 1 hr.). 1980. 9.95 (P-28) Truth Consciousness.
How we create our temptations. Going forward boldly to the next reality. How partners can help each other.

Overcoming Temptation, Pt. 1. Short Stories. Joel Osteen. 1 Cass. (Running Time: 30 Mins.). 2002. Rental 6.00 (978-1-59349-143-7(3), JA0143) J Osteen.

Overcoming Temptation, Pt. 2. Speeches. Joel Osteen. 1 Cass. (Running Time: 30 Mins.). 2002. 6.00 (978-1-59349-144-4(1), JA0144) J Osteen.

Overcoming Temptations, Tests & Trials. David T. Demola. 3 cass. (Running Time: 4 hrs. 30 mins.). 12.00 (S-1041) Faith Fellow Min.

Overcoming Test Anxiety, Vol. 3. unabr. ed. Juliette Becker. 1 cass. (Running Time: 25 min.). Dramatization. 1999. 19.95 incl. script. Postcards MindsEye.
Becker, a licensed therapist with a doctoral degree in Clinical Psychology takes the listener through a series of stress reduction exercises.

Overcoming the Barriers to Healing. Derek Prince. 1 cass. (Running Time: 25 mins.). (B-4150) Derek Prince.

Overcoming the Enemy. Kenneth E. Hagin. (How to Be an Overcomer Ser.). bk. 17.00 Faith Lib Pubns.

Overcoming the Fear of Death. Kriyananda, pseud. 1 cass. (Running Time: 90 min.). 9.95 (SC-4) Crystal Clarity.
Learn how you can overcome the fear of death & remain youthful as your age increases.

Overcoming the Influences of the Past. Albert Ellis. 1 cass. (Running Time: 89 min.). 9.95 (C017) A Ellis Institute.
REBT recognizes the important influence of past experiences. Unlike other therapies, however, it shows you how not to carry its miseries into your future! Give up your childish demandingness & grow yourself up into a happy adult.

Overcoming the Influences of the Past. Albert Ellis. 1 cass. (Running Time: 1 hr. 29 mins.). 1999. 9.95 (C017) A Ellis Institute.
Learn how to let go of past pain, give up demandingness & grow yourself up into a happy adult!.

Overcoming the Influences of the Past. Albert Ellis. 1 cass. (Running Time: 89 min.). 9.95 (C017) Inst Rational-Emotive.
REBT recognizes the important influence of past experiences. Unlike other therapies, however, it shows you how not to carry its miseries into your future! Give up your childish demandingness & grow yourself up into a happy adult.

***Overcoming the Lure of Temptation.** Created by Laura Davis. Prod. by Laura Davis. (ENG.). 2009. audio compact disk 15.00 (978-0-9843234-2-5(2)) Imm Suc Enter.

Overcoming the Past. Earnie Larsen. 1 cass. (Running Time: 1 hr.). 1989. 10.95 (978-1-56047-010-6(0), A114) E Larsen Enterprises.
Explains how to break past patterns that influence the present.

Overcoming the Problems of Life, Vol. 1. Kenneth W. Hagin, Jr. 6 cass. (Running Time: 9 hrs.). 24.00 (16J) Faith Lib Pubns.

Overcoming the Problems of Life, Vol. 2. Kenneth W. Hagin, Jr. 5 cass. (Running Time: 7 hrs. 30 mins.). 20.00 (17J) Faith Lib Pubns.

Overcoming the Spirit of Jezebel. Rick Joyner et al. (Running Time: 3600 sec.). 2005. audio compact disk 19.99 (978-1-929371-65-5(9)) Pub: Morning NC. Dist(s): Destiny Image Pubs

Overcoming the Spirit of Poverty. Creflo A. Dollar. cass. & video 25.00 (978-1-59089-121-6(X)) Pub: Creflo Dollar. Dist(s): STL Dist NA

Overcoming Twelve Tough Temptations & Nine Gospel Stress-Savers. Ed Pinegar. Read by Ed Pinegar. 1 cass. (Running Time: 1 hr.). 1993. 7.98 (978-1-55503-538-9(8), 06004709) Covenant Comms.
Young adult talks.

Overcoming Worldly Forces: The Path of the Pilgrim. Marianne Williamson. Read by Marianne Williamson. 1 cass. (Running Time: 1 hr. 30 mins.). (Lectures on a Course in Miracles). 1999. 10.00 (978-1-56170-252-7(8), M755) Hay House.

Overcoming Your Anger in the Shortest Period of Time. Michael Broder. 1 cass. (Running Time: 1 hr. 3 mins.). 14.95 (C056) A Ellis Institute.
Discusses many aspects of anger including how it is triggered & intensified. Using REBT & other exercises, you will learn to bring your anger & hostility under control by conquering the underlying low frustration tolerance.

Overcoming Your Anger in the Shortest Period of Time. Michael Broder. 1 cass. (Running Time: 1 hr. 3 mins.). 14.95 (C056) Inst Rational-Emotive.
This interactive cassette will discuss many aspects of anger including how it is triggered & intensified. Using REBT & other exercises, you will learn to bring your anger & hostility under control by conquering the underlying low frustration tolerance (LFT).

Overcoming Your Anxiety & Learn to Love Your Job! Jane K. Cleland. 1 cass. (Running Time: 1 hr.). (Improving Accounts Receivable Collections: Tape 3). 1991. 39.50 (978-1-877680-09-0(5)) Tiger Pr.
Tape 3 addresses the 6 common anxieties shared by accounts receivable collectors & gives inspirational & motivational guidance on rethinking the job so collectors end up loving their work.

Overcoming Your Anxiety in the Shortest Period of Time. Michael Broder. 1 cass. (Running Time: 1 hr. 9 mins.). 14.95 (C055) A Ellis Institute.
Visualizations & interactive exercises help you control anxiety & fear so they no longer control you.

Overcoming Your Anxiety in the Shortest Period of Time. Michael Broder. 1 cass. (Running Time: 1 hr. 9 mins.). 14.95 (C055) Inst Rational-Emotive.
This interactive cassette pinpoints the nature of your anxieties & fears & shows you how to recognize & control anxiety so it no longer controls you through exercises & visualizations.

Overcoming Your Depression in the Shortest Period of Time. Michael Broder. 1 cass. (Running Time: 1 hr. 2 mins.). 14.95 (C054) A Ellis Institute.
This interactive program enables you to moderate mood changes through exercises & visualizations.

Overcoming Your Depression in the Shortest Period of Time. Michael Broder. 1 cass. (Running Time: 1 hr. 2 mins.). 14.95 (C054) Inst Rational-Emotive.
This interactive cassette describes depression & related mood disorders; then helps you identify the factors that help moderate mood changes through exercises & visualizations.

Overcoming Your Fear of the Dentist: A Dental Office Program Guide to Controlling Dental Anxiety. 2nd unabr. ed. Leonard G. Horowitz. 2 cass. (Running Time: 3 hrs.). (Freedom from Ser.). 1987. bk. 19.95 (978-0-9609386-2-9(1)) Tetrahedron Pub.
Behavorial program for treatment of dental phobias & anxiety.

Overcoming Your Insecurites. David T. Demola. 9 cass. (Running Time: 13 hrs. 30 mins.). 45.00 Faith Fellow Min.

Overcoming Your Past How to Love Yourself. Scripts. 2 cass. (Running Time: 60 mins).Tr. of Superando Nuestro Pasado Como Quererse a Si Mismo. (SPA.). 2003. 25.00 (978-0-9744786-0-9(1)) A Nogales.
Doctor Nogales is pleased to offer this important series of psychological self-help cassettes. Although they don't replace psychological therapy, they will give you the necessary information to find your own answers and possible solutions to common difficulties and life challenges. They also include practical exercises that can help to guide listeners to a healthier life. "Overcoming Your Past""How to Love Yourself".

***Overcoming Your Shadow Mission.** unabr. ed. John Ortberg. (Running Time: 1 hr. 35 mins. 0 sec.). (Leadership Library). (ENG.). 2008. 14.99 (978-0-310-30252-0(8)) Zondervan.

Overdressed. Contrib. by Caedmon's Call. 2007. audio compact disk 13.99 (978-5-557-63544-8(0)) INO Rec.

Overeating: A Dialogue. Kenneth Wapnick. 2 CDs. 2006. audio compact disk 9.00 (978-1-59142-276-1(0), CD26) Foun Miracles.

Overeating: A Dialogue. Kenneth Wapnick. 1 CD. (Running Time: 1 hr. 27 mins. 37 secs.). 2006. 7.00 (978-1-59142-277-8(9), 3m26) Foun Miracles.

Overeating & Obesity: Program from the Award Winning Public Radio Series. Interview. Hosted by Fred Goodwin. Comment by John Hockenberry. 1 CD. (Running Time: 1 hr). 2001. audio compact disk 21.95 (978-1-932479-74-4(0), LCM 191) Lichtenstein Creat.
Three out of five Americans are overweight or obese by medical standards - it's an epidemic. Guests include Dr. Barbara Rolls, professor of Nutrition and Biobehavioral health at Pennsylvania State University; Dr. Rudolph Leibel, professor of Pediatrics and Medicine in the Institute of Human Nutrition at Columbia University's medical school; Dr. Michael Devlin, associate professor of Clinical Psychiatry at Columbia University's Medical School and

Oxford Murders. Guillermo Martinez. Read by Jonathan Davis. Tr. by Sonia Soto. (Playaway Adult Fiction Ser.).Tr. of Crimenes Imperceptibles. 2008. 39.99 (978-1-60640-766-0(X)) Find a World.

Oxford Murders. unabr. ed. Guillermo Martinez. Read by Jonathan Davis. Tr. by Sonia Soto. (Running Time: 23400 sec.).Tr. of Crimenes Imperceptibles. 2007. 34.95 (978-1-4332-0486-9(X)); audio compact disk 19.95 (978-1-4332-0490-6(8)); audio compact disk 36.00 (978-1-4332-0487-6(8)) Blckstn Audio.

Oxford Murders. unabr. ed. Guillermo Martinez. Read by Jonathan Davis. Tr. by Sonia Soto. 4 cass. (Running Time: 23400 sec.).Tr. of Crimenes Imperceptibles. 2007. 19.95 (978-1-4332-0488-3(6)); audio compact disk 19.95 (978-1-4332-0489-0(4)) Blckstn Audio.

Oxford Picture Dictionary. Jayme Adelson-Goldstein & Norma Shapiro. (Oxford Picture Dictionary Program Ser.). 2002. audio compact disk 54.95 (978-0-19-438402-5(0)) OUP.

Oxford Picture Dictionary. 2nd ed. Jayme Adelson-Goldstein & Norma Shapiro. (Oxford Picture Dictionary 2E Ser.). 2008. audio compact disk 54.95 (978-0-19-474053-1(6)) OUP.

Oxford Picture Dictionary Focused Listening Cassette. Jayme Adelson-Goldstein et al. (Oxford Picture Dictionary Program Ser.). 1998. 54.95 (978-0-19-435187-4(4)) OUP.

Oxford Picture Dictionary for Kids. Joan Ross Keyes. (Oxford Picture Dictionary for Kids Ser.). 2002. audio compact disk 54.95 (978-0-19-438401-8(2)) OUP.

Oxford Picture Dictionary for Kids, Vol. 4. Joan Ross Keyes. 4 cass. (Oxford Picture Dictionary for Kids Ser.). 1999. cass. & cass. 54.95 (978-0-19-435199-7(8)) OUP.

Oxford Picture Dictionary for the Content Areas: Cassettes. Dorothy Kauffman. 4 cass. (Oxford Picture Dictionary for the Content Areas Ser.). 2000. 54.95 (978-0-19-434341-1(3)) OUP.

Oxford Reading Tree: Stage 2 New Edition Storytapes. Roderick Hunt. cass., cass., reel tape (978-0-19-918367-8(8)) OUP.

Oxycise! On the Go Commuter Workout. 1 CD. (Running Time: 15 min.). audio compact disk (978-1-890320-05-8(6)) Oxycise Intl.
Weight Loss. Learn the Oxycise Basic Breath to increase your metabolism & lose weight. Includes 15 minute workout which can be done in a car.

Oxycise! On the Go Commuter Workout. 1 cass. (Running Time: 15 min.). 1997. (978-1-890320-06-5(4)) Oxycise Intl.
Weight Loss. learn the Oxycise Basic Breath to increase your metabolism & lose weight. Includes 15 minute workout which can be done in a car.

Oxycontin: Program from the Award Winning Public Radio Series. Interview. Hosted by Fred Goodwin. Comment by John Hockenberry. 1 CD. (Running Time: 1 hr). 2004. audio compact disk 21.95 (978-1-932479-75-1(9), LCM 313) Lichtenstein Creat.
In this hour, we explore The Double Life of OxyContin. For chronic pain patients, the drug can be a lifesaver. Says patient Mary Vargas: "That was the only thing that enabled me to finish law school, pass two bar exams, get the kind of job I dreamed of, and start thinking of having a family."But for addicts who tamper with the pills, the effects can be devastating. OxyContin is getting into the wrong hands. But who's at fault? Some doctors have even been arrested, with chilling effects. Ethicist Sandra Johnson says, "If you're a physician, you don't have to hear many stories of physicians being arrested, physicians being led away in handcuffs, to understand that the risk in numbers may be small but in terms of impact, it's devastating."We'll go beyond the headlines to explore the medical and ethical issues raised by this controversial medication, and the new federal strategy for fighting prescription drug abuse.Plus, commentator John Hockenberry wonders: when we weigh the damage caused by pain against the threat of drug abuse, can anybody ever win?.

Oxygen. Andrew Miller. Narrated by Gordon Griffin. 8 CDs. (Running Time: 9 hrs. 30 mins.). audio compact disk 82.00 (978-1-4025-2920-7(1)) Recorded Bks.

Oxygen. unabr. ed. Andrew Miller. Narrated by Gordon Griffin. 7 cass. (Running Time: 9 hrs. 30 mins.). 2002. 63.00 (978-1-84197-332-6(7)) Recorded Bks.
In the summer of 1997, Alec Valentine has returned to his childhood home to care for his terminally ill mother Alice. His elder brother Larry is also planning to visit from California, where both his acting career and marriage are failing. The brothers are wary of their boyhood rivalries resurfacing, whilst they confront their own perceived inadequacies. In contrast, Laszlo-Lazer, a Hungarian emigre in Paris (whose play Alec is translating) appears to lead a charmed life. But professional and personal success cannot obscure the memories of the 1956 uprising and the crisis of nerve that still haunts him. For all four, the time has come to take stock and reflect on risks taken and opportunities lost.

Oxygen. unabr. ed. Andrew Miller. Narrated by Gordon Griffin. 7 cass. (Running Time: 9 hrs. 30 mins.). 2002. 47.95 (978-1-4025-2224-6(X), RG054) Recorded Bks.

Oxygen. unabr. ed. John B. Olson & Randall Ingermanson. Narrated by Norman Dietz. 11 cass. (Running Time: 15 hrs. 30 mins.). 2001. 96.00 (978-1-4025-4643-3(2)) Recorded Bks.
In the year 2012, young microbial ecologist Valkerie Jansen is offered a position in the crew of a mission to Mars. As part of the NASA corps of astronauts, she can continue her research. But on the outward voyage, joy turns to horror as an explosion cripples the ship. To survive, the crew must trust each other completely, but one of them may have sabotaged the mission.

Oxygen Therapies. Ed McCabe. 1 cass. 12.00 (978-1-879323-08-7(7)) Sound Horizons AV.

Oxygen Transport in the Critically Ill Patient. Read by Arnold Aberman. 1 cass. (Running Time: 90 min.). 1985. 12.00 (C8526) Amer Coll Phys.

Oxyoke. unabr. ed. Frank Bosworth, pseud. Read by John Keyworth. 3 cass. (Running Time: 4 hrs. 30 min.). (Audio Books Ser.). 1993. 34.95 (978-1-85496-025-2(3)) Pub: UlverLrgPrint GBR. Dist(s): Ulverscroft US
Andy McGregor & Ed Leathergood, who ran the bank at Barrettsville, were good friends. When outlaws robbed the bank & killed Leathergood, McGregor went after them, but there was no trail. While everyone else searched the northward hills, Nat McCullon led McGregor's Oxyoke riders in the opposite direction where they cornered the outlaws in a barn. After a savage fight they took the outlaws back with them - all but one.

Oy Chanukah! Perf. by Klezmer Conservatory Band. 1 cass. (J). 9.98 (437); audio compact disk 17.98 (D437) MFLP CA.
Take a journey through 21 centuries of the Jewish Festival of Lights as the jubilant klezmorim music captures the essence of a rich history.

Oyasumi - Goodnight: Japanese Lullabies & Restful Melodies. Perf. by Aiko Shimada & Elizabeth Falconer. 1 CD. (Running Time: 57:33). (JPN & ENG.). (J). 2001. audio compact disk 15.00 (978-0-9770499-6-7(5)) Koto World.
Winner of a Parents' Choice GOLD award AND a 2002 NAPPA GOLD award, and nominated for "Best Asian" Music Award by Just Plain Folks Music Awards.Aiko Shimada (voice) and Elizabeth Falconer (koto) play old songs from Japan; lullabies and age-old favorites that have been used to soothe children and adults alike for centuries. Compellingly understated arrangements bring out the warmth of Shimada's voice and the ephemeral beauty of the 13-string koto. Works sung largely in Japanese, with some English lyrics artfully woven in, but no knowledge of Japanese is necessary to enjoy the beauty of these intimate, nurturing songs. "Carries listeners of any age to a place of quiet and enfolding peace." -Parents' Choice.

Oyibo, the Black Scentist Who Topped Einstein. 1 cass. (Running Time: 90 mins.). 2000. 19.99 IDA Games.

Oz. unabr. ed. L. Frank Baum. 4 cass. (J). HarperCollins Pubs.

Oz, Set. unabr. ed. L. Frank Baum. 4 cass. Incl. Land of Oz. L. Frank Baum. (Oz Ser.). (YA). (gr. 5-8). (SBC 125); Little Oz Stories. L. Frank Baum. (J). (SBC 125); Queen Zixi of Ix: Or the Story of the Magic Cloak. L. Frank Baum. (J). (SBC 125); Wizard of Oz. L. Frank Baum. (J). (SBC 125); (Oz Ser.). (YA). (gr. 5-8). 1985. 29.95 (978-0-89845-145-0(0), SBC 125) HarperCollins Pubs.

Oz Accountability, Pack. unabr. abr. ed. Tom Smith et al. 5 CDs. (Running Time: 7 hrs. 30 min.). (Smart Tapes Ser.). (ENG.). 2003. audio compact disk 24.99 (978-1-58926-179-2(8), P16J-073D) Oasis Audio.

Oz Accountability Power Pack. unabr. ed. Roger Conners et al. 5 cass. (Running Time: 7 hrs. 30 min.). 2004. 24.99 (978-1-58926-178-5(X), P16J-0730) Oasis Audio.
Using metaphors from The Wizard of Oz, the authors convey core principles that make a company successful.

Oz Power: How to Click Your Heels & Take Total Charge of Your Life. 2006. audio compact disk 25.00 (978-0-9765138-3-4(8)) Ctr Soulful.

Oz Power Presentation. Bill Bauman. 2005. audio compact disk 15.00 (978-0-9765138-2-7(X)) Ctr Soulful.

Oz Principle: Getting Results Through Individual & Organizational Accountability. abr. ed. Roger Connors et al. 2 cass. (Running Time: 3 hrs.). 2000. 17.99 (978-1-886463-83-7(2)) Oasis Audio.

Oz Principle: Getting Results Through Individual & Organizational Accountability. abr. ed. Roger Connors et al. (Running Time: 3 hrs. 9 mins. 10 sec.). (Smart Audio Ser.). (ENG.). 2003. 10.00 (978-1-60814-562-1(X), SmartTapes) Oasis Audio.

Oz Principle: Getting Results Through Individual & Organizational Accountability. abr. ed. Roger Connors et al. (Running Time: 3 hrs. 9 mins. 10 sec.). (Smart Audio Ser.). (ENG.). 2009. audio compact disk 14.99 (978-1-59859-614-4(4), SmartTapes) Oasis Audio.

Ozark Ghost Stories. Richard Young & Judy D. Young. Perf. by Judy D. Young. 1 cass. (Running Time: 45 min.). (J). (gr. 5-9). 1993. 12.00 (978-0-87483-211-2(X)) August Hse.
These scary stories from the Ozark Mountains are told by hill people everywhere. The Youngs, storytellers at the Ozark theme park Silver Dollar City, offer the stories that are most often requested of them, including "Pennywinkle! Pennywinkle!," "Frozen Charlotte," "The Vanishing Rider," & "Raw Head & Bloody Bones." Traditional music & sound effects combine with inspired storytelling to guarantee summer nights of spooky fun.

Ozark Tall Tales. Read by Richard Young & Judy D. Young. 1 cass. (Running Time: 60 min.). (American Storytelling Ser.). (J). (gr. 4 up). 1992. 12.00 (978-0-87483-212-9(8)) August Hse.
A rip-roaring collection of authentic mountain stories, gathered & retold by native Ozark storytellers & enhanced by Ozark music using such traditional instruments as the banjo, hammer dulcimer, & fiddle. Includes "The Dogs' Tale," "The Meanest Man in Arkansaw," "Cloverine Salve," & "The Great Hog Meat Swindle.".

Ozarks fiddle Music: 308 Tunes Featuring 30 Legendary Fiddlers. Drew Beisswenger & Gordon McCann. (ENG.). 2008. lib. bdg. 29.95 (978-0-7866-7730-6(9)) Mel Bay.

Ozma of Oz. L. Frank Baum. Narrated by John McDonough. 4 cass. (Running Time: 4 hrs. 45 mins.). (J). 2002. 37.75 (978-1-4025-2758-6(6)) Recorded Bks.

Ozma of Oz. unabr. ed. L. Frank Baum. Read by Flo Gibson. 3 cass. (Running Time: 4 hrs.). (Oz Ser.). (YA). (gr. 5-8). 1998. 16.95 (978-1-55685-546-7(X)) Audio Bk Con.
Dorothy is carried by a raging storm to the land of Ev & meets her old friends from Oz, plus Bellina the Hen, Tiktok, The Wheelers & Princess Langwidere. They match wits with the Nome King to save the royal family of Ev.

Ozymandias see Treasury of Percy Bysshe Shelley

Ozymandias see Poetry of Shelley

Ozzie & Harriet. 2 cass. (Running Time: 2 hrs.). 10.95 Set in vinyl album. (978-1-57816-070-9(7), OH2401) Audio File.
Includes: "September 2, 1945" A dripping faucet is keeping Harriet awake, so she nags Ozzie to get up & fix it. The problem builds as Ozzie tries to repair the faucet & winds up calling a plumber. "October 17, 1948" Ozzie gets tangled in a web of promises in the Ozzie Nelson style. "March 6, 1949" At an auction, the Nelsons buy a package they open to find a crystal ball. This program marks the first appearance on the air of David & Ricky as themselves. "November 16, 1951" All the boys, David, Ricky, Ozzie & Thorny - are fascinated by a construction job.

Ozzie & Harriet: Stretching the Truth & Sports Fans. Perf. by Ozzie Nelson & Harriet Hilliard. 1 hr. (Running Time: 1 cass.). 2001. 6.98 (2152) Radio Spirits.

P

P Vol. 1: New College Text. John Young & Kimiko Nakajima-Okano. 1984. reel tape 60.00 (978-0-8248-0980-5(7)) UH Pr.

P Vol. III: New College Text, Vol. 3. John Young & Kimiko Nakajima-Okano. 1985. reel tape 62.00 (978-0-8248-1034-4(1)) UH Pr.

P Vol. IV: New College Text, Vol. 4. John Young & Kimiko Nakajima-Okano. 1985. reel tape 60.00 (978-0-8248-1058-0(9)) UH Pr.

P. A. S. S. C. A. L. F. 8 Behaviors of Sales Success in an Agricultural Dealership. unabr. ed. Frank Lee. Read by Bobbie Gee. 2 cass. (Running Time: 2 hrs. 37 mins.). 2000. 12.95 (978-0-9701399-1-7(8)) Sales Acdmy.
Explains sales success in terms of successful behaviors & shows salespeople how to perform these behaviors consistently to achieve results.

P. A. U. S. E. - Take Control of Your Life: Be a More Conscious & Effective Decision Maker. Susan Wehrley. 2008. 29.95 (978-0-9729505-2-7(4)) Pub: Thomas & Kay. Dist(s): AtlasBooks

P & C Audio Review 1E. Ed. by Kaplan Publishing Staff. 2005. 29.00 (978-1-4195-3746-2(6)) Dearborn Financial.

P. G. Wodehouse: An Authorized Biography. unabr. ed. Frances Donaldson. Read by Frederick Davidson. 10 cass. (Running Time: 14 hrs. 30 mins.). 1999. 69.95 (978-0-7861-1639-3(0), 2467) Blckstn Audio.
Donaldson was given unique access to Wodehouse's most important private papers, including the notebooks he kept during the sad episode of his internment during the Second World War. For the first time, his beliefs, writings & actions are seen in the full context of the rest of his life.

P. G. Wodehouse: Selected Short Stories. unabr. collector's ed. P. G. Wodehouse. Read by Timothy Carlton. 6 cass. (Running Time: 6 hrs.). (Sound Idea Ser.). 1983. 36.00 (978-0-7366-3988-0(8), 9902) Books on Tape.
Titles Include: "Lord Emsworth & the Girlfriend", "Jeeves & the Yuletide Spirit," "Ukridge's Accident Syndicate," "Mulliner's Buck U Uppo," "Anselm Gets His Chance" & "The Clicking of Cuthbert".

P Is for Peril. Sue Grafton. (Kinsey Millhone Mystery Ser.). 2001. 64.00 (978-0-7366-7039-5(4)) Books on Tape.
PI Kinsey Milhone looks for a missing doctor several had motives to kill while trying to avoid a psychopathic boyfriend.

P Is for Peril. unabr. ed. Sue Grafton. Read by Liza Ross. 10 cass. (Running Time: 13 hrs.). (Kinsey Millhone Mystery Ser.). 2001. (978-0-7531-1228-1(0)) ISIS Audio GBR.
P is for Power, for Pain, for Passion and, of course, Peril . . .In the latest Kinsey Millhone adventure, our pushy, persistent, provocative heroine enters a shadow-land in which the mysterious disappearance of a prominent physician leads into a danger- filled maze of duplicity and double-dealing.

P. M. Yoga Meditations: Guided Meditations for An Evening of Relaxation & Restful Sleep, Vol. 1. Gael Chiarella. 1 CD. (Running Time: 1 hr.). 2001. audio compact disk 12.00 (93-0214) Relaxtn Co.
Come full circle, an evening of relaxation and sleep. Each CD consists of four 15-minute programs. Address releasing the day's tensions, body scanning, creative dreaming and guided breathing.

P. O. P. S. Principles of Pop Singing. Jodi Lyons & Lanelle Stevenson. 1990. spiral bd. 32.00 (978-0-02-871971-9(9)) Wadsworth Pub.

P. S. I Loathe You. unabr. ed. Lisi Harrison. (Running Time: 5 hrs.). (Clique Ser.: No. 10). (ENG.). 2009. 19.98 (978-1-60024-535-0(8)) Pub: Hachet Audio. Dist(s): HachBkGrp

P. S. I Love You. Lilian Harry. Read by Carole Boyd. 10 cass. (Sound Ser.). (J). 2002. 84.95 (978-1-84283-217-2(4)) Pub: ISIS Lrg Prnt GBR. Dist(s): Ulverscroft US

P. S. Longer Letter Later: A Novel in Letters. unabr. ed. Paula Danziger & Ann M. Martin. Read by Paula Danziger & Ann M. Martin. 3 cass. (Running Time: 4 hrs., 30 min.). (J). (gr. 1-8). 1999. 30.00 (LL 0140, Chivers Child Audio) AudioGO.

P. S. Longer Letter Later: A Novel in Letters. unabr. ed. Paula Danziger & Ann M. Martin. Read by Paula Danziger & Ann M. Martin. 3 cass. (YA). 1999. 23.98 (FS9-43381) Highsmith.

P. S. Longer Letter Later: A Novel in Letters. unabr. ed. Paula Danziger & Ann M. Martin. Read by Paula Danziger & Ann M. Martin. 3 vols. (Running Time: 3 hrs. 27 mins.). (J). (gr. 3-7). 1999. pap. bk. 36.00 (978-0-8072-8085-0(2), YA998SP, Listening Lib); 30.00 (978-0-8072-8084-3(4), YA998CX, Listening Lib) Random Audio Pubg.

P. S. Longer Letter Later Set: A Novel in Letters. abr. ed. Paula Danziger & Ann M. Martin. Read by Paula Danziger & Ann M. Martin. 2 cass. (Running Time: 3 hrs.). (J). 1999. (978-1-84032-246-0(2), HoddrStoughton) Hodder General GBR.
Elizabeth & Tara Starr are totally different & best friends. When Tara moves away, the girls continue their friendship through letters. Then life changes for both of them, & they realize they can only depend on each other & themselves.

P. T. Barnum: The Legend & the Man. unabr. collector's ed. Arthur H. Saxon. Read by Michael Prichard. 13 cass. (Running Time: 19 hrs. 30 min.). 1992. 104.00 (978-0-7366-2300-1(0), 3084) Books on Tape.
Who was the man the world knew as P. T. Barnum? Circus proprietor, discoverer of General Tom Thumb, impresario of the "Swedish nightingale" Jenny Lind, lover of practical jokes & a master of outrage, Barnum still fascinates nearly a century after his death.

P Vol. II Vol. 2: New College Text. John Young & Kimiko Nakajima-Okano. 1984. reel tape 60.00 (978-0-8248-1002-3(3)) UH Pr.

Pablo: Un Hombre de Gracia y Firmeza. (SPA.). 2005. audio compact disk 49.60 (978-1-57972-693-5(3)) Insight Living.

Pablo Neruda. Interview with Pablo Neruda. 1 cass. (Running Time: 30 min.). 1972. 13.95 (L058) TFR.
Neruda talks about his poetry, reads some of it, & discusses the interplay between writing & politics.

Pablo Neruda Lee a Pablo Neruda. unabr. ed.Tr. of Pablo Neruda Reading Pablo Neruda. (SPA.). audio compact disk 13.00 (978-958-43-0134-5(9)) YoYoMusic.

Pablo Neruda Reading His Poetry. unabr. ed. Poems. Pablo Neruda. Read by Pablo Neruda. 1 cass. Incl. Alturas de Macchu Picchu. (SWC 1215); Arte Poetica. (SWC 1215); Fabula de la Sirena y los Borrachos. (SWC 1215); Oda a los Calcetines. (SWC 1215); Solo la Muerte. (SWC 1215); Testamento de Otono. (SWC 1215); (SPA.). 1984. 12.95 (978-0-694-50162-5(X), SWC 1215) HarperCollins Pubs.

Pablo Neruda Reading Pablo Neruda see Pablo Neruda Lee a Pablo Neruda

Pablo Neruda Reading Pablo Neruda. Read by Pablo Neruda. (Running Time: 1 hr.). 2002. 14.95 (978-1-60083-138-6(9), Audiofy Corp) Iofy Corp.

Pablo Neruda Reads His Poems. Pablo Neruda. Read by Pablo Neruda. 1 cass. (Running Time: 60 mins.). (SPA.). 1992. pap. bk. 16.95 (978-0-88432-483-6(4), CSP101) J Norton Pubs.
Selections from "Residencia en la Tierra I" & "Alturas de Macchu Picchu.".

Pablum Problem: 1 Cor. 2:14-3:3. Ed Young. 1985. 4.95 (978-0-7417-1486-2(8), 486) Win Walk.

PAC Management: Capitol Learning Audio Course. Steven Billet. Prod. by TheCapitol.Net. (ENG.). 2008. 47.00 (978-1-58733-127-5(6)) TheCapitol.

Pacemakers, 1986. Moderated by Harold C. Urschel, Jr. 2 cass. (Thoracic Surgery Ser.: TH-3). 1986. 19.00 (8667) Am Coll Surgeons.

Pachebels' Canon, Level 3. (Yamaha Clavinova Connection Ser.). 2004. disk 0.82 (978-0-634-09598-6(6)) H Leonard.

Pachelbel Canon: The Meditative Classic with Ocean Waves. 2nd ed. Gordon Jeffries. 1 cass. (Running Time: 1 hr.). 1992. 9.95 (978-1-55961-161-9(8)) Relaxtn Co.

Pachelbel Canon with Ocean Sounds: Canon in D Major. 1 cass., 1 CD. (Classical Inspirations Ser.). 7.98 (CAM 922); audio compact disk 12.78 CD Jewel box. (CAM 922) NewSound.

Pacific. unabr. ed. Hugh Ambrose. Read by Mike Chamberlain. 19 CDs. (Running Time: 24 hrs.). (ENG.). (gr. 12 up). 2010. audio compact disk 49.95 (978-0-14-314565-3(7), PengAudBks) Penguin Grp USA.

Pacific. unabr. ed. Read by William Dufris. 2 pieces. 49.95 (978-0-7927-3374-4(6)); 89.95 (978-0-7927-3372-0(X)); audio compact disk 115.95 (978-0-7927-3373-7(8)) AudioGO.

Pacific Beat. unabr. ed. T. Jefferson Parker. Read by David Colacci. (Running Time: 15 hrs.). 2008. 39.25 (978-1-4233-5549-6(0), 9781423355496, Brinc Audio MP3 Lib); 24.95 (978-1-4233-5548-9(2), 9781423355489, Brilliance MP3); 39.25 (978-1-4233-5551-9(2), 9781423355519, BADLE); 24.95 (978-1-4233-5550-2(4), 9781423355502, BAD); audio compact disk 97.25 (978-1-4233-5547-2(4), 9781423355472, BriAudCD Unabrid); audio compact disk 29.99 (978-1-4233-5546-5(6), 9781423355465, Bril Audio CD Unabri) Brilliance Audio.

Pacific Blue. 1 cass. (Running Time: 60 min.). 1994. audio compact disk 15.95 CD. (2064, Creativ Pub) Quayside.
Lyrical vocabulary of the whale. Quiet piano melodies to lively arrangements. Original music by Stefan Schramm & Jonas Kvamstrom.

Pacific Blue. 1 cass. (Running Time: 60 min.). 1994. 9.95 (2062, NrthWrd Bks) TandN Child.

Pacific Blue Two. 1 cass. (Running Time: 45 min.). 1994. audio compact disk 15.95 CD. (2394, Creativ Pub) Quayside.
Stefan Schramm & Jonas Kvamstrom have created a beautiful sequel to their best selling Pacific Blue. Aquatically calming.

Pacific Blue Two. 1 cass. (Running Time: 45 min.). 1994. 9.95 (2392, NrthWrd Bks) TandN Child.

Pacific Coast. Rick Steber. Illus. by Don Gray. 1 cass. (Tales of the Wild West Ser.: Vol.2). 1987. pap. bk. 9.95 (978-0-945134-52-7(5)) Bonanza Pub.

***Pacific Coast Horns, Volume 1 - Horn Utopia: For Horn.** Pacific Coast Horns. 2009. pap. bk. 24.98 (978-1-59615-788-0(7), 1596157887) Pub: Music Minus. Dist(s): H Leonard

***Pacific Coast Horns, Volume 1 - Longhorn Serenade: For Trombone.** Pacific Coast Horns. 2009. pap. bk. 24.98 (978-1-59615-785-9(2), 1596157852) Pub: Music Minus. Dist(s): H Leonard

Pacific Coast League. rev. abr. ed. Ed. by Steven Alpert. 1 cass. 1992. bk. 15.95 (978-1-56703-010-5(6), 0010) High-Top Sports.
Sports.

Pacific Crossing. Gary Soto. Narrated by Robert Ramirez. 3 CDs. (Running Time: 3 hrs. 30 mins.). (gr. 4 up). audio compact disk 29.00 (978-1-4025-2327-4(0)) Recorded Bks.

Pacific Crossing. Gary Soto. Read by Robert Ramirez. 3 cass. (Running Time: 3 hrs. 30 mins.). (YA). 1999. pap. bk. & stu. ed. 43.25 (978-0-7887-3000-9(2), 40882) Recorded Bks.
Lincoln & Tony, barrio brothers from San Francisco, are excited about going to Japan as martial arts exchange students. To their surprise, they find baseball & jokes & people there who are a lot like their families back home.

Pacific Crossing. unabr. ed. Gary Soto. Narrated by Robert Ramirez. 3 pieces. (Running Time: 3 hrs. 30 mins.). (gr. 4 up). 1999. 28.00 (978-0-7887-2970-6(5), 95742E7) Recorded Bks.

Pacific Crossing, Class Set. Gary Soto. Read by Robert Ramirez. 3 cass. (Running Time: 3 hrs. 30 mins.). (YA). 1999. 118.80 (978-0-7887-3030-6(4), 46847) Recorded Bks.

Pacific Destiny. Scripts. Dana Fuller Ross, pseud. 5 CDs. (Running Time: 6 hrs.). (Holts, an American Dynasty Ser.: Vol. 8). 2005. 30.00 (978-1-58943-028-0(X)) Am Pubng Inc.
The nation's headlines scream for war against Spain. Newspaper publisher, Tim Holt will report the story himself from Cuba. Vanessa goes to Cuba to fight malaria and yellow fever with her husband. Frank Blake continues his Alaskan adventures while his father undertakes a dangerous secret mission in the Phillippines.

Pacific Fish. unabr. ed. Ed. by Linda Spizzirri. 1 cass. (Running Time: 90 min.). Dramatization. (Educational Coloring Book & Cassette Package Ser.). (J). (gr. k-8). 1980. pap. bk. 6.95 (978-0-86545-149-0(4)) Spizzirri.
Features some new & some familiar fish of the Pacific coast.

Pacific Islands Speaking. unabr. collector's ed. Armstrong Sperry & Dan Lazar. 6 cass. (Running Time: 6 hrs.). 1987. 36.00 (978-0-7366-1117-6(7), 2040) Books on Tape.
A history of the Pacific islands & their peoples.

Pacific Marine's Story: How It Really Was In 1943-1944. 2nd unabr. ed. Interview. Gary C. Martin. Narrated by Luke Behan & Kevin McNamara. 1 CD. (Running Time: 74 mins.). Dramatization. 2001. audio compact disk Rental 6.95 (978-0-9721444-1-4(2), 2) Audio History.
An 80 year old veteran narrates the overlooked, true stories of the men who defeated the Japanese at Roi-Namur & Saipan. Riveting & honest, it captures the power & passion of the American combat mentality in the 1940's. From the Official Marine Records & first hand accounts.

Pacific Northwest Habitats - Wetlands, Oceans, Forests & Wildlife: David Batker, Bonnie Phillips, Sean Cosgrove & Dee Arntz. Hosted by Nancy Pearlman. 1 cass. (Running Time: 28 min.). 10.00 (1414) Educ Comm CA.

Pacific Northwest Region. Compiled by Benchmark Education Staff. 2005. audio compact disk 10.00 (978-1-4108-5475-9(2)) Benchmark Educ.

Pacific Rift, unabr. ed. Michael Lewis. Narrated by Kerin McCue. 3 cass. (Running Time: 4 hrs. 30 mins.). 1992. 26.00 (978-1-55690-662-6(5), 92407E7) Recorded Bks.
An analysis of Japanese-American business practices & their cross cultural relationship - who wins, who loses.

Pacific Vortex! unabr. ed. Clive Cussler. Read by Michael Prichard. 8 cass. (Running Time: 8 hrs.). (Dirk Pitt Ser.). 1993. 64.00 (978-0-7366-2484-8(8), 3246) Books on Tape.
Dirk Pitt is put to the ultimate test as he plunges into the perilous waters of the Pacific Vortex, a fog shrouded sea zone where dozens of ships have vanished without a trace. The latest victim is the super-sub Starbuck, America's deep-diving nuclear arsenal. Pitt's job is to find & salvage the sub before the sea explodes. In a furious race against time, Pitt swirls into battle with underwater assassins & is trapped in the arms of summer Moran, the most stunningly exotic & dangerous woman ever to enter Pitt's life. As the countdown heads toward disaster, Pitt plummets into an ancient sunken island & an explosive climax.

Pacifica. Ed. by Robert A. Monroe. 1 cass. (Running Time: 30 min.). (Meta Music Ser.). 1985. 12.95 (978-1-56102-219-9(5)) Inter Indus.
As you explore the lush rain forests of your inner self, you may discover hidden memories of Polynesia & the Orient - Meta Music with a definitive "tropical" flavor.

Pacifism & Pathology in the American Left. Ward Churchill. 1 CD. (Running Time: 1 hrs. 30 min.). (AK Press Audio Ser.). (ENG.). 2003. audio compact disk 14.98 (978-1-902593-58-6(8)) Pub: AK Pr GBR. Dist(s): Consort Bk Sales

Pacifist's War: Diaries, 1939-1945. unabr. ed. Frances Partridge. Narrated by Judith Boyd. 7 cass. (Running Time: 9 hrs. 45 mins.). 2000. 62.00 (978-1-84197-058-5(1), H1053E7) Recorded Bks.
When war is declared, Frances & Ralph, both pacifists, turn their house into a sanctuary for friends more materially involved. All Allied & German manoeuvres are here recorded as they happened & the feelings of those who can only wait anxiously for news. Yet although war looms persistently over the Partridges, only a few power cuts affect them, leaving them feeling oddly isolated from it. As life goes on, Frances' diary not only chronicles events important to Britain, it also reveals an utterly different life, in which conversation, observation, literature & family are the driving forces.

Pack Es Aus. Henry Penix. (GER & ENG.). 2007. 49.99 (978-0-9772969-6-5(2)) PFC Inc.

Pack of Lies. Barbara Davoll & Dennis Hockerman. Illus. by Dennis Hockerman. 1 cass. (Christopher Churchmouse Ser.). (J). (ps-2). 1989. bk. 11.99 (978-0-89693-030-8(0), 3-1202) David C Cook.

Pack of Lies. Hugh Whitemore. Perf. by Martin Jarvis et al. 2 CDs. (Running Time: 1 hr. 52 mins.). 2005. audio compact disk 25.95 (978-1-58081-290-0(2), CDTPT208) Pub: L A Theatre. Dist(s): NetLibrary CO

Pack Rat's Day & Other Poems see Rolling Harvey down the Hill

Pack up Your Backpack Scripture Memory Tape. Paula Bussard & Christine Wyrtzen. Read by Christine Wyrtzen. 1 cass. (50-Day Spiritual Adventure Ser.). (J). (gr. k-2). 1995. 6.00 (978-1-879050-81-5(1)) Chapel of Air.

Package E see 9000 Q/A Basic Sciences Workshop: Absolutely Simple & Easy

Package Noah's Ark see Arca de Noe Paquete

Package of Praise for Kids. Alyssa Goins. 1999. 11.98 (978-0-633-00552-8(5)); audio compact disk 85.00 (978-0-633-00555-9(X)) LifeWay Christian.

Package of Praise for Kids Cassette Promo Pack. Alyssa Goins. 1999. 8.00 (978-0-633-00557-3(6)) LifeWay Christian.

Package of Praise for Kids Cd Promo Pack. Alyssa Goins. 1999. audio compact disk 12.00 (978-0-633-00558-0(4)) LifeWay Christian.

Package of Priase for Kids. Alyssa Goins. 1999. 75.00 (978-0-633-00554-2(1)); audio compact disk 16.98 (978-0-633-00553-5(3)) LifeWay Christian.

Packaging Machinery in France: A Strategic Reference 2006. Compiled by Icon Group International, Inc. Staff. 2007. ring bd. 195.00 (978-0-497-35954-6(5)) Icon Grp.

Packaging Machinery in New Zealand: A Strategic Reference 2006. Compiled by Icon Group International, Inc. Staff. 2007. ring bd. 195.00 (978-0-497-82370-2(5)) Icon Grp.

Packaging Prototypes 2: Closures. Anne Emblem & Henry Emblem. Photos by John Suett. 2001. bk. 45.00 (978-2-88046-504-9(4)) Pub: RotoVision SA CHE. Dist(s): Creat Pub Intl

***Packing for Mars: The Curious Science of Life in the Void.** unabr. ed. Mary Roach. 1 MP3-CD. (Running Time: 9 hrs.). 2010. 24.99 (978-1-4418-7664-5(2), 9781441876645, Brilliance MP3); 39.97 (978-1-4418-7667-6(7), 9781441876676, BADLE) Brilliance Audio.

***Packing for Mars: The Curious Science of Life in the Void.** unabr. ed. Mary Roach. Read by Sandra Burr. (Running Time: 9 hrs.). 2010. 24.99 (978-1-4418-7666-9(9), 9781441876669, BAD); 39.97 (978-1-4418-7665-2(0), 9781441876652, Brlnc Audio MP3 Lib); audio compact disk 29.99 (978-1-4418-7662-1(6), 9781441876621, Bril Audio CD Unabri); audio compact disk 99.97 (978-1-4418-7663-8(4), 9781441876638, BriAudCD Unabrid) Brilliance Audio.

Packing for the Long Strange Trip. Featuring Terence McKenna. 1994. 9.95 (978-1-59157-022-6(0)) Assn for Cons.

Packing Parachutes. J. Charles Plumb. Read by Charlie Plumb. 1 cass. (Running Time: 45 min.). 1991. 9.95 (978-1-881886-08-2(5)) J C Plumb.
Motivating & uplifting, Charlie Plumb, a Navy pilot & Annapolis graduate, is a former Prisoner of War in Vietnam & one of the most sought-after achievement speakers in the United States. In an upbeat, impactive style he draws upon his POW experience of nearly six years to demonstrate how to turn adversity into asset. This presentation deals with the value of inner strength in overcoming adversity & how people in their business & personal lives create their own prisons through fear of failure, negative thinking & self-pity. This presentation is sincere, straight-forward, & humorous.

Packing the Court: The Rise of Judicial Power & the Coming Crisis of the Supreme Court. unabr. ed. James MacGregor Burns. Read by Norman Dietz. (Running Time: 9 hrs. 30 mins. 0 sec.). (ENG.). 2009. 24.99 (978-1-4001-6211-6(4)); audio compact disk 69.99 (978-1-4001-4211-8(3)); audio compact disk 34.99 (978-1-4001-1211-1(7)) Pub: Tantor Media. Dist(s): IngramPubServ

Paco y el tallo grandote Audio CD. Benchmark Education Company. Based on a work by Brenda Parkes. (Shared Reading Classics Ser.). (J). (gr. k-2). 2009. audio compact disk 10.00 (978-1-60634-984-7(8)) Benchmark Educ.

Paco's Story. Larry Heinemann. Read by Larry Heinemann. 1 cass. (Running Time: 41 min.). 1988. 13.95 (978-1-55644-298-8(X), 8041) Am Audio Prose.
An experienced actor, Heinemann reads "Just One Clean Fact," the first chapter of Paco's Story.

Paco's Story. abr. unabr. ed. Larry Heinemann. Read by Richard Ferrone. 6 cass. (Running Time: 25200 sec.). 2006. 25.95 (978-0-7861-4476-1(9)); audio compact disk 25.95 (978-0-7861-7278-8(9)) Blckstn Audio.

Paco's Story. unabr. ed. Larry Heinemann. Read by Richard Ferrone. (Running Time: 25200 sec.). 2006. 54.95 (978-0-7861-4705-2(9)); audio compact disk 29.95 (978-0-7861-7705-9(5)); audio compact disk 63.00 (978-0-7861-6588-9(X)) Blckstn Audio.

Paco's Story. unabr. ed. Lenny Heinemann. Read by Richard Ferrone. (YA). 2006. 44.99 (978-1-59895-635-1(3)) Find a World.

Paco's Story. unabr. collector's ed. Larry Heinemann. Read by Walter Zimmerman. 8 cass. (Running Time: 8 hrs.). (J). 1988. 48.00 (978-0-7366-1403-0(6), 2292) Books on Tape.
Fire Base Harriette was supposed to be safe...but Alpha Company got wasted there - blown away - except for Paco, who was pretty well wasted himself. Left for dead, he lived - lone survivor of the massacre.

PACS in a Nutshell. Ed. by TheCapitol.Net. 2005. audio compact disk 107.00 (978-1-58733-025-4(3)) TheCapitol.

PACs in a Nutshell: Capitol Learning Audio Course. Ned Monroe. Prod. by TheCapitol.Net. (ENG.). 2007. 47.00 (978-1-58733-069-8(5)) TheCapitol.

***Pact.** Roberta Kray. Read by Annie Aldington. 2010. 104.95 (978-1-84652-827-9(5)); audio compact disk 109.95 (978-1-84652-828-6(3)) Pub: Magna Story GBR. Dist(s): Ulverscroft US

Pact: A Love Story. Jodi Picoult. Narrated by George Guidall. (Running Time: 61200 sec.). 2005. audio compact disk 34.99 (978-1-4193-6145-6(7)) Recorded Bks.

Pact: Three Young Men Make a Promise & Fulfill a Dream. unabr. abr. ed. Sampson Davis et al. Read by Sampson Davis et al. Told to Lisa Frazier Page. 6 CDs. (Running Time: 5 hrs. 45 mins.). (ENG.). 2002. audio compact disk 32.95 (978-1-56511-651-1(8), 1565116518) Pub: HighBridge. Dist(s): Workman Pub

Paddington. unabr. ed. Michael Bond. 4 cass. (Paddington Ser.). (J). (ps-3). HarperCollins Pubs.

Paddington & "Do It Yourself" see Paddington Turns Detective

Paddington & the Christmas Pantomine see Paddington for Christmas

Paddington & the Disappearing Trick see Paddington Set

Paddington & the Old Master see Paddington Dissappearing

Paddington Bear. unabr. ed. Michael Bond. Read by Michael Bond. 1 cass. Incl. Paddington Bear: Something Nasty in the Kitchen. Michael Bond. (Paddington Ser.). (J). (ps-3). (CP 1773); Paddington Bear & a Visit to the Dentist. Michael Bond. (Paddington Ser.). (J). (ps-3). (CP 1773); (Paddington Ser.). (J). (ps-3). 1985. 8.98 (978-0-89845-410-9(7), CP 1773) HarperCollins Pubs.
Paddington is on the prowl again in two funny stories. Paddington's eagerness to help out always turns into a tangly mess.

Paddington Bear: Something Nasty in the Kitchen see Paddington Bear

Paddington Bear & a Visit to the Dentist see Paddington Bear

Paddington Dines Out see Paddington Turns Detective

Paddington Dissappearing. unabr. ed. Michael Bond. Perf. by Michael Bond. 1 cass. Incl. Family Group. (J). (CDL5 1599); Paddington & the Old Master. Michael Bond. (Paddington Ser.). (J). (ps-3). (CDL5 1599); Spot of Decorating. (J). (CDL5 1599); (Paddington Ser.). (J). 1979. 11.00 (978-0-694-50828-0(4), CDL5 1599) HarperCollins Pubs.

Paddington for Christmas see Paddington Set

Paddington for Christmas. unabr. ed. Michael Bond. Perf. by Michael Bond. 1 cass. Incl. Everything Comes to Those Who Wait. (J). (CP 1621); Last Dance. (J). (CP 1621); Paddington & the Christmas Pantomine. Michael Bond. (Paddington Ser.). (J). (ps-3). (CP 1621); Paddington Hits the Jackpot. Michael Bond. (Paddington Ser.). (J). (ps-3). (CP 1621); (Paddington Ser.). (J). (ps-3). 1984. 8.98 (978-0-89845-178-8(7), CP 1621) HarperCollins Pubs.
Assorted escapades with Christmas themes from that best-of-bears in the worst of situations.

Paddington Hits the Jackpot see Paddington for Christmas

Paddington Makes a Bid see Paddington Turns Detective

Paddington Set. unabr. ed. Michael Bond. 4 cass. Incl. Paddington & the Disappearing Trick. Michael Bond. (Paddington Ser.). (J). (ps-3). (SBC 117); Paddington for Christmas. Michael Bond. (Paddington Ser.). (J). (ps-3). (SBC 117); Paddington Turns Detective. Michael Bond. (Paddington Ser.). (J). (ps-3). (SBC 117); (Paddington Ser.). (J). 1985. 29.95 (978-0-89845-019-4(5), SBC 117) HarperCollins Pubs.

Paddington Turns Detective see Paddington Set

Paddington Turns Detective. unabr. ed. Michael Bond. Perf. by Michael Bond. 1 cass. Incl. Paddington & "Do It Yourself" Michael Bond. (Paddington Ser.). (J). (ps-3). (CDL5 1622); Paddington Dines Out. Michael Bond. (Paddington Ser.). (J). (ps-3). (CDL5 1622); Paddington Makes a Bid. Michael Bond. (Paddington Ser.). (J). (ps-3). (CDL5 1622); (Paddington Ser.). (J). (ps-3). 1984. 9.95 (978-0-694-50720-7(2), CDL5 1622) HarperCollins Pubs.

Paddle-to-the-Sea. unabr. ed. Holling Clancy Holling. 1 cass. (Running Time: 60 min.). (J). 2004. 14.95 (978-0-9741711-3-5(1)); audio compact disk 16.95 (978-0-9741711-4-2(X)) Audio Bkshelf.
A small carved canoe and kneeling Indian travels from the Canadian wilderness to the Atlantic Ocean.

Paddy Canny: Traditional Music from the Legendary East Clare Fiddler. Contrib. by Paddy Canny. (ENG.). 1997. 13.95 (978-0-8023-7129-4(9)) Pub: Clo Iar-Chonnachta IRL. Dist(s): Dufour

Paddy Clarke Ha Ha Ha see Paddy Clarke Ha Ha Ha

Paddy Clarke Ha Ha Ha. unabr. ed. Roddy Doyle. Read by Aidan Gillen. 8 cass. (Running Time: 12 hrs.).Tr. of Paddy Clarke Ha Ha Ha. (J). 1995. 59.95 (978-0-7451-4384-2(9), CAB 1068) Pub: Chivers Audio Bks GBR. Dist(s): AudioGO
It is 1968 & Paddy Clarke is ten. He loves Geronimo & George Best. He hates kissing, zoos & the boys up the street. He can't stand his little brother & he even thinks of becoming a priest! He never picks the scabs off of his knees before they're ready & Kevin is his best friend. He wants to stop his parents from arguing all of the time. He's confused; he sees everything but understands less & less.

Paddy Tunney: The Man of Songs. 1 cass. 9.98 (C-7) Folk-Legacy.
Great Irish traditional singer from Letterkenny, Donegal.

Paddy's Lament: (Ireland 1846-1847) Prelude to Hatred. unabr. ed. Thomas Gallagher. Read by John MacDonald. 7 cass. (Running Time: 10 hrs. 30 min.). 1985. 56.00 (978-0-7366-0281-5(X), 1271) Books on Tape.
Ireland depended on the single abundant crop of potatoes but in 1846 the potato crop failed. A quarter of the population starved in less than two years. The final death toll exceeded 2 million. The history of three nations was changed & a hatred was born, a hatred that cut across the years & tears the daily fabric of life in England & Ireland, even today.

Padma Perera. abr. ed. Padma Perera. Read by Padma Perera. 1 cass. (Running Time: 29 min.). 1987. 10.00 (10) New Letters.
Originally from India, Perera demonstrates her range & discusses her work.

Padma Talwalkar (Vocal), Vol. 1. Music by Padma Talwalkar. 1 cass. (Music Today Presents Ser.). 1992. (A92034) Multi-Cultural Bks.

Padma Talwalkar (Vocal), Vol. 2. Music by Padma Talwalkar. 1 cass. (Music Today Presents Ser.). 1992. (A92035) Multi-Cultural Bks.

Padre de Amor. Read by Pablo Sierra. 2007. audio compact disk 14.99 (978-0-8297-5497-1(0)) Pub: Vida Pubs. Dist(s): Zondervan

Padre on Horseback. Herbert E. Bolton. 2 cass. 9.95 (304) Ignatius Pr.
Short portrait of Father Kino, outstanding missionary to the Southwestern U.S.

Padre Pio. unabr. ed. Mary F. Ingoldsby. Read by Christopher Codol. Ed. by Fiona Biggs. 6 cass. 24.95 set. (763) Ignatius Pr.
The holiness of this Capuchin friar became evident in 1918 with his receiving the bleeding imprint of Christ's wounds, a blessing which lasted until his death in 1968.

Padre Rico Padre Pobre / Rich Dad Poor Dad. Robert T. Kiyosaki. (SPA.). 2010. audio compact disk 24.95 (978-1-933499-86-4(9)) Fonolibro Inc.

Padres E Hijos. abr. ed. Ivan Turgueniev. Read by Hernando Iván Cano. 3 CDs. (Running Time: 3 hrs.). (SPA.). 2002. audio compact disk 17.00 (978-958-8161-36-5(3)) YoYoMusic.

Pagan Babies. Elmore Leonard. Read by Alexander Adams. 2000. audio compact disk 48.00 (978-0-7366-6175-1(1)) Books on Tape.

Pagan Babies. Elmore Leonard. Narrated by Ron McLarty. 7 CDs. (Running Time: 7 hrs. 30 mins.). 2001. audio compact disk 69.00 (978-0-7887-5355-8(X), C1373E7) Recorded Bks.
Father Terry Dunn's first mass in Rwanda ended with a bloody massacre of his Tutsi parishioners by the Hutu militia. Five years later, when Terry returns home to Detroit, he feels much more in his element. Despite a federal injunction against him & a goon looking for some money, Detroit has a great selection of people to collect charity from: sleazy restaurant owners, indicted mob bosses, ex-con stand-up comedians & dim-witted hitmen. As Terry jumps through increasingly convoluted hoops to find the perfect money-raising scam.

Pagan Babies. unabr. ed. Elmore Leonard. Read by Alexander Adams. 5 cass. (Running Time: 7 hrs. 30 mins.). 2001. 40.00 (978-0-7366-5591-0(3)); audio compact disk 48.00 Books on Tape.
Terry Dunn is the only priest for miles in the lingering aftermath of the worst massacre Rwanda has ever seen. Fr. Terry has just heard one confession too many. After exacting a chilling penance, Fr. Terry has to get out of Africa - pronto. He goes home to Detroit where a tax-fraud indictment is hanging over him. Is Dunn really a priest? Then there's Debbie Dewey. She's just been sprung from jail & is trying to make it as a stand-up comic. They hit it off beautifully. Debbie sells Terry on going in together on a con with a much bigger payoff than either could manage alone.

***Pagan Babies.** unabr. ed. Elmore Leonard. (ENG.). 2010. (978-0-06-199384-8(0), Harper Audio); (978-0-06-199761-7(7), Harper Audio) HarperCollins Pubs.

Pagan Babies. unabr. ed. Elmore Leonard. Narrated by Ron McLarty. 6 cass. (Running Time: 7 hrs. 30 mins.). 2000. 59.00 (978-0-7887-4945-2(5), 96463E7) Recorded Bks.
Father Terry Dunn's first mass in Rwanda ended with a bloody massacre of his Tutsi parishioners by the Hutu militia. Five years later, when Terry returns home to Detroit, he feels much more in his element. Despite a federal injunction against him & a goon looking for some money, Detroit has a great selection of people to collect charity from: sleazy restaurant owners, indicted mob bosses, ex-con stand-up comedians & dim-witted hitmen. As Terry jumps through increasingly convoluted hoops to find the perfect money-raising scam.

Pagan Christ & the Spirituality of Wine. Tom Harpur. (Running Time: 3600 sec.). 2005. audio compact disk 15.95 (978-0-660-19462-2(7)) Canadian Broadcasting CAN.

***Pagan Christianity.** unabr. ed. Frank Viola. Narrated by Lloyd James. (ENG.). 2008. 16.98 (978-1-59644-632-8(3), Hovel Audio) christianaud.

Pagan Christianity? Exploring the Roots of our Church Practices. unabr. ed. Frank Viola & George Barna. Narrated by Lloyd James. (Running Time: 8 hrs. 18 mins. 0 sec.). (ENG.). 2008. audio compact disk 26.98 (978-1-59644-631-1(5), Hovel Audio) christianaud.

Pagan Prayer see Poetry of Countee Cullen

Pagan Stone. abr. ed. Nora Roberts. Read by Dan John Miller. (Running Time: 6 hrs.). (Sign of Seven Trilogy: Bk. 3). 2010. audio compact disk 9.99 (978-1-4233-3791-1(3), 9781423337911, BCD Value Price) Brilliance Audio.

Pagan Stone. unabr. ed. Nora Roberts. Read by Dan John Miller. (Running Time: 11 hrs.). (Sign of Seven Trilogy: Bk. 3). 2008. 39.25 (978-1-4233-3789-8(1), 9781423337898, BADLE); 39.25 (978-1-4233-3787-4(5), 9781423337874, Brinc Audio MP3 Lib); 24.95 (978-1-4233-3788-1(3), 9781423337881, BAD); 24.95 (978-1-4233-3786-7(7), 9781423337867, Brilliance MP3); audio compact disk 97.25 (978-1-4233-3785-0(9), 9781423337850, BriAudCD Unabrid); audio compact disk 36.99 (978-1-4233-3784-3(0), 9781423337843, Bril Audio CD Unabri) Brilliance Audio.

Page. unabr. ed. Tamora Pierce. Narrated by Bernadette Dunne. 5 CDs. (Running Time: 6 hrs. 24 mins.). (Protector of the Small Ser.: No. 2). (YA). (gr. 5-8). 2007. audio compact disk 45.00 (978-0-7393-5136-9(2)) Pub: Random Audio Pubg. Dist(s): Random

Page. unabr. ed. Tamora Pierce. Read by Bernadette Dunne. (Protector of the Small Ser.: No. 2). (ENG.). (J). (gr. 5). 2008. audio compact disk 35.00 (978-0-7393-6181-8(3), Listening Lib) Pub: Random Audio Pubg. Dist(s): Random

Pages from My Life's Book. Derek Prince. 2 cass. 11.90 Set. (030-031) Derek Prince.
Prince shares his personal search for truth as a young man & his life-changing discovery that truth is a Person. Then, during three years with the British forces in WWII, the power of the Holy Spirit, combined with the Bible, began reshaping his life.

Pages of Life: Chapters I & II. Contrib. by Fred Hammond & Radical for Christ. 1 CD. 1998. audio compact disk 17.98 (978-0-7601-2277-8(6)) Provident Music.
Praise & worship with & "urban attitude".

Pai Ka Leo. Leo Punana Aha. Read by Haunani Apoliona et al. 1 cass. (J). 1989. 7.95 Bess Pr.
Original Hawaiian language songs for preschoolers.

Pai Ka Leo. Punana Leo. (J). (ps-6). 1989. bk. 6.95 (978-0-935848-63-2(0)) Bess Pr.

Pai Ka Leo. Punana Leo. Read by Haunani Apoliona et al. Photos by Lynn Martin. 1 cass. (HAW., (J). (ps-6). 1989. bk. 14.95 (978-1-880188-62-0(7)) Bess Pr.

Pai Ka Leo: A Collection of Original Hawaiian Songs for Children. Prod. by Aha Punana Leo. (HAW.). (J). 1989. pap. bk. 14.95 (978-1-57306-251-0(0)) Bess Pr.

Paid Companion. abr. ed. Amanda Quick, pseud. Read by Michael Page. (Running Time: 21600 sec.). 2007. audio compact disk 14.99 (978-1-4233-3354-8(3), 9781423333548, BCD Value Price) Brilliance Audio.

Paid Companion. unabr. ed. Amanda Quick, pseud. Read by Michael Page. (Running Time: 10 hrs.). 2004. 82.25 (978-1-59355-455-2(9), 1593554559, BrilAudUnabridg); audio compact disk 97.25 (978-1-59355-457-6(5), 1593554575, BriAudCD Unabrid); 32.95 (978-1-59355-454-5(0), 1593554540, BAU); audio compact disk 36.95 (978-1-59355-456-9(7), 1593554567, Bril Audio CD Unabri) Brilliance Audio.
The Earl of St. Merryn needs a woman. His intentions are purely practical - he simply wants someone sensible and suitably lovely to pose as his betrothed for a few weeks among polite society. He has his own agenda to pursue, and a false fiancée will keep the husband-hunters at bay while he goes about his business. The easiest solution is to hire a paid companion. However, finding the right candidate proves more of a challenge than he expected - until he encounters Miss Elenora Lodge. Her dowdy attire and pinned-up hair cannot hide her fine figure and the fire in her golden eyes. And her unfortunate circumstances, and dreams of a life of independence, make the Earl's generous offer undeniably appealing. But Elenora is unsure what this masquerade might entail. For St. Merryn is clearly hiding a secret or two, and things seem oddly amiss in his gloomy Rain Street home. She is soon to discover that his secrets are even darker than his decor, and that this lark will be a far more dangerous adventure than she's been led to believe. And Arthur, Earl of St. Merryn, is making a discovery as well: that the meek and mild companion he'd initially envisioned has become, in reality, a partner in his quest to catch a killer - and an outspoken belle of the ball who stirs a wild passion in his practical heart.

Paid Companion. unabr. ed. Amanda Quick, pseud. Read by Michael Page. (Running Time: 10 hrs.). 2004. 24.95 (978-1-59335-305-6(7), 1593353057, Brilliance MP3); 39.25 (978-1-59335-463-3(0), 1593354630, Brinc Audio MP3 Lib) Brilliance Audio.

Paid Companion. unabr. ed. Amanda Quick, pseud. Read by Michael Page. (Running Time: 10 hrs.). 2004. 39.25 (978-1-59710-556-9(2), 1597105562, BADLE); 24.95 (978-1-59710-557-6(0), 1597105570, BAD) Brilliance Audio.

Paid in Blood. abr. ed. Mel Odom. Narrated by Kevin King. (NCIS Ser.). (ENG.). 2006. 19.59 (978-1-60814-334-4(1)) Oasis Audio.

Paid in Blood. unabr. ed. Mel Odom. 2005. 25.99 (978-1-58926-868-5(7), 6868) Pub: Oasis Audio. Dist(s): TNT Media Grp

Paid in Blood. unabr. abr. ed. Mel Odom. Read by Kevin King. (Running Time: 25200 sec.). (Military NCIS Ser.). 2006. audio compact disk 27.99 (978-1-58926-867-8(9), 6867) Pub: Oasis Audio. Dist(s): TNT Media Grp

Paid in Full. Kenneth Copeland. 4 cass. 1982. bk. 20.00 Set incl. study guide. (978-0-938458-47-0(7)) K Copeland Pubns.
How Jesus paid the price for you.

Paid in Full. Kenneth Copeland. (ENG.). 2006. audio compact disk 20.00 (978-1-57562-898-1(8)) K Copeland Pubns.

Pain: Ancient Truths, Natural Remedies & the Latest Findings for Your Health Today. unabr. ed. Don Colbert. Read by Tim Lundeen. 7.99 (978-1-58926-801-2(6)) Oasis Audio.

Pain: Clinical Neurology. 1 cass. (Running Time: 1 hr.). 2001. 9.95 (CA611) Pub: VisnQst Vid Aud. Dist(s): TMW Media

Pain: Program from the Award Winning Public Radio Series. Hosted by Fred Goodwin. Comment by John Hockenberry. Contrib. by Jeanette Tracy et al. 1 cass. (Running Time: 1 hr.). (Infinite Mind Ser.). 1998. audio compact disk 21.95 (978-1-888064-32-2(3), LCM 30) Lichtenstein Creat.
What is pain? Stories from people who've learned to live with it, the latest research, and some unconventional methods anyone can use for controlling pain. Plus, people who've awakened during painful surgery campaign for better anesthesia practices.

Pain - Softening the Sensations: Relax into Healing Series (Spoken Audio CD & Booklet) Nancy Hopps. (Relax Into Healing Ser.). 2007. pap. bk. 19.95 (978-0-9785985-4-9(7), Relas into Healing) Pub: Syner Systs. Dist(s): Baker Taylor

Pain & Healing. Bruce Goldberg. (ENG.). 2005. audio compact disk 17.00 (978-1-57968-044-2(5)) Pub: B Goldberg. Dist(s): Baker Taylor

Pain & Healing. Bruce Goldberg. 1 cass. (Running Time: 20 min.). (ENG.). 2006. 13.00 (978-1-885577-10-8(9)) Pub: B Goldberg. Dist(s): Baker Taylor
This self hypnosis program trains the listener to access their natural healing forces and reduce physical pain.

Pain & the Great One. Judy Blume. 1 cass. (Running Time: 35 min.). (J). (gr. k-3). 2001. pap. bk. 15.98 (LL-118C) Kimbo Educ.
Two lighthearted stories focus on the emotions that children often feel towards their siblings - rivalry, frustration & ultimately love. Includes a book to read along with.

Pain & the Great One. unabr. ed. Judy Blume. Read by Dan Diggles. 1 cass. (Running Time: 9 mins.). (Follow the Reader Ser.). (J). (gr. k-3). 1988. pap. bk. 17.00 (978-0-8072-0122-0(7), FTR118SP, Listening Lib) Random Audio Pubg.
How will "The Great One" & her younger brother "The Pain" ever figure out which one of them their parents love more?.

Pain & the Spiritual Life. 1 cass. (Care Cassettes Ser.: Vol. 13, No. 1). 1986. 10.80 Assn Prof Chaplains.

***Pain Chronicles: Cures, Myths, Mysteries, Prayers, Diaries, Brain Scans, Healing, & the Science of Suffering.** unabr. ed. Melanie Thernstrom. (Running Time: 11 hrs. 30 mins. 0 sec.). 2010. 24.99 (978-1-4001-6854-5(6)); 34.99 (978-1-4001-9854-2(2)); 17.99 (978-1-4001-8854-3(7)); audio compact disk 83.99 (978-1-4001-4854-7(5)); audio compact disk 34.99 (978-1-4001-1854-0(9)) Pub: Tantor Media. Dist(s): IngramPubServ

Pain Control. abr. ed. Robert A. Monroe. Read by Robert A. Monroe. (Mind Food Ser.). 1983. 14.95 (978-1-56102-412-4(0)) Inter Indus.
Use the Hemi-Sync process to change the perception of pain.

Pain Control - a Drug-Free Solution. Scott Sulak. 1998. 15.00 (978-1-932659-04-7(8)) Change For Gd.

Pain Control / Relief. Created by Anne H. Spencer-Beacham. 1. 2003. audio compact disk (978-1-932163-62-9(X)) Infinity Inst.

Pain Control & Healing Response: Creative Visualizations into Self Empowerment & Spiritual Identity. (ENG.). 2009. 15.95 (978-0-9758866-9-4(X)) Awakening Pubns Inc.

Pain Control & Responsiveness to Healing: Creative Visualizations for Creating a New Reality. Created by Stanley Haluska. 1 CD. (Running Time: 70 mins). 2004. audio compact disk 15.00 (978-0-9668872-9-7(8), AP113) Awakening Pubns Inc.

Pain Control for Labor & Delivery. Luther C. Rollins, III. 1 cass. 1992. 9.95 (978-0-9635923-1-6(9)) Three Sq GA.

Pain de Menage, La Maitresse, Set. Jules Renard. Read by Claude Winter et al. 2 cass. (FRE.). 1991. 26.95 (1275-RF) Olivia & Hill.

Pain-Free Arthritis: A 7-Step Program for Feeling Better Again. abr. ed. Harris H. McIlwain & Debra Fulghum Bruce. Narrated by Simon Vance. (Running Time: 10800 sec.). 2006. audio compact disk 22.95 (978-1-933310-15-2(4)) STI Certified.

Pain Free Child Birthing: Childbirthing with Hypnosis. Mark E. Wilkins. 2006. audio compact disk 59.95 (978-0-9709302-6-2(7)) Growth Enrich.

Pain Free Childbirth Program. 2001. 59.95 (978-0-9709302-1-7(6)) Growth Enrich.

Pain Has an Element of Blank see Poems & Letters of Emily Dickinson

Pain Management. unabr. ed. Andrew Vachss. Read by Phil Gigante. (Running Time: 10 hrs.). (Burke Ser.). 2010. audio compact disk 29.99 (978-1-4418-2410-3(3), 9781441824103, Bril Audio CD Unabri) Brilliance Audio.

***Pain Management.** unabr. ed. Andrew Vachss. Read by Phil Gigante. (Running Time: 10 hrs.). (Burke Ser.). 2010. 24.99 (978-1-4418-2414-1(6), 9781441824141, BAD); 24.99 (978-1-4418-2412-7(X), 9781441824127, Brilliance MP3); 39.97 (978-1-4418-2415-8(4), 9781441824158, BADLE); 39.97 (978-1-4418-2413-4(8), 9781441824134, Brinc Audio MP3 Lib); audio compact disk 79.97 (978-1-4418-2411-0(1), 9781441824110, BriAudCD Unabrid) Brilliance Audio.

Pain Management, Relief & Control, Vol. 142. 1998. 24.95 (978-1-58557-024-9(9)) Dynamic Growth.

Pain Management with Chi Gong. Maoshing Ni. Read by Maoshing Ni. 1 cass. (Running Time: 30 min.). 1986. 9.95 (ACHIP, Shrine Eternal) SevenStar Comm.
Visualization & breathing exercises thousands of years old for overcoming pain by invigorating the flow of energies in the body releasing the blockages causing pain.

Pain Nurse. unabr. ed. Jon Talton. (Running Time: 7.5 hrs. 0 mins.). (ENG.). 2009. 29.95 (978-1-4332-6575-4(3)); 54.95 (978-1-4332-6571-6(0)); audio compact disk 60.00 (978-1-4332-6572-3(9)) Blckstn Audio.

Pain Relaxation. 1 cass. (Health Ser.). 12.98 (107) Randolph Tapes.
Use this tape to help alleviate pain. Good for migraines-neck-back-any pain.

Pain Relief. 2 CDs. 1980. audio compact disk 27.98 (978-1-56001-962-6(X)) Potentials.
Pain can arise from birth defects, disease, or negative thinking. This program contains three of Barrie's most effective techniques to provide relief. This 2-CD program from our Super Consciousness series is our newest, most powerful format. On the self-hypnosis CD, SC programs have the Subliminal Persuasion soundtrack added under Barrie?s voice. And the 17th Century Baroque music on the Subliminal CD has the same beat as your body's natural rhythm, thereby allowing the suggestions to enter deeply and effortlessly.

Pain Relief. Zoilita Grant. (ENG.). 2009. audio compact disk 16.95 (978-1-890575-47-2(X)) Zoilita Grant.

Pain Relief. Steven Gurgevich. 2005. audio compact disk 19.95 (978-1-932170-28-3(6), HWH) Tranceformation.

Pain Relief. Barrie Konicov. 1 cass. 11.98 (978-0-87082-351-0(5), 092) Potentials.
Professional hypnotist Barrie Konicov has put together three of his most effective techniques to help get rid of pains in the back, stomach, legs, arms & head which are caused by birth defects, disease or negative thinking.

Pain Relief. Barrie Konicov. 1 CD. 2004. audio compact disk 19.98 (978-1-56001-666-3(3)) Potentials.
Pain can arise from birth defects, disease, or negative thinking. This program contains three of Barrie's most effective techniques to provide relief.You will find the self-hypnosis on track 1 and the subliminal on track 2. The easy-listening music of the subliminal, together with the self-hypnosis, is the original format which most people love and with which they are most familiar.

Pain Relief. Shinzen Young. 1 CD. (Running Time: 1 hr.). (Guided Self-Healing Ser.). 2006. audio compact disk 15.95 (978-1-59179-180-5(4), W815D) Sounds True.
With Pain Relief, Shinzen Young teaches listeners how to "step outside" of pain through traditional meditation practices. Drawing from 20 years of results in the field, this widely respected teacher offers a practical program to address both chronic and short-term pain, possibly reducing the need for drugs or surgery.

***Pain Relief: Manage & Eliminate Pain, Accelerate Recovery, & Feel Better.** Martin L. Rossman. (Running Time: 2:00:00). 2010. audio compact disk 14.95 (978-1-59179-777-7(2)) Sounds True.

Pain Relief & Health Imaging. Eldon Taylor. Read by Eldon Taylor. Interview with XProgress Aware Staff. 1 cass. (Running Time: 90 min.). (Power Imaging Ser.). 16.95 incl. script. (978-1-55978-177-0(7), 8008) Progress Aware Res.
Hypnosis & soundtrack with underlying subliminal affirmations.

Pain Relief & Health Imaging: Power Imaging. Eldon Taylor. Read by Eldon Taylor. Ed. by Leslie Brice. 1 cass. (Running Time: 1 hr.). 1992. 12.95 (978-1-56705-026-4(3)) Gateways Inst.
Self improvement.

Pain to Peace: Your Deepest Pain Is Your Greatest Source of Peace. David C. Jones. 1997. 11.95 (978-1-878400-06-2(1)) Dolphin Pub.

Painful Decisions. Mary Larkin. 2009. 84.95 (978-1-4079-0480-1(9)); audio compact disk 99.95 (978-1-4079-0481-8(7)) Pub: Soundings Ltd GBR. Dist(s): Ulverscroft US

Painless Dentistry. Barrie Konicov. 1 cass. (YA). 11.98 (978-0-87082-352-7(3), 093) Potentials.
Shows how to enjoy your next trip to the dentist by putting yourself into a hypnotic sleep, & using your mind power to deaden the area where the work is to be done. No needles, no laughing gas, just the power of your mind.

Paint All Kinds of Pictures. 2004. 8.95 (978-1-56008-996-4(2)); cass. & flmstrp 30.00 (978-1-56008-740-3(4)) Weston Woods.

Paint & Construction Estimator. Ed. by Socrates Media Editors. 2005. audio compact disk 29.95 (978-1-59546-202-2(3)) Pub: Socrates Med LLC. Dist(s): Midpt Trade

Paint Animals on Rocks with Lin Wellford. Lin Wellford. 2000. reel tape 29.95 (978-0-9700713-0-9(2), 31836) Pub: ArtStone Pr. Dist(s): FplusW Media

Paint Brush Kid. unabr. ed. Clyde Robert Bulla. Narrated by Johnny Heller. 1 cass. (Running Time: 45 mins.). (J). 2001. pap. bk. & stu. ed. 23.24 Recorded Bks.
Uncle Pancho isn't really anybody's uncle, but he's everybody's friend. When the state wants to tear his house down to make room for a new freeway, his friends search for a way to help him.

Paint Brush Kid. unabr. ed. Clyde Robert Bulla. Narrated by Johnny Heller. 1 cass. (Running Time: 45 mins.). (Stepping Stone Bk.). (gr. 2 up). 2001. 10.00 (978-0-7887-4551-5(4), 96325E7) Recorded Bks.

Paint It Black. unabr. ed. Janet Fitch. Narrated by Jen Taylor. 11 cass. 2006. 94.95 (978-0-7927-4529-7(9), CSL 1011) AudioGO.

Paint It Black. unabr. ed. Janet Fitch. Narrated by Jen Taylor. 13 CDs. (Running Time: 58440 sec.). 2006. audio compact disk 112.95 (978-0-7927-4481-8(0), SLD 1011); audio compact disk 69.95 (978-0-7927-4553-2(1), CMP 1011) AudioGO.

Paint It Black. unabr. ed. Janet Fitch. Read by Jen Taylor. (YA). 2007. 79.99 (978-1-60252-852-9(7)) Find a World.

Paint It Black: A Novel. abr. ed. Janet Fitch. Read by Jennifer Jason Leigh. (Running Time: 6 hrs.). (ENG.). 2006. 14.98 (978-1-59483-569-8(1)) Pub: Hachet Audio. Dist(s): HachBkGrp

Paint It Black: A Novel. abr. ed. Janet Fitch. Read by Jennifer Jason Leigh. (Running Time: 6 hrs.). (ENG.). 2009. 19.98 (978-1-60788-145-2(4)) Pub: Hachet Audio. Dist(s): HachBkGrp

Paint the Wind. unabr. ed. Pam Muñoz Ryan. Read by Kathleen McInerney. (J). 2007. 34.99 (978-1-60252-691-4(5)) Find a World.

Paint the Wind. unabr. ed. Pam Muñoz Ryan. (Running Time: 18060 sec.). (ENG.). (J). (gr. 2-5). 2007. audio compact disk 49.95 (978-0-545-04514-8(2)) Scholastic Inc.

Paint the Wind. unabr. ed. Pam Muñoz Ryan. Read by Pam Muñoz Ryan. 4 CDs. (Running Time: 18060 sec.). (ENG.). (J). (gr. 4-7). 2007. audio compact disk 19.95 (978-0-545-04512-4(6)) Scholastic Inc.

***Painted Bird.** unabr. ed. Jerzy Kosinski. Read by Michael David Aronov & Fred Berman. (ENG.). 2010. audio compact disk 34.95 (978-1-61573-080-3(X), 161573080X) Pub: HighBridge. Dist(s): Workman Pub

Painted Drum. Louise Erdrich. Read by Anna Fields. 6 cass. (Running Time: 9 Hrs.). 2005. 69.95 (978-0-7927-3742-1(3), CSL 837, Chivers Sound Lib); audio compact disk 89.95 (978-0-7927-3743-8(1), SLD 837, Chivers Sound Lib); audio compact disk 29.95 (978-0-7927-3832-9(2), CMP 837, Chivers Sound Lib) AudioGO.

Painted Drum. unabr. ed. Louise Erdrich. Read by Anna Fields. 2005. audio compact disk 39.95 (978-0-06-082816-5(1)) HarperCollins Pubs.

***Painted Drum.** unabr. ed. Louise Erdrich. Read by Anna Fields. (ENG.). 2005. (978-0-06-088779-7(6), Harper Audio); (978-0-06-088777-3(X), Harper Audio) HarperCollins Pubs.

Painted House. John Grisham. Read by David Lansbury. 2001. 64.00 (978-0-7366-6179-9(4)); audio compact disk 64.00 (978-0-7366-8943-4(5)) Books on Tape.

Painted House. abr. ed. John Grisham. Read by David Lansbury. 5 CDs. (Running Time: 5 hrs.). (John Grisham Ser.). (ENG.). 2001. audio compact disk 31.95 (978-0-553-71252-0(7)) Pub: Random Audio Pubg. Dist(s): Random

Painted House. abr. ed. John Grisham. Read by David Lansbury. 5 CDs. (Running Time: 7 hrs. 30 mins.). 2001. audio compact disk 36.95 Books on Tape.

Painted House. unabr. ed. John Grisham. 10 CDs. (Running Time: 13 hrs.). 2001. audio compact disk 59.95 (978-0-553-71274-2(8), Random AudioBks) Random Audio Pubg.

***Painted Ladies.** unabr. ed. Robert B. Parker. Read by Joe Mantegna. (Running Time: 5 hrs. 30 mins.). 2010. audio compact disk 32.00 (978-0-7393-4392-0(0), Random AudioBks) Pub: Random Audio Pubg. Dist(s): Random

Painted Veil. unabr. ed. W. Somerset Maugham. Read by Kate Reading. 7 cass. (Running Time: 27000 sec.). 2006. 19.95 (978-0-7861-4606-2(0)); 44.95 (978-0-7861-4772-4(5)); audio compact disk 19.95 (978-0-7861-6892-7(7)); audio compact disk 29.95 (978-0-7861-7474-4(9)); audio compact disk 72.00 (978-0-7861-6395-3(X)) Blckstn Audio.

Painted Veil. unabr. ed. W. Somerset Maugham. Read by Sophie Ward. 6 cass. (Running Time: 9 hrs.). 2001. 54.95 (978-0-7540-0684-8(0), CAB 2106) Pub: Chivers Audio Bks GBR. Dist(s): AudioGO
Kitty Fane is the beautiful but shallow wife of Walter, a bacteriologist stationed in Hong Kong. Unsatisfied by her marriage, she enters an affair with Charles Townsend, a man she finds charming, attractive and exciting. When Walter discovers her deception, he exacts a strange but terrible vengeance.

Painted Word. unabr. ed. Tom Wolfe. Read by Harold N. Cropp. 2 cass. (Running Time: 2 hrs. 30 mins.). 1994. 17.95 Set. (978-0-7861-0795-7(2), 1542) Blckstn Audio.
Exposes the myths & men of modern art. From the fuliginous flatness of the fifties to the pop op minimal sixties, right on through the now-you-see-it-now-you-don't seventies, Tom Wolfe debunks the great American myth of modern art in an incandescent, hilarious & devastating blast.

Painter of Battles. unabr. ed. Arturo Pérez-Reverte. Read by Simon Vance. 7 CDs. (Running Time: 8 hrs.). (ENG.). 2008. audio compact disk 29.95 (978-0-7393-5870-2(7), Random AudioBks) Pub: Random Audio Pubg. Dist(s): Random

Painting in the Cave of the Sun, Vol. 2. Read by Stephen Dilauro. 1 cass. (Running Time: 70 min.). (YA). 1997. 11.98; 16.95 Riv Tales Prod.

Painting the Darkness. unabr. ed. Robert Goddard. Read by Michael Kitchen. 16 cass. (Running Time: 24 hrs.). 2001. 124.95 (978-0-7540-0577-3(1), CAB2000) Pub: Chivers Audio Bks GBR. Dist(s): AudioGO
On a mild autumn afternoon in 1882, William Trenchard sits smoking his pipe in the garden of his comfortable family home.When the creak of the garden gate heralds the arrival of an unexpected stranger, he is puzzled but not alarmed. He cannot know the destruction this man will wreak on all he holds most dear.

Painting the Darkness. unabr. ed. Robert Goddard. Read by Michael Kitchen. 8 CDs. (Running Time: 12 hrs.). 2001. audio compact disk 79.95 (978-0-7540-5404-7(7), CCD096) Pub: Chivers Audio Bks GBR. Dist(s): AudioGO

Paints & Coatings in France: A Strategic Reference 2006. Compiled by Icon Group International, Inc. Staff. 2007. ring bd. 195.00 (978-0-497-35955-3(3)) Icon Grp.

Pair see Twentieth-Century Poetry in English, No. 2, Recordings of Poets Reading Their Own Poetry

Pair-It Books Foundation Stage. Steck-Vaughn Staff. 2000. 45.00 (978-0-7398-4526-4(8)) SteckVau.

Pair-It Books Transition Stage Collection. Steck-Vaughn Staff. 1999. 90.00 (978-0-7398-2455-9(4)) SteckVau.

Pair-It Proficient Collection Stage 5. Steck-Vaughn Staff. (J). 1999. (978-0-7398-0938-9(5)) SteckVau.

Pair of Silk Stockings, No. 2. unabr. ed. Virginia Woolf et al. Read by Harriet Walter. 4 CDs. (Running Time: 5 hrs. 0 mins. 0 sec.). (Best of Women's Short Stories Ser.). (ENG.). 2009. audio compact disk 26.95 (978-1-934997-28-4(5)) Pub: CSAWord. Dist(s): PerseuPGW

Paix Chez Soi, la Peur des Coups. Georges Courteline. 1 cass. (FRE.). 1991. bk. 16.95 (1040-SA) Olivia & Hill.

Pajaro Dunes Tapes. R. Buckminster Fuller. 8 cass. (Running Time: 10 hrs. 29 min.). 1977. 77.00 (00704) Big Sur Tapes.
This is a complete weekend with Bucky Fuller. Two sessions outdoors; two sessions indoors. His total story & messages; nothing omitted.

Pakistan New Testament. V. Paul. 16 cass. (Running Time: 24 hrs.). (URD.). 1994. 39.98 (978-7-902030-15-1(5)) Chrstn Dup Intl.

PAL Executive Package. abr. ed. Robert A. Monroe. Read by Robert A. Monroe. 6 cass. (PAL Albums Ser.). 1988. 69.00 (978-1-56102-230-4(6)) Inter Indus.
Concentration, Retain-Recall-Release, Morning Exercise, Catnapper, Deep 10 Relaxation & Midsum mer Night.

PAL Package. abr. ed. Robert A. Monroe. Read by Robert A. Monroe. (PAL Albums Ser.). 1988. 29.95 (978-1-56102-228-1(4)) Inter Indus.
Concentration & Retain-Recall-Release.

PAL (Preliminary Achievement Level) Set: Giving Information & Socializing. Edwin T. Cornelius. Illus. by John Odam. (New Technology English Ser.: Vol. 1). 1984. pap. bk. 25.00 (978-0-89209-107-2(X)) Pace Grp Intl.

PAL (Preliminary Achievement Level) Set: Taking an Active Role in Conversations. Edwin T. Cornelius. Illus. by John Odam. (New Technology English Ser.: Vol. 2). 1984. pap. bk. 25.00 (978-0-89209-108-9(8)) Pace Grp Intl.

PAL Student Package. abr. ed. Robert A. Monroe. Read by Robert A. Monroe. 4 cass. (PAL Albums Ser.). 1988. 48.95 (978-1-56102-229-8(2)) Inter Indus.
Concentration, Retain-Recall-Release, Awake & Alert & Catnapper.

Palabra de Dios, el Mundo de Dios y Usted. Charles R. Swindoll.Tr. of God's Word, His World, & You CD. (SPA.). 2007. audio compact disk 30.00 (978-1-57972-801-4(4)) Insight Living.

Palabra de Dios Prevalecera: Himnos Sagrados Desde el Santuario Whitefield. Prod. by Foundations Bible College Staff. (SPA.). 2000. 7.95 (978-1-882542-30-7(4), 1882542304) Fndtns NC.

Palabra Eterna-RV 1960. Created by American Bible Society Staff. (Running Time: 90000 sec.). 2008. audio compact disk 39.99 (978-1-58516-873-6(4)) Am Bible.

Palabra Eterna-RV 1960. Created by American Bible Society Staff. (Running Time: 90000 sec.). 2009. audio compact disk 19.99 (978-1-58516-872-9(6)) Am Bible.

Palabras de vida Eterna: Meditaciones sobre los Evangelios. Mariano de Blas.Tr. of Words of everlasting Life. (SPA.). 2009. audio compact disk 25.00 (978-1-935405-13-9(6)) Hombre Nuevo.

Palabras y Cantos de Jesus. Paule Freeburg, Sr. et al. Read by Paule Freeburg, Sr. et al. 1 CD. (SPA.). 1996. audio compact disk 24.95 (10611) OR Catholic.
22 stories & songs from the life of Jesus in Spanish.

Palabras y Cantos de Jesus. Paule Freeburg, Sr. et al. Read by Paule Freeburg, Sr. et al. 1 cass. (SPA.). (J). (gr. k-3). 1996. 12.95 (10140) OR Catholic.

Palace Council. abr. ed. Stephen L. Carter. Read by Dominic Hoffman. 5 CDs. (Running Time: 6 hrs. 30 mins.). (ENG.). 2008. audio compact disk 29.95 (978-0-7393-4340-1(8), Random AudioBks) Pub: Random Audio Pubg. Dist(s): Random

Palace Guard. Charlotte MacLeod. Read by Mary Peiffer. 2001. 40.00 (978-0-7366-6022-8(4)) Books on Tape.

Palace of Illusions. unabr. ed. Chitra Banerjee Divakaruni. Read by Sneha Mathan. (Running Time: 45000 sec.). 2008. audio compact disk & audio compact disk 90.00 (978-1-4332-1595-7(0)) Blckstn Audio.

Palace of Illusions. unabr. ed. Chitra Banerjee Divakaruni. Read by Sneha Mathan. (Running Time: 45000 sec.). 2008. 72.95 (978-1-4332-1594-0(2)); audio compact disk & audio compact disk 29.95 (978-1-4332-1596-4(9)) Blckstn Audio.

Palace of Mirrors. unabr. ed. Margaret Peterson Haddix. Narrated by Polly Lee. (Running Time: 8 hrs. 30 mins.). (YA). (gr. 5-8). 2008. 56.75 (978-1-4361-9889-9(5)); 61.75 (978-1-4361-5934-0(2)); audio compact disk 77.75 (978-1-4361-5939-5(3)) Recorded Bks.

Palace of Mirrors. unabr. collector's ed. Margaret Peterson Haddix. Narrated by Polly Lee. 7 CDs. (Running Time: 8 hrs. 30 mins.). (YA). (gr. 5-8). 2008. audio compact disk 39.95 (978-1-4361-5943-2(1)) Recorded Bks.

Palace Tiger. Barbara Cleverly. 10 CDs. (Running Time: 11 hrs.). (Detective Joe Sandilands Ser.). (J). 2005. audio compact disk 89.95 (978-1-84559-142-7(9)) Pub: ISIS Lrg Prnt GBR. Dist(s): Ulverscroft US

Palace Tiger. unabr. ed. Barbara Cleverly. 8 cass. (Running Time: 11 hrs.). (Detective Joe Sandilands Ser.). (J). 2005. 69.95 (978-1-84559-109-0(7)) Pub: ISIS Lrg Prnt GBR. Dist(s): Ulverscroft US

Paladin of Souls. Lois McMaster Bujold. Read by Kate Reading. 11 cass. (Running Time: 16 hrs. 30 mins.). 2005. 85.95 (978-0-7861-2944-7(1), 3416); audio compact disk 108.00 (978-0-7861-8139-1(7), 3416) Blckstn Audio.

Paladin of Souls. Lois McMaster Bujold. Read by Kate Reading. (Running Time: 16 hrs. 30 mins.). 2005. 44.95 (978-1-59912-565-7(X)) Iofy Corp.

Palaeolithic of the Hampshire Basin: A Regional Model of Hominid Behaviour During the Middle Pleistocene. Robert Hosfield. (C). 1999. audio compact disk 87.50 (978-1-84171-023-5(7)) Pub: British Arch Reports GBR. Dist(s): David Brown

Palata Shest. Anton Chekhov. Read by Igor Dmitriev. 3 cass. (Running Time: 3 hrs.). (RUS.). 1996. pap. bk. 39.50 Set. (978-1-58085-563-1(6)) Interlingua VA.

Pale As the Dead. unabr. ed. Fiona Mountain. Read by Karen Cass. 8 CDs. (Running Time: 33300 sec.). (Isis (CDs) Ser.). 2006. audio compact disk 79.95 (978-0-7531-2495-6(5)) Pub: ISIS Lrg Prnt GBR. Dist(s): Ulverscroft US

Pale As the Dead. unabr. ed. Fiona Mountain. Read by Karen Cass. 7 cass. (Running Time: 34800 sec.). (Isis Cassettes Ser.). 2006. 61.95 (978-0-7531-1904-4(8)) Pub: ISIS Lrg Prnt GBR. Dist(s): Ulverscroft US

Pale Blue Dot: A Vision of the Human Future in Space. abr. ed. Carl Sagan. Read by Carl Sagan. 2 cass. (Running Time: 3 hrs.). 2000. 7.95 (978-1-57815-000-7(0), 1053, Media Bks Audio) Media Bks NJ.
The compelling sequel to Cosmos, from the Pulitzer Prize winning author. Sagan reveals how science has altered our perception of who we are & where we stand & challenges us to weigh what we will do with that knowledge with surprisingly spiritual impact.

Pale Blue Eye. Louis Bayard. Narrated by Charles Leggett. 2 CDs. (Running Time: 55740 sec.). (Sound Library). 2006. audio compact disk & audio compact disk 99.95 (978-0-7927-4237-1(0), CMP 973) AudioGO.

Pale Blue Eye: A Novel. Louis Bayard. Narrated by Charles Leggett. 13 CDs. 2006. audio compact disk 112.95 (978-0-7927-4066-7(1), SLD 973) AudioGO.

***Pale Demon.** unabr. ed. Kim Harrison. Read by Marguerite Gavin. (Running Time: 14 hrs. 5 mins.). (Hollows Ser.). 2011. 29.95 (978-1-4417-7630-3(3)); 85.95 (978-1-4417-7627-3(3)); audio compact disk 118.00 (978-1-4417-7628-0(1)) Blckstn Audio.

***Pale Demon.** unabr. ed. Kim Harrison. (ENG.). 2011. (978-0-06-202742-9(5)) HarperCollins Pubs.

***Pale Fire.** unabr. ed. Vladimir Nabokov. (Running Time: 11 hrs.). 2010. 24.99 (978-1-4418-7278-4(7), 9781441872784, Brilliance MP3); 39.97 (978-1-4418-7279-1(5), 9781441872791, Brlnc Audio MP3 Lib); 39.97 (978-1-4418-7280-7(9), 9781441872807, BADLE); audio compact disk 29.99 (978-1-4418-7276-0(0), 9781441872760, Bril Audio CD Unabri); audio compact disk 69.97 (978-1-4418-7277-7(9), 9781441872777, BriAudCD Unabrid) Brilliance Audio.

Pale Gray for Guilt: A Travis Mcgee Novel. unabr. collector's ed. John D. MacDonald. Read by Michael Prichard. 6 cass. (Running Time: 9 hrs.). (Travis McGee Ser.: Vol. 9). 1984. 48.00 (978-0-7366-0703-2(X), 1666) Books on Tape.
Tush Bannon was in the wrong place at the wrong time & the fact that he was a nice guy with a nice wife & three nice kids didn't mean a scream in hell to the jackals who had ganged together to pull him down.

Pale Horse. unabr. ed. Agatha Christie. Narrated by Hugh Fraser. (Running Time: 6 hrs. 0 mins. 0 sec.). (ENG.). 2010. audio compact disk 29.95 (978-1-60283-666-2(3)) Pub: AudioGO. Dist(s): Perseus Dist

Pale Horse. unabr. ed. Charles Todd. Narrated by Simon Prebble. 2 CDs. (Running Time: 12 hrs. 15 mins.). (Inspector Ian Rutledge Mystery Ser.: Bk. 10). 2008. audio compact disk 94.95 (978-0-7927-5346-9(1)) AudioGO.
Late on a spring night in 1920, five boys cross the Yorkshire dales to the ruins of Fountains Abbey, intent on raising the Devil. Instead, they stumble over the Devil himself, sitting there watching them. Terrified, they run for their lives, leaving behind a book on alchemy stolen from their schoolmaster. The next morning, a body is discovered in the cloisters of the abbey - a man swathed in a hooded cloak and wearing a gas mask. Scotland Yard dispatches Inspector Rutledge to find out who the man was and why he died in such mysterious circumstances. But the villagers clearly have something to hide. And what does the huge chalk sculpture of a pale horse of the Apocalypse have to do with the crime?.

Pale Horse. unabr. ed. Charles Todd. Read by Simon Prebble. (Inspector Ian Rutledge Mystery Ser.: Bk. 10). (YA). 2008. 79.99 (978-1-60514-941-7(1)) Find a World.

Pale Horse Coming. Stephen Hunter. (Earl Swagger Ser.). 2004. 15.95 (978-0-7435-1872-7(1)) Pub: S&S Audio. Dist(s): S and S Inc

Pale Horse Coming. unabr. ed. Stephen Hunter. Read by William Dufris. 2 CDs. (Running Time: 66600 sec.). (Earl Swagger Ser.). 2001. audio compact disk 49.95 (978-0-7927-2764-4(9), CMP 498, Chivers Child Audio) AudioGO.

Pale Horse Coming. unabr. ed. Stephen Hunter. Read by William Dufris. 12 vols. (Running Time: 18 hrs.). (Earl Swagger Ser.). 2002. bk. 96.95 (978-0-7927-2712-5(6), CSL 498, Chivers Sound Lib) AudioGO.

Pale Horse, Pale Rider. abr. ed. Katherine Anne Porter. Perf. by Katherine Anne Porter. 2 cass. (Running Time: 3 hrs.). 1984. 12.95 (978-0-694-50371-1(1), SWC 2007) HarperCollins Pubs.
The story of young love, with tragic complications of war & illness. Toward the end, when the heroine is at death's door, she has a vision of immortality, of heaven.

Pale Horseman. Bernard Cornwell. Read by Tom Sellwood. 9 cass. (Running Time: 52500 sec.). (Saxon Chronicles: No. 2). 2006. 79.95 (978-0-7927-3886-2(1), CSL 895) AudioGO.

Pale Horseman. Bernard Cornwell. Read by Tom Sellwood. 2 CDs. (Saxon Chronicles: No. 2). 2006. audio compact disk 29.95 (978-0-7927-3959-3(0), CMP 895) AudioGO.

***Pale Horseman.** abr. ed. Bernard Cornwell. Read by Jamie Glover. (ENG.). 2006. (978-0-06-087832-0(0), Harper Audio); (978-0-06-087831-3(2), Harper Audio) HarperCollins Pubs.

Pale Horseman. abr. ed. Bernard Cornwell. Read by Jamie Glover. (Running Time: 21600 sec.). (Saxon Chronicles: No. 2). 2006. audio compact disk 29.95 (978-0-06-078748-6(1)) HarperCollins Pubs.

Pale Horseman. abr. ed. Bernard Cornwell. Read by Jamie Glover. (Running Time: 21600 sec.). (Saxon Chronicles: No. 1). 2006. audio compact disk 14.95 (978-0-06-112657-4(8)) HarperCollins Pubs.

Pale Horseman. unabr. ed. Bernard Cornwell. Read by Tom Sellwood. 2 pieces. (Saxon Chronicles: No. 1). 2005. 49.95 (978-0-7927-3476-5(9), CMP 748); 69.95 (978-0-7927-3474-1(2), CSL 748); audio compact disk 99.95 (978-0-7927-3475-8(0), SLD 748) AudioGO.

Pale Horseman. unabr. ed. Bernard Cornwell. Read by Tom Sellwood. 12 CDs. (Running Time: 52500 sec.). (Saxon Chronicles: No. 2). 2006. audio compact disk 99.95 (978-0-7927-3887-9(X), SLD 895) AudioGO.

***Pale King.** unabr. ed. David Foster Wallace. (Running Time: 13 hrs.). (ENG.). 2011. audio compact disk & audio compact disk 34.98 (978-1-60941-975-2(8)) Pub: Hachet Audio. Dist(s): HachBkGrp

***Pale King: An Unfinished Novel.** unabr. ed. David Foster Wallace. (Running Time: 13 hrs.). (ENG.). 2011. 26.98 (978-1-60941-976-9(6)) Pub: Hachet Audio. Dist(s): HachBkGrp

Pale Kings & Princes. unabr. collector's ed. Robert B. Parker. Read by Michael Prichard. 5 cass. (Running Time: 5 hrs.). (Spenser Ser.). 1990. 40.00 (978-0-7366-1772-7(8), 2611) Books on Tape.
Wheaton is a typical New England small-college town, not the sort of place for drugs & murder. But when a reporter gets too inquisitive, he finds both - the latter his own. Spenser's call comes when the local cops work a cover. He needs help to solve this one - Hawk for back up & Susan for insight on the basics. (Trust a woman to sniff out jealousy, passion & hate!) What the trio finds is a cutthroat cocaine ring, where drugs have value supreme & human life none at all.

Pale View of Hills. collector's ed. Kazuo Ishiguro. Read by Roe Kendall. 5 cass. (Running Time: 7 hrs. 30 min.). 1999. 40.00 (978-0-7366-4826-4(7)) Books on Tape.
The moving story of Etsuko, a Japanese woman now living in England, brooding on the recet suicide of her daughter. Set against the harsh backdrop of the devastation wrought on Nagasaki by the dropping of the atomic bomb.

Pale View of Hills. unabr. ed. Kazuo Ishiguro. Read by Roe Kendall. 5 cass. (Running Time: 90 mins. per cass.). 2000. 30.00 (5172) Books on Tape.
Etsuko, a Japanese woman now living in England, dwells on the recent suicide of her daughter. Where past & present confused, she relives scenes of Japan's devastation in the wake of World War II.

Paleo Pals. unabr. ed. Aristoplay, Ltd. Staff. Read by Madeline Kotowicz & Hadley Smith. Narrated by David Zinn. 1 cass. (Running Time: 20 min.). (Play, Listen & Learn Ser.). (J). (gr. 4). 1993. pap. bk. 15.00 incl. cards. (978-1-57057-010-0(8), 4010) Talicor.
Recording of narrator "Paleo Pete" reading the text from the Paleo Pals booklet that comes with the set. Information is given on 16 prehistoric creatures. Activity book contains the text & dot to dot puzzles for readers. A deck of dinosaur playing cards completes the set.

Paleontologist. 1 cass. (J). (gr. k-4). 1997. 9.95 Learn Horizon.
Introduction to dinosaurs & other prehistoric animals, fossils & the work of a paleontologist, through songs & hands-on activities.

Paleontologist. 1 cass. (Science Ser.). (J). bk. Incl. 24p. bk. (TWIN 421) NewSound.

Palermo Ambush. unabr. ed. Colin Forbes. Read by Sean Barrett. 7 cass. (Running Time: 8 hrs. 10 min.). 2001. 61.95 (978-1-85089-854-2(5), 91062) Pub: ISIS Audio GBR. Dist(s): Ulverscroft US
A large German Army defends Sicily & reinforcements can only be brought in by a ferry from Italy. Major Petrie & fellow saboteur Ed Johnson are on a secret mission - to sink the ferry.

Palestine & the Founding of Israel: An Oral History. 1 cass. (Running Time: 25 min.). 10.95 (H0220B090, HarperThor) HarpC GBR.

Palestine Peace Not Apartheid. abr. unabr. ed. Jimmy Carter. Read by Jimmy Carter. 2006. 17.95 (978-0-7435-6348-2(4), Audioworks) Pub: S&S Audio. Dist(s): S and S Inc

Palestine, Zionism, & the Arab-Israeli Conflict, Vol. 2. Instructed by James Gelvin. 6 cass. (Running Time: 6 hrs.). 2002. 129.95 (978-1-56585-252-5(4)) Teaching Co.

Palestine, Zionism, & the Arab-Israeli Conflict: Parts I-II. Instructed by James Gelvin. 12 cass. (Running Time: 12 hrs.). 2002. 129.95 (978-1-56585-251-8(6)) Teaching Co.

Palgrave's Golden Treasury of English Poetry. abr. ed. Poems. Perf. by Claire Bloom et al. 2 cass. (Running Time: 3 hrs.). Incl. Allegro. John Milton. (SWC 2011); Constant Lover. John Suckling. (SWC 2011); Cupid & Campaspe. John Lyly. (SWC 2011); Farewell! Thou Art Too Dear for My Possessing: Sonnet 87. William Shakespeare. (SWC 2011); Fear No More the Heat o' the Sun: From "Cymbeline" William Shakespeare. (SWC 2011); Gather Ye Rose-Buds While Ye May. Robert Herrick. (SWC 2011); Go & Catch a Falling Star. John Donne. (SWC 2011); Go, Lovely Rose. Edmund Waller. (SWC 2011); Good-Morrow. John Donne. (SWC 2011); How Like a Winter Hath My Absence Been: Sonnet 97. William Shakespeare. (SWC 2011); It Was a Lover & His Lass: From "As You Like It" William Shakespeare. (SWC 2011); Mine Be a Cot Beside the Hill. Samuel Rogers. (SWC 2011); Nightingale. Richard Barnefield. (SWC 2011); O Mistress Mine: From "Twelfth Night" William Shakespeare. (SWC 2011); On a Favorite Cat, Drowned in a Tub of Goldfishes. Thomas Gray. (SWC 2011); On His Blindness. John Milton. (SWC 2011); Passionate Shepherd. Christopher Marlowe. (SWC 2011); Penseroso. John Milton. (SWC 2011); Shall I Compare Thee to a Summer's Day: Sonnet 18. William Shakespeare. (SWC 2011); Song for St. Cecilia's Day. John Dryden. (SWC 2011); That Time of Year Thou May'st in Me Behold: Sonnet 73. William Shakespeare. (SWC 2011); They Flee from Me. Thomas Wyatt. (SWC 2011); Tired with All These, for Restful Death I Cry: Sonnet 66. William Shakespeare. (SWC

2011); To Althea from Prison. Richard Lovelace. (SWC 2011); To Lucasta, Going Beyond the Seas. Richard Lovelace. (SWC 2011); When Icicles Hang by the Wall: From "Love's Labor's Lost" William Shakespeare. (SWC 2011); When in Disgrace with Fortune & Men's Eyes: Sonnet 29. William Shakespeare. (SWC 2011); When in the Chronicle of Wasted Time: Sonnet 106. William Shakespeare. (SWC 2011); When to the Sessions of Sweet Silent Thought: Sonnet 30. William Shakespeare. (SWC 2011); 1971. 22.00 (978-0-694-50374-2(6), SWC 2011) HarperCollins Pubs.

Pali. 2002. audio compact disk 10.75 (978-0-89610-486-0(9)) Island Heritage.

***Palimon-Audio: El limonero que cambio la economia de una Nacion.** Juan G. Ruelas. (SPA.). 2010. 14.00 (978-0-9825883-8-3(0)) Editorial Equipov.

***Palimpsest.** unabr. ed. Catherynne Valente. Read by Aasne Vigesaa. 1 MP3-CD. (Running Time: 11 hrs.). 2010. 24.99 (978-1-4418-7018-6(0), 9781441870186, Brilliance MP3); 24.99 (978-1-4418-7020-9(2), 9781441870209, BAD); 39.97 (978-1-4418-7019-3(9), 9781441870193, Brlnc Audio MP3 Lib); 39.97 (978-1-4418-7021-6(0), 9781441870216, BADLE); audio compact disk 29.99 (978-1-4418-7016-2(4), 9781441870162, Bril Audio CD Unabri); audio compact disk 99.97 (978-1-4418-7017-9(2), 9781441870179, BriAudCD Unabrid) Brilliance Audio.

Palindrome. abr. ed. Stuart Woods. Read by Gabrielle De Cuir. 4 cass. (Running Time: 6 hrs.). 2002. 25.00 (978-1-59040-226-9(X)) Audio Lit.
For years, Liz Barwick has been battered by her brutal husband, a famous pro football player. This time it takes an emergency room to keep her from death. Now, the beautiful and talented photographer retreats to an island paradise off Georgia's coast to find solitude - and herself. As she becomes increasingly involved with the strange and handsome twin scions of the powerful Drummond family, she feels her traumatic memories begin to fade. But when a killer launches a series of gruesome murders, Liz discovers that there is no place to hide - not even in her lover's arms.

Palindrome. unabr. ed. Stuart Woods. Read by Susan Ericksen. 6 cass. (Running Time: 8 hrs.). 2001. 29.95 (978-1-58788-146-6(2), 1587881462, BAU); 69.25 (978-1-58788-147-3(0), 1587881470) Brilliance Audio.

Palindrome. unabr. ed. Stuart Woods. Read by Susan Ericksen. (Running Time: 8 hrs.). 2005. 39.25 (978-1-59600-574-7(2), 9781596005747, BADLE); 24.95 (978-1-59600-573-0(4), 9781596005730, BAD); 39.25 (978-1-59600-572-3(6), 9781596005723, Brlnc Audio MP3 Lib); 24.95 (978-1-59600-571-6(8), 9781596005716, Brilliance MP3) Brilliance Audio.

Palindrome. unabr. ed. Stuart Woods. Read by Susan Ericksen. (Running Time: 28800 sec.). 2007. audio compact disk 92.25 (978-1-4233-3376-0(4), 9781423333760, BriAudCD Unabrid); audio compact disk 34.95 (978-1-4233-3375-3(6), 9781423333753, Bril Audio CD Unabri) Brilliance Audio.

Pallbearers. abr. ed. Stephen J. Cannell. Read by Scott Brick. 4 CDs. (Running Time: 5 hrs.). (Shane Scully Ser.: No. 9). 2010. audio compact disk 24.99 (978-1-4233-7448-0(7), 9781423374480, BACD) Brilliance Audio.

Pallbearers. abr. ed. Stephen J. Cannell. Read by Scott Brick. (Running Time: 5 hrs.). (Shane Scully Ser.: No. 9). 2010. audio compact disk 14.99 (978-1-4233-7449-7(5), 9781423374497, BCD Value Price) Brilliance Audio.

Pallbearers. unabr. ed. Stephen J. Cannell. Read by Scott Brick. 1 MP3-CD. (Running Time: 9 hrs.). (Shane Scully Ser.: No. 9). 2010. 39.97 (978-1-4233-7436-7(3), 9781423374367, Brlnc Audio MP3 Lib); 24.99 (978-1-4233-7435-0(5), 9781423374350, Brilliance MP3); 39.97 (978-1-4233-7438-1(X), 9781423374381, BADLE); 24.99 (978-1-4233-7437-4(1), 9781423374374, BAD); audio compact disk 87.97 (978-1-4233-7434-3(7), 9781423374343, BriAudCD Unabrid); audio compact disk 34.99 (978-1-4233-7433-6(9), 9781423374336, Bril Audio CD Unabri) Brilliance Audio.

Pallister-Hall Syndrome - A Bibliography & Dictionary for Physicians, Patients, & Genome Researchers. Compiled by Icon Group International, Inc. Staff. 2007. ring bd. 28.95 (978-0-497-11268-4(X)) Icon Grp.

Palm Desert: A Book by Rudy Vanderlans Based on Music & Lyrics by Van Dyke Parks. Rudy VanderLans et al. 2004. bk. 35.00 (978-0-9669409-0-9(3)) Pub: Emig. Dist(s): Gingko Press

Palm for Mrs. Pollifax. unabr. ed. Dorothy Gilman. Narrated by Barbara Rosenblat. 5 cass. (Running Time: 7 hrs. 15 mins.). (Mrs. Pollifax Mystery Ser.: Vol. 4). 1991. 44.00 (978-1-55690-401-1(0), 91403E7) Recorded Bks.
Mrs. Pollifax goes to Switzerland to investigate a plutonium hijack.

Palm Reading: On the Other Hand. Dean A. Montalbano. 6 cass. (Running Time: 5hrs 45 min). (C). 2003. 89.95 (978-1-932086-11-9(0)) L Lizards Pub Co.
An instructional Audio set designed to teach you how to read and anylize palms.

Palm Reading on CD. 2005. audio compact disk (978-1-932086-27-0(7)) L Lizards Pub Co.

Palm Record Shell Series. 2001. audio compact disk 18.99 (978-0-89610-940-7(2)) Island Heritage.

Palm Records Island Collection. 2001. audio compact disk 16.99 (978-0-89610-943-8(7)) Island Heritage.

Palm Records Island Collection Series. 2001. audio compact disk 18.99 (978-0-89610-942-1(9)) Island Heritage.

Palm Records Shell Series. 2001. audio compact disk 16.99 (978-0-89610-941-4(0)) Island Heritage.

Palmetto Symbol of Courage. Kate Sall Palmer. 2005. audio compact disk 10.95 (978-0-9667114-4-8(0)) Warbranch Pr Inc.

Paloma y sus Bromas: Audiocassette. (SPA.). (gr. k-1). 10.00 (978-0-7635-6263-2(7)) Rigby Educ.

Pals: Eddie Cantor & Georgie Jessel. Perf. by George Jessel. 1 CD. (Running Time: 73 min.). 1999. audio compact disk 15.98 (4206) Radio Spirits.

PALS Prep. 5 cass. (Running Time: 8 hrs.). 1990. 79.00 cass. & soft-bound bk. (HT107) Ctr Hlth Educ.
Are you preparing for your Pediatric Advanced Life Support (PALS) exam? Get the lastest information from the experts! Leading pediatricians & PNPs share their knowledge in pediatric critical care. Pediatric advanced life support (PALS) is essential for any nurse faced with a child in respiratory or cardiac arrest. Now you can prepare for any pediatric emergency quickly and effectively.

Pam Adams Party. Contrib. by Andrew Belling. 1 cass. (Running Time: 020 min.). (J). (ps-3). 1999. 4.99 (978-0-85953-385-0(9)) Childs Play GBR.

Pam Ayres - Poetry & Prose Collection. abr. ed. Pam Ayres. Read by Pam Ayres. 2 cass. 1999. 16.85 Set. (978-0-563-55877-4(6)) BBC WrldWd GBR.

Pam Houston. unabr. ed. Pam Houston. 1 cass. (Running Time: 29 min.). (New Letters on the Air Ser.). 1992. 10.00 (050192) New Letters.
Houston draws on her extensive experience as an outdoorswoman in her first collection of short stories, "Cowboys Are My Weakness.".

Pamdemonium. abr. ed. Pamela A. Lee & Todd Gold. Read by Pamela A. Lee. 1 cass. (Running Time: 1 hr. 30 min.). 1997. 12.98 (978-1-57042-541-7(8)) Hachet Audio.

Pamela. Samuel Richardson. Read by Anais 9000. 2008. 33.95 (978-1-60112-161-5(X)) Babblebooks.

Pamela: Or, Virtue Rewarded, Vol. 1. unabr. ed. Samuel Richardson. Narrated by Flo Gibson. 14 cass. (Running Time: 21 hrs.). 2003. 89.95 () Audio Bk Con.
This famous epistolary novel, one of the first in the English language, caused a sensation when it was published in 1740. It tells of Mr. B.'s frequent attempts to seduce his lovely maidservant. They eventually marry & their life together is described in detail.

Pamela: Or, Virtue Rewarded, Vol. 2. unabr. ed. Samuel Richardson. Narrated by Flo Gibson. 14 cass. (Running Time: 21 hrs.). 2003. 89.95 () Audio Bk Con.

Pamela (Part 2), Vol. 2. unabr. ed. Samuel Richardson. Narrated by Flo Gibson. (Running Time: 20 hrs. 51 mins.). 2001. 42.95 (978-1-55685-834-5(5)) Audio Bk Con.

Pamela (Parts 1 And 2) unabr. ed. Samuel Richardson. Narrated by Flo Gibson. (Running Time: 41 hrs. 48 mins.). 2001. 68.95 (978-1-55685-835-2(3)) Audio Bk Con.

Pamelas Prayer. 2004. DVD & audio compact disk 9.99 (978-0-01-222979-8(2)) D Christiano Films.

Pamphlet Authors. 3 cass. Incl. Pamphlet Authors: On Spiritual Growth. George Peck. 1978.; Pamphlet Authors: Southeast Asia: A Forty Year Retrospect. Thomas Silcock. 1978.; Pamphlet Authors: The Roots of My Mind. Carol Murphy. 1978.; 1978. 12.00 Set.; 4.50 ea. Pendle Hill.

Pamphlet Authors: On Spiritual Growth see Pamphlet Authors

Pamphlet Authors: Southeast Asia: A Forty Year Retrospect see Pamphlet Authors

Pamphlet Authors: The Roots of My Mind see Pamphlet Authors

Pam's Story: Program from the Award Winning Public Radio Series. Interview. Hosted by Fred Goodwin. 1 CD. (Running Time: 1 hr). 2000. audio compact disk 21.95 (978-1-932479-76-8(7), LCM 137) Lichtenstein Creat.
Modern technology has dramatically increased the chances that a pregnancy will result in a live baby, but the fact is, not all endings are happy ones. Babies still die in utero, and often there is no reason ever found for the loss. Worse yet, no one ever talks about it. In this dramatic one-hour special report, an award-winning public radio producer follows her sister through a second pregnancy as she worries: Will it happen again?.

Pan de Vida. Mariano de Blas.Tr. of bread of Life. (SPA.). 2009. audio compact disk 20.00 (978-1-935405-14-6(4)) Hombre Nuevo.

***Pan de Vida.** Padre Mariano de Blas. (SPA.). (YA). 2005. audio compact disk 19.99 (978-0-9825744-1-6(X)) Hombre Nuevo.

Pan Flutes by the Ocean. 1 cass. (Running Time: 65 min.). 1994. audio compact disk 15.95 CD. (2618, Creativ Pub) Quayside.
Originally composed by Ken Davis, a subtle blend of gentle ocean sounds with strings, pan flutes, & synthesized piano.

Pan Flutes by the Ocean. 1 cass. (Running Time: 65 min.). 1994. 9.95 (2617, NrthWrd Bks) TandN Child.

Panache Litteraire. 3rd ed. Mary J. Baker & Jean-Pierre Cauvin. (FRE & ENG.). (C). 1994. stu. ed. 64.95 (978-0-8384-5512-8(3)) Pub: Heinle. Dist(s): CENGAGE Learn

Panama. unabr. ed. Eric Zencey. Narrated by John McDonough. 11 cass. (Running Time: 15 hrs. 45 mins.). 1995. 91.00 (978-0-7887-0454-3(0), 94646E7) Recorded Bks.
For five days in 1892, the shy American historian Henry Adams follows the trail of an enigmatic woman through Paris. Soon his investigation uncovers deadly political corruption.

Panama Fever: The Epic Story of One of the Greatest Human Achievements of All Time - the Building of the Panama Canal. unabr. ed. Matthew Parker. Narrated by William Dufris. (Running Time: 63900 sec.). (ENG.). 2008. audio compact disk 39.95 (978-1-60283-356-2(7)) Pub: AudioGO. Dist(s): Perseus Dist

Panama Hattie. Contrib. by Cole Porter. 1 CD. (Running Time: 1 hr.). 2005. audio compact disk 15.95 (978-0-660-19033-4(8)) Pub: Canadian Broadcasting CAN. Dist(s): Georgetown Term
Hattie Malone is a brassy nightclub singer in Panama. She tries to adapt to the upper-class world of her fiance, Nick Bullett, who is an officer in the armed forces. He is the divorced father of an 8-year-old girl. Hattie asks that he send for the girl before the wedding. She spends most of the first act trying to gain the child's approval of her as a future stepmother. In the 2nd act, she wins over Nick's boss, Whitney, by uncovering a plan to blow up the canal.

Pancakes. Lois Young. Perf. by Lois Young. 1 cass. (Running Time: 30 min.). (J). 1992. 8.98 (978-1-56406-551-3(0)); 8.98 Incl. sleeve pack. (978-1-56406-580-3(4)); audio compact disk 13.98 CD. (978-1-56406-567-4(7)) Sony Music Ent.

Pancho. 2004. 8.95 (978-1-56008-997-1(0)); cass. & flmstrp 30.00 (978-1-56008-741-0(2)) Weston Woods.

Pancho Claus con Jose-Luis Orozco. Tr. of Christmas with Jose-Luis Orozco. (SPA.). (J). (gr. k-3). 12.00 (978-1-57417-018-4(X)) Pub: Arcoiris Recs. Dist(s): Lectorum Pubns

Pancho Claus con Jose-Luis Orozco. abr. ed. 1 CD. (Running Time: 1 hr. 30 mins.).Tr. of Christmas with Jose-Luis Orozco. (SPA.). (J). (gr. k-3). audio compact disk 14.00 (978-1-57417-007-8(4)) Pub: Arcoiris Recs. Dist(s): Lectorum Pubns

Pancreatic & Biliary Tract Surgery. Moderated by Frank G. Moody. (Postgraduate Courses Ser.). 1986. 65.00 (8603) Am Coll Surgeons.
Presents a review of the diagnosis & surgical management of hepatobiliary & pancreatic disease. 9 hour CME credit.

Panda Meets Ms. Daisy Bloom. Timothy Glass. Narrated by Allen Hite. (ENG.). (J). 2008. audio compact disk 14.95 (978-1-60031-030-0(3)) Spoken Books.

Panda's Thumb: More Reflections in Natural History. unabr. collector's ed. Stephen Jay Gould. Read by Larry McKeever. 8 cass. (Running Time: 12 hrs.). 1987. 64.00 (978-0-7366-1224-1(6), 2142) Books on Tape.
The author of "Ever Since Darwin" continues his investigation into natural selection & the evolution of animals & humans.

Pandit Jasraj (Vocal), Vol. 1. Music by Pandit Jasraj. 1 cass. (Music Today Presents Ser.). 1992. (A92032) Multi-Cultural Bks.

Pandit Jasraj (Vocal), Vol. 2. Music by Pandit Jasraj. 1 cass. (Music Today Presents Ser.). 1992. (A92033) Multi-Cultural Bks.

Pandora. unabr. ed. Anne Rice. Read by Kate Reading. 7 cass. (Running Time: 10 hrs. 30 min.). (New Tales of the Vampires Ser.: Bk. 1). 1998. 56.00 (978-0-7366-4099-2(1), 4604) Books on Tape.
The fledgling vampire David Talbot, who has set out to become the chronicler of his immortal brethren. We are in Paris; the time is now. In a crowded cafe, David meets Pandora - two thousand years old, a child of the Millennia, the first vampire ever made by the great Marius. David persuades her to write the story of her eventful life. It's an epic tale that begins in her mortal girlhood in the peaceful Rome of Caesar Augustus.

Pandora's Box: The Mystery of Memory. Manly P. Hall. 8.95 (978-0-89314-205-6(0), C880417) Philos Res.
Deals with psychology & self-help.

Pandora's Clock. abr. ed. John J. Nance. Read by John J. Nance. 4 cass. Library ed. (Running Time: 6 hrs.). 2003. 62.25 (978-1-59086-667-2(3), 1590866673, CD Lib Edit) Brilliance Audio.
Captain James Holland is the pilot on a routine flight from Frankfurt to New York, packed with people eager to be home for Christmas. When a passenger collapses from what appears to be a heart attack, Holland is forced to request an emergency landing at London's Heathrow Airport. But to his great surprise, the air traffic controllers will not let him land in England - they tell Holland that his sick passenger has contracted a dangerous new form of influenza and that the plane must return to Germany. But when German officials also refuse the landing, and other European countries follow suit, Holland begins to suspect that he's in much more trouble than anyone's letting on. In fact, his sick passenger is carrying a deadly virus accidentally released from a Bavarian laboratory, and it is feared that everyone on board is now infected. At the same time, someone with access to the CIA's computers wants to shoot the plane out of the sky, and there is a United States ambassador on board with powerful terrorist enemies who want to see him dead. While the panic on the ground spreads from the White House Situation Room to a small airport in the Ukrainian Republic, Captain Holland has only one concern: Where and when can he land?.

Pandora's Clock. abr. ed. John J. Nance. Read by John J. Nance. (Running Time: 6 hrs.). 2006. 39.25 (978-1-4233-0164-6(1), 9781423301646, BADLE); 39.25 (978-1-4233-0162-2(5), 9781423301622, Brlnc Audio MP3 Lib); audio compact disk 24.95 (978-1-4233-0161-5(7), 9781423301615, Brilliance MP3) Brilliance Audio.

Pandora's Clock. abr. ed. John J. Nance. Read by John J. Nance. (Running Time: 6 hrs.). 2006. 24.95 (978-1-4233-0163-9(3), 9781423301639, BAD) Brilliance Audio.

Pandora's Curse. Jack Du Brul. Read by J. Charles. (Playaway Adult Fiction Ser.). (ENG.). 2009. 69.99 (978-1-60775-871-6(7)) Find a World.

Pandora's Curse. unabr. ed. Jack Du Brul. Read by J. Charles. 10 cass. (Running Time: 14 hrs.). 2001. 34.95 (978-1-58788-711-6(8), 1587887118, BAU); 96.25 (978-1-58788-712-3(6), 1587887126, CD Unabrid Lib Ed) Brilliance Audio.
In northern Greenland, geologist Phillip Mercer finds a dead body hot with radiation in a 1950s U.S. Army base under the ice. Mercer is almost killed when the old base is set on fire. Geo-Research, the German team studying global warming, hustles Mercer and company out of Greenland, and Mercer vows to find out why. Surviving a bomb on the plane taking them back to Iceland, Mercer, the beautiful Anika Klein, and their fellow explorers search for the shelter of an ice cavern until they can be rescued - and that's when they learn the truth. Geo-Research is a front for Kohl AG, a German company which profited from its wartime use of slave labor. Rather than pay into the compensation fund, Kohl is trying to destroy its biggest secret - the hidden Nazi submarine base that harbored the remains of the radioactive meteorite that exploded over Tunguska, Siberia, in 1908. The Nazis contained the radiation in boxes made of looted wartime gold nicknamed "Pandora boxes." But Kohl AG's special projects director is a neo-Nazi and plans to sell the Pandora boxes to the highest bidding terrorist nation. Only Mercer and a WWII-era U-boat can stop the evil plot to hold the world hostage.

Pandora's Curse. unabr. ed. Jack Du Brul. Read by J. Charles. (Running Time: 14 hrs.). 2004. 39.25 (978-1-59710-559-0(7), 1597105597, BADLE); 24.95 (978-1-59710-558-3(9), 1597105589, BAD) Brilliance Audio.

Pandora's Curse. unabr. ed. Jack Du Brul. Read by J. Charles. (Running Time: 14 hrs.). 2004. 24.95 (978-1-59335-144-1(5), 1593351445) Soulmate Audio Bks.

Pandora's Curse. unabr. ed. Jack Du Brul. Read by J. Charles. (Running Time: 50400 sec.). 2004. audio compact disk 39.25 (978-1-59335-582-1(3), 1593355823, Brlnc Audio MP3 Lib) Brilliance Audio.

Pandora's Daughter. abr. ed. Iris Johansen. Read by Jennifer Van Dyck. (Running Time: 21600 sec.). 2008. audio compact disk 14.99 (978-1-4233-2904-6(X), 9781423329046, BCD Value Price) Brilliance Audio.

Pandora's Daughter. unabr. ed. Iris Johansen. Read by Jennifer Van Dyck. (Running Time: 11 hrs.). 2007. 39.25 (978-1-4233-2902-2(3), 9781423329022, BADLE); 24.95 (978-1-4233-2901-5(5), 9781423329015, BAD); 92.25 (978-1-4233-2896-4(5), 9781423328964, BrilAudUnabridg); audio compact disk 24.95 (978-1-4233-2899-5(X), 9781423328995, Brilliance MP3); audio compact disk 38.95 (978-1-4233-2897-1(3), 9781423328971, Bril Audio CD Unabri); audio compact disk 39.25 (978-1-4233-2900-8(7), 9781423329008, Brlnc Audio MP3 Lib); audio compact disk 97.25 (978-1-4233-2898-8(1), 9781423328988, BriAudCD Unabrid) Brilliance Audio.

Pandora's Daughter. unabr. ed. Iris Johansen. Read by Jennifer Van Dyck. (YA). 2008. 79.99 (978-1-60514-819-9(9)) Find a World.

Pandora's Legion: Harold Coyle's Strategic Solutions, Inc. unabr. ed. Harold Coyle & Barrett Tillman. Read by William Dufris. (YA). 2008. 59.99 (978-1-60514-739-0(7)) Find a World.

Pandora's Legion: Harold Coyle's Strategic Solutions, Inc. unabr. ed. Harold Coyle & Barrett Tillman. Read by William Dufris. (Running Time: 11 hrs. 0 mins. 0 sec.). (Harold Coyle's Strategic Solutions, Inc. Ser.). (ENG.). 2007. audio compact disk 37.99 (978-1-4001-0407-9(6)); audio compact disk 75.99 (978-1-4001-3407-6(2)); audio compact disk 24.99 (978-1-4001-5407-4(3)) Pub: Tantor Media. Dist(s): IngramPubServ

***Pandora's Seed: The Unforeseen Cost of Civilization.** unabr. ed. Spencer Wells. (Running Time: 6 hrs. 30 mins. 0 sec.). (ENG.). 2010. 24.99 (978-1-4001-6626-8(8)); 16.99 (978-1-4001-8626-6(9)); 34.99 (978-1-4001-9626-5(4)); audio compact disk 34.99 (978-1-4001-1626-3(0)); audio compact disk 69.99 (978-1-4001-4626-0(7)) Pub: Tantor Media. Dist(s): IngramPubServ

Pandora's Star. unabr. ed. Peter F. Hamilton. Read by John Lee. Narrated by John Lee. (Running Time: 36 hrs. 30 mins. 0 sec.). (ENG.). 2008. audio compact disk 79.99 (978-1-4001-0764-3(4)); audio compact disk 159.99 (978-1-4001-3764-0(0)); audio compact disk 49.99 (978-1-4001-5764-8(1)) Pub: Tantor Media. Dist(s): IngramPubServ

Panel Discussion, Pt. 1. Read by Thomas Neuberger et al. (120) ISI Books.

Panel Discussion Sponsored by the Committee on Young Surgeons: Surgeons Living under DRGs. 2 cass. (General Sessions Ser.: C85-SP5). 15.00 (8547) Am Coll Surgeons.

Panel: Samuel E. Konkin III, Jeff Hummel & Carol Moore: How To Protect A Free, Non-Government Community from Governments. (Running Time: 90 min.). (Freeland Ser.). 1983. 10.00 (FL5) Freeland Pr.
Konkin begins with the comment: "Anarcho-Zionism, the search for the promised gulch..." to let the audience be aware of his position & then enlarges on his ideas on agorist capitalism; Moore's solutions encompass "immense community awareness & participation in defense", which she later illustrates; Hummel's approach is to involve the community as well. He

cites such communities as Hong Kong that have sound economies & discusses the reasons why.

Panel: Victor Koman & Samuel Konkin III: Libertarian Societies in Modern Fiction. (Running Time: 60 min.). (Freeland III Ser.). 1985. 9.00 (FL13) Freeland Pr.
L. Neal Smith, Robert Heinlein, Robert Anton Wilson, & other authors are reviewed in depth by the panelists.

Pangolin. unabr. collector's ed. Peter Driscoll. Read by Rupert Keenlyside. 8 cass. (Running Time: 12 hrs.). 1983. 64.00 (978-0-7366-0517-5(7), 1491) Books on Tape.
Alan Pritchard has been a loser all his life. The opportunity to kidnap Rod Kiley, Southeast Asia's Chief CIA operative, provides his last opportunity to be some sort of success.

Panic! The Story of Modern Financial Insanity. abr. ed. Michael Lewis. Afterword by Michael Lewis. Read by Jesse Boggs & Blair Hardman. (Running Time: 7 hrs. 0 mins. 0 sec.). (ENG.). 2008. audio compact disk 29.99 (978-0-7435-8366-4(3)) Pub: S&S Audio. Dist(s): S and S Inc

Panic Attacks. Christine Ingham. 1 cass. (Running Time: 1 hr.). 2001. (978-0-00-710901-2(6), HarperThor) HarpC GBR.

Panic, Don't Panic. George Bloomer. 2. audio compact disk Whitaker Hse.

Panic in Level 4: Cannibals, Killer Viruses, & Other Journeys to the Edge of Science. unabr. ed. Richard Preston. Read by James Lurie & James James. 7 CDs. (Running Time: 8 hrs.). (ENG.). 2008. audio compact disk 34.95 (978-0-7393-2889-7(1), Random AudioBks) Pub: Random Audio Pubg. Dist(s): Random

Panic in the Stock Market: The Work on Money & Wealth. 2005. audio compact disk 15.00 (978-1-890246-29-7(8)) B Katie Int Inc.

***Panic Virus: A True Story of Medicine, Science, & Fear.** unabr. ed. Seth Mnookin. (Running Time: 10 hrs. 30 mins. 0 sec.). 2011. 24.99 (978-1-4526-5041-8(1)); 16.99 (978-1-4526-7041-6(2)); audio compact disk 34.99 (978-1-4526-0041-3(4)) Pub: Tantor Media. Dist(s): IngramPubServ

***Panic Virus (Library Edition) A True Story of Medicine, Science, & Fear.** unabr. ed. Seth Mnookin. (Running Time: 10 hrs. 30 mins.). 2011. 34.99 (978-1-4526-2041-1(5)); audio compact disk 83.99 (978-1-4526-3041-0(0)) Pub: Tantor Media. Dist(s): IngramPubServ

Panis Angelicus. Perf. by Robert Kochis & Robin Kochis. 1 cass. (Running Time: 39 mins.). 1999. 9.95 (T9185); audio compact disk 14.95 (K6920) Liguori Pubns.
Includes: "Adoro Te Devote," "Beautiful Savior," "O Lord I Am Not Worthy" & more.

Panning for Murder. unabr. ed. Jessica Fletcher & Donald Bain. Read by Cynthia Darlow. (Murder, She Wrote Ser.). (YA). 2008. 59.99 (978-1-60514-599-0(8)) Find a World.

Panorama de la Inserción Internacional de América Latina y el Caribe 2006: 2007 Trends. United Nations. (SPA.). 2008. pap. bk. 25.00 (978-92-1-323080-0(X)) Untd Nat Pubns.

Panther! unabr. ed. Roger A. Caras. Narrated by John Randolph Jones. 4 cass. (Running Time: 5 hrs. 30 mins.). 1994. 35.00 (978-0-7887-0004-0(9), 94143E7) Recorded Bks.
Roger Caras, renowned naturalist & president of the ASPCA, conveys his respect for "the great trimmer, the unrelenting reaper, the great cat of the Florida southern swamp." His talent for making the great panther come to life & detailing one man's quest to conquer the indomitable hunter, evokes powerful images of the brutal beauty of nature's relentless cycles. The listener will hear the diamondback's deadly rattle, feel the fury as the winds of hurricane Dora batter the cat's prison & in the end come away with a painful awareness of just how tragic the loss of this species would be.

Panther in the Basement. unabr. ed. Amos Oz. Tr. by Nicholas De Lange. Narrated by George Guidall. 3 cass. (Running Time: 4 hrs. 30 mins.). 2000. 26.00 (978-0-7887-1878-6(9), 95300E7) Recorded Bks.
Twelve-year-old Proffi dreams of being an underground fighter, until he is accused of treason.

Panther's Feast. unabr. ed. Robert B. Asprey. Read by John MacDonald. 7 cass. (Running Time: 10 hrs. 30 min.). 1989. 56.00 (978-0-7366-1531-0(8), 2401) Books on Tape.
On the eve of WWI, Alfred Redl was Deputy Chief of Intelligence in the Austro-Hungarian Imperial Army. He was also a spy in Russian pay, the victim of sexual blackmail. He rose from poverty to power, committed treason & finally died by his own hand.

Pantops. Ed. by Robert A. Monroe. 1 cass. (Running Time: 30 min.). (Meta Music Ser.). 1986. 12.95 (978-1-56102-220-5(9)) Inter Indus.
For those who like supportive musical form in a daydream of gentle soaring. A random drifting over snow-capped mountain peaks, up among the slow-boiling white cumulus cloud towers & then back again.

Pantothenate Kinase-Associated Neurodegeneration - A Bibliography & Dictionary for Physicians, Patients, & Genome Researchers. Compiled by Icon Group International, Inc. Staff. 2007. ring bd. 28.95 (978-0-497-11269-1(8)) Icon Grp.

Pants on Fire. unabr. ed. Maggie Alderson. Read by Katrina Baylis. 9 CDs. (Running Time: 10 hrs.). 2004. audio compact disk 93.95 (978-1-74030-953-0(7)) Pub: Bolinda Pubng AUS. Dist(s): Bolinda Pub Inc

Pants on Fire. unabr. ed. Meg Cabot. Read by Krista Sutton. 5 CDs. (Running Time: 6 hrs. 9 mins.). (YA). (gr. 9 up). 2007. audio compact disk 45.00 (978-0-7393-5085-0(4)) Pub: Random Audio Pubg. Dist(s): Random

Pants on Fire. unabr. ed. Meg Cabot. Read by Krista Sutton. (Running Time: 22140 sec.). (ENG.). (J). (gr. 8). 2007. audio compact disk 30.00 (978-0-7393-5050-8(1), Listening Lib) Pub: Random Audio Pubg. Dist(s): Random

Pants on Fire: 7 Cassettes (unabridged) unabr. ed. Maggie Alderson. Read by Katrina Baylis. 7 cass. (Running Time: 10 hrs.). 2004. 56.00 (978-1-74030-620-1(1)) Pub: Bolinda Pubng AUS. Dist(s): Bolinda Pub Inc

Panzer Soldier. abr. ed. Barry Sadler. Read by Bruce Watson. 2 vols. (Casca Ser.: No. 4). 2002. (978-1-58807-515-4(X)) Am Pubng Inc.

Panzer Soldier. abr. ed. Barry Sadler. Read by Bruce Watson. 2 vols. (Casca Ser.: No. 4). 2003. audio compact disk 25.00 (978-1-58807-278-8(9)); audio compact disk (978-1-58807-709-7(8)) Am Pubng Inc.

Panzer Soldier. abr. rev. ed. Barry Sadler. Read by Bruce Watson. 2 cass. (Running Time: 3 hrs.). (Casca Ser.: No. 4). 2004. audio compact disk 18.00 (978-1-58807-354-9(8)) Am Pubng Inc.
A Panzer soldier for the brutal Third Reich, Casca becomes entrenched in Hitler's Nazi war machine and is forced to pit his credit as a soldier against his moral judgment of humanity. Sporting the honorable Knight's Cross and a silver tanker's badge, Casca leads a tank against the hammering forces of Ivan, the throttlehold of Russia's military. Comradery, survival instinct, and highly developed German tanks keep Casca and his crew forging ahead, but when the reality of Hitler's sinister manifesto is revealed to them, they begin to question their role in the destruction of humankind.

Pap Smears - The Challenge of False Negatives & ASCUS. Contrib. by Charles J. Dunton et al. 1 cass. (American College of Obstetrics & Gynecologists UPDATE: Vol. 24, No. 1). 1998. 20.00 Am Coll Obstetric.

Papa Goriot. abr. ed. Honoré de Balzac. Read by Guillermo Piedrahita. 3 CDs. (SPA.). 2002. audio compact disk 17.00 (978-958-9494-76-9(5)) YoYoMusic.

Papa, Molly & the Great Prairie. Barbara Sobel. (J). (gr. 3-6). 1987. pap. bk. 2.95 (978-0-87386-044-4(6)) Jan Prods.

Papa Prayer. abr. ed. Larry Crabb. 2005. 19.99 (978-1-58926-875-3(X), 6875) Pub: Oasis Audio. Dist(s): TNT Media Grp

Papa Prayer. abr. ed. Larry Crabb. Narrated by Rob Lamont. (ENG.). 2006. 15.39 (978-1-60814-335-1(X)); audio compact disk 21.99 (978-1-58926-874-6(1), 6874) Oasis Audio.

Papa salvo la Fiesta: Audiocassette. (Saludos Ser.: Vol. 3). (SPA.). (gr. 2-3). 10.00 (978-0-7635-5880-2(X)) Rigby Educ.

Papacy: A Question of Authority. Jeff Cavins. (ENG.). 2007. audio compact disk 9.95 (978-1-934567-05-0(1)) Excorde Inc.

Papal Encyclical on "Faith & Reason" Leonard Peikoff. 1998. 12.95 (LPXXC79) Second Renaissance.

Papal Sin: Structures of Deceit. abr. ed. Garry Wills. Read by Garry Wills. 2 cass. (Running Time: 3 hrs.). 2000. 18.00 (978-1-55935-343-4(0)) Soundelux.
Wills traces the papacy's stubborn resistance to the truth, beginning with the challenges posed in the nineteenth century.

Papalote. Alma Flor Ada. (Cuentos Para Todo el Ano Ser.). (SPA., (J). (gr. k-3). 4.95 (978-1-58105-243-5(X)) Santillana.

***papalote de Pablo / Riley Flies a Kite.** Susan Blackaby. Illus. by Matthew Skeens. (Read-it! Readers en Español). (SPA.). 2008. audio compact disk 9.27 (978-1-4048-4589-3(5)) CapstoneDig.

Papa's Dream. Perf. by Lalo Guerrero & Los Lobos. 1 cass. (Running Time: 60 min.). (J). 1995. 9.98 (978-1-56628-047-1(8), MLP 2089B/WBMLP 2089/WB MLP D2089/WB 42562-2); 9.98 Norelco. (978-1-56628-046-4(X), MLP 2089/WB MLP D2089/WB 42562-2); audio compact disk 15.98 (978-1-56628-045-7(1), MLP D2089/WB 42562-2) MFLP CA.
A magical journey to Mexico with Lalo Guerrero & Los Lobos, story & music.

Papa's Lullaby. 1 CD. (Running Time: 1 hr.). 2001. audio compact disk 16.00 (93-0209) Relaxtn Co.
Celebrate the universal quality of a father's love. Cello, classical guitar, wooden, flutes, thumb piano and more are accompanied by tender voices of fathers from South America, Sicily, Russia and India.

Paper, Set. abr. ed. Dewey Gram. Read by Michael McKean. 2 cass. (Running Time: 3 hrs.). 1994. 16.95 (978-1-56876-024-7(8)) Soundlines Ent.
This life spirited drama follows a day in the life of four employees of "The Sun", a feisty New York newspaper, who are determined to face the task of competitive journalism. What entails is comedy, drama, murder & love, a story of everyday life.

Paper Animals. (Art Rom Create Your Own... Ser.). (J). 2004. pap. bk. 9.99 (978-1-84229-771-1(6)) Top That GBR.

***Paper Butterfly.** unabr. ed. Diane Wei Liang. Narrated by Emily Woo Zeller. 5 CDs. (Running Time: 5 hrs. 26 mins.). 2009. audio compact disk 64.95 (978-0-7927-5410-7(7)) AudioGO.

Paper Dinosaurs. (Art Rom Create Your Own... Ser.). (J). 2004. pap. bk. 9.99 (978-1-84229-770-4(8)) Top That GBR.

Paper Doll. Robert B. Parker. Read by David Dukes. (Spenser Ser.). 2008. 59.99 (978-1-60640-674-8(4)) Find a World.

Paper Doll. unabr. ed. Robert B. Parker. Read by Michael Prichard. 6 cass. (Running Time: 6 hrs.). (Spenser Ser.). 1993. 36.00 (978-0-7366-2636-1(0), 3375) Books on Tape.
Loudon Tripp, a Boston aristocrat, hires Spenser to get the facts about his wife's, Olivia's, death. Spenser distrusts Tripp's version of his perfect family. After all, no wife is a saint & something about the house feels wrong. Spenser dives into a world of grand illusion, peopled by cardboard cutouts. His search takes him to a sleepy Southern town where at last he finds somebody real. It's Olivia herself.

Paper Doll. unabr. ed. Robert B. Parker. Perf. by David Dukes. 4 cass. (Running Time: 6 hrs.). (Spenser Ser.). 2004. 25.00 (978-1-59007-207-3(3)) Pub: New Millenn Enter. Dist(s): PerseuPGW
When Boston aristocrat Loudon Tripp hires Spenser to investigate his wife's murder, Spenser uncovers high-class scandals and a corpse who might not be dead after all.

Paper Doll. unabr. ed. Robert B. Parker. Read by David Dukes. 5 CDs. (Running Time: 6 hrs.). (Spenser Ser.). 2004. audio compact disk 34.95 (978-1-59007-552-4(8)) Pub: New Millenn Enter. Dist(s): PerseuPGW

Paper Fliers. (Art Rom Create Your Own... Ser.). (J). 2004. pap. bk. 9.99 (978-1-84229-772-8(4)) Top That GBR.

Paper, I see Carl Sandburg's Poems for Children

Paper, II see Carl Sandburg's Poems for Children

Paper John. David Small. Illus. by David Small. 11 vols. (Running Time: 10 mins.). 1998. pap. bk. 18.95 (978-1-59519-066-6(X)); pap. bk. 39.95 (978-1-59519-067-3(8)); 9.95 (978-0-87499-453-7(5)); audio compact disk 12.95 (978-1-59519-065-9(1)) Live Oak Media.

Paper John. David Small. Read by David Small. 14 vols. (Running Time: 10 mins.). 1998. pap. bk. & tchr. ed. 37.95 Reading Chest. (978-0-87499-452-0(7)) Live Oak Media.

Paper John. unabr. ed. David Small. Read by David Small. 1 cass. (Running Time: 10 mins.). (J). (gr. k-3). 1998. bk. 24.95 (978-0-87499-451-3(9)); pap. bk. 16.95 (978-0-87499-450-6(0)) Live Oak Media.
A strange, gentle fellow folds paper into all sorts of shapes - flowers, kites, even houses & furniture. By accident, he catches a small grey devil on his fishing line.

***Paper Life: My Story.** abr. ed. Tatum O'neal. Read by Tatum O'neal. (ENG.). 2005. (978-0-06-079803-1(3), Harper Audio); (978-0-06-085296-2(8), Harper Audio) HarperCollins Pubs.

Paper Lion. George Plimpton. 2009. (978-1-60136-229-2(3)) Audio Holding.

Paper Lion. unabr. ed. George Plimpton. Read by Jake Gardiner. 10 cass. (Running Time: 15 hrs.). 1975. 80.00 (978-0-913369-91-3(8), 1001) Books on Tape.
"Paper Lion" recounts the adventures of George Plimpton, professional writer & weekend athlete, who joined the Detroit Lions in their summer training camp. For 4 weeks, while being groomed as quarterback, Plimpton shared all the hazards of training camp. "Paper Lion" is a quasi-insider's look at the world of big-time athletics.

Paper Men. William Golding. Read by Jonathon Oliver. 6 cass. (Running Time: 9 hrs.). 2001. 54.95 (93024) Pub: ISIS Audio GBR. Dist(s): Ulverscroft US

Paper Men. unabr. ed. William Golding. Read by Jonathan Oliver. 6 cass. (Running Time: 7 hrs. 30 min.). (Isis Ser.). 1993. 54.95 set. (978-1-85695-510-2(9), 93024) Eye Ear.
"Wilfred Barclay, curmudgeonly writer of a rich bestseller...pounds towards his end through the stations of contemporary literary success tormented & tempted by three weird sisters, Alcohol, Sex & Immortality...It moves you & at times it can shake you." - Melvyn Bragg.

Paper Money. abr. ed. Ken Follett. Perf. by John Standing. 2 cass. (Running Time: 3 hrs.). 2004. 18.00 (978-1-59007-184-7(0)) Pub: New Millenn Enter. Dist(s): PerseuPGW

Paper Money. unabr. ed. Ken Follett. Read by David Case. 6 cass. (Running Time: 6 hrs.). 36.00 (978-0-7366-1457-3(5), 2338) Books on Tape.
Felix Laski was different things to different people. To the world he was a powerful corporate raider who sent shivers through the stock market with every move he made. To Ellen Hamilton, bored wife of the head of a giant corporation, he was a masterful lover who could make her do whatever he wanted. To Tony Cox, professional criminal, he was a mastermind who could give him the keys to the strongboxes of the Bank of England & to anyone who stood in his way, Laski was sure death.

Paper Money, unabr. ed. Ken Follett. Narrated by Patrick Tull. 5 cass. (Running Time: 6 hrs. 45 mins.). 1988. 44.00 (978-1-55690-402-8(9), 88660E7) Recorded Bks.
Three seemingly unconnected events take place in a single day in London. None of them are worthy of front page treatment according to the City Desk editor, but an enterprising young reporter starts making connections. In a single day, fortunes change hands, political careers are shattered & the reporter finds the story he is uncovering too hot to print.

Paper Moon. Joe David Brown. Read by Laurel Lefkow. 10 vols. (Running Time: 15 hrs.). 2003. 84.95 (978-0-7540-8351-1(9)) Pub: Chivers Audio Bks GBR. Dist(s): AudioGO

***Paper Moon: An Inspector Montalbano Mystery.** unabr. ed. Andrea Camilleri. Read by Grover Gardner. (Running Time: 6 hrs. 0 mins.). 2010. 29.95 (978-1-4417-2189-1(4)); 44.95 (978-1-4417-2185-3(1)); audio compact disk 55.00 (978-1-4417-2186-0(X)) Blckstn Audio.

Paper Moon: Music of Nat "King" Cole. Perf. by George Shearing. 1 cass., 1 CD. 7.98 (TA 33375); audio compact disk 12.78 CD Jewel box. (TA 83375) NewSound.

Paper, Paperboard, & Newsprint in India: A Strategic Reference 2006. Compiled by Icon Group International, Inc. Staff. 2007. ring bd. 195.00 (978-0-497-36018-4(7)) Icon Grp.

Paper, Paperboard, & Newsprint in Indonesia: A Strategic Reference 2007. Compiled by Icon Group International, Inc. Staff. 2007. ring bd. 195.00 (978-0-497-36031-3(4)) Icon Grp.

Paper Towns. John Green. Read by Dan John Miller. (Playaway Young Adult Ser.). 2008. 54.99 (978-1-60640-601-4(9)) Find a World.

Paper Towns. unabr. ed. John Green. Read by Dan John Miller. 1 MP3-CD. (Running Time: 8 hrs.). 2008. 39.25 (978-1-4233-4425-4(1), 9781423344254, Brinc Audio MP3 Lib); 24.95 (978-1-4233-4424-7(3), 9781423344247, Brilliance MP3); 39.97 (978-1-4233-8003-0(7), 9781423380030, BADLE); 24.99 (978-1-4233-8002-3(9), 9781423380023, BAD); audio compact disk 71.97 (978-1-4233-4423-0(5), 9781423344230, BriAudCD Unabrid); audio compact disk 29.99 (978-1-4233-4422-3(7), 9781423344223, Bril Audio CD Unabri) Brilliance Audio.

Paperback Hero: 5 Cassettes (unabridged) unabr. ed. Antony J. Bowman. 5 cass. (Running Time: 7 hrs. 30 mins.). 2004. 40.00 (978-1-74030-259-3(1)) Pub: Bolinda Pubng AUS. Dist(s): Lndmrk Audiobks

Paperboy. 2004. bk. 24.95 (978-1-55592-054-8(3)); pap. bk. 18.95 (978-1-55592-111-8(6)); pap. bk. 38.75 (978-1-55592-640-3(1)); pap. bk. 32.75 (978-1-55592-292-4(9)); pap. bk. 32.75 (978-1-55592-293-1(7)); pap. bk. 14.95 (978-1-55592-055-5(1)); pap. bk. 14.95 (978-1-55592-667-0(3)); 8.95 (978-1-55592-997-8(4)); audio compact disk 12.95 (978-1-55592-947-3(8)) Weston Woods.

Paperboy. Dav Pilkey. Narrated by Forest Whitaker. 1 cass. (Running Time: 8 min.). (J). (gr. k-4). bk. 24.95 Weston Woods.
A father & his young daughter search for The Great Horned Owl.

Paperboy. Dav Pilkey. Narrated by Forest Whitaker. Music by Jerry Dale McFadden. 1 cass. (Running Time: 8 min.). (J). (gr. k-3). 2000. pap. bk. 12.95 (QPRA390) Weston Woods.
Every Saturday morning a paperboy & his dog get ready to leave their nice warm bed to deliver a newspaper to every house along the route they both know by heart.

Paperboy. unabr. ed. Pete Dexter. Narrated by Frank Muller. 8 CDs. (Running Time: 9 hrs. 45 mins.). 1999. audio compact disk 75.00 (978-0-7887-3714-5(7), C1071E7) Recorded Bks.
An unforgettable literary journey through the dark, swampy backroads of Florida.

Paperboy. unabr. ed. Pete Dexter. Narrated by Frank Muller. 7 cass. (Running Time: 9 hrs. 45 mins.). 1997. 60.00 (978-0-7887-0659-2(4), 94836E7) Recorded Bks.

Paperwhite Narcissus. Cynthia Riggs. (Running Time: 27000 sec.). (Martha's Vineyard Mystery Ser.). 2005. 54.95 (978-0-7861-3776-3(2)); audio compact disk 55.00 (978-0-7861-7590-1(7)); audio compact disk 29.95 (978-0-7861-7865-0(5)) Blckstn Audio.

Papi, Mami Que Es Dios? rev. ed. Patrice Karst. css. (SPA.). 1999. bk. 11.95 (978-958-96144-6-4(9)) Centauro Pub.

Papiamentu Newspaper Reader. Kate Howe. 1994. 19.00 (978-0-931745-90-4(X)) Dunwoody Pr.

Papiamentu Newspaper Reader, Set. Kate Howe & Roland DeCuba. 2 cass. (Running Time: 1 hr. 30 min. per cass.). (MIS.). 1993. 19.00 (3046) Dunwoody Pr.
The language of the Dutch Leeward Islands: Aruba, Bonaire, Curacao. Includes thirty-one selections.

Papillion. (Running Time: 60 mins.). 2002. audio compact disk 15.99 (978-1-904972-53-2(5)) Global Jrny GBR GBR.

Papillion. unabr. ed. Henri Charriere. Narrated by George Guidall. 13 cass. (Running Time: 18 hrs. 50 min.). 1996. 104.00 Set. (94695) Recorded Bks.

Papillon, unabr. ed. Henri Charriere. Narrated by George Guidall. 13 cass. (Running Time: 18 hrs. 30 mins.). 1996. 104.00 (978-0-7887-0503-8(2), 94695E7) Recorded Bks.
Chronicles Charriere's life in gripping detail, from his nine escape attempts from penal colonies in French Guyana to his sanctuary in Venezuela in 1945.

Papillon. unabr. collector's ed. Henri Charriere. Read by Michael Prichard. 12 cass. (Running Time: 18 hrs.). 1978. 96.00 (978-0-7366-0108-5(2), 1116) Books on Tape.
Twelve years in a French penal colony failed to break Charriere's spirit. He finally escaped.

Paques a New York. Poems. Blaise Cendrars. Read by Vicki Messica. 1 cass. (FRE.). 1996. 19.95 (1814-LQP) Olivia & Hill.
The series of poems written by Cendrars during his stay in New York in 1912.

Paquito y los frijoles Magicos: Audiocassette. (SPA.). (gr. k-1). 10.00 (978-0-7635-6268-7(8)) Rigby Educ.

Par Ici: Exchanges Intermediaires, Level 3-4. Robert Ariew & Anne Nerenz. (FRE.). (C). 1993. 7.16 (978-0-669-32595-9(3)) HM Harcourt.

Para Decir "Te Quiero" Prod. by Luis Antonio Reyes.Tr. of Bolero for Saying "I Love You". (SPA.). 2002. 8.95 (978-958-692-167-1(0)) Pub: Soc San Pablo COL. Dist(s): St Pauls Alba

Para Desarollar el Contexto. 1 cass. (Running Time: 1 hr.). (Scott Foresman Lectura Ser.).Tr. of Background-Building. (SPA.). (gr. k up). 2000. 44.08

(978-0-673-64444-2(8)); audio compact disk 77.28 (978-0-673-64848-8(6)) Addson-Wesley Educ.
Dialogues incorporate music and sound effects to build vocabulary and concepts, stretching children's imaginations and motivating them to read.

Para Desarollar el Contexto. 1 cass. (Running Time: 1 hr.). (Scott Foresman Lectura Ser.).Tr. of Background-Building. (SPA.). (gr. 1 up). 2000. 44.08 (978-0-673-64445-9(6)) Addson-Wesley Educ.

Para Desarollar el Contexto. 1 cass. (Running Time: 1 hr.). (Scott Foresman Lectura Ser.).Tr. of Background-Building. (SPA.). (gr. 2 up). 2000. 44.08 (978-0-673-64446-6(4)); audio compact disk 77.28 (978-0-673-64850-1(8)) Addson-Wesley Educ.

Para Desarollar el Contexto. 1 cass. (Running Time: 1 hr.). (Scott Foresman Lectura Ser.).Tr. of Background-Building. (SPA.). (gr. 3 up). 2000. 44.08 (978-0-673-64447-3(2)); audio compact disk 77.28 (978-0-673-64851-8(6)) Addson-Wesley Educ.

Para Desarollar el Contexto. 1 cass. (Running Time: 1 hr.).Tr. of Background-Building. (SPA.). (gr. 4 up). 2000. 44.08 (978-0-673-64448-0(0)); audio compact disk 77.28 (978-0-673-64852-5(4)) Addson-Wesley Educ.

Para Desarollar el Contexto. 1 cass. (Running Time: 1 hr.). (Scott Foresman Lectura Ser.).Tr. of Background-Building. (SPA.). (gr. 5 up). 2000. 44.08 (978-0-673-64449-7(9)); audio compact disk 77.28 (978-0-673-64853-2(2)) Addson-Wesley Educ.

Para Desarollar el Contexto, Grade 1. 1 CD. (Running Time: 1 hr.).Tr. of Background-Building. (J). 2001. audio compact disk 77.28 (S-Foresman) AddWesSchl.
Dialogues incorporate music and sound effects to build vocabulary and concepts - stretching children's imaginations and motivating them to read.

Para Entrenar a un Nino. Michael Pearl. 1 cass. (Running Time: 60 min). 2002. 18.00 (978-1-892112-82-8(5)) Pub: No Greater Joy. Dist(s): AtlasBooks

Para Entrenar a un Nino. Michael Pearl. 1 CD. (Running Time: 60 min). 2005. audio compact disk (978-1-892112-81-1(7)) No Greater Joy.

Para Entrenar a un Nino: To Train up a Child. Michael Pearl. 5 CDs. (Running Time: 5 hrs. 20 mins). (SPA & ENG.). 2006. audio compact disk 6.95 (978-1-892112-83-5(3)) Pub: No Greater Joy. Dist(s): STL Dist NA

Para la Conciencia Fonemica. 1 CD. (Running Time: 1 hr.). (Scott Foresman Lectura Ser.).Tr. of Phonemic Awareness. (SPA.). (gr. k up). 2000. 28.56 (978-0-673-59064-0(X)); audio compact disk 50.40 (978-0-673-59069-5(0)) Addson-Wesley Educ.
Skill-building activities develop phonemic awareness and syllable recognition by modeling letter sounds and the sound of spoken words.

Para la Conciencia Fonemica. 1 cass. (Running Time: 1 hr.). (Scott Foresman Lectura Ser.).Tr. of Phonemic Awareness. (SPA.). (gr. 1 up). 2000. 28.56 (978-0-673-59065-7(8)); audio compact disk 50.40 (978-0-673-59070-1(4)) Addson-Wesley Educ.

Para la Conciencia Fonemica. 1 cass. (Running Time: 1 hr.). (Scott Foresman Lectura Ser.).Tr. of Phonemic Awareness. (SPA.). (gr. 2 up). 2000. 28.56 (978-0-673-59066-4(6)); audio compact disk 50.40 (978-0-673-59071-8(2)) Addson-Wesley Educ.

Para la Conciencia Fonemica. 1 CD. (Running Time: 1 hr.). (Scott Foresman Lectura Ser.).Tr. of Phonemic Awareness. (SPA.). (gr. 3 up). 2000. 28.56 (978-0-673-59067-1(4)); audio compact disk 50.40 (978-0-673-59072-5(0)) Addson-Wesley Educ.

Para Mis Amigos. Read by Jaime Murrell. (SPA.). 2008. audio compact disk 14.99 (978-0-8297-6113-9(6)) Pub: Vida Pubs. Dist(s): Zondervan

Parable of the Pipeline. Burke Hedges. Ed. by Steve Price. 1 cass. (Running Time: 90 mins.). 2001. 16.95 (978-1-891279-06-5(8)) INTI.
Explains why people need to build a "pipeline" of on-going residual income instead of relying on a job to create financial freedom.

Parable of the Sower. Octavia E. Butler. Narrated by Lynne Thigpen. 10 CDs. (Running Time: 12 hrs.). 2000. audio compact disk 97.00 (978-0-7887-4760-1(6), C1253E7) Recorded Bks.
Butler gracefully combines visionary & socially realistic concepts in this story of a young female empath who braves a violent 21st-century hell to bear a needed message of hope.

Parable of the Sower. unabr. ed. Octavia E. Butler. Narrated by Lynne Thigpen. 9 cass. (Running Time: 12 hrs.). 2000. 80.00 (978-0-7887-3782-4(1), 95999E7) Recorded Bks.

Parable of the Talents. Octavia E. Butler. 11 cass. (Running Time: 16 hrs.). 94.00 (978-0-7887-4990-2(0)) Recorded Bks.

Parables. (Dovetales Ser.: Tape 11). pap. bk. 6.95 (978-0-944391-46-4(X)); 4.95 (978-0-944391-26-6(5)) DonWise Prodns.

Parables & Portraits. unabr. ed. Stephen Mitchell. Read by Stephen Mitchell. 1 cass. (Running Time: 1 hr. 30 min.). 1995. 10.95 (978-0-944993-30-9(3)) Audio Lit.
These vignettes range across the centuries to provide jewel-like portraits of some of history's most radiant men & women.

Parables from the Back Side. bk. 13.00 (978-0-687-76221-7(9)) Abingdon.

Parables in Spiritual Teachings. (203) Yoga Res Foun.

Parables in Spiritual Teachings. Swami Jyotirmayananda. 1 cass. (Running Time: 1 hr.). 1990. 12.99 Yoga Res Foun.

Parables of Jesus. abr. ed. John L. Lund. 4 cass. (Running Time: 5 hrs. 15 min.). 1996. 24.95 Set. (978-1-891114-31-1(X)) Commun Co.
Includes "The Prodigal Daughter", "The Ten Virgins", "The Kingdom of Heaven", "The Woman who Fainted Not".

Parables of Matthew 13. Warren W. Wiersbe. Read by Warren W. Wiersbe. 4 cass. (Running Time: 6 hrs.). 1987. 18.95 (978-0-8474-2303-3(4)) Back to Bible.
Presents 12 messages that give insights on the parables of the kingdom, as described in Matthew 13.

Parabolas de Jesus. Contrib. by Raphael Moreno. 2007. audio compact disk 17.00 (978-1-58459-306-5(7)) Wrld Lib Pubns.

Parachute Activities with Folk Dance Music. 2 cass. (Running Time: 2 hrs.). (YA). (gr. 2 up). 2001. pap. bk. 18.95 (KEA 9090C); pap. bk. & stu. ed. 20.95 (KEA 9090) Kimbo Educ.
Take a parachute, add some folk dance steps & you've created exciting new enthusiasm for enjoying parachute play! Do the Mushroom, Umbrella, Inside the Mountain & others to Irish Washerwoman, Seljancica, Mayim, mayim & more! Also for use with 12' or 24' parachute. Includes instructional guide.

Parachute Bank: You Alone. Perf. by Parachute Band. 1 cass., 1 CD. 1998. pap. bk. (978-1-58229-062-1(8)); audio compact disk (978-1-58229-061-4(X)) Provident Mus Dist.

Parachute Roundup. 1 cass. (Running Time: 1 hr.). (YA). (gr. 2 up). 2001. pap. bk. 10.95 (KIM 7044C); pap. bk. & stu. ed. 11.95 (KIM 7044) Kimbo Educ.
Today's popular country tunes & rhythms with simple steps & routines based on authentic country dance techniques. Designed for use with the 12' or 24' chute. Cotton Eyed Joe, Nine to Five, Thank God I'm a Country Boy & more. Includes manual.

Paraclesian Philosophy. Instructed by Manly P. Hall. 5 cass. 8.50 o.p. Pt. 1: On Natural & Unnatural Religion & Science. (11A) Philos Res.

Paraclesian Philosophy. Instructed by Manly P. Hall. 5 cass. (Running Time: 150 min.). 1999. 40.00 Set. incl album. (978-0-89314-206-3(9), S570731) Philos Res.

Paraclete: Spirit's Gift to the Church. Raymond E. Brown. 2004. 26.50 (978-1-904756-03-3(4)) STL Dist NA.

Parade see Poetry of Langston Hughes

Parade of the Wooden Soldiers. Contrib. by Johnathan Crumpton & Don Marsh. Prod. by Ed Kee. (ENG.). 2008. audio compact disk 24.99 (978-5-557-38259-5(3), Brentwood-Benson Music) Brentwood Music.

Paradigm - A Tribute to the Hits of Amy Grant. 1 cass. (Paradigm Ser.). 10.98 (C70000); audio compact disk 15.98 (CD70000) Pub: Brentwood Music. Dist(s): Provident Mus Dist
The Paradigm System transforms the familiar into something new through ambient-driven remixes of Christian music's most popular songs. Includes: That's What Love is For, Children of the World, El Shaddai, Love Will Find a Way & more.

Paradigm - A Tribute to the Hits of Michael W. Smith. 1 cass. (Paradigm Ser.). 10.98 (C70004); audio compact disk 15.98 (CD 70004) Pub: Brentwood Music. Dist(s): Provident Mus Dist
Includes; Cry for Love, Friends, I Will Be Here for You, Place in This World, I'll Lead You Home & more.

Paradigm - The Greatest Praise & Worship Choruses. 1 cass. (Paradigm Ser.). 10.98 (C70005); audio compact disk 15.98 (CD70005) Pub: Brentwood Music. Dist(s): Provident Mus Dist
Includes: Give Thanks, I Love You Lord, Majesty, Our God Reigns, Awesome God & more.

Paradigm Intermediate Keyboarding & Applications: Sessions 61-120; Instructor Resources; Instructor's CD Package. 4th ed. William Mitchell & Ronald Kapper. audio compact disk 340.00 (978-0-7638-0206-6(9)) EMC-Paradigm.

Paradigm Keyboarding Sessions: 1-30; Instructor Resources; Instructor's Guide & Software on CD. 4th rev. ed. William Mitchell et al. audio compact disk 340.00 (978-0-7638-2022-0(9)) EMC-Paradigm.

Paradigm Keyboarding Sessions 1-30: Instructor Resources; Instructor's CD. 4th ed. William Mitchell et al. audio compact disk 340.00 (978-0-7638-0145-8(3)) EMC-Paradigm.

Paradigm Keyboarding Sessions 1-30: Instructor Resources; Speech Recognition CD. 4th ed. William Mitchell et al. audio compact disk 24.95 (978-0-7638-1984-2(0)) EMC-Paradigm.

Paradigm Shift in Education. unabr. ed. 1 cass. (Running Time: 1 hr.). 1991. 10.00 (978-1-888947-52-6(7)) Sudbury Valley.
Philosophy behind Sudbury Valley School.

Paradise see Paradise

Paradise. Dante Alighieri. Read by Heathcote Williams. Tr. by Benedict Flynn from ITA. 3 cass. (Running Time: 4 hrs.). (Divine Comedy Ser.: Pt. 3). 1999. 17.98 (978-962-634-679-2(5), NA317914, Naxos AudioBooks) Naxos.
The final part of Dante's great epic trilogy, The Divine Comedy. Having said farewell to his faithful guide, Virgil, Dante is left to make the final journey to Paradise.

Paradise. abr. unabr. ed. Dante Alighieri. Read by Heathcote Williams. Tr. by Benedict Flynn from ITA. 3 CDs. (Running Time: 4 hrs.). (Divine Comedy Ser.: Pt. 3). 1999. audio compact disk 19.98 (978-962-634-179-7(3), NA317912, Naxos AudioBooks) Naxos.

Paradise. unabr. ed. Dante Alighieri. Read by Heathcote Williams. Tr. by Benedict Flynn. 4 CDs. (Running Time: 4 hr. 27 min.). audio compact disk 28.98 (978-962-634-318-0(4), NA431812) Naxos.

Paradise. unabr. ed. Toni Morrison. Narrated by Lynne Thigpen. 10 cass. (Running Time: 14 hrs.).Tr. of Paradise. 1999. 90.00 (978-0-7887-3094-8(0), 95805E7) Recorded Bks.

Paradise. unabr. ed. Toni Morrison. Narrated by Lynne Thigpen. 12 CDs. (Running Time: 14 hrs.).Tr. of Paradise. 1999. audio compact disk 108.00 (978-0-7887-3728-2(7), C1085E7) Recorded Bks.
In the mid-1070's, Ruby, an all-black Oklahoma community, is proud of its heritage. The town is also wary of five unconventional women who may be threatening its stability. Challenges listeners with such issues as civil rights, morality & racism & the drama & complexity of the human psyche.

Paradise: From the Divine Comedy. abr. ed. Dante Alighieri. Read by Heathcote Williams. (Running Time: 4 hrs.). 2003. 27.95 (978-1-60083-889-7(8)) Iofy Corp.

Paradise: From the Divine Comedy. unabr. ed. Dante Alighieri. Read by Heathcote Williams. (YA). 2007. 34.99 (978-1-60252-536-8(6)) Find a World.

Paradise: The Spirit-World Home of the Righteous. unabr. ed. Duane S. Crowther. Read by Duane S. Crowther. 1 cass. (Running Time: 90 min.). 1989. 13.98 (978-0-88290-342-2(X), 1826) Horizon Utah.
Numerous fascinating eyewitness descriptions of Paradise have been gathered & documented. They show the various abodes in the spirit world & provide a comforting view of paradise as the pre-heaven spirit-world reward for a righteous mortal life.

Paradise Alley. unabr. ed. Kevin Baker. Read by Kevin Baker. 6 cass. (Running Time: 9 hrs.). 2003. 39.95 (978-0-06-057514-4(X)) HarperCollins Pubs.

***Paradise Alley: A Novel.** unabr. ed. Kevin Baker. Read by Kevin Baker. (ENG.). 2006. (978-0-06-088931-9(4), Harper Audio); (978-0-06-088932-6(2), Harper Audio) HarperCollins Pubs.

Paradise City. abr. ed. Lorenzo Carcaterra. Read by David Colacci. (Running Time: 6 hrs.). 2005. audio compact disk 16.99 (978-1-59600-419-1(3), 9781596004191, BCD Value Price) Brilliance Audio.

Paradise City. unabr. ed. Lorenzo Carcaterra. Read by David Colacci. (Running Time: 13 hrs.). 2004. 24.95 (978-1-59335-775-7(3), 1593357753, Brilliance MP3); 39.25 (978-1-59710-560-6(0), 1597105600, BADLE); 24.95 (978-1-59710-561-3(9), 1597105619, BAD); 39.25 (978-1-59335-909-6(8), 1593359098, Brinc Audio MP3 Lib) Brilliance Audio.
As a fifteen-year-old, Giancarlo Lo Manto learned about injustice the hard way. His father was gunned down by the Camorra, the murderous clan run by Don Nicola Rossi. When his mother moved him back to his family's ancestral home in Naples, Gian found himself face-to-face with the source of the mob's strength, the spring that spawned it's deadly killers. Today, twenty-three years later, he is a dogged detective on the Naples police force, homicide division, the most dangerous beat in Europe. He is the nemesis of all who export evil, the man who stops it before it spreads overseas. His efforts have not gone unnoticed. "The strength of Naples reinforces the muscle of New York" - and now the two worlds are about to collide. In the highest towers of the most expensive streets of New York City, Pete Rossi, the son of Don Nicola, has decided to bring Gian back to America - permanently. When Gian learns his teenage niece, Paula, has gone missing in Manhattan, he cancels his much-needed vacation to Capri, to paradise, joking that "one island is just as good as the other." Gian's homecoming will be anything but smooth. Someone must always watch his back, and Detective Jennifer Fabini gets the job. A gifted officer with her own personal demons, Jennifer thinks she will be dealing with a peasant from the old country. The handsome, reserved, unrelenting Gian is a revelation: an irritant and a temptation - especially for a woman who has sworn off cops as lovers. Together the two must solve a disappearance that appears to be a kidnapping...but turns out to be a deadly trap. As they dash from the sun-struck villages of Italy to the darkest drug dens of New York, their journey links old-world honor and modern-day danger and ends in a dizzying explosion of the present and the past. Paradise City is Lorenzo Carcaterra's richest entertainment to date, a book that is at once a sensational crime novel and a provocative exploration of his trademark themes: violence and innocence, love and revenge.

Paradise City: A Novel. abr. ed. Lorenzo Carcaterra. Read by David Colacci. (Running Time: 6 hrs.). 2004. audio compact disk 74.25 (978-1-59355-949-6(6), 1593559496, BACDLib Ed) Brilliance Audio.

Paradise City: A Novel. unabr. ed. Lorenzo Carcaterra. Read by David Colacci. 9 cass. (Running Time: 13 hrs.). 2004. 34.95 (978-1-59355-946-5(1), 1593559461, BAU); 92.25 (978-1-59355-947-2(X), 159355947X, BrilAudUnabridg) Brilliance Audio.

Paradise County. unabr. ed. Karen Robards. Read by Vida Vasaitis. 12 vols. (Running Time: 12 hrs. 30 min.). 2001. bk. 96.95 (978-0-7927-2462-9(3), CSL 351, Chivers Sound Lib); audio compact disk 119.95 (978-0-7927-9903-0(8), SLD 054, Chivers Sound Lib) AudioGO.
The rolling fields of Shelby County are home to some of the finest horseflesh & bluest blood in Kentucky. But beneath the serene exterior lies a dark underside & evil that threatens everyone who touches it.

***Paradise Dislocated: Morris, Politics, Art.** Jeffrey Skoblow. (Victorian Literature & Culture Ser.). (ENG.). 27.50 (978-0-8139-2944-6(X)) U Pr of Va.

***Paradise General: Riding the Surge at a Combat Hospital in Iraq.** unabr. ed. Dave Hnida. Narrated by George K. Wilson. (Running Time: 10 hrs. 30 mins. 0 sec.). (ENG.). 2010. 24.99 (978-1-4001-6554-4(7)); 16.99 (978-1-4001-8554-2(8)); audio compact disk 34.99 (978-1-4001-1554-9(X)); audio compact disk 69.99 (978-1-4001-4554-6(6)) Pub: Tantor Media. Dist(s): IngramPubServ

Paradise Lost see Treasury of John Milton

Paradise Lost see Dylan Thomas Reading

Paradise Lost. Robert L. Heilbroner & Emma Rothschild. 1 cass. (Running Time: 56 min.). 10.95 (40052) J Norton Pubs.
Noted sociologist Dr. Hielbroner & Rothschild, author of "Paradise Lost: The Decline of the Auto-industrial Age," discuss with Heywood Hale Broun why the energy crisis will necessitate radical alterations in automotive design as well as an increased reliance upon mass transportation.

Paradise Lost. John Milton. Read by Anton Lesser. (Playaway Adult Fiction Ser.). (ENG.). 2008. 79.99 (978-1-60514-910-3(1)) Find a World.

Paradise Lost. John Milton. Read by Anton Lesser. 3 cass. (Running Time: 4 hrs. 15 mins.). 1995. 17.98 (978-962-634-502-3(0), NA300214, Naxos AudioBooks) Naxos.
Described in 1667 as one of the greatest, most noble & sublime poems which either this age or nation has produced, "Milton set himself the task of telling the story of Man's creation, fall & redemption hoping to move readers to appreciate God's wisdom & purpose.".

Paradise Lost. John Milton. Read by Graeme Malcolm. 6 cass. 2005. 14.95 (978-1-56585-991-3(X)); audio compact disk 19.95 (978-1-59803-007-5(8)) Teaching Co.

Paradise Lost. John Milton. Narrated by Flo Gibson. 2008. audio compact disk 31.95 (978-1-55685-988-5(0)) Audio Bk Con.

***Paradise Lost.** abr. ed. J. A. Jance. Read by Debra Monk. (ENG.). 2005. (978-0-06-088651-6(X), Harper Audio); (978-0-06-088652-3(8), Harper Audio) HarperCollins Pubs.

Paradise Lost. abr. ed. John Milton. Read by Anton Lesser. 3 CDs. (Running Time: 4 hrs. 15 mins.). (J). (gr. 9-12). 1994. audio compact disk 22.98 (978-962-634-002-8(9), NA300212) Naxos.
Described as one of the greatest, most noble & sublime poems which either this age or nation has produced, "Milton set himself the task of telling the story of Man's creation, fall & redemption to move readers to appreciate God's wisdom and purpose.".

Paradise Lost. unabr. ed. Kate Brian, pseud. Narrated by Cassandra Campbell. (Running Time: 6 hrs. 30 mins. 0 sec.). (Private Ser.: No. 9). (ENG.). (YA). (gr. 7-12). 2009. audio compact disk 59.99 (978-1-4001-4239-2(3)); audio compact disk 29.99 (978-1-4001-1239-5(7)) Pub: Tantor Media. Dist(s): IngramPubServ

Paradise Lost. unabr. ed. Kate Brian, pseud. Narrated by Cassandra Campbell. (Running Time: 6 hrs. 30 mins. 0 sec.). (Private Ser.: No. 9). (ENG., (YA). (gr. 7-12). 2009. audio compact disk 19.99 (978-1-4001-6239-0(4)) Pub: Tantor Media. Dist(s): IngramPubServ

Paradise Lost. unabr. ed. John Milton. Narrated by Flo Gibson. 7 cass. (Running Time: 10 hrs.). 2003. 25.95 (978-1-55685-692-1(X)) Audio Bk Con.
Considered by many to be the greatest epic poem ever written, this biblical tale concerns Adam and Eve in the Garden of Eden. Despite God's prohibition and warnings, Satan induces Eve to eat the forbidden fruit with dire consequences.

Paradise Lost. unabr. ed. John Milton. Read by Frederick Davidson. 7 cass. (Running Time: 10 hrs.). 1994. 49.95 (978-0-7861-0734-6(0), 1487) Blckstn Audio.
Often considered the greatest epic in any modern language, "Paradise Lost" tells the story of the revolt of Satan & his banishment from Heaven, & the fall of man & his expulsion from Eden. Writing in blank verse of unsurpassed majesty, Milton demonstrates his genius for imagery & cadence. His style is rich & sonorous, his characterizations are heroic, & his action is cosmic in scale. "Paradise Lost" could only be the work of a mastermind involved in the profound search for Truth.

Paradise Lost. unabr. ed. John Milton. Read by Ralph Cosham. (Running Time: 32400 sec.). 2006. 54.95 (978-0-7861-4804-2(7)) Blckstn Audio.

Paradise Lost. unabr. ed. John Milton. Read by Cosham Ralph. (Running Time: 32400 sec.). 2006. audio compact disk 29.95 (978-0-7861-7200-9(2)) Blckstn Audio.

Paradise Lost. unabr. ed. John Milton. Read by Ralph Cosham. (Running Time: 32400 sec.). 2006. audio compact disk 63.00 (978-0-7861-6233-8(3)) Blckstn Audio.

Paradise Lost. unabr. ed. John Milton. Read by Ralph Cosham. (Running Time: 32400 sec.). 2007. 19.95 (978-0-7861-4800-4(4)) Blckstn Audio.

Paradise Lost. unabr. ed. John Milton. Read by Cosham Ralph. (Running Time: 32400 sec.). 2007. audio compact disk 19.95 (978-0-7861-6237-6(6)) Blckstn Audio.

Paradise Lost. unabr. ed. John Milton. Read by Anton Lesser. (Running Time: 11 hrs.). 2004. 52.95 (978-1-60083-892-7(8)) Iofy Corp.

Paradise Lost. unabr. ed. John Milton. Read by Anton Lesser. 9 CDs. (Running Time: 38545 sec.). 2005. bk. 59.98 (978-962-634-350-0(8)) Naxos UK GBR.

Paradise Lost. unabr. ed. John Milton. 9 CDs. (Running Time: 9 hrs. 30 mins. 0 sec.). (ENG.). 2006. audio compact disk 26.98 (978-1-59644-244-3(1), Hovel Audio) christianaud.
Of Man's first disobedience and the fruitOf that forbidden tree whose mortal tasteBrought death into the world and all our woe,With loss of Eden, till on greater ManRestore us and regain the blissful seatSing, Heavenly Muse...Thus begins the epic poem, considered the greatest in the English language, as John Milton seeks to a??justify the ways of God to mena?? through relating the story of Satana??s rebellion in Heaven, the deception and fall of Man, and the presaged event of Redemption through Jesus, the Son of Goda?|the a??Second Adam.a??An English cleric with a classical education, Milton lost his eyesight in 1652, and thus the story was largely dictated by the blind poet, lending a certain quality of the ancient oral epics, which only serves to enhance the telling of the tale. Weaving classical mythology with a deep knowledge and reference to Scripture, Milton's genius for narrative unfolds what his biographer, Samuel Johnson, called his "peculiar power to astonish."Nadia May has narrated over five hundred audiobooks and has earned the prestigious AudioFile Golden Voice award, as well as fourteen Earphone awards. She is an accomplished film, TV, and theater actress. Nadiaa??s native British voice complements her graduate education in English Literature from UC Berkeley to make her delivery of John Miltona??s Paradise Lost engaging and nuanced.

Paradise Lost. unabr. ed. John Milton. Narrated by Nadia May. 1 MP3 CD. (Running Time: 9 hrs. 30 mins. 0 sec.). (ENG.). 2006. lp 19.98 (978-1-59644-246-7(8), Hovel Audio) christianaud.

***Paradise Lost.** unabr. ed. John Milton. Narrated by Nadia May. (ENG.). 2006. 16.98 (978-1-59644-245-0(X), Hovel Audio) christianaud.

Paradise Lost. unabr. abr. ed. John Milton. Narrated by Simon Vance. (Running Time: 9 hrs. 0 mins. 0 sec.). (ENG.). 2009. audio compact disk 69.99 (978-1-4001-4285-9(7)) Pub: Tantor Media. Dist(s): IngramPubServ

Paradise Lost, Bk 1. John Milton. 10.00 Esstee Audios.
A biographical introduction to Milton & a reading of the poem.

Paradise Lost, Set. unabr. ed. John Milton. Read by Frederick Davidson. 7 cass. 1999. 49.95 (FS9-51054) Highsmith.

Paradise Lost: An A+ Audio Study Guide. unabr. ed. Jayne Lewis & John Milton. (Running Time: 30 mins.). (ENG.). 2006. 5.98 (978-1-59483-718-0(X)) Pub: Hachet Audio. Dist(s): HachBkGrp

Paradise Lost - from Creation to the Fall of Mankind in Eden. 2005. 15.00 (978-1-933561-11-0(4)) BFM Books.

***Paradise Lost, with EBook.** unabr. ed. John Milton. Narrated by Simon Vance. (Running Time: 9 hrs. 0 mins.). 2009. 15.99 (978-1-4001-8285-5(9)) Tantor Media.

Paradise Lost, with EBook. unabr. abr. ed. John Milton. Narrated by Simon Vance. (Running Time: 9 hrs. 0 mins. 0 sec.). (ENG.). 2009. 24.99 (978-1-4001-6285-7(8)); audio compact disk 34.99 (978-1-4001-1285-2(0)) Pub: Tantor Media. Dist(s): IngramPubServ

Paradise News. unabr. ed. David Lodge. Read by Charles Armstrong. 8 cass. (Running Time: 9 hrs. 45 min.). (Isis Ser.). (J). 1993. 69.95 (978-1-85695-775-5(6), 931006) Pub: ISIS Lrg Prnt GBR. Dist(s): Ulverscroft US

Paradise Parade. unabr. ed. Anne Baker. Read by Michael Tudor Barnes. 14 cass. (Running Time: 20 hrs.). (Sound Ser.). (J). 2002. 99.95 (978-1-84283-137-3(2)) Pub: ISIS Lrg Prnt GBR. Dist(s): Ulverscroft US

Paradise Parade. unabr. ed. Anne Baker. Read by Julia Franklin. 16 CDs. (Running Time: 20 hrs.). (Soundings (CDs) Ser.). (J). 2005. audio compact disk 109.95 (978-1-84559-269-1(7)) Pub: ISIS Lrg Prnt GBR. Dist(s): Ulverscroft US

Paradise Regained. John Milton. Read by Anton Lesser. (Running Time: 2 hrs. 30 mins.). 2001. 20.95 (978-1-60083-893-4(6)) Iofy Corp.

***Paradise Regained.** Featuring Ravi Zacharias. 1986. audio compact disk 9.00 (978-1-61256-020-5(2)) Ravi Zach.

Paradise Regained. unabr. abr. ed. John Milton. Read by Anton Lesser. 2 CDs. (Running Time: 8169 sec.). 2006. audio compact disk 17.98 (978-962-634-399-9(0), Naxos AudioBooks) Naxos.

Paradise Restored. Dan Corner. 1 cass. 3.00 (64) Evang Outreach.

Paradise Salvage. John Fusco. Read by Brian Emerson. (Running Time: 14 hrs. 30 mins.). 2002. 41.95 (978-1-59912-567-1(6)) Iofy Corp.

Paradise Salvage. unabr. ed. John Fusco. Read by Brian Emerson. 10 cass. (Running Time: 14 hrs. 30 mins.). 2002. 69.95 (978-0-7861-2242-4(0), 2966); audio compact disk 96.00 (978-0-7861-9494-0(4), 2966) Blckstn Audio.
Each new wreck towed into Paradise Salvage is a desultory gift from Fortune, a random opportunity for discovery. Sometimes it's a handful of loose change under the upholstery or an old copy of Vue magazine with a Betty Page centerfold under the front seat. But on a hot summer day in 1979, in the trunk of an abandoned Pontiac Bonneville, Nunzio uncovers a secret that will change his life.

Paradise War. Stephen Lawhead. Read by Stuart Langston. (Running Time: 14 hrs. 30 mins.). 1991. 41.95 (978-1-59912-697-5(4)) Iofy Corp.

Paradise War. unabr. ed. Stephen Lawhead. Read by Stuart Langston. 10 cass. (Running Time: 14 hrs. 30 mins.). (Song of Albion Ser.: Bk. 1). 2002. 69.95 (978-0-7861-2323-0(0), P3006); audio compact disk 88.00 (978-0-7861-9435-3(9)) Blckstn Audio.
In an ancient cairn in the wilds of Scotland, Oxford student Simon Rawnson vanishes, seemingly into thin air. Where has he gone? Unsettling signs-a mysterious Green Man, a Celtic circle chalked on the sidewalk-point his roommate, Lewis Gillies, to an impossible answer . . . and an incredible destiny on the other side of a doorway between worlds.

Paradise War. unabr. ed. Stephen Lawhead. Read by Stuart Langston. 1 MP3. (Running Time: 5 hrs. 30 min.). (Song of Albion Ser.: Bk. 1). 2002. audio compact disk 24.95 (978-0-7861-9157-4(0)) Blckstn Audio.

***Paradise War: The Song of Albion Trilogy, Book 1.** unabr. ed. Stephen R. Lawhead. Read by Stuart Langton. (Song of Albion Ser.: Bk. 1). 2010. audio compact disk 29.95 (978-1-4417-2476-2(1)) Blckstn Audio.

Paradox of Henry Ford. Louis Untermeyer. 1 cass. (Running Time: 21 min.). 10.95 (13010) J Norton Pubs.
A critical account of the life, career, & accomplishments of Henry Ford.

Paradox of Joy & Sorrow. Thomas Merton. 1 cass. 8.95 (AA2263) Credence Commun.

Paradoxe sur le Comedien see Treasury of French Prose

Paragon English, Volume 1. Victoria Alexander. Ed. by Benjawan Poomsan. Illus. by John Main Graphics. Contrib. by Thomas L. Madden. Des. by Anne Kenyon & Doug Gordon Morton. 2006. bk. 15.00 (978-1-887521-72-7(0)) Paiboon Pubng.

Paragon Walk. unabr. ed. Anne Perry. Narrated by Davina Porter. 5 cass. (Running Time: 8 hrs. 45 mins.). (Thomas Pitt Ser.). 2001. 56.00 (978-0-7887-5959-8(0), H1182E7) Recorded Bks.
When a young woman from the upper class neighborhood of Paragon Walk is raped & murdered, Inspector Pitt is sent in on the case. Unable to believe that a killer could live among them, the residents refuse to cooperate with the investigation. He soon finds that the police society of Paragon Walk is nothing more than a mask for something much more sinister.

***Parallel.** 2010. audio compact disk (978-1-59171-171-1(1)) Falcon Picture.

Parallel. Colin B. Campbell. Contrib. by Philip Prowse. (Running Time: 44 mins.). (Cambridge English Readers Ser.). (ENG., 2004. 9.45 (978-0-521-53652-3(9)) Cambridge U Pr.

Parallel Lies. abr. ed. Ridley Pearson. Read by Dick Hill. 5 cass. Library ed. (Running Time: 6 hrs.). 2001. audio compact disk 69.25 (978-1-58788-368-2(6), 1587883686) Brilliance Audio.
Umberto Alvarez is a grieving man whose quest is to bring down the railroad company he blames for the death of his wife and children three years earlier - no matter who gets in the way. Peter Tyler is an ex-cop looking to redeem himself after being suspended from the force. Now an investigator with the National Transportations Safety Board, he will stop at nothing to catch the elusive Alvarez. But the case is more complicated than it seems. As Tyler's investigation proceeds, it becomes apparent that Alvarez is no terrorist - in fact, the more Tyler investigates, the closer he comes to the real truth. Packed with action, laced with romance, brimming with heart-stopping suspense, and marked by the intelligence and humility that make Ridley Pearson's novels stand apart from others in the genre, Parallel Lies will cause listeners to agree that he is "the best damn thriller writer on the planet" (Booklist).

Parallel Lies. unabr. ed. Ridley Pearson. Read by Ridley Pearson. (Running Time: 36000 sec.). 2001. audio compact disk 24.95 (978-1-59600-756-7(7), 9781596007567, Brilliance MP3) Brilliance Audio.

Parallel Lies. unabr. ed. Ridley Pearson. Read by Ridley Pearson. 7 cass. Library ed. (Running Time: 10 hrs.). 2001. 78.25 (978-1-58788-365-1(1), 1587883651, Unabridge Lib Edns) Brilliance Audio.

Parallel Lies. unabr. ed. Ridley Pearson. Read by Ridley Pearson. Read by Dick Hill. 7 cass. (Running Time: 10 hrs.). 2001. 32.95 (978-1-58788-364-4(3), 1587883643, BAU) Brilliance Audio.

Parallel Lies. unabr. ed. Ridley Pearson. Read by Ridley Pearson. (Running Time: 10 hrs.). 2005. 39.25 (978-1-59600-759-8(1), 9781596007598, BADLE); 24.95 (978-1-59600-758-1(3), 9781596007581, BAD); audio compact disk 39.25 (978-1-59600-757-4(5), 9781596007574, Brinc Audio MP3 Lib) Brilliance Audio.

Parallel Lies. unabr. ed. Ridley Pearson. Read by Ridley Pearson. (Running Time: 12 hrs.). 2010. audio compact disk 89.97 (978-1-4418-3577-2(6), 9781441835772, BriAudCD Unabrid); audio compact disk 29.99 (978-1-4418-3576-5(8), 9781441835765, Bril Audio CD Unabri) Brilliance Audio.

Parallels. Marilyn Muir. 1 cass. 8.95 (844) Am Fed Astrologers.

Parallels of Declination. Bonnie Armstrong. 1 cass. 8.95 (873) Am Fed Astrologers.

Paramedics to the Rescue: When Every Second Counts. (High Five Reading - Purple Ser.). (ENG.). (gr. 4-5). 2007. audio compact disk 5.95 (978-1-4296-1448-1(X)) CapstoneDig.

Paramedics to the Rescue: When Every Second Counts. Michael Silverstone. (High Five Reading Ser.). (ENG.). (gr. 4 up). 2004. audio compact disk 5.95 (978-0-7368-3854-2(6)) CapstoneDig.

Paramhansa Yogananda's World Mission: A New Dispensation. Kriyananda, pseud. (Running Time: 60 min.). 9.95 (ST-10) Crystal Clarity.
Kriyananda explores possible answers reaching conclusions that pose a key challenge for Yogananda's disciples everywhere.

Paranoia see Paranoia

Paranoia. abr. rev. ed. Joseph Finder. Read by Jason Priestley. 4 CDs. (Running Time: 5 hrs. 0 mins. 0 sec.).Tr. of Paranoia. (ENG.). 2004. audio compact disk 29.95 (978-1-55927-983-3(4)) Pub: Macmill Audio. Dist(s): Macmillan

***Paranoia on River Road.** Terry Rich Hartley. Read by Sean Pratt. (Running Time: 63). 2010. 2.99 (978-1-61114-015-6(3)); audio compact disk 2.99 (978-0-9825278-6-3(1)) Mind Wings Aud.

paranoia Plot. A. J. Butcher. Read by Sean Mangan. (Running Time: 7 hrs. 10 mins.). (Spy High Ser.). (YA). 2009. 69.99 (978-1-74214-304-0(0), 9781742143040) Pub: Bolinda Pubng AUS. Dist(s): Bolinda Pub Inc

Paranoia Plot. unabr. ed. A. J. Butcher. Read by Sean Mangan. (Running Time: 25800 sec.). (Spy High Ser.). (J). (ps-7). 2008. audio compact disk 77.95 (978-1-74093-829-7(1)) Pub: Bolinda Pubng AUS. Dist(s): Bolinda Pub Inc

Paranoia, Propaganda & Projection. unabr. ed. Sam Keen. 1 cass. (Running Time: 1 hr. 14 min.). 1983. 11.00 (05701) Big Sur Tapes.
Looks at the deeper causes of the antagonistic mind & the roots of the human capacity to wound, kill, & make enemies. He discusses what we do to dehumanize other human beings in order to allow us to kill them with a clear consciousness.

***Paranormalcy.** unabr. ed. Kiersten White. Read by Emily Eiden. (ENG.). 2010. (978-0-06-200996-8(6)); (978-0-06-206239-0(5)) HarperCollins Pubs.

Parapluie see Contes de Maupassant

Parapluie: Fabulous French Songs for Children. Lyrics by Alain Le Lait. Music by Alain Le Lait. Des. by Christy Le Lait. 1 CD. (Running Time: 31 mins.). (FRE.). (J). 2006. pap. bk. 15.95 (978-0-9747122-5-3(6)) Yadeeda.

Parapsychology: Program from Award Winning Public Radio Series. Interview. Hosted by Fred Goodwin. 1 CD. (Running Time: 1 hr). 2001. audio compact disk 21.95 (978-1-932479-77-5(5), LCM 183) Lichtenstein Creat.
Psychics, ESP, ghosts - do these things have anything to do with science? This week we look beyond the rational world to explore parapsychology - the scientific study of psychic and paranormal phenomena. Guests include intuitive psychiatrist Dr. Judith Orloff, parapsychologists Dr. Charles Tart and Dr. Marilyn Schlitz; folklore researcher Dr. Bill Ellis, author of Aliens, Ghosts and Cults: Legends We Live; and psychic Barbara Stabiner.

Parapsychology & Yoga. 1 cass. (Running Time: 1 hr.). 12.99 (171) Yoga Res Foun.

Paraworld Zero. Matthew Peterson. Narrated by Matthew Peterson. Narrated by Alicia Peterson. (Parallel Worlds Ser.: Bk. 1). (J). 2008. (978-0-9819227-4-4(0)) Para World.

Paraworld Zero. unabr. ed. Matthew Peterson. Narrated by Matthew Peterson. Narrated by Alicia Peterson. (Parallel Worlds Ser.: Bk. 1). (ENG.). (J). 2008. 29.95 (978-0-9819227-1-3(6)) Para World.

Paraworld Zero. unabr. ed. Matthew Peterson. Narrated by Matthew Peterson. Narrated by Alicia Peterson. (Parallel Worlds Ser.: Bk. 1). (J). 2008. audio compact disk 49.95 (978-0-9819227-3-7(2)) Para World.

Parcel Arrived Safely. Michael Crawford. 2 cass. (Running Time: 3 hrs.). (ENG., 1999. 16.99 (978-1-85686-682-8(3), Audiobks) Pub: Random GBR. Dist(s): Trafalgar

Parcel of Patterns. Jill Paton Walsh. Read by Brigit Forsyth. 3 cass. (Running Time: 3 hrs. 15 mins.). (J). 2000. 24.00 (978-0-7366-9155-0(3)) Books on Tape.
Young mall Percival's account of how the plague killed her family & all but destroyed her English village in 1665.

Parcel of Patterns. unabr. ed. Jill Paton Walsh. Read by Brigit Forsyth. 3 cass. (Running Time: 3 hrs.). (J). 1997. 30.00 (LL 0074, Chivers Child Audio) AudioGO.

Parcel of Patterns. unabr. ed. Jill Paton Walsh. Read by Brigit Forsyth. 3 cass. (Running Time: 4 hrs. 45 mins.). (J). (gr. 4-7). 1996. 24.00 (978-0-8072-7609-9(X), YA898CX, Listening Lib) Random Audio Pubg.

Parcel of Patterns. unabr. ed. Jill Paton Walsh. Read by Brigit Forsyth. 3 cass. (Running Time: 4 hrs. 45 mins.). (J). (gr. 5-7). 1996. pap. bk. 29.00 (978-0-8072-7610-5(3), YA892SP, Listening Lib) Random Audio Pubg.

Parcel of Patterns, Set. unabr. ed. Jill Paton Walsh. Read by Brigit Forsyth. 3 cass. (YA). 1999. 23.98 (FS9-26773) Highsmith.

Parchment of Leaves. unabr. ed. Silas House. Narrated by Kate Forbes. 7 cass. (Running Time: 9 hrs. 45 mins.). 2002. 69.75 (978-1-4025-8168-7(8), SV015MC, Griot Aud); audio compact disk 89.75 (978-1-4025-8170-0(X), CV015MC, Griot Aud) Recorded Bks.

Parcival & the Holy Grail. Joseph Campbell. 1 cass. 9.00 (A0459-86) Sound Photosyn.
Courtly love at its best according to the Mustard & Passage translation from the high German as told by the master story teller & interpreter himself. A must for Campbell fans, we were lucky to record him at this height of his inspiration.

Pardners. 1 cass. (Retro Mickey Ser.). (J). 7.99 Norelco. (978-1-55723-949-5(5)); audio compact disk 13.99 CD. (978-1-55723-950-1(9)) W Disney Records.

Pardners. unabr. ed. Rex Ellingwood Beach. Read by Jack Sondericker. 4 cass. (Running Time: 4 hrs 30 min.). Dramatization. 1990. 26.95 (978-1-55686-329-5(2), 329) Books in Motion.
Series of 11 novelettes. Included are: Pardners; The Mule Driver & the Garrulous Mute; The Colonel & the Horse Thief; The Thaw at Slisco's; Bitterroot Billings, Arbiter; The Shyness of Shorty; The Test; North of Fifty Three; Where Northern Lights Come Down O'Nights; The Scourge.

***Pardon.** abr. ed. James Grippando. Read by John Rubinstein. (ENG.). 2004. (978-0-06-079860-4(2), Harper Audio) HarperCollins Pubs.

***Pardon.** abr. ed. James Grippando. Read by John Rubinstein. (ENG.). 2004. (978-0-06-082407-5(7), Harper Audio) HarperCollins Pubs.

Pardon. unabr. ed. James Grippando. Narrated by Ron McLarty. 9 CDs. (Running Time: 10 hrs.). 2001. audio compact disk 89.00 (978-1-4025-0489-1(6), C1545) Recorded Bks.
Miami defense attorney Jack Swytek has long rebelled against his father, Harry, now Florida's governor. The two disagree on nearly everything, especially the death penalty. And when Harry allows one of Jack's clients - a man Jack believes is innocent - to die in the electric chair, their estrangement seems complete. But when a psychopath begins a twisted game of vengeance, father & son find they have nowhere to turn but to each other.

Pardon. unabr. ed. James Grippando. Narrated by Ron McLarty. 7 cass. (Running Time: 10 hrs.). 2001. 65.00 (978-0-7887-5506-4(4), 96380x7) Recorded Bks.

Pardonable Lies. Jacqueline Winspear. (Maisie Dobbs Mystery Ser.: Bk. 3). 2005. audio compact disk 29.95 (978-0-7927-3835-0(7), CMP 841, Chivers Sound Lib) AudioGO.

Pardonable Lies. Jacqueline Winspear. Read by Orlagh Cassidy. 9 CDs. (Maisie Dobbs Mystery Ser.: Bk. 3). 2005. audio compact disk 44.95 (978-0-7927-3749-0(0), SLD 841) AudioGO.

Pardonable Lies. Jacqueline Winspear. Read by Orlagh Cassidy. (Maisie Dobbs Mystery Ser.: Bk. 3). 2005. 23.95 (978-1-59397-815-0(4)) Pub: Macmill Audio. Dist(s): Macmillan

Pardonable Lies. abr. ed. Jacqueline Winspear. Read by Jacqueline Winspear. (Maisie Dobbs Mystery Ser.: Bk. 3). 2005. 14.95 (978-1-59397-813-6(8)) Pub: Macmill Audio. Dist(s): Macmillan

Pardonable Lies. abr. unabr. ed. Jacqueline Winspear. Read by Orlagh Cassidy. 9 CDs. (Running Time: 11 hrs. 0 mins. 0 sec.). (Maisie Dobbs Mystery Ser.: Bk. 3). (ENG.). 2005. audio compact disk 39.95 (978-1-59397-814-3(6)) Pub: Macmill Audio. Dist(s): Macmillan

Pardoned to Be Priests. Read by J. Gerald Harris. 2007. audio compact disk 21.95 (978-1-4276-2608-0(1)) AardGP.

Pardoner's Tale. (SAC 919) Spoken Arts.

Pardoner's Tale: The Nonnes Preeste's Tale / the Frankeleyns Tale in Middle English. unabr. ed. Geoffrey Chaucer. Read by Richard Bebb. (YA). 2007. 34.99 (978-1-60252-571-9(4)) Find a World.

Pardoners Tale/the Frankeleyns Tale/the Nonne Preestes Tale. unabr. ed. Geoffrey Chaucer. Read by Richard Bebb. (Running Time: 9532 sec.). (Complete Classics Ser.). (ENM., 2007. audio compact disk 17.98 (978-962-634-439-2(3), Naxos AudioBooks) Naxos.

Pardonnez-Moi Docteur. 1 cass. (Running Time: 60 mins.). Dramatization. (Maitres du Mystere Ser.). (FRE.). 1996. 11.95 (1384-MA) Olivia & Hill.
Popular radio thriller, interpreted by France's best actors.

Parent Adventure: Preparing Your Kid for a Life with God. Rodney Wilson & Selma Wilson. 2008. pap. bk. 97.25 (978-1-4158-6511-8(6)) LifeWay Christian.

Parent Care. Prod. by Sara Wolch. Hosted by Sara Wolch. 2 CDs. (Running Time: 2 hrs.). 2005. audio compact disk 19.95 (978-0-660-19225-3(X)) Pub: Canadian Broadcasting CAN. Dist(s): Georgetown Term

Parent-Child Dynamics. Ginger Chalford. 1 cass. (Running Time: 90 min.). 1988. 8.95 (642) Am Fed Astrologers.

Parent-Child Relationship. Elbert Willis. 1 cass. (Keys to a Successful Marriage Ser.). 4.00; 4.00 Fill the Gap.

Parent Fuel. Barry St. Clair. Prod. by Reach Out Youth Solutions Staff. (ENG.). 2008. audio compact disk 29.99 (978-1-931617-32-1(5)) Pub: Reach Out Youth. Dist(s): STL Dist NA

Parent Package of Songs: Delivered with Love. unabr. ed. Phyllis U. Hiller. 1 cass. (Running Time: 30 min.). 1992. 10.95 Incl. shell & cover. (978-1-884877-09-4(5), 199215PC) Creat Mats Lib.
Songs & poems about being a parent; coping, humor & love.

Parent Swap. unabr. ed. Terence Blacker. Read by Tom Lawrence. 6 CDs. (Running Time: 5 hrs. 59 mins.). (YA). (gr. 6-9). 2006. audio compact disk 59.95 (978-1-4056-5532-3(1), Chivers Child Audio) AudioGO.

Parent Talk with Chris Johnson: The Power of Nutrition to Shape Your Child's Life. Interview. Interview with Nancy Smorch. Featuring Chris Johnson. 1 cass. (Running Time: 60 mins.). 2001. 14.95 (978-0-9723451-1-8(6)); audio compact disk 14.95 (978-0-9723451-2-5(4)) N American Parenting Inst.
By listening to this program, you will learn: How to avoid such health issues as attention deficit disorder and hyperactivityHow to ensure your kids have a more sustained energy level throughout the dayEasy ways to make sure your kids get all of the key vitamins and minerals they needHow to utilize the power of nutrition to enhance your whole family's health and performanceAn easy to implement plan to help you make these changes part of your every day life.

Parent Traps: How to Recognize, Avoid, & Escape the Most Frequent Parental Pitfalls. Brian Sullivan. 3 CDs. 2006. audio compact disk 15.00 (978-1-57399-293-0(3)) Mac Hammond.
Parenting - It's not for cowards. Yet even for the brave, parenting isn't without its pitfalls. How can you avoid these "parent traps" so common to the family? Join Brian Sullivan as he shares what he has observed through his many years as a principal, pastor and parent. Ensure the footing of your family's future by learning to avoid these Parent Traps.

Parent You Want to Be: Who You Are Matters More Than What You Do. unabr. ed. Les Parrott, III & Leslie Parrott. (Running Time: 3 hrs. 30 mins. 0 sec.). (ENG.). 2007. 19.49 (978-0-310-27978-5(X)) Zondervan.

Parental Frustration & Family Rules. Charles B. Beckert. 1 cass. 5.98 (06003303) Covenant Comms.
Tells it like it is with insightful helps.

Parental Guidance, Vol. 33. Jayne Helle. 1 cass. (Running Time: 28 min.). 1996. 15.00 (978-1-891826-32-0(8)) Introspect.
Guides parents in helping their child develop into a healthy, happy adult.

Parental Rights & Education. Read by Charles E. Rice. 1 cass. 3.00 (123) ISI Books.

Parental Rights & Education Panel Discussion see State Intervention in the Family & Parental Rights, Pt. 2, A Psychological Assessment

Parental Rights & the Life Issues, Pt. 1. Ed. by Thomas J. Marzen. (121) ISI Books.

Parental Rights & the Life Issues, Pt. 2. Read by Thomas J. Marzen. 1 cass. 3.00 (122) ISI Books.

Parental Rights & the Life Issues Panel Discussion. Read by George S. Swan et al. (122) ISI Books.

Parental Rights in Education. Michael J. McHugh. 1 cass. (Running Time: 1 hr.). 2002. 5.00 (CLP89524) Christian Liberty.
It is very common for home educators to ask, "How do I know if home education is legal in my state?" Instructs parents regarding the topic of parental rights in education.

***Parenthood by Proxy.** abr. ed. Laura Schlessinger. Read by Laura Schlessinger. (ENG.). 2004. (978-0-06-081324-6(5), Harper Audio); (978-0-06-075570-6(9), Harper Audio) HarperCollins Pubs.

Parenthood by Proxy: Don't Have Them If You Won't Raise Them. abr. ed. Laura Schlessinger. Read by Laura Schlessinger. 2 cass. (Running Time: 3 hrs.). 2000. 18.00 (978-0-694-52145-6(0)); 20.00 (978-0-694-52321-4(6)) HarperCollins Pubs.

Parenthood by Proxy: Don't Have Them If You Won't Raise Them. unabr. ed. Laura Schlessinger. Narrated by Barbara Caruso. 7 cass. (Running Time: 10 hrs.). 2000. 65.00 (978-0-7887-4856-1(4), 96431E7) Recorded Bks.
Offering compelling evidence of widespread neglect of children the author condemns excuses given by many parents, special interest groups & professionals & she addresses the serious issues that contribute to the childhood crisis including the high divorce rate, single parenting, dual-career families & the acceptance of immoral behavior. In contrast to the prevailing culture, she exhorts us to make our children our top priority even if we must radically change our lives.

Parenthood by Proxy: Don't Have Them If You Won't Raise Them. unabr. ed. Laura Schlessinger. Narrated by Barbara Caruso. 9 CDs. (Running Time: 10 hrs.). 2001. audio compact disk 89.00 (978-0-7887-6181-2(1), C1406) Recorded Bks.
Offering compelling evidence of widespread neglect of children, the author condemns excuses given by many parents, special interest groups & professionals. And she addresses the serious issues that contribute to this childhood crisis including the high divorce rate, single parenting, dual-career families & the acceptance of immoral behavior. In contrast to the prevailing culture, she exhorts us to make our children our top priority even if we must radically change our lives. Each weekday on the country's number one radio program, Dr. Laura Schlessinger advises millions of people with her answers to tough ethical & moral questions. In this provocative book, she encourages parents as she guides them through the perils of contemporary life. Barbara Caruso's thought-provoking performance will fill you with a fresh determination to get actively involved in your children's hearts, minds & souls.

Parenting. John E. Bradshaw. (Running Time: 21600 sec.). 2008. audio compact disk 140.00 (978-1-57388-287-3(9)) J B Media.

Parenting. Pia Mellody. Read by Pia Mellody. 3 cass. 25.00 Set. (A4) Featuka Enter Inc.
Discusses healthy vs. unhealthy parenting, how to heal & reparent the inner wounded child & how to effectively parent our own children at any age.

Parenting: From Surviving to Thriving. 2006. audio compact disk 42.00 (978-1-57972-740-6(9)) Insight Living.

Parenting: Program from Award Winning Public Radio Series. Interview. Hosted by Fred Goodwin. Comment by John Hockenberry. 1 CD. (Running Time: 1 hr). 2000. audio compact disk 21.95 (978-1-932479-78-2(3), LCM 102) Lichtenstein Creat.
We all have questions about what makes a good parent. Theories come and go with every generation, but what concrete advice can experts give us? In this program, we talk to Dr. Marguerite Barratt, director of Michigan State University's Institute for Children, Youth and Families about parenting young children, and to Dr. Harold Koplowicz, director and founder of the New York University Child Study Center, about raising teenagers. We'll also hear from Judith Rich Harris, author of The Nurture Assumption, on just how much influence parents really have. Plus, a visit to a parenting workshop by popular authors Adele Faber and Elaine Mazlish, a discussion with best-selling author Annie Lamott, a performance by children's singer and songwriter Laurie Berkner, and commentary by John Hockenberry.

Parenting: When Rules & Consequences Are Not Enough. Gary Applegate. 1 cass. 1986. 10.00 Berringer Pub.
Skill Development's founder, Dr. Gary Applegate, presents the unique Skill Development approach to successful change.

Parenting: from Surviving to Thriving see Crianza de los Hijos: De Sobrevivir a Prosperar

Parenting Infants & Toddlers Without Going Nuts. Maria M. Marinakis. Perf. by Jerry Metellus. 2 cass., 1 CD. (Running Time: 2 hrs. 30 min.). 1999. CD Incl. pamphlet. Maria M Marinakis.

Parenting Is A Ministry. 6 CDs. 2004. audio compact disk (978-0-9767967-1-8(6)) Family Discipleship.

Parenting Isn't for Cowards: The 'You Can Do It' Guide for Hassled Parents from America's Best-Loved Family Advocate. James C. Dobson. Read by Mike Trout. 2 cass. (Running Time: 2 hrs.). 1988. 14.99 (978-2-01-052000-6(9)) Nelson.

Parenting Isn't for Cowards: The 'You Can Do It' Guide for Hassled Parents from America's Best-Loved Family Advocate. James C. Dobson. Narrated by John McDonough. 7 CDs. (Running Time: 7 hrs. 30 mins.). audio compact disk 69.00 (978-1-4025-3502-4(3)) Recorded Bks.

Parenting Isn't for Cowards: The 'You Can Do It' Guide for Hassled Parents from America's Best-Loved Family Advocate. unabr. ed. James C. Dobson. Narrated by John McDonough. 5 cass. (Running Time: 7 hrs. 30 mins.). 2001. 48.00 (978-0-7887-8868-0(X)) Recorded Bks.
Acknowledging that some youngsters are more challenging than others, Dr. Dobson offers valuable advice on maintaining sanity and banishing guilt.

Parenting; Marriage. H. E. Rinpoche. Read by Barry Spacks. 1 cass. (Running Time: 43 min.). (Mirror of Freedom Ser.: Nos. 6 & 7). 7.00 (PP-AVMF1) Padma Pub CA.

Parenting on Purpose: Red*Yellow*Green Framework for Respectful Discipline. 4 cassettes. 2004. 19.95 (978-0-9752599-2-4(X)) Cran Pubs.

Parenting or Adoption? A black woman's Journey. Hosted by Mardie Caldwell. (ENG.). 2008. audio compact disk 19.95 (978-1-935176-00-8(5)) Pub: Am Carrage Hse Pubng. Dist(s): STL Dist NA

Parenting outside the box Audio. As told by Diane Hawkins Summers. (ENM.). 2006. audio compact disk 24.95 (978-0-9774866-2-5(1)) summervle sprt inc.

Parenting Passages. abr. ed. David R. Veerman. Narrated by Mike Trout. 2 cass. 1994. 14.99 Set. (978-0-8423-7432-3(9)) Tyndale Hse.
Every parenting situation, just like every child, is unique. Yet this book maps out basic stages in the parenting process that any parent can expect to pass through.

Parenting Prescriptions. Scripts. Glenn I. Latham. 2 cass. (Running Time: 2 hours). 1993. 16.95 (978-0-9725742-6-6(3)) P T ink.
Illustrations of situations that arise between parents and children which commonly lead to angry confrontations. Principles are illustrated which teach a better way of responding that will achieve the desired outcome while maintaining a peaceful and loving relationship. It can be done!.

Parenting Protocol: Love, Guide, Let Go. Created by Barry Neil Kaufman et al. (ENG.). 2007. audio compact disk 150.00 (978-0-9798105-4-1(X)) Option Inst.

Parenting Skills. unabr. ed. Jennifer James. Read by Jennifer James. 1 cass. (Running Time: 1 hr. 30 min.). 1984. 9.95 (978-0-915423-10-1(3)) Jennifer J.
Parenting is one of life's most difficult jobs. Analyze your willingness to be flexible, check your parents' patterns, learn why children misbehave & develop strategies for better parenting.

Parenting Teens. JoAnn Hibbert Hamilton. 1 cass. 1999. 9.95 (978-1-57734-449-0(9), 06005926) Covenant Comms.
Fifteen keys to building better relationships with your teen.

Parenting Teens. Stephen Wood. 2 cass. (Running Time: 3 hrs.). 1997. 14.95 (978-0-9658582-9-8(4)) Family Life Ctr.

Parenting Teens with Love & Logic. 2003. audio compact disk 24.95 (978-1-930429-33-8(9)) Pub: Love Logic. Dist(s): Penton Overseas

Parenting Teens with Love & Logic. 2006. (978-1-930429-88-8(6)) Love Logic.

Parenting Teens with Love & Logic: Preparing Adolescents for Responsibile Adulthood. abr. ed. Foster W. Cline & Jim Fay. Read by Tim Kenney & Bert Gurule. 4 cass. (Running Time: 4 hrs. 30 min.). 1997. 24.95 (978-0-944634-41-7(9)) Pub: Love Logic. Dist(s): Penton Overseas
Provides parents with simple techniques & practical solutions needed for dealing with many common teenage situations since teens today are faced with pressures & influences that were unheard of in their parents' day.

Parenting Tool Kit. Dale Simpson. 1 cass. 1997. 25.00 (978-1-880892-97-8(9)) Bookmark NY.

Parenting with Intimacy Audio. 2000. (978-1-893307-05-6(0)) Intimacy Pr.

Parenting with Love & Logic. 2006. (978-1-930429-86-4(X)) Love Logic.

Parenting with Love & Logic. Foster W. Cline & Jim Fay. 4 cass. (Running Time: 5 hrs.). (Parenting Ser.). 1997. 24.95 Love Logic.

Parenting with Love & Logic: Teaching Children Responsibility. abr. ed. Jim Fay & Foster W. Cline. Read by Tim Kenney & Bert Gurule. 4 cass. (Running Time: 3 hrs. 30 min.). 1997. 24.95 (978-0-944634-38-7(9)) Pub: Love Logic. Dist(s): Penton Overseas
Puts the fun back into parenting while still raising children who are self-confident, motivated & ready for the real world.

Parenting with Love & Logic: Teaching Children Responsibility. unabr. ed. Jim Fay & Foster W. Cline. Read by Tim Kenney. 3 CDs. (Running Time: 3 hrs. 30 mins.). 2000. audio compact disk 21.95 (978-1-930429-10-9(X)) Pub: Love Logic. Dist(s): Penton Overseas

Parenting without Fear: 2007 CCEF Annual Conference. Featuring Smith Winston. (ENG.). 2007. audio compact disk 11.99 (978-1-934885-10-9(X)) New Growth Pr.

Parenting Your Adult Child: How You Can Help Them Achieve Their Full Potential. Ross Campbell & Gary Chapman. Ed. by Julie-Allyson Ieron. Prod. by Andrew Bee-Koksan. 2 cass. (ENG.). 1999. 14.99 (978-1-881273-89-9(X)) Pub: Northfield Pub. Dist(s): Moody

***Parenting 101: All We Wanted Was A Baby to Hold!** 2010. audio compact disk (978-0-9826360-1-5(6)) Mid A Bks & Tapes.

Parents & Children: Our Most Difficult Classroom. Kenneth Wapnick. 5CDs. 2005. audio compact disk 29.00 (978-1-59142-195-5(0), CD113) Foun Miracles.

Parents & Children: Our Most Difficult Classroom. Kenneth Wapnick. 1 CD. (Running Time: 4 hrs. 45 mins. 40 secs.). 2007. 23.00 (978-1-59142-318-8(X), 3m113) Foun Miracles.

Parents & Teenagers: Tuning In to Talk. Harriet Fisher. 1 cass. 10.95 (978-0-88432-232-0(7), AF1902) J Norton Pubs.
Offers a creative approach to communicating with your teenager.

Parents & Their Children: Teaching Package Teacher's Resource CD. Verdene Ryder & Celia A. Decker. (gr. 9-12). tchr. ed. 200.00 (978-1-59070-121-8(6)) Goodheart.

Parent's Guide for Raising Spiritually Mature Teenagers. Greg Grimwood. 2007. audio compact disk 19.99 (978-1-60247-939-5(9)) Tate Pubng.

Parent's Guide to Harry Potter. unabr. ed. Gina Burkhart. 2 CDs. (Running Time: 2 hrs. 36 mins. 0 sec.). (ENG.). 2005. audio compact disk 15.98 (978-1-59644-332-7(4), Hovel Audio) christianaud.
Harry Potter has captivated the imagination of millions of children. And Harry Potter has caused controversy in churches and schools. What's a parent to do with the magical, mystical world of Harry and his friends? Gina Burkart chose to read the books with her own children. As they read together, she discovered many parallels between Christian faith and the themes of these books. Indeed, the escapades of Harry Potter sparked significant conversation between Burkart and her kids. In this helpful, entertaining guide, Burkart shows how Harry Potter fits into the tradition of fairy tale writing and how this type of literature aids in building a moral framework. She highlights specific situations and emotions from Harry's world that children face in their own life, such as fear, anger, bullies, divinity and the choice of good over evil. Instead of magic words or easy answers, Burkart offers solid, practical advice for helping parents and children navigate Harry Potter's world - and our own - together.

***Parents Guide to Harry Potter.** unabr. ed. Gina Burkhart. Narrated by Kate Reading. (ENG.). 2005. 9.98 (978-1-59644-333-4(2), Hovel Audio) christianaud.

***Parent's Guide to Helping Teenagers in Crisis.** unabr. ed. Miles V. Van Pelt & Jim Hancock. (Running Time: 6 hrs. 28 mins. 0 sec.). (ENG.). 2009. 12.99 (978-0-310-77214-9(1)) Zondervan.

Parent's Guide to the College Recruiting Process. Ed. by Stephen J. Brennan. 18.95 (978-0-9619230-6-8(7)) Peak Perf Pub.

Parent's Guide to the SAT & ACT. Linda Bizer & Geraldine Markel. 2007. audio compact disk 26.95 (978-0-9791279-1-5(2)) Managing Mind.

Parents' Home Companion. Perf. by Cathy Fink & Marcy Marxer. 1 cass. (Running Time: 36 min.). (Family Ser.). (J). 1995. 9.98 (978-1-886767-01-0(7), 8031); audio compact disk 14.98 (978-1-886767-00-3(9), 8031) Rounder Records.
This recording is not simply for those new to parenthood, anyone who has ever argued across the generation gap will identify with these universal themes: the sixteen year old teen, the overwhelmed aunt or uncle, or the great-grandparent. Even those who have sworn never to have kids.

Parents in the Special Education Process Series. Reed Martin. 3 cass. (Running Time: 2 hrs. 26 min.). 1992. 37.50 Leo Media.
Tape 1: The role congress expect parents to play; Tape 2: The parent in the IEP; Tape 3: Seeking services in the least restrictive environment.

Parents Serve Children: Psalms 127-128. Ed Young. 1986. 4.95 (978-0-7417-1545-6(7), 545) Win Walk.

Parents with Special Needs Children. Wanda M. Allen. 1 cd. 2006. audio compact disk 20.00 (978-1-59971-523-0(6)) AardGP.
Parents With Special Needs Children is special to my heart. As a parent my son had Speech & Language Delays and my daughter has Developmental Delays. Many families are suffering from some type of special need and disability with their children. Whether it is Autism, Downs Syndrome, Deafness, Blindness, Mental Retardation, learning Disabilities, PDD and more. This powerful CD will pray for you and your present special need situation. You will learn to breathe and meditate on the Lord. You will hear a magnificent testimony on how good God has been in the lives of my children with special needs. You will receive information, resources, and support for your family.

Parfum, Set. Patrick Süskind. Read by G. Bejean et al. 6 cass. (FRE.). 1992. 43.95 (1629-VSL) Olivia & Hill.
The bizarre story of a man born without a sense of smell who concocts perfumes that can lead men to love or to hate.

***parfum de Printemps.** abr. ed. Thierry Gallier. (Collection Decouverte). (FRE.). 2009. audio compact disk (978-2-09-032687-1(5)) Cle Intl FRA.

Paris. pap. bk. 28.50 (978-88-7754-744-6(8)) Pub: Cideb ITA. Dist(s): Distribks Inc

Paris: St-Germain-des-Pres. Interview. 1. (Running Time: 50 mins). Dramatization. 2003. audio compact disk 10.00 (978-0-9743204-4-1(7)) Oversampling.
Each SoundWalk CD is 50 minutes of walking discovery through neighborhoods, guided by a local personality, packed full of interviews and cinematic sound effects.

Paris: The Left Bank. unabr. ed. Andrew Flack. Read by Barbara Duff & Denis J. Sullivan. 1 cass. (Running Time: 1 hr.). (Day Ranger Walking Adventures on Audio Cassette Ser.). 1989. 19.95 (978-1-877894-02-2(8)) Day Ranger.
Scripted dialogue & music to accompany an original walking route of Montparnasse & St.-Germaine. Uses first hand accounts, eyewitness stories & brief excerpts of identified literature. Detailed maps included.

Paris & the Parisians. Frances Trollope. Narrated by Flo Gibson. (ENG.). 2007. 41.95 (978-1-55685-952-6(X)) Audio Bk Con.

Paris Drake's Hypnosis for Relaxation. Scripts. Paris Drake. 1 CD. (Running Time: 40 mins.). 2004. audio compact disk 17.95 (978-0-9759752-1-3(8)) Xanadu New Age.
Hypnosis For Relaxation, Stress, & Anxiety Management. Home Use.

Paris Drake's Hypnosis for Smoking Cessation. Scripts. Paris Drake. 1 CD. (Running Time: 40 mins.). 2004. audio compact disk 17.95 (978-0-9759752-2-0(6)) Xanadu New Age.
Hypnosis To Assist listner with the desire to stop smoking. Home Use.

Paris Drake's Hypnosis for Weight Loss. Scripts. 1 CD. (Running Time: 40 mins.). 2004. 15.95 (978-0-9759752-3-7(4)) Xanadu New Age.
Hypnosis to assist listner with success in weight loss. Home use.

Paris in the Fifties, Stanley Karnow. Read by Christopher Hurt. 9 cass. (Running Time: 13 hrs.). 1998. 62.95 (978-0-7861-1350-7(2), 2253) Blckstn Audio.
"Paris in the Fifties" transports us to Latin Quarter cafes & basement jazz clubs, to unheated apartments & glorious ballrooms. We get to know illustrious intellectuals, among them Jean-Paul Sartre, Simone de Beauvoir, & Albert Camus. We meet Christian Dior, who taught Karnow the secrets of haute couture, & Prince Curnonsky, France's leading gourmet, who taught the young reporter to appreciate the complexities of haute cuisine. Karnow takes us to marathon murder trials in musty courtrooms, accompanies a group of tipsy wine connoisseurs on a tour of the Beaujolais vineyards, & recalls the famous automobile race at Le Mans when a catastrophic accident killed more than eighty spectators.

Paris Never Leaves You. unabr. ed. Adreana Robbins. Read by Lloyd James & Marguerite Gavin. 13 cass. (Running Time: 19 hrs.). 1999. 85.95 (978-0-7861-1630-0(7), 2458) Blckstn Audio.
A stunned Djuna Cortez has just inherited the estate of eccentric artist Joaquim Carlos Cortez - & learned that he is her grandfather. She falls in love with a handsome winemaker who seems to be the man of her dreams, but discovers that she is living a nightmare. She finds salvation in reading her grandfather's journals which spin a mesmerizing tale of the young artist in 1930's Paris, facing with the rest of the city the advance of Nazi forces. From her grandfather's struggles & tragedies, Djuna gathers the strength to finally break free from her abusive husband & take the steps necessary to preserve her life, her sanity, her fortune & her grandfather's powerful artistic legacy.

Paris Option. abr. ed. Robert Ludlum & Gayle Lynds. Read by Paul Michael. (Running Time: 6 hrs. 0 mins. 0 sec.). (Covert-One Ser.). (ENG.). 2006. audio compact disk 14.95 (978-1-59397-927-0(4)) Pub: Macmill Audio. Dist(s): Macmillan

Paris Option. unabr. ed. Robert Ludlum & Gayle Lynds. 12 cass. (Running Time: 18 hrs.). (Covert-One Ser.). 2002. 96.00 (978-0-7366-8664-8(9)); audio compact disk 120.00 (978-0-7366-8665-5(7)) Books on Tape.
An explosion in the middle of the night reduces part of Paris's esteemed Pasteur Institute to rubble. Among the missing is the world's top computer scientist, Emile Chambord. Many in the intelligence community suspect that the scientist was kidnapped and the bomb set to divert attention. Chambord may have been close to completing a molecular computer, which, in the wrong hands, could be the most deadly weapon in the world. Suddenly mysterious events start to occur: U.S. fighter jets disappear from radar screens, utilities across the Western states cease functioning, and telecommunications come to a halt, with devastating consequences.

Paris Option. unabr. rev. ed. Robert Ludlum & Gayle Lynds. Read by Paul Michael. 12 CDs. (Running Time: 15 hrs. 0 mins. 0 sec.). (Covert-One Ser.). (ENG., 2002. audio compact disk 48.00 (978-1-55927-712-9(2)) Pub: Macmill Audio. Dist(s): Macmillan

Paris-Paree: Claudia Hommel Dans son Cabaret. Perf. by Claudia Hommel & Duke Ellington. Contrib. by Edith Piaf et al. (J). (gr. 7-12). 1997. 10.00 (978-0-9657493-0-5(4)); audio compact disk 15.00 (978-0-9657493-1-2(2)) Maison Clobert.
Musical performance of French & American cabaret songs about Paris, France & related themes.

Paris Stories. unabr. ed. Mavis Gallant. Read by Lorna Raver & Yuri Rasovsky. (Running Time: 61200 sec.). 2006. audio compact disk 44.95 (978-0-7861-7262-7(2)) Blckstn Audio.

Paris Stories. unabr. ed. Mavis Gallant. Read by Lorna Raver & Yuri Rasovsky. Selected by Michael Ondaatje. (Running Time: 61200 sec.). 2006. 89.95 (978-0-7861-4759-5(8)); audio compact disk 120.00 (978-0-7861-6343-4(7)) Blckstn Audio.

Paris Tapes. Narrated by Juliet Stevenson. 2 cass. (Running Time: 2 hrs.). 1998. 16.95 Set, incl. map. (978-1-900652-01-8(3)) Capital VA.
Travel back in time to experience the sights, sounds & events of Paris' past at sixteen historic sites. In Paris, be roused to revolution by Desmoulins; meet Picasso & his friends while sipping coffee in Montmartre; celebrate the liberation of Paris with DeGaulle at the Arc de Triomphe.

Paris to the Moon. unabr. ed. Adam Gopnik. Read by Adam Gopnik. (YA). 2007. 34.99 (978-1-60252-510-8(2)) Find a World.

Paris to the Moon. unabr. abr. ed. Adam Gopnik. Read by Adam Gopnik. 4 CDs. (Running Time: 5 hrs.). (ENG.). 2001. audio compact disk 29.95 (978-1-56511-492-0(2), 1565114922) Pub: HighBridge. Dist(s): Workman Pub

***Paris Trout.** abr. ed. Pete Dexter. Read by Charles S. Dutton. (ENG.). 2007. (978-0-06-128736-7(9), Harper Audio); (978-0-06-128735-0(0), Harper Audio) HarperCollins Pubs.

Paris Vendetta. abr. ed. Steve Berry. Read by Scott Brick. (ENG.). 2009. audio compact disk 32.00 (978-0-7393-2916-0(2), Random AudioBks) Pub: Random Audio Pubg. Dist(s): Random

***Paris Vendetta.** abr. ed. Steve Berry. Read by Scott Brick. (ENG.). 2010. audio compact disk 14.99 (978-0-307-91422-4(4), Random AudioBks) Pub: Random Audio Pubg. Dist(s): Random

Paris Vendetta. unabr. ed. Steve Berry. Read by Scott Brick. (ENG.). 2009. audio compact disk 50.00 (978-0-7393-2918-4(9), Random AudioBks) Pub: Random Audio Pubg. Dist(s): Random

***Paris Vendetta.** unabr. ed. Steve Berry. Read by Scott Brick. 11 CDs. (Running Time: 13 hrs. 30 mins.). 2009. audio compact disk 100.00 (978-1-4159-6537-5(4), BksonTape) Pub: Random Audio Pubg. Dist(s): Random

***Paris Wife: A Novel.** unabr. ed. Paula McClain. (ENG.). 2011. audio compact disk 40.00 (978-0-307-87718-5(3), Random AudioBks) Pub: Random Audio Pubg. Dist(s): Random

Paris 1919: Six Months That Changed the World. unabr. ed. Margaret MacMillan. Narrated by Suzanne Toren. 2003. 148.00 (978-1-4025-5650-0(0)) Recorded Bks.

Paris 1919: Six Months That Changed the World. unabr. collector's ed. Margaret MacMillan. Narrated by Suzanne Toren. 18 cass. (Running Time: 26 hrs.). 2003. 69.95 (978-1-4025-5651-7(9), RG647) Recorded Bks.
At the close of WWI, between January and July of 1919, delegates from around the world converged on Paris under the auspices of peace. New countries were created, old empires were dissolved, and for six months, Paris was the center of the world. Bringing to vivid life the individuals who participated in the great Peace Conference - including Woodrow Wilson, Winston Churchill, Lawrence of Arabia, and Ho Chi Minh - Paris 1919 is a landmark work of narrative history.

Paris 1990. Aristide Bruant. Contrib. by Mouloudji. 1 cass. (Running Time: 90 mins.). (FRE.). 1991. 21.95 (1320-LQP) Olivia & Hill.
Aristide Bruant was a flamboyant figure in Paris at the turn of the century. Dressed in black, sporting a large black hat & a red scarf, he wrote about Paris street life: prostitutes, tramps, girls in caberets.

Parish Churches: East Anglia (South): Parish Churches of Suffolk & Neighbouring Districts. P. G. Lindley & A. Moseley. (English Parish Churches Ser.: Vol. 78). 2002. audio compact disk 96.00 (978-2-503-51047-7(7)) Pub: Brepols Pub BEL. Dist(s): David Brown

Parish Pastor & Chaplain. Lawrence Holst. 1986. 10.80 (0104B) Assn Prof Chaplains.

***Parish Priest.** abr. ed. Douglas Brinkley & Julie M. Fenster. Read by Julie M. Fenster. (ENG.). 2006. (978-0-06-087830-6(4), Harper Audio); (978-0-06-087829-0(0), Harper Audio) HarperCollins Pubs.

Parish Priest: Father Michael McGivney & American Catholicism. unabr. abr. ed. Douglas Brinkley & Julie M. Fenster. Read by Julie M. Fenster. (Running Time: 21600 sec.). (SPA.). 2006. audio compact disk 29.95 (978-0-06-085340-2(9)) HarperCollins Pubs.

Parish Priests & Practicing Physicians: Common Contemporary Challenges, Set. Joseph M. Champlin et al. 3 cass. (Running Time: 2 hrs. 6 min.). 1999. 29.95 (TAH424) Alba Hse Comns.
Specific topics: Is every patient or parishioner a potential enemy?; Are HMOs helping or hurting?.

Parish Retreat: A Time of Grace. Michael Sullivan. 4 cass. 34.95 (9289) Franciscan Comns.
Discussion of inspirational nature which includes the 'Healing Love of Jesus', ' The Call of the Church'. & 'Our Response to Christs Call'.

***Parisians: An Adventure History of Paris.** unabr. ed. Graham Robb. (Running Time: 12 hrs. 0 mins.). 2010. 34.99 (978-1-4001-9710-1(4)); 17.99 (978-1-4001-8710-2(9)) Tantor Media.

***Parisians: An Adventure History of Paris.** unabr. ed. Graham Robb. Narrated by Simon Vance. (Running Time: 14 hrs. 0 mins. 0 sec.). (ENG.). 2010. 24.99 (978-1-4001-6710-4(8)); audio compact disk 69.99 (978-1-4001-4710-6(7)); audio compact disk 34.99 (978-1-4001-1710-9(0)) Pub: Tantor Media. Dist(s): IngramPubServ

Pariswalks. abr. ed. Alison Landes & Sonia Landes. Prod. by Carol Shapiro. 1 cass. Sound Trvl FRA.
Travel guide - walking tour of Paris.

Pariswalks. unabr. ed. Sonia Landes & Alison Landes. Narrated by Gates McFadden. 2 cass. (Running Time: 3 hrs.). 18.00 (978-1-890489-00-7(X), 833561) Pub: Sound Trvl FRA. Dist(s): Penton Overseas
Features four walking tours and maps.

Pariswalks, Set. Sonia Landes & Alison Landes. Read by Gates McFadden. 2 cass. 1997. 18.00 Map inclu. Pub: Sound Trvl FRA. Dist(s): Penton Overseas

Park Your Car in Harvard Yard. unabr. ed. Israel Horovitz. Perf. by Judith Ivey et al. 1 cass. (Running Time: 1 hr. 40 mins.). 2001. 20.95 (978-1-58081-012-8(8), TPT22) L A Theatre.
Jacob Brackish, the toughest, meanest teacher ever to set foot in Gloucester High School is dying at home. His advertisement for a housekeeper to look after him during his final year is answered by a mousy forty year old named Katherine, a woman Jacob has forgotten he flunked years before.

Park Your Car in Harvard Yard. unabr. ed. Israel Horovitz. Read by Jason Robards & Judith Ivey. 2 CDs. (Running Time: 1 hr. 40 mins.). 2001. audio compact disk 25.95 (978-1-58081-196-5(5), CDTPT22) L A Theatre.
Jacob Brackish, a teacher straight out of a childhood nightmare, is old & alone. Kathleen Hogan, a student who he long ago failed, answers his ad for a housekeeper. Her knock at his door marks the start of a funny & touching relationship & a journey from bitterness to understanding.

Parker Pyne Investigates. unabr. ed. Agatha Christie. Narrated by Hugh Fraser. (Running Time: 6 hrs. 0 mins. 0 sec.). (ENG.). 2009. audio compact disk 29.95 (978-1-60283-665-5(5)) Pub: AudioGO. Dist(s): Perseus Dist

Parker's California Probate Code. pap. bk. 41.00 (978-0-327-04354-6(7)) LEXIS Pub.

Parking Lot Picker's Songbook - Dobro Edition. Dix Bruce & Stacy Phillips. (ENG.). 2008. spiral bd. 29.95 (978-0-7866-8018-4(0)) Mel Bay.

Parking Lot Picker's Songbook - Fiddle Edition. D. I. x. Bruce. (ENG.). 2009. spiral bd. 29.99 (978-0-7866-8145-7(4)) Mel Bay.

Parking Lot Picker's Songbook: Guitar Edition. Dix Bruce. 2007. pap. bk. 29.95 (978-0-7866-7498-5(9)) Mel Bay.

Parkinson Disease - A Bibliography & Dictionary for Physicians, Patients, & Genome Researchers. Compiled by Icon Group International, Inc. Staff. 2007. ring bd. 28.95 (978-0-497-11270-7(1)) Icon Grp.

Parkinson's Disease: How to Cope & Live with It. Jace Leach. Read by Neva Duyndam. 1 cass. 1990. 9.95 (978-1-878159-14-4(3)) Duvall Media.
If you have Parkinson's disease or have watched a family member with this progressive, debilitating illness, you will be touched by this narrative written by a man who has learned to live with it.

Parkinson's Disease: Program from the Award Winning Public Radio Series. Hosted by Fred Goodwin. Contrib. by John Hockenberry et al. 1 cass. (Running Time: 1 hr.). (Infinite Mind Ser.). 1999. audio compact disk 21.95 (978-1-888064-21-6(8), LCM 50) Lichtenstein Creat.
Join Dr. Goodwin as we explore what's new in treatment, research, and advocacy for Parkinson's Disease. Learn about tap-dancing to strengthen Parkinsonian's muscles, dogs who help patients with their balance, and the latest research indicating that for most people Parkinson's is NOT a genetic disease. Featured guests include Dr. J. William Langston of the Parkinson's Institute and Jean Samuelson, founder of the Parkinson's Action Network. With commentary from John Hockenberry.

Parkinson's Law. Barry MacGregor & Patrick Watson. Read by Albert Schultz. 1 CD. (Running Time: 3600 sec.). Dramatization. 2007. audio compact disk 15.95 (978-0-660-19673-2(5), CBC Audio) Pub: Canadian Broadcasting CAN. Dist(s): Georgetown Term
Experience this witty, hilarious and biting satire about the weird world of Management and the Workplace. Based on the best-selling book "Parkinson's Law", this one-hour dramatic adaptation is designed for anyone who has ever worked, sat on committees, hired staff or yearned to rise up the ranks of an institution! Above all, it celebrates one of the most well-known of all laws governing bureaucracies: "Work expands to fill the time available for its completion." Starring the ghost of C. Northcote Parkinson (author of the book, "Parkinson's Law") and the celebrated broadcaster Patrick Watson.

Parkinson's Law & the Law & the Profits. unabr. ed. C. Northcote Parkinson. Read by Richard Green. 8 cass. (Running Time: 8 hrs.). 1978. 48.00 (978-0-7366-0150-4(3), 1150) Books on Tape.
"Parkinson's Law" is a critique of managerial bureaucracy. In "The Law & the Profit," Parkinson concludes that there are limits to the collection revenue. He advises greatly reduced taxation to bring about an improvement in public services.

Park's Quest. Katherine Paterson. Read by Jeff Woodman. 3 cass. (Running Time: 4 hrs. 30 mins.). (J). (gr. 5-8). 2000. pap. bk. & stu. ed. 42.24 (978-0-7887-4345-0(7), 41139) Recorded Bks.
Eleven-year-old Park doesn't know much about his family. His father died in the Vietnam War & his mother refuses to talk about relatives. But when Park visits his grandfather in Virginia, instead of answers, he finds more unsettling questions.

Park's Quest. unabr. ed. Katherine Paterson. Narrated by Jeff Woodman. 3 pieces. (Running Time: 4 hrs. 30 mins.). (gr. 5 up). 2000. 29.00 (978-0-7887-4239-2(6), 96193E7) Recorded Bks.

Park's Quest, Class Set. Katherine Paterson. Read by Jeff Woodman. 3 cass. (Running Time: 4 hrs. 30 mins.). (J). (gr. 5-8). 2000. 99.70 (978-0-7887-4445-7(3), 47136) Recorded Bks.

Parler Au Quotidien. unabr. ed. 2 cass. (Running Time: 2 hrs.). (FRE.). 1992. pap. bk. 39.50 (978-0-88432-524-6(5), SFR290) J Norton Pubs.
Foreign Language Instruction. Thirty original broadcasts by Radio France Internationale.

Parler Au Quotidien, Set. 2 cass., script. (FRE.). 1995. 39.95 (1720-AF) Olivia & Hill.
Selection of 30 radio broadcasts, each one consisting of a dialogue between two radio journalists who discuss with humor the subtleties & nuances of the French language. An entertaining way to enlarge your vocabulary & improve your grammar & pronunciation.

Parler au Quotidien CDs & Text. 2 CDs. (Running Time: 2 hrs.). (FRE.). 2005. audio compact disk 39.50 (978-1-57970-123-9(X), SFR290D) J Norton Pubs.

Parliament of Fowls & Six Lyric Poems. unabr. ed. Geoffrey Chaucer. Perf. by J. B. Bessinger, Jr. 1 cass. (ENM.). 1984. 12.95 (SWC 1226) HarperCollins Pubs.

Parliament of Whores: A Lone Humorist Attempts to Explain the Entire U. S. Government. unabr. ed. P. J. O'Rourke. Read by Christopher Hurt. 6 cass. (Running Time: 8 hrs. 30 mins.). 1991. 44.95 (978-0-7861-0282-2(9), 1248) Blckstn Audio.
A guided tour of the U. S. government & a serious analysis of public policy that not only won't put you to sleep, but will make you laugh until your sides ache & may even make you go out & vote.

Parliamentary Procedure of the U. S. Senate: Capitol Learning Audio Course. Robert Dove. Prod. by TheCapitol.Net. (ENG.). 2008. 47.00 (978-1-58733-076-6(8)) TheCapitol.

***Parliamo Italiano! Secound Edition Cassettes (7)** 2nd ed. Suzanne Branciforte. 2008. 38.95 (978-0-470-43695-0(6), JWiley) Wiley US.

Parloir. 1 cass. (Running Time: 60 mins.). Dramatization. (Maitres du Mystere Ser.). (FRE.). 1996. 11.95 (1842-MA) Olivia & Hill.
Popular radio thriller, interpreted by France's best actors.

Parlons Francais, Level 1. Valentin Kameneff. 10 cass. (FRE.). 175.00 (Natl Textbk Co) M-H Contemporary.
Develops the conversational ability students need to get along comfortably in French. Using immediate classroom situations, along with real-life experiences, students quickly learn to converse & acquire the cultural awareness needed to interact with confidence in casual, social & work situations.

Parlons Francais, Level 2. Valentin Kameneff. 10 cass. (FRE.). 150.00 (978-0-8325-9668-1(X), Natl Textbk Co) M-H Contemporary.

***Parlor Games.** abr. ed. Jess Michaels & Leda Swann. Read by Erica Bell et al. (ENG.). 2006. (978-0-06-121513-1(9), Harper Audio); (978-0-06-123555-9(5), Harper Audio) HarperCollins Pubs.

Parnassus on Wheels. Christopher Morley. Read by Nadia May. 3 cass. (Running Time: 4 hrs.). 2000. 23.95 (978-0-7861-1884-7(9), 2683); audio compact disk 24.00 (978-0-7861-9806-1(0), 2683) Blckstn Audio.
The story of a marvelous man, small in stature, wiry as a cat, yet Olympic in personality.

Parnassus on Wheels. unabr. ed. Christopher Morley. Read by Flo Gibson. 3 cass. (Running Time: 3 hrs. 30 mins.). 1996. 16.95 (978-1-55685-423-1(4)) Audio Bk Con.
A horse drawn bookmobile, an eccentric literary fanatic & a middle-aged housekeeper are united by adventure & love.

Parochial & Plain Sermons. unabr. ed. John Henry Newman. Read by Rip Light et al. 60 cass. 216.00 set. (942) Ignatius Pr.
All eight volumes of Cardinal Newman's sermons are challenging & inspiring listening. In four parts, each containing two volumes.

Paroi, Set. Pierre Moustier. 3 cass. (FRE.). 1995. 34.95 (1748-LV) Olivia & Hill.
Two climbers who hate one another find themselves stuck on the face of a mountain. Only by cooperating can they survive. A cast of actors reads this winner of the Grand Prize of Books on Sports.

Paroles. Sally Sieloff Magnan. 1999. bk. 160.95 (978-0-470-00461-6(4), JWiley) Wiley US.

Paroles. Sally Sieloff Magnan. 1999. bk. 128.85 (978-0-470-00470-8(3), JWiley) Wiley US.

Paroles. Sally Sieloff Magnan et al. (FRE.). 1999. pap. bk. (978-0-03-020778-5(9)); pap. bk. & lab manual ed. (978-0-03-020794-5(0)) Harcourt Coll Pubs.

Paroles. 2nd ed. Sally Sieloff Magnan. (ENG.). (C). 2001. stu. ed. 116.95 (978-0-470-00414-2(2), JWiley) Wiley US.

Paroles. 3rd ed. Sally Sieloff Magnan et al. 2005. 12.95 (978-0-471-74113-8(2), JWiley) Wiley US.

Paroles: Tapescript. Sally Sieloff Magnan. 1999. pap. bk. 32.95 (978-0-470-00258-2(1), JWiley) Wiley US.

Paroles: Testing Program. 2nd ed. Sally Sieloff Magnan et al. (FRE.). 1999. pap. bk. (978-0-03-020753-2(3)) Harcourt Coll Pubs.

Paroles Set: Cahier d'Activites, & Video Manual. 2nd ed. Sally Sieloff Magnan et al. (SPA.). 2001. lab manual ed. 115.95 (978-0-470-00580-4(7), JWiley) Wiley US.

Paroles Set: Student Activites Manual & the Video Manual. Sally Sieloff Magnan. 1999. bk. & stu. ed. 179.80 (978-0-470-00474-6(6), JWiley) Wiley US.

Paroles 3rd Edition Lab Audio CDs. Sally Sieloff Magnan et al. (SPA.). (C). 2005. audio compact disk 30.95 (978-0-471-76892-0(8), JWiley) Wiley US.

Parotid Tumors. 2 cass. (Plastic & Maxillofacial Surgery Ser.: C85-PL3). 1985. 15.00 (8582) Am Coll Surgeons.

Parrot & Olivier in America. unabr. ed. Peter Carey. (Running Time: 13 hrs. 30 mins.). 2010. 29.95 (978-1-4417-2978-1(X)); audio compact disk 32.95 (978-1-4417-2977-4(1)) Blckstn Audio.

***Parrot & Olivier in America.** unabr. ed. Peter Carey. (Running Time: 13 hrs. 30 mins.). 2010. 79.95 (978-1-4417-2974-3(7)) Blckstn Audio.

***Parrot & Olivier in America.** unabr. ed. Peter Carey. Read by Humphrey Bower. 11 CDs. (Running Time: 13 hrs. 30 mins.). 2010. audio compact disk 109.00 (978-1-4417-2975-0(5)) Blckstn Audio.

Parrot in the Oven. Victor Martinez. Narrated by Robert Ramirez. 5 CDs. (Running Time: 5 hrs.). (gr. 8 up). audio compact disk 50.00 (978-1-4025-2328-1(9)) Recorded Bks.

Parrot in the Oven: Mi Vida, unabr. ed. Victor Martinez. Narrated by Robert Ramirez. 4 pieces. (Running Time: 5 hrs.). (gr. 8 up). 1998. 35.00 (978-0-7887-2081-9(3), 95434E7) Recorded Bks.
Growing up poor & Mexican-American in southern California is tough, but 14-year-old Manny is determined to make something of his life.

Parrot in the Peppertree. Chris Stewart. 6 vols. (Running Time: 9 hrs.). 2003. 54.95 (978-0-7540-8310-8(1)); audio compact disk 64.95 (978-0-7540-8753-3(0)) Pub: Chivers Audio Bks GBR. Dist(s): AudioGO

Parrot Who Owns Me: The Story of a Relationship. Joanna Burger. 2001. 40.00 (978-0-7366-7056-2(4)) Books on Tape.

Parrots see Gathering of Great Poetry for Children

Parrots. Walberg Pubng.

Parsi Woman: Now Sits the Autumn Cricket in the Grass see Poetry of Edna St. Vincent Millay

Parsi Woman: What Rider Spurs Him from the Darkening East see Poetry of Edna St. Vincent Millay

Parsifal Mosaic, Pt. 1. unabr. collector's ed. Robert Ludlum. Read by Michael Prichard. 9 cass. (Running Time: 13 hrs. 30 min.). 1983. 72.00 (978-0-7366-0810-7(9), 1761-A) Books on Tape.
Michael Havelock, smuggled out of Prague to America as a boy, earns his doctorate at Princeton under the tutelage of a fellow Czech immigrant, Anton Mathias, subsequently a brilliant U.S. Secretary of State. Havelock foregoes his academic career to serve as field agent specializing in espionage & defection for a clandestine branch of the U.S. State Department.

Parsifal Mosaic, Pt. 2. collector's unabr. ed. Robert Ludlum. Read by Michael Prichard. 9 cass. (Running Time: 13 hrs. 30 min.). 1983. 72.00 (978-0-7366-0811-4(7), 1761-B) Books on Tape.

Parson's Daughter. unabr. ed. Catherine Cookson. 12 cass. (Running Time: 18 hrs.). (Sound Ser.). 1994. 94.95 (978-1-85496-057-3(1)) Pub: UlverLrgPrint GBR. Dist(s): Ulverscroft US

Part of Fortune from Cyclic Perspective. Nicki Michaels. 1 cass. 8.95 (229) Am Fed Astrologers.
Integrate Sun-Moon relationship indicated by Pars position.

Part of Me: Stories of a Louisiana Family. Kimberly Willis Holt. Read by Kate Reading. 3. 2006. 24.00 (978-0-7393-3815-5(3)); audio compact disk 32.30 (978-0-7393-3786-8(6)) Pub: Books on Tape. Dist(s): NetLibrary CO

Part of the Family. Pamela Evans. Read by Annie Aldington. 12 cass. (Sound Ser.). (J). 2003. 94.95 (978-1-84283-257-8(3)) Pub: ISIS Lrg Prnt GBR. Dist(s): Ulverscroft US

Part of the Family. Pamela Evans. 11 CDs. (Running Time: 13 hrs.). (Soundings (CDs) Ser.). (J). 2005. audio compact disk 99.95 (978-1-84559-075-8(9)) Pub: ISIS Lrg Prnt GBR. Dist(s): Ulverscroft US

Part of the Furniture. unabr. ed. Mary Wesley. Read by Samuel West. 8 cass. (Running Time: 12 hrs.). 2000. 59.95 (978-0-7540-0133-1(4), CAB 1556) Pub: Chivers Audio Bks GBR. Dist(s): AudioGO
17-year-old Juno Marlowe is caught in a London air raid after saying good-bye to the two shallow men in her life. She is rescued by a frail stranger who offers her shelter. Given this respite from a bleak existence, a series of events takes her to the West Country where she finds peace and will no longer just be part of the furniture.

Part of the Sky. unabr. ed. Robert Newton Peck. Read by Terry Bregy. 2 cass. (Running Time: 3 hrs.). (YA). (gr. 7 up). 1994. 21.95 (978-1-883332-10-5(9)) Audio Bkshelf.
The sequel to A Day No Pigs Would Die, finds a boy determined to fill a man's shoes after the death of his beloved father. Young Rob Peck travels the road to mature understanding & sacrifice.

Part of, Yet Apart From: The Eternal Human Paradox. James F. Bugental. 1 cass. 9.00 (A0341-88) Sound Photosyn.
The featured speaker at the CA Association of Marriage & Family Therapists Convention.

Part-Time Lady. unabr. ed. Ann H. Workman. 3 cass. 1998. 45.95 Set. (978-1-872672-39-7(6)) Pub: Magna Story GBR. Dist(s): Ulverscroft US

Part-Time Law Practice. 1 cass. 1987. 25.00 PA Bar Inst.

Part-time Sinner. Excerpts. Featuring Martin Zender. 1. (Running Time: 62 MIN). 2004. audio compact disk 12.95 (978-0-9709849-2-0(8), 330-454-1061) Pub: Starke Hartmann. Dist(s): Baker Taylor
IN 18 GROUNDBREAKING TRACKS RECORDED LIVE IN NEWPORT NEWS, MARTIN ZENDER EXPOUNDS ON THE SUBJECT OF SIN LIKE YOU'VE NEVER HEARD IT BEFORE. PREPARE TO REST IN CHRIST AND BE FREED FROM YOUR SINS FOREVER.

Part 11 & Computer Validation: The FDA Regulations on Part 11, Electronic Records & Electronic Signatures, for Pharmaceutical, Medical Device, Food, & Cosmetics Manufacturing & GMP (Good Manufacturing Practices) Training, & for Clinical Trials & GCP (Good Clinical Practices), GMP Training Introduction to Meet FDA Regulations in the Use of Computers in Pharmaceutical, Medical Device, Food, & Cosmetics Manufacturing, Daniel Farb & Bruce Gordon. 2004. audio compact disk 299.95 (978-1-932634-57-0(6)) Pub: UnivofHealth. Dist(s): AtlasBooks

Parthenon Enigma. unabr. ed. M. C. Hawke. Read by Jerry Sciarrio. 6 cass. (Running Time: 6 hrs. 36 min.). 2001. 39.95 (978-1-58116-054-3(2)) Books in Motion.
travelling to the Parthenon replica in Nashville to do research for Jake's new international espionage novel, Jake and wife Michelle are swept into grave danger, when Jake's writing and life almost become one.

Partial Portraits, Set. unabr. ed. Henry James. Read by Flo Gibson. 7 cass. (Running Time: 10 hrs. 30 min.). 1989. 25.95 (978-1-55685-149-0(9)) Audio Bk Con.
These essays & critiques concern Emerson, the life of George Eliot, a conversation about "Daniel Deronda," Anthony Trollope, Robert Louis Stevenson, Miss Woolson, Alphonse Dauset, Guy de Mauppassant, Ivan Turgenieff, George du Maurier & a treatise on the art of fiction.

Participating & Becoming: Live Mindfulness & Marsha M. linehan, Ph. D., ABPP, SEattle INtensive 2004-2005, 3. Executive Producer Shree A. Vigil. Prod. by Behavioral Tech. 2005. audio compact disk 15.95 (978-0-9745002-6-3(7)) Behavioral Tech.

Particle Physics: Aspects of Unification Theory. Paul Davies et al. 1 cass. 1990. 12.95 (ECN221) J Norton Pubs.

Particle Physics for Non-physicists Pts. I-II: A Tour of the Microcosmos. Instructed by Steven J. Pollock. 12 cass. (Running Time: 12 hrs.). 2003. bk. 54.95 (978-1-56585-627-1(9), 1247) Teaching Co.

Particle Physics for Non-Physicists Pts. I-II: A Tour of the Microcosmos. Instructed by Steven J. Pollock. 12 CDs. (Running Time: 12 hrs.). 2003. bk. 69.95 (978-1-56585-629-5(5), 1247) Teaching Co.

Parties & Potions. unabr. ed. Sarah Mlynowski. Narrated by Ariadne Meyers. 8 CDs. (Running Time: 10 hrs. 8 mins.). (YA). (gr. 6-8). 2008. audio compact disk 55.00 (978-0-7393-7949-3(6), Listening Lib) Pub: Random Audio Pubg. Dist(s): Random

Parties & Potions. unabr. ed. Sarah Mlynowski. (Magic in Manhattan Ser.: No. 4). (ENG.). (J). (gr. 7). 2008. audio compact disk 40.00 (978-0-7393-7951-6(8), Listening Lib) Pub: Random Audio Pubg. Dist(s): Random

Parties, Predicaments, & Undercover Pets. unabr. ed. Karen McCombie. Read by Daniela Denby-Ashe. 4 CDs. (Running Time: 12600 sec.). (Ally's World Ser.). (J). (gr. 4-9). 2007. audio compact disk 34.95 (978-1-4056-5621-4(2), Chivers Child Audio) AudioGO.

Parties, Rules, & the Evolution of Congressional Budgeting. Lance T. LeLoup. (Parliaments & Legislatures Ser.). 2005. audio compact disk 9.95 (978-0-8142-9086-6(8)) Pub: Ohio St U Pr. Dist(s): Chicago Distribution Ctr

Partimos. Alma Flor Ada. 1 cass. (Running Time: 33 min.). (SPA.). (J). 1987. 3.28 incl. script. (978-0-201-16870-9(7)) Pearson ESL.

Parting. abr. ed. Beverly Lewis. Narrated by Aimee Lilly. (Courtship of Nellie Fisher Ser.: Bk. 1). (ENG.). 2007. 13.99 (978-1-60814-336-8(8)); audio compact disk 19.99 (978-1-59859-247-4(5)) Oasis Audio.

Parting. unabr. ed. Beverly Lewis. Read by Rachel Botchan. 9 cass. (Running Time: 10 hrs. 30 mins.). (Courtship of Nellie Fisher Ser.: Bk. 1). 2008. 72.75 (978-1-4281-7461-0(3)); audio compact disk 102.75 (978-1-4281-7463-4(X)) Recorded Bks.

Parting Blessing. Gary Alan Smith. 2001. bk. 5.00 (978-0-687-08540-8(3)) Abingdon.

Parting the Waters: America in the King Years, Part I - 1954-63. abr. ed. Taylor Branch. 2004. 15.95 (978-0-7435-4812-0(4)) Pub: S&S Audio. Dist(s): S and S Inc

Parting the Waters: America in the King Years, 1954-1963, Pt. 2. Taylor Branch. Read by Dick Estell. 11 cass. (Running Time: 16 hrs. 30 min.). 1999. 88.00 (978-0-7366-4553-9(5), 4953-B) Books on Tape.

Parting the Waters Pt. 1: America in the King Years, 1954-1963. unabr. ed. Read by Dick Estell. Directed By Taylor Branch. 11 cass. (Running Time: 16 hrs. 30 min.). 1999. 88.00 (978-0-7366-4552-2(7), 4953-A) Books on Tape.
Taylor Branch provides an unsurpassed portrait of Martin Luther King, Jr.'s rise to greatness & the American civil rights movement.

Parting the Waters Pt. 3: America in the King Years, 1954-1963. Taylor Branch. Read by Dick Estell. 10 cass. (Running Time: 15 hrs.). 1999. 80.00 (978-0-7366-4554-6(3), 4953-C) Books on Tape.

Parting with Pain. Harold H. LeCrone. 2 cass. 21.95 Self-Control Sys.
Learn the technique of coping with pain based on self-control & relaxation procedures.

Partly Cloudy Patriot. unabr. ed. Sarah Vowell. Read by Conan O'Brien et al. 2004. 15.95 (978-0-7435-4813-7(2)) Pub: S&S Audio. Dist(s): S and S Inc

Partner. John Grisham. Read by Frank Muller. 1997. 96.00 (978-0-7366-8896-3(X)); audio compact disk 80.00 (978-0-7366-8907-6(9)) Books on Tape.

Partner. abr. ed. John Grisham. Read by Michael Beck. 5 CDs. (Running Time: 6 hrs.). (John Grisham Ser.). (ENG.). 1997. audio compact disk 29.95 (978-0-553-45553-3(2)) Pub: Random Audio Pubg. Dist(s): Random

Partner. unabr. ed. John Grisham. Read by Frank Muller. (Running Time: 43200 sec.). (ENG.). 2007. audio compact disk 29.95 (978-0-7393-4382-1(3), Random AudioBks) Pub: Random Audio Pubg. Dist(s): Random

***Partner in Crime.** abr. ed. J. A. Jance. Read by Debra Monk & Cotter Smith. (ENG.). 2004. (978-0-06-081404-5(7), Harper Audio); (978-0-06-079802-4(5), Harper Audio) HarperCollins Pubs.

Partnering - The Key to Building Relationships; Showcasing Solutions: Leverage Yourself As a Consulting Partner Who Demonstrates True Benefits, Vol. 1. unabr. ed. Karl Walinskas. Perf. by Ted Ritsick & Beth Bloom-Wright. 1 cass. (Running Time: 50 min.). 1998. bk. 12.95 (978-0-9667084-2-4(3)) Speaking Connect.
Learn to differentiate yourself from vendors & be a Consulting Partner. Demonstrate your value now & watch your closing percentage skyrocket.

***Partnering with the Angelic.** Katie Souza. (ENG.). 2011. audio compact disk 20.00 (978-0-7684-0263-6(8)) Pub: Expected End. Dist(s): Destiny Image Pubs

Partners. unabr. ed. Louis Auchincloss. Read by Dan Lazar. 8 cass. (Running Time: 8 hrs.). 1980. 48.00 (978-0-7366-0237-2(2), 1233) Books on Tape.
A story of the small but distinguished New York law firm of Shepard, Putney & Cox, & particularly of one of the senior partners, Beekman Ehninger. It is also a group portrait of men & women whose common bond is their work. Within that bond each one pursues different answers to the search for money, power, love, revenge, or a meaning of life.

Partners In... Classics: Accompaniment/Performance. Composed by Jean Anne Shafferman. (ENG.). 2003. audio compact disk 29.95 (978-0-7390-3197-1(X)) Alfred Pub.

Partners in Crime. unabr. ed. Agatha Christie. Narrated by James Warwick. (Running Time: 28020 sec.). (Tommy & Tuppence Mystery Ser.). (ENG.). 2005. audio compact disk 29.95 (978-1-57270-471-8(3)) Pub: AudioGO. Dist(s): Perseus Dist
When the British Secret Service asks them to take over the International Detective Agency-a suspected Bolshevik spy information drop-Tommy and Tuppence jump at the chance. Told to watch for "blue letters with a Russian stamp" and visitors mentioning the number "16," they nonetheless have time for a variety of cases as they pose as the agency's director and secretary. As an amateur private detective, Tommy takes inspiration from and impersonates other great detectives from crime fiction. While fulfilling their role for British Intelligence, they breeze their way through 15 other cases, solving murder mysteries, a jewel robbery, and rounding up gangs of smugglers and counterfeiters. Originally published in 1929, this exciting whodunit is dramatically read by perennial favorite James Warwick.

Partners in Crime: A Collection. unabr. collector's ed. Read by Kate Reading. 7 cass. (Running Time: 10 hrs. 30 min.). 1995. 56.00 (978-0-7366-2951-5(3), 3645) Books on Tape.
Today's top mystery writers conjure up two imaginatively matched sleuths for each tale in a fascinating collection of nine whodunits.

Partners in Crime: Tommy & Tuppence Mysteries. unabr. ed. Agatha Christie. Read by James Warwick. 2005. 29.95 (978-1-57270-470-1(5)) Pub: Audio Partners. Dist(s): PerseuPGW
When the British Secret Service asks them to take over the International Detective Agency-a suspected Bolshevik spy information drop-Tommy and Tuppence jump at the chance. Told to watch for "blue letters with a Russian stamp" and visitors mentioning the number "16," they nonetheless have time for a variety of cases as they pose as the agency's director and secretary. As an amateur private detective, Tommy takes inspiration from and impersonates other great detectives from crime fiction. While fulfilling their role for British Intelligence, they breeze their way through 15 other cases, solving murder mysteries, a jewel robbery, and rounding up gangs of smugglers and counterfeiters. Originally published in 1929, this exciting whodunit is dramatically read by perennial favorite James Warwick.

Partners in Education: How Colleges Can Work with Schools to Improve Teaching & Learning. Theodore L. Gross. (Higher & Adult Education Ser.). 1988. bk. 36.45 (978-1-55542-089-5(3), Jossey-Bass) Wiley US.

Partners in Power: The Clintons & Their America. unabr. collector's ed. Roger Morris. Read by Jonathan Reese. 14 cass. (Running Time: 21 hrs.). 1996. 112.00 (978-0-7366-3484-7(3), 4124) Books on Tape.
No President & his First Lady have drawn more scrutiny than Bill Clinton & his wife, Hillary. This candid & controversial dual biography lays open their personal & political lives.

Partners in Spirituals: Accompaniment/Performance. Composed by Jean Anne Shafferman. (ENG.). 2002. audio compact disk 29.95 (978-0-7390-2487-4(6)) Alfred Pub.

Partners in Spirituals... Again! (6 Spectacular Partner Songs for 2-Part Voices) Accompaniment/Performance. Composed by Jean Anne Shafferman. (ENG.). 2005. audio compact disk 29.95 (978-0-7390-3696-9(3)) Alfred Pub.

Partnership. 2nd ed. Christopher H. Munch. 4 cass. (Running Time: 4 hrs. 15 mins.). (Outstanding Professors Ser.). 1997. 57.00 (978-1-57793-021-1(5), 28390, West Lglwrks) West.
Lecture given by a prominent American law school professor.

Partnership: The Making of Goldman Sachs. unabr. ed. Charles D. Ellis. Narrated by Norman Dietz. (Running Time: 32 hrs. 30 mins. 0 sec.). (ENG.). 2008. audio compact disk 119.99 (978-1-4001-4049-7(8)); audio compact disk 44.99 (978-1-4001-6049-5(9)); audio compact disk 59.99 (978-1-4001-1049-0(1)) Pub: Tantor Media. Dist(s): IngramPubServ

Partnership: The Power of Exchange. Creflo A. Dollar. 3 cass. (Running Time: 4 hrs. 30 mins.). 2000. 15.00 (978-1-931172-72-1(2), TS280, Kidz Faith) Pub: Creflo Dollar. Dist(s): STL Dist NA

Partnership: Why Should We Believe You This Time? Innovation Groups Staff. 2 cass. (Transforming Local Government Ser.). Alliance Innov.

Partnership Taxation. Nathan Bisk & Richard M. Feldheim. 4 cass. bk. 159.00 set, incl. textbk. & quizzer. (CPE0530) Bisk Educ.
Get real-world solutions to your client's partnership tax problems, & gain a better understanding of complex partnership tax issues.

Partnership Taxation - Complex Issues. James R. Hamill. 8 cass. (Running Time: 12 hrs.). 1995. 139.00 set, incl. wkbk. (741303EZ) Am Inst CPA.
Many developments in partnership taxation have occurred in recent years. Three concepts; the basis in a partner's interest in the partnership, "substantial economic effect," & liability sharing among limited & general partners, are especially confusing. This course helps you understand them & the morass of rules & regulations that apply to them.

***Partnership with God: Opening the Door to All God Has for You.** Kellie Copeland Swisher. (ENG.). 2010. audio compact disk 5.00 (978-1-60463-079-4(5)) K Copeland Pubns.

Partnerships. 1988. bk. 100.00 incl. book.; 50.00 cass. only.; 50.00 book only. PA Bar Inst.

Partnerships. Ed. by Socrates Media Editors. 2005. audio compact disk 29.95 (978-1-59546-088-2(8)) Pub: Socrates Med LLC. Dist(s): Midpt Trade

Partnerships Can Kill. unabr. ed. Connie Shelton. Read by Lynda Evans. 4 cass. (Running Time: 6 hrs.). (Charlie Parker Mystery Ser.: No. 3). 1996. 26.95 (978-1-55686-667-8(4)) Books in Motion.
An old school chum hires Charlie to prove that her dead restaurant partner didn't commit suicide.

Partnerships, LLCs, & LLPs: Uniform Acts, Taxation, Drafting, Securities, & Bankruptcy. 15 cass. (Running Time: 17 hrs. 30 min.). 1999. 395.00 Set; incl. resource matls. 884p. (AD83) Am Law Inst.
Advanced course designed as a totally integrated program on partnership & limited liability company (LLC) law, directed to general practitioners & to real estate, business, & corporate attorneys.

Partnerships Revisited: New Rules, New Entities, Old Issues, New Solutions, Tuesday, June 18, 1996, 70 Plus Cities Nationwide. American Law Institute-American Bar Association, Committee on Continuing Professional Education Staff. 3 cass. (Running Time: 3 hrs. 50 min.). 1996. 160.00 Incl. study materials. (D249) Am Law Inst.
This program examines all of the various partnership entities & compares them with the other types of business entities. The reasons for all of the recent statutory activity in partnerships also will be explored.

Parts, Accessories & Kits for Agricultural Machinery in Argentina: A Strategic Reference 2006. Compiled by Icon Group International, Inc. Staff. 2007. ring bd. 195.00 (978-0-497-35803-7(4)) Icon Grp.

Parts of a Plant Audio CD. Adapted by Benchmark Education Company Staff. Based on a work by Margaret McNamara. (Content Connections Ser.). (J). (gr. k-2). 2008. audio compact disk 10.00 (978-1-60634-895-6(7)) Benchmark Educ.

Parts of a Whole. Sundance/Newbridge, LLC Staff. (Early Math Ser.). (gr. k-1). 2000. 12.00 (978-1-58273-315-9(5)) Sund Newbrdge.

Party. unabr. ed. Short Stories. Anton Chekhov. Read by Susan McInerney. 2 cass. (Running Time: 2 hrs. 32 min.). 1993. lib. bdg. 18.95 set incl. vinyl case, notes, author's picture & biography. (978-1-883049-23-2(7)) Sound Room.
Four short works: "The Party", "Anna on the Neck", "Polinka", & "The Princess".

Party: A Guide to Adventurous Entertaining. Sally Quinn. Read by Anna Fields. 4 cass. (Running Time: 5 hrs. 30 mins.). 2000. 32.95 (978-0-7861-1578-5(5), 2407) Blckstn Audio.
A lively glimpse into the party scene but also a useful & practical guide to making your own parties a success & guaranteeing that your guests will want to come back. Includes a look at the Washington social scene.

Party Appetizers Deck & Disc. 2002. pap. bk. 14.95 (978-1-931918-02-2(3)) Compass Labs.

Party for the Alley Cats. (Sails Literacy Ser.). (gr. 2 up). 10.00 (978-0-7578-6824-5(X)) Rigby Educ.

Party Games Deck & Disc. 2002. pap. bk. 14.95 (978-1-931918-01-5(5)) Compass Labs.

Party People. Donald Davis. 1 cass. (Running Time: 56 min.). (American Storytelling Ser.). 1993. 12.00 (978-0-87483-324-9(8)) Pub: August Hse. Dist(s): Natl Bk Netwk
Two new Appalachian stories from the author of the award-winning Listening for the Crack of Dawn. These stories champion friendship without pretention & finding joy in everyday life. Includes Otto & Marguerite.

Party People. Donald Davis. 2008. audio compact disk 16.95 (978-0-87483-887-9(8)) Pub: August Hse. Dist(s): Natl Bk Netwk

Party Princess. unabr. ed. Meg Cabot. Read by Clea Lewis. 4 cass. (Running Time: 6 hrs. 5 mins.). (Princess Diaries: Vol. 7). (YA). 2006. 35.00 (978-0-307-28584-3(7), Listening Lib); audio compact disk 45.00 (978-0-307-28585-0(5), Listening Lib) Pub: Random Audio Pubg. Dist(s): Random

Party Princess. unabr. ed. Meg Cabot. Read by Clea Lewis. 5 CDs. (Running Time: 21900 sec.). (Princess Diaries: Vol. 7II). (ENG.). (J). (gr. 7). 2006. audio compact disk 30.00 (978-0-307-28411-2(5), Listening Lib) Pub: Random Audio Pubg. Dist(s): Random

Party Sing-Along. Perf. by Rick Charette et al. 1 cass. (Running Time: 90 mins.). (J). 2000. 7.98; audio compact disk 9.98 Peter Pan.
A party's not complete without the songs on this recording! Some of the best-loved children's groups perform. Danceable tunes include "Hands up!" "Braces" & Hippo Rock.".

Party Time with Old King Cole Audio CD. Adapted by Benchmark Education Company Staff. Based on a work by Jeffrey B. Fuerst. (Reader's Theater Nursery Rhymes & Songs Ser.). (J). (gr. k-1). 2008. audio compact disk 10.00 (978-1-60437-986-0(3)) Benchmark Educ.

Party to Murder. unabr. ed. Betty Rowlands. 7 CDs. (Soundings (CDs) Ser.). 2007. audio compact disk 71.95 (978-1-84559-515-9(7)) Pub: ISIS Lrg Prnt GBR. Dist(s): Ulverscroft US

Party to Murder. unabr. ed. Betty Rowlands. Read by Julia Franklin. 6 cass. (Soundings Ser.). 2007. 54.95 (978-1-84559-481-7(9)) Pub: ISIS Lrg Prnt GBR. Dist(s): Ulverscroft US

Party with the Halloween Ghosts: Whirl with the Dancing Goblins. Silvia Silk. (Grandma Jasmine Ser.). (J). 15.99 (978-0-938861-17-1(4)) Jasmine Texts.

Party's Over: The Ideas of Dr. E. F. Schumacher. E. F. Schumacher. 1 cass. 1990. 12.95 (ECN190) J Norton Pubs.
Small is beautiful.

Parure see Contes de Maupassant

Parure, Deux Amis, Le Bapteme. Short Stories. Guy de Maupassant. Read by Claude Beauclair. 1 cass. (FRE.). 1991. 13.95 (1259-OH) Olivia & Hill.
Three short stories.

***Parvana's Journey.** unabr. ed. Deborah Ellis. Read by Meera Simhan. 3 CDs. (Running Time: 3 hrs. 49 mins.). (YA). (gr. 7-10). 2009. audio compact disk 30.00 (978-0-7393-8580-7(1), Listening Lib) Pub: Random Audio Pubg. Dist(s): Random

Parvue; Un Duel; Le Bapteme. Guy de Maupassant. 1 cass. (Guy de Maupassant Ser.: Vol. I). (FRE.). bk. 16.95 (SFR451) J Norton Pubs.

Pasacalle 1: Curso de Espanol para Ninos. Equipo de Expertos 2100 Staff. 2 cass. (Running Time: 3 hrs.). (SPA & ENG.). (J). (gr. 3-7). (978-84-7143-607-8(8)) Sociedad General ESP.

Pasacalle 2: Curso de Espanol para Ninos. Isidoro Pisonero et al. 2 cass. (Running Time: 3 hrs.). (SPA & ENG.). (J). (gr. 3-7). (978-84-7143-716-7(3)) Sociedad General ESP.

Pasadena: A Novel. unabr. ed. David Ebershoff. Read by Lorna Raver. 14 cass. (Running Time: 20 hrs. 30 mins.). 2002. 89.95 (978-0-7861-2308-7(7), 2992); audio compact disk 136.00 (978-0-7861-9440-7(5), 2992); audio compact disk 39.95 (978-0-7861-9164-2(3), 2992) Blckstn Audio.
At the story's center is Linda Stamp, a fishergirl born in 1903 on a coastal onion farm in San Diego's North County, and the three men who upend her life and vie for her affection: her pragmatic farming brother, Edmund; Captain Willis Poore, a Pasadena rancher with a heroic military past; and

Bruder, the mysterious young man Linda's father brings home from World War I.

Pasadena: A Novel. unabr. ed. David Ebershoff. Read by Lorna Raver. 14 pieces. 2004. reel tape 49.95 (978-0-7861-2304-9(4)) Blckstn Audio.

Pasadena Audio Tour by Scott's L. A. Narrated by Scott Carter. Des. by Paul Whitney. (ENG.). 2006. audio compact disk 17.95 (978-0-9788500-0-5(9)) Scotts LA.

Pascal. Henri Guillemin. 1 cass. (FRE.). 1991. 22.95 (1208-VSL) Olivia & Hill.

Pascal Comelade: And His Play Toy Orchestra. Pascal Comelade. 2006. bk. 39.00 (978-84-95951-52-6(5)) Actar ESP.

Pascha: Hymns of the Resurrection. Ed. by Choirs of St Vladimir's Seminary. 1977. audio compact disk 18.00 (978-0-88141-173-7(6)) St Vladimirs.

Paseo de Rosita. Tr. of Rosie's Walk. (SPA.). 2004. 8.95 (978-0-7882-0286-5(3)) Weston Woods.

Paseo Escolar de Luis. Steck-Vaughn Staff. 1 cass. (Running Time: 1 hr. 30 min.). (SPA.). 1999. (978-0-7398-0750-7(1)) SteckVau.

***Pashto, Basic: Learn to Speak & Understand Pashto with Pimsleur Language Programs.** Pimsleur. (Running Time: 5 hrs. 0 mins. 0 sec.). (Basic Ser.). (ENG.). 2010. audio compact disk 24.95 (978-1-4423-0312-6(3), Pimsleur) Pub: S&S Audio. Dist(s): S and S Inc

***Pashto, Comprehensive: Learn to Speak & Understand Pashto with Pimsleur Language Programs.** Pimsleur. (Running Time: 16 hrs. 0 mins. 0 sec.). (Comprehensive Ser.). (ENG.). 2010. audio compact disk 345.00 (978-0-7435-9976-4(4), Pimsleur) Pub: S&S Audio. Dist(s): S and S Inc

***Pashto, Conversational: Learn to Speak & Understand Pashto with Pimsleur Language Programs.** Pimsleur. (Running Time: 8 hrs. 0 mins. 0 sec.). (Conversational Ser.). (ENG.). 2010. audio compact disk 49.95 (978-1-4423-0313-3(1), Pimsleur) Pub: S&S Audio. Dist(s): S and S Inc

Pashto Newspaper Reader. 1994. 12.00 (978-1-881265-22-1(6)) Dunwoody Pr.

Pashto Newspaper Reader. MRM, Inc. Staff. 1 cass. (Running Time: 1 hr. 30 min.). (MIS.). 1984. 12.00 (3096) Dunwoody Pr.
Fifty selections for the intermediate student, accompanied by a body of suitable lexical & grammatical aids aimed at assisting comprehension & bridging the gap between elementary Pashto & the complexities of formal journalistic style.

***Pasion por el Evangelio.** Charles R. Swindoll.Tr. of Passion for the Gospel. 2010. audio compact disk 15.00 (978-1-57972-896-0(0)) Insight Living.

Pasion Sin Fronteras. 1 cass. 16.95 (CSP320) J Norton Pubs.

Paso. Scripts. Hank Mitchum. 5CDs. (Running Time: 6 hrs.). (Stagecoach Collector's Ser.: No. 23). 2005. 14.99 (978-1-58807-810-0(8)) Am Pubng Inc.
El Paso was a commercial hub with a rough reputation, so Texas Ranger Branson Howard was called in to protect a gold shipment. More than one gang of hardcases would be waiting including Turk Killam who would stop at nothing to get the gold.

Pasos Dos: An Intermediate Course in Spanish. Rosa M. Martin & Martyn Ellis. 2 cass. (SPA & ENG., 1995. bk. 29.95 (978-0-8120-8240-1(0)) Barron.

Pasos Hacia la Cumbre del Exito. Camilo Cruz. 2 cass. (Running Time: 2 hrs.).Tr. of Reaching the Top. (SPA.). 2003. 18.00 (978-1-931059-01-5(2)) Taller del Exito.
Success has been defined as the progressive realization of a worthy goal or ideal. Success is the result of a plan put into action. In this program you'll learn the steps to turn dreams into realities.

Pass. Prod. by Laraim Associates. (Barclay Family Adventure Ser.). (J). 2003. audio compact disk (978-1-56254-985-5(5)) Saddleback Edu.

Pass & Data Cd-Coll Acct 1-29. 18th ed. (C). 2004. audio compact disk 23.95 (978-0-324-22180-0(0)) Pub: South-West. Dist(s): CENGAGE Learn

Pass Cd-Accounting. 9th ed. (C). 2004. audio compact disk 21.95 (978-0-324-20678-4(X)) Pub: South-West. Dist(s): CENGAGE Learn

Pass Key to the NTE. Albertina A. Weinlander. 1 cass. (Pass Key Ser.). 1993. pap. bk. 11.95 (978-0-8120-8040-7(8)) Barron.

Pass Key to the TOEFL: With Compact Disc. 3rd ed. Pamela J. Sharpe. CD . 1999. pap. bk. 14.95 (978-0-7641-7145-1(3)) Barron.
Short version of TOEFL - contains 4 model tests - 2 paper & pencil & 2 computer-based - all questions answered - extra practice provided.

Pass Netwrk Vers Fin/Mngrl ACC. 8th ed. (C). 2004. audio compact disk 452.95 (978-0-324-22329-3(3)) Pub: South-West. Dist(s): CENGAGE Learn

Pass On, No Pass Back. Darrell H. Y. Lum. 1 cass,. 1990. 8.00 SELECTIONS FROM PAP. BK. (978-0-910043-20-5(5)) Bamboo Ridge Pr.

Pass, Princ of Cost Acct. 13th ed. (C). 2004. audio compact disk 23.95 (978-0-324-19177-6(4)) Pub: South-West. Dist(s): CENGAGE Learn

Pass the Bread. T. D. Jakes. 1 cass. 2001. 6.00 (978-1-57855-268-9(0)) T D Jakes.

Pass the Bread: Matthew 6:11. Ed Young. (J). 1979. 4.95 (978-0-7417-1081-9(1), A0081) Win Walk.

Pass the Test - Study Diligently. unabr. ed. Dick Sutphen. Read by Dick Sutphen. 1 cass. (Running Time: 30 min.). (Quick Fix Meditations Ser.). 1998. 10.98 (978-0-87554-621-6(8), QF103) Valley Sun.
Absorb & remember all the information needed to pass the test. At test time be calm, relaxed & fully confident.

Pass-Through Entity Income Tax Refresher Course: Preparing Return for LLC's, Partnerships & S Corporations. Sidney Kess & Barbara Weltman. 6 cass. (Running Time: 6 hrs.). 1996. 185.00 Set, incl. study guide/quizzer. (0911) Toolkit Media.
Offers detailed, line-by-line instructions on the preparation of 1996 partnership income tax return, form 1065, & 1996 S Corporation income tax return, Form 1120S.

Pass Through Panic: Freeing Yourself from Anxiety & Fear. Claire Weekes. 2 cass. 1999. 17.95 Set. HighBridge.

Pass Through Panic: Freeing Yourself from Anxiety & Fear. unabr. ed. Claire Weekes. Contrib. by Claire Weekes. (Running Time: 2 hrs.). (ENG.). 2005. audio compact disk 18.95 (978-1-56511-970-3(3), 1565119703) Pub: HighBridge. Dist(s): Workman Pub

Pass Your Driving Test. Glenn Harrold. 2 CDs. (Running Time: 3612 sec.). 2006. audio compact disk 17.95 (978-1-901923-71-1(1), 247-043) Pub: Divinit Pubing GBR. Dist(s): Bookworld

Passage. abr. ed. Justin Cronin. Read by Edward Herrmann. 12 CDs. (Running Time: 14 hrs. 30 mins.). (ENG.). 2010. audio compact disk 45.00 (978-0-7393-6650-9(5), Random AudioBks) Pub: Random Audio Pubg. Dist(s): Random

Passage. unabr. ed. Lois McMaster Bujold. Read by Bernadette Dunne. (Running Time: 54000 sec.). (Sharing Knife Ser.). 2008. audio compact disk 29.95 (978-1-4332-3494-1(7)); audio compact disk & audio compact disk 99.00 (978-1-4332-3491-0(2)) Blckstn Audio.

Passage by Night. unabr. ed. Jack Higgins. Read by Barry Foster. 4 cass. (Running Time: 4 hrs.). 1993. bk. 39.95 (978-0-7451-6017-7(4), CAB 148) AudioGO.

Passage by Night. unabr. collector's ed. Jack Higgins. Read by Larry McKeever. 5 cass. (Running Time: 5 hrs.). 1985. 30.00 (978-0-7366-0505-2(3), 1479) Books on Tape.
Harry Manning, a freebooter with a past he doesn't like to talk about, runs a charter boat in the Bahamas. Also, he boozes. When his sweetheart leaves him by dying, Harry can find no relief. Except for the thought of revenge & because he is Harry, he sets out to settle the score.

***Passage for Trumpet.** 2010. audio compact disk (978-1-59171-201-5(7)) Falcon Picture.

Passage in the Life of Mr. John Oakhurst see Luck of Roaring Camp & Other Stories

Passage in the Life of Mr. John Oakhurst. unabr. ed. Bret Harte. Read by Walter Zimmerman. 1 cass. (Running Time: 48 min.). Dramatization. 1983. 7.95 (S-59) Jimcin Record.
A story concerning the code of honor in the old West.

Passage of Arms. unabr. collector's ed. Eric Ambler. Read by Richard Brown. 6 cass. (Running Time: 9 hrs.). 1989. 48.00 (978-0-7366-1487-0(7), 2363) Books on Tape.
Mr. Tan's offer had amused him. The idea of acting as front man for a Chinese pirate appealed to Nilsen's sense of humor. But call it boredom, or naivete, or greed, the American was now in the gunrunning business & Mr. & Mrs. Nilsen were running for their lives.

Passage of Gnosis to the Modern West. Stephan Hoeller. 1 cass. 1999. (40028) Big Sur Tapes.
1994 Los Angeles.

Passage of Seasons. unabr. ed. Douglas Hirt. Read by Rusty Nelson. 6 cass. (Running Time: 6 hrs. 6 min.). 2001. 39.95 (978-1-58116-143-4(3)) Books in Motion.
Cripple Creek, Colorado attracts cowboy Brad Medford. After Brad crosses a renowned gunhandler, a world-wise U.S. Marshall sets out on a daring mission of rescue where the penalty for failure is death.

***Passage on the Lady Anne.** (ENG.). 2010. audio compact disk (978-1-59171-301-2(3)) Falcon Picture.

Passage to Freedom: The Sugihara Story. Ken Mochizuki. Illus. by Dom Lee. 14 vols. (Running Time: 17 mins.). 2000. pap. bk. 35.95 (978-1-59112-544-0(8)); audio compact disk 12.95 (978-1-59112-333-0(X)) Live Oak Media.

Passage to Freedom: The Sugihara Story. Ken Mochizuki. Read by Ken Mochizuki. Illus. by Dom Lee. 1 cass. (Running Time: 17 mins.). (J). (gr. 1-6). 2000. bk. 24.95 (978-0-87499-631-9(7)); pap. bk. 16.95 (978-0-87499-630-2(9)) Pub: Live Oak Media. Dist(s): AudioGO
This true story of Chiune Sugihara, a Japanese diplomat in Lithuania in 1940, explains how Sugihara used his powers, against the orders of his own government, to help thousands of Jews escape the Holocaust.

Passage to Freedom: The Sugihara Story. Read by Ken Mochizuki. 1 cass. (Running Time: 17 mins.). (J). 2000. 9.95 (978-0-87499-629-6(5)) Live Oak Media.

Passage to Freedom, Grades 1-6: The Sugihara Story. Ken Mochizuki. Read by Ken Mochizuki. Illus. by Dom Lee. 41 vols. (Running Time: 17 mins.). (J). 2000. pap. bk. & tchr. ed. 33.95 Reading Chest. (978-0-87499-632-6(5)) Live Oak Media.
This true story of Chiune Sugihara, a Japanese diplomat in Lithuania in 1940, explains how Sugihara used his powers - against the orders of his own government - to help thousands of Jews escape the Holocaust.

Passage to India. (Running Time: 11 hrs. 30 mins.). 2005. audio compact disk 81.00 (978-0-7861-7876-6(0)) Blckstn Audio.

Passage to India. E. M. Forster. Read by Kate Reading. 1995. audio compact disk 80.00 (978-0-7366-6218-5(9)) Books on Tape.

Passage to India. E. M. Forster. Read by Meera Syal. (CSA Word Recording Ser.). (ENG.). 2009. 59.99 (978-1-60812-503-6(3)) Find a World.

Passage to India. abr. ed. E. M. Forster. Read by Meera Syal. Abr. by Rebecca Fenton. (Running Time: 5 hrs. 0 mins. 0 sec.). (ENG.). 2009. audio compact disk 26.95 (978-1-934997-21-5(8)) Pub: CSAWord. Dist(s): PerseuPGW

Passage to India. unabr. ed. Read by Sam Dastor. 9 CDs. (Running Time: 40320 sec.). (ENG.). 2005. audio compact disk 37.95 (978-1-57270-486-2(1)) Pub: AudioGO. Dist(s): Perseus Dist
Eager to know the "real" India, a group of English tourists develops a friendship with the cultivated Dr. Aziz. The veneer of trust and mutual affection is shattered during a trip to the Marabar caves, when one of the women accuses Dr. Aziz of assault. Arguably Forster's greatest novel, A Passage to India paints a troubling portrait of colonialism at its worst and, in the breach between Aziz and his English "friends," foreshadows the end of British rule in India.

Passage to India, unabr. ed. E. M. Forster. Read by Flo Gibson. 7 cass. (Running Time: 10 hrs. 30 min.). 1998. 25.95 (978-1-55685-562-7(1)) Audio Bk Con.
The difficulties of friendship & understanding between the races & religions in British-ruled India are the themes of this compassionate novel. An English lady's hallucination of an assault by an Indian causes political unrest & turmoil.

Passage to India. unabr. ed. E. M. Forster. Read by Sam Dastor. 10 cass. (Running Time: 11 hrs. 12 mins.). 2003. 34.95 (978-1-57270-329-2(6)) Pub: Audio Partners. Dist(s): PerseuPGW
What really happened in the Marabar Caves? This mystery highlights an even larger question: can an Englishman and an Indian be friends? A Passage to India is a troubling portrait of colonialism at its worst. Here the personal becomes the political, and in the breach between Aziz and his English "friends," Forster foreshadows the eventual end of British rule in India.

Passage to India. unabr. ed. E. M. Forster. Read by Frederick Davidson. 8 cass. (Running Time: 11 hrs. 30 mins.). 1992. 56.95 (978-0-7861-0350-8(7), 1307) Blckstn Audio.
This novel of society in India under the British Raj ranks high among the great literary works of the twentieth century. It is a picture of the clash between East & West, ruler & ruled & of the prejudices & misunderstandings that foredoomed Britain's "jewel in the crown.".

Passage to India. unabr. ed. E. M. Forster. Read by Frederick Davidson. 8 cass. (Running Time: 11 hrs. 30 mins.). 2005. 29.95 (978-0-7861-3465-6(8), E1307); audio compact disk 29.95 (978-0-7861-8042-4(0), ZE1307) Blckstn Audio.

Passage to India. unabr. ed. E. M. Forster. Read by Frederick Davidson. 13 vols. (Running Time: 11 hrs. 30 mins.). 2005. audio compact disk 29.95 (978-0-7861-8161-2(3), ZM1307) Blckstn Audio.

Passage to India. unabr. ed. E. M. Forster. Read by Kate Reading. 2001. audio compact disk 80.00 Books on Tape.
Misunderstanding explodes into riot as cultures clash in turn-of-the-century British India.

Passage to India. unabr. ed. E. M. Forster. Read by Kate Reading. 8 cass. (Running Time: 12 hrs.). 2001. 29.95 (978-0-7366-6765-4(2)) Books on Tape.
Misunderstanding explodes into riot as cultures clash in turn-of-the-century British India.

Passage to India. unabr. ed. E. M. Forster. Read by Sam Dastor. 10 CDs. 2000. audio compact disk 94.95 (978-0-7540-5353-8(9), CCD 044) Pub: Chivers Audio Bks GBR. Dist(s): AudioGO
Adela Quested arrived in India expecting to marry Ronny Heaslop. But Adela's desire to see the real India complicates their love. On an expedition into the heart of India, an incident occurs that divides the community sharply into racial factors.

Passage to India. unabr. ed. E. M. Forster. Read by Sam Dastor. (YA). 2007. 79.99 (978-1-60252-853-6(5)) Find a World.

Passage to India. unabr. collector's ed. E. M. Forster. Read by Kate Reading. 8 cass. (Running Time: 12 hrs.). (J). 1995. 64.00 (978-0-7366-2952-2(1), 3646) Books on Tape.
Misunderstanding explodes into riot as cultures clash in turn-of-the-century British India.

Passage to Mutiny. unabr. ed. Alexander Kent, pseud. Read by Michael Jayston. 10 cass. (Running Time: 15 hrs.). (Richard Bolitho Ser.: Bk. 7). 2000. 84.95 (978-0-7540-0466-0(X), CAB 1889) Pub: Chivers Audio Bks GBR. Dist(s): AudioGO
October 1789, New South Wales. The frigate Tempest sails into Sydney. She has been sent to police the new southern trade routes. Her captain is Richard Bolitho, who hopes to be ordered home to England, rather than dispatched to the treacherous South Sea. For he is menaced by deeper fears: the men of the Bounty have mutinied in these same waters.

Passages from the Diary of Samuel Pepys. unabr. ed. Samuel Pepys. Read by Fred Williams. 10 cass. (Running Time: 14 hrs. 30 mins.). 1997. 69.95 (978-0-7861-1151-0(8), 1917) Blckstn Audio.
To those who love vivid, unconscious writing, the diary of Samuel Pepys is infinitely delightful & precious, scarcely to be overvalued.

Passages from the Diary of Samuel Pepys. unabr. ed. Samuel Pepys. Read by Fred Williams. (Running Time: 45000 sec.). 2007. audio compact disk 29.95 (978-0-7861-6066-2(7)); audio compact disk 90.00 (978-0-7861-6065-5(9)) Blckstn Audio.

Passages from This Timeless Moment. Laura Huxley. Read by Laura Huxley. Read by Ram Dass. 1 cass. 10.00 (A0572-90) Sound Photosyn.
Laura & Ram Dass read from her book, "This Timeless Moment," about her last moments with Aldous Huxley.

***Passages in Caregiving.** unabr. ed. Gail Sheehy. Read by Gail Sheehy. (ENG.). 2010. (978-0-06-201614-0(8), Harper Audio) HarperCollins Pubs.

***Passages in Caregiving: Turning Chaos into Confidence.** unabr. ed. Gail Sheehy. Read by Gail Sheehy. (ENG.). 2010. (978-0-06-200553-3(7), Harper Audio) HarperCollins Pubs.

Passages on the Spiritual Journey. Andre Papineau. 2 cass. (Running Time: 2 hrs.). 2001. 17.95 (A7040) St Anthony Mess Pr.
Weaves biblical stories with his own contemporary stories.

Passages to Freedom. unabr. collector's ed. Joseph S. Frelinghuysen. Read by Jonathan Reese. 10 cass. (Running Time: 15 hrs.). 1993. 80.00 (978-0-7366-2438-1(4), 3203) Books on Tape.
Remarkable but true story of U. S. Army captain who escaped from an Italian POW camp during WW II.

Passages to India. unabr. ed. Julian C. Hollick. 10 cass. (Running Time: 10 hrs.). (C). 1989. spiral bd. 125.00 (978-1-56709-002-4(8), 1001) Indep Broadcast.
Presents India on its own terms & in its own words in a series of ten one hour radio documentaries. Themes covered include: the culture of India, Gandhi, Hinduism, assimilation of other cultures (English & Muslim), the oral tradition, film making, the Dharma & caste, women in India, self-reliance & democracy.

Passages 1 Class Audio CDs. 2nd rev. ed. Jack C. Richards & Chuck Sandy. (Running Time: 4 hrs. 14 mins.). (Passages Ser.). (ENG.). 2008. audio compact disk 59.00 (978-0-521-68390-6(4)) Cambridge U Pr.

Passages 2 Class Audio CDs. 2nd rev. ed. Jack C. Richards & Chuck Sandy. (Passages Ser.). (ENG.). 2008. audio compact disk 59.00 (978-0-521-68395-1(5)) Cambridge U Pr.

Passageway, Set. abr. ed. Laurel Mouritsen. 2 cass. 11.98 (978-1-55503-695-9(3), 07001002) Covenant Comms.

Passaggi-Passages: Selected Readings in English & Italian. Josephine C. Del Deo. Read by Josephine C. Del Deo. 1 cass. (Running Time: 1 hr.). 2003. pap. bk. 25.00 (978-0-9673628-3-0(0)) Three Dunes.
Readings of two stories in both English and Italian. Includes book of short stories of a travel genre about Italy.

Passamaquoddy Brief Histories. 1 cass. (Running Time: 30 min.). 16.95 (978-0-88432-494-2(X), SPS100) J Norton Pubs.

Passamaquoddy Legends: Raccoon. 1 cass. 12.95 incl. booklet, 24p. (978-0-88432-721-9(3), SPS105) J Norton Pubs.

Passenger. unabr. ed. Patrick A. Davis. Read by Jim Bond. (Running Time: 8 hrs.). 2009. 24.99 (978-1-4233-9138-8(1), 9781423391388, Brilliance MP3); 24.99 (978-1-4233-9140-1(3), 9781423391401, BAD); 39.97 (978-1-4233-9139-5(X), 9781423391395, Brinc Audio MP3 Lib); 39.97 (978-1-4233-9141-8(1), 9781423391418, BADLE) Brilliance Audio.

Passenger, Set. abr. ed. Patrick A. Davis. Read by Jim Bond. 2 cass. 1999. 17.95 (FS9-51002) Highsmith.

Passenger from Scotland Yard. H. F. Wood. Read by Walter Covell. 9 cass. (Running Time: 12 hrs.). 1989. 49.00 incl. album. (C-133) Jimcin Record.
Fascinating detective story.

Passenger from Scotland Yard. unabr. collector's ed. H. F. Wood. Read by Walter Covell. 9 cass. (Running Time: 13 hrs. 30 min.). 1984. 72.00 (978-0-7366-3901-9(2), 9133) Books on Tape.
Five men sit in a railroad compartment on the mail train from London to Dover. The same five men board the Channel steamer & cross to Calais, where they entrain for Paris. By the time the train reaches Paris, we learn that one man is a detective from Scotland Yard, on the trail of a fortune in stolen gems; one unknown man is a murderer; & another, a corpse!.

***Passenger to Frankfurt.** Agatha Christie. Narrated by Hugh Fraser. (Running Time: 7 hrs. 0 mins. 0 sec.). (ENG.). 2010. audio compact disk 29.95 (978-1-60998-010-8(7)) Pub: AudioGO. Dist(s): Perseus Dist

Passenger Transportation Services in Mexico: A Strategic Reference 2007. Compiled by Icon Group International, Inc. Staff. 2007. ring bd. 195.00 (978-0-497-82356-6(X)) Icon Grp.

***Passerby.** 2010. audio compact disk (978-1-59171-179-7(7)) Falcon Picture.

Passing Exams. Betty L. Randolph. Read by Betty L. Randolph. Read by Leonard Baron. Ed. by Success Education Institute International Staff. 1 cass. (Running Time: 60 min.). 1990. bk. 9.98 (978-1-55909-275-3(0), 53B) Randolph Tapes.
Sixty thousand messages left-right brain; male-female voice tracks. Messages subliminally parallel music. Orchestrated, specially arranged

Baroque classical music with 60 beats for accelerated learning. Exclusively recorded for Success Education Institute by a world class symphony orchestra. All messages heard audibly for 3-5 minutes before covered by music.

Passing Exams. unabr. ed. 1 cass. (Running Time: 45 min.). (Educational Ser.). 9.98 90 min. extended length stereo music. (978-1-55909-060-5(X), 53X) Randolph Tapes.
For use while studying to feel relaxed & self-confident. Subliminal messages are heard 3-5 minutes before becoming ocean sounds or music.

Passing Exams. unabr. ed. 1 cass. (Running Time: 45 min.). (Educational Ser.). 1990. 9.98 (978-1-55909-059-6(6), 53) Randolph Tapes.

Passing Gas & Getting Paid for It: The Musings of a Comic Anesthesiolosist. 2006. audio compact disk 14.95 (978-0-9779154-1-5(7)) Friend Shark.

Passing of Black Eagle see O. Henry Favorites

Passing On. unabr. ed. Penelope Lively. Read by Sheila Mitchell. 5 CDs. (Running Time: 6 hrs. 45 min.). 2000. audio compact disk 59.95 (978-0-7531-0701-0(5), 107015) Pub: ISIS Audio GBR. Dist(s): Ulverscroft US

Passing On. unabr. ed. Penelope Lively. Read by Sheila Mitchell. 7 cass. (Running Time: 7 hrs.). (Isis Ser.). (J). 2004. 61.95 (978-1-85089-786-6(7), 9007X) Pub: ISIS Lrg Prnt GBR. Dist(s): Ulverscroft US

Passing on Experience: Deut. 6:6-7, 724. Ed Young. 1989. 4.95 (978-0-7417-1724-5(7), 724) Win Walk.

Passing on the Magic: How to Fall in Love, Lose Weight & Keep It off Forever. Janet Greeson. 4 cass. (Magic of Recovery Ser.: Vol. 4). 1994. 29.95 Set. (978-0-9630955-2-7(8)) Greeson & Boyle.
Therapeutic mini workshops. Self-help - how to lose weight.

Passing Strange. Catherine Aird. Read by Bruce Montague. 2003. audio compact disk 64.95 (978-0-7540-8772-4(7)) Pub: Chivers Audio Bks GBR. Dist(s): AudioGO

Passing Strange. unabr. ed. Catherine Aird. Read by Bruce Montague. 6 cass. (Running Time: 9 hrs.). 2002. 54.95 (978-0-7540-0808-8(8), CAB 2230) AudioGO.

Passing Strange: A Gilded Age Tale of Love & Deception Across the Color Line. unabr. ed. Martha A. Sandweiss. Narrated by Lorna Raver. 12 CDs. (Running Time: 14 hrs. 30 mins. 0 sec.). (ENG.). 2009. audio compact disk 69.99 (978-1-4001-4151-7(6)); audio compact disk 24.99 (978-1-4001-6151-5(7)); audio compact disk 34.99 (978-1-4001-1151-0(X)) Pub: Tantor Media. Dist(s): IngramPubServ

Passing Strategies. Michael G. Rayel. 2002. audio compact disk 20.95 (978-0-9687816-1-6(6)); audio compact disk 24.95 (978-0-9687816-2-3(4)) Pub: Oikos Global CAN. Dist(s): IPG Chicago

Passing the Graveyard see Evening with Dylan Thomas

Passing the Money Test: How to Manage Material Resources & Position Yourself for Increase. 3 cass. (Running Time: 3 hrs.). (Passing the Test Ser.: 3). 2002. 15.00 (978-1-57399-152-0(X)) Mac Hammond.
The money test. How you relate to money and the material realm determines the amount of resource God entrusts to you as His steward. Discover the practical principles from the Word for passing the money test and becoming a faithful steward of the true riches of God.

Passing the Test Vol. I: Earthly Training for an Eternal Destiny. 5. (Running Time: 5 hrs.). (Passing the Test Ser.: 1). 2002. 25.00 (978-1-57399-124-7(4)) Mac Hammond.
In this thought-provoking series entitled Passing the Test, Mac Hammond explains that once you're born again, life is a series of tests. How well you pass or manage these eartly tests will determine the extent of you eternal rullership with Jesus.

Passing Tones. Duane Shinn. 1 cass. 19.95 (CP-13) Duane Shinn.
Discusses how to use passing tones to make a boring chord interesting; to change chords' to create an intro; to create a counter-point to the melody & so on.

Passion see Maupassant's Best Known Stories

Passion. (ENG.). 2009. audio compact disk 20.00 (978-0-9766470-2-7(8)) Guld Resource.

Passion. unabr. ed. Donna Boyd. Narrated by Paul Hecht. 10 cass. (Running Time: 13 hrs. 45 mins.). 2000. 88.00 (978-0-7887-4949-0(8), 96261E7) Recorded Bks.
A dark & sensuous world in which werewolves live undetected amidst humans. A sweeping epic that spans a century, it is the story of two werewolf brothers & Tessa, a young human woman who will reshape the destiny of both races.

***Passion.** unabr. ed. Lauren Kate. (ENG.). (J). 2011. audio compact disk 40.00 (978-0-307-70651-5(6), Listening Lib) Pub: Random Audio Pubg. Dist(s): Random

***Passion.** unabr. ed. L. J. Smith. Read by Khristine Huam & Khristine Hvam. (Running Time: 6 hrs.). (Dark Visions Ser.: Bk. 3). 2010. 19.99 (978-1-4418-5920-4(9), 9781441859204, Brilliance MP3) Brilliance Audio.

***Passion.** unabr. ed. L. J. Smith. Read by Khristine Hvam. (Running Time: 6 hrs.). (Dark Visions Ser.: Bk. 3). 2010. 39.97 (978-1-4418-5921-1(7), 9781441859211, Brinc Audio MP3 Lib); 39.97 (978-1-4418-5922-8(5), 9781441859228, BADLE) Brilliance Audio.

***Passion.** unabr. ed. L. J. Smith. Read by Khristine Huam & Khristine Hvam. (Running Time: 6 hrs.). (Dark Visions Ser.: Bk. 3). 2010. audio compact disk 19.99 (978-1-4418-5918-1(7), 9781441859181, Bril Audio CD Unabri) Brilliance Audio.

***Passion.** unabr. ed. L. J. Smith. Read by Khristine Hvam. (Running Time: 6 hrs.). (Dark Visions Ser.: Bk. 3). 2010. audio compact disk 59.97 (978-1-4418-5919-8(5), 9781441859198, BriAudCD Unabrid) Brilliance Audio.

Passion & Glory. 1 cass. (BibleQuizmania Ser.). Orig. Title: The Easter Story. (SPA.). 14.95 (978-0-97929536-17-0(7)) Emb Cassettes.

Passion & Promise: The Easter Story. Narrated by Max E. McLean. 2002. audio compact disk 9.95 (978-1-931047-25-8(1)) Fellow Perform Arts.

Passion & Purity: Learning to Bring Your Love Life under Christ's Control. unabr. ed. Elisabeth Elliot. Read by Elisabeth Elliot. 2 cass. (Running Time: 2 hrs. 20 min.). 1989. 14.95 (978-0-8474-2016-2(7)) Back to Bible.
Principles for preserving your chastity & letting God purify your love.

Passion & Purpose. John Mackey. 2009. audio compact disk 19.95 (978-1-59179-688-6(1)) Sounds True.

Passion & Resurrection Narratives of Jesus. unabr. ed. 4 cass. (Running Time: 6 hrs.). (Little Rock Scripture Study Ser.). 2002. 31.00 (978-0-8146-7616-5(2)) Liturgical Pr.
Enter into the core events of your faith. Four lessons on the Passion of Jesus will help you find meaning in the suffering and death of Jesus. Two lessons on the Resurrection will help you celebrate the new life of Easter.

Passion Dance. Perf. by Roseanna Vitro. 1 cass., 1 CD. 7.98 (TA 33385); audio compact disk 12.78 CD Jewel box. (TA 83385) NewSound.

Passion for Existence: Prem Rawat at Thammasat University in Bangkok, Thailand. Prem Rawat. (ENG.). 2006. audio compact disk 10.00 (978-1-933717-02-9(5)) P Rawat.

Passion for Holiness: Passion for Holiness Series. Ben Young. 2000. 4.95 (978-0-7417-6208-5(0), B0208) Win Walk.

Passion for Life. 2001. 10.00 (978-1-58602-074-3(9)); audio compact disk 19.99 (978-1-58602-082-8(X)) E L Long.

Passion for Life: Authentic Success & Conscious Living. unabr. ed. Liliane Fournier. Read by Liliane Fournier. (Running Time: 2 hrs.). (Quest Ser.). 2009. 39.97 (978-1-4233-8046-7(0), 9781423380467, Brlnc Audio MP3 Lib); 19.99 (978-1-4233-8045-0(2), 9781423380450, Brilliance MP3); audio compact disk 55.97 (978-1-4233-8044-3(4), 9781423380443, BriAudCD Unabrid) Brilliance Audio.

Passion for Life: Celebrity Musings from the Fairways, Set. abr. ed. Ann Liqvori. Read by Ann Liqvori. 2 cass. (Running Time: 3 hrs.). 2000. 18.00 (978-0-9668567-4-3(0)) MediaBay Audio.
Ann Liquori has collected 15 of her most fascinating interviews with celebrities, recorded as she played golf with them.

Passion for Life: The Biography of Elizabeth Taylor. unabr. ed. Donald Spoto. Read by C. M. Herbert. 9 cass. (Running Time: 13 hrs.). 1995. 62.95 (978-0-7861-0807-7(X), 1630) Blckstn Audio.
Explores the brilliant performances of her private life, in her marriage to hotel heir Nicky Hilton; her marriage to Mike Todd, who a year later died in a plane crash; & her two marriages to Richard Burton, with whom she would share a hedonistic, brash lifestyle that defined the 1960's jet set.

Passion for Souls: The Life of D. L. Moody. unabr. ed. Lyle Dorsett. 14 CDs. (Running Time: 17 hrs. 30 mins. 0 sec.). (ENG.). 2005. audio compact disk 34.98 (978-1-59644-184-2(4), Hovel Audio) christianaud.

***Passion for Souls: The Life of D. L. Moody.** unabr. ed. Lyle W. Dorsett. Narrated by Jonathan Marosz. (ENG.). 2005. 19.98 (978-1-59644-185-9(2), Hovel Audio) christianaud.

Passion for Souls: The Life of D. L. Moody. unabr. ed. Lyle W. Dorsett. Narrated by Jonathan Morosz. 2 MP3 CDs. (Running Time: 17 hrs. 30 mins. 0 sec.). (ENG.). 2005. lp 29.98 (978-1-59644-183-5(6), Hovel Audio) christianaud.

Passion for the Gospel see Pasion por el Evangelio

Passion for the Gospel. 2006. 30.00 (978-1-57972-751-2(4)); audio compact disk 30.00 (978-1-57972-750-5(6)) Insight Living.

Passion for the Possible: A Message for U. S. Churches. William S. Coffin. (Running Time: 3 hrs.). 1997. reel tape 19.95 (978-0-664-25725-5(9), 257259) Westminster John Knox.
Deals clearly & realistically with the many controversial social issues facing U. S. churches.

Passion Narratives of the Gospels. Raymond E. Brown. (Running Time: 8 hrs. 30 min.). 2004. 69.00 (978-1-904756-02-6(6)) STL Dist NA.

Passion Novena: A Scriptural Rosary on Audiocassette. Larry London & Connie London. 5 cass. (Running Time: 4 hrs. 35 min.). 1996. 24.95 Set. (978-0-87973-186-1(9)) Our Sunday Visitor.
In times of need & distress, no prayer is more comforting than the Rosary. A unique set of nine Rosary mysteries, this novena for the '90s allows you to reflect on the mysteries of salvation, while asking Mary herself to join you in your prayer of petition. Includes the Fatima Prayer.

Passion of Ayn Rand, Pt. 1. unabr. collector's ed. Barbara Branden. Read by Mary Pfeiffer. 8 cass. (Running Time: 12 hrs.). 1991. 64.00 (978-0-7366-1898-4(8), 2725 A) Books on Tape.
Ayn Rand was larger than life. She lived on an epic scale. She was intellectual & emotional, exalted but tragic, a passionate lover who could burn with hatred. She was extremely admired & savagely attacked. No one was neutral about her. Yet despite the furor, her life remained private. Her public & professional activities took place on a lighted stage, her personal life was a background. Her personal life revealed for the first time in this biography was the stuff of legend.

Passion of Ayn Rand, Pt. 2. collector's ed. Barbara Branden. Read by Mary Pfeiffer. 8 cass. (Running Time: 12 hrs.). 1991. 64.00 (978-0-7366-1899-1(6)) Books on Tape.
Ayn Rand was larger than life. She lived life on an epic scale. She was intellectual & emotional, exalted but tragic, a passionate lover who could burn with hatred. She was extremely admired & yet savagely attacked. No one was neutral about her. Yet despite her furor, her life remained private Her public & professional activities took place on a lighted stage, her personal life was the background. Her personal life, revealed here for the first time, was the stuff of legend.

Passion of Frankenstein. Thomas E. Fuller. 1 cass. (Running Time: 1 hr.). 2001. 12.95 (ARTC006) Lodestone Catalog.

Passion of Frankenstein. unabr. ed. Abr. by Thomas E. Fuller. Retold by Mary Wollstonecraft Shelley. 1 cass. (Running Time: 90 min.). Dramatization. 2002. 12.95 Centauri Express Co.

Passion of Jesus: Dramatized Audio Stories. 4 CDs. 2006. 15.00 (978-1-60079-043-0(7)) YourStory.

Passion of Love. Ellen G. White. Narrated by Eddie Hernandez. 5 CDs. 2004. audio compact disk 39.95 (978-1-883012-20-5(1)) Remnant Pubns.

Passion Principles Seven Steps to Living the Life You Love. abr. ed. Read by William Kilgore. Perf. by William Kilgore. 1 cass. (Running Time: 45 min.). (YA). 1996. cass. & video 10.00 (978-1-890896-00-3(4)) Passion Pub.
Seven principles to practice to follow your dream, discover your passion in life.

Passion, Profit & Power. Marshall Sylver. 6 cass. (Running Time: 6 hrs.). 1995. 69.95 Set, incl. wkbk. (12880PA) Nightingale-Conant.
In this mind-expanding program, you'll learn to master your inner power to create your own destiny by programming your brain to get what you want out of life.

Passion, Purpose & Cause. Mac Hammond. 2008. audio compact disk 6.00 (978-1-57399-382-1(4)) Mac Hammond.

Passion, Rejection, & Criticism. Directed By Gerald Rogers. Contrib. by Dennis C. Daley. (Living Sober 2 Ser.: Segment K). 1996. pap. bk. 89.00 NTSC. (978-1-56215-068-6(5), Jossey-Bass) Wiley US.

Passion Service. Mother Basilea Schlink. Evang Sisterhood Mary.
"Let Me Stand At Your Side", this program includes: Jesus on the Way to Gethsemane; Jesus in the Garden of Gethsemane; Jesus' Arrest: Jesus on Trial Before Annas & Caiaphas; Peter's Denial: Jesus' Path of Disgrace Through Jerusalem to Pilate; Mocked at Herod's Palace; Jesus on Trial Before Pilate's Supreme Court; Jesus Is Scourged; Jesus Crowned with Thorns; Jesus Bears the Crucifixion. Each program can be ordered separately.

Passion Test. unabr. ed. Janet Attwood & Chris Attwood. (ENG.). 2006. 24.98 (978-1-59659-115-8(3), GildAudio) Pub: Gildan Media. Dist(s): HachBkGrp

Passion Test: The Effortless Path to Discovering Your Destiny. rev. unabr. ed. Janet Bray Attwood & Chris Attwood. Read by Janet Bray Attwood & Chris Attwood. (Running Time: 6 hrs.). (ENG.). 2008. audio compact disk 29.98 (978-1-59659-132-5(3), GildAudio) Pub: Gildan Media. Dist(s): HachBkGrp

Passion to Win. Sumner Redstone. Told to Peter Knobler. 2004. 10.95 (978-0-7435-4560-0(5)) Pub: S&S Audio. Dist(s): S and S Inc

Passion to Win. abr. ed. Sumner Redstone. 3 CDs. (Running Time: 4 hrs.). 2001. audio compact disk 29.00 Books on Tape.
In this most fascinating business autobiography, Sumner Redstone tells the unvarnished story of how he overcame every obstacle to build a vast media and entertainment empire. Behind it all is the same iron will that helped him survive a fire by clinging to a third-story ledge before being rescued. Never before has Redstone revealed himself so candidly in a true life story.

***Passion Unleashed.** unabr. ed. Larissa Ione. (Running Time: 13 hrs.). (Demonica Ser.). (ENG.). 2011. 24.98 (978-1-60941-542-6(6)) Pub: Hachet Audio. Dist(s): HachBkGrp

Passion (YS Distributed) Zondervan Publishing Staff. 2005. audio compact disk 17.99 (978-0-310-66084-2(X)) Zondervan.

Passionate Life. Michael Breen & Walt Kallestad. 2005. audio compact disk 19.99 (978-1-58926-950-7(0)) Oasis Audio.

Passionate Life. abr. ed. Mike Breen & Walt Kallestad. (ENG.). 2005. 13.99 (978-1-60814-024-4(5)) Oasis Audio.

Passionate Life: Stages of Loving. Sam Keen. 3 cass. 27.00 (OC29W) Sound Horizons AV.

Passionate Motivation. unabr. ed. Dick Sutphen. Read by Dick Sutphen. 1 cass. (Running Time: 30 min.). (Quick Fix Meditations Ser.). 1998. 10.98 (978-0-87554-623-0(4), QF105) Valley Sun.
Become more inspired, energized & motivated. Be warmed by the awareness of intensifying motivation. Be persistent, ambitious & determined.

Passionate People. unabr. collector's ed. Roger Kahn. Read by Michael Russotto. 10 cass. (Running Time: 15 hrs.). 1991. 80.00 (978-0-7366-1929-5(1), 2752) Books on Tape.
What is it like to be Jewish & American? Roger Kahn, himself Jewish, had his own answer, worked out through time & experience. But he wanted to explore it with others, so he launched a professional query.

Passionate Pilgrim see Rape of Lucrece & Other Poems

Passionate Sage: The Character & Legacy of John Adams. unabr. ed. Joseph J. Ellis. Read by Tom Parker. 6 cass. (Running Time: 8 hrs. 30 mins.). 1995. 44.95 (978-0-7861-0769-8(3), 1618) Blckstn Audio.
John Adams, one of the Founding Fathers of our nation & its second president, spent nearly the last third of his life in retirement grappling with contradictory views of his place in history & fearing his reputation would not fare well in the generations after his death. Joseph Ellis explores the mind & personality of the man as well as the earlier events that shaped his thinking. Listeners will discover Adams to be both contentious & lovable, generous & petty, & the most intellectually profound of the revolutionary generation, a man who may have contributed to the earlier underestimates of his role in history, & whose perspective on America's prospects has relevance for us today.

Passionate Shepherd see Palgrave's Golden Treasury of English Poetry

Passionate Times. unabr. ed. Emma Blair. Read by Eve Karpf. 10 cass. (Running Time: 10 hrs.). 1996. 84.95 (978-0-7451-6600-1(8), CAB1216) AudioGO.
When Corporal Rieth Douglas received a head injury in Greece during World War II, he might have anticipated a hero's welcome on his return home. However, when Douglas arrives home in Glascow, his life becomes living hell. With his wife's declaration of love for one of the city's foremost villains, Douglas finds his only solace in Catie Smith. Could she possibly hold the key to recapturing the passionate times of his past?.

Passionate Woman: Hadewijch of Antwerp. Elizabeth Dreyer. 1 cass. (Running Time: 1 hr.). 1991. 7.95 (TAH233) Alba Hse Comns.
The passionate spirituality of Hadewijch is attractively presented here & will spur many listeners on to study her writings.

Passions see Treasury of Oliver Goldsmith, Thomas Gray & William Collins

Passions: Philosophy & the Intelligence of Emotions. Instructed by Robert Solomon. 12 cass. (Running Time: 12 hrs.). 54.95 (978-1-59803-052-5(3)) Teaching Co.

Passions: Philosophy & the Intelligence of Emotions. Instructed by Robert Solomon. 12 CDs. (Running Time: 12 hrs.). 2006. audio compact disk 69.95 (978-1-59803-054-9(X)) Teaching Co.

Passions & Howard Hughes. abr. ed. Terry Moore & Jerry Rivers. Read by Terry Moore. 2 cass. (Running Time: 3 hrs.). 1995. 16.95 (978-1-882071-74-6(3), 636828) B-B Audio.
In this new book by former wife and legally recognized widow, Ms. Terry Moore, the private Hughes is finally revealed.This is a compelling account of his passions for flying and his love for Hollywood's most famous starlets. Now his best friend and c.

***Passions & Prejudice.** Spindletop Productions. Read by Spindletop Productions. (Running Time: 400). (ENG.). 2010. audio compact disk 29.95 (978-0-9645617-5-5(1)) Spindletop Prod.

Passions of Chelsea Kane. abr. ed. Barbara Delinsky. Read by Karen Ziemba. 2004. 15.95 (978-0-7435-4814-4(0)) Pub: S&S Audio. Dist(s): S and S Inc

Passions of the Mind. Frances Paige. Read by Mary Gardner. 5 cass. (Storysound Ser.). (J). 2001. 49.95 (978-1-85903-382-1(2)) Pub: Mgna Lrg Print GBR. Dist(s): Ulverscroft US

Passions of the Mind: A Novel of Sigmund Freud. unabr. ed. Irving Stone. Read by Wolfram Kandinsky. 27 cass. (Running Time: 40 hrs. 30 mins.). Incl. Pt. 1. Passions of the Mind: A Novel of Sigmund Freud. 14 cass. (Running Time: 21 hrs.). Irving Stone. Read by Wolfram Kandinsky. 1981. 112.00 (1225-A); Pt. 2. Passions of the Mind: A Novel of Sigmund Freud. 13 cass. (Running Time: 19 hrs. 30 mins.). Irving Stone. Read by Wolfram Kandinsky. 1981. 104.00 (1225-B); 1984. 216.00 (978-0-7366-0228-0(3), 1225- A&B) Books on Tape.
When Freud was a young man in Vienna, the world seemed a simple place. But to Freud, growing up in the medical profession, his world was the human mind. But as his insights grew, he could not remain within bounds previously set. As he developed techniques for inquiry, conservative members of the medical profession tried to hold him in check, which meant his professional work would always be dogged by controversy.

Passive Electronics in Germany: A Strategic Reference 2007. Compiled by Icon Group International, Inc. Staff. 2007. ring bd. 195.00 (978-0-497-35979-9(0)) Icon Grp.

Passive Muscle Relaxation: A Program for Client Use. Mark S. Schwartz & Stephen N. Haynes. 1 cass. (Running Time: 38 min.). (ENG.). 1989. 16.95 (978-0-89862-817-3(2)) Guilford Pubns.

Passive Muscle Relaxation: A Program for Client Use. Mark S. Schwartz & Stephen N. Haynes. (ENG.). 2003. audio compact disk 16.95 (978-1-60623-036-7(0)) Guilford Pubns.

Passive Music for Accelerated Learning: How to Increase Your Brainpower Without Even Thinking. abr. ed. Roland Roberts. 2 cass. (Running Time: 2 hrs.). 2000. 24.95 (978-1-899836-60-4(8)) Crown Hse GBR.

Passive Parenting: Genesis 19. Ed Young. 1994. 4.95 (978-0-7417-2035-1(3), 1035) Win Walk.

***Passkey Enrolled Agent Review Audiobook: Individuals, Businesses, & Representation.** Christy Pinheiro & Kevin M. Young. (ENG.). (C). 2010. audio compact disk 79.00 (978-1-935664-00-0(X), PassKey) PasskeyPub.

Passover: Exodus 14. Ed Young. 1984. 4.95 (978-0-7417-1422-0(1), 422) Win Walk.

Passover & Easter Story/Choosing Joy. Marianne Williamson. Read by Marianne Williamson. 1 cass. (Running Time: 90 mins.). (Lectures on a Course in Miracles). (ENG.). 1998. 10.00 (978-1-56170-604-4(3), M856) Hay House.

Passover Starter Pack: Basic Items for Celebrating Your Messianic Passover Seder Dinner. 2002. pap. bk. 16.99 (978-1-880226-96-4(0)) Messianic Jewsh Pubs.

Passport: What Really Happened at Calvary. Carlisle John Peterson. 10 cass. (Running Time: 15 hrs.). 1999. pap. bk. 39.00 Set. (978-1-889448-26-8(5)) Great Hse Pub.
Foundation teachings on the full transaction of redemption, of man's soul from the powers of death, when Christ was crucified at Calvary.

Passport to Adventure. AIO Team Staff. Prod. by Focus on the Family Staff. 4 CDs. (Running Time: 6 hrs.). (Adventures in Odyssey Ser.: Vol. 19). (ENG.). (J). (gr. 3-7). 1994. audio compact disk 24.99 (978-1-56179-266-5(7), 6033) Pub: Focus Family. Dist(s): Tyndale Hse

Passport to France Travel Pak. Robert S. Kane. 1 cass. bk. & stu. ed. 29.95 (978-0-8442-9229-8(X), Passport Bks) McGraw-Hill Trade.
An introduction to the country's culture & customs, plus brief language orientation of common words, phrases & expressions.

Passport to Profits. 2000. (978-1-57042-928-6(6)) Hachet Audio.

Passport to Profits: Why the Next Investment Windfalls Will Be Found Abroad?and How to Grab Your Share. abr. ed. Mark Mobius & Stephen Fenichell. (Running Time: 3 hrs.). (ENG.). 2006. 14.98 (978-1-59483-855-2(0)) Pub: Hachet Audio. Dist(s): HachBkGrp

Passport to Purity: Guide Your Child on an Adventure to Maturity. Dennis Rainey et al. 4 cass. 2004. bk. 29.99 (978-1-57229-199-7(0)) FamilyLife.

Passport's Ingles para Ninos (English for Children) Catherine Bruzzone. 1 cass. (ENG & SPA., (J). (ps-3). 1995. pap. bk. 29.95 (978-0-8442-0787-2(X), 0787X, Passport Bks) McGraw-Hill Trade.
A wonderful beginning course for children that teaches basic language functions using songs & activities. An accompanying cassette is provided for parents & teachers with explanations on how to supplement the learning process.

Passport's Storyland Fables Series. Carol Barnett. 1 cass. (Running Time: 30 min.). 8.95 (Natl Textbk Co) M-H Contemporary.

Password: Communication for preteens 1 - Lct. Waldyr Lima. 2008. audio compact disk (978-0-7428-0057-1(1)) CCLS Pubg Hse.

Password: Communication for Preteens 2 CD. Waldyr Lima. 2009. audio compact disk (978-0-7428-0056-4(3)) CCLS Pubg Hse.

Password: Communication for Preteens 2 LCT. Waldyr Lima. 2009. audio compact disk (978-0-7428-0104-2(7)) CCLS Pubg Hse.

Password Communication for Bigger Kids Book 1 Audio CD: ELT - English Language Teaching. Waldyr Lima. 2007. audio compact disk (978-0-7428-1787-6(3)) CCLS Pubg Hse.

Password Communication for Bigger Kids Book 1 Student's Book (with CD) ELT - English Language Teaching. Waldyr Lima. 2007. spiral bd. (978-0-7428-1643-5(5)) CCLS Pubg Hse.

Password Communication for Bigger Kids Book 2 Audio CD: ELT - English Language Teaching. Waldyr Lima. (ENG.). 2007. audio compact disk (978-0-7428-0088-5(1)) CCLS Pubg Hse.

Password Communication for Bigger Kids Book 2 Student's Book (with Audio CD) ELT - English Language Teaching. Waldyr Lima. (ENG., 2007. pap. bk. (978-0-7428-0037-3(7)) CCLS Pubg Hse.

Password Communication for Kids Book 1 Audio CD: ELT - English Language Teaching. Waldyr Lima. 2006. audio compact disk (978-0-7428-1604-6(4)) CCLS Pubg Hse.
The two-book EFL/ESL series Password: Communication for Kids is designed for young learners who are about eight years old. The objective of the series is to teach children how to communicate in English. The material of each lesson takes into account the stage of the student?s development and growth within his or her particular age group. Students learn English in a pleasant way through real-life dialogues, readings, activities with picture cards, songs, and games. In the classroom, this diversity of activities creates a dynamic environment in which effective learning takes place in an enjoyable way.The interaction of the student with the teacher, with the other students, and with the material enables students to communicate naturally in English as they participate in activities which are in perfect harmony with the interests of their age group.Each book of the series contains 10 lessons.Password: Communication for Kids consists of:Student?s materialStudent?s Book (SB)CD (containing Easy Words, Lesson Situations, Reading Texts, and Songs)Teacher?s materialLesson Plan Book (LP)DVD?s Picture Card KitGame Kit.

Password Communication for Kids Book 1 Student's Book (with CD) ELT - English Language Teaching. Waldyr Lima. 2006. spiral bd. (978-0-7428-1692-3(3)) CCLS Pubg Hse.

Password Communication for Kids Book 2 Audio CD: ELT - English Language Teaching. Waldyr Lima. 2006. audio compact disk (978-0-7428-1683-1(4)) CCLS Pubg Hse.

Password Communication for Kids Book 2 Student's Book (with CD) ELT - English Language Teaching. Waldyr Lima. 2006. spiral bd. (978-0-7428-1754-8(7)) CCLS Pubg Hse.

Password communication for preteens Book 1 Audio CD. Waldyr Lima. 2008. audio compact disk (978-0-7428-0055-7(5)) CCLS Pubg Hse.

Password Communication for Preteens Book 1 Texbook (with CD) Waldyr Lima. (ENG.). 2008. spiral bd. (978-0-7428-0094-6(6)) CCLS Pubg Hse.

Password Communication for Preteens 2 Textbook (with CD) Waldyr Lima. (ENG.). 2009. spiral bd. (978-0-7428-0034-2(2)) CCLS Pubg Hse.

***Password _Effective_Communication Book 1 - Listening Comprehension Test - Audio CD: Elt - english language Teaching.** Waldyr Lima. (ENG.). 2007. audio compact disk (978-0-7428-1741-8(5)) CCLS Pubg Hse.

***Password _Effective_Communication Book 2 - Listening Comprehension Test - Audio CD.** Waldyr Lima. (ENG.). 2008. audio compact disk (978-0-7428-0048-9(2)) CCLS Pubg Hse.

***Password_Effective_Communication Book 1 CALL CD ROM: English Language Teaching.** Waldyr Lima. (ENG.). 2007. audio compact disk (978-0-7428-1693-0(1)) CCLS Pubg Hse.

Past Caring. unabr. ed. Robert Goddard. Read by Paul Shelley. 14 cass. (Running Time: 21 hrs.). 2002. 110.95 (978-0-7540-0737-1(5), CAB 2159) AudioGO.

Past Caring. unabr. ed. Robert Goddard. Read by Paul Shelley. 16 CDs. (Running Time: 24 hrs.). 2002. audio compact disk 119.95 (978-0-7540-5470-2(5), CCD 161) AudioGO.

***Past Due.** abr. ed. William Lashner. Read by Peter Francis James. (ENG.). 2004. (978-0-06-081406-9(3), Harper Audio); (978-0-06-079799-7(1), Harper Audio) HarperCollins Pubs.

Past Forgetting: Memories of the Hammer Years. unabr. ed. Peter Cushing. Read by Peter Cushing. 3 cass. (Running Time: 3 hrs. 40 min.). (Isis Ser.). (J). 2004. 34.95 (978-1-85089-618-0(6), 89111) Pub: ISIS Lrg Prnt GBR. Dist(s): Ulverscroft US

Past Is Myself. unabr. ed. Christabel Bielenberg. Read by Sheila Mitchell. 8 cass. (Running Time: 11 hrs. 23 min.). 2001. 69.95 (978-1-85695-556-0(7), 93054) Pub: ISIS Audio GBR. Dist(s): Ulverscroft US

Past-Life Interview with Titanic's Designer. unabr. ed. William Barnes & Frank Baranowski. 2 cass. (Running Time: 3 hrs.). 1999. 18.00 Set. (978-1-887010-11-5(4)) Edin Bks.
A live eyewitness account, recorded under hypnosis, from the man who holds the memories of Thomas Andrews, Titanic's historic shipbuilder.

Past Life Journey. Read by Mary Richards. 1 cass. (Running Time: 65 min.). (Series Two Thousand). 2007. audio compact disk 19.95 (978-1-56136-108-3(9)) Master Your Mind.

Past-Life Regression. 1 cass. (Ultra-Depth Hypnosis Ser.). 14.98 (978-0-87554-587-5(4), UDC801) Valley Sun.

Past Life Regression. Bettye B. Binder. Read by Bettye B. Binder. 8 cass. 29.95 SET. (978-1-879005-04-4(2)) Reincarnation Bks.
Contains exercises for distinguishing memory from imagination, how to conduct past life regressions & offers a demonstration on a past life regression on student in class. Instructional course that supplement Past Life Regression Guidebook (now in its 7th printing).

Past Life Regression. Bruce Goldberg. (ENG.). 2005. audio compact disk 17.00 (978-1-57968-031-2(0)) Pub: B Goldberg. Dist(s): Baker Taylor

Past Life Regression. Bruce Goldberg. 1 cass. (Hypnotic Time Travel Ser.). (ENG.). 2006. 13.00 (978-1-885577-03-0(6)) Pub: B Goldberg. Dist(s): Baker Taylor
Self hypnosis program that guides you back into previous lifetimes.

Past Life Regression. Barrie Konicov. Read by Barrie Konicov. 1 cass. 16.98 (978-1-56001-323-5(0), SC-II 095) Potentials.

Past Life Regression. Barrie Konicov. 2003. audio compact disk 16.98 (978-0-87082-976-5(9)) Potentials.

Past Life Regression. Barrie Konicov. 2 CDs. 2003. audio compact disk 27.98 (978-1-56001-984-8(0)) Potentials.
The experiences that we plant in our past lives are harvested in the future. Is it possible to reconstruct your present life by releasing yourself of all the negativity of the past?This 2-CD program from our Super Consciousness series is our newest, most powerful format. On the self-hypnosis CD, SC programs have the Subliminal Persuasion soundtrack added under Barrie?s voice. And the 17th Century Baroque music on the Subliminal CD has the same beat as your body's natural rhythm, thereby allowing the suggestions to enter deeply and effortlessly.

Past-Life Regression. Dick Sutphen. 1 cass. (Running Time: 1 hr.). (RX17 Ser.). 14.98 (978-0-87554-354-3(5), RX201) Valley Sun.

Past-Life Regression. Dick Sutphen. 1 cass. (Ultra-Depth Hypnosis Ser.). audio compact disk 19.98 CD. (978-0-87554-586-8(6), UD101) Valley Sun.

Past-Life Regression. Brian L. Weiss. Read by Brian L. Weiss. 2 cass. (Running Time: 3 hrs.). 1995. 16.95 (978-1-56170-140-7(8), 280) Hay House.
Learn specific techniques for exploring your past lives.

Past Life Regression - Shaman's Journey, No. 5. Kathleen Milner. 1 cass. (Running Time: 45 min.). 1995. 11.00 (978-1-886903-54-8(9)) K Milner.
Begins with a healing meditation for the physical body & concludes with a healing for the past life that was experienced. "Shaman's Journey" is a meditation with colors, symbols & the shaman's drum.

Past Life Regression & Afterlife Journey. unabr. ed. Marci Archambeault. Read by Marci Archambeault. 1 cass. (Running Time: 1 hr.). 1994. pap. bk. 14.95 (978-1-888861-01-3(0)) Quest MA.
Meditation will bring you to experience other lifetimes where you will be able to gain knowledge that will help free your life.

Past Life Regression with Mate or Lover. Barrie Konicov. 1 cass. 11.98 (978-0-87082-403-6(1), 096) Potentials.
The past often holds the key to understanding the present. Explore your past life, relationships with your mate or lover & add meaning to your present life experience.

Past-Life Regression with the Angels. Doreen Virtue. 1 CD. 2004. audio compact disk 10.95 (978-1-4019-0402-9(5)) Hay House.

Past-Life Release. 1 cass. (Tara Sutphen Meditation Tapes Ser.). 11.98 (978-0-87554-592-9(0), TS211) Valley Sun.

Past Life Therapy. Barrie Konicov. 1 CD. 2004. audio compact disk 19.98 (978-1-56001-686-1(8)) Potentials.
The experiences that we plant in our past lives are harvested in the future. Is it possible to reconstruct your present life by releasing yourself of all the negativity of the past?You will find the self-hypnosis on track 1 and the subliminal on track 2. The easy-listening music of the subliminal, together with the self-hypnosis, is the original format which most people love and with which they are most familiar.

Past-Life Therapy: Regression Album with Four Regression Sessions. Dick Sutphen. 2 cass. pap. bk. 24.98 (978-0-911842-45-6(4), AX901) Valley Sun.
Uses past-life therapy to eliminate problems by getting at the cause, either from this life or a past life.

Past Lives. Ken McClure & Ken Mcclure. 7 cass. (Running Time: 8 hrs. 30 mins.). (Isis Cassettes Ser.). 2007. 61.95 (978-0-7531-3666-9(X)) Pub: ISIS Lrg Prnt GBR. Dist(s): Ulverscroft US

Past Lives - Present Fears. Lee Carroll. Read by Lee Carroll. 1 cass. (Running Time: 1 hr. 07 min.). (Kryon Tapes Ser.). 1995. 10.00 (978-0-9636304-5-2(8)) Kryon Writings.
Live recording of channelled event.

Past Lives, Future Healing: A Psychic Reveals the Secrets to Good Health & Great Relationships. abr. ed. Sylvia Browne. Read by Sylvia Browne. 2 CDs. (Running Time: 2 hrs. 30 mins.). (ENG.). 2001. audio compact disk 22.95 (978-1-56511-481-4(7), 1565114817) Pub: HighBridge. Dist(s): Workman Pub

Past Lives Regressions Astrology. Jeanne Avery. Read by Jeanne Avery. 1 cass. (Running Time: 90 min.). 1994. 8.95 (1143) Am Fed Astrologers.

Past Lives, Soulmates & You. Edwards-Ticehur. 2001. audio compact disk 12.95 (978-0-646-19129-4(2)) Joshua Bks AUS.

Past Love. unabr. ed. Nicola Thorne. 7 cass. (Isis Ser.). (J). 2002. 61.95 (978-0-7531-1373-8(2)) Pub: ISIS Lrg Prnt GBR. Dist(s): Ulverscroft US

Past Mortem. Ben Elton. 10 CDs. (Running Time: 12 hrs. 38 mins.). (Isis (CDs) Ser.). (J). 2005. audio compact disk 89.95 (978-0-7531-2407-9(6)) Pub: ISIS Lrg Prnt GBR. Dist(s): Ulverscroft US

Past Mortem. unabr. ed. Ben Elton. 10 cass. (Running Time: 12 hrs. 38 mins.). (Isis Cassettes Ser.). (J). 2005. 84.95 (978-0-7531-2169-6(7)) Pub: ISIS Lrg Prnt GBR. Dist(s): Ulverscroft US

Past Perfect. abr. ed. Susan Isaacs. Read by Randye Kaye. (Running Time: 6 hrs.). 2008. audio compact disk 14.99 (978-1-4233-3894-9(4), 9781423338949, BCD Value Price) Brilliance Audio.

Past Perfect. unabr. ed. Susan Isaacs. Read by Randye Kaye. (Running Time: 39600 sec.). 2007. 82.25 (978-1-4233-3887-1(1), 9781423338871, BrilAudUnabridg); audio compact disk 102.25 (978-1-4233-3889-5(8), 9781423338895, BriAudCD Unabrid); audio compact disk 39.25 (978-1-4233-3891-8(X), 9781423338918, Brinc Audio MP3 Lib); audio compact disk 24.95 (978-1-4233-3890-1(1), 9781423338901, Brilliance MP3); audio compact disk 36.95 (978-1-4233-3888-8(X), 9781423338888, Bril Audio CD Unabri) Brilliance Audio.

Past Perfect. unabr. ed. Susan Isaacs. Read by Randye Kaye. (Running Time: 11 hrs.). 2007. 24.95 (978-1-4233-3892-5(8), 9781423338925, BAD) Brilliance Audio.

Past Perfect, Present Tense. unabr. ed. Richard Peck. 4 CDs. (Running Time: 4 hrs. 44 mins.). (YA). 2005. audio compact disk 45.00 (978-0-307-20699-2(8), Listening Lib); 35.00 (978-0-307-20698-5(X), Listening Lib) Random Audio Pubg.
Richard Peck treats us to a collection of all of his short stories, divided into The First, The Past, The Supernatural, and The Present.

Past Premiere Performances. As told by Andy Andrews. 2004. audio compact disk 39.99 (978-0-9776246-1-4(7)) Lightning Crown Pub.

***Past Reason Hated: A Novel of Suspense.** unabr. ed. Peter Robinson. Narrated by James Langton. (Running Time: 13 hrs. 0 mins. 0 sec.). (Inspector Banks Ser.). 2010. 24.99 (978-1-4001-6273-4(4)); 18.99 (978-1-4001-8273-2(5)); audio compact disk 37.99 (978-1-4001-1273-9(7)) Pub: Tantor Media. Dist(s): IngramPubServ

***Past Reason Hated (Library Edition) A Novel of Suspense.** unabr. ed. Peter Robinson. Narrated by James Langton. (Running Time: 13 hrs. 0 mins.). (Inspector Banks Ser.). 2010. 37.99 (978-1-4001-9273-1(0)); audio compact disk 90.99 (978-1-4001-4273-6(3)) Pub: Tantor Media. Dist(s): IngramPubServ

Past Remembering. unabr. ed. Catrin Collier. Read by Helen Griffin. 10 cass. (Running Time: 15 hrs.). 2001. 84.95 (978-0-7540-0661-9(1), CAB 2083) Pub: Chivers Audio Bks GBR. Dist(s): AudioGO
Pontypridd, 1941, and Britain stands alone. The war-torn lives of the community are burdened by rationing and fed on rumor and speculation.

Pasta, Please! Sundance/Newbridge, LLC Staff. (Early Science Ser.). (gr. k-3). 2007. audio compact disk 12.00 (978-1-4007-6334-4(7)); audio compact disk 12.00 (978-1-4007-6335-1(5)); audio compact disk 12.00 (978-1-4007-6336-8(3)) Sund Newbrdge.

Pastel de Javier, EDL Level 16. (Fonolibros Ser.: Vol. 3). (SPA.). 2003. 11.50 (978-0-7652-1023-4(1)) Modern Curr.

Pastel Shades. Perf. by Jacinta Write. Created by Matthew Manning. Prod. by Stuart Wilde. 1 cass. 10.95 (CN604) White Dove NM.
A passionate, rolling piano work that is a celebration of discovery. It encompasses many moods, delicate, gentle, bold, longing, joyful, & full of wonder. Jacinta Write is an award winning concert pianist who delights in sharing her music for relaxation & healing.

Pasteles de Manzana en Familia. Steck-Vaughn Staff. (SPA.). 1999. (978-0-7398-0743-9(9)) SteckVau.

Pasternak: Translator & Translated. Theodore Weiss. 1 cass. (Running Time: 54 min.). 11.95 (23234) J Norton Pubs.

Pasteur, l'Homme, le Savant, la Memoire, Set. 2 cass. (FRE.). 1991. 26.95 (1822-RF) Olivia & Hill.
On the 100-year anniversary of Pasteur's death, a French National Radio broadcast a series on the complex personality & scientific discoveries of the famous 19th century French scientist.

Pastime. unabr. ed. Robert B. Parker. Read by David Dukes. 4 cass. (Running Time: 6 hrs.). (Spenser Ser.). 2001. 25.00 (978-1-59040-139-2(5), Phoenix Audio) Pub: Amer Intl Pub. Dist(s): PerseuPGW

Pastime. unabr. ed. Robert B. Parker. Perf. by David Dukes. 4 cass. (Running Time: 6 hrs.). (Spenser Ser.). 2004. 25.00 (978-1-59007-208-0(1)) Pub: New Millenn Enter. Dist(s): PerseuPGW
In a sequel to Raymond Chandler's The Big Sleep, Marlowe takes on a case involving General Sternwood, who is six feet under, Vivian, who is dating a blackmailer, and Carmen, a sanitorium escapee.

Pastime. unabr. ed. Robert B. Parker. Read by David Dukes. 5 CDs. (Running Time: 6 hrs.). (Spenser Ser.). 2004. audio compact disk 34.95 (978-1-59007-553-1(6)) Pub: New Millenn Enter. Dist(s): PerseuPGW

Pastor Chuck Smith Through the Bible C-2000 Student Series on MP3. 2001. audio compact disk (978-1-931713-00-9(6)) Word For Today.

Pastor Chuck Smiths Most Requested. Chuck Smith. 6 cass. (Running Time: 9 hrs.). 2000. 21.99 (978-0-936728-84-1(1)) Word For Today.
A collection of teaching, topical teaching that have become some timeless favorites.

Pastor Chuck Smith's Most Requested Bible Studies, Pack. 2004. audio compact disk (978-1-931713-91-7(X)) Word For Today.

Pastor Chuck Smith's Most Requested Bible Studies MP3. 2004. audio compact disk (978-1-931713-92-4(8)) Word For Today.

Pastor David T. Demola's Platinum Series. David T. Demola. 6 cass. 24.00 (PLS-6) Faith Fellow Min.

Pastor in Relation to Psycho-Active Drug Use. Wayne Oates & H Wagemaker. 1986. 10.80 (0204) Assn Prof Chaplains.

Pastor in the Current Sexual Crisis. Kenneth Reed et al. 1986. 10.80 (0107) Assn Prof Chaplains.

Pastor Looks at the New Catechism. Joseph M. Champlin. 3 cass. (Running Time: 2 hrs. 52 min.). 1994. 26.95 Set. (TAH306) Alba Hse Comns.
These talks will certainly help pastors understand those important pastoral aspects of the catechism. They will clarify those sticky points & will enable the pastor to practically apply the catechism to his parish's life & activity.

Pastoral. unabr. ed. Nevil Shute. Narrated by Frank Muller. 6 cass. (Running Time: 8 hrs. 30 mins.). 1986. 51.00 (978-1-55690-403-5(7), 86190E7) Recorded Bks.
The romance of a young, bomber pilot & his girl are held in the balance during World War II in England.

Pastoral Authority. Ted Dougherty. 1986. 10.80 (0303) Assn Prof Chaplains.

Pastoral Care: Approaching the New Millennium. 1 cass. (Care Cassettes Ser.: Vol. 17, No. 8). 1990. 10.80 Assn Prof Chaplains.

Pastoral Care & Guilt. 1 cass. (Care Cassettes Ser.: Vol. 12, No. 1). 1985. 10.80 Assn Prof Chaplains.

Pastoral Care & Labor-Management Issues. 1 cass. (Care Cassettes Ser.: Vol. 12, No. 6). 1985. 10.80 Assn Prof Chaplains.

Pastoral Care & Minorities. 1 cass. (Care Cassettes Ser.: Vol. 12, No. 3). 1985. 10.80 Assn Prof Chaplains.

Pastoral Care & Substance Abuse. 1 cass. (Care Cassettes Ser.: Vol. 11, No. 1). 1984. 10.80 Assn Prof Chaplains.

Pastoral Care & the Impact of the Nuclear Crisis. 1 cass. (Care Cassettes Ser.: Vol. 12, No. 8). 1985. 10.80 Assn Prof Chaplains.

Pastoral Care for Pastors - Hazards, Hurts & Hopes in Our Calling. J. Lennart Cedarleaf. 1986. 10.80 (0511) Assn Prof Chaplains.

Pastoral Care in Home Health Care. 1 cass. (Care Cassettes Ser.: Vol. 13, No. 1). 1986. 10.80 Assn Prof Chaplains.

Pastoral Care of Children. Rudy Roder. 1986. 10.80 (0103B) Assn Prof Chaplains.

Pastoral Care of Military Veterans. Donald A. Danielson. 1986. 10.80 (0108A) Assn Prof Chaplains.

Pastoral Care of the Coronary Patient. Lynwood Swanson. 1986. 10.80 (0206B) Assn Prof Chaplains.

Pastoral Care to Vietnam Veterans. 1 cass. (Care Cassettes Ser.: Vol. 12, No. 5). 1985. 10.80 Assn Prof Chaplains.

Pastoral Care with Hospitalized Children & Families. Marvin Johnson & Joy Johnson. 1986. 10.80 (0710) Assn Prof Chaplains.

Pastoral Counseling: Methodology & Theology. Bruce Hartung et al. 1986. 10.80 (0504) Assn Prof Chaplains.

Pastoral Diagnosis. Dan McKeever. 1986. 10.80 (0212) Assn Prof Chaplains.

Pastoral Imperatives: Helping the Suffering. Timothy S. Lane et al. (ENG.). 2006. audio compact disk 29.95 (978-1-934885-68-0(1)) New Growth Pr.

Pastoral Imperatives: Helping the Suffering. unabr. ed. Timothy S. Lane et al. 3 CDs. (Running Time: 3 hrs.). 2003. audio compact disk 29.95 (978-1-930921-31-3(4)) Resources.

Pastoral Imperatives: Helping the Suffering. unabr. ed. Timothy Lane et al. 3 cass. (Running Time: 3 hrs.). 2003. 29.95 (978-1-930921-06-1(3)) Resources.

Pastoral Issues in the Care of Persons with AIDS. 1 cass. (Care Cassettes Ser.: Vol. 13, No. 6). 1986. 10.80 Assn Prof Chaplains.

Pastoral Overview of Church History. Read by Douglas Wilson. 1995. 12.00 (978-1-59128-251-8(9)); 15.00 (978-1-59128-253-2(5)) Canon Pr ID.

Pastoral Response to Disaster. F. Alvin Embry. 1986. 10.80 (0201A) Assn Prof Chaplains.

Pastoral Spanish. Romuald Zantúa & Karen Eberle-McCarthy. 12 CDs. (Running Time: 12 hrs.). (SPA.). 2005. audio compact disk 225.00 (978-1-57970-150-5(7), SSP320D) J Norton Pubs.

Pastoral Spanish, Set. Romuald Zantua & Karen Eberle-McCarthy. 12 cass. (Running Time: 12 hrs.). (SPA.). 1993. pap. bk. & stu. ed. 225.00 (978-0-88432-689-2(6), SSP320) J Norton Pubs.
This unique audio-cassette-book course provides Spanish texts for church services such as baptism, wedding, etc. More than a phrase guide, this program teaches the essentials of Spanish. Native Latin-American Spanish speakers guide the instruction with pauses for repetition & responses. No previous knowledge of Spanish is required.

Pastoral Use of Transactional Analysis. Kenneth Pepper. 1986. 10.80 (0110) Assn Prof Chaplains.

Pastoral Visiting of the Sick: Panel Discussion. 1986. 10.80 (0108B) Assn Prof Chaplains.

Pastorale des Santous de Provence. Yvan Audouard. Perf. by Michel Galabru et al. 1 cass. 1992. 16.95 (1521-RF) Olivia & Hill.
The traditional provencal tale of the Nativity told with humor & poetry.

Pastores Dabo Vobis - I Will Give You Shepherds. John O'Connor. 2 cass. (Running Time: 1 hr. 52 min.). 1995. 17.95 Set. (TAH330) Alba Hse Comns.
This pragmatic & down to earth two talk program is extremely informative & inspiring. It will help to clearly focus each priest's vision & support him in his ministry.

Pastor's & Church Finances. Larry Burkett. 1987. 25.00 (978-1-56427-085-6(8)) Crown Fin Min Inc.

Pastor's Complete Model Letter Book: More than 400 Model Letters for Ministers. Stephen R. Clark. 2004. audio compact disk 29.95 (978-0-9759893-6-4(7)) Epiphany Ln Pr.

Pastor's Experience with Cancer. Edward Mahnke et al. 1986. 10.80 (0502) Assn Prof Chaplains.

Pastor's Family of Origin: Implications for Ministry. 1 cass. (Care Cassettes Ser.: Vol. 13, No. 5). 1986. 10.80 Assn Prof Chaplains.

Pastor's Perspective on Church Finances. Jim Burgess. 1987. 8.00 (978-1-56427-086-3(6)) Crown Fin Min Inc.

Pastor's Role in Christian Television: National Association of Evangelicals, 47th Annual Convention, Columbus, Ohio, March 7-9, 1989. Jerry Rose. 1 cass. (Workshops Ser.: No. 31-Thursda). 1989. 4.25 ea. 1-8 tapes.; 4.00 ea. 9 tapes or more. Nat Assn Evan.

Pastor's Tape. Larry Burkett. 1988. 5.00 (978-1-56427-088-7(2)) Crown Fin Min Inc.

Pastor's Wives Kit. Stacia Pierce. 6 cass. (Running Time: 4 hrs. 50 mins.). 2000. 60.00 (978-1-886880-37-5(9)) Life Changers.
Practical info on the uniqueness of being a Pastors wife & how to enjoy the position.

Pasture see Robert Frost Reads

Pasture see Twentieth-Century Poetry in English, No. 6, Recordings of Poets Reading Their Own Poetry

Pastures New. J. M. Gregson & Jonathan Keeble. 2009. audio compact disk 71.95 (978-1-84652-517-9(9)) Pub: Magna Story GBR. Dist(s): Ulverscroft US

Pastures New. J. M. Gregson & Jonathan Keeble. 2009. 54.95 (978-1-84652-516-2(0)) Pub: Magna Story GBR. Dist(s): Ulverscroft US

Pastwatch: The Redemption of Christopher Columbus. unabr. ed. Orson Scott Card. Read by Stefan Rudnicki. (Running Time: 13 hrs. 50 mins.). (ENG.). 2009. 29.95 (978-1-4332-1721-0(X)); 79.95 (978-1-4332-1717-3(1)); audio compact disk 99.00 (978-1-4332-1718-0(X)) Blckstn Audio.

Pat Croce's Achieve the Impossible. Pat Croce. Read by Pat Croce. 1 cass. (Running Time: 1 hr.). 1998. 19.95 incl. script. (978-1-893714-01-4(2)) Moro Mgmt.
Metamorphosis from Philadelphia 76ers physical therapist to team owner. Learn how to foster the same passionate desire that will propell one to success.

Pat Croce's Ten Commandments of Customer Service. Pat Croce. Read by Pat Croce. 1 cass. (Running Time: 1 hr. 10 min.). 1998. 19.95 incl. script. (978-1-893714-00-7(4)) Moro Mgmt.
Sports Physical Therapists was started & built up to forty successful sports medicine centers through fierce drive, optimism & an undying belief in great customer service.

Pat Haden: Quarterback. Read by Pat Haden. 1 cass. 9.95 (978-0-89811-076-0(9), 7127) Lets Talk Assocs.
Pat Haden talks about the people & events which influenced his career, & his own approach to his speciality.

Pat Hutchins Collection. Pat Hutchins. Illus. by Pat Hutchins. 44 vols. (Running Time: 21 mins.). 1999. pap. bk. 61.95 (978-0-87499-887-0(5)) Live Oak Media.

Pat Novak, For Hire: Gambling Ring & Bookie Outfit. Perf. by Jack Webb & Ben Morris. 1 cass. (Running Time: 1 hr.). 2001. 6.98 (2066) Radio Spirits.

Pat Novak, For Hire: Go Away, Dixie & The Only Way to Make Friends Is to Die. Perf. by Jack Webb. 1 cass. (Running Time: 1 hr.). 2001. 6.98 (1935) Radio Spirits.

Pat Novak, For Hire: Jack of Clubs & Marcia Halpern. Perf. by Jack Webb. 1 cass. (Running Time: 1 hr.). 2001. 6.98 (2381) Radio Spirits.

Pat Novak, For Hire: Rory Malone & Father Lahey. Perf. by Jack Webb. 1 cass. (Running Time: 1 hr.). 2001. 6.98 (2382) Radio Spirits.

Pat Novak, For Hire: Rubin Callaway's Picture & Shirt Mix up at the Laundry. Perf. by Jack Webb. 1 cass. (Running Time: 1 hr.). 2001. 6.98 (2562) Radio Spirits.

Pat Novak, For Hire: Sam Tolliver & Go Away Dixie Gillian. Perf. by Jack Webb. 1 cass. (Running Time: 1 hr.). 2001. 6.98 (2427) Radio Spirits.

Pata del Mono y Otros Grandes Cuentos de Terror. unabr. ed. W. W. Jacobs. Read by Fabio Camero. 3 CDs.Tr. of Monkey's Paw & Other Tales of Terror. (SPA.). 2003. audio compact disk 17.00 (978-958-8218-28-1(4)) YoYoMusic.

Pataki: Myth, Magic & Mystery in the Afro-Cuban World. unabr. ed. Isabel Castellanos. Read by Raymond H. McPhee. 2 cass. (Running Time: 3 hrs.). 1996. 18.95 Set. (978-0-9646530-1-6(X)) Luna Media.
Hear the native drums & revel in the tales taken from the yellowed manuscripts of Cuba's Yoruba practitioners. Listen to stories of the transplanted African gods, & of their assimilation into the cultural & religious environment of Cuba.

***Patched Together: A Story of My Story.** unabr. ed. Brennan Manning. Narrated by Paul Michael. (Running Time: 2 hrs. 42 mins. 0 sec.). (Yasmin Peace Ser.). (ENG.). 2010. 8.98 (978-1-59644-039-5(2), christaudio); audio compact disk 12.98 (978-1-59644-038-8(4), christaudio) christianaud.

Patchwork: A Kaleidoscope of Quilts. Jocelyn Riley. 1 cass. (Running Time: 15 min.). (YA). 1989. 8.00 (978-1-877933-35-6(X)) Her Own Words.
Documentary.

Patchwork Girl of Oz. Scripts. L. Frank Baum. 6 Cds. (Running Time: 6 hrs.). Dramatization. (J). 2002. audio compact disk 25.00 (978-0-9724995-0-7(4)) Alcazar AudioWorks.
Full cast production. 36 characters. Another Oz adventure introducing the Patchwork Girl and the Glass Cat. The adventurers are searching for the ingredients for the Powder of Life to restore Unk Nunkie who has been changed into a marble statue, back to life. All the old Oz characters help, including the Wizard of Oz and Princess Dorothy and Toto, her little dog as well as Jack Pumpkinhead, the Scarecrow, the Tin Man, Princess Ozma and all the rest.

Patchwork Girl of Oz. L. Frank Baum. (Running Time: 6 hrs.). 2004. 26.95 (978-1-59912-698-2(2)) Iofy Corp.

Patchwork Girl of Oz. unabr. ed. L. Frank Baum. 6 cass. (Running Time: 8 hrs. 30 mins.). 2004. 39.95 (978-0-7861-2805-1(4), 3332); audio compact disk 48.00 (978-0-7861-8488-0(4), 3332) Blckstn Audio.
After a doll made out of a patchwork quilt is brought to life by a magician, she must find a way to break a spell that has turned two victims into motionless statues. A boy, the Patchwork Girl, and Bungle the glass cat go on a mission to find the ingredients for a charm that will transform the people back to life.

Patchwork Planet. unabr. ed. Anne Tyler. Read by Kerry Shale. 8 cass. (Running Time: 7 hrs. 30 min.). 2001. 36.95 (978-0-7540-0600-8(X), CAB2023) AudioGO.
Barnaby Gaitlin was left several years ago by his ex-wife Natalie & took their baby daughter with her. Barnaby, is in an unalterably fixed position as the black sheep of the family. The Gaitlins are rich & worthy, supposedly guided by their own special angel to do the right thing.

Patchwork Planet. unabr. ed. Anne Tyler. Read by Lloyd James. 8 cass. (Running Time: 12 hrs.). 1998. 64.00 (978-0-7366-4250-7(1), 4749) Books on Tape.
Something is wrong with Barnaby Gaitlin, a 30-year-old lovable loser. In trouble with the law since adolescence, Barnaby had this habit of breaking into other people's houses, not to steal, he just liked to sift through other people's mail & browse through their photo albums. But for the last eleven years Barnaby has been working steadily doing chores for old folks & shut-ins. Still, his family, ever mindful of what it took to buy off his victims, can't forget. With her tender perceptions on how all people, even lost souls like Barnaby, fit into the patchwork planet.

Patchwork Planet. unabr. ed. Anne Tyler. Narrated by Jeff Woodman. 7 cass. (Running Time: 9 hrs. 45 mins.). 1999. 60.00 (978-0-7887-2020-8(1), 95397E7) Recorded Bks.
Living in a basement rec room & haunted by his shady adolescent past, Barnaby Gaitlin can't seem to do anything right - until he meets kind & sensible Sophia. An ex-thief & working for Rent-A-Back, Inc. performing household chores for shut-ins & the elderly, the 30-year-old black sheep of an old Baltimore family is just trying to navigate through the perplexing world around him.

Patchwork Planet. unabr. ed. Anne Tyler. 1 cass. (Running Time: 45 mins.). 2002. 10.00; audio compact disk 15.00 (M010D) Two Kind Prods.

Patchwork Planet, Set. Anne Tyler. Read by David Morse. 4 cass. (Running Time: 4 hrs.). 1999. 24.35 (978-1-85686-711-5(0)) Ulvrscrft Audio.

Patchwork Quilt & Other Stories from Around the World. Sharon Kennedy. 1 cass. (Running Time: 70 min.). (J). (ps-4). 1998. 9.98 (978-1-57940-027-9(2), 8080); audio compact disk 14.98 (978-1-57940-026-2(4)) Rounder Records.
Storyteller shares five stories which feature children who use their wits & courage to save themselves & others.

Pate de Foie Gras see Asimov's Mysteries

Patent Antitrust. unabr. ed. Contrib. by David Bender. 7 cass. (Running Time: 9 hrs.). 1989. 50.00 course handbk. (T7-9208) PLI.

Patent Lie. unabr. ed. Paul Goldstein. Read by Paul Michael. 9 CDs. (Running Time: 10 hrs. 30 mins.). 2008. audio compact disk 90.00 (978-1-4159-4998-6(0), BksonTape) Pub: Random Audio Pubg. Dist(s): Random
Forced out of his high-powered Manhattan law firm and stuck in a dead-end solo practice, Michael Seeley, the tough-but-wounded hero of Errors and Omissions, cannot say no when his estranged brother, Leonard, head of research at upstart biotech Vaxtek, Inc., flies in from California to beg him to take over the company's lawsuit for patent infringement of its pathbreaking AIDS vaccine after the sudden death of the lead trial lawyer. The financial and moral stakes of the case are staggering, and Seeley suspects that murder cannot be ruled out as a hardball litigation tactic of big-pharma adversary St. Gall Laboratories. As Seeley travels between San Francisco and Silicon Valley to prepare for trial, dark facts surface concerning the vaccine's discovery by Vaxtek scientist Alan Steinhardt and its alleged theft by St. Gall researcher Lily Warren. Ethical quandaries deepen into mortal danger as the trial, under the stern prodding of federal judge Ellen Farnsworth, rushes to its unexpected end.

Patent Litigation 1990. 9 cass. (Running Time: 11 hrs.). bk. 95.00 incl. 1118-page course handbook. (T6-9139) PLI.

Patent Protection - A Practical Guide for Inventors. unabr. ed. H. John Rizvi. 2 cass. 2000. (978-0-9702110-0-2(7)) H J Rizvi.
Provides a common sense strategy to inventors seeking legal protection for their ideas.

Patents for the Clueless(TM) Narrated by Mike Rounds. (Running Time: 1 hr. 12 mins 21 seconds). 2004. audio compact disk 19.95 (978-1-891440-33-5(0)) CPM Systems.

Pater Noster. Peter Toon. (J). 1996. 39.95 (978-1-886412-10-1(3)) Preserv Press.

Pater Noster - "Our Father" An Exposition of Christian Prayer. Peter Toon. (Catechetical Ser.). 3.95 (978-1-886412-09-5(X)) Preserv Press.

Paternidad espiritual audio libro-Spiritual Fatherhood Audio BK. unabr. ed. Edwin Santiago. (SPA.). 2008. audio compact disk 14.99 (978-0-8297-5155-0(6)) Pub: Vida Pubs. Dist(s): Zondervan

Paterno: By the Book. unabr. ed. Joe Paterno & Bernard Asbell. Read by Joe Vincent. 6 cass. (Running Time: 8 hrs. 30 mins.). 1990. 44.95 (978-0-7861-0166-5(0), 1148) Blckstn Audio.
Here Joe Paterno tells his story, sharing his life principles & touching on a number of important subjects including: family, heroes, management, leadership, loyalty, teamwork, discipline, motivation & of course, football strategy.

Path among the Stones see Poetry & Voice of Galway Kinnell

Path Between the Seas: The Creation of the Panama Canal, 1870-1914. David McCullough. Read by Grover Gardner. 1990. 72.00 (978-0-7366-1835-9(X)) Books on Tape.

Path Between the Seas: The Creation of the Panama Canal, 1870-1914. abr. ed. David McCullough. Read by Edward Herrmann & Edward Herrmann. 5 CDs. (Running Time: 90 hrs. 0 mins. 0 sec.). (ENG.). 2003. audio compact disk 39.95 (978-0-7435-3018-7(7), Audioworks) Pub: S&S Audio. Dist(s): S and S Inc

Path Between the Seas: The Creation of the Panama Canal, 1870-1914. abr. ed. David McCullough. Read by Edward Herrmann. 2004. 21.95 (978-0-7435-4948-6(1)) Pub: S&S Audio. Dist(s): S and S Inc

Path Between the Seas: The Creation of the Panama Canal, 1870-1914, Pt. 1. unabr. ed. David McCullough. Read by Grover Gardner. 8 cass. (Running Time: 12 hrs.). 1990. 64.00 (978-0-7366-1834-2(1), 2669-A) Books on Tape.
In our lifetime the Panama Canal is taken for granted & thought of hardly at all. But once, when America was in its first century, the canal topped our list of national priorities. Why? David McCullough's book brings to life the issues that made the canal a vital concern to earlier generations. He tells the story in full, not only the engineering, but also the politics & finances. The canal made the reputations of some men, destroyed those of others. But the heart of the story is in the construction, when thousands of workers were amassed for the assault. Like war, for many it was the adventure of a lifetime.

Path Between the Seas: The Creation of the Panama Canal, 1870-1914, Pt. 2. unabr. ed. David McCullough. Read by Grover Gardner. 9 cass. (Running Time: 13 hrs. 30 min.). 1990. 72.00 (2669-B) Books on Tape.

PATH CREATING YOUR MISSION STATEMENT for WORK & for LIFE: Creating Your Mission Statement for Work & for Life. Laurie Beth Jones. 2004. 7.95 (978-0-7435-4166-4(9)) Pub: S&S Audio. Dist(s): S and S Inc

Path Is One. Swami Amar Jyoti. 1 dolby cass. 1984. 9.95 (M-50) Truth Consciousness.
There is one way Home, which must be discovered by each seeker; on this valid path, we cannot avoid meeting our blocks.

Path of Action. Illus. by Will Noffke & Jack Schwarz. 1980. 12.00 (#N1002) Aletheia Psycho.

Path of Action, 1990. Read by Jack Schwarz. 1 cass. 1978. 12.00 (#112) Aletheia Psycho.
A lecture from the "Three Jewels in the Lotus", San Francisco.

Path of Compassion: Time-honored Rules of Ethical & Spiritual Conduct, Set. unabr. ed. G. De Purucker. Pref. by Grace F. Knoche. 3 cass. (Running Time: 3 hrs. 48 min.). (ENG.). 1986. 25.00 (978-0-911500-60-8(X)) Theos U Pr.
Presented along with warnings against quick & easy methods promising enlightenment.

Path of Daggers. abr. ed. Scripts. Robert Jordan. Perf. by Mark Rolston. 10 CDs. (Running Time: 12 hrs.). (Wheel of Time Ser.: Bk. 8). 2003. 43.95 (978-1-59007-335-3(5), N Millennium Audio) Pub: New Millenn Enter. Dist(s): PerseuPGW

Path of Daggers. abr. ed. Scripts. Robert Jordan. Perf. by Mark Rolston. 8 cass. (Running Time: 12 hrs.). (Wheel of Time Ser.: Bk. 8). 2004. 39.95 (978-1-59007-334-6(7)) Pub: New Millenn Enter. Dist(s): PerseuPGW

Path of Daggers. abr. ed. Robert Jordan. Read by Mark Rolston. 8 cass. (Running Time: 5 hrs. 30 mins.). (Wheel of Time Ser.: Bk. 8). 1998. 39.95 (978-1-57511-045-5(8), 102534) Pub Mills.
The wait is over. The Seanchan invasion force is in possession of Ebon Dar. Nynaeve, Elaine & Aviendha head for Caemln, but on the way they discover an enemy much worse than the Seanchan.

Path of Daggers. unabr. ed. Robert Jordan. Narrated by Michael Kramer & Kate Reading. 19 CDs. (Running Time: 23 hrs. 30 mins. 0 sec.). (Wheel of Time Ser.: Bk. 8). (ENG.). 2008. audio compact disk 69.95 (978-1-4272-0508-7(6)) Pub: Macmill Audio. Dist(s): Macmillan

Path of Daggers. unabr. ed. Scripts. Robert Jordan. Perf. by Michael Kramer & Kate Reading. 19 CDs. (Running Time: 27 hrs.). (Wheel of Time Ser.: Bk. 8). 2003. audio compact disk 69.95 (978-1-59007-399-5(1), N Millennium Audio) Pub: New Millenn Enter. Dist(s): PerseuPGW

Path of Daggers. unabr. ed. Scripts. Robert Jordan. Perf. by Michael Kramer & Kate Reading. 16 cass. (Running Time: 22 hrs.). (Wheel of Time Ser.: Bk. 8). 2004. 49.95 (978-1-59007-398-8(3)) Pub: New Millenn Enter. Dist(s): PerseuPGW

Path of Daggers, Pt. 1. unabr. ed. Robert Jordan. Read by Michael Kramer & Kate Reading. 9 cass. (Running Time: 13 hrs. 30 min.). (Wheel of Time Ser.: Bk. 8). 1999. 72.00 (978-0-7366-4537-9(3), 4801-A) Books on Tape.
Opens with a renewed invasion by the Searchers who are now in possession of Ebou Dar, Nynaeve, Elayne & Aviendha. In Illina, Rand vows to throw the Seanchan back as he did once before. But signs of madness appearing among the Asha'man lead him to a fateful, perhaps fatal decision.

Path of Daggers, Pt. 2. unabr. ed. Robert Jordan. Read by Michael Kramer & Kate Reading. 8 cass. (Running Time: 12 hrs.). (Wheel of Time Ser.: Bk. 8). 1999. 64.00 (978-0-7366-4538-6(1), 4801-B) Books on Tape.

Path of Devotion. unabr. ed. Perf. by Eknath Easwaran. 1 cass. (Running Time: 1 hr.). 1985. 7.95 (978-1-58638-586-6(0)) Nilgiri Pr.

Path of Fate. Stephen Mark Rainey. 2009. audio compact disk 15.95 (978-1-84435-377-4(X)) Pub: Big Finish GBR. Dist(s): Natl Bk Netwk

Path of Jack Schwarz. Read by Jack Schwarz & Michael Toms. 1 cass. 15.00 (#105) Aletheia Psycho.
Autobiography oriented conversation.

Path of Light Vol. I: Meditating with the Masters. 1996. 195.00 (978-1-893027-19-0(8)) Path of Light.

Path of Light Vol. II: Opening New Channels. 1997. 59.95 (978-1-893027-20-6(1)) Path of Light.

Path of Light Vol. III: Bridge to Intuition. 1998. 69.95 (978-1-893027-21-3(X)) Path of Light.

Path of Light Vol. IV: Shamballa, Sirius & the Spiritual Sun. 1998. 59.95 (978-1-893027-22-0(8)) Path of Light.

Path of Love see Amor, Erotismo e Intimidad

Path of Love. 1 cass. (Running Time: 1 hr.). 12.99 (615) Yoga Res Foun.

Path of Nivritti (Renunciation) Swami Jyotirmayananda. 1 cass. (Running Time: 45 min.). 1990. 10.00 Yoga Res Foun.

Path of Relationship. Shakti Gawain. 2 cass. 1993. 18.00 set. (OC343-72) Sound Horizons AV.

Path of the Assassin: A Thriller. abr. ed. Brad Thor. Read by Armand Schultz. 2004. 15.95 (978-0-7435-4898-4(1)) Pub: S&S Audio. Dist(s): S and S Inc

Path of the Assassin: A Thriller. abr. ed. Brad Thor. Read by Armand Schultz. CDs 5. (Running Time: 50 hrs. 0 mins. 0 sec.). (ENG.). 2008. audio compact disk 14.99 (978-0-7435-7196-8(7)) Pub: S&S Audio. Dist(s): S and S Inc

Path of the Buddha. Osel Tendzin. 3 cass. 1981. 31.50 Vajradhatu.

Path of the Heart - Angels & Spirit Guides Meditations: Learn to heal your heart & listen to your divine Guidance. Robin Lysne. (ENG.). 2007. audio compact disk 15.95 (978-0-9778645-1-5(0)) Blue Bone Bks.

Path of the King. John Buchan. Read by John Bolen. (Running Time: 8 hrs. 30 mins.). 2001. 27.95 (978-1-60083-575-9(9), Audiofy Corp) Iofy Corp.

Path of the King. John Buchan. Read by John Bolen. (ENG.). 2005. audio compact disk 78.00 (978-1-4001-3001-6(8)) Pub: Tantor Media. Dist(s): IngramPubServ

Path of the King. unabr. ed. John Buchan. Read by John Bolen. (YA). 2007. 64.99 (978-1-60252-572-6(2)) Find a World.

Path of the King. unabr. ed. John Buchan. Narrated by John Bolen. 7 CDs. (Running Time: 8 hrs. 23 mins.). (ENG.). 2001. audio compact disk 39.00 (978-1-4001-0001-9(1)); audio compact disk 20.00 (978-1-4001-5001-4(9)) Pub: Tantor Media. Dist(s): IngramPubServ

Path of the King. unabr. ed. John Buchan. Narrated by John Bolen. (Running Time: 8 hrs. 30 mins. 0 sec.). (ENG.). 2009. audio compact disk 19.99 (978-1-4001-6090-7(1)); audio compact disk 55.99 (978-1-4001-4090-9(0)); audio compact disk 27.99 (978-1-4001-1090-2(4)) Pub: Tantor Media. Dist(s): IngramPubServ

Path of the Prototypes. Jonathan Murro. 1 cass. 1990. 7.95 A R Colton Fnd.
A lecture by Jonathan Murro on the subject as given in the title.

Path of the Rainbow Yin-Yang. Jeffrey Mishlove. 1 cass. 9.00 (A0091-86) Sound Photosyn.
ICSS '86.

Path of Transformation. Shakti Gawain. 3 cass. 1991. 27.00 set. (OC276-62) Sound Horizons AV.

Path of Wisdom & Compassion. Dalai Lama XIV. 1 cass. 1981. 10.00 Vajradhatu.
Practicing the Buddha's teaching by treading the path of mediation that he himself followed, we uncover the awakened state of mind.

Path of Zeal: Nehemiah 5:15. Ben Young. (YA). 2000. 4.95 (978-0-7417-6224-5(2), B0224) Win Walk.

Path Through Suffering. Contrib. by Elisabeth Elliot. 4 cass. (Running Time: 6 hrs.). 1992. 14.99 (978-0-8474-2047-6(7)) Loizeaux.
Inspirational.

Path to Answered Prayer. Ron Roth. 3 cass. (Running Time: 3 hrs.). 1996. 24.95 Set. (978-1-893869-07-3(5)) Celbrtng Life.

Path to Enlightenment. abr. rev. ed. Dalai Lama XIV. Read by Ken McLeod. 3 CDs. (Running Time: 3 hrs. 0 mins. 0 sec.). (ENG.). 2002. audio compact disk 19.95 (978-1-55927-708-2(4)) Pub: Macmill Audio. Dist(s): Macmillan

Path to God's Glory. Lora Allison. 2 cass. 1992. 12.00 Set. (978-1-56043-934-9(3)) Destiny Image Pubs.

Path to High Achievement. B. Eugene Griessman. 2 cass. (Running Time: 3 hrs.). 1996. 15.95 (978-1-55977-491-8(6)) CareerTrack Pubns.

Path to High Achievement. Gene Griessman. 4 cass. (Running Time: 3 hrs. 55 min.). 59.95 Set. (Q10198) CareerTrack Pubns.
Program highlights: Why Lillian Vernon Katz - head of one of the nation's largest mail-order gift businesses - credits much of her success to her lack of self-confidence; Why fashion magnate Oscar de la Renta procrastinates on purpose; How Jack Nicklaus, the world's greatest golfer, exemplifies the "10-year rule" of competency.

Path to Love: Renewing the Power of Spirit in Your Life, Set. abr. ed. Deepak Chopra. Read by Deepak Chopra. 2 CDs. (Running Time: 2 hrs. 20 mins.). (Deepak Chopra Ser.). (ENG.). 1997. audio compact disk 19.95 (978-0-679-45827-2(1), Random AudioBks) Pub: Random Audio Pubg. Dist(s): Random

Path to Peace. Joseph T. McGloin. 7 cass. 28.95 (905) Ignatius Pr.
Retreat talks given by the author that are aimed at bringing peace & meaning into your daily life.

Path to Power, Pt. 1. unabr. ed. Margaret Thatcher. Read by Donada Peters. 8 cass. (Running Time: 12 hrs.). 1996. 64.00 (978-0-7366-3421-2(5), 4067A) Books on Tape.
Lady Thatcher credits the self-reliance, thrift & respectful neighborliness she imbibed at her father's knee as the virtues that influenced her views.

Path to Power, Pt. 2. unabr. ed. Margaret Thatcher. Read by Donada Peters. 9 cass. (Running Time: 13 hrs. 30 mins.). 1996. 72.00 (4067-B) Books on Tape.

Path to Tranquility: Daily Meditations by the Dalai Lama. Dalai Lama XIV. Read by Robert Thurman et al. 2004. 10.95 (978-0-7435-1993-9(0)) Pub: S&S Audio. Dist(s): S and S Inc

Path to Tranquility: Daily Meditations by the Dalai Lama. abr. ed. Dalai Lama XIV. Read by Laurie Anderson et al. 3 CDs. (Running Time: 23 hrs. 0 mins. 0 sec.). (ENG.). 2000. audio compact disk 23.50 (978-0-7435-0629-8(4), Sound Ideas) Pub: S&S Audio. Dist(s): S and S Inc
The Dalai Lama, a living symbol of holiness and selfless triumph over tribulation, has shared his philosophy of peace with today's turbulent world. Yet rarely do we hear him speak with such directness as in this collection of quotations drawn from his own writings, teachings, and interviews. The Path To Tranquility, a fresh and accessible introduction to his inspirational wisdom, offers words of guidance, compassion, and peace that are as down to earth as they are rich in spirit. It covers almost every aspect of human life, secular and religious - happiness, intimacy, loneliness, suffering, anger, and everyday insecurities - with endearing informality, warmth, and practicality.

Path with Heart. Jack Kornfield. 3 CDs. 2004. audio compact disk 19.95 (978-1-59179-224-6(X), AW00370D) Sounds True.
A classic guide to the key principles of Buddhism's cherished vipassana (insight) tradition, complete with many special meditations and other practices.

Pathfinder. abr. adpt. ed. James Fenimore Cooper. (Bring the Classics to Life: Level 4 Ser.). (ENG.). 2008. audio compact disk 12.95 (978-1-55576-574-3(2)) EDCON Pubng.

***Pathfinder.** unabr. ed. Orson Scott Card. (Running Time: 19 hrs.). (Pathfinder Ser.). 2010. 29.99 (978-1-4418-2029-7(9), 9781441820297, BAD); 44.97 (978-1-4418-2030-3(2), 9781441820303, BADLE) Brilliance Audio.

Pathfinder. unabr. ed. Orson Scott Card. Read by Stefan Rudnicki et al. (Running Time: 18 hrs.). (Pathfinder Ser.). 2010. audio compact disk 34.99 (978-1-4418-2025-9(6), 9781441820259, Bril Audio CD Unabri) Brilliance Audio.

***Pathfinder.** unabr. ed. Orson Scott Card. Read by Scott Brick et al. (Running Time: 18 hrs.). (Pathfinder Ser.). 2010. 44.97 (978-1-4418-2028-0(0), 9781441820280, Brinc Audio MP3 Lib); 29.99 (978-1-4418-2027-3(2), 9781441820273, Brilliance MP3); audio compact disk 89.97 (978-1-4418-2026-6(4), 9781441820266, BriAudCD Unabrid) Brilliance Audio.

Pathfinder. unabr. ed. Margaret Mayhew. Read by Clive Mantle. 8 cass. (Running Time: 12 hrs.). 2003. 69.95 (978-0-7540-0901-6(7), CAB 2323) AudioGO.

***Pathfinder: Bring the Classics to Life.** adpt. ed. James Fenimore Cooper. (Bring the Classics to Life Ser.). 2008. pap. bk. 21.95 (978-1-55576-615-3(3)) EDCON Pubng.

Pathki Nana: Girl Solves a Mystery. Kenneth Thomasma. 3 cass. (Running Time: 3 hrs.). (J). 1998. 19.95 (978-1-880114-19-3(4)) Grandview.

Pathless Path to Reality. Swami Amar Jyoti. 1 cass. 1987. 9.95 (M-90) Truth Consciousness.
The Goal is universal, unlimited, unbound, beyond all our conceptions. The one who is seeking is also standing in the way. Releasing ego, merging unto Him.

Pathogenesis & Treatment of Non-Insulin-Dependent Diabetes Mellitus. Read by Ralph A. DeFronzo. 1 cass. (Running Time: 90 min.). 1986. 12.00 (C8609) Amer Coll Phys.

Pathology of Power. unabr. collector's ed. Norman Cousins. Read by Larry McKeever. 6 cass. (Running Time: 9 hrs.). 1988. 48.00 (978-0-7366-1274-6(2), 2183) Books on Tape.
Polemical attack on alleged corruption & mis-management in government, particularly in the field of defense contracts.

Pathophysiology, Diagnosis & Management of Osteoporosis. Moderated by B. Lawrence Riggs. Contrib. by Charles H. Chestnust, III et al. 1 cass. (Running Time: 90 min.). 1985. 12.00 (A8508) Amer Coll Phys.
This topic is discussed by a moderator & experts who offer differing opinions.

Pathos & Nectar of Love. unabr. ed. Swami Amar Jyoti. 1 cass. (Running Time: 1 hr. 30 min.). (Satsangs of Swami Amar Jyoti Ser.). 1998. 9.95 (978-0-933572-37-9(9), K165) Truth Consciousness.
Seeing pain in a new light, changing our mental programs. Mad love forGod. Pathos is the richness of Love.

Paths of Destiny. E. V. Thompson. Read by Trudy Harris. 9 cass. (Running Time: 12 hrs.). (Story Sound Ser.). (J). 2004. 76.95 (978-1-85903-699-0(6)) Pub: Mgna Lrg Print GBR. Dist(s): Ulverscroft US

Paths of Glory. abr. ed. Jeffrey Archer. Read by Roger Allam. 5 CDs. (Running Time: 6 hrs. 0 mins. 0 sec.). 2009. audio compact disk 29.95 (978-1-4272-0623-7(6)) Pub: Macmill Audio. Dist(s): Macmillan

Paths of Glory. unabr. ed. Jeffrey Archer. Read by Roger Allam. (Running Time: 11 hrs.). 2009. 74.95 (978-0-7927-6189-1(8), Chivers Sound Lib); 54.95 (978-0-7927-6188-4(X), Chivers Sound Lib); audio compact disk 89.95 (978-0-7927-6009-2(3), Chivers Sound Lib) AudioGO.

Paths of Glory. unabr. ed. Jeffrey Archer. Read by Roger Allam. 9 CDs. (Running Time: 11 hrs. 0 mins. 0 sec.). (ENG.). 2009. audio compact disk 39.95 (978-1-4272-0603-9(1), Rena Bks) Pub: St Martin. Dist(s): Macmillan

Paths of Yoga. 2 cass. (Running Time: 2 hrs.). (Essence of Yoga Ser.). 14.95 (ST-22S) Crystal Clarity.
Topics include: Yoga as a Religion, the interrelationships of bhakti, gyana & karma yoga; Shankya philosophy & the need for higher states of consciousness; Vedanta philosophy & the true nature of reality; how an awakened soul & calm mind help the body.

Pathway Home: A Novel. Michele Ashman Bell. 3 cass. 2004. 14.95 (978-1-59156-187-3(6)) Covenant Comms.

Pathway of A Course in Miracles: From Spirituality to Mysticism. Kenneth Wapnick. 2008. 94.00 (978-1-59142-339-3(2)); audio compact disk 106.00 (978-1-59142-338-6(4)) Foun Miracles.

Pathway of Commitment. Ruth Prince. 1 cass. (B-8002) Derek Prince.

Pathway of Forgiveness. Kenneth Wapnick. 4 CDs. 2006. audio compact disk 23.00 (978-1-59142-258-7(2), CD64) Foun Miracles.

Pathway of Forgiveness. Kenneth Wapnick. 1 CD. (Running Time: 3 hrs. 52 mins. 48 secs.). 2007. 19.00 (978-1-59142-280-8(9), 3m64) Foun Miracles.

Pathway to Destruction. Kenneth Bruce. 1 cass. (Running Time: 1 hr. 08 min.). (Excursions in History Ser.). 12.50 Alpha Tape.

Pathway to Independence. Kenneth Bruce. 1 cass. (Running Time: 1 hr.). Dramatization. (Excursions in History Ser.). 12.50 Alpha Tape.
Historically accurate story of the efforts for independence.

Pathway to Purpose¿ for Women. abr. ed. Katie Brazelton. (Running Time: 5 hrs. 0 mins. 0 sec.). (Pathway to Purpose Ser.). (ENG.). 2005. 12.99 (978-0-310-26857-4(5)) Zondervan.

***Pathway to Purpose for Women: Connecting Your to-Do List, Your Passions, & Godâ€(tm)s Purposes for Your Life.** unabr. ed. Katie Brazelton. (Running Time: 6 hrs. 13 mins. 32 sec.). (ENG.). 2010. 18.99 (978-0-310-77144-9(7)) Zondervan.

Pathway to Successful Living. Joe Alexander. 1 cass. 10.00 (SP100054) SMI Intl.
Overcoming past conditioning & taking a second look at your self-image can help remove barriers to greater success. Now you can acquire the quiet confidence of a winner, manage attitudes, build belief & get positive results.

Pathway to the Most High: From the Tabernacle to God Throne. 2005. 15.00 (978-1-933561-03-5(3)) BFM Books.

Pathway to Your Dreams: Investing in the Dreams. abr. ed. Jesse B. Brown. 6 vols. (Running Time: 240 min.). 2000. 59.95 (978-0-9659384-1-9(7)) Krystal Pr Pub.

Pathways. Jeri Taylor. (Star Trek Voyager Ser.). 2004. 15.95 (978-0-7435-4879-3(5)) Pub: S&S Audio. Dist(s): S and S Inc

Pathways. unabr. ed. Robert A. Monroe. Read by Robert A. Monroe. (Running Time: 45 min.). (Gateway Experience - Exploring Ser.). 1984. 14.95 (978-1-56113-279-9(9)) Monroe Institute.
Open the unexplored places within.

Pathways of Song: High Voice. Ed. by Alfred Publishing. (Pathways of Song Ser.). (ENG.). 2006. audio compact disk 24.99 (978-0-7390-4088-1(X)) Alfred Pub.

Pathways of Song: Low Voice. Ed. by Alfred Publishing. (Pathways of Song Ser.). (ENG.). 2006. audio compact disk 12.95 (978-0-7390-4090-4(1)) Alfred Pub.

Pathways of Song, Vol 2: High Voice. Frank LaForge & Will Earhart. (Pathways of Song Ser.). (ENG.). 2009. audio compact disk 14.99 (978-0-7390-5832-9(0)) Alfred Pub.

Pathways of Song, Vol 2: Low Voice. Frank LaForge & Will Earhart. (Pathways of Song Ser.). (ENG.). 2009. audio compact disk 14.99 (978-0-7390-5833-6(9)) Alfred Pub.

Pathways of the Pioneers MP3 CDs. Prod. by Cross View Media. (ENG.). 1998. (978-0-8280-2062-6(0)) Review & Herald.

Pathways of the Pioneers 22 CD Collection. Prod. by Cross View Media. 1998. audio compact disk (978-0-8280-2063-3(9)) Review & Herald.

Pathways to Financial Freedom. Scripts. William M. Upson & Steven F. Klamm. 3 CDs. 2007. audio compact disk 24.95 (978-0-9678982-7-8(7)) St Bernie's Pr.

Pathways to Healing. unabr. ed. La Mer Marshand. Read by La Mer Marshand. Ed. by Tomi Keitlen. (Running Time: 52 min.). (978-0-9630485-1-6(1)) In Print.
Guided Imagery to relieve stress & pain within the four lower bodies; healing through color & sound.

Pathways to Inner Peace: An Audio CD & Journal for Getting in Touch with Your Soul. Scripts. Kathryn Seifert. Executive Producer Suzanna Mallow. Music by Vinny Hazeltine. Illus. by Lisa Ali. 1 Cd. (Running Time: 1 hr.). 2004. audio compact disk 17.94 (978-0-9763972-0-5(X)) S Pub Co.
A great audio relaxation, guided imagery CD with gently soothing music background on track one. Music for peaceful meditation on track two. Accompanied by an interactive journal to record your thoughts, reactions and ideas, as well as creative work.

Pathways to Personal Power. Created by Louise LeBrun. 1999. 21.95 (978-0-9685566-6-5(3)) Par3tners Renewal CAN.

Pathways to Spirituality. 1 cass. (Running Time: 1 hr.). 2001. 10.00 (978-0-933685-32-1(7)) A A Grapevine.

Pathways to Spirituality. 1 cass. 1987. 6.50 (978-0-933685-13-0(0), TP-33) A A Grapevine.

Pathways to the Soul - Exercises of the Spirit. Thomas P. Lavin. 3 cass. (Running Time: 3 hrs. 50 min.). 1994. 24.95 set. (978-0-7822-0480-3(5), 556) C G Jung IL.
These audiotapes explore the psychological pathways of daily religious practice, & "those spiritual exercises which help us nurture our souls".

Pathways Towards Personal Progress. Brian S. Tracy. Read by Brian S. Tracy. 2 cass. (Effective Manager Seminar Ser.: No. 12). 95.00 Set, incl. 1-hr. videotape & 2 wkbks., program notes & study guide. (757VD) Nightingale-Conant.
Getting onto the "fast track." Ideas to save years in moving ahead.

Patience see Gilbert & Sullivan: The D'Oyly Carte Opera Company

Patience. David T. Demola. 3 cass. 12.00 (S-1083) Faith Fellow Min.

Patience. Thomas Merton. 1 cass. 1995. 8.95 (AA2800) Credence Commun.
Love means trials & suffering; we need to appreciate struggle while all the time relying on God.

Patience. Derek Prince. 1 cass. (Running Time: 60 min.). (B-131) Derek Prince.

Patience. unabr. ed. Garrison Keillor. (ENG.). 2008. audio compact disk 13.95 (978-1-59887-732-8(1), 1598877321) Pub: HighBridge. Dist(s): Workman Pub

Patience: Total Surrender. Marianne Williamson. Read by Marianne Williamson. 1 cass. (Running Time: 90 mins.). (Lectures on a Course in Miracles). 1999. 10.00 (978-1-56170-253-4(6), M756) Hay House.

Patience & Long-Suffering, Set. Elbert Willis. 4 cass. 13.00 Fill the Gap.

Patience & Love. Gloria Copeland. Perf. by Gloria Copeland. 1 cass. (Ingredients for Success: Faith, Patience & Love Ser.: Tape 4). 1995. cass. & video 5.00 (978-1-57562-020-6(0)) K Copeland Pubns.
Biblical teaching on success.

Patience Attains the Goal. unabr. ed. Perf. by Eknath Easwaran. 1 cass. (Running Time: 1 hr.). 1987. 7.95 (978-1-58638-587-3(9)) Nilgiri Pr.

Patience of Conversion. Thomas Merton. 1 cass. (Running Time: 60 min.). (Conversion Ser.). 8.95 (AA2232) Credence Commun.
Discussions on conversion & the necessity of choosing between the Gospel & the world.

Patience of the Spider. unabr. ed. Andrea Camilleri. Read by Grover Gardner. (Running Time: 4 hrs. 30 mins.). (Inspector Montalbano Mystery Ser.). 2010. 19.95 (978-1-4417-2213-3(0)); 34.95 (978-1-4417-2209-6(2)); audio compact disk 49.00 (978-1-4417-2210-2(6)) Blckstn Audio.

***Patience Stone.** unabr. ed. Atiq Rahimi. Read by Carolyn Seymour. (Running Time: 3 hrs. 30 mins.).Tr. of Syngué Sabour: Pierre de Patience. 2010. 29.95 (978-1-4417-5507-0(1)); 24.95 (978-1-4417-5503-2(9)); audio compact disk 24.95 (978-1-4417-5506-3(3)); audio compact disk 30.00 (978-1-4417-5504-9(7)) Blckstn Audio.

***Patience with God: Faith for People Who Don't Like Religion (or Atheism)** unabr. ed. Frank Schaeffer. (Running Time: 7 hrs. 30 mins.). (ENG.). 2010. 27.98 (978-1-59659-618-4(X), GildAudio) Pub: Gildan Media. Dist(s): HachBkGrp

Patient. Michael Palmer. Read by Michael Kramer. 2000. audio compact disk 72.00 (978-0-7366-5226-1(4)) Books on Tape.

Patient. Michael Palmer. Narrated by Paul Hecht. 10 CDs. (Running Time: 11 hrs.). 2000. audio compact disk 97.00 (978-0-7887-4893-6(9), C1268E7) Recorded Bks.
Dr. Jesse Copeland is experimenting with a tiny robot designed to remove previously inoperable brain tumors. When a notorious terrorist, suffering from a deadly tumor, hears the news, he orders Jesse to operate on him. But he demands a complete recovery or his followers will set off Boston's worst nightmare. Includes an exclusive interview with the author.

Patient. unabr. ed. Michael Palmer. Read by Michael Kramer. 9 CDs. (Running Time: 10 hrs. 48 min.). 2000. audio compact disk 72.00; 64.00 (978-0-7366-4985-8(9)) Books on Tape.
Dr. Copeland must utilize a robot she's developed to save the life of a maniac who will kill thousands if she fails.

Patient. unabr. ed. Michael Palmer. Narrated by Paul Hecht. 9 cass. (Running Time: 11 hrs.). 2000. 72.00 (978-0-7887-4306-1(6), 96222E7) Recorded Bks.
Dr. Jesse Copeland is experimenting with a tiny robot designed to remove previously inoperable brain tumors. When a notorious terrorist, suffering from a deadly tumor, hears the news, he orders Jesse to operate on him. But he demands a complete recovery or his followers will set off Boston's worst nightmare. Includes an exclusive interview with the author.

Patient Assessment & Referral. 1 cass. (Professional Issues Ser.). 1984. 9.00 (1563G) Hazelden.

Patient Care Needs. Chris Grady. (AIDS: The National Conference for Practitioners). 1986. 9.00 (978-0-932491-53-4(7)) Res Appl Inc.

***Patient Experience Boot Camp: The Mystery Shoppers Guide to Creating Loyal Fans.** Kristin Baird. (ENG.). 2010. 2495.00 (978-0-9754733-6-8(0)) Golden Lmp Pr.

Patient Grissell: The Basket-Maker's Song see Hearing Great Poetry: From Chaucer to Milton

Patient Menagment Cluster Q/A: Absolutley Simple & Easy. Ljubo Skrbic. (Running Time: 10 hrs.). 2003. bk. 150.00 (978-1-932622-08-9(X)) Postgraduate Med Rev Ed.

Patient Rights: Basic Healthcare Rights & Ethics, Concentrating on Requirements for Advance Directives & Regulatory Compliance for Doctors, Nurses, Managers, Social Workers, & Allied Health Professionals. Daniel Farb. 2004. audio compact disk 49.95 (978-1-59491-107-1(X)) Pub: UnivofHealth. Dist(s): AtlasBooks
This course is made primarily as a compliance course to teach workers in a healthcare organization about patient rights, and most importantly, the instructions for end of life care. It is useful for anyone delivering or administering patient care.

Patient Safety in the Cost-Effective Operating Room: Operating Room Environment Panel Discussion. Moderated by Donald G. McQuarrie. 2 cass. (Spring Sessions Ser.: SP-2). 1986. 19.00 (8673) Am Coll Surgeons.

Patient with COPD. Instructed by Robert Berg. 4 cass. (Running Time: 7 hrs.). 1990. 79.00 cass. & soft-bound bk. (HT09) Ctr Hlth Educ.
Here's a fresh new approach to caring for patients with COPD. There's a critical challenge to balancing oxygen delivery & maintaining breathing. It's up to you to rapidly assess & treat patients in acute respiratory distress. Prevent the downward spiral of respiratory distress, failure & cardiopulmonary arrest. Actual normal & abnormal breath sounds are included in this seminar.

***Patient Zero: A Joe Ledger Novel.** unabr. ed. Jonathan Maberry. (Running Time: 14 hrs. 30 mins.). (Joe Ledger Ser.). 2010. 29.95 (978-1-4417-6176-7(4)); 85.95 (978-1-4417-6173-6(X)); audio compact disk 32.95 (978-1-4417-6175-0(6)); audio compact disk 118.00 (978-1-4417-6174-3(8)) Blckstn Audio.

Patient's Eyes: The Dark Beginnings of Sherlock Holmes. unabr. ed. David Pirie. Read by Richard Matthews. 5 cass. (Running Time: 7 hrs. 30 mins.). 2001. 40.00 (978-0-7366-8482-8(4)) Books on Tape.
As a young medical student at Edinburgh, Sir Arthur Conan Doyle took classes with the remarkable Dr. Joseph Bell in forensic medicine. Dr. Bell exhibited many of the characteristics that Doyle would later synthesize into the personage of Sherlock Holmes: complete faith in human reason, meticulous powers of observation, and encyclopedic knowledge of the activities and methods of the criminal classes. Looking into the seamy underside of the proper Victorian world. Doyle is puzzled by the ocular symptoms of a woman in his medical practice. Bell senses that there is something criminal afoot, and...the chase is joined.

Patio de Mi Casa. (SPA.). (J). (gr. k-1). 1997. bk. 21.95 (978-1-56014-041-2(0)) Santillana.

Patito Feo. Hans Christian Andersen. 1 cass. (Running Time: 1 hrs.). (SPA.). (J). 1996. pap. bk. 19.50 (978-1-58085-253-1(X)) Interlingua VA.

Patito Feo. Created by Rigby Staff. 1992. 10.40 (978-0-435-05354-3(X), Rigby PEA) Pearson EdAUS AUS.

Patito Feo. l.t. ed. Short Stories. Illus. by Graham Percy. 1 cass. (Running Time: 10 mins.). Dramatization.Tr. of Ugly Duckling. (SPA.). (J). (ps-3). 2001. 9.95 (978-84-87650-11-6(2)) Peralt Mont ESP.

Patito Feo y Muchos Cuentos Mas, Vol. 6. abr. ed.Tr. of Ugly Duckling, the Bewitched House, Little Thumb & Many More Tales. (SPA.). 2001. audio compact disk 13.00 (978-958-9494-33-2(1)) YoYoMusic.

patito muy feo Audio CD. Benchmark Education Company. Based on a work by Brenda Parkes. (Shared Reading Classics Ser.). (J). (gr. k-2). 2009. audio compact disk 10.00 (978-1-60634-982-3(1)) Benchmark Educ.

Pato Atascado, EDL Level 10. (Fonolibros Ser.: Vol. 20). (SPA.). 2003. 11.50 (978-0-7652-1008-1(8)) Modern Curr.

Pato Paco, Set. Anna Turner & Beth Kitching. 1 cass. (Running Time: 022 mins.). (SPA., (J). (ps-5). 2000. pap. bk. 10.98 (978-0-89084-900-2(5), 078865) BJUPr.

Pato para Presidente. Doreen Cronin. Illus. by Betsy Lewin.Tr. of Duck for President. (SPA.). (J). (gr. 1-2). 8.95 (978-0-439-73610-7(2), WW32926) Lectorum Pubns.

Patriarch: George Washington & the New American Nation. unabr. ed. Richard Norton Smith. Narrated by Nelson Runger. 14 cass. (Running Time: 19 hrs. 45 mins.). 1994. 112.00 (978-0-7887-0052-1(9), 94251E7) Recorded Bks.
The life of the first president of the United States; a biographer Richard Norton Smith here confirms the judgement that it was Washington's character, & not the recently signed Constitution, that held the infant Union together.

Patriarch: The Rise & Fall of the Bingham Dynasty, Pt. 1. collector's ed. Alex S. Jones & Susan E. Tifft. Read by Frances Cassidy. 8 cass. (Running Time: 12 hrs.). 1995. 64.00 (978-0-7366-3181-5(X), 3850-A) Books on Tape.
The Binghams of Kentucky were publishing giants who had it all, but family feuding did them in.

Patriarch: The Rise & Fall of the Bingham Dynasty, Pt. 2. unabr. collector's ed. Alex S. Jones & Susan E. Tifft. Read by Frances Cassidy. 9 cass. (Running Time: 13 hrs. 30 mins.). 1995. 72.00 (978-0-7366-3182-2(8), 3850-B) Books on Tape.

Patriarch Bodhidharma's Advent in China. Contrib. by Hua. (978-0-88139-602-7(8)) Buddhist Text.

Patriarch Within. Hal Stone & Sidra Stone. 1 cass. (Running Time: 1 hr.). (Mendocino Ser.). 1993. 10.95 (978-1-56557-013-9(8), T09) Delos Inc.
The voice of the patriarch within each of us echoes the rules, values, & judgments of the outer patriarchy. This is particularly destructive in women because it allies itself with the Inner Critic. In this interview. Sidra Stone shows what this sounds like, how it impacts the lives of women, & how it can be creatively utilized.

Patriarchal Blessings & A Testimony: Collector's Edition. collector's ed. LeGrand Richards. 1 cass. 2004. 7.98 (978-1-55503-069-8(6), 0600653) Covenant Comms.

Patriarchs: Abraham, Isaac, & Jacob: Readings from the Old Testament. George B. Harrison. 1 cass. (Running Time: 33 min.). 1968. 11.95 (23119) J Norton Pubs.
Readings taken from Dr. Harrison's "The Bible for Students of Literature & Art," which have been chosen for their dramatic appeal.

Patriarchs: Moses: Readings from the Old Testament. George B. Harrison. 1 cass. (Running Time: 34 min.). 1968. 11.95 (23120) J Norton Pubs.
Selections taken from Dr. Harrison's "The Bible for Students of Art & Literature".

Patriarchs & Prophets. Ellen G. White. 25 CDs. (Running Time: 50 hrs.). 2002. audio compact disk (978-1-883012-01-4(5)) Remnant Pubns.

Patriarchs & Prophets. Ellen G. White. 2004. audio compact disk (978-1-883012-10-6(4)) Remnant Pubns.

Patriarchy in Transformation: Judaic, Christian, & Clinical Perspectives. Read by Nathan Schwartz-Salant. 1 cass. (Running Time: 90 min.). 1985. 10.95 (978-0-7822-0249-6(7), 166) C G Jung IL.

Patricia Cornwell Vol. 2: Body of Evidence - Postmortem. abr. ed. Patricia Cornwell. Read by Lindsay Crouse. (Running Time: 21600 sec.). 2006. audio compact disk 14.95 (978-0-06-112740-3(X)) HarperCollins Pubs.

Patricia Cornwell Audio Collection, Set. abr. ed. Patricia Cornwell. Read by Lindsay Crouse. Perf. by Kate Burton. 6 cass. (Running Time: 9 hrs.). 1995. 39.95 (978-0-694-51593-6(0), BGS 0009) HarperCollins Pubs.

Patricia Cornwell CD Audio Treasury: All That Remains; Cruel & Unusual. abr. ed. Patricia Cornwell. Read by Kate Burton. 5 Cds. (Running Time: 6 Hrs). 2005. audio compact disk 14.95 (978-0-06-079121-6(7)) HarperCollins Pubs.

Patricia Goedicke I. unabr. ed. Read by Patricia Goedicke. 1 cass. (Running Time: 29 min.). 1986. 10.00 New Letters.

Patricia Goedicke II: "The Poet as Lover" unabr. ed. Ed. by Patricia Goedicke. 1 cass. (Running Time: 29 min.). 1986. 10.00 New Letters.
A series of love poems.

Patricia Goedicke III. unabr. ed. Read by Patricia Goedicke & Rebekah Presson. Ed. by James McKinley. 1 cass. (Running Time: 29 min.). (New Letters on the Air Ser.). 1992. 10.00 (091892); 18.00 2-sided cass. New Letters.
Goedicke is interviewed by Rebekah Presson & reads from her book of poems, Paul Bunyon's Bearskin.

***Patricia Highsmith: Selected Novels & Short Stories.** unabr. ed. Patricia Highsmith. (Running Time: 25 hrs. NaN mins.). (ENG.). 2010. 44.95 (978-1-4417-6934-3(X)); audio compact disk 44.95 (978-1-4417-6933-6(1)); audio compact disk 140.00 (978-1-4417-6932-9(3)) Blckstn Audio.

***Patricia Highsmith: Selected Novels & Short Stories (Part 1 Of 2)** unabr. ed. Patricia Highsmith. (Running Time: 12 hrs. 5 mins.). 2010. 72.95 (978-1-4417-6931-2(5)) Blckstn Audio.

***Patricia Highsmith: Selected Novels & Short Stories (Part 2 Of 2)** unabr. ed. Patricia Highsmith. (Running Time: 12 hrs. 5 mins.). 2010. 72.95 (978-1-4417-5943-6(3)) Blckstn Audio.

Patricia Lear. unabr. ed. Read by Patricia Lear & Rebekah Presson. Ed. by James McKinley. 1 cass. (Running Time: 29 min.). (New Letters on the Air Ser.). 1992. 10.00 (111392); 18.00 2-sided cass. New Letters.
Patricia Lear is interviewed by Rebekah Presson & reads from her book of short stories Stardust, 7-Eleven, Route 57, A & W, & So Forth.

Patricia Va a California -Version Leida CD. (SPA.). (YA). 2003. audio compact disk (978-0-929724-79-9(8)) Command Performance.

Patrick. 2004. pap. bk. 14.95 (978-0-7882-0626-9(5)); 8.95 (978-1-56008-998-8(9)); cass. & flmstrp 30.00 (978-1-56008-742-7(0)) Weston Woods.

Patrick - A Rescue Mission. unabr. ed. Robert A. Monroe. Read by Robert A. Monroe. (Running Time: 45 min.). (Explorer Ser.). 1983. 12.95 (978-1-56113-016-0(8), 17) Monroe Institute.
The rescue of Patrick, who died 100 years ago.

Patrick & the Leprechaun. unabr. ed. 1 cass. (Running Time: 20 min.). Dramatization. (Magic Looking Glass Ser.). (J). (gr. 2-6). 1989. 9.95 (978-0-7810-0019-2(X), NIM-CW-126-5-C) NIMCO.
A folk story of Irish descent.

Patrick Henry: Voice of the Revolution. unabr. ed. Amy Kukla. Read by Benjamin Becker. (Running Time: 2 hrs.). (Library of American Lives & Times Ser.). 2009. 39.97 (978-1-4233-9433-4(X), 9781423394334, Brinc Audio MP3 Lib); 39.97 (978-1-4233-9434-1(8), 9781423394341, BADLE) Brilliance Audio.

Patrick Henry: Voice of the Revolution. unabr. ed. Amy Kukla. Read by Benjamin Becker. 2 CDs. (Running Time: 2 hrs.). (Library of American Lives & Times Ser.). (J). (gr. 4-8). 2009. audio compact disk 39.97 (978-1-4233-9431-0(3), 9781423394310, BriAudCD Unabrid) Brilliance Audio.

Patrick Henry: Voice of the Revolution. unabr. ed. Amy Kukla & John Kukla. Read by Benjamin Becker. (Running Time: 2 hrs.). (Library of American Lives & Times Ser.). 2009. 19.99 (978-1-4233-9432-7(1), 9781423394327, Brilliance MP3); audio compact disk 19.99 (978-1-4233-9430-3(5), 9781423394303, Bril Audio CD Unabri) Brilliance Audio.

Patrick in His Own Words. unabr. ed. Joseph Duffy. Read by Maureen O'Leary. Ed. by Fiona Biggs. 2 cass. 9.95 set. (764) Ignatius Pr.
St. Patrick's "confession" is a deeply interesting record of the genuine & intense religious experience of this great saint from boyhood to manhood, with a personal analysis by the bishop who presides over the Irish Patron's Shrine.

Patrick Kavanagh Back to John Keats. Read by Abbey Actors Staff et al. 1 cass. (Running Time: 1 hr. 06 min.). Dramatization. (Abbey Theatre Reads Ser.). (YA). (gr. 10 up). 1988. 11.95 (978-0-88432-275-7(0), ABB 004) J Norton Pubs.
Features readings of poems by Abbey actors of Kavanagh, Yeats, Tennyson, Byron & Keats, as well as Edward Lear & Brendan Behan.

Patrick Lane in Cab 43. Patrick Lane. 1 CD. (Running Time: 50 mins.). (ENG.). 2004. audio compact disk 12.95 (978-1-894177-04-7(5)) Pub: Cyclops Pr CAN. Dist(s): Literary Pr Gp
Features poems written and performed by Patrick Lane, recorded in a taxi cab, a downtown park, and in the poet's back yard. This is Lane as he was meant to be heard, a poet of the real world, a witness and chronicler of that which is most brutal and most beautiful in human experience. He looks into the darkest corners of life and presents his findings with a fierce honesty, in a voice that combines the music of speech with the unerring rhythm of the human heart.

Patrick Stewart. abr. ed. James Howard Hatfield & George Burt. 2 cass. (Running Time: 3 hrs.). 1996. 16.99 (978-1-57096-049-9(6), DAC 102) Romance Alive Audio.
This is the intimate, uncensored story of Patrick Stewart, the man who rose to super stardom as Captain Jean-Luc Picard on Star Trek: The Next Generation.

Patriot. abr. ed. Stephen Molstad. 4 cass. (Running Time: 270 min.). 2000. 24.00 (978-0-694-52359-7(3)) HarperCollins Pubs.

Patriot. abr. ed. Stephen Molstad. 2 cass. (Running Time: 3 hrs.). 2000. 18.00 (978-1-55935-347-2(3)) Soundelux.

Patriot Acts. unabr. ed. Greg Rucka. Read by Jonathan Davis. (YA). 2008. 74.99 (978-1-60252-987-8(6)) Find a World.

***Patriot Acts: Unabridged Value-Priced Edition.** Greg Rucka. Narrated by Jonathan Davis. (Running Time: 10 hrs. 0 mins. 0 sec.). (ENG.). 2010. audio compact disk 14.95 (978-1-60998-000-9(X)) Pub: AudioGO. Dist(s): Perseus Dist

Patriot Games. unabr. ed. Tom Clancy. Read by Michael Prichard. 15 cass. (Running Time: 22 hrs. 30 min.). 1987. 112.00 (978-0-7366-1237-1(8), 2155) Books on Tape.
Vacationing in London, Jack Ryan stops a terrorist attack on the duke & Duchess of Kent. His heroism earns him the hate of a very dangerous man. Can he & his family survive the payback.

Patriot Pirates. Robert H. Patton. Read by Alan Sklar. (Playaway Adult Nonfiction Ser.). 2008. 59.99 (978-1-60640-560-4(8)) Find a World.

Patriot Pirates: The Privateer War for Freedom & Fortune in the American Revolution. unabr. ed. Robert H. Patton. Narrated by Alan Sklar. (Running Time: 10 hrs. 30 mins. 0 sec.). (ENG.). 2008. audio compact disk 24.99 (978-1-4001-5660-3(2)); audio compact disk 69.99 (978-1-4001-3660-5(1)); audio compact disk 34.99 (978-1-4001-0660-8(5)) Pub: Tantor Media. Dist(s): IngramPubServ

Patriotic American Stories. unabr. ed. Read by Patrick Cullen. 3 cass. (Running Time: 4 hrs.). 2002. 23.95 (978-0-7861-2315-5(X), 3001); audio compact disk 32.00 (978-0-7861-9433-9(2), 3001) Blckstn Audio.
This recording presents a series of patriotic selections of unquestioned literary merit. The purpose is to teach patriotism. This is accomplished through stories chosen with special regard to their effectiveness as avenues through which young people may experience the patriotic sentiments and emotions upon which love of native land depends. Each story is preceded with an appropriate short poem carrying the sentiment of the selection that follows.

Patriotic & Morning Time Songs. Palmer. (J). 1989. 11.95 Ed Activities.

Patriotic Citizens Audio CD. Adapted by Benchmark Education Company Staff. Based on a work by Katherine Scraper. (Early Explorers Set C Ser.). (J). (gr. 1). 2008. audio compact disk 10.00 (978-1-60437-538-1(8)) Benchmark Educ.

Patriotic Favorites - CD Accompaniment. 2002. audio compact disk 12.95 (978-0-634-05030-5(3)) H Leonard.

Patriotic Fire: Andrew Jackson & Jean Laffite at the Battle of New Orleans. unabr. ed. Winston Groom. Read by Grover Gardner. 8 CDs. (Running Time: 10 hrs. 0 mins. 0 sec.). (ENG.). 2006. audio compact disk 34.99 (978-1-4001-0259-4(6)); audio compact disk 24.99 (978-1-4001-5259-9(3)); audio compact disk 69.99 (978-1-4001-3259-1(2)) Pub: Tantor Media. Dist(s): IngramPubServ
From the author of best-selling works of history and fiction, a fast-paced, enthralling retelling of one of the greatest battles fought on the North American continent, and of the two men who - -against all expectations and odds - -joined forces to repel the British invasion of New Orleans in December 1814. It has all the ingredients of a high-flying adventure story. Unbeknownst to the combatants, the War of l812 has ended, but Andrew Jackson, a brave, charismatic American general - -sick with dysentery and commanding a beleaguered garrison - -leads a desperate struggle to hold on to the city of New Orleans and to thwart the army that defeated Napoleon. Helping him is a devilish French pirate, Jean Laffite, who rebuffs a substantial bribe from the British and together with his erstwhile enemy saves the city from invasion . . . much to the grateful chagrin of New Orleanians, shocked to find themselves on the same side as the brazen buccaneer. Winston Groom brings his considerable storytelling gifts to the re-creation of this remarkable battle and to the portrayal of its main players. Against the richly evocative backdrop of French New Orleans, he illuminates Jackson's brilliant strategy and tactics, as well as the antics and cutthroat fighting prowess of Laffite and his men.

***Patriotic Grace.** unabr. ed. Peggy Noonan. Read by Peggy Noonan. (ENG.). 2009. (978-0-06-176097-6(8), Harper Audio); (978-0-06-176096-9(X), Harper Audio) HarperCollins Pubs.

Patriotic Grace: What It Is & Why We Need It Now. unabr. ed. Peggy Noonan. Read by Peggy Noonan. 4 CDs. (Running Time: 4 hrs.). 2008. audio compact disk 22.95 (978-0-06-175475-3(7), Harper Audio) HarperCollins Pubs.

Patriotic Songs: Intermediate Level Repertoire Cuetime. 2004. disk 34.95 (978-0-634-07852-1(6)) H Leonard.

Patriotic Songs & Marches. Dennis Buck. 1 cass. (Running Time: 1 hr.). (J). 2001. pap. bk. 10.95 (KIM 9125C); pap. bk. 14.95 (KIM9125CD); pap. bk. & pupil's gde. ed. 11.95 (KIM 9125) Kimbo Educ.
America's most famous patriotic songs & best-known marches! The marches include Pomp & Circumstance, Hail to the Chief, Sousa Greats & other famous selections. Great for group sing-alongs. Includes song guide.

Patriotic Treason: John Brown & the Soul of America. unabr. ed. Evan Carton. Narrated by Michael Prichard. (Running Time: 16 hrs. 10 mins. 12 sec.). (ENG.). 2006. audio compact disk 39.99 (978-1-4001-0316-4(9)); audio compact disk 29.99 (978-1-4001-5316-9(6)) Pub: Tantor Media. Dist(s): IngramPubServ

Patriotic Treason: John Brown & the Soul of America. unabr. ed. Evan Carton. Read by Michael Prichard. (Running Time: 16 hrs. 10 mins. 12 sec.). (ENG.). 2006. audio compact disk 79.99 (978-1-4001-3316-1(5)) Pub: Tantor Media. Dist(s): IngramPubServ

Patriotically Yours. Eastern Michigan Gospel Choir. (Running Time: 1 hr.). 2003. audio compact disk 6.98 (978-5-552-16632-9(9)) Pub: Pt of Grace Ent. Dist(s): STL Dist NA

Patriots. unabr. ed. Adam Ruthledge. 6 vols. (Running Time: 10 hrs.). (Patriot Ser.: No. 1). 2002. 30.00 (978-1-58807-085-2(9)) Am Pubng Inc.

Patriots: A Novel of Survival in the Coming Collapse. abr. ed. James Wesley Rawles. Read by Dick Hill. (Running Time: 11 hrs.). 2009. audio compact disk 19.99 (978-1-4418-3057-9(X), 9781441830579, BACD) Brilliance Audio.

Patriots: A Novel of Survival in the Coming Collapse. abr. ed. James Wesley Rawles. (Running Time: 11 hrs.). 2010. audio compact disk 14.99 (978-1-4418-3058-6(8), 9781441830586, BCD Value Price) Brilliance Audio.

Patriots: A Novel of Survival in the Coming Collapse. unabr. ed. James Wesley Rawles. Read by Dick Hill. (Running Time: 21 hrs.). 2009. 29.99 (978-1-4418-3053-1(7), 9781441830531, Brilliance MP3); 29.99 (978-1-4418-3055-5(3), 9781441830555, BAD); 44.97 (978-1-4418-3054-8(5), 9781441830548, Brinc Audio MP3 Lib); 44.97 (978-1-4418-3056-2(1), 9781441830562, BADLE); audio compact disk 39.99 (978-1-4418-3051-7(0), 9781441830517, Bril Audio CD Unabri); audio compact disk 97.97 (978-1-4418-3052-4(9), 9781441830524, BriAudCD Unabrid) Brilliance Audio.

Patriots: The Men Who Started the American Revolution. unabr. ed. A. J. Langguth. Narrated by Larry McKeever. 15 cass. (Running Time: 22 hrs.). 1989. 120.00 (978-1-55690-404-2(5), 89397E7) Recorded Bks.
An intimately detailed history of the American Revolution, following the principal & secondary actors.

Patriots' Club. Christopher Reich. 9 cass. (Running Time: 13.5 hrs.). 2005. 81.00 (978-1-4159-2023-7(0)); audio compact disk 84.15 (978-1-4159-2160-9(1)) Pub: Books on Tape. Dist(s): NetLibrary CO

Patriot's Handbook: Songs, Poems, Stories & Speeches Celebrating the Land We Love. unabr. ed. Caroline Kennedy. 2 cass. (Running Time: 3 hrs.). 2003. 18.98 (978-1-4013-9664-0(X)); audio compact disk 24.98 (978-1-4013-9665-7(8)) Pub: Hyperion. Dist(s): HarperCollins Pubs

Patriot's History of the United States: From Columbus's Great Discovery to the War on Terror. unabr. ed. Larry Schweikart. Read by Patrick G. Lawlor. (Running Time: 45 mins.). (YA). 2007. 59.95 (978-0-7861-7007-4(7)) Blckstn Audio.

***Patriot's History of the United States: From Columbus's Great Discovery to the War on Terror.** unabr. ed. Larry Schweikart. Read by Patrick G. Lawlor. (Running Time: 51 hrs. 30 mins.). 2010. audio compact disk 49.95 (978-1-4417-5602-2(7)) Blckstn Audio.

Patriot's History of the United States: From Columbus's Great Discovery to the War on Terror. unabr. ed. Larry Schweikart & Michael Allen. Read by Patrick G. Lawlor. (Running Time: 64800 sec.). 2007. 109.95 (978-0-7861-4948-3(5)) Blckstn Audio.

Patriot's History of the United States: From Columbus's Great Discovery to the War on Terror, Vol. 2. unabr. ed. Larry Schweikart & Michael Allen. Read by Patrick G. Lawlor. (Running Time: 64800 sec.). 2007. 109.95 (978-0-7861-4968-1(X)) Blckstn Audio.

Patriot's History of the United States: From Columbus's Great Discovery to the War on Terror, Vol. A. unabr. ed. Larry Schweikart. Read by Patrick G. Lawlor. (Running Time: 45 mins.). (YA). 2007. audio compact disk 130.00 (978-0-7861-5847-8(6)) Blckstn Audio.

Patriot's History of the United States: From Columbus's Great Discovery to the War on Terror, Vol. B. unabr. ed. Larry Schweikart. Read by Patrick G. Lawlor. (Running Time: 45 mins.). (YA). 2007. audio compact disk 130.00 (978-0-7861-5825-6(5)) Blckstn Audio.

Patriots vs. Tories. Joe Morecraft. 1 CD. (Running Time: 1 hr. 19 mins.). 2001. audio compact disk 10.00 (978-1-929241-68-2(2)) Pub: Vsn Forum. Dist(s): STL Dist NA

The British described the War for Independence as a "Presbyterian parson's rebellion," because of the overwhelming influence of the American clergy on our battle for freedom. But was the War biblically justified? Could the actions of the Founding Fathers be described as justifiable self-defense or as rebellion? When, if ever, is it lawful to resist authority? How should we apply the principles of submission to authority as articulated in Romans 13 and elsewhere in Scripture? In this well-reasoned lecture, Dr. Joe Morecraft presents the biblical and historical Reformation view.

Patriots vs. Tories. Joe Morecraft. 1 cass. (Running Time: 1 hr. 19 mins.). 2001. 7.00 (978-1-929241-29-3(1)) Pub: Vsn Forum. Dist(s): STL Dist NA

Patrol of the Sundance Trail. unabr. ed. Ralph Conner. Read by Gene Engene. 8 cass. (Running Time: 10 hrs.). Dramatization. 1992. 49.95 (978-1-55686-399-8(3), 892550) Books in Motion.

Sergeant Cameron, of the Royal Canadian Mounted Police, is the only person in eastern British Columbia able to match wits with old Copperhead, chief of the Sioux.

Patron Saint of Liars. unabr. ed. Ann Patchett. Read by Julia Gibson. (Running Time: 48600 sec.). 2007. audio compact disk 39.95 (978-0-06-143832-5(4), Harper Audio) HarperCollins Pubs.

***Patron Saint of Liars.** unabr. ed. Ann Patchett. Read by Julia Gibson. (ENG.). 2007. (978-0-06-155434-6(0)); (978-0-06-155436-0(7)) HarperCollins Pubs.

Patron Saint of Used Cars & Second Chances. unabr. ed. Mark Millhone. (Running Time: 8 hrs. 0 mins.). (ENG.). 2009. audio compact disk 24.95 (978-1-4332-8933-0(4)) Blckstn Audio.

Patron Saint of Used Cars & Second Chances: A Memoir. unabr. ed. Mark Millhone. (Running Time: 8 hrs. 0 mins.). (ENG.). 2009. 29.95 (978-1-4332-8934-7(2)); 54.95 (978-1-4332-8930-9(X)); audio compact disk 76.00 (978-1-4332-8931-6(8)) Blckstn Audio.

Patsy of Paradise Place. Rosie Harris. Read by Nerys Hughes. (Chivers Audio Bks.). 2003. 69.95 (978-0-7540-8413-6(2)) Pub: Chivers Audio Bks GBR. Dist(s): AudioGO

Pattern Cycles: Mastering Short Term Trading with Technical Analysis. Instructed by Alan Farley. (Trade Secrets Audio Ser.). 2000. 19.95 (978-1-883272-65-4(3)) Marketplace Bks.

***Pattern for Doomsday.** (ENG.). 2010. audio compact disk (978-1-59171-271-8(8)) Falcon Picture.

Pattern for Love. Elbert Willis. 1 cass. (Developing Ability to Love Ser.). 4.00 Fill the Gap.

Pattern for Panic. unabr. ed. Richard S. Prather. Read by Maynard Villers. 6 cass. (Running Time: 7 hrs. 30 min.). 2001. 39.95 (978-1-58116-014-7(3)) Books in Motion.

When the wife of a Mexican General becomes the victim of extortion, Detective Shell Scott agrees to take this south of the border caper. But the situation turns into more than simple blackmail, as Scott finds himself squared off against the local police and the winds of political change.

Pattern for Patience. Elbert Willis. 1 cass. (Patience & Long-Suffering Ser.). 4.00 Fill the Gap.

Pattern Man. Neville Goddard. 1 cass. (Running Time: 62 min.). 1968. 8.00 (1) J & L Pubns.

Neville taught Imagination Creates Reality. He was a powerfully influential teacher of God as Consciousness.

Pattern of AIDS. Lois Rodden. 1 cass. (Running Time: 90 min.). 1986. 8.95 (581) Am Fed Astrologers.

Pattern of Blood. unabr. ed. Rosemary Rowe. Read by Ric Jerrom. 6 cass. (Running Time: 29460 sec.). 2002. 54.95 (978-0-7540-0918-4(1), CAB 2340) Pub: Chivers Audio Bks GBR. Dist(s): AudioGO

Pattern of Shadows, Set unabr. ed. Peggy Loosemore-Jones. Read by Jean Waggoner. 2 cass. 1999. 21.95 (MRC 1029) AudioGO.

Pattern of Substance Abuse. Vince Ploscik. 1 cass. 1992. 8.95 (1082) Am Fed Astrologers.

Pattern Recognition. unabr. ed. William Gibson. (Running Time: 10 hrs. 36 mins. 0 sec.). (ENG.). 2004. audio compact disk 22.99 (978-1-4001-5095-3(7)) Pub: Tantor Media. Dist(s): IngramPubServ

Pattern Recognition. unabr. ed. William Gibson. Read by Shelly Frasier. 9 CDs. (Running Time: 10 hrs. 36 mins. 0 sec.). (ENG.). 2004. audio compact disk 29.99 (978-1-4001-0095-8(X)); audio compact disk 59.99 (978-1-4001-3095-5(6)) Pub: Tantor Media. Dist(s): IngramPubServ

Pattern Which Connects. unabr. ed. Gregory Bateson. 1 cass. (Running Time: 1 hr. 32 min.). (Informal Esalen Lectures). 1978. 11.00 (02806) Big Sur Tapes.

Patterns: Past & Future: 250th Chronicles Set, Vol. 2. Thomas Schaefer & Paul Wolfgang. 1999. bk. 95.00 (978-1-929348-04-6(5)) York County Comm.

Patterns All Around/First, Second, Third. Steck-Vaughn Staff. 2002. (978-0-7398-5912-4(9)) SteckVau.

Patterns & Solos. Jerry Hahn. (Jerry Hahn Contemporary Guitar Ser.: Vol. 2). 1998. pap. bk. 17.95 (978-0-7866-3217-6(8), 94184BCD) Mel Bay.

Patterns Everywhere. Sundance/Newbridge, LLC Staff. (Early Math Ser.). (gr. k-1). 2000. 12.00 (978-1-58273-312-8(0)) Sund Newbrdge.

Patterns in Magical Christianity: Gateways to the Mysteries of the Son of Light. deluxe exp. rev. ed. Speeches. Nicholas Whitehead. Illus. by Nicholas Whitehead. 2 cds. 2002. bk. 29.95 (978-1-928754-18-3(X)) Le Brun CAN.

Patterns of Destiny. 2006. act. bk. ed. 24.50 (978-1-60079-048-5(8)) YourStory.

Patterns of Destiny, Vol. 7. 2004. 45.00 (978-0-01-208135-8(3)) Your Story.

Patterns of Destiny Album 7: Dramatized Audio Stories. 12 cass. 2006. 45.00 (978-1-60079-006-5(2)); 45.00 (978-1-60079-029-4(1)) YourStory.

Patterns of Professions. Emma B. Donath. 1 cass. 8.95 (096) Am Fed Astrologers.

***Patti Lupone: A Memoir.** unabr. ed. Patti LuPone. Read by Patti LuPone. 2010. audio compact disk 35.00 (978-0-307-74881-2(2), Random AudioBks) Pub: Random Audio Pubg. Dist(s): Random

Pattiann Rogers. unabr. ed. Ed. by Jim McKinley. Prod. by Rebekah Presson. 1 cass. (Running Time: 29 min.). (New Letters on the Air Ser.). 1994. 10.00 (022894) New Letters.

Rogers' poetry often focuses on nature & science, sometimes finding whole ecospheres in a mudpuddle outside the author's door. Rogers reads from "Splitting & Binding," "Geocentric" & other books of poems.

Patti's Pearls. unabr. ed. Patti LaBelle & Laura Randolph Lancaster. (ENG.). 2005. 14.98 (978-1-59483-399-1(0)) Pub: Hachet Audio. Dist(s): HachBkGrp

Patton. Alan Axelrod. Read by Brian Emerson. Frwd. by Wesley K. Clark. (Running Time: 27000 sec.). (Great Generals Ser.). 2006. 54.95 (978-0-7861-4590-4(0)); audio compact disk 55.00 (978-0-7861-6998-6(2)) Blckstn Audio.

Patton. abr. unabr. ed. Alan Axelrod. Read by Brian Emerson. Frwd. by Wesley K. Clark. (Running Time: 27000 sec.). (Great Generals Ser.). 2006. audio compact disk 29.95 (978-0-7861-7669-4(5)) Blckstn Audio.

Patton. abr. unabr. ed. Alan Axelrod. Read by Brian Emerson. Frwd. by Wesley K. Clark. 6 pieces. (Running Time: 27000 sec.). (Great Generals Ser.). 2006. 25.95 (978-0-7861-4488-4(2)); audio compact disk 25.95 (978-0-7861-7241-2(X)) Blckstn Audio.

Patton: A Genius for War. Carlo D'Este. Read by Jonathan Reese. 27 cass. (Running Time: 40 hrs. 30 mins.). 1997. 216.00 (978-0-7366-3808-1(3), 4478 A&B) Books on Tape.

The general's unexpected complexities are revealed with full access to Patton's family & papers.

Patton: A Genius for War. unabr. ed. Carlo D'Este. Read by Jonathan Reese. 13 cass. (Running Time: 19 hrs. 30 mins.). 1997. 104.00 (4478-A); 112.00 (4478-B) Books on Tape.

Patton: A Study in Command. unabr. collector's ed. Herbert Essame. Read by Justin Hecht. 8 cass. (Running Time: 12 hrs.). 1982. 64.00 (978-0-7366-0303-4(4), 1291) Books on Tape.

Essame examines each of Patton's major battles, their place in winning the war, & the principles that guided Patton's strategies & decisions.

Patton: Ordeal & Triumph. collector's ed. Ladislas Farago. Read by John MacDonald. 12 cass. (Running Time: 18 hrs.). 1986. 96.00 (978-0-7366-0746-9(3), 1701-B) Books on Tape.

German Espionage in the US & Great Britain during WW II.

Patton: Ordeal & Triumph. unabr. collector's ed. Ladislas Farago. Read by John MacDonald. 9 cass. (Running Time: 13 hrs. 30 min.). 1986. 72.00 (978-0-7366-0745-2(5), 1701A) Books on Tape.

This follows George Patton from the early days in North Africa to the final battle in Europe. It concludes that the world would have been more secure & millions of Europeans would be West of the Curtain if Eisenhower & others had followed Patton's advice & counsel.

Patton: The Man Behind the Legend. unabr. ed. Martin Blumenson. Read by William Lavelle. 6 cass. (Running Time: 8 hrs. 30 mins.). 1990. 44.95 (978-0-7861-0229-7(2), 1202) Blckstn Audio.

In paying final tribute to his Third Army commander, General Eisenhower said: "He was one of those men born to be a soldier...whose gallantry & dramatic personality inspired all he commanded to great deeds of valor." Provides deep insight into one of the most fascinating & complex personalities of the Second World War & provides understanding into the contradictory elements in his character that caused him to be impossible at times but still a winning commander.

***Patton: The Pursuit of Destiny.** unabr. ed. Agostino Von Hassell. Narrated by William Dufris. (Running Time: 5 hrs. 10 mins. 52 sec.). (Generals Ser.). (ENG.). 2010. 16.09 (978-1-60814-683-3(9), SpringWater); audio compact disk 22.99 (978-1-59859-732-5(9), SpringWater) Oasis Audio.

Patton, Montgomery, Rommel: Masters of War. unabr. ed. Terry Brighton. Narrated by Mel Foster. (Running Time: 15 hrs. 0 mins. 0 sec.). (ENG.). 2009. 29.99 (978-1-4001-6497-4(4)); audio compact disk 39.99 (978-1-4001-1497-9(7)); audio compact disk 79.99 (978-1-4001-4497-6(3)) Pub: Tantor Media. Dist(s): IngramPubServ

***Patton, Montgomery, Rommel: Masters of War.** unabr. ed. Terry Brighton. Narrated by Mel Foster. (Running Time: 15 hrs. 0 mins.). 2009. 39.99 (978-1-4001-9497-1(0)); 20.99 (978-1-4001-8497-2(5)) Tantor Media.

Patton on Leadership: Strategic Lessons for Corporate Warfare. abr. ed. Alan Axelrod. Read by Bruce Winant & Robert Foxworth. 2004. 10.95 (978-0-7435-4561-7(3)) Pub: S&S Audio. Dist(s): S and S Inc

Patty Cat see Let's Read Together

Patty Cat. Created by Kane Press. (Let's Read Together Ser.). 2005. audio compact disk 4.25 (978-1-57565-170-5(X)) Pub: Kane Pr. Dist(s): Lerner Pub

Patty Horn's Desert Dwellers Fiesta! Patty Horn. Illus. by Dana Cude. (J). (gr. k-8). 1998. spiral bd. 15.95 (978-0-9644105-9-6(1)) Two Geckos Mus.

Patty Jane's House of Curl. unabr. ed. Lorna Landvik. Narrated by Christina Moore. 8 CDs. (Running Time: 9 hrs.). 1999. audio compact disk 69.00 (978-0-7887-3425-0(3), C1031E7) Recorded Bks.

When her husband abandons her in 1950s Minneapolis, Patty Jane opens her own unique beauty salon.

Patty Jane's House of Curl. unabr. ed. Lorna Landvik. Narrated by Christina Moore. 6 cass. (Running Time: 9 hrs.). 1998. 51.00 (978-0-7887-1875-5(4), 95297E7) Recorded Bks.

Pattycakes & Peekaboos. Lorraine Bayes & Dennis Westphall. Perf. by Tickle Tune Typhoon Staff. 1 cass. (Running Time: 50 min.). (J). (gr. 1). 1994. 9.98 (978-1-56628-039-6(7), MLP 2065) MFLP CA.

Side One is an active participation collection with activity songs and dances. Side Two is quiet time songs & lullabies that encourage love, joy, & the honoring of young children.

Pattysaurus & Other Tales. Short Stories. 1 CD. (Running Time: 48:30). (J). 2006. audio compact disk 15.00 (978-0-9651669-3-5(7)) Living Myth Audio.

Includes: "Pattysaurus" - a humorous family fable about sibling rivalry & dinosaur mania; "The Old Apple Tree" - a lyrical story of friendship; & "Princess Firefly" - a light-hearted adaptation of a Japanese folktale which tells of the origin of the fireflies. Each of the stories is accompanied by music on the Celtic harp or synthesizer. Honors Award from Storytelling World Magazine & Starred review in Publisher's Weekly, recommended by the Elementary School Library Collection.

Pattysaurus & Other Tales. unabr. ed. Short Stories. Diane Edgecomb. Perf. by Diane Edgecomb. Music by Tom Megan & Margot Chamberlain. 1 cass. (Running Time: 49 min.). (J). (gr. k-3). 1996. 10.00 (978-0-9651669-0-4(2)) Living Myth Audio.

Paul: A Man of Grace & Grit. 2003. 53.95 (978-1-57972-448-1(5)) Insight Living.

Paul: A Man of Grit & Grace. 2003. audio compact disk 68.00 (978-1-57972-449-8(3)) Insight Living.

Paul: A Novel. unabr. ed. Zondervan Publishing Staff & Walter Wangerin, Jr. (Running Time: 12 hrs. 0 mins. 0 sec.). (ENG.). 2003. 29.99 (978-0-310-26168-1(6)) Zondervan.

Paul: In Fresh Perspective. unabr. ed. N. T. Wright. Narrated by Simon Vance. 5 CDs. (Running Time: 7 hrs. 36 mins. 0 sec.). (ENG.). 2007. audio compact disk 23.98 (978-1-59644-503-1(3), Hovel Audio) christianaud.

Paul: The Mind of the Apostle. unabr. collector's ed. A. N. Wilson. Read by David Case. 8 cass. (Running Time: 12 hrs.). 1999. 64.00 (978-0-7366-4640-6(X), 5021) Books on Tape.

The author sheds new light on the orgin & nature of Christianity.

***Paul & Me: 53 Years of Adventures & Misadventures with My Pal Paul Newman.** unabr. ed. A. E. Hotchner. 5 CDs. (Running Time: 6 hrs.). 2010. audio compact disk 50.00 (978-0-307-71282-0(6), BksonTape) Pub: Random Audio Pubg. Dist(s): Random

Paul & Me: 53 Years of Adventures & Misadventures with Paul Newman. unabr. ed. A. E. Hotchner. Read by A. E. Hotchner. (ENG.). 2010. audio compact disk 30.00 (978-0-307-71280-6(X), Random AudioBks) Pub: Random Audio Pubg. Dist(s): Random

Paul Anderson Reminisces in His Gym. 2006. audio compact disk 4.95 (978-0-9772573-9-3(8)) P Anderson Youth Home.

Paul Anderson Speaks to You on Weightlifting. 2006. audio compact disk 4.95 (978-0-9779679-0-2(5)) P Anderson Youth Home.

Paul at Berea & Athens. Dan Corner. 1 cass. 3.00 (65) Evang Outreach.

Paul at Ephesus. Dan Corner. 1 cass. 3.00 (66) Evang Outreach.

Paul Auster. unabr. ed. Read by Paul Auster & Rebekah Presson. Ed. by James McKinley. 1 cass. (Running Time: 29 min.). (New Letters on the Air Ser.). 1994. 10.00 (092694); 18.00 2-sided cass. New Letters.

Auster is interviewed by Rebekah Presson & reads from Mr. Vertigo.

Paul Baloche DVD Guitar Songbook 2. Contrib. by Paul Baloche. 2008. pap. bk. 29.95 (978-5-557-46034-7(9)) Integrity Music.

Paul Before Felix. Dan Corner. 1 cass. 3.00 (67) Evang Outreach.

Paul Bunyan see American Tall Tales

Paul Bunyan. unabr. ed. Steven Kellogg. Read by Jerry Terheyden. 1 cass. (Running Time: 12 min.). (J). (gr. k-3). 1992. pap. bk. 17.00 (978-0-8072-6027-2(4), MR 22 SP, Listening Lib) Random Audio Pubg.

Paul Bunyan & Other American Tall Tales. Melody Warnick. Read by Steven McLaughlin. 1 CD. (Running Time: 1 hr. 0 mins. 0 sec.). (PlainTales First Tales Ser.). (ENG.). (J). (gr. k-2). 2009. audio compact disk 12.95 (978-0-9820282-3-0(7)) Pub: PlainTales. Dist(s): IPG Chicago

Paul Christensen. unabr. ed. Read by Paul Christensen. 1 cass. (Running Time: 29 min.). 1985. 10.00 New Letters.

Paul Christensen reads about the Texas landscape & about difficult relationships.

Paul Desmond: A Step-by-Step Breakdown of the Sax Styles & Techniques of a Jazz Great. Eric J. Morones. Paul Desmond. 2008. pap. bk. 19.99 (978-1-4234-2629-5(0), 1423426290) H Leonard.

Paul et Virginie, abr. ed. H. Bernardin de St. Pierre. Read by Jean Jaeg. 2 cass. (Running Time: 3 hrs.). (FRE.). 1995. 26.95 (1750-KFP) Olivia & Hill.

Idyllic novel about Paul & Virginie who grow up on an island, love one another & then are separated.

Paul Gauguin, Pt. 1. unabr. collector's ed. David Sweetman. Read by David Case. 10 cass. (Running Time: 15 hrs.). 1997. 80.00 (978-0-7366-3614-8(5), 4274-A) Books on Tape.

Paul Gauguin left his stockbroker job to pursue his dreams in Tahiti. What did he find there?.

Paul Gauguin, Pt. 2. unabr. collector's ed. David Sweetman. Read by David Case. 10 cass. (Running Time: 15 hrs.). 1997. 80.00 (978-0-7366-3615-5(3), 4274-B) Books on Tape.

Paul Gibson. 3 cass. (Running Time: 3 hrs.). (C). 15.95 Set. (978-1-57816-005-1(7), PG3501) Audio File.

Three hours from the opinionated & charming Paul Gibson talk radio broadcasts.

Paul Harris: Parents & Soccer. Read by Paul Harris. 1 cass. 9.95 (978-0-89811-072-2(6), 7123) Lets Talk Assocs.

Paul Harris talks about the people & events which influenced his career, & his own approach to his speciality.

***Paul: in Fresh Perspective.** unabr. ed. N. T. Wright. Narrated by Simon Vance. (ENG.). 2007. 14.98 (978-1-59644-504-8(1), Hovel Audio) christianaud.

***Paul Is Undead: The British Zombie Invasion.** unabr. ed. Alan Goldsher. Read by Simon Vance & Ray Porter. (Running Time: 11 hrs.). 2010. 29.95 (978-1-4417-6423-2(2)) Blckstn Audio.

***Paul Is Undead: The British Zombie Invasion.** unabr. ed. Alan Goldsher. Read by Ray Porter. (Running Time: 11 hrs.). 2010. 65.95 (978-1-4417-6420-1(8)) Blckstn Audio.

***Paul Is Undead: The British Zombie Invasion.** unabr. ed. Alan Goldsher. Read by Simon Vance. (Running Time: 11 hrs.). 2010. audio compact disk 24.95 (978-1-4417-6422-5(4)) Blckstn Audio.

***Paul Is Undead: The British Zombie Invasion.** unabr. ed. Alan Goldsher. Read by Ray Porter. (Running Time: 11 hrs.). 2010. audio compact disk 100.00 (978-1-4417-6421-8(6)) Blckstn Audio.

Paul Klein: Executive Vice President Programming, NBC TV see Scene Behind the Screen: The Business Realities of the TV Industry

Paul Laurence Dunbar. 10.00 Esstee Audios.

Paul M. Lisnek: And the Pursuit of Happiness. Paul M. Lisnek. Read by Paul M. Lisnek. 1 cass. 1992. (978-1-57654-201-9(7)) Creat Core.

Provides a refreshing & insightful look into ourselves.

Paul McCartney. abr. ed. Alan Clayson. Read by Mike Read. 3 CDs. (Running Time: 3 hrs. 36 mins.). 2003. audio compact disk (978-1-86074-534-8(2)) Sanctuary Pubng GBR.

Paul McCartney's name came second in the famed Lennon-McCartney credits on so many masterful tunes, but he has always had his own unique image and talent. Alan Clayson captures the qualities that made him so popular in this fact-based biography that covers his scrappy early years through the stormy successes of his tenure with the Beatles to more recent projects that have kept him in the limelight.

Paul McCartney: A Life. unabr. ed. Peter Ames Carlin. Narrated by John Lee. 2 MP3-CDs. (Running Time: 13 hrs. 0 mins. 0 sec.). (ENG.). 2009. 29.99 (978-1-4001-6385-4(4)); audio compact disk 39.99 (978-1-4001-1385-9(7));

audio compact disk 79.99 (978-1-4001-4385-6(3)) Pub: Tantor Media. Dist(s): IngramPubServ

***Paul McCartney: A Life.** unabr. ed. Peter Ames Carlin. Narrated by John Lee. (Running Time: 13 hrs. 0 mins.). 2009. 18.99 (978-1-4001-8385-2(5)) Tantor Media.

***Paul Mccartney: Promotional: A Life.** unabr. ed. Peter Ames Carlin. Narrated by John Lee. (Running Time: 13 hrs. 0 mins. 0 sec.). (ENG.). 2010. audio compact disk 14.95 (978-1-4001-2025-3(X)) Pub: Tantor Media. Dist(s): IngramPubServ

Paul Newman: A Life. abr. ed. Shawn Levy. Read by Marc Cashman. 5 CDs. (Running Time: 6 hrs.). 2009. audio compact disk 30.00 (978-0-307-57655-2(8), Random AudioBks) Pub: Random Audio Pubg. Dist(s): Random

Paul of Dune. unabr. ed. Brian Herbert & Kevin J. Anderson. Read by Scott Brick. 13 CDs. (Running Time: 18 hrs. 30 mins. 0 sec.). (Dune Ser.). (ENG.). 2008. audio compact disk 49.95 (978-1-4272-0484-4(5)) Pub: Macmill Audio. Dist(s): Macmillan

Paul on Trial. 8 cass. 24.95 (20134, HarperThor) HarpC GBR.

Paul Revere: Boston Patriot. unabr. ed. Augusta Stevenson. Read by Lloyd James. 4 cass. (Running Time: 5 hrs. 30 mins.). (Childhood of Famous Americans Ser.). (gr. 1-3). 2001. pap. bk. 35.95 (978-0-7861-2067-3(3), K2828) Blckstn Audio.
The bustling colorful waterfront of Boston in 1744 is the background for nine-year-old Paul Revere. Paul gets caught up in the intrigues of the time, secret meetings held by the Patriots, the colorful & sometimes dangerous sailors & their tall ships, his beginnings as a young silversmith & even a possible Indian attack on Boston. As Paul grows older, he becomes a messenger for the Patriots & has several narrow escapes.

Paul Revere & the Minutemen of the American Revolution. unabr. ed. Ryan P. Randolph. Read by Benjamin Becker. 1 MP3-CD. (Running Time: 2 hrs.). (Library of American Lives & Times Ser.). 2009. 19.99 (978-1-4233-9367-2(8), 9781423393672, Brilliance MP3); 39.97 (978-1-4233-9368-9(6), 9781423393689, Brinc Audio MP3 Lib); 39.97 (978-1-4233-9369-6(4), 9781423393696, BADLE); audio compact disk 39.97 (978-1-4233-9366-5(X), 9781423393665, BriAudCD Unabrid); audio compact disk 19.99 (978-1-4233-9365-8(1), 9781423393658) Brilliance Audio.

Paul Revere's Ride. unabr. collector's ed. David H. Fischer. Read by Dick Estell. 8 cass. (Running Time: 12 hrs.). 1996. 64.00 (978-0-7366-3328-4(6), 3980) Books on Tape.
Fischer tells how Revere, an influential politician (not just a simple silversmith), organized more than 60 people to carry the alarm with him. And because these volunteers still thought of themselves as British, the cry was: "The Regulars are coming out!" At sunrise, Revere was at Lexington when the first shots were fired.

Paul Revisited: 11 Tim. 4:9-22. Ed Young. 2000. 4.95 (978-0-7417-2261-4(5), 1261) Win Walk.

Paul Robeson: Words Like Freedom. Executive Producer Freedom Archives. (ENG.). 2008. audio compact disk 15.00 (978-0-9790789-1-0(1)) Pub: Freedom Archives. Dist(s): AK Pr Dist

Paul Spike. unabr. ed. Read by Paul Spike. 1 cass. (Running Time: 29 min.). 1985. 10.00 New Letters.
Paul Spike reads excerpts from his novel, "Vacaville", set in the 60's.

Paul Temple & the Conrad Case. unabr. ed. 4 CDs. (Running Time: 3 hrs. 45 mins.). 2008. audio compact disk 49.95 (978-0-7927-5413-8(1)) AudioGO.
From 1938 to 1969 the fictional crime novelist and detective Paul Temple, together with his Fleet Street journalist wife Steve, solved case after case in one of BBC radio's most popular series. They inhabited a sophisticated world of chilled cocktails and fast cars, where the women were chic and the men wore cravats-a world where Sir Graham Forbes, of Scotland Yard, usually needed Paul's help with his latest tricky case. The case this time involves Dr Conrad's daughter Betty, who has disappeared from her finishing school in Bavaria. Paul is invited by the police to go over there to help trace the missing girl. Initially, though, even he is baffled, since the only clue to the mystery is an unusual cocktail stick found in her bedroom. Can Paul work it out?.

Paul Temple & the Front Page Men. unabr. ed. Francis Durbridge. Read by Tom Crowe. 6 cass. 2001. (978-0-7531-0988-5(3)) ISIS Audio GBR.

***Paul Temple & the Lawrence Affair.** Francis Durbridge. Narrated by Peter Coke & Marjorie Westbury. 4 CDs. (Running Time: 3 hrs. 35 mins. 0 sec.). (ENG.). 2010. audio compact disk 34.95 (978-0-563-49411-9(5)) Pub: AudioGO. Dist(s): Perseus Dist

Paul Temple & the Madison Mystery: A BBC Radio Full-Cast Dramatization. Francis Durbridge. (Running Time: 4 hrs. 0 mins. 0 sec.). (ENG.). 2009. audio compact disk 34.95 (978-1-60283-751-5(1)) Pub: AudioGO. Dist(s): Perseus Dist

***Paul Temple Casebook, Vol. 1.** Francis Durbridge. Narrated by Anthony Head. (Running Time: 9 hrs. 0 mins. 0 sec.). (ENG.). 2010. audio compact disk 69.95 (978-1-4056-7788-2(0)) Pub: AudioGO. Dist(s): Perseus Dist

***Paul Temple Casebook: Volume Two: Four Mysteries Read by Anthony Head.** Francis Durbridge. Narrated by Anthony Head. (Running Time: 10 hrs. 0 mins. 0 sec.). (ENG.). 2011. audio compact disk 69.95 (978-1-4084-0035-7(9)) Pub: AudioGO. Dist(s): Perseus Dist

Paul Temple Mysteries. unabr. ed. Francis Durbridge. 8 vols. (Running Time: 9 hrs.). Dramatization. 2003. audio compact disk 79.95 (978-0-563-49668-7(1)) BBC Worldwide.
From 1938 to 1969, the ficitonal crime novelist and detective Paul Temple, together with his Fleet Street journalist wife Steve, solved case after case in one of BBC's most popular radio series. A collection of 3 classics.

Paul, the Dominant Disciple. Samuel Sandmel. 1 cass. (Running Time: 26 min.). 10.95 (31004) J Norton Pubs.
Portrays Paul as the shaper of Christianity, a restless & brilliant man.

Paul the Traveler. collector's ed. Ernle Bradford. Read by Walter Zimmerman. 8 cass. (Running Time: 12 hrs.). 1989. 64.00 (978-0-7366-1508-2(3), 2380) Books on Tape.
A fine biography of the man we know as St. Paul, the great Christian missionary of the first century.

Paul Van Arsdale: Dulcimer Heritage. 1 cass. 9.98 (C-87) Folk-Legacy.
The finest traditional hammered dulcimer artist ever.

Paul Weis: Failure of Organized Religion see Buckley's Firing Line

Paul Yandell Collection. Craig Dobbins. 2007. pap. bk. 19.95 (978-0-7866-7846-4(1)) Mel Bay.

Paul Zimmer. unabr. ed. Contrib. by Paul Zimmer. 1 cass. (Running Time: 29 min.). 1987. 10.00 New Letters.
Features the director of the University of Iowa Press.

Paula Deen: It Ain't All about the Cookin' abr. ed. Paula Deen. Read by Paula Deen. 6 CDs. (Running Time: 7 hrs. 0 mins. 0 sec.). (ENG.). 2007. audio compact disk 29.95 (978-0-7435-6883-8(4)) Pub: S&S Audio. Dist(s): S and S Inc

Paula Deen: It Ain't All about the Cookin' abr. ed. Paula Deen. Read by Paula Deen. (Running Time: 7 hrs. 0 mins. 0 sec.). (ENG.). 2009. audio compact disk 14.99 (978-0-7435-8083-0(4)) Pub: S&S Audio. Dist(s): S and S Inc

Paula Fox Interview with Kay Bonetti. Interview with Paula Fox & Kay Bonetti. 1 cass. 1986. 13.95 (978-1-55644-154-7(1), 6042) Am Audio Prose.
Fox talks about the main difference between writing for children, for adults, & the sources, composition, structure, & thematic concerns of her "adult" novels. She also responds to negative criticism of two books, "The Slave Dancer", & "The Servant's Tale".

Paula Spencer. unabr. ed. Roddy Doyle. Read by Ger Ryan. 1 MP3-CD. (Running Time: 6 hrs. 49 mins.). 2007. 39.95 (978-0-7927-4758-1(5)); audio compact disk 64.95 (978-0-7927-4737-6(2)); 54.95 (978-0-7927-4780-2(1)) AudioGO.
Paula Spencer begins on the eve of Paula's forty-eighth birthday. She hasn't had a drink for four months and five days. Having outlived an abusive husband and father, Paula and her four children are now struggling to live their adult lives, with two of the kids balancing their own addictions. Paula rebuilds her life slowly. As she goes about her daily routine working as a cleaning woman, and cooking for her two children at home, she re-establishes connections with her two sisters, her mother and grandchildren, expanding her world. Doyle has movingly depicted a woman, both strong and fragile, who is fighting back and finally equipped to be a mother to her children.

Paule Marshall. Interview. Interview with Paule Marshall & Kay Bonetti. 1 cass. (Running Time: 1 hr. 10 min.). 13.95 (978-1-55644-116-5(9), 4132) Am Audio Prose.
Popular black author discusses the creative process as it applies to her own work.

Paule Marshall Interview. 20.97 (978-0-13-090424-9(4)) P-H.

Pauline Instructions for a Church in Revival. As told by Frank Damazio. 6 cass. 1998. 30.00 (978-1-886849-49-5(8)) CityChristian.

Paul's Blueprint for the Church: Studies in First Timothy. Douglas Wilson. (ENG.). 2007. audio compact disk 48.00 (978-1-59128-335-5(3)) Canon Pr ID.

Paul's Case see Great American Short Stories

Paul's Case see Troll Garden

Paul's Case. 1977. (N-14) Jimcin Record.

Paul's Case. abr. ed. Willa Cather. Perf. by Carole Shelley. 1 cass. 1984. 12.95 (978-0-694-50354-4(1), SWC 1687) HarperCollins Pubs.
Adolescent rebellion & the passion for illusion are the seeds of Paul's tragic undoing.

Paul's Community & Our Spirituality. William F. Maestri. 6 cass. 1984. 46.95 incl. shelf-case & outline. (TAH151) Alba Hse Comns.
"The more things change, the more they remain the same" & we must learn from it or risk repeating our ancestors' mistakes.

Paul's Letter to the Galatians. Created by AWMI. (ENG.). 2001. audio compact disk 35.00 (978-1-59548-057-6(9)) A Wommack.

Paul's Letters to the Corinthians. Richard Rohr. 10 cass. (Running Time: 9 hrs. 20 min.). 69.95 Set. (AA2298) Credence Commun.
Rohr gives explanations of what the text meant when written & how it applies to American culture today.

Paul's Message to the City Churches: Body of Christ. unabr. ed. Mary A. Getty. 5 cass. (Running Time: 7 hrs. 51 min.). 1993. 40.95 set. (TAH288) Alba Hse Comns.
This program reveals facts that help us approach the person of St. Paul with a realistic warmth & love. It will enrich your understanding of St. Paul & supply you with those facts that really make the Acts & the Pauline Letters come alive.

Paul's Postscript: Romans 16:21-27. Ed Young. 1984. 4.95 (978-0-7417-1409-1(4), 409) Win Walk.

Paul's Thorn in the Flesh. David T. Demola. 1 cass. 4.00 (1-088) Faith Fellow Min.

Pavarotti: My World. unabr. ed. Luciano Pavarotti. Read by Barrett Whitener. 9 cass. (Running Time: 13 hrs. 30 mins.). 1996. 72.00 (978-0-7366-3297-3(2), 3952) Books on Tape.
Miami Beach officials rerouted air traffic so noise wouldn't interfere with a Pavarotti concert; in London, royalty stood in the rain at an outdoor performance. Pavarotti presents himself as a simple man who hates the limelight. He makes us believe it! Indeed, Pavarotti lays out everything like a smorgasbord: his family tragedies, his passion for horses, his health, his scandals, his friendships.

***Pavilion of Women.** unabr. ed. Pearl S. Buck. Narrated by Adam Verner. (Running Time: 15 hrs. 15 mins. 44 sec.). (ENG.). 2010. 27.99 (978-1-60814-758-8(4), SpringWater); audio compact disk 39.99 (978-1-59859-770-7(1), SpringWater) Oasis Audio.

Pavo para la Cena de Accion de Gracias? No Gracias! Alma Flor Ada. (Cuentos Para Todo el Ano Ser.). (SPA., (J). (gr. k-3). 4.95 (978-1-58105-249-7(9)) Santillana.

Paw Paw Chuck's Big Ideas in the Bible - Book. Charles R. Swindoll. (J). (ps-3). 1995. 12.99 (978-0-8499-6225-7(0)) Nelson.

Paw Paw Patch: Favorite Children's Songs. Perf. by Phil Rosenthal. 1 cass. (Running Time: 30 min.). (J). (ps-3). 1987. 9.98 (978-1-879305-03-8(8), AM-C-104) Am Melody.
Familiar folk songs & nursery rhymes with lively vocals & bluegrass accompaniment are well paced for sing alongs. 1988 ALA Notable Children's Recording.

Paw Thing. unabr. ed. Paul Jennings. 2 CDs. (Running Time: 2 hrs.). 2002. audio compact disk 22.00 (978-1-74030-601-0(5)) Pub: Bolinda Pubng AUS. Dist(s): Lndmrk Audiobks

Paw Thing. unabr. ed. Paul Jennings. Read by Stig Wemyss. 1 cass. (Running Time: 24 mins.). (Singenpoo Ser.: Bk. 1). 2002. 18.00 (978-1-74030-472-6(1)) Pub: Bolinda Pubng AUS. Dist(s): Lndmrk Audiobks

Pawing Through the Past. collector's ed. Rita Mae Brown. Narrated by Kate Forbes. Contrib. by Sneaky Pie Brown. 7 cass. (Running Time: 9 hrs. 45 mins.). (Mrs. Murphy Mystery Ser.). 2002. 42.95 (978-1-4025-1517-0(0), 96671) Recorded Bks.
"Mary Minor Harry" Haristeen is preparing for her 20th high school reunion when trouble comes to the seemingly sleepy town of Crozet, Virginia.

Pawing Through the Past. unabr. ed. Rita Mae Brown & Sneaky Pie Brown. Narrated by Kate Forbes. 7 cass. (Running Time: 9 hrs. 45 mins.). (Mrs. Murphy Mystery Ser.). 2002. 61.00 (978-1-4025-1511-8(1)) Recorded Bks.

Pawleys Island. Dorothea Benton Frank. (Lowcountry Tales Ser.). 2009. audio compact disk 9.99 (978-1-4418-2654-1(8)) Brilliance Audio.

Pawleys Island. abr. ed. Dorothea Benton Frank. Read by Dorothea Benton Frank. (Running Time: 21600 sec.). (Lowcountry Tales Ser.: No. 5). 2005. audio compact disk 16.99 (978-1-59737-176-6(9), 9781597371766) Brilliance Audio.
Of the many barrier islands that pepper the coast of South Carolina's Lowcountry, Pawleys Island, the "arrogantly shabby" family playground for generations, might be the most mysterious and charming of them all. It is here and in the surrounding area that Dorothea Benton Frank has placed her latest Lowcountry tale, Pawleys Island. Meet Huey Valentine, the owner of Gallery Valentine, catering to interior decorators and, heaven save us, tourists. Huey resides on his family plantation on the shores of the Waccamaw River, where he cares for his mother, Miss Olivia, a wise and irresistible octogenarian. And meet Huey's great friend Abigail Thurmond, retired attorney from Columbia, who has laid claim to her family's home on Pawleys Island. Huey and Abigail are complacent in their fat and sassy lives until the stormy advent of the artist Rebecca Simms. Rebecca has been catapulted from her home, her marriage, and her children. She has escaped to Pawleys Island to hide herself from herself. But after Miss Olivia pries Rebecca's secrets from her, Huey and especially Abigail are challenged to reenter life outside the dream state their idyllic geography evokes. They will see that Rebecca has her day in court, but they never expect to provoke a national forum for discussion. With characteristic humor and a full cast of eccentric and wonderfully lovable characters, Dorothea Benton Frank brings us her most honest and entertaining story to date. People have secrets they never want anyone to know. People have pasts they would prefer be left out of conversation. In Frank's nimble hands, it all comes spilling out to be examined and reconciled.

Pawleys Island. unabr. ed. Dorothea Benton Frank. Read by Dorothea Benton Frank. (Running Time: 12 hrs.). (Lowcountry Tales Ser.: No. 5). 2005. 39.25 (978-1-59737-180-3(7), 9781597371803, BADLE); 24.95 (978-1-59737-179-7(3), 9781597371797, BAD); 39.25 (978-1-59737-178-0(5), 9781597371780, Brinc Audio MP3 Lib); 24.95 (978-1-59737-177-3(7), 9781597371773, Brilliance MP3); 32.95 (978-1-59737-171-1(8), 9781597371711, BAU); audio compact disk 102.25 (978-1-59737-174-2(2), 9781597371742, BriAudCD Unabrid); audio compact disk 36.95 (978-1-59737-173-5(4), 9781597371735, Bril Audio CD Unabri) Brilliance Audio.
When Becca Sims wanders into the beautiful seaside Gallery Valentine hoping to sell some of her watercolors, she has no idea her life is about to be transformed by the gallery's owner and his best friend. With the vivid, unforgettable characters, dreamy Lowcountry setting, and authentically brazen, compulsively readable Southern voice that have made her one of today's greatest storytellers, Dorothea Benton Frank delivers her most extraordinary novel yet.

Pawnbroker's Niece. unabr. ed. June Francis. Read by Margaret Sircom. 8 cass. (Running Time: 12 hrs.). (Storysound Ser.). (J). 2003. 69.95 (978-1-85903-610-5(4)) Pub: Mgna Lrg Print GBR. Dist(s): Ulverscroft US

Paws & Tales: A Conscious Effort / Tiffany Cometh. 2004. audio compact disk 7.00 (978-1-57972-633-1(X)) Insight Living.

Paws & Tales: A Good Foundation / Grace to Hugh. 2004. audio compact disk 7.00 (978-1-57972-625-6(9)) Insight Living.

Paws & Tales: A Race Against Time / the Honey Buzz Principle. 2004. audio compact disk 7.00 (978-1-57972-630-0(5)) Insight Living.

Paws & Tales: C. J. & Ahab / Miss Helga Grissel. 2004. audio compact disk 7.00 (978-1-57972-644-7(5)) Insight Living.

Paws & Tales: C. J. Prospers / I'm Achan All Over. 2004. audio compact disk 7.00 (978-1-57972-651-5(8)) Insight Living.

Paws & Tales: Captain of My Destiny / Let It Go, Let It Go, Let It Go. 2004. audio compact disk 7.00 (978-1-57972-652-2(6)) Insight Living.

Paws & Tales: Christmas in Wildwood. 2004. audio compact disk 14.00 (978-1-57972-599-0(6)) Insight Living.

Paws & Tales: Correction Course / A Closer Look. 2004. audio compact disk 7.00 (978-1-57972-628-7(3)) Insight Living.

Paws & Tales: Cylinder 137K / Whose Name Is Jealous. 2004. audio compact disk 7.00 (978-1-57972-642-3(9)) Insight Living.

Paws & Tales: Every Good Thing / Road to Christmas. 2004. audio compact disk 7.00 (978-1-57972-646-1(1)) Insight Living.

Paws & Tales: God with the Wind / the Lighthouse. 2004. audio compact disk 7.00 (978-1-57972-629-4(1)) Insight Living.

Paws & Tales: Hullabaloo at Hunker Hill / A Pirate's Life. 2004. audio compact disk 7.00 (978-1-57972-635-5(6)) Insight Living.

Paws & Tales: If the Tooth Be Known / the Grecian Urn. 2004. audio compact disk 7.00 (978-1-57972-637-9(2)) Insight Living.

Paws & Tales: I'm a Believer. 2004. audio compact disk 7.00 (978-1-57972-639-3(9)) Insight Living.

Paws & Tales: Perfect Christmas Gift / Hold the Anchovies. 2004. audio compact disk 7.00 (978-1-57972-632-4(1)) Insight Living.

Paws & Tales: Plans in the Breaking / the Scarlet Stain. 2004. audio compact disk 7.00 (978-1-57972-636-2(4)) Insight Living.

Paws & Tales: Snake Oil / the Great Go-Cart Race. 2004. audio compact disk 7.00 (978-1-57972-631-7(3)) Insight Living.

Paws & Tales: Staci's Dilemma / Blinded by the Sight. 2004. audio compact disk 7.00 (978-1-57972-634-8(8)) Insight Living.

Paws & Tales: Story of Esther Part 2 / Story of Esther Part 3. 2004. audio compact disk 7.00 (978-1-57972-648-5(8)) Insight Living.

Paws & Tales: The Dedication / Eye of the Tiger. 2004. audio compact disk 7.00 (978-1-57972-640-9(2)) Insight Living.

Paws & Tales: The First King of Israel: the Story of Saul. 2006. audio compact disk 14.99 (978-1-57972-737-6(9)) Insight Living.

Paws & Tales: The Gift / Goliath. 2004. audio compact disk 7.00 (978-1-57972-638-6(0)) Insight Living.

Paws & Tales: The Good Shepherd / Powers & Principalities. 2004. audio compact disk 7.00 (978-1-57972-650-8(X)) Insight Living.

Paws & Tales: The Hire Principle / & Then There Were None. 2004. audio compact disk 7.00 (978-1-57972-641-6(0)) Insight Living.

Paws & Tales: The Island of Ned / Grow Your Gifts. 2004. audio compact disk 7.00 (978-1-57972-649-2(6)) Insight Living.

Paws & Tales: The Least of All / True Riches. 2004. audio compact disk 7.00 (978-1-57972-645-4(3)) Insight Living.

Paws & Tales: The Plans I Have / Story of Esther Part 1. 2004. audio compact disk 7.00 (978-1-57972-647-8(X)) Insight Living.

Paws & Tales: The Princess / Standing Alone. 2004. audio compact disk 7.00 (978-1-57972-627-0(5)) Insight Living.

Paws & Tales: The Problem with Purity Part 1 / the Problem with Purity Part 2. 2004. audio compact disk 7.00 (978-1-57972-653-9(4)) Insight Living.

Paws & Tales: The Tribe / Love Hopes. 2004. audio compact disk 7.00 (978-1-57972-643-0(7)) Insight Living.

Paws & Tales: To Have & Give Not / High Noon. 2004. audio compact disk 7.00 (978-1-57972-626-3(7)) Insight Living.

Paws & Tales Vol. 1: A Good Foundation & Other Tales. Created by Charles R. Swindoll. (Running Time: 4 hrs.). (J). 2005. audio compact disk 24.99 (978-1-4003-0228-4(5)) Nelson.
Paws & Tales is a weekly children's radio drama that teaches Biblical principles in a way that is both entertaining and life changing. Each episode includes a cast of lovable animal characters who experience exciting

adventures while learning important lessons to which kids of all ages can relate. Each Paws & Tales volume contains eight thirty-minute episodes on four CDs for hours of fun for kids. Volume 1 includes episodes #1-8. Episode/Theme: A Good Foundation - Spiritual Formation Grace to Hugh - Grace To Have and Give Not - Sharing High Noon - Overcoming Fear The Princess - Prayer Standing Alone - Standing up for truth Correction Course - Obedience A Closer Look - Using the gifts God's given us.

Paws & Tales Christmas in Wildwood. 2002. 12.99 (978-1-57972-476-4(0)); audio compact disk 18.99 (978-1-57972-475-7(2)) Insight Living.

Paws & Tales Season One. 2004. audio compact disk 50.00 (978-1-57972-605-8(4)) Insight Living.

Paws & Tales Season Two. 2004. audio compact disk 50.00 (978-1-57972-606-5(2)) Insight Living.

Paws & Tales Season 3. Charles R. Swindoll. 2007. audio compact disk 29.99 (978-1-57972-775-8(1)) Insight Living.

Paws & Tales Songs from Wildwood. 2002. 7.99 (978-1-57972-474-0(4)); audio compact disk 11.99 (978-1-57972-473-3(6)) Insight Living.

Paws & Tales the Goliath Collection: The Story of Goliath, King of Shadow Valley. 2005. audio compact disk 17.00 (978-1-57972-680-5(1)) Insight Living.

Paws Claws Scales & Tales. unabr. ed. Monty Harper. 1 CD. (Running Time: 36 mins.). (J). (gr. k-4). 2006. audio compact disk 15.00 (978-0-9701081-7-3(6)) Monty Harper.

Cleverly crafted songs featuring well-loved pets from children's literature as well as delightful new characters such as "Eleanor Gerbil," "Fred's Frog Flippy," and Lucinda, the leucistic alligator.

Pax Britannica. unabr. collector's ed. Jan Morris. Read by David Case. 13 cass. (Running Time: 19 hrs. 30 min.). (Pax Britannica Trilogy: Vol. 2). 1996. 104.00 (978-0-7366-3423-6(1), 4068) Books on Tape.

This second volume of the Pax Britannica captures Britain at its peak in 1897, Queen Victoria's Diamond Jubilee. Superbly entertaining.

Pay It Forward. Catherine Ryan Hyde. Read by Anne Pitoniak et al. 2004. 15.95 (978-0-7435-1994-6(9)) Pub: S&S Audio. Dist(s): S and S Inc

Pay It Forward. unabr. ed. Catherine Ryan Hyde. Read by William Dufris. 6 vols. (Running Time: 9 hrs.). 2000. bk. 54.95 (978-0-7927-2379-0(1), CSL 268, Chivers Sound Lib) AudioGO.

It all started with a teacher who moved to Atascadero, California, to teach social studies to junior high school students. A teacher nobody knew very well, because they couldn't get past his face. Because it was hard to look at his face. It started with a boy who could see past his teacher's face & an assignment, given out one hundred times before, with no startling results. But that assignment in the hands of that boy caused a seed to be planted & after that, nothing in the world would ever be the same.

Pay Policies that Help Prevent Lawsuits & Audits: HR Executive Answers. 2009. audio compact disk 497.00 (978-1-60029-061-9(2)) M Lee Smith.

Pay the Devil. unabr. ed. Jack Higgins. Narrated by Richard Poe. 5 cass. (Running Time: 6 hrs. 30 mins.). 2000. 45.00 (978-0-7887-4932-2(3), 96460E7) Recorded Bks.

The American Civil War is over & Colonel Clay Fitzgerald is sick of fighting. When he learns that his uncle left him an estate in rural Ireland, he sets out to find his new home & a new life but in Ireland, Clay finds the nobility cruelly mistreating the common folk. Once again, he arms himself. Disguised as a rogue, he begins to defend the weak.

Pay the Devil. unabr. ed. Jack Higgins. Narrated by Richard Poe. 6 CDs. (Running Time: 6 hrs. 30 mins.). 2001. audio compact disk 58.00 (978-0-7887-8977-9(5), C1285) Recorded Bks.

A master of many genres, his stories range from World War II adventures to espionage & political thrillers. Here he creates a swashbuckling tale set in 19th century Ireland. The American Civil War is over, & Colonel Clay Fitzgerald is sick of fighting. When he learns that his uncle left him an estate in rural Ireland, he sets out to find his new home & a new life. But in Ireland, Clay finds the nobility cruelly mistreating the common folk. Once again, he arms himself. Disguised as a rogue, he begins to defend the weak.

Pay Yourself First: A Guide to Financial Sucess. abr. ed. Jesse B. Brown. 2000. 10.00 (978-0-9659384-2-6(5)) Krystal Pr Pub.

Payback. abr. ed. Stephen Coonts & Jim DeFelice. Read by J. Charles. (Running Time: 14400 sec.). (Deep Black Ser.: No. 4). 2006. audio compact disk 14.99 (978-1-59737-343-2(5), 9781597373432, BCD Value Price) Brilliance Audio.

The Desk Three team is assigned to protect an informant traveling to the U.S. to provide secret testimony against a terrorist organization. When the man is attacked upon arriving at JFK airport, the team saves his life, but they end up losing him to what appears to be kidnappers. By launching a double-pronged operation to find and recover him, they discover that the informant has hooked up with a cell of terrorists who are plotting to assassinate the President.

Payback. abr. ed. William W. Johnstone. Abr. by Odin Westgaard. 2 cass. (Running Time: 3 hrs.). (Code Name Ser.: No. 1). 2004. 18.00 (978-1-58807-428-7(5)) Am Pubng Inc.

Today, when bomb-throwing madmen rule nations and crime cartels strangle the globe, justice demands extreme measures. For twenty years, ex-CIA operations officer John Barrone fought his country's dirty back-alley wars. Now, he leads a secret strike force of former law enforcement, intelligence, and special operations professionals against America's enemies.Code Name: Payback. Terrorists smuggle an awesome bio-weapon of mass destruction into the West Coast, setting in motion a plan to kill millions. Racing against the doomsday countdown, Barrone and his team take on the plotters in a murderous cross-country manhunt. Moving fast, striking hard, they'll do whatever it takes to win - all the way to the final battle on the streets of New York.

Payback. abr. unabr. ed. Stephen Coonts & Jim DeFelice. Read by J. Charles. (Running Time: 43200 sec.). (Deep Black Ser.: No. 4). 2005. audio compact disk 97.25 (978-1-59600-346-0(4), 9781596003460, BACDLib Ed) Brilliance Audio.

RECRUITED: A crack team of covert agents. Word is out to ex-Marine sniper Charlie Dean and his team of the National Security Agency: Infiltrate the highest stratum of Peruvian political power and derail a renegade general from acing an election. All Dean has to do is find a way inside an impenetrable bank vault protected by armed guards round the clock - it's all in a day's work for the men and women of Deep Black. ENGAGED: A violent political coup. But things get complicated when Dean and company discover the renegade general's second plot. The military madman's ruse - a nuclear weapon he claims is in the hands of Marxist guerillas, a bomb that only he can rescue...and control. IGNITED: A devastating terrorist plot. When the general and his plot are exposed, the NSA concludes the greatest threat is over. But in fact, it's only just beginning.

Payback. unabr. ed. Stephen Coonts & Jim DeFelice. Read by J. Charles. (Running Time: 12 hrs.). (Deep Black Ser.: No. 4). 2005. 39.25 (978-1-59710-840-9(5), 9781597108409, BADLE); 24.95 (978-1-59710-841-6(3), 9781597108416, BAD); 87.25 (978-1-59600-343-9(X), 9781596003439, BrilAudUnabridg); audio compact disk 39.25 (978-1-59600-348-4(0), 9781596003484, Brlnc Audio MP3 Lib); audio compact disk 24.95 (978-1-59600-347-7(2), 9781596003477, Brilliance MP3); audio compact disk 36.95 (978-1-4233-0609-2(0), 9781423306092, Bril Audio CD Unabri) Brilliance Audio.

Payback. unabr. ed. Thomas Kelly. Narrated by Ron McLarty. 9 cass. (Running Time: 12 hrs.). 1997. 78.00 (978-0-7887-1594-5(1), 95213E7) Recorded Bks.

New York in the 1980s is a boom town of construction rackets & mob action. As two Irish brothers are drawn into a fight for control in Hell's Kitchen, their loyalties are tested in an underworld powe rstruggle which threatens to demolish everything they have built.

Payback. unabr. ed. Fern Michaels. Read by Laural Merlington. (Running Time: 6 hrs.). (Sisterhood Ser.: No. 2). 2005. 39.25 (978-1-59737-547-4(0), 9781597375474, BADLE); 24.95 (978-1-59737-546-7(2), 9781597375467, BAD); 62.25 (978-1-59737-541-2(1), 9781597375412, BrilAudUnabridg); 24.95 (978-1-59737-540-5(3), 9781597375405, BAU); audio compact disk 74.25 (978-1-59737-543-6(8), 9781597375436, BriAudCD Unabrid); audio compact disk 39.25 (978-1-59737-545-0(4), 9781597375450, Brlnc Audio MP3 Lib); audio compact disk 24.95 (978-1-59737-544-3(6), 9781597375443, Brilliance MP3) Brilliance Audio.

Meet the Sisterhood - seven very different women who found one another in their darkest days and formed an indelible friendship, strong enough to heal their pasts and bring laughter and joy back into their lives. In Myra Rutledge's beautiful Virginia home, amid hugs and fresh iced tea, shrimp fritters and shell-pink tulips, the friends have gathered to embark on their second mission of sweet revenge for one of their own. Julia Webster's husband, a U.S. Senator, has used his wife's graciousness and elegance to advance his career even as he's abused her trust at every turn and left her dreams for the future in tatters. Now, on the eve of his greatest political victory, he's about to learn a serious lesson in payback. Because the senator crossed the wrong woman...and there are six more where she came from... "Revenge is a dish best served with cloth napkins and floral centerpieces...fast-paced...puts poetic justice first." - Publishers Weekly.

Payback. unabr. ed. Fern Michaels. Read by Laural Merlington. (Running Time: 21600 sec.). (Sisterhood Ser.: No. 2). 2007. audio compact disk 14.99 (978-1-4233-3362-3(4), 9781423333623, BCD Value Price) Brilliance Audio.

Payback: Debt & the Shadow Side of Wealth. Margaret Atwood. (Running Time: 18000 sec.). (CBC Massey Lectures). 2008. audio compact disk 44.95 (978-0-660-19830-9(4), CBC Audio) Canadian Broadcasting CAN.

Payback Time: Making Big Money Is the Best Revenge! abr. ed. Phil Town. Read by Phil Town. (ENG.). 2010. audio compact disk 30.00 (978-0-7393-8510-4(0), Random AudioBks) Pub: Random Audio Pubg. Dist(s): Random

***Paycheck.** unabr. ed. Philip K. Dick. Read by Keir Dullea. (ENG.). 2003. (978-0-06-079948-9(X), Harper Audio); (978-0-06-074245-4(3), Harper Audio) HarperCollins Pubs.

Payday in the Body of Christ. Creflo A. Dollar. 10.00 (978-1-59089-108-7(2)) Pub: Creflo Dollar. Dist(s): STL Dist NA

Paying Our Spiritual Debt. unabr. ed. Warren W. Wiersbe. Read by Warren W. Wiersbe. 1 cass. (Running Time: 1 hr. 10 min.). 1989. 4.95 (978-0-8474-3307-0(2)) Back to Bible.

Salvation is a free gift of God, so what debts do we have? Find out from this study in John 3:16.

Paying the Piper. unabr. ed. Sharyn McCrumb. Narrated by Davina Porter & Ian Stuart. 4 cass. (Running Time: 5 hrs.). (Elizabeth MacPherson Ser.: No. 4). 1993. 35.00 (978-1-55690-709-8(5), 93109E7) Recorded Bks.

Forensic archeologist Elizabeth McPherson, spending the summer with a small group of researchers at an isolated dig site on a Scottish Island, must thwart an unknown killer among the scientists.

Paying the Price. Rick Joyner. 1 cass. (Running Time: 90 mins.). (Call To Leadership Ser.). 2000. 5.00 (RJ01-002) Morning NC.

Rick addresses the qualities required of spiritual leaders in these times.

Paying the Price for Souls. Dan Comer. 1 cass. 3.00 (68) Evang Outreach.

Payment in Blood. unabr. ed. Elizabeth George. Read by Donada Peters. 9 cass. (Running Time: 13 hrs. 30 min.). (Inspector Lynley Ser.). 1994. 72.00 (978-0-7366-2637-8(9), 3376) Books on Tape.

Playwright Joy Sinclair's life abruptly ends on a Scottish estate. Scotland Yard's Thomas Lynley & Barbara Havers are called in on the case. Suspects include Britain's foremost actress, a successful theatrical producer & the woman Lynley loves. He & Havers pick their way through a maze of complicated relationships to solve a case rooted in the darkest past.

Payment in Blood. unabr. ed. Elizabeth George. Read by Michael McStay. 8 cass. (Running Time: 12 hrs. 29 min.). (Inspector Lynley Ser.). 2001. 69.95 (978-1-85089-779-8(4), 30691) Pub: ISIS Audio GBR. Dist(s): Ulverscroft US

Payment in Blood. unabr. ed. Elizabeth George. Narrated by Davina Porter. 10 cass. (Running Time: 14 hrs. 30 mins.). (Inspector Lynley Ser.). 1992. 85.00 (978-1-55690-762-3(1), 92426E7) Recorded Bks.

Rising playwright Joy Sinclair is killed with an 18" dagger. Aristocratic detective inspector Thomas Lynch & his lower class partner Barbara Havers are sent to the Scottish Highlands to solve this heinous crime.

Payment in Kind. unabr. ed. J. A. Jance. Read by Gene Engene. 8 cass. (Running Time: 9 hrs. 30 min.). Dramatization. (J. P. Beaumont Mystery Ser.). 1992. 49.95 (978-1-55686-410-0(8), 892515) Books in Motion.

The bloody corpses stashed in the broom closet of the Seattle School District building looked like a classic crime of passion, but 20 year old clues pointed to something much more sinister.

Payment in Kind. unabr. collector's ed. J. A. Jance. Read by Connor O'Brien. 7 cass. (Running Time: 10 hrs. 30 min.). (J. P. Beaumont Mystery Ser.). 1997. 56.00 (978-0-7366-3825-8(3), 4493) Books on Tape.

The bloody corpses in the broom closet of the Seattle School District building were lovingly entwined. Pete Kelsey admits that his dead wife was an A student in the fine art of adultery. But Pete swears he had nothing to do with the deaths.

Paz en la Tierra. unabr. ed. René González. (SPA.). 2000. 9.99 (978-0-8297-2538-4(5)) Zondervan.

Paz en la Tierra. unabr. ed. Rene Gonzalez. 2000. audio compact disk 14.99 (978-0-8297-2539-1(3)) Zondervan.

PBA Workers' Compensation Law Section: Fall Section Meeting 1998. 1998. bk. 99.00 (ACS-2076) PA Bar Inst.

The Worker's Compensation system in Pennsylvania had undergone major changes in the last couple of years. With the new regulations issued this past January, & the Third Circuit's decision in "Sullivan v. Barnett" holding case law, policy statements, & regulations.

PCAT Audiolearn: Pharmacy College Admission Test AudioLearn. 4th ed. Scripts. Shahrad Yazdani. 5 CDs & a CD-Rom. (Running Time: Over 3 Hours). (C). 2003. audio compact disk 79.00 (978-0-9704199-5-8(3)) AudioLearn.

The convenience and ease of use of recording on CD makes PCAT AudioLearn the ideal package of test revision material. AudioLearn?s finely narrated recording includes everything you need to know about the syllabus and the test itself. It covers every fact, theory, formula and equation needed by the PCAT candidate and, by helping you to memorize such huge amounts of information, can assure you the highest of scores in the PCAT. This revision course is completely mobile, by offering an unparalleled opportunity to continue your revision as easily at home as on the move, while traveling to work or driving in the car.

PDL Commuter Audio Clip Strip GM. Zondervan Publishing Staff. 2005. audio compact disk 199.90 (978-0-310-63870-4(4)) Zondervan.

PDR Electronic Library. rev. ed. Thomson PDR Staff. 2004. cd-rom & audio compact disk 99.95 (978-1-56363-499-4(6), PDR) PDRNetwork.

***PDR Electronic Library on CD-ROM: Individual Version.** PDR Staff. 2009. audio compact disk (978-1-56363-764-3(2)) PDRNetwork.

***PDR Electronic Library on CD Rom, 2011 Doc Version.** PDR Network. (ENG.). 2011. audio compact disk 9.95 (978-1-56363-792-6(8)) PDRNetwork.

***PDR Electronic Library on CD Rom, 2011 Individual Version.** PDR Network. (ENG.). 2011. audio compact disk 99.95 (978-1-56363-791-9(X)) PDRNetwork.

PD's in Depth. Edith C. Trager. 1982. (978-0-87789-216-8(4), 1601) ELS Educ Servs.

Peace. C3 Worship Staff. 2005. audio compact disk 14.99 (978-0-88368-859-5(X)) Whitaker Hse.

Peace. unabr. ed. Richard Bausch. Narrated by Michael Kramer. (Running Time: 4 hrs. 30 mins. 0 sec.). (ENG.). 2008. audio compact disk 19.99 (978-1-4001-5768-6(4)) Pub: Tantor Media. Dist(s): IngramPubServ

Peace. unabr. ed. Richard Bausch. Read by Michael Kramer. 4 CDs. (Running Time: 4 hrs. 30 mins. 0 sec.). (ENG.). 2008. audio compact disk 24.99 (978-1-4001-0768-1(7)); audio compact disk 49.99 (978-1-4001-3768-8(3)) Pub: Tantor Media. Dist(s): IngramPubServ

***Peace.** unabr. ed. Jeff Nesbit. Narrated by Robertson Dean. (Running Time: 11 hrs. 18 mins. 52 sec.). (ENG.). 2010. 24.49 (978-1-60814-773-1(8)); audio compact disk 34.99 (978-1-59859-843-8(0)) Oasis Audio.

Peace, Vol. 4. unabr. ed. Chris Yaw. Perf. by Scott Hiltzik. 1 cass. (Running Time: 1 hr.). (Living Words Ser.). 1998. 9.98 (978-1-893613-03-4(8)); audio compact disk 11.98 CD. (978-1-893613-07-2(0)) Living Wds.

Peace: A View from Abroad see Peace: The Public and Private Initiatives

Peace: Being Christian, Being Active see Peace: The Public and Private Initiatives

Peace: Can the Arms Race Be Reversed? A Washington Perspective see Peace: The Public and Private Initiatives

Peace: Children's Fears, Children's Empowerment see Peace: The Public and Private Initiatives

Peace: Feminist Perspectives in Peace Initiatives see Peace: The Public and Private Initiatives

Peace: Music to Carry Us on see Peace: The Public and Private Initiatives

Peace: Pebble or Pearl. Elbert Willis. 1 cass. (Joy & Peace Ser.). 4.00 Fill the Gap.

Peace: Program from the Award Winning Public Radio Series. Interview. Hosted by Fred Goodwin. Comment by John Hockenberry. 1 CD. (Running Time: 1 hr). (Infinite Mind Ser.). 2002. audio compact disk 21.95 (978-1-932479-11-9(2), LCM 246) Lichtenstein Creat.

It's easy to say "give peace a chance," but why is that so hard to do? In this program, we explore the art and science of resolving interpersonal conflicts peacefully, examine some common obstacles to peace, sit in on a mediation session between a landlord and his angry tenant, and probe the role of interfaith dialog in promoting peace. Guests include Robert Mnookin, director of the Harvard Negotiation Research Project; peace psychologist Dan Christie, professor of psychology at the Ohio State University; psychologist Dacher Keltner, founding director of The Berkeley Center for the Development of Peace and Well-being; storyteller Heather Forest, founding director of Story Arts; Imam Omar Abu-Namous, imam of the Islamic Cultural Center of New York; Dean James Parks Morton, president of the Interfaith Center of New York; Venerable T. Kenjitsu Nakagaki, president of the Buddhist Council of New York, and Rabbi Gerry Serotta, co-chair of Rabbis for Human Rights, North America. Plus making time for peace... commentary by John Hockenberry.

Peace: Small, Daily Acts of Courage see Peace: The Public and Private Initiatives

Peace: The Public & Private Initiatives. 9 cass. Incl. Peace: A View from Abroad. Margaret Whittle & Peter Whittle. 1984.; Peace: Being Christian, Being Active. Molly Rush. 1984.; Peace: Can the Arms Race Be Reversed? A Washington Perspective. Ed Snyder. 1984.; Peace: Children's Fears, Children's Empowerment. Harriet Heath. 1984.; Peace: Feminist Perspectives in Peace Initiatives. Ethel Jensen. 1984.; Peace: Music to Carry Us on. Marcia Taylor. 1984.; Peace: Small, Daily Acts of Courage. Jo C. Hartsig. 1984.; Peace: What Value the U. N. in Today's World. Roger Naumann. 1984.; Peace: What's New about the New Call to Peacemaking? Bob Cory. 1984.; 1984. 28.00 Set.; 4.50 ea. Pendle Hill.

Peace: What Value the U. N. in Today's World see Peace: The Public and Private Initiatives

Peace: What's New about the New Call to Peacemaking? see Peace: The Public and Private Initiatives

Peace - Serenity. Eldon Taylor. 2 cass. 29.95 Set. (978-1-55978-741-3(4), 4406) Progress Aware Res.

Peace Amidst Suffering, Talk on CD. Read by Mary Ellen Edmunds. 2007. audio compact disk 13.95 (978-1-59038-738-2(4)) Desert Bks.

Peace & Calm. Shelley L. Stockwell. 1 cass. (Running Time: 60 min.). (Self-Hynosis Ser.). 1986. 10.00 (978-0-912559-08-7(X)) Creativity Unltd Pr.

Eliminates stress with soothing music & guided imagery. Learn self-love while you relax.

Peace & Forgiveness. Read by Jefferson Glassie. 2 CDs. (Running Time: 112 mins.). 2004. audio compact disk 14.95i (978-0-9753837-1-1(X)) Peace Evltns.

Jeff Glassie reading Peace and Forgiveness.

Peace & Happiness. Speeches. As told by Swami Prabhavananda. 1. (Running Time: 50). 2003. 9.95 (978-0-87481-353-1(0)) Vedanta Pr.

INSPIRATIONAL LECTURE ON SPIRITUAL LIVING FROM THE STANDPOINT OF VEDANTA (HINDUISM).

Peace & Joy: Romans 5:1-2. Ed Young. 1984. (978-0-7417-1362-9(4), 362) Win Walk.

Peace & Justice in the Pastoral Care Movement: Pastoral Care Network for Social Responsibility. 1 cass. (Care Cassettes Ser.: Vol. 18, No. 1). 1991. 10.80 Assn Prof Chaplains.

***Peace & Plenty: Finding Your Path to Financial Serenity.** unabr. ed. Sarah Ban Breathnach. (Running Time: 10 hrs.). (ENG.). 2010. 24.98 (978-1-60788-660-0(X)); audio compact disk 34.98 (978-1-60788-659-4(6)) Pub: Hachet Audio. Dist(s): HachBkGrp

Peace & Quiet (Slow-Down) Brainstore Inc. Staff. 2002. 14.95 (978-1-890460-13-6(3)) Pub: Corwin Pr. Dist(s): SAGE

Peace & Serenity: Effective Stress Management. Created by Christine Sherborne. (ENG.). 2007. audio compact disk 19.95 (978-0-9582712-4-0(0)) Pub: Colourstory AUS. Dist(s): APG

Peace & the International Peace Academy. Ruth Young. 1 cass. 9.00 (A0166-86) Sound Photosyn.
Faustin interviews Ruth about the techniques of peace rather than of war. Major General Indar Jit Rikhye speaks on side B.

Peace Be Still. 1 cass., 1 CD. 10.98 (978-1-57908-325-0(0), 1396); audio compact disk 15.98 CD. (978-1-57908-324-3(2)) Platinm Enter.

Peace Be with You: Johann Sebastian Bach. Gloriae Dei Cantores. 2 CDs. 2000. audio compact disk 33.95 (978-1-55725-252-4(1), GDCD028) Paraclete MA.

Peace Be with You: Music CD. Thomas Ian Nicholas. (Firelight Ser.). (gr. 7-9). 2004. audio compact disk 5.99 (978-0-8066-6542-9(4)) Augsburg Fortress.

Peace Child. abr. ed. Don Richardson. Read by Brad Meeder. 6 CDs. (Running Time: 6 hrs. 30 min.). (Life of Glory Ser.). 2003. audio compact disk 25.99 Oasis Audio.

Peace Child. abr. ed. Don Richardson. Read by Brad Meeder. 4 cass. (Running Time: 6 hrs. 30 min.). (Life of Glory Ser.). 2003. 25.99 Oasis Audio.

Peace Child. unabr. ed. Don Richardson. Read by Paul Michael. (Running Time: 7 hrs. 48 mins. 0 sec.). (ENG.). 2008. audio compact disk 23.98 (978-1-59644-561-1(0)) christianaud.

***Peace Child: An Unforgettable Story of Primitive Jungle Treachery in the 20th Century.** unabr. ed. Don Richardson. Narrated by Paul Michael. (ENG.). 2008. 14.98 (978-1-59644-562-8(9), Hovel Audio) christianaud.

Peace Corps: A Twenty-Five Year Retrospective. Hosted by Bill Buzenberg. 1 cass. (Running Time: 30 min.). 9.95 (H0210B090, HarperThor) HarpC GBR.

Peace Diet: The Forty-Four Day Feast to Personal Peace. unabr. ed. Susan Corso. Read by Susan Corso. 1 cass. (Running Time: 44 min.). 1996. 12.95 (978-0-9651541-5-4(7)) Dona Nobis Pacem.
44 contemplations to personal peace.

Peace for All of Us. Wayne W. Dyer. 1 CD. (ENG.). 2005. audio compact disk 10.95 (978-1-4019-1080-8(7)) Hay House.

Peace for Such a This. Lynne Hammond. 2009. audio compact disk 6.00 (978-1-57399-422-4(7)) Mac Hammond.

Peace in Exile: Poems. David Oates. 1992. 5.00 (978-1-882291-50-2(6)) Oyster River Pr.

Peace in Our Land. Bunny Hull. 2002. audio compact disk 5.99 (978-0-9673762-8-8(9)) BrassHeart.

Peace in the Eye of the Storm. Kathy D. Crouch & Richard K. Crouch. 1 cass. 1997. CD. (978-0-9656270-1-6(2)) Three in One.
Includes contemporary Christian vocals & music, 12 songs.

Peace in the Valley. Contrib. by Bill & Gloria Gaither and Their Homecoming Friends. (Gaither Homecoming Classics Ser.). 2005. audio compact disk 17.98 (978-5-559-05728-6(2)) Gaither Music Co.

Peace in the Valley. Prod. by Michael Merriman. Directed By Michael Merriman. Contrib. by Bill & Gloria Gaither and Their Homecoming Friends et al. Prod. by Bill Gaither. (Gaither Homecoming Classics Ser.). 2005. 14.98 (978-5-559-05725-5(8)) Gaither Music Co.

Peace in the World. Swami Amar Jyoti. 1 cass. 1989. 9.95 (K-154) Truth Consciousness.
We made the world as we are. Self transformation, the only place to really start changing the world.

Peace in the World: The Secret of Loving. Swami Amar Jyoti. 1 cass. 10.95 (SAT 100) Truth Consciousness.
Simple yet profound answers to two of the most important questions asked today.

Peace Is a Blessing of God. unabr. ed. MiChelle A. Butler. 1 cass. (Running Time: 1 hr. 30 mins.). 2001. 5.00 (A115) Word Faith Pubng.

***Peace Is Every Breath: A Practice for Our Busy Lives.** unabr. ed. Thich Nhat Hanh. (ENG.). 2011. (978-0-06-202735-1(2), Harper Audio) HarperCollins Pubs.

Peace Is the Way: Bringing War & Violence to an End. abr. ed. Deepak Chopra. Read by Deepak Chopra. 3 CDs. (Running Time: 4 hrs.). (Deepak Chopra Ser.). 2005. audio compact disk 23.00 (978-0-7393-1996-3(5), RH-Aud Dim) Pub: Random Audio Pubg. Dist(s): Random

Peace Is the Way: Bringing War & Violence to an End. unabr. ed. Deepak Chopra. Read by Shishir Kurup. 6 cass. (Running Time: 8 hrs.). 2005. 64.80 (978-1-4159-2006-0(0)) Books on Tape.
From Israel to Afghanistan to Iraq to the war on terror, the world is shaken by unending conflict. There has never been a better time for a book on peace, and Deepak Chopra, drawing from a timeless wisdom tradition, shows us where the path to peace truly lies. According to Deepak Chopra, "If the way of peace is to succeed, it must offer a substitute for everything war now offers." THE SEVEN SPIRITUAL PATHS TO PEACE teaches how each of us can put an end to these things. To end war we must stop reacting out of fear. As Dr. Chopra puts it, "Violence may be innate in human nature, but so its opposite: love. The next stage of humanity, the leap to which we are poised to take, will be guided by the force of that love." This seven-step program offers a framework for changing the reader's consciousness.

Peace Is the World Smiling. Perf. by Holly Near et al. 1 cass. (Running Time: 1 hr.). (J). (gr. 1-12). 1989. 9.98 Norelco. (978-1-877737-22-0(4), MFLP #2104) MFLP CA.
Poetry & music with a "peace" theme.

Peace Is the World Smiling. Holly Near et al. 1 CD. (Running Time: 1 hr.). (J). (gr. 1-12). 1989. audio compact disk 15.98 (978-1-877737-35-0(6), MLP#D2104) MFLP CA.

Peace It Together. Mary Miche. 1 cass. (J). (ps-6). 1989. 11.50 (978-1-883505-06-6(2)) Song Trek Music.
Selection of new & traditional songs about world peace, non-violence & cooperation for children.

Peace Kills: America's Fun New Imperialism. unabr. ed. P. J. O'Rourke. Read by Dick Hill. (Running Time: 5 hrs.). 2004. 24.95 (978-1-59335-322-3(7), 1593353227, Brilliance MP3); 39.25 (978-1-59335-483-1(5), 1593354835, Brlnc Audio MP3 Lib); 62.25 (978-1-59355-713-3(2), 1593557132, BAudLibEd); audio compact disk 74.25 (978-1-59355-715-7(9), 1593557159, BACDLib Ed) Brilliance Audio.
Having unraveled the mysteries of Washington in his classic best-seller Parliament of Whores and the mysteries of economics in Eat the Rich, one of our shrewdest and most mordant foreign correspondents now turns his attention to what is these days the ultimate mystery - America's foreign policy. Although he has written about foreigners and foreign affairs for years, P.J. O'Rourke has, like most Americans, never really thought about foreign policy. Just as a dog owner doesn't have a "dog policy," says P.J., "we feed foreigners, take care of them, give them treats, and when absolutely necessary, whack them with a rolled up newspaper." But in Peace Kills, P.J. finally sets out to make sense of America's "Great Game" (no, not the slot machines in Vegas). He visits countries on the brink of conflict, in the grips of it, and still reeling from it, starting with Kosovo, where he discovers that "whenever there's injustice, oppression, and suffering, America will show up six months late and bomb the country next to where it's happening." From there, it's on to Egypt, Israel, Kuwait, Afghanistan, and Iraq, where P.J. witnesses both the start and finish of hostilities. P.J. also examines the effect of war and peace on the home front - from the absurd hassles of airport security to the hideous specter of anthrax (luckily the only threats in his mail are from credit card companies). Peace Kills is P.J. O'Rourke at his most incisive and relevant - an eye-opening look at a world much changed since he declared in his number-one national best-seller Give War a Chance that the most troubling aspect of war is sometimes peace itself.

Peace Kills: America's Fun New Imperialism. unabr. ed. P. J. O'Rourke. Read by Dick Hill. (Running Time: 5 hrs.). 2004. 39.25 (978-1-59710-562-0(7), 1597105627, BADLE); 24.95 (978-1-59710-563-7(5), 1597105635, BAD) Brilliance Audio.

Peace Kills: America's Fun New Imperialism. unabr. ed. P. J. O'Rourke. Read by Dick Hill. (Running Time: 21600 sec.). 2006. audio compact disk 16.99 (978-1-4233-1566-7(9), 9781423315667, BCD Value Price) Brilliance Audio.

Peace Like a River. Leif Enger. Read by Edward Holland. 2001. 72.00 (978-0-7366-7636-6(8)); audio compact disk 88.00 (978-0-7366-8529-0(4)) Books on Tape.

***Peace Like a River.** unabr. ed. Leif Enger. Read by Chad Lowe. (ENG.). 2005. (978-0-06-088419-2(3), Harper Audio); (978-0-06-088420-8(7), Harper Audio) HarperCollins Pubs.

Peace Like a River. unabr. ed. Leif Enger. Read by Chad Lowe. 2008. audio compact disk 29.95 (978-0-06-145787-6(6), Harper Audio) HarperCollins Pubs.

Peace Like a River: The Hymns Project. Contrib. by Chris Rice. 2007. audio compact disk 9.99 (978-5-557-58540-8(0)) INO Rec.

Peace, Locomotion. unabr. ed. Jacqueline Woodson. Read by Dion Graham. (Running Time: 2 hrs.). 2009. 19.99 (978-1-4233-9800-4(9), 9781423398004, Brilliance MP3); 39.97 (978-1-4233-9801-1(7), 9781423398011, Brlnc Audio MP3 Lib); 39.97 (978-1-4233-9803-5(3), 9781423398035, BADLE); 19.99 (978-1-4233-9802-8(5), 9781423398028, BAD); audio compact disk 19.99 (978-1-4233-9798-4(3), 9781423397984, Bril Audio CD Unabri) Brilliance Audio.

Peace, Locomotion. unabr. ed. Jacqueline Woodson. Read by Dion Graham. 2 CDs. (Running Time: 2 hrs.). (J). (gr. 4-6). 2009. audio compact disk 39.97 (978-1-4233-9799-1(1), 9781423397991, BriAudCD Unabrid) Brilliance Audio.

Peace, Love, & Baby Ducks. unabr. ed. Lauren Myracle. Read by Julia Whelan. (Running Time: 8 hrs.). 2009. 24.99 (978-1-4233-9933-9(1), 9781423399339, Brilliance MP3); 39.97 (978-1-4233-9934-6(X), 9781423399346, Brlnc Audio MP3 Lib); 24.99 (978-1-4233-9935-3(8), 9781423399353, BAD); 39.97 (978-1-4233-9936-0(6), 9781423399360, BADLE); audio compact disk 24.99 (978-1-4233-9931-5(5), 9781423399315) Brilliance Audio.

Peace, Love, & Baby Ducks. unabr. ed. Lauren Myracle. Read by Julia Whelan. 6 CDs. (Running Time: 8 hrs.). (YA). (gr. 9 up). 2009. audio compact disk 79.97 (978-1-4233-9932-2(3), 9781423399322, BriAudCD Unabrid) Brilliance Audio.

Peace Mantras: Sacred Chants from India. Dileepji. 1 CD. (Running Time: 4320 sec.). 2005. audio compact disk 16.98 (978-1-59179-254-3(1), M902D) Sounds True.

Peace Movement. 10.00 (HE812) Esstee Audios.
The great efforts of the world governments to create a world peace through disarmament & its failure to succeed.

Peace of God. Wayne Monbleau. 2 cass. (Running Time: 2 hrs.). 1992. 10.00 Set. (978-0-944648-13-1(4)) Loving Grace Pubns.
Religious.

Peace of Mind. Read by Paul Fair. 1 cass. (Running Time: 45 min.). (Relaxation Ser.). 1996. 12.95 (978-1-889896-07-6(1), S4080) Strs Les Inc.
Stress reduction.

Peace of Mind. Swami Amar Jyoti. 1 cass. 1978. 9.95 (K-19) Truth Consciousness.
Peace is needed for evolution to higher consciousness or superman. The six divine virtues, inherent attributes of God & creation.

Peace of Mind. Barrie Konicov. Read by Barrie Konicov. 1 cass. 11.98 (978-0-87082-353-4(1), 098) Potentials.
How many times have you cried out in anguish, "I would give anything for a little peace of mind!" This tape could bring you the peace you are seeking. Remove worries, problems & cares so you can live peacefully.

Peace of Mind. Created by Anne H. Spencer-Beacham. 1. 2003. audio compact disk (978-1-932163-64-3(6)) Infinity Inst.

Peace of Mind. abr. ed. Iyanla Vanzant. Read by Iyanla Vanzant. 1 CD. (Running Time: 10 hrs. 0 mins. 0 sec.). (Iyanla Live! Ser.: Vol. 10). (ENG.). 2001. audio compact disk 14.00 (978-0-7435-0754-7(1), Sound Ideas) Pub: S&S Audio. Dist(s): S and S Inc

Peace of Mind For Autism. Karen L. Simmons. 1 CD. (Running Time: 52 mins). audio compact disk 24.95 (978-0-9724682-0-6(X)) Except Resource.

Peace of Mind in a High-Tech Hurricane. Ben Saltzman. 2000. 14.95 (978-0-9671010-5-7(0)) Lifestrides Pubg.

Peace on Earth see Twentieth-Century Poetry in English, No. 4, Recordings of Poets Reading Their Own Poetry

Peace on Earth: A Christmas Musical. Contrib. by Robert Sterling. Created by Robert Sterling. Created by Deborah Craig-Claar. 2007. audio compact disk 16.98 (978-5-557-78133-6(1), Word Music); audio compact disk 90.00 (978-5-557-78132-9(3), Word Music); audio compact disk 59.95 (978-5-557-77346-1(0), Word Music) Word Enter.

Peace Prayer of St. Francis. Edd Anthony. Read by Edd Anthony. 2007. audio compact disk 16.95 (978-1-881586-13-5(8)) Canticle Cass.

Peace that Depends on Nothing: Coming to the End of All Seeking. abr. ed. Scott Morrison. 1 cass. (Running Time: 1 hr.). 1998. 7.50 (978-1-882496-24-2(8)) Twnty Frst Cntry Ren.
The process of discovering that which you are looking for is that which you are.

Peace That Failed. Kenneth Bruce. 1 cass. (Running Time: 1 hr.). (Excursions in History Ser.). 12.50 Alpha Tape.

Peace Through Work. Dave Lebre. Created by Andrew C. Jacobs. 2008. audio compact disk 9.95 (978-0-9823699-1-3(3)) Ideal Jacobs.

Peace Through World Citizenship - Garry Davis Provides Passports at the Non-Governmental Forum of the United Nations Conference on Environment & Development in Rio de Janeiro. Hosted by Nancy Pearlman. 1 cass. (Running Time: 28 min.). 10.00 (1412) Educ Comm CA.

Peace with God: The Secret Happiness. Billy Graham. 1996. (978-0-913367-54-4(0)) Billy Graham Evangelistic Association.

Peace Work. unabr. ed. Spike Milligan. Read by Spike Milligan. 6 cass. (Running Time: 8 hrs. 15 min.). (Isis Ser.). (J). 1995. 54.95 (978-1-85695-913-1(9), 950108) Pub: ISIS Lrg Prnt GBR. Dist(s): Ulverscroft US

Peaceability. Linda Eyre & Richard Eyre. 2 cass. (Running Time: 3 hrs.). (Teaching Your Children Values Ser.). (J). (ps-7). 2000. pap. bk. 16.95 (978-1-56075-788-5(7)) Penton Overseas.
Tape 1: a coaching, "how-to" program for parents; Tape 2: "Alexander's Amazing Adventures" program featuring stories, songs, sound effects & background music, that helps children ages 4-12 to develop social skills, communication skills & life skills. Includes activity cards.

Peacedreams & Other Songs of Innocence. Suzanne Renfro. 1 cass. 1995. 9.95 (978-0-9641422-0-6(1)) SuzannaSongs.

Peaceful Christmas. Contrib. by Rick Brown & Tom Calvani. Prod. by Eric Wyse & Brenda Boswell. 2006. audio compact disk 14.95 (978-1-59856-268-2(1)) Hendrickson MA.

Peaceful Driver: Steering Clear of Road Rage. Allen Liles. 1999. 10.95 (978-0-87159-854-7(X)); 15.95 (978-0-87159-857-8(4)) Unity Schl Christ.

Peaceful Easy Christmas. Prod. by Randy Ray. Composed by Ric Flauding. 1 cass. 1993. 10.98 (978-1-57919-118-4(5)); audio compact disk 14.98 CD. (978-1-57919-119-1(3)) Randolf Prod.

Peaceful Home. unabr. ed. Elisabeth Elliot. Read by Elisabeth Elliot. 2 cass. (Running Time: 2 hrs.). 1990. 9.95 (978-0-8474-2019-3(1)) Back to Bible.
Principles for being a good parent, developing a child's positive self-image & dealing with a difficult child.

Peaceful Journey-Music. 2007. audio compact disk 16.95 (978-1-56136-431-2(2)) Master Your Mind.

Peaceful Living (the Techniques & Tools For) A Stress Management Experential Series. Brian Sheen. 2003. audio compact disk 89.00 (978-1-928787-04-4(5)) Quan Pubg.

Peaceful Meadow. Read by Mary Richards. 1 cass. (Running Time: 45 min.). (Energy Break Ser.). 2007. audio compact disk 19.95 (978-1-56136-163-2(1)) Master Your Mind.

Peaceful Meditations. Patricia J. Crane. Read by Patricia J. Crane. 1 cass. (Running Time: 48 min.). 1988. 10.00 (978-1-893705-04-3(8)) Hlth Horiz.
Four peaceful meditations with extended musical interludes.

Peaceful Nights: An Aid to Dep Restful Sleep. Heraty Eugenie. 2007. 16.98 (978-1-934332-00-9(3), Heal Voice) Inter Med Pub.

Peaceful Places. D.A. Tubesing. 1 cass. (Running Time: 40 min.). (Daydreams Ser.: No. 2). 11.95 (978-0-938586-79-1(3), DD2) Whole Person.
Four poetic "visual vacations" that tap into the restorative power of nature. Eckels classical guitar accompaniment. Ocean Tides celebrates the rhythms of life & the tension-dissolving power of the sea. City Park provides a brief respite from the busy-ness of life. Hammock lets you rest & luxuriate in a safe, supportive environment. Meadow is a clean, refreshing journey of harmony, celebrating the cycles of life.

Peaceful Planet. 1 CD. (Running Time: 1 hr.). 2000. audio compact disk 15.95 (978-1-55961-619-5(9)) Relaxtn Co.

Peaceful Road to Enlightenment. Swami Amar Jyoti. 1 cass. (Satsangs of Swami Amar Jyoti Ser.). 1996. 9.95 (M-100) Truth Consciousness.
Power of Consciousness dispels darkness. A peaceful way to grow spiritually, shielded from temptation, become perfect instruments of the lord.

Peaceful Sleep. Eldon Taylor. 2 cass. (Running Time: 62 min. per cass.). (Omniphonics Ser.). 29.95 incl. script Set. (978-1-55978-807-6(0), 4008) Progress Aware Res.
3-D soundtrack with underlying subliminal affirmations, night & day versions.

Peaceful SLEEP. unabr. ed. Inna Segal. Read by Inna Segal. (Running Time: 1 hr.). (ENG.). 2009. 12.98 (978-1-59659-324-4(5), GildAudio) Pub: Gildan Media. Dist(s): HachBkGrp

***Peaceful Sleep: A Meditation on Psalms 4:8.** Deborah Kukal. (ENG.). 2009. 14.98 (978-0-9801278-3-6(1)) Hydration.

Peaceful Solution Vol. 1, Pt. 1: Yahweh's Six Hundred Thirteen Laws Will Bring Peace to All Nations. Yisrayl Hawkins. 12 cass. (Running Time: 14 hrs. 33 min.). 1999. 36.00 Set. (978-1-890967-26-0(2)) Hse of Yahweh.
Designed to clearly explain the benefits of keeping Yahweh's Laws & the curses for breaking them.

Peaceful Solution Vol. 1, Pt. 2: Yahweh's Six Hundred Thirteen Laws Will Bring Peace to All Nations. Yisrayl Hawkins. 10 cass. (Running Time: 12 hrs. 15 min.). 1999. 30.00 Set. (978-1-890967-27-7(0)) Hse of Yahweh.

Peaceful White Light: Meditation. Annette Martin. Music by Steven Halpern. 3 cass. (Running Time: 3 hrs.). 1994. 24.95 Set. (978-1-885764-00-3(6)) Artistic Visions Inc.
Metaphysical audio meditation tapes.

Peacefull Heart. Audrey Grossman. 2008. audio compact disk 19.95 (978-1-4276-3433-7(5)) AardGP.

Peacegiver: How Christ Offers to Heal Hearts & Homes. James L. Ferrell. 2005. audio compact disk 19.95 (978-1-59038-451-0(2)) Deseret Bk.

Peacekeeper. unabr. ed. Jeffrey A. Poston. Read by Rusty Nelson. 4 cass. (Running Time: 4 hrs. 54 min.). 1998. 26.95 (978-1-55686-819-1(7)) Books in Motion.
Gunfighter Jason Pearses is a dark-skinned stranger seeking a quiet life in the west. He tries to make peace between homesteaders & wealthy land speculator, which causes danger, treachery, prejudice, & even love as he comes to terms with being a black man in the American West.

Peacekeepers. abr. ed. Ben Bova. Read by Theodore Bikel. 4 cass. (Running Time: 6 hrs.). 2002. 25.00 (978-1-57453-535-8(8)) Audio Lit.
The U.S. and Russia have joined forces to form the International Peacekeeping Force. Assigned control of every nation's orbiting nuclear hardware, the International Peacekeeping Force's brief is to prevent any military action across national borders, anywhere in the world. But, when super-terrorist Jamal Shamar makes off with the world's last half-dozen nuclear warheads, a new force is needed. Mercenaries.

Peacemaker. Gordon Kent. Narrated by George Guidall. 17 CDs. (Running Time: 19 hrs.). audio compact disk 160.00 (978-1-4025-1760-0(2)) Recorded Bks.

Peacemaker. collector's ed. Gordon Kent. Read by George Guidall. 14 cass. (Running Time: 19 hrs.). 2002. 59.95 (978-0-7887-8895-6(7)) Recorded Bks.
U.S. Navy Lt. Alan Craik has an impossible mission. He and a former Navy SEAL must rescue a kidnapped friend from Central Africa just as the region explodes in violence. Making a desperate dash on foot, the men are pursued by ruthless mercenaries. Meanwhile, a Navy ship faces mortal danger as it prepares to test-launch Peacemaker - a top-secret weapon disguised as a spy satellite.

Peacemaker. unabr. ed. Gordon Kent. Narrated by George Guidall. 14 cass. (Running Time: 19 hrs.). 2002. 117.00 (978-0-7887-5264-3(2)) Recorded Bks.

Peacemaker: A Biblical Guide to Resolving Personal Conflict. 3rd abr. ed. Ken Sande. (Running Time: 4 hrs. 50 mins.). 2005. audio compact disk 29.99 (978-0-8010-3037-6(4)) Pub: Baker Bks. Dist(s): Baker Pub Grp

Peacemaker: Power of the Enneagram Individual Type Audio Recording. Scripts. Based on a work by Enneagram Institute Staff. 1 CD. (Running Time: 60 mins.). 2004. audio compact disk 10.00 (978-0-9755222-8-8(0)) Enneagr.
Type Nine Individual Type Audio Recording (ITAR) in CD format from the audio tapeset The Power of the Enneagram. Includes a 25 minute introduction to the system as a whole, as well as a 35 minute exposition on Type Nine. An excellent way for therapists or business consultants to introduce the Enneagram to clients, or to work with the Enneagram in ongoing situations.

Peacemakers. Francis Frangipane. 1 cass. (Running Time: 90 mins.). (Seeing the Multitudes Ser.: Vol. 7). 2000. 5.00 (FF07-007) Morning NC.
From the beatitudes, Francis draws applications for ministry to those who need Jesus.

Peacemakers. unabr. ed. Perf. by Eknath Easwaran. 1 cass. (Running Time: 1 hr.). 1986. 7.95 (978-1-58638-588-0(7)) Nilgiri Pr.

Peacemaker's Journey. abr. ed. Perf. by Jake Swamp. 1 cass. (Running Time: 1 hr. 10 min.). 1996. 11.95 (978-1-57453-070-4(4)) Audio Lit.
The myth of a messenger form the Great Creator who convinced five warring nations to unite as the Iroquois Confederacy.

Peacemaking: How to Be It, How to Do It. unabr. ed. Thich Nhat Hanh. 2 CDs. (Running Time: 2 hrs 30 min). 2002. audio compact disk 24.95 (978-1-56455-987-6(4)) Sounds True.
Zen master returns to the theme that first brought him to the world's attention: peace, and how to embody it. Looking deeply into the roots of anger, Thich Nhat Hanh emerges with real solutions to the violence we commit against ourselves and each other.

Peacemaking in the International Area: The Role of the Church: National Association of Evangelicals, 47th Annual Convention, Columbus, Ohio, March 7-9, 1989. Brian O'Connell. 1 cass. (Workshops Ser.: No. 32-Thursda). 1989. 4.25 ea. 1-8 tapes.; 4.00 ea. 9 tapes or more. Nat Assn Evan.

Peacemaking Skills for Little Kids. (J). 1998. audio compact disk 16.00 (978-1-878227-64-5(5)) Peace Educ.

Peacemaking Skills for Little Kids, Concept Book. 2nd ed. Fran Schmidt & Alice Friedman. (FRE., 1993. tchr. ed. & ring bd. 23.95 (978-1-878227-16-4(5)) Peace Educ.

Peacock in Flight. unabr. ed. Katharine Gordon. 6 cass. 2001. 49.46 (978-1-86042-293-5(4)) Pub: Soundings Ltd GBR. Dist(s): ISIS Pub

Peak. unabr. ed. Roland Smith. Narrated by Ramon de Ocampo. 6 CDs. (Running Time: 7 hrs. 30 mins.). (YA). (gr. 6 up). 2007. audio compact disk 66.75 (978-1-4281-6356-0(5)); 51.75 (978-1-4281-6351-5(4)) Recorded Bks.
Peak Marcello is a 14-year-old who loves to climb things. Unfortunately, living in New York City makes his hobby difficult. After a run-in with the law, Peak is presented two options: endure Juvenile Detention or reconnect with his estranged father, who runs a climbing operation in Thailand. The choice is easy for Peak, but his father has an ulterior motive for their reunion - he wants his son to risk his life and become the youngest person to ever scale Mount Everest.

Peak: How Great Companies Get Their Mojo from Maslow. unabr. ed. Chip Conley. Read by Chip Conley. (Running Time: 7 hrs. 30 mins.). (ENG.). 2008. 24.98 (978-1-59659-243-8(5), GildAudio) Pub: Gildan Media. Dist(s): HachBkGrp

Peak: How Great Companies Get Their Mojo from Maslow. unabr. ed. Chip Conley. Read by Chip Conley. 9 CDs. (Running Time: 7 hrs. 30 mins.). (ENG.). 2009. audio compact disk 39.98 (978-1-59659-218-6(4)) Pub: Gildan Media. Dist(s): HachBkGrp

Peak Experience: Harness the Energy of the Body-Mind-Spirit Connection. Lloyd Glauberman. 2000. 12.00 (978-1-929043-02-6(3)) Psycho-tech.

Peak Experience at Will. Colin Wilson. 4 cass. 36.00 (OC94) Sound Horizons AV.

Peak Learning. Read by Mary Richards. (Subliminal Impact Ser.). 12.95 (608) Master Your Mind.
Explores how to have the intelligence, creativity, & insight to learn anything you set your mind to.

Peak Learning. Read by Mary Richards. 2007. audio compact disk 19.95 (978-1-56136-003-1(1)) Master Your Mind.

Peak Performance: The Personal Side of Management. unabr. ed. Jennifer James. Read by Jennifer James. 1 cass. (Running Time: 42 min.). 1986. 9.95 (978-0-915423-22-4(7)) Jennifer J.
Explores the qualities essential for leadership. Teaches how to feel at your peak & stay there whether you are at work or at home.

Peak Performance for Christ. Tommy Newberry. Read by Tommy Newberry. 2 cass. (Running Time: 1 hr. 34 min.). 20.00 Set. (978-1-886669-03-1(1)) One Percent Club.

Peak Performance Sports: Hypnotic & Subliminal Learning. David Illig. 1985. 14.99 (978-0-86580-007-6(3)) Success World.

Peak Performance Woman. Brian S. Tracy. 6 cass. (Running Time: 6 hrs.). 1995. bk. 49.95 Set. (13480PAX) Nightingale-Conant.
Learn how to achieve financial independence, increase your productivity, easily influence & persuade others, negotiate & communicate more effectively, & maximize the quality of your life.

Peak Performance 8 CD Set: David Wolfe on Weight Loss. David Wolfe. 2007. 97.00 (978-0-9790648-5-2(6)) Sunfood MaulBros.

Peak Performers in Business. Charles Garfield. 1 cass. (Running Time: 53 min.). 8.95 (978-0-88684-096-9(1)) Listen USA.
Learn how you can identify, assess & train yourself & others to perform at your peak-regardless of profession, age or position.

Peaks & Valleys: Making Good & Bad Times Work for You - At Work & in Life. unabr. ed. Spencer Johnson. Read by John Dossett. 2 CDs. (Running Time: 2 hrs. 0 mins. 0 sec.). (ENG.). 2009. audio compact disk 19.99 (978-0-7435-8307-7(8)) Pub: S&S Audio. Dist(s): S and S Inc

Peanut & Phelonious. John Davis. Read by John Davis. 1 CD. (Running Time: 67min 59sec). 2003. pap. bk. 12.95 (978-1-932226-18-8(4)) Pub: Wizard Acdmy. Dist(s): Baker Taylor
A gift. A game. A decision.In Peanut & Phelonious, you will take an emotional journey with characters who have no names. The story promotes the virtue of assistance through the tale of two brothers and their love for a granddaughter. It tells of a lifestyle committed to personal values rarely shared in modern society and allows you to glimpse the power of love - the way things should be.Hear "Learning to Fly,"an original song composed and performed by the author, at the beginning and the end of this audio performance of Peanut & Phelonious.Cover Photo courtesy of Wendy McNally.

Peanut Butter & Jelly Big Book Audiotext. 3rd ed. Harcourt School Publishers Staff. (Trophies Reading Program Ser.). (J). 2002. 14.00 (978-0-15-325457-4(2)) Harcourt Schl Pubs.

Peanut Butter Kid Audio Book. Gertrude Stonesifer. (ENG.). (J). 2008. audio compact disk 9.95 (978-1-932278-49-1(4)) Pub: Mayhaven Pub. Dist(s): Baker Taylor

Peanut Butter Pie. Tom Paxton. Perf. by Tom Paxton. 1 cass. (Running Time: 30 min.). (J). 1992. 8.98 (978-1-56406-560-5(X)); 8.98 Incl. sleeve pack. (978-1-56406-586-5(3)); audio compact disk 13.98 CD. (978-1-56406-573-5(1)) Sony Music Ent.

Peanut Butter, Tarzan & Roosters. Perf. by Jackie Silberg. 1 cass. (J). 1988. 10.95 (978-0-939514-15-1(X)) Miss Jackie.
Includes Miss Jackie's own compositions & favorite folk & nursery tunes.

Peanut Man. 1 cass. (Running Time: 43:07 min.). (J). 2004. 5.98 (978-1-56628-412-7(0)); audio compact disk 9.98 (978-1-56628-411-0(2)) MFLP CA.

PEAR Process (2 CD Set) Personal Enlightenment & Release Process. Olivia Stephanino. (ENG.). 2009. 34.95 (978-1-890405-05-2(1)) Pub: LightLines. Dist(s): New Leaf Dist

Pearl. unabr. ed. John Steinbeck. Narrated by Frank Muller. 2 cass. (Running Time: 2 hrs. 45 mins.). 1947. 20.00 (978-0-7887-3122-8(X), 95787E7) Recorded Bks.
An ancient legendary pearl found by a poor fisherman reflects man's preoccupation with materialism, money & power.

Pearl. unabr. abr. ed. John Steinbeck. Read by Hector Elizondo. Contrib. by Hector Elizondo. 2 cass. (Running Time: 3 hrs.). (ENG.). 1993. 16.00 (978-0-453-00875-4(5), 0453008755) Pub: Penguin-HghBrdg. Dist(s): Workman Pub
A pearl brings tragedy to a pearl-fisher's family.

Pearl: Lady Pokingham. abr. ed. Lady Pokingham. Read by Evangeline Anthurium. 2 cass. (Running Time: 2 hrs. 45 min.). 17.95 set. (978-0-9636240-1-7(6), Clivia) The Studio.
A reading of the Victorian erotic classic.

Pearl: Lady Pokingham, Vol. 2. abr. ed. Read by Evangeline Anthuriam. 2 cass. (Running Time: 2 hrs. 30 min.). 1993. 17.95 set. (978-0-9636240-2-4(4)) The Studio.
Classic Victorian erotica.

Pearl: My Grandmother's Tale. abr. ed. Read by Licentia Tittlesworth. 2 cass. (Running Time: 3 hrs.). 1994. 17.95 set. (978-0-9636240-3-1(2)) The Studio.

***Pearl Buck in China: Journey to the Good Earth.** unabr. ed. Hilary Spurling. Narrated by Hilary Spurling. (Running Time: 9 hrs. 14 mins. 13 sec.). (ENG.). 2010. 24.49 (978-1-60814-723-6(1)); audio compact disk 34.99 (978-1-59859-771-4(X)) Oasis Audio.

***Pearl Cove.** unabr. ed. Elizabeth Lowell. Read by Robin Rowan. (ENG.). 2009. (978-0-06-196722-1(X), Harper Audio); (978-0-06-182981-9(1), Harper Audio) HarperCollins Pubs.

Pearl Cove, Set. unabr. ed. Elizabeth Lowell. Read by Dick Hill. 7 cass. (Running Time: 9 hrs.). 1999. 73.25 (FS9-51046) Highsmith.

Pearl Diver. Jeff Talarigo. Read by Jenny Sterlin. 5 cass. (Running Time: 7 hrs. 30 mins.). 2004. 24.99 (978-1-4025-7277-7(8), 03974) Recorded Bks.

Pearl Diver. unabr. ed. Jeff Talarigo. Read by Jenny Ikeda. 7 CDs. (Running Time: 7 hrs. 30 mins.). 2004. audio compact disk 74.75 (978-1-4025-8663-7(9)); 49.75 (978-1-4025-8661-3(2)) Recorded Bks.
This lyrical novel sweeps listeners away to an ignoble period from Japanese history, when lives were shattered by intolerance and for one group of societal outcasts, survival hinged on the determination of the human spirit. In 1948, a 19-year-old pearl diver with leprosy is forced to erase her name from family records and move to an island leprosarium. Mere miles from the home she can never return to, she must accept that her life will never be the same.

Pearl Harbor. Braun Media. (ENG.). 2007. 7.95 (978-1-59987-635-1(3)) Braun Media.

Pearl Harbor. Dan Martin. 2004. audio compact disk 4.95 (978-1-57306-200-8(6)) Bess Pr.

Pearl Harbor. unabr. ed. Randall Wallace. Read by Barrett Whitener. 8 CDs. (Running Time: 12 hrs.). 2001. audio compact disk 79.95 (978-0-7927-9865-1(1), SLD 116, Chivers Sound Lib) AudioGO.
Childhood friends Rafe McCawley and Danny Walker are daring young pilots in the U.S. Army Air Corps. Rafe has fallen in love with Evelyn Stewart, a beautiful U.S. Navy nurse. But when the sounds of war begin to rumble on the horizon, Rafe decides he must leave to join Europe's fight. Meanwhile, Evelyn and Danny are transferred to Hawaii's peaceful paradise - Pearl Harbor - unaware of the approach of devastating forces that soon will forever change their lives - and the fate of the entire world.

Pearl Harbor. unabr. ed. Randall Wallace. Read by Barrett Whitener. 6 vols. (Running Time: 9 hrs.). 2001. bk. 54.95 (978-0-7927-2491-9(7), CSL 380, Chivers Sound Lib) AudioGO.

Pearl Harbor: A Novel of December 8th. unabr. ed. Newt Gingrich & William R. Forstchen. Read by William Dufris. (Running Time: 12 hrs. 30 mins. 0 sec.). (ENG.). 2007. audio compact disk 39.95 (978-1-4272-0127-0(7)) Pub: Macmill Audio. Dist(s): Macmillan

Pearl Harbor: Reflections & Notes. 1 cass. (Running Time: 71 min.). 11.95 (H0090B090, HarperThor) HarpC GBR.

Pearl Harbor: The Verdict of History, Pt. 1. unabr. collector's ed. Gordon W. Prange et al. Read by Wolfram Kandinsky. 10 cass. (Running Time: 15 hrs.). 1991. 80.00 (978-0-7366-1930-1(5), 2753-A) Books on Tape.
Pearl Harbor: The Verdict of History is the sequel to Prange's earlier book, At Dawn We Slept. Verdict sorts out the responsibility for Pearl Harbor. It deals not with action, but with reaction. It is the definitive analysis of the acts, failures to act, & the mental attitudes that made the Japanese attack on Pearl Harbor possible & so successful.

Pearl Harbor: The Verdict of History, Pt. 2. collector's ed. Gordon W. Prange. Read by Wolfram Kandinsky. 10 cass. (Running Time: 15 hrs.). 1991. 80.00 (978-0-7366-1931-8(3), 2753-B) Books on Tape.

Pearl Harbor Murders. Max Allan Collins. Narrated by Jeff Woodman. 6 CDs. (Running Time: 6 hrs. 30 mins.). 2002. audio compact disk 58.00 (C1642) Recorded Bks.
On the night of December 5, 1941, Tarzan author Edgar Rice Burroughs discovers the body of Pearl Harada, a gorgeous Japanese-American nightclub singer, on the beach. Although one of her lovers is charged with the murder, a police detective asks Burroughs to investigate further. Two days later, before Burroughs can unravel the clues, bombs fall on Pearl Harbor. But as the dust clears, so does the evidence: there must be a connection between Pearl's death and the Japanese attack.

Pearl Harbor Murders. Max Allan Collins. Read by Charlie O'Dowd. 2001. 25.00 (978-1-58807-063-0(8)) Am Pubng Inc.

Pearl Harbor Murders. Max Allan Collins. Narrated by Jeff Woodman. 6 CDs. (Running Time: 6 hrs. 30 mins.). audio compact disk 58.00 (978-1-4025-1546-0(4)) Recorded Bks.

Pearl Harbor Murders. abr. ed. Max Allan Collins. Read by Charlie O'Dowd. 4 vols. 2000. (978-1-58807-580-2(X)) Am Pubng Inc.

Pearl Harbor Murders. unabr. ed. Max Allan Collins. Narrated by Jeff Woodman. 5 cass. (Running Time: 6 hrs. 30 mins.). 2002. 48.00 (978-1-4025-1345-9(3), 96668) Recorded Bks.

***Pearl in a Cage.** unabr. ed. Joy Dettman. Read by Deidre Rubenstein. (Running Time: 20 hrs. 42 mins.). 2010. audio compact disk 123.95 (978-1-74214-497-9(7), 9781742144979) Pub: Bolinda Pubng AUS. Dist(s): Bolinda Pub Inc

***Pearl in the Sand.** unabr. ed. Tessa Afshar. Narrated by Laural Merlington. (Running Time: 11 hrs. 0 mins. 0 sec.). (ENG.). 2011. audio compact disk 34.99 (978-1-59859-876-6(7)) Oasis Audio.

Pearl Jam: The Unauthorized Biography of Pearl Jam. Andrea Thorn. (Maximum Ser.). (ENG.). 2001. audio compact disk 14.95 (978-1-84240-072-2(X)) Pub: Chrome Dreams GBR. Dist(s): IPG Chicago

Pearl of Great Price. Neville Goddard. 1 cass. (Running Time: 62 min.). 1963. 8.00 (30) J & L Pubns.
Neville taught Imagination Creates Reality. He was a powerfully influential teacher of God as Consciousness.

Pearl of Great Price. Read by Basilea Schlink. 1 cass. (Running Time: 30 min.). 1985. Evang Sisterhood Mary.
Talks about fulfillment of our deepest longings & the Commandments of God-a gift & blessing today.

Pearl of Greatest Price: Volume 1, Vol. 1. Speeches. Bhagat Singh Thind. (Running Time: 60 mins.). (ENG., 2003. 6.50 (978-1-932630-25-1(2)) Pub: Dr Bhagat Sin. Dist(s): Baker Taylor

Pearl of Greatest Price: Volume 1, Vol. 1. collector's ed. Speeches. Narrated by Bhagat Singh Thind. Based on a work by Bhagat Singh Thind. Clark Walker. (Running Time: 60 mins). (ENG.). 2003. audio compact disk 12.00 (978-1-932630-02-2(3)) Pub: Dr Bhagat Sin. Dist(s): Baker Taylor

Pearl of Patmos. Jeffrey Lord. Read by Lloyd James. Abr. by Odin Westgaard. 2 vols. 2004. 18.00 (978-1-58807-362-4(9)) Am Pubng Inc.

Pearl of Patmos. abr. ed. Jeffrey Lord. Read by Lloyd James. Abr. by Odin Westgaard. 2 vols. No. 7. 2004. (978-1-58807-780-6(2)) Am Pubng Inc.

Pearls see Winter's Tales

Pearls & Peril, Set. Lynn Gardner. 2 cass. 1996. 11.98 Set. (978-1-55503-933-2(2), 07001371) Covenant Comms.
The action-packed romantic sequel to "Emeralds & Espionage".

Pearls Before Swine. unabr. ed. Mary Clayton. Read by Simon J. Williamson. 6 cass. (Running Time: 8 hrs.). 1999. 69.95 (978-1-85903-257-2(5)) Ulvrscrft Audio.
Murder visits the Cornish village of St. Breddaford. A headless corpse is found in a pigsty & ex-inspector Reynolds is soon involved whether he likes it or not.

Pearls Before Swine. unabr. ed. Ann Drysdale. Read by Ann Drysdale. 4 cass. (Running Time: 5 hrs. 18 mins.). (Isis Audio Reminiscence Ser.). (J). 2002. 44.95 (978-0-7531-1279-3(5)) Pub: ISIS Lrg Prnt GBR. Dist(s): Ulverscroft US
Leaving London and a promising Fleet Street career, Ann Drysdale came to a ramshackle moorland farmhouse at the end of the 1960s, bewildered by a broken marriage and determined to find self-reliance and a worthwhile life for her children. She stayed on to create the incredible "shoestring" enterprise that became Hagg House Farm. This book, her third idiosyncratic account of her life among Yorkshire's hill farmers, continues the stories.

Pearls from My Memory Box. Mary M. Slappey. Read by Mary M. Slappey. (Running Time: 30 min). 1986. 10.00 Interspace Bks.

***Pearls of Great Price: 366 Daily Devotional Readings.** unabr. ed. Joni Eareckson Tada. (Running Time: 15 hrs. 5 mins. 30 sec.). (ENG.). 2010. 19.99 (978-0-310-77160-9(9)) Zondervan.

Pearls of Wisdom: African & Caribbean Folktales. Raouf Mama & Mary Romney. 2 cass. 2001. 20.00 (978-0-86647-135-0(9)) Pro Lingua.

Pearls of Wisdom: African & Caribbean Folktales. Raouf Mama & Mary Romney. 2001. pap. bk. & wbk. ed. 24.00 (978-0-86647-137-4(5)); pap. bk. & wbk. ed. 39.00 (978-0-86647-162-6(6)) Pro Lingua.

Pearls of Wisdom: African & Caribbean Folktales. Raouf Mama & Mary Romney. 2 CDs. (gr. 4-12). 2005. pap. bk., stu. ed., wbk. ed. 39.00 (978-0-86647-201-2(0)); audio compact disk 20.00 (978-0-86647-200-5(2)) Pro Lingua.

Pearls of Wisdom: African & Caribbean Folktales. Raouf Mama & Mary Romney. Illus. by Siri Webber-Feeney. 2 CDs. (gr. 4-12). 2005. pap. bk. & stu. ed. 28.00 (978-0-86647-218-0(5)) Pro Lingua.

Peasant Prince: The True Story of Mao's Last Dancer. unabr. ed. Li Cunxin. Read by Paul English. 1 CD. (Running Time: 15 mins.). (J). (gr. 1-5). 2008. audio compact disk 39.95 (978-1-74214-102-2(1), 9781742141022) Pub: Bolinda Pubng AUS. Dist(s): Bolinda Pub Inc

Pebbles & Pearls. Jon Kabat-Zinn. 2 CDs. (Running Time: 1 Hrs 45 Mins). 2005. audio compact disk 19.95 (978-1-59179-391-5(2), AB00138D) Sounds True.
Across America, people in search of inner peace and better health know Jon Kabat-Zinn as the clinical researcher and teacher who dared to bring mindfulness practice out of the meditation hall and into the most respected pain management center in the country. On Pebbles and Pearls, Kabat-Zinn turns his attention to another challenge - how ordinary people can use meditation in the arenas of the workplace and the family. Join Jon Kabat-Zinn as he shares a host of insights and methods that you can apply to real-life situations: how to use work as a contemplative practice; advice on mindful parenting; grounding yourself in your body; how to work with overwhelming emotions; and much more. "In the yogic tradition," teaches Kabat-Zinn, "the world is described as a spinning grindstone. You can be completely chewed up by it - or you can position yourself so that you hone yourself, like a blade." On Pebbles and Pearls, you will learn how to take the wiser path, at the side of this pioneering expert on meditation and mind/body healing.

Pebbles in the Roadway: Tales & Essays, Bits & Pieces. James McEachin. 1 cass. (Running Time: 1 hr. 12 min.). 2003. 18.95 (978-0-9656661-2-1(3)); 21.95 (978-0-9656661-1-4(5)) Rharl Pub.
Selected readings of short stories involving life in the USA.

Pecheur d'Islande, Set. Pierre Loti. Read by C. Deis & G. Bejean. 4 cass. (FRE.). 1991. 32.95 (1468-VSL) Olivia & Hill.
The ill-starred love of Yann, a Breton fisherman who spends the spring & summer months fishing off the coast of Iceland & Guad, the young & beautiful girl he met at the Paimpol pardon. A novel of Breton life describing the eternal struggle between man & sea & the anxiety of the ones left behind.

Peckham's Marbles. unabr. ed. Peter De Vries. Read by Multivoice Production Staff. (Running Time: 7 hrs.). 2008. 39.25 (978-1-4233-5846-6(5), 9781423358466, BADLE); 24.95 (978-1-4233-5845-9(7), 9781423358459, BAD) Brilliance Audio.

Peckham's Marbles. unabr. ed. Peter De Vries. Read by George Ralph et al. (Running Time: 25200 sec.). 2008. audio compact disk 39.25 (978-1-4233-5844-2(9), 9781423358442, Brinc Audio MP3 Lib); audio compact disk 24.95 (978-1-4233-5843-5(0), 9781423358435, Brilliance MP3) Brilliance Audio.

Pecos Bill see American Tall Tales

Pecos Bill. 1 cass. (Running Time: 26 min.). (J). 9.98 Windham Hill.

***Pecos Billy & Sue Dance Suite.** Perf. by R. A. Zuckerman. Composed by R. A. Zuckerman. 2010. 12.95 (978-1-891083-14-3(7)) ConcertHall.

Pecos River. unabr. ed. Frederic Bean. Read by Michael Taylor. 6 cass. (Running Time: 8 hrs. 30 min.). (Rivers West Ser.: Bk. 10). 2001. 39.95 (978-1-55686-770-5(0)) Books in Motion.
The trail to peace is long, hard and stained in blood for Buck Wallace, as he carves out a home in Pecos River Comanche country.

Peculiar - In a Good Way! Mary Ellen Edmunds. 2006. audio compact disk 14.95 (978-1-59038-698-9(1)) Desert Bks.

Peculiar Grace. unabr. ed. Jeffrey Lent. Narrated by Todd McLaren. (Running Time: 14 hrs. 30 mins. 0 sec.). (ENG.). 2007. audio compact disk 39.99 (978-1-4001-0543-4(9)); audio compact disk 79.99 (978-1-4001-3543-1(5)); audio compact disk 29.99 (978-1-4001-5543-9(6)) Pub: Tantor Media. Dist(s): IngramPubServ

Peculiar Love of the Lord Jesus. Dan Corner. 1 cass. 3.00 (69) Evang Outreach.

Peculiar Treasure. Edna Ferber. 11 cass. (Running Time: 16 hrs. 30 mins.). 88.00 Audio Bk Con.
Edna Ferber gave us a series of great books. Her autobiography reveals how she did it.

Peculiar Treasure. unabr. ed. Edna Ferber. Read by Flo Gibson. 11 cass. (Running Time: 1 hr. 30 min. per cass.). (Classic Books on Cassettes Coll.). 1998. 88.00 Set. Audio Bk Con.
The autobiography of Edna Ferber revealing how she gave us a series of great books.

Peculiar Treasure. unabr. collector's ed. Edna Ferber. Read by Flo Gibson. 11 cass. (Running Time: 16 hrs. 30 mins.). 1984. 88.00 (978-0-7366-0666-0(1), 1628) Books on Tape.
Edna Ferber minces no words in expressing her love & broad knowledge of the United States, her feelings & experiences as a Jew, with a world perspective on Judaism & the discipline, habits, trials & rewards & politicians of an era.

Peculiar Treasure, Set. Edna Ferber. 11 cass. (Running Time: 16 hrs. 30 min.). 88.00 Audio Bk Con.
She gave us a series of great books, Her autobiography reveals how she did it.

***Peculiar Treasures.** unabr. ed. Robin Jones Gunn. (Running Time: 8 hrs. 47 mins. 0 sec.). (Katie Weldon Ser.). (ENG.). 2009. 14.99 (978-0-310-77205-7(2)) Zondervan.

Pedagogy of Freedom: Ethics, Democracy & Civic Courage. unabr. ed. Paulo Freire. Read by Julius Wong Loi Sing. 2 cass. (Running Time: 4 hrs.). 2001. 24.95 (978-0-9660180-6-6(0)) Rowman.
This profound book by one of the world's most influential educators shows why an engaged way of learning & teaching is central to the creation of the individual & culture.

Pedestrian see Fantastic Tales of Ray Bradbury

Pediatric AIDS. Mary Boland. (AIDS: The National Conference for Practitioners). 1986. 9.00 (978-0-932491-55-8(3)) Res Appl Inc.

Pediatric Airway Management V D. Gausche. 2004. 270.95 (978-0-7637-3284-4(2)) Jones Bartlett.

Pediatric & Adolescent Gynecology. Contrib. by S. Jean Emans et al. 1 cass. (American Academy of Pediatrics UPDATE: Vol. 18, No. 7). 1998. 20.00 Am Acad Pediat.

Pediatric Board Review, Vol. A160. unabr. ed. 44 cass. (Running Time: 45 hrs.). 1994. 650.00 set. (978-1-57664-356-3(5)) CME Info Svcs.
Continuing medical education home-study. Complete package contains audiotapes, syllabus, self-assessment examination to earn CME Category 1 credit.

Pediatric Education for Prehospital Professionals, Second Edition Classroom DVD. 2nd rev. ed. American Academy of Pediatrics (AAP). 2009. 250.95 (978-0-7637-6627-6(5)) Jones Bartlett.

Pediatric Emergency Care: Where Do We Go from Here? David Wagner & Martha Bushore. (Pediatric Emergencies: The National Conference for Practioners Ser.). 1986. 9.00 (978-0-932491-63-3(4)) Res Appl Inc.

Pediatric First Aid for Caregivers & Teachers DVD, Revised First Edition. American Academy of Pediatrics (AAP). 2007. 63.95 (978-0-7637-5442-6(0)) Jones Bartlett.

Pediatric Nursing, Pt. 1. Patricia Hoefler. (Complete Q & A Ser.). 2002. (978-1-56533-131-0(1)) MEDS Pubng.

Pediatric Nursing, Pt. 2. Patricia Hoefler. (Complete Q & A Ser.). 2002. (978-1-56533-132-7(X)) MEDS Pubng.

Pediatric Ophthalmology & Glaucoma. (Postgraduate Programs Ser.: C84-PG15). 1984. 65.00 (8495) Am Coll Surgeons.
Discusses developments in pediatric ophthalmology. Emphasis is placed on current implications & technique for cataract surgery in children & on aspects of strabismus diagnosis & surgical technique. Also discusses pediatric glaucoma, with emphasis on indications & techniques for management of these diseases.

Pediatric Sleep Disorders. Contrib. by Richard A. Ferber et al. 1 cass. (American Academy of Pediatrics UPDATE: Vol. 18, No. 6). 1998. 20.00 Am Acad Pediat.

Pediatric Sports Medicine. Contrib. by Paul R. Stricker et al. 1 cass. (American Academy of Pediatrics UPDATE: Vol. 17, No. 5). 1998. 20.00 Am Acad Pediat.

Pediatric Surgery: The Injured Child. (Postgraduate Programs Ser.: C84-PG9). 1984. 45.00 (8489) Am Coll Surgeons.
Addresses recent advances & controversies in the diagnosis & treatment of the injured child. 6 hours CME category 1 credit.

Pediatric Surgery: Ulcerative Colitis & Hirschsprung's Disease. Moderated by Lester W. Martin. (Postgraduate Courses Ser.: C86-PG9). 1986. 57.00 (8619) Am Coll Surgeons.
This course brings into perspective the many recent developments in ulcerative colitis & Hirschsprung's disease. 6 hours CME credit.

Pediatric Trauma. unabr. ed. Instructed by JoAnn C. Tess-Piburn. (Running Time: 7 hrs.). 1990. 79.00 cass. & soft-bound bk. (HT52) Ctr Hlth Educ.
If you treat children you know how quickly they can go into shock. This insightful, highly detailed course will teach you how to do a 60 second assessment quickly & effectively. Learn patterns of injury, what complications to expect, & emergency treatment of trauma patients.

Pediatric Urology: Reconstructive Surgery of the External Genitalia. Moderated by John W. Duckett, Jr. 2 cass. (Urologic Surgery Ser.: UR-3). 1986. 19.00 (8670) Am Coll Surgeons.

Pedir deseos con monedas Audio CD: Emergent Set A. Benchmark Education Staff. Ed. by Cynthia Swain. (Early Explorers Ser.). (J). 2008. audio compact disk 10.00 (978-1-60437-255-7(9)) Benchmark Educ.

Pedlar's Pack & Other Stories. unabr. collector's ed. Elizabeth Goudge. Read by Donada Peters. 7 cass. (Running Time: 10 hrs. 30 mins.). 1988. 56.00 (978-0-7366-1334-7(X), 2237) Books on Tape.
Includes "A Shepard & a Shepardess," "Doing Good," "Sweet Herbs," "Cloud-Capped Towers," "Picnic with Albert," "Escape for Jane" & "Rabbits in a Hat".

Pedrin, el Conejo Travieso. Tr. of Tale of Peter Rabbit, the. (SPA.). 2004. 8.95 (978-0-7882-0266-7(9)) Weston Woods.

Pedrito y el Lobo - Cuento para Aprender Musica. unabr. ed. Sergei Prokofiev. Read by Jose Ferrer.Tr. of Peter & the Wolf - Tale to Learn Music. (SPA.). 2002. audio compact disk 13.00 (978-958-43-0148-2(9)) YoYoMusic.

Pedro y Juan. unabr. ed. Guy de Maupassant. Read by Pedro J. Vega. 3 CDs.Tr. of Peter & John. (SPA.). 2002. audio compact disk 17.00 (978-958-8161-30-3(4)) YoYoMusic.

Pee-Wee Harris. Percy Keese Fitzhugh. Narrated by Erik Sellin. (ENG.). 2009. audio compact disk (978-1-935513-11-7(7)) C CD Bks.

Peef the Christmas Bear. unabr. ed. Tom Hegg. Read by Tom Hegg. Perf. by Warren Hanson. 1 cass. (Running Time: 13 mins.). (J). (ps-3). 1997. 6.95 (978-0-931674-33-4(6)) Waldman Hse Pr.
Peef, Santa's own hand-made teddy bear dreams of belonging to a little girl or boy. Then one Christmas Eve Santa is one toy short & Peef gets his wish. This little bear shows us the treasure of belonging.

Peek-a-Boo. Perf. by Hap Palmer. 1 cass. (Running Time: 1 hr.). (J). 2001. 9.95 (HP 95); audio compact disk 14.95 (HP 95) Hap-Pal Music.
A light-hearted look at the world of young children-waking, eating, getting dressed, taking a bath, hearing favorite bedtime stories & most importantly... PLAY. Messages of self acceptance & pride ring out with compassion & gentle humor. Twenty One classic songs including: "Gettin' Up Time," "My Mommy Comes Back," "Today I Took My Diapers Off," "Don't Wash My Blanket," "Walking," "Daddy Be a Horsie," "Piggie Toes," "What a Miracle" & many more!.

Peek-a-Boo. Hap Palmer. 1 read-along cass. (J). bk. 11.95 (EA 645C) Kimbo Educ.
Light hearted songs look at the world of children - waking up, eating, getting dressed, bathing, hearing a bedtime story & playing.

Peek-a-Boo, I Love You! Families & School. 1 cass. (Running Time: 60 min.). (J). 2000. 10.00 Moonlight Rose.

Peek-a-Boogie: Hand Motion, Fingerplay & Movement Songs - Music That Children Can Do! Pamela Ott. 1 cass. (Teaching Tunes Ser.). 14.95 (978-1-886655-10-2(3), 85082); audio compact disk 14.95 (978-0-8039-6875-2(2), 85081) Corwin Pr.

Peek Between the Sheets: Writing the Sex. Brenda Wilbee. (Running Time: 45 min.). (How to Write Best-Selling Romance Ser.: Tape 4). 1988. 7.95 (978-0-943777-11-5(9)) byBrenda.
Teaches writing and Building sexual tension in the romance novel.

Peeled. unabr. ed. Joan Bauer. Read by Kathe Mazur. 5 CDs. (Running Time: 5 hrs. 38 mins.). (YA). (gr. 6-9). 2008. audio compact disk 45.00 (978-0-7393-6791-9(9), Listening Lib) Pub: Random Audio Pubg. Dist(s): Random
Hildy Biddle is a high school reporter eager to stand up for the truth. She's just waiting for a chance to prove herself as a journalist, and yearning for a big story. The trouble is, the town's biggest story stars . . . a ghost. Not a very easy interview! This ghost has the town in a tizzy, and the local paper is playing up people's fears with shocking headlines of eerie happenings and ghostly sightings. Hildy's determined to discover what's really going on, but her desire to uncover the truth is making some people awfully nervous. Does the truth have a chance of being heard over all the buzz?.

Peeling the Onion. Wendy Orr. Read by Kate Hosking. (Running Time: 4 hrs. 30 mins.). (YA). 2009. 59.99 (978-1-74214-352-1(0), 9781742143521) Pub: Bolinda Pubng AUS. Dist(s): Bolinda Pub Inc

Peeling the Onion. unabr. ed. Wendy Orr. Read by Kate Hosking. 4 cass. (Running Time: hrs.). 1999. (590805) Bolinda Pubng AUS.
Finding yourself in a hospital, in a bed full of shattered glass, is traumatic. Coming to terms with multiple fractures & probably long-term difficulties is something else again-slow, painful, full of obstacles & questions with no clear answers. Anna is used to being athletic, popular, 'normal'. Now she feels the layers of her familiar self being peeled away. Nothing is normal or easy. Can she pick up the pieces of her life? What part will Hayden & Luck play? Who, now, is Anna Duncan?.

Peeling the Onion. unabr. ed. Wendy Orr. Read by Kate Hosking. (Running Time: 4 hrs. 30 mins.). (YA). 2007. audio compact disk 57.95 (978-1-74093-918-8(2), 9781740939188) Pub: Bolinda Pubng AUS. Dist(s): Bolinda Pub Inc

Peeling the Onion: A Memoir. unabr. ed. Günter Grass. Read by Norman Dietz. 12 CDs. (Running Time: 15 hrs. 30 mins. 0 sec.). (ENG.). 2007. audio compact disk 37.99 (978-1-4001-0506-9(4)); audio compact disk 75.99 (978-1-4001-3506-6(0)); audio compact disk 24.99 (978-1-4001-5506-4(1)) Pub: Tantor Media. Dist(s): IngramPubServ

***Peeper Pizzaazzz!** Created by Storytellin' Time. (ENG.). (YA). 2008. audio compact disk 15.00 (978-0-9722213-6-8(0)) Storytellin Time.

Peeping Beauty. Mary Jane Auch. 1 cass. (Running Time: 35 min.). (J). (ps-3). 2001. pap. bk. 15.95 (VX-52C) Kimbo Educ.
Starstruck Poulette, the hen, is nearly taken in by a slick talent scout (a fox). Includes a read along book.

Peeping Beauty. Mary Jane Auch. Read by Jerry Terheyden. (Live Oak Readalong Ser.). pap. bk. 18.95 (978-1-59519-335-3(9)) Pub: Live Oak Media. Dist(s): AudioGO

Peeping Beauty. Mary Jane Auch. Illus. by Mary Jane Auch. (Running Time: 9 mins.). 1995. 9.95 (978-1-59112-098-6(5)) Live Oak Media.

Peeping Beauty. Mary Jane Auch. Illus. by Mary Jane Auch. Read by Jerry Terheyden. 14 vols. (Running Time: 9 mins.). (J). 1995. pap. bk. & tchr. ed. 37.95 Reading Chest. (978-0-87499-328-8(8)) Live Oak Media.
Starstruck by her dream of becoming a famous ballerina, Poulette the hen is nearly taken in by a slick talent scout (a fox) who offers her the lead in his production of "Peeping Beauty." Poulette cleverly uses her ballet skills to avoid becoming a chicken dinner.

Peeping Beauty. Mary Jane Auch. Illus. by Mary Jane Auch. Read by Jerry Terheyden. 11 vols. (Running Time: 9 mins.). (J). (gr. k-3). 1995. bk. 25.95 (978-0-87499-327-1(X)); pap. bk. 16.95 (978-0-87499-326-4(1)) Live Oak Media.

Peer Gynt. Henrik Ibsen. 1 cass. (Running Time: 1 hr.). (Radiobook Ser.). 1987. 4.98 (978-0-929541-47-1(2)) Radiola Co.

Peer Gynt. unabr. ed. Henrik Ibsen. Narrated by Flo Gibson. (Running Time: 5 hrs.). 2000. 19.95 (978-1-55685-734-8(9)) Audio Bk Con.

Peer Gynt. unabr. ed. Henrik Ibsen. Narrated by Flo Gibson. 4 cass. (Running Time: 5 hrs. 30 mins.). (YA). 2003. 29.95 Audio Bk Con.
In this poetical and satirical play of Norse folklore, Peer Gynt has many adventures all over the world which feed his braggadocio. When death threatens he returns to his love for salvation.

Peer Mediation Training for Young People: A Video Training Resource. rev. ed. Hilary Stacey. 2001. 55.95 (978-1-873942-58-1(3)) Pub: P Chapman GBR. Dist(s): SAGE

Peer Pressure. 3 cass. (Running Time: 3 hrs.). (Adventures in Odyssey). (J). (gr. k-4). 2001. 12.99 Pub: Focus Family. Dist(s): Tommy Nelson
Adventures in Odyssey stories packaged by theme.

Peer Pressure. Focus on the Family Staff. 3 cass. (Running Time: 3 hrs.). (Adventures in Odyssey). (J). (gr. 1-7). 2001. 9.99 (978-1-58997-020-5(9)) Pub: Focus Family. Dist(s): Tommy Nelson

Peer Pressure: The Art of Being an Individual. unabr. ed. Christina Clement. Read by Thomas Amshay. 1 cass. (Running Time: 45 min.). (YA). (gr. 10-12). 1989. 9.00 (978-0-939401-04-8(5)) RFTS Prod.
Discusses why people are afraid to be themselves & how to make sure it doesn't happen.

Peer Pressure Vol. 5. AIO Team Staff. Created by Focus on the Family Staff. (Running Time: 1 hr. 10 mins. 0 sec.). (Adventures in Odyssey Life Lessons Ser.). (ENG.). (J). 2005. audio compact disk 5.99 (978-1-58997-222-3(8)) Pub: Focus Family. Dist(s): Tyndale Hse

Peer-Reviewed Journal: A Comprehensive Guide Through the Editorial Process - Book & CD, Set. 3rd ed. Gary Michael Smith. Orig. Title: Replaces 0965838072 (book) And 0965838056 (CD). 2000. audio compact disk 70.00 (978-0-9658380-6-1(4)) Chatgris Pr.

Peg Clancy Power. 1 cass. 9.98 (C-8) Folk-Legacy.
Unaccompanied traditional songs & ballads from a lovely Irish singer.

Peg Leg Meg. unabr. ed. Nan Bodsworth. (Aussie Bites Ser.). (YA). 2003. audio compact disk 39.95 (978-1-74030-963-9(4)) Pub: Bolinda Pubng AUS. Dist(s): Bolinda Pub Inc

Pegasus. Narrated by Mia Farrow. (What's a Good Story? Ser.). (YA). 1991. pap. bk. & stu. ed. 99.00 (60794) Phoenix Films.
Serves to introduce the myth genre, a form to be found in many cultures. Before there was science to explain nature & human phenomena, there was myth.

Pegasus. unabr. ed. Doris Orgel. Narrated by Mia Farrow. 1 cass. (Running Time: 50 min.). (Stories to Remember Ser.). (J). (gr. 1-5). 1991. 8.98 (978-1-879496-12-5(7)); audio compact disk 13.98 CD. (978-1-56896-034-0(4)) Lightyear Entrtnmnt.
Mia Farrow narrates the story of Pegasus, the fabled winged horse from Greek mythology, accompanied by twelve-piece orchestration & elaborate effects.

Pegasus. unabr. ed. Doris Orgel. Narrated by Mia Farrow. 1 cass. (Running Time: 50 min.). (Stories to Remember Ser.). (J). (gr. 1-5). 1993. pap. bk. 8.98 incl. long box. (978-1-879496-13-2(5)) Lightyear Entrtnmnt.

Pegasus Bridge: June 6, 1944. unabr. collector's ed. Stephen E. Ambrose. Read by Dick Estell. 6 cass. (Running Time: 6 hrs.). 1988. 48.00 (978-0-7366-1335-4(8), 2238) Books on Tape.
Pegasus Bridge was the first engagement of D-Day. The Allies knew that the bridges over the Orne River & the adjacent canal were the key to D-Day & so did the Germans. This is the story of Major John Howard & the 181 troops under his command. It was their task to seize Pegasus Bridge.

Pegasus Descending. abr. ed. James Lee Burke. Read by Will Patton. (Dave Robicheaux Ser.). 2006. 17.95 (978-0-7435-6461-8(8), Audioworks) Pub: S&S Audio. Dist(s): S and S Inc

Pegasus Descending. abr. ed. James Lee Burke. Read by Will Patton. CDs 5. (Running Time: 6 hrs. 0 mins. 0 sec.). (Dave Robicheaux Ser.). 2008. audio compact disk 14.99 (978-0-7435-7619-2(5)) Pub: S&S Audio. Dist(s): S and S Inc

Pegasus Descending. unabr. ed. James Lee Burke. Read by Will Patton. 10 cass. (Running Time: 12 hrs.). (Dave Robicheaux Ser.). 2006. 94.75 (978-1-4281-0289-7(2)); audio compact disk 119.75 (978-1-4281-0291-0(4)) Recorded Bks.
In Pegasus Descending, Burke delivers a gritty episode in the life of Dave Robicheaux, as the detective struggles with psychological demons. Haunted for 25 years by a friend's murder, Dave might have a chance at redemption when the victim's daughter arrives in town and gets herself in trouble. Just why is she baiting the very thug who is responsible for her father's death? And what can Dave do to avoid a catastrophe? The sensual, southern tones of narrator Will Patton vividly define the cast of characters that emerge from the rich fabric of Burke's novel.

Pegasus Descending. unabr. ed. James Lee Burke. Read by Will Patton. (Dave Robicheaux Ser.). 2006. 29.95 (978-0-7435-6462-5(6), Audioworks); audio compact disk 49.95 (978-0-7435-5423-7(X), Audioworks) Pub: S&S Audio. Dist(s): S and S Inc

***Pegasus in Space.** abr. ed. Anne McCaffrey. Read by Sharon Williams. (Running Time: 6 hrs.). (Talents Ser.). 2010. audio compact disk 9.99 (978-1-4418-6707-0(4), 9781441867070, BCD Value Price) Brilliance Audio.

Pegasus in Space. unabr. ed. Anne McCaffrey. Read by Sharon Williams. 9 cass. (Running Time: 13 hrs.). (Saga of the Talents Ser.). 2000. 35.95 (978-1-58788-060-5(1), 1587880601, BAU) Brilliance Audio.
For an overpopulated Earth, whose resources are strained to the breaking point, there is only one place to look for relief: straight up. With the successful completion of the Padrugoi Space Station, humanity has at last achieved its first large-scale permanent presence in space. Additional bases are feverishly being built on the Moon and on Mars, stepping-stones to the greatest adventure in all history: the colonization of alien worlds. Already long-range telescopes have identified a number of habitable planets orbiting the stars and distant galaxies. Now it's just a question of getting there. But there are those who, for selfish motives of their own, want Padrugoi and the other outposts to fail. People who will stop at nothing to maintain their power or to avenge its loss. Standing in their way are the Talented, men and women gifted with extraordinary mental powers that have made them as feared as they are respected - and utterly indispensable to the colonization effort. There is Peter Reidinger, a teenage paraplegic who is the strongest telekinetic ever, his mind capable of teleporting objects and people thousands of miles in the blink of an eye. Yet all his power cannot repair his damaged spine or allow him to feel the gentle touch of a loved one . . . Rhyssa Owne, the pwerful telepath and mother hen to Peter, and the rest of her "children" - and a fierce, unrelenting fighter against the prejudice that would deny the Talented the right to lead happy and productive lives . . . and Amariyah, an orphan girl who loves two things in the world above all others: gardening and Peter Reidinger. And woe to anyone who harms either one of them - for the young girl's talent may prove to be the most amazing of all. Now, as sabotage and attempted murder strike the Station, it's up to the Talented to save the day. Only, who's going to save the Talented?.

Pegasus in Space. unabr. ed. Anne McCaffrey. Read by Sharon Williams. (Running Time: 13 hrs.). (Talents Ser.). 2005. 39.25 (978-1-59600-624-9(2), 9781596006249, Brlnc Audio MP3 Lib); 24.95 (978-1-59600-623-2(4), 9781596006232, Brilliance MP3); 49.97 (978-1-59600-626-3(9), 9781596006263, BADLE); 24.95 (978-1-59600-625-6(0), 9781596006256, BAD) Brilliance Audio.

***Pegasus in Space.** unabr. ed. Anne McCaffrey. Read by Sharon Williams. (Running Time: 14 hrs.). (Talents Ser.). 2010. audio compact disk 29.99

(978-1-4418-4103-2(2), 9781441841032, Bril Audio CD Unabri); audio compact disk 89.97 (978-1-4418-4104-9(0), 9781441841049, BriAudCD Unabrid) Brilliance Audio.

Peggy's Violin: A Butterfly in Time: Teacher's Guide with CD. Contrib. by Peggy M. Hills. 2007. audio compact disk 32.98 (978-1-897166-45-1(1)) Child Group CAN.

Peines de Coeur d'une Chatte Anglaise, Guide-Ane a l'Usage des Animaux qui Veulent Parvenir aux Honneurs. Honoré de Balzac. Read by C. Grandi & G. Bejean. 1 cass. (FRE.). 1991. 21.95 (1151-VSL) Olivia & Hill.

"Peines de coeur" - A cat living in an aristocratic family in London compares English & French manners. "Guide-ane" - A charming satire of the burgeoning scientific institutes in the Europe of the 1830s.

Peking Target. unabr. collector's ed. Adam Hall. Read by Richard Brown. 6 cass. (Running Time: 9 hrs.). (Quiller Ser.). 1987. 48.00 (978-0-7366-1194-7(0), 2112) Books on Tape.

At a state funeral in Pekin, the deceased's coffin blows up in the face of mourners.

***PelÃ-cula.** Pablo Olivares. (SPA.). 2010. audio compact disk 15.99 (978-0-8297-5440-7(7)) Pub: CanZion. Dist(s): Zondervan

Pele: The Hawaiian Legend of Pele. Scripts. As told by Dietrich Varez. Narrated by Wong Kaupena. 1 CD. (Running Time: 25 mins). Dramatization. (HAW.). 2002. cass. & cd-rom 16.95 (978-1-929317-25-7(5)) Coco Info.

Pelene. Egle Zalcic. 1 cass. (Running Time: 18 mins.). (LIT., bk. 22.95 (SLT102) J Norton Pubs.

The tory of Cinderella, her bad sisters & the handsome prince. Worksheets & a game board are included. Lithuanian-English glossary.

Pelican see Sampler of American Humor

Pelican at Blandings. abr. ed. P. G. Wodehouse. Read by Martin Jarvis. (Running Time: 5 hrs. 0 mins. 0 sec.). (Blandings Castle Saga Ser.). (ENG.). 2008. audio compact disk 26.95 (978-1-934997-04-8(8)) Pub: CSAWord. Dist(s): PerseuPGW

Pelican at Blandings. unabr. ed. P. G. Wodehouse. Read by Frederick Davidson. 5 cass. (Running Time: 7 hrs.). 1997. 39.95 (978-0-7861-1050-6(3), 1822) Blckstn Audio.

There are tricky corners to be rounded & assorted godsons, impostors & pretty girls to be paired off. Fortunately, many years' membership in the old Pelican Club means the Hon. Galahad Threepwood is able to keep cool.

Pelican Brief. John Grisham. Read by Alexander Adams. 1992. audio compact disk 72.00 (978-0-7366-8911-3(7)) Books on Tape.

Pelican Brief. l.t. ed. John Grisham. Read by Michael Shannon. 8 cass. (Running Time: 12 hrs.). (Audio Bks.). 1992. bk. 69.95 set. (978-0-7838-8001-3(4), Macmillan Ref) Gale.

John Grisham's latest bestseller begins with the simultaneous assassinations of two Supreme Court Justices. When Darby Shaw, a brilliant law student, finds an obscure connection between the death of a ninety-four year old liberal legend, & the youngest most conservative justice, she quickly realizes - the hard way - that her suspect has powerful friends, & one of them has apparently read her brief.

Pelican Brief. unabr. ed. John Grisham. Read by Alexander Adams. 8 cass. (Running Time: 12 hrs.). 1992. 64.00 (978-0-7366-2204-2(7), 2999) Books on Tape.

Abe Rosenberg, at 91 the Supreme Court's liberal legend, has little in common with Myron Jensen, the court's youngest & most conservative member. Yet each is murdered within two hours of the other, leaving the country in shock & its law enforcement agencies stupified.

Pelican Brief, unabr. ed. John Grisham. Narrated by George Guidall. 9 cass. (Running Time: 13 hrs.). 1992. 78.00 (978-1-55690-753-1(2), 92137E7) Recorded Bks.

A law student compiles a brief explaining two shocking murders. Her theory, "The Pelican Brief," could incriminate powerful people, including the current president of the United States. Now she finds herself a target for assassination.

Pella's Angel. Meredith Bean McMath. 11 cass. (Running Time: 12 hrs.). (YA). (gr. 7 up). 2002. (978-0-9724158-1-1(5)) Run Rabbit Run Prod.

Based on true stories from a Civil War Virginia border country, Pella's Angel traces the story of Annabelle McBain, a southern girl who must choose between love and pride.

Pellucidar. Edgar Rice Burroughs. Read by Patrick G. Lawlor. (Running Time: 6 hrs.). 2003. 25.95 (978-1-60083-637-4(2), Audiofy Corp) Iofy Corp.

Pellucidar. unabr. ed. Edgar Rice Burroughs. Read by Patrick G. Lawlor. 5 CDs. (Running Time: 5 hrs. 58 mins.). (Pellucidar Ser.). (ENG.). 2003. audio compact disk 33.00 (978-1-4001-0069-9(0)); audio compact disk 20.00 (978-1-4001-5069-4(8)) Pub: Tantor Media. Dist(s): IngramPubServ

In this sequel to At the Earth's Core, David Innes vows revenge and returns to the Inner World of Pellucidar to rescue the beautiful Dian, who had been torn from his arms by trickery. However, his return trip places him far from the land of his beloved and he is forced to undertake a desperate journey thousands of miles across the fierce inner earth to reach her. David's epic voyage takes him through the many strange lands of Pellucidar, including the pendant moon and Land of Awful Shadow. His heart pounding encounters with primeval beasts and extraordinary peoples makes Pellucidar one of the best adventure stories ever penned by Edgar Rice Burroughs.

Pellucidar. unabr. ed. Edgar Rice Burroughs. Read by Patrick G. Lawlor. (Pellucidar Ser.). (ENG.). 2003. audio compact disk 66.00 (978-1-4001-3069-6(7)) Pub: Tantor Media. Dist(s): IngramPubServ

Pellucidar, with EBook. unabr. ed. Edgar Rice Burroughs. Narrated by Patrick G. Lawlor. (Running Time: 6 hrs. 0 mins. 0 sec.). (Pellucidar Ser.). (ENG.). 2009. audio compact disk 22.99 (978-1-4001-1116-9(1)); audio compact disk 19.99 (978-1-4001-6116-4(9)) Pub: Tantor Media. Dist(s): IngramPubServ

Pellucidar, with eBook. unabr. ed. Edgar Rice Burroughs. Narrated by Patrick G. Lawlor. (Running Time: 6 hrs. 0 mins. 0 sec.). (Pellucidar Ser.). (ENG.). 2009. audio compact disk 45.99 (978-1-4001-4116-6(8)) Pub: Tantor Media. Dist(s): IngramPubServ

Pelo en la Leche. Rescate VanPelt. 1 CD. (Running Time: 1 hr. 30 min.). (SPA.). 2002. audio compact disk 9.99 (978-0-8297-3832-2(0)) Pub: Vida Pubs. Dist(s): Zondervan

Pelo en la Leche. Rescate VanPelt. 2002. 2.00 (978-0-8297-3835-3(5)); audio compact disk 3.60 (978-0-8297-3833-9(9)) Zondervan.

Pelo en la Leche. unabr. ed. Rescate VanPelt. 2002. 9.99 (978-0-8297-3834-6(7)) Pub: Vida Pubs. Dist(s): Zondervan

Peloponnesian War. Instructed by Kenneth W. Harl. 2007. 199.95 (978-1-59803-368-7(9)); audio compact disk 99.95 (978-1-59803-369-4(7)) Teaching Co.

***Peloponnesian War.** unabr. ed. Donald Kagan. (Running Time: 18 hrs. 30 mins.). 2010. 44.95 (978-1-4417-6920-6(X)); 99.95 (978-1-4417-6917-6(X)); audio compact disk 39.95 (978-1-4417-6919-0(6)); audio compact disk 123.00 (978-1-4417-6918-3(8)) Blckstn Audio.

Pelvic Fractures. (Postgraduate Programs Ser.: C84-PG7). 1984. 45.00 (8487) Am Coll Surgeons.

Discusses recent developments in the management of fractures of the pelvis.

Pema Chodron & Alice Walker in Conversation: On the Meaning of Suffering & the Mystery of Joy. Pema Chödrön & Alice Walker. 1 CD. (Running Time: 71 Mins). 2005. audio compact disk 14.95 (978-1-59179-392-2(0), AW00411D) Sounds True.

The seed of joy lies in the heart of suffering. Pulitzer Prize-winning author Alice Walker discovered this revolutionary truth when she first heard the teachings of Pema Chodron, an American-born Buddhist nun whose popular books have helped to awaken and spread the practice of compassion in the West. On Pema Chodron and Alice Walker in Conversation, you will learn about the life-changing impact on both women of tonglen meditation: an ancient Tibetan meditation that transforms pain into compassion through the medium of your own breath. With honesty and humor, Chodron and Walker reflect on anger, joy, fear, and the union of spirituality and social activism. A deeply courageous vision of the human journey unfolds as these two thinkers from different worlds come together in a provocative exchange of insight and personal revelation. Ultimately, their combined wisdom illuminates the realm, available to us all, where the barriers between self and others dissolve. Recorded live at San Francisco's Palace of Fine Arts, Pema Ch"dr"n and Alice Walker in Conversation includes a lively question-and-answer session available nowhere else. Complete with a booklet including Ane Pema's tonglen instructions, suggestions for further readings, and more.

Pema Chodron Collection. Pema Chödrön. 6 CDs. (Running Time: 7 hrs.). 2004. audio compact disk 39.95 (978-1-59179-159-1(6), W846D) Sounds True.

Pema Chödrön is one of the West's most beloved teachers of Buddhism, making the Tibetan vajrayana tradition accessible in today's world. Now, three of her most popular teachings are available in one boxed set. The Pema Chödrön Collection includes: Pure Meditation - step-by-step instruction in Tibetan Buddhism's pinnacle practice for transformation and letting go; Good Medicine - teachings in tonglen, an elegant meditation that allows us to use our troubles to befriend ourselves and widen our circle of compassion; and From Fear to Fearlessness - offers an antidote to fear in the four noble aspirations - maitri (lovingkindness), compassion, joy, and equanimity.

Pen Pals. abr. ed. Olivia Goldsmith. 4 cass. (Running Time: 6 hrs.). 2002. 24.95 (Nova Audio Bks) Brilliance Audio.

Valerie Molaro has broken through the glass ceiling and into the ranks of Wall Street's elite. When her boss is caught playing fast and loose with SEC rules, she agrees to take the rap since he promises to protect her. Abandoned by both her boss and her fiance, Valerie finds herself in a filthy prison. After falling into depression the other prisoners come together to revive her spirits. Jolted into action, Valerie takes a better look at her drab surroundings and transforms both the prison and herself.

Pen Pals. unabr. ed. Olivia Goldsmith. 9 cass. (Running Time: 13 hrs.). 2002. 34.95 (BAU) Brilliance Audio.

Pen Pals. unabr. ed. Olivia Goldsmith. Read by Joyce Bean. 9 cass. (Running Time: 13 hrs.). 2002. 34.95 (978-1-58788-862-5(9), 1587888629, BAU); 96.25 (978-1-58788-863-2(7), 1587888637, Unabridge Lib Edns) Brilliance Audio.

Meet Jennifer - a smart, sexy woman who has made good in a man's world. A major player on The Street, Jennifer agrees to take the fall when her boss is caught playing fast and loose with the SEC. After all, her fiance is a lawyer with the connections to get her off. Instead, Jennifer ends up in Jennings Correctional Facility for Women, a world a whole lot tougher than Wall Street. Inside she meets a lively group of smart, tough women: crew leader Movita, crazy Cher, blindly optimistic Theresa, and the adorable Suki. While Jennifer waits in vain for the rescue that her fiance has promised, Movita makes her an offer she can't refuse.

Pen Pals. unabr. ed. Olivia Goldsmith. Read by Joyce Bean. (Running Time: 13 hrs.). 2004. 39.25 (978-1-59335-453-4(3), 1593354533, Brlnc Audio MP3 Lib) Brilliance Audio.

Pen Pals. unabr. ed. Olivia Goldsmith. Read by Joyce Bean. (Running Time: 13 hrs.). 2004. 39.25 (978-1-59710-565-1(1), 1597105651, BADLE); 24.95 (978-1-59710-564-4(3), 1597105643, BAD) Brilliance Audio.

Pen Pals. unabr. ed. Olivia Goldsmith. Read by Joyce Bean. (Running Time: 13 hrs.). 2004. 24.95 (978-1-59335-107-6(0), 1593351070) Soulmate Audio Bks.

Pen to Change America. Upton Sinclair. 1 cass. (Running Time: 40 min.). 1964. 11.95 (23050) J Norton Pubs.

The author gives students at the City College of New York an engrossing talk about his life & his thoughts.

Pen to Change America. Upton Sinclair. 2007. audio compact disk 12.95 (978-1-57970-477-3(8), Audio-For) J Norton Pubs.

Penacho de Moctezuma. Mario Moya Pelencia. Narrated by Francisco Rivela. 8 cass. (Running Time: 11 hrs.). 74.00 (978-1-4025-1667-2(3)) Recorded Bks.

***Penalty.** unabr. ed. Mal Peet. (Running Time: 6 hrs.). 2011. 19.99 (978-1-4558-0077-3(5), 9781455800773, Candlewick Bril); 39.97 (978-1-4558-0078-0(3), 9781455800780, Candlewick Bril); 19.99 (978-1-4558-0074-2(0), 9781455800742, Candlewick Bril); 39.97 (978-1-4558-0075-9(9), 9781455800759, Candlewick Bril); audio compact disk 22.99 (978-1-4558-0072-8(4), 9781455800728, Candlewick Bril); audio compact disk 49.97 (978-1-4558-0073-5(2), 9781455800735, Candlewick Bril) Brilliance Audio.

Penalty Shootout. Bill Knox. 2008. 44.95 (978-0-7531-3290-6(7)); audio compact disk 59.95 (978-0-7531-3291-3(5)) Pub: Isis Pubng Ltd GBR. Dist(s): Ulverscroft US

Penance & Indulgences in the Catechism. Jerome Fasano. 1 cass. (Inspiring Presentations from the National Rosary Congress Ser.). 2.50 (978-1-56036-089-6(5)) AMI Pr.

Penderwicks: A Summer Tale of Four Sisters, Two Rabbits, & a Very Interesting Boy. unabr. ed. Jeanne Birdsall. Read by Susan Denaker. (J). 2006. 44.99 (978-0-7393-7521-1(0)) Find a World.

Penderwicks: A Summer Tale of Four Sisters, Two Rabbits, & a Very Interesting Boy. unabr. ed. Jeanne Birdsall. Read by Susan Denaker. 6 CDs. (Running Time: 6 hrs. 45 mins.). (Penderwick Ser.). (J). (ps-3). 2006. audio compact disk 42.50 (978-0-307-28577-5(4), Listening Lib); 35.00 (978-0-307-28576-8(6), Listening Lib) Pub: Random Audio Pubg. Dist(s): Random

This summer the Penderwick sisters have a wonderful surprise: a holiday on the grounds of a beautiful estate called Arundel. Soon they are busy discovering the summertime magic of Arundel's sprawling gardens, treasure-filled attic, tame rabbits, and the cook who makes the best gingerbread in Massachusetts. But the best discovery of all is Jeffrey Tifton, son of Arundel's owner, who quickly proves to be the perfect companion for their adventures. The icy-hearted Mrs. Tifton is not as pleased with the Penderwicks as Jeffrey is, though, and warns the new friends to stay out of trouble. Which, of course, they will - won't they? One thing's for sure: it will be a summer the Penderwicks will never forget.

Penderwicks: A Summer Tale of Four Sisters, Two Rabbits, & a Very Interesting Boy. unabr. ed. Jeanne Birdsall. Read by Susan Denaker. 6 CDs. (Running Time: 6 hrs. 45 mins.). (Penderwick Ser.). (ENG.). (J). (gr. 1). 2006. audio compact disk 39.00 (978-0-307-28451-8(4), Listening Lib) Pub: Random Audio Pubg. Dist(s): Random

***Penderwicks at Point Mouette.** unabr. ed. Jeanne Birdsall. (ENG.). (J). 2011. audio compact disk 34.00 (978-0-307-91531-3(X), Listening Lib) Pub: Random Audio Pubg. Dist(s): Random

Penderwicks on Gardam Street. unabr. ed. Jeanne Birdsall. Read by Susan Denaker. 6 CDs. (Running Time: 7 hrs. 41 mins.). (J). (gr. 4-7). 2008. audio compact disk 50.00 (978-0-7393-6501-4(0), Listening Lib) Pub: Random Audio Pubg. Dist(s): Random

THE PENDERWICK SISTERS are home on Gardam Street and ready for an adventure! But the adventure they get isn't quite what they had in mind. Mr. Penderwick's sister has decided it's time for him to start dating - and the girls know that can only mean one thing: disaster. Enter the Save-Daddy Plan - a plot so brilliant, so bold, so funny, that only the Penderwick girls could have come up with it. It's high jinks, big laughs, and loads of family warmth as the Penderwicks triumphantly return.

Penderwicks on Gardam Street. unabr. ed. Jeanne Birdsall. Read by Susan Denaker. (Running Time: 27660 sec.). (Penderwick Ser.). (ENG.). (J). (gr. 3-7). 2008. audio compact disk 34.00 (978-0-7393-6499-4(5), Listening Lib) Pub: Random Audio Pubg. Dist(s): Random

Pendle Hill Idea: A Joint Search: Education in Community see Pendle Hill Idea: A Quaker Experiment in Work, Study, Worship

Pendle Hill Idea: A Quaker Experiment in Work, Study, Worship. 8 cass. Incl. Pendle Hill Idea: A Joint Search: Education in Community. Parker J. Palmer. 1980.; Pendle Hill Idea: All Life Has An Intrinsic Worth: Readings from a Forty Year Journal. Mary Morrison. 1980.; Pendle Hill Idea: An Attitude of Mind Which Permits the New to Emerge: The Integrated Life. Marian Sanders. 1980.; Pendle Hill Idea: Quakers & the Way of the Cross. Parker J. Palmer. 1980.; Pendle Hill Idea: The God-Indwelt Society: The Life of the Spirit at Pendle Hill. Janet Sheperd. 1980.; Pendle Hill Idea: The Idea Seeking Embodiment in the Written Word: Writers & Writing at Pendle Hill. Helen Brooks. 1980.; Pendle Hill Idea: The Power of An Idea Should Reside in Its Potentiality: The Second Fifty Years. Edwin A. Sanders. 1980.; Pendle Hill Idea: To Embody the Reluctant Stuff of the Real World: Housing the Pendle Hill Idea. Mather Lippincott. 1980.; 1980. 26.00 Set.; 4.50 ea. Pendle Hill.

Pendle Hill Idea: All Life Has An Intrinsic Worth: Readings from a Forty Year Journal see Pendle Hill Idea: A Quaker Experiment in Work, Study, Worship

Pendle Hill Idea: An Attitude of Mind Which Permits the New to Emerge: The Integrated Life see Pendle Hill Idea: A Quaker Experiment in Work, Study, Worship

Pendle Hill Idea: Quakers & the Way of the Cross see Pendle Hill Idea: A Quaker Experiment in Work, Study, Worship

Pendle Hill Idea: The God-Indwelt Society: The Life of the Spirit at Pendle Hill see Pendle Hill Idea: A Quaker Experiment in Work, Study, Worship

Pendle Hill Idea: The Idea Seeking Embodiment in the Written Word: Writers & Writing at Pendle Hill see Pendle Hill Idea: A Quaker Experiment in Work, Study, Worship

Pendle Hill Idea: The Power of An Idea Should Reside in Its Potentiality: The Second Fifty Years see Pendle Hill Idea: A Quaker Experiment in Work, Study, Worship

Pendle Hill Idea: To Embody the Reluctant Stuff of the Real World: Housing the Pendle Hill Idea see Pendle Hill Idea: A Quaker Experiment in Work, Study, Worship

Pendragon. abr. ed. Catherine Coulter. Read by Anne Flosnik. (Running Time: 21600 sec.). (Bride Ser.). 2007. audio compact disk 14.99 (978-1-59737-848-2(8), 9781597378482, BCD Value Price) Brilliance Audio.

Pendragon. unabr. ed. Catherine Coulter. Read by Anne Flosnik. (Running Time: 11 hrs.). (Bride Ser.). 2006. 39.25 (978-1-59737-846-8(1), 9781597378468, BADLE); 24.95 (978-1-59737-845-1(3), 9781597378451, BAD); 82.25 (978-1-59737-840-6(2), 9781597378406, BrilAudUnabridg); audio compact disk 39.25 (978-1-59737-844-4(5), 9781597378444, Brlnc Audio MP3 Lib); audio compact disk 97.25 (978-1-59737-842-0(9), 9781597378420, BriAudCD Unabrid); audio compact disk 36.95 (978-1-59737-841-3(0), 9781597378413, Bril Audio CD Unabri); audio compact disk 24.95 (978-1-59737-843-7(7), 9781597378437, Brilliance MP3) Brilliance Audio.

Dear Reader: It's time for a bit of cat racing, a sinister mystery, and a light touch of gothic menace. Add the signature Sherbrooke grit and wit and voila, you have Pendragon. Here's to the next generation - Tysen Sherbrooke now has four sons and Meggie, age nineteen. Her almost-cousin Jeremy Stanton-Greville - Sophia Sherbrooke's brother, and the man Meggie has held in silent adoration since she was thirteen years old - unknowingly breaks her guileless heart. Deeply depressed, she rallies with a hasty marriage to Thomas Malcombe, the earl of Lancaster and a brand-new card in the Sherbrooke deck, in the spring of 1824, despite a very nasty rumor involving a local girl. Thomas takes his bride to Pendragon, a castle on the southeastern coast of Ireland. A monstrous old place, filled with very eccentric folk, Pendragon nonetheless charms Meggie, until she discovers that she's there for a reason that could lead to disaster. I hope you like Meggie Sherbrooke's story and getting together with the Sherbrooke clan again. Feel free to email me at ReadMoi@aol.com or write me at P.O. Box 17, Mill Valley, CA. 94942. Catherine Coulter.

Pendragon, unabr. ed. Stephen R. Lawhead. Read by Frederick Davidson. 10 cass. (Running Time: 15 hrs.). (Pendragon Cycle Ser.: Bk. 4). 1996. 69.95 (978-0-7861-0986-9(6), 1763) Blckstn Audio.

Arthur is King - but treachery runs rampant throughout the beleaguered Isle of the Mighty. Darkest evil descends upon Britain's shore in many guises. Fragile alliances fray & tear, threatening all the noble liege has won with his wisdom & his blood. His most trusted counselor - the warrior, bard & kingmaker whom legend will name Merlin - is himself to be tested on a mystical journey back through his own extraordinary past. So in a black time of plague & pestilence, it is Arthur who must stand alone against a great & terrible adversary. For only this way can he truly win immortality - & the name to treasure above all others: "Pendragon.".

Pendred Syndrome - A Bibliography & Dictionary for Physicians, Patients, & Genome Researchers. Compiled by Icon Group International, Inc. Staff. 2007. ring bd. 28.95 (978-0-497-11271-4(X)) Icon Grp.

Pendulum - How Does It Work? George King. 2005. audio compact disk 12.50 (978-0-937249-21-5(1)) Aetherius Soc.

Penelope's Pen Pal - Book & Audio Cassette. 1 read-along cass. (J). (ps-3). 1986. bk. 9.98 (978-0-89544-153-9(5), NO. 153) Silbert Bress.

Penelope learns that a person's character is more important than outward appearances.

Penelopiad: The Myth of Penelope & Odysseus. unabr. ed. Margaret Atwood. Read by Laural Merlington. (Running Time: 3 hrs.). (Myths Ser.). 2005. 39.25 (978-1-4233-0782-2(8), 9781423307822, BADLE); 24.95 (978-1-4233-0781-5(X), 9781423307815, BAD); 44.25 (978-1-4233-0776-1(3), 9781423307761, BrilAudUnabridg); 19.95 (978-1-4233-0775-4(5), 9781423307754, BAU); audio compact disk 39.25 (978-1-4233-0780-8(1), 9781423307808, Brlnc Audio MP3 Lib); audio compact disk 62.25 (978-1-4233-0778-5(X), 9781423307785, BriAudCD Unabrid); audio compact disk 19.95 (978-1-4233-0777-8(1), 9781423307778, Bril Audio CD Unabri); audio compact disk 24.95 (978-1-4233-0779-2(8), 9781423307792, Brilliance MP3) Brilliance Audio.
In Homer's account in The Odyssey, Penelope - wife of Odysseus and cousin of the beautiful Helen of Troy - is portrayed as the quintessential faithful wife, her story a salutary lesson through the ages. Left alone for twenty years when Odysseus goes off to fight in the Trojan war after the abduction of Helen, Penelope manages, in the face of scandalous rumours, to maintain the kingdom of Ithaca, bring up her wayward son, and keep over a hundred suitors at bay, simultaneously. When Odysseus finally comes home after enduring hardships, overcoming monsters and sleeping with goddesses, he kills her suitors and - curiously - twelve of her maids. In a splendid contemporary twist to the ancient story, Margaret Atwood has chosen to give the telling of it to Penelope and to her twelve hanged Maids, asking: "What led to the hanging of the maids, and what was Penelope really up to?" In Atwood's dazzling, playful retelling, the story becomes as wise and compassionate as it is haunting, and as wildly entertaining as it is disturbing. With wit and verve, drawing on the storytelling and poetic talent for which she herself is renowned, she gives Penelope new life and reality - and sets out to provide an answer to an ancient mystery.

***Penetrating the Darkness: Discovering the Power of the Cross Against Unseen Evil.** unabr. ed. Jack Hayford. (Running Time: 6 hrs. 0 mins. 0 sec.). (ENG.). 2011. audio compact disk 21.98 (978-1-61045-070-6(1)) christianaud.

Penetrating the Darkness: How to Become a Bright Light in a Dark World. 1. (Running Time: 47 mins.). 2002. 15.00 (978-1-57399-122-3(8)) Mac Hammond.
A major portion of the body of Christ poses little or no threat to the kingdom of darkness. In her message Penetrating the Darkness, Lynne Hammond reveals why this is so and how believers can change their prespective and truly become-dangerous to darkness!.

***Pengarron Dynasty.** Gloria Cook. Read by Patricia Gallimore. 8 cass. 2010. 69.95 (978-1-84559-538-8(6)) Pub: Soundings Ltd GBR. Dist(s): Ulverscroft US

Pengarron Land. Gloria Cook. Read by Patricia Gallimore. 14 cass. (Running Time: 18 hrs. 30 mins.). (Soundings Ser.). (J). 2005. 99.95 (978-1-84283-600-2(5)) Pub: ISIS Lrg Prnt GBR. Dist(s): Ulverscroft US

Pengarron Pride. Gloria Cook. 12 cass. (Running Time: 50400 sec.). (Soundings Ser.). 2005. 94.95 (978-1-84283-601-9(3)) Pub: ISIS Lrg Prnt GBR. Dist(s): Ulverscroft US

Pengarron Rivalry. Gloria Cook. 2007. 69.95 (978-1-84559-539-5(4)) Pub: Soundings Ltd GBR. Dist(s): Ulverscroft US

Penguin Island. unabr. ed. Anatole France. Read by Frederick Davidson. 7 cass. (Running Time: 10 hrs.). 1999. 49.95 (978-0-7861-1673-7(0), 2501) Blckstn Audio.
The story of the strutting penguins & their virtues & vices is not merely a burlesque allegory of French history; it is a satire of the history of mankind. With gentle yet biting irony, France challenges the Spencerian belief in the ultimate perfectibility of man, though his irony reveals his sympathy for man's weaknesses & his need for social institutions.

Penguin Parade. 1 cass. (Running Time: 42 min.). (J). 1996. 9.98 (978-1-56628-088-4(5)); audio compact disk 15.98 (978-1-56628-087-7(7)) MFLP CA.
An eclectic mix of musical styles & instruments focus on the animal kingdom.

Penguins. Linda Allison. Read by Jerry Kay. Illus. by Bill Wells. (Running Time: 20 min.). (Science in Action Learning Ser.). (J). (ps-6). 1988. bk. 9.95 Kay Productions.

Penguins. unabr. ed. Read by Linda Spizzirri. 48 cass. (Running Time: 15 min.). Dramatization. (Educational Coloring Book & Cassette Package Ser.). (J). (gr. k-8). 1989. pap. bk. 6.95 (978-0-86545-147-6(8)) Spizzirri.
Features a visit to Antartica, home of the Rock Hopper, Emperor, Adelie, King & other penguins.

Penguins Family: Story of a Humboldt Penguin Trade Paper. Kathleen Hollenbeck. Illus. by Daniel Stegos. (ENG.). (J). (ps-2). 2005. 8.95 (978-1-59249-350-0(5), SC4027) Soundprints.

Penguins on the Go/Day at a Time. Steck-Vaughn Staff. 2002. (978-0-7398-5911-7(0)) SteckVau.

Penguins Stopped Play. Harry Thompson & Harry Thompson. (Isis Cassettes Ser.). 2007. 61.95 (978-0-7531-3691-1(0)) Pub: ISIS Lrg Prnt GBR. Dist(s): Ulverscroft US

Penguins Stopped Play: Eleven Village Cricketers Take on the World. Harry Thompson & Harry Thompson. Read by Glen McCready. (Running Time: 33900 sec.). (Isis (CDs) Ser.). 2007. audio compact disk 79.95 (978-0-7531-2658-5(3)) Pub: ISIS Lrg Prnt GBR. Dist(s): Ulverscroft US

Penis Dialogues: The Work on Gender/Privacy. 2005. audio compact disk 24.00 (978-1-890246-32-7(8)) B Katie Int Inc.

Pennies on a Dead Woman's Eyes. unabr. ed. Marcia Muller. Read by Bernadette Dunne. 7 cass. (Running Time: 10 hrs. 30 mins.). (Sharon McCone Mystery Ser.: No. 12). 2000. 56.00 (978-0-7366-5105-9(5), 5248) Books on Tape.
Convicted of murder in 1956, Lis Benedict has served her long sentence and just been released from jail. Her daughter, Judy, convinced of her mother's innocence, persuades All Souls Legal Cooperative to reinvestigate her mother's case. Sharon McCone loves a challenge but has little affection for the cold and unlikable Lis. Then, suddenly, the woman in question is dead, a vicious threat is scrawled in red paint across the front of Sharon's house, and San Francisco's #1 PI is following a fresh trail of death that leads back to the '50s in search of a killer who has engineered a fatal cover-up and built a brilliant career on murder.

Pennillion Singing (Welsh Music) 1 cass. 10.95 (C11061) J Norton Pubs.
The best performers of Cerdd Dant/pennillion singing from the heartland of Welsh culture.

Pennsylvania: Historic Philadelphia Walking Tour. 1 cass. (Running Time: 90 min.). 12.95 (CC205) Comp Comms Inc.
Explore Philadelphia's Independence National Historic Park & see the Liberty Bell, Independence Hall, a Colonial Tavern & capture the magic of Ben Franklin.

Pennsylvania: Philadelphia - A Guide Through Independence Park. (Running Time: 90 min.). 1990. 12.95 (CC208) Comp Comms Inc.
The story of how we started our severence from England that climaxed in the War of 1812.

Pennsylvania A Workers' Compensation Practice & Procedure. 1987. 75.00 book only. PA Bar Inst.

Pennsylvania AIDS Confidentiality Act of Nineteen Ninety: Impact on Litigation & Treatment. Read by Bruce E. Cooper. 1 cass. 1991. 20.00 (AL-106) PA Bar Inst.

Pennsylvania Appellate Advocacy & Procedure. 1990. 50.00 (AC-594) PA Bar Inst.

Pennsylvania Avenue: Profiles in Backroom Power. unabr. ed. John Harwood & Gerald Seib. Read by William Hughes. 7 CDs. (Running Time: 27000 sec.). 2008. audio compact disk & audio compact disk 29.95 (978-1-4332-1388-5(5)) Blckstn Audio.

Pennsylvania Avenue: Profiles in Backroom Power. unabr. ed. John Harwood & Gerald F. Seib. Read by William Hughes. (Running Time: 27000 sec.). 2008. 29.95 (978-1-4332-1387-8(7)); 54.95 (978-1-4332-1385-4(0)); audio compact disk 29.95 (978-1-4332-1389-2(3)) Blckstn Audio.

Pennsylvania Avenue: Profiles in Backroom Power. unabr. ed. Harwood John & Gerald F. Seib. Read by William Hughes. (Running Time: 27000 sec.). 2008. audio compact disk & audio compact disk 70.00 (978-1-4332-1386-1(9)) Blckstn Audio.

Pennsylvania Civil Practice & Procedure. 1988. bk. 95.00 book.; 40.00 cass. only.; 55.00 book only. PA Bar Inst.

Pennsylvania Dutch Country: A Journey Through Lancaster County. Bill McCoy. 2001. 19.95 (978-1-931739-04-7(8)) Travelog Corp.

Pennsylvania Dutch Night Before Christmas. Narrated by Chet Williamson. Illus. by James Rice. (Running Time: 024 min.). (Night Before Christm Ser.). (ENG.). (J). (gr. k-3). 2000. 9.95 (978-1-56554-839-8(6)) Pelican.

Pennsylvania Election Law. 1988. 35.00 (AC-455) PA Bar Inst.

Pennsylvania Escheat Act. 1 cass. (Running Time: 1 hr.). 1983. 15.00 PA Bar Inst.

Pennsylvania Evidence. 1998. bk. 99.00 (ACS-2078); bk. 99.00 (ACS-2078) PA Bar Inst.
Approved by the Pennsylvania Supreme Court, the official Pennsylvania Rules of Evidence go into effect on October 1,1998. How will these new Rules affect your practice? What changes have been made to the substantive law of evidence? How do the Pennsylvania rules differ for the Federal rules?.

Pennsylvania Hazardous Sites Clean-Up Act. Read by John P. Krill, Jr. 1 cass. 1989. 20.00 (AL-65) PA Bar Inst.

Pennsylvania Human Relations Commission. 1 cass. (Running Time: 1 hr.). (Advocacy Before Administrative Agencies Ser.). 1985. 20.00 PA Bar Inst.

Pennsylvania Inheritance Tax. 1990. 45.00 (AC-560) PA Bar Inst.

Pennsylvania Land Recycling & Reclamation. 1997. bk. 99.00 (ACS-1370) PA Bar Inst.
The Environmental Quality Board, on June 17,1997, approved the final regulations to Act 2, the Pa. Land Recycling & Environmental Remediation Standards Act. In the two years that it has been in existence, Act 2 is credited with boosting the number of brownfields recycled, decreasing the obstacles to overcome & reducing the time it takes to get the job done.

Pennsylvania Legal Practice Course. 20 cass. 1991. 325.00 set. (AC-PLP-1991) PA Bar Inst.

Pennsylvania Limited Partnerships. 1990. 75.00 (AC-583) PA Bar Inst.

Pennsylvania Public Utility Law. 1990. 80.00 (AC-589) PA Bar Inst.

Pennsylvania Realty Transfer Taxes. 1987. bk. 80.00; 45.00 PA Bar Inst.

Pennsylvania Superfund Update. 1999. bk. 99.00 (ACS-2155) PA Bar Inst.
Designed to cover the latest developments in the Pennsylvania Superfund program & the Hazardous sites Clean-up Act. Legal & practical solutions are given for liability & government enforcement, response actions & settlements, & private actions.

Pennsylvania Takeover Act of Nineteen Ninety. 1990. 60.00 (AC-573) PA Bar Inst.

Pennsylvania Wage-Hour Law. Read by Richard C. Lengler. 1 cass. 1989. 20.00 (AL-78) PA Bar Inst.

Pennsylvania Wetlands Regulation. Read by Joel R. Burcat. 1 cass. 1990. 20.00 (AL-98) PA Bar Inst.

Pennsylvania Workers' Compensation Practice & Procedure. 1987. bk. 125.00 incl. book.; bk. 125.00; 50.00 cass. only.; 50.00 PA Bar Inst.

Penny. abr. ed. Joyce Meyer & Deborah Bedford. Read by Ellen Archer. (Running Time: 6 hrs.). (ENG.). 2007. 14.98 (978-1-59483-936-8(0)) Pub: Hachet Audio. Dist(s): HachBkGrp

Penny a Day. Lilian Harry. 2009. 84.95 (978-1-84559-998-0(5)); audio compact disk 89.95 (978-1-84559-999-7(3)) Pub: Soundings Ltd GBR. Dist(s): Ulverscroft US

Penny Changes the Day/Money Riddles. Steck-Vaughn Staff. (J). 1999. (978-0-7398-2440-5(6)) SteckVau.

***Penny for Your Thoughts.** 2010. audio compact disk (978-1-59171-283-1(1)) Falcon Picture.

Penny for Your Thoughts. Short Stories. Diane Ferlatte. Perf. by Diane Ferlatte. Perf. by Erik Pearson. (Running Time: 60 mins.). (YA). 2005. audio compact disk 15.00 (978-0-9760432-6-3(2)) D Ferlatte.
Upon sharing some of my personal stories at storytelling festivals, colleges, & similar venues, I have often been asked if those stories are on any of my recordings. Up to now the answer had always been no. Since so many people seemed interested, this CD is a result of those requests. These stories are from experiences in my life. They show the beauty of friendship, the character of courage, and how one's reactions to racial, cultural, & generational barriers or conflicts can completely transform the outcome & may even transform the participants. I didn't search out these stories or events - they simply occurred as part of my everyday living - but they all left a strong impression on me. They all contributed to the person I am today, & I think they also very much affected some of the others involved in these stories. When I think of these stories, two proverbs jump to mind: Talking with one another is loving one anotherA stranger is just a friend you haven't met yetI sincerely hope that these stories will be meaningful & perhaps even inspirational for you as they were for me.Diane Ferlatte.

Penny from Heaven. unabr. ed. Jennifer L. Holm. Read by Amber Sealey. 5 CDs. (Running Time: 5 hrs. 36 mins.). (J). (gr. 4-7). 2006. audio compact disk 45.00 (978-0-7393-3596-3(0), Listening Lib); 35.00 (978-0-7393-3595-6(2), Listening Lib) Pub: Random Audio Pubg. Dist(s): Random
It's 1953 and 11-year-old Penny dreams of a summer of butter pecan ice cream, swimming, and baseball. But nothing's that easy in Penny's family. For starters, she can't go swimming because her mother's afraid she'll catch polio at the pool. To make matters worse, her favorite uncle is living in a car. Her Nonny cries every time her father's name is mentioned. And the two sides of her family aren't speaking to each other! Inspired by Newbery Honor winner Jennifer Holm's own Italian American family, Penny from Heaven is a shining story about the everyday and the extraordinary, about a time in America's history, not all that long ago, when being Italian meant that you were the enemy. But most of all, it's a story about families - about the things that tear them apart and bring them together. And Holm tells it with all the richness and the layers, the love and the laughter of a Sunday dinner at Nonny's. So pull up a chair and enjoy the feast! Buon appetito!.

Penny from Heaven. unabr. ed. Jennifer L. Holm. Read by Amber Sealey. 5 CDs. (Running Time: 20160 sec.). (ENG.). (J). (gr. 5). 2006. audio compact disk 35.00 (978-0-7393-3111-8(6), Listening Lib) Pub: Random Audio Pubg. Dist(s): Random

Penny Hen see Let's Read Together

Penny Hen. Created by Kane Press. (Let's Read Together Ser.). 2005. audio compact disk 4.25 (978-1-57565-171-2(8)) Pub: Kane Pr. Dist(s): Lerner Pub

Penny Mining Stocks. Sam Parks. 1 cass. (Running Time: 1 hr. 10 min.). 11.95 (415) J Norton Pubs.

Penny Pollard in Print. unabr. ed. Robin Klein. Read by Rebecca Macauley. (Running Time: 4800 sec.). (Penny Pollard Ser.). (J). (gr. 3-8). 2005. audio compact disk 39.95 (978-1-74093-685-9(X)) Pub: Bolinda Pubng AUS. Dist(s): Bolinda Pub Inc

Penny Pollard's Diary. unabr. ed. Robin Klein. Read by Rebecca Macauley. 1 cass. (Running Time: 1 hr.). (Penny Pollard Ser.). (J). 2000. 18.00 (978-1-74030-103-9(X), 500223) Pub: Bolinda Pubng AUS. Dist(s): Bolinda Pub Inc

Penny Pollard's Diary. unabr. ed. Robin Klein. (Running Time: 1 hr.). (Penny Pollard Ser.). (J). 2004. audio compact disk 39.95 (978-1-74093-337-7(0)) Pub: Bolinda Pubng AUS. Dist(s): Bolinda Pub Inc

Penny Pollard's Letters. unabr. ed. Robin Klein. Read by Rebecca Macauley. 1 cass. (Running Time: 1 hr. 15 mins.). (Penny Pollard Ser.). (J). 2004. 18.00 (978-1-74030-150-3(1), 500535); audio compact disk 39.95 (978-1-74093-333-9(8)) Pub: Bolinda Pubng AUS. Dist(s): Bolinda Pub Inc

Penny Pollard's Passport. unabr. ed. Robin Klein. 1 cass. (Running Time: 1 hr. 45 mins.). 2002. (978-1-74030-593-8(0)) Bolinda Pubng AUS.

Penny Pollard's Passport. unabr. ed. Robin Klein. Read by Rebecca Macauley. (Running Time: 6300 sec.). (Penny Pollard Ser.). (J). (gr. 6). 2006. audio compact disk 43.95 (978-1-74093-791-7(0)) Pub: Bolinda Pubng AUS. Dist(s): Bolinda Pub Inc

Penny Pollard's Scrapbook. unabr. ed. Robin Klein. 2 Cass. (Running Time: 1 hr. 30 mins.). 2002. (978-1-74030-571-6(X)) Bolinda Pubng AUS.

Penny Town Justice. unabr. ed. A. L. McWilliams. Read by Maynard Villers. 6 cass. (Running Time: 8 hrs. 30 min.). 2001. 39.95 (978-1-55686-803-0(0)) Books in Motion.
Ex-army scout Lane Devens becomes a 19th century private investigator. Hired by businessmen to uncover a crooked land deal, Lane is taken into custody after his clients are found dead.

Penny's Fourth of July. Timothy Glass. Narrated by Allen Hite. (ENG.). (J). 2008. audio compact disk 14.95 (978-1-60031-031-7(1)) Spoken Books.

Penny's Pantry. Penny J. Stucki. 1 cass. (Running Time: 60 min.). 1989. 9.95 (978-1-877681-00-4(8)) Townsend Consulting.
Discusses economical food shopping. Features an interview with a mother of six who feeds her family for $100.00 a month.

Pennywhistle for Beginners. Excerpts. Bill Ochs. Read by Bill Ochs. 1 CD. (Running Time: 74 mins.). (J). 2004. audio compact disk 12.95 (978-0-9727516-1-2(0)) Pub: Pnnywhstlrs Pr. Dist(s): Bk Clearing Hse
CD includes spoken instruction, plus every tune and musical exercise in the book. Most tracks have guitar accompaniment. CD includes also two bonus tracks, the music for which can be found at www.pennywhistle.com.

Pennywhistle for Beginners Learn-to-Play Pennywhistle Set: Includes Clarke Meg D Pennywhistle in Clamshell Pack: Book, Whistle & Compact Disc. Excerpts. Bill Ochs. Instructed by Bill Ochs. Jim Keyes. 1 CD. (Running Time: 44 minutes). (J). 2004. audio compact disk 15.95 (978-0-9727516-3-6(7)) Pub: Pnnywhstlrs Pr. Dist(s): Bk Clearing Hse
CD includes spoken instruction, plus all tunes and musical exercises. Most tracks include guitar accompaniment. CD also includes two bonus tracks, the music for which can be found at www.pennywhistle.com.

Pennywhistle Learning Tape. Ryan J. Thomson. 1 cass. (Running Time: 60 min.). 1987. 11.95 (978-0-931877-12-4(1)) Captain Fiddle Pubns.
Instructional tape in traditional Pennywhistle playing for those with no experience.

Penrod, Set. Booth Tarkington. Read by Flo Gibson. 5 cass. (Running Time: 7 hrs. 30 min.). (J). 1990. 20.95 (978-1-55685-172-8(3)) Audio Bk Con.
The hilarious story of the escapades of twelve-year-old Penrod Schofield. His active imagination keeps him in hot water at home & at school.

Pensees see Treasury of French Prose

Pensees. Blaise Pascal. Read by William Sutherland. Tr. by H. F. Stewart. 8 CDs. (Running Time: 13 hrs.). 2001. audio compact disk 88.00 (2807) Blckstn Audio.
The book begins with an analysis of the difference between mathematical and intuitive thinking and continues the discussion, in later sections, by considering the value of skepticism, contradictions, feeling, memory and imagination.

Pensees. Blaise Pascal. Read by William Sutherland. Tr. by H. F. Stewart. (Running Time: 45000 sec.). 2008. audio compact disk 29.95 (978-1-4332-0459-3(2)) Blckstn Audio.

Pensees. unabr. ed. Blaise Pascal. Read by William Sutherland. Tr. by H. F. Stewart. 9 cass. (Running Time: 13 hrs.). 2001. 62.95 (978-0-7861-2047-5(9), 2807) Blckstn Audio.

Pensées. unabr. ed. Blaise Pascal & William Sutherland. Tr. by H. F. Stewart. (Running Time: 12 hrs. 5 mins.). 2008. audio compact disk 90.00 (978-0-7861-9698-2(X)) Blckstn Audio.

Penser Vite. unabr. ed. Robert A. Monroe. Read by Roland Simon. 1 cass. (Running Time: 30 min.). (Human Plus Ser.). (FRE.). 1993. 14.95 (978-1-56102-102-4(4)) Inter Indus.
Speed up thought processes at will.

Penseroso see Treasury of John Milton

Penseroso see Poetry of John Milton

Penseroso see Palgrave's Golden Treasury of English Poetry

Pension Benedict. 1 cass. (Running Time: 60 mins.). Dramatization. (Maitres du Mystere Ser.). (FRE.). 1996. 11.95 (1839-MA) Olivia & Hill.
Popular radio thriller, interpreted by France's best actors.

Pension Plan Investments: Confronting Today's Legal Issues. 11 cass. (Running Time: 15 hrs.). 1991. 175.00 (T7-9337) PLI.

Pension Plan Update after TEFRA. Contrib. by Leonard J. Witman. (Running Time: 4 hrs.). 1984. 70.00 incl. program handbook. NJ Inst CLE.
Covers such topics as: testing for top heavy states, top heavy group-key employees defined, aggregation tests, accelerated vesting, minimum benefit requirements.

Pension, Profit-Sharing, Welfare, & Other Compensation Plans. 13 cass. (Running Time: 19 hrs.). 1999. 395.00 Set; incl. study guide 1541p. (MD56) Am Law Inst.
Advanced course includes recent developments.

Pent up Anxieties Spill over into the Body: Volume 19, Vol. 20. Speeches. Bhagat Singh Thind. (Running Time: 60 mins.). (ENG., 2003. audio compact disk 12.00 (978-1-932630-21-3(X)) Pub: Dr Bhagat Sin. Dist(s): Baker Taylor

Pent up Anxieties Spill over into the Body: Volume 20, Vol. 20. Speeches. As told by Bhagat Singh Thind. (Running Time: 60 mins.). (ENG., 2003. 6.50 (978-1-932630-44-2(9)) Pub: Dr Bhagat Sin. Dist(s): Baker Taylor

Pentateuch on Cassette. Read by Robert Baram. 16 cass. (Running Time: 60 min. per cass.). 37.95 (978-0-8198-5845-0(5)) Pauline Bks.

***Pentatonic Soloing Strategies for Guitar: Modern Ideas for All Styles.** Erik Halbig. (Improv Ser.). (ENG., 2010. pap. bk. (978-0-7390-7096-3(7)) Alfred Pub.

Pentecost: Music of Taize. 1 cass. (Running Time: 60 min.). 9.95 (AA2480) Credence Commun.
The beautiful music of Taize you loved on Laudate is here sung & played by the ecumenical choir at Christ the King University Church in London.

Pentecost: Taize Chants with English Verses. 1 cass. (Running Time: 60 mins.). 1999. 9.95 (T9215) Liguori Pubns.
Songs include: "Psallite Deo," "Gloria Tibi Domine," "Eat This Bread" & more.

Pentecost-a Great Promise! 1985. (0211) Evang Sisterhood Mary.

Pentecostalism. Vincent M. Walsh. 1 cass. 1985. 4.00 Key of David.
Personal stories & examples told to promote a full understanding of the basic powers of the Renewal.

Pentecostalism in Catholic Church. Vincent M. Walsh. 1 cass. 1986. 4.00 Key of David.

Penthouse. unabr. collector's ed. Elleston Trevor. Read by Mary Woods. 7 cass. (Running Time: 10 hrs. 30 min.). 1987. 56.00 (978-0-7366-1159-6(2), 2084) Books on Tape.
At nine o'clock on a mild October night two men are shot in the lobby of Manhattan's luxury Park Tower. Minutes later, a police chief listens to a voice on the telephone from the penthouse. "I've jammed the elevators & stacked 40 pounds of explosives against the stairway door. Break it open & you'll blow this building right across Central Park." Tina St. Clair, who never had to fight for anything in her life, must fight for her life itself.

Penultimate Chance Saloon. Simon Brett & Simon Brett. Read by Simon Brett. 5 cass. (Running Time: 24600 sec.). 2007. 49.95 (978-0-7531-3675-1(9)); audio compact disk 64.95 (978-0-7531-2635-6(4)) Pub: ISIS Audio GBR. Dist(s): Ulverscroft US

Penultimate Peril. abr. ed. Lemony Snicket, pseud. Read by Tim Curry. (Series of Unfortunate Events Ser.: Bk. 12). (J). 2005. audio compact disk 25.95 (978-0-06-057949-4(8), HarperChildAud) HarperCollins Pubs.

Penultimate Peril. abr. ed. Lemony Snicket, pseud. Read by Tim Curry. (Series of Unfortunate Events Ser.: Bk. 12). (J). (gr. 5 up). 2005. 20.00 (978-0-06-057948-7(X), HarperChildAud) HarperCollins Pubs.

Penwyth Curse. unabr. ed. Catherine Coulter. Read by Anne Flosnik. 9 CDs. (Running Time: 10 hrs.). (Song Ser.: Vol. 6). 2002. audio compact disk 97.25 (978-1-59086-641-2(X), 159086641X, BriAudCD Unabrid); 82.25 (978-1-58788-897-7(1), 1587888971, Unabridge Lib Edns); 32.95 (978-1-58788-896-0(3), 1587888963, BAU); audio compact disk 38.95 (978-1-59086-640-5(1), 1590866401) Brilliance Audio.
Eighteen years old and four times a widow? This is the Penwyth Curse. Become acquainted with two sets of heroes and heroines as their stories overlap. History, romantic suspense, magic, and mayhem ensue.

Penwyth Curse. unabr. ed. Catherine Coulter. Read by Anne Flosnik. (Running Time: 10 hrs.). (Song Novels Ser.). 2004. 39.25 (978-1-59335-594-4(7), 1593355947, Brlnc Audio MP3 Lib) Brilliance Audio.

Penwyth Curse. unabr. ed. Catherine Coulter. Read by Anne Flosnik. (Running Time: 10 hrs.). (Song Novels Ser.). 2004. 39.25 (978-1-59710-567-5(8), 1597105678, BADLE); 24.95 (978-1-59710-566-8(X), 159710566X, BAD) Brilliance Audio.

Penwyth Curse. unabr. ed. Catherine Coulter. Read by Anne Flosnik. (Running Time: 10 hrs.). (Song Novels Ser.). 2004. 24.95 (978-1-59335-145-8(3), 1593351453) Soulmate Audio Bks.

***Peony: A Novel of China.** unabr. ed. Pearl S. Buck. Narrated by Kirsten Potter. (Running Time: 16 hrs. 0 mins. 0 sec.). (ENG.). 2011. audio compact disk 39.99 (978-1-59859-854-4(6), SpringWater) Oasis Audio.

Peony in Love. abr. ed. Lisa See. Read by Jodi Long. (Running Time: 21600 sec.). (ENG.). 2008. audio compact disk 14.99 (978-0-7393-2873-6(5), Random AudioBks) Pub: Random Audio Pubg. Dist(s): Random

Peony in Love. unabr. ed. Lisa See. Read by Janet K. Song. 9 CDs. (Running Time: 10 hrs. 30 mins.). 2007. audio compact disk 90.00 (978-1-4159-3934-5(9)); 90.00 (978-1-4159-4199-7(8)) Books on Tape.
For young Peony, betrothed to a suitor she has never met, these lyrics from The Peony Pavilion mirror her own longings. In the garden of the Chen Family Villa, a small theatrical troupe is performing scenes from this epic opera, a live spectacle few females have ever seen. Like the heroine in the drama, Peony is the cloistered daughter of a wealthy family, trapped like a good-luck cricket in a bamboo-and-lacquer cage. Though raised to be obedient, Peony has dreams of her own. Peony's mother is against her daughter's attending the production. But Peony's father assures his wife that proprieties will be maintained, and that the women will watch the opera from behind a screen. Yet even hidden from view, Peony catches sight of an elegant, handsome man - and is immediately overcome with emotion.

People: A Musical Celebration of Diversity. Perf. by Peabo Bryson et al. 1 cass., 1 CD. 1995. 10.98 (978-1-56896-115-6(4), 54150-4); audio compact disk 16.98 CD. (978-1-56896-116-3(2), CD54150-2) Lightyear Entrtnmnt.
Other performers include: Sounds of Blackness, Grover Washington, Jr. & Vanessa Williams. Features 11 original songs performed by major artists, including stars of the 4 most recent Disney soundtrack smashes!.

People & Activities Around the World. unabr. ed. University of Iowa, CEEDE Staff. 5 cass. (YA). 1986. 8.95 ea. Triumph Learn.
A cultural awareness program.

People & Activities Around the World: Complete English Set. unabr. ed. University of Iowa, CEEDE Staff. 1 cass. 1989. 70.00 incl. tchr's. guide, student text, filmstrip & CAI disk. (978-0-7836-0758-0(X), 8961) Triumph Learn.
English readings describing the work of people in various parts of the world.

People & Change: Cambodian Cassette Tape. unabr. ed. University of Iowa, CEEDE Staff. 1 cass. (CAM.). 1988. 8.95 (978-0-7836-0669-9(9), 8819) Triumph Learn.
Cambodian readings of everyday episodes in the life of one family. A problem solving program.

People & Change: Complete Vietnamese Set. unabr. ed. University of Iowa, CEEDE Staff. 1 cass. (VIE.). 1989. 59.00 incl. tchr's. guide, student text, CAI disk & activity masters. (978-0-7836-0743-6(1), 8939) Triumph Learn.
A problem solving program. Vietnamese readings of episodes in the life of one family.

People & Change: English Cassette Tape. unabr. ed. University of Iowa, CEEDE Staff. 1 cass. 1988. 8.95 (978-0-7836-0670-5(2), 8820) Triumph Learn.
English readings of everyday episodes in the life of one family. A problem solving program.

People & Change: Lao Cassette Tape. unabr. ed. University of Iowa, CEEDE Staff. 1 cass. (LAO.). 1988. 8.95 (978-0-7836-0671-2(0), 8821) Triumph Learn.
Lao readings of everyday episodes in the life of one family. A problem solving program.

People & Change: Spanish Cassette Tape. unabr. ed. University of Iowa, CEEDE Staff. 1 cass. (SPA.). 1988. 8.95 (978-0-7836-0672-9(9), 8822) Triumph Learn.
Spanish readings of everyday episodes in the life of one family. A problem solving program.

People & Change: Vietnamese Cassette Tape. unabr. ed. University of Iowa, CEEDE Staff. 1 cass. (VIE.). 1988. 8.95 (978-0-7836-0673-6(7), 8823) Triumph Learn.
Vietnamese readings of everyday episodes in the life of one family. A problem solving program.

People & Places. (Laubach Way to Reading Ser.). 1993. 12.00 (978-0-88336-940-1(0)) New Readers.

People & the Ballot. Joshua Kaplan. 2008. audio compact disk 29.99 (978-1-4361-7435-0(X)) Recorded Bks.

***People are Alike All Over.** 2010. audio compact disk (978-1-59171-225-1(4)) Falcon Picture.

People Are Idiots & I Can Prove It! The 10 Ways You Are Sabotaging Yourself & How You Can Overcome Them. unabr. ed. Larry Winget. 5 CDs. (Running Time: 6 hrs.). (ENG.). (gr. 8 up). 2008. audio compact disk 29.95 (978-0-14-314424-3(3), PengAudBks) Penguin Grp USA.

People Around You. Dahia Shabaka. (Living & Working Together Ser.). (J). (gr. k). 2000. 7.98 (978-1-58120-975-4(4)) Metro Teaching.

People at Work. unabr. ed. 3 cass. bk. 49.50 incl. student workbook, teacher's manual/Independent study supplement. (SEN215) J Norton Pubs.

People at Work: Listening/Communicative Skills/Vocabulary Building. Edgar Sather et al. 3 CDs. (gr. 9-12). 2005. pap. bk. & tchr. ed. 39.00 (978-0-86647-211-1(8)) Pro Lingua.

People at Work: Listening/Communicative Skills/Vocabulary Building. Edgar Sather et al. 3 CDs. (gr. 9-12). 2005. pap. bk. & stu. ed. 28.00 (978-0-86647-210-4(X)) Pro Lingua.

People at Work 3. Edgar Sather et al. 3 CDs. 2005. audio compact disk 20.00 (978-0-86647-209-8(6)) Pro Lingua.

People Code: A New Way to See Yourself, Your Relationships, & Life. Taylor Hartman. 2004. 10.95 (978-0-7435-4289-0(4)) Pub: S&S Audio. Dist(s): S and S Inc

People Could Fly: American Black Folktales. As told by Virginia Hamilton. (ENG.). (J). 2008. 59.99 (978-1-60514-911-0(X)) Find a World.

People Could Fly: American Black Folktales. unabr. ed. Virginia Hamilton. Read by Virginia Hamilton. 4 cass. (Running Time: 4 hrs.). 2005. 24.95 (978-0-9741711-7-3(4)); audio compact disk 39.95 (978-0-9741711-8-0(2)) Audio Bkshelf.

People for the Ethical Treatment of Animals' Ingrid Newkirk Shares Undercover Footage about Animals in Laboratories & the Animal Liberation Front. Hosted by Nancy Pearlman. 1 cass. (Running Time: 29 min.). 10.00 (1016) Educ Comm CA.

People Get Ready: Luke 3:1-18. Ed Young. 1996. 4.95 (978-0-7417-2087-0(6), 1087) Win Walk.

People Get Screwed All the Time: Protecting Yourself from Scams, Fraud, Identity Theft, Fine Print, & More. Robert Massi. Read by Todd McLaren. (Playaway Adult Nonfiction Ser.). 2008. 64.99 (978-1-60640-696-0(5)) Find a World.

People Get Screwed All the Time: Protecting Yourself from Scams, Fraud, Identity Theft, Fine Print, & More. unabr. ed. Robert Massi. Narrated by Todd McLaren. (Running Time: 10 hrs. 30 mins. 0 sec.). (ENG.). 2007. audio compact disk 34.99 (978-1-4001-0476-5(9)); audio compact disk 69.99 (978-1-4001-3476-2(5)) Pub: Tantor Media. Dist(s): IngramPubServ

People Get Screwed All the Time: Protecting Yourself from Scams, Fraud, Identity Theft, Fine Print, & More. unabr. ed. Robert Massi. Read by Todd McLaren. (Running Time: 10 hrs. 30 mins. 0 sec.). (ENG.). 2007. audio compact disk 24.99 (978-1-4001-5476-0(6)) Pub: Tantor Media. Dist(s): IngramPubServ

People Go to the Movies: The Cows of Dolo Ken Paye. Directed By Marvin Silverman. 1 cass. 1996. cass. & video 89.00 (72286) Phoenix Films.

People in a Process: Therapy As Concept & Experience. Read by Judith Hubback. 1 cass. (Running Time: 2 hrs.). 1986. 12.95 (978-0-7822-0095-9(8), 196) C G Jung IL.

People in High Places. 1 cass. (Running Time: 30 min.). 8.00 (C0060B090, HarperThor) HarpC GBR.

People in My Head: Concrete Poetry on the Psychology of Surviving the Game. 2008. audio compact disk (978-0-9642175-2-2(X)) N W Commun.

People in Our Neighborhood. Lyrics by Ron Hiller & Judy Hiller. 1 cass. (Running Time: 40 min.). (J). (ps-1). 1996. pap. bk. 10.95 (KIM 9144); pap. bk. 14.95 CD. (KIM 9144CD) Kimbo Educ.
Introduce children to community helpers & workers. Songs about nurses, doctors, computer programmers, astronauts, construction workers, politicians, teachers, athletes & more. Includes safety reminders & movement activities! Guide with lyrics. (Community Helpers, Singable Songs).

People in the News. Katherine De Jersey. 1 cass. 8.95 (511) Am Fed Astrologers.
Why public cares about one person & not the other.

People Like Us, No. 2. Roy Mallard. Read by Roy Mallard. 2 cass. (Running Time: 3 hrs.). 1998. 15.00 Set. (978-0-563-55825-5(3)) BBC WrldWd GBR.
Interviews offer a series of ground-breaking reports based around the working lives of ordinary people.

***People Like Us: Life with Rob Lacey.** Zondervan. (ENG.). 2011. 14.99 (978-0-310-41254-0(4)) Zondervan.

People Love to Buy. William H. Gove. 1 cass. (Running Time: 30 min.). 10.95 (13001) J Norton Pubs.
Selling is not talking someone into doing something he doesn't want to do. People love to buy. Selling is making it easy for people to do what they enjoy doing. Give deals in specifics & words that help make someone easier to buy from.

People Matter Most & Choices. Jack R. Christianson. 1 cass. 7.98 (978-1-55503-140-4(4), 06003672) Covenant Comms.
New stories, great spirit, for youth & adults.

People Need the Lord. Contrib. by Steve Green. (Mastertrax Ser.). 2006. audio compact disk 9.98 (978-5-558-01637-6(X)) Pt of Grace Ent.

People Need the Lord. Contrib. by Steve Green. (Ultimate Tracks (Word Tracks) Ser.). 2006. audio compact disk 8.98 (978-5-558-26936-9(7), Word Music) Word Enter.

People of Darkness. Tony Hillerman. Read by Nelson Runger. 5 cass. (Running Time: 6 hrs. 20 min.). (Joe Leaphorn & Jim Chee Novel Ser.). 1993. 44.20 Set. (978-1-56544-037-1(4), 250034); Rental 7.80 30 day rental Set. (250034) Literate Ear.
B.J. Vines is missing a box with keepsakes important only to him. He is also one of the richest men in New Mexico. Because he befriended the People of Darkness, a peyote-eating Indian sect, Sergeant Jim Chee is called in on the case.

People of Darkness. unabr. ed. Tony Hillerman. Read by Jonathan Marosz. 6 cass. (Running Time: 6 hrs.). (Joe Leaphorn & Jim Chee Novel Ser.). 1994. 48.00 (978-0-7366-2725-2(1), 3455) Books on Tape.
Jim Chee learns about "People of Darkness" when cult Indians turn up dead.

People of Darkness. unabr. ed. Tony Hillerman. Narrated by George Guidall. 5 cass. (Running Time: 7 hrs.). (Joe Leaphorn & Jim Chee Novel Ser.). 1990. 44.00 (978-1-55690-405-9(3), 90087E7) Recorded Bks.
Sergeant Jim Chee knew one thing for sure - someone was trying to kill him. What he couldn't figure out was why.

People of Destiny. Speeches. Joel Osteen. 4 audio cass. (J). 2001. 16.00 (978-1-931877-08-4(4)); audio compact disk 16.00 (978-1-931877-25-1(4), JCS004) J Osteen.

People of Heaven. unabr. ed. Beverley Harper. Read by Jerome Pride. 11 cass. (Running Time: 16 hrs. 10 mins.). 2004. 88.00 (978-1-74030-110-7(2), 500218) Pub: Bolinda Pubng AUS. Dist(s): Lndmrk Audiobks

People of Israel. 10.00 (RME105) Esstee Audios.

People of Lavender Court. unabr. ed. Kathleen Dayus. Read by Diana Bishop. 8 cass. (Running Time: 8 hrs.). 2000. 69.95 (978-0-7531-0685-3(X), 991003) Pub: ISIS Audio GBR. Dist(s): Ulverscroft US
Aggie, orphaned at ten, whose life is to see violent changes of fortune; Florrie, the good-hearted neighbor whose reckless daughter throws two households into scandalous uproar; & Annie, who manages to carve out a life of some dignity. Frank & unsentimental, Kathleen /Dayus takes us into the slums of turn-of-the-century Birmingham, a harsh world made bearable by kindness, courage & laughter.

People of Lavender Court. unabr. ed. Kathleen Dayus. Read by Diana Bishop. 8 CDs. (Running Time: 15 hrs.). 2001. audio compact disk 89.95 (978-0-7531-0797-3(X), 0797-X) Pub: ISIS Audio GBR. Dist(s): ISIS Pub
Aggie, orphaned at ten, whose life is to see violent changes of fortune; Florrie, the good-hearted neighbor whose feckless daughter throws two households into scandalous uproar & Annie, who manages to carve out a life of some dignity. Frank & unsentimental, Kathleen Dayus takes us into the slums of turn-of-the-century Birmingham - a harsh world made bearable by kindness, courage & laughter.

People of Preparation. Elbert Willis. 1 cass. (Victory of Surrender Ser.: Vol. 2). 4.00 Fill the Gap.

People of Presence. Richard D. Dobbins. 4 cass. (Running Time: 2 hrs.). 1997. 19.95 Set. (978-1-890329-57-0(6)) Totally Alive.
Ministry tapes designed to help you tap into your full God-given potential...expressing His life.

People of Promise: How to Be an Authentic Believer. unabr. ed. Dan Lupton. 3 cass. (Running Time: 2 hrs.). (Fifty Day Spiritual Adventure 1999 Ser.). 13.00 Set. (978-1-57849-112-4(6)) Mainstay Church.

People of Refuge. Charles R. Swindoll. 1 cass. 1985. 10.99 (978-2-01-019873-1(5)) Nelson.

People of Sparks. Jeanne DuPrau. 4 cass. (Running Time: 6 hrs. 30 mins.). (Books of Ember Ser.: Bk. 2). (J). (gr. 5 up). 2004. 36.00 (978-1-4000-8489-0(X), Listening Lib); audio compact disk 46.75 (978-1-4000-8990-1(5), Listening Lib) Pub: Random Audio Pubg. Dist(s): NetLibrary CO

People of Sparks. unabr. ed. Jeanne DuPrau. Read by Wendy Dillon. 7 CDs. (Running Time: 28500 sec.). (Books of Ember Ser.: Bk. 2). (ENG.). (J). (gr. 5-8). 2006. audio compact disk 30.00 (978-0-7393-3169-9(8), Listening Lib) Pub: Random Audio Pubg. Dist(s): Random

People of the Abyss. Jack London. Read by Anais 9000. 2008. 27.95 (978-1-60112-145-5(8)) Babblebooks.

People of the Black Circle. Robert E. Howard. 2008. audio compact disk 29.95 (978-1-897304-08-2(0)) Pub: AudioRealms CN CAN. Dist(s): Natl Bk Netwk

People of the Book. Geraldine Brooks. Contrib. by Edwina Wren. (Running Time: 14 hrs.). (ENG.). (gr. 12 up). 2008. audio compact disk 39.95 (978-0-14-314298-0(4), PengAudBks) Penguin Grp USA.

People of the Book. unabr. ed. Geraldine Brooks. Read by Edwina Wren. 10 cass. (Running Time: 14 hrs.). 2008. 79.95 (978-1-4332-1268-0(4)); audio compact disk 29.95 (978-1-4332-1270-3(6)); audio compact disk & audio compact disk 99.00 (978-1-4332-1269-7(2)) Blckstn Audio.

People of the Dark. Robert E. Howard. (Running Time: 5 mins.). 2009. audio compact disk 29.95 (978-1-897304-13-6(7)) Dorch Pub Co.

People of the Deer. unabr. ed. Farley Mowat. Read by Wolfram Kandinsky. 8 cass. (Running Time: 12 hrs.). 1994. 64.00 (978-0-7366-2848-8(7), 3556) Books on Tape.
Two summers spent in the barrens west of Hudson's Bay with the Ihalmiut.

People of the Lie Vol. 1: Toward a Psychology of Evil. M. Scott Peck. 2004. 7.95 (978-0-7435-4168-8(5)) Pub: S&S Audio. Dist(s): S and S Inc

People of the Lie Vol. 2: The Hope for Healing Human Evil. M. Scott Peck. 2004. 7.95 (978-0-7435-4170-1(7)) Pub: S&S Audio. Dist(s): S and S Inc

People of the lie vol. 3 possession & group Evil: Possession & Group Evil. M. Scott Peck. 2004. 7.95 (978-0-7435-4171-8(5)) Pub: S&S Audio. Dist(s): S and S Inc

***People of the Longhouse.** unabr. ed. W. Michael Gear & Kathleen O'Neal Gear. (Running Time: 10 hrs. 0 mins.). 2010. 16.99 (978-1-4001-8813-0(X)); 34.99 (978-1-4001-9813-9(5)) Tantor Media.

***People of the Longhouse.** unabr. ed. W. Michael Gear & Kathleen O'Neal Gear. Narrated by Joshua Swanson. (Running Time: 12 hrs. 0 mins. 0 sec.). (ENG.). 2010. 24.99 (978-1-4001-6813-2(9)); audio compact disk 34.99 (978-1-4001-1813-7(1)); audio compact disk 83.99 (978-1-4001-4813-4(8)) Pub: Tantor Media. Dist(s): IngramPubServ

People of the Whale. unabr. ed. Linda Hogan. Narrated by Stefan Rundicki. 1 MP3-CD. (Running Time: 10 hrs. 30 mins.). 2008. 29.95 (978-1-4332-4431-5(4)) Blckstn Audio.

People of the Whale. unabr. ed. Linda Hogan. Narrated by Stefan Rudnicki. (Running Time: 9.5 hrs. 0 mins.). 2008. cass. & cass. 29.95 (978-1-4332-4429-2(2)); cass. & audio compact disk 29.95 (978-1-4332-4430-8(6)) Blckstn Audio.

People of the Whale. unabr. ed. Linda Hogan. Narrated by Stefan Rundicki. 9 CDs. (Running Time: 10 hrs. 30 mins.). 2008. audio compact disk 80.00 (978-1-4332-4428-5(4)) Blckstn Audio.

People of the Whale. unabr. ed. Linda Hogan & Stefan Rundicki. (Running Time: 9.5 hrs. NaN mins.). 2008. 59.95 (978-1-4332-4427-8(6)) Blckstn Audio.

People of Vision. Speeches. Joel Osteen. 1 cass. (Running Time: 30 Mins.). 2001. 6.00 (978-1-59349-097-3(6), JA0097) J Osteen.

People, Places & Change. Holt, Rinehart and Winston Staff. 2001. audio compact disk 204.80 (978-0-03-054899-4(3)) Holt McDoug.

People, Places & Change. 3rd ed. Holt, Rinehart and Winston Staff. (SPA.). 2002. audio compact disk 208.73 (978-0-03-067166-1(3)) Holt McDoug.
Watch the culture, land, and life of different regions come alive with student interviews, absorbing visuals, and active-learning strategies. Your students will get to know the people and places of the world in a way that is relevant to their own lives and experiences.

People, Places & Change. 3rd ed. Holt, Rinehart and Winston Staff. 2002. audio compact disk 208.73 (978-0-03-068171-4(5)) Holt McDoug.

People, Places & Change, Set. 3rd ed. Helgren. 2003. audio compact disk 598.33 (978-0-03-035907-1(4)) Holt McDoug.

People, Places & Change: Audio CD Program. 5th ed. Holt, Rinehart and Winston Staff. (SPA.). 2005. audio compact disk 208.73 (978-0-03-037468-5(5)) Holt McDoug.

People, Places & Change: Audio CD Summaries. 5th ed. Holt, Rinehart and Winston Staff. (SPA.). 2005. audio compact disk 212.93 (978-0-03-038464-6(8)); audio compact disk 212.93 (978-0-03-038471-4(0)) Holt McDoug.

People, Places & Things (audio, text, illustrations, & cover with player Included) Judy Litman. Ed. by Judy Litman. (ENG., 2009. 2.99 (978-0-9672800-0-4(1)) J Litman Pubn.

People, Places, & Things 1: Audio CD. Lin Lougheed. 2005. audio compact disk 39.95 (978-0-19-430233-3(4)) OUP.

People, Places, & Things 2: Audio CD. Lin Lougheed. 2006. audio compact disk 39.95 (978-0-19-430234-0(2)) OUP.

People, Places, & Things 3: Audio CD. Lin Lougheed. 2006. audio compact disk 39.95 (978-0-19-430235-7(0)) OUP.

People Problems: Neh. 4:1-9. Ed Young. 1990. 4.95 (978-0-7417-1808-2(1), 808) Win Walk.

People Skills, Set. Abe Wagner. 6 cass. (Running Time: 55 min. per cass.). 39.95 (978-0-926632-03-5(5)) A Wagner & Assocs.
Discusses how to understand yourself & others, how to communicate & argues that recognition is the best motivation.

***People Speak: American Voices, Some Famous, Some Littl.** unabr. ed. Howard Zinn. Read by James Earl Jones. (ENG.). 2004. (978-0-06-081335-2(0), Harper Audio) HarperCollins Pubs.

People Speak: American Voices, Some Famous, Some Little Known, from Columbus to the Present. unabr. ed. Howard Zinn. Read by James Earl Jones. 2004. audio compact disk 19.95 (978-0-06-058983-7(3)) HarperCollins Pubs.

People That Time Forgot. Edgar Rice Burroughs. Read by Brian Emerson. 3 cass. (Running Time: 4 hrs. 30 min.). 2000. 23.95 (2395) Blckstn Audio.
In uncharted Caprona, a continent lost from the map of the Earth, where time has stopped & all the primeval creatures of long-gone ages still prowl, Bowen Tyler is lost. To find Tyler, Thomas Billigs travels across the world to Caprona, with all the weaponry the modern world afforded.

People That Time Forgot. Edgar Rice Burroughs. (Running Time: 4 mins.). 2009. audio compact disk 35.95 (978-1-897304-34-1(X)) Dorch Pub Co.

***People that Time Forgot.** Edgar Rice Burroughs. (Running Time: 4 mins.). 2009. 19.95 (978-1-897331-21-7(5), AudioRealms) Dorch Pub Co.

People That Time Forgot. unabr. ed. Edgar Rice Burroughs. Read by Brian Emerson. 3 cass. (Running Time: 1 hr. 30 min. per cass.). 1999. 23.95 Set. (978-0-7861-1564-8(5)) Blckstn Audio.
In uncharted Caprona, a continent lost from the map of the Earth, where Time has stopped & all the primeval creatures of long-gone ages still prowl, Bowen Tyler is lost.

People vs. Abe Latham, Colored see Erskine Caldwell

People vs. Kirk. unabr. collector's ed. Robert Traver. Read by John MacDonald. 9 cass. (Running Time: 9 hrs.). 1985. 54.00 (978-0-7366-0734-6(X), 1691) Books on Tape.
Set in rural Michigan, this tale of a love triangle resolves its tensions in mortal violence.

People Who Walk in Darkness. unabr. ed. Stuart M. Kaminsky. Narrated by Daniel Oreskes. 7 CDs. (Running Time: 7 hrs. 45 mins.). 2008. 49.95 (978-0-7927-5531-9(6), Chivers Sound Lib); audio compact disk 79.95 (978-0-7927-5442-8(5), Chivers Sound Lib) AudioGO.
Inspector Rostnikov is a Russian bear of a man, an honest policeman in a very dishonest post-Soviet Russia. Known as "The Washtub," Rostnikov is one of the most engaging and relevant characters in crime fiction, a sharp and caring policeman as well as the perfect tour guide to a changing (that is, disintegrating) Russia. Surviving pogroms and politburos, he has solved crimes, mostly in spite of the powers that rule his world. In The People Who Walk in Darkness, Rostnikov travels to Siberia to investigate a murder at a diamond mine, where he discovers an old secret - and an even older personal problem. His compatriots head to Kiev on a trail of smuggled diamonds and kidnapped guest workers, and what they discover leads them to a vast conspiracy that not only has international repercussions but threatens them on a very personal level.

People Will Say We're in Love (from Oklahoma) - ShowTrax. Arranged by Kirby Shaw. 1 CD. (Running Time: 5 mins.). 2000. audio compact disk 19.95 (08742191) H Leonard.
This charming duet from the Rogers & Hammerstein classic in a medium swing setting for vocal jazz groups.

People with One Heart. Michael Pinder. 1996. audio compact disk (978-1-888057-05-8(X)) One Step Recs.

People with One Heart. Narrated by Mike Pinder. Music by Mike Pinder. 1 cass. (J). 9.98; audio compact disk 15.98 CD. One Step Recs.

People with One Heart: Stories from Around the World for the Child Within Us All. Mike Pinder. 1 cass. (J). 1996. (978-1-888057-01-0(7)) One Step Recs.
Mike Pinder, singer-songwriter of the Moody Blues narrates seven uplifting & imaginative stories for children over a musical atmosphere created by Mike.

People With Special Needs: Love's Finest Hour: John 9:1-3, 1022. Ed Young. 1994. 4.95 (978-0-7417-2022-1(1)) Win Walk.

People Work in Our Community Audio CD. Adapted by Benchmark Education Company Staff. Based on a work by Katherine Scraper. (Early Explorers Set C Ser.). (J). (gr. 1). 2008. audio compact disk 10.00 (978-1-60437-532-9(9)) Benchmark Educ.

People, Yes, Set. abr. ed. Carl Sandburg. Read by Carl Sandburg. 2 cass. 1984. 19.95 (978-0-694-50383-4(5), SWC 2023) HarperCollins Pubs.

People You Meet. 2 cass. (Running Time: 3 hrs.). 19.50 (SEN152) J Norton Pubs.

People's Act of Love. James Meek. Read by Gordon Griffin. (Running Time: 52200 sec.). 2005. audio compact disk 39.99 (978-1-4193-6548-5(7)) Recorded Bks.

Peoples & Cultures of the World, Vol. I-II. Instructed by Edward Fischer. 12 cass. (Running Time: 12 hrs.). bk. 54.95 (978-1-56585-917-3(0), 4617) Teaching Co.

Peoples & Cultures of the World, Vol. I-II. Instructed by Edward Fischer. 12 CDs. (Running Time: 12 hrs.). 2004. bk. 69.95 (978-1-56585-919-7(7), 4617) Teaching Co.

Peoples & Empires: A Short History of European Migration, Exploration, & Conquest, from Greece to the Present. Anthony Pagden. Narrated by Robert O'Keefe. 5 cass. (Running Time: 6 hrs. 30 mins.). 49.00 (978-1-4025-1360-2(7)) Recorded Bks.

People's Democratic Dictatorship. Mao Tse-Tung. Anno. by Li Tien-Yi. 1 cass. 1951. 8.95 incl. suppl. materials. (978-0-88710-053-6(8)) Yale Far Eastern Pubns.

***People's History of the United States.** abr. ed. Howard Zinn. Read by Matt Damon. (ENG.). 2004. (978-0-06-075414-3(1), Harper Audio) HarperCollins Pubs.

***People's History of the United States.** abr. ed. Howard Zinn. Read by Matt Damon. (ENG.). 2004. (978-0-06-081336-9(9), Harper Audio) HarperCollins Pubs.

***People's History of the United States.** unabr. ed. Howard Zinn. Read by Jeff Zinn. (ENG.). 2009. (978-0-06-196924-9(9), Harper Audio) HarperCollins Pubs.

People's History of the United States: A Lecture at Reed College, Set. abr. ed. Howard Zinn. 2 CDs. (Running Time: 060 min.). (AK Press Audio Ser.). (ENG.). 1998. audio compact disk 20.00 (978-1-873176-95-5(3)) Pub: AK Pr GBR. Dist(s): Consort Bk Sales

People's History of the United States: Highlights from the Twentieth Century. abr. ed. Howard Zinn. Read by Matt Damon. 4 cass. (Running Time: 6 hrs.). 2003. audio compact disk 29.95 (978-0-06-053006-8(5)) HarperCollins Pubs.

***People's History of the United States: 1492 to Present.** unabr. ed. Howard Zinn. Read by Jeff Zinn. (ENG.). 2009. (978-0-06-196835-8(8), Harper Audio) HarperCollins Pubs.

People's History Project 1: Collected Lectures of Howard Zinn. Howard Zinn. (AK Press Audio Ser.). (ENG., 2004. audio compact disk 45.00 (978-1-902593-95-1(2)) Pub: AK Pr GBR. Dist(s): Consort Bk Sales

***people's Train.** Tom Keneally. Read by David Tredinnick. (Running Time: 17 hrs.). 2010. 114.99 (978-1-74214-604-1(X), 9781742146041) Pub: Bolinda Pubng AUS. Dist(s): Bolinda Pub Inc

people's Train. unabr. ed. Tom Keneally. Read by David Tredinnick. (Running Time: 17 hrs.). 2009. audio compact disk 118.95 (978-1-74214-390-3(3), 9781742143903) Pub: Bolinda Pubng AUS. Dist(s): Bolinda Pub Inc

Peopleware Productive Projects & Teams. unabr. ed. Tom DeMarco & Timothy Lister. Read by Tom Scott. 4 cass. (Running Time: 4 hrs. 2 min.). 1993. 32.00 set. (978-1-884387-00-5(4)) Tech Bks-On-Tape.
Unabridged reading of Peopleware.

PEP Financial Breakthrough: Beyond the First Strike. Charles Moore. 2010. 19.99 (978-0-914391-37-1(2)) Comm People Pr.

Pepins & Their Problems. Polly Horvath. Read by Julie Halston. 4 cass. 2004. 23.00 (978-1-4000-9073-0(3), Listening Lib) Random Audio Pubg.

Pepins & Their Problems. Polly Horvath. Read by Julie Halston. 6 cds. (J). 2004. audio compact disk 30.00 (978-1-4000-9490-5(9), Listening Lib) Random Audio Pubg.

Pepita Jimenez. Juan Valera. Read by Laura García. (Running Time: 3 hrs.). 2001. 16.95 (978-1-60083-177-5(X), Audiofy Corp) Iofy Corp.

Pepita Jimenez. abr. ed. Juan Valera. Read by Laura García. 3 CDs. (SPA.). 2001. audio compact disk 17.00 (978-958-9494-20-2(X)) YoYoMusic.

Peppe the Lamplighter. unabr. ed. Elisa Bartone. 1 cass. (Running Time: 11 min.). (J). (gr. k-4). 1994. pap. bk. 16.90 (978-0-8045-6829-6(4), 6829) Spoken Arts.
A job as a lamplighter was not what his father had dreamed of for Peppe. One night, with his youngest daughter missing in the dark, lamp lighting becomes "the best job in America".

Pepper. (J). Pepper Jelly.

***Pepper: A Snowy Search.** Liam O'Donnell. Illus. by Cathy Diefendorf. (Pet Tales Ser.). (ENG.). (J). 2009. pap. bk. 12.95 (978-1-59249-561-0(3)) Soundprints.

Pepper Jelly. (J). Pepper Jelly.

***Peppermint-Filled PiÃ±atas: Breaking Through Tolerance & Embracing Love.** unabr. ed. Eric Michael Bryant. (Running Time: 5 hrs. 19 mins. 0 sec.). (ENG.). 2008. 12.99 (978-0-310-30932-1(8)) Zondervan.

Peppermint Goose; Beano: Moon-Star Records. Sandi Johnson & Flora Fefie. Narrated by Lynette Louise & Van Buchanan. 1 CD. (J). (ps-6). 1996. audio compact disk 12.99 (978-1-929063-26-0(1), 126) Moons & Stars.
Story 1: Two geese visit a sick friend in the hospital. Story 2: A jumping bean creates adventures back to fantasy land. Includes Beano song.

Peppermint Pig. unabr. ed. Nina Bawden. Read by Carole Boyd. 3 cass. (Running Time: 4 hrs., 30 min.). (J). (gr. 1-8). 1999. 30.00 (LL 3067, Chivers Child Audio) AudioGO.

Peppermint Pig. unabr. ed. Nina Bawden. Read by Carole Boyd. 3 cass. (J). 1994. 23.98 Set. (978-0-8072-7283-1(3), LL 3067, Listening Lib) Random Audio Pubg.
When Poll & her mother moved out to the country at the turn of the century, life became much more exciting. There was the butcher shop where Granny Greengrass had her finger chopped off, fascinating gypsies & lots of haunted places! But best of all there was Johnnie, the baby peppermint pig! And when Johnnie grew up, he became a very special pig whose antics made him the talk of the town.

Peppermint Wings. Linda Arnold. 1 cass. (Running Time: 38 min.). (J). (ps-3). 1990. 9.98 Incl. lyrics. (978-1-889212-02-9(4), CAAR3) Ariel Recs.
Original children's songs composed & performed by Linda Arnold & a children's chorus.

Peppermint Wings. Perf. by Linda Arnold. 1 cass. (J). (ps-7). 9.98 (2184) MFLP CA.
Linda's heartwarming tunes & fresh, effervescent voice connect us with the innocence of childhood & its simple joys. Songs include: "Mr. Wizard Lizard," "I Am a Pizza," "Let's Play," "Treehouse," & many more.

Peppermint Wings. Perf. by Linda Arnold. 1 cass. (J). 10.98 (978-1-57471-450-0(3), YM123-CD) Youngheart Mus.
Songs include: "Monster Day"; "Mr. Wizard"; "I Am a Pizza"; "Please Please Hercules"; "Let's Play"; "Pasta"; "Treehouse"; "Yam Jam"; "Read a Book"; "Hello"; "Teddy Bear King"; "Peppermint Wings"; "I Wish I Was Magic" & more.

Peppermint Wings: Magical Songs for Children. Linda Arnold. Arranged by John Lee Sanders. Illus. by Catharine Gallagher. 1 cass. (J). 1990. audio compact disk 13.98 (978-1-57471-454-8(6), YM123-CD) Youngheart Mus.

Peppermints in the Parlor. unabr. ed. Barbara Brooks Wallace. Read by Angela Lansbury. 3 cass. (Running Time: 5 hrs.). 2000. 22.00 (Random AudioBks) Random Audio Pubg.
Emily Luccock is looking forward to living at Sugar Hill Hall. She remembers her aunt & uncle's grand old mansion well but this time things are different. Her aunt's once bright & lively home is now dead with silence. Evil lurks in every corner & the dark, shadowed walls watch & whisper late at night. Emily is desperate to uncover the truth about what is happening at Sugar Hill Hall but time is running out & she must find a way to save the people & home she cares so much about.

Peppermints in the Parlor. unabr. ed. Barbara Brooks Wallace. Read by Angela Lansbury. 3 cass. (Running Time: 5 hrs. 6 mins.). (J). (gr. 3-7). 2004. 30.00 (978-0-8072-8784-2(9), YA267CX, Listening Lib) Random Audio Pubg.
Emily Luccock is looking forward to living at Sugar Hill Hall. She remembers her aunt & uncle's grand old mansion well. But this time things are different. Her aunt's once bright & lively home is now dead with silence. Evil lurks in every corner & the dark, shadowed walls watch & whisper late at night.

Peppermints in the Parlor. unabr. ed. Barbara Brooks Wallace. Read by Angela Lansbury. 3 vols. (Running Time: 5 hrs. 6 mins.). (J). (gr. 3-7). 2004. pap. bk. 36.00 (978-0-8072-8785-9(7), YA267SP, Listening Lib) Random Audio Pubg.

Pepys' Diary. abr. ed. Samuel Pepys. Read by Kenneth Branagh. (Running Time: 30600 sec.). (ENG.). 2006. audio compact disk 29.95 (978-1-59887-026-8(2), 1598870262, HighBridge Classics) Pub: HighBridge. Dist(s): Workman Pub

Pequeno Faro Rojo Y el Gran Puente Gris. Tr. of Little Red Lighthouse, the. (SPA.). 2004. 8.95 (978-0-7882-0262-9(6)) Weston Woods.

Pequeno Vals Vienes see Poesia y Drama de Garcia Lorca

Pera Pera. 1 cass. (Running Time: 1 hr.). (Yoroshiku Ser.: Stages 3 and 4). (JPN.). (YA). (gr. 9-12). EducServs AUS.

Perceiving the Arts. 6th ed. Dennis J. Sporre. 2002. 12.97 (978-0-13-022556-6(8), Prentice Hall) P-H.

Percepcion. Carlos Gonzalez. 1 cass. (Running Time: 40 mins). (SPA.). 2004. audio compact disk 15.00 (978-1-56491-104-9(7)) Imagine Pubs.

Perception, Dispassion & Freedom. Swami Amar Jyoti. 1 cass. 1989. 9.95 (K-115) Truth Consciousness.
Why do we all perceive differently? Mutual freedom to be ourselves. Ingredients for detachment. A higher, wiser view of life.

Perceptual Motor Activities: Actividades para la Percepcion Motor. Georgiana Stewart. 1 cass. (Running Time: 35 min.). (SPA & ENG.). (J). (ps-3). 2001. pap. bk. 10.95 (KMS 9078C) Kimbo Educ.
Develop skills using multicultural rhythm instruments. Side A - English translation. Side B - Spanish narration. Manual in English with narration script in Spanish.

Perch Hill: A New Life. unabr. ed. Adam Nicolson. Read by Raymond Sawyer. 8 cass. (Running Time: 12 hrs.). 2000. 69.95 (978-0-7531-0747-8(3), 000216) Pub: ISIS Audio GBR. Dist(s): Ulverscroft US
Without knowing one end of a hay baler from the other, the author, fed up with London & with life, escapes with his family to a run-down farm in the Sussex Weald. Looking for Arcadia, but finding a mixture of intense beauty & chaos, he struggles with bloody-minded sheep & his neighbors before eventually arriving at some sort of equilibrium.

***Perchance to Dream.** 2010. audio compact disk (978-1-59171-233-6(5)) Falcon Picture.

Perchance to Dream. Chandler & Parker. Read by Elliott Gould. 2 cass. (Running Time: 3 hrs.). 2001. 18.00 (978-1-59040-163-7(8), Phoenix Audio) Pub: Amer Intl Pub. Dist(s): PerseuPGW

Perchance to Dream. Gilbert Highet. Read by Gilbert Highet. 1 cass. (Running Time: 30 min.). 11.95 (23317-A) J Norton Pubs.

Perchance to Dream. Sally Malcolm. 2009. audio compact disk 15.95 (978-1-84435-347-7(8)) Pub: Big Finish GBR. Dist(s): Natl Bk Netwk

Perchance to Dream. abr. ed. Robert B. Parker. Perf. by Elliott Gould. 2 cass. (Running Time: 3 hrs.). 2004. 18.00 (978-1-59007-209-7(X)) Pub: New Millenn Enter. Dist(s): PerseuPGW

Perchance to Dream. abr. ed. Robert B. Parker. Read by Elliott Gould. 3 CDs. (Running Time: 3 hrs.). 2004. audio compact disk 24.95 (978-1-59007-554-8(4)) Pub: New Millenn Enter. Dist(s): PerseuPGW

Perchance to Dream. unabr. ed. Robert B. Parker. Read by Jonathan Marosz. 5 cass. (Running Time: 5 hrs.). 1994. 30.00 (978-0-7366-2694-1(8), 3428) Books on Tape.
A Philip Marlowe thriller & sequel to Raymond Chandler's The Big Sleep, written by the creator of Spenser.

Percival Keene. unabr. ed. Frederick Marryat. Read by William Sutherland. 10 cass. (Running Time: 15 hrs.). 2000. 69.95 (978-0-7861-1851-9(2), 2650) Blckstn Audio.
The adventures of the mischievous young midshipman. Percival Keene, the son of a Royal Marine & a lowborn shopkeeper, take place on board HMS Calliope, one of the great men-of-war in Nelson's fleet. On his first cruise, Keene learns that the demanding Captain Delmar, a member of the wealthy & titled De Versely family, is actually his natural father, but refuses to acknowledge him. As Keene sets about to win his father's love & acceptance, he survives a shipwreck, captured by murderous pirates, duels of honor with fellow officers & battles against the French.

***Percival Keene.** unabr. ed. Frederick Marryat. Read by William Sutherland. (Running Time: 14 hrs. 5 mins.). (ENG.). 2011. 29.95 (978-1-4417-8498-8(5)); audio compact disk 118.00 (978-1-4417-8496-4(9)) Blckstn Audio.

***Percival's Planet: A Novel.** unabr. ed. Michael Byers. Narrated by William Dufris. (Running Time: 17 hrs. 30 mins. 0 sec.). (ENG.). 2010. audio compact disk 83.99 (978-1-4001-4841-7(3)) Pub: Tantor Media. Dist(s): IngramPubServ

***Percival¿s Planet: A Novel.** unabr. ed. Michael Byers. (Running Time: 14 hrs. 0 mins.). 2010. 19.99 (978-1-4001-8841-3(5)) Tantor Media.

***Percival¿s Planet: A Novel.** unabr. ed. Michael Byers. Narrated by William Dufris. (Running Time: 17 hrs. 30 mins. 0 sec.). (ENG.). 2010. 29.99 (978-1-4001-6841-5(4)); audio compact disk 39.99 (978-1-4001-1841-0(7)) Pub: Tantor Media. Dist(s): IngramPubServ

Percussion. Robert W. Smith et al. (Band Expressions Ser.). 2005. spiral bd. 29.95 (978-0-7579-4053-8(6)) Alfred Pub.

Percussion Set. Created by Mel Bay Publications Inc. 2006. 39.95 (978-3-8024-0531-0(5)) Mel Bay.

***Percy Jackson & the Olympians.** Rick Riordan. (Percy Jackson & the Olympians Ser.: Bks. 1-5). (J). 2010. audio compact disk, audio compact disk, audio compact disk 174.99 (978-0-7393-5268-7(7), Listening Lib) Pub: Random Audio Pubg. Dist(s): Random

***Percy Jackson & the Olympians.** unabr. ed. Rick Riordan. Read by Jesse Bernstein. 9 CDs. (Running Time: 11 hrs.). (Percy Jackson & the Olympians Ser.: Bk. 5). (YA). (gr. 5-8). 2009. audio compact disk 65.00 (978-0-7393-8035-2(4), Listening Lib) Pub: Random Audio Pubg. Dist(s): Random

Percy Jackson & the Olympians. unabr. ed. Rick Riordan. Read by Jesse Bernstein. (Percy Jackson & the Olympians Ser.: Bk. 5). (ENG.). (J). (gr. 4). 2009. audio compact disk 44.00 (978-0-7393-8033-8(6), Listening Lib) Pub: Random Audio Pubg. Dist(s): Random

Perdido. unabr. ed. Jill Robinson. Read by Connie Stothart. 10 cass. 59.50 (A-107) Audio Bk.
Wonderful novel about a true Hollywood Princess living in one of the stately homes at the beginning of the end of the old Hollywood.

Pere Goriot see Treasury of French Prose

Pere Goriot. unabr. ed. Honoré de Balzac. Read by Walter Covell. 9 cass. (Running Time: 13 hrs. 30 min.). 1991. 63.00 set. (C-229) Jimcin Record.
The most famous & the best of all the novels in Balzac's "Human Comedy".

Pere Goriot, Set. Honoré de Balzac. Read by J. Castalo. 3 cass. (FRE.). 1995. 31.95 (1766-VSL) Olivia & Hill.
Pere Goriot's excessive love for his two daughters leads to their downfall & his own death.

Peregrine Worsthorne: British Conservatism see Buckley's Firing Line

Peregrine's Saga. unabr. collector's ed. Henry Williamson. Read by Donada Peters. 7 cass. (Running Time: 7 hrs.). 1986. 42.00 (978-0-7366-0905-0(9), 1848) Books on Tape.
In the story the young author, recovering like many of his generation from the scars of W. W. I escapes to the Devon countryside of a still rural England & becomes a wandering observer & chronicler of the intertwinded lives of field, cliff & hedgerow.

Perelandra. unabr. ed. C. S. Lewis. Read by Geoffrey Howard. 1 CD. (Running Time: 8 hrs. 30 mins.). 2000. audio compact disk 19.95 (2614) Blckstn Audio.
Perelandra is a planet of pleasure. An unearthly, misty world of strange desires, sweet smells & delicious tastes, where beasts are friendly & naked beauty is unashamed, a new Garden of Eden.

Perelandra. unabr. ed. C. S. Lewis. Read by Geoffrey Howard. 6 CDs. (Running Time: 7 hrs. 40 min.). 2000. audio compact disk 56.00 (978-0-7861-9790-3(0), z2614) Blckstn Audio.

Perelandra. unabr. ed. C. S. Lewis. Read by Geoffrey Howard. (Running Time: 8 hrs. 30 mins.). 2001. 24.95 (978-0-7861-9366-0(2)) Blckstn Audio.

Perelandra. unabr. collector's ed. C. S. Lewis. Read by Grover Gardner. 6 cass. (Running Time: 9 hrs.). 1983. 48.00 (978-0-7366-0845-9(1), 1796) Books on Tape.
Dr. Ransom is ordered to Perelandra by the Supreme Being. There he finds a new Garden of Eden. This story is of his encounter with the new Adam & Eve & his battle with the insinuating force of evil, in the shape of English physicist, Dr. Weston.

Perelandra Microbial Balancing Program Workshop: The Introduction. 2 cass. (Running Time: 2 hrs.). 2004. 14.95 (978-0-927978-47-7(4), WT-110) Perelandra Ltd.
Machaelle talks about the world of microbes, what they do to us, what they do for us and why the program works.

Perelandra Nature Workshop. 3 cass. (Running Time: 4 hrs. 30 mins.). 2004. 19.95 (978-0-927978-14-9(8), WT-104) Perelandra Ltd.

Perelandra Seasons: Screen Saver. Photos by Clarence Wright. 2001. audio compact disk 12.95 (978-0-927978-50-7(4)) Perelandra Ltd.

Perelandru. unabr. ed. C. S. Lewis. Read by Geoffrey Howard. 6 CDs. (Running Time: 32400 sec.). (Space Trilogy). 2000. 44.95 (978-0-7861-1815-1(6), 2614) Blckstn Audio.
Perelandra is a planet of pleasure. An unearthly, misty world of strange desires, sweet smells & delicious tastes, where beasts are friendly & naked beauty is unashamed, a new Garden of Eden.

Perennial Knowledge. Swami Amar Jyoti. 1 cass. 1985. 9.95 (K-81) Truth Consciousness.
The foundation of genuine spirituality. Sanatana, the classic eternal path for all. Master shows the path. Prana, energy & transformation.

Perennial Philosophy. Aldous Huxley. 2 cass. (Running Time: 2 hrs. 40 min.). 1995. 17.95 Set. (978-1-879557-29-1(0)) Audio Scholar.
A religious classic filtered through the great intellectual mind of Aldous Huxley. Identifying the spiritual beliefs of various religious traditions, Huxley recast them in terms which are personally meaningful.

Perennial Questions, Current Answers. Robert A. Wilson. 2 cass. 18.00 Set. (A0151-84) Sound Photosyn.

Perennial Winter 04: Audio Sampler. 2003. (978-0-06-058782-6(2)) HarperCollins Pubs.

Peretti's Prayer Cover: 11 Cor, 1:1-11. Ed Young. 1990. 4.95 (978-0-7417-1775-7(1), 775) Win Walk.

Perez & Martina. 1 cass. (Bilingual Fables). 59.95 (Natl Textbk Co) M-H Contemporary.
Presents a story in Spanish & English.

Perfect. unabr. ed. Natasha Friend. Narrated by Danielle Ferland. 4 CDs. (Running Time: 4 hrs. 30 mins.). (YA). (gr. 6-9). 2005. audio compact disk 48.75 (978-1-4193-7018-2(9), C3536); 28.75 (978-1-4193-7013-7(8), 98262) Recorded Bks.
First-time novelist Natasha Friend is a writer with a talent for realistically expressing the fears and uncertainties of today's adolescents in a good story. Perfect has received the Milkweed Prize for Children's Literature and is a Book Sense "Winter Picks" selection. This is the moving story of a young girl who develops a dangerous eating disorder while dealing with intense grief.

***Perfect.** unabr. ed. Harry Kraus. (Running Time: 9 hrs. 4 mins. 0 sec.). (ENG.). 2009. 14.99 (978-0-310-29353-8(7)) Zondervan.

Perfect ABC Songbook. Jeffrey McFarland-Johnson. Perf. by Karen May & John Kelley. 1 cass. (Running Time: 38 min.). (J). (gr. k-3). 1998. 25.00 (978-1-892397-02-7(1));; 30.00 overhead transparencies (lyrics only).; cass. & trans. 30.00 sheet music for piano vocal/guitar.; audio compact disk 15.00 CD. (978-1-892397-01-0(3)) JohnSong.
Collection of 26 little original one-minute songs designed to teach the primary phonetic sound of each letter of the English alphabet (United States).

Perfect Angel. unabr. collector's ed. Seth J. Margolis. Read by Edward Lewis. 7 cass. (Running Time: 10 hrs. 30 min.). 1997. 56.00 (978-0-913369-90-6(X), 4390) Books on Tape.

Perfect Arrangement: A Novel. unabr. ed. Suzanne Berne. Narrated by Alexandra O'Karma. 9 cass. (Running Time: 12 hrs. 15 mins.). 2002. 42.95 (978-0-7887-9623-4(2), RF413) Recorded Bks.
The thought provoking story of a typical, small-town family entering a confusing time in their lives. When the Cook-Goldmans hire a new nanny for their children, but fail to check her references carefully, their convenient arrangement soon leads to a string of troubling events.

Perfect Arrangment. Suzanne Berne. Narrated by Alexandra O'Karma. 9 cass. (Running Time: 12 hrs. 15 mins.). 83.00 (978-0-7887-9609-8(7)) Recorded Bks.

Perfect Beast. unabr. ed. Kay Gregory. Read by Lynda Evans. 4 cass. (Running Time: 5 hrs. 36 min.). 2001. 26.95 (978-1-55686-837-5(5)) Books in Motion.
School teacher Rosemary Reid had always handled irate parents well... until meeting widower, Jonathan Riordan. First impressions aside, somehow, this man was different.

Perfect Brightness of Hope. George W. Pace. 1 cass. 9.95 (978-1-57734-352-3(2), 06005888) Covenant Comms.
Keys to following Christ.

Perfect Business: How to Make A Million from Home with No Payroll No Debts No: How to Make A Million from Home with No Payroll No Employee Headaches No Debt. Michael Leboeuf. 2004. 10.95 (978-0-7435-4562-4(1)) Pub: S&S Audio. Dist(s): S and S Inc

***Perfect Chemistry.** unabr. ed. Simone Elkeles. Read by Roxanne Hernandez and Blas Kisic. (Running Time: 9 hrs.). (YA). 2010. 24.99 (978-1-4418-8852-5(7), 9781441888525, Brilliance MP3); 39.97 (978-1-4418-8853-2(5), 9781441888532, Brlnc Audio MP3 Lib); 39.97 (978-1-4418-8854-9(3), 9781441888549, BADLE); audio compact disk 24.99 (978-1-4418-8850-1(0), 9781441888501, Bril Audio CD Unabri); audio compact disk 54.97 (978-1-4418-8851-8(9), 9781441888518, BriAudCD Unabrid) Brilliance Audio.

Perfect Christmas. Debbie Macomber. Contrib. by Tavia Gilbert. (Playaway Adult Fiction Ser.). (ENG.). 2009. 54.99 (978-1-4418-1033-5(1)) Find a World.

***Perfect Christmas.** Debbie Macomber. 2010. audio compact disk 9.99 (978-1-4418-6132-0(7)) Brilliance Audio.

Perfect Christmas. unabr. ed. Debbie Macomber. Read by Tavia Gilbert. 1 MP3-CD. (Running Time: 4 hrs.). 2009. 24.99 (978-1-4418-0577-5(X), 9781441805775, Brilliance MP3); 39.97 (978-1-4418-0578-2(8), 9781441805782, Brlnc Audio MP3 Lib); 24.99 (978-1-4418-0579-9(6), 9781441805799, BAD); 39.97 (978-1-4418-0580-5(X), 9781441805805, BADLE); audio compact disk 74.97 (978-1-4418-0576-8(1), 9781441805768, BriAudCD Unabrid); audio compact disk 26.99 (978-1-4418-0575-1(3), 9781441805751, Bril Audio CD Unabri) Brilliance Audio.

Perfect Christmas Gift. (Paws & Tales Ser.: Vol. 15). (J). 2001. audio compact disk 5.99 (978-1-57972-386-6(1)) Insight Living.

Perfect Christmas Gift. unabr. ed. 1 cass. (Running Time: 30 min.). (Paws & Tales Ser.: Vol. 15). 2001. 3.99 (978-1-57972-356-9(X)) Insight Living.
While the entire town of Wildwood is preparing for what they expect to be their Best Christmas ever most of the town is overcome with an epidemic that they don?t know how to treat.

Perfect Compassion of Vedanta. Swami Amar Jyoti. 1 cass. 1986. 9.95 (R-82) Truth Consciousness.
Freedom from the basic cause of suffering, the great promise of Vedanta. Gems from 'Mundaka Upanishad'.

Perfect Crime. unabr. ed. Peter Abrahams. Read by Sharon Williams. (Running Time: 10 hrs.). 2009. 24.99 (978-1-4233-9074-9(1), 9781423390749, Brilliance MP3); 24.99 (978-1-4233-9076-3(8), 9781423390763, BAD); 39.97 (978-1-4233-9075-6(X), 9781423390756, Brlnc Audio MP3 Lib); 39.97 (978-1-4233-9077-0(6), 9781423390770, BADLE) Brilliance Audio.

***Perfect Crime.** unabr. ed. Peter Abrahams. Read by Sharon Williams. (Running Time: 11 hrs.). 2010. audio compact disk 29.99 (978-1-4418-4089-9(3), 9781441840899, Bril Audio CD Unabri); audio compact disk 89.97 (978-1-4418-4090-5(7), 9781441840905, BriAudCD Unabrid) Brilliance Audio.

Perfect Crime, Set. abr. ed. Peter Abrahams. Read by Sharon Williams. 2 cass. 1999. 17.95 (FS9-40110) Highsmith.

Perfect Dark: Initial Vector. Greg Rucka. 2005. 11.95 (978-1-59397-883-9(9)) Pub: Macmill Audio. Dist(s): Macmillan

Perfect Daughter. unabr. ed. Gillian Linscott. Read by Lin Sagovsky. 8 cass. (Running Time: 8 hrs. 30 mins.). 2002. 69.95 (978-0-7540-0741-8(3), CAB 2163) AudioGO.
At nineteen, Verona North was talented and attractive. But only a few months after leaving home to study art in London, she is found hanging in the family boathouse in Devon, apparently a suicide. It seems that the perfect daughter had plunged rapidly into leftwing politics, drugs, and depravity. Her father, Ben, has no doubt who's to blame, his cousin, the suffragette, Nell Bray. Nell is sure she's not responsible, and yet.

Perfect Daughters: Adult Daughters of Alcoholics. Robert J. Ackerman. 1 cass. (Running Time: 60 min.). 1990. 9.95 (978-1-55874-081-5(3)) Health Comm.
In this tape, Dr. Robert Ackerman discusses the effects on these women of being raised in dysfunctional homes & discusses how they are learning to live with the legacies of their childhood.

Perfect Day. Contrib. by Josh Bates. Prod. by Mark A. Miller & Dale Oliver. Contrib. by Terry Hemmings. 2005. audio compact disk 11.97 (978-5-558-83394-2(7)) Pt of Grace Ent.

Perfect Enough. (ENG.). 2007. 197.00 (978-0-9792996-2-9(4)) Summit Dynamics.

***Perfect Evil.** unabr. ed. Alex Kava. Read by Richard Rowan. (Running Time: 11 hrs.). (Maggie O'Dell Ser.). 2011. 39.97 (978-1-4418-8511-1(0), 9781441885111, BADLE); 39.97 (978-1-4418-8510-4(2), 9781441885104, Brlnc Audio MP3 Lib); 19.99 (978-1-4418-8509-8(9), 9781441885098, Brilliance MP3); audio compact disk 69.97 (978-1-4418-8508-1(0), 9781441885081, BriAudCD Unabrid) Brilliance Audio.

***Perfect Evil.** unabr. ed. Alex Kava. Read by Richard Rowan. (Running Time: 11 hrs.). (Maggie O'Dell Ser.: Bk. 1). 2011. audio compact disk 19.99 (978-1-4418-8507-4(2), 9781441885074, Bril Audio CD Unabri) Brilliance Audio.

Perfect Gallows. unabr. ed. Peter Dickinson. Read by Stephen Thorne. 8 cass. (Running Time: 7 hrs. 30 min.). 2001. 69.95 (978-1-85089-777-4(8), 88102) Pub: ISIS Audio GBR. Dist(s): Ulverscroft US
"From the marvelous first chapter...when we encounter the hanging body in the dovecote, we know that we are once again in the safe hands of a master." - P.D. James.

Perfect Gift: John 1:14. Ed Young. (J). 1979. 4.95 (978-0-7417-1098-7(6), A0098) Win Walk.

Perfect Girl. unabr. ed. Mary Hogan. Read by Ann Marie Lee. 4 CDs. (Running Time: 4 hrs. 36 mins.). (YA). (gr. 6-9). 2007. audio compact disk 28.00 (978-0-7393-3796-7(3), Random AudioBks) Pub: Random Audio Pubg. Dist(s): Random

Perfect Harmony: The Intertwining Lives of Animals & Humans Throughout History. unabr. ed. Roger A. Caras. Read by Michael Mitchell. 7 cass. (Running Time: 10 hrs. 30 min.). 1998. 56.00 (978-0-7366-3999-6(3), 4499) Books on Tape.
An expert on animals presents a history of man that acknowledges the contributions of beasts.

Perfect Health. Paul R. Scheele. Read by Paul R. Scheele. 1 cass. (Running Time: 17 min.). (Paraliminal Tapes Ser.). 1991. 14.91 (978-0-925480-16-3(9)) Learn Strategies.
Helps align listeners body & mind to create better health.

Perfect Health Audio Series: Mind Body Solution. Deepak Chopra. 3 cass. 39.98 ea. Gaiam Intl.
An innovative home study course that teaches you how to harness your body's own intelligence & employ the enormous healing power inside you to be healthy, joyful & alive. The "Perfect Health Audio Series" is completely attuned to people's increasing focus on prevention, self-care & longevity.

Perfect Husband. unabr. ed. Lisa Gardner. Read by Jennifer Wydra. 8 vols. (Running Time: 12 hrs.). 1998. bk. 69.95 (978-0-7927-2257-1(4), CSL 146, Chivers Sound Lib) AudioGO.
Jim Beckett was everything Tess had ever dreamed of, but two years after she married him, she helped put him behind bars for savagely murdering ten women. Even locked up in a maximum security prison, he vowed to make her pay. Now that the cunning killer has escaped, Tess decides to fight back with the help of a burned-out ex-marine. The clock winds down to the terrifying reunion between husband & wife.

Perfect Husband. unabr. ed. Lisa Gardner. Read by Jennifer Wydra. 8 cass. (Running Time: 12 hrs.). 2000. 59.95 (CSL 146) Pub: Chivers Audio Bks GBR. Dist(s): AudioGO
Jim Beckett was everything Tess had ever dreamed of... But two years after Tess married him, she helped put him behind bars for savagely murdering ten women. Even locked up in a maximum security prison, he vowed to make her pay. Now the cunning killer has escaped... Tess decides to fight back with the help of a burned out ex-marine. The clock soon winds down to the terrifying reunion between husband and wife.

Perfect Job: Finding a New Career. Richard Jafolla & Mary-Alice Jafolla. Read by Richard Jafolla & Mary-Alice Jafolla. (Career Ser.). 1986. 12.95 (220) Stppng Stones.
Motivational tapes that work on the subconscious mind (subliminal) & conscious mind to bring about self-improvement.

***Perfect Joy.** unabr. ed. Stephanie Perry Moore. Narrated by Debora Raell. (Running Time: 2 hrs. 30 mins. 0 sec.). (Carmen Browne Ser.). (ENG.). 2010. audio compact disk 12.98 (978-1-61045-085-0(X), christaudio) christianaud.

Perfect Just as You Are: Buddhist Practices on the Four Limitless Ones - Loving-Kindness, Compassion, Joy, & Equanimity. unabr. ed. Pema Chödrön. 8 CDs. (ENG.). 2009. audio compact disk 69.95 (978-1-59030-628-4(7)) Pub: Shambhala Pubns. Dist(s): Random

Perfect Justice. unabr. ed. William Bernhardt. Read by Jonathan Marosz. 7 cass. (Running Time: 10 hrs. 30 min.). (Ben Kincaid Ser.: No. 4). 1998. 56.00 (978-0-7366-4108-1(4), 4613) Books on Tape.
The question is: Was it a racially motivated killing or something less exotic-like simple revenge? A young Vietnamese immigrant is brutally slaughtered by a crossbow. The police wast no time. They're certain that they've got the perpetrator: a ruthless member of a white supremacist group. Attorney Ben Kincaid reluctantly agrees to confer with the presumed murderer. But his attitude changes when he encounters a chilling certainty: an innocent man has been cast as a scapegoat. The real killer is still at large. The odds are stacked against Kincaid as he enters an incendiary murder trial with more twists than a dustbowl tornado.

Perfect Law. Swami Amar Jyoti. 1 cass. 1988. 9.95 (F-19) Truth Consciousness.
God is compassionate; law is just law. "As we do, so it happens. "Keeping awake, seeing clearly. Transcending mind. Focus on the Goal.

Perfect Liberation. Swami Amar Jyoti. 1 cass. 1975. 9.95 (M-55) Truth Consciousness.
Keeping head & heart open, realizing universal Oneness. Meditate & realize thou art That.

Perfect Life. Swami Amar Jyoti. 1 cass. 1987. 9.95 (A-36) Truth Consciousness.
Seeing what really matters behind all the nonessentials. Smoothly flowing awakened living, in tune with reality & truth, creates the higher qualities. The contagion of imbalance.

Perfect Little Girls see Petites Filles Modeles

Perfect Love. 6 cass. 19.95 (2047, HarperThor) HarpC GBR.

Perfect Love. Perf. by Lori Wilke. 1 cass. (Running Time: 5 min.). 1998. 9.98 Music sound track. (978-1-891916-41-0(6)) Spirit To Spirit.

Perfect Love. unabr. ed. Elizabeth Buchan. Read by Sian Thomas. 10 cass. (Running Time: 10 hrs.). 1996. 84.95 (978-0-7451-6637-7(7), CAB 1253) AudioGO.
Despite their 20-year age gap, Prue & Max have enjoyed two decades of marriage. But what Prue had forgotten was Violet, her rebellious step-daughter from Max's first marriage. Now, with a husband, baby & a successful career in New York, Violet has returned & Prue must deal with her.

Perfect Love: Reflections on God's Love. Narrated by Max E. McLean. 2002. audio compact disk 9.95 (978-1-931047-24-1(3)) Fellow Perform Arts.

***Perfect Love Song: A Holiday Story.** unabr. ed. Patti Callahan Henry. Read by Emily Durante. (Running Time: 5 hrs.). 2010. 19.99 (978-1-4418-6996-8(4), 9781441869968, BAD); 39.97 (978-1-4418-6997-5(2), 9781441869975, BADLE); 39.97 (978-1-4418-6995-1(6), 9781441869951, Brlnc Audio MP3 Lib); 19.99 (978-1-4418-6994-4(8), 9781441869944, Brilliance MP3); audio compact disk 19.99 (978-1-4418-6992-0(1), 9781441869920, Bril Audio CD Unabri); audio compact disk 69.97 (978-1-4418-6993-7(X), 9781441869937, BriAudCD Unabrid) Brilliance Audio.

Perfect Lover see Amante Perfecto (DigVer): El Tao del Amor y el Sexo

Perfect Lover see Amante Perfecto: El Tao del Amor y el Sexo

***Perfect Lover.** abr. ed. Stephanie Laurens. Read by Katie Carr. (ENG.). 2004. (978-0-06-078653-3(1), Harper Audio); (978-0-06-082452-5(2), Harper Audio) HarperCollins Pubs.

Perfect Lover. abr. ed. Stephanie Laurens. Read by Katie Carr. (Running Time: 18000 sec.). (Cynster Family Ser.: Bk. 10). 2006. audio compact disk 14.95 (978-0-06-087729-3(4)) HarperCollins Pubs.

Perfect Match. unabr. ed. Jodi Picoult. Read by Nancy Black. 12 CDs. (Running Time: 55800 sec.). 2005. audio compact disk 108.95 (978-1-74093-687-3(6)) Pub: Bolinda Pubng AUS. Dist(s): Bolinda Pub Inc

Perfect Mess: The Hidden Benefits of Disorder - How Crammed Closets, Cluttered Offices, & On-the-Fly Planning Make the World a Better Place. abr. ed. Eric Abrahamson & David H. Freedman. 3 CDs. (Running Time: 3 hrs.). (ENG.). 2007. audio compact disk 24.98 (978-1-59483-615-2(9)) Pub: Hachet Audio. Dist(s): HachBkGrp

Perfect Mess: The Hidden Benefits of Disorder ? How Crammed Closets, Cluttered Offices, & on-the-Fly Planning Make the World a Better Place. abr. ed. Eric Abrahamson & David H. Freedman. (Running Time: 3 hrs.). (ENG.). 2007. 14.98 (978-1-59483-616-9(7)) Pub: Hachet Audio. Dist(s): HachBkGrp

Perfect Mess: The Hidden Benefits of Disorder ? How Crammed Closets, Cluttered Offices, & on-the-Fly Planning Make the World a Better Place. abr. ed. Eric Abrahamson & David H. Freedman. (Running Time: 3 hrs.). (ENG.). 2009. 39.98 (978-1-60788-290-9(6)) Pub: Hachet Audio. Dist(s): HachBkGrp

Perfect Mess: The Hidden Benefits of Disorder? How Crammed Closets, Cluttered Offices, & On-the-Fly Planning Make the World a Better Place. unabr. ed. Eric Abrahamson & David H. Freedman. Read by Scott Brick. 9 CDs. (Running Time: 10 hrs.). 2007. audio compact disk 90.00 (978-1-4159-3627-6(7)) Books on Tape.

Perfect Mile. unabr. ed. Neal Bascomb. Read by Nelson Runger. 12 CDs. (Running Time: 14 hrs. 30 mins.). 2004. audio compact disk 99.75 (978-1-4025-8374-2(5)); 89.75 (978-1-4025-8333-9(8)) Recorded Bks.
In the tradition of Seabiscuit, this nostalgic audiobook reaches back to the golden age of sport for an utterly captivating narrative of what may be the most remarkable athletic feat of all time. They said no human could ever run a mile in less than four minutes. In 1952, three amazing athletes begged to differ.

Perfect Mile: Three Athletes. One Goal. & Less Than Four Minutes to Achieve It. Neal Bascomb. Narrated by Nelson Runger. 12 CDs. (Running Time: 14 hrs. 15 mins.). 2004. audio compact disk 29.99 (978-1-4025-7561-7(0), 01532) Recorded Bks.

Perfect Mistake. unabr. ed. Kate Brian, pseud. Narrated by Justine Eyre. (Running Time: 6 hrs. 0 mins.). (Privilege Ser.: No. 3). 2009. 13.99 (978-1-4001-8244-2(1)); 29.99 (978-1-4001-9244-1(7)) Tantor Media.

Perfect Mistake. unabr. ed. Kate Brian, pseud. Narrated by Justine Eyre. (Running Time: 6 hrs. 0 mins. 0 sec.). (Privilege Ser.: No. 3). (ENG.). 2010. 19.99 (978-1-4001-6244-4(0)); audio compact disk 29.99 (978-1-4001-1244-9(3)); audio compact disk 59.99 (978-1-4001-4244-6(X)) Pub: Tantor Media. Dist(s): IngramPubServ

***Perfect Mistress.** unabr. ed. Victoria Alexander. (Running Time: 11 hrs.). 2011. 39.97 (978-1-61106-442-1(2), 9781611064421, BADLE); 24.99 (978-1-61106-441-4(4), 9781611064414, BAD); 14.99 (978-1-61106-439-1(2), 9781611064391, Brilliance MP3); 39.97 (978-1-61106-440-7(6), 9781611064407, Brinc Audio MP3 Lib); audio compact disk 24.99 (978-1-61106-437-7(6), 9781611064377, Bril Audio CD Unabri); audio compact disk 69.97 (978-1-61106-438-4(4), 9781611064384, BriAudCD Unabrid) Brilliance Audio.

Perfect Murder. unabr. ed. H. R. F. Keating. Read by Frederick Davidson. 6 cass. (Running Time: 8 hrs. 30 mins.). (Inspector Ghote Mystery Ser.: No. 1). 1995. 44.95 (978-0-7861-0813-8(4), 1636) Blckstn Audio.
It is just Inspector Ghote's luck to be landed with the case of The Perfect Murder at the start of his career with the Bombay Police. For in this baffling of crimes there is the cunning & important tycoon Lala Varde to contend with. And as if this were not enough, he finds himself having to investigate the mysterious theft of one rupee from the desk of the Minister of Police Affairs & the Arts. Frustrated, he struggles through the quagmires of incompetence & corruption to solve these curious crimes.

Perfect Murder. unabr. ed. H. R. F. Keating. Read by Frederick Davidson. (Running Time: 7 hrs. 30 mins.). 2009. 29.95 (978-1-4332-9541-6(5)); audio compact disk 69.00 (978-1-4332-9540-9(7)) Blckstn Audio.

***Perfect Murder, Perfect Town.** abr. ed. Lawrence Schiller. Read by Ron Mclarty. (ENG.). 2006. (978-0-06-113538-5(0), Harper Audio); (978-0-06-113539-2(9), Harper Audio) HarperCollins Pubs.

Perfect Murder, Perfect Town, Set. abr. ed. Lawrence Schiller. Read by Ron McLarty. 4 cass. 1999. 25.00 (FS9-43338) Highsmith.

Perfect Nightmare. abr. ed. John Saul. Read by Dick Hill & Susie Breck. (Running Time: 21600 sec.). 2006. audio compact disk 16.99 (978-1-59737-700-3(7), 9781597377003, BCD Value Price) Brilliance Audio.
Every parent's nightmare becomes reality for Kara Marshall when her daughter, Lindsay, vanishes from her bedroom during the night. The police suspect that the girl is just another moody teenage runaway, angry over leaving behind her school and friends because her family is moving. But Lindsay's recent eerie claim - that someone invaded her room when the house was opened to prospective buyers - drives Kara to fear the worst: a nameless, faceless stalker has walked the halls of her home in search of more than a place to live. Patrick Shields recognizes Kara's pain - and carries plenty of his own since he lost his wife and two children in a devastating house fire. But more than grief draws Patrick and Kara together. He, too, senses the hand of a malevolent stranger in this tragedy. And as more people go missing from houses up for sale, Patrick's suspicion, like Kara's, blooms into horrified certainty. Someone is trolling this peaceful community - undetected and undeterred - harvesting victims for a purpose no sane mind can fathom. Someone Kara and Patrick, alone and desperate, are determined to unmask. Someone who is even now watching, plotting, keeping a demented diary of unspeakable deeds . . . and waiting until the time is ripe for another fateful visit.

Perfect Nightmare. unabr. ed. John Saul. Read by Dick Hill & Susie Breck. (Running Time: 10 hrs.). 2005. 39.25 (978-1-59710-896-6(0), 9781597108966, BADLE); 24.95 (978-1-59710-897-3(9), 9781597108973, BAD); 32.95 (978-1-59355-646-4(2), 9781593556464, BAU); 82.25 (978-1-59355-647-1(0), 9781593556471, BrilAudUnabridg); audio compact disk 36.95 (978-1-59355-648-8(9), 9781593556488, Bril Audio CD Unabri); audio compact disk 97.25 (978-1-59355-649-5(7), 9781593556495, BriAudCD Unabrid); audio compact disk 24.95 (978-1-59335-747-4(8), 9781593357474, Brilliance MP3); audio compact disk 39.25 (978-1-59335-881-5(4), 9781593358815, Brinc Audio MP3 Lib) Brilliance Audio.

Perfect Paragon. M. C. Beaton, pseud. Read by Donada Peters. (Agatha Raisin Mystery Ser.: Bk. 16). 2005. audio compact disk 53.55 (978-1-4159-2204-0(7)) Pub: Books on Tape. Dist(s): NetLibrary CO

Perfect Partners. unabr. collector's ed. Jayne Ann Krentz. Read by Mary Peiffer. 7 cass. (Running Time: 10 hrs. 30 mins.). 1996. 56.00 (978-0-7366-3353-6(7), 894283) Books on Tape.
Letitia Thornquist, a librarian in the Midwest, just inherited the family sporting goods business, an industry giant. She's green in business & in the dark about sports, but at least she's enthusiastic. How will she learn?.

Perfect Pitch. unabr. ed. Brendan Guy Alimo. Read by Brendan Guy Alimo. 2 CDs. (Running Time: 2 hrs.). 2003. audio compact disk 29.95 (978-0-9724806-2-8(5)) BGA Stories.
For the first time, the true story of sport and spirit for all ages! From a million-to-one chance encounter on an airliner, John Lopez, a 29 year old medical salesman, is offered the chance to try out as a batting practice pitcher for the Texas Rangers!. He has only 12 days to prepare for his ultimate trial on Memorial Day weekend, 1974, while the Vietnam War is about to reach its terrible end. For years, John has dreamed of pitching in the colors of several Major League Baseball Teams.

Perfect Pitch. unabr. ed. Brendan Guy Alimo. Read by Brendan Guy Alimo. 2 cass. (Running Time: 2 hrs.). 2003. 24.95 (978-0-9724806-7-3(6)) BGA Stories.

Perfect Pitch: Program from Award Winning Public Radio Series. Interview. Hosted by Fred Goodwin. 1 CD. (Running Time: 1 hr). 2000. audio compact disk 21.95 (978-1-932479-79-9(1), LCM 135) Lichtenstein Creat.
Why can some people name a note as soon as they hear it when others can't tell one from another? In this hour, we'll explore the mysterious ability known as perfect pitch. A cellist with perfect pitch will give a guided tour through the notes and keys. We'll also hear from a psychologist and geneticist who have different ideas about how many people have perfect pitch and why. And a report on Williams Syndrome, a rare genetic disorder which can cause physical and mental problems - and a sensitivity to music and pitch. Guests include: Gordon Grubb, a cellist with the Grossmont Symphony; Dr. Dan Levitin, a record producer and psychology professor at McGill University; Dr. Peter Gregersen, Chief of the Division of Biology and Human Genetics North Shore University Hospital; Dr. Ursula Bellugi, professor and director of the laboratory for cognitive neuroscience at the Salk Institute; Dr. Glen Schellenberg, professor of psychology at the University of Toronto; and Dr. Howard Lenhoff, professor emeritus at the University of California at Irvine.

Perfect Pitch Ear Training SuperCourse. 3rd ed. 2004. audio compact disk 169.00 (978-0-942542-58-5(4)) EarTraining.

Perfect Pitch for Children: A Message to Parents & Teachers. David Lucas Burge. 1 CD. (J). 1999. audio compact disk 14.95 (978-0-942542-92-9(4)) EarTraining.
Supplement to the "Perfect Pitch Ear Training SuperCourse.".

Perfect Pitch for Children: A Message to Parents & Teachers. unabr. ed. David Lucas Burge. 1 cass. (Running Time: 60 min.). 1999. 14.95 (978-0-942542-96-7(7)) EarTraining.
Supplement to the Perfect Pitch Ear Training SuperCourse.

Perfect Pitch Supercourse Old Version, Set. Harvey Smith. 8 CDs. 1999. 145.00 (978-0-942542-90-5(8)) EarTraining.
Learn to recognize exact tones & chords by ear.

Perfect Poison. abr. ed. Amanda Quick, pseud. Read by Anne Flosnik. (Running Time: 5 hrs.). (Arcane Society Ser.). 2010. audio compact disk 14.99 (978-1-4233-4082-9(5), 9781423340829, BCD Value Price) Brilliance Audio.

Perfect Poison. unabr. ed. Amanda Quick, pseud. Read by Anne Flosnik. (Running Time: 10 hrs.). (Arcane Society Ser.). 2009. 39.97 (978-1-4233-4080-5(9), 9781423340805, BADLE); 24.99 (978-1-4233-4079-9(5), 9781423340799, BAD); 24.99 (978-1-4233-4077-5(9), 9781423340775, Brilliance MP3); 39.97 (978-1-4233-4078-2(7), 9781423340782, Brinc Audio MP3 Lib); audio compact disk 34.99 (978-1-4233-4075-1(2), 9781423340751); audio compact disk 92.97 (978-1-4233-4076-8(0), 9781423340768, BriAudCD Unabrid) Brilliance Audio.

Perfect Poison: A Female Serial Killer's Deadly Medicine. abr. ed. M. William Phelps. Read by J. Charles. (Running Time: 6 hrs.). 2008. audio compact disk 14.99 (978-1-4233-4931-0(8), 9781423349310, BCD Value Price) Brilliance Audio.

Perfect Poison: A Female Serial Killer's Deadly Medicine. unabr. ed. M. William Phelps. Read by J. Charles. (Running Time: 14 hrs.). 2008. 39.25 (978-1-4233-4929-7(6), 9781423349297, BADLE); 24.95 (978-1-4233-4928-0(8), 9781423349280, BAD); 107.25 (978-1-4233-4923-5(7), 9781423349235, BrilAudUnabridg); audio compact disk 39.25 (978-1-4233-4927-3(X), 9781423349273, Brinc Audio MP3 Lib); audio compact disk 112.25 (978-1-4233-4925-9(3), 9781423349259, BriAudCD Unabrid); audio compact disk 38.95 (978-1-4233-4924-2(5), 9781423349242, Bril Audio CD Unabri) Brilliance Audio.

Perfect Poison: They Called Her the Angel of Death. unabr. ed. M. William Phelps. Read by J. Charles. 1 MP3-CD. (Running Time: 50400 sec.). 2008. audio compact disk 24.95 (978-1-4233-4926-6(1), 9781423349266, Brilliance MP3) Brilliance Audio.

***Perfect Promise.** Stephen Swisher. (ENG.). 2010. audio compact disk 5.00 (978-1-60463-078-7(7)) K Copeland Pubns.

Perfect Relaxation. Swami Amar Jyoti. 1 cass. 1980. 9.95 (P-33) Truth Consciousness.
How may we come to that perfect relaxation where a new consciousness is born? The direct way between Him & us.

Perfect Scent: A Year Behind the Scenes of the Perfume Industry in Paris & New York. unabr. ed. Chandler Burr. (Running Time: 12 hrs. 0 mins. 0 sec.). (ENG.). 2008. audio compact disk 24.99 (978-1-4001-5657-3(2)) Pub: Tantor Media. Dist(s): IngramPubServ

Perfect Scent: A Year Behind the Scenes of the Perfume Industry in Paris & New York. unabr. ed. Chandler Burr. Read by Mel Foster. (Running Time: 12 hrs. 0 mins. 0 sec.). (ENG.). 2008. audio compact disk 69.99 (978-1-4001-3657-5(1)); audio compact disk 34.99 (978-1-4001-0657-8(5)) Pub: Tantor Media. Dist(s): IngramPubServ

Perfect Season: Why 1998 Was Baseball's Greatest Year, unabr. ed. Tim McCarver & Danny Peary. Narrated by Richard M. Davidson. 6 cass. (Running Time: 7 hrs. 30 mins.). 1999. 53.00 (978-0-7887-3484-7(9), 95893E7) Recorded Bks.
McCarver uses his knowledge and experience to relate the 1998 season, one that broke records, made history and reestablished baseball as the great American pastime.

Perfect Soldier. unabr. ed. Ralph Peters. Read by David Hilder. 8 cass. (Running Time: 11 hrs. 30 mins.). 1995. 56.95 (978-0-7861-0874-9(6), 1674) Blckstn Audio.
Deliberately maimed on a goodwill mission to a former Soviet republic, Major Christopher Ritter is headed for another land of intrigue: Washington, D.C. From the Pentagon to the Senate, he's entering a different kind of war, in which sex, money & influence are wielded like laser-bombs. At stake are a series of photographs said to depict the KGB murder of American POWs & the success of a secret, multi-billion dollar oil deal. Major Ritter, the perfect soldier & the perfect pawn, stands on the firing line, seeking a measure of atonement in a city without shame.

Perfect Soldier. unabr. ed. Ralph Peters. Read by David Hilder. (Running Time: 11 hrs. 30 mins.). 2010. 29.95 (978-1-4417-1344-5(1)); audio compact disk 100.00 (978-1-4417-1341-4(7)) Blckstn Audio.

Perfect Spy. unabr. ed. John le Carré. Read by David Case. 15 cass. (Running Time: 22 hrs. 30 min.). (George Smiley Novels Ser.). 1993. 120.00 (978-0-7366-2536-4(4), 3288) Books on Tape.

Perfect Spy. unabr. ed. John le Carré. Narrated by Frank Muller. 12 cass. (Running Time: 18 hrs.). (George Smiley Novels Ser.). 1987. 97.00 (978-1-55690-406-6(1), 87800E7) Recorded Bks.
Magnus Pym, a British spy, goes missing & his whereabouts becomes the primary concern of everyone.

Perfect Storm: A True Story of Men Against the Sea. unabr. ed. Sebastian Junger. Read by Richard M. Davidson. 6 cass. (Running Time: 9 hrs.). 2000. 42.50 (978-0-7366-5470-8(4), 5341) Books on Tape.
It was "the perfect storm", a nor'easter created by so rare a combination of weather conditions that it could not possibly have been worse. Creating waves one hundred feet high and winds of 120 miles an hour, the storm whipped the sea to inconceivable levels. Tragically, the six-man crew of the Andrea Gail headed directly towards the storm's center. working from published material, radio dialogues, eye-witness accounts, and the experience of people caught in similar storms, Junger re-creates the last moments of the Andrea Gail as well as the heart-stopping rescues of other victims of the storm.

Perfect Storm: A True Story of Men Against the Sea. unabr. ed. Sebastian Junger. Narrated by Richard M. Davidson. 8 CDs. (Running Time: 9 hrs. 30 mins.). 1999. audio compact disk 75.00 (978-0-7887-3427-4(X), C1033E7) Recorded Bks.
In October 1991, three separate storm systems converged to create a monster. One hundred foot seas & gale-force winds upended boats, tossing them around like children's toys. Describes the men caught in this storm, their fate & the fate of their vessels, the heroic efforts to rescue them & the once in a century "perfect storm." Includes interview with the author.

Perfect Storm: A True Story of Men Against the Sea, unabr. ed. Sebastian Junger. Narrated by Richard M. Davidson. 7 cass. (Running Time: 9 hrs. 30 mins.). 1998. 66.00 (978-0-7887-1970-7(X), 95357E7) Recorded Bks.

Perfect Strangers. unabr. ed. Robyn Sisman. 8 cass. (Isis Ser.). (J). 2002. 69.95 (978-0-7531-1372-1(4)) Pub: ISIS Lrg Prnt GBR. Dist(s): Ulverscroft US

Perfect Tax. G Edward Griffin. Read by G Edward Griffin. 1 cass. 1999. (978-0-912986-36-4(0)) Am Media.

Perfect Thing: How the iPod Shuffles Commerce, Culture, & Coolness. abr. ed. Steven Levy. Read by Anthony Rapp. 2006. 17.95 (978-0-7435-6125-9(2)) Pub: S&S Audio. Dist(s): S and S Inc

Perfect Time. Perf. by Maire Brennan. 1 cass., 1 CD. 8.78 (EPIC 69143); audio compact disk 12.78 CD Jewel box. (EPIC 69143) NewSound.

Perfect Timing. Jill Mansell. 2008. 76.95 (978-0-7531-3222-7(2)); audio compact disk 99.95 (978-0-7531-3223-4(0)) Pub: Isis Pubng Ltd GBR. Dist(s): Ulverscroft US

Perfect Union. Catherine Allgor. Narrated by Anne Twomey. 13 CDs. (Running Time: 57420 sec.). (Sound Library). 2006. audio compact disk 112.95 (978-0-7927-4021-6(1), SLD 939) AudioGO.

Perfect Weight. Hilary Jones. Read by Hilary Jones. (Running Time: 0 hr. 45 mins.). 2000. 16.95 (978-1-59912-930-3(2)) Iofy Corp.

Perfect Weight: Perfect Body. Dick Sutphen. 1 cass. (Running Time: 1 hr.). (RX17 Ser.). 1986. 14.98 (978-0-87554-302-4(2), RX111) Valley Sun.
You have the power & ability to attain the perfect weight & body. You now control your weight. Every day you become thinner. You eat healthy foods & smaller portions at meals. You stick to your diet. You live a healthy lifestyle. You now attain your weight goals & the body you desire. You have the power & ability to take total control of your body & your life. "Thin" is your conditioned response key word.

Perfect Witness, unabr. ed. Barry Siegel. Narrated by Paul Hecht. 9 cass. (Running Time: 12 hrs.). 1998. 78.00 (978-0-7887-1976-9(9), 95363E7) Recorded Bks.
The tale of deception & murder in a courtroom.

Perfect World: Logos October 3, 1999. Ben Young. 1999. 4.95 (978-0-7417-6150-7(5), B0150) Win Walk.

***Perfect 10 Diet: 10 Key Hormones That Hold the Secret to Losing Weight & Feeling Great-Fast!** Michael Aziz. Contrib. by Fred Stella. (Playaway Adult Nonfiction Ser.). 2010. 59.99 (978-1-4418-3791-2(4)) Find a World.

Perfect 10 Diet: 10 Key Hormones That Hold the Secret to Losing Weight & Feeling Great-Fast! unabr. ed. Michael Aziz. Read by Fred Stella. (Running Time: 10 hrs.). 2010. 24.99 (978-1-4418-3427-0(3), 9781441834270, Brilliance MP3); 24.99 (978-1-4418-3429-4(X), 9781441834294, BAD); 39.97 (978-1-4418-3428-7(1), 9781441834287, Brinc Audio MP3 Lib); 39.97 (978-1-4418-3430-0(3), 9781441834300, BADLE); audio compact disk 29.99 (978-1-4418-3425-6(7), 9781441834256, Bril Audio CD Unabri); audio compact disk 82.97 (978-1-4418-3426-3(5), 9781441834263, BriAudCD Unabrid) Brilliance Audio.

Perfected in Love: Cultivating Our Relationships Through the Love of God, Vol. 1. Mac Hammond. (ENG.). 2007. audio compact disk 20.00 (978-1-57399-327-2(1)) Mac Hammond.

Perfected in Love: Expanding Your Boundaries, Vol 3. Mac Hammond. (ENG.). 2007. audio compact disk 25.00 (978-1-57399-329-6(8)) Mac Hammond.

Perfected in Love: How to Express Love Effectively in Different Types of Relationships. 3 cass. (Running Time: 3 hrs.). (Perfected in Love Ser.: 2). 2002. 15.00 (978-1-57399-115-5(5)) Mac Hammond.
Anything you want out of life by the hand of God is going to come to you only by the degree to which you've been perfected in love. In Volume II of the Perfected in Love series, Mac Hammond lays out the three fundamental ways we are to love (or give to) people differently, depending on whether they are under our authority, we are under their authority, or we are their peer.

Perfected in Love: How to Express Love Effectively in Different Types of Relationships, Vol. 2. Mac Hammond. (ENG.). 2007. audio compact disk 15.00 (978-1-57399-328-9(X)) Mac Hammond.

Perfected in Love Vol. 1: Cultivating Our Relationships Through the Love of God. 4 cass. (Running Time: 4 hrs.). (Perfected in Love Ser.: 1). 2001. 20.00 (978-1-57399-113-1(9)) Mac Hammond.
Almost everything God does in our life, He does through people, and He's made it clear that the only people He can use are the ones that we walk in love toward. When we purposely choose to base our lives on the love of God, we'll begin to experience the presence and power of God in ways we've never dreamed of.

Perfected in Love Vol. III: Expanding Your Boundaries. 5. (Running Time: 5 hrs.). (Perfected in Love Ser.: 3). 2001. 25.00 (978-1-57399-116-2(3)) Mac Hammond.
In Volume III of Perfected in Love, Mac Hammond sheds light on the very interesting topic of boundaries, reveals that it is possible to expand your boundaries of love, and then gives you bibical steps on how to do just that!.

Perfecting a Man of God. unabr. ed. R. Edward Miller. Read by R. Edward Miller. 5 cass. (Running Time: 7 hrs. 30 min.). 1997. 22.50 Set. (978-0-945818-13-7(0)) Peniel Pubns.
Formation of God's glorified sons.

Perfecting Connecting: An Interview with Sarah Michel: Learning to Speak the Language with Others. Narrated by Sarah Michel. (ENG.). 2003. 14.95 (978-0-9743751-2-0(8)) Telos Pubns.

Perfecting Presentations. Arch Lustberg. Read by Arch Lustberg. 1 cass. (Running Time: 50 min.). 1994. 12.00 (978-1-56641-013-7(4)) Library Video.
Renowned media coach Arch Lustberg discusses how to give memorable & interesting speeches. His proven techniques will improve anyone's public speaking abilities.

Perfection: He Is There. Dennis R. Deaton. 1 cass. 3.95 (978-1-57734-378-3(6), 34441174) Covenant Comms.

Perfection - He Is There! Dennis R. Deaton. 1 cass. 7.98 (978-1-55503-782-6(8), 06005047) Covenant Comms.
Keeping focused on what's important.

Perfection Is Hard to Come By. Instructed by Manly P. Hall. 8.95 (978-0-89314-207-0(7), C860713) Philos Res.

Perfection of Being. Swami Amar Jyoti. 1 cass. 1989. 9.95 (K-114) Truth Consciousness.
God, the highest perfection of form, can assume any form. Living without ego. On simplicity & faith.

Perfection of Krishna. Swami Amar Jyoti. 1 dolby cass. 1986. 9.95 (K-85) Truth Consciousness.
Many charming episodes & heroic exploits illustrate Lord Krishna's perfect manifestation of Being, the love & wisdom of Supremacy in every facet of life.

Perfection of Love: Genesis 17:1. Ed Young. (J). 1980. 4.95 (978-0-7417-1149-6(4), A0149) Win Walk.

Perfectionism & Self-Worth. unabr. ed. Jennifer James. Read by Jennifer James. 1 cass. (Running Time: 52 min.). 1985. 9.95 (978-0-915423-06-4(5)) Jennifer J.
Understand perfectionism, learn to relax, & put value back into your life to find a new balance.

Perfectionist & Other Plays. unabr. ed. Joyce Carol Oates. Perf. by Barbara Bosson et al. 1 cass. (Running Time: 1 hr. 54 min.). 1994. 25.95 (978-1-58081-013-5(6), TPT48) Pub: L A Theatre. Dist(s): NetLibrary CO
Tobias Harte; a man obsessed with perfection in everything from ethics to egg salad. Rollicking comedy ensues as Harte struggles with his highly imperfect family & friends.

Perfectionnement Allemand. 1 cass. (Running Time: 1 hr., 30 min.).Tr. of Using German. (FRE & GER.). 2000. bk. 75.00 (978-2-7005-1029-4(1)); bk. 95.00 (978-2-7005-1099-7(2)) Pub: Assimil FRA. Dist(s): Distribks Inc

Perfectionnement Anglais. Assimil Staff. 1 cass. (Running Time: 1 hr., 30 min.).Tr. of Using English. 1999. bk. 75.00 (978-2-7005-1028-7(3)); bk. 95.00 (978-2-7005-1075-1(5)) Pub: Assimil FRA. Dist(s): Distribks Inc

Perfectionnement Espagnol. 1 cass. (Running Time: 1 hr., 30 min.). (FRE & SPA.). 2000. bk. 75.00 (978-2-7005-1030-0(5)) Pub: Assimil FRA. Dist(s): Distribks Inc

Perfectionnement Italien. Equipo de Expertos 2100 Staff. 1 cass. (Running Time: 1 hr., 30 min.). (FRE, ITA & SPA.). 2000. 75.00 (978-2-7005-1031-7(3)) Pub: Assimil FRA. Dist(s): Distribks Inc

Perfectly Good Family. unabr. ed. Lionel Shriver. Read by Susan Ericksen. (Running Time: 13 hrs.). 2009. 39.97 (978-1-4233-6083-4(4), 9781423360834, BADLE); 39.97 (978-1-4233-6081-0(8), 9781423360810, Brlnc Audio MP3 Lib); 24.99 (978-1-4233-6080-3(X), 9781423360803, Brilliance MP3); 24.99 (978-1-4233-6082-7(6), 9781423360827, BAD); audio compact disk 97.97 (978-1-4233-6079-7(6), 9781423360797, BriAudCD Unabrid); audio compact disk 36.99 (978-1-4233-6078-0(8), 9781423360780, Bril Audio CD Unabri) Brilliance Audio.

***Perfectly Imperfect: A Life in Progress.** unabr. ed. Lee Woodruff. Read by Lee Woodruff. Intro. by Bob Woodruff. 5 CDs. (Running Time: 6 hrs. 30 mins.). 2009. audio compact disk 80.00 (978-1-4159-6169-8(7), BksonTape) Pub: Random Audio Pubg. Dist(s): Random

Perfectly Imperfect: A Life in Progress. unabr. ed. Lee Woodruff. Read by Lee Woodruff. Intro. by Bob Woodruff. (ENG.). 2009. audio compact disk 29.95 (978-0-7393-8218-9(7), Random AudioBks) Pub: Random Audio Pubg. Dist(s): Random

Perfectly Positioned. Read by Francis Anfuso. 2007. audio compact disk 10.00 (978-0-9791957-2-3(1)) Pilot Comm.

Perfectly Pure & Good. unabr. ed. Frances Fyfield. Read by Rula Lenska. 6 cass. (Running Time: 6 hrs.). (Attorney Sarah Fortune Mysteries Ser.). 1994. 54.95 (978-0-7451-4340-8(7), CAB 1023) AudioGO.
Sarah Fortune travels to the seaside town of Norfolk to sort out the inheritance problems of the Pardoes. She soon finds that guilt, insecurity, unrequited love & a touch of insanity afflict the family & the town. The townspeople claim that years before, a woman with an uncanny resemblance to Sarah walked into the sea & never came back.

Perfectly Reasonable Deviations from the Beaten Track: The Letters of Richard P. Feynman. Richard Phillips Feynman. 2005. audio compact disk 34.99 (978-1-4193-4322-3(X)) Recorded Bks.

Perfezionamento dell'Inglese. Assimil Staff. 1 CD. (Running Time: 1 hr. 30 min.).Tr. of Using English. 1999. pap. bk. 95.00 (978-2-7005-1096-6(8)); pap. bk. 75.00 (978-2-7005-1359-2(2)) Pub: Assimil FRA. Dist(s): Distribks Inc

Perfidious Parrot. unabr. ed. Janwillem Van de Wetering. Narrated by George Guidall. 6 cass. (Running Time: 8 hrs. 30 mins.). (Grijpstra & DeGier Mystery Ser.). 2000. 53.00 (978-0-7887-3106-8(8), 95817) Recorded Bks.
Although detectives Grijpstra & de Gier are retired, they still take on an occasional investigation. But when cases involving blackmail, a looted ship & murder arrive on their doorstep in rapid succession, the two Dutchmen wonder if they shouldn't close up shop for good.

Perfil y Gratitud. unabr. ed. Hector David Aguilar. (SPA.). 1999. 4.99 (978-0-8297-2210-9(6)) Pub: Vida Pubs. Dist(s): Zondervan

Perfil y Gratitud. unabr. ed. Hector David Aguilar. 1999. audio compact disk 11.99 (978-0-8297-2211-6(4)) Zondervan.

Perform Perfect Katas. 1 cass. (Martial Arts Programming Ser.). 12.50 (978-0-87554-195-2(X), K105) Valley Sun.
You move with relaxed power in your kata. You move with even, flowing speed. Your kata forms are precise & accurate. You project power in every movement you make. You are focused on your individual movements. You are not distracted by your surroundings. You perform powerful, flowing katas.

Performance at Hog Theater. Russell Edson. Read by Russell Edson. 1 cass. (Running Time: 54 min.). (Watershed Tapes of Contemporary Poetry Ser.). 1978. 11.95 (23619) J Norton Pubs.
Edson coaxes the listener into his upside-down world.

Performance Characteristics of Total Quality People! unabr. ed. Earling Vining. Read by Earling Vining. 2 cass. (Running Time: 1 hr. 54 min.). 1998. 29.95 Set. (978-1-893603-10-3(5)) Exec Dev Syst.
"It's not where you are but where you're going that counts." With this simple truth, Vining went from picking cotton to reaching for the stars. Achieve successs & develop that "winning spirit" through implementation of her program - how to get along with others, how to improve your self-image & communications abilities, how to think, act & look a winner. Assertive positive situation control.

Performance Coaching. Lanny Bassham. 4 CDs. (Running Time: 3 hrs. 30 mins). 2004. 75.00 (978-1-934324-11-0(6)) Mental Mgmnt.

Performance Driver Selling. Jeff Magee. audio compact disk 49.95 (978-0-9641240-5-9(X)) J Magee Intl.

Performance Edge. Robert K. Cooper. Read by Robert K. Cooper. 6 cass. 1991. 59.95 set incl. performance cards. (249A) Nightingale-Conant.
Dr. Robert Cooper identifies the "turning points" in your life & shows how exercise, nutrition & mental attitude can keep you at your best during these critical moments.

Performance Management & Appraisal: A How-to-Do-It Manual for Librarians. G. Edward Evans. (How-To-Do-It Manuals for Libraries Ser.: Vol. 132). 2004. audio compact disk 75.00 (978-1-55570-498-8(0)) Neal-Schuman.

Performance Measurement & Evaluation Series. Incl. Performance Measurement & Evaluation Series: Does Team Trading Make Any Real Difference? D. Mitchell.; Performance Measurement & Evaluation Series: Financial Evaluation of Brokerage Firms. R. Rosenthal.; Performance Measurement & Evaluation Series: Mistakes You Can Make in Evaluating Performance. F. Pusateri.; Performance Measurement & Evaluation Series: New Mathematical Tools for Technical Trading. D. Iglehart.; Performance Measurement & Evaluation Series: New Ways to Compare Performance of Trading Advisors. R. Oberuc.; Performance Measurement & Evaluation Series: Performance Evaluation. P. Shouse.; Performance Measurement & Evaluation Series: Projecting Performance: Risk-Reward Tradeoffs. W. Dunn.; Performance Measurement & Evaluation Series: Should Trading Systems Be Altered As Money Grows? Kevin Campbell.; Performance Measurement & Evaluation Series: The Costs & Benefits of Trading Research. F. Gehm.; Performance Measurement & Evaluation Series: Uses & Abuses of Performance Data. C. Starkey & R. Isaacson.; 100.00 Set. (Mngd Acct Reprts); 15.00 ea. Futures Pub.

Performance Measurement & Evaluation Series: Does Team Trading Make Any Real Difference? see Performance Measurement & Evaluation Series

Performance Measurement & Evaluation Series: Financial Evaluation of Brokerage Firms see Performance Measurement & Evaluation Series

Performance Measurement & Evaluation Series: Mistakes You Can Make in Evaluating Performance see Performance Measurement & Evaluation Series

Performance Measurement & Evaluation Series: New Mathematical Tools for Technical Trading see Performance Measurement & Evaluation Series

Performance Measurement & Evaluation Series: New Ways to Compare Performance of Trading Advisors see Performance Measurement & Evaluation Series

Performance Measurement & Evaluation Series: Performance Evaluation see Performance Measurement & Evaluation Series

Performance Measurement & Evaluation Series: Projecting Performance: Risk-Reward Tradeoffs see Performance Measurement & Evaluation Series

Performance Measurement & Evaluation Series: Should Trading Systems Be Altered As Money Grows? see Performance Measurement & Evaluation Series

Performance Measurement & Evaluation Series: The Costs & Benefits of Trading Research see Performance Measurement & Evaluation Series

Performance Measurement & Evaluation Series: Uses & Abuses of Performance Data see Performance Measurement & Evaluation Series

Performance Plus, Vol. 11. Alfred Publishing Staff. (Performance Plus Ser.). (ENG.). 1997. audio compact disk 12.95 (978-0-7692-1560-0(2), Warner Bro) Alfred Pub.

Performance Plus Digital Orchestrations, Vol. 12. Alfred Publishing Staff. 1 cass. (Performance Plus Ser.). (ENG.). 1997. audio compact disk 12.95 (978-0-7692-1569-3(6), Warner Bro) Alfred Pub.

Performance Reviews with Less Stress & Better Results. PUEI. 2007. audio compact disk 199.00 (978-1-934147-64-1(8), Fred Pryor) P Univ E Inc.

Performer's Edge. 2002. audio compact disk 14.95 (978-0-9728185-5-1(3)) InGenius Inc.

Performer's Edge. Edward Strachar. 1997. (978-0-9717185-3-1(9)) InGenius Inc.

Performer's Edge. abr. ed. Speeches. Edward Strachar. 1 cass. (Running Time: 60 mins.). 2002. 14.95 (978-0-9723168-1-1(7)) InGenius Inc.

Performing a Single Audit for State & Local Governments. Robert H. Werner. 2 cass. 1994. 119.00 incl. wkbk. (747032VC) Am Inst CPA.
This course shows how to conduct audits complying with the Single Audit Act of 1984. It has been completely revised in the light of SOP 92-7, which synthesizes the requirements of a variety of federal government & AICPA pronouncements. This course also reflects the AICPA's Audit & Accounting Guide, Audits of State & Local Governmental Units, SAS No. 68, GAO's Yellow Book, & OMB's Compliance Supplement for Single Audits of State & Local Governments.

Performing & Responding. John Howard. Contrib. by Roy Bennett. 1 CD. (Running Time: 1 hr. 12 mins.). (Cambridge Assignments in Music Ser.). (ENG.). 1995. audio compact disk 58.00 (978-0-521-42230-7(2)) Cambridge U Pr.

Perfume from Provence. unabr. ed. Winifred Fortesque. Read by Patricia Hughes. 5 cass. (Running Time: 7 hrs. 30 min.). 1998. 34.95 (978-0-7531-0338-8(9), 980315) Pub: ISIS Audio GBR. Dist(s): Ulverscroft US
In the early 1930's, Winifred Fortesque & her husband, Sir John Fortesque, settled in Provence, in a small house amid olive groves, on the border of Grasse. Almost at once they were bewitched, by the scenery, by their garden - a terraced landscape of vines, wild flowers, roses & lavender - & by the charming, infuriating, warm-hearted Provencals. The house, called the Domaine, was tiny & plans were drawn up to extend it over mountain terraces. This account of life is a tribute to the stonemasons, builders, craftsmen, gardeners & Provencal village life.

Perfume of the Lady in Black. unabr. ed. Gaston Leroux. Read by Flo Gibson. 7 cass. (Running Time: 9 hrs. 30 min.). 1998. 25.95 (978-1-55685-589-4(3)) Audio Bk Con.
Melodrama takes place on the Riviera & is a sequel to "The Mystery of the Yellow Room.".

***Pericles.** abr. ed. William Shakespeare. (ENG.). 2006. (978-0-06-112638-3(1), Caedmon); (978-0-06-112637-6(3), Caedmon) HarperCollins Pubs.

Pericles. unabr. ed. William Shakespeare. Read by Nigel Terry & John Gielgud. (Running Time: 8220 sec.). (Arkangel Shakespeare Ser.). (ENG.). 2006. audio compact disk 19.95 (978-1-932219-27-2(7)) Pub: AudioGO. Dist(s): Perseus Dist

Pericles. unabr. ed. William Shakespeare. Read by Audio Partners Staff. 2 cass. (Running Time: 2 hrs. 17 mins.). (Arkangel Shakespeare Ser.). 2004. 17.95 (978-1-932219-67-8(6), Atlntc Mnthly) Pub: Grove-Atltc. Dist(s): PerseuPGW
Pericles undergoes shipwreck, storm, and a tyrant's fury. He wins love only to have his family torn asunder, but what is lost may also be found. This strange and powerful tale of loss and recovery is the first of Shakespeare's late romances. Performed by Sir John Gielgud, Nigel Terry, and the Arkangel cast.

***Peril.** abr. ed. Christine Feehan. Read by Natalie Ross Gigante & Phil Gigante. (Running Time: 7 hrs.). (Dark Ser.). 2010. audio compact disk 24.99 (978-1-4418-1542-2(2), 9781441815422, BACD) Brilliance Audio.

***Peril.** unabr. ed. Christine Feehan. Read by Natalie Rose Ross. (Running Time: 14 hrs.). (Dark Ser.). 2010. 24.99 (978-1-4418-1538-5(4), 9781441815385, Brilliance MP3) Brilliance Audio.

***Peril.** unabr. ed. Christine Feehan. Read by Ross Natalie & Phil Gigante. (Running Time: 14 hrs.). (Dark Ser.). 2010. 39.97 (978-1-4418-1539-2(2), 9781441815392, Brlnc Audio MP3 Lib) Brilliance Audio.

***Peril.** unabr. ed. Christine Feehan. Read by Phil Gigante. (Running Time: 14 hrs.). (Dark Ser.). 2010. 39.97 (978-1-4418-1541-5(4), 9781441815415, BADLE) Brilliance Audio.

***Peril.** unabr. ed. Christine Feehan. Read by Ross Natalie & Phil Gigante. (Running Time: 14 hrs.). (Dark Ser.). 2010. 24.99 (978-1-4418-1540-8(6), 9781441815408, BAD) Brilliance Audio.

***Peril.** unabr. ed. Christine Feehan. Read by Natalie Ross Gigante & Phil Gigante. (Running Time: 14 hrs.). (Dark Ser.). 2010. audio compact disk 92.97 (978-1-4418-1537-8(6), 9781441815378, BriAudCD Unabrid); audio compact disk 38.99 (978-1-4418-1536-1(8), 9781441815361, Bril Audio CD Unabri) Brilliance Audio.

Peril: Three Hunted Men & Killers. 1 cass. (Running Time: 1 hr.). 2001. 6.98 (1693) Radio Spirits.

Peril & Promise: A Commentary on America. John Chancellor. Read by John Chancellor. 2 cass. (Running Time: 90 min. per cass.). 1990. 15.95 HarperCollins Pubs.

Peril at End House. unabr. ed. Agatha Christie. Read by Hugh Fraser. (Running Time: 20640 sec.). (Hercule Poirot Mystery Ser.). 2005. 25.95 (978-1-57270-462-6(4)) Pub: Audio Partners. Dist(s): PerseuPGW
Vacationing in St. Loo, Hercule Poirot meets a beautiful young woman named Nick Buckley, who tells him about three accidents she's had in the past few days, none of which sound much like accidents to the detective. During a chat, Nick complains of a bothersome wasp. After she leaves, Poirot finds a bullet on the ground and a bullet hole in the hat Nick had been wearing and left behind. He offers her his protection and help and she accepts. Another attempt on her life results in the death of another person, and Poirot spirits Nick away for safekeeping. When even this doesn't stop Nick's would-be killer - and it becomes clear that several "friends" could benefit greatly from her death - Poirot stages an unusual séance. Reader Hugh Fraser finds all the mystery and drama in this colorful whodunit first published as a book in 1932.

Peril at End House. unabr. ed. Agatha Christie. Read by Hugh Fraser. Contrib. by Hugh Fraser. 5 CDs. (Running Time: 20640 sec.). (Hercule Poirot Mystery Ser.). (ENG.). 2005. audio compact disk 27.95 (978-1-57270-463-3(2)) Pub: AudioGO. Dist(s): Perseus Dist

Peril at End House: A BBC Full-Cast Radio Drama. unabr. ed. Agatha Christie. Narrated by Full Cast. (Running Time: 2 hrs. 0 mins. 0 sec.). (ENG.). 2010. audio compact disk 24.95 (978-1-60283-811-6(9)) Pub: AudioGO. Dist(s): Perseus Dist

Peril in the Mist. unabr. ed. Robert Swindells. Read by Andy Crane. 2 cass. (Dinner Ladies Adventures Ser.). (J). (gr. 1-8). 1999. 18.95 (CCA 3490, Chivers Child Audio) AudioGO.

Perilous Friends. collector's ed. Carole Epstein. Read by Kate Reading. 8 cass. (Running Time: 12 hrs.). 2000. 64.00 (978-0-7366-4997-1(2)) Books on Tape.
Barbara Simons & her friend Susan break into the apartment of Susan's ex-husband, Frank, to snoop around. They find his dead body & a stash of high grade heroin that they have to take with them for safe-keeping. Then Barbara's friend Joanne convinces her to pose as a lesbian hooker trying to raise money for her AIDS-stricken friends to help investigate a cigarette smuggling gang. Meanwhile, the fact that she's an Anglophone in French Montreal is doing nothing to raise her spirits. All told, in the space of a few days, she's lost her job, sold out a friend, tampered with evidence, convinced her neighbors she's a hooker, & probably lost the love of her life. Things are not going well for Barbara.

Perilous Gard, unabr. ed. Elizabeth M. Pope. Narrated by Jill Tanner. 7 cass. (Running Time: 9 hrs. 15 mins.). (gr. 8 up). 1992. 60.00 (978-1-55690-597-1(1), 92202E7) Recorded Bks.
When Kate Sutton, lady-in-waiting to Princess Elizabeth, is banished to a mysterious old castle, she discovers the secrets, both magical & horrible, of the Fairy Folk.

Perilous Relations. collector's ed. Carole Epstein. Read by Kate Reading. 6 cass. (Running Time: 9 hrs.). 2000. 48.00 (978-0-7366-5083-0(0)) Books on Tape.
Barbara Simmons, who loves poking her nose into other people's business, has her hands full when she tries to solve the mystery surrounding the death of her former boss.

Perilous Road. William O. Steele. Read by Ramon De Ocampo. (Running Time: 4 hrs.). 2005. 19.95 (978-1-59912-909-9(4)) Iofy Corp.

Perilous Road. William O. Steele. Read by Ramon de Ocampo. 4 CDs. (Running Time: 14400 sec.). (J). (gr. 4-7). 2005. audio compact disk 27.95 (978-1-59316-040-1(2), LL132) Listen & Live.
Chris Brabson hates the Union troops. Yankee riders in the Tennessee mountains have stolen his family's newly harvested crops and their only horse. In spite of this, Chris' brother joins the Union army, and his parents refuse to take either side. But Chris has no doubts - he would fight for the Confederacy. This Newbery Honor book powerfully illustrates the senseless waste of war and the true meaning of courage and tolerance.

Perilous Road. unabr. ed. William O. Steele. Read by Ramon de Ocampo. (J). 2008. 39.99 (978-1-60514-740-6(0)) Find a World.

Perils of Peppermints. Barbara Brooks Wallace. Narrated by Suzanne Toren. 4 CDs. (Running Time: 6 hrs.). (J). 2003. audio compact disk 39.75 (978-1-4193-1809-2(8)) Recorded Bks.

Perils of Peppermints. unabr. ed. 4 cass. (Running Time: 6 hrs.). (J). 2003. 37.00 (978-1-4025-4487-3(1)) Recorded Bks.

Perimeter & Area Audio CD Set. Adapted by Benchmark Education Company Staff. (Math Explorers Ser.). (J). (gr. 3-8). 2008. audio compact disk 75.00 (978-1-60634-142-1(1)) Benchmark Educ.

Perimeter at the Arena Audio CD: Set B. Benchmark Education Co. (Math Explorers Ser.). (J). (gr. 3-8). 2009. audio compact disk 10.00 (978-1-935441-70-0(1)) Benchmark Educ.

Perimeter at the Zoo Audio CD: Set B. Benchmark Education Co. (Math Explorers Ser.). (J). (gr. 3-8). 2009. audio compact disk 10.00 (978-1-935441-71-7(X)) Benchmark Educ.

Perimeter in the Classroom Audio CD: Set B. Benchmark Education Co. (Math Explorers Ser.). (J). (gr. 3-8). 2009. audio compact disk 10.00 (978-1-935441-72-4(8)) Benchmark Educ.

Period Piece: A Cambridge Childhood. Gwen Raverat. 2005. bk. 39.95 (978-1-904555-15-5(2)); bk. 39.95 (978-1-904555-16-2(0)) Pub: Clear Bks GBR GBR. Dist(s): Intl Pubs Mktg

Period Piece: A Cambridge Childhood. Gwen Raverat. (Soundings (CDs) Ser.). (J). 2006. audio compact disk 71.95 (978-1-84559-316-2(2)) Pub: ISIS Lrg Prnt GBR. Dist(s): Ulverscroft US

Period Piece: A Cambridge Childhood. unabr. ed. Gwen Raverat. Read by Diana Bishop. 8 cass. (Soundings Ser.). (J). 2005. 69.95 (978-1-84559-113-7(5)) Pub: ISIS Lrg Prnt GBR. Dist(s): Ulverscroft US

Peripheral Vascular Surgery. Moderated by Welsley S. Moore. (Postgraduate Courses Ser.: C86-PG17). 1986. 85.00 (8627) Am Coll Surgeons.
Reviews advances in the scientific investigation, clinical application & postgraduate education as it applies to general vascular surgery. 9 hours CME credit.

Periquin. Tr. of Lentil. (SPA.). 2004. 8.95 (978-0-7882-0261-2(8)) Weston Woods.

Perish in Penzance. unabr. ed. Jeanne M. Dams. Read by Kate Reading. 5 cass. (Running Time: 7 hrs. 30 mins.). (Dorothy Martin Mystery Ser.: Vol. 7). 2001. 40.00 (978-0-7366-8484-2(0)) Books on Tape.
A thirty-year-old death haunts Alan Nesbitt, former Chief Constable in Cornwall. Back in 1968, a beautiful twenty-year-old girl was found dead on the rocks, presumably having jumped from the cliffs. All that was known about her was her age, that she had had a child six months earlier, and that she weighed about ninety pounds. Nesbitt got nowhere with the investigation, and he regrets it. Fortunately, he is now married to sleuth Dorothy Martin, who gets on the case directly. Only a few days later, a model she's just met meets a similar end, and the parallels between the two cases begin to add up. The drug dealing and smuggling that are Penzance's heritage as a coastal maritime town play a part.

Perishables Category Management: Meat Department. 1 cass. (America's Supermarket Showcase '96 Ser.). 1996. 11.00 (NGA96-038) Sound Images.

Perkins Goes Out. Read by Odds Bodkin. Created by Odds Bodkin. Contrib. by Perkins School for the Blind. (Running Time: 31 mins.). (J). 2002. (978-0-9743510-4-9(0)) Perkins Schl Blind.
This tape builds on the book also titled "Perkins Goes Out." Perkins gets ready then goes out to meet some friends. They go on a picnic, to the playground, and across the street to the library. There is a song titled "Magic World" (about sounds and exploring the world outside) and portions of songs introduced in the "Belly Button" and "Doing, Doing, Doing" cassettes.This tape is also designed to accompany the Perkins Goes Out Activity Guide that provides activities that parents and other caregivers can do with children with visual impairments - especially focusing on exploring the outside world.

Perks of Being a Wallflower. Stephen Chbosky. Narrated by Johnny Heller. (Running Time: 23400 sec.). (YA). (gr. 7-12). 2006. audio compact disk 19.99 (978-1-4193-8724-1(3)) Recorded Bks.

Perks of Being a Wallflower. unabr. ed. Stephen Chbosky. Read by Eric Cazenove. 5 cass. (Running Time: 7 hrs. 30 mins.). (YA). (gr. 9-12). 2000. 40.00 (978-0-7366-4904-9(2)) Books on Tape.
Story of what it's like to grow up in high school. More intimate than a diary, Charlie's letters are singular & unique, hilarious & devastating. We may not know where he lives. We may not know to whom he is writing. All we know is the world he shares. Caught between trying to live his life & trying to run from it puts him on a strange course through uncharted territory.

Perks of Being a Wallflower. unabr. ed. Stephen Chbosky. Read by Eric Cazenove. 5 cass. (Running Time: 7 hrs. 30 min.). (YA). 2001. 24.95 (978-0-7366-4936-0(0)) Books on Tape.

Perky Otter see Let's Read Together

Perky Otter. Created by Kane Press. (Let's Read Together Ser.). 2005. audio compact disk 4.25 (978-1-57565-183-5(1)) Pub: Kane Pr. Dist(s): Lerner Pub

Perloo the Bold. unabr. ed. Avi. Narrated by John McDonough. 5 pieces. (Running Time: 6 hrs. 30 mins.). (gr. 7 up). 1999. 45.00 (978-0-7887-3526-4(8), 95267E7) Recorded Bks.
Perloo, a studious unadventurous Montmer (rabbit-like creature) reluctantly responds to a summons from Jolaine, the Montmer "granter" & finds himself plunged into political intrigue & adventure.

Perloo the Bold. unabr. ed. Avi. Narrated by Avi. 5 cass. (Running Time: 6 hrs. 30 mins.). (YA). (gr. 7 up). 2000. pap. bk. & stu. ed. 58.24 (978-0-7887-3651-3(5), 41016X4) Recorded Bks.
Perloo, one of those mouse-like creatures known as Montmers, is an historian & something of a homebody. When the dying queen names him her successor, he is hardly ready to have greatness thrust upon him, especially when the queen's conniving son is out for vengeance. A touching lesson about integrity.

Perloo the Bold, Class Set. unabr. ed. Avi. Narrated by Avi. 5 cass. (Running Time: 6 hrs. 30 mins.). (YA). 1999. 115.70 (978-0-7887-3679-7(5), 95843X4) Recorded Bks.

Perls Reads from "In & Out the Garbage Pail" unabr. ed. Fritz Perls. 1 cass. (Running Time: 1 hr.). 1969. 11.00 (04404) Big Sur Tapes.
Reading from his autobiography which is a many-faceted mosaic of memories & reflections on his life.

Permafrost. Ed. by Marcia Phillips et al. 2004. audio compact disk 167.95 (978-90-5809-690-6(4)) Taylor and Fran.

Permafrost, MN. Stearns and Price Staff. 2001. audio compact disk 15.95; audio compact disk 15.95 Lodestone Catalog.
You wouldn't want much northern exposure in this town, where a permanent temperature inversion keeps winter around all year long.

Permanent Books. (23334) J Norton Pubs.

Permanent Conversion to God. Thomas Merton. 1 cass. (Running Time: 60 min.). (Conversion Ser.). 8.95 (AA2231) Credence Commun.
Discussions on conversion & the necessity of choosing between the Gospel & the world.

Permanent Errors see Long & Happy Life

Permanent Rose. unabr. ed. Hilary McKay. Read by Sophie Aldred. 3 cass. (Running Time: 4 hrs. 28 mins.). (Casson Family Ser.: Bk. 3). (J). (gr. 4-7). 2006. 30.00 (978-0-307-28463-1(8), Listening Lib); audio compact disk 38.00 (978-0-307-28464-8(6), Listening Lib) Pub: Random Audio Pubg. Dist(s): Random

Permanent War for Permanent Peace. Robert A. Wilson. 2 cass. 18.00 (OC75) Sound Horizons AV.

Permanent Waving. Milady Publishing Company Staff. 1 cass. (Standard Ser.: Chapter 11). 1995. 17.95 (978-1-56253-283-3(9), Milady) Pub: Delmar. Dist(s): CENGAGE Learn

Permanent Weight Control for Busy People. Bob Griswold. Read by Deirdre M. Griswold. 2000. 11.98 (978-1-55848-210-4(5)) EffectiveMN.

Permanent Weight Loss. Emmett Miller. (ENG.). 2007. audio compact disk 16.95 (978-1-55841-140-1(2)) Emmett E Miller.

Permanent Weight Loss. abr. ed. Roger W. Bretemitz. 1 cass. (Running Time: 45 min.). 1985. pap. bk. 9.95 (978-1-893417-08-3(5)) Vector Studios.
Hypnosis that changes belief system to truly realize that one can lose the weight & keep it off. Turns hunger into a friend that says "you're being successful at losing weight.".

Permanent Weight Loss, Set. Clark Cameron. 6 cass. 59.95 (1291AX) Nightingale-Conant.
Featuring the lastest in psychological training, this incredible program addresses the source of weight loss problems - not just the symptoms. Using a breakthrough technique called the Releasing Strategy, Dr. Clark Cameron shows you how to let go of negative ideas & beliefs that are the root cause of weight problems. Dr. Cameron's system is easy to learn & use. Best of all, it can be applied not only to weight loss & weight control, but to all other areas of your life as well. People who've used this revolutionary approach say it has changed their entire attitude about themselves - & life itself! Includes 24 Flash Cards featuring Releasing Statements.

Permanent Weight Loss & Management. 1998. 24.95 (978-1-58557-000-3(1)) Dynamic Growth.

Permissible Limits. unabr. ed. Graham Hurley. Read by Shirley Dixon. 12 cass. (Running Time: 18 hrs.). 2000. 94.95 (978-0-7531-0810-9(0), 000616) Pub: ISIS Audio GBR. Dist(s): Ulverscroft US
When Ellie Bruce loses her husband, in an unexplained flying accident over the English Channel, her life is torn apart. Their business is on the point of collapse. And it seems Adam was having an affair.

Permission Marketing: Turning Strangers into Friends & Friends into Customers. Seth Godin. Narrated by Richard M. Davidson. 5 cass. (Running Time: 7 hrs.). 50.00 (978-1-4025-0175-3(7)) Recorded Bks.

Permission Marketing: Turning Strangers into Friends & Friends into Customers. Seth Godin. Read by Seth Godin. 2004. 10.95 (978-0-7435-1995-3(7)) Pub: S&S Audio. Dist(s): S and S Inc

Permission Marketing: Turning Strangers into Friends & Friends into Customers. unabr. ed. Seth Godin. 2001. 45.00 (T1004L8) Recorded Bks.

Permission Slips: Every Woman's Guide to Giving Herself a Break. unabr. ed. Sherri Shepherd. Read by Sherri Shepherd. Told to Laurie Kilmartin. (Running Time: 8 hrs.). (ENG.). 2009. 24.98 (978-1-60024-751-4(2)); audio compact disk 34.98 (978-1-60024-750-7(4)) Pub: Hachet Audio. Dist(s): HachBkGrp

Permission to Be Precious. Pia Mellody. Read by Pia Mellody. 6 cass. 50.00 Set. (A1) Featuka Enter Inc.
Pia describes in detail the nature of codependence, how it manifests itself in our adult life & how to recover.

***Permission to Speak Freely: Essays & Art on Fear, Confession, & Grace.** unabr. ed. Anne Jackson. (ENG.). 2010. 10.98 (978-1-59644-917-6(9)); audio compact disk 15.98 (978-1-59644-916-9(0)) christianaud.

Perpetual Care & Flaubert in Miami Beach. Short Stories. Sheila Ballantyne. Read by Sheila Ballantyne. 1 cass. (Running Time: 68 min.). 1988. 13.95 (978-1-55644-286-5(6), 8021) Am Audio Prose.
Two short stories from her acclaimed collection Life on Earth.

Perpetual Motivation: How to Light Your Fire & Keep It Burning in Your Career & in Life. Dave Durand. Read by Dave Durand. 3 CDs. (Running Time: 14400 sec.). 2007. audio compact disk 24.95 (978-0-86716-836-5(6)) St Anthony Mess Pr.

Perri O'Shaughnessy: Breach of Promise, Acts of Malice, Move to Strike. abr. ed. Perri O'Shaughnessy. Read by Laural Merlington. (Running Time: 12 hrs.). (Nina Reilly Ser.). 2006. audio compact disk 34.95 (978-1-59737-717-1(1), 9781597377171, BACD) Brilliance Audio.
Breach of Promise: At glitzy Lake Tahoe, couples break up every day, but none quite so glamorous or successful as Lindy and Mike Markov. The scenario starts off in the standard way: Mike's met a younger woman and wants out. The problem? Mike and Lindy built a $200-million business together and Mike claims he doesn't owe Lindy a dime since they never married. Acts of Malice: Set amid the darker side of Lake Tahoe's glamorous ski resorts, Acts of Malice has Nina taking on the case of Jim Strong, a member of South Lake Tahoe's most prominent families and the owners of the posh Paradise Ski Resort. With his brother Alex recently killed in a headline-making accident that occurred while they were skiing together, Jim fears he may be indicted in the death. When the coroner announces that Alex died from injuries unrelated to the accident, Jim is charged with murder. Move to Strike: Nina's recovering from a great loss, haunted by a killer who may still be tracking her, and working on a tough new case. Her client is a sixteen-year-old girl charged with first-degree murder. Did Nikki Zack steal something from her uncle, a prominent plastic surgeon, and then kill him with an ancient samurai sword? To help find out, Nina calls in private investigator Paul Van Wagoner, her ex-lover and constant ally.

Perri O'Shaughnessy: Obstruction of Justice, Breach of Promise & Acts of Malice. abr. ed. Perri O'Shaughnessy. Narrated by Laural Merlington. 6 cass. (Running Time: 9 hrs.). (Nina Reilly Ser.). 2002. 19.95 (978-1-59086-225-4(2), 1590862252, Nova Audio Bks) Brilliance Audio.
Obstruction of Justice Two people have died in macabre accidents, one struck by lightning on Tahoe's highest mountain and one mowed down by a hit-and-run driver. In the middle of a controversial procedure to exhume one of the bodies, powerful businessman Quentin de Beers is killed. Charged with murder, Quentin's angry grandson won't talk, even to Nina Reilly, his defense attorney. Breach of Promise At glitzy Lake Tahoe, couples break up every day, but none quite so glamorous or successful as Lindy and Mike Markov. The scenario starts off in the standard way: Mike's met a younger woman and wants out. The problem? Mike and Lindy built a $200-million business together and Mike claims he doesn't owe Lindy a dime since they never married. Acts of Malice Set amid the darker side of Lake Tahoe's glamorous ski resorts, Acts of Malice has Nina taking on the case of Jim Strong, a member of South Lake Tahoe's most prominent families and the owners of the posh Paradise Ski Resort. With his brother Alex recently killed in a headline-making accident that occurred while they were skiing together, Jim fears he may be indicted in the death. When the coroner announces that Alex died from injuries unrelated to the accident, Jim is charged with murder.

Perri O'Shaugnessy Collection: Invasion of Privacy, Move to Strike, Unfit to Practice. abr. ed. Perri O'Shaughnessy. Read by Laural Merlington. 12 cass. (Running Time: 18 hrs.). (Nina Reilly Ser.). 2003. 29.95 (978-1-59086-540-8(5), 1590865405, Nova Audio Bks) Brilliance Audio.
Invasion of Privacy (Luann Kindem, engineer) Twelve years ago, a young girl disappeared. Now a filmmaker has made a movie about it. The girl's parents call it invasion of privacy. A woman lawyer calls it murder. The bloodstains on the courtroom floor belong to attorney Nina Reilly. Months earlier she'd been shot during a heated murder trial. She should have died that day. Instead, Nina has returned to the same Lake Tahoe court. Her only concession to her lingering fear is to give up criminal law. She figures an invasion of privacy lawsuit is a nice, safe civil action that will help her support her young son and pay the bills for her one-woman law office. She figures wrong. Move to Strike (Luann Kindem, engineer) Nina's not sleeping much these days. She's recovering from a great loss, haunted by a killer who may still be tracking her, and working on a tough new case. Her client is a sixteen-year-old girl charged with first-degree murder. Nikki Zack is a rebel, a thief, and the best friend of Nina's son, Bob. Did she steal something from her uncle, a prominent plastic surgeon, and then kill him with an ancient samurai sword? To help find out, Nina calls in private investigator Paul Van Wagoner, her ex-lover and constant ally, whose bravado doesn't betray his own sleepless nights. As they work through the twisting lies surrounding Nikki, it becomes brutally clear to Nina that she must pull an ace out of her sleeve in the courtroom to save her client, and solve the mystery surrounding Paul to save herself. Unfit to Practice (Melissa Coates, engineer) As an attorney championing desperate people, Nina Reilly has skirted the edges of legal ethics in pursuit of a just result but she has never before broken the rule of absolute protection of her clients' secrets. One September night at Lake Tahoe when her unlocked truck is stolen, her life changes forever. Inside are her most sensitive cases, complete with the sometimes brutally candid notes she took while interviewing her clients. It's the event that every attorney most fears - one careless moment that undoes a lifetime of building trust and respect. The worst has happened - the secrets are being revealed one by one, in ways that will cause the greatest harm. Nina's own clients complain to the State Bar of California, and suddenly Nina is fighting for her license and her livelihood in a Kafkaesque legal proceeding that may ultimately lead to her disbarment.

***Perricone Prescription.** abr. ed. Nicholas Perricone. Read by Robb Webb. (ENG.). 2005. (978-0-06-084292-5(X), Harper Audio); (978-0-06-084291-8(1), Harper Audio) HarperCollins Pubs.

Perricone Prescription: A Physician's 28-Day Program for Total Body & Face Rejuvenation. abr. ed. Nicholas Perricone. Read by Robb Webb. (Running Time: 10800 sec.). 2008. audio compact disk 14.95 (978-0-06-146773-8(1), Harper Audio) HarperCollins Pubs.

Perricone Promise: Look Younger, Live Longer in Three Easy Steps. abr. ed. Nicholas Perricone. Read by Lloyd Sherr. (ENG.). 2005. 14.98 (978-1-59483-128-7(9)) Pub: Hachet Audio. Dist(s): HachBkGrp

Perricone Promise: Look Younger, Live Longer in Three Easy Steps. abr. ed. Nicholas Perricone. Read by Lloyd Sherr. (Running Time: 2 hrs. 30 mins.). (ENG.). 2009. 34.98 (978-1-60788-030-1(X)) Pub: Hachet Audio. Dist(s): HachBkGrp

Perro Vagabundo. Marc Simont. 14 vols. (Running Time: 6 mins.). (Picture Book Readalong in Spanish Ser.). (J). 2004. pap. bk. 37.95 (978-1-59112-937-0(0)) Live Oak Media.

Perro Vagabundo. Marc Simont. Read by David Cromett. 11 vols. (Running Time: 6 mins.). (Picture Book Readalong in Spanish Ser.). (SPA., (J). 2004. pap. bk. 16.95 (978-1-59112-935-6(4)) Pub: Live Oak Media. Dist(s): AudioGO

Perro Vagabundo. Marc Simont. Illus. by Marc Simont. (Running Time: 6 mins.). (J). 2004. 9.95 (978-1-59112-934-9(6)); audio compact disk 12.95 (978-1-59112-938-7(9)) Live Oak Media.

Perro Vagabundo. Marc Simont. 1 CD. (Running Time: 5:51 min.). (Picture Book Readalong in Spanish Ser.). (SPA.). (J). 2005. pap. bk. 18.95 (978-1-59112-939-4(7)) Pub: Live Oak Media. Dist(s): AudioGO

***Perry Mason -Case of Velvet Claws.** Erle Stanley Gardner. 2010. audio compact disk 9.99 (978-1-4418-9217-1(6)) Brilliance Audio.

Persecution. Dan Corner. 1 cass. 3.00 (70) Evang Outreach.

***Persecution.** abr. ed. David Limbaugh. Read by David Limbaugh. (ENG.). 2004. (978-0-06-078649-6(3), Harper Audio) HarperCollins Pubs.

***Persecution.** abr. ed. David Limbaugh. Read by David Limbaugh. (ENG.). 2004. (978-0-06-081407-6(1), Harper Audio) HarperCollins Pubs.

Persecution: Why in the World Do They Hate Us? George Pearsons. (ENG.). 2008. audio compact disk 30.00 (978-1-57562-970-4(4)) K Copeland Pubns.

Persephone & the Pomegranate Seed. Bradley Clark. 1 cass. 8.95 (053) Am Fed Astrologers.
An AFA Convention workshop tape.

Persephone's Beauty Box & Psyche's Failure: The Tale of Eros & Psyche Re-Explored. Read by Nathan Schwartz-Salant. 1 cass. (Running Time: 90 min.). 1982. 10.95 (978-0-7822-0248-9(9), 125) C G Jung IL.

Perservering in Love. Eknath Easwaran. 1 cass. (Running Time: 53 min.). 1989. 7.95 (978-1-58638-589-7(5), PL) Nilgiri Pr.
Includes many primary topics such as: attentiveness to the eight-points, family life as a suitable context, the importance of spiritual reading before bed, & falling asleep in the mantram.

Perseus, Nos. 67, 68 & 69. Carl Faber. 3 cass. (Running Time: 3 hrs. 45 min.). 1987. 28.50 (978-0-918026-46-0(6), SR 85-970) Perseus Pr.

***Perseus & Medusa.** Eve & Sebastian Facio. Illus. by Daniel Perez. Retold by Blake A. Hoena. (Mythology Ser.). (ENG.). 2010. audio compact disk 14.60 (978-1-4342-2573-3(9)) CapstoneDig.

Perseus & the Gorgon's Head, Level 1. 2 cass. (Running Time: 1 hr. 30 mins.). (SmartReader Ser.). (J). 1999. pap. bk. & tchr. ed. 19.95 (978-0-7887-0784-1(1), 79352T3) Recorded Bks.
Greek mythology has all the action & excitement of the best adventure stories. Watch Perseus as he faces monsters & dragons on his quest to fulfill a prophecy.

Perseus & the Gorgon's Head, Level 2. 2 cass. (Running Time: 1 hr. 50 mins.). (SmartReader Ser.). (J). 1999. pap. bk. & tchr. ed. 19.95 (978-0-7887-0786-5(8), 79353T3) Recorded Bks.

Perseverance, Vol. 6. AIO Team Staff. Prod. by Focus on the Family Staff. (Running Time: 1 hr. 10 mins. 0 sec.). (Adventures in Odyssey Life Lessons Ser.). (ENG.). (J). 2005. audio compact disk 5.99 (978-1-58997-223-0(6)) Pub: Focus Family. Dist(s): Tyndale Hse

***Perseverance: Hanging on to Jesus through Hebrews.** John M. Oakes. (ENG.). 2010. 10.00 (978-0-9844974-3-0(9)) Illumination MA.

Perseverance & Fruitfulness. Dan Corner. 1 cass. 3.00 (71) Evang Outreach.

Perseverance of God: Psalm 46:7; Gen. 32:1-32. Ed Young. 1990. 4.95 (978-0-7417-1831-0(6), 831) Win Walk.

Perseverence. Swami Jyotirmayananda. 1 cass. (Running Time: 1 hr.). 1990. 12.99 Yoga Res Foun.

Pershing: Great General Series. unabr. ed. Jim Lacey & Wesley K. Clark. Read by Tom Weiner. (Running Time: 6.5 hrs. 0 mins.). 2008. 29.95 (978-1-4332-4982-2(0)); 44.95 (978-1-4332-4980-8(4)); audio compact disk 60.00 (978-1-4332-4981-5(2)) Blckstn Audio.

Persian. 2 cass. (Running Time: 80 min.). (Language - Thirty Library). bk. 16.95 set in vinyl album. Moonbeam Pubns.
Using the proven method based on the famous U.S. Military accelerated language learning program, Language/30 courses stress conversationally useful words & phrases.

Persian. Ed. by Charles Berlitz. 2 cass. (Running Time: 1 hr. 30 mins.). (Language/30 Brief Course Ser.). pap. bk. 21.95 (AF1038) J Norton Pubs.
Quick, highly condensed introduction to the words & phrases you'll need to communicate effectively in the country you're visiting. Cassettes & phrase guide book are in a vinyl album.

Persian. abr. ed. Barry Sadler. Read by Charlton Griffin. 2 vols. (Casca Ser.: No. 6). 2003. (978-1-58807-523-9(0)); audio compact disk 25.00 (978-1-58807-280-1(0)); audio compact disk (978-1-58807-711-0(X)) Am Pubng Inc.

Persian. abr. ed. Barry Sadler. Read by Charleton Griffin. 2 cass. (Running Time: 3 hrs.). (Casca Ser.: No. 6). 2003. 18.00 (978-1-58807-106-4(5)) Am Pubng Inc.
Inducted into Shapur IIs royal forces as a commander, Casca enters the volatile lands of the Persian Empire to battle the military force of the equestrian Huns. However, other powers are teaming to plot Cascas demise; Rasheed, trusted advisor to the king, seeks a death sentence for Casca. Though cursed to journey an immortal life of a soldier, can Casca survive burning at the stake?Fraught with religious zealots, the Brotherhood of the Lamb brands Casca a heretic. Battling a secretive, radical Christian sect, Casca must not only save his life, but that of a political dynastyas CASCA: THE PERSIAN.

Persian: Language 30. Educational Services Corporation Staff. 2004. audio compact disk 21.95 (978-1-931850-14-8(3)) Educ Svcs DC.

Persian Boy. unabr. ed. Mary Renault. Read by Peter MacDonald. 11 cass. (Running Time: 16 hrs. 30 min.). (Alexander Trilogy). 1984. 88.00 (978-0-7366-0871-8(0), 1821) Books on Tape.
The sequel to Mary Renault's earlier novel about Alexander the Great, "Fire from Heaven." It follows the story of Alexander from his victory over the Persian King Darius to his death seven years later.

Persian Boy. unabr. ed. Mary Renault. Narrated by Aviva Skell. 10 cass. (Running Time: 15 hrs.). 1983. 85.00 (978-1-55690-407-3(X), 83060E7) Recorded Bks.
Sixteen year old Bagoas, eunuch slave & lover, was an actual historical character. He relates the career of the greatest conqueror of all time - Alexander.

Persian Expedition. Xenophon. Read by Pat Bottino. 7 cass. (Running Time: 10 hrs.). 1999. 49.95 (978-0-7861-1568-6(8), 2397) Blckstn Audio.
In speeches to the army of mercenaries you can find humor, delight in an exact analysis of a situation, sensitive understanding of men - all of which qualities the Spartans sorely lacked.

Persian Expedition. unabr. ed. Xenophon & Xenophon. Read by Pat Bottino. Tr. by Rex Warner. (Running Time: 36000 sec.). 2008. audio compact disk 29.95 (978-1-4332-4517-6(5)); audio compact disk & audio compact disk 80.00 (978-1-4332-4516-9(7)) Blckstn Audio.

Persian, Farsi: Language/30. rev. ed. Educational Services Corporation Staff. Intro. by Charles Berlitz. 2 cass. (PER.). 1994. pap. bk. 21.95 (978-0-910542-75-3(9)) Educ Svcs DC.
Persian (Farsi) self-teaching language course.

Persian Fiction Reader, Set. rev. ed. Michael C. Hillmann & Mohammad M. Khorrami. 3 cass. (Running Time: 1 hr. 30 min. per cass.). (PER.). 1995. 24.00 (3115) Dunwoody Pr.
Thirty-two texts cover a range of subjects such as city, village, & domestic life, commercial transactions, war, & reflections on life.

Persian Gulf States. unabr. ed. Joseph Stromberg. Read by Peter Hackes. (Running Time: 10800 sec.). (World's Political Hot Spots Ser.). 2006. audio compact disk 25.95 (978-0-7861-6475-2(1)) Pub: Blckstn Audio. Dist(s): NetLibrary CO

Persian Gulf States. unabr. ed. Joseph Stromberg. Read by Peter Hackes. Ed. by Wendy McElroy. 2 cass. (Running Time: 3 hrs.). Dramatization. (World's Political Hot Spots Ser.). (YA). (gr. 11 up). 1992. 17.95 (978-0-938935-95-7(X), 10360) Knowledge Prod.
More than half of the world's oil comes from Persian Gulf states. Political instability & religious strife here threaten to interrupt economic routines throughout the world.

Persian Letters, Set. unabr. ed. Charles de Secondat Montesquieu. Read by Robert L. Halvorson. 7 cass. (Running Time: 10 hr. 30 min.). 49.95 (92) Halvorson Assocs.

Persian Literature, Modern: The Beginning & Early Writers. Hassan Kamshad. 1 cass. (Running Time: 22 min.). 1968. 11.95 (23122) J Norton Pubs.
A study of the imaginative prose literature written in Iran during the past hundred years.

Persian Newspaper Reader, Set. Michael C. Hillmann & Ramin Sarraf. 2 cass. (Running Time: 1 hr. 30 min. per cass.). (PER.). 1996. 19.00 (3150) Dunwoody Pr.
Fifty-two selections from Iranian newspapers are designed for the student who has completed at least one semester of study & is ready to begin reading simple natural language text.

Persian Night: Iran under the Khomeinist Revolution. unabr. ed. Amir Taheri. Read by Robertson Dean. (Running Time: 14 hrs. 0 mins.). (ENG.). 2009. 29.95 (978-1-4332-7496-1(5)); 79.95 (978-1-4332-7492-3(2)); audio compact disk 99.00 (978-1-4332-7493-0(0)) Blckstn Audio.

Persian Pickle Club, Set. abr. ed. Sandra Dallas. Perf. by Maira Kelly. 4 cass. (Running Time: 6 hrs.). 1995. 22.95 (978-1-56876-047-6(7), 693294) Soundlines Ent.
It is the 1930's, & hard times have hit Harveyville, Kansas, where the crops are burning up. For Queenie Bean, a young farmwife, the highlight of each week is the gathering of the Persian Pickle Club, a group of local women dedicated to improving their minds, exchanging gossip, & putting well honed quilting skills to use. Then the club gains a new member, a city girl from Denver with a penchant for investigative journalism, & the Pickles face the revelation of a long-kept secret involving the disappeamce of one of their husbands. Audie Award winner1996.

Persian Radif Music, Set. Perf. by Dariush Tala'i. 5 CD. 1999. audio compact disk 65.00 (978-1-56859-073-8(3)) Mazda Pubs.
Recordings were made at the University of Washington in Seattle in 1992 while he was a visiting professor in the school of music.

Persian Vol. 1 (Contemporary Spoken Persian) CDs & Text. Mehdi Marashi. 8 CDs. (Running Time: 8 hrs.). (PER.). 2005. audio compact disk 225.00 (978-1-57970-136-9(1), AFPE01D) J Norton Pubs.

Persian Vol. 2 (Contemporary Spoken Persian) CDs & Etxt. Mehdi Marashi. 8 CDs. (Running Time: 8 hrs.). (PER.). 2005. audio compact disk 225.00 (978-1-57970-265-6(1), AFPE20D, Audio-For) J Norton Pubs.

Persian War: From the Histories. abr. ed. Herodotus. Read by Roy Marsden. 3 CDs. (Running Time: 3 hrs. 55 mins.). 1996. audio compact disk 22.98 (978-962-634-084-4(3), NA308412, Naxos AudioBooks) Naxos.
The heroic tale of the Greek's resistance to the vast invading force assembled by Xerxes, King of Persia. Here, not only are the great battles, but also peneterating human insight and a powerful sense of epic destiny at work.

Persian War: From the Histories. abr. ed. Herodotus. Read by Roy Marsden. 3 cass. (Running Time: 3 hrs. 55 mins.). 1996. 17.98 (978-962-634-584-9(5), NA308414, Naxos AudioBooks) Naxos.

persimmon Tree. Bryce Courtenay. Read by Humphrey Bower. (Running Time: 28 hrs. 15 mins.). 2009. 114.99 (978-1-74214-217-3(6), 9781742142173) Pub: Bolinda Pubng AUS. Dist(s): Bolinda Pub Inc

persimmon Tree. unabr. ed. Bryce Courtenay. Read by Humphrey Bower. (Running Time: 28 hrs. 15 mins.). 2008. audio compact disk 123.95 (978-1-921334-72-6(X), 9781921334726) Pub: Bolinda Pubng AUS. Dist(s): Bolinda Pub Inc

Persimmon Tree. unabr. ed. Bryce Courtenay. Read by Humphrey Bower. (Running Time: 100800 sec.). 2008. audio compact disk 54.95 (978-1-921334-73-3(8)) Pub: Bolinda Pubng AUS. Dist(s): Bolinda Pub Inc

Persistant Prayer & Intercession. Frank Damazio. 2 cass. (Running Time: 3 hrs.). 2000. (978-1-886849-50-1(1)) CityChristian.

Persistence: Luke 11:5-13. Ed Young. 1993. 4.95 (978-0-7417-1970-6(3), 970) Win Walk.

Persistence - an Iron Will, Vol. 5. Richard Gorham & Orison Swett Marden. Narrated by Richard Gorham. (ENG.). 2006. audio compact disk 14.95 (978-0-9791934-4-6(3)) LshipTools.

Persistence Is for Suckers (an Essay from Things I've Learned from Women Who've Dumped Me) abr. ed. David Wain. Read by David Wain. Ed. by Ben Karlin. (Running Time: 15 mins.). (ENG.). 2008. 1.98 (978-1-60024-332-5(0)) Pub: Hachet Audio. Dist(s): HachBkGrp

***Persistence of Desire.** unabr. ed. John Updike. Read by John Updike. (ENG.). 2009. (978-0-06-196251-6(1), Caedmon) HarperCollins Pubs.

***Persistence of Desire: A Selection from the John Updike Audio Collection.** unabr. ed. John Updike. Read by John Updike. (ENG.). 2009. (978-0-06-196252-3(X), Caedmon) HarperCollins Pubs.

Person & Gifts of the Holy Spirit. 2003. audio compact disk (978-1-931713-87-0(1)) Word For Today.

Person from England. unabr. collector's ed. Fitzroy Maclean. Read by Richard Brown. 12 cass. (Running Time: 18 hrs.). 1992. 96.00 (978-0-7366-2192-2(X), 2987) Books on Tape.
In the 19th century, Englishmen, Russians & others contended for Central Asia - from the Caspian to the Karakoram, the Khyber Pass to Siberia. Maclean recalls the romantic fascination of this contest.

Person in Charge of Child Care. Dora C. Fowler. 4 cass. (Running Time: 6 hrs.). 1985. pap. bk. 59.00 Set, incl. bk., 20p. (978-1-57323-020-9(0)) Natl Inst Child Mgmt.
Child care management training materials.

Person of Interest. unabr. ed. Susan Choi. Read by Bernadette Dunne. (Running Time: 57600 sec.). 2008. 29.95 (978-1-4332-0859-1(8)); audio compact disk 29.95 (978-1-4332-0860-7(1)) Blckstn Audio.

Person of Interest. unabr. ed. Susan Choi. Read by Bernadette Dunne. (Running Time: 57600 sec.). 2008. audio compact disk & audio compact disk 29.95 (978-1-4332-0861-4(X)) Blckstn Audio.

Person of Interest. unabr. ed. Suzanne Choi. Read by Bernadette Dunne. (Running Time: 57600 sec.). 2008. 72.95 (978-1-4332-0862-1(8)); audio compact disk & audio compact disk 99.00 (978-1-4332-0863-8(6)) Blckstn Audio.

Person of Interest. unabr. ed. Theresa Schwegel. Narrated by Cristine McMurdo-Wallis. 11 CDs. (Running Time: 12 hrs. 45 mins.). 2008. audio compact disk 123.75 (978-1-4361-2037-1(3)); audio compact disk 56.95 (978-1-4361-2038-8(1)) Recorded Bks.
Author Theresa Schwegel's debut won the Edgar Award for Best First Novel and was also shortlisted for the Anthony Award. Person of Interest is an astute slice of suspenseful crime fiction offering an intense portrait of the complicated lives of an undercover police officer and his family. As Schwegel steadily ratchets up the tension, the McHugh family faces mounting internal and external pressures that threaten to shred the very fabric of their domestic life.

Person of Jesus Christ. Lester Sumrall. 3 cass. (Running Time: 4 hrs. 30 mins). 1999. 40.00 (978-1-58568-103-7(2)) Sumrall Pubng.

Person of the Holy Spirit. Lester Sumrall. 12 cass. (Running Time: 18 hrs.). 1999. 48.00 (978-1-58568-101-3(6)) Sumrall Pubng.

Person of the Holy Spirit, Pack. 2003. audio compact disk (978-1-931713-85-6(5)) Word For Today.

Person of the Holy Spirit Series. Kenneth W. Hagin, Jr. 4 cass. 1994. 16.00 Set. (31J) Faith Lib Pubns.

Person of Tomorrow. unabr. ed. Carl Ransom Rogers. 1 cass. (Running Time: 90 min.). 1970. 11.00 Big Sur Tapes.

***Person or Persons Unknown.** (ENG.). 2010. audio compact disk (978-1-59171-262-6(9)) Falcon Picture.

Person or Persons Unknown. Anthea Fraser. Read by Jacqueline Tong. 6 cass. (Running Time: 28140 sec.). (Rona Parish Mysteries Ser.). 2006. 54.95 (978-0-7927-3944-9(2), CSL 924); audio compact disk 74.95 (978-0-7927-3945-6(0), SLD 924) AudioGO.

Person or Persons Unknown. unabr. ed. Bruce Alexander. Read by Stuart Langton. 7 cass. (Running Time: 10 hrs. 30 min.). (Sir John Fielding Mystery Ser.). 1999. 56.00 (978-0-7366-4337-5(0), 4826) Books on Tape.
In eighteenth century London prostitutes are being brutally murdered in Covent Garden. Sir John Fielding, the blind magistrate who cofounded London's first place force, must call upon his keen intellect & uncommon detecting skills to solve this shocking series of crimes with a plan that is a daring as it is desperate.

Person to Person. 1 cass. 7.95 student bk. (BEN130) J Norton Pubs.

Person to Person. 3rd rev. ed. Jack Richards et al. 2005. audio compact disk 39.95 (978-0-19-430222-7(9)) OUP.

Person to Person. 3rd rev. ed. Jack Richards et al. 2005. audio compact disk 39.95 (978-0-19-430221-0(0)) OUP.

Person to Person. 3rd rev. ed. Jack Richards et al. 2 cds. 2005. audio compact disk 39.95 (978-0-19-430223-4(7)) OUP.

Person to Person (Andrew) John 1:40-42. Ed Young. 1985. 4.95 (978-0-7417-1466-4(3), 466) Win Walk.

Persona & Shadow. Read by John Van Eenwyk. 2 cass. (Running Time: 1 hr. 45 min.). 1991. 16.95 Set. (978-0-7822-0320-2(5), 441) C G Jung IL.

Persona & Shadow in Dreams. Read by James Wyly. 2 cass. (Running Time: 2 hrs. 30 min.). 1988. 18.95 Set. (978-0-7822-0336-3(1), 342) C G Jung IL.

Persona Non Grata. unabr. ed. Ruth Downie. Narrated by Simon Vance. (Running Time: 10 hrs. 30 mins. 0 sec.). (Roman Empire Ser.). (ENG.). 2009. audio compact disk 79.99 (978-1-4001-4418-1(3)) Pub: Tantor Media. Dist(s): IngramPubServ

Persona Non Grata: A Novel of the Roman Empire. unabr. ed. Ruth Downie. Narrated by Simon Vance. (Running Time: 10 hrs. 30 mins. 0 sec.). (Roman Empire Ser.). (ENG.). 2009. 29.99 (978-1-4001-6418-9(4)); audio compact disk 39.99 (978-1-4001-1418-4(7)) Pub: Tantor Media. Dist(s): IngramPubServ

***Persona Non Grata: A Novel of the Roman Empire.** unabr. ed. Ruth Downie. Narrated by Simon Vance. (Running Time: 10 hrs. 30 mins.). (Roman Empire Ser.). 2009. 16.99 (978-1-4001-8418-7(5)) Tantor Media.

Personagges de Contes en Chanson pour les Petits et les Grandes. 1 CD. (Running Time: 1 hr. 30 mins.). (Prelude Ser.).Tr. of Fairy Tale Characters in Songs for Children of All Ages. (FRE., (J). 2000. pap. bk. 19.95 (978-2-7005-0217-6(5)) Pub: Assimil FRA. Dist(s): Distribks Inc

Personal Achievement. Shad Helmstetter. 1 cass. (Self-Talk Cassettes Ser.). 10.95 (978-0-937065-39-6(0)) Grindle Pr.

Personal Ads, Why Not? Lynn Davis. Read by Lynn Davis. Ed. by Trudy Meehan. Illus. by Tony Portello. 1 cass. (Running Time: 1 hr.). 1983. pap. bk. 9.95 (978-0-9610742-0-3(5)) Purcell Prods.
Takes you step-by-step through the ins & outs, the do's & don'ts of personal ads. Learn how to choose the right publication; how to write your ad; how to get the most for your money; how to describe yourself effectively; how to answer other people's ads; telephone techniques; who picks up the tab; screening for safety; handling rejection.

Personal Ads, Why Not? Davis Lynn. Read by Lynn Davis. 1 cass. (Running Time: 1 hr.). 1984. pap. bk. 16.95 Purcell Prods.

Personal & Collective Dreambody in Disease. Joseph Goodbread. 2 cass. 18.00 (OC137) Sound Horizons AV.

Personal & Collective Healing. W. Brugh Joy. Read by W. Brugh Joy. 2 cass. (Running Time: 2 hrs. 15 min.). 1989. 11.95 Set. Tigers Nest Aud.
Educational aid which teaches the listener about self nourishment & the dynamics of healing illness. Recorded live public presentation.

Personal & Impersonal God. Swami Amar Jyoti. 1 cass. 1989. 9.95 (K-119) Truth Consciousness.
Ending the age-old controversy regarding God with form & the Formless Absolute. The Prophets differ in method but not in Principle. A more enlightened view of worship.

Personal & Planetary Peace: Guided Imagery for Conscious Co-Creation of Universal Peace. 1 cass. (Running Time: 1 hr. 30 mins.). 1999. 19.95 (978-1-893087-23-1(9)) Awaken Vis.

Personal & Professional Disappointment. Harriet Hensley. Read by Harriet Hensley. Ed. by Ellen Harkins & Patricia Magerkurth. 1 cass. (Running Time: 31 min.). (Life Stages Ser.). 1991. 10.00 (978-1-56948-016-8(8)) Menninger Clinic.
Harriet Hensley, MSW, offers insights into the life stages & how our expectations can create times of disappointment. She explores the ways to manage & understand the events that may create difficulties as people balance both a professional & private life.

Personal Best Balancing Fitness & Nutrition CD: Individual License. Contrib. by Nutrition Company Staff. (gr. 6-12). 2004. audio compact disk 88.00 (978-1-59070-242-0(5)) Goodheart.

Personal Best Balancing Fitness & Nutrition CD: Site License. Contrib. by Nutrition Company Staff. (gr. 6-12). 2004. audio compact disk 264.00 (978-1-59070-243-7(3)) Goodheart.

Personal BrandStorming, Vol. 2. Mark Victor Hansen. 1 CD. 2002. audio compact disk 25.00 (978-0-9674506-3-6(2)) Personal Brand Pr.

Personal BrandStorming Vol. 1: Learn the Personal Branding Insights from Those Who Lived Them. 1 CD. 2002. audio compact disk 25.00 (978-0-9674506-2-9(4)) Personal Brand Pr.

Personal BrandStorming Vol. 3: A Conversation with Wyland. 1 CD. (Running Time: 75 Min). 2002. audio compact disk 25.00 (978-0-9674506-4-3(0)) Personal Brand Pr.

Personal Celebration Series. unabr. ed. Paul R. Scheele. 4 cass. 1991. 29.95 set. (978-0-925480-23-1(1)) Learn Strategies.
Four cassettes with affirmations for people to gain satisfaction & purpose in their lives.

Personal Demon. unabr. ed. Kelley Armstrong. Narrated by Laural Merlington & Todd McLaren. (Running Time: 12 hrs. 30 mins. 0 sec.). (Women of the Otherworld Ser.: Bk. 8). (ENG.). 2008. audio compact disk 39.99 (978-1-4001-0551-9(X)); audio compact disk 29.99 (978-1-4001-5551-4(7)) Pub: Tantor Media. Dist(s): IngramPubServ

Personal Demon. unabr. ed. Kelley Armstrong. Narrated by Todd McLaren & Laural Merlington. (Running Time: 12 hrs. 30 mins. 0 sec.). (Women of the Otherworld Ser.: Bk. 8). (ENG.). 2008. audio compact disk 79.99 (978-1-4001-3551-6(6)) Pub: Tantor Media. Dist(s): IngramPubServ

***Personal Demons.** unabr. ed. Lisa Desrochers. Read by Sara Barnett, Michael Nathanson. (Running Time: 10 hrs.). 2010. 39.97 (978-1-4418-8238-7(3), 9781441882387, BADLE) Brilliance Audio.

***Personal Demons.** unabr. ed. Lisa Desrochers. Read by Michael Nathanson & Sara Barnett. (Running Time: 11 hrs.). 2010. audio compact disk 19.99 (978-1-4418-8234-9(0), 9781441882349, Bril Audio CD Unabri) Brilliance Audio.

***Personal Demons.** unabr. ed. Lisa DesRochers & Lisa Desrochers. Read by Sara Barnett, Michael Nathanson. (Running Time: 11 hrs.). 2010. 19.99 (978-1-4418-8236-3(7), 9781441882363, Brilliance MP3); 39.97 (978-1-4418-8237-0(5), 9781441882370, Brlnc Audio MP3 Lib) Brilliance Audio.

***Personal Demons.** unabr. ed. Lisa DesRochers & Lisa Desrochers. Read by Sara Barnett & Michael Nathanson. (Ru[illegible]ng Time: 11 hrs.). 2010. audio compact disk 49.97 (978-1-4418-8235[illegible], [illegible]9781441882356, BriAudCD Unabrid) Brilliance Audio.

Personal Development. unabr. ed. Robert A. Monroe. Read by Robert A. Monroe. (Running Time: 45 min.). (Explorer Ser.). 1986. 12.95 (978-1-56113-029-0(X), 30) Monroe Institute.
Exercises about altering the concept of time.

Personal Development Series. 9 cass. 46.00 set, 6 progs.; 60.00 set, 8 progs.; 67.00 set, 9 progs. (831; 832; 83 839) Direction Dynamics.
Most topics from book: "It's All in Your Head".

Personal Devil. Roberta Gellis. Read by Nadia May. 8 cass. (Running Time: 11 hrs.). 2005. 65.95 (978-0-7861-2934-8(4), 3409); audio compact disk 81.00 (978-0-7861-8188-9(5), 3409) Blckstn Audio.

Personal Digital Storage Equipment in United Kingdom: A Strategic Reference 2007. Compiled by Icon Group International, Inc. Staff. 2007. ring bd. 195.00 (978-0-497-82455-6(8)) Icon Grp.

Personal Discipline Against Prejudiced Thinking. Instructed by Manly P. Hall. 8.95 (978-0-89314-208-7(5), C820620) Philos Res.

Personal Ecology: The Complete Self-Esteem Program. Lloyd Glauberman. 2 cass. (Hypno-Peripheral Processing Tapes Ser.). 34.95 Set. (851PA-2M) Nightingale-Conant.
This breakthrough psychotechnology program combines the methods of hypnotherapy with the latest teachings of Neuro-Linguistic Programming. Each high-impact tape gently overloads your conscious mind with messages on two channels at once, creating a synergistic whole that unleashes both hemispheres of your brain.

Personal Efficiency Program: How to Get Organized to Do More Work in Less Time. 3rd unabr. rev. ed. Kerry Gleeson. Read by Barrett Whitener. (Running Time: 9 hrs.). (ENG.). 2007. audio compact disk 29.98 (978-1-59659-078-6(5), GildAudio) Pub: Gildan Media. Dist(s): HachBkGrp

Personal Efficiency Program, 4th Edition: How to Stop Feeling Overwhelmed & Win Back Control of Your Work! unabr. ed. Kerry Gleeson. Read by Erik Synnesvetd. (Running Time: 7 hrs. 20 mins.). (ENG.). 2009. 24.98 (978-1-59659-337-4(7), GildAudio) Pub: Gildan Media. Dist(s): HachBkGrp

Personal Empowering. D.A. Tubesing. 1 cass. (Running Time: 43 min.). (Guided Meditation Ser.: No. 4). 11.95 (978-0-938586-81-4(5), PE) Whole Person.
Side A: My Gifts discloses a box of special gifts from within the "heart's house." As listeners unwrap their gifts, they unlock inner resources for meeting life's challenges. Side B: Hidden Strengths provide a quiet visit to a timeless desert canyon that restores a sense of perspective, power, & strength.

Personal Empowerment CD Album. Bruce Goldberg. (ENG.). 2005. audio compact disk 75.00 (978-1-57968-025-1(9)) Pub: B Goldberg. Dist(s): Baker Taylor

Personal Empowerment Program Cassette Album, Set. Bruce Goldberg. Read by Bruce Goldberg. 6 cass. (Running Time: 3 hrs.). (ENG.). 2006. 65.00 (978-1-885577-77-1(X)) Pub: B Goldberg. Dist(s): Baker Taylor
Through self-hypnosis learn to overcome procrastination and take charge of life.

Personal Energy Power. Eldon Taylor. 2 cass. (Running Time: 62 min. per cass.). (Omniphonics Ser.). 29.95 incl. script Set. (978-1-55978-812-0(7), 4013) Progress Aware Res.
3-D soundtrack with underlying subliminal affirmations, night & day versions.

Personal Evolution: The Art of Living with Purpose. Veronica Ray. 1 cass. (Running Time: 60 min.). bk. 10.00 (978-0-89486-825-2(X)) Hazelden.
Through stories & narratives, listeners are invited to sort through the stories & beliefs that have been given meaning to their lives.

Personal Evolution "Stop Smoking" Patrick K. Porter. 1 cass. (978-1-887630-08-5(2)) Renaissnce Pub.
Psychology self-help.

Personal Evolution "Success" Patrick K. Porter. 2 cass. Set. (978-1-887630-00-9(7)) Renaissnce Pub.

Personal Evolution "Weight Control" Patrick K. Porter. 1 cass. (978-1-887630-07-8(4)) Renaissnce Pub.

Personal Excellence: Where Achievement & Fulfillment Meet. unabr. ed. Ken Blanchard. Read by Ken Blanchard. Ed. by Dan Strutzel. 6 cass. (Running Time: 6 hrs.). 1993. 49.95 Set, incl. wkbk. (662A) Nightingale-Conant.
Develop your personal mission statement, identify your values, set goals & lead a balanced life.

Personal Experience of the Christian Mystery. Instructed by Manly P. Hall. 8.95 (978-0-89314-209-4(3), C861221) Philos Res.

Personal Finance. Carol S. Mull. 1 cass. 8.95 (455) Am Fed Astrologers.
What does your chart show re:work, etc.

Personal Finance. abr. ed. Eric Tyson. 1 cass. 9.95 (51666) Books on Tape.
For those who don't know the difference between the commodities market & the supermarket, this expert & trustworthy advice will cut through the jungle of statistic complexity and show how to make easy work of your own finances, no matter what the income or experience level.

Personal Finance. 5th rev. abr. ed. Eric Tyson. Read by Brett Barry. (Running Time: 12600 sec.). (For Dummies Ser.). 2006. audio compact disk 14.95 (978-0-06-115325-9(7)) HarperCollins Pubs.

***Personal Finance for Dummies.** abr. ed. Eric Tyson. Read by Brett Barry. (ENG.). 2006. (978-0-06-123034-9(0), Harper Audio); (978-0-06-123033-2(2), Harper Audio) HarperCollins Pubs.

Personal Finances. Gary V. Whetstone. Adapted by Gif Wilson. (Practics Ser.: Vol. PR 201). 1997. 170.00 (978-1-58866-064-0(8)) Gary Whet Pub.

Personal Financial Planning for Lawyers. Contrib. by Joan Tucker et al. (Running Time: 3 hrs.). 1985. 85.00 incl. program handbook. NJ Inst CLE.
The speakers analyze retirement & security plans, what investment choices remain available, how to evaluate lifestyle, objectives & risk tolerance.

Personal Financial Planning in a Crisis Situation. Suzanne Clark-James. 1 cass. 119.00 incl. wkbk. (740050KQ) Am Inst CPA.
You'll find a wealth of practical tips here to help you deal with emotionally stressed people, especially those confronting divorce, death & disability. Through basic communication principles, nonverbal communication & active listening, you'll discover methods of presenting information to clients in crisis...How to make such clients feel more comfortable...How to help them finacially weather their traumas. Technical skills are discussed in conjunction with communication skills, covering: money management, savings & investments, asset transfer issues, taxes, insurance & employee benefits.

Personal Genius. Paul R. Scheele. Read by Paul R. Scheele. 1 cass. (Running Time: 17 min.). (Paraliminal Tapes Ser.). 1990. 14.95 (978-0-925480-14-9(2)) Learn Strategies.
Helps activate listeners hidden intelligence & use more of true, natural genius.

Personal Goals. Virgil B. Smith. 1 cass. (Running Time: 12 min.). 1972. 5.95 (978-1-878507-04-4(4), 23C) Human Grwth Services.
Reasons for goals; types of goals; ways of organizing goals by both importance priority & time priority; reorganizing goals when needs & interests change.

***Personal God: Can You Really Know the One Who Made the Universe?** unabr. ed. Tim Stafford. (Running Time: 2 hrs. 49 mins. 0 sec.). (ENG.). 2009. 14.99 (978-0-310-77211-8(7)) Zondervan.

Personal Growth. unabr. ed. Judith L. Powell. Read by Judith L. Powell. 1 cass. (Running Time: 40 min.). (Successful Living Ser.). 1987. pap. bk. 12.95 (978-0-914295-27-3(6)) Top Mtn Pub.
Side A presents exercises designed to magnify personal growth potential, motivate creative solutions to personal problems, & realize dreams & ideals. Side B presents subliminal attitude suggestions hidden in New Age Music.

Personal Growth Series. 8 cass. 52.00 incl. vinyl storage album. (LS-5) Crystal Clarity.
Focuses on: Achieving Emotional Maturity; How to Work with Your Emotions; How to Change Your Destiny; Magnetism & personal Growth; Self-acceptance.

Personal Healing. Perf. by Caroline Myss. 1 CD. (Running Time: 1.25 Hrs.). 2003. audio compact disk 15.95 (978-1-59179-060-0(3)) Sounds True.

Personal History, Pt. 1. unabr. collector's ed. Katharine Graham. Read by Frances Cassidy. 11 cass. (Running Time: 16 hrs. 30 mins.). 1997. 88.00 (978-0-7366-3697-1(8), 4379-A) Books on Tape.
The legendary publisher of the Washington Post recounts a fascinating life led in the limelight & the editorial room.

Personal History, Pt. 2. unabr. collector's ed. Katharine Graham. Read by Frances Cassidy. 11 cass. (Running Time: 16 hrs. 30 mins.). 1997. 88.00 (978-0-7366-3698-8(6), 4379-B) Books on Tape.
A frank autobiography, the legendary publisher of the Washington Post recounts a fascinating life led in the limelight & the editorial room.

Personal History of Samuel Johnson. unabr. ed. Christopher Hibbert. Read by David Case. 10 cass. (Running Time: 15 hrs.). 2001. 80.00 (978-0-7366-8263-3(5)) Books on Tape.
Samuel Johnson, the father of English letters, had his official biography. This work is much smaller and nimbler, but scarcely less important. It ranges from the eccentric schoolboy in Lichfield, to the Grub Street hack, and finally to the legendary figure of Fleet Street. Johnson comes off still larger than life, but with a profoundly human side to him as well.

Personal Holiness in Times of Temptation Audio Album. Instructed by Bruce Wilkinson. 4 cass. 2000. 19.95 (978-1-885447-83-8(3)) Walk Thru the Bible.
It's getting tougher every day! From the television to the newsstand to the internet, today's Christian man is constantly pressured to give up his standards. Give in to temptation. And become morally impure. Yet nothing in our walk with God is more important - or more rewarding - than personal holiness.

Personal Injuries. Scott Turow. Read by Ken Howard. 1999. 72.00 (978-0-7366-4745-8(7)) Books on Tape.

Personal Injuries. abr. ed. Scott Turow. 4 cass. (Running Time: 6 hrs.). 1999. 25.95 (FS9-51026) Highsmith.

Personal Injuries. abr. ed. Scott Turow. Read by Joe Mantegna. 5 CDs. (Running Time: 21600 sec.). (ENG.). 2005. audio compact disk 14.99 (978-0-7393-2262-8(1), Random AudioBks) Pub: Random Audio Pubg. Dist(s): Random

Personal Injuries. unabr. ed. Scott Turow. Read by Ken Howard. 9 cass. (Running Time: 13 hrs. 30 min.). 1999. 54.95 (5083) Books on Tape.
A gripping, suspenseful novel about corruption, deceit. & love.

Personal Injuries. unabr. ed. Scott Turow. Read by Joe Mantegna. 8 cass. (Running Time: 12 hrs.). 1999. 49.95 (FS9-51027) Highsmith.

Personal Injury Cases: Evaluation; Negotiation; Settlement; Alternative Dispute Resolution. 1988. 50.00 (AC-467) PA Bar Inst.

Personal Injury Litigation - Workplace-Related Injuries. (Running Time: 5 hrs.). 1993. 92.00 Incl. 299p. coursebk. (29310) NYS Bar.
The presentations on this recording provides an update on traditional worksite personal injury claims, explore "new" areas where workplace litigation is mushrooming & highlight key litigation techniques in the handling of these cases. The speakers discuss not only the substantive & procedural aspects of such claims, but also the insurance coverage aspects of the cases.

Personal Insight of Children with Attention Deficit Hyperactivity Disorder from a Positive Parenting Perspective. Vicki Carlson. 1 cass. (Running Time: 55 min.). 1997. bk. 20.00 (978-1-58111-007-4(3)) Contemporary Medical.
Discusses the three important aspects of ADHD, provides suggestions for school accommodations, gives valuable insights, shares personal experience as parent, schoolparent advocate.

Personal Insights on Children with ADHD from a Positive Parenting Perspective. Contrib. by Vicki Carlson. 1 cass. (Running Time: 1 hrs.). 20.00 (19-001A) J W Wood.
Discusses three important aspects of ADHD, provides suggestions for school accomodations, gives valuable insights that parents & professionals need to be aware of when working together, shares personal experiences as a parent, school/parent advocate, & teacher of positive parenting.

Personal Integrity & Professional Responsibility: Ethics in Occupational Therapy, Set. Gerald Winslow. 2 cass. (Running Time: 1 hrs. 40 min.). 1997. bk. 25.00 (978-1-58111-032-6(4)) Contemporary Medical.
Focuses on the purposes of ethics in today's practice of occupational therapy; defines ethics & describes the role of ethics in a time of rapid change in health care.

Personal Keys to Winning Series. Created by Laura Boynton King. 6 CD's. 2002. audio compact disk 109.95 (978-0-9748885-2-1(4)) Summit Dynamics.
A 6-volume series of Self-Hypnosis CD's designed to help individuals achieve and maintain a more positive balance in life.

Personal Law Library. Ed. by Socrates Media Editors. 2005. audio compact disk 49.95 (978-1-59546-113-1(2)) Pub: Socrates Med LLC. Dist(s): Midpt Trade

Personal Legal Forms & Agreements. Ed. by Socrates Media Editors. 2005. audio compact disk 29.95 (978-1-59546-093-6(4)) Pub: Socrates Med LLC. Dist(s): Midpt Trade

Personal Liability for Environmental Violations: Avoiding & Defending Civil Suits & Criminal Prosecutions. 5 cass. (Running Time: 6 hrs. 30 min.). 125.00 (T7-9323) PLI.
This recording of the April 1991 program reviews the dramatic expansion of individual criminal & civil liability resulting from improper management of hazardous waste & other environmental violations.

Personal Magic: The Role & the True Self. Marion Weinstein. 2 cass. (Running Time: 1 hrs. 30 min.). 1997. 17.95 Set. (978-0-9604128-9-1(1)) Earth Magic.
Differentiate & identify the cocietal role which most of us play in our lives, & the inner true self that lies hidden. Once assessed & understood, the true self can liberate & guide our lives.

Personal Management: Self Study Course. 2nd ed. William Smercak. 1 cass. (Running Time: 1 hrs. 30 min.). 1998. 22.00 (978-1-890786-01-4(2)) Visions-Srvs.
Guides the listener through a series of exercises to teach visually impaired persons new skills.

Personal Mastery Program: Discovering Passion & Purpose in Your Life & Work. Srikumar S. Rao. (Running Time: 21600 sec.). 2008. audio compact disk 69.95 (978-1-59179-948-1(1)) Sounds True.

Personal Meditations. unabr. ed. Richard O'Connor. Read by Rick Kleit. 3 CDs. (Running Time: 2 hrs. 30 mins. 0 sec.). (ENG.). 2005. audio compact disk 19.95 (978-1-59397-821-1(9)) Pub: Macmill Audio. Dist(s): Macmillan

Personal Memoirs of U. S. Grant, Pt. 1. unabr. collector's ed. Ulysses S. Grant. Read by Jonathan Reese. 10 cass. (Running Time: 15 hrs.). 1992. 80.00 (978-0-7366-2260-8(8), 3049-A) Books on Tape.
During the last year of his life, when he was dying of cancer, Grant recalled his Ohio boyhood, his West Point years & the grim military campaign in Mexico that ended in a victory Grant thought shameful.

Personal Memoirs of U. S. Grant, Pt. 2. collector's ed. Ulysses S. Grant. Read by Jonathan Reese. 8 cass. (Running Time: 12 hrs.). 1992. 64.00 (978-0-7366-2261-5(6), 4379-B) Books on Tape.

Personal Memoirs of U. S. Grant Pt. 1: The Early Years, West Point, Mexico. unabr. ed. Ulysses S. Grant. Narrated by Peter Johnson. 4 cass. (Running Time: 5 hrs.). 1988. 35.00 (978-1-55690-532-2(7), 88400E7) Recorded Bks.
The early years, West Point & Mexico.

Personal Memoirs of U. S. Grant Pt. 2: The Vicksburg Campaign. unabr. ed. Ulysses S. Grant. Narrated by Peter Johnson. 7 cass. (Running Time: 9 hrs. 30 mins.). 1987. 60.00 (978-1-55690-531-5(9), 87300E7) Recorded Bks.
Declaration of War to General Commanding.

Personal Memoirs of U. S. Grant Pt. 3: The Wilderness Campaign: Surrender at Appomattox. unabr. ed. Ulysses S. Grant. Narrated by Peter Johnson. 6 cass. (Running Time: 9 hrs.). 1988. 51.00 (978-1-55690-533-9(5), 88550E7) Recorded Bks.
The Wilderness Campaign; Surrender at Appomattox.

***Personal Memoirs of Ulysses S. Grant: Ulysses S. Grant.** unabr. ed. Robin Field. Read by Robin Field. (Running Time: 19 hrs.). 2010. 44.95 (978-1-4417-6677-9(4)); 99.95 (978-1-4417-6674-8(X)); audio compact disk 123.00 (978-1-4417-6675-5(8)) Blckstn Audio.

Personal Mythology. Stanley Krippner & David Feinstein. 1 cass. 9.00 (A0425-89) Sound Photosyn.

Personal Odyssey. unabr. ed. Thomas Sowell. Narrated by Jeff Riggenbach. 8 cass. (Running Time: 11 hrs. 30 mins.). 2001. 56.95 (978-0-7861-2144-1(0), 2895) Blckstn Audio.
Here is the gritty, powerful story of Thomas Sowell's life-long education in the school of hard knocks, as the journey took him from Harlem to the Marines, the Ivy League, and a career as a controversial writer, teacher, and economist in government and private industry.

***Personal Odyssey.** unabr. ed. Thomas Sowell. Read by Jeff Riggenbach. (Running Time: 11 hrs. 5 mins.). (ENG.). 2011. 29.95 (978-1-4417-8411-7(X)); audio compact disk 100.00 (978-1-4417-8409-4(8)) Blckstn Audio.

Personal Peace. Eldon Taylor. Read by Eldon Taylor. Interview with Progress Aware Staff. 1 cass. (Running Time: 1 hr. 30 min.). (Power Imaging Ser.). 16.95 incl. script. (978-1-55978-184-8(X), 8009) Progress Aware Res.
Hypnosis & soundtrack with underlying subliminal affirmations.

Personal Peace Meditation. Eldon Taylor. Read by Eldon Taylor. Ed. by Leslie Brice. 1 cass. (Running Time: 1 hr.). 1992. 12.95 (978-1-56705-364-7(5)) Gateways Inst.
Self improvement.

Personal Power. Lisa Ford. 2 cass. (Running Time: 3 hrs.). 1995. 15.95 (978-0-943066-35-6(2)) CareerTrack Pubns.

Personal Power. Arleen LaBella. 1986. 9.75 (978-0-932491-38-1(3)) Res Appl Inc.
Learn strategies to influence people to follow your lead, win cooperation & support, move your career in the right direction, & get what you want in negotiations.

Personal Power. unabr. ed. Dianthus. 1 cass. (Running Time: 1 hr. 23 min.). (ENG.). 1996. 10.00 (978-1-890372-06-4(4)) Dianthus.
Does personal power mean confidence & freedom, or does it mean more than you can imagine? Our relationship with soul, or the unknown of ourself, belongs at the core of this discussion.

Personal Power! A Thirty-Day Program for Unlimited Success. unabr. ed. Anthony Robbins. 24 cass. 1995. 179.95 Set. (644AM) Nightingale-Conant.
Personal Power! is a 30-day program designed to take you to new levels of personal & professional success. It's based on proven techniques developed by Anthony Robbins, one of the foremost peak-performance consultants in the country. Includes a Success Journal & Summary Cards, plus an Introductory Issue of Powertalk!.

Personal Power: Discover Your Full Potential. Lloyd Glauberman. 1999. 12.00 (978-1-929043-01-9(5)) Psycho-tech.

Personal Power Thru Cosmobiology. Eleonora Kimmel. 1 cass. 8.95 (196) Am Fed Astrologers.

Personal Preparation for Revival: National Association of Evangelicals, 47th Annual Convention, Columbus, Ohio, March 7-9, 1989. Evelyn Christenson. 1 cass. (Workshops Ser.: No. 16-Wednesd). 1989. 4.25 ea. 1-8 tapes.; 4.00 ea. 9 tapes or more. Nat Assn Evan.

Personal Problem-Solving. Frank L. Natter. 4 cass. (Improving Your Personal Problem-Solving Ser.: Pt. 1). 1989. 29.95 Set in album. (978-1-878287-61-8(3), ATAF) Type & Temperament.
Starts with the basics of type as related to problem-solving. A full side covers Temperament & problem-solving; another, vocational choice - a vital area for many. Life cycles are reviewed in the fourth tape, along with an overview of personality profiles as related to problem-solving. Unique & powerful material. Includes; Meeting the world/Seeing the world (Extraversion/Introversion, & Sensing/Intuition); Decision-Making/Life Styles (Thinking/Feeling, & Judging/Perceiving) Temperament/Vocational Choice; Life Cycles/Personality Profiles.

Personal Public Relations. Frank S. Farrington. 1 cass. (Running Time: 22 min.). 10.95 (13012) J Norton Pubs.
Suggestions for developing the art of personal public relations & the improvement of personal performance.

Personal Recollections of Joan of Arc, abr. ed. Perf. by St. Charles Players. 2 cass. (Running Time: 120 min.). (Adventure Theatre Ser.). (gr. 5-9). 1999. 16.95 (978-1-56994-524-7(1), 316644, Monterey SoundWorks) Monterey Media Inc.
Toward the end of The Hundred Years War between France & England, as Merlin predicted, a great warrior emerged, uniting a beleaguered nation & leading it to improbable victories. It was said this warrior was a messenger of God. And it may have been, for a country was saved & a kingdom restored. This great leader of men, this messenger who united a nation, was a 17 year-old maiden named Joan. This is her story as recounted by her secretary & page.

Personal Recollections of Joan of Arc, unabr. ed. Mark Twain. Read by Michael Anthony. 11 cass. (Running Time: 16 hrs.). 1992. 76.95 (978-0-7861-0119-1(9), 1105) Blckstn Audio.
This is a fascinating & remarkably accurate biography of the life & mission of Joan of Arc told by one of this country's greatest storytellers.

Personal Recollections of Joan of Arc. unabr. ed. Mark Twain. Read by Mark Taheny. 11 cass. 43.95 set. (768) Ignatius Pr.
Few people know that Twain considered this not only his most important but also his best work. This is a fascinating & remarkably accurate biography of the life & mission of Joan of Arc told by one of this country's greatest storytellers.

Personal Recollections of Joan of Arc. unabr. collector's ed. Mark Twain. Read by Wolfram Kandinsky. 14 cass. (Running Time: 21 hrs.). 1992. 112.00 (978-0-7366-2254-7(3), 3043) Books on Tape.
Twain was fascinated by Joan. He spent 12 years in research & made many attempts before finally getting the story right. He wanted to laud Joan for her unique role in history. He was able to do so after studying contemporary accounts written by both sides, the French & the English.

Personal Recollections of Joan of Arc, Set. Mark Twain. Read by Grover Gardner. 10 cass. (Running Time: 15 hrs.). 1991. 44.95 (978-1-55685-211-4(8)) Audio Bk Con.
Joan of Arc as seen through the eyes of her childhood friend & secretary, Louis le Conte, told with irony & brilliant insight into human nature.

Personal Record. Joseph Conrad. Read by Anais 9000. 2008. 27.95 (978-1-60112-022-9(2)) Babblebooks.

Personal Reflections & Meditations. abr. ed. Bernie S. Siegel. Read by Bernie S. Siegel. 1 cass. (Running Time: 1 hr. 05 min.). 1991. 12.00 (978-1-55994-430-4(7), CPN 1886) HarperCollins Pubs.

Personal Relations: At the Office. Adrian S. Palmer et al. 1 cass. 12.95; 31.85 incl. bk., tchr's. handbk., cass. Alemany Pr.
Program provides dialogs, activities, exercises, & games focusing on specific speech arts, such as asking-telling, agreeing-refusing & suggesting-insisting.

Personal Relations: Schooldays. Adrian S. Palmer et al. 1 cass. 12.95; 31.85 incl. bk., tchr's. handbk., cass. Alemany Pr.
Program provides dialogs, activities, exercises, & games focusing on specific speech arts, such as asking-telling, agreeing-refusing, & suggesting-insisting.

Personal Relationships. Theresa Gurlacz. 1 cass. 8.95 (137) Am Fed Astrologers.

Personal Restoration. Derek Prince. 1 cass. (B-4095) Derek Prince.

Personal Revelation, Set. JoAnn Hibbert Hamilton. 2 cass. 2004. 11.95 (978-1-57734-236-6(4), 07001746) Covenant Comms.

Personal Revelation: Receiving & Responding to the Voice of the Lord. Gerald Lund. 2009. audio compact disk 14.99 (978-1-60641-194-0(2)) Deseret Bk.

Personal Safety Nets Audiobook. Judy Pigott & John W. Gibson. Read by Lynne Compton et al. Music by Timothy Michaels. Prod. by s: A Voice With a View. 2009. audio compact disk 29.95 (978-0-9779226-6-6(9)) Taking Flight.

Personal Safety Nets Download. John W. Gibson & Judy Pigott. Read by Judy Pigott et al. Music by Timothy Michaels. Prod. by Mount View Productions: A Voice With a View. 2009. 29.95 (978-0-9779226-0-4(X)) Taking Flight.

Personal Safety Nets Workbook with Audio. Read by Judy Pigott et al. Based on a book by John W. Gibson & Judy Pigott. Music by Timothy Michaels. Prod. by Mount View Productions: A Voice with a View. 2009. pap. bk. 39.95 (978-0-9779226-4-2(2)) Taking Flight.

Personal Safety Songs. unabr. ed. Phyllis U. Hiller. 1 cass. (Running Time: 50 min.). (J). (ps-2). 1991. 10.95 (978-1-884877-08-7(7), 8609) Creat Mats Lib.
Selected for the Department of Human Services curriculum for sex abuse prevention. Twenty-two short songs that correlate with personal safety curriculum: self esteem, relationships, body parts, feelings, problem solving, keeping safe.

Personal Security in a Troubled World. Instructed by Manly P. Hall. 8.95 (978-0-89314-210-0(7), C800104) Philos Res.

Personal Sharing by Mother Angelica. Interview with Mother Angelica. 1 cass. (Running Time: 60 min.). 10.00 (978-1-55794-050-6(9), T1) Eternal Wrd TV.

Personal Shielding: To Deflect Hostility. Richard Driscoll. (Running Time: 32 min). 2002. per. 20.00 (978-0-9634126-2-1(0), Westside Psych) Westside Pubng.

Personal Shorthand for the Journalist. Walter Blum & C. Theo Yerian. (J). 1980. pap. bk. 237.20 (978-0-89420-225-4(1), 242000) Natl Book.

Personal Side of Management. unabr. ed. Jennifer James. Read by Jennifer James. 1 cass. (Running Time: 1 hr.). 9.95 Jennifer J.
The human edge is how being described as the capital of the future. Global markets changing workforce expectations, increasing stress & diversity require new personal & professional strategies. The ability to manage others & maintain your energy is dependent upon knowing why you do what you do. What are the qualities essential for balance & how do we maintain them at work & at home.

Personal Stand: Observations & Opinions from a Freethinking Roughneck. Trace Adkins. Read by Alan Sklar. (Playaway Adult Nonfiction Ser.). (ENG.). 2009. 59.99 (978-1-60775-768-9(0)) Find a World.

Personal Stand: Observations & Opinions from a Freethinking Roughneck. unabr. ed. Trace Adkins. Narrated by Alan Sklar. (Running Time: 8 hrs. 0 mins. 0 sec.). (ENG.). 2008. audio compact disk 29.99 (978-1-4001-0601-1(X)); audio compact disk 19.99 (978-1-4001-5601-6(7)) Pub: Tantor Media. Dist(s): IngramPubServ

Personal Stand: Observations & Opinions from a Freethinking Roughneck. unabr. ed. Trace Adkins. Read by William Dufris. (Running Time: 8 hrs. 0 mins. 0 sec.). (ENG.). 2008. audio compact disk 59.99 (978-1-4001-3601-8(6)) Pub: Tantor Media. Dist(s): IngramPubServ

Personal Stress Management: Turning Challenges into Opportunities. Michael Hayes Samuelson. 2001. audio compact disk 14.95 (978-0-9710216-4-8(3)) Green Glass Prod.

Personal Struggles, Conflict & Spiritual Growth. Carole Riley. 2 cass. (Running Time: 2 hrs.). 2001. 16.95 (A6750) St Anthony Mess Pr.
Helps us attain spiritual growth in the struggles and conflicts of everyday life.

Personal Success: Win! Win! Ed Pinegar. 1 cass. 7.98 (978-1-55503-667-6(8), 06004881) Covenant Comms.
The true nature of success.

Personal transformation Meditation: The Chakras. Diane Zimberoff. 2002. audio compact disk 18.00 (978-0-9622728-4-4(1)) Wellness Pr.

Personality & Intuition Training. Helen Palmer. 2 cass. 14.00 Set. (A0098-87) Sound Photosyn.

Personality Code. Travis Bradberry. Read by Lloyd James. (Playaway Adult Nonfiction Ser.). (ENG.). 2009. 49.99 (978-1-60812-587-6(4)) Find a World.

Personality Code. unabr. ed. Travis Bradberry. (Running Time: 4 hrs. 0 mins. 0 sec.). (ENG.). 2007. audio compact disk 24.99 (978-1-4001-0413-0(0)) Pub: Tantor Media. Dist(s): IngramPubServ

Personality Code: Unlock the Secret to Understanding Your Boss, Your Colleagues, Your Friends... & Yourself! unabr. ed. Travis Bradberry. Read by Lloyd James. (Running Time: 4 hrs. 0 mins. 0 sec.). (ENG.). 2007. audio compact disk 19.99 (978-1-4001-5413-5(8)); audio compact disk 49.99 (978-1-4001-3413-7(7)) Pub: Tantor Media. Dist(s): IngramPubServ

Personality of Achievers: How to Go Beyond Your Goals. Roger Dawson. 6 cass. (Running Time: 6 hrs.). 1993. 59.95 set. (2741A) Nightingale-Conant.

Personality of Joyce. (23301-A) J Norton Pubs.

Personality Plus: Some Experiences of Emma Mcchesney & Her Son, Jock. unabr. ed. Edna Ferber. Read by Flo Gibson. 2 cass. (Running Time: 2 hrs. 30 min.). 1997. 14.95 (978-1-55685-479-8(X), 479-X) Audio Bk Con.
A successful, charming business woman watches & encourages her handsome, delightful son as he faces the challenges & pressures of the advertising world.

Personality Testing. Joseph L. Felix. 1 cass. (Running Time: 21 min.). 1968. (29232) J Norton Pubs.
Presentation of arguments for & against the use of personality tests in the schools.

Personality Types & How to Cope. Frank Minirth & Paul Meier. Read by Frank Minirth & Paul Meier. 2 cass. (Running Time: 1 hr. 56 min.). (Minirth & Meier Home Counseling Audio Library). 1994. 14.95 set. (978-1-56707-032-3(9)) Dallas Christ Recs.
Understanding how people handle the pressures of contemporary living.

Personalized Direct Mail Program. Somers H. White. 4 cass. (Running Time: 30 min. per cass.). 80.00 (C102) S White.
Learn how to start a mail list, how to use mail lists, show you techniques to stay in touch with present customers in a non-commerical way and how to contact others.

Personally Speaking, Vol. 2. (Running Time: 1 hr.). 2005. audio compact disk 15.95 (978-0-660-19381-6(7)) Canadian Broadcasting CAN.

Personally Yours the Seven Churches of Revelation. 2007. 10.00 (978-0-9758688-9-8(6)) E Heskett.

Personally Yours the Seven Spirits of Revelation. (ENG.). 2007. 10.00 (978-0-9758688-8-1(8)) E Heskett.

Personnel Forms. Ed. by Socrates Media Editors. 2005. audio compact disk 29.95 (978-1-59546-016-5(0)) Pub: Socrates Med LLC. Dist(s): Midpt Trade

Personnel Law for Managers & Supervisors, Set. abr. ed. Rod Murrow. Read by Rod Murrow. 2 cass. (Running Time: 1 hrs. 39 min.). 1998. bk. 21.95 (978-1-57294-117-5(0),) SkillPath Pubns.
Learn the essentials of what should & shouldn't be done when hiring & firing. Answers vital employment questions.

Persons Unknown. unabr. ed. Judy Chard. 4 cass. (Running Time: 6 hrs.). (Audio Books Ser.). 1992. 44.95 (978-1-85496-689-6(8)) Pub: UlverLrgPrint GBR. Dist(s): Ulverscroft US
When her West End stage play closes, Clare Martin decides to explore Britain. A strange compulsion takes her to a Scottish village, Fasnich, & to the Carnegie House Hotel. Her stay is cut short by a terrifying feeling of deja vu, & gradually, Clare realizes that she had been there before as a child ... & some terrible occurrence has erased her memory of it. As the drama of love & death unfolds, Clare realizes that she is in grave danger, & only one man can save her.

Perspective in Advocacy: Trial & Appellate. Myron H. Bright et al. 5 cass. (Running Time: 5 hrs.). 1989. 395.00 Set. (978-1-55917-500-5(1), 9430) Natl Prac Inst.
Discussion of jury selection, direct & cross examination of the expert & non-expert witness, final arguments to the jury & more.

Perspectives are Precipices see Twentieth-Century Poetry in English, No. 24, Recordings of Poets Reading Their Own Poetry

Perspectives on Joint Tortfeasor Releases. Gerald A. McHugh. (Running Time: 1 hr.). 1988. 20.00 PA Bar Inst.

Perspectives on Parenting. E. Kent Hayes. Read by E. Kent Hayes. Ed. by Patricia Magerkurth. 1 cass. (Running Time: 1 hr.). 1991. 10.00 (978-1-56948-002-1(8)) Menninger Clinic.
E. Kent Hayes discusses understanding your child's needs, setting limits, & the importance of parents' availability & involvement in a child's life.

Perspectives on Pastoral Care with Surgical Patients. 1 cass. (Care Cassettes Ser.: Vol. 11, No. 1). 1984. 10.80 Assn Prof Chaplains.

Perspectives 2000: Intermediate English, Level 1. 3rd ed. Rachel Lee et al. (J). 1992. 23.95 (978-0-8384-4233-3(1)) Heinle.

Perspectives 2000: Intermediate English, Level 1. 3rd ed. Rachel Lee et al. (J). 1993. pap. bk. 56.95 (978-0-8384-4199-2(8)) Heinle.

Persuaded, Live in D. C. Contrib. by Richard Smallwood with Vision. (Running Time: 2 hrs. 20 mins.). 2007. 14.98 (978-5-557-92774-1(3), Verity) Brentwood Music.

Persuader. Lee Child. Read by Dick Hill. (Jack Reacher Ser.). 2009. 79.99 (978-1-60775-697-2(8)) Find a World.

Persuader. abr. ed. Lee Child. Read by Dick Hill. (Running Time: 21600 sec.). (Jack Reacher Ser.). 2005. audio compact disk 16.99 (978-1-59600-409-2(6), 9781596004092, BCD Value Price) Brilliance Audio.
Jack Reacher. The ultimate loner. An elite ex-military cop who left the service years ago, he's moved from place to place...without family ... without possessions... without commitments. And without fear. Which is good, because trouble -big, violent, complicated trouble - finds Reacher wherever he goes. And when trouble finds him, Reacher does not quit, not once...not ever. But some unfinished business has now found Reacher. And Reacher is a man who hates unfinished business. Ten years ago, a key investigation went sour and someone got away with murder. Now a chance encounter brings it all back. Now Reacher sees his one last shot. Some would call it vengeance. Some would call it redemption. Reacher would call it...justice.

Persuader. unabr. ed. Lee Child. Read by Dick Hill. 9 cass. (Running Time: 13 hrs.). (Jack Reacher Ser.). 2003. 32.95 (978-1-59086-405-0(0), 1590864050, BAU); 92.25 (978-1-59086-406-7(9), 1590864069, CD Unabrid Lib Ed) Brilliance Audio.
Jack Reacher. The ultimate loner. An elite ex-military cop who left the service years ago, he's moved from place to place...without family ... without possessions... without commitments. And without fear. Which is good, because trouble -big, violent, complicated trouble - finds Reacher wherever he goes. And when trouble finds him, Reacher does not quit, not once...not ever. But some unfinished business has now found Reacher. And Reacher is a man who hates unfinished business. Ten years ago, a key investigation went sour and someone got away with murder. Now a chance encounter brings it all back. Now Reacher sees his one last shot. Some would call it vengeance. Some would call it redemption. Reacher would call it...justice.

Persuader. unabr. ed. Lee Child. Read by Dick Hill. (Running Time: 46800 sec.). (Jack Reacher Ser.). 2004. audio compact disk 39.25 (978-1-59335-380-3(4), 1593353804, Brlnc Audio MP3 Lib) Brilliance Audio.
Jack Reacher. The ultimate loner. An elite ex-military cop who left the service years ago, he's moved from place to place...without family ... without possessions... without commitments. And without fear. Which is good, because trouble -big, violent, complicated trouble - finds Reacher wherever he goes. And when trouble finds him, Reacher does not quit, not once...not ever. But some unfinished business has now found Reacher. And Reacher is a man who hates unfinished business. Ten years ago, a key investigation went sour and someone got away with murder. Now a chance encounter brings it all back. Now Reacher sees his one last shot. Some would call it vengeance. Some would call it redemption. Reacher would call it...justice.

Persuader. unabr. ed. Lee Child. Read by Dick Hill. (Running Time: 13 hrs.). (Jack Reacher Ser.). 2004. 39.25 (978-1-59710-568-2(6), 1597105686, BADLE); 24.95 (978-1-59710-569-9(4), 1597105694, BAD) Brilliance Audio.

Persuader. unabr. ed. Lee Child. Read by Dick Hill. (Running Time: 46800 sec.). (Jack Reacher Ser.). 2007. audio compact disk 107.25 (978-1-4233-3404-0(3), 9781423334040, BriAudCD Unabrid); audio compact disk 38.95 (978-1-4233-3403-3(5), 9781423334033, Bril Audio CD Unabri) Brilliance Audio.

Persuader. unabr. ed. Lee Child. Read by Dick Hill. (Running Time: 13 hrs.). (Jack Reacher Ser.). 2004. 24.95 (978-1-59335-116-8(X), 159335116X) Soulmate Audio Bks.

***Persuasion.** Jane Austen. Narrated by Greta Scaachi. (Running Time: 9 hrs. 0 mins. 0 sec.). (Cover to Cover Ser.). (ENG.). 2011. audio compact disk 29.95 (978-1-60283-882-6(8)) Pub: AudioGO. Dist(s): Perseus Dist

***Persuasion.** Jane Austen. Read by Amy von Lecteur. 2009. 27.95 (978-1-60112-972-7(6)) Babblebooks.

Persuasion. Jane Austen. Read by Nadia May. (Running Time: 28800 sec.). 2006. audio compact disk 29.95 (978-0-7861-7353-2(X)) Blckstn Audio.

Persuasion. Jane Austen. 6 cass. (Running Time: 9 hrs.). 2001. 48.00 (978-0-7366-6187-4(5)) Books on Tape.
In Persuasion, the book's heroine, Anne Elliot, was earlier engaged to Frederick Wentworth, a young naval officer, now become a captain. Anne is 27, & the early bloom of youth is past when she & Captain Wentworth are thrown together again. This book is often thought to be the story of Jane Austen's own lost love. In it, she seems mellowed & more philosophical, touched perhaps by the sentiment of a story in which she saw herself as heroine but in whose happy outcome she had a premonition that she would never play a part.

Persuasion. Jane Austen. Read by Anna Massey. 6 cass. (Running Time: 8 hrs.). 44.95 (CC/022) C to C Cassettes.
Sir Walter Elliot of Kellynch-Hall... "considered the blessing of beauty as inferior only to the blessing of a baronetcy; & the Sir Walter Eliot who united these gifts, was the constant object of his warmest respect & devotion".

Persuasion. Jane Austen. Narrated by Jill Masters. (Running Time: 8 hrs. 30 mins.). 1982. 24.95 (978-1-59912-811-5(X)) Iofy Corp.

Persuasion. Jane Austen. Read by Juliet Stevenson. 3 cass. (Running Time: 3 hrs. 30 mins.). (Works of Jane Austen). 1996. 17.98 (978-962-634-607-5(8), NA310714, Naxos AudioBooks) Naxos.

Persuasion. abr. ed. Jane Austen. Read by Amanda Root. Abr. by Derek Webb. 3 CDs. (Running Time: 0 hr. 60 mins. 0 sec.). (ENG., 2002. audio compact disk 25.00 (978-1-84456-035-6(X), HoddrStoughton) Pub: Hodder General GBR. Dist(s): IPG Chicago

Persuasion. abr. ed. Jane Austen. Read by Alison Fiske. Contrib. by Donald Bancroft. 5 cass. 25.95 (SCN 010) J Norton Pubs.
The story of Anne Elliot & Captain Wentworth, a more mature couple.

Persuasion. abr. ed. Jane Austen. Read by Juliet Stevenson. 3 CDs. (Running Time: 3 hrs. 30 mins.). (Works of Jane Austen). 1996. audio compact disk 22.98 (978-962-634-107-0(6), NA310712, Naxos AudioBooks) Naxos.

Persuasion. abr. ed. Jane Austen. Perf. by Glenda Jackson. 4 cass. (Running Time: 6 hrs.). 2004. 25.00 (978-1-59007-131-1(X)) Pub: New Millenn Enter. Dist(s): PerseuPGW
The last novel completed by Jane Austen before she died unmarried in her early forties, Persuasion is thought to be the story of the author's own lost love. The happy ending is not one in which Austen would ever play a part.

Persuasion. abr. ed. Abr. by Laurie A. Knox. Based on a book by Jane Austen. 2007. 5.00 (978-1-60339-129-0(0)); audio compact disk 5.00 (978-1-60339-130-6(4)) Listenr Digest.

Persuasion. unabr. ed. Jane Austen. Read by Ann Mavrolean. 6 cass. 35.70 (C-127) Audio Bk.
A novel of the second chance, from one of the great master of romantic fiction. Another classic by the author of "Pride & Prejudice".

Persuasion. unabr. ed. Jane Austen. Read by Anna Massey. 6 cass. (Running Time: 8 hrs.). (gr. 9-12). 1999. 29.95 (978-1-57270-105-2(6), F61105u) Pub: Audio Partners. Dist(s): PerseuPGW
A delightful social satire of England's landed gentry & a moving tale of lovers separated by class distinction.

Persuasion. unabr. ed. Jane Austen. Read by Nadia May. 6 cass. (Running Time: 8 hrs. 30 mins.). 2000. 44.95 (978-0-7861-1849-6(0), 2648) Blckstn Audio.
Often thought to be the story of the author's own lost love. Anne Elliot encounters Frederick Wentworth, the man to whom she was once engages when he was a young naval officer. Now a captain, Wentworth is courting the rash young Louisa Musgrove.

Persuasion. unabr. ed. Jane Austen. Read by Nadia May. (Running Time: 28800 sec.). 2006. audio compact disk 63.00 (978-0-7861-6636-7(3)) Blckstn Audio.

Persuasion. unabr. ed. Jane Austen. Read by Donada Peters. 6 cass. (Running Time: 9 hrs.). 2001. 29.95 (978-0-7366-6781-4(4)) Books on Tape.
A woman in her late twenties finds happiness in love after she had resigned herself to life as an old maid.

Persuasion. unabr. ed. Jane Austen. Read by Michael Page. 6 cass. (Running Time: 9 hrs.). (Bookcassette Classic Collection). 1997. 57.25 (978-1-56100-820-9(6), 1561008206, Unabridge Lib Edns) Brilliance Audio.
Anne Elliot is a young woman of perfect breeding and unwavering integrity. Austen wrote of her, "She is almost too good for me." Persuasion is the story of Anne and Captain Wentworth and their long awaited union. The world of country gentry in Regency England serves as a setting while portraying the many aspects of proper society - its failings and humor.

Persuasion. unabr. ed. Jane Austen. Read by Michael Page. (Running Time: 9 hrs.). 2006. 39.25 (978-1-4233-1099-0(3), 9781423310990, BADLE); 24.95 (978-1-4233-1098-3(5), 9781423310983, BAD); audio compact disk 34.95 (978-1-4233-1094-5(2), 9781423310945, Bril Audio CD Unabri); audio compact disk 24.95 (978-1-4233-1096-9(9), 9781423310969, Brilliance MP3); audio compact disk 92.25 (978-1-4233-1095-2(0), 9781423310952, BriAudCD Unabrid); audio compact disk 39.25 (978-1-4233-1097-6(7), 9781423310976, Brlnc Audio MP3 Lib) Brilliance Audio.

Persuasion. unabr. ed. Jane Austen. Read by Nadia May. (YA). 2008. 59.99 (978-1-60514-912-7(8)) Find a World.

Persuasion. unabr. ed. Jane Austen. Read by Jill Masters. 6 cass. (Running Time: 10 hrs.). Dramatization. 1982. 34.00 (C-83) Jimcin Record.
This book features Jane Austen's most memorable heroine - Anne Eliot. It is often thought to be the story of Austen's own lost love.

Persuasion. unabr. ed. Jane Austen. Read by Juliet Stevenson. 7 CDs. (Running Time: 31417 sec.). (Complete Classics Ser.). 2007. audio compact disk 47.98 (978-962-634-436-1(9), Naxos AudioBooks) Naxos.

Persuasion. unabr. ed. Jane Austen. Narrated by Flo Gibson. 6 cass. (Running Time: 9 hrs.). 1984. 51.00 (978-1-55690-408-0(8), 84750E7) Recorded Bks.
Anne Elliot finds her path to lifelong happiness obstructed by the misguided intentions of a friend.

Persuasion. unabr. ed. Jane Austen. Read by Anne Flosnik. Narrated by Anne Flosnik. (Running Time: 9 hrs. 30 mins. 0 sec.). (Tantor Unabridged Classics Ser.). (ENG.). 2008. 22.99 (978-1-4001-5686-3(6)); audio compact disk 65.99 (978-1-4001-3686-5(5)); audio compact disk 32.99 (978-1-4001-0686-8(9)) Pub: Tantor Media. Dist(s): IngramPubServ

Persuasion. unabr. collector's ed. Jane Austen. Read by Jill Masters. 6 cass. (Running Time: 9 hrs.). 1982. 48.00 (978-0-7366-3873-9(3), 9083) Books on Tape.
Anne Elliot, was earlier engaged to Frederick Wentworth, a young naval officer, now become a captain. Anne is 27, & the early bloom of youth is past when she & Captain Wentworth are thrown together again.

Persuasion, Set. unabr. ed. Jane Austen. Read by Flo Gibson. 6 cass. (Running Time: 8 hrs. 30 min.). 1993. 24.95 (978-1-55685-303-6(3)) Audio Bk Con.
Gentle, charming, sensitive Anne Elliott is persuaded to break her engagement to Captain Wentworth. Eight years later they meet again. Can their love survive numerous obstacles?.

Persuasion, Set. unabr. ed. Jane Austen. Read by Jill Masters. 6 cass. 1999. 44.95 (FS9-24902) Highsmith.

Persuasion: The Art of Getting What You Want. rev. unabr. ed. Dave Lakhani. 5 CDs. (Running Time: 5 hrs.). (ENG.). 2008. audio compact disk 29.98 (978-1-59659-139-4(0), GildAudio) Pub: Gildan Media. Dist(s): HachBkGrp

Persuasion in the Courtroom. Joseph V. Guastaferro. 6 cass. (Running Time: 5 hrs. 30 min.). 1990. 165.00 incl. manual. PEG MN.

Persuasion in the Courtroom. rev. ed. Joseph V. Guastaferro. 1989. pap. bk. 185.00 (978-0-943380-33-9(2)) PEG MN.

Persuasion IQ: The 10 Skills You Need to Get Exactly What You Want. unabr. abr. ed. Kurt W. Mortensen. Read by Jim Bond. (Running Time: 8 hrs.). 2008. 39.25 (978-1-4233-6412-2(0), 9781423364122, BADLE); 24.95 (978-1-4233-6411-5(2), 9781423364115, BAD); audio compact disk 82.25 (978-1-4233-6408-5(2), 9781423364085, BriAudCD Unabrid); audio compact disk 24.95 (978-1-4233-6409-2(0), 9781423364092, Brilliance MP3); audio compact disk 39.25 (978-1-4233-6410-8(4), 9781423364108, Brlnc Audio MP3 Lib); audio compact disk 29.95 (978-1-4233-6407-8(4), 9781423364078, Bril Audio CD Unabri) Brilliance Audio.

Persuasion Power Skills. Roger Burgraff. 6 cass. 1991. pap. bk. 79.50 incl. bklt. (978-0-88432-436-2(2), S03040) J Norton Pubs.
Provides proven & positive ways to communicate with greater impact & influence people.

Persuasions. Douglas M. Jones. Read by John Currie. 2 cass. 1998. 20.00 (978-1-59128-550-2(X)) Canon Pr ID.

Persuasions AudioBook: A Dream of Reason Meeting Unbelief. Douglas J. Wilson. Read by Gene Helsel. 2 CDs. (ENG.). 1998. audio compact disk 20.00 (978-1-59128-549-6(6)) Canon Pr ID.

Persuasive Expert Testimony. 1 cass. (Running Time: 60 min.). (Complete Audiotape Ser.). 1990. 39.95 (FAZ050S) Natl Inst Trial Ad.

Persuasive Expert Testimony. Intro. by David M. Malone. 1 cass. (Running Time: 1 hr.). 1990. 43.95 (AUDZO5OS) NITA.
Describes how to present expert testimony that will compel your jury to make the "leap of faith" to adopt your expert's opinions even if they do not fully understand the bases for these opinions.

Persuasive Platform Presentations. Lilly Walters. Read by Lilly Walters. 4 cass. (Running Time: 4 hrs. 30 min.). 1989. pap. bk. 89.95 Set. (978-0-934344-33-3(7)) Royal Pub.
Secrets of successful speakers: Find the right topic for the right audience, overcome fear of the platform, become an expert, make your presentation desirable, motivate the audience, present a good image, voice production. Includes 84-page workbook.

***Persuasive Selling & Power Negotiation: Develop Unstoppable Sales Skills & Close ANY Deal.** unabr. ed. Made for Success. Read by Zig, Brian; Ziglar Tracy. (Running Time: 12 hrs.). (Made for Success Ser.). 2010. audio compact disk 32.95 (978-1-4417-6094-4(6)) Blckstn Audio.

***Persuasive Selling & Power Negotiation (Library Edition) Develop Unstoppable Sales Skills & Close ANY Deal.** unabr. ed. Made for Success. Read by Zig Tracy. (Running Time: 12 hrs.). (Made for Success Ser.). 2010. audio compact disk 123.00 (978-1-4417-6092-0(X)) Blckstn Audio.

Pertinent Players. unabr. ed. Joseph Epstein. Read by Michael Russotto. 11 cass. (Running Time: 16 hrs. 30 min.). 1995. 88.00 (3851) Books on Tape.
How does a writer achieve prominence? And with what inner resources or against what adversities? How does a writer fail, despite advantages? In his third collection of critical essays, Mr. Epstein explores these questions with characteristic humor. He reveals the cultural contributions & the personal foibles of 18 literary greats, including Henry James, George Orwell, Robert Louis Stevenson & H. L. Mencken.

Peru: Preserving the Adobe. Prod. by Betty Rogers. 1 cass. (Running Time: 30 min.). 9.95 (B0190B090, HarperThor) HarpC GBR.

Peruvian Ayahuasca Session. Luis E. Luna. 1 cass. 9.00 (A0124-84) Sound Photosyn.
Another Luna recording of an actual shamanic experience.

Pervaya Lubov. Ivan Turgenev. 5 cass. (RUS.). 1996. bk. 59.50 set. (978-1-58085-573-0(3)) Interlingua VA.
Includes Russian text. The combination of written text & clarity & pace of diction will open the door for intermediate & advanced students to genuine comprehension & the use of literary texts for advancement in rapid understanding of written & oral language materials. The audio text plus written text concept makes foreign languages accessible to a much wider range of students than books alone.

***Pesado y liviano Audio CD.** April Barth. Adapted by Benchmark Education Co., LLC. (Content Connections Ser.). (SPA.). (J). 2010. audio compact disk 10.00 (978-1-61672-205-0(3)) Benchmark Educ.

Pescador. unabr. ed. Marcos Vidal. 2002. 14.99 (978-0-8297-3242-9(X)) Zondervan.

Pescao Vivo. Pescao Vivo. 2008. audio compact disk 14.99 (978-0-8297-6103-0(9)) Pub: Vida Pubs. Dist(s): Zondervan

Peste see Albert Camus: Reading from His Novel and Essays

Pesticide Hazards. Hosted by Nancy Pearlman. 1 cass. (Running Time: 29 min.). 10.00 (112) Educ Comm CA.

Pesticides: Effectiveness & Health Risks. 1 cass. (Running Time: 50 min.). 10.95 (I0270B090, HarperThor) HarpC GBR.

Pet Day/Plenty of Pets. Steck-Vaughn Staff. (Running Time: 523 sec.). (Primary Take-Me-Home Books Level A Ser.). 1998. 9.80 (978-0-8172-8658-3(6)) SteckVau.

***Pet for Petunia.** unabr. ed. Paul Schmid. Illus. by Paul Schmid. (ENG.). 2011. (978-0-06-203650-6(5)) HarperCollins Pubs.

Pet Masterclass. Annette Capel & Rosemary Nixon. 2009. audio compact disk 25.95 (978-0-19-451404-0(8)) OUP.

PET PARENTHOOD Adopting the Right Animal Companion for You. Diane Pomerance. Read by Diane Pomerance. (ENG.). 2007. audio compact disk 7.95 (978-0-9795218-6-7(6)) Polaire Pubna.

Pet Sematary. abr. ed. Stephen King. 3 CDs. (Running Time: 4 hrs. 30 mins.). 2001. audio compact disk 28.50 Books on Tape.
Dr. Louis Creed and his wife chose rural Maine to settle his family and bring up his children. It was a better place than smog-covered Chicago - or so he thought. But that was before he discovered the old pet burial ground located in the backwoods of the quiet community of Ludlow.

Pet Show! 2004. bk. 24.95 (978-0-89719-680-2(5)); pap. bk. 32.75 (978-1-55592-294-8(5)); pap. bk. 14.95 (978-0-7882-0662-7(1)); 8.95 (978-1-56008-421-1(9)) Weston Woods.

Pet Show! Ezra Jack Keats. 1 cass. (Running Time: 11 min.). (J). (ps-3). pap. bk. 12.95 (RAC349); pap. bk. 32.75 Weston Woods.
Archie needs to come up with a pet in a hurry for the neighborhood pet show.

Pet Show! Ezra Jack Keats. 1 cass. (J). (ps-4). bk. 24.95 (HRA349) Weston Woods.

***Pet Show.** Weston Woods Staff. (J). audio compact disk 12.95 (978-0-439-72273-5(X)) Weston Woods.

Pet Supplies & Veterinary Services in Italy: A Strategic Reference 2006. Compiled by Icon Group International, Inc. Staff. 2007. ring bd. 195.00 (978-0-497-36042-9(X)) Icon Grp.

Pet Supplies & Veterinary Services in United Kingdom: A Strategic Reference 2006. Compiled by Icon Group International, Inc. Staff. 2007. ring bd. 195.00 (978-0-497-82456-3(6)) Icon Grp.

Petals on the Wind. unabr. ed. V. C. Andrews. Read by Donada Peters. 12 cass. (Running Time: 18 hrs.). 1988. 96.00 (978-0-7366-1361-3(7), 2260) Books on Tape.
The lives of four innocent children are locked away from the world by a selfish mother scheming for an inheritance. Cathy knew what to do. She knew it was time to show her mother & grandmother that the pain & terror of the attic could not be forgotten.

Petals on the Wind, unabr. ed. V. C. Andrews. Narrated by Alyssa Bresnahan. 14 cass. (Running Time: 19 hrs. 15 mins.). 1996. 112.00 (978-0-7887-0578-6(4), 94756E7) Recorded Bks.
This sequel to "Flowers in the Attic" follows the Dollaganger children into adulthood & deeper into the curse that still haunts their family.

Petaybee Trilogy: Powers That Be, Power Lines & Power Play. abr. ed. Anne McCaffrey & Elizabeth Ann Scarborough. Read by Marina Sirtis. 6 cass. (Running Time: 9 hrs.). 2002. 32.00 (978-1-57453-529-7(3)) Audio Lit.
Strange things are happening on the icy planet of Petaybee. Unauthorized genetically engineered species have been spotted and yet the locals are deliberately hiding something - perhaps even plotting rebellion.

Pete & P. J. Sing, Dance & Read with Me, Read-Along with Big Book, CD & Instrument. Cindy Bousman. 1 CD. (Running Time: 1 hr). (J). (ps-3). 2000. pap. bk. 29.95 (978-1-931127-38-7(7), 986-006) Kindermusik Intl.
This softcover whimsical, rhythmical book is about a small boy & his dog taking a bath. The CD contains three readings of the story, two with page-turn signals, as well as music for singing, dancing & listening.

Pete Rose. 1 cass. (Reading with Winners: Ser. 1). 1984. 32.95 (978-0-89811-121-7(8), 8801C); Lets Talk Assocs.

Pete Rose: Hitting. Read by Pete Rose. 1 cass. 9.95 (7116) Lets Talk Assocs.
Pete Rose talks about the people & events which influenced his career, & his approach to his speciality.

Pete Seeger: For Kids & Just Plain Folks. Perf. by Pete Seeger. 1 cass. (Family Heritage Ser.). (J). 1997. 7.98 Incl. cass. blisterpak. (Sony Wonder); audio compact disk 11.98 CD. (Sony Wonder) Sony Music Ent.
Includes: If I Had a Hammer, What Did You Learn in School Today?, Michael, Row the Boat Ashore, Be Kind to Your Parents & This Old Car.

Pete Seeger's Family Concert. Pete Seeger. Perf. by Pete Seeger. 1 cass. (Running Time: 30 min.). (J). 1992. 8.98 (978-1-56406-550-6(2)); 8.98 Incl. sleeve pack. (978-1-56406-579-7(0)); audio compact disk 13.98 CD. (978-1-56406-566-7(9)) Sony Music Ent.

Peter - Before & After. unabr. ed. Read by Gayle D. Erwin. 1 cass. (Running Time: 1 hr.). 1992. 4.95 (978-1-56599-520-8(1), C-20) Yahshua Pub.

Peter Alsop: Live Solo Recording. Perf. by Peter Alsop. 1 cass. 11.00; audio compact disk Moose Schl Records.
Adult oriented songs that address social issues such as parenting, sexuality & drugs. They are currently being enjoyed by thousands of adult-type humans & teens.

Peter Alsop's Chris Moose Holidays. Perf. by Peter Alsop. 1 CD. (J). audio compact disk Moose Schl Records.
A new Christmas classic - diversity & fun for kids of all religions all year long.

Peter Alsop's Chris Moose Holidays. Scripts. Perf. by Peter Alsop. 1 cass. (Running Time: 1 hr. 10 min.). (J). 1994. 11.00 (MS 505) Moose Schl Records.

Peter Alsop's Sing-Along Songs, Set. Perf. by Peter Alsop. 5 cass. pap. bk. 69.00 Incl. 2 live video concerts & sing-along bk. Moose Schl Records.
Includes: Wha'D'Ya' Wanna Do!?, Take Me with You!, Staying Over, Plugging Away, & Family Roles (for parents & teachers). Live video concerts include: Wake Up (abuse & abduction prevention skills) & Costume Party (outdoor family concert). Sing-along booklet contains musical chords, exercises, questions & discussion topics for each of the songs in this package.

Peter & John see Pedro y Juan

Peter & John. Guy de Maupassant. Read by Pedro J. Vega. (Running Time: 3 hrs.). 2002. 16.95 (978-1-60083-240-6(7), Audiofy Corp) Iofy Corp.

Peter & Max: A Fables Novel. unabr. ed. Bill Willingham. (Running Time: 9 hrs.). (Fables Ser.). 2009. 24.99 (978-1-4418-3693-9(4), 9781441836939, BAD); 39.97 (978-1-4418-3694-6(2), 9781441836946, BADLE) Brilliance Audio.

Peter & Max: A Fables Novel. unabr. ed. Bill Willingham. Read by Wil Wheaton. (Running Time: 8 hrs.). (Fables Ser.). 2009. 24.99 (978-1-4418-3691-5(8), 9781441836915, Brilliance MP3); 39.97 (978-1-4418-3692-2(6), 9781441836922, Brlnc Audio MP3 Lib); audio compact disk 29.99 (978-1-4418-3689-2(6), 9781441836892, Bril Audio CD Unabri) Brilliance Audio.

Peter & Max: A Fables Novel. unabr. ed. Bill Willingham. (Running Time: 9 hrs.). (Fables Ser.). 2011. audio compact disk 14.99 (978-1-4418-3695-3(0), 9781441836953, BCD Value Price) Brilliance Audio.

Peter & Max: A Fables Novel. unabr. ed. Bill Willingham & Wil Wheaton. (Running Time: 8 hrs.). (Fables Ser.). 2009. audio compact disk 99.97 (978-1-4418-3690-8(X), 9781441836908, BriAudCD Unabrid) Brilliance Audio.

Peter & Max (Collector's Edition) A Fables Novel. unabr. ed. Bill Willingham. Read by Wil Wheaton. (Running Time: 8 hrs.). (Fables Ser.). 2010. audio compact disk 29.99 (978-1-4418-4737-9(5), 9781441847379, Bril Audio CD Unabri) Brilliance Audio.

Peter & the Secret of Rundoon. Dave Barry & Ridley Pearson. Contrib. by Jim Dale. (Peter & the Starcatchers Ser.: No. 3). (J). (gr. k). 2009. 69.99 (978-1-60775-878-5(4)) Find a World.

Peter & the Secret of Rundoon. unabr. ed. Dave Barry & Ridley Pearson. 9 cass. (Running Time: 39600 sec.). (Peter & the Starcatchers Ser.: No. 3). (J). 2007. 92.25 (978-1-4233-3864-2(2), 9781423338642, BrilAudUnabridg); 29.95 (978-1-4233-3863-5(4), 9781423338635, BAU); audio compact disk 97.25 (978-1-4233-3866-6(9), 9781423338666, BriAudCD Unabrid) Brilliance Audio.

Peter & the Secret of Rundoon. unabr. ed. Dave Barry & Ridley Pearson. 1 MP3-CD. (Running Time: 39600 sec.). (Peter & the Starcatchers Ser.: No. 3). (J). (gr. 4-7). 2007. audio compact disk 39.25 (978-1-4233-3868-0(5), 9781423338680, Brlnc Audio MP3 Lib); audio compact disk 24.95 (978-1-4233-3867-3(7), 9781423338673, Brilliance MP3); audio compact disk 36.95 (978-1-4233-3865-9(0), 9781423338659, Bril Audio CD Unabri) Brilliance Audio.

Peter & the Secret of Rundoon. unabr. ed. Dave Barry & Ridley Pearson. Read by Jim Dale. (Running Time: 11 hrs.). (Peter & the Starcatchers Ser.: No. 3). 2007. 39.25 (978-1-4233-3870-3(7), 9781423338703, BADLE); 24.95 (978-1-4233-3869-7(3), 9781423338697, BAD) Brilliance Audio.

Peter & the Shadow Thieves. Dave Barry & Ridley Pearson. Contrib. by Jim Dale. (Peter & the Starcatchers Ser.: No. 2). (J). 2009. 69.99 (978-1-60775-686-6(2)) Find a World.

Peter & the Shadow Thieves. unabr. ed. Dave Barry & Ridley Pearson. 7 cass. (Running Time: 36000 sec.). (Peter & the Starcatchers Ser.: No. 2). (J). 2006. 82.25 (978-1-59737-457-6(1), 9781597374576, BrilAudUnabridg); audio compact disk 24.95 (978-1-59737-460-6(1), 9781597374606, Brilliance MP3) Brilliance Audio.
Please enter a Synopsis.

Peter & the Shadow Thieves. unabr. ed. Dave Barry & Ridley Pearson. 9 CDs. (Running Time: 36000 sec.). (Peter & the Starcatchers Ser.: No. 2). (J). (gr. 5-8). 2006. audio compact disk 97.25 (978-1-59737-459-0(8), 9781597374590, BriAudCD Unabrid) Brilliance Audio.

Peter & the Shadow Thieves. unabr. ed. Dave Barry & Ridley Pearson. Read by Jim Dale. 9 CDs. (Running Time: 36000 sec.). (Peter & the Starcatchers Ser.: No. 1). (J). 2006. audio compact disk 29.95 (978-1-59737-458-3(X), 9781597374583, Bril Audio CD Unabri) Brilliance Audio.

Peter & the Shadow Thieves. unabr. ed. Dave Barry & Ridley Pearson. Read by Jim Dale. 7 cass. (Running Time: 36000 sec.). (Peter & the Starcatchers Ser.: No. 2). (J). 2006. 29.95 (978-1-59737-456-9(3), 9781597374569, BAU) Brilliance Audio.

Peter & the Shadow Thieves. unabr. ed. Dave Barry & Ridley Pearson. Read by Jim Dale. (Running Time: 10 hrs.). (Peter & the Starcatchers Ser.: No. 2). 2006. 39.25 (978-1-59737-463-7(6), 9781597374637, BADLE); 24.95 (978-1-59737-462-0(8), 9781597374620, BAD); 39.25 (978-1-59737-461-3(X), 9781597374613, Brlnc Audio MP3 Lib) Brilliance Audio.

Peter & the Starcatchers. Dave Barry & Ridley Pearson. Contrib. by Jim Dale. (Peter & the Starcatchers Ser.: No. 1). (J). (gr. 4-7). 2009. 65.00 (978-1-60775-518-0(1)) Find a World.

Peter & the Starcatchers. unabr. ed. Dave Barry & Ridley Pearson. Read by Jim Dale. Contrib. by Dave Barry. 6 CDs. (Running Time: 9 hrs.). (Peter & the Starcatchers Ser.: No. 1). 2004. audio compact disk 29.95 (978-1-59355-978-6(X), 159355978X, Bril Audio CD Unabri); 29.95 (978-1-59355-976-2(3), 1593559763, BAU); 74.25 (978-1-59355-977-9(1), 1593559771, BrilAudUnabridg); audio compact disk 87.25 (978-1-59355-979-3(8), 1593559798, BriAudCD Unabrid) Brilliance Audio.
In an evocative and fast-paced adventure on the high seas and on a faraway island an orphan boy named Peter and his mysterious new friend, Molly, overcome bands of pirates and thieves in their quest to keep a fantastical secret safe and save the world from evil. Bestselling authors Dave Barry and Ridley Pearson have turned back the clock and revealed a wonderful story that precedes J. M. Barrie's beloved Peter Pan. Peter and the Starcatchers is brimming with richly developed characters from the scary but somehow familiar Black Stache and the ferocious Mister Grin to the sweet but sophisticated Molly and the fearless Peter. Riveting adventure takes listeners on a journey from a harsh orphanage in old England to a treacherous sea in a decrepit old tub. Aboard the Never Land is a trunk that holds a magical substance with the power to change the fate of the world - just a sprinkle and wounds heal and just a dusting and people can fly. Towering seas and a violent storm are the backdrop for battles at sea. Bone-crushing waves eventually land our characters on Mollusk Island - where the action really heats up.

Peter & the Starcatchers. unabr. ed. Dave Barry & Ridley Pearson. Read by Jim Dale. 1 MP3-CD. (Running Time: 9 hrs.). (Peter & the Starcatchers Ser.: No. 1). (gr. 3-6). 2004. 24.95 (978-1-59335-780-1(X), 159335780X, Brilliance MP3); 39.25 (978-1-59335-914-0(4), 1593359144, Brlnc Audio MP3 Lib) Brilliance Audio.

Peter & the Starcatchers. unabr. ed. Dave Barry & Ridley Pearson. Read by Jim Dale. (Running Time: 9 hrs.). (Peter & the Starcatchers Ser.: No. 1). 2004. 39.25 (978-1-59710-571-2(6), 1597105716, BADLE); 24.95 (978-1-59710-570-5(8), 1597105708, BAD) Brilliance Audio.

Peter & the Sword of Mercy. Dave Barry & Ridley Pearson. Contrib. by Jim Dale. (Peter & the Starcatchers Ser.: No. 4). (J). 2009. 49.99 (978-1-4418-2830-9(3)) Find a World.

Peter & the Sword of Mercy. unabr. ed. Dave Barry & Ridley Pearson. Read by Jim Dale. (Running Time: 2 hrs.). (Peter & the Starcatchers Ser.: No. 4). 2008. 9.99 (978-1-4233-0976-5(6), 9781423309765, Brilliance MP3); audio compact disk 14.99 (978-1-4233-0974-1(X), 9781423309741, Bril Audio CD Unabri) Brilliance Audio.

Peter & the Sword of Mercy. unabr. ed. Dave Barry & Ridley Pearson. Read by Jim Dale. 10 CDs. (Running Time: 12 hrs.). (Peter & the Starcatchers Ser.). (YA). (gr. 5-8). 2009. audio compact disk 69.97 (978-1-4418-0225-5(8), 9781441802255, BriAudCD Unabrid) Brilliance Audio.

Peter & the Sword of Mercy. unabr. ed. Dave Barry & Ridley Pearson. Read by Jim Dale. (Running Time: 2 hrs.). (Peter & the Starcatchers Ser.: No. 4). 2009. 25.97 (978-1-4233-0979-6(0), 9781423309796, BADLE); 9.99 (978-1-4233-0978-9(2), 9781423309789, BAD); 25.97 (978-1-4233-0977-2(4), 9781423309772, Brlnc Audio MP3 Lib); 39.97 (978-1-4418-0227-9(4), 9781441802279, Brlnc Audio MP3 Lib); 24.99 (978-1-4418-0226-2(6), 9781441802262, Brilliance MP3); 24.99 (978-1-4418-0228-6(2), 9781441802286, BAD); 39.97 (978-1-4418-0229-3(0), 9781441802293, BADLE); audio compact disk 25.97 (978-1-4233-0975-8(8), 9781423309758, BriAudCD Unabrid); audio compact disk 29.99 (978-1-4418-0224-8(X), 9781441802248, Bril Audio CD Unabri) Brilliance Audio.

Peter & the Symphony. Comment by Eric Friesen & Peter Oundjian. (ENG.). 2009. audio compact disk 79.95 (978-0-660-19916-0(5), CBC Audio) Canadian Broadcasting CAN.

Peter & the Wolf see Pierre et le Loup

Peter & the Wolf. 1 cass. (Talking Mother Goose Ser.). (J). (ps up). 1986. 9.95 (978-0-934323-33-8(X)) Alchemy Comms.

Peter & the Wolf. Adapted by Carin Dewhirst. Illus. by Naomi Howland. (CD Ser.). (J). (ps-3). 1997. bk. 14.98 (978-1-56799-540-4(3), Friedman-Fairfax) M Friedman Pub Grp Inc.

Peter & the Wolf. Sergei Prokofiev. Read by Peter Fernandez. (Live Oak Readalong Ser.). pap. bk. 18.95 (978-1-59519-339-1(1)) Pub: Live Oak Media. Dist(s): AudioGO

Peter & the Wolf. Sergei Prokofiev. Interview with Charles Mikloayck. 1 cass. (Running Time: 7 min.). (J). (ps up). 1987. 9.95 Live Oak Media.
A brave boy defies his grandfather's warning & captures a fierce wolf.

Peter & the Wolf. Sergei Prokofiev. Illus. by Charles Mikloayck. (Running Time: 7 mins.). 1987. 9.95 (978-0-59112-099-5(3)) Live Oak Media.

Peter & the Wolf. unabr. ed. Sergei Prokofiev. Read by Peter Fernandez. Tr. by Maria Carlson. Illus. by Charles Mikolaycak. Interview with Charles Mikloayck. 11 vols. (Running Time: 7 mins.). (J). (gr. 1-6). 1987. pap. bk. 16.95 (978-0-87499-073-7(4)) Live Oak Media.

Peter & the Wolf, Level 4. Carin Dewhirst. (J). 1996. bk. 16.98 (978-1-56799-303-5(6)) Friedman Pub.

Peter & the Wolf: A new Classic for Narrator & Symphony Orchestra: Stories in Music. Prod. by Stephen Simon. Conducted by Stephen Simon & Bonnie Simon. (J). 2007. audio compact disk 16.98 (978-1-932684-12-4(3)) Simon Simon.

Peter & the Wolf: Classical Symphony, March in B-Flat, Overture on Hebrew Themes. Narrated by Sting. 1 cass. (J). (gr. 4 up). 9.98 (2291); 18.98 compact disc. (D2291) MFLP CA.
A natural way to introduce children to the exciting possibilities of classical music. Sting's narration is lively & absolutely faithful to the original story.

Peter & the Wolf: Pedro y el Lobo. Narrated by Jose Carreras. 1 cass. (SPA.). (J). (gr. 4 up). 9.98 (2292); 18.98 compact disc. (D2292) MFLP CA.
A natural way to introduce children to the exciting possibilities of classical music. Wonderful Spanish language version by opera superstar Jose Carreras.

Peter & the Wolf - Tale to Learn Music see Pedrito y el Lobo - Cuento para Aprender Musica

Peter & the Wolf - Tale to Learn Music. Sergei Prokofiev. Read by José Ferrer. (Running Time: 1 hr.). 2002. 14.95 (978-1-60083-143-0(5), Audiofy Corp) Iofy Corp.

Peter & the Wolf & Young Person's Guide to the Orchestra. Perf. by Philadelphia Orchestra & Eugene Ormandy. 1 cass. (J). (ps-7). 7.98 (385) MFLP CA.
Without narration, the lively music for full symphony orchestra showcases each group of instruments in turn, making a delightful learning experience for the whole family.

Peter & the Wolf; Carnival of the Animals. Perf. by Philharmonia Orchestra, The. Narrated by Jonathan Winters. 1 cass. (Running Time: 54 min.). (J). (ps-7). 10.98 (341); audio compact disk 19.98 (D341) MFLP CA.
Jonathan Winters brings new life to these wonderful classical pieces with distinctive voices for each of the characters in "Peter & the Wolf" & brilliant innovations for the verses written by Ogden Nash for Saint-Saens "Carnival of the Animals.".

Peter & the Wolf, Grades 1-6. Sergei Prokofiev. Read by Peter Fernandez. Tr. by Maria Carlson. Illus. by Charles Mikolaycak. Interview with Charles Mikloayck. 14 vols. (Running Time: 7 mins.). (J). 1987. pap. bk. & tchr. ed. 33.95 Reading Chest. (978-0-87499-075-1(0)) Live Oak Media.
A brave boy defies his grandfather's warning & captures a fierce wolf.

Peter & Wee & Other Folk Tales. Donna Dettman. (Running Time: 45 min.). (J). (ps-12). 1996. 10.00 (UPC 76186401944) D Dettman.
Storyteller provides her versions of four folktales.

Peter & Wendy. J. M. Barrie. 2 CDs. (Running Time: 2 hrs. 30 mins.). (J). 2003. audio compact disk 17.99 (978-1-58926-165-5(8), C05M-0030, Oasis Kids) Oasis Audio.

Peter & Wendy. unabr. ed. 1 cass. (Running Time: 45 mins.). 1999. 18.95 (CART001) CA Artists.

Peter Benchley. Interview. Interview with Peter Benchley. 1 cass. (Running Time: 25 min.). 1978. 10.95 (L010) TFR.
Benchley says he's horrified at the popularity of "Jaws" & he defends himself against charges by Jacques Cousteau that the effect of "Jaws" will be to downgrade the environment. In second interview, Jacques Cousteau reviews his career, his global exploration of the deep, & trades barbs with Peter Benchley.

Peter Block, Set. Innovation Groups Staff. 5 cass. (Running Time: 6 hrs. 30 min.). (Transforming Local Government Ser.). 1997. 74.99 Set. (978-1-882403-36-3(3)) Alliance Innov.
Training information for those working in or with local government.

Peter Bursch's Rock Guitar. Peter Bursch. 2001. pap. bk. 17.95 (978-3-8024-0365-1(7)) Voggenreiter Pubs DEU.

Peter Commentary. Chuck Missler. 1 CD- ROM. (Running Time: 8 hrs +). (Chuck Missler Commentaries). 2001. cd-rom & audio compact disk 29.95 (978-1-57821-132-6(8)) Koinonia Hse.

Peter Cooley. unabr. ed. Read by Peter Cooley. 1 cass. (Running Time: 29 min.). 1987. 10.00 New Letters.
Poet reads a selection of elergies & poems.

Peter Cooper. 10.00 Esstee Audios.
Discusses how a man changed the nature of American industry.

Peter Cushing: An Autobiography. unabr. ed. Peter Cushing. Read by Peter Cushing. 6 cass. (Running Time: 6 hrs. 13 mins.). (Isis Ser.). 1994. 54.95 (978-1-85089-781-1(6), 89021) Eye Ear.
Peter Cushing's life story is a fascinating account of the development of one of Britain's most distinguished actors & reveals the frequent perils of an actor's life.

Peter Davison. unabr. ed. Read by Peter Davison. 1 cass. (Running Time: 29 min.). 1985. 10.00 New Letters.
The Massachusetts poet reads from Walking The Boundaries & A Voice in The Mountain.

Peter Fleming: Tennis. Read by Peter Fleming. 1 cass. 9.95 (978-0-89811-119-4(6), 7177) Lets Talk Assocs.
Peter Fleming talks about the people & events which influenced his career, & his own approach to his speciality.

Peter Gunn. Arranged by Rob Goldsmith. (Warner Bros. Publications 21st Century Guitar Ensemble Ser.). (ENG.). 2002. audio compact disk 19.95 (978-0-7579-9981-9(6), Warner Bro) Alfred Pub.

***Peter I & II Commentary.** Chuck Missler. (ENG.). 2009. audio compact disk 44.95 (978-1-57821-434-1(3)) Koinonia Hse.

Peter Jeppson Story. Peter Jeppson. 1 cass. 2004. 3.95 (978-1-57734-385-1(9), 34441247) Covenant Comms.

Peter Meinke: "A Decent Life" unabr. ed. Read by Peter Meinke. 1 cass. (Running Time: 29 min.). 1986. 10.00 New Letters.
A short story set in the 'not-so-distant' future in a police state.

Peter Nabokov. unabr. ed. Ed. by Jim McKinley. Prod. by Rebekah Presson. 1 cass. (Running Time: 29 min.). (New Letters on the Air Ser.). 1994. 10.00 (030593) New Letters.
Nabokov's new book, "Native American Testimony" tells the story of 500 years of white - Indian relations through the voices of dozens of Native Americans whose speeches & writings Nabokov has collected. Native American actors read from the text & Nabokov talks about his struggle to find material that tells a good & true story, free of stereotype.

Peter Pan. J. M. Barrie. Narrated by Flo Gibson. (J). 2009. audio compact disk 24.95 (978-1-60646-100-6(1)) Audio Bk Con.

Peter Pan. J. M. Barrie. Narrated by Full Cast. (Running Time: 2 hrs. 0 mins. 0 sec.). (ENG.). 2010. audio compact disk 24.95 (978-1-60283-849-9(6)) Pub: AudioGO. Dist(s): Perseus Dist

Peter Pan. J. M. Barrie. Narrated by Roe Kendall. (Running Time: 5 hrs. 30 mins.). 2000. 24.95 (978-1-59912-568-8(4)) Iofy Corp.

Peter Pan. J. M. Barrie. Read by Carlos Muñoz. (Running Time: 3 hrs.). (YA). 2002. 16.95 (978-1-60083-276-5(8), Audiofy Corp) Iofy Corp.

Peter Pan. J. M. Barrie. Read by Vanessa Maroney. (Running Time: 5 hrs. 55 mins.). (J). 2002. 22.95 (978-1-59912-101-7(8), Audiofy Corp) Iofy Corp.

Peter Pan. J. M. Barrie. Read by John Chatty. 4 cass. (Running Time: 4 hrs.). (J). 1987. 28.00 incl. albums. (C-172) Jimcin Record.
Join Peter, Captain Hook, Wendy & all the other characters in this children classic.

Peter Pan. J. M. Barrie. Read by Samuel West. 2 cass. (Running Time: 2 hrs. 30 mins.). (J). 1996. 13.98 (978-962-634-602-0(7), NA210214, Naxos AudioBooks) Naxos.
The story of a little boy who refused to grow up. Join Peter Pan, Wendy, John and Michael as they fly away to endless adventures in the magical Neverland, where they meet the wicked Captain Hook and a host of other characters.

Peter Pan. J. M. Barrie. Narrated by Vanessa Maroney. (Running Time: 21300 sec.). (Unabridged Classics in MP3 Ser.). (J). 2008. audio compact disk 24.00 (978-1-58472-532-9(X), In Aud) Sound Room.

Peter Pan. J. M. Barrie. Read by Donada Peters. (Running Time: 17460 sec.). (ENG.). (J). (ps-7). 2004. audio compact disk 19.99 (978-1-4001-5102-8(3)); audio compact disk 24.99 (978-1-4001-0102-3(6)) Pub: Tantor Media. Dist(s): IngramPubServ

Peter Pan. J. M. Barrie. 1 cass. (Read & Sing Alongs Ser.). (J). bk. 12.99 (978-0-7634-0371-3(7)); 11.99 (978-0-7634-0379-9(2)); 11.99 Norelco. (978-0-7634-0378-2(4)); audio compact disk 19.99 CD. (978-0-7634-0380-5(6)); audio compact disk 19.99 (978-0-7634-0381-2(4)) W Disney Records.

Peter Pan. J. M. Barrie. 1 cass. (Read-Along Ser.). (J). (ps-3). 1990. bk. 7.99 (978-1-55723-009-6(9)) W Disney Records.

Peter Pan. Read by Famous Theater Company Staff. 1 cass. (J). (ps-2). 2.98 (978-1-55886-022-3(3)); 3.98 incl. poster. (978-1-55886-026-1(6)) Smarty Pants.
A children's fairy tale about a boy who flies.

Peter Pan. Perf. by Mary Martin. 1 cass. (Running Time: 1 hr. 40 min.). (J). (ps up). 9.98 (284) MFLP CA.
The magic of the child who would not grow up.

Peter Pan. abr. ed. J. M. Barrie. Perf. by St. Charles Players. 2 cass. (Running Time: 1 hr. 15 min.). Dramatization. (Story Theatre for Young Readers Ser.). (J). (gr. 4-7). 1999. 16.95 (978-1-56994-518-6(7), 337354, Monterey SoundWorks) Monterey Media Inc.
Imagine a place where dreams come true, where Pirates fight lost boys & Indians; where a fairy named Tinkerbell sprinkles magic dust & adventures fill your days & nights; where a young boy is your leader & he can fly & crow, & he'll never grow up to be a man . . . because he's Peter Pan.

Peter Pan. abr. ed. J. M. Barrie. Read by Samuel West. 2 CDs. (Running Time: 2 hrs. 30 mins.). (Junior Classics Ser.). (J). (gr. 3-5). 1996. audio compact disk 17.98 (978-962-634-102-5(5), NA210212) Naxos.
The story of a little boy who refused to grow up. Join Peter Pan, Wendy, John and Michael as they fly away to endless adventures in the magical Neverland, where they meet the wicked Captain Hook and a host of other characters.

Peter Pan. unabr. ed. J. M. Barrie. Read by Roe Kendall. 4 cass. (Running Time: 5 hrs. 30 mins.). (gr. 5-9). 2000. 32.95 (978-0-7861-1786-4(9), 2585); audio compact disk 40.00 (978-0-7861-9872-6(9), 2585) Blckstn Audio.
As a baby, Peter Pan fell out of his carriage & was taken by fairies to Never-Never Land. There he can fly & is the champion of the Lost Boys & a friend to the fairy Tinker Bell. Revisiting England, Peter becomes involved with Wendy Darling & her younger brothers, all of whom accompany Peter to Never-Never Land.

Peter Pan. unabr. ed. J. M. Barrie. Read by Roe Kendall. (Running Time: 5 hrs. 30 mins.). 2004. audio compact disk 24.95 (978-0-7861-9502-2(9), 2585) Blckstn Audio.

Peter Pan. unabr. ed. J. M. Barrie. Read by Christopher Cazenove. (Running Time: 5 hrs. 0 mins.). 2010. 19.95 (978-1-4417-1550-0(9)); 34.95 (978-1-4417-1546-3(0)); audio compact disk 49.00 (978-1-4417-1547-0(9)) Blckstn Audio.

Peter Pan. unabr. ed. Short Stories. J. M. Barrie. Read by Patrick Treadway. 4 cass. (Running Time: 4 hrs. 15 min.). Dramatization. (J). 1992. 26.95 (978-1-55686-439-1(6), 439) Books in Motion.

Peter Pan. unabr. ed. J. M. Barrie. 4 cass. (Running Time: 4 hrs.). (Classic Literature Ser.). 1997. pap. bk. 21.95 (978-1-55656-201-3(2)) Pub: Dercum Audio. Dist(s): APG
First published as "Peter & Wendy." Allows the listener to fully experience anew the wonder of flight & the promise of eternal youth.

Peter Pan. unabr. ed. J. M. Barrie. Read by Vanessa Maroney. (J). 2006. 49.99 (978-1-59895-173-8(4)) Find a World.

Peter Pan. unabr. ed. J. M. Barrie. Read by Jim Dale. 3 cass. (Running Time: 5 hrs. 14 mins.). (J). (ps-3). 2006. 30.00 (978-0-7393-3811-7(0), Listening Lib) Pub: Random Audio Pubg. Dist(s): Random

Peter Pan. unabr. ed. J. M. Barrie. Read by Jim Dale. 5 CDs. (Running Time: 5 hrs. 14 mins.). (J). (ps-3). 2006. audio compact disk 38.25 (978-0-7393-3780-6(7), Listening Lib) Pub: Random Audio Pubg. Dist(s): NetLibrary CO
Fly away with Peter Pan to the enchanted island of Neverland! This first chapter book adaptation of the classic novel, originally published in 1911, tells the story of the boy who never grows up. And when they join Peter on his magical island, Wendy and her brothers are in for exciting encounters with mermaids, an Indian princess, and pirates! Let the amazing adventures begin!.

Peter Pan, unabr. ed. J. M. Barrie. Narrated by Donal Donnelly. 5 pieces. (Running Time: 6 hrs. 30 mins.). (gr. 4 up). 1991. 44.00 (978-1-55690-409-7(6), 91105E7) Recorded Bks.
Peter, Wendy & the boys fly to Never-Never Land for a rendezvous with Captain Hook in this classic of fantasy literature.

Peter Pan. unabr. ed. J. M. Barrie. Read by Tim Curry. (J). 2006. 17.95 (978-0-7435-6427-4(8)) Pub: S&S Audio. Dist(s): S and S Inc

Peter Pan. unabr. ed. J. M. Barrie. Read by Vanessa Maroney. 5 cds. (Running Time: 5 hrs 54 mins). (J). 2002. audio compact disk 29.95 (978-1-58472-300-4(9), 067, In Aud) Pub: Sound Room. Dist(s): Baker Taylor
The adventures of the three Darling children in Never-Never Land, featuring Captain Hook and his gang of pirates, the fairy Tinkerbell, and Peter Pan, the boy who would never grow up.

Peter Pan. unabr. ed. J. M. Barrie. Read by Vanessa Maroney. 1 cd. (Running Time: 5 hrs 53 mins). (J). 2002. audio compact disk 18.95 (978-1-58472-392-9(0), In Aud) Pub: Sound Room. Dist(s): Baker Taylor
MP3 format.

Peter Pan. unabr. ed. J. M. Barrie. Narrated by Donada Peters. (Running Time: 5 hrs. 0 mins. 0 sec.). (ENG.). (J). (gr. 4-7). 2008. 19.99 (978-1-4001-5866-9(4)); audio compact disk 39.99 (978-1-4001-3866-1(3)) Pub: Tantor Media. Dist(s): IngramPubServ

Peter Pan. unabr. ed. J. M. Barrie. Narrated by Donada Peters. (Running Time: 5 hrs. 0 mins. 0 sec.). (ENG.). (J). (gr. 4-7). 2008. audio compact disk 19.99 (978-1-4001-0866-4(7)) Pub: Tantor Media. Dist(s): IngramPubServ

Peter Pan. unabr. ed. J. M. Barrie. Read by Jim Dale. 5 CDs. (Running Time: 18840 sec.). (ENG.). (J). (gr. 3-7). 2006. audio compact disk 29.95 (978-0-7393-3690-8(8), Listening Lib) Pub: Random Audio Pubg. Dist(s): Random

Peter Pan. unabr. ed. J. M. Barrie & Roe Kendall. 4 cass. 2004. reel tape 24.95 (978-0-7861-2829-7(1)); audio compact disk 29.95 (978-0-7861-8384-5(5)) Blckstn Audio.

Peter Pan. unabr. ed. Read by Tim Curry & J. M. Barrie. 5 CDs. (Running Time: 5 hrs. 0 mins. 0 sec.). (ENG.). (J). (gr. 4-9). 2006. audio compact disk 29.95 (978-0-7435-6452-6(9)) Pub: S&S Audio. Dist(s): S and S Inc

Peter Pan. unabr. abr. ed. J. M. Barrie. 3 CDs. (Running Time: 3 hrs.). (SPA.). 2002. audio compact disk 17.00 (978-958-43-0193-2(4)) YoYoMusic.
Uno de los más amados personajes de toda la literatura infantil es Peter Pan, el niño que no quería crecer y que hacía realidad todas las aventuras con que los niños de todas las edades sueñan. Por eso, en esta bella novela, que no solo es para niños sino también para adultos, está el Hada celosa, el capitán pirata en busca de vengarse, la familia pobre que tiene que usar un perro en lugar de una niñera y las feroces tribus indígenas todos haciendo marco a los niños perdidos que siguen las órdenes de Peter Pan. Con una gran dosis de humor, Peter Pan no solo ha sido un libro predilecto sino que en innumerables ocasiones ha sido llevado al cine y el teatro.

Peter Pan. unabr. collector's ed. J. M. Barrie. Read by Donada Peters. 5 cass. (Running Time: 5 hrs.). (J). 1993. 30.00 (978-0-7366-2537-1(2), 3289) Books on Tape.
Peter Pan is the boy who doesn't want to grow up.

Peter Pan, Set. J. M. Barrie. Read by Sophie Arthuys et al. 2 cass. (J). 1992. bk. 35.95 (1GA067) Olivia & Hill.
Peter Pan, the story of the little boy who refused to grow up & his adventures in Never Never Land where he meets Captain Hook.

Peter Pan, Set. unabr. ed. J. M. Barrie. Read by Flo Gibson. 4 cass. (Running Time: 5 hrs. 30 min.). (J). (gr. 3-5). 1987. 19.95 (978-1-55685-075-2(1)) Audio Bk Con.
The adventures of the boy who would not grow up, with Wendy, the lost boys of Neverland, Captain Hook & the pirates.

Peter Pan - Grow up, Peter Pan! Alvin Granowsky. 1 cass. (Point of View Stories Ser.). (J). (gr. 4-6). 1993. 8.49 (978-0-8114-2218-5(6)) SteckVau.
Two versions of the traditional story & a retelling from the viewpoint of a story character motivate students to read & analyze literature through critical thinking. Flip-book presentation emphasizes the difference in the two story versions & encourages students to complete both & compare.

Peter Pan in Kensington Gardens. unabr. ed. J. M. Barrie. Read by Flo Gibson. 2 cass. (Running Time: 2 hrs.). (J). (gr. 1 up). 1994. 14.95 (978-1-55685-337-1(8)) Audio Bk Con.
A fanciful tour of the gardens with birds, fairies & little Peter Pan. Narrator's note: The sudden deaths of two babies are unexpectedly mentioned in the last two pages.

Peter Pan in Scarlet. unabr. ed. Geraldine McCaughrean. Read by Tim Curry. 8 CDs. (Running Time: 9 hrs.). (YA). (gr. 5 up). 2006. audio compact disk 64.75 (978-1-4281-2153-9(6)); 39.75 (978-1-4281-2148-5(X)) Recorded Bks.
In August 2004 the Special Trustees of Great Ormond Street Children's Hospital launched a worldwide search for a writer to create a sequel to J.M. Barrie's timeless masterpiece. The Special Trustees own the copyright to Peter Pan and to mark the work's centenary they authorized the creation of a new work that would share the same enriching characters as the original, and bring as much pleasure to the children and adults universally as Peter Pan has done. Set in the 1930s, Peter Pan in Scarlet takes readers flying back to Neverland in an adventure filled with tension, danger, and swashbuckling derring-do!.

Peter Pan in Scarlet. unabr. ed. Geraldine McCaughrean. Read by Tim Curry. 2006. 17.95 (978-0-7435-6428-1(6)) Pub: S&S Audio. Dist(s): S and S Inc

Peter Pan in Scarlet. unabr. ed. Geraldine McCaughrean. Read by Tim Curry. 6 CDs. (Running Time: 6 hrs. 30 mins. 0 sec.). (ENG.). (gr. 4-9). 2006. audio compact disk 29.95 (978-0-7435-6453-3(7)) Pub: S&S Audio. Dist(s): S and S Inc

Peter Pan Read & Sing-Along. 1 cass. (Running Time: 25 min.). (Disney Ser.). (J). bk. 11.98 Blisterpack. (DISN 60962) NewSound.

Peter Pan Syndrome: Hebrews 5:11; 6:3. Ed Young. 1991. 4.95 (978-0-7417-1891-4(X), 891) Win Walk.

Peter, Paul & Mary. Perf. by Peter, Paul and Mary. 1 cass. (J). (ps up). 9.98 (283); audio compact disk 15.98 (D283) MFLP CA.
Wonderful music that folksingers Peter, Paul & Mary have shared over the years, includes "Puff the Magic Dragon", "The Marvelous Toy", "I Have a Song", & nine more timeless favorites.

Peter, Paul & Mary Magdalene: The Followers of Jesus in History & Legend. unabr. ed. Bart D. Ehrman. Read by Grover Gardner. 12 CDs. (Running Time: 12 hrs. 30 mins. 0 sec.). (ENG.). 2006. audio compact disk 79.99 (978-1-4001-3236-2(3)); audio compact disk 29.99 (978-1-4001-5236-0(4)); audio compact disk 39.99 (978-1-4001-0236-5(7)) Pub: Tantor Media. Dist(s): IngramPubServ
Vibrantly written and leavened with many colorful stories, Peter, Paul, and Mary Magdalene will appeal to anyone curious about the early Christian church and the lives of these important figures.

Peter, Paul & Mommy Too. Perf. by Peter, Paul and Mary. 1 cass. (Running Time: 52 min.). (J). 1993. pap. bk. 10.98 (978-1-880528-14-3(2), 4-45216) Warner Bros.
Live concert recorded from PBS special by the singing trio - Peter, Paul & Mary. Also comes with complete lyric booklet.

Peter Penny's Dance. 2004. 8.95 (978-1-56008-999-5(7)); cass. & flmstrp 30.00 (978-1-56008-743-4(9)) Weston Woods.

Peter Piper Picks & Pickles Peppers Audio CD. Adapted by Benchmark Education Company Staff. Based on a work by Jeffrey B. Fuerst. (Reader's Theater Nursery Rhymes & Songs Ser.). (J). (gr. k-1). 2008. audio compact disk 10.00 (978-1-60437-994-5(4)) Benchmark Educ.

Peter Prescription. unabr. ed. Laurence J. Peter. Read by Emile Jalbert. 4 cass. 23.80 (E-207) Audio Bk.
"The Peter Prescription" is a book on "How to make things right." Before the discovery of the Peter Principle, escalation was considered profitable. The author goes beyond his best selling "Peter Principle" to offer solutions for the incompetence treadmill.

Peter Rabbit see Ten All Time Favorite Stories

Peter Rabbit & Friends. Beatrix Potter. Read by Pauline Brailsford. 1 cass. (Running Time: 38 min.). (Picture Book Parade Ser.). (J). (ps-4). 1986. 8.95 Jeremy Fisher Doll. (978-0-89719-930-8(8), WW733C) Weston Woods.
Collection of Beatrix Potter favorites including "the Tale of Peter Rabbit," "the Tale of Mr. Jeremy Fisher," "the Tale of Tom Kitten," "the Tale of Benjamin Bunny," & "the Tale of Two Bad Mice".

Peter Rabbit & Other Beatrix Potter Favorites. (J). 2005. audio compact disk (978-1-933796-47-5(2)) PC Treasures.

Peter Rabbit & Other Stories. Beatrix Potter. Read by Vanessa Maroney. (Running Time: 2 hrs.). (J). 2002. 15.95 (978-1-59912-102-4(6), Audiofy Corp) Iofy Corp.

Peter Rabbit & Other Stories. Beatrix Potter. Narrated by Vanessa Maroney. (Running Time: 6900 sec.). (Unabridged Classics in MP3 Ser.). (ENG.). (J). 2008. audio compact disk 24.00 (978-1-58472-631-9(8), In Aud) Sound Room.

Peter Rabbit & Other Stories. unabr. ed. Short Stories. Beatrix Potter. Read by Vanessa Maroney. 2 cds. (Running Time: 1 hr 54 mins). (J). 2002. pap. bk. (978-1-58472-304-2(1), In Aud) Sound Room.
Includes The Tale of Peter Rabbit, The Tale of Jeremy Fisher, The Tale of Benjamin Bunny, The Tale of Two Bad Mice, The Tale of the Flopsy Bunnies, The Tailor of Gloucester, The Tale of Squirrel Nutkin, The Tale of Mrs. Tiggy-Winkle, The Tale of Jemima Puddle-Duck, The Tale of Tom Kitten, The Tale of Ginger and Pickles, The Tale of Mrs. Tittlemouse, and Appley Dapply's Nursery Rhymes.

Peter Rabbit & Other Stories. unabr. ed. Beatrix Potter. Read by Vanessa Maroney. 2 cds. (Running Time: 1 hr 54 mins). (J). 2002. audio compact disk 18.95 (978-1-58472-302-8(5), 064, In Aud) Pub: Sound Room. Dist(s): Baker Taylor
The Tale of Peter Rabbit, The Tale of Jeremy Fisher, The Tale of Benjamin Bunny, The Tale of Two Bad Mice, The Tale of the Flopsy Bunnies, The Tailor of Gloucester, The Tale of Squirrel Nutkin, The Tale of Mrs. Tiggy-Winkle, The Tale of Jemima Puddle-Duck, The Tale of Tom Kitten, The Tale of Ginger and Pickles, The Tale of Mrs. Tittlemouse, Appley Dapply's Nursery Rhymes.

Peter Rabbit's Second Tale. Vera Sharp. (J). V Sharp.
This audio is a charming poem for young children. Peter's second tale is nothing like his first, & is sure to delight youngsters & their parents.

Peter Schlemihls Wundersame Geschichte. Chamisso. audio compact disk 12.95 (978-0-8219-3803-4(7)) EMC-Paradigm.

Peter Shaffer: Equus. Perf. by Peter Barkworth & Ian Sharrock. 2 cass. 15.95 (SCN 209) J Norton Pubs.
The relationship between Martin Dysart, a psychiatrist & that of his patient, Alan Strang, a boy who worships the "Godslave" Equus & then blinds his horse as well as five others.

Peter Simple. unabr. ed. Frederick Marryat. Read by Frederick Davidson. 13 cass. (Running Time: 19 hrs. 30 min.). 2000. 85.95 (978-0-7861-1753-6(2), 2557) Blckstn Audio.
In this seminal story of naval life during the Napoleonic War, Marryat's young hero embarks upon a life at sea & finds it to be a rough school indeed. Simple's trials & triumphs, alongside his faithful mentor, Terence O'Brien, mirror Marryat's person experience, from the hand-to-hand combat of cutting-out missions to the devastating hurricane off St. Pierre & the mutiny aboard the "Rattlesnake.".

Peter Stuyvesant: New Amsterdam & the Origins of New York. unabr. ed. L. J. Krizner and Lisa Sita. Read by Roscoe Orman. (Running Time: 1 hr.). (Library of American Lives & Times Ser.). 2009. 39.97 (978-1-4233-8181-5(5), 9781423381815, Brlnc Audio MP3 Lib); 39.97 (978-1-4233-8182-2(3), 9781423381822, BADLE); 19.99 (978-1-4233-8180-8(7), 9781423381808, Brilliance MP3); audio compact disk 39.97 (978-1-4233-8179-2(3), 9781423381792, BriAudCD Unabrid); audio compact disk 19.99 (978-1-4233-8178-5(5), 9781423381785) Brilliance Audio.

Peter Taylor: "Instruction of a Mistress" see Peter Taylor: "Three Heroines" and "Instruction of a Mistress"

Peter Taylor: "Three Heroines" & "Instruction of a Mistress", Set. unabr. ed. Read by Peter Taylor. 2 cass. (Running Time: 29 min. per cass.). Incl. Peter Taylor: "Instruction of a Mistress"; 1986. 10.00 ea.; 13.00 double-sided. New Letters.
This southern writer calls "Three Heroines" a 'broken line prose' account.

Peter the Great. unabr. ed. Henri Troyat. Read by Wolfram Kandinsky. 11 cass. (Running Time: 16 hrs. 30 mins.). 88.00 (978-0-7366-1549-5(0), 2418) Books on Tape.
Like Stalin after him, Peter permanently changed the destiny of Russia. He destroyed the Swedish empire, built St. Petersburg & opened Russia to the West. He was a visionary, but he was cruel, gargantuan in his appetite for debauchery, secretive & paranoid.

Peter the Great, Pt. 1. collector's ed. Robert K. Massie. Read by Wolfram Kandinsky. 11 cass. (Running Time: 16 hrs. 30 mins.). 1983. 88.00 (978-0-7366-0435-2(9), 1406-A) Books on Tape.
Robert Massie depicts the life & times of one of civilization's most extraordinary rulers, Peter I, Czar of Russia. The first Czar to travel outside his own country, he was insatiably curious & fired by Western ideas.

Peter the Great, Pt. 2. collector's ed. Robert K. Massie. Read by Wolfram Kandinsky. 9 cass. (Running Time: 13 hrs. 30 mins.). 1983. 72.00 (978-0-7366-0436-9(7), 1406-B) Books on Tape.

Peter the Great, Pt. 3. collector's ed. Robert K. Massie. Read by Wolfram Kandinsky. 12 cass. (Running Time: 18 hrs.). 1983. 96.00 (978-0-7366-0437-6(5), 1406-C) Books on Tape.

Peter the Great: Abridged: His Life & World. (ENG.). 2007. (978-1-60339-079-8(0)); cd-rom & audio compact disk (978-1-60339-080-4(4)) Listenr Digest.

***Peter the Great: His Life & World.** unabr. ed. Robert K. Massie. Read by Frederick Davidson. (Running Time: 46 hrs.). 2010. 59.95 (978-1-4417-4450-0(9)); audio compact disk 160.00 (978-1-4417-4447-0(9)) Blckstn Audio.

Peter the Great Pt. 1: His Life & World, Part 1 Of 2. unabr. ed. Robert K. Massie. Read by Frederick Davidson. 16 cass. (Running Time: 55 hrs. 30 mins.). 1991. 99.95 (978-0-7861-0266-2(7), 1233A,B) Blckstn Audio.
Massie gives us, full scale, this man of enormous energy & complexity - impetuous & stubborn, bawdy & stern, relentless in his perseverance, constantly on the move, inspecting, organizing, encouraging, criticizing, commanding, capable of the greatest generosity & the greatest cruelty.

Peter the Great Pt. 2: His Life & World, Part 2 Of 2. unabr. ed. Robert K. Massie. Read by Frederick Davidson. 15 cass. (Running Time: 55 hrs. 30 mins.). 1991. 95.95 (978-0-7861-0267-9(5), 1233A,B) Blckstn Audio.

Peter Viereck. Read by Peter Viereck. 1 cass. (Running Time: 29 min.). Incl. Archer in the Marrow. 1987.; 1987. 10.00 New Letters.
Viereck reads from his poem that takes the reader on a journey from the Garden of Eden to the Auschwitz death camp & talks about using formal technique without resorting to "formalism".

Peter Weiss Reading from His Works. abr. ed. Peter Weiss. Perf. by Peter Weiss. 1 cass. 1984. 12.95 (SWC 1131) HarperCollins Pubs.

Peterkin Papers. 4 Cds. (Running Time: 4 hrs. 30 minutes). (J). 2004. audio compact disk (978-0-9755663-8-1(5)) Alcazar AudioWorks.
A most charming and entertaining story of a family totally devoid of common sense who muddle through their adventures with life's challenges with love and cooperation, but find when they come to their wits' end, it is time to consult the wise, sensible "Lady from Philadelphia" who manages to extricate them from their troubles with sensible commonplace but boring solutions.

Peterkin Papers. abr. ed. Lucretia P. Hale. Perf. by Cathleen Nesbitt. 1 cass. Incl. Peterkin Papers: About Elizabeth Eliza's Piano. (J). (CDL5 1377); Peterkin Papers: The Lady Who Put Salt in Her Coffee. (J). (CDL5 1377); Peterkin Papers: The Peterkins at Home. (J). (CDL5 1377); Peterkin Papers: The Peterkin's Picnic. (J). (CDL5 1377); Peterkin Papers: The Peterkins Showed-up. (J). (CDL5 1377); Peterkin Papers: The Peterkins Try to Become Wise. (J). (CDL5 1377); (J). 1984. 9.95 (978-0-694-50888-4(8), CDL5 1377) HarperCollins Pubs.

Peterkin Papers: About Elizabeth Eliza's Piano see Peterkin Papers

Peterkin Papers: The Lady Who Put Salt in Her Coffee see Peterkin Papers

Peterkin Papers: The Peterkins at Home see Peterkin Papers

Peterkin Papers: The Peterkin's Picnic see Peterkin Papers

Peterkin Papers: The Peterkins Showed-up see Peterkin Papers

Peterkin Papers: The Peterkins Try to Become Wise see Peterkin Papers

Peterkin Papers & Selected Stories, Set. unabr. ed. Lucretia P. Hale. Read by Flo Gibson. 2 cass. (Running Time: 2 hrs. 58 min.). (J). (gr. 1-2). 1987. 14.95 (978-1-55685-102-5(2)) Audio Bk Con.
The misadventures of Agamemnon, Solomon John, Elizabeth Eliza, Mr. & Mrs. & the little Peterkin boys whose problems are invariably solved by the kind lady from Philadelphia.

Peter's Advice on Christian Living. Dan Corner. 1 cass. 3.00 (72) Evang Outreach.

Peter's Chair see Silla de Pedro

Peter's Chair. 2004. bk. 24.95 (978-0-89719-681-9(3)); pap. bk. 18.95 (978-1-55592-810-0(2)); pap. bk. 18.95 (978-1-55592-776-9(9)); pap. bk. 38.75 (978-1-55592-760-8(2)); pap. bk. 38.75 (978-1-55592-723-3(8)); pap. bk. 32.75 (978-1-55592-295-5(3)); pap. bk. 32.75 (978-1-55592-296-2(1)); pap. bk. 14.95 (978-1-56008-071-8(X)); pap. bk. 14.95 (978-1-55592-668-7(1)); 8.95 (978-1-56008-635-2(1)); 8.95 (978-1-56008-422-8(7)); cass. & flmstrp 30.00 (978-0-89719-555-3(8)); audio compact disk 12.95 (978-1-55592-879-7(X)) Weston Woods.

Peter's Chair. Ezra Jack Keats. 1 cass., 5 bks. (Running Time: 6 min.). (J). pap. bk. 32.75 Weston Woods.
Peter wants to run away when his new baby sister arrives.

Peter's Chair. Ezra Jack Keats. (J). (ps-3). bk. 24.95; pap. bk. 12.95 (RAC107); pap. bk. 12.95 (PRA107) Weston Woods.
Peter wants to run away when his new baby sister arrives.

Peter's Message on Pentecost. Dan Corner. 1 cass. 3.00 (73) Evang Outreach.

Peter's Pence. unabr. ed. Jon Cleary. Read by Christopher Kay. 6 cass. (Running Time: 9 hrs.). 1999. 54.95 (60482) Pub: Soundings Ltd GBR. Dist(s): Ulverscroft US

Peter's Pence. unabr. ed. Jon Cleary. 6 cass. (Sound Ser.). 2004. 54.95 (978-1-85496-048-1(2)) Pub: UlverLrgPrint GBR. Dist(s): Ulverscroft US

Pete's a Pizza. 2004. bk. 24.95 (978-1-55592-068-5(3)) Weston Woods.

Pete's a Pizza. William Steig. Illus. by William Steig. (Running Time: 5 mins.). 2000. audio compact disk 12.95 (978-1-59112-738-3(6)) Live Oak Media.

Pete's a Pizza. William Steig. Illus. by William Steig. Read by George Guidall. Narrated by Chevy Chase. 11 vols. (Running Time: 5 mins.). (J). (ps-3). 2000. bk. 25.95 (978-0-87499-683-8(X)) Live Oak Media.
Steig, inspired by a game he used to play with his daughter, turns a rainy day into a pizza party, starring a caring father & his feeling-blue son, Pete.

Pete's a Pizza. unabr. ed. William Steig. 1 cass. (Running Time: 5 mins.). (J). (gr. k-2). 2000. 9.95 (978-0-87499-681-4(3), LK31016) Live Oak Media.
Pete is in a terrible state, and it is his father who has the wisdom to humor him back to his usual self by making Pete into a pizza pie. The giggles of Pete and the listeners increase as Pete is kneaded, stretched, spread, baked, and (almost) sliced." -.

Petey. Ben Mikaelsen. Narrated by L. J. Ganser. 6 CDs. (Running Time: 6 hrs. 15 mins.). (gr. 4 up). audio compact disk 58.00 (978-1-4025-2330-4(0)) Recorded Bks.

Petey. unabr. ed. Ben Mikaelsen. Narrated by L. J. Ganser. 5 pieces. (Running Time: 6 hrs. 15 mins.). (gr. 4 up). 2001. 37.00 (978-0-7887-4557-7(3), 96331E7) Recorded Bks.
When Petey Corbin grew up in the 1920s, no one knew about cerebral palsy. Few people looked beyond his twisted body to see the intelligence in his eyes.

Petey. unabr. ed. Ben Mikaelsen. Narrated by L. J. Ganser. 5 cass. (Running Time: 6 hrs. 15 mins.). (J). 2001. pap. bk. & stu. ed. 53.24 Recorded Bks.

Petit Chaperon Rouge see Contes de Perrault

Petit Chaperon Rouge. Tr. of Little Red Riding Hood. (FRE.). (J). pap. bk. 12.95 (978-2-89558-051-5(0)) Pub: Coffragants CAN. Dist(s): Penton Overseas

Petit Chaperon Rouge. 1 cass. (Running Time: 1 hr., 30 mins.). (Musicontes Ser.).Tr. of Little Red Riding Hood. (FRE.). (J). bk. 24.95 (978-2-09-230468-6(2)) Pub: F Nathan FRA. Dist(s): Distribks Inc

Petit Chaperon Rouge. 1 cass.Tr. of Little Red Riding Hood. (FRE.). (J). (gr. 3 up). 1991. bk. 14.95 (1AD030) Olivia & Hill.
The Little Red Riding Hood.

Petit Chaperon Rouge. adpt. ed. Charles Perrault. Illus. by Lara Barrington. Adapted by Marie Eykel. 1 cass., bklet. (Running Time: 50 mins.). (Best-Sellers Ser.). Orig. Title: Little Red Riding Hood. (FRE.). (J). (ps-2). 2000. 9.95 (978-2-921997-00-3(2)) Pub: Coffragants CAN. Dist(s): Penton Overseas
Features classic children's fables recorded completely in French by well-known artists.

Petit Chose, Set. Alphonse Daudet. Read by Roger Messie. 2 cass. (FRE.). 1995. 26.95 (1757-KFP) Olivia & Hill.
Touching autobiography describing Daudet's childhood & difficult beginnings as a writer.

Petit Poucet. 1 cass.Tr. of Tom Thumb. (FRE.). (J). (gr. 3 up). 1991. bk. 14.95 (1AD032) Olivia & Hill.
French version of Hansel & Gretel.

Petit Prince see Principito

Petit Prince. Antoine de Saint-Exupéry. 1 cass., bklet. (Running Time: 90 mins.). (FRE., (J). (gr. 1-7). cass. & audio compact disk 12.95 (978-2-921997-41-6(X)) Pub: Coffragants CAN. Dist(s): Penton Overseas
Recorded by well-know actors or speakers. Includes compact plastic case & booklet with text in French.

Petit Prince. Antoine de Saint-Exupéry. 1 CD . (Running Time: 1 hr. 30 mins.). (FRE.). (J). (gr. 1-7). 2000. 16.95 (978-2-921997-42-3(8)) Pub: Coffragants CAN. Dist(s): Penton Overseas
Features classic children's fables recorded completely in French by well-known artists.

Petit Prince. Antoine de Saint-Exupéry. 1 CD. (Running Time: 1 hr. 30 mins.). (FRE.). 2000. pap. bk. 35.95 (978-2-07-051666-7(0)) Pub: Gallimard Edns FRA. Dist(s): Distribks Inc

Petit Prince. Antoine de Saint-Exupéry. 1 cass. (Running Time: 1 hr. 30 mins.). (FRE., 2000. pap. bk. 27.95 (978-2-07-051645-2(8)) Pub: Gallimard Edns FRA. Dist(s): Distribks Inc

Petit Prince. Antoine de Saint-Exupéry. 2 cass. (FRE.). (J). 2001. 22.50 (978-0-8442-1383-5(7)) Glencoe.
Presents the story of the Little Prince.

Petit Prince. Antoine de Saint-Exupéry. Perf. by Gerard Philipe. 1 cass. (FRE.). 1991. 14.95 (1284) Olivia & Hill.
The story of a pilot who, one evening, has to make a forced landing in the middle of the Sahara desert. When he awakens the following morning, he is astounded to hear the voice of a young boy who asks: "S'il vous plait, dessinemoi un mouton." Thus begins a wonderful friendship & a touching story.

Petit Prince Cannibale, Set. Francoise Lefevre. Read by Marie-Christine Letort. 3 cass. (FRE.). 1996. 34.95 Set. (1862-LV) Olivia & Hill.
The story of a mother who gives up her singing career to devote herself to her autistic son.

Petit Reconstituant. l.t. ed. Elizabeth George. (French Ser.).Tr. of Suitable Vengeance. (FRE., 2001. bk. 30.99 (978-2-84011-437-6(2)) Pub: UlverLrgPrint GBR. Dist(s): Ulverscroft US

Petit Somme. unabr. ed. Robert A. Monroe. Read by Sylvestre Gomiak. 1 cass. (Running Time: 30 min.). (Mind Food Ser.). 1991. 14.95 (978-1-56102-426-1(0)) Inter Indus.
Compresses 90 minute sleep cycle into 30 minutes.

Petit Vieux des Batignolles, Set. Emile Gaboriau. Read by G. Bejean et al. 2 cass. (FRE.). 1995. 26.95 (1679-VSL) Olivia & Hill.
A vicious crime, a guilty victim, a very beautiful woman, a motive. Who killed "le petit vieux"? Inspector Mechinet is on the case. Gaboriau is the father of French mystery stories.

Petite Fadette. George Sand. pap. bk. 21.95 (978-88-7754-748-4(0)) Pub: Cideb ITA. Dist(s): Distribks Inc

Petite Fadette, Set. George Sand. Read by K. Faraoun & G. Faraoun. 4 cass. (FRE.). 1991. 34.95 (1288-VSL) Olivia & Hill.
A simple, idylicized romance of country life placed in Berrichon at the beginning of the 19th century. Fadette, a poor peasant girl, meets young Landry, the son of a prosperous farmer, who falls in love with her.

Petite Fille Aux Allumettes. Tr. of Little Match Girl. (FRE.). pap. bk. 12.95 (978-2-89558-068-3(5)) Pub: Coffragants CAN. Dist(s): Penton Overseas

Petite Fille Aux Allumettes. Felicia Cavalieri. 1 cass., bklet. (Running Time: 50 mins.). (Best-Sellers Ser.).Tr. of Little Match Girl. (FRE., (J). (ps-2). 2000. cass. & audio compact disk 9.95 (978-2-921997-31-7(2)) Pub: Coffragants CAN. Dist(s): Penton Overseas

Petite Marchande d'Allumettes. 1 cass.Tr. of Little Match Girl. (FRE.). (J). (gr. 3 up). 1991. bk. 14.95 (1AD035) Olivia & Hill.

Petite Rouge. unabr. ed. Sheila Hebert Collins. Read by Sheila Hebert Collins. 1 cass. (Running Time: 020 min.). (Cajun Tall Tales Ser.). (J). (gr. k-3). 1999. 9.95 (978-1-56554-400-0(5)) Pelican.

Petite Rouge: A Cajun Red Riding Hood. Mike Artell. Narrated by Vernel Bagneris. (Running Time: 15 mins.). (J). 2003. 10.75 (978-1-4193-1627-2(3)) Recorded Bks.

Petite Sirene. Tr. of Little Mermaid. (FRE.). (J). pap. bk. 12.95 (978-2-89558-071-3(5)) Pub: Coffragants CAN. Dist(s): Penton Overseas

Petite Sirene. Based on a story by Hans Christian Andersen. 1 cass.Tr. of Little Mermaid. (FRE.). (J). (gr. 3 up). 1991. bk. 14.95 (1AD027) Olivia & Hill.

Petite Sirene. Axelle Laffont. 1 cass., bklet. (Running Time: 50 mins.). (Best-Sellers Ser.). (FRE., (J). (ps-2). audio compact disk 9.95 (978-2-89517-042-6(8)) Pub: Coffragants CAN. Dist(s): Penton Overseas

Petites Filles Modeles. Sophie Comtesse De Segur. Adapted by Anne-Marie Deraspe. Illus. by Anne Cote. 1 CD . (Running Time: 90 mins.).Tr. of Perfect Little Girls. (FRE.). (J). (gr. 1-7). 1998. 16.95 (978-2-921997-23-2(1)) Pub: Coffragants CAN. Dist(s): Penton Overseas
Features classic children's fables recorded completely in French by well-known artists.

Petites Filles Modeles. Sophie Comtesse De Segur. Adapted by Anne-Marie Deraspe. Illus. by Anne Cote. 1 cass. (Running Time: 90 mins.). (Collection Comtesse de Segur: Vol. 2).Tr. of Perfect Little Girls. (FRE.). (J). (gr. 1-7). 1998. cass. & audio compact disk 12.95 (978-2-921997-18-8(5)) Pub: Coffragants CAN. Dist(s): Penton Overseas

petites filles Modeles. unabr. ed. Comtesse de Segur. Read by Béatrice Pasquier. 2007. 69.99 (978-2-35569-049-5(9)) Find a World.

Petitte Bijou. l.t. ed. Patrick Modiano. (French Ser.). (FRE., 2001. bk. 30.99 (978-2-84011-440-6(2)) Pub: UlverLrgPrint GBR. Dist(s): Ulverscroft US

PetMassage: Doggie Songs for Kids. Perf. by Charlie Oswanski. Arranged by Charlie Oswanski. Lyrics by Jonathan Rudinger. (J). 2005. audio compact disk 12.95 (978-0-9664826-8-3(9)) PetMassage Ltd.

PetMassage: Energy Work with Dogs: Accessing the Magnificent Body Language & Body Wisdom of the Dog Through Acupressure, Chakra Balancing & Positional Release. Jonathan Rudinger. Photos by Cheryl Hall Photography Staff. 5 cds. (PetMassage for Dogs Ser.). 2003. audio compact disk 44.95 (978-0-9664826-4-5(6)) PetMassage Ltd.

Petra en Alabanza. Contrib. by Petra. Prod. by Bob Hartman & John Lawry. 1994. audio compact disk 9.99 (978-7-01-422462-2(X), Word Records) Word Enter.

Petra: the Early Years. Contrib. by Petra & Jonathan Watkins. (Early Years (EMI-Cmg) Ser.). 2006. audio compact disk 7.99 (978-5-558-24618-6(9)) Pt of Grace Ent.

Petrakis Reads Petrakis. Short Stories. Harry Mark Petrakis. 1 cass. 1995. 14.95 (978-0-941702-31-7(6)) Lake View Pr.
Short stories.

Petrified Forest see Theatre Highlights

Petrified Forest National Park & Painted Desert. Patrick T. Houlihan & Betsy Houlihan. 1 cass. (Running Time: 1 hr). 2000. 12.00 (978-1-931544-10-8(7)) Walkabout Audio.
The description of the driving tour through the Petrified Forest National Park & the Painted Desert. Also the discussion of geological causes for the land forms ancient dinosaur inhabitants, formation processes of petrified wood & archeological finds.

Petrified Forest National Park & the Painted Desert: Northbound - Walkabout Audio Tours. Patrick T. Houlihan & Betsy Houlihan. 1 CD. (Running Time: 1 hr). 2000. audio compact disk 19.00 (978-1-931544-11-5(5)) Walkabout Audio.
The description of the driving tour through the Petrified Forest National Park & the Painted Desert. Also the discusion of geological causes for the land forms ancient dinosaur inhabitants, formation processes of petrified wood & archeological finds.

Petrified Forest National Park & the Painted Desert: Southbound - Walkabout Audio Tours. Patrick T. Houlihan & Betsy Houlihan. 1 CD. (Running Time: 1 hr.). 2000. audio compact disk 19.00 (978-1-931544-12-2(3)) Walkabout Audio.
The description of the driving tour through the Petrified Forest National Park & the Painted Desert. Also the discussion of geological causes for the land forms ancient dinosaur inhabitants, formation processes of petrified wood & archeological finds.

Petrified Man. (J). (SWC 1626) HarperCollins Pubs.

Petro Breath. Poems. John M. Bennett & Screamin Popeyes. 1 cass. 1993. 6.00 (978-0-935350-51-7(9)) Luna Bisonte.
Surrealist poetry performed with avant-pop sound art.

Petrochemicals in Venezuela: A Strategic Reference 2007. Compiled by Icon Group International, Inc. Staff. 2007. ring bd. 195.00 (978-0-497-82470-9(1)) Icon Grp.

Petrodollar Investments, Criteria For. Phillip Bradley. 1 cass. (Running Time: 53 min.). 10.95 (455) J Norton Pubs.

Petronov Plan, Set. unabr. ed. James Pattinson. 4 cass. 1986. 44.95 (978-1-85496-177-8(2), US0062) Ulvrscrft Audio.

Petrouchka: Stravinsky. (YA). 1994. 17.00 (978-0-89898-795-9(4), BMR05095, Warner Bro) Alfred Pub.

Petrukian. Jay O'Callahan. As told by Jay O'Callahan. (ENG.). (J). 2008. audio compact disk 15.00 (978-1-877954-56-6(X)) Pub: Artana Prodns. Dist(s): High Windy Audio

Petrukian. Jay O'Callahan. Perf. by Jay O'Callahan. 1 cass. (Running Time: 1 hr. 04 min.). (YA). (gr. 2 up). 1994. 10.00 (978-1-877954-11-5(X)) Artana Prodns.
In the fantastic land of Artana a blacksmith hides a dark secret. Only the answer to a strange riddle can save him.

Pets! Gail Godwin et al. Read by Jane Curtin et al. 3 CDs. (Running Time: 3 hrs. 0 mins. 0 sec.). (Selected Shorts Ser.). (ENG.). 2007. audio compact disk 28.00 (978-1-934033-01-2(4)) Pub: Symphony Space. Dist(s): IPG Chicago

***Petting Zoo: A Novel.** unabr. ed. Jim Carroll. (Running Time: 9 hrs. 30 mins. 0 sec.). (ENG.). 2010. 24.99 (978-1-4001-6877-4(5)); 34.99 (978-1-4001-9877-1(1)); 16.99 (978-1-4001-8877-2(6)); audio compact disk 83.99 (978-1-4001-4877-6(4)) Pub: Tantor Media. Dist(s): IngramPubServ

***Petting Zoo: A Novel.** unabr. ed. Jim Carroll. Narrated by Scott Brick. (Running Time: 9 hrs. 30 mins. 0 sec.). (ENG.). 2010. audio compact disk 34.99 (978-1-4001-1877-9(8)) Pub: Tantor Media. Dist(s): IngramPubServ

Petty Crimes. Gary Soto. Narrated by Robert Ramirez. 4 CDs. (Running Time: 3 hrs. 45 mins.). (gr. 6 up). 1998. audio compact disk 39.00 (978-1-4025-1482-1(4), C1607) Recorded Bks.
10 stories about the dangerous little scams faced by young people growing up in the city. Soto's sometimes funny, sometimes tragic tales show inner-city youth striving for more from their lives, and confronting the limitations of their futures.

Petty Crimes. unabr. ed. Short Stories. Gary Soto. Narrated by Robert Ramirez. 3 pieces. (Running Time: 3 hrs. 45 mins.). (gr. 6 up). 2001. 28.00 (978-0-7887-5373-2(8)) Recorded Bks.
Ten stories show inner-city youth striving for more from their lives - and confronting the limitations of their futures.

Petunia. 2004. bk. 24.95 (978-1-56008-237-8(2)); pap. bk. 14.95 (978-0-7882-0603-0(6)); 8.95 (978-1-56008-632-1(7)); cass. & flmstrp 30.00 (978-1-56008-744-1(7)) Weston Woods.

Petunia. Roger Duvoisin. 1 cass. (Running Time: 10 min.). (J). (ps-3). 2000. bk. 24.95 (QHBC045) Weston Woods.
A silly goose learns that carrying a book under her wing doesn't necessarily make her knowledgeable.

Petunia. unabr. ed. Roger Duvoisin. Read by Julie Harris. 1 cass. Incl. Petunia: Petunia & the Song. (J). (CP 1489); Petunia: Petunia, I Love You. (J). (CP 1489); Petunia: Petunia Takes a Trip. (J). (CP 1489); Petunia: Petunia's Christmas. (J). (CP 1489); Petunia: Petunia's Treasure. (J). (CP 1489); Petunia: Petunia's Treasure. (J). (CP 1489); (J). 1984. 8.98 (978-0-89845-180-1(9), CP 1489) HarperCollins Pubs.

Petunia: Petunia & the Song see Petunia

Petunia: Petunia, I Love You see Petunia

Petunia: Petunia Takes a Trip see Petunia

Petunia: Petunia's Christmas see Petunia

Petunia: Petunia's Treasure see Petunia

Petunia & Her Playmates. (J). 2005. audio compact disk (978-1-933796-05-5(7)) PC Treasures.

Petunia Takes a Trip. Roger Duvoisen. (J). 1989. 22.66 (978-0-394-03685-4(9)) SRA McGraw.

Peu, Beaucoup, Passionnement. I.t. ed. Martine Angela Monupet. (French Ser.). (FRE., 2001. bk. 30.99 (978-2-84011-443-7(7)) Pub: UlverLrgPrint GBR. Dist(s): Ulverscroft US

Peur see Treasury of Guy de Maupassant: Contes Choisis

Peur - La Ficelle. Guy de Maupassant. 1 cass. (Guy de Maupassant Ser.: Vol. III). (FRE.). bk. 16.95 (SFR453) J Norton Pubs.

Peutz-Jeghers Syndrome - A Bibliography & Dictionary for Physicians, Patients, & Genome Researchers. Compiled by Icon Group International, Inc. Staff. 2007. ring bd. 28.95 (978-0-497-11272-1(8)) Icon Grp.

Peyote & the NAC. unabr. ed. Bob Bergman. 1 cass. (Running Time: 1 hr. 30 min.). 1975. 11.00 (13501) Big Sur Tapes.
Psychiatrist Bergman went to work for the Indian Health Service on the Navajo Reservation in 1966, where at that time more than 30,000 Navajos were members of the Native American Church. Expecting to find a clinic full of "peyote addicts," Bergman found instead a thriving spiritual practice that used peyote as a sacrament. Here he speaks movingly of his personal experience with the NAC.

Peyote Songs. Sung by Billy & Wayne Turtle. unabr. ed. Billy Turtle & Wayne Turtle. 1 cass. (Running Time: 90 min.). 1980. 11.00 (11001) Big Sur Tapes.
Southern Cheyennes Billy & Wayne Turtle sing 32 intertribal peyote songs. Their great-grandparents, Dog Woman & John Turtle, led the meetings for the first chapter of The Native American Church in 1918. Billy Turtle is a roadman (ceremonial leader) in the Church & is highly respected as a medicine man & for his singing.

Peyton Place. unabr. ed. Grace Metalious. Read by Tim O'Connor. 12 cass. (Running Time: 18 hrs.). 2001. 96.00 (978-0-7366-8315-9(1)) Books on Tape.
the story of a repressive New England town known for its high standards of public morality, and the steamy sexual activities that take place behind its bedroom doors. While the town's rigid mores lead to hypocrisy and repression, the earthy characters have an unbelievably high level of sexual functioning, especially the playboy Rodney Harrington and the profoundly round-heeled Betty Anderson. In this environment, Allison McKenzie, a dreamy girl coming to womanhood, must make her way without a father, living with her frigid mother Constance McKenzie.

Pez Maravilloso. Steck-Vaughn Staff. 1 cass. (Running Time: 90 mins.). (SPA.). 1999. (978-0-7398-0746-0(3)) SteckVau.

***Pfeffernut County Audio CD Complete Set.** (Pfeffernut County Ser.). (ENG.). 2008. audio compact disk 47.72 (978-1-4048-5489-5(4)) CapstoneDig.

Pfeiffer Syndrome - A Bibliography & Dictionary for Physicians, Patients, & Genome Researchers. Compiled by Icon Group International, Inc. Staff. 2007. ring bd. 28.95 (978-0-497-11273-8(6)) Icon Grp.

Pflum's Greatest Hits. Poems. Richard Pflum. 1 CD. (Running Time: 60 minutes). 2002. audio compact disk 9.95 (978-0-9713615-3-9(3)) Muse Rules Pr.
32 of the best poems by Indianapolis writer Richard Pflum, author of A Dream of Salt, A Strange Juxtapositionn of parts, and other collections. The poet is known for his interests in music and surreal imagery. Read by the author and accompanied by a booklet of the poems.

PgMP Exam Review: Processes Audio CD. 2007. audio compact disk (978-0-9787230-7-1(4)) Crosswind Proj Manag.

PgMP Exam Review: Terminology & Processes Mp3 Audio CD. 2007. audio compact disk 39.95 (978-0-9787230-8-8(2)) Crosswind Proj Manag.

PgMP Exam Review: Terminology Audio CD. 2007. audio compact disk (978-0-9787230-9-5(0)) Crosswind Proj Manag.

PGT-CD 2000: Everything from Planned Giving Today. Ed. by G. Roger Schoenhals. 2000. audio compact disk Rental 129.00 (978-1-929029-01-3(2)) Planned Giving.

Phaedo, Set. unabr. ed. Plato. Read by Robert L. Halvorson. 4 cass. (Running Time: 360 min.). 28.95 (70) Halvorson Assocs.

Phaedrus. unabr. ed. Plato. Read by Robert L. Halvorson. 4 cass. (Running Time: 360 min.). Incl. Laches. (68); Lysis. (68); 28.95 (68) Halvorson Assocs.

Phallus in Wonderland. abr. ed. O'Connell Mary. 2 CDs. (Running Time: 7200 sec.). 2007. audio compact disk 19.95 (978-0-660-19685-5(9), CBC Audio) Pub: Canadian Broadcasting CAN. Dist(s): Georgetown Term
Men have celebrated the penis for millennia, and often used their organ as a symbol of power and dominance. In Ancient Greece it was common for men to pursue teenage boys for sexual gratification. In Ancient Rome, it was said, generals sometimes promoted soldiers based on penis size.Throughout history, the pursuit of the perfect penis has fuelled the search for cures for impotence. In the eleventh century a recipe involved sparrows and billy-goats. When honey was added, the ingredients were cooked until the mixture became hard. It was made into pills and men would take one before intercourse. Today men pop Viagra. IDEAS producer Mary O?Connell takes us on a 2-CD historical tour of male sexuality.

Phantas see Widdershins: The First Book of Ghost Stories

Phantastes. unabr. ed. George MacDonald. Read by Rob Gregory. 6 cass. (Running Time: 9 hrs.). 1999. 44.95 (978-0-7861-0143-6(1), 1128) Blckstn Audio.
Presents the narrator's dream-like adventures into fantasyland where he confronts tree-spirits & the shadow, sojourns to the palace of the fairy queen, & searches for the spirit of earth.

Phantom. abr. ed. Terry Goodkind. Read by Sam Tsoutsouvas. (Running Time: 32400 sec.). (Sword of Truth: Bk. 2). 2007. audio compact disk 19.99 (978-1-59600-877-9(6), 9781596008779, BCD Value Price) Brilliance Audio.
Please enter a Synopsis.

Phantom. unabr. ed. Terry Goodkind. Read by Sam Tsoutsouvas. (Running Time: 23 hrs.). (Sword of Truth Ser.). 2006. 29.95 (978-1-59710-330-5(6), 9781597103305, BAD) Brilliance Audio.

Phantom. unabr. ed. Terry Goodkind. Read by Sam Tsoutsouvas. (Running Time: 23 hrs.). (Sword of Truth: Bk. 2). 2006. 44.25 (978-1-59710-331-2(4), 9781597103312, BADLE); 46.95 (978-1-59086-313-8(5), 9781590863138, BAU); 122.25 (978-1-59086-314-5(3), 9781590863145, BrilAudUnabridg); audio compact disk 145.25 (978-1-59086-316-9(X), 9781590863169, BriAudCD Unabrid); audio compact disk 49.95 (978-1-59086-315-2(1), 9781590863152, Bril Audio CD Unabri); audio compact disk 29.95 (978-1-59335-687-3(0), 9781593356873, Brilliance MP3); audio compact disk 44.25 (978-1-59335-821-1(0), 9781593358211, Brinc Audio MP3 Lib) Brilliance Audio.
On the day she awoke remembering nothing but her name, Kahlan Amnell became the most dangerous woman alive. For everyone else, that was the day that the world began to end. As her husband, Richard, desperately searches for his beloved, whom only he remembers, he knows that if she doesn't soon discover who she really is, she will unwittingly become the instrument that will unleash annihilation. But Kahlan learns that if she ever were to unlock the truth of her lost identity, then evil itself would finally possess her, body and soul. If she is to survive in a murky world of deception and betrayal, where life is not only cheap but fleeting, Kahlan must find out why she is such a central figure in the war-torn world swirling around her. What she uncovers are secrets darker than she could ever have imagined.

Phantom. unabr. ed. Roy Lewis. Read by Gordon Griffin. 6 cass. (Running Time: 23400 sec.). (Soundings Ser.). 2006. 54.95 (978-1-84283-604-0(8)) Pub: ISIS Lrg Prnt GBR. Dist(s): Ulverscroft US

Phantom Bark see Poetry of Hart Crane

Phantom Coach. unabr. ed. Amelia B. Edwards. Read by Jim Killavey. 1 cass. (Running Time: 80 min.). Dramatization. 1981. 7.95 (S-4) Jimcin Record.
Two classics of horror & the supernatural.

***Phantom Evil.** unabr. ed. Heather Graham. (Running Time: 11 hrs.). 2011. audio compact disk 32.99 (978-1-4418-9618-6(X), 9781441896186, Bril Audio CD Unabri) Brilliance Audio.

Phantom Falcon. Anne Schraff. Narrated by Larry A. McKeever. (Sport Ser.). (J). 2000. audio compact disk 14.95 (978-1-58659-290-5(4)) Artesian.

Phantom Falcon. abr. ed. 1 cass. (Running Time: 40 min.). 1999. 10.95 (54116) Artesian.

Phantom Falcon. unabr. ed. Anne Schraff. Narrated by Larry A. McKeever. 1 cass. (Running Time: 40 min.). (Take Ten Ser.). (J). 2000. 10.95 (978-1-58659-036-9(7), 54117) Artesian.

Phantom Hag see Classic Ghost Stories, Vol. 2, A Collection

Phantom Horsewoman see Poetry of Thomas Hardy

Phantom in the Mirror. John R. Erickson. 2 cass. (Running Time: 2 hrs.). Dramatization. (Hank the Cowdog Ser.: No. 20). (J). (gr. 2-5). 1993. 16.95 Set. (978-0-87719-233-6(2), 9233) Lone Star Bks.

Phantom in the Mirror. unabr. ed. John R. Erickson. Read by John R. Erickson. 2 cass. (Running Time: 3 hrs.). (Hank the Cowdog Ser.: No. 20). (J). (gr. 2-5). 2001. 16.95 (978-0-7366-6909-2(4)) Books on Tape.
Hank finds the meanest, toughest, stupidest dog he's ever seen in the machine shed. How does he get rid of this unwanted visitor?.

Phantom in the Mirror. unabr. ed. John R. Erickson. Read by John R. Erickson. 2 cass. (Running Time: 3 hrs.). (Hank the Cowdog Ser.: No. 20). (J). 2002. 17.99 (978-1-59188-320-3(2)) Maverick Bks.

Phantom in the Mirror. unabr. ed. John R. Erickson. Read by John R. Erickson. 2 CDs. (Running Time: Approx. 3 hours). (Hank the Cowdog Ser.: No. 20). (J). 2002. audio compact disk 19.99 (978-1-59188-620-4(1)) Maverick Bks.
After Pete the Barncat starts a rumor about a Phantom Dog in the machine shed, Hank the Cowdog?the Head of Ranch Security?decides that he better check it out. And sure enough, when Hank takes a peek into the shadows, he sees the meanest, toughest, stupidest dog he?s ever seen. Hank tries all of his tricks to outwit the Phantom in the Mirror?but each time, the phantom dog matches him step for step. Hank?s got to find a way to rid the ranch of this uninvited visitor?but how?Two new songs ?Poor Me? and ?Gloria? are featured in this hilarious adventure for the whole family.

Phantom in the Mirror. unabr. ed. John R. Erickson. Read by John R. Erickson. 2 cass. (Hank the Cowdog Ser.: No. 20). (J). (gr. 2-5). 1998. 17.00 (21628B3) Recorded Bks.

Phantom in the Mirror. unabr. collector's ed. John R. Erickson. 1 CD. (Running Time: 3 hrs.). (Hank the Cowdog Ser.: Bk. 20). (J). 2001. audio compact disk 19.99 Books on Tape.
Hank finds the meanest, toughest stupidest dog he's ever seen in the machine shed. How does he get rid of this unwanted visitor?.

Phantom in the Mirror. unabr. collector's ed. John R. Erickson. 2 cass. (Running Time: 3 hrs.). (Hank the Cowdog Ser.: No. 20). (J). 2001. 24.00 (978-0-7366-6153-9(0)) Books on Tape.

Phantom in the Mirror. unabr. collector's ed. John R. Erickson. 2 cass. (Running Time: 3 hrs.). (Hank the Cowdog Ser.: No. 20). (J). 2001. 24.00 (978-0-7366-7542-0(6)) Books on Tape.

Phantom Island see Great American Short Stories, Vol. II, A Collection

Phantom Island. 1986. (S-73) Jimcin Record.

Phantom Island. Washington Irving. Read by Lloyd Battista. Contrib. by Brad Hill. Intro. by Joyce Carol Oates & Peter Benchley. 1 cass. 14.95 (978-1-56268-005-3(6)) Spencer Library.
A mysterious place that exists without question in the hearts & minds of poets, musicians & artists, "The Phantom Island" becomes an obsession for the hero of Washington Irving's strange tale. Mortgaged to the hilt to finance his lofty quest, Don Fernando sets sail & embarks on a voyage that tests faith, commitment & good sense. The reward of such an enterprise is yours for the listening.

Phantom Major: The Story of David Sterling & the SAS Regiment. unabr. ed. Virgina Crowle. Narrated by Robert Whitfield. 7 cass. (Running Time: 8 hrs. 30 mins.). 2001. 49.95 (978-0-7861-2148-9(3), 2922); audio compact disk 64.00 (978-0-7861-9593-0(2), 2922) Blckstn Audio.
In the dark and uncertain days of 1941 and 1942, when Rommel's tanks were sweeping towards Suez, a handful of daring raiders were making history for the Allies. They operated deep behind the German lines, often driving hundreds of miles through the deserts of North Africa. They hid by day and struck by night, destroying aircraft, blowing up ammunition dumps, derailing trains, and killing many times their own number. These were the SAS, Stirling's desert raiders, the brainchild of a deceptively mild-mannered man with a brilliant idea. Small teams of resourceful, highly trained men would penetrate beyond the front lines of the opposing armies and wreak havoc where the Germans least expected it.

Phantom Menace. Terry Brooks. Read by Alexander Adams. 1999. audio compact disk 72.00 (978-0-7366-5176-9(4)) Books on Tape.

Phantom Menace. unabr. ed. Terry Brooks. Read by Alexander Adams. Based on a story by George Lucas. 7 cass. (Running Time: 10 hrs. 30 min.). 1999. 56.00 (978-0-7366-4511-9(X), 4943) Books on Tape.
In barren desert lands & seedy spaceports, in visit underwater cities & in the blackest depths of space, unfolds a tale of good & evil, of myth & magic, of innocence & power. At last the saga that captured the imagination of millions turns back in time to reveal its cloaked origins, the start f a legend, the story of Star Wars.

Phantom Menace. unabr. ed. Terry Brooks. Read by Alexander Adams. Based on a story by George Lucas. 9 CDs. (Running Time: 13 hrs. 30 mins.). 2001. audio compact disk 72.00 Books on Tape.
In barren desert lands and seedy spaceports... in vast underwater cities and in the blackest depths of space... unfolds a tale of good and evil, of myth and magic, of innocence and power. At last the saga that captured the imagination of millions turns back in time to reveal its cloaked origins - the start of a legend - the story of Star Wars.

Phantom Mudder. unabr. ed. Darrel and Sally Odgers. Read by Alan King. (Running Time: 50 mins.). (Jack Russell: Dog Detective Ser.). (J). 2006. audio compact disk 39.95 (978-1-74093-787-0(2)) Pub: Bolinda Pubng AUS. Dist(s): Bolinda Pub Inc

Phantom of Billy Bantam & the Ghoul of Bodger O'Toole. Read by Richard Mitchley. (Running Time: 6600 sec.). (J). 2001. audio compact disk 21.95 (978-0-7540-6772-6(6)) AudioGo GBR.

Phantom of Manhattan. unabr. ed. Frederick Forsyth. Read by Roger R. Reese et al. 4 cass. (Running Time: 5 hrs.). 2001. 25.00 (978-1-59040-040-1(2), Phoenix Audio) Pub: Amer Intl Pub. Dist(s): PerseuPGW
It is 1906. Erik, the creature with the hideous face but poetic heart, has escaped to America, to a life that begins in misery, but in time makes him incredibly wealthy and brutally powerful. When he learns that his beloved Christine - now an international opera star - has a son, he is determined to learn the truth.

Phantom of Manhattan. unabr. collector's ed. Frederick Forsyth. Read by Stefan Rudnicki. 4 cass. (Running Time: 6 hrs.). 1999. 22.95 (978-0-7366-4735-9(X), 5073) Books on Tape.
The Phantom of the Opera escapes to the U.S. & becomes a ruthless mutimillionaire, still masked & obsessed with the singer Christine.

Phantom of the Opera see Fantasma de la Opera

Phantom of the Opera. Gaston Leroux. Read by Barrett Whitener. (Running Time: 9 hrs. 22 mins.). 2003. 29.95 (978-1-59912-103-1(4), Audiofy Corp) Iofy Corp.

Phantom of the Opera. Gaston Leroux. Narrated by Ralph Cosham. (Running Time: 8 hrs.). (C). 2004. 27.95 (978-1-59912-699-9(0)) Iofy Corp.

Phantom of the Opera. Gaston Leroux. Narrated by Walter Zimmerman. (Running Time: 7 hrs. 30 mins.). 2006. 25.95 (978-1-59912-148-2(4)) Iofy Corp.

Phantom of the Opera. Gaston Leroux. Read by Walter Zimmerman. 7 cass. (Running Time: 10 hrs.). 1989. 36.00 incl. album. (C-188) Jimcin Record.
This thriller is now a Broadway play.

Phantom of the Opera. Gaston Leroux. Read by Alexander Adams. (Running Time: 28800 sec.). (Unabridged Classics in Audio Ser.). (ENG.). 2006. audio compact disk 29.99 (978-1-4001-0276-1(6)); audio compact disk 59.99 (978-1-4001-3276-8(2)) Pub: Tantor Media. Dist(s): IngramPubServ

Phantom of the Opera. Gaston Leroux. Read by Fabio Camero. (Running Time: 3 hrs.). 2002. 16.95 (978-1-60083-269-7(5), Audiofy Corp) Iofy Corp.

Phantom of the Opera. Gaston Leroux. Narrated by Barrett Whitener. (Running Time: 33780 sec.). (Unabridged Classics in MP3 Ser.). (ENG.). 2008. audio compact disk 24.00 (978-1-58472-446-9(3), In Aud) Sound Room.

Phantom of the Opera. Gaston Leroux. Narrated by Flo Gibson. (ENG.). 2008. audio compact disk 29.95 (978-1-60646-063-4(3)) Audio Bk Con.

Phantom of the Opera. Composed by Andrew Lloyd Webber. 1 cass. 6.98; audio compact disk 9.98 Lifedance.
Sung by members of various British productions. Includes "All I Ask of You," "Angel of Music," "Masquerade," "Music of the Night," "Overture," "The Phantom of the Opera," "Point of No Return," "Prima Donna," "Think of Me" & "Wishing You Were Somehow Here Again." Demo CD or cassette available.

Phantom of the Opera. Read by Jeremy Nicholas & Peter Yapp. 2 CDs. (Running Time: 9537 sec.). 2006. audio compact disk 17.98 (978-962-634-374-6(5), Naxos AudioBooks) Naxos.

Phantom of the Opera. abr. ed. Gaston Leroux. Read by Jeremy Nicholas & Peter Yapp. 2 cass. (Running Time: 2 hrs. 30 mins.). 1997. 13.98 (978-962-634-618-1(3), NA211814, Naxos AudioBooks) Naxos.
This 19th century French thriller tells of the mysterious Erik, a grotesque & elusive "phantom," who hides himself in the bowels of the Paris Opera & entices, with his angelic voice, the beautiful Christine. Her abduction prompts a dramatic search for her & the truth.

Phantom of the Opera. abr. ed. Gaston Leroux. Perf. by Christopher Cazenove. 2 cass. (Running Time: 3 hrs.). 2004. 18.00 (978-1-59007-031-4(3)) Pub: New Millenn Enter. Dist(s): PerseuPGW
A baffling series of incidents at the majestic Paris Opera sparks frightening rumors about a mysterious "opera ghost." A young and beautiful prima donna is visited by a masked "Angel of Music" who teaches her to sing and jealously demands her devotion. Is it a ghost... an angel... or a man? And what does the mask conceal?.

Phantom of the Opera. unabr. ed. Gaston Leroux. Read by Ralph Cosham. 6 cass. (Running Time: 8 hrs.). 2004. 54.95 (978-0-7861-2844-0(5), 3376) Blckstn Audio.

Phantom of the Opera. unabr. ed. Gaston Leroux. Read by Geoffrey Howard. 13 vols. (Running Time: 8 hrs.). 2004. audio compact disk 24.95 (978-0-7861-8364-7(0), 3376) Blckstn Audio.

Phantom of the Opera. unabr. ed. Gaston Leroux. Read by Ralph Cosham. 7 CDs. (Running Time: 8 hrs.). 2004. audio compact disk 63.00 (978-0-7861-8331-9(4), 3376) Blckstn Audio.

Phantom of the Opera. unabr. ed. Gaston Leroux. Read by Geoffrey Howard. 8 CDs. 2004. audio compact disk 32.95 (978-0-7861-8332-6(2)) Blckstn Audio.

Phantom of the Opera. unabr. ed. Gaston Leroux. Read by Alexander Adams. 7 CDs. (Running Time: 8 hrs. 12 mins.). 2001. audio compact disk 56.00 Books on Tape.
A madman inhabits the catacombs under the Paris Opera House & wreaks havoc on the world above.

Phantom of the Opera. unabr. ed. Gaston Leroux. Narrated by Henry Butler. 7 cass. (Running Time: 9 hrs. 45 mins.). 1988. 60.00 (978-1-55690-410-3(X), 88991E7) Recorded Bks.
The legend that excited all of Parisian upper classes: the kidnapping of Christine Daae, the disappearance of the Vicomte de Chagny & the death of his elder brother, Count Philippe, whose body was found on the banks of the lake in the lower cellars of the Paris Opera House.

Phantom of the Opera. unabr. ed. Gaston Leroux. Read by Barrett Whitener. 1 cd. (Running Time: 9 hrs 23 mins). 2002. audio compact disk 18.95 (978-1-58472-393-6(9), In Aud) Pub: Sound Room. Dist(s): Baker Taylor
MP3 format.

Phantom of the Opera. unabr. ed. Gaston Leroux. Read by Geoffrey Howard. 7 cass. 2004. reel tape 29.95 (978-0-7861-2846-4(1)) Blckstn Audio.

Phantom of the Opera. unabr. ed. Gaston Leroux. Read by Barrett Whitener. (YA). 2006. 74.99 (978-1-59895-174-5(2)) Find a World.

Phantom of the Opera. unabr. ed. Gaston Leroux. Narrated by Alexander Adams. (Running Time: 8 hrs. 0 mins. 0 sec.). (ENG.). 2008. 19.99 (978-1-4001-5899-7(0)); audio compact disk 27.99 (978-1-4001-0899-2(3)) Pub: Tantor Media. Dist(s): IngramPubServ

Phantom of the Opera. unabr. collector's ed. Gaston Leroux. Read by Alexander Adams. 6 cass. (Running Time: 9 hrs.). 1998. 48.00 (978-0-7366-4154-8(8), 4657) Books on Tape.
A madman inhabits the catacombs under the Paris Opera House & wreaks havoc on the world above.

Phantom of the Opera. unabr. collector's ed. Gaston Leroux. Read by Alexander Adams. 7 cass. (Running Time: 7 hrs.). 2000. 56.00 (978-0-7366-5139-4(X), 9188) Books on Tape.
In L'Opera de Paris a beautiful woman disappears. In a moment the opera's facade falls away, not only away but into a pit where all the perverse impulses of art grow visible & manifest.

Phantom of the Opera, Level 2. (Yamaha Clavinova Connection Ser.). 2004. disk 1.04 (978-0-634-09591-7(9)) H Leonard.

Phantom of the Opera, Set. unabr. ed. Gaston Leroux. Read by Flo Gibson. 6 cass. (Running Time: 9 hrs.). (Classic Books on Cassettes Ser.). 1988. 24.95 (978-1-55685-118-6(9)) Audio Bk Con.
Who is the mysterious ghost who titillates & terrifies the staff, performers & patrons of the Paris Opera House?.

Phantom of the Opera, with eBook. unabr. ed. Gaston Leroux. Narrated by Alexander Adams. (Running Time: 8 hrs. 0 mins. 0 sec.). (ENG.). 2008. audio compact disk 55.99 (978-1-4001-3899-9(X)) Pub: Tantor Media. Dist(s): IngramPubServ

Phantom of the Temple. unabr. ed. Robert H. Van Gulik. Narrated by Frank Muller. 4 cass. (Running Time: 5 hrs.). (Judge Dee Mysteries Ser.). 1986. 35.00 (978-1-55690-411-0(8), 86880E7) Recorded Bks.
Looking for an interesting birthday present for his First Wife, Judge Dee spots a small ebony box in a store with a very curious price tag.

Phantom Prey. John Sandford, pseud. Read by Richard Ferrone. (Running Time: 6 hrs.). (ENG.). (gr. 12 up). 2009. audio compact disk 14.95 (978-0-14-314475-5(8), PengAudBks) Penguin Grp USA.

Phantom Prey. abr. ed. John Sandford, pseud. Read by Richard Ferrone. 5 CDs. (Running Time: 6 hrs.). (ENG.). (gr. 8). 2008. audio compact disk 29.95 (978-0-14-314312-3(3), PengAudBks) Penguin Grp USA.

Phantom Prey. unabr. ed. John Sandford, pseud. Read by Richard Ferrone. 9 CDs. (Running Time: 11 hrs.). (ENG.). (gr. 8). 2008. audio compact disk 39.95 (978-0-14-314311-6(5), PengAudBks) Penguin Grp USA.

Phantom Tollbooth. unabr. ed. Norton Juster. Read by Pat Carroll. 1 cass. (Running Time: 51 min.). (J). (gr. 4-6). 1989. 9.95 (978-0-89845-903-6(6), CPN 1703) HarperCollins Pubs.
A bored boy, a phantom tollbooth, tokens & we're off to a world of wordplay & wonder.

Phantom Tollbooth. unabr. ed. Norton Juster. 1 read-along cass. (Running Time: 1 hr.). (Middle Grade Cliffhangers Ser.). (J). (gr. 5-6). 1982. 15.98 (978-0-8072-1096-3(X), SWR 29 SP, Listening Lib); (Listening Lib) Random Audio Pubg.
Milo drives his electric car through the tollbooth in his bedroom & into the lands beyond. Then the magic begins.

Phantom Tollbooth, unabr. ed. Norton Juster. Narrated by Norman Dietz. 4 pieces. (Running Time: 5 hrs. 15 mins.). (gr. 5 up). 1993. 35.00 (978-1-55690-876-7(8), 93318E7) Recorded Bks.
Milo, bored with everything, discovers a Phantom Tollbooth in his room & when he drives through he embarks upon a series of adventures that open his mind. This mischievous, magical tale is a treasure for any child who has ever struggled with grammar, spelling & mathematics.

Phantom Tollbooth. unabr. ed. Norton Juster. Narrated by Norman Dietz. 5 CDs. (Running Time: 5 hrs. 15 mins.). (gr. 5 up). 2000. audio compact disk 40.00 (978-0-7887-3735-0(X), C1106E7) Recorded Bks.

Phantom Waltz. Catherine Anderson. Narrated by Julia Gibson. 10 cass. (Running Time: 14 hrs. 45 mins.). 88.00 (978-0-7887-9962-4(2)) Recorded Bks.

Phantom Woman see Classic Ghost Stories, Vol. 2, A Collection

Phantoms. unabr. ed. Dean Koontz. Read by Buck Schimer. (Running Time: 15 hrs.). 2008. 39.25 (978-1-4233-3931-1(2), 9781423339311, BADLE); 24.95 (978-1-4233-3930-4(4), 9781423339304, BAD); 107.25 (978-1-4233-3925-0(8), 9781423339250, BrilAudUnabridg); audio compact disk 39.25 (978-1-4233-3929-8(0), 9781423339298, Brinc Audio MP3 Lib); audio compact disk 112.25 (978-1-4233-3927-4(4), 9781423339274, BriAudCD Unabrid); audio compact disk 24.95 (978-1-4233-3928-1(2), 9781423339281, Brilliance MP3); audio compact disk 40.95 (978-1-4233-3926-7(6), 9781423339267, Bril Audio CD Unabri) Brilliance Audio.

Phantoms Afoot: Helping the Spirits among Us. abr. ed. Mary S. Rain. Read by Nancy Fish. 2 cass. (Running Time: 3 hrs.). 1997. 17.95 (978-1-57453-171-8(9)) Audio Lit.

Phantoms in the Night. Les Savage, Jr. 2009. (978-1-60136-231-5(5)) Audio Holding.

Phantoms of the High Seas. Nox Arcana. Composed by Joseph Vargo. (ENG.). 2008. audio compact disk 13.99 (978-0-9788857-7-9(5)) Monolith.

Pharmaceutical Additives Electronic Handbook. Michael Ash & Irene Ash. (Gower Chemical Reference Ser.). 1996. audio compact disk 450.00 (978-0-566-07602-2(0)); audio compact disk 450.00 (978-0-566-07597-1(0)) Ashgate Pub Co.

Pharmaceutical Computer Validation Introduction: GMP (Good Manufacturing Practices) Training Introduction to Meet FDA Regulations in the Use of Computers in Pharmaceutical, Medical Device, Food, & Cosmetics Manufacturing, with Emphasis on Computer System Validation & Part 11. Daniel Farb & Bruce Gordon. 2004. audio compact disk 99.95 (978-0-9743674-8-4(6)) Pub: UnivofHealth. Dist(s): AtlasBooks

Pharmaceutical Computer Validation Introduction 10 Users. Daniel Farb & Bruce Gordon. 2005. audio compact disk 299.95 (978-1-59491-183-5(5)) Pub: UnivofHealth. Dist(s): AtlasBooks

Pharmaceutical Computer Validation Introduction, 5 Users. Daniel Farb & Bruce Gordon. (ENG.). 2005. 199.95 (978-1-59491-153-8(3)) Pub: UnivofHealth. Dist(s): AtlasBooks

Pharmaceutical Drugs AudioLearn. 6 CD's. (Running Time: 6.7 hrs.). 2008. audio compact disk 99.99 (978-1-59262-015-9(9)) AudioLearn.

Pharmaceutical Industry: Chemistry & Concepts. Harold A. Wittcoff & Bryan G. Reuben. 10 cass. (Running Time: 9 hrs. 42 min.). 655.00 incl. manual. (978-0-8412-1036-3(5), 78); 46.00 manual. (978-0-8412-1037-0(3)) Am Chemical.
Introduces the scientist to the pharmaceutical industry. Describes the characteristics of this important industry & includes discussions of economics, government regulation & competition.

Pharmaceutical Quality Control Lab: GMP (Good Manufacturing Practices) Training for Pharmaceutical Manufacturing, Covering FDA Regulations of Laboratory Results, SOPs (Standard Operating Procedures), & OOS (Out of Standard) & OOT (Out of Trend) Results. Daniel Farb et al. 2004. audio compact disk 149.95 (978-0-9743674-9-1(4)) Pub: UnivofHealth. Dist(s): AtlasBooks

Pharmaceutical Quality Control Lab 10 Users. Daniel Farb et al. 2005. audio compact disk 449.95 (978-1-59491-184-2(3)) Pub: UnivofHealth. Dist(s): AtlasBooks

Pharmaceutical Quality Control Lab 5 Users. Daniel Farb et al. 2005. audio compact disk 299.95 (978-1-59491-154-5(1)) Pub: UnivofHealth. Dist(s): AtlasBooks

Pharmaceutical Regulatory Documents: A Reference of Federal Documents Pertaining to Major Pharmaceutical, Medical Device, Sales, Manufacturing, Electronic Records, & Clinical Trials FDA Regulations, Including GMPs (Good Manufacuring Practices), GCPs (Good Clinical Practices), & GLPs (Good Laboratory Practices) with HIPAA Regulations Included, As an Aid to Compliance. Daniel Farb. 2004. audio compact disk 59.95 (978-1-59491-100-2(2)) Pub: UnivofHealth. Dist(s): AtlasBooks

Pharmaceuticals & Personal Injury Litigation. 1988. bk. 120.00 incl. book.; 65.00 cass. only.; 55.00 book only. PA Bar Inst.

Pharmaceuticals in Germany: A Strategic Reference 2007. Compiled by Icon Group International, Inc. Staff. 2007. ring bd. 195.00 (978-0-497-35980-5(4)) Icon Grp.

Pharmacokinetics: Principles & Applications. Peter G. Welling. 9 cass. (Running Time: 9 hrs. 36 min.). 590.00 incl. manual. (978-0-8412-1042-4(X), 84); 48.00 manual. (978-0-8412-1043-1(8)) Am Chemical.
Provides both the conceptual basis for an understanding of pharmacokinetics as well as the mathematics essential for practical application.

Pharmacology Made Easy: Analgesic Drugs. Patricia Hoefler. 2002. (978-1-56533-116-7(8)) MEDS Pubng.

Pharmacology Made Easy: Antimicrobial Drugs. Patricia Hoefler. 2002. (978-1-56533-118-1(4)) MEDS Pubng.

Pharmacology Made Easy: Cardiovascular Drugs. Patricia Hoefler. 2002. (978-1-56533-117-4(6)) MEDS Pubng.

Pharmacology Made Easy: Endocrine Drugs. Patricia Hoefler. 2002. (978-1-56533-119-8(2)) MEDS Pubng.

Pharmacology Made Easy: Labor & Delivery Drugs. Patricia Hoefler. 2002. (978-1-56533-122-8(2)) MEDS Pubng.

Pharmacology Made Easy: Psychiatric Drugs. Patricia Hoefler. 2002. (978-1-56533-099-3(4)) MEDS Pubng.

Pharmacology Made Easy Pt. 1: Respiratory Drugs. Patricia Hoefler. 2002. (978-1-56533-120-4(6)) MEDS Pubng.

Pharmacology Made Easy Pt. 2: Respiratory Drugs. Patricia Hoefler. 2002. (978-1-56533-121-1(4)) MEDS Pubng.

Pharmacology Made Easy Audio Series. Patricia A. Hoefler. 1992. audio compact disk (978-1-56533-134-1(6)) MEDS Pubng.
Audio review solution.

Pharmacology Made Insanely Easy CD Review. 2009. audio compact disk 89.00 (978-0-9761029-9-1(4)) ICAN.

Pharmacology Recall Audio. Anand Ramachandran. (Recall Ser.). (ENG.). 2007. 37.95 (978-0-7817-6659-3(1)) Lppncott W W.

Pharmacy & Drug Information Section - Back to the Future: A Modern Perspective on Herbals & Their Relation to Alternative Medicine (The EMBASE Lecture) 1 cass. (Medical Library Association 1998 Annual Meeting & Exhibit Ser.). 1998. 12.00 (06) Med Lib Assn.

***Pharmacy Certified Technician Calculations Workbook Answer Key CD.** 2010. audio compact disk (978-0-941174-01-5(8)) Mich Pharm.

Pharmacy Practice For Technicians: Text with Encore CD. 3rd ed. Don A. Ballington & Robert J. Anderson. 2007. audio compact disk 38.95 (978-0-7638-2223-1(X)) Paradigm MN.

Pharmacy Technician Certification Exam Review. audio compact disk 31.95 (978-0-7638-2215-6(9)) Paradigm MN.

Phases & Warning Signs of Relapse. 1 cass. (Overcoming Roadblocks in Recovery Ser.). 7.95 (7571) Hazelden.

Phedre: Dual Language Edition, Set. Jean Racine. Perf. by Emmanuele Riva & Paul Emile Deiber. 2 CDs. (FRE.). 1995. 44.95 (1391-H) Olivia & Hill.
The tragic consequences of Phedre's love for the young Hippolyte, the son of her husband, Thesee. This gem of the French classical theater is performed by leading actors.

Phenomena see Poetry of Robinson Jeffers

Phenomenology of Possession: An Ambiguous Flight? Etzel Cardena. 1 cass. 9.00 (A0363-88) Sound Photosyn.
Recorded at the 5th annual ICSS '88. As Etzel gets nearer his Ph.D., he gets more concise & the subjects of his talks are always interesting if you want to explore shamanism, theater, & psychology.

Phenomenon: Everything You Need to Know about the Paranormal. abr. ed. Sylvia Browne & Lindsay Harrison. Read by Jeanie Hackett. (Running Time: 5 hrs.). (ENG.). 2005. audio compact disk 29.95 (978-1-56511-983-3(5), 1565119835) Pub: HighBridge. Dist(s): Workman Pub

Phenylketonuria - A Bibliography & Dictionary for Physicians, Patients, & Genome Researchers. Compiled by Icon Group International, Inc. Staff. 2007. ring bd. 28.95 (978-0-497-11274-5(4)) Icon Grp.

Phiem: Her Beauty Her Messages. Phiem. 2003. audio compact disk 17.99 (978-0-9744299-0-8(2)) PHIEM.

Phil Becomes City Fire Chief. (CC-5005) Natl Recrd Co.

Phil Byrnes Mysteries. Sable Jak. (ENG.). 2008. audio compact disk 12.95 (978-1-60245-161-2(3)) GDL Multimedia.

Phil Donahue: TV Talk Show Host. Interview. Interview with Phil Donahue. 1 cass. (Running Time: 30 min.). 9.95 (A0220B090, HarperThor) HarpC GBR.

Phil Gordon's Little Green Book: Lessons & Teachings in No Limit Texas Hold'em. abr. ed. Phil Gordon. Read by Phil Gordon. 2005. 12.95 (978-0-7435-5242-4(3)); audio compact disk 21.00 (978-0-7435-5182-3(6), Audioworks) Pub: S&S Audio. Dist(s): S and S Inc

Phil Harris/Alice Faye Show: Lawn Party & Buying a Boat. Perf. by Phil Harris & Alice Faye. 1 cass. (Running Time: 1 hr.). 2001. 6.98 (2386) Radio Spirits.

Phil Harris-Alice Faye Show: Explain the Beer. Perf. by Phil Harris et al. 2009. audio compact disk 39.98 (978-1-57019-884-7(5)) Radio Spirits.

Phil Harris-Alice Faye Show: Money, Brains & Beauty. Perf. by Phil Harris & Alice Faye. (ENG.). 2008. audio compact disk 39.98 (978-1-57019-859-5(4)) Radio Spirits.

***Phil Harris-Alice Faye Show: Private Lives.** Perf. by Phil Harris et al. 2010. audio compact disk 39.98 (978-1-57019-929-5(9)) Radio Spirits.

Phil Harris/Alice Faye. 2 cass. (Running Time: 2 hrs.). 10.95 Set in vinyl album. (978-1-57816-072-3(3), PH2401) Audio File.
Includes: "January 9, 1949" Phil accidentally drops Willie's engagement ring down the kitchen sink drain, so he asks Frankie to help him retrieve it. "May 15, 1949" Mr. Scott, the sponsor, throws a party, but Remley is not invited. Scott's swimming pool is the scene of disaster. "January 19, 1950" Alice wants a new car, but can't decide which one to buy. Hans Conried appears as the automobile salesman. Phil & Remley try their hand at auto repair. "April 16, 1950" When the Harris' daughters are invited to the birthday party for the sponsor's little girl. Mr. Scott asks Phil to provide the entertainment for the party.

Phil Harris/Alice Faye Christmas Show of 1949. Perf. by Elliott Lewis. 1954. (CC-8080) Natl Recrd Co.

Phil Harris/Alice Faye Show. collector's ed. Perf. by Phil Harris et al. 6 cass. (Running Time: 9 hrs.). 2000. bk. 34.98 (4553) Radio Spirits.
Situation comedy based on the home life of Phil Harris, bandleader on "The Jack Benny Program" and his real-life wife, Alice Faye. Phil was the rough-cut, lovable egomaniac & Alice was the movie star who gave up fame to be a wife and mother. Their domestic life was full of Phil's wild predicaments, which grew wilder with the help of Frankie Remley. 18 episodes.

Phil Harris/Alice Faye Show: A Brawl at the Grocery Store & Phil Decides to Do Some Home Repairs. Perf. by Phil Harris & Alice Faye. 1 cass. (Running Time: 1 hr.). 2001. 6.98 (2428) Radio Spirits.

Phil Harris/Alice Faye Show: A Job for Willy & The Babysitter. Perf. by Phil Harris & Alice Faye. 1 cass. (Running Time: 1 hr.). 2001. 6.98 (2467) Radio Spirits.

Phil Harris/Alice Faye Show: Band Not Invited to Ball & Inaugural Ball. Perf. by Phil Harris et al. 1 cass. (Running Time: 1 hr.). 2001. 6.98 (1788) Radio Spirits.

Phil Harris/Alice Faye Show: Cinderella & Male Secretary. Perf. by Phil Harris & Alice Faye. 1 cass. (Running Time: 1 hr.). 2001. 6.98 (1964) Radio Spirits.

Phil Harris/Alice Faye Show: Foster Parent & Father's Day. Perf. by Phil Harris & Alice Faye. 1 cass. (Running Time: 1 hr.). 2001. 6.98 (2387) Radio Spirits.

Phil Harris/Alice Faye Show: Game Show Appearance & No Money for Cab Driver. Perf. by Phil Harris & Alice Faye. 1 cass. (Running Time: 1 hr.). 2001. 6.98 (1875) Radio Spirits.

Phil Harris/Alice Faye Show: Is Phil Being Drafted? & Willie Engaged to Miss O'Conner. Perf. by Phil Harris & Alice Faye. 1 cass. (Running Time: 1 hr.). 2001. 6.98 (1787) Radio Spirits.

Phil Harris/Alice Faye Show: Julius' Marriage & Alice Buys a Car. Perf. by Phil Harris & Alice Faye. 1 cass. (Running Time: 1 hr.). 2001. 6.98 (1916) Radio Spirits.

Phil Harris/Alice Faye Show: Jury Duty & Remley Moves in. Perf. by Phil Harris & Alice Faye. 1 cass. (Running Time: 1 hr.). 2001. 6.98 (2385) Radio Spirits.

Phil Harris/Alice Faye Show: Little Alice's First Date & The Romance of Alice & Phil. Perf. by Phil Harris & Alice Faye. 1 cass. (Running Time: 1 hr.). 2001. 6.98 (2608) Radio Spirits.

Phil Harris/Alice Faye Show: Mr. Alice Faye & A Car for Alice. Perf. by Phil Harris & Alice Faye. 1 cass. (Running Time: 1 hr.). 2001. 6.98 (2389) Radio Spirits.

Phil Harris/Alice Faye Show: No Presents from Rexall & Getting a Christmas Tree in the Mountains. Perf. by Phil Harris & Alice Faye. 2001. 6.98 (2446) Radio Spirits.

Phil Harris/Alice Faye Show: Phil & Alice Plead for Frankie & Wallpaper the Bedroom. Perf. by Phil Harris & Alice Faye. 1 cass. (Running Time: 1 hr.). 2001. 6.98 (1789) Radio Spirits.

Phil Harris/Alice Faye Show: Phil Gets a Part in a Movie & An Older Man. Perf. by Phil Harris & Alice Faye. 1 cass. (Running Time: 1 hr.). 2001. 6.98 (1948) Radio Spirits.

Phil Harris/Alice Faye Show: Red Paint on Poodle & Fixing the Furnace. Perf. by Phil Harris & Alice Faye. 1 cass. (Running Time: 1 hr.). 2001. 6.98 (2586) Radio Spirits.

Phil Harris/Alice Faye Show: Remley is Fired & Valentine's Day Flowers. Perf. by Phil Harris & Alice Faye. 1 cass. (Running Time: 1 hr.). 2001. 6.98 (2384) Radio Spirits.

Phil Harris/Alice Faye Show: The Birthday Gift & Jessica, Your Draggin' Your Neck. Perf. by Phil Harris & Alice Faye. 1 cass. (Running Time: 1 hr.). 2001. 6.98 (2623) Radio Spirits.

Phil Harris/Alice Faye Show: The Flying Saucer & Three Easter Bunnies. Perf. by Phil Harris & Alice Faye. 1 cass. (Running Time: 1 hr.). 2001. 6.98 (1987) Radio Spirits.

Phil Harris/Alice Faye Show: The Live Steer & Health Food Diet. Perf. by Phil Harris & Alice Faye. 1 cass. (Running Time: 1 hr.). 2001. 6.98 (2485) Radio Spirits.

Phil Harris/Alice Faye Show: The Option & Phil Returns. Perf. by Phil Harris & Alice Faye. 1 cass. (Running Time: 1 hr.). 2001. 6.98 (2388) Radio Spirits.

Phil Harris/Alice Faye Show: The Used Trunk & Mother's Day Treat. Perf. by Phil Harris & Alice Faye. 1 cass. (Running Time: 1 hr.). 2001. 6.98 (1936) Radio Spirits.

Phil Harris/Alice Faye Show: TV Show Audition & The Electricians. Perf. by Phil Harris & Alice Faye. 1 cass. (Running Time: 1 hr.). 2001. 6.98 (2125) Radio Spirits.

Phil Harris/Alice Faye Show: What's A Rexall? & Frankie in Charge. Perf. by Phil Harris & Alice Faye. 1 cass. (Running Time: 1 hr.). 2001. 6.98 (2383) Radio Spirits.

Phil Harris/Alice Faye Show: Woman Wrestler Working for Phil & Buying Alice a Fur Coat. Perf. by Phil Harris & Alice Faye. 1 cass. (Running Time: 1 hr.). 2001. 6.98 (1694) Radio Spirits.

Phil Harris/Alice Faye Show & Duffy's Tavern. unabr. ed. Perf. by Frank Remley et al. 1 cass. (Running Time: 60 min.). Dramatization. 7.95 Norelco box. (CC3049) Natl Recrd Co.
Phil Harris-Alice Faye: Phil can't understand why his daughter, Phyllis, won't introduce him to her new boyfriend. He thinks it may be the way he dresses & he impulsively gives away his entire wardrobe. Phil sings one of his special numbers from "Alice in Wonderland." Duffy's Tavern: "Hello, Duffy's Tavern, where the elite meet to eat. Archie the manager speaking, Duffy ain't here." Archie's in love with Marie & wants to marry her, but he gets nervous when she says yes to his proposal.

Philadelphia, Set. unabr. ed. Christopher Davis. Read by Charles Napier. 4 cass. (Running Time: 6 hrs.). 1993. 22.95 (978-1-56876-014-8(0), 692285) Soundlines Ent.
Trial lawyer Andrew Beckett, having just been assigned the case of his career, keeps his AIDS condition secret from his associates. When he is fired for his illness, he pursues a suit against his firm, challenging a black lawyer to take up his case.

Philadelphia All the Time. Charles Hardy, III. 1 cass. (Running Time: 1 hr. 19 min.). 1992. bk. 13.95 (978-0-9635344-0-8(8), SD-1231) Spinning Disc.
Songs, performers, & speakers associated with Philadelphia (1896-1947). Descriptive fifty page book (illustrated) includes Marian Anderson, Russell Conwell, Leopold Stokowski, Jeanette MacDonald & Nelson Eddy.

Philadelphia Discovery Practice. 1996. bk. 99.00 (ACS-1105) PA Bar Inst.
Provides lawyers with the expertise required to successfully pursue & supervise discovery in Philadelphia County & the Eastern District. Contains practical forms for everyday use as well as the Pennsylvania & Federal Rules of Discovery.

Philadelphia Discovery Practice & Supplement: Pennsylvania Rules of Depositions & Discovery Pa. R.C.P. 4001-4025 & Pennsylvania Rules of Professional Conduct. 1990. 70.00 (AC-591) PA Bar Inst.

Philadelphia Experiment. Al Bielek. 1 cass. (Running Time: 2 hrs.). 16.95 (AT-5610) Lghtwrks Aud & Vid.
Al Bielek, a survivor of the now famous Navy invisibility experiments carried out in the late 40's, where sailors were teleported & a destroyer made optically invisible, relates the incredible details of his bizarre experiences in this rare first-person interview.

Philadelphia Local Taxes. 1991. 55.00 (AC-608) PA Bar Inst.

Philadelphia Motion Court Practice & Procedure. Read by Samuel M. Lehrer. 1 cass. 1991. 20.00 (AL-115) PA Bar Inst.

***Philadelphia Report: The Philadelphia Investigating Grand Jury Report into Allegations of Clergy Sexual Abuse in the Archdiocese of Philadelphia.** Lynne Abraham. Read by Various. (ENG.). 2010. 19.95 (978-0-9843759-2-9(9)) Cherry Hill Pubng.

***Philadelphia Report: The Philadelphia Investigating Grand Jury Report into Allegations of Clergy Sexual Abuse in the Archdiocese of Philadelphia.** abr. ed. Lynne Abraham. Read by Matt Anthony et al. Frwd. by Marci A. Hamilton. (ENG.). 2010. audio compact disk 29.95 (978-0-9843759-1-2(0)) Cherry Hill Pubng.

***Philadelphia Report: The Philadelphia Investigating Grand Jury Report into Allegations of Clergy Sexual Abuse in the Archdiocese of Philadelphia.** unabr. ed. Lynne Abraham. Read by Marci A. Hamilton et al. Frwd. by Marci A. Hamilton. (ENG.). 2010. audio compact disk 39.95 (978-0-9843759-3-6(7)) Cherry Hill Pubng.

***Philanthropy.** unabr. ed. George Soros. (Running Time: 10 hrs. 0 mins.). 2010. 34.99 (978-1-4001-9719-4(8)); 16.99 (978-1-4001-8719-5(2)) Tantor Media.

***Philanthropy.** unabr. ed. George Soros. (Running Time: 10 hrs. 0 mins. 0 sec.). (ENG.). 2011. 24.99 (978-1-4001-6719-7(1)); audio compact disk 69.99 (978-1-4001-4719-9(0)); audio compact disk 34.99 (978-1-4001-1719-2(4)) Pub: Tantor Media. Dist(s): IngramPubServ

Philco Radio Time. collector's ed. Perf. by Bing Crosby et al. 6 cass. (Running Time: 9 hrs.). 2000. bk. 34.98 (4544) Radio Spirits.
Musical variety program. 18 episodes.

Philco Radio Time: Dinah Shore & Phil Harris & Elliot Lewis. Perf. by Dinah Shore et al. Hosted by Bing Crosby. 1 cass. (Running Time: 1 hr.). 2001. 6.98 (1521) Radio Spirits.

Philco Radio Time: George Burns & Ester Williams, Red Engle. Perf. by George Burns & Esther Williams. Hosted by Bing Crosby. 1 cass. (Running Time: 1 hr.). 2001. 6.98 (1917) Radio Spirits.

Philip Dacey. Read by Philip Dacey. 1 cass. (Running Time: 29 min.). 1985. 10.00 New Letters.
One of a weekly half-hour radio program with authors talking & presenting their own works.

Philip Dow. Read by Philip Dow. 1 cass. (Running Time: 29 min.). 1985. 10.00 New Letters.
One of a weekly half-hour radio program with authors talking & presenting their works. Philip Dow reads from Paying Back The Sea & Potlach.

Philip Hall Likes Me. Bette Greene. (J). 1978. 21.33 (978-0-394-77096-3(X)) SRA McGraw.

Philip Hall Likes Me: I Reckon Maybe. unabr. ed. Bette Greene. Narrated by Andrea Johnson. 3 cass. (Running Time: 3 hrs. 20 mins.). (YA). 2001. pap. bk. & stu. ed. 47.24 Recorded Bks.
Beth Lambert thinks Philip Hall is the cutest boy in sixth grade. But Mama thinks Philip invites Beth over to his farm just do his chores & only hangs out with her when his friends aren't around.

Philip Hall Likes Me: I Reckon Maybe. unabr. ed. Bette Greene. Narrated by Andrea Johnson. 3 pieces. (Running Time: 3 hrs. 15 mins.). (gr. 5 up). 2001. 32.00 (978-0-7887-4561-4(1), 96332E77) Recorded Bks.

Philip Levine. Poems. Philip Levine. Read by Philip Levine. 1 cass. Incl. At the Fillmore. 1985. (SWC 1503); Baby Villon. 1985. (SWC 1503); Blasting from Heaven. (SWC 1503); Breath. 1985. (SWC 1503); Clouds. 1985. (SWC 1503); For the Poets of Chile Who Died with Their Country. 1985. (SWC 1503); Grandmother in Heaven. 1985. (SWC 1503); Heaven. 1985. (SWC 1503); Holding On. 1985. (SWC 1503); Horse. (SWC 1503); New Day. (SWC 1503); On the Edge. (SWC 1503); On the Murder of Lieutenant Jose Del Castillo by the Falangist Bravo Martinez, July 12, 1936. 1985. (SWC 1503); Poem Circling Hamtramek, Michigan All Night in Search of You. 1985. (SWC 1503); Salami. 1985. (SWC 1503); Saturday Sweeping. 1985. (SWC 1503); They Feed the Lion. 1985. (SWC 1503); To My God in His Sickness. 1985. (SWC 1503); To P. L., 1916-1937. 1985. (SWC 1503); Zaydee. 1985. (SWC 1503); 1976. 14.00 (978-0-694-50281-3(2), SWC 1503) HarperCollins Pubs.

Philip Levine. Read by Philip Levine. 1 cass. (Running Time: 29 min.). 1985. 10.00 New Letters.
A reading by American Book Award-winning poet from California.

Philippians Commentary. Chuck Missler. 1 MP3 CD-ROM. (Running Time: 8 hours). (Chuck Missler Commentaries). 2001. cd-rom 29.95 (978-1-57821-168-5(9)) Koinonia Hse.
Paul wrote this highly relevant letter whose theme is "joy through suffering" while imprisoned in Rome. There may never have been a time when this letter could mean more to some of the families which have been impacted by the tragic events of the recent past. Paul knew suffering; and Paul knew true joy. And he knew joy through suffering. In his darkest hour, he wrote a letter to encourage his most intimate friends.

Philippine Model. Serafin Lanot. 1 cass. 8.95 (757) Am Fed Astrologers.

Philippine Psychic Surgery. Jaime T. Licuaco. 1 cass. 9.00 (A0201-87) Sound Photosyn.
From ICSS '87 with slides.

Philippines, Set. unabr. ed. Joseph Stromberg. Read by Harry Reasoner et al. 2 cass. (Running Time: 3 hr.). (World's Political Hot Spots Ser.). 1991. 17.95 (978-0-938935-92-6(5), 10357) Knowledge Prod.
Strategically located, the Philippine Islands have been one of the keys to American policy in the Pacific. But this loose island chain has a bitter history, vacillating between oppression & rebellion.

Philippines: Knowledge Products. unabr. ed. McElroy Wendy. Read by Reasoner Harry. 2006. audio compact disk 25.95 (978-0-7861-6693-0(2)) Pub: Blckstn Audio. Dist(s): NetLibrary CO

Philippines' Senator Helena Benitez, United Nations Consultant Eric Carlson & Philippines' Rural Development Leader Mr. Horacio Morales Share Concerns at the Habitat Summit. Hosted by Nancy Pearlman. 1 cass. (Running Time: 28 min.). 10.00 (1503) Educ Comm CA.

***Philistines.** Guy Mccrone. 2010. 54.95 (978-1-4079-0822-9(7)); audio compact disk 64.95 (978-1-4079-0823-6(5)) Pub: Soundings Ltd GBR. Dist(s): Ulverscroft US

Phillip Lopate. unabr. ed. Phillip Lopate. 1 cass. (Running Time: 29 min.). (New Letters on the Air Ser.). 1992. 10.00 (112911) New Letters.
In "Against Joie de Vivre," Lopate takes on such subjects as the "good life," dating a smoker, his own childhood & the nearly lost art of essay writing.

Phillis Wheatley: Make Her Black & Bid Her Sing (CD) Perf. by Dorothy Mains Prince. (YA). 2007. audio compact disk 12.95 (978-1-4276-1581-7(0)) AardGP.

Philly Stakes. unabr. ed. Gillian Roberts. Narrated by Diane Warren. 6 cass. (Running Time: 8 hrs.). (Amanda Pepper Mystery Ser.). 1994. 51.00 (978-1-55690-994-8(2), 94133E7) Recorded Bks.
With Christmas approaching, Amanda shelves her plans to teach "A Christmas Carol" & decides to have her spoiled scholars cook & serve a meal for the homeless, a noble notion until her parental co-host, one of the wealthiest businessmen in town, decides to cater the meal & have it in his home. When, later that night, the genteel St. Nick is found murdered in his home it's up to Amanda to solve the crime.

***Philo Vance.** Perf. by Jackson Beck. 2010. audio compact disk 35.95 (978-1-57019-930-1(2)) Radio Spirits.

Philo Vance, Detective. Contrib. by Jackson Beck. (Running Time: 10800 sec.). 2004. 9.98 (978-1-57019-553-2(6)) Radio Spirits.

Philo Vance, Detective: Full Dress Murder Case & Prize Ring Murder Case. Perf. by Jackson Beck. 1 cass. (Running Time: 1 hr.). 2001. 6.98 (2609) Radio Spirits.

Philo Vance, Detective: Indentical Murder & Tip Top Murder. Perf. by Jackson Beck. 1 cass. (Running Time: 1 hr.). 2001. 6.98 (2072) Radio Spirits.

Philo Vance, Detective: Peacock Murder Case & One Cent Murder Case. Perf. by Jackson Beck. 1 cass. (Running Time: 1 hr.). 2001. 6.98 (2544) Radio Spirits.

Philo Vance, Detective: Shower Bath Murder Case & The Rooftop Murder Case. Perf. by Jackson Beck. 1 cass. (Running Time: 1 hr.). 2001. 6.98 (2267) Radio Spirits.

Philo Vance, Detective: The Church Murder & The Mathematical Murder. Perf. by Jackson Beck. 1 cass. (Running Time: 1 hr.). 2001. 6.98 (2044) Radio Spirits.

Philo Vance, Detective: The Herrignbone Murder Case & The Listless Murder Case. Perf. by Jackson Beck. 1 cass. (Running Time: 1 hr.). 2001. 6.98 (2189) Radio Spirits.

Philo Vance, Detective: The Ivory Murder Case & The Golden Key Murder Case. Perf. by Jackson Beck. 1 cass. (Running Time: 1 hr.). 2001. 6.98 (2249); 6.98 (2249) Radio Spirits.

Philo Vance, Detective: The Movie Murder & The Green Girl's Murder. Perf. by Jackson Beck. 1 cass. (Running Time: 1 hr.). 2001. 6.98 (2052) Radio Spirits.

Philo Vance, Detective: Whirlaround Murder Case & The Alibi Murder Case. Perf. by Jackson Beck. 1 cass. (Running Time: 1 hr.). 2001. 6.98 (2563) Radio Spirits.

Philo Vance, Private Detective. collector's ed. Perf. by Jackson Beck et al. 6 cass. (Running Time: 9 hrs.). 1999. bk. 34.98 (4190) Radio Spirits.
18 episodes of this detective melodrama with Vance, his secretary Ellen Deering & District Attorney Markham.

***Philo Vance, Volume 1.** RadioArchives.com. (Running Time: 600). (ENG.). 2009. audio compact disk 29.98 (978-1-61081-088-3(0)) Radio Arch.

Philodendron see Twentieth-Century Poetry in English, No. 29, Recordings of Poets Reading Their Own Poetry

Philomena Wonderpen Collection: (Philomena Wonderpen Is a very naughty teacher / Teeny Weeny coll / School camp Star. Ian Bone. Read by Melissa Chambers. (J). 2009. 39.99 (978-1-74214-364-4(4), 9781742143644) Pub: Bolinda Pubng AUS. Dist(s): Bolinda Pub Inc

Philomena Wonderpen Is a School Camp Star. unabr. ed. Ian Bone. Read by Melissa Chambers. Illus. by Janine Dawson. 2 CDs. (Running Time: 1 hr. 31 mins.). (J). (gr. 2-4). 2008. audio compact disk 39.95 (978-1-921415-48-7(7), 9781921415487) Pub: Bolinda Pubng AUS. Dist(s): Bolinda Pub Inc

Philomena Wonderpen Is a Teeny Weeny Doll. unabr. ed. Ian Bone. Read by Melissa Chambers. (Running Time: 1 hr. 15 mins.). (Philomena Wonderpen Ser.). (J). 2007. audio compact disk 39.95 (978-1-74093-964-5(6), 9781740939645) Pub: Bolinda Pubng AUS. Dist(s): Bolinda Pub Inc

Philomena Wonderpen Is a very naughty Teacher. unabr. ed. Ian Bone. Read by Melissa Chambers. (Running Time: 1 hr. 10 mins.). (Philomena Wonderpen Ser.). (J). 2007. audio compact disk 39.95 (978-1-74093-909-6(3)) Pub: Bolinda Pubng AUS. Dist(s): Bolinda Pub Inc

Philosopher Enthroned. Gilbert Highet. Read by Gilbert Highet. 1 cass. (Running Time: 30 min.). 11.95 (23307-A) J Norton Pubs.

Philosopher Looks at the O. J. Verdict. Leonard Peikoff. (Running Time: 1 hr. 30 min.). 1996. 14.95 (978-1-56114-578-2(5), LP30C) Second Renaissance.
A brilliant analysis of the real-life consequences of "ivory tower" ideas.

Philosopher of the Atom. Gilbert Highet. Read by Gilbert Highet. 1 cass. (Running Time: 30 min.). 11.95 (23306-A) J Norton Pubs.

Philosophers of Investing & Financial Economics. Narrated by Louis Rukeyser. Contrib. by JoAnn Skousen & Mark Skousen. 2 cass. (Running Time: 2 hrs. 30 mins.). (Secrets of the Great Investors Ser.: Vol. 3). 2003. 17.95 (978-1-56823-055-9(9)) Pub: Knowledge Prod. Dist(s): APG
Saving, budgeting, & investing are keys to creating wealth - but there are many different philosophies about how to approach this essential task. The "investment philosophers" offer systematic beliefs about investing that often parallel other systems of human contact (e.g. Taoism, the hunter-warrior, etc.). The financial economists (e.g. Fisher, Keynes) offer insights about how human behavior is collectively expressed in markets.

Philosopher's Stone. Franklyn M. Wolff. 1 cass. (Running Time: 20 min.). 7.00 (A0155-82) Sound Photosyn.
A twenty minute video produced by SP to save Dr. Wolff's mountain ashram (it succeeded!) including footage from the forties of his school at work.

Philosophia Perennis: Osho Speaking on the Golden Verses of Pythagoras. abr. ed. Read by Osho Oshos. 2 cass. (Running Time: 2 hrs.). 1996. 17.95 (978-1-57453-061-2(5)) Audio Lit.
Osho shows that Pythagoras was not only one of the greatest philosophical & scientific minds of ancient Greece, but a towering spiritual master as well.

Philosophic & Literary Integration in "Atlas Shrugged" Andrew Bernstein. 7 cass. (Running Time: 8 hrs.). 1995. 79.95 Set. (978-1-56114-422-8(3), MB05D) Second Renaissance.
Shows how Ayn Rand's philosophic breakthroughs are dramatized by a mystery story & how plot & theme are perfectly united.

Philosophic & Literary Integration in "The Fountainhead" Andrew Bernstein. 4 cass. (Running Time: 4 hrs.). 1994. 39.95 Set. (978-1-56114-304-7(9), MB02D) Second Renaissance.
Analysis of "The Fountainhead" by Ayn Rand.

Philosophic Basis of a Woman's Right to Abortion. Andrew Bernstein. (Running Time: 90 min.). 12.95 (CB08C) Second Renaissance.

Philosophic Basis of Capitalism. Leonard Peikoff. Read by Leonard Peikoff. 1 cass. (Running Time: 60 min.). 1981. 9.95 (978-1-56114-063-3(5), LP02C) Second Renaissance.
Aimed at businessmen, this talk presents the philosophical prerequisites for a defense of the free market.

Philosophic Basis of Capitalism - Questions & Answers. Leonard Peikoff. Read by Leonard Peikoff. 1 cass. (Running Time: 50 min.). 1981. 8.95 (978-1-56114-156-2(9), LP15C) Second Renaissance.

Philosophic Corruption of Physics. David Harriman. 5 cass. (Running Time: 6 hrs. 30 min.). 69.95 Set. (CH54D) Second Renaissance.
Topics include: Newton to Kant (Newton's physics & his philosophic legacy); Kant's Physics & the Early 19th Century (Kant deduces the principles of physics from his "categories"); The Death of Classical Physics (the transition of Kantian empiricism); Relativity: The Physics of Appearances (Einstein's subjectivism & rationalism); Quantum Theory: The Physics of Nihilism (Kantian nihilism takes over in Germany).

Philosophic Death of Free Speech. Robert Garmong. 1 cass. (Running Time: 1 hr. 40 min.). 1996. 12.95 (978-1-56114-533-1(5), HG40C) Second Renaissance.
A discussion of the precarious state of the principle of free speech.

Philosophic State of Economics. Richard M. Salsman. 1 cass. (Running Time: 1 hr. 30 min.). 1996. 12.95 (978-1-56114-600-0(5), DS41C) Second Renaissance.
An examination of the three dominant schools: the Marxists; the Consumptionists; & the New Classicals.

Philosophical Dictionary. unabr. ed. Francois Voltaire, pseud. Narrated by Donal Donnelly. 3 cass. (Running Time: 4 hrs. 30 mins.). 1988. 26.00 (978-1-55690-412-7(6), 88300E7) Recorded Bks.
A collection of Voltaire's ideas & thoughts that were too short for pamphlets but worth saving for later development - wise & witty entries on subjects as diverse as atheism & kissing.

Philosophical Evaluation of Divorce. Instructed by Manly P. Hall. 8.95 (978-0-89314-211-7(5), C841202) Philos Res.

Philosophical Investigation. unabr. collector's ed. Philip Kerr. Read by Geoffrey Howard. 8 cass. (Running Time: 12 hrs.). 1995. 64.00 (978-0-7366-2953-9(X), 3647) Books on Tape.
In 2013 AD London, Detective "Jake"™ Jacowics pits her smarts & intuition against a high-minded sociopath intent on killing potential murderers.

Philosophical Reflections on the Use & Abuse of Money. Instructed by Manly P. Hall. 8.95 (978-0-89314-212-4(3), C810329) Philos Res.

Philosophies of Asia. Alan Watts. Read by Alan Watts. 1 cass. 59.95 ElectronicUniv.

Philosophies of Asia, Vol. 1. Alan Watts. 3 cass. (Running Time: 2 hrs. 38 min.). 1995. 29.95 Set. Tuttle Pubng.
These audio books bring to life the dramatic words of Alan Watts & demonstrate that his philosophical insights, & interpretations are as relevant today as they were twenty to thirty years ago. Titles in this volume include: The Relevance of Oriental Philosophy; The Mythology of Hinduism; Ecozen; A Ball of Hot Iron.

Philosophies of Asia, Vol. 2. Alan Watts. 3 cass. (Running Time: 2 hrs. 48 min.). 1995. 29.95 Set. Tuttle Pubng.

Philosophies of India. unabr. ed. Doug Allen. Read by Lynn Redgrave. (Running Time: 10800 sec.). (World of Philosophy Ser.). 2006. audio compact disk 25.95 (978-0-7861-6380-9(1)) Pub: Blckstn Audio. Dist(s): NetLibrary CO

Philosophy. 1 cass. (Berkeley University Weekly Broadcasts Ser.). 13.95 (23702) J Norton Pubs.
"Common Ground" about the theologian Paul Tillich; "To Be or Not to be" on existentialism; "The Great Greeks" on the golden age of imperial Athens; "The Distant Drummer" about the life of Henry Thoreau.

Philosophy. unabr. ed. Read by Marvin Miller & Thomas Mitchell. 8 cass. 47.60 (B-703) Audio Bk.
The complete writings of Marcus Aurelius, philosopher & emperor, & two dialogues of Plato, with an account of the death of Socrates.

Philosophy: A Very Short Introduction. abr. ed. Edward Craig. Read by Maurice West. 3 CDs. 2005. audio compact disk 22.98 (978-962-634-344-9(3)) Naxos UK GBR.

Philosophy: Clinbush vs. Jefferson. Leonard Peikoff. 1 cass. (Philosophy: Who Needs It? Ser.). 1997. 12.95 Set. (LPXXC21) Second Renaissance.

Philosophy: Cloning. Leonard Peikoff. 1 cass. (Philosophy: Who Needs It? Ser.). 1997. 12.95 (LPXXC15) Second Renaissance.

Philosophy: Infant Intelligence vs. Hillary. Leonard Peikoff. 2 cass. (Philosophy: Who Needs It? Ser.). 1997. 25.95 Set. (LPXXC19) Second Renaissance.

Philosophy: Interview Akhil Amar, Yale Law Professor: 4th, 5th & 6th Amendments. Leonard Peikoff. 1 cass. (Philosophy: Who Needs It? Ser.). 1997. 12.95 (LPXXC18) Second Renaissance.

Philosophy: Interview Robert Park, Physicist: Assault on Science. Leonard Peikoff. 1 cass. (Philosophy: Who Needs It? Ser.). 1997. 12.95 (LPXXC13) Second Renaissance.

Philosophy: San Diego Mass Suicide - Cult or Religion? Leonard Peikoff. 2 cass. (Philosophy: Who Needs It? Ser.). 1997. 25.95 Set. (LPXXC17) Second Renaissance.

Philosophy: Tie-in Contest (FCC, Animal Rights, Augustine) Leonard Peikoff. 1 cass. (Philosophy: Who Needs It? Ser.). 1997. 12.95 (LPXXC16) Second Renaissance.

Philosophy: Who Needs It? Ayn Rand. Read by Ayn Rand. 1 cass., 1 CD. (Running Time: 70 min.). 1974. 14.95 (978-1-56114-022-0(8), AR21C); audio compact disk 16.95 CD. Second Renaissance.
Addressing the graduating class of the U. S. Military Academy at West Point, Ayn Rand dramatically demonstrates why everyone urgently requires a knowledge of philosophy. Presupposing little prior knowledge of or interest in philosophy, she explains how philosophic ideas exert an omnipresent, usually unrecognized, influence upon all men's lives, & thus why philosophic ideas should be regarded with utmost gravity. Ayn Rand concludes this talk with an inspiring salute to the moral spirit of America's founding principles preserved & symbolized by West Point.

Philosophy: Who Needs It. Ayn Rand. Read by Lloyd James. (Running Time: 39600 sec.). 2006. 65.95 (978-0-7861-2545-6(4)); audio compact disk 81.00 (978-0-7861-9028-7(0)) Blckstn Audio.

Philosophy: Who Needs It. unabr. ed. Ayn Rand. Read by Anna Fields & Lloyd James. (Running Time: 11 hrs. NaN mins.). (ENG.). 2010. audio compact disk 29.95 (978-0-7861-8853-6(7)) Blckstn Audio.

***Philosophy: Who Needs It.** unabr. ed. Ayn Rand. Read by Lloyd James. (Running Time: 11 hrs. NaN mins.). (ENG.). 2010. audio compact disk 29.95 (978-0-7861-9029-4(9)) Blckstn Audio.

Philosophy & Niscience (Side One); East & West Consciousness (Side Two) Ann Ree Colton. 1 cass. 1990. 7.95 A R Colton Fnd.
Lectures by Ann Ree Colton, an Illumined Teacher of the Higher Life for nearly 60 years.

Philosophy & Religion in the West. Phillip Cary. 16 cass. (Running Time: 16 hrs.). 69.95 Set; 32 lectures in 3 pts.; incl. course guide. (625) Teaching Co.
Begin with Socrates & the prophets of ancient Israel, all the way up to philosophers & theologians who are alive & writing today. Also includes Plato, Aristotle, Plotinus, Origen, Augustine, Aquinas, Maimonides, Luther, Calvin, Descartes, Leibniz, Locke, Hume, Schleiermacher, Kant, Hegel, Kierkegaard, Nietsche, Marx, Freud, Martin Buber, Karl Barth, & more.

Philosophy & Religion in the West, Pts. I-III. Instructed by Phillip Cary. 16 cass. (Running Time: 16 hrs.). 79.95 (978-1-56585-169-6(2)) Teaching Co.

Philosophy & Religion in the West, Pts. I-III, Vol. 1. Instructed by Phillip Cary. 16 CDs. (Running Time: 16 hrs.). 1999. audio compact disk 99.95 (978-1-56585-720-9(8)) Teaching Co.

Philosophy & Religion in the West, Vol. 2. Instructed by Phillip Cary. 5 cass. (Running Time: 5 hrs.). 1999. 199.95 (978-1-56585-170-2(6)); audio compact disk 269.95 (978-1-56585-721-6(6)) Teaching Co.

Philosophy & Religion in the West, Vol. 3. Instructed by Phillip Cary. 5 cass. (Running Time: 5 hrs.). 1999. 199.95 (978-1-56585-171-9(4)); audio compact disk 269.95 (978-1-56585-722-3(4)) Teaching Co.

Philosophy & Science in the 17th & 18th Century Vol. 6: Multilingual Books Literature on Tape/cd. Excerpts. Ed. by Maurizio Falyhera & Cristina Giocometti. 1 cass. (Running Time: 90). (Audio Anthology of Italian Literature Ser.: 6). (ITA.). 1999. spiral bd. 19.95 (978-1-58214-109-1(6)) Language Assocs.

Philosophy & Science in the 17th & 18th Century on Cd: Multilingual Books Literature on Tape/cd, 6. Excerpts. Ed. by Maurizio Falyhera & Cristina Giocometti. 1 CD. (Running Time: 90 mins.). (Audio Anthology of Italian Literature Ser.: 6). (ITA.). 1999. audio compact disk 29.95 (978-1-58214-110-7(X)) Language Assocs.

Philosophy & the Real World Out There. Leonard Peikoff. 1 cass. (Running Time: 90 min.). 1990. 12.95 (978-1-56114-158-6(5), LP25C) Second Renaissance.

Philosophy as a Guide to Living. Instructed by Stephen Erickson. 12 cass. (Running Time: 12 hrs.). 2006. 129.95 (978-1-59803-134-8(1)); audio compact disk 69.95 (978-1-59803-136-2(8)) Teaching Co.

Philosophy for Studs- the Alpha Male Guide. Anthony Leccisi. Read by Anthony Leccisi. 1 mp3 cd. (Running Time: 4 hrs.). 2005. audio compact disk 12.99 (978-0-9781009-1-9(3)) Academic Audiobks CAN.
History's greatest thinkers- Epicurus, Socrates, Plato, Aristotle, Sun Tzu, Seneca, Beaudelaire, Sir Francis Bacon, George Bernard Shaw, Oscar Wilde, Winston Churchill and others expound their philosophies on wine, women, song, love, lust, life, living, manners, character, sex, marriage, death and laughter. Everything you need to know to be a world class male in today's modern world.WARNING: This audiobook contains mature subject matter. It is suitable for males 14 years of age and older.This is the ultimate and final authority on etiquette, health, fitness, manners, culture, the arts, sports, social skills and mostly, how to enjoy the company of women. By buying this book you are thinking with your head, and not your dick.That will get you laid!Happy hunting.

Philosophy of Action, No. 1. Swami Jyotirmayananda. 1 cass. (Running Time: 45 min.). 1990. 10.00 Yoga Res Foun.

Philosophy of Action, No. 2. Swami Jyotirmayananda. 1 cass. (Running Time: 45 min.). 1990. 10.00 Yoga Res Foun.

Philosophy of Ayn Rand Refuted. John Robbins. 1 cass. (Blue Banner Lectures Ser.: No. 6). 5.00 Trinity Found.

Philosophy of Beauty. Swami Jyotirmayananda. 1 cass. (Running Time: 45 min.). 1990. 10.00 Yoga Res Foun.

Philosophy of Bioenergetics. unabr. ed. Stanley Keleman. 1 cass. (Running Time: 90 min.). 1970. 11.00 (06801) Big Sur Tapes.
Bioenergetic analysis views the life of the body as an energetic process & attempts to understand the life of the body through its expression of vitality, gesture, emotion, feeling, & relationship. Bioenergetics seeks to develop an individual's range of expression & feels that man's physical processes & his state of consciousness are one & the same.

Philosophy of Christian Home Education. Michael J. McHugh. 1 cass. (Running Time: 1 hr.). 2002. 5.00 (CLP89530) Christian Liberty.
Explores the commitment of home education from a distinctly biblical viewpoint. The tape will be of help to parents who are considering home education and to parents who wish to share their views on Christian home education with other adults.

Philosophy of Conservatism. Frank Meyer. 1 cass. (Running Time: 1 hr. 29 min.). 11.95 (128) J Norton Pubs.

Philosophy of Desires. Swami Jyotirmayananda. 1 cass. (Running Time: 45 min.). 1990. 10.00 Yoga Res Foun.

Philosophy of Education. Leonard Peikoff. Read by Leonard Peikoff. 6 cass. 1985. 89.00 (978-1-56114-049-7(X), LP01D) Second Renaissance.
In this path-breaking, five-lecture work, Dr. Peikoff argues that the central purpose of schooling is to give the child the cognitive tools for making full use of his conceptual consciousness. He incisively explains how to teach a child to think for himself & why today's educational establishment is failing miserably at this task. Includes: Purpose of Education; Teaching Thinking Methods; A Proper Curriculum; The Skill of Teaching.

Philosophy of History, Set. unabr. ed. Georg Wilhelm Friedrich Hegel. Read by Robert L. Halvorson. 15 cass. (Running Time: 22 hrs.). 105.95 (28) Halvorson Assocs.

Philosophy of Mind. Instructed by John Searle. 6 cass. (Running Time: 7 hrs. 30 mins.). 1996. 39.95 (978-1-56585-096-5(3)) Teaching Co.

Philosophy of Mind: Brains, Consciousness, & Thinking Machines. Instructed by Patrick Grim. (ENG.). 2008. 129.95 (978-1-59803-422-6(7)); audio compact disk 69.95 (978-1-59803-423-3(5)) Teaching Co.

Philosophy of Motivation. unabr. ed. Darryl Wright. 6 cass. (Running Time: 7 hrs.). 1997. 69.95 Set. (978-1-56114-311-5(1), CW500) Second Renaissance.
Exploration of the distinction between "motivation by fear" & "motivation by love".

Philosophy of Objectivism. Leonard Peikoff. 24 cass. (Running Time: 33 hrs.). 1976. 199.00 Set. (978-1-56114-157-9(7), LP24D) Second Renaissance.

Philosophy of Relative Existences see Classic Ghost Stories, Vol. 2, A Collection

Philosophy of Religion, Parts I-III. Instructed by James Hall. 18 CDs. (Running Time: 18 hrs.). 2003. bk. 99.95 (978-1-56585-602-8(3), 4680) Teaching Co.

Philosophy of Religion, Pts. I-III. Instructed by James Hall. 18 cass. (Running Time: 18 hrs.). 2003. bk. 79.95 (978-1-56585-601-1(5), 4680) Teaching Co.

Philosophy of Romantic Fiction. Andrew Bernstein. 6 cass. (Running Time: 5 hrs. 30 min.). 1996. 49.95 Set. (978-1-56114-386-3(3), MB14D) Second Renaissance.
The themes & philosophies of "Les Miserables", "The Brothers Karamazov" & "Atlas Shrugged".

Philosophy of Science. Instructed by Jeffrey L. Kasser. 18 CDs. (Running Time: 18 hrs.). 2006. 99.95 (978-1-59803-238-3(0)); 199.95 (978-1-59803-237-6(2)) Teaching Co.

Philosophy of the Austrian School of Economics. Richard M. Salsman. 6 cass. (Running Time: 7 hrs.). 1995. 69.95 Set. (978-1-56114-372-6(3), DS08D) Second Renaissance.
Discussion of Carl Menger, Ludwin von Mises & Friedrich Hayek.

Philosophy of the Practice of Dentistry. Lindsey D. Pankey & William J. Davis. Ed. by Veronica Sanitate. Illus. by Linda Byhardt & Tim Worachelk. Frwd. by F. Harold Wirth. 1987. 127.50 (978-0-944742-02-0(5)) Med Coll of OH Pr.

Philosophy of Value. Manly P. Hall. 5 cass. (Running Time: 150 min.). 1999. 40.00 set incl. album. (978-0-89314-213-1(1), S800174) Philos Res.

Philosophy of War. 4 cass. 45.00 set. (8511) MEA A Watts Cass.

Philosophy Open-Line: Does Deep Blue Think? Etc. Leonard Peikoff. 1 cass. (Philosophy: Who Needs It? Ser.). 1997. 12.95 (LPXXC23) Second Renaissance.

Philosophy, Religion, & the Meaning of Life. Instructed by Francis J. Ambrosio. 2009. 199.95 (978-1-59803-579-7(7)); audio compact disk 269.95 (978-1-59803-580-3(0)) Teaching Co.

Philosophy: Tie-in Contest (Tonya Harding, a Compulsive Gambler, an Obnoxious Braggart) Leonard Peikoff. 1 cass. (Philosophy: Who Needs It? Ser.). 1997. 12.95 (LPXXC12) Second Renaissance.

Philosophy: Volunteerism: Three Student Interviews. Leonard Peikoff. 1 cass. (Philosophy: Who Needs It? Ser.). 1997. 12.95 Set. (LPXXC20) Second Renaissance.

Philosophy: Why I Quit the Republican Party (Including Interview with Michael Reagan) Leonard Peikoff. 1 cass. (Philosophy: Who Needs It? Ser.). 1997. 12.95 Set. (LPXXC22) Second Renaissance.

Phil's Tonsils Must Come Out. Perf. by Phil Harris & Alice Faye. 1 cass. (Running Time: 60 min.). 7.95 (CC-5005) Natl Recrd Co.
In the story "Phil's Tonsils Must Come Out," Phil is scared when he learns he must have an operation; & of course, Frank Remley & Julius really help! Phil gets in the wrong hospital waiting room, & it is a riot of misunderstanding with another waiting patient. In the story "Phil Becomes the City Fire Chief," when Phil agrees to become the City Volunteer Fire Chief, Frank Remley is right there with his useful suggestions.

Phineas Finn, unabr. ed. Anthony Trollope. Read by Flo Gibson. 16 cass. (Running Time: 24 hrs.). 1993. 46.95 (978-1-55685-267-1(3)) Audio Bk Con.
The handsome Phineas Finn's political & romantic entanglements are explored with zest when he becomes an Irish member of the House of Commons. How will the Reform Bill fare & will Lady Laura Standish, Violet Effingham, Mary Flood Jones, or Marie Goesler win his hand.

Phineas Finn. unabr. ed. Anthony Trollope. Read by Robert Whitfield. 16 cass. (Running Time: 23 hrs. 30 mins.). 2000. 99.95 (978-0-7861-1782-6(6), 2581) Blckstn Audio.
Phineas Finn is an Irish M.P.A. climbing the political ladder, largely through the assistance of his string of lovers. The questions he is forced to ask himself about honesty, independence & parliamentary democracy are questions still asked today.

Phineas Finn, Pt. 1. unabr. collector's ed. Anthony Trollope. Read by David Case. 9 cass. (Running Time: 13 hrs. 30 min.). 1994. 72.00 (978-0-7366-2618-7(2), 3359-A) Books on Tape.
With the Reform Bill of 1867 as background, Trollope's story pits ambition & public life against the unreasonable demands of love. The author tackles themes that continue to fascinate. For example, an Irish member of Commons personifies the dilemma that England & Ireland in their relationship face even to the present day. Phineas Finn (1869), the second of the Palliser novels, follows Can You Forgive Her?.

Phineas Finn, Pt. 2. collector's ed. Anthony Trollope. Read by David Case. 9 cass. (Running Time: 13 hrs. 30 min.). 1994. 72.00 (978-0-7366-2619-4(0), 3359-B) Books on Tape.

***Phineas Finn: The Irish Member.** unabr. ed. Anthony Trollope. Read by Simon Vance. (Running Time: 22 hrs. 5 mins.). (Palliser Novels Ser.). (ENG.). 2011. 44.95 (978-1-4417-8067-6(X)); audio compact disk 123.00 (978-1-4417-8065-2(3)) Blckstn Audio.

Phineas Redux, Pt. 1. unabr. collector's ed. Anthony Trollope. Read by David Case. 9 cass. (Running Time: 13 hrs. 30 min.). 1994. 72.00 (978-0-7366-2790-0(1), 3506-A) Books on Tape.
Disenchanted by a scandal & a murder trial, Finn abandons the charmed inner circle of power. Fourth of Palliser novels.

Phineas Redux, Pt. 2. Anthony Trollope. 9 cass. (Running Time: 13 hrs. 30 mins.). 1999. 59.95 Audio Bk Con.
After his Irish wife dies, Phineas Finn returns to his parliamentary career. rumors of scandal damaged his reputation & a trial for murder forces him out of the inner circle of power he had longed for, however he gains self wisdom.

Phineas Redux, Pt. 2. collector's unabr. ed. Anthony Trollope. Read by David Case. 9 cass. (Running Time: 13 hrs. 30 min.). 1994. 72.00 (978-0-7366-2791-7(X), 3506-B) Books on Tape.
Disenchanted by a scandal & a murder trial, Finn abandons the charmed inner circle of power. Fourth of Palliser novels.

Phineas Redux (Part 1) unabr. ed. Anthony Trollope. Read by Flo Gibson. 9 cass. (Running Time: 12 hrs. 30 min.). 1994. 28.95 (978-1-55685-312-8(2)) Audio Bk Con.
After his Irish wife dies, Phineas Finn returns to his parliamentary career. Rumors of scandal damage his reputation & a trial for murder forces him out of the inner circle of power he had longed for, but he gains in self wisdom.

Phineas Redux (Part 2), Vol. 2. unabr. ed. Anthony Trollope. Narrated by Flo Gibson. (Running Time: 12 hrs.). 1994. 28.95 (978-1-55685-836-9(1)) Audio Bk Con.

Phineas Redux (Parts 1 And 2) unabr. ed. Anthony Trollope. Narrated by Flo Gibson. (Running Time: 24 hrs. 25 mins.). 1994. 53.95 (978-1-55685-837-6(X)) Audio Bk Con.

Phizzog see Carl Sandburg's Poems for Children

Phobias. Bruce Goldberg. (ENG.). 2005. audio compact disk 17.00 (978-1-57968-084-8(4)) Pub: B Goldberg. Dist(s): Baker Taylor

Phobias. Bruce Goldberg. Read by Bruce Goldberg. 1 cass. (Running Time: 25 min.). (ENG.). 2006. 13.00 (978-1-885577-49-8(4)) Pub: B Goldberg. Dist(s): Baker Taylor
Through self-hypnosis remove these irrational fears once and for all.

Phobias & How to Overcome Them: Understanding & Beating Your Fears. abr. ed. James Gardner & Arthur H. Bell. Read by Ron Hippe. (Running Time: 14400 sec.). 2008. audio compact disk 23.95 (978-1-59316-110-1(7)) Listen & Live.

Phoenix see Twentieth-Century Poetry in English, No. 5, Recordings of Poets Reading Their Own Poetry

Phoenix. abr. ed. Barry Sadler. Read by Charlton Griffin. Abr. by Odin Westgaard. 2 vols. (Casca Ser.: No. 14). 2003. 18.00 (978-1-58807-114-9(6)); (978-1-58807-545-1(1)) Am Pubng Inc.

Phoenix. abr. ed. Barry Sadler. Read by Charlton Griffin. Abr. by Odin Westgaard. 2 vols. (Casca Ser.: No. 14). 2004. audio compact disk 25.00 (978-1-58807-288-7(6)); audio compact disk (978-1-58807-719-6(5)) Am Pubng Inc.

Phoenix: Chinese Feng Shui Music. Jian-ming Wang. Perf. by Shanghai Chinese Traditional Orchestra. Conducted by Xia Fei-yun. 1 CD. (Running Time: 1 hr.). audio compact disk (978-1-57606-050-6(0)) Wind Recs.
Based on the theories of the I Ching & the five Chinese tones, this feng shui music is designed to help people improve their life through the energy released from music. Phoenix is beneficial for the heart & blood circulation, as well as for those whose homes are located in murky, cold or humid environments, near a river, or near a bridge, or in homes facing north. Detailed liner notes.

Phoenix & the Carpet. abr. ed. E. Nesbit. Read by Anna Bentinck. 2 CDs. audio compact disk 17.98 (978-962-634-320-3(6), Naxos AudioBooks) Naxos.

Phoenix & the Carpet. unabr. ed. E. Nesbit. Read by Johanna Ward. 5 cass. (Running Time: 7 hrs. 30 min.). (J). 1994. 39.95 (978-0-7861-0832-9(0), 1532) Blckstn Audio.
Cyril, Robert, Anthea, Jane, & the Lamb (their baby brother) discover that a second-hand carpet bought for the nursery is a flying one. And there is more: from an egg that falls out of the carpet hatches a flame-colored bird, the Phoenix, whose advice & assistance prove valuable. They find hidden treasure in France & with it they are able to restore the fortunes of a little boy. Their own house is invaded by a thousand Persian cats, a cow, & a burglar who eventually marries the cook on an island in the South Seas.

Phoenix & the Carpet, Set. E. Nesbit. Narrated by Flo Gibson. 5 cass. (Running Time: 7 hrs.). (J). 1985. 20.95 (978-1-55685-063-9(8)) Audio Bk Con.
Five children find a magic carpet able to journey through time & space, & a phoenix, an honorable bird, who help them to have adventures which never turn out exactly as planned.

Phoenix & the Water Faucet Vision. Ursula K. Le Guin & Jen Gish. 1 cass. (Running Time: 1 hr.). 12.95 (978-1-57677-097-9(4), OWME006) Lodestone Catalog.

Phoenix & the Water Faucet Vision. Ursula K. Le Guin & Jen Gish. 1 CD. (Running Time: 1 hr.). 2001. audio compact disk 15.95 (OWME008) Lodestone Catalog.

Phoenix & Turtle see Rape of Lucrece & Other Poems

Phoenix Endangered. unabr. ed. Mercedes Lackey & James Mallory. Narrated by William Dufris. 2 MP3-CDs. (Running Time: 17 hrs. 30 mins. 0 sec.). (Enduring Flame Ser.: Bk. 2). (ENG.). 2008. 29.99 (978-1-4001-5786-0(2)); audio compact disk 39.99 (978-1-4001-0786-5(5)) Pub: Tantor Media. Dist(s): IngramPubServ

Phoenix Endangered. unabr. ed. Mercedes Lackey & James Mallory. Read by William Dufris. 14 CDs. (Running Time: 17 hrs. 30 mins. 0 sec.). (Enduring Flame Ser.: Bk. 2). (ENG.). 2008. audio compact disk 79.99 (978-1-4001-3786-2(1)) Pub: Tantor Media. Dist(s): IngramPubServ

Phoenix on the Sword. Robert E. Howard. 2007. audio compact disk 24.95 (978-0-8095-6276-3(6)) Diamond Book Dists.

Phoenix on the Sword. Robert E. Howard. 2006. audio compact disk 19.95 (978-0-8095-6275-6(8)) Pub: Wildside. Dist(s): Diamond Book Dists

***Phoenix Rising.** unabr. ed. Karen Hesse. (Running Time: 4 hrs.). 2010. 39.97 (978-1-4418-1822-5(7), 9781441818225, BADLE); 24.99 (978-1-4418-1821-8(9), 9781441818218, BAD); audio compact disk 62.97 (978-1-4418-1818-8(9), 9781441818188, BriAudCD Unabrid) Brilliance Audio.

***Phoenix Rising.** unabr. ed. Karen Hesse. (Running Time: 5 hrs.). (YA). 2010. audio compact disk 24.99 (978-1-4418-1817-1(0), 9781441818171, Bril Audio CD Unabri) Brilliance Audio.

***Phoenix Rising.** unabr. ed. Karen Hesse. Read by Julia Whelan. (Running Time: 5 hrs.). 2010. 24.99 (978-1-4418-1819-5(7), 9781441818195, Brilliance MP3); 39.97 (978-1-4418-1820-1(0), 9781441818201, Brinc Audio MP3 Lib) Brilliance Audio.

Phoenix Rising. unabr. ed. John J. Nance. Read by Brian Emerson. 9 cass. (Running Time: 13 hrs.). 1995. 62.95 (978-0-7861-0700-1(6), 1577) Blckstn Audio.
The "Big Three" U.S. airlines have achieved national dominance - with high prices & poor service. Challenging them comes a new, visionary airline, one that combines a great name from aviation's recent past with new standards of comfort & elegance. This billion-dollar start-up was engineered by Elizabeth Sterling, a bright young investment banker (& single parent). When she assumes the post of chief financial officer for this upstart carrier, she finds herself masterminding a frantic defense against a sinister campaign by powerful, unknown forces determined to destroy her proud creation.

***Phoenix Rising.** unabr. ed. John J. Nance. Read by Brian Emerson. (Running Time: 13 hrs.). 2010. 29.95 (978-1-4417-4210-0(7)); audio compact disk 109.00 (978-1-4417-4207-0(7)) Blckstn Audio.

Phoenix Rising: No-Eyes' Vision of the Changes to Come. abr. ed. Mary S. Rain. Read by Nancy Fish. 2 cass. (Running Time: 3 hrs.). 1997. 17.95 (978-1-57453-172-5(7)) Audio Lit.
No-Eyes reveals her compelling visions of the future.

Phoenix Rising: Rising above Limitations. Denise Linn. 2 cass. (Running Time: 2 hrs.). 2000. 16.95 (978-1-56170-698-3(1), 4027) Hay House.
Meditations for recreating your self & your life.

Phoenix Soul Vol. VII: One Man's Search for Love & Inner Peace. unabr. ed. David Essel. Read by David Essel. 1 cass. (Running Time: 1 hr. 30 mins.). (David Essel's Dynamic Living Ser.: Vol. 7). 2000. 9.95 (978-1-893074-09-5(9)) D Essel Inc.
Selected readings by David from his book, performed live. Inspirational reflections to help you rise above life's intimate challenges.

Phoenix Taoist Center Meditation with Taoist Chant CD. Created by Phoenix Taoist Center. (ENG.). 2007. audio compact disk 9.95 (978-1-889633-27-5(5)) Valley SpiritA.

Phoenix to Tucson on I-10. unabr. ed. Joy Wake. Read by Elaine West. 1 cass. (Running Time: 1 hr. 17 min.). (Triptape Ser.). 1994. 12.95 (978-1-883605-50-6(4)) Pub: Echo Peak Prods. Dist(s): Bookpeople
Describes historical sights & other points of interest along I-10 between Phoenix & Tucson. Features excerpts of Native Americans, historians & naturalists telling about the area as you drive through it.

Phoenix Transformed. unabr. ed. Mercedes Lackey & James Mallory. Narrated by William Dufris. (Running Time: 25 hrs. 0 mins. 0 sec.). (Enduring Flame Ser.: Bk. 3). (ENG.). 2009. 39.99 (978-1-4001-6280-2(7)); audio compact disk 59.99 (978-1-4001-1280-7(X)); audio compact disk 119.99 (978-1-4001-4280-4(6)) Pub: Tantor Media. Dist(s): IngramPubServ

***Phoenix Transformed.** unabr. ed. Mercedes Lackey & James Mallory. Narrated by William Dufris. (Running Time: 25 hrs. 0 mins.). (Enduring Flame Ser.: Bk. 3). 2009. 59.99 (978-1-4001-9280-9(3)); 27.99 (978-1-4001-8280-0(8)) Tantor Media.

Phoenix Tree. unabr. ed. Jon Cleary. Read by Gordon Griffin. 12 cass. (Running Time: 18 hrs.). 1999. 94.95 (68599) Pub: Soundings Ltd GBR. Dist(s): Ulverscroft US

Phoenix Unchained. unabr. ed. Mercedes Lackey. Read by William Dufris. (Running Time: 13 hrs. 30 mins. 0 sec.). (Enduring Flame Ser.: Bk. 1). (ENG.). 2007. audio compact disk 37.99 (978-1-4001-0574-8(9)) Pub: Tantor Media. Dist(s): IngramPubServ

Phoenix Unchained. unabr. ed. Mercedes Lackey & James Mallory. Read by William Dufris. (Running Time: 13 hrs. 30 mins. 0 sec.). (Enduring Flame Ser.: Bk. 1). (ENG.). 2007. audio compact disk 75.99 (978-1-4001-3574-5(5)); audio compact disk 24.99 (978-1-4001-5574-3(6)) Pub: Tantor Media. Dist(s): IngramPubServ

Phone French. Valerie Dumonuy. (TY: Short Courses Ser.). 2008. audio compact disk 12.95 (978-0-07-159169-0(9), 9780071591690) McGraw.

Phone German. Paul Stocker. (TY: Short Courses Ser.). 2008. audio compact disk 12.95 (978-0-07-159173-7(7), 9780071591737, Tch Yourself) Pub: McGraw-Hill Trade. Dist(s): McGraw

Phone Italian. Clelia Boscolo. (TY: Short Courses Ser.). 2008. audio compact disk 12.95 (978-0-07-159178-2(8), 9780071591782) McGraw.

Phone Japanese. Haruko Laurie. (TY: Short Courses Ser.). 2008. audio compact disk 12.95 (978-0-07-159182-9(6), 9780071591829) McGraw.

Phone Mandarin Chinese. Qian Kan. (TY: Short Courses Ser.). 2008. audio compact disk 12.95 (978-0-07-159186-7(9), 9780071591867) McGraw.

Phone Power. George Walter. 2004. 7.95 (978-0-7435-4178-7(2)) Pub: S&S Audio. Dist(s): S and S Inc

Phone Power. George Walther. Read by George Walther. 13 cass. 189.95 Set, incl. video cassette. (918T) Nightingale-Conant.

Phone Power: For Dealing with Difficult People. George Walther. Read by George Walther. 1 cass. 15.95 (914T) Nightingale-Conant.

Phone Power: For Effective Communication. George Walther. Read by George Walther. 1 cass. 15.95 (906T) Nightingale-Conant.

Phone Power: For Getting Appointments. George Walther. Read by George Walther. 1 cass. 15.95 (917T) Nightingale-Conant.

Phone Power: For Negotiation. George Walther. Read by George Walther. 1 cass. 15.95 (913T) Nightingale-Conant.

Phone Power: For the Accounts Receivable Collector. George Walther. Read by George Walther. 1 cass. 15.95 (910T) Nightingale-Conant.

Phone Power: For the Customer Service Professional. George Walther. Read by George Walther. 1 cass. 15.95 (915T) Nightingale-Conant.

Phone Power: For the Inbound Telemarketer. George Walther. Read by George Walther. 1 cass. 15.95 (912T) Nightingale-Conant.

Phone Power: For the Outbound Telemarketer. George Walther. Read by George Walther. 1 cass. 15.95 (911T) Nightingale-Conant.

Phone Power: For the Person Who Manages. George Walther. Read by George Walther. 1 cass. 15.95 (905T) Nightingale-Conant.

Phone Power: For the Receptionist. George Walther. Read by George Walther. 1 cass. 15.95 (907T) Nightingale-Conant.

Phone Power: For the Salesperson. George Walther. Read by George Walther. 1 cass. 15.95 (916T) Nightingale-Conant.

Phone Power: For the Secretary. George Walther. Read by George Walther. 1 cass. 15.95 (909T) Nightingale-Conant.

Phone Power: For the Switchboard Operator. George Walther. Read by George Walther. 1 cass. 15.95 (908T) Nightingale-Conant.

Phone Recruiting: How to Turn Phone Recruiting into a Downline Organization. Dave Johnson. 6 cass. (Dave Johnson Program of Sales Seminars). 65.00 D Johnson.
Shows how to say just enough to sincerely interest the caller on a one-on-one recruiting interview. Explains how to not say too much which gives them too much information with which to make a negative decision.

Phone Spanish. Juan Kattan-Ibarra. (TY: Short Courses Ser.). 2008. audio compact disk 12.95 (978-0-07-159190-4(7), 9780071591904) McGraw.

Phonemic Awareness see Para la Conciencia Fonemica

Phonemic Awareness. 1 cass. (Running Time: 1 hr.). (Scott Foresman Reading Ser.). (gr. k up). 2004. stu. ed. 25.50 (978-0-673-63964-6(9)); stu. ed. 45.00 (978-0-673-65057-3(X)) Addson-Wesley Educ.
Recordings model letter sounds and syllables with demonstrations of blending and word segmentation.

Phonemic Awareness. 1 cass. (Running Time: 1 hr.). (Scott Foresman Reading Ser.). (gr. 1 up). 2004. 25.50 (978-0-673-63965-3(7)); audio compact disk 45.00 (978-0-673-65058-0(8)) Addson-Wesley Educ.

Phonemic Awareness. 1 cass. (Running Time: 1 hr.). (Scott Foresman Reading Ser.). (gr. 2 up). 2004. 25.50 (978-0-673-63966-0(5)); audio compact disk 45.00 (978-0-673-65059-7(6)) Addson-Wesley Educ.

Phonemic Awareness. 1 cass. (Running Time: 1 hr.). (Scott Foresman Reading Ser.). (gr. 3 up). 2004. 25.50 (978-0-673-63967-7(3)); audio compact disk 45.00 (978-0-673-65060-3(X)) Addson-Wesley Educ.

Phonemic Awareness - Phonics Strategies That Work, Set. Janiel M. Wagstaff. 6 cass. (Running Time: 4 hrs. 44 min.). (J). (gr. k-2). 1999. 75.00 Incl. hdbk. (978-1-886397-28-6(7)) Bureau of Educ.
Workshop for educators.

Phonetic Practice. 1 cass. (Running Time: 1 hr.). 2000. 15.95 Prof Pride.
A series of famous & not so famous names spelled phonetically, gets faster & faster. For a fun time learning how to use the alphabet in that strange way we do.

Phonetic Zoo A. Created by Andrew Pudewa. (J). 2002. audio compact disk 99.00 (978-0-9840990-4-7(2)) Institute for Ex.

Phonetic Zoo B. Created by Andrew Pudewa. (YA). 2002. audio compact disk 99.00 (978-0-9840990-5-4(0)) Institute for Ex.

Phonetic Zoo C. Created by Andrew Pudewa. (YA). 2002. audio compact disk 99.00 (978-0-9840990-6-1(9)) Institute for Ex.

Phoney Boloney: 11 Cor. 11:1-15. Ed Young. 1990. 4.95 (978-0-7417-1798-6(0), 798) Win Walk.

Phonics. 1 cass. (Learn to Read Ser.). (J). Incl. 24 p. bk. set. (TWIN 405) NewSound.
Teach initial consonant sounds, the hard & soft sound of "c" & "g", & short & long vowel sounds - including "y" as a vowel, with animated characters, rhyming lyrics & rhythmic sounds!.

Phonics. Kim Mitzo Thompson & Karen Mitzo Hilderbrand. (J). 1989. audio compact disk 12.99 (978-1-57583-240-1(2), Twin 105CD) Twin Sisters.

Phonics. Kim Mitzo Thompson & Karen Mitzo Hilderbrand. Arranged by Hal Wright. (J). 1989. pap. bk. 13.99 (978-1-57583-295-1(X), Twin 405CD) Twin Sisters.

Phonics. unabr. ed. Twin Sisters Productions. Read by Twin Sisters. (J). 2007. 44.99 (978-1-60252-692-1(3)) Find a World.

Phonics, Vol. 1. unabr. ed. Brad Caudle & Richard Caudle. Perf. by Brad Caudle et al. 1 cass. (Running Time: 50 min.). (J). (gr. 1 up). 1994. pap. bk. 12.95 Deluxe set. (978-1-878489-50-0(X), RL950) Rock N Learn.
"Top 40" type songs with educational lyrics teach phonetic basics for learning to read. Covers short vowels, consonants, blends, & more. Includes illustrated activity book with worksheets.

Phonics, Vol. I. unabr. ed. Brad Caudle & Richard Caudle. Perf. by Brad Caudle et al. Illus. by Bart Harlan. 1 cass. (Running Time: 50 min.). (Rock 'N Learn Ser.). (YA). (gr. 1-12). 1994. pap. bk. 9.95 (978-1-878489-30-2(5), RL930) Rock N Learn.

Phonics, Vol. 2. unabr. ed. Brad Caudle & Richard Caudle. Perf. by Brad Caudle et al. 1 cass. (Running Time: 50 min.). (J). (gr. 1 up). 1994. pap. bk. 12.95 Deluxe Set. (978-1-878489-51-7(8), RL951) Rock N Learn.
"Top 40" type songs with educational lyrics teach phonic concepts. Covers long vowels, vowel combinations, "rule breakers," & more. Includes illustrated activity book with worksheets. Picks up where Rock 'n Learn "Phonics," Vol. 1 leaves off.

Phonics, Vol. II. unabr. ed. Brad Caudle & Richard Caudle. Perf. by Brad Caudle et al. Illus. by Bart Harlan. 1 cass. (Running Time: 50 min.). (Rock 'N Learn Ser.). (YA). (gr. 1-12). 1994. pap. bk. 9.95 (978-1-878489-31-9(3), RL931) Rock N Learn.

Phonics, Vols. I & II, Set. Brad Caudle & Richard Caudle. Illus. by Bart Harlan. 2 cass. (Running Time: 1 hr. 40 min.). (Rock 'N Learn Ser.). (J). (gr. 1 up). 1990. pap. bk. 15.95 (978-1-878489-00-5(3), RL900) Rock N Learn.
Teaches everything needed to sound out unfamiliar words, from short & long vowel sounds to complex blends. High-interest, musical format for all ages. Includes activity book with reproducible worksheets.

Phonics: Consonants & Vowels. 1 cass. (Running Time: 1 hr.). (J). (gr. k-6). 2001. pap. bk. 9.98 (TS 405C) Kimbo Educ.
A captivating program for teaching initial consonant sounds & short & long vowel sounds. Catchy choruses, rhyming stories & an activity book filled with puzzles. Includes book.

Phonics: Consonants & Vowels. 1 CD. (Running Time: 1 hr.). (J). (gr. 2-10). 2001. pap. bk. 14.95 (TS 405CD) Kimbo Educ.

Phonics: First Grade. (On Our Way to English Ser.). (gr. 1 up). audio compact disk 9.95 (978-0-7578-1475-4(1)) Rigby Educ.

Phonics: Kindergarten. (On Our Way to English Ser.). (gr. k up). audio compact disk 9.95 (978-0-7578-1563-8(4)) Rigby Educ.

Phonics: Second Grade. (On Our Way to English Ser.). (gr. 2 up). audio compact disk 9.95 (978-0-7578-1387-0(9)) Rigby Educ.

Phonics: Third Grade. (On Our Way to English Ser.). (gr. 3 up). audio compact disk 9.95 (978-0-7578-4287-0(9)) Rigby Educ.

Phonics & English 1 Listening. audio compact disk 15.50 (978-1-59166-293-8(1)) BJUPr.

Phonics, Consonants & Vowels. Contrib. by Twin Sisters Productions Staff. 1 CD. (J). 1997. bk. 19.95 (978-1-57583-028-5(0)) Pub: Twin Sisters. Dist(s): Carson Dellos

Phonics Fun. Ed. by Publications International Staff. 2004. bk. & wbk. ed. 12.98 (978-0-7853-8958-3(X)) Pubns Intl Ltd.

Phonics in Context, Set 1. 7 cass. (J). (gr. 2-4). 89.00 incl. worksheets. (978-0-89525-180-0(9), AMC 321) Ed Activities.
Thirteen different skills lessons are taught in this program, including, initial consonants, final consonants, digraphs, blends, short vowels, long vowel patterns (vowel-consonant-final e), long vowel patterns (double vowel combinations), vowel plus a combinations.

Phonics in Context, Set 2. 7 cass. (J). (gr. 4-6). 79.00 Set, incl. worksheets. (978-0-89525-063-6(2), AMC 328) Ed Activities.
Thirteen different skills lessons are taught in this program, including; initial consonants, final consonants, digraphs, blends, short vowels, long vowel patterns (vowel-consonant-final e), long vowel patterns (double vowel combinations), irregular vowel patterns, vowel plus r combinations.

Phonics Museum Kindergarten Kit. Marlin Detweiler et al. 2000. audio compact disk 105.00 (978-1-930710-56-6(9)) Veritas Pr PA.

Phonics Songs - Long Vowels. 1 cass. (Learning Beat Ser.). (J). bk. (LB104) NewSound.
Teach consonants, consonant blends & word families.

Phonics Songs - Short Vowels. 1 cass. (Running Time: 1 hr.). (J). (gr. k-6). 2001. wbk. ed. 10.95 (THR 103C) Kimbo Educ.
12 rhyming word families including short vowel sounds, consonants & blends are taught through snappy songs with amusing lyrics. Reproducible workbook & lyrics included.

Phonics Songs - Short Vowels. 1 cass. (Learning Ser.). (J). bk. (LB103) NewSound.
Teach consonants, consonant blends & word families.

Phonics Songs & Rhymes see Rimas y Canciones de Fonetica

Phonics Songs & Rhymes. 1 cass. (Running Time: 1 hr.). (J). 2001. stu. ed. 39.36 (978-0-673-62199-3(5), S-Foresman); stu. ed. 69.00 (978-0-673-62203-7(7), S-Foresman) AddWesSchl.
Original songs/rhymes help introduce each lesson's phonetic element and develop phonemic awareness. Also provides the instrumental track for all the songs.

Phonics Songs & Rhymes. (Scott Foresman Reading Ser.). (gr. k up). 2004. 39.96 (978-0-328-02528-2(3)); audio compact disk 69.00 (978-0-328-02529-9(1)) Addson-Wesley Educ.

Phonics Songs & Rhymes. 1 cass. (Running Time: 1 hr.). (gr. 1 up). 2004. 39.36 (978-0-673-62200-6(2)); audio compact disk 69.00 (978-0-673-62204-4(5)) Addson-Wesley Educ.

Phonics Songs & Rhymes. 1 cass. (Running Time: 1 hr.). (gr. 2 up). 2004. 39.36 (978-0-673-62201-3(0)) Addson-Wesley Educ.

Phonics Songs & Rhymes. 1 cass. (Running Time: 1 hr.). (gr. 3 up). 2004. 39.36 (978-0-673-62202-0(9)); audio compact disk 69.00 (978-0-673-62206-8(1)) Addson-Wesley Educ.

Phonograms - Build-a-Word. Steck-Vaughn Staff. 1 cass. (Running Time: 1 hr. 30 min.). (J). 2001. (978-0-7398-4659-9(0)) SteckVau.

Phonograph & the Graft see Great American Short Stories, Vol. II, A Collection

Phonograph & the Graft. unabr. ed. O. Henry. Read by Cindy Hardin & Walter Zimmerman. 1 cass. (Running Time: 48 min.). Dramatization. 1983. 7.95 (S-55) Jimcin Record.
Two delightful stories by the acknowledged master of the surprise ending.

Phonograph & the Graft & The Lotus & the Bottle. O. Henry. 1 cass. 1989. 7.95 (S-55) Jimcin Record.
Surprise endings in far away lands.

Phonothek: Lehr- und Ubungsmaterial Zur Deutschen Phonetik. E. Stock & U Hirschfeld. 2 cass. (Running Time: 1 hr. 30 mins.). 2005. 36.50 (978-3-468-49458-1(0)) Langenscheidt.

Phony Seance Racket & Hollywood Blackmailer. Perf. by Dick Powell. 1 cass. (Running Time: 60 min.). Dramatization. (Richard Diamond, Private Detective Ser.). 6.00 Once Upon Rad.
Radio broadcasts - mystery & suspense.

Photo of a Robber & New Easter Outfit. 1 cass. (Running Time: 60 min.). Dramatization. (Amos 'n' Andy Ser.). 1949. 6.00 Once Upon Rad.
Radio broadcasts - humor.

Photo Op! Images of World Culture. Heinle and Heinle Staff et al. (SPA., (C). 1998. audio compact disk 66.95 (978-0-8384-1024-0(3)) Pub: Heinle. Dist(s): CENGAGE Learn

Photograph. unabr. ed. Penelope Lively. Read by Daniel Gerroll & Patricia Kalember. (YA). 2006. 44.99 (978-1-59895-540-8(3)) Find a World.

Photographic Equipment in Germany: A Strategic Reference 2007. Compiled by Icon Group International, Inc. Staff. 2007. ring bd. 195.00 (978-0-497-35981-2(2)) Icon Grp.

Photography for Beginners: No. 3 in the River Road Poetry Series. Stephen Edgar. Read by Stephen Edgar. Executive Producer Carol Jenkins. (ENG.). 2008. audio compact disk 18.00 (978-0-9804148-2-0(2)) RivRoad AUS.

PhotoReading Personal Learning Course. Paul R. Scheele. Read by Paul R. Scheele. 9 cass. (Running Time: 8 hrs.). 1995. 245.00 Set, incls. 4 bks. (978-0-925480-61-3(4), 9PLC) Learn Strategies.
Use your "whole mind" to read with greater speed, increased comprehension, & more enjoyment.

Photoshop for Wedding Photographers Personal Seminar: Interactive DVD Training & Guide. Scott Kelby. (KW Personal Seminar Ser.). (ENG., 2005. audio compact disk 45.00 (978-0-321-35673-4(X)) Pub: Peachpit Pr. Dist(s): Pearson Educ

Photosynthesis CD: Changing Sunlight into Food. Bobbie Kalman & Rebecca Sjonger. (ENG.). (J). 2008. audio compact disk 10.00 (978-0-7787-7715-1(4)) CrabtreePubCo CAN.

Photovoltaic (PV) Solar Energy Equipment in Mexico: A Strategic Reference 2007. Compiled by Icon Group International, Inc. Staff. 2007. ring bd. 195.00 (978-0-497-82357-3(8)) Icon Grp.

Phowa. Perf. by Lama Wangdu Rinpoche. 1 CD. (Running Time: 28 mins.). (TIB.). 2004. audio compact disk 15.00 (978-0-915801-97-8(3)) Rudra Pr.

Phrasal Verb Affair. Scripts. Keith Kohnhorst. 1 CD. (Running Time: 63 mins.). Dramatization. (gr. 9-12). 2003. audio compact disk 19.00 (978-0-86647-169-5(3)) Pro Lingua.
The dramatic reading of the story on the CD give your students the chance to hear the phrasal verbs as they appear naturally in context when native speakers talk.

Phrasal Verb Affair. Scripts. Keith Kohnhorst & Shrewsbury Nadel Nancy. 1 CD. (Running Time: 63 mins.). Dramatization. (gr. 9-12). 2003. pap. bk. & stu. ed. 28.00 (978-0-86647-170-1(7)) Pro Lingua.

Phrase-a-Day English for Hispanic Children. 2 CDs. (Umbrella Parade Ser.). (J). 2005. audio compact disk 34.95 (978-1-57970-172-7(8), SEN850D) J Norton Pubs.

Phrase-a-Day English for Young Children. Judith White. Read by Judith White. Illus. by Carol Macbain. 2 cass. (Running Time: 1 hrs.). (Umbrella Parade Ser.). (J). (gr. k-6). 1993. pap. bk. 24.95 Set. (978-0-88432-500-0(8), BEN850) J Norton Pubs.
Conversations between parents & children in French or Spanish or English.

Phrase-a-Day French for Young Children. Foreign Language for Young Children Staff & Judith White. 2 cass. (Running Time: 2 hrs.). (J). (gr. k-6). 1989. pap. bk. & act. bk. ed. 24.95 (978-0-88432-284-9(X), SFR850) J Norton Pubs.
Children learn a variety of everyday expressions by listening & coloring. Organized by season of year. Native speakers, original music & sound effects. All the voices on the tapes are native speakers; the music & sound effects are original.

Phrase-a-Day French for Young Children. Judith K. White. 2 CDs. (Umbrella Parade Ser.). (FRE.). (J). 2005. audio compact disk 24.95 (978-1-57970-186-4(8), SFR850D) J Norton Pubs.

Phrase-a-Day Spanish for Young Children. Judith K. White. 2 CDs. (Umbrella Parade Ser.). (SPA., (J). 2005. audio compact disk 24.95 (978-1-57970-213-7(9), SSP850D) J Norton Pubs.

Phrase-a-Day Spanish for Young Children, Set 2. Foreign Language for Young Children Staff & Judith White. 2 cass. (Running Time: 180 mins.). (J). (gr. k-6). 1989. bk. 24.95 (978-0-88432-283-2(1), SSP850) J Norton Pubs.
Children learn a varitey of everyday expressions by listening & coloring, in this creative way to learn a foreign language. Organized by season of year. Native speakers, original music & sound effects.

Phyllis Curtin - Opera Arias (1960-1968) Phyllis Curtin. 1 cass. 1997. 16.99 Stereo/Mono. (VA1A 1152) VAI Audio.
The celebrated American soprano in live performances arias & scenes from "Nozze di Figaro," "Cosi' Fan Tutte," "Louise," "La Traviata," "Andrea Chenier," "La Rondine," "Gianni Schicchi," "Susannah," & "Saloome".

Phyllis Curtin Sings Faure & Debussy. Perf. by Phyllis Curtin & Ryan Edwards. Composed by Bernard Faure & Claude Debussy. 1 CD. 1999. 16.99 INCL. BKLET. (VAIA 1186) VAI Audio.
Features Faure's "La Chanson d'Eve" & both Faure's & Debussy's settings of six poems of Verlaine. Recorded in 1964. Includes complete texts & translations.

Phyllis Janik. unabr. ed. Phyllis Janik. Read by Phyllis Janik. 1 cass. (Running Time: 29 min.). 1986. 10.00 New Letters.
Chicago author Phyllis Janik reads new poems & an excerpt from a novel, "Ending Up".

Phyllis Naylor Interview with Kay Bonetti. Phyllis Reynolds Naylor. (Running Time: 59 min.). 13.95 (978-1-55644-191-2(6), 7063) Am Audio Prose.
Good in-depth discussion on writing for readers of all ages.

Physical: An American Checkup. James McManus. Read by James McManus. 5 cass. (Running Time: 27480 sec.). 2006. 49.95 (978-0-7927-3884-8(5), CSL 889) AudioGO.

Physical: An American Checkup. James McManus. Read by James McManus. 2005. 17.95 (978-1-59397-811-2(1)) Pub: Macmill Audio. Dist(s): Macmillan

Physical Abuse, Pt. 6. (D035CB090) Natl Public Radio.

Physical Abuse of the Child. Stephen Ludwig. (Pediatric Emergencies: The National Conference for Practioners Ser.). 1986. 9.00 (978-0-932491-74-9(X)) Res Appl Inc.

Physical Activity & Health Instructor's Toolkit. Kelli McCormack-Brown et al. (C). 2001. audio compact disk 204.95 (978-0-7637-1886-2(6), 1886-6) Jones Bartlett.

Physical Becomes Mental: Program from the Award Winning Public Radio Series. Hosted by Fred Goodwin. Comment by John Hockenberry. Contrib. by Caroline Carney-Doebbeling et al. 1 cass. (Running Time: 1 hr.). (Infinite Mind Ser.). 1999. audio compact disk 21.95 (978-1-888064-08-7(0)) Lichtenstein Creat.
Sometimes psychological symptoms like depression, psychosis or mania aren't a sign of mental illness, but a sign of physical illness. Diseases like thyroid disorders, multiple sclerosis and AIDS can have symptoms that might make you questions your mental health, and often these symptoms are the first signs of physical illness. In this hour, we hear about such illnesses from physicians who try to spot them and people who suffer from them. The guests are Dr. Caroline Carney-Doebbeling, Assistant Professor of Psychiatry and Internal Medicine at the University of Iowa College of Medicine and an expert in the area of combined illness, Dr. Tom Wise, Chairman of the Department of Psychiatry at Inova/Fairfax Hospital in Falls Church, Virginia and Professor and Vice Chairman at Georgetown University, Dr. Bradford Navia, an Associate Professor of Neurology and Psychiatry at Tufts University Medical School in Boston, and Camille Chatterjee, the news editor of Psychology Today.

Physical Body As a Universal Symbol. Manly P. Hall. 1 cass. 8.95 (978-0-89314-214-8(X), C890604) Philos Res.

Physical Changes with Aging. unabr. ed. Charlotte Eliopoulos. Read by Charlotte Eliopoulos. 1 cass. (Running Time: 30 min.). 1991. 15.00 (978-1-882515-07-3(2)) Hlth Educ Netwk.
Describes age-related changes to all body systems & nursing implications.

Physical Chemistry of Polymers. James E. Mark. 4 cass. (Running Time: 3 hrs.). 395.00 incl. 156 pp. manual. (89); 18.00 manual. (978-0-8412-1253-4(8)) Am Chemical.
Provides a survey of physical polymer chemistry for chemists & technicians without formal training in this area.

Physical Ed. 1 cass. (Running Time: 1 hr.). (J). (ps-5). 2001. 10.95 (KIB 1100C); audio compact disk 14.95 (KUB 1100CD) Kimbo Educ.
Let's get physical! A healthy collection of 16 fun fitness songs, group games & activities. Walk, hop, skip, jump, run, gallop & leap! Can You Keep Your Balance, Stretching With Ed, Marching Game, Monkey in the Middle & more.

Physical Effects of Aging. 1989. 9.95 (978-1-877843-10-5(5)) Elder Care Solutions.
What happens to our bodies as we grow older. Eight major body systems & how they age.

Physical Evidence. unabr. ed. Thomas T. Noguchi & Arthur Lyons. Narrated by George Guidall. 5 cass. (Running Time: 7 hrs.). 1993. 44.00 (978-1-55690-893-4(8), 93335E7) Recorded Bks.
Dr. Eric Parker, formerly of the L.A. Coroner's office, investigates a cryonic suspension clinic which is freezing wealthy clients with the promise of thawing them out sometime in the medically improved future.

Physical Existence: Perceptions from the Other Side. unabr. ed. Robert A. Monroe. Read by Robert A. Monroe. (Running Time: 45 min.). (Explorer Ser.). 1983. 12.95 (978-1-56113-009-2(5), 10) Monroe Institute.
A meeting with several entities who have passed over to the other side.

Physical Fitness & Wellness Presentation Package. 3rd rev. ed. Jerrold Greenberg et al. 2004. audio compact disk 245.00 (978-0-7360-5227-6(5)) HumanKinUSA.

Physical Healing. Carol Rios. 2007. audio compact disk 18.95 (978-1-4276-2341-6(4)) AardGP.

Physical Properties of Polymers: Current Concepts in the Characterization & Preparation of Useful Polymers. Instructed by James E. Mark et al. 8 cass. (Running Time: 7 hrs. 30 min.). 595.00 incl. 165pp. manual. (82) Am Chemical.
Designed to keep practicing polymer scientists abreast of the recent advances in important areas of polymeric materials.

Physical Rehabilitation: A Service of Celebration & Affirmation. 1 cass. (Care Cassettes Ser.: Vol. 11, No. 6). 1984. 10.80 Assn Prof Chaplains.

Physical Science: Spanish Section Summaries. David Frank et al. audio compact disk 59.47 (978-0-13-166263-6(5)) PH School.

Physical Stress. Manly P. Hall. 1 cass. 8.95 (978-0-89314-215-5(8), C900722) Philos Res.

Physical Therapy. Steven C. Eggleston. 1 cass. 1987. 6.95 SCE Prod & List & Lrn.
Instructions on physical therapy modalities for doctors, nurses & physical therapists.

Physical Universe. Poems. Louis Simpson. Read by Louis Simpson. 1 cass. (Running Time: 57 min.). 1985. 10.95 (23663) J Norton Pubs.
Retrospective album covering almost 30 years of work from this major American poet.

Physical Well-Being. unabr. ed. Judith L. Powell. Read by Judith L. Powell. 1 cass. (Running Time: 40 min.). (Successful Living Ser.). 1987. pap. bk. 12.97 (978-0-914295-26-6(8)) Top Mtn Pub.
Side A presents exercises designed to improve physical well-being & enjoy changes in health, beauty & strength. Side B presents subliminal health-related suggestions hidden in New Age Music.

Physician Assisted Suicide: Compassion or Collapse? Richard McCormick. 1 cass. (Running Time: 1 hr.). 1997. 9.95 (TAH382) St Pauls Alba.
Examining the highly visible public issue of physician assisted suicide as it affects the health, growth & direction of society raises questions of moral, legal & philosophical dimensions.

Physician Liability after DiMarco. 1 cass. (Running Time: 30 min.). 1991. 25.00 (AL-119) PA Bar Inst.
The audio package includes DiMarco & Dunkle opinions.

Physician Reimbursement. Moderated by George F. Sheldon. 2 cass. (General Sessions Ser.: GS-3). 1986. 19.00 (8631) Am Coll Surgeons.

Physicians, Dentists, & Veterinarians (Services to Clients) Richard J. Vargo & Greg Gates. 3 cass. (Running Time: 8 hrs.). 1995. 119.00 set, incl. wkbk. (745336EZ) Am Inst CPA.
With this course, you can help your doctor clients boost their collections without losing patients, handle their automobile & employee business expenses for maximum savings, make tax-wise plans for retirement, cope with stricter fee limits, & avoid a stack of uncollectible bills. You will also get thorough answers to such questions as: what useful tax strategies can you recommend for the business organization of a solo health care practitioner or group of practitioners; how can you incorporate cost controls in the accounting & informations systems of your doctor clients; & what internal control methods can you suggest.

Physicist. 1 cass. (Science Ser.). (J). bk. Incl. 24p. bk. (TWIN 427) NewSound.

Physick Book of Deliverance Dane. unabr. ed. Katherine Howe. Read by Katherine Kellgren. 11 CDs. (Running Time: 13 hrs.). 2009. audio compact disk 39.99 (978-1-4013-9305-2(5), Hyperion Audio) Pub: Hyperion. Dist(s): HarperCollins Pubs

***Physick Book of Deliverance Dane.** unabr. ed. Katherine Howe. Read by Katherine Kellgren. 2010. audio compact disk 19.99 (978-1-4013-9515-5(5)) Pub: Hyperion. Dist(s): HarperCollins Pubs

***Physick Book of Deliverance Dane.** unabr. ed. Katherine Howe. Read by Katherine Kellgren. 11 CDs. (Running Time: 12 hrs. 45 mins.). 2009. audio compact disk 100.00 (978-0-307-70197-8(2), BksonTape) Pub: Random Audio Pubg. Dist(s): Random

Physics, Set. 2004. act. bk. ed. 13.99 (978-1-57583-363-7(8)) Twin Sisters.

Physics: Instructor's Resource CD W/Testing Software. 2nd rev. ed. Walker. audio compact disk 49.97 (978-0-13-101481-7(1)) PH School.

Physics Vol. 127: Get Kids Excited about Physics! unabr. ed. Kim Mitzo Thompson & Karen Mitzo Hilderbrand. 1 CD. (Running Time: 40 min.). (Get Kids Excited about Ser.). (J). (ps-4). 1999. audio compact disk 12.99 (978-1-57583-207-4(0)) Twin Sisters.
Through 12 clever, informative songs, children will learn how physics relates to the real world.

Physics - Mind & Matter. Read by F. David Peat et al. 1 cass. (Running Time: 54 min.). 14.95 (CBC1015) MMI Corp.
Discusses human understanding of the Universe; how the theory of evolution, quantum theory & theory of relativity have revolutionized man's knowledge.

Physics & Meditation. Arthur Zajonc. 1 cass. 9.00 (OC87) Sound Horizons AV.

Physics & the Theory of Consciousness. unabr. ed. Arthur Young. 1 cass. 1982. 7.00 (978-1-56964-111-8(0), A0165-82) Sound Photosyn.

Physics, eGrade Plus Demo. 6th ed. John D. Cutnell & Kenneth W. Johnson. 2003. audio compact disk 128.95 (978-0-471-46323-8(X)) Wiley US.

Physics Experiments on File. Diagram Group. (gr. 6-12). 2004. audio compact disk 149.95 (978-0-8160-5579-1(3)) Facts On File.

Physics for Scientists & Engineers: a Strategic Approach: Computerized Test Bank. Andrew Knight. audio compact disk 49.97 (978-0-8053-8995-1(4)) Addson-Wesley Educ.

Physics Matters: Resource CD. James Trefil & Robert M. Hazen. (YA). 2004. audio compact disk (978-0-471-52776-3(9)) Wiley US.

***Physics of star Trek.** abr. ed. Lawrence M. Krauss. Read by Lawrence M. Krauss. (ENG.). 2006. (978-0-06-113531-6(3), Harper Audio); (978-0-06-113530-9(5), Harper Audio) HarperCollins Pubs.

Physics of Star Trek. unabr. ed. Lawrence M. Krauss. Read by Larry McKeever. 7 cass. (Running Time: 7 hrs.). 1996. 42.00 (978-0-7366-3380-2(4), 4030) Books on Tape.
What warps when you travel at warp speed? What happens when you get beamed up? Are time loops really possible & can I kill my grandmother before I'm born? How does the Star Trek universe stack up to the real universe? Get the answers to these questions & find out what the series creators got right - & wrong - about science.

***Physics of the Future: How Science Will Change Civilization & Daily Life by the Year 2100.** unabr. ed. Michio Kaku. (Running Time: 12 hrs.). (ENG.). 2011. audio compact disk 40.00 (978-0-307-87705-5(1), Random AudioBks) Pub: Random Audio Pubg. Dist(s): Random

Physics of the Impossible: A Scientific Exploration into the World of Phasers, Force Fields, Teleportation, & Time Travel. unabr. ed. Michio Kaku. Read by Feodor Chin. 10 CDs. (Running Time: 11 hrs. 45 mins.). 2008. audio compact disk 90.00 (978-1-4159-4683-1(3)) Random.

Physics Reprints. Ed. by Marco A. V. Bitetto. 1 cass. 2000. (978-1-58578-056-3(1)) Inst of Cybernetics.

Physics Smarts by Dancing Beetle. Eugene Ely et al. 1 cass. (Running Time: 80 min.). (J). 1995. 10.00 Erthvilbz.
Physics facts & theories come together when Ms. Orangutan & the spunky musical humans read & sing with Dancing Beetle.

Physics Suite Cd for Understanding Physics, Fi Rst Edition. Cummings. (YA). 2004. tchr. ed. (978-0-471-46443-3(0)) Wiley US.

Physics Suite CD T/A Understanding Physics 1e. Cummings. (YA). 2004. audio compact disk (978-0-471-48775-3(9)) Wiley US.

Physik. unabr. ed. Angie Sage. Read by Gerard Doyle. 11 cass. (Running Time: 12 hrs. 25 mins.). (Septimus Heap Ser.: Bk. 3). (J). (gr. 4-6). 2007. 88.75 (978-1-4281-4574-0(5)); audio compact disk 108.75 (978-1-4281-4579-5(6)) Recorded Bks.

Physiologic Adaptation of Space. Moderated by Sam L. Pool. Contrib. by Michael W. Bungo et al. 1 cass. (Running Time: 90 min.). 1985. 12.00 (A8505) Amer Coll Phys.
This topic is discussed by a moderator & experts who offer differing opinions.

Physiological Quieting. Janet Hulmel. (Running Time: 25 min.). 10.00 (0476-97, Ther Ed) Adv Rehab Therapy.
Designed to decrease sympathetic nervous system activity, the Physiological Quieting audiotape combines: Breathing Retraining, Autogenics, Positive Imagery, & Self Statements. Accompanying background music matches the voice rhythm & facilitates physiological changes. Physiological Quieting is an essential component of treatment for: Fibromyalgia, Chronic Pain, Headaches Incontinence, Pregnancy/Delivery, Pre/Post Surgery.

Phytoestrogen Estrogens in Foods to Help Relieve: Menopausal Symptoms. Calista Hunter. 1 cass. (Running Time: 49 min.). 1998. bk. 20.00 (978-1-58111-053-1(7)) Contemporary Medical.

Piaf mon Amie. unabr. ed. Ginou Richer. Read by Selena Hernandez. (YA). 2007. 99.99 (978-2-35569-101-0(0)) Find a World.

Piano & Organ Without a Teacher One. Vladislav Celik. 1 cass. (Running Time: 60 min.). (Music Instructional Ser.). 4.95 (978-1-883993-01-6(6)) Music Inst CA.

Piano & Organ Without a Teacher One. Vladislav Celik. 1 cass. (Running Time: 60 min.). (Music Instructional Ser.). pap. bk. 12.95 (978-0-9624062-4-9(4)) Music Inst CA.
Intended to be used with the book of the same title. It is for self teaching how to play music.

Piano & Organ Without a Teacher Two. Vladislav Celik. 1 cass. (Running Time: 72 min.). (Music Instructional Ser.). pap. bk. 12.95 (978-0-9624062-5-6(2)); 4.95 (978-1-883993-02-3(4)) Music Inst CA.

Piano Arranging: How to Do It on the Spot. Duane Shinn. Read by Duane Shinn. 6 cass. (Running Time: 6 hrs.). 139.95 Set, incl. songbk. & 72 cards. (PA-1) Duane Shinn.

Piano Course 2 for the Visually Impaired, Set. unabr. ed. William M. Brown, Jr. 4 cass. 2000. 37.00 (978-0-9700478-2-3(7)) Valdosta Mus.

Piano Ensemble, Bk. 4. Phillip Keveren. (Hal Leonard Piano Library). 1998. pap. bk. 5.95 (978-0-7935-9406-1(5), 0793594065) H Leonard.

Piano Ensembles, Level 1. Phillip Keveren. (Hal Leonard Student Piano Library). 1998. pap. bk. 5.95 (978-0-7935-9400-9(6), 0793594006) H Leonard.

Piano Ensembles, Level 2. Phillip Keveren. (Hal Leonard Student Piano Library). 1998. pap. bk. 5.95 (978-0-7935-9402-3(2), 0793594022) H Leonard.

Piano Ensembles, Level 3. Phillip Keveren. (Hal Leonard Student Piano Library). 1998. pap. bk. 5.95 (978-0-7935-9404-7(9), 0793594049) H Leonard.

Piano Ensembles: Level 5. Phillip Keveren. (Hal Leonard Student Piano Library). 1999. audio compact disk 5.95 (978-0-634-00254-0(6), 0634002546) H Leonard.

Piano for All Times. Mark Hayes. 1993. 11.98 (978-0-7673-1307-0(0)) LifeWay Christian.

Piano for All Times. Mark Hayes. 1993. audio compact disk 16.98 (978-0-7673-1285-1(6)) LifeWay Christian.

Piano Hymns. Transcribed by Paul Howard. 1997. pap. bk. 22.96 (978-0-7866-3221-3(6), 96648CDP) Mel Bay.

Piano Improvisation from Ragtime to Contemporary. Duane Shinn. 1 cass. 19.95 (MU-4) Duane Shinn.
Traces the development of piano improvising from ragtime to the present.

***Piano in the House.** 2010. audio compact disk (978-1-59171-291-6(2)) Falcon Picture.

Piano in the Pyrenees. Tony Hawks. 2007. 69.95 (978-0-7531-3733-8(X)) Pub: ISIS Audio GBR. Dist(s): Ulverscroft US

Piano in the Pyrenees. Tony Hawks. Read by Tony Hawks. (Running Time: 36000 sec.). 2007. audio compact disk 84.95 (978-0-7531-2699-8(0)) Pub: ISIS Audio GBR. Dist(s): Ulverscroft US

Piano Lessons, Bk. 5. Phillip Keveren. (Hal Leonard Student Piano Library). 1998. pap. bk. 5.95 (978-0-7935-8471-0(X), 079358471X) H Leonard.

Piano Lessons - French Edition Bk. 3: Hal Leonard Student Piano Library. Phillip Keveren. 2001. audio compact disk 6.99 (978-90-431-1155-3(4), 9043111554) H Leonard.

Piano Lessons - French Edition Bk. 4: Hal Leonard Student Piano Library. Phillip Keveren. 2001. audio compact disk 6.99 (978-90-431-1156-0(2), 9043111562) H Leonard.

Piano Lessons - French Edition Bk. 5: Hal Leonard Student Piano Library. Phillip Keveren. 2001. audio compact disk 6.99 (978-90-431-1157-7(0), 9043111570) H Leonard.

Piano Lessons French Edition Bk. 2: Hal Leonard Student Piano Library. Phillip Keveren. 2001. audio compact disk 6.99 (978-90-431-1154-6(6), 9043111546) H Leonard.

Piano Lessons International. Hal Leonard Publications Staff. 2004. audio compact disk 10.95 (978-0-634-08426-3(7)); audio compact disk 10.95 (978-0-634-08427-0(5)) H Leonard.

Piano Lessonsm French Edition Bk. 1: Hal Leonard Student Piano Library. Phillip Keveren. 2001. audio compact disk 6.99 (978-90-431-1153-9(8), 9043111538) H Leonard.

Piano Man's Daughter. abr. ed. Timothy Findley & Timothy Findley. Narrated by Colm Feore. 4 cass. (Running Time: 5 hrs.). (ENG.). 2001. 24.95 (978-0-86492-255-7(8)) Pub: BTC Audiobks CAN. Dist(s): U Toronto Pr
A young piano tuner pieces together the identity of his mad yet talented mother Lily. The love child of a piano player, Lily travels from turn-of-the-century Toronto to an assylum in the 1930s.

Piano Man's Daughter. abr. ed. Timothy Findley & Timothy Findley. Narrated by Colm Feore. Prod. by CBC Radio Staff. 4 CDs. (Running Time: 5 hrs.). (ENG.). 2001. audio compact disk 24.95 (978-0-86492-257-1(4)) Pub: BTC Audiobks CAN. Dist(s): U Toronto Pr

Piano Man's Daughter. abr. collector's ed. Timothy Findley & Timothy Findley. Narrated by Colm Feore. 4 cass. (Running Time: 5 hrs.). (Between the Covers Collection). (ENG.). (gr. 3-6). 2005. 24.95 (978-0-86492-203-8(5));

audio compact disk 24.95 (978-0-86492-201-4(9)) Pub: BTC Audiobks CAN. Dist(s): U Toronto Pr

Piano Method for Young Beginners, Bk. 2. Andrew Scott & Gary Turner. 1 CD. (Running Time: 90 mins.). (Progressive Ser.). 1997. pap. bk. 14.95 (978-0-947183-27-1(2), 256-188) Kolala Music SGP.

Piano Praise: Worship Songs for Piano & Optional Instruments. Jeff Bennett. 2005. pap. bk. 19.95 (978-0-634-07797-5(X), 063407797X) H Leonard.

Piano School, Vol. 3 & 4. Shinichi Suzuki. (Suzuki Method Core Materials Ser.). (ENG.). 1995. audio compact disk 15.95 (978-0-87487-462-4(9), Warner Bro) Alfred Pub.

Piano School Vol. 1 & 2: Watts. Shinichi Suzuki. (Suzuki Method Core Materials Ser.). (ENG.). 1996. audio compact disk 15.95 (978-0-87487-896-7(9), Warner Bro) Alfred Pub.

Piano School Vol. 3 & 4: Watts. Shinichi Suzuki. (Suzuki Method Core Materials Ser.). (ENG.). 1996. audio compact disk 15.95 (978-0-87487-897-4(7), Warner Bro) Alfred Pub.

Piano School Aide, Vol. 5. Shinichi Suzuki. (Suzuki Method Core Materials Ser.). (ENG.). 1995. audio compact disk 15.95 (978-0-87487-463-1(7), Warner Bro) Alfred Pub.

Piano School Aide, Vol. 6. Shinichi Suzuki. (Suzuki Method Core Materials Ser.). (ENG.). 1994. audio compact disk 15.95 (978-0-87487-464-8(5), Warner Bro) Alfred Pub.

Piano School CD V-2 Kataoka. Shinichi Suzuki. (Suzuki Method Core Materials Ser.). (ENG.). 1993. audio compact disk 15.95 (978-0-87487-498-3(X), Warner Bro) Alfred Pub.

Piano School CD V-3 Kataoka. Shinichi Suzuki. (Suzuki Method Core Materials Ser.). (ENG.). 1993. audio compact disk 15.95 (978-0-87487-499-0(8), Warner Bro) Alfred Pub.

Piano School CD V 6 Watts. Shinichi Suzuki. (Suzuki Method Core Materials Ser.). (ENG.). 1996. audio compact disk 15.95 (978-0-87487-899-8(3), Warner Bro) Alfred Pub.

Piano School CD V-7 Aide. Shinichi Suzuki. (Suzuki Method Core Materials Ser.). (ENG.). 1996. audio compact disk 15.95 (978-0-87487-465-5(3), Warner Bro) Alfred Pub.

Piano School Watts, Vol. 7. Shinichi Suzuki. (Suzuki Method Core Materials Ser.). (ENG.). 1996. audio compact disk 15.95 (978-0-87487-900-1(0), Warner Bro) Alfred Pub.

Piano Shop on the Left Bank: Discovering a Forgotten Passion in a Paris Atelier. unabr. ed. Thaddeus E. Carhart. Read by Dan Cashman. 6 cass. (Running Time: 9 hrs.). 2002. 48.00 (978-0-7366-8618-1(5)) Books on Tape.
In this engaging memoir, an American writer living in Paris recounts his experiences in a piano shop tucked into an out-of-the-way street on the Rive Gauche. Walking his two young children to school every morning, Thad Carhart passes an unassuming little storefront in his Paris neighborhood. Intrigued by its simple sign - Desforges Pianos - he enters, only to have his way barred by the shop's imperious owner. Unable to stifle his curiosity, he finally lands the proper introduction, and a world previously hidden is brought into view. As he earns the trust of the atelier's music lovers, he shows us a life in which the serious pursuit of music is as natural as breathing.

Piano Solos Book 1 - CD - French Edition: Hal Leonard Student Piano Library. Phillip Keveren. 2001. audio compact disk 6.99 (978-90-431-1158-4(9), 9043111589) H Leonard.

Piano Solos Book 2 - CD - French Edition: Hal Leonard Student Piano Library. Phillip Keveren. (ENG.). 2001. audio compact disk 6.99 (978-90-431-1159-1(7), 9043111597) H Leonard.

Piano Solos Book 3 - CD - French Edition: Hal Leonard Student Piano Library. Phillip Keveren. 2001. audio compact disk 6.99 (978-90-431-1160-7(0), 9043111600) H Leonard.

Piano Solos Book 4 - CD - French Edition: Hal Leonard Student Piano Library. Phillip Keveren. 2001. audio compact disk 6.99 (978-90-431-1161-4(9), 9043111619) H Leonard.

Piano Solos Book 5 - CD - French Edition: Hal Leonard Student Piano Library. Phillip Keveren. 2001. audio compact disk 5.95 (978-90-431-1162-1(7), 9043111627) H Leonard.

Piano Teacher. unabr. ed. Janice Y. K. Lee. (Running Time: 10 hrs. 5 mins.). 2009. 29.95 (978-1-4332-5673-8(8)); audio compact disk 65.95 (978-1-4332-5669-1(X)) Blckstn Audio.

Piano Teacher. unabr. ed. Janice Y. K. Lee. Narrated by Orlagh Cassidy. 9 CDs. (Running Time: 10 hrs. 30 mins.). 2009. audio compact disk 90.00 (978-1-4332-5670-7(3)) Blckstn Audio.

Piano Teacher. unabr. ed. Janice Y. K. Lee. Contrib. by Orlagh Cassidy. 9 CDs. (Running Time: 11 hrs.). (ENG.). (gr. 12 up). 2009. audio compact disk 39.95 (978-0-14-314441-0(3), PengAudBks) Penguin Grp USA.

Piano Tricks & Licks. Robert Laughlin. Read by Robert Laughlin. 1 cass. (Running Time: 1 hr.). 1995. 12.00 (978-0-929983-04-2(1)) New Schl Am Music.
Demonstration of Laughlin's favorite pop piano tricks & licks - like having a private lesson.

Piano Tuner. unabr. ed. Daniel Mason. 8 cass. (Running Time: 12 hrs.). 2002. 72.00 (978-0-7366-8782-9(3)) Books on Tape.

Pianoforte Praise. Don Wyrtzen. 2001. 11.98 (978-0-633-01699-9(3)); audio compact disk 16.98 (978-0-633-01700-2(0)) LifeWay Christian.

Piast Tas - Fiesta Time. Perf. by Ron Joaquin & Southern Scratch. 1 cass., 1 CD. 7.98 (CANR 8111) NewSound.

Piazza see Melville: Six Short Novels

Piazzolla - Histoire du Tango & Other Latin Classics for Guitar & Flute Duet. Composed by Astor Piazzolla. 2006. pap. bk. 34.98 (978-1-59615-384-4(9), 1596153849) Pub: Music Minus. Dist(s): H Leonard

Picasso: A Biography. unabr. ed. Patrick O'Brian. Read by Richard Brown. 10 cass. (Running Time: 15 hrs.). 1993. 80.00 (3290-A); 72.00 (3290-B) Books on Tape.
Epic artist emerges as a man of contradictions wielding great influence over the world around him.

Picasso: A Biography. unabr. ed. Patrick O'Brian. Read by Richard Brown. 19 cass. (Running Time: 28 hrs. 30 min.). 1993. 152.00 (3290A/B) Books on Tape.

Picasso: Creator & Destroyer. abr. ed. Arianna S. Huffington. Read by Natascha McElhone. 2 cass. (Running Time: 3 hrs.). 1996. 17.95 (978-1-57453-092-6(5)) Audio Lit.
Here is Picasso as never seen before, the indefatigable painter, the bohemian, the seducer, the father & ultimately, the man sacrificed on the altar of his own contradictions.

Picasso: Creator & Destroyer. unabr. ed. Arianna S. Huffington. Read by Nadia May. 14 cass. (Running Time: 20 hrs. 30 mins.). 1994. 89.95 (978-0-7861-0642-4(5), 1454) Blckstn Audio.
Picasso was a man whose burning passions - for painting, for women, for ideas - were matched by his compulsion to invent reality in his life no less than in his art. Here is the tragic story of a man who, unable to love, was driven to dominate & humiliate the women & the many men who fell under his hypnotic spell. Drawing on a wealth of startling revelations, the author has stripped bare the romantic myths to reveal, in all its volatile complexity, Picasso's lifelong struggle between his power to create & his compulsion to destroy.

Picasso: Creator & Destroyer. unabr. collector's ed. Arianna S. Huffington. Read by Kimberly Schraf. 15 cass. (Running Time: 22 hrs. 30 min.). 1997. 120.00 (978-0-7366-3576-9(9), 4228) Books on Tape.
The world knows him simply as Picasso, this century's towering artistic genius, a man whose creativity & magnetism made him a legend.

Picasso: Music of His Time. Hugh Griffith. 1 CD. (Running Time: 1 hr. 30 min.). (Art & Music Ser.). 2003. audio compact disk (Naxos AudioBooks) Naxos.

Picasso & Dora: A Personal Memoir. unabr. collector's ed. James Lord. Read by John Edwardson. 10 cass. (Running Time: 15 hrs.). 1997. 80.00 (978-0-7366-4043-5(6), 4542) Books on Tape.
An art historian recounts his experiences with the great painter & his mistress, also an artist.

Picasso Flop. Vince VanPatten & Robert J. Randisi. Read by Tom Weiner. (Running Time: 23400 sec.). (Texas Hold'em Mysteries Ser.). 2007. 59.95 (978-0-7861-6913-9(3)); audio compact disk 63.00 (978-0-7861-6912-2(5)) Blckstn Audio.

Picasso Flop. unabr. ed. Vince Van Patten & Robert J. Randisi. Read by Tom Weiner. (Running Time: 23400 sec.). (Texas Hold'em Mysteries Ser.). 2007. 27.95 (978-0-7861-4911-7(6)); audio compact disk 27.95 (978-0-7861-5935-2(9)) Blckstn Audio.

Picasso Flop. unabr. ed. Vince Van Patten & Robert J. Randisi. Read by Tom Weiner. (Running Time: 23400 sec.). 2007. audio compact disk 29.95 (978-0-7861-7061-6(1)) Blckstn Audio.

Picasso Scam. Stuart Pawson & Andrew Wincott. 2009. 54.95 (978-1-84652-375-5(3)); audio compact disk 71.95 (978-1-84652-376-2(1)) Pub: Magna Story GBR. Dist(s): Ulverscroft US

Picasso's Rembrandt's Elephant's Eye. James Wyly. Read by James Wyly. 1 cass. (Running Time: 48 min.). 1994. 9.95 (978-0-7822-0471-1(6), 548) C G Jung IL.

Picasso's War: The Destruction of Guernica & the Masterpiece That Changed the World. Russell Martin. Read by Oliver Wyman. (Playaway Adult Nonfiction Ser.). 2009. 54.99 (978-1-60775-731-3(1)) Find a World.

Piccadilly Jim, P. G. Wodehouse. Read by Flo Gibson. 6 cass. (Running Time: 8 hrs.). 1999. 24.95 (978-1-55685-396-8(3)) Audio Bk Con.
This romantic romp involves four cases of mistaken identity & outlandish & hilarious behavior on both sides of the Atlantic.

Piccadilly Jim. abr. ed. P. G. Wodehouse. Read by Martin Jarvis. (Running Time: 5 hrs. 0 mins. 0 sec.). (ENG.). 2009. audio compact disk 26.95 (978-1-934997-19-2(6)) Pub: CSAWord. Dist(s): PerseuPGW

Piccadilly Jim. unabr. ed. P. G. Wodehouse. Read by Frederick Davidson. 6 cass. (Running Time: 8 hrs. 30 mins.). 1994. 44.95 (978-0-7861-0496-3(1), 1447) Blckstn Audio.
He was a gossip columnist's dream. Picadilly Jim's life was a collage of broken promises & drunken brawls. And his straight-laced Victorian aunt was not amused. So, she decided to reform him. Unfortunately, her reform project started at a time when Jim had fallen in love & had already decided to reform himself. Thus, life became complicated. Jim pretends to be himself - a beautiful display of Wodehousean logic; hilarious indeed!.

Piccolo & Annabelle Volume 1: The Very Messy Inspection. unabr. ed. Stephen Axelsen. Read by Stanley McGeagh. (Running Time: 8100 sec.). (Piccolo & Annabelle Ser.). (J). 2006. audio compact disk 43.95 (978-1-74093-803-7(8)) Pub: Bolinda Pubng AUS. Dist(s): Bolinda Pub Inc

Piccolo Principe. Antoine de Saint-Exupéry. 1 cass. (Running Time: 1 hr. 30 mins.).Tr. of Little Prince. (ITA.). (J). 2000. pap. bk. 33.95 (978-88-452-3835-2(0)) Pub: Fabbri ITA. Dist(s): Distribks Inc

Pick a Pack of Praise. (J). (gr. 3-6). 1988. bk. 12.99 (978-0-685-68213-5(7), TA-9100C) Lillenas.

Pick a Pack of Praise: 50 Songs of Fun & Faith for Kids. Contrib. by Nan Allen. Arranged by Dennis Allen. 1 cass. (Running Time: 1 hr.). (J). (gr. 3-6). 1988. 12.99 (TA-9100C) Lillenas.
Fifty songs of fun & faith for kids. A sequel to Sing a Song of Scripture, this collection featured both general & seasonal selections, designed for use anytime children sing Compiled by a committee of experienced children's music workers, these songs are meaningful yet fun to sing. Included are contemporary & traditional favorites, along with memorable new songs. A double-length split-channel cassette features all 50 songs; suitable for listening or performance.

Pick Me up! (Music & ASL) Fun Songs for Learning Signs. Created by Sign2Me. Executive Producer Bob Tarcea. Music by Roger Treece. Lyrics by Nancy Stewart. (ENG., 2003. bk. & act. bk. ed. 36.95 (978-0-9668367-8-3(2), Sign Two Me) Northlight Commns.
Pick Me Up! is compilation of 20 original songs and an American Sign Language (ASL) Activity Guide that provides a step by step, fun and easy way to learn ASL signs for young hearing children. Studies show that combining music and movement is a powerful tool for language learning, and using ASL signs simultaneously with spoken English can significantly improve the signer?s English literacy skills. Composed by Grammy? Nominee Roger Treece, the songs have a creative flair that adults will enjoy as much as the children. More than 230 ASL signs are illustrated in full color in the activity guide.

***Pick-up Game: A Full Day of Full Court.** unabr. ed. Marc Aronson and Charles R. Smith Jr. (Running Time: 3 hrs.). 2011. 19.99 (978-1-4558-0084-1(8), 9781455800841, Candlewick Bril); 39.97 (978-1-4558-0085-8(6), 9781455800858, Candlewick Bril); 19.99 (978-1-4558-0081-0(3), 9781455800810, Candlewick Bril); 39.97 (978-1-4558-0082-7(1), 9781455800827, Candlewick Bril); audio compact disk 22.99 (978-1-4558-0079-7(1), 9781455800797, Candlewick Bril); audio compact disk 49.97 (978-1-4558-0080-3(5), 9781455800803, Candlewick Bril) Brilliance Audio.

Picked-up Pieces, Pt. 1. unabr. collector's ed. John Updike. Read by John MacDonald. 7 cass. (Running Time: 10 hrs. 30 min.). 1984. 56.00 (978-0-7366-0986-9(5), 1926-A) Books on Tape.
Updike proves his mastery of the short form with this selection of book reviews, essays & reflections on life, love, art, & the IRS, for contrast.

Picked-up Pieces, Pt. 2. collector's ed. John Updike. Read by John MacDonald. 7 cass. (Running Time: 10 hrs. 30 min.). 1984. 56.00 (978-0-7366-0987-6(3), 1926-B) Books on Tape.

Pickering Manuscript see Poetry of William Blake

Pickett's Charge: A Microhistory of the Final Attack at Gettysburg. unabr. ed. George R. Stewart. Narrated by Nelson Runger. 8 cass. (Running Time: 10 hrs. 30 mins.). 1992. 70.00 (978-1-55690-714-2(1), 92337E7) Recorded Bks.
To quote the author: "If we grant that the Civil War furnishes the great dramatic episode of the history of the U.S. & that Gettysburg provides the climax of the war, then the climax of the climax...must be Pickett's Charge".

Pickett's Charge in History & Memory. unabr. ed. Carol Reardon. Read by Anna Fields. 7 cass. (Running Time: 10 hrs. 30 mins.). 2001. 56.00 (978-0-7366-6200-0(6)) Books on Tape.
A study of how Pickett's Charge has evolved from an historic event into a legend that fits the country's changing needs.

Pickin' on Neil Young. 1 cass., 1 CD. 7.98 (CMH 8025); audio compact disk 11.18 CD Jewel box. (CMH 8025) NewSound.

Picking a Professional. Bruce Williams. Read by Bruce Williams. 1 cass. (Insider's Report Ser.). 9.95 (978-0-944305-09-6(1)) Bonneville Media.
Features advice on choosing a lawyer, a doctor, an insurance company, & servicemen.

Picking Cotton: Our Memoir of Injustice & Redemption. unabr. ed. Jennifer Thompson-Cannino & Ronald Cotton. Read by Richard Allen & Karen White. Told to Erin Torneo. 1 MP3-CD. (Running Time: 8 hrs. 0 mins. 0 sec.). (ENG.). 2009. 19.99 (978-1-4001-6152-2(5)) Pub: Tantor Media. Dist(s): IngramPubServ

Picking Cotton: Our Memoir of Injustice & Redemption. unabr. ed. Jennifer Thompson-Cannino et al. Narrated by Richard Allen & Karen White. 7 CDs. (Running Time: 8 hrs. 0 mins. 0 sec.). (ENG.). 2009. audio compact disk 59.99 (978-1-4001-4152-4(4)) Pub: Tantor Media. Dist(s): IngramPubServ

Picking Cotton: Our Memoir of Injustice & Redemption. unabr. ed. Jennifer Thompson-Cannino et al. Read by Richard Allen & Karen White. Told to Erin Torneo. 7 CDs. (Running Time: 8 hrs. 0 mins. 0 sec.). (ENG.). 2009. audio compact disk 29.99 (978-1-4001-1152-7(8)) Pub: Tantor Media. Dist(s): IngramPubServ

***Picking Dandelions: A Search for Eden among Lifeâ€(tm)s Weeds.** unabr. ed. Sarah Cunningham. (Running Time: 5 hrs. 44 mins. 20 sec.). (ENG.). 2010. 14.99 (978-0-310-77346-7(6)) Zondervan.

Picking Up. Kate Fenton. Read by Jan Francis. 10 vols. (Running Time: 15 hrs.). 2003. 84.95 (978-0-7540-8368-9(3)) Pub: Chivers Audio Bks GBR. Dist(s): AudioGO

Picking up Girls Made Easy. 2nd ed. Eric Weber. 1 cass. (Running Time: 45 min.). 1995. 20.95 (978-0-914094-70-8(X)) Symphony Pr.
Interpersonal relationships.

Pickle Puss. unabr. ed. Patricia Reilly Giff. Read by Suzanne Toren. 1 cass. (Running Time: 48 mins.). (Follow the Reader Ser.). (J). (gr. 1-2). 1987. pap. bk. 17.00 incl. pap. bk. & guide. (978-0-8072-0145-9(6), FTR 115SP, Listening Lib) Random Audio Pubg.
Emily Arrow's plan for August is to read more books than Dawn Bosco. If she wins the book reading contest, she gets to keep Pickle Puss, a stray cat that both girls want.

Pickles to Pittsburgh: The Sequel to Cloudy with a Chance of Meatballs. Judi Barrett. Illus. by Ron Barrett. 14 vols. (Running Time: 15 mins.). 1999. pap. bk. 37.95 (978-0-87499-539-8(6)); pap. bk. 39.95 (978-1-59112-751-2(3)); audio compact disk 12.95 (978-1-59112-748-2(3)) Live Oak Media.

Pickles to Pittsburgh: The Sequel to Cloudy with a Chance of Meatballs. Judi Barrett. Read by Bonnie Kelly-Young et al. 11 vols. (Running Time: 15 mins.). (J). (gr. 1-6). 1999. bk. 25.95 (978-0-87499-538-1(8)) Live Oak Media.
A postcard from their grandfather's peculiar vacation spot sparks Kate's dream about the oddly familiar town of Chewandswallow.

Pickles to Pittsburgh: The Sequel to Cloudy with a Chance of Meatballs. Judi Barrett. Illus. by Ron Barrett. (Running Time: 15 mins.). (J). (gr. k-3). 1999. 9.95 (978-0-87499-540-4(X)) Live Oak Media.

Pickles to Pittsburgh: The Sequel to Cloudy with a Chance of Meatballs. Judi Barrett. Read by Bonnie Kelly-Young & George Guidall. 11 vols. (Running Time: 15 mins.). (J). 2005. pap. bk. 16.95 (978-0-87499-537-4(X)); pap. bk. 18.95 (978-1-59112-749-9(1)) Pub: Live Oak Media. Dist(s): AudioGO

Pickles to Pittsburgh & Cloudy with a Change of Meaballs. Judi Barrett. Illus. by Ron Barrett. 22 vols. (Running Time: 29 mins.). 1999. pap. bk. 30.95 (978-0-87499-819-1(0)); pap. bk. 34.95 (978-1-59112-842-7(0)) Live Oak Media.

Pickup. Nadine Gordimer. Narrated by Lisette Lecat. 8 CDs. (Running Time: 9 hrs.). audio compact disk 82.00 (978-1-4025-3287-0(3)) Recorded Bks.

Pickup. unabr. ed. Nadine Gordimer. Narrated by Lisette Lecat. 6 cass. (Running Time: 9 hrs.). 2002. 58.00 (978-1-84197-333-3(5)) Recorded Bks.
Part cross-cultural love affair, part glimpse into an unnamed Arab village in the twenty-first century (complete with TV, cell phones, and a marketplace filled with the world's neon plastic discards). It is also a condemnation of stereotyping, piety, and prejudice. Nadine Gordimer's prose is hypnotic. Her use of image repetition lends a dreamlike quality to this fable for our time.

Pickup: A Novel. unabr. ed. Nadine Gordimer. Narrated by Lisette Lecat. 6 cass. (Running Time: 9 hrs.). 2002. 34.95 (978-1-4025-2217-8(7), RG047) Recorded Bks.
Julie is from an affluent white family and is always searching for new ideas and adventures. When her car breaks down in a South African city she is immediately drawn to Abdu the mechanic who comes to her aid. He has left his home and family in the north to find work in the new South Africa. As their relationship develops into passionate love, they must both confront the prejudices of their past and the uncertainties of the future.

***Pickup Artist: The New & Improved Art of Seduction.** unabr. ed. Mystery. Narrated by Alan Sklar. (Running Time: 9 hrs. 30 mins.). 2010. 34.99 (978-1-4001-9414-8(8)); 16.99 (978-1-4001-8414-9(2)) Tantor Media.

Pickup Artist: The New & Improved Art of Seduction. unabr. ed. Mystery. (Running Time: 9 hrs. 30 mins. 0 sec.). ([illegible]). 2010. audio compact disk 34.99 (978-1-4001-1414-6(4)) Pub: Ta[illegible] Media. Dist(s): IngramPubServ

Pickup Artist: The New & Improved Art of Seduction. unabr. ed. Mystery. Narrated by Alan Sklar. (Running Time: 9 hrs. 30 mins. 0 sec.). (ENG.). 2010. 24.99 (978-1-4001-6414-1(1)); audio compact disk 69.99 (978-1-4001-4414-3(0)) Pub: Tantor Media. Dist(s): IngramPubServ

Pickwick Papaers (Parts 1 And 2) unabr. ed. Charles Dickens. Narrated by Flo Gibson. (Running Time: 32 hrs. 14 mins.). 2002. 61.95 (978-1-55685-840-6(X)) Audio Bk Con.

Pickwick Papers see Cambridge Treasury of English Prose: Dickens to Butler

Pickwick Papers see Works of Charles Dickens

Pickwick Papers. Charles Dickens. Read by Walter Zimmerman. 25 cass. (Running Time: 90 min. per cass.). 1987. 120.00 incl. albums. (C-176) Jimcin Record.
Dickens' first best-seller. Sam Weller & friends in & out of trouble in London.

Pickwick Papers. Charles Dickens. Read by Anton Lesser. 4 cass. (Running Time: 4 hrs. 45 mins.). (Works of Charles Dickens). 1998. 22.98 (978-962-634-666-2(3), NA416614, Naxos AudioBooks) Naxos.
Dickens' first best-selling novel traces the story of the immortal Mr. Samuel Pickwick & his travels on behalf of the Pickwick Club. A comic romance novel in the traditional Dickens' style.

Pickwick Papers. abr. ed. Charles Dickens. Read by Anton Lesser. 3 CDs. (Running Time: 4 hrs. 45 mins.). (Works of Charles Dickens). 1998. audio compact disk 28.98 (978-962-634-166-7(1), NA416612, Naxos AudioBooks) Naxos.

Pickwick Papers. abr. ed. Charles Dickens. Perf. by Paul Scofield. 2 cass. (Running Time: 3 hrs.). (Ultimate Classics Ser.). 2004. 18.00 (978-1-931056-65-6(X), N Millennium Audio) New Millenn Enter.
Abetted by Pickwick's faithful manservant, Sam Weller, the Pickwickians bumble through hilarious romantic misadventures & other twists of plot, encountering many delightfully Dickensian characters along the way.

Pickwick Papers. abr. ed. Charles Dickens. Read by Paul Scofield. 3 CDs. (Running Time: 3 hrs.). 2004. audio compact disk 24.95 (978-1-59007-581-4(1)) Pub: New Millenn Enter. Dist(s): PerseuPGW

***Pickwick Papers.** unabr. ed. Charles Dickens. Read by Simon Prebble. (Running Time: 30 hrs. 30 mins.). 2010. 44.95 (978-1-4417-2405-2(2)); 85.95 (978-1-4417-3273-6(X)); 85.95 (978-1-4417-2401-4(X)); audio compact disk 160.00 (978-1-4417-2402-1(8)) Blckstn Audio.

Pickwick Papers, Part II. unabr. ed. Charles Dickens. Narrated by Flo Gibson. 10 cass. (Running Time: 14 hrs. 30 mins.). (YA). 2003. 65.95 Audio Bk Con.
The comic novel includes letters and manuscripts about the Pickwick Club's activities and romances. The benevolent business man Pickwick and fellow members Sodgrass the poet, Tupman the lover, and Winkle the sportsman with loyal valet Samuel Weller, his father, Alfred Jingle, Sargent Buzfuz, and jilted Mrs. Bardell are a few of the characters or caricatures who made this book an immediate success.

Pickwick Papers, Pt. 1. unabr. ed. Charles Dickens. Narrated by Patrick Tull. 12 cass. (Running Time: 18 hrs.). 1988. 97.00 (978-1-55690-413-4(4), 88920E7) Recorded Bks.
The first day's journey; A field-day & bivouac; An old-fashioned card-party; The Eatanswill election; The action of Bardell against Pickwick.

Pickwick Papers, Pt. 2. unabr. ed. Charles Dickens. Narrated by Patrick Tull. 9 cass. (Running Time: 13 hrs.). 1988. 78.00 (978-1-55690-414-1(2), 88887E7) Recorded Bks.
How Mr. Pickwick is confined to Fleet Prison; An important conference between Pickwick & Samuel Weller; How the Pickwick Club is finally dissolved & everything is resolved to the satisfaction of everybody.

Pickwick Papers, Pt. C. collector's unabr. ed. Charles Dickens. Read by Walter Zimmerman. 9 cass. (Running Time: 13 hrs. 30 min.). 1987. 72.00 (978-0-7366-3936-1(5), 9176-C) Books on Tape.
Sam Weller & friends in & out of trouble in London.

Pickwick Papers, Pt. A. unabr. collector's ed. Charles Dickens. Read by Walter Zimmerman. 8 cass. (Running Time: 12 hrs.). 1987. 64.00 (978-0-7366-3934-7(9), 9176-A) Books on Tape.
Dickens' first best-seller. Sam Weller & friends in & out of trouble in London.

Pickwick Papers, Pt. B. collector's unabr. ed. Charles Dickens. Read by Walter Zimmerman. 8 cass. (Running Time: 12 hrs.). 1987. 64.00 (978-0-7366-3935-4(7), 9176 B) Books on Tape.
Sam Weller & friends in & out of trouble in London.

Pickwick Papers: The Posthumous Papers of the Pickwick Club. Charles Dickens. Narrated by Walter Zimmerman. (Running Time: 32 hrs.). 1987. 29.95 (978-1-59912-872-6(1)) Iofy Corp.

Pickwick Papers (Part 1), Part I. unabr. ed. Charles Dickens. Narrated by Flo Gibson. 12 cass. (Running Time: 18 hrs.). 2003. 39.95 (978-1-55685-705-8(5)) Audio Bk Con.
This comic novel includes letters and manuscripts about the Pickwick Club's activities and romances. The benevolent business man Pickwick and fellow members Sodgrass the poet, Tupman the lover, and Winkle the sportsman with loyal valet Samuel Weller, his father, Alfred Jingle, Sargent Buzfuz, and jilted Mrs. Bardell are a few of the characters or caricatures who made this book an immediate success.

Pickwick Papers (Part 2), Vol. 2. unabr. ed. Charles Dickens. Narrated by Flo Gibson. (Running Time: 14 hrs. 21 mins.). 2002. 29.95 (978-1-55685-838-3(8)) Audio Bk Con.

Picnic. 2004. bk. 24.95 (978-0-7882-0583-5(8)); pap. bk. 14.95 (978-0-7882-0651-1(6)); 8.95 (978-0-89719-953-7(7)); cass. & flmstrp 30.00 (978-0-89719-565-2(5)) Weston Woods.

Picnic. Based on a book by Emily Arnold McCully. Directed By Jim Bresnahan. 1 cass. (Running Time: 4 min.). (Story Hour Collection). (J). (ps-3). 195.00 (PMP306) Weston Woods.

Picnics: Picnic Recipes from Summer Music Festivals, Classic Ragtime Music. Sharon O'Connor. (Sharon O'Connor's Menus & Music Ser.). 1994. bk. 24.95 (978-1-883914-08-0(6)) Menus & Music.

Picnics & BBQ Deck & Disc. 2002. pap. bk. 14.95 (978-1-931918-06-0(6)) Pub: Compass Labs. Dist(s): Andrews McMeel

Picolo-Ecolo. Audio. 1 cass. (Running Time: 90 mins.).Tr. of Ecological Picolo. (FRE.). 1998. cass. & audio compact disk 9.95 (978-2-921997-09-6(6)) Penton Overseas.
Recorded by well-know actors or speakers. Includes compact plastic case & booklet with text in French.

Picture Book about George Washington. 1 cass. (J). (gr. k-3). 15.95 (VX-81C) Kimbo Educ.
Our first president & the America of his time are both brought to life in this picture biography of George Washington.

Picture Book Biography Series. bk. Live Oak Media.

Picture Book Biography Series: Remarkable Women. unabr. ed. David A. Adler. Read by Randye Kaye & Charles Turner. Illus. by Robert Casilla. 33 vols. (Running Time: 35 mins.). (J). (gr. 1-6). 1999. pap. bk. 45.95 (978-0-87499-574-9(4)) Live Oak Media.
Includes: "A Picture Book of Anne Frank," "A Picture Book of Eleanor Roosevelt" & "A Picture Book of Rosa Parks.".

Picture Book of Abraham Lincoln. David A. Adler. 1 cass. (Running Time: 35 min.). (J). (gr. k-3). 2001. pap. bk. 15.95 (VX-57C) Kimbo Educ.
Capture all the facts of the life, times & importance of our 16th President. Read along book.

Picture Book of Abraham Lincoln. David A. Adler. Illus. by John Wallner. 14 vols. (Running Time: 9 mins.). 1990. pap. bk. 39.95 (978-1-59112-779-6(3)); 9.95 (978-1-59112-158-9(2)) Live Oak Media.

Picture Book of Abraham Lincoln. David A. Adler. Illus. by John Wallner. (Running Time: 9 mins.). (J). (gr. k-3). 1990. audio compact disk 12.95 (978-1-59112-776-5(9)) Live Oak Media.

Picture Book of Abraham Lincoln. unabr. ed. David A. Adler. Read by Melinda Herring. Illus. by John Wallner. Interview with John Wallner. Illus. by Alexandra Wallner. Interview with Alexandra Wallner. 11 vols. (Running Time: 9 mins.). (Picture Book Biography Ser.). (J). (gr. 1-3). 1990. bk. 25.95 (978-0-87499-159-8(5)); pap. bk. 16.95 (978-0-87499-158-1(7)); pap. bk. & tchr. ed. 37.95 Reading Chest. (978-0-87499-160-4(9)) Live Oak Media.
The life, times, & importance of the sixteenth president of the United States are presented in a simple, straightforward text accompanied by clear, colorful illustrations that capture the flavor of the 1800's.

Picture Book of Anne Frank. David A. Adler. Illus. by Karen Ritz. 14 vols. (Running Time: 9 mins.). 1995. pap. bk. 39.95 (978-1-59112-783-3(1)); 9.95 (978-1-59112-101-5(9)); audio compact disk 12.95 (978-1-59112-780-2(7)) Live Oak Media.

Picture Book of Anne Frank. David A. Adler. Read by Randye Kaye. Illus. by Karen Ritz. 14 vols. (Running Time: 9 mins.). (Picture Book Biography Ser.). (J). 1995. pap. bk. & tchr. ed. 37.95 Reading Chest. (978-0-87499-348-6(2)) Live Oak Media.
The short, tragic life of a young girl caught up in the hatred that was Germany in the 1930's & 1940's is detailed for the young reader. Anne's innocence & courage, made poignantly evident in her now famous diary, are seen to transcend both her death & the evil that brought it about.

Picture Book of Anne Frank. unabr. ed. David A. Adler. Read by Randye Kaye. Illus. by Karen Ritz. 11 vols. (Running Time: 9 mins.). (Picture Book Biography Ser.). (J). (gr. 1-6). 1995. bk. 25.95 (978-0-87499-347-9(4)); pap. bk. 16.95 (978-0-87499-346-2(6)) Pub: Live Oak Media. Dist(s): AudioGO

Picture Book of Benjamin Franklin. David A. Adler. Narrated by Patrick Collins. 1 CD. (Running Time: 11 mins.). (J). (gr. k-3). 2008. pap. bk. 18.95 (978-1-4301-0339-4(6)); pap. bk. 39.95 (978-1-4301-0341-7(8)) Live Oak Media.

Picture Book of Benjamin Franklin. David A. Adler. Read by Patrick Collins. Illus. by John Wallner & Alexandra Wallner. 1 cass. (Running Time: 11 mins.). (Picture Book Biography Ser.). (J). (gr. k-3). 2008. bk. 25.95 (978-1-4301-0337-0(X)); bk. 28.95 (978-1-4301-0340-0(X)); pap. bk. 16.95 (978-1-4301-0336-3(1)) Live Oak Media.

Picture Book of Benjamin Franklin, Set. David A. Adler. Read by Patrick Collins. Illus. by John Wallner & Alexandra Wallner. 1 cass. (Running Time: 11 mins.). (Picture Book Biography Ser.). (J). (gr. k-3). 2008. pap. bk. 37.95 (978-1-4301-0338-7(8)) Live Oak Media.

Picture Book of Christopher Columbus see Libro Ilustrado Sobre Cristobal Colon

Picture Book of Christopher Columbus. David A. Adler. Illus. by John Wallner. 14 vols. (Running Time: 12 mins.). 1992. pap. bk. 39.95 (978-1-59112-759-8(9)); 9.95 (978-1-59112-156-5(6)) Live Oak Media.

Picture Book of Christopher Columbus. David A. Adler. Illus. by John Wallner. (Running Time: 12 mins.). (J). (gr. k-3). 1992. audio compact disk 12.95 (978-1-59112-756-7(4)) Live Oak Media.

Picture Book of Christopher Columbus. unabr. ed. David A. Adler. Read by Linda Terheyden. Illus. by John Wallner & Alexandra Wallner. 11 vols. (Running Time: 12 mins.). (Picture Book Biography Ser.). (J). (gr. k-3). 1992. pap. bk. 16.95 (978-0-87499-262-5(1)) AudioGO.
An appreciation of the life, times, & accomplishments of Christopher Columbus.

Picture Book of Christopher Columbus. unabr. ed. David A. Adler. Read by Linda Terheyden. Illus. by John Wallner & Alexandra Wallner. 11 vols. (Running Time: 12 mins.). (Picture Book Biography Ser.). (J). (gr. k-3). 1992. bk. 25.95 (978-0-87499-263-2(X)); pap. bk. & tchr. ed. 37.95 Reading Chest. (978-0-87499-264-9(8)) Live Oak Media.

Picture Book of Christopher Columbus. unabr. ed. David A. Adler. 1 cass. (Running Time: 12 min.). (J). (gr. 2-4). 1992. 9.95 Live Oak Media.

Picture Book of Eleanor Roosevelt. David A. Adler. Illus. by Robert Casilla. 14 vols. (Running Time: 9 mins.). 1997. pap. bk. 39.95 (978-1-59112-755-0(6)) Live Oak Media.

Picture Book of Eleanor Roosevelt. David A. Adler. Read by Randye Kaye. Illus. by Robert Casilla. 14 vols. (Running Time: 9 mins.). (Picture Book Biography Ser.). (gr. 1-6). 1997. pap. bk. & tchr. ed. 37.95 Reading Chest. (978-0-87499-401-8(2)) Live Oak Media.
Eleanor Roosevelt went from being a sad, shy child to becoming an adult who reached out to people everywhere. She was an important, beloved figure of her time & is remembered as one of America's greatest women.

Picture Book of Eleanor Roosevelt. David A. Adler. Illus. by Robert Casilla. (Running Time: 9 mins.). (J). (gr. k-3). 1997. audio compact disk 12.95 (978-1-59112-936-3(2)) Live Oak Media.

Picture Book of Eleanor Roosevelt. David A. Adler. Illus. by Robert Casilla. (Running Time: 9 mins.). (J). (gr. k-3). 1997. 9.95 (978-1-59112-105-3(1)) Live Oak Media.

Picture Book of Eleanor Roosevelt. unabr. ed. David A. Adler. Read by Randye Kaye. Illus. by Robert Casilla. 1 cass. (Running Time: 9 mins.). (Picture Book Biography Ser.). (J). (gr. 1-6). 1997. bk. 25.95 (978-0-87499-400-1(4)); pap. bk. 16.95 (978-0-87499-399-8(7)) Pub: Live Oak Media. Dist(s): AudioGO

Picture Book of Frederick Douglas. David A. Adler. Read by Charles Turner. Illus. by Samuel Byrd. (J). 2005. audio compact disk 12.95 (978-1-59519-375-9(8)) Live Oak Media.

Picture Book of Frederick Douglass. David A. Adler. Read by Charles Turner. Illus. by Samuel Byrd. 1 cass. (Running Time: 18 mins.). (Picture Book Readalongs Ser.). (J). (ps-3). 2005. pap. bk. 16.95 (978-1-59519-372-8(3)) Pub: Live Oak Media. Dist(s): AudioGO

Picture Book of Frederick Douglass. unabr. ed. David A. Adler. Read by Charles Turner. Illus. by Samuel Byrd. 1 CD. (Running Time: 18 mins.). (Picture Book Readalongs Ser.). (J). (gr. k-4). 2005. bk. 25.95 (978-1-59519-373-5(1)); pap. bk. 28.95 (978-1-59519-377-3(4)) Live Oak Media.
Frederick Douglass, born into slavery in 1818, escaped to freedom in 1838 and became a great leader in the abolitionist movement. His struggles and determination, as well as his accomplishments as a writer, orator and important figure of the nineteenth century are outlined in this beginning biography for young children.

Picture Book of Frederick Douglass, Set. unabr. ed. David A. Adler. Read by Charles Turner. Illus. by Samuel Byrd. 1 cass. (Running Time: 18 mins.). (Picture Book Readalongs Ser.). (J). (gr. k-4). 2005. pap. bk. 37.95 (978-1-59519-374-2(X)); pap. bk. 39.95 (978-1-59519-378-0(2)) Live Oak Media.

Picture Book of George Washington. 9.95 (978-1-59112-160-2(4)) Live Oak Media.

Picture Book of George Washington. David A. Adler. Interview with John Wallner & Alexandra Wallner. 1 readalong cass. (Running Time: 7 min.). (J). (ps-4). 1990. 9.95 Live Oak Media.
The life, times, & importance of the first president of the United States are introduced through simple, straightforward text complemented by illustrations that capture the flavor of the period.

Picture Book of George Washington. David A. Adler. Illus. by John Wallner. 14 vols. (Running Time: 7 mins.). 1990. pap. bk. 39.95 (978-1-59112-767-3(X)) Live Oak Media.

Picture Book of George Washington. David A. Adler. Read by Rick Adamson. Illus. by John Wallner. Interview with John Wallner. Illus. by Alexandra Wallner. Interview with Alexandra Wallner. 14 vols. (Running Time: 7 mins.). (Picture Book Biography Ser.). (J). (gr. 1-3). 1990. pap. bk. & tchr. ed. 37.95 Reading Chest. (978-0-87499-163-5(3)) Live Oak Media.

Picture Book of George Washington. David A. Adler. Illus. by John Wallner. (Running Time: 7 mins.). (J). (gr. k-3). 1990. 9.95 (978-1-59112-106-0(X)); audio compact disk 12.95 (978-1-59112-764-2(5)) Live Oak Media.

Picture Book of George Washington. unabr. ed. David A. Adler. Read by Rick Adamson. Illus. by John Wallner. Interview with John Wallner. Illus. by Alexandra Wallner. Interview with Alexandra Wallner. 11 vols. (Running Time: 7 mins.). (Picture Book Biography Ser.). (J). (gr. 1-3). 1990. bk. 25.95 (978-0-87499-162-8(5)); pap. bk. 16.95 (978-0-87499-161-1(7)) Pub: Live Oak Media. Dist(s): AudioGO

Picture Book of George Washington Carver. David A. Adler. 1 cass. (Running Time: 16 mins.). (J). (ps-2). 2008. pap. bk. 16.95 (978-1-4301-0344-8(2)); pap. bk. 18.95 (978-1-4301-0347-9(7)); pap. bk. 39.95 (978-1-4301-0349-3(3)) Live Oak Media.

Picture Book of George Washington Carver. David A. Adler. Read by Nathan Hinton. Illus. by Dan Brown. 1 cass. (Running Time: 16 mins.). (Picture Book Biography Ser.). (J). (ps-2). 2008. bk. 25.95 (978-1-4301-0345-5(0)); bk. 28.95 (978-1-4301-0348-6(5)) Live Oak Media.

Picture Book of George Washington Carver. David A. Adler. Illus. by Dan Brown. Narrated by Nathan Hinton. (J). 2008. audio compact disk 12.95 (978-1-4301-0343-1(4)) Live Oak Media.

Picture Book of George Washington Carver, Set. David A. Adler. 1 cass. (Running Time: 16 mins.). (J). (ps-2). 2008. pap. bk. 37.95 (978-1-4301-0346-2(9)) Live Oak Media.

Picture Book of Harriet Tubman. David A. Adler. Illus. by Samuel Byrd. Narrated by Gail Nelson. (J). (gr. k-4). 2005. 9.95 (978-1-59519-379-7(0)) Live Oak Media.

Picture Book of Harriet Tubman. David A. Adler. Read by Charles Turner. Illus. by Samuel Byrd. (J). (gr. k-4). 2005. audio compact disk 12.95 (978-1-59519-383-4(9)) Live Oak Media.

Picture Book of Harriet Tubman. unabr. ed. David A. Adler. Read by Gail Nelson. Illus. by Samuel Byrd. 1 CD. (Running Time: 15 mins.). (Picture Book Readalong Ser.). (J). (gr. k-4). 2005. bk. 28.95 (978-1-59519-385-8(5)) Live Oak Media.

Picture Book of Harriet Tubman. unabr. ed. David A. Adler. Read by Gail Nelson. Illus. by Samuel Byrd. 1 cass. (Running Time: 15 mins.). (Picture Book Readalong Ser.). (J). (gr. k-4). 2005. bk. 25.95 (978-1-59519-381-0(2)) Live Oak Media.

Picture Book of Harriet Tubman, Set. David A. Adler. Read by Gail Nelson. Illus. by Samuel Byrd. 1 cass. (Running Time: 15 mins.). (Picture Book Readalong Ser.). (J). (gr. k-4). 2005. pap. bk. 37.95 (978-1-59519-382-7(0)) Live Oak Media.

Picture Book of Harriet Tubman, Set. unabr. ed. David A. Adler. Read by Gail Nelson. Illus. by Samuel Byrd. 1 CD. (Running Time: 15 mins.). (Picture Book Readalong Ser.). (J). (gr. k-4). 2005. pap. bk. 39.95 (978-1-59519-386-5(3)) Live Oak Media.

Picture Book of King. 9.95 (978-1-59112-157-2(4)) Live Oak Media.

Picture Book of Martin Luther King, Jr. see Libro Ilustrado Sobre Martin Luther King, Hijo

Picture Book of Martin Luther King, Jr. David A. Adler. Illus. by Robert Casilla. 14 vols. (Running Time: 10 mins.). 1990. pap. bk. 39.95 (978-1-59112-775-8(0)) Live Oak Media.

Picture Book of Martin Luther King, Jr. David A. Adler. Illus. by Robert Casilla. (Running Time: 10 mins.). (J). (gr. k-3). 1990. 9.95 (978-1-59112-102-2(7)); audio compact disk 12.95 (978-1-59112-772-7(6)) Live Oak Media.

Picture Book of Martin Luther King, Jr. unabr. ed. David A. Adler. Read by Charles Turner. Illus. by Robert Casilla. 14 vols. (Running Time: 10 mins.). (Picture Book Biography Ser.). (J). (gr. k-3). 1998. pap. bk. & tchr. ed. 37.95 Reading Chest. (978-0-87499-167-3(6)) Live Oak Media.
An appreciation of the life, times, & accomplishments of Dr. King.

Picture Book of Martin Luther King, Jr., unabr. ed. David A. Adler. Tr. by Teresa Mlawer. Illus. by Robert Casilla. 22 vols. (Running Time: 20 mins.). (J). 1999. pap. bk. 33.95 (978-0-87499-569-5(8)) Live Oak Media.

Picture Book of Martin Luther King, Jr. unabr. rev. ed. David A. Adler. Read by Charles Turner. Illus. by Robert Casilla. 11 vols. (Running Time: 10 mins.). (Picture Book Biography Ser.). (J). (gr. k-3). 1998. bk. 25.95 (978-0-87499-166-6(8)); pap. bk. 16.95 (978-0-87499-165-9(X)) Pub: Live Oak Media. Dist(s): AudioGO

Picture Book of Rosa Parks. 9.95 (978-1-59112-159-6(0)) Live Oak Media.

Picture Book of Rosa Parks. David A. Adler. (J). (gr. k-3). 2001. pap. bk. 15.95 (VX-59C) Kimbo Educ.
Travel back to 1955 & learn how Rosa Parks protests & helps to mark the beginning of the civil rights movement in America. Includes read along book.

Picture Book of Rosa Parks. David A. Adler. Illus. by Robert Casilla. (Running Time: 17 mins.). (J). (gr. k-3). 1997. 9.95 (978-1-59112-104-6(3)); audio compact disk 12.95 (978-1-59112-760-4(2)) Live Oak Media.

Picture Book of Rosa Parks. unabr. ed. David A. Adler. Read by Charles Turner. Illus. by Robert Casilla. 14 vols. (Running Time: 17 mins.). (Picture Book Biography Ser.). (gr. 1-6). 1997. pap. bk. & tchr. ed. 37.95 Reading Chest. (978-0-87499-398-1(9)) Live Oak Media.
In 1895, Rosa Parks was riding home from work by bus in Montgomery Alabama. The driver asked her to give up her seat to a white passenger. When she refused, Rosa was arrested. In protest, blacks throughout the city boycotted the city's buses. For many people this marked the beginning of the civil rights movement in America.

Picture Book of Rosa Parks. unabr. ed. David A. Adler. Read by Charles Turner. Illus. by Robert Casilla. 11 vols. (Running Time: 17 mins.). (Picture Book Biography Ser.). (J). (gr. 1-6). 1997. bk. 25.95 (978-0-87499-397-4(0)); pap. bk. & tchr. ed. 16.95 (978-0-87499-396-7(2)) Pub: Live Oak Media. Dist(s): AudioGO

Picture Book of Thomas Jefferson. David A. Adler. Illus. by John Wallner. 11 vols. (Running Time: 11 mins.). 1999. bk. 28.95 (978-1-59112-770-3(X)); pap. bk. 39.95 (978-1-59112-771-0(8)) Live Oak Media.

Picture Book of Thomas Jefferson. David A. Adler. Illus. by John Wallner. (Running Time: 11 mins.). (J). (gr. k-3). 2000. 9.95 (978-0-87499-650-0(3)); audio compact disk 12.95 (978-1-59112-768-0(8)) Live Oak Media.

Picture Book of Thomas Jefferson. unabr. ed. David A. Adler. Illus. by John Wallner & Alexandra Wallner. 11 vols. (Running Time: 11 mins.). (J). (gr. 1-6). 1999. pap. bk. 16.95 (978-0-87499-651-7(1)); pap. bk. & tchr. ed. 37.95 Reading Chest. (978-0-87499-653-1(8)) Live Oak Media.
An appealing package with simple language & detailed drawings conveys information about the life & accomplishments of Thomas Jefferson.

Picture Book of Thomas Jefferson. unabr. ed. David A. Adler. Illus. by John Wallner & Alexandra Wallner. 11 vols. (Running Time: 11 mins.). (J). (gr. 1-6). 1999. bk. 25.95 (978-0-87499-652-4(X)) Live Oak Media.

Picture Descriptions see Descriptions de Dessins: French Picture Descriptions

Picture Dictionary. abr. ed. Norma Shapiro & Jayme Adelson-Goldstein. (Oxford Picture Dictionary Program Ser.). 1998. 54.95 (978-0-19-470061-0(5)) OUP.

Picture for Harold's Room. 2004. bk. 24.95 (978-0-7882-0559-0(5)) Weston Woods.

Picture for Harold's Room. (J). 2004. pap. bk. 14.95 (978-0-7882-0624-5(9)); 8.95 (978-1-56008-638-3(6)); cass. & flmstrp 30.00 (978-0-89719-527-0(2)) Weston Woods.

Picture for Harold's Room. Crockett Johnson. 1 cass. (Running Time: 6 min.). (J). pap. bk. 12.95 Weston Woods.
With his purple crayon, Harold draws a picture for his room & then becomes part of it.

Picture for Harold's Room. Crockett Johnson. 1 cass. (Running Time: 6 min.). (J). (ps-3). pap. bk. 12.95 Weston Woods.
Harold draws himself a castle in an enchanted garden & fills it with a king, a giant, a fairy & himself.

Picture for Harold's Room, A; Clocks & More Clocks; Leopold the See-Through Crumbpicker; Surprize Party. 2004. (978-0-89719-832-5(8)); cass. & flmstrp (978-0-89719-740-3(2)) Weston Woods.

Picture Has a Special Look. (J). 2004. 8.95 (978-1-56008-633-8(5)); cass. & flmstrp 30.00 (978-1-56008-745-8(5)) Weston Woods.

Picture Is Not an Argument II. Leonard Peikoff. 1 cass. (Philosophy: Who Needs It? Ser.). 1998. 12.95 (LPXXC61) Second Renaissance.

Picture Lessons Cards & Albums Fall 2002. 2002. 2.29 (978-1-59185-009-0(6)) CharismaLife Pub.

Picture of a Nativity see Poetry of Geoffrey

Picture of Dorian Gray. 2 cass. (Read-along Ser.). bk. 34.95 Set, incl. learner's guide & exercises. (S23936) J Norton Pubs.

***Picture of Dorian Gray.** Oscar Wilde. Narrated by Edward Petherbridge. (Running Time: 9 hrs. 30 mins. 0 sec.). (Cover to Cover Ser.). (ENG.). 2010. audio compact disk 29.95 (978-1-60283-878-9(X)) Pub: AudioGO. Dist(s): Perseus Dist

Picture of Dorian Gray. Oscar Wilde. 2007. 16.95 (978-1-60112-017-5(6)) Babblebooks.

Picture of Dorian Gray. Oscar Wilde. Read by Rupert Graves. 2002. pap. bk. (978-1-901768-72-5(4)) CSA Telltapes GBR.

Picture of Dorian Gray. Oscar Wilde. Read by Rupert Graves. 2 cass. (Running Time: 3 hrs.). 12.00 Set. (978-1-878427-43-4(1), XC425) Cimino Pub Grp.
Combines sparkling wit, social satire & indulgently luxurious description with heavy intensity. It is Wilde's only published novel & like many first novels contains elements of autobiography. As read by Rupert Graves, a versatile young actor, who takes on each character with zest giving them identities of their own thus bringing a brilliant new interpretation to this classic story.

Picture of Dorian Gray. Oscar Wilde. 2 cass. (Running Time: 3 hrs.). 2001. 17.99 (978-0-00-105460-8(0)) Pub: HarpC GBR. Dist(s): Trafalgar
Oscar Wilde's tale of the beautiful young man who 'sold himself to the devil for a pretty face' follows the fortunes of Dorian Gray when his prayer for eternal youth as he contemplates his newly finished portrait is answered.

Picture of Dorian Gray. Oscar Wilde. Read by Michael Sheen. 3 cass. (Running Time: 3 hrs. 15 mins.). 1995. 17.98 (978-962-634-574-0(8), NA307414, Naxos AudioBooks) Naxos.

Picture of Dorian Gray. Oscar Wilde. Narrated by Steven Crossley. 8 CDs. (Running Time: 9 hrs.). audio compact disk 78.00 (978-1-4025-2100-3(6)) Recorded Bks.

Picture of Dorian Gray. abr. ed. Oscar Wilde. Read by Marvin Miller. 2 cass. 10.95 (978-0-89926-214-7(7)) Audio Bk.
A man sells his soul for eternal youth.

Picture of Dorian Gray. abr. ed. Oscar Wilde. (Classics Collection). 2001. 7.95 (978-1-57815-239-1(9), Media Bks Audio) Media Bks NJ.

Picture of Dorian Gray. abr. ed. Oscar Wilde. Read by Michael Sheen. 3 CDs. (Running Time: 3 hrs.15 mins.). (J). (gr. 9-12). 1995. audio compact disk 22.98 (978-962-634-074-5(6), NA307412) Naxos.

Picture of Dorian Gray. abr. ed. Oscar Wilde. Read by Stephen Fry. 4 cass. (Running Time: 6 hrs.). (Ultimate Classics Ser.). 2004. 25.00 (978-1-931056-71-7(4), N Millennium Audio) New Millenn Enter.
The story of a man who sells his soul to the devil in exchange for eternal youth. As Basil Hallward, an aspiring artist, puts a few touches on a portrait of his handsome young friend Dorian Gray, Gray wishes that the portrait might grow old while he remains forever young. While Dorian Gray spends his life pursuing fresh experiences and new sensations, his looks do not change. However, the portrait, secretly hidden in the attic of his residence and with which he has grown increasingly obsessed, does. More and more, as Dorian struggles to hide his true identity, the portrait reveals his progressive pathway to dissolution.

Picture of Dorian Gray. abr. adpt. ed. Oscar Wilde. (Bring the Classics to Life: Level 4 Ser.). (ENG.). 2008. audio compact disk 12.95 (978-1-55576-590-3(4)) EDCON Pubng.

Picture of Dorian Gray. unabr. ed. Oscar Wilde. Read by Marvin Miller. 7 cass. 41.65 (B-123) Audio Bk.
This novel, in a wide sense, covers the growth, education & development of an exceptional youth. It is the study of a soul, or more particularly of a young man who sells his soul for eternal youth. This was Wilde's only novel & is a classic of English literature.

Picture of Dorian Gray. unabr. ed. Oscar Wilde. Read by Simon Vance. (Running Time: 27000 sec.). (Classic Collection (Blackstone Audio) Ser.). 2009. audio compact disk 19.95 (978-1-4332-0916-1(0)) Blckstn Audio.

Picture of Dorian Gray. unabr. ed. Oscar Wilde. Read by Simon Vance. (Running Time: 27000 sec.). (Classic Collection (Blackstone Audio) Ser.). 2008. 24.95 (978-1-4332-0913-0(6)); audio compact disk 19.95 (978-1-4332-0917-8(9)); audio compact disk & audio compact disk 27.00 (978-1-4332-0914-7(4)) Blckstn Audio.

Picture of Dorian Gray. unabr. ed. Oscar Wilde. Read by Simon Vance. (Running Time: 27000 sec.). (Classic Collection (Blackstone Audio) Ser.). 2008. 19.95 (978-1-4332-0915-4(2)) Blckstn Audio.

Picture of Dorian Gray. unabr. ed. Oscar Wilde. Read by Tim Behrens. 6 cass. (Running Time: 8 hrs. 30 min.). 1989. 39.95 (978-1-55686-254-0(7), 254) Books in Motion.
As time goes by, a portrait ages horribly while the man who is its subject appears unravaged by age.

Picture of Dorian Gray. unabr. ed. Oscar Wilde. Read by Michael Page. (Running Time: 7 hrs.). 2005. 39.25 (978-1-59737-008-0(8), 9781597370080, BADLE); 24.95 (978-1-59737-007-3(X), 9781597370073, BAD); audio compact disk 39.25 (978-1-59737-006-6(1), 9781597370066, Brinc Audio MP3 Lib); audio compact disk 24.95 (978-1-59737-005-9(3), 9781597370059, Brilliance MP3); audio compact disk 87.25 (978-1-59737-004-2(5), 9781597370042, BriAudCD Unabrid); audio compact disk 32.95 (978-1-59737-003-5(7), 9781597370035, Bril Audio CD Unabri) Brilliance Audio.

***Picture of Dorian Gray.** unabr. ed. Oscar Wilde. Read by Don Hagen. (Running Time: 9 hrs.). (ENG.). 2010. 9.98 (978-1-59659-518-7(3), GildAudio) Pub: Gildan Media. Dist(s): HachBkGrp

Picture of Dorian Gray, unabr. ed. Oscar Wilde. Narrated by Steven Crossley. 6 cass. (Running Time: 9 hrs.). 1997. 51.00 (978-0-7887-0575-5(X), 94753E7) Recorded Bks.
The classic story of a young man who sells his soul in exchange for eternal beauty & youth.

Picture of Dorian Gray. unabr. ed. Oscar Wilde. Narrated by Simon Prebble. (Running Time: 8 hrs. 0 mins. 0 sec.). (Tantor Unabridged Classics Ser.). (ENG.). 2008. 19.99 (978-1-4001-5948-2(2)); audio compact disk 27.99 (978-1-4001-0948-7(5)); audio compact disk 55.99 (978-1-4001-3948-4(1)) Pub: Tantor Media. Dist(s): IngramPubServ

Picture of Dorian Gray. unabr. collector's ed. Oscar Wilde. Read by Dan Lazar. 8 cass. (Running Time: 8 hrs.). 1980. 48.00 (978-0-7366-0418-5(9), 1390) Books on Tape.

Picture of Dorian Gray, Set. unabr. ed. Oscar Wilde. Read by Flo Gibson. 5 cass. (Running Time: 7 hrs. 30 min.). 1992. 20.95 (978-1-55685-253-4(3)) Audio Bk Con.
In this brilliant allegorical novel, the vain Dorian Gray's prayer is answered when he retains his handsome youthful appearance while his portrait grows old & shows the ravages of corruption. There are horrifying consequences.

Picture of Dorian Gray: A BBC Full-Cast Radio Drama. Oscar Wilde. Narrated by Full Cast. (Running Time: 2 hrs. 0 mins. 0 sec.). (BBC Radio Ser.). (ENG.). 2010. audio compact disk 14.95 (978-1-60283-873-4(9)) Pub: AudioGO. Dist(s): Perseus Dist

***Picture of Dorian Gray: Bring the Classics to Life.** adpt. ed. Oscar Wilde. (Bring the Classics to Life Ser.). 2008. pap. bk. 21.95 (978-1-55576-619-1(6)) EDCON Pubng.

Picture of Dorian Gray & Camile. Oscar Wilde & Alexandre Dumas. Contrib. by Lucio Agostini. 2 cass. (Running Time: 2 hrs.). (Stage Ser.). 2004. 18.99 (978-1-894003-18-6(7)) Pub: Scenario Prods CAN. Dist(s): PerseuPGW

Picture of the Year. Clive Egleton. Read by Christopher Kay. 8 CDs. (Sound Ser.). (J). 2002. audio compact disk 79.95 (978-1-84283-236-3(0)) Pub: ISIS Lrg Prnt GBR. Dist(s): Ulverscroft US

Picture Perfect. abr. ed. Jodi Picoult. Read by multivoice. (Running Time: 4 hrs.). 2009. audio compact disk 9.99 (978-1-4418-0139-5(1), 9781441801395, BCD Value Price) Brilliance Audio.

Picture Perfect. unabr. ed. Jodi Picoult. (Running Time: 14 hrs.). 2009. 24.99 (978-1-4233-9066-4(0), 9781423390664, Brilliance MP3) Brilliance Audio.

Picture Perfect. unabr. ed. Jodi Picoult. Read by multivoice. (Running Time: 14 hrs.). 2009. 39.97 (978-1-4233-9069-5(5), 9781423390695, BADLE) Brilliance Audio.

Picture Perfect. unabr. ed. Jodi Picoult. Read by Bruce Reizen & Sandra Burr. (Running Time: 14 hrs.). 2009. 24.99 (978-1-4233-9068-8(7), 9781423390688, BAD); audio compact disk 24.99 (978-1-4418-0137-1(5), 9781441801371, Bril Audio CD Unabri) Brilliance Audio.

Picture Perfect. unabr. ed. Jodi Picoult. Read by Multivoice Production Staff et al. (Running Time: 14 hrs.). 2009. 39.97 (978-1-4233-9067-1(9), 9781423390671, Brinc Audio MP3 Lib) Brilliance Audio.

Picture Perfect. unabr. ed. Jodi Picoult & Bruce Reizen. Read by Multivoice Production Staff & Sandra Burr. (Running Time: 14 hrs.). 2009. audio compact disk 87.97 (978-1-4418-0138-8(3), 9781441801388, BriAudCD Unabrid) Brilliance Audio.

Picture Pyramids. Art Freifeld. Illus. by Paul Leung. 1988. 9.95 (978-0-916177-36-2(X)) Am Eng Pubns.

Picture This. Perf. by Jim Brickman. 1 cass. 9.98; audio compact disk 16.98 Lifedance.
Brickman's romantic style of music is delicate & simple, yet it stirs the soul gently & deeply. The one vocal number, "Valentine," is worthy of attention. Demo CD or cassette available.

Picture This: Guided Imagery for Circle Time. Murray White. 2004. 24.95 (978-1-873942-62-8(1)) Pub: P Chapman GBR. Dist(s): SAGE

Picture This! Learning English Through Pictures, 2. Tim Harris & Allan Rowe. 2006. (978-0-13-170342-1(0)) Longman.

Picture This for Families: Guided Imagery to Build Self-Esteem for All the Family. Murray White. Illus. by Philippa Drakeford. 2004. 14.95 (978-1-904315-38-4(0)) Pub: P Chapman GBR. Dist(s): SAGE

Picture to Remember, Level 2. Sarah Scott-Malden. Contrib. by Philip Prowse. (Running Time: 1 hr. 18 mins.). (Cambridge English Readers Ser.). (ENG., 2000. 9.45 (978-0-521-66476-9(4)) Cambridge U Pr.

Pictures & Patterns. Prod. by Zobeida Perez. (J). 1994. 17.00 (978-0-89898-745-4(8), BMR05066, Warner Bro) Alfred Pub.

Pictures at a Revolution: Five Movies & the Birth of the New Hollywood. Mark Harris. Read by Lloyd James. (Playaway Adult Nonfiction Ser.). 2008. 69.99 (978-1-60640-711-0(2)) Find a World.

Pictures at a Revolution: Five Movies & the Birth of the New Hollywood. unabr. ed. Mark Harris. Read by Lloyd James. 14 CDs. (Running Time: 17 hrs. 30 mins. 0 sec.). (ENG.). 2008. audio compact disk 39.99 (978-1-4001-0625-7(7)); audio compact disk 79.99 (978-1-4001-3625-4(3)); audio compact disk 29.99 (978-1-4001-5625-2(4)) Pub: Tantor Media. Dist(s): IngramPubServ

Pictures Don't Lie see X Minus One

Pictures from the Fire. unabr. ed. Gaye Hicilmaz. Read by Richard Aspel. 8 CDs. (Running Time: 33600 sec.). (YA). (gr. 7-13). 2005. audio compact disk 87.95 (978-1-74093-561-6(6)) Pub: Bolinda Pubng AUS. Dist(s): Bolinda Pub Inc

Pictures in the Hallway: Cat in Cage see Sean O'Casey Reading Juno & the Paycock & Other Works

Pictures of His Glory: Stories of His Presence That Will Ignite Your Spirit. Lynne Hammond. 2 CDs. 2006. audio compact disk 10.00 (978-1-57399-355-5(7)) Mac Hammond.

Pictures of Hollis Woods. Patricia Reilly Giff. Read by Hope Davis. 3 CDs. (Running Time: 2 hrs. 18 mins.). (J). (gr. 4-7). 2004. audio compact disk 20.40 (978-0-8072-1786-3(7), Listening Lib) Pub: Random Audio Pubg. Dist(s): NetLibrary CO

Pictures of Hollis Woods. unabr. ed. Patricia Reilly Giff. Read by Hope Davis. 2 cass. (Running Time: 2 hrs. 18 mins.). (J). (gr. 4-7). 2004. 23.00 (978-0-8072-0920-2(1), S YA 396 CX, Listening Lib) Random Audio Pubg.

Pictures of Hollis Woods. unabr. ed. Patricia Reilly Giff. Read by Hope Davis. (Running Time: 12960 sec.). (ENG.). (J). (gr. 3-7). 2007. audio compact disk 25.00 (978-0-7393-5968-6(1), Listening Lib) Pub: Random Audio Pubg. Dist(s): Random

***Pictures of You.** unabr. ed. Caroline Leavitt. (ENG.). 2011. audio compact disk 34.95 (978-1-61573-655-3(7), 1615736557) Pub: HighBridge. Dist(s): Workman Pub

Pictures on the Fridge. Norman Foote. 1 cass., 1 CD. (J). 8.78 (YR 43); audio compact disk 11.18 CD Jewel box. (YR 43) NewSound.
Reflects Foote's sense of humor & the magic of everyday life.

Pictures on the Fridge. Norman Foote. 1 cass. (J). (ps-7). 1998. 10.98 (978-0-945267-73-7(8), YM043-CN); audio compact disk 13.98 (978-0-945267-74-4(6), YM043-CD) Youngheart Mus.
Songs include: "Everybody Pitchin' in"; "Spider Dan"; "Magic Penny"; "Skip a Rock"; "Mr. Wind"; "Singing Policeman"; "Get up"; "Sister-My Brother"; "Simon Smith & His Amazing Dancing Bear"; "Safest Dog"; "Pictures on the Fridge"; "Bye Bye Black Bird" & "Goodnight.".

Piece by Piece. Calvin Trillin. Read by Calvin Trillin. (Playaway Adult Nonfiction Ser.). (ENG.). 2009. 34.99 (978-1-60775-723-8(0)) Find a World.

Piece of Cake: A Memoir. unabr. ed. Cupcake Brown. Read by Bahni Turpin. 17 CDs. (Running Time: 21 hrs.). 2006. audio compact disk 102.00 (978-1-4159-2693-2(X)); 96.00 (978-1-4159-2692-5(1)) Books on Tape.
A Piece of Cake is unlike any memoir you'll ever read. Moving and almost transgressive in its frankness, it is a relentlessly gripping tale of a resilient spirit who took on the worst of contem-porary urban life and survived it with a furious wit and unyielding determination. Cupcake Brown is a dynamic and utterly original storyteller who will guide you on the most satisfying, startlingly funny, and genuinely affecting tour through hell you'll ever take.

Piece of Heaven. unabr. ed. Barbara Samuel. 9 cass. (Running Time: 13 hrs. 30 min.). 2003. 72.00 (978-0-7366-9224-3(X)) Books on Tape.
Luna McGraw struggles to rebuild a relationship with her daughter while opening up to a world of possibilities with Thomas Coyote.

Piece of Justice. unabr. ed. Jill Paton Walsh. Read by Brigit Forsyth. 6 cass. (Running Time: 9 hrs.). (Imogen Quy Mystery Ser.). 2000. 49.95 (978-0-7451-6648-3(2), CAB 1264) Pub: Chivers Audio Bks GBR. Dist(s): AudioGO
Deceptively quiet, Imogene Quy has developed the unexpected passion of quilt-making. Her lodger, Fran, has been hired to finish a biography of the late great mathematician, Gideon Summerfield. But why have precious biographers had such a hard time writing the book? When Fran finds herself in danger, Imogen must act before it's too late.

Piece of My Heart. Peter Robinson. 2 CDs. (Running Time: 54360 sec.). (Inspector Banks Mystery Ser.). 2006. audio compact disk & audio compact disk 49.95 (978-0-7927-4249-4(4), CMP 975) AudioGO.

Piece of My Heart. Peter Robinson. Narrated by Ron Keith. 13 CDs. (Running Time: 54360 sec.). (Inspector Banks Mystery Ser.). 2006. audio compact disk 112.95 (978-0-7927-4068-1(8), SLD 975) AudioGO.

Piece of Steak see Call of the Wild & Other Stories

Piece of String see Great French & Russian Stories, Vol. 1, A Collection

Piece of String see De Maupassant Short Stories

Piece of String see Maupassant's Best Known Stories

Piece of String see Favorite Stories by Guy de Maupassant

Piece of String, Vol. 10. unabr. ed. Guy de Maupassant. Read by Nelita B. Castillo. Narrated by Nelita B. Castillo. 1 cass. (Running Time: 43 min.). Incl. Doer of Good. Oscar Wilde. (J). 1984.; Dusk. Saki. (J). 1984.; Federigo & the Falcon. Giovanni Boccaccio. Narrated by Amato Petale. (J). 1984.; Great Weep. Saki. (J). 1984.; (Fantasies Ser.). (J). 1984. 17.95 Incl. holder, scripts, lesson plans, & tchr's. guide. (978-0-86617-051-2(0)) Multi Media TX.
Comprehensive lesson plans that use classic short stories to develop skills in listening, reading, vocabulary, following details, making inferences, visualization, drawing conclusions, critical appreciation & comparison. This module's objective is to formulate & illustrate a statement of theme with reference to the story.

Piece of the Action: How the Middle Class Joined the Money Class. unabr. ed. Joseph Nocera. Read by Michael Prichard. 15 cass. (Running Time: 22 hrs. 30 min.). 1996. 120.00 (978-0-7366-3230-0(1), 3891) Books on Tape.
The credit card & mutual fund revolution opened the doors of the financial world to the middle class. How did it come about.

Piece of Work. abr. ed. Laura Zigman. Read by Emily Durante. (Running Time: 14400 sec.). 2007. audio compact disk 14.99 (978-1-4233-1351-9(8), 9781423313519, BCD Value Price) Brilliance Audio.

Piece of Work. unabr. ed. Laura Zigman. Read by Emily Durante. (Running Time: 8 hrs.). 2006. 39.25 (978-1-59737-435-4(0), 9781597374354, BADLE); 24.95 (978-1-59737-434-7(2), 9781597374347, BAD); 39.25 (978-1-59737-433-0(4), 9781597374330, Brinc Audio MP3 Lib); 24.95 (978-1-59737-432-3(6), 9781597374323, Brilliance MP3); 74.25 (978-1-59737-429-3(6), 9781597374293, BrilAudUnabridg); audio compact disk 87.25 (978-1-59737-431-6(8), 9781597374316, BriAudCD Unabrid); audio compact disk 32.95 (978-1-59737-430-9(X), 9781597374309, Bril Audio CD Unabri) Brilliance Audio.
Please enter a Synopsis.

Pieces of Glass: A Moment of Tragedy, a Lifetime of Faith. unabr. ed. Sarah Kay. (Running Time: 4 hrs. 5 mins. 0 sec.). (ENG.). 2008. 9.99 (978-0-310-27874-0(0)) Zondervan.

Pieces of Justice. Margaret Yorke. Read by Maureen O'Brien. 8 cass. (Running Time: 12 hrs.). 2002. 69.95 (978-0-7540-0890-3(8), CAB 2312) Pub: Chivers Audio Bks GBR. Dist(s): AudioGO

***Pieces of My Heart.** abr. ed. Robert J. Wagner. Read by Robert J. Wagner. (ENG.). 2008. (978-0-06-170615-8(9)); (978-0-06-170618-9(3)) HarperCollins Pubs.

Pieces of My Heart: A Life. Robert J. Wagner. Read by Robert J. Wagner. Told to Scott Eyman. (Playaway Adult Nonfiction Ser.). (ENG.). 2009. 59.99 (978-1-60812-712-2(5)) Find a World.

Pieces of My Heart: A Life. abr. ed. Robert J. Wagner. Read by Robert J. Wagner. 2009. audio compact disk 14.99 (978-0-06-190626-8(3), Harper Audio) HarperCollins Pubs.

Pieces of the Frame. unabr. ed. John McPhee. Read by Walter Zimmerman. 8 cass. (Running Time: 12 hrs.). 1989. 64.00 (978-0-7366-1550-1(4), 2419) Books on Tape.
Subjects familiar to McPhee's readers - sport, Scotland, conservation - are central to this gathering of 11 factual stories. From the backwoods of Georgia to Ruidoso Downs in New Mexico to the rivers of the Perthshire & Banff, McPhee's peregrinations & encounters become our own.

Pieces of the Puzzle. unabr. ed. Robert Stanek, pseud. Narrated by Karl Fehr. (Running Time: 6 hrs. 58 mins.). (ENG.). 2008. 22.95 (978-1-57545-354-5(1), RP Audio Pubng) Pub: Reagent Press. Dist(s): OverDrive Inc

Pied Beauty see Gathering of Great Poetry for Children

Pied Leger. unabr. ed. Robert A. Monroe. Read by Roland Simon. 1 cass. (Running Time: 30 min.). (Human Plus Ser.). (FRE.). 1993. 14.95 (978-1-56102-069-0(9)) Inter Indus.
Make walking, jogging, running easier.

Pied Piper. Perf. by Donovan Leitch & Aine Whelan. 1 cass. (J). 2002. 10.98; audio compact disk 16.98 MFLP CA.

Pied Piper. abr. ed. Ridley Pearson. Read by Dale Hull. 3 CDs. (Running Time: 3 hrs.). (Lou Boldt/Daphne Matthews Ser.). 2002. audio compact disk 14.99 (978-1-59086-461-6(1), 1590864611); audio compact disk 62.25 (978-1-59086-462-3(X), 159086462X, CD Lib Edit) Brilliance Audio.

***Pied Piper.** abr. ed. Ridley Pearson. Read by Dale Hull. (Running Time: 3 hrs.). (Lou Boldt/Daphne Matthews Ser.). 2010. audio compact disk 9.99 (978-1-4418-5642-5(0), 9781441856425, BCD Value Price) Brilliance Audio.

Pied Piper. unabr. ed. Perf. by Keith Baxter. 1 cass. Incl. Colony of Cats. Andrew Lang. (J). (CDL5 1397); Thumbelina. Illus. by Hans Christian Andersen. (J). (CDL5 1397); Thumbelina. Illus. by Hans Christian Andersen. (J). (CDL5 1397); (J). 1972. 11.00 (978-0-694-50900-3(0), CDL5 1397) HarperCollins Pubs.

Pied Piper. unabr. ed. Ridley Pearson. Read by Michael Mitchell. 11 cass. (Running Time: 16 hrs. 30 min.). 1999. 88.00 (4773) Books on Tape.
In Seattle, they're calling him the Pied Piper - someone who comes in the night & takes children away. To Lieutenant Lou Boldt & forensic pathologist Daphne Matthews, it's clear these aren't random kidnappings. They must work together to track the Pied Piper before anther child is taken. And when another child is taken, it hits close to home for Lou Boldt.

Pied Piper. unabr. ed. Ridley Pearson. Read by Dale Hull. (Running Time: 15 hrs.). (Lou Boldt/Daphne Matthews Ser.). 2007. 39.25 (978-1-4233-3072-1(2), 9781423330721, BADLE); 24.95 (978-1-4233-3071-4(4), 9781423330714, BAD) Brilliance Audio.

Pied Piper. unabr. ed. Ridley Pearson. Read by Dale Hull. (Running Time: 15 hrs.). (Lou Boldt/Daphne Matthews Ser.). 2007. 39.25 (978-1-4233-3070-7(6), 9781423330707, Brinc Audio MP3 Lib); 24.95 (978-1-4233-3069-1(2), 9781423330691, Brilliance MP3) Brilliance Audio.

***Pied Piper.** unabr. ed. Ridley Pearson. Read by Dale Hull. (Running Time: 16 hrs.). (Lou Boldt/Daphne Matthews Ser.). 2010. audio compact disk 89.97 (978-1-4418-4011-0(7), 9781441840110, BriAudCD Unabrid) Brilliance Audio.

***Pied Piper.** unabr. ed. Ridley Pearson. Read by Dale Hull. (Running Time: 16 hrs.). (Lou Boldt/Daphne Matthews Ser.). 2010. audio compact disk 29.99 (978-1-4418-4010-3(9), 9781441840103) Brilliance Audio.

Pied Piper. unabr. collector's ed. Nevil Shute. Read by Richard Brown. 7 cass. (Running Time: 10 hrs. 30 min.). 1991. 56.00 (978-0-7366-1900-4(3), 2726) Books on Tape.
It is the summer of 1940 & in Europe the time of Blitzkreig. John Howard, a 70-year-old Englishman vacationing in France, cuts short his tour & heads for home. He agrees to take two children with him. But war closes in. Trains fail, roads clog with refugees. And as if things are not difficult enough, other children join Howard's little band. At last they reach the coast & find not deliverance but desperation. The old Englishman's greatest test lies ahead of him.

Pied Piper of Hamelin see Flautista de Hamelin

Pied Piper of Hamelin. l.t. ed. Short Stories. Illus. by Graham Percy. 1 cass. (Running Time: 10 mins.). Dramatization. (J). (ps-3). 2001. bk. 8.99 (978-84-86154-38-7(3)) Pub: Peralt Mont ESP. Dist(s): imaJen

Pied Piper of Hamelin. unabr. ed. Robert Browning. Perf. by Boris Karloff. 1 cass. (J). 1984. 9.95 (978-0-694-50775-7(X), CDL5 1075) HarperCollins Pubs.

Pied Piper of Hamelin & Other Favorite Poems. Read by Anton Lesser et al. Selected by Jan Fielden & John Mole. 2 cass. (Running Time: 1 hr. 57 mins.). (J). (ps-3). 1995. 13.98 (978-962-634-545-0(4), NA204514, Naxos AudioBooks) Naxos.
From Coleridge to Ted Hughes via Wordsworth, Yeats, Lear, de la Mare and a a fair sprinkling of Anons, this charming collection includes such well-loved poems as Hiawatha, The Pied Piper of Hamlin and The Jumblies.

Pied Piper of Hamelin & Other Favorite Poems. unabr. ed. Poems. Read by Anton Lesser et al. Selected by Jan Fielden & John Mole. 2 CDs. (Running Time: 1 hr. 57 mins.). (J). (ps-3). 1995. audio compact disk 17.98 (978-962-634-045-5(2), NA204512, Naxos AudioBooks) Naxos.
From Coleridge to Ted Hughes via Wordsworth, Yeats, Lear, de la Mane and a fair sprinkling of Anons, this charming collection includes such well-loved poesm as Hiawatha, The Pied Piper of Hamelin, and The Jumblies.

Piel de Zapa. abr. ed. Honoré de Balzac. Read by Laura García. 3 CDs. (SPA.). 2002. audio compact disk 17.00 (978-958-8161-46-4(0)) YoYoMusic.

***Piensa lo bueno y se te Dara.** Conny Mendez. Prod. by FonoLibro Inc. Narrated by Isabel Varas. (SPA.). 2010. audio compact disk 11.95 (978-1-61154-002-4(X)) Fonolibro Inc.

Piense Para Obtener un Cambio. unabr. ed. John C. Maxwell. (SPA.). 2010. audio compact disk 16.99 (978-987-557-189-1(X)) Pub: Peniel ARG. Dist(s): Zondervan

Pierce with a Pin, Set. unabr. ed. Kenneth Hopkins. 6 cass. 1998. 69.95 (978-1-85903-039-4(4)) Pub: Magna Story GBR. Dist(s): Ulverscroft US

***Pierced by the Word: Thirty One Meditations for Your Soul.** unabr. ed. John Piper. Narrated by Michael Kramer. (ENG.). 2005. 10.98 (978-1-59644-165-1(8), Hovel Audio) christianaud.

Pierced by the Word: Thirty-One Meditations for Your Soul. unabr. ed. John Piper. Narrated by Michael Kramer. 3 CDs. (Running Time: 3 hrs. 15 mins. 0 sec.). (ENG.). 2005. audio compact disk 18.98 (978-1-59644-164-4(X), Hovel Audio) christianaud.

Pierced Ear: Jude 1:4. Ed Young. 1989. 4.95 (978-0-7417-1740-5(9), 740) Win Walk.

Piercing Cry of a Rooster: Luke 22:1-53. Ed Young. 1996. 4.95 (978-0-7417-2096-2(5), 1096) Win Walk.

Piercing the Darkness. Frank E. Peretti. Read by Frank E. Peretti. 3 cds. (Running Time: 3 hrs.). Dramatization. 2005. audio compact disk 19.99 (978-1-58134-524-7(0), Crossway Bibles) CrosswayIL.
A spiritual struggle breaks out in a small town-and a young woman is caught in the middle. Top-selling novel of forgiveness and the power of prayer.

Piercing the Darkness. Frank E. Peretti. Narrated by Richard Ferrone. 15 cass. (Running Time: 21 hrs.). 122.00 (978-0-7887-5341-1(X)) Recorded Bks.

Piercing the Darkness. unabr. ed. Frank E. Peretti. Read by Kevin Foley. 15 cass. (Running Time: 18 hrs.). 2001. 74.95 (978-1-55686-740-8(9)) Books in Motion.
Across a vast panorama of heart-stopping action, Sally Roe flees for her life. Her journey is a penetrating portrayal of our times, and a vivid reminder of the redemptive power of the Cross.

Piercing the Knots-Granthis: A Mantra & Vizualization Meditation. Thomas Ashley-Farrand. Voice by Thomas Ashley-Farrand. (ENG.). 2009. audio compact disk 18.00 (978-0-615-29415-5(4)) SaraswaPubns.

Piercing the Veil of Unconsciousness. Swami Amar Jyoti. 1 cass. 9.95 (R-96) Truth Consciousness.
Steps to consciousness. In peace we grow, not otherwise. Angelic & demonic ways. Subjective living. Yoga Maya, conscious Divine Play.

Piercing the Veil of Unconsciousness. unabr. ed. Swami Amar Jyoti. 1 cass. (Running Time: 1 hr. 30 min.). (Satsangs of Swami Amar Jyoti Ser.). 1998. 9.95 (978-0-933572-30-0(1), M-109) Truth Consciousness.
Encountering the dark night. Rules & rituals in sadhana. On faith & understanding.

Pierna Lastimada, Set. (Coleccion Chiquilines - Imagen y Sonido). (SPA.). (J). bk. 15.95 (978-950-11-0625-1(X), SGM25X) Pub: Sigmar ARG. Dist(s): Continental Bk

Pierre. 2004. bk. 24.95 (978-0-7882-0566-8(8)); pap. bk. 14.95 (978-0-7882-0631-3(1)); 8.95 (978-1-56008-640-6(8)); cass. & flmstrp 30.00 (978-1-56008-746-5(3)) Weston Woods.

Pierre: A Cautionary Tale. Maurice Sendak. 1 cass. (Running Time: 6 min.). (J). (ps-3). 2000. pap. bk. 12.95 Weston Woods.
Pierre flaunts an "I don't care" attitude until an encounter with a lion changes everything.

Pierre & Jean. unabr. ed. Guy de Maupassant. Read by Walter Zimmerman. 4 cass. (Running Time: 5 hrs. 30 mins.). 1990. 32.95 (978-0-7861-0630-1(1), 2120) Blckstn Audio.
First published in 1888 in France, this novel is usually considered Maupassant's greatest novel. It is a piercing study of jealousy, suspicion, & family love. Pierre & Jean are the sons of a retired Parisian jeweller M. Roland, living in Le Havre, a colorful & busy seaport. Pierre is a doctor, whose temperment is somewhat nervous & unsteady. Jean, the younger, has a placid nature & is a lawyer. Both love the widowed young Mme Rosemilly, who seems to prefer Jean. When Jean inherits a fortune from M. Marechal, an old family friend, Pierre - who gets nothing - is puzzled, jealous, & suspicious of his mother's one-time sin of adultry. She reads his thoughts & both live in torture.

Pierre & Jean. unabr. ed. Guy de Maupassant. Read by Walter Zimmerman. 4 cass. (Running Time: 5 hrs. 30 mins.). 1991. 28.00 set. (C-213) Jimcin Record.
Best short novel of famous French author.

Pierre et le Loup. 1 cass. (Running Time: 1 hr., 30 mins.). (Musicontes Ser.).Tr. of Peter & the Wolf. (FRE.). (J). 2000. bk. 24.95 (978-2-09-230475-4(5)) Pub: F Nathan FRA. Dist(s): Distribks Inc

Pierre; One Was Johnny; Alligators All Around; Chicken Soup with Rice. 2004. (978-0-89719-840-0(9)); cass. & flmstrp (978-0-89719-748-9(8)) Weston Woods.

Pierre Salinger: President & the Press see Buckley's Firing Line

Pierres de Sang. l.t. ed. Andre-Jean Arnaud. (French Ser.). (FRE., 2000. bk. 30.99 (978-2-84011-349-2(X)) Pub: UlverLrgPrint GBR. Dist(s): Ulverscroft US

Pig in a Park. unabr. ed. Pauline Baird Jones. Read by Juanita Parker. 6 cass. (Running Time: 7 hrs.). 2001. 39.95 (978-1-55686-923-5(1)) Books in Motion.
Sparks and bullets fly as Isabel Stanley and her CIA mystery man try to stop anti-government operatives from blowing up Congress.

Pig Pig Grows Up. 2004. bk. 24.95 (978-0-7882-0578-1(1)); pap. bk. 14.95 (978-0-7882-0639-9(7)); 8.95 (978-1-56008-641-3(6)); cass. & flmstrp 30.00 (978-1-56008-747-2(1)) Weston Woods.

Pig Pig Grows Up. David M. McPhail. 1 readalong cass. (Running Time: 6 min.). (Pig Pig Ser.). (J). (gr. k-2). 2000. pap. bk. 12.95 Weston Woods.
A big pig refuses to grow up, until one day, when he surprises everyone, including himself.

Pig Pig Grows Up. unabr. ed. David M. McPhail. Illus. by David M. McPhail. Read by Peter Fernandez. 1 cass. (Running Time: 8 mins.). (Pig Pig Ser.). (J). (gr. k-2). 1985. pap. bk. 15.95 (978-0-941078-94-8(9)) Live Oak Media.
A young pig is determined to remain a baby.

Pig Pig Grows Up. unabr. ed. David M. McPhail. Illus. by David M. McPhail. 1 cass. (Running Time: 8 min.). (Pig Pig Ser.). (J). (gr. k-2). 1985. 9.95 Live Oak Media.

Pig Pig Grows Up, Grades K-2. unabr. ed. David M. McPhail. Illus. by David M. McPhail. Read by Peter Fernandez. 14 vols. (Running Time: 8 mins.). (Pig Pig Ser.). (J). 1985. pap. bk. & tchr. ed. 31.95 Reading Chest. (978-0-941078-95-5(7)) Live Oak Media.

Pig Scrolls. Paul Shipton. Read by Robert Llewellyn. (Running Time: 25200 sec.). (J). (gr. 5-9). 2001. audio compact disk 59.95 (978-0-7540-6753-5(X)) AudioGo GBR.

Pig Who Sang to the Moon: The Emotional World of Farm Animals. abr. ed. Jeffrey Moussaieff Masson. Read by Tim Jerome. 6 CDs. (Running Time: 7 hrs. 30 mins.). 2003. audio compact disk 29.95 (978-1-57270-372-8(5), 890560) Pub: Audio Partners. Dist(s): PerseuPGW
Jeffrey Moussaieff Masson's groundbreaking When Elephants Weep explored emotions in the animal kingdom, particularly those of wild animals. Now, in a book that is as fascinating - and sure to be as controversial - as his earlier work, Masson reveals startling evidence that barnyard creatures have complex feelings too, such as love, loyalty, friendship, sadness, grief, and sorrow. Weaving together history, literature, science, and his own vivid experiences observing pigs, cows, sheep, goats, and chickens, Masson bears witness to the emotions and intelligence of these remarkable animals, each possessing distinct qualities. Shattering the lingering myth of the "dumb animal without feelings," the author has written a revolutionary book that is sure to stir human emotions far and wide. Reader Tim Jerome's extensive theatrical background enhances Masson's penetrating prose.

Pig Who Sang to the Moon: The Emotional World of Farm Animals. abr. ed. Jeffrey Moussaieff Masson. Read by Tim Jerome. 5 cass. (Running Time: 7 hrs. 30 mins.). 2003. 27.95 (978-1-57270-371-1(7), 750711) Pub: Audio Partners. Dist(s): PerseuPGW

Piggies. Audrey Wood & Don Wood. Read by Audrey Wood. Perf. by Carl Shaylen & Jennifer Shaylen. Illus. by Don Wood. Contrib. by Carl Shaylen & Jennifer Shaylen. 1 cass. (Running Time: 17 min.). (J). (ps-1). 1994. pap. bk. 14.00 (978-0-15-200191-9(3)) Harcourt.
Seven original songs by children's musicians Carl & Jennifer Shaylen bring this nighttime fantasy to young children in a whole new way. Each pair of piggies - fat, smart, long, silly, & wee - has its own spirited voice. And the songs tell us just what happens when these little piggies get hot, cold, clean, dirty, & finally, all cozy & ready for bed.

Piggins & Picnic with Piggins. unabr. ed. Roddy McDowall. 1 cass. (Running Time: 26 min.). (J). (gr. 1-4). 1988. 9.95 (978-0-89845-765-0(3), CPN 1822) HarperCollins Pubs.

Piggyback Songs: Singable Poems Set to Favorite Tunes. 1 CD. (Running Time: 1 hr.). (J). (ps-1). 2001. pap. bk. 10.95 (KIM 9141C); pap. bk. 11.95 (KIM 9141); pap. bk. 14.95 (KIM 9141CD) Kimbo Educ.
This collection of songs is sung to classics such as, Mary Had a Little Lamb, Row, Row, Row Your Boat & Frere Jacques. Great for schools, parties, car trips & story hours. The song themes include seasons, school, feelings, animals & fun. Includes guide with lyrics, finger plays & gross motor activities.

Pigman. unabr. ed. Paul Zindel. Read by Eden Riegel & Charlie McWade. 4 CDs. (Running Time: 4 hrs. 30 mins.). (YA). (gr. 8 up). 2009. audio compact disk 24.95 (978-1-935169-00-0(9)) Graymalkin.

Pigman & Me, unabr. ed. Paul Zindel. Read by Jeff Woodman. 3 pieces. (Running Time: 3 hrs. 15 mins.). (gr. 5 up). 1994. 27.00 (978-0-7887-0141-2(X), 94366E7) Recorded Bks.
Author Paul Zindel tells how, when a teenager living in Staten Island, he met an old Italian man who changes his whole outlook on life.

Pigman & Me. unabr. ed. Paul Zindel. Read by Jeff Woodman. 3 cass. (Running Time: 3 hrs. 15 min.). (J). (gr. 1). 1994. 9.50 Set. Recorded Bks.

Pigman & Me. unabr. ed. Paul Zindel. Narrated by Jeff Woodman. 3 CDs. (Running Time: 3 hrs. 15 mins.). (gr. 5 up). 2000. audio compact disk 29.00 (978-0-7887-4966-7(8), C1311E7) Recorded Bks.
A teenager living in Staten Island, met an old Italian man who changes his whole outlook on life.

Pigman's Legacy. unabr. ed. Paul Zindel. Read by Eden Riegel & Charlie McWade. 4 CDs. (Running Time: 4 hrs.). (YA). (gr. 8 up). 2009. audio compact disk 24.95 (978-1-935169-07-9(6)) Graymalkin.

Pigments & Dyes in China: A Strategic Reference 2007. Compiled by Icon Group International, Inc. Staff. 2007. ring bd. 195.00 (978-0-497-35889-1(1)) Icon Grp.

Pignocchio/On with the Show! Steck-Vaughn Staff. 1997. (978-0-8172-7385-9(9)) SteckVau.

Pigs & Pirates. 2004. 8.95 (978-1-56008-637-6(8)); cass. & flmstrp 30.00 (978-1-56008-748-9(X)) Weston Woods.

Pigs at the Trough: How Corporate Greed & Political Corruption Are Undermining America. abr. ed. Arianna S. Huffington. Read by Alison Fraser. 2009. 44.99 (978-1-60812-724-5(9)) Find a World.

Pigs Have Wings. P. G. Wodehouse. Read by Martin Jarvis. (ENG.). 2009. audio compact disk 33.07 (978-1-906147-39-6(6), CSAW) CSA Telltapes GBR.

***Pigs in Heaven.** abr. ed. Barbara Kingsolver. Read by Barbara Kingsolver. (ENG.). 2005. (978-0-06-089457-3(1), Harper Audio); (978-0-06-089456-6(3), Harper Audio) HarperCollins Pubs.

Pigs in Heaven. unabr. ed. Barbara Kingsolver. Narrated by C. J. Critt. 12 CDs. (Running Time: 13 hrs. 30 mins.). 1999. audio compact disk 104.00 (978-0-7887-3712-1(0), C1069E7) Recorded Bks.
A woman struggles to officially adopt the little Cherokee Indian girl who was abandoned into her care two years previously.

Pigs in Heaven, Set. unabr. ed. Barbara Kingsolver. Narrated by C. J. Critt. 9 cass. (Running Time: 13 hrs. 30 mins.). 1993. 95.00 (978-1-55690-936-8(5), 93432E5) Recorded Bks.

Pigs is Pigs see Sampler of American Humor

Pigs' Wedding. 2004. pap. bk. 14.95 (978-0-7882-0591-0(9)); 8.95 (978-1-56008-397-9(2)); cass. & flmstrp 30.00 (978-0-89719-583-6(3)) Weston Woods.

Pigs' Wedding. Helme Heine. 1 cass. (J). (ps-3). pap. bk. 12.95 (PRA325) Weston Woods.
How the bride & groom help their friends prepare for the wedding celebration.

Pigs' Wedding. Helme Heine. 1 cass. (J). (ps-3). 2004. 8.95 (978-0-89719-971-1(5), RAC325) Weston Woods.

Pigs'Wedding. 2004. bk. 24.95 (978-0-89719-789-2(5)) Weston Woods.

Pigtown. unabr. ed. William J. Caunitz. Read by David Colacci. (Running Time: 10 hrs.). 2008. 24.95 (978-1-4233-5423-9(0), 9781423354239, Brilliance MP3); 24.95 (978-1-4233-5425-3(7), 9781423354253, BAD); 39.25 (978-1-4233-5424-6(9), 9781423354246, Brinc Audio MP3 Lib); 39.25 (978-1-4233-5426-0(5), 9781423354260, BADLE) Brilliance Audio.

Pigtown, unabr. ed. William J. Caunitz. Narrated by Frank Muller. 7 cass. (Running Time: 9 hrs. 45 mins.). 1995. 60.00 (978-0-7887-0347-8(1), 94539E7) Recorded Bks.
Detective Matt Stuart works a shabby beat where homicides are his daily paper work. Tracking down an elusive killer, he is forced to face some critical decisions.

Pike see Poetry & Voice of Ted Hughes

Pikovaya Dama. Alexander Pushkin. 1 cass. (Running Time: 90 min.). (RUS.). 1996. pap. bk. 24.50 (978-1-58085-561-7(X)) Interlingua VA.
Includes Russian text, intermediate/advanced level. The combination of written text & clarity & pace of diction will open the door for intermediate & advanced students to genuine comprehension & the use of literary texts for advancement in rapid understanding of written & oral language materials. The audio text plus written text concept makes foreign languages accessible to a much wider range of students than books alone.

Pilgrim at Tinker Creek, unabr. ed. Annie Dillard. Read by Grace Conlin. 7 cass. (Running Time: 10 hrs.). 1993. 49.95 (978-0-7861-0490-1(2), 1441) Blckstn Audio.
A personal narrative. It highlights one year's explorations on foot in the author's own neighborhood, one year's assaults & curiosities. Here are both beauty & terror: the vision of a cedar tree charged with light, & the sight of a crippled moth crawling on the ground, his wings crumpled & glued to his back. In the summer, Annie Dillard stalks muskrats in the creek & thinks about wave mechanics; in the fall, she watches a monarch butterfly migration & dreams of Arctic caribou. She tries to con a coot; she collects pond water & examines it under a microscope on her kitchen table; she frightens frogs. She unties a snakeskin, witnesses a flood, & plays "King of the Meadow" with a field of grasshoppers. Throughout the year, she brings anecdotes & bizarre bits of information to bear on what she experiences.

Pilgrim at Tinker Creek. unabr. ed. Annie Dillard. (Running Time: 8 hrs. 0 mins.). 2009. audio compact disk 19.95 (978-1-4332-6126-8(X)) Blckstn Audio.

Pilgrim at Tinker Creek. unabr. ed. Annie Dillard. (Running Time: 9.5 hrs. 0 mins.). (ENG.). 2009. 29.95 (978-1-4332-6127-5(8)) Blckstn Audio.

Pilgrim at Tinker Creek. unabr. ed. Annie Dillard. Read by Tavia Gilbert. (Running Time: 9.5 hrs. 0 mins.). (ENG.). 2009. 59.95 (978-1-4332-6123-7(5)); audio compact disk 80.00 (978-1-4332-6124-4(3)) Blckstn Audio.

Pilgrim at Tinker Creek, unabr. ed. Annie Dillard. Narrated by Barbara Rosenblat. 8 cass. (Running Time: 10 hrs. 45 mins.). 1994. 70.00 (978-0-7887-0001-9(4), 94140E7) Recorded Bks.
This Pulitzer Prize winner invites the listener to "look at my world!" Reflections on life & nature inspired by a year in an isolated valley in western Virginia's Blue Ridge Mountains.

Pilgrim of Hate. Ellis Peters. Read by Vanessa Benjamin. 6 cass. (Running Time: 8 hrs. 30 mins.). (Chronicles of Brother Cadfael Ser.: Vol. 10). 2000. 44.95 (978-0-7861-1881-6(4), 2680); audio compact disk 56.00 (978-0-7861-9834-4(6), 2680) Blckstn Audio.
The year of our Lord 1141, a civil war over England's throne leaves a legacy of violence & the murder of a knight dear to Brother Cadfael.

Pilgrim of Hate. Ellis Peters, pseud. Read by Derek Jacobi. 2 cass. (Running Time: 3 hrs.). (Chronicles of Brother Cadfael Ser.: Vol. 10). 1998. (978-1-84032-160-9(1), HoddrStoughton) Hodder General GBR.
In distant Winchester, a knight, supporter of the Empress Maud, has been murdered - not apparently an event of importance to those seeking miraculous cures at the saint's shrine. But among the throng some strange customers indeed begin to puzzle Brother Cadfael - & as the story unfolds it becomes evident that the murder is a much less remote affair than it first seemed.

Pilgrim of Hate. unabr. ed. Ellis Peters, pseud. Read by Stephen Thorne. 6 cass. (Running Time: 7 hrs.). (Chronicles of Brother Cadfael Ser.: Vol. 10). 2000. 29.95 (978-1-57270-127-4(7), N61127u) Pub: Audio Partners. Dist(s): PerseuPGW
In 1141 A.D., the celebration of Saint Winifred brought a flood of pilgrims & possibly a murderer, to town. Brother Cadfael, who has taken religious vows, discovers a plot of evil.

Pilgrim of Hate. unabr. ed. Ellis Peters, pseud. Read by Stephen Thorne. 6 cass. (Running Time: 9 hrs.). (Chronicles of Brother Cadfael Ser.: Vol. 10). 2000. 49.95 (978-0-7451-4148-0(X), CAB 831) Pub: Chivers Audio Bks GBR. Dist(s): AudioGO
Pilgrims gather from far and wide at the Benedictine Abbey seeking miraculous cures. In distant Winchester, a supporter of Empress Maud has been murdered. Among the throng of pilgrims, some begin to question Brother Cadfael. And, as the story unfolds, it becomes evident that the murder is much less a remote affair than it first seemed.

Pilgrim of Hate. unabr. ed. Ellis Peters, pseud. Narrated by Patrick Tull. 6 cass. (Running Time: 8 hrs.). (Chronicles of Brother Cadfael Ser.: No. 10). 1994. 51.00 (978-0-7887-0005-7(7), 94144E7) Recorded Bks.
As England's civil war draws to a slow & painful close, Shrewsbury prepares for the Feast of Saint Winifred, an annual celebration that attracts pilgrims from all across England who come seeking after miracles. Two such seekers arrive at the abbey & Cadfael's herbarium door: the dark-eyed Ciaran who has vowed to walk to Wales unshod as a kind of penance & close on his heels, his sullen companion, Matthew. When Cadfael's old friend Sir Olivier arrives with a tale of murder, the youth's puzzling association becomes darker & more inscrutable.

Pilgrim of the Heart. Krishna Das. 2006. audio compact disk 24.95 (978-1-59179-495-0(1)) Sounds True.

Pilgrim on Earth. Contrib. by Peter B. Allen. (Running Time: 30 min.). 2004. 14.95 (978-5-559-78161-7(4)); audio compact disk 16.95 (978-5-559-78371-0(4)) Pub: Pt of Grace Ent. Dist(s): STL Dist NA

Pilgrim Pope: Messages for the World. Karol Wojtyla. Read by Michael Prichard. Ed. by Achille Silvestrini. 10 cass. (Running Time: 15 hrs.). 1999. 80.00 (978-0-7366-4695-6(7), 5089) Books on Tape.
Pope John Paul II has made it his mission to carry the word of Jesus Christ to the world. The most widely traveled pope in the history of the Catholic Church, he has redefined the role of the papacy by being an active, living presence in the lives of the diverse faithful worldwide.

Pilgrim Pope: Messages for the World. collector's ed. Karol Wojtyla. Read by Michael Prichard. 10 cass. (Running Time: 15 hrs.). 1999. 80.00 (978-0-7366-4751-9(1), 5089) Books on Tape.

Pilgrim Saga. abr. ed. Perf. by Philip L. Barbour et al. 1 cass. 1984. 12.95 (978-0-694-50216-5(2), SWC 1336) HarperCollins Pubs.
Letters, diaries & documents of the settlers tell the story of the pilgrims from their departure from Europe to the establishment of their settlement.

Pilgrimage. Perf. by Robert Gass & Denver Symphony Orchestra. 1 cass. (Running Time: 1 hr.). 9.98 (MT048) White Dove NM.
The first instrumental recording by Robert Gass features him on piano & the strings of the Denver Symphony Orchestra. The all-acoustic timbres breathe with aliveness & passion.

***Pilgrimage.** unabr. ed. Paulo Coelho. Read by Sean Runnette. (ENG.). 2009. (978-0-06-180599-8(8), Harper Audio); (978-0-06-180600-1(5), Harper Audio) HarperCollins Pubs.

Pilgrimage: Nine Songs of Ecstasy. Perf. by Simon Cloquet & Eric Calvi. 1 cass., 1 CD. 8.78 (PHI 536201); audio compact disk 13.58 CD Jewel box. (PHI 536201) NewSound.

***Pilgrimage to Beethoven.** Richard Wagner. Tr. by Anita Conrade. Contrib. by Edward Asner et al. Adapted by Bernard Da Costa. (Running Time: 3480 sec.). (L. A. Theatre Works Audio Theatre Collections). (ENG.). 2010. audio compact disk 18.95 (978-1-58081-719-6(X)) L A Theatre.

Pilgrimage to Beethoven. unabr. ed. Bernard Da Costa. Perf. by Edward Asner et al. 1 cass. (Running Time: 1 hr. 01 min.). 1994. 19.95 (978-1-58081-071-5(3)) L A Theatre.
Beethoven's music soars in the background as a poor, young composer named Richard Wagner struggles towards Vienna to meet the composer he idolizes. Hampering him every step of the way is an annoying Englishman, who claims he's just trying to help. A comic & touching exploration of the soul of the artist, & the revolutionary thinking that created Wagnerian opera.

Pilgrimage to Medina & Mecca - Excerpts. unabr. ed. Excerpts. Richard F. Burton. Narrated by Patrick Tull. 3 cass. (Running Time: 4 hrs. 30 mins.). 1992. 26.00 (978-1-55690-763-0(X), 92434E7) Recorded Bks.
Excerpts from renowned soldier, scholar, spy Sir Richard Burton's account of his pilgrimage, disguised as a Muslim to the holy cities of Mecca & Medina in 1853.

Pilgrims. unabr. ed. Elizabeth Gilbert. Narrated by Coleen Marlo. (Running Time: 6 hrs.). (ENG.). (gr. 12 up). 2008. audio compact disk 29.95 (978-0-14-314335-2(2), PengAudBks) Penguin Grp USA.

Pilgrims, No. I. unabr. ed. Orion's Gatel Hark. 6 cass. (Running Time: 6 hrs.). 1995. 24.99 HARK Ent.

Pilgrim's Inn. unabr. collector's ed. Elizabeth Goudge. Read by Wanda McCaddon. 10 cass. (Running Time: 15 hrs.). (Eliot Family Ser.). Orig. Title: The Herb of Grace. 1983. 80.00 (978-0-7366-0484-0(7), 1459) Books on Tape.
The story focuses on a soldier, George Eliot, his wife Nadine, & their five children. At the heart of the story is their acquisition of an ancient pilgrims' inn on the river.

Pilgrims Laid the Foundation. Derek Prince. 1 cass. (I-4032) Derek Prince.

Pilgrims of Plimoth. 2004. 8.95 (978-0-7882-0052-6(6)); cass. & flmstrp 30.00 (978-0-89719-608-6(2)) Weston Woods.

Pilgrims of Plimoth: Struggle for Survival. Marcia Sewall. 1 cass. (Running Time: 10 min.). (J). 2000. bk. 24.95 Weston Woods.
The arrival of the Pilgrims in the new world is chronicled in this dramatic reenactment of their daily activities during those first trying years in the colony they called Plimoth.

Pilgrims of Plimouth. Marcia Sewall. 1 cass. (Running Time: 25 min.). (J). (gr. k-6). 1989. bk. 24.95 (978-1-56008-010-7(8), HRA330); 8.95 (978-0-89719-992-6(8), RAC330) Weston Woods.
The coming of the pilgrims to the New World.

Pilgrims of Rayne. unabr. ed. Read by William Dufris. (Running Time: 57600 sec.). (Pendragon Ser.: Bk. 8). (J). (gr. 5-9). 2007. 92.25 (978-1-59737-292-3(7), 9781597372923, BrilAudUnabridg); audio compact disk 44.25 (978-1-59737-296-1(X), 9781597372961, Brinc Audio MP3 Lib) Brilliance Audio.
Please enter a Synopsis.

Pilgrims of Rayne. unabr. ed. Read by William Dufris. (Running Time: 57600 sec.). (Pendragon Ser.: Bk. 8). (J). (gr. 5-9). 2007. audio compact disk 29.95 (978-1-59737-295-4(1), 9781597372954, Brilliance MP3) Brilliance Audio.

Pilgrims of Rayne. unabr. ed. D. J. MacHale. Read by William Dufris. (Running Time: 16 hrs.). (Pendragon Ser.: Bk. 8). 2007. 44.25 (978-1-59737-298-5(6), 9781597372985, BADLE); 29.95 (978-1-59737-297-8(8), 9781597372978, BAD) Brilliance Audio.

Pilgrims of Rayne. unabr. ed. D. J. MacHale. Read by William Dufris. (Running Time: 16 hrs.). (Pendragon Ser.: Bk. 8). 2009. audio compact disk 19.99 (978-1-4233-9909-4(9), 9781423399094); audio compact disk 49.97 (978-1-4233-9910-0(2), 9781423399100, BriAudCD Unabrid) Brilliance Audio.

Pilgrim's Praise. Music by Judy Rogers. 1 cass. (Running Time: 1 hr.). 2002. 8.50 (JR00007) Christian Liberty.
Filled with a rich blend of thought provoking praise to the Lord Jesus Christ. Many of the songs remind us that we are all pilgrims on the earth and need to look to God daily as our Good Shepherd.

Pilgrim's Progress. John Bunyan. 2 cass. (Running Time: 164 min.). (YA). (gr. 8 up). 2000. 10.95 (978-0-89084-912-5(9), 045906) BJUPr.

Pilgrim's Progress. John Bunyan. 1 cass. (Running Time: 96 min.). (Christian Audio Classics Ser.). 1996. 4.97 (978-1-55748-717-9(0)) Barbour Pub.

Pilgrim's Progress. John Bunyan. Narrated by Gary Martin. (Running Time: 6 hrs.). 1990. 34.95 (978-1-59912-838-2(1)) Iofy Corp.

Pilgrim's Progress. John Bunyan. 2005. audio compact disk 29.99 (978-0-89051-449-8(6), 303-208) Pub: Master Bks. Dist(s): Spring Arbor Dist

Pilgrim's Progress. John Bunyan. Read by Edward De Souza. 4 cass. (Running Time: 5 hrs. 15 mins.). 1999. 22.98 (978-962-634-671-6(X), NA417114, Naxos AudioBooks) Naxos.
This great religious allegory, dating from the late 1670's, is presented as a dream in which Christian undertakes a journey through the Slough of Despond to the Celestial City. Features 17th century music for violins & organ.

***Pilgrim's Progress.** John Bunyan. Narrated by Michael Russotto. (ENG.). 2010. audio compact disk 34.95 (978-1-60646-139-6(7)) Audio Bk Con.

Pilgrim's Progress. abr. ed. John Bunyan. Narrated by Max McLean. 5 CDs. (Running Time: 19320 sec.). (Listener's Collection of Classic Christian Literature Ser.). 2007. audio compact disk 29.95 (978-1-931047-56-2(1)) Fellow Perform Arts.

Pilgrim's Progress. abr. ed. John Bunyan. Read by Edward De Souza. 4 CDs. (Running Time: 5 hrs. 15 mins.). 1999. audio compact disk 28.98 (978-962-634-171-1(8), NA417112, Naxos AudioBooks) Naxos.
The great religious allegory of Christian's journey through the Slough of Despond to the Celestial City in search of Truth. (Multi-Voice Recording).

***Pilgrim's Progress.** abr. ed. John Bunyan. Narrated by Veronica Murphy. (Running Time: 3 hrs. 18 mins. 0 sec.). (ENG.). 2004. 10.98 (978-1-59644-034-0(1), Hovel Audio) christianaud.

***Pilgrim's Progress.** abr. ed. John Bunyan. Narrated by Paul Michael. (Running Time: 3 hrs. 0 mins. 0 sec.). (ENG.). 2010. audio compact disk 5.98 (978-1-59644-714-1(1), christaudio) christianaud.

Pilgrim's Progress. unabr. ed. John Bunyan. Read by Robert Whitefield. 7 cass. (Running Time: 10 hrs.). 1998. 49.95 (978-0-7861-1273-9(5), 2208) Blckstn Audio.
Is considered by most critics as the greatest allegory in any language. It was written by a jailed tinker who received very little formal education.

Pilgrim's Progress. unabr. ed. John Bunyan. Read by Robert Whitfield. 9 CDs. (Running Time: 10 hrs.). 2000. audio compact disk 72.00 (978-0-7861-9931-0(8), 2208) Blckstn Audio.
Tale is also a Christian's epic journey. After Christian reads a book that tells him that the city in which he & his family dwell will be set ablaze, he flees from the City of Destruction. His journeys take him to the Slough of Despond, the Interpreter's House, the House Beautiful, the Valley of Humiliation, the Valley of the Shadow of Death, Vanity Fair, Doubting Castle, the Delectable Mountains & finally to the Celestial City.

Pilgrim's Progress. unabr. ed. John Bunyan. Read by Robert Whitfield. (Running Time: 10 hrs.). 2010. 24.95 (978-0-7861-9365-3(4), 2208) Blckstn Audio.

Pilgrim's Progress. unabr. ed. John Bunyan. Read by Gary Martin. 5 cass. (Running Time: 7 hrs. 5 min.). 1991. 32.00 set. (C-216) Jimcin Record.
Inspirational journey to salvation.

Pilgrim's Progress. unabr. ed. John Bunyan. 1 cass. 10.95 (SAC 7121) Spoken Arts.

Pilgrim's Progress. unabr. ed. John Bunyan. 9 CDs. (Running Time: 10 hrs. 30 mins. 0 sec.). (ENG.). 2006. audio compact disk 28.98 (978-1-59644-361-7(8), Hovel Audio) christianaud.
John Bunyan was a simple maker and mender of pots and pans who received very little education. In spite of that, he penned the most successful allegory ever written. Embark on a perilous journey with Christian, the lead character, from the City of Destruction to the luminous safe haven of the Celestial City. The journey will encourage you to a??set your hope fully on the grace to be given youa?? amidst the obstacles of life.

Pilgrim's Progress. unabr. ed. John Bunyan. Narrated by Nadia May. 1 MP3CD. (Running Time: 10 hrs. 30 mins. 0 sec.). (ENG.). 2006. lp 19.98 (978-1-59644-363-1(4), Hovel Audio) christianaud.

Pilgrim's Progress. unabr. ed. John Bunyan. Read by Michael Russotto. 8 cass. (Running Time: 11 hrs.). 1994. 26.95 (978-1-55685-321-0(1)) Audio Bk Con.
Christian's progress from this world to that which is to come is a dream of a dangerous journey fraught with doubt & struggles with sin leading to eventual conversion & faith. Part II concerns his wife, Christiana & children as they travel the same road.

***Pilgrim's Progress.** unabr. ed. John Bunyan. Read by Robert Whitfield. (Running Time: 10 hrs.). 2010. audio compact disk 29.95 (978-1-4417-4768-6(0)) Blckstn Audio.

***Pilgrim's Progress.** unabr. ed. John Bunyan. Narrated by James Langton. (Running Time: 6 hrs. 30 mins. 0 sec.). 2010. 19.99 (978-1-4001-6808-8(2)); audio compact disk 66.99 (978-1-4001-4808-0(1)); audio compact disk 27.99 (978-1-4001-1808-3(5)) Pub: Tantor Media. Dist(s): IngramPubServ

***Pilgrim's Progress.** unabr. ed. John Bunyan. Narrated by Paul Michael. (ENG.). 2010. 5.98 (978-1-59644-715-8(X), christaudio) christianaud.

***Pilgrim's Progress.** unabr. ed. John Bunyan. Narrated by James Langton. (Running Time: 6 hrs. 30 mins.). 2010. 14.99 (978-1-4001-8808-6(3)) Tantor Media.

Pilgrim's Progress, Pt. 1. Contrib. by John Bunyan. 1 cass. 1995. 34.99 (978-5-901797-08-2(6)) Bible Games Co.
Christian literature.

Pilgrim's Progress, Pt. 2. Contrib. by John Bunyan. 1 cass. 1995. 39.99 (978-5-901797-09-9(4)) Bible Games Co.

Pilgrim's Progress, Vol. 1. adpt. ed. John Bunyan. Adapted by Jim Pappas. 6 cass. (Running Time: 6 hrs.). Dramatization. 1999. 24.99 (978-7-901280-00-7(X)) HARK Ent.
Accompany Christian on his diverse adventures as he passes through the Slough of Despond, escapes from prison & encounters lions & others.

Pilgrims Progress, Vol. 2. unabr. adpt. ed. 6 cass. (Running Time: 8 hrs.). Dramatization. 1995. 24.99 (978-7-901280-07-6(7)) HARK Ent.
Christiana & her four sons & Mercy are in for an adventure. Together they travel & gather wisdom & confront internal & external dangers along their path of faith.

Pilgrim's Progress: From This World to That Which Is to Come. unabr. ed. John Bunyan. Ed. by C. J. Lovik. Narrated by Tim Lundeen. (Running Time: 6 hrs. 1 mins. 26 sec.). (ENG.). 2009. 17.49 (978-1-60814-612-3(X)); audio compact disk 24.99 (978-1-59859-665-6(9)) Oasis Audio.

Pilgrim's Progress: Retold for the Modern Reader. abr. ed. John Bunyan. Narrated by Veronica Murphy. 3 CDs. (Running Time: 3 hrs. 18 mins. 0 sec.). (ENG.). 2004. audio compact disk 18.98 (978-1-59644-033-3(3), Hovel Audio) christianaud.
This is an updated version for all ages retold in wonderful storytelling fashion. John Bunyan was a simple maker and mender of pots and pans who received very little education. In spite of that, he penned the most successful allegory ever written. Embark on a perilous journey with Christian, the lead character, from the City of Destruction to the luminous safe haven of the Celestial City. The journey will encourage you to a??set your hope fully on the grace to be given youa?? amidst the obstacles of life.

***Pilgrim's Progress (Library Edition)** unabr. ed. John Bunyan. Narrated by James Langton. (Running Time: 6 hrs. 30 mins.). 2010. 27.99 (978-1-4001-9808-5(9)) Tantor Media.

***Pilgrim's Progress Unabridged.** unabr. ed. John Bunyan. Narrated by Nadia May. (ENG.). 2006. 16.98 (978-1-59644-362-4(6), Hovel Audio) christianaud.

Pilgrim's Regress: An Allegorical Apology for Christianity, Reason, & Romanticism. unabr. ed. C. S. Lewis. Read by Robert Whitfield. 5 cass. (Running Time: 7 hrs.). 2001. 39.95 (978-0-7861-1960-8(8), 2731); audio compact disk 48.00 (978-0-7861-9764-4(1), 2731) Blckstn Audio.
The story of John & his odyssey to an enchanting island that has created in him an intense longing - a mysterious, sweet desire. John's pursuit of this desire takes him through adventures with such people as Mr. Enlightenment, Media Halfways, Mr. Mammon, Mother Kirk, Mr. Sensible & Mr. Humanist & through such cities as Thrill & Eschropolis, as well as the Valley of Humiliation.

Pilgrim's Report. Henri J. M. Nouwen. Read by Henri J. M. Nouwen. 1 cass. (Running Time: 56 min.). 7.95 Credence Commun.
Focuses on the spiritual dimension of the political & economic turmoil.

Pilgrims vs. Indians. Douglas W. Phillips. 1 cass. (Running Time: 1 hr. 18 mins.). 2001. 7.00 (978-1-929241-27-9(5)) Pub: Vsn Forum. Dist(s): STL Dist NA

Pilgrims vs. Indians. Douglas W. Phillips. 1 CD. (Running Time: 1 hr. 18 mins.). 2001. audio compact disk 10.00 (978-1-929241-65-1(8)) Pub: Vsn Forum. Dist(s): STL Dist NA
The Pilgrims did more to promote a godly vision of Christian / Indian relations than any other group in American history. They signed a peace treaty with local natives which lasted unbroken for more than fifty years. In all, the relations between the two communities represented the high water mark of Christian / Indian relations in North America. THis tape seeks to answer questions like: Should we respect pagan cultures or seek to transform them? Is paganism noble? Did the Pilgrims steal land from the Indians?.

***Pili the Iwa Bird Flies Again.** (ENG.). (J). 2010. audio compact disk (978-1-933835-20-4(6)) Part Dev.

Pill Hill Quartet. Short Stories. Jay O'Callahan. Perf. by Jay O'Callahan. 1 CD. (Running Time: 1 hr. 1 min.). Dramatization. 2002. audio compact disk 15.00 (978-1-877954-33-7(0)) Pub: Artana Prodns. Dist(s): Yellow Moon
Jay O'Callahan grew up in the neighborhood of Brookline, Massachusetts called Pill Hill because so many doctors lived there. The magical house and grounds and the dramas and tragedies of the eccentric neighbors inpired these colorful stories about Norwegians in the attic, a sausage dog who spoke only Portuguese, and salmon in the bathtub.

Pill Hill Quartet. abr. ed. Short Stories. Jay O'Callahan. Perf. by Jay O'Callahan. 1 cass. (Running Time: 1 hr. 1 min.). Dramatization. 2002. 10.00 (978-1-877954-34-4(9)) Pub: Artana Prodns. Dist(s): High Windy Audio

Pillage. Obert Skye. 2008. audio compact disk 39.95 (978-1-59038-937-9(9), Shadow Mount) Deseret Bk.

Pillar of Fire. unabr. ed. Judith Tarr. Read by Anna Fields. 15 cass. (Running Time: 22 hrs.). 1996. 95.95 (978-0-7861-1061-2(9), 1832) Blckstn Audio.
This is a monumental novel of Ancient Egypt - of the turbulent years of the reigns of the Pharaoh Akhenaten & his successors.

Pillar of Fire: America in the King Years, Part II - 1963-64. abr. ed. Taylor Branch. 2004. 15.95 (978-0-7435-4815-1(9)) Pub: S&S Audio. Dist(s): S and S Inc

Pillar of Fire: America in the King Years, 1963-1965, Pt. 1, set. Taylor Branch. Read by Dick Estell. 11 cass. (Running Time: 90 mins. per cass.). 2000. 88.00 (5131-A) Books on Tape.
Captures the intensity of the legendary King years in all their glory & intensity.

Pillar of Fire: America in the King Years, 1963-1965, Pt. 2, set. Taylor Branch. Read by Dick Estell. 11 cass. (Running Time: 90 mins. per cass.). 2000. 88.00 (5131-B) Books on Tape.

Pillars of Creation. unabr. ed. Terry Goodkind. Read by Jim Bond. 13 cass. (Running Time: 23 hrs.). (Sword of Truth Ser.: Bk. 7). 2001. 44.95 (978-1-58788-936-3(6), 1587889366, BAU); 146.25 (978-1-58788-937-0(4), 1587889374, Unabridge Lib Edns) Brilliance Audio.
Tormented her entire life by inhuman voices, Jennsen seeks to end her intolerable agony. She at last discovers a way to silence the voices. For everyone else, the torment is about to begin. Richard Rahl and his wife, Kahlan, have been reunited after their long separation, but with winter descending and the paralyzing dread of an army of annihilation occupying their homeland, they must venture deep into a strange and desolate land. Their quest turns to terror when they find themselves the helpless prey of a tireless hunter. Exploited by those intent on domination, Jennsen finds herself drawn into the center of a violent struggle for conquest and revenge. Worse yet, she finds her will seized by dark forces more abhorrent than anything she ever envisioned. Only then does she come to realize that the voices were real. Staggered by loss and increasingly isolated, Richard and Kahlan desperately struggle to survive. But if they are to live, they must stop the relentless, unearthly threat that comes out of the darkest night of the human soul. To do so, Richard will be called upon to face the demons stalking among the Pillars of Creation.

Pillars of Creation. unabr. ed. Terry Goodkind. Read by Jim Bond. (Running Time: 23 hrs.). (Sword of Truth Ser.: Bk. 7). 2004. 29.95 (978-1-59335-302-5(2), 1593353022, Brilliance MP3); audio compact disk 44.25 (978-1-59335-535-7(1), 1593355351, Brinc Audio MP3 Lib) Brilliance Audio.

Pillars of Creation. unabr. ed. Terry Goodkind. Read by Jim Bond. (Running Time: 23 hrs.). (Sword of Truth Ser.). 2004. 44.25 (978-1-59710-572-9(4),

1597105724, BADLE); 29.95 (978-1-59710-573-6(2), 1597105732, BAD) Brilliance Audio.

Pillars of Creation. unabr. ed. Terry Goodkind. Read by Jim Bond. (Running Time: 23 hrs.). (Sword of Truth Ser.: Bk. 7). 2007. audio compact disk 38.95 (978-1-4233-2171-2(5), 9781423321712, Bril Audio CD Unabri); audio compact disk 112.25 (978-1-4233-2172-9(3), 9781423321729, BriAudCD Unabrid) Brilliance Audio.

Pillars of Hercules: A Grand Tour of the Mediterranean, Pt. I. unabr. ed. Paul Theroux. Read by Michael Prichard. 8 cass. (Running Time: 12 hrs.). 1996. 64.00 (4192-A) Books on Tape.
On this trip of exploration to the Mediterranean coast, Theroux had no commitment to any particular destination or schedule. His only prohibition - no travel by airplane.

Pillars of Hercules: A Grand Tour of the Mediterranean, Pt. II. unabr. ed. Paul Theroux. Read by Michael Prichard. 8 cass. (Running Time: 12 hrs.). 1996. 64.00 (4192-B) Books on Tape.

Pillars of Hercules: A Grand Tour of the Mediterranean, Pts. I-II. unabr. ed. Paul Theroux. Read by Michael Prichard. 16 cass. (Running Time: 24 hrs.). 1996. 128.00 (978-0-7366-3545-5(9), 4192) Books on Tape.

Pillars of Midnight. unabr. collector's ed. Elleston Trevor. Read by David Case. 7 cass. (Running Time: 7 hrs.). 1992. 42.00 (978-0-7366-2115-1(6), 2918) Books on Tape.
Two epidemics take their toll on a small English town - one mortal, the other moral. Both devastate.

Pillars of the Earth. Ken Follett. Read by John Lee. (Running Time: 41 hrs.). (ENG.). (gr. 8 up). 2007. audio compact disk 59.95 (978-0-14-314237-9(2), PengAudBks) Penguin Grp USA.

Pillars of the Earth. abr. ed. Ken Follett. Read by Richard E. Grant. 8 CDs. (Running Time: 10 hrs.). (ENG.). (gr. 8 up). 2007. audio compact disk 29.95 (978-0-14-314238-6(0), PengAudBks) Penguin Grp USA.

Pillars of the Earth. unabr. ed. Ken Follett. Read by David Case. 28 cass. (Running Time: 42 hrs.). 1989. 216.00 (2501-A/B/C) Books on Tape.
Ken Follett is a master of detail & split-second suspense. Now, in The Pillars of the Earth, he reaches beyond the expected to 12th century feudal England. The creation of a cathedral is at the center of this drama. And it is a drama, building a great church. Around its construction Follett weaves a story of betrayal, revenge & love. It begins with the public hanging of an innocent man & ends with the humiliation of a king.

Pillars of the Earth. unabr. ed. Ken Follett. Read by George Ralph. 10 cass. (Running Time: 30 hrs.). 1989. 39.95 set, library ed. Brilliance Audio.
Not-so-noble knights, righteous heroes, valiant heroines & both virtuous & immoral men of God highlight this story.

Pillars of the Earth. unabr. ed. Ken Follett. 2000. 15.99 (978-0-7435-0563-5(8), Audioworks) S&S Audio.
About a man and his evolution as a stone mason/ architect / builder - his dream to see a cathedral thru to completion (that he has worked on), and all he encounters throughout his lifetime.

Pillars of the Earth, Pt. 1. unabr. ed. Ken Follett. Read by David Case. 11 cass. (Running Time: 16 hrs. 30 min.). 1989. 88.00 (2501-A); 88.00 (978-0-7366-1649-2(7), 2501-A) Books on Tape.
Reach beyond the expected to 12th century feudal England. It begins with the public hanging of an innocent man and ends with the humiliation of a king.

Pillars of the Earth, Pt. 2. unabr. ed. Ken Follett. Read by David Case. 9 cass. (Running Time: 13 hrs. 30 mins.). 1989. 72.00 (978-0-7366-1651-5(9), 2501-C) Books on Tape.

Pillars of the Earth, Pt. 3. unabr. ed. Ken Follett. Read by David Case. 8 cass. (Running Time: 12 hs.). 1989. 64.00 (978-0-7366-1650-8(0), 2501-B) Books on Tape.

Pillars of the Earth, Set. unabr. ed. Ken Follett. Read by George Ralph. 20 cass. 1999. 178.50 (FS9-34261) Highsmith.

Pillow Full of Wishes. Cathy Fink & Marcy Marxer. 1 cass. (J). 2000. 9.98 (978-1-57940-049-1(3), 8086); audio compact disk 14.98 Rounder Records.
Includes: "Rainbow's End/Pot of Gold," "Make a Wish," "The Banana Wish Song," "All Around the World" & others.

Pillow Talk: Listen Your Way to Better Sleep. Created by Janet Fontana. Voice by Janet Fontana. Des. by Gunston Hope. Prod. by Spectrum SleepWorks. (ENG.). 2007. 79.95 (978-0-9817862-0-9(0)) Spectrum Sleep.

Pills & Skills: Using Medication Treatment Effectively. John F. Taylor. 1 cass. (Running Time: 45 min.). (Answers to ADD Ser.). 1993. 9.95 (978-1-883963-06-4(0)) ADD Plus.
Lecture tape.

Pilot down, Presumed Dead. unabr. ed. Marjorie Phleger. 1 read-along cass. (Running Time: 26 min.). (Middle Grade Cliffhangers Ser.). (J). (gr. 5-6). 1980. 15.98 (978-0-8072-1064-2(1), SWR 9 SP, Listening Lib); (Listening Lib) Random Audio Pubg.
When Steve Ferris' plane is forced down on an uncharted island, he realizes that rescue may be years away. He survives with skill & determination, & keeps alive the hope of returning to civilization.

Pilot's Wife. abr. ed. Anita Shreve. Read by Blair Brown. (Running Time: 18000 sec.). (ENG.). 2007. audio compact disk 14.99 (978-0-7393-5736-1(0), Random AudioBks) Pub: Random Audio Pubg. Dist(s): Random

Pilot's Wife. unabr. ed. Anita Shreve. Read by Mary Peiffer. 7 CDs. (Running Time: 9 hrs.). 2001. audio compact disk 34.95 (978-0-7366-5708-2(8)) Books on Tape.
Being married to a pilot means you have to be a bit of a fatalist, but nothing has prepared Kathryn Lyons for the news of her husband's fatal crash.

Pilot's Wife. unabr. ed. Anita Shreve. Read by Mary Peiffer. 6 cass. (Running Time: 9 hrs.). 1999. 29.95 (978-0-7366-4478-5(4)) Books on Tape.

Pilot's Wife, unabr. collector's ed. Anita Shreve. Read by Mary Peiffer. 6 cass. (Running Time: 9 hrs.). 1998. 48.00 (978-0-7366-4245-3(5), 4744) Books on Tape.

Pilot's Wife. unabr. collector's ed. Anita Shreve. Read by Mary Peiffer. 7 CDs. (Running Time: 9 hrs.). (New Core Collections). 2000. audio compact disk 56.00 (978-0-7366-5148-6(9)) Books on Tape.

Pimps, Hos, Playas, & My Other Hollywood Friends: A Life. John Leguizamo. 2006. audio compact disk 29.95 (978-0-06-114236-9(0)) HarperCollins Pubs.

Pimsleur Albanian (Compact) Paul Pimsleur. (Running Time: 5 hrs.). 2004. 49.95 (978-1-933092-70-6(X), Audiofy Corp) Iofy Corp.

Pimsleur Arabic (Eastern) I, 2nd Ed. Paul Pimsleur. (Running Time: 15 hrs.). 2003. 159.95 (978-1-933092-35-5(1), Audiofy Corp) Iofy Corp.

Pimsleur Arabic (Egyptian) I. Paul Pimsleur. (Running Time: 15 hrs.). 2001. 159.95 (978-1-933092-36-2(X), Audiofy Corp) Iofy Corp.

Pimsleur Armenian (Eastern) (Compact) Paul Pimsleur. (Running Time: 5 hrs.). 2004. 49.95 (978-1-933092-71-3(8), Audiofy Corp) Iofy Corp.

Pimsleur Armenian (Western) (Compact) Paul Pimsleur. (Running Time: 5 hrs.). 2004. 49.95 (978-1-933092-72-0(6), Audiofy Corp) Iofy Corp.

Pimsleur Basic Arabic (Eastern) Paul Pimsleur. (Running Time: 5 hrs.). 2005. 29.95 (978-1-60083-384-7(5), Audiofy Corp) Iofy Corp.

Pimsleur Basic Arabic (Egyptian) Paul Pimsleur. (Running Time: 5 hrs.). 2005. 29.95 (978-1-60083-344-1(6), Audiofy Corp) Iofy Corp.

Pimsleur Basic Chinese (Cantonese) Paul Pimsleur. (Running Time: 5 hrs.). 2005. 29.95 (978-1-60083-385-4(3), Audiofy Corp) Iofy Corp.

Pimsleur Basic Chinese (Mandarin) Paul Pimsleur. (Running Time: 5 hrs.). 2005. 29.95 (978-1-60083-386-1(1), Audiofy Corp) Iofy Corp.

Pimsleur Basic Czech. Paul Pimsleur. (Running Time: 5 hrs.). 2005. 29.95 (978-1-60083-387-8(X), Audiofy Corp) Iofy Corp.

Pimsleur Basic Farsi (Persian) Paul Pimsleur. (Running Time: 5 hrs.). 2005. 29.95 (978-1-60083-388-5(8), Audiofy Corp) Iofy Corp.

Pimsleur Basic French. Paul Pimsleur. (Running Time: 5 hrs.). 2005. 29.95 (978-1-60083-389-2(6), Audiofy Corp) Iofy Corp.

Pimsleur Basic German. Paul Pimsleur. (Running Time: 5 hrs.). 2005. 29.95 (978-1-60083-390-8(X), Audiofy Corp) Iofy Corp.

Pimsleur Basic Greek. Paul Pimsleur. (Running Time: 5 hrs.). 2005. 29.95 (978-1-60083-391-5(8), Audiofy Corp) Iofy Corp.

Pimsleur Basic Hebrew. Paul Pimsleur. (Running Time: 5 hrs.). 2005. 29.95 (978-1-60083-392-2(6), Audiofy Corp) Iofy Corp.

Pimsleur Basic Italian. Paul Pimsleur. (Running Time: 5 hrs.). 2005. 29.95 (978-1-60083-393-9(4), Audiofy Corp) Iofy Corp.

Pimsleur Basic Japanese. Paul Pimsleur. (Running Time: 5 hrs.). 2005. 29.95 (978-1-60083-394-6(2), Audiofy Corp) Iofy Corp.

Pimsleur Basic Korean. Paul Pimsleur. (Running Time: 5 hrs.). 2005. 29.95 (978-1-60083-414-1(0), Audiofy Corp) Iofy Corp.

Pimsleur Basic Ojibwe. Paul Pimsleur. (Running Time: 5 hrs.). 2005. 29.95 (978-1-60083-415-8(9), Audiofy Corp) Iofy Corp.

Pimsleur Basic Polish. Paul Pimsleur. (Running Time: 5 hrs.). 2005. 29.95 (978-1-60083-395-3(0), Audiofy Corp) Iofy Corp.

Pimsleur Basic Portuguese (Brazilian) Paul Pimsleur. (Running Time: 5 hrs.). 2005. 29.95 (978-1-60083-396-0(9), Audiofy Corp) Iofy Corp.

Pimsleur Basic Russian. Paul Pimsleur. (Running Time: 5 hrs.). 2005. 29.95 (978-1-60083-397-7(7), Audiofy Corp) Iofy Corp.

Pimsleur Basic Spanish. Paul Pimsleur. (Running Time: 5 hrs.). 2005. 29.95 (978-1-60083-398-4(5), Audiofy Corp) Iofy Corp.

Pimsleur Basic Thai. Paul Pimsleur. (Running Time: 5 hrs.). 2005. 29.95 (978-1-60083-413-4(2), Audiofy Corp) Iofy Corp.

Pimsleur Basic Vietnamese. Paul Pimsleur. (Running Time: 5 hrs.). 2005. 29.95 (978-1-60083-416-5(7), Audiofy Corp) Iofy Corp.

Pimsleur Beginner German. unabr. ed. Pimsleur Staff. 1 cass. (GER.). 1990. 25.00 (978-0-671-52163-9(2), Pimsleur) S&S Audio.

Pimsleur Beginner Italian. unabr. ed. Henry N. Raymond. 4 cass. (Running Time: 4 hrs.). 1990. 25.00 (978-0-671-52165-3(9), 492442, Pimsleur) S&S Audio.

Pimsleur Beginner Japanese. unabr. ed. Pimsleur Staff. 1 cass. 1989. 25.00 (978-0-671-52164-6(0), Pimsleur) S&S Audio.

Pimsleur Beginner Portuguese (Brazilian) unabr. ed. Pimsleur Staff. 1 cass. 1989. 25.00 (978-0-671-56263-2(0), Pimsleur) S&S Audio.

Pimsleur Beginner Russian. unabr. ed. Pimsleur Staff. 1 cass. 1987. 25.00 (978-0-671-52166-0(7), Pimsleur) S&S Audio.

Pimsleur Brazilian Portuguese I & II. Paul Pimsleur. (Running Time: 30 hrs.). 2005. 289.95 (978-1-59912-878-8(0), Audiofy Corp) Iofy Corp.

Pimsleur Brazilian Portuguese I, II & III, Set. Paul Pimsleur. (Running Time: 45 hrs.). 2005. 399.95 (978-1-59912-842-9(X), Audiofy Corp) Iofy Corp.

Pimsleur Chinese (Cantonese) I. Paul Pimsleur. (Running Time: 16 hrs.). 2005. 159.95 (978-1-933092-37-9(8), Audiofy Corp) Iofy Corp.

Pimsleur Chinese (Mandarin) I. Paul Pimsleur. (Running Time: 15 hrs.). 2000. 139.95 (978-1-933092-38-6(6), Audiofy Corp) Iofy Corp.

Pimsleur Chinese (Mandarin) I & II. Paul Pimsleur. (Running Time: 30 hrs.). 2005. 289.95 (978-1-59912-883-2(7), Audiofy Corp) Iofy Corp.

Pimsleur Chinese Mandarin I, II & III. Paul Pimsleur. (Running Time: 45 hrs.). 2005. 399.95 (978-1-59912-847-4(0), Audiofy Corp) Iofy Corp.

Pimsleur Chinese (Mandarin) II. Paul Pimsleur. (Running Time: 15 hrs.). 2002. 159.95 (978-1-933092-39-3(4), Audiofy Corp) Iofy Corp.

Pimsleur Chinese (Mandarin) III. Paul Pimsleur. (Running Time: 15 hrs.). 2003. 159.95 (978-1-933092-40-9(8), Audiofy Corp) Iofy Corp.

Pimsleur Compact Arabic (Eastern), Set. unabr. ed. Pimsleur Staff. 5 cass. (ARA.). 1997. 95.00 (978-0-671-57905-0(3), Pimsleur) S&S Audio.

Pimsleur Conversational Arabic (Eastern) Paul Pimsleur. (Running Time: 8 hrs.). 2007. 49.95 (978-1-60083-072-3(2), Audiofy Corp) Iofy Corp.

Pimsleur Conversational Arabic (Egyptian) Paul Pimsleur. (Running Time: 8 hrs.). 2007. 49.95 (978-1-60083-076-1(5), Audiofy Corp) Iofy Corp.

Pimsleur Conversational Chinese (Cantonese) Paul Pimsleur. (Running Time: 8 hrs.). 2007. 49.95 (978-1-60083-074-7(9), Audiofy Corp) Iofy Corp.

Pimsleur Conversational Chinese (Mandarin) Paul Pimsleur. (Running Time: 8 hrs.). 2007. 49.95 (978-1-60083-086-0(2), Audiofy Corp) Iofy Corp.

Pimsleur Conversational Czech. Paul Pimsleur. (Running Time: 8 hrs.). 2007. 49.95 (978-1-60083-075-4(7), Audiofy Corp) Iofy Corp.

Pimsleur Conversational ESL for Spanish Speakers. Paul Pimsleur. (Running Time: 8 hrs.). 2007. 49.95 (978-1-60083-092-1(7), Audiofy Corp) Iofy Corp.

Pimsleur Conversational Farsi (Persian) Paul Pimsleur. (Running Time: 8 hrs.). 2007. 49.95 (978-1-60083-077-8(3), Audiofy Corp) Iofy Corp.

Pimsleur Conversational French. Paul Pimsleur. (Running Time: 8 hrs.). 2007. 49.95 (978-1-60083-078-5(1), Audiofy Corp) Iofy Corp.

Pimsleur Conversational German. Paul Pimsleur. (Running Time: 8 hrs.). 2007. 49.95 (978-1-60083-079-2(X), Audiofy Corp) Iofy Corp.

Pimsleur Conversational Greek (Modern) Paul Pimsleur. (Running Time: 8 hrs.). 2007. 49.95 (978-1-60083-080-8(3), Audiofy Corp) Iofy Corp.

Pimsleur Conversational Hebrew (Modern) Paul Pimsleur. (Running Time: 8 hrs.). 2007. 49.95 (978-1-60083-081-5(1), Audiofy Corp) Iofy Corp.

Pimsleur Conversational Italian. Paul Pimsleur. (Running Time: 8 hrs.). 2007. 49.95 (978-1-60083-083-9(8), Audiofy Corp) Iofy Corp.

Pimsleur Conversational Japanese. Paul Pimsleur. (Running Time: 8 hrs.). 2007. 49.95 (978-1-60083-084-6(6), Audiofy Corp) Iofy Corp.

Pimsleur Conversational Korean. Paul Pimsleur. (Running Time: 8 hrs.). 2007. 49.95 (978-1-60083-085-3(4), Audiofy Corp) Iofy Corp.

Pimsleur Conversational Polish. Paul Pimsleur. (Running Time: 8 hrs.). 2007. 49.95 (978-1-60083-087-7(0), Audiofy Corp) Iofy Corp.

Pimsleur Conversational Portuguese (Brazilian) Paul Pimsleur. (Running Time: 8 hrs.). 2007. 49.95 (978-1-60083-073-0(0), Audiofy Corp) Iofy Corp.

Pimsleur Conversational Russian. Paul Pimsleur. (Running Time: 8 hrs.). 2006. 49.95 (978-1-60083-088-4(9), Audiofy Corp) Iofy Corp.

Pimsleur Conversational Spanish. Paul Pimsleur. (Running Time: 8 hrs.). 2007. 49.95 (978-1-60083-089-1(7), Audiofy Corp) Iofy Corp.

Pimsleur Conversational Thai. Paul Pimsleur. (Running Time: 8 hrs.). 2007. 49.95 (978-1-60083-090-7(0), Audiofy Corp) Iofy Corp.

Pimsleur Conversational Vietnamese. Paul Pimsleur. (Running Time: 8 hrs.). 2007. 49.95 (978-1-60083-091-4(9), Audiofy Corp) Iofy Corp.

Pimsleur Croatian (Compact) Paul Pimsleur. (Running Time: 5 hrs.). 2003. 49.95 (978-1-933092-73-7(4), Audiofy Corp) Iofy Corp.

Pimsleur Czech I. Paul Pimsleur. (Running Time: 16 hrs.). 2006. 159.95 (978-1-59912-886-3(1), Audiofy Corp) Iofy Corp.

Pimsleur Danish (Compact) Paul Pimsleur. (Running Time: 5 hrs.). 2003. 49.95 (978-1-933092-75-1(0), Audiofy Corp) Iofy Corp.

Pimsleur Dutch (Compact) Paul Pimsleur. (Running Time: 5 hrs.). 1997. 49.95 (978-1-933092-76-8(9), Audiofy Corp) Iofy Corp.

Pimsleur ESL Arabic. Paul Pimsleur. (Running Time: 16 hrs.). 2001. 159.95 (978-1-933092-51-5(3), Audiofy Corp) Iofy Corp.

Pimsleur ESL Chinese (Cantonese) Paul Pimsleur. (Running Time: 16 hrs.). 2001. 159.95 (978-1-933092-52-2(1), Audiofy Corp) Iofy Corp.

Pimsleur ESL Chinese (Mandarin) Paul Pimsleur. (Running Time: 16 hrs.). 2001. 159.95 (978-1-933092-53-9(X), Audiofy Corp) Iofy Corp.

Pimsleur ESL French. Paul Pimsleur. (Running Time: 16 hrs.). 2002. 159.95 (978-1-933092-54-6(8), Audiofy Corp) Iofy Corp.

Pimsleur ESL German. Paul Pimsleur. (Running Time: 16 hrs.). 2001. 159.95 (978-1-933092-55-3(6), Audiofy Corp) Iofy Corp.

Pimsleur ESL Haitian. Paul Pimsleur. (Running Time: 16 hrs.). 2002. 159.95 (978-1-933092-56-0(4), Audiofy Corp) Iofy Corp.

Pimsleur ESL Italian I. Paul Pimsleur. (Running Time: 16 hrs.). 2002. 139.95 (978-1-933092-57-7(2), Audiofy Corp) Iofy Corp.

Pimsleur ESL Italian II. Paul Pimsleur. (Running Time: 16 hrs.). 1999. 159.95 (978-1-933092-58-4(0), Audiofy Corp) Iofy Corp.

Pimsleur ESL Korean. Paul Pimsleur. (Running Time: 16 hrs.). 2001. 159.95 (978-1-933092-63-8(7), Audiofy Corp) Iofy Corp.

Pimsleur ESL Portuguese (Brazilian) Paul Pimsleur. (Running Time: 15 hrs.). 2001. 159.95 (978-1-933092-64-5(5), Audiofy Corp) Iofy Corp.

Pimsleur ESL Russian. Paul Pimsleur. (Running Time: 16 hrs.). 2001. 139.95 (978-1-933092-65-2(3), Audiofy Corp) Iofy Corp.

Pimsleur ESL Spanish I. Paul Pimsleur. (Running Time: 16 hrs.). 2001. 139.95 (978-1-933092-66-9(1), Audiofy Corp) Iofy Corp.

Pimsleur ESL Spanish II. Paul Pimsleur. (Running Time: 15 hrs.). 2001. 159.95 (978-1-933092-67-6(X), Audiofy Corp) Iofy Corp.

Pimsleur ESL Spanish III. Paul Pimsleur. (Running Time: 15 hrs.). 2001. 159.95 (978-1-933092-68-3(8), Audiofy Corp) Iofy Corp.

Pimsleur ESL Vietnamese. Paul Pimsleur. (Running Time: 16 hrs.). 2002. 159.95 (978-1-933092-69-0(6), Audiofy Corp) Iofy Corp.

Pimsleur Farsi (Persian) I. Paul Pimsleur. (Running Time: 5 hrs.). 2005. 159.95 (978-1-59912-389-9(4), Audiofy Corp) Iofy Corp.

Pimsleur French I. Paul Pimsleur. (Running Time: 16 hrs.). 2002. 139.95 (978-1-933092-01-0(7), Audiofy Corp) Iofy Corp.

Pimsleur French I & II. Paul Pimsleur. (Running Time: 31 hrs. 30 mins.). 2005. 289.95 (978-1-59912-879-5(9), Audiofy Corp) Iofy Corp.

Pimsleur French I, II & III. Paul Pimsleur. (Running Time: 46 hrs. 30 mins.). 2005. 399.95 (978-1-59912-843-6(8), Audiofy Corp) Iofy Corp.

Pimsleur French II. Paul Pimsleur. (Running Time: 15 hrs. 30 mins.). 2004. 159.95 (978-1-933092-02-7(5), Audiofy Corp) Iofy Corp.

Pimsleur French III, 2nd Ed. Paul Pimsleur. (Running Time: 15 hrs.). 2005. 159.95 (978-1-60083-094-5(3), Audiofy Corp) Iofy Corp.

Pimsleur German I. Paul Pimsleur. (Running Time: 15 hrs. 30 mins.). 2002. 139.95 (978-1-933092-04-1(1), Audiofy Corp) Iofy Corp.

Pimsleur German I & II. Paul Pimsleur. (Running Time: 30 hrs. 30 mins.). 2005. 289.95 (978-1-59912-880-1(2), Audiofy Corp) Iofy Corp.

Pimsleur German I, II & III. Paul Pimsleur. (Running Time: 44 hrs. 30 mins.). 2005. 399.95 (978-1-59912-844-3(6), Audiofy Corp) Iofy Corp.

Pimsleur German II. Paul Pimsleur. (Running Time: 15 hrs.). 2003. 159.95 (978-1-933092-05-8(X), Audiofy Corp) Iofy Corp.

Pimsleur German III, 2nd Ed. Paul Pimsleur. (Running Time: 15 hrs. 30 mins.). 2006. 159.95 (978-1-59912-948-8(5), Audiofy Corp) Iofy Corp.

Pimsleur German Plus. Paul Pimsleur. (Running Time: 5 hrs.). 2001. 84.95 (978-1-933092-98-0(X), Audiofy Corp) Iofy Corp.

Pimsleur Greek (Modern) I. Paul Pimsleur. (Running Time: 15 hrs.). 2002. 159.95 (978-1-933092-41-6(6), Audiofy Corp) Iofy Corp.

Pimsleur Haitian Creole (Compact) Paul Pimsleur. (Running Time: 5 hrs.). 2004. 49.95 (978-1-933092-78-2(5), Audiofy Corp) Iofy Corp.

Pimsleur Hebrew. unabr. ed. Pimsleur Staff. 16 cass. (Pimsleur Language Program Ser.). (HEB.). 1997. 295.00 (978-0-671-57932-6(0), Pimsleur) S&S Audio.
30 lessons.

Pimsleur Hebrew I. Paul Pimsleur. (Running Time: 15 hrs.). 2001. 159.95 (978-1-933092-42-3(4), Audiofy Corp) Iofy Corp.

Pimsleur Hindi (Compact) Paul Pimsleur. (Running Time: 5 hrs.). 2003. 49.95 (978-1-933092-79-9(3), Audiofy Corp) Iofy Corp.

Pimsleur Indonesian (Compact) Paul Pimsleur. (Running Time: 5 hrs.). 2003. 49.95 (978-1-933092-80-5(7), Audiofy Corp) Iofy Corp.

Pimsleur Instant Conversation Arabic Eastern: The Simplest, Most Effective Language Course Ever Developed! unabr. ed. Pimsleur Staff. 8 cass. (Running Time: 9 hrs.). (ARA.). 2003. 49.95 (978-0-7607-4469-7(6), Pimsleur); audio compact disk 49.95 (978-0-7607-4470-3(X), Pimsleur) Pub: S&S Audio. Dist(s): S and S

Pimsleur Intermediate French. unabr. ed. Pimsleur Staff. 1 cass. 1996. 25.00 (978-0-671-56267-0(3), Pimsleur) S&S Audio.

Pimsleur Intermediate German. unabr. ed. Pimsleur Staff. 1 cass. 1996. 25.00 (978-0-671-56266-3(5), Pimsleur) S&S Audio.

Pimsleur Intermediate Italian. unabr. ed. Pimsleur Staff. 1 cass. 1996. 25.00 (978-0-671-56265-6(7), Pimsleur) S&S Audio.

Pimsleur Intermediate Japanese. unabr. ed. Pimsleur Staff. 1 cass. 1996. 25.00 (978-0-671-56269-4(X), Pimsleur) S&S Audio.

Pimsleur Intermediate Russian. unabr. ed. Pimsleur Staff. 1 cass. 1995. 25.00 (978-0-671-56270-0(3), Pimsleur) S&S Audio.

Pimsleur Intermediate Spanish. unabr. ed. Pimsleur Staff. 1 cass. 1995. 25.00 (978-0-671-56268-7(1), Pimsleur) S&S Audio.

Pimsleur Irish (Quick&Simple) Paul Pimsleur. (Running Time: 4 hrs.). 2001. 19.95 (978-1-59912-000-3(3), Audiofy Corp) Iofy Corp.

Pimsleur Italian I. Paul Pimsleur. (Running Time: 15 hrs. 30 mins.). 2002. 139.95 (978-1-933092-07-2(6), Audiofy Corp) Iofy Corp.

Pimsleur Italian I & II. Paul Pimsleur. (Running Time: 31 hrs.). 2005. 289.95 (978-1-59912-881-8(0), Audiofy Corp) Iofy Corp.

Pimsleur Italian I, II & III. Paul Pimsleur. (Running Time: 46 hrs.). 2005. 399.95 (978-1-59912-845-0(4), Audiofy Corp) Iofy Corp.

Pimsleur Italian II. Paul Pimsleur. (Running Time: 15 hrs. 30 mins.). 2004. 159.95 (978-1-933092-08-9(4), Audiofy Corp) Iofy Corp.

Pimsleur Italian III. Paul Pimsleur. (Running Time: 15 hrs.). 2005. 159.95 (978-1-933092-09-6(2), Audiofy Corp) Iofy Corp.

Pimsleur Japanese I. Paul Pimsleur. (Running Time: 15 hrs. 30 mins.). 2002. 139.95 (978-1-933092-10-2(6), Audiofy Corp) Iofy Corp.

Pimsleur Japanese I & II. Paul Pimsleur. (Running Time: 31 hrs.). 2005. 289.95 (978-1-59912-882-5(9), Audiofy Corp) Iofy Corp.

Pimsleur Japanese I, II & III. Paul Pimsleur. (Running Time: 46 hrs. 30 mins.). 2005. 399.95 (978-1-59912-846-7(2), Audiofy Corp) Iofy Corp.

Pimsleur Japanese II. Paul Pimsleur. (Running Time: 15 hrs. 30 mins.). 2004. 159.95 (978-1-933092-11-9(4), Audiofy Corp) Iofy Corp.

Pimsleur Japanese III. Paul Pimsleur. (Running Time: 15 hrs. 30 mins.). 2005. 159.95 (978-1-933092-12-6(2), Audiofy Corp) Iofy Corp.

Pimsleur Korean I. Paul Pimsleur. (Running Time: 15 hrs.). 2005. 159.95 (978-1-933092-81-2(5), Audiofy Corp) Iofy Corp.

Pimsleur Lithuanian (Compact) Paul Pimsleur. (Running Time: 5 hrs.). 2004. 49.95 (978-1-933092-82-9(3), Audiofy Corp) Iofy Corp.

Pimsleur Norwegian: Learn to Speak & Understand Norwegian with Pimsleur Language Programs. unabr. ed. Allison DuBois et al. 5 CDs. (Running Time: 50 hrs. 0 mins. 0 sec.). (Compact Ser.). (NOR & ENG.). 2005. audio compact disk 49.95 (978-0-7435-5055-0(2), Fireside) Pub: S and S. Dist(s): S and S Inc

Pimsleur Norwegian (Compact) Paul Pimsleur. (Running Time: 5 hrs.). 2003. 49.95 (978-1-933092-83-6(1), Audiofy Corp) Iofy Corp.

Pimsleur Ojibwe I. Paul Pimsleur. (Running Time: 15 hrs.). 1997. 159.95 (978-1-933092-43-0(2), Audiofy Corp) Iofy Corp.

Pimsleur Polish I. Paul Pimsleur. (Running Time: 15 hrs.). 2004. 159.95 (978-1-933092-84-3(X), Audiofy Corp) Iofy Corp.

Pimsleur Portuguese (Brazillian) I. Paul Pimsleur. (Running Time: 15 hrs.). 2001. 139.95 (978-1-933092-44-7(0), Audiofy Corp) Iofy Corp.

Pimsleur Portuguese (Brazillian) II. Paul Pimsleur. (Running Time: 15 hrs.). 2001. 159.95 (978-1-933092-45-4(9), Audiofy Corp) Iofy Corp.

Pimsleur Portuguese (Brazillian) III. Paul Pimsleur. (Running Time: 15 hrs.). 2002. 159.95 (978-1-933092-46-1(7), Audiofy Corp) Iofy Corp.

Pimsleur Portuguese (Continental) (Compact) Paul Pimsleur. (Running Time: 5 hrs.). 2005. 49.95 (978-1-933092-85-0(8), Audiofy Corp) Iofy Corp.

Pimsleur Romanian (Compact) Paul Pimsleur. (Running Time: 5 hrs.). 2003. 49.95 (978-1-933092-86-7(6), Audiofy Corp) Iofy Corp.

Pimsleur Russian I. Paul Pimsleur. (Running Time: 15 hrs.). 2001. 139.95 (978-1-933092-47-8(5), Audiofy Corp) Iofy Corp.

Pimsleur Russian I & II. Paul Pimsleur. (Running Time: 30 hrs.). 2005. 289.95 (978-1-59912-884-9(5), Audiofy Corp) Iofy Corp.

Pimsleur Russian I, II & III. Paul Pimsleur. (Running Time: 45 hrs.). 2005. 399.95 (978-1-59912-848-1(9), Audiofy Corp) Iofy Corp.

Pimsleur Russian II. Paul Pimsleur. (Running Time: 15 hrs.). 2003. 159.95 (978-1-933092-48-5(3), Audiofy Corp) Iofy Corp.

Pimsleur Russian III. Paul Pimsleur. (Running Time: 15 hrs.). 2004. 159.95 (978-1-933092-49-2(1), Audiofy Corp) Iofy Corp.

Pimsleur Spanish I. Paul Pimsleur. (Running Time: 16 hrs.). 2002. 139.95 (978-1-933092-13-3(0), Audiofy Corp) Iofy Corp.

Pimsleur Spanish I & II. Paul Pimsleur. (Running Time: 32 hrs.). 2005. 289.95 (978-1-59912-885-6(3), Audiofy Corp) Iofy Corp.

Pimsleur Spanish I, II & III. Paul Pimsleur. (Running Time: 48 hrs.). 2005. 399.95 (978-1-59912-849-8(7), Audiofy Corp) Iofy Corp.

Pimsleur Spanish II. Paul Pimsleur. (Running Time: 16 hrs.). 2003. 159.95 (978-1-933092-14-0(9), Audiofy Corp) Iofy Corp.

Pimsleur Spanish III. Paul Pimsleur. (Running Time: 16 hrs.). 2004. 159.95 (978-1-933092-15-7(7), Audiofy Corp) Iofy Corp.

Pimsleur Spanish Plus. Paul Pimsleur. (Running Time: 5 hrs.). 2001. 84.95 (978-1-933092-99-7(8), Audiofy Corp) Iofy Corp.

Pimsleur Swahili (Compact) Paul Pimsleur. (Running Time: 5 hrs.). 2003. 49.95 (978-1-933092-87-4(4), Audiofy Corp) Iofy Corp.

Pimsleur Swedish (Compact) Paul Pimsleur. (Running Time: 5 hrs.). 2003. 49.95 (978-1-933092-88-1(2), Audiofy Corp) Iofy Corp.

Pimsleur Swiss German (Compact) Paul Pimsleur. (Running Time: 5 hrs.). 2004. 49.95 (978-1-933092-89-8(0), Audiofy Corp) Iofy Corp.

Pimsleur Thai I. Paul Pimsleur. (Running Time: 15 hrs.). 2006. 159.95 (978-1-59912-947-1(7), Audiofy Corp) Iofy Corp.

Pimsleur Twi (Compact) Paul Pimsleur. (Running Time: 5 hrs.). 1997. 49.95 (978-1-933092-91-1(2), Audiofy Corp) Iofy Corp.

Pimsleur Vietnamese I. Paul Pimsleur. (Running Time: 15 hrs.). 2004. 159.95 (978-1-933092-92-8(0), Audiofy Corp) Iofy Corp.

Pinal County. unabr. ed. Stan Howe. Read by Maynard Villers. 8 cass. (Running Time: 11 hrs. 36 min.). 1996. 49.95 (978-1-55686-661-6(5)) Books in Motion.
Forty-four year old Justin Davidson lives in the Arizona desert in his camper. He gets involved in deadly S. American politics when two desert-stressed wet-backs wander into his camp.

Pinata & More! Bilingual Songs for Children. 2nd rev. ed. Sarah Barchas. Illus. by Elizabeth Gething & David Hoffman. 1 cass.; 1 CD. (Running Time: 45 min.). (ENG & SPA.). (J). (gr. k-6). 1997. pap. bk. 12.95 (978-1-889686-06-6(9)); pap. bk. 15.98 (978-1-889686-07-3(7)) High Haven Mus.
Twenty original & traditional songs celebrating Hispanic culture, history, traditions, foods, holidays, festivities, contributions, & joy in being bilingual.

Pinata Vacia. Alma Flor Ada. (Cuentos Para Todo el Ano Ser.). (SPA., (J). (gr. k-3). 4.95 (978-1-58105-253-4(7)) Santillana.

Pinballs. Betsy Byars. Narrated by Christina Moore. 3 CDs. (Running Time: 2 hrs. 45 mins.). (gr. 4 up). audio compact disk 29.00 (978-1-4025-0464-8(0)) Recorded Bks.

Pinballs. unabr. ed. Betsy Byars. 1 cass. (Running Time: 90 mins.). (J). (gr. 4-6). 1999. pap. bk. 15.98 (978-0-8072-1800-6(6), JJRH100SP, Listening Lib) Random Audio Pubg.
After being bounced from foster home to foster home, can the children finally learn to be a real family with the Masons? Narrated word-for-word up to an exciting point in the story. When the narrator stops, listeners finish reading story on their own.

Pinballs. unabr. ed. Betsy Byars. Read by Rita Gardner. 2 vols. (Running Time: 2 hrs. 51 mins.). (J). (gr. 5-9). 1989. pap. bk. 29.00 (978-0-8072-8536-7(6), LB2SP, Listening Lib); 23.00 (978-0-8072-8503-9(X), LB2CX, Listening Lib) Random Audio Pubg.
Harvey, Thomas J & Carlie bounce around foster homes, until the Masons take them in. Also available in Cliffhanger cassette & book.

Pinballs. unabr. ed. Betsy Byars. Read by Rita Gardner. 2 cass. (J). 1995. 16.98 Set. (978-0-8072-8528-2(5), LL 0008, Listening Lib); 23.00 t. (LL 0008, Listening Lib) Random Audio Pubg.
Life in & out of foster homes has been tough for Harvey, Thomas J., & Charlie. In fact, they've been knocking around from place to place for so long, they feel like pinballs! But things change when the Masons take them in, & slowly the children begin to feel like a family again.

Pinballs, unabr. ed. Betsy Byars. Narrated by Christina Moore. 2 pieces. (Running Time: 2 hrs. 45 mins.). (gr. 4 up). 1997. 19.00 (978-0-7887-0434-5(6), 94626E7) Recorded Bks.
Introduces young listeners to three adolescents overcoming personal tragedy together in a foster home.

Pinballs, Set. unabr. ed. Betsy Byars. Read by Rita Gardner. 2 cass. (J). (gr. 1-8). 1999. 16.98 (LL 0008, Chivers Child Audio) AudioGO.

Pinballs, Set. unabr. ed. Betsy Byars. Read by Rita Gardner. 2 cass. (YA). 1999. 16.98 (FS9-34153) Highsmith.

Pinch to Grow On. Miss Dee. 1 cass. 8.95 (269) Am Fed Astrologers.
Reach your highest potential & love yourself.

***Pinchbeck Bride.** unabr. ed. Stephen Anable. Read by To be Announced. (Running Time: 8 hrs. NaN mins.). (Sequel to the Fisher Boy Ser.). (ENG.). 2011. 29.95 (978-1-4417-7780-5(6)); 54.95 (978-1-4417-7777-5(6)); audio compact disk 76.00 (978-1-4417-7778-2(4)) Blckstn Audio.

Pincher Martin. unabr. ed. William Golding. Read by Richard Earthy. 6 cass. (Running Time: 6 hrs. 29 min.). Orig. Title: Two Deaths of Christopher Martin. 2001. 54.95 (978-1-85089-652-4(6), 30491) Pub: ISIS Audio GBR. Dist(s): Ulverscroft US
"Prose more tightly packed, more jaggedly concrete, I can't imagine: & the shock ending...is technical wizardry of the first order." - Kenneth Tynan in "The Observer".

Pine Apple Farm. (ENG.). 2009. audio compact disk (978-0-933173-13-2(X)) Chging Church Forum.

Pine Barrens. unabr. ed. John McPhee. Read by Dan Lazar. 4 cass. (Running Time: 4 hrs.). 1986. 24.00 (978-0-7366-1066-7(9), 1993) Books on Tape.
Discusses the vast expanse of bog, swamp & piney woods in central New Jersey.

Pinecrest Rest Haven. Poems. Grace Cavalieri. Read by Grace Cavalieri. Music by Mike Sokol. Illus. by Cynthia Comitz. 1 cass. 1997. 10.00 (978-0-938572-23-7(7)) Bunny Crocodile.
In the Pinecrest Rest Haven, Mr. & Mrs. P. no longer remember they're married & meet to fall in love (& hate) again & again.

Ping: A Frog in Search of a New Pond. unabr. ed. Stuart Avery Gold. Read by Christopher Lane. (Running Time: 1 hr.). 2008. 14.95 (978-1-4233-7528-9(9), 9781423375289, BAD) Brilliance Audio.

Ping: A Frog in Search of a New Pond. unabr. ed. Stuart Avery Gold. Read by Christopher A. Lane. (Running Time: 1 hr.). 2008. 14.95 (978-1-4233-7526-5(2), 9781423375265, Brilliance MP3); 39.25 (978-1-4233-7529-6(7), 9781423375296, BADLE); 39.25 (978-1-4233-7527-2(0), 9781423375272, Brinc Audio MP3 Lib) Brilliance Audio.

Ping: A Frog in Search of a New Pond. unabr. ed. Stuart Avery Gold. Read by Christopher Lane. (Running Time: 1 hr.). 2008. audio compact disk 14.95 (978-1-4233-7524-1(6), 9781423375241, Bril Audio CD Unabri) Brilliance Audio.

Ping: A Frog in Search of a New Pond. unabr. ed. Stuart Avery Gold. Read by Christopher A. Lane. (Running Time: 1 hr.). 2008. audio compact disk 39.25 (978-1-4233-7525-8(4), 9781423375258, BriAudCD Unabrid) Brilliance Audio.

Ping & the Way of Ping Unabridged CD Collection: Ping, the Way of Ping. unabr. ed. Stuart Avery Gold. Read by Christopher Lane. (Running Time: 2 hrs.). 2010. audio compact disk 29.99 (978-1-4418-1881-2(2), 9781441818812, Bril Audio CD Unabri) Brilliance Audio.

***Pinheads & Patriots: Where You Stand in the Age of Obama.** unabr. ed. Bill O'Reilly. Read by Bill O'Reilly. 2010. (978-0-06-200995-1(8), Harper Audio); (978-0-06-204191-3(6), Harper Audio) HarperCollins Pubs.

***Pinheads & Patriots: Where You Stand in the Age of Obama.** unabr. ed. Bill O'Reilly. 2010. 29.99 (978-0-06-195074-2(2), Harper Audio) HarperCollins Pubs.

Pinhoe Egg. unabr. ed. Diana Wynne Jones. Read by Gerard Doyle. 9 cass. (Running Time: 10 hrs. 25 mins.). (Chrestomanci Ser.). (J). (gr. 4-8). 2007. 67.75 (978-1-4281-3487-4(5)); audio compact disk 97.75 (978-1-4281-3492-8(1)) Recorded Bks.

Pink & Say. Patricia Polacco. Narrated by Patricia Polacco. 1 cass. (Running Time: 15 min.). (J). 2001. bk. 27.95 (978-0-8045-6835-7(9), 6835) Spoken Arts.
Two boys who meet while fighting in the Civil War.

Pink Flamingo Murders. abr. ed. Elaine Viets. 4 cass. (Running Time: 6 hrs.). (Francesca Vierling Mystery Ser.: No. 3). 2000. 25.00 (978-1-58807-052-4(2)) Am Pubng Inc.
Ever wish you could get rid of your obnoxious neighbors: the drug dealer, the rude guy with the yappy dog, the person who paints his house purple? Someone is killing off the neighborhood pests on North Dakota Place, a once-posh city street. Even die-hard preservationists will admit four murders are taking neighborhood beautification a little too far, especially when a socialite is whacked with a pink plastic lawn flamingo.

***Pink Floyd - Dark Side of the Moon: Drum Play-along Volume 24.** Pink Floyd. (ENG.). 2010. pap. bk. 14.99 (978-1-4234-9255-9(2), 1423492552) H Leonard.

Pink Floyd - Ultimate Minus One: Guitar Tab. audio compact disk 21.95 (978-88-507-0107-0(1), ML2160) Nuova Carisch ITA.

Pink Forest: A Woman's Intimate Confessions. Dana Dorfman. (ENG.). 2008. (978-0-9798592-2-9(0)) Banderae.

Pink Hotel Burns Down. Perf. by Firesign Theatre. Text by Firesign Theatre. 1 CD. (Running Time: 68 mins). Dramatization. 2005. audio compact disk 15.95 (978-1-59938-021-6(8), FTR) Lode Cat.

Pink Hotel Burns Down: A Collection of Rare & Unreleased Material. Firesign Theatre Firesign Theatre Staff. Prod. by Richard Fish. 1 cass. (Running Time: 60 min.). 1996. 12.95 (978-1-57677-052-8(4), MSUG006) Lodestone Catalog.
Includes: "The Pink Hotel Burns Down" (originally a demo for an interactive computer program); "Nick Danger Meets the Hut" (a collection of radio ads from the past 30 years); "Exorcism in Your Daily Life" (a longstanding favorite & one of their first parodies of The Classroom Film); & "Over the Edge" (a side-splitting parody of soap operats) - & more!.

Pink Hotel Burns Down: A Collection of Rare & Unreleased Material. Perf. by Firesign Theatre Firesign Theatre Staff. 1 CD. 1998. audio compact disk 15.95 (978-1-57677-103-7(2), MSUG008) Lodestone Catalog.

Pink Madness: Why Does Aphrodite Drive People Crazy with Pornography? James Hillman. Read by James Hillman. 1 cass. (Running Time: 1 hr.). 1995. pap. bk. 11.95 (978-1-879816-15-2(6)) Pub: Spring Audio. Dist(s): Daimon Verlag
James Hillman explores and explodes many of the myths and fantasies about pornography.

***Pinkalicious.** unabr. ed. Victoria Kann & Elizabeth Kann. Read by Kathleen Mcinerney. Illus. by Victoria Kann. (ENG.). 2008. (978-0-06-172878-5(0)); (978-0-06-172964-5(7)) HarperCollins Pubs.

Pinkerton, Behave! 2004. bk. 24.95 (978-0-89719-683-3(X)); pap. bk. 32.75 (978-1-55592-297-9(X)); pap. bk. 14.95 (978-1-56008-072-5(8)); 8.95 (978-0-89719-915-5(4)); 8.95 (978-1-56008-423-5(5)); cass. & filmstrp 30.00 (978-0-89719-515-7(9)) Weston Woods.

Pinkerton, Behave! Steven Kellogg. 1 cass., 5 bks. (Running Time: 6 min.). (J). pap. bk. 32.75 Weston Woods.
Although Pinkerton gets commands mixed up, he manages to fetch the burglar at just the right time.

Pinkerton, Behave! Steven Kellogg. 1 cass. (Running Time: 6 min.). (J). (ps-3). bk. 24.95 Weston Woods.

Pinkerton, Behave! Steven Kellogg. 1 cass. (Running Time: 5 min.). (J). (ps-3). 1999. pap. bk. 12.95 (QRAC278) Weston Woods.

Pinkerton's Gold. unabr. ed. Tom Nichols. Read by Rusty Nelson. 8 cass. (Running Time: 8 hrs. 36 min.). 1998. 49.95 (978-1-55686-763-7(8)) Books in Motion.
A banished Englishman turned detective investigates a series of deadly robberies.

Pinky & Rex. unabr. ed. James Howe. Narrated by Christina Moore. 1 cass. (Running Time: 15 mins.). (Pinky & Rex Ser.). (gr. 2 up). 1997. 10.00 (978-0-7887-1348-4(5), 95197E7) Recorded Bks.
The first book in a series filled with fun & friendship. A trip to the museum with Pinky's dad & his sister, Amanda, puts Pinky & Rex's friendship to the test. Will their friendship survive when both youngsters set their sights on the same stuffed animal at the museum gift shop?.

Pinky & Rex & the Bully, unabr. ed. James Howe. Narrated by Christina Moore. 1 cass. (Running Time: 15 mins.). (Pinky & Rex Ser.). (gr. 2 up). 1997. 10.00 (978-0-7887-1684-3(0), 95208E7) Recorded Bks.

Pinky & Rex & the Bully, unabr. ed. James Howe. Read by Christina Moore. Illus. by Melissa Sweet. 1 cass. (Running Time: 15 min.). (Pinky & Rex Ser.). (J). (gr. 1-4). 1997. bk. 22.24 (978-0-7887-1825-0(8), 40605) Recorded Bks.

Pinky & Rex & the Double-Dad Weekend, unabr. ed. James Howe. Narrated by Christina Moore. 1 cass. (Running Time: 15 mins.). (Pinky & Rex Ser.). (gr. 2 up). 1997. 10.00 (978-0-7887-1683-6(2), 95207E7) Recorded Bks.

Pinky & Rex & the Double-Dad Weekend, unabr. ed. James Howe. Read by Christina Moore. Illus. by Melissa Sweet. 1 cass. (Running Time: 15 min.). (Pinky & Rex Ser.). (J). (gr. 1-4). 1997. bk. 22.24 (978-0-7887-1824-3(X), 40604) Recorded Bks.

Pinky & Rex & the Just-Right Pet. James Howe. Narrated by Christina Moore. (Running Time: 15 mins.). (Pinky & Rex Ser.: Vol. 12). (gr. 2 up). 10.00 (978-0-7887-5354-1(1)) Recorded Bks.

Pinky & Rex & the Mean Old Witch. unabr. ed. James Howe. Narrated by Christina Moore. 1 cass. (Running Time: 15 mins.). (Pinky & Rex Ser.). (gr. 2 up). 1997. 10.00 (978-0-7887-1774-1(X), 95209E7) Recorded Bks.
Pinky & Rex don't throw the ball into Mrs. Morgan's yard on purpose. It just happens by accident. But every time it does, she flies out the door & screams at them. Will Pinky & Rex get revenge, or will they have a change of heart?.

Pinky & Rex & the New Baby, unabr. ed. James Howe. Narrated by Christina Moore. 1 cass. (Running Time: 15 mins.). (Pinky & Rex Ser.:). (J). (gr. 1-4). 10.00 (978-0-7887-1823-6(1), 95210) Recorded Bks.
Available to libraries only.

Pinky & Rex & the New Baby. unabr. ed. James Howe. Narrated by Christina Moore. 1 cass. (Running Time: 15 mins.). (Pinky & Rex Ser.). (gr. 2 up). 1997. 10.00 (978-0-7887-1682-9(4), 95210E7) Recorded Bks.

Pinky & Rex & the New Neighbors, unabr. ed. James Howe. Narrated by Christina Moore. 1 cass. (Running Time: 15 mins.). (Pinky & Rex Ser.). (gr. 2 up). 10.00 (978-0-7887-1685-0(9), 95206E7) Recorded Bks.

Pinky & Rex & the New Neighbors. unabr. ed. James Howe. Read by Christina Moore. Illus. by Melissa Sweet. 1 cass. (Running Time: 15 min.). (Pinky & Rex Ser.). (J). (gr. 1-4). 1997. bk. 22.24 (978-0-7887-1826-7(6), 40606) Recorded Bks.

Pinky & Rex & the Perfect Pumpkin. James Howe. Read by Christina Moore. 1 cass. (Running Time: 15 mins.). (Pinky & Rex Ser.). (J). (gr. 1-4). 2000. pap. bk. & stu. ed. 23.24 (978-0-7887-4459-4(3), 41149) Recorded Bks.
Pinky & Rex are excited. It's pumpkin-picking weekend with Pinky's Grandma & Grandpa. Pinky's sister & cousin are coming along too. But when Pinky's cousin arrives, she does her best to keep Rex out of the fun. What should Rex do?.

Pinky & Rex & the Perfect Pumpkin. unabr. ed. James Howe. Narrated by Christina Moore. 1 cass. (Running Time: 15 mins.). (Pinky & Rex Ser.). (gr. 2 up). 2000. 11.00 (978-0-7887-3987-3(5), 96256E7) Recorded Bks.

Pinky & Rex & the Perfect Pumpkin, Class set. James Howe. Read by Christina Moore. 1 cass. (Running Time: 15 mins.). (Pinky & Rex Ser.). (J). (gr. 1-4). 2000. 71.70 (978-0-7887-4460-0(7), 47146) Recorded Bks.

Pinky & Rex & the School Play. James Howe. Read by Christina Moore. 1 cass. (Running Time: 15 mins.). (Pinky & Rex Ser.). (J). (gr. 1-4). 1999. pap. bk. & stu. ed. 22.24 (978-0-7887-2984-3(5), 40866) Recorded Bks.
Pinky wants to try out for the lead in the school play. Rex, on the other hand, is terrified of being on stage. But when Pinky talks Rex into going with him to audition, everything changes.

Pinky & Rex & the School Play. unabr. ed. James Howe. Narrated by Christina Moore. 1 cass. (Running Time: 15 mins.). (Pinky & Rex Ser.). (gr. 2 up). 1999. 10.00 (978-0-7887-2213-4(1), 95211E7) Recorded Bks.

Pinky & Rex & the School Play, Class Set. James Howe. Read by Christina Moore. 1 cass. (Running Time: 15 mins.). (Pinky & Rex Ser.). (J). (gr. 1-4). 1999. 70.70 (978-0-7887-3014-6(2), 46831) Recorded Bks.

Pinky & Rex & the Spelling Bee. unabr. ed. James Howe. Narrated by Christina Moore. 1 cass. (Running Time: 15 mins.). (Pinky & Rex Ser.:). (gr. 2 up). 1997. 10.00 (978-0-7887-1773-4(1), 95205E7) Recorded Bks.
Rex, who knows she is a terrible speller, is worried that she will embarrass herself in today's spelling bee. Pinky, on the other hand, is a great speller. Will Pinky win the championship again, or will something unexpected keep him from the title?.

Pinky & Rex Boxed Set, unabr. ed. James Howe. Read by Christina Moore. 1 cass. (Running Time: 15 min.). (Pinky & Rex Ser.). (J). (gr. 1-4). 1997. bk. 70.70 (978-0-7887-3587-5(X), 46590) Recorded Bks.

Pinky & Rex Get Married. unabr. ed. James Howe. Narrated by Christina Moore. 1 cass. (Running Time: 15 mins.). (Pinky & Rex Ser.). (gr. 2 up). 1997. 10.00 (978-0-7887-1772-7(3), 95204E7) Recorded Bks.
When Pinky discovers that Rex is away for the day, his disappointment quickly turns to loneliness. None of the usual things seem any fun without Rex. Realizing how much he misses her, Pinky comes up with a solution to ensure that they will never be apart again.

Pinky & Rex Go to Camp. unabr. ed. James Howe. Narrated by Christina Moore. 1 cass. (Running Time: 15 mins.). (Pinky & Rex Ser.:). (gr. 2 up). 1997. 10.00 (978-0-7887-1775-8(8), 95198E7) Recorded Bks.
Pinky & his best friend Rex are going away to camp for the first time. Rex is excited about it, but Pinky definitely is not. He's really worried that his pesky sister Amanda will raid his room while he's gone & that the camp counselors will turn into monsters at night. Can a letter to "Dear Amie" help him enjoy the camp?.

Pinned. unabr. ed. Alfred C. Martino. Read by Mark Shanahan. (YA). 2007. 39.99 (978-1-60252-488-0(2)) Find a World.

Pinned: There Can Be Only One Winner. unabr. ed. Alfred C. Martino. 6 CDs. (Running Time: 025200 sec.). (J). 2005. audio compact disk 29.95 (978-1-59316-044-9(5), LL136) Listen & Live.
Pinned follows Ivan Korske and Bobby Zane, two high school seniors, as they embark on the most important winter of their lives in a quest for the New Jersey state high school wrestling championship.Ivan Korske is the pride of Lennings, a rural town tucked away in the farmlands of western Jersey, and the odds-on favorite to be crowned state champion in the 129-pound weight class. For Ivan, the stakes are impossibly high. A state championship fulfills a promise he made to his mother before she passed away nine months earlier and will, perhaps, stem his father?s continued withdrawal from life. But mostly, Ivan dreams of getting a scholarship to a college far from his dreary hometown. To him, anything short of the title is failure.In Short Hills, a wealthy town on the other side of the state, Bobby Zane protects his younger brother Christopher from the fallout of their parents? impending divorce, while searching for comfort from Carmelina Carrillo, a girl from a depressed part of Newark. Despite the distractions from the intense pressures of adolescent love and the family?s breakup, Bobby realizes his quest for the coveted 129-pound state title may be his only hope for salvation.Pinend follows Ivan and Bobby?s season-long efforts toward overcoming forces within and beyond their control toward a title that only one of them can capture!.

Pinned: A Novel: A Novel. Alfred C. Martino. Read by Mark Shanahan. (Running Time: 7 hrs.). 2005. 19.95 (978-1-59912-913-6(2)) Iofy Corp.

Pinocchio see Pinocho

Pinocchio. 1 cass. (Running Time: 12 min.). (Talking Bear Tape Ser.). (J). 1986. 4.95 (978-0-89926-205-5(8), 918-D) Audio Bk.

Pinocchio, 6 cass. (ITA.). (YA). 1985. pap. bk. 79.50 (978-1-57970-006-5(3), SIT100) J Norton Pubs.
Advanced-level program in the language of the original story.

Pinocchio. 1 cass. (J). 11.99 (978-1-55723-330-1(6)); 11.99 Norelco. (978-1-55723-329-5(2)); audio compact disk 19.99 CD. (978-1-55723-331-8(4)); audio compact disk 19.99 (978-1-55723-439-1(6)) W Disney Records.

Pinocchio. 1 cass. (Read-Along Ser.). (J). 1993. bk. 7.99 (978-1-55723-363-9(2)) W Disney Records.

Pinocchio. Carlo Collodi. Read by Carlos Muñoz. (Running Time: 3 hrs.).Tr. of Avventure di Pinocchio. (J). 2002. 16.95 (978-1-60083-262-8(8), Audiofy Corp) Iofy Corp.

Pinocchio. Carlo Collodi. Read by Vanessa Maroney. (Running Time: 4 hrs. 46 mins.).Tr. of Avventure di Pinocchio. (J). 2002. 22.95 (978-1-59912-104-8(2), Audiofy Corp) Iofy Corp.

Pinocchio. Carlo Collodi. Narrated by Vanessa Maroney. (Running Time: 17160 sec.). (Unabridged Classics in MP3 Ser.).Tr. of Avventure di Pinocchio. (ENG.). (J). 2008. audio compact disk 14.95 (978-1-58472-597-8(4), In Aud); audio compact disk 24.00 (978-1-58472-534-3(6), In Aud) Sound Room.

Pinocchio. Carlo Collodi. Read by Rebecca C. Burns. (Running Time: 12240 sec.).Tr. of Avventure di Pinocchio. (ENG.). (J). (ps-7). 2004. audio compact disk 16.99 (978-1-4001-5108-0(2)) Pub: Tantor Media. Dist(s): IngramPubServ

Pinocchio. Carlo Collodi. Read by Rebecca C. Burns. (Running Time: 12240 sec.).Tr. of Avventure di Pinocchio. (ENG.). (J). (ps-7). 2005. audio compact disk 39.99 (978-1-4001-3108-2(1)) Pub: Tantor Media. Dist(s): IngramPubServ

Pinocchio. Carlo Collodi & Katie Daynes. Read by Jonathan Kydd. Illus. by Mauro Evangelista. (Young Reading CD Packs Ser.).Tr. of Avventure di Pinocchio. (J). (gr. k-3). 2006. pap. bk. 9.99 (978-0-7945-1204-0(6), UsborneU) EDC Pubng.

Pinocchio. Read by Maggie Smith. 1 cass. (J). (ps-2). 2.98 (978-1-55886-021-6(5)); 3.98 (978-1-55886-025-4(8)) Smarty Pants.
A children's fairy tale about a wooden boy.

Pinocchio. abr. ed. Carlo Collodi. Narrated by Marvin Miller. 2 cass. (Running Time: 2 hrs. 4 min.).Tr. of Avventure di Pinocchio. (J). 12.95 (978-0-89926-134-8(5), 822) Audio Bk.
Excerpts from this timeless classic of the wooden puppet who longs to be a real boy.

Pinocchio. abr. ed. Carlo Collodi. Read by Martin Jarvis. 2 cass. (Running Time: 3 hrs.).Tr. of Avventure di Pinocchio. (J). 12.00 Set. (978-1-878427-48-9(2), XC448) Cimino Pub Grp.
The listener soon becomes caught up with Carlo Collodi's impish creation as they are swept along at a cracking action-packed pace from the day when Geppetto first carves the puppet from a piece of wood to the final happy ending with many exciting & dangerous adventures on the way.

Pinocchio. abr. ed. Carlo Collodi. Read by John Sessions. 2 cass. (Running Time: 2 hrs.).Tr. of Avventure di Pinocchio. (J). 1997. 13.98 (978-962-634-619-8(1), NA211914, Naxos AudioBooks) Naxos.
Pinocchio is a naughty, disobedient wooden puppet who longs to grow up and become a real boy, but as long as he misbehaves and disappoints his father, old Gepetto, he is doomed and his dream will never be realized.

Pinocchio. abr. ed. Carlo Collodi. Read by John Sessions. 2 CDs. (Running Time: 2 hrs. 38 mins.).Tr. of Avventure di Pinocchio. (J). (gr. k-2). 1997. audio compact disk 17.98 (978-962-634-119-3(X), NA211912) Naxos.
Pinocchio is a naughty, disobedient wooden puppet who longs to become a real boy, but as long as he misbehaves and disappoints his father, old Gepetto, he is doomed never to become one.

Pinocchio. unabr. ed. 4 CDs. (Running Time: 4 hrs. 46 mins.). (J). 2002. audio compact disk 43.00 (978-1-58472-151-2(0), Commuters Library) Sound Room.

Pinocchio. unabr. ed. Carlo Collodi. Read by Susan O'Malley. 3 cass. (Running Time: 4 hrs.).Tr. of Avventure di Pinocchio. (gr. k-5). 1997. 23.95 (978-0-7861-1180-0(1), 1939) Blckstn Audio.
The tale of a mischievous puppet who longs to be a human boy.

Pinocchio. unabr. ed. Carlo Collodi. Read by Susan O'Malley. (Running Time: 4 hrs. 0 mins.).Tr. of Avventure di Pinocchio. 2009. 19.95 (978-1-4417-0792-5(1)); audio compact disk 49.00 (978-1-4417-0789-5(1)) Blckstn Audio.

Pinocchio. unabr. ed. Carlo Collodi. Read by Laurie Klein. 4 cass. (Running Time: 5 hrs. 15 min.). Dramatization.Tr. of Avventure di Pinocchio. (J). (gr. 2-7). 1991. 26.95 (978-1-55686-350-9(0), 350) Books in Motion.
Classic story of a puppet who comes to life.

Pinocchio. unabr. ed. Carlo Collodi. Read by Vanessa Maroney.Tr. of Avventure di Pinocchio. (J). 2006. 39.99 (978-1-59895-175-2(0)) Find a World.

Pinocchio. unabr. ed. Carlo Collodi. Narrated by Donal Donnelly. 4 cass. (Running Time: 6 hrs.).Tr. of Avventure di Pinocchio. (gr. 4 up). 1991. 35.00 (978-1-55690-415-8(0), 91221E7) Recorded Bks.
Introduces children to the famous Italian classic behind the movie. A delightfully imaginative tale of a naughty wooden puppet who longs to become a boy.

Pinocchio. unabr. ed. Carlo Collodi. Read by Vanessa Maroney. 4 cds. (Running Time: 4 hrs 44 mins).Tr. of Avventure di Pinocchio. (J). 2002. audio compact disk 26.95 (978-1-58472-306-6(8), 068, In Aud) Pub: Sound Room. Dist(s): Baker Taylor
The famous story of the wooden puppet who wants to be a real boy.

Pinocchio. unabr. ed. Carlo Collodi. Narrated by Rebecca C. Burns. (Running Time: 3 hrs. 30 mins. 0 sec.).Tr. of Avventure di Pinocchio. (ENG.). (J). (gr. 4-7). 2008. 17.99 (978-1-4001-5885-0(0)); audio compact disk 17.99 (978-1-4001-0885-5(3)); audio compact disk 35.99 (978-1-4001-3885-2(X)) Pub: Tantor Media. Dist(s): IngramPubServ

Pinocchio. unabr. collector's ed. Carlo Collodi. Read by Rebecca C. Burns. 4 cass. (Running Time: 4 hrs.).Tr. of Avventure di Pinocchio. (J). 1996. 24.00 (978-0-7366-3369-7(3), 4019) Books on Tape.
Classical tale of the mischievous puppet who longs to be a flesh-&-blood little boy. Ranges from highest adventure to deepest despair, with many lessons to be learned in between. These are the trials Pinocchio must endure on his way to becoming a real little boy.

Pinocchio: Baby Snooks & Daddy. (J). 1946. (CC-5075) Natl Recrd Co.

Pinocchio: Storia di un Burattino. Carlo Collodi. Read by Elsa Proverbio. 6 cass. (Running Time: 6 hrs.). (ITA.). (J). 1996. pap. bk. 79.50 dual language bk. (978-1-58085-451-1(6)) Interlingua VA.
Includes dual language Italian-English transcription. The combination of written text & clarity & pace of diction will open the door for intermediate & advanced students to genuine comprehension & the use of literary texts for advancement in rapid understanding of written & oral language materials. The audio text plus written text concept makes foreign languages accessible to a much wider range of students than books alone.

Pinocchio: The Story Teller. 1 cass. (J). 24.95 1 cass. & 10 bks. (978-0-8442-6837-8(2), Natl Textbk Co) M-H Contemporary.
Teaches to develop skills in another language.

Pinocchio; The Hunting of the Snark. unabr. ed. Lewis Carroll, pseud & Carlo Collodi. Narrated by Flo Gibson. 3 cass. (Running Time: 4 hrs. 30 min.). (J). 1985. 16.95 (978-1-55685-064-6(6)) Audio Bk Con.
The adventures of a naughty wooden puppet who learns to mend his ways; also includes a humorous poem about an elusive snark.

Pinocho. abr. ed. Carlo Collodi. Read by Carlos Muñoz. 3 CDs.Tr. of Pinocchio. (SPA.). 2002. audio compact disk 17.00 (978-958-43-0000-3(8)) YoYoMusic.

Pinocho - La Historica de un Muneco: Pinocchio - Story of a Puppet. Carlo Collodi. Read by Juan Camacho. 6 cass. (Running Time: 9 hrs.). (SPA.). (J). pap. bk. 69.50 Set, incl. transcript. (978-1-58085-260-9(2)); pap. bk. 79.50 Set, incl. Spanish transcript with English translation. (978-1-58085-261-6(0)) Interlingua VA.

Pinpointing Entry & Exit Points. Instructed by John Clayburg. (Trade Secrets Audio Ser.). 2000. 19.95 (978-1-883272-63-0(7)) Marketplace Bks.

Pinpointing Forecasting. Robert Donath. 1 cass. 8.95 (099) Am Fed Astrologers.
Synthesize transits and directions on 90 dgree dial.

Pio Peep. Selected by Alma Flor Ada & F. Isabel Campoy. Illus. by Vivi Escrivá.Tr. of Traditional Spanish Nursery Rhymes. (ENG & SPA.). (J). (gr. 1-2). audio compact disk 15.95 (978-1-58186-227-0(X), DSP32521) Pub: Del Sol Pub. Dist(s): Lectorum Pubns

***Pioneer Woman: Black Heels to Tractor Wheels - A Love Story.** unabr. ed. Ree Drummond. (ENG.). 2011. (978-0-06-202725-2(5), Harper Audio) HarperCollins Pubs.

Pioneer Women Set: Selections from Their Journals. abr. ed. Perf. by Sandy Dennis & Eileen Heckart. 2 cass. 1984. 19.95 (SWC 2060) HarperCollins Pubs.

Pioneers. James Fenimore Cooper. Read by Jim Killavey. 13 cass. (Running Time: 21 hrs.). 1989. 69.00 incl. album. (C-156) Jimcin Record.
Natty Bumpo vs. civilization.

Pioneers. abr. adpt. ed. James Fenimore Cooper. (Bring the Classics to Life: Level 4 Ser.). (ENG.). 2008. audio compact disk 12.95 (978-1-55576-577-4(7)) EDCON Pubng.

Pioneers, unabr. ed. James Fenimore Cooper. Read by Jim Killavey. 13 cass. (Running Time: 19 hrs.). 1986. 85.95 (978-0-7861-0543-4(7), 2038) Blckstn Audio.
This is the fourth in Cooper's series of five books known as the Leatherstocking Tales, which were arranged according to the chronology of their hero, Natty Bumppo. While portraying life in a new settlement on New York's Lake Otsego in the final years of the eighteenth century, Cooper deftly explores the cultural & philosophical underpinnings of the American experience. He contrasts the natural codes of the hunter & woodsman, Natty Bumppo & his Indian friend John Mokegan with the more rigid structure of law required by a more complex society.

Pioneers. unabr. ed. Ed. by Linda Spizzirri. 48 cass. (Running Time: 15 min.). Dramatization. (Educational Coloring Book & Cassette Package Ser.). (J). (gr. k-8). 1989. pap. bk. 6.95 (978-0-86545-151-3(6)) Spizzirri.
Over the Cumberland Gap, into new uncharted place. A close Look at those people & how they lived.

Pioneers, Set. unabr. ed. James Fenimore Cooper. Read by Jim Killavey. 13 cass. 1999. 85.95 (FS9-34208) Highsmith.

***Pioneers: Bring the Classics to Life.** adpt. ed. James Fenimore Cooper. (Bring the Classics to Life Ser.). 2008. pap. bk. 21.95 (978-1-55576-618-4(8)) EDCON Pubng.

Pioneers in Petticoats: The Women of the Old West. unabr. ed. Jimmy Gray. Narrated by Cathy Martindale. Prod. by Joe Loesch. 1 cass. (Running Time: 1 hr.). (Wild West Ser.). (YA). 1999. 12.95 (978-1-887729-64-2(X)) Toy Box Prods.
They came from everywhere & from every walk of life. Belle Starr, Calamity Jane, Annie Oakley, Baby Doe, the homesteader, the rancher, the preacher's wife, those intrepid pioneers in petticoats. This is their story.

Pioneers in Petticoats: Women of the West. unabr. ed. Jimmy Gray. Read by Cathy Martindale. Ed. by Joe Loesch. 1 cass. (Running Time: 60 min.). (Americana Ser.). 1995. 9.95 (978-1-887262-03-3(2), AudioMagazine) Natl Tape & Disc.
An original documentary that tells the story of women in the Old West with a host narrator, a number of character voices, background music & sound effects.

Pioneers of Science Fiction & Adventure. unabr. ed. H. G. Wells et al. 6 cass. (Running Time: 4 hrs. 19 min.). 1987. 55.00 (978-0-8045-0032-6(0), PCC 32) Spoken Arts.
Here Is Where the Major Concepts of Science Fiction Began, but These Stories Are Also Uniquely Stirring. Titles Include: The Time Machine, the Sentinel, Around the World in 80 Days, the Lost World, 20,000 Leagues under the Sea & Facts in the Case of M. Valdemar.

Pious Agent. unabr. collector's ed. John Braine. Read by Stuart Courtney. 7 cass. (Running Time: 10 hrs. 30 min.). 1984. 56.00 (978-0-7366-0495-6(2), 1469) Books on Tape.
This is a novel of deception & treachery in the British Secret Service. Its hero is Xavier Flynn, a devout Catholic, & one of a group of agents recruited to eliminate England's internal enemies - most of whom are members of the Secret Service staff.

Pipe Dream. unabr. ed. Solomon Jones. Narrated by Kevin R. Free. 7 cass. (Running Time: 9 hrs. 15 mins.). 2001. 69.75 (978-1-4193-1258-8(8), F0200MC, Griot Aud) Recorded Bks.

Pipe Layin' Dan. Perf. by La Wanda Page. 2001. audio compact disk 16.98 (978-1-929243-30-3(8)) Uproar Ent.

Pipe of Wine. Charletta Brunson. Narrated by Chris Mezolesta. (ENG.). 2007. audio compact disk 14.95 (978-0-9786553-2-7(X)) Dreamervision Pub.

Pipe of Wine. Charletta Brunson. Read by Chris Mezzolesta. (ENG.). 2008. 9.95 (978-1-934965-09-2(X)) Pub: Dreamervision Pub. Dist(s): Dreamervision Dist

Pipe Up - Overcoming Anxiety about Speaking in Groups. Mitchell W. Robin. 1 cass. 1999. 14.95 (C071) A Ellis Institute.

Pipeline at Sparrow Ridge. unabr. ed. Sandy Laurence. 1 cass. (Running Time: 20 min.). (J). (gr. 4-8). 1983. bk. 16.99 (978-0-934898-52-2(9)); pap. bk. 9.95 (978-0-934898-20-1(0)) Jan Prods.
"Exciting" & "dangerous" are the key words to describe the experiences of teenagers who uncover a plot to blow up a natural gas pipline.

Pipelines 2002: Proceedings of the Pipeline Division Specialty Conference held in Cleveland, Ohio, August 4-7, 2002. Ed. by George Kurz. 2002. audio compact disk 109.00 (978-0-7844-0641-0(3), 40641) Am Soc Civil Eng.

Pipelines 2007: Advances & Experiences with Trenchless Pipeline Projects. Ed. by Lynn Osborn & Mohammad Najafi. 2007. audio compact disk 120.00 (978-0-7844-0934-3(X)) Am Soc Civil Eng.

Piper on the Mountain. unabr. ed. Ellis Peters, pseud. Narrated by Simon Prebble. 5 cass. (Running Time: 7 hrs.). (Inspector George Felse Mystery Ser.: Vol. 5). 44.00 (978-1-55690-716-6(8), 92344E7) Recorded Bks.
Dominic Felse, precocious son of a renowned detective George Felse, investigates, without aid of his father, the death of an Englishman in Czechoslovakia. Available to libraries only.

***Piper Reed Gets a Job.** unabr. ed. Kimberly Willis Holt. Read by Emily Janice Card. 2 CDs. (Running Time: 1 hr. 52 mins.). (Piper Reed Ser.: No. 3). (J). (gr. 3-5). 2009. audio compact disk 24.00 (978-0-7393-6191-7(0), Listening Lib) Pub: Random Audio Pubg. Dist(s): Random

Piper Reed Gets a Job. unabr. ed. Kimberly Willis Holt. Read by Emily Janice Card. (J). (gr. 3). 2009. audio compact disk 22.00 (978-0-7393-6187-0(2), Listening Lib) Pub: Random Audio Pubg. Dist(s): Random

Piper's Tune. unabr. ed. Jessica Stirling. Read by Eve Karpf. 12 CDs. (Running Time: 12 hrs.). 2000. audio compact disk 110.95 (978-0-7540-5374-3(1), CCD065) AudioGO.
At eighteen, Arthur Franklin's cosseted daughter, Lindsay, has left her Glasgow school & finds her role as a marriagable young lady more than agreeable. And the source of the family's wealth, the Franklin's shipbuilding yard on Clydeside, is prospering. But unexpectedly, Lindsay acquires a share in the business & she decides she must master that business as carefully as her male cousins.

Piper's Tune. unabr. ed. Jessica Stirling. Read by Eve Karpf. 12 cass. (Running Time: 18 hrs.). 2000. 96.95 (978-0-7540-0470-7(8), CAB 1893) Pub: Chivers Audio Bks GBR. Dist(s): AudioGO
At eighteen, Lindsay Franklin enjoys her life along with her widowed father. But when her grandfather retires & hands the family ship-building business over to the new generation, Lindsay decides that she must master the business like her male cousins. But several eligible men decide that it is time to master Lindsay.

Pippa Passes see Browning's Last Duchess

Pippa Passes. unabr. ed. Rumer Godden. Read by Patricia Jones. 4 cass. (Running Time: 5 hrs 30 min.). (Isis Ser.). (J). 2004. 44.95 (978-1-85695-933-9(3), 950412) Pub: ISIS Lrg Prnt GBR. Dist(s): Ulverscroft US

Pippi Goes on Board. unabr. ed. Astrid Lindgren. 1 read-along cass. (Running Time: 27 min.). (Pippi Longstocking Ser.). (J). (gr. 3-5). 1980. 15.98 (978-0-8072-1054-3(4), SWR 3 SP, Listening Lib); (Listening Lib) Random Audio Pubg.
The purchase & consumption of 36 pounds of candy...& defeat of the village bully are a few of the things with which Pippi occupies herself & her friends during Captain Longstocking's absence.

Pippi in the South Seas. unabr. ed. Astrid Lindgren. 1 read-along cass. (Running Time: 16 min.). (Pippi Longstocking Ser.). (J). (gr. 3-5). 1980. 15.98 (978-0-8072-1052-9(8), SWR 2 SP, Listening Lib); (Listening Lib) Random Audio Pubg.
Pippi helps out her father, the king of Kurrekuredutt Island.

Pippi Is a Thing Finder, TheTurtle Who Could not Stop Talking, the Lad Who Went to the North Wind, Five Hundred Hat-Audio CD: Classic Children Tales Volume 2. Created by Edcon Publishing. (Classic Children's Tales Ser.). (ENG.). (J). 2009. audio compact disk 12.95 (978-1-55576-627-6(7)) EDCON Pubng.

Pippi Longstocking. abr. ed. Astrid Lindgren. 11 vols. (Running Time: 53 mins.). Dramatization. (Pippi Longstocking Ser.). (J). (gr. 3-5). 1973. bk. 24.95 incl. cloth bk. in bag. (978-0-670-55744-8(7)); pap. bk. 15.95 incl. paper bk. in bag. (978-0-670-55743-1(9)); 9.95 (978-0-670-55748-6(X)) Live Oak Media.
The irrepressible Pippi delights youngsters with her madcap adventures & uninhibited actions.

Pippi Longstocking. unabr. ed. Astrid Lindgren. Read by Esther Benson. 2 cass. (Running Time: 3 hrs.). (Pippi Longstocking Ser.). (J). (gr. 3-5). 1999. 23.00 (LL 0007, Chivers Child Audio) AudioGO.

Pippi Longstocking. unabr. ed. Astrid Lindgren. Read by Esther Benson. 2 cass. (Running Time: 3 hrs.). (Pippi Longstocking Ser.). (J). (gr. 3-5). 1999. 17.95 (L189) Blckstn Audio.
Pippi - in her oversized shoes & mismatched stockings - lives with her monkey, Mr. Nilsson, & her horse in a house named Villa Villekulla. She has no adults to tell her what to do or where to go.

Pippi Longstocking. unabr. ed. Astrid Lindgren. Read by Esther Benson. 2 cass. (Running Time: 2 hrs. 37 min.). (Pippi Longstocking Ser.). (J). (gr. 3-5). 1990. 15.95 Set. (978-0-8072-7388-3(0), YA 807 CXR, Listening Lib) Random Audio Pubg.
Imagine two carrot-colored gravity-defying braids attached to the nine-year-old "strongest kid in the world" & you've conjured up Pippi. Pippi lives with a monkey & a horse.

Pippi Longstocking. unabr. ed. Astrid Lindgren. Read by Esther Benson. 2 vols. (Running Time: 2 hrs. 37 mins.). (J). (gr. 3-7). 1990. pap. bk. 29.00 (978-0-8072-7307-4(4), YA807SP, Listening Lib); 23.00 (978-0-8072-7214-5(0), TYA 807 CX, Listening Lib) Random Audio Pubg.

Pippi Longstocking. unabr. ed. Astrid Lindgren. Read by Esther Benson. (Running Time: 9420 sec.). (ENG.). (J). (gr. 3-2). 2007. audio compact disk 14.99 (978-0-7393-4890-1(6), Listening Lib) Pub: Random Audio Pubg. Dist(s): Random

Pippi Longstocking. unabr. ed. Astrid Lindgren. Transcribed by Florence Lamborn. Narrated by Christina Moore. 2 pieces. (Running Time: 2 hrs. 45 mins.). (Pippi Longstocking Ser.). (J). (gr. 3 up). 1998. 19.00 (978-0-7887-1911-0(4), 95332E7) Recorded Bks.
A vison of days free from chores, bedtime hours, & homework.

Pippi Longstocking. unabr. ed. Astrid Lindgren. Read by Christina Moore. 2 cass. (Running Time: 2 hr. 45 min.). (Pippi Longstocking Ser.). (J). (gr. 3-5). 1998. 31.24 HMWK SET . (978-0-7887-1939-4(4), 40646) Recorded Bks.
This classic story tells of a child's dream life with absolute freedom: no chores, no bedtime hour, no homework.

Pique-niquers. R. de Roussy De Sales. (Drole d'Equipe Ser.). 15.00 (978-0-8442-1349-1(7), Natl Textbk Co) M-H Contemporary.
Features short dialogue designed for intermediate students.

Piranha to Scurfy: And Other Stories. unabr. ed. Ruth Rendell. Read by Donada Peters. 6 cass. (Running Time: 9 hrs.). 2001. 29.95 (978-0-7366-5692-4(8)) Books on Tape.
Tells of a singular curmudgeon who devotes his life to writing scathing letters to newly published authors, pointing out their errors. He does so in memory of his mother, who lies buried in the garden, for reasons that emerge to haunting effect. "The Wink" recounts the story of a woman, raped years ago in a small English town, who waits a lifetime for a perfectly satisfying moment of revenge. Nine stories grace this collection, each one an achievement of the very highest order.

Piranha to Scurfy: And Other Stories. unabr. ed. Ruth Rendell. Narrated by Jenny Sterlin. 8 cass. (Running Time: 9 hrs. 15 mins.). 2000. 71.00 (978-0-7887-5464-7(5), 96599K8) Recorded Bks.
The first in a collection of nine gems from the grand mistress of suspense.

Piranha to Scurfy: And Other Stories. unabr. ed. Ruth Rendell. Narrated by Jenny Sterlin. 9 CDs. (Running Time: 9 hrs. 15 mins.). 2001. audio compact disk 78.00 (978-1-4025-0491-4(8), C1547) Recorded Bks.
How frightening can a book be? Ambrose Ribbon, self-appointed editor and grammar police, is about to find out. He has spent years pointing out mistakes to writers and their publishers. So when he picks up the latest supernatural thriller from a best-selling author, its typos and lapses of logic are no surprise. Its story, however, slyly begins to poison Ribbon's life. "Piranha to Scurfy" is just the first story in this collection of nine gems from the grand mistress of suspense.

Piranha to Scurfy: And Other Stories. unabr. collector's ed. Ruth Rendell. Read by Donada Peters. 6 cass. (Running Time: 9 hrs.). 2000. 48.00 (978-0-7366-6104-1(2)) Books on Tape.
Tells of a singular curmudgeon who devotes his life to writing scathing letters to newly published authors, pointing out their errors. He does so in memory of his mother, who lies buried in the garden, for reasons that emerge to haunting effect. "The Wink" recounts the story of a woman, raped years ago in a small English town, who waits a lifetime for a perfectly satisfying moment of revenge. Nine stories grace this collection, each one an achievement of the very highest order.

Piratas del Caribe Book on CD. Carol Gaab. (SPA.). 2009. audio compact disk 20.00 (978-1-934958-55-1(7)) TPRS.

Pirate. abr. ed. Ted Bell. Read by John Shea. (Running Time: 6 hrs.). (Hawke Ser.). 2010. audio compact disk 9.99 (978-1-4418-0840-0(X), 9781441808400, BCD Value Price) Brilliance Audio.

Pirate. abr. ed. Fabio. Read by Hilary Alexander. 1 cass. (Running Time: 90 min.). 1993. 5.99 (978-1-57096-004-8(6), RAZ 905) Romance Alive Audio.
Fabio's first swashbuckling, passionate romance throws fragile child-woman Christina Abbott together with lusty adventurer & pirate, Marco Glaviano. As she blossoms into lovely womanhood, Marco discovers it is useless to resist her charms.

Pirate. abr. ed. Barry Sadler. Read by Charlton Griffin. Abr. by Odin Westgaard. 2 vols. (Casca Ser.: No. 15). 2003. 18.00 (978-1-58807-115-6(4)); (978-1-58807-555-0(9)) Am Pubng Inc.

Pirate. abr. ed. Barry Sadler. Read by Charlton Griffin. Abr. by Odin Westgaard. 2 vols. (Casca Ser.: No. 15). 2004. audio compact disk 25.00 (978-1-58807-289-4(4)); audio compact disk (978-1-58807-720-2(9)) Am Pubng Inc.

Pirate. unabr. ed. Ted Bell. Read by John Shea. (Running Time: 17 hrs.). (Hawke Ser.). 2005. 39.25 (978-1-59737-380-7(X), 9781597373807, BADLE); 24.95 (978-1-59737-379-1(6), 9781597373791, BAD); 39.25 (978-1-59737-378-4(8), 9781597373784, Brlnc Audio MP3 Lib); 24.95 (978-1-59737-377-7(X), 9781597373777, Brilliance MP3); 107.25 (978-1-59737-372-2(9), 9781597373722, BrilAudUnabridg); 39.95 (978-1-59737-371-5(0), 9781597373715, BAU); audio compact disk 122.25 (978-1-59737-374-6(5), 9781597373746, BriAudCD Unabrid); audio compact disk 39.95 (978-1-59737-373-9(7), 9781597373739, Bril Audio CD Unabri) Brilliance Audio.
In Ted Bell's scorching follow-up to his New York Times bestseller Assassin, intrepid intelligence operative Alex Hawke must thwart a secret, deadly alliance between China and France before they annihilate everything and everyone in their headlong rush toward world domination. Aboard the Star of Shanghai in the south of France, an American spy is held captive. He possesses vital, explosive intelligence linking two nations and one horrifying plot. If he is not rescued, he faces certain torture and inevitable death. Nearby, in a seaside hotel, a man still haunted by the loss of his wife two years earlier finds comfort in the arms of a beautiful Chinese actress - but is she to be trusted? So begins Pirate, an electrifying thriller marking the return of international counterterrorist Alex Hawke. In Paris, a ruthless descendant of Napoleon has risen to power, hell-bent on restoring France's former glory. His fiery ambitions are cynically stoked by a coterie of cold-blooded Mandarins, plotting behind the gates of Beijing's Forbidden City. Cloaked in secrecy, this unholy alliance devises a twisted global plan, backed by China's growing nuclear arsenal, that will send America and the world to the brink of a gut-wrenching showdown. With the aid of his old friend and former Navy SEAL, Stokely Jones, Hawke sets out to investigate the deadly connections that bind the French-Chinese axis. Together, they discover that a powerful German industrialist may hold the key, somewhere inside the walls of his Bavarian mountain lair. Meanwhile, clues to an old and gruesome murder in Paris lead to New York City, where horrifying evidence could finally bring a madman to his knees. In the end, as American and British forces prepare to defend a sovereign and oil-rich Gulf nation against unwilling occupation, the terror is all too real. The world is once more balanced on the knife-edge of a full-blown nuclear confrontation. Hawke must once more prepare to hurl himself deep into the nightmare visions of madmen. He must garner every ounce of strength, courage, and useful pain from his past. He must defeat this enemy or else forfeit the lives of untold thousands, including his own, to an axis of evil no historian could have ever predicted. Packed with unrelenting action, glamour, and high style, and featuring the spectacular Alex Hawke, who time and again transports readers to the edge of danger, Pirate is a spellbinding thriller. Be prepared for Alex Hawke's most daunting and heart-pounding mission yet. Here is an author who gets you in the palm of his hand . . . and then clenches his fist!.

Pirate & the Pagan. abr. ed. Virginia Henley. Read by Deborah McLiam. 1 cass. (Running Time: 90 min.). 1993. 5.99 (978-1-57096-002-4(X), RAZ 903) Romance Alive Audio.
Penniless Lady Summer St. Catherine snares wealthy magistrate Lord Ruark Helford in marriage to save her family's fortunes, then falls for his dashing brother Rory, the pirate known as Black Jack Flash. How will she ever choose between these two men in her life?.

Pirate at Fifty. abr. ed. Jimmy Buffett. Read by Jimmy Buffett. 4 cass., 3 CDs. (Running Time: 4 hrs.). 1998. 24.00 Set. (978-0-679-45157-0(9), Random AudioBks); audio compact disk 27.50 CD Set. (978-0-679-46061-9(6), Random AudioBks) Random Audio Pubg.
Jimmy leaves Frank Bama sitting at a bar in Margaritaville & does some soul-searching in a personal journal that is funnier & more adventurous than anything he has ever written. Jimmy digs deep into his trunk full of cocktail napkins from almost every Corona he's had yet & shares the stories that go along with them. He offers treasured advice & insights on how to survive a plane crash, make it through therapy sessions as a traditional Southern male, start a band, & most of all, have a great time getting it all done.

Pirate Coast: Thomas Jefferson, the First Marines, & the Secret Mission of 1805. Richard Zacks. Read by Raymond Todd. (Running Time: 14 hrs. 30 mins.). 2005. reel tape 79.95 (978-0-7861-3502-8(6)); audio compact disk 99.00 (978-0-7861-7936-7(8)) Blckstn Audio.

Pirate Coast: Thomas Jefferson, the First Marines, & the Secret Mission Of 1805. unabr. ed. Richard Zacks. 10 cass. (Running Time: 14 hrs. 30 mins.). 2005. 32.95 (978-0-7861-3447-2(X)) Blckstn Audio.

Pirate Coast: Thomas Jefferson, the First Marines, & the Secret Mission Of 1805. unabr. ed. Richard Zacks. Read by Raymond Todd. 13 vols. (Running Time: 48600 sec.). 2005. audio compact disk 29.95 (978-0-7861-8110-0(9)) Blckstn Audio.

Pirate Coast: Thomas Jefferson, the First Marines, & the Secret Mission Of 1805. unabr. ed. Richard Zacks. Read by Raymond Todd. 11 CDs. (Running Time: 48600 sec.). 2005. audio compact disk 34.95 (978-0-7861-7977-0(5)) Blckstn Audio.

Pirate Hunter. Richard Zacks. Read by Michael Prichard. (Running Time: 19 hrs. 6 mins.). 2003. 34.95 (978-1-60083-654-1(2), Audiofy Corp) Iofy Corp.

Pirate Hunter: The True Story of Captain Kidd. unabr. ed. Richard Zacks. Narrated by Michael Prichard. 16 CDs. (Running Time: 19 hrs. 7 mins. 12 sec.). (ENG.). 2003. audio compact disk 59.99 (978-1-4001-0088-0(7)); audio compact disk 25.99 (978-1-4001-5088-5(4)); audio compact disk 119.99 (978-1-4001-3088-7(3)) Pub: Tantor Media. Dist(s): IngramPubServ

***Pirate Latitudes.** unabr. ed. Michael Crichton. Read by John Bedford Lloyd. 2009. (978-0-06-193026-3(1), Harper Audio); (978-0-06-196723-8(8), Harper Audio) HarperCollins Pubs.

***Pirate Latitudes.** unabr. ed. Michael Crichton. Read by John Bedford Lloyd. 2010. audio compact disk 19.99 (978-0-06-204676-5(4), Harper Audio) HarperCollins Pubs.

Pirate Queen. unabr. ed. Susan Ronald. Read by Josephine Bailey. (YA). 2007. 79.99 (978-1-60252-854-3(3)) Find a World.

Pirate Queen: Queen Elizabeth I, Her Pirate Adventurers, & the Dawn of Empire. unabr. ed. Susan Ronald. Narrated by Josephine Bailey. (Running Time: 14 hrs. 0 mins. 0 sec.). (ENG.). 2007. audio compact disk 39.99 (978-1-4001-0533-5(1)); audio compact disk 29.99 (978-1-4001-5533-0(9)) Pub: Tantor Media. Dist(s): IngramPubServ

Pirate Queen: Queen Elizabeth I, Her Pirate Adventurers, & the Dawn of Empire. unabr. ed. Susan Ronald. Read by Josephine Bailey. (Running Time: 14 hrs. 0 mins. 0 sec.). (ENG.). 2007. audio compact disk 79.99 (978-1-4001-3533-2(8)) Pub: Tantor Media. Dist(s): IngramPubServ

Pirate Round. James Nelson. Read by Peter Wickham. 12 cass. (Sound Ser.). (J). 2003. 94.95 (978-1-84283-398-8(7)) Pub: ISIS Lrg Prnt GBR. Dist(s): Ulverscroft US

Pirate Round. unabr. ed. James Nelson. Read by Peter Wickham. 11 CDs. (Running Time: 16 hrs.). (Sound Ser.). (J). 2003. audio compact disk 99.95 (978-1-84283-585-2(8)) Pub: ISIS Lrg Prnt GBR. Dist(s): Ulverscroft US

Pirated Emerald. unabr. ed. Vickie Britton & Loretta Jackson. Read by Stephanie Brush. 8 cass. (Running Time: 8 hrs. 36 min.). (Ardis Cole Ser.: Bk. 7). 2001. 49.95 (978-1-58116-148-9(4)) Books in Motion.
Ardis takes over the retrieval of The Fortune, a clipper ship sunk with a valuable gem as cargo. While securing the valuable "Sea Star Emerald," Ardis Cole falls victim to modern-day treasure hunters, and must prove her innocence.

Pirates. Russell Punter. (Young Reading Cd Packs Ser.). (J). 2005. audio compact disk 9.99 (978-0-7945-0947-7(9), UsborneU) EDC Pubng.

Pirates! Celia Rees. Read by Jennifer Wiltsie. 6 cass. (Running Time: 8 hrs. 54 mins.). (J). (gr. 7 up). 2004. 45.00 (978-0-8072-2073-3(6), Listening Lib); audio compact disk 51.00 (978-1-4000-8622-1(1), Listening Lib) Pub: Random Audio Pubg. Dist(s): NetLibrary CO

Pirates! unabr. ed. Celia Rees. Read by Jennifer Wiltsie. (Running Time: 32040 sec.). (ENG.). (J). (gr. 3-12). 2007. audio compact disk 50.00 (978-0-7393-3905-3(2), Listening Lib) Pub: Random Audio Pubg. Dist(s): Random

Pirates: All Aboard for Hours of Puzzling Fun! Anna Nilsen. 2006. pap. bk. (978-1-921049-71-2(5)) Little Hare Bks AUS.

Pirate's Daughter. unabr. ed. Robert Girardi. Read by Arthur Addison. 7 cass. (Running Time: 10 hrs. 30 mins.). 1997. 56.00 (978-0-7366-3665-0(X), 4340) Books on Tape.
Adventure & romance thrive in this tale of piracy, abduction & greed in plundered Africa.

Pirate's Life. (Paws & Tales Ser.: Vol. 22). (J). 2002. 3.99 (978-1-57972-428-3(0)) Insight Living.

Pirate's Life. (Paws & Tales Ser.: Vol. 22). (J). 2002. audio compact disk 5.99 (978-1-57972-429-0(9)) Insight Living.

Pirate's Life for Me! Julie Thompson & Brownie Macintosh. Illus. by Patrick O'Brien. 1 cass. (J). 1996. pap. bk. 13.95 (978-0-88106-835-1(7)) Charlesbridge.
Historical.

***Pirates of Barbary: Corsairs, Conquests & Captivity in the Seventeenth-Century Mediterranean.** unabr. ed. Adrian Tinniswood. (Running Time: 11 hrs. 30 mins. 0 sec.). (ENG.). 2010. 24.99 (978-1-4001-6924-5(0)); 17.99 (978-1-4001-8924-3(1)); audio compact disk 34.99 (978-1-4001-1924-0(3)) Pub: Tantor Media. Dist(s): IngramPubServ

***Pirates of Barbary (Library Edition) Corsairs, Conquests & Captivity in the Seventeenth-Century Mediterranean.** unabr. ed. Adrian Tinniswood. (Running Time: 11 hrs. 30 mins.). 2010. 34.99 (978-1-4001-9924-2(7)); audio compact disk 83.99 (978-1-4001-4924-7(X)) Pub: Tantor Media. Dist(s): IngramPubServ

Pirates of Penzance see Gilbert & Sullivan: The D'Oyly Carte Opera Company

Pirates of Pompeii. unabr. collector's ed. Caroline Lawrence. Read by Justine Eyre. 3 cass. (Running Time: 4 hrs. 16 mins.). (Roman Mysteries Ser.: Bk. 3). (J). (gr. 4-7). 2005. 30.00 (978-0-307-20657-2(2), BksonTape) Random Audio Pubg.
Following the eruption of Mount Vesuvius and the destruction of Pompeii, thousands of people huddle in refugee camps along the Bay of Naples. Among them are Flavia Gemina and her friends who discover that children are being taken from the camps.

Pirates of the I Don't Care -Ibbean: A Kids' Musical about Storing up Treasures in Heaven. Contrib. by Barny Robertson. Created by Jeff Smith. 2007. audio compact disk 12.00 (978-5-557-54388-0(0)); audio compact disk 90.00 (978-5-557-54334-7(1)); audio compact disk 90.00 (978-5-557-54335-4(X)) Lillenas.

***Pirates of the Levant.** unabr. ed. Arturo Pérez-Reverte. (Running Time: 9 hrs. 0 mins. 0 sec.). (ENG.). 2010. 29.99 (978-1-4001-6786-9(8)); 19.99 (978-1-4001-8786-7(9)); audio compact disk 39.99 (978-1-4001-1786-4(0)); audio compact disk 95.99 (978-1-4001-4786-1(7)) Pub: Tantor Media. Dist(s): IngramPubServ

Pirates Past Noon. unabr. ed. Mary Pope Osborne. Read by Mary Pope Osborne. 1 cass. (Magic Tree House Ser.: No. 4). (J). (gr. k-3). 2000. pap. bk. 17.00 (FTR211SP, Listening Lib) Random Audio Pubg.

Pirates Past Noon. unabr. ed. Mary Pope Osborne. 1 cass. (Running Time: 45 mins.). (Magic Tree House Ser.: No. 4). (J). (gr. k-3). 2004. pap. bk. 17.00 (978-0-8072-0333-0(5), Listening Lib) Random Audio Pubg.

Pirates Who Don't Do Anything: A VeggieTales Movie: Music CD. Thomas Nelson Publishing Staff. (J). 2008. audio compact disk 9.99 (978-1-4003-1243-6(4)) Nelson.

Pirlie Pig. Anne Forsyth. 2008. 54.95 (978-1-84559-992-8(6)); audio compact disk 64.95 (978-1-84559-993-5(4)) Pub: Soundings Ltd GBR. Dist(s): Ulverscroft US

Pisa Y Ve! Level 6, Vol. 10. 2003. 11.50 (978-0-7652-0997-9(7)) Modern Curr.

Pisces. Narrated by Patricia G. Finlayson. Music by Mike Cantwell. Contrib. by Marie De Seta & TMY Communications Staff. 1 cass. (Running Time: 30 min.). (Astrologer's Guide to the Personality Ser.: Vol. 12). 1994. 7.99 (978-1-878535-23-8(4)) De Seta-Finlayson.
Astrological description of the sign of Pisces; individually customized, covering love, money, career, relationships & more.

Pisces: February Eighteen - March Twenty. Barrie Konicov. 1 cass. 11.98 (978-0-87082-096-0(6), 099) Potentials.
The author, Barrie Konicov, explains how each sign of the Zodiac has its positive & negative aspect, & that as individuals, in order to master our own destiny, we must enhance our positive traits.

Pisces: February Nineteen-March Twenty. Barrie Konicov. 1 cass. 2000. 16.98 (978-1-56001-572-7(1)) Potentials.

Pisces: Unleash the Power of Your True Self. 1 cass. (Running Time: 1 hr.). 1999. 9.99 (978-1-928996-11-8(6)) MonAge.

Pisces: Your Relationship with the Energy of the Universe. Loy Young. 1993. 9.95 (978-1-882888-24-5(3)) Aquarius Hse.

Pisces Rising: Return of the Goddess. Maria K. Simms. 1 cass. 8.95 (428) Am Fed Astrologers.
Age of Aquarius=Emerging feminine.

Pistachio Prescription. unabr. ed. Paula Danziger. Read by Pat Starr. 3 cass. (Running Time: 3 hrs.). (J). 1997. 30.00 (LL 3046, Chivers Child Audio) AudioGO.

Pistachio Prescription. unabr. ed. Paula Danziger. 1 cass. (Running Time: 1 hr. 19 min.). (Young Adult Cliffhangers Ser.). (YA). (gr. 4-6). 1985. 15.98 incl. bk. & guide. (978-0-8072-1836-5(7), JRH 120SP, Listening Lib) Random Audio Pubg.
Cassie Stephens, the first "teenage bomb in captivity", thinks she might explode at any minute. There's trouble at home, she's got asthma & a host of other problems, real & imaginary. But eating pistachios, the red ones, can cure any problem.

Pistachio Prescription. unabr. ed. Paula Danziger. 3 cass. (Running Time: 3 hrs. 21 min.). (Young Adult Cassette Library). (YA). (gr. 4-6). 1988. 23.98 set. (978-0-8072-7204-6(3), YA808CX, Listening Lib) Random Audio Pubg.

Pistachio Prescription. unabr. ed. Paula Danziger. Read by Paula Danziger. 3 cass. (Running Time: 3 hrs. 36 mins.). (Young Adult Cassette Library). (J). (gr. 4-6). 1988. 30.00 (978-0-8072-8003-4(8), YA964CX, Listening Lib) Random Audio Pubg.
Identify with her dilemmas.

Pistachio Prescription. unabr. ed. Paula Danziger. Read by Paula Danziger. 3 cass. (Running Time: 3 hrs.36 mins.). (Young Adult Cassette Library). (YA). (gr. 4-6). 1988. pap. bk. 35.00 (978-0-8072-8004-1(6), YA964SP, Listening Lib) Random Audio Pubg.

Pistachio Prescription, Set. unabr. ed. Paula Danziger. Read by Pat Starr. 3 cass. (YA). 1999. 23.98 (FS9-25207) Highsmith.

Pistas de Animales. (SPA.). (gr. k-1). 10.00 (978-0-7635-6269-4(6)) Rigby Educ.

Pistol: The Life of Pete Maravich. unabr. ed. Mark Kriegel. Read by Lloyd James. (Running Time: 12 hrs. 30 mins. 0 sec.). (ENG.). 2007. audio compact disk 34.99 (978-1-4001-0486-4(6)); audio compact disk 24.99 (978-1-4001-5486-9(3)); audio compact disk 69.99 (978-1-4001-3486-1(2)) Pub: Tantor Media. Dist(s): IngramPubServ

Pistoleer: A Novel of John Wesley Hardin. abr. ed. James Carlos Blake. Read by Scott Brick et al. 4 cass. (Running Time: 6 hrs.). 2001. 25.00 (978-1-59040-075-3(5), Phoenix Audio) Pub: Amer Intl Pub. Dist(s): PerseuPGW

Pit. Frank Norris. Read by Anais 9000. 2008. 27.95 (978-1-60112-199-8(7)) Babblebooks.

Pit & the Pendulum see Invisible Man & Selected Short Stories of Edgar Allan Poe

Pit & the Pendulum see Tales of Terror

Pit & the Pendulum see Best of Edgar Allan Poe

Pit & the Pendulum see Edgar Allan Poe

Pit & the Pendulum see Mind of Poe

Pit & the Pendulum. Edgar Allan Poe. 1 cass. (Running Time: 37 min. per cass.). 1978. 10.00 (LSS1103) Esstee Audios.

Pit & the Pendulum. Edgar Allan Poe. Ed. by Raymond Harris. Illus. by Robert J. Pailthorpe. (Classics Ser.). (YA). (gr. 6-12). 1982. pap. bk. 17.96 (978-0-89061-267-5(6), 472) Jamestown.

Pit & the Pendulum. Edgar Allan Poe. Read by Alexander Scourby. 1 cass. 10.95 (978-0-8045-0830-8(5), SAC 830) Spoken Arts.

Pit & the Pendulum. abr. ed. Edgar Allan Poe. Read by Basil Rathbone. 1 cass. Incl. Cask of Amontillado. (CPN 1115); Facts in the Case of M. Valdemar. (CPN 1115); 1995. 9.95 (978-1-55994-100-6(6), CPN 1115) HarperCollins Pubs.

Pit & the Pendulum. unabr. ed. Edgar Allan Poe. Read by John Chatty & Walter Zimmerman. 1 cass. (Running Time: 58 min.). Dramatization. 1979. 7.95 (N-24) Jimcin Record.
Horror stories from the master of the macabre.

Pit & the Pendulum. unabr. ed. Edgar Allan Poe. 1 cass. (Running Time: 54 mins.). (Creative Short Story Audio Library Ser.). (YA). (gr. 7-12). 1995.

11.00 (978-0-8072-6112-5(2), CS940CX, Listening Lib) Random Audio Pubg.

Pit & the Pendulum, Vol. 2. unabr. ed. Edgar Allan Poe. Narrated by Amato Petale. 1 cass. (Running Time: 42 min.). (Fantasies Ser.). (J). 1984. 17.95 Incl. holder, scripts, lesson plans, & tchr's. guide. (978-0-86617-043-7(X)) Multi Media TX.
Comprehensive lesson plans that use classic short stories to develop skills in listening, reading, vocabulary, following details, making inferences, visualization, drawing conclusion, critical appreciation & comparison. This module's objective is to specify the effect probably intended by the author with an explanation as to how the effect was achieved.

Pit & the Pendulum & The Tell-Tale Heart. Edgar Allan Poe. 1 cass. (Running Time: 1 hr.). (Radiobook Ser.). 1987. 4.98 (978-0-929541-37-2(5)) Radiola Co.
Two complete stories.

Pit Bull: Lessons from Wall Street's Champion Trader. Martin Schwartz. Read by Ian Esmo. Told to Dave Morine & Paul Flint. (Running Time: 39600 sec.). 2006. audio compact disk 81.00 (978-0-7861-6887-3(0)) Blckstn Audio.

Pit Bull: Lessons from Wall Street's Champion Trader. unabr. ed. Martin Schwartz. Read by Ian Esmo. Told to Dave Morine & Paul Flint. (Running Time: 39600 sec.). 2006. audio compact disk 29.95 (978-0-7861-7468-3(4)) Blckstn Audio.

Pit Bull: Lessons from Wall Street's Champion Trader. unabr. ed. Martin Schwartz et al. Read by Ian Esmo. 8 cass. (Running Time: 11 hrs. 30 mins.). 1998. 56.95 (978-0-7861-1450-4(9), 2312) Blckstn Audio.
True story of how the Champion Trader became the best of the best on Wall Street, of the people & places he discovered along the way & of the trader's tricks & techniques he used to make his millions.

Pitch Pack. (ENG.). 2006. audio compact disk 39.95 (978-0-9769097-2-9(3)) Fade.

Pitching in a Pinch: Baseball from the Inside. Christy Mathewson. Read by Adams Morgan. 4 cass. (Running Time: 5 hrs. 30 mins.). 2000. 32.95 (978-0-7861-1580-8(7), 2409) Blckstn Audio.
Originally published in 1912, this is an insider's account blending anecedote, biography, instruction, & social history. It celebrates baseball as it was played in the first decade of the twentieth century by famous contemporaries like Honus Wagner & Ruby Marquand, managers like John McGraw & Connie Mack, & many others.

Pitching in a Pinch: Baseball from the Inside. unabr. ed. Christy Mathewson. Read by Adams Morgan. (Running Time: 19800 sec.). 2008. audio compact disk & audio compact disk 50.00 (978-1-4332-3430-9(0)); audio compact disk & audio compact disk 29.95 (978-1-4332-3431-6(9)) Blckstn Audio.

Pitfalls & Benefits of Tax Shelters. 5 cass. (Running Time: 3 hrs. 30 min.). 50.00 (471-475) J Norton Pubs.
Discusses the advantages of each type of shelter & potential problems & how to avoid them.

Pitfalls of Asset Protection. 2 cass. (Running Time: 1 hrs. 40 min.). (Asset Protection Ser.). 1998. pap. bk. 120.00 Set. (YB82) Am Law Inst.

Pitfalls of Christian Liberty. John MacArthur, Jr. 5 cass. (John MacArthur's Bible Studies). 17.25 (HarperThor) HarpC GBR.

Pitfalls of Formula. SERCON Panel. 1 cass. 9.00 (A0116-87) Sound Photosyn.
At the Science Fiction writers convention featuring Silverberg, Fowler, Lupoff, Feder, Tarbro.

Pitman's Brat. Una Horne. Read by Anne Dover. 7 cass. (Running Time: 9 hrs. 15 mins.). (Story Sound Ser.). (J). 2005. 61.95 (978-1-85903-865-9(4)) Pub: Mgna Lrg Print GBR. Dist(s): Ulverscroft US

Pixar Touch: The Making of a Company. David A. Price. Read by David Drummond. (Playaway Adult Nonfiction Ser.). (ENG.). 2009. 64.99 (978-1-60812-590-6(4)) Find a World.

Pixar Touch: The Making of a Company. unabr. ed. David A. Price. Narrated by David Drummond. (Running Time: 9 hrs. 0 mins. 0 sec.). (ENG.). 2008. audio compact disk 24.99 (978-1-4001-5765-5(X)); audio compact disk 69.99 (978-1-4001-3765-7(9)) Pub: Tantor Media. Dist(s): IngramPubServ

Pixar Touch: The Making of a Company. unabr. ed. David A. Price. Narrated by David A. Drummond. (Running Time: 9 hrs. 0 mins. 0 sec.). (ENG.). 2008. audio compact disk 34.99 (978-1-4001-0765-0(2)) Pub: Tantor Media. Dist(s): IngramPubServ

Pixiewater: The Miracle of the Pixie Pool. Brian J. Helsaple. 1 cass. (Running Time: 30 min.). (Life Lessons Ser.). (gr. k-5). 1999. bk. 20.95 (978-1-928714-00-2(5)) Two Brians.
Reminds children to drink a lot of good clean water.

Pizza Boogie. Joanne O. Hammil. (J). 1992. bk. 10.00 (978-0-9626239-1-2(1)) JHO Music.

Pizza Delivery Millionaire. Rick Vazquez. 2008. audio compact disk 19.95 (978-1-4276-3167-1(0)) AardGP.

Pizza Mystery. Gertrude Chandler Warner. (Running Time: 5400 sec.). (Boxcar Children Ser.: No. 33). (J). 2005. audio compact disk 14.95 (978-0-7861-7491-1(9)) Blckstn Audio.

Pizza Mystery. unabr. ed. Gertrude Chandler Warner. Narrated by Aimee Lilly. (Boxcar Children Ser.). (ENG.). (J). 2003. 10.49 (978-1-60814-089-3(X)) Oasis Audio.

Pizza Party: A Team-Building Guide. 2006. (978-0-9773129-6-2(8)) Opt Inc.

Pizza Perfecta de Pura, EDL Level 3. (Fonolibros Ser.: Vol. 16). (SPA.). 2003. 11.50 (978-0-7652-1003-6(7)) Modern Curr.

Pizza Pokey/Pizza for Everyone. Steck-Vaughn Staff. (J). 1997. (978-0-8172-7364-4(6)) SteckVau.

Pizza Tastes Great: Dialogues & Stories. William P. Pickett. 1 cass. (C). 1988. pap. bk. 22.00 (978-0-13-677683-3(3)) Longman.

Pizza the Size of the Sun. Jack Prelutsky. Read by Jack Prelutsky. 1 CD. (Running Time: 54 mins.). (J). 2000. audio compact disk 15.00 (978-0-7366-9005-8(0)) Books on Tape.
Poems set to music. Includes: "Rat for Lunch!" "I Met a Dozen Duhduhs," & "We're Loudies!".

Pizza the Size of the Sun. abr. ed. Jack Prelutsky. Read by Jack Prelutsky. (Running Time: 3600 sec.). (J). (gr. k). 2007. 14.95 (978-0-06-135945-3(9), HarperChildAud) HarperCollins Pubs.

Pizza the Size of the Sun, unabr. ed. Jack Prelutsky. Read by Jack Prelutsky. 1 cass. (J). (gr. 1-8). 1999. 9.98 (LL 0152, Chivers Child Audio) AudioGO.

***Pizza the Size of the Sun.** unabr. ed. Jack Prelutsky. Read by Jack Prelutsky. (ENG.). 2007. (978-0-06-144895-9(8), GreenwillowBks); (978-0-06-144894-2(X), GreenwillowBks) HarperCollins Pubs.

Pkl2009 INTL Residen. ICC & Steve Note. 2009. audio compact disk (978-1-4390-5619-6(6)) Delmar.

Place see Richard Eberhart Reading His Poetry

Place: Program from the Award Winning Public Radio Series. Interview. Hosted by Fred Goodwin. Comment by John Hockenberry. 1 CD. (Running Time: 1 hr). 2003. audio compact disk 21.95 (978-1-932479-80-5(5), LCM 297) Lichtenstein Creat.
We look at what connects us to certain places and not to others, and what happens when we lose that special relationship to our surroundings.Guests include Dr. Susan Ossman, visiting professor of anthropology at Georgetown University and an expert on media and migration; Dr. Kent Curtis, director of education at the Walden Woods Project, a land conservancy based on the environmental philosophy of writer Henry David Thoreau; and Dr. Roberta Feldman, architect, psychologist, and director of the City Design Center in Chicago.We also hear from a New York office worker whose sense of place was shattered by the World Trade Center attacks, attend a "feng shui" design session at our production facilities, and learn about life in cyberspace with reporter Ellen Horne. Plus, commentary by John Hockenberry.

Place at Whitton. unabr. ed. Thomas Keneally. Read by Geoff Hiscock. 4 cass. (Running Time: 5 hrs.). 2004. 32.00 (978-1-74030-091-9(2), 500217) Pub: Bolinda Pubng AUS. Dist(s): Lndmrk Audiobks

Place Beyond Courage. Elizabeth Chadwick. 2008. 99.95 (978-1-4079-0084-1(6)); audio compact disk 104.95 (978-1-4079-0085-8(4)) Pub: Soundings Ltd GBR. Dist(s): Ulverscroft US

***Place Called Alive - Music: Music from the Film.** 2009. audio compact disk 10.00 (978-0-9800664-3-2(3)) Erie Chapman.

Place Called Freedom. unabr. ed. Ken Follett. Read by Sean Barrett. 10 cass. (Running Time: 15 hrs.). 2000. 84.95 (978-0-7451-6741-1(1), CAB 1357) Pub: Chivers Audio Bks GBR. Dist(s): AudioGO
Powerful landlords rule the coal-fields in 18th century Scotland. Jay Jamisson presides over the mine where men, women, and children toil. Rebel miner, Mack McAsh, challenges the Jamisson family. When James enforces the law binding him to the mine, Mack flees to London to help lead the famous poor uprising of 1768. Finding himself sentenced to death for a crime he did not commit, Mack is rescued and transported to America, where again he struggles to find a place called freedom.

Place Called Freedom. unabr. ed. Ken Follett. Narrated by Simon Prebble. 10 cass. (Running Time: 14 hrs. 30 mins.). 85.00 (978-0-7887-0839-8(2), 94985E7) Recorded Bks.
A tale of Mack McAsh & Lizzie Hallim's passionate search for freedom. United in America, their only chance for freedom lies beyond the western frontier, if they're brave enough to take it. Available to libraries only.

Place Called Hope. unabr. ed. Audrey Howard. Read by Carole Boyd. 12 cass. (Running Time: 18 hrs.). 2002. 96.95 (978-0-7540-0813-2(4), CAB 2235) AudioGO.

Place Called Morning. unabr. ed. Ann Tatlock. Narrated by Barbara Caruso. 6 cass. (Running Time: 8 hrs. 30 mins.). 1999. 51.00 (978-0-7887-3760-2(0), 95931E7) Recorded Bks.
Mae Demaray is a cheerful widow who delights in helping others & spending time with her young grandson. But when a tragic accident takes the child's life, all faith & joy fly from Mae's heart. Filled with spiritual struggle, this inspirational novel follows Mae's journey toward a new beginning.

Place Called Sweet Shrub. unabr. ed. Jane Roberts Wood. Narrated by C. J. Critt. 8 cass. (Running Time: 12 hrs.). 1999. 70.00 (978-0-7887-0318-8(8), 94510E7) Recorded Bks.
After a year on the Texas frontier, Lucy Richards returns to her mother's home on the outskirts of Dallas. Life is quite-and lonely-until an irreverent, poetry-loving principal from Lucy's past drives into town to win her heart & her hand.

Place Called Sweet Shrub, Set. unabr. ed. Jane Roberts Wood. Narrated by C. J. Critt. 8 cass. (Running Time: 12 hrs.). 1996. 67.00 (94510) Recorded Bks.

Place Cards: Gen. 43:15-34. Ed Young. 1988. 4.95 (978-0-7417-1685-9(2), 685) Win Walk.

Place de la Concorde Suisse. John McPhee. 2 cass. (Running Time: 3 hrs.). 1989. 30.00 (978-0-7366-1497-9(4), 2373) Books on Tape.
McPhee spent weeks with the Swiss National Guard on maneuvers & this is his story.

Place for Keeping. Lucille Clifton. Read by Lucille Clifton. 1 cass. (Running Time: 45 min.). (Watershed Tapes of Contemporary Poetry). 11.95 (23615) J Norton Pubs.
A retrospective, compiled from two live readings.

Place for the Wicked. unabr. collector's ed. Elleston Trevor. Read by Peter McDonald. 8 cass. (Running Time: 8 hrs.). 1987. 48.00 (978-0-7366-1225-8(4), 2143) Books on Tape.
A small group of friends, a flight to the South of France marks the beginning of a well-earned holiday, a place they have come to love - the sun, the sea, the palms. But this year it will be different. It only takes a split second of panic on one of their parts to compromise all of them.

***Place for Weakness: Preparing Yourself for Suffering.** unabr. ed. Michael S. Horton. (Running Time: 6 hrs. 46 mins. 1 sec.). (ENG.). 2010. 14.99 (978-0-310-58706-4(9)) Zondervan.

Place in Normandy. unabr. ed. Nicholas Kilmer. Narrated by John McDonough. 6 cass. (Running Time: 8 hrs.). 1998. 51.00 (978-0-7887-1995-0(5), 95382E7) Recorded Bks.
Taking over the family's aging French farmhouse causes struggles & collisions with plumbers, owls & the country culture.

Place in the Country. unabr. ed. Laura Shaine Cunningham. Narrated by Suzanne Toren. 8 cass. (Running Time: 11 hrs.). 2000. 65.00 (978-0-7887-4930-8(7), 96459E7) Recorded Bks.
The author captures the dreams of city dwellers who long for a simpler life. As a child, she vows to exchange her crowded new York City apartment for a place in the country but her rural adulthood home brings constant surprises, deer dine on the garden, the neighbor's Holsteins stampede through the yard & the local college paints the night sky with a neon glow.

Place in the Hills. unabr. ed. Michelle Paver. 12 cass. (Isis Ser.). (J). 2002. 94.95 (978-0-7531-1417-9(8)) Pub: ISIS Lrg Prnt GBR. Dist(s): Ulverscroft US

Place in the Sun. Judith Saxton. Read by Anne Dover. 4 cass. (Running Time: 6 hrs.). (Sound Ser.). (J). 2003. 44.95 (978-1-84283-296-7(4)) Pub: ISIS Lrg Prnt GBR. Dist(s): Ulverscroft US

Place of Conscience in Daily Living. Instructed by Manly P. Hall. 8.95 (978-0-89314-216-2(6), C801207) Philos Res.

Place of Execution. unabr. ed. Val McDermid. Read by Paddy Glynn. 10 cass. Library ed. (Running Time: 14 hrs.). 2001. 107.25 (978-1-58788-621-8(9), 1587886219, Unabridge Lib Edns) Brilliance Audio.
Winter 1963: two children have disappeared off the streets of Manchester; the murderous careers of Myra Hindley and Ian Brady have begun. On a freezing day in December, another child goes missing: thirteen-year-old Alison Carter vanishes from her town, an insular community that distrusts the outside world. For the young George Bennett, a newly promoted inspector, it is the beginning of his most difficult and harrowing case: a murder with no body, an investigation with more dead ends and closed faces than he'd have found in the anonymity of the inner city, and an outcome which reverberates through the years. Decades later he finally tells his story to journalist Catherine Heathcote, but just when the book is poised for publication, Bennett unaccountably tries to pull the plug. He has new information which he refuses to divulge, new information that threatens the very foundations of his existence. Catherine is forced to re-investigate the past, with results that turn the world upside down. A Greek tragedy in modern England, A PLACE OF EXECUTION is a taut psychological thriller that explores, exposes and explodes the border between reality and illusion in a multi-layered narrative that turns expectations on their head and reminds us that what we know is what we do not know.

Place of Execution. unabr. ed. Val McDermid. Read by Paddy Glynn. (Running Time: 14 hrs.). 2004. 39.25 (978-1-59335-646-0(3), 1593356463, Brlnc Audio MP3 Lib); 24.95 (978-1-59335-294-3(8), 1593352948, Brilliance MP3) Brilliance Audio.

Place of Execution. unabr. ed. Val McDermid. Read by Paddy Glynn. (Running Time: 14 hrs.). 2004. 39.25 (978-1-59710-576-7(7), 1597105767, BADLE); 24.95 (978-1-59710-577-4(5), 1597105775, BAD) Brilliance Audio.

***Place of Execution.** unabr. ed. Val McDermid. Read by Paddy Glynn. (Running Time: 15 hrs.). 2010. audio compact disk 89.97 (978-1-4418-4060-8(5), 9781441840608, BriAudCD Unabrid); audio compact disk 29.99 (978-1-4418-4059-2(1), 9781441840592, Bril Audio CD Unabri) Brilliance Audio.

Place of Execution. unabr. ed. Val McDermid. Read by Paddy Glynn. 14 CDs. (Running Time: 21 hrs.). 2001. audio compact disk 104.95 (978-0-7531-1247-2(7), 1247-7) Pub: ISIS Audio GBR. Dist(s): ISIS Pub
For the young George Bennett, newly promoted to inspector, thirteen-year-old Alison Carter's disappearance is the beginning of his most difficult & harrowing case. Decades later he tells his story to journalist Catherine Heathcote, but inexplicably pulls the plug just before publication. Catherine is forced to reinvestigate the past with results that turn the world upside down.

Place of Execution. unabr. ed. Val McDermid. Read by Paddy Glynn. 14 cass. (Running Time: 21 hrs.). (Isis Ser.). (J). 2001. 99.95 (978-0-7531-0668-6(X), 991009) Pub: ISIS Lrg Prnt GBR. Dist(s): Ulverscroft US

Place of Happiness, Set unabr. ed. Judith Hagar. Read by Valerie Georgeson. 2 cass. 1999. 21.95 (MRC 1025) AudioGO.

***Place of Healing: Wrestling with the Mysteries of Suffering, Pain, & God's Sovereignty.** unabr. ed. Joni Eareckson Tada. (ENG.). 2010. 12.98 (978-1-59644-351-8(0)); audio compact disk 21.98 (978-1-59644-350-1(2)) christianaud.

Place of Healing in Religion. William Beachy. 1986. 10.80 (0105B) Assn Prof Chaplains.

Place of Hiding. abr. ed. Elizabeth George. Read by Simon Jones. (Running Time: 21600 sec.). (ENG.). 2007. audio compact disk 14.99 (978-0-7393-4376-0(9), Random AudioBks) Pub: Random Audio Pubg. Dist(s): Random

Place of Hiding. unabr. ed. Elizabeth George. 16 cass. (Running Time: 24 hrs.). 2003. 117.00 (978-0-7366-9486-5(2)) Books on Tape.

Place of Israel in God's Purposes. Derek Prince. 1 cass. 5.95 (4381) Derek Prince.
It is important for the Christian to know why Israel is mentioned so often in the Old & New Testaments. We cannot fully understand the Bible until we understand its significance.

Place of Knowing: A Spiritual Autobiography. Emma Lou Warner Thayne. 7 CD Set. (Running Time: 8 hrs 40 mins). 2006. audio compact disk 39.95 (978-0-9786864-0-6(3)) E L Thayne.

Place of Knowledge & Wisdom. Swami Amar Jyoti. 1 cass. 1992. 9.95 (M-88) Truth Consciousness.
Intelligent seeking: amid all the indirect knowledge, keeping focus on the Source of all knowledge. Readiness for seeking.

***Place of My Own: The Architecture of Daydreams.** unabr. ed. Michael Pollan. Read by Michael Pollan. (Running Time: 10 hrs.). 2010. 39.97 (978-1-4418-3686-1(1), 9781441836861, Brlnc Audio MP3 Lib); 24.99 (978-1-4418-3685-4(3), 9781441836854, Brilliance MP3); 24.99 (978-1-4418-3687-8(X), 9781441836878, BAD); 39.97 (978-1-4418-3688-5(8), 9781441836885, BADLE); audio compact disk 29.99 (978-1-4418-3683-0(7), 9781441836830, Bril Audio CD Unabri); audio compact disk 92.97 (978-1-4418-3684-7(5), 9781441836847, BriAudCD Unabrid) Brilliance Audio.

Place of Pain; Finding the Good Feelings. Myron Madden & Wilbur Schwartz. 1986. 10.80 (0210B) Assn Prof Chaplains.

***Place of Peace: A Novel.** Zondervan. (Kauffman Amish Bakery Ser.). (ENG.). 2010. 12.99 (978-0-310-41306-6(0)) Zondervan.

Place of Repentance. Elbert Willis. 1 cass. (Developing Stability Ser.). 4.00 Fill the Gap.

Place of Safety. unabr. ed. Caroline Graham. Read by Hugh Ross. 10 CDs. (Running Time: 15 hrs.). (Chief Inspector Barnaby Ser.: Bk. 6). 2003. audio compact disk 94.95 (978-0-7540-5550-1(7), CCD 241) AudioGO.

Place of Safety. unabr. ed. Caroline Graham. Read by Hugh Ross. 8 cass. (Running Time: 12 hrs.). (Chief Inspector Barnaby Ser.: Bk. 6). 2000. 69.95 (978-0-7540-0452-3(X), CAB 1875) Pub: Chivers Audio Bks GBR. Dist(s): AudioGO
Ex-vicar Lionel Lawrence has opened his rectory to rehabilitate young offenders. However, he has no idea that the consequences will include blackmail & murder. The disappearance of wild Carlotta seems to involve both. Chief Inspector Barnaby must now find the violent person behind Carlotta's disappearance.

Place of Wonder. AIO Team Staff. Read by Hal Smith et al. (Running Time: 5 hrs.). (Adventures in Odyssey Gold Ser.). (ENG.). (J). (gr. 1-7). 2006. audio compact disk 24.99 (978-1-58997-291-9(0), Tyndale Ent) Tyndale Hse.

***Place of Yes: 10 Rules for Getting Everything You Want Out of Life.** abr. ed. Bethenny Frankel. Read by Bethenny Frankel. (Running Time: 6 hrs. 0 mins. 0 sec.). (ENG.). 2011. audio compact disk 29.99 (978-1-4423-3544-8(0)) Pub: S&S Audio. Dist(s): S and S Inc

Place on Earth. unabr. ed. Wendell Berry. (Running Time: 12 hrs. 18 mins. 0 sec.). (ENG.). 2007. audio compact disk 28.98 (978-1-59644-485-0(1), christaudio) christianaud.

***Place on Earth: A Novel.** unabr. ed. Wendell Berry. Narrated by Paul Michael. (Yasmin Peace Ser.). (ENG.). 2007. 16.98 (978-1-59644-486-7(X), christaudio) christianaud.

Place on the Water: An Angler's Reflections on Home. unabr. ed. Jerry Dennis. Narrated by Ed Sala. 5 cass. (Running Time: 6 hrs. 45 mins.). 46.00 (978-0-7887-2942-3(X), 95658E7) Recorded Bks.
In these anecdote-filled essays, the author shares all the outdoors has to offer, casting his words with the natural grace & rhythm of a fly fisherman. Available to libraries only.

Place to Be. Jay Ungar & Lyn Hardy. (J). 1981. audio compact disk 14.95 (978-0-939065-98-1(3)) Gentle Wind.

Place to Be. Jay Ungar & Lyn Hardy. 1 cass. (Running Time: 28 min.). (J). (ps-5). 1981. 9.95 (978-0-939065-06-6(1), GW 1006) Gentle Wind.
Features philosophy of Malvina Reynolds'songs.

Place to Call Home. June Francis. 8 cass. (Running Time: 10 hrs. 35 mins.). (Story Sound Ser.). (J). 2005. 69.95 (978-1-85903-806-2(9)) Pub: Mgna Lrg Print GBR. Dist(s): Ulverscroft US

Place to Hide. abr. ed. Johnny Ray Barnes, Jr. & Julian Barnes. Read by Multivoice Production Staff. (Running Time: 2 hrs.). (Strange Matter Ser.). 2006. audio compact disk 9.95 (978-1-4233-0846-1(8), 9781423308461, BACD) Brilliance Audio.
Trey Porter and his friends have been chased from their campsite by bullies, and are searching for a new one. One that's absolutely bully-proof. They decide on the legendary fort of Widow Hill, a Revolutionary War relic hidden deep in the forests of Fairfield. The path to the fort is not an easy one, however, as someone or something is trying to stop them any way it can. A dark secret awaits Trey Porter. A secret guarded for over two hundred years and desired by every dark creature that lurks in the forest. Trey promises not to reveal the secret. . . over his dead body.

Place to Hide. abr. ed. Engle & Barnes. (Running Time: 2 hrs.). (Strange Matter Ser.). 2006. 9.95 (978-1-4233-0848-5(4), 9781423308485, BAD) Brilliance Audio.

Place to Hide. abr. ed. Engle & Julian Barnes. Read by Multivoice Production Staff. (Running Time: 2 hrs.). (Strange Matter Ser.). 2006. 25.25 (978-1-4233-0849-2(2), 9781423308492, BADLE) Brilliance Audio.

Place to Hide. unabr. ed. Johnny Ray Barnes, Jr. Read by Multivoice Production Staff. 2 CDs. (Running Time: 2 hrs.). (Strange Matter Ser.: Bk. 4). (J). (gr. 3-5). 2006. audio compact disk 25.25 (978-1-4233-0847-8(6), 9781423308478, BACDLib Ed) Brilliance Audio.

Place Value Mysteries/Time Flies. Created by Steck-Vaughn Staff. (Running Time: 2432 sec.). (Shutterbug Bks.). 2003. (978-0-7398-7798-2(4)) SteckVau.

Placebo Effect: Program from the Award Winning Public Radio Series. Interview. Hosted by Fred Goodwin. Comment by John Hockenberry. 1 CD. (Running Time: 1 hr.). 2000. audio compact disk 21.95 (978-1-932479-81-2(3), LCM 116) Lichtenstein Creat.
The "placebo effect" is astonishingly large. Between 35 and 75 percent of patients report feeling better from taking an inert pill during trials of new drugs. But what is the placebo effect, and how does it work. And if placebos can help so many people feel better, should they be used as treatment? Guests include Dr. Jon Levine , professor of medicine and the director of the National Institutes of Health Pain Center at the University of California, San Francisco Medical Center; Dr. Walter Brown, clinical professor of psychiatry at Brown University School of Medicine and Tufts University School of Medicine; Dr. Fred Quitkin, professor of Clinical Psychiatry at Columbia University; comedian David Brenner; New York Post columnist Gersh Kuntzman; and commentator John Hockenberry.

Placebo Effect in Healing. 1 cass. (Care Cassettes Ser.: Vol. 9, No. 11). 1982. 10.80 Assn Prof Chaplains.

Placenta: To Know Me Is to Love Me. A Reference Guide for Gross Placental Examination with Companion Atlas. Doris Schuler-Maloney & Steve Lee. Illus. by Marty Boesenberg. 2004. audio compact disk 109.00 (978-0-9670354-1-3(4)) D S M.

Placenta: To Know Me Is to Love Me Companion Atlas. Doris Schuler-Maloney. 2004. audio compact disk 69.00 (978-0-9670354-2-0(2)) D S M.

Places I Have Been. Terence McKenna. 1 cass. 9.00 (A0365-88) Sound Photosyn.
Terence the traveler.

Places in Between. Rory Stewart. Read by Rory Stewart. (Running Time: 32400 sec.). 2006. audio compact disk 34.99 (978-1-4281-1670-2(2)) Recorded Bks.

Places in Between. unabr. ed. Rory Stewart. 8 CDs. (Running Time: 9 hrs.). 2006. audio compact disk 92.75 (978-1-4281-1673-3(7)) Recorded Bks.

Places in Between. unabr. ed. Rory Stewart. Read by Rory Stewart. 8 cass. (Running Time: 9 hrs.). 2006. 61.75 (978-1-4281-1671-9(0)) Recorded Bks.

Places in the Dark. unabr. ed. Thomas H. Cook. Narrated by George Guidall. 6 cass. (Running Time: 8 hrs.). 2000. 54.00 (978-0-7887-4924-7(2), 96409) Recorded Bks.
In 1937, Dora March, a mysterious young woman, arrives in a small Maine town. Soon the tragedies begin, a house fire, a murder, a suicide. Within a year, Dora vanishes, leaving behind dark, unanswered questions. Now, obsessed with knowing who she really is, the town's lawyer sets out to find her.

Places in the Dark. unabr. ed. Thomas H. Cook. Narrated by George Guidall. 7 CDs. (Running Time: 8 hrs.). 2001. audio compact disk 69.00 (978-0-7887-7168-2(X), C1421) Recorded Bks.
In 1937, a slender young woman arrived in a small Maine town. Dora March was lovely, quiet & mysterious. Soon the tragedies began: a house fire, a murder, a suicide. Within a year, Dora vanished, leaving behind dark, unanswered questions. But before she disappeared, the town's newspaperman was stabbed to death. Now Cal, the slain man's brother, must tear off the emotional veil clouding his judgement & find Dora March. The scenes in are not graphic, but they are the stuff of nightmares. As the suspense in this haunting work increases with each chapter, it urges the listener toward a final, shocking revelation.

Places in the Heart: Hebrews 4:12-16. Ed Young. 1991. Rental 4.95 (978-0-7417-1887-7(1), 887) Win Walk.

Places of the Dead Road. William S. Burroughs. Read by William S. Burroughs. 1 cass. (Running Time: 30 min.). 8.95 (AMF-5) Am Audio Prose.
Burroughs reads from "Places of the Dead Road" & talks about dreams, ESP, his relation to his audience, space travel & death.

Places of the Spirit: Music & Images Inspired by the Berkshires. Ed. by Jeanne Gressler. Music by Paula Robison. Illus. by Jim Schantz. Contrib. by Cyro Baptista. Prod. by Adam Abeshouse. Intro. by Bernard Pucker. 1 CD. (Running Time: 100 mins.). 2003. audio compact disk 25.00 (978-1-879985-11-7(X)) Pucker Gallery.
World reknown flautist Paula Robison performs extant pieces of music, inspired by the artwork of Jim Schantz. This artwork describes the fields, rivers and forests of the Berkshire area.

Places That Scare You: A Guide to Fearlessness in Difficult Times. unabr. ed. Pema Chödrön. Read by Joanna Rotte. (ENG.). 2008. audio compact disk 19.95 (978-1-59030-585-0(X)) Pub: Shambhala Pubns. Dist(s): Random

Plague Dogs. unabr. collector's ed. Richard Adams. Read by Grover Gardner. 11 cass. (Running Time: 16 hrs. 30 mins.). 1991. 88.00 (978-0-7366-1988-2(7), 2804) Books on Tape.
Snitter & Rowf, escapees from a vivisection lab, make for the desolate heaths & the windy countryside of England's Lake District. There, aided by a crafty fox, they raid chicken coops, kill sheep & forage for sustenance. They hide out in abandoned caves & mine shafts. Local farmers, incensed by their losses, set traps & organize hunts. A reporter announces that Snitter & Rowf may be carrying bubonic plague. Panic follows. The hunt intensifies, driving the dogs deeper into a wilderness bereft of hope.

Plague of Angels. unabr. ed. P. F. Chisholm. Read by Christopher Kay. 10 cass. (Running Time: 15 hrs.). 2001. 84.95 (978-1-86042-519-6(4), 25194) Pub: Soundings Ltd GBR. Dist(s): Ulverscroft US

***Plague of Doves.** unabr. ed. Louise Erdrich. Read by Peter Francis James & Kathleen Mcinerney. (ENG.). 2008. (978-0-06-163252-5(X)); (978-0-06-163253-2(8)) HarperCollins Pubs.

Plague of Doves. unabr. ed. Louise Erdrich. Read by Peter Francis James & Kathleen McInerney. 10 CDs. (Running Time: 12 hrs.). 2009. audio compact disk 19.99 (978-0-06-178024-0(3), Harper Audio) HarperCollins Pubs.

Plague of Doves. unabr. ed. Louise Erdrich. Narrated by Peter Francis James. (Running Time: 11 hrs. 15 mins.). 2008. 56.75 (978-1-4361-3923-6(6)); 82.75 (978-1-4361-0722-8(9)); audio compact disk 123.75 (978-1-4361-0724-2(5)) Recorded Bks.
Louise Erdrich, NBA finalist and NBCCA winner, pens distinctly American novels evoking the complex heritage and character of her native Midwest. The Boston Globe says Erdrich is "at the peak of her powers as a writer." In 1911, a terrible, blood-chilling crime was committed at the edge of the Ojibwe Reservation, east of the predominantly white town of Pluto, North Dakota. As time passes and memories fade, the past lies buried - until destiny comes calling.

Plague of Secrets. abr. ed. John Lescroart. Read by David Colacci. (Running Time: 6 hrs.). (Dismas Hardy Ser.: No. 13). 2009. audio compact disk 26.99 (978-1-4233-3983-0(5), 9781423339830, BACD) Brilliance Audio.

Plague of Secrets. abr. ed. John Lescroart. Read by David Colacci. (Running Time: 6 hrs.). (Dismas Hardy Ser.: No. 13). 2010. audio compact disk 14.99 (978-1-4233-3984-7(3), 9781423339847, BCD Value Price) Brilliance Audio.

Plague of Secrets. unabr. ed. John Lescroart. (Running Time: 14 hrs.). (Dismas Hardy Ser.: No. 13). 2009. 39.97 (978-1-4233-3982-3(7), 9781423339823, BADLE) Brilliance Audio.

Plague of Secrets. unabr. ed. John Lescroart. Read by David Colacci. (Running Time: 14 hrs.). (Dismas Hardy Ser.: No. 13). 2009. 39.97 (978-1-4233-3980-9(0), 9781423339809, Brlnc Audio MP3 Lib); 24.99 (978-1-4233-3981-6(9), 9781423339816, BAD); 24.99 (978-1-4233-3979-3(7), 9781423339793, Brilliance MP3); audio compact disk 92.97 (978-1-4233-3978-6(9), 9781423339786, BriAudCD Unabrid); audio compact disk 38.99 (978-1-4233-3977-9(0), 9781423339779, Bril Audio CD Unabri) Brilliance Audio.

Plague Ship. Clive Cussler & Jack Du Brul. (Running Time: 7 hrs.). No. 5. (ENG.). (gr. 8). 2009. audio compact disk 14.95 (978-0-14-314443-4(X), PengAudBks) Penguin Grp USA.

Plague Ship. abr. ed. Clive Cussler & Jack Du Brul. Read by Jason Culp. 5 CDs. (Running Time: 7 hrs.). No. 5. (ENG.). (gr. 8). 2008. audio compact disk 29.95 (978-0-14-314309-3(3), PengAudBks) Penguin Grp USA.

Plague Ship. unabr. ed. Clive Cussler & Jack Du Brul. Read by Scott Brick. 13 CDs. (Running Time: 16 hrs.). No. 5. (ENG.). (gr. 8). 2008. audio compact disk 39.95 (978-0-14-314308-6(5), PengAudBks) Penguin Grp USA.

Plague Ship. unabr. ed. Clive Cussler & Jack Du Brul. Read by Scott Brick. 9 cass. (Oregon Files Ser.: No. 5). 2008. 129.00 (978-1-4159-5615-1(4), BksonTape); audio compact disk 129.00 (978-1-4159-5599-4(9), BksonTape) Pub: Random Audio Pubg. Dist(s): Random
For four novels, Clive Cussler has charted the exploits of the Oregon, a covert ship completely dilapidated on the outside but on the inside packed with sophisticated weaponry and intelligence-gathering equipment. Captained by the rakish, one-legged Juan Cabrillo and manned by a crew of former military and spy personnel, it is a private enterprise, available for any government agency that can afford it - and now Cussler sends the Oregon on its most extraordinary mission yet. The crew has just completed a top secret mission against Iran in the Persian Gulf when they come across a cruise ship adrift at sea. Hundreds of bodies litter its deck, and, as Cabrillo tries to determine what happened, explosions rack the length of the ship. Barely able to escape with his own life and that of the liner's sole survivor, Cabrillo finds himself plunged into a mystery as intricate - and as perilous - as any he has ever known and pitted against a cult with monstrously lethal plans for the human race . . . plans he may already be too late to stop.

Plague Ship. unabr. collector's ed. Frank G. Slaughter. Read by Dick Estell. 7 cass. (Running Time: 10 hrs. 30 min.). 1987. 56.00 (978-0-7366-1090-2(1), 2014) Books on Tape.
High in the Andes, an archaeologist stumbles on an ancient tomb & unwittingly releases germs from a civilization doomed by plague over 5000 years ago.

***Plain & Simple Christmas.** unabr. ed. Amy Clipston. (Running Time: 4 hrs. 43 mins. 53 sec.). (ENG.). 2010. 14.99 (978-0-310-59039-2(6)) Zondervan.

Plain Brown Wrapper. Karen Grigsby Bates. Narrated by Robin Miles. 8 cass. (Running Time: 11 hrs. 30 mins.). 74.00 (978-1-4025-2856-9(6)) Recorded Bks.

Plain, Honest Men: The Making of the American Constitution. unabr. ed. Richard Beeman. Narrated by Paul Boehmer & Michael Prichard. (Running Time: 19 hrs. 30 mins. 0 sec.). (ENG.). 2009. audio compact disk 49.99 (978-1-4001-0985-2(X)) Pub: Tantor Media. Dist(s): IngramPubServ

Plain, Honest Men: The Making of the American Constitution. unabr. ed. Richard Beeman. Narrated by Paul Boehmer. (Running Time: 19 hrs. 30 mins. 0 sec.). (ENG.). 2009. audio compact disk 34.99 (978-1-4001-5985-7(7)); audio compact disk 99.99 (978-1-4001-3985-9(6)) Pub: Tantor Media. Dist(s): IngramPubServ

***Plain Jane.** abr. ed. Fern Michaels. Read by Laural Merlington. (Running Time: 6 hrs.). 2010. audio compact disk 9.99 (978-1-4418-6704-9(X), 9781441867049, BCD Value Price) Brilliance Audio.

Plain Jane. unabr. ed. Fern Michaels. Read by Laural Merlington. (Running Time: 11 hrs.). 2004. 39.25 (978-1-59335-431-2(2), 1593354312, Brlnc Audio MP3 Lib) Brilliance Audio.

Plain Jane. unabr. ed. Fern Michaels. Read by Laural Merlington. (Running Time: 11 hrs.). 2004. 49.97 (978-1-59710-578-1(3), 1597105783, BADLE); 24.95 (978-1-59710-579-8(1), 1597105791, BAD) Brilliance Audio.

***Plain Jane.** unabr. ed. Fern Michaels. Read by Laural Merlington. (Running Time: 11 hrs.). 2010. audio compact disk 29.99 (978-1-4418-4093-6(1), 9781441840936, Bril Audio CD Unabri); audio compact disk 89.97 (978-1-4418-4094-3(X), 9781441840943, BriAudCD Unabrid) Brilliance Audio.

Plain Jane. unabr. ed. Fern Michaels. Read by Laural Merlington. (Running Time: 11 hrs.). 2004. 24.95 (978-1-59335-117-5(8), 1593351178) Soulmate Audio Bks.

***Plain Kate.** unabr. ed. Erin Bow. Read by Cassandra Campbell. (Running Time: 7 hrs.). 2010. 24.99 (978-1-4418-2137-9(6), 9781441821379, BAD); 39.97 (978-1-4418-2138-6(4), 9781441821386, BADLE); 24.99 (978-1-4418-2135-5(X), 9781441821355, Brilliance MP3); 39.97 (978-1-4418-2136-2(8), 9781441821362, Brlnc Audio MP3 Lib); audio compact disk 59.97 (978-1-4418-2134-8(1), 9781441821348, BriAudCD Unabrid) Brilliance Audio.

Plain Kate. unabr. ed. Erin Bow. Read by Cassandra Campbell. 8 CDs. (Running Time: 9 hrs.). (YA). 2010. audio compact disk 24.99 (978-1-4418-2133-1(3), 9781441821331, Bril Audio CD Unabri) Brilliance Audio.

Plain Murder. unabr. collector's ed. C. S. Forester. Read by Bill Kelsey. 7 cass. (Running Time: 7 hrs.). 1988. 42.00 (978-0-7366-1308-8(0), 2215) Books on Tape.
Novel whose central character is an underworld psychopath; from the author of "The African Queen" & "Hornblower".

Plain Old Man. Charlotte MacLeod. Read by Mary Peiffer. 2000. 40.00 (978-0-7366-5640-5(5)) Books on Tape.

Plain Paradise. unabr. ed. Beth Wiseman. Narrated by Renee Ertl. (Running Time: 9 hrs. 4 mins. 52 sec.). (Daughters of the Promise Ser.: Bk. 4). (ENG.). 2010. 19.59 (978-1-60814-644-4(8)); audio compact disk 27.99 (978-1-59859-701-1(9)) Oasis Audio.

Plain Perfect. unabr. ed. Beth Wiseman. Narrated by Renee Ertl. (Running Time: 8 hrs. 46 mins. 14 sec.). (Daughters of the Promise Ser.: Bk. 1). (ENG.). 2009. 19.59 (978-1-60814-559-1(X)) Oasis Audio.

Plain Perfect. unabr. ed. Beth Wiseman. Read by Aimee Lilly. Narrated by Renee Ertl. (Running Time: 8 hrs. 46 mins. 14 sec.). (Daughters of the Promise Ser.: Bk. 1). (ENG.). 2009. audio compact disk 27.99 (978-1-59859-536-9(9)) Oasis Audio.

Plain Promise. unabr. ed. Beth Wiseman. Narrated by Renee Ertl. (Running Time: 9 hrs. 47 mins. 45 sec.). (Daughters of the Promise Ser.: Bk. 3). (ENG.). 2009. 20.99 (978-1-60814-600-0(6)); audio compact disk 29.99 (978-1-59859-648-9(9)) Oasis Audio.

***Plain Proposal.** unabr. ed. Beth Wiseman. Narrated by Renee Ertl. (Running Time: 8 hrs. 0 mins. 0 sec.). (Daughters of the Promise Novel Ser.). (ENG.). 2011. audio compact disk 27.99 (978-1-59859-855-1(4)) Oasis Audio.

Plain Pursuit. unabr. ed. Beth Wiseman. Narrated by Renee Ertl. (Running Time: 9 hrs. 37 mins. 2 sec.). (Daughters of the Promise Ser.: Bk. 2). (ENG.). 2009. 19.59 (978-1-60814-560-7(3)) Oasis Audio.

Plain Pursuit. unabr. ed. Beth Wiseman. Read by Aimee Lilly. Narrated by Renee Ertl. (Running Time: 9 hrs. 37 mins. 2 sec.). (Daughters of the Promise Ser.: Bk. 2). (ENG.). 2009. audio compact disk 27.99 (978-1-59859-537-6(7)) Oasis Audio.

Plain Speaker: Opinions on Books, Men, & Things see Cambridge Treasury of English Prose: Austen to Bronte

Plain Speaking. unabr. ed. Merle Miller. Read by Michael Prichard. 10 cass. (Running Time: 15 hrs.). 1978. 80.00 (978-0-7366-0147-4(3), 1148) Books on Tape.
Harry Truman gave us an example of how far you can go by taking the simple, direct line.

Plain Tales from the Hills. Rudyard Kipling. Read by Martin Jarvis. (CSA Word Recording Ser.). (ENG.). 2009. 59.99 (978-1-60775-709-2(5)) Find a World.

Plain Tales from the Hills. Rudyard Kipling. Read by Martin Jarvis. 4 cass. (Running Time: 6 hrs.). 1994. 19.95 Boxed set. (978-1-878427-40-3(7), XC603) Cimino Pub Grp.
Contains twenty-eight short stories about people living in India at the time of the British Raj. Kipling's genius as a storyteller, the raciness of his narrative & the humor & vitality of the characters contribute to ensuring that these stories are as timeless as India itself.

Plain Tales from the Hills. abr. ed. Rudyard Kipling. Read by Martin Jarvis. 2 cass. (Running Time: 3 hrs.). 1998. 16.85 Set. (978-1-901768-23-7(6)) Pub: CSA Telltapes GBR. Dist(s): Ulverscroft US

Plain Tales from the Hills. unabr. ed. Rudyard Kipling. Narrated by Martin Jarvis. 4 CDs. (Running Time: 5 hrs.). 2009. audio compact disk 26.95 (978-1-934997-49-9(8)) Pub: CSAWord. Dist(s): PerseuPGW

Plain Tales from the Hills. unabr. ed. Rudyard Kipling. 2001. Rental 12.99 (978-1-57815-251-3(8), Media Bks Audio) Media Bks NJ.

Plain Tales from the Hills, No. 2. Rudyard Kipling. Read by Martin Jarvis. 2 cass. 1998. 16.85 Set. (978-1-901768-24-4(4)) Pub: CSA Telltapes GBR. Dist(s): Ulverscroft US

Plain Tales of the Afghan Border. unabr. ed. John Bowen. Read by Garard Green. 3 cass. (Running Time: 3 hrs. 45 min.). 2001. 34.95 (978-1-85089-708-8(5), 89122) Pub: ISIS Audio GBR. Dist(s): Ulverscroft US
When John Bowen took over the administration of a remote area of India he could not know that his friendship with an Afridi of noble birth would introduce him to the enchanted world of Pushtu storytelling.

Plain Truth. unabr. ed. Jodi Picoult. Narrated by Christina Moore & Suzanne Toren. 12 cass. (Running Time: 17 hrs.). 2008. 59.95 (978-1-4193-8943-6(2)); audio compact disk 64.95 (978-1-4193-8945-0(9)); audio compact disk 123.75 (978-1-4193-8944-3(0)) Recorded Bks.

Plain Truth. unabr. ed. Jodi Picoult. Narrated by Suzanne Toren & Christina Moore. 12 cass. (Running Time: 17 hrs.). 2006. 113.75 (978-1-4193-8942-9(4)) Recorded Bks.

Plains Chippewa - Metis Music from Turtle Mountain: Drums, Fiddles, Chansons, & Rock & Roll. Anno. by Nicholas C. P. Vrooman. 1 cass. 1992. (0-9307-404110-9307-40411-2-3); audio compact disk (0-9307-40411-2-3) Smithsonian Folkways.
From traditional drum songs to French children's songs & from Scottish fiddle dance tunes to contemporary country & rock 'n' roll, presents music heard on the Turtle Mountain Reservation.

Plains Indians. 1 cass. Dramatization. (J). pap. bk. 6.95 (978-0-86545-089-9(7)) Spizzirri.
Illustrates the life of the Plains Tribes.

Plains of Passage. Jean M. Auel. Read by Sandra Burr. (Playaway Adult Fiction Ser.). (ENG.). 2009. 130.00 (978-1-60775-546-3(7)) Find a World.

Plains of Passage. unabr. ed. Jean M. Auel. Read by Sandra Burr. 24 cass. (Running Time: 34 hrs.). (Earth's Children Ser.: Vol. 4). 1999. 59.95 (978-1-56740-474-6(X), 156740474X, BAU) Brilliance Audio.

Plains of Passage. unabr. ed. Jean M. Auel. Read by Sandra Burr. 28 CDs. (Running Time: 34 hrs.). (Earth's Children Ser.: Vol. 4). 2002. audio compact disk 69.95 (978-1-59086-092-2(6), 1590860926, CD Unabridged); audio compact disk 184.25 (978-1-59086-093-9(4), 1590860934, CD Unabrid Lib Ed) Brilliance Audio.
In The Plains of Passage, orphaned Ayla and wandering Jondalar search for a place on Earth they can call home. Ayla and Jondalar set out on horseback across the windswept grasslands of Ice Age Europe. To the hunter gatherers of their world - who have never seen tame animals - Ayla and Jondalar appear enigmatic and frightening. The mystery surrounding the woman, who speaks with a strange accent and talks to animals with their own sounds, is heightened by her control of a large, menacing wolf. The tall, yellow-haired man who rides by her side is also held in awe, not only for the magnificent stallion he commands, but for his skill as an artificer of stone tools, and for the new weapon he devises that makes hunting less perilous. In the course of their cross-continental odyssey, Ayla and Jondalar encounter both savage enemies and brave friends. Together they learn that the vast and unkown world can be difficult and dangerous, but breathtakingly beautiful and enlightening as well.

Plains of Passage. unabr. ed. Jean M. Auel. Read by Sandra Burr. (Running Time: 34 hrs.). (Earth's Children Ser.: Vol. 4). 2004. 29.95

(978-1-59335-319-3(7), 1593353197, Brilliance MP3); audio compact disk 44.25 (978-1-59335-478-7(9), 1593354789, Brlnc Audio MP3 Lib) Brilliance Audio.

Plains of Passage. unabr. ed. Jean M. Auel. Read by Sandra Burr. (Running Time: 34 hrs.). (Earth's Children Ser.). 2004. 44.25 (978-1-59710-581-1(3), 1597105813, BADLE); 24.99 (978-1-59710-580-4(5), 1597105805, BAD) Brilliance Audio.

***Plains of Passage.** unabr. ed. Jean M. Auel. Read by Sandra Burr. (Running Time: 34 hrs.). (Earth's Children Ser.). 2011. 19.99 (978-1-61106-458-2(9), 9781611064582, Brilliance MP3); audio compact disk 29.99 (978-1-61106-456-8(2), 9781611064568, Bril Audio CD Unabri); audio compact disk 99.97 (978-1-61106-457-5(0), 9781611064575, BriAudCD Unabrid) Brilliance Audio.

Plains of Passage, Pt. 1. unabr. ed. Jean M. Auel. Narrated by Barbara Rosenblat. 15 cass. (Running Time: 21 hrs. 30 mins.). (Earth's Children Ser.: Vol. 4). 1991. 100.00 (978-1-55690-416-5(9), 91212E7) Recorded Bks.
The fourth in the series of pre-historic fantasies featuring Ayla & Jondalar.

Plains of Passage, Pt. 1. unabr. collector's ed. Jean M. Auel. Read by Donada Peters. 12 cass. (Running Time: 18 hrs.). (Earth's Children Ser.: Vol. 4). 1991. 96.00 (978-0-7366-1941-7(0), 2763-A) Books on Tape.
Ayla & Jondalar set out on horseback over the grasslands of Ice-Age Europe. They traverse a vast continent, difficult & treacherous, but pristine & breathtakingly beautiful, full of enchantment. Their trek is a search for something that calls them, that special place that can be their home.

Plains of Passage, Pt. II. Nicholas Kilmer. Read by John McDonough. 82.00 (91213) Recorded Bks.

Plains of Passage, Pt. 2. collector's ed. Jean M. Auel. Read by Donada Peters. 11 cass. (Running Time: 16 hrs. 30 min.). (Earth's Children Ser.: Vol. 4). 1991. 96.00 (978-0-7366-1942-4(9), 2763-B) Books on Tape.
Ayla & Jondalar set out on horseback over the grasslands of Ice-Age Europe. They traverse a vast continent, difficult and treacherous, but pristine and breathtakingly beautiful, full of enchantment. Their trek is a search for something that calls them, that special place that can be their home.

Plains of Passage, Pt. 2. unabr. ed. Jean M. Auel. Narrated by Barbara Rosenblat. 11 cass. (Running Time: 15 hrs. 30 mins.). (Earth's Children Ser.: Vol. 4). 1991. 82.00 (978-1-55690-417-2(7), 91213E7) Recorded Bks.
The fourth in the series of pre-historic fantasies featuring Ayla & Jondalar.

Plains of Passage, Set. unabr. ed. Jean M. Auel. Read by Sandra Burr. 24 cass. (Earth's Children Ser.: Vol. 4). 1999. 189.55 (FS9-51024) Highsmith.

Plainsong. unabr. ed. Kent Haruf. Narrated by Tom Stechschulte. 6 cass. (Running Time: 9 hrs. 30 mins.). 1999. 56.00 (978-0-7887-3765-7(1), 95982E7) Recorded Bks.
A hymn to the breadth of human spirit, tracing the growth of an unlikely extended family which includes a high school teacher, a pregnant teenager & two elderly ranchers.

Plainsong, Set. unabr. ed. Kent Haruf. Narrated by Tom Stechschulte. 8 CDs. (Running Time: 9 hrs. 30 mins.). 2000. audio compact disk 75.00 (978-0-7887-4202-6(7), C1131E5) Recorded Bks.
A hymn to the breadth of human spirit, this traces the growth of an unlikely extended family which includes a high school teacher, a pregnant teenager & two elderly ranchers.

Plainswoman. unabr. ed. Irene Bennett Brown. Read by Stephanie Brush. 12 cass. (Running Time: 13 hrs. 12 min.). 2001. 64.95 (978-1-55686-805-4(7)) Books in Motion.
Desperate for funds when her Kansas homestead is ravaged by sun and drying winds, Amy Whitford sets out to gain the job of school head, and the love of Chalk Holden.

Plan. abr. ed. Stephen J. Cannell. Read by Stephen J. Cannell. 4 cass. (Running Time: 6 hrs.). 2001. 25.00 (978-1-59040-150-7(6), Phoenix Audio) Pub: Amer Intl Pub. Dist(s): PerseuPGW

Plan B: Audio Book on CD. unabr. ed. Pete Wilson. 2010. audio compact disk 24.99 (978-1-4003-1631-1(6)) Nelson.

Plan B: Further Thoughts on Faith. unabr. ed. Anne Lamott. Read by Anne Lamott. 4 cass. (Running Time: 5 hrs.). 2005. 36.00 (978-1-4159-1784-8(1)) Books on Tape.
From the bestselling author of BIRD BY BIRD and OPERATING INSTRUCTIONS comes the much-anticipated follow-up to her 1999 runaway bestseller TRAVELING MERCIES. In PLAN B: FURTHER THOUGHTS ON FAITH, Anne Lamott offers a spiritual antidote to anxiety and despair in today's troubling world. In the midst of terrorism, war, and environmental devastatiion - not to mention personal crises - it is difficult to find comfort and peace. Here, with her trademark wisdom, humor, and honesty, Lamott offers a collection of essays about finding faith and love during these turbulent times.

Plan B: Further Thoughts on Faith. unabr. ed. Anne Lamott. (ENG.). (gr. 8). 2005. audio compact disk 29.95 (978-0-14-305734-5(0), PengAudBks) Penguin Grp USA.

Plan for Peace. Elbert Willis. 1 cass. (Joy & Peace Ser.). 4.00 Fill the Gap.

Plan for Perfection. Elbert Willis. 1 cass. (Victory of Surrender Ser.: Vol. 2). 4.00 Fill the Gap.

Plan is the Man. Reuven Doron. 1 cass. (Running Time: 90 mins.). (Ways of God Ser.: Vol. 3). 2000. 5.00 (RD04-003) Morning NC.
Through the teaching in this eight-part series, Reuven does an excellent job of explaining God's ways versus man's ways.

***Plan of Attack.** abr. ed. Dale Brown. Read by J. K. Simmons. (ENG.). 2005. (978-0-06-085677-9(7), Harper Audio); (978-0-06-085676-2(9), Harper Audio) HarperCollins Pubs.

Plan of Attack. abr. ed. Bob Woodward. Read by Boyd Gaines. 2004. 15.95 (978-0-7435-3963-0(X)) Pub: S&S Audio. Dist(s): S and S Inc

***Plan of Attack.** unabr. ed. Dale Brown. Read by William Dufris. (ENG.). 2005. (978-0-06-085664-9(5), Harper Audio); (978-0-06-085665-6(3), Harper Audio) HarperCollins Pubs.

Plan of Attack. unabr. ed. Bob Woodward. Narrated by Richard Poe. 12 cass. (Running Time: 16 hrs. 30 mins.). 2004. 79.75 (978-1-4193-0748-5(7), 97869MC) Recorded Bks.

Plan of Attack: A Novel. Dale Brown. Read by William Dufris. 12 vols. 2004. bk. 55.95 (978-0-7927-3253-2(7), SLD 668, Chivers Sound Lib); bk. 69.95 (978-0-7927-3254-9(5), CMP 668, Chivers Sound Lib) AudioGO.

Plan of Salvation. Matthew B. Brown. 4 cass. 2004. 19.95 (978-1-59156-089-0(6)); audio compact disk 19.95 (978-1-59156-090-6(X)) Covenant Comms.

Plan Your Estate Right: Or the IRS Will Plan It for You. Brian Reeves. 2 cass. (Running Time: 3 hr. 30 min.). (RPL Audio Books Ser.). 1998. 16.95 (978-1-879755-02-4(5), 502) Recorded Pubns.
Learn about all aspects of estate planning.

Plan Your Own Future. Donna Moore. 1 cass. (Running Time: 50 min.). 1986. 10.95 D J Moore.
Describes two easy ways to set personal goals.

Plane Truth about Christmas. Jimmy Travis Getzen. 2000. 75.00 (978-0-633-00754-6(4)); 11.98 (978-0-633-00751-5(X)); audio compact disk 85.00 (978-0-633-00753-9(6)); audio compact disk 16.98 (978-0-633-00752-2(8)) LifeWay Christian.

Planescape Player's Primer. TSR Inc. Staff. (Advanced Dungeons & Dragons Ser.). 1995. bk. 15.00 (978-0-7869-0121-0(7)) Pub: Wizards Coast. Dist(s): Macmillan

Planet America. abr. ed. Mack Maloney. Read by Charlton Griffin. 2 vols. No. 2. 2003. (978-1-58807-549-9(4)) Am Pubng Inc.

Planet America. abr. ed. Mack Maloney. Read by Charleton Griffin. 4 cass. (Running Time: 6 hrs.). (Starhawk Ser.: No. 2). 2003. 25.00 (978-1-58807-137-8(5)) Am Pubng Inc.
Earth has become the center of the galaxya vast militaristic empire governed by an extended family of near-immortals who rule with brutal efficiency and stern repression. In nearly two millennia, no one has dared oppose their will. Except for one man: enigmatic rogue pilot Hawk Hunter has gone AWOL from the Empire's elite X-Forces to search for the mythical Home Planets.Battling his way across the most dangerous regions of the galaxy, Hunter believes he may have finally found his goalthe planet called Americathe possible birthplace of all humanity. Or is he too caught up in the legends of the Home Planets to see the truth? True or not, Hunter knows that America is a peaceful planet with no weapons of warand war is coming, for an alien armada has targeted America for invasionand Hawk Hunter will have to summon all of his inborn skills as a pilot, commander, and warrior to stop them.

Planet Architecture: Eric Owen Moss - Recent Works. Ed. by Dana Hutt. Prod. by Timothy Sakamoto. (C). 2000. audio compact disk 30.00 (978-1-893801-04-2(7)) in-D.

Planet Architecture: Will Bruder - Recent Works. Ed. by Dana Hutt. Prod. by Timothy Sakamoto. (C). 2000. audio compact disk 29.99 (978-1-893801-03-5(9)) Pub: in-D. Dist(s): Amazon Com

Planet Doom. Anne Schraff. 1 cass. (Running Time: 3788 sec.). (PageTurner Adventure Ser.). (J). 2002. 10.95 (978-1-56254-481-2(0), SP 4810) Saddleback Edu.
Word-for-word read-along of Planet Doom.

Planet Earth in the Chart. Helen Garrett. 1 cass. 1992. 8.95 (1031) Am Fed Astrologers.

Planet Earth Speaks. unabr. ed. Dean Marshall & Marie Kirkendoll. 3 cass. (Running Time: 3 hrs.). 1986. 29.95 incl. bklet. (978-1-55585-080-7(4)) Quest NW Pub.
Communicate with the Angelic Beings who oversee & manage each mountain, river, waterfall & lake, of the earth.

Planet Google: One Company's Audacious Plan to Organize Everything We Know. unabr. ed. Randall Stross. (Running Time: 7.5 hrs. NaN mins.). 2008. 29.95 (978-1-4332-5534-2(0)); 54.95 (978-1-4332-5531-1(6)); audio compact disk 19.95 (978-1-4332-5533-5(2)); audio compact disk 60.00 (978-1-4332-5532-8(4)) Blckstn Audio.

Planet India: How the World's Fastest Growing Democracy Is Transforming America & the World. unabr. ed. Mira Kamdar. Read by Shelly Frasier. (Running Time: 11 hrs. 30 mins. 0 sec.). (ENG.). 2007. audio compact disk 34.99 (978-1-4001-0377-5(0)); audio compact disk 69.99 (978-1-4001-3377-2(7)); audio compact disk 24.99 (978-1-4001-5377-0(8)) Pub: Tantor Media. Dist(s): IngramPubServ

Planet Jazz. Perf. by Ed Hamilton. 1 cass. 7.98 (TA 33387); 7.98 (TA 33387); audio compact disk 12.78 Jewel box. (TA 83387); audio compact disk 12.78 CD Jewel box. (TA 83387) NewSound.

Planet Jupiter. 1 cass. (Running Time: 23 min.). 14.95 (23240) MMI Corp.
Covers size, distance, gravitation, satelites, sounds from Jupiter, surface details & more.

***Planet Man, Volume 1.** RadioArchives.com. (Running Time: 600). (ENG.). 2004. audio compact disk 29.98 (978-1-61081-023-4(6)) Radio Arch.

***Planet Man, Volume 2.** RadioArchives.com. (Running Time: 390). (ENG.). 2004. audio compact disk 14.98 (978-1-61081-024-1(4)) Radio Arch.

Planet Mars. Read by Fred Heiss. 1 cass. (Running Time: 24 min.). 14.95 (23319) MMI Corp.
Comparison of size, density, orbit to that of earth. Can Mars sustain life?.

Planet Mars & Its Inhabitants. Eros Urides. Narrated by Peter Jahns. (ENG.). 2005. audio compact disk 20.00 (978-0-9820380-1-7(1)) CoolBeat.

Planet Mars & its Inhabitants. unabr. ed. Eros Urides. Read by Peter Jahns. (YA). 2007. 34.99 (978-1-60252-931-1(0)) Find a World.

Planet Meditation Kit Set: How to Harness the Energy of the Planets for Good Fortune, Health, & Well-Being. Harish Johari. 5 cass. (Running Time: 1 hr.). 1999. bk. 35.00 (978-0-89281-759-7(3), Heal Arts VT) Inner Tradit.

Planet of Exile. unabr. ed. Ursula K. Le Guin. Read by Carrington MacDuffie. (Running Time: 4 hrs. 0 mins.). 2010. 19.95 (978-1-4417-1739-9(0)); 24.95 (978-1-4417-1735-1(8)); audio compact disk 49.00 (978-1-4417-1736-8(6)) Blckstn Audio.

Planet of Junior Brown. unabr. ed. Virginia Hamilton. Narrated by Peter Francis James. 4 pieces. (Running Time: 5 hrs. 30 mins.). (gr. 6 up). 1994. 35.00 (978-0-7887-0071-2(5), 94304E7) Recorded Bks.
Junior, a lonely musical prodigy & Buddy, a street-smart homeless boy, build a model of the solar system in the school basement. When their secret world is discovered, Buddy must use all his resources to save a devastated Junior.

Planet of the Blind. unabr. ed. Stephen Kuusisto. Narrated by Brian Keeler. 5 CDs. (Running Time: 5 hrs. 45 mins.). 2000. audio compact disk 48.00 (978-1-84197-046-2(8), C1207E7) Recorded Bks.
Stephen Kuusisto is 'legally blind'. His sight is a kaleidoscope of colors & shapes, ordered only by his imagination. Blindness in the 1950's was a social stigma, Stephen's mother wanted a normal life for him, so he fought desperately to uphold the illusion of sight. Each day was a an exhausting pretence. He managed to ride a bike, even when reading involved pressing his nose to the page & painfully forcing his eyes to concentrate. Head up, he strode through a carefully memorized labyrinth of streets, hoping to fool passer-by that he could actually see.

Planet of the Blind. unabr. ed. Stephen Kuusisto. Narrated by Brian Keeler. 4 cass. (Running Time: 5 hrs. 45 mins.). 2000. 39.00 (978-1-84197-070-7(0), H1093E7) Recorded Bks.

***Planet of the Spiders.** Terrance Dicks. Narrated by Elisabeth Sladen. (Running Time: 4 hrs. 0 mins. 0 sec.). (Doctor Who Ser.). (ENG.). 2010. audio compact disk 34.95 (978-1-4056-8768-3(1)) Pub: AudioGO. Dist(s): Perseus Dist

Planet Pirates. Anne McCaffrey et al. Read by Constance Towers. 6 cass. (Running Time: 8 hrs.). 2003. 32.00 (978-1-57453-538-9(2)) Brilliance Audio.

Planet Salt Spring. unabr. ed. Arthur Black. 1 CD. (Running Time: 1 hr. 6 mins.). 2009. audio compact disk 18.95 (978-1-55017-470-0(3)) Pub: Harbour Pub Co CAN. Dist(s): IngramPubServ

Planet Sleeps. 2 cass. (Running Time: 40 min.). (J). (ps-3). 1997. 8.98 Set, incl. insert. (Sony Wonder); audio compact disk 17.98 CD. Sony Music Ent.
Sixteen exquisite lullabies from all the world's quadrants are sung in a variety of the world's languages & accompanied by indigenous instruments. Insert is rich in information about the cultures represented & includes translations of the lyrics.

Planet Sleeps. David Field. Perf. by Rankin Family et al. 1 cass. (Running Time: 40 min.). 1997. 8.98; audio compact disk 17.98 CD. Sony Music Ent.
Collection of lullabies recorded in countries around the world.

Planet Squeezebox: Accordion Music from Around the World, Vol. 1. Contrib. by Michal Shapiro. 3 CDs. (Running Time: 3 hrs.). 1995. bk. 44.95 (978-1-55961-319-4(X), CD3470, Ellipsis Arts); bk. 34.95 (978-1-55961-320-0(3), CD3470) Relaxtn Co.

Planet with One Mind. Mike Pinder. 1 cass. (J). 9.98 (978-1-888057-04-1(1)); audio compact disk 15.98 CD. One Step Recs.
Features the following inspiring children's stories: "The Legend of the Indian Paintbrush" - the story of a young native American who follows & fulfills his Dream-Vision by Tomie dePaola; "A Spark in the Dark" - a story about a star, the earth, the light we come from & the light we bring into the world by Richard Tichnor & Jenny Smith; "The Rajah's Rice" - set in ancient India, the story of a young girl, her love of elephants, mathematics & her people by David Barry; "The Butterfly Boy" - the beautiful & thoughtful story of the boy who thought he was a butterfly - inspired by the writings of Chinese Philosopher, Chuang Tzu; "All of You Was Singing" - the Mayan & Aztec story of how music came to the earth, & the profound importance of music to the well-being of life by Richard Lewis; "Old Turtle" - enchanting fable promoting deeper understanding of the earth & all beings who inhabit it by Douglas Wood & "Why the Sky Is Far Away" by Mary-Joan Gerson.

Planet with One Mind: Stories from Around the World for the Child Within Us All. Mike Pinder. 1 cass. (J). 1995. (978-1-888057-00-3(9)) One Step Recs.
Mike Pinder, singer-songwriter of the Moody Blues narrates seven uplifting & imaginative stories for children over a musical atmosphere created by Mike.

Planet with One Mind; A People with One Heart; An Earth with One Spirit: Stories from Around the World for the Child Within Us All. Mike Pinder. 3 cass. (J). Set. (978-1-888057-03-4(3)) One Step Recs.
Mike Pinder, singer-songwriter of the Moody Blues narrates twenty-one uplifting & imaginative stories for children over a musical atmosphere created by Mike.

Planeta: Level Ia. M. Cerrolaza et al. 2 cass. (Running Time: 3 hrs.). (SPA.). 2001. 54.95 (978-84-7711-224-2(X), ED11224X) Pub: Edelsa ESP. Dist(s): Continental Bk
A new program designed for adolescents and adults. Each level contains five thematic units in which language function, grammatical usage, activities, exercises, civilization and review are found.

Planetary Chronicles. Perf. by Jonn Serrie. 1 cass. 9.98 (MPC2004); audio compact disk 14.98 CD. Miramar Images.
An impressive selection from his planetarium portfolio, each song on this release was chosen to represent a specific era of his music. Planetary Chronicles is a compilation of Serrie's full range of talent with emphasis on earlier compositions.

Planetary Emphasis in Vocational Astrology. Julie O'Toole. 1 cass. 8.95 (266) Am Fed Astrologers.
What angular planets say about the use of energy.

Planetary Lovers in Myth. Bradley Clark. 1 cass. 8.95 (054) Am Fed Astrologers.
Gain deeper awareness by looking at "primary pairs".

Planetary Nodes, 1984. Gwen Steifbold. 1 cass. 8.95 (332) Am Fed Astrologers.
Nodes are stranger than planets themselves.

Planetary Nodes, 1986. Gwen Steifbold. 1 cass. 8.95 (588) Am Fed Astrologers.
How do they work? Examples.

Planets. 1 cass. Dramatization. (J). pap. bk. 6.95 (978-0-86545-112-4(5)) Spizzirri.
Journey to the surface of the planets & their moons.

Planets. Dorling Kindersley Publishing Staff. Narrated by Andrew Sachs. (Eyewitness Videos Ser.). (ENG.). (J). (gr. 1-12). 2007. 12.99 (978-0-7566-3890-0(9)) DK Pub Inc.

Planets. unabr. ed. Dava Sobel. Read by Lorna Raver. 5 CDs. 2005. audio compact disk 38.25 (978-1-4159-2454-9(6)) Pub: Books on Tape. Dist(s): NetLibrary CO

Planets. unabr. ed. Dava Sobel. Read by Lorna Raver. 4 cass. 2005. 36.00 (978-1-4159-2453-2(8)) Books on Tape.
After the huge national and international success of Longitude and Galileo's Daughter, Dava Sobel tells the human story of the nine planets of our solar system. THE PLANETS tells the story of each member of our solar family, from their discovery, both mythic and historic, to the latest data from the modern era's robotic space probes and images from the Hubble Space Telescope. Whether revealing what hides behind Venus' cocoon of acid clouds, describing Jupiter's 'Technicolor lightning bolts and shimmering sheets of auroras,' or capturing first-hand the excitement at the Jet Propulsion Laboratory when the first pictures from Voyager were beamed to earth, Dava Sobel's unique tour of the solar family is filled with fascination and poetry.

Planets in Progression. Mohan Koparkar. 1 cass. (Running Time: 90 min.). 1988. 8.95 (686) Am Fed Astrologers.

Planets Out of Bound. C. Hannan & L. Hannan. 1 cass. 1992. 8.95 (1039) Am Fed Astrologers.

Planned Businesshood: You Can Plan & Manage Your Own Successful Small Business. Robert Wardrick. (Small Business Headstart Ser.). 1996. 5.95 (978-0-9652744-1-8(1)) Authors Wkshp.

Planned Reading Program As a Help to Personal Growth. Instructed by Manly P. Hall. 8.95 (978-0-89314-217-9(4), C821121) Philos Res.

Planning for the Closely Held Business: Tax, Non-Tax & Personal Considerations. 5 cass. (Running Time: 5 hrs. 30 min.). 1990. bk. 55.00 incl. 303-page course handbook. (T6-9148) PLI.

Planning for the Closely Held Business: Tax, Non-Tax & Personal Considerations. unabr. ed. Contrib. by Sanford J. Schlesinger. 4 cass. (Running Time: 6 hrs.). 1989. 50.00 course handbk. (T7-9199) PLI.
This recording of PLI's February 1989 program examines all aspects tax, non-tax & personal of planning for the closely held business. Topics include: planning techniques, structuring & restructuring closely held entities, closely held business freeze, tax elections under applicable IRC Sections, pension, profit-sharing & Section 401(k) plans.

Planning for the Professional. 1987. bk. 95.00; 60.00 PA Bar Inst.

Planning Techniques for Large Estates. 20 cass. (Running Time: 30 hrs.). 1998. 545.00 Set; incl. study guide 1802p. (MD33) Am Law Inst.
Advanced course deals with the most sophisticated problems & considerations, approached on a transactional basis.

Planning the Small Estate. Read by Arthur Bredenbeck et al. (Running Time: 2 hrs. 30 min.). 1992. 89.00 Incl. Ethics: 5 hrs.; Law Practice Management: 0.15 min., & 153p. tape materials. (ES-55250) Cont Ed Bar-CA.
Three practitioners discuss non-estate tax aspects of planning of small (under $600.000) estates. Focuses on trusts, POD arrangements, joint tenancy, beneficiary designations, life insurance, IRAs, property tax, & ethical considerations.

Planning Your Financial Future. Moderated by Harold Kamens. Contrib. by Charles M. Aulino et al. (Running Time: 6 hrs. 30 min.). 1984. 105.00 incl. program handbook. NJ Inst CLE.
The speakers devote particular attention to Social Security, Medicare, health insurance, life insurance, trusts, investments, pension planning, tax planning.

Planning Your Future. abr. ed. Linda L. McNeil. Read by Linda L. McNeil. 2 cass. (Running Time: 1 hrs. 20 min.). 1996. pap. bk. 49.95 Set; incl. computer disk. (978-1-891446-06-1(1)) Open Mind.
Specifically for physical therapists. Leads user through the process of business planning & marketing strategy in a one day do-it-yourself format. Includes the 10 keys for successful planning.

Planning Your Unique Wedding Freeway Guide. Randie Pellegrini. Read by Randie Pellegrini. (Playaway Adult Nonfiction Ser.). (ENG.). 2009. 34.99 (978-1-60812-575-3(0)) Find a World.

Plans I Have. (Paws & Tales Ser.: No. 44). 2002. 3.99 (978-1-57972-506-8(6)); audio compact disk 5.99 (978-1-57972-507-5(4)) Insight Living.

Plans in the Breaking. (Paws & Tales Ser.: Vol. 23). (J). 2002. 3.99 (978-1-57972-430-6(2)); audio compact disk 5.99 (978-1-57972-431-3(0)) Insight Living.

Plans, Purposes, & Pursuits. Kenneth E. Hagin. 24.00 (C8128) Faith Lib Pubns.
Experience the true moving of God's Spirit.

Plant. Dorling Kindersley Publishing Staff. (Eyewitness Videos Ser.). (ENG.). (J). (gr. 1-12). 2006. 12.99 (978-0-7566-2830-7(X)) DK Pub Inc.

Plant a Tree with Mickey the Clown & the Bamboo Kazoo. 1 cass. (J). 9.98 (978-1-885654-01-4(4)); audio compact disk 12.98 CD. (978-1-885654-02-1(2)) Real Folks Mus.
A joyous & fun collection of original songs from America's premier musical clown & the most unique entertainment personality to come along in quite a while. This collection is a sure bet to delight both the young & the young at heart. Each song is designed to enrich your curriculum (Preschool to Early Elementary) & can easily be incorporated into lesson plans & learning activities. The songs on "Plant a Tree" are written to develop motor skills, build character, encourage self-esteem, promote cooperative learning, enhance social awareness & interpersonal relationships & reinforce language & listening proficiencies while at the same time having "Fun".

Plant & Animal Fossils. Compiled by Benchmark Education Staff. 2005. audio compact disk 10.00 (978-1-4108-5498-8(1)) Benchmark Educ.

Plant & Horticulture Therapy, Vol. 8. Jonathan Parker. 2 cass. (Running Time: 2 hrs.). 1998. 17.00 Set. (978-1-58400-007-5(4)) QuantumQuests Intl.

Plant Has Needs Audio CD. Adapted by Benchmark Education Company Staff. Based on a work by Cynthia Swain. (Early Explorers Set C Ser.). (J). (gr. k). 2008. audio compact disk 10.00 (978-1-60437-507-7(8)) Benchmark Educ.

Plant Has Parts: Early Explorers Emergent Set A Audio CD. Benchmark Education Staff. (J). 2006. audio compact disk 10.00 (978-1-4108-7589-1(X)) Benchmark Educ.

Plant Messengers & Brain Evolution. Dennis J. McKenna. 3 cass. 1992. 27.00 set. (OC294-65) Sound Horizons AV.

Plant People. abr. ed. Engle & Barnes. (Running Time: 2 hrs.). (Strange Matter Ser.). 2007. 9.95 (978-1-4233-0852-2(2), 9781423308522, BAD) Brilliance Audio.

Plant People. abr. ed. Engle & Julian Barnes. Read by Multivoice Production Staff. (Running Time: 2 hrs.). (Strange Matter Ser.). 2007. 25.25 (978-1-4233-0853-9(0), 9781423308539, BADLE) Brilliance Audio.

Plant People. abr. ed. Marion Engle & J. Barnes. Read by Full Cast Production Staff. (Running Time: 7200 sec.). (Strange Matter Ser.). (J). (gr. 4-7). 2007. audio compact disk 25.25 (978-1-4233-0851-5(4), 9781423308515, BACDLib Ed) Brilliance Audio.

Plant People. abr. ed. Marion Engle & Rudol Barnes. Read by Full Cast Production Staff. (Running Time: 7200 sec.). (Strange Matter Ser.). (J). (gr. 4-7). 2007. audio compact disk 9.95 (978-1-4233-0850-8(6), 9781423308508, BACD) Brilliance Audio.

Plant Realm: Language of the Greenworld. Susan Hecker. 1 cass. (Running Time: 1 hr. 33 min.). (Language & Life of Symbols Ser.). 1995. 10.95 (978-0-7822-0489-6(9), 565) C G Jung IL.

Plant Resources of South-East Asia: Edible Fruits & Nuts. Ed. by E. W. Verheij et al. (World Biodiversity Database Ser.). 2000. audio compact disk 160.00 (978-3-540-14845-6(0)) Spri.

Plant Resources of South-East Asia: Timber Trees. R. H. Lemmens et al. (World Biodiversity Database CD-ROM Ser.). 2000. audio compact disk 399.00 (978-3-540-14773-2(X)) Spri.

Plant Resources of South-East Asia: Timber Trees. R. H. Lemmens et al. 2000. audio compact disk 399.00 (978-3-540-14771-8(3)) Spri.

Plant Spirit Medicine: Healing with the Power of Plants. Eliot A. Cohen. 6. (Running Time: 12 hrs.). 2004. 25.00 (978-1-893183-29-2(7), Swan Raven) Granite Pub.
This is a trailblazing book on tape that explores an old way of healing through the spirit of plants! Eliot Cowen learned that it wasn't the plant that healed a person, but the spirit in the plant. Learning to contact the spirit of the plant was to ask it directly to heal the person. This ancient practice of plant spirit medicine, long forgotten in the West, has now been remembered, revitalized and reintroduced by this American healer. This book opens the reader to the real and ancient world of contact with plant spirits, how to make that contact for oneself, as well as wonderful stories of Indian shaman healers and their respect and alliance with plant spirits. This is a wonderful psychic and spiritual approach to holistic healing. As seen in Yoga Journal, Natural Health, New Age Journal and now a One Spirit Book-of-the-Month Club Selection This is the audio tape version of the ever-popular book by the same title. Very high quality production with original indigenous music in the background, sound effects, sensitive reading.

***Plant Spirit Medicine: Healing with the Power of Plants.** Eliot Cowan. 2010. audio compact disk 19.99 (978-1-893183-30-8(0)) Pub: Granite Pub. Dist(s): AtlasBooks

Plant Story Rhymes. unabr. ed. Alfreda C. Doyle. Read by Alfreda C. Doyle. 1 cass. (Running Time: 35 min.). (Alfreda's Radio Ser.: Vol. 3). (J). (gr. 5-9). 1998. 16.95 (978-1-56820-307-2(1)) Story Time.
Stories that educate, entertain, inform & rhyme.

Plant That Ate Dirty Socks. unabr. ed. Read by Rick Adamson. Ed. by Nancy McArthur. 2 vols. (Running Time: 3 hrs. 3 mins.). (J). (gr. 3-7). 1997. pap. bk. 29.00 (978-0-8072-7751-5(7), YA909SP, Listening Lib) Random Audio Pubg.

Plant That Ate Dirty Socks. unabr. ed. Nancy McArthur. Read by Rick Adamson. 2 cass. (Running Time: 3 hrs.). (Plant That Ate Dirty Socks Ser.: Bk. 1). (J). (gr. k-3). 1999. 23.00 (LL 0092, Chivers Child Audio) AudioGO.

Plant That Ate Dirty Socks. unabr. ed. Nancy McArthur. Read by Rick Adamson. 2 cass. (Running Time: 3 hrs. 3 mins.). (J). (gr. 3-7). 1997. 23.00 (978-0-8072-7750-8(9), YA909CX, Listening Lib) Random Audio Pubg.

planta tiene partes Audio CD: Emergent Set A. Benchmark Education Staff. Ed. by Cynthia Swain. (Early Explorers Ser.). (J). 2008. audio compact disk 10.00 (978-1-60437-238-0(9)) Benchmark Educ.

***Plantas en Sus HáBitats Audio Cd.** Debra Castor. Adapted by Benchmark Education Company, LLC. (Content Connections Ser.). (SPA.). (J). 2009. audio compact disk 10.00 (978-1-935472-65-0(8)) Benchmark Educ.

Plantation. abr. ed. Dorothea Benton Frank. Read by Susie Breck. 4 cass. (Running Time: 6 hrs.). (Lowcountry Tales Ser.: No. 2). 2001. 53.25 (978-1-58788-979-0(X), 158788979X, Lib Edit) Brilliance Audio.
The follow-up to Frank's debut novel, Sullivan's Island, this colorful contemporary romance effortlessly evokes the lush beauty of the South Carolina Lowcountry while exploring the complexities of family relationships. When Caroline Wimbley Levine learns that her mother, Miss Lavinia, has supposedly gone mad, she leaves the big city bustle of Manhattan and returns to Tall Pines Plantation. Caroline originally left Tall Pines to escape her feisty, eccentric mother and her drunken brother, Trip, but when Miss Lavinia dies, Caroline is forced to come to terms with her family's troubled history as well as her failing relationship with her husband. As Caroline reminisces about her past rebelliousness and her childhood, she realizes that her father's sudden and tragic death many years before served as a catalyst for the family's disintegration. Caroline and Trip also learn that their seemingly selfish and self-assured mother was not so uncaring after all.

Plantation. abr. ed. Dorothea Benton Frank. Read by Susie Breck. (Running Time: 6 hrs.). (Lowcountry Tales Ser.: No. 2). 2006. 39.25 (978-1-4233-0168-4(4), 9781423301684, BADLE); 24.95 (978-1-4233-0167-7(6), 9781423301677, BAD); 39.25 (978-1-4233-0166-0(8), 9781423301660, Brlnc Audio MP3 Lib); audio compact disk 24.95 (978-1-4233-0165-3(X), 9781423301653, Brilliance MP3) Brilliance Audio.
When Caroline Wimbley Levine learns that her mother, Miss Lavinia, has supposedly gone mad, she leaves the big city bustle of Manhattan and returns to Tall Pines Plantation. She had left to escape her feisty mother and her drunken brother, Trip, but when Miss Lavinia dies, Caroline is forced to come to terms with her family's troubled history as well as her failing relationship with her husband.

Plantation. unabr. ed. Chris Kuzneski. Read by Dick Hill. (Running Time: 13 hrs.). (Payne & Jones Ser.: Bk. 1). 2009. 24.99 (978-1-4233-8970-5(0), 9781423389705, Brilliance MP3); 24.99 (978-1-4233-8972-9(7), 9781423389729, BAD); 39.97 (978-1-4233-8971-2(9), 9781423389712, Brlnc Audio MP3 Lib); 39.97 (978-1-4233-8973-6(5), 9781423389736, BADLE); audio compact disk 29.99 (978-1-4233-8968-2(9), 9781423389682, Bril Audio CD Unabri); audio compact disk 92.97 (978-1-4233-8969-9(7), 9781423389699, BriAudCD Unabrid) Brilliance Audio.

Plantations of River Road Self Guided Audio Tour (2 CD Set) Pamela Pipes. Prod. by Tours BaYou. 2008. audio compact disk (978-0-9801321-1-3(8)) Tours Bayou.

***Plants.** Perf. by Millmark Education Staff. (ConceptLinks Ser.). 2007. audio compact disk 28.00 (978-1-4334-0047-6(2)) Millmark Educ.

Plants. Steck-Vaughn Staff. 2002. 9.00 (978-0-7398-6208-7(1)) SteckVau.

***Plants: CD add-on Set.** Perf. by Millmark Education Staff. (ConceptLinks Ser.). 2009. audio compact disk 50.00 (978-1-61618-344-8(6)) Millmark Educ.

Plants & Animals in Different Seasons Audio CD. Adapted by Benchmark Education Company Staff. Based on a work by Kira Freed. (Early Explorers Set C Ser.). (J). (gr. 2). 2008. audio compact disk 10.00 (978-1-60437-544-2(2)) Benchmark Educ.

Plants & Compounds. Alexander Shulgin. 1 cass. (Running Time: 60 Min.). 1999. 11.00 (13702) Big Sur Tapes.
1979 Mill Valley, CA.

Plants & the Seasons Audio CD. Adapted by Benchmark Education Company Staff. Based on a work by Margaret McNamara. (Content Connections Ser.). (J). (gr. k-2). 2008. audio compact disk 10.00 (978-1-60634-899-4(X)) Benchmark Educ.

Plants in Their Habitats Audio CD. Adapted by Benchmark Education Company Staff. Based on a work by Margaret McNamara. (Content Connections Ser.). (J). (gr. k-2). 2008. audio compact disk 10.00 (978-1-60634-894-9(9)) Benchmark Educ.

Plants of Hawaii. Bess Press. 2004. audio compact disk 4.95 (978-1-57306-203-9(0)) Bess Pr.

Plants, People & Environmental Quality: Syllabus. (J). 1977. 70.90 (978-0-89420-173-8(5), 140000) Natl Book.

***Plants SB1 Audio CD Important Producers.** Perf. by Millmark Education Staff. (Content Literacy Libraries Ser.). 2008. audio compact disk (978-1-4334-0400-9(1)) Millmark Educ.

***Plants SB2 Audio CD Structure & Function.** Perf. by Millmark Education Staff. (Content Literacy Libraries Ser.). 2008. audio compact disk (978-1-4334-0401-6(X)) Millmark Educ.

***Plants SB3 Audio CD Growing & Using Energy.** Perf. by Millmark Education Staff. (Content Literacy Libraries Ser.). 2008. audio compact disk (978-1-4334-0402-3(8)) Millmark Educ.

***Plants SB4 Audio CD Reproduction in Flowering Plants.** Perf. by Millmark Education Staff. (Content Literacy Libraries Ser.). 2008. audio compact disk (978-1-4334-0403-0(6)) Millmark Educ.

Plants That Never Ever Bloom. unabr. ed. Ruth Heller. 1 cass. (Running Time: 6 min.). (J). (gr. 1-4). 1989. bk. 20.90 (6551-D) Spoken Arts.

Plants Theme Audio CD. ed. (J). 2004. audio compact disk (978-1-4108-1837-9(3)) Benchmark Educ.

Plants, Visions & History. unabr. ed. Terence McKenna. 1 cass. 1988. 9.00 (978-1-56964-048-7(3), A0324-89) Sound Photosyn.
At the L.A. Whole Life Expo.

Plastic. (Materials Ser.). (ENG.). 2009. audio compact disk 5.95 (978-1-4329-3251-0(9), AcornHR) Heinemann Rai.

Plastic & Maxillofacial Surgery. (Post Graduate Surgery Ser.: C84-PG13). 1984. 45.00 (8493) Am Coll Surgeons.
Presents methods of management of acute injuries of the upper extremity.

Plastic & Maxillofacial Surgery: Aesthetic & Reconstructive Surgery of the Nose. Moderated by John M. Goin. (Postgraduate Courses Ser.). 1986. 57.00 (8623 (C86-PG13)) Am Coll Surgeons.
Provides information concerning concepts of patient selection, preoperative planning & surgical techniques related to nasal surgery. 6 hours CME credit.

Plastic & Maxillofacial Surgery: Reconstruction & Rehabilitation of the Burn Patient. (Postgraduate Programs Ser.: C85-PG13). 45.00 (8523) Am Coll Surgeons.
Focuses on concepts of postburn reconstruction & total patient rehabilitation. 6 hours CME category 5 credits.

Plastic Recycling; Geographical Information Systems; & United Nations Restructuring. Hosted by Nancy Pearlman. 1 cass. (Running Time: 30 min.). 10.00 (512) Educ Comm CA.

Plastic Surgery Equipment & Services in Taiwan: A Strategic Reference 2007. Compiled by Icon Group International, Inc. Staff. 2007. ring bd. 195.00 (978-0-497-82433-4(7)) Icon Grp.

Plastics Machinery in China: A Strategic Reference 2006. Compiled by Icon Group International, Inc. Staff. 2007. ring bd. 195.00 (978-0-497-35890-7(5)) Icon Grp.

Plastics Materials & Equipment in Kenya: A Strategic Reference 2006. Compiled by Icon Group International, Inc. Staff. 2007. ring bd. 195.00 (978-0-497-82341-2(1)) Icon Grp.

Plastics Resins in Malaysia: A Strategic Reference 2006. Compiled by Icon Group International, Inc. Staff. 2007. ring bd. 195.00 (978-0-497-82346-7(2)) Icon Grp.

Platanos Verdes. Created by Rigby Staff. 1993. 10.40 (978-0-435-05945-3(9), Rigby PEA) Pearson EdAUS AUS.

Plates of Gold: The Book of Mormon Comes Forth. Matthew Brown. 3 cass. 2004. 14.95 (978-1-59156-371-6(2)); audio compact disk 15.95 (978-1-59156-372-3(0)) Covenant Comms.

Platinum. 1997. 9.98 (Sony Wonder); audio compact disk 13.98 CD. Sony Music Ent.
Features fun favorites such as "Caribbean Amphibian, & "Just Happy to Be Me".

Platinum Rule: Discover the Four Basic Business Personalities - and How They Can Lead You to Success. abr. ed. Tony Alessandra & Michael J. O'Connor. (ENG.). 2006. 14.98 (978-1-59483-742-5(2)) Pub: Hachet Audio. Dist(s): HachBkGrp

Platiquemos Spanish Course Lev. 1-4 CS: Multilingual Books Language Course. 2nd ed. Don Casteel. 25 cass. (Multilingual Books Intensive Cassette Foreign Language Ser.). (SPA.). (C). 2004. per. 349.00 (978-1-58214-142-8(8)) Language Assocs.

Platiquemos Spanish Course Level 1 CD Level 1: Multilingual Books Language Course. Don Casteel. 8 CD's. (Multilingual Books Intensive Language Courses). (SPA.). (C). 2000. per. 99.00 (978-1-58214-290-6(4)) Language Assocs.

Platiquemos Spanish Course Level 2 CD Level 2: Multilingual Books Language Course. Don Casteel. 8 CD's. (Multilingual Books Intensive Language Courses). (SPA.). (C). 2000. per. 99.00 (978-1-58214-291-3(2)) Language Assocs.

Platiquemos Spanish Course Level 3 CD Level 3: Multilingual Books Language Course. Don Casteel. 7 CD's. (Multilingual Books Intensive Language Courses). (SPA.). (C). 2000. per. 99.00 (978-1-58214-292-0(0)) Language Assocs.

Platiquemos Spanish Course Level 4 CD Level 4: Multilingual Books Language Course. Don Casteel. 6 CD. (Multilingual Books Intensive Language Courses). (SPA.). (C). 2000. per. 99.00 (978-1-58214-293-7(9)) Language Assocs.

Platiquemos Spanish Course Level 5-8: Multilingual Books Language Course. 2nd ed. Don Casteel. 25 CDs. (Multilingual Books Intensive Language Courses). (SPA.). (C). 2004. per. 349.00 (978-1-58214-140-4(1)) Language Assocs.

Platiquemos Spanish Course Level 7 CD Level 7: Multilingual Books Language Course. Don Casteel. 6 CD's. (Multilingual Books Intensive Language Courses). (SPA.). (C). 2000. per. 99.00 (978-1-58214-288-3(2)) Language Assocs.

Platiquemos Spanish Course Level 8 CD Level 8: Multilingual Books Language Course. Don Casteel. 6 CDs. (Multilingual Books Intensive Language Courses). (SPA.). (C). 2000. per. 99.00 (978-1-58214-289-0(0)) Language Assocs.

Platiquemos Spanish Level 1 Cassette Level 1: Multilingual Books Language Course. Don Casteel. 8 cass. (Multilingual Books Intensive Cassette Foreign Language Ser.). (SPA.). (C). 2000. per. 79.00 (978-1-58214-275-3(0)) Language Assocs.

Platiquemos Spanish Level 2 Cassette Course Level 2: Multilingual Books Language Course. Don Casteel. 8 cass. (Multilingual Books Intensive Language Courses). (SPA.). (C). 2000. per. Rental 99.00 (978-1-58214-279-1(3)) Language Assocs.

Platiquemos Spanish Level 3 Cassette Course Level 3: Multilingual Books Language Course. Don Casteel. 7 cass. (Multilingual Books Intensive Language Courses). (SPA.). (C). 2000. per. 99.00 (978-1-58214-280-7(7)) Language Assocs.

Platiquemos Spanish Level 4 Cassette Course Level 4: Multilingual Books Language Course. Don Casteel. 6 cass. (Multilingual Books Intensive Language Courses). (SPA.). (C). 2000. per. 99.00 (978-1-58214-281-4(5)) Language Assocs.

Platiquemos Spanish Level 5 CD Level 5: Multilingual Books Language Course. Don Casteel. 6 CD's. (Multilingual Books Interactive Language Courses Ser.). (SPA.). (C). 2000. per. 99.00 (978-1-58214-287-6(4)) Language Assocs.

Platiquemos Spanish Level 6 CD Level 6: Multilingual Books Language Course. Don Casteel. 7 CDs. (Multilingual Books Intensive Language Courses). (SPA.). (C). 2000. per. 99.00 (978-1-58214-286-9(6)) Language Assocs.

Plato. 10.00 Esstee Audios.
The Greek thinker tells why we do what we do.

Plato: Greece (CA. 428-348 B. C.) Berel Lang. Read by Charlton Heston. Ed. by George H. Smith & Wendy McElroy. 2 cass. (Running Time: 3 hrs.). (Giants of Philosophy Ser.). 1990. 17.9[illegible]78-0-938935-17-9(8), 10301) Pub: Knowledge Prod. Dist(s): APG
The first great philosopher of the West, [illegible]ght that existing things are modeled on changeless, eternal forms. To Plato, human beings consist of an immortal soul & a mortal body, the soul ha a love for the eternal, the good, the true & the beautiful; these give life purpose, stability & meaning.

Plato: Greece (CA. 428-348 B. C.) abr. ed. Narrated by Charlton Heston. (Running Time: 8226 sec.). (Audio Classics: the Giants of Philosophy Ser.). 2006. audio compact disk 25.95 (978-0-7861-6941-2(9)) Pub: Blckstn Audio. Dist(s): NetLibrary CO

Plato: Greece (CA. 428-348 B. C.) abr. ed. Narrated by Charlton Heston. 2 CDs. (Running Time: 2 hrs. 16 mins.). (Giants of Philosophy Ser.). 1990. audio compact disk 16.95 (978-1-56823-067-2(2)) Pub: Knowledge Prod. Dist(s): APG

Plato: Greece (CA. 428-348 B. C.), Set. unabr. ed. Read by Charlton Heston. 2 cass. (Giants of Philosophy Ser.). 17.95 (K117) Blckstn Audio.
See how one of the world's most important philosophers created a complete system of thought, including his views on ethics, metaphysics, politics & aesthetics. Learn about his epistemology - how we know what we know.

Plato & a Platypus Walk into a Bar: Understanding Philosophy Through Jokes. Daniel Klein & Thomas Cathcart. Narrated by Johnny Heller. (Running Time: 15300 sec.). 2007. audio compact disk 19.99 (978-1-4281-7376-7(5)) Recorded Bks.

Plato in 90 Minutes. Paul Strathern. Narrated by Robert Whitfield. (Running Time: 1 hr. 30 mins.). (C). 2003. 17.95 (978-1-59912-569-5(2)) Iofy Corp.

Plato in 90 Minutes. unabr. ed. Paul Strathern. Read by Robert Whitfield. 1 CD. (Running Time: 1 hr. 30 mins.). (Philosophers in 90 Minutes Ser.). 2004. audio compact disk 14.95 (978-0-7861-9287-8(9)) Blckstn Audio.
In an age when philosophers had scarcely glimpsed the horizons of the mind, a boy named Aristocles decided to forgo his ambitions as a wrestler. Adopting the nickname Plato, he embarked instead on a life in philosophy. In 387 B.C. he founded the Academy, the world's first university, and taught his students that all we see is not reality but merely a reproduction of the true source. And in his famous Republic he described the politics of "the highest form of state.".

Plato in 90 Minutes. unabr. ed. Paul Strathern. Read by Robert Whitfield. (Running Time: 1 hr. 30 mins.). (Philosophers in 90 Minutes Ser.). 2001. reel tape 14.95 (978-0-7861-2471-8(7)) Blckstn Audio.

Plato in 90 Minutes. unabr. ed. Paul Strathern. Read by Robert Whitfield. 1 cass. (Running Time: 1 hr. 30 mins.). 2003. 14.95 (978-0-7861-2392-6(3), 3069); audio compact disk 16.00 (978-0-7861-9279-3(8), 3069) Blckstn Audio.

Plato, Socrates, & the Dialogues. Michael Sugrue. 8 cass. (Running Time: 1 hrs. 30 min. per cass.). 49.95 Set; 16 lectures; incl. course guide. (463) Teaching Co.
Socrates refused to write down any of his thoughts. But among his pupils was Plato, who immortalized his teacher's life & thought in more than 30 dialogues that laid the basis for Western civilization. These dialogues breathe with the feeling, the tension, & even the humor of great theater, & testify to Plato's artistic gifts as well as to the loyalty, friendship, & dauntless love of learning that he shared with his beloved master.

Plato, Socrates, & the Dialogues. Instructed by Michael Sugrue. 16 CDs. (Running Time: 12 hrs.). 1996. audio compact disk 179.95 (978-1-59803-139-3(2)) Teaching Co.

Plato, Socrates & the Dialogues, Pts. I-II. Instructed by Michael Sugrue. 8 cass. (Running Time: 12 hrs.). 1996. 129.95 (978-1-56585-121-4(8)) Teaching Co.

Plato, Socrates & the Dialogues, Vol. 2. Instructed by Michael Sugrue. 4 cass. (Running Time: 6 hrs.). 1996. 129.95 (978-1-56585-122-1(6)) Teaching Co.

Plato Sucks. abr. ed. Andrei Codrescu. Read by Andrei Codrescu. 2 cass. (Running Time: 3 hrs.). 2001. 18.00 (978-1-59040-166-8(2), Phoenix Audio) Pub: Amer Intl Pub. Dist(s): PerseuPGW

Plato told him see Twentieth-Century Poetry in English, No. 5, Recordings of Poets Reading Their Own Poetry

Plato's Euthyphro, Apology & Crito. unabr. ed. Plato. Voice by Albert A. Anderson. 2 CDs. (Running Time: 2 hrs.). Dramatization. (Theater of the Mind Ser.: Vol. II). 1998. audio compact disk 25.00 CD & text Set. (978-1-887250-14-6(X)) Agora Pubns.
What is the proper relationship between religion & ethics? As Socrates enters the court to defend himself against the charge of atheism, he meets Euthyphro, an expert on religious matters. Euthyphro believes that ethics should be based on religion. Socrates examines that belief. What do human beings need to know to live the best possible life? During his trial, Socrates seeks to justify his own life by responding to that question. Is it better to suffer injustice & die or commit injustice & live? Socrates faces that choice. The conversation with his friend Crito probes the foundations of civil & moral law.

Plato's Gorgias. unabr. ed. Plato. Ed. by Albert A. Anderson. Tr. by Benjamin Jowett. Contrib. by Ray Munro. 2 cass. (Running Time: 3 hrs.). Dramatization. (Theater of the Mind Ser.: Vol. I). (J). 1994. 25.00 (978-1-887250-00-9(X)) Agora Pubns.
Gorgias of Leontini, a famous teacher of rhetoric, has come to Athens to recruit students, promising to teach them how to become leaders in politics & business. A group has gathered at Callicles' house to hear Gorgias demonstrate the power of his art. This dialogue blends comic & serious discussion of the best human life, providing a penetrating examination of ethics.

Plato's Gorgias. unabr. ed. Plato. Albert A. Anderson. 3 CDs. (Running Time: 3 hrs.). Dramatization. (Theater of the Mind Ser.). 1998. audio compact disk 30.00 CD & text Set. (978-1-887250-13-9(1)) Agora Pubns.

Plato's Ion & Meno. Plato. Ed. by Lieselotte Anderson. Illus. by Donald Krueger. Adapted by Albert A. Anderson. 2 cass. (Running Time: 2 hrs.). Dramatization. (Theater of the Mind Ser.: Vol. 3). (J). (gr. 7 up). 1997. bk. 37.50 Set. Agora Pubns.
Socrates questions Ion about his ability to interpret the epic poetry of Homer & about the nature of his art. A similar discussion between Socrates & Meno probes the nature of morality, especially its origin & how it is known. These conversations illuminate two fundamental issues of our activities as human beings.

Plato's Ion & Meno. unabr. ed. Plato. Ed. by Albert A. Anderson. Tr. by Benjamin Jowett from GEC. 2 cass. (Running Time: 2 hrs.). Dramatization. (Theater of the Mind Ser.). 1998. audio compact disk 12.50 (978-1-887250-10-8(7)) Agora Pubns.

Plato's Ion & Meno. unabr. ed. Plato. Albert A. Anderson. 2 CDs. (Running Time: 2 hrs.). Dramatization. (Theater of the Mind Ser.). 1998. audio compact disk 25.00 CD Set. (978-1-887250-12-2(3)) Agora Pubns.

Plato's Phaedrus. (Theater of the Mind Ser.). (ENG.). 2009. audio compact disk 25.00 (978-1-887250-55-9(7)) Agora Pubns.

Plato's Portrait of Sokrates. Read by Stephen G. Daitz. Ed. by Stephen G. Daitz. 2 cass. (Running Time: 2 hrs.). (Living Voice of Greek & Latin Ser.). (GRE.). 1988. pap. bk. 39.95 (978-0-88432-254-2(8), S23695) J Norton Pubs.
Includes Apology, Krito, Phaido.

Plato's Republic. Albert A. Anderson. 10 cass. (Running Time: 12.5 hrs.). Dramatization. (gr. 12 up). 2001. 125.00 (978-1-887250-27-6(1)) Agora Pubns.
Performance of Plato's dialogue treating the idea of justice in the context of the best possible human society and human life.

Plato's Republic. unabr. ed. Simon Blackburn. Narrated by Simon Vance. (Running Time: 4 hrs. 30 mins. 0 sec.). (Books That Changed the World Ser.). (ENG.). 2007. audio compact disk 24.99 (978-1-4001-0390-4(8)); audio compact disk 49.99 (978-1-4001-3390-1(4)); audio compact disk 19.99 (978-1-4001-5390-9(5)) Pub: Tantor Media. Dist(s): IngramPubServ

Plato's Republic, Bks. 1-2. unabr. ed. Plato. 2 cass. Dramatization. (Theater of the Mind Ser.: Vol. 4). (J). (gr. 7 up). 1997. bk. 37.50 Set. Agora Pubns.
Plato's most comprehensive dialogue, treats ethics, politics, epistemology, metaphysics, & the arts. The conversation begins with attempts to define the nature of justice, centering on Thrasymachus' explanation of justice as power. Then Plato's brothers, Glaucon & Adeimantus, propose a social contract theory of values, challenging Socrates to defend justice as intrinsically good. The investigation continues in an effort to imagine a society in which true justice can be manifested.

Plato's Republic, Bks. 5-6. unabr. ed. Ed. by Albert A. Anderson. (Theater of the Mind Ser.: Vol. IX). 2001. audio compact disk 25.00 (978-1-887250-19-1(0)) Agora Pubns.

Plato's Republic, I-II. Instructed by David Roochnik. 12 CDs. (Running Time: 12 hrs.). 2005. audio compact disk 69.95 (978-1-59803-044-0(2), 4537) Teaching Co.

Plato's Republic, Vol. I-II. Instructed by David Roochnik. 12 cass. (Running Time: 12 hrs.). 2005. 54.95 (978-1-59803-042-6(6), 4537) Teaching Co.

Plato's Republic: Bks 7&8. unabr. ed. Plato. Ed. by Albert A. Anderson. 2 CDs. (Running Time: 2 hrs. 30 min.). (Theater of the Mind Ser.). 1999. audio compact disk 25.00 (978-1-887250-22-1(0)) Agora Pubns.
Book Seven begins with the Allegory of the Cave, an exploration of the process of being educated. Socrates and Glaucon probe the meaning of this story both as it relates to the discussion of knowledge and reality developed earlier and to the concept of dialectic, the overall method of Plato's dialogues. Throughout Plato's Republic we confront the ways in which the republic and the individual mirror and create each other. In Book Eight Socrates and Plato's brothers explore five different kinds of republic and five different kinds of individual, showing how aristocracy becomes timocracy and how oligarchy spawns democracy, ending with the evolution of tyranny.

Plato's Republic: Bks 9&10. unabr. ed. Plato. Ed. by Albert A. Anderson. 2 CDs. (Running Time: 2 hrs. 30 min.). Dramatization. (Theater of the Mind Ser.). 2000. audio compact disk 25.00 (978-1-887250-24-5(7)) Agora Pubns.
The concluding books of Plato?s Republic reveal the entire dialogue in a new perspective. The nature and goodness of the soul and its true relationship to public life are considered in Book Nine. Socrates returns to Glaucon?s earlier challenge to justify the claim that a just life is superior to an unjust life. He does that by showing the life of tyrants compared to a life devoted to the love of wisdom. In Book Ten the role of poetry and the other arts is examined and placed in the overall context of the best human life. The dialogue concludes with the Myth of Er, a story about a warrior who is killed in battle, travels to another world, and returns to tell a wonderful tale about life and death.

Plato's Republic: Books One & Two, Vol. 12. unabr. ed. Plato. Albert A. Anderson. 2 CDs. (Running Time: 2 hrs. 30 min.). Dramatization. (Theater of the Mind Ser.). (gr. 7 up). 1998. audio compact disk 25.00 CD Set. (978-1-887250-15-3(8)) Agora Pubns.
Plato's most comprehensive dialogue, treats ethics, politics, epistemology, metaphysics, & the arts. The conversation begins with attempts to define the nature of justice, centering on Thrasymachus' explanation of justice as power. Then Plato's brothers, Glaucon & Adeimantus, propose a social contract theory of values, challenging Socrates to defend justice as intrinsically good. The investigation continues in an effort to imagine a society in which true justice can be manifested.

Plato's Republic, Books 3&4. unabr. ed. Plato. Ed. by Albert A. Anderson. Tr. by Benjamin Jowett from GEC. Directed By Raymond Munro. 2 CDs. (Running Time: 2.5). Dramatization. (Theater of the Mind Ser.). 2001. audio compact disk 25.00 (978-1-887250-17-7(4)) Agora Pubns.
Socrates, Glaucon, and Adeimantus are discussing the best way to educate leaders for a just republic. In the course of their dialogue, the meaning of justice in individuals and in society shifts from external order imposed through rules and regulations to the harmony and balance internal to every person in the republic. Only then will an individual be ready to act-whether in acquiring wealth, in the care of the body, or in any public or private affairs.

Plato's Republic (complete) unabr. ed. Plato. Albert A. Anderson. 10 CDs. (Running Time: 12.5 hrs). Dramatization. (Theater of the Mind Ser.). 2001. audio compact disk 125.00 (978-1-887250-26-9(3)) Agora Pubns.

Plato's Symposium. Ed. by Albert A. Anderson. 2 CDs. (Running Time: 2.5 hours). Dramatization. (Theater of the Mind Ser.). 2003. audio compact disk 25.00 (978-1-887250-29-0(8)) Agora Pubns.
The dramatic nature of Plato's dialogues is delightfully evident in the Symposium. The marriage between character and thought bursts forth as the guests gather at Agathon's house to celebrate the success of his first tragedy. With wit and insight, they each present their ideas about love-from Erixymachus's scientific naturalism to Aristophanes' comic fantasy. The unexpected arrival of Alcibiades breaks the spell cast by Diotima's ethereal climb up the staircase of love to beauty itself. Ecstasy and intoxication clash as Plato concludes with one of his most skillful displays of dialectic.

Plausible Prejudices: Essays on American Writing. unabr. ed. Joseph Epstein. Read by Michael Russotto. 11 cass. (Running Time: 16 hrs. 30 min.). 1990. 88.00 (978-0-7366-1773-4(6), 2612) Books on Tape.
As editor of the American Scholar, Joseph Epstein has all the requisite intellectual credentials, but it is a quirky & stubborn individuality that gives his writing its glow. He brings language, reading, literary biography & authors such as Edmund Wilson, Norman Mailer, John Irving & Philip Roth up for scrutiny & asks questions that help us form our own judgments & opinions. The title comes from H. L. Mencken, who wrote "Criticism is a prejudice made plausible." Epstein is in Mencken's irreverent tradition, but gentler, & a fine essayist for our time.

Play. unabr. ed. Daniel Greenberg. 1 cass. (Running Time: 1 hr.). 1993. 10.00 (978-1-888947-54-0(3)) Sudbury Valley.
Learning & education from play.

Play a Li'l Song for Me. Perf. by Ben Tankard. 2003. audio compact disk Verity Records.

Play Acoustic Guitar with Eric Clapton: Six of His Greatest Hits. Contrib. by Eric Clapton. 2002. pap. bk. 16.95 (978-0-634-04150-1(9), 00695686) H Leonard.

Play All Day. Perf. by Timmy Abell. 1 cass. (J). (ps-2). 1992. (978-0-9665740-4-3(4), UP925) Upstream Prodns.
Collection of songs from traditional to original & from English ballad to playful Reggae words of wisdom. Timmy uses a variety of acoustic instruments in this entertaining & inspirational recording.

Play-along Christmas: 27 Christmas Favorites. Arranged by Sandy Feldstein. 2004. audio compact disk 14.95 (978-0-8258-4516-1(5)); audio compact disk 14.95 (978-0-8258-4517-8(3)); audio compact disk 14.95 (978-0-8258-4520-8(3)); audio compact disk 14.95 (978-0-8258-4521-5(1)); audio compact disk 14.95 (978-0-8258-4522-2(X)); audio compact disk 14.95 (978-0-8258-4523-9(8)) Fischer Inc NY.

Play & Praise. 1999. 11.98 (978-0-7673-9721-6(5)) LifeWay Christian.

Play & Praise. 2003. audio compact disk 84.95 (978-0-633-09329-7(7)); audio compact disk 12.00 (978-0-633-09323-5(8)) LifeWay Christian.

Play & Praise. Barney Robertson. 2000. 79.95 (978-0-633-01211-3(4)) LifeWay Christian.

Play & Praise. Barney Robertson. 2001. audio compact disk 84.95 (978-0-633-01626-5(8)) LifeWay Christian.

Play & Praise. Barny Robertson. 2000. 11.98 (978-0-633-00768-3(4)); audio compact disk 16.98 (978-0-633-00769-0(2)); audio compact disk 84.95 (978-0-633-00767-6(6)) LifeWay Christian.

Play & Praise. Barny Robertson. 2001. audio compact disk 16.98 (978-0-633-01628-9(4)) LifeWay Christian.

Play & Praise, Vol. 1. 1999. audio compact disk 16.98 (978-0-7673-9722-3(3)); audio compact disk 12.00 (978-0-7673-9662-2(6)) LifeWay Christian.

Play & Praise, Vol. 3. Barny Robertson. 2001. 11.98 (978-0-633-01627-2(6)); 79.95 (978-0-633-01625-8(X)) LifeWay Christian.

Play & Praise, Vol. 5. Genevox Music Staff. 2003. 11.98 (978-0-633-09295-5(9)); audio compact disk 16.98 (978-0-633-09313-6(0)) LifeWay Christian.

Play & Sincerity. 1 cass. (Running Time: 28 min.). 12.00 (L430) MEA A Watts Cass.

Play Bach! 1 cass. or CD. (Running Time: 57 min.). (J). (gr. 4-6). 1996. 10.98; audio compact disk 14.98 CD. (978-0-9651869-0-2(3)) Classic Raps.
Energetic & informative "radio play" that successfully sprinkles facts about Bach's life & music into a cute modern day story.

Play Ball! Perf. by Erich Kunzel et al. 1 cass., 1 CD. 7.98 (TA 30468); audio compact disk 12.78 CD Jewel box. (TA 80468) NewSound.

Play Ball, Amelia Bedelia. Peggy Parish. 1 read-along cass. (Running Time: 15 min.). (I Can Read Bks.). (J). (gr. 1-3). HarperCollins Pubs.

Play Ball, Amelia Bedelia. abr. ed. Peggy Parish. Illus. by Wallace Tripp. 1 cass. (Running Time: 90 min.). (Amelia Bedelia Ser.). (J). (ps-3). 2005. 9.99 (978-0-06-074108-2(2), HarperFestival) HarperCollins Pubs.

Play Ball, Amelia Bedelia. unabr. abr. ed. Peggy Parish. Illus. by Wallace Tripp. 1 cass. (I Can Read Bks.). (J). (ps-3). 1990. 8.99 (978-1-55994-241-6(X)) HarperCollins Pubs.

***Play Ballads with a Band: For B-flat Clarinet.** Brian Ogilvie. 2009. pap. bk. 24.98 (978-1-59615-795-8(X), 159615795X) Pub: Music Minus. Dist(s): H Leonard

***Play Ballads with a Band: Music Minus One Alto Sax.** Created by Hal Leonard Corporation Staff. 2009. pap. bk. 24.98 (978-1-59615-797-2(6), 1596157976) Pub: Music Minus. Dist(s): H Leonard

***Play Ballads with a Band: Music Minus One Bb Trumpet.** Created by Hal Leonard Corporation Staff. 2009. pap. bk. 24.98 (978-1-59615-794-1(1), 1596157941) Pub: Music Minus. Dist(s): H Leonard

***Play Ballads with a Band: Music Minus One Tenor Sax.** Created by Hal Leonard Corporation Staff. 2009. pap. bk. 24.98 (978-1-59615-623-4(6), 1596156236) Pub: Music Minus. Dist(s): H Leonard

***Play Ballads with a Band: Music Minus One Trombone.** Roy Agee. 2009. pap. bk. 24.98 (978-1-59615-798-9(4), 1596157984) Pub: Music Minus. Dist(s): H Leonard

Play Banjo Today! Level One: A Complete Guide to the Basics. Colin O'Brien. 2008. pap. bk. 9.95 (978-1-4234-1993-8(6), 1423419936) H Leonard.

Play Before God: Instrumental Music for Worship, Prayer & Reflection. Bobby Fisher. 1989. audio compact disk 15.95 (216) GIA Pubns.

***PLAY Beginning Blues Guitar: The Ultimate Multimedia Instructor, CD-ROM.** Alfred Publishing Staff. (Play Ser.). (ENG.). 2009. audio compact disk 19.99 (978-0-7390-6560-0(2)) Alfred Pub.

***PLAY Beginning Electric Guitar: The Ultimate Multimedia Instructor, CD-ROM.** Alfred Publishing Staff. (Play Ser.). (ENG.). 2009. audio compact disk 19.99 (978-0-7390-6561-7(0)) Alfred Pub.

***PLAY Beginning Rock Guitar: The Ultimate Multimedia Instructor, CD-ROM.** Alfred Publishing Staff. (Play Ser.). (ENG.). 2009. audio compact disk 19.99 (978-0-7390-6563-1(7)) Alfred Pub.

Play by the Rules: Early Explorers Early Set B Audio CD. Mary Butenhoff. Adapted by Benchmark Education Staff. (J). 2007. audio compact disk 10.00 (978-1-4108-8228-8(4)) Benchmark Educ.

Play Dates. unabr. ed. Leslie Carroll. (Running Time: 12 hrs. 5 mins.). 2008. 29.95 (978-1-4332-4937-2(5)); 72.95 (978-1-4332-4934-1(0)); audio compact disk 90.00 (978-1-4332-4935-8(9)) Blckstn Audio.

Play Daze Audio. H. McCormick. (ENG.). (J). 2008. audio compact disk 11.00 (978-0-9818619-4-4(6)) TBT Pub.

***Play Dead.** abr. ed. Harlan Coben. Read by Scott Brick. (Running Time: 10 hrs.). 2010. 9.99 (978-1-4418-9348-2(2), 9781441893482, BAD); audio compact disk 14.99 (978-1-4418-5886-3(5), 9781441858863, BACD) Brilliance Audio.

***Play Dead.** unabr. ed. Ryan Brown. Read by MacLeod Andrews. (Running Time: 9 hrs.). 2010. 24.99 (978-1-4418-5320-2(0), 9781441853202, Brilliance MP3); 24.99 (978-1-4418-5322-6(7), 9781441853226, BAD); 39.97 (978-1-4418-5323-3(5), 9781441853233, BADLE); audio compact disk 29.99 (978-1-4418-5318-9(9), 9781441853189, Bril Audio CD Unabri); audio compact disk 79.97 (978-1-4418-5319-6(7), 9781441853196, BriAudCD Unabrid) Brilliance Audio.

***Play Dead.** unabr. ed. Harlan Coben. Read by Scott Brick. (Running Time: 15 hrs.). 2010. 17.99 (978-1-4418-5399-8(5), 9781441853998, BAD); 39.97 (978-1-4418-5400-1(2), 9781441854001, BADLE); 17.99 (978-1-4418-5397-4(9), 9781441853974, Brilliance MP3); 39.97 (978-1-4418-5398-1(7), 9781441853981, Brinc Audio MP3 Lib); audio compact disk 29.99 (978-1-4418-5395-0(2), 9781441853950, Bril Audio CD Unabri); audio compact disk 79.97 (978-1-4418-5396-7(0), 9781441853967, BriAudCD Unabrid) Brilliance Audio.

Play Dead. unabr. ed. David Rosenfelt. Read by Grover Gardner. (YA). 2007. 44.99 (978-1-60252-855-0(1)) Find a World.

Play Dead. unabr. ed. David Rosenfelt. Read by Grover Gardner. 6 CDs. (Running Time: 28800 sec.). 2007. audio compact disk 29.95 (978-1-59316-097-5(6)) Listen & Live.

***Play Dead: A Thriller.** unabr. ed. Ryan Brown. Read by MacLeod Andrews. (Running Time: 9 hrs.). 2010. 39.97 (978-1-4418-5321-9(9), 9781441853219, Brinc Audio MP3 Lib) Brilliance Audio.

Play Dirty. abr. ed. Sandra Brown. Read by Victor Slezak. (Running Time: 6 hrs. 0 mins. 0 sec.). 2009. audio compact disk 14.99 (978-0-7435-8299-5(3)) Pub: S&S Audio. Dist(s): S and S Inc

Play Dirty. unabr. ed. Sandra Brown. Read by Victor Slezak. 12 cass. (Running Time: 14 hrs.). 2007. 98.75 (978-1-4281-5337-0(3)); audio compact disk 123.75 (978-1-4281-5338-7(1)) Recorded Bks.

Play Dirty. unabr. ed. Sandra Brown. Read by Victor Slezak. 12 CDs. (Running Time: 14 hrs. 0 mins. 0 sec.). 2007. audio compact disk 49.95 (978-0-7435-6146-4(5)) Pub: S&S Audio. Dist(s): S and S Inc

Play Drums Today! Level 2: A Complete Guide to the Basics. Scott Schroedl. 2001. pap. bk. 9.95 (978-0-634-02850-2(2), 0634028502) H Leonard.

Play Famous Blues Guitar Rhythms in 60 Minutes. Pat Conway. 1 CD. (Running Time: 1 hr.). 1998. pap. bk. 8.95 (978-0-7119-5630-8(8), AM 936089) Music Sales.

Play for a Kingdom. unabr. ed. Thomas Dyja. Read by Ian Esmo. 10 cass. (Running Time: 14 hrs. 30 mins.). 1998. 69.95 (978-0-7861-1302-6(2), 2214) Blckstn Audio.

In a moment of quiet during the endgame between Grant & Lee, a Union & a Confederate company meet - not entirely by accident. Left behind on picket duty to guard their army's flank, the soldiers decide to relax with a baseball & bat, when, as if by magic, a company of Alabama infantry appears from the woods. These ordinary soldiers determine to play baseball with the enemy.

Play Great Chord Riffs in 60 Minutes. Music Sales Corporation Staff. 1 CD. (Running Time: 1 hr.). 1998. pap. bk. 5.95 (978-0-7119-5636-0(7)) Music Sales.

Play Great Golf. Glenn Harrold. 2 CDs. (Running Time: 3 hrs.). 2002. audio compact disk 17.95 (978-1-901923-36-0(3)) Pub: Divinit Pubing GBR. Dist(s): Bookworld

Play Great Golf. Glenn Harrold. 2003. 11.95 (978-1-901923-16-2(9)) Pub: Divinit Pubing GBR. Dist(s): Bookworld

Play Guitar in 60 Minutes. Pat Conway. 1 CD. (Running Time: 1 hr.). 1998. pap. bk. 5.95 (978-0-7119-5632-2(4), AM 936100) Music Sales.

Play Guitar with AC-DC. 2004. bk. 21.95 (978-0-7119-7434-0(9), AM955900) Pub: Music Sales. Dist(s): H Leonard

Play It Again: Bill's Favorites (& One New Story) unabr. ed. Bill Harley. Read by Bill Harley. 1 cass., 1 CD. (Running Time: 53 min.). (J). (gr. k-6). 1999. 10.00 (978-1-878126-33-7(4), RRR115); audio compact disk 15.00 CD. (978-1-878126-34-4(2), RRR115J) Round Riv Prodns.

Bill's humor, empathy, & award-winning songwriting shine through on this compilation of his favorite songs. With fourteen tracks from "Monsters in the Bathroom" to "You're in Trouble," to an updated version of "50 Ways to Fool Your Mother." Also includes the previously unrecorded classic story of Charlene, the skunk in the middle, "You're Not the Boss of Me.".

Play It Again II Set: The Duke University 1992 NCAA Basketball National Championship Run. unabr. ed. Read by Bob Harris & Mike Waters. 2 cass. (Running Time: 2 hr.). 1994. 9.95 (978-1-885408-06-8(4)) Listen & Live.

For the second year in a row, Duke topped college basketball. Relive Christian Laettner's last-second shot to beat the Kentucky Wildcats in the Final Four & the Blue Devil's victory over Michigan's Fab Five in the national title game.

Play It Safe. unabr. ed. Sandra Robbins. 1 cass. (Running Time: 32 min.). Dramatization. (See-More Ser.). (J). (ps-2). 1992. 7.95 (978-1-882601-00-4(9)) See-Mores Wrkshop.

Created for children based on Shadow Box Theatre's Production. Audio Soundtrack of show.

Play Keyboard Scales. Darryl Winston. (Step One Ser.). 1997. audio compact disk 9.95 (978-0-8256-1612-9(3)) Pub: Music Sales. Dist(s): H Leonard

***Play Like You Mean It.** abr. ed. Rex Ryan. (Running Time: 5 hrs.). (ENG.). 2011. audio compact disk 30.00 (978-0-307-91473-6(9), Random AudioBks) Pub: Random Audio Pubg. Dist(s): Random

Play of the Mind. Swami Amar Jyoti. 1 dolby cass. 1986. 9.95 (J-51) Truth Consciousness.

The greatest journey is through our own mind. The Raja Yoga path. On materialism & spiritual materialism. The duty of the seeker.

Play on Words. unabr. ed. Deric Longden. Read by Deric Longden. 6 cass. (Running Time: 9 hrs.). 2000. 54.95 (978-0-7531-0748-5(1), 000306) Pub: ISIS Audio GBR. Dist(s): Ulverscroft US

Further episodes in the life of Deric Longden, his wife Aileen Armitage & their small army of cats.

Play on Words. unabr. ed. Deric Longden. Read by Deric Longden. 6 CDs. (Running Time: 6 hrs.). (Isis Ser.). (J). 2002. audio compact disk 64.95 (978-0-7531-1580-0(8)) Pub: ISIS Lrg Prnt GBR. Dist(s): Ulverscroft US

Further episodes in the life of Deric Longden, his wife Aileen Armitage, and their small army of cats. Ever since Dame Thora Hird breathed life into the role of Deric Longden's mother in 'Wide Eyed and Legless', she had been on at him to write a play based on the sequel. Among other things, Deric here describes the unique experience of seeing at close hand his book - and an important part of his own life - turn into a film. Despite the usual hilarious interruptions, his own work gets done, influenced by such matters as rag-and-bone men, the Moscow State Circus and crinkle-cut beetroot.

Play Pennywhistle Now! Peter Pickow. 2004. bk. 179.50 (978-0-8256-1780-5(4)) Music Sales.

Play Pennywhistle Now! The Fun & Easy Way to Play Pennywhistle. Peter Pickow. bk. 10.95 (978-0-8256-1765-2(0)) Music Sales.

Play Pennywhistle Now! The Fun & Easy Way to Play Pennywhistle. Peter Pickow. 1989. pap. bk. 17.95 (978-0-8256-1779-9(0), AM962270, Amsco Music) Pub: Music Sales. Dist(s): H Leonard

***Play Poker Like the Pros.** unabr. ed. Phil Hellmuth. Read by Phil Hellmuth. (ENG.). 2006. (978-0-06-128404-5(1), Harper Audio); (978-0-06-128405-2(X), Harper Audio) HarperCollins Pubs.

Play Poker Like the Pros: The Greatest Poker Player in the World Today Reveals His Million-Dollar-Winning Strategies to the Most Popular Tournament, Home, & Online Games. unabr. ed. Phil Hellmuth & Phil Hellmuth, Jr. Read by Phil Hellmuth, Jr. (Running Time: 37800 sec.). 2006. audio compact disk 39.95 (978-0-06-123880-2(5)) HarperCollins Pubs.

Play Recorder Today! Book/CD Packaged with a Recorder. Created by Hal Leonard Corporation Staff. 2009. pap. bk. 9.99 (978-1-4234-8093-8(7), 1423480937) H Leonard.

Play Room/Mitch in the Morning. Jay Bonansinga. 1 CD. (Running Time: 1 hr.). 2001. audio compact disk 15.95 (MEBT003) Lodestone Catalog.

Can two Chicago cops catch the killer before becoming the next targets? Mitch in the Morning is a radio shock jock, whose show comes unglued when a disturbed female caller promises revenge on her cheating husband on the air.

Play Solo Flamenco Guitar with Juan Martin. Juan Martin. (ENG.). 2005. spiral bd. 29.95 (978-0-7866-6238-8(7), 20838SET) Mel Bay.

Play Solo Flamenco Guitar with Juan Martin. Juan Martin & Patrick Campbell. (ENG & SPA.). 2002. spiral bd. 29.95 (978-0-7866-6458-0(4)) Mel Bay.

Play the Great Masters! 18 Favorite Classics for Young Players - Alto Sax/Baritone Sax. Created by Hal Leonard Corporation Staff. James Curnow. 2007. pap. bk. 12.95 (978-90-431-2414-0(1), 9043124141) H Leonard.

Play the Great Masters! 18 Favorite Classics for Young Players - Bassoon/Trombone/Euphonium BC/TC. Created by Hal Leonard Corporation Staff. James Curnow. 2007. pap. bk. 12.95 (978-90-431-2418-8(4), 9043124184) H Leonard.

Play the Great Masters! 18 Favorite Classics for Young Players - Clarinet. Created by Hal Leonard Corporation Staff. James Curnow. 2007. pap. bk. 12.95 (978-90-431-2413-3(3), 9043124133) H Leonard.

Play the Great Masters! 18 Favorite Classics for Young Players - F/Eb Horn. Created by Hal Leonard Corporation Staff. James Curnow. 2007. pap. bk. 12.95 (978-90-431-2417-1(6), 9043124176) H Leonard.

Play the Great Masters! 18 Favorite Classics for Young Players - Flute/Oboe. Created by Hal Leonard Corporation Staff. James Curnow. 2007. pap. bk. 12.95 (978-90-431-2421-8(4), 9043124214) H Leonard.

Play the Great Masters! 18 Favorite Classics for Young Players - Recorder. Created by Hal Leonard Corporation Staff. James Curnow. 2007. pap. bk. 12.95 (978-90-431-2419-5(2), 9043124192) H Leonard.

Play the Great Masters! 18 Favorite Classics for Young Players - Soprano Sax/Tenor Sax. Created by Hal Leonard Corporation Staff. James Curnow. 2007. pap. bk. 12.95 (978-90-431-2415-7(X), 904312415X) H Leonard.

Play the Great Masters! 18 Favorite Classics for Young Players - Trumpet. Created by Hal Leonard Corporation Staff. James Curnow. 2007. pap. bk. 12.95 (978-90-431-2416-4(8), 9043124168) H Leonard.

Play the Great Masters! 18 Favorite Classics for Young Players - Violin. Created by Hal Leonard Corporation Staff. James Curnow. 2007. pap. bk. 12.95 (978-90-431-2420-1(6), 9043124206) H Leonard.

Play the Jaw Harp Now! unabr. ed. David Holt. Perf. by David Holt. 1 cass. (Running Time: 60 min.). 1991. 9.98 (978-0-942303-25-4(3), HW1250) Pub: High Windy Audio. Dist(s): August Hse

A complete mini-course teaching the listener how to play the jaw harp & have fun doing it. Step by step instructions. Side two features the world's best jaw harp music. Comes with free jaw harp.

Play the World: The 101 World Instrument Primer. Randy Raine-Reusch. (ENG.). 2008. per. 22.95 (978-0-7866-7678-1(7)) Mel Bay.

Play Their First Big Game: The Bugville Critters. unabr. ed. Robert Stanek, pseud. Narrated by Victoria Charters. (Running Time: 19 mins.). (ENG.). (J). 2008. 5.95 (978-1-57545-355-2(X), RP Audio Pubng) Pub: Reagent Press. Dist(s): OverDrive Inc

***Play Their Hearts Out: A Coach, His Star Recruit, & the Youth Basketball Machine.** unabr. ed. George Dohrmann. (Running Time: 14 hrs.). 2010. 29.95 (978-1-4417-6337-2(6)); 79.95 (978-1-4417-6334-1(1)); audio compact disk 32.95 (978-1-4417-6336-5(8)); audio compact disk 109.00 (978-1-4417-6335-8(X)) Blckstn Audio.

Play to Rest. 1 cass. (Running Time: 1 hr.). (J). 2001. 10.95 (KUB 3000C) Kimbo Educ.

Songs & activities useful from clean-up time to quiet time. Clean-Up is Fun, Daydreams, Lullaby Rock, Sandman, Relax With Me & more.

***Play Ukulele Today! Level Two.** John King. 2010. pap. bk. 9.95 (978-1-4234-6601-7(2), 1423466012) H Leonard.

***Play Violin Today! - Level 2: A Complete Guide to the Basics.** Created by Hal Leonard Corp. (ENG.). 2010. pap. bk. 9.99 (978-1-4234-9434-8(2), 1423494342) H Leonard.

Play with a Pro: Trombone Music & CD. Bugs Bower. 1 CD. 2004. bk. 14.95 (978-0-8256-2737-8(0), NM10096) Music Sales.

Play with a Pro: Trumpet Music. Bugs Bower. 2004. audio compact disk 14.95 (978-0-8256-1921-2(1), NM10080) Music Sales.

Play with Fire. collector's ed. Dana Stabenow. Read by Marguerite Gavin. 5 cass. (Running Time: 7 hrs. 30 min.). (Kate Shugak Ser.). 2000. 40.00 (978-0-7366-4994-0(8), 5252) Books on Tape.

A female Alaskan investigator checks into the mysterious disappearance of the son of a local preacher.

Play with Me. 2004. bk. 24.95 (978-1-56008-238-5(0)); pap. bk. 14.95 (978-0-7882-0604-7(4)); 8.95 (978-1-56008-310-8(7)); cass. & flmstrp 30.00 (978-1-56008-749-6(8)) Weston Woods.

Play with Me. Marie Hall Ets. 11 vols. (Running Time: 6 mins.). (J). (gr. k-3). 1976. pap. bk. 16.95 (978-0-670-55985-5(7)) Live Oak Media.

Play with Me. Marie Hall Ets. (Running Time: 6 mins.). 1982. 9.95 (978-1-59112-108-4(6)) Live Oak Media.

Play with Me. Marjorie Hall Ets. Read by Jenna Whidden. (Live Oak Readalong Ser.). pap. bk. 18.95 (978-1-59519-342-1(1)) Pub: Live Oak Media. Dist(s): AudioGO

Play with Me. unabr. ed. Marie Hall Ets. 1 read along cass. (Running Time: 6 min.). (J). 1975. 9.95 Live Oak Media.

A little girl discovers that patience is needed to attract animals as playmates.

Play with Me, Set. unabr. ed. Marie Hall Ets. Read by Jenna Whidden. 1 read along cass. (Running Time: 6 min.). (J). (gr. k-3). 1975. pap. bk. 15.95 Live Oak Media.

Play with Me: Program from the Award Winning Public Radio Series. Interview. Hosted by Fred Goodwin. Comment by John Hockenberry. 1 CD. (Running Time: 1 hr.). 2000. audio compact disk 21.95 (978-1-932479-82-9(1), LCM 138) Lichtenstein Creat.

Play, the silly stuff of life, turns out to be more than just a good time. This hour of The Infinite Mind looks at the importance of play to both children and adults. We hear from a play therapist who explains how she uses play to help children, the director of a play room at a hospital's pediatric ward, as well as a toy designer and toy critic who discuss the role of technology in toys. Guests include: singer/songwriter Suzanne Vega; Dr. Diane Frey, Professor of Counseling at Wright State University; Sue Bratton, Clinical Director of the Counseling Department at the University of North Texas; and Cynthia Walter-Glickman, of the social work staff of Bronx-Lebanon Hospital Center. Commentary by John Hockenberry.

Play with Me Set: Grades K-3. unabr. ed. Marie Hall Ets. Read by Jenna Whidden. 14 vols. (Running Time: 6 mins.). (J). (gr. k-3). 1975. pap. bk. & tchr. ed. 33.95 INCL. 4 BKS. & GUIDE. (978-0-670-55979-4(2)) Live Oak Media.

A little girl finds a playmate among the meadow creatures when she finally learns to sit quietly & not frighten them.

Play Your First Blues Riffs in 60 Minutes. Pat Conway. 1 CD. (Running Time: 1 hr.). 1998. bk. 8.95 (978-0-7119-5639-1(1), Am 936177) Pub: Music Sales. Dist(s): H Leonard

Play Your First Rock Riffs in 60 Minutes. Pat Conway. 1 CD. (Running Time: 1 hr.). 1998. pap. bk. 8.95 (978-0-7119-5638-4(3), AM 936166) Music Sales.

Play Your Instruments. Ella Jenkins. 1 CD. (Running Time: 1 hr.). (J). 2001. audio compact disk 15.00 (FC 45018CD) Kimbo Educ.

Play Your Instruments & Make a Pretty Sound. Perf. by Ella Jenkins. 1 cass. (J). (ps-4). 1994. (0-9307-450180-9307-45018-2-5); audio compact disk (0-9307-45018-2-5) Smithsonian Folkways.

Ella encourages children to play rhythm instruments either provided by the teacher or homemade. After she sings "Put Your Instruments Away," a jazz band introduces the trombone, clarinet, drum, trumpet, etc. Ten songs include "Follow the Leader," "Let's Listen to the Band" & harmonica Happiness".

Playa Step Your Game Up. Pretty Tony. Read by Pretty Tony. 2008. 12.95 (978-1-934965-04-7(9)); audio compact disk 14.95 (978-1-934965-03-0(0)) Dreamervision Pub.

Playalong Cello: Classical Tunes. 2004. bk. 25.95 (978-0-7119-9638-0(5), 0711996385) H Leonard.

Playaology: Playa Step Your Game Up, Vol. 2. Pretty Tony. Read by Pretty Tony. 2008. 12.95 (978-1-934965-07-8(3)); audio compact disk 14.95 (978-1-934965-06-1(5)) Dreamervision Pub.

Playaway Presents - Children's Stories from Africa: The Chameleon & the Hare; Mfoso's Beautiful Daughters; Ears, Eyes, Legs & Arms; the Princess Who Lost Her Hair. unabr. ed. Caroline Wheal. Read by Janet Suzman. (J). 2007. 34.99 (978-1-60252-621-1(4)) Find a World.

Playaway Presents - Children's Stories from Africa: The Hippo & the Lion; Mpempe the Faithful Dog; Monsoor & the Donkey. unabr. ed. Caroline Wheal. Read by Janet Suzman. (J). 2007. 34.99 (978-1-60252-620-4(6)) Find a World.

Playaway Presents - Children's Stories from China: The Daughter of the Dragon King; the Crane Girl; the Emperor & the Nightingale; the Wishing Star. unabr. ed. Caroline Wheal. Read by David Yip. (J). 2007. 34.99 (978-1-60252-651-8(6)) Find a World.

Playaway Presents - Children's Stories from China: The Magical Dog Panhu; the Archer Yi; the Wise Emperor Shun; Dragon's Gate. unabr. ed. Caroline Wheal. Read by David Yip. (J). 2007. 34.99 (978-1-60252-650-1(8)) Find a World.

Playaway Presents - Children's Stories from India: Crocodile & Monkey; Satyavan & Savitri; Good Advice. unabr. ed. Joanna Whiteley. Read by Nina Wadia. (J). 2007. 34.99 (978-1-60252-693-8(1)) Find a World.

Playaway Presents - Children's Stories from India: The Feast; Rama; the Potter; Ahmad & Shehernaz. unabr. ed. Joanna Whiteley. Read by Nina Wadia. (J). 2007. 34.99 (978-1-60252-694-5(X)) Find a World.

Playaway Presents - Children's Stories from Japan: Mariko & her Beautiful Long Hair; the Moon Maiden; the Black Bowl. unabr. ed. Caroline Wheal. Read by Duncan Law & Cast. (J). 2007. 34.99 (978-1-60252-653-2(2)) Find a World.

Playaway Presents - Children's Stories from Japan: Mr Rat's Daughter; the Journey of the Jelly Fish; the Rice-Box Warrior. unabr. ed. Caroline Wheal. Read by Duncan Law & Cast. (J). 2007. 34.99 (978-1-60252-652-5(4)) Find a World.

Playaway Presents - Italian Fairy Tales: Angiola & her Beautiful Hair; the Three Fools; Strega Nona. unabr. ed. Caroline Wheal. Read by Kate Gielgud & Cast. (J). 2007. 34.99 (978-1-60252-623-5(0)) Find a World.

Playaway Presents - Stories from Ancient Egypt: In the Beginning; the Children of Ra Atum; Isis & Osiris; Horus & Seth. unabr. ed. David Angus. Read by Janet Suzman. (J). 2007. 34.99 (978-1-60252-624-2(9)) Find a World.

Playaway Presents - Stories from Ancient Egypt: The Wisdom of Imhotep; the Glory of the Pharaohs; the Book of Thoth; the Last Pharaohs. unabr. ed. David Angus. Read by Janet Suzman. (J). 2007. 34.99 (978-1-60252-625-9(7)) Find a World.

Playaway Presents - Stories of the Native Americans: The Dun Horse; Waupee & the Birds; the Story of Scarface; Ball Player & the Wizard. unabr. ed. Nigel Forde. Read by David Jarvis & Cast. (J). 2007. 34.99 (978-1-60252-695-2(8)) Find a World.

Playaway Presents - Stories of the Native Americans: White Feather; Waupee & the Birds; the Red Swan; Feather Woman & the Morning Star. unabr. ed. Nigel Forde. Read by David Jarvis & Cast. (J). 2007. 34.99 (978-1-60252-696-9(6)) Find a World.

Playaway Presents - the Arabian Nights: Sinbad the Porter & Sinbad the Sailor; the Ebony Horse; the Fisherman & the Genie; the Good Doctor of Damascus; the Tale of the One-Eyed Beggar; the Tale of the Generous Man. unabr. ed. David Angus. Read by Kate Gielgud. (J). 2007. 34.99 (978-1-60252-654-9(0)) Find a World.

Playaway Presents: Italian Fairy Tales: Marco & the Cloud; Oraggio & Bianchinetta; the Merchant's Beautiful Wife. unabr. ed. Caroline Wheal. Read by Kate Gielgud & Cast. (J). 2007. 34.99 (978-1-60252-622-8(2)) Find a World.

Playback. abr. ed. Raymond Chandler. Read by Elliott Gould. 4 cass. (Running Time: 3 hrs.). 2004. 18.00 (978-1-59007-097-0(6)); audio compact disk 21.95 (978-1-59007-098-7(4)) Pub: New Millenn Enter. Dist(s): PerseuPGW

***Playbook: Suit up. Score Chicks. Be Awesome.** unabr. ed. Barney Stinson. Read by Neil Patrick Harris as Barney Stinson. Told to Matt Kuhn. (Running Time: 2 hrs. 0 mins. 0 sec.). (ENG.). 2010. audio compact disk 14.99 (978-1-4423-3655-1(2)) Pub: S&S Audio. Dist(s): S and S Inc

Playboy. Carly Phillips. Read by William Dufris. 8 CDs. 2004. audio compact disk 79.95 (978-0-7927-3176-4(X), SLD 638, Chivers Sound Lib); 54.95 (978-0-7927-3175-7(1), CSL 638, Chivers Sound Lib) AudioGO.

There isn't a woman in town who's immune to the legendary Chandler charm. So far single cop Rick Chandler has managed to fend off the marriage-minded advances of Yorkshire Falls' entire female population. A past mistake has taught him never to put his heart on the line... until he answers the SOS of a real-life runaway bride. In spite of her pearly gown and tiara, Kendall Sutton vows to never wed-making her the ideal pretend lover who can ward off Rick's legion of admirers. When their passionate charade flames into the real thing, Rick is suddenly thinking about two words that spell forever after, but will Kendall ever say "I do?" Can a woman who's had it with weddings tie the knot with the town's most popular playboy?.

Playboy of the Western World. J. M. Synge. Read by Cyril Cusack & Siobhan McKenna. (Playaway Young Adult Ser.). (ENG.). 2008. 34.99 (978-1-60640-535-2(7)) Find a World.

Playboy of the Western World. John Millington Synge. Perf. by Siobhan McKenna & Eamonn Keanne. 1 cass. 10.95 (ECN 087) J Norton Pubs.

Realistic portrayal of Irish life in which an Irish peasant harbours a murderer.

Playboy of the Western World. unabr. ed. John Millington Synge. Perf. by Orson Bean et al. 2 cass. (Running Time: 1 hr. 39 mins.). 2001. 22.95 (978-1-58081-160-6(4), TPT137) L A Theatre.

Playboy of the Western World. unabr. ed. John Millington Synge. Perf. by Orson Bean et al. 2 CDs. (Running Time: 1 hr. 39 mins.). 2001. audio compact disk 25.95 (978-1-58081-194-1(9), CDTPT137) Pub: L A Theatre. Dist(s): NetLibrary CO

In a wayside pub near a village in County Mayo in western Ireland, Christopher Mahon becomes a local hero when he announces to the patrons that he's killed his father.

Player on the Other Side. unabr. ed. Ellery Queen. Read by David Edwards. 6 vols. (Running Time: 9 hrs.). (Ellery Queen Mystery Ser.). 2000. bk. 54.95 (978-0-7927-2232-8(9), CSL 121, Chivers Sound Lib) AudioGO.

A card with the letter "J" on it appeared in Robert York's mail, and a day later he was dead. Then another card showed up, and Ellery Queen knew he was up against a brilliant killer who made a game of death by warning his victims. The only clue was the signature "Y" and Ellery had to find him and stop his remorseless vendetta.

Player on the Other Side. unabr. ed. Ellery Queen. Read by David Edwards. 8 CDs. (Running Time: 12 hrs.). 2004. audio compact disk 79.95 (978-0-7927-3228-0(6), SLD 321, Chivers Sound Lib) AudioGO.
A card with the letter "J" on it appeared in Robert York's mail and a day later he was dead. Then another card showed up and Ellery Queen knew he was up against a brilliant killer who made a game of death by warning his victims. The only clue was the signature "Y" and Ellery Queen had to find him and stop his remorseless vendetta before "Y" won his mad game.

Players in Pigtails. 2004. bk. 24.95 (978-0-7882-0517-0(X)); 8.95 (978-0-7882-0515-6(3)); audio compact disk 12.95 (978-0-7882-0516-3(1)) Weston Woods.

Playful & Passionate Relationships. Jonathan Robinson. Read by Jonathan Robinson. 1 cass. (Running Time: 45 min.). 1991. 9.95 (978-1-57328-789-0(X)) Focal Pt Calif.
Why do most relationships lose the playfulness & passion with which they begin? It's because the partners fail to do things which keep romance & fun alive. This tape presents the seven key behaviors couples can do to keep their love for each other strong, playful, & passionate. Includes many simple, fun & romantic ideas you can use right away to add spice to your relationship.

Playful Child for Happy Dreams. unabr. ed. Mary Richards. 1 cass. (Running Time: 45 min.). (Children's I Am Ser.). (J). (gr. k-5). 2007. audio compact disk 19.95 (978-1-56136-202-8(6)) Master Your Mind.
An imaginative adventure with dolphins, a ride on a unicorn to the elves & a dream castle. Then create a wondrous garden for imaginative play.

Playground. Perf. by Tony Bennett & Rosie O'Donnell. 1 cass. (Family Artist Ser.). (J). 1998. 16.98 (Sony Wonder); 9.98 CD. Sony Music Ent.
Includes family favorites & kids'songs with characters from Sesame Street. Recommended for kids of all ages.

Playground. Crazy Curt. 1 cass. (Running Time: 32 min.). (J). (ps-1). 1995. 9.98 (978-1-893967-09-0(3), EKCT5009); audio compact disk 14.98 (978-1-893967-08-3(5), EKCD5009) Emphasis Ent.
Collection of songs that teach & entertain, in a context that is musically diverse - rock, blues, folk, country, a smattering of jazz & even a rap song.

Playground to Podium: A Parents Guide: Building Confidence for Public Speaking. Ted McIlvain. Read by Rebecca Rodriquez. (Running Time: 9900 sec.). 2007. audio compact disk 19.99 (978-1-60462-126-6(5)) Tate Pubng.

Playin' Favorites. Music by Greg Scelsa & Steve Millang. 1 cass. (Running Time: 1 hr.). (J). 1992. pap. bk. 10.95 (YM10C); pap. bk. 14.95 (YM10CD) Kimbo Educ.
Includes I've Been Working on the Railroad, Join in the Game, The Three Pig Blues, Down by the Bay, Heavenly Music & more. Includes guide.

Playin' in the Band: A Qualitative Study of Poplular Music Styles as Clinical Improvisation. Kenneth Aigen. (C). 2002. per. 39.00 (978-1-891278-30-3(4)) Barcelona Pubs.

Playin' the Blues. Robben Ford. (ITA & SPA.). audio compact disk 24.95 (978-88-7207-552-4(1), ML1443) Portraits & Prayer Pubng Hse.

Playing a Role: Scripted vocational role play Program. Gary Sigler & Darla Kay Fitzpatrick. 2000. spiral bd. 29.00 (978-1-57861-107-2(5), IEP Res) Attainment.

Playing Around. unabr. ed. Gilda O'Neill. Read by Carole Boyd. 10 cass. (Running Time: 15 hrs.). 2000. 84.95 (978-0-7540-0557-5(7), CAB 1980) Pub: Chivers Audio Bks GBR. Dist(s): AudioGO
A seventeen year old, named Angie, with the help of a mini skirt, a pair of false lashes & pink lipstick, has made herself into a beauty of the Swinging Sixties. Angie has the world at her feet, but all this was before that rainy night, when Angie got into the big car, leaving her friend Jackie in Soho to find her own way home.

Playing Beatie Bow. unabr. ed. Ruth Park. Read by Cate Milte. 5 cass. (Running Time: 7 hrs.). 1999. 39.95 (978-0-7861-1626-3(9), 2454) Blckstn Audio.
An Australian children's favorite, this is a fantasy combining Australian history, Victorian sensibilities & the changes a lonely girl from a divided family can go through when something magical happens. Abigail Kirk babysits a young girl, Samantha, who points out a ghostly looking girl to Abigail when playing a game called "Beatie Bow." Abigail chases the apparition & touches her.

Playing Blues, Boogie & R&B on the Piano. Duane Shinn. 1 cass. 19.95 (PS-4) Duane Shinn.
Shows how the 12-bar blues is formed. Allows you to play along as a blues bass line is played for you. Talks about the old "barrel-house" styles, & works through a basic boogie pattern. Then gets into some specific technique used in blues playing, & close by jamming together on some blues riffs.

Playing by Heart. Jacquelyn Ross. Narrated by Richard Ferrone. 11 cass. (Running Time: 15 hrs. 30 mins.). 94.00 (978-1-4025-3437-9(X)) Recorded Bks.

Playing Cards Only-Fall 2002. 2002. 0.99 (978-1-59185-010-6(X)) CharismaLife Pub.

Playing Chords in Rhythm. Duane Shinn. 1 cass. 39.95 incl. chart incl. chart. (HAR-12) Duane Shinn.
This course is built around a unique chart which slips behind the keys & shows what notes to play in various chords, & also shows how to create a "rhythm bass" by playing a bass note followed by a chord.

Playing Dulcimer in the Chord Melody Style. Rosamond Campbell. 2001. spiral bd. 24.95 (978-0-7866-5113-9(X), 97533BCD) Mel Bay.

Playing Favorites. 1998. 14.99 (978-1-60689-165-0(0)) Pub: Youngheart Mus. Dist(s): Creat Teach Pr

Playing Favorites. Perf. by Greg Scelsa. Music by Steve Millang. 1 cass. (J). 1992. 10.98 (978-1-57471-520-0(8), YM012-CN); lp 12.98 (YM012-R); audio compact disk 13.98 CD. (978-1-57471-496-8(1), YM012-CD) Youngheart Mus.
Songs include: "I've Been Working on the Railroad"; "Join in the Game"; "It Ain't Gonna Rain"; "Down by the Bay"; "This Old Man"; "Did You Ever See a Lassie?"; "We've Got the Whole World" & more.

Playing for Keeps: Michael Jordan & the World He Made. unabr. ed. David Halberstam. Narrated by Richard M. Davidson. 15 cass. (Running Time: 20 hrs. 15 mins.). 1999. 125.00 (978-0-7887-3247-8(1), 95851E7) Recorded Bks.
Michael Jordan is more than a great basketball player, he is a cultural phenomenon. Full of human drama & penetrating insights, this puts Jordan's epic career in the context of sweeping changes in the world of sports. Conveys Jordan's intelligence & personal style & brings home the astonishing power of his life story.

Playing for Pizza. John Grisham. 2007. audio compact disk 34.99 (978-1-60252-230-5(8)) Find a World.

Playing for Pizza. unabr. ed. John Grisham. Read by Christopher Evan Welch. (YA). 2007. 49.99 (978-0-7393-7523-5(7)) Find a World.

Playing for Pizza. unabr. ed. John Grisham. Read by Christopher Evan Welch. 6 CDs. (Running Time: 7 hrs.). 2007. audio compact disk 60.00 (978-1-4159-4663-3(9), BksonTape) Pub: Random Audio Pubg. Dist(s): Random

Playing for Pizza. unabr. ed. John Grisham & Christopher Evan Welch. (ENG.). 2008. audio compact disk 14.99 (978-0-7393-8319-3(1), Random AudioBks) Pub: Random Audio Pubg. Dist(s): Random

Playing for the Ashes. Elizabeth George. Read by Donada Peters. (Inspector Lynley Ser.). 1994. 72.00 (978-0-7366-2886-0(X)) Books on Tape.

Playing for the Ashes, Pt. 1. unabr. ed. Elizabeth George. Read by Donada Peters. 8 cass. (Running Time: 12 hrs.). (Inspector Lynley Ser.). 1994. 64.00 (978-0-7366-2885-3(1), 3587-A) Books on Tape.
When a fire kills a cricket star, it looks like the perfect crime. Can Thomas Lynley & Barbara Havers solve it?.

Playing for the Ashes, Pt. 2. Elizabeth George. Read by Donada Peters. 9 cass. (Running Time: 13 hrs. 30 min.). (Inspector Lynley Ser.). 1994. 72.00 (3587-B) Books on Tape.
When a fire kills a cricket star, it looks like the perfect crime. Can Thomas Lynley and Barbara Havers solve it?.

Playing God. unabr. ed. Charles L. Mee, Jr. Read by James Armstrong. 7 cass. (Running Time: 10 hrs.). 1997. 49.95 (978-0-7861-1159-6(3), 1930) Blckstn Audio.
Paints a fascinating picture of great men at great moments. They imagine themselves to be Zeus, hurling thunderbolts here, there, everywhere & Mee is a master storyteller who catches you in their web, only to learn afterward that they made a lot of noise & provided a brilliant but fleeting flash of light.

Playing Honky Tonk & Ragtime on the Piano. Duane Shinn. 1 cass. 19.95 (PS-3) Duane Shinn.
Focuses on the sound of "rinky-tink" or "honky-tonk" piano - the sound that brought cowboys pouring into cabarets of the old West. Talks about "bending" notes, & gives the basic formula for this style.

Playing Hymns & Gospel Songs on the Piano. Duane Shinn. 1 cass. 19.95 (PS-5) Duane Shinn.
Discusses playing the kawai grand piano. Plays & explains what's going on & how you can do it too.

Playing in the Water Audio CD. Adapted by Benchmark Education Company Staff. Based on a work by Francisco Blane. (My First Reader's Theater Ser.). (J). (gr. k-1). 2008. audio compact disk 10.00 (978-1-60634-090-5(5)) Benchmark Educ.

Playing It by Heart: Taking Care of Yourself No Matter What. abr. ed. Melody Beattie. Read by Melody Beattie. 2 cass. (Running Time: 3 hrs.). 2001. 18.00 Audio Lit.
The effects of codependency described in the author's work are pervasive & people often fall back into old, familiar ways that only serve to increase the problem. She focuses on fear & how it controls people's lives through victim behavior & repeated patterns of self-defeating action. As one who has lived through what she describes, Beattie is a recovering alcoholic & codependent, she speaks authoritatively about building inner resources & developing the basis for truly sound relationships.

Playing It by Heart: Taking Care of Yourself No Matter What. abr. ed. Melody Beattie. 2 cass. (Running Time: 3 hrs.). 1999. 17.95 (978-1-57453-304-0(5)) Audio Lit.
Beattie helps listeners understand that fear is the common denominator that draws people back into controlling or victim patterns of behavior. With her unique combination of compassion & common sense, she helps listeners navigate the course between fear of involvement on one hand & entanglement in relationships on the other.

Playing It by Heart: Taking Care of Yourself No Matter What. unabr. ed. Melody Beattie. Read by Melody Beattie. 6 cass. (Running Time: 9 hrs.). 2001. 35.00 (978-1-57453-394-1(0)) Audio Lit.

Playing Life's Game by God's Rules. unabr. ed. Swami Amar Jyoti. 1 cass. (Running Time: 1 hr. 30 min.). (Satsangs of Swami Amar Jyoti Ser.). 1998. 9.95 (978-0-933572-32-4(8), M108) Truth Consciousness.
Reaching the final veil. Love, longing & unconditional surrender.

Playing Our Roles. Swami Amar Jyoti. 1 cass. 1976. 9.95 (G-2) Truth Consciousness.
The need to be real, to play our roles with spiritual consciousness as Karma Yoga. The success trap. Selfless service.

Playing Piano for a Gospel Quartet. 1 cass. bk. 29.95 (CP-19) Duane Shinn.
Specialized course designed for those who are or will be playing for a gospel quartet. Certain techniques are necessary, & Duane demonstrates these techniques in detail.

Playing Politics Pt. 1: Acts 25:1-27. Ed Young. 2000. 4.95 (978-0-7417-2252-2(6), 1252) Win Walk.

Playing Politics Pt. 2: Acts 26:1-31. Ed Young. 2000. 4.95 (978-0-7417-2254-6(2), 1254) Win Walk.

Playing Second Fiddle: John 1:40. Ed Young. (J). 1978. 4.95 (978-0-7417-1024-6(2), A0024) Win Walk.

Playing Standard Ballads on the Piano. Duane Shinn. 1 cass. 19.95 (PS-2) Duane Shinn.
Teaches how to create an "orchestral pad" under your melody line. You'll learn the "block-chord" technique, & the secret of getting a full, lush sound.

***Playing the Blues: Blues Rhythm Guitar.** Steve Trovato & Nick Stoubis. 2010. pap. bk. 14.99 (978-0-7866-8234-8(5)) Mel Bay.

***Playing the Game.** unabr. ed. Barbara Taylor Bradford. Read by Katherine Kellgren. (Running Time: 13 hrs. 0 mins. 0 sec.). 2010. audio compact disk 39.99 (978-1-4272-1077-7(2)) Pub: Macmill Audio. Dist(s): Macmillan

Playing the Game of Teamsmanship. Arynne Simon. 1 cass. 1995. 9.95 (978-1-882389-14-8(X)) Wilarvi Communs.

Playing with Boys. Alisa Valdes-Rodriguez. Read by Isabel Keating. 10 cass. 84.95 (978-0-7927-3297-6(9), CSL 685); audio compact disk 112.95 (978-0-7927-3298-3(7), SLD 685); audio compact disk 49.95 (978-0-7927-3299-0(5), CMP 685) AudioGO.

Playing with Fire see Tales of the Supernatural

Playing with Fire. Emily Blake. Read by Kirsten Kairos. (Running Time: 13560 sec.). (Little Secrets Ser.). (J). 2006. audio compact disk 24.95 (978-0-439-89551-4(0), Scholastic Pr) Scholastic Inc.

Playing with Fire. abr. ed. Nigel Havers. Read by Nigel Havers. (Running Time: 2 hrs. 24 mins. 0 sec.). (ENG.). 2009. audio compact disk 19.95 (978-1-4055-0619-9(9)) Pub: Little BrownUK GBR. Dist(s): IPG Chicago

Playing with Fire. unabr. ed. Mary A. Larkin. Read by Anne Dover. 10 cass. (Running Time: 13 hrs. 15 min.). (Storysound Ser.). (J). 2003. 84.95 (978-1-85903-598-6(1)) Pub: Mgna Lrg Print GBR. Dist(s): Ulverscroft US

Playing with Fire. unabr. ed. Peter Robinson. 10 cass. (Running Time: 14 hrs.). (Inspector Banks Mystery Ser.). 2004. bk. 89.00 (978-1-4025-7546-4(7)) Recorded Bks.

Playing with Fire. unabr. ed. Peter Robinson. Narrated by Ron Keith. 8 cass. (Running Time: 14 hrs.). (Inspector Banks Mystery Ser.). 2004. 34.99 (978-1-4025-7370-5(7), 03994) Recorded Bks.
Two barges moored side-by-side in a canal are destroyed by fire, and Banks knows the devastating blaze is no accident. On board one barge, a young junkie girl perishes. On board the other, an odd and secretive artist is burned beyond recognition. Not long after, another raging inferno engulfs a trailer and its occupant. Before the body count can climb any higher, Banks must determine whether he's dealing with a serial arsonist or with a far more devious individual who is lighting fires to incinerate evidence of further crimes. Packed with shocking surprises, Playing with Fire is a suspenseful masterwork.

Playing with Fire: The Dangers of Sexual Sin. Creflo A. Dollar. 2009. audio compact disk 28.00 (978-1-59944-747-6(9)) Creflo Dollar.

Playing with the Band at Christmas: For Solo Instruments & Play-along CD with Concert Band. 2004. audio compact disk 12.95 (978-0-8258-5257-2(9)); audio compact disk 12.95 (978-0-8258-5258-9(7)); audio compact disk 12.95 (978-0-8258-5259-6(5)); audio compact disk 12.95 (978-0-8258-5260-2(9)); audio compact disk 12.95 (978-0-8258-5261-9(7)) Fischer Inc NY.

Playing with the Enemy: A Baseball Prodigy, a World at War, & a Field of Broken Dreams. unabr. ed. Gary Moore. Read by Gary Moore. Read by Toby Moore. (YA). 2008. 54.99 (978-1-60514-835-9(0)) Find a World.

Playing with the Enemy: A Baseball Prodigy, a World at War, & a Field of Broken Dreams. unabr. ed. Gary Moore. Narrated by Toby Moore. (ENG.). 2008. 18.19 (978-1-60814-337-5(6), SpringWater) Oasis Audio.

Playing with the Enemy: A Baseball Prodigy, a World at War, & a Field of Broken Dreams. unabr. ed. Gary W. Moore. Read by Gary W. Moore. Narrated by Toby Moore. Frwd. by Jim Morris. (Running Time: 9 hrs. 23 mins. 8 sec.). (ENG.). 2008. audio compact disk 25.99 (978-1-59859-372-3(2)) Oasis Audio.

Playing with the Moon. Eliza Graham. 2009. 69.95 (978-1-4079-0692-8(5)); audio compact disk 79.95 (978-1-4079-0693-5(3)) Pub: Soundings Ltd GBR. Dist(s): Ulverscroft US

Playland. unabr. ed. Athol Fugard. Perf. by Lou Ferguson et al. 1 cass. (Running Time: 1 hr. 20 min.). 1996. 19.95 (978-1-58081-084-5(5), CTA51) L A Theatre.
Set in a traveling South African amusement park on New Year's Eve, Playland explores the possiblities for blacks & whites to find understanding in a racially divided world. A volatile dialogue begins when two men, a former soldier & a night watchman, meet at Playland. The show takes an explosive turn when these men delve into their sordid pasts.

Playmates. unabr. collector's ed. Robert B. Parker. Read by Michael Prichard. 5 cass. (Running Time: 5 hrs.). (Spenser Ser.). 1990. 40.00 (978-0-7366-1774-1(4), 2613) Books on Tape.
Spenser smells corruption in college town. Taft University's hottest basketball star is shaving points for quick cash. All manner of sleaze - from corrupt academics to hoods with graduate degrees - have their fingers in the pot. Spenser's search takes him from lecture halls to blue collar bars &, finally, into a bloody confrontation with almost certain death. But Spenser saves an arrogant young athlete - even though it nearly kills him to do it.

Plays & Memories see Sound of Modern Drama: The Crucible

Plays the Thing. Valerie Whiteson & Nava Horovitz. 1998. (978-0-312-17796-6(8)) St Martin.

Plays the Thing Audio Sampler: A Whole Language Approach to Learning English. Valerie Whiteson & Nava Horovitz. 1 cass. (Running Time: 1 hr.). pap. bk. Cambridge U Pr.

Play's the Thing - The Grey Lady. adpt. ed. Focus on the Family Staff. Prod. by Dave Arnold. Adapted by Paul McCusker. (Running Time: 240 hrs. 0 mins.). (Radio Theatre Ser.). (ENG.). (J). (gr. 3). 2007. audio compact disk 14.97 (978-1-58997-509-5(X), Tyndale Ent) Tyndale Hse.

Plays Well with Others. unabr. collector's ed. Allan Gurganus. Read by Barrett Whitener. 12 cass. (Running Time: 18 hrs.). 1998. 96.00 (978-0-7366-4206-4(4), 4702) Books on Tape.

Playtime Album. 1 cass. (J). 1996. 10.98 Consort Bk Sales.

Playtime Music Box. Created by Walt Disney Records Staff. Prod. by Bill Weisbach. (Baby Einstein Ser.). (J). (ps-k). 2005. audio compact disk 7.98 (978-5-558-86506-6(7)) W Disney Records.

Playtime Parachute Fun. Perf. by Jill Gallina. 1 cass. (Running Time: 40 min.). (J). (ps-3). 2001. pap. bk. 10.95 Incl. manual. (KIM 7056C); pap. bk. 14.95 (KIM7056CD); pap. bk. & stu. ed. 11.95 (KIM 7056) Kimbo Educ.
Turn kids on to teamwork as their gross motor skills develop while playing parachute routines. Parachute Rollerball, Merry-Go-Round, Floating Cloud, Mountain High & more. Guide with lyrics & instructions. (Fitness & Dancing with Parachutes).

Playtime Playmate. Perf. by Fritzie Locke. 1 cass. (Running Time: 45 mins.). (J). (ps-5). 2003. bk. 8.95 (978-0-9650258-1-2(0), Persnickety Pr) Pub: DBP & Assocs. Dist(s): Penton Overseas
A fun-filled resource of children's sing-alongs & playtime activities. Sons include: "The Wheels on the Bus," "Pop Goes the Weasel," "Bingo" & Five Little Monkeys.".

Playtime Rhymes for Little People. Clare Beaton. 1 CD. (Running Time: 28 mins. 14 sec.). (J). 2002. audio compact disk 15.99 (978-1-84148-975-9(1)) BarefootBksMA.
Designed to help children develop language and counting skills while improving their coordination and encouraging them to interact.

Playtime Songs. Penton Overseas, Inc. Staff. 1 cass. (Running Time: 62m). (J). 2002. audio compact disk 14.95 (978-1-58467-014-8(2)) Pub: Gentle Wind. Dist(s): Rounder Kids Mus Dist

Playtime Songs. Penton Overseas, Inc. Staff. 1 CD. (Running Time: 1 hr.). (Ready-Set-Sing Collection). (ENG.). (J). (ps-7). 2003. audio compact disk 4.99 (978-1-56015-232-3(X)) Penton Overseas.
These four new collections of kids favorite sing-along songs include fun activity songs to get everyone up, moving & having great fun.

Playtime with Beethoven. Composed by Ludwig van Beethoven. 1 cass. (Running Time: 1 hr.). (Classical Babies Ser.). (J). 2002. 7.99 (978-1-894677-21-9(8)); audio compact disk 9.99 (978-1-894677-20-2(X)) Pub: Kidzup CAN. Dist(s): Penton Overseas
Introduce children to one of the great figures of history who remains the most popular classical composer, Ludwig van Beethoven.

Playway to English. Günter Gerngross & Herbert Puchta. (ENG.). 1999. 24.15 (978-0-521-65689-4(3)) Cambridge U Pr.

Playway to English. Günter Gerngross & Herbert Puchta. Contrib. by Günter Gerngross & Herbert Puchta. (Running Time: 2 hrs. 4 mins.). (ENG.). 1999. 40.00 (978-0-521-65668-9(0)) Cambridge U Pr.

Playway to English. Günter Gerngross & Herbert Puchta. (Running Time: hrs. mins.). (ENG.). 2000. act. bk. ed. 24.15 (978-0-521-66582-7(5)) Cambridge U Pr.

Playway to English, Bk. 3. Günter Gerngross & Herbert Puchta. (Running Time: 1 hr. 23 mins.). (ENG.). 1999. act. bk. ed. 24.15

(978-0-521-66583-4(3)); act. bk. ed. 24.15 (978-0-521-66584-1(1)) Cambridge U Pr.

Playway to English Junior a Class, Set. Suzanne Antonaros et al. Contrib. by Günter Gerngross & Herbert Puchta. (Playway to English Ser.). 2000. tchr. ed. 12.00 (978-0-521-65517-0(X)) Cambridge U Pr.
1. What's your name?; 2. Shopping; 3. In the house; 4. Clothes; 5. Christmas; 6. Family; 7. Time; 8. The magician; 9. My body; 10. Breakfast; 11. Travelling; 12. On a farm; 13. Water; 14. Holiday.

Playway to English Level 1 Class Audio CDs (3) 2nd rev. ed. Günter Gerngross & Herbert Puchta. (Running Time: 3 hrs. 45 mins.). (ENG.). 2009. audio compact disk 24.15 (978-0-521-12984-8(2)) Cambridge U Pr.

Playway to English Level 2 Class Audio CDs (3) 2nd rev. ed. Günter Gerngross & Herbert Puchta. (Running Time: 3 hrs. 45 mins.). (ENG.). 2009. audio compact disk 24.15 (978-0-521-13106-3(5)) Cambridge U Pr.

Playway to English Level 3 Class Audio CDs (3) 2nd rev. ed. Günter Gerngross & Herbert Puchta. (Running Time: 2 hrs. 21 mins.). (ENG.). 2009. audio compact disk 58.80 (978-0-521-13128-5(6)) Cambridge U Pr.

Playway to English Level 4 Class Audio CDs (3) 2nd rev. ed. Günter Gerngross & Herbert Puchta. (Running Time: 2 hrs. 49 mins.). (ENG.). 2009. audio compact disk 58.80 (978-0-521-13152-0(9)) Cambridge U Pr.

Playway to English Pre-Junior Class. Suzanne Antonaros et al. Contrib. by Günter Gerngross & Herbert Puchta. (Running Time: 56 mins.). (Playway to English Ser.). 1999. tchr. ed. 6.00 (978-0-521-65528-6(5)) Cambridge U Pr.
1. What's your name?; 2. School; 3. Fruit; 4. Pets; 5. Toys; 6. Christmas; 7. Winter; 8. Health; 9. Party time; 10. Food and drink; 11. Easter; 12. Weather; 13. Animals; 14. Holidays.

Playway to English Stories. Günter Gerngross & Herbert Puchta. Contrib. by Günter Gerngross & Herbert Puchta. (ENG.). 1999. 24.15 (978-0-521-65685-6(0)) Cambridge U Pr.

Playway to English 1. Günter Gerngross. (ENG.). 1999. audio compact disk 24.15 (978-0-521-65496-8(3)) Cambridge U Pr.

Playway to English 1. Günter Gerngross & Herbert Puchta. Contrib. by Günter Gerngross & Herbert Puchta. (ENG.). 1999. act. bk. ed. 23.00 (978-0-521-65502-6(1)) Cambridge U Pr.

Playway to English 1. Herbert Puchta & Günter Gerngross. (Running Time: 3455 sec.). (ENG.). 1999. audio compact disk 23.00 (978-0-521-65688-7(5)) Cambridge U Pr.

Playway to English 1: Activity Book. Herbert Puchta & Günter Gerngross. (ENG.). 1999. act. bk. ed. 24.15 (978-0-521-65501-9(3)) Cambridge U Pr.

Playway to English 2. 2nd ed. Günter Gerngross. (ENG.). 1999. act. bk. ed. 24.15 (978-0-521-65494-4(7)) Cambridge U Pr.

Playway to English 2, Set. Günter Gerngross & Herbert Puchta. Contrib. by Günter Gerngross & Herbert Puchta. (ENG.). 1999. 42.00 (978-0-521-65678-8(8)) Cambridge U Pr.

Playway to English 2: Class Audio CD Set, Set. Günter Gerngross. (Running Time: 1 hr. 24 mins.). (ENG.). 1999. audio compact disk 42.00 (978-0-521-65677-1(X)) Cambridge U Pr.

Playway to English 2: Stories. 2nd ed. Günter Gerngross. 1 CD. (Running Time: 1 hr. 30 mins.). (ENG.). 1999. audio compact disk 24.15 (978-0-521-65491-3(2)) Cambridge U Pr.

Playway to English 2 Stories. Günter Gerngross & Herbert Puchta. Contrib. by Günter Gerngross & Herbert Puchta. (ENG.). 1999. 23.00 (978-0-521-65674-0(5)) Cambridge U Pr.

Playway to English 3. Günter Gerngross. 3 Cass. (Running Time: hrs. mins.). (ENG.). 1999. audio compact disk 42.00 (978-0-521-65667-2(2)) Cambridge U Pr.

Playway to English 4, Set. Günter Gerngross & Herbert Puchta. Contrib. by Günter Gerngross & Herbert Puchta. 3 cass. (Running Time: 2 hrs. 47 mins.). (ENG.). 2000. 42.00 (978-0-521-65658-0(3)) Cambridge U Pr.

Playway to English 4: Activity Book. Herbert Puchta & Günter Gerngross. (Running Time: 32 mins.). (ENG.). 2000. act. bk. ed. 24.15 (978-0-521-66581-0(7)) Cambridge U Pr.

Playway to English 4: Class Audio CD Set, Set. Günter Gerngross. 3 CDs. (Running Time: hrs. mins.). (ENG.). 2000. audio compact disk 42.00 (978-0-521-65657-3(5)) Cambridge U Pr.

Play2music Classic Rock: Easy to Use & Quick to Master. 2004. audio compact disk 19.95 (978-0-634-07928-3(X)) H Leonard.

Plaza Suite. Neil Simon. Contrib. by Edward Asner et al. 2 CDs. (Running Time: 1 hr. 30 mins.). audio compact disk 25.95 (978-1-58081-237-5(6), CDRDP7) L A Theatre.

Plaza Suite. unabr. ed. Neil Simon. Perf. by Edward Asner et al. 2 cass. (Running Time: 1 hr. 30 mins.). 1989. 22.95 (978-1-58081-085-2(3), RDP7) L A Theatre.
Set of three brief encounters in the same suite at the famed Plaza Hotel in New York.

Plazas. Rolle. 2000. audio compact disk 32.75 (978-0-8384-1135-3(5)) Heinle.

Plazas: Lugar de Encuentros. Robert Hershberger. stu. ed. (978-0-8384-1112-4(6)) Heinle.

Plazas: Lugar de Encuentros. Robert Hershberger. (C). bk. 120.95 (978-0-8384-6573-8(0)); bk. 166.95 (978-0-8384-6574-5(9)); bk. 119.95 (978-0-8384-6995-8(7)); bk. 143.95 (978-0-8384-7519-5(1)); bk. 108.95 (978-0-8384-7776-2(3)); bk. 149.95 (978-0-8384-8058-8(6)); bk. 126.95 (978-0-8384-8084-7(5)); bk. 116.95 (978-0-8384-8086-1(1)); bk. 106.95 (978-0-8384-8129-5(9)); bk. 134.95 (978-0-8384-8147-9(7)); bk. 151.95 (978-0-8384-8173-8(6)); bk. 175.95 (978-0-8384-8174-5(4)); bk. 82.95 (978-0-8384-8209-4(0)); bk. 130.95 (978-0-8384-8270-4(8)); bk. 98.95 (978-0-8384-8524-8(3)); bk. 69.95 (978-0-8384-8667-2(3)); bk. 58.95 (978-0-8384-8749-5(1)); bk. 114.95 (978-0-8384-8785-3(8)); bk. 84.95 (978-0-8384-8794-5(7)) Heinle.

Plazas: Lugar de Encuentros. Robert Hershberger. (C). 2002. bk. 71.95 (978-0-8384-8489-0(1)) Heinle.
PLAZAS is based on the premise that true, authentic communication takes place where language and culture meet. In the real world, plazas are about meeting and connecting and are at the very heart of each and every Hispanic city. Likewise, PLAZAS was designed to bring you and your students together to communicate and interact. Invoking the metaphor of the plaza, PLAZAS intends to be a meeting place, a lugar de encuentro, for the Spanish-speaking world both in and outside of the classroom.

Plazas: Lugar de Encuentros. Robert Hershberger. 2000. bk. 52.00 (978-0-8384-1110-0(X)) Heinle.

Plazas: Lugar de Encuentros. 2nd ed. Robert Hershberger et al. 2003. bk. (978-0-8384-0857-5(5)) Heinle.

Plazas: Rovia Passcard. Hershberger. (C). bk. 95.95 (978-0-8384-8644-3(4)); bk. 114.95 (978-0-8384-8653-5(3)); bk. 95.95 (978-0-8384-8662-7(2)); bk. 110.95 (978-0-8384-8671-9(1)); bk. 89.95 (978-0-8384-8680-1(0)); bk. 77.95 (978-0-8384-8689-4(4)); bk. 88.95 (978-0-8384-8698-6(3)); bk. 170.95 (978-0-8384-8707-5(6)); bk. 120.95 (978-0-8384-8725-9(4)); bk. 135.95 (978-0-8384-8734-1(3)); bk. 130.95 (978-0-8384-8743-3(2)); bk. 96.95 (978-0-8384-8752-5(1)); bk. 115.95 (978-0-8384-8761-7(0)); bk. 115.95 (978-0-8384-8716-7(5)) Heinle.
Based on the premise that true, authentic communication takes place where language and culture meet. In the real world, plazas are about meeting and connecting and are at the very heart of each and every Hispanic city.

Plazas: Rovia Passcard. annot. ed. Hershberger. (C). 2001. bk. & tchr. ed. 54.25 (978-0-8384-4768-0(6)) Heinle.

Plazas: Testbank. Postma-Cartter. 2001. audio compact disk 21.75 (978-0-8384-1185-8(1)) Heinle.

Plea of Insanity. unabr. ed. Jilliane Hoffman. Narrated by Karen White. (Running Time: 13 hrs. 0 mins. 0 sec.). (ENG.). 2009. audio compact disk 37.99 (978-1-4001-1137-4(4)); audio compact disk 24.99 (978-1-4001-6137-9(1)); audio compact disk 75.99 (978-1-4001-4137-1(0)) Pub: Tantor Media. Dist(s): IngramPubServ

Pleading Guilty. Scott Turow. Narrated by Ron McLarty. 9 cass. (Running Time: 13 hrs. 30 mins.). 1993. 86.00 (978-1-4025-3583-3(X)) Recorded Bks.

Pleading Guilty. abr. ed. Scott Turow. 2004. 15.95 (978-0-7435-4816-8(7)) Pub: S&S Audio. Dist(s): S and S Inc

Pleading Guilty. unabr. ed. Scott Turow. Read by Grover Gardner. 8 cass. (Running Time: 12 hrs.). 1993. 64.00 (978-0-7366-2605-7(0), 3348) Books on Tape.
Mack Malloy, 50-ish ex-cop & partner-on-the-wane at a top-notch law firm, dreads his assignment. Their star litigator is missing - so is 5.6 million dollars. Malloy's search leads to the firm's inner sanctum, then to the dark heart of the city. What waits is a corpse, cold & lifeless.

Pleading Guilty. unabr. ed. Scott Turow. Read by Robert Petkoff. (Running Time: 14 hrs. 30 mins.). (ENG.). 2010. 24.98 (978-1-60788-381-4(3)); audio compact disk 29.98 (978-1-60788-380-7(5)) Pub: Hachet Audio. Dist(s): HachBkGrp

Pleading Your Case. Lynne Hammond. 2009. audio compact disk 6.00 (978-1-57399-421-7(9)) Mac Hammond.

Pleasant Home: A Bible Study for Young Mothers. Read by Nancy Wilson. 5. 2005. 15.00 (978-1-59128-551-9(8)); 20.00 (978-1-59128-553-3(4)) Canon Pr ID.

***Please.** Edwin Torres. 2002. audio compact disk 19.95 (978-0-9710371-6-8(7)) Pub: Faux Pr. Dist(s): SPD-Small Pr Dist

Please Come to Order. Edwin C. Bliss. 6 cass. 69.50 incl. chart of motions. (S1840) J Norton Pubs.
Learn the art of managing meetings. Includes dramatizations of the right & wrong ways of handling motions, how to get a motion passed, answers to frequently-asked questions, & tests & quizzes.

Please Come to Order!, Set. Edward Bliss. 6 CDs. (Running Time: 3 hrs. 40 mins.). 2006. audio compact disk 49.50 (978-1-57970-364-6(X), S01840D, Audio-For) J Norton Pubs.
This program by certified parliamentarian Ed Bliss provides everything you need to know to preside or participate more effectively at formal meetings. And, because "knowledge is power," your influence within the organizations to which you belong will increase dramatically. Skits are used throughout to add interest and emphasize major points. You'll especially appreciate the author's approach to Rules of Procedure, with his emphasis on fairness and understanding. There's no sense that procedure should be used for manipulation.

Please Don't Eat the Daisies. abr. ed. Jean Kerr. Perf. by Jean Kerr. 2 cass. (Running Time: 3 hrs.). 2000. 7.95 (978-1-57815-189-9(9), 1129, Media Bks Audio) Media Bks NJ.
The author captures the perils of motherhood, wifehood, selfhood & other assorted challenges.

Please Don't Eat the Daisies. unabr. ed. Jean Kerr. Read by Marni Webb. 2 cass. (Running Time: 3 hrs.). 1998. 17.95 (978-1-57270-057-4(2), M21057u, Audio Editions) Pub: Audio Partners. Dist(s): PerseuPGW
Based on the real-life adventures of a '50s family, these stories make fun of a woman's dilemma with rambunctious sons, slick magazine advice, & a celebrity husband.

Please Enjoy Your Breathing! Thich Nhat Hanh et al. 1 cass. 9.00 (A0136-83) Sound Photosyn.
Benefit for Thich Nhat Hanh, put on by the San Francisco Zen Center in Berkeley. A touching occasion with readings by three foremost talents in poetry.

Please Forgive Them. Perf. by Lori Wilke. 1 cass. (Running Time: 4 min.). 1992. 9.98 Sound track. (978-1-891916-25-0(4)) Spirit To Spirit.

Please Have Dinner with Me Tonight. unabr. ed. H. Ann Myers. Read by H. Ann Myers. 1 cass. (Running Time: 45 min.). (Think Fit Ser.). 1992. 9.95 (978-1-887011-00-6(5)) Fresh Aer Hlth.
This tape focuses on the attitude & thoughts that you digest when you eat. Listen to this tape while eating.

Please, I'd Rather Manage Myself. Marsha Haigh Arend. 6 CDs. (Running Time: 8 hrs.). 2005. audio compact disk Rental 30.00 (978-0-9743176-7-8(X)) Roll Bay Pub.

***Please Listen to Me (Part 1)** 2010. audio compact disk (978-0-9826360-4-6(0)) Mid A Bks & Tapes.

***Please Listen to Me (Part 2)** 2010. audio compact disk (978-0-9826360-5-3(9)) Mid A Bks & Tapes.

***Please Look after Mom.** unabr. ed. Kyung-Sook Shin. Tr. by Chi-Young Kim. (Running Time: 7 hrs.). (ENG.). 2011. audio compact disk 35.00 (978-0-307-74736-5(0), Random AudioBks) Pub: Random Audio Pubg. Dist(s): Random

Please Pass the Guilt. unabr. ed. Rex Stout. Read by Michael Prichard. (Running Time: 19020 sec.). (Nero Wolfe Ser.). 2005. 27.95 (978-1-57270-479-4(9)) Pub: Audio Partners. Dist(s): PerseuPGW
A bomb explodes in the desk drawer of a top TV executive. But was the death trap intended for him or for the man who opened the drawer? Each man had a host of enemies, so was it the ambitious business partner, the jealous wife, the office secretary, or the man with blood on his hands? Nero Wolfe finds himself up to his corpulent neck as he and Archie Goodwin sort their way through secrets, over-the-top ambition, and a long list of suspects to find the truth and the guilty party.

Please Pass the Guilt. unabr. ed. Rex Stout. Narrated by Michael Prichard. (Running Time: 19020 sec.). (Nero Wolfe Ser.). (ENG.). 2005. audio compact disk 27.95 (978-1-57270-480-0(2)) Pub: AudioGO. Dist(s): Perseus Dist

Please Pass the Guilt. unabr. collector's ed. Rex Stout. Read by Michael Prichard. 4 cass. (Running Time: 6 hrs.). (Nero Wolfe Ser.). 1999. 32.00 (978-0-7366-4456-3(3), 4901) Books on Tape.
When a boorish millionaire & a Mets fan with a phony name show up at his door with a tempting case, Nero Wolfe finds himself investigating corporate treachery, domestic intrigue & worse.

Please Please Please, unabr. ed. Renee Swindle. Read by Marjorie Johnson. 8 vols. (Running Time: 10 hr.). 1999. bk. 69.95 (978-0-7927-2324-0(4), CSL 213, Chivers Sound Lib) AudioGO.
For weeks, Babysister has hidden her affair with Darren Forrest Wilson from her family, her friends & especially her best friend Deborah, whom Darren was dating before Babysister stole him away. What starts out as lust, quickly turns into the real thing. But when Darren changes his mind about Babysister, it looks like wedding bells for he & Deborah. Babysister is out in the cold until, of course, Darren returns begging forgiveness.

Please Stay a Baby. Julie Chapman. 1 cass., 1 CD. (J). 5.58 (LY 9585); 5.58 (LY9585 320 1LY9588); 5.58 (LY9585 320 1LY9588) NewSound.

Please Understand Me: Character & Temperament Types. unabr. ed. Marilyn Bates & David Keirsey. 6 cass. (Running Time: 8 hrs.). 1994. 29.95 set. (978-1-885705-00-6(X)) Prometheus Nemesis.
A description of four styles of attitude & action, based on the work of Myers-Briggs & Jung: used by corporations, colleges, & families to promote productive & cooperative interpersonal relations.

Pleaser. Hal Stone & Sidra Stone. 1 cass. (Running Time: 1 hrs.). (Mendocino Ser.: Vol. 13). 1997. 10.95 (978-1-56557-053-5(7), T13) Delos Inc.
Our much maligned Pleasers truly care about others & want to make them happy. Unfortunately, they are somewhat less concerned with us. This tape will help you to separate from your own Pleaser without losing the gifts it brings.

Pleasing God. Swami Amar Jyoti. 1 cass. 9.95 (K-104) Truth Consciousness.
Prasanna - when God is pleased with us, all is well. He sees what we are. Why is it difficult to follow Truth in our lives?.

Pleasing God. Ed Pinegar. 1 cass. 3.95 (978-1-57734-397-4(2), 34441387) Covenant Comms.

Pleasing God, Vol. 1. 2003. audio compact disk (978-1-931713-76-4(6)) Word For Today.

Pleasing God, Vol. 1. 2003. (978-1-931713-70-2(7)) Word For Today.

Pleasing God, Vol. 2. 2003. audio compact disk (978-1-931713-77-1(4)) Word For Today.

Pleasing God, Vols. 1 & 2. 2003. audio compact disk (978-1-931713-78-8(2)) Word For Today.

Pleasing God, Volume 2 2003. (978-1-931713-71-9(5)) Word For Today.

Pleasing God; Faith. Ed Pinegar. 1 cass. 7.98 (978-1-55503-397-2(0), 06004652) Covenant Comms.
Applying the atonement unto repentance.

Pleasing Hour: A Novel. Lily King. Narrated by Suzanne Toren. 8 CDs. (Running Time: 9 hrs.). audio compact disk 78.00 (978-1-4025-2078-5(6)) Recorded Bks.

Pleasing Hour: A Novel. Lily King. Narrated by Suzanne Toren. 6 cass. (Running Time: 9 hrs.). 1999. 54.00 (978-0-7887-9423-0(X), 96772) Recorded Bks.
Based on her travels in Europe while working as an au pair. Having suffered a tremendous loss, 17-year-old Rosie becomes a nanny on a houseboat to paris, filling the void with a new family. Discovering the secrets of the detached mother, Rosie realizes that they share eerily similar demons.

Pleasing the Dead. unabr. ed. Deborah Turrell Atkinson. (Running Time: 9 hrs. NaN mins.). 2009. 29.95 (978-1-4332-6432-0(3)); audio compact disk 59.95 (978-1-4332-6428-3(5)); audio compact disk 80.00 (978-1-4332-6429-0(3)) Blckstn Audio.

Pleasing the Ghost, unabr. ed. Sharon Creech. Narrated by Johnny Heller. 1 cass. (Running Time: 1 hr. 30 mins.). (gr. 3 up). 2000. 12.00 (978-0-7887-3820-3(8), 96062E7) Recorded Bks.
Every time the wind blows, a ghost appears in nine-year-old Dennis' room. One day the ghost of Uncle Arvie appears, needing Dennis' help. But Arvie had a stroke before he died, so when he asks "Fraggle pin Heartfoot a wig pasta?" he's definitely asking something else. And Mom doesn't believe in ghosts, so she's no help.

Pleasing the Ghost, unabr. ed. Sharon Creech. Read by Johnny Heller. 2 cass. (Running Time: 1 hr. 30 mins.). (J). (gr. 3 up). 2000. pap. bk. & stu. ed. 25.20 (978-0-7887-3852-4(6), 41050X4) Recorded Bks.

Pleasing the Ghost, Class Set. unabr. ed. Sharon Creech. Read by Johnny Heller. 2 cass. (Running Time: 1 hr. 30 mins.). (J). 1999. 82.30 (978-0-7887-3878-4(X)) Recorded Bks.

Pleasing Your Hard-to-Please Customers: How to Serve Their Needs - & Save Your Sanity. Rick Brinkman. 4 cass. (Running Time: 4 hrs. 10 min.). 59.95 Set, incl. wkbk., 28p. (Q10157) CareerTrack Pubns.
You'll learn how to gracefully take charge of difficult or uncomfortable situations...discover new ways to "connect" with customers...& develop strategies that lead to a positive resolution. When you gain the skills to recognize problem customers & meet their needs, you're on your way to finding common ground, solving problems & pleasing even your toughest customers. This is proactive problem solving at its best.

Pleasing Your Hard-to-Please Customers: How to Serve Their Needs & Save Your Sanity. Rick Brinkman. 2 cass. (Running Time: 3 hrs.). 1997. 15.95 (978-1-55977-674-5(9)) CareerTrack Pubns.

Pleasure. J. Krishnamurti. 1 cass. (Running Time: 1 hr.). (Krishnamurti with Dr. Allan W. Anderson Ser.: No. 8). 8.50 (APA748) Krishnamurti.
These 1974 dialogues cover the entire spectrum of Krishnamurti's teaching in a series highly regarded for its depth of inquiry into each particular subject.

Pleasure. abr. ed. Eric Jerome Dickey. Read by Susan Spain. (Running Time: 6 hrs.). 2009. audio compact disk 14.99 (978-1-4233-4565-7(7), 9781423345657) Brilliance Audio.

Pleasure. unabr. ed. Eric Jerome Dickey. Read by Susan Spain. (Running Time: 15 hrs.). 2008. 24.95 (978-1-4233-4562-6(2), 9781423345626, BAD); 39.25 (978-1-4233-4563-3(0), 9781423345633, BADLE); audio compact disk 24.95 (978-1-4233-4560-2(6), 9781423345602, Brilliance MP3); audio compact disk 38.95 (978-1-4233-4558-9(4), 9781423345589, Bril Audio CD Unabri); audio compact disk 39.25 (978-1-4233-4561-9(4), 9781423345619, Brinc Audio MP3 Lib); audio compact disk 117.25 (978-1-4233-4559-6(2), 9781423345596, BriAudCD Unabrid) Brilliance Audio.

Pleasure & Social Metaphysics, The Psychology Of. Nathaniel Branden. 1 cass. (Running Time: 47 min.). 10.95 (553) J Norton Pubs.
Branden explains why pleasure is not just a luxury, but a profound psychological need. He analyzes those individuals whose lives depend upon social acceptance, including their thoughts & action.

Pleasure Boats & Leisure Marine Equipment & Services in United Kingdom: A Strategic Reference 2007. Compiled by Icon Group International, Inc. Staff. 2007. ring bd. 195.00 (978-0-497-82457-0(4)) Icon Grp.

Pleasure Boats in France: A Strategic Reference 2006. Compiled by Icon Group International, Inc. Staff. 2007. ring bd. 195.00 (978-0-497-35956-0(1)) Icon Grp.

***Pleasure Control.** abr. ed. Cathryn Fox. Read by Erica Bell. (ENG.). 2006. (978-0-06-123009-7(X), Harper Audio); (978-0-06-121510-0(4), Harper Audio) HarperCollins Pubs.

***Pleasure of Challenge... the Challenge of Pleasure.** Created by Uncommon Sensing LLC. (ENG.). 2001. audio compact disk 60.00 (978-0-9826724-3-3(8)) Uncommon Sens.

Pleasure of Finding Things Out: The Best Short Works of Richard P. Feynman. collector's unabr. ed. Richard Phillips Feynman. Read by Dan Cashman. 8 CDs. (Running Time: 12 hrs.). 2000. audio compact disk 64.00 (978-0-7366-5230-8(2)) Books on Tape.
An unparalleled collection of the timeless writings of one of science's most beloved & original thinkers.

Pleasure of Finding Things Out: The Best Short Works of Richard P. Feynman. unabr. ed. Richard Phillips Feynman. Read by Dan Cushman. 6 cass. (Running Time: 9 hrs.). 2001. 29.95 (978-0-7366-4953-7(0)) Books on Tape.

Pleasure of Finding Things Out: The Best Short Works of Richard P. Feynman. unabr. collector's ed. Richard Phillips Feynman. Read by Don Cashman. 6 cass. (Running Time: 9 hrs.). 2000. 48.00 (978-0-7366-5005-2(9)) Books on Tape.

pleasure of Living see Por el placer a Vivir

Pleasure of My Company. unabr. ed. Steve Martin. Read by Steve Martin. 2007. audio compact disk 14.95 (978-1-4013-9033-4(1)) Pub: Hyperion. Dist(s): HarperCollins Pubs

Pleasure Principle: Discovering a New Way to Health. Dr. paul Pearsall. 2004. 10.95 (978-0-7435-4600-3(8)) Pub: S&S Audio. Dist(s): S and S Inc

Pleasure Principle: Discovering a New Way to Health, Set. Paul P. Pearsall. 6 cass. 1994. 49.95 Set, incl. planner. (10960AX) Nightingale-Conant.
With this program, you'll understand the natural pleasure processes of your brain & body - & how to use them as keys to open the neurochemical "locks" on your brain's health maintenance system. It will show you how - & why - pleasure is the best way to enhance the mind/body connection necessary for better health. In an engaging combination of live lecture tapes, studio records & Hawaiian music - interspersed with audio "tests" & exercises - Dr. Pearsall calls for a life of "healthy hedonism." It's an approach to living that harnesses the most important & natural process in human evolution. Includes planner.

Pleasure Principle in Literature. Lionel Trilling. 1 cass. (Running Time: 55 min.). 1963. 11.95 (23222) J Norton Pubs.
Trilling, a dean of literary critics, traces with scholarly insight from the 18th century to the present what Wadsworth called the "grand elementary principle of pleasure".

Pleasure Principle; Interior Knowledge. Ann Ree Colton. 1 cass. 7.95 A R Colton Fnd.

***Pleasure Unbound: A Demonica Novel.** unabr. ed. Larissa Ione. (Running Time: 10 hrs. 30 mins.). (Demonica Ser.). (ENG.). 2011. 24.98 (978-1-60941-472-6(1)) Pub: Hachet Audio. Dist(s): HachBkGrp

Pleasures & Pains. Barry Milligan. (ENG.). 2003. 22.50 (978-0-8139-2235-5(6)) U Pr of Va.

Pleasures & Sorrows of Work. unabr. ed. Alain de Botton. Read by David Colacci. 1 MP3-CD. (Running Time: 7 hrs.). 2009. 39.97 (978-1-4233-9292-7(2), 9781423392927, Brlnc Audio MP3 Lib); 24.99 (978-1-4233-9291-0(4), 9781423392910, Brilliance MP3); 39.97 (978-1-4233-9294-1(9), 9781423392941, BADLE); 24.99 (978-1-4233-9293-4(0), 9781423392934, BAD); audio compact disk 24.99 (978-1-4233-9289-7(2), 9781423392897, Bril Audio CD Unabri); audio compact disk 74.97 (978-1-4233-9290-3(6), 9781423392903, BriAudCD Unabrid) Brilliance Audio.

***Pleasures of God: Meditations on God's Delight in Being God.** unabr. ed. John Piper. Narrated by Grover Gardner. (ENG.). 2005. 16.98 (978-1-59644-110-1(0), Hovel Audio) christianaud.

Pleasures of God: Meditations on God's Delight in Being God. unabr. ed. John Piper. Narrated by Grover Gardner. 1 MP3CD. (Running Time: 12 hrs. 0 mins. 0 sec.). (ENG.). 2005. lp 19.98 (978-1-59644-111-8(9), Hovel Audio); audio compact disk 28.98 (978-1-59644-112-5(7), Hovel Audio) christianaud.

Pleasures of Love. unabr. ed. Jean Plaidy. Read by Diana Bishop. 10 cass. (Running Time: 15 hrs.). 2001. 84.95 (978-0-7531-0996-0(4), 010311) Pub: ISIS Audio GBR. Dist(s): Ulverscroft US

Pleasures of Reading, Pt. 2. (23335) J Norton Pubs.

Pledge. Chris Brown & Dave Earley. 4 cass. 99.95 Incls. planning agenda, Pledge Sunday sermon & promotional materials, teaching guide & handouts, personal ministry & youth spiritual gifts inventories, recommended resources. (459) Chrch Grwth VA.
Lead your teens to a life of maturity, purity & ministry.

Pledge, Set. abr. ed. Rob Kean. Read by Robert Lawrence. 2 cass. 1999. 17.95 (FS9-51020) Highsmith.

Pledge of Allegiance in Translation: What It Really Means. Elizabeth Raum. Contrib. by Miles Tagmeyer & Scott Combs. (Kids' Translations Ser.). (ENG.). (gr. 3-4). 2008. audio compact disk 17.32 (978-1-4296-3226-3(7)) CapstoneDig.

Pleiades. 1 cass. (Running Time: 26 min.). 14.95 (23355) MMI Corp.
Story of a famous star group in constellation Taurus. Discovery, brightness, other characteristics are covered.

Pleiadian Agenda: A New Cosmology for the Age of Light. abr. ed. Barbara H. Clow. Read by Kitt Weagant. 2 cass. (Running Time: 3 hrs.). 1997. 17.95 (978-1-57453-096-4(8)) Audio Lit.
Barbara Hand Clow channels the voice of Satya, a Pleiadian goddess. Satya describes the huge cosmic drama taking place simultaneously in nine dimensions, with Earth as the chosen theater.

Pleins Pouvoirs. unabr. ed. Robert A. Monroe. Read by Roland Simon. 1 cass. (Running Time: 30 min.). (Human Plus Ser.). (FRE.). 1993. 14.95 (978-1-56102-064-5(8)) Inter Indus.
Redirect mental & physical states to express your best.

Plenary I - John P. McGovern Award Lecture: Perspectives on Medicine & Microbes. Moderated by Frieda Weise. 1 cass. (Medical Library Association 1998 Annual Meeting & Exhibit Ser.). 1998. 12.00 (GS2) Med Lib Assn.
Includes: Preserving Traditional Values & Changing Paradigms of Medical Education & Practice...Kenneth Ludmerer, MD; Emerging Diseases Behind the former Iron Curtain...Laurie Garrett.

Plenary II - the Janet Doe Lecture: Strategies & Measures for Our Next Century. Perf. by Wayne J. Peay. 1 cass. (Medical Library Association 1998 Annual Meeting & Exhibit Ser.). 1998. 12.00 (GS3) Med Lib Assn.

Plenary III - the Digital Estate: Strategies for Surviving & Thriving in an Interactive Age. Perf. by Charles L. Martin, Jr. 1 cass. (Medical Library Association 1998 Annual Meeting & Exhibit Ser.). 1998. 12.00 (GS5) Med Lib Assn.

Plenary IV - Laugh for the Health of It. Perf. by John Morreall. 1 cass. (Medical Library Association 1998 Annual Meeting & Exhibit Ser.). 1998. 12.00 (GS7) Med Lib Assn.

***Plenitude: The New Economics of True Wealth.** unabr. ed. Juliet B. Schor. Narrated by Karen White. (Running Time: 7 hrs. 30 mins. 0 sec.). (ENG.). 2010. 19.99 (978-1-4001-6733-3(7)); 29.99 (978-1-4001-9733-0(3)); 14.99 (978-1-4001-8733-1(8)); audio compact disk 71.99 (978-1-4001-4733-5(6)); audio compact disk 29.99 (978-1-4001-1733-8(X)) Pub: Tantor Media. Dist(s): IngramPubServ

Plenty of People! Hosted by Nancy Pearlman. 1 cass. (Running Time: 28 min.). 10.00 (501) Educ Comm CA.

Plenty of Pretty Good Jokes. unabr. ed. Paula Poundstone. Told to Garrison Keillor. 4 CDs. (Running Time: 4 hrs. 30 mins.). (ENG.). 2004. audio compact disk 39.95 (978-1-56511-917-8(7), 1565119177) Pub: HighBridge. Dist(s): Workman Pub

Plight of the Untouchables; Culture of Violence. unabr. ed. Julian C. Hollick. 1 cass. (Running Time: 30 min.). 1991. 12.50 (978-1-56709-028-4(1), 1059) Indep Broadcast.
Side A: Victims of the caste system, India's Untouchables are now organizing to seize political power for themselves. Side B: The assassination of Rajiv Gandhi brought to the surface the issue of violence in public life in India & the fear of many that using violence to settle issues will destroy Indian democracy.

Plimoth Adventure - Voyage of Mayflower. Jerry Robbins. Perf. by Colonial Radio Theatre Staff. 1 cass. (Running Time: 1 hr.). Dramatization. (J). 1999. 12.98 (978-1-929244-06-5(1)) Pub: Colonial Radio. Dist(s): Penton Overseas
From the actual pages of William Bradford's journal, details the pilgrims' epic struggle to find religious freedom in the New World. Many have heard what these brave souls endured after they landed, now hear what persecution & betrayals led to their fateful voyage.

Ploo & the Terrible Gnobbler. Mick Inkpen. Read by Samantha Bond. (Running Time: 0 hr. 30 mins. 0 sec.). (Blue Nose Island Ser.: Bk. 1). (ENG., (J). (gr. k-2). 2004. audio compact disk 5.95 (978-1-84032-673-4(5), HoddrStoughton) Pub: Hodder General GBR. Dist(s): IPG Chicago

Ploo & the Terrible Gnobbler. Mick Inkpen. Read by Samantha Bond. (Blue Nose Island Ser.: Bk. 1). (ENG., (J). (ps). 2006. audio compact disk 11.95 (978-1-84032-988-9(2), HoddrStoughton) Pub: Hodder General GBR. Dist(s): Trafalgar

Plot Against America. unabr. ed. Philip Roth. Read by Ron Silver. (Running Time: 13 hrs. 0 mins.). 2004. audio compact disk 45.00 (978-0-618-50929-4(1)) HM Harcourt.

Plot Against America. unabr. ed. Philip Roth. Narrated by Ron Silver. 9 cass. (Running Time: 13 hrs. 30 mins.). 2004. 89.75 (978-1-4193-1891-7(8), 97933MC) Recorded Bks.

Plot It Yourself. unabr. ed. Rex Stout. 4 cass. (Running Time: 5 hrs. 45 mins.). (Nero Wolfe Ser.). 2003. 24.95 (978-1-57270-301-8(6)) Pub: Audio Partners. Dist(s): PerseuPGW
Two of America's foremost novelists, a world-famous playwright, and the heads of three great publishing companies hire Nero Wolfe to discover how they have been framed for plagiarism. Soon the discerning Wolfe must solve a murder case by analyzing nuances of literary style while legman Archie Goodwin canvasses the literary scene for glamorous women.

Plot It Yourself. unabr. ed. Rex Stout. Narrated by Michael Prichard. (Nero Wolfe Mystery Ser.). (ENG.). 2008. audio compact disk 29.95 (978-1-60283-490-3(3)) Pub: AudioGO. Dist(s): Perseus Dist

Plot It Yourself. unabr. collector's ed. Rex Stout. Read by Michael Prichard. 6 cass. (Running Time: 6 hrs.). (Nero Wolfe Ser.). 1996. 48.00 (978-0-7366-3354-3(5), 4005) Books on Tape.
It's bad enough to steal someone's idea; but it takes real guts to claim it is your own, then sue the originator. That's just what a gang of hack writers do, ingeniously planting evidence to back up their claims. The frustrated authors call on Nero Wolfe for help. But when someone dies, Wolfe realizes it's no simple extortion scheme. He'll have to draw on his critical skills to close the book on a killer well-versed in the ABCs of murder.

Plot to Overcome Christmas. Perf. by Orson Welles. (CC8060) Natl Recrd Co.

Plot to Save Socrates. Paul Levinson. Read by Mark Shanahan. (Running Time: 9 hrs.). 2005. 23.95 (978-1-60083-339-7(X)) Iofy Corp.

Plot to Save Socrates. unabr. ed. Paul Levinson. Read by Mark Shanahan. 7 CDs. (Running Time: 36000 sec.). 2006. audio compact disk 24.95 (978-1-59316-074-6(7), LL166) Listen & Live.

Plots of Opportunity: Representing Conspiracy in Victorian England. Albert D. Pionke. 2004. audio compact disk 9.95 (978-0-8142-9037-8(X)) Pub: Ohio St U Pr. Dist(s): Chicago Distribution Ctr

Plotting the Short Story. Elizabeth R. Bills. 1 cass. (Running Time: 30 min.). (Secrets of Successful writers Ser.). 1963. 11.95 (23023) J Norton Pubs.
Conflict, resolution of conflict, & alteration of character are discussed as the three elements of a good plot.

Plug Yourself into the Frequency of Happiness. Rhegina Sinozich. (ENG.). 2008. audio compact disk 24.95 (978-0-9706297-1-5(0)) Abrezia Pr.

Pluggin' Away. Perf. by Peter Alsop. 1 CD. (Running Time: 46 min.). (J). (gr. k-8). audio compact disk Moose Schl Records.
Includes: Wha'D'Ya' Wanna Do!?, Take Me with You!, Staying Over, Plugging Away, & Family Roles (for parents & teachers). Live video concerts include: Wake Up (abuse & abduction prevention skills) & Costume Party (outdoor family concert). Sing-along booklet contains musical chords, exercises, questions & discussion topics for each of the songs in this package.

Pluggin' Away. Perf. by Peter Alsop. 1 cass. (Running Time: 46 min.). (J). (gr. k-8). 1991. 11.00 (MS 504) Moose Schl Records.

***Pluid Dhorcha Leara.** Coil Neaine Phaidin. (ENG.). 11.95 (978-0-8023-7017-4(9)) Pub: Clo Iar-Chonnachta IRL. Dist(s): Dufour

Pluirin na mBan / A Woman's Love. (ENG.). 1993. audio compact disk 20.95 (978-0-8023-8091-3(3)) Pub: Clo Iar-Chonnachta IRL. Dist(s): Dufour

Pluirin na mBan / A Woman's Love: A Womans Love. (ENG.). 1993. 13.95 (978-0-8023-7091-4(8)) Pub: Clo Iar-Chonnachta IRL. Dist(s): Dufour

Plum Boy! & other tales from Japan: Musical Adventures with Elizabeth Falconer. Perf. by Elizabeth Falconer. 1 CD. (Running Time: 61:08). (J). 2000. audio compact disk 15.00 (978-0-9770499-2-9(2)) Koto World.
"An unusual, entertaining tour-de-force performance by a gifted artist." - Parents' ChoiceSteeped in the culture and language of Japan, Elizabeth Falconer is a storyteller with a feather-light touch. Weaving Japanese words into each story, she's also a master of the 13-string, Japanese koto, and accompanies these colorful Japanese folk tales on that eloquent instrument. In the title story, a boy, born from a plum, becomes a hero when he and his friends-a dog, a monkey and a pheasant-divert a pack of demon thieves from evil-doing and rescue a village. "Kumo the Spider" repays a farmer's good deed and spins not only cloth but clouds. "Issunboshi" is about a boy who's an inch tall and follows his dream to become a Samurai, with magical results, and in "Shiro and Kuro," a monkey teaches a couple of quarrelsome kitties a lesson in sharing. "The Tale of a Snail" paints vivid word pictures of a husband and wife planting and harvesting their rice fields and adopting a little snail, who comes to them courtesy of the Water God, as their son-with rewarding results. It's an unusual, entertaining tour-de-force performance by a gifted artist. -Parents' Choice Review.

Plum Gatherer (poem) see Poetry of Edna St. Vincent Millay

***Plum Island.** unabr. ed. Nelson DeMille. Read by Scott Brick. (Running Time: 19 hrs. 30 mins.). (ENG.). 2010. 24.98 (978-1-60788-973-1(0)) Pub: Hachet Audio. Dist(s): HachBkGrp

Plum Lovin' unabr. ed. Janet Evanovich. Narrated by Lorelei King. 3 cass. (Running Time: 3 hrs. 15 mins.). (Between-the-Numbers Novel Ser.). 2007. 34.95 (978-0-7927-4770-3(4), Chivers Sound Lib); audio compact disk 39.95 (978-0-7927-4679-9(1), Chivers Sound Lib) AudioGO.
Stephanie's wannabe lover, Diesel, ropes her into playing Cupid, promising to help Stephanie get her man, er, woman, a bond-jumping Annie Hart, during Valentine's week. Diesel manipulates Stephanie into playing matchmaker and providing romantic support to a cast of misfits who prove to be more troublesome than crooks. The pace is fast with cameo appearances of all the usual eccentrics.

Plum Lovin' unabr. ed. Janet Evanovich. Read by Lorelei King. 3 CDs. (Running Time: 3 hrs. 30 mins. 0 sec.). (Between-the-Numbers Novel Ser.). (ENG.). 2007. audio compact disk 19.95 (978-1-4272-0053-2(X)) Pub: Macmill Audio. Dist(s): Macmillan

Plum Lucky. unabr. ed. Janet Evanovich. Narrated by Lorelei King. 1 MP3-CD. (Running Time: 3 hrs. 30 mins.). (Between-the-Numbers Novel Ser.). 2008. 24.95 (978-0-7927-5298-1(8)); audio compact disk 39.95 (978-0-7927-5226-4(0)) AudioGO.
Stephanie Plum has a way of attracting danger, lunatics, oddballs, bad luck . . . and mystery men. And no one is more mysterious than the unmentionable Diesel. He's back and hot on the trail of a little man in green pants who's lost a giant bag of money. Problem is, the money isn't exactly lost. Stephanie's Grandma Mazur has found it, and like any good Jersey senior citizen, she's hightailed it in a Winnebago to Atlantic City and hit the slots. With Lula and Connie in tow, Stephanie attempts to bring Grandma home, but the luck of the Irish is rubbing off on everyone: Lula's found a job modeling plus-size lingerie. Connie's found a guy. Diesel's found Stephanie. And Stephanie has found herself in over her head with a caper involving thrice-stolen money, a racehorse, a car chase, and a bad case of hives. Plum Lucky is an all-you-can-eat buffet of thrills, chills, shrimp cocktail, plus-size underwear, and scorching hot men.

Plum Lucky. unabr. ed. Janet Evanovich. Read by Lorelei King. 3 CDs. (Running Time: 3 hrs. 30 mins. 0 sec.). (Between-the-Numbers Novel Ser.). (ENG.). 2008. audio compact disk 19.95 (978-1-4272-0266-6(4)) Pub: Macmill Audio. Dist(s): Macmillan

Plum Spooky. abr. ed. Janet Evanovich. Read by Lorelei King. 3 CDs. (Running Time: 4 hrs. 0 mins. 0 sec.). (Between-the-Numbers Novel Ser.). (ENG.). 2009. audio compact disk 19.95 (978-1-4272-0601-5(5)) Pub: Macmill Audio. Dist(s): Macmillan

Plum Spooky. unabr. ed. Janet Evanovich. Read by Lorelei King. (Running Time: 6 hrs. 30 mins.). (Between-the-Numbers Novel Ser.). 2009. 44.95 (978-0-7927-6212-6(6), Chivers Sound Lib) AudioGO.

Plum Spooky. unabr. ed. Janet Evanovich. Read by Lorelei King. (Running Time: 6 hrs. 30 mins.). (Between-the-Numbers Novel Ser.). 2009. 64.95 (978-0-7927-6165-5(0), Chivers Sound Lib); 44.95 (978-0-7927-6164-8(2), Chivers Sound Lib); audio compact disk 74.95 (978-0-7927-5999-7(0), Chivers Sound Lib) AudioGO.

Plum Spooky. unabr. ed. Janet Evanovich. Read by Lorelei King. 7 CDs. (Running Time: 6 hrs. 30 mins. 0 sec.). (Between-the-Numbers Novel Ser.). (ENG.). 2009. audio compact disk 34.95 (978-1-4272-0599-5(X)) Pub: Macmill Audio. Dist(s): Macmillan

Plum Village Meditations. Thich Nhat Hanh & Jina Van Hengel. 1 cass. (Running Time: 90 min.). 2003. 11.00 (55011) Parallax Pr.
A recording of four practices enjoyed at Plum Village, including a forty-five-minute bell meditation.

Plum Village Meditations. unabr. ed. Thich Nhat Hanh. 1 CD. (Running Time: 60 min.). 2004. audio compact disk 15.95 (978-1-59179-222-2(3), AW00347D) Sounds True.
Brings four authentic meditations just as they are taught at this celebrated Zen sanctuary and peace center in southern France. These direct teachings from Plum Village include a 45-minute bell-sounding meditation introduced and rung by Thich Nhat Hanh, plus three additional guided meditations led by Sister Jina: conscious breathing for calming the mind and cultivating joy; body appreciation and attunement practice, and more.

Plumb. Contrib. by Matt Bronleewe & Dan Haseltine. 1997. 10.98 (978-0-7601-1029-4(8), C70008); audio compact disk 15.98 (978-0-7601-1030-0(1), CD70008) Pub: Brentwood Music. Dist(s): Provident Mus Dist
Combines powerful vocals with issue oriented lyrics, edgy guitars & infectious rhythms on their exciting self titled debut.

Plumb: Candy Coated Water Drops. Perf. by Plumb. Prod. by Matt Bronleewe & Glenn Rosenstein. 1 cass. 1998. 10.98 (978-0-7601-2447-5(7)); audio compact disk 16.98 (978-0-7601-2448-2(5)) Provident Music.
Focuses on the hope that can only be found through Christ.

Plumber. Joseph Salerno & Stephen Rivele. Read by Robert Foxworth. 2 cass. (Running Time: 3 hrs.). 1991. 15.95 set. (978-1-879371-00-2(6), 20070) Pub Mills.
This is the true story of how Joe Salerno, a young plumber, inadvertently became mixed up with the Atlantic City mob, witnessed the murder of one of his friends, & turned state's witness. He entered the Federal Witness Protection Program & lost his identity, & put himself & his family in grave danger. After ten years of hardship, his testimony was responsible for the conviction & incarceration of the key Mafia murderers.

Plumbing Projects 1-2-3 (Dvd) Meredith Books Staff. 2008. 14.95 (978-0-696-24109-3(9), Home Depot) Meredith Bks.

Plume Empoisonnee. 1 cass. (Running Time: 60 mins.). Dramatization. (Maitres du Mystere Ser.). (FRE.). 1996. 11.95 (1826-MA) Olivia & Hill.
Popular radio thriller, interpreted by France's best actors.

Plunkitt of Tammany Hall. Read by Anais 9000. As told by Plunkitt George Washington. Told to William L. Riordon. 2008. 27.95 (978-1-60112-025-0(7)) Babblebooks.

Plus Grosse Proie de Ming. Patricia Highsmith. Read by Madeleine Barbulee. 1 cass. 1992. 16.95 (1540-RF) Olivia & Hill.
The hero of this mystery is a cat who avenges the death of her mistress.

Plus Pk CD, C21 Accounting. 8th ed. (C). 2005. audio compact disk 175.95 (978-0-538-44229-9(8)) Pub: South-West. Dist(s): CENGAGE Learn

Plus Polarity. unabr. ed. Robert A. Monroe. Read by Robert A. Monroe. (Running Time: 45 min.). (Gateway Experience - Prospecting Ser.). 1984. 14.95 (978-1-56113-289-8(6)) Monroe Institute.
Go thru the Null Point to the opposite polarity.

Plus Proche Voisin (Nearest Neighbor) Helene Vachon. 1 cass., bklet. (Running Time: 50 mins.). (Best-Sellers Ser.). (FRE.). (J). (ps-2). 2000. cass. & audio compact disk 9.95 (978-2-921997-36-2(3)) Pub: Coffragants CAN. Dist(s): Penton Overseas

Plutarch's Lives see Cambridge Treasy Malory

Plutarch's Lives. unabr. ed. Plutarch. Read by Bernard Mayes. Tr. by John Dryden. 16 cass. (Running Time: 55 hrs. 30 mins.). 2000. 99.95

(978-0-7861-1040-7(6), 1812A,B); 95.95 (978-0-7861-1055-1(4), 1812A,B) Blckstn Audio.

Plutarch's Lives, Pt. 2. unabr. ed. Plutarch. Read by Bernard Mayes. Tr. by John Dryden. 15 cass. (Running Time: 22 hrs. 30 min.). 1996. 95.95 (1812B) Blckstn Audio.
One of two books Mary Shelley chose for the blind hermit to use for Frankenstein's monster's education and a principal source for Shakespeare. Originally comprised a series of books that gave an account of one Greek and one Roman life, followed by a comparison of the two.

Plutarch's Lives, Vol. 2. unabr. ed. Plutarch. Read by Bernard Mayes. Tr. by John Dryden. 14 cass. (Running Time: 42 hrs. 30 mins.). 1996. 89.95 (978-0-7861-1096-4(1), 1868A,B) Blckstn Audio.

Plutarch's Lives, Vol. 2. unabr. ed. Plutarch. Read by Bernard Mayes. Tr. by John Dryden. 15 cass. (Running Time: 42 hrs. 30 mins.). 2000. 95.95 (978-0-7861-1097-1(X), 1868A,B) Blckstn Audio.

Plutarch's Lives Vol. 2, Pt. 1. unabr. ed. Plutarch. Read by Bernard Mayes. 14 cass. (Running Time: 21 hrs.). 1996. 89.95 (1868A) Blckstn Audio.
Comprised of a series of books that gave an account of one Greek & one Roman life. Compares Theseus & Romulus; Pericles & Fabius; Alcibiades & Coriolanus; Aristides & Marcus Cato, & Lysander with Sylla, among others.

Plutarch's Lives Vol. 2, Pt. 2. unabr. ed. Plutarch. Read by Bernard Mayes. 15 cass. (Running Time: 22 hrs. 30 min.). 1999. 95.95 (1868B) Blckstn Audio.

Plutarch's Lives - Excerpts. unabr. ed. Plutarch. Narrated by Ray Atherton. 5 cass. (Running Time: 7 hrs. 30 mins.). 1990. 44.00 (978-1-55690-418-9(5), 90050E7) Recorded Bks.
Accounts of the lives of Mark Antony, Cicero, Theseus & Romulus.

Plutarch's Lives, Vol. 1. unabr. ed. Plutarch & Translated by Dryden. Read by Bernard Mayes. (Running Time: 42 hrs. 50 mins.). 2008. 69.95 (978-1-4332-5190-0(6)) Blckstn Audio.

Plutarch's Lives, Vol. 1- Part A. unabr. ed. Plutarch & Translated by Dryden. Read by Bernard Mayes. (Running Time: 21 hrs. 50 mins.). 2008. audio compact disk 130.00 (978-1-4332-5188-7(4)) Blckstn Audio.

Plutarch's Lives, Vol. 1- Part B. unabr. ed. Plutarch & Translated by Dryden. Read by Bernard Mayes. (Running Time: 21 hrs. 0 mins.). 2008. audio compact disk 130.00 (978-1-4332-5189-4(2)) Blckstn Audio.

Plutarch's Lives, Vol. 2. unabr. ed. Plutarch & Translated by Dryden. Read by Bernard Mayes. (Running Time: 41 hrs. 0 mins.). 2008. 69.95 (978-1-4332-5042-2(X)) Blckstn Audio.

Plutarch's Lives, Vol. 2- Part A. unabr. ed. Plutarch & Translated by Dryden. Read by Bernard Mayes. (Running Time: 20 hrs. 0 mins.). 2008. audio compact disk 125.00 (978-1-4332-5040-8(3)) Blckstn Audio.

Plutarch's Lives, Vol. 2- Part B. unabr. ed. Plutarch & Translated by Dryden. Read by Bernard Mayes. (Running Time: 21 hrs. 0 mins.). 2008. audio compact disk 130.00 (978-1-4332-5041-5(1)) Blckstn Audio.

Pluto. Dale Richardson. 1 cass. 8.95 (295) Am Fed Astrologers.
Power, money & sex in individual & mundane charts.

Pluto: Death or Transformation. J. Lavine. 1 cass. 1992. 8.95 (1058) Am Fed Astrologers.

Pluto: Evolutionary Journey of the Soul. Jeff Green. 1 cass. 8.95 (529) Am Fed Astrologers.
Evolutionary intent & karmic purpose.

Pluto: The Shadow or the Light. Joyce Levine. Read by Joyce Levine. 1 cass. (Running Time: 40 min.). (Integrating Astrological Cycles Ser.). 1994. 11.95 (978-1-885856-06-7(7)) Vizualizations.
Side 1 - informational; Side 2 - guided meditation.

Pluto - Spiritual Pipeline to the Solar System. Carol Hemingway. 1 cass. 8.95 (418) Am Fed Astrologers.
An AFA Convention workshop tape.

Pluto - Vulcan: Guided Visualizations. Luisa De La Lama. Narrated by Leila Gomez Bear & Jaques Bourquin. Music by Summa. 6 cass. (Running Time: 30 min.). (Power Planets Inner Journeys Ser.). 1994. 11.95 set. (978-1-883381-05-9(3)) White Dragon.
Guided visualizations to contact the archetypal powers of Pluto & Vulcan using Greek mythological figures. Theme narrated from the book "Power Planets".

Pluto Files: The Rise & Fall of America's Favorite Planet. unabr. ed. Neil deGrasse Tyson. (Running Time: 5 hrs. 0 mins.). 2009. audio compact disk 19.95 (978-1-4332-4409-4(8)) Blckstn Audio.

Pluto Files: The Rise & Fall of America's Favorite Planet. unabr. ed. Neil deGrasse Tyson. Read by Mirron Willis. (Running Time: 5 hrs. NaN mins.). 2009. 19.95 (978-1-4332-4410-0(1)); audio compact disk 34.95 (978-1-4332-4406-3(3)); audio compact disk 50.00 (978-1-4332-4407-0(1)) Blckstn Audio.

Pluto, Planet of Magic & Power. Ginger Chalford. 1 cass. 8.95 (048) Am Fed Astrologers.
Pluto's house location a key to recovering your lost power.

Pluto-Saturn Conjunction in Birth Charts with Transits. Martha Frohlinger. 1 cass. 8.95 (121) Am Fed Astrologers.
Their aspects in the chart by transits through life.

Pluto, the Bulldozer (Phoenix Bird) Ruth Eichler. 1 cass. 8.95 (105) Am Fed Astrologers.
Pluto's transformative effects on planets by transit.

Plutonium Murders. unabr. collector's ed. Robert Davis. Read by Michael Prichard. 9 cass. (Running Time: 13 hrs. 30 min.). 1997. 72.00 (978-0-7366-3792-3(3), 4466) Books on Tape.
Dr. Alex Seacourt, a mild-mannered internist, bumps into a man on a busy New York street & unwittingly he gets involved in a plot to hold the world hostage through the threat of plutonium poisoning.

Plygain Carols (Welsh Music) 1 cass. 10.95 incl. bklt. (C11059) J Norton Pubs.
Old Welsh carol sung in the close harmony style of the midnight "Plygain" carol services.

Plymouth Adventure of the Mayflower. Perf. by Colonial Radio Theatre Staff. 1 cass. (Running Time: 51 mins.). 2001. 12.95 (COLR004) Lodestone Catalog.
In 1620, the Pilgrims were a small, devout band crossing a vast ocean in a very small ship.

PM Story Books: Turquoise Level. Created by Rigby. (PM Collection). (J). 2000. audio compact disk 33.50 (978-0-7635-7555-7(0), Rigby PEA) Pearson EdAUS AUS.

PM Yoga Mediatations. (Running Time: 1:00:00). 2001. audio compact disk 11.95 (978-1-55961-661-4(X)) Sounds True.

PMA Easy Plan: De techniek voor jouw persoonlijke ontploiing en het verhogen van de kwaliteit van je Leven. Speeches. Jacob Korthuis. 8 CDs. (Running Time: 15 hrs. 40 mins.).Tr. of PMA Easy Plan: the technique for your personal development & increasing the quality of your Life. (DUT., 2009. audio compact disk 395.00 (978-0-9786598-8-2(0)) BCE Inst Inc.

PMA Easy Plan: The technique for your personal development & increasing the quality of your Life. Jacob Korthuis. 8 CDs. (Running Time: 15 hrs. 40 mins.).Tr. of PMA Easy Plan: de techniek voor jouw persoonlijke ontplooiing en het verhogen van de kwaliteit van je Leven. (ENG., 2009. audio compact disk 395.00 (978-0-9786598-9-9(9)) BCE Inst Inc.

PMA Easy Plan: de techniek voor jouw persoonlijke ontplooiing en het verhogen van de kwaliteit van je Leven see PMA Easy Plan: The technique for your personal development & increasing the quality of your Life

PMA Easy Plan: the technique for your personal development & increasing the quality of your Life see PMA Easy Plan: De techniek voor jouw persoonlijke ontplooiing en het verhogen van de kwaliteit van je Leven

PMBOK Audio Digest: PMP Exam Training: PMBOK Essentials (12 Audio CD Cased Set), Vol. 1. 2008. ring bd. 99.00 (978-1-934579-01-5(7)) Praizion Medis.

PMBOK Guide Audio Digest: PMP Exam Audio Prep. (ENG., 2009. ring bd. 149.00 (978-1-934579-07-7(6)) Praizion Medis.

PMP Bootcamp. (ENG.). 2009. 49.00 (978-1-934579-96-1(3)) Praizion Medis.

***PMP Exam: A Project Manager's Experience.** Prod. by Praizion Media. 2008. audio compact disk 14.99 (978-1-934579-08-4(4)) Praizion Medis.

PMP Exam Audio Flashcards. 2009. audio compact disk 24.99 (978-1-934579-10-7(6)) Praizion Medis.

***Pmp exam Bootcamp: Pmp exam Prep.** Prod. by Praizion Media. (ENG.). 2009. audio compact disk 39.99 (978-1-934579-13-8(0)) Praizion Medis.

***Pmp exam drive Time.** Prod. by Praizion Media. 2010. 24.99 (978-1-934579-09-1(2)) Praizion Medis.

***Pmp exam readiness Review.** Prod. by Praizion Media. (ENG.). 2010. audio compact disk 14.99 (978-1-934579-17-6(3)) Praizion Medis.

***PMP Exam Secrets.** Prod. by Praizion Media. 2010. audio compact disk 14.99 (978-1-934579-12-1(2)) Praizion Medis.

***Pmp exam study Strategy.** Prod. by Praizion Media. 2010. 14.99 (978-1-934579-21-3(1)) Praizion Medis.

PMP Exam Success Series: Terminology & Processes Mp3 Audio CD. (J). 2007. audio compact disk 39.95 (978-0-9787032-7-1(8)) Crosswind Proj Manag.

PMP Exam Success Series: Terms & Definitions Audio CD. 2005. audio compact disk 24.95 (978-0-9748761-0-8(0)) Crosswind Proj Manag.

PMP Flash Cards: Audio Flash Cards for the PMP & CAPM Exam. Praizion Media Staff. Narrated by P. AKINWALE. 1 CD. (Running Time: 1hr. 11mins 54 seconds). 2006. audio compact disk 40.00 (978-1-59971-405-9(1)) AardGP.
PMP Flash Cards is designed to test your knowledge of the 9 knowledge areas, 44 PMBOK processes and their numerous inputs, outputs, tools and techniques of Project Management as described in the PMBOK Third Edition. These flash cards will help you memorize all the the 44 processes and their inputs, outputs, tools and techniques. Questions are categorized by knowledge area. You have approximately 10 - 15 seconds to answer each question correctly. The correct answer will be read at the end of each question. CD is in regular audio CD format. You can play it in your car for great drive time study or at home as you relax. Refresh your memory with ease. Once you have mastered the contents of this CD you will have a strong base to build on. This CD will also help PMPs wishing to familiarize themselves with changes in the PMBOK Third Edition. Details on PMP Flash cards are available at www.microsoftprojecttraining.info.

Pmp Flashcards 1&2. Praizion Media. (ENG.). 2005. audio compact disk 24.99 (978-1-934579-00-8(9)) Praizion Medis.

***Pmp Flashcards 3.** Prod. by Praizion Medai. 2010. audio compact disk 14.99 (978-1-934579-20-6(3)) Praizion Medis.

PMP Success Series: Terms & Definitions. Scripts. Tony Johnson. 1. (Running Time: 72 mins.). 2004. audio compact disk 24.95 (978-0-9748761-5-3(1)) Crosswind Proj Manag.
The PMP Success Series: Terms and Definitions Audio CD is a key tool for anyone preparing for the PMP Exam. This CD has Terms and Definitions for all 39 Proces areas covered on the PMP and CAPM exams. The format allows you to listen to the term, think of the answer, and then hear the correct answer. It's perfect for quizzing yourself or memorization during that late night study session, or that long commute to the office.

PMP Success Series: Understanding the Processes. 2nd ed. Scripts. Tony Johnson. 1 CD. (Running Time: 60 mins.). 2004. audio compact disk 24.95 (978-0-9748761-6-0(X)) Crosswind Proj Manag.
The PMP Success Series: Understanding the Processes Audio CD is a key tool for anyone preparing for the PMP Exam. This CD has descriptions of all 39 process areas covered on the PMP and CAPM exams. The format describes each of the processes, where they occur and have impact, as well as a description of the process and key inputs, tools and outputs. It's perfect for memorizing how all the pieces of the PMBOK fit together during that long commucate to the office or that late night study session.

PMP Understanding the Processes Audio CD 3rd Ed. PMBOK. 2005. audio compact disk 24.95 (978-0-9748761-3-9(5)) Crosswind Proj Manag.

PMS. (Running Time: 45 min.). (Health Ser.). 9.98 (978-1-55909-130-5(4), 106) Randolph Tapes.
Helps alleviate some of the ups & downs when your body hormones make changes.

PMS. Rick Brown. Read by Rick Brown. Ed. by John Quatro. 1 cass. (Running Time: 30 min.). (Subliminal - New Age Ser.). 1993. 10.95 (978-1-57100-061-3(5), N132); 10.95 (978-1-57100-085-9(2), S132); 10.95 (978-1-57100-109-2(3), W132); 10.95 (978-1-57100-133-7(6), H132) Sublime Sftware.
PMS reduces the physical effects of the monthly cycle.

PMS, No. E132. Rick Brown. Read by Rick Brown. Ed. by John Quatro. 1 cass. (Running Time: 30 min.). (Subliminal - Easy Listening Ser.). 1993. 10.95 (978-1-57100-013-2(5)) Sublime Sftware.
"PMS" reduces the physical effects of the monthly cycle.

PMS, No. J132. Rick Brown. Read by Rick Brown. Ed. by John Quatro. 1 cass. (Running Time: 30 min.). (Subliminal - Jazz Ser.). 1993. 10.95 (978-1-57100-037-8(2)) Sublime Sftware.

PMS & Mood Swings. unabr. ed. Don Colbert. Read by Greg Wheatley. 1 cass. (Running Time: 1 hr.). 2003. 7.99; audio compact disk 9.99 Oasis Audio.

PMS Outlaws. Sharyn McCrumb. Narrated by Barbara Rosenblat. 8 CDs. (Running Time: 8 hrs. 45 mins.). (Elizabeth MacPherson Ser.: No. 9). audio compact disk 78.00 (978-1-4025-1564-4(2)) Recorded Bks.

PMS Outlaws. unabr. ed. Sharyn McCrumb. Narrated by Barbara Rosenblat. 6 cass. (Running Time: 8 hrs. 45 mins.). (Elizabeth MacPherson Ser.: No. 9). 2002. 57.00 (978-0-7887-5012-0(7)) Recorded Bks.
Elizabeth, deeply troubled by the death of her husband, has checked into a mental institution for treatment. There, she meets a host of colorful patients, each with their own quirky point of view. Meanwhile, trouble is brewing at her brother Bill's law firm. He has just bought a mansion for himself and his partner, A.P. Hill, to set up their practice in. But A.P. cannot enjoy the new building as she is becoming obsessed with finding two women calling themselves the "PMS Outlaws".

PMS Relief. Eldon Taylor. 1 cass. (Running Time: 62 min.). (Inner Talk Ser.). 16.95 incl. script. (978-1-55978-143-5(2), 5364C) Progress Aware Res.
Soundtrack - Musical Themes with underlying subliminal affirmations.

PMS Relief: Babbling Brook. Eldon Taylor. 1 cass. 16.95 (978-1-55978-487-0(3), 5364F) Progress Aware Res.

PMS Relief: Harmonies. Eldon Taylor. Read by Eldon Taylor. Ed. by Leslie Brice. 1 cass. (Running Time: 1 hr.). 1992. 16.95 (978-1-56705-342-5(4)) Gateways Inst.
Self improvement.

PMS Relief: Ocean. Eldon Taylor. Read by Eldon Taylor. Ed. by Leslie Brice. 1 cass. (Running Time: 1 hr.). 1992. 16.95 (978-1-56705-343-2(2)) Gateways Inst.

***Pnin.** unabr. ed. Vladimir Nabokov. Read by Stefan Rudnicki. (Running Time: 6 hrs.). 2010. 39.97 (978-1-4418-7274-6(4), 9781441872746, Brinc Audio MP3 Lib); 39.97 (978-1-4418-7275-3(2), 9781441872753, BADLE); 19.99 (978-1-4418-7273-9(6), 9781441872739, Brilliance MP3); audio compact disk 59.97 (978-1-4418-7272-2(8), 9781441872722, BriAudCD Unabrid); audio compact disk 19.99 (978-1-4418-7271-5(X), 9781441872715, Bril Audio CD Unabri) Brilliance Audio.

Poacher's Son. unabr. ed. Paul Doiron. Read by John Bedford Lloyd. 7 CDs. (Running Time: 8 hrs. 30 mins. 0 sec.). 2010. audio compact disk 29.99 (978-1-4272-0896-5(4)) Pub: Macmill Audio. Dist(s): Macmillan

Pobre Ana -Song. (SPA.). (YA). 2003. audio compact disk (978-0-929724-77-5(1)) Command Performance.

***Pobre Ser Humano.** Charito Siuta. 2010. 20.00 (978-1-4507-1680-2(6)) Indep Pub IL.

Pocahontas. Melissa Manchester. 1 cass. (J). 5.58 Blisterpack. (DOVE 531) NewSound.

Pocahontas. Carole Marsh. 1 cass. (Read-Along Ser.). (J). bk. 7.99 (978-1-55723-739-2(5)); 11.99 Norelco. (978-1-55723-741-5(7)); audio compact disk 19.99 (978-1-55723-743-9(3)) W Disney Records.

Pocahontas. Carole Marsh. 1 cass. (Sing-Along Ser.). (J). (ps-3). 1995. bk. 11.99 (978-1-55723-745-3(X)); 11.99 (978-1-55723-740-8(9)); audio compact disk 19.99 CD. (978-1-55723-742-2(5)) W Disney Records.

Pocahontas. unabr. ed. Ingri Parin D'Aulaire & Edgar Parin D'Aulaire. 1 cass. (Running Time: 6 min.). (J). (gr. 3-5). 1992. pap. bk. 15.00 (6512-A) Spoken Arts.

Pocahontas: My Own Story. unabr. ed. John E. Smith. Narrated by Jonathan Reese. (Running Time: 3 hrs. 0 mins. 0 sec.). (Tantor Unabridged Classics Ser.). (ENG.). 2008. audio compact disk 17.99 (978-1-4001-0798-8(9)); audio compact disk 35.99 (978-1-4001-3798-5(5)) Pub: Tantor Media. Dist(s): IngramPubServ

Pocahontas: My Own Story. unabr. ed. John E. Smith. Read by Jonathan Reeser. (Running Time: 3 hrs. 0 mins. 0 sec.). (ENG.). 2008. audio compact disk 17.99 (978-1-4001-5798-3(6)) Pub: Tantor Media. Dist(s): IngramPubServ

Pocahontas: My Own Story. unabr. collector's ed. John E. Smith. Read by Jonathan Reese. 3 cass. (Running Time: 3 hrs.). 1995. 18.00 (978-0-7366-3105-1(4), 3781) Books on Tape.
Originally published in 1624, & modernized in 1907, Smith's account exposes the harsh realities that the settlers faced to survive: agitated Indians, & long, paralyzing winters.

Pocahontas: The Life & the Legend. unabr. ed. Frances Mossiker. Narrated by Flo Gibson. 11 cass. (Running Time: 14 hrs. 30 mins.). 1982. 91.00 (978-1-55690-419-6(3), 82045E7) Recorded Bks.
The story of America's First Lady, from the first fateful encounter to her ignominious death.

Pocahontas: The Spirit of Christmas. 1 cass. (J). (ps-3). 1995. 6.98 (978-1-55723-776-7(X)) W Disney Records.

Pocahontas: Who's Making that Sound? 1 cass. (My First Read Along Ser.). (J). bk. 7.99 (978-1-55723-961-7(4)) W Disney Records.

Pocahontas Play-Along. 1 cass. (J). (ps-3). 1995. bk. 22.78 (978-1-55723-744-6(1)) W Disney Records.

Pocahontas Read-Along. 1 cass. (J). 1995. 7.98 (978-1-55723-778-1(6)) W Disney Records.

Pocket Computer Primer. Hank Librach. 1982. 8.95 (978-0-686-87024-1(7)) Micro Text Pubns.

Pocket for Corduroy. Don Freeman. Illus. by Don Freeman. Read by Linda Terheyden. 1 cass. (Running Time: 30 mins.). (Corduroy Ser.). (J). (gr. k-1). 2000. pap. bk. 19.97 (978-0-7366-9202-1(9)) Books on Tape.
Tale of the further adventures of Corduroy, the popular stuffed teddy bear accompanies Lisa to a laundromat where he realizes that while he now has a button, he is missing a pocket.

Pocket for Corduroy. Don Freeman. Illus. by Don Freeman. 11 vols. (Running Time: 13 mins.). 1982. pap. bk. 35.95 (978-1-59112-795-6(5)); 9.95 (978-1-59112-109-1(4)); audio compact disk 12.95 (978-1-59112-792-5(0)) Live Oak Media.

Pocket for Corduroy. Don Freeman. Illus. by Don Freeman. 11 vols. (Running Time: 13 mins.). (J). 2004. pap. bk. 18.95 (978-1-59112-793-2(9)) Live Oak Media.

Pocket for Corduroy. Don Freeman. (Corduroy Ser.). (J). (gr. k-1). 1986. bk. 35.55 (978-0-676-31898-2(3)) SRA McGraw.

Pocket for Corduroy. unabr. ed. Don Freeman. 1 read-along cass. (Running Time: 13 min.). (Corduroy Ser.). (J). (gr. k-1). 1982. 9.95 Live Oak Media.
The further adventures of Corduroy. The stuffed teddy bear accompanies Lisa to a laundromat where he realizes that while he now has a button, he is missing a pocket.

Pocket for Corduroy. unabr. ed. Don Freeman. Illus. by Don Freeman. Read by Linda Terheyden. 11 vols. (Running Time: 13 mins.). (Corduroy Ser.). (J). (gr. k-1). 1982. bk. 25.95 (978-0-941078-17-7(5)); pap. bk. 16.95 (978-0-941078-15-3(9)); pap. bk. & stu. ed. 33.95 Reading Chest. (978-0-941078-16-0(7)) Live Oak Media.

Pocket for Corduroy & Corduroy. Don Freeman. Illus. by Don Freeman. 22 vols. (Running Time: 24 mins.). 1982. pap. bk. 34.95 (978-1-59112-843-4(9)) Live Oak Media.

Pocket Full of Miracles. Don J. Black. 2004. 9.95 (978-1-57734-666-1(1)) Covenant Comms.

Pocket Full of Miracles, Pt. 1. Don J. Black. 1 cass. 7.98 (978-1-55503-894-6(8), 06005187) Covenant Comms.
A collection of heart-warming true stories.

Pocket Full of Rye. Agatha Christie. Read by Rosalind Ayres. (Running Time: 24480 sec.). (Miss Marple Ser.: No. 8). 2007. 27.95 (978-1-57270-558-6(2)) Pub: Audio Partners. Dist(s): PerseuPGW

***Pocket Full of Rye.** Agatha Christie. Narrated by June Whitfield. 2 CDs. (Running Time: 1 hr. 30 mins. 0 sec.). (ENG., 2010. audio compact disk 24.95 (978-0-563-51035-2(8)) Pub: AudioGO. Dist(s): Perseus Dist

Pocket Full of Rye. unabr. ed. Agatha Christie. Narrated by Rosalind Ayres. 6 CDs. (Running Time: 24480 sec.). (Miss Marple Ser.: No. 8). (ENG.). 2007. audio compact disk 29.95 (978-1-57270-557-9(4)) Pub: AudioGO. Dist(s): Perseus Dist

Pocket Guide to Meditation Fundamentals. John J. Kelly & N. Tracy Childers. Read by John J. Kelly & N. Tracy Childers. 1 cass. (Running Time: 1 hr. 30 min.). 1997. 9.95 Incl. bk. scripts. (978-1-890639-01-3(X)) eSpirit Pub.

Pocket Idiot's Guide to Golf Rules & Etiquette. abr. ed. Jim Corbett. Narrated by Jonathon Marosz. (Running Time: 4 hrs. 0 mins. 0 sec.). (Pocket Idiot Guides). (ENG.). 2007. 11.19 (978-1-60814-338-2(4)); audio compact disk 15.99 (978-1-59859-219-1(X)) Oasis Audio.

Pocket Idiot's Guide to Investing in Mutual Funds. abr. ed. Lita Epstein. Read by Grover Gardner. (Pocket Idiot's Guides (Playaway) Ser.). 2007. 34.99 (978-1-60252-777-5(6)) Find a World.

Pocket Idiot's Guide to Investing in Mutual Funds. abr. ed. Lita Epstein. Narrated by Grover Gardner & Jonathon Marosz. (Pocket Idiot Guides). (ENG.). 2007. 11.19 (978-1-60814-339-9(2)) Oasis Audio.

Pocket Magic: Graphic Games for the Pocket Computer. Bill L. Behrendt. (YA). 1982. 8.95 (978-0-686-87025-8(5)) Micro Text Pubns.

Pocket Medical French. Russell Dollinger. 1997. 9.95 (978-0-945585-10-7(1)) Booksmythe.

Pocket Medical French Compact Disc. abr. ed. Russell K. Dollinger. (Running Time: 3600 sec.). (Pocket Medical Ser.). 2007. audio compact disk 10.95 (978-0-945585-26-8(8)) Booksmythe.

Pocket Medical Russian Compact Disc. abr. ed. Russell K. Dollinger. (Running Time: 3600 sec.). (Pocket Medical Ser.). 2007. audio compact disk 10.95 (978-0-945585-28-2(4)) Booksmythe.

Pocket Medical Spanish. Russell Dollinger. 1997. 9.95 (978-0-945585-08-4(X)) Booksmythe.

Pocket Medical Spanish Album. Russell Dollinger. 1992. bk. 19.95 (978-0-945585-09-1(8)) Booksmythe.

Pocket Medical Spanish Compact Disc. abr. ed. Russell K. Dollinger. (Running Time: 3600 sec.). (Pocket Medical Ser.). 2007. audio compact disk 10.95 (978-0-945585-24-4(1)) Booksmythe.

Pocket Proof of Facts: Proof of Facts & How to Deal with the Difficult Judge. Ronald Carlson. 1993. bk. 95.00 (978-0-614-06018-8(4)) Natl Prac Inst.

Pocket Proof of Facts: Proof of Facts & How to Deal with the Difficult Judge. Ronald Carlson. 1 cass. 1995. 29.95 bk. (4324) Natl Prac Inst.

Pocket Rhythms for Drums. Dirk Brand. 2005. spiral bd. 19.95 (978-3-89922-020-9(X)) AMA Verlag DEU.

Pocket Voice Bible: New Testament - NIV. Narrated by Steven B. Stevens. 2001. audio compact disk 89.99 (978-0-9718267-0-0(6)) Theo Tech Inc.

Pocketful of Praise. Arranged by Ken Bible. 1 cass. (Running Time: 1 hr.). (J). (gr. 3-7). 1987. 12.99 (TA-9085C) Lillenas.
A handy kids' songbook packed with 50 contemporary & traditional favorites. It is ideal as a group songbook anytime children sing - for Sunday School, children's church, Vacation Bible School, Christian schools or home use. All songs based on Scripture, with scripture references listed. The cassette is split-channel, thus making it suitable for listening, rehearsal or performance.

Poco. Perf. by Fred Penner. 1 cass. (J). (ps-5). 10.98 (978-0-945267-54-6(1), YM085-CN); audio compact disk 13.98 (978-0-945267-55-3(X), YM085-CD) Youngheart Mus.
Songs include: "If I Knew You Were Coming I'd Have Baked a Cake"; "Li'l Liza Jane"; "The Cat Came Back" (again); "Piggy Back Ride"; "The Bump"; "Poco"; "Ka-Lim-Ba"; "Never Smile at a Crocodile"; "Roller Skating"; "Joshua"; "The Rattlin' Bog" & more.

Poco a Poco. James M. Hendrickson. bk., stu. ed., lab manual ed. 110.05 (978-0-8384-0690-8(4)) Heinle.

Poco a Poco. 4th ed. James M. Hendrickson. 1.00 (978-0-8384-0941-1(5)); audio compact disk 23.25 (978-0-8384-0920-6(2)) Heinle.

Poco a Poco. 4th ed. James M. Hendrickson. (C). 30.95 (978-0-8384-8133-2(7)) Heinle.

Poco a Poco: Atajo 3.0. James M. Hendrickson. (C). bk. & lab manual ed. 169.95 (978-0-8384-8240-7(6)) Heinle.

Pod King: Uttered Thought Climatology. Poems. John M. Bennett. 1 cass. (Running Time: 60 min.). 1992. 6.00 (978-0-935350-35-7(7)) Luna Bisonte.
Audio performance of poetry with music & sound art - Avant Garde.

¿Podemos tener una mascota? Emergent Set A. Benchmark Education Staff. Ed. by Cynthia Swain. (Early Explorers Ser.). (J). 2008. audio compact disk 10.00 (978-1-60437-251-9(6)) Benchmark Educ.

Podemos usar monedas Audio CD: Emergent Set A. Benchmark Education Staff. Ed. by Tammy Jones. (Early Explorers Ser.). (J). 2008. audio compact disk 10.00 (978-1-60437-256-4(7)) Benchmark Educ.

Poder de la Mente. Carlos Gonzales & Dina Gonzales. 4 cass. (Running Time: 3 hrs.). (SPA.). 2000. 39.00 (978-1-56491-051-6(2)) Imagine Pubs.
Mental drills that enable the person to concentrate better, recall, sleep better & increase his emotional level.

Poder de la Mente. 4th ed. Carlos Gonzalez. 4 CDs. (Running Time: 2 hrs).Tr. of Power of the Mind. (SPA.). 2004. audio compact disk 49.00 (978-1-56491-121-6(7)) Imagine Pubs.

Poder de la Palabra. Louise L. Hay. 1 cass. (Running Time: 57 min.).Tr. of Power of Your Spoken Word: Change Your Negative Self-Talk & Create the Life You Want. (SPA.). 1994. 10.95 (978-84-7953-057-0(X), 234S) Hay House.
In her comfortable manner, Louise shows you how negative self-talk can create a mental atmosphere that attracts negative experiences. See how changing your words & thoughts can change your life for the better.

Poder de la Sensacion. Carlos Gonzalez. 4 CDs. (Running Time: 2 hrs.).Tr. of Power of Sensation. (SPA.). 2005. audio compact disk 49.00 (978-1-56491-125-4(X)) Imagine Pubs.

Poder de Mantenerse Enfocado. abr. ed. Jack L. Canfield et al. 5 cds. (Running Time: 18000 sec.). (SPA.). 2007. audio compact disk 24.95 (978-1-933499-61-1(3)) Fonolibro Inc.

Poder de Mantenerse Enfocado: Lo Que Saben los Mas Grandes Triunfadores Acerca de para la Seguridad Financiera y el Exito. abr. ed. Jack L. Canfield et al. Narrated by Jose Duarte. (SPA.). 2009. 59.99 (978-1-61545-561-4(2)) Find a World.

Poder del Ahora: Un Camino Hacia la Realizacion Espiritual. Eckhart Tolle. Read by Jose Manuel Vieira.Tr. of Power of Now: a Guide to Spiritual Enlightment. (SPA.). 2009. 59.99 (978-1-60775-711-5(7)) Find a World.

Poder del Ahora: Un Camino Hacia la Realizacion Espiritual. Eckhart Tolle. 6.Tr. of Power of Now: a Guide to Spiritual Enlightment. (SPA.). 2008. audio compact disk 24.95 (978-1-933499-66-6(4)) Fonolibro Inc.

Poder del Metabolismo. (SPA.). 2008. 29.95 (978-0-9788437-4-8(6)) F Suarez.

Poder del Pensamiento. Carlos Gonzalez. 1 CD. (Running Time: 40 mins). (SPA.). 2003. audio compact disk 15.00 (978-1-56491-110-0(1)) Imagine Pubs.

Poder del Pensamiento: (Power of Thought) Carlos González. Read by Carlos González. Ed. by Dina Gonzalez. 1 cass. (Running Time: 32 min.). (SPA.). 1991. 10.00 (978-1-56491-027-1(X)) Imagine Pubs.
In Spanish. It explains how thoughts act upon the persons life.

Poder del Pensamiento Positivo: El Programa Original Para el Exito Personal. Norman Vincent Peale. 5 cass. (Running Time: 6 hrs. 35 min.). (SPA.). 1997. 29.95 Set. (978-0-924967-38-2(2)) Intl Ctr Creat Think.

Poder en Contraste a la Fuerza: Los Determinantes Ocultos del Comportamiento Humano. David R. Hawkins. (SPA & ENG.). 2004. 14.95 (978-1-4019-0177-6(8), 1778) Hay House.

Poder en tu Boca. Victor Richards. 2007. audio compact disk 5.99 (978-1-933172-37-8(1)) Jayah Producc.

Poder Está en Ti. René González. 2002. 3.00 (978-0-8297-3555-0(0)); audio compact disk 4.00 (978-0-8297-3553-6(4)) Zondervan.

Poder Está en Ti. unabr. ed. René González. (SPA.). 2002. 9.99 (978-0-8297-3554-3(2)) Pub: Vida Pubs. Dist(s): Zondervan

Poder sin Limite en las Ventas. unabr. ed. Camilo Cruz. 3 cass. (Running Time: 3 hrs.). (SPA.). 2003. 26.00 (978-1-931059-03-9(9)) Taller del Exito.
In this program, which is directed mainly to the field of sales,you will discover different strategies and techniques to better sell your ideas, talents, products or services. Discover how to develop the qualities of successful sales professionals.

Poder y la Gloria. abr. ed. Graham Greene.Tr. of Power & the Glory. (SPA.). 2006. audio compact disk 17.00 (978-958-8218-67-0(5)) Pub: Yoyo Music COL. Dist(s): YoYoMusic

Podkayne of Mars. unabr. ed. Robert A. Heinlein. Read by Emily Janice Card. (Running Time: 6 hrs. 0 mins.). (ENG.). 2009. 29.95 (978-1-4332-5163-4(9)); 44.95 (978-1-4332-5160-3(4)); audio compact disk 55.00 (978-1-4332-5161-0(2)) Blckstn Audio.

Podre ser Lo Que Quiera. Steck-Vaughn Staff. (SPA.). 1999. (978-0-7398-0749-1(8)) SteckVau.

Poe & Irving. unabr. ed. Edgar Allan Poe & Washington Irving. Read by Lloyde Battista. Hosted by Peter Benchley. 2 cass. (Running Time: 2 hrs.). (Spencer Audio Theater Ser.). 1995. 20.95 Set, library ed. (978-1-883049-65-2(2)) Sound Room.
Musically scored dramatic readings of two classic stories: "The Fall of the House of Usher" & "The Phantom Island".

Poe by Dancing Beetle. Eugene Ely et al. 1 cass. (Running Time: 89 min.). (J). 1992. 10.00 Erthviibz.
Edgar Allen Poe, parody & nature sounds come together when Ms. Fire Toad & the spunky musical humans read & sing with Dancing Beetle.

Poe: Collected Stories & Poems: Collected Stories & Poems. Edgar Allan Poe. Read by Ralph Cosham. (Running Time: 6 hrs 30 mins.). 2004. 26.95 (978-1-59912-105-5(0), Audiofy Corp) Iofy Corp.

Poe Masterpieces. Edgar Allan Poe. Read by Edward Blake. 2 cass. (Running Time: 1 hr. 24 min.). 15.95 Set. (12157FA) Filmic Archives.
Includes: "The Pit & the Pendulum," & "The Fall of the House of Usher".

Poe Masterpieces, Set. unabr. ed. Edgar Allan Poe. Read by Edward Blake. 2 cass. (Cassette Bookshelf Ser.). 1987. 15.98 (978-0-8072-3466-2(4), CB122CX, Listening Lib) Random Audio Pubg.
Selections include: "The Pit & the Pendulum", "The Fall of the House of Usher".

Poe Shadow. abr. ed. Matthew Pearl. Read by Erik Singer. 2006. 17.95 (978-0-7435-5579-1(1), Audioworks) Pub: S&S Audio. Dist(s): S and S Inc

Poe Shadow. unabr. ed. Matthew Pearl. Read by Erik Singer. 13 CDs. (Running Time: 14 hrs.). 2006. audio compact disk 119.75 (978-1-4193-8042-6(7), C3633); 109.75 (978-1-4193-8040-2(0), 98296) Recorded Bks.
In this intricately crafted thriller, most people in 1849 Baltimore believe Edgar Allan Poe drank himself to death. But attorney Quentin Clark is determined to restore Poe's reputation, and he knows Poe's fictional detective, Auguste Dupin, was based on a real man. Putting everything on the line, Clark travels to France to track down the sleuth who can determine the true cause of Poe's death.

Poe Shadow. unabr. ed. Matthew Pearl. Read by Erik Singer. 2006. 29.95 (978-0-7435-5580-7(5), Audioworks) Pub: S&S Audio. Dist(s): S and S Inc

Poem see Poetry & Voice of Muriel Rukeyser

Poem see Gathering of Great Poetry for Children

Poem As Mask see Poetry & Voice of Muriel Rukeyser

Poem Circling Hamtramek, Michigan All Night in Search of You see Philip Levine

Poem in October see Dylan Thomas Reading His Poetry

Poem in October see Evening with Dylan Thomas

Poem in Prose see Twentieth-Century Poetry in English, No. 29, Recordings of Poets Reading Their Own Poetry

Poem on His Birthday see Dylan Thomas Reading: And Death Shall Have No Dominion and Other Poems

Poem on His Birthday see Dylan Thomas Reading His Poetry

Poem to a Rose see Twentieth-Century Poetry in English, No. 24, Recordings of Poets Reading Their Own Poetry

Poem to My Son: To Juan at the Winter Solstice see Caedmon Treasury of Modern Poets Reading Their Own Poetry

Poem to Negroes & Whites see Twentieth-Century Poetry in English, No. 24, Recordings of Poets Reading Their Own Poetry

Poem, What & How Does a Mean. Joseph Schwartz. 1 cass. (Running Time: 26 min.). 1969. 10.95 (23150) J Norton Pubs.
Schwartz encourages the reader of poetry to begin his understanding of a poem by attempting to paraphrase it.

Poemas del Alma, No. 3. Prod. by Luis Antonio Reyes.Tr. of Poems of the Soul. (SPA.). 2002. 8.95 (978-958-692-174-9(3)) Pub: Soc San Pablo COL. Dist(s): St Pauls Alba

Poemas y Palabras para la Reflexion, No. 3. Prod. by Luis Antonio Reyes.Tr. of Poems & Words to Reflect Upon. (SPA.). 2002. 8.95 (978-958-692-176-3(X)) Pub: Soc San Pablo COL. Dist(s): St Pauls Alba

Poemes Choisis. Poems. Paul Verlaine. Read by Marianne Valery. 1 cass. (FRE.). 1995. 19.95 (1729-LQP) Olivia & Hill.
Selection of poems including: Never More; Apres trois ans; Voeux; Lassitude; Mon reve familier; A une femme; L'Angoisse; Croquis parisien; Marines; Crepuscule du soir mystique; Promenade sentimentale; Chanson d'automne; L'Heure du berger, Le Rossignol; Sub urbe; En sourdine; Colloque sentimental; Ariettes oubliees; Sagesse; Kaliedoscope; Le Squelette; Art poetique; Langueur; Crimen amoris; Un Conte; Lucien Lelinois; Impression fausse; Autre; Tantalized; A Arthur Rimbaud.

Poemes Choisis, Set. Poems. Arthur Rimbaud. Read by Roger Blin et al. 2 cass. (FRE.). 1992. 26.95 (1605-RF); audio compact disk 44.95 CD. (1606-RF) Olivia & Hill.

Poems & Discussion. Jon Klimo. 1 cass. 9.00 (A0357-89) Sound Photosyn.
Ecstatic articulation, once improvised, now examined.

Poems & Hymn Tunes As Songs: Metrical Partners. Joseph Jones. 2 cass. 24.50 incl. wkbk & 1 blank cass. (S01560) J Norton Pubs.
This imaginative & innovative program employs well-known, "classic" poems in combination with hymn tunes & other tunes of various meters to demonstrate a creative method for new songs composition.

Poems & Letters of Emily Dickinson. abr. ed. Emily Dickinson. Read by Julie Harris. 1 cass. Incl. Because I Could Not Stop for Death. (CPN 1119); Before I Got My Eye Put Out. (CPN 1119); Bird Came down the Walk. (CPN 1119); Hope Is the Thing with Feathers. (CPN 1119); I Cannot Live with You. (CPN 1119); I Cautiously Scanned My Little Life. (CPN 1119); I Died for Beauty, but Was Scarce. (CPN 1119); I Heard a Fly Buzz When I Died. (CPN 1119); I Like to See It Lap up Miles. (CPN 1119); I Never Lost As Much but Twice. (CPN 1119); I Never Saw a Moor. (CPN 1119); I Reason, Earth Is Short. (CPN 1119); I Years Had Been from Home. (CPN 1119); If You Were Coming in the Fall. (CPN 1119); I'll Tell You How the Sun Rose. (CPN 1119); I'm Nobody! Who Are You? Poems of Emily Dickinson for Young People. Emily Dickinson. (CPN 1119); Love Is Anterior to Life. (CPN 1119); My Life Closed Twice Before Its Close. (CPN 1119); My River Runs to Thee. (CPN 1119); Narrow Fellow in the Grass. (CPN 1119); Pain Has an Element of Blank. (CPN 1119); Safe in Their Alabaster Chambers. (CPN 1119); Soul Selects Her Own Society. (CPN 1119); There Came a Wind, Like a Bugle. (CPN 1119); This Is My Letter to the World. (CPN 1119); To Fight Aloud Is Very Brave. (CPN 1119); To Make a Prairie It Takes a Clover & One Bee. (CPN 1119); Toad Can Die of Light! (CPN 1119); What Soft, Cherubic Creatures. (CPN 1119); 1991. 12.00 (978-0-89845-595-3(2), CPN 1119) HarperCollins Pubs.

Poems & Letters of Emily Dickinson. unabr. ed. Emily Dickinson. Read by Julie Harris. 1 cass. Incl. After Great Pain a Formal Feeling Comes. (CDL5 1119); Besides the Autumn Poets Sing. (CDL5 1119); Heart Asks Pleasure First. (CDL5 1119); I Dwell in Possibility. (CDL5 1119); I Felt a Funeral in My Brain. (CDL5 1119); I Taste a Liquor Never Brewed. (CDL5 1119); Letter to Dr. & Mrs. J. G. Holland, Summer 1862. (CDL5 1119); Letter to John L. Graves, April 1856. (CDL5 1119); Letter to Louise & Frances Norcross, July 1879. (CDL5 1119); Letter to Maria Whitney, Summer 1883. (CDL5 1119); Letter to Mrs. J. G. Holland, June 1884. (CDL5 1119); Letter to Otis P. Lord, December 3, 1882. (CDL5 1119); Letter to Sally Jenkins, December 1880. (CDL5 1119); Letter to Susan Gilbert Dickinson, October 1883. (CDL5 1119); Letter to T. W. Higginson, April 15, 1862. (CDL5 1119); Letter to T. W. Higginson, April 25, 1862. (CDL5 1119); Sky Is Low, the Clouds Are Mean. (CDL5 1119); There's a Certain Slant of Light. (CDL5 1119); 1985. 8.98 (CDL5 1119) HarperCollins Pubs.

Poems & Memories. W. B. Yeats. Read by Lennox Robinson. 1 cass. 10.95 (978-0-8045-0751-6(1), SAC 46-1) Spoken Arts.

Poems & Oratory Theme: Reader's Theater Classics Set A Read Aloud Think Aloud CD Rom. Compiled by Benchmark Education Staff. 2007. audio compact disk 10.00 (978-1-4108-8556-2(9)) Benchmark Educ.

Poems & Songs of Middle Earth. abr. ed. J. R. R. Tolkien. Perf. by J. R. R. Tolkien. 1 cass. 1984. 8.98 (978-0-89845-224-2(4), CP 1231) HarperCollins Pubs.

Poems & Words to Reflect Upon see Poemas y Palabras para la Reflexion

Poems by Emily Dickinson. Emily Dickinson. Read by Flo Gibson. 2 cass. (Running Time: 1 hr. per cass.). 1986. 7.95 Set, 30-day. Audio Bk Con.
This collection of poems by Emilly Dickinson is her "Letter to the World"; life, love, nature, time, & eternity are explored with keen insight.

Poems by Emily Dickinson. Emily Dickinson. Narrated by Flo Gibson. 2008. audio compact disk 16.95 (978-1-60646-027-6(7)) Audio Bk Con.

Poems by Emily Dickinson. Emily Dickinson. Narrated by Flo Gibson. 2008. audio compact disk 22.95 (978-1-60646-227-0(X)) Audio Bk Con.

Poems by Emily Dickinson. unabr. ed. Emily Dickinson. Read by Flo Gibson. 2 cass. (Running Time: 2 hrs.). 1986. (978-1-55685-024-0(7)) Audio Bk Con.
This collection of poems by Emilly Dickinson is her "Letter to the World"; life, love, nature, time & eternity are explored with keen insight.

Poems by the Bronte Sisters, Set. unabr. ed. Emily Brontë & Charlotte Brontë. Narrated by Flo Gibson. 2 cass. (Running Time: 2 hrs.). 1984. 14.95 (978-1-55685-023-3(9)) Audio Bk Con.
Charlotte, Emily & Anne examine life on the moors, romance & death in a series of lyric poems.

Poems for Patriarchs. Poems. Featuring Douglas W. Phillips. 3 cass. (Running Time: 3 hrs.). 2003. 21.00 (978-1-929241-58-3(5)) STL Dist NA.

Poems for Patriarchs. Douglas W. Phillips. 2003. audio compact disk 26.00 (978-1-929241-79-8(8)) STL Dist NA.

Poems for Piano: Poems (with Descriptive Music) Karla Carey. (Reflections in Thought, from Dawn to Dusk Ser.). 1988. 8.00 (978-1-55768-538-4(X)) LC Pub.

Poems for Refugees. Ed. by Pippa Haywood. 2 cass. 2002. (978-1-901768-76-3(7)); audio compact disk (978-1-901768-78-7(3)) CSA Telltapes GBR.

Poems for the Unborn Child see Poetry & Voice of Muriel Rukeyser

Poems from a Light in the Attic. Shel Silverstein. Perf. by Shel Silverstein. 1 cass. (J). 5.50 HarperCollins Pubs.
A cassette with foldout of poems & drawings.

Poems from Almost Tomorrow: The Poetry of Ray Nargis. Excerpts. Nargis Ray. Narrated by Nargis Ray. 1 CD. (Running Time: 1 hour). (ENG.). 2008. audio compact disk 15.95 (978-0-9801045-2-3(1)) Pub: Raven Prod MN. Dist(s): Adventure Pubns

Poems from an Ex-Queen of England. 2nd ed. Royalty Patrenia Turner. (Running Time: 30 mins.). 2006. 10.00 (978-1-59975-705-6(2)) Indep Pub IL.

Poems from Black Africa. unabr. ed. Read by James Earl Jones. Ed. by Langston Hughes. 1 cass. Incl. Africa's Plea. Roland Tombekai Dempster. (SWC 1315); Damage You Have Done. Ellis Ayitey Komey. (SWC 1315); Independence. Adebayo Faletti. (SWC 1315); Meaning of Africa. Abioseh Nicol. (SWC 1315); My Africa. Michael Dei-Anang. (SWC 1315); Oral Traditionals: Congolese: Paddling Song. Richard Rive. (SWC 1315); Oral Traditionals: Ethiopian: Trousers of Wind. Richard Rive. (SWC 1315); Oral Traditionals: Gabonese: The Little Bird. Richard Rive. (SWC 1315); Oral Traditionals: Ghanian: Foolish Child. Richard Rive. (SWC 1315); Oral Traditionals: Ghanian: Prayer for Every Day. Richard Rive. (SWC 1315); Oral Traditionals: Liberian: Nana Kru. (SWC 1315); Oral Traditionals: Malagasy: Half Sigh. Richard Rive. (SWC 1315); Oral Traditionals: Nigerian: O Lamb Give Me My Salt. Richard Rive. (SWC 1315); Oral Traditionals: South African: Absent Lover. Richard Rive. (SWC 1315); Oral Traditionals: South African: Keep It Dark. Richard Rive. (SWC 1315); Oral Traditionals: South African: Pass Office Song. Richard Rive. (SWC 1315); Oral Traditionals: South African: Shaka, King of the Zulus. Richard Rive. (SWC 1315); Oral Traditionals: South African: Six to Six. Richard Rive. (SWC 1315); Stanley Meets Mutesa. James D. Rubadin. (SWC 1315); Three Phases of Africa. Francis E. Parkes. (SWC 1315); Where the Rainbow Ends. Richard Rive. (SWC 1315); Poems from Black Africa. Read by James Earl Jones. Ed. by Langston Hughes. (SWC 1315); 1984. 12.95 (978-0-694-50210-3(3), SWC 1315) HarperCollins Pubs.

Poems from Doctor Zhivago. Boris Pasternak. Read by Tatiana Pobers. 1 cass., bklet. (Running Time: 60 mins.). (RUS.). 2000. 16.95 (SRU110) J Norton Pubs.
Twenty poems among the most imaginative in modern literature by a great artist equal in creative power to T. S. Eliot, Rilke & Paul Valery.

Poems from Doctor Zhivago. Boris Pasternak. Read by Tatiana Pobers. (RUS.). 11.95 (978-0-8045-0756-1(2), SAC 756) Spoken Arts.

Poems from Italy see Twentieth-Century Poetry in English, No. 27, Recordings of Poets Reading Their Own Poetry

Poems from Prison see Etheridge Knight

Poems from the Heart. Poems. Sandy Rochelle. Read by Sandy Rochelle. 1 cass. (Running Time: 25 min.). Dramatization. 1989. pap. bk. 10.00 (1-229-208); 6.00 (978-0-9635809-0-0(6)) S Rochelle Pub.
Sandy Rochelle, accomplished actress & award winning poet reveals through her relationships with her autistic, deaf son, her husband, father & self an intimate look at life exploring every emotion.

Poems from the Like Free Zone. Poems. Taylor Mali. 1 cass. (Running Time: 1 hr.). 2000. 10.00 (978-0-9648118-1-2(2)) Words Worth Ink.
Thirteen poems about teaching & love. Some explicit language.

Poems from the Shoebox. Nell Wiser. Narrated by Sonja Lanzener. (ENG.). 2007. audio compact disk 9.95 (978-1-60031-025-6(7)) Spoken Books.

Poems in Shapes: A Collection of Poetry in Shapes by Themes. Karen Jean Matsko Hood. 2006. audio compact disk 24.95 (978-1-59434-786-3(7)) Whsprng Pine.

Poems of D. H. Lawrence. unabr. ed. D. H. Lawrence. Read by Wendy Hiller. 1 cass. (Running Time: 36 min.). 10.95 (978-0-8045-1062-2(8), SAC 1062) Spoken Arts.
Twenty-four of Lawrence's poems are read.

Poems of Edna St. Vincent Millay. unabr. ed. Poems. Edna St. Vincent Millay. Read by David Frost & Dorothy Jacobson. 1 cass. (Running Time: 60 min.). (Poetic Heritage Ser.). 1981. 10.00 (103150) Summer Stream.

Poems of Elinor Wylie & Amy Lowell. unabr. ed. Poems. Elinor Wylie & Amy Lowell. Read by David Frost & Dorothy Jacobson. 1 cass. (Running Time: 60 min.). (Poetic Heritage Ser.). 1981. 10.00 (102180) Summer Stream.

Poems of Emily Dickinson. Emily Dickinson. Read by Nancy Wickwire. 1 cass. 10.95 (978-0-8045-0761-5(9), SAC 761) Spoken Arts.
These poems speak of the human endeavor.

Poems of Emily Dickinson & Lizette Woodworth Reese. unabr. ed. Poems. Emily Dickinson & Lizette Reese. Read by David Frost & Dorothy Jacobson. 1 cass. (Running Time: 60 min.). (Poetic Heritage Ser.). 1981. 10.00 (103290) Summer Stream.

Poems of Federico García Lorca. unabr. ed. Federico García Lorca. 2 cass. (Running Time: 3 hrs.). (SPA.). 1994. 22.95 (978-0-88432-513-0(X), SSP250) J Norton Pubs.
For the advanced listener. Includes notes.

Poems of James Dickey. James Dickey. Read by James Dickey. 1 cass. 10.95 (978-0-8045-0984-8(0), SAC 984) Spoken Arts.

Poems of Kabir. abr. ed. Poems. Read by Robert Bly. Tr. by Robert Bly. 2 cass. (Running Time: 2 hrs.). 1995. 16.95 (978-0-944993-04-0(4)) Audio Lit.
Kabir, a 15th-century Indian spiritual master, embraced both the Hindu & Sufi traditions, the poems are both provocative & intensely religious.

Poems of Lauris Edmond. Lauris Edmond. Read by Frances Edmonds. Music by Dorothy Buchanan. (ENG.). 2000. audio compact disk 24.95 (978-1-86940-234-1(0)) Pub: Auckland UniPr NZL. Dist(s): IPG Chicago

Poems of Love & Beauty. abr. ed. Read by Marvin Miller. 2 cass. 10.95 (978-0-89926-215-4(5)) Audio Bk.
A collection of 40 poems from the pens of Marlow, Milton, Browning, Shelly, Keates & Tennyson.

Poems of Miller Williams. Miller Williams. Read by Miller Williams. 10.95 (978-0-8045-1185-8(3), SAC 1160) Spoken Arts.

Poems of Mirabai. unabr. ed. Poems. Read by Robert Bly. Selected by Robert Bly. 1 cass. (Running Time: 1 hr. 30 min.). 1996. 12.95 (978-1-57453-079-7(8)) Audio Lit.
Mirabi was a much-beloved 16th-century Hindu mystic whose songs & poems declare her ecstatic love of God.

Poems of Patriotism. Mary M. Slappey. Read by Mary M. Slappey. (Running Time: 30 min). 1986. 10.00 Interspace Bks.

Poems of Richard Wilbur. Richard Wilbur. Read by Richard Wilbur. 1 cass. 10.95 (978-0-8045-0747-9(3), SAC 747) Spoken Arts.

Poems of Rumi. unabr. ed. Poems. Read by Robert Bly & Coleman Barks. Tr. by Robert Bly & Coleman Barks. 2 cass. (Running Time: 2 hrs. 30 min.). 1995. 16.95 (978-0-944993-10-1(9)) Audio Lit.
Versions of Rumi, accompanied by a group of creative musicians.

Poems of Sam Ragan. unabr. ed. Sam Ragan. Read by Sam Ragan. Ed. by Christopher King. Contrib. by Arthur L. Klein. 1 cass. (Running Time: 50 min.). 1986. 10.95 (978-0-8045-1170-4(5)) Spoken Arts.
Ragan reads from his three prize-winning collections of poetry: "The Tree in the Far Pasture," "To the Water's Edge," & "Journey into Morning".

Poems of Sara Teasdale & Margaret Widdemer. unabr. ed. Poems. Sara Teasdale & Margaret Widdemer. Read by David Frost & Dorothy Jacobson. 1 cass. (Running Time: 60 min.). (Poetic Heritage Ser.). 1981. 10.00 (103010) Summer Stream.

***Poems of St Therese of Lisieux.** unabr. ed. Narrated by Tavia Gilbert. (ENG.). 2010. 12.98 (978-1-59644-860-5(1), Hovel Audio); audio compact disk 12.98 (978-1-59644-933-6(0), Hovel Audio) christianaudio.

Poems of the Orient. 2 cass. (Running Time: 2 hrs.). 1998. 16.85 Set. (962634656-6) Ulvrscrft Audio.
The Rubaiyat of Omar Khayyam, with other poems by Rumi, Jami, Rabindranath Tagore, Byron, Shelley & Thomas Moore. The Rubaiyat, in the famous translation by Edward Fitzgerald, remains one of the most popular poems, expressing the fascination of Victorian England with the Orient.

Poems of the Orient. unabr. ed. Poems. Read by David Timson et al. Arranged by Naxos Audio Staff. 2 CDs. (Running Time: 2 hrs. 35 mins.). 1998. audio compact disk 15.98 (978-962-634-156-8(4), NA215612, Naxos AudioBooks) Naxos.
Vast in extent and inspired by, or from the Orient, includes the "Ruba' Iya't of Omar Khayyam" with other poems by Rumi, Sa'di, Hafiz, Jami, Baligh, Faiz, Iqbal, Sen, Tagore, Byron and Thomas Moore.

Poems of the Soul see Poemas del Alma

Poems of W. B. Yeats: A New Selection. W. B. Yeats. Read by W. B. Yeats. Perf. by Siobhan McKenna & Michael MacLiammoir. 1 cass. 10.95 (978-0-8045-0753-0(8), SAC 755) Spoken Arts.
Includes: "The Lake Isle of Innisfree" & "The Song of the Old Mother".

Poems on Slavery. Henry Wadsworth Longfellow. 2007. 22.95 (978-1-60402-361-9(9)) Indep Pub IL.

Poems, Selected. Nicolás Guillén. Read by Nicolás Guillén. 1 cass. (Running Time: 1 hr.). (Watershed Tapes of Contemporary Poetry). 1979. 11.95 (23624) J Norton Pubs.
One of Cuba's major poet reads his poems in Spanish.

Poems to a Brown Cricket see Poetry & Voice of James Wright

Poems to Love & the Body. Poems. Dave Malone. 1 CD. audio compact disk 12.00 (978-0-9667744-1-2(8)) Bliss Sta.

Poe's Children: The New Horror - An Anthology. unabr. abr. ed. Peter Straub. 12 CDs. (Running Time: 15 hrs. 30 mins.). (ENG.). 2008. audio compact disk 49.95 (978-0-7393-7599-0(7), Random AudioBks) Pub: Random Audio Pubg. Dist(s): Random

***Poe's Detective: The Detective Stories of Edgar Allan Poe.** Edgar Allan Poe. Narrated by Bronson Pinchot. (Running Time: 4 hrs. 0 mins. 0 sec.). (ENG.). 2011. audio compact disk 19.95 (978-1-60998-162-4(6)) Pub: AudioGO. Dist(s): Perseus Dist

Poe's Greatest Hits: Tales & Poems by the Master of Horror. Edgar Allan Poe. Read by Norman George. 2 cass. (Running Time: 2 hrs. 30 mins.). 2001. 19.95 (978-0-9711753-1-0(4)); audio compact disk 24.95 (978-0-9711753-0-3(6)) Logofon Record.
The best loved tales & poems.

Poe's Heart & the Mountain Climber: Exploring the Effect of Anxiety On. Richard Restak. Read by Scott Brick. 6 CDs. (Running Time: 1 hr.). 2004. audio compact disk 63.00 (978-1-4159-0776-4(5)) Books on Tape.

Poe's Heart & the Mountain Climber: Exploring the Effects of Anxiety. unabr. ed. Richard Restak. Read by Scott Brick. 5 cass. (Running Time: 7 hrs. 30 min.). 2004. 54.00 (978-1-4159-0365-0(4)) Books on Tape.
Bombarded by media feed about terrorism, war, and rising unemployment rates, and by an array of ads that urge us to "ask our doctor" about anti-anxiety medication, it feels as if this country is having a collective anxiety attack. In fact, anxiety is one.

Poesia para Oir. unabr. ed. Read by Carlos J. Vega. 3 CDs.Tr. of Poetry to Hear. (SPA.). 2002. audio compact disk 17.00 (978-958-9494-69-1(2)) YoYoMusic.

Poesia y Drama de Garcia Lorca. unabr. ed. Poems. Federico García Lorca. Perf. by Maria Douglas & Raul Dantes. 1 cass. Incl. Aire de Nocturno. (SWC 1067); Bodas de Sangre: Act Three, Part One, Last Scene. (SWC 1067); Burla de Don Pedro a Caballo. (SWC 1067); Cancion de Jinete. (SWC 1067); Ciudad sin Sueno. (SWC 1067); Encina. (SWC 1067); Encuentros de un Caracol Aventurero. (SWC 1067); Hora de Estrellas. (SWC 1067); Manana. (SWC 1067); Muerto de Amor. (SWC 1067); Narciso. (SWC 1067); Oda a Walt Whitman. (SWC 1067); Pequeno Vals Vienes. (SWC 1067); Prendimiento de Antonito el Camborio en el Camino de Sevilla. (SWC 1067); Romance de la Luna, Luna. (SWC 1067); Romance de la Pena Negra. (SWC 1067); Romance del Emplazado. (SWC 1067); Romance Sonambula. (SWC 1067); Sombra de Mi Alma. (SWC 1067); Vals en las Ramas. (SWC 1067); (SPA.). 1984. 12.95 (978-0-694-50054-3(2), SWC 1067) HarperCollins Pubs.

Poesies Choisies de Stéphane Mallarmé. Poems. Stephane Mallarmé. Read by A. Deviegue & A. Faraoun. 1 cass. (FRE.). 1991. 22.95 (1420-VSL) Olivia & Hill.
Reading of Mallarme's poetry.

Poet. abr. ed. Michael Connelly. Read by Buck Schirner. 3 CDs, Library ed. (Running Time: 3 hrs.). (Jack McEvoy Ser.: No. 1). 2003. audio compact disk 62.25 (978-1-59086-558-3(8), 1590865588, BAU) Brilliance Audio.
With his four Harry Bosch novels, Michael Connelly joined "the top rank of a new generation of crime writers" (Los Angeles Times). Now Connelly returns with his most searing thriller yet - a major new departure that recalls the best work of Thomas Harris ("Red Dragon," "Silence of the Lambs") and James Patterson ("Along Came a Spider"). Our hero is Jack McEvoy, a Rocky Mountain News crime-beat reporter. As the novel opens, Jack's twin brother, a Denver homicide detective, has just killed himself. Or so it seems. But when Jack begins to investigate the phenomenon of police suicides, a disturbing pattern emerges, and soon suspects that a serial murderer is at work - a devious cop killer who's left a coast-to-coast trail of "suicide notes" drawn from the poems of Edgar Allan Poe. It's the story of a lifetime - except that "the Poet" already seems to know that Jack is trailing him. . . Here is definitive proof that Michael Connelly is among the best suspense novelist working today.

Poet. abr. ed. Michael Connelly. Read by Buck Schirner. (Running Time: 3 hrs.). (Jack McEvoy Ser.: No. 1). 2010. audio compact disk 9.99 (978-1-4418-0829-5(9), 9781441808295, BCD Value Price) Brilliance Audio.

Poet. unabr. ed. Michael Connelly. Read by Buck Schirner. (Running Time: 15 hrs.). (Jack McEvoy Ser.: No. 1). 2004. 39.25 (978-1-59335-401-5(0), 1593354010, Brlnc Audio MP3 Lib) Brilliance Audio.

Poet. unabr. ed. Michael Connelly. Read by Buck Schirner. (Running Time: 15 hrs.). (Jack McEvoy Ser.: No. 1). 2004. 39.25 (978-1-59710-582-8(1), 1597105821, BADLE); 24.95 (978-1-59710-583-5(X), 159710583X, BAD) Brilliance Audio.

Poet. unabr. ed. Michael Connelly. Read by Buck Schirner. (Running Time: 54000 sec.). (Jack McEvoy Ser.: No. 1). 2006. audio compact disk 112.25 (978-1-4233-2324-2(6), 9781423323242, BriAudCD Unabrid); audio compact disk 38.95 (978-1-4233-2323-5(8), 9781423323235, Bril Audio CD Unabri) Brilliance Audio.

Poet. unabr. ed. Michael Connelly. Read by Buck Schirner. (Running Time: 15 hrs.). (Jack McEvoy Ser.: No. 1). 2004. 24.95 (978-1-59335-146-5(1), 1593351461) Soulmate Audio Bks.

Poet among Scientists. Robert Graves. 1 cass. (Running Time: 59 min.). 1965. 11.95 (33021) J Norton Pubs.
The poet discusses the difference between the scientist, who focuses on analysis & classification of external fact, & the poet, who concentrates on the discovery of internal truth.

Poet & His Vulture. Gilbert Highet. Read by Gilbert Highet. 1 cass. (Running Time: 30 min.). 11.95 (23288-A) J Norton Pubs.

Poet & the Lunatics. unabr. ed. G. K. Chesterton. Read by Frederick Davidson. 5 cass. (Running Time: 7 hrs. 30 min.). 1989. 39.95 (978-0-7861-0085-9(0), 1078) Blckstn Audio.
Gabriel Gale is a poet. He is also remarkably similar to the "late" Father Brown, whose apparent simple-mindedness masks his extraordinary mental percipience. He solves complex crimes by following moral clues & interpreting moral atmospheres. When various "lunatics" threaten to throw him into a lunatic asylum, one of his "mad" friends holds these scientists & modernists at bay while Gale escapes only to indulge in painting some satiric & entertaining portraits of his enemies.

Poet & the Lunatics. unabr. ed. G. K. Chesterton. Read by Peter Joyce. 5 cass. 1998. 47.95 Set. (978-1-86015-443-0(3)) T T Beeler.
A collection of stories, linked by hero Gabriel Gale, that deal with the struggle against bureaucratic monoliths.

Poet & the Musician. Gilbert Highet. Read by Gilbert Highet. 1 cass. (Running Time: 30 min.). 11.95 (23294-A) J Norton Pubs.

Poet & the Poem: Bastian Boettcher Poetry Rap Special. Ed. by William Gilcher & Cindy Comitz. Tr. by William Gilcher. Des. by Cindy Comitz. Intro. by Grace Cavalieri. 1 CD. (Running Time: 90 mins.). 2000. pap. bk. 15.00 (978-0-938572-29-9(6)) Bunny Crocodile.

Poet & the Urn. (23288-A) J Norton Pubs.

Poet As Translator: To Traduce or Transfigure. George Steiner. 1 cass. (Running Time: 1 hr. 7 min.). 1970. 13.95 (23149) J Norton Pubs.
Discussion of poetry as a language in itself.

Poet in Italy. (23284-A) J Norton Pubs.

Poet Josephine Miles see I'm Too Busy to Talk Now: Conversations with American Artists Over 70 Series

Poet of Sierra Flat see Luck of Roaring Camp & Other Stories

Poet of Tolstoy Park. unabr. ed. Sonny Brewer. Narrated by Rick Bragg. 10 CDs. (Running Time: 38700 sec.). 2006. audio compact disk 29.99 (978-1-4193-9720-2(6)) Recorded Bks.
This book is based on the true life of Henry Stuart. When the 67-year-old former professor finds out he is dying of tuberculosis, he vows to "learn in solitude how to save myself." He sets off for Fairhope, Alabama, with only the writings of his beloved Tolstoy for company. There, the barefoot poet builds himself a small hut and slowly becomes an inspiration for the rest of the utopian town. When his last few months become his last few years, Henry's attempt to understand death becomes a lesson on life.

***Poet Prince.** unabr. ed. Kathleen McGowan, pseud. Narrated by Cassandra Campbell. (Running Time: 15 hrs. 30 mins.). (Magdalene Line Ser.: Bk. 3). 2010. 20.99 (978-1-4001-8827-7(X)) Tantor Media.

***Poet Prince.** unabr. ed. Kathleen McGowan, pseud. Narrated by Cassandra Campbell. (Running Time: 16 hrs. 0 mins. 0 sec.). (Magdalene Line Ser.: Bk. 3). (ENG.). 2010. 29.99 (978-1-4001-6827-9(9)); audio compact disk 39.99 (978-1-4001-1827-4(1)) Pub: Tantor Media. Dist(s): IngramPubServ

***Poet Prince.** unabr. ed. Kathleen McGowan, pseud. Narrated by Cassandra Campbell. (Running Time: 16 hrs. 0 mins. 0 sec.). (Magdalene Line Ser.: Bk. 3). (ENG., 2010. audio compact disk 95.99 (978-1-4001-4827-1(8)) Pub: Tantor Media. Dist(s): IngramPubServ

***Poet Slave of Cuba: A Biography of Juan Francisco Manzano.** unabr. ed. Margarita Engle. 2 CDs. (Running Time: 2 hrs. 5 mins.). (YA). (gr. 7 up). 2009. audio compact disk 24.00 (978-0-307-58307-9(4), Listening Lib) Pub: Random Audio Pubg. Dist(s): Random

Poet Slave of Cuba: A Biography of Juan Francisco Manzano. unabr. ed. Margarita Engle. Read by Yesenia Cabrero et al. (ENG.). (J). (gr. 7). 2009. audio compact disk 22.00 (978-0-307-58305-5(8), Listening Lib) Pub: Random Audio Pubg. Dist(s): Random

Poet Stanley Kunitz see I'm Too Busy to Talk Now: Conversations with American Artists Over 70 Series

Poet the Dreamer. 1. 2002. audio compact disk 8.99 (978-0-9767430-0-2(0)) Museum Pr.

Poetas del Amor - Antologia de los Mas Bellos Poemas. unabr. ed. Read by Gaspar Ospina & Adelaida Espinoza. 3 CDs.Tr. of Poets of Love - An Anthology of the Most Beautiful Poems. (SPA.). 2001. audio compact disk 17.00 (978-958-9494-60-8(9)) YoYoMusic.

Poetas Románticos de América. abr. ed. Guillermo Valencia et al. Read by Fabio Camero. (SPA.). 2007. audio compact disk 17.00 (978-958-8218-97-7(7)) YoYoMusic.

Poetastic Ur-text. Poems. Lake Bob. 1 cass. 2002. 15.95 (978-0-9622531-2-6(X)) American Segment.

Poetic Forms: The List Poem, The Ode, The Prose Poem, The Sonnet, The Haiku, The Blues Poem, The Villanelle, The Ballad, The Acrostic, Free Verse. Hosted by Ron Padgett. 5 cass. (Running Time: 5 hrs.). 1988. 47.95 (978-0-915924-25-7(0)) Tchrs & Writers Coll.
Features interviews with contemporary poets on ten poetic forms ranging from the Sonnet to free verse.

Poetic Journey. Kelly Ryan. 2001. 12.95 (978-0-660-18322-0(6)) Canadian Broadcasting CAN.

Poetic Ministry (1999) 1999. 27.00 (978-1-59128-344-7(2)); 40.00 (978-1-59128-346-1(9)) Canon Pr ID.

Poetic Ribology CD Set. J/Vincent Washington. Music by George Hicks. 2007. audio compact disk 25.00 (978-1-4276-3175-6(1)) AardGP.

Poetic Sound 'n' Riddlins. Eric Fortmeyer, Sr.. Read by Eric Fortmeyer, Sr. 1 CD. (C). (gr. 6-12). 1999. audio compact disk 19.95 (978-1-928620-13-6(2), EFX-9991045-0388) AGI Prods.

Poetic Vision & Modern Literature. Stephen Spender. 1 cass. (Running Time: 53 min.). 1953. 11.95 (23001) J Norton Pubs.
A discussion of the view that the writers of the 20th century have been preoccupied with the endeavor to organize experience or to interpret contemporary life in visionary patterns.

***Poetic Wisdom (Audio Book)** Katherine Rodriquez. 2010. audio compact disk 12.95 (978-1-60031-077-5(X)) Infinity PubPA.

Poetical Sketches see Poetry of William Blake

Poetics of Peace: Vital Voices in Troubled Times. Michael Meade. Contrib. by Luis Rodriguez et al. 2 CDs. 2003. audio compact disk 23.95 (978-0-9716011-5-4(1)) Mosaic Multicult Found.

Poetry. 1 cass. (Running Time: 30 min.). (POR.). 11.95 (PR607) J Norton Pubs.
The words of contemporary Brazilian poets.

Poetry Album: A Collection of Works by Major Romantic & Victorian Poets. Narrated by Flo Gibson. (ENG.). 2007. audio compact disk 19.95 (978-1-55685-947-2(3)) Audio Bk Con.

Poetry Album Set: A Collection of Major British & American Poems. Read by Flo Gibson. 3 cass. (Running Time: 4 hrs.). 1996. 16.95 (978-1-55685-434-7(X)) Audio Bk Con.
Major works by thirty-seven great poets such as Browning, Burns, Byron, Coleridge, Dryden, Emerson, Goldsmith, Jonson, Keats, Milton, Pope, Tennyson, Whitman, Wordsworth, & Yeats.

Poetry Alive! Act 1. Poems. 1 cass. 1999. 17.95 Poetry Alive.
Twenty classic poems vigorously performed in digital sound with sizzling sound effects.

Poetry Alive! Act 2. Poems. 1 cass. 1999. 17.95 Poetry Alive.
Twenty-three classic poems vigorously performed in digital sound with sizzling sound effects.

Poetry & Imagination. Thomas Merton. 1 cass. (Running Time: 60 min.). (Rilke - Poet of Inwardness Ser.). 8.95 (AA2076) Credence Commun.
How the experience of inwardness in the poet is what the contemplative seeks.

Poetry & Reflections. unabr. ed. Langston Hughes. Perf. by Langston Hughes. 1 cass. Incl. Ballad of the Gypsy. (V1640); Cultural Exchange. (V1640); Dinner Guest: Me. (V1640); In Explanation of Our Times. (V1640); Intern at Provident Hospital. (V1640); Ku-Klux-Klan. (V1640); Mama & Daughter. (V1640); Merry Go-Round. 9 cass. (Running Time: 13 hrs. 30 min.). (V1640); Migrant. (V1640); Mulatto. (V1640); Negro Speaks of Rivers. (V1640); One Way Ticket. (V1640); Out of Work. (V1640); Puzzled. (V1640); Reads Kid Sleepy. (V1640); South. (V1640); Southern Mammy Sings. (V1640); Sylvester's Dying Bed. (V1640); Trumpet Player, Fifty-Second Street. (V1640); 1984. 11.95 (978-1-55994-092-4(1), V1640) HarperCollins Pubs.

Poetry & Religion, Set. Poems. George Santayana. Read by Robert L. Halvorson. 6 cass. (Running Time: 540 min.). 42.95 (84) Halvorson Assocs.

Poetry & Religious Experience. Thomas Merton. 1 cass. 1995. 8.95 (AA2804) Credence Commun.
Merton suggests that poetic experience is like religious experience. Without poetic experience we miss a lot of religious experience. Poetry enriches our interior life & our capacity to respond to God.

Poetry & the Unconscious. Duncan Howie. 1 cass. (Running Time: 20 min.). 1960. 11.95 (23152) J Norton Pubs.
Poetic creativity is discussed in terms of Freudian dreamwork.

Poetry & Voice of Galway Kinnell. unabr. ed. Poems. Galway Kinnell. Read by Galway Kinnell. 1 cass. Incl. Book of Nightmares: Under the Maud Moon. (SWC 1502); Call Across the Valley of Not-Knowing. (SWC 1502); Dead Shall Be Raised Incorruptible. (SWC 1502); Dear Stranger Extant in Memory by the Blue Juniata. (SWC 1502); Hen Flower. (SWC 1502); In the Hotel of Lost Light. (SWC 1502); Lastness. (SWC 1502); Little Sleep's-Head Sprouting Hair in the Moonlight. (SWC 1502); Path among the Stones. (SWC 1502); Shoes of Wandering. Galway Kinnell. (SWC 1502); 1984. 12.95 (978-0-694-50280-6(4), SWC 1502) HarperCollins Pubs.

Poetry & Voice of James Wright. unabr. ed. Poems. James Wright. 1 cass. Incl. As I Step over a Puddle. (SWC 1538); At Thomas Hardy's Birthplace. (SWC 1538); Autumn Begins. (SWC 1538); Before a Cashier's Window. (SWC 1538); Best Days. (SWC 1538); Blessing. (SWC 1538); Centenary Ode. (SWC 1538); City of Evenings. (SWC 1538); First Days. (SWC 1538); Hook. (SWC 1538); Lifting Legal Nets. (SWC 1538); Lights in the Hallway. (SWC 1538); Lying in a Hammock. (SWC 1538); Milkweed. (SWC 1538); Minneapolis Poem. (SWC 1538); My Grandmother's Ghost. (SWC 1538); Names in Monterchi: To Rachel. (SWC 1538); Northern Pike. (SWC 1538); Poems to a Brown Cricket. (SWC 1538); Saint Judas. (SWC 1538); Silent Angel. (SWC 1538); Stages on a Journey Westward. (SWC 1538); To the Evening Star. (SWC 1538); Trouble. (SWC 1538); Two Poems about President Harding. (SWC 1538); 1984. 12.95 (978-0-694-50293-6(6), SWC 1538) HarperCollins Pubs.

Poetry & Voice of Margaret Atwood. unabr. ed. Poems. Margaret Atwood. Read by Margaret Atwood. 1 cass. Incl. Animals in That Country. Margaret Atwood. (SWC 1537); At First I Was Given Centuries. (SWC 1537); At the Tourist Center in Boston. (SWC 1537); Book of Ancestors. (SWC 1537); Cyclops. (SWC 1537); Dreams of the Animals. (SWC 1537); Foundling. (SWC 1537); Game after Supper. (SWC 1537); Girl & Horse, 1928. (SWC 1537); Landlady. (SWC 1537); Late August. (SWC 1537); Midwinter, Presolstice. (SWC 1537); My Beautiful Wooden Leader. (SWC 1537); Power Politics. (SWC 1537); Roominghouse, Winter. (SWC 1537); Six A. M., Boston, Summer Sublet. (SWC 1537); Small Cabin. (SWC 1537); There Is Only One of Everything. (SWC 1537); They Are Hostile Nations. (SWC 1537); They Eat Out. (SWC 1537); They Were All Inaccurate. (SWC 1537); Tricks with Mirrors. (SWC 1537); We Are Hard on Each Other. (SWC 1537); You Are Happy. Margaret Atwood. (SWC 1537); You Refuse to Own Yourself. (SWC 1537); Younger Sister, Going Swimming. (SWC 1537); 1984. 12.95 (978-0-694-50292-9(8), SWC 1537) HarperCollins Pubs.

Poetry & Voice of Marilyn Hacker. unabr. ed. Poems. Marilyn Hacker. Read by Marilyn Hacker. 1 cass. Incl. Art of the Novel. (SWC 1501); Before the War. (SWC 1501); Cities. (SWC 1501); Conte. (SWC 1501); Dark Twin. (SWC 1501); Elegy for Janis Joplin. (SWC 1501); Exiles. (SWC 1501); For Elektra. (SWC 1501); Geographer (for Luther Thomas Cupp, 1947-1974) (SWC 1501); Navigators. (SWC 1501); Nightsong. (SWC 1501); Presentation Piece. (SWC 1501); Sea Coming Indoors. (SWC 1501); Somewhere in a Turret. (SWC 1501); 1984. 12.95 (978-0-694-50279-0(0), SWC 1501) HarperCollins Pubs.

Poetry & Voice of Muriel Rukeyser. abr. ed. Poems. Muriel Rukeyser. Read by Muriel Rukeyser. 1 cass. Incl. Are You Born? (SWC 1536); Ballad of Orange & Grape. (SWC 1536); Burning the Dreams. (SWC 1536); Columbus. (SWC 1536); Dam. (SWC 1536); Despisals. (SWC 1536); Dream Drumming. (SWC 1536); How We Did It. (SWC 1536); In Our Time. (SWC 1536); Looking at Each Other. (SWC 1536); Mother As Pitchfork. (SWC 1536); Night Feeding. (SWC 1536); No One Ever Walking. (SWC 1536); Orpheus. (SWC 1536); Poem. (SWC 1536); Poem As Mask. (SWC 1536); Poems for the Unborn Child. (SWC 1536); Rune. (SWC 1536); Song. (SWC 1536); Speed of Darkness. (SWC 1536); St. Roach. (SWC 1536); Then. (SWC 1536); This Morning. (SWC 1536); This Our Only Earth. (SWC 1536); To Be a Jew in the Twentieth Century. (SWC 1536); Waterlily: Fragile. (SWC 1536); Waterlily: The Long Body. (SWC 1536); 1984. 12.95 (978-0-694-50291-2(X), SWC 1536) HarperCollins Pubs.

Poetry & Voice of Ted Hughes. abr. ed. Ted Hughes. 1 cass. Incl. Bang-a Burning. 1985. (SWC 1535); Bride & Groom. 1985. (SWC 1535); Calves. 1985. (SWC 1535); Collision with the Earth. 1985. (SWC 1535); Dead Man Lies. 1985. (SWC 1535); Every Day the World. 1985. (SWC 1535); Hawk Roosting. 1985. (SWC 1535); His Legs Ran About. 1985. (SWC 1535); Icecrust & Snowflake. 1985. (SWC 1535); Jaguar. 1985. (SWC 1535); Mayday on Holderness. 1985. (SWC 1535); Once I Said Lightly. 1985. (SWC 1535); Otter. 1985. (SWC 1535); Pike. 1985. (SWC 1535); Primrose Petal's Edge. 1985. (SWC 1535); Retired Colonel. 1985. (SWC 1535); Sea Grieves. 1985. (SWC 1535); Six Young Men. 1985. (SWC 1535); Sunstroke. 1985. (SWC 1535); This Is the Maneater's Skull. 1985. (SWC 1535); Thought Fox: And Other Poems. Ted Hughes. 1985. (SWC 1535); View of a Pig. 1985. (SWC 1535); Waving Goodbye. 1985. (SWC 1535); What Will You Make of Half a Man. 1985. (SWC 1535); When the Still-Soft Eyelid. 1985. (SWC 1535); Wind. 1985. (SWC 1535); Pt. I. Sheep. 1985. (SWC 1535); 1984. 12.95 (978-0-694-50290-5(1), SWC 1535) HarperCollins Pubs.

***Poetry by elaine Gareis LIFE.** Elaine Gareis. 2008. audio compact disk (978-1-61584-591-0(7)) Indep Pub IL.

Poetry Collection, Vol. 1. unabr. ed. Poems. John Franklyn-Robbins et al. Narrated by William Blake et al. 1 cass. (Running Time: 1 hr.). 1997. 10.00 (978-0-7887-0540-3(7), 95215E7) Recorded Bks.
Brings out the power & music of poetry. Selections include immortal poems by 16th & 17th century British poets like Milton & Donne, & Romantic poets from Blake to Keats.

Poetry Collection, Vol. 2. unabr. ed. Poems. John Franklyn-Robbins et al. 2 cass. (Running Time: 1 hr. 45 mins.). 1998. 18.00 (978-0-7887-0660-8(8), 95216E7) Recorded Bks.
Enjoy works by the major Victorian poets & North America's greatest 19th century writers.

Poetry East & West. Robert Bly. Read by Robert Bly. 2 cass. (Running Time: 2 hrs. 22 min.). 1983. 18.00 (00302) Big Sur Tapes.
The first part of this reading focuses closely on the idea of the "Unborn Mind" and "the It", & their possible relationships to one another. The second half is a reading by the author accompanying himself on the Greek instrument, the bazouki.

Poetry Explained by Karla Kuskin. 2004. 8.95 (978-0-89719-924-7(3)); cass. & flmstrp 30.00 (978-0-89719-524-9(8)) Weston Woods.

Poetry-Face Off. Created by CBC Audio. (Running Time: 3600 sec.). (ENG.). 2007. audio compact disk 16.95 (978-0-660-19726-5(X)) Canadian Broadcasting CAN.

Poetry Face-off. Mary Pinkoski et al. (Running Time: 3600 sec.). (ENG.). 2008. audio compact disk 17.95 (978-0-660-19795-1(2), CBC Audio) Canadian Broadcasting CAN.

Poetry Face-off 2004. 2005. audio compact disk 15.95 (978-0-660-19317-5(5)) Canadian Broadcasting CAN.

Poetry Face-off 2006. Poems. 1 CD. (Running Time: 1 hr.). 2006. audio compact disk 16.95 (978-0-660-19555-1(0), CBC Audio) Canadian Broadcasting CAN.

Poetry for Children: Selected Poems by Lewis Carroll & Charles & Mary Lamb. Lewis Carroll, pseud et al. Narrated by Nita Moyer. 1 CD. (Running Time: 4 hrs. 17 mins.). (J). 2005. audio compact disk Rental 19.95 (978-0-9748692-3-0(6)) Access Dig Des.

Poetry for the Winter Season. abr. ed. Read by Sandra Douglas Weir et al. Ed. by Christina Hardyment. (Running Time: 8514 sec.). 2006. audio compact disk 17.98 (978-962-634-426-2(1), Naxos AudioBooks) Naxos.

***Poetry in Pink Fundraiser.** Karen Jean Matsko Hood. (ENG.). 2011. audio compact disk 24.95 (978-1-59434-311-7(X)) Whsprng Pine.

Poetry in Quest of God. Robert F. Morneau. 3 cass. (Running Time: 2 hrs. 41 min.). 1995. 27.95 Set. (TAH344) Alba Hse Comns.
Many notable authors are quoted, using examples of their works, to lead the listener to discover the intersection of spirituality & poetry found at the crossroads of these transcendentals. Magnificently evocative material for anyone wishing to discover & cultivate a fresh approach to the gifts of the spirit through the radiance of the imagination.

Poetry in Shapes: A Collection of Poetry in Shapes by Themes. Karen Jean Matsko Hood. 2006. 29.95 (978-1-59434-785-6(9)) Whsprng Pine.

Poetry in Spanish: An Anthology. Julio Cortázar. Read by Julio Cortázar. 8.95 avail. LP. (HPL 4) Lib Congress.
Recorded at the University of Oklahoma at Norman, Oklahoma, November 20, 1975 for the Archive of Hispanic Literature on Tape. Included are selections from Historia de cronopios y de famas.

Poetry in Spanish: An Anthology. Gabriela Mistral. Read by Gabriela Mistral. 8.95 (HPL 2) Lib Congress.
Poems read by the author at the Library of Congress, December 12, 1950, for the Archive of Hispanic Literature on Tape. Included are: Merciendo; Apegado a mi; Dormida; La casa; Una palabra & others.

Poetry in Spanish: An Anthology: El Contemplado: Tema con Variaciones. Read by Pedro Salinas. 8.95 (HPL 1) Lib Congress.
Read by its author, the famed Spanish poet, Pedro Salinas (1891-1951), this poem was originally recorded in the Library of Congress on December 24, 1946, for the Archive of Hispanic Literature on Tape.

Poetry in Spanish: An Anthology: Two Colombian Poets. Eduardo Carranza & German P. Garcia. Read by Eduardo Carranza & German P. Garcia. 8.95 avail. LP. (HPL 3) Lib Congress.
Eduardo Carranza, reading poetry in Bogota, Colombia, November 9, 1961. Included are Hacia la soledad; Los Angeles; Es el tiempo; El extranjero; & others & German Pardo Garcia, reading his poetry in Mexico City, May 5, 1960. Included are Clamor ante Edgar Poe; Signo de Espana; Honda amistad; Desnudez & others.

Poetry in the Making. George Baker & British Library Staff. (British Library - British Library Sound Archive Ser.). 2009. audio compact disk 25.00 (978-0-7123-0554-9(8)) Pub: Britis Library GBR. Dist(s): Chicago Distribution Ctr

Poetry in the 1950s Vol. 1: Homage to the Beat Generation. Poems. Robert Briggs. Read by Robert Briggs. Music by Stuart Fessant. Contrib. by Chelsea Johnson & Chel White. 1 cass., 1 CD. (Running Time: 1 hr. 16 min.). 1998. 9.95 (978-0-931191-16-9(5)) Rob Briggs.
A lecture & jazz-poetry reading.

Poetry, Music & Freedom, & Other Lectures. Jacques Cassidy. 3 cass. (Running Time: 3 hrs. 45 min.). (Of Man, the Island & the Continent Ser.: Vol. 2). (YA). 1993. 40.00 (978-1-889954-69-1(1)) J Cassidy Prodns.
Three lectures in aesthetics, the first two in poetry & song, the third, a lecture & poetic recital in song of the human spirit.

Poetry-Music of the Soul. John Bradshaw. (Running Time: 2640 sec.). 2008. audio compact disk 50.00 (978-1-57388-145-6(7)) J B Media.

Poetry of A Dramatic Presentation. Robinson Jeffers. Read by Rex Campbell et al. 2 cass. (Running Time: 2 hrs.). Dramatization. 1972. 18.00 (06101) Big Sur Tapes.
This 1972 celebration in Carmel, California contains many selections of Jeffers' poetry as well as insights & data on Jeffers the poet & Jeffers the man.

Poetry of Adrienne Rich. Adrienne Rich. Read by Adrienne Rich. 1 cass. (Running Time: 36 min.). (YM-YWHA Poetry Center Ser.). 1968. 10.95 (23203) J Norton Pubs.

Poetry of Allen Tate. Allen Tate. Read by Allen Tate. 1 cass. (Running Time: 19 min.). (YM-YWHA Poetry Center Ser.). 1964. 10.95 (23220) J Norton Pubs.

Poetry of Anne Sexton. Anne Sexton. Read by Anne Sexton. 1 cass. (Running Time: 35 min.). (YM-YWHA Poetry Center Ser.). 1964. 10.95 (23212) J Norton Pubs.

Poetry of Anthony Burgess. Anthony Burgess. Read by Anthony Burgess. 1 cass. (Running Time: 57 min.). (YM-YWHA Poetry Center Ser.). 1966. 10.95 (23246) J Norton Pubs.

Poetry of Barbara Howes. Barbara Howes. Read by Barbara Howes. 1 cass. (Running Time: 28 min.). (YM-YWHA Poetry Center Ser.). 1963. 10.95 (23175) J Norton Pubs.

Poetry of Benet. abr. ed. Stephen Vincent Benet. Perf. by Joseph Wiseman. 1 cass. Incl. Difference. (SWC 1401); Metropolitan Nightmare. (SWC 1401); Nightmare at Noon. (SWC 1401); Nightmare for Future Reference. (SWC 1401); Nightmare, with Angel. Stephen Gallagher. (SWC 1401); Notes to Be Left in a Cornerstone. (SWC 1401); Ode to Walt Whitman. (SWC 1401); Short Ode. (SWC 1401); Thomas Jefferson. (SWC 1401); 1985. 12.95 (978-0-694-50244-8(8), SWC 1401) HarperCollins Pubs.

Poetry of Benet. abr. ed. Stephen Vincent Benet. Read by Stephen Vincent Benet. Read by Joseph Wiseman. 1 cass. Incl. American Names. (SWC 1337); Ballad of William Sycamore. 1985. (SWC 1337); Daniel Boone. (SWC 1337); Death of Stonewall Jackson. 1985. (SWC 1337); Do You Remember Springfield? (SWC 1337); Dulce Ridentem. (SWC 1337); John James Audobon. (SWC 1337); Litany for Dictatorships. 1985. (SWC 1337); Minor Litany. (SWC 1337); Mountain Whippoorwill. (SWC 1337); Nightmare Number Three. (SWC 1337); Opening of the Battle of Gettysburg. 1985. (SWC 1337); Western Wagons. (SWC 1337); 1985. 12.95 (978-0-694-50217-2(0), SWC 1337) HarperCollins Pubs.

Poetry of Byron. unabr. ed. Poems. Byron. Perf. by Tyrone Power. 1 cass. Incl. Childe Harold's Pilgrimage: Cantos III & IV. (SWC 1042); Don Juan: Canto I. (SWC 1042); On This Day I Complete My Thirty-Sixth Year. (SWC 1042); She Walks in Beauty. (SWC 1042); 1984. 12.95 (978-0-694-50033-8(X), SWC 1042) HarperCollins Pubs.

Poetry of C. Day Lewis. Cecil Day Lewis. Read by Cecil Day Lewis. 1 cass. (Running Time: 53 min.). (YM-YWHA Poetry Center Ser.). 1965. 10.95 (23184) J Norton Pubs.

Poetry of Coleridge. unabr. ed. Samuel Taylor Coleridge. Perf. by Ralph Richardson. 1 cass. Incl. Dejection: An Ode. (SWC 1092); Frost at Midnight. (SWC 1092); Kubla Khan. (SWC 1092); Rime of the Ancient Mariner. (SWC 1092); This Lime-Tree Bower My Prison. (SWC 1092); 1984. 12.95 (978-0-694-50071-0(2), SWC 1092) HarperCollins Pubs.

Poetry of Countee Cullen. abr. ed. Countee Cullen. Perf. by Ruby Dee & Ossie Davis. 1 cass. Incl. Black Christ. (SWC 1400); For a Poet. (SWC 1400); For Paul Laurence Dunbar. (SWC 1400); Heritage. (SWC 1400); Incident. (SWC 1400); Karenge ya Marenge. (SWC 1400); Pagan Prayer. (SWC 1400); Saturday's Child. (SWC 1400); Scottsboro, Too, Is Worth Its Song. (SWC 1400); Simon the Cyrenian Speaks. (SWC 1400); Tableau. (SWC 1400); To Certain Critics. (SWC 1400); Yet Do I Marvel. (SWC 1400); 1984. 12.95 (SWC 1400) HarperCollins Pubs.

Poetry of Dan Jacobson. Dan Jacobson. Read by Dan Jacobson. 1 cass. (Running Time: 37 min.). (YM-YWHA Poetry Center Ser.). 1966. 10.95 (23177) J Norton Pubs.

Poetry of Dannie Abse. Dannie Abse. Read by Dannie Abse. 1 cass. (Running Time: 50 min.). (YM-YWHA Poetry Center Ser.). 1964. 10.95 (23156) J Norton Pubs.

Poetry of Daryl Hine. Daryl Hine. Read by Daryl Hine. 1 cass. (Running Time: 27 min.). (YM-YWHA Poetry Center Ser.). 1967. 10.95 (23172) J Norton Pubs.

Poetry of Denise Levertov. Denise Levertov. Read by Denise Levertov. 1 cass. (Running Time: 37 min.). (YM-YWHA Poetry Center Ser.). 1965. 10.95 (23183) J Norton Pubs.

Poetry of Dennis Schmitz. Dennis Schmitz. Read by Dennis Schmitz. 1 cass. (Running Time: 20 min.). (YM-YWHA Poetry Center Ser.). 1968. 10.95 (23210) J Norton Pubs.

Poetry of Donald Hall. Donald Hall. Read by Donald Hall. 1 cass. (Running Time: 26 min.). (YM-YWHA Poetry Center Ser.). 1964. 10.95 (23169) J Norton Pubs.

Poetry of Earth - Robinson Jeffers. unabr. ed. Robinson Jeffers. Read by William Everson. 1 cass. (Running Time: 47 min.). 1970. 10.95 (06103) Big Sur Tapes.
Everson pays tribute to Jeffers' influence in the literary world & to the relevance of his thought & insight to mounting ecological dilemma.

Poetry of Edgar Allan Poe, Vol. 2. unabr. abr. ed. Edgar Allan Poe. Perf. by Christopher Cazenove et al. 1 cass. (Running Time: 90 mins.). 2004. 15.00 (978-1-59007-032-1(1)); 15.00 (978-1-59007-033-8(X)) Pub: New Millenn Enter. Dist(s): PerseuPGW
Poe's poems, more personal than his prose, explore the themes of love, death and despair, reflecting the anguish he suffered throughout his own short, troubled life.

Poetry of Edna St. Vincent Millay. abr. ed. Edna St. Vincent Millay. Perf. by Judith Anderson. 1 cass. Incl. Anguish. (SWC 1024); Assault. (SWC 1024); Cap d'Antibes: Let You Not Say of Me When I Am Old. (SWC 1024); Cap d'Antibes: Moon, That Against the Lintel of the West. (SWC 1024); City Trees. (SWC 1024); Curse. (SWC 1024); I Know I Am But Summer to Your Heart. (SWC 1024); Love Is Not All. (SWC 1024); Mindful of You the Sodden Earth in Spring. (SWC 1024); Moriturus. (SWC 1024); New England Spring, 1942. (SWC 1024); Not in This Chamber Only at My Birth. (SWC 1024); Now by the Path I Climbed I Journey Back. (SWC 1024); O Think Not I Am Faithful to a Vow. (SWC 1024); Parsi Woman: Now Sits the Autumn Cricket in the Grass. (SWC 1024); Parsi Woman: What Rider Spurs Him from the Darkening East. (SWC 1024); Plum Gatherer (poem) (SWC 1024); Renascence. (SWC 1024); Spring: Where Can the Heart Be Hidden in the Ground. (SWC 1024); Thou Art Not Lovelier Than Lilacs, No. (SWC 1024); Wild Swans. (SWC 1024); 1984. 12.95 (978-0-694-50020-8(8), SWC 1024) HarperCollins Pubs.

Poetry of Edward Dahlberg. Edward Dahlberg. Read by Edward Dahlberg. 1 cass. (Running Time: 41 min.). (YM-YWHA Poetry Center Ser.). 10.95 (23252) J Norton Pubs.

Poetry of Galway Kinnell. Galway Kinnell. Read by Galway Kinnell. 1 cass. (Running Time: 33 min.). (YM-YWHA Poetry Center Ser.). 1965. 10.95 (23179) J Norton Pubs.

Poetry of Geoffrey. unabr. ed. Geoffrey Hill. 1 cass. Incl. After Cumae. (SWC 1597); Annunciations. (SWC 1597); Canticle for Good Friday. (SWC 1597); Distant Battle of Drake's Drum. (SWC 1597); Funeral Music. (SWC 1597); Genesis. 1996. (SWC 1597); God's Little Mountain. (SWC 1597); Guardians. (SWC 1597); Imaginative Life. (SWC 1597); Locust Songs. (SWC 1597); Mercia Hymns. (SWC 1597); Merlin. (SWC 1597); Of Commerce & Society. (SWC 1597); Orpheus & Eurydice. (SWC 1597); Ovid in the Third Reich. (SWC 1597); Picture of a Nativity. (SWC 1597); Prayer to the Sun. (SWC 1597); Requiem for the Plantagenet Kings. (SWC 1597); Soliloquies. (SWC 1597); Solomon's Mines. (SWC 1597); Songbook of Arrurruz. (SWC 1597); Three Baroque Meditations. (SWC 1597); To the Supposed Patron. (SWC 1597); Two Formal Elegies. (SWC 1597); Wreaths. (SWC 1597); 1979. 14.00 (978-0-694-50322-3(3), SWC 1597) HarperCollins Pubs.

Poetry of George Oppen. George Oppen. Read by George Oppen. 1 cass. (Running Time: 29 min.). (YM-YWHA Poetry Center Ser.). 1967. 10.95 (23196) J Norton Pubs.

Poetry of George P. Elliott. George P. Elliott. Read by George P. Elliott. 1 cass. (Running Time: 32 min.). (YM-YWHA Poetry Ser.). 1964. 10.95 (23258) J Norton Pubs.

Poetry of Hart Crane. unabr. ed. Poems. Hart Crane. Perf. by Tennessee Williams. 1 cass. Incl. Bridge: To Brooklyn Bridge. (SWC 1206); Broken Tower. (SWC 1206); Cutty Sark. (SWC 1206); Eternity. (SWC 1206); Hurricane. (SWC 1206); Key West. (SWC 1206); My Grandmother's Love Letters (poem) (SWC 1206); O Carib Isle. (SWC 1206); Phantom Bark. (SWC 1206); Powhatan's Daughter: The Harbor Dawn, The Dance, Indiana. (SWC 1206); Praise for an Urn. (SWC 1206); Royal Palm. (SWC 1206); Three Songs (Southern Cross) (SWC 1206); White Buildings: Legend. (SWC 1206); Pts. III & IV. Voyages. (SWC 1206); 1984. 12.95 (978-0-694-50156-4(5), SWC 1206) HarperCollins Pubs.

Poetry of Hortense Calisher. Hortense Calisher. Read by Hortense Calisher. 1 cass. (Running Time: 1 hr. 10 min.). (YM-YWHA Poetry Center Ser.). 1963. 13.75 (23246) J Norton Pubs.

Poetry of Howard Moss. Howard Moss. Read by Howard Moss. 1 cass. (Running Time: 38 min.). (YM-YWHA Poetry Center Ser.). 1967. 10.95 (23192) J Norton Pubs.

Poetry of Howard Nemerov, Pt. I. Howard Nemerov. Read by Howard Nemerov. 1 cass. (Running Time: 1 hr. 14 min.). (YM-YWHA Poetry Center Ser.). 1962. 13.75 (23194) J Norton Pubs.

Poetry of Howard Nemerov, Pt. II. Howard Nemerov. Read by Howard Nemerov. 1 cass. (Running Time: 39 min.). (YM-YWHA Poetry Center Ser.). 1965. 10.95 (23195) J Norton Pubs.

Poetry of Hugh Macdiarmid. Hugh MacDiarmid. Read by Hugh MacDiarmid. 1 cass. (Running Time: 23 min). (YM-YWHA Poetry Center Ser.). 1967. 11.95 (23189) J Norton Pubs.

Poetry of Irving Feldman. Irving Feldman. Read by Irving Feldman. 1 cass. (Running Time: 43 min.). (YM-YWHA Poetry Center Ser.). 1965. 10.95 (23260) J Norton Pubs.

Poetry of Isabella Gardner. Isabella Gardner. Read by Isabella Gardner. 1 cass. (Running Time: 15 min.). (YM-YWHA Poetry Center Ser.). 1964. 10.95 (23164) J Norton Pubs.

Poetry of Isabella Gardner. Isabella Gardner. Read by Isabella Gardner. 1 cass. (Running Time: 36 min.). (YM-YWHA Poetry Ser.). 1967. 10.95 (23165) J Norton Pubs.

Poetry of Jack Marshall. Jack Marshall. Read by Jack Marshall. 1 cass. (Running Time: 23 min.). (YM-YWHA Poetry Center Ser.). 1964. 10.95 (23191) J Norton Pubs.

Poetry of James T. Farrell. James T. Farrell. Read by James T. Farrell. 1 cass. (Running Time: 44 min.). (YM-YWHA Poetry Center Ser.). 1964. 10.95 (25259) J Norton Pubs.

Poetry of James Tate. James Tate. Read by James Tate. 1 cass. (Running Time: 27 min.). (YM-YWHA Poetry Center Ser.). 1967. 10.95 (23221) J Norton Pubs.

Poetry of Jean Garrigue. Jean Garrigue. Read by Jean Garrigue. 1 cass. (Running Time: 28 min.). (YM-YWHA Poetry Center Ser.). 1965. 10.95 (23166) J Norton Pubs.

Poetry of John Ashbery. John Ashbery. Read by John Ashbery. 1 cass. (Running Time: 39 min.). (YM-YWHA Poetry Center Ser.). 1967. 10.95 (23157) J Norton Pubs.

Poetry of John Barth. John Barth. Read by John Barth. 1 cass. (Running Time: 38 min.). (YM-YWHA Poetry Ser.). 1967. 10.95 (23162) J Norton Pubs.

Poetry of John Cheever. John Cheever. Read by John Cheever. 1 cass. (Running Time: 27 min.). (YM-YWHA Poetry Center Ser.). 1964. 10.95 (23249) J Norton Pubs.

Poetry of John Ciardi. John Ciardi. Read by John Ciardi. 1 cass. (Running Time: 56 min.). (YM-YWHA Poetry Center Ser.). 1964. 10.95 (23250) J Norton Pubs.

Poetry of John Dryden. unabr. ed. John Dryden. Perf. by Paul Scofield. 1 cass. Incl. Absalom & Achitophel. (SWC 1125); Alexander's Feast, or, The Power of Music: An Ode in Honor of St. Cecilia's Day. (SWC 1125); Evening's Love: Prologue. (SWC 1125); I Feed a Flame Within. (SWC 1125); Man of Mode: Epilogue. (SWC 1125); To the Memory of Mr. Oldham. (SWC 1125); Whilst Alexis Lay Press'd. (SWC 1125); Zambra Dance. (SWC 1125); (J). 1984. 12.95 (978-0-694-50092-5(5), SWC 1125) HarperCollins Pubs.

Poetry of John Hall Wheelock. John H. Wheelock. Read by John H. Wheelock. 1 cass. (Running Time: 55 min.). (YM-YWHA Poetry Center Ser.). 1964. 10.95 (23235) J Norton Pubs.

Poetry of John Hollander. John Hollander. Read by John Hollander. 1 cass. (Running Time: 29 min.). (YM-YWHA Poetry Center Ser.). 1967. 10.95 (23173) J Norton Pubs.

Poetry of John Malcolm Brinnin. John M. Brinnin. Read by John M. Brinnin. 1 cass. (Running Time: 38 min.). (YM-YWHA Poetry Ser.). 1964. 10.95 (23244) J Norton Pubs.

Poetry of John Milton. unabr. ed. Poems. John Milton. Perf. by Anthony Quayle. 1 cass. Incl. Allegro. (SWC 1259); How Soon Hath Time... (SWC 1259); Lycidas. (SWC 1259); On Shakespeare. (SWC 1259); On the Morning of Christ's Nativity. (SWC 1259); Penseroso. (SWC 1259); When I Consider How My Light is Spent (Sonnet on His blindness) (SWC 1259); Lines 1-109. Samson Agonistes. (SWC 1259); Lines 976-1023. Comus. (SWC 1259); 1984. 12.95 (978-0-694-50183-0(2), SWC 1259) HarperCollins Pubs.

Poetry of John Updike. John Updike. Read by John Updike. 1 cass. (Running Time: 47 min.). (YM-YWHA Poetry Center Ser.). 1967. 10.95 (23225) J Norton Pubs.

Poetry of John Wain. John Wain. Read by John Wain. 1 cass. (Running Time: 29 min.). (YM-YWHA Poetry Center Ser.). 1965. 11.95 (23229) J Norton Pubs.

Poetry of John Wieners. John Wieners. Read by John Wieners. 1 cass. (Running Time: 55 min.). (YM-YWHA Poetry Center Ser.). 1966. 10.95 (23236) J Norton Pubs.

Poetry of Kathleen Fraser. Kathleen Fraser. Read by Kathleen Fraser. 1 cass. (Running Time: 15 min.). (YM-YWHA Poetry Center Ser.). 1964. 10.95 (23262) J Norton Pubs.

Poetry of Keats. abr. ed. Poems. John Keats. Read by Ralph Richardson. 1 cass. (Running Time: 90 min.). 1996. 12.00 (978-0-694-51706-0(2), CPN 1087) HarperCollins Pubs.

Poetry of Keats. unabr. ed. Poems. John Keats. Perf. by Ralph Richardson. 1 cass. Incl. Belle Dame sans Merci. (SWC 1087); Bright Star! Would I Were As Steadfast As Thou Art. (SWC 1087); Endymion: Hymn to Pan. (SWC 1087); Eve of St. Agnes. (SWC 1087); Keen, Fitful Gusts Are Whispering. (SWC 1087); Lines on the Mermaid Tavern. (SWC 1087); Ode on a Grecian Urn. (SWC 1087); Ode on Melancholy. (SWC 1087); Ode to a Nightingale. (SWC 1087); On First Looking into Chapman's Homer. (SWC 1087); Song about Myself. (SWC 1087); When I Have Fears That I May Cease to Be. (SWC 1087); 1984. 12.95 (978-0-694-50069-7(0), SWC 1087) HarperCollins Pubs.

Poetry of Langston Hughes. unabr. ed. Poems. Langston Hughes. Perf. by Ruby Dee & Ossie Davis. 1 cass. Incl. Aunt Sue's Stories. (SWC 1272); Ballad of the Landlord. (SWC 1272); Dead in There. (SWC 1272); Deferred. (SWC 1272); Dream Boogie. (SWC 1272); Dream Variations. (SWC 1272); Juke Box Love Song. (SWC 1272); Life Is Fine. (SWC 1272); Lincoln Theatre. (SWC 1272); Little Old Letter. (SWC 1272); Madam & the Census Man. (SWC 1272); Madam & the Rent Man. (SWC 1272); Me & the Mule. (SWC 1272); Midwinter Blues. (SWC 1272); Motto. (SWC 1272); Negro Servant. (SWC 1272); Negro Speaks of Rivers. (SWC 1272); Night: Four Songs. (SWC 1272); Not a Movie. (SWC 1272); Parade. (SWC 1272); Puzzled. (SWC 1272); Refugee in America. (SWC 1272); Song for a Dark Girl. (SWC 1272); Song for Billie Holliday. (SWC 1272); Southern Mammy Sings. (SWC 1272); Too Blue. (SWC 1272); Vari-Colored Song. (SWC 1272); When Sue Wears Red. (SWC 1272); Who But the Lord? (SWC 1272); 1984. 8.98 (978-0-694-50189-2(1), SWC 1272) HarperCollins Pubs.

Poetry of Laurence Lieberman. Laurence Lieberman. Read by Laurence Lieberman. 1 cass. (Running Time: 28 min.). (YM-YWHA Poetry Center Ser.). 1969. 11.95 (23185) J Norton Pubs.

Poetry of Loren Eiseley. Loren C. Eiseley. Read by Loren C. Eiseley. 1 cass. (Running Time: 51 min.). (YM-YWHA Poetry Center Ser.). 1968. 10.95 (23257) J Norton Pubs.

Poetry of Louis Untermeyer. Louis Untermeyer. Read by Louis Untermeyer. 1 cass. (Running Time: 40 min.). (YM-YWHA Poetry Center Ser.). 1966. 10.95 (23224) J Norton Pubs.

Poetry of Madness. unabr. ed. Poems. Alan Watts et al. 2 cass. (Running Time: 1 hr. 57 min.). 1968. 18.00 Set. (02509) Big Sur Tapes.
Beat poet Ginsberg gives a fiery poetic presentation of madness; Watts & John Perry, through poetic prose, make comprehensible the fluid, non-ordinary nature of madness as a means to growth & integration. Naranjo warns against embracing wild madness uncritically.

Poetry of May Swenson. May Swenson. Read by May Swenson. 1 cass. (Running Time: 32 min.). (YM-YWHA Poetry Center Ser.). 1963. 10.95 (23239) J Norton Pubs.

Poetry of Melville Cane. Melville Cane. Read by Melville Cane. 1 cass. (Running Time: 38 min.). (YM-YWHA Poetry Center Ser.). 10.95 (23248) J Norton Pubs.

Poetry of Michael Goldman. Michael Goldman. Read by Michael Goldman. 1 cass. (Running Time: 40 min). (YM-YWHA Poetry Center Ser.). 1965. 10.95 (23168) J Norton Pubs.

Poetry of Michael Hamburger. Michael Hamburger, pseud. Read by Michael Hamburger, pseud. 1 cass. (Running Time: 30 min.). (YM-YWHA Poetry Center Ser.). 1966. 10.95 (23170) J Norton Pubs.

Poetry of Micheal Dennis Browne. Micheal D. Browne. Read by Micheal D. Browne. 1 cass. (Running Time: 23 min.). (YM-YWHA Poetry Center Ser.). 1968. 10.95 (23245) J Norton Pubs.

Poetry of Miller Williams. Miller Williams. Read by Miller Williams. 1 cass. (Running Time: 26 min). (YM-YWHA Poetry Center Ser.). 1969. 10.95 (23237) J Norton Pubs.

Poetry of Muriel Rukeyser, Pt. I. Muriel Rukeyser. Read by Muriel Rukeyser. 1 cass. (Running Time: 45 min.). (YM-YWHA Poetry Center Ser.). 1964. 10.95 (23207) J Norton Pubs.

Poetry of Muriel Rukeyser, Pt. II. Muriel Rukeyser. Read by Muriel Rukeyser. 1 cass. (Running Time: 42 min.). (YM-YWHA Poetry Center Ser.). 1964. 10.95 (23208) J Norton Pubs.

Poetry of Paradise. Thomas Merton. 1 cass. 8.95 (AA2368) Credence Commun.

Poetry of Pasternak. abr. ed. Poems. Boris Pasternak & Merrill Sparks. Perf. by Yevgeny Yevtushenko & Morris Carnovsky. Tr. by Eugene M. Kayden et al. 1 cass. Incl. Autumn. (SWC 1232); From a Poem. (SWC 1232); Oh Had I Known It Once for All. (SWC 1232); On Early Trains. (SWC 1232); Sublime Malady. (SWC 1232); Testament. (SWC 1232); To a Friend. (SWC 1232); Trembling Piano. (SWC 1232); Wind. 1985. (SWC 1232); Winter Night. (SWC 1232); (RUS & ENG.). 1977. 14.00 (978-0-694-50169-4(7), SWC 1232) HarperCollins Pubs.

Poetry of Philip Booth. Philip Booth. Read by Philip Booth. 1 cass. (Running Time: 30 min.). (YM-YWHA Poetry Center Ser.). 1965. 10.95 (23243) J Norton Pubs.

Poetry of Rainer Maria Rilke. unabr. ed. Poems. Rainer Maria Rilke. Perf. by Lotte Lehmann. 1 cass. Incl. Marienleben. (SWC 1128); Weise von Liebe und Tod. (SWC 1128); (GER.). (J). 1984. 12.95 (978-0-694-50095-6(X), SWC 1128) HarperCollins Pubs.

Poetry of Ralph Waldo Emerson. unabr. ed. Poems. Ralph Waldo Emerson. Perf. by Archibald Macleish. 1 cass. Incl. Bacchus. (SWC 1359); Brahma. (SWC 1359); Concord Hymn. (SWC 1359); Days. (SWC 1359); Each & All. (SWC 1359); Fragments. (SWC 1359); Give All to Love. (SWC 1359); Hamatreya. (SWC 1359); Merlin I & II. (SWC 1359); Music. Running Press Staff. (SWC 1359); Ode. (SWC 1359); Problem. (SWC 1359); Rhodora. (SWC 1359); Snow Storm. (SWC 1359); Terminus. (SWC 1359); Threnody. (SWC 1359); Two Rivers. (SWC 1359); Woodnotes. (SWC 1359); 1972. 14.00 (978-0-694-50229-5(4), SWC 1359) HarperCollins Pubs.

Poetry of Randall Jarrell. Randall Jarrell. Read by Randall Jarrell. 1 cass. (Running Time: 1 hr. 7 min.). (YM-YWHA Poetry Center Ser.). 1963. 10.95 (23178) J Norton Pubs.

Poetry of Revelation. Thomas Merton. 1 cass. 8.95 (AA2369) Credence Commun.

Poetry of Richard Geller. Richard Geller. Read by Richard Geller. 1 cass. (Running Time: 25 min.). (YM-YWHA Poetry Center Ser.). 1968. 10.95 (23167) J Norton Pubs.

Poetry of Richard Howard. Richard Howard. Read by Richard Howard. 1 cass. (Running Time: 25 min.). (YM-YWHA Poetry Center Ser.). 1968. 10.95 (23174) J Norton Pubs.

Poetry of Richard Weber. Richard Weber. Read by Richard Weber. 1 cass. (Running Time: 25 min.). (YM-YWHA Poetry Center Ser.). 1967. 10.95 (23230) J Norton Pubs.

Poetry of Robert Bly. Robert Bly. Read by Robert Bly. 1 cass. (Running Time: 38 min.). (YM-YWHA Poetry Ser.). 1966. 10.95 (23242) J Norton Pubs.

Poetry of Robert Browning. unabr. ed. Robert Browning. Perf. by James Mason. 1 cass. Incl. Andrea del Sarto. (SWC 1048); Bishop Orders His Tomb. (SWC 1048); Fra Lippo Lippi. (SWC 1048); 1984. 12.95 (978-0-694-50037-6(2), SWC 1048) HarperCollins Pubs.

Poetry of Robert Burns & Border Ballads. unabr. ed. Poems. Robert Burns. Perf. by Frederick Worlock & C. R. Brookes. 1 cass. Incl. Auld Lang Syne. (SWC 1103); Banks o'Doon. (SWC 1103); Border Ballads: Sir Patrick Spense. (SWC 1103); Clerk Saunders. (SWC 1103); Edward, Edward. (SWC 1103); For A'That & A'That. (SWC 1103); Get Up & Bar the Door. (SWC 1103); John Anderson, My Jo. (SWC 1103); Lament of the Border Widow. (SWC 1103); Mary Morison. (SWC 1103); Sic a Wife As Willie Had. (SWC 1103); Tam O'Shanter. Robert Burns. (SWC 1103); Thomas the Rhymer. (SWC 1103); To a Louse (On Seeing One on a Lady's Bonnet at Church) (SWC 1103); To a Mouse (On Turning Her up in Her Nest with the Plough, November 1785) (SWC 1103); Two Corbies. (SWC 1103); Wee Wee Man. (SWC 1103); Wife of Usher's Well. (SWC 1103); (J). 1984. 12.95 (978-0-694-50079-6(8), SWC 1103) HarperCollins Pubs.

Poetry of Robert Creeley. Robert Creeley. Read by Robert Creeley. 1 cass. (Running Time: 25 min.). (YM-YWHA Poetry Ser.). 1966. 10.95 (23251) J Norton Pubs.

Poetry of Robert Frost: The Collected Poems, Complete & Unabridged. unabr. abr. ed. Robert Frost. Read by Susan Anspach et al. 1 cass. (Running Time: 90 mins.). 2004. 15.00 (978-1-59007-034-5(8)) Pub: New Millenn Enter. Dist(s): PerseuPGW
Drawing upon everyday incidents, common situations and rural imagery, Frost fashioned poetry of great lyrical beauty and potent symbolism. The language is simple, clear and colloquial, yet dense with meaning and wider significance.

Poetry of Robert Huff. Robert Huff. Read by Robert Huff. 1 cass. (Running Time: 56 min.). (YM-YWHA Poetry Center Ser.). 1962. 10.95 (23176) J Norton Pubs.

Poetry of Robert Lowell. Robert Lowell. Read by Robert Lowell. 1 cass. (Running Time: 28 min.). (YM-YWHA Poetry Center Ser.). 1968. 10.95 (23187) J Norton Pubs.

Poetry of Robert W. Service. unabr. ed. Poems. Robert Service. Read by Ed Begley. 1 cass. Incl. Ballad of Pious Pete. (SWC 1218); Call of the Yukon. (SWC 1218); Clancy of the Mounted Police. (SWC 1218); Cremation of Sam McGee. (SWC 1218); Law of the Yukon. (SWC 1218); Men That Don't Fit In. (SWC 1218); Rhyme of the Remittance Man. (SWC 1218); Shooting of Dan McGrew. (SWC 1218); Spell of the Yukon. (SWC 1218); Trail of Ninety-Eight. (SWC 1218); 1984. 12.95 (978-0-694-50165-6(4), SWC 1218) HarperCollins Pubs.

Poetry of Robinson Jeffers. unabr. ed. Poems. Robinson Jeffers. Perf. by Judith Anderson. 1 cass. Incl. Ante Mortem. (SWC 1297); Apology for Bad Dreams. (SWC 1297); Ave Caesar. (SWC 1297); Beauty of Things. (SWC 1297); Bed by the Window. M. Scott Peck. (SWC 1297); Birth - Dues. (SWC 1297); Boats in a Fog. (SWC 1297); Divinely Superfluous Beauty. (SWC 1297); Granite & Cypress. (SWC 1297); House Dog's Grave. (SWC 1297); Hungerfield. 2 cass. (SWC 1297); Hurt Hawks. (SWC 1297); Love the Wild Swan. (SWC 1297); Night. (SWC 1297); November Surf. (SWC 1297); Old Stonemason. (SWC 1297); Phenomena. Ed. by Virginia Carrieri-Kohlman. (SWC 1297); Rearmament. (SWC 1297); Rock & Hawk. (SWC 1297); Science. (SWC 1297); Shine, Perishing Republic. (SWC 1297); Summer Holiday. (SWC 1297); Their Beauty Has More Meaning. (SWC 1297); To the Stone-Cutters. (SWC 1297); Pt. XII. Women at Point Sur. (SWC 1297); 1984. 12.95 (978-0-694-50202-8(2), SWC 1297) HarperCollins Pubs.

Poetry of Samuel Hazo. Samuel Hazo. Read by Samuel Hazo. 1 cass. (Running Time: 37 min.). (YM-YWHA Poetry Center Ser.). 1965. 10.95 (23171) J Norton Pubs.

Poetry of Self Compassion. Speeches. Featuring David Whyte. one. 1991. audio compact disk 15.00 (978-1-932887-08-2(3)) Many Rivers Pr.
While this recording is over ten years old, it continues to be our perennial bestseller.....Compassion is a form of faith: a faith in the way each of us is made for this world. Innocence is the ability to look at that world with fresh eyes. On "The Poetry of Self Compassion", David Whyte looks at innocence as a faculty of exploration and a source of courage, compassion and self knowledge.

Poetry of Shelley. abr. ed. Poems. Percy Bysshe Shelley. Perf. by Vincent Price. 1 cass. Incl. Adonais. (SWC 1059); Hymn to Intellectual Beauty. (SWC 1059); Music, When Soft Voices Die. (SWC 1059); My Soul Is an Enchanted Boat. (SWC 1059); Ode to the West Wind. (SWC 1059); Ozymandias. (SWC 1059); Prometheus Unbound. (SWC 1059); To a Skylark. (SWC 1059); With a Guitar, to Jane. (SWC 1059); 1984. 12.95 (978-0-694-50048-2(8), SWC 1059) HarperCollins Pubs.

Poetry of Silence, Program 9. Read by Colleen Dewhurst. (F007EB090) Natl Public Radio.

Poetry of St. John of the Cross. Poems. Joan Wagner. 1 cass. (Running Time: 44 min.). 1992. 7.95 (TAH245) Alba Hse Comns.
This cassette, spoken with feeling & a profound sense of what the text means, conveys a new & moving vision of St. John's tremendous experience. Combined with a good commentary, it can soothe minds & hearts tired of the emptiness of life & reaching out for the Life that knows no end.

Poetry of Stephen Spender. Stephen Spender. Read by Stephen Spender. 1 cass. (Running Time: 56 min.). (YM-YWHA Poetry Center Ser.). 1964. 10.95 (23215) J Norton Pubs.

Poetry of Sterling A. Brown. Sterling A. Brown. Read by Sterling A. Brown. Anno. by Joanne Gabbin. Contrib. by Yusef Jones. 1 cass. 1995. Incl. notes & biography. (0-9307-470020-9307-47002-2-8); audio compact disk (0-9307-47002-2-8) Smithsonian Folkways.
The music of the life Sterling saw around him resonates in these verses - the blues sung to lost loves, chants of saints praying to be in the number, tragic-comic cries in the face of hatred & injustice & jubilant songs of endurance & perseverance.

Poetry of the Early Seventeenth Century. Jonson et al. 1 cass. 10.95 (978-0-8045-0994-7(8), SAC 7122) Spoken Arts.

Poetry of the Holy Spirit. Robert F. Morneau. 1 cass. (Running Time: 1 hr.). 2001. 8.95 (A6911) St Anthony Mess Pr.
Poets offer us a whole new set of images which can shape and transform our lives, because they have insight into the Trinity and the Incarnation.

Poetry of the Soul. Paul Ferrini. Read by Paul Ferrini. Perf. by Suzi Kesler. 1 cass. (Running Time: 65 min.). 1997. audio compact disk 10.00 (978-1-879159-26-6(0)) Heartways Pr.
A selection of original love poems with piano accompaniment.

Poetry of Theodore Roethke. Theodore Roethke. Read by Theodore Roethke. 1 cass. (Running Time: 36 min.). (YM-YWHA Poetry Center Ser.). 10.95 (23205) J Norton Pubs.

Poetry of Thomas Hardy. unabr. ed. Poems. Thomas Hardy. Read by Richard Burton. 1 cass. Incl. After a Journey. (CPN 1140); At Casterbridge Fair. (CPN 1140); At Castle Boterel. (CPN 1140); Beyond the Last Lamp. (CPN 1140); Channel Firing. (CPN 1140); Great Things. (CPN 1140); I Found Her out There. (CPN 1140); In Tenebris I. (CPN 1140); Let Me Enjoy. (CPN 1140); Old Furniture. (CPN 1140); Phantom Horsewoman. (CPN 1140); Reminiscences of a Dancing Man. (CPN 1140); Shut Out That Moon. (CPN 1140); Souls of the Slain. (CPN 1140); Sunshade. (CPN 1140); Timing Her. (CPN 1140); Voice. (CPN 1140); Weathers. (CPN 1140); Wessex Heights. (CPN 1140); (J). 1989. 9.95 (978-1-55994-052-8(2), CPN 1140) HarperCollins Pubs.

Poetry of Tony Towle. Tony Towle. Read by Tony Towle. 1 cass. (Running Time: 33 min.). (YM-YWHA Poetry Center Ser.). 1968. 10.95 (23223) J Norton Pubs.

Poetry of Vachel Lindsay. unabr. ed. Poems. Vachel Lindsay. Perf. by Nicholas C. Lindsay. 1 cass. Incl. Abraham Lincoln Walks at Midnight. (SWC 1216); Blacksmith's Serenade. (SWC 1216); Congo. (SWC 1216); Daniel. (SWC 1216); Drunkard's Funeral. (SWC 1216); Eagle That Is Forgotten. (SWC 1216); Flower-Fed Buffaloes. (SWC 1216); Ghosts of the Buffaloes. (SWC 1216); Kallyope Yell. (SWC 1216); Lion. (SWC 1216); Moon's the North Wind's Cooky. (SWC 1216); Mouse That Gnawed the Oak-Tree Down. (SWC 1216); Potatoes' Dance. (SWC 1216); Sea Serpent Chantey. (SWC 1216); Simon Legree: A Negro Sermon. (SWC 1216); Sorceress. (SWC 1216); Two Old Crows. (SWC 1216); What the Hyena Said. (SWC 1216); 1984. 12.95 (978-0-694-50163-2(8), SWC 1216) HarperCollins Pubs.

Poetry of W. H. Auden, Pt. 1. W. H. Auden. Read by W. H. Auden. 1 cass. (Running Time: 50 min.). (YM-YWHA Poetry Center Ser.). 1953. 10.95 (23158) J Norton Pubs.

Poetry of W. H. Auden, Pt. 2. W. H. Auden. Read by W. H. Auden. 1 cass. (Running Time: 59 min.). (YM-YWHA Poetry Center Ser.). 1966. 10.95 (23159) J Norton Pubs.

Poetry of Wallace Stevens see Inner Ear

Poetry of Walt Whitman. unabr. abr. ed. Walt Whitman. Read by Joan Allen et al. 1 cass. (Running Time: 90 mins.). 2004. 15.00 (978-1-59007-035-2(6)) Pub: New Millenn Enter. Dist(s): PerseuPGW
Walt Whitman's poetry, idealistic, romantic and utterly new in form and structure, participates in the complex vitality and variety of American life, whether elegizing the fallen president, exalting modern achievements, or evoking the tragedies of war.

Poetry of Walt Whitman: An A+ Audio Study Guide. unabr. ed. Walt Whitman. Read by Peter Strauss. (Running Time: 1 hr.). (ENG.). 2006. 5.98 (978-1-59483-559-9(4)) Pub: Hachet Audio. Dist(s): HachBkGrp

Poetry of Walt Whitman: An A+ Audio Study Guide. unabr. ed. Walt Whitman. Read by Peter Strauss. (Running Time: 1 hr.). (ENG.). 2009. 14.98 (978-1-60788-264-0(7)) Pub: Hachet Audio. Dist(s): HachBkGrp

Poetry of Wendell Berry. Wendell Berry. Read by Wendell Berry. 1 cass. (Running Time: 30 min.). (YM-YWHA Poetry Center Ser.). 1966. 10.95 (23241) J Norton Pubs.

Poetry of William Blake. William Blake. Read by Wendy Hiller et al. 1 cass. Incl. Everlasting Gospel. (SAC 1061); Gates of Paradise. (SAC 1061); Jerusalem. (SAC 1061); Milton. (SAC 1061); Notebook. (SAC 1061); Pickering Manuscript. (SAC 1061); Poetical Sketches. (SAC 1061); Songs of Experience. (SAC 1061); Songs of Innocence. (SAC 1061); 10.95 (978-0-8045-1061-5(X), SAC 1061) Spoken Arts.

Poetry of William Butler Yeats. unabr. ed. Poems. W. B. Yeats. Perf. by Siobhan McKenna & Cyril Cusack. 1 cass. Incl. Broken Dreams. (SWC 1081); Byzantium. (SWC 1081); Cat & the Moon. (SWC 1081); Crazed Moon. (SWC 1081); Crazy Jane & Jack the Journeyman. (SWC 1081); Crazy Jane & the Bishop. (SWC 1081); Crazy Jane Grown Old Looks at the Dancers. (SWC 1081); Crazy Jane on God. (SWC 1081); Crazy Jane on the Day of Judgement. (SWC 1081); Crazy Jane Reproved. (SWC 1081); Crazy Jane Talks with the Bishop. (SWC 1081); Cuchulain Comforted. (SWC 1081); Dialogue of Self & Soul. (SWC 1081); Girl's Song. (SWC 1081); Lake Isle of Innisfree. (SWC 1081); Lapis Lazuli. (SWC 1081); Last Confession. (SWC 1081); Leda & the Swan. (SWC 1081); Man Young & Old: First Love, Human Dignity, The Mermaid (poem) (SWC 1081); News for the Delphic Oracle. (SWC 1081); No Second Troy. (SWC 1081); Sailing to Byzantium. (SWC 1081); Second Coming. (SWC 1081); Song of Wandering Aengus. (SWC 1081); Those Dancing Days Are Gone. (SWC 1081); Why Should Not Old Men Be Mad? (SWC 1081); Wild Old Wicked Man. (SWC 1081); Wild Swans at Coole: Manuscript Materials. W. B. Yeats. (SWC 1081); Young Man's Song. (SWC 1081); 1984. 12.95 (978-0-694-50063-5(1), SWC 1081) HarperCollins Pubs.

Poetry of William Dickey. William Dickey. Read by William Dickey. 1 cass. (Running Time: 28 min.). (YM-YWHA Poetry Center Ser.). 1965. 10.95 (23256) J Norton Pubs.

Poetry of William Jay Smith. Jay S. William. Read by Jay S. William. 1 cass. (Running Time: 37 min). (YM-YWHA Poetry Center Ser.). 1963. 10.95 (23214) J Norton Pubs.

Poetry of Winfield Townley Scott. Winfield Townley Scott. Read by Winfield Townley Scott. 1 cass. (Running Time: 39 min.). (YM-YWHA Poetry Center Ser.). 1965. 10.95 (23211) J Norton Pubs.

Poetry on Record: 98 Poets Read Their Work (1888-2006) unabr. ed. 4 CDs. (Running Time: 5 hrs.). 2006. audio compact disk 49.98 (978-0-7389-3443-3(7)) Sony Music Ent.
Poetry On Record: 98 Poets Read Their Work (1888-2006) is an engrossing collection of poems read by the people who wrote them, from the dawn of sound recording to the current day. Over the course of four CDs and an info-packed book, it tells the story of the past 120 years of poetry in English, from Romanticism (Dylan Thomas) to Modernism (T.S. Eliot), from the Harlem Renaissance (Langston Hughes) to Black Arts (Amiri Baraka), from rhyme and meter (Alfred, Lord Tennyson) to free verse (Adrienne Rich), and beyond. Equally important, it allows listeners to understand exactly how the poets intended their poems to be read aloud. Poetry On Record is the most comprehensive collection of its kind and is a must-have for any fan of poetry, or for anyone who wants an expertly chosen overview as a starting point.

Poetry Please. 3 cass. (Running Time: 9 hrs.). 1998. bk. 37.45 Set, slipcase. (978-0-563-38205-8(8)) BBC WrldWd GBR.
One of Radio 4's most popular programmes - listeners select the poems they want to hear.

Poetry Please. 25th unabr. anniv. ed. Compiled by British Broadcasting Corporation Staff. (Running Time: 2 hrs. 0 mins. 0 sec.). (ENG.). 2010. audio compact disk 24.95 (978-1-60283-845-1(3)) Pub: AudioGO. Dist(s): Perseus Dist

Poetry Please, No. 3. abr. ed. Poems. 2 cass. (Running Time: 2 hrs.). 1998. 16.85 Set. (978-0-563-38199-0(X)) BBC WrldWd GBR.
Marks the eightieth anniversary of Armistice Day. This compilation will be themed along such lines as Home Front, Hope, Despair, & Battle Poems.

Poetry Poster Audio. Compiled by Benchmark Education Staff. 2005. audio compact disk 10.00 (978-1-4108-3927-5(3)) Benchmark Educ.

Poetry Power - A Giant Lies Sleeping. Mary M. Slappey. Read by Mary M. Slappey. (Running Time: 60 min). 1986. 20.00 Interspace Bks.

Poetry Quartets, Vol. 1. Simon Armitage et al. (ENG., 1999. 24.95 (978-1-85224-468-2(2)) Pub: Bloodaxe Bks GBR. Dist(s): Dufour

Poetry Quartets, Vol. 2. Fleur Adcock et al. (ENG., 1999. 24.95 (978-1-85224-469-9(0)) Pub: Bloodaxe Bks GBR. Dist(s): Dufour

Poetry Quartets, Vol. 3. James Fenton et al. (ENG., 1999. 26.95 (978-1-85224-470-5(4)) Pub: Bloodaxe Bks GBR. Dist(s): Dufour

Poetry Quartets, Vol. 6. British Council Staff & Bloodaxe Books Staff. (ENG., 2000. 26.95 (978-1-85224-519-1(0)) Pub: Bloodaxe Bks GBR. Dist(s): Dufour

Poetry Quartets, Vol. 7. John Burnside et al. (ENG., 2000. 26.95 (978-1-85224-520-7(4)) Pub: Bloodaxe Bks GBR. Dist(s): Dufour

Poetry Quartets, Vol. 8. Andrew Motion et al. Ed. by British Council. (SPA & ENG., 2004. 26.95 (978-1-85224-550-4(6)) Pub: Bloodaxe Bks GBR. Dist(s): Dufour

Poetry Quartets, Vol. 9. Benjamin Zephaniah et al. Ed. by British Council. (SPA & ENG., 2004. 26.95 (978-1-85224-551-1(4)) Pub: Bloodaxe Bks GBR. Dist(s): Dufour

Poetry Quartets 4: Irish Poets. Paul Durcan et al. 1 cass. (Running Time: 90 mins.). (Poetry Quartets Ser.). (ENG., 1999. 26.95 (978-1-85224-498-9(4)) Pub: Bloodaxe Bks GBR. Dist(s): Dufour

Poetry Quartets 5: Women Poets. Helen Dunmore et al. 1 cass. (Running Time: 90 mins.). (Poetry Quartets Ser.). (ENG., 1999. 26.95 (978-1-85224-499-6(2)) Pub: Bloodaxe Bks GBR. Dist(s): Dufour

Poetry Reading: An Ancient Tradition. Robert Bly. 2 cass. (Running Time: 2 hrs.15 min.). 1983. 18.00 (00305) Big Sur Tapes.
The author reminisces on his introduction to poetry & speaks on the nature of poetry reading.

Poetry Smarts World-Wide by Dancing Beetle. Eugene Ely et al. 1 cass. (Running Time: 83 min.). (J). 1991. 10.00 Erthviibz.
Poetry classics world-wide & nature sounds come together when Ms. Jabiru & the spunky musical humans read & sing with Dancing Beetle.

Poetry Therapy. Leland Roloff. Read by Leland Roloff. 6 cass. (Running Time: 9 hrs.). 1992. 45.95 set. (978-0-7822-0395-0(7), 488) C G Jung IL.
Poetry Therapy is an inclusive expressive arts therapy that attempts to utilize verbal expressions in all their symbolic & metaphoric resonances. It is a poetry that both listens to poetry & creates it. It is a therapy which gives psychological life a vital & profound immediacy through "speaking" the lost & found languages of dreams, reveries, observations, meditations. This course explores the "poetic mind," the "mythic mind," & the intellectual foundations for these modes.

Poetry to Hear see Poesia para Oir

Poetry to Hear. Read by Carlos J. Vega. (Running Time: 3 hrs.). (C). 2002. 16.95 (978-1-60083-190-4(7), Audiofy Corp) Iofy Corp.

Poets & Conflict. 1 cass. 10.00 Esstee Audios.

Poets & Human Nature. 1 cass. 10.00 Esstee Audios.

Poets & Painters of Greenwich Village. unabr. ed. Andrew Flack. Read by Barbara Duff & Greg Michaels. 1 cass. Dramatization. (Day Ranger Walking Adventures on Audio Cassette Ser.). 1989. 19.95 (978-1-877894-00-8(1)) Day Ranger.
Scripted dialogue & music to accompany an original walking route of Greenwich Village; uses first hand accounts, eyewitness stories & brief excerpts of identified literature. Two detailed maps included.

Poets & Prophets: Poems of Sanai & Sa'di. Poems. Hakim Sanai & Sa'di. Read by Coleman Barks. 1 cass. (Running Time: 62 min.). (Handbook of Poetry Audio Book Ser.: Vol. 1). 1997. 12.00 (978-0-930872-58-8(4)) Omega Pubns NY.

Poets' Corner: The One-and-Only Poetry Book for the Whole Family. unabr. ed. John Lithgow. Read by Morgan Freeman et al. (Running Time: 6 hrs. 30 mins.). (ENG.). 2007. 24.98 (978-1-60024-054-6(2)) Pub: Hachet Audio. Dist(s): HachBkGrp

Poets Eleven - Audible Number 2. Brian Groth et al. 1 cass. (Running Time: 90 min.). 1986. 5.75 (978-0-932593-11-5(9)) Black Bear.
Poetry reading featuring Brian Groth, J.K. Durick, Jane Ransom, Kevin Zepper, David Radavich, Stephen Unsino, Belinda Subraman, A.D. Winans, Tom House, Jake Berry & Patrick McKinnon.

Poets Eleven - Audible Number 3. Sheila Brown et al. (Running Time: 90 min.). 1986. 5.75 (978-0-932593-12-2(7)) Black Bear.
Poetry reading featuring Brian Groth, Sheila Brown, Richard Weekley, Brian Clemons, Jack Foley, (Tony Moffeit, Ric Soos & Connie VanMatre in song), Nancy Scott & Patsy Bickerstaff.

Poets Giftpack. Keats. 45.00 (978-1-85998-271-6(9), HoddrStoughton) Pub: Hodder General GBR. Dist(s): Trafalgar

Poet's Gold, Poetry Reading. unabr. ed. Poems. Perf. by David Ross. 1 cass. 1984. 8.98 (CDL5 1741) HarperCollins Pubs.
Anthology of selected radio broadcasts of poetry readings by Ross.

Poets in Person: A Series on American Poets & Their Art. unabr. ed. Hosted by Joseph Parisi. 7 cass. (Running Time: 30 min.). 1991. 65.00 Set. (978-1-881505-00-6(6)) Poet Found.
Thirteen poets in conversation - reading their poems, discussing their lives, their work, & the changing styles in contemporary American poetry. Joseph Parisi, editor of "Poetry" is host.

Poets in Person: A Series on American Poets & Their Art, No. 1. unabr. ed. Hosted by Joseph Parisi. 1 cass. (Running Time: 30 min.). 1991. 9.95 (978-1-881505-01-3(4)) Poet Found.
Side 1: Introduction - Includes clips from other programs in the series to outline the evolution of American poetry since the 1950s. Side 2: Allen Ginsberg with Lewis Hyde - Reading his poems, discussing his life, his work, & the changing styles in contemporary American poetry.

Poets in Person: A Series on American Poets & Their Art, No. 2. unabr. ed. Interview with Karl Jay Shapiro & Maxine Kumin. Hosted by Joseph Parisi. 1 cass. (Running Time: 30 min.). 1991. 9.95 (978-1-881505-02-0(2)) Poet Found.
Side 1: Karl Shapiro in Conversation with Joseph Parisi & Side 2: Maxine Kumin in Conversation with Alicia Ostriker - Reading their poems, discussing their lives, their work, & the changing styles in contemporary American poetry.

Poets in Person: A Series on American Poets & Their Art, No. 3. unabr. ed. Interview with W. S. Merwin & Gwendolyn Brooks. Hosted by Joseph Parisi. 1 cass. (Running Time: 30 min.). 1991. 9.95 (978-1-881505-03-7(0)) Poet Found.
Side 1: W. S. Merwin with James Richardson & Side 2: Gwendolyn Brooks with Alice Fulton - Reading their poems, discussing their lives, their work, & the changing styles in contemporary American poetry.

Poets in Person: A Series on American Poets & Their Art, No. 4. unabr. ed. Interview with James Merrill & Adrienne Rich. Hosted by Joseph Parisi. 1 cass. (Running Time: 30 min.). 1991. 9.95 (978-1-881505-04-4(9)) Poet Found.
Side 1: James Merrill in Conversation with J. D. McClatchy & Side 2: Adrienne Rich in Conversation with Diane Wood Middlebrook - Reading their poems, discussing their lives, their work, & the changing styles in contemporary American poetry.

Poets in Person: A Series on American Poets & Their Art, No. 5. unabr. ed. Interview with John Ashbery & Sharon Olds. Hosted by Joseph Parisi. 1 cass. (Running Time: 30 min.). 1991. 9.95 (978-1-881505-05-1(7)) Poet Found.
Side 1: John Ashbery in Conversation wtih David Bromwich & Side 2: Sharon Olds in Conversation with Alicia Ostriker - Reading their poems, discussing their lives, their work, & the changing styles in contemporary American poetry.

Poets in Person: A Series on American Poets & Their Art, No. 6. Poems. Ed. by Joseph Parisi. Interview with Charles Wright & Rita Dove. 1 cass. (Running Time: 30 min.). 1991. 9.95 (978-1-881505-06-8(5)) Poet Found.
Side 1: Charles Wright in Conversation with J. D. McClatchy & Side 2: Rita Dove in Conversation with Helen Vendler - Reading their poems, discussing their lives, their work & the changing styles in contemporary American poetry.

Poets in Person: A Series on American Poets & Their Art, No. 7. Interview with Gary Soto & A. R. Ammons. Hosted by Joseph Parisi. 1 cass. (Running Time: 30 min.). 1991. 9.95 (978-1-881505-07-5(3)) Poet Found.
Side 1: Gary Soto in Conversation with Joseph Parisi & Side 2: A. R. Ammons in Conversation with Alice Fulton - Reading their poems, discussing their lives, their work, & the changing styles in contemporary American poetry.

Poets Look at War. 10.00 Esstee Audios.
From Sassoon's pacifism to Kipling's jingoism.

Poets of Love - An Anthology of the Most Beautiful Poems see Poetas del Amor - Antologia de los Mas Bellos Poemas

Poets of Love - an Anthology of the Most Beautiful Poems. Read by Gaspar Y. Ospina & Adelaidia Espinoza. (Running Time: 3 hrs.). 2001. 16.95 (978-1-60083-180-5(X), Audiofy Corp) Iofy Corp.

Poets of Nature: A Meditation on the Human Connection with Earth. Anne Brontë et al. Read by Jonathan Epstein et al. 2008. audio compact disk 25.00 (978-0-9818091-0-6(3)) BMA Studios.

Poets of the Great War. Poems. Read by Michael Maloney et al. Ed. by Adrian Barlow & Perry Keenlyside. 2 cass. (Running Time: 1 hr. 52 mins.). 1997. 13.98 (978-962-634-609-9(4), NA210914, Naxos AudioBooks) Naxos.
Collection from a generation who fought through a war of unprecedented destructive power and who had to find new voices to express the horror of what they discovered. 62 poems by 29 great poets of the period.

Poets of the Great War. unabr. ed. Poems. Read by Michael Maloney et al. Ed. by Adrian Barlow & Perry Keenlyside. 2 CDs. (Running Time: 1 hr. 52 mins.). 1997. audio compact disk 17.98 (978-962-634-109-4(2), NA210912, Naxos AudioBooks) Naxos.

***Poet's Wife.** Judith Allnatt. 2010. 84.95 (978-1-4450-0182-1(9)); audio compact disk 99.95 (978-1-4450-0183-8(7)) Pub: Isis Pubng Ltd GBR. Dist(s): Ulverscroft US

Poil de carotte, Set. Jules Renard. Read by Christine Authier. 2 cass. (FRE.). 1991. bk. 35.95 (1GA058) Olivia & Hill.
The sad & tender story of Poil de carotte ("carrot top"), a lonely little redheaded boy who is bullied by his mother & neglected by his father.

Poinciana. unabr. ed. Phyllis A. Whitney. Read by Beth Porter. 10 cass. (Running Time: 10 hrs.). 1999. 84.95 (978-0-7540-0276-5(4), CAB1699) AudioGO.
The palm beach home of Ross Logan contains his enigmatic past, a celebrated collection of oriental art & a prized new possession, his terrified young bride. Saga of love betrayed & a woman trapped by the past.

***Poingo Reader with 3-Book Disney Library: Toy Story, Mickey Mouse Clubhouse, Finding Nemo.** Ed. by Publications International Staff. (J). 2009. 74.98 (978-1-4127-4519-2(5)) Pubns Intl Ltd.

***Poingo 2-Book Disney Princess Library: Magical World; Cinderella.** Ed. by Publications International Staff. (J). 2009. 13.98 (978-1-4127-7872-5(7)) Pubns Intl Ltd.

***Poingo 2 Pack: Sesame Street: Meet the People in Your Neighborhood; Thomas & Friends: Thomas & the New Carousel.** Ed. by Publications International Staff. (J). 2009. 13.98 (978-1-4127-6808-5(X)) Pubns Intl Ltd.

Point Blank. abr. ed. Catherine Coulter. Read by Dick Hill. (Running Time: 21600 sec.). (FBI Thriller Ser.: No. 10). 2006. audio compact disk 16.99 (978-1-59600-855-7(5), 9781596008557, BCD Value Price) Brilliance Audio.
The explosive action kicks off as FBI agent Ruth Warnecki hunts for Confederate gold in a West Virginia cave. She never expects to encounter the grisly murder that catapults her into a horrific plague of death, all centered on the prestigious Stanislaus School of Music. And at Hooter's Motel in Maryland, FBI agents Savich and Carver are nearly killed while attempting to rescue a kidnap victim. Instead of a hostage, all they see is a glowing-red timer and then a catastrophic explosion. They are then led to Arlington National Cemetery, but the search for the kidnap victim is cut short when Savich takes a fateful call on his cell, as a mysterious voice threatens to kill him and his wife. Pitted against an insane killer and his psychotic teenage girlfriend, Savich and Sherlock find themselves fighting a hate-driven villain with a very long memory. Point Blank is a nail-biting, edge-of-your-seat thriller, as exhilarating and terrifying as anything Catherine Coulter has ever written.

Point Blank. unabr. ed. Catherine Coulter. Read by Dick Hill. (Running Time: 10 hrs.). (FBI Thriller Ser.: No. 10). 2005. 39.25 (978-1-59710-847-8(2), 9781597108478, BADLE); 24.95 (978-1-59710-846-1(4), 9781597108461, BAD) Brilliance Audio.

Point Blank. unabr. ed. Catherine Coulter. Read by Dick Hill. (Running Time: 36000 sec.). (FBI Thriller Ser.: No. 10). 2005. 82.25 (978-1-59355-717-1(5), 9781593557171, BrilAudUnabridg); audio compact disk 36.95 (978-1-59355-719-5(1), 9781593557195, Bril Audio CD Unabri); audio compact disk 97.25 (978-1-59355-720-1(5), 9781593557201, BriAudCD Unabrid); audio compact disk 24.95 (978-1-59335-752-8(4), 9781593357528, Brilliance MP3); audio compact disk 39.25 (978-1-59335-886-0(5), 9781593358860, Brlnc Audio MP3 Lib) Brilliance Audio.
Please enter a Synopsis.

Point Blank. unabr. ed. Catherine Coulter. Read by Dick Hill. (Running Time: 36000 sec.). (FBI Thriller Ser.: No. 13). 2005. 32.95 (978-1-59355-716-4(7), 9781593557164, BAU) Brilliance Audio.

Point Blank. unabr. ed. Anthony Horowitz. Narrated by Simon Prebble. 4 pieces. (Running Time: 5 hrs. 45 mins.). (Alex Rider Ser.: Bk. 2). (gr. 7 up). 2002. 42.00 (978-1-4025-2474-5(9)) Recorded Bks.
Recently recruited and trained as a special agent by MI6, the British secret service, 14-year-old West Londoner Alex Rider is sent to infiltrate an ultra-private school where the rich and powerful send their uncontrollable, rebellious sons. What he discovers in the mountaintop fortress of the campus are enough armed guards to repel an invasion-and new classmates who have become eerie copies of each other in their compliant attitudes and actions.

Point Deception. unabr. ed. Marcia Muller. Read by Ray Gautreau Laural Merlington. (Running Time: 8 hrs.). 2005. 39.25 (978-1-59600-763-5(X), 9781596007635, BADLE); 24.95 (978-1-59600-762-8(1), 9781596007628, BAD) Brilliance Audio.

Point Deception. unabr. ed. Marcia Muller. Read by Laural Merlington & Ray Gautreau. (Running Time: 28800 sec.). 2005. audio compact disk 39.25 (978-1-59600-761-1(3), 9781596007611, Brlnc Audio MP3 Lib); audio compact disk 24.95 (978-1-59600-760-4(5), 9781596007604, Brilliance MP3) Brilliance Audio.
A bestselling journalist, Guy Newberry is known for his articles on the plight of troubled communities. Shortly after his arrival in the small seaside community of Signal Port, California, a town that has never recovered from the unsolved murder of two young families 13 years ago, another nightmare begins. An unidentified woman's body washes up at nearby Point Deception, immediately stirring up old feelings of fear and suspicion. Relentless in pursuing his story, and haunted by a tragedy in his own past, Newberry does not let up, instilling fear in the town's sheriff, Rhoda Swift, who fears his prying will destroy her town. But as more women die and public panic sets in, Newberry and Swift form an uneasy alliance and unite in a confrontation with a killer whose motives are not as random as they seem.

Point Last Seen. unabr. ed. Hannah Nyala. 4 cass. (Running Time: 6 hrs.). 1997. 25.95 Audio Lit.

Point Last Seen: A Woman Tracker's Story. unabr. ed. Hannah Nyala. Read by Hannah Nyala. 4 cass. (Running Time: 6 hrs.). 1997. 25.95 (978-1-57453-230-2(8)) Audio Lit.
Nyala uses her search & rescue team skills to find her children, who had been taken away by her abusive husband. Compelling, frightening & ultimately redemptive, one woman's harrowing journey to physical & spiritual safety for herself & her children.

***Point Man: How a Man Can Lead His Family.** unabr. ed. Steve Farrar. Narrated by Raymond Todd. (ENG.). 2008. 16.98 (978-1-59644-582-6(3), christianSeed) christianaud.

Point Man: How a Man Can Lead His Family. unabr. ed. Steve Farrar. Read by Raymond Todd. (Running Time: 6 hrs. 18 mins. 0 sec.). (ENG.). 2008. audio compact disk 26.98 (978-1-59644-581-9(5)) christianaud.

Point of Origin. Patricia Cornwell. Read by Kate Reading. 8 cass. (Running Time: 12 hrs.). (Kay Scarpetta Ser.: No. 9). 1998. 64.00 (978-0-7366-4175-3(0), 4674) Books on Tape.
She's the sharpest investigator in crime fiction today. Now Kay Scarpetta meets a master of arson. Nineteen horses have perished in a suspicious fire at the farm of an African-American publisher, Kenneth Sparkes. Among the rubble lies another fatality, the body of Sparkes's former lover. But there's no sign of how the fire started, no trace of gas or other accelerant. Kay's meticulous forensic work turn up evidence that leads back to a series of

equally inexplicable arson-murders. Amid the tangled circumstances, Kay gains on a killer who's weapon of choice is fire. But in a showdown between good & evil, can she prevail.

Point of Origin. Patricia Cornwell. Read by Elizabeth McGovern. 2 cass. (Kay Scarpetta Ser.: No. 9). 1998. 16.85 Set. (978-0-00-105539-1(9)) Ulvrscrft Audio.

Point of Origin. collector's unabr. ed. Patricia Cornwell. Read by Kate Reading. 10 CDs. (Running Time: 15 hrs.). (Kay Scarpetta Ser.: No. 9). 2000. audio compact disk 80.00 (978-0-7366-5141-7(1)) Books on Tape.
Kay Scarpetta, Virginia's chief medical examiner, investigates an arson-murder & discovers evidence that sheds light on a series of unsolved crimes.

Point of Origin, Set. abr. ed. Patricia Cornwell. Read by Joan Allen. 4 cass. (Kay Scarpetta Ser.: No. 9). 1999. 24.95 (FS9-43229) Highsmith.

Point of Origin, Set. unabr. ed. Patricia Cornwell. Read by Kate Reading. 8 cass. (Kay Scarpetta Ser.: No. 9). 1999. 39.95 (FS9-43194) Highsmith.

Point of Self Cylic Astrology. Clara Darr. 1 cass. 8.95 (075) Am Fed Astrologers.
Analysis of ages from cradle to grave.

Point of the Deal: How to Negotiate When Yes Is Not Enough. unabr. ed. Danny Ertel & Mark Gordon. Read by Erik Synnestvedt. (Running Time: 8 hrs.). (ENG.). 2008. 24.98 (978-1-59659-197-4(8), GildAudio) Pub: Gildan Media. Dist(s): HachBkGrp

Point of the Deal: How to Negotiate When Yes Is Not Enough. unabr. ed. Danny Ertel & Mark Gordon. Read by Erik Synnestvedt. 6 CDs. (Running Time: 8 hrs.). (ENG.). 2008. audio compact disk 29.98 (978-1-59659-168-4(4), GildAudio) Pub: Gildan Media. Dist(s): HachBkGrp

Point of View, Set. Steck-Vaughn Staff. (C). 1998. pap. bk. (978-0-8172-6874-9(X)) SteckVau.

Point of View Stories, Set. Alvin Granowsky. 6 cass. (J). (gr. 4-6). 1993. pap. bk. 98.15 (978-0-8114-2230-7(5)) SteckVau.
Two versions of the traditional story & a retelling from the viewpoint of a story character motivate students to read & analyze literature through critical thinking. Flip-book presentation emphasizes the difference in the two story versions & encourages students to complete both & compare. Titles include: Cinderella/That Awful Cinderella, Rumpelstiltskin/A Deal Is a Deal, Snow White/The Unfairest of Them All, Robin Hood/The Sheriff Speaks, Peter Pan/Grow up, Peter Pan, Rip Van Winkle/Wake up, Rip Van Winkle. Includes Teacher's Guide. Classroom library includes 5 copies of all 6 titles, plus 6 cassettes & teacher's guide.

Point Omega. unabr. ed. Don DeLillo. Read by Campbell Scott. 3 CDs. (Running Time: 3 hrs.). 2010. audio compact disk 19.99 (978-1-4423-0054-5(X)) Pub: S&S Audio. Dist(s): S and S Inc

Point to Point Navigation: A Memoir 1964 to 2006. Gore Vidal. Read by Gore Vidal. (Running Time: 32400 sec.). 2006. audio compact disk 34.99 (978-1-4281-1297-1(9)) Recorded Bks.

Pointe Aux Tortues. l.t. ed. Catherine Hermary-Vieille. (French Ser.). 1994. bk. 30.99 (978-2-84011-086-6(5)) Pub: UlverLrgPrint GBR. Dist(s): Ulverscroft US

Pointing from the Grave. Samantha Weinberg. Narrated by Nadia May. (Running Time: 13 hrs.). 2003. 41.95 (978-1-59912-571-8(4)) Iofy Corp.

Pointing from the Grave. unabr. ed. Samantha Weinberg. Read by Nadia May. 8 CDs. 2004. audio compact disk 49.95 (978-0-7861-9193-2(7)) Blckstn Audio.

Pointing from the Grave: A True Story of Murder & DNA. unabr. ed. Samantha Weinberg. Read by Nadia May. 10 CDs. (Running Time: 13 hrs.). 2003. audio compact disk 80.00 (978-0-7861-9246-5(1), 3082); audio compact disk 24.95 (978-0-7861-9012-6(4), 3082); 62.95 (978-0-7861-2416-9(4), 3082) Blckstn Audio.
This is not only a riveting true-crime story but also a fascinating history of the development of DNA research and its role in forensics, taking the reader on a virtual history of DNA with hard science presented in a very accessible and exciting way. It is also an unforgettable story about an unforgettable woman.

Pointing from the Grave: A True Story of Murder & DNA. unabr. ed. Samantha Weinberg. 7 pieces. (Running Time: 12 hrs. 30 mins.). 2004. reel tape 39.95 (978-0-7861-2414-5(8)) Blckstn Audio.

***Points of Departure.** Pat Murphy. 2009. (978-1-60136-491-3(1)) Audio Holding.

Points of Light. 1 cass. (Running Time: 1 hr.). 9.95 (978-1-55961-338-5(6)) Relaxtn Co.

Points of Light. Boris Mourashkin. 1 CD. (Running Time: 1 hr.). audio compact disk 13.95 (978-1-55961-307-1(6)) Relaxtn Co.

Poirot Collection: Radio Dramatization. unabr. ed. Agatha Christie. 6 CDs. (Running Time: 9 hrs.). Dramatization. 2002. audio compact disk 64.95 (978-0-563-53048-0(0), BBCD 002) BBC Worldwide.

Poirot Investigates: Eleven Complete Mysteries. unabr. ed. Agatha Christie. Read by David Suchet. 4 cass. (Running Time: 5 hrs. 45 mins.). 2003. 25.95 (978-1-57270-320-9(2)) Pub: Audio Partners. Dist(s): PerseuPGW
Two things bind this sampler of thrillers: the diminutive Poirot's deductive brilliance and his partner Hasting's obtuseness. The cases here involve film stars, valuable jewels, and abductions as Poirot stylishly uncovers the truth.

Poirot Investigates: Eleven Complete Mysteries. unabr. ed. Agatha Christie. Narrated by David Suchet. 5 CDs. (Running Time: 6 hrs.). (Mystery Masters Ser.). (ENG.). 2003. audio compact disk 27.95 (978-1-57270-321-6(0)) Pub: AudioGO. Dist(s): Perseus Dist
This captivating collection includes: The Adventure of 'The Western Star', The Tragedy at Marsdon Manor, The Adventure of the Cheap Flat, The Million-Dollar Bond Robbery, & more.

Poirot's Early Cases: 18 Hercule Poirot Mysteries. unabr. ed. Agatha Christie. Narrated by David Suchet & Hugh Fraser. (Mystery Masters Ser.). (ENG.). 2005. audio compact disk 27.95 (978-1-57270-472-5(1)) Pub: AudioGO. Dist(s): Perseus Dist
The unabridged tales in this Mystery Masters audiobook include all the ones in the print book first published in 1974. With each case, Poirot further proves his reputation as the greatest mind in detective fiction. In "The Plymouth Express," the body of the daughter of a wealthy American industrialist is found stuffed under a train seat. "Problem at Sea" finds a disliked rich woman murdered in a locked room on a ship. "The King of Clubs" involves a prince, his dancer fiancée, and a fiendish bit of blackmail. These gems are alternately read by David Suchet and Hugh Fraser, whose roles as, respectively, Poirot and his sidekick, Captain Hugh Hastings, in PBS's Mystery! series and the Arts and Entertainment's Poirot series are considered definitive.

Poirot's Early Cases: 18 Unabridged Stories. unabr. ed. Agatha Christie. Read by David Suchet & Hugh Fraser. 2003. 29.95 (978-1-57270-293-6(1)) Pub: Audio Partners. Dist(s): PerseuPGW

Poison. Ed McBain, pseud. Read by Jonathan Marosz. (87th Precinct Ser.: Bk. 39). 2001. 64.00 (978-0-7366-5935-2(8)) Books on Tape.

Poison. unabr. ed. Kathryn Harrison. Read by Barbara Caruso. 4 CDs. (Running Time: 4 hrs. 30 mins.). (J). 2006. audio compact disk 84.75 (978-1-4193-9911-4(X)); 65.75 (978-1-4193-9906-0(3), 94613) Recorded Bks.
In this richly textured historical novel, best-selling author Kathryn Harrison spins a mesmerizing tale of forbidden passion and terrifying superstition in 17th-century Spain. As the Spanish Inquisition conducts its ruthless reign of terror, the lives of two women - one, the free spirited daughter of a poor silk farmer; the other, the French princess doomed to marry the deformed King of Spain - unravel like the cocoons of silkworms. A nationally-acclaimed writer of exquisite talents, Kathryn Harrison will leave you breathless.

Poison. unabr. ed. Kathryn Harrison. Narrated by Barbara Caruso. 9 cass. (Running Time: 13 hrs. 15 mins.). 1995. 78.00 (978-0-7887-0421-5(4), 94613E7) Recorded Bks.
As the Spanish Inquisition conducts its ruthless reign of terror, the lives of two women - one, the free spirited daughter of a poor silk farmer; the other, the French princess doomed to marry the deformed King of Spain - unravel like the cocoons of silkworms.

Poison Belt: Being an Account of Another Amazing Adventure of Professor Challenger. Arthur Conan Doyle. Read by Fred Williams. 5 CDs. (Running Time: 6 hrs.). 2000. audio compact disk 40.00 (978-0-7861-9890-0(7), z2381) Blckstn Audio.

Poison Belt: Being an Account of Another Amazing Adventure of Professor Challenger. unabr. ed. Arthur Conan Doyle. Read by Fred Williams. 4 cass. (Running Time: 6 hrs.). 1999. 32.95 (978-0-7861-1531-0(9), 2381) Blckstn Audio.

Poison Belt: Being an Account of Another Amazing Adventure of Professor Challenger. unabr. ed. Arthur Conan Doyle. Read by Fred Williams. 4 cass. (Running Time: 6 hrs..). 1999. audio compact disk 24.95 (978-0-7861-1698-0(6)) Pub: Blckstn Audio. Dist(s): Penton Overseas

Poison Belt: Being an Account of Another Amazing Adventure of Professor Challenger. unabr. ed. Arthur Conan Doyle. Read by Fred Williams. 1 CD. (Running Time: 5 hrs. 30 min.). 2001. audio compact disk 19.95 (zm2381) Blckstn Audio.

Poison Belt: Being an Account of Another Amazing Adventure of Professor Challenger. unabr. ed. Arthur Conan Doyle. Narrated by Paul Hecht. 3 cass. (Running Time: 3 hrs. 30 mins.). 1996. 26.00 (978-0-7887-0495-6(8), 94687E7) Recorded Bks.
Challenger summons Professor Summerlee, Lord John Roxton & E. D. Malone to his sitting room with one unusual request: bring your own oxygen.

Poison Belt & Other Stories. unabr. ed. Arthur Conan Doyle. Read by Fred Williams. (Running Time: 5 hrs. 30 mins.). 1999. 24.95 (978-0-7861-9620-3(3)) Blckstn Audio.

***Poison Diaries.** unabr. ed. Maryrose Wood. Illus. by The Duchess Of Northumberland. (ENG.). 2010. (978-0-06-204074-9(X)) HarperCollins Pubs.

***Poison Diaries.** unabr. ed. Maryrose Wood. Read by Violet Mathieson. Illus. by The Duchess Of Northumberland. (ENG.). 2010. (978-0-06-203273-7(9)) HarperCollins Pubs.

Poison Flowers. unabr. ed. Natasha Cooper. 8 cass. 1998. 83.95 Set. (978-1-85903-128-5(5)) Pub: Magna Story GBR. Dist(s): Ulverscroft US

Poison Heart. unabr. ed. Mary Logue. Read by Joyce Bean. (Running Time: 7 hrs.). (Claire Watkins Ser.). 2005. 24.95 (978-1-59710-980-2(0), 9781597109802, BAD) Brilliance Audio.

Poison Heart. unabr. ed. Mary Logue. Read by Joyce Bean. (Running Time: 7 hrs.). (Claire Watkins Ser.: Bk. 5). 2005. 39.25 (978-1-59710-981-9(9), 9781597109819, BADLE); 69.25 (978-1-59355-435-4(4), 9781593554354, BrilAudUnabridg); 29.95 (978-1-59355-434-7(6), 9781593554347, BAU); audio compact disk 29.95 (978-1-59600-056-8(2), 9781596000568, Bril Audio CD Unabri); audio compact disk 82.25 (978-1-59600-057-5(0), 9781596000575, BriAudCD Unabrid); audio compact disk 24.95 (978-1-59335-721-4(4), 9781593357214, Brilliance MP3); audio compact disk 39.25 (978-1-59335-855-6(5), 9781593358556, Brlnc Audio MP3 Lib) Brilliance Audio.
Deputy Sheriff Claire Watkins is the sole female deputy in Fort St. Antoine, Wisconsin, a quiet Mississippi River town an hour and a half from the Twin Cities. The official population in Fort St. Antoine is now 142, but it's a figure that is about to be reduced dramatically as several suspicious deaths are reported. Claire's investigations focus on a local woman with a suspicious history of serial widowhood.

Poison in the Pen, unabr. ed. Patricia Wentworth. Read by Nadia May. 5 cass. (Running Time: 7 hrs.). 1992. 39.95 (978-0-7861-0320-1(5), 1281) Blckstn Audio.
When a mysterious suicide follows an outbreak of poison pen letters in the quiet village of Tilling Green, Detective Inspector Frank Abbott of Scotland Yard dispatches Miss Silver to investigate. Disguised as a vacationer, the retired governess learns of the marital & financial difficulties among the Reptons at the Manor House as well as all the petty details of life among the other village inhabitants. It soon becomes apparent to Miss Silver that the suicide was murder & that there is a vicious & demented killer at work. The officious letters still come & the terror mounts with two more seemingly unconnected murders. Miss Silver almost becomes a fourth victim, but outwits the killer with her usual straight-spined aplomb.

Poison Pages. Michael Dahl. Illus. by Martin Blanco. (Library of Doom Ser.). (gr. 1-3). 2008. audio compact disk 14.60 (978-1-4342-0605-3(X)) CapstoneDig.

***Poison Throne.** unabr. ed. Celine Kiernan. Read by Ellen Grafton & Kate Rudd. (Running Time: 14 hrs.). (Moorehawke Trilogy). 2010. 24.99 (978-1-4418-9177-8(3), 9781441891778, BAD); 39.97 (978-1-4418-9178-5(1), 9781441891785, BADLE); 24.99 (978-1-4418-9175-4(7), 9781441891754, Brilliance MP3); 39.97 (978-1-4418-9176-1(5), 9781441891761, Brlnc Audio MP3 Lib); audio compact disk 89.97 (978-1-4418-9174-7(9), 9781441891747, BriAudCD Unabrid); audio compact disk 34.99 (978-1-4418-9173-0(0), 9781441891730, Bril Audio CD Unabri) Brilliance Audio.

Poisoned Chalice: Being the Second Journal of Sir Roger Shallot Concerning Wicked Conspiracies & Horrible Murders Perpetrated in the Reign of King Henry VIII. unabr. ed. Michael Clynes, pseud. 7 cass. 1998. 76.95 Set. (978-1-85903-137-7(4)) Pub: Magna Story GBR. Dist(s): Ulverscroft US

Poisoned Cherries. unabr. ed. Quintin Jardine. Read by Joe Dunlop. 8 cass. (Running Time: 12 hrs.). (Sound Ser.). (J). 2003. 69.95 (978-1-84283-482-4(7)) Pub: ISIS Lrg Prnt GBR. Dist(s): Ulverscroft US

Poisoned Cherries. unabr. ed. Quintin Jardine. Read by Joe Dunlop. 9 CDs. (Running Time: 34200 sec.). (Sound Ser.). 2003. audio compact disk 84.95 (978-1-84283-530-2(0)) Pub: ISIS Lrg Prnt GBR. Dist(s): Ulverscroft US

Poisoned Rose. unabr. ed. Leann Sweeney. Read by Stephanie Brush. 8 cass. (Running Time: 9 hrs. 30 min.). 2001. 49.95 (978-1-58116-036-9(4)) Books in Motion.
When yardman Ben Garrison is found poisoned on the Rose estate, Abby Rose discovers Ben was not the man he claimed to be. In a search for the truth, Abby unearths a generation of deceit, forgery, and blackmail, which places her in grave danger.

***Poisoner's Handbook: Murder & the Birth of Forensic Medicine in Jazz Age New York.** unabr. ed. Deborah Blum. Narrated by Coleen Marlo. (Running Time: 10 hrs. 0 mins.). 2010. 34.99 (978-1-4001-9550-3(0)); 16.99 (978-1-4001-8550-4(5)) Tantor Media.

***Poisoner's Handbook: Murder & the Birth of Forensic Medicine in Jazz Age New York.** unabr. ed. Deborah Blum. Narrated by Coleen Marlo. 1 MP3-CD. (Running Time: 10 hrs 0 mins. 0 sec.). (ENG.). 2010. 24.99 (978-1-4001-6550-6(4)); audio compact disk 69.99 (978-1-4001-4550-8(3)); audio compact disk 34.99 (978-1-4001-1550-1(7)) Pub: Tantor Media. Dist(s): IngramPubServ

Poisoning in the Pub. Simon Brett. 2009. audio compact disk 79.95 (978-0-7531-4353-7(4)) Pub: Isis Pubng Ltd GBR. Dist(s): Ulverscroft US

Poisoning in the Pub: The Fethering Mysteries. Simon Brett. 2009. 61.95 (978-0-7531-4352-0(6)) Pub: Isis Pubng Ltd GBR. Dist(s): Ulverscroft US

Poisonist. unabr. ed. Jonathan Hickman. Narrated by Jonathan Hickman. (Running Time: 8 hrs. 40 mins.). 2009. audio compact disk 29.95 (978-1-57545-356-9(8), RP Audio Pubng) Pub: Reagent Press. Dist(s): OverDrive Inc

Poisonous Snakes. unabr. ed. Ed. by Linda Spizzirri. 1 cass. (Running Time: 15 min.). Dramatization. (Educational Coloring Book & Cassette Package Ser.). (J). (gr. k-8). 1989. pap. bk. 6.95 (978-0-86545-158-2(3)) Spizzirri.
Explores the world's largest, fastest, deadliest poisonous snakes.

Poisonwood Bible. unabr. ed. Barbara Kingsolver. Read by Dean Robertson. 10 cass. (Running Time: 16 hrs.). 1998. 44.95 (978-1-56740-408-1(1), 1567404081, BAU) Brilliance Audio.

Poisonwood Bible, unabr. ed. Barbara Kingsolver. Read by Dean Robertson. 10 cass. (Running Time: 16 hrs.). 1998. 89.25 (978-1-56740-610-8(6), 1567406106, Unabridge Lib Edns) Brilliance Audio.
The Poisonwood Bible is a story told by the wife and four daughters of Nathan Price, a fierce evangelical Baptist who takes his family and mission to the Belgian Congo in 1959. They carry with them all they believe they will need from home, but soon find that all of it - from garden seeds to Scripture - is calamitously transformed on African soil. This tale of one family's tragic undoing and remarkable reconstruction, over the course of three decades in postcolonial Africa, is set against history's most dramatic political parables. The Poisonwood Bible dances between the darkly comic human failings and inspiring poetic justices of our times. In a compelling exploration of religion, conscience, imperialist arrogance, and the many paths to redemption, Barbara Kingsolver has brought forth her most ambitious work ever.

Poisonwood Bible. unabr. ed. Barbara Kingsolver. Read by Dean Robertson. (Running Time: 16 hrs.). 2004. 19.99 (978-1-59335-902-7(0), 1593359020, Brilliance MP3); 39.25 (978-1-59335-903-4(9), 1593359039, Brlnc Audio MP3 Lib) Brilliance Audio.

Poisonwood Bible. unabr. ed. Barbara Kingsolver. Read by Dean Robertson. (Running Time: 16 hrs.). 2004. 39.25 (978-1-59710-585-9(6), 1597105856, BADLE); 24.95 (978-1-59710-584-2(8), 1597105848, BAD) Brilliance Audio.

***Poisonwood Bible.** unabr. ed. Barbara Kingsolver. Read by Dean Robertson. (Running Time: 16 hrs.). 2010. audio compact disk 19.99 (978-1-4558-0093-3(7), 9781455800933, Bril Audio CD Unabri); audio compact disk 79.97 (978-1-4558-0094-0(5), 9781455800940, BriAudCD Unabrid) Brilliance Audio.

Poke Salad. Kay McFarland. 2006. audio compact disk 17.99 (978-1-59886-905-7(1)) Tate Pubng.

Pokemon - Showtrax. Arranged by Mark Brymer. 1 CD. 2000. audio compact disk 19.95 H Leonard.
Combines the TV theme & the irresistible PokeRAP into a package your choir will love to perform.

Pokemon Diamond & Pearl Tin-02. Pokemon. 2008. 14.99 (978-1-60438-042-2(X)) Pub: Upper Dck Co. Dist(s): Diamond Book Dists

Pol Pot: Why? Hosted by Leonard Peikoff. 1 cass. (Philosophy: Who Needs It? Ser.). 1998. 12.95 (LPXXC54) Second Renaissance.

Pola Chapelle Sings Italian Folk Songs. Perf. by Pola Chapelle. Music by Raphael Boguslaw. (Running Time: 38 mins). (ITA.). 2005. audio compact disk 16.00 (978-0-9763967-4-1(2)) Hallelujah.

Poland. James A. Michener. Read by Larry McKeever. 1993. 88.00 (978-0-7366-2350-6(7)) Books on Tape.

Poland. unabr. ed. Victoria Varga. Read by Peter Hackes. Ed. by Wendy McElroy. Prod. by Pat Childs. (Running Time: 10800 sec.). (World's Political Hot Spots Ser.). 2006. audio compact disk 25.95 (978-0-7861-6447-9(6)) Pub: Blckstn Audio. Dist(s): NetLibrary CO

Poland. unabr. ed. Victoria Varga. Read by Peter Hackes. Ed. by Wendy McElroy. 2 cass. (Running Time: 3 hrs.). Dramatization. (World's Political Hot Spots Ser.). (YA). (gr. 11 up). 1992. 17.95 (978-0-938935-99-5(2), 10363) Knowledge Prod.
The breakdown of Europe's Eastern Bloc proves that its map of Europe cannot be redrawn merely to serve political ends. Perhaps no country illustrates this more clearly than Poland, whose borders often have been a negotiating tool of the Big Powers.

Poland, Pt. A. unabr. ed. James A. Michener. Read by Larry McKeever. 11 cass. (Running Time: 16 hrs. 30 min.). 1993. 88.00 (978-0-7366-2349-0(3), 3127A) Books on Tape.
Poland's history, skillfully portrayed, in this multi-generational novel that moves from the 13th century to the present.

Poland, Pt. B. unabr. ed. James A. Michener. Read by Larry McKeever. 11 cass. (Running Time: 16 hrs. 30 min.). 1993. 88.00 (3127B) Books on Tape.

Polar Bear, Polar Bear, Audiocassette. Bill Martin. (Metro Reading Ser.). (J). (gr. k). 2000. 8.46 (978-1-58120-981-5(9)) Metro Teaching.

Polar Bears of Blue Hill: Fighting Cancer Through Visualization. Interview with Erik Esselstyn. 1 cass. (Running Time: 1 hr.). 10.95 (OP-80-12-25, HarperThor) HarpC GBR.

Polar Bears Past Bedtime. unabr. ed. Mary Pope Osborne. 1 cass. (Running Time: 45 mins.). (Magic Tree House Ser.: No. 12). (J). (gr. k-3). 2004. pap. bk. 17.00 (978-0-8072-0537-2(0), Listening Lib) Random Audio Pubg.

Polar Bear's Welcome. unabr. ed. Ramona du Houx. Voice by Ramona du Houx et al. 1 cass. (Running Time: 1 hr.). Dramatization. (J). 1991. 4.95 (978-1-882190-01-0(7)) Polar Bear ME.
Greek Legends & American Lore come together in a mythological tale of hope, wisdom & love. Come & discover Polar Bear's wishing well. Children are calmed & inspired by the stories.

Polar Express. Chris Van Allsburg. Illus. by Chris Van Allsburg. (J). (ps-3). 1987. 18.66 (978-0-676-31743-5(X)) SRA McGraw.

Polar Express. unabr. ed. Chris Van Allsburg. Read by William Hurt. 1 cass. (Running Time: 11 mins.). (J). (ps-3). 1990. 11.00 (978-0-8072-0193-0(6), FTR 138 CX, Listening Lib) Random Audio Pubg.
With a flawless storyline, Chris Van Allsburg's Polar Express evokes all the drama, mystery & poignancy of a Christmas classic. The masterfully rendered full color art adds a quiet elegance & subtle dimension to the powerful narrative. In this new recording, William Hurt's narration masterfully blends with the rhythms & cadences of the beautifully orchestrated music. "For all who truly believe," this is indeed a story for a lifetime.

Polar Habitats Audio CD. Adapted by Benchmark Education Company Staff. Based on a work by Kira Freed. (Early Explorers Set C Ser.). (J). (gr. 2). 2008. audio compact disk 10.00 (978-1-60437-554-1(X)) Benchmark Educ.

Polar Shift. Clive Cussler & Paul Kemprecos. 12 CDs. (Running Time: 15 hrs.). (NUMA Files Ser.: No. 6). 2005. audio compact disk 96.00 (978-1-4159-0760-3(9)) Books on Tape.

Polar Shift. abr. ed. Clive Cussler. Read by Ron McLarty. Told to Paul Kemprecos. (Running Time: 6 hrs.). No. 6. (ENG.). (gr. 8). 2007. audio compact disk 14.95 (978-0-14-314221-8(6), PengAudBks) Penguin Grp USA.

Polar Shift. unabr. ed. Clive Cussler & Paul Kemprecos. 10 cass. (Running Time: 15 hrs.). (NUMA Files Ser.: No. 6). 2005. 90.00 (978-1-4159-0759-7(5)) Books on Tape.

Polar Star. unabr. ed. Martin Cruz Smith. Narrated by Frank Muller. 8 cass. (Running Time: 10 hrs. 45 mins.). (Arkady Renko Ser.: No. 2). 1990. 70.00 (978-1-55690-420-2(7), 90002E7) Recorded Bks.
Ex-Chief Investigator Renko is in deep on the "slime line," the fish-gutting station in a Soviet fish factory ship of some 250 souls. Almost as many secrets & a dangerous shipboard sub-culture that cares little for the Party & less for human life.

Polar Star. unabr. collector's ed. Martin Cruz Smith. Read by Wolfram Kandinsky. 10 cass. (Running Time: 15 hrs.). (Arkady Renko Ser.: No. 2). 1989. 80.00 (978-0-7366-1620-1(9), 2480) Books on Tape.
Arkady Renko, the moody & brooding hero of Gorky Park, is back after an absence of eight years. He has not prospered. We don't envy his circumstances. Forced out of the Moscow hierarchy, he exists in the lonely, dirty, twilight of a Soviet factory ship, Polar Star. He wants only to avoid the limelight, but when murder is done, he can't stay on the sidelines. In Renko, Martin Cruz Smith has created a character not only vivid & memorable, but believable. He has a stubborn, unheroic streak of individualism that makes us like & identify with him. He's like all of us, as we wish we were.

Polarities; The Call to Service. Ann Ree Colton & Jonathan Murro. 1 cass. 7.95 A R Colton Fnd.

Pole to Pole. Michael Palin. Contrib. by Michael Palin. 6 CDs. (Running Time: 5 hrs. 38 mins.). 2006. audio compact disk 64.95 (978-0-7927-4339-2(3), BBCD 166) AudioGO.

Pole to Pole. unabr. ed. Michael Palin. Narrated by Michael Palin. (Running Time: 5 hrs. 40 mins. 0 sec.). (ENG.). 2010. audio compact disk 49.95 (978-1-60283-833-8(X)) Pub: AudioGO. Dist(s): Perseus Dist

Policarpa Salavarrieta. unabr. ed. Abuelo Historias Del. (SPA.). 2007. audio compact disk 13.00 (978-958-8318-03-5(3)) Pub: Yoyo Music COL. Dist(s): YoYoMusic

Police at the Funeral. unabr. ed. Margery Allingham. Read by Francis Matthews. 8 cass. (Running Time: 12 hrs.). (Albert Campion Ser.: Bk. 4). 2000. 59.95 (978-0-7451-5729-0(7), CAB 434) Pub: Chivers Audio Bks GBR. Dist(s): AudioGO
Uncle Andrew is dead, Aunt Julia is poisoned and Uncle William is attacked... and once again, Albert Campion comes to the rescue. Bland, blue-eyed and deceptively vague, he encounters the formidable Great Aunt Caroline and her bizarre household of horror as he searches for clues through a delightful mess of intrigue.

Policeman's Ball. Harry Cole. 5 cass. (Isis Cassettes Ser.). (J). 2006. 49.95 (978-0-7531-2104-7(2)) Pub: ISIS Lrg Prnt GBR. Dist(s): Ulverscroft US

Policeman's Lot. unabr. ed. Harry Cole. Read by Christopher Scott. 6 cass. (Running Time: 7 hrs. 5 mins.). (Isis Cassettes Ser.). (J). 2006. 54.95 (978-1-85695-272-9(X)) Pub: ISIS Lrg Prnt GBR. Dist(s): Ulverscroft US

Policeman's Patch. unabr. ed. Harry Cole. Read by Christopher Scott. 6 cass. (Isis Cassettes Ser.). 2006. 54.95 (978-1-85695-277-4(0)) Pub: ISIS Lrg Prnt GBR. Dist(s): Ulverscroft US

Policeman's Patrol: More Hilarious Tales of Life on the Beat. unabr. ed. Harry Cole. Read by Christopher Scott. 5 cass. (Running Time: 7 hrs. 30 mins.). 2001. 49.95 (978-0-7531-0840-6(2), 000610) Pub: ISIS Audio GBR. Dist(s): Ulverscroft US

Policeman's Prelude. unabr. ed. Harry Cole. 5 cass. (Isis Cassettes Ser.). (J). 2005. 49.95 (978-0-7531-1761-3(4)) Pub: ISIS Lrg Prnt GBR. Dist(s): Ulverscroft US

Policeman's Progress. unabr. ed. Harry Cole. Read by Christopher Scott. 6 cass. (Running Time: 7 hrs. 30 mins.). (Isis Cassettes Ser.). (J). 1995. 54.95 (978-1-85695-282-8(7)) Pub: ISIS Lrg Prnt GBR. Dist(s): Ulverscroft US

Policeman's Story. unabr. ed. Harry Cole. Read by Chrstopher Scott. 6 cass. (Isis Cassettes Ser.). (J). 2005. 54.95 (978-0-7531-1564-0(6)) Pub: ISIS Lrg Prnt GBR. Dist(s): Ulverscroft US

Policeman's Travels. unabr. ed. Harry Cole. Read by Christopher Scott. 6 cass. (Running Time: 7 hrs. 52 mins.). (Isis Cassettes Ser.). (J). 2004. 54.95 (978-0-7531-1884-9(X)) Pub: ISIS Lrg Prnt GBR. Dist(s): Ulverscroft US

Policing Patents for Infringement - Best Practices for Protection & Prosecution. Ed. by ReedLogic Staff. 2006. audio compact disk 249.95 (978-1-59701-090-0(1)) Aspatore Bks.

Policing the City: Crime & Legal Authority in London, C. 1780-1840. Andrew T. Harris. (History of Crime & Criminal Justice Ser.). 2004. audio compact disk 9.95 (978-0-8142-9046-0(9)) Pub: Ohio St U Pr. Dist(s): Chicago Distribution Ctr

***Policy.** unabr. ed. Patrick Lynch. Read by Sandra Burr. (Running Time: 13 hrs.). 2010. 24.99 (978-1-4418-4149-0(0), 9781441841490, Brilliance MP3); 39.97 (978-1-4418-4150-6(4), 9781441841506, Brlnc Audio MP3 Lib); 39.97 (978-1-4418-4152-0(0), 9781441841520, BADLE); 24.99 (978-1-4418-4151-3(2), 9781441841513, BAD) Brilliance Audio.

Polihale & Other Kaua'i Legends. Frederick B. Wichman. 1 cass. 1992. pap. bk.; 8.00 SELECTIONS FROM PAP. BK. (978-0-910043-29-8(9)) Bamboo Ridge Pr.

Polish. 2 cass. (Running Time: 80 min.). (Language - Thirty Library). bk. 16.95 set in vinyl album. Moonbeam Pubns.
Using the proven method based on the famous U.S. Military accelerated language learning program, Language/30 courses stress conversationally useful words & phrases.

Polish. Created by Berlitz. (Berlitz in 60 Minutes Ser.). (POL & ENG., 2008. audio compact disk 9.95 (978-981-268-390-8(9)) Pub: Berlitz Pubng. Dist(s): Langenscheidt

Polish. Ed. by Charles Berlitz. 2 cass. (Running Time: 1 hr. 30 mins.). (Language/30 Brief Course Ser.). pap. bk. 21.95 (AF1053) J Norton Pubs.
Quick, highly condensed introduction to the words & phrases you'll need to communicate effectively in the country you're visiting. Cassettes & phrase guide book are in a vinyl album.

Polish. Hania Forss & Collins UK Staff. Contrib. by Rosi McNab. (Running Time: 3 hrs. 0 mins. 0 sec.). (Collins Easy Learning Audio Course Ser.). (ENG.). 2009. audio compact disk 18.95 (978-0-00-727177-1(8)) Pub: HarpC GBR. Dist(s): IPG Chicago

Polish: Language 30. Educational Services Corporation Staff. 2004. audio compact disk 21.95 (978-1-931850-15-5(1)) Educ Svcs DC.

Polish: Language/30. rev. ed. Educational Services Corporation Staff. Intro. by Charles Berlitz. 2 cass. (POL.). 1995. pap. bk. 21.95 (978-0-910542-83-8(X)) Educ Svcs DC.
Polish self-teaching language course.

Polish: Learn to Speak & Understand Polish with Pimsleur Language Programs. Pimsleur Staff. (Running Time: 40 hrs. 0 mins. 0 sec.). (Quick & Simple Ser.). (ENG.). 2004. audio compact disk 19.95 (978-0-7435-2887-0(5), Pimsleur) Pub: S&S Audio. Dist(s): S and S Inc

Polish: Learn to Speak & Understand Polish with Pimsleur Language Programs. Pimsleur Staff & Pimsleur. (Running Time: 160 hrs. 0 mins. 0 sec.). (Comprehensive Ser.). (POL & ENG.). 2004. audio compact disk 345.00 (978-0-7435-2889-4(1), Pimsleur) Pub: S&S Audio. Dist(s): S and S Inc

Polish: Learn to Speak & Understand Polish with Pimsleur Language Programs. unabr. ed. Pimsleur Staff. 5 CDs. (Running Time: 50 hrs. 0 mins. 0 sec.). (Basic Ser.). (POL & ENG.). 2006. audio compact disk 24.95 (978-0-7435-5081-9(1), Pimsleur) Pub: S&S Audio. Dist(s): S and S Inc

Polish: Short Course, Set. Paul Pimsleur. 5 cass. (Pimsleur Language Learning Ser.). 1996. 149.95 Set, incl. study guide. (0671-57942-8) SyberVision.

Polish: Textbook of the Polish Language for English-Speaking People. Joseph Wira. (C). 1987. (978-0-9618215-2-4(3)) Belweder Pr.

Polish-American - Puerto Rican American. Joe Giordano. Narrated by George Guidall. Contrib. by Nydia Garcia-Preto et al. 6 cass. (Running Time: 30 min.). (Growing Up in America Ser.: Vol. 5). 1997. 12.00 Set. (978-1-891207-05-1(9)) Ethnic Prods.

Polish Folk Legends. Florence Waszkelewicz-Clowes. 1 cass. (Running Time: 1 hr. 40 min.). 1993. 11.95 (978-0-9634152-1-9(2)) Polish-Amer Jrnl.

Polish for Speakers of English, Compact. unabr. ed. 5 cass. (Running Time: 5 hrs.). (Pimsleur Tapes Ser.). (POL.). 1996. 129.00 Set. (19250, Pimsleur) S&S Audio.
A ten-lesson-unit program based upon the Pimsleur Spoken Language Programmed Instructional Method, providing basic beginning language training to the ACTFL Novice Level.

Polish Officer. collector's ed. Alan Furst. Read by Stuart Langton. 7 cass. (Running Time: 10 hrs. 30 min.). 2000. 56.00 (978-0-7366-5512-5(3)) Books on Tape.
In 1939, as the German army ravages his country, Captain Alexander de Milja enlists in the newly formed Polish underground & takes his first act of defiance: hiding Poland's gold reserves on a refugee train & moving them beyond the German grasp. As the war continues, he moves from Warsaw to Paris & on the the frozen Ukraine... living in the shadows, always on the run, always just one step away from discovery & ruin.

Polish Officer. unabr. ed. Alan Furst. Read by George Guidall. (Running Time: 11 hrs. 45 mins.). 2008. 56.75 (978-1-4361-1556-8(6)); audio compact disk 123.75 (978-1-4193-1675-3(3), Clipper Audio) Recorded Bks.

Polish Phrase Book. Created by Berlitz Publishing Staff. (Berlitz Phrase Books & CD Ser.). (POL & ENG., 2007. audio compact disk 14.95 (978-981-268-193-5(0)) Pub: Berlitz Pubng. Dist(s): Langenscheidt

Polish Readings & Conversations. Maria Swiecicka-Ziemianek. 1 CD. (Running Time: 60 MIN.). (POL.). 2005. audio compact disk 29.50 (978-1-57970-229-8(5), AFP600D) J Norton Pubs.

Polish with Ease see Polnisch Ohne Muhe

Polishing Professional Style. Shad Helmstetter. 1 cass. (Self-Talk Ser.). 10.95 (978-0-937065-54-9(4)) Grindle Pr.
Companion Self-Talk Cassettes as mentioned in the book, "What To Say When You Talk To Your Self".

Political & Social Consequences of Price Inflation. Lawrence Fertig et al. 1 cass. (Running Time: 1 hr. 24 min.). 11.95 (286) J Norton Pubs.

Political Astrology in Divisional Harmonics. H. M. Ishikawa. 1 cass. 8.95 (172) Am Fed Astrologers.
Rectification of Presidential candidates' birth times.

Political Brain: The Role of Emotion in Deciding the Fate of the Nation. unabr. ed. Drew Westen. Read by Anthony Heald. (Running Time: 59400 sec.). 2007. 85.95 (978-1-4332-0889-8(X)); 29.95 (978-1-4332-0891-1(1)); audio compact disk 29.95 (978-1-4332-0893-5(8)); audio compact disk 108.00 (978-1-4332-0890-4(3)); audio compact disk 29.95 (978-1-4332-0892-8(X)) Blckstn Audio.

Political Creed & Character. Robert Lindner. 1 cass. (Running Time: 25 min.). 10.95 (27015) J Norton Pubs.
An analysis of the personality dynamics of those individuals who join communist & fascist political groups.

Political Death. unabr. ed. Antonia Fraser. Read by Patricia Hodge. 6 cass. (Running Time: 9 hrs.). (Jemima Shore Mystery Ser.: Bk. 8). 2000. 49.95 (CAB 1199) Pub: Chivers Audio Bks GBR. Dist(s): AudioGO
Summoned by Lady Imogen Swain, Jemima Shore is entrusted with the diaries she kept in 1964, diaries that contain an account of Imogen's passionate affair with Burgo Smyth, now a foreign secretary. Jemima's meeting with Imogen is just the first step in a series of sinister events that lead to political scandal, blackmail and murder.

Political Death: A Jemima Shore Mystery. unabr. ed. Antonia Fraser. Read by Patricia Hodge. 6 cass. (Running Time: 6 hrs.). 1996. 54.95 (978-0-7451-6583-7(4), CAB1199) AudioGO.

Political Death: A Jemima Shore Mystery. unabr. ed. Antonia Fraser. Read by Donada Peters. 5 cass. (Running Time: 7 hrs. 30 min.). 1994. 40.00 (5109) Books on Tape.
A TV reporter has just recovered juicy bits involving the current Foreign Secretary when this discovery shifts from scandal to murder.

Political Fund Raising. 4 cass. (Running Time: 4 hrs.). 38.00 (27025-27028) J Norton Pubs.
Specialists in various fields of political fund raising discuss their methods & assess their profession.

Political Incorrections: The Best Opening Monologues from Politically Incorrect with Bill Maher. Bill Maher. 2004. 7.95 (978-0-7435-4179-4(0)) Pub: S&S Audio. Dist(s): S and S Inc

Political Mind: Why You Can't Understand 21st-Century American Politics with an 18th-Century Brain. George Lakoff. Read by Kent Cassella. (Playaway Adult Nonfiction Ser.). (ENG.). 2009. 64.99 (978-1-60812-547-0(5)) Find a World.

Political Mind: Why You Can't Understand 21st Century American Politics with an 18th Century Brain. unabr. ed. George Lakoff. Narrated by Kent Cassella. 7 CDs. (Running Time: 8 hrs. 30 mins. 0 sec.). (ENG.). 2008. audio compact disk 69.99 (978-1-4001-3809-8(4)) Pub: Tantor Media. Dist(s): IngramPubServ

Political Mind: Why You Can't Understand 21st Century American Politics with an 18th Century Brain. unabr. ed. George Lakoff. Read by Kent Cassella. 7 CDs. (Running Time: 8 hrs. 30 mins. 0 sec.). (ENG.). 2008. audio compact disk 34.99 (978-1-4001-0809-1(8)); audio compact disk 24.99 (978-1-4001-5809-6(5)) Pub: Tantor Media. Dist(s): IngramPubServ

Political Savvy. Susan Dellinger. 4 cass. (Running Time: 4 hrs.). 49.95 CareerTrack Pubns.
A discussion of the nature of power & politics, as well as many tips on how to build power within the organizational structure.

Political Thought of the Roman State-Church. John Robbins. 1 cass. (Conference on Christianity & Roman Catholicism Ser.: No. 7). 5.00 Trinity Found.

Political Wives. 1 cass. (Running Time: 30 min.). 9.95 (G0300B090, HarperThor) HarpC GBR.

Political Zoo. abr. ed. Michael Savage. Narrated by Tim Lundeen. (ENG.). 2006. 18.19 (978-1-60814-340-5(6)) Oasis Audio.

Politically Correct Holiday Stories For an Enlightened Yultide Season. James Finn Garner. 2004. 5.95 (978-0-7435-4150-3(2)) Pub: S&S Audio. Dist(s): S and S Inc

Politically Incorrect Guide to American History. Thomas E. Woods, Jr. (Running Time: 32400 sec.). 2005. 54.95 (978-0-7861-3534-9(4)); audio compact disk 63.00 (978-0-7861-7792-9(6)) Blckstn Audio.

Politically Incorrect Guide to American History. unabr. ed. Thomas E. Woods, Jr. 1 MP3. (Running Time: 28800 sec.). 2005. audio compact disk 29.95 (978-0-7861-8011-0(0), ZM3508) Blckstn Audio.

Politically Incorrect Guide to American History. unabr. ed. Thomas E. Woods, Jr. Read by Barrett Whitener. 6 cass. (Running Time: 8 hrs.). 2005. 29.95 (978-0-7861-3758-9(4), E3508); audio compact disk 29.95 (978-0-7861-7636-6(9), ZE3508) Blckstn Audio.

Politically Incorrect Guide to Capitalism. unabr. ed. Robert P. Murphy. Read by Perry Richards. (Running Time: 21600 sec.). (Politically Incorrect Guides). 2007. 25.95 (978-0-7861-4922-3(1)); audio compact disk 25.95 (978-0-7861-5899-7(9)) Blckstn Audio.

Politically Incorrect Guide to Capitalism. unabr. ed. Robert P. Murphy. Read by Perry Richards. (Running Time: 21600 sec.). (Politically Incorrect Guides). 2007. 54.95 (978-0-7861-6871-2(4)); audio compact disk 63.00 (978-0-7861-6870-5(6)); audio compact disk 29.95 (978-0-7861-7050-0(6)) Blckstn Audio.

Politically Incorrect Guide to Darwin & Intelligent Design. unabr. ed. Jonathan Wells. Read by Tom Weiner. 6 CDs. (Running Time: 21600 sec.). 2006. audio compact disk 25.95 (978-0-7861-6840-8(4)) Blckstn Audio.

Politically Incorrect Guide to Darwin & Intelligent Design. unabr. ed. Jonathan Wells. Read by Tom Weiner. (Running Time: 21600 sec.). 2006. 44.95 (978-0-7861-4769-4(5)); audio compact disk 29.95 (978-0-7861-7454-6(4)) Blckstn Audio.

Politically Incorrect Guide to Darwinism & Intelligent Design. unabr. ed. Jonathan Wells. Read by Tom Weiner. 5 cass. (Running Time: 21600 sec.). 2006. 25.95 (978-0-7861-4628-4(1)) Blckstn Audio.

Politically Incorrect Guide to Darwinism & Intelligent Design. unabr. ed. Jonathan Wells. Read by Tom Weiner. (Running Time: 21600 sec.). 2006. audio compact disk 55.00 (978-0-7861-6375-5(5)) Blckstn Audio.

Politically Incorrect Guide to English & American Literature. unabr. ed. Elizabeth Kantor. Read by James Adams. 7 cass. (Running Time: 28800 sec.). 2006. 25.95 (978-0-7861-4626-0(5)); 72.95 (978-0-7861-4832-5(2)); audio compact disk 25.95 (978-0-7861-6838-5(2)); audio compact disk 29.95 (978-0-7861-7452-2(8)); audio compact disk 90.00 (978-0-7861-6138-6(8)) Blckstn Audio.

Politically Incorrect Guide to Global Warming. Christopher C. Horner. Read by Jeff Riggenbach. (Running Time: 41400 sec.). 2007. audio compact disk 63.00 (978-0-7861-6177-5(9)) Blckstn Audio.

Politically Incorrect Guide to Global Warming: (and Environmentalism) Christopher C. Horner. Read by Jeff Riggenbach. (Running Time: 41400 sec.). 2007. 54.95 (978-0-7861-4824-0(1)) Blckstn Audio.

Politically Incorrect Guide to Global Warming (and Environmentalism) unabr. ed. Christopher C. Horner. Read by Jeff Riggenbach. (Running Time: 41400 sec.). 2007. 29.95 (978-0-7861-4823-3(3)); audio compact disk 29.95 (978-0-7861-6176-8(0)); audio compact disk 29.95 (978-0-7861-7166-8(9)) Blckstn Audio.

Politically Incorrect Guide to Islam. unabr. ed. Robert Spencer. Read by Jeff Riggenbach. 6 cass. (Running Time: 10 hrs.). (YA). 2005. 29.95 (978-0-7861-4416-7(5)) Blckstn Audio.

Politically Incorrect Guide to Islam: And the Crusades. unabr. ed. Robert Spencer. Read by Jeff Riggenbach. 7 CDs. (Running Time: 30600 sec.). 2005. audio compact disk 29.95 (978-0-7861-7395-2(5)) Blckstn Audio.

Politically Incorrect Guide to Islam (and the Crusades) Robert Spencer. (Running Time: 30600 sec.). 2005. 59.95 (978-0-7861-3777-0(0)); audio compact disk 72.00 (978-0-7861-7589-5(3)) Blckstn Audio.

Politically Incorrect Guide to Islam (and the Crusades) unabr. ed. Robert Spencer. Read by Tom Weiner. (Running Time: 30600 sec.). 2005. audio compact disk 29.95 (978-0-7861-7864-3(7)) Blckstn Audio.

Politically Incorrect Guide to the Bible. unabr. ed. Robert J. Hutchinson. Read by Tom Weiner. (Running Time: 30600 sec.). (Politically Incorrect Guides). 2007. 24.95 (978-1-4332-0523-1(8)); audio compact disk 24.95 (978-1-4332-0524-8(6)) Blckstn Audio.

Politically Incorrect Guide to the Bible. unabr. ed. Robert J. Hutchinson. Read by Tom Weiner. (Running Time: 30600 sec.). 2007. 44.95 (978-1-4332-0521-7(1)); audio compact disk & audio compact disk 55.00 (978-1-4332-0522-4(X)) Blckstn Audio.

Politically Incorrect Guide to the Bible. unabr. ed. Robert J. Hutchinson & Tom Weiner. (Running Time: 30600 sec.). (Politically Incorrect Guides). 2007. audio compact disk 29.95 (978-1-4332-0525-5(4)) Blckstn Audio.

Politically Incorrect Guide to the Civil War. unabr. ed. H. W. Crocker, III. (Running Time: 7.5 hrs. NaN mins.). 2008. audio compact disk 29.95 (978-1-4332-5124-5(8)) Blckstn Audio.

Politically Incorrect Guide to the Civil War. unabr. ed. H. W. Crocker, III. (Running Time: 7 hrs. 0 mins.). 2008. audio compact disk & audio compact disk 19.95 (978-1-4332-5123-8(X)) Blckstn Audio.

Politically Incorrect Guide to the Civil War. unabr. ed. H. W. Crocker, III. (Running Time: 7.5 hrs. NaN mins.). 2008. 54.95 (978-1-4332-5121-4(3)); audio compact disk 60.00 (978-1-4332-5122-1(1)) Blckstn Audio.

Politically Incorrect Guide to the Constitution. unabr. ed. Kevin R. C. Gutzman. Read by Tom Weiner. (Running Time: 23400 sec.). (Politically Incorrect Guides). 2007. 19.95 (978-0-7861-4981-0(7)); audio compact disk 19.95 (978-0-7861-5783-9(6)) Blckstn Audio.

Politically Incorrect Guide to the Constitution. unabr. ed. Kevin R. C. Gutzman. Read by Tom Weiner. (Running Time: 23400 sec.). (Politically Incorrect Guides). 2007. 44.95 (978-0-7861-6803-3(X)); audio compact disk 29.95 (978-0-7861-6956-6(7)); audio compact disk 55.00 (978-0-7861-6802-6(1)) Blckstn Audio.

Politically Incorrect Guide to the Founding Fathers. unabr. ed. Brion McClanahan. (Running Time: 8 hrs. 0 mins.). 2009. 29.95 (978-1-4332-7933-1(9)); audio compact disk 24.95 (978-1-4332-7932-4(0)) Blckstn Audio.

Politically Incorrect Guide to the Great Depression & the New Deal. unabr. ed. Robert Murphy. (Running Time: 7 hrs. 30 mins.). (ENG.). 2009. 29.95

(978-1-4332-9360-3(9)); audio compact disk 24.95 (978-1-4332-9359-7(5)) Blckstn Audio.

Politically Incorrect Guide to the Middle East. unabr. ed. Martin Sieff. (Running Time: 23400 sec.). (Politically Incorrect Guides). 2008. audio compact disk 29.95 (978-1-4332-0826-3(1)) Blckstn Audio.

Politically Incorrect Guide to the Middle East. unabr. ed. Martin Sieff. Read by Tom Weiner. (Running Time: 23400 sec.). (Politically Incorrect Guides). 2008. 29.95 (978-1-4332-0824-9(5)); 54.95 (978-1-4332-0827-0(X)); audio compact disk 29.95 (978-1-4332-0825-6(3)); audio compact disk & audio compact disk 63.00 (978-1-4332-0828-7(8)) Blckstn Audio.

***Politically Incorrect Guide to the Sixties.** unabr. ed. Jonathan Leaf. Narrated by Rick Silversmith. 1 Playaway. (Running Time: 5 hrs. 30 mins.). 2009. 59.99 (978-1-4332-9154-8(1)) Blckstn Audio.

Politically Incorrect Guide to the Sixties. unabr. ed. Jonathan Leaf. Narrated by Rick Silversmith. 1 MP3-CD. (Running Time: 5 hrs. 30 mins.). 2009. 29.95 (978-1-4332-5451-2(4)); 54.95 (978-1-4332-5448-2(4)); audio compact disk 29.95 (978-1-4332-5450-5(6)); audio compact disk 76.00 (978-1-4332-5449-9(2)) Blckstn Audio.

Politically Incorrect Guide to the South: (and Why It Will Rise Again) unabr. ed. Clint Johnson. Narrated by Dianna Dorman. (Running Time: 32400 sec.). 2007. audio compact disk 29.95 (978-0-7861-7211-5(8)) Blckstn Audio.

Politically Incorrect Guide to the South: (and Why It Will Rise Again) unabr. ed. Clint Johnson. Read by Dianna Dorman. (Running Time: 32400 sec.). 2007. 54.95 (978-0-7861-4785-4(7)); audio compact disk 63.00 (978-0-7861-6278-9(3)) Blckstn Audio.

Politically Incorrect Guide to the Vietnam War. unabr. ed. Phillip Jennings. (Running Time: 10 hrs. 0 mins.). 2010. 29.95 (978-1-4332-7119-9(2)); audio compact disk 24.95 (978-1-4332-7118-2(4)) Blckstn Audio.

Politically Incorrect Guide(tm) to the Vietnam War. unabr. ed. Phillip Jennings. (Running Time: 10 hrs. 0 mins.). 2010. 59.95 (978-1-4332-7115-1(X)); audio compact disk 90.00 (978-1-4332-7116-8(8)) Blckstn Audio.

Politically Incorrect Guide to Western Civilization. unabr. ed. Anthony Esolen. (Running Time: 39600 sec.). (Politically Incorrect Guides). 2008. 24.95 (978-1-4332-1468-4(7)) Blckstn Audio.

Politically Incorrect Guide to Western Civilization. unabr. ed. Anthony Esolen. Read by Malcolm Hillgartner. (Running Time: 7.5 hrs. 0 mins.). 2008. 29.95 (978-1-4332-1470-7(9)); 59.95 (978-1-4332-1466-0(0)); audio compact disk 70.00 (978-1-4332-1467-7(9)); audio compact disk & audio compact disk 24.95 (978-1-4332-1469-1(5)) Blckstn Audio.

Politically Incorrect Guide to Women, Sex, & Feminism. unabr. ed. Carrie Lukas. Read by Dianna Dorman. (Running Time: 25200 sec.). 2006. 44.95 (978-0-7861-4690-1(7)); audio compact disk 55.00 (978-0-7861-6643-5(6)) Blckstn Audio.

Politically Incorrect Guide to Women, Sex, & Feminism. unabr. ed. Carrie L. Lukas. Read by Dianna Dorman. 6 cass. (Running Time: 19800 sec.). 2006. 24.95 (978-0-7861-4548-5(X)); audio compact disk 25.95 (978-0-7861-7130-9(8)); audio compact disk 29.95 (978-0-7861-7570-3(2)) Blckstn Audio.

Politically Incorrect Guidetrade; to the Founding Fathers. unabr. ed. Brion McClanahan. (Running Time: 8 hrs. 0 mins.). (ENG.). 2009. 54.95 (978-1-4332-7929-4(0)); audio compact disk 76.00 (978-1-4332-7930-0(4)) Blckstn Audio.

Politically Incorrect Guidetrade; to the Great Depression & the New Deal. unabr. ed. Robert Murphy. (Running Time: 7.5 hrs. 0 mins.). (ENG.). 2009. 54.95 (978-1-4332-9356-6(0)); audio compact disk 69.00 (978-1-4332-9357-3(9)) Blckstn Audio.

Politically Incorrect Guide#8482; to the South (and Why It Will Rise Again) unabr. ed. Clint Johnson. (Running Time: 10 hrs. 4 mins.). (J). 2007. 26.95 (978-0-7861-4791-5(1)); audio compact disk 26.95 (978-0-7861-6284-0(8)) Blckstn Audio.

***Politician: An Insider's Account of John Edwards's Pursuit of the Presidency & the Scandal That Brought Him Down.** unabr. ed. Andrew Young. (Running Time: 12 hrs. 0 mins.). 2010. 17.99 (978-1-4001-8650-1(1)) Tantor Media.

***Politician: An Insider's Account of John Edwards's Pursuit of the Presidency & the Scandal That Brought Him Down.** unabr. ed. Andrew Young. Narrated by Kevin Foley. 1 MP3-CD. (Running Time: 11 hrs. 30 mins. 0 sec.). 2010. 24.99 (978-1-4001-6650-3(0)); audio compact disk 34.99 (978-1-4001-1650-8(3)); audio compact disk 69.99 (978-1-4001-4650-5(X)) Pub: Tantor Media. Dist(s): IngramPubServ

Politicians, Partisans, & Parasites: My Adventures in Cable News. unabr. ed. Tucker Carlson. Read by Tucker Carlson. (Running Time: 5 hrs.). 2004. 39.25 (978-1-59335-509-8(2), 1593355092, Brlnc Audio MP3 Lib) Brilliance Audio.

Every weeknight, millions of Americans tune in to see Tucker Carlson anchor the right side of the aisle on CNN's Crossfire. Named by New York magazine as the journalist most likely to succeed in the Years of Bush, he has charmed liberals and roused conservatives with his singular brand of acerbic wit and razor-sharp insight. Tossed by fate (and the O.J. Simpson murder trial) into the trenches of electronic journalism, Carlson learned early that "television brings out the crazy in people." Naturally, he started taking notes. The result is a hilarious and brilliantly revealing look at the most powerful and weirdest medium there is. Carlson has not only seen television from the inside, but dares to describe it. In this book, he takes you behind the curtain of a political talk show: The hosts. The guests. The stalkers. From the heroic to the imprisoned to Monica Lewinsky's sex therapist, Carlson has interviewed them all. Not always edifying, but "definitely more fun than playing Scrabble with the shut-ins," it's a portrait you won't forget.

Politicians, Partisans, & Parasites: My Adventures in Cable News. unabr. ed. Tucker Carlson. Read by Tucker Carlson. (Running Time: 5 hrs.). 2004. 39.25 (978-1-59710-587-3(2), 1597105872, BADLE); 24.95 (978-1-59710-586-6(4), 1597105864, BAD) Brilliance Audio.

Politicians, Partisans, & Parasites: My Adventures in Cable News. unabr. ed. Tucker Carlson. Read by Tucker Carlson. (Running Time: 5 hrs.). 2006. audio compact disk 16.99 (978-1-4233-1563-6(4), 9781423315636, BCD Value Price) Brilliance Audio.

Politicians, Partisans, & Parasites: My Adventures in Cable News. unabr. ed. Tucker Carlson. Read by Tucker Carlson. (Running Time: 5 hrs.). 2004. 24.95 (978-1-59335-235-6(2), 1593352352) Soulmate Audio Bks.

Politicians, Partisans & Parasites: My Adventures in Cable News. unabr. ed. Tucker Carlson. Read by Tucker Carlson. (Running Time: 5 hrs.). 2003. 62.25 (978-1-59355-295-4(5), 1593552955, BrilAudUnabridg) Brilliance Audio.

Politician's Wife. unabr. ed. Shirley Lowe. Read by Judith Franklin. 6 cass. (Running Time: 9 hrs.). (Storysound Ser.). (J). 1996. 64.95 (978-1-85903-112-4(9), 31129) Pub: Mgna Lrg Print GBR. Dist(s): Ulverscroft US

Flora Matlock appears to be the perfect wife when she faces a sex scandal & finds herself caught up in a damage limitation exercise. As she starts to uncover the extent of the lies, she vows to take revenge.

Politics. Aristotle. Narrated by Jim Killavey. (Running Time: 10 hrs.). 1990. 27.95 (978-1-59912-841-2(1)) Iofy Corp.

Politics. Aristotle. Narrated by Bernard Mayes. (Running Time: 10 hrs. 30 mins.). (C). 2000. 30.95 (978-1-59912-572-5(2)) Iofy Corp.

Politics Vol. 5-6. unabr. ed. Aristotle. Read by Bernard Mayes. 7 cass. (Running Time: 10 hrs.). 2001. 49.95 (978-0-7861-1942-4(X), 2713); audio compact disk 72.00 (978-0-7861-9777-4(3), 2713) Blckstn Audio.

Aristotle's succinct & thoughtful analysis is based on his study of over 150 city constitutions & covers the gamut of political issues in order to establish which types are best.

Politics Vol. 5-6. unabr. ed. Aristotle. Read by Jim Killavey. 8 cass. (Running Time: 11 hrs. 50 min.). 1991. 49.00 set. (C-221) Jimcin Record.

Treatise on forms & organizations of government.

Politics Vol. 5-6, Set. abr. ed. Aristotle. Read by Robert L. Halvorson. 6 cass. (Running Time: 360 min.). 42.95 (30) Halvorson Assocs.

***Politics - According to the Bible: A Comprehensive Resource for Understanding Modern Political Issues in Light of Scripture.** unabr. ed. Wayne A. Grudem. (ENG.). (C). 2010. 39.99 (978-0-310-41359-2(1)) Zondervan.

Politics & Society in 20th Century America Series. Eugene Lieber. (ENG.). 2006. audio compact disk 200.00 (978-1-935069-19-5(5)) IAB Inc.

Politics as Experience. unabr. ed. R. D. Laing. 1 cass. (Running Time: 59 min.). 1967. 11.00 (07001) Big Sur Tapes.

Tells us that the schizophrenic is imprisoned by members of a "normal" society because he does not conform to standard patterns of communication & behavior. He has lost his ability to play the deadening social game of lie & counter-lie.

Politics: Corinne McLaughlin & Gordon Davidson in Conversation with Michael Toms: Integrating the Spiritual & the Political. Corinne McLaughlin & Gordon Davidson. 1 cass. (Running Time: 60 min.). 1995. 9.95 (2488) New Dimen Found.

Politics of Bad Faith: The Radical Assault on America's Future. David Horowitz. Read by Jeff Riggenbach. (Running Time: 27000 sec.). 2007. audio compact disk 55.00 (978-0-7861-0362-1(0)) Blckstn Audio.

Politics of Bad Faith: The Radical Assault on America's Future. unabr. ed. David Horowitz. Read by Jeff Riggenbach. 6 cass. (Running Time: 8 hrs. 30 mins.). 2000. 44.95 (978-0-7861-1724-6(9), 2529) Blckstn Audio.

Brings into the open the refusal of the political Left - to learn from the past, specifically from the checkered history of progressive movements for social justice & equal outcomes. This refusal shapes agendas that Horowitz describes as part of a new "cold war" against America - a culture war that pits "progressives" & "multi-culturists" against America's founding principles & ideas.

Politics of Bad Faith: The Radical Assault on America's Future. unabr. ed. David Horowitz. (Running Time: 27000 sec.). 2007. audio compact disk 29.95 (978-0-7861-0364-5(7)) Blckstn Audio.

Politics of Cancer Therapy. Read by G Edward Griffin. 1 cass. (Running Time: 60 min.). 10.00 (978-0-912986-30-2(1), AC11) Am Media.

Reveals who is holding back a control for cancer & why. An expose of the I.G. Farben drug cartel & the use of tax-exempt foundations to control medical schools.

Politics of Diplomacy. abr. ed. James A. Baker, III & DeFrank. Read by James A. Baker, III & James A. Baker, III. (Running Time: 3 hrs.). 2009. 24.99 (978-1-4233-9134-0(9), 9781423391340, Brilliance MP3); 24.99 (978-1-4233-9136-4(5), 9781423391364, BAD); 39.97 (978-1-4233-9135-7(7), 9781423391357, Brlnc Audio MP3 Lib); 39.97 (978-1-4233-9137-1(3), 9781423391371, BADLE) Brilliance Audio.

Politics of Liberty. John Hospers. 1 cass. (Running Time: 1 hr. 22 min.). 11.95 (220) J Norton Pubs.

Hospers presents his interpretation of libertarian philosophy, & lists what he feels are the major warning signs along the road to totalitarianism.

Politics of Pragmatism. Peter Schwartz. Read by Peter Schwartz. 2 cass. (Running Time: 90 min. per cass.). 1987. 24.95 (978-1-56114-033-6(3), HS03D) Second Renaissance.

The dominance of pragmatic, anti-principled "solutions" in politics today: supply-side economics on the right & neoliberalism on the left.

Politics of Psychosurgery. Peter Breggin. 1 cass. (Running Time: 53 min.). 10.95 (192) J Norton Pubs.

Breggin attacks the practice of psychosurgery - "brain mutilation used to control emotions or behavior." He exposes deceptive statements made by its defenders, & analyzes use of the technique for the purpose of mind control, particularly of minorities. Redefinition of our freedoms in psychological terms so as to eliminate them is a growing danger.

Politics of Sodomy. Douglas Wilson. 4 CDs. (ENG.). 2004. audio compact disk 14.00 (978-1-59128-501-4(1)) Canon Pr ID.

Politics of Sodomy. Read by Douglas Wilson. 4. 2004. 11.00 (978-1-59128-500-7(3)); 14.00 (978-1-59128-502-1(X)) Canon Pr ID.

Politics of Virtue. unabr. ed. David Kelley. Read by David Kelley. 1 cass. (Running Time: 1 hr. 30 min.). 1996. 14.95 (978-1-57724-005-1(7), Prncpal Srce Audio) Objectivist Ctr.

Explanation of why the current idealogical battle is shifting from economics & politics to ethics & culture & why this creates a tremendous opportunity for Objectivism.

Politika. abr. ed. Read by Jay O'Sanders. Created by Tom Clancy & Martin Greenberg. 2 CDs. (Running Time: 2 hrs.). (Tom Clancy's Power Plays Ser.: No. 1). 2002. audio compact disk 23.50 (978-0-7435-0426-3(7), Audioworks) S&S Audio.

The sudden death of Russia's president has thrown the Russian Federation into chaos. Devastating crop failures have left millions in the grip of famine, and an uprising seems inevitable.

Polk Presidency. Ernest Yaniger. 1 cass. (Running Time: 33 min. per cass.). 1982. 10.00 (HP519) Esstee Audios.

Polk was America's first dark-horse candidate, best remembered for his land acquisitions through a war with Mexico. Profiled also are his generals, who would distinguish themselves in the Civil War.

Polk the Man Who Transformed. Walter Borneman. 2008. audio compact disk 39.99 (978-1-4281-8535-7(6)) Recorded Bks.

Polka Dots on Crow Mountain: Tall Tales & True Stories Inspired by a Southern Childhood. unabr. ed. Joy Steiner. 1 cass. (Running Time: 52 min.). (J). (ps up). 1996. 10.00 (978-0-9654155-0-7(3)) Pickle Juice.

Humorous stories, rich with visual imagery & rhythmic word play, about the escapades & encounters of the folks in a small southern town.

***Polka Favorites: Accordion Play-along Volume 1.** Created by Hal Leonard Corp. (ENG.). 2011. pap. bk. 14.99 (978-1-4234-9557-4(8), 1423495578) H Leonard.

pollita Vivita: Audiocassette. (SPA.). (gr. k-1). 10.00 (978-0-7635-6270-0(X)) Rigby Educ.

Pollution Control Equipment & Services in Saudi Arabia: A Strategic Reference 2007. Compiled by Icon Group International, Inc. Staff. 2007. ring bd. 195.00 (978-0-497-82409-9(4)) Icon Grp.

Pollution Control Equipment in Peru: A Strategic Reference 2007. Compiled by Icon Group International, Inc. Staff. 2007. ring bd. 195.00 (978-0-497-82382-5(9)) Icon Grp.

Pollution from Non-Point Sources, Pt. 1. Hosted by Nancy Pearlman. 1 cass. (Running Time: 30 min.). 10.00 (606) Educ Comm CA.

Pollution from Non-Point Sources, Pt. 2. Hosted by Nancy Pearlman. 1 cass. (Running Time: 29 min.). 10.00 (607) Educ Comm CA.

Pollution in Puget Sound, Washington, U. S. A. & Reef Protection in Australia. Hosted by Nancy Pearlman. 1 cass. (Running Time: 28 min.). 10.00 (813) Educ Comm CA.

Pollution in Santa Monica Bay. Hosted by Nancy Pearlman. 1 cass. (Running Time: 29 min.). 10.00 (242) Educ Comm CA.

Pollution of the Great Lakes. 1 cass. (Running Time: 1 hr. 30 min.). 11.95 (G0490B090, HarperThor) HarpC GBR.

Pollution Solution: Keeping Earth a Beautiful Place. Peter Enns. Illus. by Lock Wolverton. 1 cass. (J). (ps-6). 1992. 5.98 (978-0-943593-76-0(X)) Kids Intl Inc.

Pollution Solutions with California's Berkeley Ecology Center, El Cerrito's Recycling Center, & Alameda's West County Toxic Coalition. Hosted by Nancy Pearlman. 1 cass. (Running Time: 28 min.). 10.00 (1404) Educ Comm CA.

Polly Wolly Doodle (from Through the Eyes of a Child) - ShowTrax. Arranged by John Leavitt. 1 CD. (Running Time: 1 hr. 30 mins.). 2000. audio compact disk 49.95 (08742483) H Leonard.

All four movements of this choral suite available separately.

Pollyanna. Eleanor H. Porter. Read by S. Patricia Bailey. (Running Time: 6 hrs. 30 mins.). 1996. 27.95 (978-1-59912-573-2(0)) Iofy Corp.

Pollyanna. Eleanor H. Porter. Read by Laurel Lefkow. 3. (Running Time: 13284 sec.). (Junior Classics Ser.). (J). (gr. 3-8). 2007. audio compact disk 22.98 (978-962-634-469-9(5), Naxos AudioBooks) Naxos.

Pollyanna. Eleanor H. Porter. Read by Rebecca C. Burns. (Running Time: 21600 sec.). (ENG.). (J). (ps-7). 2005. audio compact disk 49.99 (978-1-4001-3130-3(8)); audio compact disk 19.99 (978-1-4001-5130-1(9)); audio compact disk 24.99 (978-1-4001-0130-6(1)) Pub: Tantor Media. Dist(s): IngramPubServ

Pollyanna. unabr. ed. Eleanor H. Porter. Read by S. Patricia Bailey. 5 cass. (Running Time: 7 hrs.). (gr. 5 up). 1997. 39.95 (978-0-7861-1103-9(8), 1867) Blckstn Audio.

As Pollyanna arrives in Beldingsville to live with her strict & dutiful maiden aunt, she exclaims, "Oh, Aunt Polly, I don't know how to be glad enough that you let me come to live with you!" And from this point she begins to bring cheer into everybody's life, including the sick, the lonely, & the just plain miserable. All are transformed - until one day when something so terrible happens that even Pollyanna doesn't know how to feel glad anymore.

Pollyanna. unabr. ed. Eleanor H. Porter. Read by S. Patricia Bailey. 5 cass. (Running Time: 1 hr. 30 mins. per cass.). (J). 1997. 39.95 (1867) Blckstn Audio.

Pollyanna. unabr. ed. Eleanor H. Porter. Read by Rebecca Burns. (J). 2006. 39.99 (978-1-59895-679-5(5)) Find a World.

Pollyanna. unabr. ed. Eleanor H. Porter. Narrated by Barbara Caruso. 5 pieces. (Running Time: 6 hrs. 45 mins.). (gr. 7 up). 1997. 44.00 (978-0-7887-1335-4(3), 95184E7) Recorded Bks.

An orphan girl cheers lonely & miserable people with her glad game. Then something so terrible happens that she can't find a reason to play it anymore.

Pollyanna. unabr. ed. Eleanor H. Porter. Narrated by Rebecca C. Burns. (Running Time: 6 hrs. 0 mins. 0 sec.). (ENG.). (J). (gr. 4-7). 2008. 19.99 (978-1-4001-5884-3(2)); audio compact disk 45.99 (978-1-4001-3884-5(1)) Pub: Tantor Media. Dist(s): IngramPubServ

Pollyanna. unabr. ed. Eleanor H. Porter. Read by Rebecca C. Burns. (Running Time: 6 hrs. 0 mins. 0 sec.). (ENG.). (J). (gr. 4-7). 2008. audio compact disk 22.99 (978-1-4001-0884-8(5)) Pub: Tantor Media. Dist(s): IngramPubServ

Pollyanna. unabr. collector's ed. Eleanor H. Porter. Read by Rebecca C. Burns. 4 cass. (Running Time: 6 hrs.). (J). 1998. 32.00 (978-0-7366-4182-1(3), 4680) Books on Tape.

Pollyanna is an expert at bringing cheer into everybody's life, until something terrible happens so that even she doesn't feel glad anymore.

Pollyanna, Set. Eleanor H. Porter. Read by Flo Gibson. 4 cass. (Running Time: 6 hrs.). (J). 1995. 19.95 (978-1-55685-355-5(6)) Audio Bk Con.

The hard hearts of Aunt Polly, Mrs. Snow, & "the man" are gradually softened by the appealing ways of eternally optimistic Pollyanna.

Pollyanna: A BBC Radio Full-Cast Dramatization. Eleanor H. Porter. (Running Time: 2 hrs. 0 mins. 0 sec.). (ENG.). 2009. audio compact disk 24.95 (978-1-60283-757-7(0)) Pub: AudioGO. Dist(s): Perseus Dist

Polly's Angel. Katie Flynn. 14 CDs. (Sound Ser.). 2003. audio compact disk 104.95 (978-1-84283-174-8(7)) Pub: UlverLrgPrint GBR. Dist(s): Ulverscroft US

Polly's Angel. unabr. ed. Katie Flynn. Read by Julia Franklyn. 16 cass. (Running Time: 24 hrs.). 2001. 104.95 (978-1-86042-955-2(6), 2-955-6) Pub: Soundings Ltd GBR. Dist(s): Ulverscroft US

When war is declared in 1939, Polly O'Brady is working in a shop in Liverpool. Her friend Tad in Dublin joins the Navy, however, her pal Sunny is in the Air Force, so Polly decides when she is old enough she will join up too. Polly's father has had a stroke & she tries to persuade her mother to take him back to Dublin, where there is no war. Then Polly could leave home. But she has reckoned without the Luftwaffe. The city is bombed & Polly's parents refuse to cut & run when their adopted city - & their family - are in mortal danger.

Polnisch Ohne Muhe. 1 cass. (Running Time: 1 hr. 30 min.).Tr. of Polish with Ease. (GER & POL.). 2000. bk. 75.00 (978-3-89625-103-9(1)); bk. 95.00 (978-3-89625-209-8(7)) Pub: Assimil DEU. Dist(s): Distribks Inc

Polo. unabr. ed. Jilly Cooper. Read by Lindsay Sandison. 16 cass. (Running Time: 20 hr.). (Isis Ser.). (J). 1998. 104.95 (978-1-85695-782-3(9), 940607) Pub: ISIS Lrg Prnt GBR. Dist(s): Ulverscroft US

Polo Is My Life. 2000. audio compact disk 25.00 (978-0-7435-0049-4(0), Audioworks) S&S Audio.

Polonais sans Peine. 1 cass. (Running Time: 1 hr. 30 min.). (FRE & POL.). 2000. bk. 75.00 (978-2-7005-1316-5(9)); bk. 95.00 (978-2-7005-2019-4(X)) Pub: Assimil FRA. Dist(s): Distribks Inc

Polycystic Kidney Disease - A Bibliography & Dictionary for Physicians, Patients, & Genome Researchers. Compiled by Icon Group International, Inc. Staff. 2007. ring bd. 28.95 (978-0-497-11275-2(2)) Icon Grp.

Polycystic Ovary Syndrome. Contrib. by Roger A. Lobo et al. 1 cass. (American College of Obstetrics & Gynecologists UPDATE: Vol. 24, No. 2). 1998. 20.00 Am Coll Obstetric.

Polyeucte, Set. Corneille. Perf. by Paul Emile Deiber & Michel Bouquet. 2 CDs. 1992. 44.95 (1642-H) Olivia & Hill.
In the early days of Christianity, Pauline, the daughter of a pagan emperor, is torn between her allegiance to her husband Polyeucte, who is about to be baptized & her love for her former lover, a pagan named Servus.

Polygons Around the World. Based on a book by Margaret McNamara. (J). 2008. audio compact disk 10.00 (978-1-4108-8084-0(2)) Benchmark Educ.

Polygons Around the World E-Book: Set A. Benchmark Education Staff. Ed. by Margaret McNamara. (Math Explorers Ser.). (J). 2008. audio compact disk 15.00 (978-1-60437-166-6(8)) Benchmark Educ.

Polygons Around Town. Based on a book by Kira Freed. (J). 2008. audio compact disk 10.00 (978-1-4108-8078-9(8)) Benchmark Educ.

Polygons Around Town E-Book: Set A. Benchmark Education Staff. Ed. by Kira Freed. (Math Explorers Ser.). (J). 2008. audio compact disk 15.00 (978-1-60437-160-4(9)) Benchmark Educ.

Polygons at School. Based on a book by Margaret McNamara. (J). 2008. audio compact disk 10.00 (978-1-4108-8082-6(6)) Benchmark Educ.

Polygons at School E-Book: Set A. Benchmark Education Staff. Ed. by Margaret McNamara. (Math Explorers Ser.). (J). 2008. audio compact disk 15.00 (978-1-60437-164-2(1)) Benchmark Educ.

Polygons in Communities. Based on a book by Margaret McNamara. (J). 2008. audio compact disk 10.00 (978-1-4108-8083-3(4)) Benchmark Educ.

Polygons in Communities E-Book: Set A. Benchmark Education Staff. Ed. by Margaret McNamara. (Math Explorers Ser.). (J). 2008. audio compact disk 15.00 (978-1-60437-165-9(X)) Benchmark Educ.

Polygons in Puzzles. Based on a book by Kira Freed. (J). 2008. audio compact disk 10.00 (978-1-4108-8080-2(X)) Benchmark Educ.

Polygons in Puzzles E-Book: Set A. Benchmark Education Staff. Ed. by Kira Freed. (Math Explorers Ser.). (J). 2008. audio compact disk 15.00 (978-1-60437-162-8(5)) Benchmark Educ.

Polygons on Maps. Based on a book by Kira Freed. (J). 2008. audio compact disk 10.00 (978-1-4108-8079-6(6)) Benchmark Educ.

Polygons on Maps E-Book: Set A. Benchmark Education Staff. Ed. by Kira Freed. (Math Explorers Ser.). (J). 2008. audio compact disk 15.00 (978-1-60437-161-1(7)) Benchmark Educ.

Polymer Chemistry & Technology: An Introduction to the Practical Side of Polymer Chemistry. Instructed by Raymond B. Seymour. 5 cass. (Running Time: 4 hrs. 48 min.). 175.00 incl. 385pp. manual. (61) Am Chemical.
Introduces the chemistry & technology that is relevant to polymer production & use.

Polymer Rheology. unabr. ed. Read by Hershel Markovitz. 7 cass. (Running Time: 7 hrs. 30 min.). 625.00 Set, incl. 245p. manual. (A7) Am Chemical.

Polymer Synthesis. 2nd rev. ed. 5 cass. (Running Time: 5 hrs. 30 min.). 37.00 addt'l. manual. (B5) Am Chemical.

Polynesia on the Edge. 1 CD. (Running Time: 30 min). (Luau Celebration Ser.: 1). 2000. audio compact disk 16.95 (978-1-58513-099-3(0)) Dance Fantasy.
The companion music for a variety of Polynesian choreographies described in our dance books, including the songs: Otamu Malia, Bora Bora, Papaya, Raarotonga, Pakakina, Vikilani, Tamure Rumba, Birthday Singalong, Taualuga, Kana Naka, Tinikling, Jingle Bells Singalong, Here Comes Santa, and Kang Ding Ku'ipo.

Polynesia on the Edge. 1. (Running Time: 30 mins). (Luau Celebration Ser.). 2002. 14.95 (978-1-58513-084-9(2), 3/Poly-Cass) Dance Fantasy.
Side A features live drumming selections for Cook and Society Island dances: Otamu Malia, Bora Bora, Papaya, Rarotonga, Pakakina, Vikilani, Tamure Rumba, and a primal Happy Birthday audience singalong. Side B honors the songs and dances of Hawaii and her cross-cultural communities: Taualuga (Samoa), Kana Naka (vintage Hawaiian), Tinikling (the Philippines), primitive drum and flute Jingle Bells (Europe), Here Comes Santa (vintage Hawaiian), and Kang Ding Ku'ipo (China).

Polynesian Choreographies Booklet w/Companion Music CD. Vicki Corona. Music by Vicki Corona. (Celebrate the Cultures Ser.: 2-32A). 1991. pap. bk. 24.95 (978-1-58513-132-7(6)) Dance Fantasy.

Pomaikai. Ronald J. Loo & Pila Nahenahe. 1 cass. 1991. (978-1-885332-00-4(9)) P Nahenahe.
Hawaiian slack key guitar music & vocals.

Pomegranate Seeds see Tanglewood Tales

Pomegranate Seeds. unabr. ed. Nathaniel Hawthorne. Read by Walter Zimmerman. 1 cass. (Running Time: 78 min.). Dramatization. 1981. 7.95 (S-27) Jimcin Record.
A classic myth from Hawthorne's Tanglewood Tales.

Pomes Penyeach see James Joyce Reads James Joyce

Pomp & Pizazz. Perf. by Erich Kunzel & Cincinnati Pops Orchestra. 1 cass., 1 CD. 7.98 (TA 30122); audio compact disk 12.78 CD Jewel box. (TA 80122) NewSound.

Pompe Disease - A Bibliography & Dictionary for Physicians, Patients, & Genome Researchers. Compiled by Icon Group International, Inc. Staff. 2007. ring bd. 28.95 (978-0-497-11276-9(0)) Icon Grp.

Pompeii. Contrib. by Time-Life Audiobooks Staff. (Lost Civilizations Ser.). 1999. (978-1-57042-724-4(0)) Hachet Audio.

Pompeii. abr. ed. Robert Harris. Read by Michael Cumpsty. (Running Time: 21600 sec.). (ENG.). 2006. audio compact disk 14.99 (978-0-7393-4177-3(4), Random AudioBks) Pub: Random Audio Pubg. Dist(s): Random

Ponder Heart. unabr. ed. Eudora Welty. Narrated by Sally Darling. 3 cass. (Running Time: 4 hrs.). 1994. 27.00 (978-0-7887-0029-3(4), 94228E7) Recorded Bks.
The slightly wacky bachelor son of a rich Southern family suddenly marries a poor hillbilly girl, leading to mayhem for his relatives & amusement for the town.

Ponder on This. unabr. ed. Alice A. Bailey. Read by Vivian Harte. (YA). 2007. 49.99 (978-1-60252-943-4(4)) Find a World.

***Ponder on This: Writings of Alice Bailey & the Tibetan Master Djwhal Khul.** Alice A. Bailey. (ENG.). 2007. audio compact disk 25.00 (978-0-85330-231-5(6)) Lucis Pr GBR.

Ponds Audio CD. Adapted by Benchmark Education Company Staff. Based on a work by Katherine Scraper. (Early Explorers Set C Ser.). (J). (gr. k-1). 2008. audio compact disk 10.00 (978-1-60437-524-4(8)) Benchmark Educ.

Pondy Woods see Robert Penn Warren Reads Selected Poems

Poney Rouge, Set. John Steinbeck. Read by Michel Duchaussoy. 2 cass. 1992. bk. 35.95 (1GA074) Olivia & Hill.
One morning, Jody discovers a red pony in the stables. It is a present from his father. But when he has trained him & is finally able to ride him, the pony falls sick.

Ponga Boy. Philip Reed & Phil Lebherz. Illus. by Philip Reed. Narrated by Tony Plana. Prod. by Jessica Kaye. (ENG.). 2009. 29.95 (978-0-615-18957-4(1)) Epic CA.

Pongwiffy: A Witch of Dirty Habits. unabr. ed. Kaye Umansky. Read by Prunella Scales. 3 cass. (Running Time: 4 hrs., 30 min.). (J). (gr. 1-8). 1999. 24.95 (CCA 3165, Chivers Child Audio) AudioGO.

Pongwiffy: A Witch of Dirty Habits. unabr. ed. Kaye Umansky. Read by Prunella Scales. 3 CDs. (Running Time: 4 hrs. 30 mins.). (J). 2002. audio compact disk 29.95 (978-0-7540-6528-9(6), CHCD 028, Chivers Child Audio) AudioGO.

Pongwiffy & the Pantomime. unabr. ed. Kaye Umansky. Read by Prunella Scales. 4 cass. (Running Time: 6 hrs.). (J). (gr. 1-8). 1999. 32.95 (CCA 3492, Chivers Child Audio) AudioGO.

PONS (Profile of Nonverbal Sensitivity) Test Manual. Robert Rosenthal et al. 1979. 14.00 (978-0-8290-0753-4(9)) Ardent Media.

Pont de la Riviere Kwai, Set. Pierre Boulle. Read by Jean Rochefort. 5 cass. (FRE.). 1991. 39.95 (1319-AV) Olivia & Hill.
The cruel destiny of Colonel Nicholson, an English prisoner of the Japanese during WW II. The genesis of the film starring Alec Guiness.

***Ponte Al Dia, Set.** 2nd rev. ed. Mike Thacker et al. 2008. cd-rom 225.00 (978-0-340-96893-2(1)) Pub: Hodder Edu GBR. Dist(s): Trans-Atl Phila

Pontoon. unabr. ed. Garrison Keillor. Read by Garrison Keillor. (ENG.). 2009. audio compact disk 19.99 (978-1-59887-934-6(0), 1598879340) Pub: HighBridge. Dist(s): Workman Pub

Pony Engine & Other Stories for Children. Perf. by David Wayne et al. 1 cass. Incl. Country Mouse & the Town Mouse. Aesop. (J). (CP 1355); Little Boy with the Long Name. Bryna Ivens Untermeyer. (J). (CP 1355); Old Woman & Her Pig. Bryna Ivens Untermeyer. (J). (CP 1355); Silly Billy. Bryna Ivens Untermeyer. (J). (CP 1355); Six Foolish Fishermen. Benjamin Elkin. (J). (CP 1355); Story of Minikin & Manikin. Louis Untermeyer. (J). (CP 1355); Three Billy-Goats-Gruff. Bryna Ivens Untermeyer. (J). (CP 1355); (J). 1984. 8.98 (978-0-89845-642-4(8), CP 1355) HarperCollins Pubs.

Pony Express War. unabr. ed. Gary McCarthy. Read by Gene Engene. 6 cass. (Running Time: 6 hrs. 24 min.). (Derby Man Ser.: Bk. 4). 1994. 39.95 (978-1-55686-537-4(6)) Books in Motion.
Darby Buckingham sides with the pony express when he throws himself into a bloody war between the pony express, Paiute warriors & murderous saboteurs led by a sadistic giant.

***Pony Girl.** unabr. ed. Laura Lippman. Read by Linda Emond & Francois Battiste. (ENG.). 2008. (978-0-06-176312-0(8), Harper Audio); (978-0-06-176309-0(8), Harper Audio) HarperCollins Pubs.

Ponzi's Scheme: The True Story of a Financial Legend. unabr. ed. Mitchell Zuckoff. Read by Grover Gardner. 7 cass. (Running Time: 5 hrs.). 2005. 99.00 (978-1-4159-1580-6(6)); audio compact disk 88.40 (978-1-4159-1630-8(6)) Pub: Books on Tape. Dist(s): NetLibrary CO
The true story of an Italian immigrant in the 1920s who parlayed investments in 2 cent stamps into a $15 million fraud.

Poodle: A Basic Guide to This Canine Breed. Karen Jean Matsko Hood. 2006. 29.95 (978-1-59808-877-9(7)) Whspmg Pine.

Poodle Springs. abr. unabr. ed. Raymond Chandler. Read by Elliott Gould. 2 cass. (Running Time: 3 hrs.). 2004. 18.00 (978-1-59007-105-2(0)); 25.00 (978-1-59007-106-9(9)) Pub: New Millenn Enter. Dist(s): PerseuPGW
When Chandler died he left "behind the opening chapters of this PhilipMarlowe private investigator novel set in the 1950s, which Parker has completed. Here, Marlowe has a rich wife . And has moved from Los Angeles to the bright-buck community of Poodle Springs, where he is hired by the area crime boss to track down a missing local who has run out on a gambling debt.

Poodle's Broken E. Laura Brightwood. Instructed by Laura Brightwood. Created by 3-C Institute for Social Development. (J). 2009. (978-1-934409-12-1(X)) 3C Institute.

Poofin. (J). 1991. 8.00 Family Life.

Pooh Goes Visiting & Other Stories. A. A. Milne. Contrib. by Judi Dench et al. 1 cass. (Running Time: 60 min.). Dramatization. (ENG.). (J). 1998. 8.99 (978-1-84032-047-3(8), HoddrStoughton) Pub: Hodder General GBR. Dist(s): Trafalgar

Pooh Invents a New Game: And Other Stories. A. A. Milne. Read by Judi Dench et al. 2 cass. (Running Time: 3600 sec.). (J). (ps-3). 1997. 7.99 (978-1-84032-226-2(8), HoddrStoughton) Pub: Hodder General GBR. Dist(s): Trafalgar
This excellent dramatization of some of Milne's favorite stories from The House at Pooh Corner is problematic for American ears because of the strong British accents of the actors and the actor's adult voices. In addition to the title story, there are three others: "In Which Rabbit Has a Busy Day," "In Which Tigger Is Unbounced," and "In Which Piglet Does a Very Grand Thing.".

Pooh Invents a New Game & Other Stories. abr. ed. A. A. Milne. Read by Judi Dench et al. (Running Time: 0 hr. 60 mins. 0 sec.). (ENG., (J). (ps-4). 2007. audio compact disk (978-1-84456-293-0(X), HoddrStoughton) Hodder General GBR.

Pooh Learning Series: Read-Along. 1 CD; 1 Cass. (Pooh Learning Ser.). (J). audio compact disk 9.98 (978-0-7634-1956-1(7)) W Disney Records.

Pooh Travelpak: Winnie the Pooh & Winnie the Pooh & Some Bees. unabr. ed. A. A. Milne. Read by Peter Dennis. 2 cass. (Running Time: 2 hrs.). (J). 1999. 34.95 (978-0-929071-59-6(X)) B-B Audio.
Plugn Play Travelpaks contain everything your customers will need for many hours of audiobook listening. 2 Fantastic Audiobooks with1 Portable Cassette Player plus1 Comfortable Headset plus 2 Batteriers POOH TRAVELPAK 2 Hours WINNIE THE POOH Written.

Pooh's Grand Adventure. Kathie Lee Gifford. (J). 1997. 11.99 Norelco. (978-0-7634-0325-6(3)); audio compact disk 19.99 CD. (978-0-7634-0327-0(X)); audio compact disk 19.99 (978-0-7634-0328-7(8)) W Disney Records.
Contains Pooh-related songs from the direct-to-home video release of the same name.

Pooh's Grand Adventure. Kathie Lee Gifford. (J). (ps-3). 1997. 11.99 (978-0-7634-0326-3(1)) W Disney Records.

Pooka & the Fiddler. Mick Bolger. Music by Colcannon. 1 CD. (Running Time: 57 mins). (J). 2005. audio compact disk (978-0-9769518-0-3(0)) Oxford Road.

Pooki Dot's New Friends. deluxe ed. Gail Gonzalez & Stacey Lorea. Perf. by Stacey Lorea et al. Des. by Gail Gonzalez. Voice by Mattie Marino. Illus. by Jorge Lorea. Prod. by Tune Platoon Incorporated Staff. Arranged by Luci Dow. (J). 2000. bk. 39.99 (978-0-9707357-3-7(1)) Tune Plat.

Pooki Dot's New Friends. deluxe ed. Gail Gonzalez & Stacey Lorea. Perf. by Stacey Lorea et al. Prod. by Tune Platoon Incorporated Staff. Des. by Gail Gonzalez. Voice by Mattie Marino. Illus. by Jorge Lorea. Arranged by Luci Dow. (J). 2000. bk. 39.99 (978-0-9707357-4-4(X)) Tune Plat.

Pool Boy. Michael Simmons. Read by Chad Lowe. 3 cass. (Running Time: 3 hrs. 40 mins.). (J). (gr. 7 up). 2004. 30.00 (978-0-8072-2323-9(9), Listening Lib) Random Audio Pubg.

Pool of Dreams. Perf. by Oracle. 1 cass., 1 CD. 8.78 (RCA 68796); audio compact disk 12.78 CD Jewel box. (RCA 68796) NewSound.

Poop-Eaters: Dung Beetles in the Food Chain. Deirdre A. Prischmann. Contrib. by Patrick Olson & Charity Jones. (Extreme Life Ser.). (ENG.). (gr. 3-4). 2008. audio compact disk 12.99 (978-1-4296-3212-6(7)) CapstoneDig.

Poor Butterfly. unabr. ed. Stuart M. Kaminsky. Narrated by George Guidall. 4 cass. (Running Time: 5 hrs. 45 mins.). (Toby Peters Mystery Ser.: No. 15). 1997. 35.00 (978-0-7887-0833-6(3), 94978E7) Recorded Bks.
Famed conductor Leopold Stokowski is reopening the San Francisco Metropolitan Opera in 1942, but a suspicious accident & mysterious threats plague the company.

Poor Caroline. unabr. ed. Winifred Holtby. Read by Frances Jeater. 8 cass. (Running Time: 9 hrs. 35 min.). 1994. 69.95 (978-1-85089-729-3(8), 90111) Pub: ISIS Audio GBR. Dist(s): Ulverscroft US
Caroline sees herself as a pioneer, she is definitely an eccentric, with her trailing beads & feathers. She dreams of the reforms she will effect through her Christian Cinema Company, which has a motley crew of unusual characters.

***Poor Little Bitch Girl.** unabr. ed. Jackie Collins. Read by Jackie Collins. Read by Allison Daugherty et al. 1 Playaway. (Running Time: 11 hrs. 30 mins.). 2010. 94.95 (978-0-7927-7007-7(2)); 59.95 (978-0-7927-7006-0(4)); audio compact disk 94.95 (978-0-7927-6906-4(6)) AudioGO.

Poor Little Bitch Girl. unabr. ed. Jackie Collins. Read by Jackie Collins. Read by Katherine Kellgren et al. (Running Time: 11 hrs. 30 mins. 0 sec.). (ENG.). 2010. audio compact disk 39.99 (978-1-4272-0868-2(9)) Pub: Macmill Audio. Dist(s): Macmillan

***Poor-Mouth Jubilee.** Michael Chitwood. (ENG.). 2010. audio compact disk 12.00 (978-1-932195-91-0(2)) Tupelo Pr Inc.

Poor Old Lu: Chrono 1993-1998. 1999. audio compact disk 16.98 (KMGD8682) Provident Mus Dist.

Poor Old Lu: In Their Final Performance. 1 cass. 1999. 10.98 (KMGC8670); audio compact disk 10.98 (KMGD8670) Provident Mus Dist.

Poor Old Lu: Sin. 1 CD. 1999. audio compact disk 16.98 (KMGD9496) Provident Mus Dist.

Poor Old Lu: Star Studded Super Step. 1 cass. 1999. 10.98 (KMGC8640); audio compact disk 16.98 (KMGD8640) Provident Mus Dist.

Poor People. Fyodor Dostoyevsky. Read by Patrick Cullen & Julia Emlen. (Running Time: 5 hrs. 30 mins.). 2004. 24.95 (978-1-59912-574-9(9)) Iofy Corp.

Poor People. unabr. ed. Fyodor Dostoyevsky. 4 cass. (Running Time: 5 hrs. 30 mins.). 2004. 32.95 (978-0-7861-2626-2(4), 3234) Blckstn Audio.

Poor People. unabr. ed. Fyodor Dostoyevsky. Read by Patrick Cullen & Julia Emlen. 5 CDs. (Running Time: 5 hrs. 30 mins.). 2001. audio compact disk 40.00 (978-0-7861-8743-0(3), 3234) Blckstn Audio.

Poor People. unabr. ed. Fyodor Dostoyevsky. Read by Patrick Cullen & Julia Emlen. (YA). 2008. 39.99 (978-1-60514-913-4(6)) Find a World.

Poor Richard's Almanac see Ten All Time Favorite Stories

***Poor Will Be Glad: Joining the Revolution to Lift the World Out of Poverty.** unabr. ed. Peter Greer & Phil Smith. (Running Time: 6 hrs. 18 mins. 0 sec.). (ENG.). 2009. 19.99 (978-0-310-77366-5(0)) Zondervan.

Poor You Will Always Have, & the Ten Percent Will Never Fall, Vol. 2. Poems. David Jedidiah. Read by Rael Jedidiah. Ed. by Rael Jedidiah. 1 cass. (YA). 1999. pap. bk. (978-1-892981-01-1(7), BK02PA) Divinity Seven.

Poorhouse Fair. unabr. collector's ed. John Updike. Read by Jack Hrkach. 6 cass. (Running Time: 6 hrs.). 1984. 36.00 (978-0-7366-0691-2(2), 1654) Books on Tape.
Novel concerns the events surrounding a fair put on by members of a poorhouse & is an allegory about charity.

Pop. Gordon Korman. Read by Nick Podehl. (ENG.). (J). 2009. 54.99 (978-1-4418-1098-4(6)) Find a World.

Pop. unabr. ed. Gordon Korman. Read by Tom Parks & Nick Podehl. (Running Time: 6 hrs.). 2009. 24.99 (978-1-4233-9970-4(6), 9781423399704, Brilliance MP3); 39.97 (978-1-4233-9971-1(4), 9781423399711, Brlnc Audio MP3 Lib); 24.99 (978-1-4233-9972-8(2), 9781423399728, BAD); 39.97 (978-1-4233-9973-5(0), 9781423399735, BADLE); audio compact disk 24.99 (978-1-4233-9968-1(4), 9781423399681) Brilliance Audio.

Pop. unabr. ed. Gordon Korman. Read by Tom Parks & Nick Podehl. 5 CDs. (Running Time: 6 hrs.). (YA). (gr. 7-10). 2009. audio compact disk 74.97 (978-1-4233-9969-8(2), 9781423399698, BriAudCD Unabrid) Brilliance Audio.

***Pop Art.** unabr. ed. Joe Hill. (ENG.). 2007. (978-0-06-155233-5(X)); (978-0-06-155234-2(8)) HarperCollins Pubs.

Pop Ballads: Easy Rhythm Guitar Series Volume 8. Created by Hal Leonard Corporation Staff. 2007. pap. bk. 14.99 (978-1-4234-1972-3(3), 1423419723) H Leonard.

Pop Chronicles: The Lively Story of Pop Music in the '40s. unabr. ed. John Gilliland. 4 cass. (Running Time: 6 hrs.). 1994. 21.95 (978-1-55935-147-8(0), 692290) Soundelux.
Rare interviews, commentary & music. An historical collection of the Radio Series.

Pop Formulas: Hamonic Tools of the Hit Makers. Volkmar Kramarz. 2007. pap. bk. 19.95 (978-3-8024-0620-1(6)) Voggenreiter Pubs DEU.

Pop Goes the Weasel. James Patterson. Read by Michael Kramer. (Alex Cross Ser.: No. 5). 1999. audio compact disk 72.00 (978-0-7366-5205-6(1)) Books on Tape.

Pop Goes the Weasel. abr. ed. James Patterson. Read by Keith David & Roger Rees. (Running Time: 6 hrs.). (Alex Cross Ser.: No. 5). (ENG.). 2006. 14.98 (978-1-59483-612-1(4)); audio compact disk 14.98 (978-1-59483-611-4(6)) Pub: Hachet Audio. Dist(s): HachBkGrp

Pop Goes the Weasel. unabr. ed. James Patterson. Read by Michael Kramer. 7 cass. (Running Time: 10 hrs. 30 min.). (Alex Cross Ser.: No. 5). 1999. 56.00 (978-0-7366-4792-2(9), 5140); audio compact disk 72.00 Books on Tape.
Here is a dangerous villian, a love story of great tenderness & a plot of relentless suspense & heart-pounding pace.

Pop Goes the Weasel. unabr. ed. James Patterson. (Alex Cross Ser.: No. 5). (ENG.). 2005. 16.98 (978-1-59483-674-9(4)) Pub: Hachet Audio. Dist(s): HachBkGrp

Pop Goes the Weasel, Set. abr. ed. James Patterson. Read by Keith David & Roger R. Reese. 4 cass. (Alex Cross Ser.: No. 5). 1999. 25.98 (FS9-51077) Highsmith.

Pop Partners: 10 Tremendous Partner Songs for Young Singers. Composed by Sally K. Albrecht & Tim Hayden. (ENG.). 2009. audio compact disk 39.95 (978-0-7390-5977-7(7)) Alfred Pub.

Pop Piano Playing Simplified. Duane Shinn. 1 cass. 19.95 (CP-6) Duane Shinn.
Discusses how to play "pop" piano in three interrelated steps. Explains how to read the melody line only (the tune) of sheet music; teaches how to learn to read chord signs & play chords; explains how to create a "rhythm bass" in the left hand with chords.

Pop Plant 3. Martyn Geraint. 2005. 8.81 (978-0-00-087275-3(X)) Zondervan.

Pop Rock Parachute. 1 cass. (YA). (gr. 2 up). 2001. pap. bk. 10.95 (KEA 6025C) Kimbo Educ.
Set to motivating, original contemporary music, these parachute activities are designed to develop endurance, general strength & flexibility. Use the routines as one continuous program or individually to suit your needs. Stimulate kids' sense of rhythm & timing using a 12' or 24' parachute. Includes Bombs Away, Bubble House, Disappear & more. Includes manual.

Pop Showcase for Strings (for Solo or String Orchestra) For Solo or String Orchestra. Composed by Jack Bullock. (ENG.). 2001. audio compact disk 10.95 (978-0-7579-8150-0(X)) Alfred Pub.

Popcorn! Rick Charette. 1 cass. (Running Time: 46 min.). (J). (gr. k-5). 1996. 9.98 (978-1-884210-13-6(9)); audio compact disk 12.98 CD. (978-1-884210-14-3(7)) Pine Pt Record.
Original, singable songs featuring light, upbeat accompaniment. Includes creative movement activities. Wonderful songs to reinforce language education. Includes: "Amos the Moose," "Popcom," & "Going Through the Car Wash," & more.

Popcorn Report. Faith Popcorn. 2004. 7.95 (978-0-7435-4180-0(4)) Pub: S&S Audio. Dist(s): S and S Inc

Pope Don't Know about This: Black Catholics. 1 cass. (Running Time: 30 min.). 9.95 (F0530B090, HarperThor) HarpC GBR.

Pope John & the Popes John Paul. Bernard R. Bonnot. 4 cass. (Running Time: 3 hrs. 20 min.). 24.95 incl. shelf-case. (TAH011) Alba Hse Comns.
Discusses the impact of John XXIII as an able pastoral leader.

Pope John Paul II: A Prophetic Humanist. Avery Dulles. 1 cass. (Running Time: 1 hr. 10 min.). 1995. 8.95 (TAH333) Alba Hse Comns.
An excellent study on the Holy Father's positions & insights throughout his life & during his papacy. Good motivational material. Highly informative. Intensely pastoral.

Pope John Paul II: The Biography. unabr. ed. Tad Szulc. Read by John Edwardson. 13 cass. (Running Time: 19 hrs. 30 mins.). 1995. 104.00 (978-0-7366-3198-3(4), 3862) Books on Tape.
Nearly a billion believers consider Pope John Paul II to be God's mouthpiece on earth. He wields extraordinary influence as a world statesman. An uprecendented interview with the pontiff as well as access to private documents.

Pope John Paul II: The Biography. unabr. ed. Tad Szulc. Narrated by Nelson Runger. 17 cass. (Running Time: 23 hrs.). 1995. 136.00 (978-0-7887-0438-3(9), 94630E7) Recorded Bks.
Tad Szulc, veteran news correspondent, paints a fascinating, unbiased portrait of the leader of the largest Christian church on earth.

Pope John Paul II: The Pope of the Rosary. 2 cass. (Running Time: 2 hrs.). (LAT.). 1999. 14.98 (T9285); audio compact disk 19.98 (K6930) Liguori Pubns.
Let the inspirational words of Pope John Paul II captivate your imagination & reaffirm your belief in this compilation of Rosary broadcasts & homily excerpts.

Pope John Paul II the Biography. Tad Szulc. 2004. 15.95 (978-0-7435-4817-5(5)) Pub: S&S Audio. Dist(s): S and S Inc

Pope John Paul the Second's Letter to Families. Comment by George Rutler. 3 cass. 1995. 19.95 Set. (5505-C) Ignatius Pr.
Fr. Rutler takes you through each section of this letter, adding his own incisive commentary.

Pope John XXIII. unabr. ed. Thomas Cahill. Read by Grover Gardner. 6 cass. (Running Time: 9 hrs.). 2002. 48.00 (978-0-7366-8585-6(5)) Books on Tape.
Elected to the papacy at the age of 76, Pope John XXIII was to have a brief but important reign. Although he had a doctorate in theology, his gifts were pastoral - reaching out to the people of the Church. After his doctorate, he spent nine years working for the socially-minded bishop of Bergamo, acquiring a broad understanding of the problems of the working class. This pastoral sympathy for ordinary people was brought out in his papacy. Vatican II, which he convened, brought forth the idea of a church as a community, in which all God's people are a sign of redemption for the human race.

Popes & the Papacy: A History. Instructed by Thomas Noble. 12 cass. (Running Time: 12 hrs.). 54.95 (978-1-59803-155-3(4)) Teaching Co.

Popes & the Papacy: A History. Instructed by Thomas Noble. 12 CDs. (Running Time: 12 hrs.). 2005. audio compact disk 69.95 (978-1-59803-157-7(0)) Teaching Co.

***Pope's Maestro.** unabr. ed. Sir Gilbert Levine. Narrated by Sir Gilbert Levine. Intro. by John Tagliabue. (ENG.). 2010. 18.98 (978-1-61045-066-9(3), MissionAud); audio compact disk 29.98 (978-1-61045-065-2(5), MissionAud) christianaud.

***Popol Vuh.** abr. ed. Read by Yadira Sanchez. (SPA.). 2008. audio compact disk 17.00 (978-958-8318-41-7(6)) Pub: Yoyo Music COL. Dist(s): YoYoMusic

Popped. abr. ed. Carol Higgins Clark. (Regan Reilly Mystery Ser.: No. 7). 2004. 15.95 (978-0-7435-4818-2(3)) Pub: S&S Audio. Dist(s): S and S Inc

Poppy. Perf. by W. C. Fields. 1 cass. 10.00 (MC1013) Esstee Audios.
Radio drama.

Poppy. unabr. ed. Avi. Narrated by John McDonough. 4 CDs. (Running Time: 4 hrs.). (gr. 3 up). audio compact disk 39.00 (978-0-7887-9527-5(9)) Recorded Bks.

Poppy, unabr. ed. Avi. Narrated by John McDonough. 3 pieces. (Running Time: 4 hrs.). (gr. 3 up). 1997. 27.00 (978-0-7887-0606-6(3), 94785E7) Recorded Bks.
A tiny deer mouse's battle against a menacing owl provides a hearty lesson about bullies & celebrates the strength of a courageous spirit.

***Poppy & Ereth.** unabr. ed. Avi. Narrated by John McDonough. 1 Playaway. (Running Time: 4 hrs. 15 mins.). (J). (gr. 3-5). 2009. 59.75 (978-1-4407-3874-6(2)); 33.75 (978-1-4407-3864-7(5)); audio compact disk 46.75 (978-1-4407-3868-5(8)) Recorded Bks.

***Poppy & Ereth.** unabr. collector's ed. Avi. Narrated by John McDonough. 4 CDs. (Running Time: 4 hrs. 15 mins.). (J). (gr. 3-5). 2009. audio compact disk 44.95 (978-1-4407-3872-2(6)) Recorded Bks.

Poppy & Rye, unabr. ed. Avi. Narrated by John McDonough. 4 pieces. (Running Time: 5 hrs.). (gr. 3 up). 2000. 37.00 (978-0-7887-3163-1(7), 95836E7) Recorded Bks.
In this sequel to "Poppy," the spirited deermouse teams up with Ragweed's dreamy brother Rye to save his family's home from greedy, dambuilding beavers.

Poppy & Rye, unabr. ed. Avi. Narrated by John McDonough. 4 cass. (Running Time: 5 hrs.). (J). (gr. 8). 2000. pap. bk. & stu. ed. 50.24 (978-0-7887-3185-3(8), 40920E5) Recorded Bks.

Poppy & Rye, Class Set. unabr. ed. Avi. Read by John McDonough. 4 cass. (Running Time: 5 hrs.). (J). (gr. 3). 1999. 107.70 (978-0-7887-3231-7(5), 46887) Recorded Bks.

Poppy Day. unabr. ed. Annie Murray. Read by Judith Porter. 12 cass. (Running Time: 15 hrs.). (Sound Ser.). 2002. 94.95 (978-1-86042-852-4(5)) Pub: UlverLrgPrint GBR. Dist(s): Ulverscroft US
Jessica Hart's life is changed forever with the death of her mother. Her manipulative new stepmother tries to force her into marrying an older man, but to Jess,the idea of being trapped in a loveless marriage is unthinkable. So she escapes to Birmingham, to her Aunt Olive, the last remaining connection with her mother. Then Jess's security is threatened when she meets a friend of the family and falls passionately in love. for handsome ned Green is not only already married, but about to become a father any day.

Poppy Field. unabr. ed. Christine Marion Fraser. Read by Lesley Mackie. 5 cass. (Running Time: 7 hrs.). 2000. 49.95 (978-1-86042-677-3(8), 26778) Pub: Soundings Ltd GBR. Dist(s): Ulverscroft US
Sixteen-year-old Velana Domingo's world is turned upside down when her childhood sweetheart announces he is leaving the small town of Olhao in Southern Portugal to become a priest in Paris. At the same time, her mother confesses that the man Velana has always known as her beloved Papa is not her true father. Velana embarks on a musical career, taking her across Europe where she falls in love & searches for her real father.

Poppy Orchard. unabr. ed. Mary Withall. Read by James Bryce. 16 cass. (Running Time: 19 hrs.). (Sound Ser.). 2002. 104.95 (978-1-86042-779-4(0)) Pub: UlverLrgPrint GBR. Dist(s): Ulverscroft US
It is 1938. When Stephen Beaton's childhood sweetheart, Ellen McDougal, arrives from Australia to take up a research post in a veterinary surgery, the pair barely have time to renew their friendship before Stephen is posted as a doctor to Manston Air Base in Kent. There, Stephen's boredom is relieved by the promise of meeting the delectable Grace Dobie. But everything changes when Hitler's bombers attack.

Poppy Seeds. unabr. ed. Clyde Robert Bulla. Narrated by Robert Ramirez. 1 cass. (Running Time: 15 mins.). (gr. 2 up). 1998. 10.00 (978-0-7887-2212-7(3), 95511E7) Recorded Bks.
Tale of a boy's dream to bring beauty to his dusty Mexican village.

Poppy Seeds, Class Set. unabr. ed. Clyde Robert Bulla. Read by Robert Ramirez. 1 cass., 10 bks. (Running Time: 20 min.). (J). 1998. bk. 70.70 (978-0-7887-2534-0(3), 46704) Recorded Bks.
A tale of a boy's dream to bring beauty to his dusty Mexican village.

Poppy Seeds, Homework. unabr. ed. Clyde Robert Bulla. Read by Robert Ramirez. 1 cass. (Running Time: 20 min.). (J). (gr. 2). 1998. bk. 22.24 (978-0-7887-2229-5(8), 40713) Recorded Bks.

Poppy Silk. unabr. ed. Michael Taylor. Read by Maggie Mash. 13 cass. (Running Time: 17 hrs. 15 mins.). (Story Sound Ser.). (J). 2004. 99.95 (978-1-85903-658-7(9)) Pub: Mgna Lrg Print GBR. Dist(s): Ulverscroft US

Poppy's Return. unabr. ed. Avi. Read by John McDonough. 3 cass. (Running Time: 4 hrs. 30 mins.). 2006. 29.75 (978-1-4193-7118-9(5), 98272) Recorded Bks.
Avi is the recipient of the Newbery Medal, Newbery Honor and the Boston Globe/Horn Book Award. He pens the fifth book in his extremely popular Poppy series. When her sister suddenly shows up with a summons from their father, Poppy learns that he is not well and the old family home is about to be demolished by a bulldozer. Poppy decides to travel with her rebellious son Junior in the hope of salvaging their relationship.

Poprygunya, a Lady Hopper. Anton Chekhov. 1 cass. (Running Time: 1 hrs. 30 min.). (RUS.). 1996. pap. bk. 24.50 (978-1-58085-568-6(7)) Interlingua VA.

Pops Plays Puccini. Perf. by Erich Kunzel & Cincinnati Pops Orchestra. 1 cass., 1 CD. 7.98 (TA 30260); audio compact disk 12.78 CD Jewel box. (TA 80260) NewSound.

PopShowcase for Solo or Band. Composed by Jack Bullock. (Belwin 21st Century Band Method Ser.). (ENG.). 2000. audio compact disk 12.95 (978-0-7579-2528-3(6)) Alfred Pub.

Popular Chord Style Piano: Introductory Course. Robert Laughlin. 1 cass. 1986. pap. bk. 25.00 (978-0-929983-05-9(X)) New Schl Am Music.
Teaches chord piano basics - major, minor & 7th chords, how to read lead sheets & make substitutions. Seven songs are included.

Popular Classical Piano. 1999. audio compact disk 24.95 (978-0-634-01112-2(X), 00451028) Pub: iSong. Dist(s): H Leonard

Popular Guitar Styles - Samba & Bossa Nova. Burkhard Buck Wolters. 2008. pap. bk. 17.95 (978-0-7866-7777-1(5)) Mel Bay.

Popular Music. Colin Cripps. Contrib. by Roy Bennett. (Cambridge Assignments in Music Ser.). (ENG.). 1988. 38.99 (978-0-521-26828-8(1)) Cambridge U Pr.

Popular Piano Solos. Phillip Keveren. (Hal Leonard Student Piano Library). 1999. audio compact disk 10.95 (978-0-634-00256-4(2), 0634002562) H Leonard.

Popular Piano Solos. Phillip Keveren. (Hal Leonard Student Piano Library). 1999. pap. bk. 10.95 (978-0-634-00261-8(9), 0634002619) H Leonard.

Popular Piano Solos, Level 4. Phillip Keveren. (Hal Leonard Student Piano Library). 1999. audio compact disk 10.95 (978-0-634-00266-3(X), 063400266X) H Leonard.

Popular Piano Solos, Level 5. Phillip Keveren. (Hal Leonard Student Piano Library). 2000. audio compact disk 10.95 (978-0-634-02533-4(3), 0634025333) H Leonard.

Popular Piano Solos: Level 2. Created by Hal Leonard Corporation Staff. (Hal Leonard Student Piano Library). (ENG.). 1999. audio compact disk 10.95 (978-0-634-00258-8(9), 0634002589) H Leonard.

Popular Poetry, Popular Verse. unabr. ed. Poems. Read by Anton Lesser & Simon Russell Beale. Ed. by Duncan Steen. 2 cass. (Running Time: 2 hrs. 39 mins.). 1994. 67.98 (978-962-634-516-0(0), NA201614, Naxos AudioBooks) Naxos.
Eighty-Four poems complete this collection by some of the greatest writers in the English language, such as Shakespeare, Blake, Wordsworth, Byron, Keats, Yeats, Lear, Hardy and many others.

Popular Solos for Young Singers. Created by Hal Leonard Corporation Staff. 2005. audio compact disk 12.95 (978-0-634-09487-3(4), 0634094874) H Leonard.

Popular Songs: Orchestra Play-along Volume 1. Created by Hal Leonard Corporation Staff. 2008. pap. bk. 14.99 (978-1-4234-4573-9(2), 1423445732) H Leonard.

Popularity. 1 cass. 10.00 (978-1-58506-030-6(5), 62) New Life Inst OR.
You can have a personality that attracts all the friends you want.

Population. Milton Diamond. 1 cass. (Running Time: 1 hr.). (Human Sexuality Ser.). 11.95 (34012) J Norton Pubs.

Population Crisis USA, Pt. 1. Hosted by Nancy Pearlman. 1 cass. (Running Time: 31 min.). 10.00 (1117) Educ Comm CA.

Population Crisis USA, Pt. 2. Hosted by Nancy Pearlman. 1 cass. (Running Time: 32 min.). 10.00 (1118) Educ Comm CA.

Population Crisis USA (Special) Hosted by Nancy Pearlman. 1 cass. (Running Time: 59 min.). 10.00 (1100A); 10.00 (1100B) Educ Comm CA.

Population Explosion. unabr. ed. Aldous Huxley. 1 cass. (Running Time: 1 hr.). (Human Situation Ser.). 1959. 11.00 (01109) Big Sur Tapes.

***Population: 485.** abr. ed. Michael Perry. Read by Michael Perry. (ENG.). 2005. (978-0-06-084306-9(3), Harper Audio); (978-0-06-084305-2(5), Harper Audio) HarperCollins Pubs.

Por amor a las Tortugas. (Saludos Ser.: Vol. 1). (SPA.). (gr. 2-3). 10.00 (978-0-7635-5882-6(6)) Rigby Educ.

Por Camino de Swann. unabr. ed. Proust Marcel. Read by Daniel Quintero. (SPA.). 2007. audio compact disk 17.00 (978-958-8318-15-8(7)) Pub: Yoyo Music COL. Dist(s): YoYoMusic

Por el Amor de Nuestros Hijos. Wayne W. Dyer. 2003. (978-1-931059-33-6(0)) Taller del Exito.

Por el Avance de la Fe: Himnos Sagrados Desde el Santuario Whitefield. Prod. by Foundations Bible College Staff. (SPA.). 2000. 7.95 (978-1-882542-29-1(0), 1882542290) Fndtns NC.

Por el placer a Vivir. Cesar Lozano.Tr. of pleasure of Living. (SPA.). 2009. audio compact disk 17.00 (978-1-935405-47-4(0)) Hombre Nuevo.

Por la Vida. unabr. ed. Marcos Vidal. (SPA.). 2000. 9.99 (978-0-8297-2575-9(X)) Pub: Vida Pubs. Dist(s): Zondervan

Por Que los Hombres Se Casan con las Cabronas. Sherry Argov. Narrated by Anna Silvetti. (SPA.). 2009. 59.99 (978-1-61545-568-3(X)) Find a World.

Por que soplan los vientos Salvajes: Audiocassette. (Saludos Ser.: Vol. 1). (SPA.). (gr. 3-5). 10.00 (978-0-7635-1846-2(8)) Rigby Educ.

Por qué soy Católico: Y por qué quiero seguirlo Siendo. Juan Rivas.Tr. of Why Catholic?. (SPA.). 2009. 18.95 (978-1-935405-02-3(0)) Hombre Nuevo.

Por que soy Catolico: Y por que quiero seguirlo Siendo. Juan Rivas.Tr. of Why Catholic?. (SPA.). 2009. audio compact disk 12.95 (978-1-935405-01-6(2)) Hombre Nuevo.

***¿Por Qué Tenemos Reglas? Audio Cd.** Margaret Mcnamara. Adapted by Benchmark Education Company, LLC. (Content Connections Ser.). (SPA.). (J). 2009. audio compact disk 10.00 (978-1-935472-75-9(5)) Benchmark Educ.

Por Quién Doblan Las Campanas. abr. ed. Ernest Hemingway. Read by Laura García. 3 CDs.Tr. of For Whom the Bell Tolls. (SPA.). 2002. audio compact disk 17.00 (978-958-8161-39-6(8)) YoYoMusic.

Por Tu Gracia. unabr. ed. Heriberto Hermosillo & Zondervan Publishing Staff. (SPA.). 2003. 9.99 (978-0-8297-4144-5(5)) Pub: Zondervan. Dist(s): Vida Pubs

Por un Día Más. Mitch Albom. Read by Jose Manuel Vieira.Tr. of For One More Day. (SPA.). 2009. 59.99 (978-1-61545-569-0(8)) Find a World.

Por un Día Más. abr. ed. Mitch Albom. 5 cds. (Running Time: 14400 sec.).Tr. of For One More Day. (SPA.). 2007. audio compact disk 24.95 (978-1-933499-60-4(5)) Fonolibro Inc.

Porcupine Year. unabr. ed. Louise Erdrich. Narrated by Christina Moore. 4 cass. (Running Time: 4 hrs. 15 mins.). (YA). (gr. 5-8). 2008. 33.75 (978-1-4361-5890-9(7)); audio compact disk 46.75 (978-1-4361-5895-4(8)) Recorded Bks.

Porgue la Gracia to do lo Cambia. Chuck Smith & Merrie Destefano. (SPA.). 2000. pap. bk. 8.99 (978-0-936728-82-7(5)) Word For Today.

Pork Pie Hat. unabr. ed. Peter Straub. Read by Peter Marinker. 2 cass. (Running Time: 2 hrs.). 2000. 24.95 (978-0-7531-0754-6(6), 991220) Pub: ISIS Audio GBR. Dist(s): Ulverscroft US
When a graduate student with a passion for jazz arrived in New York to discover that a legendary saxophonist he had assumed long dead is not only still alive but playing in an East Village club, he spends night after night in awe-struck attendance. When the legend grants him an interview on Halloween, he jumps at the opportunity. What unfolds is an endless night filled with an extraordinary story told by a dying master: a story centered upon the Halloween night of his eleventh year, a white woman screaming in a shanty town, a killer & an unidentified man fleeing with a strange bundle in his arms.

Pork Pie Hat. unabr. ed. Peter Straub. Read by Peter Marinker. 3 CDs. (Running Time: 2 hrs. 56 mins.). (Isis Ser.). 2002. audio compact disk 38.95 (978-0-7531-1400-1(3)) Pub: ISIS Audio GBR. Dist(s): Ulverscroft US

Porkbarrel. Randy Fitzgerald & Gerald Lipson. 1 cass. (Running Time: 60 min.). 1987. 9.95 (978-0-945999-06-5(2)) Independent Inst.
Government Waste Is Abundant via Congress's Porkbarreling of Water Projects, Military Bases, etc. Here Is the Uncensored Report of the Grace Commission.

Porky & the Gato. unabr. ed. Connie Robinson. 1 cass. (Running Time: 10 mins.). (J). (gr. k-3). 2001. 10.95 (978-1-928632-56-6(4)) Writers Mrktpl.
English and Spanish book about Porky (the Pig) and his day celebrating the Day of the Dead and meeting a new American friend a cat.

Pornography & Fantasy. Milton Diamond. 1 cass. (Running Time: 1 hr.). (Human Sexuality Ser.). 11.95 (34017) J Norton Pubs.

Pornography Plague. Jeff Cavins. 2004. audio compact disk 7.95 (978-1-932927-44-3(1)) Ascensn Pr.

Porphyria - A Bibliography & Dictionary for Physicians, Patients, & Genome Researchers. Compiled by Icon Group International, Inc. Staff. 2007. ring bd. 28.95 (978-0-497-11277-6(9)) Icon Grp.

***Porque el Cambio Es Necesario para Crecer.** Tr. of Why Change Is Necessary for Growth. (SPA.). 2005. audio compact disk 24.00 (978-0-944129-26-5(9)) High Praise.

Porque los Hombres aman las Cabronas. Sherry Argov. 5 CDs. (SPA.). 2007. audio compact disk 24.95 (978-1-933499-40-6(0)) Pub: Fonolibro Inc. Dist(s): Giron Bks

Porque los Hombres de Casan con Cabronas. abr. ed. Sherry Argov. (Running Time: 21600 sec.). (SPA.). 2007. audio compact disk 24.95 (978-1-933499-44-4(3)) Fonolibro Inc.

Porque Morir Joven: Secretor de la Salud. unabr. ed. Tito Alvarez. Read by Tito Alvarez. 1 cass. (Running Time: 45 min.). (SPA.). 1997. 9.99 (978-0-9662427-0-6(X)) T A Enterprises.
Preventative medicine.

Port Authority. Conor McPherson. Featuring Jim Norton et al. 2 cass. (Running Time: 1 hr. 30 mins.). 2002. 13.98 (978-962-634-743-0(0), NA224314); audio compact disk 17.98 (978-962-634-243-5(9), NA224314) Naxos.
With three Dublin men of different ages simply telling their stories to the audience, it is a spare document. But the wit, insight and pathos so skillfully woven by this major dramatist, makes it unforgettable.

Port Handling Equipment in Ecuador: A Strategic Reference 2007. Compiled by Icon Group International, Inc. Staff. 2007. ring bd. 195.00 (978-0-497-35926-3(X)) Icon Grp.

Port Handling Equipment in Singapore: A Strategic Reference 2006. Compiled by Icon Group International, Inc. Staff. 2007. ring bd. 195.00 (978-0-497-82417-4(5)) Icon Grp.

***Port Mortuary.** Patricia Cornwell. (Running Time: 13 hrs.). (Scarpetta Novel Ser.). (ENG.). 2010. audio compact disk 39.95 (978-0-14-242871-9(X), PengAudBks); audio compact disk 29.95 (978-0-14-242872-6(8), PengAudBks) Penguin Grp USA.

Port Mungo. Patrick McGrath. Read by Jennifer Van Dyck. 2004. 32.95 (978-0-7927-3251-8(0), SLD 667, Chivers Sound Lib) AudioGO.

Port na Coille. (ENG.). 1994. 13.95 (978-0-8023-7102-7(7)); audio compact disk 21.95 (978-0-8023-8102-6(2)) Pub: Clo Iar-Chonnachta IRL. Dist(s): Dufour

Port Security Equipment & Services in Japan: A Strategic Reference 2006. Compiled by Icon Group International, Inc. Staff. 2007. ring bd. 195.00 (978-0-497-82332-0(2)) Icon Grp.

Port Vila Blues. unabr. ed. Garry Disher. Read by David Tredinnick. 5 cass. (Running Time: 7 hrs. 30 mins.). 1998. (978-1-86340-706-9(5), 570321) Bolinda Pubng AUS.

Wyatt snatches the cash, bypasses the alarm system, eludes the cops, & makes it safely to his bolthole in Hobart. It's the diamond-studded Tiffany brooch - & perhaps the girl - that brings him undone. Now some very hard people want to put Wyatt & that brooch out of circulation. But this is Wyatt's game & Wyatt sets the rules - even if it means a reckoning somewhere far from home.

Portable Brazilian Portuguese. Prod. by Travel Linguist Inc. & Joe Mefford. (ENG & POR.). 2009. DVD 29.95 (978-0-9745935-6-2(7)) Big Sc Soft.

Portable Chinese: Mandarin Chinese. (ENG & CHI.). 2009. DVD 29.95 (978-0-9745935-8-6(3)) Big Sc Soft.

Portable Coach: Twenty-Eight Sure-Fire Strategies for Business & Personal Success. Thomas Leonard. Told to Byron Laursen. 2004. 10.95 (978-0-7435-4563-1(X)) Pub: S&S Audio. Dist(s): S and S Inc

Portable Do It! One Hundred Seventy-Two Essential Excerpts Plus 190 Quotations from the Number One New York Times Bestseller "Do It! Let's Get off Our Buts" Peter McWilliams. 1993. 8.95 (978-0-931580-80-2(3)) Mary Bks.

Portable Door. unabr. ed. Tom Holt. 10 cass. (Isis Cassettes Ser.). (J). 2005. 84.95 (978-0-7531-2021-7(6)) Pub: ISIS Lrg Prnt GBR. Dist(s): Ulverscroft US

Portable Door. unabr. ed. Tom Holt. Read by Raymond Sawyer. 11 CDs. (Running Time: 43200 sec.). (Isis (CDs) Ser.). 2005. audio compact disk 99.95 (978-0-7531-2334-8(7)) Pub: ISIS Lrg Prnt GBR. Dist(s): Ulverscroft US

Portable German. Prod. by Travel Linguist Inc. & Joe Mefford. (ENG & GER.). 2009. DVD 29.95 (978-0-9745935-5-5(9)) Big Sc Soft.

Portable Italian. Prod. by Travel Linguist Inc. & Joe Mefford. (ENG & FRE.). 2009. DVD 29.95 (978-0-9745935-7-9(5)) Big Sc Soft.

Portable Japanese. Prod. by Travel Linguist Inc. & Joe Mefford. (ENG & JPN.). 2009. DVD 29.95 (978-0-9745935-3-1(2)) Big Sc Soft.

Portable MBA in Economics. abr. ed. Read by David Ackroyd. 4 cass. (Running Time: 6 hrs.). 2001. 25.00 (978-1-59040-084-5(4), Phoenix Audio) Pub: Amer Intl Pub. Dist(s): PerseuPGW

Portable MBA in Entrepreneurship. abr. ed. William Bygrave. Read by David Ackroyd. 4 cass. (Running Time: 6 hrs.). 2001. 25.00 (978-1-59040-093-7(3), Phoenix Audio) Pub: Amer Intl Pub. Dist(s): PerseuPGW

Portable MBA in Marketing. abr. ed. Alexander Hiam & Charles Schewe. 4 cass. (Running Time: 6 hrs.). 2001. 25.00 (978-1-59040-127-9(1), Phoenix Audio) Pub: Amer Intl Pub. Dist(s): PerseuPGW

***Portable Patriot.** unabr. ed. Joel Miller & Kristen Parrish. Narrated by Sean Runnette & Joanna P. Adler. (ENG.). 2010. 14.98 (978-1-61045-068-3(X), MissionAud); audio compact disk 24.98 (978-1-61045-067-6(1), MissionAud) christianaud.

Portable Russian. Prod. by Travel Linguist Inc. & Joe Mefford. (ENG & RUS.). 2009. DVD 29.95 (978-0-9745935-4-8(0)) Big Sc Soft.

Portable Sounds. Contrib. by Tobymac. Prod. by Toby McKeehan et al. 2007. audio compact disk 17.99 (978-5-557-94934-7(8)) FF Rcds.

Portable Sounds. Contrib. by Tobymac. 2007. 14.99 (978-5-557-57022-0(5)) FF Rcds.

***Portal in the Park.** Cricket Casey & Melle Mel. Perf. by Lady Gaga. (ENG.). (J). 2010. audio compact disk 12.99 (978-1-934814-23-9(7)) Red Planet Au.

Portals of Heaven. John Belt. (Sounds of Worship Ser.). 2003. audio compact disk 15.00 (978-0-9748236-1-4(9)) Pub: Live in His Presence. Dist(s): STL Dist NA

Porte Etroite, Set. André Gide. Read by Marianne Epin. 3 cass. (FRE.). 1995. 34.95 (1648-TH) Olivia & Hill.

There is no reason why Alissa should not marry her cousin Jerome, except for her fear that marriage may be profane love. This fear takes control of her, consuming her spirit & flesh. She turns her back on love, joy, human contact & finally life itself.

Porterhouse Blue. unabr. ed. Tom Sharpe. Read by David Case. 6 cass. (Running Time: 9 hrs.). 1990. 48.00 (978-0-7366-1775-8(2), 2614) Books on Tape.

To Porterhouse College - bastion of conservatism, repository of a famous dining hall & wine cellar, center of hopeless academic standards - comes a crusading new master. The prig, afire with liberal zeal, upsets everyone's digestion with his plans for the admission of women, a cafeteria & contraceptive dispensers. The shock of the new & modern particularly rattles the college retainers, hidebound Royalists to a man. The head porter, Skullion, rallies supporters & launches a counterattack. Their counterrevolutionary efforts result in an escalation of threats, bluffs & maneuvers to shame the shadiest of politicians. It also leads to an investigative documentary that precipitates scandal of the highest order & an utterly unforeseeable conclusion.

Portes Ouvertes. Haggstrom. (C). bk. 101.95 (978-0-8384-8111-0(6)) Heinle.

Portes Tordues: The Scariest Way in the World to Learn French! Kathie S. Dior. Tr. by Kathie S. Dior. Narrated by Lydie Guijarro. Illus. by Krista Buuck & Andrew Edmonds. 1 CD. (Running Time: 51 mins). Dramatization.Tr. of Twisted Doors. (FRE & ENG.). 2005. per. 34.95 (978-0-9710227-1-3(2)) Dior.

Portfolio Management in Practice: Essential Capital Markets. Christine Brentani. (Corporate Finance Essentials Ser.). (ENG., (C). 2003. 65.95 (978-0-7506-5906-2(8), Butter Sci Hein) Sci Tech Bks.

Portfolios Art Program: Technology. (gr. 1 up). 1998. audio compact disk (978-1-58079-054-3(2), Scott Frsmn) Addson-Wesley Educ.

***Portions of You.** L. Ron Hubbard. 2010. audio compact disk 15.00 (978-1-4031-6811-5(3)); audio compact disk 15.00 (978-1-4031-6812-2(1)); audio compact disk 15.00 (978-1-4031-6802-3(4)); audio compact disk 15.00 (978-1-4031-6803-0(2)); audio compact disk 15.00 (978-1-4031-6810-8(5)); audio compact disk 15.00 (978-1-4031-6800-9(8)); audio compact disk 15.00 (978-1-4031-6809-2(1)); audio compact disk 15.00 (978-1-4031-6805-4(9)); audio compact disk 15.00 (978-1-4031-6813-9(X)); audio compact disk 15.00 (978-1-4031-6807-8(5)); audio compact disk 15.00 (978-1-4031-6806-1(7)); audio compact disk 15.00 (978-1-4031-6808-5(3)); audio compact disk 15.00 (978-1-4031-6801-6(6)); audio compact disk 15.00 (978-1-4031-6799-6(0)); audio compact disk 15.00 (978-1-4031-6804-7(0)) Bridge Pubns Inc.

Portnoy's Complaint. unabr. ed. Philip Roth. Read by Ron Silver. 2009. audio compact disk 34.99 (978-0-06-198641-3(0), Harper Audio) HarperCollins Pubs.

Portofino. unabr. ed. Frank Schaeffer. Read by Christopher Lane. 5 cass. (Running Time: 7 hrs.). 1994. 39.95 (978-0-7861-0474-1(0), 1426) Blckstn Audio.

Ten-year-old Calvin Becker, his two sisters, & his parents - fundamentalist missionaries trying to convert Roman Catholics in Switzerland - come down from the Alps to vacation on the Mediterranean. His mother & father try to convert everyone they meet on the beach, but when alone in the hotel room, they bicker continually between themselves. His two sisters survive the parental conflict. The boy turns outward: He learns his way around the colorful resort town of Portofino, makes pagan friends, helps beach boys haul boats, befriends a whiskey-sipping painter, & even visits a Roman Catholic church. And Calvin falls in love. Together with Jennifer, he goes through most of the motions of puberty. A bloody beach accident & its aftermath seem to bond the two children forever...or at least until another summer.

Portrait see Portret

Portrait & Biographical Record of Lehigh, Northampton & Carbon Counties, Pennsylvania: Containing Biographical Sketches of Prominent & Representative Citizens of the Counties. Chapman Publishing Co. Staff. 2002. audio compact disk 24.50 (978-0-7884-2168-6(9)) Heritage Bk.

Portrait de Dorian Gray, Set. Oscar Wilde. Read by Jacques Roland. 6 cass. 1992. 52.95 (1634-LPQ) Olivia & Hill.

Wilde's classic story of a young man of extraordinary beauty who never grows old.

Portrait in Brownstone. Louis Auchincloss. Read by C. M. Herbert. 8 cass. (Running Time: 11 hrs. 30 mins.). 1999. 56.95 (978-0-7861-1597-6(1), 2426) Blckstn Audio.

Tale of a New York family dynasty opens with the suicide of Geraldine Brevoort, a woman whose pride & envy fed her alcoholism, & kept her alone, & leads the listener through an odyssey, told in flashbacks by Geraldine's plain yet bright cousin, Ida, & Ida's husband, Derrick - also Geraldine's lover, unbeknownst to Ida - & other family members. What unfolds is the story of the intertwining of families from different ethnic & social backgrounds, & the misapprehensions that result when such families are brought together through love, marriage & adultery.

Portrait in Brownstone. unabr. ed. Louis Auchincloss. Read by Dan Lazar. 8 cass. (Running Time: 12 hrs.). 1978. 64.00 (978-0-7366-0111-5(2), 1118) Books on Tape.

The book begins with Cousin Geraldine's suicide in 1950, & concludes with son Hugh's wedding a year later. In the interval, Ida Dennison Hartley journeys into the past to retrieve the childhood values & traditions she needs to order her present & protect her family's future.

Portrait in Death. abr. ed. J. D. Robb, pseud. Read by Susan Ericksen. (Running Time: 21600 sec.). (In Death Ser.). 2007. audio compact disk 14.99 (978-1-4233-1756-2(4), 9781423317562, BCD Value Price) Brilliance Audio.

Portrait in Death. unabr. ed. J. D. Robb, pseud. Read by Susan Ericksen. 7 cass. (Running Time: 10 hrs.). (In Death Ser.). 2003. 30.95 (978-1-59086-719-8(X), 159086719X, BAU) Brilliance Audio.

After a tip from a reporter, Eve Dallas finds the body of a young woman in a Delancey Street dumpster. Just hours before, the news station had mysteriously received a portfolio of professional portraits of the woman. The photos seemed to be nothing out of the ordinary for any pretty young woman starting a modeling career. Except that she wasn't a model. And that these photos were taken after she had been murdered. Now Dallas is on the trail of a killer who's a perfectionist and an artist. He carefully observes and records his victim's every move. And he has a mission: to own every beautiful young woman's innocence, to capture her youth and vitality - in one fateful shot.

Portrait in Death. unabr. ed. J. D. Robb, pseud. Read by Susan Ericksen. 7 cass. (Running Time: 10 hrs.). (In Death Ser.:). 2003. 82.25 (978-1-59086-720-4(3), 1590867203) Brilliance Audio.

Portrait in Death. unabr. ed. J. D. Robb, pseud. Read by Susan Ericksen. (Running Time: 10 hrs.). (In Death Ser.). 2004. 39.25 (978-1-59335-591-3(2), 1593355912, Brlnc Audio MP3 Lib) Brilliance Audio.

Portrait in Death. unabr. ed. J. D. Robb, pseud. Read by Susan Ericksen. (Running Time: 12 hrs.). (In Death Ser.). 2004. 39.25 (978-1-59710-588-0(0), 1597105880, BADLE); 24.95 (978-1-59710-589-7(9), 1597105899, BAD) Brilliance Audio.

Portrait in Death. unabr. ed. J. D. Robb, pseud. Read by Susan Ericksen. (Running Time: 12 hrs.). (In Death Ser.). 2007. audio compact disk 36.95 (978-1-4233-1753-1(X), 9781423317531, Bril Audio CD Unabri); audio compact disk 102.25 (978-1-4233-1754-8(8), 9781423317548, BriAudCD Unabrid) Brilliance Audio.

Portrait in Death. unabr. ed. J. D. Robb, pseud. Read by Susan Ericksen. (Running Time: 10 hrs.). (In Death Ser.). 2004. 24.95 (978-1-59335-129-8(1), 1593351291) Soulmate Audio Bks.

Portrait in Sepia. unabr. ed. Isabel Allende. Read by Blair Brown. 8 cass. (Running Time: 12 hrs.).Tr. of Retrato en Sepia. 2001. 39.95 (978-0-694-52599-7(5)) HarperCollins Pubs.

Portrait in Shadows. unabr. ed. John William Wainwright. Read by Peter Joyce. 6 cass. 1999. 41.21 (978-1-86015-415-7(8)) T T Beeler.

A thriller that details the life of a brutal killer from his first murder at age !5 to a life spent as a contract assassin.

Portrait of a Foolish Woman. 2001. (978-0-940110-28-1(8)) Life Action Publishing.

Portrait of a Girl. unabr. ed. Mary Williams. Read by Patricia Gallimore. 6 cass. (Running Time: 7 hrs. 30 min.). (Sound Ser.). (J). 2003. 54.95 (978-1-84283-494-7(0)); audio compact disk 71.95 (978-1-84283-694-1(3)) Pub: ISIS Lrg Prnt GBR. Dist(s): Ulverscroft US

Portrait of a Girl with Comic Book see Twentieth-Century Poetry in English, No. 29, Recordings of Poets Reading Their Own Poetry

Portrait of a Groove. Perf. by Bluezeum Staff. 1 cass., 1 CD. 7.98 (TA 33331); audio compact disk 12.78 CD Jewel box. (TA 83331) NewSound.

Portrait of a Killer: Jack the Ripper - Case Closed. Patricia Cornwell. 2003. 104.00 (978-0-7366-8685-3(1)) Books on Tape.

Portrait of a Killer: Jack the Ripper - Case Closed. unabr. ed. Patricia Cornwell. Read by Kate Reading. 9 cass. (Running Time: 13 hrs. 30 mins.). 2002. audio compact disk 88.00 (978-0-7366-8676-1(2)) Books on Tape.

Explores the psychological and evidential clues surrounding this elusive serial killer. Out of the swirling fog, the killer strikes at the downtrodden of London's slums: five hapless prostitutes. After every crime, he disappears. The final time, he disappears forever. An architect of masterfully engineered trails of clues and a sleuth of motivation.

Portrait of a Lady. Henry James. Contrib. by Miriam Margolyes. 4 CDs. (Running Time: 4 hrs. 30 mins.). 2006. audio compact disk 29.95 (978-0-7927-4328-6(8), BBCD 156) AudioGO.

Portrait of a Lady. Henry James. Retold by Blanche Malvern. Illus. by Anna Balbusso & Elena Balbusso. Contrib. by Kenneth Brodey. (Reading & Training: Step 5 Ser.). 2005. pap. bk. 21.95 (978-88-530-0168-9(2), BlackCat) Grove-Atltic.

Portrait of a Lady. abr. ed. Henry James. Read by Elizabeth McGovern. 4 cass. (Running Time: 5 hrs. 15 mins.). 1996. 22.98 (978-962-634-600-6(0), NA410014, Naxos AudioBooks) Naxos.

Isabel Archer is an independent, spirited & good-looking American woman in Europe, intent on leading a life according to her own wishes. She inherits a considerable fortune after the death of her uncle & her potential seems limitless.

Portrait of a Lady. abr. ed. Henry James. Read by Elizabeth McGovern. 4 CDs. (Classic Literature with Classical Music Ser.). 2006. audio compact disk 28.98 (978-962-634-376-0(1), Naxos AudioBooks) Naxos.

Portrait of a Lady. abr. ed. Henry James. Perf. by Nina Foch. 4 cass. (Running Time: 6 hrs.). 2004. 25.00 (978-1-59007-023-9(2)) Pub: New Millenn Enter. Dist(s): PerseuPGW

Isabel Archer is a young American orphan who receives an inheritance from an uncle. Under the wing of an aunt, she meets Madame Merle, her aunt's sophisticated friend, who instills in her the sense of European sophistication which overpowers her common sense. Isabel marries widower Gilbert Osmond, a friend of Madame Merle, who projects refined tastes & intellectual detachment. She is utterly captivated by Osmond's languid charm. He is thrilled to have his superior prize. But in the end, Isabel discovers that her husband & Madame Merle are both exemplars of an appalling, complex depravity that has become a central issue in her life.

Portrait of a Lady. unabr. ed. Henry James. 6 cass. (Running Time: 9 hrs.). 1999. 53.95 Audio Bk Con.

Portrait of a Lady. unabr. ed. Henry James. Read by Nadia May. 16 cass. (Running Time: 24 hrs.). 1995. 99.95 (978-0-7861-0899-2(1), 1675) Blckstn Audio.

An American heiress newly arrived in Europe, Isabel does not look to a man to furnish her with destiny; instead she desires, with grace & courage, to find it herself. Two eligible suitors approach her & are refused. She then becomes utterly captivated by the languid charms of Gilbert Osmond. To him, she represents a superior prize worth at least seventy thousand pounds; through him, she faces a tragic choice. Numerous critics regard "The Portrait of a Lady" as James' masterpiece. F. R. Leavis declared that "we can't ask for a finer exhibition of James' peculiar gifts".

Portrait of a Lady. unabr. ed. Henry James. Read by Nadia May. (Running Time: 82800 sec.). 2007. audio compact disk 130.00 (978-0-7861-6151-5(5)) Blckstn Audio.

Portrait of a Lady. unabr. ed. Henry James. Read by Nadia May. (Running Time: 82800 sec.). 2007. audio compact disk 44.95 (978-0-7861-6152-2(3)) Blckstn Audio.

Portrait of a Lady. unabr. ed. Henry James. Read by Laural Merlington. (Running Time: 22 hrs.). 2006. 44.25 (978-1-4233-1081-5(0), 9781423310815, BADLE); 29.95 (978-1-4233-1080-8(2), 9781423310808, BAD); audio compact disk 44.25 (978-1-4233-1079-2(9), 9781423310792, Brlnc Audio MP3 Lib); audio compact disk 112.25 (978-1-4233-1077-8(2), 9781423310778, BriAudCD Unabrid); audio compact disk 29.95 (978-1-4233-1078-5(0), 9781423310785, Brilliance MP3); audio compact disk 44.95 (978-1-4233-1076-1(4), 9781423310761, Bril Audio CD Unabri) Brilliance Audio.

The heroine of this powerful novel is the spirited young American Isabel Archer. Blessed by nature and fortune, she journeys to Europe to seek her future, but what she finds may prove to be her undoing. She is courted by three men: an English aristocrat, an American gentleman, and a sensitive expatriate. Her invalid cousin becomes her benefactor and adviser. But it is after the ingenuous Isabel falls prey to the schemes of an infinitely more sophisticated older woman that her life takes shape. Rich in character and the interplay of tensions, The Portrait of a Lady is a brilliant, timeless, and essential American novel.

Portrait of a Lady. unabr. ed. Henry James. Read by Wanda McCaddon. Narrated by Wanda McCaddon. (Running Time: 25 hrs. 0 mins. 0 sec.). (Tantor Unabridged Classics Ser.). (ENG.). 2008. 34.99 (978-1-4001-5697-9(1)); audio compact disk 45.99 (978-1-4001-0697-4(4)); audio compact disk 91.99 (978-1-4001-3697-1(0)) Pub: Tantor Media. Dist(s): IngramPubServ

Portrait of a Lady, Vol. 1 & 2. unabr. ed. Henry James. (Running Time: 10 hrs. 49 mins.). 39.95 (978-1-4142-2715-3(9)) Audio Bk Con.

Portrait of a Lady (Part 1), Vol. 1. unabr. ed. Henry James. Read by Flo Gibson. 6 cass. (Running Time: 9 hrs.). 1989. 26.95 (978-1-55685-131-5(6)) Audio Bk Con.

Isabel Archer, an american Heiress, strikes out for independence in search of her destiny in Europe, while pursued by eligible suiters.

Portrait of a Lady (Parts 1 And 2) unabr. ed. Henry James. Narrated by Flo Gibson. (Running Time: 21 hrs. 27 mins.). 1989. 46.95 (978-1-55685-841-3(8)) Audio Bk Con.

Portrait of a Marriage. collector's ed. Nigel Nicolson. Read by David Case & Donada Peters. 6 cass. (Running Time: 9 hrs.). 2000. 48.00 (978-0-7366-5649-8(9)) Books on Tape.

The story of Harold Nicolson & Vita Sackville-West as told by their son, Nigel.

Portrait of a President: John F. Kennedy in Profile. unabr. collector's ed. William Manchester. Read by John MacDonald. 7 cass. (Running Time: 7 hrs.). 1984. 42.00 (978-0-7366-0715-5(3), 1678) Books on Tape.

"Portrait of a President" by William Manchester is an inside look at the man who was our 35th president, John Fitzgerald Kennedy.

Portrait of a Radical. Interview. Houston Smith et al. 2 cassettes. (Running Time: 90 minutes each). 2001. 15.95 (978-0-9719336-1-3(8)) Four Season Prod.

Enjoy select, unedited segments of the interviews that were conducted for the documentary film "Portrait of a Radical / The Jesus Movement". Here more of the insight and passion that three of the country's most respected and dynamic theologians have for their favorite subject. Much of this material is not found in the video. The interviewees are Houston Smith, Richard Rohr, and Allen Dwight Callahan.

Portrait of a Traitor: Arnold. Perf. by Basil Rathbone. 1 cass. 10.00 (MC1024) Esstee Audios.

Radio drama.

Portrait of a Woman Used by God. 2001. (978-0-940110-27-4(X)) Life Action Publishing.

Portrait of an Addict as a Young Man: A Memoir. unabr. ed. Bill Clegg. (Running Time: 6 hrs.). (ENG.). 2010. 24.98 (978-1-60788-358-6(9)) Pub: Hachet Audio. Dist(s): HachBkGrp

Portrait of an Artist. unabr. ed. Laurie Lisle. Read by Grace Conlin. 10 cass. (Running Time: 14 hrs. 30 mins.). 1995. 69.95 (978-0-7861-0804-6(5), 1627) Blckstn Audio.

Here is the story of a great romance - between the extraordinary painter & her much older mentor, lover & husband, Alfred Stieglitz. Renowned for her fierce independence, iron determination & unique artistic vision, Georgia

O'Keeffe is a twentieth century legend. Her dazzling career spans virtually the entire history of modern art in America.

Portrait of an Unknown Woman. unabr. ed. Vanora Bennett. Read by Josephine Bailey. (YA). 2007. 59.99 (978-1-60252-856-7(X)) Find a World.

Portrait of an Unknown Woman. unabr. ed. Vanora Bennett. Narrated by Josephine Bailey. 12 CDs. (Running Time: 15 hrs. 0 mins. 0 sec.). (ENG.). 2007. audio compact disk 39.99 (978-1-4001-0469-7(6)); audio compact disk 29.99 (978-1-4001-5469-2(3)) Pub: Tantor Media. Dist(s): IngramPubServ

Portrait of an Unknown Woman. unabr. ed. Vanora Bennett. Read by Josephine Bailey. (Running Time: 15 hrs. 0 mins. 0 sec.). (ENG.). 2007. audio compact disk 79.99 (978-1-4001-3469-4(2)) Pub: Tantor Media. Dist(s): IngramPubServ

Portrait of Chloe. Elvi Rhodes. Read by Anne Dover. 12 CDs. (Running Time: 14 hrs.). (Sound Ser.). (J). 2003. audio compact disk 99.95 (978-1-84283-524-1(6)) Pub: ISIS Lrg Prnt GBR. Dist(s): Ulverscroft US

Portrait of Chloe. unabr. ed. Elvi Rhodes. Read by Anne Dover. 12 cass. (Running Time: 14 hrs.). (Sound Ser.). (J). 2003. 94.95 (978-1-86042-340-6(X)) Pub: ISIS Lrg Prnt GBR. Dist(s): Ulverscroft US

Portrait of Dorian Gray see Retrato de Dorian Gray

Portrait of Dorian Gray. Oscar Wilde. Read by Fabio Camero. (Running Time: 3 hrs.). 2002. 16.95 (978-1-60083-214-7(8), Audiofy Corp) Iofy Corp.

Portrait of Jesus. Joseph F. Girzone. Narrated by Aelred Rosser. 4 cass. (Running Time: 5 hrs. 45 mins.). 2000. 41.00 (978-0-7887-4841-7(6), K0003E7) Recorded Bks.
A warm, folksy look at the life & times of Jesus. Drawing from the synoptic gospels, he portrays Jesus as the man his contemporaries would have known. He also reiterates Jesus' original message of love, forgiveness & fellowship giving listeners a complete picture of His life & message.

Portrait of Jesus. unabr. ed. Joseph F. Girzone. Read by Raymond Todd. 4 cass. (Running Time: 5 hrs. 30 mins.). 1999. 32.95 (978-0-7861-1661-4(7), 2489) Blckstn Audio.
Recaptures the truth of Jesus that is presented to us in the Gospels & gives a compelling vision of the person Jesus' contemporaries must have known.

Portrait of Jesus. unabr. ed. Joseph F. Girzone. Read by Raymond Todd. 5 CDs. (Running Time: 7 hrs. 30 min.). 2000. audio compact disk 40.00 (z2489) Blckstn Audio.

Portrait of Jesus. unabr. ed. Joseph F. Girzone. Read by Raymond Todd. 5 CDs. (Running Time: 5 hrs. 30 mins.). 2006. audio compact disk 40.00 (978-0-7861-9908-2(3), 2489) Blckstn Audio.

Portrait of Jesus. unabr. ed. Joseph F. Girzone. Read by Raymond Todd. (Running Time: 1 hr. 0 mins.). (ENG.). 2009. 29.95 (978-1-4417-0062-9(5)) Blckstn Audio.

Portrait of Rose. Pamela Street. Read by Jane Jermyn. 4 cass. (Running Time: 6 hrs.). 1999. 44.95 (61896) Pub: Soundings Ltd GBR. Dist(s): Ulverscroft US

Portrait of the Artist see James Joyce Soundbook

Portrait of the Artist. James Joyce. Narrated by John Lynch. (Running Time: 3 hrs.). 2006. 14.95 (978-1-59912-985-3(X)) Iofy Corp.

Portrait of the Artist as a Young Man. James Joyce. Narrated by Jim Killavey. (Running Time: 10 hrs.). 1994. 21.95 (978-1-59912-851-1(9)) Iofy Corp.

Portrait of the Artist As A Young Man. James Joyce. Read by Hernando Iván Cano. (Running Time: 3 hrs.). 2002. 16.95 (978-1-60083-239-0(3), Audiofy Corp) Iofy Corp.

Portrait of the Artist as a Young Man. abr. ed. James Joyce. 2 cass. (Running Time: 3 hrs.). 2000. 17.99 (978-0-00-104667-2(5)) Pub: HarpC GBR. Dist(s): Trafalgar
Follows the progress of Stephen Dedalus from infancy to early manhood. The richness of the language and Joyce's mastery of literary style as he describes the Dedalus family, young Stephen's education by the Jesuits, his sexual awakening, his intellectual development and his eventual revolt against the religion in which he has been raised.

Portrait of the Artist as a Young Man. abr. ed. James Joyce. Read by Jim Norton. 3 CDs. (Running Time: 13500 sec.). (Works of James Joyce). (gr. 9-12). 1995. audio compact disk 22.98 (978-962-634-070-7(3), NA307012) Naxos.

Portrait of the Artist as a Young Man. unabr. ed. Joyce James. Read by Jim Norton. (YA). 2007. 69.99 (978-1-60252-714-0(8)) Find a World.

Portrait of the Artist as a Young Man. unabr. ed. James Joyce. Read by Frederick Davidson. 7 cass. (Running Time: 10 hrs. 30 min.). (J). (gr. 9-12). 1995. 49.95 (978-0-7861-0655-4(7), 1559) Blckstn Audio.
In this largely autobiographical novel, James Joyce introduces us to the life of a middle-class Irish boy named Stephen Dedalus, who later appears as a leading character in Ulysses. The story describes Stephen's development from his early boyhood, through bullying at school & an adolescent crisis of faith - partially inspired by the famous "hellfire sermon" preached by Father Arnall, & partly by the guilt of his own precocious sexual adventures - to his days as a student & ultimate destiny as a poet.

Portrait of the Artist as a Young Man. unabr. ed. James Joyce. Read by Jim Killavey. 7 cass. (Running Time: 7 hrs.). 1993. 28.00 set. (C-230) Jimcin Record.
Few novels have had such an impact as this starkly realistic psychological drama.

Portrait of the Artist as a Young Man. unabr. ed. James Joyce. Read by Jim Norton. 7 CDs. 2005. audio compact disk 47.98 (978-962-634-366-1(4)) Naxos UK GBR.

Portrait of the Artist as a Young Man, unabr. ed. James Joyce. Narrated by Donal Donnelly. 8 cass. Library ed. (Running Time: 11 hrs. 30 mins.). 1999. 70.00 (978-1-55690-421-9(5), 91106E7) Recorded Bks.
Joyce's landmark fiction debut recounts the internal & external events in a young artist's life & the evolution he takes in his discovery of a vocation.

Portrait of the Artist as a Young Man. unabr. ed. James Joyce. Read by John Lee. Narrated by John Lee. (Running Time: 8 hrs. 0 mins. 0 sec.). (Tantor Unabridged Classics Ser.). (ENG.). 2008. 22.99 (978-1-4001-5696-2(3)); audio compact disk 65.99 (978-1-4001-3696-4(2)); audio compact disk 32.99 (978-1-4001-0696-7(6)) Pub: Tantor Media. Dist(s): IngramPubServ

***Portrait of the Artist as a Young Man.** unabr. ed. James Joyce. Read by Frederick Davidson. (Running Time: 10 hrs.). 2010. 29.95 (978-1-4417-4603-0(X)); audio compact disk 90.00 (978-1-4417-4600-9(5)) Blckstn Audio.

Portrait of the Artist as a Young Man. unabr. collector's ed. James Joyce. Read by David Case. 7 cass. (Running Time: 10 hrs. 30 mins.). (J). 1992. 56.00 (978-0-7366-2301-8(9), 3085) Books on Tape.
While it is not an autobiography, it does convey elements of Joyce's own life.

Portrait of the Artist as a Young Man. unabr. collector's ed. James Joyce. Narrated by Donal Donnelly. 10 CDs. (Running Time: 11 hrs. 30 mins.). 2004. audio compact disk 39.95 (978-1-4025-9809-8(2)) Recorded Bks.
Published in Dublin in 1916, the novel recounts the internal and external events in a young artist?s life, and the evolution he takes in his discovery of a vocation.

Portrait of the Artist as a Young Man, Set. unabr. ed. James Joyce. Read by Flo Gibson. 6 cass. (Running Time: 8 hrs. 30 min.). 1994. 24.95 (978-1-55685-317-3(3)) Audio Bk Con.
The forerunner of "Ulysses", this autobiographical novel deals with Stephen Dedalus' childhood, adolescence & early manhood. His growing rebellion against Catholicism & his family background, his first love affairs, & his interest in art, literature, metaphysics & aesthetics are explored in stream of consciousness sequences.

Portrait of the New Vietnam. Alex Chadwick. Read by Alex Chadwick. 1 cass. (Running Time: 1 hr.). 11.95 (H0070B090, HarperThor) HarpC GBR.

Portraits of Christ. unabr. ed. Read by Gayle D. Erwin. 1 cass. (Running Time: 1 hr.). 1992. 4.95 (978-1-56599-524-6(4), C-24) Yahshua Pub.

Portraits of Crisis: Experience & Theory. Read by Robert Moore. 2 cass. (Running Time: 4 hrs.). 1986. 21.95 Set. (978-0-7822-0174-1(1), 214) C G Jung IL.

Portraits of Praise, Vol. 1. Perf. by James White & Calvary Temple Choir and Orchestra Staff. 1 cass. 1999. (978-0-7601-3085-8(X)); audio compact disk (978-0-7601-3084-1(1)) Brentwood Music.
Live concert that offers a blend of your favorite praise & worship choruses along with fresh new songs birthed in the church. Songs include: "Let Everything Praise the Lord," "When Jesus Lifts a Load," "Bless the Lord," "We Give You Glory" & more.

Portraits of Praise, Vol. 2. Perf. by Mark Condon & Turnpoint Church Choir. 1 cass. 1999. (978-0-7601-3087-2(6)); audio compact disk (978-0-7601-3086-5(8)) Brentwood Music.
Live concert offers a blend of your favorite praise & worship choruses along with fresh new songs birthed in the church. Songs include: "Let Everything Praise the Lord," "When Jesus Lifts a Load," "Bless the Lord," "We Give You Glory" & many more.

Portraits of Worship, Vol. 1. Perf. by Geron Davis et al. 1 cass. 1999. (978-0-7601-3089-6(2)); audio compact disk (978-0-7601-3088-9(4)) Brentwood Music.
Live concert offers a blend of your favorite praise & worship choruses along with fresh new songs birthed in the church. Songs include: "Holy Ground," "You Alone are Worthy," "Peace Speaker," "Worship Christ the Lord" & many more.

Portraits of Worship, Vol. 2. Perf. by Dave Williamson & Newsong Christian Fellowship Choir. 1 cass. 1999. (978-0-7601-3091-9(4)); audio compact disk (978-0-7601-3090-2(6)) Brentwood Music.

Portray of the Artist as a Young Man see Retrato del Artista Joven

Portret. Nikolai Gogol. 1 cass. (Running Time: 1 hrs.).Tr. of Portrait. (RUS.). 1996. pap. bk. 19.50 (978-1-58085-555-6(5)) Interlingua VA.

Portugues Basico para Estrangeiros (Basic Portuguese for Foreigners) Set C: Advanced. 2nd rev. ed. Rejane De Oliveira Slade. 4 CDs. 1999. audio compact disk 64.00 (978-0-9638790-7-3(3)) Braminas.
Portuguese language course which contains dialogues, exercises, vocabulary and music.

Portugues Basico para Estrangeiros (Basic Portuguese for Foreigners) Set A: Beginners. Rejane De Oliveira Slade. 4 CDs. 1999. audio compact disk 64.00 (978-0-9638790-5-9(7)) Braminas.
Portuguese language course which contains dialogues, exercises, vocabulary and music of the textbook Portugues Basico para Estrangeiros.

Portugues Basico para Estrangeiros (Basic Portuguese for Foreigners) Set B: Intermediate. 2nd ed. Rejane De Oliveira Slade. 4 CDs. 1999. audio compact disk 64.00 (978-0-9638790-6-6(5)) Braminas.

Portugues Contemporaneo, No. 1. Maria Isabel Abreu & Clea Rameh. 1972. 100.00 (978-0-87840-048-5(6)) GeorgetownUPr.

Portugues Contemporaneo, No. 2. Maria Isabel Abreu & Clea Rameh. 1972. 115.00 (978-0-87840-049-2(4)) GeorgetownUPr.

Portuguese. Created by Berlitz. (Berlitz in 60 Minutes Ser.). (POR & ENG., 2008. audio compact disk 9.95 (978-981-268-391-5(7)) Pub: Berlitz Pubng. Dist(s): Langenscheidt

Portuguese. Ed. by Charles Berlitz. 2 cass. (Running Time: 1 hr. 30 mins.). (Language/30 Brief Course Ser.). pap. bk. 21.95 (AF1028) J Norton Pubs.
Quick, highly condensed introduction to the words & phrases you'll need to communicate effectively in the country you're visiting. Cassettes & phrase guide book are in a vinyl album.

Portuguese. Margaret Clarke & Collins Educational Staff. Contrib. by Rosi McNab. (Running Time: 3 hrs. 0 mins. 0 sec.). (Collins Easy Learning Audio Course Ser.). (POR & ENG.). 2009. audio compact disk 19.95 (978-0-00-731364-8(0)) Pub: HarpC GBR. Dist(s): IPG Chicago

Portuguese, Vol. 1. 24 CDs. (Running Time: 19 hrs.). (Foreign Service Institute Language Ser.). (POR.). 2005. audio compact disk 275.00 (978-1-57970-202-1(3), AFP151D) J Norton Pubs.

Portuguese: Culture Capsules. 1 cass. (Running Time: 1 hr.). 12.95 (978-0-88432-508-6(3), AFP167) J Norton Pubs.
The brief culture capsules recorded in English at the end of each lesson unit of the introductory courses are available as separate cassettes.

Portuguese: Language 30. rev. ed. Educational Services Corporation Staff. Intro. by Charles Berlitz. 2 cass. (POR.). 1995. pap. bk. 21.95 (978-0-910542-73-9(2)) Educ Svcs DC.
Portuguese self-teaching language course.

Portuguese: Learn to Speak & Understand Portuguese with Pimsleur Language Programs. 2nd ed. Pimsleur Staff. (Running Time: 500 hrs. 0 mins. NaN sec.). (Compact Ser.). (ENG.). 2005. audio compact disk 115.00 (978-0-7435-3690-5(8), Pimsleur) Pub: S&S Audio. Dist(s): S and S Inc

Portuguese: Learn to Speak & Understand Portuguese with Pimsleur Language Programs. 2nd unabr. ed. Pimsleur Staff. 5 CDs. (Running Time: 50 hrs. 0 mins. 0 sec.). (Compact Ser.). (POR & ENG.). 2006. audio compact disk 49.95 (978-0-7435-5066-6(8), Pimsleur) Pub: S&S Audio. Dist(s): S and S Inc

Portuguese Bible. Contrib. by Danillo Nunes. 16 cass. (POR.). 1994. 39.98 Set. (978-7-902033-36-7(7)) Chrstn Dup Intl.

Portuguese Bible - New Testament (Spoken Word) Almeida Versao Atualizada. Read by Davi Nunes. 16 cass. 1994. 39.97 (978-1-58968-070-8(7), 7001A) Chrstn Dup Intl.

Portuguese Bible - Psalms (Spoken Word) Almeida Versao Atualizada. Read by Davi Nunes. 4 cass. 1994. 12.97 (978-1-58968-071-5(5), 7020A) Chrstn Dup Intl.

Portuguese (Brazilian) 2 cass. (Running Time: 90 min. per cass.). (Basic Courses Ser.). 1993. bk. 20.00 set incl. 2 bks. (LivingLang) Random Info Grp.

Portuguese (Brazilian), Set Paul Pimsleur. 16 cass. (Pimsleur Language Learning Ser.). 1996. 345.00 Set, incl. study guide. (0671-57286-5) SyberVision.

Portuguese (Brazilian) Learn to Speak & Understand Portuguese with Pimsleur Language Programs. 2nd ed. Pimsleur Staff. 4 cass. (Running Time: 400 hrs. 0 mins. NaN sec.). (Quick & Simple Ser.). (ITA & ENG.). 2000. audio compact disk 19.95 (978-0-7435-1769-0(5), Pimsleur) Pub: S&S Audio. Dist(s): S and S Inc

Portuguese (Brazilian) Basic. Paul Pimsleur. 8 lessons on 4 cass. (Pimsleur Language Learning Ser.). 1996. 29.95 (56263-1) SyberVision.

Portuguese (Brazilian) for Speakers of English, One. abr. ed. 16 cass. (Running Time: 15 hrs.). (Pimsleur Tapes Ser.). (POR.). 1997. 345.00 set. (18387, Pimsleur) S&S Audio.
Spoken foreign-language proficiency training. Thirty, half-hour, intensive, spoken-language lesson units to be completed at the rate of one lesson per day for 30 days. By achieving eighty-percent correct answers to the questions in each unit, the Pimsleur Spoken Language Programmed Instructional Method will enable the learner to achieve the ACTFL Intermediate-Low Spoken Proficiency Level.

Portuguese (Brazilian) for Speakers of English, Two. unabr. ed. 16 cass. (Running Time: 15 hrs.). (Pimsleur Tapes Ser.). (POR & ENG.). 1997. 345.00 Set. (18379, Pimsleur) S&S Audio.
An additional thirty-lesson-unit program, accomplished at the same rate as a Pimsleur I. Will enable the learner to achieve the ACTFL Intermediate-Mid Spoken Proficiency Level.

Portuguese (Brazilian) I: Learn to Speak & Understand Portuguese with Pimsleur Language Programs. 2nd rev. ed. Pimsleur Staff. 16 CDs. (Running Time: 160 hrs. 0 mins. 0 sec.). (Comprehensive Ser.). (ENG.). 2001. audio compact disk 345.00 (978-0-7435-0019-7(9), Pimsleur) Pub: S&S Audio. Dist(s): S and S Inc

Portuguese (Brazilian) III: Learn to Speak & Understand Brazilian Portuguese with Pimsleur Language Programs. unabr. ed. Pimsleur Staff & Pimsleur. 16 CDs. (Running Time: 160 hrs. 0 mins. 0 sec.). (Comprehensive Ser.). (ENG.). 2002. audio compact disk 345.00 (978-0-7435-0505-5(0), Pimsleur) Pub: S&S Audio. Dist(s): S and S Inc

Portuguese (Continental) 2 cass. (Running Time: 90 min. per cass.). (Basic Courses Ser.). 1993. bk. 20.00 set incl. 2 bks. (LivingLang) Random Info Grp.

Portuguese (Continental) Short Course, Set. Paul Pimsleur. 16 cass. (Pimsleur Language Learning Ser.). pap. bk. & stu. ed. 149.95 SyberVision.

Portuguese (Continental) for Speakers of English, Compact. unabr. ed. 5 cass. (Running Time: 5 hrs.). (Pimsleur Tapes Ser.). (POR.). 1994. 129.00 set. (18385, Pimsleur) S&S Audio.
A ten-lesson-unit program based upon the Pimsleur Spoken Language Programmed Instructional Method, providing basic beginning language training to the ACTFL Novice Level.

Portuguese for Beginners: Total Bilingual Book in English & Portuguese for English Native Speakers - Beginners, Intermediate & Advance Level. 3rd ed. Short Stories. Lourdes Gallagher. Des. by Lourdes Gallagher. Tr. by Alex Alfinito. Voice by Valerie James. Rev. by Christopher Perry. Voice by Alex Alfinito. 2 CD. (Running Time: 2 Hrs 30 min). Dramatization. (POR & ENG.). (C). 1998. audio compact disk 39.99 (978-0-9720962-6-3(4)) BES.

Portuguese for Beginners Level 1 & 2: Total Bilingual Book in English & Portuguese for English Native Speakers - Beginners, Intermediate & Advanced. 3rd ed. Short Stories. Lourdes Gallagher. Des. by Lourdes Gallagher. Ed. by Alexandre Alfinito. Tr. by Alexandre Alfinito. Anno. by Valerie James. Voice by Valerie James. Rev. by Christopher Perry. 2 CD. (Running Time: 2 hrs. 30 min). Dramatization. (ENG & POR.). 1998. cass. & video 78.00 (978-0-9720962-7-0(2)) BES.

Portuguese in a Minute. Cimino. 1 cass. (Language in a Minute Cassette Ser.). 1990. 5.95 (978-1-878427-01-4(6), XC1026) Cimino Pub Grp.
Feel at home in any foreign country with these 101 esssential words & phrases. Hear each word introduced in English, hear them pronounced by a Voice of America instructor. Practice at your own pace, you can check yourself with the wallet sized dictionary included.

Portuguese Indispensables. unabr. ed. 1 cass. (Running Time: 25 min.). 1996. 11.95 (978-0-88432-950-3(X), CPG104) J Norton Pubs.
50 useful phrases for foreign travel.

Portuguese Irregular Verbs. Alexander McCall Smith. 3 CDs. (Running Time: 4 hrs.). (von Igelfeld Ser.). 2004. audio compact disk 22.99 (978-1-4193-0506-1(9)) Recorded Bks.

Portuguese Irregular Verbs. unabr. ed. Alexander McCall Smith. Narrated by Paul Hecht. 3 cass. (Running Time: 4 hrs.). (von Igelfeld Ser.). 2004. 26.75 (978-1-4025-9048-1(2)) Recorded Bks.
This is the first novel starring distinguished philologist Professor Doctor Moritz-Maria von Igelfeld. Von Igelfeld is the world?s leading scholar on Portuguese irregular verbs. But in other matters such as tennis against equally dreadful opponents and the arranging of fencing duels he is not nearly so skilled. Yet that does not stop him from having a go at life, and the results are always humorous.

Portuguese Prose & Poetry. 1 cass. (Running Time: 1 hr.). 1994. 14.95 (978-0-88432-652-6(7), PR0610) J Norton Pubs.

Portuguese Psalms. Contrib. by Danillo Nunes. 4 cass. (POR.). 1994. 12.98 Set. (978-7-902033-43-5(X)) Chrstn Dup Intl.
Bible.

Portuguese Vocabulary Builder. unabr. ed. 1 cass. 14.95 (SPGO10) J Norton Pubs.
Dictionary providing 101 essential words & phrases for the traveler.

***Poseidon Adventure.** abr. ed. Paul Gallico. Read by Dylan Baker. (ENG.). 2006. (978-0-06-115441-6(5), Harper Audio); (978-0-06-115442-3(3), Harper Audio) HarperCollins Pubs.

Poseidon's Gold. unabr. ed. Lindsey Davis. Narrated by Donal Donnelly. 12 cass. (Running Time: 16 hrs. 30 mins.). (Marcus Didius Falco Ser.). 1995. 97.00 (978-0-7887-0391-1(9), 94583E7) Recorded Bks.
To clear his name, Falco must find a sunken ship, an ancient statue & murderer.

***Poser: God's Dismantling of the False Self.** John Eldredge. (ENG.). 2011. audio compact disk 14.99 (978-1-933207-43-8(4)) Ransomed Heart.

***Poser: My Life in Twenty-Three Yoga Poses.** unabr. ed. Claire Dederer. Read by To be announced. (Running Time: 11 hrs. NaN mins.). (ENG.). 2010. 29.95 (978-1-4417-8151-2(X)) Blckstn Audio.

***Poser: My Life in Twenty-Three Yoga Poses.** unabr. ed. Claire Dederer. Read by To Be Announced. (Running Time: 11 hrs. NaN mins.). (ENG.). 2010. 65.95 (978-1-4417-8148-2(X)) Blckstn Audio.

***Poser: My Life in Twenty-Three Yoga Poses.** unabr. ed. Claire Dederer. Read by To be announced. (Running Time: 11 hrs. NaN mins.). 2010. audio compact disk 29.95 (978-1-4417-8150-5(1)) Blckstn Audio.

***Poser: My Life in Twenty-Three Yoga Poses.** unabr. ed. Claire Dederer. Read by To Be Announced. (Running Time: 11 hrs. NaN mins.). (ENG.). 2010. audio compact disk 100.00 (978-1-4417-8149-9(8)) Blckstn Audio.

Poshli Dal'she. Michael Ransome. 1 cass. (RUS., (C). 1990. bk. 75.00 (978-0-569-09250-0(7)) St Mut.
Language: Russian-English Level 4 recorded by native speakers.

Position Before Practice. Elbert Willis. 1 cass. (Resurrection Living Ser.). 4.00 Fill the Gap.

Position to Receive. Michael Matthews & Ed Montgomery. 2 Cds. (Running Time: 7200 sec.). (ENG.). 2007. audio compact disk 19.95 (978-0-9787492-0-0(0)) Dom Global.

Position to Receive Presents 5 PS for Success! Michael Matthews. (ENG.). 2007. audio compact disk 12.95 (978-0-9787492-2-4(7)) Dom Global.

Position Your Expertise for High Fee Markets. 2000. 25.00 (978-1-930039-08-7(5)) Morgan Seminar.

Positioned for Power: Yielding to the Master's Plan. Phillip Halverson & Fern Halverson. 1 cass. 1997. 18.00 (978-1-57399-037-0(X)) Mac Hammond.
Teaching about prayer.

Positioned for Power: Yielding to the Master's Plan. Phillip Halverson & Fern Halverson. 2 CDs. 2006. audio compact disk 10.00 (978-1-57399-361-6(1)) Mac Hammond.
When Phillip and Fern cried out for more of God's power, He answered in unexpected ways. Find out how you can be in position for the Holy Spirit to manifest in your life and ministry. (Note: Phillip went home to be with the Lord in 1985 and Fern in 2003.).

Positioned for Prosperity: Developing the Six Attributes of a Heaven-Blessed Man or Woman. Mac Hammond. 1 cass. (LAWS That Govern Prosperity Ser.: Vol. 5). 1997. 36.00 (978-1-57399-043-1(4)) Mac Hammond.

Positioning. Nido R. Qubein. Read by Nido R. Qubein. 6 cass. 49.95 Set. (508AD) Nightingale-Conant.
How to be sure you're always in the right place at the right time.

Positioning: An audio series on Ephesians. Prod. by Influencial Productions. Voice by Tracy M. Boyd. 2008. 25.00 (978-0-9822763-1-0(1)) Influent Prod.

Positioning: The Battle for Your Mind. Al Ries & Jack Trout. 2 cass. (Running Time: 3 hrs.). 2004. 24.00 (978-1-932378-24-5(3)); audio compact disk 28.00 (978-1-932378-25-2(1)) Pub: A Media Intl. Dist(s): Natl Bk Netwk
This business classic deals with the problems of communicating to a skeptical, media-blitzed public.

Positioning Ourselves in Prayer. Francis Frangipane. 1 cass. (Running Time: 90 mins.). (Basics of Spiritual Warfare Ser.: Vol. 5). 2000. 5.00 (FF02-005) Morning NC.
Francis combines years of practical experience with a soundbiblical perspective in this popular & important series.

Positioning Success: Do You Know What You Don't Know? Bill Lisowski & John Mengelson. (Running Time: 12300 sec.). 2007. audio compact disk 24.99 (978-1-60247-635-6(7)) Tate Pubng.

Positive Affirmations see Afirmaciones Positivas

Positive Affirmations for Mind & Body Healing. Perf. by John Daniels. 1 cass., 1 CD. 7.98 (CMH 2013); audio compact disk 9.58 CD Jewel box. (CMH 2013) NewSound.

Positive & Successful Children with Mind Power, Vol. 37, set. Jonathan Parker. Read by Jonathan Parker. 2 CDs. (Running Time: 2 hrs.). (Success Ser.: Vol. 3). (J). (gr. k-8). 1999. audio compact disk (978-1-58400-036-5(8)) QuantumQuests Intl.
Disc 1 contains several guided visualizations. Disc 2 contains audible & subliminal positive affirmations with music.

Positive Attitude. 1 cass. (Running Time: 45 min.). (Success Ser.). 9.98 (978-1-55909-031-5(6), 37); 9.98 90 min. extended length stereo music. (37X) Randolph Tapes.
Promotes positive, dynamic, energies. Subliminal messages are heard 3-5 minutes before becoming ocean sounds or music.

Positive Attitude. Rick Brown. Read by Rick Brown. Ed. by John Quatro. 1 cass. (Running Time: 30 min.). (Subliminal - New Age Ser.). 1993. 10.95 (978-1-57100-062-0(3), N135); 10.95 (978-1-57100-086-6(0), S135); 10.95 (978-1-57100-110-8(7), W135); 10.95 (978-1-57100-134-4(4), H135) Sublime Sftware.
More than 300 positive affirmations.

Positive Attitude, No. E135. Rick Brown. Read by Rick Brown. Ed. by John Quatro. 1 cass. (Running Time: 30 min.). (Subliminal - Easy Listening Ser.). 1993. 10.95 (978-1-57100-014-9(3)) Sublime Sftware.
"Positive Attitude" - More than 300 positive affirmations.

Positive Attitude, No. J135. Rick Brown. Read by Rick Brown. Ed. by John Quatro. 1 cass. (Running Time: 30 min.). (Subliminal - Jazz Ser.). 1993. 10.95 (978-1-57100-038-5(0)) Sublime Sftware.

Positive Attitude Training. Michael Border. Read by Michael Border. 1 cass. (Running Time: 1 hr.). 1999. 16.85 (978-0-671-03341-5(7)) S and S Inc.
How to design new attitudes that can become the cornerstones of a new positive personality.

Positive Attitude Training. Michael Broder. Read by Michael Broder. 6 cass. 1992. 59.95 set incl. bonus booster tape. (254A) Nightingale-Conant.
You become what you think about. Here's a scientifically proven method for changing your life by changing your attitude.

Positive Attitude Training: Self-Mastery Made Easy. abr. ed. Michael Broder. Read by Michael Broder. 2 CDs. (Running Time: 2 hrs. 0 mins. 0 sec.). (ENG.). 2006. audio compact disk 19.95 (978-0-7435-5195-3(8), Sound Ideas) Pub: S&S Audio. Dist(s): S and S Inc

Positive Black Images. Rex A. Barnett. (Running Time: 45 min.). (YA). 16.99 (978-0-924198-08-3(7)) Hist Video.

Positive Black Role Models. Rex A. Barnett. Interview with James Wood. (YA). 16.99 (978-0-924198-14-4(1)) Hist Video.
Atlanta bank official talks about his career to motivate others to high achievement.

Positive Care Giver. Eldon Taylor. 1 CD. (Running Time: 52 min.). (Whole Brain Innertalk Ser.). 1998. audio compact disk (978-1-55978-850-2(X)) Progress Aware Res.

Positive Choices - From Stress to Serenity. Gail McMeekin. 1 cass. (Running Time: 1 hr. 30 mins.). 1992. 15.00 (978-0-9678271-1-7(6)) Creative Suc.
A unique approach to stress management & personal/professional growth.

Positive Discipline see Disciplina Positiva

Positive Discipline. Jane Nelsen. Read by Jane Nelsen. Ainge Katie. Prod. by Ainge Kenneth, Jr. (ENG.). 2008. 14.95 (978-0-9821210-0-9(8), StoneVista) EmpoweringUT.

Positive Discipline: As read by Dr. Jane Nelsen. Jane Nelsen. Read by Jane Nelsen. Prod. by Kenneth Ainge, Jr. 2008. audio compact disk 39.95 (978-0-9816250-4-1(5)) EmpoweringUT.

Positive Discipline for Teenagers the Workshop: A workshop with Jane Nelsen & Lynn Lott. Jane Nelsen & Lott Lynn. Ed. by Kenneth Ainge, Jr. 2007. audio compact disk 39.95 (978-0-9816250-2-7(9)) EmpoweringUT.

Positive Discipline Workshop 5 CD Set: An audio workshop with Jane Nelsen. Jane Nelsen. Prod. by Ainge Kenneth, Jr. 2007. audio compact disk 39.95 (978-0-9816250-3-4(7)) EmpoweringUT.

Positive Discpline Birth to Five. Perf. by Jane Nelsen. 2 CDs. (Running Time: 2.00 hrs.). 2006. audio compact disk 19.95 (978-0-9606896-5-1(6)) EmpoweringUT.

Positive Energy. unabr. ed. Judith H. Orloff. 9 cass. (Running Time: 13 hrs. 30 min.). 2004. 90.00 (978-0-7366-9859-7(0)) Books on Tape.
Judith Orloff, M.D. shows readers how to use the new science of "energy psychiatry" to bring about enhanced vitality and well being.

Positive Energy: 10 Extraordinary Prescriptions for Transforming Fatigue, Stress, & Fear into Vibrance, Strength, & Love. abr. ed. Judith Orloff. Read by Judith Orloff. (Running Time: 3 hrs.). (ENG.). 2004. audio compact disk 20.00 (978-0-7393-0911-7(0)) Pub: Random Audio Pubg. Dist(s): Random

Positive Energy Practices: How to Attract Uplifting People & Combat Energy Vampires. Judith Orloff. 2 CDs. (Running Time: 10800 sec.). 2006. audio compact disk 19.95 (978-1-59179-405-9(6), W989D) Sounds True.

Positive Expectancy to Win. 1977. audio compact disk (978-0-89811-287-0(7)) Meyer Res Grp.

Positive Expectancy to Win. Paul J. Meyer. 1 cass. (Running Time: 30 min.). 11.00 (978-0-89811-053-1(X), 7103) Meyer Res Grp.
Direct your life, achieve success, & reach goals by taking responsibility for the expectations which affect your life.

Positive Expectancy to Win. Paul J. Meyer. 1 cass. 10.00 (SP100023) SMI Intl.
What you expect of yourself becomes a powerful self-fulfilling prophecy that determines what you will become. Learn to direct your life, to achieve success, & to reach your goals by taking responsibility for the expectations which affect your life.

Positive Experiential Awareness, Purposeful Relaxation, & Differentiated Bodily Feeling States, Set-PA. Russell E. Mason. Read by Russell E. Mason. 3 cass. (Running Time: 2 hrs. 51 min.). (Train-Ascendance Cassettes Ser.). 1975. pap. bk. 23.00 set. (978-0-89533-012-3(1), GT-PA) F I Comm.
Explanations & practice for awareness of positive feeling states, including purposeful relaxation, significance (excitement), joy, & sexual bodily feeling states.

Positive Family Dynamics: The Geometry of Being - Geometry in Motion. Eldon Taylor. Directed By Eldon Taylor. 1 cass. (Running Time: 30 min.). (Sacred Geometry Ser.). 1997. cass. & video 29.95 (978-1-55978-699-7(X), V106) Progress Aware Res.
Geometry in motion developing from fractals, forming mandalas, absolutely mesmerizing with tones & frequencies.

Positive Health. Hilary Jones. Read by Hilary Jones. (Running Time: 0 hr. 30 mins.). 2000. 16.95 (978-1-59912-931-0(0)) Iofy Corp.

Positive Imagery for People with Cancer. 1 cassette. (Running Time: 57:09 mins.). 1989. 12.95 (978-1-55841-029-9(5)) Emmett E Miller.
The healing imagery from Healing Journey helps you grow stronger, while Side 2 helps you empower your army of white cells ridding your body of unwelcome guests. Designed to help strengthen your immune and healing responses.

Positive Imaging. Norman Vincent Peale. 1 cass. (Running Time: 42 min.). 11.00 (978-0-89811-213-9(3), 9420) Meyer Res Grp.
Dr. Peale's method puts you in command of your life by releasing your potential for finding solutions to any problem.

Positive Imaging. Norman Vincent Peale. 1 cass. 10.00 (SP100047) SMI Intl.
The man who taught the world to think positively tells how you can use your imagination & ability to visualize to reach goals. Dr. Peale's method puts you in command of your life by releasing your potential for finding solutions to any problem.

***Positive Leadership: Strategies for Extraordinary Performance.** unabr. ed. Kim Cameron. Narrated by David Drummond. 3 CDs. (Running Time: 3 hrs.). 2009. audio compact disk 39.95 (978-0-7927-6054-2(9)) AudioGO.

***Positive Life: Living with HIV as a Pastor, Husband, & Father.** unabr. ed. Shane Stanford. (Running Time: 5 hrs. 27 mins. 0 sec.). (ENG.). 2010. 19.99 (978-0-310-77355-9(5)) Zondervan.

Positive Mental Attitude see Actitud Mental Positiva

Positive Mental Attitude. Michael P. Kelly. 1 cass. 1992. 14.95 (978-1-883700-09-6(4)) ThoughtForms.
Self help.

Positive Mental Attitude. Eldon Taylor. 1 cass. (Running Time: 62 min.). (Inner Talk Ser.). 16.95 (978-1-55978-081-0(9), 5302A) Progress Aware Res.
Soundtrack - Tropical Lagoon with underlying subliminal affirmations.

Positive Mental Attitude: Easy. Eldon Taylor. Read by Eldon Taylor. Ed. by Leslie Brice. 1 cass. (Running Time: 1 hr.). 1992. 16.95 (978-1-56705-038-7(7)) Gateways Inst.
Self improvement.

Positive Mental Attitude: Environmental Theme. Eldon Taylor. 1 cass. 16.95 (978-1-55978-452-8(0), 5302F) Progress Aware Res.

Positive Mental Attitude: Harmonies. Eldon Taylor. Read by Eldon Taylor. Ed. by Leslie Brice. 1 cass. (Running Time: 1 hr.). 1992. 16.95 (978-1-56705-039-4(5)) Gateways Inst.

Positive Mental Attitude: Music Theme. Eldon Taylor. 1 cass. 16.95 (978-1-55978-083-4(5), 5302C) Progress Aware Res.

Positive Mental Attitude: Ocean. Eldon Taylor. Read by Eldon Taylor. Ed. by Leslie Brice. 1 cass. (Running Time: 1 hr.). 1992. 16.95 (978-1-56705-040-0(9)) Gateways Inst.

Positive Mental Attitude: Stream. Eldon Taylor. Read by Eldon Taylor. Ed. by Leslie Brice. 1 cass. (Running Time: 1 hr.). 1992. 16.95 (978-1-56705-041-7(7)) Gateways Inst.

Positive Ministry of the Holy Spirit. 3 CDs. 2004. audio compact disk (978-1-59548-021-7(8)) A Wommack.

Positive Ministry of the Holy Spirit. Created by AWMI. (ENG.). 2006. 25.00 (978-1-59548-084-2(6)); audio compact disk 25.00 (978-1-59548-085-9(4)) A Wommack.

Positive Music for Today's Kids! Bright Smiles & Blue Skies. unabr. ed. Lisa M. Nelson. 1 cass. (Running Time: 40 min.). (J). (gr. k-6). 1990. pap. bk. 9.95 (978-0-9627863-0-3(6)) Brght Ideas CA.
A series of audio cassette tapes created specifically for the elementary school-aged child (5-12). The tapes are designed to promote self-esteem & positive life values, The approach is fun, the music is hip, upbeat & current. "Bright Smiles & Blue Skies" also includes a full-color illustrated lyric book.

Positive Parenting. 1 cass. (Running Time: 45 min.). (Relationship Ser.). 1989. 9.98 (978-1-55909-197-8(5), 64S) Randolph Tapes.
Designed for parents, step-parents etc., to feel more secure, decisive, & be more effective. Subliminal messages are heard 3-5 minutes before becoming ocean sounds or music.

Positive Parenting. 2 cass. set. (978-0-9626359-2-2(8)) S McDaniel Enter.
Specific "how-to" techniques for positive parenting. The age range is birth through teens. Fun, funny & very practical.

Positive Parenting. Shad Helmstetter. 1 cass. (Self-Talk Ser.). 10.95 (978-0-937065-47-1(1)) Grindle Pr.
Companion Self-Talk Cassettes as mentioned in the book, "What To Say When You Talk To Your Self".

Positive Parenting. Eldon Taylor. 2 cass. (Running Time: 62 min.). (Inner Talk Ser.). 16.95 (978-0-940699-91-5(5), 5320A) Progress Aware Res.
Soundtrack - Tropical Lagoon with underlying subliminal affirmations.

Positive Parenting: Easy. Eldon Taylor. Read by Eldon Taylor. Ed. by Leslie Brice. 1 cass. (Running Time: 1 hr.). 1992. 16.95 (978-1-56705-099-8(9)) Gateways Inst.
Self improvement.

Positive Parenting: Environmental Theme. Eldon Taylor. 1 cass. 16.95 (978-1-55978-468-9(7), 5320F) Progress Aware Res.

Positive Parenting: Ocean. Eldon Taylor. Read by Eldon Taylor. Ed. by Leslie Brice. 1 cass. (Running Time: 1 hr.). 1992. 16.95 (978-1-56705-100-1(6)) Gateways Inst.

Positive Parenting: Soundtrack: Leisure Listening. Eldon Taylor. 1 cass. (Running Time: 62 min.). 16.95 (978-0-940699-50-2(8), 5320B) Progress Aware Res.
Musical soundtrack with underlying subliminal affirmations.

Positive Parenting: Soundtrack: Musical Themes. Eldon Taylor. 1 cass. (Running Time: 62 min.). 16.95 incl. script. (978-0-940699-51-9(6), 5320C) Progress Aware Res.

Positive Parenting: Stream. Eldon Taylor. Read by Eldon Taylor. Ed. by Leslie Brice. 1 cass. (Running Time: 1 hr.). 1992. 16.95 (978-1-56705-101-8(4)) Gateways Inst.
Self improvement.

Positive Parenting in Spanish. Tr. by Maria Teran from ENG. 1 cass. (978-0-9626359-3-9(6)) S McDaniel Enter.
Spanish translation adapted to meet the needs of the Hispanic community in raising children in a way that is non-abusive both physically & emotionally.

Positive Parenting Series. 5 progs. on 6 cass. 40.00 set. (870; 871; 872; 873; 874; 875) Direction Dynamics.
Topics from book: "Beyond the Cornucopia Kids".

Positive Paul's Philosophy. Paul Stanyard. 1 cass. 12.50 Alpha Tape.

Positive Personality Fulfillment, Set-PPF. Russell E. Mason. Read by Russell E. Mason. 2 cass. (Running Time: 1 hr. 58 min.). (Train-Ascendance Cassettes Ser.). 1975. bk. 16.00 (978-0-89533-048-2(2), 71 GT-PF) F I Comm.
Practice & applications for purposeful relaxation, meditative relaxation & desired feeling states for problem solutions & goal attainments.

Positive Philosophy. unabr. ed. August Comte. Read by Robert L. Halvorson. 4 cass. (Running Time: 360 min.). 28.95 (36) Halvorson Assocs.

Positive Power of Change. 1995. 20.00 (978-0-9713440-5-1(1)) Cornelia Pr.

Positive Power Thinking. abr. ed. Robert A. Robinson. Read by Robert Anthony Robinson. 1 cass. (Running Time: 20 min.). (Magic Magnifying Mind Ser.). 1991. pap. bk. 7.95 (978-1-884780-03-5(2)) Phoenix Pubng.
Personal achievement, self help & success motivation recording.

Positive Reinforcement for Cats. abr. ed. Nina Mattikow. 1 cass. (Running Time: 60 min.). Dramatization. (Pet Cassettes Ser.). 1992. 9.95 (978-1-55569-550-7(7), 41004) Great Am Audio.
You can boost your cat's overall sense of well being. A happier cat means a happier you!.

Positive Reinforcement for Dogs. abr. ed. Nina Mattikow. 1 cass. (Running Time: 60 min.). Dramatization. (Pet Cassettes Ser.). 1992. 9.95 (978-1-55569-547-7(7), 41001) Great Am Audio.
You can let your best friend know just how special he is. Lend support for those dog day afternoons.

Positive Relationships: Easy. Eldon Taylor. Read by Eldon Taylor. Ed. by Leslie Brice. 1 cass. (Running Time: 1 hr.). 1992. 16.95 (978-1-56705-130-8(8)) Gateways Inst.
Self improvement.

Positive Relationships: Environmental Theme. Eldon Taylor. 1 cass. 16.95 (978-1-55978-484-9(9), 5355F) Progress Aware Res.

Positive Relationships: Harmonies. Eldon Taylor. Read by Eldon Taylor. Ed. by Leslie Brice. 1 cass. (Running Time: 1 hr.). 1992. 16.95 (978-1-56705-131-5(6)) Gateways Inst.

Positive Relationships: Music, Meditation, & Prayer. Marianne Williamson. 1 cass. (Running Time: 1 hrs. 30 min.). 1998. 10.95 (978-1-56170-439-2(3), M822) Hay House.
Helps enhance the relationships you have with everyone.

Positive Relationships: Music Theme. Eldon Taylor. 1 cass. 16.95 (978-1-55978-126-8(2), 5355C) Progress Aware Res.

Positive Relationships: Ocean. Eldon Taylor. Read by Eldon Taylor. Ed. by Leslie Brice. 1 cass. (Running Time: 1 hr.). 1992. 16.95 (978-1-56705-132-2(4)) Gateways Inst.
Self improvement.

Positive Relationships: Stream. Eldon Taylor. Read by Eldon Taylor. Ed. by Leslie Brice. 1 cass. (Running Time: 1 hr.). 1992. 16.95 (978-1-56705-133-9(2)) Gateways Inst.

Positive Risk Taking. Shad Helmstetter. 1 cass. (Self-Talk Cassettes Ser.). 10.95 (978-0-937065-06-8(4)) Grindle Pr.

Positive Role Models. Rex A. Barnett. (YA). 16.99 (978-0-924198-12-0(5)) Hist Video.
Shares his journey to stellor archievements as a motivator for people.

Positive Self Change: Self Help Tape. 1 cass. 8.95 (978-0-9626664-1-4(6)) Halt Counseling.
A mind re-programming tape to help people change their life & accomplish goals. It will reprogram your mind to be the winner that you can be. This tape will motivate you to get the wealth & success you deserve.

Positive Self Image & Confidence wtih Tropical Ocean, Vol. 13. Jonathan Parker. Read by Jonathan Parker. 1 CD. (Running Time: 1 hr.). (Subliminal Ser.: Vol. 4). 1999. audio compact disk (978-1-58400-069-3(4)) QuantumQuests Intl.
1 compact disc with subliminal affirmations & tropical ocean.

Positive Self Image & Self Confidence, Vol. 7. Jonathan Parker. Read by Jonathan Parker. 1 CD. (Running Time: 1 hr.). (Subliminal Ser.: Vol. 4). 1999. audio compact disk (978-1-58400-048-8(1)) QuantumQuests Intl.
1 compact disc with subliminal affirmations & easy listening music.

Positive Self-Talk for Teens. Shad Helmstetter. 1 cass. (Self-Talk Cassettes Ser.). 10.95 (978-0-937065-34-1(X)) Grindle Pr.

Positive Strokes for Little Folks. Catherine Wiands. 1 cass. (Running Time: 1 hr.). (J). (gr. 1-6). 1984. 12.00 (978-0-943262-01-7(1)) Chngng Attitudes.

Positive Substitution, Purposeful Relaxation, & Goal Achievement Training: A Systematic Positive Beginning, Set-PS. Russell E. Mason. 1975. pap. bk. 60.00 (978-0-89533-014-7(8)) F I Comm.

Positive Supervisory Skills: How to Get Results Through People. William H. Halbert. Read by William H. Halbert. 6 cass. album. (Running Time: 5 hrs. 37 min.). 1989. 59.95 incl. wkbk. (978-1-878542-12-0(5), 11-0601) SkillPath Pubns.
Focuses on management skills essential to success, including setting clear-cut goals, planning vs. reacting, cultivating leadership skills,

understanding & handling stress, creating positive expectations, managing conflict, & others.

Positive Therapy: Be More Positive. Coby Zvikler. (Running Time: 1 hr.). 2002. audio compact disk 15.99 (978-1-904451-19-8(5)) Global Jrny GBR GBR.

Positive Therapy: Build Self Confidence. Coby Zvikler. (Running Time: 1 hr.). 2002. audio compact disk 15.99 (978-1-904451-18-1(7)) Global Jrny GBR GBR.

Positive Therapy: Care Free Flying. C Zuikler. (Running Time: 1 hr.). 2002. audio compact disk 15.99 (978-1-904451-23-5(3)) Global Jrny GBR GBR.

Positive Therapy: Improve Your Memory. Coby Zvikler. (Running Time: 1 hr.). 2002. audio compact disk 15.99 (978-1-904451-24-2(1)) Global Jrny GBR GBR.

Positive Therapy: Interview Confidence. Coby Zvikler. (Running Time: 1 hr.). 2002. audio compact disk 15.99 (978-1-904451-20-4(9)) Global Jrny GBR GBR.

Positive Therapy: Learn to Relax. Coby Zvikler. (Running Time: 1 hr.). 2002. audio compact disk 15.99 (978-1-904451-14-3(4)) Global Jrny GBR GBR.

Positive Therapy: Lose Weight. Coby Zvikler. (Running Time: 1 hr.). 2002. audio compact disk 15.99 (978-1-904451-17-4(9)) Global Jrny GBR GBR.

Positive Therapy: Overcoming Phobias. Coby Zvikler. (Running Time: 1 hr.). 2002. audio compact disk 15.99 (978-1-904451-25-9(X)) Global Jrny GBR GBR.

Positive Therapy: Relieve Stress & Anxiety. Coby Zvikler. (Running Time: 1 hr.). 2002. audio compact disk 15.99 (978-1-904451-15-0(2)) Global Jrny GBR GBR.

Positive Therapy: Sleep Well. Coby Zvikler. (Running Time: 1 hr.). 2002. audio compact disk 15.99 (978-1-904451-22-8(5)) Global Jrny GBR GBR.

Positive Therapy: Stop Smoking. Coby Zvikler. (Running Time: 1 hr.). 2002. audio compact disk 15.99 (978-1-904451-16-7(0)) Global Jrny GBR GBR.

Positive Therapy: Stress Free Exams. Coby Zvikler. (Running Time: 1 hr.). 2002. audio compact disk 15.99 (978-1-904451-21-1(7)) Global Jrny GBR GBR.

Positive Thinking see Actitudes Positivas

Positive Thinking. Betty L. Randolph. 1 stereo cass. (Running Time: 45 min.). (Self-Hypnosis Ser.). 9.98 (102) Randolph Tapes.
Discusses how a positive attitude makes good things happen!.

Positive Thinking. Dick Sutphen. 1 cass. (Running Time: 1 hr.). (RX17 Ser.). 14.98 (978-0-87554-384-0(7), RX148) Valley Sun.

Positive Thinking, No. 1. Swami Jyotirmayananda. Read by Swami Jyotirmayananda. 1 cass. (Running Time: 60 min.). 12.99 (727) Yoga Res Foun.

Positive Thinking, No. 2. Swami Jyotirmayananda. 1 cass. (Running Time: 1 hr.). 1990. 12.99 Yoga Res Foun.

Positive Thinking, No. 3. Swami Jyotirmayananda. 1 cass. (Running Time: 1 hr.). 1990. 12.99 Yoga Res Foun.

Positive Thinking, No. 4. Swami Jyotirmayananda. 1 cass. (Running Time: 1 hr.). 1990. 12.99 Yoga Res Foun.

Positive Thinking, No. 5. Swami Jyotirmayananda. Read by Swami Jyotirmayananda. 1 cass. (Running Time: 60 min.). 12.99 (728) Yoga Res Foun.

Positive Thinking, No. 6. Swami Jyotirmayananda. 1 cass. (Running Time: 1 hr.). 1990. 12.99 Yoga Res Foun.

Positive Thinking, No. 7. Swami Jyotirmayananda. 1 cass. (Running Time: 1 hr.). 1990. 12.99 Yoga Res Foun.

Positive Thinking, No. 8. Swami Jyotirmayananda. 1 cass. (Running Time: 1 hr.). 1990. 12.99 Yoga Res Foun.

Positive Thinking: Tap into the Power of Your Subconscious Mind. Kelly Howell. 1 CD. (Running Time: 60 mins.). (ENG.). 2004. audio compact disk 14.95 (978-1-881451-84-6(4)) Brain Sync.
Positive thoughts produce positive results. The only problem is some of our most persistent, self-defeating beliefs are stored deep in the unconscious, where they have the power to undermine our happiness and sabotage our success. Now you can effortlessly change those negative beliefs to produce the results you want. A special combination of brain wave frequencies are harmonically layered in soothing music to trigger heightened states of receptivity. Here the unconscious is primed to receive and act on a new set of ideas. Subliminal messages are deeply absorbed by the unconscious to immediately impact your sense of self, your creativity and dynamic expression of your power in the world. The results are profound.

Positive Thinking: Tap the power of positive Thinking. Kelly Howell. 1 cass. (Running Time: 1 hr.). (Brain Wave Subliminal Ser.). 1996. 9.95 (978-1-881451-38-9(0)) Brain Sync.
You feel refreshed and invigorated as positive information is absorbed by your subconscious mind.

Positive Thinking & Actions. Bruce Goldberg. (ENG.). 2005. audio compact disk 17.00 (978-1-57968-092-3(5)) Pub: B Goldberg. Dist(s): Baker Taylor

Positive Thinking & Actions. Bruce Goldberg. Read by Bruce Goldberg. 1 cass. (Running Time: 25 min.). (ENG.). 2007. 13.00 (978-1-885577-57-3(5)) Pub: B Goldberg. Dist(s): Baker Taylor
Through self-hypnosis eliminate defeatist & negative thinking. Become a doer & achiever, free of procrastination.

Positive Thinking & Happiness, Set. unabr. ed. Trenna Daniells. 2 cass. (Running Time: 80 min.). Dramatization. (One to Grow On Ser.). (J). (ps-7). 1999. 19.95 (978-0-918519-24-5(1)) Trenna Prods.
Four stories that promote positive thinking & happiness. Action packed stories that promote self-esteem, self responsibility, morals & values.

Positive Thinking Made Easy - Instant Mood Brightener. Robert E. Griswold. Read by Robert E. Griswold. 1 cass. (Super Strength Ser.). 1993. 10.95 (978-1-55848-311-8(X)) EffectiveMN.
Don't need insomnia to benefit, helps you to enjoy a peaceful night's sleep & wake up feeling better than ever.

***Positive Thinking Made Easy Instant Mood Brightener: 2 Complete Bestsellers on One CD.** Bob Griswold. Contrib. by Effective Learning Systems. (Running Time: 51). (Super Strength Ser.). (ENG.). 2004. audio compact disk 14.95 (978-1-55848-111-4(7)) EffectiveMN.

Positive Thinking Power for Busy People. Bob Griswold. Read by Deirdre M. Griswold. 2000. 11.98 (978-1-55848-211-1(3)) EffectiveMN.

Positive Thoughts for Successful Living. Gary N. Arnold et al. 1998. bk. 12.95 (978-1-57867-031-4(4)) Windhorse Corp.

Positive Thoughts for Successful Living. unabr. ed. Gary Arnold et al. 1 cass. 1997. pap. bk. 12.95 (978-1-57867-034-5(9)) Windhorse Corp.
A cornucopia of life affirming thought.

Positive Use of Negative Aspects. Capel McCutcheon. 1 cass. 8.95 (563) Am Fed Astrologers.
Show clients how to do it.

Positive Words, Powerful Results: Simple Ways to Honor, Affirm, & Celebrate Life. abr. ed. Hal Urban. 2004. 11.95 (978-0-7435-3944-9(3)) Pub: S&S Audio. Dist(s): S and S Inc

Positively Singable Songs. Perf. by Ronno. 1 LP. (J). pupil's gde. ed. 11.95 (KIM 9137) Kimbo Educ.

Positively Singable Songs. Perf. by Ronno. 1 cass. (Running Time: 40 min.). (J). 2000. pap. bk. 10.95 (KIM 9137C); pap. bk. 14.95 (KIM 9137CD) Kimbo Educ.

Positively Young! How to Live, Love, Laugh & Let Go of Inner Wrinkles at Any Age. abr. ed. Julia M. Busch. Read by Julia M. Busch. 2 cass. Dramatization. 1993. 24.95 set. (978-0-9632907-3-1(8)) Anti Aging Pr.
Stress releasing, pain releasing, age reversing games, stories & questions. Allows the listener to get in touch with his or her hopes, dreams & goals by playing youth games, letting go (of pain & stumbling blocks) to grow games, self-love games & laugh lessons. Reviewers give it "a ten smile rating!".

Positively 4th Street. unabr. ed. David Hajdu. Read by Susan O'Malley. 9 cass. (Running Time: 13 hrs.). 2002. 62.95 (978-0-7861-2321-6(4), 3004); audio compact disk 80.00 (978-0-7861-9442-1(1), 3004) Blckstn Audio.
When something amazing happens, Hajdu puts you right there. The unknown Baez barefoot in the rain, bedazzling the Newport Jazz Festival and becoming immortal overnight. The irresistibly irresponsible Farina talking his folk-star wife out of shooting him dead with his own pistol. The little spastic gnome Dylan transmogrified into greatness onstage, bashing Joan with the searing lyrics of She Belongs to Me. A stoned Farina advising Dylan to cynically hitch his wagon to Joan's rising star and "start a whole new genre. Poetry set to music, but not chamber music or beatnik jazz, man, poetry you can dance to.

Positivity: Groundbreaking Research Reveals How to Embrace the Hidden Strength of Positive Emotions, Overcome Negativity, & Thrive. abr. unabr. ed. Barbara Fredrickson. Read by Kimberly Farr. (ENG.). 2009. audio compact disk 34.95 (978-0-7393-8182-3(2), Random AudioBks) Pub: Random Audio Pubg. Dist(s): Random

Positivity: Groundbreaking Research Reveals How to Embrace the Hidden Strength of Positive Emotions, Overcome Negativity, & Thrive. unabr. ed. Barbara Fredrickson. Narrated by Kimberly Farr. 8 CDs. (Running Time: 9 hrs.). 2009. audio compact disk 70.00 (978-1-4159-6044-8(5), BksonTape) Pub: Random Audio Pubg. Dist(s): Random

Positivity... The Power to Choose Your Actions, Feelings & Thoughts. Paul Stanyard. 4 cass. (Tapes by Positive Paul Stanyard Ser.). 12.50 Set. Alpha Tape.

Positronic Man. Isaac Asimov & Robert A. Silverberg. Read by Kristofer Batho. 7 CDs. 2004. audio compact disk 37.95 (978-0-7927-3266-2(9), SLD 311, Chivers Sound Lib) AudioGO.

Positronic Man. unabr. ed. Isaac Asimov & Robert A. Silverberg. Read by Kristofer Batho. 8 cass. (Running Time: 12 hrs.). 2001. 69.95 (978-0-7862-9975-1(4), CSL 080, Chivers Sound Lib) AudioGO.
A technological breakthrough leads to the development of an extraordinary robot named Andrew, who can create, learn, and even feel. But when U.S. Robots and Mechanical Men, Inc. learn of his talents, they terminate this new line of robots, frightened of its implications. But Andrew has other ideas, as he struggles to attain his freedom and dignity.

Posse, Set. unabr. ed. Ahrgus Juilliard. Read by Melvin Van Peebles. 2 cass. (Running Time: 3 hrs.). 1993. 16.95 (978-1-56876-006-3(X)) Soundlines Ent.
A historic epic set in the wild untamed West, about a group of desperados who ride & fight together seeking justice where it is not given.

Possess or Perish. Kenneth W. Hagin, Jr. 1 cass. 4.95 (SJ02) Faith Lib Pubns.

Possess the Land. Tsea. 2008. audio compact disk (978-0-9797500-4-5(0)) TSEA.

***Possessed.** unabr. ed. L. J. Smith. Read by Khristine Huam & Khristine Hvam. (Running Time: 6 hrs.). (Dark Visions Ser.: Bk. 2). 2010. 19.99 (978-1-4418-5915-0(2), 9781441859150, Brilliance MP3) Brilliance Audio.

***Possessed.** unabr. ed. L. J. Smith. Read by Khristine Hvam. (Running Time: 6 hrs.). (Dark Visions Ser.: Bk. 2). 2010. 39.97 (978-1-4418-5916-7(0), 9781441859167, Brlnc Audio MP3 Lib); 39.97 (978-1-4418-5917-4(9), 9781441859174, BADLE) Brilliance Audio.

***Possessed.** unabr. ed. L. J. Smith. Read by Khristine Huam & Khristine Hvam. (Running Time: 6 hrs.). (Dark Visions Ser.: Bk. 2). 2010. audio compact disk 19.99 (978-1-4418-5913-6(6), 9781441859136, Bril Audio CD Unabri) Brilliance Audio.

***Possessed.** unabr. ed. L. J. Smith. Read by Khristine Hvam. (Running Time: 6 hrs.). (Dark Visions Ser.: Bk. 2). 2010. audio compact disk 59.97 (978-1-4418-5914-3(4), 9781441859143, BriAudCD Unabrid) Brilliance Audio.

Possessing the Heart of the Ministry. Alfred D. Harvey, Jr. 10 cass in album. (Running Time: 9 hrs. 10 mins.). 2003. 50.00 (978-1-932508-18-5(X)) Doers Pub.

Possessing the Land. Kenneth E. Hagin. (How to Be an Overcomer Ser.). 17.00 Faith Lib Pubns.
Discover how you can unite with other believers to see the supernatural power of God overcome strife & division as God demonstrates Himself mightily in your midst.

Possessing Your Birthright: Regaining Total Prosperity. Creflo A. Dollar & Taffi L. Dollar. 4 cass. (Running Time: 6 hrs.). 2001. 20.00 (978-1-931172-84-4(6), TS218, Kidz Faith) Pub: Creflo Dollar. Dist(s): STL Dist NA

***Possession.** unabr. ed. A. S. Byatt. Read by Virginia Leishman. (ENG.). 2005. (978-0-06-082960-5(5), Harper Audio); (978-0-06-079794-2(0), Harper Audio) HarperCollins Pubs.

Possession: A Romance. unabr. ed. A. S. Byatt. Narrated by Virginia Leishman. 16 cass. (Running Time: 23 hrs.). 1999. 128.00 (978-0-7887-3104-4(1), 95815E7) Recorded Bks.
When a young scholar discovers a curious letter hidden in a dusty book, it sends him in quest of the mysterious 19th century woman who inspired it. A wonderful mix of poetry & posturing literary criticism, part mystery, part romance & an entertaining juxtaposition of the 19th & 20th centuries.

***Possession in Death.** unabr. ed. J. D. Robb, pseud. Read by Susan Ericksen. (Running Time: 3 hrs.). (In Death Ser.). 2010. audio compact disk 19.99 (978-1-4418-9185-3(4), 9781441891853, Bril Audio CD Unabri) Brilliance Audio.

***Possession in Death.** unabr. ed. J. D. Robb, pseud. Read by Susan Ericksen. (Running Time: 3 hrs.). (In Death Ser.). 2010. 19.99 (978-1-4418-9187-7(0), 9781441891877, Brilliance MP3); 39.97 (978-1-4418-9188-4(9), 9781441891884, Brlnc Audio MP3 Lib); audio compact disk 62.97 (978-1-4418-9186-0(2), 9781441891860, BriAudCD Unabrid) Brilliance Audio.

Possessions. unabr. ed. Judith Michael. Read by Multivoice Production Staff. (Running Time: 18 hrs.). 2009. 44.97 (978-1-4233-8599-8(3), 9781423385998, Brlnc Audio MP3 Lib); 29.99 (978-1-4233-8598-1(5), 9781423385981, Brilliance MP3); 44.97 (978-1-4233-8601-8(9), 9781423386018, BADLE); 29.99 (978-1-4233-8600-1(0), 9781423386001, BAD) Brilliance Audio.

Possibilities. 6 cass. 2002. 29.99 (978-1-58602-128-3(1)); audio compact disk 49.99 (978-1-58602-129-0(X)) E L Long.

Possibilities & Probabilities. 10.00 (RME119) Esstee Audios.

Possibilities for over One Hundredfold More Spiritual Information: The Humble Approach in Theology & Science. John Templeton. Read by Randy Cheramie. 6 CDs. (Running Time: 21900 sec.). 2005. audio compact disk 14.95 (978-1-932031-84-3(7)) Pub: Templeton Pr. Dist(s): Chicago Distribution Ctr

Possibilities of Sainthood. Donna Freitas. Read by Emily Bauer. (YA). (gr. 7). 2008. 59.99 (978-1-60640-602-1(7)) Find a World.

Possibilities of Sainthood. unabr. ed. Donna Freitas. Read by Emily Bauer. (Running Time: 7 hrs.). 2008. 39.25 (978-1-4233-7273-8(5), 9781423372738, BADLE); 39.25 (978-1-4233-7271-4(9), 9781423372714, Brlnc Audio MP3 Lib); 24.95 (978-1-4233-7272-1(7), 9781423372721, BAD); 24.95 (978-1-4233-7270-7(0), 9781423372707, Brilliance MP3); audio compact disk 29.95 (978-1-4233-7268-4(9), 9781423372684, Bril Audio CD Unabri) Brilliance Audio.

Possibilities of Sainthood. unabr. ed. Donna Freitas. Read by Emily Bauer. 6 CDs. (Running Time: 7 hrs.). (YA). (gr. 7-10). 2008. audio compact disk 60.97 (978-1-4233-7269-1(7), 9781423372691, BriAudCD Unabrid) Brilliance Audio.

Possibility Faith. Kenneth W. Hagin, Jr. 4 cass. 16.00 (06J) Faith Lib Pubns.

Possibility Living: Add Years to Your Life & Life to Your Years with God's Health Plan. abr. ed. Robert A. Schuller. Read by Robert A. Schuller. 2 cass. (Running Time: 3 hrs.). 2000. 18.00 HarperCollins Pubs.

Possibility of Everything. unabr. ed. Hope Edelman. (Running Time: 12 hrs. 0 mins.). (ENG.). 2009. 29.95 (978-1-4417-0658-4(5)); 72.95 (978-1-4417-0654-6(2)); audio compact disk 34.95 (978-1-4417-0657-7(7)); audio compact disk 105.00 (978-1-4417-0655-3(0)) Blckstn Audio.

Possible Human. unabr. ed. Jean Houston. 2 cass. (Running Time: 1 hr. 47 min.). 1979. 18.00 Set. (01001) Big Sur Tapes.
A personal approach through biographical anecdotes to knowing what it can be like to be fully human.

Possible Side Effects: True Stories. Augusten Burroughs. Narrated by Augusten Burroughs. 8 CDs. (Running Time: 35940 sec.). 2006. audio compact disk 79.95 (978-0-7927-4015-5(7), SLD 936) AudioGO.

Possible Side Effects: True Stories. unabr. ed. Augusten Burroughs. Read by Augusten Burroughs. 8 CDs. (Running Time: 32400 sec.). (ENG.). 2006. audio compact disk 29.95 (978-1-59397-892-1(8)) Pub: Macmill Audio. Dist(s): Macmillan

Possible You. Louise L. Hay. 6 cass. 59.95 Set. (669PAB) Nightingale-Conant.
Use your own thoughts to transform your life. Learn how to free yourself from self-limitations...cherish the miracle you are...gain wealth...develop fulfilling relationships...& communicate more effectively.

Possum Magic. 2004. bk. 24.95 (978-1-55592-075-3(6)); bk. 24.95 (978-1-55592-076-0(4)); pap. bk. 32.75 (978-1-55592-298-6(8)) Weston Woods.

Possum Magic. Mem Fox. Illus. by Julie Vivas. 1 cass. (Running Time: 1 hr.). (J). 2001. bk. 24.95; pap. bk. 12.75 (BPRA575) Weston Woods.

Possum Magic. Mem Fox. 1 cass. (Running Time: 8 min.). (J). (gr. k-2). 2004. 8.95 (978-1-55592-980-0(X)) Weston Woods.
An Australian possum named Hush used to think that the magic made by Grandma Poss to make her invisible was fun - until one day, Hush wants to know what she looks like. Tour Australia with these two possums as they sample food that will one day make Hush's wish come true.

***Post-American Presidency: The Obama Administration's War on America.** unabr. ed. Pamela A. Geller & Robert Spencer. (Running Time: 12 hrs. 0 mins. 0 sec.). 2010. 24.99 (978-1-4001-6835-4(X)); 17.99 (978-1-4001-8835-2(0)); 34.99 (978-1-4001-9835-1(6)); audio compact disk 83.99 (978-1-4001-4835-6(9)); audio compact disk 34.99 (978-1-4001-1835-9(2)) Pub: Tantor Media. Dist(s): IngramPubServ

Post-American World. unabr. ed. Fareed Zakaria. Read by Fareed Zakaria. 7 CDs. (Running Time: 8 hrs. 30 mins. 0 sec.). (ENG.). 2008. audio compact disk 39.95 (978-0-7435-7685-7(3)) Pub: S&S Audio. Dist(s): S and S Inc

Post-Birthday World. unabr. ed. Lionel Shriver. Read by Tanya Eby. 2 MP3-CDs. (Running Time: 21 hrs.). 2009. 29.99 (978-1-4233-6094-0(X), 9781423360940, Brilliance MP3); 29.99 (978-1-4233-6096-4(6), 9781423360964, BAD); 44.97 (978-1-4233-6095-7(8), 9781423360957, Brlnc Audio MP3 Lib); 44.97 (978-1-4233-6097-1(4), 9781423360971, BADLE); audio compact disk 29.99 (978-1-4233-6092-6(3), 9781423360926, Bril Audio CD Unabri); audio compact disk 97.97 (978-1-4233-6093-3(1), 9781423360933, BriAudCD Unabrid) Brilliance Audio.

Post Captain. Patrick O'Brian. Read by Patrick Tull. 12 Cass. (Running Time: 19.5 Hrs). (Aubrey-Maturin Ser.). 39.95 (978-1-4025-0221-7(4)); audio compact disk 49.95 (978-1-4025-2827-9(2)) Recorded Bks.

Post Captain. Patrick O'Brian & Simon Vance. 11 cass. (Running Time: 16 hrs.). (Aubrey-Maturin Ser.). 2002. 76.95 (978-0-7861-2670-5(1), 3228) Blckstn Audio.

Post Captain. unabr. ed. Patrick O'Brian. Read by Simon Vance. 13 CDs. (Running Time: 16 hrs.). (Aubrey-Maturin Ser.). 2001. audio compact disk 104.00 (978-0-7861-8833-8(2), 3228) Blckstn Audio.

Post Captain. unabr. ed. Patrick O'Brian. Read by Simon Vance. 13 pieces. (Running Time: 19 hrs. 30 mins.). (Aubrey-Maturin Ser.). 2004. reel tape 49.95 (978-0-7861-2764-1(3)); audio compact disk 69.95 (978-0-7861-8628-0(3)); audio compact disk 39.95 (978-0-7861-8703-4(4), 3228) Blckstn Audio.

Post Captain. unabr. ed. Patrick O'Brian. Read by John Lee. 12 cass. (Running Time: 18 hrs.). (Aubrey-Maturin Ser.). 2004. 104.00 (978-1-4159-0244-8(5)) Books on Tape.
In 1803 Napoleon smashed the Peace of Amiens and plunged Europe into war again. The second in the Aubrey/Maturin series.

Post Captain. unabr. ed. Patrick O'Brian. Read by Richard Brown. 13 cass. (Running Time: 19 hrs. 30 mins.). (Aubrey-Maturin Ser.). 1992. 104.00 (978-0-7366-2224-0(1), 3014) Books on Tape.
Aubrey & Maturin take to the sea in pursuit of French & Spanish enemies.

Post Captain. unabr. ed. Patrick O'Brian. Narrated by Patrick Tull. 17 CDs. (Running Time: 19 hrs. 30 mins.). (Aubrey-Maturin Ser.). 2001. audio compact disk 139.00 (978-0-7887-7202-3(3), C1443) Recorded Bks.
The Peace of Amiens has left Aubrey with no ship, no enemy to pursue & no possibility of prize money to supplement his meager income. His decision to seek refuge from his troubles & creditors in France proves doubly disastrous.

Post Captain. unabr. ed. Patrick O'Brian. Narrated by Patrick Tull. 14 cass. (Running Time: 19 hrs. 30 mins.). (Aubrey-Maturin Ser.: No. 2). 1992. 112.00 (978-1-55690-718-0(4), 92340E7) Recorded Bks.
British Captain Jack Anbrey, taking refuge in France from his creditors, is imprisoned when war breaks out with Napoleon in 1803.

Post Captain. unabr. ed. Patrick O'Brian. Read by Simon Vance. (YA). 2007. 79.99 (978-1-59895-865-2(8)) Find a World.

***Post Catastrophe Economy: Rebuilding America & Avoiding the Next Bubble.** unabr. ed. Eric Janszen. (Running Time: 8 hrs. 0 mins.). 2010. 15.99 (978-1-4001-8654-9(4)) Tantor Media.

***Post Catastrophe Economy: Rebuilding America & Avoiding the Next Bubble.** unabr. ed. Eric Janszen. Narrated by John Pruden. (Running Time: 8 hrs. 0 mins. 0 sec.). (ENG.). 2010. 19.99 (978-1-4001-6654-1(3)); audio compact disk 29.99 (978-1-4001-1654-6(6)); audio compact disk 59.99 (978-1-4001-4654-3(2)) Pub: Tantor Media. Dist(s): IngramPubServ

Post-Death Tax Elections. Read by John McDonnell, Jr. & Betty J. Orvell. (Running Time: 2 hrs. 30 min.). 1992. 89.00 Incl. 88p. tape materials. (ES-55251) Cont Ed Bar-CA.
Covers the decedent's final income tax, the federal estate tax, & the fiduciary income tax of the estate. Includes moneysaving techniques; selecting the best tax year; & IRS rules & deadlines.

Post Disaster Trauma & Its Theological Implications. 1 cass. (Care Cassettes Ser.: Vol. 10, No. 5). 1983. 10.80 Assn Prof Chaplains.

Post Divorce Reconstruction: Rebuilding Your Life While Avoiding the Pitfalls. unabr. ed. Christine Smith. 1 cass. (Running Time: 1 hr. 20 min.). 1996. 19.95 (978-0-9653423-1-5(X)); 39.95 Incl. wkbk. & planner. (978-0-9653423-0-8(1)) Post Dvrce Recon.
Practical self help program to reconstruct your life after divorce.

Post-Exilic Period: Ezra, Nehemiah & Esther. Robert (Bob) James Utley. (ENG.). 2006. spiral bd. 15.00 (978-1-892691-41-5(8)) Bible Lessons.

Post Grad. unabr. ed. Emily Cassel. (Running Time: 5 hrs. 30 mins. 0 sec.). (ENG.). 2009. audio compact disk 24.99 (978-1-4272-0838-5(7)) Pub: Macmill Audio. Dist(s): Macmillan

Post Millenialism: Logos 03/07/99. Ben Young. 1999. 4.95 (978-0-7417-6122-4(X), B0122) Win Walk.

Post Modernism: Logos March 15, 1998. Ben Young. 1998. 4.95 (978-0-7417-6076-0(2), B0076) Win Walk.

Post Mortem. unabr. ed. Guy Cullingford. Read by John Rye. 7 cass. (Running Time: 7 hrs. 50 min.). 2001. 61.95 (978-1-85695-400-6(5), 92054) Pub: ISIS Audio GBR. Dist(s): Ulverscroft US
Who killed Gilbert Worth? Many things call for an explanation: the position of the fatal gun, a half-written letter & a missing manuscript. Worth's family & mistress all had motives & opportunity. And there is one person in particular who has the very best reason for wanting to identify the killer.

Post-Mortem Estate Planning. 1990. 45.00 (AC-593) PA Bar Inst.

Post-Mortem Estate Planning. (Running Time: 4 hrs.). 1999. bk. 99.00 (ACS-2254) PA Bar Inst.
A checklist of creative planning techniques for protecting family business interests, a detailed look at elections & a brush-up on income tax issues this manual offers a convenient & practical update for estate & financial planners.

Post-Mortem Planning & Estate Administration. 10 cass. (Running Time: 15 hrs.). 1998. 395.00 Set; incl. study guide 535p. (MD12) Am Law Inst.
Designed for experienced practitioners, advanced course deals with the major problem areas in administering a decedent's estate.

Post-Mortem Planning & Estate Administration. 1 cass. (Running Time: 15 hrs. 30 min.). 1999. 395.00 Incl. study guide. (AE20) Am Law Inst.

Post Office: Basic Terms. Douglas Moore. Illus. by Sydney M. Baker. (All about Language Ser.). 1987. pap. bk. 22.00 (978-0-939990-52-8(0)) Intl Linguistics.

Post Office Cat. 2004. bk. 24.95 (978-0-7882-0571-2(4)); 8.95 (978-1-56008-311-5(5)); cass. & flmstrp 30.00 (978-1-56008-750-2(1)) Weston Woods.

Post-Polio Syndrome: Program from the Award Winning Public Radio Series. Hosted by Fred Goodwin. Contrib. by John Hockenberry et al. 1 cass. (Running Time: 1 hr.). (Infinite Mind Ser.). 1999. audio compact disk 21.95 (978-1-888064-18-6(8), LCM 53) Lichtenstein Creat.
Forty-four years ago this April, Jonas Salk developed the Polio vaccine and the terrible epidemic was eliminated. Or was it? for more than 1.6 million Americans there has been no cure. Survivors of polio who believed they had put the disease behind them forever find they are once again struggling with chronic symptoms. Along with the debilitating physical aspects, survivors also face the emotional devastation of Post-Polio Syndrome. Later in the program, a study on "contagious" emotions is discussed, with commentary by John Hockenberry.

Post-Secondary Education & Career Development: A Resource Guide for the Blind, Visualy Impaired. 1 cass. (Running Time: 1 hr.). 2003. Natl Fed Blind.

Post Traumatic Stress Disorder: Program from the Award Winning Public Radio Series. Hosted by Fred Goodwin. Contrib. by Matthew Friedman et al. 1 cass. (Running Time: 1 hr.). (Infinite Mind Ser.). 1999. audio compact disk 21.95 (978-1-888064-09-4(9), LCM 67) Lichtenstein Creat.
Psychological trauma can leave hidden landmines in the psyche. Dr. Goodwin speaks with Dr. Matthew Friedman, director of the National Center for PTSD, about the impact of trauma on combat veterans and others. Later in the program, a discussion about a ground-breaking program treating Vietnam veterans with PTSD who are addicted to drugs and alcohol. Dr. Goodwin talks with Dr. Beverly Donovan, who directs the program, and to Belleruth Naparstek, creator of the best-selling Health Journeys guided imagery tape series. Commentary by John Hockenberry.

Post-Traumatic Stress Disorder: 2007 CCEF Annual Conference. Featuring Tim Lane. (ENG.). 2007. audio compact disk 11.99 (978-1-934885-17-8(7)) New Growth Pr.

Post War Syndrome. Eldon Taylor. 1 cass. (Running Time: 62 min.). (Inner Talk Ser.). 14.95 incl. script. (978-1-55978-162-6(9), 5388C) Progress Aware Res.
Soundtrack - Musical Themes with underlying subliminal affirmations.

Postal, Set. abr. ed. Jonathan Lowe. Read by Frank Muller. 6 cass. (Running Time: 9 hrs.). 1999. 29.95 (978-1-57511-046-2(6)) Pub Mills.
A lonely & embittered postal clerk slips into madness.

***Postcard.** abr. ed. Beverly Lewis. Narrated by Aimee Lilly. (Amish Country Crossroads Ser.). (ENG.). 2010. 12.98 (978-1-59644-999-2(3), christaudio) christianaud.

Postcard. unabr. ed. Tony Abbott. Read by Lincoln Hoppe. 6 CDs. (Running Time: 7 hrs. 27 mins.). (YA). (gr. 5-8). 2008. audio compact disk 45.00 (978-0-7393-6364-5(6), Listening Lib) Pub: Random Audio Pubg. Dist(s): Random
One phone call changes Jason's summer vacation - and life! - forever. When Jason's grandmother dies, he's sent down to her home in Florida to help his father sort through her things. At first he gripes about spending the summer miles away from his best friend, doing chores, and sweating in the Florida heat, but he soon discovers a mystery surrounding his grandmother's murky past. An old, yellowed postcard . . . a creepy phone call with a raspy voice at the other end asking, "So how smart are you?" . . . an entourage of freakish funeral-goers . . . a bizarre magazine story - all contain clues that will send Jason on a thrilling journey to uncover family secrets.

Postcard. unabr. ed. Tony Abbott. Read by Lincoln Hoppe. (Running Time: 26820 sec.). (ENG.). (J). (gr. 3-7). 2008. audio compact disk 34.00 (978-0-7393-6362-1(X), Listening Lib) Pub: Random Audio Pubg. Dist(s): Random

Postcard from Madison, Vol. 1. UW Sch of Music Staff. Prod. by Stephanie Jutt. 1998. audio compact disk 14.95 (978-0-9658834-3-6(4)) Pub: U of Wis Pr. Dist(s): Chicago Distribution Ctr

Postcard from Madison, Vol. 2. UW Sch of Music Staff. Prod. by Stephanie Jutt. 1999. audio compact disk 14.95 (978-0-9658834-4-3(2)) Pub: U of Wis Pr. Dist(s): Chicago Distribution Ctr

***Postcard Killers.** James Patterson & Liza Marklund. Read by Katherine Kellgren et al. (Running Time: 7 hrs. 30 mins.). (ENG.). 2011. audio compact disk & audio compact disk 14.98 (978-1-60941-378-1(4)) Pub: Hachet Audio. Dist(s): HachBkGrp

Postcard Killers. unabr. ed. James Patterson & Liza Marklund. Read by Katherine Kellgren et al. (Running Time: 7 hrs. 30 mins.). (ENG.). 2010. 24.98 (978-1-60788-383-8(X)); audio compact disk 34.98 (978-1-60788-382-1(1)) Pub: Hachet Audio. Dist(s): HachBkGrp

Postcards for Peaceful Parenting: Creative Stress Management, Vol. 3. unabr. ed. Scripts. Juliette Becker. Read by Juliette Becker. 1 cass. (Running Time: 45 min.). Dramatization. 1999. 19.95 (978-1-928667-05-6(8)) Postcards MindsEye.
A recording for parents of new babies & toddlers. Dr. Barker, a mother of five, teaches you how to relax & take daily "mini-vacations" to relieve the stress of care-giving.

Postcards for Peaceful Parenting Vol. 3: Creative Stress Management. unabr. ed. Scripts. Juliette Becker. Read by Juliette Becker. 1 CD. (Running Time: 45 min.). Dramatization. 1999. 19.95 (978-1-928667-04-9(X)) Postcards MindsEye.
A recording for parents of new babies & toddlers. Dr. Baker, a mother of five, teaches you how to relax & take daily "mini-vacations" to relieve the stress of care-giving.

Postcards from Around the Globe. unabr. ed. Read by Noah Adams. Contrib. by N.P.R-National Public Radio Staff. 1 CD. (Running Time: 1 hr.). (ENG.). 2009. audio compact disk 14.95 (978-1-59887-857-8(3), 1598878573) Pub: HighBridge. Dist(s): Workman Pub

Postcards from Europe: 25 Years of Travel Tales from America's Favorite Guidebook Writer. unabr. ed. Rick Steves & Audio Literature Staff. Read by Rick Steves. 2 cass. (Running Time: 3 hrs.). 2001. reel tape 18.00 (978-1-57453-426-9(2)) Audio Lit.
A journal of Rick's favorite European stories, his traveling life and how he started his business. Complete with the sights, sounds, tastes and people of Europe - without ever leaving that comfy sofa or the relative safety of your own car.

Postcards from Heaven: Messages of Love from the Other Side. unabr. ed. Dan Gordon. Read by Anthony Heald. (Running Time: 3 hrs. 0 mins.). 2008. audio compact disk 19.95 (978-1-4332-6529-7(X)) Blckstn Audio.

Postcards from Heaven: Messages of Love from the Other Side. unabr. ed. Dan Gordon. (Running Time: 3 hrs. NaN mins.). 2009. audio compact disk 33.00 (978-1-4332-6527-3(3)); audio compact disk 24.95 (978-1-4332-6526-6(5)) Blckstn Audio.

Postcards from Heaven: Messages of Love from the Other Side. unabr. ed. Dan Gordon. Read by Anthony Heald. (Running Time: 3 hrs. NaN mins.). 2009. 19.95 (978-1-4332-6530-3(3)) Blckstn Audio.

Postcards from Wits End. Sarah Harvey. Read by Ruth Sillers. (Chivers Audio Bks.). 2003. 96.95 (978-0-7540-8414-3(0)) Pub: Chivers Audio Bks GBR. Dist(s): AudioGO

Postcards from Your Mindseye... Creative Stress Management, Vol. 2. unabr. ed. Scripts. Juliette Becker. Read by Juliette Becker. 1 cass. (Running Time: 40 min.). Dramatization. 1999. 19.95 (978-1-928667-03-2(1)); 19.95 (978-1-928667-01-8(5)) Postcards MindsEye.
During the first half of this recording, Dr. Barker takes you on an imaginative journey & teaches you how to relax when faced with overwhelming circumstances. The 2nd half teaches you how to create your own journey using " mental postcards.".

Posted Missing. unabr. collector's ed. Alan Villiers. Read by Dan Lazar. 8 cass. (Running Time: 12 hrs.). 1979. 64.00 (978-0-7366-0160-3(0), 1161) Books on Tape.
"On the face of it, it would seem difficult to mislay a battleship & yet a 20,000 ton battleship is missing in the North Atlantic, gone without a vestige remaining, sunk in the sea somewhere off the Azores with not even a floating lifebuoy left as a temporary mark above the watery grave." Thus the "Sao Paulo" joined the list of ships "posted missing" by Lloyds of London during the first half of the 20th century. Lloyds conducted official inquiries into these disappearances. Alan Villiers attended these hearings & presents his findings in this study.

***Poster Girl, No-Work Spanish 2: A Spanish Language Learning Story.** Anne Emerick. Read by Michelle Thorson. (ENG & SPA.). 2010. audio compact disk 19.99 (978-0-9754649-5-3(7)) Aboon Books.

Postern of Fate. unabr. ed. Agatha Christie. Narrated by Bill Wallis. 6 CDs. (Running Time: 7 hrs. 22 mins.). (Mystery Masters Ser.). (ENG.). 2004. audio compact disk 29.95 (978-1-57270-366-7(0)) Pub: AudioGO. Dist(s): Perseus Dist
After closing their detective agency, Tommy and Tuppence Beresford move to the resort town of Hollowquay for their retirement - which is quickly postponed. Tuppence discovers a children's book signed with a child's name, "Alexander Parkinson." Scrawled inside is a cryptic message: "Mary Jordan did not die naturally. It was one of us. I think I know which one." Tommy joins her in trying to solve the old mystery, but danger looms as they get closer to finding what really happened in this town years ago.

Postern of Fate. unabr. ed. Agatha Christie & Bill Wallis. 5 cass. (Running Time: 7 hrs. 22 mins.). 2004. 27.95 (978-1-57270-365-0(2)) Pub: Audio Partners. Dist(s): PerseuPGW

Postgraduate Course in Federal Securities Law. 11 cass. (Running Time: 15 hrs.). 1998. 315.00 Set; incl. study guide. (MD11) Am Law Inst.
Provides an opportunity to improve expertise in order to counsel & serve clients at an advanced, specialized leve l.

Postillion Struck by Lightning. unabr. ed. Dirk Bogarde. Read by Dirk Bogarde. 8 cass. (Running Time: 8 hrs.). (Autobiography Ser.: Vol. 2). 1994. 69.95 (978-0-7451-4319-4(9), CAB 1002) AudioGO.
The second volume in Dirk Bogarde's autobiogpahy series captures the middle years of his life as an aspiring artist & his first steps as an actor, on the road to Hollywood. Bogarde's many fans will be delighted by his superlative memoir.

Postillion Struck by Lightning. unabr. collector's ed. Dirk Bogarde. Read by David Case. 7 cass. (Running Time: 10 hrs. 30 mins.). 1989. 56.00 (978-0-7366-1509-9(1), 2381) Books on Tape.
Bogarde was trained as an artist. Indeed, he has a drawing in the collection of the British Museum, But acting was in his blood & this is the story of how he answered its call.

Postive Philosophy, August Comte. Read by Robert L. Halvorson. 4 cass. (Running Time: 6 hrs.). Incl. Critique of Pure Reason. Immanuel Kant. Read by Robert L. Halvorson. (36); 28.95 (36) Halvorson Assocs.

***Postman Always Rings Twice.** unabr. ed. James Cain. Read by Stanley Tucci. (ENG.). 2005. (978-0-06-084078-5(1), Harper Audio); (978-0-06-084077-8(3), Harper Audio) HarperCollins Pubs.

Postman Always Rings Twice. unabr. ed. James M. Cain. Read by Stanley Tucci. 3 CDs. (Running Time: 3 hrs.). 2005. audio compact disk 22.95 (978-0-06-075667-3(5)) HarperCollins Pubs.

Postman Pat: Big Surprise. John Cunliffe. (Postman Pat Ser.: Vol. 9). (J). 12.99 (978-1-85998-916-6(0), HoddrStoughton) Pub: Hodder General GBR. Dist(s): Trafalgar

Postman Pat: Following the Trail. John Cunliffe. (Postman Pat Ser.: Vol. 5). (J). 12.99 (978-1-85998-912-8(8), HoddrStoughton) Pub: Hodder General GBR. Dist(s): Trafalgar

Postman Pat: Follows a Trail. John Cunliffe. (Postman Pat Ser.: Vol. 5). (J). 1996. pap. bk. 22.00 (978-1-85998-753-7(2), HoddrStoughton) Pub: Hodder General GBR. Dist(s): Trafalgar

Postman Pat: Hole in the Road. John Cunliffe. (Postman Pat Ser.: Vol. 1). (J). 1996. bk. 22.00 (978-1-85998-702-5(8), HoddrStoughton) Pub: Hodder General GBR. Dist(s): Trafalgar

Postman Pat: Suit of Armour. John Cunliffe. (Postman Pat Ser.: Vol. 2). (J). 1999. 12.99 (978-1-85998-904-3(7), HoddrStoughton) Pub: Hodder General GBR. Dist(s): Trafalgar

Postman Pat: Suit of Armour. John Cunliffe. (Postman Pat Ser.: Vol. 2). (J). 1996. bk. (978-1-85998-701-8(X), HoddrStoughton) Hodder General GBR.

Postman Pat: The Robot. John Cunliffe. (Postman Pat Ser.: Vol. 10). (J). 12.99 (978-1-85998-917-3(9), HoddrStoughton) Pub: Hodder General GBR. Dist(s): Trafalgar

Postman Pat Has Too Many Parcels. John Cunliffe. (Postman Pat Ser.: Vol. 8). (J). 1997. bk. (978-1-85998-915-9(2), HoddrStoughton) Hodder General GBR.

Postman Pat Misses the Show. John Cunliffe. (Postman Pat Ser.: Vol. 4). (J). 1997. pap. bk. 22.00 (978-1-85998-752-0(4), HoddrStoughton) Pub: Hodder General GBR. Dist(s): Trafalgar

Postman Pat Special Delivery. John Cunliffe. (J). pap. bk. 16.99 (978-1-84032-216-3(0), HoddrStoughton) Pub: Hodder General GBR. Dist(s): Trafalgar

Postman Pat Takes Flight. John Cunliffe. (J). 1999. 11.99 (978-1-85998-905-0(5), HoddrStoughton) Pub: Hodder General GBR. Dist(s): Trafalgar

Postmistress. unabr. ed. Sarah Blake. Read by Orlagh Cassidy. (Running Time: 10 hrs. 30 mins.). 2010. 29.95 (978-1-4417-2574-5(1)); 65.95 (978-1-4417-2570-7(9)); audio compact disk 100.00 (978-1-4417-2571-4(7)) Blckstn Audio.

Postmistress. unabr. ed. Sarah Blake. Contrib. by Orlagh Cassidy. 9 CDs. (Running Time: 11 hrs.). (ENG.). (gr. 12 up). 2010. audio compact disk 39.95 (978-0-14-314544-8(4), PengAudBks) Penguin Grp USA.

Postmistress of Laurel Run. Bret Harte. Read by Joe Knight. 1 cass. (Running Time: 51 min. per cass.). 1981. 10.00 (LSS1130) Esstee Audios.
Colorful & sentimental story of larceny & love out of the Old West.

Postmodern Spiritual Practices: The Construction of the Subject & the Reception of Plato in Lacan, Derrida, & Foucault. Paul Allen Miller. (Classical Memories/Modern Identities Ser.). 2007. audio compact disk 9.95 (978-0-8142-9147-4(3)) Pub: Ohio St U Pr. Dist(s): Chicago Distribution Ctr

***Postmodernism & Philosophy.** Featuring Ravi Zacharias. 2007. audio compact disk 9.00 (978-1-61256-068-7(7)) Ravi Zach.

Postmortem. Patricia Cornwell. Narrated by C. J. Critt. 10 CDs. (Running Time: 11 hrs. 30 mins.). (Kay Scarpetta Ser.: No. 1). 2000. audio compact disk 97.00 (978-0-7887-4463-1(1), C1160E7) Recorded Bks.
Chief Medical Examiner Kay Scarpetta is in a race against time, gathering clues to track down a serial killer before he strikes again.

Postmortem. unabr. ed. Patricia Cornwell. Narrated by C. J. Critt. 8 cass. (Running Time: 11 hrs. 30 mins.). (Kay Scarpetta Ser.: No. 1). 1993. 70.00 (978-1-55690-892-7(X), 93334E7) Recorded Bks.

Postmortem. unabr. collector's ed. Patricia Cornwell. Read by Donada Peters. Narrated by Donada Peters. 7 cass. (Running Time: 10 hrs. 30 min.). (Kay Scarpetta Ser.: No. 1). 1991. 56.00 (978-0-7366-2071-0(0), 2879) Books on Tape.
Four Richmond women with little in common have been brutally murdered. Using her forensic expertise & state-of-the-art technology, Chief Medical Examiner Kay Scarpetta joins forces with the police in tracking the murderer. Laden with forensic details, this mystery is not for the squeamish.

Postmortem, Set. abr. ed. Patricia Cornwell. Perf. by Lindsay Crouse. 2 cass. (Running Time: 3 hrs.). (Kay Scarpetta Ser.: No. 1). 1992. 16.00 (978-1-55994-528-8(1), DCN 2268) HarperCollins Pubs.
A serial killer loose in Richmond, Virginia. The female victims have nothing in common except for two things: their murderer, & Kay Scarpetta, Virginia's newly appointed Chief Medical Examiner. As she threads her way through the grisly labyrinth of postmortem clues, she reaches a chilling conclusion: the killer is already closing in on his next intended victim - Scarpetta himself.

Postmortem, Set. unabr. ed. Patricia Cornwell. Read by Sheila Hart. 8 cass. (Kay Scarpetta Ser.: No. 1). 1999. 73.25 (FS9-31564) Highsmith.

Postmortem Elections & the Marital Deduction. Read by Edna R. Alvarez. (Running Time: 2 hrs. 15 min.). 1990. 65.00 Incl. 291p. tape materials. (ES-53239) Cont Ed Bar-CA.
Learn to use postmortem tax planning to take maximum advantage of the marital deduction. Also covers coordination of estate & income tax returns.

Postpartum Healing & Recovery: Heal, Balance & Restore Our Body, Mind & Emotions. Mark Bancroft. Read by Mark Bancroft. 1 cass., bklet. (Running Time: 1 hr.). (Pregnancy & Childbirth Ser.). 1999. 12.95 (978-1-58522-034-2(5), 506) EnSpire Pr.
Two complete sessions plus printed instructionmanual/guidebook. With healing music soundtrack.

Postpartum Healing & Recovery: Heal, Balance, & Restore Your Body, Mind, & Emotions. Mark Bancroft. Read by Mark Bancroft. 1 CD, 1 bklet. (Running Time: 1 hr.). (Pregnancy & Childbirth Ser.). 2006. audio compact disk 20.00 (978-1-58522-058-8(2)) EnSpire Pr.

Postpartum Husband. Karen Kleiman. Narrated by Sharon Eisenhour. (ENG.). 2008. audio compact disk 12.95 (978-1-60031-052-2(4)) Spoken Books.

Postscript see Ship That Died of Shame

***Postulate Out of a Golden Age.** L. Ron Hubbard. (ENG.). 2002. audio compact disk 15.00 (978-1-4031-1533-1(8)) Bridge Pubns Inc.

***Postulates of a Golden Age.** L. Ron Hubbard. 2010. audio compact disk 15.00 (978-1-4031-7480-2(6)); audio compact disk 15.00 (978-1-4031-7492-5(X)); audio compact disk 15.00 (978-1-4031-7483-3(0)); audio compact disk 15.00 (978-1-4031-7489-5(X)); audio compact disk 15.00 (978-1-4031-7481-9(4)); audio compact disk 15.00 (978-1-4031-7494-9(6)); audio compact disk 15.00 (978-1-4031-7484-0(9));

audio compact disk 15.00 (978-1-4031-7490-1(3)); audio compact disk 15.00 (978-1-4031-7491-8(1)); audio compact disk 15.00 (978-1-4031-7487-1(3)); audio compact disk 15.00 (978-1-4031-7485-7(7)); audio compact disk 15.00 (978-1-4031-7486-4(5)); audio compact disk 15.00 (978-1-4031-7493-2(8)); audio compact disk 15.00 (978-1-4031-7482-6(2)); audio compact disk 15.00 (978-1-4031-7488-8(1)); audio compact disk 15.00 (978-1-4031-7479-6(2)) Bridge Pubns Inc.

***Postures of the Mind, Affections of the Heart.** Featuring Ravi Zacharias. 1993. audio compact disk 9.00 (978-1-61256-058-8(X)) Ravi Zach.

***Postwar: A History of Europe Since 1945.** unabr. ed. Tony Judt. Read by Ralph Cosham. (Running Time: 31 hrs. 5 mins.). (ENG.). 2011. 44.95 (978-1-4417-7822-2(5)); 85.95 (978-1-4417-7819-2(5)); 85.95 (978-1-4417-0233-3(4)); audio compact disk 44.95 (978-1-4417-7821-5(7)); audio compact disk 160.00 (978-1-4417-7820-8(9)) Blckstn Audio.

Postwar World & Its Culture. 10.00 (HE814) Esstee Audios.
The new outlooks which were the forerunners of a new day & new philosophies.

Pot: What It Is, What It Does. unabr. ed. Ann Tobias. Read by Peter Fernandez. Illus. by Tom Huffman. 14 vols. (Running Time: 15 mins.). 1992. pap. bk. & tchr. ed. 31.95 Reading Chest. (978-0-87499-267-0(2)) Live Oak Media.
An objective examination of all facets of marijuana & its use.

Pot: What It Is, What It Does. unabr. ed. Ann Tobias. Read by Peter Fernandez. Illus. by Tom Huffman. 1 cass. (Running Time: 15 mins.). (J). (gr. 1-6). 1992. pap. bk. 24.95 (978-0-87499-266-3(4)); pap. bk. 15.95 (978-0-87499-265-6(6)) Live Oak Media.

Pot: What It Is, What It Does. unabr. ed. Ann Tobias. 1 cass. (Running Time: 15 min.). (J). (gr. 3-6). 1992. 9.95 Live Oak Media.

Pot Luck Astrology. Rose Cosentino. 1 cass. 8.95 (503) Am Fed Astrologers.
Tidbits the books won't tell you about.

Pot of Broth see Five One Act Plays

Pot of Gold. Judith Michael. Read by Margaret Whitton. 2004. 10.95 (978-0-7435-4564-8(8)) Pub: S&S Audio. Dist(s): S and S Inc

Pot That Jaun Built. 2004. bk. 24.95 (978-0-7882-0335-0(5)); 8.95 (978-0-7882-0337-4(1)); audio compact disk 12.95 (978-0-7882-0338-1(X)) Weston Woods.

Potato Factory. Bryce Courtenay. Narrated by Humphrey Bower. 16 cass. (Running Time: 23 hrs. 30 mins.). 2004. 128.00 (978-1-876584-83-2(1)) Pub: Bolinda Pubng AUS. Dist(s): Lndmrk Audiobks

potato Factory. Bryce Courtenay. Read by Humphrey Bower. (Running Time: 23 hrs. 30 mins.). 2009. 114.99 (978-1-74214-209-8(5), 9781742142098) Pub: Bolinda Pubng AUS. Dist(s): Bolinda Pub Inc

Potato Factory. unabr. ed. Bryce Courtenay. 20 CDs. (Running Time: 23 hrs. 30 mins.). 2001. audio compact disk 123.95 (978-1-74030-392-7(X)) Pub: Bolinda Pubng AUS. Dist(s): Bolinda Pub Inc

potato Factory. unabr. ed. Bryce Courtenay. Read by Humphrey Bower. (Running Time: 23 hrs. 30 mins.). 2009. 54.95 (978-1-74214-111-4(0), 9781742141114) Pub: Bolinda Pubng AUS. Dist(s): Bolinda Pub Inc

Potatoes' Dance see Poetry of Vachel Lindsay

Potencia Sexual. unabr. ed. Carlos González. 3 cass. (Running Time: 1 hr. 34 min.). (SPA.). 1996. bk. 29.95 Set. (978-1-56491-064-6(4)) Imagine Pubs.
Improves the quality & the idea of sex - marital drills to feel better about sex with the couple.

Potential Absolute Surrender. Elbert Willis. 1 cass. (Because of Calvary Ser.). 4.00 Fill the Gap.

Potential of a Human Birth. Swami Amar Jyoti. 1 cass. 1990. 9.95 (K-125) Truth Consciousness.
Mankind is a crossroads in evolution; human birth is sacred. Refining the raw material of mind. Perfection of faith.

Potential Pitfalls of Ministry. 2001. (978-0-940110-29-8(6)) Life Action Publishing.

Potentially of the Soul. Swami Jyotirmayananda. 1 cass. (Running Time: 45 min.). 1990. 10.00 Yoga Res Foun.

Potomac Fever, Set. unabr. ed. Henry Horrock. Read by Brian O'Neill. 8 vols. (Running Time: 12 hrs.). 2000. bk. 69.95 (978-0-7927-2334-9(1), CSL 223, Chivers Sound Lib) AudioGO.
Cal Terrell & Bobbie Short are homicide detectives in Washington, D.C. When Mary Jeanne Turner's cocaine racked body bobs up in Chesapeake Bay, Cal & Bobbie think it's just another overdose. For them, the real action is the Reggae Club massacre, where a drive by machine gun attack on teenagers has exposed the government's inability to protect the young in its capital. But the investigation into Mary Jeanne's death leads Cal & Bobbie into Washington's notorious political machine, where men & women are consumed by Potomac Fever: that unique Washington obsession with power & what it can achieve.

Potpourri of Bob & Ray. (Running Time: 52 min.). 1958. 10.95 (485) J Norton Pubs.
Four different Bob & Ray shows. Includes the Armed Forces Talent Program, the Adventures of Sherlock Sage & Dr. Clyde, the Good Neighbor Award, & more.

potpourri of bob & Ray: 4 different shows From 1958. (ENG.). 2008. audio compact disk 12.95 (978-1-57970-519-0(7), Audio-For) J Norton Pubs.

Potpourri of Poetry: An Introduction to Great Poets. Poems. Robert Louis Stevenson. Audio Bk Con.

Potpourri of Poetry: An Introduction to Great Poets, Set. Robert Louis Stevenson. 2 cass. (Running Time: 2 hrs.). (J). 1983. 20.95 Audio Bk Con.
"Daffodils," "To a Mouse," "The Pied Piper of Hamlin," "Paul Revere's Ride," "The Highwayman," & "Twas the Night Before Christmas.".

Potrait of a Radical: An Evening with Richard Rohr. Richard Rohr. 1 cassette. (Running Time: 90 minutes). 2001. 9.95 (978-0-9719336-2-0(6)) Four Season Prod.
Join us for an evening lecture with one of the most dynamic and sometimes controversial personalities in the Church today. Listen as Franciscan Father Richard Rohr, the most popular cassette author in the Catholic Church, offers a view of Jesus that will likely be from a perspective you have not yet heard.

Potsdam Bluff, unabr. ed. Jack D. Hunter. Read by Brian Emerson. 7 cass. (Running Time: 10 hrs.). 1995. 49.95 (978-0-7861-0914-2(9), 1722) Blckstn Audio.
It's 1945 and Stalin's army stands poised to conquer all of Europe. The only way to stop him is for Truman to bluff him down. To make the bluff work, C. G. Brandt, America's ultra-professional but very human American spymaster, is forced to risk everything on Alex Lukas, an untrained but bilingual secret agent. Lukas must escort a Soviet defector who will parachute into Bavaria with crucial information. But the defector's plane crashes; there is a gorgeous Communist spy in the drop area; and Lukas can't believe the amount of well-armed interest in his movements. Against all odds, Lukas manages to get out with his skin intact. Then he's given new orders: To proceed to New Mexico, to a place called Los Alamos, pick up a crate and deliver it to our Moscow embassy. And, the crate happens to be the key to the great bluff and the biggest card in Harry Truman's hand as he faces off with Joseph Stalin.

***Potsdam Bluff.** unabr. ed. Jack D. Hunter. Read by Brian Emerson. (Running Time: 10 hrs.). 2010. 29.95 (978-1-4417-4191-2(7)); audio compact disk 90.00 (978-1-4417-4188-2(7)) Blckstn Audio.

Potshot. Robert B. Parker. Read by Joe Mantegna. (Spenser Ser.). 2001. 32.00 (978-0-7366-6208-6(1)) Books on Tape.

Potter's Field. unabr. ed. Ellis Peters, pseud. 6 cass. (Running Time: 7 hrs.). 2003. 29.95 (978-1-57270-298-1(2)) Pub: Audio Partners. Dist(s): PerseuPGW

Potter's Field. unabr. ed. Ellis Peters, pseud. Read by Stephen Thorne. 6 cass. (Running Time: 9 hrs.). (Chronicles of Brother Cadfael Ser.: Vol. 17). 2000. 49.95 (978-0-7451-6513-4(3), CAB 1129) Pub: Chivers Audio Bks GBR. Dist(s): AudioGO
During the plowing of the Potter's Field in October of 1143, the grizzly remains of a woman's body are unearthed. The tenant potter had only recently left to become a monk at the Benedictine Abbey, and had abandoned his wife after 15 years of marriage. Rumor had it that the Welsh woman had returned to her homeland, perhaps with her lover. Who could tell? But the discovery of the corpse impels Brother Cadfael to piece together some cryptic clues and solve a baffling crime.

Potter's Field. unabr. ed. Ellis Peters, pseud. Narrated by Patrick Tull. 6 cass. (Running Time: 7 hrs. 30 mins.). (Chronicles of Brother Cadfael Ser.: Vol. 17). 1997. 51.00 (978-0-7887-1089-6(3), 95092E7) Recorded Bks.
The abbey at Shrewsbury has added a nearby field to their holdings. The monks rejoice, until they plow it for a winter planting & discover a corpse.

Potter's House. Rosie Thomas. Read by Rula Lenska. 12 CDs. (Running Time: 18 hrs.). 2002. audio compact disk 110.95 (978-0-7540-5527-3(2), CCD 218) Pub: Chivers Audio Bks GBR. Dist(s): AudioGO

Potter's House. unabr. ed. Rosie Thomas. Read by Rula Lenska. 2002. 84.95 (978-0-7540-0859-0(2), CAB 2281) Pub: Chivers Pr GBR. Dist(s): AudioGO

Potters House Classics Cass. 2004. 15.00 (978-1-57855-609-0(0)) T D Jakes.

Potty Proud. unabr. ed. Patricia Giangrande & Stephanie Olen. Read by Actis, Stella, and Company Staff. Illus. by William Callaghan. 1 cass. (Running Time: 30 min.). (J). (gr. 6). 1991. bk. 19.95 (978-0-9629701-0-8(7)) Anton Enter.
30 minutes of entertaining & instructional songs & narration covering various aspects of toilet training.

Potty Training for Toddlers. 1 cass. (Running Time: 60 min.). 10.95 (C-1) Psych Res Inst.
Positive suggestions for children 18 mo. to 3 years.

Potty Training Your Toddler. Judith Cohen et al. 1 cass. (Running Time: 20 min.). (Potti Pets Ser.). 1997. Incl. charts, stickers, diploma, 3 Potti Pets products. (978-0-9664396-4-9(3)) PPP Enterp.

Poul Anderson: Promise & Problems. (Running Time: 60 min.). (Freeland II Ser.). 1984. 9.00 (FL9) Freeland Pr.
As technology advances in our lifetime our opportunites increase. These & other criteria are disucssed.

Poultry Equipment in India: A Strategic Reference 2006. Compiled by Icon Group International, Inc. Staff. 2007. ring bd. 195.00 (978-0-497-36019-1(5)) Icon Grp.

Poultry in the Pulpit. unabr. ed. Alexander Cameron. Read by Christopher Scott. 8 cass. (Running Time: 12 hrs.). 2001. 69.95 (978-1-86042-893-7(2), 2-893-2) Pub: Soundings Ltd GBR. Dist(s): Ulverscroft US
Biography of a life as a minister, both in his native Ayrshire & in Nairnshire. Perfectly reflects the reality of life in a rural community. "Farmyard manner" & uncompromisingly honest & straightforward approach to life's problems were to make him one of Scotland's most popular ministers.

Pounce: How to Seize Profit in Today's Chaotic Markets. abr. ed. Ken Stern. Read by William Dufris. (Running Time: 5 hrs. 0 mins. 0 sec.). (ENG.). 2009. audio compact disk 24.95 (978-1-4272-0708-1(9)) Pub: Macmill Audio. Dist(s): Macmillan

Pound: A Biography. unabr. ed. David Sinclair. Narrated by Gordon Griffin. 7 cass. (Running Time: 9 hrs. 30 mins.). 2001. 63.00 (978-1-84197-273-2(8)) Recorded Bks.
The British pound has been in existence since the Dark Ages. Sinclair, a journalist and biographer, surveys its history from that time tot he present, where, in his last chapter, its future may be determined by the influence of the Eurodollar. He discusses the presence of early coinage including silver pennies of the eighth century and many other types of coins that led to the development of the pound as it is known. During the reign of King Henry VII in the late 15th century, the pound took on greater visibility s it became the financial basis for exploration/colonization in the new world.

Pour Out Your Holy Spirit. Perf. by Singletons, The. 2002. audio compact disk Provident Mus Dist.

Pouring the Sun: An Immigrant's Journey. Jay O'Callahan. Perf. by Jay O'Callahan. 1 cass. (Running Time: 1 hr. 15 mins.). Dramatization. 2000. 10.00 (978-1-877954-29-0(2)); audio compact disk 15.00 (978-1-877954-30-6(6)) Pub: Artana Prodns. Dist(s): Yellow Moon
Story of an immigrant woman who, like the molten metal in a blast furnace, is transformed into steel.

Pouring Water on a Drowning Man: Hebrews 3:12-13. Ed Young. (J). 1982. 4.95 (978-0-7417-1256-1(3), 256) Win Walk.

Poursuite Inattendue. Christiane Szeps-Fralin. wbk. ed. 59.95 (978-0-8219-3627-6(1)) EMC-Paradigm.

Poursuite Inattendue. Christiane Szeps-Fralin. 3 cass. (Running Time: 3 hrs.). (Mystery Thrillers in French Ser.). (FRE.). pap. bk. 49.95 (SFR113) J Norton Pubs.
Short-episode thriller, intermediate level, in a radio-play format, especially created to develop listening comprehension skills. Accompanying book provides a transcript of the recording, exercises & French vocabulary.

Pourtant, Quand Je Reve... (But, When I Dream...) Audio. 1 cass. (Coffragants Ser.). (FRE.). cass. & audio compact disk 11.95 Plastic case, incl. text bklet. (978-2-921997-06-5(1)) Penton Overseas.

Poustinia: Encountering God in Silence, Solitude & Prayer. abr. ed. Catherine Doherty. Read by Emile Briere. 4 cass. (Running Time: 5 hrs. 30 mins.). 24.95 (978-0-921440-53-6(7)) Madonna Hse CAN.
Poustinia, a Russian word, means "desert," a place to meet Christ in silence, solitude and prayer. Catherine Doherty combines her insights into the great spiritual traditions of the Russian Church with her very personal experience of life with Christ. Men and women who desire communion with God can discover how the poustinia powerfully fulfills their yearning. Readers are invited to leave the noise and harried pace of daily life to enter a place of silence and solitude. Catherine writes from her own experience with refreshing and startling Christian authenticity and a strong personal sense of spiritual authority. Catherine emphasizes 'poustinia of the heart,' an interiorized poustinia, a silent chamber carried always and everywhere in which to contemplate God within. Learn how our desert can be in the marketplace, in the midst of countless conferences, traffic jams, bus trips-or a hospital ward. Written by one who knows by experience, Poustinia brings consolation with its vision of a personal desert that can bloom in simple prayer. A timeless best-seller, published in 16 foreign editions around the world, Poustinia won the prestigious French Academy Award, and has become a worldwide phenomenon.

Pouvant: A Semester Course in Self-Esteem, Vol. 1. Frank Dane. 1 cass. 1990. 79.50 (978-0-87562-102-9(3)) Spec Child.

Poverty: The Vocation to Work. Thomas Merton. 1 cass. 1995. 8.95 Credence Commun.
Hard work is a gift from God. We are born to move from work to gratitude & then finally to charity.

Poverty - A Framework for Understanding & Working with Students & Adults from Poverty see Framework for Understanding Poverty

Poverty & Promise: One Volunteer's Experience of Kenya. abr. ed. Narrated by Cindi Brown. Based on a book by Cindi Brown. Donny Soeder. Engineer RavenPheat Productions. Music by Sule Greg Wilson. 2 CDs. (Running Time: 4 hrs.). 2009. audio compact disk 10.95 (978-0-9800620-1-4(2)) Voice Pr.

Poverty & the First Agriculture Secretary. Robert LeFevre. 1 cass. (Running Time: 56 min.). 10.95 (1014) J Norton Pubs.
How to decrease hunger & unemployment. The Bible & its startling parallels today.

Poverty Bay. unabr. ed. Earl Emerson. Narrated by Richard Poe. 6 cass. (Running Time: 9 hrs.). (Thomas Black Mystery Ser.: Vol. 2). 1994. 51.00 (978-1-55690-980-1(2), 94119E7) Recorded Bks.
Seattle private eye Thomas Black investigates the disappearance of the young heir to a $15 million fortune.

Poverty in America: Its Cause & Extent. 1 cass. (Urban Problems Ser.). 10.00 Esstee Audios.
What is the American view of poverty?.

Povesti Belkina. Alexander Pushkin. 4 cass. (Running Time: 4 hrs.). (RUS.). 1996. bk. 49.50 set. (978-1-58085-559-4(8)) Interlingua VA.
Includes English vocabulary & notes. The combination of written text & clarity & pace of diction will open the door for intermediate & advanced students to genuine comprehension & the use of literary texts for advancement in rapid understanding of written & oral language materials. The audio text plus written text concept makes foreign languages accessible to a much wider range of students than books alone.

***Powan & the Kuan-yan.** Anonymous. 2009. (978-1-60136-580-4(2)) Audio Holding.

Powder & Patch. Georgette Heyer. Narrated by Flo Gibson. 2008. audio compact disk 24.95 (978-1-60646-042-9(0)) Audio Bk Con.

Powder & Patch, Set. unabr. ed. Georgette Heyer. Read by Flo Gibson. 4 cass. (Running Time: 5 hrs.). 1998. bk. 19.95 (978-1-55685-524-5(9)) Audio Bk Con.
The unrefined country-bred Philip goes to Paris to become a fashionable, elegant fop to please the lovely Cleone. However, he returns to England hoping to win her as his true self.

Powder Puff Puzzle. unabr. ed. Patricia Reilly Giff. 1 read-along cass. (Running Time: 48 min.). (Polka Dot Private Eye Ser.). (J). (gr. 1-2). 1989. 15.98 incl. bk. & guide. (978-0-8072-0172-5(3), FTR 137 SP, Listening Lib) Random Audio Pubg.
The poor meow has jumped from her arms into a car, & before Dawn can do anything, the car drives away. Will Dawn ever find Powder Puff?.

Powder River. unabr. ed. Winfred Blevins. Read by Michael Taylor. 8 cass. (Running Time: 11 hrs. 6 min.). 2001. 49.95 (978-1-58116-056-7(9)) Books in Motion.
The northern Cheyenne tribe leaves Indian Territory to return to their ancestral home 1,500 miles north. Joining this proud group being pursued by thousands of well-armed soldiers, is half-breed Adam McLean and his wife Elaine, a strong-willed New Englander determined to stand by her husband and his people.

Powder River. unabr. ed. Gary McCarthy. Read by Laurie Klein. 12 cass. (Running Time: 15 hrs.). 1994. 64.95 (978-1-55686-567-1(8)) Books in Motion.
Here is the sequel to "Wind River," a powerful novel of the West in the mid-1800s. Two sisters stretch the limits of what a woman's will can accomplish in a man's world.

Powder River Complete Collection Volume 1. Jerry Robbins. (ENG.). 2008. audio compact disk 49.95 (978-1-60245-164-3(8)) GDL Multimedia.

Powder River Complete Collection Volume 2. Jerry Robbins. (ENG.). 2008. audio compact disk 49.95 (978-1-60245-165-0(6)) GDL Multimedia.

Powder River Season Four, Volume 1. Jerry Robbins. (ENG.). 2008. audio compact disk 9.95 (978-1-60245-155-1(9)) GDL Multimedia.

Powder River Season Four, Volume 2. Jerry Robbins. (ENG.). 2008. audio compact disk 9.95 (978-1-60245-156-8(7)) GDL Multimedia.

Powder River Season Four, Volume 3. Jerry Robbins. (ENG.). 2008. audio compact disk 9.95 (978-1-60245-157-5(5)) GDL Multimedia.

Powder River Season One, Volume Three. Jerry Robbins. (ENG.). 2008. audio compact disk 9.95 (978-1-60245-113-1(3)) GDL Multimedia.

Powder River Season One Volume 1. (ENG.). 2008. audio compact disk 9.95 (978-1-60245-111-7(7)) GDL Multimedia.

Powder River Season One Volume 2. (ENG.). 2008. audio compact disk 9.95 (978-1-60245-112-4(5)) GDL Multimedia.

Powder River Season Three, Volume 1. Jerry Robbins. (ENG.). 2008. audio compact disk 9.95 (978-1-60245-152-0(4)) GDL Multimedia.

Powder River Season Three, Volume 2. Jerry Robbins. (ENG.). 2008. audio compact disk 9.95 (978-1-60245-153-7(2)) GDL Multimedia.

Powder River Season Three, Volume 3. Jerry Robbins. (ENG.). 2008. audio compact disk 9.95 (978-1-60245-154-4(0)) GDL Multimedia.

Powder River Season Two, Volume 1. Jerry Robbins. (ENG.). 2008. audio compact disk 9.95 (978-1-60245-149-0(4)) GDL Multimedia.

Powder River Season Two, Volume 2. Jerry Robbins. (ENG.). 2008. audio compact disk 9.95 (978-1-60245-150-6(8)) GDL Multimedia.

Powder River Season Two, Volume 3. Jim French. (ENG.). 2008. audio compact disk 9.95 (978-1-60245-151-3(6)) GDL Multimedia.

Powderkeg. unabr. ed. Larry D. Names. Read by Maynard Villers. 8 cass. (Running Time: 8 hrs. 36 min.). (Creed Ser.: Bk. 3). 2001. 49.95 (978-1-55686-807-8(3)) Books in Motion.
Willing to risk his life by going home to the girl and the land he loved, Creed finds himself caught between a town's angry citizens and Union soldiers sent to occupy their town.

Power. Neville Goddard. 1 cass. (Running Time: 62 min.). 1968. 8.00 (6) J & L Pubns.
Neville taught Imagination Creates Reality. He was a powerfully influential teacher of God as Consciousness.

Power. Michael Korda. 2004. 5.95 (978-0-7435-4151-0(0)) Pub: S&S Audio. Dist(s): S and S Inc

Power. Phil Proctor & Peter Bergman. Read by Phil Proctor & Peter Bergman. 1 CD. (Running Time: 1 hr.). audio compact disk 15.95 (978-1-57677-109-9(1), PROB002) Lodestone Catalog.

Power. collector's ed. Linda Hogan. Read by Tonya Jordan. 6 cass. (Running Time: 9 hrs.). 1999. 48.00 (978-0-7366-4774-8(0), 5118) Books on Tape.
Based on a true story, this coming of age novel reveals the powerful forces that endanger Native Americans & the survival of their spirituality.

***Power.** unabr. ed. Rhonda Byrne. Read by Rhonda Byrne. (Running Time: 6 hrs. 0 mins. 0 sec.). (ENG.). 2010. audio compact disk 29.95 (978-1-4423-3796-1(6)) Pub: S&S Audio. Dist(s): S and S Inc

Power: The Twelve Steps to Personal Power. J. Kennedy Shultz. 1 cass. 1989. 18.95 (978-0-924687-04-4(5)) Rel Sci Vision Pr.
A talk based on the 12-step Alcoholics Anonymous program that teaches people how to overcome any problem & build a life of personal power.

Power Vol. 2: Training in the Zone. Kelly Howell. 1 cass. (Running Time: 1 hr.). 1995. 11.95 (978-1-881451-42-6(9)) Brain Sync.
The music is paced to peak training flowing from soft jazz to fast trance dance, to rhythmic tribal beats. You are transported to the planet Zone II - where the inhabitants have transcended the limits of the body & reveal the secrets of "essential ecstasy". You experience a state of profound well-being marked by moments of freedom, euphoria & power, as your workout moves into the magical dimensions of the The Zone.

Power - The Practice: The Practice of Spiritual Mind Healing. J. Kennedy Shultz. 1 cass. 1989. 18.95 (978-0-924687-02-0(9)) Rel Sci Vision Pr.
How to use the power of the mind to improve life.

Power - The Principle: The Basic Ideas of the Science of Mind. J. Kennedy Shultz. 1 cass. 1989. 18.95 (978-0-924687-00-6(2)) Rel Sci Vision Pr.
Teaches the basic ideas of The Science of Mind.

Power - The Product: Applying the Principles of Science of Mind for Health, Wealth, Love & Self-Expression. J. Kennedy Shultz. 1 cass. 1989. 18.95 (978-0-924687-01-3(0)) Rel Sci Vision Pr.
How to apply the basic ideas of The Science of Mind to everyday situations.

Power, Ambition, Glory: The Stunning Parallels Between Great Leaders of the Ancient World & Today... & the Lessons You Can Learn. unabr. ed. John Prevas & Steve Forbes. Narrated by Alan Sklar. 1 MP3-CD. (Running Time: 12 hrs. 30 mins. 0 sec.). (ENG.). 2009. 24.99 (978-1-4001-6247-5(5)); audio compact disk 34.99 (978-1-4001-1247-0(8)); audio compact disk 69.99 (978-1-4001-4247-7(4)) Pub: Tantor Media. Dist(s): IngramPubServ

Power & Intimacy. Pia Mellody. Read by Pia Mellody. 1 cass. 10.00 (A7) Featuka Enter Inc.
An example of how boundaries are used to create true intimacy & power sharing.

Power & Intimacy. unabr. ed. Jennifer James. Read by Jennifer James. 1 cass. (Running Time: 1 hr.). 9.95 (978-0-915423-53-8(7)) Jennifer J.

Power & Passion of Beethoven. unabr. abr. ed. Jeffrey Siegel. (Running Time: 3600 sec.). (Keyboard Conversations Ser.). (ENG.). 2006. audio compact disk 14.95 (978-0-7393-3269-6(4), Random AudioBks) Pub: Random Audio Pubg. Dist(s): Random

Power & Place of Poetry: An Irish radio Interview. Poems. Featuring David Whyte. 1 CD. 2004. audio compact disk 15.00 (978-1-932887-10-5(5)) Pub: Many Rivers Pr. Dist(s): Partners-West
Mary Curtain of Radio Telefis Eireann offers a penetrating interview with David Whyte. Drawn by her questions, he speaks persuasively to the role of poet and poetry in the life of individuals and society. He makes it clear that what we are truly yearning for can only be found through our imagination.

Power & Possibility in the Structure of Gender Relations. Caroline Stevens. Read by Caroline Stevens. 1 cass. (Running Time: 75 min.). 1993. 10.95 (978-0-7822-0450-6(3), 528) C G Jung IL.

Power & Precision Version 2. BORENSTEIN. 2001. audio compact disk 395.00 (978-1-56321-212-3(9)) Pub: L Erlbaum Assocs. Dist(s): Taylor and Fran

Power & Purity. Jack Deere. 1 cass. (Running Time: 90 mins.). (Intimacy with God & the End-Time Church Ser.: Vol. 1). 2000. 5.00 (JD09-001) Morning NC.
Oneness with the Father is essential for every believer in these last days & the teaching in this six-tape series will impart a heartfelt hunger for intimate fellowship with Him.

Power & the Glory see Poder y la Gloria

Power & the Glory. Graham Greene. Read by Fabio Camero. (Running Time: 3 hrs.). 2005. 8.95 (978-1-60083-321-2(7), Audiofy Corp) Iofy Corp.

Power & the Glory. unabr. ed. Graham Greene. Read by Bernard Mayes. 7 cass. (Running Time: 10 hrs.). 1990. 49.95 (978-0-7861-0104-7(0), 1097) Blckstn Audio.
It is the story of a whiskey priest who is hunted by Communist authorities during the religious persecution in Mexico.

Power & the Glory. unabr. ed. Graham Greene. Read by Andrew Sachs. 8 cass. (Running Time: 12 hrs.). 2000. 59.95 (SAB 014) Pub: Chivers Audio Bks GBR. Dist(s): AudioGO
In a poor and barren Mexican state, the Red Shirts have gained control, outlawed God, and murdered priests. But one still lives, the whisky priest, who has an illegitimate daughter and believes he has lost his soul. While avoiding his executioners, he tramps anonymously across the countryside, and it's quite a while before he is able to stop running and find God.

Power & the Glory. unabr. ed. Graham Greene. Narrated by John Aulicino. 7 cass. (Running Time: 9 hrs. 45 mins.). 1990. 60.00 (978-1-55690-422-6(3), 90060E7) Recorded Bks.
In 1938, police are lining up priests in front of firing squads. A "whiskey priest" flees through the jungles. An American bank robber & killer are also on the run. The three come together in the climax.

***Power & the Glory.** unabr. ed. Graham Greene. Read by Bernard Mayes. (Running Time: 10 hrs.). 2010. audio compact disk 90.00 (978-1-4417-0408-5(6)) Blckstn Audio.

***Power & the Glory.** unabr. ed. Graham Greene. Read by Bernard Mayes. (Running Time: 9.5 hrs. NaN mins.). 2010. 29.95 (978-1-4417-0411-5(6)); audio compact disk 29.95 (978-1-4417-0410-8(8)) Blckstn Audio.

Power & the Shadow of Power in Inter- & Intrapersonal Relationships. Read by Marilyn Matthews. 1 cass. (Running Time: 90 min.). 1987. 10.95 (978-0-7822-0165-9(2), 248) C G Jung IL.

Power & Use of Humor. Ben Bissell. 1 cass. (Running Time: 35 min.). 15.00 C Bissell.
This live presentation identifies how we lose our humor power & then examines five ways to regain it.

Power & Wisdom. by Osel Tendzin. 3 cass. 1984. 31.50 (A072) Vajradhatu.
Three talks. The Buddhist teachings, as transmitted by the Kagyu lineage of Tibet, provide a path to the realization of enlightened mind in everyday life.

Power, Anger, Trust & Communication. unabr. ed. Marty Klein. 3 cass. (Running Time: 4 hrs. 5 mins.). 1999. 39.95 (978-0-9704526-1-0(6)) CA Sex Ed Assocs.
Helps you deal with clients who are passive-aggressive, who break agreements or withhold sex. You'll learn how to work more effectively with couples who refuse to compromise, partners who lie or keep secrets & relationships that lack the good will needed for negotiation & self-soothing. You'll learn when "better communication" makes things worse.

Power Bowling. 1 cass. 10.00 (978-1-58506-046-7(1), 91) New Life Inst OR.
No matter what your present bowling skill, here's an easy, natural way to improve.

Power Broker. Stephen Frey. Read by Holter Graham. (Running Time: 40560 sec.). 2006. audio compact disk 37.95 (978-1-57270-559-3(0)) Pub: Audio Partners. Dist(s): PerseuPGW

Power Broker. unabr. ed. Stephen Frey. Narrated by Holter Graham. 7 cass. (Running Time: 40560 sec.). (Sound Library). 2006. 59.95 (978-0-7927-4030-8(0), CSL 944); audio compact disk 89.95 (978-0-7927-4031-5(9), SLD 944); audio compact disk & audio compact disk 29.95 (978-0-7927-4253-1(2), CMP 944) AudioGO.

Power Broker Pt. C: Robert Moses & the Fall of New York. collector's ed. Robert A. Caro. Read by Jonathan Reese. 13 cass. (Running Time: 19 hrs. 30 min.). 1991. 104.00 (978-0-7366-2074-1(5)) Books on Tape.
The story of Robert Moses & the New York he controlled. Pulitzer winning story of power in America's imperial city.

Power Broker Pt. A: Robert Moses & the Fall of New York. unabr. collector's ed. Robert A. Caro. Read by Jonathan Reese. 15 cass. (Running Time: 22 hrs. 30 mins.). 1991. 120.00 (978-0-7366-2072-7(9), 2880 A) Books on Tape.

Power Broker Pt. B: Robert Moses & the Fall of New York. collector's ed. Robert A. Caro. Read by Jonathan Reese. 15 cass. (Running Time: 22 hrs. 30 min.). 1991. 120.00 (978-0-7366-2073-4(7)) Books on Tape.

Power Business Writing, Set. Patricia Westheimer. 2 cass. (Running Time: 1 hr. 30 mins.). (Discovery Ser.). 1991. pap. bk. 15.95 (978-1-56015-202-6(8)) Penton Overseas.
There are a number of beneficial suggestions about business writing in this program. The focus is more on proper style & grammatical errors than on the content of what is written.

Power Canvassing: Master the art of cold Calling. Gavin Ingham. 1 cd. (Running Time: 55 min). 2004. audio compact disk 97.00 (978-1-59971-680-0(1)) AardGP.
Gavin Ingham's Power Canvassing cold calling audio is a motivational blend of mindset, motivation and skills that will focus on helping you to master the art of cold calling. By following this structured approach anyone with average communication skills will eliminate the fear of cold calling and feel confident to make more calls, create a stronger impact with clients and explode their sales results, fast. If you have ever wanted to line up more new client meetings and win more new business then this is for you.

Power Centers. 1994. bk. 99.00 (ACS-950) PA Bar Inst.
One of the hottest trends in today's commercial real estate market is the emergence of power shopping centers. This explores where these entities are developed, how they are coordinated, the problems that arise in their creation, & what parties are involved in the process.

Power Channel. Told to Reinhard Bonnke. 3. (Running Time: Approx: 55 min per CD.). 2004. audio compact disk 7.00 (978-1-933106-04-5(2)) E-R-Productions.
Join Reinhard Bonnke and discover the principles of power learned from over thirty years of ministry in Africa and around the world. You'll learn why prayer and intercession is what "Christ for All Nations" was built on.

Power Charged for Life. Jeff Magee. 2001. audio compact disk 19.95 (978-0-9641240-4-2(1)) J Magee Intl.

Power Chord Rock: Essential Elements Guitar Songs Mid-Beginner. Created by Hal Leonard Corporation Staff. 2008. pap. bk. 12.99 (978-1-4234-3343-9(2), 1423433432) H Leonard.

Power Chords. Robert Laughlin. Read by Robert Laughlin. 1 cass. (Running Time: 1 hr.). 1989. pap. bk. 23.00 (978-0-929983-13-4(0), 160) New Schl Am Music.
Presents advanced keyboard chords - how to make them & how to use them. Includes sections on voicings, inversions, slash chords, & jazz voicings.

Power Closing. (Specialized Sales Ser.). 1989. bk. 14.98 (978-1-55909-234-0(3), 200P) Randolph Tapes.

Power Communication Skills. Susan Baile. 4 cass. (Running Time: 4 hrs. 39 min.). 49.95 CareerTrack Pubns.
Presents, step-by-step, the skills that will make one stronger personally & more effective on the job.

Power Connections for Women - An Introduction: Basic Tools for Building Powerful Connections with Men. Gigi Tomasek Sage et al. Interview with Beth Ellenby. 2000. 19.95 (978-0-9671516-1-8(9)) Rest of Your Life.

Power Day Trading: Successful Strategies to Increase Profits. Instructed by Marc Friedfertig. (Trade Secrets Audio Ser.). 2000. 19.95 (978-1-883272-09-8(2)) Marketplace Bks.

***Power Down.** unabr. ed. Ben Coes. (Running Time: 16 hrs. 0 mins. 0 sec.). (ENG.). 2010. audio compact disk 39.99 (978-1-4272-1037-1(3)) Pub: Macmill Audio. Dist(s): Macmillan

Power English: WHAT to Say, & HOW to Say It. Scripts. Natasha Cooper. 14 CDs. (Running Time: 15 hrs. 45 mins.). Dramatization. (ENG & RUS.). 2003. pap. bk. 269.99 (978-1-932521-24-5(0)) Cooper Learn Syst.
175 real-life dialogues and scenarios, 2500 phrases, and jokes. Telephoning, making appointments and reservations, resolving problems and emergencies, obtaining info, goods, and services.

Power English: WHAT to Say, & HOW to Say It. Scripts. Natasha Cooper. 12 cass. (Running Time: 16 hrs.15 mins.). Dramatization. (ENG & RUS.). 2003. pap. bk. 229.99 (978-1-932521-23-8(2)) Cooper Learn Syst.
Phrases, scenarios and real-life dialogues for telephoning, appointments and reservations, resolving problems and emergencies, obtaining info, goods, and services, etc. Etiquette with humorous examples.

Power English: WHAT to Say, & HOW to Say It. Scripts. Natasha Cooper. 14 CDs. (Running Time: 15 hrs. 45 mins.). Dramatization. 2003. pap. bk. 269.99 (978-1-932521-26-9(7)) Cooper Learn Syst.
4 multimedia vinyl albums: Audio CDs with accompanying books: "Telephone in Business and Daily Life", "Appointments and Reservations", "Resolving Problems and Emergencies", "Obtaining Information, Goods, and Services".

Power English: WHAT to Say, & HOW to Say It: Guide to Real-Life Communication for Non-Native Speakers of American English. Scripts. Natasha Cooper. 12 cass. (Running Time: 16 hrs. 15 mins.). Dramatization. 2003. pap. bk. 229.99 (978-1-932521-25-2(9)) Cooper Learn Syst.
Phrases, dialogues and exercises for telephoning, appointments and reservations, resolving problems and emergencies, obtaining info, goods, and services and more.

Power English & Word Command Total Program. Margaret M. Bynum. (YA). (gr. 10-12). 1986. 69.95 (978-0-913286-96-8(6), 2022, Lrn Inc) Oasis Audio.
Features methods in improving one's English.

Power, Faith & Fantasy: America in the Middle East, 1776 to the Present. unabr. ed. Michael B. Oren. Read by Norman Dietz. (YA). 2008. 84.99 (978-1-60514-673-7(0)) Find a World.

Power, Faith & Fantasy: America in the Middle East, 1776 to the Present. unabr. ed. Michael B. Oren. Narrated by Norman Dietz. (Running Time: 28 hrs. 30 mins. 0 sec.). (ENG.). 2007. audio compact disk 39.99 (978-1-4001-5444-9(8)) Pub: Tantor Media. Dist(s): IngramPubServ

Power, Faith & Fantasy: America in the Middle East, 1776 to the Present. unabr. ed. Michael B. Oren. Read by Norman Dietz. 22 CDs. (Running Time: 28 hrs. 30 mins. 0 sec.). (ENG.). 2007. audio compact disk 49.99 (978-1-4001-0444-4(0)); audio compact disk 99.99 (978-1-4001-3444-1(7)) Pub: Tantor Media. Dist(s): IngramPubServ

Power for Submission. 4 cass. 1996. 20.00 (978-0-00-519080-7(0)) Majestic Mda.

Power for the Abandoned Woman Vol. 1: Confronting the Victim Illusion. Carolyn Gabriel. Perf. by Tim Underwood. 1 cass. (Running Time: 46 min.). 1999. pap. bk. 9.95 (978-1-888368-04-8(7)) RUSA.
How to regain personal power after a relationship betrayal or abandonment. Emotional first-aid, how to take care of yourself.

Power Game, Pt 1. unabr. ed. Hedrick Smith. Read by Michael Wells. 11 cass. (Running Time: 16 hrs.). 1990. 76.95 (978-0-7861-0176-4(8), 1157-A,B) Blckstn Audio.
Smith takes us inside America's power center to reveal how the game of governing is played in Washington in the 1980s. He shows how a revolutionary explosion of power in the mid-1970s has turned Washington inside out.

Power Game, Pt. 2. unabr. ed. Hedrick Smith. Read by Michael Wells. 12 cass. (Running Time: 16 hrs.). 1990. 83.95 (978-0-7861-0177-1(6), 1157-A,B) Blckstn Audio.

Power Games: A Kate Power Novel. unabr. ed. Judith Cutler. Narrated by Patricia Gallimore. 6 cass. (Running Time: 8 hrs.). 2001. 56.00 (978-1-84197-185-8(5), H1169E7) Recorded Bks.
Although Detective Sergeant Kate Power's house is now at least habitable, the same cannot be said for her garden. In the process of having it cleared, she alights upon a rather unusual discovery. In the meantime, there is also the spate of arson attacks hitting Birmingham, a body at her local tennis club &, of course, the attentions of DCI Graham Harvey to keep her occupied.

Power Generation Equipment in Australia: A Strategic Reference 2007. Compiled by Icon Group International, Inc. Staff. 2007. ring bd. 195.00 (978-0-497-35811-2(5)) Icon Grp.

Power Gifts of the Spirit. Kenneth E. Hagin. 4 cass. 16.00 (05H) Faith Lib Pubns.

Power-Glide English As a Second Language Spanish. Robert W. Blair. 6. (Running Time: 5 hrs 30 min). (SPA.). (YA). 2002. audio compact disk 69.95 (978-1-58204-260-2(8)) Power-Glide.

Power-Glide English As a Second Language Spanish Course. Robert W. Blair. 6. (Running Time: 5 hrs 30 min). 2002. pap. bk. 149.95 (978-1-58204-087-5(7)) Power-Glide.

Power-Glide French Children's Course Upgrade. l.t. ed. Robert W. Blair. 4 CDs. (Running Time: 5 hrs. 18 min.). (J). 2001. pap. bk. 59.95 (978-1-58204-211-4(X)) Power-Glide.

Power-Glide French Junior. Robert W. Blair. 8 CDs. (Running Time: 8 hrs 18 min). (J). 2002. audio compact disk 39.95 (978-1-58204-148-3(2)) Power-Glide.

Power-Glide French Lower Elementary. l.t. ed. Robert W. Blair. 9 cds. (Running Time: 8 hours 18 Mins). 2002. pap. bk. 99.95 (978-1-58204-207-7(1)) Power-Glide.

Power-Glide French Ultimate. Robert W. Blair. 9 CDs. (Running Time: 6 hrs 6 min). (YA). 2000. audio compact disk Rental 69.95 (978-1-58204-064-6(8)) Power-Glide.

Power-Glide French Ultimate Adventure Course. Created by Robert W. Blair. 9. (Running Time: 6 hrs 6 min). (YA). 2002. pap. bk. 149.95 (978-1-58204-201-5(2)) Power-Glide.

Power-Glide French Ultimate Year One Course. l.t. ed. Robert W. Blair. 4 CDs. (Running Time: 4 hours 24 mins). 2003. pap. bk. 129.95 (978-1-58204-230-5(6)) Power-Glide.

Power-Glide French Year One. Told to Robert W. Blair. 4 CDs. (Running Time: 4 hrs 24 min). (YA). 2003. audio compact disk 39.95 (978-1-58204-252-7(7)) Power-Glide.

Power-Glide German Children's Course. l.t. rev. ed. Robert W. Blair. 4 CDs. (Running Time: 5 hrs. 36 min.). (J). 2001. pap. bk. 59.95 (978-1-58204-212-1(8)) Power-Glide.

Power-Glide German Junior. Robert W. Blair. 8 CDs. (Running Time: 8 hrs 12 min). (J). 2002. audio compact disk 39.95 (978-1-58204-145-2(8)) Power-Glide.

Power-Glide German Lower Elementary. l.t. ed. Robert W. Blair. 8 CDs. (J). 2002. pap. bk. 119.95 (978-1-58204-221-3(7)) Power-Glide.

Power-Glide German Lower Elementary. l.t. ed. Robert W. Blair. 8. (Running Time: 8 hours 12mins). 2002. pap. bk. 99.95 (978-1-58204-208-4(X)) Power-Glide.

Power-Glide German Ultimate. Robert W. Blair. 7 CDs. (Running Time: 7 hrs 12 min). (YA). 2000. audio compact disk 69.95 (978-1-58204-072-1(9)) Power-Glide.

Power-Glide German Ultimate Adventure Course. Robert W. Blair. 7 CDs. (Running Time: 7 hrs 12 min). (YA). 2002. pap. bk. 149.95 (978-1-58204-202-2(0)) Power-Glide.

Power-Glide German Ultimate Year One Course. 2003. pap. bk. 129.95 (978-1-58204-231-2(4)) Power-Glide.

Power-Glide Japanese Ultimate Adventure Course. Robert W. Blair. 6 CDs. (Running Time: 2 hrs 36 min). (YA). 2002. pap. bk. 149.95 (978-1-58204-204-6(7)) Power-Glide.

Power-Glide Japanese Ultimate Adventure Course Audio CD Set. Robert W. Blair. 6 CDs. (Running Time: 2 hrs 36 min). (YA). 2002. audio compact disk 69.95 (978-1-58204-259-6(4)) Power-Glide.

Power-Glide Latin Lower Elementary. l.t. ed. Robert W. Blair. 4. (Running Time: 2 hours 54 mins). (YA). 2000. pap. bk. 149.95 (978-1-58204-209-1(8)) Power-Glide.

Power-Glide Latin Ultimate. Told to Robert W. Blair. 7 CDs. (Running Time: 6 hrs 20 min). (YA). 2000. audio compact disk 69.95 (978-1-58204-089-9(3)) Power-Glide.

Power-Glide Latin Ultimate Adventure Course. Robert W. Blair. 7 CDs. (Running Time: 6 hrs 20 min). (YA). 1999. pap. bk. 149.95 (978-1-58204-203-9(9)) Power-Glide.

Power-Glide Russian Ultimate Adventure Course. Robert W. Blair. 7 CDs. (Running Time: 7 hrs 10 min). (YA). 1999. pap. bk. 149.95 (978-1-58204-205-3(5)) Power-Glide.

Power-Glide Russian Ultimate Course. Robert W. Blair. 7 CDs. (Running Time: 7 hrs 10 min). (YA). 2000. audio compact disk 69.95 (978-1-58204-258-9(6)) Power-Glide.

Power-Glide Spanish Children's Course Upgrade. l.t. ed. Robert W. Blair. 4. (Running Time: 6 hrs 6 min). (J). 2001. pap. bk. 59.95 (978-1-58204-210-7(1)) Power-Glide.

Power-Glide Spanish Junior. Robert W. Blair. 8. (Running Time: 12 hrs 10 min). (J). 2002. audio compact disk 39.95 (978-1-58204-144-5(X)) Power-Glide.

Power-Glide Spanish Junior Adventure Course, Grades PS-7 Lower Elementary. Robert W. Blair. 8 CDs. (Running Time: 12 hrs. 10 mins). 2002. pap. bk., tchr. ed., wbk. ed. 99.95 (978-1-58204-206-0(3)) Power-Glide.

Power-Glide Spanish Junior Adventure Guide. Created by Robert W. Blair. 8 CDs. (gr. 8-12). 2002. pap. bk. 39.95 (978-1-58204-219-0(5)) Power-Glide.

Power-Glide Spanish Ultimate. 2nd ed. Robert W. Blair. 9 CDs. (Running Time: 9 hrs 45 min). (YA). 1998. audio compact disk 69.95 (978-1-58204-055-4(9)) Power-Glide.

Power-Glide Spanish Ultimate Adventure Course. l.t. ed. Robert W. Blair. 9 audio CDs. (Running Time: 9 hours 45 mins). (YA). 2002. pap. bk. 149.95 (978-1-58204-200-8(4)) Power-Glide.

Power-Glide Spanish Ultimate Year One. Robert W. Blair. 4 CDs. (Running Time: 3 hrs 42 min). (YA). 2003. audio compact disk 39.95 (978-1-58204-250-3(0)) Power-Glide.

Power-Glide Spanish Ultimate Year 1 Course. l.t. ed. Robert W. Blair. 4. (Running Time: 3 hours 42 mins). (YA). 2003. pap. bk. 99.95 (978-1-58204-229-9(2)) Power-Glide.

Power Golf. 1 cass. 10.00 (978-1-58506-047-4(X), 92) New Life Inst OR.
Whatever your present handicap, this program will knock strokes off your game.

Power Golf. abr. ed. Roger W. Breternitz. 1 cass. (Running Time: 45 min.). 1985. pap. bk. 9.95 Vector Studios.
Hypnosis implants suggestions of concentration, perception & a winning attitude to one's score & make the game more enjoyable.

Power Grab: How Obama's Green Policies Will Steal Your Freedom & Bankrupt America. unabr. ed. Christopher C. Horner. (Running Time: 8 hrs. 30 mins.). 2010. 29.95 (978-1-4417-2970-5(4)); audio compact disk 29.95 (978-1-4417-2969-9(0)) Blckstn Audio.

***Power Grab: How Obama's Green Policies Will Steal Your Freedom & Bankrupt America.** unabr. ed. Christopher C. Horner. (Running Time: 8 hrs. 30 mins.). 2010. 54.95 (978-1-4417-2966-8(6)); audio compact disk 76.00 (978-1-4417-2967-5(4)) Blckstn Audio.

Power Healing. John Wimber. Read by John Wimber. Read by Kevin Springer. 1 cass. (Running Time: 60 min.). 9.95 HarperCollins Pubs.

Power Hiring: How to Find, Assess, Hire & Keep Great Talent. Lou Adler. 6 cass. (Running Time: 6 hrs.). 1998. (978-1-55525-061-4(0), 19100A) Nightingale-Conant.
Win the talent war.

Power-House. unabr. ed. John Buchan. Read by Peter Joyce. 3 cass. 1998. 34.95 (978-1-86015-401-0(8)) Pub: UlverLrgPrint GBR. Dist(s): Ulverscroft US
A man discovers a plan for worldwide domination & struggles to defeat the sinister master-mind behind it.

Power Immune System: Easy. Eldon Taylor. Read by Eldon Taylor. Ed. by Leslie Brice. 1 cass. (Running Time: 1 hr.). 1992. 16.95 (978-1-56705-117-9(0)) Gateways Inst.
Self improvement.

Power in Praise. 5 cass. 11.95 Incl. album. (978-0-943026-16-9(4), A2) Carothers.

Power in the Life of the Believer. unabr. ed. Chuck Smith. 4 cass. (Running Time: 3 hrs.). 2001. 12.95 Word For Today.
This collection of messages was designed to grant insight into the role of the Holy Spirit.

Power in the Name of Jesus. Featuring Bill Winston. 4 Cass. 2004. 20.00 (978-1-59544-000-6(3)); audio compact disk 32.00 (978-1-59544-001-3(1)) Pub: B Winston Min. Dist(s): Anchor Distributors

Power Intuition: A Self Guided Tour to Success. Raymond Justice & Marjorie Baker Price. 3 cass. (Running Time: 3 hrs.). 2001. bk. & wbk. ed. 59.95 (978-1-890679-18-7(6)) Micheles.

Power Is Within You. Louise L. Hay. 6 CDs. 2004. audio compact disk 23.95 (978-1-4019-0394-7(0)) Hay House.

Power Is Within You. abr. ed. Louise L. Hay. 2 cass. (Running Time: 2 hrs.). 1996. 16.95 (978-1-56170-328-9(1), 336) Hay House.
Louise Hay expands on her philosophy of "loving the self" & shows how to overcome emotional barriers.

Power Is Within You. unabr. ed. Louise L. Hay. Read by Louise L. Hay. Ed. by Linda Tomchin. 6 cass. (Running Time: 8 hrs.). 1992. 30.00 (978-1-56170-047-9(9), 311) Hay House.
Louise Hay expands on her philosophies of "loving the self" & shows you how to overcome emotional barriers. Includes a series of beautiful meditations & a printed listing of "Self-Help Resources" for recovery options.

Power Learning. 4 cass. (Running Time: 4 hrs.). 29.95 Set. (PL4) Psych Res Inst.
Designed to provide maximum learning effectiveness for all ages.

Power Learning. Eldon Taylor. Read by Eldon Taylor. Interview with Progress Aware Staff. 1 cass. (Running Time: 62 min.). 16.95 incl. script. (978-1-55978-297-5(8), 020111) Progress Aware Res.
Verbal coaching soundtrack with underlying subliminal affirmations & sound matrix frequencies for brain entrainment.

Power Learning & Memory. Eldon Taylor. Read by Eldon Taylor. Ed. by Leslie Brice. 1 cass. (Running Time: 1 hr.). 1992. 12.95 (978-1-56705-022-6(0)) Gateways Inst.
Self improvement.

Power Learning & Memory. Eldon Taylor. Read by Eldon Taylor. Interview with Progress Aware Staff. 1 cass. (Running Time: 1 hr. 30 min.). (Power Imaging Ser.). 16.95 incl. script. (978-1-55978-180-0(7), 8004) Progress Aware Res.
Hypnosis & soundtrack with underlying subliminal affirmations.

Power Lines: A Completely Practical Guide to Communicating with Confidence & Power. unabr. ed. Diana Morris. Read by Diana Morris. Comment by Eric Conqer. 1 cass. (Running Time: 18 min.). 1997. bk. 14.95 (978-1-891019-09-8(0)) New HeightsMed.
Six communication strategies for jump-starting your communications effectiveness.

Power Listening. abr. ed. 1 CD. 2005. audio compact disk 16.00 (978-1-891966-06-4(5)) Bus Efficacy.

Power Listening: Easy to Use Tools for Improved Communication. unabr. ed. Rochelle Devereaux. Read by Rochelle Devereaux. 1 cass. (Running Time: 36 min.). 1997. 14.95 (978-1-891966-00-2(6)) Bus Efficacy.
Outlines barriers to effective communication & techniques to overcome them. Targets business people wanting to increase their communication skills.

Power Listening for Parents. unabr. ed. Rochelle Devereaux. Read by Rochelle Devereaux. 1 cass. (Running Time: 46 min.). 1998. 14.95 (978-1-891966-01-9(4)) Bus Efficacy.
Provides listening techniques for parents to use & demonstrate to their children & identifies some barriers parents or children create to block communications.

Power Listening for Problem Solvers. unabr. ed. Rochelle Devereaux. Read by Rochelle Devereaux. 1 cass. (Running Time: 54 min.). 1999. 17.95 (978-1-891966-02-6(2)) Bus Efficacy.
Skills to avoid problems & resolve conflicts.

Power Listening for Sales. unabr. ed. Rochelle Devereaux. Read by Rochelle Devereaux. 1 cass. (Running Time: 53 mins.). 2000. 14.95 (978-1-891966-03-3(0)) Bus Efficacy.
Covers benefits & methods to increase listening effectiveness.

Power Marketing: Book Two in the Series; Building Business in the 21st Century. John DePuy. Narrated by Todd Walters. (ENG.). 2007. audio compact disk (978-0-9795480-6-2(3)) Palm Tree.

Power Marketing for Attorneys. Cindy Speaker. 3 CDs. (Running Time: 3 hrs.). 1999. audio compact disk 59.00 (978-0-9702051-0-0(4)) C Speaker.
Comprehensive marketing program for attorneys.

Power Memory. Alan Butkowsky. Read by Alan Butkowsky. 6 cass. 59.95 Set. (218A) Nightingale-Conant.

Power Negotiating for Salespeople. Roger Dawson. 6 cass. (Running Time: 6 hrs.). 1994. 59.95 Set. (11750A) Nightingale-Conant.

Power Networking. Donna Fisher. 4 cass. (Running Time: 6 hrs.). (CareerTrack Audio Ser.). 1995. 19.95 Set. (978-1-55977-358-4(8)) CareerTrack Pubns.
Where the real "power" in power networking resides. How to develop a networking outlook people respect & respond to. Breaking down the barriers that keep you from meeting new people. Ways to introduce yourself that make people eager to call on you.

Power of a Controlled Mind. Elbert Willis. 1 cass. (Controlling Your Mind Guidelines Ser.). 4.00 Fill the Gap.

Power of a Free Mind: Finding Inner Harmony & Awakening to Your True Self. Guy Finley. 6 cass. (Running Time: 6 hrs.). 1992. 59.95 set. (270A) Nightingale-Conant.

Power of A Man: Using Your Influence as a Man of Character. Rick Johnson. (ENG.). 2009. 24.99 (978-1-934384-23-7(2)) Pub: Treasure Pub. Dist(s): STL Dist NA

***Power of a Plate of Cookies.** Elizabeth Craig. 2009. audio compact disk 14.99 (978-1-60641-253-4(1)) Deseret Bk.

Power of a Positive Attitude: Discovering the Key to Success. Roger Fritz. Read by Christopher Lee. (Playaway Adult Nonfiction Ser.). 2008. 44.99 (978-1-60640-891-9(7)) Find a World.

Power of a Positive Attitude: Discovering the Key to Success. unabr. ed. Roger Fritz. Read by Christopher Lane. (Running Time: 3 hrs.). 2008. 39.25 (978-1-4233-6447-4(3), 9781423364474, BADLE); 24.95 (978-1-4233-6446-7(5), 9781423364467, BAD); audio compact disk 24.95 (978-1-4233-6444-3(9), 9781423364443, Brilliance MP3); audio compact disk 39.25 (978-1-4233-6445-0(7), 9781423364450, Brinc Audio MP3 Lib); audio compact disk 62.25 (978-1-4233-6443-6(0), 9781423364436, BriAudCD Unabrid); audio compact disk 19.95 (978-1-4233-6442-9(2), 9781423364429, Bril Audio CD Unabri) Brilliance Audio.

Power of a Positive Friend. abr. ed. Ladd Karol. 4 cass. (Running Time: 6 hrs.). 2004. 24.99 (978-1-58926-698-8(6), 6698); audio compact disk 27.99 (978-1-58926-699-5(4), 6699) Oasis Audio.
Through seven biblical principles, Ladd and Kelly's bold insight on subjects, such as "Building on Your Common Interests," "Attitudes and Actions That Divide Relationships," "Encouraging Ways to Enjoy Your Friendships," and "Sacrifice and Trust¿a Must," will help you grow positive friendships.

Power of a Positive Mom. gif. ed. Karol Ladd. (ENG.). 2005. audio compact disk 24.99 (978-1-58229-473-5(9)) Pub: S and S. Dist(s): S and S Inc

Power of a Positive Mom & the Power of a Positive Woman. abr. ed. Karol Ladd. 6 CDs. (Running Time: 6 hrs.). 2003. audio compact disk 26.99 (978-1-58926-247-8(6), H69M-001D); 24.99 (978-1-58926-246-1(8), H69M-0010) Oasis Audio.
Offers seven time-tested principles that will transform your role, to make you not just a mother but a Positive Mom.

Power of a Positive No: How to Say No & Still Get to Yes. unabr. ed. William Ury. Read by William Ury. (Running Time: 25200 sec.). (ENG.). 2007. audio compact disk 29.95 (978-0-7393-4214-5(2), Random AudioBks) Pub: Random Audio Pubg. Dist(s): Random

***Power of a Praying Life: Finding the Freedom, Wholeness, & True Success God Has for You.** unabr. ed. Stormie Omartian. (Running Time: 8 hrs. 0 mins. 0 sec.). (Power of Praying Ser.). (ENG.). 2011. audio compact disk 27.99 (978-1-59859-862-9(7)) Oasis Audio.

Power of a Praying Wife. Stormie Omartian. 2008. audio compact disk 199.95 (978-1-933376-81-3(3)) Sampson Res.

Power of a Praying Wife. abr. ed. Stormie Omartian. Read by Stormie Omartian. 3 CDs. (Running Time: 3 hrs.). 2002. audio compact disk 16.99 (978-0-7369-0933-4(8)) Harvest Hse.
Today's challenges and presssures can make a fulfilling marriage seem like an impossible dream. Stormie Omartian shares how God has strengthened her own marriage since she began to pray for her husband concerning key areas of his life.

Power of a Praying Wife. abr. ed. Stormie Omartian. Narrated by Aimee Lilly. (Running Time: 10800 sec.). 2007. audio compact disk 18.99 (978-0-7369-1986-9(4)) Harvest Hse.

Power of a Praying Woman. Stormie Omartian. Narrated by Cynthia Darlow. 5 cass. (Running Time: 7 hrs. 30 mins.). 2002. 48.00 (978-1-4025-4417-0(0)) Recorded Bks.

***Power of a Whisper: Hearing God, Having the Guts to Respond.** unabr. ed. Bill Hybels. (Running Time: 8 hrs. 3 mins. 2 sec.). (ENG.). 2010. 22.99 (978-0-310-59195-5(3)); audio compact disk 37.99 (978-0-310-32934-3(5)) Zondervan.

Power of a Wise Woman. 2000. 6.00 (978-1-58602-047-7(1)) E L Long.

Power of a Wise Woman. 2001. audio compact disk 10.00 (978-1-58602-077-4(3)) E L Long.

Power of a Woman. unabr. ed. Barbara Taylor Bradford. Read by Kate Reading. 7 cass. (Running Time: 10 hrs. 30 mins.). 1998. 56.00 (978-0-7366-4075-6(4), 4584) Books on Tape.
A remarkable woman must confront her life's greatest tragedy; a random act of violence which injures her daughter. On her journey, she learns about family secrets, betrayals, revenge, redemption & the healing power of love.

Power of Acknowledgment. Judith W. Umlas. 2007. 12.95 (978-0-9792153-4-6(X)) IIL Pub NY.

Power of Agreement. Mark Crow. 4 cass. (Running Time: 4 hrs.). 2001. (978-1-931537-15-5(1)) Vision Comm Creat.

Power of Agreement in Marriage. Leroy Tompson, Sr. 2002. 15.00 (978-1-931804-09-7(5)) Ever Increase Wd Min.

Power of Ambition. Jim Rohn. 6 cass. (Running Time: 6 hrs.). 1994. 59.95 Set. (10950A) Nightingale-Conant.

Power of Ambition: Unleashing the Conquering Drive Within You! Jim Rohn. 6 cass. (Running Time: 6 hrs.). 1994. 59.95 incl. Quotation bk. (978-1-55525-076-8(9), 10950A) Nightingale-Conant.
Now, Jim Rohn - one of the world's most sought-after inspirational speakers - reveals the way to focus the ambitions & dreams that are at the core of your being. His dynamic program points the way to achieving great wealth & success, not through selfish means, but by working with others to achieve mutual goals.

Power of an Hour: Business & Life Mastery in One Hour a Week. rev. unabr. ed. Dave Lakhani. (Running Time: 4 hrs.). (ENG.). 2007. audio compact disk 29.98 (978-1-59659-127-1(7), GildAudio) Pub: Gildan Media. Dist(s): HachBkGrp

Power of an Hour: Business & Life Mastery in One Hour a Week. unabr. ed. Dave Lakhani. (Running Time: 4 hrs.). (ENG.). 2007. 29.98 (978-1-59659-118-9(8), GildAudio) Pub: Gildan Media. Dist(s): HachBkGrp

Power of Attraction: How to Tap into the Energy of Intention to Create a Healthier, Happier, More Abundant Life. Denise Hedges & Tom Waldenfels. 2006. audio compact disk 37.95 (978-0-9778813-1-4(8)) LifeWork Coach.

Power Of Beads. unabr. ed. Judith Weston. (YA). 1999. 4.95 (978-0-929071-70-1(0)) B-B Audio.

Power of Being Good & Loving Thy Neighbor & God. Jack R. Christianson. 1 cass. 7.98 (978-1-55503-183-1(8), 06003923) Covenant Comms.
Great stories, new perspectives for youth.

Power of Brokenness. Don Nori. 4 cass. 25.00 Set. (978-1-56043-392-7(2)) Destiny Image Pubs.

Power of Character. abr. ed. Michael Josephson. 2 cass. (Running Time: 3 hrs.). 2001. 18.00 (978-1-59040-088-3(7), Phoenix Audio) Pub: Amer Intl Pub. Dist(s): PerseuPGW

Power of Choice: Initating Change in Your Life. Caroline Myss. (Power of Choice). 2001. 55.00 (978-1-893869-62-2(8)) Celbrtng Life.

Power of Choice & Self Determinism. unabr. ed. L. Ron Hubbard. 1 cass. (Running Time: 1 hr.). 2001. 20.00 (978-0-88404-533-5(1)) Bridge Pubns Inc.

Power of Clarity: Find Your Focal Point, Maximize Your Income & Minimize Your Effort. 2001. 69.95 (978-1-55525-101-7(3)); audio compact disk 79.95 (978-1-55525-102-4(1)) Nightingale-Conant.

Power of Classical Music. Narrated by Victoria Rowell. 1 cass. (Running Time: 60 min.). (J). (gr. 7). 1999. 8.99 Twin Sisters.
Stimulates creative thought, critical thinking skills, & developmental skills.

Power of Classical Music. Executive Producer Twin Sisters Productions Staff. 1 CD. (Running Time: 61 mins). (Growing Minds with Music Ser.: TW 3050CD). (J). 2003. audio compact disk 12.99 (978-1-57583-640-9(8)) Twin Sisters.
Award-winning, best-selling collection of fourteen musical masterpieces performed with unique solo instruments and Nashville's finest 16-piece string ensemble.

Power of Classical Music. unabr. ed. Twin Sisters Productions. Read by Twin Sisters. (YA). 2007. 59.99 (978-1-60252-697-6(4)) Find a World.

Power of Communication & Persuasion. Michael Wickett. Read by Michael Wickett. 4 cass. 49.95 Set, incl. Progress Guide. (877AD) Nightingale-Conant.
In this dynamic audio adaptation of Michael Wickett's live seminar, you'll learn how to communicate instinctively to your listeners' fundamental needs & desires.

Power of Compassion. Dalai Lama XIV. 2 cass. 2002. (978-0-00-711439-9(7), HarperThor) HarpC GBR.

Power of Confessions: Making God's Word a Reality. Speeches. Creflo A. Dollar. 2 cassette. (Running Time: 2 hrs. 20 mins.). 2006. 10.00 (978-1-59944-051-4(2)); audio compact disk 11.00 (978-1-59944-052-1(0)) Creflo Dollar.

Power of Conscious Dreaming. Rudy Noel & Judy Lehn. 1988. CN Video Creations.
Stress & anxiety reduction tape.

Power of Conscious Dreaming. abr. ed. Rudy Noel. 1 cass. (Running Time: 90 mins.). 1988. (978-0-925332-02-8(X)) CN Video Creations.
Stress & anxiety reduction audio.

Power of Customer Service. Hosted by Paul Timm. 1 cass. (Running Time: 45 mins.). pap. bk. 99.95 (1002AV); pap. bk. 99.95 (1002AV); pap. bk. 99.95 (1002SAV); pap. bk. 99.95 (1002SAV) J Wilson & Assocs.

Power of Desire: Unleashing the Conquering Force Within You. Jack M. Zufelt. Read by Jack M. Zufelt. 6 cass. 59.95 Set. (740AD) Nightingale-Conant.
If you have a "Core Desire" - if you want something with all your heart & soul - the very strength of your wish can release a "Conquering Force" that will overcome any obstacle. Jack Zufelt's powerful techniques help you to release your Conquering Force to realize those desires...starting now!.

Power of Devotion. Swami Jyotirmayananda. Read by Swami Jyotirmayananda. 1 cass. (Running Time: 45 min.). 10.00 (806) Yoga Res Foun.

Power of Discrimination. Swami Amar Jyoti. 1 cass. 1979. 9.95 (K-27) Truth Consciousness.
Our vibrations, auras, & the Master's working. He stands by Principle always. The power of discrimination. Following the middle path.

Power of Divine Love. 1999. 69.95 (978-1-893027-32-9(5)) Path of Light.

Power of E-Thinking: Getting More of What You Want, by Using More of What You Have! Speeches. Featuring Melvin J. Gravely, 2nd. 2 cass. 1999. 25.95 (978-0-9656194-3-1(5)) Impact Grp.

Power of Effective Listening. Jim Cairo. 4 cass. 49.95 Set, incl. wkbk. (811-C47); 4.95 addtl. wkbk. (811WB); 22.95 business user's manual, 200p. (446-C47) Natl Seminars.
Does your mind wander while others are talking? For most of us, listening is one of the most difficult things we have to do. Learn to listen & you'll hear what's really being said. Whether you want to learn new techniques or sharpen the ones you already have, this series will make a difference.

Power of Effective Listening. unabr. ed. Jim Cairo. 2 cass. (Running Time: 3 hrs.). (Smart Audio Ser.). 19.99 (978-1-58926-335-2(9)); audio compact disk 19.99 (978-1-58926-336-9(7)) Oasis Audio.

Power of Effective Listening, Set. Jim Cairo. Read by Jim Cairo. 2 cass. (Running Time: 1 hr. 30 mins. per cass.). (National Seminars Ser.). 1998. 17.95 (978-1-886463-48-6(4)) Oasis Audio.
Learn the art of effective listening & how to hear what is really said.

Power of Emotion. unabr. ed. Almine. 2006. audio compact disk 13.95 (978-0-9724331-1-2(2), 397-005) SpiritJmys.

Power of Everybody. unabr. ed. Bill Hybels. 2003. 29.99 (978-0-310-25310-5(1)) Zondervan.

Power of Expectation. Mac Hammond. 2008. audio compact disk 6.00 (978-1-57399-381-4(6)) Mac Hammond.

Power of Faith. John MacArthur, Jr. 5 cass. 16.95 (20158, HarperThor) HarpC GBR.

Power of Faith & Patience: Activating God's Promises in Your Life. Mac Hammond. 4 cass. (Running Time: 4 hours). 2005. 10.00 (978-1-57399-180-3(5)); audio compact disk 20.00 (978-1-57399-181-0(3)) Mac Hammond.
In this four-message series by Mac Hammond, you'll discover how you can embrace and employ the two simple truths of faith and patience. When these two truths work together, they produce the promise of God...every time!.

Power of Faith Audio CD (MP3 Disk) Change Defeat to Victory Using the Ingredients of Faith. Orig. Title: Believing what you can't See. 2007. 13.99 (978-0-9794870-1-9(3)) P Cook.

Power of Faith Paperback book & MP3 Audio CD: Change Defeat to Victory Using the Ingredients of Faith. Orig. Title: Believing what you can't See. 2007. (978-0-9794870-3-3(X)) P Cook.

Power of Faithful Stewardship. Creflo A. Dollar. 2008. audio compact disk 21.00 (978-1-59944-721-6(5)) Creflo Dollar.

Power of Forgiveness. Mark Crow. 2 cass. (Running Time: 2 hrs.). 2001. (978-1-931537-17-9(8)) Vision Comm Creat.

Power of Forgiveness, John Gray. 2 cass. (Running Time: 2 hrs.). 1996. 17.95 (978-1-886095-16-8(7)) Genesis Media Grp.

Power of Forgiveness. unabr. ed. Almine & Almine. (Running Time: 3480 sec.). 2006. audio compact disk 13.95 (978-0-9724331-7-4(1), 397-008) SpiritJrnys.

Power of Forgiving. Everett L. Worthington, Jr. 2006. audio compact disk 12.95 (978-1-59947-093-1(4)) Pub: Templeton Pr. Dist(s): Chicago Distribution Ctr

Power of Full Engagement: Managing Energy, Not Time, Is the Key to High Performance & Personal Renewal. abr. ed. Jim Loehr & Tony Schwartz. Read by Jim Loehr & Tony Schwartz. 4 CDs. (Running Time: 43 hrs. 0 mins. 0 sec.). (ENG.). 2003. audio compact disk 30.00 (978-0-7435-2843-6(3), Sound Ideas) Pub: S&S Audio. Dist(s): S and S Inc

Power of Ghandi. Steck-Vaughn Staff. 2003. (978-0-7398-8421-8(2)) SteckVau.

Power of Goal Setting. 1982. audio compact disk (978-0-89811-284-9(2)) Meyer Res Grp.

Power of Goal Setting. Paul J. Meyer. 1 cass. 10.00 (SP100016) SMI Intl.
"If you are not making the progress you would like to & are capable of making, it is simply because your goals are not clearly defined," says Paul J. Meyer, one of America's foremost authorities on goal setting. Listen & put the ideas to use today. Recorded live, the cassette catches Meyer's enthusiastic spirit & excitement.

Power of Goal Setting. abr. ed. Paul J. Meyer. 1 cass. (Running Time: 1 hr. 2 min.). 11.00 (978-0-89811-016-6(5), 5153); Meyer Res Grp.
Inspires you with self-confidence & tells you how to use a logical, well-defined process to set & achieve your goals.

Power of God: Matt. 27:29-31; 1 Cor. 1:23-24. Ed Young. 1990. 4.95 (978-0-7417-1827-3(8), 827) Win Walk.

Power of God's Prophetic Purpose. Gary V. Whetstone. 6 cass. (Running Time: 9 hrs.). (Empowerment Ser.). 1998. pap. bk. 50.00 (978-1-58866-196-8(2), VEO29A); pap. bk. 25.00 (978-1-58866-197-5(0), VEO30A) Gary Whet Pub.
The world is on the threshold of the greatest days in god's prophetic timetable. What is your part in His plan?.

***Power of Half.** unabr. ed. Kevin Salwen & Hannah Salwen. Read by Fred Sanders. (ENG.). 2010. (978-0-06-196933-1(8), Harper Audio); (978-0-06-196932-4(X), Harper Audio) HarperCollins Pubs.

Power of Half: One Family's Decision to Stop Taking & Start Giving Back. unabr. ed. Kevin Salwen & Hannah Salwen. Read by Fred Sanders. 2010. audio compact disk 34.99 (978-0-06-182496-8(8), Harper Audio) HarperCollins Pubs.

Power of His Touch. Contrib. by Dave Williamson. 1997. 11.98 (978-0-7601-2013-2(7), 75700064); 4.00 (978-0-7601-2019-4(6), 75700071); 4.00 (978-0-7601-2020-0(X), 75700073) Pub: Brentwood Music. Dist(s): H Leonard

Power of His Touch. Contrib. by Dave Williamson. 1997. audio compact disk 85.00 (978-0-7601-2015-6(3), 75700063) Pub: Brentwood Music. Dist(s): H Leonard

Power of His Word & Inspiration. Voice by Eddie Long. (ENG.). 2008. 25.00 (978-1-58602-372-0(1)) Pub: E L Long. Dist(s): Anchor Distributors

Power of Holiness. Featuring Bill Winston. 2. 2002. audio compact disk 16.00 (978-1-59544-062-4(3)) Pub: B Winston Min. Dist(s): Anchor Distributors
Jesus Christ the "Anointed-One" lives on the inside of the Believer, and there are characteristics that flow out of the anointing which causes you to act and operate above the levelof the unsaved.

Power of Holy Habits. bk. 2.00 (978-0-687-76224-8(3)) Abingdon.

Power of Illusions. unabr. ed. J. Krishnamurti & David Shainberg. Read by J. Krishnamurti & David Shainberg. Ed. by Krishnamurti Foundation of America Staff. 1 cass. (Running Time: 60 min.). 1991. 8.50 (ADS83) Krishnamurti.
J. Krishnamurti & Dr. David Shainberg discuss the power of illusions on our conditioning. This discussion was recorded in NYC, April 11,1983.

Power of Imagery: Creating Wellness. Martin L. Rossman. 2005. audio compact disk 15.95 (978-0-9773494-4-9(6)) The Heal Mind Inc.

Power of Imagery: Creating Wellness Beyond Cancer. Martin L. Rossman. 2005. audio compact disk 15.95 (978-0-9773494-9-4(7)) The Heal Mind Inc.

Power of Imagery: Healing Cancer from Within. Martin L. Rossman. 2005. audio compact disk 15.95 (978-0-9773494-6-3(2)) The Heal Mind Inc.

Power of Imagery: Healing through Awareness. Martin L. Rossman. 2005. audio compact disk 15.95 (978-0-9773494-2-5(X)) The Heal Mind Inc.

Power of Imagery: Optimizing Cancer Treatments. Martin L. Rossman. 2005. audio compact disk 15.95 (978-0-9773494-8-7(9)) The Heal Mind Inc.

Power of Imagery: Pain Relief. 2005. audio compact disk 15.95 (978-0-9773494-0-1(3)) The Heal Mind Inc.

Power of Imagery: Relaxing into Healing. Martin L. Rossman. 2005. audio compact disk 15.95 (978-0-9773494-1-8(1)) The Heal Mind Inc.

Power of Imagery: Successful Cancer Surgery. Martin L. Rossman. 2005. audio compact disk 15.95 (978-0-9773494-7-0(0)) The Heal Mind Inc.

Power of Imagery: Tools to Change Your Life. Martin L. Rossman. 2005. audio compact disk 15.95 (978-0-9773494-3-2(8)) The Heal Mind Inc.

Power of Imagery: Transforming Your Fear of Cancer. Martin L. Rossman. 2005. audio compact disk 15.95 (978-0-9773494-5-6(4)) The Heal Mind Inc.

Power of Images in Sickness & Health. Read by Russell Lockhart. 1 cass. (Running Time: 90 min.). 1980. 10.95 (978-0-7822-0147-5(4), 111) C G Jung IL.

Power of Imprinting. unabr. ed. Timothy Leary. 2 cass. (Running Time: 2 hrs. 41 min.). 1982. 18.00 (01501) Big Sur Tapes.

Power of Innovative Thinking: Let New Ideas Lead You to Success. Jim Wheeler. Read by Patrick G. Lawlor. (Running Time: 10800 sec.). 2008. audio compact disk 23.95 (978-1-59316-108-8(5)) Listen & Live.

Power of Intention: Learning to Co-Create Your World Your Way. Wayne W. Dyer. 2 CDs. (ENG.). 2007. audio compact disk 19.95 (978-1-4019-0355-8(X), 3541) Hay House.
This will be a PBS special, and then sold in retail stores in 3 years.

Power of Intention: Learning to Co-Create Your World Your Way. abr. ed. Wayne W. Dyer. 4 CDs. (Running Time: 4 hrs.). 2004. audio compact disk 23.95 (978-1-4019-0217-9(0), 2170) Hay House.

Power of Intention: Learning to Co-create Your World Your Way. abr. ed. Wayne W. Dyer. Read by Wayne W. Dyer. (YA). 2008. 54.99 (978-1-60252-988-5(4)) Find a World.

Power of Intuition. Judith Orloff & Deepak Chopra. 1 CD. 2005. audio compact disk 10.95 (978-1-4019-0622-1(2), 6222) Hay House.

Power of Intuition. unabr. ed. Anne Armstrong & Jim Armstrong. 1 cass. (Running Time: 1 hr. 28 min.). 1987. 11.00 (00101) Big Sur Tapes.

Power of Joy: How the Deliberate Pursuit of Pleasure Can Heal Your Life. Christiane Northrup. 2008. audio compact disk 15.00 (978-1-4019-2308-2(9)) Hay House.

Power of Kabbalah. Yehuda Berg. 2002. 18.95 (978-1-58872-022-1(5)) Jodere Grp.

Power of Kabbalah: The Art of Spiritual Transformation. unabr. ed. Rav Berg. Contrib. by Moskovitz. 2 cass. (Running Time: 4 hrs.). 2001. 59.99 (978-1-57189-180-8(3)) Jodere Grp.
Introduction to the basic principles of Kabbalah. Learn how to bring the light of the Creator and all of its beneficience into your life.

Power of Kabbalah: The Art of Spiritual Transformation: How to Remove Chaos & Find True Fulfillment. 1 CD. (Running Time: 1 hr. 30 mins.). 2000. audio compact disk 79.95 (978-1-55525-097-3(1)) Nightingale-Conant.

Power of Less: The Fine Art of Limiting Yourself to the Essential... In Business & in Life. unabr. ed. Leo Babauta. Read by Fred Stella. (Running Time: 4 hrs.). 2009. 39.97 (978-1-4233-7857-0(1), 9781423378570, Brlnc Audio MP3 Lib); 39.97 (978-1-4233-7859-4(8), 9781423378594, BADLE); 24.99 (978-1-4233-7856-3(3), 9781423378563, Brilliance MP3); 24.99 (978-1-4233-7858-7(X), 9781423378587, BAD); audio compact disk 69.97 (978-1-4233-7855-6(5), 9781423378556, BriAudCD Unabrid); audio compact disk 19.99 (978-1-4233-7854-9(7), 9781423378549, Bril Audio CD Unabri) Brilliance Audio.

Power of Life & Death. Jack Deere. 1 cass. (Running Time: 90 mins.). (Proverbs Ser.: Vol. 2). 2000. 5.00 (JD08-002) Morning NC.
Practical wisdom for everyday living is brought to life in Jack's thorough exposition of this important book of the Bible.

Power of Light: Eight Stories for Hanukkah. unabr. ed. Short Stories. Isaac Bashevis Singer. Narrated by George Guidall. 2 pieces. (Running Time: 1 hr. 45 mins.). (gr. 1 up). 1997. 19.00 (978-0-7887-1799-4(5), 95271E7) Recorded Bks.
Whether it is the spirit of a young girl extinguishing the Hanukkah candles, or a parakeet that serves as a match-maker, these delightful stories are infused with the power of love.

Power of Light: Eight Stories for Hanukkah, Class Set. unabr. ed. Isaac Bashevis Singer. Read by George Guidall. 2 cass., 10 bks. (Running Time: 1 hr. 45 min.). (J). (gr. 2). 1997. bk. 129.30 (978-0-7887-2904-1(7), 46402) Recorded Bks.
These enchanting stories unlock the mysteries of Hanukkah.

Power of Light: Eight Stories for Hanukkah, Homework Set. unabr. ed. Isaac Bashevis Singer. Read by George Guidall. 2 cass. (Running Time: 1 hr. 45 min.). (J). 1997. bk. & pap. bk. 36.20 (978-0-7887-1842-7(8), 40622) Recorded Bks.

Power of Limits: Harmony & Proportions Etc. Gyorgy Doczi. 3 cass. 24.00 (OC99) Sound Horizons AV.

Power of Love. Kenneth Copeland. (ENG.). 2006. audio compact disk 5.00 (978-1-57562-895-0(3)) K Copeland Pubns.

Power of Love. Kenneth Copeland. 1 cass. 1988. 5.00 (978-0-88114-809-1(1)) K Copeland Pubns.
Biblical teaching on love's power.

Power of Love. Elbert Willis. 1 cass. (Oasis of Love Guidelines Ser.). 4.00 Fill the Gap.

Power of Love: A Dr. Laura Audio Collection. unabr. abr. ed. Laura Schlessinger. Read by Laura Schlessinger. 5 CDs. (Running Time: 7 hrs.). 2004. audio compact disk & audio compact disk 29.95 (978-0-06-075598-0(9)) HarperCollins Pubs.

Power of Love for Jesus. 1985. (0250) Evang Sisterhood Mary.

***Power of Love, the: A Dr. Laura Audio Collection.** abr. ed. Laura Schlessinger. Read by Laura Schlessinger. (ENG.). 2004. (978-0-06-081490-8(X), Harper Audio); (978-0-06-078429-4(6), Harper Audio) HarperCollins Pubs.

Power of Mind. Swami Jyotirmayananda. 1 cass. (Running Time: 1 hr.). 1990. 12.99 Yoga Res Foun.

Power of Motherhood: Exodus 1 & 2, Selected. Ed Young. 1995. 4.95 (978-0-7417-2058-0(2), 1058) Win Walk.

***Power of Multisensory Preaching & Teaching: Increase Attention, Comprehension, & Retention.** Zondervan. (Running Time: 8 hrs. 14 mins. 27 sec.). (ENG.). 2010. 9.99 (978-0-310-86936-8(6)) Zondervan.

Power of Music. Don Campbell. 5 cass. (Running Time: 5 hrs.). 1996. bk. 49.95 Set. (13640AZ) Nightingale-Conant.
This deeply moving program will lift you & inspire you as it teaches you how to benefit from the most subtle, delicate & potent medium for altering emotions.

Power of Music. David Glen Hatch. 1 cass. 9.95 (978-1-57734-249-6(6), 06005480) Covenant Comms.
Inspiring stories & beautiful music teaches about the power of music.

Power of Music: How to Use Sound for Relaxation, Concentration & Healing. Don Campbell. 4 cass. (Running Time: 4 hrs.). 1999. 59.95 Set. (83-0049) Explorations.
Shows how to improve your emotional intelligence & mental IQ with music; raise your performance level; create a sound environment for your office, home & commute to work; use your voice to release stress & energize your brain & use music to promote psychological & physiological healing.

Power of Myth. unabr. ed. Joseph Campbell & Bill Moyers. 6 CDs. (Running Time: 6 hrs.). (ENG.). 2001. audio compact disk 36.95 (978-1-56511-510-1(4), 1565115104) Pub: HighBridge. Dist(s): Workman Pub

Power of Myth: Programs 1-6. Bill Moyers. (Playaway Adult Nonfiction Ser.). 2009. 59.99 (978-1-60812-738-2(9)) Find a World.

Power of Myth Vol. 3: The First Storytellers. unabr. ed. Joseph Campbell. 1 cass. (Running Time: 1 hr.). 1992. 10.95 Pub: HighBridge. Dist(s): Workman Pub

Power of Narrative: Poetic Stories & Stories of Poets. Robert F. Morneau. 4 cass. (Running Time: 4 hrs. 44 min.). 1993. 32.95 Set. (TAH295) Alba Hse Comns.
Bishop Morneau in his unique classical literary style will reach into your heart & life through four poets who transcend the years with their poetic stories. He expounds on the power of the narrative through such poets as Gerard Manley Hopkins; George Herbert & Emily Dickenson. Excellent for person interested in good literature & the one searching for life's deeper meanings.

Power of Natural Hair Growth. Robert I. Berrick. 1 cass. (Running Time: 60 min.). 1989. 29.95 (978-0-9622637-0-5(2)) Inner Visions.
Presents a self-help program utilizing mental imagery to stop hair loss and promote hair growth.

Power of Nice: How to Conquer the Business World with Kindness. unabr. ed. Linda Kaplan Thaler & Robin Koval. Narrated by Linda Kaplan Thaler & Robin Koval. (Running Time: 3 hrs. 0 mins. 0 sec.). (ENG.). 2006. 12.59 (978-1-60814-341-2(4)) Oasis Audio.

Power of Nice: How to Conquer the Business World with Kindness. unabr. ed. Robin Koval & Linda Kaplan Thaler. Narrated by Robin Koval. Frwd. by Jay Leno. (Running Time: 3 hrs. 0 mins. 0 sec.). (ENG.). 2006. audio compact disk 17.99 (978-1-59859-169-9(X)) Oasis Audio.

Power of Nice: How to Conquer the Business World with Kindness. unabr. ed. Linda Kaplan Thaler & Robin Koval. Read by Linda Kaplan Thaler & Robin Koval. Frwd. by Jay Leno. (Running Time: 10800 sec.). 2007. audio compact disk 36.00 (978-0-7861-5844-7(1)) Blckstn Audio.

Power of Nice: How to Negotiate So Everyone Wins - Especially You! Ronald M. Shapiro & Mark A. Jankowski. (Running Time: 2 hr. 20 min.). 1999. 39.95 INCL. BKLET. (978-0-9675965-0-1(5)) Shapiro Negot.
One of the most successful deal makers in sports & business presents his unique negotiating strategies.

Power of Now: A Guide to Spiritual Enlightenment. abr. ed. Narrated by Eckhart Tolle. 2 cass. (Running Time: 3 hrs.). 2002. (978-1-84032-489-1(9)) Bolinda Pubng AUS.
One of the greatest spiritual books written in recent times. These tapes show us how to invoke the profound, enlightening power from the present moment, for creating a liberated life.

Power of Now: A Guide to Spiritual Enlightenment. unabr. ed. Eckhart Tolle. Read by Eckhart Tolle. (YA). 2008. 59.99 (978-1-60252-927-4(2)) Find a World.

Power of Now: A Guide to Spiritual Enlightenment. unabr. ed. Eckhart Tolle. Read by Eckhart Tolle. 7 CDs. (Running Time: 7 hrs. 35 mins. 0 sec.). (ENG.). 2001. audio compact disk 39.95 (978-1-57731-208-6(2)) Pub: New Wrld Lib. Dist(s): PerseuPGW

Power of Now: a Guide to Spiritual Enlightment see Poder del Ahora: Un Camino Hacia la Realizacion Espiritual

power of One. Bryce Courtenay. Read by Humphrey Bower. (Running Time: 21 hrs. 30 mins.). 2009. 114.99 (978-1-74214-210-4(9), 9781742142104) Pub: Bolinda Pubng AUS. Dist(s): Bolinda Pub Inc

Power of One. David Litchford. 1 cass. 7.98 (978-1-55503-756-7(9), 069406) Covenant Comms.
You can make a difference for good.

Power of One. unabr. ed. Bryce Courtenay. Read by Humphrey Bower. 18 CDs. (Running Time: 21 hrs. 30 mins.). 2002. audio compact disk 123.95 (978-1-74030-390-3(3)) Pub: Bolinda Pubng AUS. Dist(s): Bolinda Pub Inc

Power of One. unabr. ed. Bryce Courtenay. 7 cass. (Running Time: 9 hrs. 15 mins.). (YA). 2003. 56.00 (978-1-74030-703-1(8)) Pub: Bolinda Pubng AUS. Dist(s): Bolinda Pub Inc

Power of One. unabr. ed. Bryce Courtenay. 15 cass. (Running Time: 21 hrs. 30 mins.). 2004. 120.00 (978-1-876584-85-6(8)) Bolinda Pubng AUS.

Power of One. unabr. ed. Bryce Courtenay. Read by Humphrey Bower. 2 CDs. (Running Time: 77400 sec.). 2005. audio compact disk 54.95 (978-1-74093-680-4(9)) Pub: Bolinda Pubng AUS. Dist(s): Bolinda Pub Inc

Power of One: Romans 5:12-21. Ben Young. 1996. 4.95 (978-0-7417-6003-6(7), B0003) Win Walk.

Power of One - ShowTrax. Music by Kirby Shaw. 1 CD. (Running Time: 5 mins.). 2000. audio compact disk 19.95 (08711247) H Leonard.
Each person makes a difference! That's the message of this inspirational original that cooks from beginning to end. What a great message for kids & adults everywhere!.

Power of One Thing: How to Intentionally Change Your Life. unabr. ed. Randy Carlson. Narrated by Randy Carlson. (Running Time: 5 hrs. 33 mins. 22 sec.). (ENG.). 2009. 16.09 (978-1-60814-583-6(2)); audio compact disk 22.99 (978-1-59859-629-8(2)) Oasis Audio.

power of one young readers' Edition. Bryce Courtenay. Read by Humphrey Bower. (Running Time: 9 hrs. 15 mins.). (YA). 2009. 79.99 (978-1-74214-311-8(3), 9781742143118) Pub: Bolinda Pubng AUS. Dist(s): Bolinda Pub Inc

power of one young reader's Edition. unabr. ed. Bryce Courtenay. Read by Humphrey Bower. (Running Time: 9 hrs. 15 mins.). (YA). 2007. audio compact disk 87.95 (978-1-74093-931-7(X), 9781740939317) Pub: Bolinda Pubng AUS. Dist(s): Bolinda Pub Inc

Power of Oneness: To Lose Weight & Be Loved for Who I Am. Janet Greeson. 4 cass. 1994. cass. & video 29.95 Set. (978-0-9630955-3-4(6)) Greeson & Boyle.
Self discovery tapes capturing the 7 unique qualities of being lovable. Weight loss.

Power of Optimism. Alan L. McGinnis. Read by Alan L. McGinnis. 6 cass. 1990. 59.95 set. (742A) Nightingale-Conant.
Take problems & turn them into opportunities & challenges, raise your level of motivation, learn how to maintain a cheerful disposition & change mental habits that bring happiness & genuine contentment.

Power of Outrageous Marketing: Using the 10 Time-Tested Secrets of Titans, Tycoons & Billionaires to Get Rich in Your Own Business. abr. ed. Joe Vitale, Jr. & Joe Vitale. Read by Joe Vitale, Jr. & Joe Vitale. (Running Time: 2 hrs. 0 mins. 0 sec.). (ENG.). 2007. audio compact disk 19.95 (978-0-7435-6969-9(5), Nightgale) Pub: S&S Audio. Dist(s): S and S Inc

Power of Paradox: Using Contradiction, Conflict & Chaos to Achieve the Impossible. H. Evan Woodhead. Contrib. by Hasley Enterprises Worldwide Inc. (ENG., 2006. pap. bk. (978-0-9739858-3-2(6)) Hasley EnterCN CAN.

Power of Partnership. 2 cass. (Running Time: 2 hrs.). 2003. audio compact disk 14.00 (978-1-881541-90-5(8)) A Wommack.

Power of Partnership. 2 Audio Cassette Tap. 2005. (978-1-59548-048-4(X)) A Wommack.

***Power of Pause: Audiobook Version.** Terry Hershey. Read by Terry Hershey. (Running Time: 360). (ENG.). 2010. audio compact disk 25.95 (978-0-9826247-0-8(0)) Hershey Assoc.

Power of Persistence. Speeches. Joel Osteen. 1 Cass. (Running Time: 30 Mins.). 2001. 6.00 (978-1-59349-096-6(8), JA0096) J Osteen.

Power of Persistence. Dick Sutphen. 1 cass. (Running Time: 1 hr.). (RX17 Ser.). 1986. 14.98 (978-0-87554-320-8(0), RX129) Valley Sun.
You are persistent, ambitious & determined. You strive until you've accomplished your goals. You keep at it until the job is done. Persistence is the power of winners. You have the will power and ability to keep going. You are a success-oriented winner who persists until the task is complete. You are relentless in the fulfillment of your desires. "Persistence power" are your key words for conditioned response.

Power of Personal Mission. James W. Huber. Read by James W. Huber. 6 cass. 1991. 39.95 Set, incl. wkbk. (862A) Nightingale-Conant.
Bring vigor to your work-life by discovering your core passion - that which you care most about doing with your career.

Power of Persuasion. Harry Hazel. 1 cass. 10.00 (SP100075) SMI Intl.
Sharing the secrets of the most effective leaders down through history. Harry Hazel amplifies the vital components of powerful persuasion. To the degree you give others what they want, they will give you what you want. He elaborates on this premise of successful persuasion, emphasizing a strong sensitivity to others & persuasion skills founded on integrity.

Power of Persuasion. Betty L. Randolph. Read by Betty L. Randolph. Read by Leonard Baron. Ed. by Success Education Institute International. 1 cass. (Success Ser.). 1989. bk. 14.98 Ocean Format. (978-1-55909-231-9(9), 190P); bk. 14.98 Music Format. (978-1-55909-232-6(7), 190PM) Randolph Tapes.
Includes 60,000 messages with the left-right brain.

Power of Persuasion: Getting It, Using It & Defending Yourself Against It, Set. G. Ray Funkhouser. 6 cass. 49.95 (442AX) Nightingale-Conant.
Highly acclaimed expert & scholar G. Ray Funkhouser describes the four kinds of persuasion power, how to recognize each & how to use them all. He then relates the natural six-step decision-making process; how to determine where any individual is in that process & which techniques are best-suited to persuade.

Power of Pluto. Lee Yelenics. 1 cass. 8.95 (373) Am Fed Astrologers.
Interpret natal & transit.

Power of Politeness; the Ladder of Grace. Jonathan Murro & Ann Ree Colton. 1 cass. 7.95 A R Colton Fnd.

Power of Positive Confession. David T. Demola. 12 cass. 48.00 (S-1071) Faith Fellow Min.

Power of Positive Confrontation: The Skills You Need to Know to Handle Conflicts at Work, at Home & in Life. unabr. ed. Susan Barbara & Magee Pachter. (Running Time: 7 hrs. 30 mins.). (ENG.). 2009. 24.98 (978-1-59659-412-8(8), GildAudio) Pub: Gildan Media. Dist(s): HachBkGrp

Power of Positive Doing. Ivan Burnell. 1 cass. (Running Time: 47 min.). 1991. 11.00 (978-0-89811-271-9(0), SP100076) Meyer Res Grp.
Workable strategies for accomplishing whatever you want in all areas of your life. How to plant positive seeds in your life & the lives of others.

Power of Positive Doing. Ivan Burnell. 1 cass. 10.00 (SP100076) SMI Intl.
Learn how to plant positive seeds in your life & the lives of others. "The Power of Positive Doing" builds on the foundation of positive thinking & talking & offers a set of workable strategies for accomplishing whatever you want to do in all areas of your life.

Power of Positive Feelings a 3 Hour Event: Conquering Negative Feelings Forever. (ENG.). 2009. audio compact disk 50.00 (978-0-925640-13-0(1)) Outcomes Unltd.

Power of Positive Habits: Put Your Mind & Body on Autopilot in 21 Days & Reach Your Goals Automatically! Excerpts. Dan Robey. 2 cass. (Running Time: 120 min). 2004. 19.95 (978-0-9725219-8-7(4)) Abritt Pubng.
The Power Of Positive Habits Put your mind and body on autopilot in 21 days and reach your goals automatically with this simple to follow audio program,.

Power of Positive Intimidation in Selling. Dave Johnson. (Dave Johnson Educational Library). D Johnson.
Discusses how to get others to positively do what one wants them to do.

Power of Positive Parenting: How to Raise Positive Children in Today's World. Barbara J. Smyly. 12 cass. (Running Time: 12 hrs.). 1994. pap. bk. 89.95 Set. (978-0-9616707-9-5(7)) Alivening Pubns.
Information to shift limiting perspectives & to change ineffective methods of child rearing.

Power of Positive Playing. unabr. ed. Frank Scoblete. 1 cass. (Running Time: 1 hr.). 1997. audio compact disk 16.95 CD. (978-1-882173-07-5(4)) Paone Pr.
How to beat the casinos at their own games. How to avoid the pitfalls of casino play & how to overcome the casino's three-tiered strategy.

Power of Positive Thinking. Peale. 1958. 16.95 (978-1-55927-442-5(5)) Macmill Audio.

Power of Positive Thinking. Norman Vincent Peale. 10 cass. (Running Time: 6 hrs. 40 min.). 1995. pap. bk. 99.95 Set. Intl Ctr Creat Think.
These inspirational & motivational tapes & guidebooks will allow you to explore positive ways to achieve personal success, self-fulfillment, optimism, entusiasm & contentment in your life & point the way to greater happiness.

Power of Positive Thinking. Norman Vincent Peale. 5 cass. (Running Time: 6 hrs. 35 min.). 1996. 29.95 Set. (978-0-924967-37-5(4)) Intl Ctr Creat Think.

Power of Positive Thinking. Norman Vincent Peale. 6 cass. 59.95 set. (427AX) Nightingale-Conant.
This pioneering work by Dr. Norman Vincent Peale is the all-time motivational classic on harnessing the power of a positive outlook on life. Based on a life-affirming message of renewed energy & enthusiasm, this program will help you discover what Dr. Peale calls the "inherent power which partakes of the divine...that extra inborn power which accompanies challenge." Don't think your way to failure & misery - discover this remarkable guide to happiness & a better life.

Power of Positive Thinking. unabr. ed. Norman Vincent Peale. Read by Norman Vincent Peale. 6 cass. (Running Time: 4 hrs.). 1988. 59.95 Set. (978-0-671-64223-5(5)) S&S Audio.

Power of Positive Thinking: A Practical Guide to Mastering the Problems of Everyday Living. abr. ed. Norman Vincent Peale. Read by Norman Vincent Peale. 1 CD. (Running Time: 10 hrs. 0 mins. 0 sec.). (ENG.). 1999. audio compact disk 14.00 (978-0-671-58186-2(4)) Pub: S&S Audio. Dist(s): S and S Inc
Dr. Peale shows listeners how to eliminate self-doubt & how to free oneself from worry, stress & resentment. Rich with anecdotes, this powerful program will allow every listener to achieve the happiness & success that Dr. Peale has already delivered to millions.

Power of Positive Thinking: A Practical Guide to Mastering the Problems of Everyday Living. abr. ed. Norman Vincent Peale. Read by Norman Vincent Peale. 4 CDs. (Running Time: 40 hrs. 0 mins. 0 sec.). (ENG.). 2001. audio compact disk 30.00 (978-0-7435-0780-6(0), Sound Ideas) Pub: S&S Audio. Dist(s): S and S Inc

Power of Positive Thinking in Business: Ten Traits for Maximum Results. Scott W. Ventrella. Read by Scott W. Ventrella. 2004. 10.95 (978-0-7435-1996-0(5)) Pub: S&S Audio. Dist(s): S and S Inc

Power of Praise. Kenneth Copeland. 1 cass. (Running Time: 1 hr.). 1987. 5.00 (978-0-88114-800-8(8), 02-0037) K Copeland Pubns.

Power of Praise. Speeches. Creflo A. Dollar. 5 cass. (Running Time: 6 hrs.). 2003. 25.00 (978-1-59089-781-2(1)); audio compact disk Rental 34.00 (978-1-59089-782-9(X)) Creflo Dollar.

Power of Praise. Caryl Krueger. Read by Caryl Krueger. 2 cass. (Running Time: 3 hrs.). 2001. 17.00 Belleridge.
Enjoy the illuminating story of the book of Psalms as well as the importance of praise in our daily lives. Also included is the story of a famous king: David, a life of praise. These cassettes are filled with Biblical and present-day stories about the merits of praise in challenging times.

Power of Prayer. Mark Crow. 5 cass. (Running Time: 5 hrs.). 2001. (978-1-931537-08-7(9)) Vision Comm Creat.

Power of Prayer. Creflo A. Dollar. 2008. audio compact disk 50.00 (978-1-59944-740-7(1)) Creflo Dollar.

Power of Prayer. Larry Dossey. 6 cass. (Running Time: 6 hrs.). 1994. 59.95 Set. (11260A) Nightingale-Conant.

Power of Prayer. Briege McKenna. 8 cass. (Running Time: 8 hrs.). 24.95 (978-0-8198-5835-1(8)) Pauline Bks.
Contents: Witnessing to Jesus, Eucharist, Do You Really Believe?, Not By Bread Alone, Living with the Resurrected Christ, Bloom Where You're Planted, The Cross in Our Lives, Jesus is Alive.

Power of Prayer: Connecting with the Wisdom of the Universe. Larry Dossey. 6 cass. (Running Time: 6 hrs.). 1994. 59.95 (978-1-55525-079-9(3), 11260A) Nightingale-Conant.
According to Dr. Larry Dossey, a practicing physician who has extensively researched & tested this amazing phenomenon, prayer is now being proven in medicine & in the laboratory as a universal force that is no longer an exclusive matter of faith alone. In this program, Dr. Dossey explains the scientific evidence supporting this force, which he calls "a process of communicating with the transcendent".

Power of Prayer to Change Your Marriage. Stormie Omartian. 2009. audio compact disk 18.99 (978-0-7369-2514-3(7)) Harvest Hse.

Power of Praying for Your Adult Children. Stormie Omartian. 2009. audio compact disk 19.99 (978-0-7369-2668-3(2)) Harvest Hse.

Power of Praying Together Audiobook: Where Two or More Are Gathered. Stormie Omartian & Jack Hayford. 2003. (978-0-7369-1070-5(0)) Harvest Hse.

Power of Premonitions: How Knowing the Future Can Shape Our Lives. unabr. ed. Larry Dossey. Read by Jim Bond. 1 MP3-CD. (Running Time: 10 hrs.). 2008. 39.97 (978-1-4233-9298-9(1), 9781423392989, Brlnc Audio MP3 Lib) Brilliance Audio.

Power of Premonitions: How Knowing the Future Can Shape Our Lives. unabr. ed. Larry Dossey. Read by Jim Bond. 1 MP3-CD. (Running Time: 10 hrs.). 2009. 24.99 (978-1-4233-9297-2(3), 9781423392972, Brilliance MP3); 24.99 (978-1-4233-9299-6(X), 9781423392996, BAD); 39.97 (978-1-4233-9300-9(7), 9781423393009, BADLE); audio compact disk 29.99 (978-1-4233-9295-8(7), 9781423392958); audio compact disk 97.97 (978-1-4233-9296-5(5), 9781423392965, BriAudCD Unabrid) Brilliance Audio.

Power of Preparation. Elbert Willis. 1 cass. (Developing Stability Ser.). 4.00 Fill the Gap.

Power of Presence. Peter Senge. 2008. audio compact disk 19.95 (978-1-59179-528-5(1)) Sounds True.

Power of Prevailing Prayer. 2004. (978-1-59024-130-1(4)); audio compact disk (978-1-59024-129-5(0)) B Hinn Min.

Power of Prevention. Ralph Alan Dale. Read by Ralph Alan Dale. 1 cass. 1981. pap. bk. 14.00; 9.00 (5) Dialectic Pubng.
How we came to lose the power of prevention of illness & how we are now regaining that power.

Power of Proclamation. Derek Prince. 1 cass. 1990. 5.95 (I-4320) Derek Prince.
You can use your Bible as Moses used his rod: to extend God's authority into every area where Satan opposes the purposes & the people of God.

Power of Prophetic Vision. Michael-Liberte Lattiboudeaire. 8 cass. (Running Time: 8 hrs.). (ENG.). 2008. pap. bk. 14.95 (978-1-889448-27-5(3), Great House) Pub: Great Hse Pub. Dist(s): Spring Arbor Dist
Two or more components of organization brought together in a harmonious relationship for the purpose of achieving a goal, purpose or destiny in which each cannot achieve by itself.

Power of Psalm 23. Mark Crow. 2 cass. (Running Time: 2 hrs.). 2001. (978-1-931537-00-1(3)) Vision Comm Creat.

Power of Publicity. Bonnie Weiss. 2 cass. (Running Time: 2 hr.). 1985. 29.95 (978-0-931143-01-4(2)); Catalyst Pubns.
Step-by-step guidance on how to effectively & inexpensively publicize your product, service, event or organization. It is designed for small business owners, authors, lecturers, non-profit & others on limited budgets. Includes major sources for contacting media personnel in the U. S. & Canada.

Power of Purpose: Creating Meaning in Your Life & Work. abr. ed. Richard J. Leider. Read by Richard J. Leider. 2 cass. (Running Time: 3 hrs.). 1997. 17.95 (978-1-57453-215-9(4)) Audio Lit.
A remarkable program for helping us to discover our purpose. It is based on many interviews with people of all ages & acts as a guide to finding one's calling in life & creating a life filled with meaning.

Power of Purpose: How to Create the Life You Always Wanted. Les Brown. 6 cass. (Running Time: 6 hrs.). 1998. 59.95 (978-1-55525-080-5(7), 17780A) Nightingale-Conant.
Live your dreams.

Power of Qi: Quigong Meditations for Better Health & Spiritual Well-Being. Ken Cohen. 2 CDs. (Running Time: 2 hrs. 30 min.). 2000. audio compact disk 24.95 (978-1-56455-799-5(5), AE00500) Sounds True.
An information-packed collection with the West's leading authority on qigong. Three titles include Taoist Healing Imagery, Qigong Meditations & Healthy Breathing.

Power of Radical Forgiveness. Colin Tipping. 2009. audio compact disk 69.95 (978-1-59179-678-7(4)) Sounds True.

Power of Real Choice. Jackie Woods. 2003. audio compact disk 14.95 (978-0-9659665-6-6(9)) Adawehi Pr.

Power of Resilience: Achieving Balance, Confidence & Personal Strength in Your Life. abr. ed. Robert Brooks. 3 cass. (Running Time: 4 hrs. 30 mins.). 2004. 24.00 (978-1-932378-60-3(X)) Pub: A Media Intl. Dist(s): Natl Bk Netwk

Power of Resilience: Achieving Balance, Confidence & Personal Strength in Your Life. abr. ed. Robert Brooks. 4 CDs. (Running Time: 4 hrs. 30 mins.). 2005. audio compact disk 28.00 (978-1-932378-61-0(8)) Pub: A Media Intl. Dist(s): Natl Bk Netwk

Power of Revelation-CIY. Featuring Bill Winston. 4. 2002. audio compact disk 32.00 (978-1-59544-085-3(2)) Pub: B Winston Min. Dist(s): Anchor Distributors
Pastor Bill Winston teaches in this powerful (4) four cassette series profound truths necessary for the Believer in this end time. In this series, you will be given insight on RevelationKnowledge like never before.

Power of Self-Coaching: The Five Essential Steps to Creating the Life You Want. abr. ed. Joseph J. Luciani. 4 CDs. (Running Time: 6 hrs.). (ENG.). 2004. audio compact disk 24.95 (978-1-57270-427-5(6)) Pub: AudioGO. Dist(s): Perseus Dist

Power of Self-Coaching: The Five Essential Steps to Creating the Life You Want. abr. ed. Joseph J. Luciani. 4 cass. (Running Time: 5 hrs.). 2004. 24.95 (978-1-57270-426-8(8), Atlntc Mnthly) Pub: Grove-Atltc. Dist(s): PerseuPGW
This empowering guide shows people who are experiencing emotional turmoil how to reconnect with their innate capacity for genuine happiness before more serious emotional problems develop. The Power of Self-Coaching offers five simple steps toward reclaiming one's natural and spontaneous potential, the inner power that can transform one's life. Using the author's proven technique of self-talk, listeners can liberate themselves from reflexive, destructive thinking and begin to create a life of happiness and empowerment.

Power of Self Confidence. Jeff Davidson. 2005. audio compact disk 14.95 (978-1-60729-120-6(7)) Breath Space Inst.

Power of Self-Confidence. Jeff Davidson. 2005. 13.95 (978-1-60729-229-6(7)) Breath Space Inst.

Power of Self-Esteem, Set. Nathaniel Branden. 8 CDs. (Running Time: 9 hrs.). 2005. audio compact disk 49.50 (978-1-57970-266-3(X), S00858D, Audio-For) J Norton Pubs.
High self-esteem can empower life with new energy, improve personal relationships, enhance careers, and give a sense of joy in living. This series of lectures presents the four key elements of healthy self-esteem: self-awareness, self-acceptance, self-responsibility, and self-assertion.

Power of Self-Esteem: Powerful Techniques That Will Change Your Life! Joe Hodowanes. Read by Joe Hodowanes. 1 cass. (Running Time: 1 hr. 15 min.). 1998. 14.95 (978-0-9664427-1-7(7)) J M Wanes.
Designed to identify the 14 best steps you can take to strengthen & nurture your self-esteem & self-esteem of others.

Power of Self-Esteem: The Path to Success. Nathaniel Branden. Read by Nathaniel Branden. 6 cass. (Running Time: 6 hrs.). vinyl bd. 49.50 (978-0-88432-173-6(8), S00858) J Norton Pubs.
Discusses what self-esteem is & why it is our most urgent need. Shows how it affects virtually every aspect of our existence: our work, our ambition, our ability to love. Presents the 4 key elements of healthy self-esteem: self-awareness, self-acceptance, self-responsibility & self-assertion.

Power of Self-Love. Caren Croxen. 1981. 6.95 (978-0-944955-01-7(0)) Wissmann Pub.

Power of Self-Reliance. unabr. ed. Almine. 2006. audio compact disk 13.95 (978-0-9724331-5-0(5), 397-006) SpiritJrnys.

Power of Sensation see Poder de la Sensacion

Power of Sex. Doug Fields. (Super-Ser.). 2006. audio compact disk 60.00 (978-5-558-25706-9(7)) Group Pub.

Power of Silence. unabr. ed. Almine. 2006. audio compact disk 13.95 (978-0-9724331-6-7(3), 397-007) SpiritJrnys.

Power of Silence: A Weekend Inquiry with Adyashanti - February 25-26 2006. Featuring Adyashanti. 7 CDs. (Running Time: Approx 8 hrs.). 2006. audio compact disk 65.00 (978-0-9763788-8-4(4), 7POS) Open Gate Pub.
"Our deepest nature is silence: that space which is beyond the known, understanding, and imagination. True silence is not a dead or static state; it is a state of unity, creative response, and deep love. Salvation lies within the heart of silence and nowhere else. Be still and know." ~ AdyashantiThis 7-CD album was recorded live at a weekend intensive with Adyashanti on February 25-26, 2006, in Los Altos, CA. It offers a profound and intimate investigation into the freedom of spiritual awakening. Included are satsang talks, questions from the audience, and powerful direct inquiry dialogues.

Power of Simple Prayer: How to Talk with God about Everything. abr. ed. Joyce Meyer. Read by Sandra McCollom. Told to Beth Clark. (Running Time: 6 hrs.). (ENG.). 2007. 14.98 (978-1-59483-891-0(7)) Pub: Hachet Audio. Dist(s): HachBkGrp

Power of Simple Prayer: How to Talk with God about Everything. abr. ed. Joyce Meyer. Read by Sandra McCollom. 5 CDs. (Running Time: 6 hrs.). (ENG., 2007. audio compact disk 29.98 (978-1-59483-078-5(9)) Pub: Hachet Audio. Dist(s): HachBkGrp

Power of Simplicity. PUEI. 2000. audio compact disk 89.95 (978-1-934147-06-1(0), CareerTrack) P Univ E Inc.

Power of Six Sigma. unabr. ed. Subir Chowdhury. 2 CDs. (Running Time: 3 hrs.). (YA). 2001. audio compact disk 19.95 (978-0-929071-77-0(8)) B-B Audio.
Six Sigmanever before has a business initiative transformed corporations so dramatically. While it has been credited with improving productivity, slashing costs, and improving profit margins, it can cause much angst among employees who need to change th.

Power of Slow: Inding Balance & Fulfillment beyond the Cult of Speed. unabr. ed. Carl Honore. (Running Time: 3:06:38). 2009. audio compact disk 24.95 (978-1-59179-685-5(7)) Sounds True.

Power of Small: Why Little Things Make All the Difference. unabr. ed. Robin Koval & Linda Kaplan Thaler. Read by Robin Koval & Linda Kaplan Thaler. (ENG.). 2009. audio compact disk 21.00 (978-0-7393-8188-5(1), Random AudioBks) Pub: Random Audio Pubg. Dist(s): Random

Power of Soul: The Way to Heal, Rejuvenate, Transform, & Enlighten All Life. abr. unabr. ed. Zhi Gang Sha. Read by Zhi Gang Sha. (Running Time: 13 hrs. 0 mins. 0 sec.). (ENG.). 2009. audio compact disk 39.99 (978-0-7435-7491-4(5)) Pub: S&S Audio. Dist(s): S and S Inc

Power of Speaking God's Word. Creflo A. Dollar. 2008. audio compact disk 28.00 (978-1-59944-736-0(3)) Creflo Dollar.

Power of Storms. Compiled by Benchmark Education Staff. 2005. audio compact disk 10.00 (978-1-4108-5465-0(5)) Benchmark Educ.

Power of Style Dvd: Berlin Stylewriting. True to the Game Staff. 2007. audio compact disk 24.95 (978-3-939566-15-1(2)) Pub: Publikat Verlags DEU. Dist(s): Gingko Press

Power of Submission. abr. ed. 4 cass. (Running Time: 6 hrs.). 1997. 20.00 (978-0-00-525749-4(2)) Majestic Mda.

Power of Suffering. Steve Thompson. 1 cass. (Running Time: 90 mins.). (Power of Suffering Ser.: Vol. 3). 2000. 5.00 (ST04-003) Morning NC.
The author's messages offer helpful instruction on an often misunderstood pathway which can release spiritual power in our lives.

Power of Suffering Series. unabr. ed. Steve Thompson. 4 cass. (Running Time: 6 hrs.). 2000. 20.00 (ST04-000) Morning NC.
Includes: "God's Heart for Healing," "How to be Anointed," "The Power of Suffering" & "The Power of Weakness." Steve's messages offer helpful

instruction on an often misunderstood pathway which can release spiritual power in our lives.

Power of Thanksgiving. unabr. ed. Myrtle Smith. Prod. by David Keyston. 1 cass. (Running Time: 1 hrs. 15 min.). (Myrtle Smyth Audiotapes Ser.). 1998. , CD. (978-1-893107-16-8(7), M16, Cross & Crown) Healing Unltd.

Power of the Anointing. Kenneth Copeland. 2 CDs. (BVOV Ser.). 2006. audio compact disk 10.00 (978-1-57562-892-9(9)) K Copeland Pubns.

Power of the Anointing. Kenneth Copeland. Perf. by Kenneth Copeland. . 1996. cass. & video 10.00 Set. (978-0-88114-984-5(5)) K Copeland Pubns.
Biblical teaching on the Anointing.

Power of the Blood. 2003. (978-1-59024-093-9(6)); audio compact disk (978-1-59024-092-2(8)) B Hinn Min.

Power of the Book You Can TRUST - Unleashing the Inspired Word into Your Life: Why I Believe the Bible Is True. 2005. 15.00 (978-1-933561-09-7(2)) BFM Books.

Power of the Chun Bu Kyung CD: The Heavenly Code. Perf. by Ilchi Lee. Prod. by Arang Park. Arranged by Arang Park. Narrated by Judy Lebeau. Ji-in Kim. (ENG.). 2007. audio compact disk 19.95 (978-1-935127-06-2(3)) Pub: BEST Life. Dist(s): SCB Distributors

***Power of the Corporate Anointing: How to Appropriate the Miracle-Working Power of God.** Mac Hammond. 2010. audio compact disk 6.00 (978-1-57399-460-6(X)) Mac Hammond.

Power of the Cross: A Musical Praising Christ, the Risen Lamb. Contrib. by Marty Parks. 2007. audio compact disk 16.99 (978-5-557-56379-6(2)); audio compact disk 12.00 (978-5-557-56378-9(4)); audio compact disk 60.00 (978-5-557-56374-1(1)); audio compact disk 90.00 (978-5-557-56372-7(5)) Lillenas.

Power of the Dog. unabr. ed. Don Winslow. Read by Ray Porter. (Running Time: 72000 sec.). 2008. 95.95 (978-1-4332-4544-2(2)); 44.95 (978-1-4332-4546-6(9)); audio compact disk & audio compact disk 120.00 (978-1-4332-4545-9(0)) Blckstn Audio.

Power of the Enneagram: A New Technology of Self-Discovery. Don Richard Riso. 6 cass. (Running Time: 6 hrs.). 1995. 59.95 Set, incl. wkbk. (12930AS) Nightingale-Conant.
You'll learn to evaluate your own personality from the nine basic personality types. You will be able to assess your weaknesses & turn them into strengths & be able to improve your productivity & increase job satisfaction.

Power of the Imagination: Creating Positive Change. abr. ed. Patricia W. Carson. Read by Patricia W. Carson. 1 cass. (Running Time: 60 min.). 1999. 10.00 (978-1-928652-05-2(0)) Motivational OH.

Power of the Lord's Blessing. Gary V. Whetstone. 4 cass. (Running Time: 6 hrs.). (Freedom Ser.). 1994. pap. bk. 35.00 (978-1-58866-222-4(5), VROO9A) Gary Whet Pub.
Many believers are not experiencing God's blessing. This series reveals how to free yourself from barriers of frustration & self effort set up by Satan.

Power of the Mantram. unabr. ed. Eknath Easwaran. 1 cass. (Running Time: 25 mins.). 1992. 7.95 (978-1-58638-590-3(9), PM) Nilgiri Pr.
Lucid and straightforward instructions for choosing and using a mantram in daily life.

Power of the Mind see Poder de la Mente

Power of the Mind to Heal. Joan Borysenko. 1 cass. 59.95 Aquarius Prods.
This seven-part series offers thought-provoking exercises & guided meditations. Joan is the author of several New York Times best-sellers & the co-founder & directory of the Mind Body Clinic at New England Deaconess in Boston.

Power of the Mind to Heal. abr. ed. Joan Borysenko & Miroslav Borysenko. 1 cass. (Running Time: 2 hrs.). 1999. 16.00 (80481) Courage-to-Change.
How to heal the physical & emotional ailments that afflict us.

Power of the Mind to Heal. unabr. ed. Joan Borysenko. 2 cass. 13.95 set. (89263) Books on Tape.
The subject of bestsellers by such authors as Bill Moyers & Deepak Chopra, the "mind/body connection" is among the most exciting areas in the field of health & healing. Now, Harvard-trained physician & bestselling author Joan Borysenko reveals that healing is really the simplest of matters - & can be accomplished with her practical pragmatic approach.

Power of the Mind to Heal: Renewing Body, Mind, & Spirit. 1993. 59.95 (978-1-55525-094-2(7)) Nightingale-Conant.

Power of the Mind to Heal: Renewing Body, Mind & Spirit. Joan Borysenko. 6 cass. (Running Time: 6 hrs.). 1993. suppl. ed. 59.95 (978-1-55525-016-4(5), 10410A) Nightingale-Conant.
You hold the key to physical, emotional & spiritual healing within your remarkable mind. Healing is the simplest of matters. We heal by becoming truly ourselves, by discovering our wholeness.

Power of the Mountain Man. unabr. ed. William W. Johnstone. Read by Doug van Liew. 4 cass. (Running Time: 6 hrs.). (Mountain Man Ser.: No. 15). 2001. 24.95 (978-1-890990-65-7(5)) Otis Audio.
Smoke Jensen is summoned to San Francisco, only to find his friend Francie dead & the wealthy plotting to take control of the gold mines. Smoke heads to the High Sierras to recruit all the prospectors, ranchers & farmers he can gather to stop them.

Power of the Plus Factor. Norman Vincent Peale. 1 cass. 1986. 9.95 (978-0-07-040888-3(2)) Zondervan.

Power of the Resurrection. 2003. (978-1-59024-101-1(0)); audio compact disk (978-1-59024-100-4(2)) B Hinn Min.

Power of the Resurrection. Alfred D. Harvey, Jr. 1 Cass. 2003. 10.00 (978-1-932508-26-0(0)) Doers Pub.

Power of the Spirit. Eldon Taylor. 1 cass. (Running Time: 62 min.). (Inner Talk Ser.). 16.95 incl. script. (978-1-55978-012-4(6), 5412C) Progress Aware Res.
Soundtrack - Musical Themes with underlying subliminal affirmations.

Power of the Spirit: Babbling Brook. Eldon Taylor. 1 cass. 16.95 (978-1-55978-762-8(7), 5412F) Progress Aware Res.

Power of the Sword. Wilbur Smith. Read by Tim Pigott-Smith. 2 cass. (Running Time: 4 hrs.). (ENG.). 2001. 16.99 (978-0-333-78164-7(3)) Pub: Macmillan UK GBR. Dist(s): Trafalgar

Power of the Sword, Pt. 1. unabr. collector's ed. Wilbur Smith. Read by Richard Brown. 11 cass. (Running Time: 16 hrs. 30 min.). (Courtney Novels). 1988. 88.00 (978-0-7366-1378-1(1), 2272-A) Books on Tape.
The story of two half-brothers, both sons of Centaine, Shasa by an English father, Manfred De La Rey by a Boer. Their struggle, set in the 1930s & 1940s, portends Africa's current crisis.

Power of the Sword, Pt. 2. collector's ed. Wilbur Smith. Read by Richard Brown. 10 cass. (Running Time: 15 hrs.). (Courtney Novels). 1988. 80.00 (978-0-7366-1379-8(X), 2272-B) Books on Tape.

Power of the Tithe. Bill Winston. 2 cass. (Running Time: 0hr.53min.). 2002. 10.00 (978-1-931289-68-9(9)) Pub: B Winston Min. Dist(s): Anchor Distributors

Power of the Tongue. Kenneth Copeland. 2006. audio compact disk 5.00 (978-1-57562-867-7(8)) K Copeland Pubns.

Power of the Tongue. Kenneth Copeland. 1 cass. 1981. 5.00 (978-0-88114-740-7(0)) K Copeland Pubns.
Biblical teaching on the words we speak.

Power of the Tongue. Featuring Bill Winston. 6 CDs. 2005. audio compact disk 48.00 (978-1-59544-136-2(0)) Pub: B Winston Min. Dist(s): Anchor Distributors

Power of the Tongue, Vol. 166. Bill Winston. 6 cass. (Running Time: 5hr.27min.). (C). 2003. 35.00 (978-1-931289-12-2(3)) Pub: B Winston Min. Dist(s): Anchor Distributors

Power of True Self-Esteem. 1 CD. 1990. audio compact disk 16.95 (978-1-55841-121-0(6)) Emmett E Miller.
Dr. Miller, co-convener of the historic California Task Force on Self-Esteem, Personal and Social Responsibility, is interviewed by Michael Toms of New Dimensions radio. An entertaining exploration of the myths and truths about Self-Esteem and how Self-Esteem can lead to our cultural transformation.

Power of True Self-Esteem: Discovering the Beauty of your Essential Nature. 1 cassette. 1990. 12.95 (978-1-55841-037-4(6)) Emmett E Miller.

Power of Truth: A Leading with Emotional Intelligence Conversation with Warren Bennis. unabr. ed. Daniel Goleman et al. (Running Time: 3600 sec.). (ENG.). 2006. audio compact disk 14.95 (978-1-59397-974-4(6)) Pub: Macmill Audio. Dist(s): Macmillan

Power of Truth Thinking. Elbert Willis. 1 cass. (Truth Thinking Ser.). 4.00 Fill the Gap.

Power of Two with One Heart. Lisa Bevere. 2008. 14.99 (978-1-933185-39-2(2)) Messengr Intl.

Power of Unity, Set. Bobby Hilton. 4 cass. (Running Time: 6 hrs.). 1999. 18.00 (978-1-930766-03-7(3)) Bishop Bobby.
Religious ministry program.

Power of Visualization. Lee Pulos. 6 cass. (Running Time: 6 hrs.). 1993. 59.95 set. (610A) Nightingale-Conant.

Power of Weakness. Steve Thompson. 1 cass. (Running Time: 90 mins.). (Power of Suffering Ser.: Vol. 4). 2000. 5.00 (ST04-004) Morning NC.
the aurhor's messages offer helpful instruction on an often misunderstood pathway which can release spiritual power in our lives.

***Power of Who: You Already Know Everyone You Need to Know.** unabr. ed. Bob Beaudine. (Running Time: 5 hrs.). (ENG.). 2010. 27.98 (978-1-59659-511-8(6), GildAudio) Pub: Gildan Media. Dist(s): HachBkGrp

Power of Will. Frank C. Haddock. 6 cass. 1992. 59.95 set incl. wkbk. (695A) Nightingale-Conant.
First published as a book in 1907, this classic work on developing & using will power to achieve greatness is sure to have a major impact in the lives of all who listen.

Power of Women: Harness Your Unique Strengths at Home, at Work, & in Your Community. abr. ed. Susan Nolen-Hoeksema. Read by Susan Nolen-Hoeksema. 4 CDs. (Running Time: 5 hrs.). 2010. audio compact disk 19.99 (978-1-4272-0916-0(2)) Pub: Macmill Audio. Dist(s): Macmillan

Power of Wonder. unabr. ed. Gerald Heard. 1 cass. (Running Time: 29 min.). 1954. 11.00 (09202) Big Sur Tapes.
Speaks of the sense of "wonder" - the pure passion, the pure wish to understand outside of ourselves & outside of personal motives.

Power of Word Filled Prayers: Asking in the Name of Jesus. 2006. 15.00 (978-1-933561-22-6(X)) BFM Books.

Power of Words. Speeches. Joel Osteen. 6 audio cass. (J). 2001. 24.00 (978-1-931877-15-2(7), JAS011) J Osteen.

Power of Words. Speeches. Joel Osteen. 3 CDs. (J). 2002. audio compact disk 24.00 (978-1-931877-32-9(7), JCS011) J Osteen.

Power of Words, Pt. 1. Speeches. Joel Osteen. 1 Cass. (Running Time: 30 Mins.). 2001. 6.00 (978-1-59349-119-2(0), JA0119) J Osteen.

Power of Words, Pt. 2. Speeches. Joel Osteen. 1 Cass. (Running Time: 30 Mins.). 2001. 6.00 (978-1-59349-120-8(4), JA0120) J Osteen.

Power of Words: Overcoming Discouraging Words, Pt. 6. Speeches. Told to Joel Osteen. 1 Cass. (Running Time: 30 Mins.). 2001. Rental 6.00 (978-1-59349-124-6(7), JA0124) J Osteen.

Power of Words: Speak to Your Mountains, Pt. 5. Speeches. Told to Joel Osteen. 1 Cass. (Running Time: 30 Mins.). 2001. 6.00 (978-1-59349-123-9(9), JA0123) J Osteen.

Power of Words: Speaking with Wisdom & Grace. Nancy Leigh DeMoss. (ENG.). 2003. audio compact disk 16.00 (978-0-940110-71-7(7)) Life Action Publishing.

***Power of Your Spirit: Use it Now!** unabr. ed. Sonia Choquette. (ENG.). 2011. audio compact disk 29.95 (978-1-4019-2811-7(0)) Hay House.

Power of Your Spoken Word: Change Your Negative Self-Talk & Create the Life You Want. Instructed by Louise L. Hay. 1 cass. (Running Time: 1 hr.). (Conversations on Living Lecture Ser.). 1991. 10.95 (978-0-937611-25-8(5), 234) Hay House.
In this engaging & spirited lecture, Louise helps us to discover our own power, wisdom, & inner strengths through the mastery of the words we speak. Most of us are not aware of how influential our spoken words are. When we say anything, we are, in fact, extending our own inner self-talk to create a similar world around us.

Power of Your Spoken Word: Change Your Negative Self-Talk & Create the Life You Want! Louise L. Hay. 1 CD. 2005. audio compact disk 10.95 (978-1-4019-0441-8(6)) Hay House.

Power of Your Spoken Word: Change Your Negative Self-Talk & Create the Life You Want see Poder de la Palabra

Power of Your Subconscious Mind. Joseph Murphy. 3 cass. 1989. 39.95 (978-0-13-687013-5(9)) P-H.
Shows today's audience how to achieve success, improve health, find wealth, & deepen relationships through the power of suggestion-visualization subconscious mind.

Power of your Voice. Laraine Flemming & Carol Fleming. 2004. 5.95 (978-0-7435-4152-7(9)) Pub: S&S Audio. Dist(s): S and S Inc

Power of Your Words Pt. 3: Keep Your Tongue from Speaking Evil. Speeches. Told to Joel Osteen. 1 Cass. (Running Time: 30 Mins). 2001. 6.00 (978-1-59349-121-5(2), JA0121) J Osteen.

Power of Your Words Pt. 4: The Blessing. Speeches. Told to Joel Osteen. 1 Cass. (Running Time: 30 Mins.). 2001. Rental 6.00 (978-1-59349-122-2(0), JA0122) J Osteen.

Power of 45 Strategy. Jeffrey Zalewski. (ENG.). 2007. audio compact disk 19.95 (978-1-934722-03-9(0)) Direct Sell Acad.

Power on Her Own: A Kate Power Novel. unabr. ed. Judith Cutler. Narrated by Patricia Gallimore. 7 cass. (Running Time: 10 hrs.). 2000. 63.00 (978-1-84197-114-8(6), H1110E7) Recorded Bks.
Personal tragedy convinced Kate Power she'd had enough of working for the men in London. However, when she relocates to Birmingham CID, a whole new host of troubles is waiting to swamp her.

Power on the Edge: Mastering Energetic Boundaries. Interview. Kelle Eli. 8 CDs. (Running Time: 8 hours). 2004. 150.00 (978-0-9758777-0-8(4)) k Eli.

Power on with Jesus (Cassette) Compiled by Sunday School Publishing Board. (J). 2005. 3.99 (978-1-932972-11-5(0)) Townsnd-Pr.

Power over People, Pts. I-II. 2nd rev. ed. Instructed by Dennis Dalton. 16 CDs. (Running Time: 12 hrs.). 1991. audio compact disk 69.95 (978-1-56585-346-1(6), 443) Teaching Co.

Power over People, Vol. I, Pts. I-II. 2nd rev. ed. Instructed by Dennis Dalton. 8 cass. (Running Time: 12 hrs.). 54.95 (978-1-56585-101-6(3), 443) Teaching Co.

Power over People: Classical & Modern Political Theory, Vol. 2. 2nd rev. ed. Instructed by Dennis Dalton. 4 cass. (Running Time: 6 hrs.). 1991. 129.95 (978-1-56585-102-3(1)); audio compact disk 179.95 (978-1-56585-347-8(4)) Teaching Co.

Power over Sin Provided. Elbert Willis. 1 cass. (Because of Calvary Ser.). 4.00 Fill the Gap.

Power Pack: Power Listening for Sales Professionals, Set. unabr. ed. Rochelle Devereaux. Read by Rochelle Devereaux. 3 cass. (Running Time: 4 hr. 30 min.). 2000. 29.95 (978-1-891966-04-0(9)) Bus Efficacy.
Covers ways to increase effectiveness of sales presentations using power listening techniques.

Power, Passion & Pain of Black Love. Jawanza Kunjufu. 1 cass. (Running Time: 60 mins.). 1999. 29.95 (AT13) African Am Imag.
Learn the secrets of staying together & how to be selective when choosing a mate. Discusses how to develop & improve your relationships.

Power Passion & Persuasion: Advocacy Inside & Out. Dominic J. Gianna. 1996. pap. bk. 185.00 (978-0-943380-96-4(0)) PEG MN.

Power Persuasion Sales, Set. abr. ed. Roger W. Breternitz. 2 cass. (Running Time: 45 min.). 1985. pap. bk. 39.95 Vector Studios.
Tape 1: Parameters of top closers, techniques to selling in every arena. Tape 2: Hypnosis implants suggestions of how to communicate subliminally to make bigger sales & more sales.

Power Planets Vol. 1: Inner Journeys: Sun - Moon. Luisa De La Lama. 1 cass. (Running Time: 60 min.). 1994. 11.95 White Dragon.
Sun: Meet Apollo & contact your guardian angel. Moon: Contact the goddess Isis & heal your relationship with the Great Mother.

Power Planets Vol. 2: Inner Journeys: Mercury - Venus. Luisa De La Lama. 1 cass. (Running Time: 60 min.). 1994. 11.95 White Dragon.
Mercury: Merge with Hermes & activate your mind's potential. Venus: Commune with Eros & Aphrodite. Awaken your unconditional love.

Power Planets Vol. 3: Inner Journeys: Mars - Jupiter. Luisa De La Lama. 1 cass. (Running Time: 60 min.). 1994. 11.95 White Dragon.
Mars: Contact Ares & be a winner. Jupiter: Meet Zeus, king of Olympus. Become abundant & royal.

Power Planets Vol. 4: Inner Journeys: Saturn - Chiron. Luisa De La Lama. 1 cass. (Running Time: 60 min.). 1994. 11.95 White Dragon.
Saturn: Merge with Sanat Kumara, Lord of the World. Learn to use your limitations to further your ideals & activate your manifesting potential. Chiron: Contact Chiron, the Healer & Teacher. Heal your inner wounds & gain wholeness.

Power Planets Vol. 5: Inner Journeys: Uranus - Neptune. Luisa De La Lama. 1 cass. (Running Time: 60 min.). 1994. 11.95 White Dragon.
Uranus: Meet Uranus, the Sky god, & activate your inner giant. Neptune: Merge with Poseidon & enhance your creative potential & divine inspiration.

Power Planets Vol. 6: Inner Journeys: Pluto - Volcan. Luisa De La Lama. 1 cass. (Running Time: 60 min.). 1994. 11.95 White Dragon.
Pluto: Commune with Hades & Persephone. Activate your spiritual power & the riches awaiting you in the depth of your being. Volcan: Meet Hephaestos the divine blacksmith & tap into the power of your Soul.

Power Play. abr. ed. Joseph Finder. Read by Dennis Boutsikaris. (ENG.). 2007. audio compact disk 24.95 (978-1-4272-0125-6(0)) Pub: Macmill Audio. Dist(s): Macmillan

Power Play. unabr. ed. Joseph Finder. 1 MP3-CD. (Running Time: 11 hrs.). 2007. 54.95 (978-0-7927-4917-2(0), Chivers Sound Lib); audio compact disk 89.95 (978-0-7927-4873-1(5), Chivers Sound Lib); 59.95 (978-0-7927-4935-6(9), Chivers Sound Lib) AudioGO.
It was the perfect retreat for a troubled company. No cell phones. No BlackBerrys. No cars, just a deluxe lodge surrounded by thousands of miles of wilderness and a desolate seacoast. Jake Landry is a junior executive at the Hammond Aerospace Corporation, a steady, modest, and taciturn guy with a gift for keeping his head down - and a turbulent past he prays he's put behind him. Ordered to fill in for his boss at the annual offsite, he's out of his element. He's uncomfortable with the lavish accommodations and swaggering men who run the company and the only person he knows there is the new special assistant to the CEO - who happens to be Jake's ex. Then a band of hunters, apparently lost in the woods, crash the opening-night festivities. Soon the execs of a billion-dollar company, cut off from the rest of the world, find themselves at the mercy of a group of men with guns...and a cunning plan to take Hammond Aerospace for all it's worth. But the hostage takers aren't who they appear to be and neither is Jake Landry.

Power Play. unabr. ed. Joseph Finder. Read by Dennis Boutsikaris. 7 CDs. (Running Time: 8 hrs. 30 mins. 0 sec.). (ENG.). 2007. audio compact disk 29.95 (978-1-4272-0123-2(4)) Pub: Macmill Audio. Dist(s): Macmillan

Power Plays. unabr. ed. Collin Wilcox. Read by Larry McKeever. 8 cass. (Running Time: 8 hrs.). (Frank Hastings Ser.). 1997. 48.00 (978-0-7366-3737-4(0), 4414) Books on Tape.
On the face of it, it was only a minor traffic accident, a fender bender between a Buick & a Mercedes. But when Lt. Frank Hastings shows up it seems that something more's at stake.

Power Plays Collection: Politika; Ruthless.com; Shadow Watch. abr. ed. Tom Clancy & Martin H. Greenburg. Read by Jay O. Sanders & J. K. Simmons. Created by Tom Clancy. 9 CDs. (Running Time: 9 hrs.). (ENG.). 2000. audio compact disk 49.95 (978-0-7435-0699-1(5), Audioworks) Pub: S&S Audio. Dist(s): S and S Inc

Power Points & Sacred Sites on Every Continent. Hosted by Nancy Pearlman. 1 cass. (Running Time: 29 min.). 10.00 (1034) Educ Comm CA.

Power Politics see Poetry & Voice of Margaret Atwood

Power, Politics, & Possessions: Building the Instruments of Peace: Witnessing in the Community see Power, Politics, & Possessions: Five Lectures on the Christian Conscience

Power, Politics, & Possessions: By Whose Authority?: The Politics of God & the Politics of the World see Power, Politics, & Possessions: Five Lectures on the Christian Conscience

Power, Politics, & Possessions: Five Lectures on the Christian Conscience. William Durland. 5 cass. Incl. Power, Politics, & Possessions: Building the Instruments of Peace: Witnessing in the Community. 1979.; Power, Politics, & Possessions: By Whose Authority?: The Politics of God & the Politics of the World. 1979.; Power, Politics, & Possessions: The Economics of Peacemaking: Simplicity & Voluntary Poverty. 1979.; Power, Politics, & Possessions: The Role of the Church Community: Must Modern Christians Be Peacemakers? 1979.; Power, Politics, & Possessions: The Scriptural Basis of Peacemaking. 1979.; 1979. 17.50 Set.; 4.50 ea. Pendle Hill.

Power, Politics, & Possessions: The Economics of Peacemaking: Simplicity & Voluntary Poverty see Power, Politics, & Possessions: Five Lectures on the Christian Conscience

Power, Politics, & Possessions: The Role of the Church Community: Must Modern Christians Be Peacemakers? see Power, Politics, & Possessions: Five Lectures on the Christian Conscience

Power, Politics, & Possessions: The Scriptural Basis of Peacemaking see Power, Politics, & Possessions: Five Lectures on the Christian Conscience

Power Potion. unabr. ed. Wendelin Van Draanen. Read by Marc Cashman. (Gecko & Sticky Ser.: Bk. 3). (ENG.). (J). 2010. audio compact disk 25.00 (978-0-7393-7930-1(5), Listening Lib) Pub: Random Audio Pubg. Dist(s): Random

Power Principles of Prayer. Gary V. Whetstone. (Practical Ministry Ser.). 1996. 260.00 (978-1-58866-034-3(6)) Gary Whet Pub.

Power Reading. (gr. k-9). 2003. bk. & vinyl bd. (978-1-883186-37-1(4), PPS 25); vinyl bd. (978-1-883186-35-7(8), PPS 25) Natl Read Styles Inst.

Power Reading. Bob Cole. Illus. by David Ford. 20 cass. (Running Time: 20 hrs.). (J). (gr. 2-5). 2002. pap. bk. 129.95 (978-1-883186-18-0(8), PP03C) Natl Read Styles Inst.

Power Reading: Power Pak Primer A. Sandra Dutton & Robin Conner. (J). (gr. k-2). 2002. pap. bk. 129.95 (978-1-883186-12-8(9), PP0PA) Natl Read Styles Inst.

Power Reading: Power Pak Primer B. Sandra Dutton. Illus. by Robin Conner. (J). (gr. k-2). 2002. pap. bk. 129.95 (978-1-883186-13-5(7), PP0PB) Natl Read Styles Inst.

Power Reading: Power Pak-1C. I.t. ed. Lynea Bowdish. Illus. by Robin Conner. 20 cass. (Running Time: 30 hrs.). (J). (ps-3). 2002. pap. bk. 129.95 (978-1-883186-17-3(X)) Natl Read Styles Inst.

Power Reading: Power Pak-2B. I.t. ed. Lynea Bowdish. Illus. by Robin Connors. 20 cass. (Running Time: 30 hrs.). (J). (gr. k-3). 2002. pap. bk. 129.95 (978-1-883186-15-9(3), PP02B) Natl Read Styles Inst.

Power Reading: Power Pak 7A. Robert Cole & Barbara Larkin. Illus. by David Ford. (YA). (gr. 1-7). 2002. pap. bk. 129.95 (978-1-883186-10-4(2), PP07A) Natl Read Styles Inst.

Power Reading: Power Pak 8A. Robert Cole & Elaine Marie Alphin. Illus. by David Ford. (YA). (gr. 1-8). 2002. pap. bk. 129.95 (978-1-883186-11-1(0), PP08A) Natl Read Styles Inst.

Power Reading: Power Paks K-8. (Power Reading Ser.). (J). (gr. k-8). 2002. 2878.20 (978-1-883186-32-6(3), PPS18) Natl Read Styles Inst.
360 high-interest, reproducible, stories accompanied by questions based on state standards and language-arts games that provide practice in vocabulary and comprehension.

Power Rhythms: 100 African & Afro Caribbean Rhythms. Bill Matthews. 2005. audio compact disk 16.50 (978-0-9765971-5-5(2)) Fremont Drum.

Power Selling: Twenty-One Psychological Principles for Closing the Sale. Loretta Malandro. Read by Loretta Malandro. 6 cass. 59.95 Set. (732AD) Nightingale-Conant.
Provides you with the 21 most current psychological principles of persuasion - new, powerful discoveries about human behavior & why people buy now. You'll learn how to create the "Eureka Factor" - the buyer's sense of "feeling" that everything is just right.

Power Speech. Ed. by Alfred Publishing. (ENG.). 2006. audio compact disk 24.95 (978-0-944200-15-5(X)) Alfred Pub.

Power Speech: How You Can Unleash the Hidden Persuasive Powers in Your Voice. Geoffrey G. Forward. Read by Geoffrey G. Forward. Read by Elisabeth Howard. 1 cass. (Running Time: 2 hrs.). 1994. 24.95 (978-0-944200-01-8(X)) Perfom Arts Global.
How to improve your speaking voice. How to communicate more clearly & effectively. How to improve your image.

Power Spots, Vestments, & Rituals. Fern Shafer. 1 cass. 9.00 (A0355-88) Sound Photosyn.
1988 ICSS '88, with Suzanne Palmer & Sarah Dubin-Vaughn.

Power Surge: Singing the Marks of Discipleship. 1999. audio compact disk 8.00 (978-0-933173-77-4(6)) Chging Church Forum.

Power Surge Thematic Programming. 2000. pap. bk. 35.00 (978-0-933173-88-0(1)) Chging Church Forum.

Power Talk. Sarah Myers McGinty. 2002. 17.98 (978-1-58621-131-8(5)) Hachet Audio.

Power Talk: Standard American English. unabr. ed. Bettye P. Zoller et al. Read by Bettye P. Zoller & Hugh Lampman. Frwd. by Edward Asner. 2 cass. (Running Time: 3 hrs.). 1993. pap. bk. 39.95 (978-1-884643-02-6(7), AMSP 2 PT) Pub: Voicesvoices. Dist(s): Penton Overseas
Using a broad-based approach to voice & speech patterns, these tapes offer techniques for improving vocal quality, vocabulary, & articulation, & minimizing or eliminating regional accents. The audios combine self-directed listen/repeat practice with target sounds, words, & phrases; they are sup ported by a detailed instruction book that includes assessment procedures & encouragement.

Power Talk: Using Language to Build Authority & Influence. abr. ed. Sarah Myers McGinty. (ENG.). 2005. 14.98 (978-1-59483-437-0(7)) Pub: Hachet Audio. Dist(s): HachBkGrp

Power Talk: Standard American English, Grades 6-12: Your Ladder to Success! Bettye P. Zoller & John A. Watleins. Read by Bettye P. Zoller & Hugh Lampman. Ed. by John A. Watleins. Frwd. by Edward Asner. 2 cass. (Running Time: 3 hrs.). 1995. lib. bdg., tchr. ed., stu. ed. 24.95 (978-1-884643-11-8(6), SPP95) Voicesvoices.

Power Talking Skills: Say What You Mean & Get What You Want. George R. Walther. 6 cass. (Running Time: 6 hrs. 28 min.). 79.95 Set incl. participant's kit. (V50170) CareerTrack Pubns.
Power Talking Skills will help you speak, think & behave more effectively. You'll replace powerless language with powerful alternatives. You'll see the difference immediately - as you become more positive, persuasive & powerful in every situation.

Power Tennis. 1 cass. 10.00 (978-1-58506-048-1(8), 93) New Life Inst OR.
The hidden part of your mind has a tremendous potential to improve your tennis.

Power Tennis. abr. ed. Roger W. Breternitz. 1 cass. (Running Time: 45 min.). 1985. pap. bk. 9.95 (978-1-893417-24-3(7)) Vector Studios.
Hypnosis: Implants suggestions of strength, endurance, depth perception, concentration, & a winning attitude. Helps instill the basics of good tennis form, & visualization of winning.

Power That Delivers Us. Rick Joyner. 1 cass. (Running Time: 90 mins.). (Foundation Ser.: Vol 5). 2000. 5.00 (RJ04-005) Morning NC.
Firmly establishing basic Christian principles, these messages also illuminate some of the primary enemies of truth, such as legalism & the control spirit.

Power, the Life of the Believer. Smith Chuck. (ENG.). 2001. audio compact disk 22.99 (978-1-932941-10-4(X)) Word For Today.

***Power Thoughts: 12 Strategies for Winning the Battle of the Mind.** unabr. ed. Joyce Meyer. Read by Sandra McCollom. (Running Time: 9 hrs. 30 mins.). (ENG.). 2010. 24.98 (978-1-60788-632-7(4)); audio compact disk 29.98 (978-1-60788-631-0(6)) Pub: Hachet Audio. Dist(s): HachBkGrp

***Power Through Prayer.** unabr. ed. E. M. Bounds. Narrated by Doren Elias. (ENG.). 2004. 9.98 (978-1-59644-047-0(3), Hovel Audio) christianaud.

Power Through Prayer. unabr. ed. E. M. Bounds. Narrated by Doren Elias. 2 CDs. (Running Time: 2 hrs. 36 mins. 0 sec.). (ENG.). 2004. audio compact disk 15.98 (978-1-59644-048-7(1), Hovel Audio) christianaud.
In a penetrating and forthright style, Edward M. Bounds offers stimulating advice to Christian servants. a??The preaching that kills may have insight and grasp of principles, may be scholarly and critical in taste, may have every minutia of the derivation and grammar of the lettera?|.and yet may be like a frost, a killing frost. Preaching which kills is prayerless preaching. Without prayer, the preacher creates death, and not life.

Power to Achieve. Allan Cox. 1 cass. (Running Time: 50 min.). 8.95 (978-0-88684-085-3(6)) Listen USA.
Shows how achievers become leaders.

Power to Change. Marianne Williamson. 4 cass. (Running Time: 4 hrs.). 1997. reel tape 30.00 (978-1-56170-437-8(7), M820) Hay House.
Lectures based on "A Course in Miracles" includes: No. 1: "Internal Power - The Balance of Conciousness;" No. 2: "Creating the World - Tough Mind, Tender Heart;" No. 3: "Undoing Terrorism - Rebirth & Transformation;" & No. 4: "The Living Temple".

Power to Change. Marianne Williamson. 4 CDs. (Running Time: 14400 sec.). 2006. audio compact disk 23.95 (978-1-4019-0668-9(0)) Hay House.

Power to Change Perception: Forgiveness. Marianne Williamson. Read by Marianne Williamson. 1 cass. (Running Time: 90 mins.). (Lectures on a Course in Miracles). 1999. 10.00 (978-1-56170-254-1(4), M757) Hay House.

Power to Change Your Life. unabr. ed. Rick Warren. (Running Time: 4 hrs. 49 mins. 41 sec.). (Living with Purpose Ser.). (ENG.). 2006. 12.99 (978-0-310-27554-1(7)) Zondervan.

Power to Get In: A Step-by-Step System to Get in Anyone's Door So You Have the Best Chance to... Present Your Offer... Make the Sale... Grow Your Business. Michael A. Boylan. 6 cass. (Running Time: 6 hrs.). 1998. pap. bk. (978-1-55525-081-2(5), 19460A) Nightingale-Conant.
Get faster access to a better future.

Power to Let Go & Live in the Now. Guy Finley. (ENG.). 2006. 7.49 (978-1-929320-59-2(0)) Life of Learn.

Power to Play Winning Soccer: Mental Rehearsal C. D. for Soccer Players. (YA). 2001. 14.99i (978-0-9713586-0-7(5)) Next Level Suc.

Power to Please Set: Delivering Quality Customer Service. George Walther. 6 cass. 59.95 (15050AX) Nightingale-Conant.
Every time you make contact with a customer, you're practicing customer service & building a relationship. This program shows how to build long-lasting & highly profitable relationships. Learn to create an effective referral system...make current customers nine times more likely to buy...& win back ex-customers, your biggest source of untapped profits. Apply these principles to your own career & see your own profits increase automatically.

Power to Predict: How Real Time Businesses Anticipate Customer Needs, Create Opportunities, & Beat the Competition. abr. ed. Vivek Ranadive. Read by Chris Ryan. Frwd. by Frederick W. Smith. (Running Time: 16200 sec.). 2006. audio compact disk 28.00 (978-1-933309-51-4(2)) Pub: A Media Intl. Dist(s): Natl Bk Netwk

Power to Prosper. Kenneth Copeland. 1 cass. 1987. 5.00 (978-0-88114-782-7(6)) K Copeland Pubns.
Biblical teaching on prosperity.

Power to Prosper: The Inner Path to Success. Ruth Ross. Read by Ruth Ross. 6 cass. (Running Time: 50 min. per cass.). 1992. bk. 49.95 set in binder, incl. guide. (978-0-9622313-3-9(9)) Prosper Natural.
Dr. Ruth Ross leads a six-part program for clearing your mind of negative thinking that can block your path to prosperity & abundance.

***Power to Prosper: 21 Days to Financial Freedom.** Michelle Singletary. (Running Time: 6 hrs. 42 mins. 9 sec.). (ENG.). 2010. 14.99 (978-0-310-40647-1(1)) Zondervan.

Power to Stand. Eugene Waller. Read by Peggy Faulkner. 4 cass. 1995. 29.95 Set. (978-0-9648073-0-3(0)) Accente.
Spiritual, religious sermons.

Power to the People. Laura Ingraham. Narrated by Laura Ingraham. (Running Time: 39600 sec.). 2007. audio compact disk 34.99 (978-1-4281-6618-9(1)) Recorded Bks.

Power to Vote Audio CD. Adapted by Benchmark Education Company Staff. Based on a work by Katherine Scraper. (Early Explorers Set C Ser.). (J). (gr. 1). 2008. audio compact disk 10.00 (978-1-60437-528-2(0)) Benchmark Educ.

Power Tool Box Full Year. 4 cass. (Running Time: 4 hrs.). (J). (gr. 1-6). 1998. bk. & ring bd. 619.99 (978-1-57405-042-4(7)) CharismaLife Pub.

Power Tool Box Praise & Worship, Qtr. 1-4, set 3 CD . (J). (gr. 1-7). 1998. audio compact disk 59.95 (978-1-57405-435-4(X)) CharismaLife Pub.

Power Tool Box Praise & Worship, Qtr. 2. 1 CD. (Power Tool Box Ser.). (J). (gr. 1-7). 1998. audio compact disk 15.99 (978-1-57405-430-9(9)) CharismaLife Pub.

Power Tool Box Praise & Worship, Qtr. 3. 1 CD. (Power Tool Box Ser.). (J). (gr. 1-7). 1998. audio compact disk 15.99 (978-1-57405-431-6(7)) CharismaLife Pub.

Power Tool Box Praise & Worship, Qtr. 4. 1 CD. (Power Tool Box Ser.). (J). (gr. 1-7). 1998. audio compact disk 15.99 (978-1-57405-432-3(5)) CharismaLife Pub.

Power Tools for Four-String Bass, Vol. 1. Fred Cockfield. 2001. per. 19.95 (978-0-7866-5124-5(5)) Mel Bay.

Power Tools for Missionaries No. 1: Teaching Investigators to Make & Keep Commitments. Ed Pinegar. 1 cass. 4.98 (978-1-57734-153-6(8), 06005616) Covenant Comms.

Power Tools for Missionaries No. 2: Open Your Mouth & Share the Gospel. Ed Pinegar. 1 cass. 2004. 4.95 (978-1-57734-154-3(6), 06005624) Covenant Comms.

Power Tools for Missionaries No. 3: The Worth of Souls-Activation. Ed Pinegar. 1 cass. 2004. 4.98 (978-1-57734-155-0(4), 06005632) Covenant Comms.

Power Tools for Missionaries No. 4: Staying Motivated as a Missionary. Ed Pinegar. 1 cass. 4.98 (978-1-57734-156-7(2), 06005640) Covenant Comms.

Power Tools Recharged: 125+ Essential Forms & Presentations for Your School Library Information Program. rev. ed. Joyce Kasman Valenza. 2004. pap. bk. 55.00 (978-0-8389-0880-8(2), 0880-2-2700) ALA.

Power Training in the Zone: Increase Energy & Motivation. Kelly Howell. 1 CD. (Running Time: 60 mins.). (ENG.). 2004. audio compact disk 14.95 (978-1-881451-99-0(2)) Brain Sync.
Just slip on your headphones, and start your workout. Within minutes you'll feel an exciting surge of power and energy as your mind transcends daily clutter. An intoxicating fusion of high-beta brain wave frequencies and primal rhythms stimulate your body to:-Blast through blocks-Boost beta-endorphin production-Burn more fat-Dramatically increase heart health.

Power Trio Blues. Dave Rubin. (Inside the Blues Ser.). (ENG.). 1996. 19.99 (978-0-7935-4589-6(7), 0793545897) H Leonard.

Power Twin. Roberto Orellana. 2003. 2.00 (978-0-8297-3935-0(1)); audio compact disk 3.60 (978-0-8297-3933-6(5)) Zondervan.

Power Twins. unabr. ed. Ken Follett. Read by David Case. 4 cass. (Running Time: 1 hr. per cass.). (J). 1992. 24.00 set. (2952); Rental 9.95 set. (2952) Books on Tape.
Two tales for young readers.

Power Twins & the Mystery Hideout. unabr. ed. Ken Follett. Read by David Case. 4 cass. (Running Time: 4 hrs.). 1992. 24.00 (978-0-7366-2153-3(9), 2952) Books on Tape.

Power under Pressure. Robert Kriegel. Read by Robert Kriegel. 6 cass. 1991. 59.95 Set. (1801A) Nightingale-Conant.
Learn to reach new performance peaks & make stress work for you in a positive way.

Power up Collection, Level 1. (J). 2002. (978-0-7398-5096-1(2)) SteckVau.

Power up Collection, Level 2. 2002. (978-0-7398-5131-9(4)) SteckVau.

Power up Collection, Level 3. 2002. (978-0-7398-5166-1(7)) SteckVau.

Power up Collection, Level 4. 2002. (978-0-7398-5201-9(9)) SteckVau.

Power up your Mind: Learn faster, work Smarter. Bill Lucas. Read by Francis Greenslade. (Running Time: 8 hrs. 40 mins.). 2009. 79.99 (978-1-74214-259-3(1), 9781742142593) Pub: Bolinda Pubng AUS. Dist(s): Bolinda Pub Inc

Power up Your Mind: Learn Faster, Work Smarter. unabr. ed. Bill Lucas. Read by Fancis Greenslade. (Running Time: 31200 sec.). 2007. audio compact disk 87.95 (978-1-921334-41-2(X), 9781921334412) Pub: Bolinda Pubng AUS. Dist(s): Bolinda Pub Inc

Power up your Mind: Learn faster, work Smarter. unabr. ed. Bill Lucas. Read by Francis Greenslade. (Running Time: 8 hrs. 40 mins.). 2009. 43.95 (978-1-921415-55-5(X), 9781921415555) Pub: Bolinda Pubng AUS. Dist(s): Bolinda Pub Inc

Power Weight Loss. Betty L. Randolph. Read by Betty L. Randolph. Read by Leonard Baron. Ed. by Success Education Institute International. 1 cass. (Health Ser.). 1989. bk. 14.98 Ocean Format. (978-1-55909-209-8(2), 2P); bk. 14.98 Music Format. (978-1-55909-210-4(6), 2PM); bk. 14.98 Ocean Format. (978-1-55909-207-4(6), 1P); bk. 35.00 Music Format. (978-1-55909-208-1(4), 1PM) Randolph Tapes.
Includes 60,000 messages with the left-right brain.

Power Weight Loss Plus. Prod. by Betty L. Randolph. 1 cass. (Power Weight Loss Works! Ser.). 19.95 (2) Randolph Tapes.

Power Weight Loss Works! Prod. by Betty L. Randolph. 3 cass. 49.95 Set. (TV3P) Randolph Tapes.
This special program is layered & compressed for state-of-the-art programming. Good for your entire family - fast results.

Power Within Us! unabr. ed. Kathleen Gage. Read by Kathleen Gage. 3 cass. 1995. 24.95 set. (978-1-57294-035-2(2), 11-0302) SkillPath Pubns.
NLP is based on mastering a series of techniques designed to tap your full potential & to make the kinds of changes that will produce lasting results.

Power Within You. Pat Williams & Jerry B. Jenkins. 1 cass. 10.00 (SP100055) SMI Intl.
Shed a whole new light on the process of self-motivation. You may begin thinking differently about your priorities & what you want out of life. You will discover greater satisfaction within yourself!.

Power Workout. abr. ed. Roger W. Breternitz. 1 cass. (Running Time: 45 min.). 1985. pap. bk. 9.95 (978-1-893417-25-0(5)) Vector Studios.
Hypnosis: Helps to get the most out of a work-out. Gives new desire to work out more, implants suggestions that one is getting stronger, has more endurance & building muscle.

Power Writing. rev. ed. Robert R. Max & Sarah P. Cerny. 4 cass. (J). (gr. 10-12). 1988. spiral bd. 120.00 incl. wkbk & 3 ref. bks. (978-1-55678-006-6(0), 3000, Lrn Inc) Oasis Audio.
Designed to enable executives, professionals, supervisors, secretaries, salespersons & technicians write clearer & more persuasive letters, memos & reports.

Power 99 Real Estate Vocabulary Builder. 1. 2004. audio compact disk (978-0-9760359-2-3(8)) M Sauer.

Power 99 Vocabulary Builder. Created by Martin Sauer. 1 cass. 2004. (978-0-9760359-0-9(1)) M Sauer.

Powered by Instinct: 5 Rules for Trusting Your Guts. 2007. (978-0-9717999-0-5(3)) Monumentus Pr.

Powerful Communication Skills for Women. Kay Keller. 6 cass. 59.95 Set, incl. wkbk. (137-C47) Natl Seminars.
The way you communicate may be the single most important factor in your success. This program will show you how to build your self-esteem & deal more confidently with problems. You'll learn to communicate effectively in even the most difficult situations.

Powerful Communication Skills for Women, Set. abr. ed. Kay Keller. 2 cass. (Running Time: 3 hrs.). 2000. 17.95 (978-1-886463-87-5(5)) Oasis Audio.

Powerful Communication Techniques: The Foundation of Success. Paul M. Lisnek. Read by Paul M. Lisnek. Ed. by Robert L. Sandidge. 2 cass. (Running Time: 2 hrs.). 1993. SET. (978-1-57654-204-0(1), CPA209) Creat Core.
Presents the fundamentals of effective communication in an educational & entertaining manner.

Powerful Discipline Strategies That Reduce Behavior Problems. abr. ed. Contrib. by Mark Boybton. 4 CDs. (Running Time: 4 hrs. 1 min.). (gr. 6-12). 2005. audio compact disk 89.00 (978-1-886397-68-2(6)) Bureau of Educ.

Powerful Early Intervention Strategies to Help Students Struggling with Reading & Writing: Grades K-2. Perf. by Joan Aldrich Knight. 6 cass. (Running Time: 4 hrs. 26 min.). (J). (gr. k-2). 2003. 89.00 (978-1-886397-55-2(4)) Bureau of Educ.

Powerful Entrepreneur - Hypnosis. 1 CD. (Running Time: 50 minutes). (LBR Relaxation Ser.: No. 5). 1999. audio compact disk (978-0-9749845-4-4(X)) L Rubinstein.
Hypnosis CD. Track 1 is used as a power nap which will wake you up at the end. Track 2 is a used to fall asleep to.

Powerful Esteem. Eldon Taylor. 2 cass. (Running Time: 62 min. per cass.). (Omniphonics Ser.). 29.95 Set. (978-1-55978-808-3(9), 4009) Progress Aware Res.
3-D soundtrack with underlying subliminal affirmations, night & day versions.

Powerful Golf. Speeches. As told by Michael Russ. 1. (Running Time: 77 mins.). 2002. audio compact disk 14.95 (978-0-9720234-0-5(2)) Russ Invis.
"Powerful Living" is living life in your most powerful state of mind. A strong, energetic and confident state where you can accomplish anything you set your mind too. At the heart of the Powerful Living program are several concepts that will assist you in reaching and maintaining this powerful state. These concepts will show you a different way to perceive and respond to the adversity and drama you face in everyday life and help you re-program

An Asterisk (*) at the beginning of an entry indicates that the title is appearing for the first time.

yourself for the life you envision. A life filled with love, joy, success, energy, self-confidence and more. "Powerful Golf" is the first project by Powerful Living International, LLC, and represents an opportunity for every golfer to use the Powerful Living concepts to sharpen the mental side of their golf game. Thereby achieving a lower score and a more enjoyable experience. Golf is a great metaphor for life and provides the perfect proving ground for the Powerful Golf concepts because within a round of golf, you experience much of the same adversity and drama of life, but in a more compressed period of time. Once you have applied the Powerful Golf concepts on the course, experiencing lower scores and playing with more enthusiasm, you can take them into your everyday life and see dramatic improvement there as well."You can take lessons, practice and become the best ball striker on the planet, but your mastery of golf's mental game is what gives you the opportunity to play to your potential".

Powerful Immune System. Eldon Taylor. 1 cass. (Running Time: 62 min.). (Inner Talk Ser.). 16.95 (978-1-55978-300-2(1), 5338A); 16.95 incl. script. (978-1-55978-474-0(1), 5338F) Progress Aware Res.
Soundtrack - Brook with underlying subliminal affirmations.

Powerful Immune System: Classic. Eldon Taylor. Read by Eldon Taylor. Ed. by Leslie Brice. 1 cass. (Running Time: 1 hr.). 1992. 16.95 (978-1-56705-116-2(2)) Gateways Inst.
Self improvement.

Powerful Immune System: Harmonies. Eldon Taylor. Read by Eldon Taylor. Ed. by Leslie Brice. 1 cass. (Running Time: 1 hr.). 1992. 16.95 (978-1-56705-118-6(9)) Gateways Inst.

Powerful Immune System: Ocean. Eldon Taylor. Read by Eldon Taylor. Ed. by Leslie Brice. 1 cass. (Running Time: 1 hr.). 1992. 16.95 (978-1-56705-119-3(7)) Gateways Inst.

Powerful Immune System: Pastoral Theme. Eldon Taylor. 1 cass. 16.95 (978-1-55978-050-6(9), 5338M) Progress Aware Res.

Powerful Immune System: Stream. Eldon Taylor. Read by Eldon Taylor. Ed. by Leslie Brice. 1 cass. (Running Time: 1 hr.). 1992. 16.95 (978-1-56705-120-9(0)) Gateways Inst.

Powerful Leadership Secrets. Roger Burgraff. 8 cass. 1992. 89.50 incl. bklt. (978-0-88432-438-6(9), SO3060) J Norton Pubs.
Teaches skills necessary for successful leadership.

Powerful Life. 2009. audio compact disk 10.99 (978-1-933207-40-7(X)) Ransomed Heart.

Powerful Medical Device Sales 5 Users. Daniel Farb et al. 2005. audio compact disk 349.95 (978-1-59491-277-1(7)) Pub: UnivofHealth. Dist(s): AtlasBooks

Powerful Memory & Concentration, Vol. 5. Jonathan Parker. Read by Jonathan Parker. 1 CD. (Running Time: 1 hr.). (Subliminal Ser.: Vol. 4). 1999. audio compact disk (978-1-58400-046-4(5)) QuantumQuests Intl.
Subliminal affirmations with classical music on compact disc.

Powerful People in Hindu Chart System. Barbara Cameron. 1 cass. 8.95 (043) Am Fed Astrologers.

Powerful Person. Dick Sutphen. 1 cass. (Running Time: 1 hr.). (RX17 Ser.). 1986. 14.98 (978-0-87554-292-8(1), RX101) Valley Sun.
Every day, you become more aware of your inner strength. You now unleash your potential to direct & lead others. You have the power & ability to attain your goals. You are a powerful negotiator & you get what you want. You are as forceful & dynamic as you need to be. Your posture & voice project self-confidence & power. "Power" is your key word for conditioned response.

Powerful Pharmaceutical Sales 5 Users. Daniel Farb et al. 2005. audio compact disk 299.95 (978-1-59491-276-4(9)) Pub: UnivofHealth. Dist(s): AtlasBooks

Powerful Praying: John 15: 6-7. Ed Young. (J). 1978. 4.95 (978-0-7417-1020-8(X), A0020) Win Walk.

Powerful Presentation Skills: How to Get a Group's Attention, Hold People's Interest & Persuade Them to Act. Read by Debra Smith. Perf. by Debra Smith. 4 cass. (Running Time: 6 hrs.). wbk. ed. 59.95 (V10153) CareerTrack Pubns.

Powerful Presentation Skills: How to Get a Group's Attention, Hold People's Interest & Persuade Them to Act. Debra Smith. Read by Debra Smith. 4 cass. (Running Time: 3 hrs. 48 min.). 1998. 59.95 Set incl. 48p. wkbk. (978-1-55977-702-5(8), V10153) CareerTrack Pubns.
With the skills you'll learn in just a few hours, you & your staff will discover proven ways to: increase your visibility & clout...boost your confidence & poise...& get people solidly behind you. You'll learn effective ways to practice your presentations, how to control nervousness, & techniques that will help you project the self-assurance you need to put an audience in the palm of your hand.

Powerful Presentations: A Practical Skills Audio Tape Seminar. unabr. ed. James B. Hightshoe. 5 cass. (Running Time: 3 hrs. 20 min.). 1994. 59.95 Set. (978-1-893039-00-1(5), Speechmasters) Integratd Commns Inc.

Powerful Presentations Skills, Set. Neil Poindexter. Read by Neil Poindexter. 2 cass. (Running Time: 1 hr. 30 mins. per cass.). (National Seminars Ser.). 1998. 17.95 (978-1-886463-45-5(X)) Oasis Audio.
Does the prospect of public speaking strike fear into your heart? This will give you the time-tested fundamentals you will need to be an effective speaker.

Powerful Proofreading & Editing Skills. Michelle Fairfield Poley. Read by Michelle Fairfield Poley. 6 cass. (Running Time: 2 hrs. 6 min.). 1990. 59.95 Set, incl. wkbk. (978-1-878542-23-6(0), 11-0605) SkillPath Pubns.
Program helps listeners develop precise, faster proofreading skills, richer language & style, & professional editing techniques.

Powerful Sales. Read by Michael Russ. Text by Michael Russ. 1 CD. (Running Time: 80 mins.). 2003. audio compact disk 18.95 (978-0-9720234-8-1(8)) Russ Invis.
Achieving success in Professional Sales requires more than mastering fundamental techniques. Sales technique is most powerful when an energetic and confident presence is behind it. Maintaining this powerful presence, however, can be a challenge when negative events and circumstances continually undermine your productivity and success. "Powerful Sales" will empower you by showing you how to overcome adverse situations while maintaining a high level of energy, confidence and attitude! Leading to increased productivity and the time you need to achieve your goals. "Powerful Sales" accomplishes this by describing six life concepts that you can embrace and use right now! Topic include: fine-tuning your "awareness", aligning your "self-talk" with your vision, how the choices you make affect your energy, goal setting, a successful response technique and more. Each concept stands on it's own and has the potential to send your life and career into a whole new direction.

Powerful Self-Talk: Change Your Self-Talk, Change Your Life. Michael Russ. Read by Michael Russ. 1 CD. (Running Time: 30 mins.). 2002. audio compact disk 9.95 (978-0-9720234-5-0(3)) Russ Invis.
Self-Talk is what you think and say about yourself and what you do. You can choose self-talk that is positive and supportive or negative and self-defeating. Powerful Self-Talk provides useful tools and specific steps that you can use to change the direction of your life right now. Use it to help you lose weight, work through an illness, make a sale, achieve better job performance, increase your confidence and self-esteem, achieve any goal and much, much more!!!.

Powerful Selling & Closing. Eldon Taylor. 1 cass. (Running Time: 62 min.). (Inner Talk Ser.). 16.95 incl. script. (978-1-55978-062-9(2), 5309C) Progress Aware Res.
Soundtrack - Musical Themes with underlying subliminal affirmations.

Powerful Selling & Closing: Babbling Brook. Eldon Taylor. 1 cass. 16.95 (978-1-55978-458-0(X), 5309F) Progress Aware Res.

Powerful Selling & Closing: Classic. Eldon Taylor. Read by Eldon Taylor. Ed. by Leslie Brice. 1 cass. (Running Time: 1 hr.). 1992. 16.95 (978-1-56705-066-0(2)) Gateways Inst.
Self improvement.

Powerful Selling & Closing: Easy. Eldon Taylor. Read by Eldon Taylor. Ed. by Leslie Brice. 1 cass. (Running Time: 1 hr.). 1992. 16.95 (978-1-56705-067-7(0)) Gateways Inst.

Powerful Selling & Closing: Ocean. Eldon Taylor. Read by Eldon Taylor. Ed. by Leslie Brice. 1 cass. (Running Time: 1 hr.). 1992. 16.95 (978-1-56705-068-4(9)) Gateways Inst.

Powerful Selling & Closing: Rhythm. Eldon Taylor. Read by Eldon Taylor. Ed. by Leslie Brice. 1 cass. (Running Time: 1 hr.). 1992. 16.95 (978-1-56705-069-1(7)) Gateways Inst.

Powerful Selling & Closing: Stream. Eldon Taylor. Read by Eldon Taylor. Ed. by Leslie Brice. 1 cass. (Running Time: 1 hr.). 1992. 16.95 (978-1-56705-070-7(0)) Gateways Inst.

Powerful Strategies for Dealing with Difficult Parents. abr. ed. Contrib. by Randy Fortenbary. 4 CDs. 2005. audio compact disk 89.00 (978-1-886397-69-9(4)) Bureau of Educ.

Powerful Tools for Activating the Law of Attraction: A Practical Guide to Transform your Life. Christine Sherborne. (ENG.). 2009. audio compact disk 19.95 (978-0-9804386-4-2(0)) Pub: Colourstory AUS. Dist(s): APG

Powerful Witness Preparation. Ronald J. Cohen & Paula M. Demore. 1995. pap. bk. 185.00 (978-0-943380-97-1(9)) PEG MN.

Powerful Witness Preparation. unabr. ed. Ronald J. Cohen. Read by Ronald Jay Cohen. 6 cass. (Running Time: 6 hrs.). pap. bk. 165.00 Set. PEG MN.
Trail-proven strategies that help prepare expert & lay witnesses.

Powerful World of Energy with Max Axiom, Super Scientist. Agnieszka Biskup. Contrib. by Dennis Spears & Colleen Buckman. (Graphic Science Ser.). (ENG.). (gr. 3-4). 2009. audio compact disk 6.95 (978-1-4296-4221-7(1)) CapstoneDig.

Powerhouse: An Intermediate Business English Coursebook. David Evans & David Strutt. 2002. bk. & stu. ed. 15.70 (978-0-582-32542-5(0)); 16.75 (978-0-582-32557-9(9)) AddisonWesley.

Powerhouse: An Intermediate Business English Coursebook. David Evans & David Strutt. 2002. bk. & stu. ed. 15.70 (978-0-582-42086-1(5)); 16.75 (978-0-582-42087-8(3)) Longman.

Powerlessness & Unmanageability & Higher Power, Manipulating & Intellectualizing. 1 cass. (Recovery - The New Life Ser.). 1979. 8.95 (1594G) Hazelden.

PowerLines: How to Communicate with Power & Precision. unabr. ed. Diana Morris. Read by Diana Morris. Perf. by Eric Conger. 1 cass. (Running Time: 1 hrs. 18 min.). 1997. (978-1-891019-01-2(5)) New HeightsMed.
Six communication strategies for jumpstarting your communications effectiveness - in business & in life.

Powermind System: Inspirational Highlights. Michael M. Kiefer. Read by Michael Monroe Kiefer. 2 cass. (Running Time: 2 hrs.). 1995. 18.00 Set. (978-0-9645934-1-1(6)) Kiefer Enterprises.
Inspirational highlights from the book "The Powermind System." Tapes include; the author's story, determining life values, goals, natural talents, the conscious, subconscious & superconscious minds, & 4 personality traits of high achievers.

PowerPoint with Sales Tips: A Thorough & Interactive Guide to PowerPoint Success for Businesspeople That Teaches the Technical Use of PowerPoint Plus Sales & Presentation Applications in an Interactive Program with a Touch of Humor. Daniel Farb & Bruce Gordon. 2004. bk. 79.95 (978-1-59491-112-5(6)) Pub: UnivofHealth. Dist(s): AtlasBooks
PowerPoint with Sales Tips covers thoroughly in one interactive program all the major program features common to all Windows versions that an average business person will need in order to make great presentations and increase sales.

Powerpuff Girls: City of Soundsville - Music from the Powerpuff Girls. 1 cass. (Running Time: 1 hr. 30 mins.). (J). 2002. 9.98 (978-0-7379-0202-0(7), R4 74329); audio compact disk 13.98 (978-0-7379-0204-4(3), R2 74330) Rhino Enter.
Soundtrack to the Powerpuff Girls series, with a twist. The theme music from the show expanded to make "a sweet, tasty, easy to swallow musical treat that you can dance to".

Powerpuff Girls: Heroes & Villains. 1 cass. (Running Time: 1 hr. 30 mins.). (J). 2001. 10.98 (978-0-7379-0119-1(5), R4 75847); 10.98 (978-0-7379-0136-8(5), R2 75847) Rhino Enter.
A sonic powerpuff adventure, with all new songs about Bubbles, Blossom, Buttercup and the infamous villain MoJo JoJo. The album features new music by the Apples in Stereo, Bis, Frank Black, Cornelius, Devo, The Bill Doss, Dressy Bessy, Komeda, Optiganally Yours, Shonen Knife, and the Sugarplastic.

Powerpuff Girls: Heroes & Villains. Perf. by Apples, The et al. 2002. audio compact disk 17.98 (978-0-7379-0179-5(9), 75848) Rhino Enter.
Heroes and Villains is a "sonic Powerpuff adventure," with all new songs about Bubbles, Blossom, Buttercup, and the infamous Villain MoJo JoJo.

Powerpuff Girls: MoJo JoJo's Rising. Adapted by Laura Dower. 1 cass. (Running Time: 1 hr. 30 mins.). (J). 2002. pap. bk. 7.98 (978-0-7379-0177-1(2), R4 76728) Rhino Enter.
Blossom, Bubbles and Buttercup save the world before bedtime. The story chronicles the creation of the Powerpuff Girls' arch-rival MoJo JoJo.

Powers. unabr. ed. Ursula K. Le Guin. Read by Andy Paris. 12 CDs. (Running Time: 14 hrs.). (YA). (gr. 5-8). 2007. audio compact disk 108.75 (978-1-4281-7261-6(0)); 88.75 (978-1-4281-7256-2(4)) Recorded Bks.
Ursula K. Le Guin's haunting epic of survival, selfdiscovery, and hope is third in a sequence that begins with her PEN Award-winning Gifts. Young Gavie sometimes "remembers" the future. But as a slave living among those who feel threatened by the powers of the Marsh people, Gavie must hide his abilities. And then tragic events force the grief-stricken Gavie to flee the only world he's ever known. In his perilous quest for freedom, Gavie must learn to harness his unique gifts or he may never find a place he can call home.

Powers of Attorney. unabr. ed. Louis Auchincloss. Read by Dan Lazar. 8 cass. (Running Time: 8 hrs.). 1980. 48.00 (978-0-7366-0238-9(0), 1234) Books on Tape.
Twelve short stories all centering on members of the fictional law firm of Tower, Tilney, & Webb. The main interest in most of the stories is the vying for position & the search for status that take place within the firm itself. Often a certain character appears in several different stories, each time with a different facet of his personality emphasized.

Powers of Mantras. Sivananda Radha. 1 cass. (Running Time: 90 min.). 1974. 9.95 (978-0-931454-47-9(6)) Timeless Bks.
Guidance is given on the nature & use of Mantra. Detailed instructions on chanting & advice on how to quiet the mind.

Powers That Be. Read by Heywood Hale Broun & David Halberstam. 1 cass. (Running Time: 56 min.). 11.95 (40372) J Norton Pubs.
A talk with David Halberstam about newspaper empires.

Powerscripts Interactive Audio Sales Training: For Automotive Sales, Car Sales. Tony Baricevic. 2008. 149.98 (978-1-61539-139-4(8)) Indep Pub IL.

Powerscripts Interactive Audio Sales Training: For Mortgage Professionals. Tony Baricevic. 2008. 149.98 (978-1-61539-138-7(X)) Indep Pub IL.

PowerStudy , Version 1.5 for Plotnik's Introduction to Psychology. 7th ed. Rod Plotnik & Tony Doyle. 2003. cd-rom 32.95 (978-0-534-58049-0(1)) Wadsworth Pub.

PowerTalk, Bk. 1. Edwin T. Cornelius. 1988. 12.00 (978-0-89209-946-7(1)); 12.00 (978-0-89209-947-4(X)); 12.00 (978-0-89209-948-1(8)) Pace Grp Intl.

PowerTalk, Bk. 2. Edwin T. Cornelius. 1988. 12.00 (978-0-89209-949-8(6)); 12.00 (978-0-89209-950-4(X)); 12.00 (978-0-89209-951-1(8)) Pace Grp Intl.

PowerTalk, Bk. 3. Edwin T. Cornelius. 1988. 12.00 (978-0-89209-952-8(6)); 12.00 (978-0-89209-953-5(4)); 12.00 (978-0-89209-954-2(2)) Pace Grp Intl.

PowerTalk, Bk. 4. Edwin T. Cornelius. 1988. 12.00 (978-0-89209-955-9(0)); 12.00 (978-0-89209-956-6(9)); 12.00 (978-0-89209-957-3(7)); 12.00 (978-0-89209-958-0(5)) Pace Grp Intl.

PowerTapping Other Lifetimes: Your Hidden Resources. Galexis. 2 cass. (Running Time: 3 hrs.). 1995. 17.95 Set. (978-1-56089-036-2(3)) Visionary FL.
Retrieve power lost in other lifetimes by other "yous" to become whole. Release obstacles in your current life. Includes meditation on Side 4.

PowerWords SAT Verbal Prep Cartoon Series: SAT Verbal Prep in Rhythm, Rhyme & Rap. unabr. ed. Edith L. Sennet. Perf. by Myles MacMillan. Illus. by Keith Monse. 1 cass. (Running Time: 1 hr.). (YA). (gr. 7 up). 1992. bk. 11.95 (978-1-879871-08-3(4)) Sennet Lrn Sys.
120 "must know" words. Rap beat, sound effects, funny lyrics & raps for every 10 words. 60 words/20 pix on a side. Interactive reinforcement exercises & cartoon booklet offer multisensory approach to vocabulary. No memorization.

PowerWords SAT VerbalPrep Cartoon Series Set 2: PowerWords SAT Verbal Prep Cartoon Flashcards. Edith L. Sennet. Voice by Edith L. Sennet. (Rhthym Rhyme & Rap). (YA). 1991. 11.95 (978-1-879871-03-8(3)) Sennet Lrn Sys.

PowerXpress Barnabas. bk. 9.95 (978-0-687-03944-9(4)) Abingdon.

PowerXpress Beatitude Attitude. 2008. bk. 9.95 (978-0-687-03963-0(0)) Abingdon.

PowerXpress Dance for Joy. bk. 9.95 (978-0-687-09517-9(4)) Abingdon.

PowerXpress Esther. bk. 9.95 (978-0-687-09514-8(X)) Abingdon.

PowerXpress Feasts & Festivals. bk. 9.95 (978-0-687-07922-3(5)) Abingdon.

PowerXpress Fruits of the Spirit. bk. 9.95 (978-0-687-04033-9(7)) Abingdon.

PowerXpress Here Comes the Judges. bk. 9.95 (978-0-687-04043-8(4)) Abingdon.

PowerXpress into the Bible Adam & Eve. 2004. bk. 9.95 (978-0-687-04151-0(1)) Abingdon.

PowerXpress into the Bible Jesus at the Synagogue. bk. 9.95 (978-0-687-04181-7(3)) Abingdon.

PowerXpress into the Bible Living as Caretakers. 2004. bk. 9.95 (978-0-687-04141-1(4)) Abingdon.

PowerXpress into the Bible Who Is Jesus. bk. 9.95 (978-0-687-04191-6(0)) Abingdon.

PowerXpress into the Bible 3,000 More. bk. 9.95 (978-0-687-03942-5(8)) Abingdon.

PowerXpress into the Promised Land. bk. 9.95 (978-0-687-02039-3(5)) Abingdon.

PowerXpress Jesus Calms the Storm. bk. 9.95 (978-0-687-09457-8(7)) Abingdon.

PowerXpress Jesus in the Temple. bk. 9.95 (978-0-687-09348-9(1)) Abingdon.

PowerXpress Journey to the Cross. bk. 9.95 (978-0-687-09288-8(4)) Abingdon.

PowerXpress Kingdom Parables. bk. 9.95 (978-0-687-04153-4(8)) Abingdon.

PowerXpress Life in Bible Times. bk. 9.95 (978-0-687-09437-0(2)) Abingdon.

PowerXpress Living God's Word Honesty. bk. 9.95 (978-0-687-05661-3(6)) Abingdon.

PowerXpress Living God's Word Peer Pressure Music. 2004. bk. 9.95 (978-0-687-05671-2(3)) Abingdon.

PowerXpress Living God's Word Self-Esteem. 2004. bk. 9.95 (978-0-687-05691-0(8)) Abingdon.

PowerXpress Livng God's Word Sharing & Kindness. 2005. bk. 9.95 (978-0-687-05811-2(2)) Abingdon.

PowerXpress Namaan & the Servant Girl. bk. 9.95 (978-0-687-04073-5(6)) Abingdon.

PowerXpress Noah's Ark. bk. 9.95 (978-0-687-09398-4(8)) Abingdon.

PowerXpress Occupations in Bible Times. bk. 9.95 (978-0-687-09504-9(2)) Abingdon.

PowerXpress Paul's Journey. bk. 9.95 (978-0-687-03954-8(1)) Abingdon.

PowerXpress Peacemakers. bk. 9.95 (978-0-687-09492-9(5)) Abingdon.

PowerXpress Philip & the Ethiopian. bk. 9.95 (978-0-687-04133-6(3)) Abingdon.

PowerXpress Pilate's Plight. bk. 9.95 (978-0-687-04183-1(X)) Abingdon.

PowerXpress Proverbs. bk. 9.95 (978-0-687-04063-6(9)) Abingdon.

PowerXpress Psalm 23. bk. 9.95 (978-0-687-04053-7(1)) Abingdon.

PowerXpress Resurrection & Road to Emmaus. bk. 9.95 (978-0-687-07842-4(3)) Abingdon.

PowerXpress Ruth. 2004. bk. 9.95 (978-0-687-07396-2(0)) Abingdon.

PowerXpress Samuel. Abingdon. 2003. bk. 9.95 (978-0-687-07462-4(2)) Abingdon.

PowerXpress Signs of Faith. bk. 9.95 (978-0-687-07446-4(0)) Abingdon.

PowerXpress Ten Lepers. bk. 9.95 (978-0-687-08101-1(7)) Abingdon.

PowerXpress the Easter Message. bk. 9.95 (978-0-687-04193-0(7)) Abingdon.

PowerXpress the Four Friends. bk. 9.95 (978-0-687-09798-2(3)) Abingdon.

PowerXpress the Golden Rule. bk. 9.95 (978-0-687-03934-0(7)) Abingdon.

PowerXpress the Sower. bk. 9.95 (978-0-687-04163-3(5)) Abingdon.

PowerXpress the Ten Commandments. bk. 9.95 (978-0-687-04192-3(9)) Abingdon.

PowerXpress Triumphal Entry. bk. 9.95 (978-0-687-09474-5(7)) Abingdon.

PowerXpress Two by Two. bk. 9.95 (978-0-687-04083-4(3)) Abingdon.

PowerXpress upon this Rock. bk. 9.95 (978-0-687-03924-1(X)) Abingdon.

PowerXpress Washing Feet. bk. 9.95 (978-0-687-07326-9(X)) Abingdon.

Powhatan's Daughter: The Harbor Dawn, The Dance, Indiana see Poetry of Hart Crane

Powwow Highway. rev. ed. David Seals. (Seven Council Fires of Sweet Medicine Ser.: Act 1). 1996. pap. bk. 17.00 (978-1-887786-27-0(9)) Sky & Sage Bks.

Pox Party. unabr. ed. M. T. Anderson. Read by Peter Francis James. 7 CDs. (Running Time: 8 hrs. 19 mins.). (Astonishing Life of Octavian Nothing, Traitor to the Nation Ser.: Bk. 1). (YA). (gr. 7 up). 2007. audio compact disk 55.00 (978-0-7393-4846-8(9), Listening Lib) Pub: Random Audio Pubg. Dist(s): Random
He is a boy dressed in silks and white wigs and given the best of classical educations. Raised by a mysterious group of rational philosophers known only by numbers, the boy and his mother - a princess in exile from a faraway land - are the only people in their household assigned names. As the boy's regal mother, Cassiopeia, entertains the house scholars with her beauty and wit, young Octavian begins to question the purpose behind his guardians' fanatical studies. Only after he dares to open a forbidden door does he learn the hideous nature of their experiments - and his own chilling role in them.

Pox Party. unabr. ed. M. T. Anderson. Read by Peter Francis James. 7 CDs. (Running Time: 29940 sec.). (Astonishing Life of Octavian Nothing, Traitor to the Nation Ser.: Bk. 1). (ENG.). (J). (gr. 9-12). 2007. audio compact disk 45.00 (978-0-7393-3862-9(5), Listening Lib) Pub: Random Audio Pubg. Dist(s): Random

Poyson Garden: An Elizabethan Mystery. unabr. ed. Karen Harper. Narrated by Davina Porter. 6 cass. (Running Time: 9 hrs.). 1999. 53.00 (978-0-7887-3755-8(4), 95727E7) Recorded Bks.
You've never met a sleuth quite like Elizabeth, the future queen of England. Forced to wait out her ascendancy in the English countryside, the 25-year-old princess has the wit & the courage to make the most of her exile, even when she becomes a target for murde.

Praatpaal: Dutch for Beginners. A. Schoenmakers. 1 cass. (DUT.). 1989. 42.00 Pub: S T Pubng GBR. Dist(s): AK Pr Dist
This audio tape goes with the "Praatpaal," Dutch for beginners. It contains the dialogues together with pronunciation guidance & three songs.

Prabhupada Bhajanas. 1 cass.; 1 CD. 4.95 (CD-5); audio compact disk 14.95 CD. Bhaktivedanta.

Pracital Strategies for Accelerating the Literacy Skills & Content Learning of Your ESL Students, Set. abr. ed. Perf. by Joe Gusman. 6 cass. (Running Time: 4 hrs. 6 mins.). 2000. tchr. ed. 75.00 (978-1-886397-31-6(7)) Bureau of Educ.

Practical Application of Astrological Degrees. Fayette Cometti. 1 cass. 8.95 (058) Am Fed Astrologers.
Fine-tune and/or rectify with practical use of degree interpretations.

Practical Approach to Attitudinal Healing. Thomas Pinkson. 3 cass. 27.00 set. (A0412-88) Sound Photosyn.
A great set to give some one who needs help in the healing process. Strong, supportive, informative & effective.

Practical Approach to Fated Astrology. Jan Popelka. 1 cass. 8.95 (282) Am Fed Astrologers.
Interpret fated indicators & use them in today's world.

Practical Approach to Liens on Real Estate. 1986. bk. 50.00; 25.00 PA Bar Inst.

Practical Approach to Liens on Real Estate. 1998. bk. 99.00 (ACS-2126); bk. 99.00 (ACS-2126) PA Bar Inst.
For those who handle real estate transactions & for the general practitioner as well, the importance of understanding liens on property is crucial. In this concentrated book, the experienced authors highlight the liens you encounter & the procedures necessary to devise prompt solutions to problems you may face.

Practical Approach to Mechanics' Liens. 1999. bk. 99.00 (ACS-1228) PA Bar Inst.
In any real estate market it is vital to have mastered the current issues under the Pennsylvania Mechanics' Lien Law to solve your clients' problems. This explains elements necessary to establish & perfect a lien & also provides tips on waiver & discharge, enforcing the lien & defending against enforcements.

Practical Approach to Success. collector's ed. Jim Cathcart & Tony Alessandra. Read by Jim Cathcart & Tony Alessandra. 14 cass. (Running Time: 14 hrs.). 1984. Rental 14.95 (978-0-7366-0849-7(4), 1800) Books on Tape.
Teaches us how success can be attained in the business world of human relationships.

Practical Approach to Wrongful Termination. Read by Maureen McClain et al. (Running Time: 2 hrs.). 1991. 65.00 Incl. tape materials. (MI-54300) Cont Ed Bar-CA.
Using a sample case, experts conduct initial client interviews, preliminary discovery, & early negotiations. Topics include: witness credibility & appeal; client interview checklists; personnel policies; potential causes of action in contract & tort; mitigation of damages; punitive damages; preparation for depositions; fee arrangements; discrimination & public policy claims; alternative dispute resolution; & negotiation strategies.

Practical Beginning Theory. 7th ed. Bruce Benward & Barbara S. Jackson. (C). 1991. 19.00 (978-0-697-10637-7(3)) Brown & Benchmark.

Practical Benefits of Christianity. unabr. ed. David Barton. Read by David Barton. 1 cass. (Running Time: 1 hrs.). 1996. bk. (978-0-925279-53-8(6)) Wallbuilders.
Most individuals understand the eternal importance of Christianity; but what are its benefits in this world? Discover the specific attributes of Christianity identified by the Founding Fathers as foundational to the preservation of any civil society.

Practical Business Chinese. Wei Hong. 1997. reel tape 9.95 (978-0-8351-2592-5(0), PRBUCT); reel tape 24.95 (978-0-8351-2591-8(2), PRBUBT) China Bks.

Practical Chinese Reader Bk. 1: Traditional & Simplified Character Editions. Beijing Language Institute Staff. 7 cass. (Running Time: 10 hrs. 30 mins.). 49.95 (978-0-88727-086-4(7)) Cheng Tsui.

Practical Chinese Reader Bk. 2: Traditional & Simplified Character Editions. Beijing Language Institute Staff. 7 cass. (Running Time: 10 hrs. 30 mins.). 49.95 (978-0-88727-087-1(5)) Cheng Tsui.

Practical Chinese Reader Bk. 3: Traditional & Simplified Character Editions. Beijing Language Institute Staff. 3 cass. (Running Time: 4 hrs. 30 mins.). 29.50 (978-0-88727-105-2(7)) Cheng Tsui.

Practical Chinese Reader Bk. 4: Traditional & Simplified Character Editions. Beijing Language Institute Staff. 4 cass. (Running Time: 6 hrs.). 34.95 (978-0-88727-106-9(5)) Cheng Tsui.

Practical Christian Life. Read by Wayne Monbleau. 6 cass. (Running Time: 8 hrs.). 1983. 45.00 Set. (978-0-944648-20-9(7), 302) Loving Grace Pubns. *Religious.*

Practical Christian Living. Charles R. Swindoll. 2008. audio compact disk 38.00 (978-1-57972-823-6(5)) Insight Living.

Practical Christian Living. Read by Douglas Wilson. 1989. 9.50 (978-1-59128-230-3(6)); 12.00 (978-1-59128-232-7(2)) Canon Pr ID.

Practical Christian Living: Volume 1. Read by Douglas Wilson. 4 CDs. (ENG.). 2007. audio compact disk 32.00 (978-1-59128-231-0(4)) Canon Pr ID.

Practical Christian Living: Volume 2. Douglas Wilson. (ENG.). 2008. audio compact disk 32.00 (978-1-59128-233-4(0)) Canon Pr ID.

Practical Christianity: Old Testament Principles for Our New Life in Christ. 2001. 23.00 (978-1-57972-376-7(4)) Insight Living.

Practical Christianity: Old Testament Principles for Our New Life in Christ. 2002. audio compact disk 34.00 (978-1-57972-518-1(X)) Insight Living.

Practical Classroom Strategies for Making Inclusion Work (Grades 6 - 12) Narrated by Sonya Heineman Kunkel. 6 cass. (Running Time: 4 hrs. 12 mins.). 2001. 89.00 (978-1-886397-43-9(0)) Bureau of Educ.
A live audio program that includes a comprehensive resource handbook.

Practical Coaching Skills for Managers. Rick Seymour. 4 cass. (Running Time: 5 hrs. 27 min.). 59.95 Set, incl. wkbk., 34p. (Q10183) CareerTrack Pubns.
How to help your people excel in all they do, spark individual achievement, lead a collaborative team effort, & reach group goals.

***Practical Computing.** 2nd ed. Lynn Hogan. (ENG., 2009. pap. bk. 87.67 (978-0-558-21751-8(6)) Pearson Custom.

Practical Conservation in English 2. Eugene J. Hall. (YA). (gr. 9-12). 1981. 45.00 (978-0-686-86691-6(6), 40028) Prentice ESL.

Practical, Creative Strategies for Strengthening Your First Grade Program. abr. ed. Contrib. by Bridget Dwyer. 6 cass. (Running Time: 3 hrs. 20 mins.). 2002. pap. bk. 89.00 (978-1-886397-46-0(5)) Bureau of Educ.
Live audio program including a comprehensive resource handbook.

Practical Demonkeeping. unabr. ed. Christopher Moore. (Running Time: 8.5 hrs. 0 mins.). 2009. 29.95 (978-1-4332-9305-4(6)); 54.95 (978-1-4332-9301-6(3)); audio compact disk 76.00 (978-1-4332-9302-3(1)) Blckstn Audio.

Practical Demonkeeping. unabr. ed. Christopher Moore. Read by Oliver Wyman. 2009. audio compact disk 24.99 (978-0-06-177050-0(7), Harper Audio) HarperCollins Pubs.

***Practical Demonkeeping.** unabr. ed. Christopher Moore. Read by Oliver Wyman. (ENG.). 2009. (978-0-06-190268-0(3), Harper Audio); (978-0-06-190269-7(1), Harper Audio) HarperCollins Pubs.

Practical Discipline Strategies for the Dufficult Young Child. Gene Bedley. 2007. audio compact disk 95.00 (978-1-886397-81-1(3)) Bureau of Educ.

Practical English, No. 3. 2nd ed. Tim Harris & Allan Rowe. 5 cass. (Running Time: 7 hrs. 30 mins.). (ENG.). (C). (ps). 1988. 36.95 (978-0-15-570935-5(6)) Pub: Heinle. Dist(s): CENGAGE Learn

Practical English for Arabic Speakers. 2 CDs. (Running Time: 2 hrs.). 2005. audio compact disk 35.00 (978-1-57970-173-4(6), SEN415D) J Norton Pubs.

Practical English 1, Bk. 1. 2nd ed. Tim Harris & Allan Rowe. 3 cass. (ENG.). (C). 1986. 36.95 (978-0-15-570919-5(4)) Pub: Harcourt Coll Pubs. Dist(s): CENGAGE Learn

Practical English 2. 2nd ed. Tim Harris & Allan Rowe. 1 cass. (Running Time: 90 mins.). (ENG.). (C). 1987. 36.95 (978-0-15-570927-0(5)) Pub: Harcourt Coll Pubs. Dist(s): CENGAGE Learn

Practical ESL Teaching Techniques, Set. J. William McVey. 2 CDs. (Running Time: 2 hrs.). 2005. audio compact disk 59.50 (978-1-57970-182-6(5), S07013) J Norton Pubs.

Practical Everyday Spelling. 3 cass. wbk. ed. 34.95 (GW1055, Natl Textbk Co) M-H Contemporary.
Designed for intermediate level students to practice spelling patterns & sound-letter correspondence while expanding their vocabulary.

Practical Eveyday Spelling Workbook: 3 CDs. Elaine Kirn. 2005. audio compact disk 35.00 (978-1-891077-56-2(2)) Authors Editors.

Practical Evidence. (Running Time: 5 hrs. 30 min.). 1994. 92.00 Incl. 365p. coursebk. (20411) NYS Bar.
Practical summary of the evidentiary principles used at trial. The presentations afford the opportunity to review the basics & to keep up on the changes occurring in the realm of evidentiary rules & procedures at trial.

Practical Exercises for Inner Harmony. 2006. 19.95 (978-0-911203-99-8(0)) New Life.

Practical Exercises for Inner Harmony (Tape Album) 2006. audio compact disk 19.95 (978-0-911203-98-1(2)) New Life.

Practical Geostatistics 2000 Book & CD. Isobel Clark & William V. Harper. (C). 2000. spiral bd. 100.00 (978-0-9703317-2-4(X)) Ecosse NA.

Practical Guide to Estate Planning. Ray Madaff. 2005. audio compact disk 175.00 (978-0-8080-8945-2(5)) Toolkit Media.

Practical Guide to Federal Evidence: Objections, Responses, Rules & Practice Commentary. Contrib. by Anthony J. Bocchino & David A. Sonenshein. 3 cass. 1996. 43.95 Set. (AUDZ290S) NITA.
A working knowledge of the Federal Rules of Evidence & an understanding of their underlying concepts.

Practical Guide to Jazz Band Guitar. David Frackenpohl. 2008. spiral bd. 19.95 (978-0-7866-7690-3(6)) Mel Bay.

Practical Guide to Negotiation. Contrib. by Thomas F. Guernsey. 4 cass. 1996. 53.95 Set. (978-1-55681-511-9(5), AUDZ300S) NITA.
Describes all the basics of a successful negotiation & leads you step by step through the stages & pitfalls.

Practical Guide to Quality Control. James W. Pattillo. 6 cass. 159.00 Incl. wkbk. & quizzer. (CPE2280) Bisk Educ.
Illustrates and explains cost-effective QC policies and procedures and provides practical guidance for developing, implementing, and maintaining a system tailored to your practice.

Practical Guide to US Taxation of International Transactions: 5th Edition Study Problems. rev. ed. Michael S. Schadewald & Robert J. Misey, Jr. (C). 2006. reel tape (978-0-8080-1479-9(X), 90087350) Toolkit Media.

Practical Handbook for the Boyfriend: For Every Guy Who Wants to Be One for Every Girl Who Wants to Build One! unabr. ed. Felicity Huffman & Patricia Wolff. Read by Shelly Frasier. (Running Time: 4 hrs. 30 mins. 0 sec.). (ENG.). 2007. audio compact disk 19.99 (978-1-4001-5332-9(8)) Pub: Tantor Media. Dist(s): IngramPubServ

Practical Handbook for the Boyfriend: For Every Guy Who Wants to Be One for Every Girl Who Wants to Build One. unabr. ed. Felicity Huffman & Patricia Wolff. Read by Shelly Frasier. 4 CDs. (Running Time: 4 hrs. 30 mins. 0 sec.). (ENG.). 2007. audio compact disk 24.99 (978-1-4001-0332-4(0)) Pub: Tantor Media. Dist(s): IngramPubServ
Most dating books are written for women-what a mistake that is. Women know how to date. . .It's men who need the help! At last: a blithe, bold, and bawdy guide to building a better boyfriend. At some point, every guy-player, geek, mama's boy, "regular Joe"-meets a woman who makes him want to be a boyfriend. A good boyfriend. Problem is, unless he's had some first-rate training (by a previous girlfriend, a sister, a mom), he probably doesn't even know what that means. Felicity Huffman and Patricia Wolff come to the rescue with a rollicking-and whip-smart-handbook to navigating the minefield of male-female relationships.

Practical Handbook for the Boyfriend: For Every Guy Who Wants to Be One/for Every Girl Who Wants to Build One. unabr. ed. Felicity Huffman & Patricia Wolff. Read by Shelly Frasier. (Running Time: 4 hrs. 30 mins. 0 sec.). (ENG.). 2007. audio compact disk 49.99 (978-1-4001-3332-1(7)) Pub: Tantor Media. Dist(s): IngramPubServ

Practical Healthcare Self-Massage along Meridians & Acupoints. (CHI.). 2003. 16.95 (978-7-88718-070-4(8), PRHESE) China Bks.

Practical Heart: Four Novellas. unabr. ed. Allan Gurganus. Read by Dan Cashman. 11 cass. (Running Time: 16 hrs. 30 mins.). 2001. 88.00 (978-0-7366-8317-3(8)) Books on Tape.
The works trace how far people will go - through social pretense, sexual and racial secrets - to preserve their own dignity, a necessary mythology. In "The Practical Heart," the narrator's great-aunt, deprived of the family fortune, becomes the young boy's guide to life outside provincial North Carolina. In "Preservation News," a well-born matron eulogizes a gay preservationist who saved everything but his own life. "He's One, Too" chronicles an admired local businessman accused of child molestation. "Saint Monster" reveals a son's memories of a man truly Christ-like and therefore utterly endangered.

Practical Helps for a Hurting Church: A Study of 1 Corinthians 6:12-11:34. 1998. 30.95 (978-1-57972-263-0(6)) Insight Living.

Practical Intuition. Thomas R. Condon. 1 cass. (Expanded Intuition Training Tape Ser.). 12.95 (978-1-884305-72-6(5)) Changeworks.
How to recognize & interpret your hunches, insights & little voices. Hypnotic exercises to apply intuition to practical everyday outcomes. Getting to know the language of your intuitive part.

Practical Issues: Money, Decisions, Housework. Joseph Selbie & Kirtani Selbie. 1 cass. (Ananda Talks about Marriage Ser.). 9.95 (DM-5) Crystal Clarity.
Deals with What we learn by being parents; karkmic implications of having a child; why we need to have fun with our children; the unwanted child; the special role of fathering.

Practical Laboratory Skills Training Guides, Set. E. Prichard. 2003. pap. bk. (978-0-85404-493-1(0)) Royal Soc Chem GBR.

Practical Life of Faith. 1998. 48.95 (978-1-57972-270-8(9)) Insight Living.

Practical Magic. Alice Hoffman. Read by Cherry Jones. 2004. 10.95 (978-0-7435-4565-5(6)) Pub: S&S Audio. Dist(s): S and S Inc

Practical Magic. unabr. ed. Alice Hoffman. Narrated by Christina Moore. 8 CDs. (Running Time: 9 hrs. 30 mins.). 1999. audio compact disk 73.00 (978-0-7887-3396-3(6), C1002E7) Recorded Bks.
Gillian & Sally Owens were brought up by their elderly guardian aunts in a small New England town. But when a grown Gillian returns with her dead husband in the trunk of the car, the sisters must conjure up some real magic to keep Gillian out of jail.

Practical Magic. unabr. ed. Alice Hoffman. Narrated by Christina Moore. 7 cass. (Running Time: 9 hrs. 30 mins.). 1995. 60.00 (978-0-7887-0337-9(4), 94529E7) Recorded Bks.

Practical Medical Spanish, Set. 2nd ed. AMR Staff. 4 cass. (Running Time: 5 hrs.). (AMR Language Ser.). (SPA.). 1999. pap. bk. 49.95 (978-1-886463-39-4(5)) Oasis Audio.
Spanish language learning for medical professionals.

Practical Miracles for Mars & Venus: Nine Principles for Lasting Love, Increasing Success & Vibrant Health in the Twenty-First Century. unabr. ed. John Gray. Read by John Gray. 6 cass. (Running Time: 9 hrs.). 2000. 29.95 (978-0-694-52372-6(0)) HarperCollins Pubs.

Practical Mysticism. unabr. ed. Evelyn Underhill. Narrated by Marni Green. 2006. audio compact disk 19.95 (978-0-9790364-3-9(7)) A Audiobooks.
In Practical Mysticism, Evelyn Underhill distills the essential (and comprehensible) steps that comprise the process of achieving mystical understanding. Though she uses the pantheon of Christian mystics as her guide, her methodology transcends any particular faith, and offers a common-sense approach to self-improvement and enhanced awareness.

Practical Mysticism in Modern Living. Manly P. Hall. 5 cass. (Running Time: 150 min.). 1999. 40.00 set incl. album. (978-0-89314-218-6(2), S800173) Philos Res.

Practical Newspaper Readings. Li Chen-Ch'ing. 5 cass. (Running Time: 5 hrs.). (CHI.). 1988. pap. bk. 61.70 set.; 8.95 ea. Yale Far Eastern Pubns.
Presents recent articles from Taiwan newspapers.

Practical Newspaper Readings. Li Chen-Ch'ing. 5 cass. (Running Time: 5 hrs.). (CHI.). (C). 1988. 44.75 set. (978-0-88710-159-5(3)) Yale Far Eastern Pubns.

Practical Parenting: Giving Your Kids the Tools to Navigate Life's Rough Waters. Montel Williams & Jeffrey Gardere. Read by Montel Williams & Jeffrey Gardere. 2 cass. (Running Time: 3 hrs.). 2000. 18.95 (978-1-58825-003-2(2), 4082) Hay House.

Practical Philosophy Pts. I-II: The Greco-Roman Moralists. Instructed by Luke Timothy Johnson. 12 CDs. (Running Time: 12 hrs.). 2002. bk. 69.95 (978-1-56585-537-3(X), 4473) Teaching Co.

Practical Philosophy Pts. I-II: The Greco-Roman Moralists. Instructed by Luke Timothy Johnson. 12 cass. (Running Time: 12 hrs.). 2002. bk. 54.95 (978-1-56585-539-3), 4473) Teaching Co.

Practical Power of Yoga- Audio Book. Yee Rodney & Coleen Saidman. 2009. 14.98 (978-0-7662-4088-9(6)) Gaiam Intl.

Practical Prayer: Making Space for God in Everyday Life. Anne Tanner. Read by Anne Tanner. Read by Peter Gardiner-Harding. (ENG.). 2002. audio compact disk 18.95 (978-1-55126-348-9(3), 1700) Pub: ANG CAN. Dist(s): U Toronto Pr

Practical Problem Solving. Arynne Simon. 1 cass. 1995. 14.95 (978-1-882389-18-6(2)) Wilarvi Communs.
Learning & building this precise skill. Also a device for measuring accurately the distress in one's life & how to relieve it.

Practical Psychology of the Eternal Mind & Everyday Health. Roger C. Mills. 5 cass. 45.00 set. (A0711-90) Sound Photosyn.
Workshop on the psycho-spiritual principles of Eastern & Western Philosophies which have been developed for application to prevention programs.

Practical Reviews in Anesthesiology. 12 cass. (Anesthesiology Ser.). 245.00 set, 1 cass. per month with 1 yr. subscript. (0896-5315) Ed Reviews.
Digests of the most important articles from the current journals, edited & discussed by experts.

Practical Reviews in Cancer Management. 12 cass. (Cancer Management Ser.). 245.00 set, 1 cass. per month with 1 yr. subscript. (0896-5307) Ed Reviews.

Practical Reviews in Cardiology. 12 cass. (Cardiology Ser.). 245.00 set, 1 cass. per month with 1 yr. subscript. (0896-5463) Ed Reviews.

Practical Reviews in Dermatology. 6 cass. (Dermatology Ser.). 120.00 set, 6 cassettes per year (one every other month) with 1 yr. subscript. (0896-7076) Ed Reviews.

Practical Reviews in Emergency Medicine. 12 cass. (Emergency Medicine Ser.). 245.00 set, 1 cass. per month with 1 yr. subscript. (0896-5382) Ed Reviews.

Practical Reviews in Family Practice. 12 cass. (Family Practice Ser.). 245.00 set, 1 cass. per month with 1 yr. subscript. (0896-5412) Ed Reviews.

Practical Reviews in Gastroenterology. 12 cass. (Gastroenterology Ser.). 245.00 set, 1 cass. per month with 1 yr. subscript. (0896-5439) Ed Reviews.

Practical Reviews in General Surgery. 12 cass. (General Surgery Ser.). 245.00 set, 1 cass. per month with 1 yr. subscript. (0896-5404) Ed Reviews.

Practical Reviews in Internal Medicine. 24 cass. (Internal Medicine Ser.). 285.00 set, 2 cass. per month with 1 yr. subscript. (0896-5323) Ed Reviews.

Practical Reviews in Nuclear Medicine. 12 cass. (Nuclear Medicine Ser.). 245.00 set, 1 cass. per month with 1 yr. subscript. (0896-5331) Ed Reviews.

Practical Reviews in Obstetrics & Gynecology. 12 cass. (Obstetrics & Gynecology Ser.). 245.00 set, 1 cass. per month with 1 yr. subscript. (0896-5390) Ed Reviews.

Practical Reviews in Ophthalmology. 12 cass. (Ophthalmology Ser.). 245.00 set, 1 cass. per month with 1 yr. subscript. (0896-5366) Ed Reviews.

Practical Reviews in Oral & Maxillofacial Surgery. 12 cass. (Oral & Maxillofacial Surgery Ser.). 245.00 set, 1 cass. per month with 1 yr. subscript. (0896-5447) Ed Reviews.

Practical Reviews in Orthodontics. 12 cass. (Orthodontics Ser.). 245.00 set, 1 cass. per month with 1 yr. subscript. (1046-7106) Ed Reviews.

Practical Reviews in Pathology. 12 cass. (Pathology Ser.). 245.00 set, 1 cass. per month with 1 yr. subscript. (0896-534X) Ed Reviews.
Practical Reviews in Pathology - Digests of the most important articles from the current journals, edited & discussed by experts.

Practical Reviews in Pediatric Dentistry. 6 cass. (Pediatric Dentistry Ser.). 145.00 set, 6 cassettes per year (one every other month). (1051-0265) Ed Reviews.
Digests of the most important articles from the current journals, edited & discussed by experts.

Practical Reviews in Pediatrics. 12 cass. (Pediatrics Ser.). 245.00 set, 1 cass. per month with 1 yr. subscript. (0896-5455) Ed Reviews.

Practical Reviews in Psychiatry. 12 cass. (Psychiatry Ser.). 245.00 set, 1 cass. per month with 1 yr. subscript. (0896-5358) Ed Reviews.

Practical Reviews in Radiology. 24 cass. (Radiology Ser.). 285.00 set, 2 cass. per month with 1 yr. subscript. (0896-5374) Ed Reviews.

Practical Reviews in Urology. 12 cass. (Urology Ser.). 245.00 set, 1 cass. per month with 1 yr. subscript. (0896-5420) Ed Reviews.

Practical Solution to Loneliness: Ecc. 4:9-16. Ed Young. 1993. 4.95 (978-0-7417-1984-3(3), 984) Win Walk.

Practical Spanish for Policemen & Firemen see Spanish for Police & Firefighters

Practical Strategies for Achieving Success with Difficult & at Risk Students (Grades 6-12) abr. ed. Narrated by Gail S. Dusa. 6 cass. (Running Time: 3 hrs. 51 mins.). 2001. 85.00 (978-1-886397-39-2(2)) Bureau of Educ.
Live audio program & a comprehensive resource handbook.

Practical Strategies for Achieving Success with Struggling Readers & Writers (Grades 6-12) Contrib. by Larry Lewin. 2008. audio compact disk 89.00 (978-1-886397-80-4(5)) Bureau of Educ.

Practical Strategies for Creating an Outstanding Fifth Grade Program. abr. ed. Perf. by Tarry Lindquist. 6 cass., handbk. (Running Time: 4 hrs. 24 mins.). 2000. 85.00 (978-1-886397-33-0(3)) Bureau of Educ.
Live educator's workshop includes a comprehensive resource handbook.

Practical Strategies for Working Successfully with Difficult Students. abr. ed. Contrib. by Jane Bluestein. 4 CDs. (Running Time: 4 hrs. 40 mins.). 2005. audio compact disk 89.00 (978-1-886397-66-8(X)) Bureau of Educ.

Practical Strategies for Working with Students with Asperger Syndrome & High-Functioning Autism. abr. ed. Contrib. by Kathy Morris. 4 CDs. (Running Time: 3 hrs. 45 mins.). (gr. k-12). 2005. audio compact disk 89.00 (978-1-886397-70-5(8)) Bureau of Educ.

Practical Strategies that Build Literacy in Kindergarten Classrooms. abr. ed. Contrib. by Charlene Sutler Arvizu. 6 cass. (Running Time: 4 hrs. 34 mins.). 2003. 89.00 (978-1-886397-51-4(1)) Bureau of Educ.
Live audio program including a comprehensive resource book.

Practical Tips for Beating Depression. Eknath Easwaran. 1 cass. (Running Time: 54 min.). 1989. 7.95 (978-1-58638-591-0(7), PT) Nilgiri Pr.
Discusses the mechanics of depression & suggests practical strategies for banishing it from our lives. No life is free from trouble, but we can train our minds to be steady in all situations. Learn to meet life's ups & downs with grace & wisdom.

Practical Truth. Ed Rabel. Read by Bill Bell. 2 cass. (Running Time: 3 hrs.). 2000. 13.95 (978-0-87159-826-4(4)) Unity Schl Christ.

Practical Vedanta One. unabr. ed. Vivekananda. Read by Bruce Robertson. 1 cass. (Running Time: 53 min.). 1987. 7.95 (978-1-882915-03-3(8)) Vedanta Ctr Atlanta.
The nature & description of Vedanta philosophy & practices.

Practical View of Egolessness. Swami Amar Jyoti. 1 cass. 1976. 9.95 (K-76) Truth Consciousness.
Spirituality applied to commerce, professions & relationships. The fully perfect practicality of the egoless ones. Easy to accept a guru, difficult to follow the master's discipline.

Practical Ways to Help When Tragedy Strikes: 2007 CCEF Annual Conference. Featuring Paul Randolph. (ENG.). 2007. audio compact disk 11.99 (978-1-934885-08-6(8)) New Growth Pr.

Practical Ways to Improve Your Communication. Robert Phillips & Rob Phillips. 6 cass. (Running Time: 9 hrs.). 1990. pap. bk. 49.50 incl. wkbk. (978-0-88432-182-8(7), S08100) J Norton Pubs.
This program will help improve listening ability, task-oriented reading & basic writing style. Specific techniques show how to make the most of information sources, avoid the paperwork morass & organize ideas so they can be effectively presented.

Practical Ways to Improve Your Communication, Set. Rob Phillips. 4 CDs. (Running Time: 4 hrs.). 2006. audio compact disk 49.50 (978-1-57970-380-6(1), S08100D, Audio-For) J Norton Pubs.
Get beyond basics with this practical program focusing on the critical importance of good communications in your personal and professional life. The first thing this program teaches is how to improve your listening skills. Although we spend more time listening than in any other communications activity, we never receive any training. Read better and faster, no matter what your reading habits are now. You'll find out how to identify central ideas quickly and to scan to find specific facts fast. Write clearly with real impact. Begin by learning to identify and avoid the 4 biggest problems: being too wordy, using the wrong voice, hiding behind formality, and skimping on specifics. This program will help you identify your bad habits and teach you some good ones. No theory here, just practical tips and plenty of practice.

Practical Web Research in a Nutshell: Capitol Learning Audio Course. Peggy Garvin. Prod. by TheCapitol.Net. (ENG.). 2008. 47.00 (978-1-58733-086-5(5)) TheCapitol.

Practical Wisdom. Jack Deere. 1 cass. (Running Time: 90 mins.). (Proverbs Ser.: Vol. 1). 2000. 5.00 (JD08-001) Morning NC.
Practical wisdom for everyday living is brought to life in Jack's thorough exposition of this important book of the Bible.

***Practical Wisdom.** unabr. ed. Barry Schwartz & Kenneth Sharpe. Read by Barry Schwartz. (Running Time: 11 hrs. 0 mins. 0 sec.). (ENG.). 2010. audio compact disk 39.99 (978-1-4423-3948-4(9)) Pub: S&S Audio. Dist(s): S and S Inc

Practical Wisdom Set: Making the Most of Every Moment. Dan Millman. 6 cass. 1994. 59.95 (10680AX) Nightingale-Conant.
In this program, Dan Millman - martial arts expert, world champion athlete & best-selling author of Way of the Peaceful Warrior - reveals specific practices & principles for improving your mental clarity, emotional serenity & physical vitality. He shows you how to tap into your unlimited powers of expression, creativity & courage. And he provides practical wisdom for manifesting your hopes & dreams & making the most of every moment of your life. Includes workbook.

***Practically Radical: Not-So-Crazy Ways to Transform Your Company, Shake up Your Industry, & Challenge Yourself.** unabr. ed. William C. Taylor. (ENG.). 2011. (978-0-06-202721-4(2), Harper Audio) HarperCollins Pubs.

Practically Shameless: How Shadow Work Helped Me Find My Voice, My Path, & My Inner Gold. Alyce Barry. Frwd. by Cliff Barry. Illus. by Cindy Kalman. (ENG.). 2008. audio compact disk 24.95 (978-0-9798326-2-8(4)) Prac Shame.

Practicas: Preparacion al Diploma del Espanol como Lengua Extranjera: Basico. J. Arribas & R. De Castro. 1 cass. (Running Time: 1 hr. 30 min.). (SPA.). 2001. 26.95 (978-84-7711-089-7(1), EDI891) Pub: Edelsa ESP. Dist(s): Continental Bk
This review contains exercises in oral comprehension, written expression, grammar and vocabulary. Each unit has a cultural theme so the students will be learning both the language and the lifestyle. An excellent preparation for the exam or for perfection of the language.

Practicas: Preparacion al Diploma del Espanol como Lengua Extranjera: Inicial. J. Arribas & R. De Castro. 1 cass. (Running Time: 1 hr. 30 min.). (SPA.). 2001. 26.95 (978-84-7711-091-0(3), EDI913E) Pub: Edelsa ESP. Dist(s): Continental Bk

Practicas: Preparacion al Diploma del Espanol como Lengua Extranjera: Superior. J. Arribas & R. De Castro. 1 cass. (Running Time: 1 hr. 30 min.). (SPA.). 2001. 26.95 (978-84-7711-087-3(5), EDI875E) Pub: Edelsa ESP. Dist(s): Continental Bk

Practicas De Audicion, Vol. 1. audio compact disk 35.95 (978-88-536-0014-1(4)) EMC-Paradigm.

Practicas De Audicion, Vol. 2. audio compact disk 35.95 (978-88-536-0138-4(8)) EMC-Paradigm.

Practicas y Oraciones de la Iglesia Catolica: De un Manual para el Catolico de Hoy en Audio, No. 2. Redemptorist Pastoral Communications Staff. 1 cass. (Running Time: 62 min.). (SPA.). 1992. 9.95 (978-0-89243-443-5(0)) Liguori Pubns.
This two-tape series in Spanish presents the basic beliefs, practices, & prayers of the living Catholic tradition. Tape 2 focuses on time-honored practices that guide Catholics in living according to Church teaching. It offers practical information on sacraments, holy days, & the liturgical seasons.

Practice. unabr. ed. Myrtle Smyth. Prod. by David Keyston. 1 cass. (Running Time: 69 mins.). (Myrtle Smyth Audiotape Ser.). 2000. 8.95 (978-1-893107-37-3(X), M29) Healing Unltd.
Lecture of metaphysical content on the subject - the practice of Christian Science healing.

Practice & Improve Your English. Saxon Penne. 4 cass. (Running Time: 60 min.). (Practice & Improve Ser.). 1988. pap. bk. 39.95 (978-0-8442-5682-5(X), 5682X, Contemporary) McGraw-Hill Trade.
Features listening program to help master conversational English.

Practice & Improve Your English Plus. Saxon Penne. 4 cass. (Running Time: 4 hrs.). (Practice & Improve Ser.). 1988. pap. bk. (978-0-8442-5696-2(X), 5696X, Contemporary) McGraw-Hill Trade.
Features a listening program to help master conversational English-Advanced program.

Practice & Improve Your German Plus. Ruth Rach. 4 cass. (Running Time: 4 hrs.). (Practice & Improve Ser.). 1995. pap. bk. 39.95 (978-0-8442-2569-2(X), Natl Textbk Co) M-H Contemporary.

Practice & Improve Your Italian. 4 cass. (Running Time: 4 hrs.). (Practice & Improve Ser.). 1991. 39.95 Set. (Passport Bks) McGraw-Hill Trade.

Practice & Improve Your Italian Plus. 4 cass. (Running Time: 4 hrs.). (Practice & Improve Ser.). 1991. 39.95 Set. (Passport Bks) McGraw-Hill Trade.

Practice & Procedure in PA.'s Appellate Courts. (Running Time: 4 hrs.). 1999. bk. 99.00 (ACS-2271) PA Bar Inst.
Read the "ins & outs" of the appeals process in Pennsylvania from those who know it firsthand.

Practice Before the Pennsylvania Human Relations Commission. 1999. bk. 99.00 (ACS-2326) PA Bar Inst.
Whether an employment or housing lawyer who practices before the PHRC every day, or a business, government or general practice lawyer who is there on occasion, you need to understand the Commission's unique structure & procedures in order to represent your clients effectively.

Practice Book on English Stress & Intonation. Kenneth Croft. (J). (gr. 9-12). 1961. 90.00 (978-0-87789-125-3(7), 1181) ELS Educ Servs.

***Practice Books for the Flute: Omnibus Edition Books 1-5.** Trevor Wye. (ENG.). 2006. pap. bk. 45.95 (978-1-84609-625-9(1), 1846096251) Pub: Novello & Co GBR. Dist(s): H Leonard

Practice Continuation Agreements: A Practice Survival Kit. 2nd ed. John Eads. 2007. audio compact disk 43.75 (978-0-87051-682-5(5)) Am Inst CPA.

Practice Exercises for the TOEFL. 5th ed. Sharpe. (Toefl Test Preparation Ser.). 2003. audio compact disk 21.95 (978-0-7641-7740-8(0)) Barron.

Practice Exercises for the TOEFL, Pack. 6th rev. ed. Pamela J. Sharpe. 2007. audio compact disk 21.99 (978-0-7641-9316-3(3)) Barron.

***Practice Exercises for the TOEFL Audio CD Pack.** 7th rev. ed. Pamela Sharpe. (ENG.). 2011. audio compact disk 21.99 (978-1-4380-7032-2(2)) Barron.

Practice Exercises in a Manual of Modern Greek 1. 7 cass. (Running Time: 6 hrs. 40 min.). 95.00 Set. (GRO430) J Norton Pubs.

Practice in the Philidelphia Court of Common Pleas. 1987. bk. 105.00 incl. book.; 40.00 cass. only.; 65.00 book only. PA Bar Inst.

Practice in Uninsured Motorist Cases. 1986. bk. 60.00 incl. book.; 35.00 cass. only.; 25.00 book only. PA Bar Inst.

Practice Makes Perfect for Rotten Ralph. Jack Gantos. Read by Jack Gantos. Illus. by Nicole Rubel. (J). (gr. k-3). 2006. audio compact disk 12.95 (978-1-59519-924-9(1)) Live Oak Media.

Practice Makes Perfect for Rotten Ralph: A Rotten Ralph Rotten Reader. unabr. ed. Jack Gantos. Read by Jack Gantos. Illus. by Nicole Rubel. 1 CD. (Running Time: 13 mins.). (J). (ps-2). 2007. bk. 28.95 (978-1-59519-926-3(8)) Live Oak Media.

Practice Music Cha Cha Cha. Conversa-Phone Institute Staff & Betty White. 1 cass. (Running Time: 55 min.). (Betty White Practice Dance Music Ser.). 1990. 9.95 (978-1-56752-112-2(6)) Conversa-phone.
Big Band music with tempos to practice specific Ballroom Dance. Slow medium & fast tempos are provided for each dance.

Practice Music Fourteen Different Dances. Conversa-Phone Institute Staff & Betty White. 1 cass. (Running Time: 55 min.). (Betty White Practice Dance Music Ser.). 1990. 9.95 (978-1-56752-119-1(3)) Conversa-phone.

Practice Music Fox Trot. Conversa-Phone Institute Staff & Betty White. 1 cass. (Running Time: 55 min.). (Betty White Practice Dance Music Ser.). 1990. 9.95 (978-1-56752-109-2(6)) Conversa-phone.

Practice Music Hustle. Conversa-Phone Institute Staff & Betty White. 1 cass. (Running Time: 55 min.). (Betty White Practice Dance Music Ser.). 1990. 9.95 (978-1-56752-110-8(X)) Conversa-phone.

Practice Music Latin Dances. Conversa-Phone Institute Staff & Betty White. 1 cass. (Running Time: 55 min.). (Betty White Practice Dance Music Ser.). 1990. 9.95 (978-1-56752-116-0(9)) Conversa-phone.

Practice Music Lindy (Swing) Conversa-Phone Institute Staff & Betty White. 1 cass. (Running Time: 55 min.). (Betty White Practice Dance Music Ser.). 1990. 9.95 (978-1-56752-113-9(4)) Conversa-phone.

Practice Music Merengue. Conversa-Phone Institute Staff & Betty White. 1 cass. (Running Time: 55 min.). (Betty White Practice Dance Music Ser.). 1990. 9.95 (978-1-56752-118-4(5)) Conversa-phone.

Practice Music Rhumba. Conversa-Phone Institute Staff & Betty White. 1 cass. (Running Time: 55 min.). (Betty White Practice Dance Music Ser.). 1990. 9.95 (978-1-56752-114-6(2)) Conversa-phone.

Practice Music Tango. Conversa-Phone Institute Staff & Betty White. 1 cass. (Running Time: 55 min.). (Betty White Practice Dance Music Ser.). 1990. 9.95 (978-1-56752-117-7(7)) Conversa-phone.

Practice Music Waltz. Conversa-Phone Institute Staff & Betty White. 1 cass. (Running Time: 55 min.). (Betty White Practice Dance Music Ser.). 1990. 9.95 (978-1-56752-115-3(0)) Conversa-phone.

Practice of Austerity. Swami Jyotirmayananda. Read by Swami Jyotirmayananda. 1 cass. (Running Time: 60 min.). 12.99 (724) Yoga Res Foun.

Practice of Detachment. Swami Jyotirmayananda. 1 cass. (Running Time: 1 hr.). 1990. 12.99 Yoga Res Foun.

***Practice of Godliness.** unabr. ed. Jerry Bridges. Narrated by Lloyd James. (ENG.). 2005. 14.98 (978-1-59644-107-1(0), Hovel Audio) christianaud.

Practice of Godliness: Godliness Has Value for All Things. unabr. ed. Jerry Bridges. Read by Lloyd James. (Running Time: 27000 sec.). 2006. audio compact disk 55.00 (978-0-7861-6633-6(9)) Blckstn Audio.

Practice of Godliness: Godliness Has Value for All Things. unabr. ed. Jerry Bridges. Narrated by Lloyd James. 6 CDs. (Running Time: 7 hrs. 18 mins. 0 sec.). (ENG.). 2005. audio compact disk 24.98 (978-1-59644-109-5(7), Hovel Audio); lp 19.98 (978-1-59644-108-8(9), Hovel Audio) christianaud.
What makes someone Godly? Scripture tells us that God has given us "everything we need for life and godliness." But what makes a Christian godly? In The Practice of Godliness, Jerry Bridges examines what it means to grow in Christian character and helps us establish the foundation upon which that character is built. Bridges opens our eyes to see how character formation affects the way we relate to God, to ourselves, and to others. In order to live godly lives, we need an inward foundation of God-centeredness. This book will help you establish that foundation and then build an outward structure of Godlikeness.

Practice of Humility. Swami Jyotirmayananda. 1 cass. (Running Time: 45 min.). 1990. 10.00 Yoga Res Foun.

Practice of Meditation, No. 1. Swami Jyotirmayananda. 1 cass. (Running Time: 45 min.). 1990. 10.00 Yoga Res Foun.

Practice of Meditation, No. 2. Swami Jyotirmayananda. 1 cass. (Running Time: 45 min.). 1990. 10.00 Yoga Res Foun.

Practice of Meditation, No. 3. Swami Jyotirmayananda. 1 cass. (Running Time: 45 min.). 1990. 10.00 Yoga Res Foun.

Practice of Pranayama: An In-Depth Guide to the Yoga of Breath. unabr. ed. Richard Rosen. (ENG.). 2010. 59.95 (978-1-59030-778-6(X)) Pub: Shambhala Pubns. Dist(s): Random

Practice of Psychotherapy: Foundations - Mythology & the Shamanic Tradition, Nos. 13, 14, 15. Carl Faber. 3 cass. (Running Time: 3 hrs. 45 min.). 1982. 28.50 (978-0-918026-48-4(2), SR 53-526) Perseus Pr.

Practice of Psychotherapy: Foundations - Phenomenology & Existential Philosophy, Nos. 25, 26 & 27. Carl Faber. 3 cass. (Running Time: 3 hrs. 45 min.). 1984. 24.50 (978-0-918026-47-7(4), SR 60-183); 5.00 cass. No. 25. Perseus Pr.

Practice of the Presence of God. Brother Lawrence. Narrated by Edward Lewis. (Running Time: 3 hrs.). (C). 2002. 20.95 (978-1-59912-701-9(6)) Iofy Corp.

Practice of the Presence of God. Prod. by InSpirit Tapes and CDs. 1 CD. (Running Time: 63 mins.). 2007. audio compact disk 9.95 (978-1-932758-00-9(3)) InSpirit Tapes.

Practice of the Presence of God. unabr. ed. Brother Lawrence. Read by Edward Lewis. 2 cass. (Running Time: 2 hrs. 30 mins.). 2002. 17.95 (978-0-7861-2355-1(9), 3014); audio compact disk 16.00 (978-0-7861-9397-4(2), 3014) Blckstn Audio.
A record of the conversations and letters exchanged between Brother Lawrence and people in his community, who came to him for advice once they noticed his passionate living for God.

Practice of the Presence of God: Being Conversations & Letters of Nicholas Herman of Lorraine. unabr. ed. Brother Lawrence. 1. (Running Time: 1 hr. 6 mins. 0 sec.). (ENG.). 2004. audio compact disk 12.98 (978-1-59644-001-2(5), Hovel Audio) christianaud.
Nicholas Herman (c. 1605-1691) was born in Lorraine, France and served as a cook and shoe repairer at a Carmelite monastery. He was only a lay member of the order, and walked with a limp from injuries incurred as a soldier, yet his private thoughts provide a wellspring of devotional insight and refreshment.

***Practice of the Presence of God: Being Conversations & Letters of Nicholas Hermann of Lorraine.** unabr. ed. Brother Lawrence. Narrated by Scott Brick. (ENG.). 2004. 8.98 (978-1-59644-000-5(7), Hovel Audio) christianaud.

Practice of the Presence of God: Pure Gold Audio Classics. John Wesley & Brother Lawrence. Read by Charlie Glaize. 2008. 19.99 (978-1-4245-0193-9(8)) Tre Med Inc.

Practice of the Wild: Essays. abr. ed. Gary Snyder. Read by Gary Snyder. 2 cass. (Running Time: 3 hrs.). 1991. 16.95 (978-0-939643-33-2(2), NrthWrd Bks) TandN Child.
The author reads from a new collection of essays.

Practice of Tibetan Buddhism. unabr. ed. Lama A. Govinda. 1 cass. (Running Time: 47 min.). 1960. 11.00 (06303) Big Sur Tapes.

Practice of Vichar (Enquiry) Swami Jyotirmayananda. 1 cass. (Running Time: 1 hr.). 1990. 12.99 Yoga Res Foun.

Practice of Yoga in the World. (112) Yoga Res Foun.

Practice of Yoga in the World. Swami Jyotirmayananda. 1 cass. (Running Time: 1 hr.). 1990. 12.99 Yoga Res Foun.

***Practice Resurrection: A Conversation on Growing up in Christ.** unabr. ed. Eugene H. Peterson. Narrated by Grover Gardner. (ENG.). 2010. 16.98 (978-1-59644-060-9(0), Hovel Audio); audio compact disk 26.98 (978-1-59644-059-3(7), Hovel Audio) christianaud.

***Practice Tests for IGCSE English as a Second Language Extended Level Book 2 Audio CDs (2) Listening & Speaking.** Marian Barry & Susan Daish. (Running Time: 2 hrs. 39 mins.). (Georgian Press Ser.). (ENG.). 2010. audio compact disk 24.00 (978-0-521-18633-9(1)) Cambridge U Pr.

***Practice Tests for IGCSE English as a Second Language: Listening & Speaking, Core Level Audio CDs (2)** Marian Barry. (Georgian Press Ser.). (ENG.). 2010. audio compact disk 33.00 (978-0-521-14058-4(7)) Cambridge U Pr.

***Practice Tests for IGCSE English as a Second Language: Listening & Speaking, Extended Level Audio CDs (2)** Marian Barry. (Georgian Press Ser.). (ENG.). 2010. audio compact disk 33.00 (978-0-521-14054-6(4)) Cambridge U Pr.

Practice These Principles. 1 cass. (Running Time: 1 hr. 30 min.). 1989. 6.50 (978-0-933685-18-5(1), TP-36) A A Grapevine.
Features personal experiences of Alcoholics Anonymous members with the Twelve Traditions of AA.

Practice to Deceive. unabr. ed. David Housewright. Read by Brian Emerson. 6 cass. (Running Time: 8 hrs. 30 mins.). 1998. 44.95 (978-0-7861-1421-4(5), 2297) Blckstn Audio.
The brash & resourceful St. Paul private investigator Holland Taylor takes on an unpromising embezzlement case, with the help of his elegant attorney lady love & an eccentric computer-genius friend. Someone seems anxious to derail his investigation. The game becomes serious when an unscrupulous businessman is found dead & Taylor first is suspected of the crime & then is shot at himself. Millions of dollars are at stake, as well as the reputations of the most powerful people in the cities. As the killer pursues him, Taylor races to put together the last pieces of the puzzle, find the money, & catch the people who are willing to do anything to stop him.

Practice to Deceive: A Holland Taylor Mystery. unabr. ed. David Housewright. Read by Brian Emerson. (Running Time: 28800 sec.). 1991. audio compact disk 29.95 (978-0-7861-0231-0(4)) Blckstn Audio.

Practice with Pictures Learn through Pictures. Akiko Adachi. 2004. pap. bk. 40.95 (978-4-89358-576-9(2)) Pub: Bonjinsha JPN. Dist(s): Cheng Tsui

Practicing Catholic. unabr. ed. James Carroll. Read by Bill Weideman. 1 MP3-CD. (Running Time: 15 hrs.). 2009. 39.97 (978-1-4233-8732-9(5), 9781423387329, Brinc Audio MP3 Lib); 24.99 (978-1-4233-8731-2(7), 9781423387312, Brilliance MP3); 39.97 (978-1-4233-8734-3(1), 9781423387343, BADLE); 24.99 (978-1-4233-8733-6(3), 9781423387336, BAD); audio compact disk 99.97 (978-1-4233-8730-5(9), 9781423387305, BriAudCD Unabrid); audio compact disk 34.99 (978-1-4233-8729-9(5), 9781423387299) Brilliance Audio.

Practicing Catholic. unabr. ed. Daniel E. Pilarczyk. Read by Daniel E. Pilarczyk. 2 cass. (Running Time: 3 hrs.). 1998. 14.95 (978-0-86716-374-2(7), A3747) St Anthony Mess Pr.
Pilarcyzk says "Being Catholic involves certain specific religious practices which arise from Catholic faith & tradition & which, taken together, constitute a way of being religious in a truly Catholic fashion".

Practicing Golf: A System for Generating the Best Golf You Can Play. Chuck Hogan. Ed. by Mike Altman. 1991. pap. bk. 24.95 (978-0-9624504-2-6(1)) Sports Enhance.

Practicing History: Selected Essays. unabr. ed. Barbara W. Tuchman. Read by Pam Ward. (Running Time: 11 hrs. 30 mins.). 2009. 29.95 (978-1-4417-0617-1(8)); 72.95 (978-1-4417-0613-3(5)); audio compact disk 105.00 (978-1-4417-0614-0(3)) Blckstn Audio.

Practicing History: Selected Essays. unabr. ed. Barbara W. Tuchman. Read by Walter Zimmerman. 9 cass. (Running Time: 13 hrs. 30 min.). 1988. 72.00 (978-0-7366-1362-0(5), 2261) Books on Tape.
A collection of the authors best essays & articles from forty-five years of writing.

Practicing History: Selected Essays. unabr. ed. Barbara W. Tuchman. Narrated by Aviva Skell. 7 cass. (Running Time: 9 hrs. 45 mins.). 1987. 60.00 (978-1-55690-423-3(1), 87510E7) Recorded Bks.
Essays on history from Vietnam, Israel & the Great war to writing history & its meaning. Includes: When Does History Happen? How We Entered World War I, etc.

Practicing in California under the New Rules of Professional Conduct. Read by Karen A. Betzner & Ronald E. Mallen. (Running Time: 45 min.). 1989. 19.00 Incl. 48p. tape materials. (MI-52920) Cont Ed Bar-CA.
Learn about which employees of the opposing parties you are allowed to contact, & how; who is a client when representing a corporation; conflict of interest in your relations with an opposing party's counsel; what kind of client marketing is allowed; when you may sell your law practice, & more. Includes a valuable summary of the changes, new rules, & charts which cross-reference the old & new rules.

Practicing Mind: Bringing Discipline & Focus into Your Life. unabr. ed. Thomas M. Sterner. Ed. by Lin Bloom McDowell. (ENG.). 2007. audio compact disk 23.95 (978-0-9776572-1-6(3)) Mountain Sage.

Practicing Peace in Times of War: A Buddhist Perspective. unabr. ed. Pema Chödrön. (Running Time: 5400 sec.). (ENG.). 2006. audio compact disk 19.95 (978-1-59030-414-3(4), Shamb Audio) Pub: Shambhala Pubns. Dist(s): Random

Practicing the Power of Now: Essential Teachings, Meditations, & Exercises from the Power of Now. Eckhart Tolle. Read by Eckhart Tolle. (Playaway Adult Nonfiction Ser.). (ENG.). 2009. 40.00 (978-1-60775-590-6(4)) Find a World.

***Practicing Your Energy Skills for Life & Relationships: Meditations, Real-life Applications, & More.** John Friedlander. (Running Time: 10 hrs.). (Psychic Psychology Ser.). (ENG.). 2011. audio compact disk 75.00 (978-1-58394-277-2(7)) Pub: North Atlantic. Dist(s): Random

Practitioner's Clinic: Structuring Partnerships & Business Succession Plans. Instructed by Thomas Langdon & Frank Rainaldi. 4 CDs. (Running Time: 270 mins.). 2004. audio compact disk 39.95 (978-1-59280-137-4(4)) Marketplace Bks.
It's not the size of your prospect list that's the secret to success for financial professionals - it's your ability to bring creative solutions to the individualized needs of clients. Now, this comprehensive practitioner's "clinic" can take your problem-solving skills to exciting new levels. Two top industry experts introduce a wealth of powerful strategies for structuring business succession plans and partnerships that aid clients by avoiding big tax hits and meeting both existing and future contingencies. Using an extensive "Case Study" format, Frank Rainaldi addresses the most prevalent partnership arrangements, the vast array of scenarios each presents, and it's recommended planning solution. Tom Langdon then assesses every scenario from a legal perspective - highlighting what questions you need to ask in each situation, and which choices best suit individual cases. By evaluating each situation from a planning and legal perspective - you'll be prepared to service almost any client that walks through your door, while guiding existing clients on to increased success and savings as their circumstances change over time. And these two pros cover - it all - including:- Virtually every type of partnership & corporation - and the unique aspects of each. S-corps, C-corps, family-corps, limited liability partnerships and more - all are explored in exceptional detail.- "What If" scenarios for any situation imaginable - so you can easily alter your advice to accommodate a multitude of unexpected conditions.- The benefits and disadvantages of everything from cross-purchase agreements, stock-redemption plans, hybrid buy-sell agreements - and a great deal more.Nearly 5 hours of in-depth, case-by-case analysis make this "clinic" an invaluable leaming and reference tool for any financial professional.

Prader-Willi Syndrome - A Bibliography & Dictionary for Physicians, Patients, & Genome Researchers. Compiled by Icon Group International, Inc. Staff. 2007. ring bd. 28.95 (978-0-497-11278-3(7)) Icon Grp.

Prague Counterpoint. abr. ed. Bodie Thoene & Brock Thoene. 2 cass. (Running Time: 3 hrs.). (Zion Covenant Ser.: Bk. 2). 2001. 22.99 (978-1-58926-001-6(5)) Oasis Audio.
She had escaped the Nazi terror. But a nation's priceless treasures were compelling her to return. In Vienna Prelude, Elisa Lindheim risked her life helping others escape pre-World War II Austria. The climactic ending finds her safely in Czechoslovakia, but not for long. A million other lives are endangered & she cannot still their silent cry for help. Prague Counterpoint finds Elisa watching in horror as Hitler's forces sweep through her beloved Vienna & he directs his ambition toward the takeover of Czechoslovakia. As Europe slides irrevocably toward the brink of war, Elisa is torn between the Underground's lofty political goals & the safety of two little boys & underneath it all, her heart yearns for John. Will she ever see him again?.

Prague Counterpoint. unabr. ed. Bodie Thoene & Brock Thoene. Narrated by Susan O'Malley. 11 cass. (Running Time: 16 hrs.). (Zion Covenant Ser.: Bk. 2). 2002. 76.95 (978-0-7861-2167-0(X), 2917); audio compact disk 112.00 (978-0-7861-9548-0(7), 2917) Blckstn Audio.
She has escaped the Nazi Terror. But a nation's priceless treasures are compelling her to return. Prague Counterpoint finds Elisa watching in horror as Hitler's forces sweep through her beloved Vienna; he then directs his ambition toward the takeover of Czechoslovakia. As Europe slides irrevocably toward the brink of war, Elisa is torn between the Underground's lofty political goals and the safety of two little boys and underneath it all, her heart yearns for John. Will she ever see him again.

Prague Orgy. Philip Roth. Narrated by George Guidall. 2 cass. (Running Time: 2 hrs. 15 mins.). 1985. 22.00 (978-1-4025-0764-9(X)) Recorded Bks.

Prague Walks. unabr. ed. Ivana Edwards. Read by Ivana Edwards. 2 cass. (Running Time: 3 hrs.). 2001. 18.00 Penton Overseas.

Prague Walks Audio Guide. Ivana Edwards. Prod. by Carol Shapiro. 1 cass. (Running Time: 3 hrs.). (Audiowalks Ser.: Vol. 6). 2000. (978-1-890489-05-2(0)) Sound Trvl FRA.
Audio version of the travel guidebook.

Praire Home Companion's. 25th anniv. ed. Perf. by Garrison Keillor. 4 cass., 4 CDs. (Running Time: 6 hrs.). audio compact disk 44.95 CD. HighBridge.
Includes highlights from other recordings plus new, never-before-available material.

Prairie. unabr. ed. James Fenimore Cooper. Read by Noah Waterman. 11 cass. (Running Time: 16 hrs.). 1995. 76.95 (978-0-7861-0911-1(4), 1705) Blckstn Audio.
The final chapter in James Fenimore Cooper's great saga of American frontiersman Natty Bumppo. Though nearly 90 in 1804, Bumppo is still competent as a frontiersman & trapper, now on the Great Plains. Once more he is drawn into conflict with society in the form of an emigrant party led by the surly Ishmael Bush & his miscreant brother-in-law Abiram White. And once again this great man of nature is called upon to exhibit his courage & resourcefulness to rescue the innocent.

Prairie, Set. unabr. ed. James Fenimore Cooper. Read by Noah Waterman. 11 cass. 1999. 76.95 (FS9-34209) Highsmith.

Prairie Cabin: A Norwegian Pioneer Woman's Story. Jocelyn Riley. 1 cass. (Running Time: 17 min.). (YA). 1991. 8.00 (978-1-877933-38-7(4)) Her Own Words.
Documentary.

Prairie Dawn's Purple Book. Jane Zion Brauer. 1986. 24.50 (978-0-19-434174-5(7)) OUP.

Prairie Home Companion. unabr. ed. Garrison Keillor. (ENG., 2008. audio compact disk 19.95 (978-1-59887-603-1(1), 1598876031) Pub: HighBridge. Dist(s): Workman Pub

Prairie Home Companion. 20th abr. anniv. unabr. ed. Garrison Keillor. 4 CDs. (Running Time: 6 hrs.). (ENG.). 1994. audio compact disk 36.95 (978-1-56511-106-6(0), 1565111060) Pub: HighBridge. Dist(s): Workman Pub

Prairie Home Companion. 25th anniv. unabr. abr. ed. Garrison Keillor. Contrib. by Garrison Keillor. 5 CDs. (Running Time: 5 hrs. 30 mins.). 1999. audio compact disk 39.95 (978-1-56511-325-1(X), 156511325X) Pub: HighBridge. Dist(s): Workman Pub

Prairie Home Companion: It's Only a Show. unabr. ed. Garrison Keillor. Told to Garrison Keillor. 2 CDs. (Running Time: 2 hrs.). (ENG.). 2006. audio compact disk 24.95 (978-1-59887-027-5(0), 1598870270) Pub: HighBridge. Dist(s): Workman Pub

Prairie Home Companion: July 6-7 1984. 10th anniv. abr. ed. Garrison Keillor. 2 cass. (Running Time: 17 hrs. 32 mins.). (ENG.). 1991. 17.95 (978-0-942110-07-4(2)) Pub: HighBridge. Dist(s): Workman Pub
One of the best live radio shows recorded. Includes a special anniversary edition of "News from Lake Wobegon".

Prairie Home Companion: 2nd Annual Farewell Performance. unabr. ed. Garrison Keillor. (ENG., 2008. audio compact disk 19.95 (978-1-59887-602-4(3), 1598876023) Pub: HighBridge. Dist(s): Workman Pub

Prairie Home Companion Anniversary Album: The First Five Years. abr. unabr. ed. Garrison Keillor. Contrib. by Garrison Keillor. (Running Time: 5400 sec.). (ENG., 2008. audio compact disk 19.95 (978-1-59887-600-0(7), 1598876007) Pub: HighBridge. Dist(s): Workman Pub

Prairie Home Companion English Majors: A Comedy Collection for the Highly Literate. unabr. ed. Garrison Keillor. Contrib. by Garrison Keillor. 2 CDs. (Running Time: 2 hrs. 30 mins.). (ENG., 2008. audio compact disk 24.95 (978-1-59887-588-1(4), 1598875884) Pub: HighBridge. Dist(s): Workman Pub

Prairie Home Companion Never Better: Stories from Lake Wobegon. unabr. ed. Garrison Keillor. (Running Time: 8100 sec.). (ENG.). 2007. audio compact disk 24.95 (978-1-59887-094-7(7), 1598870947) Pub: HighBridge. Dist(s): Workman Pub

Prairie Home Companion the Final Performance. unabr. ed. Garrison Keillor. (ENG., 2008. audio compact disk 19.95 (978-1-59887-601-7(5), 1598876015) Pub: HighBridge. Dist(s): Workman Pub

Prairie Home Companion the 4th Annual Farewell Performance. unabr. ed. Garrison Keillor. (ENG., 2008. audio compact disk 19.95 (978-1-59887-604-8(X), 159887604X) Pub: HighBridge. Dist(s): Workman Pub

Prairie Home Companion 10th Anniversary: Was Ten Years on the Prairie. unabr. ed. Read by Garrison Keillor. (Running Time: 1 hr. 45 mins.). (ENG.). 2006. audio compact disk 19.95 (978-1-59887-048-0(3), 1598870483) Pub: HighBridge. Dist(s): Workman Pub

Prairie Home Companion's 25th Anniversary Collection. unabr. ed. Garrison Keillor. 4 cass. (Running Time: 6 hrs.). 2000. 35.95 (P241) Blckstn Audio.
We should, from time to time, divert ourselves from meatier audio books & like a kid in a pie eating contest, plunge our face into satisfying humor. Includes 23 songs & jingles plus 15 monologues about Lake Wobegon, including Truckstop & The Living Flag.

***Prairie Home: the Early Stuff.** unabr. ed. Garrison Keillor. Contrib. by Garrison Keillor. (ENG.). 2010. audio compact disk 24.95 (978-1-61573-522-8(4), 1615735224) Pub: HighBridge. Dist(s): Workman Pub

Prairie Prose... And Cons. 2nd ed. Illus. by Antoinette Clark. Photos by Bobbie Evans-Truesdale. 1999. audio compact disk 13.00 (978-0-9700848-1-1(1)) J Hilderbrant Enter.

Prairie Quilts. Jocelyn Riley. 1 cass. (Running Time: 15 min.). (YA). 1990. 8.00 (978-1-877933-36-3(8)) Her Own Words.
Documentary.

Prairie Waters by Night see Carl Sandburg Reading Cool Tombs & Other Poems

***Prairie Yuletide.** Ernest Haycox. 2009. (978-1-60136-456-2(3)) Audio Holding.

Prairie Yuletide. Ernest Haycox. (Running Time: 0 hr. 30 mins.). 2000. 10.95 (978-1-60083-547-6(3)) Iofy Corp.

Prairyerth. abr. ed. William Least Heat-Moon. Read by Cotter Smith. 4 cass. (Running Time: 4 hrs.). 25.00 Set. S&S Audio.

Praise! Robert Laughlin. Read by Robert Laughlin. 1 cass. (Running Time: 1 hr.). 1994. pap. bk. 25.00 (978-0-929983-19-6(X), SR 207 463) New Schl Am Music.
Weaves basic course in Chord Piano around songs of inspiration.

Praise. Derek Prince. 1 cass. (B-4081); 5.95 (033) Derek Prince.
We need never approach God empty-handed, since the fruit of our lips is a sacrifice always acceptable to him.

Praise: Psalms, Proverbs & Praise with Integrity's Hosanna! 12 cass. 24.97 (978-0-529-06984-9(9), WBC-30) Nelson.

Praise Adonai: Celebrating 40 Years of Jerusalem Reunited. Contrib. by Paul Wilbur & Don Moen. 2007. audio compact disk 13.99 (978-5-557-63541-7(6)) Integrity Music.

Praise Album One. Merlin R. Carothers. Read by Merlin R. Carothers. 6 cass. (Running Time: 6 hrs.). (Merlin R. Carothers Tape Ser.: Vol. I). 1980. 11.95 (978-0-943026-11-4(3)) Carothers.
Selected sermons by Merlin R. Carothers, author of "Prison to Praise".

Praise Album Two. Merlin R. Carothers. Read by Merlin R. Carothers. 6 cass. (Running Time: 6 hrs.). (Merlin R. Carothers Tape Ser.: Vol. II). 1980. 11.95 (978-0-943026-12-1(1)) Carothers.
Selected sermons.

Praise & Intercession. Don Potter. 3 cass., 3 videos. 15.00 Set. (DP01-000) Morning NC.
Provides a deeper understanding of praise & intercession. Don shares his heart & demonstrates the principles behind the different Hebrew words for worship.

Praise & Worship. 1 CD. audio compact disk 5.98 (978-1-57908-467-7(2), 5342) Platinm Enter.

Praise & Worship, Set. 1 cass., 1 CD. audio compact disk 4.98 (978-1-57908-468-4(0), 5342) Platinm Enter.

Praise & Worship, Vol. 1. Prod. by Randy Ray. Narrated by Ron Jenson. Intro. by Bill Bright. 1 cass. 1984. 9.98 (978-1-57919-115-3(0)) Randolf Prod.

Praise & Worship 2002: Gospel Heroes. 2002. audio compact disk Provident Mus Dist.

Praise Be to God: Uplift in Scripture & Song. Karla Carey. 1 cass. (Running Time: 60 min.). (Inspiration in Words & Music Ser.). 1988. 10.00 (978-1-55768-536-0(3)) LC Pub.

Praise Christmas Prime Mover Cd Combo Listening Cd. Dennis Allen & Nan Allen. 2000. audio compact disk 5.00 (978-0-633-01557-2(1)) LifeWay Christian.

Praise Every Morning: Intermediate-Advanced Level. Laurindo Almeida. Contrib. by Didi Almeida. 1996. pap. bk. 19.95 (978-0-7866-2100-2(1), 95983BCD) Mel Bay.

Praise for an Urn see Poetry of Hart Crane

Praise God, the Sun Still Rises see Tales of the Desert

Praise Her in the Gates AudioBook: The Calling of Christian Motherhood. Nancy Wilson. Read by Karen Hieronymus. 4. (ENG.). 2008. audio compact disk 20.00 (978-1-59128-575-5(5)) Canon Pr ID.

Praise Him: Campmeetin' Live. Perf. by Oak Ridge Boys, The et al. 1 CD. (Running Time: 60 mins.). 2000. audio compact disk 7.99

(978-0-7601-3459-7(6), SO33210) Pub: Brentwood Music. Dist(s): Provident Mus Dist
Songs include: "Heaven's Jubilee," "He Did It All for Me," "Homeland," "Roses Will Bloom Again," "He's Got the Whole World in His Hands" & more.

Praise Him! Praise Him! Dennis Allen. 1999. 11.98 (978-0-633-03948-6(9)); 75.00 (978-0-633-03947-9(0)); audio compact disk 16.98 (978-0-633-03946-2(2)); audio compact disk 85.00 (978-0-633-03945-5(4)) LifeWay Christian.

Praise Hymn Wedding Songbook. Brentwood-Benson Music Publishing Staff & Praise Hymn. 2007. pap. bk. 39.95 (978-5-557-61413-9(3), Brentwood-Benson Music) Brentwood Music.

Praise Hymns & Songs. O. D. Hall. 2000. audio compact disk 85.00 (978-0-633-00526-9(6)) LifeWay Christian.

Praise Hymns & Songs Collection for Blended Worship Choral Cd. O. D. Hall. 2000. audio compact disk 16.98 (978-0-633-00522-1(3)) LifeWay Christian.

Praise in His Presence Live. 2002. audio compact disk Provident Mus Dist.

Praise in the Dance: Stepping into God's Glory. Regina Evans. Contrib. by Jim Walton. 1 CD. (Running Time: 22 mins.). 2001. audio compact disk 10.00 (978-0-9718329-0-9(0)) R Evans.
A unified line dance that is captivating, fun and easy to learn.

Praise Keeper. Perf. by Bill Murk. 1 Tape. (Running Time: 45 min). 1997. 9.99 (978-0-9725443-3-7(X)); audio compact disk 14.99 (978-0-9725443-2-0(1)) Pub: Myrrh Pub. Dist(s): STL Dist NA
Voilin and orchestra like you've never heard it before! Christian radios across the country list this as one of their favorite and most frequently played intrumental CDs.

Praise Lift Him Up. 1 CD. (Running Time: 38 mins.). 2002. audio compact disk 6.99 (978-1-57583-533-4(9), 3003CD) Twin Sisters.
Whenever one comes into the presence of God, their life is forever changed. With these all new, original praise and worship songs kids, and adults, may experience the life, changing love of Jesus Christ as they bow down and worship the One most worthy of praise.

Praise on the Inside. Contrib. by J. Moss. (Soundtraks Ser.). 2007. audio compact disk 8.99 (978-5-557-60866-4(4)) Christian Wrld.

Praise Singer. unabr. ed. Mary Renault. Read by Grover Gardner. 7 cass. (Running Time: 10 hrs. 30 min.). 1986. 56.00 (978-0-7366-0872-5(9), 1822) Books on Tape.
In this novel of ancient Greece, Renault turns to the world of the port - the bard since the time of the tyrants, the Persian wars & a great flowering of the arts.

Praise Song for The Land: Poems of Hope & Love & Care. Kofi Anyidoho. 2002. (978-9988-550-45-5(6)) Sub-Saharan GHA.

Praise Songs. David C. Cook Publishing Company Staff. (VBS 2009 Ser.). (ENG.). (J). 2009. audio compact disk 12.99 (978-2-608-00878-7(X)) David C Cook.

***Praise Songs by Children of Faith: Sing A Long Songs.** unabr. ed. Harry H. Harrison, Jr. 2001. audio compact disk 6.98 (978-7-472-02295-2(0)) Nelson.

Praise the King. Perf. by Cindy Morgan. 1 cass. 1999. 7.98 (978-0-7601-2799-5(9)) Brentwood Music.

Praise the Lord! Gospel Music in Washington D. C. Perf. by Herbert Jackson et al. 1 CD. (Running Time: 60 min.). 1999. 9.99 Smithsonian Folkways.
Notes include history of performers.

Praise the Lord: Litanies, Prayers & Occasional Services. Gennifer Brooks. 1997. audio compact disk 10.95 (978-0-7880-0854-2(4)) CSS OH.

Praise the Lord Together. Prod. by Twin Sisters Productions Staff. 1 CD. (Running Time: 30 mins). (J). 2005. audio compact disk 6.99 (978-1-57583-812-0(5)) Twin Sisters.
Bring kids and their friends together in worship with this contemporary collection of Bible songs and favorite choruses. Celebrate God's mighty power and His amazing love for us all! Praise the Lord together singing, "Alleluia, Alleluia!" BONUS! The ENHANCED CD includes 81 pages of sheet music that can be printed from your own computer!.

Praise the Risen Lord: (An Easter Musical) Mary Kay Beall. 2000. audio compact disk 59.95 (978-0-634-02594-5(5)) H Leonard.

Praise to the Lord! Roger Hoffman & Melanie Hoffman. 1 cass.; 1 CD. 1998. 10.95 (978-1-57008-535-2(8), Bkcraft Inc); audio compact disk 15.95 CD. (978-1-57008-546-8(3), Bkcraft Inc) Deseret Bk.

Praise to the Lord: Great Hymns of the Church. Schola Cantorum of St. Peter the Apostle Staff. Directed By J. Michael Thompson. 2005. 14.95 (978-0-8146-7930-2(7)); audio compact disk 16.95 (978-0-8146-7931-9(5)) Liturgical Pr.

Praise to the Man. Michael Ballam. 1 cass. 9.98 (978-1-55503-752-9(6), 1100556) Covenant Comms.
A portrait of the prophet Joseph in word & song.

Praise to You. Contrib. by Virtue. (Christian World Soundtraks Ser.). 2007. audio compact disk 8.99 (978-5-557-60863-3(X)) Christian Wrld.

Praise Works! 5 cass. 11.95 Incl. album. (978-0-943026-27-5(X), A4) Carothers.

Praise Worship: Revelation. 1 cass. 6.98 (978-0-529-07152-1(5), WBC-35) Nelson.

Praise You: Satb. Contrib. by Johnathan Crumpton et al. Prod. by Ed Kee. (ENG.). 2008. audio compact disk 24.99 (978-5-557-47020-9(4), Brentwood-Benson Music) Brentwood Music.

Praise You in the Storm. Contrib. by Casting Crowns. (Sound Performance Soundtracks Ser.). 2005. audio compact disk 5.98 (978-5-558-78693-4(0)) Pt of Grace Ent.

Praise Your Way Through. 1998. 6.00 (978-1-58602-058-3(7)) E L Long.

Praisesong for the Widow. Paule Marshall. (4131) Am Audio Prose.

Praising Yahweh: Twenty-One Years in the Top Nation of All Nations. 1 cass. (Running Time: 47 min.). 1999. 8.00 (978-1-890967-41-3(6)); audio compact disk 12.00 (978-1-890967-42-0(4)) Hse of Yahweh.
Songs expressing sheer delight in Father Yahweh & His Laws. He is declared beautiful, wonderful, & awe-inspiring among His people.

Praising Your Way to Victory. Speeches. Joel Osteen. 1 Cass. (Running Time: 30 Mins). 2000. 6.00 (978-1-59349-084-3(4), JA0084) J Osteen.

Prana & Pranic Healing: Experience of Breath & Energy. Swami Shankardev Saraswati & Jayne Stevenson. (ENG.). 2005. audio compact disk 33.00 (978-0-9803496-3-4(X)) Big Shakti AUS.

Prana, Power & Transformation. Swami Amar Jyoti. 1 dolby cass. 1986. 9.95 (O-26) Truth Consciousness.
Relaxation, control & right use of Prana. Repaying the debts we incur on earth. Stepping stones to higher transformation. Maintaining the balance of Nature.

Prana Upasana, No. 1. Swami Jyotirmayananda. 1 cass. (Running Time: 1 hr.). 1990. 12.99 Yoga Res Foun.

Prana Upasana, No. 2. Swami Jyotirmayananda. 1 cass. (Running Time: 1 hr.). 1990. 12.99 Yoga Res Foun.

Pranayama: May Our Breath Be Our Prayer. Nubia Teixeira. Told to Jai Uttal & Ben Leinbach. 2 CDs. (Running Time: 7200 sec.). 2005. audio compact disk 24.95 (978-1-59179-250-5(9), M898D) Sounds True.

Pranayama: The Breath of Life. Scripts. Richard Cushing Miller. 3 cassettes. (Running Time: 180 Minutes). (ENG.). 1996. 24.95 (978-1-893099-07-4(5)) Anahata Pr.
The practice of pranayama presented in the nondual wisdom tradition. Recorded live during an actual workship presentation. Includes discussion, practie and questions and aswers.

Prancer. Stephen Cosgrove. Illus. by Carol Heyer. (J). (gr. k-7). 1989. pap. bk. 12.95 (978-1-55868-041-8(1)) Gr Arts Ctr Pub.

Praneshhacharya's Dilemma. unabr. ed. Julian C. Hollick. 1 cass. (Running Time: 60 min.). (Passages to India Ser.). 1991. 15.00 (978-1-56709-015-4(X), 1015) Indep Broadcast.
Since Indians operate within circles of dependence & interdependence of family, caste, language & religion, the modernization of sections of Indian society has created new tensions & contradictions between individual & community roles & identities.

Prarieblomman: The Prairie Blossoms for an Immigrant's Daughter. Linda K. Hubalek. 1 cass. (Butter in the Well Ser.: Bk. 2). 1994. 9.95 (978-1-886652-05-7(8)) Butterfld Bks.

Prater Violet. unabr. ed. Christopher Isherwood. Read by J. Paul Boehmer. (ENG.). 2010. audio compact disk 22.95 (978-1-61573-074-2(5), 1615730745) Pub: HighBridge. Dist(s): Workman Pub

Pratique du Neerlandais. 1 cass. (Running Time: 1 hr., 30 min.). (DUT & FRE.). 2000. bk. 75.00 (978-2-7005-1349-3(5)) Pub: Assimil FRA. Dist(s): Distribks Inc

Pray. Contrib. by CeCe Winans. 2005. audio compact disk 8.99 (978-5-558-75060-7(X)) Christian Wrld.

Pray: Your Path to Every Victory. Kenneth Copeland. 12 cass. 1982. 60.00 Set. (978-0-938458-20-3(5)) K Copeland Pubns.
Biblical teaching on prayer.

Pray-along Rosary. Music by Sheldon Cohen. 2004. audio compact disk 12.95 (978-0-87946-255-0(8), 413) ACTA Pubns.

Pray-Along Rosary. abr. ed. Prod. by Sheldon Cohen. (Running Time: 096 min.). 2001. 9.95 (978-0-87946-222-2(1)) ACTA Pubns.

Pray-along Rosary: (Including the Mysteries of Light) Arranged by Sheldon Cohen. 1 cass. (Running Time: 65 mins.). 2004. 9.95 (978-0-87946-242-0(6), 317) ACTA Pubns.

Pray & Be Rich: The Bible's 7 Secrets of Success. 2001. (978-0-9704029-7-4(X)) NewsMax Media.

Pray & Die. unabr. ed. Stella Whitelaw. 6 cass. (Running Time: 8 hrs.). (Soundings Ser.). (J). 2006. 54.95 (978-1-84283-899-0(7)) Pub: ISIS Lrg Prnt GBR. Dist(s): Ulverscroft US

Pray & Play Songs for Young Children. Prod. by Group Publishing Staff. 1 cass. (J). 1997. 9.99 (978-0-7644-3045-9(9)) Group Pub.

***Pray for Silence.** unabr. ed. Linda Castillo. Narrated by Kathleen McInerney. 9 CDs. (Running Time: 11 hrs. 30 mins.). 2010. audio compact disk 89.95 (978-0-7927-7161-6(3)) AudioGO.

***Pray for Silence.** unabr. ed. Linda Castillo. Read by Kathleen McInerney. 9 CDs. (Running Time: 11 hrs.). (Kate Burkholder Ser.). 2010. audio compact disk 39.99 (978-1-4272-0971-9(5)) Pub: Macmill Audio. Dist(s): Macmillan

***Pray for the Land: How to Pray for Israel.** Lynne Hammond. 2010. audio compact disk 6.00 (978-1-57399-469-9(3)) Mac Hammond.

Pray for the Peace of Jerusalem. Contrib. by Don Moen & Chris Thomason. Prod. by Mark Gasbarro & Paul Mills. 2002. audio compact disk 16.98 (978-5-550-14677-4(0)) Integrity Music.

Pray Hard. Pam Walker. Read by Marguerite Gavin. 2 CDs. (Running Time: 9000 sec.). (J). (ps-7). 2005. audio compact disk 24.00 (978-0-7861-7881-0(7)) Blckstn Audio.

Pray Hard. Pamela Walker. Read by Marguerite Gavin. (Running Time: 7 hrs. 0 mins.). 2005. 29.95 (978-0-7861-8064-6(1)) Blckstn Audio.

Pray Hard. Pamela Walker. Read by Marguerite Gavin. 2 cass. (Running Time: 7 hrs. 0 mins.). (J). 2005. 22.95 (978-0-7861-3499-1(2)) Blckstn Audio.

Pray Hard. Pamela Walker. Narrated by Marguerite Gavin. (Running Time: 2 hrs. 30 mins.). 2005. 17.95 (978-1-59912-575-6(7)) Iofy Corp.

Pray On. Contrib. by Babbie Mason. 2001. audio compact disk 9.99 (978-5-551-04275-4(8)) Sprg Hill Music Group.

Pray the Price. Terry Teykl. 2 cass. 1998. 10.00 (978-1-57892-048-8(5)) Prayer Pt Pr.
Sermon teaching call to prayer for mainline churches.

Pray the Rosary. Wayne Weible. 1 cass. (Running Time: 1 hr. 18 mins.). 1994. 10.95 (978-1-881788-01-0(6)) Weible Columns.

Pray the Rosary with Daughters of St Paul. Daughters of St Paul. 2001. audio compact disk 19.95 (978-0-8198-5944-0(3), 332-291) Pauline Bks.

Prayer. Lawrence Paolicelli. 1 cass. (Inspiring Presentations from the National Rosary Congress Ser.). 2.50 (978-1-56036-095-7(X)) AMI Pr.

Prayer. Lester Sumrall. 10 cass. (Running Time: 15 hrs.). 1999. 40.00 (978-1-58568-105-1(9)) Sumrall Pubng.

***Prayer.** unabr. ed. Richard J. Foster. (ENG.). 2007. (978-0-06-137610-8(8), Harper Audio) HarperCollins Pubs.

Prayer: A Closer Walk with God. Fred Faller. 3 cass. 2006. 16.00 (978-1-57782-205-9(6)) Discipleshp.

Prayer: A History. abr. ed. Interview. Susan Mahoney & Marieke Meyer. 1 CD. (Running Time: 2400 sec.). 2006. audio compact disk 15.95 (978-0-660-19621-3(2), CBC Audio) Canadian Broadcasting CAN.

Prayer: Does It Make Any Difference? unabr. ed. Philip Yancey. (Running Time: 12 hrs. 0 mins. 0 sec.). (ENG.). 2006. 21.99 (978-0-310-27252-6(1)) Zondervan.

***Prayer: Finding the Heart's True Home.** unabr. ed. Richard Foster. Narrated by Terence Aselford. (ENG.). 2007. 16.98 (978-1-59644-452-2(5), Hovel Audio) christianaud.

Prayer: Finding the Heart's True Home. unabr. ed. Richard J. Foster. (ENG.). 2007. (978-0-06-133750-5(1), Harper Audio) HarperCollins Pubs.

Prayer: Finding the Heart's True Home. unabr. ed. Richard J. Foster. Read by Terence Aselford. (Running Time: 36000 sec.). 2007. audio compact disk 29.95 (978-0-06-133749-9(8), Harper Audio) HarperCollins Pubs.

Prayer: Finding the Heart's True Home. unabr. ed. Richard J. Foster. Read by Terence Aselford. (Running Time: 9 hrs. 30 mins. 0 sec.). (ENG.). 2007. audio compact disk 29.98 (978-1-59644-451-5(7)) christianaud.

Prayer: Learning the God Language. Maureen Schuler. 3 cass. (Running Time: 2 hrs. 53 min.). 1995. 27.95 Set. (TAH325) Alba Hse Comns.
Excellent for those trying to develop a realistic relationship with God who calls us into balance. Soothing for those trying to understand the hard things of life.

Prayer: Let's Communicate. 1 CD. (Running Time: 60 mins.). 2007. audio compact disk 9.95 (978-0-9717687-7-2(3)) Excorde Inc.

Prayer: Long Distance Is the Next Best Thing to Being There & Family Fiasco? Jack Marshall. 1 cass. 7.98 (978-1-55503-307-1(5), 06004296) Covenant Comms.
Youth talk.

Prayer: Manifest a State of Grace. unabr. ed. Kelly Howell. 1 cass. (Running Time: 60 min.). 1998. 11.95 (978-1-881451-58-7(5)) Brain Sync.
Scientific evidence has revealed that prayer influences the world in unexpected and extraordinary ways. It is a medium of communication that connects us to each other and the Power of Creation. Through prayer we can overcome challenges and transform reality in ways we might never have dreamed were possible. Kelly Howell guides you to establish a deeply personal connection with your creator and use the power of prayer to overcome even the most difficult challenges.

Prayer: Manifest a State of Grace. unabr. ed. Kelly Howell. 1 CD. (Running Time: 60 min.). 2000. audio compact disk 14.95 (978-1-881451-72-3(0)) Brain Sync.

Prayer: Speaking God's Language. Speeches. Creflo A. Dollar. 4 cass. (Running Time: 4 hrs. 30 mins.). 2006. 20.00 (978-1-59944-033-0(4)); audio compact disk 28.00 (978-1-59944-034-7(2)) Creflo Dollar.

Prayer: The Power Plant of the Church Series. Kenneth W. Hagin, Jr. 3 cass. 1993. 12.00 Set. (28J) Faith Lib Pubns.

Prayer: The Search for Inner Rest. Thomas Merton. 1 cass. 8.95 (AA2262) Credence Commun.

Prayer: The Way to a Transparent Life. Henri J. M. Nouwen. Read by Henri J. M. Nouwen. 1 cass. (Running Time: 38 min.). 7.95 (AA0261) Credence Commun.
Shows how prayer reveals the true nature of life & the world.

Prayer Vol. 1: Developing Your Prayer Life. Veronica Winston & Bill Winston. 2 cass. (C). 1997. 10.00 (978-1-931289-69-6(7)) Pub: B Winston Min. Dist(s): Anchor Distributors

Prayer - The Way of Love. Carole M. Troskowski. 1 cass. 4.00 (95C3) IRL Chicago.

Prayer A Day: A Collection of 365 Prayers with Bible Verses. Karen Jean Matsko Hood. 2008. 29.95 (978-1-59434-527-2(9)) Whsprng Pine.

Prayer & Active Life. Read by Thomas Merton. 1 cass. (Running Time: 60 min.). (Thomas Merton Ser.). 7.95 (AA2072) Credence Commun.

Prayer & Fasting. 2003. (978-1-59024-151-6(7)); audio compact disk (978-1-59024-152-3(5)) B Hinn Min.

Prayer & Fasting. 2001. (978-1-59024-021-2(9)); audio compact disk (978-1-59024-023-6(5)) B Hinn Min.

Prayer & Fasting. Kingsley Fletcher. 4 cass. 1992. 25.00 Set. (978-0-938612-89-6(1)) Destiny Image Pubs.

Prayer & Fasting - Biblical Keys to Prayer that Creates Results. 2004. audio compact disk (978-1-59024-125-7(8)) B Hinn Min.

Prayer & Forgiveness. Mother Angelica & Father Michael. 1 cass. (Running Time: 60 min.). (Mother Angelica Live Ser.). 1989. 10.00 (978-1-55794-119-0(X), T70) Eternal Wrd TV.
The author describes his personal experiences in the war torn land of Lebanon & how these experiences led him to deeper prayer.

***Prayer & Forgiveness: The Key to Making Your Life Bitter or Better.** Mac Hammond. 2010. audio compact disk 6.00 (978-1-57399-466-8(9)) Mac Hammond.

Prayer & Human Liberation in Teresa's "Interior Castle" Vilma Seelaus. 4 cass. 1986. 32.95 incl. shelf case. (TAH169) Alba Hse Comns.
Using the wisdom of Teresa's writings as a guide, the authoress treats of the pressing human need of liberation.

Prayer & Meditation. Jack Boland. 1 cass. 8.00 (BW05) Master Mind.

Prayer & Politics. Lynne Hammnod. 1 CD. 2006. audio compact disk 5.00 (978-1-57399-358-6(1)) Mac Hammond.

***Prayer & Praying Men.** unabr. ed. E. M. Bounds. Narrated by Simon Vance. (ENG.). 2006. 10.98 (978-1-59644-273-3(5), Hovel Audio) christianaud.

Prayer & Praying Men. unabr. ed. E. M. Bounds. Narrated by Simon Vance. 4 CDs. (Running Time: 4 hrs. 30 mins. 0 sec.). (ENG.). 2006. audio compact disk 18.98 (978-1-59644-272-6(7), Hovel Audio) christianaud.

Prayer & Self-Growth. Thomas Merton. 1 cass. 8.95 (AA2260) Credence Commun.

Prayer & Temperament. Chester P. Michael. 1985. 15.00 (978-0-940136-14-4(7)) Open Door Inc.

Prayer & the Active Life. Thomas Merton. 1 cass. (Running Time: 60 min.). (Origins of Prayer Ser.). 8.95 (AA2072) Credence Commun.
Merton at his richest, sharing the best of monastic contemplation.

Prayer & the Heavenlies. Mark Hanby. 3 cass. 1992. 18.00 Set. (978-0-938612-72-8(7)) Destiny Image Pubs.

Prayer & the Nation. Stephen Mansfield. 1 cass. (Running Time: 90 mins.). (Studies in Church History Ser.: Vol. 2). 2000. 5.00 (SM02-002) Morning NC.
An in-depth look at different philosophies that have influenced church history, this series provides excellent keys for understanding how to effectively confront the important issues of our times.

Prayer & Your Life in God. Lynne Hammond. 6 CDs. (Running Time: 6 hours). 2005. audio compact disk 30.00 (978-1-57399-197-1(X)) Mac Hammond.
Learn how to stop being dominated by your head and start being led by your heart, why prayer lists don't work, and how to pick up on "cues" from the Holy Spirit so you can pray supernaturally.

Prayer & Your Life in God, Set. Lynne Hammond. 6 cass. (Running Time: 6 hrs.). 1995. (978-1-57399-011-0(6)) Mac Hammond.

Prayer as a Therapeutic Tool for Spiritual Healing. Ron Roth. 3 cass. (Running Time: 3 hrs.). 1995. 24.95 Set. (978-1-893869-03-5(2)) Celbrtng Life.
Defines his term in relationship to the spiritual concepts as "Laying on of Hands" - anointing with oil, etc., & how to effectively use them in everyday living.

Prayer as a Weapon. Creflo A. Dollar. 2 cass. (Running Time: 3 hrs.). 2000. 10.00 (978-1-931172-60-8(9), TS241, Kidz Faith) Pub: Creflo Dollar. Dist(s): STL Dist NA

Prayer as Energy Medicine. Ron Roth. 2 cass. (Running Time: 2 hrs.). 1995. 16.95 Set. (978-1-893869-08-0(3)) Celbrtng Life.
Explore the fundamentals of prayer-power as well as the myths which surround the world of "Communion with God".

Prayer as Love: John of the Cross. Keith J. Egan. 4 cass. (Running Time: 3 hrs. 46 min.). 1991. 33.95 set. (TAH249) Alba Hse Comns.
This workshop looks to John of the Cross poetry, letters & commentaries as a way of imagining what he would counsel us in our day as we struggle to pray.

Prayer Chest. Joel, August & Fotinos Gold. 2007. reel tape 14.95 (978-1-4332-0448-7(7)); audio compact disk 14.95 (978-1-4332-0449-4(5)) Blckstn Audio.

Prayer Chest. unabr. ed. August Gold & Joel Fotinos. Narrated by Jack Garrett. (Running Time: 19200 sec.). (ENG.). 2007. audio compact disk 29.95 (978-1-60283-299-2(4)) Pub: AudioGO. Dist(s): Perseus Dist

Prayer Chest - A Novel about Receiving All of Life's Riches. unabr. ed. August Gold & Joel Fotinos. Read by Jack Garrett. (YA). 2008. 54.99 (978-1-60252-989-2(2)) Find a World.

Prayer Command Center. Gary V. Whetstone. 4 cass. (Running Time: 6 hrs.). (Empowerment Ser.). 1996. pap. bk. 35.00 (978-1-58866-198-2(9), 4VEO24A) Gary Whet Pub.
In these end times, God's mandate is for His people to pray. Learn how you can set up a Prayer Command Center in your home, school, office, business, or public building.

Prayer Confessions to Dominate in the New Millennium. Veronica Winston. 3 CDs. (Running Time: 2hr.42min.). (C). 2000. audio compact disk 24.00 (978-1-931289-14-6(X)) Pub: B Winston Min. Dist(s): Anchor Distributors

Prayer Confessions to Dominate in the New Millennium. Veronica Winston. 3 cass. (C). 2003. 15.00 (978-1-931289-55-9(7)) Pub: B Winston Min. Dist(s): Anchor Distributors

Prayer Evangelism. Terry Teykl. 6 cass. 19.99 Set. (978-1-57892-100-3(7)) Prayer Pt Pr.
Sermon/teaching.

Prayer Flag. Sudeep Sen. (BEN & ENG., 2003. audio compact disk 25.00 (978-0-930324-97-1(8)) Pub: Wings Pr. Dist(s): IPG Chicago

Prayer for a Friend. Contrib. by Casting Crowns. (Mastertrax Ser.). 2007. audio compact disk 9.98 (978-5-557-60316-4(6)) Beach St.

Prayer for an Angel. Ben Young. 1998. 4.95 (978-0-7417-6108-8(4), B0108) Win Walk.

Prayer for Awakening. Swami Amar Jyoti. 1 cass. 1991. 9.95 (P-55) Truth Consciousness.
Arise, Awake! Praying to awaken from the slumber of ego. Melting into Joy - what holds us back?.

Prayer for Courage. Eknath Easwaran. 1 cass. (Running Time: 1 hr.). (Easwaran on Tape Ser.). 1989. 7.95 (978-1-58638-592-7(5)) Nilgiri Pr.

Prayer for Owen Meany. unabr. ed. John Irving. Read by Joe Barrett. (Running Time: 24 hrs.). 2009. 29.99 (978-1-4233-9165-4(9), 9781423391654, Brilliance MP3); 44.97 (978-1-4233-9166-1(7), 9781423391661, Brlnc Audio MP3 Lib); 29.99 (978-1-4233-9167-8(5), 9781423391678, BADLE); audio compact disk 49.99 (978-1-4233-9163-0(2), 9781423391630); audio compact disk 99.97 (978-1-4233-9164-7(0), 9781423391647, BriAudCD Unabrid) Brilliance Audio.

Prayer for Spiritual Workers & The New Lord's Prayer. George King. 2009. audio compact disk (978-0-937249-52-9(1)) Aetherius Soc.

Prayer for the Ship. Douglas Reeman. Read by David Rintoul. 5 cass. 49.95 (978-0-7927-3320-1(7), CSL 694); audio compact disk 74.95 (978-0-7927-3321-8(5), SLD 694) AudioGO.

Prayer from the Heart. Liz Smith. 1 cass. 9.95 (10001174); audio compact disk 14.95 (2800810) Covenant Comms.
A voice comparable to the late Karen Carpenter.

Prayer from Your Heart. Lynne Hammond. 2005. 5.00 (978-1-57399-222-0(4)) Mac Hammond.

Prayer from Your Heart. Lynne Hammond. (ENG.). 2007. audio compact disk 5.00 (978-1-57399-337-1(9)) Mac Hammond.

Prayer Habits. Lynne Hammond. 1 cass. (Running Time: 1 hr.). 2005. 5.00 (978-1-57399-221-3(6)); audio compact disk 5.00 (978-1-57399-270-1(4)) Mac Hammond.

Prayer, Healing, & the Mind: Program from the Award Winning Public Radio Series. Hosted by Fred Goodwin. Comment by John Hockenberry. Contrib. by Larry Dossey et al. 1 cass. (Running Time: 1 hr.). (Infinite Mind Ser.). 1998. audio compact disk 21.95 (978-1-888064-54-4(4), LCM 1) Lichtenstein Creat.
New, scientific research says prayer does heal. Medical researchers, clergy, and patients provide startling new insights into these "miracles of medicine." Guests include Dr. Larry Dossey, who has written six books on the subject, including the best-selling Healing Words. In addition, "Is a smile the best medicine?" - The Infinite Mind's David Furst reports from a convention of therapists who specialize in humor.

Prayer in the Twenty-First Century. David Steindl-Rast. 1 cass. (Running Time: 1 hr. 10 min.). 1992. 8.95 (AA2566) Credence Commun.
Leads you to conclusions about spirituality & prayer that are revolutionary.

Prayer Is . Robert L. Ferring. 3 cass. 25.95 incl. shelf-case. (TAH072) Alba Hse Comns.
Examines one's prayer relationship with God.

Prayer Is Good Medicine. Contrib. by Anna-Liza Kozma. 1 CD. (Running Time: 1 hr.). 2005. audio compact disk 15.95 (978-0-660-19046-4(X)) Pub: Canadian Broadcasting CAN. Dist(s): Georgetown Term

Prayer Is Good Medicine Set: How to Reap the Healing Benefits of Prayer. abr. ed. Larry Dossey. 2 cass. (Running Time: 3 hrs.). 1996. 18.00 (978-0-694-51751-0(8), CPN 2616) HarperCollins Pubs.
The author discusses the practice of healing & prayer, when, why, how & where your faith might be put to work for you. He examines spoken & silent prayers, seeking guidance or specific requests, false hopes, the power of belief & destructive prayers.

Prayer Journal. unabr. ed. Terry Teykl. 6 cass. 1996. 25.00 Set. (978-1-57892-035-8(3)) Prayer Pt Pr.
Sermon/teaching on prayer.

Prayer Matrix: Plugging into the Unseen Reality. unabr. ed. David Jeremiah. (Running Time: 2 hrs. 0 mins. 0 sec.). (ENG.). 2007. audio compact disk 15.98 (978-1-59644-511-6(4), Hovel Audio) christianaud.

***Prayer Matrix: Plugging into the Unseen Reality.** unabr. ed. David Jeremiah. Narrated by Lloyd James. (ENG.). 2007. 9.98 (978-1-59644-512-3(2), Hovel Audio) christianaud.

Prayer of Faith: Strength for that Special Need. Richard Jafolla & Mary-Alice Jafolla. Read by Richard Jafolla & Mary-Alice Jafolla. (Special Spiritual Ser.). 1986. 12.95 (390) Stppng Stones.
Motivational tapes that work on the subconscious mind (subliminal) & conscious mind to bring about self-improvement.

Prayer of Hours. rev. ed. Monks of Utah Staff & Frank L. Hicks, Jr. 1 cass. 2000. 15.95 (978-1-929179-07-7(3)) Solitude Solace.

Prayer of Jabez. Bruce Wilkinson. Voice by Bruce Wilkinson. 4 cassettes. (Audio Curriculum Ser.). 2002. 19.99 (978-0-9720074-5-0(8)) Pub: Glob Vision. Dist(s): STL Dist NA

Prayer of Jabez. Bruce Wilkinson. Voice by Bruce Wilkinson. 4 CDs. (Running Time: 360 mins.). (Audio Curriculum Ser.). 2003. 19.99 (978-0-9720074-9-8(0)) Pub: Glob Vision. Dist(s): STL Dist NA

Prayer of Jabez: Breaking Through to the Blessed Life. Bruce Wilkinson. (Breakthrough Ser.). (ENG.). 2001. audio compact disk 12.99 (978-1-57673-907-5(4), Mltnmah) Pub: Doubday Relig. Dist(s): Random

Prayer of Jabez: Breaking Through to the Blessed Life. abr. ed. Bruce Wilkinson. Read by Bruce Wilkinson. 1 cass. (Running Time: 1 hr.). (Breakthrough Ser.: Vol. 1). (ENG.). 2000. 8.99 (978-1-57673-842-9(6), Mltnmah) Pub: Doubday Relig. Dist(s): Random

Prayer of Jabez for Women. Darlene Wilkinson. Voice by Darlene Wilkinson. 2 CDs. (Running Time: 106 mins.). (Audio Curriculum Ser.). 2002. 16.99 (978-0-9720074-6-7(6)) Pub: Glob Vision. Dist(s): STL Dist NA

Prayer of Jabez for Women: Darlene Live in Atlanta! Darlene Wilkinson. 2 cassettes. (Running Time: 106 mins.). 2002. 14.99 (978-0-9720074-7-4(4)) Pub: Glob Vision. Dist(s): STL Dist NA

Prayer of Jesus: Secrets to Real Intimacy with God. Hank Hanegraaff. Read by Hank Hanegraaff. 2 cass. (Running Time: 3 hrs.). 2001. 12.99 (978-0-9712492-1-9(0)); audio compact disk 14.99 (978-0-9712492-0-2(2)) Christ Res Inst.

Prayer of Petition & Supplication. Kenneth Copeland. 1 cass. 1983. 5.00 (978-0-88114-008-8(2)) K Copeland Pubns.
Indepth biblical study on prayer.

Prayer of St. Francis. unabr. ed. Eknath Easwaran. 1 cass. (Running Time: 57 mins.). 1989. 7.95 (978-1-58638-593-4(3), PSF) Nilgiri Pr.
Line-by-line commentary on the prayer Easwaran recommends as the first passage to use in meditation.

Prayer of the Night Shepherd. Phil Rickman. (Merrily Watkins Ser.). 2007. 104.95 (978-0-7531-3595-2(7)); audio compact disk 109.95 (978-0-7531-2681-3(8)) Pub: ISIS Audio GBR. Dist(s): Ulverscroft US

Prayer Orchestra. Derek Prince. 1 cass. (Running Time: 60 min.). 5.95 (I-4127) Derek Prince.

***Prayer Posies.** Barbee Lux. Illus. by Cherish Flieder & Benjamin Hummel. (ENG.). (J). 2009. pap. bk. 15.99 (978-1-59879-695-7(X), Livevst) Lifevest Pub.

***Prayer Posies.** Barbee Lux. Illus. by Cherish Flieder & Benjamin Hummen. (ENG.). (J). 2009. bk. 24.99 (978-1-59879-696-4(8), Livevst) Lifevest Pub.

Prayer Puzzle: Romans 8:26-30. Dan Hayden. 1 CD. (Running Time: 2 hrs. 13 mins.). 2004. audio compact disk 14.95 (978-1-932691-07-8(3)) Pub: Sola Scriptura. Dist(s): STL Dist NA

Prayer School Vol. 1: Teaching & Prayer with Lynne Hammond. Lynne Hammond. 1 cass. 1996. 12.50 (978-1-57399-027-1(2)) Mac Hammond.

Prayer School Vol. 1: Teaching & Prayer with Lynne Hammond. Lynne Hammond. 1 cass. 1997. 30.00 (978-1-57399-044-8(2)) Mac Hammond.
Teaching on prayer.

Prayer School Vol. 3: Teaching & Prayer with Lynne Hammond. Lynne Hammond. 7 cass. (Running Time: 1 hr.). 1998. 17.50 (978-1-57399-063-9(9)) Mac Hammond.

Prayer School, Vol 1: Teaching & Prayer with Lynne Hammond. Lynne Hammond. 5 CDs. 2006. audio compact disk 25.00 (978-1-57399-309-8(3)) Mac Hammond.
In this series of teaching and prayer times, Lynne Hammond reveals why, when, and how "praying through" should be done. This is more than a teaching series, it's an experience.

Prayer School, Vol 2: Teaching & Prayer with Lynne Hammond. Lynne Hammond. 5 CDs. 2006. audio compact disk 25.00 (978-1-57399-310-4(7)) Mac Hammond.
In these anointed sessions, you'll learn the three ingredients that make up a strong foundation of effective prayer. You'll also discover powerful ways to "minister to the Lord" and why doing so can effect your prayer life like nothing else.

Prayer School, Vol 3: Teaching & Prayer with Lynne Hammond. Lynne Hammond. 7 CDs. 2006. audio compact disk 35.00 (978-1-57399-311-1(5)) Mac Hammond.
Many believers are tired of their stagnant, go-nowhere prayer lives. But as Lynne Hammond points out in these remarkable live sessions of teaching, worship, and prayer, if you really want to move out in prayer, you must learn to travel by faith.

***Prayer Selections.** unabr. ed. Richard J. Foster. Read by Rick Adamson. (ENG.). 2004. (978-0-06-078455-3(5), Harper Audio) HarperCollins Pubs.

***Prayer Selections.** unabr. ed. Richard J. Foster. Read by Rick Adamson. (ENG.). 2004. (978-0-06-081480-9(2), Harper Audio) HarperCollins Pubs.

Prayer, Soul of the Apostolate. Mother M. Bernard. 1 cass. (National Meeting of the Institute, 1990 Ser.). 4.00 (90N6) IRL Chicago.

***Prayer Storm Audio Book: Tap Your Prayer Storm Power!** James W. Goll. (ENG.). 2010. audio compact disk 29.99 (978-1-936081-20-2(2)) Pub: Casscomm. Dist(s): Destiny Image Pubs

Prayer That Changes Everything: The Hidden Power of Praising God. Stormie Omartian. 3 CDs. (Running Time: 3 hrs.). 2004. audio compact disk 16.99 (978-0-7369-1380-5(7)) Harvest Hse.

Prayer That Changes Things. Kenneth Copeland. 4 cass. 1982. bk. 20.00 Set incl. study guide. (978-0-938458-45-6(0)) K Copeland Pubns.
Principles of prayer.

Prayer That Changes Things, Vol. 2. Bill Winston & Veronica Winston. 2 cass. (C). 2000. 10.00 (978-1-931289-70-2(0)) Pub: B Winston Min. Dist(s): Anchor Distributors

Prayer That Heals. unabr. ed. Myrtle Smith. Prod. by David Keyston. 1 cass. (Running Time: 54 min.). (Myrtle Smith Audiotapes Ser.). 1998. , CD. (978-1-893107-20-5(5), M20, Cross & Crown) Healing Unltd.

Prayer That Prepares the Way: Taking Your Place in God's End-Time Plan. Patsy Cameneti. 8. (Running Time: 6 hrs.). 2002. 35.00 (978-1-57399-162-9(7)) Mac Hammond.
In these last days, God is using people all over the world to prepare the way for the Second Coming of Christ. As Patsy Cameneti beautifully explains, you can play an active role in the work force that constructed the highway for the Lord's return. In this insightful series, you'll learn how God responds to the prayers of the saints by the strategic positioning of governments, kings, and military leaders. get this series and learn how you can help in Prayer That Prepares tghe Way.

Prayer, the Life of the Believer. Smith Chuck. (ENG.). 2001. audio compact disk 22.99 (978-1-932941-12-8(6)) Word For Today.

Prayer to Divine Mother. Swami Amar Jyoti. 1 cass. 1987. 9.95 (K-99) Truth Consciousness.
All-prevading Shakti, Divine Power. The male-female aspect of God. Strength to unite the distracted mind. Our borrowed light. One focus in light solves everything.

Prayer to the Sun see Poetry of Geoffrey

***Prayer: Your Letter to God.** unabr. ed. AndrÃ(c) K. Dugger. (Running Time: 4 hrs. 52 mins. 15 sec.). (ENG.). 2010. 14.99 (978-0-310-40883-3(0)) Zondervan.

Prayer 101: How to Talk to God, Luke 11:1-13;18:1-14. Ed Young. 1996. 4.95 (978-0-7417-2095-5(7), 1095) Win Walk.

Prayerbook Hebrew Companion Set. Narrated by Rhoda Leah Agin. Contrib. by Debby Graudenz & Jerry Isaak-Shapiro. 1 cass. 1998. 34.95 (978-0-939144-29-7(8)) EKS Pub Co.
Features vocabulary, exercises, & prayers. Sephardic pronunciation.

Prayerful Pauses with Jesus & Mary. Robert Peffley. Read by Andrea Star. 3 cass. (Running Time: 1 hr. 30 min.). (YA). (gr. 9 up). 1987. 19.95 (978-0-89622-341-7(8)) Twenty-Third.
Poetic reflections.

Prayer/Meditation Toward Enlightenment. unabr. ed. Swami Amar Jyoti. 1 cass. (Running Time: 90 mins.). (Satsangs of Swami Amar Jyoti Ser.). 1999. 9.95 (978-0-933572-47-8(6), P-67) Truth Consciousness.
What is prayer & do we ever stop needing to pray? Minding the pitfalls on the spiritual path. Four stages of meditation.

Prayers. unabr. ed. Sylvia Browne. 2002. audio compact disk 10.95 (978-1-4019-0106-6(9), 1069) Hay House.

***Prayers & Personal Devotions of Mother Angelica.** unabr. ed. Raymond Arroyo. Narrated by Lorna Raver. (Running Time: 5 hrs. 30 mins. 0 sec.). (ENG.). 2010. 19.99 (978-1-4001-6582-7(2)); 11.99 (978-1-4001-8582-5(3)); audio compact disk 19.99 (978-1-4001-1582-2(5)) Pub: Tantor Media. Dist(s): IngramPubServ

***Prayers & Personal Devotions of Mother Angelica.** unabr. ed. Raymond Arroyo. Narrated by Lorna Raver. (Running Time: 5 hrs. 30 mins. 0 sec.). (ENG., 2010. audio compact disk 39.99 (978-1-4001-4582-9(1)) Pub: Tantor Media. Dist(s): IngramPubServ

Prayers & Promises When Facing a Life-Threatening Illness. unabr. ed. Ed Dobson. (Running Time: 4 hrs. 0 mins. 0 sec.). (ENG.). 2007. 12.99 (978-0-310-27612-8(8)) Zondervan.

Prayers for All People. unabr. ed. Read by Andrew Harvey. Ed. by Mary Ford-Grabowsky. 2 cass. (Running Time: 3 hrs.). 1996. 17.95 (978-1-57453-014-8(3), 330051) Audio Lit.
Gathers an extraordinary range of sacred poetry & prayers from around the world from ancient Persia to contemporary America. From the joys & struggles of the spiritual search, to the richness of relationships, to the encounter with suffering & death, these poems touch on all the major passages & experiences of life.

Prayers for Dark People. unabr. ed. W. E. B. Du Bois. Read by Ameria Jones. 1 cass. (Running Time: 1 hr. 30 min.). 1997. bk. 16.95 (978-0-9645593-9-4(0)) MasterBuy Audio Bks.
Non-denominational prescriptions for daily living by the noted African-American educator/scholar/activist. Includes biographical information & insight into how the prayers came to be.

Prayers for Rain, Set. abr. ed. Dennis Lehane. Read by Thomas J. Brown. 2 cass. (Patrick Kenzie/Angela Gennaro Ser.: Bk. 5). 1999. 17.95 (FS9-50896) Highsmith.

Prayers for Rain, Set. unabr. ed. Dennis Lehane. Read by Thomas J. Brown. 6 cass. (Patrick Kenzie/Angela Gennaro Ser.: Bk. 5). 1999. 35.95 (FS9-43907) Highsmith.

Prayers for Sale. unabr. ed. Sandra Dallas. Read by Maggi-Meg Reed. 8 CDs. (Running Time: 9 hrs. 0 mins. 0 sec.). (ENG.). 2009. audio compact disk 39.95 (978-1-4272-0615-2(5), Rena Bks) Pub: St Martin. Dist(s): Macmillan

Prayers for the Assassin: A Novel. abr. ed. Robert Ferrigno. Read by Armand Schultz. 2006. 17.95 (978-0-7435-5571-5(6)) Pub: S&S Audio. Dist(s): S and S Inc

Prayers for the Dead. unabr. ed. Faye Kellerman. Read by Kathleen O'Malley. 10 cass. (Running Time: 15 hrs.). 1997. 80.00 (4275) Books on Tape.
Someone has murdered Azor Sparks, a well-known heart surgeon & Lt. Peter Decker must work overtime to unravel a mysterious tangle.

***Prayers for Those Who Grieve.** unabr. ed. Jill Kelly. (Running Time: 1 hr. 0 mins. 0 sec.). (ENG.). 2011. audio compact disk 9.99 (978-1-59859-910-7(0)) Oasis Audio.

Prayers of a God Chaser: Passionate Prayers of Pursuit. unabr. ed. Tommy Tenney. Read by Jim Bond. 2 cass. (Running Time: 3 hrs.). 2002. 17.95 (978-1-59086-679-5(7), 1590866797); 44.25 (978-1-59086-680-1(0), 1590866800); audio compact disk 24.95 (978-1-59086-681-8(9), 1590866819); audio compact disk 62.25 (978-1-59086-682-5(7), 1590866827) Brilliance Audio.
Tommy Tenney's passion for God and His kingdom is turned here to the arena of prayer. The benefits of prayer are an often-discussed concept, but many Christians have not yet experienced them. In this book, Tenney dives deep into the riches of intimate and rewarding conversation with the Almighty. A thorough study of biblical, historical and contemporary prayers will lead the listener into life-changing and purposeful prayer. Tommy has a unique gift to lead hungry people into the presence of God. He understands the value of intimacy with God and humility in serving God's people.

Prayers of a God Chaser: Passionate Prayers of Pursuit. unabr. ed. Tommy Tenney. Read by Jim Bond. (Running Time: 3 hrs.). 2004. 39.25 (978-1-59335-572-2(6), 1593355726, Brlnc Audio MP3 Lib) Brilliance Audio.

Prayers of a God Chaser: Passionate Prayers of Pursuit. unabr. ed. Tommy Tenney. Read by Jim Bond. (Running Time: 3 hrs.). 2005. 39.25 (978-1-59600-825-0(3), 9781596008250, BADLE); 24.95 (978-1-59710-610-8(0), 9781597106108, BAD) Brilliance Audio.

Prayers of a God Chaser: Passionate Prayers of Pursuit. unabr. ed. Tommy Tenney. Read by Jim Bond. (Running Time: 3 hrs.). 2004. 24.95 (978-1-59335-127-4(5), 1593351275) Soulmate Audio Bks.

Prayers of an Omega: Facing the Transitions of Aging. Katie Funk Wiebe. Narrated by Rosalie Loeppky. Contrib. by Herb Hammond. 1 cass. (Running Time: 60 mins.). 9.95 (978-0-921788-25-6(8)) Kindred Prods.

Prayers of Christ in the Passion: Words & Meditations for Good Friday. Benedict J. Groeschel. 2 cass. (Running Time: 2 hrs. 7 min.). 1998. 19.95 Set. (TAH395) Alba Hse Comns.
Through scripture readings & reflections from Fr. Groeschel we may develop a greater awareness of Christ's love for us which was never better expressed than in his passion & death on the cross of Calvary. Can be used for Lenten meditations.

Prayers of Intercession for the Holy Souls. Benedict J. Groeschel et al. 2004. reel tape 9.95 (978-1-59276-054-1(6)); audio compact disk 14.95 (978-1-59276-055-8(4)) Our Sunday Visitor.
CONTAINS THE MOST POPULAR DEVOTIONS TO THE HOLY SOULS - ROSARY, WAY OF THE CROSS AND THE LITANY. CONVENIENT FORMAT. USES A VARIETY OF PEOPLE FOR THE RECORDING - PRIESTS, RELIGIOUS MEN AND NOVICES AND LAY MEN AND WOMEN. LISTENER CAN SLIP INTO A CHAPEL AND JOIN WITH OTHERS PRAYING FOR THE HOLY SOULS ALL IN THE COMFORT OF THEIR OWN HOME.

Prayers of My Heart. unabr. ed. Twin Sisters Productions. Read by Twin Sisters. (YA). 2008. 44.99 (978-1-59922-322-3(8)) Find a World.

Prayers of Steel see Carl Sandburg Reading Cool Tombs & Other Poems

Prayers of the People Rehearsal. bk. 5.00 (978-0-687-04773-4(0)) Abingdon.

***Prayers that Bring Healing: Overcome Sickness, Pain & Disease. God's Healing Is for You!** unabr. ed. John Eckhardt. Narrated by Mirron Willis. (ENG.). 2010. 10.98 (978-1-59644-927-5(6)); audio compact disk 15.98 (978-1-59644-926-8(8)) christianaud.

***Prayers That Matter.** Robert Millett. 2010. audio compact disk 14.99 (978-1-60641-773-7(8)) Deseret Bk.

***Prayers that Release Heaven on Earth.** unabr. ed. John Eckhardt. Narrated by Mirron Willis. (ENG.). 2010. 10.98 (978-1-59644-925-1(X)); audio compact disk 15.98 (978-1-59644-924-4(1)) christianaud.

Prayers That Rout Demons. unabr. ed. John Eckhardt. Narrated by John Eckhardt. Narrated by Rick Lance & Tim Lundeen. (Running Time: 3 hrs. 2

mins. 42 sec.). (ENG.). 2010. 12.59 (978-1-60814-635-2(9)); audio compact disk 17.99 (978-1-59859-692-2(6)) Oasis Audio.

Praying: Finding Our Way Through Duty to Delight. abr. ed. J. I. Packer & Caroline Nystrom. (ENG.). 2007. 9.09 (978-1-60814-343-6(0)) Oasis Audio.

Praying: Finding Our Way Through Duty to Delight. abr. ed. J. I. Packer & Carolyn Nystrom. Read by Rob Lamont. (Running Time: 7200 sec.). (ENG.). 2007. audio compact disk 12.99 (978-1-59859-233-7(5)) Oasis Audio.

Praying for Financial Success. audio compact disk 12.95 (978-1-56229-029-0(0), Christian Livng) Pneuma Life Pub.

Praying for Healthy Pregnancy. audio compact disk 12.95 (978-1-56229-030-6(4), Christian Livng) Pneuma Life Pub.

***Praying for Purpose for Women: A Prayer Experience That Will Change Your Life Forever.** unabr. ed. Katie Brazelton. (Running Time: 5 hrs. 8 mins. 0 sec.). (Pathway to Purpose Ser.). (ENG.). 2009. 12.99 (978-0-310-77172-2(2)) Zondervan.

Praying for Sleep. unabr. ed. Jeffery Deaver. Read by Connor O'Brien. 9 cass. (Running Time: 13 hrs. 30 min.). 1999. 72.00 (978-0-7366-4310-8(9), 4636) Books on Tape.
When he breaks out of a hospital for the criminally insane, Michael Hrubek wants one thing: Lis Atcheson, the woman who identified him as a rapist & murderer. Atcheson has good reason to be terrified. The hospital director, more concerned with minimizing the escape than finding the escapee, hires an out of work cop to trail Hrubek. It is up to Lis to save herself, not only from Hrubek, but from a dark secret in her own past, a secret Hrubek knows all too well.

Praying for Troubled Teenager. audio compact disk 12.95 (978-1-56229-028-3(2), Christian Livng) Pneuma Life Pub.

Praying for Unsaved Husband. audio compact disk 12.95 (978-1-56229-022-1(3), Christian Livng) Pneuma Life Pub.

Praying for Weight Loss. 1 CD. (Running Time: 1 hr.). 2004. audio compact disk 12.95 (978-1-56229-033-7(9), Christian Livng) Pneuma Life Pub.

Praying for Your Children. audio compact disk 12.95 (978-1-56229-025-2(8), Christian Livng) Pneuma Life Pub.

Praying for Your Marriage. 1 CD. (Running Time: 1 hr.). 2004. audio compact disk 12.95 (978-1-56229-024-5(X), Christian Livng) Pneuma Life Pub.

Praying for Your Nation. Lynne Hammond. 1 cass. 1996. 10.00 (978-1-57399-024-0(8)) Mac Hammond.
Teaching on the importance of praying for your nation.

Praying for Your Nation. Lynne Hammond. 2008. audio compact disk 12.00 (978-1-57399-407-1(3)) Mac Hammond.

Praying for Your Workplace & Career. audio compact disk 12.95 (978-1-56229-026-9(6), Christian Livng) Pneuma Life Pub.

Praying God's Will for Your Life. unabr. ed. Stormie Omartian. 4 cass. (Running Time: 5 hrs.). 2003. 25.99 (978-1-58926-238-6(7), T10M-0100) Oasis Audio.
A guide to a life of prayer that will direct your steps toward spititual well being.

Praying God's Will for Your Life. unabr. ed. Stormie Omartian. Narrated by Stormie Omartian. (ENG.). 2003. 12.59 (978-1-60814-342-9(2)); audio compact disk 17.99 (978-1-58926-239-3(5), T10M-010D) Oasis Audio.

Praying God's Word: Breaking Free from Spiritual Strongholds. Beth Moore. 19.99 (978-0-8054-2348-8(6)) BH Pubng Grp.

Praying God's Word: Breaking Free from Spiritual Strongholds. abr. ed. Beth Moore. Read by Cynthia Holloway. 2 cass. (Running Time: 3 hrs.). 2003. 17.95 (978-1-59086-925-3(7), 1590869257, Brill Audio); 44.25 (978-1-59086-926-0(5), 1590869265, BAudLibEd); audio compact disk 19.95 (978-1-59086-927-7(3), 1590869273, BACD); audio compact disk 62.25 (978-1-59086-928-4(1), 1590869281, BACDLib Ed) Brilliance Audio.
How do we practice II Corinthians 10:3-5, "tearing down strongholds by captivating our minds with the knowledge of God"? Beth Moore shows you how in Praying God's Word. A topical prayer guide addressing fourteen common strongholds and what Scripture reveals about each of them, Praying God's Word presents Scriptures in prayer form to be incorporated into your daily prayer life. God's Word, through prayer, helps you overcome bitterness, anger, and unforgiveness, setting you free from each and every stronghold which claims your life, and replacing it with the mind of Christ.

Praying God's Word: Breaking Free from Spiritual Strongholds. abr. ed. Beth Moore. Read by Cynthia Holloway. (Running Time: 3 hrs.). 2006. 39.25 (978-1-4233-0384-8(9), 9781423303848, BADLE); 24.95 (978-1-4233-0383-1(0), 9781423303831, BAD); 39.25 (978-1-4233-0382-4(2), 9781423303824, Brlnc Audio MP3 Lib); audio compact disk 24.95 (978-1-4233-0381-7(4), 9781423303817, Brilliance MP3) Brilliance Audio.

Praying God's Word: Breaking Free from Spiritual Strongholds. abr. ed. Beth Moore. Read by Cynthia Holloway. (Running Time: 3 hrs.). 2009. audio compact disk 9.99 (978-1-4418-2487-5(1), 9781441824875, BCD Value Price) Brilliance Audio.

Praying God's Word: Breaking Free from Spiritual Strongholds. unabr. ed. Beth Moore. (Running Time: 10 hrs.). 2009. 19.99 (978-1-4418-2520-9(7), 9781441825209, Brilliance MP3) Brilliance Audio.

Praying God's Word: Breaking Free from Spiritual Strongholds. unabr. ed. Beth Moore. Read by Joyce Bean. (Running Time: 10 hrs.). 2009. 39.97 (978-1-4418-2521-6(5), 9781441825216, Brlnc Audio MP3 Lib); 39.97 (978-1-4418-2523-0(1), 9781441825230, BADLE); 19.99 (978-1-4418-2522-3(3), 9781441825223, BAD); audio compact disk 97.97 (978-1-4418-2519-3(3), 9781441825193, BriAudCD Unabrid); audio compact disk 19.99 (978-1-4418-2518-6(5), 9781441825186, Bril Audio CD Unabri) Brilliance Audio.

Praying in the Spirit. Lynne Hammond. 1 cass. (Running Time: 1 hr.). 2005. 5.00 (978-1-57399-223-7(2)) Mac Hammond.

Praying in Tongues. 1986. Key of David.

***Praying Life: Connecting with God in a Distracting World.** unabr. ed. Paul Miller. Narrated by Arthur Morey. (ENG.). 2009. 16.98 (978-1-59644-846-9(6), Hovel Audio); audio compact disk 26.98 (978-1-59644-845-2(8), Hovel Audio) christianaud.

Praying Man. Contrib. by Brian Free & Assurance. (Soundtraks Ser.). 2007. audio compact disk 8.99 (978-5-557-52829-0(6)) Christian Wrld.

Praying Mysteries: Understanding the Purpose of Tongues, 3 of prayer series. Lynne Hammond. 5 cass. (Running Time: 5 hrs). 2005. 12.50 (978-1-57399-240-4(2)) Mac Hammond.
Tongues. It's the doorway to the supernatural. It will bring revelation from heaven that will revolutionize your life and release God's plans and purposes for you in a way nothing else can. Get this series and start tapping the awesome power of this God-given gift.

Praying Mysteries: Understanding the Purpose of Tongues, 3 of prayer series. Lynne Hammond. 5 CDs. (Running Time: 5 hrs). 2006. audio compact disk 25.00 (978-1-57399-304-3(2)) Mac Hammond.

Praying Our Goodbyes. Joyce Rupp. Read by Sherry Kennedy Brownrigg. 3 CDs. (Running Time: 14400 sec.). 2006. audio compact disk 24.95 (978-0-86716-822-8(6)) St Anthony Mess Pr.

Praying Out Your Destiny: Understanding the Hope of Your Calling. Terri Copeland Pearsons. (ENG.). 2006. audio compact disk 15.00 (978-1-57562-907-0(0)) K Copeland Pubns.

Praying the Franciscan Crown. Edd Anthony. Read by Edd Anthony. audio compact disk 16.95 (978-1-881586-27-2(8)) Canticle Cass.

***Praying the Names of God: A Daily Guide.** unabr. ed. Ann Spangler. (Running Time: 7 hrs. 31 mins. 0 sec.). (ENG.). 2009. 16.99 (978-0-310-30259-9(5)) Zondervan.

Praying the Our Father with Teresa of Avila. Steven Payne. 1 cass. (Running Time: 49 min.). 8.95 I C S Pubns.
Fr. Steven Payne, O.C.D. shows how Jesus was Teresa's "book" on prayer & how it was to the prayer he taught that she spontaneously turned when her sisters asked her to teach them to pray.

Praying the Psalms. Roland E. Murphy. 4 cass. (Running Time: 5 hrs. 13 min.). 1996. 34.95 Set. (TAH361) Alba Hse Comns.
Exposes the listener to the vital essence of the spirituality found within the Psalter. A thorough course in the Psalms, this series will prove to be an elucidating experience for all, & bring a fresh vitality into the Christian prayer life.

Praying the Scriptures. Mother Angelica & Father Michael. 1 cass. (Running Time: 60 min.). (Mother Angelica Live Ser.). 1988. 10.00 (978-1-55794-113-8(0), T64) Eternal Wrd TV.
Explains how to pray the Scriptures.

Praying Through the Deeper Issues of Marriage Audiobook: Protecting Your Relationship So It Will Last a Lifetime. Stormie Omartian. 2007. audio compact disk 18.99 (978-0-7369-2053-7(6)) Harvest Hse.

Praying to Change History. Derek Prince. 6 cass. 29.95 (I-EP1) Derek Prince.

Praying to Heal Memories. Kevin M. Cronin. 1 cass. (Running Time: 1 hr.). 2001. 8.95 (A6821) St Anthony Mess Pr.
Discusses the mystery of pain and suffering in our daily lives.

Praying to the Lord. 1983. Archae Edns.

Praying with the Anabaptists: The Secret of Bearing Fruit. Marlene Kropf & Eddy Hall. 1994. bk. & pap. bk. 19.95 (978-0-87303-248-3(9)) Faith & Life.

Praying Without Paying: Matt 6:19-21. Ed Young. (J). 1981. 4.95 (978-0-7417-1163-2(X), A0163) Win Walk.

Pre- & Postoperative Care: Biology of Aging: Implications for the Surgeon. (Postgraduate Programs Ser.: C84-PG1). 1984. 85.00 (8481) Am Coll Surgeons.
Provides the practicing surgeon with an understanding of the aging process & its clinical implications. 12 hours CME category 1 credit.

Pre- & Postoperative Care: Management of the Critically Ill Surgical Patient. (Postgraduate Programs Ser.: C85-PG1). 85.00 (8511) Am Coll Surgeons.
Discusses the institution & withdrawal of therapy in the critically ill surgical patient. (12 hours CME category 1 credit).

Pre- & Postoperative Care: Perioperative Care of the Compromised Patient. Moderated by Richard L. Simmons. (Postgraduate Courses Ser.). 1986. 115.00 (8611(C86-PG1)) Am Coll Surgeons.
12 Hours CME credit provides an understanding of the role of the normal host defenses against infections, how these are disturbed by Trauma or surgical operation & how to manage patients with best defense deficiencies.

Pre- & Postoperative Care in Ambulatory Surgery. 2 cass. (General Sessions Ser.: C85-SP7). 15.00 (8549) Am Coll Surgeons.

Pre-Algebra. Elizabeth Alden & John Blackwood. 5 cass. 69.00 incl. 8 activity bks., guide. (978-0-89525-193-0(0), AMC 357) Ed Activities.
An Introduction to the basics including addition, subtraction, multiplication, & division of integers, evaluating expressions & the solution of equation in one variable. Translating from English to algebra & simple word problems are also included.

Pre-Algebra: Chapter Audio Summaries. (gr. 6-12). 2005. audio compact disk (978-0-618-43348-3(1), 2-05821); audio compact disk (978-0-618-43350-6(3), 2-05823); audio compact disk (978-0-618-43349-0(X), 2-05822) Holt McDoug.

Pre-Algebra Concepts. America's Math Teacher. (Mastering Essential Math Skills Ser.). (J). (gr. 6-13). 2008. pap. bk. 34.95 (978-0-9821901-2-8(3)) Math Essentials.

Pre & Post Operative: Babbling Brook. Eldon Taylor. 1 cass. 16.95 (978-1-55978-546-4(2), 5506F) Progress Aware Res.

Pre & Post Operative: Music Theme. Eldon Taylor. 1 cass. 16.95 (978-1-55978-246-3(3), 5506C) Progress Aware Res.

Pre & Post Operative: Ocean. Eldon Taylor. Read by Eldon Taylor. Ed. by Leslie Brice. 1 cass. (Running Time: 1 hr.). 1992. 16.95 (978-1-56705-345-6(9)) Gateways Inst.
Self improvement.

Pre & Post Operative: Stream. Eldon Taylor. Read by Eldon Taylor. Ed. by Leslie Brice. 1 cass. (Running Time: 1 hr.). 1992. 16.95 (978-1-56705-346-3(7)) Gateways Inst.

Pre-Ballet for the Young Dancer (Ages 4-6) Constance Reynolds. 1 cass. (J). (ps-1). 15.00 incl. guide. (KIM 1015C); lp 15.00 (KIM 1015) Kimbo Educ.
Rhythmic exercises develop poise, coordination, flexibility & grace within the young student. Children learn to share, accept discipline, are motivated to move, & encouraged to dance.

Pre-Band Instrument Method. John Brimhall. Ed. by Debbie Cavalier. (C). 1997. 12.95 (978-0-7692-1776-5(1), 0196B, Warner Bro) Alfred Pub.

Pre-Cognitive Re-Education. Rick Moss. 15 cass. 2001. 160.00 (978-0-9670896-3-8(8)) Plickity Plunk.

Pre-Consult Cardiology. Contrib. by William A. Lutin et al. 1 cass. (American Academy of Pediatrics UPDATE: Vol. 19, No. 1). 1998. 20.00 Am Acad Pediat.

Pre-Convention Professional Seminar, Series I. Thomas Armstrong. 1 cass. (Running Time: 90 mins.). 1999. 14.00 (P60WA) Torah Umesorah.

Pre-Convention Professional Seminar: Fundraising, Series 2. Mark Gadson. 1 cass. (Running Time: 90 mins.). 1999. 12.00 (P60WB) Torah Umesorah.

Pre-Design. 2003. audio compact disk 45.00 (978-0-7931-8638-9(2)) Kaplan Pubng.

Pre-Existence. Neville Goddard. 1 cass. (Running Time: 62 min.). 1969. 8.00 (18) J & L Pubns.
Neville taught Imagination Creates Reality. He was a powerfully influential teacher of God as Consciousness.

Pre Genesis. Scripts. Glenn Kimball & Chase Kimball. Prod. by John Fassett. Engineer Bob Karp. 2 CDs. (Running Time: 02:14:06). 2005. audio compact disk 18.95 (978-1-59772-044-1(5), Your Own Wrld Bks) Your Own Wrld.
There are many texts, including the Holy Bible, which speak of human civilizations before Adam and Eve. Ancient texts and legends speak of five great, successful epochs of time, the first four of which ended in cataclysm because of the wickedness of the people.Any single text or tradition reads today, because it has come to us from thousands of years ago, like a silly tabloid tale. However, by combining the texts, legends and histories together, we see that the story in the middle makes a great deal of sense. God didn?t waste the time and space of the earth. He used it for exactly the same purpose over and over again.The previous civilizations looked forward to the coming of a Messianic figure that would come into the world, die on a cross and bring resurrection to us all. They spoke of the return of paradise in the end, where governments would no longer be divided and religions would be as one. This CD is designed to bring science and religion to the same table after having been fragmented by discoveries of ancient human civilizations before Adam and Eve. Best of all, we introduce quotes from the Kolbrin Bible, the Bible of Joseph of Arimathea, which tells us the rest of the story of the creation and the coming of Adam and Eve into the world.

Pre-Geometrical Dynamics: A Quantum Mechanical Perspective. Geoffrey Chew. 2 cass. 18.00 set. (A0424-89) Sound Photosyn.
The Dean of Physics at UC Berkeley gives his own interpretation of how it's laid out.

Pre-Hospital Trauma Care - Trauma Care in the ED. Gary Fleisher. (Pediatric Emergencies: The National Conferenc for Practioners Ser.). 1986. 9.00 (978-0-932491-64-0(2)) Res Appl Inc.

Pre-K Hooray! Action Songs to Learn & Grow By. 1 cass. (Running Time: 1 hr.). (J). (ps). 2001. pap. bk. 10.95 (KIM 9134C); pap. bk. 14.95 (KIM 9134CD); pap. bk. & pupil's gde. ed. 11.95 (KIM 9134) Kimbo Educ.

Pre-Op, Tape 1. abr. ed. Robert A. Monroe. Read by Robert A. Monroe. 6 cass. (Emergency Ser.). 1983. 69.00 Set. (978-1-56102-700-2(6)); Inter Indus.
Play before surgery for relaxation & coding Hemi-Sync signals.

Pre-Raphaelite Art of the Victorian Novel: Narrative Challenges to Visual Gendered Boundaries. Sophia Andres. 2004. audio compact disk 9.95 (978-0-8142-9049-1(3)) Pub: Ohio St U Pr. Dist(s): Chicago Distribution Ctr

Pre-Spar Win Program. 1 cass. (Martial Arts Programming Ser.). 12.50 (978-0-87554-196-9(8), K106) Valley Sun.
You are now totally confident in your sparring ability. You are relaxed & focused whenever you spar. You are confident & enjoy the challenge of sparring. You draw on your total awareness in sparring. Your mind is calm & focused whenever you spar. You are now physically relaxed but energized when you spar.

Pre surgical Hypnosis: Preparing the body-mind for speedy healing & Ease. Carol S. Rios. 2007. audio compact disk 19.99 (978-1-4276-2344-7(9)) AardGP.

Preach on Sister, Preach On. Perf. by La Wanda Page. 2001. audio compact disk 16.98 (978-1-929243-28-0(6)) Uproar Ent.

Preach the Word. Contrib. by Gold City. (Mastertrax Ser.). 2007. audio compact disk 9.98 (978-5-557-71914-8(8)) Pt of Grace Ent.

***Preach the Word Prophecy Conference.** unabr. ed. Tim F. LaHaye et al. (Running Time: 8 hrs. 0 mins. 0 sec.). (ENG.). 2011. audio compact disk 27.99 (978-1-59859-884-1(8)) Oasis Audio.

Preacher & the Presidents: Billy Graham in the White House. unabr. abr. ed. Nancy Gibbs & Michael Duffy. Read by L. J. Ganser. (Running Time: 11 hrs.). (ENG.). 2007. 26.98 (978-1-59483-973-3(5)) Pub: Hachet Audio. Dist(s): HachBkGrp

Preacher's Boy. Katherine Paterson. Narrated by Johnny Heller. 4 CDs. (Running Time: 4 hrs. 30 mins.). (gr. 5 up). 1999. audio compact disk 39.00 (978-1-4025-1495-1(6), C1620) Recorded Bks.
The year 1900 is fast approaching, and the high spirited Robbie Burns Hewitt plans to live live to the fullest, because the world is going to end anyway! No more living by The Ten Commandments, since he ":ain't got the knack for holiness." But before long, Robbie must choose between the truth and a lie while a man's life hangs in the balance.

Preacher's Boy. unabr. ed. Katherine Paterson. Narrated by Johnny Heller. 3 pieces. (Running Time: 4 hrs. 30 mins.). (gr. 5 up). 1999. 28.00 (978-0-7887-9789-7(1), 96835) Recorded Bks.
Willful and high-spirited, exerting his independence at every turn, 10-year-old Robert "Robbie" Burns Hewitt plans to live life to the fullest - because the world is going to end at the turn of the century anyway! The year 1900 is fast approaching. Robbie decides that living by The Ten Commandments, which have been drilled into his head by his preacher father, is not meant for him - since he "ain't got the knack for holiness." On his quest to be his own person, he stirs up trouble daily. Before long, he must choose between the truth and a lie while a man's life hangs in the balance.

***Preacher's Bride.** unabr. ed. Jody Hedlund. Narrated by Mimi Black. (Running Time: 11 hrs. 0 mins. 0 sec.). (ENG.). 2011. audio compact disk 32.99 (978-1-59859-863-6(5)) Oasis Audio.

Preacher's Daughter. unabr. ed. Beverly Lewis. Read by Stina Nelsen. 9 CDs. (Running Time: 11 hrs.). (Annie's People Ser.: No. 1). 2006. audio compact disk 119.75 (978-1-4193-8170-6(9), CK184); 79.75 (978-1-4193-8168-3(7), K1188) Recorded Bks.
Beverly Lewis continues her tradition of Amish stories with the Annie's People series. In the first book, Lewis addresses young Annie Zook's inner conflict between the strong bonds of her family and faith and the allurement of her talent. Her love of drawing has thus prevented her from choosing a husband, much to her Old Order preacher father's consternation. Annie's feelings grow further convoluted when her longtime pen pal from the outside world Louisa Stratford comes to visit and encourages her to cultivate her gift.

Preacher's Son. unabr. ed. Elizabeth Gill. Contrib. by Rachel Bavidge. 6 cass. (Story Sound Ser.). (J). 2006. 54.95 (978-1-85903-921-2(9)) Pub: Mgna Lrg Print GBR. Dist(s): Ulverscroft US

Preacher's Son. unabr. ed. Elizabeth Gill & Rachel Bavidge. Contrib. by Rachel Bavidge. 6 vols. (Story Sound CD Ser.). (J). 2006. audio compact disk 64.95 (978-1-85903-957-1(X)) Pub: Mgna Lrg Print GBR. Dist(s): Ulverscroft US

Preaching Plagues: Exodus 7-10. Ed Young. 1984. 4.95 (978-0-7417-1421-3(3), 421) Win Walk.

Preadolescent Determinants of Sexuality. Contrib. by Robert Rosenfield et al. 1 cass. (American Academy of Pediatrics UPDATE: Vol. 19, No. 9). 1998. 20.00 Am Acad Pediat.

Prealgebra. 3rd ed. Created by Pearson. (Math XL Ser.). 2005. audio compact disk 20.00 (978-0-321-27927-9(1)) P-H.

Prealgebra: Chapter Test Prep. 3rd ed. Jamie Blair et al. 2005. audio compact disk 17.80 (978-0-13-149130-4(X)) Pearson Educ CAN CAN.

Prealgebra & Introductory Algebra: Digital Video Tutor. Marvin L. Bittinger & Alex Ellenbogen. 2003. audio compact disk 34.00 (978-0-321-25725-3(1)) AddisonWesley.

Precalc Math Space. audio compact disk 7.95 (978-0-618-41308-9(1), 309067) Pub: Brooks-Cole. Dist(s): CENGAGE Learn

Precalculus. 7th rev. ed. Sullivan & Sullivan. (Math XL Ser.). 2004. audio compact disk 20.00 (978-0-13-147949-4(0)) PH School.

Precalculus Enhanced with Graphing Utilities: MathXL(r) CD. 4th ed. Sullivan. audio compact disk 20.00 (978-0-13-154352-2(0)) PH School.

Precepts for Living, 2002-2003: The UMI Annual Sunday School Lesson Commentary. Ed. by A. Okechukwu Ogbonnaya. Contrib. by A. Okechukwu Ogbonnaya. Contrib. by Deborah Branker-Harrod et al. Illus. by

Carter Fred. 1 CD. (C). 2002. stu. ed. & per. 16.25 (978-0-940955-80-6(6), 11-2003, UMI) Urban Ministries.
This in-depth CD-ROM Biblical expository includes: Comprehensive word and topic searches, Internet connectivity which links you to on-line Precepts discussion groups, and Complete Bible in The New Living Translation and the traditional King James Version.

Precio del Exito: Conozca y Practique los Secretos del Exito Que Usan los Triunfadores. Carlos Cuauhtemoc Sanchez. (Running Time: 3000 sec.). 2004. audio compact disk 15.95 (978-968-7277-54-7(8)) Pub: EdSelect MEX. Dist(s): Giron Bks

Precious. abr. ed. Sapphire. Read by Sapphire. (ENG.). 2009. audio compact disk 15.00 (978-0-307-57811-2(9), Random AudioBks) Pub: Random Audio Pubg. Dist(s): Random

Precious Baby (I Welcome You) Read by Mary Richards. 1 cass. (Running Time: 60 min.). (J). 2007. audio compact disk 19.95 (978-1-56136-176-2(3)) Master Your Mind.

Precious Bane, unabr. ed. Mary Webb. Read by Flo Gibson. 6 cass. (Running Time: 8 hrs. 30 min.). 1998. 24.95 (978-1-55685-568-9(0)) Audio Bk Con.
Set in the wild hills of Shropshire, the harsh farming life is explored & Prudence Sam, due to her harelip, is cursed as a witch by fierce, morose neighbors. Only the weaver, Kester Woodseaves, can see her real beauty.

Precious Bane. unabr. collector's ed. Mary Webb. Read by Jill Masters. 8 cass. (Running Time: 12 hrs.). (J). 1989. 64.00 (978-0-7366-1468-9(0), 2348) Books on Tape.
Prue Sam triumphs over a physical handicap to win her heart's desire.

Precious Blood of Jesus. Kenneth E. Hagin. 1 cass. 4.95 (SH22) Faith Lib Pubns.

Precious Blood of Jesus. Read by Basilea Schlink. 1 cass. (Running Time: 30 min.). 1985. (0280) Evang Sisterhood Mary.
Discusses how we can experience its power in our lives & Jesus' suffering has the power to transform the fearful into true disciples of the cross.

Precious Door. Short Stories. (2061) Am Audio Prose.

Precious in God's Sight. Dan Comer. 1 cass. 3.00 (106) Evang Outreach.

Precious Lord! How to Play Soul Gospel, Tape 1. Robert L. Jefferson. 1992. 9.95 (978-1-880549-02-5(6)) Pensacola Pubns.

***Precious Memories: Gospel Songs for Easy Guitar.** Created by Hal Leonard Corp. (ENG.). 2010. pap. bk. 12.99 (978-1-4234-9770-7(8), 1423497708) H Leonard.

Precious Peace: Relaxation & Guided Imagery for Expectant Mothers. Mary Lee B. Simpson & Susan Boyes. Read by Susan Boyes. 1 cass. (Running Time: 60 min.). 1998. 12.95 (978-0-9665650-1-0(0)); audio compact disk 15.95 CD. (978-0-9665650-0-3(2)) PeaceWrks.
Meditations for expectant mothers include guided imagery & relaxation exercises to still fears & uncertainties related to pregnancy & childbirth.

Precious Sons. unabr. ed. George Furth. Perf. by Judith Ivey et al. 1 cass. (Running Time: 1 hr. 39 min.). 1995. 25.95 (978-1-58081-014-2(4), TPT65) Pub: L A Theatre. Dist(s): NetLibrary CO
An eccentric mother on Chicago's South Side rules her family with wisecracks & a will of iron. When she squares off against her husband over the fate of their "precious sons," shattering family secrets come to light.

Precious Stones in Lore & Legend. Instructed by Manly P. Hall. 8.95 (978-0-89314-219-3(0), C610507) Philos Res.

Precious Time. Erica James. (Isis (CDs) Ser.). (J). 2005. audio compact disk 104.95 (978-0-7531-2398-0(3)) Pub: ISIS Lrg Prnt GBR. Dist(s): Ulverscroft US

Precious Time. unabr. ed. Erica James. Read by Julia Sands. 14 cass. (Running Time: 16 hrs.). (Isis Ser.). (J). 2002. 99.95 (978-0-7531-1292-2(2)) Pub: ISIS Lrg Prnt GBR. Dist(s): Ulverscroft US
In order to spend some precious time with her four-year-old son Ned before he starts school, single mother Clara Costello trades in her secure, well-paid job abd two-seater sports car for a camper van and sets off with Ned on a mystery tour of England. But you know what they say about the best-laid plans? Clara and Ned get no furhter than Deaconsbridge, a small market town on the edge of the Peak District, where fate and some colourful local characters conspire to keep them for a while.

Precipice. abr. ed. Read by William Franklyn. Contrib. by Colin Forbes. 2 cass. (Running Time: 3 hrs.). (ENG., 2001. 16.95 (978-0-333-66952-5(5)) Pub: Macmillan UK GBR. Dist(s): Trafalgar
Britain's best secret agents Tweed, Paula Grey and international foreign correspondent Bob Newman are back once again. In this 1996 thriller, they are on the trail of billionnaire Leopold Brazil, a communications tycoon. Tweed suspects he has a major world-threatening plan after seeing photographs of a rogue satellite being launched from French Guiana on the Ariane rocket delivery system. Brazil, with a base in Switzerland and a residence in Dorset, England, hides behind heavies and devious lawyers alike. Tweed's trail takes him and his team to Dorset, Geneva, Zurich and also the Swiss Valais canyon. Paula Grey is almost kidnapped and battle erupts on a mountainside when Brazil's plan to disable global communications and bring back Russia.

Precipice. unabr. ed. Ben Bova et al. Read by Amanda Karr & Scott Sowers. 10 CDs. (Running Time: 12 hrs. 0 mins. 0 sec.). (Grand Tour Ser.). (ENG.). 2005. audio compact disk 44.95 (978-1-59397-490-9(6)) Pub: Macmill Audio. Dist(s): Macmillan

Precision & Flexibility. unabr. ed. Jeannie Deva. 1 cass. (Running Time: 1 hr.). (Deva Method Advanced Vocal Exercises Ser.: Vol. 2). 1996. 12.00 (978-1-882224-16-6(7)) Jeannie Deva.
Second of a series of vocal exercise tapes that complement "The Contemporary Vocalist Improvement Course".

Precision Tools for Metalworking in Germany: A Strategic Reference 2006. Compiled by Icon Group International, Inc. Staff. 2007. ring bd. 195.00 (978-0-497-35982-9(0)) Icon Grp.

Predator. (Song Box Ser.). (gr. 1-2). bk. 8.50 (978-0-7802-2261-8(X)) Wright Group.

***Predator.** Terri Blackstock. (Running Time: 8 hrs. 55 mins. 25 sec.). (ENG.). 2010. 19.99 (978-0-310-28913-5(0)) Zondervan.

Predator. unabr. ed. Terri Blackstock. (Running Time: 8 hrs. 55 mins. 25 sec.). (ENG.). 2011. audio compact disk 32.99 (978-0-310-28911-1(4)) Zondervan.

Predator. unabr. ed. Patricia Cornwell. 13 CDs. (Running Time: 16 hrs.). (Kay Scarpetta Ser.: No. 14). 2005. audio compact disk 104.00 (978-1-4159-2547-8(X)) Books on Tape.

Predator. unabr. collector's ed. Patricia Cornwell. Read by Kate Reading. 11 cass. (Running Time: 16 hrs.). (Kay Scarpetta Ser.: No. 14). 2005. 99.00 (978-1-4159-0758-0(7)) Books on Tape.

Predator: 1 Big Book, 6 Each of 1 Student Book, & 1 Cassette. (Song Box Ser.). (gr. 1-2). 68.95 (978-0-7802-3205-1(4)) Wright Group.

Predator State: How Conservatives Abandoned the Free Market & Why Liberals Should Too. unabr. ed. James K. Galbraith. (Running Time: 7.5 hrs. 0 mins.). (ENG.). 2009. 29.95 (978-1-4332-8779-4(X)); 54.95 (978-1-4332-8775-6(7)); audio compact disk 24.95 (978-1-4332-8778-7(1)); audio compact disk 69.00 (978-1-4332-8776-3(5)) Blckstn Audio.

Predators. unabr. ed. Frederick Ramsay. (Running Time: 8 hrs. 0 mins.). 2009. 29.95 (978-1-4417-1404-6(9)); 54.95 (978-1-4417-1400-8(6)); audio compact disk 76.00 (978-1-4417-1401-5(4)) Blckstn Audio.

Predators & Prey. Sundance/Newbridge, LLC Staff. (Early Science Ser.). (gr. k-3). 2007. audio compact disk 12.00 (978-1-4007-6544-7(7)); audio compact disk 12.00 (978-1-4007-6543-0(9)); audio compact disk 12.00 (978-1-4007-6542-3(0)) Sund Newbrdge.

Predestination: Is God for You or Against You? Romans 8:29-34. Ben Young. 1996. 4.95 (978-0-7417-6007-4(X), B0007) Win Walk.

Predestined Glory. Neville Goddard. 1 cass. (Running Time: 62 min.). 1970. 8.00 (87) J & L Pubns.
Neville taught Imagination Creates Reality. He was a powerfully influential teacher of God as Consciousness.

Predestined Love. Dick Sutphen. Read by Dick Sutphen. 2 cass. (Running Time: 3 hrs.). (New Age Nonfiction Ser.). 1991. 14.95 Set. (978-0-87554-454-0(1), N107) Valley Sun.
True cases of reincarnation & people who discovered, through regressive hypnosis, how each lifetime opens the door to a new, more enlightened love.

Predictability with Transits. Sylvia Sherman. 1 cass. 8.95 (314) Am Fed Astrologers.
Analyzing happenings through "now" planets.

Predictable Communication Strategies: Powerful Strategies for Predictable Outcomes. (ENG.). 2009. audio compact disk 125.00 (978-0-925640-03-1(4)) Outcomes Unltd.

Predictable Results in Unpredictable Times. abr. unabr. ed. Stephen R. Covey et al. (Running Time: 3 hrs. 0 mins. 0 sec.). (ENG.). 2010. audio compact disk 19.99 (978-1-936111-01-5(2)) Pub: Franklin Covey. Dist(s): S and S Inc

Predictable Results in Unpredictable Times E-Audio. Stephen R. Covey. (ENG.). 2009. (978-1-936111-02-2(0)) Franklin Covey.

Predictably Irrational: The Hidden Forces That Shape Our Decisions. unabr. ed. Dan Ariely & Michael D'Orso. Read by Simon Jones. (Running Time: 27000 sec.). 2008. audio compact disk 34.95 (978-0-06-145785-2(X), Harper Audio) HarperCollins Pubs.

Predicting the Weather Audio CD. Adapted by Benchmark Education Company Staff. Based on a work by Katherine Scraper. (Early Explorers Set C Ser.). (J). (gr. 1). 2008. audio compact disk 10.00 (978-1-60437-533-6(7)) Benchmark Educ.

Predictive Astrology. Sophia Mason. 5 cass. 1992. 8.95 ea. Am Fed Astrologers.

Predictive Compatibility Readings. Howard S. Berg. 1 cass. 8.95 (636) Am Fed Astrologers.
An AFA Convention workshop tape.

Predictive Power of Options. Instructed by Larry McMillan. (Running Time: 110 mins.). 2005. audio compact disk 19.95 (978-1-59280-158-9(7)) Marketplace Bks.
Recorded at the International Online Trading Expo 4A. One of the country's top experts in options trading offers the very latest strategies in option trading techniques, covering hedging, volatility, and pricing concepts, plus his own options philosophy. You will learn how to incorporate the predictive power of options in your daily trading.

Predictive Techniques. Laura Des Jardins. 1 cass. (Running Time: 90 min.). 1984. 8.95 (085) Am Fed Astrologers.

Predictors of Preterm Labor. Contrib. by Charles J. Lockwood et al. 1 cass. (American College of Obstetrics & Gynecologists UPDATE: Vol. 24, No. 9). 1998. 20.00 Am Coll Obstetric.

Preeminence of Truth. Dan Comer. 1 cass. 3.00 (74) Evang Outreach.

Preeminent Person of Christ: A Study of Hebrews 1-10. 1998. 57.95 (978-1-57972-271-5(7)) Insight Living.

Preeminente Persona de Cristo. 2005. audio compact disk 522.80 (978-1-57972-673-7(9)) Insight Living.

Preface see Osbert Sitwell Reading His Poetry

Preface to the Holographic Mind. unabr. ed. Karl Pribram. 1 cass. (Running Time: 90 min.). 1978. 11.00 (04601) Big Sur Tapes.

Prefaces to Shakespeare's Plays. unabr. ed. A. L. Rowse. Read by Bill Kelsey. 7 cass. (Running Time: 10 hrs. 30 min.). 1992. 56.00 (978-0-7366-2154-0(7), 2953) Books on Tape.
An authority on Elizabethan England, the author throws new light on the circumstances behind the plays.

Preferential Policies. unabr. ed. Thomas Sowell. Read by Michael Wells. 4 cass. (Running Time: 5 hrs. 30 mins.). 1990. 32.95 (978-0-7861-0193-1(8), 1169) Blckstn Audio.
By "preferential policies" the author means government-mandated policies concerning government-designated groups, policies which legally mandate that citizens are not all judged by the same criteria or subjected to the same procedures. In this work, he analyzes the mechanisms & consequences of these legalized preferences in an international context, paying particular attention to programs in India, Malaysia, Sri Lanka & the United States.

Preferred Provider Organization & Alternative Health Care Delivery Systems. 1984. bk. 90.00; 55.00 PA Bar Inst.

Pregnancy. Bruce Goldberg. Read by Bruce Goldberg. 1 cass. (Running Time: 25 min.). (ENG.). 2006. 13.00 (978-1-885577-38-2(9)) Pub: B Goldberg. Dist(s): Baker Taylor
Reduce the discomforts of confinement through self-hypnosis.

Pregnancy & Birth. Milton Diamond. 1 cass. (Running Time: 1 hr.). (Human Sexuality Ser.). 11.95 (34011) J Norton Pubs.

Pregnancy & Childbirth. Steven Gurgevich. (ENG.). 2002. audio compact disk 19.95 (978-1-932170-11-5(1), HWH) Tranceformation.

Pregnancy & the Mind: Program from the Award Winning Public Radio Series. Interview. Hosted by Fred Goodwin. Comment by John Hockenberry. 1 CD. (Running Time: 1 hr.). 2004. audio compact disk 21.95 (978-1-932479-83-6(X), LCM 311) Lichtenstein Creat.
We think about pregnancy as a time when women glow, right? Full of happy expectation for the future. But for many women, that's simply not the case. We'll break through the myths to explore the truth about pregnancy and mental illness. We'll also look at the way a baby's mind develops, and ask: just how much does a fetus pick up from the outside?Guests include Dr. Shari Lusskin and Dr. Zachary Stowe, both experts in reproductive psychiatry, and developmental psychologist Dr. Janet DiPietro. All this, plus a reading of Oh Baby the Places You'll Go: A Book to Be Read in Utero adapted by author Tish Rabe from the works of Dr. Seuss, and Irish singer-songwriter Susan McKeown performs a ballad of motherhood.Plus commentary by John Hockenberry describing his wife's two pregnancies - which resulted in four children.

Pregnancy & the Vegetarian Diet. unabr. ed. Michael Klaper. Read by Michael Klaper. 1 cass. (Running Time: 30 min.). (Help Yourself to Health Ser.). 1987. 7.00 (978-0-929274-08-9(3)); 3.40 Gentle World.
An overview of nutrition & pregnancy & the role of pure vegetarian nutrition in producing optimal health.

***Pregnant Widow.** Martin Amis. Narrated by Steven Pacey. (Running Time: 14 hrs. 10 mins. 0 sec.). (ENG.). 2010. audio compact disk 29.95 (978-1-60998-136-5(7)) Pub: AudioGO. Dist(s): Perseus Dist

Prego! An Invitation to Italian. 5th ed. Graziana Lazzarino & Janice Aski. 1 cass. (Running Time: 1 hr.). (ITA.). (C). 2000. 16.56 (978-0-07-231032-0(4), 9780072310320, Mc-H Human Soc); audio compact disk 13.43 (978-0-07-233991-8(8), Mc-H Human Soc) Pub: McGrw-H Hghr Educ. Dist(s): McGraw

Prego! An Invitation to Italian. 5th ed. Graziana Lazzarino et al. 1 CD. (Running Time: 90 min.). (C). 2000. bk. & stu. ed. 91.87 (978-0-07-234221-5(8), Mc-H Human Soc); bk. & stu. ed. 58.00 (978-0-07-235004-3(0), Mc-H Human Soc) McGrw-H Hghr Educ.

Prego! Vol. 1: Student Program, Vol. 1. 4th ed. Graziana Lazzarino. 1 cass. (Running Time: 90 min.). (C). 1995. 47.81 (978-0-07-911937-7(9), Mc-H Human Soc) Pub: McGrw-H Hghr Educ. Dist(s): McGraw

Prego! An Invitation to Italian Pt. B. 5th ed. Graziana Lazzarino & Janice Aski. 1 cass. (Running Time: 90 min.). (C). 2000. stu. ed. 31.56 (978-0-07-230900-3(8), Mc-H Human Soc) Pub: McGrw-H Hghr Educ. Dist(s): McGraw

Prego! Listening Comprehension. 4th ed. Lazzarino. 1 cass. (Running Time: 1 hr.). 1995. 15.00 (978-0-07-037766-0(9), Mc-H Human Soc) Pub: McGrw-H Hghr Educ. Dist(s): McGraw

***Preguntas que Hacen los Cristianos.** Charles R. Swindoll.Tr. of Questions Christians Ask. 2010. audio compact disk 34.00 (978-1-57972-894-6(4)) Insight Living.

Prehistoric Birds. 1 cass. (Running Time: 45 min.). Dramatization. (J). pap. bk. 4.98 (978-0-86545-084-4(6)) Spizzirri.
Interesting facts about the first reptile bird, the giant fround birds & the first flying birds of the prehistoric world.

Prehistoric Birds. Ed. by Linda Spizzirri. Illus. by Peter M. Spizzirri. 1 cass. (Running Time: 45 min.). Dramatization. (J). (gr. 1-8). pap. bk. 4.98 incl. educational coloring bk. (978-0-86545-023-3(4)) Spizzirri.

Prehistoric Fish. unabr. ed. Peter M. Spizzirri. Read by Charles Fuller. Ed. by Linda Spizzirri. (Running Time: 15 min.). (Educational Coloring Book & Cassette Ser.). (J). (gr. 1-8). pap. bk. 6.95 (978-0-86545-086-8(2)) Spizzirri.
The Jawless Fish, giant duncleosteus & many other dwellers of ancient oceans are featured.

Prehistoric Life. Dorling Kindersley Publishing Staff. (Eyewitness Videos Ser.). (ENG.). (J). (gr. 3). 2009. 12.99 (978-0-7566-5546-4(3)) DK Pub Inc.

Prehistoric Mammals. unabr. ed. Peter M. Spizzirri. Read by Charles Fuller. Ed. by Linda Spizzirri. 1 cass. (Running Time: 15 min.). Dramatization. (Educational Coloring Book & Cassette Ser.). (J). (gr. 1-8). pap. bk. 4.98 (978-0-86545-087-5(0)) Spizzirri.
The cave bear, saber-toothed cat & mastodon are a few of the mammals that you will meet in this book.

Prehistoric Sea Life. 1 cass. Dramatization. (J). pap. bk. 6.95 (978-0-86545-083-7(8)) Spizzirri.
Interesting data about Mesosaurs, Fish Lizards, Tylosaurs Proniger & many more.

Prehistoric Sea Life. Ed. by Linda Spizzirri. Illus. by Arnie Kohn. 1 cass. Dramatization. (J). (gr. 1-8). pap. bk. 4.98 incl. educational coloring bk. (978-0-86545-020-2(X)) Spizzirri.

Prehistory: The Making of the Human Mind. unabr. ed. Colin Renfrew. Narrated by Robert Ian MacKenzie. 8 cass. (Running Time: 9 hrs. 15 mins.). 2009. 82.75 (978-1-4361-9222-4(6)); audio compact disk 123.75 (978-1-4361-9223-1(4)) Recorded Bks.

Prehistory: The Making of the Human Mind. unabr. collector's ed. Colin Renfrew. Narrated by Robert Ian MacKenzie. 8 CDs. (Running Time: 9 hrs. 15 mins.). 2009. audio compact disk 49.95 (978-1-4361-9224-8(2)) Recorded Bks.

Prejudice: Program from the Award Winning Public Radio Series. Interview. Hosted by Fred Goodwin. 1 CD. (Running Time: 1hr). (Infinite Mind Ser.). 2002. audio compact disk 21.95 (978-1-888064-84-1(6), LCM 214) Lichtenstein Creat.
In this hour, we explore the topic of Prejudice. Why do human beings so often divide the world into "us" and "them?" Whether it's black or white, young or old, gay or straight, people often make irrational presumptions about others. This week, we explore the psychology of prejudice with social psychologists Dr. Mahzarin Banaji of Harvard University, Dr. Susan Fiske of Princeton University and Dr. Gregory Herek of the University of California at Davis. And we talk to writer Esmeralda Santiago, journalist Ellis Cose, and filmmakers Marco Williams and Whitney Dow about the psychological effects of prejudice.

Prejudice to Purity (Nathaniel) John 1:46-47. Ed Young. 1985. 4.95 (978-0-7417-1470-1(1), 470) Win Walk.

Prelude, or, Growth of a Poet's Mind: Book Fifth: While I Was Seated in a Rocky Cave see Selected Poetry of William Wordsworth

Prelude, or, Growth of a Poet's Mind: Book First: Oh, Many a Time Have I, a Five-Year's Child see Selected Poetry of William Wordsworth

Prelude to a Kiss. unabr. ed. Craig Lucas. Perf. by Charles Durning et al. 1 cass. (Running Time: 1 hr. 25 mins.). 2000. 20.95 (978-1-58081-167-5(1), TPT143) L A Theatre.

Prelude to Foundation. unabr. ed. Isaac Asimov. Read by Larry McKeever. 12 cass. (Running Time: 18 hrs.). 1994. 96.00 (978-0-7366-2831-0(2), 3539) Books on Tape.
A young Outworld mathematician's theory of prediction makes him the most sought-after man in the Galactic Empire. Why? He holds the key to the future!.

Prelude to Glory Vol. 1: Our Sacred Honor. Ron Carter. 14 cass. (Running Time: 16 hrs.). 1998. 39.95 Set. (978-1-57008-572-7(2), Bkcraft Inc) Deseret Bk.
Presents the early events of the Revolutionary War through the eyes of common people. We meet the heroes, but we see them through the eyes and hearts of the soldiers and the sailors, men and women, who came out of the shops, fields, and forests and paid the price.

Prelude to Glory Vol. 2: The Times That Try Men's Souls. unabr. ed. Ron Carter. 6 cass. (Running Time: 9 hrs.). 2003. 39.95 (978-1-57008-671-7(0)) Deseret Bk.
Focusing primarily on events between June and December 1776, this installment in the series follows Billy Weems (friend of Matthew Dunson from volume 1) to the battlefields in the New York area, where General George Washington commands the Continental army. Early on, Billy meets and befriends Eli Stroud, a white man raised by Iroquois Indians, who lends his unusual talents to the Revolutionary cause.

Prelude to Glory Vol. 6: The World Turned Upside Down. abr. ed. Ron Carter. Read by Ron Carter. 2 cass. (Running Time: 3 hrs.). 2003. 15.95 (978-1-57008-848-3(9)) Deseret Bk.
Having underestimated the resolve and strength of the Continental Army in New England, Great Britain adopts a new strategy in the war to subdue the American rebels.

Prelude to Glory Vol. 7: The Impending Storm. abr. ed. Ron Carter. 2 cass. (Running Time: 3 hrs.). 2003. 19.95 (978-1-59038-173-1(4), 995-103, Shadow Mount) Pub: Deseret Bk. Dist(s): Bookworld
October 19, 1781: The great guns at Yorktown fell silent, British General Cornwallis surrendered, and England conceded the war. For one euphoric moment a shout of jubilation rolled forth in America - and then harsh reality gripped the country. America was thirteen separate countries, each with its own money, political organization, culture, and history. Congress was essentially powerless.

Prelude to Pearl Harbor. Kenneth Bruce. 1 cass. (Running Time: 1 hr.). Dramatization. (Excursions in History Ser.). 12.50 Alpha Tape.

Prelude to Terror. unabr. collector's ed. Helen MacInnes. Read by Donada Peters. 9 cass. (Running Time: 13 hrs. 30 min.). 1997. 72.00 (978-0-7366-4025-1(8), 4524) Books on Tape.
The art world meets cloak-&-dagger intrigue in a Cold War thriller.

Prelude to World War I. Kenneth Bruce. 1 cass. (Running Time: 1 hr.). Dramatization. (Excursions in History Ser.). 12.50 Alpha Tape.

Preludes for Memnon XIV, XIX, LXIII, III, XXIX see Twentieth-Century Poetry in English: Recordings of Poets Reading Their Own Poetry

Preludes I see Gathering of Great Poetry for Children

Premarital Institute: A Partnership Ministry. 1 cass. (Care Cassettes Ser.: Vol. 17, No. 5). 1990. 10.80 Assn Prof Chaplains.

Premature Burial see Great American Short Stories, Vol. II, A Collection

Premature Burial. Edgar Allan Poe. 1983. (S-53) Jimcin Record.

Premature Burial. unabr. ed. Edgar Allan Poe. Perf. by David Ely. 1 cass. (Running Time: 76 min.). Dramatization. 1986. 8.95 (S-75) Jimcin Record.

Premature Burial & Other Stories. unabr. ed. Edgar Allan Poe. Read by Carol Mazer. 2 cass. (Running Time: 2 hrs. 30 min.). Dramatization. 1991. 16.95 Set. (978-1-55686-378-3(0), 378) Books in Motion.
Included: The Premature Burial, A Tale of the Ragged Mountains, The Oval Portrait, Ms. Found in a Bottle, & The Facts in the Case of M. Valdemar.

Premature Burial & The Oblong Box. Edgar Allan Poe. 1 cass. 1989. 7.95 (S-75) Jimcin Record.
More visions of the macabre.

Premenstrual Syndrome. Barrie Konicov. 1 cass. 11.98 (978-0-87082-354-1(X), 100) Potentials.
Many studies point to the fact that chemical changes in a woman's body during her period make her more prone to anger, accidents, & extreme mood changes. Begin using this cassette five days before the menstrual cycle begins &, according to the author, all that will change.

Premier. unabr. collector's ed. Georges Simenon. Read by Michael Prichard. 5 cass. (Running Time: 5 hrs.). 1983. 30.00 (978-0-7366-0537-3(1), 1511) Books on Tape.
An elderly French statesman, former premier of the nation, retires to a small farmhouse in Normandy at the edge of the sea. Left alone with his thoughts & memories, this once-powerful manipulator of people & events contemplates a past in which he traded a lifetime of humanity for a moment at the summit.

Premier Celebration of the Gods in Every Man. Jean S. Bolen. 1 cass. 9.00 (A0232-89) Sound Photosyn.
At the Palace of Fine Arts in San Francisco.

Premiere Comparution. 1 cass. (Running Time: 60 mins.). Dramatization. (Maitres du Mystere Ser.). (FRE.). 1996. 11.95 (1383-MA) Olivia & Hill.
Popular radio thriller, interpreted by France's best actors.

Premiere Enquete de Maigret, Set. Georges Simenon. Read by Moulouji & Vanina Michel. 2 cass. (FRE.). 1995. 28.95 (1626-LQP) Olivia & Hill.
A young, newly-married, Maigret shows the methods & insights that will make him famous as he investigates a murder involving an influential family.

Premiere Ligne. l.t. ed. Jean-Marie Laclavetine. (French Ser.). (FRE., 2000. bk. 30.99 (978-2-84011-357-7(0)) Pub: UlverLrgPrint GBR. Dist(s): Ulverscroft US

Premiers Poemes. Ruth P. Weinreb. (J). (gr. 8-10). 1982. 31.96 (978-0-8013-0147-6(5), 75810) Longman.

Premises Liability & Construction Work Site Accidents. (Running Time: 4 hrs.). 1995. 92.00 Incl. 209p. coursebk. (20571) NYS Bar.
This series of presentations dealing with construction site incidents explores the elements, defenses & obstacles to the actions brought by plaintiffs against defendants as well as claims brought by the defendants against the employer in third-party actions. The coverage available to a third-party defendant for the various theories of recovery is also discussed.

Prenatal Eclipse: A Key to Karmic Needs. Rose Lineman. 1 cass. (Running Time: 90 min.). 1994. 8.95 (214) Am Fed Astrologers.

Prendimiento de Antonito el Camborio en el Camino de Sevilla see Poesia y Drama de Garcia Lorca

Prentice Alvin. Orson Scott Card. Read by Ray Verna. 8 cass. (Running Time: 11 hrs. 10 min.). (Tales of Alvin Maker Ser.: No. 3). 1993. 50.60 Set. (978-1-56544-047-0(1), 550005); Rental 10.50 Set, 30-day. (550005) Literate Ear.
Alvin finally begins his apprenticeship. Who can guess that the blacksmith's new apprentice is actually preparing himself for a higher calling, as a Maker?.

Prentice Alvin. unabr. ed. Orson Scott Card. Read by Orson Scott Card. Read by Stefan Rudnicki & Gabrielle De Cuir. (Running Time: 50400 sec.). (Tales of Alvin Maker Ser.). 2007. 79.95 (978-1-4332-0236-0(0)); audio compact disk 29.95 (978-1-4332-0238-4(7)); audio compact disk 99.00 (978-1-4332-0237-7(9)) Blckstn Audio.

Prentice Hall Jazz Collection. Compiled by David Cutler. 2003. audio compact disk 20.60 (978-0-13-111674-0(6), P-H) Pearson Educ CAN CAN.

Prentice Hall Literature: ExamView(r) Textbank Software. (J). (gr. 6 up). audio compact disk 129.97 (978-0-13-165150-0(1)) PH School.

Prentice Hall Literature: ExamView(r) Textbank Software. (YA). (gr. 7 up). audio compact disk 129.97 (978-0-13-165151-7(X)) PH School.

Prentice Hall Literature: ExamView(r) Textbank Software. (YA). (gr. 8 up). audio compact disk 129.97 (978-0-13-165152-4(8)) PH School.

Prentice Hall Literature: Listening to Literature Audio CD. cass. & audio compact disk 188.97 (978-0-13-165087-9(4)) PH School.

Prentice Hall Literature: Listening to Literature Audio CD. (YA). (gr. 10 up). cass. & audio compact disk 188.97 (978-0-13-165065-7(3)) PH School.

Prentice Hall Literature: Listening to Literature Audio CD. (YA). (gr. 11 up). cass. & audio compact disk 188.97 (978-0-13-165066-4(1)) PH School.

Prentice Hall Literature: Listening to Literature Audio CD. (YA). (gr. 12 up). cass. & audio compact disk 188.97 (978-0-13-165067-1(X)) PH School.

Prentice Hall Literature: Listening to Literature Audio CD. (J). (gr. 6 up). cass. & audio compact disk 188.97 (978-0-13-165061-9(0)) PH School.

Prentice Hall Literature: Listening to Literature Audio CD. (YA). (gr. 7 up). cass. & audio compact disk 188.97 (978-0-13-165062-6(9)) PH School.

Prentice Hall Literature: Listening to Literature Audio CD. (YA). (gr. 8 up). cass. & audio compact disk 188.97 (978-0-13-165063-3(7)) PH School.

Prentice Hall Literature: Listening to Literature Audio CD. (YA). (gr. 9 up). cass. & audio compact disk 188.97 (978-0-13-165064-0(5)) PH School.

Prentice Hall Literature: Listening to Literature Audiocassettes. (YA). (gr. 10 up). 65.47 (978-0-13-065145-7(1)) PH School.

Prentice Hall Literature: Listening to Literature Audiocassettes. (YA). (gr. 11 up). 81.97 (978-0-13-065137-2(0)) PH School.

Prentice Hall Literature: Listening to Literature Audiocassettes. (YA). (gr. 12 up). 81.97 (978-0-13-065111-2(7)) PH School.

Prentice Hall Literature: Listening to Literature Audiocassettes. (J). (gr. 6 up). 65.47 (978-0-13-065335-2(7)) PH School.

Prentice Hall Literature: Listening to Literature Audiocassettes. (YA). (gr. 7 up). 65.47 (978-0-13-065327-7(6)) PH School.

Prentice Hall Literature: Listening to Literature Audiocassettes. (YA). (gr. 8 up). 65.47 (978-0-13-065319-2(5)) PH School.

Prentice Hall Literature: Listening to Literature Audiocassettes. (YA). (gr. 9 up). 65.47 (978-0-13-065293-5(8)) PH School.

Prentice Hall Literature: Listening to Literature: Book on CD. (YA). (gr. 12 up). audio compact disk 188.97 (978-0-13-180273-5(9)) PH School.

Prentice Hall Literature: Listening to Literature: Book on Tape. (YA). (gr. 10 up). reel tape 188.97 (978-0-13-063508-2(1)) PH School.

Prentice Hall Literature: Listening to Literature: Book on Tape. (YA). (gr. 11 up). reel tape 188.97 (978-0-13-063506-8(5)) PH School.

Prentice Hall Literature: Listening to Literature: Book on Tape. (YA). (gr. 12 up). reel tape 188.97 (978-0-13-063507-5(3)); reel tape 188.97 (978-0-13-180267-4(4)) PH School.

Prentice Hall Literature: Listening to Literature: Book on Tape. (J). (gr. 6 up). reel tape 188.97 (978-0-13-063490-0(5)) PH School.

Prentice Hall Literature: Listening to Literature: Book on Tape. (YA). (gr. 7 up). reel tape 188.97 (978-0-13-063501-3(4)) PH School.

Prentice Hall Literature: Listening to Literature: Book on Tape. (YA). (gr. 8 up). reel tape 188.97 (978-0-13-063502-0(2)) PH School.

Prentice Hall Literature: Listening to Literature: Book on Tape. (YA). (gr. 9 up). reel tape 188.97 (978-0-13-063503-7(0)) PH School.

Prentice Hall Literature: Reader's Companion Adapted & English Learner's Version Audio Program. (YA). (gr. 12 up). 49.97 (978-0-13-180276-6(3)) PH School.

Prentice Hall Literature: Reader's Companion Audio Program. (YA). (gr. 12 up). 49.97 (978-0-13-180275-9(5)) PH School.

Prentice Hall Literature: Reader's Notebook Adapt/English Learner's Version. cass. & audio compact disk 49.97 (978-0-13-165189-0(7)) PH School.

Prentice Hall Literature: Reader's Notebook Adapt/English Learner's Version. (YA). (gr. 10 up). cass. & audio compact disk 49.97 (978-0-13-165147-0(1)) PH School.

Prentice Hall Literature: Reader's Notebook Adapt/English Learner's Version. (YA). (gr. 11 up). cass. & audio compact disk 49.97 (978-0-13-165148-7(X)) PH School.

Prentice Hall Literature: Reader's Notebook Adapt/English Learner's Version. (YA). (gr. 12 up). cass. & audio compact disk 49.97 (978-0-13-165149-4(8)) PH School.

Prentice Hall Literature: Reader's Notebook Adapt/English Learner's Version. (J). (gr. 6 up). cass. & audio compact disk 49.97 (978-0-13-165143-2(9)) PH School.

Prentice Hall Literature: Reader's Notebook Adapt/English Learner's Version. (YA). (gr. 7 up). cass. & audio compact disk 49.97 (978-0-13-165144-9(7)) PH School.

Prentice Hall Literature: Reader's Notebook Adapt/English Learner's Version. (YA). (gr. 8 up). cass. & audio compact disk 49.97 (978-0-13-165145-6(5)) PH School.

Prentice Hall Literature: Reader's Notebook Adapt/English Learner's Version. (YA). (gr. 9 up). cass. & audio compact disk 49.97 (978-0-13-165146-3(3)) PH School.

Prentice Hall Literature: Spanish/English Summaries. cass. & audio compact disk 53.97 (978-0-13-165188-3(9)) PH School.

Prentice Hall Literature: Spanish/English Summaries. (YA). (gr. 10 up). cass. & audio compact disk 53.97 (978-0-13-165139-5(0)) PH School.

Prentice Hall Literature: Spanish/English Summaries. (YA). (gr. 11 up). cass. & audio compact disk 53.97 (978-0-13-165140-1(4)) PH School.

Prentice Hall Literature: Spanish/English Summaries. (YA). (gr. 12 up). cass. & audio compact disk 53.97 (978-0-13-165141-8(2)) PH School.

Prentice Hall Literature: Spanish/English Summaries. (J). (gr. 6 up). cass. & audio compact disk 53.97 (978-0-13-165135-7(8)) PH School.

Prentice Hall Literature: Spanish/English Summaries. (YA). (gr. 7 up). cass. & audio compact disk 53.97 (978-0-13-165136-4(6)) PH School.

Prentice Hall Literature: Spanish/English Summaries. (YA). (gr. 8 up). cass. & audio compact disk 53.97 (978-0-13-165137-1(4)) PH School.

Prentice Hall Literature: Spanish/English Summaries. (YA). (gr. 9 up). cass. & audio compact disk 53.97 (978-0-13-165138-8(2)) PH School.

Prentice Hall Rock & Roll Compilation: Volume 1, v.ume I. 3rd ed. Compiled by Reebee Garofalo. 2003. audio compact disk 27.40 (978-0-13-189784-7(5), P-H) Pearson Educ CAN CAN.

Prentice Hall World Explorer: Program Videotapes (8) with Teacher's Guides. 8 pieces. tchr. ed. 347.97 (978-0-13-434130-9(9)) PH School.

Prentice Hall World Explorer: Eastern Hemisphere: Guided Reading Audiotapes. (ENG & SPA.). 95.97 (978-0-13-115949-5(6)) PH School.

Prentice Hall World Explorer: Western Hemisphere: Guided Reading Audiotapes. (ENG & SPA.). 71.97 (978-0-13-115951-8(8)) PH School.

Prentice Hall's Observations in Child Development: Volume 1. David B. Daniel. 2002. audio compact disk 9.20 (978-0-13-048111-5(4), P-H) Pearson Educ CAN CAN.

Prenuptial Agreements. 1995. bk. 99.00 (ACS-948) PA Bar Inst.
Receive practical tips for negotiating & drafting prenuptial agreements, including what financial information must be provided under "Simeone.".

Prenuptial & Postnuptial Agreements after Simeone. 1 cass. (Running Time: 30 min.). 1990. 25.00 (AL-104) PA Bar Inst.

Prep. Curtis Sittenfeld. 2005. audio compact disk 39.99 (978-1-4193-4383-4(1)) Recorded Bks.

Prep for ACLS. unabr. ed. Instructed by Jill S. Flateland. 3 cass. (Running Time: 10 hrs.). 1993. 99.00 cass. & soft-bound bk. (HT35) Ctr Hlth Educ.
If you're dreading the ACLS exam & can't seem to plow through the ACLS book, this course is for you. Learn what you need to know to pass the ACLS exam. It's easy! Using the cassette seminar, you will learn: airway management; detailed algorithms; dysrhythmia interpretation; legal & ethical considerations; 1st & 2nd line drugs; PALS & NALS & more!.

Preparandonos para la victoria see Bible Boot Camp

Preparate para Amar: Solo para Jovenes. Angel Espinosa de los Monteros.Tr. of Prepare to Love. (SPA.). (YA). 2009. audio compact disk 15.00 (978-1-935405-28-3(4)) Hombre Nuevo.

***Preparation & Portrait of a Prophet.** Featuring Ravi Zacharias. 1998. audio compact disk 9.00 (978-1-61256-009-0(1)) Ravi Zach.

Preparation & Trial of a Medical Malpractice Case. Robert L. Conason. Read by Robert L. Conason. (Running Time: 3 hrs.). 1990. 85.00 NY Law Pub.
Expert guidance on subjects including the initial interview; case selectivity; investigation/obtaining records; finding & using experts; commencing litigation; pleadings; interrogatories; document discovery; & depositions. Also includes information about the physical examination of the plaintiff; settlement; organizing the presentation/order of proof; jury selection; the opening statement; direct examination; lawyer's demeanor & objections, cross examination & closing arguments.

Preparation for Remarriage. Howard B. Lyman. 1 cass. (Running Time: 25 min.). 10.95 (35022) J Norton Pubs.

Preparation for Rising Higher. Swami Amar Jyoti. 1 dolby cass. 1985. 9.95 (M-63) Truth Consciousness.
Importance of human birth. When ego's work is over. Self-purification. The higher school.

Preparation for Samadhi. Swami Amar Jyoti. 1 cass. 1976. 9.98 (P-5) Truth Consciousness.
Readiness comes through seeing our mind realistically. On complacency & forgetfulness. The need for precision.

Preparation for Successful Surgery. Created by Ellen Chernoff Simon. 1 CD. (Running Time: 70 min.). 2004. audio compact disk 18.00 (978-0-9765587-2-9(6)) Imadulation.
This audio contains guided imagery and medical hypnosis to help you experience a comfortable, successful surgery and recovery. Many studies have demonstrated that listening to a guided imagery recording prior to surgery can help speed recovery, reduce bleeding, lessen anxiety, reduce the amount of medication used, lessen the hospital stay, and increase feelings of comfort and ease.

Preparation for the New Catechism. Fr. Hardon. 7 cass. 28.00 Set. (93A) IRL Chicago.

Preparation of Mind & Heart. Swami Amar Jyoti. 1 cass. 1987. 9.95 (J-55) Truth Consciousness.
Stages of spiritual unfoldment. Readiness needed for the higher stages. Precise auto-reflection, self-analysis. Each soul has its own journey.

Preparation of the Bride. Derek Prince. 1 cass. (Running Time: 1 hr.). 1991. 5.95 (I-4327) Derek Prince.
The marriage supper of the Lamb is being prepared for His Bride. Will you be ready? How can you prepare?.

Preparation of the Fiduciary Income Tax Return. unabr. ed. Contrib. by Samuel H. Laitman. 8 cass. (Running Time: 11 hrs.). 1989. 50.00 course handbk. (T7-9201) PLI.
Designed to acquaint practitioners with how to prepare a Form 1041 return, this recording of PLI's February 1989 program examines the complicated concepts & pitfalls facing the practitioner.

Preparatory Course for the JLPT: Level 1. Setsuko Matsumoto & Keiko Hoshino. 2004. pap. bk. 39.95 (978-4-89689-431-8(6)) Cheng Tsui.

Prepare for Race Day Go Grab Your Shoes. Created by Ellen Chernoff Simon. 1 CD. (Running Time: 70 min.). 2004. audio compact disk 18.00 (978-0-9765587-8-1(5)) Imadulation.
This slef hypnosis CD is designed to condition your powerful subconscious mind to maintain a healthy regimen priorto your race day. You will hear suggestions and ideas that enhance your personal goals and support intelligent respect for your body and an awareness of your inter fitness and strength.

Prepare for Surgery, Heal Faster: Relaxation/Healing Process. Peggy Huddleston. 1 cass. 2004. 9.95 (978-0-9645757-3-8(6)) Angel River Pr.

Prepare for your Operation: Helps your child relax preparing them for a hospital Procedure. Lynda Hudson. Adam Skinner. (J). 2007. audio compact disk 29.50 (978-1-905557-25-7(6)) First Way Forward GBR.

Prepare for 2012 & Beyond (Double CD) Meditations, Exercises & Invocations. Diana Cooper & Rosemary Stephenson. (Running Time: 1 hr. 41 mins. 5 sec.). (ENG.). 2009. audio compact disk 21.95 (978-1-84409-188-1(0)) Pub: Findhorn Pr GBR. Dist(s): IPG Chicago

Prepare the Way. Morningstar. 1998. 10.99 (978-7-5124-0169-3(8)) Destiny Image Pubs.

Prepare to Be Healed: Mediatations for Before & After Medical Treatments. Michael Moran. 1 cass. (Running Time: 90 mins.). 1999. 10.95 (978-0-87159-817-2(5)) Unity Schl Christ.

Prepare to Copy. 1 cass. (Running Time: 1 hr.). 2000. 15.95 Prof Pride.
Four radio ATL's used. Students learn.

Prepare to Love see Preparate para Amar: Solo para Jovenes

Prepare to Meet Your God: Scriptural Meditations for the Terminally Ill & Their Caregivers. Glenn A. Pearson. 4 CDs. (Running Time: 4 hrs). 2007. audio compact disk 24.95 (978-0-9765222-2-5(5), Trestle Press) Ekklesia Pr.
This is an unabridged audio version of Prepare To Meet Your God, which Genesis Press has made available so that more people can be helped. The book, Prepare To Meet Your God, has the feel of Glenn being present with the person reading. This audio book actually brings Glenn in as direct contact with the person listening because Glenn reads the prayers and scriptures for each section. Glenn?s writing style is direct from his personal candor, as you will hear. Terminal illness is an unpopular subject, even in Christian circles. Few books deal with the emotional/spiritual questions people face with terminal illness. Prepare To Meet Your God is a pastoral book that will comfort, encourage and help the terminally ill and their caregivers deal with an expected death and the complications that lead up to it. This book is written with authority and sensibility but with compassion and delicacy. Few audio books will be as practical and spiritually uplifting on this subject as this one.

Prepare to Praise. Gloria Copeland. 1 cass. 1986. 5.00 (978-0-88114-691-2(9)) K Copeland Pubns.
Biblical teaching on praising God.

Prepared for Rage. unabr. ed. Dana Stabenow. Narrated by Lorelei King. 8 CDs. (Running Time: 9 hrs. 45 mins.). 2008. audio compact disk 79.95 (978-0-7927-5237-0(6)) AudioGO.

Prepared for Rage. unabr. ed. Dana Stabenow. Read by Lorelei King. 8 CDs. (Running Time: 10 hrs. 0 mins. 0 sec.). (ENG.). 2008. audio compact disk 39.95 (978-1-4272-0297-0(4)) Pub: Macmill Audio. Dist(s): Macmillan

Preparing a Case for Trial: The Last 180 Days. Read by Charles Breyer et al. (Running Time: 3 hrs.). 1992. 89.00 Incl. 77p. tape materials & Action Guide. (CP-55246) Cont Ed Bar-CA.
Higly respected litigators & legal lecturers offer practical advice on the mechanics of getting to trial (at-issue memorandum; trial-setting & status conferences; pre-trial motions; final discovery) & trial preparation (stipulations; preparing documentary evidence; oral testimony; & motions in limine & trial brief).

Preparing a Habitation for God. Rick Joyner. 1 cass. (Running Time: 90 mins.). (Foundation Ser.: Vol. 3). 2000. 5.00 (RJ05-003) Morning NC.
As an overview of God's plan for His church, this series contains essential truths for everyone who wants to see the church become all that she is called to be.

Preparing a Talk Vol. I: Fulton J. Sheen. unabr. ed. Fulton J. Sheen. 7 cass. (Running Time: 30 min.). (Life Is Worth Living Ser.: 0006). 1985. 29.95 F Sheen Comm.
The late Bishop Sheen explains his approach to the preparation & delivery of his television talks.

Preparing & Trying the Medical Malpractice Case. 1996. bk. 68.00 (AC-1061) PA Bar Inst.
This will explain how to utilize discovery techniques to ensure full disclosure, identify & analyze the major statutes that impact the area of medical malpractice & assist you in preparing your cases to maximize success.

Preparing & Trying the Medical Malpractice Case. 1991. 65.00 PA Bar Inst.

Preparing Black Children for Leadership. Rex A. Barnett. (Running Time: 18 min.). (YA). 1990. 16.99 (978-0-924198-07-6(9)) Hist Video.
How to prepare black children for leadership is discussed.

Preparing Clients for a Successful Reading. Elbert Wade. 1 cass. 8.95 (359) Am Fed Astrologers.
An AFA Convention workshop tape.

Preparing for A+ Certification: Instructor Resources; Instructor's Guide CD. Faithe Wempen. (Pc Maintenance Ser.). 2005. audio compact disk 69.95 (978-0-7638-1909-5(3)) EMC-Paradigm.

Preparing for A+ Certification: Student Courseware; Text with Encore! Companion CD & Workbook. Faithe Wempen. (Pc Maintenance Ser.). 2005. audio compact disk 70.95 (978-0-7638-1906-4(9)) EMC-Paradigm.

Preparing for a Forensic Mental Health Practice. Thomas Grisso. (Running Time: 60 min.). 1988. 13.95 (978-0-943158-27-3(3), PFP-TBP, Prof Resc Pr) Pro Resource.
Guides listeners through a process of self-examination concerning their preparedness for doing forensic evaluations & then describes concrete steps for listeners to prepare themselves for work in the legal arena.

Preparing for a Mission. Ed Pinegar. 1 cass. 2004. 9.95 (978-1-57734-232-8(1), 06005772) Covenant Comms.
An inspirational tape for prospective missionaries.

Preparing for Adolescence: Caution Changes Ahead. James C. Dobson. (Running Time: 8 hrs. 5 mins.). 2004. audio compact disk 39.99 (978-0-8307-3115-2(6), Gospel Light) Gospel Lght.

Preparing for Adolescence: How to Survive the Coming Years of Change. James C. Dobson. 8 cass. (Running Time: 8 hrs.). 2004. 39.99 (978-0-8307-2635-6(7), Gospel Light) Gospel Lght.

Preparing for Adolescence Pack: How to Survive the Coming Years of Change. James C. Dobson. (ENG.). 1999. audio compact disk 39.99 (978-0-8307-3830-4(4), Regal Bks) Gospel Lght.

Preparing for Adolescence Family Tape Pack. Perf. by James C. Dobson. 8 cass. 1999. 39.99 Set. Gospel Lght.
Six tapes for parents & kids to listen to together & 2 tapes just for parents.

Preparing for & Conducting a Winning Deposition. Ronald J. Cohen & Paula M. Demore. 1995. pap. bk. 185.00 (978-0-943380-99-5(5)) PEG MN.

Preparing for & Handling Child Custody Disputes. Moderated by Dennis Brown. (Running Time: 6 hrs. 30 min.). 1985. 110.00 incl. program handbook. NJ Inst CLE.
Discusses developing a strategy, selecting & preparing an expert, the court's increasing reliance on experts.

Preparing for & Trying the Personal Injury Case. Contrib. by William O. Barnes, Jr. et al. (Running Time: 7 hrs.). 1984. 90.00 incl. program handbook. NJ Inst CLE.
Topics covered include: recognizing the cause of action & its elements, discovery & demonstrative evidence, selection & use of expert witnesses, use of hypothetical questions.

Preparing for Career Success Instructor's CD. 3rd ed. Jerry Ryan & Roberta Ryan. (YA). audio compact disk 59.95 (978-1-59357-210-5(7), J2107) JIST Pubng.

Preparing for Childbirth. Martin Rossman. 1 CD. (Running Time: 1 hr. 15 mins.). 2006. audio compact disk 15.95 (978-1-59179-141-6(3), W772D) Sounds True.

Preparing for Christmas with Richard Rohr: Daily Reflections for Advent. Richard Rohr. 2 cass. (Running Time: 2 hrs.). 1992. vinyl bd. 17.95 (978-0-00-540786-8(9), A5200) St Anthony Mess Pr.
Challenges our traditional understanding of Advent and Christmas.

Preparing for Congressional Oversight & Investigation: Capitol Learning Audio Course: A How-to for Agency Officials & Members of the Private Sector. Eleanor Hill. Prod. by TheCapitol.Net. (ENG.). 2007. 47.00 (978-1-58733-064-3(4)) TheCapitol.

Preparing for Exams: Learning Skill III. Marianne L. McManus. 1 cass. (Running Time: 18 min.). (How to Ser.). 10.95 (17036) J Norton Pubs.
Ways in which the student can approach tests with a maximum of confidence.

Preparing for Messiah's Coming. Derek Prince. 1 cass. (I-4115) Derek Prince.

Preparing for Remarriage. Elizabeth A. Einstein. Read by Elizabeth A. Einstein. 1 cass. (Stepfamily Living Ser.: No. 3). 1992. 9.95 (978-1-884944-09-3(4)) E Einstein.
Explores the four tasks of remarriage preparation: Resolving, Rebuilding, Relinking & Remarrying.

Preparing for Surgery. Martin Rossman. 1 CD. (Running Time: 1 hr. 15 mins.). 2006. audio compact disk 15.95 (978-1-59179-140-9(5), W771D) Sounds True.

Preparing for, Taking, & Using Depositions. Read by H. Sinclair Kerr, Jr. et al. (Running Time: 6 hrs.). 1990. 97.00 Incl. 215p. tape materials. (CP-53262) Cont Ed Bar-CA.

Preparing for the SAT Exam. Audrey Troy. 1 cass. 10.00 (SP100057) SMI Intl.
Scoring well on the Scholastic Aptitude Test depends upon being prepared. Audrey Troy explains how students can take steps that will improve their scores. Explains different types of questions & a strategy for answering them plus other hints that will help students who plan college careers.

Preparing, Not over-Preparing, for Sales. Jeff Davidson. 2005. 14.95 (978-1-60729-223-4(8)) Breath Space Inst.

Preparing, Not over-Preparing, for Sales. Jeff Davidson. (ENG.). 2005. audio compact disk 14.95 (978-1-60729-116-9(9)) Breath Space Inst.

Preparing the Fiduciary Income Tax Return: Form 1041. Contrib. by Charles M. Aulino. (Running Time: 4 hrs.). 1985. 85.00 incl. program handbook. NJ Inst CLE.
Topics covered include distributable net income, trust accumulations, the throw-back rule, rules for grantor trusts, tiers, distributions in kind.

Preparing the Lord's Missionary. Ed Pinegar & Patricia Pinegar. 2004. audio compact disk 10.95 (978-1-57734-808-5(7)) Covenant Comms.

Preparing the Way: The Reopening of the John G. Lake Healing Rooms in Spokane, Washington. Cal Pierce. 2 cass. 2001. 14.99 (978-1-58158-054-9(1)) McDougal Pubng.

Preparing the Way for Jesus: Based on the Gospel of Luke. Cindy Holtrop & Shirley Cooman. (Running Time: 50 mins.). (Noel Ser.). 15.95 (978-1-56212-259-1(2), 416100) FaithAliveChr.

Preparing to Meet the Gods: The Soul Turned Inward. Read by John Van Eenwyk. 1 cass. (Running Time: 90 min.). (Facing the Gods Ser.: No. 1). 1987. 10.95 (978-0-7822-0315-8(9), 285) C G Jung IL.

Preparing to Meet the Savior. Steven A. Cramer. 1 cass. 7.98 (978-1-55503-413-9(6), 06004598) Covenant Comms.
Fireside drawn from second half of his book In the Arms of His Love.

Preparing YOU to WIN see Richard Harvey's Blackjack PowerPrep Session

Preparing Your Mind for Knee Surgery: A Proven Technique to Reduce Stress. 1 cass. (Running Time: 1 hr.). 1999. 10.00 (978-0-9673422-2-1(8)) Med Empathy.

Preparing Your Teen for Life. abr. ed. Dennis Rainey. Ed. by Keith Lynch. 6 cass. (Running Time: 6 hrs.). 1996. 29.95 Set. (978-1-57229-037-2(4)) FamilyLife.

Presbyterian Worship Planner. 1 CD. 1999. audio compact disk 99.95 (978-0-664-50103-7(6)) Pub: Geneva Press. Dist(s): Westminster John Knox
Resource for ministers and others who plan Presbyterian Worship.

Presbyterian Worship Planner: Version 2. 0. Created by Presbyterian Publishing Corporation. 2005. audio compact disk 149.95 (978-0-664-50280-5(6)) Pub: Presbyterian Pub. Dist(s): Westminster John Knox

Preschool Action Time. 1 cass. (Running Time: 1 hr.). (J). (ps). 2001. pap. bk. 10.95 (KIM 9110C); pap. bk. 14.95 (KIM 9110CD) Kimbo Educ.
This recording features gross & fine motor skills. Finger plays include Where Is Thumbkin?, Miss Mary Mack & Open, Shut Them. Action songs include Clean-Up Time, Miss Mary Mack, Dinosaur Visit, Ten Little Pumpkins, Tiny Tim & more. You'll even find a singing song! Includes guide.

Preschool Aerobic Fun. Georgiana Stewart. 1 LP. (J). (ps). 2001. pap. bk. & pupil's gde. ed. 11.95 (KIM 7052) Kimbo Educ.
Exciting musical activities provide exercises that pave the way to aerobic fitness skills. Warm-ups, stretches, continuous & vigorous activities & cool down. Includes guide.

Preschool Aerobic Fun. Georgiana Stewart. 1 CD. (J). (ps-3). 2001. pap. bk. 14.95 CD. (KIM7052CD) Kimbo Educ.

Preschool Aerobic Fun. Georgiana Stewart. 1 cass. (J). (ps-8). 2001. pap. bk. 10.95 (KIM 7052C) Kimbo Educ.

Preschool Favorites. Georgiana Stewart. 1 cass. (J). (ps). 2001. pap. bk. 10.95 (KIM 9122C); pap. bk. & pupil's gde. ed. 11.95 (KIM 9122) Kimbo Educ.
Give kids Get Up & Grow Power. Activities include bean bag play, finger plays, shapes, rhythm sticks, dances, games & pre-aerobics. Kids will love it!. Includes guide.

Preschool Favorites. abr. ed. 1 cass. (Running Time: 30 mins.). (J). 2002. 7.99 (978-1-894677-26-4(9)) Kidzup Prodns.
Includes "The Alphabet Song," "Wheels on the Bus," "Boom Boom Ain't It Great to Be Crazy," and others.

Preschool Favorites. abr. ed. Kidzup Productions Staff. 1 CD. (Running Time: 30 mins.). (Toddler Ser.). (J). 2003. audio compact disk 9.99 (978-1-894677-25-7(0)) Pub: Kidzup Prodns. Dist(s): Penton Overseas

Preschool Musical: The Little Red Hen; Mary & Her Little Lambs; Goldilocks & the Three Bears. unabr. ed. Tammy Carder. Read by Twin Sisters Productions. (J). 2008. 44.99 (978-1-60252-990-8(6)) Find a World.

Preschool Musical 2: A Catepillar's Voice; the Oversized, Overripe Turnip; the Lost Mitten. Karen Mitzo Hilderbrand & Kim Mitzo Thompson. (ENG.). (J). 2008. 44.99 (978-1-60514-656-0(0)) Find a World.

Preschool Play Songs. William Janiak. 1 LP. (Running Time: 1 hr.). (J). 2001. pap. bk. 11.95 (KIM 9118) Kimbo Educ.
More basic skills & fun that teach imaginative play, body identification, rhythmic awareness & more. Kids will love Alphabet Notion, March Around the Circle, Jack in the Box & other activity songs. Includes guide.

Preschool Play Songs. William Janiak. 1 cass. (Running Time: 30 min.). (J). (gr. 1). 2001. pap. bk. 10.95 (KIM 9118C) Kimbo Educ.

Preschool Playtime Band. 1 cass. (Running Time: 1 hr.). (J). (ps). 2001. pap. bk. 10.95 (KIM 9099C); pap. bk. 11.95 (KIM 9099); pap. bk. 14.95 (KIM 9099CD) Kimbo Educ.
Kids love a rhythm band & parade! Ragtime to rock melodies will have children marching while learning about rhythm. Lyrics, activities & suggestions for making simple rhythm instruments are included Follow the Band, Alexander's Ragtime Band, Yankee Doodle Dandy, Stars & Stripes, I Love a Piano, Entry of the Gladiators & Hey Look Me Over will start the band rolling.

Preschool Praise. Arranged by Jospeh Linn. 1 cass. (Running Time: 1 hr.). (J). 1988. 12.99 (TA-9096C) Lillenas.
A sequel to the best-selling collection Songs to Grow On, here is a terrific resource for all who work with preschoolers. 100 songs on a variety of topics, all in a songbook & matching split-channel cassette. The split-channel format of the cassette makes it suitable for listening, rehearsal or performance. Parents & grandparents, put this cassette in the hands of your preschoolers & make Christian learning a fun experience.

Preschool Songs. Perf. by Cedarmont Kids. 1 cass. (J). 1999. 3.99 (978-0-00-512659-2(2)) Provident Music.

Prescription for Advertising: A Common Sense Guide for Understanding the Complex & Confusing World of Advertising. unabr. ed. Edmond A. Bruneau. Read by Dick Estell. 3 cass. (Running Time: 4 hrs. 30 min.). 1986. bk. 37.95 incl. cass. & hardcover. (978-0-9616683-1-0(8)); pap. bk. 29.95 incl. cass. & paperback. (978-0-9616683-2-7(6)); pap. bk. 19.95 (978-0-9616683-3-4(4)) Boston Bks.
The do's & dont's of advertising. A presentation for the businessperson who wants to capitalize on the power of advertising but doesn't know the ropes.

Prescription for Anxiety: John 1:40. Ed Young. (J). 1978. 4.94 (978-0-7417-1025-3(0), A0025) Win Walk.

Prescription for Destruction: 11 Peter 3:10-18. Ed Young. 1983. 4.95 (978-0-7417-1350-6(0), 350) Win Walk.

Prescription for the Future: How the Technology Revolution Is Changing the Pulse of Global Health. Gwendolyn B. Moore et al. 1 cass. (Running Time: 60 min.). 1996. bk. 12.00 (978-1-888232-11-0(0)) Pub: Spurge ink. Dist(s): Natl Bk Netwk

Prescription to Grow Your GM-HBC Sales. 1 cass. (America's Supermarket Showcase '96 Ser.). 1996. 11.00 (NGA96-016) Sound Images.

Prescriptions for: Extraverts & Introverts, Sensers, Intuitives, Thinkers, Feelers, Judgers & Preceivers. William G. Murray & Rosalie R. Murray. 1 cass. (Running Time: 60 min.). (Type Communications Ser.). 1987. 10.00 (978-1-878287-54-0(0), ATAL) Type & Temperament.
Practical hints & prescriptions translating type theories into useful day-to-day action.

Presence. abr. ed. Duncan B. Campbell & T. Austin Sparks. 4 CDs. (Running Time: 4 hrs.). 2000. 24.99 (978-0-9677402-6-3(6)) Pub: Mercy Place. Dist(s): Destiny Image Pubs

Presence. unabr. ed. Eve Bunting. 4 cass. (Running Time: 5 hrs.). (YA). (gr. 6-10). 2004. 38.00 (978-1-4025-7351-4(0)) Recorded Bks.
Eve Bunting's thriller fairly crackles with suspense and danger as 17-year-old Catherine encounters a Presence at her grandmother's church whom she at first identifies simply as a handsome and very sensitive young man. Yet he seems to sense her terrible guilt and psychological distress over a fatal car accident in which her best friend was killed in way s she comes to recognize as supernatural..

Presence. unabr. ed. Bill Myers. (Running Time: 8 hrs. 1 mins. 0 sec.). (Soul Tracker Ser.). (ENG.). 2005. 12.99 (978-0-310-26890-1(7)) Zondervan.

Presence. unabr. ed. John Saul. Read by Phil Gigante. (Running Time: 10 hrs.). 2008. 24.95 (978-1-4233-5590-8(3), 9781423355908, Brilliance MP3); 39.25 (978-1-4233-5593-9(8), 9781423355939, BADLE); 39.25 (978-1-4233-5591-5(1), 9781423355915, Brinc Audio MP3 Lib); 24.95 (978-1-4233-5592-2(X), 9781423355922, BAD); audio compact disk 102.25 (978-1-4233-5589-2(X), 9781423355892, BriAudCD Unabrid); audio compact disk 38.95 (978-1-4233-5588-5(1), 9781423355885, Bril Audio CD Unabri) Brilliance Audio.

Presence, unabr. ed. John Saul. Narrated by Richard Ferrone. 8 cass. (Running Time: 11 hrs. 15 mins.). 1998. 75.00 (978-0-7887-1868-7(1), 95290E7) Recorded Bks.
Strange skeletal remains, mysterious deaths, secret underground experiments make this a suspenseful plot & nonstop action as the author offers an unusual theory about our place in the universe.

Presence: Adagio music for Healing. 2005. audio compact disk (978-1-59250-620-0(8)) Gaiam Intl.

Presence of Christmas. unabr. abr. ed. Read by Bruce Heighley. Contrib. by Harry Nilsson. (Running Time: 3600 sec.). 2007. audio compact disk 36.00 (978-1-4332-0555-2(6)) Blckstn Audio.

Presence of Christmas. unabr. abr. ed. Read by Bruce Heighley. (Running Time: 3600 sec.). 2007. audio compact disk 19.95 (978-1-4332-0556-9(4)) Blckstn Audio.

Presence of Christmas: A Heartwarming Anthology of Stories, Poems & Songs of the Holiday Season. unabr. ed. Perf. by Harry Nilsson. Narrated by Bruce Heighley. 1 CD. (Running Time: 1 hr.). 2004. audio compact disk 15.98 (978-1-59007-469-5(6)) Pub: New Millenn Enter. Dist(s): PerseuPGW

Presence of God. Reuven Doron. 1 cass. (Running Time: 90 mins.). (Desperate for God Ser.: Vol. 1). 2000. 5.00 (RD03-001) Morning NC.
In this series, Reuven stresses the importance of developing true dependency on God.

Presence of God. Swami Jyotirmayananda. 1 cass. (Running Time: 45 min.). 1990. 10.00 Yoga Res Foun.

Presence of Mind. Swami Amar Jyoti. 1 cass. 1990. 9.95 (P-53) Truth Consciousness.
Being truly present everywhere, each moment, teaches us what we need, leads to full Consciousness. Our "adult" sand castles.

Presence of the Past. Rupert Sheldrake. 8 cass. 72.00 (OC122) Sound Horizons AV.
The hypothesis of formative causation provides a revolutionary alternative to the orthodox theories of science. Also predicts that when some members of a species learn something new, the ability to learn it should increase all over the world.

Presence of the Past. unabr. ed. Julian C. Hollick. 1 cass. (Running Time: 60 min.). (Passages to India Ser.). 1991. 15.00 (978-1-56709-005-5(2), 1005) Indep Broadcast.
Life in India is dominated & shaped by its past. The program uses the example of the political career of Mahatma Gandhi to show how Gandhi consciously blended past & present for deliberate political ends.

Presence of the Past: The Hypothesis of Formative Causation. Charles Muses. 2 cass. 18.00 set. (A0092-83) Sound Photosyn.
With Rupert Sheldrake on tape.

Presence of the Past: The Hypothesis of Formative Causation. Rupert Sheldrake. 2 cass. 18.00 set. (A0130-83) Sound Photosyn.
With Charles Muses.

Present. unabr. ed. Johanna Lindsey. Read by Laural Merlington. (Running Time: 5 hrs.). (Malory Ser.). 2008. 39.25 (978-1-4233-6605-8(0), 9781423366058, Brinc Audio MP3 Lib); 39.25 (978-1-4233-6607-2(7), 9781423366072, BADLE); 24.95 (978-1-4233-6604-1(2), 9781423366041, Brilliance MP3); 24.95 (978-1-4233-6606-5(9), 9781423366065, BAD); audio compact disk 69.25 (978-1-4233-6603-4(4), 9781423366034, BriAudCD Unabrid); audio compact disk 19.99 (978-1-4233-6602-7(6), 9781423366027, Bril Audio CD Unabri) Brilliance Audio.

Present, Set. unabr. ed. Johanna Lindsey. Read by Laural Merlington. 3 cass. (Malory Ser.). 1999. 36.25 (FS9-43359) Highsmith.

Present: Enjoying Your Work & Life in Changing Times. unabr. ed. Spencer Johnson. Read by Dennis Boutsikaris. (Running Time: 1 hr.). (ENG.). 2003. audio compact disk 9.99 (978-0-7393-1056-4(9)) Pub: Random Audio Pubg. Dist(s): Random

Present & the Past. unabr. ed. Ivy Compton-Burnett. Read by Elizabeth Proud. 7 cass. (Running Time: 7 hrs.). 2001. 61.95 (978-1-85089-828-3(6), 21291) Pub: ISIS Audio GBR. Dist(s): Ulverscroft US
Nine years after her divorce from Cassius Clare, Catherine decides to re-enter his life. Cassius's second wife Flavia initially feels resentment. But as friendship develops between the two women, it is Cassius who is excluded & whose self-pity intensifies, erupting in a shocking, unexpected way.

Present at the Creation, Vol. 1. collector's ed. Dean Acheson. Read by Arthur Addison. 15 cass. (Running Time: 22 hrs. 30 min.). 2000. 120.00 (978-0-7366-5650-4(2)) Books on Tape.
Dean Acheson was not only present at the creation of the postwar world, he was one of its chief architects. He joined the State Department in 1941 as an assistant secretary & with brief intermissions, was continuously involved until 1953, when he left office as Secretary of State. Throughout that time, Acheson's was one of the most influential minds & strongest wills at work. His career spanned World War II, the reconstruciton of Europe, the Korean War, the development of nuclear power & the formation of the United Nations & NATO.

Present at the Creation, Vol. 2. collector's ed. Dean Acheson. Read by Arthur Addison. 15 cass. (Running Time: 22 hrs. 30 min.). 2000. 120.00 (978-0-7366-5665-8(0)) Books on Tape.

Present-Day Thoughts on the Quality of Life. Jacques Barzun. 10.95 (35001) J Norton Pubs.
How industry, democracy, science, & technology limit the special quality of life for individuals today.

***Present Future: Six Tough Questions for the Church.** unabr. ed. Reggie McNeal. Narrated by Lloyd James. (ENG.). 2007. 14.98 (978-1-59644-457-7(6), Hovel Audio) christianaud.

Present Future: Six Tough Questions for the Church. unabr. ed. Reggie McNeal. Read by Lloyd James. (Running Time: 6 hrs. 0 mins. 0 sec.). (ENG.). 2007. audio compact disk 23.98 (978-1-59644-456-0(8)) christianaud.

Present Laughter. Noel Coward. Contrib. by Ian Ogilvy et al. 2 CDs. (Running Time: 5220 sec.). 1996. audio compact disk 25.95 (978-1-58081-328-0(3)) Pub: L A Theatre. Dist(s): NetLibrary CO

Present Laughter. Noel Coward. Contrib. by Ian Ogilvy et al. (Playaway Adult Fiction Ser.). (ENG.). 2009. 39.99 (978-1-60775-741-2(9)) Find a World.

Present Laughter. unabr. ed. Noel Coward. Perf. by Jon Matthews et al. 1 cass. (Running Time: 1 hr. 24 min.). 1996. 19.95 (978-1-58081-030-2(6), TPT75) L A Theatre.
In this delicious comedy, a gallery of friends, lovers, relatives & theatre acolytes buzz around stage star Garry Essendine like bubbles in fine champagne. While Garry struggles to plan his upcoming tour to Africa, his elegant London flat is invaded by a love-struck ingenue, an adulterous producer & a married seductress - not to mention Garry's estranged wife & the memorable Roland Maule, an aspiring playwright who is quite, quite mad.

***Present Laughter: Act II, Scene I.** abr. ed. Noel Coward. Read by Simon Jones. (ENG.). 2006. (978-0-06-125301-0(4), Harper Audio) HarperCollins Pubs.

Present Moment: A Retreat on the Practice of Mindfulness. Thich Nhat Hanh. 6 cass. (Running Time: 7 hrs. 30 min.). 2003. stu. ed. 40.00 (93000) Parallax Pr.

Present Moment: A Retreat on the Practice of Mindfulness. Thich Nhat Hanh. 2003. audio compact disk 69.95 (978-1-59179-126-3(X)) Sounds True.

Present Perfect: Finding God in the Now. Gregory A. Boyd. Ed. by Jim Reimann. (Running Time: 3 hrs. 33 mins. 18 sec.). (ENG.). 2010. 19.99 (978-0-310-77304-7(0)) Zondervan.

Present Time, No. 6. 6 cass. 10.00 ea. (978-1-893165-57-1(4)) Rational Isl.
The quarterly journal for everyone using re-evaluation counseling, or interested in doing so.

Present Time, No. 11. 2 cass. (Running Time: 3 hrs.). 10.00 ea. (978-1-893165-58-8(2)) Rational Isl.
The quarterly journal for everyone using re-evaluation counseling or interested in doing so.

Present Time, No. 12. 2 cass. 10.00 ea. (978-1-893165-59-5(0)) Rational Isl.

Present Time, No. 13. 2 cass. 10.00 ea. (978-1-893165-60-1(4)) Rational Isl.

Present Time, No. 17. 2 cass. 10.00 ea. (978-1-893165-62-5(0)) Rational Isl.

Present Time, No. 18. 2 cass. 10.00 ea. (978-1-893165-64-9(7)) Rational Isl.

Present Time, No. 22. 4 cass. 10.00 ea. (978-1-893165-65-6(5)) Rational Isl.

Present Time, No. 26. 3 cass. 10.00 ea. (978-1-893165-66-3(3)) Rational Isl.

Present Time, No. 33. 5 cass. 10.00 ea. (978-1-893165-67-0(1)) Rational Isl.
The quarterly journal for everyone using re-evaluation counseling or intersted in doing so.

Present Time, No. 34. 3 cass. 10.00 ea. (978-1-893165-68-7(X)) Rational Isl.
The quarterly journal for everyone using re-evaluation counseling or interested in doing so.

Present Time, No. 39. 3 cass. 10.00 ea. (978-1-893165-69-4(8)) Rational Isl.

Present Time, No. 40. 5 cass. 10.00 ea. (978-1-893165-70-0(1)) Rational Isl.

Present Time, No. 43. 4 cass. 10.00 ea. (978-1-893165-71-7(X)) Rational Isl.

Present Time, No. 44. 4 cass. 10.00 ea. (978-1-893165-72-4(8)) Rational Isl.
The quarterly journal for everyone using re-evaluation counsleing or interested in doing so.

Present Time, No. 45. 5 cass. 10.00 ea. (978-1-893165-73-1(6)) Rational Isl.
The quarterly journal for everyone using re-evaluation counseling or interested in doing so.

Present Time, No. 46. 6 cass. 10.00 ea. (978-1-893165-74-8(4)) Rational Isl.

Present Time, No. 48. 5 cass. 10.00 ea. (978-1-893165-75-5(2)) Rational Isl.

Present Time, No. 53. 6 cass. 10.00 ea. (978-1-893165-76-2(0)) Rational Isl.
The quarterly journal for everyone using re-evaluation counseling, or interested in doing so.

Present Time, No. 56. 3 cass. 10.00 ea. (978-1-893165-77-9(9)) Rational Isl.
The quarterly journal for everyone using re-evaluation counseling or interested in doing so.

Present Time, No. 57. 5 cass. 10.00 ea. (978-1-893165-78-6(7)) Rational Isl.

Present Time, No. 60. 5 cass. 10.00 ea. (978-1-893165-79-3(5)) Rational Isl.

Present Time, No. 61 (18.4) 4 cass. 10.00 ea. (978-1-893165-63-2(9)) Rational Isl.
The quarterly journal for everyone using re-evaluation counseling or interested in it.

Present Time, No. 65 (17.4) 5 cass. 10.00 ea. (978-1-893165-61-8(2)) Rational Isl.
The quarterly journal for everyone using re-evaluation counseling or interested in doing so.

Present with Confidence: Fear No More! Neil Poindexter. 4 cass. 49.95 Set, incl. wkbk. (124-C47) Natl Seminars.
No matter what your role, the power & impact of a clear, persuasive presentation style is your most effective business ally...whether you're in front of one or 100 people. Learn to skillfully present your ideas...one-on-one, in meetings & before groups...with impact & confidence!.

***Presentation Masters: Communication Mastery in Speeches, Meetings, & the Media.** unabr. ed. Made for Success. Read by Various Readers. (Running Time: 7 hrs. NaN mins.). (Made for Success Ser.). 2011. audio compact disk 32.95 (978-1-4417-7257-2(X)); audio compact disk 118.00 (978-1-4417-7256-5(1)) Blckstn Audio.

Presentation of a Case to a Zoning Hearing Board. 1995. bk. 99.00 (ACS-1004) PA Bar Inst.
Highlights those methods which experienced zoning lawyers use to win cases from detailed preparation to calming angry crowds.

Presentation Piece see Poetry & Voice of Marilyn Hacker

Presenting the Fatima Message to Youth. 1 cass. 1991. 2.50 (978-1-56036-056-8(9)) AMI Pr.

Presenting with Impact. Arleen LaBella. 1986. 9.75 (978-0-932491-39-8(1)) Res Appl Inc.
Will help you make powerful, interesting, & effective presentations. Increase your confidence while you develop your skills for getting your message across.

Presents the Gyuto Monks Multiphonic Choir's "Music of Tibet" Huston Smith. 1 cass. 10.50 (A0171-86) Sound Photosyn.
This tape benefits the Monks & Tibetan refugees & does not get sold wholesale. The original, on location, recording of multiphonic chanting by the monks.

Preservation & Archiving Technology. 2 cass. 1990. 16.00 set. Recorded Res.

Preservationist. unabr. ed. David Maine. Read by Ensemble Cast. (YA). 2008. 54.99 (978-1-60252-991-5(4)) Find a World.

Preserve & Protect. unabr. collector's ed. Allen Drury. Read by Dan Lazar. 12 cass. (Running Time: 18 hrs.). 1979. 96.00 (978-0-7366-0241-9(0), 1237) Books on Tape.
The setting is Washington, D.C. The action begins when President Harley Hudson is killed in an air crash. The Speaker of the House becomes president & calls for a national committee to select new nominees for the coming election. Washington is filled with an atmosphere of dangerous violence as the committe undertakes this serious decision.

Preserver. William Shatner. Read by William Shatner. 2004. 10.95 (978-0-7435-1954-0(X)) Pub: S&S Audio. Dist(s): S and S Inc

Preserving Private Lands for the Common Good. Hosted by Nancy Pearlman. 1 cass. (Running Time: 29 min.). 10.00 (318) Educ Comm CA.

President & Other Myths, Program 5. Read by Miguel Angel Asturias. (F007CB090) Natl Public Radio.

***President Barack Obama's Inaugural Address.** annot. ed. Compiled by Dt Qi Hua. (CHI.). 2009. pap. bk. 12.00 (978-957-710-529-5(1)) DTPC Ltd TWN.

President Franklin D. Roosevelt. Read by Franklin D. Roosevelt. (Running Time: 44 min.). 1941. 10.95 (19560) J Norton Pubs.
Speeches before Congress of September 21, 1939 & December 8, 1941. The first, calling for repeal of the 1935 Neutrality Act; the second asking for a declaration of war between America & Japan.

President Franklin D. Roosevelt. Read by Franklin D. Roosevelt. (Running Time: 49 min.). 1943. 10.95 (19542) J Norton Pubs.
Two Fireside Chats; one on the federal seizure of the coal mines & how one faction can interrupt the march to victory; the other talking about the first crack in the Axis & progress of the war.

President from Hawaii. Carolan. Illus. by Joanna Carolan. 2009. audio compact disk 18.95 (978-0-9800063-0-8(9)) Banana Patch.

President Lincoln: The Duty of a Statesman. unabr. ed. William Lee Miller. Read by Lloyd James. 2 MP3-CDs. (Running Time: 19 hrs. 30 mins. 0 sec.). (ENG.). 2008. 34.99 (978-1-4001-5639-9(4)); audio compact disk 99.99 (978-1-4001-3639-1(3)); audio compact disk 49.99 (978-1-4001-0639-4(7)) Pub: Tantor Media. Dist(s): IngramPubServ

President Reagan: The Triumph of Imagination. Richard Reeves. Narrated by George K. Wilson. (Running Time: 93600 sec.). 2005. audio compact disk 39.99 (978-1-4193-7781-5(7)) Recorded Bks.

President Richard Nixon's - the Watergate Tapes: Selected. aut. ed. As told by Richard Nixon. (ENG.). 2009. lthr. 389.00 (978-1-934304-08-2(5)) Flatsigned Pr.

President Speaks off the Record. unabr. collector's ed. Harold Brayman. Read by Victor Rumbellow. 7 cass. (Running Time: 10 hrs. 30 min.). 1980. 56.00 (978-0-7366-0256-3(9), 1251-A) Books on Tape.
This is a history of the Gridiron Club, an exclusive organization of Washington reporters. For nearly a century this club has hosted dinners at which presidents, Cabinet members, party brass & assorted political fauna have taken turns roasting each other, always entirely off-the-record.

Presidential Address: National Association of Evangelicals, 47th Annual Convention, Columbus, Ohio, March 7-9, 1989. John H. White. 1 cass. (General Sessions Ser.: No. 104). 1989. 4.25 ea. 1-8 tapes.; 4.00 ea. 9 tapes or more. Nat Assn Evan.

Presidential Address: Proceedings of the 45th Annual Convention National Association of Evangelicals Buffalo New York. Read by Ray H. Hughes. 1 cass. (Running Time: 60 min.). 1987. 4.00 (317) Nat Assn Evan.

Presidential Agenda: Sources of Executive Influence in Congress. Roger T. Larocca. (Parliaments & Legislatures Ser.). 2006. audio compact disk 9.95 (978-0-8142-9110-8(4)) Pub: Ohio St U Pr. Dist(s): Chicago Distribution Ctr

Presidential Assortment. 311.40 (978-1-55927-971-0(0)) Pub: Macmill Audio. Dist(s): Macmillan

Presidential Campaign Songs, 1789-1996. Oscar Brand. 1 cass. (Running Time: 69 min.). (YA). (gr. 7 up). 1999. 8.50; 14.00 Smithsonian Folkways.
Extensive notes, discography, song notes & images of campaign memorabilia.

Presidential-Congressional Relations: Capitol Learning Audio Course. Chuck Cushman. Prod. by TheCapitol.Net. (ENG.). 2008. 47.00 (978-1-58733-075-9(X)) TheCapitol.

Presidential Courage: Brave Leaders & How They Changed America, 1789-1989. abr. ed. Michael R. Beschloss. Read by Michael R. Beschloss. 2007. 17.95 (978-0-7435-6179-2(1)) Pub: S&S Audio. Dist(s): S and S Inc

Presidential Courage: Brave Leaders & How They Changed America 1789-1989. abr. ed. Michael R. Beschloss. Read by Michael R. Beschloss. 5 CDs. (Running Time: 6 hrs. 0 mins. 0 sec.). (ENG.). 2007. audio compact disk 29.95 (978-0-7435-6178-5(3)) Pub: S&S Audio. Dist(s): S and S Inc

Presidential Deal, Les Standiford. Narrated by Ron McLarty. 9 cass. (Running Time: 12 hrs.). 1998. 80.00 (978-0-7887-2503-6(3), 95575E7) Recorded Bks.
Johnny Deal is about to receive a presidential award for rescuing 20 people from Miami waters. At the ceremony, however, terrorists attack the stage. Now Johnny & the First Lady are hostages & his chances to be a hero are rapidly slipping away.

Presidential Resignation. 1 cass. (Running Time: 60 min.). 1974. 6.00 Once Upon Rad.
A brief history of the Watergate story & President Nixon's farewell speech.

Presidential Styles: Some Giants & a Pygmy. Samuel Rosenman & Dorothy Rosenman. 1 cass. (Running Time: 56 min.). 10.95 (40244) J Norton Pubs.

Presidents: Abraham Lincoln, Sixteenth, 1861-1865; Andrew Johnson, Seventeenth, 1865-1869. 1 cass. (Running Time: 30 min.). Dramatization. (American Presidents Ser.: No. 11). 12.50 Alpha Tape.
Describes time in office & accomplishments.

Presidents: Andrew Jackson, Seventh, 1829-1837; Martin Van Buren, Eighth, 1837-1841. 1 cass. (Running Time: 30 min.). Dramatization. (American Presidents Ser.: No. 5). 12.50 Alpha Tape.

Presidents: Chester A. Arthur, Twenty-First, 1881-1885. 1 cass. (Running Time: 30 min.). Dramatization. (American Presidents Ser.: No. 14). 12.50 Alpha Tape.

Presidents: Dwight D. Eisenhower, Thirty-Fourth, 1953-1961. 1 cass. (Running Time: 30 min.). Dramatization. (American Presidents Ser.: No. 22). 12.50 Alpha Tape.

Presidents: Franklin D. Roosevelt, Thirty-Second, 1933-1945; Harry S. Truman, Thirty-Third, 1945-1953. 1 cass. (Running Time: 30 min.). Dramatization. (American Presidents Ser.: No. 21). 12.50 Alpha Tape.

Presidents: George Washington, First, 1789-1797; John Adams, Second, 1797-1801. 1 cass. (Running Time: 30 min.). Dramatization. (American Presidents Ser.: No. 1). 12.50 Alpha Tape.

Presidents: Grover Cleveland, Twenty-Second, 1885-1889, 1893-1897; Benjamin Harrison, Twenty-Third, 1889-1893. 1 cass. (Running Time: 30 min.). Dramatization. (American Presidents Ser.: No. 15). 12.50 Alpha Tape.

Presidents: Herbert Hoover, Thirty-First, 1929-1933. 1 cass. (Running Time: 30 min.). Dramatization. (American Presidents Ser.: No. 20). 12.50 Alpha Tape.

Presidents: James Buchanan, Fifteenth, 1857-1861. 1 cass. (Running Time: 30 min.). Dramatization. (American Presidents Ser.: No. 10). 12.50 Alpha Tape.

Presidents: James Madison, Fourth, 1809-1817; James Monroe, Fifth, 1817-1825. 1 cass. (Running Time: 30 min.). Dramatization. (American Presidents Ser.: No. 3). 12.50 Alpha Tape.

Presidents: John F. Kennedy, Thirty-Fifth, 1961-1963; Lyndon B. Johnson, Thirty-Sixth, 1963-1969. 1 cass. (Running Time: 30 min.). Dramatization. (American Presidents Ser.: No. 23). 12.50 Alpha Tape.

Presidents: John Quincy Adams, Sixth, 1825-1829. 1 cass. (Running Time: 30 min.). Dramatization. (American Presidents Ser.: No. 4). 12.50 Alpha Tape.

Presidents: John Tyler, Tenth, 1821-1845; James Polk, Eleventh, 1845-1849. 1 cass. (Running Time: 30 min.). Dramatization. (American Presidents Ser.: No. 7). 12.50 Alpha Tape.

Presidents: Millard Fillmore, Thirteenth, 1850-1853. 1 cass. (Running Time: 30 min.). Dramatization. (American Presidents Ser.: No. 9). 12.50 Alpha Tape.

Presidents: Rutherford B. Hayes, Nineteenth, 1877-1881; James A. Garfield, Twentieth, 1881. 1 cass. (Running Time: 30 min.). Dramatization. (American Presidents Ser.: No. 13). 12.50 Alpha Tape.

Presidents: Theodore Roosevelt, Twenty-Sixth, 1901-1909; William Howard Taft, Twenty-Seventh, 1909-1913. 1 cass. (Running Time: 30 min.). Dramatization. (American Presidents Ser.: No. 17). 12.50 Alpha Tape.

Presidents: Thomas Jefferson, Third, 1801-1809. 1 cass. (Running Time: 30 min.). Dramatization. (American Presidents Ser.: No. 2). 12.50 Alpha Tape.

Presidents: Ulysses S. Grant, Eighteenth, 1869-1877. 1 cass. (Running Time: 30 min.). Dramatization. (American Presidents Ser.: No. 12). 12.50 Alpha Tape.

Presidents: Warren Harding, Twenty-Ninth, 1921-1923; John Calvin Coolidge, Thirtieth, 1923-1929. 1 cass. (Running Time: 30 min.). Dramatization. (American Presidents Ser.: No. 19). 12.50 Alpha Tape.

Presidents: William Harrison, Ninth, 1841. 1 cass. (Running Time: 30 min.). Dramatization. (American Presidents Ser.: No. 6). 12.50 Alpha Tape.

Presidents: William McKinley, Twenty-Fifth, 1897-1901. 1 cass. (Running Time: 30 min.). Dramatization. (American Presidents Ser.: No. 16). 12.50 Alpha Tape.

Presidents: Woodrow Wilson, Twenty-Eighth, 1913-1921. 1 cass. (Running Time: 30 min.). Dramatization. (American Presidents Ser.: No. 18). 12.50 Alpha Tape.

Presidents: Zachary Taylor, Twelfth, 1849-1850. 1 cass. (Running Time: 30 min.). Dramatization. (American Presidents Ser.: No. 8). 12.50 Alpha Tape.

Presidents & U. S. Government: Rock n' Learn. 1 CD. (Running Time: 37 min.). (J). (gr. 2-4). 2001. pap. bk. & tchr. ed. 12.99 (978-1-878489-14-2(3)) Rock N Learn.
Through songs and raps, learn the presidents of the U. S. through George W. Bush, plus facts about our government. Includes lyrics.

Presidents Collection: Ulysses S. Grant/George Washington/Thomas Jefferson. unabr. ed. Michael Korda et al. Read by Sam Tsoutsouvas. 11 CDs. (Running Time: 46800 sec.). 2006. audio compact disk 39.95 (978-0-06-087875-7(4)) HarperCollins Pubs.

President's Daughter. Jack Higgins. Contrib. by Patrick Macnee. (Sean Dillon Ser.). 2008. 64.99 (978-1-60640-675-5(2)) Find a World.

President's Daughter. abr. ed. Jack Higgins. Perf. by Patrick Macnee. 4 cass. (Running Time: 6 hrs.). (Sean Dillon Ser.). 2004. 25.00 (978-1-59007-195-3(6)) Pub: New Millenn Enter. Dist(s): PerseuPGW
Begins in 1969 in Vietnam, where an American army officer saves a French woman's life. She thinks her husband is dead, she and the American officer have a night of passion, and then her husband is found alive. Advance to 1997, when the former officer becomes president of the U.S., the French woman dies, and their daughter (the result of that night of passion) is now 28 years old. The young woman is kidnapped and will be killed if the president doesn't comply with the kidnappers' demands; he has 10 days to decide.

President's Daughter. unabr. ed. Jack Higgins. Read by Patrick Macnee. 6 cass. (Running Time: 9 hrs.). (Sean Dillon Ser.). 2001. 32.00 (978-1-59040-041-8(0), Phoenix Audio) Pub: Amer Intl Pub. Dist(s): PerseuPGW
The President's daughter has been kidnapped; only two men command the President's confidence to act in this matter, Sean Dillon, a seasoned, former IRA enforcer and Blake Johnson, a decorated Marine and FBI agent. High-tension action and harrowing twists of a powerful man facing the most momentous decision of his life.

***President's Daughter.** unabr. ed. Jack Higgins. Read by Michael Page. (Running Time: 8 hrs.). (Sean Dillon Ser.). 2010. 24.99 (978-1-4418-4335-7(3), 9781441843357, BAD); 39.97 (978-1-4418-4334-0(5), 9781441843340, Brlnc Audio MP3 Lib); 39.97 (978-1-4418-4336-4(1), 9781441843364, BADLE); 24.99 (978-1-4418-4333-3(7), 9781441843333, Brilliance MP3); audio compact disk 87.97 (978-1-4418-4332-6(9), 9781441843326, BriAudCD Unabrid); audio compact disk 29.99 (978-1-4418-4331-9(0), 9781441843319, Bril Audio CD Unabri) Brilliance Audio.

President's Daughter. unabr. ed. Jack Higgins. Read by Patrick Macnee. 6 cass. (Sean Dillon Ser.). 1999. 35.00 (FS9-34527) Highsmith.

President's House: A First Daughter Shares the History & Secrets of the World's Most Famous Home. unabr. ed. Margaret Truman. Read by Sandra Burr. (Running Time: 12 hrs.). 2003. 87.25 (978-1-59355-161-2(4), 1593551614, BrilAudUnabridg); audio compact disk 97.25 (978-1-59355-163-6(0), 1593551630, BriAudCD Unabrid); 32.95 (978-1-59355-106-3(1), 1593551061, BAU); audio compact disk 36.95 (978-1-59355-162-9(2), 1593551622, Bril Audio CD Unabri) Brilliance Audio.
As Margaret Truman knows from firsthand experience, living in the White House can be exhilarating and maddening, alarming and exhausting, but it is certainly never dull. Part private residence, part goldfish bowl, and part national shrine, the White House is both the most important address in America and the most intensely scrutinized. In The President's House, Margaret Truman takes us behind the scenes as she reveals what it feels like to live in the White House. Here are hilarious stories of Teddy Roosevelt's rambunctious children tossing spitballs at presidential portraits

and a heartbreaking account of the tragedy that befell President Coolidge's young son John. Here, too, is the real story of the Lincoln Bedroom - as well as the thrilling narrative of how first lady Dolley Madison rescued the priceless portrait of George Washington and a copy of the Declaration of Independence before British soldiers torched the White House in 1814. Today the 132-room White House operates as an exotic combination of first-class hotel and fortress, with 1600 dedicated workers and an annual budget over $1 billion. But ghosts of the past still walk the august corridors, including the phantom whose visit President Harry S. Truman described to his daughter in eerie detail. From the basement swarming with reporters to the "Situation Room" crammed with sophisticated technology to the Oval Office where the President receives the world's leaders, the White House is a beehive of relentless activity, deal-making, intrigue, gossip, and, of course, history in the making.

President's House: A First Daughter Shares the History & Secrets of the World's Most Famous Home. unabr. ed. Margaret Truman. Read by Sandra Burr. (Running Time: 12 hrs.). 2004. 39.25 (978-1-59335-520-3(3), 1593355203, Brlnc Audio MP3 Lib) Brilliance Audio.

President's House: A First Daughter Shares the History & Secrets of the World's Most Famous Home. unabr. ed. Margaret Truman. Read by Sandra Burr. (Running Time: 12 hrs.). 2004. 39.25 (978-1-59710-592-7(9), 1597105929, BADLE) Brilliance Audio.

President's House: A First Daughter Shares the History & Secrets of the World's Most Famous Home. unabr. ed. Margaret Truman. Read by Sandra Burr. (Running Time: 12 hrs.). 2004. 24.95 (978-1-59335-249-3(2), 1593352492) Soulmate Audio Bks.

President's House: A First Daughter Shares the History & Secrets of the World's Most Famous Home. unabr. ed. Margaret Truman. Read by Sandra Burr. (Running Time: 12 hrs.). 2004. 24.95 (978-1-59710-593-4(7), 1597105937, BAD) Brilliance Audio.

President's Lady: A Novel about Rachel & Andrew Jackson. unabr. ed. Irving Stone. Read by John MacDonald. 9 cass. (Running Time: 13 hrs. 30 mins.). 1983. 72.00 (978-0-7366-0670-7(X), 1632) Books on Tape.
Andrew Jackson is one of the most colorful characters in American history. The dramatic story of his life & the era in which he lived read like fiction . He dominated events & the people around him. Jackson's principal source of strength was his wife Rachel, as dedicated to him as he was to his own career.

Presidents' Rap. Sarah Jordan Educational Audio Staff. 1 cass. (Running Time: 1 hr.). (J). 2001. pap. bk. 14.95; pap. bk. 16.95 Penton Overseas.
More than 12 songs in different musical styles introduce fun facts about our nation's presidents, including George W. Bush.

Presidents' Rap. abr. ed. Blaine Selkirk. (J). (gr. 4-7). 1992. audio compact disk (978-1-895523-61-4(3)) S Jordan Publ.

Presidents' Rap: From Washington to George W. Bush. Blaine Selkirk. Prod. by Sara Jordan. (Running Time: 47 minutes). (J). 2001. audio compact disk 11.95 (978-1-894262-50-7(6), JMP121CD) Jordan Music.
Over a dozen songs in different musical styles complementing each historical period. Teaches Presidential history from Washington to George W. Bush Grades: 3 - 7.

Presidents' Rap: Washington to Clinton. Sara Jordan. 1 cass. (Running Time: 1 hr.). (J). (gr. 1 up). 2001. pap. bk. 14.95 (RT 107KC); pap. bk. 16.95 (RT 107KCD) Kimbo Educ.
A great way to learn American history using classical, gospel, rock, pop & rap. 11 catchy songs written in the style of each historical period. Includes lyric book.

Presidents' Rap: Washington to George W. Bush. Blaine Selkirk. Lyrics by Blaine Selkirk. Ed. by Sara Stratton. Prod. by Sara Jordan. Composed by Sara Jordan. Engineer Mark Shannon. 1 cass. (Running Time: 41 min. 12 secs.). (J). (gr. 3-7). 2001. pap. bk. 14.95 (978-1-894262-51-4(4), JMP121K) Jordan Music.
Relive the history of our past Presidents in this treasure trove of tid-bits of knowledge about our Presidents packaged neatly into over a dozen catchy songs written within the musical style of each historical period. Comprehensive, illustrated, encyclopaedic summary of the history of the American Presidents from Washington to George W. Bush. More than 45 minutes of upbeat music packed tightly with information.

President's Wife: Mrs. Lincoln. 1 cass. 10.00 Esstee Audios.
The story of a troubled woman.

Press Conferences & Media Interviews for Scientists & Engineers: Capitol Learning Audio Course. Bill Noxon. Prod. by TheCapitol.Net. (ENG.). 2007. 47.00 (978-1-58733-057-5(1)) TheCapitol.

Press Corpse. Ron Nessen et al. 5 cass. (Running Time: 7 hrs.). 2002. 39.95 (978-0-7861-1043-8(0), 1815) Blckstn Audio.

Press Corpse. unabr. ed. Ron Nessen & Johanna Neuman. Read by Christopher Lane. 5 cass. (Running Time: 7 hrs. 30 min.). 1999. 39.95 (1815) Blckstn Audio.
Reunites the dynamic twosome of Jerry Knight, the "Night Talker" - the brash & opinionated right-wing host of America's most popular all-night talk show - & Jane Day, a thoroughly liberated & just as opinionated leftist reporter for "The Washington Post." When a well-known journalist is killed at an event where the President is speaking, Knight & Day can't help getting involved. It soon becomes apparent that the bad guys may have hit the wrong target. And the President might be next.

Press in a Free Society. Ayn Rand. 1 cass. (Running Time: 60 min.). 1990. 12.95 (978-1-56114-113-5(5), AR28C) Second Renaissance.

Press On. 2006. 17.99 (978-0-9772573-2-4(0)) P Anderson Youth Home.

Press On. Aaron Angton. 2002. 11.98 (978-0-9727644-6-9(1)); audio compact disk 16.98 (978-0-9727644-5-2(3)) Pub: Pt of Grace Ent. Dist(s): STL Dist NA

Press On. Contrib. by Selah. (Ultimate Tracks (Word Tracks) Ser.). 2006. audio compact disk 8.99 (978-5-558-26937-6(5), Word Music) Word Enter.

Press the Battle to the Gates. Derek Prince. 1 cass. (Running Time: 60 min.). 5.95 (I-4245) Derek Prince.

Pressing Toward the Mark. Gloria Copeland. 2 cass. 1992. 10.00 Set. (978-0-88114-863-3(6)) K Copeland Pubns.
Biblical teaching on victorious living.

Pressure: 11 Samuel 12. Ed Young. 1982. 4.95 (978-0-7417-1240-0(7), 240) Win Walk.

Pressure of Being a Mother: Exodus 1 & 2, 730. Ed Young. 1989. 4.95 (978-0-7417-1730-6(1), 730) Win Walk.

Pressure of Sex: 1 Thes. 4:1-8. Ed Young. 1989. 4.95 (978-0-7417-1737-5(9), 737) Win Walk.

Pressures Gifted Children Feel & Why They Underachieve. unabr. ed. Sylvia Rimm. Read by Sylvia Rimm. 1 cass. (Running Time: 53 min.). 1993. 10.95 (978-0-937891-17-9(7), SR31A) Apple Pub Wisc.
Identifies characteristics of underachievement syndrome & the underlying psychological pressures that make gifted children vulnerable to the problem.

Prestekragen, Vol. 101. unabr. ed. Ed. by Janne Lillestol. Tr. by Janne Lillestol. Illus. by Scott Zins. Prod. by Scott Zins. 1 cass. (Running Time: 18 min.). (Listen & Learn Language Audio Ser.: Vol. LL0399).Tr. of Daisy. (ENG & NOR.). 1999. pap. bk. 9.95 (978-1-892623-07-2(2)) Intl Book.
English & Norwegian bilingual text with the Norwegian narration.

Prester John. unabr. ed. John Buchan. Read by Frederick Davidson. 6 cass. (Running Time: 8 hrs. 30 mins.). 1994. 44.95 (978-0-7861-0744-5(8), 1496) Blckstn Audio.
On a seashore hideaway, three young truants observe a huge black man who is muttering incantations & performing weird rites. When the black man discovers the children, he chases them with a knife. In defense, Davy Crawfurd flings a rock at him, & they narrowly escape. Years later he comes face to face with that same black man in Africa.

Prestige. unabr. ed. Christoper Priest. Read by Simon Vance. 10 cass. (Running Time: 45000 sec.). 2006. 25.95 (978-0-7861-4629-1(X)); audio compact disk 25.95 (978-0-7861-6841-5(2)); audio compact disk 29.95 (978-0-7861-7455-3(2)) Blckstn Audio.

Prestige. unabr. ed. Christopher Priest. Read by Simon Vance. (Running Time: 45000 sec.). 2006. 79.95 (978-0-7861-4750-2(4)); audio compact disk 90.00 (978-0-7861-6394-6(1)) Blckstn Audio.

Presto Change-O & Tooth Fairy. Audrey Wood. (J). 10.97 (978-0-85953-374-4(3)) Childs Play GBR.

Presumed Guilty. unabr. ed. James Scott Bell. (Running Time: 8 hrs. 5 mins. 0 sec.). (ENG.). 2008. 12.99 (978-0-310-27819-1(8)) Zondervan.

***Presumed Guilty.** unabr. ed. Tess Gerritsen. Read by Jennifer Van Dyck. (Running Time: 8 hrs.). 2011. 19.99 (978-1-4418-7582-2(4), 9781441875822, Brilliance MP3); 39.97 (978-1-4418-7584-6(0), 9781441875846, BADLE); 39.97 (978-1-4418-7583-9(2), 9781441875839, Brlnc Audio MP3 Lib); audio compact disk 19.99 (978-1-4418-7580-8(8), 9781441875808, Bril Audio CD Unabri); audio compact disk 59.97 (978-1-4418-7581-5(6), 9781441875815, BriAudCD Unabrid) Brilliance Audio.

Presumed Innocent. Scott Turow. Read by Scott Turow. 2 cass. 1989. 13.95 (978-1-55644-337-4(4), 9061) Am Audio Prose.
The author reads excerpts from his thriller.

Presumed Innocent. abr. ed. Scott Turow. Read by John Heard. 2004. 10.95 (978-0-7435-4566-2(4)) Pub: S&S Audio. Dist(s): S and S Inc

Presumed Innocent. unabr. ed. Scott Turow. Read by Edward Herrmann. (Running Time: 16 hrs.). (ENG.). 2010. 24.98 (978-1-60788-377-7(5)); audio compact disk 29.98 (978-1-60788-376-0(7)) Pub: Hachet Audio. Dist(s): HachBkGrp

Presumed Innocent. unabr. collector's ed. Scott Turow. Read by Grover Gardner. 10 cass. (Running Time: 15 hrs.). 1988. 80.00 (978-0-7366-1336-1(6), 2239) Books on Tape.
Rusty Sabich, Kindle County's longtime chief deputy prosecutor, has been asked to investigate the murder of one of his colleagues, Carolyn Polhemus. What Horgan, Sabich's boss, doesn't know is that Carolyn & Rusty had been lovers.

Presumption: An Entertainment Sequel to Jane Austen's Pride & Prejudice. unabr. collector's ed. Julia Barrett, pseud. Read by Kate Reading. 8 cass. (Running Time: 12 hrs.). 1995. 48.00 (978-0-7366-2954-6(8), 3648) Books on Tape.
The witty, well-crafted sequel to Jane Austen's "Pride & Prejudice" serves up juicy new developments in the life of the Bennet clan. Jane would have approved.

Presumption of Death. Jill Paton Walsh & Dorothy L. Sayers. Read by Edward Petherbridge. 8 vols. (Running Time: 12 hrs.). (Lord Peter Wimsey Mystery Ser.). 2003. 69.95 (978-0-7540-8309-2(8)); audio compact disk 79.95 (978-0-7540-8752-6(2)) Pub: Chivers Audio Bks GBR. Dist(s): AudioGO

Presumption of Death. unabr. ed. Perri O'Shaughnessy. Read by Laural Merlington. 8 cass. (Running Time: 13 hrs.). (Nina Reilly Ser.: Vol. 9). 2003. 34.95 (978-1-59086-986-4(9), 1590869869, BAU); 87.25 (978-1-59086-987-1(7), 1590869877, BrilAudUnabridg); audio compact disk 38.95 (978-1-59086-989-5(3), 1590869893, Bril Audio CD Unabri); audio compact disk 102.25 (978-1-59086-990-1(7), 1590869907, BriAudCD Unabrid) Brilliance Audio.
Nina Reilly needs a fresh start. In three years, she's taken on some of Lake Tahoe's most controversial cases and has turned her struggling one-woman law firm into a thriving practice. Now she's ready to sort out her complex relationship with her boyfriend, Monterey P.I. Paul van Wagoner. So she's heading to the Carmel Valley, the place where she began her career and where her estranged father lives. It's also a place of dramatic contradictions and hidden tensions, of new wealth and old families. And, within days of her arrival, Nina is already feeling the heat, as a case of arson exposes some of the darkest secrets of her hometown. Two suspicious fires have already raged through the valley this summer, igniting suspicions of arson. When a third blaze ends in a fatality, police zero in on a suspect: Wish, the son of Sandy Whitefeather, Nina's ex-assistant. The dead man is identified as Wish's childhood friend, a troubled local auto mechanic who hated the changes wealthy newcomers had brought to the valley. Nina and Paul are certain that there is more to this strange case than meets the eye. As they work together to clear Wish, new, more frightening questions are raised, and another fire is set. And out of the flames a terrifying picture emerges: a community steeped in secrets and rage, a tangled history between two men, and a killer whose motives are dark and wrenching.

Presumption of Death. unabr. ed. Perri O'Shaughnessy. Read by Laural Merlington. (Running Time: 13 hrs.). (Nina Reilly Ser.). 2004. 39.25 (978-1-59335-617-0(X), 159335617X, Brlnc Audio MP3 Lib) Brilliance Audio.

Presumption of Death. unabr. ed. Perri O'Shaughnessy. Read by Laural Merlington. (Running Time: 13 hrs.). (Nina Reilly Ser.). 2004. 39.25 (978-1-59710-595-8(3), 1597105953, BADLE); 24.95 (978-1-59710-594-1(5), 1597105945, BAD) Brilliance Audio.

Presumption of Death. unabr. ed. Perri O'Shaughnessy. Read by Laural Merlington. (Running Time: 13 hrs.). (Nina Reilly Ser.). 2004. 24.95 (978-1-59335-210-3(7), 1593352107) Soulmate Audio Bks.

Presumption of Death. unabr. ed. Jill Paton Walsh & Dorothy L. Sayers. 6 cass. (Running Time: 9 hrs.). (Lord Peter Wimsey Mystery Ser.). 2003. 29.95 (978-1-57270-322-3(9)) Pub: Audio Partners. Dist(s): PerseuPGW

Presumption of Death. unabr. ed. Jill Paton Walsh & Dorothy L. Sayers. Narrated by Edward Petherbridge. 8 CDs. (Running Time: 9 hrs. 2 mins.). (Lord Peter Wimsey Mystery Ser.). (ENG.). 2003. audio compact disk 34.95 (978-1-57270-323-0(7)) Pub: AudioGO. Dist(s): Perseus Dist

Presumption of Guilt. Terri Blackstock. 2 cass. (Running Time: 90 min. per cass.). (Sun Coast Chronicles Ser.: Bk. 4). 1997. 14.99 (978-0-310-21085-6(2)) Zondervan.
Weaves suspense, mystery & faith-in-action.

***Presumption of Guilt: Book 4.** abr. ed. Terri Blackstock. (Running Time: 3 hrs. 0 mins. 0 sec.). (Sun Coast Chronicles Ser.). (ENG.). 2003. 10.99 (978-0-310-26088-2(4)) Zondervan.

Pretend. Perf. by Hap Palmer. 1 cass. (J). 11.95 (EA 563C); lp 11.95 (EA 563) Kimbo Educ.
Rag Doll - Guitar Player - The Friendly Giant - Little Ants & more.

Pretend Wife. unabr. ed. Bridget Asher. (Running Time: 8 hrs. 0 mins.). (ENG.). 2009. 29.95 (978-1-4332-8889-0(3)); 54.95 (978-1-4332-8885-2(0)); audio compact disk 76.00 (978-1-4332-8886-9(9)) Blckstn Audio.

Pretend You Don't See Her. abr. ed. Mary Higgins Clark. Read by Randy Graff. (Running Time: 30 hrs. 0 mins. 0 sec.). (ENG.). 2009. audio compact disk 9.99 (978-0-7435-8350-3(7)) Pub: S&S Audio. Dist(s): S and S Inc

Pretend You Don't See Her. unabr. ed. Mary Higgins Clark. Read by Mary Peiffer. 6 cass. (Running Time: 9 hrs.). 1997. 48.00 (978-0-7366-3711-4(7), 4395) Books on Tape.
Lacey Farrell, a high-powered Manhattan realtor, is placed in the Witness Protection Program after witnessing a murder. But she soon realizes that her sanctuary is not safe & she is caught in a race against time as she tries to uncover the truth.

Pretend You Don't See Her. unabr. ed. Mary Higgins Clark. Read by Cecelia Riddett. 7 CDs. (Running Time: 8 hrs. 30 mins.). 2004. audio compact disk 74.75 (978-1-4193-0803-1(3)) Recorded Bks.
This #1 New York Times best-seller enthralls with the tale of Lacey Farrell, a promising young real estate agent. When Lacey sees a murder she must enter the witness protection program until the killer comes to justice. But she has clues that the police don?t know about. Soon she must return to New York City to blow the top off the case before she becomes the next victim.

Pretend You Don't See Her. unabr. ed. Mary Higgins Clark. Narrated by Cecelia Riddett. 6 cass. (Running Time: 8 hrs. 30 mins.). 1997. 59.75 (978-1-4025-3537-6(6), 97237MC, Griot Aud) Recorded Bks.

Pretender to Love. unabr. ed. Zabrina Faire. Read by Jean DeBarbieris. 4 cass. (Running Time: 5 hrs. 30 min.). 26.95 (978-1-55686-108-6(7), 108) Books in Motion.
The scene is nineteenth century England. The heroine is young, strikingly beautiful Julia Cavanaugh. Julia's father, a physician, dies & she is bilked out of his estate by greedy bankers. Left penniless, she agrees to act as fiancee for a friend named Frederick. Frederick needs a fiancee in order to inherit wealth from his dying uncle, the Earl. The story becomes complicated when all the characters go on a sea voyage.

Preterial Civil Practice: Current Issues & Strategies. 1987. bk. 75.00 incl. book.; 35.00 cass. only.; 40.00 book only. PA Bar Inst.

Pretties. unabr. ed. Scott Westerfeld. Read by Carine Montbertrand. 10 CDs. (Running Time: 9 hrs.). (Uglies Ser.: Bk. 2). (YA). (gr. 9 up). 2006. audio compact disk 104.75 (978-1-4281-1123-3(9)); 75.75 (978-1-4281-1118-9(2)) Recorded Bks.
Tally Youngblood never felt like the other Pretties - she almost didn't become one. But Tally isn't the only one who feels like she's missing a part of herself. After uncovering sinister clues about the Pretty surgery, she stumbles upon a possible cure for Pretty-mindedness and a possible escape from the city. But the cure could have deadly consequences.

Pretty Boy Floyd. unabr. ed. Larry McMurtry & Diana Ossana. 8 cass. 19.95 Set. (51892) Books on Tape.
In 1925 Charley Floyd, a sweet-smiling country boy, robbed his first armored car. He rocketed to fame, but paid the price. A tragic story.

Pretty Face. John Escott et al. (Dominoes Ser.). 2003. 14.25 (978-0-19-424373-5(7)) OUP.

Pretty Fire. unabr. ed. Charlayne Woodard. 1 cass. (Running Time: 1 hr. 35 mins.). (gr. 7 up). 2001. 20.95 (978-1-58081-137-8(X), TPT131) L A Theatre.
In five autobiographical vignettes, Charlayne Woodard tells the moving tale of her African-American family through three generations of love, struggle & triumph.

Pretty Fire. unabr. ed. Charlayne Woodard. Read by Charlayne Woodard. 2 CDs. (Running Time: 1 hr. 35 mins.). 2001. audio compact disk 25.95 (978-1-58081-191-0(4), CDTPT131) Pub: L A Theatre. Dist(s): NetLibrary CO

Pretty Good Bits: From a Prairie Home Companion to Garrison Keillor. unabr. ed. Garrison Keillor & Prairie Home Companion Staff. 1 CD. (Running Time: 1 hr.). (ENG.). 2003. audio compact disk 6.99 (978-1-56511-815-7(4), 1565118154) Pub: HighBridge. Dist(s): Workman Pub

Pretty Good Joke. unabr. ed. Garrison Keillor. 2 CDs. (Running Time: 2 hrs. 30 mins.). (ENG.). 2000. audio compact disk 24.95 (978-1-56511-388-6(8), 1565113888) Pub: HighBridge. Dist(s): Workman Pub

Pretty in Plaid: A Life, a Witch, & a Wardrobe, or, the Wonder Years Before the Condescending, Egomanical, Self-Centered Smart Ass Phase. Jen Lancaster. 2009. audio compact disk 39.95 (978-1-4406-4104-6(8), PengAudBks) Penguin Grp USA.

Pretty in Plaid: A Life, a Witch, & a Wardrobe, or, the Wonder Years Before the Condescending, Egomanical, Self-Centered Smart Ass Phase. unabr. ed. Jen Lancaster. Read by Jamie Heinlein. 7 CDs. (Running Time: 8 hrs.). (ENG.). (gr. 12 up). 2009. audio compact disk 32.95 (978-0-14-314477-9(4), PengAudBks) Penguin Grp USA.

Pretty Lady. unabr. ed. Arnold Bennett. Read by Alistair Maydon. 8 cass. (Running Time: 10 hrs.). 1994. 69.95 (978-1-85695-424-2(2), 89075) Pub: ISIS Audio GBR. Dist(s): Ulverscroft US
The coincidental meetings of a young French courtesan & a respectable, middle-aged Englishman seem somehow fated. Against the backdrop of London at the outset of the First World War, Arnold Bennett charts the development of their relationship.

***Pretty Little Liars.** unabr. ed. Sara Shepard. Read by Cassandra Morris. (ENG.). 2010. (978-0-06-201618-8(0)); (978-0-06-201411-5(0)) HarperCollins Pubs.

***Pretty Little Liars #2: Flawless.** unabr. ed. Sara Shepard. Read by Cassandra Morris. (ENG.). 2010. (978-0-06-201412-2(9)); (978-0-06-201615-7(6)) HarperCollins Pubs.

***Pretty Little Liars #3: Perfect.** unabr. ed. Sara Shepard. Read by Cassandra Morris. (ENG.). 2010. (978-0-06-201616-4(4)); (978-0-06-201413-9(7)) HarperCollins Pubs.

***Pretty Little Liars #4: Unbelievable.** unabr. ed. Sara Shepard. Read by Cassandra Morris. (ENG.). 2010. (978-0-06-201414-6(5)); (978-0-06-201617-1(2)) HarperCollins Pubs.

***Pretty Little Liars #5: Wicked.** unabr. ed. Sara Shepard. Read by Cassandra Morris. (ENG.). 2010. (978-0-06-204130-2(4)); (978-0-06-201415-3(3)) HarperCollins Pubs.

***Pretty Little Liars #6: Killer.** unabr. ed. Sara Shepard. Read by Cassandra Morris. (ENG.). 2010. (978-0-06-201416-0(1)); (978-0-06-204131-9(2)) HarperCollins Pubs.

***Pretty Little Liars #7: Heartless.** unabr. ed. Sara Shepard. Read by Cassandra Morris. (ENG.). 2010. (978-0-06-204132-6(0)); (978-0-06-201417-7(X)) HarperCollins Pubs.

***Pretty Little Liars #8: Wanted.** unabr. ed. Sara Shepard. Read by Cassandra Morris. (ENG.). 2010. (978-0-06-204133-3(9)); (978-0-06-201418-4(8)) HarperCollins Pubs.

***Pretty Monsters.** unabr. ed. Kelly Link. Narrated by Christina Moore. 1 Playaway. (Running Time: 13 hrs. 15 mins.). (YA). (gr. 8 up). 2009. 59.75 (978-1-4407-0401-7(5)); 78.75 (978-1-4361-9748-9(1)); audio compact disk 108.75 (978-1-4361-9752-6(X)) Recorded Bks.

***Pretty Monsters.** unabr. collector's ed. Kelly Link. Narrated by Christina Moore. 11 CDs. (Running Time: 13 hrs. 15 mins.). (YA). (gr. 8 up). 2009. audio compact disk 56.95 (978-1-4407-2555-5(1)) Recorded Bks.

Pretty Pink Shroud. unabr. ed. E. X. Ferrars. Read by Sheila Mitchell. 5 cass. (Running Time: 5 hrs. 45 min.). 1996. 49.95 (978-1-85695-984-1(8), 950908) Pub: ISIS Audio GBR. Dist(s): Ulverscroft US
Lady Guest always donated good quality clothes to her favorite charity shop, but the day they received a gorgeous pink dress, bloodstained & pierced with a bullet hole, had them all confused, especially as she had worn it at a masquerade, the previous night & hadn't been seen since.

Pretty Sister of José. unabr. ed. Frances Hodgson Burnett. Read by Laurie Klein. 2 cass. (Running Time: 2 hrs. 15 min.). Dramatization. (J). 1992. 16.95 (978-1-55686-429-2(9), 429) Books in Motion.
Pepita; young, beautiful, & completely spoiled by her adoring brother, Jose, sees Sebastiano for the first time in the bull ring. Sebastiano, the handsome & rich hero to all of Spain, cares only for the love of the sport, & never for a woman.

Pretty Woman. abr. ed. Fern Michaels. Read by Laural Merlington. 2005. 14.95 (978-0-7435-5030-7(7)) Pub: S&S Audio. Dist(s): S and S Inc

Pretty Woman. abr. ed. Fern Michaels. Read by Laural Merlington. (Running Time: 43 hrs. 0 mins. 0 sec.). (ENG.). 2008. audio compact disk 14.99 (978-0-7435-7100-5(2)) Pub: S&S Audio. Dist(s): S and S Inc

Prevailing Christ. Mark Chironna. 2 cass. 1992. 12.00 Set. (978-1-56043-916-5(5)) Destiny Image Pubs.

Prevent Mental Abnormalities. Swami Jyotirmayananda. 1 cass. (Running Time: 45 min.). 1990. 10.00 Yoga Res Foun.

Prevent Sexual Harassment in the Work Place. 1 cass. (Running Time: 30 mins.). 2000. pap. bk. 99.95 (1045AV); pap. bk. 99.95 (1045AV) J Wilson & Assocs.

Preventing & Handling Trouble in Closely Held Corporations. Robert C. Clark. 1989. 115.00 (978-1-55917-555-5(9)) Natl Prac Inst.

Preventing Career Burnout. Bruce A. Baldwin. Read by Bruce A. Baldwin. (Running Time: 60 min.). 1983. 8.95 (978-0-933583-10-8(9), PDC831) Direction Dynamics.
A revealing & helpful framework for preventing or reversing the burnout syndrome.

Preventing Divorces. Elbert Willis. 1 cass. (Relationship Ser.). 4.00 Fill the Gap.

Preventing Power Struggles. 2001. audio compact disk 25.95 (978-1-889609-13-3(7)) Loving Guidnce.

Preventing Power Struggles. unabr. ed. Becky Bailey. 2 cass. (Running Time: 2 hrs.). 1995. 16.95 Set. (978-1-889609-01-0(3), AT-102) Loving Guidnce.
Learn how to prevent power struggles between children & adults, 1998 Parent's Choice Award.

Preventing Strategic Gridlock: Leading Over, Under & Around Organizational Jams to Achieve High Performance Results. Interview. Pamela S. Harper. 1 CD. (Running Time: 1hr). 2002. audio compact disk 15.95 (978-0-9715739-5-6(6), 1-866-372-2636) Cameo Pubns.

Prevention. (Running Time: 45 min.). (Health Ser.). 12.98 (978-1-55909-097-1(9), 82) Randolph Tapes.
This powerful tape strengthens & activates your immune system.

Prevention & Management of Transient Cerebral Ischemia & Stroke. Read by Bruce Dobkin. 1 cass. (Running Time: 90 min.). 1986. 12.00 (C8628) Amer Coll Phys.

Prevention & Managment of Stroke. Moderated by Robert C. Griggs. Contrib. by Robert W. Brennan & Louis R. Caplan. 1 cass. (Running Time: 90 min.). 1986. 12.00 (A8618) Amer Coll Phys.
This topic is discussed by a moderator & experts who offer differing opinions.

Prevention & Treatment of Athletic Injuries. Robert Kerlan. 4 cass. (Running Time: 2 hrs.). (Exceptional Teachers in Sports Ser.). 39.95 Lets Talk Assocs.

Preview of Guide Book for Correct Teachings of Jesus Christ. Anthony W. Agee. 14.00 (978-0-9715017-1-3(8)) Anthony Agee.

Previsions. Ted Neather et al. 3 cass. (ENG.). 1998. 176.00 Set. (978-0-7487-2773-5(6)) St Mut.

Prey. abr. ed. Michael Crichton. Read by Robert Sean Leonard. 4 cass. (Running Time: 6 hrs.). 2002. 26.95 (978-0-06-053694-7(2)) HarperCollins Pubs.

***Prey.** abr. ed. Michael Crichton. Read by Robert Sean Leonard. (ENG.). 2004. (978-0-06-079367-8(8), Harper Audio); (978-0-06-081458-8(6), Harper Audio) HarperCollins Pubs.

Prey. abr. ed. Michael Crichton. Read by Robert Sean Leonard. 2005. audio compact disk 14.95 (978-0-06-087477-3(5)) HarperCollins Pubs.

***Prey.** unabr. ed. Michael Crichton. Read by Robert Sean Leonard. (ENG.). 2003. (978-0-06-073562-3(7), Harper Audio); (978-0-06-079915-1(3), Harper Audio) HarperCollins Pubs.

Prey. unabr. ed. Michael Crichton. Narrated by George Wilson. 9 cass. Library ed. (Running Time: 13 hrs.). 2002. 84.00 (978-1-4025-3593-2(7)) Recorded Bks.

Prey. unabr. collector's ed. Michael Crichton. Narrated by George Wilson. 9 cass. (Running Time: 13 hrs.). 2003. 42.95 (978-1-4025-3594-9(5)) Recorded Bks.
Combining themes from Jurassic Park and Andromeda Strain, Michael Crichton weaves a superbly suspenseful bio-thriller. Fast-paced novel mixes primitive vivid creatures and startling future developments.

Prey Dancing. unabr. ed. Jonathan Gash. Narrated by Richard Greenwood. 7 cass. (Running Time: 11 hrs.). 2000. 63.00 (978-1-84197-151-3(0), H1145E7) Recorded Bks.
Clare's life may not be ideal, but at least it's endurable. She is unable to forgive her unscrupulous husband for exploting her innocence, but at least she has her hired lover. But everything is about to change. Cullokin, an AIDs victim, was a patient who faced death with unusual courage.

***Prey on Patmos.** unabr. ed. Jeffrey Siger. (Running Time: 8 hrs. 30 mins.). (Chief Inspector Kaldis Novels Ser.). 2011. 29.95 (978-1-4417-7036-4(9)); 54.95 (978-1-4417-7036-3(4)); audio compact disk 76.00 (978-1-4417-7037-0(2)) Blckstn Audio.

Preyed on or Prayed For. unabr. ed. Terry Teykl. 1 cass. 1996. 5.00 (978-1-57892-037-2(X)) Prayer Pt Pr.
The pitfalls of ministry & how the congregation can support in prayer.

Priapus. Read by Rafael Lopez-Pedraza. 1 cass. (Running Time: 2 hrs.). 1984. 12.95 (978-0-7822-0149-9(0), ND7702) C G Jung IL.

Price. Arthur Miller. Perf. by Richard Dreyfuss et al. 2 CDs. (Running Time: 1 hr. 58 mins.). (L. A. Theatre Works). 2001. audio compact disk 25.95 (978-1-580801-208-5(2), CDRDP8) Pub: L A Theatre. Dist(s): NetLibrary CO
Two long estranged middle-aged brothers reunite. Nostalgia and recrimination erupt as they sell off an attic full of furniture, their last link to a family and a world that no longer exist.

Price. Arthur Miller. Contrib. by Harris Yulin et al. (Playaway Adult Fiction Ser.). (ENG.). 2009. 39.99 (978-1-60775-742-9(7)) Find a World.

Price. abr. ed. Joan Johnston. Read by Stevie Ray Dallimore. 2004. 15.95 (978-0-7435-4827-4(2)) Pub: S&S Audio. Dist(s): S and S Inc

Price. unabr. ed. Arthur Miller. Read by Richard Dreyfuss & Amy Irving. 2 CDs. (Running Time: 2 hrs.). 2001. audio compact disk 24.95 L A Theatre.

Price: 11 Cor. 11:16-33. Ed Young. 1990. 4.95 (978-0-7417-1799-3(9), 799) Win Walk.

Price Controls. Murray Newton Rothbard. 2 cass. (Running Time: 2 hrs. 14 min.). 19.95 (304) J Norton Pubs.
Covers farm price supports; foreign aid; rationing; the energy crisis; rent control; & zoning laws.

Price of a Child. Lorene Cary. Narrated by Lorene Cary. 10 cass. (Running Time: 12 hrs.). 1997. 74.00 (978-1-4025-4604-4(1)) Recorded Bks.

Price of a Temper: Numbers 20:1-13. Ed Young. 1985. 4.95 (978-0-7417-1442-8(6), 442) Win Walk.

Price of Admiralty: The Evolution of Naval Warfare. unabr. collector's ed. John Keegan. Read by Bill Kelsey. 10 cass. (Running Time: 15 hrs.). 1991. 80.00 (978-0-7366-2075-8(3), 2881) Books on Tape.
Keegan illuminates naval operations from Nelson's day to our own. He does this by dissecting four benchmark sea battles: Trafalgar, wooden ships of the line; Jutland, ironclads; Midway, aircraft carriers; & the Battle of the Atlantic, which saw the perfection of submarines. Keegan believes that "...by looking at its past we may know the future of naval warfare".

Price of Darkness. Graham Hurley. 2008. 94.95 (978-0-7531-3143-5(9)); audio compact disk 99.95 (978-0-7531-3144-2(7)) Pub: Isis Pubng Ltd GBR. Dist(s): Ulverscroft US

Price of Desire: Three Novellas from Transgressions. Ed McBain, pseud et al. Read by Richard Ferrone et al. Ed. by Ed McBain. 2005. 20.95 (978-1-59397-737-5(9)) Pub: Macmill Audio. Dist(s): Macmillan

Price of Desire: Three Novellas from Transgressions. unabr. ed. Lawrence Block et al. Ed. by Stephen King et al. 4 CDs. 2005. bk. 69.95 (978-0-7927-3630-1(3), CMP 798) AudioGO.

***Price of Everything: And the Hidden Logic of Value.** unabr. ed. Eduardo Porter. Read by Don Hagen. (Running Time: 9 hrs.). (ENG.). 2011. 34.00 (978-1-59659-641-2(4), GildAudio); audio compact disk 39.98 (978-1-59659-626-9(0), GildAudio) Pub: Gildan Media. Dist(s): HachBkGrp

Price of Experience Pt. A: Power, Money, Image & Murder in Los Angeles. unabr. collector's ed. Randall Sullivan. Read by Michael Prichard. 13 cass. (Running Time: 19 hrs. 30 min.). 1997. 104.00 (978-0-7366-3616-2(1), 4276-A) Books on Tape.
In this true crime story of the notorious "Billionaire Boys Club," Randall Sullivan examines a whiz-kid named Joe Hunt.

Price of Experience Pt. B: Power, Money, Image & Murder in Los Angeles. unabr. collector's ed. Randall Sullivan. Read by Michael Prichard. 12 cass. (Running Time: 18 hrs.). 1997. 96.00 (978-0-7366-3617-9(X), 4276-B) Books on Tape.

Price of Fame. unabr. ed. Carolyne Aarsen. Narrated by Sherri Berger. (Running Time: 7 hrs. 18 mins. 51 sec.). (Grace Chapel Inn Ser.). (ENG.). 2009. 18.19 (978-1-60814-531-7(X)); audio compact disk 25.99 (978-1-59859-591-8(1)) Oasis Audio.

***Price of Fear: Classic BBC Radio Horror.** Broadcasting Corp. British. Narrated by Vincent Price & Full Cast. (Running Time: 2 hrs. 0 mins. 0 sec.). (ENG.). 2011. audio compact disk 24.95 (978-1-4084-6702-2(X)) Pub: AudioGO. Dist(s): Perseus Dist

Price of Freedom. unabr. ed. Alex Domokos & Rita Y. Toews. Ed. by Vanessa Benjamin. 9 CDs. (Running Time: 11 hrs. 30 mins.). 2004. audio compact disk 72.00 (978-0-7861-8337-1(3), 3370); 56.95 (978-0-7861-2838-9(0), 3370) Blckstn Audio.
When a tech rep in charge of an avionics retrofit at a U.S. air base in Germany comes up missing, Jake Adams, a former Air Force intelligence and CIA officer, is hired to find him. Was the man selling vital technology for the new Joint Strike Fighter?.

Price of Glory: Verdun, 1916. collector's ed. Alistair Horne. Read by Bill Kelsey. 11 cass. (Running Time: 16 hrs. 30 min.). 2000. 88.00 (978-0-7366-5459-3(3)) Books on Tape.
Verdun was the battle that lasted ten months. The battle in which at least 700,000 men fell along a fifteen mile front, the battle which aimed to defeat the enemy rather than bleed him to death. Understanding the First World War, the key to the minds of those who waged it, to the traditions that bound them & to the world that gave them the opportunity.

Price of Guilt. unabr. ed. Margaret Yorke. Read by Rula Lenska. 8 cass. (Running Time: 8 hrs.). 2000. 69.95 (978-0-7540-0517-9(8), CAB1940) AudioGO.
When journalist Andrew Sherwood witnesses an assault on a woman, he wants to find out more about her. Louise Widdows is on the run from a tyrannical husband. She moves into a vacant cottage & is befriended by Andrew & his young son. She is drawn to the freedom so long denied, while Andrew is drawn to her by the mystery of her sudden flight & the secret he suspects she is hiding.

Price of Guilt. unabr. ed. Margaret Yorke. Read by Rula Lenska. 8 CDs. (Running Time: 12 hrs.). 2002. audio compact disk 79.95 (978-0-7540-5515-0(9), CCD 206) Pub: Chivers Pr GBR. Dist(s): AudioGO

Price of Love. unabr. ed. Anne Baker. Narrated by Judith Boyd. 10 cass. (Running Time: 13 hrs.). 2000. 92.00 (978-1-84197-141-4(3), H1135E7) Recorded Bks.
Life at home was unbearable for Kate McGlory. Kate got a live-in job as a shop assistant & life is certainly better for her. When rich Jack Courtney starts paying Kate attention, she feels she has everything she could wish for.

Price of Love. unabr. ed. Elisabeth Elliot. Read by Elisabeth Elliot. 4 cass. (Running Time: 4 hrs. 5 min.). 1989. 18.95 (978-0-8474-2012-4(4)) Back to Bible.
Elisabeth tells how your home can be a tabernacle for God, through forgiveness, prayer, sacrifice & obedience.

***Price of Love & Other Stories.** unabr. ed. Peter Robinson. Read by John Lee et al. (ENG.). 2009. (978-0-06-196261-5(9), Harper Audio); (978-0-06-190090-7(7), Harper Audio) HarperCollins Pubs.

Price of Murder. unabr. ed. Bruce Alexander. 7 cass. (Running Time: 10 hrs. 30 min.). 2003. 63.00 (978-0-7366-9576-3(1)) Books on Tape.

Price of Nice. John E. Bradshaw. (Running Time: 6000 sec.). 2008. audio compact disk 70.00 (978-1-57388-225-5(9)) J B Media.

Price of Nice. unabr. ed. John Bradshaw. 2 cass. (Running Time: 2 hrs.). 16.00 Set. (978-1-57388-066-4(3)) J B Media.
This lecture is for people pleasers & sweethearts who use "nice" as a disguise to cover shame. John offers practical insights into how we can learn to be kindly but firmly direct.

Price of Power. James W. Huston. Narrated by Adams Morgan. (Running Time: 16 hrs.). (C). 1999. 44.95 (978-1-59912-702-6(4)) Iofy Corp.

Price of Power. unabr. ed. James W. Huston. Read by Adams Morgan. 11 cass. (Running Time: 16 hrs.). 1999. 76.95 (978-0-7861-1656-0(0), 2484) Blckstn Audio.
The action sweeps from the Oval Office to a Navy SEAL assault on a remote Indonesian Island, from the court-martial of an admiral to the impeachment hearings of a peacenik President.

Price of Power. unabr. ed. James W. Huston. Read by Adams Morgan. 14 CDs. (Running Time: 14 hrs.). 2001. audio compact disk 112.00 (z2484) Blckstn Audio.
Sweeps from the Oval Office to a Navy SEAL assault on a remote Indonesian Island, from the court-martial of an admiral to the impeachment hearings of a peacenik President.

Price of Power. unabr. ed. James W. Huston. Read by Adams Morgan. 14 CDs. (Running Time: 16 hrs.). 2000. audio compact disk 112.00 (978-0-7861-9710-1(2), 2484) Blckstn Audio.

***Price of Power.** unabr. ed. James W. Huston. Read by Adams Morgan. (Running Time: 15 hrs. 15 mins.). 2010. audio compact disk 29.95 (978-1-4417-3591-1(7)) Blckstn Audio.

Price of Power, Set. abr. ed. James W. Huston. Read by Timothy Enos. 2 cass. (Running Time: 3 hr.). 1999. 17.95 (978-1-55935-314-4(7), 393399) Soundelux.
Sequel to Huston's "Balance of Power" sweeps from the Oval Office to a Navy Seal assault on a remote Indonesian island.

Price of Prosperity: A realistic Appraisal of the Future of Our National Economy. unabr. ed. Peter L. Bernstein. Read by Walter Dixon. (Running Time: 3 hrs. 10 mins.). (ENG.). 2009. 24.98 (978-1-59659-329-9(6), GildAudio) Pub: Gildan Media. Dist(s): HachBkGrp

Price of Silence. Kate Wilhelm. Read by Anna Fields. (Running Time: 34200 sec.). 2006. 59.95 (978-0-7861-4502-7(1)); audio compact disk 72.00 (978-0-7861-7227-6(4)) Blckstn Audio.

Price of Silence. unabr. ed. Kate Wilhelm. Read by Anna Fields. (Running Time: 34200 sec.). 2006. audio compact disk 29.95 (978-0-7861-7661-8(X)) Blckstn Audio.

***Price of Stones: Building a School for My Village.** unabr. ed. Twesigye Jackson Kaguri & Susan Urbanek Linville. (Running Time: 8 hrs. 0 mins.). 2010. 15.99 (978-1-4001-8572-6(6)) Tantor Media.

***Price of Stones: Building a School for My Village.** unabr. ed. Twesigye Jackson Kaguri & Susan Urbanek Linville. Narrated by Richard Allen. 1 MP3-CD. (Running Time: 9 hrs. 30 mins. 0 sec.). 2010. 19.99 (978-1-4001-6572-8(5)) Pub: Tantor Media. Dist(s): IngramPubServ

***Price of Stones: Building a School for My Village.** unabr. ed. Twesigye Jackson Kaguri & Susan Urbanek Linville. Narrated by Richard Allen voc. 8 CDs. (Running Time: 9 hrs. 30 mins. 0 sec.). 2010. audio compact disk 29.99 (978-1-4001-1572-3(8)); audio compact disk 59.99 (978-1-4001-4572-0(4)) Pub: Tantor Media. Dist(s): IngramPubServ

Priceless Gift of Faith. Instructed by Manly P. Hall. 8.95 (978-0-89314-220-9(4), C850317) Philos Res.

Priceless Gifts, Set. Gracia Jones. 2 cass. 2004. 12.95 (978-1-57734-343-1(3), 07001967) Covenant Comms.

Priceless Memories. abr. unabr. ed. Digby Diehl & Bob Barker. Read by Digby Diehl & Bob Barker. (Running Time: 7 hrs.). (ENG.). 2009. 19.98 (978-1-60024-554-1(4)) Pub: Center St. Dist(s): HachBkGrp

Priceless Memories. unabr. ed. Digby Diehl & Bob Barker. Read by Digby Diehl & Bob Barker. 6 CDs. (Running Time: 7 hrs.). (ENG.). 2009. audio compact disk 29.98 (978-1-60024-553-4(6)) Pub: Hachet Audio. Dist(s): HachBkGrp

Pricing of the Factors of Production. Murray Newton Rothbard. 1 cass. (Running Time: 1 hr. 18 min.). 11.95 (307) J Norton Pubs.
Covers taxes; production costs; the classical theory of distribution; the Law of Diminishing Returns; & marginal productivity theory.

Pride. (712) Yoga Res Foun.

Pride. Swami Jyotirmayananda. 1 cass. (Running Time: 1 hr.). 1990. 12.99 Yoga Res Foun.

Pride: The Charley Pride Story, Set. abr. ed. Charley Pride & Jim Henderson. Read by Charley Pride. 2 cass. (Running Time: 3 hrs.). 1994. 16.95 (978-1-879371-71-2(5)) Pub Mills.
One of the most enduring figures in country music, Charley Pride, recounts his struggle from an impoverished childhood in Mississippi to his career as one of the top twenty bestselling recording artists of all time.

Pride & Ownership: A Firefighter's Love of the Job. Rick Lasky. Narrated by Jack Shook. 2008. audio compact disk 49.00 (978-1-59370-152-9(7), Fire Eng Bks & Vid) PennWell Corp.

***Pride & Ownership: A Firefighter's Love of the Job - Audio Book.** Rick Lasky. (ENG.). 2008. audio compact disk 49.00 (978-1-59370-171-0(3)) Pub: Fire Eng. Dist(s): PennWell Corp

Pride & Predjudice: An A+ Audio Study Guide. unabr. ed. Jane Austen & Sheila Allen. (Running Time: 30 mins.). (ENG.). 2006. 5.98 (978-1-59483-720-3(1)) Pub: Hachet Audio. Dist(s): HachBkGrp

Pride & Prejudice see Orgullo y Prejuicio

Pride & Prejudice see Orgullo y Perjurio

Pride & Prejudice. Jane Austen. Narrated by Anne Flosnik. (ENG.). 2007. 12.95 (978-0-9801087-2-9(1)) Alpha DVD.

Pride & Prejudice. Jane Austen. Narrated by Flo Gibson. (ENG.). 2008. audio compact disk 34.95 (978-1-60646-026-9(9)) Audio Bk Con.

Pride & Prejudice. Jane Austen. Read by Irene Sutcliffe. 10 cass. (Running Time: 11 hrs. 30 min.). 59.95 (CC/001) C to C Cassettes.

***Pride & Prejudice.** Jane Austen. Read by Helen Lisanti. (ENG.). 2010. 19.95 (978-0-9843759-7-4(X)); audio compact disk 29.95 (978-0-9843759-6-7(1)) Cherry Hill Pubng.

Pride & Prejudice. Jane Austen. Read by Juliet Stevenson. (Running Time: 3 hrs.). (ENG., 2005. audio compact disk 25.00 (978-1-84456-033-2(3), HoddrStoughton) Pub: Hodder General GBR. Dist(s): Trafalgar

Pride & Prejudice. Jane Austen. Read by Laura Garcia. (Running Time: 3 hrs.). 2002. 16.95 (978-1-60083-224-6(5), Audiofy Corp) Iofy Corp.

Pride & Prejudice. Jane Austen. Read by Kate Redding. (Running Time: 12 hrs.). 2003. 34.95 (978-1-59912-106-2(9), Audiofy Corp) Iofy Corp.

Pride & Prejudice. Jane Austen. Narrated by Jane Lapotaire. (Running Time: 3 hrs.). 2006. 14.95 (978-1-60083-041-9(2)) Iofy Corp.

Pride & Prejudice. Jane Austen. Read by Allison Green. 8 cass. (Running Time: 11 hrs.). 1993. 50.60 Set. (978-1-56544-019-7(6), 350003); Rental 9.50 30 day rental Set. (350003) Literate Ear.
Bright & spirited Elizabeth Bennett, considered one of the most delightful heroines of all time, spars with her proud beau, Mr. Darcy, throughout

Austen's superb comedy of manners. Pride must be set aside & prejudice thawed in this nineteenth century precursor of the romance novels of our day.

Pride & Prejudice. Jane Austen. Narrated by Ronald Colman. 1 cass. (Running Time: 60 min.). 7.95 (LS-4338) Natl Recrd Co.

Pride & Prejudice. Jane Austen. Read by Jenny Agutter. 3 cass. (Running Time: 3 hrs. 45 mins.). (Works of Jane Austen). 1996. 17.98 (978-962-634-604-4(3), NA310414, Naxos AudioBooks) Naxos.
Not only a wonderful love story, contains dialogue that sparkles with wit and irony, an ingenious and compelling plot and some of the most unforgettable characters ever created.

Pride & Prejudice. Jane Austen. Contrib. by Joanna David. 4 cass. (Running Time: 6 hrs.). (Classics on Audio Ser.). (ENG.). (gr. 12 up). 2003. 16.95 (978-0-14-086060-3(6), 693102, PenGlobal) Penguin Grp USA.
Elizabeth Bennett, the second of five daughters whom Mrs. Bennett is anxious to dispose of in marriage, is the most intelligent & delightful of all Austen's heroines.

Pride & Prejudice. Jane Austen. 1 cass. (Running Time: 1 hr.). (Radiobook Ser.). 1987. 4.98 (978-0-929541-27-3(8)) Radiola Co.

Pride & Prejudice. Jane Austen. Narrated by Flo Gibson. 10 CDs. (Running Time: 11 hrs.). 2000. audio compact disk 97.00 (978-0-7887-4914-8(5), C1295E7) Recorded Bks.
With five grown daughters & not one yet married, the business of Mrs. Bennets life 'was to get her daughters married." So when Mr. Bingley, a most eligible bachelor, takes up residence at nearby Netherfield park, Mrs. Bennet wastes time in displaying her daughters to the best possible advantage. Flighty Lydia, thoughtful Jane, studious Mary, the youngest Kitty & light of her father's life, Elizabeth.

Pride & Prejudice. Jane Austen. 2001. audio compact disk 21.45 (978-1-903342-03-9(1)) Wordsworth Educ GBR.

Pride & Prejudice. abr. ed. Jane Austen. Read by Claire Bloom. 1 cass. 1984. 8.98 (CDL5 1595) HarperCollins Pubs.

Pride & Prejudice. abr. ed. Jane Austen. Narrated by Juliet Stevenson. 2 cass. (Running Time: 3 hrs.). 1999. 16.95 (978-1-85998-013-2(9), HoddrStoughton) Pub: Hodder General GBR. Dist(s): Trafalgar
In a remote Hertfordshire village, far off the good coach roads of George III's England, Mr. and Mrs. Bennet - a country squire of no great means and his scatterbrained wife - must marry off their five vivacious daughters. At the heart of this all-consuming enterprise are the headstrong second daughter Elizabeth and her aristocratic suitor Fitzwilliam Darcy, two lovers in whom pride and prejudice must be overcome before love can bring the novel to its magnificent conclusion.

Pride & Prejudice. abr. ed. Jane Austen. Read by Susannah York. 3 vols. (Classics Collection). (YA). 1987. audio compact disk 11.99 (978-1-57815-525-5(8), Media Bks Audio) Media Bks NJ.

Pride & Prejudice. abr. ed. Jane Austen. Read by Susannah York. 2 cass. (Running Time: 3 hrs.). 2000. 7.95 (978-1-57815-123-3(6), 1085, Media Bks Audio) Media Bks NJ.
Elizabeth Bennett & Mr. Darcy dislike each other & are blinded by pride & by prejudice.

Pride & Prejudice. abr. ed. Jane Austen. Read by Jenny Agutter. 3 CDs. (Running Time: 3 hrs. 45 mins.). (Works of Jane Austen). (J). (gr. 9-12). 1996. audio compact disk 22.98 (978-962-634-104-9(1), NA310412) Naxos.
Not only a wonderful love story, contains dialogue that sparkles with wit and irony, an ingenious and compelling plot and some of the most unforgettable characters ever created.

Pride & Prejudice. abr. ed. Jane Austen. Perf. by Glenda Jackson. 4 cass. (Running Time: 6 hrs.). 2004. 25.00 (978-1-59007-132-8(8)) New Millenn Enter.
This timeless satire on English manners traces the fortunes and foibles of a family of marriageable young women and their suitors.

Pride & Prejudice. abr. ed. Jane Austen & Joanna David. (Running Time: 6 hrs.). (ENG.). (gr. 12 up). 2005. audio compact disk 16.95 (978-0-14-305817-5(7), PengAudBks) Penguin Grp USA.

Pride & Prejudice. abr. ed. Abr. by Laurie A. Knox. Based on a book by Jane Austen. 2007. 5.00 (978-1-60339-127-6(4)); audio compact disk 5.00 (978-1-60339-128-3(2)) Listenr Digest.

Pride & Prejudice. unabr. ed. Jane Austen. Read by Irene Sutcliffe. 8 cass. (Running Time: 11 hrs. 30 mins.). (gr. 9-12). 2004. 34.95 (978-1-57270-055-0(6), F81055u) Pub: Audio Partners. Dist(s): PerseuPGW
The tale of how three of the five daughters of the bookish & indolent Mr. Bennett find themselves husbands, in a timeless pattern of courtship, property, marriage & love.

Pride & Prejudice. unabr. ed. Jane Austen. Read by Lindsay Duncan. 10 cass. (Running Time: 90 mins. per cass.). 1998. 84.95 (978-0-7540-0149-2(0), CAB 1572) AudioGO.

Pride & Prejudice. unabr. ed. Jane Austen. Narrated by Irene Sutcliffe. 9 CDs. (Running Time: 11 hrs 30 min). (Cover to Cover Ser.). (ENG.). 2005. audio compact disk 37.95 (978-1-57270-500-5(0)) Pub: AudioGO. Dist(s): Perseus Dist
One of the best-loved works of English literature, Pride and Prejudice follows Elizabeth Bennet (Austen's favorite of all her creations) and her four sisters through a series of romantic adventures - and misadventures. Affections, affectations, and shenanigans abound due to Mrs. Bennet's relentless matchmaking, the devious Wickham, and Elizabeth's tempestuous relationship with the snobbish Mr. Darcy, which the meddlesome Lady Catherine de Bourgh is determined to crush out. In addition to being Austen's most popular novel, Pride and Prejudice also contains some of her most astringent comments on manners and morals.

Pride & Prejudice, unabr. ed. Jane Austen. Read by Nadia May. 8 cass. (Running Time: 11 hrs. 30 mins.). 1989. 56.95 (978-0-7861-0057-6(5), 1054) Blckstn Audio.
The story of the Bennet's efforts to secure suitable marriages for their five daughters.

Pride & Prejudice. unabr. ed. Jane Austen. Read by Nadia May. 11 CDs. (Running Time: 11 hrs. 30 mins.). 2000. audio compact disk 88.00 (978-0-7861-9894-8(X), 1054) Blckstn Audio.
The story of the Bennet's efforts to secure suitable marriages for their five daughters.

Pride & Prejudice. unabr. ed. Jane Austen. Read by Nadia May. 8 cass. (Running Time: 11 hrs.). 2005. 29.95 (978-0-7861-3503-5(4)); audio compact disk 29.95 (978-0-7861-7848-3(5)); audio compact disk 29.95 (978-0-7861-8967-0(3), 1054) Blckstn Audio.

***Pride & Prejudice.** unabr. ed. Jane Austen. (Running Time: 9 hrs. NaN mins.). (ENG.). 2011. 29.95 (978-1-4417-7469-9(6)); audio compact disk 29.95 (978-1-4417-7468-2(8)) Blckstn Audio.

Pride & Prejudice. unabr. ed. Jane Austen. Read by Sharon Williams. 8 cass. (Running Time: 11 hrs.). 2002. 29.95 (978-1-59086-151-6(5), 1590861515, BAU) Brilliance Audio.
A delightful novel about "how girls catch husbands." Listen in to find out: What will happen to sister Lydia? Will the arrogant Lady Catherine de Burgh's intrigues be foiled? Will sister Jane marry Mr. Bingley? And especially, will Elizabeth, cured of her prejudice, and Mr. Darcy, cured of his pride, fall into each other's arms? Listeners will also savor the wit, the sly irony and satire and comedy that Miss Austen crowds into almost every quiet, well-bred line of this novel. There is great sanity, common sense and worldly wisdom to be found in her exploration of human nature. Sir Walter Scott said, Jane Austen had "that exquisite touch which renders ordinary commonplace things and characters interesting." This quality provides today's listeners of Pride and Prejudice with a fascinating trip into the lives of the privileged in England during the eighteenth century.

Pride & Prejudice. unabr. ed. Jane Austen. Read by Sharon Williams. (Running Time: 11 hrs.). 2004. 39.25 (978-1-59335-423-7(1), 1593354231, Brlnc Audio MP3 Lib) Brilliance Audio.

Pride & Prejudice. unabr. ed. Jane Austen. Read by Sharon Williams. (Running Time: 11 hrs.). 2004. 39.25 (978-1-59710-597-2(X), 159710597X, BADLE); 24.95 (978-1-59710-596-5(1), 1597105961, BAD) Brilliance Audio.

Pride & Prejudice. unabr. ed. Jane Austen. Read by Sharon Williams. (Running Time: 11 hrs.). 2005. audio compact disk 97.25 (978-1-59737-142-1(4), 9781597371421, BriAudCD Unabrid); audio compact disk 36.95 (978-1-59737-141-4(6), 9781597371414, Bril Audio CD Unabri) Brilliance Audio.

Pride & Prejudice. unabr. ed. Jane Austen. Read by Lindsay Duncan. 10 cass. (Running Time: 15 hrs.). 2001. 69.95 (CAB 1572) Pub: Chivers Audio Bks GBR. Dist(s): AudioGO
Few readers have failed to be charmed by the witty and independent spirit of Elizabeth Bennet. Her early determination to dislike Mr. Darcy, possibly the most eligible bachelor in the whole of English literature, is a misjudgement matched in folly by Darcy's arrogant pride. Their first impressions give way to truer feelings in a comedy profoundly concerned with achieving happiness.

Pride & Prejudice. unabr. ed. Jane Austen. Read by Lindsay Duncan. 10 CDs. 2000. audio compact disk 94.95 (978-0-7540-5338-5(5), CCD 029) Pub: Chivers Audio Bks GBR. Dist(s): AudioGO
Few readers have failed to be charmed by the witty & independent spirit of Elizabeth Bennet. Her early determination to dislike Mr. Darcy, possibly the most eligible bachelor in the whole of English literature, is a misjudgment matched in folly by Darcy's arrogant pride.

Pride & Prejudice. unabr. ed. Jane Austen. Read by Kate Redding. (YA). 2006. 54.99 (978-1-59895-176-9(9)) Find a World.

Pride & Prejudice. unabr. ed. Jane Austen. Read by Emilia Fox. 11 CDs. (Running Time: 13 hrs. 2 min.). bk. 67.98 (978-962-634-356-2(7), NAX35612) Naxos.

Pride & Prejudice, unabr. ed. Jane Austen. Narrated by Flo Gibson. 8 cass. (Running Time: 11 hrs.). 1980. 70.00 (978-1-55690-424-0(X), 80020E7) Recorded Bks.
Mother & unwed daughters pursue an eligible bachelor in the intimate domesticity of Jane Austen's England.

Pride & Prejudice. unabr. ed. Jane Austen. 10 CDs. (Running Time: 11 Hrs). 2005. audio compact disk 34.95 (978-1-4193-2357-7(1)) Recorded Bks.

Pride & Prejudice. unabr. ed. Jane Austen. Read by Sharon Williams. (Running Time: 11 hrs.). 2004. 24.95 (978-1-59335-191-5(7), 1593351917) Soulmate Audio Bks.
A delightful novel about "how girls catch husbands." Listen in to find out: What will happen to sister Lydia? Will the arrogant Lady Catherine de Burgh's intrigues be foiled? Will sister Jane marry Mr. Bingley? And especially, will Elizabeth, cured of her prejudice, and Mr. Darcy, cured of his pride, fall into each other's arms? Listeners will also savor the wit, the sly irony and satire and comedy that Miss Austen crowds into almost every quiet, well-bred line of this novel. There is great sanity, common sense and worldly wisdom to be found in her exploration of human nature. Sir Walter Scott said, Jane Austen had "that exquisite touch which renders ordinary commonplace things and characters interesting." This quality provides today's listeners of Pride and Prejudice with a fascinating trip into the lives of the privileged in England during the eighteenth century.

Pride & Prejudice. unabr. ed. Jane Austen. Read by Kate Reading. 1 cd. (Running Time: 11 hrs 49 mins). 2002. audio compact disk 18.95 (978-1-58472-394-3(7), In Aud) Pub: Sound Room. Dist(s): Baker Taylor
MP3 format.

Pride & Prejudice. unabr. ed. Jane Austen. Narrated by Josephine Bailey. (Running Time: 11 hrs. 30 mins. 0 sec.). (Unabridged Classics in Audio Ser.). (ENG.). 2008. 24.99 (978-1-4001-5633-7(5)); audio compact disk 75.99 (978-1-4001-3633-9(4)); audio compact disk 37.99 (978-1-4001-0633-2(8)) Pub: Tantor Media. Dist(s): IngramPubServ

***Pride & Prejudice.** unabr. ed. Jane Austen. (Running Time: 9 hrs. NaN mins.). 2011. 59.95 (978-1-4417-7466-8(1)); audio compact disk 90.00 (978-1-4417-7467-5(X)) Blckstn Audio.

Pride & Prejudice. unabr. ed. Christina Calvit. Perf. by Kate Burton et al. Adapted by Jane Austen. 1 cass. (Running Time: 2 hrs. 6 min.). 1997. 22.95 (978-1-58081-052-4(7), CTA55) L A Theatre.
The sparkling tale of the Bennett's, a family blessed with five daughters & a mother desperate to marry them off. The tempestuous pairing of the witty, independent Elizabeth & her arrogant but honorable suitor, Mr. Darcy, set the standard for all great couples of the stage & screen.

Pride & Prejudice. unabr. collector's ed. Jane Austen. Read by Kate Reading. 9 cass. (Running Time: 13 hrs. 30 mins.). 1996. 72.00 (978-0-7366-3370-3(7), 4020) Books on Tape.
"Pride & Prejudice" has delighted generations of readers with its ingenious plot, brilliant dialogue, inventive assortment of unique characters & wealth of humor. The central theme is the romantic clash of two opinionated young people. In one corner, we have Elizabeth Bennet, our highly vivacious heroine; in the other, the arrogant but captivating Mr. Darcy. Their destinies interweave in a timeless pattern of courtship, love, property & marriage.

Pride & Prejudice, Set. unabr. ed. Jane Austen. Read by Flo Gibson. 8 cass. (Running Time: 12 hrs.). 1986. 26.95 (978-1-55685-025-7(5)) Audio Bk Con.
While Mrs. Bennett pursues husbands for her daughter. The course of the courtship of proud Darcy for prejudiced Elizabeth never runs smoothly.

Pride & Prejudice, Set. unabr. ed. Jane Austen. Read by Nadia May. 8 cass. 1999. 56.95 (FS9-50921) Highsmith.

Pride & Prejudice: Dramatic Reading. Pamela Robinson. 1 cass. (Running Time: 46 min.). 1968. 11.95 (23082) J Norton Pubs.
A dramatic presentation of the 19th century classic by an instructor in oral interpretation of literature at the University of Cincinnati.

Pride & Prejudice: Dramatized play based on the Novel. unabr. ed. Christina Calvit & Jane Austen. Read by A. Full Cast. (YA). 2008. 34.99 (978-1-60514-985-1(3)) Find a World.

***Pride & Prejudice: (Unabridged Audiobook)** Read by Wendy Mullen. 2010. audio compact disk 24.95 (978-1-4276-4633-0(3)) AardGP.

Pride & Prejudice (A) abr. ed. Jane Austen. (Running Time: 4 hrs.). 2009. audio compact disk 22.98 (978-962-634-957-1(3), Naxos AudioBooks) Naxos.

Pride & Prejudice & Zombies. unabr. ed. Jane Austen & Seth Grahame-Smith. Read by Katherine Kellgren. (Running Time: 11 hrs.). (Quirk Classic Ser.). 2009. 24.99 (978-1-4418-1678-8(X), 9781441816788, Brilliance MP3); 39.97 (978-1-4418-1679-5(8), 9781441816795, Brlnc Audio MP3 Lib); 39.97 (978-1-4418-1680-1(1), 9781441816801, BADLE); audio compact disk 29.99 (978-1-4418-1676-4(3), 9781441816764, Bril Audio CD Unabri); audio compact disk 97.97 (978-1-4418-1677-1(1), 9781441816771, BriAudCD Unabrid) Brilliance Audio.

***Pride & Prejudice & Zombies: Dreadfully Ever After: Dreadfully Ever After.** unabr. ed. Steve Hockensmith. (Running Time: 9 hrs.). 2011. 39.97 (978-1-4558-0388-0(X), 9781455803880, BADLE); 24.99 (978-1-4558-0386-6(3), 9781455803866, Brilliance MP3); 39.97 (978-1-4558-0387-3(1), 9781455803873, Brlnc Audio MP3 Lib); audio compact disk 29.99 (978-1-4558-0384-2(7), 9781455803842, Bril Audio CD Unabri); audio compact disk 92.97 (978-1-4558-0385-9(5), 9781455803859, BriAudCD Unabrid) Brilliance Audio.

Pride & the Anguish. unabr. ed. Douglas Reeman. Read by David Rintoul. 8 cass. (Running Time: 8 hrs.). 1996. 69.95 (978-0-7451-6645-2(8), CAB 1261) AudioGO.
It is November 1941, & Lt. Ralph Trewin arrives as second-in-command of the HMS Porcupine. To Trewin, the gunboat seems to symbolize the ignorance he finds in Singapore. The following month the Japanese invade Malaya, & in three months Singapore knows the humiliation of surrencer. Through the despair of the bloody campaign, the little gunboat becomes a symbol of bravery.

PRIDE Methodologies for IRM. abr. ed. 2006. 54.00 (978-0-9786182-1-6(1)) M Bryce Assocs.

Pride of a Champion. unabr. ed. Read by Bob Richards. 1 cass. (Running Time: 30 min.). 15.00 B R Motivational.
A recorded live speech by Bob Richards on the most important motivational quality in America today - pride.

Pride of Place, Set. unabr. ed. Judith Glover. 8 cass. (Storysound Ser.). (J). 1997. 69.95 (978-1-85903-161-2(7)) Pub: Mgna Lrg Print GBR. Dist(s): Ulverscroft US

Pride of Polly Perkins. unabr. ed. Joan Jonker. Read by Melanie Hill. 10 cass. (Running Time: 10 hrs.). 1998. 84.95 (978-0-7540-0126-3(1), CAB1549) AudioGO.
It is 1934 & the Perkins family struggles to make ends meet. When Polly's father is taken ill, the family is faced with being turned out into the street. Now her mother must manage the family. Polly earns some money selling flowers, but little does she know that her life will change completely when she meets Charles Denholme.

Pride of the West. John Wynne & John McEvoy. (ENG.). 2008. audio compact disk 25.95 (978-0-8023-8165-1(0)) Pub: Clo Iar-Chonnachta IRL. Dist(s): Dufour

Pride of the Yankees: Gary Cooper As Lou Gehrig. unabr. ed. Hosted by Cecil B. DeMille. 1 cass. (Running Time: 60 min.). Dramatization. 1943. 7.95 Norelco box. (DD-5700) Natl Recrd Co.
This is the true story of one of baseball's all-time great athletes, "The Iron Man of Baseball," Lou Gehrig...his boyhood, his days at Columbia University, his happy marriage & his final speech before a crowd of 60,000 baseball fans who came out to pay him tribute. Gary Cooper is featured as the beloved baseball player, with Virginia Bruce as his wife, Ellie, & Edgar Buchanan as his friend & sportswriter-narrator, Sam Blake.

Pride of the Yankees; It Happens Every Spring. collector's ed. Perf. by Gary Cooper & Ray Milland. 2 cass. (Running Time: 2 hrs.). (AMC's Audio Movies to Go Ser.). 2000. bk. 9.98 (6012) Radio Spirits.
Original scores and sound effects create an audio version of movie classics. Digitally remastered with intermissions featuring the original commercials.

Pride vs. Humility. Derek Prince. 2 cass. 11.90 Set. (053-054) Derek Prince.
Though this vast theme spans time & eternity, it also applies in the lives of each one of us.

Pride's Harvest. unabr. ed. Jon Cleary. Read by Gordon Griffin. 8 cass. (Running Time: 12 hrs.). (Sound Ser.). 2004. 69.95 (978-1-85496-811-1(4), 68114) Pub: UlverLrgPrint GBR. Dist(s): Ulverscroft US
When the Inspector is called to the scene of a murder in an Australian country town, the locals resent his inquiries into the easy-going corruption of the establishment. As the list of suspects grows, tensions escalate.

Priest. Ken Bruen. (Jack Taylor Ser.: Bk. 5). 2008. audio compact disk 64.95 (978-0-7531-2543-4(9)) Pub: ISIS Audio GBR. Dist(s): Ulverscroft US

Priest. unabr. ed. Ken Bruen. Read by Gerry O'Brien. 5 cass. (Running Time: 6 hrs. 15 mins.). (Jack Taylor Ser.: BK. 5). 2008. 49.95 (978-0-7531-3552-5(3)) Pub: ISIS Audio GBR. Dist(s): Ulverscroft US

Priest: Aaron. unabr. ed. Francine Rivers. Read by Chris Fabry. 5 CDs. (Running Time: 6 hrs.). (Sons of Encouragement Ser.: Vol. 1). 2004. audio compact disk 40.00 (978-0-7861-8480-4(9), 3323) Blckstn Audio.

Priest: Aaron. unabr. ed. Francine Rivers. Read by Chris Fabry. 4 cass. (Running Time: 6 hrs.). (Sons of Encouragement Ser.: Vol. 1). 25.99 (978-1-58926-628-5(5)) Oasis Audio.

Priest: Aaron. unabr. ed. Francine Rivers. Narrated by Chris Fabry. 5 CDs. (Running Time: 6 hrs.). (Sons of Encouragement Ser.: Vol. 1). (ENG.). 2004. audio compact disk 19.99 (978-1-58926-629-2(3)) Oasis Audio.

Priest: Aaron. unabr. ed. Francine Rivers. Narrated by Chris Fabry. (Sons of Encouragement Ser.: Vol. 1). (ENG.). 2009. 13.99 (978-1-60814-344-3(9)) Oasis Audio.

Priest: Affective & Authentic. Andrew Cusack. 2 cass. (Running Time: 1 hr. 50 min.). 1997. 18.95 Set. (TAH381) St Pauls Alba.
The clergy today face issues in parish ministry that require them to be thoroughly formed & informed in order to minister in effective, authentic ways. Great material for personal reflection, renewal, retreat or someone looking for a boost in their ministerial life.

Priest: In Touch with Oneself. Loughlan Sofield. 3 cass. (Running Time: 2 hrs. 24 min.). 1996. 28.95 Set. (TAH362) Alba Hse Comns.
Bro. Loughlan looks at the issues of clergy morale, feelings, the critical stages in the life of the priest, & discusses leadership issues as they affect ministry & values. Greatly informative material for personal renewal or meditation.

Priest: Person of Christ. Paul Hinnebusch. 2 cass. (Running Time: 2 hrs. 40 min.). 1997. 18.95 Set. (TAH377) St Pauls Alba.
Pastoral action becomes the specific nature of the priesthood lived out through the aspects of worship of God & evangelization of people.

Priest: Witness of God's Presence. Donald W. Wuerl. 5 cass. (Running Time: 5 hrs.). 37.95 incl. shelf-case. (TAH070) Alba Hse Comns.
Provides a picture of the priest in today's world.

Priest Describes Medjugorje. Interview with Mother Angelica & Father Pervan. 1 cass. (Running Time: 60 min.). (Mother Angelica Live Ser.). 1987. 10.00 (978-1-55794-091-9(6), T42) Eternal Wrd TV.

Priest Fainted. unabr. ed. Catherine Temma Davidson. Narrated by Alyssa Bresnahan. 7 cass. (Running Time: 9 hrs. 15 mins.). 1998. 60.00 (978-0-7887-2606-4(4), 95450E7) Recorded Bks.
Blends memories, Greek myths, recipes & family gossip in this multi layered story of one woman's year in Greece.

***Priest-Kings of Gor.** unabr. ed. John Norman. Read by Ralph Lister. (Running Time: 13 hrs.). (Gorean Saga Ser.). 2010. 24.99 (978-1-4418-4905-2(X), 9781441849052, Brilliance MP3); 39.97 (978-1-4418-4906-9(8), 9781441849069, Brlnc Audio MP3 Lib); 24.99 (978-1-4418-4907-6(6), 9781441849076, BAD); audio compact disk 29.99 (978-1-4418-4902-1(5), 9781441849021, Bril Audio CD Unabri); audio compact disk 79.97 (978-1-4418-4904-5(1), 9781441849045, BriAudCD Unabrid) Brilliance Audio.

Priest Prepares for Death. Interview with Mother Angelica & Rick Arkfield. 1 cass. (Running Time: 60 min.). (Mother Angelica Live Ser.). 1987. 10.00 (978-1-55794-093-3(2), T44) Eternal Wrd TV.

Priest, the Pilgrim, & the Pope. Contrib. by Anna-Liza Kozma. 1 CD. (Running Time: 1 hr. 30 mins.). 2005. audio compact disk 19.95 (978-0-660-19047-1(8)) Pub: Canadian Broadcasting CAN. Dist(s): Georgetown Term

Priestess of Avalon. Marion Zimmer Bradley. Read by Bernadette Dunne. 2001. 80.00 (978-0-7366-7047-0(5)) Books on Tape.

***Priestess of Avalon.** unabr. ed. Marion Zimmer Bradley & Diana L. Paxson. Narrated by Rosalyn Landor. (Running Time: 15 hrs. 0 mins. 0 sec.). (Avalon Ser.). 2010. 29.99 (978-1-4001-6779-1(5)); audio compact disk 39.99 (978-1-4001-1779-6(8)); audio compact disk 95.99 (978-1-4001-4779-3(4)) Pub: Tantor Media. Dist(s): IngramPubServ

Priestly Morale. Neal Quartier. Read by Neal Quartier. 1 cass. (Running Time: 90 min.). 1992. 9.95 (978-7-900783-06-6(7), AA2547) Credence Commun.
Quartier, a priest & psychologist, blends the great themes of scripture with the finest in contemporary psychology.

Priestly Prerogative see Son of the Wolf

Priestly-Prophetic Balance in a Pastoral Ministry. William Hulme. 1986. 10.80 (0609A) Assn Prof Chaplains.

Priestly Sins. unabr. ed. Andrew M. Greeley. 8 cass. (Running Time: 12 hrs.). 2004. 72.00 (978-1-4159-0211-0(9)) Books on Tape.
A young, innocent Catholic priest finds himself caught up in the scandal of clerical abuse.

Priests Alive. Loughlin Sofield. 3 cass. (Running Time: 2 hrs. 24 min.). 1994. 27.95 Set. (TAH319) Alba Hse Comns.
Excellent for priests who are searching for ways of handling & understanding their own & others' anger & hostility. This program will most certainly point the way to healthy intimacy & give the ins & outs of a very practical spirituality.

Priests & Ambassadors. David T. Demola. 1 cass. 4.00 (1-092) Faith Fellow Min.

Priests & Mary. Interview with Mother Angelica et al. 1 cass. (Running Time: 60 min.). (Mother Angelica Live Ser.). 1987. 10.00 (978-1-55794-089-6(4), T40) Eternal Wrd TV.

Priests & Nuns Newsletter. 1 cass. 10.00 (978-1-893165-80-9(9)) Rational Isl.
Shared experiences of people working in the Catholic church, using re-evaluation counseling.

***Priest's Graveyard.** unabr. ed. Ted Dekker. (Running Time: 14 hrs.). (ENG.). 2011. 24.98 (978-1-60941-994-3(4)); audio compact disk & audio compact disk 34.98 (978-1-60941-992-9(8)) Pub: Hachet Audio. Dist(s): HachBkGrp

Priest's Madonna. Amy Hassinger. Read by Anna Fields. (Running Time: 36000 sec.). 2006. audio compact disk 24.95 (978-1-59316-071-5(2)) Listen & Live.

Priest's Madonna. unabr. ed. Amy Hassinger. Read by Anna Fields. (YA). 2007. 39.99 (978-1-60252-778-2(4)) Find a World.

Prima Bette. abr. ed. Honoré de Balzac. 3 CDs. (SPA.). 2002. audio compact disk 17.00 (978-958-8161-43-3(6)) YoYoMusic.

Prima Latina Pronunciation: Introduction to Christian Latin. 2nd ed. Scripts. Voice by Leigh Lowe. 1 CD. (Running Time: 60 min). (J). 2003. audio compact disk 4.95 (978-1-930953-50-5(X)) Memoria.
The Prima Latina Set (teacher, student, CD) includes an audio CD with pronunciation direction for each lesson and four beautiful Gregorian chant hymns.

Primacy of Consciousness vs. the Objectivist Ethics. Andrew Bernstein. 5 cass. (Running Time: 5 hrs.). 1994. 49.95 Set. (978-1-56114-318-4(9), CB09D) Second Renaissance.
An examination of the distinction between the primacy of consciousness & the primacy of existence.

***Primal: A Quest for the Lost Soul of Christianity.** unabr. ed. Mark Batterson. (Running Time: 5 hrs. 45 mins. 0 sec.). (ENG.). 2010. audio compact disk 21.98 (978-1-61045-053-9(1)) christianaud.

Primal Branding: Create Zealots for Your Brand, Your Company, & Your Future. unabr. ed. Patrick Hanlon. Narrated by Alan Sklar. (Running Time: 8 hrs. 0 mins. 0 sec.). (ENG.). 2006. audio compact disk 59.99 (978-1-4001-3219-5(3)); audio compact disk 19.99 (978-1-4001-5219-3(4)) Pub: Tantor Media. Dist(s): IngramPubServ

Primal Branding: Create Zealots for Your Brand, Your Company, & Your Future. unabr. ed. Patrick Hanlon. Read by Alan Sklar. (Running Time: 8 hrs. 0 mins. 0 sec.). (ENG.). 2006. audio compact disk 29.99 (978-1-4001-0219-8(7)) Pub: Tantor Media. Dist(s): IngramPubServ

Primal Leadership: Realizing the Power of Emotional Intelligence. Daniel Goleman. 8 CDs. (Running Time: 10 hrs. 30 min.). 2002. audio compact disk 64.00 (978-0-7366-8734-8(3)) Books on Tape.
After having interviewed some 3,429 corporate executives, the author has come to the conclusion that a true leader is one who makes his subordinates feel good. This may have some obvious counter-examples, one could imagine a company in which the leader makes his subordinates feel good but fails to achieve business goals, but Goleman's careful research methodology reveals that many executives who are most successful in the business world have this quality as well.

Primal Leadership: Realizing the Power of Emotional Intelligence. abr. rev. ed. Daniel Goleman et al. Read by Daniel Goleman. 3 CDs. (Running Time: 3 hrs. 30 mins. 0 sec.). (ENG.). 2002. audio compact disk 20.00 (978-1-55927-744-0(0)) Pub: Macmill Audio. Dist(s): Macmillan

Primal Leadership: Realizing the Power of Emotional Intelligence. unabr. ed. Richard Boyatzis et al. Read by Arthur Morey. (Running Time: 9 hrs. 0 mins. 0 sec.). (ENG.). 2006. audio compact disk 29.95 (978-1-59397-929-4(0)) Pub: Macmill Audio. Dist(s): Macmillan

Primal Leadership: Realizing the Power of Emotional Intelligence. unabr. ed. Daniel Goleman. 7 cass. (Running Time: 10 hrs. 30 mins.). 2002. 56.00 (978-0-7366-8589-4(8)) Books on Tape.
After having interviewed some 3,429 corporate executives, the author has come to the conclusion that a true leader is one who makes his subordinates feel good. This may have some obvious counter-examples, one could imagine a company in which the leader makes his subordinates feel good but fails to achieve business goals, but Goleman's careful research methodology reveals that many executives who are most successful in the business world have this quality as well.

Primal Love. abr. ed. Douglas M. Gillette. Read by Douglas M. Gillette. 2 cass. (Running Time: 3 hrs.). 1997. 16.95 (978-1-882071-54-8(9)) B-B Audio.
Douglas Gillette shows us how to use our evolutionary past to solve our romantic mysteries of today. How the patterns of nature evolved in the past make our love lives both wonderfully joyful & miserably intolerable is the substance of a book that, like.

Primal Screams. Dahmer Bart. Narrated by Ralph Wallace. (ENG.). 2009. 11.99 (978-0-9815403-7-5(6)) Innovo Pub.

Primal Wish. Neville Goddard. 1 cass. (Running Time: 62 min.). 1967. 8.00 (38) J & L Pubns.
Neville taught Imagination Creates Reality. He was a powerfully influential teacher of God as Consciousness.

Primary Activity Box: Games & Activities for Younger Learners. Caroline Nixon & Michael Tomlinson. (Running Time: 1 hr. 10 mins.). (Cambridge Copy Collection). (ENG., 2001. 25.00 (978-0-521-77966-1(9)) Cambridge U Pr.

***Primary Activity Box Audio CD: Games & Activities for Younger Learners.** Caroline Nixon et al. (Running Time: 1 hr. 10 mins.). (Cambridge Copy Collection). (ENG.). 2009. audio compact disk 24.00 (978-0-521-15628-8(9)) Cambridge U Pr.

Primary Aeronautical Language Manual. Aviation Language School, Inc. Staff. Intro. by Deborah J. Balter. 1 cass. (Running Time: 1 hr. 30 mins.). 1994. pap. bk. 60.00 (978-0-941456-00-5(5)) Aviation Lang Sch.

Primary Biliary Cirrhosis: Pathogenesis & Management. Read by Marshall M. Kaplan. 1 cass. (Running Time: 90 min.). 1985. 12.00 (C8530) Amer Coll Phys.

Primary Care in the Office Setting. Contrib. by Vicki L. Seltzer et al. 1 cass. (American College of Obstetrics & Gynecologists UPDATE: Vol. 21, No. 2). 1998. 20.00 Am Coll Obstetric.

Primary care medicine recommendations for pda powered by skyscape Inc-e02. Allan Goroll & Albert Mulley. 2005. audio compact disk 49.95 (978-0-7817-8232-6(5)) Lppncott W W.

Primary Colors: A Novel of Politics. unabr. ed. Read by Lloyd James. 11 cass. (Running Time: 16 hrs.). 1997. 76.95 (978-0-7861-1091-9(0), 1869) Blckstn Audio.
Young Henry Burton, a former congressional aide of mixed race & the grandson of a legendary civil rights leader, is going through a precocious midlife crisis. Tired of the back-scratching & back-stabbing of legislative politics, he's wondering what to do next with his Beltway experience & abilities when Jack Stanton, the governor of a small southern state who has set his sights on the presidency, half flatters, half shanghais him into a campaign staff job. What follows for Henry - & the reader - is an education in modern American electoral politics.

Primary Colors: A Novel of Politics. unabr. ed. Narrated by Peter Francis James. 11 cass. (Running Time: 16 hrs.). 1997. 96.00 (978-0-7887-0609-7(8), 94809E7) Recorded Bks.
Story of a governor-from-a-small-state's quest for the presidency & a jaded Beltway insider searching for a leader to believe in.

Primary Colours. Andrew Littlejohn & Diana Hicks. (Running Time: hrs. mins.). (ENG.). 2002. 42.00 (978-0-521-66722-7(4)) Cambridge U Pr.

Primary Colours: Songs Starter. Andrew Littlejohn & Diana Hicks. (Running Time: hrs. mins.). (ENG.). 2002. 15.75 (978-0-521-66719-7(4)) Cambridge U Pr.

Primary Colours Class Starter. Diana Hicks & Andrew Littlejohn. (Running Time: hrs. mins.). (ENG.). 2002. audio compact disk 40.00 (978-0-521-75096-7(2)) Cambridge U Pr.

Primary Colours Italy Level 1 Class Cassette. Diana Hicks & Andrew Littlejohn. (Primary Colours Ser.). 2004. (978-88-8433-336-0(9)) Cambridge U Pr.

Primary Colours Italy Level 1/2 Songs. Diana Hicks & Andrew Littlejohn. (Primary Colours Ser.). 2004. audio compact disk (978-88-8433-905-8(7)) Cambridge U Pr.

Primary Colours Italy Level 2 Class Cassette. Diana Hicks & Andrew Littlejohn. (Primary Colours Ser.). 2004. (978-88-8433-339-1(3)) Cambridge U Pr.

Primary Colours Italy, 3 Class Cassettes. Diana Hicks & Andrew Littlejohn. (Primary Colours Ser.). 2004. (978-88-8433-325-4(3)) Cambridge U Pr.

Primary Colours Italy, 4 Class Cassettes. Diana Hicks & Andrew Littlejohn. (Primary Colours Ser.). 2004. (978-88-8433-329-2(6)) Cambridge U Pr.

Primary Colours, Level 1. Diana Hicks & Andrew Littlejohn. (Running Time: hrs. mins.). (ENG.). 2002. audio compact disk 42.00 (978-0-521-75098-1(9)) Cambridge U Pr.

Primary Colours, Level 1: Songs & Stories. Diana Hicks & Andrew Littlejohn. (Running Time: hrs. mins.). (ENG.). 2002. audio compact disk 15.75 (978-0-521-75101-8(2)) Cambridge U Pr.

Primary Colours, Level 2. Diana Hicks & Andrew Littlejohn. (ENG.). 2003. audio compact disk 43.05 (978-0-521-75099-8(7)) Cambridge U Pr.

Primary Colours, Level 2. Andrew Littlejohn & Diana Hicks. (ENG., 2003. 41.00 (978-0-521-66721-0(6)) Cambridge U Pr.

Primary Colours, Level 2: Songs & Stories. Diana Hicks & Andrew Littlejohn. (ENG.). 2003. audio compact disk 24.15 (978-0-521-75102-5(0)) Cambridge U Pr.

Primary Colours, Level 2: Songs & Stories. Andrew Littlejohn & Diana Hicks. (ENG., 2003. 23.00 (978-0-521-66717-3(8)) Cambridge U Pr.

Primary Colours: Level 3: Songs & Stories. Diana Hicks & Andrew Littlejohn. (ENG.). 2003. audio compact disk 24.15 (978-0-521-75103-2(9)) Cambridge U Pr.

Primary Colours: Level 3: Songs & Stories. Andrew Littlejohn & Diana Hicks. (ENG.). 2003. 24.15 (978-0-521-66716-6(X)) Cambridge U Pr.

Primary Colours Level 4 Class Audio Cassettes. Diana Hicks & Andrew Littlejohn. (Running Time: 2 hrs. 20 mins.). (ENG.). 2007. 41.00 (978-0-521-69986-0(X)) Cambridge U Pr.

Primary Colours Level 4 Class Audio CDs. Diana Hicks & Andrew Littlejohn. (Running Time: 2 hrs. 20 mins.). (ENG.). 2007. audio compact disk 43.05 (978-0-521-69985-3(1)) Cambridge U Pr.

Primary Colours Level 5 Class Audio Cassettes. Diana Hicks & Andrew Littlejohn. (Running Time: 2 hrs. 20 mins.). (ENG.). 2007. 42.00 (978-0-521-69993-8(2)) Cambridge U Pr.

Primary Colours Level 5 Class Audio CDs. Diana Hicks & Andrew Littlejohn. (Running Time: 2 hrs. 20 mins.). (ENG.). 2007. audio compact disk 42.00 (978-0-521-69992-1(4)) Cambridge U Pr.

Primary Colours Songs Audio CD Starter. Diana Hicks & Andrew Littlejohn. (Running Time: 33 mins.). (ENG., 2002. audio compact disk 15.00 (978-0-521-75097-4(0)) Cambridge U Pr.

Primary Colours Starter. Andrew Littlejohn & Diana Hicks. (Running Time: hrs. mins.). (ENG.). 2002. 42.00 (978-0-521-66723-4(2)) Cambridge U Pr.

Primary Colours 1: Songs & Stories. Andrew Littlejohn & Diana Hicks. (Running Time: hrs. mins.). (ENG.). 2002. 15.75 (978-0-521-66718-0(6)) Cambridge U Pr.

Primary Colours 3. Diana Hicks & Andrew Littlejohn. (ENG.). 2003. audio compact disk 43.05 (978-0-521-75100-1(4)) Cambridge U Pr.

Primary Colours 3. Andrew Littlejohn & Diana Hicks. (ENG.). 2003. 43.05 (978-0-521-66720-3(8)) Cambridge U Pr.

Primary English see Ingles Primario

Primary Hyperoxaluria - A Bibliography & Dictionary for Physicians, Patients, & Genome Researchers. Compiled by Icon Group International, Inc. Staff. 2007. ring bd. 28.95 (978-0-497-11279-0(5)) Icon Grp.

Primary Inversion. Catherine Asaro. Read by Anna Fields. 8 cass. (Running Time: 12 hrs.). 2000. 56.95 (978-0-7861-1868-7(7), 2667) Blckstn Audio.
The Skolian Empire rules a third of the civilized galaxy through its mastery of faster-than-light communication. But war with the rival empire of the Traders seems imminent, a war that can only lead to slavery for the Skolians or the destruction of both sides. Destructive skirmishes have already occurred. A desperate attempt must be made to avert total disaster.

Primary Inversion. Asaro Catherine. Narrated by Anna Fields. (Running Time: 11 hrs. 30 mins.). 2000. 34.95 (978-1-59912-576-3(5)) Iofy Corp.

Primary Justice: A Novel of Suspense. unabr. ed. William Bernhardt. Read by Jonathan Marosz. 6 cass. (Running Time: 9 hrs.). (Ben Kincaid Ser.: No. 1). 1998. 48.00 (978-0-7366-4105-0(X), 4610) Books on Tape.
For as long as he can remember, Ben Kincaid has wanted to be a lawyer. Strange as it seems, his motives are pure. He's not in it for the money & the prestige; he just wants to do the right thing. Then, opportunity knocks & he leaves the DA's office for Raven, Tucker & Tubb, one of Tulsa's most prestigious law firms. But Ben is about to make a life-changing discovery about legal ethics: Doing the right thing & representing the client's interests can be mutually exclusive. It's time to play hardball in the courtroom. And what an amnesiac eight-year-old girl can't remember explodes into a case of corporate manipulation of millions, child abandonment & murder.

Primary Justice: A Novel of Suspense. unabr. ed. William Bernhardt. Read by Larry Block. 10 cass. (Running Time: 15 hrs.). (Ben Kincaid Ser.: No. 1). 2001. (GKT 036) Chivers Audio Bks GBR.
Ben Kincaid becomes a lawyer in order to protect truth and justice. But once he gets a position in a Tulsa law firm, Ben finds out that on the fast track, deals are struck, secrets are kept, and justice is compromised.

***Primary Kid's Box Level 3 Pupil's Book with Songs CD & Parents' Guide Polish Edition.** Caroline Nixon et al. (ENG.). 2010. pap. bk. & pap. bk. 12.00 (978-0-521-74993-0(X)) Cambridge U Pr.

Primary Praise: 60 Scripture Songs for Kids. Contrib. by Joseph Linn. Prod. by Joseph Linn. 2007. audio compact disk 19.99 (978-5-557-61408-5(7)) Lillenas.

Primary Process Thinking (Companion CD-ROM) Theory, Measurement, & Research. unabr. ed. Robert R. Holt. 2005. audio compact disk (978-0-8236-4192-5(9), BN 24192) Intl Univs Pr.

Primary pulmonary hypertension - A Bibliography & Dictionary for Physicians, Patients, & Genome Researchers. Compiled by Icon Group International, Inc. Staff. 2007. ring bd. 28.95 (978-0-497-11280-6(9)) Icon Grp.

Primary Resources: Winter 99-2000. 1 cass. (J). (gr. 1-2). 1999. pap. bk. 10.99 (978-1-57405-616-7(6)) CharismaLife Pub.

***Primary Source History of the Colony of Connecticut.** unabr. ed. Ann Malaspina. Read by Jay Snyder. (Running Time: 1 hr.). 2011. audio compact disk 24.99 (978-1-61106-986-0(6), 9781611069860, Bril Audio CD Unabri); audio compact disk 29.97 (978-1-61106-987-7(4), 9781611069877, BriAudCD Unabrid) Brilliance Audio.

Primary Source History of the Colony of Georgia. unabr. ed. Liz Sonneborn. (Running Time: 1 hr.). (Primary Sources of the Thirteen Colonies Ser.). 2009. 14.99 (978-1-4233-9412-9(7), 9781423394129, Brilliance MP3); 39.97 (978-1-4233-9413-6(5), 9781423394136, Brlnc Audio MP3 Lib); 39.97 (978-1-4233-9414-3(3), 9781423394143, BADLE); audio compact disk 14.99 (978-1-4233-9410-5(0), 9781423394105, Bril Audio CD Unabri) Brilliance Audio.

Primary Source History of the Colony of Georgia. unabr. ed. Liz Sonneborn. Read by Jay Snyder. (Running Time: 1 hr.). (Primary Sources of the Thirteen Colonies Ser.). 2009. audio compact disk 39.97 (978-1-4233-9411-2(9), 9781423394112, BriAudCD Unabrid) Brilliance Audio.

***Primary Source History of the Colony of Maryland.** unabr. ed. Liz Sonneborn. Read by Eileen Stevens. (Running Time: 1 hr.). 2011. audio compact disk 24.99 (978-1-4558-0184-8(4), 9781455801848, Bril Audio CD Unabri); audio compact disk 29.97 (978-1-61106-487-2(2), 9781611064872, BriAudCD Unabrid) Brilliance Audio.

Primary Source History of the Colony of Massachusetts. unabr. ed. Jeri Freedman. Read by Jay Snyder. 1 MP3-CD. (Running Time: 1 hr.). (Primary Sources of the Thirteen Colonies Ser.). 2009. 14.99 (978-1-4233-9362-7(7), 9781423393627, Brilliance MP3); 39.97 (978-1-4233-9363-4(5), 9781423393634, Brlnc Audio MP3 Lib); 39.97 (978-1-4233-9364-1(3), 9781423393641, BADLE); audio compact disk 39.97 (978-1-4233-9361-0(9), 9781423393610, BriAudCD Unabrid); audio compact disk 14.99 (978-1-4233-9360-3(0), 9781423393603, Bril Audio CD Unabri) Brilliance Audio.

***Primary Source History of the Colony of New Jersey.** unabr. ed. Tamra Orr. Read by Jay Snyder. (Running Time: 1 hr.). 2011. audio compact disk 24.99 (978-1-61106-483-4(X), 9781611064834, Bril Audio CD Unabri); audio compact disk 29.97 (978-1-61106-491-9(0), 9781611064919, BriAudCD Unabrid) Brilliance Audio.

Primary Source History of the Colony of New York. unabr. ed. Paul Kupperberg. Read by Jay A. Snyder. (Running Time: 1 hr.). (Primary Sources of the Thirteen Colonies Ser.). 2009. 39.97 (978-1-4233-8187-7(4), 9781423381877, BADLE); 39.97 (978-1-4233-8186-0(6), 9781423381860, Brlnc Audio MP3 Lib); 14.99 (978-1-4233-8185-3(8), 9781423381853, Brilliance MP3); audio compact disk 39.97 (978-1-4233-8184-6(X), 9781423381846, BriAudCD Unabrid); audio compact disk 14.99 (978-1-4233-8183-9(1), 9781423381839) Brilliance Audio.

Primary Source History of the Colony of North Carolina. unabr. ed. Philip Margulies. Read by Jay Snyder. (Running Time: 1 hr.). (Primary Sources of the Thirteen Colonies Ser.). 2009. 14.99 (978-1-4233-9417-4(8), 9781423394174, Brilliance MP3); 39.97 (978-1-4233-9418-1(6), 9781423394181, Brlnc Audio MP3 Lib); 39.97 (978-1-4233-9419-8(4), 9781423394198, BADLE); audio compact disk 14.99 (978-1-4233-9415-0(1), 9781423394150, Bril Audio CD Unabri); audio compact disk 39.97 (978-1-4233-9416-7(X), 9781423394167, BriAudCD Unabrid) Brilliance Audio.

***Primary Source History of the Colony of Pennsylvania.** unabr. ed. G. S. Prentzas. Read by Jay Snyder. (Running Time: 1 hr.). 2011. audio compact disk 24.99 (978-1-4558-0183-1(6), 9781455801831, Bril Audio CD Unabri); audio compact disk 29.97 (978-1-61106-488-9(0), 9781611064889, BriAudCD Unabrid) Brilliance Audio.

Primary Source History of the Colony of South Carolina. unabr. ed. Heather Hasan. Read by Eileen Stevens. (Running Time: 1 hr.). (Primary Sources of the Thirteen Colonies Ser.). 2009. 14.99 (978-1-4233-9392-4(9), 9781423393924, Brilliance MP3); 39.97 (978-1-4233-9393-1(7), 9781423393931, Brlnc Audio MP3 Lib); 39.97 (978-1-4233-9394-8(5), 9781423393948, BADLE); audio compact disk 14.99 (978-1-4233-9390-0(2), 9781423393900, Bril Audio CD Unabri); audio compact disk 39.97 (978-1-4233-9391-7(0), 9781423393917, BriAudCD Unabrid) Brilliance Audio.

Primary Source History of the Colony of Virginia. unabr. ed. Sandra Whiteknact. Read by Eileen Stevens. 1 MP3-CD. (Running Time: 1 hr.). (Primary Sources of the Thirteen Colonies Ser.). 2009. 39.97 (978-1-4233-8206-5(4), 9781423382065, Brlnc Audio MP3 Lib); 39.97 (978-1-4233-8207-2(2), 9781423382072, BADLE); 14.99 (978-1-4233-8205-8(6), 9781423382058, Brilliance MP3); audio compact disk 39.97 (978-1-4233-8204-1(8), 9781423382041, BriAudCD Unabrid); audio compact disk 14.99 (978-1-4233-8203-4(X), 9781423382034, Bril Audio CD Unabri) Brilliance Audio.

Primary Stories for Children of All Ages. Narrated by Dale Bulla. 1 cass. (Running Time: 60 min.). (J). (gr. k-3). 1990. 9.95 (978-1-884197-01-7(9)) N Horizon Educ.
A collection of five folktales told by storyteller Dale Bulla. No. 1 The Wolf & the 7 Kids, No. 2 How Stories Come to Earth, No. 3 The Gunniwolf, No. 4 The Magic Box, No. 5 How Spider Got His Thin Waist.

Primary Themes Clip Art. (Timesaving Software Tools for Teachers Ser.). 2004. audio compact disk 19.99 (978-1-57690-693-4(0)) Tchr Create Ma.

Primates. unabr. ed. Ed. by Linda Spizzirri. 48 cass. (Running Time: 15 min.). Dramatization. (Educational Coloring Book & Cassette Package Ser.). (J). (gr. k-8). 1989. pap. bk. 6.95 (978-0-86545-157-5(5)) Spizzirri.
Features courage of various species from the Gorilla to the Titi Monkey.

***primavera Audio CD.** Francisco Blane. Adapted by Benchmark Education Company, LLC. (My First Reader's Theater Ser.). (SPA.). (J). 2009. audio compact disk 10.00 (978-1-935470-78-6(7)) Benchmark Educ.

Prime Candidate, unabr. ed. Gordon Cotler. Narrated by Richard Poe. 6 cass. (Running Time: 9 hrs.). 1996. 51.00 (978-0-7887-0516-8(4), 94711E7) Recorded Bks.
When an attractive female real estate agent is found dead in highly respected liberal senator Morton Beaufoy's car, his media consultant Jock Caprisi must try to save the senator's campaign & career.

Prime Cut. unabr. ed. Diane Mott Davidson. Narrated by Barbara Rosenblat. 9 CDs. (Running Time: 10 hrs. 45 mins.). (Goldy Schulz Culinary Mysteries Ser.: No. 8). 1999. audio compact disk 83.00 (978-0-7887-3432-8(6), C1038E7) Recorded Bks.
When caterer-turned-sleuth Goldy Schulz finds her least-favorite general contractor dead, she uses her many talents to uncover the perfect recipe for murder.

Prime Cut. unabr. ed. Diane Mott Davidson. Narrated by Barbara Rosenblat. 8 cass. (Running Time: 10 hrs. 45 mins.). (Goldy Schulz Culinary Mysteries Ser.: No. 8). 1999. 72.00 (978-0-7887-2922-5(5), 95647E7) Recorded Bks.

Prime Directive. Garfield Reeves-Stevens. (Star Trek Ser.). 2004. 10.95 (978-0-7435-4662-1(8)) Pub: S&S Audio. Dist(s): S and S Inc

***Prime Minister.** 2010. audio compact disk (978-1-59171-290-9(4)) Falcon Picture.

***Prime Minister.** Anthony Trollope. Read by Anais 9000. 2009. 33.95 (978-1-60112-256-8(X)) Babblebooks.

Prime Minister, Pt. 1. unabr. collector's ed. Anthony Trollope. Read by David Case. 10 cass. (Running Time: 15 hrs.). 1994. 80.00 (978-0-7366-2887-7(8), 3588-A) Books on Tape.
As the Duke of Omnium, the new prime minister & his wife move to the center of society, Ferdinand Lopez moves to influence them.

Prime Minister, Pt. 2. collector's ed. Anthony Trollope. Read by David Case. 10 cass. (Running Time: 15 hrs.). 1994. 80.00 (978-0-7366-2888-4(6), 3588-B) Books on Tape.

Prime Minister (Part 1), unabr. ed. Anthony Trollope. Read by Flo Gibson. 9 cass. (Running Time: 13 hrs. 30 min.). 1993. 28.95 (978-1-55685-300-5(9)) Audio Bk Con.
Plantagenet Palliser, the Duke of Omnium, & his wife, Lady Glencora, approach his political duties & their social lives in often divergent ways. Ferdinand Lopez & Emily Wharton's tragic marriage tests the constancy of the charming Arthur Fletcher.

Prime Minister (Part 2), Vol. 2. unabr. ed. Anthony Trollope. Narrated by Flo Gibson. (Running Time: 12 hrs. 47 mins.). 1993. 28.95 (978-1-55685-842-0(6)) Audio Bk Con.

Prime Minister (Parts 1 And 2) unabr. ed. Anthony Trollope. Narrated by Flo Gibson. (Running Time: 25 hrs. 32 mins.). 1993. 53.95 (978-1-55685-843-7(4)) Audio Bk Con.

Prime Ministers of Canada. Blaine Selkirk & Ed Butts. Composed by Mark Shannon. Prod. by Sara Jordan. (Running Time: 68 minutes). (J). 2001. audio compact disk 11.95 (978-1-894262-57-6(3), JMP122CD) Jordan Music.
Sing and learn about Canadian history and Canada's Prime Ministers with this wonderful collection of then songs starting with Sir John A. Mcdonald through to Chretien. The musical tyle of each song reflects the corresponding historical period. Grades: 3-7.

Prime Ministers of Canada. Blaine Selkirk & Ed Butts. Ed. by Ed Butts & John Zeman. Lyrics by Blaine Selkirk. Prod. by Sara Jordan. Composed by Mark Shannon. Engineer Mark Shannon. 1 cass. (Running Time: 66 mins. 48 secs.). (J). 2001. pap. bk. 14.95 (978-1-894262-59-0(X), JMP122K) Jordan Music.
Ten songs in different musical styles representing each historical period. This kit teaches Canadian history and about Canada's Prime Ministers from Macdonald to Chrétien. A bonus complement of music accompaniment tracks makes class performances a breeze. Grades: 3 - 7.

Prime Ministers of Canada. Blaine Selkirk & Ed Butts. Ed. by Ed Butts et al. Lyrics by Blaine Selkirk. Prod. by Sara Jordan. Composed by Mark Shannon. Engineer Mark Shannon. 1 CD. (Running Time: 66 mins. 48 secs.). (J). 2001. pap. bk. 16.10 (978-1-894262-58-3(1), JMP122CDK) S Jordan Publ.

Prime of Miss Jean Brodie. unabr. ed. Muriel Spark. (Running Time: 14400 sec.). 2007. audio compact disk 19.95 (978-1-4332-0615-3(3)) Blckstn Audio.

Prime of Miss Jean Brodie. unabr. ed. Muriel Spark. Read by Nadia May. (Running Time: 14400 sec.). 2007. 24.95 (978-1-4332-0613-9(7)); audio compact disk 36.00 (978-1-4332-0614-6(5)) Blckstn Audio.

Prime of Miss Jean Brodie & the Girls of Slender Means, Set unabr. ed. Muriel Spark. Read by Geraldine McEwan. 6 cass. 1999. 44.98 (LL 0047) AudioGO.

Prime Time. unabr. ed. Sandra Brown. Read by Joyce Bean. (Running Time: 6 hrs.). 2005. 39.25 (978-1-59710-599-6(6), 9781597105996, BADLE); 24.95 (978-1-59710-598-9(8), 9781597105989, BAD); 24.95 (978-1-59355-980-9(1), 9781593559809, BAU); 62.25 (978-1-59355-981-6(X), 9781593559816, BrilAudUnabridg); audio compact disk 74.25 (978-1-59355-983-0(6), 9781593559830, BriAudCD Unabrid); audio compact disk 24.95 (978-1-59335-781-8(8), 9781593357818, Brilliance MP3); audio compact disk 39.25 (978-1-59335-915-7(2), 9781593359157, Brlnc Audio MP3 Lib) Brilliance Audio.
More than anything else, cable TV reporter Andrea Malone wanted a network job. And it could be hers if she gained a coveted interview with the aging General Ratiff - especially if she uncovered the secret that drove him into seclusion at his Texas ranch. One obstacle was Lyon Ratiff, the general's watchdog of a son. Andrea had a plan, but had no way of knowing how Lyon's unexpected, undeniable effect on her would change everything, how they both would face a storm of suspicion and betrayal - and how Andrea Malone would have to choose between the ruthless demands of her profession and the equally strong dictates of the heart.

Prime Time. unabr. ed. Sandra Brown. Read by Joyce Bean. (Running Time: 21600 sec.). 2007. audio compact disk 14.99 (978-1-4233-3361-6(6), 9781423333616, BCD Value Price) Brilliance Audio.

Prime Time Aerobics. Leslie Johnson & Charlene Schade. Illus. by Steve Pileggi. Orig. Title: Rhythmic Aerobex. 1985. bk. 17.95 incl. wkbk. (978-0-9610234-0-9(6)) Exer Fun.
Fitness fun for Seniors. Based on aerobic exercise theory, it includes a complete cardiovascular workout. Written & choreographed by professionals in the field of gerontology & physical fitness.

Prime Time Christmas. Karen Dean & Don Marsh. 1994. 75.00 (978-0-7673-0804-5(2)) LifeWay Christian.

Prime Time Christmas. Karen Dean & Don Marsh. 1994. 11.98 (978-0-7673-0803-8(4)) LifeWay Christian.

Prime Time Christmas (Stereo/Split Acc Cd0. Karen Dean & Don Marsh. 1994. audio compact disk 85.00 (978-0-7673-0805-2(0)) LifeWay Christian.

Prime Witness. Steve Martini. Narrated by George Guidall. 9 cass. (Running Time: 13 hrs.). (Paul Madriani Ser.: No. 2). 1993. 86.00 (978-1-4025-3878-0(2)) Recorded Bks.

Prime Witness. abr. ed. Steve Martini. Read by Joe Mantegna. 2 cass. (Running Time: 3 hrs.). (Paul Madriani Ser.: No. 2). 2001. 18.00 (978-1-59040-141-5(7), Phoenix Audio) Pub: Amer Intl Pub. Dist(s): PerseuPGW

Primer Curso, Selected Readings with Program Notes. Holt, Rinehart and Winston Staff. (SPA.). 1997. 34.20 (978-0-03-095169-5(0)) Holt McDoug.

primer día de Bill Audio CD: Emergent Set A. Benchmark Education Staff. Ed. by Cynthia Swain. (Early Explorers Ser.). (J). 2008. audio compact disk 10.00 (978-1-60437-247-2(8)) Benchmark Educ.

Primer for Mideast Investment. 6 cass. (Running Time: 5 hrs.). 55.00 (451-456) J Norton Pubs.

Primer Lesson see Carl Sandburg's Poems for Children

Primer Nivel: Acordeon. Tr. of Level One: Accordion. (SPA.). 2004. audio compact disk 15.95 (978-0-8256-2728-6(1)) Pub: Music Sales. Dist(s): H Leonard

Primer Nivel: Armonia. Tr. of Level One: Harmony. (SPA.). 2004. pap. bk. 14.95 (978-0-8256-2793-4(1), Schirmer Trade Bks) Pub: Music Sales. Dist(s): H Leonard

Primer Nivel: Bajo. Tr. of Level One: Bass. (SPA.). 2004. audio compact disk 17.95 (978-0-8256-2729-3(X)) Pub: Music Sales. Dist(s): H Leonard

Primer Nivel: Bajo Sexto. Tr. of Level One: Six String Bass. (SPA.). 2004. audio compact disk 14.95 (978-0-8256-2730-9(3)) Pub: Music Sales. Dist(s): H Leonard

Primer Nivel: Bateria. Tr. of Level One: Drums. (SPA.). 2004. audio compact disk 17.95 (978-0-8256-2731-6(1)) Pub: Music Sales. Dist(s): H Leonard

Primer Nivel: Canto. Tr. of Level One: Chorus/Singing. (SPA.). 2004. audio compact disk 15.95 (978-0-8256-2732-3(X)) Pub: Music Sales. Dist(s): H Leonard

Primer Nivel: Saxofon. Tr. of Level One: Saxophone. (SPA.). 2004. pap. bk. 14.95 (978-0-8256-2794-1(X), Schirmer Trade Bks) Pub: Music Sales. Dist(s): H Leonard

Primer Nivel: Solfeo. Tr. of Level One: Reading/Writing Music. (SPA.). 2004. audio compact disk 15.95 (978-0-8256-2734-7(6)) Pub: Music Sales. Dist(s): H Leonard

Primer Nivel: Trompeta. Tr. of Level One: Trumpet. (SPA.). 2004. pap. bk. 14.95 (978-0-8256-2792-7(3), Schirmer Trade Bks) Pub: Music Sales. Dist(s): H Leonard

Primer Nivel: Violin. Tr. of Level One: Violin. (SPA.). 2004. pap. bk. 15.95 (978-0-8256-2791-0(5), Schirmer Trade Bks) Pub: Music Sales. Dist(s): H Leonard

Primer of Newspaper Chinese. rev. ed. Yu-Ju Chih. 4 cass. 1982. 8.95 ea. incl. suppl. materials. (978-0-88710-057-4(0)) Yale Far Eastern Pubns.

Primer on Criminal Tax Fraud Litigation. 1989. 40.00 (AC-525) PA Bar Inst.

Primer on Jungian Psychology. Read by Thomas P. Lavin. 1 cass. (Running Time: 90 min.). 1989. 10.95 (978-0-7822-0142-0(3), 391) C G Jung IL.

Primer on Money, Banking, & Gold. unabr. ed. Peter L. Bernstein. Read by Sean Pratt. (Running Time: 5 hrs. 20 mins.). (ENG.). 2008. 24.98 (978-1-59659-322-0(9), GildAudio) Pub: Gildan Media. Dist(s): HachBkGrp

Primer on Organization Development. Read by Fred Nader. 1 cass. (Running Time: 90 min.). 1989. 10.95 (978-0-7822-0219-9(5), 392) C G Jung IL.

Primer on Postmodernism. unabr. ed. Stanley Grenz. 6 CDs. (Running Time: 7 hrs. 0 mins. 0 sec.). (ENG.). 2005. audio compact disk 24.98 (978-1-59644-292-4(1), Hovel Audio) christianaud.
From the academy to pop culture, our society is in the throes of change rivaling the birth of modernity out of the decay of the Middle Ages. We are now moving from the modern to the postmodern era.But what is postmodernism? How did it arise? What characterizes the postmodern ethos? What is the postmodern mind and how does it differ from the modern mind? Who are its leading advocates? Most important of all, what challenges does this cultural shift present to the church, which must proclaim the gospel to the emerging postmodern generation?Stanley Grenz here charts the postmodern landscape. He shows the threads that link art and architecture, philosophy and fiction, literary theory and television. He shows how the postmodern phenomenon has actually been in the making for a century and then introduces readers to the gurus of the postmodern mind-set. What he offers here is truly an indispensable guide for understanding todaya??s culture.

***Primer on Postmodernism.** unabr. ed. Stanley Grenz. Narrated by Nadia May. (ENG.). 2005. 14.98 (978-1-59644-293-1(X), Hovel Audio) christianaud.

Primer to Postmodernism - DELETED. unabr. ed. Stanley J. Grenz. Narrated by Nadia May. 6 CDs. (Running Time: 7 hrs). 2005. 19.98 (978-1-59644-291-7(3), Hovel Audio) christianaud.

Primero lo Primero. Stephen R. Covey. 4 cass. (Running Time: 4 hrs.).Tr. of First Things First. (SPA.). 2002. 25.95 (978-970-05-1013-2(1)) Taller del Exito.
Manage your time by learning how to balance your life. Time management suggests that working harder, smarter, and faster will help you gain control over your life, and that increased control will bring peace and fulfillment.

Primordial Tones: The Tones of the Earth, the Sun, the Moon & Shiva - Shakti Sound. Joachim-Ernst Berendt. 2 CDs. (Running Time: 2 hrs.). 1994. audio compact disk 29.95 (978-0-89281-416-9(0)) Inner Tradit.
Brings the listener's consciousness into harmony with archetypal primordial energies of the particular heavenly bodies.

Primrose see William Carlos Williams Reads His Poetry

Primrose Petal's Edge see Poetry & Voice of Ted Hughes

Prince see Principe

Prince see Principe

Prince. Read by Andrew Julow. (ENG.). 2007. audio compact disk 9.99 (978-0-9801132-0-4(2)) ejunto.

Prince. Niccolo Machiavelli. Read by Shelly Frasier. (Running Time: 4 hrs.). 2003. 25.95 (978-1-60083-628-2(3), Audiofy Corp) Iofy Corp.

Prince. Niccolo Machiavelli. Read by Shelly Frasier. (ENG.). 2003. audio compact disk 58.00 (978-1-4001-3059-7(X)) Pub: Tantor Media. Dist(s): IngramPubServ

Prince. Nicolo Maquiavelo. Read by Pedro Montoya. (Running Time: 3 hrs.). 2002. 16.95 (978-1-60083-261-1(X), Audiofy Corp) Iofy Corp.

Prince. unabr. ed. Niccolo Machiavelli. Read by Shelly Frasier. (Running Time: 4 hrs. 0 mins. 0 sec.). (Tantor Unabridged Classics Ser.). (ENG.). 2008. audio compact disk 19.99 (978-1-4001-0843-5(8)) Pub: Tantor Media. Dist(s): IngramPubServ

Prince. unabr. ed. Niccolo Machiavelli. Read by Patrick Cullen. Tr. by Daniel Donno. 3 cass. (Running Time: 16200 sec.). 2006. 19.95 (978-0-7861-4398-6(3)); audio compact disk 19.95 (978-0-7861-7440-9(4)); audio compact disk 29.95 (978-0-7861-7771-4(3)) Blckstn Audio.

Prince. unabr. ed. Niccolo Machiavelli. Read by Shelly Frasier. (J). 2008. 44.99 (978-1-60514-674-4(9)) Find a World.

Prince. unabr. ed. Niccolo Machiavelli. Read by Fritz Weaver. Tr. by George Bull. 3. (Running Time: 4 hrs.). (ENG.). 2006. audio compact disk 19.95 (978-1-59887-081-7(5), 1598870815) Pub: HighBridge. Dist(s): Workman Pub

Prince. unabr. ed. Niccolo Machiavelli. Read by Walter Zimmerman. 5 cass. (Running Time: 5 hrs. 46 min.). 1989. 36.00 (C-184) Jimcin Record.
Treatise on the use & misuse of power.

Prince. unabr. ed. Niccolo Machiavelli. Read by Fritz Weaver. Tr. by George Bull. 4 cass. (Running Time: 6 hrs.). (Classics on Cassette). 1994. 24.00 (978-0-453-00893-8(3)) Pub: Penguin-HghBrdg. Dist(s): Penguin Grp USA
The famous treatise on statecraft.

Prince. unabr. ed. Niccolo Machiavelli. Narrated by Nelson Runger. 3 cass. (Running Time: 3 hrs. 30 mins.). 1987. 26.00 (978-1-55690-426-4(6), 87200E7) Recorded Bks.
Political analysis of the attributes required by a Renaissance ruler.

Prince. unabr. ed. Niccolo Machiavelli. Read by Shelly Frasier. (Running Time: 4 hrs. 0 mins. 0 sec.). (ENG.). 2008. audio compact disk 39.99 (978-1-4001-3843-2(4)); audio compact disk 19.99 (978-1-4001-5843-0(5)) Pub: Tantor Media. Dist(s): IngramPubServ

Prince. unabr. ed. Narrated by Ian Richardson. (Running Time: 3 hrs. 0 mins. 0 sec.). (ENG.). 2008. audio compact disk 22.95 (978-1-934997-03-1(X)) Pub: CSAWord. Dist(s): PerseuPGW

Prince. unabr. collector's ed. Niccolo Machiavelli. Read by Walter Zimmerman. 6 cass. (Running Time: 6 hrs.). 1988. 36.00 (978-0-7366-3940-8(3), 9184) Books on Tape.
Describes how a leader could unite Italy & put a stop to the senseless conflict.

Prince, Set. Niccolo Machiavelli. Read by Michel Galabru. 2 cass. (FRE.). 1995. 28.95 (1772-TH) Olivia & Hill.
Political treatise, written in 1513, which has become a classic.

Prince, Set. unabr. ed. Niccolo Machiavelli. Read by Robert L. Halvorson. 4 cass. (Running Time: 360 min.). 28.95 (27) Halvorson Assocs.

Prince: Jonathan. unabr. ed. Francine Rivers. Narrated by Chris Fabry. (Sons of Encouragement Ser.: Vol. 3). (ENG.). 2005. 13.99 (978-1-60814-345-0(7)); audio compact disk 19.99 (978-1-59859-047-0(2)) Oasis Audio.

Prince: Unabridged. Niccolo Machiavelli. Narrated by Ross M. Armetta. 3 CDs. (Running Time: 190 minutes approx.). 2005. audio compact disk 16.99 (978-1-59733-207-1(0), Martial Strat) InfoFount.
This is the newest and best version of The Prince on the market. It has the complete and UNABRIDGED text by Machiavelli on 3 Disks with the bonus short title Mencius on the third disk. It has music and it is clearly and energetically narrated by the actor Ross Armetta.This audiobook will help you understand what people mean when they say "Machiavellian". It will help you protect you from dangerous and unscrupulous people (ignorance is not bliss and knowledge is power) and take advantage of the theories of The Prince that many use to obtain power and develop competitive superiority.The Prince is a real world study of how power is gained and maintained. The Prince describes the process of gaining and administering power. Machiavelli outlines "the game rules" between competitive humans. It is readily applied with a little imagination to a team, company, group, institutional, or governmental context.The Prince is one of the true classics of Western Civilization and its principles have been used by a numerous and diverse group of Western (and probably Eastern) leaders including, undoubtedly Abraham Lincoln, Hitler, and many Presidents and CEO's of Western Corporations.It is a blue print of how to top others and gain power, and to secure and enlarge power. More than just theory The Prince is a study of strategy as applied with politics and cunning to gain power.The Prince portrays the chaotic, tumultuous world of 16th century Europe and of earlier periods to provide context to his theories. Machiavelli clearly imparts his belief that mal deeds may be required by a leader for the greater good of all. Machiavelli imparts that religious and moral values are inappropriate in competition. The most desirable choice is circumstantially dependent. Machiavelli essentially theorizes that decency, honesty, and religion can not be observed by "a prince" as it may imperil their state. The realization of goals are more important than any other consideration - the end is more important than the means "it is better to be feared than loved."The Prince also relates to psychology and depicts methods of gaining and staying in power, to maintain a fair and stable governance. Machiavelli expresses that the ruler must be loved or feared. The Prince has been lauded and defiled as a theoretical study of amoral beliefs and political trickery.Machiavelli was a savvy Italian politician and lady's man with much of the information being quite useful in the most difficult competition / war and complex political negotiation:. Most of the concepts of this book are still true and applicable today and readily applied to modern business and competition. It is an essential study for those in competitive environments and situations. Success can certainly be achieved in ways other than Machiavelli depicts;

However, if for only self-protection it is prudent to know the Machiavellian theories so you can recognize it and protect yourself from those who use it.

Prince - Discourse on Voluntary Servitude Set: Machiavelli-La Boetie. unabr. ed. George H. Smith & Wendy McElroy. Perf. by Don Jones & Jonathan Lutz. Narrated by Craig Deitschmann. 2 cass. (Running Time: 75 mins. per cass.). Dramatization. (Audio Classics Ser.: Vol. 6). 1986. 17.95 (978-0-938935-06-3(2), 390285) Knowledge Prod.
With the Renaissance came new ideas on man & his relationship to government & society. Machiavelli wanted to expand governmental power over men, & La Boetie sought to limit it. This presentation includes the essential ideas of these classic works, with a narrative explanation of the author's character, his times, the controversies he faced & the opinions of critics & supporters.

***Prince & the Donkey's Ears.** Anonymous. 2009. (978-1-60136-611-5(6)) Audio Holding.

Prince & the Pauper see Principe y el Mendigo

Prince & the Pauper. Retold by Jerry Stemach. Mark Twain. (Classic Literature Ser.). 2000. audio compact disk 18.95 (978-1-4105-0160-8(4)) D Johnston Inc.

Prince & the Pauper. Mark Twain. Ed. by Jerry Stemach. Retold by Alan Venable. Narrated by Nick Sandys. 2000. audio compact disk 200.00 (978-1-58702-515-0(9)) D Johnston Inc.

Prince & the Pauper. Short Stories. Mark Twain. As told by Jim Weiss. 1 cass. (Running Time: 1 hr.). Dramatization. (YA). (gr. k up). 2003. 10.95 (978-1-882513-54-3(1)); audio compact disk 14.95 (978-1-882513-79-6(7)) Greathall Prods.

Prince & the Pauper. Mark Twain. Read by Carlos J. Vega. (Running Time: 3 hrs.). 2002. 16.95 (978-1-60083-201-7(6), Audiofy Corp) Iofy Corp.

Prince & the Pauper. Mark Twain. 2 cass. (Running Time: 2 hrs. 30 mins.). (YA). (gr. 3 up). 2002. 16.95 (978-1-56994-537-7(3)) Monterey Media Inc.
The dreamings and readings of the pauper Tom Canty set off the cascade of mistaken identities that comprise Twain's famous tale.

Prince & the Pauper. Mark Twain. Read by Kenneth Jay. 2 cass. (Running Time: 2 hrs. 30 min.). (Junior Classics Ser.). (J). (gr. 6-12). 2001. 13.98 (978-962-634-726-3(0), NA222614) Naxos.
The hilarious adventures of Tom Canty, a ragged street urchin who bears a striking resemblance to Edward VI, son of Henry VIII. Longing to experience the fun and excitement of the outside world, the young prince persuades Tom to exchange clothes, and in doing so, the two exchange places in society.

Prince & the Pauper. Mark Twain. Read by Kenneth Jay. 2 CDs. (Running Time: 2 hrs. 30 min.). (Junior Classics Ser.). (J). (gr. 9-12). 2001. audio compact disk 17.98 (978-962-634-226-8(9), NA222612) Naxos.

Prince & the Pauper. Mark Twain. 1 cass. (J). 3.98 Clamshell. (978-1-55886-114-5(9), BB/PT 441) Smarty Pants.

Prince & the Pauper. abr. ed. Mark Twain. Read by Ian Richardson. 1 cass. (Running Time: 56 min.). (J). (gr. 4-6). 1991. 10.95 (978-1-55994-373-4(4), CPN 1542) HarperCollins Pubs.

Prince & the Pauper. abr. ed. Mark Twain. Read by Carl Reiner. 4 cass. (Running Time: 6 hrs.). (Ultimate Classics Ser.). 2004. 25.00 (978-1-931056-47-2(1), N Millennium Audio) New Millenn Enter.
On the same day in 16th century London were born Tom Canty, destined to become a street beggar & Edward Tudor, son of Henry VII, a future king. Several years later, young Canty Canty invades the royal precincts hoping to see the Prince. The boys discover they are identical in appearance & exchange clothes. Mistaken for the beggar boy, Prince Edward thrown into the streets. Tom Canty, too frightened to confess his true identity, assumes the mantle of the Prince of Wales.

Prince & the Pauper. abr. ed. Mark Twain & St. Charles Players. 1 cass. (Running Time: 1 hr. 30 min.). Dramatization. 2002. 16.95 (Monterey SoundWorks) Monterey Media Inc.

Prince & the Pauper. abr. adpt. ed. Mark Twain. (Bring the Classics to Life: Level 2 Ser.). (ENG.). (gr. 2-16). 2008. audio compact disk 12.95 (978-1-55576-460-9(6)) EDCON Pubng.

Prince & the Pauper, unabr. ed. Mark Twain. Read by Flo Gibson. 5 cass. (Running Time: 7 hrs. 30 min.). (J). (gr. 4-8). 1987. 20.95 (978-1-55685-084-4(0)) Audio Bk Con.
With the Coronation approaching & the Prince & the Pauper's role reversed many puzzling & often frightening events take place.

Prince & the Pauper. unabr. ed. Mark Twain. Read by Wolfram Kandinsky. 7 cass. (Running Time: 10 hrs.). 1994. 49.95 (978-0-7861-0466-6(X), 1418) Blckstn Audio.
They look alike but they are in very different worlds. Tom Canty, impoverished & abused by his father, is fascinated with royalty. Edward Tudor, heir to the throne of England, is kind & generous but wants to run free & play in the river - just once. Just how insubstantial their differences are becomes all too clear when a chance encounter leads to an exchange of clothing - & roles; the pauper finds himself caught up in the pomp & folly of the royal court, a role which is further complicated when the king dies soon after the switch; & the prince wanders horror-stricken through the lower strata of English society.

Prince & the Pauper. unabr. ed. Mark Twain. Read by Jack Sondericker. 6 cass. (Running Time: 6 hrs. 30 min.). (J). 1989. 39.95 (978-1-55686-300-4(4), 300) Books in Motion.
Tom Canty, a boy of the London slums & Edward Tudor, destined to be the King of England were born on the same day. A chance encounter brings them together, the two boys exchange clothes & ironically are mistaken one for the other.

Prince & the Pauper. unabr. ed. Mark Twain. Read by Michael Prichard. 8 cass. (Running Time: 12 hrs.). 2001. 29.95 (978-0-7366-6798-2(9)) Books on Tape.
A young prince in Tudor England meets a beggar boy who is his look-alike. When they exchange clothes, they find themselves in real trouble.

Prince & the Pauper. unabr. ed. Mark Twain. Narrated by Norman Dietz. 6 cass. (Running Time: 8 hrs. 45 mins.). (gr. 8). 1994. 53.00 (978-1-55690-989-4(6), 94128E7) Recorded Bks.
Twain's tall tale about a bedraggled street urchin who becomes king-for-a-day & his twin, the pampered Prince of Wales, left to fend among his seedier subjects.

***Prince & the Pauper.** unabr. ed. Mark Twain. Narrated by Dick Hill. (Running Time: 7 hrs. 30 mins. 0 sec.). 2010. 19.99 (978-1-4526-5044-9(6)); 14.99 (978-1-4526-7044-7(7)); audio compact disk 27.99 (978-1-4526-0044-4(9)) Pub: Tantor Media. Dist(s): IngramPubServ

Prince & the Pauper. unabr. collector's ed. Mark Twain. Read by Michael Prichard. 8 cass. (Running Time: 8 hrs.). (J). 1981. 48.00 (978-0-7366-0232-7(1), 1228) Books on Tape.
On the same day in 16th century London were born Tom Canty, destined to become a street beggar, & Edward Tudor, son of Henry VIII, a future king. Several years later young Canty invades the royal precincts hoping to see the Prince. The boys exchange garments & discover they are identical in appearance. Mistaken for the beggar boy, Prince Edward is thrown into the streets. Tom Canty, too frightened to confess his true identity, assumes the mantle of Prince of Wales.

Prince & the Pauper, Set. unabr. ed. Mark Twain. Read by Robert L. Halvorson. 4 cass. (Running Time: 360 min.). (J). 28.95 (82) Halvorson Assocs.

Prince & the Pauper, Vol. 4. Mark Twain. Ed. by Gail Portnuff Venable & Dorothy Tyack. Retold by Alan Venable & Jerry Stemach. Illus. by Jeff Ham. Narrated by Nick Sandys. Contrib. by Ted S. Hasselbring. (Start-to-Finish Books). (J). (gr. 2-3). 2000. 35.00 (978-1-58702-516-7(7)) D Johnston Inc.

Prince & the Pauper, Vol. 4. Mark Twain. Ed. by Gail Portnuff Venable & Dorothy Tyack. Retold by Alan Venable & Jerry Stemach. Illus. by Jeff Ham. Contrib. by Ted S. Hasselbring. (Start-to-Finish Books). (J). (gr. 2-3). 2002. 100.00 (978-1-58702-951-6(0)) D Johnston Inc.

Prince & the Pauper, Vol. 4. abr. ed. Mark Twain. Ed. by Gail Portnuff Venable & Dorothy Tyack. Retold by Alan Venable & Jerry Stemach. Illus. by Jeff Ham. Narrated by Nick Sandys. Contrib. by Ted S. Hasselbring. 1 cass. (Running Time: 1 hr.). (Start-to-Finish Books). (J). (gr. 2-3). 2000. 7.00 (978-1-58702-373-6(3), F33K2) D Johnston Inc.
In 16th century England, two boys are born on the same day into very different circumstances. Tom Canty is a pauper who dreams of being a Prince. Young Edward is a prince who covets the freedom of being a pauper. When the two boys decide to trade places, they both get more than they bargained for.

***Prince & the Pauper: Bring the Classics to Life.** adpt. ed. Mark Twain. (Bring the Classics to Life Ser.). 2008. pap. bk. 21.95 (978-1-55576-497-5(5)) EDCON Pubng.

***Prince & the Pauper (Library Edition)** unabr. ed. Mark Twain. Narrated by Dick Hill. (Running Time: 7 hrs. 30 mins.). 2010. 27.99 (978-1-4526-2044-2(X)); audio compact disk 66.99 (978-1-4526-3044-1(5)) Pub: Tantor Media. Dist(s): IngramPubServ

Prince & the Pauper Read Along. Prod. by Saddleback Educational Publishing. (Saddleback's Illustrated Classics Ser.). (YA). 2005. audio compact disk 24.95 (978-1-56254-931-2(6)) Saddleback Edu.

Prince Caspian see Principe Caspian: Las Crinicas de Narnia

Prince Caspian. unabr. ed. C. S. Lewis. Read by Lynn Redgrave. (Running Time: 014400 sec.). 2005. audio compact disk 29.95 (978-0-06-079335-7(X)) HarperCollins Pubs.

Prince Caspian. abr. ed. C. S. Lewis. Read by Claire Bloom. Illus. by Pauline Baynes. 1 cass. (Running Time: 1 hr. 4 min.). (Chronicles of Narnia Ser.: Bk. 2). (J). (gr. 3 up). 1989. 12.00 (978-0-89845-090-3(X), CPN 1603) HarperCollins Pubs.

Prince Caspian. adpt. ed. Read by Paul Scofield et al. C. S. Lewis. (Running Time: 240 hrs. 0 mins.). (Radio Theatre: Chronicles of Narnia Ser.). (ENG.). (J). (gr. 3). 2007. audio compact disk 14.97 (978-1-58997-512-5(X), Tyndale Ent) Tyndale Hse.

***Prince Caspian.** unabr. ed. C. S. Lewis. Read by Lynn Redgrave. 2005. (978-0-06-085441-6(3)); (978-0-06-085442-3(1)) HarperCollins Pubs.

Prince Caspian. unabr. abr. ed. C. S. Lewis. Read by Lynn Redgrave. 4 CDs. (Running Time: 9 hrs.). (Chronicles of Narnia Ser.). (J). (gr. 6-8). 2003. audio compact disk 27.50 (978-0-06-056440-7(7)) HarperCollins Pubs.

Prince Caspian & The Voyage of the Dawn Treader. Bridgestone Staff. 2004. DVD & audio compact disk 24.95 (978-0-7800-2601-8(2)) Public Media Inc.

Prince Charming. Julie Garwood. Read by Harriet Walter. 2004. 10.95 (978-0-7435-4568-6(0)) Pub: S&S Audio. Dist(s): S and S Inc

Prince Charming. unabr. ed. Julie Garwood. Read by Deborah Hall. 12 vols. (Running Time: 18 hrs.). 2002. bk. 96.95 (978-0-7927-2715-6(0), CSL 501, Chivers Sound Lib) AudioGO.
Only her beloved grandmother, Lady Esther, knows how devasted Taylor Stapleton has been since her fiance eloped with Taylor's cousin. Now dear Esther - one of London's richest and most formidable matriarchs - lies dying. But first she is going to help Taylor pull off the scam of the season. To escape becoming a ward of her unscrupulous uncle, Taylor will wed Lucas Ross, a rugged American rancher.

Prince Charming, Set. abr. ed. Julie Garwood. Read by Harriet Walter. 2 cass. (Running Time: 3 hrs. 0 mins. 0 sec.). (ENG., 1994. 17.00 (978-0-671-89174-9(X), 391402, Audioworks) Pub: S&S Audio. Dist(s): S and S Inc

Prince Darling. unabr. ed. 1 cass. (Running Time: 20 min.). Dramatization. (Magic Looking Glass Ser.). (J). (gr. 2-6). 1989. 9.95 (978-0-7810-0030-7(0), NIM-CW-128-2-C) NIMCO.
A French folk tale.

Prince Heureux et Autres Contes. Oscar Wilde. Read by Claude Villers. 1 cass. (FRE.). 1992. bk. 26.95 (1GA065) Olivia & Hill.
Story about the statue of the Prince who watched over his town & who cried over the misery surrounding him.

***prince of Bagram Prison.** unabr. ed. Alex Carr. Read by Caroline Lee. (Running Time: 9 hrs. 46 mins.). 2010. audio compact disk 87.95 (978-1-74214-656-0(2), 9781742146560) Pub: Bolinda Pubng AUS. Dist(s): Bolinda Pub Inc

Prince of Beverly Hills. unabr. ed. Stuart Woods. Read by Guerin Barry. (Running Time: 9 hrs.). (Rick Barron Ser.). 2004. 24.95 (978-1-59710-600-9(3), 1597106003, BAD) Brilliance Audio.

Prince of Beverly Hills. unabr. ed. Stuart Woods. Read by Guerin Barry. (Running Time: 9 hrs.). (Rick Barron Ser.: No. 1). 2004. 39.25 (978-1-59710-601-6(1), 1597106011, BADLE); 39.25 (978-1-59335-844-0(X), 159335844X, BriAudCD Unabrid); 24.95 (978-1-59335-710-8(9), 1593357109, Brilliance MP3); 29.95 (978-1-59355-216-9(5), 1593552165, BAU); 74.25 (978-1-59355-217-6(3), 1593552173, BAudLibEd); audio compact disk 33.95 (978-1-59355-218-3(1), 1593552181, Bril Audio CD Unabri); audio compact disk 92.25 (978-1-59355-219-0(X), 159355219X, Bril Audio CD Unabri) Brilliance Audio.
Stuart Woods' new novel is a sexy, action-packed thriller in the tradition of his best. As the Cleveland Plain Dealer wrote about his last novel, Capital Crimes, "Woods knows how to deliver a taut, well-told tale...The last two paragraphs will make any reader gulp." In The Prince of Beverly Hills, set in Hollywood's Golden Age of the 1930s, Woods introduces a new character that possesses the kind of suave confidence, take-charge manner, and clever wit-under-pressure that his fans will recognize and love at first sight. Rick Barron, a sharp, capable detective on the Beverly Hills force, finds himself demoted after a run-in with his captain, but soon lands a job on the security detail for Centurion Pictures, one of the hottest studios. As the protector of the studio's interests, Barron looks after the cream of the crop of filmdom's stars - Clete Barrow, the British leading man with a penchant for parties; and Glenna Gleason, a peach of a talent on the verge of superstardom. Rick's easy charm has society columnists dubbing him "the Prince of Beverly Hills," the white knight of movie stars, until he uncovers a murder cover-up and a blackmail scam that threatens the studio's business and may originate with the West Coast mob. When two suspicious deaths begin to look like double-murder, and an attempt is made on Glenna Gleason's life, Barrow knows he is up against wise guys whose stakes are do-or-die. A dicey war of nerves is on.

Prince of Chaos. Roger Zelazny. Read by Bruce Watson. 2 vols. (Chronicles of Amber: Bk. 10). 2004. audio compact disk 25.00 (978-1-58807-262-7(2)) Am Pubng Inc.

Prince of Chaos. abr. ed. Roger Zelazny. Read by Bruce Watson. 2 vols. (Chronicles of Amber: Bk. 10). 2003. (978-1-58807-538-3(9)) Am Pubng Inc.

Prince of Chaos. abr. ed. Roger Zelazny. 2 vols. (Running Time: 3 hrs.). (Chronicles of Amber: Bk. 10). 2003. 18.00 (978-1-58807-135-4(9)) Am Pubng Inc.
Having survived the blackest betrayal and a near assassination, Merle Corey, aka Merlin, discovers he is third in line to occupy the throne of Chaos. However, his ascension is aided by a series of conveniently fatal "accidents" engineered by Dana, his mother, and his uncle Mandor. But Merlin's trials are far from over. Deadly plots and dark enchantments await Merlin on the road to ultimate rule. Yet, he has determined to triumph and silence the murderous discord between Amber and Chaos...for the moment, at least. And at the end of his visionary quest lies an unsettling destiny: his father, Corwin, who was long believed to be dead, had been secretly imprisoned by a villain's magic.

Prince of Chaos. abr. ed. Roger Zelazny. Read by Bruce Watson. 3 vols. (Chronicles of Amber: Bk. 10). 2004. audio compact disk (978-1-58807-693-9(8)) Am Pubng Inc.

Prince of Egypt. Music by Stephen Schwartz. Prod. by Hans Zimmer. 1 cass. 1999. 10.98; audio compact disk 17.98 Provident Mus Dist.
Sharing the message of faith, hope & freedom in God through songs performed by the all-star cast, plus artists such as Amy Grant, Whitney Houston & Mariah Carey. The Original Motion Picture Soundtrack.

Prince of Egypt: Inspirational. 1 cass. 1999. 10.98 (978-0-7601-2637-0(2)); audio compact disk 16.98 (978-0-7601-2638-7(0)) Provident Music.

Prince of Egypt: Inspirational. Music by Stephen Schwartz. Contrib. by Hans Zimmer. 1 cass., 1 CD. 1998. 10.98 (0044-50050-40044-50050-2 CD); audio compact disk 16.98 CD. (0044-50050-2 CD) Brentwood Music.
Music's most popular artists from gospel, pop & R&B celebrate with songs inspired by the film. Includes: "The River" by Cece Winans, "Just As Long" by Trin-i-Tee 5:7, "I Will Get There" by Boyz II Men, "Power" by Fred Hammond & Radical for Christ, "Stay with Me" by Bebe Winans, "God Will Take Care of Me" by Carman, "Let My People Go" by Kirk Franklin, "I Am" by Donnie McClurkin, "Didn't I" by Christian, "Everything in Between" by Jars of Clay, "Yo Pharaoh" by Tyrone Tribbett & Greater Anointing, "My Deliverer" by dcTalk & "Moses the Deliverer" by Shirley Caesar.

Prince of Egypt: Inspirational. Music by Stephen Schwartz. Prod. by Hans Zimmer. 1 cass. 1999. 10.98; audio compact disk 16.98 Provident Mus Dist.
Music's most popular artists from gospel, pop & R&B celebrate with songs inspired by the film. Featuring performances by Jars of Clay, Kirk Franklin, dcTalk, CeCe Winans & more.

Prince of Egypt: Nashville. 1 cass. 1999. 10.98 (978-0-7601-2635-6(6)); audio compact disk 16.98 (978-0-7601-2636-3(4)) Provident Music.

Prince of Egypt: Nashville. Music by Stephen Schwartz. Contrib. by Hans Zimmer. 1 cass., 1 CD. 1998. 10.98 (0044-50045-40044-50045-2); audio compact disk 16.98 CD. (0044-50045-2) Brentwood Music.
Inspired by the epic drama, includes songs by contemporary Christian & country artists: "Freedom" by Wynonna, "Make It Through" by Randy Travis & Linda Davis, "I Give You to His Heart" by Alison Krauss, "Heartbeat of Hope" by Steven Curtis Chapman, "Milk & Honey" by Pam Tillis, "Once in Awhile" by Vince Gill, "Walk in Glory" by Mindy McCready, "Somewhere Down the Road" by Faith Hill, "Please Be the One" by Reba, "Slavery Deliverance & Faith" by Clint Black, "Godspeed" by Beth Nielsen Chapman, "The Voice" by Alabama, "You Are My Light" by Gary Chapman, "The Moving of the Mountain" by Mac McAnally, "I Will Be There for You" by Jessica Andrews, "I Can't Be a Slave" by Toby Keith & "Could It Be Me" by Charlie Daniels.

Prince of Egypt: Nashville. Music by Stephen Schwartz. Prod. by Hans Zimmer. 1 cass. 1999. 10.98; audio compact disk 16.98 Provident Mus Dist.
Inspired by the epic drama, includes songs by contemporary christian & country artists as Steven Curtis Chapman, Vince Gill, Reba, Gary Chapman & more.

Prince of Egypt: Original Soundtrack. 1 cass. 1999. 11.98 (978-0-7601-2633-2(X)); audio compact disk 17.98 (978-0-7601-2634-9(8)) Provident Music.

Prince of Egypt: The Original Motion Picture Soundtrack. Voice by Val Kilmer et al. 1 cass., 1 CD. Dramatization. 1998. 11.98 (0044-50041-40044-50041-2); audio compact disk 17.98 CD. (0044-50041-2) Brentwood Music.
Inspired by the Biblical story of Moses, a man chosen by God to lead his people to freedom. Follows Moses from the time he is a baby & set adrift in a basket on the Nile to the pivotal moment when he delivers his people from Egypt into the Promised Land. Sharing the message of faith, hope & freedom in God through songs performed by the all-star cast, plus artists such as Amy Grant, Whitney Houston & Mariah Carey.

***Prince of Fenway Park.** unabr. ed. Julianna Baggott. Read by William Dufris. (ENG.). 2009. (978-0-06-180953-8(5)); (978-0-06-188262-3(3)) HarperCollins Pubs.

Prince of Fire. abr. ed. Daniel Silva. Read by Guerin Barry. (Running Time: 21600 sec.). (Gabriel Allon Ser.: No. 5). 2006. audio compact disk 16.99 (978-1-59600-809-0(1), 9781596008090, BCD Value Price) Brilliance Audio.
Few recent thriller writers have elicited the kind of critical praise that Daniel Silva has received, with his "provocative and deeply satisfying" (The Miami Herald) novels featuring art restorer and sometime spy Gabriel Allon, "a man whose depth and passion make him one of the most fascinating characters in the genre" (Chicago Sun-Times). Now Allon is back in Venice, when a terrible explosion in Rome leads to a disturbing personal revelation: the existence of a dossier in terrorist hands that strips away his secrets, lays bare his history. Hastily recalled home to Israel, drawn once more into the heart of a service he had once forsaken, Allon finds himself stalking an elusive master terrorist across a landscape drenched with generations of blood, the trail turning on itself until, finally, he can no longer be certain who is stalking whom. And when at last the showdown comes, it will not be Gabriel alone who is threatened with destruction - for it is not his history alone that has been laid bare. A knife-edged thriller of astonishing intricacy and feeling, filled with exhilarating prose, this is Daniel Silva's finest novel yet.

Prince of Fire. unabr. ed. Daniel Silva. Read by Guerin Barry. (Running Time: 10 hrs.). (Gabriel Allon Ser.: No. 5). 2005. 39.25 (978-1-59710-603-0(8), 9781597106030, BADLE); 24.95 (978-1-59710-602-3(X), 9781597106023, BAD); 24.95 (978-1-59335-784-9(2), 9781593357849, Brilliance MP3); 39.25 (978-1-59335-918-8(7), 9781593359188, Brinc Audio MP3 Lib); 32.95 (978-1-59600-020-9(1), 9781596000209, BAU); 82.25 (978-1-59600-021-6(X), 9781596000216, BrilAudUnabridg); audio compact disk 36.95 (978-1-59600-023-0(6), 9781596000230, Bril Audio CD Unabri);

audio compact disk 97.25 (978-1-59600-024-7(4), 9781596000247, BriAudCD Unabrid) Brilliance Audio.
Please enter a Synopsis.

Prince of Fire, the Messenger, the Secret Servant. abr. ed. Daniel Silva. (Running Time: 18 hrs.). (Gabriel Allon Ser.: Nos. 5-7). 2008. audio compact disk 34.95 (978-1-4233-5246-4(7), 9781423352464, BACD) Brilliance Audio.

Prince of Fools. unabr. ed. Philip Caveney. Read by Maxwell Caulfield. 7 CDs. (Running Time: 8 hrs. 25 mins.). (YA). (gr. 7 up). 2008. audio compact disk 55.00 (978-0-7393-6318-8(2), Listening Lib) Pub: Random Audio Pubg. Dist(s): Random
"The Lord of Laughter, the Monarch of Mirth, the King of Comedy" - if only bumbling Sebastian Darke could live up to these epithets and be a successful jester like his father. The problem is, Sebastian's never been very funny. But after his father's death, with no choice but to beg in the streets, the half-human, half-elf teen sets off with Max, his father's slightly cynical and fully self-important Buffalope, to offer his services as a jester to King Septimus of Keladon - rumored to be one of the richest monarchs in the world. On the way, the pair meets Captain Cornelius Drummel, small in stature but the fiercest of fighters. The three rescue the fair princess and soon-to-be-queen, Kerin, who's being held captive by brigands, and happily escort her back home. If only Sebastian knew that the kidnapping was part of a plot engineered by the evil King Septimus. A plot that poor Sebastian has now foiled. No one would dare challenge the king. No one but a fool.

Prince of Fools. unabr. ed. Philip Caveney. Read by Maxwell Caulfield. (ENG.). (J). (gr. 7). 2008. audio compact disk 37.00 (978-0-7393-6316-4(6), Listening Lib) Pub: Random Audio Pubg. Dist(s): Random

Prince of Frogtown. unabr. ed. Rick Bragg. Read by Rick Bragg. 7 CDs. (Running Time: 8 hrs.). (ENG.). 2008. audio compact disk 34.95 (978-0-7393-6839-8(7), Random AudioBks) Pub: Random Audio Pubg. Dist(s): Random

***Prince of Mist.** unabr. ed. Carlos Ruiz Zafón. Narrated by Jonathan Davis. 5 CDs. (Running Time: 5 hrs.). 2010. audio compact disk 44.99 (978-1-60788-767-6(3)) Pub: Hachet Audio. Dist(s): HachBkGrp

Prince of Mist. unabr. ed. Carlos Ruiz Zafón. Read by Jonathan Davis. (Running Time: 6 hrs.). (ENG.). 2010. 16.98 (978-1-60788-373-9(2)); audio compact disk 24.98 (978-1-60788-372-2(4)) Pub: Hachet Audio. Dist(s): HachBkGrp

Prince of Peace. 1 cass., 1 CD. 1999. 10.98 (978-0-7601-2775-9(1)); audio compact disk 15.98 CD. (978-0-7601-2774-2(3)) Brentwood Music.
Seventeen timeless inspirational performances.

Prince of Peace: A Christmas Presentation of 5 Songs in Unison/2 Part. Created by Marty Parks. (ENG.). 2008. audio compact disk 12.00 (978-5-557-42036-5(3)) Lillenas.

***Prince of Peace: A Christmas Presentation of 5 Songs in Unison/2 Part.** Created by Marty Parks. (ENG.). 2008. audio compact disk 59.99 (978-5-557-42037-2(1)); audio compact disk 12.99 (978-5-557-42034-1(7)) Lillenas.

Prince of Peace: Isiah 9:1-7. Ed Young. 1989. 4.95 (978-0-7417-1772-6(7), 772) Win Walk.

Prince of the City: Giuliani, New York & the Genius of American Life. Fred Siegel. Read by Brian Emerson. Told to Harry Siegel. (Running Time: 52200 sec.). 2006. 79.95 (978-0-7861-4517-1(X)); audio compact disk 99.00 (978-0-7861-7187-3(1)) Blckstn Audio.

Prince of the City: Giuliani, New York & the Genius of American Life. unabr. ed. Fred Siegel. Read by Brian Emerson. Told to Harry Siegel. (Running Time: 52200 sec.). 2006. audio compact disk 29.95 (978-0-7861-7621-2(0)) Blckstn Audio.

Prince of the City: Giuliani, New York & the Genius of American Life. unabr. ed. Fred Siegel. Read by Brian Emerson. Told to Harry Siegel. (Running Time: 52200 sec.). 2007. 32.95 (978-1-4332-0333-6(2)); audio compact disk 32.95 (978-1-4332-0334-3(0)) Blckstn Audio.

Prince of Thieves. unabr. ed. Brian D. Boyer. Read by Dan Lazar. 8 cass. (Running Time: 8 hrs.). 1976. 48.00 (978-0-7366-0026-2(4), 1038) Books on Tape.
In the jargon of the criminal underworld, a master forger is called "the prince of thieves." Such a man is Peter "Tony" Milano. "The Prince of Thieves" is a fictionalized biography of the world's greatest forger.

Prince of Thieves: A Novel. abr. ed. Chuck Hogan. Read by Donnie Wahlberg. 2004. 15.95 (978-0-7435-3994-4(X)) Pub: S&S Audio. Dist(s): S and S Inc

Prince of Thieves: A Novel. abr. ed. Chuck Hogan. Read by Donnie Wahlberg. (Running Time: 6 hrs. 0 mins. 0 sec.). (ENG.). 2007. audio compact disk 14.95 (978-0-7435-6423-6(5), S&S Encore) Pub: S&S Audio. Dist(s): S and S Inc

Prince of Tides. Pat Conroy. Read by Pat Conroy. 1 cass. (Running Time: 30 min.). 8.95 (AMF-12) Am Audio Prose.
The author reads from "Prince of Tides," talks about the South, the military, his relationship with his parents, & its impact on his develpment as a writer.

Prince of Tides. abr. ed. Pat Conroy. Read by Dan John Miller. (Running Time: 13 hrs.). 2009. audio compact disk 35.99 (978-1-4418-0785-4(3), 9781441807854, Bril Audio CD Unabri) Brilliance Audio.

Prince of Tides. abr. ed. Pat Conroy. Read by Dan John Miller. (Running Time: 13 hrs.). 2010. audio compact disk 14.99 (978-1-4418-0792-2(6), 9781441807922, BCD Value Price) Brilliance Audio.

Prince of Tides. abr. ed. Pat Conroy. Read by Richard Thomas. 2002. 21.00 (978-0-553-71336-7(1)) Random.

Prince of Tides. unabr. ed. Pat Conroy. Read by Frank Muller. (Running Time: 23 hrs.). 2009. 29.99 (978-1-4418-0787-8(X), 9781441807878, Brilliance MP3); 29.99 (978-1-4418-0789-2(6), 9781441807892, BAD); 44.97 (978-1-4418-0788-5(8), 9781441807885, Brinc Audio MP3 Lib); 44.97 (978-1-4418-0790-8(X), 9781441807908, BADLE); audio compact disk 49.99 (978-1-4418-0791-5(8), 9781441807915, BACD); audio compact disk 107.97 (978-1-4418-0786-1(1), 9781441807861, BriAudCD Unabrid) Brilliance Audio.

Prince of Tides. unabr. ed. Pat Conroy. Narrated by Frank Muller. 18 cass. (Running Time: 23 hrs.). 1988. 144.00 (978-1-55690-425-7(8), 88020E7) Recorded Bks.
The story of Tom Wingo, his gifted & troubled twin sister Savannah & the dark & violent past of the extraordinary family in which they were born.

Prince of Tides, Pt. A. unabr. ed. Pat Conroy. Read by Wolfram Kandinsky. 12 cass. (Running Time: 18 hrs.). 1988. 88.00 (978-0-7366-1458-0(3), 2339-A) Books on Tape.
Tom Wingo, a high school coach whose marriage & career are crumbling, flies from South Carolina to New York after learning of his twin sister's suicide attempt. His twin, Savannah, is one of the most gifted poets of her generation. The cadenced beauty of her art & the jumbled cries of her illness are clues to the long-hidden story of her wounded family. Tom meets with Savannah's psychiatrist. Together they unravel a family history of violence, abandonment & love & Tom realizes that trying to save his sister is the last chance to save himself.

Prince of Tides, Pt. B. unabr. ed. Pat Conroy. Read by Wolfram Kandinsky. 11 cass. (Running Time: 16 hrs. 30 mins.). 1988. 88.00 (978-0-7366-1459-7(1), 2339-B) Books on Tape.

Prince of Warwood & the King's Key: Teacher's Tool Kit. J. Noel Clinton. (ENG.). 2007. spiral bd. 19.99 (978-0-9773115-0-7(3)) C2 Pubng.

Prince Rabbit & Other Stories. unabr. ed. A. A. Milne. Read by Tammy Grimes. 1 cass. Incl. Magic Hill. (J). (CDL5 1490); Princess & the Apple Tree. (J). (CDL5 1490); Princess Who Could Not Laugh. (J). (CDL5 1490); (J). 1984. 9.95 (978-0-694-50842-6(X), CDL5 1490) HarperCollins Pubs.
Here are 4 of Milne's stories for children, headed by a rabbit who imagined he was as smart as any human, & a princess whose funny bone needed tickling.

Prince Talkalot. (J). 2003. audio compact disk 7.99 (978-0-9740847-1-8(9)) GiGi Bks.
Do actions really speak louder than words? Prince Talkalot knows the answer. This adventurous story takes place in medieval times and features princes, princesses, damsels in distress and a dragon with one very sore jaw.

Prince William Sound Environmental Reader. Ed. by Nancy Lethcoe & Lisa Nurnberger. (J). 1989. pap. bk. 12.00 (978-0-9613146-9-9(9)) Prince W Sound.

Prince/Discourse on Voluntary Servitude. Niccolo Machiavelli et al. Read by Craig Deitschmann. (Running Time: 10800 sec.). (Giants of Political Thought Ser.). 2006. audio compact disk 25.95 (978-0-7861-6983-2(4)) Pub: Blckstn Audio. Dist(s): NetLibrary CO

Princeling. unabr. ed. Cynthia Harrod-Eagles. Read by Elizabeth Proud. 10 cass. (Running Time: 12 hr. 30 min.). (Morland Dynasty Ser.: No. 3). (J). 1998. 84.95 (978-0-7531-0448-4(2), 980912) Pub: ISIS Lrg Prnt GBR. Dist(s): Ulverscroft US
In the turbulent reign of Elizabeth I, the Catholic Morlands are threatened by the upsurge of Protestantism & forced to seek new spheres of influence through marriage. John, heir to Morland Place, rides north to win the daughter of Black Will Percy, the Borderland cattle lord, but she will not have him. Lettice, the second Morland, enters the court of Mary, Queen of Scots & weds the harsh, ambitious Lord Robert Hamilton.

Princeps' Fury. unabr. ed. Jim Butcher. (Running Time: 18 hrs.). Bk. 5. (ENG.). (gr. 8). 2008. audio compact disk 49.95 (978-0-14-314375-8(1), PengAudBks) Penguin Grp USA.

Princes. unabr. ed. Sonya Hartnett. Read by Francis Greenslade. 3 cass. (Running Time: 4 hrs. 40 mins.). 2002. (978-1-74030-736-9(4)) Bolinda Pubng AUS.

Princes. unabr. ed. Sonya Hartnett. Read by Francis Greenslade. 4 CDs. (Running Time: 4 hrs. 40 mins.). (YA). 2005. audio compact disk 57.95 (978-1-74093-404-6(0)) Pub: Bolinda Pubng AUS. Dist(s): Bolinda Pub Inc

Princes of Ireland: The Dublin Saga. abr. ed. Edward Rutherfurd. Read by John Keating. 8 CDs. (Running Time: 32400 sec.). (ENG.). 2005. audio compact disk 19.95 (978-0-7393-2450-9(0), Random AudioBks) Pub: Random Audio Pubg. Dist(s): Random

Prince's Poison Cup. R. C. Sproul. Narrated by R. C. Sproul. (J). (ps-3). 2008. audio compact disk 10.00 (978-1-56769-117-7(X), ReformTrust) Ligonier Minist.

***princesa del Guisante: VersiÃ³n del cuento de Hans Christian Anderson.** Susan Blackaby. Tr. by Patricia Abello. Illus. by Charlene Delage. (Read-it! Readers en Español). (SPA.). 2008. audio compact disk 9.27 (978-1-4048-4465-0(1)) CapstoneDig.

Princese Palatine. l.t. ed. Claude Pasteur. (French Ser.). (FRE., 2001. bk. 30.99 (978-2-84011-444-4(5)) Pub: UlverLrgPrint GBR. Dist(s): Ulverscroft US

Princess. (Paws & Tales Ser.: Vol. 5). (J). 2001. 3.99 (978-1-57972-394-1(2)); audio compact disk 5.99 (978-1-57972-395-8(0)) Insight Living.

***Princess: A Lucky Kitten.** Barbie Heit Schwaeber. Illus. by Catherine Huerta. (Pet Tales Ser.). (ENG.). (J). 2009. audio compact disk 12.95 (978-1-59249-803-1(5)) Soundprints.

Princess Academy. unabr. ed. Shannon Hale. Read by Laura Credidio & The Full Cast Family. (J). 2007. 49.99 (978-1-60252-538-2(2)) Find a World.

Princess Album. 1 cass. (Classic Collections). (J). 10.99 (978-0-7634-0001-9(7)); 10.99 Norelco. (978-0-7634-0000-2(9)); audio compact disk 16.99 (978-0-7634-0003-3(3)) W Disney Records.

Princess Album. 1 cass. (Classic Collections). (J). (ps-3). 1996. audio compact disk 16.99 CD. (978-0-7634-0002-6(5)) W Disney Records.

Princess & Curdie. George MacDonald. Read by Ian Whitcomb. (Running Time: 6 hrs.). 2006. 25.95 (978-1-60083-651-0(8), Audiofy Corp) Iofy Corp.

Princess & Curdie. George MacDonald. Read by Jim Killavey. 5 cass. (Running Time: 7 hrs.). 1989. 35.00 incl. album. (C-205) Jimcin Record.

Princess & Curdie. George MacDonald. Read by Ian Whitcomb. (Running Time: 21660 sec.). (ENG.). (J). (gr. 4-7). 2005. audio compact disk 66.00 (978-1-4001-3085-6(9)) Pub: Tantor Media. Dist(s): IngramPubServ

Princess & Curdie. unabr. ed. George MacDonald. Read by Michael Low. 5 cass. (Running Time: 7 hrs. 30 min.). (J). 1989. 39.95 (978-0-7861-0081-1(8), 1075) Blckstn Audio.
This story occurs approximately one year after Curdie, the miner's son, saved princess Irene from the subterranean city of goblins situated under her father's palace.

Princess & Curdie. unabr. ed. George MacDonald. Read by Laurie Klein. 4 cass. (Running Time: 5 hrs. 30 min.). Dramatization. (J). (gr. 1-6). 1991. 26.95 (978-1-55686-355-4(1), 355) Books in Motion.
This sequel to The Princess & the Goblin finds Princess Irene & Curdie involved in saving the life of the king from evil forces within the kingdom.

Princess & Curdie. unabr. ed. George MacDonald. Narrated by Ian Whitcomb. 5 CDs. (Running Time: 6 hrs. 1 min.). (ENG.). (J). 2003. audio compact disk 33.00 (978-1-4001-0085-9(2)); audio compact disk 20.00 (978-1-4001-5085-4(X)) Pub: Tantor Media. Dist(s): IngramPubServ

Princess & Curdie. unabr. ed. George MacDonald. Read by Ian Whitcomb. (J). 2008. 54.99 (978-1-60514-602-7(1)) Find a World.

Princess & Curdie. unabr. ed. George MacDonald. Narrated by Ian Whitcomb. (Running Time: 6 hrs. 0 mins. 0 sec.). (ENG.). (J). (gr. 4-7). 2009. 19.99 (978-1-4001-5930-7(X)); lab manual ed. 45.99 (978-1-4001-3930-9(9)); audio compact disk 22.99 (978-1-4001-0930-2(2)) Pub: Tantor Media. Dist(s): IngramPubServ

Princess & Curdie. unabr. collector's ed. George MacDonald. Read by Rebecca C. Burns. 4 cass. (Running Time: 6 hrs.). (J). (gr. 4-7). 1998. 32.00 (978-0-7366-4535-5(7), 4728) Books on Tape.
When Princess Irene's great-grandmother summons Curdie to her room in the dove tower, she gives him not only a great task but also a traveling companion - the oldest & ugliest creature Curdie has ever seen - who soon becomes his best & most loyal friend. But just what is Curdie's task? And what lessons is he to learn along the way?.

Princess & Curdie, Set. George MacDonald. Read by Flo Gibson. 4 cass. (Running Time: 5 hrs.). (J). (gr. 2-4). 1997. 19.95 (978-1-55685-486-6(2)) Audio Bk Con.
Gurdie, the miner's son, embarks on a magical & mysterious adventure to perform a great task at the King's court. A Princess, the odd creature Lina, the Uglies & many more accompany him through his trials.

Princess & Frog. (Ladybird Bks.). (J). bk. 12.95 (978-0-86685-634-8(X)) Intl Bk Ctr.

Princess & the Apple Tree see Prince Rabbit & Other Stories

Princess & the Castle/Castles. Steck-Vaughn Staff. (J). 1999. (978-0-7398-2446-7(5)) SteckVau.

Princess & the Goblin. George MacDonald. Read by Ian Whitcomb. (Running Time: 5 hrs. 24 mins.). 2003. 25.95 (978-1-60083-650-3(X), Audiofy Corp) Iofy Corp.

Princess & the Goblin. George MacDonald. Read by Jim Killavey. 6 cass. (Running Time: 6 hrs.). (J). 1989. 42.00 (C-180); 47.00 incl. album. Jimcin Record.
Delightful children's tale.

Princess & the Goblin. George MacDonald. Read by Ian Whitcomb. (ENG.). 2005. audio compact disk 66.00 (978-1-4001-3084-9(0)) Pub: Tantor Media. Dist(s): IngramPubServ

Princess & the Goblin. unabr. ed. George MacDonald. Read by Frederick Davidson. 4 cass. (Running Time: 6 hrs.). (J). 1988. 32.95 (978-0-7861-0027-9(3), 1026) Blckstn Audio.
This is an ageless tale of courage and loyalty, beauty and honor, mystery and divinity and above all, the conflict of good and evil.

Princess & the Goblin. unabr. ed. George MacDonald. Read by Laurie Klein. 4 cass. (Running Time: 5 hrs.). Dramatization. (J). (gr. 1-6). 1991. 26.95 (978-1-55686-354-7(3), 354) Books in Motion.
Eight year old Princess Irene escapes from the Goblins with the help from Curdie, a miners son, & her magical great-great grandmother.

Princess & the Goblin. unabr. ed. George MacDonald. Narrated by Ian Whitcomb. 5 CDs. (Running Time: 5 hrs. 19 mins.). (ENG.). (J). 2003. audio compact disk 33.00 (978-1-4001-0084-2(4)); audio compact disk 20.00 (978-1-4001-5084-7(1)) Pub: Tantor Media. Dist(s): IngramPubServ
Young Princess Irene is sent to the country to be raised in a half farmhouse, half castle located in the side of a mountain. While exploring the top of the castle, Irene becomes lost and inexplicably finds her way to a mystifying and beautiful woman spinning a thread. Princess Irene is drawn to the woman whom she discovers is her great-great grandmother. But after she returns, her nurse, Lootie, refuses to believe in the old woman's existence and the young Princess cannot find the way back to her great-great grandmother.Days later, while on an outing with Lootie, Princess Irene believes that she detects a Goblin. They meet a young miner, Curdie, who confirms her sighting. Soon Curdie discovers Goblins lurking under the castle that have constructed an evil plot against the king and his palace. Princess Irene's belief in her great-grandmother's powers becomes essential as she and Curdie work to foil the sinister Goblin plan. As the Princess tells Curdie, "sometimes you must believe without seeing".

Princess & the Goblin. unabr. ed. George MacDonald. Read by Ian Whitcomb. (J). 2008. 54.99 (978-1-60514-603-4(X)) Find a World.

Princess & the Goblin. unabr. ed. George MacDonald. Narrated by Ian Whitcomb. (Running Time: 5 hrs. 30 mins. 0 sec.). (ENG.). (J). (gr. 4-7). 2009. 19.99 (978-1-4001-5940-6(7)); audio compact disk 45.99 (978-1-4001-3940-8(6)); audio compact disk 22.99 (978-1-4001-0940-1(X)) Pub: Tantor Media. Dist(s): IngramPubServ

Princess & the Goblin. unabr. collector's ed. George MacDonald. Read by Rebecca C. Burns. 4 cass. (Running Time: 6 hrs.). (J). (gr. 4-7). 1998. 32.00 (978-0-7366-4536-2(5), 4729) Books on Tape.
The adventures of Irene, the beautiful royal child who dares to climb the stairs of worm-eaten oak to reach the secluded chambers of her ancient yet ageless great-great-grandmother.

Princess & the Goblin, Set. unabr. ed. George MacDonald. Read by Flo Gibson. 4 cass. (Running Time: 5 hrs. 30 min.). (J). (gr. 2-3). 1987. 19.95 (978-1-55685-082-0(4)) Audio Bk Con.
The Princess & Curdie, the miner's son, foil the evil plans of the goblins with the aid of her magical great great grandmother.

Princess & the Kiss. Jennie Bishop. Ed. by Jennie Bishop. (J). 2009. 15.99 (978-1-59317-380-7(6)) Warner Pr.

Princess & the Pea see Storytime Favorites

Princess & the Pea. Hans Christian Andersen. (Ladybird Bks.).Tr. of Prindsessen Paa Aerten. (ARA., (J). (gr. 4-6). 1989. bk. 12.95 (978-0-86685-633-1(1)) Intl Bk Ctr.

Princess & the Pea. Read by Larry Robinson. Adapted by Janet Stevens. Illus. by Janet Stevens. Based on a story by Hans Christian Andersen. 11 vols. (Running Time: 8 mins.).Tr. of Prindsessen Paa Aerten. (J). (gr. k-3). 1996. bk. 25.95 (978-0-87499-353-0(9)); pap. bk. 16.95 (978-0-87499-352-3(0)) Live Oak Media.
In this rendition of Hans Christian Andersen's well-known tale, a tiger is proven to be a princess.

Princess & the Pea. Janet Stevens. Illus. by Janet Stevens. 11 vols. (Running Time: 8 mins.).Tr. of Prindsessen Paa Aerten. 1996. bk. 28.95 (978-1-59519-262-2(X)); pap. bk. 18.95 (978-1-59519-261-5(1)); pap. bk. 39.95 (978-1-59519-263-9(8)); 9.95 (978-1-59112-111-4(6)); audio compact disk 12.95 (978-1-59519-260-8(3)) Live Oak Media.

Princess & the Pea, Pack. Susanna Davidson. (Usborne Young Reading: Series One Ser.). (J). (ps-3). 2006. pap. bk. 9.99 (978-0-7945-1155-5(4), UsborneU) EDC Pubng.

Princess & the Pea & Other Children's Favorites. (J). 2005. audio compact disk (978-1-933796-25-3(1)) PC Treasures.

Princess & the Pea, Grades K-3. Read by Larry Robinson. Adapted by Janet Stevens. Illus. by Janet Stevens. Based on a story by Hans Christian Andersen. 14 vols. (Running Time: 8 mins.). 1996. pap. bk. & tchr. ed. 37.95 Reading Chest. (978-0-87499-354-7(7)) Live Oak Media.

Princess & the Puma see Great American Short Stories

Princess & the Puma see Favorite Stories by O. Henry

Princess Bean's Messy World: A Rock 'n Roll Fairytale. Perf. by Rachel Bean Resnikoff. Created by Rachel Bean Resnikoff. Created by Eric Stephens. 1 cass. (Running Time: 49 mins.). (YA). (gr. k up). 2000. 9.98 BeanStar Ent.
Princess Bean is a spunky, pink-haired girl in high-top boots whose skills include saving princes in distress & learning to whistle in 107 different languages. She lives inside a book at the library with her friends Dragon & Prince. Princess Bean's foibles will amuse children while helping them navigate the ever-turbulent waters of childhood with a sense of joy, wonder & confidence. Every day is a heroic adventure for her as she explores important issues like integrity & self-confidence.

Princess Bean's Messy World: A Rock 'n Roll Fairytale. Perf. by Rachel Bean Resnikoff. Created by Rachel Bean Resnikoff. Created by Eric Stephens. 1 CD. (Running Time: 49 mins.). (YA). (ps). 2000. audio compact disk 14.98 BeanStar Ent.

Princess Bella-Flor. unabr. ed. 1 cass. (Running Time: 20 min.). Dramatization. (Magic Looking Glass Ser.). (J). (gr. 2-6). 1989. 9.95 (978-0-7810-0045-1(9), NIM-CW-130-3-C) NIMCO.
A Spanish folk tale.

Princess Ben: Being a Wholly Truthful Account of Her Various Discoveries & Misadventures, Recounted to the Best of Her Recollection, in Four Parts. Catherine Gilbert Murdock. Read by Catherine Gilbert Murdock. (Playaway Children Ser.). (J). 2008. 59.99 (978-1-60640-793-6(7)) Find a World.

Princess Ben: Being a Wholly Truthful Account of Her Various Discoveries & Misadventures, Recounted to the Best of Her Recollection, in Four Parts. unabr. ed. Catherine Gilbert Murdock. (Running Time: 7 hrs.). 2008. 39.25 (978-1-4233-7324-7(3), 9781423373247, BADLE); 24.95 (978-1-4233-7323-0(5), 9781423373230, BAD) Brilliance Audio.

Princess Ben: Being a Wholly Truthful Account of Her Various Discoveries & Misadventures, Recounted to the Best of Her Recollection, in Four Parts. unabr. ed. Catherine Gilbert Murdock. Read by Catherine Gilbert Murdock. 1 MP3-CD. (Running Time: 7 hrs.). 2008. 39.25 (978-1-4233-7322-3(7), 9781423373223, Brinc Audio MP3 Lib); 24.95 (978-1-4233-7321-6(9), 9781423373216, Brilliance MP3); audio compact disk 82.25 (978-1-4233-7319-3(7), 9781423373193, BriAudCD Unabrid); audio compact disk 29.99 (978-1-4233-7320-9(0), 9781423373209, Bril Audio CD Unabri) Brilliance Audio.

Princess Bride. abr. unabr. ed. William Goldman. Perf. by Rob Reiner. 2 cass. (Running Time: 6 hrs.). 2004. 25.00 (978-1-59007-187-8(5)) Pub: New Millenn Enter. Dist(s): PerseuPGW
A grandfather reads a bedtime story to his grandson that has been passed down through the generations. As he reads, the story comes to life. The beautiful Buttercup is kidnapped and held against her will to marry the horrible Prince Humperdinck, and Westley (her childhood sweetheart, and now the Dread Pirate Roberts) tries to save her. Along the way, he meets an accomplished swordsman and a huge and strong giant who vow to help him rescue the hostage Buttercup.

Princess Casamassima, Set. Henry James. Read by Flo Gibson. 14 cass. (Running Time: 21 hrs.). 1995. 42.95 (978-1-55685-365-4(3)) Audio Bk Con.
Hyacinth Robinson, drawn into the London underworld of revolutionary politics, vows to assassinate an enemy of the people. His exposure to the Princess Cassamassima's world of art, nobility & beauty causes him to lose faith in his cause.

Princess Charming. unabr. ed. Jane Heller. Narrated by C. J. Critt. 9 cass. (Running Time: 12 hrs. 30 mins.). 1998. 78.00 (978-0-7887-1927-1(0), 95348E7) Recorded Bks.
Elaine, a PR manager, is wondering how her Two best friends talked her into joining them on a cruise. Not long out of port Elaine discovers she is sailing towards romance & danger.

***Princess Club.** unabr. ed. Catherine Marshall. Adapted by C. Archer. Narrated by Jaimee Draper. (Catherine Marshall's Christy Ser.). (ENG.). 2010. 7.00 (978-1-60814-707-6(X), SpringWater) Oasis Audio.

Princess Collection Two: A Dream Come True for Every Little Princess. Prod. by Walt Disney Records Staff. 1 CD. (J). 1998. bk. 16.98 (978-0-7634-0450-5(0)) W Disney Records.

Princess Collection Two: A Dream Come True for Every Little Princess. Prod. by Walt Disney Records Staff. 1 cass. (J). (ps-3). 1998. 10.98 (978-0-7634-0449-9(7)) W Disney Records.

Princess Diana. abr. ed. Katherine Krohn. Read by Josephine Bailey. 1 cass. (Running Time: 1 hr. 30 mins.). (YA). (gr. 5-12). 2000. 9.95 (978-0-7366-4708-3(2), 5229) Books on Tape.
The story of this extraordinary woman from her childhood to the tragic accident that took her life.

Princess Diana. collector's unabr. ed. Katherine Krohn. Read by Josephine Bailey. 2 CDs. (Running Time: 3 hrs.). (J). 2000. audio compact disk 12.95 (978-0-7366-5223-0(X), 5229) Books on Tape.

Princess Diana. unabr. collector's ed. Katherine Krohn. Read by Josephine Bailey. 1 cass. (Running Time: 1 hr. 30 mins.). (Biography Ser.). (YA). (gr. 5-12). 2000. 9.95 (978-0-7366-5037-3(7), 5229) Books on Tape.
She tells the story of this extraordinary woman from her childhood to the tragic accident that took her life.

Princess Diaries. unabr. ed. Meg Cabot. 5 CDs. (Running Time: 5 hrs. 54 mins.). (Princess Diaries: Vol. I). (J). (gr. 7 up). 2004. audio compact disk 40.00 (978-0-8072-1164-9(8), S YA 311 CD, Listening Lib) Random Audio Pubg.
"She's just a New York City girl living with her artist mom. Dad is the prince of Genovia and can't have any more kids. Like it or not, Mia is heir to the throne.".

Princess Diaries. unabr. ed. Meg Cabot. Read by Anne Hathaway. 4 vols. (Running Time: 5 hrs. 54 mins.). (Princess Diaries: Vol. I). (J). (gr. 7 up). 2004. pap. bk. 38.00 (978-0-8072-0669-0(5), Listening Lib); 32.00 (978-0-8072-0514-3(1), LL0224, Listening Lib) Random Audio Pubg.
A young girl living in New York City with her artist mother discovers her real father is Prince of Genovia. Now that he is unable to have any more children, she becomes a Princess, heir to the throne.

Princess Diaries. unabr. ed. Meg Cabot. Read by Anne Hathaway. 5 CDs. (Running Time: 5 hrs. 54 mins.). (Princess Diaries: Vol. I). (ENG.). (J). (gr. 7). 2005. audio compact disk 19.99 (978-0-307-24326-3(5), Listening Lib) Pub: Random Audio Pubg. Dist(s): Random

Princess Furball. 2004. bk. 24.95 (978-1-56008-093-0(0)); pap. bk. 18.95 (978-1-55592-457-7(3)); pap. bk. 18.95 (978-1-55592-459-1(X)); pap. bk. 38.75 (978-1-55592-458-4(1)); pap. bk. 38.75 (978-1-55592-460-7(3)); pap. bk. 32.75 (978-1-55592-299-3(6)); pap. bk. 32.75 (978-1-55592-300-6(3)); pap. bk. 14.95 (978-0-7882-0663-4(X)); pap. bk. 14.95 (978-0-7882-0397-8(5)); 8.95 (978-1-56008-312-2(3)); 8.95 (978-1-56008-424-2(3)); cass. & flmstrp 30.00 (978-0-89719-639-0(2)); audio compact disk 12.95 (978-1-55592-921-3(4)) Weston Woods.

Princess Furball. Charlotte S. Huck. 1 cass. (Running Time: 17 min.). (J). (gr. k-4). pap. bk. 12.95 (RAC347) Weston Woods.
A king falls in love with a princess in a coat of a thousand furs after she hides her identity in some delicious soup.

Princess Furball. Read by Charlotte S. Huck. Illus. by Anita Lobel. 1 cass. (Running Time: 17 min.). (J). bk. 24.95; pap. bk. 32.75 Weston Woods.

Princess Furball. Read by Charlotte S. Huck. Illus. by Anita Lobel. 1 cass. (J). (ps-4). pap. bk. 12.95 (PRA347) Weston Woods.
From the book by Charlotte Huck.

Princess Gwenevere & the Jewel Riders (Play-a-sound) abr. unabr. ed. Nancy L. McGill & Catherine Coulter. Read by Anne Flosnik. 5 CDs. (Running Time: 10 hrs.). (Bride Ser.). 2004. audio compact disk 36.95 (978-1-59086-908-6(7), 1590869087, BACD) Brilliance Audio.
Dear Reader: The Sherbrooke family saga continues with James and Jason Sherbrooke, identical male twins who look exactly like their beautiful Aunt Melissande, and not at all like their father, the earl, which riles him no end. James, twenty-eight minutes older than his brother, is the heir. He is solid, is James. He's a student of astronomy, rides like a centaur, and, unlike his brother, Jason, enjoys learning the ropes of managing his father's estates. He no longer sows excessive wild oats, as his neighbor, Corrie Tybourne Barrett, a brat he's known since she was three-years-old, looks forward to doing since she turned eighteen. When she nearly shoves him off a cliff, sneering all the while, James hauls off and spanks her. A promising start. Then, unfortunately, the earl, Douglas Sherbrooke, is shot at. This leads to Georges Cadoudal, a Frenchman in the employ of the English war ministry with whom Douglas had dealings with some years before. But Cadoudal died in 1815, fifteen years before. Were there children who might want revenge against Douglas? But the question is why: Georges and Douglas parted friends, at least Douglas believed that they had. Adventures compound; Corrie hurls herself into the thick of things. As for Jason, not quite a half an hour younger, he loves horses, wants to start a stud farm, still sows more oats than a man should be allowed, but finally meets a girl who stops him in his tracks. And then what happens? You will have to listen to the book to find out. I hope you enjoy yourself. The characters are rich, colorful, and a hoot to boot. The mystery will confound you. Do let me know what you think. Write me at P.O. Box 17, Mill Valley, CA., 94942 or email me at readmoi@aol.com. Keep an eye on my web site at www.CatherineCoulter.com. Catherine Coulter [signature].

Princess Gwenevere & the Jewel Riders (Play-a-sound) unabr. ed. Nancy L. McGill & Catherine Coulter. Read by Anne Flosnik. 6 cass. (Running Time: 10 hrs.). (Bride Ser.). 2004. 82.25 (978-1-58788-901-1(3), 1587889013, BrilAudUnabridg); 32.95 (978-1-58788-900-4(5), 1587889005, BAU) Brilliance Audio.

Princess Gwenevere & the Jewel Riders (Play-a-sound) unabr. ed. Nancy L. McGill & Catherine Coulter. Read by Anne Flosnik. (Running Time: 10 hrs.). (Bride Ser.). 2004. 39.25 (978-1-59335-540-1(8), 1593355408, Brinc Audio MP3 Lib); 24.95 (978-1-59335-279-0(4), 1593352794, Brilliance MP3) Brilliance Audio.

Princess in Love. Meg Cabot. Read by Anne Hathaway. 3 vols. (Running Time: 5 hrs. 4 mins.). (Princess Diaries: Vol. 3). (J). (gr. 7 up). 2004. pap. bk. 38.00 (978-0-8072-2284-3(4), Listening Lib); audio compact disk 38.25 (978-0-8072-2002-3(7), Listening Lib) Pub: Random Audio Pubg. Dist(s): NetLibrary CO

Princess in Love. unabr. ed. Meg Cabot. 3 cass. (Running Time: 5 hrs. 4 mins.). (Princess Diaries: Vol. 3). (J). (gr. 7 up). 2004. 30.00 (978-0-8072-0712-3(8), Listening Lib) Random Audio Pubg.

Princess in Pink. Meg Cabot. Read by Clea Lewis. 5 cass. (Running Time: 7 hrs.). (Princess Diaries: Vol. 5). (J). 2004. 50.00 (978-0-8072-2085-6(X), Listening Lib); audio compact disk 46.75 (978-1-4000-8617-7(5), Listening Lib) Pub: Random Audio Pubg. Dist(s): NetLibrary CO

Princess in the Spotlight, Meg Cabot. Read by Anne Hathaway. 4 CDs. (Running Time: 4 hrs. 54 mins.). (Princess Diaries: Vol. 2). (J). (gr. 7 up). 2004. audio compact disk 32.30 (978-0-8072-1770-2(0), Listening Lib) Pub: Random Audio Pubg. Dist(s): NetLibrary CO

Princess in the Spotlight. unabr. ed. Meg Cabot. Read by Anne Hathaway. 4 cass. (Running Time: 4 hrs. 54 mins.). (Princess Diaries: Vol. 2). (J). (gr. 7 up). 2004. 32.00 (978-0-8072-0584-6(2), Listening Lib) Random Audio Pubg.
Just when Mia thought she had the whole Princess thing under control... things get out of hand, fast! There's the havoc of the interview's aftermath and her dreaded princess lessons at the Plaza.

Princess in the Spotlight, unabr. ed. Meg Cabot. Read by Anne Hathaway. 4 vols. (Running Time: 4 hrs. 54 mins.). (Princess Diaries: Vol. 2). (J). (gr. 7 up). 2004. pap. bk. 38.00 (978-0-8072-1197-7(4), S YA 332 SP, Listening Lib) Random Audio Pubg.

Princess in Training. unabr. collector's ed. Meg Cabot. Read by Clea Lewis. 4 cass. (Running Time: 6 hrs. 17 mins.). (Princess Diaries: Vol. 6). (YA). 2005. 35.00 (978-1-4000-9876-7(9), BksonTape); audio compact disk 42.50 (978-0-307-20670-1(X), BksonTape) Pub: Random Audio Pubg. Dist(s): NetLibrary CO
It's an all new school year for Princess Mia, with all new classes, all new challenges... and all new worries. With a baby brother at home who won't stop crying and a potential eco-disaster in her native land that has all of Europe in an uproar, Mia's got a lot more on her mind than just a case of the sophomore slumps: There's Ms. Martinez, the new English teacher who can't seem to stand Mia - or her writing. Michael, so busy with his new classes at Columbia, barely has time to IM, let alone make out. Lana, who has some disturbing information on just what college boys expect from their girlfriends. Lilly, who seems to think Mia has plenty of time in between flunking geometry and her princess lessons to run for student body president. And of course Grandmere, who has a plan to keep Genovia from being thrown out of the EU that seems to include making unscheduled appearances in the hallways of Albert Einstein High in her tiara, and forcing her only granddaughter to fondle the body parts of long deceased saints... Really, it's almost more than a princess in training can bear.

Princess in Waiting. Meg Cabot. Read by Clea Lewis. 4 vols. (Running Time: 5 hrs. 21 mins.). (Princess Diaries: Vol. 4). (J). 2004. 38.00 (978-1-4000-9010-5(5), Listening Lib); audio compact disk 38.25 (978-1-4000-8610-8(8), Listening Lib) Pub: Random Audio Pubg. Dist(s): NetLibrary CO

Princess in Waiting. unabr. ed. Judith Saxton. Read by Pippa Sparkes. 6 cass. (Running Time: 8 hrs.). 1999. 69.95 (978-1-85903-252-7(4)) Pub: Magna Story GBR. Dist(s): Ulverscroft US
Katherine of Aragon was little more than a child when she arrived in Plymouth. She was not to know that the most powerful and handsome man in England had vowed to make her his own.

Princess Margaret. Tim Heald. 2008. 76.95 (978-0-7531-3148-0(X)); audio compact disk 99.95 (978-0-7531-3149-7(8)) Pub: Isis Pubng Ltd GBR. Dist(s): Ulverscroft US

Princess Mia. unabr. ed. Meg Cabot. Narrated by Clea Lewis. 6 CDs. (Running Time: 6 hrs. 45 mins.). (Princess Diaries: Bk. 9). (YA). (gr. 7-10). 2008. audio compact disk 66.75 (978-1-4361-0358-9(4)) Recorded Bks.
New York Timesbest-selling author Meg Cabot's charming and witty Princess Diaries series is a megahit with young listeners. Being the crown princess of Genovia has never been easy for Mia. And if ruling a tiny country wasn't enough, she also has to deal with a broken heart after her true love Michael breaks up with her. So her parents send her to a therapist to at least get her out of bed. And just when she thinks things couldn't get any worse, she discovers a long buried secret that could affect her family forever.

Princess of Landover. abr. ed. Terry Brooks. Read by Dick Hill. 5 CDs. (Running Time: 6 hrs.). (Magic Kingdom of Landover Ser.: No. 6). 2009. audio compact disk 24.99 (978-1-4233-9851-6(3), 9781423398516) Brilliance Audio.

Princess of Landover. abr. ed. Terry Brooks. Read by Dick Hill. (Running Time: 6 hrs.). (Magic Kingdom of Landover Ser.: No. 6). 2010. audio compact disk 14.99 (978-1-4233-9852-3(1), 9781423398523, BCD Value Price) Brilliance Audio.

Princess of Landover. unabr. ed. Terry Brooks. Read by Dick Hill. 1 MP3-CD. (Running Time: 12 hrs.). (Magic Kingdom of Landover Ser.: No. 6). 2009. 24.99 (978-1-4233-9847-9(5), 9781423398479, Brilliance MP3); 39.97 (978-1-4233-9848-6(3), 9781423398486, Brinc Audio MP3 Lib); 24.99 (978-1-4233-9849-3(1), 9781423398493, BAD); 39.97 (978-1-4233-9850-9(5), 9781423398509, BADLE); audio compact disk 99.97 (978-1-4233-9846-2(7), 9781423398462, BriAudCD Unabrid); audio compact disk 38.99 (978-1-4233-9845-5(9), 9781423398455) Brilliance Audio.

Princess of Mars. Edgar Rice Burroughs. (Running Time: 7 mins.). 2009. audio compact disk 31.95 (978-1-897304-45-7(5)) Dorch Pub Co.

Princess of Mars. Edgar Rice Burroughs. Narrated by Jim Killavey. (Running Time: 6 hrs. 30 mins.). 1988. 27.95 (978-1-59912-820-7(9)) Iofy Corp.

Princess of Mars. Edgar Rice Burroughs. Narrated by Dennis McKee. (Running Time: 7 hrs. 30 mins.). 2000. 27.95 (978-1-59912-396-7(7)) Iofy Corp.

Princess of Mars. Edgar Rice Burroughs. Read by John Bolen. (Running Time: 6 hrs. 45 mins.). 2001. 27.95 (978-1-60083-590-2(2), Audiofy Corp) Iofy Corp.

Princess of Mars. Edgar Rice Burroughs. Read by John Bolen. (Mars Ser.). (ENG.). 2001. audio compact disk 72.00 (978-1-4001-3018-4(2)) Pub: Tantor Media. Dist(s): IngramPubServ

***Princess of Mars.** Edgar Rice Burroughs. (Running Time: 7 mins.). 2009. 19.95 (978-1-897331-00-2(2), AudioRealms) Dorch Pub Co.

Princess of Mars. abr. ed. Edgar Rice Burroughs. Read by Stan Winiarski. 2 cass. (Running Time: 3 hrs.). (Mars Ser.). (YA). (gr. 8-12). 1999. 16.95 (978-1-882071-51-7(4), 393368) B-B Audio.
I stood on the Arizona bluff with my attention drawn to the large red star, Mars. I closed my eyes, stretched out my arms and was drawn through the trackless immensity of space. I opened my eyes upon a strange landscape.Suddenly projected to.

Princess of Mars. unabr. ed. Edgar Rice Burroughs. Narrated by Jared Field. (Running Time: 6 hrs. 36 mins.). (J). (gr. 3-9). 2001. 20.95 (978-1-55685-655-6(5)) Audio Bk Con.

Princess of Mars. unabr. ed. Edgar Rice Burroughs. Narrated by Jared Field. 5 cass. (Running Time: 7 hrs. 30 mins.). 2000. 35.95 Audio Bk Con.
John, an adventurous soldier & gentleman of Virginia, finds himself mysteriously transported to Mars. There he is captured, befriends his captors, fights great battles & falls in love with the beautiful prisoner, the Princess Dejah Thoris.

Princess of Mars. unabr. ed. Edgar Rice Burroughs. 1 CD. (Running Time: 7 hrs.). 2001. audio compact disk 25.00; audio compact disk 51.00 Books on Tape.
John Carter, facing death at the hands of the Apaches, wills his transmigration to Mars. There he finds the dying civilization of Barsoom.

Princess of Mars. unabr. ed. Edgar Rice Burroughs. Read by Jim Killavey. 6 cass. (Running Time: 8 hrs.). 1989. 36.00 incl. album. (C-191) Jimcin Record.
Adventures of John Carter.

Princess of Mars. unabr. ed. Edgar Rice Burroughs. Narrated by John Bolen. 1 CD (MP3). (Running Time: 6 hrs. 45 mins.). (Mars Ser.: Vol. 1). (ENG.). 2001. audio compact disk 20.00 (978-1-4001-5018-2(3)) Pub: Tantor Media. Dist(s): IngramPubServ
Ex-confederate army captain John Carter finds himself unwittingly transported to Mars, while fleeing Apache Indians. Ferocious Martians whose culture is based on the ability to fight for their race populate this new world. Fortunately for John, the gravitational difference between Mars and Earth has endowed him with the superhuman strength that he will need for survival on this hostile planet. John Carter battles monstrous Martian creatures but gains the respect and friendship of the Barsoomians. He also encounters the beautiful Dejah Thoris, Princess of Helium, and earns her everlasting devotion.

Princess of Mars. unabr. ed. Edgar Rice Burroughs. Read by John Bolen. (Running Time: 7 hrs. 0 mins. 0 sec.). (Barsoom Ser.). (ENG.). 2008. 19.99 (978-1-4001-5910-9(5)); audio compact disk 55.99 (978-1-4001-3910-1(4)) Pub: Tantor Media. Dist(s): IngramPubServ

Princess of Mars. unabr. ed. Edgar Rice Burroughs. Read by John Bolen. (Running Time: 7 hrs. 0 mins. 0 sec.). (Barsoom Ser.). (ENG.). 2008. audio compact disk 27.99 (978-1-4001-0910-4(8)) Pub: Tantor Media. Dist(s): IngramPubServ

***Princess of Mars.** unabr. ed. Edgar Rice Burroughs. Read by William Dufris. (Running Time: 7 hrs. 30 mins.). (Martian Ser.). 2010. 29.95 (978-1-4417-1867-9(2)); 54.95 (978-1-4417-1863-1(X)); audio compact disk 24.95 (978-1-4417-1866-2(4)); audio compact disk 69.00 (978-1-4417-1864-8(8)) Blckstn Audio.

Princess of Mars. unabr. collector's ed. Edgar Rice Burroughs. Read by Jim Killavey. 6 cass. (Running Time: 9 hrs.). 1988. 48.00 (978-0-7366-3945-3(4), 9191) Books on Tape.
John Carter, facing death at the hands of the Apaches, wills his transmigration to Mars. There he finds the dying civilization of Barsoom.

Princess of Mars, Bk. 1. unabr. ed. Edgar Rice Burroughs. Read by Jack Sondericker. 6 cass. (Running Time: 6 hrs. 42 mins.). Dramatization. (Mars Ser.: Bk. 1). 1993. 39.95 (978-1-55686-482-7(5), 482) Books in Motion.
I stand on the Arizona bluff with my attention drawn to the large red star, Mars. I closed my eyes, stretched out my arms & was drawn through the trackless immensity of space. I opened my eyes upon a strange landscape. I knew I was on Mars.

Princess on the Brink. unabr. ed. Meg Cabot. Read by Clea Lewis. 5 CDs. (Running Time: 5 hrs. 16 mins.). (Princess Diaries: Vol. 8). (YA). (gr. 7-10). 2007. audio compact disk 50.00 (978-0-7393-4857-4(4), Listening Lib) Pub: Random Audio Pubg. Dist(s): Random

***Princess Plot.** unabr. ed. Kirsten Boie. Narrated by Polly Lee. 1 Playaway. (Running Time: 10 hrs. 15 mins.). (YA). (gr. 5-8). 2009. 59.75 (978-1-4407-1739-0(7)); 67.75 (978-1-4407-1731-4(1)); audio compact disk 97.75 (978-1-4407-1735-2(4)) Recorded Bks.

***Princess Plot.** unabr. collector's ed. Kirsten Boie. Narrated by Polly Lee. 9 CDs. (Running Time: 10 hrs. 15 mins.). (YA). (gr. 5-8). 2009. audio compact disk 51.95 (978-1-4407-2551-7(9)) Recorded Bks.

Princess Pocahontas. Virginia Watson. Read by Vanessa Benjamin. (Running Time: 25200 sec.). (J). (gr. 4-7). 2006. 44.95 (978-0-7861-4501-0(3)); audio compact disk 55.00 (978-0-7861-7228-3(2)) Blckstn Audio.

Princess Pocahontas. unabr. ed. Virginia Watson. Read by Vanessa Benjamin. (Running Time: 25200 sec.). (J). (gr. 4-7). 2006. audio compact disk 29.95 (978-0-7861-7662-5(8)) Blckstn Audio.

Princess Posy: Knight in Training. Alex Gutteridge. Read by Sophie Aldred. (Running Time: 5400 sec.). (J). 2001. audio compact disk 21.95 (978-0-7540-6794-8(7)) AudioGo GBR.

Princess Royal. Perf. by Carrie Crompton. 1 cass. 9.98 incl. Norelco pkg. (978-1-877737-40-4(2), EB 2219); audio compact disk 12.98 CD. (978-1-877737-55-8(0)) MFLP CA.

Princess Scargo & the Birthday Pumpkin. As told by Geena Davis. Music by Michael Hedges. Illus. by Karen Barbour. 1 cass. (Running Time: 1 hr.). (J). 9.95 Weston Woods.
A touching story, based on a popular Native American legend, about a young Native American girl who gives up a precious birthday gift in order to save her village.

Princess, the Dragon & Scaredy Cats. Audrey Wood. (J). 10.97 (978-0-85953-375-1(1)) Childs Play GBR.

Princess Who Could Not Laugh see Prince Rabbit & Other Stories

Princess Who Never Laughed, the Fairy Shoemaker,Miss Molly Squeak,Sleeping Beauty,the Tinderbox-Audio CD. EDCON Publishing Group Staff. (ENG.). 2008. audio compact disk 12.95 (978-0-8481-0416-0(1)) EDCON Pubng.

***Princess Who Wanted a Crown of Dew.** Anonymous. 2009. (978-1-60136-613-9(2)) Audio Holding.

Princess with a Purpose(tm) Music CD. Kelly Chapman. Illus. by Tammie Lyon. 2010. audio compact disk 14.99 (978-0-7369-2746-8(8)) Harvest Hse.

Princessa: Machiavelli for Women, abr. ed. Harriet Rubin. Read by Harriet Rubin. 2 cass. (Running Time: 2 hrs. 30 min.). 1997. 17.95 (978-1-57453-216-6(2)) Audio Lit.
Study of the great female heroes & the ability of women acting more like women & not like men.

Princesse de Babylone, Set. Francois Voltaire, pseud. Read by Bernard Merle. 2 cass. (FRE.). 1995. 26.95 (1756-KFP) Olivia & Hill.
The tale of a Babylonian princess who searches the world looking for her lover gives Voltaire the opportunity to paint the mores of ten nations. An oriental fantasy.

Princesse de Cleves see Treasury of French Prose

Princesse de Cleves, Set. Madame De Lafayette. Read by Michele Morgan. 2 cass. (FRE.). 1991. 38.95 (1069-EF) Olivia & Hill.
The Princesse de Cleves, whose marriage was arranged by her mother, does not love her husband, but she remains loyal to him despite her love for the Duc de Nemours.

Princeton Review Word Smart & Grammar Smart CD. unabr. l.t. ed. Adam Robinson & Julian Fleisher. 6 CDs. (Running Time: 6 hrs.). (Princeton Review Ser.). (ENG.). 2001. audio compact disk 39.95 (978-0-609-81111-5(8), LivingLang) Pub: Random Info Grp. Dist(s): Random
The words people use say a lot about them. Some words say that they're smart, persuasive, and informed. Others say that they don't know what they're talking about. Knowing which words to use, though, is only half the battle: Once they've found le mot juste, they have to know how to use it correctly. Expanding one's vocabulary and learning basic grammar rules are two guaranteed ways to improve one's speaking, reading, and writing skills. Not only are these skills critical on standardized tests such as the SAT or GRE, they will also open doors for students professionally and even socially. The Princeton Review is recognized as the nation's leader in test preparation and vocabulary- building courses. This audio program is based on the best-selling books Word Smart and Grammar Smart by The Princeton Review. Four 60-minute Word Smart CDs include: • 200 essential words grouped by topic • Concise, accurate definitions and funny examples that listeners will remember Two 60-minute Grammar Smart CDs include: • Parts of speech and sentence components • Grammar pitfalls - misplaced modifiers and subject-verb agreement • Lots of fun examples illustrating correct usage.

Princeton Review Word Smart Audio Program. Julian Fleisher et al. 4 cass. (Running Time: 4 hrs.). 1993. 25.00 (LivingLang) Random Info Grp.

Princeton Review Word Smart Genius, Vol. 2. Julian Fleisher. 4 cass. 1997. 25.00 (LivingLang) Random Info Grp.

Princeton Review Word Smart II: Building an Even More Educated Vocabulary. unabr. l.t. ed. Adam Robinson & Julian Fleisher. 5 CDs. (Running Time: 5 hrs.). (Princeton Review on Audio Ser.). (ENG.). 2001. audio compact disk 29.95 (978-0-609-81108-5(8), LivingLang) Pub: Random Info Grp. Dist(s): Random
Some interesting word facts: • The word "noisome" had nothing whatsoever to do with noise. • "Ordinance" and "ordnance" have two distinct meanings. • An "errant" fool is a fool who is lost, while and "arrant" fool is one whose foolishness is obvious. Word Smart II exposes hundreds of examples like these, so readers will never be surprised by vocabulary again. More than 70,000 people have improved their vocabularies with the original Word Smart, but an educated and powerful vocabulary doesn't stop growing with one book. All of the 848 entries in Word Smart II belong in an impressive vocabulary. Learning and using these words effectively can help readers to get better grades, score higher on tests, and communicate more confidently at work. Includes: • Concise, accurate definitions • Great examples and stories that teach words in context • Mnemonics to make it all stick Here's what Publishers Weekly had to say about the first Word Smart audio vocabulary building program: "An engaging, supportive means of instruction... Just hearing words used conversationally makes them seem accessible and real. This lively production has broad appeal, suitable for high schoolers trying to boost their verbal SAT scores or for the business person who wants to add polish to presentations. The Princeton Review's overall approach is refreshing." The Word Smart II audio program takes up where Word Smart left off. Based on the best-selling Word Smart and Word Smart II books (more than 200,000 copies sold), this four-hour CD course (plus one extra bonus CD) continues the education. Word Smart II introduces more words that people truly need to know to do well in school and in their careers.

Principal as a Generalist & a Specialist. Heshy Glass. 1 cass. (Running Time: 90 mins.). 1999. 6.00 (P60FD) Torah Umesorah.

Principal Navigations, Voyages & Discoveries of the English Nation see Cambridge Treasy Malory

Principal's on the Roof. unabr. ed. Elizabeth Levy. Read by Christine Marshall. Illus. by Mordicai Gerstein. 1 CD. (Running Time: 3120 sec.). (First Chapter Bks.). (YA). (gr. 7-11). 2006. audio compact disk 15.95 (978-1-59519-751-1(6)); 12.95 (978-1-59519-750-4(8)) Live Oak Media.
The principal has promised to read aloud from the school's roof if the students read 1000 books during their reading marathon. When he agrees to read a story by Fletcher's owner Gwen, she is thrilled - until the principal starts sneezing uncontrollably as he's reading her science fiction story about aliens who live on rooftops and make humans sneeze! Can Fletcher and Jasper solve the mystery before the principal falls off the roof and Gwen gets blamed?.

Principe. Niccolo Machiavelli. 1 cass. (Running Time: 1 hrs.).Tr. of Prince. (ITA.). 1997. pap. bk. 19.50 (978-1-58085-467-2(2)) Interlingua VA.

Principe. unabr. ed. Nicolas Maquiavelo. 2 cass. (Running Time: 3 hrs.). 2003. 12.00 (978-958-43-0132-1(2)) Pub: Yoyo Music COL. Dist(s): Mich St U Pr

Principe. unabr. ed. Nicolás Maquiavelo. Read by Pedro Montoya. 3 CDs.Tr. of Prince. (SPA.). 2002. audio compact disk 17.00 (978-958-43-0001-0(6)) YoYoMusic.

Principe, Vol. 4. Niccolo Machiavelli. Ed. by Maurizio Falyhera & Cristina Giocometti. (ITA.). 1999. bk. 29.95 (978-1-58214-107-7(X)) Language Assocs.

Principe Vol. 4: Multilingual Books Literature. Excerpts. Niccolo Machiavelli. Ed. by Maurizio Falyhera & Cristina Giocometti. 1 cass. (Running Time: 90). (Audio Anthology of Italian Literature Ser.: 4). (ITA.). 1999. spiral bd. 19.95 (978-1-58214-106-0(1)) Language Assocs.

Principe Caspian. C. S. Lewis. Narrated by Karl Hofmann. (Cronicas de Narnia (Playaway) Ser.). (SPA.). (J). 2009. 59.99 (978-1-61545-562-1(0)) Find a World.

***Principe Caspian.** C. S. Lewis. 2010. audio compact disk 17.95 (978-1-933499-94-9(X)) Fonolibro Inc.

Principe Caspian: Las Crinicas de Narnia. C. S. Lewis. 5 cds. (Running Time: 21600 sec.). (Cronicas de Narnia Ser.).Tr. of Prince Caspian. (SPA.). (J). (ps). 2007. audio compact disk 24.95 (978-1-933499-58-1(3)) Fonolibro Inc.

Principe Feliz - El Fantasma de Canterville - El Crimen de Lord Arturo Saville. abr. ed. Oscar Wilde. Read by Carlos Zambrano. 3 CDs.Tr. of Happy Prince - The Canterville Ghost - Lord Arthur Saville's Crime. (SPA.). 2002. audio compact disk 17.00 (978-958-8161-20-4(7)) YoYoMusic.

Principe y el Mendigo. abr. ed. Mark Twain. Read by Carlos J. Vega. 3 CDs.Tr. of Prince & the Pauper. (SPA.). 2002. audio compact disk 17.00 (978-958-9494-85-1(4)) YoYoMusic.

Principia Ethica, Set. unabr. ed. George Edward Moore. Read by Robert L. Halvorson. 8 cass. (Running Time: 720 min.). 56.95 (98) Halvorson Assocs.

Principios del Exito: Como Llegar de Donde Esta a Donde Quiere Ir. abr. ed. Jack L. Canfield. Narrated by Jose Duarte. 6 cds. (Running Time: 21600 sec.).Tr. of Success Principles. (SPA.). 2007. audio compact disk 24.95 (978-1-933499-51-2(6)) Fonolibro Inc.

Principito. Antoine de Saint-Exupéry.Tr. of Petit Prince. (SPA.). 2002. bk. 11.90 (978-956-201-479-3(7), 1620) Dolmen Ediciones CHL.

Principito. abr. ed. Antoine de Saint-Exupéry.Tr. of Petit Prince. (SPA.). 2002. audio compact disk 13.00 (978-958-43-0143-7(8)) YoYoMusic.

Principito. unabr. ed. Antoine de Saint-Exupéry. 3 CDs. (Running Time: 3 hrs.).Tr. of Petit Prince. (SPA.). 2002. audio compact disk 17.00 (978-958-9494-72-1(2)) YoYoMusic.
En El Principito, que Antoine de Saint-Exupéry escribió poco años antes de su muerte, pareciera que el autor hubiera profetizado el que habría de ser su final. En efecto, el autor, un piloto durante la guerra, un día desapareció durante una misión y nunca se volvió a saber de él. Dejó una herencia literaria breve pero de alta calidad, y entre ella, El Principito ha sido considerado, desde su publicación como una pequeña obra, muestra, que bajo el manto de un cuento infantil, apela a todas las edades por su ternura y su bello fondo filosófico. En efecto, aquí hay una fábula que muestra que las ilusiones se pueden llevar a cabo, que las cosas esenciales no son las que se ven a primera vista y que un mundo de ilusión tiene tanta validez como el real.

Principle Approach: Christian Philosophy & Methodology of Education. Instructed by Stephen McDowell. 2000. 5.95 (978-1-887456-29-6(5)) Providence Found.

Principle-Centered Leadership see Liderazgo Centrado en Principios

Principle Centered Leadership. Stephen R. Covey. 6 cass. 69.95 Set, incl. wkbk. (268-C47) Natl Seminars.
Learn from one of today's most respected leadership experts as he teaches you to apply the "natural laws" of leadership to all aspects of your life.

Principle Centered Leadership. Stephen R. Covey. 6 cass. (Running Time: 6 hrs.). 1994. 69.95 Set incl. 12p. wkbk. (774PAX) Nightingale-Conant.
Covey identifies four levels of natural laws which control our lives: Personal, Interpersonal, Managerial & Organizational. And he gives you a more complete way of thinking about how to operate on each of these levels: Trustworthiness at the personal level, trust at the interpersonal level, empowerment at the managerial level & alignment at the organizational level. Includes workbook.

Principle-Centered Leadership. abr. ed. Stephen R. Covey. Read by Stephen R. Covey. 3 CDs. (Running Time: 33 hrs. 0 mins. 0 sec.). (ENG.). 2002. audio compact disk 29.95 (978-1-929494-61-3(0)) Pub: Franklin Covey. Dist(s): S and S Inc

Principle-Centered Leadership. abr. ed. Stephen R. Covey. 2006. 17.95 (978-1-933976-30-3(6)) Pub: Franklin Covey. Dist(s): S and S Inc

Principle Centered Leadership. abr. ed. Stephen R. Covey. Read by Stephen R. Covey. 1 cass. (Running Time: 1 hr.). 1999. 16.85 (978-0-671-01113-0(8)) S and S Inc.
How to achieve a wise & renewing balance between work & family in the midst of constant pressures & crises.

Principle Centered Leadership. abr. ed. Stephen R. Covey. Read by Stephen R. Covey. 1 CD. (Running Time: 11 hrs. 20 mins. 0 sec.). (ENG.). 2000. audio compact disk 14.00 (978-0-671-31703-4(2), Sound Ideas) Pub: S&S Audio. Dist(s): S and S Inc

Principle of Growth. Elbert Willis. 1 cass. (Developing Stability Ser.). 4.00 Fill the Gap.

Principle of Teaching. Robin McMillan. 1 cass. (Running Time: 90 mins.). (He Still Heals Ser.: Vol. 3). 2000. 5.00 (SA01-003) Morning NC.
Learn about the healing power of God that is available to believers today.

Principle of the Path: How to Get from Where You Are to Where You Want to Be. unabr. ed. Andy Stanley. Narrated by Jon Gauger. (Running Time: 5 hrs. 4 mins. 50 sec.). (ENG.). 2009. 16.09 (978-1-60814-540-9(9)) Oasis Audio.

Principle of the Path: How to Get from Where You Are to Where You Want to Be. unabr. ed. Andy Stanley. Narrated by Jon Gauger. (Running Time: 5 hrs. 4 mins. 50 sec.). (ENG.). 2009. audio compact disk 22.99 (978-1-59859-517-8(2)) Oasis Audio.

Principle Woods Book of Courage. Short Stories. Jennifer Whitlock. Dramatization. (J). 2001. 9.95 (978-0-9700601-7-4(3)) Principle.

Principle Woods Book of Honesty. Short Stories. Jennifer Whitlock. Dramatization. (J). 2001. audio compact disk 12.95 (978-0-9700601-8-1(1)) Principle.

Principle Woods Book of Work. Short Stories. Jennifer Whitlock. Dramatization. (J). 2000. 9.95 (978-0-9700601-4-3(9)) Principle.

Principle Woods Singin' & Dancin' #1. 2000. audio compact disk 9.95 (978-0-9700601-2-9(2)) Principle.

Principle Woods the Book of Courage. Short Stories. Jennifer Whitlock. Dramatization. (J). 2001. audio compact disk 12.95 (978-0-9700601-5-0(7)) Principle.

Principle Woods Work. Narrated by Lisa Valdini. 1 CD. (Running Time: 1 hr.). (J). (gr. k-2). 2000. audio compact disk 12.95 (978-0-9700601-3-6(0)) Principle.

Principles & Practice of Formation in Religious Life, Pt. 3. Fr. Hardon. 10 cass. 60.00 Set. (XXC) IRL Chicago.

Principles & Practice of Formation in Religious Life, Pt. 4. Fr. Hardon. 10 cass. 60.00 Set. (XXD) IRL Chicago.

Principles & Practice of Formation in Religious Life, Pts. 1A & 1B. Fr. Hardon. 20 cass. 115.00 Set. (XXA) IRL Chicago.

Principles & Practice of Formation in Religious Life, Pts. 2A & 2B. Fr. Hardon. 18 cass. 115.00 Set. (XXB) IRL Chicago.

Principles & Practice of Prayer. Fr. Hardon. 9 cass. 45.00 Set. (92P) IRL Chicago.

Principles & Practice of the Yogic Path. Ole Nydahl. 2 cass. 18.00 set. (A0408-89) Sound Photosyn.

Principles for a Life-Style: Col. 3:1-17. Ed Young. (J). 1982. 4.95 (978-0-7417-1257-8(1), 257) Win Walk.

Principles for Building Strong Faith. Kenneth W. Hagin, Jr. 3 cass. 1983. 12.00 Set. (23J) Faith Lib Pubns.

Principles for Choosing a Mate: Proverbs 3:6. Ed Young. (J). 1981. 4.95 (978-0-7417-1158-8(3), A0158) Win Walk.

Principles for Living on the Edge. Douglas Pittman. 3 cass. (Running Time: 2 hrs. 45 min.). 1997. 29.95 Set. (978-1-890225-01-8(0), PLE-CT) Sundancer Graphics.
Explores 7 universal principles: attraction polarity, cause & effect, correspondence, vibration, flow, & connection, & supports the listener in integrating them into a daily routine.

Principles of a Free Society. Interview with Ayn Rand. 1 cass. (Running Time: 30 min.). 14.95 (AR53C) Second Renaissance.
Addresses such issues as: the link between the political & economic systems of a society; does a free society need a constitution?; government financing in a free society; is federalism a necessity of a free society?; limitations on suffrage; should there be popular referendums for laws?.

Principles of Child Development. unabr. ed. Hosted by Ruth Strang. 1 cass. (Famous Authorities Talk about Children Ser.). 12.95 (C29128) J Norton Pubs.

Principles of Conscience: Romans 14:1-12. Ed Young. 1984. 4.95 (978-0-7417-1401-5(9), 401) Win Walk.

Principles of Disability & Workers' Compensation Case Management. Featuring Deborah V. DiBenedetto. 2001. 149.95 (978-0-9712831-3-8(3)) A B Haag.

Principles of Dreams. Soozi Holbeche. (978-0-7225-3838-8(3), HarperThor) HarpC GBR.

Principles of Efficient Thinking (CD Set) Barbara Branden. (ENG.). 2007. audio compact disk 89.50 (978-1-57970-486-5(7), Audio-For) J Norton Pubs.

Principles of Equine Osteosynthesis: Combination Book. L. R. Bramlage et al. Ed. by G. E. Fackelman et al. 2000. audio compact disk (978-3-13-116671-5(1)) G Thieme DEU.

Principles of Esoteric Astrology. Margie Herskovitz. 1 cass. 8.95 (160) Am Fed Astrologers.
Soul growth, purpose of life, karma, and age of soul.

Principles of Feng Shui. Simon Brown. 2001. (978-0-7225-3835-7(9), HarperThor) HarpC GBR.

Principles of Finance: An Interactive Approach. Steve Wyatt. (FB - Introduction to Finance Ser.). 1998. audio compact disk 43.95 (978-0-538-84377-5(2)) Pub: South-West. Dist(s): CENGAGE Learn

Principles of Food Science. Janet D. Ward. (gr. 9-13). tchr. ed. 188.00 (978-1-56637-795-9(1)) Goodheart.

Principles of Grammar. Leonard Peikoff. Read by Leonard Peikoff. 16 cass. 1993. 149.00 (978-1-56114-050-3(3), LP05D) Second Renaissance.
Discover how the normally dry subject of grammar can be transformed into an engrossing epistemological field of study. Learn why a mastery of the principles of grammar is essential for anyone who values precision in thinking & writing. Includes: Basic Grammatical Concepts; Subordination & Coordination; Verbs & Pronouns; Punctuation; Choosing the Right Word.

Principles of Healing. Kriyananda, pseud. 1 cass. (Running Time: 2 hrs.). 14.95 (ST-17) Crystal Clarity.
Includes: healing as an energy process; how attitudes, ego, prayer, colors, metals & crystals affect healing energy; the importance of willingness; how to counsel people.

Principles of Healing, Pts. 1 & 2. Marianne Williamson. Read by Marianne Williamson. 1 cass. (Running Time: 90 mins.). (Lectures on a Course in Miracles). 1999. 10.00 (978-1-56170-255-8(2), M758) Hay House.

Principles of Holotropic Therapy. unabr. ed. Stanislav Grof. 1 cass. (Running Time: 90 min.). 1985. 11.00 (00803) Big Sur Tapes.

Principles of Manifestation: Praying for Changes. Marianne Williamson. Read by Marianne Williamson. 1 cass. (Running Time: 90 mins.). (Lectures on a Course in Miracles). 1999. 10.00 (978-1-56170-256-5(0), M759) Hay House.

Principles of Prayer. Benny Hinn. 5 cass. 1993. 30.00 Set. (978-1-881256-07-6(3)) Wrld Outreach Church.

Principles of Prayer: Incorrect Prayer. Alfred D. Harvey, Jr. 4 Cass. 2003. 20.00 (978-1-932508-08-6(2)) Doers Pub.

Principles of Prayer: The Name of Jesus in Prayer. Alfred D. Harvey, Jr. 6 Cass. 2003. 30.00 (978-1-932508-07-9(4)) Doers Pub.

Principles of Prayer Pt. 1: Overview of the Eight Types of Prayer. Alfred D. Harvey, Jr. 6 cass in album. (Running Time: 5 hrs. 30 mins.). 2003. 30.00 (978-1-932508-01-7(5)) Doers Pub.
Correct and incorrect ways to get your prayers answered.

Principles of Prayer Pt. 2: What Is Prayer? Alfred D. Harvey, Jr. 5 cass in album. (Running Time: 2 hrs. 35 mins.). 2003. 25.00 (978-1-932508-02-4(3)) Doers Pub.
Correct and incorrect ways to getting your prayers answered.

Principles of Prayer Pt. 3: The Will of God in Prayer/The Importance of the Word in Prayer. Alfred D. Harvey, Jr. 6 cass in album. (Running Time: 5 hrs. 30 mins.). 2003. 30.00 (978-1-932508-03-1(1)) Doers Pub.

Principles of Prayer Pt. 4: Prayer Must Be a Habit. Alfred D. Harvey, Jr. 1 cass in album. (Running Time: 55 mins.). 2003. 5.00 (978-1-932508-04-8(X)) Doers Pub.

Principles of Prayer Pt. 5: Learning to Pray (the Basics) Alfred D. Harvey, Jr. 2 cass in album. (Running Time: 1 hr. 50 mins.). 2003. 10.00 (978-1-932508-05-5(8)) Doers Pub.

Principles of Prayer Pt. 6: The Importance of Faith in Prayer. Alfred D. Harvey, Jr. 4 cass in album. (Running Time: 3 hrs. 40 mins.). 2003. 20.00 (978-1-932508-06-2(6)) Doers Pub.

Principles of Purpose. Myles Munroe. 8 cass. 1992. 42.00 Set. (978-1-56043-908-0(4)) Destiny Image Pubs.

Principles of Self-Counseling. Ginger Chalford. 1 cass. (Personal Growth "How to" Ser.). 1989. bk. 9.95 (978-1-56089-014-0(2)) Visionary FL.
Explains how to discover significant personal emotional patterns & choose an appropriate technique to release negative patterns while replacing them with positive, freer patterns that create more success & fulfillment.

Principles of Self-Healing. Ginger Chalford. 1 cass. (Personal Health Ser.). 1988. bk. 9.95 (978-1-56089-019-5(3)) Visionary FL.
Features an explanation of hidden emotional messages of various illnesses, how to find them, how to choose appropriate treatment; also explains how

healing works in general & gives healing techniques to aid recovery through visualizations.

Principles of Self Hypnosis: Pathways to the Unconscious. C. Alexander Simpkins & Annellen M. Simpkins. (Frontiers of Consciousness Ser.). 1991. reel tape 42.95 (978-0-8290-2465-4(4)) Irvington.

Principles of Spiritual Warfare. Rick Joyner. 1 cass. (Running Time: 90 mins.). (Combating Principalities Ser.: Vol. 1). 2000. 5.00 (RJ09-001) Morning NC.
"Principles of Spiritual Warfare" & "Putting on the Full Armor of God." These tapes highlight practical truths that lead to certain victory in spirtual warfare.

Principles of Transformation, Set. Ariel Kane & Shya Kane. Contrib. by Helene DeLillo. 2 cass. (Running Time: 2 hrs. 26 min.). (Being in the Moment Ser.). 1995. (978-1-888043-08-2(3)) ASK Prodns.
Live seminar investigating the fundamental principles that facilitate personal transformation.

Principles, Philosphy & Rules of Encounter. unabr. ed. Will Schutz. 2 cass. (Running Time: 3 hrs.). 1970. 16.00 Set. (04901) Big Sur Tapes.
Gives an historical overview of the encounter movement, the philosophy behind it, & the general guidelines for running encounter groups.

Principles to Successful Recovery. Cardwell C. Nuckols. Read by Cardwell C. Nuckols. Ed. by Dick Ulett & JoAnn Moore. 1 cass. (Running Time: 1 hr.). 1995. 10.95 (978-1-56168-006-1(0), A9407) GWC Inc.
An overview of working a good program with suggestions as to ways to keep centered in a program of recovery.

Principles with Promise. Don J. Black. 1 cass. 7.98 (978-1-55503-043-8(2), 060076) Covenant Comms.
On faith, the atonement & morality by this master storyteller.

Prindsessen Paa Aerten see Princess & the Pea

Printed Circuit Boards (PCB) Production Equipment in Germany: A Strategic Reference 2006. Compiled by Icon Group International, Inc. Staff. 2007. ring bd. 195.00 (978-0-497-35983-6(9)) Icon Grp.

***Printer's Devil.** 2010. audio compact disk (978-1-59171-235-0(1)) Falcon Picture.

Printer's Devil. unabr. ed. Paul Bajoria. Read by Katherine Kellgren. 8 CDs. (Running Time: 9 hrs 15 mins.). (J). 2006. audio compact disk 84.75 (978-1-4193-6623-9(8), C3485); 65.75 (978-1-4193-6618-5(1), 98234) Recorded Bks.
This entertaining novel is right at home alongside Charles Dickens' Oliver Twist and Leon Garfield's Smith. In Victorian London, 12-year-old orphan Mog Winter prints wanted posters about all the dangerous villains. When a brute named Cockburn escapes prison, the ink on the posters is barely dry before Mog gets caught up in the criminal underworld. Soon thieves, crooked schemers - even murderers - are hunting Mog, but he doesn't know why.

Printing & Publishing in Italy: A Strategic Reference 2006. Compiled by Icon Group International, Inc. Staff. 2007. ring bd. 195.00 (978-0-497-36043-6(8)) Icon Grp.

Prion Disease - A Bibliography & Dictionary for Physicians, Patients, & Genome Researchers. Compiled by Icon Group International, Inc. Staff. 2007. ring bd. 28.95 (978-0-497-11281-3(7)) Icon Grp.

Prior Bad Acts. abr. ed. Tami Hoag. Read by Erik Bergmann. (Running Time: 21600 sec.). (ENG.). 2007. audio compact disk 14.99 (978-0-7393-4160-5(X), Random AudioBks) Pub: Random Audio Pubg. Dist(s): Random

Prior Bad Acts. unabr. ed. Tami Hoag. Read by Holter Graham. 12 CDs. (Running Time: 15 hrs.). 2006. audio compact disk 81.60 (978-1-4159-2756-4(1)); 90.00 (978-1-4159-2755-7(3)) Books on Tape.
It was a crime so brutal, it changed the lives of even the most hardened homicide cops. The Haas family murders left a scar on the community nothing can erase, but everyone agrees that convicting the killer, Karl Dahl, is a start. Only Judge Carey Moore seems to be standing in the way. Her ruling that Dahl's prior criminal record is inadmissible raises a public outcry - and puts the judge in grave danger. When an unknown assailant attacks Judge Moore in a parking garage, two of Minneapolis's top cops are called upon to solve the crime and keep the judge from further harm. Detective Sam Kovac is as hard-boiled as they come, and his wisecracking partner, Nikki Liska, isn't far behind. Neither one wants to be on this case, but when Karl Dahl escapes from custody, everything changes, and a seemingly straightforward case cartwheels out of control. The stakes go even higher when the judge is kidnapped - snatched out of her own bed even as the police sit outside, watching her house. Now Kovac and Liska must navigate through a maze of suspects that includes the stepson of a murder victim, a husband with a secret life, and a rogue cop looking for revenge where the justice system failed.

Prior Bad Acts. unabr. ed. Tami Hoag. Read by Holter Graham. 12 CDs. (Running Time: 41400 sec.). (ENG.). 2006. audio compact disk 44.95 (978-0-553-50285-5(9)) Pub: Random Audio Pubg. Dist(s): Random

Prioridad de la Iglesia: National Association of Evangelicals, 47th Annual Convention, Columbus, Ohio, March 7-9, 1989. Jose A. Reyes. 1 cass. (Workshops Ser.: No. 11-Wednesd). 1989. 4.25 ea. 1-8 tapes.; 4.00 ea. 9 tapes or more. Nat Assn Evan.

Priorities for Prosperity: Joshua 1:1-18. Ed Young. 1985. 4.95 (978-0-7417-1447-3(7), 447) Win Walk.

Priory School see Return of Sherlock Holmes

Priory School: A Sherlock Holmes Adventure. (ENG.). 2007. (978-1-60339-065-1(0)); cd-rom & audio compact disk (978-1-60339-066-8(9)) Listenr Digest.

Prisionera. unabr. ed. Proust Marcel. Read by Santiago Munevar. (SPA.). 2007. audio compact disk 17.00 (978-958-8318-19-6(X)) Pub: Yoyo Music COL. Dist(s): YoYoMusic

Prisionero de Zenda. abr. ed. Anthony Hope-Hawkins. 3 CDs. (SPA.). 2002. audio compact disk 17.00 (978-958-8161-12-9(6)) YoYoMusic.

***Prism.** unabr. ed. Faye Kellerman. Read by Jenna Lamia. Illus. by Aliza Kellerman. (ENG.). 2009. (978-0-06-190243-7(8)); (978-0-06-190242-0(X)) HarperCollins Pubs.

Prism. unabr. ed. Faye Kellerman. Read by Jenna Lamia. Illus. by Aliza Kellerman. 5 CDs. (Running Time: 6 hrs.). (J). (gr. 7 up). 2009. audio compact disk 27.99 (978-0-06-176102-7(8), HarperChildAud) HarperCollins Pubs.

Prism: The Choral Artistry of Gloriae Dei Cantores. Conducted by Elizabeth C. Patterson. 2003. audio compact disk 12.99 (978-1-55725-350-7(1), GDC109) Paraclete MA.

Prism for Use with Understanding Psychology & Essentials of Understanding Psychology. 5th ed. Robert S. Feldman. 1 CD. (Running Time: 1 hr.). 1998. stu. ed. 25.00 (978-0-07-229774-4(3), Mc-H Human Soc) Pub: McGrw-H Hghr Educ. Dist(s): McGraw

Prism Lecture. Robert A. Wilson. 1 cass. (Running Time: 1 hr. 25 min.). 1982. 11.00 (05501) Big Sur Tapes.
Futurist...libertarian...satirist...former Playboy editor, author of "The Widow's Son" & "The Illuminati" series.

Prisms. Ed. by Robert A. Monroe. 1 cass. (Running Time: 30 min.). (Meta Music Artist Ser.). 1992. 14.95 (978-1-56102-245-8(4)) Inter Indus.
An experience of color through soum - a sparkling acoustic spectrum.

Prison Bars Do Not a Prison Make: Acts 12:1-25. Ed Young. 1998. 4.95 (978-0-7417-2170-9(8), A1170) Win Walk.

Prison Diary. unabr. ed. Jeffrey Archer. Read by Martin Jarvis. 7 CDs. (Running Time: 10 hrs. 30 min.). 2004. audio compact disk 45.00 (978-1-59007-416-9(5)) Pub: New Millenn Enter. Dist(s): PerseuPGW

Prison Diary. unabr. abr. ed. Jeffrey Archer. Read by Martin Jarvis. 6 cass. (Running Time: 10 hrs. 30 min.). 2004. 32.95 (978-1-59007-415-2(7)) Pub: New Millenn Enter. Dist(s): PerseuPGW

Prison Door Is Open. Kenneth W. Hagin, Jr. 1 cass. 4.95 (SJ03) Faith Lib Pubns.

Prison Industrial Complex. Angela Y. Davis. (ENG.). 1999. audio compact disk 14.98 (978-1-902593-22-7(7)) Pub: AK Pr GBR. Dist(s): Consort Bk Sales

Prison Meditations of Father Alfred Delp. 8 cass. 32.95 (902) Ignatius Pr.
Stirring reflections on life's meaning as he awaits his execution by the Nazis.

Prison of Personality. Swami Amar Jyoti. 1 cass. 1983. 9.95 (J-44) Truth Consciousness.
Choosing between our personality & freedom of the soul. Letting go the habits of unconsciousness. Results of spiritual & of worldy values.

Prison of Shaking Truth. 2004. 20.00 (978-1-57855-603-8(1)) T D Jakes.

Prison to Praise. 3 cass. 9.95 Incl. album. (978-0-943026-15-2(6), A1) Carothers.

Prison Work: A Tale of Thirty Years in the California Department of Corrections. William Richard Wilkinson et al. (History of Crime & Criminal Justice Ser.). 2005. audio compact disk 9.95 (978-0-8142-9079-8(5)) Pub: Ohio St U Pr. Dist(s): Chicago Distribution Ctr

Prisoner. Short Stories. Tom McAfee. Read by Tom McAfee. 1 cass. (Running Time: 55 min.). Incl. Merry Month of May. (1111); This is My Living Room. (1111); 12.95 (978-1-55644-019-9(7), 1111) Am Audio Prose.

Prisoner: Released. unabr. ed. Brian Brookheart. 2 cass. 1997. pap. bk. 10.00 Set. B Brookheart.
The dramatic story of a young man's journey through poverty, juvenile delinquency, prison life & God's restoration.

***Prisoner in the Third Cell.** unabr. ed. Gene Edwards. (ENG.). 2011. 8.98 (978-1-61045-111-6(2), Hovel Audio); audio compact disk 12.98 (978-1-61045-110-9(4), Hovel Audio) christianaud.

Prisoner of Birth. abr. ed. Jeffrey Archer. Read by Roger Allam. (Running Time: 6 hrs. 0 mins. 0 sec.). 2008. audio compact disk 29.95 (978-1-4272-0305-2(9)) Pub: Macmill Audio. Dist(s): Macmillan

Prisoner of Birth. unabr. ed. Jeffrey Archer. Narrated by Roger Allam. 2 MP3-CDs. (Running Time: 16 hrs.). 2008. 69.95 (978-0-7927-5301-8(1)) AudioGO.

Prisoner of Birth. unabr. ed. Jeffrey Archer. Read by Roger Allam. 13 CDs. (Running Time: 16 hrs.). 2008. audio compact disk 112.95 (978-0-7927-5247-9(3)) AudioGO.
Danny Cartwright and Spencer Craig never should have met. One evening, Danny, an East End cockney who works as a garage mechanic, takes his fiancee up to the West End to celebrate their engagement. He crosses the path of Spencer Craig, a West End barrister posed to be the youngest Queen's Counsel of his generation. A few hours later, Danny is arrested for murder and later is sentenced to twenty-two years in prison, thanks to irrefutable testimony from Spencer, the prosecution's main witness. Danny spends the next few years in a high-security prison while Spencer Craig's career as a lawyer goes straight up. All the while Danny plans to escape and wreak his revenge. This suspenseful novel takes the listener through so many twists and turns that no one will guess the ending.

Prisoner of Birth. unabr. ed. Jeffrey Archer. Narrated by Roger Allam. 13 CDs. (Running Time: 16 hrs. 30 mins. 0 sec.). 2008. audio compact disk 44.95 (978-1-4272-0283-3(4)) Pub: Macmill Audio. Dist(s): Macmillan

Prisoner of Chillon see Treasury of George Gordon, Lord Byron

***Prisoner of Conscience.** Zondervan. (ENG.). 2010. 22.99 (978-0-310-39553-9(4)) Zondervan.

Prisoner of Guantanamo. Dan Fesperman. Read by David Colacci. (Playaway Adult Fiction Ser.). 2008. 79.99 (978-1-60640-916-9(6)) Find a World.

Prisoner of Guantanamo. abr. ed. Dan Fesperman. Read by David Colacci. (Running Time: 21600 sec.). 2007. audio compact disk 14.99 (978-1-4233-1781-4(5), 9781423317814, BCD Value Price) Brilliance Audio.

Prisoner of Guantánamo. unabr. ed. Dan Fesperman. Read by David Colacci. (Running Time: 12 hrs.). 2006. 39.25 (978-1-4233-1779-1(3), 9781423317791, BADLE); 24.95 (978-1-4233-1778-4(5), 9781423317784, BAD) Brilliance Audio.

Prisoner of Guantanamo. unabr. ed. Dan Fesperman. Read by David Colacci. (Running Time: 43200 sec.). 2006. 87.25 (978-1-4233-1773-9(4), 9781423317739, BrilAudUnabridg); audio compact disk 107.25 (978-1-4233-1775-3(0), 9781423317753, BriAudCD Unabrid); audio compact disk 39.25 (978-1-4233-1777-7(7), 9781423317777, Brinc Audio MP3 Lib); audio compact disk 24.95 (978-1-4233-1776-0(9), 9781423317760, Brilliance MP3); audio compact disk 38.95 (978-1-4233-1774-6(2), 9781423317746, Bril Audio CD Unabri) Brilliance Audio.
Please enter a Synopsis.

Prisoner of Second Avenue. unabr. ed. Neil Simon. Perf. by Richard Dreyfuss & Marsha Mason. 2 CDs. (Running Time: 1 hr. 38 mins.). (L. A. Theatre Works). 2000. audio compact disk 25.95 (978-1-58081-182-8(5), CDTPT139) Pub: L A Theatre. Dist(s): NetLibrary CO

Prisoner of Second Avenue. unabr. ed. Neil Simon. Read by Richard Dreyfuss & Marsha Mason. 2 cass. (Running Time: 1 hr. 38 mins.). Dramatization. 2000. 23.95 (978-1-58081-162-0(0), TPT139) L A Theatre.

Prisoner of the Daleks. unabr. ed. Trevor Baxendale. Narrated by Nicholas Briggs. (Running Time: 6 hrs. 0 mins. 0 sec.). (Doctor Who Ser.). (ENG.). 2010. audio compact disk 39.95 (978-1-60283-822-2(4)) Pub: AudioGO. Dist(s): Perseus Dist

Prisoner of the State: The Secret Journal of Premier Zhao Ziyang. unabr. ed. Bao Pu et al. Narrated by Norman Dietz. 2 MP3-CDs. (Running Time: 13 hrs. 0 mins. 0 sec.). (ENG.). 2009. 24.99 (978-1-4001-6336-6(6)); audio compact disk 37.99 (978-1-4001-1336-1(9)); audio compact disk 75.99 (978-1-4001-4336-8(5)) Pub: Tantor Media. Dist(s): IngramPubServ

Prisoner of the Vatican. David I. Kertzer. Read by Alan Sklar. (Playaway Adult Nonfiction Ser.). 2008. 59.99 (978-1-60640-562-8(4)) Find a World.

Prisoner of the Vatican: The Popes' Secret Plot to Capture Rome from the New Italian State. unabr. ed. David I. Kertzer & David Kertzer. Narrated by Alan Sklar. (Running Time: 14 hrs. 0 mins. 0 sec.). (ENG.). 2004. audio compact disk 22.99 (978-1-4001-5142-4(2)) Pub: Tantor Media. Dist(s): IngramPubServ

Prisoner of the Vatican: The Popes' Secret Plot to Capture Rome from the New Italian State. unabr. ed. David I. Kertzer & David Kertzer. Read by Alan Sklar. (Running Time: 14 hrs. 0 mins. 0 sec.). (ENG.). 2004. audio compact disk 75.99 (978-1-4001-3142-6(1)) Pub: Tantor Media. Dist(s): IngramPubServ

Prisoner of Vatican. unabr. ed. David Kertzer. Narrated by Alan Sklar. 6 CDs. (Running Time: 14 hrs. 0 mins. 0 sec.). (ENG.). 2004. audio compact disk 37.99 (978-1-4001-0142-9(5)) Pub: Tantor Media. Dist(s): IngramPubServ

Prisoner of Zenda. Perf. by Ronald Colman. (DD-8170) Natl Recrd Co.

Prisoner of Zenda. Anthony Hope-Hawkins. Read by Alfred von Lecteur. 2009. 27.95 (978-1-60112-992-5(0)) Babblebooks.

Prisoner of Zenda. Anthony Hope-Hawkins. Read by Santiago Munévar. (Running Time: 3 hrs.). 2002. 16.95 (978-1-60083-225-3(3), Audiofy Corp) Iofy Corp.

Prisoner of Zenda. Anthony Hope-Hawkins. Read by Jim Roberts. 5 cass. (Running Time: 5 hrs. 30 min.). 1989. 35.00 incl. album. (C-13) Jimcin Record.
Swashbuckling adventure story.

Prisoner of Zenda. unabr. ed. Anthony Hope-Hawkins. Read by Bernard Mayes. 5 cass. (Running Time: 7 hrs. 30 min.). 1997. 39.95 (978-0-7861-1049-0(X), 1821) Blckstn Audio.
Rudolf Rassendyll ponders his life's purpose. Promising relatives he'll collect material for a book, he sets out for the tiny kingdom of Ruritania. He discovers he bears a resemblance to the king. Adventures ensue when he decides to impersonate the king to defeat a plot to dethrone him.

Prisoner of Zenda. unabr. ed. Anthony Hope-Hawkins. Read by Jack Sondericker. 4 cass. (Running Time: 5 hrs. 30 min.). 1989. 26.95 (978-1-55686-298-4(9), 298) Books in Motion.
Rudolf Rassendyll is the spitting image of Rudolf III of Ruritania. When he goes to see his famous twin crowned, he becomes involved in a fantastic plot to steal the throne through an amazing impersonation of the king.

Prisoner of Zenda. unabr. ed. Anthony Hope-Hawkins & Bernard Mayes. (Running Time: 6.5 hrs. NaN mins.). 2008. 29.95 (978-1-4332-5396-6(8)); audio compact disk 60.00 (978-1-4332-5395-9(X)) Blckstn Audio.

Prisoner of Zenda. unabr. collector's ed. Anthony Hope-Hawkins. Read by Jim Roberts. 6 cass. (Running Time: 6 hrs.). (J). 1982. 36.00 (978-0-7366-3847-0(4), 9013) Books on Tape.
The hero, Rudolf Rassendyll, an indolent young Englishman, decides to visit the kingdom of Ruritania to witness the coronation of its new king. He discovers that crown prince is nearly his exact double. On coronation day, the king is taken prisoner by his evil brother, Ruppert. Rassendyll is suddenly compelled to impersonate the monarch.

Prisoners. abr. ed. Matthew S. Hart. Read by Charlton Griffin. Abr. by Odin Westgaard. 2 vols. No. 9. 2004. (978-1-58807-746-2(2)) Am Pubng Inc.

Prisoners. abr. ed. Matthew S. Hart. Read by Charlton Griffin. Abr. by Odin Westgaard. 2 vols. No. 9. 2004. 18.00 (978-1-58807-251-1(7)) Am Pubng Inc.

Prisoner's Base. unabr. ed. Rex Stout. Read by Michael Pritchard. 6 cass. (Running Time: 6 hrs. 30 min.). (Nero Wolfe Ser.). 2001. 29.95 (978-1-57270-191-5(9), N61191u) Pub: Audio Partners. Dist(s): PerseuPGW

Prisoner's Base. unabr. ed. Rex Stout. Narrated by Michael Prichard. (Nero Wolfe Ser.). (ENG.). 2008. audio compact disk 29.95 (978-1-60283-426-2(1)) Pub: AudioGO. Dist(s): Perseus Dist

Prisoner's Base. unabr. collector's ed. Rex Stout. Read by Michael Prichard. 7 cass. (Running Time: 7 hrs.). (Nero Wolfe Ser.). 1995. 56.00 (978-0-7366-3137-2(2), 3812) Books on Tape.
Nero Wolfe sorts through dirty laundry to find killer of towel company heiress.

Prisoners of Hell. unabr. ed. John S. Jones. Read by Gene Engene. 6 cass. (Running Time: 6 hrs.). Dramatization. 1991. 39.95 (978-1-55686-365-3(9), 365) Books in Motion.
The author recounts, in gripping & moving prose, his own W.W.II experiences, from his captures at Corregidor to his release four years later.

Prisoners of Honor: The Dreyfus Affair. unabr. collector's ed. David Levering Lewis. Read by Alexander Adams. 8 cass. (Running Time: 12 hrs.). 1996. 64.00 (978-0-7366-3424-3(X), 4069) Books on Tape.
The Dreyfus Affair, the cause celebre of the late Nineteenth Century, led to a titanic clash that divided France, embroiled all of Europe & skewered Captain Alfred Dreyfus, a promising Jewish army officer.

Prisoners of Hope. abr. ed. Dayna Curry et al. 3 CDs. (Running Time: 3 hrs.). 2004. audio compact disk 19.99 (978-1-58926-073-3(2), D52L-010D) Oasis Audio.
Two ordinary young women left the comforts of the United States to serve God by helping the poor in Afghanistan. They soon found themselves in the midst of an international war on terrorism;and in a Taliban prison. In Prisoners of Hope, Dayna and Heather describe their sudden arrest, captivity and dramatic rescue. They also discuss their work with the destitute women and children of Afghanistan, whom they grew to love.

Prisoners of Our Own Thoughts. Instructed by Manly P. Hall. 8.95 (978-0-89314-221-6(2), C8105311) Philos Res.

Prisoners of Our Thoughts: Viktor Frankl's Principles at Work. unabr. ed. Alex Pattakos. (Running Time: 4 hrs. 30 mins.). (ENG.). 2008. 24.98 (978-1-59659-190-5(0), GildAudio) Pub: Gildan Media. Dist(s): HachBkGrp

Prisoners of Our Thoughts: Viktor Frankl's Principles for Discovering Meaning in Life & Work. unabr. ed. Alex Pattakos. Read by Alex Pattakos. 6 CDs. (Running Time: 4 hrs. 30 mins.). (ENG.). 2008. audio compact disk 29.98 (978-1-59659-169-1(2), GildAudio) Pub: Gildan Media. Dist(s): HachBkGrp

Prisoners of Santo Tomas. unabr. collector's ed. Celia Lucas. Read by Wanda McCaddon. 7 cass. (Running Time: 10 hrs. 30 min.). 1983. 56.00 (978-0-7366-0690-5(4), 1650) Books on Tape.
Among the casualties of war in the Pacific were thousands of American & British civilians who fell into the Japanese net. Their internment was not benign: by the war's end, some had been shot, many had died from starvation & most were weak & badly undernourished. Two who survived were a courageous English woman, Isla Corfield & her teenage daughter Gill. Through 3 years of privation & despair, Isla kept a diary, recorded secretly in notebooks which she hid. These notebooks give a first-hand account of what it was like to live in the nightmare world of internment.

Prisoners of the Mahdi. unabr. ed. Byron Farwell. Read by Bill Kelsey. 10 cass. (Running Time: 15 hrs.). 1994. 80.00 (978-0-7366-2889-1(4), 3589) Books on Tape.
When Mohammed Ahmed captured Khartoum, three Europeans suffered a long & terrible captivity. Has anything changed?.

Prisoners of War: A Story of Four American Soldiers. Interview. Prod. by Erica Heilman & Gregory L. Sharrow. Engineer Scott Gillette. 1 CD. (Running Time: 58 mins). 2004. audio compact disk 14.95 (978-0-916718-28-2(X)) VT Folklife Ctr.

Prisonniere see Stolen Lives: Twenty Years in a Desert Jail

Prisonniere, Pt. 1, set. Marcel Proust. Read by Andre Dussollier. 4 cass. (FRE.). 1995. 39.95 (1776-TH) Olivia & Hill.
Published a year after Proust's death, this is the first of three texts which conclude "A la Recherche du temps perdu" (the other two being "Albertine disparue" & "Le Temps retrouve").

Prisonniere, Pt. 2. Marcel Proust. Read by Andre Dussollier. 4 cass. (FRE.). 1994. 39.95 Set. (1777-TH) Olivia & Hill.
Published a year after Proust's death, La Prisonniere is the first of three texts which conclude A la Recherche du temps perdu (the other two being Albertine disparue, & Le Temps retrouve).

Prisonniere, Pts. 1-2, set. Marcel Proust. Read by Andre Dussollier. 8 cass. (FRE.). 1995. 69.95 (1776/7) Olivia & Hill.
Published a year after Proust's death, this is the first of three texts which conclude "A la Recherche du temps perdu" (the other two being "Albertine disparue" & "Le Temps retrouve").

Prisons on Fire: George Jackson, Attica, & Black Liberation. Anita Johnson et al. 1 CD. (Running Time: 1 hr. 30 mins.). (AK Press Audio Ser.). (ENG.). 2002. audio compact disk 14.98 (978-1-902593-52-4(9)) Pub: AK Pr GBR. Dist(s): Consort Bk Sales

Prisons We Choose to Live Inside. Doris Lessing. 5 CDs. (Running Time: 18000 sec.). (Massey Lectures). 2007. audio compact disk 39.95 (978-0-660-19670-1(0), CBC Audio) Pub: Canadian Broadcasting CAN. Dist(s): Georgetown Term
In these five Massey lectures, Doris Lessing addresses the question of personal freedom and individual responsibility in a world increasingly prone to political rhetoric, mass emotions and inherited structures of unquestionable belief. In her remarkable subtle yet forthright style, Lessing attacks inhumanity and ignorance, urging the individual to rise above the constraints of our society, to build a better world.

Pritikin Weight Loss Breakthrough: Five Easy Steps to Outsmart Your Fat Instinct. abr. ed. Robert Pritikin. Read by Russ Wheeler. 2 cass. 1998. 17.95 set. (978-1-55935-274-1(4)) Soundelux.
Four simple principles that can be used to defeat the fat instinct & fifteen practical tips that will help implement the Pritikin Program on a daily basis.

Privacy in the Workplace: Unreasonable Intrusion or Legitimate Interest? 1 cass. (Running Time: 50 min.). (CLE TV: The Lawyers' Video Magazine Ser.). 1992. 95.00 incl. study guide. (Y161) Am Law Inst.
Covers privacy issues in the workplace including searches, psychological testing, medical exams & records, & surveillance.

Privacy or Liberty: Which is Your Right? Leonard Peikoff. 1998. 12.95 (LPXXC83) Second Renaissance.

Privacy Survival Kit. 2001. ring bd. 99.00 (978-1-932214-06-2(2)) Privacy Council Inc.

Private. unabr. ed. Kate Brian, pseud. Narrated by Cassandra Campbell. (Running Time: 6 hrs. 0 mins. 0 sec.). (Private Ser.: No. 1). (ENG.). (J). (gr. 9-12). 2009. audio compact disk 49.99 (978-1-4001-4231-6(8)) Pub: Tantor Media. Dist(s): IngramPubServ

Private. unabr. ed. Kate Brian, pseud. Narrated by Cassandra Campbell. (Running Time: 6 hrs. 0 mins. 0 sec.). (Private Ser.: No. 1). (ENG.). (YA). (gr. 9-12). 2009. 19.99 (978-1-4001-6231-4(9)); audio compact disk 24.99 (978-1-4001-1231-9(1)) Pub: Tantor Media. Dist(s): IngramPubServ

Private. unabr. ed. James Patterson & Maxine Paetro. Read by Peter Hermann. (Running Time: 7 hrs.). (ENG.). 2010. 24.98 (978-1-60788-449-1(6)); audio compact disk 34.98 (978-1-60788-448-4(8)) Pub: Hachet Audio. Dist(s): HachBkGrp

***Private.** unabr. ed. James Patterson & Maxine Paetro. Read by Peter Hermann. 6 CDs. (Running Time: 7 hrs.). (ENG.). 2011. audio compact disk 19.98 (978-1-60788-690-7(1)) Pub: Hachet Audio. Dist(s): HachBkGrp

Private Eye: Golden Satiricals 1. 2 cass. 1998. 15.00 Set. (978-1-86117-165-8(X)) Ulvrscrft Audio.
These recordings were originally issued in the 60's & 70's & featured the classic sketches & songs that such an incredible array of talent could create.

Private Eye: Golden Satiricals 2. abr. ed. 2 cass. 1998. 15.00 Set. Ulvrscrft Audio.
Includes the infamous 1971 Private Eye Album-"Ho, Ho Very Satirical" that was banned at the time because of its strong political content.

Private Eyes. Jonathan Kellerman. Read by John Rubinstein. 2 cass. (Alex Delaware Ser.: No. 6). 15.99 Set. RandomHse Pub.

Private Eyes. abr. ed. Jonathan Kellerman. Read by John Rubinstein. (Running Time: 3 hrs.). (Alex Delaware Ser.: No. 6). (ENG.). 2004. audio compact disk 14.99 (978-0-7393-1223-0(5), Random AudioBks) Pub: Random Audio Pubg. Dist(s): Random

Private Eyes. unabr. ed. Jonathan Kellerman. Read by Alexander Adams. 11 cass. (Running Time: 16 hrs. 30 min.). (Alex Delaware Ser.: No. 6). 1993. 88.00 (978-0-7366-2351-3(5), 3128) Books on Tape.
The voice belongs to a woman, but Alex Delaware remembers a little girl. It's been 11 years since Melissa Dickinson, then a fearful seven-year-old, dialed a hospital help line & spoke to psychologist Delaware. Now she's a beautiful young heiress whose future should be filled with hope. Instead her worst childhood fear has returned. Twenty years ago Melissa's mother was left scarred & crippled by an attacker who is now free & on the streets of L.A. Melissa calls to tell Delaware that her mother has vanished. Can he help find her & protect Melissa.

Private Eyes. unabr. ed. Contrib. by Susan Musleh. 1 cass. (Running Time: 3 min.). (Susan's Romantic Adventures - A Secret Admirer's Kit Ser.). (C). 1998. 24.95 (978-1-893494-02-2(0), PE-300) Susans Romantic Adv.

Private Eye's Blue Record. abr. ed. 2 cass. 1998. 15.00 Set. (978-1-86117-173-3(0)) Ulvrscrft Audio.
These recordings were originally issued in the 60's & 70's & feature the classic songs & sketches that such an incredible array of talent could create.

Private Files of Rex Saunders: Concerning Gambling & Counterfeit Ring. 1 cass. (Running Time: 1 hr.). 2001. 6.98 (1695) Radio Spirits.

Private Healing Island. Steven Gurgevich. (ENG.). 2005. audio compact disk 19.95 (978-1-932170-26-9(X), HWH) Tranceformation.

Private History of a Campaign That Failed: A Performance. (ENG.). 2007. (978-1-60339-027-9(8)); cd-rom & audio compact disk (978-1-60339-028-6(6)) Listenr Digest.

Private History of a Campaign that Failed, Unabridged: Narrated by Richard Henzel. Narrated by Richard Henzel. 2009. audio compact disk 9.99 (978-0-9747237-6-1(2)) R Henzel.

Private Inquiry. unabr. ed. Jessica Mann. Read by Anita Wright. 6 cass. (Running Time: 9 hrs.). (Isis Ser.). (J). 2004. 54.95 (978-0-7531-0197-1(1), 970807) Pub: ISIS Lrg Prnt GBR. Dist(s): Ulverscroft US
Barbara's young son Toby, is cared for by his retired father, who has recently made a friend of Clarissa Trelawney, an attractive but mysterious newcomer to town. Clarissa's murder sends shock waves through the community. Could Barbara Pomeroy have killed her in a fit of jealous rage?.

Private Justice. Terri Blackstock. Narrated by John McDonough. 9 cass. (Running Time: 12 hrs.). (Newpointe 911 Ser.: Vol. 1). 81.00 (978-1-4025-1172-1(8)) Recorded Bks.

***Private Justice.** Terri Blackstock. (Running Time: 11 hrs. 4 mins. 0 sec.). (Newpointe 911 Ser.). (ENG.). 2009. 14.99 (978-0-310-30490-6(3)) Zondervan.

Private Justice. unabr. ed. Terri Blackstock. Read by Juanita Parker. 8 cass. (Running Time: 11 hrs.). (Newpointe 911 Ser.: Bk. 1). 2001. 49.95 (978-1-55686-971-6(1)) Books in Motion.
A dark shadow of fear has fallen over Newpointe, LA. First one then another of the town's firemen's wives have been murdered, and a third barely escaped. A serial killer is stalking this sleepy community.

Private Lessons with Julie Goodnight¿CD. Julie Goodnight. (ENG.). 2002. 24.99 (978-0-9720513-1-6(7)) Goodnght Trning Stables.

***Private Life.** unabr. ed. Jane Smiley. Narrated by Kate Reading. 11 CDs. (Running Time: 13 hrs. 45 mins.). 2010. audio compact disk 40.00 (978-0-307-71533-3(7), BksonTape) Pub: Random Audio Pubg. Dist(s): Random

Private Life. unabr. ed. Jane Smiley. Read by Kate Reading. 11 CDs. (Running Time: 13 hrs. 30 mins.). (ENG.). 2010. audio compact disk 40.00 (978-0-307-71531-9(0), Random AudioBks) Pub: Random Audio Pubg. Dist(s): Random

Private Life of Chairman Mao, Pt. 1. unabr. ed. Li. Read by Geoffrey Howard. 11 cass. (Running Time: 16 hrs. 30 mins.). 1996. 88.00 (4122-A) Books on Tape.

Private Life of Chairman Mao, Pt. 2. unabr. ed. Li Zhisui. Read by Geoffrey Howard. 7 cass. (Running Time: 10 hrs. 30 mins.). 1999. 56.00 (4122-B) Books on Tape.
During his lifetime, Mao was idolized by millions of his countrymen more as a symbol than a person & today, 20-plus years after his death, still is. But Dr. Li, Mao's personal physician, saw him close up & knows how little he cared for those who trusted & revered him.

Private Life of Chairman Mao, Pt. A&B. unabr. ed. Li. Read by Geoffrey Howard. 11 cass. (Running Time: 16 hrs. 30 mins.). 1996. 144.00 (978-0-7366-3480-9(0), 4122A/B) Books on Tape.

Private Life of the Cat Who... Tales of Koko & Yum Yum from the Journal of James Mackintosh Qwilleran. Lilian Jackson Braun. Narrated by George Guidall. (Running Time: 1 hr. 15 mins.). (Cat Who... Ser.). 2004. 9.99 (978-1-4025-6340-9(X), 03764) Recorded Bks.

Private Lives. unabr. ed. Noel Coward. Perf. by Rosalind Ayres et al. 1 cass. (Running Time: 1 hr. 13 min.). 1995. 19.95 (978-1-58081-031-9(4), TPT47) L A Theatre.
The French Riviera, where the lights of a yacht are reflected in the water & in the eyes of four lovers, hilariously mismatched. Wit, romance, desire & bittersweet truth.

Private Lives: An Intimate Comedy. Noel Coward. 2 CDs. (Running Time: 4380 sec.). 2005. audio compact disk 25.95 (978-1-58081-239-9(2), CDTPT47) Pub: L A Theatre. Dist(s): NetLibrary CO

Private Lives: An Intimate Comedy. Noel Coward. Contrib. by Rosalind Ayres & Ian Ogilvy. (Playaway Adult Fiction Ser.). (ENG.). 2009. 39.99 (978-1-60812-511-1(4)) Find a World.

***Private Lives: Classic Radio Theatre Series.** Noel Coward. Told to Paul Scofield & Patricia Routledge. (Running Time: 1 hr. 30 mins. 0 sec.). (ENG.). 2010. audio compact disk 24.95 (978-1-4084-2694-4(3)) Pub: AudioGO. Dist(s): Perseus Dist

Private Lives of Pippa Lee. unabr. ed. Rebecca Miller. (Running Time: 7.5 hrs. 0 mins.). 2008. cass. & cass. 29.95 (978-1-4332-4415-5(2)); audio compact disk 26.95 (978-1-4332-4416-2(0)) Blckstn Audio.

Private Lives of Pippa Lee. unabr. ed. Rebecca Miller. Read by Bernadette Dunne. 6 CDs. (Running Time: 7 hrs. 30 mins.). 2008. audio compact disk 60.00 (978-1-4332-4414-8(4)) Blckstn Audio.

Private Lives of Pippa Lee. unabr. ed. Rebecca Miller & Bernadette Dunne. (Running Time: 7.5 hrs. NaN mins.). 2008. 29.95 (978-1-4332-4417-9(9)); 54.95 (978-1-4332-4413-1(6)) Blckstn Audio.

Private Papers of Henry Ryecroft. George R. Gissing. Read by Anais 9000. 2009. 27.95 (978-1-60112-220-9(9)) Babblebooks.

Private Papers of Henry Ryecroft, Set. George R. Gissing. Narrated by Grover Gardner. 4 cass. (Running Time: 6 hrs.). 1988. 19.95 (978-1-55685-124-7(3)) Audio Bk Con.
Out of a life of poverty & turmoil, Gissing wrote this idyllic fantasy of comfort & good books amidst the English countryside.

Private Patient. unabr. ed. P. D. James. Read by Rosalyn Landor. 12 CDs. 2008. audio compact disk 110.00 (978-1-4159-5964-0(1), BksonTape) Pub: Random Audio Pubg. Dist(s): Random
When the notorious investigative journalist, Rhoda Gradwyn, books into Mr. Chandler-Powell's private clinic in Dorset for the removal of a disfiguring, long-standing facial scar, she has every prospect of a successful operation by a distinguished surgeon, a week's peaceful convalescence in one of Dorset's most beautiful manor houses and the beginning of a new life. She will never leave Cheverell Manor alive. When Adam Dalgliesh and his team are called in to investigate the murder - and a second death occurs - even more complicated problems than the question of innocence or guilt arise.

Private Patient. unabr. ed. P. D. James. Read by Rosalyn Landor. 12 CDs. (Running Time: 15 hrs.). (Adam Dalgliesh Mystery Ser.). (ENG.). 2008. audio compact disk 44.95 (978-0-7393-7691-1(8), Random AudioBks) Pub: Random Audio Pubg. Dist(s): Random

Private Peaceful. unabr. ed. Michael Morpurgo. Read by Jeff Woodman. 5 CDs. (Running Time: 5 hrs. 15 mins.). (YA). (gr. 7 up). 2005. audio compact disk 51.75 (978-1-4193-5614-8(3)); 39.75 (978-1-4193-2977-7(4), 97975) Recorded Bks.
When he was 15, Thomas Peaceful lied about his age and followed his older brother into the English army to fight in World War I. Now two years have passed, and Thomas? duty for the night is to stay awake and watch the battlefields. He will be shot if he falls asleep. As the night goes on, Thomas reflects on home, his family, his first love and the horrors of the war. And all the while, a shattering truth comes closer to the surface.

Private Pilot & Recreational Pilot FAA Written Exam Audio Review. Irvin N. Gleim. 2000. 60.00 (978-0-917539-81-7(8)) Gleim Pubns.

Private Placements: Current Developments in Private Financings. Moderated by Paul E. Kreutz et al. 7 cass. (Running Time: 9 hrs. 30 min.). 1988. 60.00 (T7-9163) PLI.
Discusses the interaction of state & federal regulations including Regulations D & state securities laws issuers' problems in the current regulatory atmosphere: the offering process; integration & disclosure issues.

Private Placements after Rule 144A. 3 cass. (Running Time: 3 hrs. 30 min.). 60.00 set three audiocass. plus 675-page course handbook. (T6-9170) PLI.

Private Placements & Other Private Financings. unabr. ed. Contrib. by Paul E. Kreutz et al. 4 cass. (Running Time: 5 hrs. 30 min.). 1988. pap. bk. 60.00 PLI.
This recording of PLI's October 1988 satellite program focuses on developments in private placements resulting from changing conditions in financial markets, innovative financial products & growth of state regulation & SEC regulatory action after Regulation D.

Private Pleasures. Lawrence Sanders. 2004. 10.95 (978-0-7435-4570-9(2)) Pub: S&S Audio. Dist(s): S and S Inc

Private Practices. abr. ed. Stephen White. Read by Dick Hill. (Running Time: 7 hrs.). (Dr. Alan Gregory Ser.). 2006. 24.95 (978-1-4233-0171-4(4), 9781423301714, BAD); audio compact disk 24.95 (978-1-4233-0169-1(2), 9781423301691, Brilliance MP3) Brilliance Audio.
Dr. Alan Gregory is a practicing psychologist with a few little problems to work through. He has an office filled with bloody corpses. He has a teenage patient who may be a sad victim or a savage killer. He has a beautiful estranged wife who wants him back in the worst way, and a lovely lover doing her best to keep him. He has a co- who wants him off the case, and an unknown enemy who wants him pe- -ntly out of action. To round out his many dilemmas, the list of suspects -s like a Who's Who of his posh Colorado community. And as a Rocky M- -tain winter wonderland is swept by a nightmare blizzard of evil, secret sins leave a trail of blood leading to their hiding place deep in the heart and mind of a monstrous murderer.

Private Practices. abr. ed. Stephen White. Read by Dick Hill. (Running Time: 7 hrs.). (Dr. Alan Gregory Ser.). 2008. audio compact disk 14.99 (978-1-4233-6230-2(6), 9781423362302, BCD Value Price) Brilliance Audio.

Private Practices. unabr. collector's ed. Stephen White. Read by Michael Kramer. 10 cass. (Running Time: 15 hrs.). (Dr. Alan Gregory Ser.). 1993. 80.00 (978-0-7366-2592-0(5), 3337) Books on Tape.
A madman pushes into psychologist Alan Gregory's office, his pistol against a young woman's head. He demands his wife, Claire. She's in the next office, in session with Gregory's partner, Diane Estevez. The cops save Diane, but not Claire or the hostage. Claire was to testify before a grand jury. Curiously, another witness in the same case dies, also in front of Gregory. Sam Purdy, a detective with the Boulder police, figures Gregory may be able to help with the case. But Gregory himself needs help. With his own life at risk, he & Diane ransack their files for clues. In this race for truth, life itself is the prize.

Private Revenge. Richard Woodman. 8 cass. (Running Time: 9 hrs. 30 mins.). (Nathaniel Drinkwater Ser.: Bk. 9). (J). 2005. 69.95 (978-1-84283-978-2(0)) Pub: ISIS Lrg Prnt GBR. Dist(s): Ulverscroft US

Private Revenge. Richard Woodman & Richard Woodman. 8 CDs. (Running Time: 9 hrs. 30 mins.). (Nathaniel Drinkwater Ser.: Bk. 9). (J). 2005. audio compact disk 79.95 (978-1-84559-014-7(7)) Pub: ISIS Lrg Prnt GBR. Dist(s): Ulverscroft US

Private Scandals. unabr. ed. Nora Roberts. Read by Julie Finneran. (Running Time: 16 hrs.). 2008. 39.25 (978-1-4233-7895-2(4), 9781423378952, BADLE); 39.25 (978-1-4233-7893-8(8), 9781423378938, Brinc Audio MP3 Lib); 24.95 (978-1-4233-7894-5(6), 9781423378945, BAD); 24.95 (978-1-4233-7892-1(X), 9781423378921, Brilliance MP3); audio compact disk 117.25 (978-1-4233-7891-4(1), 9781423378914, BriAudCD Unabrid); audio compact disk 34.95 (978-1-4233-7890-7(3), 9781423378907, Bril Audio CD Unabri) Brilliance Audio.

Private Scores. unabr. ed. Anne T. Wallach. Read by Ruth Stokesberry. 10 cass. (Running Time: 15 hrs.). 1988. 80.00 (978-0-7366-1275-3(0), 2184) Books on Tape.
Novel concerning a single mother whose daughter is victimized at a prestigious private school.

Private Sector. abr. ed. Brian Haig. Read by John Rubinstein & Michael Emerson. (ENG.). 2005. 14.98 (978-1-59483-343-4(5)) Pub: Hachet Audio. Dist(s): HachBkGrp

Private Undergraduate & Graduate Level Education in Poland: A Strategic Reference 2006. Compiled by Icon Group International, Inc. Staff. 2007. ring bd. 195.00 (978-0-497-82394-8(2)) Icon Grp.

Private View. collector's ed. Irene M. Selznick. Read by Anna Fields. 12 cass. (Running Time: 18 hrs.). 2000. 96.00 (978-0-7366-5635-1(9)) Books on Tape.
Irene Mayer came to Hollywood when she was ten. Her childhood was populated with legendary names as her father, Louis B., practically created the movie industry. This is her story: about being her father's daughter, her husband's wife, & finally, herself.

Private View. unabr. ed. Anita Brookner. Read by Judith Whale. 6 cass. (Running Time: 9 hrs.). (Isis Ser.). (J). 2004. 54.95 (978-1-85695-941-4(4), 950511) Pub: ISIS Lrg Prnt GBR. Dist(s): Ulverscroft US

Private World of Dreams. Instructed by Manly P. Hall. 8.95 (978-0-89314-222-3(0), C850519) Philos Res.

Privateersman. Richard Woodman. Read by Joe Dunlop. 8 cass. (Running Time: 10 hrs.). (William Kite Trilogy: Bk. 2). (J). 2004. 69.95 (978-1-84283-394-0(4)) Pub: ISIS Lrg Prnt GBR. Dist(s): Ulverscroft US

Privilege. unabr. ed. Kate Brian, pseud. Narrated by Justine Eyre. (Running Time: 8 hrs. 0 mins. 0 sec.). (Privilege Ser.: No. 1). (ENG.). (YA). (gr. 9-12). 2009. audio compact disk 29.99 (978-1-4001-1242-5(7)); audio compact disk 59.99 (978-1-4001-4242-2(3)); audio compact disk 19.99 (978-1-4001-6242-0(4)) Pub: Tantor Media. Dist(s): IngramPubServ

Privilege Beyond Compare. 1 cass. (Running Time: 30 min.). Incl. Privilege Beyond Compare: The Battle of Gethsemane - Yesterday & Today. 1985. (0289); 1985. (0289) Evang Sisterhood Mary.
Jesus' true disciples - one with Him in suffering & in glory; Jesus' victory in Gethsemane shows us the way to victory in dark times.

Privilege Beyond Compare: The Battle of Gethsemane - Yesterday & Today see Privilege Beyond Compare

Privilege of Suffering: 1 Peter 11-19. Ed Young. 1983. 4.95 (978-0-7417-1295-0(4), 295) Win Walk.

Privilege of Youth: A Teenager's Story of Longing for Acceptance & Friendship. unabr. ed. Dave Pelzer. Read by J. Charles. 5 cass. (Running Time: 7 hrs.). 2004. 29.95 (978-1-59355-228-2(9), 1593552289); 69.25 (978-1-59355-229-9(7), 1593552297); audio compact disk 29.95 (978-1-59355-230-5(0), 1593552300); audio compact disk 82.25 (978-1-59355-231-2(9), 1593552319) Brilliance Audio.
More than six million readers can attest to the heartbreak and courage of Dave Pelzer's story of growing up in an abusive home. His inspirational books have helped countless others triumph over hardship and misfortune. Now this former lost boy who defeated insurmountable odds to emerge whole and happy at last takes us on his incredible odyssey toward healing and forgiveness. In The Privilege of Youth, Pelzer supplies the missing chapter of his life: as a boy on the threshold of adulthood. With his usual sensitivity and insight, he recounts the relentless taunting he endured from bullies; but he also describes the joys of learning and the thrill of making his first real friends - some of whom he still shares close relationships with today. He writes about the simple pleasures of exploring a neighborhood he was just beginning to get to know while trying to forget the hell he had endured as a child. From high school to a world beyond the four walls that were his prison for so many years, The Privilege of Youth charts this crucial turning point in Dave Pelzer's life. This brave and compassionate memoir from the man who has journeyed far will inspire a whole new generation of readers.

Privilege of Youth: A Teenager's Story of Longing for Acceptance & Friendship. unabr. ed. Dave Pelzer. Read by J. Charles. (Running Time: 6 hrs.). 2004. 39.25 (978-1-59335-498-5(3), 1593354983, Brlnc Audio MP3 Lib) Brilliance Audio.

Privilege of Youth: A Teenager's Story of Longing for Acceptance & Friendship. unabr. ed. Dave Pelzer. Read by J. Charles. (Running Time: 6 hrs.). 2004. 39.25 (978-1-59710-604-7(6), 1597106046, BADLE); 24.95 (978-1-59710-605-4(4), 1597106054, BAD) Brilliance Audio.

Privilege of Youth: A Teenager's Story of Longing for Acceptance & Friendship. unabr. ed. Dave Pelzer. Read by J. Charles. (Running Time: 6 hrs.). 2004. 24.95 (978-1-59335-262-2(X), 159335262X) Soulmate Audio Bks.

Privileged Communications. Edwin Hoover. 1986. 10.80 (0601) Assn Prof Chaplains.

Privileged Conversation. unabr. ed. Evan Hunter. Read by Barrett Whitener. 6 cass. (Running Time: 9 hrs.). 1996. 48.00 (978-0-7366-3425-0(8), 4070) Books on Tape.

David Chapman, a New York psychiatrist who should know better, plays out his sexual fantasies with Kate Duggan, a Broadway dancer. But unknown to David, someone else fantasizes about Kate, someone who will kill to satisfy his dementia.

Privileged Conversation, Set. abr. ed. Evan Hunter. Read by Eric Goldner. 4 cass. (Running Time: 6 hrs.). 1996. 21.95 (978-1-55935-195-9(0), 693519) Soundelux.

Privileged Information. abr. ed. Stephen White. Read by Dick Hill. (Running Time: 6 hrs.). (Dr. Alan Gregory Ser.). 2006. 24.95 (978-1-4233-0175-2(7), 9781423301752, BAD); audio compact disk 24.95 (978-1-4233-0173-8(0), 9781423301738, Brilliance MP3) Brilliance Audio.

Alan Gregory is a clinical psychologist with a thriving practice in Boulder, Colorado. His life begins to unravel when one of his female patients is found in an apparent suicide and the local paper begins printing accusations from an unnamed source of sexual impropriety between the woman and Dr. Gregory. He launches a psychological and personal quest for the truth that rapidly intensifies when more of his patients die untimely deaths, and Gregory suspects not only that the deaths are related but that another one of his patients may be somehow involved. Lacking facts but roused by suspicion and troubled by seemingly random acts of terror around him, Gregory starts to fear for the safety of the people he loves. The question of the inviolability of confidential disclosures made to Gregory by his patients - privileged information - becomes crucial as the psychologist pursues an unsettling romance with Lauren Crowder, a lovely deputy district attorney investigating one of the deaths. Bound to silence, Gregory follows the psychological tracks of someone he fears may be a cunning and disturbed killer, while turning to his enigmatic but supportive partner, Diane Estevez, for counsel, and to his tart-tongued female urologist neighbor for support. The sinister, surprising drama unfolds against Boulder's Rocky Mountain backdrop, in the arresting natural beauty of Aspen, and in the midst of a baroque Halloween costume party in downtown Boulder. Finally, in a lonely mountain lodge enshrouded in menace, the story comes to its breathtaking climax.

Privileged Information. abr. ed. Stephen White. Read by Dick Hill. (Running Time: 6 hrs.). (Dr. Alan Gregory Ser.). 2008. audio compact disk 14.99 (978-1-4233-6229-6(2), 9781423362296, BCD Value Price) Brilliance Audio.

Privileged Information. unabr. collector's ed. Stephen White. Read by Michael Kramer. 9 cass. (Running Time: 13 hrs. 30 min.). (Dr. Alan Gregory Ser.). 1992. 72.00 (978-0-7366-2262-2(4), 3050) Books on Tape.

Psychologist Alan Gregory has great style & enjoys a thriving Rocky Mountain practice until his life begins to unravel. It happens this way: one of his patients apparently commits suicide & the local paper accuses Gregory of an improper sexual relationship with the deceased.

Prize. abr. ed. Julie Garwood. Read by Anne Flosnik. (Running Time: 6 hrs.). 2009. audio compact disk 19.99 (978-1-4418-1210-0(5), 9781441812100, BACD) Brilliance Audio.

Prize. abr. ed. Julie Garwood. Read by Anne Flosnik. (Running Time: 6 hrs.). 2010. audio compact disk 9.99 (978-1-4418-4801-7(0), 9781441848017, BCD Value Price) Brilliance Audio.

Prize. unabr. ed. Julie Garwood. Read by Anne Flosnik. (Running Time: 12 hrs.). 2009. 24.99 (978-1-4418-1206-3(7), 9781441812063, Brilliance MP3); 24.99 (978-1-4418-1208-7(3), 9781441812087, BAD); 39.97 (978-1-4418-1207-0(5), 9781441812070, Brlnc Audio MP3 Lib); 39.97 (978-1-4418-1209-4(1), 9781441812094, BADLE); audio compact disk 29.99 (978-1-4418-1201-8(6), 9781441812018, Bril Audio CD Unabri); audio compact disk 87.97 (978-1-4418-1205-6(9), 9781441812056, BriAudCD Unabrid) Brilliance Audio.

Prize: The Epic Quest for Oil, Money & Power. Daniel Yergin. Read by Grover Gardner. 1991. 120.00 (978-0-7366-2022-2(2)) Books on Tape.

Prize: The Epic Quest for Oil, Money & Power, Pt. 1. unabr. ed. Daniel Yergin. Read by Grover Gardner. 14 cass. (Running Time: 21 hrs.). 1991. 112.00 (978-0-7366-2021-5(4), 2837-A) Books on Tape.

Reveals how & why oil has become the largest industry in the world, a game of huge risks & monumental rewards. The personalities are fascinating & diverse - Dad Joiner, John D. Rockefeller, Winston Churchill, George Bush & Saddam Hussein. In a way the story of oil is the story of the 20th century.

Prize: The Epic Quest for Oil, Money & Power, Pt. 2. Daniel Yergin. Read by Grover Gardner. 15 cass. (Running Time: 22 hrs. 30 min.). 1991. 120.00 (2837-B) Books on Tape.

Prize: The Epic Quest for Oil Money & Power the Battery for World Mastery. abr. ed. Daniel Yergin. 2006. 9.95 (978-0-7435-6269-0(0)) Pub: S&S Audio. Dist(s): S and S Inc

Prize for Sister Catherine. Kathleen Rowntree. Narrated by Diana Bishop. 6 cass. (Running Time: 8 hrs.). 56.00 (978-1-84197-261-9(4)) Recorded Bks.

Prize for Sister Catherine. unabr. ed. Kathleen Rowntree. Narrated by Diana Bishop. 7 CDs. (Running Time: 8 hrs.). 2001. audio compact disk 69.00 (978-1-4025-1012-0(8), C1590) Recorded Bks.

The Prioress at Albion Priory is old and in poor health, and must name her successor. But her fruitless management has led to spiritual discontent and financial peril. There are two very different candidates to choose between. Sister Margaret is bold and bossy, stopping at nothing to get her own way, while Sister Catherine has a more innate spirituality that may benefit the group in the long run. Only sweeping reforms can save the convent from ruin.

Prize Murder. Nicholas Rhea. Read by Graham Padden. 7. 2007. 61.95 (978-1-84652-062-4(2)); audio compact disk 79.95 (978-1-84652-063-1(0)) Pub: ISIS Audio GBR. Dist(s): Ulverscroft US

Prize Winner of Defiance, Ohio: How My Mother Raised 10 Kids on 25 Words or Less. unabr. ed. Terry Ryan. Read by Carrington MacDuffie. 6 vols. (Running Time: 9 hrs.). 2001. 54.95 (978-0-7927-2510-7(7), CSL 399, Chivers Sound Lib) AudioGO.

Terry Ryan tells the miraculous story of how her mother kept the family afloat by writing jingles. Mom's winning ways defied the church, her alcoholic husband, and antiquated views of housewives. Evelyn Ryan composed her jingles not in the boardroom, but at the ironing board. It wasn't just the winning that was miraculous; it was the timing. Graced with a rare appreciation for life's inherent hilarity, Evelyn turned every financial challenge into an opportunity for fun and profit.

***Prized Possessions.** unabr. ed. Avery Corman. Read by Jean Reed Bahle. (Running Time: 9 hrs.). 2010. 24.99 (978-1-4418-4153-7(9), 9781441841537, Brilliance MP3); 39.97 (978-1-4418-4154-4(7), 9781441841544, Brlnc Audio MP3 Lib); 24.99 (978-1-4418-4155-1(5), 9781441841551, BAD); 39.97 (978-1-4418-4156-8(3), 9781441841568, BADLE) Brilliance Audio.

Prized Possessions, Set. unabr. ed. Jessica Stirling. Read by Vivien Heilbron. 10 cass. 1999. 84.95 (978-0-7540-0387-8(6), CAB1810) AudioGO.

Lizzie Conway has clawed her way out of the Gorbals slum despite the debt left by her husband. She would do anything to protect Polly, Babs & Rosie. But now they are grown up & Lizzie's strength & determination cannot protect her girls from falling in love with men as feckless as their father.

Prizzi's Family. unabr. collector's ed. Richard Condon. Read by Michael Prichard. 5 cass. (Running Time: 7 hrs. 30 mins.). 1991. 40.00 (978-0-7366-2009-3(5), 2825) Books on Tape.

By day Charley Partanna is a hit man for the Prizzis. By night he works on his high school diploma. Except when he's juggling two gorgeous women. But these days two are more than even Charley can handle!.

Prizzi's Glory. unabr. collector's ed. Richard Condon. Read by Michael Prichard. 8 cass. (Running Time: 8 hrs.). 1991. 48.00 (978-0-7366-2076-5(1), 2882) Books on Tape.

Tired, depressed & bored, Charley Partenna marries Maerose..."for the change." But he needn't have bothered. Don Corrado has a bigger change in mind...respectability for the Prizzis.

Prizzi's Honor. Richard Condon. 2009. (978-1-60136-163-9(7)) Audio Holding.

Prizzi's Honor. unabr. collector's ed. Richard Condon. Read by Christopher Hurt. 7 cass. (Running Time: 10 hrs. 30 mins.). 1985. 56.00 (978-0-7366-0837-4(0), 1788) Books on Tape.

This is no ordinary story of boy-meets-girl. Charley is a faithful lieutenant for the Prizzis, New York's most powerful Mafia family. The object of his affection is Irene Walker, a Los Angeles-based tax consultant. But it's her freelancing that pays - she's a hit man for the mob. She has also cheated the Prizzis out of a large sum of money. This places Charley's oldest loyalties in conflict with his newest one. Which wins?.

***Pro Charts for Jazz Guitar.** Ed. by Dan Libertino. (ENG.). 2010. pap. bk. 14.99 (978-1-4234-9771-4(6), 1423497716) H Leonard.

***Pro Charts for Jazz Singers: Medium High Voice.** Nick Fryman. (ENG.). 2010. pap. bk. 14.99 (978-1-4234-9776-9(7), 1423497767) H Leonard.

***Pro Charts for Jazz Singers: Medium Low Voice.** Nick Fryman. (ENG.). 2010. pap. bk. 14.99 (978-1-4234-9777-6(5), 1423497775) H Leonard.

Pro-Cite Software. 2 cass. 1990. 16.00 set. Recorded Res.

Pro Drummer's Handbook. Pete Sweeney. (ENG.). 2001. audio compact disk 10.00 (978-0-7390-1131-7(6)) Alfred Pub.

Pro-Fidelitate et Virtute Award to Bishop Hogan. 1 cass. (National Meeting of the Institute, 1992 Ser.). 4.00 (92N5) IRL Chicago.

Pro Guitarist's Handbook. Paul Lidel. (ENG.). 2001. audio compact disk 10.00 (978-0-7390-1125-6(1)) Alfred Pub.

Pro Keyboardist's Handbook. Jon Dryden. (ENG.). 2001. audio compact disk 10.00 (978-0-7390-1127-0(8)) Alfred Pub.

Pro-Life Primer, Set. Instructed by Gregory Koukl. 2 cass. 1999. 14.95 (978-0-9673584-2-0(6)) Stand to Reason.

Pro-Life Work & the Gospel of Life. Frank Pavone. 1 cass. 4.00 (95E) IRL Chicago.

Pro Secrets. Duane Shinn. Read by Duane Shinn. 36 cass. (Running Time: 36 hrs.). 360.00 set, incl. 36 printed summary cards. (PS-36) Duane Shinn.

Pro Speech. Geoffrey G. Forward. (ENG.). 2006. audio compact disk 49.95 (978-0-944200-14-8(1)) Alfred Pub.

***Proactive Parenting CD Set.** Tracy Marie Boyd. Prod. by Influential Productions. (ENG.). 2010. (978-0-9822763-9-6(7)) Influent Prod.

Proactive Strategies for Antitrust Clients Susceptible to More Aggressive Enforcement Policies: Billable Opportunities Antitrust Lawyers. Peter Sullivan. 2009. 250.00 (978-1-59701-496-0(6)) ReedLogic.

Proactive Strategies to Help Clients Prevent Lawsuits by Fired Employees: Billable Opportunities for Labor & Employment Lawyers. Alfred Kline & Patrick Cain. 2009. 250.00 (978-1-59701-498-4(2)) ReedLogic.

Proactively Planning for a Career in Academic Advising: NACADA Webinar Series 18. Featuring Jennifer Bloom. Albert Matheny. (ENG.). 2008. audio compact disk 140.00 (978-1-935140-60-3(4)) Nat Acad Adv.

Probability & Statistics for Chemists: Fundamental Techniques for the Analysis of Experimental Results. Instructed by Charles L. Perrin. 8 cass. (Running Time: 7 hrs. 12 min.). 260.00 incl. 112pp. manual. (42) Am Chemical.

Provides basis in probability & statistics while avoiding complex mathematical derivations.

Probable Future. abr. ed. Alice Hoffman. Read by Susan Ericksen. (Running Time: 6 hrs.). 2009. audio compact disk 14.99 (978-1-4418-1262-9(8), 9781441812629, BCD Value Price) Brilliance Audio.

Probable Future. unabr. ed. Alice Hoffman. Read by Susan Ericksen. 7 cass. Library ed. (Running Time: 11 hrs.). 2003. 87.25 (978-1-59086-039-7(X), 159086039X, Unabridge Lib Edns); 32.95 (978-1-59086-038-0(1), 1590860381, BAU); audio compact disk 36.95 (978-1-59086-040-3(3), 1590860403, BriAudCD Unabrid); audio compact disk 102.25 (978-1-59086-269-8(4), 1590862694, CD Unabrid Lib Ed) Brilliance Audio.

Women of the Sparrow family have unusual gifts. Elinor can detect falsehood. Her daughter, Jenny, can see people's dreams when they sleep. Granddaughter Stella has a mental window to the future - a future that she might not want to see. In Alice Hoffman's latest tour de force, this vivid and intriguing cast of characters confronts a haunting past - and a very current murder - against the evocative backdrop of small-town New England. By turns chilling and enchanting, The Probable Future chronicles the Sparrows' legacy as young Stella struggles to cope with her disturbing clairvoyance. Her potential to ruin or redeem becomes unbearable when one of her premonitions puts her father in jail, wrongly accused of homicide. Yet this ordeal also leads Stella to the grandmother she was forbidden to meet, and to an historic family home full of talismans from her ancestors.

Probable Future. unabr. ed. Alice Hoffman. Read by Susan Ericksen. (Running Time: 11 hrs.). 2004. 39.25 (978-1-59335-616-3(1), 1593356161, Brlnc Audio MP3 Lib) Brilliance Audio.

Probable Future. unabr. ed. Alice Hoffman. Read by Susan Ericksen. (Running Time: 11 hrs.). 2004. 39.25 (978-1-59710-607-8(0), 1597106070, BADLE); 24.95 (978-1-59710-606-1(2), 1597106062, BAD) Brilliance Audio.

Probable Future. unabr. ed. Alice Hoffman. Read by Susan Ericksen. (Running Time: 11 hrs.). 2004. 24.95 (978-1-59335-209-7(3), 1593352093) Soulmate Audio Bks.

Probable Tomorrows: How Science & Technology Will Transform Our Lives in the Next Twenty Years. unabr. ed. Marvin Cetron & Owen Davies. Read by C. M. Herbert. 8 cass. (Running Time: 11 hrs. 30 mins.). 1997. 56.95 (978-0-7861-1181-7(X), 1940) Blckstn Audio.

What will our world be like in the year 2010? Where will we work? How will we travel? What kind of advances can we expect in medicine & technology? These questions are answered in this book.

Probate Practice. Contrib. by Daniel I. Lubetkin. (Running Time: 4 hrs.). 1985. 70.00 incl. Basic Estate Administration Skills Text. NJ Inst CLE.

Covers pre-probate through post-probate prodecures & includes a discussion of recent legislation.

***Probe 7-over & Out.** 2010. audio compact disk (978-1-59171-296-1(3)) Falcon Picture.

Probing the Inner Sky. Steven Forrest. 2 cass. 1993. 18.00 set. (OC340-72) Sound Horizons AV.

Probing the Mystery of Creation. Swami Amar Jyoti. 1 cass. 1989. 9.95 (O-30) Truth Consciousness.

Can we ever find out how creation began, our forgotten beginning? Glimpses of the ultimate answer.

Problem see Poetry of Ralph Waldo Emerson

Problem at Pollensa Bay: And 7 Other Mysteries. unabr. ed. Agatha Christie. Read by Jonathan Cecil. 4 cass. (Running Time: 5 hrs. 3 mins.). 2003. 25.95 (978-1-57270-334-6(2)) Pub: Audio Partners. Dist(s): PerseuPGW

Problem at Pollensa Bay: And 7 Other Mysteries. unabr. ed. Agatha Christie. Narrated by Jonathan Cecil. 4 CDs. (Running Time: 5 hrs. 3 mins.). (Mystery Masters Ser.). (ENG.). 2003. audio compact disk 25.95 (978-1-57270-335-3(0)) Pub: AudioGO. Dist(s): Perseus Dist

Problem Child. unabr. ed. Michael Buckley. Read by L. J. Ganser. 6 CDs. (Running Time: 6 hrs. 45 mins.). (Sisters Grimm Ser.: Bk. 3). (J). (gr. 4-6). 2006. audio compact disk 64.75 (978-1-4281-1015-1(1)); 39.75 (978-1-4281-1010-6(0)) Recorded Bks.

The Sisters Grimm books are hits with young readers and critics. In their third outing, Sabrina and Daphne confront the menace behind the family's troubles, Little Red Riding Hood. After meeting their recently returned uncle Jake, the girls embark on a harrowing quest to reconstruct the mythical vorpal blade, the only weapon capable of killing Red's pet and bodyguard, the dreaded Jabberwocky.

Problem Is the Solution: How to Use Sympton Pnenomena to Generate Solution. Stephen G. Gilligan. 10 cass. (Running Time: 15 hrs. 45 mins.). 2000. 129.95 (978-1-884605-12-3(5)) Genesis II.

Learn to apply hypnotic techniques to use symtom pnenomena to generate solutions.

Problem of Alienation CD. Adam Schaff. 1 CD. (Running Time: 45 mins.). 2006. audio compact disk 12.95 (978-1-57970-411-7(5), C35120D, Audio-For) J Norton Pubs.

In Part 1 of this lecture, Schaff explains the concept of alienation as a specific relation between humans and their products, material and spiritual. Part 2 elaborates the problems of alienation. Topics include self and social alienation and the impact of this concept in life.

Problem of Cell Thirteen. unabr. ed. Jacques Futrelle. Read by Walter Covell. (Running Time: 82 min.). Dramatization. 1980. 7.95 (N-45) Jimcin Record.

Professor Van Dusen, the "Thinking Machine" makes a bet that he can escape from an "escape-proof" prison in one week. Will he succeed?.

Problem of Cell 13 see Classic Detective Stories, Vol. I, A Collection

Problem of Cell 13. Jacques Futrelle. (Reading & Training, Intermediate Ser.). (J). (gr. 4-7). 2005. pap. bk. 21.95 (978-88-7754-759-0(6)) Cideb ITA.

Problem of Evil. Kenneth Wapnick. 4 CDs. 2005. audio compact disk 25.00 (978-1-59142-178-8(0), CD82) Foun Miracles.

Problem of Evil: The Question of Job. Prod. by Paul Kennedy. Hosted by Paul Kennedy. (Running Time: 60 mins.). 2005. audio compact disk 15.95 (978-0-660-19220-8(9)) Pub: Canadian Broadcasting CAN. Dist(s): Georgetown Term

Problem of Immortality see Twentieth-Century Poetry in English, No. 5, Recordings of Poets Reading Their Own Poetry

Problem of Lawsuits: 1 Cor. 6:1-11. Ed Young. 1986. 4.95 (978-0-7417-1493-0(0), 493) Win Walk.

Problem of Lust. unabr. ed. William MacDonald. Read by William MacDonald. 1 cass. (Running Time: 43 min.). (Upward Call Ser.: Vol. 7). 1995. 8.95 (978-1-884833-02-1(0)) Lumen Prodns.

Provides biblical advice for Godly living in our sex-obsessed society.

Problem of Myself: Romans 7:15-25. Ed Young. (J). 1980. 4.95 (978-0-7417-1122-9(2), A0122) Win Walk.

Problem of Pain. C. S. Lewis. Narrated by Robert Whitfield. (Running Time: 4 hrs.). 1999. 22.95 (978-1-59912-703-3(2)) Iofy Corp.

Problem of Pain. abr. unabr. ed. Read by Robert Whitfield. 3 cass. (Running Time: 14400 sec.). 2006. 19.95 (978-0-7861-4474-7(2)); audio compact disk 19.95 (978-0-7861-7244-3(4)) Blckstn Audio.

Problem of Pain. unabr. ed. C. S. Lewis. Read by Robert Whitfield. 1 CD. (Running Time: 14400 sec.). 2001. audio compact disk 24.95 (978-0-7861-9573-2(8), 2609) Blckstn Audio.

For centuries Christians have been tormented by one question above all. "If God is good & all-powerful, why does he allow his creatures to suffer pain?" Lewis sets out to disentangle this knotty issue, but wisely adds that in the end no intellectual solution can dispense with the necessity for patience & courage.

Problem of Pain. unabr. ed. C. S. Lewis. Read by Robert Whitfield. 3 cass. (Running Time: 4 hrs.). 2000. 23.95 (978-0-7861-1810-6(5), 2609); audio compact disk 32.00 (978-0-7861-9851-1(6), 2609) Blckstn Audio.

Problem of Pain. unabr. ed. C. S. Lewis. Read by James Simmons. 2004. audio compact disk 25.95 (978-0-06-075748-9(5)) HarperCollins Pubs.

Problem of Sin. Swami Jyotirmayananda. 1 cass. (Running Time: 45 min.). 1990. 10.00 Yoga Res Foun.

Problem Solving. 1 cass. (Running Time: 45 min.). (Educational Ser.). 1989. bk. 9.98 (978-1-55909-205-0(X), 77S) Randolph Tapes.

Tap into your inner resources for the answers, put your subconscious mind to work for you. Subliminal messages are heard 3-5 minutes before becoming ocean sounds or music.

Problem Solving. Barrie Konicov. 1 cass. (YA). 11.98 (978-0-87082-437-1(6), 101) Potentials.

Explains creative problem solving which requires imaginative thinking & using your head.

Problem Solving. Barrie Konicov. 1 CD. 2004. audio compact disk 19.98 (978-1-56001-680-9(9)) Potentials.

Solving problems by patching negative areas is not the answer - the solution is creative problem solving. That requires imaginative thinking, which is where this program begins. You will find the self-hypnosis on track 1 and the subliminal on track 2. The easy-listening music of the subliminal, together with the self-hypnosis, is the original format which most people love and with which they are most familiar.

Problem Solving. Judith A. Tindall. 1987. audio compact disk 21.95 (978-1-55959-000-6(9)) Taylor and Fran.

Problem Solving. unabr. ed. Robert A. Monroe. Read by Robert A. Monroe. (Running Time: 45 min.). (Gateway Experience - Threshold Ser.). 1983. 14.95 (978-1-56113-257-7(8)) Monroe Institute.
Ask for & receive creative solutions.

Problem-Solving Arts Pt. 1: Syllabus. Norman H. Crowhurst. 1976. 227.10 (978-0-89420-175-2(1), 256000) Natl Book.

Problem-Solving Arts Pt. 2: Syllabus. Norman H. Crowhurst. 1977. 195.80 (978-0-89420-176-9(X), 256050) Natl Book.

Problem-Solving Arts Pt. 3: Syllabus. Norman H. Crowhurst. 1978. 196.20 (978-0-89420-177-6(8), 256090) Natl Book.

Problem Solving for Corporate Counsel. 1990. 65.00 (AC-546) PA Bar Inst.

Problem with Immorality. Blaine Yorgason & Brenton Yorgason. Read by Marvin Payne. 1 cass. (Gospel Power Ser.). 6.95 (978-0-929985-47-3(8)) Jackman Pubng.
A father's letter to his son regarding lust & immorality.

***Problem with the Puddles.** unabr. ed. Kate Feiffer. Read by Halley Feiffer. 3 CDs. (Running Time: 3 hrs.). (J). (gr. 2-4). 2009. audio compact disk 30.00 (978-0-7393-8129-8(6), Listening Lib) Pub: Random Audio Pubg. Dist(s): Random

Problem with the Puddles. unabr. ed. Kate Feiffer. Read by Halley Feiffer. (ENG.). (J). 2009. audio compact disk 25.00 (978-0-7393-8127-4(X), Listening Lib) Pub: Random Audio Pubg. Dist(s): Random

Problemas del Trabajo: Scientolgy Aplicada al Mundo del Trabajo Cotidiano. L. Ron Hubbard. (Running Time: 3 hrs. 25 mins. 0 sec.). (SPA.). 2007. audio compact disk 20.00 (978-1-4031-5658-7(1)) Bridge Pubns Inc.

Probleme der Leistungsmessung. Sybille Bolton. 1 cass. (Running Time: 1 hr. 20 mins.). (Fernstudienangebot Ser.: Vol. 10). (GER.). 1996. 11.95 (978-3-468-49669-1(9)) Langenscheidt.

Problems in a Different Light. 1 cass. (Running Time: 30 min.). 1985. (0242) Evang Sisterhood Mary.
Topics include; Who Is Really Happy?; Not my Will; But Thine, O Lord; In The Footsteps of Christ.

Problems in Antarctica; Earth Day Nineteen Years Later; & Not Building in Flood Plains. Hosted by Nancy Pearlman. 1 cass. (Running Time: 29 min.). 10.00 (815) Educ Comm CA.

Problems in Obesity Surgery. Moderated by Joel B. Freeman. (Postgraduate Courses Ser.). 1986. 65.00 (8602) Am Coll Surgeons.
Discusses aspects of the morbidly obese patient. 9 hours CME credit.

Problems in Reproductive Endocrinology. William F. Crowley, Jr. 1 cass. (Running Time: 90 min.). 1985. 12.00 (C8551) Amer Coll Phys.

Problems in the Area of Sex. Nathaniel Branden. 1 cass. (Running Time: 1 hr. 15 min.). 11.95 (615) J Norton Pubs.
Covers impotence & premature ejaculation; the nonorgasmic woman; & common misconceptions concerning sex.

Problems in the Diagnosis & Management of the Acquired Immunodeficiency Syndrome. Moderated by Merle A. Sande. Contrib. by Harold W. Jaffe et al. 1 cass. (Running Time: 90 min.). 1986. 12.00 (A8640) Amer Coll Phys.
This topic is discussed by a moderator & experts who offer differing opinions.

Problems of a Journalist. Nicholas Von Hoffman. 1 cass. (Running Time: 1 hr. 28 min.). 11.95 (195) J Norton Pubs.

Problems of Human Nature. unabr. ed. Aldous Huxley. 1 cass. (Running Time: 52 min.). (Human Situation Ser.). 1959. 11.00 (01114) Big Sur Tapes.
Traces how cultural frames of reference have shifted through the ages, even though the fundamental experiences they address have remained the same.

Problems of Marriage. Nathaniel Branden. 1 cass. (Running Time: 43 min.). 10.95 (813) J Norton Pubs.
Love is not enough for success, & people's own self-doubts are largely responsible for the failures of marriages. There are too many unanswered questions, such as; why do I want to get married? What do I want from marriage.

Problems of Marriage. Nathaniel Branden. 1 CD. (Running Time: 43 mins.). 2005. audio compact disk 10.95 (978-1-57970-247-2(3), AF0813D, Audio-For) J Norton Pubs.
Have you ever asked yourself these qustions: "Why do I want to get married?" "What do I want from a marriage?" The answers to these questions could help solve or avoid problems in marriage. Nathaniel Branden, Ph.D., discusses why love is not enough and how people's own self-doubts are largely responsible for failures in marriage.

Problems of Preaching. 1 cass. (Running Time: 16 min.). 12.00 (L260) MEA A Watts Cass.

Problems of Satori. unabr. ed. John Lilly. 2 cass. (Running Time: 1 hr. 56 min.). 1971. 18.00 Set. (03906) Big Sur Tapes.
Recounts his work with Sufi Oscar Ichazo at his "esoteric" school in Chile. Oscar teaches that satori is "natural, simple, easy, obvious & continuous." Lilly talks about how esoteric schools are no longer only for the elite, anyone can have access to satori.

***Problems of Work.** L. Ron Hubbard. (FRE.). 2007. audio compact disk 20.00 (978-1-4031-5647-1(6)); audio compact disk 20.00 (978-1-4031-5656-3(5)); audio compact disk 20.00 (978-1-4031-5645-7(X)); audio compact disk 20.00 (978-1-4031-5649-5(2)); audio compact disk 20.00 (978-1-4031-5650-1(6)); audio compact disk 20.00 (978-1-4031-5651-8(4)); audio compact disk 20.00 (978-1-4031-5654-9(9)); audio compact disk 20.00 (978-1-4031-5653-2(0)); audio compact disk 20.00 (978-1-4031-5659-4(X)); audio compact disk 20.00 (978-1-4031-5657-0(3)); audio compact disk 20.00 (978-1-4031-5694-5(8)); audio compact disk 20.00 (978-1-4031-5652-5(2)); audio compact disk 20.00 (978-1-4031-5655-6(7)); audio compact disk 20.00 (978-1-4031-5648-8(4)); audio compact disk 20.00 (978-1-4031-5646-4(8)) Bridge Pubns Inc.

***Problems of Work.** L. Ron Hubbard. (ENG.). 2008. 14.00 (978-1-4031-5860-4(6)); 14.00 (978-1-4031-5862-8(2)); 14.00 (978-1-4031-5864-2(9)); 14.00 (978-1-4031-5863-5(0)); 14.00 (978-1-4031-5861-1(4)); 14.00 (978-1-4031-5865-9(7)) Bridge Pubns Inc.

***Problems of Work.** L. Ron Hubbard. 2010. audio compact disk 20.00 (978-1-4031-6949-5(7)); audio compact disk 20.00 (978-1-4031-6953-2(5)); audio compact disk 35.00 (978-1-4031-6960-0(8)); audio compact disk 20.00 (978-1-4031-6955-6(1)); audio compact disk 20.00 (978-1-4031-6954-9(3)); audio compact disk 20.00 (978-1-4031-6959-4(4)); audio compact disk 20.00 (978-1-4031-6950-1(0)); audio compact disk 20.00 (978-1-4031-6962-4(4)); audio compact disk 20.00 (978-1-4031-6948-8(9)); audio compact disk 20.00 (978-1-4031-6952-5(7)); audio compact disk 20.00 (978-1-4031-6870-2(9)); audio compact disk 20.00 (978-1-4031-6957-0(8)); audio compact disk 20.00 (978-1-4031-6951-8(9)); audio compact disk 20.00 (978-1-4031-6961-7(6)); audio compact disk 20.00 (978-1-4031-6956-3(X)); audio compact disk 20.00 (978-1-4031-6958-7(6)) Bridge Pubns Inc.

Problems of Work: Scientology Applied to the Workaday World. abr. ed. L. Ron Hubbard. Read by Harry Chase. (Running Time: 2 hrs. 58 mins. 0 sec.). (ENG.). 2007. audio compact disk 20.00 (978-1-4031-5544-3(5)) Bridge Pubns Inc.

***ProBlogger: Secrets for Blogging Your Way to a Six-Figure Income.** unabr. ed. Darren Rowse & Chris Garrett. Read by Erik Synnestvedt. (Running Time: 7 hrs.). (ENG.). 2010. 27.98 (978-1-59659-620-7(1), GildAudio) Pub: Gildan Media. Dist(s): HachBkGrp

Proceed, Sergeant Lamb. unabr. collector's ed. Robert Graves. Read by Bill Kelsey. 8 cass. (Running Time: 12 hrs.). 1990. 64.00 (978-0-7366-1722-2(1), 2563) Books on Tape.
In this sequel to Sergeant Lamb of the Ninth, Lamb, along with 3000 others of Burgoyne's army, is in a prison camp near Boston, awaiting repatriation. But the American Congress refuses to ratify the agreement & Lamb plans an escape. He manages to make his way through General Washington's lines & rejoins the British in New York. From there he joins Cornwallis in the Carolinas, fighting with him until Yorktown. Again he makes a remarkable escape to rejoin the British in New York, accompanied by eight Fusiliers.

Proceedings: "The Game's Afloat III" Sherlockian Conference, October 30 - November 1, 1998. unabr. ed. 3 cass. (Running Time: 3 hrs.). 12.50 Set. (978-1-888728-10-1(8)) Clssic Spclties.
Includes presentation on: "Jack the Ripper" & Conan Doyle's "Lost World" as well as Irish songs & Sherlock Holmes' possible wives.

Proceedings of AVSP 2001: Auditory Visual Speech Processing. 2nd ed. 2001. audio compact disk 20.00 (978-0-9712714-1-8(0)) Fuzzy Bks.

Proceedings of OCEANS '07 MTS/IEEE Vancouver. MTS/IEEE Oceans 2007 presenters. 2007. audio compact disk (978-0-933957-35-0(1)) Marine Tech Soc.

Proceedings of the American Society for Composites: Twenty-First Technical Conference. Created by Destech Publications. 2006. audio compact disk Rental 195.00 (978-1-932078-60-2(6)) DEStech Pubns.

Proceedings of the American Society for Composites, 17th Technical Conference. C. T. Sun. 2002. audio compact disk 404.95 (978-0-8493-1501-5(8), 1501) Pub: CRC Pr. Dist(s): Taylor and Fran

Proceedings of the Conference on Sustainable Range Management. Ed. by Bruce Alleman & Steven Downes. 2004. audio compact disk 195.00 (978-1-57477-144-2(2)) Battelle.

Proceedings of the Second International Conference on Remediation of Contaminated Sediments. Ed. by Marco Pellei & Augusto Porta. 2004. audio compact disk 195.00 (978-1-57477-143-5(4)) Battelle.

Proceedings of the Seventh International in Situ & on-Site Bioremediation Symposium. Ed. by Victor S. Magar & Mark E. Kelley. 2003. audio compact disk 295.00 (978-1-57477-139-8(6)) Battelle.

Proceedings of the Singaporean-French Ipal Symposium 2009 - Sinfra'09. Wee Kheng Leow. 2009. audio compact disk 47.00 (978-981-4277-55-6(X)) World Scientific Pub.

Proceedings of the Twenty-Fourth Annual Conference of the Cognitive Society. Ed. by Wayne Gray. 2002. audio compact disk 39.95 (978-0-8058-4583-9(6)) Pub: L Erlbaum Assocs. Dist(s): Taylor and Fran

Proceedings of the Twenty-Sixth Annual Conference of the Cognitive Science Society, Pts. 1 & 2. Ed. by Kenneth Forbus et al. 2005. audio compact disk 200.00 (978-0-8058-5464-0(9)) Pub: L Erlbaum Assocs. Dist(s): Taylor and Fran

Proceedings of the WICON WORKSHOPS: ConWiN 2005, ESAS 2005, MeshNets 2005, SensorFusion 2005. 2005. audio compact disk 25.00 (978-0-9767294-1-9(5)) I Comn S & Tech.

Proceedings of the 25th International Conference of the System Dynamics Society. Ed. by John Sterman et al. (ENG.). 2007. audio compact disk 25.00 (978-0-9745329-8-1(3)) Sys Dynam Soc.

Proceedings of the 26th International Conference of the System Dynamics Society. Ed. by Brian C. Dangerfield. Prod. by Jennifer I. Rowe et al. (ENG.). 2008. audio compact disk 25.00 (978-1-935056-01-0(8)) Sys Dynam Soc.

Proceedings of the 28th Annual Conference of the Cognitive Science Society. Ed. by Ron Sun & Naomi Miyake. 2006. audio compact disk 39.95 (978-0-8058-6296-6(X)) Pub: L Erlbaum Assocs. Dist(s): Taylor and Fran

Proceedings 27th annual cognitive society Society 2005. 2005. audio compact disk 195.00 (978-0-8058-5991-1(8)) Pub: L Erlbaum Assocs. Dist(s): Taylor and Fran

Proceso. abr. ed. Franz Kafka. Read by Carlos Zambrano. 3 CDs. (SPA.). 2001. audio compact disk 17.00 (978-958-9494-59-2(5)) YoYoMusic.

Process: The Way of the Tarot Reader. Dan/M Pelletier. Read by Dan/M Pelletier. Ed. by Leisa/Anne ReFalo. Prod. by Leisa/Anne ReFalo. (ENG.). 2008. 45.00 (978-1-935194-99-6(2)) Tarot Connect.

Process (CD) The Way of the Tarot Reader. Dan/M Pelletier. Read by Dan/M Pelletier. Ed. by Leisa/Anne ReFalo. Prod. by Leisa/Anne ReFalo. (ENG.). 2008. audio compact disk 60.00 (978-1-935194-98-9(4)) Tarot Connect.

Process Measurement & Control. unabr. ed. Read by Marvin D. Weiss. 4 cass. (Running Time: 5 hrs.). 455.00 Set, incl. 280p. manual. (A8) Am Chemical.

Process of Change. Jack Boland. (Super Ser.). 8.00 (BI13A) Master Mind.

Process of Individuation. Read by Diane Martin. 1 cass. (Running Time: 2 hrs.). 1986. 12.95 (978-0-7822-0155-0(5), 207) C G Jung IL.

Process of Making Medical Record. David Belgum. 1986. 10.80 (0205) Assn Prof Chaplains.

Process of Preparation. Elbert Willis. 1 cass. (Victory of Surrender Ser.: Vol. 1). 4.00 Fill the Gap.

Process of Purification. Swami Amar Jyoti. 1 dolby cass. 1986. 9.95 (M-65) Truth Consciousness.
Freedom from limitations, leaving off our false masks & images. Cleaning of mind & heart on the various paths.

Process of Raising Capital from Angel Investors. Ed. by Ellen Sandles. 2006. audio compact disk 49.95 (978-1-59701-096-2(0)) Aspatore Bks.

Process of Relaxation. Swami Amar Jyoti. 2 cass. 1978. 12.95 (J-15) Truth Consciousness.
In relaxation, giving ourselves up to the laws of Nature, healing power is released. Opening up everything.

Process Phonics: ABACADABA Song. Cecelia Pollack. Perf. by Linda Rogers & Terri Laureta. 1 cass. (Running Time: 5 min.). (J). (gr. 4-6). 1995. 10.00 (978-1-892272-05-8(9)) Procss Phncs.
Alphabet song, sings the sounds of the letters.

Processes. Lee Lefebre. Read by Lee Lefebre. 1 cass. (Running Time: 45 min.). 1992. 6.00 (978-1-57838-039-8(1)) CrossLife Express.
Christian living.

Processes, Vol. 2. unabr. ed. Esther Hicks & Jerry Hicks. 4 CDs. (Running Time: 4 hrs.). 2005. audio compact disk 23.95 (978-1-4019-0735-8(0)) Hay House.

Processing a Civil Suit, Side A; Criminal Defense, Traffic, DUI, Side B. Frank L. Natter. 1 cass. (Running Time: 90 min.). (Type Law Tapes Ser.: No. 2). 1989. 10.00 (978-1-878287-57-1(5), ATA-2) Type & Temperament.
Implications & insights to understanding one's own personal legal & financial planning on the given subject.

Processing Interventions for the Child with NLD: Central Auditory Processing Disorder (CAPD) Judith Paton. 1 cass. (Running Time: 1 hr. 22 min.). 1998. bk. 20.00 (978-1-58111-062-3(6)) Contemporary Medical.
Describes audiology testing, organic basis of NLD diagnosing & treating NLD, hearing & communication accomodations.

Processing into the Promise. 4 cass. 2002. 20.00 (978-1-58602-122-1(2)); audio compact disk 34.99 (978-1-58602-127-6(3)) E L Long.

Proclaiming the Theology of the Body: A Seminar for Priests. Christopher West. 2006. audio compact disk 29.95 (978-1-932927-71-9(9)) Ascensn Pr.

Proclamare Tu Amor. Contrib. by Don Moen et al. 2001. audio compact disk 10.99 (978-5-553-85668-7(X)) Integrity Music.

Proclamare Tu Amor 2. Contrib. by Don Moen et al. Created by Integrity Music. 2002. audio compact disk 10.98 (978-5-550-14686-6(X)) Integrity Music.

Proclamation - for the King & His Kingdom. Eric Claybon & Reign's. 2004. audio compact disk 16.98 (978-5-553-36406-9(X)) Pub: Pt of Grace Ent. Dist(s): STL Dist NA

Procrastinate No More. 2002. 24.95 (978-1-58557-053-9(2)) Dynamic Growth.

Procrastination. 1 cass. (Running Time: 60 min.). 10.95 (010) Psych Res Inst.
Increase productivity by becoming a do it now type of person.

Procrastination: Beating the Manana Habit! Bruce A. Baldwin. Read by Bruce A. Baldwin. (Running Time: 60 min.). 1983. 8.95 (978-0-933583-09-2(5), PDC835) Direction Dynamics.
Teaches the eight major personal conflicts that cause procrastination & diagnostic clues to identify each.

Procrastinator's Handbook: Mastering the Art of Doing It Now. abr. ed. Rita Emmett. Read by Rita Emmett. 3 CDs. (Running Time: 3 hrs. 0 mins. 0 sec.). (ENG.). 2005. audio compact disk 19.95 (978-1-59397-847-1(2)) Pub: Macmill Audio. Dist(s): Macmillan

Procurer & Other Erotic Stories see Alcahuete y Otras Historias Eroticas

Procurer & Other Erotic Stories. Marquis de Sade. Read by Laura García. (Running Time: 1 hr.). 2002. 14.95 (978-1-60083-139-3(7), Audiofy Corp) Iofy Corp.

Prodigal Daughter. Jeffrey Archer. Narrated by Barbara Rosenblat. 15 CDs. (Running Time: 17 hrs.). audio compact disk 144.00 (978-0-7887-9859-7(6)) Recorded Bks.

Prodigal Daughter. Rachel Moore & Trudy Harris. 2008. audio compact disk 84.95 (978-1-84652-200-0(5)) Pub: Magna Story GBR. Dist(s): Ulverscroft US

Prodigal Daughter. Rachel Moore & Trudy Harris. 2008. 69.95 (978-1-84652-199-7(8)) Pub: Magna Story GBR. Dist(s): Ulverscroft US

Prodigal Daughter. abr. ed. Jeffrey Archer. Read by Paula Prentiss. 2 cass. (Running Time: 3 hrs.). 2000. 16.99 (978-0-00-104765-5(5)) Zondervan.
Florentyna Kane has finally achieved her goal of becoming president of the United States, but a deadly conspiracy led by a senator threatens to silence her and her dreams forever.

Prodigal Daughter. abr. rev. ed. Jeffrey Archer. Read by Lorelei King. 3 CDs. (Running Time: 3 hrs. 45 mins. 0 sec.). 2004. audio compact disk 14.95 (978-1-59397-412-1(4)) Pub: Macmill Audio. Dist(s): Macmillan

Prodigal Daughter. unabr. ed. Jeffrey Archer. Narrated by Barbara Rosenblat. 12 cass. (Running Time: 17 hrs.). 1994. 97.00 (978-0-7887-0089-7(8), 94329E7) Recorded Bks.
The daughter of a Polish immigrant & self-made millionaire aspires to the highest office in the land of her birth, the United States of America.

Prodigal God: Recovering the Heart of the Christian Faith. unabr. ed. Timothy Keller. (Running Time: 3 hrs.). (ENG.). (gr. 8 up). 2008. audio compact disk 24.95 (978-0-14-314380-2(8), PengAudBks) Penguin Grp USA.

Prodigal Heirs: Israel & the Church. Chuck Missler. 2 cass. (Running Time: 1 hr. 30 mins. per cass.). (Briefing Packages by Chuck Missler). 1995. vinyl bd. 14.95 Incl. notes. (978-1-880532-45-4(X)) Koinonia Hse.
Has God abandoned Israel? Has the Church "replaced" Israel? The Bible is very clear about the different origins, roles, and destinies of Israel and the Church. It also describes how God feels about people who "say they are Jews but are not."It is dangerous, as well as destructive, to automatically transfer the promises that God gave Israel to the Church.Chuck Missler explores the controversies and misunderstandings of these two prophetically relevant groups, as well as a big surprise on our near horizon! He also reviews popular myths such as: 1. Replacement Theology 2. Israel rejected her messiah; therefore she forfeited the promises to her 3. The Church, thus, replaces Israel, becoming "spiritual Israel," etc. 4. The Lost Ten Tribes TheoryThe myth of the "Ten Lost Tribes" is the basis for "British-Israelism" and similar legends, but has no real Biblical basis. It is based upon misconceptions derived from the misreading of passages such as II Kings 17:7-23, II Chronicles 6:6-11, and so on.

Prodigal Mage. unabr. ed. Karen Miller. (Running Time: 13 hrs.). (Fisherman's Children Ser.). (ENG.). 2009. 29.98 (978-1-60024-695-1(8), Orbit LitBrn) Pub: Little. Dist(s): HachBkGrp

Prodigal Mind. Swami Amar Jyoti. 1 dolby cass. 1985. 9.95 (J-48) Truth Consciousness.
The Yogic way of dealing with the wandering mind. Uses & pitfalls of mind control. Genesis of asceticism. Pride & arrogance. What needs are.

Prodigal Project: Exodus. abr. ed. Ken Abraham & Daniel Hart. Read by Dick Hill. 2 cass. (Running Time: 3 hrs.). (Prodigal Project Ser.). 2003. audio compact disk 62.25 (978-1-59355-015-8(4), 1593550154, BACDLib Ed); 17.95 (978-1-59355-012-7(X), 159355012X); audio compact disk 19.95 (978-1-59355-013-4(8), 1593550138, BACD) Brilliance Audio.
In the twinkling of an eye, their lives changed forever. Husbands, wives, children, all lost in what was first called "the disappearance." Now many understand that with millions of Christians called home, the Rapture has irrevocably torn the fabric of their lives. They wander, rootless and searching, in the wake of events nearly too powerful, too overwhelming to comprehend. Some set out on a personal odyssey to reconnect with family, their past, with some semblance of order in a world menaced by the Muslim mujahideen. Offering hope, Azul Dante and his Prodigal Project remain a beacon in the swirling maelstrom of uncertainty that threatens to engulf nations, ideologies, and faiths. While on quiet street corners, in darkened homes, abandoned offices, wherever two or more are gathered, a small band of believers begin again to spread the Word.

Prodigal Project: Exodus. unabr. ed. Ken Abraham & Daniel Hart. Read by Dick Hill. 5 cass. (Running Time: 7 hrs.). (Prodigal Project Ser.). 2003. 29.95 (978-1-59355-129-2(0), 1593551290, BAU); 69.25 (978-1-59355-014-1(6), 1593550146, BrilAudUnabridg) Brilliance Audio.

Prodigal Project: Exodus. unabr. ed. Ken Abraham & Daniel Hart. Read by Dick Hill. (Running Time: 7 hrs.). (Prodigal Project Ser.). 2004. 39.25 (978-1-59335-502-9(5), 1593355025, Brlnc Audio MP3 Lib) Brilliance Audio.

Prodigal Project: Exodus. unabr. ed. Ken Abraham & Daniel Hart. Read by Dick Hill. (Running Time: 7 hrs.). (Prodigal Project Ser.). 2004. 24.95 (978-1-59335-229-5(8), 1593352298) Soulmate Audio Bks.

Prodigal Project: Genesis. abr. ed. Ken Abraham & Daniel Hart. Read by Dick Hill. 2 cass. (Running Time: 3 hrs.). (Prodigal Project Ser.). 2003. audio compact disk 19.95 (978-1-59355-008-0(1), 1593550081, BACD); 17.95 (978-1-59355-007-3(3), 1593550073) Brilliance Audio.
On just another Sunday, a man joins a group of friends for a golf game. A working mother, trying to balance career and home, skips weekly services. An Internet junkie scours the Web looking for some comforting news but finds only unrest. Ordinary people who live their lives in an unsettled time, like most too overwhelmed by their own concerns to register the groundswell of changes taking place everywhere-until the instance when millions around the world disappear. Immediately, life after the Rapture becomes a chaotic battle for survival. Into the void steps Azul Dante, the charismatic leader of the Prodigal Project. He shines a light in the darkness of the End Times, his new world order representing a return to the promised land of the past. And in the beginning, seven hopeful men and women set out separately to find salvation in the Prodigal Project. Instead, they initiate a series of personal trials that will ultimately prove to be the sternest test of their souls.

Prodigal Project: Genesis. unabr. ed. Ken Abraham & Daniel Hart. Read by Dick Hill. 6 cass. (Running Time: 8 hrs.). (Prodigal Project Ser.). 2003. 29.95 (978-1-59355-128-5(2), 1593551282, BAU); 74.25 (978-1-59355-009-7(X), 159355009X, BrilAudUnabridg) Brilliance Audio.

Prodigal Project: Genesis. unabr. ed. Ken Abraham & Daniel Hart. Read by Dick Hill. (Running Time: 10 hrs.). (Prodigal Project Ser.). 2004. 39.25 (978-1-59335-343-8(X), 159335343X, Brlnc Audio MP3 Lib) Brilliance Audio.

Prodigal Project: Genesis. unabr. ed. Ken Abraham & Daniel Hart. Read by Dick Hill. (Running Time: 10 hrs.). (Prodigal Project Ser.). 2004. 24.95 (978-1-59335-023-9(6), 1593350236) Soulmate Audio Bks.

Prodigal Project: Genesis. unabr. ed. Ken Abraham & Daniel Hart. Read by Dick Hill. 2 cass. (Running Time: 3 hrs.). (Prodigal Project Ser.). 2003. audio compact disk 62.25 (978-1-59355-010-3(3), 1593550103, BACDLib Ed) Brilliance Audio.

Prodigal Project: Kings. abr. ed. Ken Abraham & Daniel Hart. Read by Dick Hill. (Running Time: 4 hrs.). (Prodigal Project Ser.). 2004. audio compact disk 21.95 (978-1-59355-135-3(5), 1593551355); audio compact disk 69.25 (978-1-59355-136-0(3), 1593551363, BACDLib Ed) Brilliance Audio.
Based on a Biblical interpretation of the Rapture, Kings continues the story of those caught up in the events following this world-upending event. Azul Dante, the increasingly controversial figure whom some nations hope will restore order to the world, recovers from a recent assassination attempt. Behind the scenes, another and even more sinister force exerts its powerful influence at a gathering of ten world leaders. While they meet, other events prefiguring the start of the last days have armies poised for battle. Meanwhile, the members of the seven set out to spread the good news of Christianity and salvation in a world desperate for answers and assurance. "Do not fear, for those who are with us are more than those who are with them." - 2 Kings 6:16.

Prodigal Project: Numbers. abr. ed. Ken Abraham & Daniel Hart. Read by Dick Hill. (Running Time: 3 hrs.). (Prodigal Project Ser.). 2003. 17.95 (978-1-59355-017-2(0), 1593550170); audio compact disk 62.25 (978-1-59355-020-2(0), 1593550200, BACDLib Ed); audio compact disk 19.95 (978-1-59355-018-9(9), 1593550189, BACD) Brilliance Audio.
Special Agent John Jameson has been assigned a daunting task - to take out the vicious leader of the militant Islamic mujahideen that has been menacing the world in the wake of the Rapture. Caught between his duty to country and his newfound faith, Jameson has learned a terrible secret. Desperate to relay this information to the highest level of the American government, Jameson enlists the aid of journalist Cat Early. Caught up in chaotic events that neither could have imagined, the pair struggle to have their voices heard in the tumult of a world on the brink of catastrophic global warfare. Only one man seemingly holds the power to bring peace - the charismatic world leader Azul Dante.

Prodigal Project: Numbers. unabr. ed. Ken Abraham & Daniel Hart. Read by Dick Hill. 6 cass. (Running Time: 7 hrs.). (Prodigal Project Ser.). 2003. 74.25 (978-1-59355-019-6(7), 1593550197, BrilAudUnabridg) Brilliance Audio.

Prodigal Project: Numbers. unabr. ed. Ken Abraham & Daniel Hart. Read by Dick Hill & Breck Susie. 5 cass. (Running Time: 7 hrs.). (Prodigal Project Ser.). 2003. 29.95 (978-1-59355-130-8(4), 1593551304, BAU) Brilliance Audio.

Prodigal Project: Numbers. unabr. ed. Ken Abraham & Daniel Hart. Read by Dick Hill & Susie Breck. (Running Time: 8 hrs.). (Prodigal Project Ser.). 2004. 39.25 (978-1-59335-507-4(6), 1593355076, Brlnc Audio MP3 Lib) Brilliance Audio.

Prodigal Project: Numbers. unabr. ed. Ken Abraham & Daniel Hart. Read by Dick Hill & Susie Breck. (Running Time: 8 hrs.). (Prodigal Project Ser.). 2005. 39.25 (978-1-59600-828-1(8), 9781596008281, BADLE); 24.95 (978-1-59710-613-9(5), 9781597106139, BAD) Brilliance Audio.

Prodigal Project: Numbers. unabr. ed. Ken Abraham & Daniel Hart. Read by Dick Hill & Susie Breck. (Running Time: 8 hrs.). (Prodigal Project Ser.). 2004. 24.95 (978-1-59335-239-4(5), 1593352395) Soulmate Audio Bks.

Prodigal Project CD Collection: Genesis, Exodus, Numbers, Kings. abr. ed. Ken Abraham & Daniel Hart. (Running Time: 13 hrs.). 2009. audio compact disk 34.99 (978-1-4233-7736-8(2), 9781423377368, BACD) Brilliance Audio.

Prodigal Project, the: Exodus: Exodus. unabr. ed. Ken Abraham & Daniel Hart. Read by Dick Hill. (Running Time: 7 hrs.). (Prodigal Project Ser.). 2005. 39.25 (978-1-59600-827-4(X), 9781596008274, BADLE); 24.95 (978-1-59710-612-2(7), 9781597106122, BAD) Brilliance Audio.

Prodigal Project, the: Genesis: Genesis. unabr. ed. Ken Abraham & Daniel Hart. Read by Dick Hill. (Running Time: 10 hrs.). (Prodigal Project Ser.). 2005. 24.95 (978-1-59710-611-5(9), 9781597106115, BAD) Brilliance Audio.

Prodigal Project, the: Genesis: Genesis. unabr. ed. Ken Abraham & John Hart. Read by Dick Hill. (Running Time: 10 hrs.). (Prodigal Project Ser.). 2005. 39.25 (978-1-59600-826-7(1), 9781596008267, BADLE) Brilliance Audio.

Prodigal Son. Kenneth Wapnick. 4 CDs. 2005. audio compact disk 23.00 (978-1-59142-201-3(9), CD79) Foun Miracles.

Prodigal Son. Kenneth Wapnick. 2009. 18.00 (978-1-59142-378-2(3)) Foun Miracles.

Prodigal Son. abr. ed. Danielle Steel. (Running Time: 6 hrs.). 2012. audio compact disk 19.99 (978-1-4233-8862-3(3), 9781423388623, BACD) Brilliance Audio.

Prodigal Son. abr. ed. Danielle Steel. (Running Time: 6 hrs.). 2013. audio compact disk 14.99 (978-1-4233-8863-0(1), 9781423388630, BCD Value Price) Brilliance Audio.

Prodigal Son. unabr. ed. Dean Koontz & Kevin J. Anderson. 8 cass. (Running Time: 12 hrs.). (Dean Koontz's Frankenstein Ser.: Bk. 1). 2005. 96.00 (978-1-4159-1561-5(X)); audio compact disk 68.85 (978-1-4159-1648-3(9)) Pub: Books on Tape. Dist(s): NetLibrary CO

Prodigal Son. unabr. ed. Danielle Steel. (Running Time: 10 hrs.). 2012. 39.97 (978-1-4233-8859-3(3), 9781423388593, Brlnc Audio MP3 Lib); 39.97 (978-1-4233-8861-6(5), 9781423388616, BADLE); 24.99 (978-1-4233-8858-6(5), 9781423388586, Brilliance MP3); 24.99 (978-1-4233-8860-9(7), 9781423388609, BAD); audio compact disk 92.97 (978-1-4233-8857-9(7), 9781423388579, BriAudCD Unabrid); audio compact disk 38.99 (978-1-4233-8856-2(9), 9781423388562, Bril Audio CD Unabri) Brilliance Audio.

Prodigal Son's Brother. Kenneth Wapnick. 2008. 18.00 (978-1-59142-362-1(7)); audio compact disk 22.00 (978-1-59142-361-4(9)) Foun Miracles.

Prodigal Spy. Joseph Kanon. Read by Michael Kramer. 1999. 96.00 (978-0-7366-4560-7(8)) Books on Tape.

Prodigal Spy. unabr. ed. Joseph Kanon. Read by Michael Kramer. 12 cass. (Running Time: 18 hrs.). 1999. 96.00 (4967) Books on Tape.
Washington, 1950. Walter Kotlar, a high-level State Department official, is under scrutiny from the HOuse Un-American Activities Committee. When the chief witness against him dies, Kotler flees the country. His son, Nick, is told to think of him as dead. But twenty years later Walter Kotlar is still alive & enlists a young journalist to bring Nick a message; he badly wants to see his son. Nick agrees to accompany the journalist to Soviet-occupied Czechoslovakia for the painful reunion. Once in Prague, Nick learns of his father's impossible request; he wants to come home. He also has a valuable secret about what really happened the night he walked out of Nick's life.

Prodigal Spy, Set. abr. ed. Joseph Kanon. Read by Boyd Gaines. 4 cass. 1999. 26.00 (FS9-43313) Highsmith.

***Prodigal Summer.** unabr. ed. Barbara Kingsolver. Read by Barbara Kingsolver. (ENG.). 2005. (978-0-06-089463-4(6), Harper Audio); (978-0-06-089462-7(8), Harper Audio) HarperCollins Pubs.

Prodigal Summer. unabr. ed. Barbara Kingsolver. Narrated by Barbara Kingsolver. 13 CDs. (Running Time: 15 hrs.). 2001. audio compact disk 108.00 (978-0-7887-7182-8(5), C1432) Recorded Bks.
The author turns her magical talents to three intertwined stories of a single lush Appalachian summer. A reclusive biologist watches with excitement as coyotes move onto the isolated mountain she patrols, unaware of the personal changes in store for her when she lets another stranger into her own most private spaces. On a farm down the mountain, a bookish city girl finds herself suddenly widowed, her life full of ghosts from the past & her future clouded in uncertainty. Down the road from the widow's farm, two elderly neighbors feud over everything from pesticides to God, gradually becoming aware of bonds that connect the two of them beneath their arguments. In a pattern as delicate as a moth's wings, Kingsolver weaves these three stories into a moving tapestry showing the fragile, unexpected ways that all of nature's aspects, including human lives, are intricately connected.

Prodigal Summer. unabr. ed. Barbara Kingsolver. Narrated by Barbara Kingsolver. 10 cass. (Running Time: 15 hrs.). 2001. 94.00 (978-0-7887-5208-7(1), 96516) Recorded Bks.
Three stories that come together during a lush Appalachian summer: A biologist lets a stranger into her most private areas, a bookish girl finds herself suddenly widowed on her husband's farm & a couple of elderly neighbors feud over everything from pesticides to God.

Prodigal Who Stayed Home: Luke 15:25, A0021. Ed Young. (J). 1978. 4.95 (978-0-7417-1021-5(8), A0021) Win Walk.

Prodigal's Prodigal Father: Luke 15. Ed Young. 1979. 4.95 (978-0-7417-1064-2(1), A0065) Win Walk.

Prodigy. unabr. ed. Dave Kalstein. Read by Paul Michael Garcia. (Running Time: 46800 sec.). 2007. 72.95 (978-1-4332-0724-2(9)); audio compact disk 29.95 (978-1-4332-0726-6(5)); audio compact disk 81.00 (978-1-4332-0725-9(7)) Blckstn Audio.

Producer: A Memoir. unabr. ed. David Wolper. 10 cass. (Running Time: 14 hrs. 30 mins.). 2004. 37.95 (978-1-59007-508-1(0)) Pub: New Millenn Enter. Dist(s): PerseuPGW

Producer: A Memoir. unabr. ed. David Wolper & David Fisher. Read by David Wolper & Mark A. Cross. Intro. by Art Buchwald & Mike Wallace. 12 CDs. (Running Time: 14 hrs. 30 mins.). 2004. audio compact disk 69.95 (978-1-59007-509-8(9)) Pub: New Millenn Enter. Dist(s): PerseuPGW

***Producer: John Hammond & the Soul of American Music.** unabr. ed. Dunstan Prial. Read by Ray Porter. (Running Time: 12 hrs. 5 mins.). (ENG.). 2011. 29.95 (978-1-4332-2721-9(5)); 72.95 (978-1-4332-2717-2(7)); audio compact disk 32.95 (978-1-4332-2720-2(7)); audio compact disk 105.00 (978-1-4332-2718-9(5)) Blckstn Audio.

Producers Pack. 2005. audio compact disk 69.95 (978-0-9769097-3-6(1)) Fade.

Producing & Selling Your Own Audio Cassettes. unabr. ed. Gordon Burgett. Read by Gordon Burgett. 1 cass. (Running Time: 1 hr.). 1992. 9.95 Set. (978-0-910167-12-3(5)) Comm Unltd CA.
Explains making ones own tape, then selling it widely to others.

Producing Faith. Elbert Willis. 1 cass. (Faith School Ser.: Vol. 2). 4.00 Fill the Gap.

Producing Shakespeare. Jonathon Miller. 1 cass. (Running Time: 40 min.). 1976. 11.95 (23501) J Norton Pubs.
The eminent British director discusses the problems of the producer in the theater, his relationship to the classics, & the tasks that are imposed on the interpreter of the classics in the modern theater.

Producing Your Own CDs: A Handbook. Christian W. Huber. 2004. pap. bk. 14.95 (978-0-7119-9805-6(1), AM976338, Amsco Music) Music Sales.

Product Design for Key Stage 3: Teacher Support Pack. Andy Biggs et al. (Design & Make It Ser.). (YA). (gr. 6-9). 2000. audio compact disk 187.50 (978-0-7487-5455-7(5)) Pub: NelsonThorne GBR. Dist(s): Trans-Atl Phila

Product Development: 2 Day. Compiled by Ignite! Learning. (ENG.). (YA). 2008. (978-1-934763-92-6(6)) Ignite.

Product Distribution & Marketing. 13 cass. (Running Time: 18 hrs.). 1999. 395.00 Set; incl. study guide 1117p. (MD62) Am Law Inst.
Advanced course covers a wide spectrum of legal issues, trends, & business approaches regarding product distribution & marketing. Takes into account the advent of Internet distribution & marketing, consolidations at all levels of distribution chains, & new forms of relationships between suppliers & distributors.

Product Liability. 2nd ed. Steven Finz. 1999. Sum & Substance.

Product Liability Litigation - Post Daubert: A "Nuts & Bolts" Analysis in a New Era. (Running Time: 4 hrs. 30 min.). 1994. 92.00 Incl. 244p. coursebk. (2017) NYS Bar.
These focused presentations concentrate on the implications & strategic considerations arising from the recent U.S. Supreme Court decision of Daubert v. Merrell-Dow dealing with the use of expert testimony in product liability litigation. Each segment of the trial of a product liability action is also reviewed in light of this development.

Product Strategies - A Strategy for the New Milenium. Juan A. Gutierrez. Read by Juan Alejandro Gutiérrez Hurtado. (Running Time: 1 hr.). (C). 2003. 14.95 (978-1-60083-299-4(7), Audiofy Corp) Iofy Corp.

Product Strategies - A Strategy for the New Millenium see Estrategias de Producto - una Estrategia del Nuevo Milenio

Production & Post-Production Equipment for the Film Industry in Nigeria: A Strategic Reference 2006. Compiled by Icon Group International, Inc. Staff. 2007. ring bd. 195.00 (978-0-497-82374-0(8)) Icon Grp.

Production Music Library. Prod. by Extreme Music Library Plc. (YA). 1999. audio compact disk 319.95 (978-0-7365-1483-5(X)) Films Media Grp.

Production Music Library, Set. Prod. by Extreme Music Library Plc. (YA). 1998. audio compact disk 189.95 (978-0-7365-1484-2(8)) Films Media Grp.

Productive Bankers Achieving the Three P's. Janet L. Myers. 6 cass. 1993. 99.95 Set. (978-1-880023-19-8(9)) Dearborn Busn Pr.
Business subjects - bank management, banks & banking, negotiation, performance, performance standards, productivity, profit & sales management.

Productive Conflict Skills. Pat Heim. 1 cass. (Running Time: 50 min.). 1995. 12.95 (978-1-891531-03-3(4)) Heim Gp.
Covers fifteen strategies to make difficult discussions more productive.

Productive Dialogue. Ann Seagrave & Faison Covington. Read by Ann Seagrave & Faison Covington. (Anxiety Treatment Ser.). 15.50 CHAANGE.
Designed for those who want & need help in identifying & changing non-productive self-statements & dialogue.

Productive Workplaces: Relflections on the Function of the Inner Dialogue in Managing Change. Read by Marvin Weisbord. 1 cass. (Running Time: 90 min.). 1989. 10.95 (978-0-7822-0323-3(X), 393) C G Jung IL.

Productivity & Cost-Efficiencies: Experiences Worldwide. 1 cass. 1990. 8.50 Recorded Res.

Products Liability. 9 cass. (Running Time: 10 hrs. 30 min.). 1996. 275.00 Set; incl. study guide 331p. (MB16) Am Law Inst.
Advanced course provides the experienced lawyer with a comprehensive & multifaceted examination of products liability law & practice.

Products Liability. 1985. bk. 55.00 incl. book.; 40.00 cass. only.; 15.00 book only. PA Bar Inst.

Products Liability. Steven Finz. 2 cass. (Running Time: 3 hrs.). (Outstanding Professors Ser.). 1996. 33.50 (978-0-940366-64-0(9), 28421) West.
Lecture given by a prominent American law school professor.

Products Liability: Update on the Law & Trial Strategy. David S. Shrager. 1 cass. (Running Time: 1 hr.). 1987. 20.00 PA Bar Inst.

Products Liability Law: Child Restraint Systems. 1 cass. 1994. 175.00 (43256) Natl Prac Inst.

Products Liability Law: Crashworthiness. 1 cass. 1993. 175.00 (33267) Natl Prac Inst.

Products Liability Law: Failure to Warn. 1 cass. 1994. 175.00 (5331) Natl Prac Inst.

Products of Truth Thinking. Elbert Willis. 1 cass. (Truth Thinking Ser.). 4.00 Fill the Gap.

Products that Kill & Maim. Robert S. Sigman. Read by Robert S. Sigman. 1 cass. (Running Time: 60 min.). (Law for the Layman Ser.). 1990. 16.95 (978-1-878135-05-6(8)) Legovac.
What you need to know before you see an attorney.

Profecia Celestina. James Redfield. 2 cass. (Running Time: 2 hrs.). (SPA.). 2002. 20.00 (978-970-05-1025-5(5)) Taller del Exito.
Compelling story of intrigue, suspense, and religious revelation centered around an ancient manuscript.

Professional. unabr. ed. Robert B. Parker. Read by Joe Mantegna. (Spenser Ser.). (ENG.). 2009. audio compact disk 30.00 (978-0-7393-4389-0(0), Random AudioBks) Pub: Random Audio Pubg. Dist(s): Random

Professional Baseball Player Database, Vol. 4. 2000. audio compact disk 39.00 (978-0-9707326-0-6(0)) Old Time Dat.

Professional by Choice: Milady's Career Development Guide. Harper. 1 cass. (SalonOvations Ser.). 1995. 10.95 (978-1-56253-302-1(9), Milady) Pub: Delmar. Dist(s): CENGAGE Learn

Professional Ethics for the Chaplain. 1 cass. (Care Cassettes Ser.: Vol. 13, No. 1). 1986. 10.80 Assn Prof Chaplains.

Professional Foul. Perf. by Peter Barkworth & John Shrapnel. 2 cass. 15.95 (SCN 114) J Norton Pubs.
This play, set in Czechoslovakia, makes a telling statement about human rights & the treatment of dissidents.

Professional Horoscope Interpretation. John Soric. 1 cass. 8.95 (585) Am Fed Astrologers.
Accurate, intimate knowledge of client.

Professional Image. Richard Flint. 6 cass. Incl. Professional Image: Beginnings. 1983.; Professional Image: Is the Golden Rule Really Golden? 1983.; Professional Image: The Professional Ethic. 1983.; Professional Image: This Is a Test. 1983.; Pt. I. Professional Image: What Is a Professional? 1983.; Pt. II. Professional Image: What Is a Professional? 1983.; 1983. 70.00 (978-0-937851-09-8(4)) Pendelton Lane.
This cassette album is dedicated to the subject of ethics. It defines what a professional is & includes nine rules that should govern a professional.

Professional Image: Beginnings see Professional Image

Professional Image: Is the Golden Rule Really Golden? see Professional Image

Professional Image: The Professional Ethic see Professional Image

Professional Image: This Is a Test see Professional Image

Professional Image: What Is a Professional? see Professional Image

Professional Liability. 2 cass. (Spring Meeting Philadelphia, PA Ser.: S87-GS1). 19.00 (8701) Am Coll Surgeons.
Discusses area of liability including preparation, expert witnesses & trials of malpractice.

Professional Liability. 2 cass. (General Sessions Ser.: GS-2). 1986. 19.00 (8630) Am Coll Surgeons.

Professional Prospecting & Closing. Mark Victor Hansen. 4 cass. 60.00 (3) M V Hansen.
Obtain unlimited prospecting ideas of the professionals.

Professional Rescuer CPR. 2nd ed. National Safety Council (NSC) Staff. (C). 2001. tchr. ed. 194.95 (978-0-7637-1840-4(8), 1840-8) Jones Bartlett.

Professional Rescuer CPR DVD. 3rd rev. ed. American Academy of Orthopaedic Surgeons (AAOS). 2006. 86.50 (978-0-7637-4377-2(1)) Jones Bartlett.

Professional Responsibilities in Tax Practice. unabr. ed. Sharon E. Bossung & Wanda G. Spruill. 1 cass. (Running Time: 90 min.). 119.00 incl. wkbk. (742500KQ) Am Inst CPA.
As a CPA tax practitioner, you want to live up to the high standards of the profession while giving clients excellent value. You also want to be in the best position to avoid sanctions & penalties, some of which might affect your right to practice. If you don't know what your obligations to tax clients & to the tax system are, your right to practice might be at risk. This course gives you clear-cut answers to all of this & much more.

Professional Responsibility. Erwin Chemerinsky. (Running Time: 10800 sec.). (Law School Legends Ser.). 2007. audio compact disk 47.95 (978-0-314-17964-7(X), gilbert) West.

*__Professional Responsibility.__ 10th rev. ed. Erwin Chemerinsky. (Law School Legends Audio Ser.). 2010. audio compact disk 52.00 (978-0-314-90542-0(1)) West.

Professional Responsibility: Avoiding Malpractice & State Bar Complaints. Read by Lise M. Pearlman & Tim Hallahan. (Running Time: 3 hrs.). 1992. 89.00 Incl. 144p. tape materials. (MI-55400) Cont Ed Bar-CA.
Dramatized episodes in the life of a law firm to illustrate ethical situations causing the most State Bar complaints & malpractice suits. They cover: rules & standards; sources of information; former representation; competence; abandonment; client communication; supervision of non-attorneys; legal vs. personal ethics; sharing fees with non-lawyers; attorney as witness; restriction of practice; advertising & more.

Professional Responsibility & Code of Ethics for Financial Planners. Philip Roitman. 2 cass. 1995. 69.00 Set. (0945) Toolkit Media.
Defines key terminology contained in the code & provides in-depth analysis of issues.

Professional Responsibility, 2005 ed. (Law School Legends Audio Series) 2005th rev. ed. Erwin Chemerinsky. 2005. 46.95 (978-0-314-16105-5(8)); audio compact disk 46.95 (978-0-314-16106-2(6)) West.

Professional Screenwriters Series, Vol. I. 2005. audio compact disk 69.95 (978-0-9769097-1-2(5)) Fade.

Professional Screenwriters Series V2, Vol 2. As told by James Mangold et al. (ENG.). 2006. audio compact disk 69.96 (978-0-9769097-7-4(4)) Fade.

*__Professional Secretary.__ Linda Maytum-Wilson. 1995. 65.80 (978-1-85811-109-4(9)) Pub: EMIS GBR. Dist(s): Intl Spec Bk

Professional Selling. Somers H. White. 4 cass. (Running Time: 60 min. per cass.). 80.00 (C116) S White.
Assists the sales professional in setting priorites, planning, organizing & time management. Helps you in handling the beginning & ending of a sales situation, giving you confidence.

Professional Selling Techniques. unabr. ed. Nido R. Qubein. Read by Grover Gardner. 7 cass. (Running Time: 7 hrs.). 1987. 42.00 (978-0-7366-1226-5(2), 2144) Books on Tape.
Sales strategies are examined & suggestions offered for improvement.

Professional Speaker Training System. Paul Hartunian. 15 audio CDs. (Running Time: 15 hours). 2006. per. 1497.00 (978-0-939038-47-3(1)) Clifford Pubns.
Professional Speaker Training System is a packaged kit that provides complete training for anyone interested in starting out in the speaking business or growing their current speaking business.

Professional Supervision Skills: How to Bring Out the Best in Your People - & the Leader in You. Jack M. Everitt. 6 cass. (Running Time: 5 hrs. 1 min.). 59.95 Set incl. 24p. wkbk. (V10120) CareerTrack Pubns.
If you're a new supervisor, this program will break you in fast. If you're a good supervisor now - but want to be even better - invest a few hours with Professional Supervision Skills. You'll gain new skills to lead people, manage your time & contribute to your organization.

Professional Telephone Collectors' Techniques: (ptct) 2006. 604.98 (978-1-933960-04-3(3)) ACA Intl.

Professional Telephone Skills. PUEI. 1994. 69.95 (978-1-933328-77-5(0), CareerTrack) P Univ E Inc.

Professional Telephone Skills. Debra Smith. 2 cass. (Running Time: 3 hrs.). 1995. 15.95 (978-0-943066-39-4(5)) CareerTrack Pubns.

Professional Thief. unabr. collector's ed. Edwin H. Sutherland. Read by Michael Owens. 5 cass. (Running Time: 7 hrs. 30 min.). 1983. 40.00 (978-0-7366-0339-3(5), 1325) Books on Tape.
A journey into the hidden world of the professional thief.

Professional Writer. A. E. Van Vogt. 1 cass. (Running Time: 1 hr.). 11.95 (1019) J Norton Pubs.
A. E. Van Vogt shares the techinques developed during the fifty years he has been a professional writer.

Professionalism & Ethics for Today's Law Practice. Prod. by Advantage Legal Seminars. 2008. 177.00 (978-0-9795737-4-3(2)) Anzman Publg.

Professionalism in Astrology. ACT Staff. 1 cass. 8.95 (481) Am Fed Astrologers.
What are problems of professional astrologers?.

Professionalism in Counseling. 1 cass. (Professional Issues Ser.). 1984. 8.95 (1564G) Hazelden.

Professor. Charlotte Brontë. Narrated by Frederick Davidson. (Running Time: 10 hrs.). 1999. 30.95 (978-1-59912-704-0(0)) Iofy Corp.

Professor. Charlotte Brontë. 2001. pap. bk. 89.95 (978-1-86015-009-8(8)) Ulverscroft US.

Professor, unabr. ed. Charlotte Brontë. Read by Grover Gardner. 6 cass. (Running Time: 9 hrs.). 1999. 24.95 (978-1-55685-026-4(3), 1985) Audio Bk Con.
Based loosely on Charlotte Bronte's love for Professor Heger in Brussels & a forerunner to "Villette.".

Professor. unabr. ed. Charlotte Brontë. Read by Frederick Davidson. 7 cass. (Running Time: 10 hrs.). 2000. 49.95 (978-0-7861-1752-9(4), 2556); audio compact disk 64.00 (978-0-7861-9899-3(0), 2556) Blckstn Audio.
This work formulated a new aesthetic that questioned many of the presuppositions of Victorian society. Bronte's hero escapes from a humiliating clerkship in a Yorkshire mill to find work as a teacher in Belgium, where he falls in love with an impoverished student-teacher, who is perhaps the author's most realistic feminist heroine.

Professor. unabr. ed. Charlotte Brontë. Read by Frederick Davidson. (YA). 2008. 59.99 (978-1-60514-741-3(9)) Find a World.

Professor, Set. unabr. ed. Charlotte Brontë. Read by James Wilby. 8 cass. 2000. 69.95 (978-0-7540-0420-2(1), CAB 1843) AudioGO.
This is the story of William Crimsworth, who goes to Brussels to seek his fortune, but falls in love with Frances, a school teacher & lace-maker. This is a subtle portrayal of a self-made man & his relationships in a society that worships property & propriety.

*__Professor & Other Writings.__ unabr. ed. Terry Castle. Read by Maggi-Meg Reed. (ENG.). 2010. (978-0-06-199292-6(5), Harper Audio); (978-0-06-199151-6(1), Harper Audio) HarperCollins Pubs.

*__Professor & the Madman.__ abr. ed. Simon Winchester. Read by Simon Jones. (ENG.). 2004. (978-0-06-075633-8(0), Harper Audio); (978-0-06-079966-3(8), Harper Audio) HarperCollins Pubs.

*__Professor & the Madman.__ unabr. ed. Simon Winchester. Read by Simon Winchester. (ENG.). 2004. (978-0-06-079969-4(2), Harper Audio) HarperCollins Pubs.

Professor & the Madman: A Tale of Murder, Insanity, & the Making of the Oxford English Dictionary. Simon Winchester. Read by David Case. 1999. audio compact disk 48.00 (978-0-7366-5160-8(8)) Books on Tape.

Professor & the Madman: A Tale of Murder, Insanity, & the Making of the Oxford English Dictionary. unabr. ed. Simon Winchester. Read by David Case. 5 cass. (Running Time: 7 hrs. 30 min.). 1999. 40.00 (978-0-7366-4421-1(0), 4882) Books on Tape.
When the editors of the Oxford English Dictionary put out a call during the late 19th century pleading for "men of letters" to contribute entries, hundreds of responses came forth. Has a murderer helped compile the dictionary.

Professor & the Madman: A Tale of Murder, Insanity, & the Making of the Oxford English Dictionary. unabr. ed. Simon Winchester. Read by David Case. 6 CDs. (Running Time: 7 hrs. 12 mins.). 2001. audio compact disk 48.00 Books on Tape.

*__Professor & the Madman: A Tale of Murder, Insanity, & the Making of the Oxford English Dictionary.__ unabr. ed. Simon Winchester. Read by Simon Winchester. (ENG.). 2004. (978-0-06-075632-1(2), Harper Audio) HarperCollins Pubs.

Professor & the Madman: A Tale of Murder, Insanity, & the Making of the Oxford English Dictionary. unabr. ed. Simon Winchester. Read by Simon Winchester. Read by Elizabeth Winchester. 2005. audio compact disk 14.95 (978-0-06-083626-9(1)) HarperCollins Pubs.

Professor Bernard Siegan: Economic Liberties. (Running Time: 60 min.). (Cal State Univ., Long Beach). 1984. 9.00 (F164) Freeland Pr.
Discusses contracts & court protection: Is there protection? What can citizens do to ensure their freedom in this matter? Cites historical cases to illustrate his talk.

Professor John Hospers: The Future of Democracy. (Running Time: 60 min.). (Cypress College). 1980. 9.00 (F101) Freeland Pr.
Discusses the problems of a democracy & its pitfalls when it violates individual rights.

Professor Judith Jacobsen & Daniel Luecke on Regional Growth & U. S. Optimum Population Concerns; Rattlesnake Venom; Fish Kill in Texas; Lake Cleanup. Hosted by Nancy Pearlman. 1 cass. (Running Time: 27 min.). 10.00 (1510) Educ Comm CA.

Professor Milton P. Siegel Speaks Out about the Vatican Control of the World Health Organization. Hosted by Nancy Pearlman. 1 cass. (Running Time: 29 min.). 10.00 (1107) Educ Comm CA.

Professor of Desire. unabr. ed. Philip Roth. Read by David Colacci. (Running Time: 9 hrs.). 2009. 39.97 (978-1-4418-0548-5(6), 9781441805485, Brinc Audio MP3 Lib); 24.99 (978-1-4418-0547-8(8), 9781441805478, Brilliance MP3); 39.97 (978-1-4418-0550-8(8), 9781441805508, BADLE); 24.99 (978-1-4418-0549-2(4), 9781441805492, BAD); audio compact disk 29.99 (978-1-4418-0545-4(1), 9781441805454, Bril Audio CD Unabri); audio compact disk 92.97 (978-1-4418-0546-1(X), 9781441805461, BriAudCD Unabrid) Brilliance Audio.

Professor Paradox. (23296-A) J Norton Pubs.

Professor Tibor Machan: Libertarianism vs. Marxism. (Running Time: 60 min.). (Cal State Univ., Long Beach). 1984. 9.00 (F160) Freeland Pr.

Professor Was a Thief. L. Ron Hubbard. Read by Jim Meskimen et al. Narrated by R. F. Daley. 2 CDs. (Running Time: 2 hrs.). (Stories from the Golden Age Ser.). (ENG.). (gr. 6). 2009. audio compact disk 9.95 (978-1-59212-324-7(4)) Gala Pr LLC.

*__Professors' Guide: Acing Exams.__ abr. ed. Lynn F. Jacobs & Jeremy S. Hyman. Read by Lynn F. Jacobs & Jeremy S. Hyman. (ENG.). 2006. (978-0-06-136531-7(9), Harper Audio) HarperCollins Pubs.

*__Professors' Guide: Going to See the Professor.__ abr. ed. Lynn F. Jacobs & Jeremy S. Hyman. Read by Lynn F. Jacobs & Jeremy S. Hyman. (ENG.). 2006. (978-0-06-136532-4(7), Harper Audio) HarperCollins Pubs.

*__Professors' Guide: Taking Excellent Lecture Notes.__ abr. ed. Lynn F. Jacobs & Jeremy S. Hyman. Read by Lynn F. Jacobs & Jeremy S. Hyman. (ENG.). 2006. (978-0-06-136530-0(0), Harper Audio) HarperCollins Pubs.

*__Professors' Guide (TM) to Getting Good Grades in College.__ abr. ed. Lynn F. Jacobs & Jeremy S. Hyman. Read by Lynn F. Jacobs & Jeremy S. Hyman. (ENG.). 2006. (978-0-06-117395-0(9), Harper Audio); (978-0-06-122904-6(0), Harper Audio) HarperCollins Pubs.

Professor's House. Willa Cather. Narrated by Flo Gibson. 2009. audio compact disk 24.95 (978-1-60646-071-9(4)) Audio Bk Con.

Professor's House, unabr. ed. Willa Cather. Narrated by Flo Gibson. 4 cass. (Running Time: 5 hrs.30 mins.). (gr. 10 up). 1999. 19.95 (978-1-55685-624-2(5)) Audio Bk Con.
St. Peter resists moving into his new & better house in order to work & keep his dreams & true self within the shabby walls of his old home.

Professor's Yarn see $30,000 Bequest & Other Stories

Profeta. abr. ed. Kahlil Gilbran. Narrated by Ramon Morell. 5 cds. (Running Time: 7200 sec.). (SPA.). 2008. audio compact disk 24.95 (978-1-933499-59-8(1)) Fonolibro Inc.

*__Profeta.__ abr. ed. Khalil Gilbran. Read by Hernando Ivan Cano. (SPA.). 2008. audio compact disk 17.00 (978-958-8318-40-0(8)) Pub: Yoyo Music COL. Dist(s): YoYoMusic

Proficiency Masterclass. Kathy Gude. 2009. audio compact disk 39.95 (978-0-19-432922-4(4)) OUP.

Profile of a Prophet & God Is the Gardener. Hugh B. Brown. 1 CD. 2004. audio compact disk 10.98 (978-1-55503-965-3(0), 2500728) Covenant Comms.
Two all-time classic general authority talks.

Profile of a Prophet & God Is the Gardener: Collector's Edition. collector's ed. Hugh B. Brown. 1 cass. 2004. 7.98 (978-1-55503-320-0(2), 0600343) Covenant Comms.
Two of his most beloved talks.

Profile Plus 2005 for Hoeger/Hoeger's Lifetime Physical Fitness & Wellness, 9th. 9th ed. (C). 2006. audio compact disk 23.95 (978-0-495-01738-7(8)) Pub: Wadsworth Pub. Dist(s): CENGAGE Learn

Profile 2006 Cd-Prin/Lab Ser. (C). 2005. audio compact disk 23.95 (978-0-534-60497-4(8)) Pub: Brooks-Cole. Dist(s): CENGAGE Learn

*__Profiles in Audacity: Great Decisions & How They Were Made.__ unabr. ed. Alan Axelrod. Read by Scott Peterson. (Running Time: 10 hrs.). (ENG.). 2010. 49.98 (978-1-59659-656-6(2), GildAudio) Pub: Gildan Media. Dist(s): HachBkGrp

Profiles in Courage. John F. Kennedy. 1975. audio compact disk 9.99 (978-0-06-074352-9(2)) HarperCollins Pubs.

Profiles in Courage. John F. Kennedy. Read by Kennedy John F. 1975. 9.99 (978-0-06-074351-2(4)) HarperCollins Pubs.

Profiles in Courage. unabr. abr. ed. John F. Kennedy. Read by Caroline Kennedy. 2003. audio compact disk 22.00 (978-0-06-053323-6(4)) HarperCollins Pubs.

*__Profiles in Folly: History's Worst Decisions & Why They Went Wrong.__ unabr. ed. Alan Axelrod. Read by Scott Peterson. (Running Time: 11 hrs. 30 mins.). (ENG.). 2010. 39.98 (978-1-59659-669-6(4), GildAudio) Pub: Gildan Media. Dist(s): HachBkGrp

Profit from Real Estate. Betty L. Randolph. Read by Betty L. Randolph. Read by Leonard Baron. Ed. by Success Education Institute International Staff. 1 cass. (Running Time: 60 min.). (Specialized Sales Ser.). 1989. bk. 14.98 (978-1-55909-214-2(9), 80PM) Randolph Tapes.
60,000 messages left-right brain. Male-female voice tracks with Megafonic Subliminals. Ocean (P) & Music (PM).

Profit Motive. Murray Newton Rothbard. 1 cass. (Running Time: 35 min.). 10.95 (305) J Norton Pubs.
The "owner vs. managers" theory; conglomerates; nonprofit corporation; & government.

Profit Sharing: The Chapman Guide to Making Money an Asset in Your Marriage. unabr. ed. Gary Chapman. Narrated by Maurice England. (Marriage Savers Ser.). (ENG.). 2007. 9.79 (978-1-60814-346-7(5)); audio compact disk 13.99 (978-1-59859-249-8(1)) Oasis Audio.

Profitable Spare-Time Hours: Great Home Businesses. 2 cass. 19.95 (978-0-88432-234-4(3), S00940) J Norton Pubs.
Presents ideas that will help you find a profitable, home-based business which can both satisfy community needs & help you make money for yourself.

Profitable Spare-Time Hours: How to Supplement Your Income. 1 cass. 10.95 (966) J Norton Pubs.
Shows how to supplement your income from 15 categories of part-time & free-lance opportunities.

Profitable Telemarketing. George Walther. Read by George Walther. 6 cass. 69.95 Set. (726A) Nightingale-Conant.

Profits Aren't Everything, They're the Only Thing: No-Nonsense Rules from the Ultimate Contrarian & Small Business Guru. unabr. ed. George Cloutier & Samantha Marshall. Narrated by Erik Synnestvedt. (Running Time: 5 hrs. 0 mins. 0 sec.). (ENG.). 2009. 19.99 (978-1-4001-6526-1(1)); 13.99 (978-1-4001-8526-9(2)); audio compact disk 29.99 (978-1-4001-1526-6(4)); audio compact disk 59.99 (978-1-4001-4526-3(0)) Pub: Tantor Media. Dist(s): IngramPubServ

Profound Differences Between Prayer, Contemplation, & Meditation. unabr. ed. Stan Kendz. Read by Stan Kendz. 1 cass. (Running Time: 50 min.). 1995. 10.00 (978-1-57582-006-4(4)) HAPPE Progs.
Learn why prayer, meditation, & contemplation are not the same & do not effect the body in the same way. Learn which is more beneficial to self-awareness & growth.

Profscam. unabr. ed. Charles J. Sykes. Read by Michael Wells. 6 cass. (Running Time: 8 hrs. 30 mins.). 1991. 44.95 (978-0-7861-0227-3(6), 1200) Blckstn Audio.
Sykes examines the academic culture of the American professoriate & finds it distinctly lacking in redeeming traits. What the American university professor is trying to do,he argues, is to turn American universities into professional clubs where deviation from the party line means expulsion & exile, where perks are paramount & where taxpayers, parents & students - who pay the bills - are treated with the utmost contempt.

Program. Gregg Hurwitz. Read by Erik Steele. 9 cass. 79.95 (978-0-7927-3792-6(X), CSL 862); audio compact disk 49.95 (978-0-7927-3845-9(4), CMP 862) AudioGO.

Program. Gregg Hurwitz. Read by Eric Steele. 12 CDs. (Running Time: 54540 sec.). 2005. audio compact disk 110.95 (978-0-7927-3793-3(8), SLD 862) AudioGO.

*__Program.__ abr. ed. Gregg Hurwitz. (ENG.). 2004. (978-0-06-078642-7(6), Harper Audio) HarperCollins Pubs.

Program. abr. ed. Gregg Hurwitz. Read by Dylan Baker. 2004. audio compact disk 29.95 (978-0-06-075776-2(0)) HarperCollins Pubs.

*__Program.__ abr. ed. Gregg Hurwitz. Read by Dylan Baker. (ENG.). 2004. (978-0-06-081428-1(4), Harper Audio) HarperCollins Pubs.

*__Program.__ abr. ed. Stephen White. Read by Sandra Burr. (Running Time: 6 hrs.). (Dr. Alan Gregory Ser.). 2010. audio compact disk 9.99 (978-1-4418-6691-2(4), 9781441866912) Brilliance Audio.

Program. unabr. ed. Stephen White. Read by Sandra Burr. 8 cass. (Running Time: 11 hrs.). (Dr. Alan Gregory Ser.). 2001. 34.95 (978-1-58788-357-6(0), 1587883570, BAU); 87.25 (978-1-58788-358-3(9), 1587883589) Brilliance Audio.
Take a character as multi-dimensional as Tony Soprano. Pair him with a mother and daughter in peril and on the run. Add a clinical psychologist tasked with helping them negotiate their new lives - a program with an agenda all its own - and the result is a book that Stephen White's peers are already calling "one of the best thrillers you will ever read" (William Bernhardt) and "an exciting ride through a dark region of law enforcement." (Peter Abrahams). When New Orleans District Attorney Kirsten Lord and her nine-year-old daughter are imperiled by a chillingly believable death threat, Lord has no other choice but to accept the Witness Protection Program's offer to hide them in Boulder, Colorado. There, they meet program veteran Carl Luppo, a solitary mob hit man who is tormented by his former life and has nothing but time for regret. Sensing that Lord and her daughter's safety has been compromised, Luppo takes on the role of sentinel, fully realizing this might be his last shot at redemption. While Lord suspects that Luppo's warnings about the program's dark side are for her own protection and that she should believe the former assassin's instincts, the only person she can really trust is nine-years-old.

Program. unabr. ed. Stephen White. Read by Sandra Burr. (Running Time: 11 hrs.). (Dr. Alan Gregory Ser.). 2005. 39.25 (978-1-59600-767-3(2), 9781596007673, BADLE); 24.95 (978-1-59600-766-6(4), 9781596007666, BAD); audio compact disk 39.25 (978-1-59600-765-9(6), 9781596007659, Brinc Audio MP3 Lib) Brilliance Audio.

Program. unabr. ed. Stephen White. Read by Sandra Burr. (Running Time: 39600 sec.). (Dr. Alan Gregory Ser.). 2005. audio compact disk 24.95 (978-1-59600-764-2(8), 9781596007642, Brilliance MP3) Brilliance Audio.

*__Program.__ unabr. ed. Stephen White. Read by Sandra Burr. (Running Time: 12 hrs.). (Dr. Alan Gregory Ser.). 2010. audio compact disk 29.99 (978-1-4418-4023-3(0), 9781441840233); audio compact disk 89.97 (978-1-4418-4024-0(9), 9781441840240, BriAudCD Unabrid) Brilliance Audio.

Program: The Brain-Smart Approach to the Healthiest You - The Life-Changing 12-Week Method. unabr. ed. Kelly Traver. (Running Time: 13 hrs. 30 mins.). 2009. audio compact disk 34.95 (978-1-4417-1156-4(2)) Blckstn Audio.

Program: The Brain-Smart Approach to the Healthiest You - The Life-Changing 12-Week Method. unabr. ed. Kelly Traver. Read by Cassandra Campbell. (Running Time: 13 hrs. 30 mins.). 2009. 29.95

(978-1-4417-1157-1(0)); 79.95 (978-1-4417-1153-3(8)); audio compact disk 109.00 (978-1-4417-1154-0(6)) Blckstn Audio.

Program for a Healthy Planet. (J). 1990. 9.95 (978-1-887028-56-1(0)) Slim Goodbody.

Program for Better Vision. 3 cass. (Running Time: 20 min. per cass.). 1999. 59.95 Set, incl. prog. guide 80p., 2 vision charts, fusion string & toll-free support line. (83-0068) Explorations.
Techniques for exercise, relaxation, visualization & perception to improve eyesight & reduce, postpone or eliminate the need for corrective lenses. Addresses nearsightedness, farsightedness, astigmatism & eye imbalance.

Program for Your Tape Album: A Guide to the Big Book's Design for Living. Created by James Hubal & Joanne Hubal. 4 cass. (Running Time: 90 min.). 35.00 set. (978-0-89486-745-3(8), 5638) Hazelden.
An amazing mix of humor & intensity brings the Twelve Steps to new life on these powerful tapes. Multiply the impact of A Program for You whenever you turn on these tapes.

Program Notes: Elements of Literature. Holt, Rinehart and Winston Staff. 1997. 92.00 (978-0-03-095575-4(0)); 92.00 (978-0-03-095576-1(9)); 92.00 (978-0-03-095577-8(7)); 92.00 (978-0-03-095578-5(5)); 92.00 (978-0-03-095580-8(7)) Holt McDoug.

Program Notes: Elements of Literature. 5th ed. Holt, Rinehart and Winston Staff. 1997. 92.00 (978-0-03-095581-5(5)) Holt McDoug.

Program Notes: Elements of Literature. 6th ed. Holt, Rinehart and Winston Staff. 1997. 92.00 (978-0-03-095582-2(3)) Holt McDoug.

Program of Spiritual Development for Cancer Patients. 1 cass. (Care Cassettes Ser.: Vol. 14, No. 6). 1987. 10.80 Assn Prof Chaplains.

Programa de Idiomas Ahora Con Musica: Aprenda Ingles Sisema de Aprendizaje Innovador y Dinamico see VocabuLearn Spanish - English 2: Music-Enhanced

Programa Nacioal de Capacitacion Para el Proveedor Voluntario de Salud. Michael Karpinski. Prod. by Michael Karpinski. 2002. per. 399.00 (978-0-9718597-8-4(7)) Medifecta Hlth.

Programa Nacional de Cuidadores de Enfermos. Excerpts. 1. (Running Time: 30 mins). Dramatization. 2002. per. (978-0-9726833-0-2(5)) Medifecta Hlth.

Programmable Logic Controllers. 3rd rev. ed. W. Bolton. (C). 2003. 29.95 (978-0-7506-5986-4(6), NewSci) Sci Tech Bks.

Programmatic Portuguese, Vol. 2. Foreign Service Institute Staff. 18 cass. (Running Time: 16 hrs.). 2001. pap. bk. 225.00 (AFP180) J Norton Pubs.
Introduces Portuguese as it is spoken by educated Brazilians. Emphasis is on spoken Portuguese, distinguishing the nasal & the non-nasal vowels. There are dialogs of natural, everyday conversations between native speakers, emphasizing the difference between Portuguese spelling & speech. Dialogs for memorization are presented in three steps: pronunciation, fluency & participation.

Programmatic Spanish: Book Course, Vol. I. Foreign Service Institute Staff. 12 cass. (Running Time: 17 hrs.). (SPA.). 1967. pap. bk. 225.00 (978-0-88432-015-9(4), AFS101) J Norton Pubs.
Learn from this course by listening & repeating & repeating again, a process very similar to the way you learned to speak English. The FSI basic course provides three to four times more recorded material than courses offered elsewhere! Brief culture capsules (2-3 mins.) recorded in English at the end of each lesson unit are a unique added feature. Provides useful & entertaining insights into the language usage & customs of native speakers of Spanish. Includes manual.

Programmed Arabic Islamic Reader, Vol. 1. 6 cass. 57.43 Set. U MI Lang Res.

Programmed Arabic Islamic Reader, Vol. 2. 10 cass. 81.98 Set. U MI Lang Res.

Programmed Arabic Islamic Reader, Vols. 1 & 2. 16 cass. 107.05 Set. U MI Lang Res.

Programmed Arabic-Islamic Reader I. Raji M. Rammuny. 5 cass. (Running Time: 450 min.). 1991. 65.00 (978-0-86685-545-7(9)) Intl Bk Ctr.

Programmed Arabic-Islamic Reader II. Raji M. Rammuny. 10 cass. (Running Time: 900 min.). (ARA & ENG.). 1994. 99.95 (978-0-86685-546-4(7)) Intl Bk Ctr.

Programmed Course in Modern Literary Arabic Phonology & Script. Ernest N. McCarus & Raji Mahmud Rammuny. 6 cass. 1974. 57.43 Set. U MI Lang Res.

Programmed Ear Training: Intervals, Melody & Rhythm. 2nd ed. Leo Horacek & Gerald Lefkoff. (C). 1989. bk. (978-0-318-64535-3(1)) Harcourt Coll Pubs.

Programmed Relaxation. George W. Kisker. 10.95 (29095) J Norton Pubs.
Discussion & demonstration of a new therapeutic approach utilizing progressive relaxation, psychological programming & operant shaping.

Programmed Weight Gain. 1 cass. (Running Time: 60 min.). 10.95 (028) Psych Res Inst.
Induces a change in eating habits to correspond to physical requirements.

Programming & Problem Solving ADA 95. 2nd ed. Suzanne Levy. (C). 2000. audio compact disk 101.00 (978-0-7637-1389-8(9), 1389-9) Jones Bartlett.

Programming & Problem Solving with C++ 2nd ed. Nell B. Dale et al. (C). 1999. audio compact disk 101.00 (978-0-7637-1189-4(6), 1189-6) Jones Bartlett.

Programming Awareness. unabr. ed. John Lilly. 1 cass. 1983. 10.00 (978-1-56964-619-9(8), A0068-83) Sound Photosyn.
From Dr. Lilly's personal collection.

Programming for the Hypnotherapist. Gil Boyne. Read by Gil Boyne. 1 cass. 12.50 (117) Westwood Pub Co.
Instills confidence in your ability to use hypnosis creatively, & to build a successful practice.

Programming in BASIC. unabr. ed. William R. Parks. 4 cass. (Running Time: 1 hr. 20 min.). (Computer Science Ser.: Ser. I). 1977. 49.95 (CA-1) Tape Text.
An introduction to BASIC computer language. A self-paced approach allows you to proceed at your own pace & can be used on PC computer systems at home, in schools, business & industry.

Programming in C++ 2nd ed. Nell B. Dale et al. (C). 2000. audio compact disk 101.00 (978-0-7637-1545-8(X), 1545-X) Jones Bartlett.

Programming In-House Database Software Applications. 2 cass. 1990. 16.00 set. Recorded Res.

Programming Nonverbal Behavior. unabr. ed. B. F. Skinner. 4 cass. (Running Time: 4 hrs. 6 min.). 1966. 36.00 Set. (10601) Big Sur Tapes.

Programming Pearls. Ed. by Marco A. V. Bitetto. 1 cass. 1999. (978-1-58578-104-1(5)) Inst of Cybernetics.

Programming Right from the Start with Visual BasicNET & Student CD: Instructor's Resource CD. Crews & Daniel Murphy. audio compact disk 18.97 (978-0-13-141698-7(7)) PH School.

Programs, Babies & Shrinkage: Jeremiah 1:3-4. Ed Young. (J). 1980. 4.95 (978-0-7417-1145-8(1), A0145) Win Walk.

Programs for Digital Signal Processing. Ed. by Digital Signal Processing Committee. 1979. bk. 85.00 (978-0-686-96748-4(8)) IEEE.

Progress. Tom Hutchinson. 1999. 17.50 (978-0-19-435248-2(X)) OUP.

Progress & Evolution. Swami Amar Jyoti. 1 cass. 1991. 9.95 (K-132) Truth Consciousness.
Growth within one's self is a right, but not at the cost of others. On competition, cooperation & human potential.

Progress & How to Promote It. 1 cass. (Running Time: 1 hr.). 12.99 (189) Yoga Res Foun.

Progress & Performance. Edwin T. Cornelius. Illus. by John Odam. (New Technology English Ser.: Vol. 3). 1984. 17.00 (978-0-89209-165-2(7)) Pace Grp Intl.

Progress of Love. Alice Munro. Read by Alice Munro. 1 cass. (Running Time: 71 min.). 1987. 13.95 (978-1-55644-186-8(X), 7051) Am Audio Prose.
Munro reads the title story from her collection The Progress of Love & brings her characters rural Ontario idiom vividly to life.

Progress of the Seasons: Forty Years of Baseball in Our Town. unabr. ed. George V. Higgins. Read by Ian Esmo. 5 cass. (Running Time: 7 hrs. 30 min.). 1998. 39.95 (1909) Blckstn Audio.
Story of the Boston Red Sox. Beyond the games, there's a moment when mythic Emily is called to check the all-time lineup with deceased forebears. By then you've come to know what the author's values have in common with those in "Our Town" & why certain professional athletes achieve immortality & others don't.

Progress of the Seasons: Forty Years of Baseball in Our Town. unabr. ed. George V. Higgins. Read by Ian Esmo. 5 cass. (Running Time: 7 hrs.). 2006. 39.95 (978-0-7861-1145-9(3), 1909) Blckstn Audio.

Progress Report. Maxine Kumin. Perf. by Maxine Kumin. 1 cass. (Running Time: 42 min.). (Watershed Tapes of Contemporary Poetry). 1976. 11.95 (23629) J Norton Pubs.
Recorded in performance at the Folger Shakespeare Library.

Progress Thru Ego-Centered - Planned Chaos: Volume 10, Vol. 10. Speeches. As told by Bhagat Singh Thind. 1 cass. (Running Time: 60 mins.). (ENG., 2003. 6.50 (978-1-932630-34-3(1)) Pub: Dr Bhagat Sin. Dist(s): Baker Taylor

Progress to Perfection. Derek Prince. 2 cass. 11.90 Set. (043-044) Derek Prince.
Perfection is our goal because Jesus commanded it. It is possible because His Word shows us seven successive steps to attain it.

Progress Without Loss of Soul. Read by Theo Abt. 1 cass. (Running Time: 90 min.). 1987. 10.95 (978-0-7822-0007-2(9), 240) C G Jung IL.

Progressed Chart Comparison. Lynne Palmer. 1 cass. 8.95 (274) Am Fed Astrologers.
Natal & progressed charts of Queen Elizabeth & Prince Charles.

Progressed Moon. Karen McCoy. 1 cass. (Running Time: 90 min.). 1988. 8.95 (698) Am Fed Astrologers.

Progressions. Karen Johns. 1 cass. 8.95 (178) Am Fed Astrologers.

Progressions: Changes in Body, Mind & Spirit. Dee Wynne. 1 cass. 8.95 (371) Am Fed Astrologers.
Three outer planets change body, mind, spirit.

Progressive Accelerated Learning, Set. Monroe Institute Staff. 6 cass. 1994. 69.00 (10630PAX) Nightingale-Conant.
This program uses the hemispheric synchronization (Hemi-Sync) sound technology developed by Robert Monroe, a pioneer responsible for some of today's most innovative research in human consciousness. Unlike subliminal self-improvement programs, Progressive Accelerated Learning keeps you in control at all times. This sound technology teaches you how to use your own resources to their full capacity. Your results are strengthened over time. Includes: Tape 1: Concentration; Tape 2: Retain/Recall/Release; Tape 3: Morning Exercise; Tape 4: Catnapper; Tape 5: Deep 10 Relaxation; Tape 6: Midsummer Night.

Progressive Around the Drums with Syncopation. Jim Latta. (Progressive Ser.). 1997. pap. bk. 19.95 (978-0-947183-69-1(8), 256-054) Kolala Music SGP.

Progressive Classical Solos. Nathaniel Gunod. (ENG.). 1997. audio compact disk 9.95 (978-0-7390-2610-6(0)) Alfred Pub.

Progressive Commitment. Derek Prince. 1 cass. (I-4076) Derek Prince.

Progressive Complete Learn to Play Drums Manual. Craig Lauritsen. 2003. pap. bk. 29.95 (978-1-86469-258-7(8), 256-018) Kolala Music SGP.

Progressive Drum Grooves. Craig Lauritsen. (Progressive Ser.). 1997. pap. bk. 19.95 (978-1-875726-31-8(4), 256-052) Kolala Music SGP.

Progressive Era Triple Alliance: Governments As a Cartelizer. Murray Newton Rothbard. 2 cass. (Running Time: 2 hrs. 36 min.). 19.95 (213) J Norton Pubs.
Big business attempts to freeze out new competition - a significant factor in passage of much of the era's legislation.

Progressive Excitement. Jack Schwarz. 10.00 (503) Aletheia Psycho.

Progressive Guitar Chords. Gary Turner & Brenton White. (Progressive Ser.). 1997. pap. bk. 24.95 (978-0-947183-09-7(4), 256-046) Kolala Music SGP.

Progressive Muscle Relaxation, Confidence & Positive Thinking: Morning Mind Exercise & Relaxing at the Beach. Michael S. Prokop. (Running Time: 46 min.). (J). 1999. 9.95 (978-0-933879-29-4(6)) Alegra Hse Pubs.

Progressive Relaxation & Breathing. Matthew McKay & Patrick Fanning. (Running Time: 50 mins). (Relaxation Skills CD Ser.). (ENG.). 2008. audio compact disk 13.95 (978-1-57224-639-3(1)) New Harbinger.

Progressive Rock Drumming & Soloing Methods. Rob Leytham. 1997. pap. bk. 9.95 (978-0-7866-2854-4(5), 96670BCD) Mel Bay.

Progressuve Muscle Relaxation: Guided Imagery for Well-Being. Catherine Sheen. 1 CD. (Running Time: 41 minutes). 2005. audio compact disk 14.95 (978-0-9773381-5-3(0)) Reach In.
Progressive Muscle Relaxation is a guided imagery that promotes relaxation and stress reduction by guiding you to tense, then relax one muscle group at a time, from your feet to your face and head. This guided imagery can help you let go of stress, release pain from contracted muscles, and achieve a lasting sense of inner peace and freedom. The CD includes a Preparation for Guided Imagery track.

Prohibition & Al Capone. 10.00 (HT409) Esstee Audios.

Project. Perf. by Michael W. Smith. 1 cass. 1983. audio compact disk Brentwood Music.
This debut release, now certified gold, features the classic hit, Friends, written by Michael & his wife, Debbie. Also features Great is the Lord.

Project: A Perfect World. unabr. ed. Gary Paulsen. Narrated by Jeff Woodman. 1 cass. (Running Time: 1 hr.). (Gary Paulsen's World of Adventure Ser.: Bk. 9). (gr. 4 up). 1997. 10.00 (978-0-7887-1161-9(X), 95121E7) Recorded Bks.
Young Jim Stanton's father has been given a wonderful job at Folsom National Laboratories in New Mexico. The company has provided the Strantons with everything they need, including a fabulous house & even a brand new car. The only trouble is that it all seems a little too perfect.

Project Alexandria: WorldWide Astrological Library. ACT Staff. 1 cass. (Workshop Ser.). 8.95 (010) Am Fed Astrologers.

Project Charisma - Attract Love. 1 cass. (Sleep Programming Tapes Ser.). 12.98 (978-0-87554-547-9(5), 1121) Valley Sun.

Project Cost Estimating: Principles & Practice. Jack Sweeting. 1997. bk. 40.00 (978-0-85295-380-8(1), 53801) Pub: IChemE GBR. Dist(s): Gulf Pub

Project Delta: After Action Reports Det B-52 (1964-1970) Stephen Sherman. 1999. bk. 59.99 (978-1-929932-01-6(4)) RADIX Pr.

Project Financing: Power Generation, Waste Recovery & Other Industrial Facilities. 8 cass. (Running Time: 10 hrs. 30 min.). 1991. 175.00 Set. (T7-9321) PLI.
This recording of the March 1991 PLI program focuses on project financing where there is no creditworthy borrower or lessee.

Project Management. Larry Johnson. 4 cass. 79.95 set incl. workbook. (C10107) CareerTrack Pubns.
This audio will help you develop the crucial skills needed to put a project together. You'll learn to take a project successfully from start to finish - without wasting time or money.

Project Management, Set. Fred Pryor Seminars Staff. 6 cass. 1994. 59.95 (10540AX) Nightingale-Conant.
Project management is a key skill for the '90s & beyond. In this targeted seminar, you'll learn the five-step project management style. Find out how to incorporate the traits of a successful project manager & design an efficient team.

Project Management: Bring Your Projects in on Time & on Budget - Consistently. Larry Johnson. 4 cass. (Running Time: 4 hrs. 14 min.). 1994. 59.95 Set incl. 64p. wkbk. (V10144) CareerTrack Pubns.
Complete with easy-to-follow graphics, this program helps you chart a successful course to meet your own project goals & outlines the steps you need to take to become a trusted project leader in your own organization.

Project Management: Guaranteed to Help You Complete Your Projects on Time, on Budget, & on Target. Fred Pryor. 6 cass. 59.95 Set plus wkbk. (10540AS) Pryor Resources.
Competent, creative project management is a key professional skill. This seminar is based on extensive surveys and interviews, & it pinpoints & clarifies the specific abilities needed by today's successful project managers.

***Project management Basics.** Prod. by Praizion Media. (ENG.). 2010. audio compact disk 14.99 (978-1-934579-18-3(1)) Praizion Medis.

***Project Management for Dummies.** abr. ed. Stanley Portny. (ENG.). 2008. (978-0-06-176486-8(8), Harper Audio); (978-0-06-176487-5(6), Harper Audio) HarperCollins Pubs.

Project Management for the Clueless(r). Narrated by Mike Rounds. 1 CD. (Running Time: 42 mins., 52 seconds). 2004. audio compact disk 19.95 (978-1-891440-37-3(3)) CPM Systems.

Project Management Tools Cd Version 40. 2004. audio compact disk 139.95 (978-1-890367-36-7(2)) Pub: ESI Int. Dist(s): Taylor and Fran

Project Mulberry. unabr. collector's ed. Linda Sue Park. Read by Mina Kim. 3 cass. (Running Time: 4 hrs. 33 mins.). (J). (gr. 4-7). 2005. 30.00 (978-0-307-24535-9(7), BksonTape); audio compact disk 32.30 (978-0-307-24536-6(5), BksonTape) Pub: Random Audio Pubg. Dist(s): NetLibrary CO
Julia Song and her friend Patrick would love to win a blue ribbon, maybe even two, at the state fair. They've always done projects together, and they work well as a team. This time, though, they're having trouble coming up with just the right plan. Then Julia's mother offers a suggestion: They can raise silkworms, as she did when she was a girl in Korea. Patrick thinks it's a great idea. Of course there are obstacles-for example, where will they get mulberry leaves, the only thing silkworms eat?-but nothing they can't handle. Julia isn't so sure. The club where kids do their projects is all about traditional American stuff, and raising silkworms just doesn't fit in. Moreover, the author, Ms. Park, seems determined to make Julia's life as complicated as possible, no matter how hard Julia tries to talk her out of it. In her first novel with a contemporary setting, Linda Sue Park delivers a funny, lively story that illuminates both the process of writing a novel and the meaning of growing up American.

Project Mulberry: Includes Author Interview. unabr. ed. Linda Sue Park. Read by Mina Kim. 4 CDs. (Running Time: 4 hrs. 33 mins.). (ENG.). (J). (gr. 3-7). 2005. audio compact disk 28.00 (978-0-307-24534-2(9), Listening Lib) Pub: Random Audio Pubg. Dist(s): Random

Project: Peace (Musical) What Kids Can Do to Build a More Tolerant World - ShowTrax. Roger Emerson. 1 CD. (Running Time: 30 mins.). 2000. audio compact disk 59.95 H Leonard.
From the stirring opening to its powerful conclusion, this unique pop-style revue can help young people tackle the serious issues facing them in their world today.

Project Scapegoats: Lessons from the Titanic Project. Speeches. Mark Kozak-Holland. 1 CD. (Running Time: 65). 2006. audio compact disk 14.87 (978-1-897326-32-9(7)) Multi-Media ON CAN.
We?ve all heard about them?projects where things go so wrong that they make the newspapers. Sometimetimes the project fails during its design stage, sometimes during its build stage, or sometimes during its post-launch operational stage. Whatever the case, these projects fail, and fail BIG. But do any come close to the track- record of the cruise ship Titanic: four years in development (1909-1912) and only 4 days in operation?Facing a financial loss that could bankrupt the company, plusthousands of potential lawsuits, the company that owned the shipwas eager to participate in two official government inquiries thatsought out who to blame for the disaster.Learn from this historical project so that YOU don?t get caught as the Project Scapegoat if one of your projects fails.

***Project Third Dynamic.** L. Ron Hubbard. (ENG.). 2002. audio compact disk 15.00 (978-1-4031-3677-0(7)) Bridge Pubns Inc.

Project Xanadu: The World Library. Ted Nelson. 1 cass. 9.00 (A0328-88) Sound Photosyn.
A great concept coming directly from the horse's mouth.

Projecting a Powerful, Confident Presence. Patricia Smith-Pierce. 3 cass. (Running Time: 5 hrs.). bk. 49.00 Set. (5007) Natl Inst Child Mgmt.
Examines vocal & verbal communication patterns that fit the needs & demands of a child care director. Negative patterns particularly associated with lack of competence & credibility will be highlighted.

Projecting a Professional Image in Child Care. Dora C. Fowler. 1 cass. (Running Time: 60 min.). 9.95 (978-1-57323-013-1(8)) Natl Inst Child Mgmt.

Projectionist's Nightmare see Brian Patten Reading His Poetry

Projective Use of the Wechsler-Bellevue Test. Molly Harrower. 1 cass. (Running Time: 16 min.). 1952. (29242) J Norton Pubs.
The qualitative analysis of Wechsler-Bellevue test items as a method for discovering underlying personality dynamics.

Projekt Alphabet: Audio Cass. to use W/Kursbuch. C. Volkmar-Clark. (Running Time: 1 hr.). 2005. 16.50 (978-3-468-49898-5(5)) Langenscheidt.

Projekt Alphabet: Audio CD to use W/Kursbuch. C. Volkmar-Clark. (Running Time: 1 hr.). 2005. audio compact disk 16.50 (978-3-468-49899-2(3)) Langenscheidt.

***Prokofiev - Visions Fugitives, Op. 22.** Composed by Sergei Prokofiev. (ENG.). 2011. pap. bk. 12.99 (978-1-4234-9413-3(X), 142349413X, G Schirmer) H Leonard.

Prokofiev: Violin Concerto No. 1 in D Major, Op. 19: Book/2-CD Pack. Composed by Sergei Prokofiev. Mila Georgieva. 2009. pap. bk. 34.98 (978-1-59615-203-8(6), 1596152036) Pub: Music Minus. Dist(s): H Leonard

Prokop Divorce Adjustment Inventory: Divorce Test for Children. Michael S. Prokop. 1986. 10.40 (978-0-933879-30-0(X)) Alegra Hse Pubs.

Prolactinoma: Diagnosis & Management. Contrib. by Michael O. Thorner et al. 1 cass. (Running Time: 90 min.). 1985. 12.00 (A8511) Amer Coll Phys.
This topic is discussed by a moderator & experts who offer differing opinions.

Prologue. (SAC 919) Spoken Arts.

Prologue to the Legend of Good Women see Hearing Great Poetry: From Chaucer to Milton

Prom. unabr. ed. Laurie Halse Anderson. Narrated by Katherine Kellgren. 5 CDs. (Running Time: 5 hrs. 45 mins.). (YA). 2005. audio compact disk 48.75 (978-1-4193-5610-0(0), C3416); 39.75 (978-1-4193-5097-9(8), 98119) Recorded Bks.
New York Times best-selling author Laurie Halse Anderson is a National Book Award finalist and recipient of a Michael L. Printz Honor. Young adults will identify strongly with Prom's main character, Ashley, a senior who doesn't care about the big dance until the faculty advisor steals all the funds. Suddenly Ash has an urge to make the Prom happen somehow - no matter what it takes.

Promesa de Amor. 1. (YA). 2003. audio compact disk 10.00 (978-1-59305-051-1(8)) Good News Prod Intl.

Promesa de Amor (Gustavo Velázquez) 1. (YA). 2003. 10.00 (978-1-59305-052-8(6)); audio compact disk 10.00 (978-1-59305-050-4(X)) Good News Prod Intl.

Promessi Sposi (Beginning Chapters) Alessandro Manzoni. Read by Francesco Noli. 1 cass. (Running Time: 1 hrs. 30 min.). 1996. pap. bk. 24.50 (978-1-58085-457-3(5)) Interlingua VA.

Prometheus see Don Juan

Prometheus, Nos. 40, 41 & 42. Carl Faber. 3 cass. (Running Time: 3 hrs. 45 min.). 1985. 28.50 (978-0-918026-49-1(0), SR 64-518) Perseus Pr.

Prometheus & Gilgamesh. 1 cass. (Running Time: 1 hr.). Dramatization. 2001. audio compact disk 15.95 (HEAD002) Lodestone Catalog.
A musical dramatization about the rebellious god who dared to give humankind fire.

Prometheus Deception. Robert Ludlum. Narrated by Carol Bilger. 16 CDs. (Running Time: 18 hrs. 30 mins.). audio compact disk 154.00 (978-0-7887-9851-1(0)) Recorded Bks.

Prometheus Deception. abr. ed. Robert Ludlum. Read by Frank Muller. (Running Time: 6 hrs. 0 mins. 0 sec.). (ENG.). 2007. audio compact disk 14.95 (978-1-4272-0129-4(3)) Pub: Macmill Audio. Dist(s): Macmillan

Prometheus Deception. unabr. ed. Robert Ludlum. Read by Michael Prichard. 14 cass. (Running Time: 21 hrs.). 2001. 112.00 (978-0-7366-6352-6(5)) Books on Tape.
Nicholas Bryson spent years as a deep-cover operative for a secret intelligence group, the Directorate. After a critical undercover mission went drastically wrong, Bryson was retired to a new identity. Years later, his closely held cover cracks & Bryson learns that the Directorate was not what it claimed.

Prometheus Deception. unabr. ed. Robert Ludlum. Narrated by Paul Michael & Carol Bilger. 12 cass. (Running Time: 18 hrs. 30 mins.). 2000. 98.00 (978-0-7887-7153-8(1), 96711K8) Recorded Bks.
After a critical undercover mission goes horribly wrong, American intelligence operative Nicholas Bryson is forced to retire to a new identity. But when his cover is blown, Bryson learns that his former job was not what it seemed, & he's been a pawn in a deadly game of international intrigue. With everything he thought he knew about his own life in question, Bryson is all alone in a wilderness of mirrors - with millions of lives in the balance!.

Prometheus Unbound see Poetry of Shelley

Prometo Amarte. unabr. ed. Jaime Murrell, Sr. (SPA.). 2000. 9.99 (978-0-8297-2279-6(3)) Pub: Vida Pubs. Dist(s): Zondervan

Prometo Amarte. unabr. ed. Jaime Murrell, Sr. 2000. audio compact disk 14.99 (978-0-8297-2280-2(7)) Zondervan.

Promise. Donna Boyd. Narrated by Paul Hecht. 10 CDs. (Running Time: 11 hrs. 30 mins.). audio compact disk 97.00 (978-1-4025-1556-9(1)) Recorded Bks.

Promise. Douglas W. Phillips. 1 cass. (Running Time: 1 hr.). 2000. 7.00 (978-1-929241-14-9(3)) Pub: Vsn Forum. Dist(s): STL Dist NA

Promise. Douglas W. Phillips. 1 CD. (Running Time: 1 hr.). 2000. audio compact disk 10.00 (978-1-929241-76-7(3)) Pub: Vsn Forum. Dist(s): STL Dist NA
"Honor your father and mother" is the first command with a promise. This compact disc addresses the blessings associated with honor, how to install honor in the hearts of your children, and even how adults may honor renegade authority figures.

Promise. Denise Robertson. 2009. 61.95 (978-0-7531-4434-3(4)); audio compact disk 84.95 (978-0-7531-4435-0(2)) Pub: Isis Pubng Ltd GBR. Dist(s): Ulverscroft US

Promise. unabr. ed. Donna Boyd. Narrated by Paul Hecht. 8 cass. (Running Time: 11 hrs. 30 mins.). 2001. 68.00 (978-0-7887-5455-5(6), L1009x7) Recorded Bks.
Donna Boyd returns to the lives of the Devoncroix family, powerful rulers of the werewolves. Hannah, a researcher in Alaska studying wolves, rescues an injured wolf & a diary from a plane crash. With this act of compassion, she is drawn into a world she never dreamed existed.

Promise: How God Works All Things Together for Good. unabr. ed. Robert Morgan. Read by Scott Brick. (Running Time: 6 hrs. 30 mins. 0 sec.). (ENG.). 2008. audio compact disk 21.98 (978-1-59644-569-7(6)) christianaud.

***Promise: How God Works All Things Together for Good.** unabr. ed. Robert J. Morgan. Narrated by Scott Brick. (ENG.). 2008. 12.98 (978-1-59644-570-3(X), christianSeed) christianaud.

***Promise: President Obama, Year One.** unabr. ed. Jonathan Alter. Read by Jonathan Alter. 18 CDs. (Running Time: 21 hrs.). 2010. audio compact disk 49.99 (978-1-4423-3445-8(2)) Pub: S&S Audio. Dist(s): S and S Inc

Promise & Honor. Kim Murphy. Read by Dianna Dorman. (Running Time: 41400 sec.). 2006. 65.95 (978-0-7861-4589-8(7)) Blckstn Audio.

Promise & Honor: A Civil War Novel. Kim Murphy. Read by Dianna Dorman. (Running Time: 41400 secs.). 2006. audio compact disk 81.00 (978-0-7861-6999-3(0)) Blckstn Audio.

Promise & Honor: A Civil War Novel. unabr. ed. Kim Murphy. Read by Dianna Dorman. (Running Time: 41400 sec.). 2006. audio compact disk 29.95 (978-0-7861-7514-7(1)) Blckstn Audio.

Promise & Praise. 3 cass. 9.99 (978-0-529-07121-7(5), WBC-70) Nelson.

Promise for Ellie. abr. ed. Lauraine Snelling. Narrated by Renee Ertl. (Running Time: 9 hrs. 8 mins. 26 sec.). (Daughters of Blessing Ser.). (ENG.). 2008. 19.59 (978-1-60814-347-4(3)) Oasis Audio.

Promise for Ellie. abr. ed. Lauraine Snelling. Narrated by Renee Ertl. (Running Time: 9 hrs. 8 mins. 26 sec.). (Daughters of Blessing Ser.). (ENG.). 2008. audio compact disk 27.99 (978-1-59859-440-9(0)) Oasis Audio.

Promise for Spring. abr. ed. Kim Vogel Sawyer. Narrated by Traci Svensgaard. (Running Time: 6 hrs. 15 mins. 0 sec.). (ENG.). (YA). 2009. audio compact disk 24.98 (978-1-59644-706-6(0), christaudio) christianaud.

***Promise for Spring.** abr. ed. Kim Vogelsawyer. Narrated by Traci Svensgaard. (ENG.). 2009. 14.98 (978-1-59644-707-3(9), christaudio) christianaud.

Promise for This Day & Age. Read by Basilea Schlink. 1 cass. (Running Time: 30 min.). 1985. (0277) Evang Sisterhood Mary.
A new outpouring of the Holy Spirit awaits us in the end times; those who humble themselves before God & man experience the fulfilment of a tremendous promise.

Promise Is a Promise: An Almost Unbelievable Story of a Mother's Unconditional Love & What It Can Teach Us. unabr. ed. Wayne W. Dyer. 2 cass. (Running Time: 2 hrs.). 1996. 15.95 (978-1-56170-404-0(0), 386) Hay House.
True story of Kaye O'Bara, who has cared for her comatose daughter for over 25 years. This an amazing story that will warm your heart & inpsire you.

Promise Keepers Live Worship. audio compact disk 13.99 Provident Mus Dist.

Promise Me. abr. ed. Harlan Coben. Read by Harlan Coben. (Running Time: 6 hrs.). (Myron Bolitar Ser.: No. 8). 2007. audio compact disk 14.99 (978-1-59737-634-1(5), 9781597376341, BCD Value Price) Brilliance Audio.

Promise Me. unabr. ed. Harlan Coben. (Running Time: 11 hrs.). (Myron Bolitar Ser.: No. 8). 2006. 24.95 (978-1-59737-631-0(0), 9781597376310, BAD) Brilliance Audio.

Promise Me. unabr. ed. Harlan Coben. Read by Harlan Coben. (Running Time: 11 hrs.). (Myron Bolitar Ser.: No. 8). 2006. 39.25 (978-1-59737-632-7(9), 9781597376327, BADLE); 82.25 (978-1-59737-626-6(4), 9781597376266, BrilAudUnabridg); 32.95 (978-1-59737-625-9(6), 9781597376259); audio compact disk 97.25 (978-1-59737-628-0(0), 9781597376280, BriAudCD Unabrid); audio compact disk 39.25 (978-1-59737-630-3(2), 9781597376303, Brlnc Audio MP3 Lib); audio compact disk 24.95 (978-1-59737-629-7(9), 9781597376297, Brilliance MP3); audio compact disk 36.95 (978-1-59737-627-3(2), 9781597376273) Brilliance Audio.
It has been six years since entertainment agent Myron Bolitar last played superhero. In six years he hasn't thrown a punch. He hasn't held, much less fired, a gun. He hasn't called his friend Win, still the scariest man he knows, to back him up or get him out of trouble. All that is about to change . . . because of a promise. The school year is almost over. Anxious families await word of college acceptances. In these last pressure-cooker months of high school, some kids will make the all-too-common and all-too-dangerous mistake of drinking and driving. But Myron is determined to help keep his friends' children safe, so he makes two neighborhood girls promise him: If they are ever in a bind but are afraid to call their parents, they must call him. Several nights later, the call comes at 2:00 am, and true to his word, Myron picks up one of the girls in midtown Manhattan and drives her to a quiet cul-de-sac in New Jersey where she says her friend lives. The next day, the girl's parents discover that their daughter is missing. And that Myron was the last person to see her. Desperate to fulfill a well-intentioned promise turned nightmarishly wrong, Myron races to find her before she's gone forever. But his past will not be buried so easily - for trouble has always stalked him, and his loved ones often suffer. Now Myron must decide once and for all who he is and what he will stand up for if he is to have any hope of saving a young girl's life. "Harlan Coben is the modern master of the hook-and-twist - luring you in on the first page, only to shock you on the last." - Dan Brown, author of The Da Vinci Code.

***Promise Me.** unabr. ed. Richard Paul Evans. Read by Michele Pawk. (Running Time: 5 hrs. 0 mins. 0 sec.). 2010. audio compact disk 29.99 (978-1-4423-3533-2(5)) Pub: S&S Audio. Dist(s): S and S Inc

***Promise Me: How a Sister's Love Launched the Global Movement to End Breast Cancer.** unabr. ed. Nancy G. Brinker & Joni Rodgers. Narrated by Coleen Marlo. (Running Time: 14 hrs. 0 mins.). 2010. 19.99 (978-1-4001-8974-8(8)); 29.99 (978-1-4001-6974-0(7)); audio compact disk 95.99 (978-1-4001-4974-2(6)); audio compact disk 39.99 (978-1-4001-1974-5(X)) Pub: Tantor Media. Dist(s): IngramPubServ

Promise Me Forever. abr. ed. Janelle Taylor. Read by Jessica Arden. 1 cass. (Running Time: 90 min.). 1994. 5.99 (978-1-57096-007-9(0), RAZ 908) Romance Alive Audio.
In 1875 Savannah the "Black Widow," Rachel McCandless, has now buried her third husband under mysterious circumstances & Captain Daniel Slade intends to expose her in her own web or find the real killer. What he finds is a love that flourishes despite intrigue, deceit & danger.

Promise Me; The Woods; Hold Tight. unabr. ed. Harlan Coben. (Running Time: 35 hrs.). 2009. audio compact disk 39.99 (978-1-4233-8651-3(5), 9781423386513) Brilliance Audio.

Promise of a Lie. unabr. ed. Howard Roughan. 7 cass. (Running Time: 10 hrs. 30 min.). 2004. 72.00 (978-1-4159-0162-5(7)) Books on Tape.

Promise of Forever, Set. Anita Stansfield. 2 cass. 1996. 11.98 Set. (978-1-57734-074-4(4), 07001460) Covenant Comms.

Promise of Glory. C. X. Moreau. Read by Tom Parker. (Running Time: 11 hrs. 30 mins.). 2002. 34.95 (978-1-59912-577-0(3)) Iofy Corp.

Promise of Glory. unabr. ed. C. X. Moreau. Read by Tom Parker. 8 cass. (Running Time: 12 hrs.). 2002. 56.95 (978-0-7861-2160-1(2), 2910); audio compact disk 80.00 (978-0-7861-9526-8(6), 2910); audio compact disk 24.95 (978-0-7861-9212-0(7), 2910) Blckstn Audio.
In the battle of Antietam, Union casualties topped 12,000 and Confederate casualties exceeded 11,000. Such memorable military figures as Lee and McClellan, as well as Burnside, Longstreet, Hooker, and Jackson, all took part in the single bloodiest day of the Civil War.

Promise of Glory. unabr. ed. C. X. Moreau. Read by Tom Parker. 8 pieces. 2004. reel tape 39.95 (978-0-7861-2290-5(0)) Blckstn Audio.

Promise of Glory: A Novel on Antietam. unabr. ed. C. X. Moreau. Read by Tom Parker. (Running Time: 39600 sec.). 2007. audio compact disk 29.95 (978-0-7861-7433-1(1)) Blckstn Audio.

Promise of Healing. Speeches. Creflo A. Dollar. 7 cass. (Running Time: 6 hrs.). 2005. 25.00 (978-1-59089-909-0(1)); audio compact disk 34.00 (978-1-59089-910-6(5)) Creflo Dollar.

Promise of His Appearing AudioBook: The Shroud of Turin. Peter J. Leithart. Read by Aaron Wells. (ENG.). 2009. audio compact disk 20.00 (978-1-59128-434-5(1)) Canon Pr ID.

Promise of Hope. Amy Clipston. (Running Time: 8 hrs. 12 mins. 22 sec.). (Kauffman Amish Bakery Ser.). (ENG.). 2010. 12.99 (978-0-310-77332-0(6)) Zondervan.

Promise of Sleep: A Pioneer in Sleep Medicine Explores the Vital Connection Between Health, Happiness, & A Good Night's Sleep. William C. Dement & Christopher Vaughan. Read by Jeff McCarthy. 2004. 15.95 (978-0-7435-4900-4(7)) Pub: S&S Audio. Dist(s): S and S Inc

Promise of the Morning. Grace Goodwin. Read by Elizabeth Henry. 4 cass. (Running Time: 6 hrs.). 1999. 44.95 (64194) Pub: Soundings Ltd GBR. Dist(s): Ulverscroft US

***Promise of the Valley.** Zondervan. (Running Time: 8 hrs. 26 mins. 38 sec.). (Westward Dreams Ser.). (ENG.). 2010. 9.99 (978-0-310-86941-2(2)) Zondervan.

Promise to Believe In. abr. ed. Tracie Peterson. Narrated by Aimee Lilly. (Running Time: 6 hrs. 19 mins. 7 sec.). (Brides of Gallatin County Ser.). (ENG.). 2008. 18.19 (978-1-60814-348-1(1)) Oasis Audio.

Promise to Believe In. abr. ed. Tracie Peterson. Narrated by Aimee Lilly. (Running Time: 6 hrs. 19 mins. 7 sec.). (Brides of Gallatin County Ser.: No. 1). (ENG.). 2008. audio compact disk 25.99 (978-1-59859-354-9(4)) Oasis Audio.

Promise to Keep. Lilian Harry. Read by Carole Boyd. 12 cass. (Soundings Ser.). (J). 2005. 94.95 (978-1-84283-656-9(0)); audio compact disk 99.95 (978-1-84283-726-9(5)) Pub: ISIS Lrg Prnt GBR. Dist(s): Ulverscroft US

Promised Blessings of the Book of Mormon, Set. 3 cass. 2004. 17.95 (978-1-57734-593-0(2), 06006221) Covenant Comms.
Four timeless talks by beloved LDS speakers.

Promised Child. 1 cass. (BibleQuizmania Ser.). (SPA.). 14.95 (978-0-929536-14-9(2)) Emb Cassettes.

Promised Land. unabr. collector's ed. Robert B. Parker. Read by Michael Prichard. 6 cass. (Running Time: 6 hrs.). (Spenser Ser.). 1989. 48.00 (978-0-7366-1551-8(2), 2420) Books on Tape.
Spenser's client Harvey Shepard has lost his pretty wife - and a very pretty quarter million in real estate. Now a loan shark is putting on the bite. Spenser finds himself doing a slow burn in the Cape Cod sun when the wife turns up as a murder one suspect & her husband has 24 hours before the mob kills him.

Promised Land: Pillar of Fire. unabr. ed. David G. Woolley. 10 cass. 2004. 39.95 (978-1-57734-723-1(4)); audio compact disk 39.95 (978-1-57734-944-0(X)) Covenant Comms.

Promised Land: Place of Refuge, Vol. 3. David G. Woolley. 10 cass. 2004. 39.95 (978-1-59156-412-6(3)) Covenant Comms.

Promised Land: The Power of Deliverance, Vol. 2. David G. Woolley. 14 cass. 2004. 39.95 (978-1-57734-942-6(3)) Covenant Comms.

Promised Land Vol. 2: The Power of Deliverance. David G. Woolley. 16 CDs. 2004. audio compact disk 39.95 (978-1-57734-943-3(1)) Covenant Comms.

Promised Land Vol. 3: Place of Refuge. David G. Woolley. 12 CDs. 2004. audio compact disk 39.95 (978-1-59156-413-3(1)) Covenant Comms.

Promised Land of Vocation: Knowing if you're called to marriage, religious life, or the Priesthood. 2009. audio compact disk 24.95 (978-0-9769197-4-2(5)) N Smith Pub.

Promised World. Lisa Tucker. 2009. audio compact disk 34.99 (978-1-4423-9832-0(9)) Brilliance Audio.

Promised World. unabr. ed. Lisa Tucker. Read by Tanya Eby. (Running Time: 11 hrs.). 2009. 24.99 (978-1-4233-9834-9(3), 9781423398349, Brilliance MP3); 39.97 (978-1-4233-9835-6(1), 9781423398356, Brlnc Audio MP3 Lib); 24.99 (978-1-4233-9836-3(X), 9781423398363, BAD); 39.97 (978-1-4233-9837-0(8), 9781423398370, BADLE); audio compact disk 34.99 (978-1-4233-9832-5(7), 9781423398325, Bril Audio CD Unabri); audio compact disk 87.97 (978-1-4233-9833-2(5), 9781423398332, BriAudCD Unabrid) Brilliance Audio.

Promises. (Dovetales Ser.: Tape 2). pap. bk. 6.95; 4.95 (978-0-944391-17-4(6)) DonWise Prodns.

Promises. unabr. ed. Belva Plain. Narrated by Barbara Rosenblat. 9 cass. (Running Time: 13 hrs. 25 min.). Rental 17.50 Set. (94803) Recorded Bks.

Promises. unabr. ed. Belva Plain. Narrated by Barbara Rosenblat. 9 cass. (Running Time: 13 hrs. 15 mins.). 1996. 78.00 (978-0-7887-0629-5(2), 94803E7) Recorded Bks.
Margaret & Adam Crane are happy with their lives. But when a woman from Adam's past suddenly appears, problems arise.

Promises & Perils of New Approaches to Hospital Chaplaincy. 1 cass. (Care Cassettes Ser.: Vol. 17, No. 6). 1990. 10.80 Assn Prof Chaplains.

Promises & Pitfalls of the Spiritual Path. Ram Dass. 1 cass. 9.00 (A0659-81) Sound Photosyn.

***Promises Broken: Courtship, Class, & Gender in Victorian England.** Ginger S. Frost. (Victorian Literature & Culture Ser.). (ENG.). 27.50 (978-0-8139-2934-7(2)) U Pr of Va.

Promises for the Imperfect. Contrib. by Number One Gun. Prod. by Aaron Sprinkle. 2005. audio compact disk 13.98 (978-5-558-92593-7(0)) Tooth & Nail.

Promises from God. unabr. ed. Jay Brice & Matt Allen. Read by Keith Showalter. Contrib. by Cathy Frizzell. 1 cass. (Running Time: 39 min.). 1996. 9.97 (978-1-889704-00-5(8)) Ripe Unto Harvest.
Devotional.

Promises in Death. abr. ed. J. D. Robb, pseud. Read by Susan Ericksen. 5 CDs. (Running Time: 6 hrs.). (In Death Ser.). 2009. audio compact disk 26.99 (978-1-4233-6518-1(6), 9781423365181, BACD) Brilliance Audio.

Promises in Death. abr. ed. J. D. Robb, pseud. (Running Time: 6 hrs.). (In Death Ser.). 2009. audio compact disk 14.99 (978-1-4233-6519-8(4), 9781423365198) Brilliance Audio.

Promises in Death. unabr. ed. J. D. Robb, pseud. Read by Susan Ericksen. 1 MP3-CD. (Running Time: 12 hrs.). (In Death Ser.). 2009. 39.97 (978-1-4233-6515-0(1), 9781423365150, Brlnc Audio MP3 Lib); 39.97 (978-1-4233-6517-4(8), 9781423365174, BADLE); 24.99 (978-1-4233-6514-3(3), 9781423365143, Brilliance MP3); 24.99 (978-1-4233-6516-7(X), 9781423365167, BAD); audio compact disk 102.97 (978-1-4233-6513-6(5), 9781423365136, BriAudCD Unabrid); audio compact disk 38.99 (978-1-4233-6512-9(7), 9781423365129, Bril Audio CD Unabri) Brilliance Audio.

Promises Live @ Saddleback. Perf. by Rick Muchow. 1 cass., 1 CD. 1999. audio compact disk 16.98 CD. (978-1-58229-065-2(2), Howard Bks) Pub: S and S. Dist(s): S and S Inc
Praise & worship music.

Promises of God. Mark Crow. 3 cass. (Running Time: 3 hrs.). 2001. (978-1-931537-10-0(0)) Vision Comm Creat.

Promises of Grace: Logos June 7, 1998. Ben Young. 1998. 4.95 (978-0-7417-6085-2(1), B0085) Win Walk.

***Promises She Keeps.** unabr. ed. Erin Healy. 2011. audio compact disk 29.99 (978-1-4003-1712-7(6)) Nelson.

***Promises to Keep.** Jane Green. Contrib. by Cassandra Campbell. (Running Time: 12 hrs.). (ENG.). 2010. audio compact disk 39.95 (978-0-14-242767-5(5), PengAudBks) Penguin Grp USA.

Promises to Keep: Joshua 14:6-15. Ed Young. 1985. 4.95 (978-0-7417-1456-5(6), 456) Win Walk.

Promises to Keep: On Life & Politics. unabr. ed. Joe Biden. Read by Mark Deakins. (ENG.). 2008. audio compact disk 29.95 (978-0-7393-8389-6(2), Random AudioBks) Pub: Random Audio Pubg. Dist(s): Random

Promote Yourself & Your Business with Writing. Eric Gelb. 1 cass. (Running Time: 43 mins.). 2003. 10.00 (978-1-890158-16-3(X), Small Busn); audio compact disk 15.00 (978-1-890158-15-6(1), Small Busn) Career Advan.
Leapfrog you competition. Position yourself as the expert in your field. This explains how you can write, publish and distribute how-to information products. How to get free publicity.

Promoting Environmental Messages Through the Arts, Pt. 1. Hosted by Nancy Pearlman. 1 cass. (Running Time: 30 min.). 10.00 (702) Educ Comm CA.

Promoting Environmental Messages Through the Arts, Pt. 2. Hosted by Nancy Pearlman. 1 cass. (Running Time: 30 min.). 10.00 (703) Educ Comm CA.

Promoting Student Development Through Intentionally Structured Groups: Principles, Techniques & Applications. Roger B. Winston, Jr. et al. (Higher Education Ser.). 1988. bk. 41.45 (978-1-55542-113-7(X), Jossey-Bass) Wiley US.

Promoting Yourself in the Workplace: How to Quietly Help Yourself by Helping Others. Jeffrey L. Magee. 2 cass. (Running Time: 120 min.). 1997. 15.95 (978-1-55977-663-9(3)) CareerTrack Pubns.

Prononciation Arabe. 1 cass. (Running Time: 1 hr., 30 min.). (ARA & FRE.). 2000. bk. 75.00 (978-2-7005-0092-9(X)) Pub: Assimil FRA. Dist(s): Distribks Inc

Pronounce It Perfectly in French. Christopher Kendris. 2 cass. (Pronounce It Perfectly Ser.). (FRE & ENG.). 1994. pap. bk. 19.95 (978-0-8120-8038-4(6)) Barron.

Pronouncing American English. Gertrude Orion. 16 cass. (YA). (gr. 9 up). pap. bk. 20.95 (978-0-06-632441-8(6)) Heinle.
Overview of the sounds of American English.

Pronouncing American English: Sample Tape. 2nd ed. Orion. (College ESL Ser.). (J). 1997. suppl. ed. 5.00 (978-0-8384-6335-2(5)) Heinle.

Pronouncing American English Vowels: An Accent Guide for Native Mandarin Chinese Speakers. Sarah Hoefflin. 2004. per. (978-0-9753816-0-1(1)) Logical Learn.

Pronouncing Computer Terminology. Ford Language Institute Staff. Read by Carol Ford. 1 cass. (Running Time: 1 hr.). 25.00 incl. txtbk. (978-1-877878-26-8(X)) Ford Lang Inst.
Proper pronunciation of computer terms in American English.

Pronouncing Medical Terminology. Ford Language Institute Staff. Read by Carol Ford. 2 cass. (Running Time: 2 hrs.). 39.00 set, incl. txtbk. (978-1-877878-25-1(1)) Ford Lang Inst.
Proper pronunciation of medical terms in American English.

Pronto. unabr. ed. Elmore Leonard. Read by Alexander Adams. 7 cass. (Running Time: 7 hrs.). 1994. 56.00 (978-0-7366-2640-8(9), 3378) Books on Tape.
For 20 years Harry Arno's scam was a sports book in Miami Beach. And for 20 years Harry's been skimming the profits, shortchanging his partners. Harry's ready to retire when the FBI sets him up in a sting. Harry runs - to the Italian Riviera, where mob enforcers & a determined U.S. Marshall lob him like a shuttlecock.

***Pronto.** unabr. ed. Elmore Leonard. Read by Alexander Adams. (ENG.). 2010. (978-0-06-199763-1(3), Harper Audio); (978-0-06-199381-7(6), Harper Audio) HarperCollins Pubs.

Pronto Guide: Spanish for Banking with Audio CD. Compiled by Tara Bradley Williams. Pronto Spanish. (ENG & SPA.). 2007. pap. bk. 15.95 (978-1-934467-21-3(9)) Pronto Spanish.

Pronto Guide: Spanish for Construction. Tara Bradley Williams. (SPA.). 2007. 15.95 (978-1-934467-02-2(2)) Pronto Spanish.

Pronto Guide: Spanish for Educators. Tara Bradley Williams. (SPA.). 2007. 15.95 (978-1-934467-03-9(0)) Pronto Spanish.

Pronto Guide: Spanish for Food Service. Tara Bradley Williams. (SPA.). 2007. 15.95 (978-1-934467-06-0(5)) Pronto Spanish.

Pronto Guide: Spanish for Health Care. Tara Bradley Williams. (SPA.). 2007. 15.95 (978-1-934467-07-7(3)) Pronto Spanish.

Pronto Guide: Spanish for Hospitality. Tara Bradley Williams. (SPA.). 2007. 15.95 (978-1-934467-05-3(7)) Pronto Spanish.

Pronto Guide: Spanish for Human Resources. Tara Bradley Williams. (SPA.). 2007. 15.95 (978-1-934467-04-6(9)) Pronto Spanish.

Pronto Guide: Spanish for Law Enforcement with Audio CD. Compiled by Tara Bradley Williams. Pronto Spanish. (ENG & SPA.). 2007. pap. bk. 15.95 (978-1-934467-23-7(5)) Pronto Spanish.

Pronto Guide: Spanish for Manufacturing with Audio CD. Compiled by Tara Bradley Williams. Pronto Spanish. (ENG & SPA.). 2007. pap. bk. 15.95 (978-1-934467-22-0(7)) Pronto Spanish.

Pronto Guide: Spanish for the Workplace with Audio CD. Compiled by Tara Bradley Williams. Pronto Spanish. (ENG & SPA.). 2007. pap. bk. 15.95 (978-1-934467-20-6(0)) Pronto Spanish.

ProntoPass Drug Pronunciation CD Software: 700+ Drugs. Created by ProntoPass Solutions. (ENG.). 2008. audio compact disk 12.99 (978-0-9822278-1-7(7)) ProntoPass.

ProntoPass NAPLEX(r) Review Combo: Pharmacy. Created by ProntoPass Solutions. (ENG., 2008. 479.00 (978-0-9822278-0-0(9)) ProntoPass.

ProntoPass See & Say Pronunciation Combo: Pharmacist, Pharmacy Technician. Created by ProntoPass Solutions. (ENG., 2008. 19.99 (978-0-9822278-4-8(1)) ProntoPass.

ProntoPass Top 200 Drugs Pronunciation Audio CD: Pharmacy. Created by ProntoPass Solutions. (ENG.). 2008. 9.99 (978-0-9822278-2-4(5)) ProntoPass.

Pronunciation: Practice Through Interaction. Martin Hewings & Sharon Goldstein. 2 cass. (Running Time: 5 hrs. 24 mins.). (ENG.). 1998. stu. ed. 59.00 (978-0-521-57795-3(0)) Cambridge U Pr.

Pronunciation Activies: Vowels in Limericks. Arlene Egelberg. Illus. by Tom Milutinovic. 1 CD. (gr. 5-12). 2005. audio compact disk 18.00 (978-0-86647-207-4(X)) Pro Lingua.

Pronunciation Activities: Vowels in Limericks. Arlene Egelberg. Illus. by Tom Milutinovic. 1 CD. (gr. 5-12). 2005. pap. bk. & stu. ed. 28.00 (978-0-86647-208-1(8)) Pro Lingua.

Pronunciation Activities Package: Vowels in Limericks from Adam to Ursula. Arlene Egelberg. Illus. by Tom Milutinovic. (gr. 7-12). 2001. pap. bk. & stu. ed. 28.00 (978-0-86647-117-6(0)); 16.50 (978-0-86647-116-9(2)) Pro Lingua.

Pronunciation & Reading of Ancient Greek. Stephen G. Daitz. 2 CDs. (Running Time: 2 hrs. 2 mins.). (GEC.). 2003. audio compact disk 39.95 (978-1-57970-096-6(9), SGK660) J Norton Pubs.

Pronunciation & Reading of Ancient Greek: A Practical Guide. 2nd rev. ed. Read by Stephen G. Daitz. Ed. by Stephen G. Daitz. 2 cass. (Running Time: 2 hrs.). (Living Voice of Greek & Latin Ser.). 1985. pap. bk. 38.50 (978-0-88432-083-8(9), S23660) J Norton Pubs.
Includes selections from Homer & Plato.

Pronunciation & Reading of Classical Latin. Stephen G. Daitz. 2 CDs. (Running Time: 1 hr. 45 min.). (LAT.). 2003. pap. bk. 39.95 (978-1-57970-097-3(7), SLT675) J Norton Pubs.

Pronunciation & Reading of Classical Latin: A Practical Guide. Read by Robert P. Sonkowsky. Ed. by Stephen G. Daitz. 2 cass. (Living Voice of Greek & Latin Ser.). 1984. pap. bk. 91.00 (978-0-88432-125-5(8), S23675) J Norton Pubs.

Pronunciation Exercises for Beginning Chinese. James Liang. 2 cass. 1978. 8.95 ea. incl. suppl. materials. (978-0-88710-060-4(0)) Yale Far Eastern Pubns.

Pronunciation Exercises in English. M. Elizabeth Clarey & Robert James Dixson. 2 cass. (C). 1987. 53.00 (978-0-13-730870-5(1)) Longman.

Pronunciation for Advanced Learners of English. David Brazil. 2 cass. (Running Time: 2 hrs. 46 mins.). (ENG.). 1994. 45.00 (978-0-521-38420-9(6)) Cambridge U Pr.

***Pronunciation for Advanced Learners of English Audio CDs (3)** David Brazil. (Running Time: 2 hrs. 46 mins.). (ENG.). 2010. audio compact disk 41.00 (978-0-521-16672-0(1)) Cambridge U Pr.

Pronunciation for Success Student Course: 31 Days to a More Successful North American English Accent. 2nd ed. Colleen Meyers & Sheryl Holt. 3 CD's. (Running Time: Over 3 hours). 2000. video & audio compact disk 119.00 (978-0-9663107-1-9(3)); DVD & audio compact disk 129.00 (978-0-9663107-2-6(1)) ESL Videos.
Every workbook comes with a 3-CD set of follow-along and listening exercises from the book.

Pronunciation in American English. Kathy L. Hans. 2000. pap. bk. & wbk. ed. 50.00 (978-0-9678379-1-8(X)) AmEnglish.

Pronunciation Matters: Communicative, Story-Based Activities for Mastering the Sounds of North American English. Lynn E. Henrichsen et al. (C). 1999. 75.00 (978-0-472-00292-4(9)) U of Mich Pr.

Pronunciation Pairs. 4 cass. 66.95 New Readers.

Pronunciation Pairs: An Introduction to the Sounds of English. 2nd rev. ed. Ann Baker & Sharon Goldstein. (ENG.). 2007. audio compact disk 56.00 (978-0-521-67811-7(0)) Cambridge U Pr.

Pronunciation Pairs: An Introductory Course for Students of English. Ann Baker & Sharon Goldstein. 4 cass. 62.95 Set. Midwest European Pubns.
Teaches how to recognize & produce the sounds of American English, providing practice with individual sounds, word stress, intonation, & sound-spelling relationships.

Pronunciation Pairs Audio Cassettes. Ann Baker & Sharon Goldstein. (Running Time: 6 hrs. 20 mins.). (ENG.). 2007. 56.00 (978-0-521-67810-0(2)) Cambridge U Pr.

Pronunciation Plus: Practice Through Interaction: North American English. Martin Hewings & Sharon Goldstein. (ENG.). 2001. stu. ed. 61.00 (978-0-521-78522-8(7)) Cambridge U Pr.

Pronunciation Practice: 4 Audiotapes/CDs. Elaine Kirn. 2007. audio compact disk 35.00 (978-1-891077-52-4(X)) Authors Editors.

Pronunciation Sampler. (Running Time: 15 mins.). 1998. 0.01 (978-0-521-65934-5(5)) Cambridge U Pr.

Pronunciation Tasks. Martin Hewings. 2 cass. (Running Time: 2 hrs. 44 mins.). (ENG., 1993. 45.00 (978-0-521-38453-7(2)) Cambridge U Pr.

***Pronunciation Tasks Audio CDs (3) A Course for Pre-intermediate Learners.** Martin Hewings. (Running Time: 2 hrs. 44 mins.). (ENG.). 2010. audio compact disk 41.00 (978-0-521-18354-3(5)) Cambridge U Pr.

Proof. Dick Francis. Contrib. by Nigel Havers. 3 CDs. (Running Time: 3 hrs. 5 mins.). 2006. audio compact disk 39.95 (978-0-7927-4333-0(4), BBCD 160) AudioGO.

Proof. Jeremy Pearsons. (ENG.). 2007. audio compact disk 5.00 (978-1-57562-952-0(6)) K Copeland Pubns.

Proof. unabr. ed. Dick Francis. Read by Tony Britton. 8 cass. (Running Time: 8 hrs.). 1993. 69.95 (978-0-7451-4114-5(5), CAB 797) AudioGO.
At a party celebrating the success of the racing season, a runaway horse cart plows into the marquee. Wine merchant Tony Beach, a witness to the death & destruction, claims it's a fluke accident. But when his expert advice is called into account over sub-standard alcohol in a local night club, connections start to click & another person dies.

Proof. unabr. ed. Dick Francis. Read by Tony Britton. 8 cass. (Running Time: 12 hrs.). 2000. 59.95 (CAB 797) Pub: Chivers Audio Bks GBR. Dist(s): AudioGO
At a party to celebrate the racing season, a runaway horse plows into the marquee. Wine merchant Tony Beach, a witness to the terrible death, believes it's just a terrible accident. But when his expert advice is called into account over sub-standard alcohol in a local night club, another person dies.

Proof. unabr. ed. Dick Francis. Narrated by Simon Prebble. 7 cass. (Running Time: 10 hrs.). 1985. 60.00 (978-0-7887-3485-4(7), 95768E7) Recorded Bks.
As wine merchant Tony Beach searches for the source of fraudulent whiskey, he finds himself pulled into a world of greed, deception and unspeakable murder.

Proof of Damages. unabr. ed. Contrib. by Robert L. Conason. 8 cass. (Running Time: 10 hrs.). 1989. 125.00 (T7-9218) PLI.
A distinguished panel of plaintiff's & defendant's attorneys analyzes the approaches to proving damages in a personal injury case. Emphasis is placed on effectively marshalling the evidence to present the recoverable elements of damages. Areas covered in this recording of PLI's August 1989 program include: role of damages in voir dire, lost profits, tax consequences & inflationary spirals, valuation of a "going business", future loss of earnings, damage witnesses (medical & economic), discovery of documents, evaluating personal injury & wrongful death claims, present value determination & jury charges.

Proof of Your Love. Elbert Willis. 1 cass. (Prosperity Insights Ser.). 4.00 Fill the Gap.

Proof Positive. Phillip Margolin. Narrated by Nanette Savard. (Running Time: 34200 sec.). 2006. audio compact disk & audio compact disk 29.95 (978-0-7927-4242-5(7), CMP 957) AudioGO.

Proof Positive. Phillip Margolin. Read by Nanette Savard. 8 cass. (Running Time: 34200 sec.). 2006. 54.95 (978-0-7927-4241-8(9), CSL 957); audio compact disk 79.95 (978-0-7927-4051-3(3), SLD 957) AudioGO.

***Proof Positive.** abr. ed. Phillip Margolin. Read by Margaret Whitton. (ENG.). 2006. (978-0-06-113471-5(6), Harper Audio); (978-0-06-113472-2(4), Harper Audio) HarperCollins Pubs.

***Proof Positive.** unabr. ed. Phillip Margolin. Read by Nanette Savard. (ENG.). 2006. (978-0-06-113470-8(8), Harper Audio); (978-0-06-113469-2(4), Harper Audio) HarperCollins Pubs.

Proof Positive. unabr. ed. Phillip Margolin. Read by Nanette Savard. (Running Time: 34200 sec.). 2006. audio compact disk 39.95 (978-0-06-089797-0(X)) HarperCollins Pubs.

***Prop Master: A Comprehensive Video for Theatrical Prop Management.** Amy Mussman. 1. (Running Time: 1hr 16 min). 2010. 29.95 (978-1-56608-170-2(X)) Meriwether Pub.

Propaganda & Control of the Public Mind. Noam Chomsky. 2 cass. (Running Time: 120 min.). (AK Press Audio Ser.). (ENG.). 1998. audio compact disk 20.00 (978-1-873176-68-9(6)) Pub: AK Pr GBR. Dist(s): Consort Bk Sales

Propaganda & Poetry. (23293-A) J Norton Pubs.

Propaganda Broadcast (WWII) Read by Douglas Chandler. (Running Time: 15 min.). 10.95 (#19025) J Norton Pubs.
Douglas Chandler (Paul Revere) delivers a propaganda commentary from Germany on the eve of the third Axis Pact. From the U. S. General Records of the Department of Justice.

Propeller One-Way Night Coach. unabr. ed. John Travolta. (ENG.). 2005. 9.99 (978-1-59483-675-6(2)) Pub: Hachet Audio. Dist(s): HachBkGrp

Proper Believing. Elbert Willis. 1 cass. (Secret to Believing Prayer Ser.). 4.00 Fill the Gap.

***Proper Care & Feeding of Husbands.** abr. ed. Laura Schlessinger. Read by Laura Schlessinger. (ENG.). 2004. (978-0-06-075417-4(6), Harper Audio) HarperCollins Pubs.

***Proper Care & Feeding of Husbands.** abr. ed. Laura Schlessinger. Read by Laura Schlessinger. (ENG.). 2004. (978-0-06-081327-7(X), Harper Audio) HarperCollins Pubs.

Proper Care & Feeding of Husbands. unabr. abr. ed. Laura Schlessinger. Read by Laura Schlessinger. 3 CDs. (Running Time: 3 hrs.). 2004. audio compact disk 22.00 (978-0-06-056675-3(2)) HarperCollins Pubs.

Proper Care & Feeding of Marriage. abr. ed. Laura Schlessinger. Read by Laura Schlessinger. Read by Lily LoBianco. 2007. audio compact disk 25.95 (978-0-06-122711-0(0)) HarperCollins Pubs.

Proper Care & Feeding of Marriage. unabr. ed. Laura Schlessinger. Read by Lily Lobianco. 6 CDs. (Running Time: 23400 sec.). 2007. audio compact disk 34.95 (978-0-06-123399-9(4)) HarperCollins Pubs.

***Proper Care & Feeding of Marriage: Preface & Introduction read by Dr. Laura Schlessinger.** abr. ed. Laura Schlessinger. Read by Lily Lobianco. (ENG.). 2007. (978-0-06-125734-6(6), Harper Audio); (978-0-06-125735-3(4), Harper Audio) HarperCollins Pubs.

***Proper Care & Feeding of Marriage: Preface & Introduction read by Dr. Laura Schlessinger.** unabr. ed. Laura Schlessinger. Read by Lily Lobianco. (ENG.). 2007. (978-0-06-125736-0(2), Harper Audio); (978-0-06-125737-7(0), Harper Audio) HarperCollins Pubs.

Proper Care & Feeding of Your Pastor. George Pearsons. 1 CD. 2006. audio compact disk (978-1-57562-887-5(2)) K Copeland Pubns.

***Proper Care & Maintenance of Friendship.** unabr. ed. Lisa Verge Higgins. (Running Time: 11 hrs. 5 mins.). (ENG.). 2011. 29.95 (978-1-4417-7385-2(1)); 72.95 (978-1-4417-7382-1(7)); audio compact disk 32.95 (978-1-4417-7384-5(3)); audio compact disk 105.00 (978-1-4417-7383-8(5)) Blckstn Audio.

Proper Husband Role. Elbert Willis. 1 cass. (Keys to a Successful Marriage Ser.). 4.00 Fill the Gap.

Proper Pursuit. unabr. ed. Lynn Austin. Read by Jenny Ikeda. 14 cass. (Running Time: 16 hrs.). 2008. 98.75 (978-1-4281-7465-8(6)) Recorded Bks.

Proper Woman. unabr. ed. Lillian Beckwith. Read by Hannah Gordon. 6 cass. (Running Time: 6 hrs.). 2001. 54.95 (978-0-7540-0616-9(6), CAB2039) Pub: Chivers Audio Bks GBR. Dist(s): AudioGO
For Anna, a carefree & gentle child living in a remote community in the Hebrides, a chance meeting with the mysterious & romantic "Jimmy Pearl" is to take on a dream-like quality as she grows to womanhood & encounters a hard & often cruel world. Anna is forced into a loveless marriage to cold & hearless "Black Fergus." But life has surprises in store for them, including the reappearance of "Jimmy Pearl".

Properties of Hazardous Industrial Materials. Andre R. Cooper, Sr. 1998. audio compact disk 250.00 (978-1-56670-236-2(4), L1236) CRC Pr.

Properties of Materials. Sundance/Newbridge, LLC Staff. (Early Science Ser.). (gr. k-3). 2007. audio compact disk 12.00 (978-1-4007-6580-5(3)); audio compact disk 12.00 (978-1-4007-6579-9(X)); audio compact disk 12.00 (978-1-4007-6578-2(1)) Sund Newbrdge.

***Properties of Matter: CD add-on Set.** Perf. by Millmark Education Staff. (ConceptLinks Ser.). 2009. audio compact disk 50.00 (978-1-61618-353-0(5)) Millmark Educ.

***Properties of Matter Audio CD.** Perf. by Millmark Education Staff. (ConceptLinks Ser.). 2007. audio compact disk 28.00 (978-1-4334-0061-2(8)) Millmark Educ.

Properties of Matter Audio CD: Physical & Chemical Changes. Saxe. Perf. by Millmark Education Staff. 1997. audio compact disk (978-1-4334-0406-1(0)) Millmark Educ.

***Properties of Matter SB1 Audio CD Describing & Measuring Matter.** Perf. by Millmark Education Staff. (Content Literacy Libraries Ser.). 2008. audio compact disk (978-1-4334-0404-7(4)) Millmark Educ.

***Properties of Matter SB2 Audio CD Atoms, Elements, & Compounds.** Perf. by Millmark Education Staff. (Content Literacy Libraries Ser.). 2008. audio compact disk (978-1-4334-0405-4(2)) Millmark Educ.

***Properties of Matter SB4 Audio CD Chemical Reactions.** Perf. by Millmark Education Staff. (Content Literacy Libraries Ser.). 2008. audio compact disk (978-1-4334-0407-8(9)) Millmark Educ.

Properties of Organic Compounds: Version 6.0. 6th rev. ed. David R. Lide. 2000. audio compact disk 1360.00 (978-0-8493-9762-2(6), 9762) Pub: CRC Pr. Dist(s): Taylor and Fran

Properties of Planets. 1 cass. (Running Time: 34 min.). 14.95 (13495) MMI Corp.
Moon's gravity, satellites of Jupiter, clouds of Venus, properties of planets are discussed by astronomers.

Properties of the Scalp & Hair. Milady Publishing Company Staff. 1 cass. (Standard Ser.: Chapter 4). 1995. 12.95 (978-1-56253-276-5(6), Milady) Delmar.

Property. unabr. ed. Ray Frey. Read by Cliff Robertson. Ed. by John Lachs & Mike Hassell. 2 cass. (Running Time: 3 hrs.). Dramatization. (Morality in Our Age Ser.). 1995. 17.95 Set. (978-1-56823-027-6(3), 10506) Knowledge Prod.
Ownership has long been a basic principle of western society. Yet during the last century property rights have been increasingly curbed by courts & legislatures as they grapple with collective vs. individual control of physical & human assets. To what degree can society interfere with an owner's decision regarding bodily organs, wetlands, new life forms, jobs, & ideas? How are possessions legitimately acquired, used, & sold? Are property

rights based on human agreement, on the natural order of things, or on a divine law?.

Property. unabr. abr. ed. Read by Cliff Robertson. (Running Time: 10800 sec.). (Morality in Our Age Ser.). 2006. audio compact disk 25.95 (978-0-7861-6632-9(0)) Pub: Blckstn Audio. Dist(s): NetLibrary CO

Property & Ownership. Robert LeFevre. 1 cass. (Running Time: 1 hr. 52 min.). 12.50 (1003) J Norton Pubs.
Ways of owning property & who is responsible in collective ownership?.

Property Rights & the Birth of the State. Murray Newton Rothbard. 1 cass. (Running Time: 1 hr. 28 min.). 11.95 (183) J Norton Pubs.

Prophecies. Perf. by Dik Darnell & Steven Halpern. 1 cass., 1 CD. 7.98 (EC 7007); audio compact disk 12.78 CD Jewel box. (EC 7007) NewSound.

Prophecies: Book of Daniel & Revelations. Narrated by George Vafiadis. (Running Time: 8700 sec.). (Unabridged Classics in MP3 Ser.). (ENG.). 2008. audio compact disk 24.00 (978-1-58472-650-0(4), In Aud) Sound Room.

Prophecies: Daniel & Revelations: Directly from the Holy Bible, King Hames Version. Contrib. by George Vafiadis. (Playaway Adult Nonfiction Ser.). 2008. 39.99 (978-1-60640-830-8(5)) Find a World.

Prophecy. Vincent M. Walsh. 1 cass. 1986. 4.00 Key of David.
Personal stories & examples told to promote a full understanding of the basic powers of the Renewal.

Prophecy: What the Future Holds for You. abr. ed. Sylvia Browne & Lindsay Harrison. Read by Jeanie Hackett. (Running Time: 5 hrs.). (ENG.). 2004. audio compact disk 26.95 (978-1-56511-873-7(1), 1565118731) Pub: HighBridge. Dist(s): Workman Pub

Prophecy & Extraordinary Religious Phenomena. Carroll Stuhlmueller. Read by Carroll Stuhlmueller. 1 cass. (Running Time: 90 min.). 7.95 (TAH213) Alba Hse Comns.

Prophecy & Social Issues. Carroll Stuhlmueller. 1 cass. 1990. 9.95 (TAH227) Alba Hse Comns.
Fr. Stuhlmueller answers many questions by giving a careful analysis of the role & nature of prophecy in the Scriptures. He explains the complex relationship of the prophets towards the institutions of Israel, the defense of the poor, & the messianic vision of a better tomorrow.

Prophecy & the Messianic Era: The Secret Prophecies of the Torah-Moshiach. unabr. ed. Shmuel Irons. Read by Shmuel Irons. 2 cass. (Running Time: 3 hrs.). 19.95 Set. (978-1-889648-18-7(3)) Jwish Her Fdtn.
A clear view of ancient history based on the Bible & Talmud & other ancient primary sources. A new way of looking at the past.

***Prophecy Answer Book.** unabr. ed. David Jeremiah. (Running Time: 6 hrs. 30 mins.). 2010. 14.99 (978-1-4001-8763-8(X)); audio compact disk 47.99 (978-1-4001-4763-2(8)) Pub: Tantor Media. Dist(s): IngramPubServ

***Prophecy Answer Book.** unabr. ed. David Jeremiah. Narrated by John Allen Nelson. (Running Time: 3 hrs. 0 mins. 0 sec.). (ENG.). 2010. 19.99 (978-1-4001-6763-0(9)); audio compact disk 19.99 (978-1-4001-1763-5(1)) Pub: Tantor Media. Dist(s): IngramPubServ

Prophecy Be Damned. unabr. ed. Patricia Lucas White. Read by Bernadette Dunne. (Running Time: 41400 sec.). (Tales of the Penitent Ser.). 2006. 65.95 (978-0-7861-4883-7(7)); audio compact disk 81.00 (978-0-7861-5997-0(9)); audio compact disk 29.95 (978-0-7861-7117-0(0)) Blckstn Audio.

Prophecy for a Queen, Dilys Gater. Read by Hazel Temperley. 3 cass. (Running Time: 4 hrs. 30 min.). (Sound Ser.). 1989. 34.95 (978-1-85496-264-5(7), 62647) Pub: UlverLrgPrint GBR. Dist(s): Ulverscroft US

Prophecy of Daniel & Revelation Audio Tapes, Vol. 5. Speeches. Ronald G. Fanter. 8 cass. (Running Time: 90 mins.). 2003. 40.00 (978-1-931215-43-5(X)) Cut Edge Min.
Tapes Included In This VolumeThe Wrath Of GodSeventy Weeks Are DeterminedThe Babylonian CultApproaching Hoof BeatsReturn Of The NephilimThe Gospel Of The KingdomThe Avenger Of BloodDaniel's Fourth Beast.

Prophecy of Peace: The Choral Music of Samuel Adler. Glori Dei Cantores. 2004. audio compact disk 16.95 (978-1-55725-366-8(8), GDCD036) Paraclete MA.

Prophecy of the Sisters. unabr. ed. Michelle Zink. (Running Time: 8 hrs.). (ENG.). 2009. 24.98 (978-1-60024-657-9(5)) Pub: Hachet Audio. Dist(s): HachBkGrp

Prophecy of the Sisters. unabr. ed. Michelle Zink. Read by Eliza Dushku. 7 CDs. (Running Time: 8 hrs.). (ENG.). 2009. audio compact disk 29.98 (978-1-60024-656-2(7)) Pub: Hachet Audio. Dist(s): HachBkGrp

Prophecy of the Soul Sorcerer, Bk. 2. Ed. by Eric Dean Seaton. Photos by Patrick Broome & Mat Broome. 1 cass. (Running Time: 90 mins.). (YA). 2000. 10.95 (978-1-930315-27-3(9)) Arcane.

Prophecy of the Stones. unabr. ed. 7 cassettes. (Running Time: 10 hrs). (J). 2004. 61.75 (978-1-4193-0372-2(4)) Recorded Bks.

Prophecy Portfolio. Jack Van Impe. 1982. 30.00 (978-0-934803-37-3(4)) J Van Impe.
Contains all of Dr. Van Impe's prophecy cassettes.

Prophecy Update. Chuck Smith. 2 cass. (Running Time: 1 hr. 30 mins.). 2001. 6.75 (978-0-936728-83-4(3), tppup01) Word For Today.
Messages discussing what the Bible has to say regarding the subject of prophecy.

Prophecy vs. Spirituality. Swami Jyotirmayananda. 1 cass. (Running Time: 45 min.). 1990. 10.00 Yoga Res Foun.

Prophecy 101: What Is the World Coming To? Chuck Missler. 1 MP3 CD-ROM. (Running Time: 4 hours). 2001. cd-rom 19.95 (978-1-57821-169-2(7)) Koinonia Hse.
The Bible contains 8,362 predictive verses about 737 different matters and yet prophecy is one of the most neglected subjects in the Church today. Understanding prophecy is an essential and fundamental issue for every serious Christian. But where do we start?This series has been designed to give you a strategic overview of prophecy; past, present and future. This series will encourage the new believer and strengthen the faith of all who study it. Now, more than ever, it is important that we have answers for people who are seeking the truth. We need to equip ourselves to be ready to give an answer to every man for the hope that lies within us. This new updated version includes diagrams and visual aids that auto-advance as Chuck gives the presentation!.

Prophecy 101: What Is the World Coming To? Chuck Missler. 4 audio CDs. (Running Time: 4 hours). 2006. audio compact disk 29.95 (978-1-57821-358-0(4)) Koinonia Hse.

Prophesies of Black Elk. William Lyon. 1 cass. 9.00 (A0204-87) Sound Photosyn.
ICSS '87.

Prophesy. unabr. ed. Chris Kuzneski. (Running Time: 11 hrs.). (Payne & Jones Ser.). 2010. 24.99 (978-1-4233-8964-4(6), 9781423389644, Brilliance MP3); 24.99 (978-1-4233-8966-8(2), 9781423389668, BAD); 39.97 (978-1-4233-8967-5(0), 9781423389675, BADLE) Brilliance Audio.

Prophesy. unabr. ed. Chris Kuzneski. Read by Dick Hill. (Running Time: 11 hrs.). (Payne & Jones Ser.). 2010. 39.97 (978-1-4233-8965-1(4), 9781423389651, Brlnc Audio MP3 Lib); audio compact disk 29.99 (978-1-4233-8962-0(X), 9781423389620, Bril Audio CD Unabri); audio compact disk 92.97 (978-1-4233-8963-7(8), 9781423389637, BriAudCD Unabrid) Brilliance Audio.

Prophet see Prophete

Prophet. Frank E. Peretti. Narrated by Richard Ferrone. 14 cass. (Running Time: 21 hrs.). 114.00 (978-0-7887-5339-8(8)) Recorded Bks.

Prophet. unabr. ed. Khalil Gibran. Read by Paul Sparer & Becky Ann Baker. (Running Time: 5400 sec.).Tr. of Prophète. 2006. audio compact disk 19.95 (978-0-7393-3328-0(3), Random AudioBks) Pub: Random Audio Pubg. Dist(s): Random

Prophet, Vol.. I. Jerry Ahern. Read by Charlie O'Dowd. 2 vols. 2004. 18.00 (978-1-58807-312-9(2)) Am Pubng Inc.

Prophet, Vol.. I. Jerry Ahern. Read by Charlie O'Dowd. 2 vols. No. 7. 2004. (978-1-58807-871-1(X)) Am Pubng Inc.

Prophet, Vol.. II. Jerry Ahern. Read by Charlie O'Dowd. 2 vols. No. 7. 2004. 18.00 (978-1-58807-313-6(0)); (978-1-58807-872-8(8)) Am Pubng Inc.

Prophet: Amos. unabr. ed. Francine Rivers. Narrated by Chris Fabry. (Sons of Encouragement Ser.: Vol. 4). (ENG.). 2006. 13.99 (978-1-60814-349-8(X)); audio compact disk 19.99 (978-1-59859-101-9(0)) Oasis Audio.

Prophet: And Other Stories. unabr. ed. Khalil Gibran. Read by Jonathan Reese. (Running Time: 10800 sec.). 2007. audio compact disk 19.95 (978-0-7861-6145-4(0)) Blckstn Audio.

Prophet & Other Writings, unabr. ed. Khalil Gibran. Read by Jonathan Reese. 2 cass. (Running Time: 3 hrs.). 1999. 17.95 (978-0-7366-4435-8(0), 4808) Books on Tape.
He was a man whose fame & influence spread far beyond the Near East. His poetry has been translated into more than twenty languages.

Prophet & Other Writings. unabr. ed. Khalil Gibran. Narrated by Jonathan Reese. (Running Time: 3 hrs. 0 mins. 0 sec.). (ENG.). 2008. audio compact disk 17.99 (978-1-4001-5794-5(3)); audio compact disk 35.99 (978-1-4001-3794-7(2)) Pub: Tantor Media. Dist(s): IngramPubServ

Prophet & Other Writings. unabr. ed. Khalil Gibran. Narrated by Jonathan Reese. (Running Time: 3 hrs. 0 mins. 0 sec.). (Tantor Unabridged Classics Ser.). (ENG.). 2008. audio compact disk 17.99 (978-1-4001-0794-0(6)) Pub: Tantor Media. Dist(s): IngramPubServ

Prophet & Other Writings. unabr. collector's ed. Khalil Gibran. Read by Jonathan Reese. 2 cass. (Running Time: 3 hrs.). 1998. 16.00 (978-0-7366-4348-1(6), 4808) Books on Tape.
The author's poetry has been translated into more than twenty languages. His drawings & paintings have been exhibited in the great capitals of the world & compared by Auguste Rodin to the work of William Blake. In the United States, which he made his home during the last twenty years of his life, he began to write in English.

Prophet & the Garden of the Prophet. unabr. ed. Khalil Gibran. Read by Garard Green. 3 cass. (Running Time: 3 hrs. 15 min.). (Isis Ser.). (J). 2001. 34.95 (978-1-85695-602-4(4), 8911X) Pub: ISIS Lrg Prnt GBR. Dist(s): Ulverscroft US

Prophet & the Plates: Evidences of the Divine Mission of Joseph Smith & the Book of Mormon. abr. ed. Brad Wilcox. (Running Time: 119 Mins.). 2003. audio compact disk 12.95 (978-1-59038-200-4(5)) Deseret Bk.

Prophet & the Wanderer. Read by Robert Glenister. 3. (Running Time: 13402 sec.). (Classic Fiction Ser.). 2007. audio compact disk 22.98 (978-962-634-463-7(6), Naxos AudioBooks) Naxos.

***Prophet Marries a Prostitute.** Featuring Ravi Zacharias. 2001. audio compact disk 9.00 (978-1-61256-007-6(5)) Ravi Zach.

Prophet of Purpose: The Inside Story of Rick Warren & His Rise to Global Prominence. unabr. ed. Jeffrey L. Sheler. Read by Danny Campbell. (ENG.). 2009. audio compact disk 35.00 (978-0-7393-5833-7(2), Random AudioBks) Pub: Random Audio Pubg. Dist(s): Random

Prophet of Yonwood. unabr. ed. Jeanne DuPrau. Read by Becky Ann Baker. 5 CDs. (Running Time: 6 hrs. 19 mins.). (Books of Ember Ser.: Bk. 3). (J). 2005. audio compact disk 38.25 (978-0-7393-3585-7(5), Listening Lib); 35.00 (978-0-7393-3584-0(7), Listening Lib) Pub: Random Audio Pubg. Dist(s): Random
It's 50 years before the settlement of the city of Ember, and the world is in crisis. War looms on the horizon as 11-year-old Nickie and her aunt travel to the small town of Yonwood, North Carolina. There, one of the town's respected citizens has had a terrible vision of fire and destruction. Her garbled words are taken as prophetic instruction on how to avoid the coming disaster. If only they can be interpreted correctly... As the people of Yonwood scramble to make sense of the woman's mysterious utterances, Nickie explores the oddities she finds around town - her great-grandfather's peculiar journals and papers, a reclusive neighbor who studies the heavens, a strange boy who is fascinated with snakes - all while keeping an eye out for ways to help the world. Is this vision her chance? Or is it already too late to avoid a devastating war?.

Prophet of Yonwood. unabr. ed. Jeanne DuPrau. Read by Becky Ann Baker. (Running Time: 22740 sec.). (Books of Ember Ser.: Bk. 3). (ENG.). (J). (gr. 5-8). 2006. audio compact disk 30.00 (978-0-7393-3109-5(4), Listening Lib) Pub: Random Audio Pubg. Dist(s): Random

Prophet, Priest & King: Logos November 2, 1997. Ben Young. 1997. 4.95 (978-0-7417-6054-8(1), B0054) Win Walk.

Prophète see Prophet

Prophete. Khalil Gibran. 1 cass. (Running Time: 1 hr.).Tr. of Prophet. 2001. 18.95 (978-2-89558-021-8(9)) Pub: Coffragants CAN. Dist(s): Penton Overseas

Prophete. Khalil Gibran. 1 cass. (Running Time: 90 mins.). (French Audiobooks Ser.).Tr. of Prophet. 2000. bk. 14.95 (978-2-89517-050-1(9)) Pub: Coffragants CAN. Dist(s): Penton Overseas

Prophetess. unabr. ed. Barbara Wood. Read by Susie Breck. (Running Time: 16 hrs.). 2008. 24.95 (978-1-4233-5403-1(6), 9781423354031, Brilliance MP3); 24.95 (978-1-4233-5405-5(2), 9781423354055, BAD); 39.25 (978-1-4233-5404-8(4), 9781423354048, Brlnc Audio MP3 Lib); 39.25 (978-1-4233-5406-2(0), 9781423354062, BADLE) Brilliance Audio.

Prophetic & Priesthood Ministry. Rick Joyner. 1 cass. (Running Time: 90 mins.). (Prophetic Ministry & Gifts Ser.: Vol. 5). 2000. 5.00 (RJ06-005) Morning NC.
These messages contain advanced teaching on the prophetic ministry, including discussion of strongholds & hindrances.

Prophetic Books. Read by Frederick Ryan. 16 cass. (Running Time: 60 min. per cass.). 37.95 (978-0-8198-5844-3(7)) Pauline Bks.

Prophetic Books: From the King James Bible, Vol. 5. Read by Eric Martin. 5 cass. 22.95 Set. (978-1-891320-04-0(1)) Jodacom Intl.

Prophetic Character. Steve Thompson. 1 cass. (Running Time: 90 mins.). (Prophetic Ministry Ser.: Vol. 6). 2000. 5.00 (ST01-006) Morning NC.
Now updated & expanded, this popular series combines insights from the Scriptures & personal experience to explain how we can more effectively hear from God & minister prophetically.

Prophetic Church Seminar. Frank Damazio. 7 cass. (Running Time: 10 hrs. 30 min.). 2000. 39.99 (978-1-886849-51-8(X)) CityChristian.

Prophetic Commission. Rick Joyner. 1 cass. (Running Time: 90 mins.). (Prophetic Ministry & Gifts Ser.: Vol. 4). 2000. 5.00 (RJ06-004) Morning NC.
These messages contain advanced teaching on the prophetic ministry, including discussion of strongholds & hindrances.

Prophetic Destiny, Set. Paul Thomas Smith. 2 cass. 1996. 11.98 (978-1-55503-919-6(7), 07001320) Covenant Comms.
The Saints in the Rocky Mountains.

Prophetic Gifts. Rick Joyner. 2004. 19.99 (978-0-7684-0215-5(8)) Destiny Image Pubs.

Prophetic Guide to the End Times Series. Derek Prince. 4 cass. 19.95 Set. (PGE1) Derek Prince.
Are you perplexed or fearful as you contemplate the chaotic, threatening world around us? Biblical prophecy will equip you for all that lies ahead.

Prophetic Life: Powerful Truths for Powerful Leadership. Michael Lattiboudeaire. 16 cass. (Running Time: 24 hrs.). 1998. 54.95 Dramatized. (978-1-889448-13-8(3)) Great Hse Pub.
The power of the prophetic life that produces reality.

Prophetic Life: Powerful Truths for Powerful Leadership, Set. Michael Lattiboudeaire. 16 cass. (Running Time: 24 hrs.). 1998. 99.99 (978-1-889448-14-5(1)); audio compact disk 48.95 (978-1-889448-15-2(X)) Great Hse Pub.

Prophetic Ministry. abr. ed. Rick Joyner. 2004. 19.99 (978-0-7684-0213-1(1)) Destiny Image Pubs.

Prophetic Ministry & Gifts Series. Rick Joyner. 8 cass. (Running Time: 12 hrs.). 2000. 40.00 (RJ07-000) Morning NC.
These messages contain advanced teaching on the prophetic ministry, including discussion of strongholds & hindrances.

Prophetic Ministry in the Health Care Setting. 1 cass. (Care Cassettes Ser.: Vol. 14, No. 1). 1987. 10.80 Assn Prof Chaplains.

Prophetic Ministry Series. unabr. ed. Steve Thompson. 6 cass. (Running Time: 9 hrs.). 2000. 30.00 (ST01-000) Morning NC.
Now updated & expanded, this popular series combines insights from the Scriptures & personal experience to explain how we can more effectively hear from God & minister prophetically.

Prophetic Ministry Training Series. Steve Thompson. 6 cass. 30.00 Set. (ST01-000) Morning NC.
Combines insights from the Scriptures & personal experience to explain how we can more effectively hear from God & minister prophetically.

Prophetic Perspective on Today's World. Derek Prince. 1 cass. (I-4170) Derek Prince.

Prophetic Sketches. Neville Goddard. 1 cass. (Running Time: 62 min.). 1968. 8.00 (52) J & L Pubns.
Neville taught Imagination Creates Reality. He was a powerfully influential teacher of God as Consciousness.

Prophetic Vision of America: Henry James' The American Scene. Leon Edel. (Running Time: 27 min.). 1968. 11.95 (23041) J Norton Pubs.
Discussion of Henry James' novel about his homeland written after a long absence from the United States.

Prophetic Voice of Malcolm X. unabr. ed. 2 cass. (Running Time: 1 hr. 52 min.). 1963. 19.95 Set. (978-1-57970-031-7(4)) J Norton Pubs.
Presents two speeches: "Black Man's History" given on December 23, 1962, & "The Black Revolution" given on June 23, 1963.

Prophetic Warrior: Prophetic Atmospheres. John Belt. 2003. audio compact disk 15.00 (978-0-9748236-2-1(7)) Pub: Live in His Presence. Dist(s): STL Dist NA

Prophetie des Andes. 2 CDs. (Running Time: 2 hrs.).Tr. of Celestine Prophecy. 2001. pap. bk. 18.95 (978-2-89558-016-4(2)) Pub: Coffragants CAN. Dist(s): Penton Overseas

Prophetie des Andes. Audio. 1 cass., bklet. (Running Time: 90 mins.). (FRE.). 16.95 (978-2-921997-17-1(7)) Pub: Coffragants CAN. Dist(s): Penton Overseas
Recorded completely in international French language by well-known actors or speakers.

Prophets. Richard Rohr. 9 cass. (Running Time: 8 hrs. 56 min.). 69.95 Set. (AA2339) Credence Commun.
Rohr explains what the text meant when written & how it applies to American culture today.

Prophets, Vol. 1. Read by George W. Sarris. 1 cass. (World's Greatest Stories Ser.). 1995. 10.98 (978-1-57919-101-6(0)); audio compact disk 10.98 CD. (978-1-57919-096-5(0)) Randolf Prod.
Dramatic word-for-word readings of excerpts from the New International Version of the Bible. Includes passages about Daniel in the Lions' Den, Fiery Furance, Handwriting on the Wall, Elijah & Prophets of Baal, & Prophecy of Jonah.

Prophets: Coughlin, Townshend, Long. 10.00 (HD423) Esstee Audios.

Prophets: Pure Spirit Embodied. Swami Amar Jyoti. 1 cass. 1987. 9.95 (K-94) Truth Consciousness.
The work of the Prophets, Avatars. How does the Supreme take embodiment? Why they appear in human form. Whenever you utter the name of the Prophets...bow your head down.

Prophets & Kings. Ellen G. White. 2 MP3 disks. 2004. audio compact disk 39.95 (978-1-883012-16-8(3)); audio compact disk 39.95 (978-1-883012-15-1(5)) Remnant Pubns.

Prophets & Prophecy. Stephen Doyle. 5 cass. (Running Time: 7 hrs. 14 min.). 1994. 40.95 Set. (TAH301) Alba Hse Comns.
An excellent introduction for beginners, perfect for updating your knowledge on the prophets & the biblical history of those important times. Good for CCD classes as well as adult education. An excellent 10 week study. Also an exceptional source of biblical facts & trivia.

Prophets Before You. Francis Frangipane. 1 cass. (Running Time: 90 mins.). (Seeing the Multitudes Ser.: Vol. 8). 2000. 5.00 (FF07-008) Morning NC.
From the beatitudes, Francis draws applications for ministry to those who need Jesus.

Prophet's Good Idea see Brian Patten Reading His Poetry

Prophets KJV. Perf. by George W. Sarris. 5 CD's. (Running Time: about 1 hour each). (World's Greatest Stories Ser.: Volume 1). (J). 1989. audio compact disk 7.95 (978-0-9767744-5-7(3)) GWSPubs.
Bible stories read dramatically by George W. Sarris. The texts for all the stories are taken directly, word for word, from the King James Version Bible, with the addition of carefully selected music and sound effects. Vol 1 contains The Burning Fiery Furnace, The Handwriting on the Wall, Daniel in the Lions' Den, Elijah and the Prophets of Baal, and the complete book of Jonah.

Prophets NIV. Perf. by George W. Sarris. 5 CD's. (Running Time: about 1 hour). (World's Greatest Stories Ser.: Volume 1). (J). 1988. audio compact disk 7.95 (978-0-9767744-0-2(2)) GWSPubs.
Bible stories read dramatically by George W. Sarris. The texts for all the stories are taken directly, word for word, from the New International Version

Bible, with the addition of carefully selected music and sound effects. Vol. 1 contains The Blazing Furnace, The Handwriting on the Wall, Daniel in the Lions' Den, Elijah and the Prophets of Baal, and the complete book of Jonah.

Prophets of Antiquity Versus the Profits of Today. Instructed by Manly P. Hall. 8.95 (978-0-89314-223-0(9), C830522) Philos Res.

Prophets of Joy. Steven C. Warner. 1 cass., 1 CD. 1996. 11.00 (978-0-937690-70-3(8), 7216) Wrld Lib Pubns.
Religious music from Advent through the Feast of the Assumption.

Prophets of Joy. Steven C. Warner. 1 cass., 1 CD. (Running Time: 1 hr. 11 mins.). 1996. audio compact disk 17.00 CD. (978-0-937690-69-7(4), 7218) Wrld Lib Pubns.

Prophets of the Bible: Mighty Men Who Changed the World. Lester Sumrall. 9 cass. (Running Time: 13 hrs. 30 mins.). 1999. 36.00 (978-1-58568-109-9(1)) Sumrall Pubng.

Prophet's Reward. Tsea. 2008. audio compact disk (978-0-9797500-7-6(5)) TSEA.

Prophylactic Pastoral Care with Heart Patients. Joe Abbott. 1986. 10.80 (0305B) Assn Prof Chaplains.

Propionic Acidemia - A Bibliography & Dictionary for Physicians, Patients, & Genome Researchers. Compiled by Icon Group International, Inc. Staff. 2007. ring bd. 28.95 (978-0-497-11282-0(5)) Icon Grp.

***Proposal.** unabr. ed. Catherine Marshall. Adapted by C. Archer. Narrated by Jaimee Draper. (Catherine Marshall's Christy Ser.). (ENG.). 2010. 7.00 (978-1-60814-705-2(3), SpringWater) Oasis Audio.

Proposed New Rules of Criminal Procedure. 1 cass. (Running Time: 1 hr. 30 min.). 1988. 15.00 PA Bar Inst.

Proposition. Judith Ivory. Narrated by Steven Crossley. 10 cass. (Running Time: 13 hrs. 30 mins.). 88.00 (978-0-7887-9547-3(3)); audio compact disk 116.00 (978-1-4025-2925-2(2)) Recorded Bks.

Propósito de Celebrar la Navidad. unabr. ed. Rick Warren. Read by George Bass. (Running Time: 1 hr. 30 mins. 0 sec.). (ENG.). 2008. audio compact disk 19.99 (978-0-7435-8192-9(X)) Pub: S&S Audio. Dist(s): S and S Inc

Pros & Cons of Lay Ministry: A Protestant Prospective. 1 cass. (Care Cassettes Ser.: Vol. 10, No. 3). 1983. 10.80 Assn Prof Chaplains.

Pros & Cons of Lay Ministry: A Roman Catholic Perspective. 1 cass. (Care Cassettes Ser.: Vol. 10, No. 3). 1983. 10.80 Assn Prof Chaplains.

Pros Speak about Success, Set. abr. ed. Speakers Roundtable Staff. Read by Speakers Roundtable Staff. 20 cass. (Running Time: 20 hrs.). 129.95 (978-1-57294-148-9(0), 11-2001) SkillPath Pubns.
Full of practical tactics & personal tips from the world's leading consultants, authors & self-development experts.

Prose. 1 cass. (Running Time: 31 min.). (POR.). 11.95 (PR608) J Norton Pubs.
Brief readings about colorful situations of Brazilian everyday life.

Prose & Poetry. Stephen Spender. Read by Stephen Spender. 1 cass. (Running Time: 30 min.). 1968. 11.95 (23083) J Norton Pubs.
The noted British poet reads a number of his poems & a selection from his autobiography.

Prose & Poetry Anthology. Read by Jean-Gabriel Gaussens. 1 cass. (FRE.). bk. 16.95 (SFR460) J Norton Pubs.

Prosecution & Defense of Shareholder Litigation Against Directors & Officers. 8 cass. (Running Time: 11 hrs.). 1992. 225.00 Set; incl. study guide 503p. (M910) Am Law Inst.
Basic course provides a comprehensive study from the viewpoint of both plaintiffs' & defendants' counsle, with emphasis on the practical, including tactics, judgement calls, & the impact of insurance coverage.

Prosecution of George W. Bush for Murder. unabr. ed. Vincent Bugliosi. Narrated by Marc Cashman. 11 CDs. (Running Time: 13 hrs.). 2008. audio compact disk 104.95 (978-0-7927-5606-4(1)) AudioGO.
Bestselling author Vincent Bugliosi has written the most important and thought-provoking book of his prolific career. In a meticulously researched and clearly presented legal case that puts George W. Bush on trial for murder after he leaves his presidency, Bugliosi delivers a searing indictment of the President and his administration. With what he believes is overwhelming evidence that President Bush took the nation to war in Iraq under false pretenses-a war that has caused great loss of life, cost this nation close to $1 trillion, and alienated most of our allies in the Western world-Bugliosi argues that it is George W. Bush who must be held accountable for what Bugliosi considers to be monumental crimes. In this groundbreaking book, Bugliosi, in his inimitable style, presents a powerful case against the man in the oval office.

Prosecution of George W. Bush for Murder. unabr. ed. Vincent Bugliosi. Read by Marc Cashman. 1 MP3-CD. (Running Time: 13 hrs.). 2008. 64.95 (978-0-7927-5607-1(X)) AudioGO.

Prosecution of George W. Bush for Murder. unabr. ed. Vincent Bugliosi. Narrated by Marc Cashman. (Running Time: 38700 sec.). (ENG.). 2008. audio compact disk 34.95 (978-1-60283-468-2(7)) Pub: AudioGO. Dist(s): Perseus Dist

Prosecutors. Gary Delsohn. Read by Gary Delsohn. (Running Time: 4 hrs. 30 mins.). 2005. 21.95 (978-1-60083-323-6(3)) Iofy Corp.

Prosecutors: A Year in the Life of a District Attorney's Office. abr. ed. Gary Delsohn. 4 CDs. (Running Time: 4 hrs. 30 mins.). 2003. audio compact disk 27.95 (978-1-59316-010-4(0)); 22.95 (978-1-59316-009-8(7)) Listen & Live.
A riveting, behind-the-scenes look at how America's overburdened judicial system really functions.

Prosecutors: A Year in the Life of a District Attorney's Office. unabr. ed. Gary Delsohn. 7 cass. (Running Time: 10 hrs.). 2003. 34.95 (978-1-59316-011-1(9)) Listen & Live.

Prospect Park West. unabr. ed. Amy Sohn. Narrated by Kate Reading. 2 MP3-CDs. (Running Time: 13 hrs. 30 mins. 0 sec.). (ENG.). 2009. 29.99 (978-1-4001-6346-5(3)); audio compact disk 79.99 (978-1-4001-4346-7(2)) Pub: Tantor Media. Dist(s): IngramPubServ

Prospect Park West. unabr. ed. Amy Sohn. Read by Kate Reading. 11 CDs. (Running Time: 13 hrs. 30 mins. 0 sec.). (ENG.). 2009. audio compact disk 39.99 (978-1-4001-1346-0(6)) Pub: Tantor Media. Dist(s): IngramPubServ

Prospecting Album. unabr. ed. Robert A. Monroe. Read by Robert A. Monroe. 6 cass. (Running Time: 9 hrs.). (Gateway Experience - Prospecting Ser.). 1989. 72.00 (978-1-56113-285-0(3)) Monroe Institute.
Prospecting album for six cassettes.

Prospecting for Murder. unabr. ed. Larry D. Names. Read by Maynard Villers. 6 cass. (Running Time: 7 hrs. 30 min.). 1999. 39.95 (978-1-55686-882-5(0)) Books in Motion.
Harqua Hala, Arizona ain't what it used to be. After all it is 1912, & shoot-outs in the street are now a thing of the past. This new found civility does not seem to help Marshal Walt Philips, though, for he is found murdered. A pair of his old friends, former Pinkerton man Charlie Siringo & former peace officer Wyatt Earp, are left to find the killer. With the help of a young army lieutenant named George Patton, Siringo & Earp soon discover more than they bargained for, including a plot to kill the president.

Prospecting for Successful Selling. abr. ed. Mark Victor Hansen. Read by Mark Victor Hansen. 1 cass. (Self-Help Ser.). 1989. 9.95 (978-0-07-026054-2(0), TDM 1111) McGraw.
the author explains the techniques that should be basic to all selling campaigns, ones that will allow the salesperson to discover & profit from the hidden prospects to be found everywhere & rise above being just an average sales person.

Prospects for Democracy. Noam Chomsky. Read by Noam Chomsky. 1 CD. (Running Time: 74 mins.). (AK Press Audio Ser.). (ENG.). 2000. audio compact disk 14.98 (978-1-873176-38-2(4)) Pub: AK Pr GBR. Dist(s): Consort Bk Sales

Prospects for Gold & Silver. Jerome Smith. 1 cass. (Running Time: 1 hr. 25 min.). 11.95 (413) J Norton Pubs.

ProSpeech: American Diction for Men & Women in Business. How to Speak for Success. Geoffrey G. Forward. Read by Geoffrey G. Forward. Read by Elisabeth Howard. 2 cass. (Running Time: 2 hrs.). 24.95 set. (978-0-944200-05-6(2)) Perfom Arts Global.
How to pronounce the speech sounds of Standard American Speech. How to link them together into words & sentences. How to find & give correct spoken emphasis.

Prospering in the Japanese Market. unabr. ed. David K. Luhman. Read by David K. Luhman. 1 cass. (Running Time: 45 min.). (Doing Busines in Japan Ser.: Vol. 2). 1993. 10.00 (978-1-889297-01-9(1)) Numen Lumen.
Obtaining office space, human resources, salary systems, health insurance, corporate taxation, Japan's legal system, copyrights, patents.

Prosperity. Rick Brown. Read by Rick Brown. Ed. by John Quatro. 1 cass. (Running Time: 30 min.). (Subliminal - Soft Sounds Ser.). 1993. 10.95 (978-1-57100-089-7(5), S143); 10.95 (978-1-57100-113-9(1), W143); 10.95 (978-1-57100-137-5(9), H143) Sublime Sftware.
Reduces the self-sabotage factor.

Prosperity. Richard Jafolla & Mary-Alice Jafolla. Read by Richard Jafolla & Mary-Alice Jafolla. (Career Ser.). 1986. 12.95 (210) Stppng Stones.
Motivational tapes that work on the subconscious mind (subliminal) & conscious mind to bring about self-improvement.

Prosperity. Paul R. Scheele. 1 cass. (Paraliminal Tapes Ser.). 1988. 24.95 (978-0-925480-02-6(9)) Learn Strategies.
Reprogram the negative beliefs you may have about financial success & open your life to abundance.

Prosperity, No. E143. Rick Brown. Read by Rick Brown. Ed. by John Quatro. 1 cass. (Running Time: 30 min.). (Subliminal - Easy Listening Ser.). 1993. 10.95 (978-1-57100-017-0(8)) Sublime Sftware.
"Prosperity" reduces the self-sabatoge factor.

Prosperity, No. J143. Rick Brown. Read by Rick Brown. Ed. by John Quatro. 1 cass. (Running Time: 30 min.). (Subliminal - Jazz Ser.). 1993. 10.95 (978-1-57100-041-5(0)) Sublime Sftware.
"Prosperity" reduces the self-sabatoge factor.

Prosperity: A Blessing or Curse? Creflo A. Dollar. 2008. audio compact disk 28.00 (978-1-59944-711-7(8)) Creflo Dollar.

Prosperity: Promises & Conditions. Derek Prince. 1 cass. (B-4014) Derek Prince.

Prosperity Pt. 1: The Principles. Kenneth Copeland. 6 cass. 1986. 30.00 Set incl. study guide. (978-0-88114-819-0(9)) K Copeland Pubns.
In-depth study of biblical prosperity.

Prosperity Pt. 2: God's Will, God's Why, God's Way. Kenneth Copeland. 6 cass. 1986. 30.00 Set incl. study guide. (978-0-88114-820-6(2)) K Copeland Pubns.

Prosperity Affirmations. Created by Sunny Dawn Johnston. Music by Kris Voelker. Deb McGowan. 2008. audio compact disk 14.00 (978-0-9798119-8-2(8)) Sunlight.

Prosperity Album: How to Apply Spiritual Laws to Create, Health, Wealth & Abundance in Your Life. Randy Gage. 8CD's. 2002. audio compact disk 97.00 (978-0-9715578-2-6(9)) Prime Concepts Grp.

Prosperity & Abundance. Michael P. Marshall. Read by Michael P. Marshall. Ed. by Jonathan C. Renaud. Music by Ted Crook. 1 cass. (Running Time: 52 min.). 1995. 9.00 (978-0-912403-02-1(0)) Prod Renaud.
Michael Marshall reveals how to overcome life-long programs that get in the way of true prosperity. He helps you to remove any guilt or negativity, replacing them with only positive reinforcement & realization of what is truly needed to achieve complete & total prosperity in life.

Prosperity & Abundance. Eldon Taylor. 1 cass. (Running Time: 62 min.). (Inner Talk Ser.). 16.95 (978-1-55978-089-6(4), 5304A) Progress Aware Res.
Soundtrack - Tropical Lagoon with underlying subliminal affirmations.

Prosperity & Abundance: Attracting Abundance into your Life. Created by Christine Sherborne. (ENG.). 2007. audio compact disk 19.95 (978-0-9582712-0-2(8)) Pub: Colourstory AUS. Dist(s): APG

Prosperity & Abundance: Babbling Brook. Eldon Taylor. 1 cass. 16.95 (978-1-55978-454-2(7), 5304F) Progress Aware Res.

Prosperity & Abundance: Music Theme. Eldon Taylor. 1 cass. 16.95 (978-1-55978-091-9(6), 5304C) Progress Aware Res.

Prosperity & Manifestation. Thomas A. Hensel & Kevin R. Emery. 2 cass. 1996. 19.95 (978-1-890405-00-7(0)) LightLines.
Practical how-to guide to identify & release blocks to abundance & magnetize yourself to prosperity in all areas of life.

Prosperity Consciousness. Martha B. Beveridge. 1 cass. (Running Time: 60 min.). 1994. 9.95 (978-1-889237-27-5(2)) Options Now.
A loving cassette on how you think about money, time, health & well-being.

Prosperity Consciousness. Fredric Lehrman. 6 cass. (Running Time: 6 hrs.). 1994. 59.95 Set incl. Affirmation Brochure. (11250AM) Nightingale-Conant.
Are you really willing to be wealthy? On a deep level, most people are not willing to be wealthy because of predisposed attitudes & conditioning. Nobody can build real wealth until they've mastered the true source of wealth - the mind. Learn to develop a "prosperity consciousness," align money with personal values, progress through the four stages of money mastery & plant the seeds in your mind for building a fortune. Fredric Lehrman used his formula to multiply his income 16 times. You can, too.

Prosperity God's Way. Lester Sumrall. 5 cass. (Running Time: 7 hrs. 30 mins.). 1999. 20.00 (978-1-58568-111-2(3)) Sumrall Pubng.

Prosperity Insights Series, Set. Elbert Willis. 4 cass. 13.00 Fill the Gap.

Prosperity Is Ours. Kenneth Copeland. 1 cass. (Living in Prosperity Ser.: No. 3). 1983. 5.00 (978-0-88114-171-9(2)) K Copeland Pubns.
Biblical study on Living in Prosperity.

Prosperity Magnet: Magnetize Yourself to Attract Riches, Vol. 12. Jonathan Parker. 2 cass. (Running Time: 1 hr. 45 min.). 1992. 17.00 Set. (978-1-58400-011-2(2)) QuantumQuests Intl.

Prosperity Plus. unabr. ed. Edwene Gaines. (ENG.). 2006. 14.98 (978-1-59659-108-0(0), GildAudio) Pub: Gildan Media. Dist(s): HachBkGrp

Prosperity Principle - Audio Book. Gay Hendricks. 2009. 14.98 (978-0-7662-4154-1(8)) Gaiam Intl.

Prosperity Principles That Work. Jack Boland. 12 cass. 1975. 59.95 (978-0-88152-002-6(0)) Master Mind.
Prosperity is natural & easily achieved. Techniques are taught that bring immediate results.

Prosperity Profile. Creflo A. Dollar. 20.00 (978-1-59089-102-5(3)) Pub: Creflo Dollar. Dist(s): STL Dist NA

Prosperity Programming. Liah Kraft-Kristaine. Read by Liah Kraft-Kristaine. 1 cass. (Running Time: 62 min.). 1989. 9.95 (978-1-878095-04-6(8)) LMI Prodns.
Self-programming for greater expectation of wealth.

Prosperity Secrets of the Zodiac. Glenda Tomosovich. 1 cass. 8.95 (349) Am Fed Astrologers.
Understanding blocks to prosperity with the chart.

Prosperity Through Self-Love: A Workshop. 2000. 15.00 (978-1-58937-000-5(7)) Quantum Sprituality.

Prosperity vs. Materialism. Creflo A. Dollar. cass. & video 25.00 (978-1-59089-124-7(4)) Pub: Creflo Dollar. Dist(s): STL Dist NA

Prospero's Daughter. unabr. ed. Elizabeth Nunez. Narrated by Simon Vance. 8 cass. (Running Time: 45360 sec.). 2006. 69.95 (978-0-7927-3938-8(8), Chivers Sound Lib); audio compact disk 94.95 (978-0-7927-3939-5(6), Chivers Sound Lib) AudioGO.

Prosperous Attitude. Eldon Taylor. 2 cass. (Running Time: 62 min. per cass.). (Omniphonics Ser.). 29.95 incl. script Set. (978-1-55978-811-3(9), 4012) Progress Aware Res.
3-D soundtrack with underlying subliminal affirmations, night & day versions.

Prosperous Thinking: How to Bring Your Thoughts, Choices & Imagination in Line with God's Will for Your Wealth. Mac Hammond. 1 cass. (LAWS That Govern Prosperity Ser.: Vol. 3). 1996. 18.00 (978-1-57399-032-5(9)) Mac Hammond.
Teaching on controlling & having the right thoughts.

Prospice see Browning's Last Duchess

Prospice & Home Thoughts from Abroad see Treasury of Robert Browning

***Prostitutes' Ball.** abr. ed. Stephen J. Cannell. Read by Scott Brick. (Running Time: 5 hrs.). (Shane Scully Ser.). 2010. 9.99 (978-1-4418-9397-0(0), 9781441893970, BAD); audio compact disk 19.99 (978-1-4233-7446-6(0), 9781423374466, BACD) Brilliance Audio.

***Prostitutes' Ball.** unabr. ed. Stephen J. Cannell. Read by Scott Brick. (Running Time: 8 hrs.). (Shane Scully Ser.). 2010. 24.99 (978-1-4233-7444-2(4), 9781423374442, BAD); 39.97 (978-1-4233-7443-5(6), 9781423374435, Brinc Audio MP3 Lib); 39.97 (978-1-4233-7445-9(2), 9781423374459, BADLE); 24.99 (978-1-4233-7442-8(8), 9781423374428, Brilliance MP3); audio compact disk 87.97 (978-1-4233-7441-1(X), 9781423374411, BriAudCD Unabrid); audio compact disk 29.99 (978-1-4233-7440-4(1), 9781423374404, Bril Audio CD Unabri) Brilliance Audio.

Protagoras, Set. unabr. ed. Plato. Read by Robert L. Halvorson. 2 cass. (Running Time: 180 min.). 14.95 (69) Halvorson Assocs.

Protect & Defend. Richard North Patterson. Read by Patricia Kalember. 2000. 96.00 (978-0-7366-5921-5(8)) Books on Tape.

Protect & Defend: A Thriller. abr. ed. Vince Flynn. Read by Armand Schultz. (Running Time: 6 hrs. 0 mins. 0 sec.). No. 8. 2009. audio compact disk 14.99 (978-0-7435-9756-2(7)) Pub: S&S Audio. Dist(s): S and S Inc

Protect & Defend: A Thriller. unabr. ed. Vince Flynn. Read by George Guidall. 9 CDs. (Running Time: 11 hrs. 0 mins. 0 sec.). No. 8. 2007. audio compact disk 49.95 (978-0-7435-6823-4(0)) Pub: S&S Audio. Dist(s): S and S Inc

Protect It Now. Anthony J. Battaglia, Jr. 1992. pap. bk. & stu. ed. 15.00 (978-1-880254-04-2(2)) Vista.

Protect your achilles heel: crafting armor for the new age at work Cassette: Crafting Armor for the New Age at Work. Wess Roberts. 2004. 10.95 (978-0-7435-4572-3(9)) Pub: S&S Audio. Dist(s): S and S Inc

Protect Your Life Savings: Your Nest Egg Is Harder to Keep Than Create. Michael A. Rome & Hal S. Hammond. 2 cass. (Running Time: 2 hr.). (RPL Audio Books Ser.). 1998. 16.95 (978-1-879755-01-7(7), 501) Recorded Pubns.
Protect & maximize your life savings.

Protected: An audio CD on Psalm 91. Prod. by Influencial Productions. Voice by Tracy M. Boyd. 2008. (978-0-9822763-2-7(X)) Influent Prod.

Protected in Judgment. 1985. (0232) Evang Sisterhood Mary.

Protecting Employer Confidential Information & Business Relationships. 1 cass. 1989. bk. 35.00 (AC-488) PA Bar Inst.

Protecting Employers Against Unfair Competition. Burt Whitt. 2006. audio compact disk 99.95 (978-1-59701-092-4(8)) Aspatore Bks.

Protecting Minority Shareholders from "Squeeze Out" Attempts. Contrib. by Barry N. Shinberg. (Running Time: 4 hrs.). 1984. 75.00 incl. program handbook. NJ Inst CLE.
Examines the nature of squeeze outs & other types of oppression, major & minor causes, duties owed to minority shareholders, techniques commonly employed to squeeze out or to oppress minority shareholders.

Protecting Our Groundwater Resources. Hosted by Nancy Pearlman. 1 cass. (Running Time: 29 min.). 10.00 (1105) Educ Comm CA.

Protecting the Diamond Vol. 1: Communication Skills to Create & Maintain Intimacy in Your Life. unabr. ed. Bill E. Goldberg. Read by Bill E. Goldberg. Read by Erin McLaughin. Perf. by Rob Whitesides-Woo. 1 cass. (Running Time: 1 hr. 10 min.). 1997. 9.95 (978-0-9661461-1-0(5)) B E Goldberg.
Describes concepts & skills regarding communication & related topics.

Protecting the Gift: Keeping Children & Teenagers Safe (and Parents Sane) abr. ed. Gavin De Becker. 4 cass., 5 CDs. (Running Time: 6 hrs.). 1999. (Random AudioBks) Random Audio Pubg.
Taking his much-acclaimed theory about the empowering nature of intuition one step further, de Becker has created a program packed with insight about parents' fears (& their common misconceptions), while offering priceless wisdom & prescriptive action they can take to protect their children.

Protecting the Mind. Read by Osel Tendzin. 3 cass. 1977. 34.00 (A058) Vajradhatu.
Three talks. Discipline Beyond Hope & Fear. 1) Mind As It Is; 2) Experiencing Mind As it Is: Knowledge; 3) Allowing Mind To Be As It Is: Protection.

Protecting Trade Secrets & Confidential Business Information. Read by Warren Krauss et al. (Running Time: 2 hrs. 30 min.). 1992. 89.00 Incl. tape materials. (BU-55125) Cont Ed Bar-CA.
Compares trade secrets with patents & copyrights. Explains defenses including independent conception; reverse engineering; & disclosure. Reviews assignments, licensing, & the use of customer lists. Covers remedies including injunctions, TROs, & damages. Discusses internal procedures to safeguard information from competitors & unauthorized employees. Tells you ways to protect confidential business knowledge & sensitive operation information.

Protecting Your Mental Health Practice: How to Minimize Legal & Financial Risk. Robert H. Woody. (Social & Behavioral Science Ser.). 1988. bk. 43.50 (978-1-55542-111-3(3), Jossey-Bass) Wiley US.

Protecting Your PC. Ian Barile. 2005. bk. 39.95 (978-1-58450-375-0(0)) Chrles River Media.

Protection Against the Hand of Glory see Graveyard of Ghost Tales

Protection from Deception. Derek Prince. 3 cass. 14.95 Set. (PD1) Derek Prince.
Navigating through the minefield of signs & wonders. In the midst of confusion & deception, God's Word provides a clear path on which to walk in peace & safety.

Protection of Children from Sexual Exploitation in Tourism: Youth Module for Ages 12-16. Contrib. by World Tourism Organization Staff. 2002. ring bd. 40.00 (978-92-844-0499-5(1)) Pub: Wrld Tourism Org ESP. Dist(s): Renouf Publ

***Protector.** David Morrell. Read by Stefan Rudnicki. (Playaway Adult Fiction Ser.). (ENG.). 2010. 59.99 (978-1-4417-1787-0(0)) Find a World.

Protector. unabr. ed. David Morrell. Read by Stefan Rudnicki. 2003. reel tape 40.00 (978-1-57453-562-4(5)) Audio Lit.
In the tradition of David Morrell's bestselling The Fifth Profession, this tale of a super-bodyguard hunting down a rogue client who controls a new and powerful weapon promises to be the most imitated thriller for years to come. Based on extensive interviews with special ops agents around the world, it confirms Morrell as the master of high-action suspense.

Protector. unabr. ed. David Morrell. (Running Time: 11 hrs. 0 mins.). (ENG.). 2009. 29.95 (978-1-4332-1913-9(1)); 65.95 (978-1-4332-1909-2(3)); audio compact disk 100.00 (978-1-4332-1910-8(7)) Blckstn Audio.

Protector. unabr. ed. Larry Niven. Read by Mark Sherman. 6 CDs. (Running Time: 7 hrs.). 2003. audio compact disk 48.00 (978-0-7861-9281-6(X), 3067); 39.95 (978-0-7861-2390-2(7), 3067) Blckstn Audio.
Phssthpok the Pak had been traveling for most of his thirty-two thousand years. His mission: to protect the group of Pak breeders sent out into space on a Pak ship some two and a half million years before. But Brennan, one of the rebel Belters, planned to meet that ship first.

Protector. unabr. collector's ed. Larry Niven. Read by Connor O'Brien. 8 cass. (Running Time: 8 hrs.). 1998. 48.00 (978-0-7366-4082-4(7), 4591) Books on Tape.
An alien being is assigned to protect the colonies of his people sent into space millions of years before.

Protector: A Vindication. unabr. ed. J. H. D'Aubigne. Read by Frederick Davidson. 7 cass. (Running Time: 10 hrs.). 1992. 49.95 (978-0-7861-0356-0(6), 1313) Blckstn Audio.
Whether viewed as subjugator or protector, Oliver Cromwell was a titan of 17th Century England. Working from Cromwell's letters & speeches, D'Aubigne revealed the Protector to be a man of prayer & Bible study, exceedingly devout, consecrated to God, a devoted family man. Included are Cromwell's tender letters to his children, his response to the proposal that he be crowned, & his thoughts at the end of his life, as well as observations by George Fox & Milton & the death warrant of Charles.

Protector: A Vindication. unabr. ed. J. H. Merle d'Aubigné. Read by Frederick Davidson. (Running Time: 10 hrs. 0 mins.). (ENG.). 2009. 29.95 (978-1-4417-0576-1(7)); audio compact disk 90.00 (978-1-4417-0573-0(2)) Blckstn Audio.

Protector's War. unabr. ed. S. M. Stirling. Read by Todd McLaren. Narrated by Todd McLaren. (Running Time: 22 hrs. 30 mins. 0 sec.). (Emberverse Ser.). (ENG.). 2008. audio compact disk 34.99 (978-1-4001-5677-1(7)); audio compact disk 99.99 (978-1-4001-3677-3(6)) Pub: Tantor Media. Dist(s): IngramPubServ

Protector's War. unabr. ed. S. M. Stirling. Narrated by Todd McLaren. (Running Time: 22 hrs. 30 mins. 0 sec.). (Emberverse Ser.). (ENG.). 2008. audio compact disk 49.99 (978-1-4001-0677-6(X)) Pub: Tantor Media. Dist(s): IngramPubServ

Protégé. Stephen Frey. Read by Holter Graham. 9 CDs. 2006. audio compact disk 89.95 (978-0-7927-3861-9(6), SLD 883); audio compact disk 29.95 (978-0-7927-3954-8(X), CMP 883) AudioGO.

Protege. Stephen Frey. Read by Holter Graham. 8 cass. (Running Time: 39660 sec.). (Sound Library). 2006. 69.95 (978-0-7927-3860-2(8), CSL 883) AudioGO.

Protege. unabr. ed. Stephen Frey. 9 CDs. (Running Time: 39360 sec.). (Audio Editions Mystery Masters Ser.). 2005. audio compact disk 37.95 (978-1-57270-504-3(3), Audio Edits Mystry) Pub: Audio Partners. Dist(s): PerseuPGW

Protege. unabr. ed. Stephen Frey. Read by Holter Graham. 8 cass. (Running Time: 39360 sec.). (Audio Editions Mystery Masters Ser.). 2006. 37.95 (978-1-57270-506-7(X), Audio Edits Mystry) Pub: Audio Partners. Dist(s): PerseuPGW

Protein Power Life Plan. abr. ed. Michael R. Eades & Mary Dan Eades. (ENG.). 2005. 14.98 (978-1-59483-476-9(8)) Pub: Hachet Audio. Dist(s): HachBkGrp

Protestant Christianity. unabr. ed. Dale A. Johnson. Read by Ben Kingsley. Ed. by Walter Harrelson & Mike Hassell. Prod. by Pat Childs. (Running Time: 10800 sec.). (Religion, Scriptures, & Spirituality Ser.). 2006. audio compact disk 25.95 (978-0-7861-6484-4(0)) Pub: Blckstn Audio. Dist(s): NetLibrary CO

Protestant Christianity. unabr. ed. Dale A. Johnson. Read by Ben Kingsley. Ed. by Walter Harrelson & Mike Hassell. 2 cass. (Running Time: 3 hrs.). Dramatization. (Religion, Scriptures & Spirituality Ser.). 1993. 17.95 (978-1-56823-009-2(5), 10452) Knowledge Prod.
Since the sixteenth century, Christianity has flourished in a third form called Protestantism. In the Protestant Reformation four distant forms of religious expression emerged: Lutheran, Reformed, Anglican, & some radical extensions of these initial movements. Succeeding Protestant developments extended this variety as they also attempted to live out their understanding of Protestant foundation principles.

Protestant Reformation. Ian R. K. Paisley. 4 CDs. (Running Time: 6 hrs.). 1999. audio compact disk 24.99 (978-1-889893-35-8(8)) Emerald House Group Inc.

Protoctist Glossary. Lynn Margulis et al. 1995. audio compact disk 96.00 (978-3-540-14510-3(9)) Spri.

Protoctist Glossary. Lynn Margulis et al. 1997. audio compact disk 88.95 (978-3-540-14199-0(5)) Spri.

Proud Allies. 3 cass. 10.00 ea. (978-1-893165-81-6(7)) Rational Isl.
Shared experiences of gay people, about being lesbian & gay & about using re-evaluation counseling.

Proud My Bed Is Dry for Happy Dreams. Read by Mary Richards. 1 cass. (Running Time: 50 min.). (J). 2007. audio compact disk 19.95 (978-1-56136-175-5(5)) Master Your Mind.

Proud Ones. unabr. collector's ed. Verne Athanas. Read by Rob McQuay. 7 cass. (Running Time: 7 hrs.). 1997. 42.00 (978-0-7366-3618-6(8), 4277) Books on Tape.
Taking a bullet for Sheriff Cass Silver leaves cattleman Thad Ogilvie with a bum leg. Now he's useless on the ranch. But Ogilvie is tough, shrewd & a quick draw, so Silver deputizes him - a just reward.But Thad soon discovers just how demanding his new job is. His boss is waging a one-man war against Martin Dupre, a powerful businessman who owns just about everything & everyone in town. When Dupre's men ambush Silver, Ogilvie must avenge the death of an honorable man. But in his condition, is he any match for Dupre?.

Proud Rooster & Little Hen. Short Stories. Carl Sommer. Narrated by Carl Sommer. 1 cass. Dramatization. (Another Sommer-Time Story Ser.). (J). (gr. 1-4). 2003. bk. 16.95 (978-1-57537-559-5(1)) Advance Pub.

Proud Rooster & Little Hen. Carl Sommer. Narrated by Carl Sommer. 1 cass. Dramatization. (Another Sommer-Time Story Ser.). (J). 2003. lib. bdg. 23.95 (978-1-57537-760-5(8)) Advance Pub.
Character Education story with character song by Karacter Kidz.

***Proud Rooster & Little Hen / Gallito Orgulloso Y Gallinita.** ed. Carl Sommer. Illus. by Greg Budwine. (Another Sommer-Time Story Bilingual Ser.). (ENG & SPA.). (J). 2009. bk. 26.95 (978-1-57537-189-4(8)) Advance Pub.

Proud Tower: A Portrait of the World Before the War, 1890-1914. Barbara W. Tuchman. Read by Nadia May. (Running Time: 19 hrs. 30 mins.). 2005. reel tape 99.95 (978-0-7861-3530-1(1)) Blckstn Audio.

Proud Tower: A Portrait of the World Before the War 1890-1914. Barbara W. Tuchman. Read by Nadia May. (Running Time: 79200 sec.). 2005. audio compact disk 120.00 (978-0-7861-7797-4(7)); audio compact disk 44.95 (978-0-7861-8013-4(7)) Blckstn Audio.

Proud Tower: A Portrait of the World Before the War, 1890-1914, Pt. 1. unabr. ed. Barbara W. Tuchman. Read by Walter Zimmerman. 8 cass. (Running Time: 12 hrs.). 1987. 64.00 (978-0-7366-1144-2(4), 2069-A) Books on Tape.
The fateful years, 1890-1914, leading up to the Great War come to life. It was a time when the world of Privilege still existed in Olympian luxury. Immersed in complacency after a century of remarkable improvements in their charges, Europe's rulers were blind to the coming storm.

Proust: A Biography. unabr. ed. Ronald Hayman. Read by David Case. 15 cass. (Running Time: 22 hrs. 30 mins.). 1992. 120.00 (978-0-7366-2234-9(9), 3024) Books on Tape.
"Proust" reveals a sensitive & intelligent young writer working his craft, while tracking the development of his ideas about time & memory. Ideas developed even as he went into seclusion to complete his monumental novel before he died.

Proust & the Squid: The Story & Science of the Reading Brain. unabr. ed. Maryanne Wolf. Read by Kirsten Potter. (ENG., 2008. audio compact disk 32.95 (978-1-59887-736-6(4), 1598877364) Pub: HighBridge. Dist(s): Workman Pub

Proust Was a Neuroscientist. unabr. ed. Jonah Lehrer. Read by Dan John Miller. (Running Time: 7 hrs.). 2008. 39.25 (978-1-4233-7425-1(8), 9781423374251, BADLE); 39.25 (978-1-4233-7423-7(1), 9781423374237, Brlnc Audio MP3 Lib); 24.95 (978-1-4233-7422-0(3), 9781423374220, Brilliance MP3); 24.95 (978-1-4233-7424-4(X), 9781423374244, BAD); audio compact disk 87.25 (978-1-4233-7421-3(5), 9781423374213, BriAudCD Unabrid); audio compact disk 29.95 (978-1-4233-7420-6(7), 9781423374206, Bril Audio CD Unabri) Brilliance Audio.

Prove All Things; Fullness. Ann Ree Colton & Jonathan Murro. 1 cass. 7.95 A R Colton Fnd.

Proven Chart Patterns: Key Indicators for Success in Today's Markets. Instructed by Chris Manning. 1 cassett. (Running Time: 90 minutes). (Trade Secrets Audio Ser.). 2001. 19.95 (978-1-931611-40-4(8)) Marketplace Bks.
In this audio tape, master trader Chris Manning presents proven, reliable chart patterns that pinpoint buy/sell signals for short and longer-term investors - plus precise indicators for developing each pattern. Manning's clear, comprehensive style is easy enough, even for those new to technical analysis. With a focus on using chart patterns to profit from today's markets - and seizing market turns before the 'crowd' does.

Proven Collection Strategies: Using the Mail, Phone & Outside Agencies to Retrieve Lost Dollars. Mickey Kinder. 4 cass. (Running Time: 3 hrs. 13 min.). 59.95 Set incl. 48p. wkbk. (V10158) CareerTrack Pubns.
Gain the skills for setting accounts quickly & easily - without alienating your customers in the process. You'll get powerful insights into the psychology of collections...learn how to get better results with your letters & telephone calls...& discover how to work more effectively with outside collection agencies.

Proven Guilty. unabr. ed. Jim Butcher. (Running Time: 16 hrs.). Bk. 8. (ENG.). (gr. 12 up). 2009. audio compact disk 49.95 (978-0-14-314474-8(X), PengAudBks) Penguin Grp USA.

Proven Wisdom for Financial Security. Read by James Earl Jones. Prod. by Mark Warner. (Proven Wisdom Ser.). 2004. 9.99 (978-1-58926-675-9(7)) Oasis Audio.

Proven Wisdom for Financial Security. unabr. ed. Mark Warner. Narrated by Mark Warner. Read by James Earl Jones. 1 CD. (Running Time: 1 hr.). (Proven Wisdom Ser.). (ENG.). 2004. audio compact disk 9.99 (978-1-58926-676-6(5)) Oasis Audio.

Proven Wisdom for Stronger Relationships. Read by James Earl Jones. Prod. by Mark Warner. (Proven Wisdom Ser.). 2004. 9.99 (978-1-58926-677-3(3)) Oasis Audio.

Proven Wisdom for Stronger Relationships. Mark Warner. Read by Mark Warner. (Running Time: 1 hr.). 2005. audio compact disk 17.00 (978-0-7861-8183-4(4), 3414) Blckstn Audio.

Proven Wisdom from the Life of Jesus. Read by James Earl Jones. Prod. by Mark Warner. (Proven Wisdom Ser.). 9.99 (978-1-58926-679-7(X)) Oasis Audio.

Proven Wisdom from the Life of Jesus. unabr. ed. Read by James Earl Jones. Prod. by Mark Warner. 1 CD. (Running Time: 1 hr.). (Proven Wisdom Ser.). 2004. audio compact disk 9.99 (978-1-58926-680-3(3)) Oasis Audio.

Provence see Twentieth-Century Poetry in English, No. 1, Recordings of Poets Reading Their Own Poetry

Proverbios. Charles R. Swindoll.Tr. of Proverbs. (SPA.). 2006. audio compact disk 42.00 (978-1-57972-734-5(4)) Insight Living.

Proverbs see Proverbios

Proverbs. 2003. 48.00 (978-1-57972-562-4(7)); audio compact disk 48.00 (978-1-57972-561-7(9)) Insight Living.

Proverbs. Narrated by Samuel Montoya. 2 cass. (SPA.). 1994. 8.98 Set. (978-7-902032-45-2(X)) Chrstn Dup Intl.

Proverbs. unabr. ed. Read by George Vafiadis. 2 cds. (Running Time: 1 hr 56 mins). 2002. audio compact disk 18.95 (978-1-58472-308-0(4), 032, In Aud) Pub: Sound Room. Dist(s): Baker Taylor
King James Version.

Proverbs: Wit & Wisdom. 1 cass. (Running Time: 30 min.). 9.95 (F0230B090, HarperThor) HarpC GBR.

Proverbs - Our Daily Wisdom. Gloria Copeland. (ENG.). 2008. audio compact disk 30.00 (978-1-57562-979-7(8)) K Copeland Pubns.

Proverbs Commentary. Chuck Missler. 1 CD Rom. (Running Time: 8 hours aprox). (Chuck Missler Commentaries). 2006. cd-rom 29.95 (978-1-57821-329-0(0)); audio compact disk 44.95 (978-1-57821-328-3(2)) Koinonia Hse.
The Book of Proverbs could be titled, "Wise Up" and Live. Beyond simply obeying laws, this book focuses on leading an aggressively dynamic life, giving examples of proper and improper attitudes, conduct, and characteristics in succinct, penetrating ways. A proverb can be thought of as "a short sentence from long experience"; it is easy to remember, yet it condenses much wisdom into a small space. "All Scripture is given by inspiration of God and is profitable" in four ways: for doctrine - what?s right; for reproof - what?s not right; for correction - how to get right; and for instruction in righteousness - how to stay right (2 Timothy 3:16). This book touches on all four of these.

Proverbs, Ecclesiastes & Song of Solomon from the King James Bible, Vol. 3. Read by Eric Martin. 3 cass. (Running Time: 2 hrs. 57 min.). 1997. 12.95 (978-1-891320-03-3(3)) Jodacom Intl.

Proverbs for the People. unabr. ed. 17 cass. (Running Time: 21 hrs. 15 mins.). 2003. 99.75 (978-1-4025-5716-3(7), F0130MC, Griot Aud) Recorded Bks.

Proverbs Our Daily Wisdom. Gloria Copeland. 6 cass. 1989. 30.00 Set. (978-0-88114-928-9(4)) K Copeland Pubns.
Biblical teaching on wisdom.

Proverbs Series. unabr. ed. Jack Deere. 8 cass. (Running Time: 12 hrs.). 2000. 40.00 (JD08-000) Morning NC.
Practical wisdom for everyday living is brought to life in Jack's thorough exposition of this important book of the Bible.

Provide, Provide see Robert Frost Reads

Provide, Provide see Twentieth-Century Poetry in English, No. 6, Recordings of Poets Reading Their Own Poetry

***Provide World Class Service at the Local Level.** (ENG.). 2010. audio compact disk 25.00 (978-0-9766470-5-8(2)) Guld Resource.

Providence. Geoffrey Wolff. Read by Geoffrey Wolff. 1 cass. (Running Time: 30 min.). 8.95 (AMF 23) Am Audio Prose.
The author reads from his book & talks about the place, people, & concept of Providence.

Providence. unabr. ed. Anita Brookner. Read by Judith Whale. 6 cass. (Running Time: 6 hrs. 30 min.). (Isis Ser.). (J). 2004. 54.95 (978-1-85695-401-3(3), 92055) Pub: ISIS Lrg Prnt GBR. Dist(s): Ulverscroft US

Providence of God: Matt. 6:33; Romans 8:26-30. Ed Young. 1990. 4.95 (978-0-7417-1824-2(3), 824) Win Walk.

Providential Battles: Twenty Battles That Changed the World. William Potter. Read by William Potter. (Running Time: 15420 sec.). 2006. audio compact disk 25.00 (978-1-933431-30-7(X)) Vsn Forum.

Providential Battles II: Epic Conflicts That Changed the World. William Potter. 2008. audio compact disk 25.00 (978-1-933431-45-1(8)) Vsn Forum.

Providing Data, Information & Knowledge to the Virtual Office: Organizational Support for Remote Workers. Claire R. McInerney. 1 cass. 1999. 54.00 (978-0-87111-503-4(4)) SLA.

Provinces of Night. abr. unabr. ed. William Gay. Read by Dick Hill. 7 cass. (Running Time: 11 hrs.). 2000. 32.95 (978-1-58788-170-1(5), 1587881705, BAU) Brilliance Audio.

Provinces of Night. unabr. ed. William Gay. Read by Dick Hill. 7 cass. (Running Time: 11 hrs.). 2000. 32.95 Brilliance Audio.

Provinces of Night. unabr. ed. William Gay. Read by Dick Hill. (Running Time: 11 hrs.). 2005. 39.25 (978-1-59600-594-5(7), 9781596005945, BADLE); 24.95 (978-1-59600-593-8(9), 9781596005938, BAD); 24.95 (978-1-59600-591-4(2), 9781596005914, Brilliance MP3); 39.25 (978-1-59600-592-1(0), 9781596005921, Brlnc Audio MP3 Lib) Brilliance Audio.
The year is 1952, and E.F. Bloodworth has returned to his home - a forgotten corner of Tennessee - after twenty years of roaming. The wife he walked out on has withered and faded, his three sons are grown and angry. Warren is a womanizing alcoholic, Boyd is driven by jealousy to hunt down his wife's lover, and Brady puts hexes on his enemies from his mamma's porch. Only Fleming, the old man's grandson, treats him with the respect his age commands, and sees past all the hatred to realize the way it can posion a man's soul. It is ultimately the love of Raven Lee, a sloe-eyed beauty from another town, that gives Fleming the courage to reject this family curse.

Provincials: A Personal History of Jews in the South. unabr. ed. Eli N. Evans. Read by Wolfram Kandinsky. 12 cass. (Running Time: 18 hrs.). 96.00 (978-0-7366-2749-8(9), 3474) Books on Tape.
When we think of the Jewish immigration to the U.S. from 1880 to 1920, New York comes to mind. Surely not the South, where, Evans reminds us, "Jews languished as the provincials, the Jews of the periphery, not destined to triumph but just to survive. "Not only a warm, personal chronicle by a Jew raised in Durham, North Carolina, but a social history: Of the 400,000 Jews scattered across 11 Southern states, of the south itself, & of the whole country.

Proving & Defending Damages. (Running Time: 5 hrs. 30 min.). 1995. 92.00 Incl. 388p. coursebk. (20561) NYS Bar.
Focuses on the presentation & defense of damages in the trial of a personal injury case. All facets of the recoverable elements of damages are addressed by plaintiffs' & defendants' attorneys. Successful, proven techniques utilized during voir dire, opening statements & summations are highlighted by the experienced panelists.

Proving Damages in Personal Injury & Death Cases. 1985. bk. 60.00 incl. book.; 35.00 cass. only.; 25.00 book only. PA Bar Inst.

Proving Damages in Personal Injury & Death Cases. 1995. bk. 99.00 (ACS-965) PA Bar Inst.
An arsenal of practice tips to help get the compensation due the client. Successful litigators from around the state share their techniques.

Proving Damages in Personal Injury & Death Cases - A Statewide Institute. 1989. 50.00 (AC-526) PA Bar Inst.

Proving Earnings Loss in Personal Injury Litigation. Contrib. by Robert P. Wolfe. (Running Time: 4 hrs.). 1985. 75.00 incl. program handbook. NJ Inst CLE.
Discusses what constitutes a vocational-earnings loss expert; interrelationship of medical, vocational & economic factors in earnings loss; nature of a vocational evalution, work traits vs. worker skills; vocational interviews.

Proving Ground: The Inside Story of the 1998 Sydney-to-Hobart Race. G. Bruce Knecht. Read by Michael Kramer. 2001. 48.00 (978-0-7366-7161-3(7)) Books on Tape.

Proving Ground: The Inside Story of the 1998 Sydney-to-Hobart Race. unabr. collector's ed. G. Bruce Knecht. Read by Michael Kramer. 6 cass. (Running Time: 9 hrs.). 2001. 48.00 Books on Tape.
The dramatic story of the 1998 race from Sydney to Hobart, one of the worst sailing disasters in modern history.

Proving It. unabr. ed. Andrew Vachss. Read by Burt Reynolds. 4 cass. (Running Time: 6 hrs.). 2001. 24.95 (978-1-57511-086-8(5)) Pub Mills.
Author surveys a desolate landscape of losers. An adolescent who is shunned by his peers exacts a terrible revenge; a teenage "escort" is hired for a devious plan & used as a human shield; a terminally ill woman hires a hit man to put her out of her misery; a young man discovers the shattering truth about the identity of his sister's rapist.

Proving Your Case: Using McElhaney's Trial Notebook Method of Advocacy. unabr. ed. James McElhaney. Read by James McElhaney. 3 cass. (Running Time: 3 hrs.). (Jim McElhaney's Master Advocate Ser.). pap. bk. 85.00 Set. PEG MN.
Shows you how to use a system that works simply logically & easily to prove your case.

Proyecto. unabr. ed. Marcos Witt. 2003. 9.99 (978-0-8297-4394-4(4)) Zondervan.

Prune. unabr. ed. Ramon Royal Ross. 4 cass. (Running Time: 5 hrs.). (YA). (gr. 5-8). 1984. 37.00 (978-1-4025-2066-2(6), 96621) Recorded Bks.
The hero of this book is a prune. His journey begins in an ordinary way: he is picked, packed in a box with the rest of the crop, and carried off to the packing shed. But along the way, his life takes an unexpected turn. When his crate tips over, Prune meets Pica, a magpie. As they travel together, they meet Muskrat. The three soon become friends and begin an epic quest that will teach them much about loyalty, adventure, and courage.

Prussian Officer. unabr. ed. Short Stories. D. H. Lawrence. Narrated by Jill Tanner. 6 cass. (Running Time: 9 hrs. 15 mins.). 1999. 51.00 (978-1-55690-427-1(4), 89440E7) Recorded Bks.
Includes: "The Prussian Officer"; "Goose Fair"; "The Thorn in the Flesh"; "The Shades of Spring"; "Daughters of the Vicar"; "A Fragment of Stained Glass"; "Second Best"; "The Shadow in the Rose Garden"; "The White Stocking"; "A Sick Collier"; "The Christening" & "Odour of Chrysanthemums".

***Pryde & the Infernal Device.** Malcolm Archibald. 2010. 69.95 (978-1-4079-0782-6(4)); audio compact disk 84.95 (978-1-4079-0783-3(2)) Pub: Soundings Ltd GBR. Dist(s): Ulverscroft US

Pryde's Rock. Malcolm Archibald. 2008. 61.95 (978-1-84559-963-8(2)); audio compact disk 79.95 (978-1-84559-964-5(0)) Pub: Soundings Ltd GBR. Dist(s): Ulverscroft US

PS, I Love You. Cecelia Ahern. Read by Bernadette Dunne. 2004. audio compact disk 90.00 (978-0-7366-9870-2(1)) Books on Tape.

PS, I Love You. abr. ed. Cecelia Ahern. Read by Rupert Degas & Victoria Smurfit. 5 CDs. (Running Time: 21600 sec.). 2006. audio compact disk 14.98 (978-1-4013-8334-3(3), Hyperion Audio) Pub: Hyperion. Dist(s): HarperCollins Pubs

PS, I Love You. abr. movie tie-in ed. Cecelia Ahern. Read by Victoria Smurfit. Told to Rupert Degas. (Running Time: 21600 sec.). 2007. audio compact disk 14.95 (978-1-4013-8901-7(5), Hyperion Audio) Pub: Hyperion. Dist(s): HarperCollins Pubs

Psalm Meditations, Vol. 1, Set. Joan Chittister. 1 cass. (Running Time: 59 min.). 1988. 8.95 (AA2122) Credence Commun.
Reads a passage from the psalms the comments briefly & prayerfully.

Psalm Meditations, Vol. 2. Joan Chittister. 1 cass. (Running Time: 59 min.). 1998. 8.95 (AA2123) Credence Commun.

Psalm Meditations, Vol. 3. Joan Chittister. 1 cass. (Running Time: 1 hr. 15 min.). 8.95 (AA2238) Credence Commun.
A passage from Psalms, brief commentary & music for meditation.

Psalm Meditations, Vol. 4. Joan Chittister. 1 cass. (Running Time: 1 hr. 18 min.). 8.95 (AA2239) Credence Commun.

Psalm Meditations, Vol. 5. Joan Chittister. 1 cass. (Running Time: 1 hr. 05 min.). 8.95 (AA2389) Credence Commun.
A passage from Psalms, brief commentary, & music for meditation.

Psalm Meditations, Vol. 6. Joan Chittister. 1 cass. (Running Time: 1 hr. 07 min.). 8.95 (AA2390) Credence Commun.
The format is simple & lovely, the content is profound. Sr. Joan reads a passage from the psalms. She then comments briefly & prayerfully. The words are followed by beautiful chamber music. Chittister's literary range, her psychological depth & scriptural sophistication are inspiring. The music creates a space & a mood for you to move into your own reflections.

Psalm of Hope. Felix Goebal-Komala. 1995. 10.95 (352); audio compact disk 15.95 (352) GIA Pubns.

Psalm of Life see Best Loved Poems of Longfellow

Psalm of Life (A Poem from the Poets' Corner) The One-and-Only Poetry Book for the Whole Family. unabr. ed. Henry Wadsworth Longfellow & John Lithgow. Read by John Lithgow. (Running Time: 10 mins.). (ENG.). 2008. 0.99 (978-1-60024-323-3(1)) Pub: Hachet Audio. Dist(s): HachBkGrp

Psalm Twenty-Three. Perf. by Kathy Troccoli. 1 cass. 1999. (751-321-3631) Brentwood Music.

Psalm 100. Warren W. Wiersbe. Read by Warren W. Wiersbe. 1 cass. (Running Time: 1 hr. 30 min.). 1987. 4.95 (978-0-8474-2314-9(X)) Back to Bible.
These four messages discusses praise: who should praise, how one should praise, & why one should praise.

Psalm 101 (Psalms Across the Universe) NRSV English & Polish. Narrated by Natalie Kozdra & Jadwiga Kozdra. (ENG.). 2009. 0.99 (978-0-9799446-8-0(6)) Groark Audio.

Psalm 108 (Psalms Across the Universe) NRSV English & Portuguese. Narrated by Eileen Groark et al. (ENG.). 2009. 0.99 (978-0-9799446-9-7(4)) Groark Audio.

Psalm 119, Vol. 1. 1 cass. (Running Time: 55 min.). 1997. 8.00 (978-1-890967-37-6(8)); audio compact disk 12.00 (978-1-890967-39-0(4)) Hse of Yahweh.
The words of this Psalm offers a refreshing hope to the Saints of Yahweh that through patient endurance & the keeping of his laws, peace will rest upon the earth.

Psalm 119, Vol. 2. 1 cass. (Running Time: 90 mins.). 1997. 8.00 (978-1-890967-38-3(6)); audio compact disk 12.00 (978-1-890967-40-6(8)) Hse of Yahweh.

Psalm 23. Perf. by Eddie James, and Color Blind. 1 cass. 10.98 (978-1-57908-263-5(7), 1357); audio compact disk 15.98 CD. (978-1-57908-262-8(9), 1357) Platinm Enter.

Psalm 23. Perf. by Kathy Troccoli. 1 cass. 1999. 8.98 (978-0-7601-2725-4(5)) Brentwood Music.

Psalm 51: Rebellion to Revival. Voddie Baucham, Jr. (YA). 2002. audio compact disk 15.00 (978-0-633-09033-3(6)) LifeWay Christian.

Psalm 55 (Psalms Across the Universe) NRSV English & Russian. Narrated by Marc Sengin & Ksenenya Bakhrakh. (ENG.). 2009. 0.99 (978-0-9799446-4-2(3)) Groark Audio.

Psalm 63 (Psalms Across the Universe) NRSV (English & French) Narrated by Gregoire Rosia. (ENG.). 2009. 0.99 (978-0-9799446-5-9(1)) Groark Audio.

Psalm 97 (Psalms Across the Universe) NRSV English & Yoruba. Narrated by Oluremi Olabinjo. (ENG.). 2009. 0.99 (978-0-9799446-6-6(X)) Groark Audio.

Psalm 99 (Psalms Across the Universe) NRSV English & Tigrigna. Narrated by Teclezghi Ucbaghiorghis. (ENG.). 2009. 0.99 (978-0-9799446-7-3(8)) Groark Audio.

Psalms. 1 cass. 1997. 10.98 (978-0-7601-1292-2(4), C70018); audio compact disk 15.98 (978-0-7601-1293-9(2), CD70018) Pub: Brentwood Music. Dist(s): Provident Mus Dist
Based upon the writings of David, Psalms soothes the soul with the most sacred of worship choruses. Uses the voice as an instrument of soaring praise as ethereal melodies & stirring harmonies are delicately blended with sound & rhythm to capture the range of emotion the Psalmist conveys.

Psalms. Narrated by E. W. Jeffries. 4 cass. (Running Time: 6 hrs.). 1994. 10.99 (978-7-902033-02-2(2)) Chrstn Dup Intl.

Psalms. Read by Paul Mims. 1994. 9.99 (978-7-902032-95-7(6)) Chrstn Dup Intl.

Psalms. Chuck Missler. 24 audio CDs. (Running Time: 24 hours aprox). (Chuck Missler Commentaries). 2007. audio compact disk 89.95 (978-1-57821-374-0(6)) Koinonia Hse.

Psalms. Chuck Missler. 1 CD Rom. (Running Time: 24 hours aprox). (Chuck Missler Commentaries). 2007. cd-rom 44.95 (978-1-57821-375-7(4)) Koinonia Hse.

Psalms. Narrated by Samuel Montoya. 4 cass. (SPA.). 1994. 12.98 Set. (978-7-902032-38-4(7)) Chrstn Dup Intl.

Psalms. unabr. ed. Read by Alex Jennings. 4 CDs. 2005. audio compact disk 28.98 (978-962-634-352-4(4)) Naxos UK GBR.

Psalms. unabr. ed. Poems. Read by George Vafiadis. 4 cds. (Running Time: 4 hrs 59 mins). 2002. audio compact disk 26.95 (978-1-58472-309-7(2), 031, In Aud) Pub: Sound Room. Dist(s): Baker Taylor
King James Version.

Psalms. unabr. ed. Read by Michael Knox York. 4 cass. (Bible Ser.). 2004. 24.95 (978-1-59007-474-9(2)); audio compact disk 39.95 (978-1-59007-475-6(0)) Pub: New Millenn Enter. Dist(s): PerseuPGW

Psalms: A Biblical Interpretation. Concept by Ermance Rejebian. (ENG.). 2007. 5.99 (978-1-60339-155-9(X)); audio compact disk 5.99 (978-1-60339-156-6(8)) Listenr Digest.

Psalms: The First Decade. Douglas Wilson. 11 CDs. (ENG.). 2000. audio compact disk 34.00 (978-1-59128-498-7(8)) Canon Pr ID.

Psalms: The First Decade. Read by Douglas Wilson. 11. 2000. 28.00 (978-1-59128-497-0(X)); 34.00 (978-1-59128-499-4(6)) Canon Pr ID.

Psalms: The Fourth Decade. Douglas Wilson. 10 CDs. (ENG.). 2006. audio compact disk Rental 34.00 (978-1-59128-528-1(3)) Canon Pr ID.

Psalms: The Fourth Decade. Read by Douglas Wilson. 10. 2006. 28.00 (978-1-59128-527-4(5)); 34.00 (978-1-59128-529-8(1)) Canon Pr ID.

Psalms: The Second Decade. Douglas Wilson. 10 CDs. (ENG.). 2002. audio compact disk 34.00 (978-1-59128-504-5(6)) Canon Pr ID.

Psalms: The Second Decade. Read by Douglas Wilson. 10. 2002. 28.00 (978-1-59128-503-8(8)); 34.00 (978-1-59128-505-2(4)) Canon Pr ID.

Psalms: The Third Decade. Read by Douglas Wilson. 10. 2004. 28.00 (978-1-59128-506-9(2)); 34.00 (978-1-59128-508-3(9)) Canon Pr ID.

Psalms & Proverbs. 2000. 14.99 (978-7-902032-26-1(3)) Chrstn Dup Intl.

Psalms & Proverbs. Contrib. by E. W. Jeffries. 5 cass. 1998. 21.98 Set. (978-7-902031-49-3(6)) Chrstn Dup Intl.

Psalms & Proverbs. Contrib. by Paul Mims. 6 cass. 1997. 14.98 Set. (978-7-902030-98-4(8)) Chrstn Dup Intl.
Bible.

Psalms & Proverbs. Contrib. by Paul Mims. 5 cass. 1998. 19.98 Set. (978-7-902031-42-4(9)) Chrstn Dup Intl.

Psalms & Proverbs. Narrated by Samuel Montoya. (SPA.). 1999. audio compact disk 19.98 (978-7-902031-77-6(1)) Chrstn Dup Intl.

Psalms & Proverbs: King James Version. abr. ed. 16.95 Trinity Tapes.

Psalms & Proverbs: King James Version. unabr. ed. 6 cass. (Running Time: 4 hrs. 30 min.). 1983. 29.95 (PP-C-EZ) Trinity Tapes.

Psalms & Proverbs 31 Days to Get the Message. unabr. ed. Eugene H. Peterson. Read by Kelly Ryan Dolan. Prod. by Oasis Audio staff. 6 cass. (Running Time: 7 hrs. 30 mins.). 2001. 48.00 (978-0-7861-8398-2(5), 3357) Blckstn Audio.

Psalms & Selahs. Read by Marquis Laughlin. Perf. by Steve Turley. 1 CD. (Running Time: 40 min. 53 sec.). 2002. audio compact disk 12.95 (978-0-9726331-1-6(1)) Pub: Sola Scriptura. Dist(s): STL Dist NA
"Combining beautifully read selections from the Psalms with favorite hymns played on classical guitar, Psalms & Selahs provides a wonderful way to reflect on the power of God's Word and the moving melodies of the Christian faith. Includes Amazing Grace, Be Thou My Vision, and A Mighty Fortress Is Our God as well as a complete reading of Psalm 23.".

Psalms & the Tales of David. abr. ed. Perf. by Judith Anderson. 1 cass. 1984. 12.95 (978-0-694-50042-0(9), SWC 1053) HarperCollins Pubs.

Psalms Fifty-Six - Sixty-Three. unabr. ed. Warren W. Wiersbe. Read by Warren W. Wiersbe. 2 cass. (Running Time: 2 hrs. 25 min.). 1989. 9.95 (978-0-8474-2355-2(7)) Back to Bible.
This study directs your attention to the outcome of danger & battles through prayer & praise.

Psalms for Leaders: Psalms Across the Universe, Vol. 3. Narrated by Various Artists. (ENG.). 2009. 10.00 (978-0-9799446-3-5(5)) Groark Audio.

Psalms for Life Living Audio Cassette. D. N. Sutton. Read by D. N. Sutton. (ENG.). 2001. 6.00 (978-0-940361-32-4(9)) Sherwood-Spencer Pub.

Psalms for Life Living CD. D. N. Sutton. Read by D. N. Sutton. (ENG.). 2001. audio compact disk 12.00 (978-0-940361-42-3(6)) Sherwood-Spencer Pub.

Psalms for Life Living CD & Book: Modern poems singing praises to God. D. N. Sutton. Read by D. N. Sutton. (ENG.). 2001. per. 20.00 (978-0-940361-52-2(3)) Sherwood-Spencer Pub.

Psalms for the Church Year, Vol. 7. John Foley. 1995. 10.95 (343); audio compact disk 15.95 (343) GIA Pubns.

Psalms for the Church Year, Vol. 8. David Haas. 1 cass. 1996. 10.95 (CS-387); audio compact disk 15.95 (CD-387) GIA Pubns.

Psalms for the Church Year, Vol. 9. David Haas. 1 cass. 1998. 10.95 (CS-430); 10.95 (CS-430); audio compact disk 15.95 (CD-430); audio compact disk 15.95 (CD-430) GIA Pubns.

Psalms for the Church Year, Vol. 10. Malcolm Kogut. 1 cass. 1999. 10.95; 10.95; audio compact disk 15.95; audio compact disk 15.95 GIA Pubns.

Psalms for the 21st Century. Poems. Errol Strider. Composed by Charles Moselle. 1 cd. (Running Time: 45 mins). Dramatization. 2005. audio compact disk 15.95 (978-1-878868-06-0(3)) Strider Inner.

Psalms for Warriors: Selections from the Psalms Project. Executive Producer Barbara Groark. (ENG.). 2007. 12.99 (978-0-9799446-1-1(9)) Groark Audio.

Psalms Forty-Two - Fifty-Five. unabr. ed. Warren W. Wiersbe. Read by Warren W. Wiersbe. 4 cass. (Running Time: 4 hrs. 50 min.). 1989. 18.95 (978-0-8474-2354-5(9)) Back to Bible.
Provides insights for handling life's daily trials & directs our thoughts toward God for victory.

Psalms from the Heart. 2002. (978-0-940110-24-3(5)); audio compact disk (978-0-940110-19-9(9)) Life Action Publishing.

Psalms in French. Read by Charles Guillot. 4 cass. (Running Time: 4 hrs.). 2001. 34.95 (S50014) J Norton Pubs.

Psalms in German. Read by Edwin Auchenbach. 5 cass. (Running Time: 5 hrs.). 27.95 (S50013) J Norton Pubs.

Psalms in Many Tongues. unabr. ed. Perf. by Eknath Easwaran. 1 cass. (Running Time: 1 hr.). 1990. 7.95 (978-1-58638-594-1(1)) Nilgiri Pr.

Psalms in Portuguese. Narrated by David Nunes. 4 cass. (Running Time: 4 hrs.). vinyl bd. 34.95 (S50015) J Norton Pubs.

Psalms in Spanish. Read by Samuel Montoya. 4 cass. (Running Time: 4 hrs.). vinyl bd. 34.95 (S50011) J Norton Pubs.

Psalms Now. Leslie Brandt. 2 cass. (Running Time: 12 min.). (J). (ps-3). 12.99 (978-0-570-09051-9(2), 79KM9990) Concordia.

Psalms of David. 4 CDs. 2004. audio compact disk (978-1-883012-11-3(2)) Remnant Pubns.

Psalms of David & the Song of Solomon Vol. 4: From the King James Bible. Eric Martin. Read by Eric Martin. 5 CD's. (Running Time: 5 hrs. 30 min.). (J). (gr. 6 up). 1997. audio compact disk 18.95 CD Set. (978-1-891320-02-6(5)) Jodacom Intl.

Psalms of David, Songs of Mary. John L. Bell. 1 cass., 1 CD. 1997. 10.95 (CS-403); audio compact disk 15.95 (CD-403) GIA Pubns.

Psalms of Islam. Imam Ali Hussain. Tr. by Al Ansarian Publications. Created by Khaled Sharafuddin. Narrated by Chris Hawes. 2007. audio compact disk 39.95 (978-1-4276-2872-5(6)) AardGP.

Psalms of King David part One see Salmos del Rey David: Primera Parte - Salmos 1 al 87

Psalms of King David Part One. Read by Pedro Montoya. (Running Time: 3 hrs.). 2002. 16.95 (978-1-60083-208-6(3), Audiofy Corp) Iofy Corp.

Psalms of King David part Two see Salmos del Rey David - Segunda Parte - Salmos 88 Al 150

Psalms of King David Part Two. Read by Pedro Montoya. (Running Time: 3 hrs.). 2002. 16.95 (978-1-60083-209-3(1), Audiofy Corp) Iofy Corp.

Psalms of Praise: Psalm 149-150. Ed Young. 1989. 4.95 (978-0-7417-1767-2(0), 767) Win Walk.

Psalms of the Notre Dame Folk Choir. Composed by Steven C. Warner. Directed By Karen Schneider-Kirner. Contrib. by The Notre Dame Folk Choir. (Running Time: 4200 sec.). 2006. audio compact disk 17.00 (978-1-58459-305-8(9)) Wrld Lib Pubns.

Psalms, Proverbs & Ecclesiastes. Gary V. Whetstone. Instructed by June Austin. (Old Testament Ser.: Vol. OT 202). (C). 1997. 80.00 (978-1-58866-014-5(1)) Gary Whet Pub.

Psalms, Songs, & Spiritual Songs. bk. 10.00 (978-0-687-04886-1(9)) Abingdon.

Psalms Thirty-Four - Forty-One. unabr. ed. Warren W. Wiersbe. Read by Warren W. Wiersbe. 4 cass. (Running Time: 4 hrs. 55 min.). 1989. 18.95 (978-0-8474-2352-1(2)) Back to Bible.
Encouragement in daily living, through God's peace, protection, chastening & spiritual experiences.

Psalter. unabr. ed. Narrated by Flo Gibson. 4 cass. (Running Time: 4 hrs.). 2003. 19.95 (978-1-55685-751-5(9)) Audio Bk Con.

***Psam 10.** Tics. 2010. audio compact disk (978-1-4507-1556-0(7)) Indep Pub IL.

Pscho-Epistemology I. Harry Binswanger. 3 cass. (Running Time: 3 hrs. 30 min.). 32.95 Set. (IB01D) Second Renaissance.
Two lectures in which Dr. Binswanger presents Ayn Rand's revolutionary theories & offers his own observations on the role of the subconscious in thinking & on the specific operations by which one "programs" one's subconscious. Includes Q&A.

Pseudo. Perf. by Wooky. 1 CD. 1999. audio compact disk 16.98 (978-1-57908-477-6(X), 5323) Platinm Enter.

Pseudo-Egoism of Thomas Hobbes. John Ridpath. 1 cass. (Running Time: 1 hr. 30 min.). 1995. 12.95 (978-1-56114-516-4(5), CR01C) Second Renaissance.
An explanation of the 19th century's altruist-statist doctrines.

Pseudoxanthoma Elasticum - A Bibliography & Dictionary for Physicians, Patients, & Genome Researchers. Compiled by Icon Group International, Inc. Staff. 2007. ring bd. 28.95 (978-0-497-11283-7(3)) Icon Grp.

PSI Cops. unabr. ed. Michael Bracken. Read by Maynard Villers. 4 cass. (Running Time: 5 hrs. 36 min.). 1995. 26.95 (978-1-55686-570-1(8)) Books in Motion.
A sex-crazed killer who mutilates his victims with an electronic laser knife is pursued by 21st century PSI cops that are able to read the psychic residue at a crime scene.

P'Sicha Address. Shmuel Kamenetsky. 1 cass. (Running Time: 90 mins.). 1999. 6.00 (T60TA) Torah Umesorah.

Psicobelleza: Un Camino Hacia la Autentica Belleza. Roberto Tirigall & Viviana Accornero Tirigall. 2008. pap. bk. 15.99 (978-958-04-9930-5(6)) Pub: Norma S A COL. Dist(s): Distr Norma

Psicomeditacion: 10 Tecnicas para Armonizar Mente y Cuerpo. 3rd ed. Roberto Tirigall. 2006. pap. bk. 15.99 (978-958-04-9058-6(9)) Grupo Ed Norma ARG.

PSM Relaxation Experience: Personalized Stress Management. Joseph L. Gill. 2002. audio compact disk 14.95 (978-0-910819-04-6(1)) Counsel & Consult.

Psmith in the City. unabr. ed. P. G. Wodehouse. Read by Frederick Davidson. 4 cass. (Running Time: 5 hrs. 30 mins.). 1996. 32.95 (978-0-7861-0945-6(9), 1697) Blckstn Audio.
Psmith & his friend, Mike Jackson, have been pressed into jobs in the city. Psmith intends to keep his knowledge of work limited to hearsay, & uses his wit & sangfroid to smooth over the world of business for Mike & himself.

Psmith in the City, Set. unabr. ed. P. G. Wodehouse. Read by Flo Gibson. 4 cass. (Running Time: 5 hrs. 30 min.). 1997. 19.95 (978-1-55685-456-9(0), 456-0) Audio Bk Con.
Sent by their fathers to work in a bank in the city, the flippant, irresponsible Psmith & his friend Mike, who would rather be playing cricket, cope as best they can.

Psmith Journalist. P. G. Wodehouse. Read by Anais 9000. 2008. 27.95 (978-1-60112-195-0(4)) Babblebooks.

Psmith Journalist. unabr. ed. P. G. Wodehouse. Read by Frederick Davidson. 5 cass. (Running Time: 7 hrs.). 1995. 39.95 (978-0-7861-0819-0(3), 1641) Blckstn Audio.
Psmith, journalist working for Cosy Moments, usually is not a controversial writer. Falling in with its deputy editor Billy Windsor, Psmith allows his literary aspirations to run riot & soon Cosy Moments is not cosy at all. With biting

attacks on the New York slum problem, the circulation goes up, but the owner of the tenements is not amused. Unable to "buy" the magazine's cooperation, the villain tries to quiet the writing duo permanently.

Psoas & Back Pain. (ENG.). (J). 2008. 15.00 (978-0-9657944-9-7(0)) Guinea Pig.

PSYCH-K & the Realm of the Subconscious: Conversations with Rob Williams - the Originator of PSYCH-K with Host Laura Lee. Interview. Robert M. Williams. Created by Robert M. Williams. Hosted by Laura Lee. 3 cass. (Running Time: 3 hours). 2003. 24.95 (978-1-889071-25-1(0), 6316) Radio Bookstore.
Originally recorded for Conversation for Exploration - hosted by Laura Lee, lauralee.com - this insightful, wide-ranging conversation with Rob Williams reveals his philosophy on life, reality, and the nature of the mind. "These interviews are an honest, no-holds-barred look at my philosophy of life and its connection to PSYCH-K?. Laura Lee asks the important questions that bring out the meaningful and revealing answers from her guests. Of course you don?t have to agree with my philosophy to benefit from PSYCH-K?, but so many people have asked me to elaborate on my world view and how it has developed as a result of years of working in the realm of the subconscious. These interviews are an answer to that request." - Rob Williams.

Psyche: Structure & Dynamics. Read by Murray Stein. 1 cass. (Running Time: 2 hrs.). 1986. 12.95 (978-0-7822-0267-0(5), 199) C G Jung IL.

Psyche & Eros. 1 cass. (Running Time: 1 hr. 17 min.). (J). (gr. 6-12). 1988. 10.00 (978-1-879846-05-0(5)) Cloudstone NY.
An enchanting rendition of how beautiful mortal Psyche became the bride of Eros...a myth of love, adventure, amusement...dramatic & detailed. 2 Greek songs.

Psyched to Sell. Art Mortell. Read by Art Mortell. 6 cass. (Running Time: 6 hrs.). 1993. pap. bk. 79.95 set incl. action guide. (2022) Dartnell Corp.
Shows you how to capitalize on the most threatening sales situation. Use Art Mortell's unique mental game plan & transform virtually any setback into a positive sales opportunity.

Psychedelic Conference 1983. 6 cass. (AA & A Symposium Ser.). 60.00 set. (A0104-83) Sound Photosyn.
Features Andrew Weil, Carl Ruck, Jonathan Ott, Osmond, Terence McKenna, Alexander Shulgin, Albert Hoffman, Ralph Metzner, & Houston Clark, presenting a wealth of concise & stimulating information.

Psychedelics: Program from the Award Winning Public Radio Series. Interview. Hosted by Fred Goodwin. Comment by John Hockenberry. 1 CD. (Running Time: 1 hr). (Infinite Mind Ser.). 2003. audio compact disk 21.95 (978-1-932479-04-1(X), LCM 259) Lichtenstein Creat.
LSD, psilocybin, mescaline... they're listed as schedule one narcotics, right up there with heroin, amphetamines, and marijuana. But today, 35 years after "turn on, tune in, drop out," we explore what scientists are learning about the potential of psychedelic drugs to treat disorders ranging from obsessive compulsive disorder to addiction. Plus, seeing God... and the DEA: "Psychedelics" features a report on a religious group called the UDV that's suing the federal government for the right to drink huasca, a sacramental tea that contains DMT. Guests include Dr. Mark Geyer, professor of psychiatry at the University of California, San Diego; Dr. Debra Mash, professor of neurology, University of Miami School of Medicine; Dr. Charles Schuster, director of the substance abuse clinical research division at Wayne State School of Medicine in Detroit and former director of the National Institute on Drug Abuse; Jeffrey Bronfman, the North American representative of the UDV (Uniao do Vegetal) church; and Bill Lichtenstein speaks with Nick Bromell, author of "Tomorrow Never Knows: Rock and Psychedelics in the 1960s." The program concludes with commentary from John Hockenberry.

Psychedelics & Paranormal Phenomena. unabr. ed. James Fadiman & Hastings. 1 cass. (Running Time: 90 min.). 1971. 11.00 (03201) Big Sur Tapes.

Psychedelics & the Inner World. unabr. ed. Ralph Metzner. 1 cass. (Running Time: 1 hr. 20 min.). 1968. 11.00 (01603) Big Sur Tapes.
Reviews psychedelic compounds & their effects, explores the relationship between the psychedelic experience & Eastern philosophy & practice, & speaks of the rituals of traditional peoples who carefully design & control psychedelic use.

Psychedelics & Why I Study Them. Alexander Shulgin. 1 cass. (Running Time: 30 Min.). 1999. 11.00 (13703) Big Sur Tapes.
1983 Santa Barbara, CA.

Psychedelics Before & after History. unabr. ed. Terence McKenna. 1 cass. 1987. 10.00 (978-1-56964-007-4(6), A0227-87) Sound Photosyn.
A rousing intro to an ethnobotanical & philosophical approach to life through Terence's eyes.

Psychedelics in the 1990s. 8 cass. (AA & A Symposium Ser.). 75.00 set. (A0600-90) Sound Photosyn.
Complete conference! These videos display the leading spokespersons for a psychedelic perspective in a daylong celebration organized by Alise Agar.

Psychedelics in the 1990s Vol. 1: Plants & Native Cultures. 2 cass. (AA & A Symposium Ser.). 18.00 set. (A0560-90) Sound Photosyn.
A powerful opening expressing the strong cultural & historical roots of the light gathering plants.

Psychedelics in the 1990s Vol. 2: Legal & Practical Challenges to Research. 2 cass. (AA & A Symposium Ser.). 20.00 set. (A0570-90) Sound Photosyn.
In contrast information is generated. Hear Tim Leary remind us of our friends, listen to his subtle & not-so-subtle suggestions, play fully, cheer lead, & evoke true heartfelt expressions of camaraderie within historic relationships.

Psychedelics in the 1990s Vol. 3: MDMA - Facts & Fantasies. 2 cass. (AA & A Symposium Ser.). 18.00 set. (A0560-90) Sound Photosyn.
Dr. McKenna has the definitive word on MDMA ("adam" or "ecstasy") & here is the most scientific talk delivered to the conference.

Psychedelics in the 1990s Vol. 4: Passages from "This Timeless Moment" & Evening Session on Entheogens. 2 cass. (AA & A Symposium Ser.). 20.00 set. (A0573-90) Sound Photosyn.
Laura Huxley & Ram Dass perform a dramatic reading from her book about the last moments with her husband, Aldous. Then the exuberent group, Timothy Leary, Ralph Metzner, Andrew Weil, Terence McKenna, Mark Kleiman, Robert Zanger, Rick Doblin, & Emerson Jackson, regathers to reaffirm the health & good cheer brought forth by the topic.

Psyche's Workshop: An Exploration of the Transcendent Function. Read by Peter Mudd. 8 cass. (Running Time: 7 hrs.). 1990. 48.95 Set. (978-0-7822-0213-7(6), 416S) C G Jung IL.

Psychiatric Nursing, Pt. 1. Patricia Hoefler. (Complete Q & A Ser.). 2002. (978-1-56533-127-3(3)) MEDS Pubng.

Psychiatric Nursing, Pt. 2. Patricia Hoefler. (Complete Q & A Ser.). 2002. (978-1-56533-128-0(1)) MEDS Pubng.

Psychiatric Oppression & Personal Liberation. Peter Breggin. 1 cass. (Running Time: 52 min.). 10.95 (191) J Norton Pubs.

***Psychiatry: The Science of Lies.** unabr. ed. Thomas Szasz. (Running Time: 5 hrs.). 2010. 19.95 (978-1-4417-6365-5(1)); 34.95 (978-1-4417-6362-4(7)); audio compact disk 24.95 (978-1-4417-6364-8(3)); audio compact disk 49.00 (978-1-4417-6363-1(5)) Blckstn Audio.

Psychiatry & the Free Market. Peter Breggin. 1 cass. (Running Time: 43 min.). 10.95 (334) J Norton Pubs.

Psychiatry, CD-ROM 2009 Edition. Rhoda K. Hahn et al. 2008. audio compact disk 28.95 (978-1-934323-11-3(X)) Pub: Current Clin Strat. Dist(s): Baker Taylor

***Psychic.** unabr. ed. Sylvia Browne. Read by Hillary Huber. (ENG.). 2010. (978-0-06-199762-4(5), Harper Audio) HarperCollins Pubs.

***Psychic: My Life in Two Worlds.** unabr. ed. Sylvia Browne. Read by Hillary Huber. (ENG.). 2010. (978-0-06-198873-8(1), Harper Audio) HarperCollins Pubs.

Psychic Abilities: Dreams & Physics. Russell Targ. 1 cass. 9.00 (A0142-86) Sound Photosyn.

Psychic Aspect of Intuition. unabr. ed. Helen Palmer. 1 cass. (Running Time: 58 min.). 1991. 11.00 (08603) Big Sur Tapes.
Explores the systematic development of intuition & its many advantages for vastly improving contact with other people. The development of intuition thus becomes a staging ground for moving into the many other worlds of experience.

Psychic Awareness. Read by Mary Richards. 1 cass. (Running Time: 60 min.). (Series Two Thousand). 2007. audio compact disk 19.95 (978-1-56136-097-0(X)) Master Your Mind.

Psychic Centers - Their Significance & Development. George King. 2007. audio compact disk (978-0-937249-42-0(4)) Aetherius Soc.

Psychic Children: Revealing the Intuitive Gifts & Hidden Abilities of Boys & Girls. abr. ed. Sylvia Browne. Read by Jeanie Hackett. (YA). 2007. 49.99 (978-1-60252-779-9(2)) Find a World.

Psychic Children: Revealing the Intuitive Gifts & Hidden Abilities of Boys & Girls. abr. ed. Sylvia Browne. Read by Jeanie Hackett. (ENG.). 2007. audio compact disk 26.95 (978-1-59887-088-6(2), 1598870882) Pub: HighBridge. Dist(s): Workman Pub

Psychic Detective. unabr. ed. George Khoury. 1 cass. (Running Time: 20 min.). (J). (gr. 4-8). 1983. bk. 16.99 (978-0-934898-51-5(0)); pap. bk. 9.95 (978-0-934898-19-5(7)) Jan Prods.
A teenager, known & respected for her special psychic powers, has been asked to assist the police in tracking down members of a "gang" accused of committing several crimes.

Psychic Development, Vol. 7, set. Jonathan Parker. Read by Jonathan Parker. 2 CDs. (Running Time: 2 hrs.). (Guided Meditation Ser.: Vol. 6). 1999. audio compact disk (978-1-58400-062-4(7)) QuantumQuests Intl.

Psychic Dimensions of Sport. unabr. ed. Michael Murphy et al. 1 cass. (Running Time: 90 min.). 1972. 11.00 (07203) Big Sur Tapes.
Athletics as an educational, mental, & spiritual force with a de-emphasis on traditional concepts of competitiveness is examined by the co-founder of Esalen, an ex-pro football player, & an innovator of body techniques.

Psychic Empowerment. Christopher Love. Read by Christopher Love. 1 cass. (Running Time: 30 min.). 1997. 10.95 World Sangha Pubg.
Self-hypnosis meditation for healing, self-improvement & realizing our full & powerful potential as spiritual beings.

Psychic Factors that Affect Health. Geoffrey Hodson et al. Read by Geoffrey Hodson et al. 2 cass. (Running Time: 2 hrs.). 1988. 14.95 (978-0-8356-2093-2(X)) Pub: Theos Pub Hse. Dist(s): Natl Bk Netwk
Based on esoteric lectures & radio interviews.

Psychic Healing. 1 cass. 10.00 (978-1-58506-045-0(3), 87) New Life Inst OR.
Within your own body is a strength & power capable of helping effect seemingly "miraculous" cures of many problems.

Psychic Healing. 2 CDs. 1982. audio compact disk 27.98 (978-1-56001-963-3(8)) Potentials.
Your thoughts, actions, and beliefs have a profound effect upon people around you who suffer from illness. Become a positive influence for them.This 2-CD program from our Super Consciousness series is our newest, most powerful format. On the self-hypnosis CD, SC programs have the Subliminal Persuasion soundtrack added under Barrie?s voice. And the 17th Century Baroque music on the Subliminal CD has the same beat as your body's natural rhythm, thereby allowing the suggestions to enter deeply and effortlessly.

Psychic Healing. Barrie Konicov. 1 CD. 2004. audio compact disk 19.98 (978-1-56001-681-6(7)) Potentials.
Your thoughts, actions, and beliefs have a profound effect upon people around you who suffer from illness. Become a positive influence for them.You will find the self-hypnosis on track 1 and the subliminal on track 2. The easy-listening music of the subliminal, together with the self-hypnosis, is the original format which most people love and with which they are most familiar.

Psychic Healing. Read by Mary Richards. 1 cass. (Running Time: 60 min.). (Series Two Thousand). 2007. audio compact disk 19.95 (978-1-56136-098-7(8)) Master Your Mind.

Psychic Healing: Using the Tools of a Medium to Cure Whatever Ails You. Sylvia Browne. 2 CDs. 2009. audio compact disk 18.95 (978-1-4019-1089-1(0)) Hay House.

Psychic Opening. unabr. ed. Helen Palmer. 1 cass. (Running Time: 1 hr. 24 min.). 1988. 11.00 (HP001) Big Sur Tapes.
Palmer's early experiences with spontaneous clairvoyance, with accounts of the practices that stabilized her access to that state of mind.

Psychic or Charlatan? How to Interpret a Psychic Reading. abr. ed. Bruce Way. Read by Bruce Way. 2 cass. (Running Time: 2 hrs. 30 min.). 1997. 17.95 (978-1-57453-165-7(4)) Audio Lit.
Show how to tell if you are dealing with a genuine psychic, different methods psychics use & how to prepare before a reading.

Psychic Protection. Ted Andrews. Read by Ted Andrews. 1 cass. (Running Time: 45 min.). 1995. 10.00 (978-1-888767-04-9(9)) Life Magic Ent.
Music & guided meditations to provide two powerful exercises for balance, health & protection. Contains exercises of "The Middle Pillar" & "Banishing Ritual of Pentagram".

Psychic Protection. Barrie Konicov. 2 CDs. 2003. audio compact disk 27.98 (978-1-56001-985-5(9)) Potentials.
When you open your psychic self, you become exposed to certain negative influences. Learn techniques to safe-guard your mind.You will find the self-hypnosis on track 1 and the subliminal on track 2. The easy-listening music of the subliminal, together with the self-hypnosis, is the original format which most people love and with which they are most familiar.

Psychic Protection. Barrie Konicov. 1 CD. 2004. audio compact disk 19.98 (978-1-56001-682-3(5)) Potentials.

Psychic Protection: Be Positive. Barrie Konicov. 1 cass. 11.98 (978-0-87082-406-7(6), 106) Potentials.
Techniques & methods that are necessary to safe guard the integrity of your mind. When you open up physically, you also open the doors to certain negative forces & influences. You must be able to protect yourself against these unwanted intruders.

Psychic Protection from Negativity. Bruce Goldberg. (ENG.). 2005. audio compact disk 17.00 (978-1-57968-043-5(7)) Pub: B Goldberg. Dist(s): Baker Taylor

Psychic Protection from Negativity. Bruce Goldberg. Read by Bruce Goldberg. 1 cass. (Running Time: 25 min.). (ENG.). 2007. 13.00 (978-1-885577-29-0(X)) Pub: B Goldberg. Dist(s): Baker Taylor
Use self-hypnosis as a protection from all kinds of psychic attacks from outside forces.

Psychic Reading Tape. 1 cass. 11.98 (978-0-87554-575-2(0), PR01) Valley Sun.

Psychic Self-Defense. George King. 2006. audio compact disk (978-0-937249-33-8(5)) Aetherius Soc.

Psychic Self-Destruction: Releasing the Mind from Regrets & Self-Censure. Instructed by Manly P. Hall. 8.95 (978-0-89314-224-7(7), C800116) Philos Res.

Psychic Smog: Its Cause & Cure. Manly P. Hall. 8.95 (978-0-89314-225-4(5), C880724) Philos Res.
Beliefs of nature.

Psychic Stress. Manly P. Hall. 1 cass. 8.95 (978-0-89314-226-1(3), C900923) Philos Res.

Psychic Training Program. unabr. ed. A[illegible]mstrong & Jim Armstrong. 2 cass. (Running Time: 2 hrs. 16 min.). 1[illegible]18.00 Set. (00103) Big Sur Tapes.
The Armstrongs present exercises & training to teach us to trust the intuitive input we normally receive & to identify & recognize our own style of receiving it.

Psycho. Robert Block. Narrated by Kevin McCarthy. (Running Time: 2 hrs. 30 mins.). 2006. 14.95 (978-1-59912-987-7(6)) Iofy Corp.

Psycho. unabr. ed. Robert Bloch. Read by Paul Michael Garcia. (Running Time: 5.5 hrs. NaN mins.). 2009. 29.95 (978-1-4332-5709-4(2)); audio compact disk 34.95 (978-1-4332-5705-6(X)); audio compact disk 50.00 (978-1-4332-5706-3(8)) Blckstn Audio.

Psycho-Cybernetics. abr. rev. ed. Maxwell Maltz. Read by Maxwell Maltz. 2 CDs. (Running Time: 2 hrs. 0 mins. 0 sec.). (ENG.). 2001. audio compact disk 20.00 (978-1-55927-665-8(7)) Pub: Macmill Audio. Dist(s): Macmillan

Psycho-Cybernetics. unabr. abr. rev. ed. Maxwell Maltz. Read by Maxwell Maltz. 2 cass. (Running Time: 2 hrs. 0 mins. 0 sec.). (ENG.). 1988. 15.95 (978-0-940687-47-9(X)) Pub: Macmill Audio. Dist(s): Macmillan

Psycho-Cybernetics: How to Use the Power of Self-Image Psychology for Success. 2nd rev. unabr. ed. Maxwell Maltz & Dan S. Kennedy. Read by Paul Michael. (Running Time: 11 hrs. 30 mins. 0 sec.). (ENG.). 2006. audio compact disk 39.95 (978-1-59397-930-0(4)) Pub: Macmill Audio. Dist(s): Macmillan

Psycho-Cybernetics for Winners. 1984. audio compact disk (978-0-89811-289-4(3)) Meyer Res Grp.

Psycho-Cybernetics for Winners. Paul J. Meyer. 1 cass. 11.00 (978-0-89811-250-4(8), 9443) Meyer Res Grp.
Use the powers of your mind to achieve your goals through the technique of Psycho-Cybernetics. Also available in Spanish.

Psycho-Cybernetics for Winners. Paul J. Meyer. 1 cass. 10.00 (SP100059) SMI Intl.
Winning, in all areas of life, is dependent on motivation & mental attitude. By applying the principles of Psycho-Cybernetics, you, too, can improve your life. Regardless of your age & status in life, it's never too late to start getting what you want out of life.

Psycho-Epistemology. Harry Binswanger. 3 cass. (Running Time: 3 hrs.). 1995. 32.95 Set. (978-1-56114-352-8(9), IB01D) Second Renaissance.
A discussion of the role of the subconscious in thinking & on the specific operations by which one "programs" one's subconscious.

Psycho-Epistemology II. unabr. ed. Harry Binswanger. 2 cass. (Running Time: 3 hrs.). 1997. 29.95 Set. (978-1-56114-519-5(X), CB51D) Second Renaissance.
Operating your mental software.

Psycho-Epistemology of the Arab World. Edwin Locke. 1 cass. (Running Time: 90 min.). 1994. 12.95 (978-1-56114-404-4(5), IL08C) Second Renaissance.

Psycho-Geometrics: The Science of Understanding People & the Art of Influencing Them. Susan Dellinger. 2 cass. (Running Time: 120 min.). 1997. 15.95 (978-1-55977-704-9(4)) CareerTrack Pubns.

Psycho-Linguistics: Personal Evolution. Patrick K. Porter. Ed. by Mark Horowitz. 1 cass. 1995. 16.00 (978-0-9637611-2-5(9)) Positive Chngs Hypnosis.
Self-help guided imagery.

Psycho-Linguistics Workshop, Vol. I. Patrick K. Porter. 2 cass. Set. (978-1-887630-09-2(0)) Renaissnce Pub.
Psychology self-help.

Psycho-Oncology: Program from the Award Winning Public Radio Series. Interview. Hosted by Fred Goodwin. Comment by John Hockenberry. 1 CD. (Running Time: 1 hr.). 2000. audio compact disk 21.95 (978-1-932479-84-3(8), LCM 100) Lichtenstein Creat.
"You've got cancer" are some of the most frightening words anyone can hear. In this hour of The Infinite Mind, we'll talk about the psychology of cancer, a relatively new field called psycho-oncology. Drs. Jimmie Holland and David Payne of Memorial Sloan-Kettering Cancer Center will talk about helping people cope with cancer diagnosis and treatment. These pioneers in this field will also discuss whether or not a positive attitude can help a person's prognosis. Plus, a visit to Gilda's Club, poetry from breast cancer survivors, helping kids cope with cancer, and commentary by John Hockenberry.

Psycho-Spiritual Intuition: The Transformative Effect of Inner Knowing. unabr. ed. M. Teri Daunter. Read by M. Teri Daunter. 1 cass. (Running Time: 60 min.). 1996. 10.00 (978-0-9643646-3-9(8)) Mobius Pubng.
On this daring audio session, Dr. Daunter is your instructor in the language of energy & the body's intuitive language system. She teaches you to access "past life" episodes by learning to interpret the energy signals we constantly receive within the body in order to prevent illness from developing in the physical/mental body or assist in the treatment of an illness that has already developed. With many examples of her own relivings, she demonstrates how intuition is trainable & your birthright.

Psychoactive Drugs. 1 cass. (Introduction to Chemical Dependency Ser.). 8.95 (1491G) Hazelden.

Psychoactive Drugs Through Human History. unabr. ed. Andrew Weil. 1 cass. (Running Time: 51 min.). 1983. 11.00 (02601) Big Sur Tapes.
Keynote address at 1983 Santa Barbara conference on "Entheogens: The Spiritual Psychedelics".

Psychoactive Drugs Through Human History. unabr. ed. Andrew Weil. 1 cass. 1983. 9.00 (978-1-56964-820-9(4), A0150-83) Sound Photosyn.
At the 1983 Psychedelic Conference.

Psychoanalysis: Program from the Award Winning Public Radio Series. Interview. Hosted by Fred Goodwin. 1 CD. (Running Time: 1hr). (Infinite Mind Ser.). 2002. audio compact disk 21.95 (978-1-888064-82-7(X), LCM 216) Lichtenstein Creat.
In this hour, we explore Psychoanalysis, including what's new since Freud's day, new theories on the unconscious, and the role of the analyst's couch in movies.Guests include: Dr. Glen Gabbard, Professor of Psychiatry and Director of the Baylor Psychiatry Clinic at the Baylor College of Medicine and author of "Love and Hate in the Analytic Setting" and "Psychiatry and the Cinema;" Dr. Susan Vaughan, author of "The Talking Cure: The Science Behind Psychotherapy;" Dr. Elisabeth Young-Bruehl, a philosopher and psychoanalyst whose books include "Cherishment: A Psychology of the Heart" and "Anna Freud: A Biography." Plus, we'll talk to writer, director and producer David Grubin about his new film "Young Dr. Freud" and to psychoanalyst Dr. Frederick Levenson about the new matchmaking service, Theradate.

Psychoanalytic View of Marriage. Read by Rudolf Ekstein. 1 cass. (Running Time: 55 min.). 10.95 J Norton Pubs.

Psychoimmunity & the Healing Process. Jason Serrinus. 2 cass. 18.00 (OC79) Sound Horizons AV.

Psycholinguistic Aspects of Foreign Accents. Daniel P. Dato. 6 cass. pap. bk. 69.95 Set. (978-1-881336-05-1(0)) Bilingual Cl.
Personalized program for achieving a clear, pleasaant-sounding speech.

Psycholinguistics. 2nd ed. Jean Berko Gleason & Nan Bernstein Ratner. (978-0-15-508296-0(5)) Wadsworth Pub.

Psychological Adaptation Syndromes (P.A.S.) Walter Kempler. Read by Walter Kempler. 1 cass. (Running Time: 1 hr.). 1989. 8.50 Kempler Inst.
Discusses four fundamental possible patterns from which all behavior and diagnosis emerge.

Psychological Allergies. Instructed by Manly P. Hall. 8.95 (978-0-89314-227-8(1), C820425) Philos Res.

Psychological Approach to the Bible, Pt. I. Read by Murray Stein. 7 cass. (Running Time: 7 hrs.). 1988. 44.95 (978-0-7822-0283-0(7), 359S) C G Jung IL.
A study of the Bible for its insight into psychological questions about the ego, self, individuation & the shadow.

Psychological Approach to the Bible, Pt. II. Read by Murray Stein. 7 cass. (Running Time: 7 hrs.). 1989. 44.95 Set. (978-0-7822-0289-2(6), 371S) C G Jung IL.
A study of the Bible for its insight into psychological questions about the role of the anima & animus in individuation, & the problems of narcissism & envy.

Psychological Aspects of Creative Writing. Charles K. Hofling. 1 cass. (Running Time: 43 min.). 1968. 11.95 (23006) J Norton Pubs.
0Discussion of motivations, imaginativeness, role of life frustrations, & relationship of neurosis to creativity.

Psychological Causes of Inefficient Thinking. Barbara Branden. 1 cass. (Running Time: 1 hr. 34 min.). (Principles of Effective Thinking Ser.). 12.50 (710) J Norton Pubs.
The surrender of the will to efficacy; failure of self-esteem; the "malevolent universe" premise; social metaphysics; emotional repression; & the source & conditions of intellectual certainty.

Psychological Contracts. Jerry Johnson. Read by Jerry Johnson. Ed. by Patricia Magerkurth. 1 cass. (Running Time: 24 min.). (Management Ser.). 1992. 10.00 (978-1-56948-012-0(5)) Menninger Clinic.
Early life experiences, family configuration & cultural heritage are several of the basic human components that create our assumptions & expectations. People bring their assumptions & expectations into the workplace & they have a profound impact on their relationships at work. Jerry Johnson, MPA discusses how these factors interact to influence the working environment & how managers can more effectively understand this process.

Psychological Death - Spiritual Rebirth. Claudio Naranjo. 2 cass. 18.00 (OC76) Sound Horizons AV.

Psychological Death & the Emptying of the Mind. J. Krishnamurti. 1 cass. (Running Time: 1 hr.). (Transformation of Man Ser.: No. 5). 8.50 (ATOM 765) Krishnamurti.
This well-liked series between J. Krishnamurti, Professor David Bohm, & psychiatrist, Dr. David Shainberg, explores the conditions of human life & the need to bring about a deep, radical, fundamental change in human consciousness if mankind is to emerge from its misery & conflict.

Psychological Development in Men. 16 cass. (Running Time: 15 hrs.). 1992. 83.95 set. (978-0-7822-0387-5(6), MEN) C G Jung IL.
How men change & develop through their whole life span is the subject of much interest & concern. This intensive course, taught by the faculty of the Jung Institute, examines the major way stations in a man's development & the conflicts that are spawned in his quest for individuation. While these developmental stages give the course a structure, many of the speakers draw upon mythological & archetypal images to help illuminate the many faces of the masculine. Included are lively discussions about gender identity & masculine initiation, two issues particularly relevant to men's experience today. Includes the following tapes: Stein No. 475, Moore No. 476, Wyly No. 477, Dalrymple No. 478, Lavin No. 479, Stein No. 480, Moore No. 481, & Roloff No. 482.

Psychological Development in Men: Fatherhood. Thomas P. Lavin. Read by Thomas P. Lavin. 2 cass. (Running Time: 2 hrs.). 1992. 16.95 set. (978-0-7822-0390-5(6), 479) C G Jung IL.
Part of the set "Psychological Development in Men" (No. MEN).

Psychological Development in Men: Forming the Male Self. Robert Moore. Read by Robert Moore. 2 cass. (Running Time: 2 hrs.). 1992. 16.95 set. (978-0-7822-0384-4(1), 476) C G Jung IL.

Psychological Development in Men: Individuation & the Midlife Crisis. Murray Stein. Read by Murray Stein. 2 cass. (Running Time: 1 hr. 45 min.). 1992. 16.95 set. (978-0-7822-0391-2(4), 480) C G Jung IL.

Psychological Development in Men: Integrity & the Achievement of Wholeness. Robert Moore. Read by Robert Moore. 2 cass. (Running Time: 1 hr. 50 min.). 1992. 16.95 set. (978-0-7822-0389-9(2), 481) C G Jung IL.

Psychological Development in Men: Marriage & the Problem of Intimacy. David Dalrymple. Read by David Dalrymple. 2 cass. (Running Time: 2 hrs.). 1992. 16.95 set. (978-0-7822-0351-6(5), 478) C G Jung IL.

Psychological Development in Men: Seats of Wisdom. Leland Roloff. Read by Leland Roloff. 2 cass. (Running Time: 1 hr. 45 min.). 1992. 16.95 set. (978-0-7822-0392-9(2), 482) C G Jung IL.

Psychological Development in Men: Sons & Mothers. Murray Stein. Read by Murray Stein. 2 cass. (Running Time: 1 hr. 45 min.). 1992. 16.95 set. (978-0-7822-0356-1(6), 475) C G Jung IL.

Psychological Development in Men: The Hero's Quest. James Wyly. Read by James Wyly. 2 cass. (Running Time: 1 hr. 45 min.). 1992. 16.95 set. (978-0-7822-0385-1(X), 477) C G Jung IL.

Psychological Effects of Aging. 1989. 9.95 (978-1-877843-08-2(3)) Elder Care Solutions.
Personality changes. Mental illnesses. Confusion & suspicion. Communicating & dealing with these areas.

Psychological Effects of Religion. Nathaniel Branden. 2 cass. (Running Time: 1 hr. 28 min.). 19.95 (840-841) J Norton Pubs.
The examination of why most people are religious; the Freudian view of equating father with god; & Branden's belief that religious teachings & beliefs are psychologically destructive.

Psychological Effects of Religion (audio CD Set) Nathaniel Branden. (ENG.). 2007. audio compact disk 19.95 (978-1-57970-463-6(8), Audio-For) J Norton Pubs.

Psychological Examination of Novel-Construction. Thomas H. Pear. 1 cass. (Running Time: 27 min.). 1968. 11.95 (23011) J Norton Pubs.
A psychological examination of some of the writings of Dickens, Galsworthy, Scott, Fitzgerald, & others.

Psychological Genius of D. H. Lawrence. Malcolm Brown. 1 cass. 1999. 11.00 (05901) Big Sur Tapes.
1971 Esalen Institute.

Psychological Importance of Classroom Challenge for Gifted Children's Achievement. unabr. ed. Sylvia Rimm. Read by Sylvia Rimm. 1 cass. (Running Time: 42 min.). 1993. 10.95 (978-0-937891-20-9(7), SR32A) Apple Pub Wisc.
Dr. Rimm aids you in realizing the importance of appropriate challenge in the classroom as part of fostering achievement in gifted students.

Psychological Interventions for the Child with Nonverbal Learning Disorders. Kathryn Stewart. 1 cass. (Running Time: 88 min.). 1997. bk. 15.00 (978-1-58111-014-2(6)) Contemporary Medical.
Overview of NLD, including definition, academic, perceptual & social/emotional areas; discussion of treatment; use of cognitive behavioral interventions.

Psychological Interventions for the Child with Nonverbal Learning Disorders. Contrib. by Kathryn Stewart. 1 cass. (Running Time: 1 hrs. 30 min.). 20.00 (19-008A) J W Wood.
Overview of NLD, differentiating &/or overlapping with other diagnoses, discussion of treatment issues & use of cognitive behavioral interventions for impulsivity training, intrusive thoughts & games.

Psychological Knower. Hal Stone & Sidra Stone. 1 cass. (Running Time: 1 hrs.). (Mendocino Ser.: Vol. 15). 1997. 10.95 (978-1-56557-055-9(3), T15) Delos Inc.
An Authority on all psychological & spiritual matters & happy to share this knowledge with everyone. Unhappily, not everyone is interested in listening. Learn how to use its insights & information without driving others away.

Psychological Preparedness & Disaster Stress Reduction: What to do Before, During & after Any Critical Incident to Prevent Post Traumatic Stress Disorders. Speeches. Donald E. Dossey. Prod. by Outcomes Unlimited Press. Created by Donald Dossey. 4 CDs. (Running Time: 3 hrs. 30 mins.). 2006. audio compact disk 45.00 (978-0-925640-10-9(7)) Outcomes Unltd.
Psychological Preparedness & Disaster Stress ReductionWith Dr. Donald DosseyWhat to do Before, During, & After Any Critical IncidentTo Prevent Post Traumatic Stress Disorders Life Stresses and Critical IncidentsCan Cause Permanent Mental, Emotional and Physical Damage!The threat of traumatic events faces us daily.Prepare for possible mental and emotional scars from a future disaster.Remedy the psychological damage that past traumas may have created.Complete check-off list for psychological preparedness. Simple and complete self-tests to identify the signposts of mental, emotional and physical symptoms of Psychological Aftershock (PTSD), phobias and panic attacks. Learn the necessary steps to safeguard you and your family from needless suffering and pain.

Psychological Roots of Illness. Zipporah P. Dobyns. 1 cass. 8.95 (090) Am Fed Astrologers.
An AFA Convention workshop tape.

Psychological Science: Mind, Brain, & Behavior: Norton Media Library. Michael S. Gazzaniga & Todd Heatherton. (YA). 2002. audio compact disk (978-0-393-10457-8(5)) Norton.

Psychological Seduction. unabr. ed. William K. Kilpatrick. Read by Mark Taheny. 5 cass. 22.95 set. (110) Ignatius Pr.
This witty & hard-hitting expose of modern psychology pulls no punches about the damage that can be inflicted on one's faith as a result of "believing" in psychology. The author, a psychologist & a Catholic, reveals these hidden dangers with humor & perspective.

Psychological Slaves to Time. abr. ed. Jiddu Krishnamurti. 1 CD. (Running Time: 1 hr. 16 mins.). (Living Life Without Conflict Ser.). 2008. audio compact disk 16.95 (978-1-888004-60-1(6)) Pub: K Publications GBR. Dist(s): SCB Distributors
Can time ever end? Or, is it something that is a continuous movement? Time by the sun is one thing; time psychologically is another. We are bound to the psychological time. We are slaves to that time and perhaps we are also bound to the sun as yesterday, today, and tomorrow. I think it is very important to understand this question: whether time can ever come to an end?.

Psychological Theory & Practice. Instructed by Manly P. Hall. 5 cass. 8.50 ea. o.p. Pt. 1: Defense Mechansims in Daily Conduct. (800166-A) Philos Res.

Psychological Theory & Practice. Instructed by Manly P. Hall. 5 cass. (Running Time: 150 min.). 1999. 40.00 Set. incl. album. (978-0-89314-228-5(X), S800166) Philos Res.

Psychological Type & Weight Loss. Frank L. Natter. 1 cass. (Running Time: 90 min.). 1989. 10.00 (978-1-878287-74-8(5), ATA-H) Type & Temperament.
Recording of a seminar given recently by Natter. Understanding why we put on those pounds helps empower us to shed them. Helpful hints for waist-watchers.

Psychological Types. Read by John Giannini. 1 cass. (Running Time: 2 hrs.). 1991. 16.95 (978-0-7822-0078-2(8), 440) C G Jung IL.

Psychological Types. Read by Thomas P. Lavin. 2 cass. (Running Time: 2 hrs.). 1986. 16.95 (978-0-7822-0134-5(2), 200) C G Jung IL.

Psychological Types. unabr. ed. Joseph Wheelwright. 1 cass. (Running Time: 90 min.). 1971. 11.00 (08301) Big Sur Tapes.
Concerns the Jungian psychological personality types from which the Gray-Wheelwright test was developed. After fully describing types & combinations, he talks about how anyone may move towards the point of transcending limitations.

Psychological War on Fat. Franklin D. Cordell & Gale R. Giebler. 1 cass. (Running Time: 50 min.). 11.00 (978-0-89811-146-0(3), 7187) Meyer Res Grp.
Lose weight & keep it off by understanding the psychological reasons for being overweight.

Psychological War on Fat. Gale R. Giebler & Franklin D. Cordell. 1 cass. 10.00 (SP100035) SMI Intl.
Lose weight & keep it off by understanding the psychological reasons for being overweight. Modify your behavior & design a new eating pattern to win the battle once & for all.

Psychologically Battered Child: Strategies for Identification, Assessment, & Intervention. James Garbarino et al. (Social & Behavioral Science Ser.). 1986. bk. 40.50 (978-1-55542-002-4(8), Jossey-Bass) Wiley US.

Psychology. Donald Baucum. (Running Time: 30600 sec.). (Barron's EZ-101 Study Keys Ser.). 2005. 54.95 (978-0-7861-3771-8(1)); audio compact disk 63.00 (978-0-7861-7599-4(0)) Blckstn Audio.

Psychology. Nathaniel Branden. 11 cass. (Running Time: 8 hrs.). 90.00 (826-836) J Norton Pubs.

Psychology. Contrib. by Discover America. Prod. by Chris Staples. Contrib. by J R McNeely. 2005. audio compact disk 13.98 (978-5-559-10360-0(8)) Tooth & Nail.

Psychology. Ed. by J. Bruce Overmier & Judith A. Overmier. 2000. cd-rom 190.00 (978-1-84169-210-4(7), Pysch Press) Pub: Tay Francis Ltd GBR. Dist(s): Taylor and Fran

Psychology, Set. unabr. ed. John Dewey. Read by Robert L. Halvorson. 9 cass. (Running Time: 810 min.). 63.95 (12) Halvorson Assocs.

Psychology: An Introduction with Student Practice Test. Benjamin B. Lahey. 1995. stu. ed. (978-0-614-03037-2(4)) Brown & Benchmark.

Psychology: Norton Media Library. 6th ed. Henry Gleitman et al. (YA). 2003. audio compact disk (978-0-393-10607-7(1)) Norton.

Psychology & Astrology. ACT Staff. 1 cass. 8.95 (482) Am Fed Astrologers.
What are similarities?.

Psychology & Esthetic of High-Speed Race Driving. Stirling Moss. 1 cass. (Running Time: 50 min.). 1987. 10.95 (35064) J Norton Pubs.
A discussion of what motivates the men who routinely drive at speeds in excess of 170 MPH. Moss suggests that not only are there significant differences between American & European styles of driving, but also between the types of men who belong to each tradition.

Psychology & New Astrology. Bruno Huber. 1 cass. (Running Time: 60 min.). 1989. 8.95 (166) Am Fed Astrologers.
Transpersonal function of outer planets.

Psychology Applied to Teaching. 5th ed. Robert F. Biehler & Jack Snowman. (C). 1985. 5.00 (978-0-395-40823-0(7)) HM.

Psychology in the Dental Office. Marsha Freeman. 2 cass. (Running Time: 90 min.). 1997. Set. (978-0-910167-42-0(7)) Freemn Assoc.
How psychology - & knowledge of it - plays a key role in providing excellent, safe service.

Psychology of a Course in Miracles. Frances Vaughan. 2 cass. 18.00 (OC80) Sound Horizons AV.

Psychology of Achievement. Brian S. Tracy. 6 cass. 59.95 Set, incl. wkbk. (270-C47) Natl Seminars.
In this program, renowned achievement expert Brian Tracy tells you the specific techniques you need to become more successful than you ever dreamed possible.

Psychology of Achievement. Brian S. Tracy. 6 CDs. (Running Time: 6 hrs.). audio compact disk 69.95 (978-1-55525-083-6(1), 5031CD) Nightingale-Conant.
Grow with this classic program.

Psychology of Achievement. Brian S. Tracy. Read by Brian S. Tracy. 6 cass. (Running Time: 6 hrs.). 59.95 (978-1-55525-082-9(3), 503AD) Nightingale-Conant.
Keys to personal power, influence & self-confidence.

Psychology of Achievement: Develop the Top Achiever's Mindset. abr. ed. Brian S. Tracy & Brian Tracy. Read by Brian S. Tracy & Brian Tracy. 2 CDs. (Running Time: 20 hrs. 0 mins. 0 sec.). (ENG.). 2002. audio compact disk 19.95 (978-0-7435-2658-6(9), Nightgale) Pub: S&S Audio. Dist(s): S and S Inc

Psychology of Adventure. Tristan Jones. 9.00 (OC52) Sound Horizons AV.

Psychology of Altruism: Selfishness as a Virtue. Ayn Rand. 1 cass. (Running Time: 45 min.). 1993. 12.95 (978-1-56114-120-3(8), AR42C) Second Renaissance.

Psychology of Dependence. Nathaniel Branden. 1 cass. (Running Time: 1 hr. 25 min.). (Basic Principles of Objectivism Ser.). 11.95 (568) J Norton Pubs.

Psychology of Freedom. Peter Breggin. 1 cass. (Running Time: 72 min.). 1987. 9.95 (978-0-945999-17-1(8)) Independent Inst.
Explains How to Achieve Greater Freedom & Happiness for Individuals Through Overcoming Psychological Restrictions, Including Reliance on Government.

Psychology of Hate. unabr. ed. Gilbert Highet. Read by Gilbert Highet. 1 cass. (Running Time: 30 min.). 9.95 (23292-A) J Norton Pubs.

Psychology of High Self-Esteem. Nathaniel Branden. Read by Nathaniel Branden. 6 cass. 39.95 Set, incl. interactive wkbk. (185AD) Nightingale-Conant.
How to become the real, worthy you.

Psychology of Hope/Boundaries. Marianne Williamson. Read by Marianne Williamson. 1 cass. (Running Time: 90 mins.). (Lectures on a Course in Miracles). 1999. 10.00 (978-1-56170-257-2(9), M760) Hay House.

Psychology of Human Behavior. Instructed by David W. Martin. 18 cass. (Running Time: 18 hrs.). 79.95 (978-1-59803-178-2(3)) Teaching Co.

Psychology of Human Behavior. Instructed by David W. Martin. 18 CDs. (Running Time: 18 hrs.). 2006. audio compact disk 99.95 (978-1-59803-180-5(5)) Teaching Co.

Psychology of Human Motivation. Denis Waitley. Read by Denis Waitley. 8 cass. 1991. 64.95 set incl. wkbk. (689A) Nightingale-Conant.
Learn the ability to get motivated & stay motivated & develop an internal passion for excellence.

Psychology of Illness. Bernie S. Siegel. 6 cass. 54.00 (OC113) Sound Horizons AV.
Siegel shares some amazingly heart-warming stories about his techniques and experiences treating cancer patients.

Psychology of Illness Meditation. Bernie S. Siegel. 1 cass. 9.00 (OC113M) Sound Horizons AV.

Psychology of Individualism, Set. Interview. Nathaniel Branden. 2 CDs. (Running Time: 87 mins.). 2005. audio compact disk 12.95 (978-1-57970-250-2(3), AF0852D, Audio-For) J Norton Pubs.
Nathaniel Branden, Ph.D., takes us behind the scenes of his book "Honoring the Self," and discusses how his childhood influenced his lifelong interest in the issue of self-esteem, elaborating on many of the themes covered in his book, chapter by chapter: selfishness, individualism, politics, economics, and much more are discussed.

Psychology of Individualism: An Interview. Nathaniel Branden. 1 cass. (Running Time: 87 min.). 12.95 (852) J Norton Pubs.
Branden takes us behind the scenes of Honoring the Self. He talks about how his childhood influenced his lifelong interest in the issue of self-esteem & elaborates on many of the themes covered in his book, chapter by

chapter. Selfishness, individualism, politics, economics & much more are discussed.

Psychology of Money Set: Healing Your Emotional Issues with Money. David Grudermeyer & Rebecca Grudermeyer. 2 cass. 18.95 INCL. HANDOUTS. (T-29) Willingness Wrks.

Psychology of Negotiating. Neil Rackham. Intro. by A. E. Whyte. 1 cass. (Running Time: 45 min.). (Listen & Learn USA! Ser.). 8.95 (978-0-88684-024-2(4)) Listen USA.
Shows how understanding your opponent can put you in the superior negotiating position.

Psychology of Persuasion: How to Persuade Others to Your Way of Thinking. Kevin Hogan & Zig Ziglar. Narrated by Kevin Hogan & Zig Ziglar. (Running Time: 345 hrs. NaN mins.). (ENG.). 2009. audio compact disk 19.95 (978-1-58980-726-6(X)) Pelican.

Psychology of Persuasion Set: How to Persuade Others to Your Way of Thinking. unabr. ed. Narrated by Kevin Hogan. 2 cass. (Running Time: 120 min.). (ENG.). 1999. 18.00 (978-1-56554-431-4(5)) Pelican.

Psychology of Psychic Experiences & the Integration of Them Into Everyday Life. Charles Tart. 1 cass. 9.00 (A0143-86) Sound Photosyn.

Psychology of Religious Awareness. unabr. ed. Abraham H. Maslow. 1 cass. (Running Time: 1 hr.). 1967. 11.00 (01402) Big Sur Tapes.

Psychology of Romantic Love. Nathaniel Branden. 16 cass. (Running Time: 19 hrs.). 144.00 (601-616) J Norton Pubs.

Psychology of Romantic Love CD Set. Nathaniel Branden. 18 CDs. (Running Time: 19 hrs.). 2005. audio compact disk 144.00 (978-1-57970-252-6(X), AFNB03D, Audio-For) J Norton Pubs.
In this 16-lecture course, Nathaniel Branden, Ph.D., has chosen to deal with one of the most crucially important aspects of human life. What is romantic love? Why is it so difficult to achieve and sustain? What are the common errors men and women make by which they deny themselves the possibility of romantic fulfillment? These lectures provide invaluable information on how to improve the quality of a successful relationship, how to understand and appreciate the meaning and value of romantic love, and the conditions necessary for its continual growth.

Psychology of Sales Success. unabr. ed. 3 cass. (Running Time: 5 hrs.). 2001. 49.00 Personal Selling.
A tested program that can help with the most important and most difficult psychological challenges you encounter in selling. Program covers everything from building a positive attitude to dealing with lies and deception, managing adversity, disappointment, and much more.

Psychology of Satan: Encountering the Dark Side of the Self. Read by Robert Moore. 8 cass. (Running Time: 7 hrs.). 1989. 48.95 Set. (978-0-7822-0187-1(3), 379S) C G Jung IL.
An examination of the archetypal shadow - that part of the shadow which cannot be integrated into the individuating ego - providing insight into the nature & dynamics of human destructiveness & evil on a personal as well as a social level.

Psychology of Self-Esteem. Julie White. 6 cass. 89.95 set. (C10113) CareerTrack Pubns.
Dr. Julie White has surveyed the latest psychological research about self-esteem. In this audio, she goes beyond "feel-good" remedies. She reveals the truths behind why self-esteem is such a fragile & changing state of mind.

Psychology of Selling: The Art of Closing Sales. abr. ed. Brian S. Tracy. 2 CDs. (Running Time: 20 hrs. 0 mins. 0 sec.). (ENG., 2002. audio compact disk 19.95 (978-0-7435-2069-0(6), Nightgale) Pub: S&S Audio. Dist(s): S and S Inc

Psychology of Selling: The Art of Closing Sales. unabr. ed. Brian S. Tracy. 6 cass. (Running Time: 6 hrs.). 1992. audio compact disk 79.65 (978-1-55525-018-8(1), 1651cd) Nightingale-Conant.
Is it possible to triple your income within twelve months? Absolutely with this program!.

Psychology of Selling: The Art of Closing Sales. unabr. ed. Brian S. Tracy. Read by Brian S. Tracy. 6 cass. (Running Time: 6 hrs.). 1992. 69.95 (978-1-55525-017-1(3), 1651A) Nightingale-Conant.
Is it possible to triple you income within twelve months? Absolutely with this program.

Psychology of Selling Set: How to Read Your Customer. 6 cass. pap. bk. 155.00 Incl. 2 multiple choice tests. (978-0-7612-0905-8(0), 80154); pap. bk. & wbk. ed. 30.00 (978-0-7612-0906-5(9), 80155) AMACOM.
You'll learn how to: Understand the number one factor that determines what customers buy & who they buy it from - fulfilling a personal or professional need; Deal effectively with buyer doubt & complacency; Recognize the five types of questions buyers use to signal they're ready to make a deal.

Psychology of Separation & Loss: Perspectives on Development, Life Transitions, & Clinical Practice. Jonathan Bloom-Feshbach et al. (Social & Behavioral Science Ser.). 1987. bk. 65.00 (978-1-55542-040-6(0), Jossey-Bass) Wiley US.

Psychology of Sex. Nathaniel Branden. 1 cass. (Running Time: 74 min.). 11.95 (576) J Norton Pubs.
A person's sexual choices as the expression of his deepest values - Sex & self-esteem.

Psychology of Success. Lawrence T. Markson. 1 cass. (Running Time: 41 min.). 1986. 11.00 (978-0-89811-264-1(8), SP100069) Meyer Res Grp.
Success can be yours! More success than you have ever experienced...more than you ever dreamed! It's just a matter of adopting the attitudes of success & then pushing forward the goals that are important to you. Step by step to help you take charge of your life, set challenging goals, & become the achiever you were meant to be.

Psychology of Success: Ten Proven Principles for Winning. Brian S. Tracy. Read by Brian S. Tracy. 6 cass. 49.95 Set. (191AD) Nightingale-Conant.
The practical approach to winning big.

Psychology of the Divine: Numinosity, Archetype & Symbol. Murray Stein. Read by Murray Stein. 3 cass. (Running Time: 3 hrs. 45 min.). 1991. 24.95 set. (978-0-7822-0352-3(3), 449) C G Jung IL.

Psychology of the Orphan Archetype. Read by Lucille Klein. 3 cass. (Running Time: 3 hrs. 30 min.). 1990. 22.95 Set. (978-0-7822-0130-7(X), 419) C G Jung IL.

Psychology of the Ruling Class. Karl Hess. 1 cass. (Running Time: 54 min.). 10.95 (422) J Norton Pubs.
Hess makes a perceptive analysis of power & those who wield it. He discusses the psychological traits which distinguish the "power elite" from the rest of us & provides some startling new evidence to support the old dictum that "power corrupts absolutely".

Psychology of the Transference & Countertransference. Read by Lionel Corbett. 2 cass. (Running Time: 4 hrs.). 1987. 21.95 Set. (978-0-7822-0040-9(0), 270) C G Jung IL.

Psychology of the Wild by Dancing Beetle. Eugene Ely et al. 1 cass. (Running Time: 83 min.). (J). 1994. 10.00 Erthviibz.
Mother nature's creatures have stress release principals that can be rediscovered & utilized in our unbalanced world. Infotainment by Ms. Coyote & Dancing Beetle.

Psychology of Tournament Golf. David L. Cook. (ENG.). 2003. audio compact disk 34.95 (978-0-9742650-0-1(4)) Sacred Story.

Psychology of Weight Loss. Carol Landesman et al. (Running Time: 1 hr. 30 min.). 1985. 11.95 (978-0-944831-09-0(5)) Health Life.

Psychology of Winning. Denis Waitley. 6 cass. 59.95 Set, incl. wkbk. (259SP) Natl Seminars.
Build your self-esteem, your motivation & your self-discipline while you develop the 10 qualities of a total winner.

Psychology of Winning: Learn the 10 Qualities of Winners. unabr. ed. Denis Waitley. 6 cass. (Running Time: 6 hrs.). 1992. pupil's gde. ed. 69.95 (978-1-55525-023-2(8), 7161cd) Nightingale-Conant.
Build self-esteem, motivation, and self discipline while developing the 10 qualities of a total winner?.

Psychology of Winning: Learn the 10 Qualities of Winners. unabr. ed. Denis Waitley. Read by Denis Waitley. 6 cass. (Running Time: 6 hrs.). 1992. pupil's gde. ed. 59.95 (978-1-55525-002-7(5), 7161A) Nightingale-Conant.

Psychology of Winning: Ten Qualities of a Total Winner. abr. ed. Denis Waitley. Read by Denis Waitley. 2 CDs. (Running Time: 20 hrs. 0 mins. 0 sec.). (ENG.). 2005. audio compact disk 19.95 (978-0-7435-4473-3(0), Nightgale) Pub: S&S Audio. Dist(s): S and S Inc

Psychology of Winning (Hypnosis), Vol. 16. Jayne Helle. 1 cass. (Running Time: 28 min.). 1997. 15.00 (978-1-891826-15-3(8)) Introspect.
Being a winner is an attitude & belief system from within. Overcome sabotaging habits & become the winner you are.

Psychology of Winnng for the 21st Century. unabr. ed. Denis Waitley. 2 cass. (Running Time: 3 hrs.). (YA). 2001. 17.95 (978-0-929071-74-9(3)) B-B Audio.
Time is the only resource or gift distributed equally to everyone while they are alive. How you spend your time is far more important than all the material possessions you may own. Dr. Waitley explains how the new millennium gives us new opportunities to.

Psychology, Spirituality & True Happiness. Cardwell C. Nuckols. Perf. by Cardwell C. Nuckols. Ed. by Charles Hodge. Executive Producer Dennis S. Miller. Dennis S. Miller. Engineer Charles Hodge. (ENG.). 2009. audio compact disk 55.00 (978-1-55982-020-2(9)) Grt Lks Training.

Psychomentry - the Art of Divination Through Objects. George King. 2007. audio compact disk (978-0-937249-43-7(2)) Aetherius Soc.

Psychometry - the Art of Divination Through Objects. George King. 2007. audio compact disk (978-0-937249-47-5(5)) Aetherius Soc.

Psychoneuroimmunlogy: The Geometry of Being - Geometry in Motion. Eldon Taylor. Directed By Eldon Taylor. 1 cass. (Running Time: 30 min.). (Sacred Geometry Ser.). 1997. cass. & video 39.95 (978-1-55978-670-6(1), V108) Progress Aware Res.
Geometry in motion developing from fractals, forming mandalas, absolutely mesmerizing with tones & frequencies.

Psychopathology & the Boy Lover. Read by Robert Moore. 2 cass. (Running Time: 2 hrs.). 1990. 14.00 Set. (978-0-7822-0202-1(0), 403-3) C G Jung IL.

Psychopath's Lullaby. Music by Craig Steven Quiter. Concept by Christopher S. Hyatt. 2008. audio compact disk 14.95 (978-1-935150-03-9(0)) Orig Falcon.

Psychoses. Robert Stone. 1 cass. 1983. 10.00 (978-0-938137-09-2(3)) Listen & Learn.
Symptoms; Hallucinations, Delusions, Psychomotor & Thought Disturbances; Classifications: Paranoid, Catatonic, Residual, Hebephrenic, Schizo-affective, Latent, Simple, Chronic & Acute Undifferentiated, Childhood.

Psychosis: Program from the Award Winning Public Radio Series. Interview. Hosted by Fred Goodwin. 1 CD. (Running Time: 1 hr.). 2000. audio compact disk 21.95 (978-1-932479-85-0(6), LCM 103) Lichtenstein Creat.
It's the frightening state of mind that most of us equate with "madness": delusions, paranoia, hearing voices. In truth, as many as 120 different conditions can cause psychosis, including drug and alcohol abuse, metabolic disorders, thyroid malfunction, head injuries, Alzheimer's and reactions to prescription medication. In this hour, we'll hear from an actively psychotic person, from successful individuals who've experienced psychosis and recovered, and from experts. Later in the program, we change directions to hear about new developments in neuroscience. Guests include: singer/songwriter Dory Previn, political consultant and former New York Times reporter Bob Boorstin, psychiatrist Dr. Murray Claytor; graduate student Leslie Greenblat, Dr. Wayne Fenton of the National Institute of Mental Health and Nature Neuroscience editor Dr. Charles Jennings.

Psychosis: Treating Beyond Positive Symptoms, Vol. 4. Interview. Featuring Daniel Weinberger. Interview with Stephen M. Stahl. 1 CD. 2004. audio compact disk (978-1-4225-0015-6(2)) NEI Pr.

Psychosis of Wealth Is Self-Destruct. Instructed by Manly P. Hall. 8.95 (978-0-89314-229-2(8), C860615) Philos Res.

Psychosocial Support & Community Networking. Rosemary Moynihan. (AIDS: The National Conference for Practitioners). 1986. 9.00 (978-0-932491-56-5(1)) Res Appl Inc.

Psychosomatic Wellness: Guided Meditations, Affirmations & Music to Heal Your Bodymind. Candace Pert. (Running Time: 3540 sec.). 2008. audio compact disk 17.95 (978-1-59179-793-7(4)) Sounds True.

Psychosurgery, Psychiatry & Nazism. Peter Breggin. 1 cass. (Running Time: 1 hr. 26 min.). 11.95 (199) J Norton Pubs.
In this speech on the political implications of psychosurgery, Breggin analyzes psychiatric oppression in Nazi Germany & reveals how some of the same techniques & attitudes are being fostered today in America.

Psychotheological Dynamics of Religious Experience. Carole Riley. 3 cass. (Running Time: 3 hrs.). 1993. 26.95 Set. (TAH294) Alba Hse Comns.
This program discusses: corporeal, imaginative & intellectual visions; interior touches; tears; spiritual feelings; raptures; revelations; flame of love; levitation; sweet orors; ecstasy; ligature; etc. Excellent for Directors & those wishing to ground their prayer life on a sound psychological foundation.

Psychotherapeutic Humor: Applications in Practice. Waleed A. Salameh. (Running Time: 40 min.). 1987. 13.95 (978-0-943158-36-5(2), HUM-TBP, Prof Resc Pr) Pro Resource.
Provides an overview of psychtherapeutic humor & offers numerous examples of practice applications.

Psychotherapy. Comment by Margo Adler. 1 cass. (Running Time: 30 min.). 9.95 (I0280B090, HarperThor) HarpC GBR.

Psychotherapy. Nathaniel Branden. 4 cass. (Running Time: 2 hr. 58 min.). 39.00 (816-819) J Norton Pubs.
Psychotherapy is both an intellectual & emotional process of treatment, with not one system or approach right for every person, no one ideal therapist for a given individual. An evaluation of self-esteem, & breaking free of repressed pains & memories.

Psychotherapy: Purpose, Process & Practice. Kenneth Wapnick. 8CDs. 2004. audio compact disk 53.00 (978-1-59142-129-0(2), CD93) Foun Miracles.
The pamphlet, "Psychotherapy: Purpose, Process and Practice," was the subject of this 2003 line-by-line commentary.

Psychotherapy & Healing. Kenneth Wapnick. 6 CDs. 2006. audio compact disk 37.00 (978-1-59142-230-3(2), CD120) Foun Miracles.

Psychotherapy & Healing. Kenneth Wapnick. 2009. 30.00 (978-1-59142-455-0(0)) Foun Miracles.

Psychotherapy & Objectivist Ethics. Nathaniel Branden. 1 cass. (Running Time: 48 min.). 10.95 (551) J Norton Pubs.
Dr. Branden demonstrates why effective psychotherapy requires a rational, conscious code of ethics & explores the nature of such an ethical system.

Psychotropic Music. Acoustic Research Staff & Boris Mourashkin. 2 cass. (Running Time: 2 hrs.). 1995. 16.95 (978-1-55961-292-0(4)); audio compact disk 19.95 (978-1-55961-291-3(6)) Relaxtn Co.

PT 109: JFK in WWII. unabr. ed. Robert Donovan. Narrated by Matthew Modine. 7 cass. (Running Time: 10 hrs.). 2002. 35.95 (2C328) Recorded Bks.
Vividly recreates the events of August 2, 1943, when a japanese destroyer sliced an American PT boat in two. In the wake of this disaster, John F. Kennedy, the boat's skipper, risked his life again and again to bring his crew to safety.

***Pteranodon Soars.** Dawn Bentley. Illus. by Karen Carr. (Smithsonian Prehistoric Pals Ser.). (ENG.). (J). 2009. bk. 19.95 (978-1-59249-542-9(7)) Soundprints.

Pterodactyl Rose: Poems of Ecology. William Heyen. 1991. 12.95 (978-1-877770-27-2(2)) Time Being Bks.

Ptolemy's Gate. unabr. ed. Jonathan Stroud. Read by Simon Jones. 10 cass. (Running Time: 15 hrs. 32 mins.). (Bartimaeus Trilogy: Bk. 3). (J). (gr. 4-7). 2006. 65.00 (978-0-307-28571-3(5), Listening Lib) Pub: Random Audio Pubg. Dist(s): Random

Ptolemy's Gate. unabr. ed. Jonathan Stroud. Read by Simon Jones. 13 CDs. (Running Time: 15 hrs. 32 mins.). (Bartimaeus Trilogy: Bk. 3). (J). (gr. 4-7). 2007. audio compact disk 72.25 (978-0-307-28572-0(3), Listening Lib) Pub: Random Audio Pubg. Dist(s): NetLibrary CO
Three years have passed since the magician Nathaniel helped prevent a cataclysmic attack on London. Now an important member of the British government, he grapples with numerous problems: foreign wars are going badly, Britain's enemies are mounting attacks close to London, and rebellion is growing among the commoners. Increasingly imperious and distracted, Nathaniel is treating Bartimaeus worse than ever. The long-suffering djinni is growing weak and vulnerable from too much time in this world, and his patience is nearing its end. Meanwhile, undercover in London, Nathaniel's longtime rival Kitty has been stealthily completing her research on magic, demons, and Bartimaeus's past. She has a daring plan that she hopes will break the endless cycle of conflict between djinn and humans. But will anyone listen to what she has to say? In this glorious conclusion to the Bartimaeus Trilogy, the destinies of Bartimaeus, Nathaniel, and Kitty converge once more. For the first time, we will learn the secrets of Bartimaeus's past, and catch a glimpse into the mysterious Other Place "the world of demons" as together, the threesome faces treacherous magicians, a complex conspiracy, and a rebellious faction of demons. To survive, they must test the limits of this world and question the deepest parts of themselves. And most difficult of all - they will have to learn to trust one another.

Ptolemy's Gate. unabr. ed. Jonathan Stroud. Read by Simon Jones. 14 CDs. (Running Time: 55800 sec.). (Bartimaeus Trilogy: Bk. 3). (ENG.). (J). (gr. 7-12). 2005. audio compact disk 57.00 (978-0-8072-1981-2(9), Listening Lib) Pub: Random Audio Pubg. Dist(s): Random

***PTP 2010 Deacons Set.** Arranged by Polishing the Pulpit. 2010. audio compact disk 25.00 (978-1-60644-097-1(7)) Heart Heart.

***PTP 2010 Elders Volume 1.** Arranged by Polishing the Pulpit. 2010. audio compact disk 25.00 (978-1-60644-086-5(1)) Heart Heart.

***PTP 2010 Elders Volume 2.** Arranged by Polishing the Pulpit. 2010. audio compact disk 25.00 (978-1-60644-087-2(X)) Heart Heart.

***PTP 2010 Elders Volume 3.** Arranged by Polishing the Pulpit. 2010. audio compact disk 25.00 (978-1-60644-088-9(8)) Heart Heart.

***PTP 2010 Members Volume 1.** Arranged by Polishing the Pulpit. 2010. audio compact disk 25.00 (978-1-60644-095-7(0)) Heart Heart.

***PTP 2010 Members Volume 2.** Arranged by Polishing the Pulpit. 2010. audio compact disk 25.00 (978-1-60644-096-4(9)) Heart Heart.

***PTP 2010 Preachers Volume 1.** Arranged by Polishing the Pulpit. 2010. 25.00 (978-1-60644-076-6(4)) Heart Heart.

***PTP 2010 Preachers Volume 10.** Arranged by Polishing the Pulpit. 2010. 25.00 (978-1-60644-085-8(3)) Heart Heart.

***PTP 2010 Preachers Volume 2.** Arranged by Polishing the Pulpit. 2010. audio compact disk 25.00 (978-1-60644-077-3(2)) Heart Heart.

***PTP 2010 Preachers Volume 3.** Arranged by Polishing the Pulpit. 2010. audio compact disk 25.00 (978-1-60644-078-0(0)) Heart Heart.

***PTP 2010 Preachers Volume 4.** Arranged by Polishing the Pulpit. 2010. audio compact disk 25.00 (978-1-60644-079-7(9)) Heart Heart.

***PTP 2010 Preachers Volume 5.** Arranged by Polishing the Pulpit. 2010. 25.00 (978-1-60644-080-3(2)) Heart Heart.

***PTP 2010 Preachers Volume 6.** Arranged by Polishing the Pulpit. 2010. audio compact disk 25.00 (978-1-60644-081-0(0)) Heart Heart.

***PTP 2010 Preachers Volume 7.** Arranged by Polishing the Pulpit. 2010. audio compact disk 25.00 (978-1-60644-082-7(9)) Heart Heart.

***PTP 2010 Preachers Volume 8.** Arranged by Polishing the Pulpit. 2010. audio compact disk 25.00 (978-1-60644-083-4(7)) Heart Heart.

***PTP 2010 Preachers Volume 9.** Arranged by Polishing the Pulpit. 2010. 25.00 (978-1-60644-084-1(5)) Heart Heart.

***PTP 2010 Sermon Swap.** Arranged by Polishing the Pulpit. (YA). 2010. audio compact disk 15.00 (978-1-60644-102-2(7)) Heart Heart.

***PTP 2010 Spanish Set.** Arranged by Polishing the Pulpit. 2010. audio compact disk 25.00 (978-1-60644-100-8(0)) Heart Heart.

***PTP 2010 Teen MP3 CD.** Arranged by Polishing the Pulpit. 2010. audio compact disk 15.00 (978-1-60644-101-5(9)) Heart Heart.

***PTP 2010 Women Volume 1.** Arranged by Polishing the Pulpit. 2010. audio compact disk 25.00 (978-1-60644-089-6(6)) Heart Heart.

***PTP 2010 Women Volume 2.** Arranged by Polishing the Pulpit. 2010. 25.00 (978-1-60644-090-2(X)) Heart Heart.

***PTP 2010 Women Volume 3.** Arranged by Polishing the Pulpit. 2010. 25.00 (978-1-60644-091-9(8)) Heart Heart.

***PTP 2010 Women Volume 4.** Arranged by Polishing the Pulpit. 2010. audio compact disk 25.00 (978-1-60644-092-6(6)) Heart Heart.

***PTP 2010 Women Volume 5.** Arranged by Polishing the Pulpit. 2010. audio compact disk 25.00 (978-1-60644-093-3(4)) Heart Heart.

***PTP 2010 Women Volume 6.** Arranged by Polishing the Pulpit. 2010. audio compact disk 25.00 (978-1-60644-094-0(2)) Heart Heart.

***PTP 2010 Youth Workers Volume 1.** Arranged by Polishing the Pulpit. 2010. audio compact disk 25.00 (978-1-60644-098-8(5)) Heart Heart.

***PTP 2010 Youth Workers Volume 2.** Arranged by Polishing the Pulpit. 2010. audio compact disk 25.00 (978-1-60644-099-5(3)) Heart Heart.

Pt1 Anna Karenina. Leo Tolstoy. Read by Nadia May. 15 CDs. (Running Time: 25 hrs.). 2005. audio compact disk 120.00 (978-0-7861-8391-3(8), 1397A,B) Blckstn Audio.

Pt2 Anna Karenina. Leo Tolstoy. Read by Nadia May. 15 CDs. (Running Time: 25 hrs.). 2005. audio compact disk 96.00 (978-0-7861-8390-6(X), 1397A,B) Blckstn Audio.

Pt2 Don Quixote de la Mancha. Miguel de Cervantes Saavedra. Read by Robert Whitfield. 15 CDs. (Running Time: 19 hrs.). 2005. audio compact disk 120.00 (978-0-7861-8178-0(8)) Blckstn Audio.

Puberty Blues. unabr. ed. Gabrielle Carey & Kathy Lette. Read by Rebecca Macauley. 3 CDs. (Running Time: 3 hrs.). 2009. audio compact disk 54.95 (978-1-74093-650-7(7)) Pub: Bolinda Pubng AUS. Dist(s): Bolinda Pub Inc

Public Affairs Primer for Nonprofits & Associations: Capitol Learning Audio Course. Paul Powell. Prod. by TheCapitol.Net. (ENG.). 2007. 47.00 (978-1-58733-058-2(X)) TheCapitol.

Public Confessions of a Middle-Aged Woman Aged 55 3/4. unabr. ed. Sue Townsend. Narrated by Carolyn Oldershaw. 6 cass. (Running Time: 8 hrs.). 2002. 56.00 (978-1-84197-423-1(4)) Recorded Bks.
For over ten years, Sue Townsend has written a monthly column for Sainsbury's Magazine, which covers everything from hosepipe bans and Spanish restaurants to writer's block. Collected now for the first time, they form a set of funny, perceptive and touching pieces from one of Britain's most popular and acclaimed writers.

Public Education see Great American Speeches: 1898-1918

Public Election Laws. 1986. bk. 55.00; 35.00 PA Bar Inst.

Public Enemies. abr. ed. Bryan Burrough. Read by Campbell Scott. 2004. 15.95 (978-0-7435-3991-3(5)) Pub: S&S Audio. Dist(s): S and S Inc

***Public Enemies.** unabr. ed. Bryan Burrough. Narrated by Richard M. Davidson. 1 Playaway. (Running Time: 26 hrs. 45 mins.). 2009. 69.75 (978-1-4407-0804-6(5)); audio compact disk 123.75 (978-1-4025-9375-8(9)) Recorded Bks.

Public Enemies. unabr. ed. Bryan Burrough. Narrated by Richard M. Davidson. 18 cass. (Running Time: 26 hrs. 45 mins.). 2004. 99.75 (978-1-4025-9373-4(2), 97766MC, Griot Aud) Recorded Bks.

***Public Enemies.** unabr. collector's ed. Bryan Burrough. Narrated by Richard M. Davidson. 22 CDs. (Running Time: 26 hrs. 45 mins.). 2009. audio compact disk 87.95 (978-1-4025-9376-5(7)) Recorded Bks.

Public Enemies: America's Greatest Crime Wave & the Birth of the FBI 1933-1934. abr. movie tie-in ed. Bryan Burrough. Bryan Burrough. Read by Campbell Scott. 5 CDs. (Running Time: 60 hrs. 0 mins. 0 sec.). (ENG.). 2009. audio compact disk 14.99 (978-0-7435-8292-6(6)) Pub: S&S Audio. Dist(s): S and S Inc

Public Enemies: America's Greatest Crime Wave & the Birth of the FBI, 1933-34. abr. ed. Bryan Burrough. 2004. 26.00 (978-0-7435-3807-7(2), Audioworks) Pub: S&S Audio. Dist(s): S and S Inc

Public Enemy, Vol. 1. Ben Young. 2000. 4.95 (978-0-7417-6176-7(9), B0176) Win Walk.

Public Enemy #2. Ben Young. 2000. 4.95 (978-0-7417-6177-4(7), B0177) Win Walk.

Public Enemy #3. Ben Young. 2000. 4.95 (978-0-7417-6178-1(5), B178) Win Walk.

Public Enemy #4. Ben Young. 2000. 4.95 (978-0-7417-6179-8(3), B0179) Win Walk.

Public Fire Education Planning: Instructor Package. pap. bk. & tchr. ed. 235.00 (AVA09905SS00AIF) Natl Tech Info.

Public Like a Frog: Entering the Lives of Three Great Americans. Jean Houston. Read by Jean Houston. 2 cass. (Running Time: 3 hrs.). 1995. 16.00 (978-0-8356-2102-1(2), 2102, Quest) Pub: Theos Pub Hse. Dist(s): Natl Bk Netwk
Self-transformational exercises that dramatize the creative breakthroughs of Emily Dickinson, Thomas Jefferson, & Helen Keller.

Public Relations: Do It Yourself. 6 cass. 59.50 (978-0-88432-433-1(8), S01675) J Norton Pubs.
Learn how to obtain free publicity for those important events or accomplishments that will advance your business, your career, or an organization you care about.

Public Relations for the Local Church: A Practical Guide for Ministry Leaders. Joel B. Curry. Ed. by Cindy G. Spear. 3 cass. (C). 1991. stu. ed. & rng bd. 89.95 Set, incl. resource pkt. (978-0-941005-36-4(4)) Chrch Grwth VA.
Helps any pastor have more productive relationships with local news media & show how to develop & take advantage of opportunities for positive publicity for the local church. And many times, at no cost to the church!.

Public Relations in Support of Development. Julian Padowicz. Read by Julian Padowicz. 1 cass. (Running Time: 1 hr. 11 min.). 1989. 14.95 (978-1-881288-05-3(6), BFI AudioBooks) BusnFilm Intl.
A guide to building a climate conducive to fundraising, both inside & outside a non-profit agency - excellent guide to public relations skills & techniques.

Public School. 1 cass. (Urban Problems Ser.). 10.00 (UP702) Esstee Audios.
Mary Antin takes a look at what the public school did for the immigrant.

Public Speaking. Douglas M. Fraleigh. 1 cass. 10.00 (978-1-58506-037-5(2), 69) New Life Inst OR.
You can learn to relax & overcome stage fright. Gain a new self-confidence in speaking before any group.

Public Speaking. Speeches. Edward Strachar. 1 cass. (Running Time: 60 mins.). 2002. 14.95 (978-0-9719358-8-4(2)) InGenius Inc.

Public Speaking Made Easy. Created by Anne H. Spencer-Beacham. 1. 2003. audio compact disk (978-1-932163-66-7(2)) Infinity Inst.

***Public Speaking Superstar: Overcome Stage Fright, Develop Compelling Stories & Riveting Presentations.** unabr. ed. Made For Success. (Running Time: 9 hrs.). (Made for Success Ser.). 2010. audio compact disk 29.95 (978-1-4417-5282-6(X)) Blckstn Audio.

***Public Speaking Superstar (Library Edition) Overcome Stage Fright, Develop Compelling Stories & Riveting Presentations.** unabr. ed. Made for Success. (Running Time: 9 hrs. 0 mins.). (Made for Success Ser.). 2010. lib. bdg. 118.00 (978-1-4417-5280-2(3)) Blckstn Audio.

Publicizing Your Book. SERCON Panel. 1 cass. 9.00 (A0128-87) Sound Photosyn.
A presentation by Bridge Publications at the SF writers convention.

Publish & Be Murdered. Ruth Dudley Edwards. Read by Bill Wallis. 6 CDs. (Running Time: 9 hrs.). 2001. audio compact disk 64.95 (978-0-7540-5431-3(4), CCD 122) Pub: Chivers Audio Bks GBR. Dist(s): AudioGO
Amiss is not entirely happy with his job - managing a right-wing, 22-year-old English magazine. When the drunken deputy editor is found drowned in a punch bowl, suspicions of foul play are brushed aside. After another death, they begin to wonder.

Publish & Be Murdered. unabr. ed. Ruth Dudley Edwards. Read by Bill Wallis. 6 cass. (Running Time: 9 hrs.). 2000. 49.95 (CAB 1661) Pub: Chivers Audio Bks GBR. Dist(s): AudioGO
Amiss is unhappy with his job managing a right-wing, 200-year-old English magazine; for the atmosphere is poisoned with egocentricity. And when the deputy editor is found drowned in a bowl of punch, suspicions of foul play are brushed aside by the police. But after another death, it appears that something wicked is at play among the magazine staff.

Publish & Be Murdered. unabr. ed. Ruth Dudley Edwards. Read by Bill Wallis. 6 cass. (Running Time: 6 hrs.). 1999. 54.95 (978-0-7540-0238-3(1), CAB1661) Pub: Chivers Audio Bks GBR. Dist(s): AudioGO
Something wicked is at play among the staff of a right-wing 200-year-old English magazine.

***Publisher: Henry Luce & His American Century.** unabr. ed. Alan Brinkley. Narrated by Sean Runnette. (Running Time: 21 hrs. 30 mins.). 2010. 24.99 (978-1-4001-8759-1(1)); 34.99 (978-1-4001-6759-3(0)); 49.99 (978-1-4001-9759-0(7)); audio compact disk 49.99 (978-1-4001-1759-8(3)); audio compact disk 119.99 (978-1-4001-4759-5(X)) Pub: Tantor Media. Dist(s): IngramPubServ

Publishing & Communications. Incl. Publishing & Communications: Bob: Radio TV Talk Show Moderator; Publishing & Communications: JoAnn: Corporate Communications - Industrial T.V.; Publishing & Communications: Mary: Corporate Business Editor; Publishing & Communications: Milt: Managing Editor - Magazines; Publishing & Communications: Phil: Associate Editor - Business Press; Publishing & Communications: Sally: Production - Publishing; (Selections from the Career Strategy Cassette Library). 11.95 per cass. J Norton Pubs.
In-depth interviews of young men & women with 5 - 10 years job experience. Guides to career planning for college students making intelligent decisions about their future careers.

Publishing & Communications: Bob: Radio TV Talk Show Moderator see Publishing & Communications

Publishing & Communications: JoAnn: Corporate Communications - Industrial T.V. see Publishing & Communications

Publishing & Communications: Mary: Corporate Business Editor see Publishing & Communications

Publishing & Communications: Milt: Managing Editor - Magazines see Publishing & Communications

Publishing & Communications: Phil: Associate Editor - Business Press see Publishing & Communications

Publishing & Communications: Sally: Production - Publishing see Publishing & Communications

Publishing Timeline 2000: A Chronology of Publishing & Graphic Arts Events. unabr. ed. Richard Sasso. Intro. by Carl Schlesinger. 1 CD. (Running Time: 90 mins.). 2000. audio compact disk 49.95 (978-0-9679051-2-9(5)) QBC Pubng.

Puccini - Arias for Tenor & Orchestra Volume 1. Composed by Giacomo Puccini. 2007. pap. bk. 34.98 (978-1-59615-545-9(0), 1596155450) Pub: Music Minus. Dist(s): H Leonard

Puccini arias for soprano & orchestra, vol. II, Vol. 2. Maldjanska Zvetelina. 2001. pap. bk. 39.98 (978-1-59615-563-3(9), 586-092) Pub: Music Minus. Dist(s): Bookworld

Puccini Arias for Soprano with Orchestra - Volume III. Composed by Giacomo Puccini. Zvetelina Maldjanska. 2008. pap. bk. 34.98 (978-1-4234-5925-5(3), 1423459253) Pub: Music Minus. Dist(s): H Leonard

Puccini's Ghosts. Morag Joss. Read by Jacqueline King & Jonathan Hackett. 10 cass. (Running Time: 12 hrs. 30 mins.). (Isis Cassettes Ser.). 2006. 84.95 (978-0-7531-3656-0(2)) Pub: ISIS Lrg Prnt GBR. Dist(s): Ulverscroft US

Puccini's Ghosts. Morag Joss. Read by Joan Walker & Jonathan Hackett. (Running Time: 45000 sec.). (Isis (CDs) Ser.). 2006. audio compact disk 99.95 (978-0-7531-2621-9(4)) Pub: ISIS Lrg Prnt GBR. Dist(s): Ulverscroft US

Puck of Pook's Hill. unabr. ed. Rudyard Kipling. Read by Flo Gibson. 4 cass. (Running Time: 6 hrs.). (J). 1990. 19.95 (978-1-55685-161-2(8)) Audio Bk Con.
The magic of Puck transports little Una & Dan to centuries past, where they witness the making of myth & history that created the heritage of England.

Puck of Pook's Hill. unabr. ed. Rudyard Kipling. Read by Nadia May. 4 cass. (Running Time: 5 hrs. 30 mins.). 1994. 32.95 (978-0-7861-0679-0(4), 1459) Blckstn Audio.
Dan & Una acted "Midsummer Night's Dream" three times over on Midsummer's Eve, in the middle of a Ring - & right under Pook's Hill. That was how they met Puck, "the oldest Old Thing in England," & the last of the People of the Hills. With Puck, they were introduced to the nearly forgotten pages of old England's history & to the people who had lived near Pook's Hill & helped to make that history. This story of Dan & Una & their adventures has the feel & spirit of Old England. It is told with whimsical reality & understanding & in the years since its publication has become one of the lasting books for boys & girls the world over.

Puck of Pook's Hill. unabr. ed. Rudyard Kipling. Narrated by Steven Crossley. 6 cass. (Running Time: 9 hrs.). (gr. 7 up). 1997. 51.00 (978-0-7887-1338-5(8), 95187E7) Recorded Bks.
On Midsummer Eve in a Sussex meadow, Dan & Una act out their version of Shakespeare's "A Midsummer Night's Dream." Suddenly, Puck, as old as Time itself, miraculously appears. The youngsters are swept into the past as Puck conjures up villages of long ago.

Puck of Pook's Hill, Set. unabr. ed. Rudyard Kipling. Read by Steven Crossley. 6 cass. (Running Time: 9 hrs.). (YA). 1997. pap. bk. 67.20 (978-0-7887-1719-2(7), 40587) Recorded Bks.
Puck appears on Midsummer's Eve & sweeps two youngsters into the past.

Puddlejumpers. unabr. ed. Mark Jean & Christopher Carlson. Read by Sean Kenin. 6 CDs. (Running Time: 6 hrs. 39 mins.). (YA). (gr. 7 up). 2008. audio compact disk 55.00 (978-0-7393-6339-3(5), Listening Lib) Pub: Random Audio Pubg. Dist(s): Random
Ernie Banks, named for the legendary Chicago Cubs shortstop, is a troubled, thirteen-year-old juvenile delinquent. Abandoned on the doorstep of the Lakeside Home for Boys when he was three years old, his only proof that he once belonged to somebody is a vintage Ernie Banks baseball card, a crystal acorn he wears on a string around his neck, and a strange spiral birthmark on the bottom of his right foot. As a last reprieve before being sent to a juvenile detention facility, Ernie is allowed to spend three weeks on a working farm. When Ernie arrives at the home of Russ Frazier, he learns that the widower's baby was kidnapped years before. Ernie is determined to solve the case. He teams up with Joey, a local tomboy, to investigate clues that lead them on a dangerous journey into a forbidden world of dark secrets, magic puddles, and the cavernous underground kingdom of the Puddlejumpers - eleven-inch-tall water creatures with whom Ernie has a mysterious connection.

Pudd'nhead Wilson. Mark Twain. Narrated by Flo Gibson. (ENG.). 2007. 19.95 (978-1-55685-911-3(2)) Audio Bk Con.

Pudd'nhead Wilson. Mark Twain. Read by Michael Prichard. (Running Time: 6 hrs. 30 mins.). 2003. 27.95 (978-1-60083-636-7(4), Audiofy Corp) Iofy Corp.

Pudd'nhead Wilson. Mark Twain. Read by Jim Killavey. 4 cass. (Running Time: 5 hrs. 30 min.). 1989. 24.00 incl. album. (C-78) Jimcin Record.
Satire on slavery.

Pudd'nhead Wilson. Mark Twain. Read by Ray Verna. 4 cass. (Running Time: 5 hrs.). 1993. 35.20 Set. (978-1-56544-015-9(3), 350040); Rental 7.30 30 day rental Set. (350040) Literate Ear.
All the magical elements of Mark Twain's unique feel for the Old South, combined here with mystery & comedy.

Pudd'nhead Wilson. unabr. ed. Mark Twain. Read by Jim Killavey. 4 cass. (Running Time: 5 hrs.). Dramatization. 1982. 24.00 (C-78) Jimcin Record.
The story is set in pre-Civil War America. The story line concerns the exchange of a slave woman's child for a judge's son.

Pudd'nhead Wilson. unabr. ed. Mark Twain. Narrated by Norman Dietz. 5 cass. (Running Time: 6 hrs. 45 mins.). 1999. 46.00 (978-1-55690-687-9(0), 92342E7) Recorded Bks.
The darkly humorous story of two babies, one white & one black, switched at birth & the humble country lawyer who discovers the truth.

Pudd'nhead Wilson. unabr. ed. Mark Twain. 4 cass. 1996. 44.95 (978-1-86015-428-7(X)) Pub: UlverLrgPrint GBR. Dist(s): Ulverscroft US
Mark Twain's novel of satirical wit was aimed at the injustices in the southern states of America in the middle of the 19th century. It tells the story of two children, one born free, the other a slave. When the slave's mother Roxana switches the infants in the cradles, she is not the only one who lives to regret the action. This tale has many facets to it, it is a murder mystery, a social commentary on the manners & beliefs of the time & a detective novel.

Pudd'nhead Wilson. unabr. collector's ed. Mark Twain. Read by Jim Roberts. 6 cass. (Running Time: 6 hrs.). 1982. 36.00 (978-0-7366-3870-8(9), 9078) Books on Tape.
A slave woman's child is swapped for a judge's son. Take Southern prejudice, a switch in identities, a bizarre murder & the exuberant characters of Twain's youth, mix them with his mature wit & social sensibilities & you have a first-rate yarn.

***Puddnhead Wilson & Those Extraordinary Twins, by Mark Twain: Narrated by Richard Henzel.** Narrated by Richard Henzel. 2010. audio compact disk 39.99 (978-0-9826688-3-2(X)) R Henzel.

Pudd'nhead Wilson, Unabridged: Read by Richard Henzel. 6 CDs. (Running Time: 5 hrs. 45 mins.). Orig. Title: The Tragedy of Pudd'nhead Wilson by Mark Twain. (ENG.). 2002. audio compact disk 29.99 (978-0-9747237-0-9(3)) R Henzel.
Richard Henzel reads Mark Twain's Pudd'nhead Wilson, unabridged.

Puddocky. unabr. ed. 1 cass. (Running Time: 20 min.). Dramatization. (Magic Looking Glass Ser.). (J). (gr. 2-6). 1989. 9.95 (978-0-7810-0022-2(X), NIM-CW-127-1-C) NIMCO.
A folk tale of German descent.

Pueblos Audio CD Program. Sheri Spaine Long. (YA). 2007. cd-rom 35.56 (978-0-618-15056-4(0), 333269) CENGAGE Learn.

Puedes clasificar botes Audio CD: Emergent Set A. Benchmark Education Staff. Ed. by Katherine Scraper. (Early Explorers Ser.). (J). 2008. audio compact disk 10.00 (978-1-60437-252-6(4)) Benchmark Educ.

Puedes Subir: Level 3, Vol. 8. (Fonolibros Ser.). 2003. 11.50 (978-0-7652-0995-5(0)) Modern Curr.

Puedo Quedarme en Casa? Created by Rigby Staff. 1993. 10.40 (978-0-435-05953-8(X), Rigby PEA) Pearson EdAUS AUS.

Puentes. 3rd ed. Marinelli & Laughlin. (C). bk. 111.95 (978-0-8384-8285-8(6)); bk. 101.95 (978-0-8384-8713-6(0)); bk. & stu. ed. 92.95 (978-0-8384-7503-4(5)); bk. & stu. ed. 145.95 (978-0-8384-7772-4(0)); bk. & stu. ed. 90.95 (978-0-8384-7819-6(0)); bk. & stu. ed. 117.95 (978-0-8384-8571-2(5)) Heinle.

Puentes. 3rd ed. Marinelli & Laughlin. 2001. audio compact disk 10.50 (978-0-8384-2440-7(6)) Heinle.

Puentes. 3rd ed. Marinelli & Laughlin. (C). 2001. lab manual ed. 10.50 (978-0-8384-2443-8(0)) Heinle.

Puentes. 3rd ed. Marinelli & Laughlin. (C). 2001. bk., wbk. ed., lab manual ed. 31.50 (978-0-8384-2448-3(1)) Heinle.

Puentes. 3rd ed. Marinelli & Laughlin. (C). 2001. bk. & tchr. ed. 57.75 (978-0-8384-2499-5(6)) Heinle.

Puertas a la Lengua Espanola: An Introductory Course. John G. Copeland et al. 1990. tchr. ed. & stu. ed. (978-0-318-67200-7(6)) McGraw.

Puertas Abiertas see Puertas Abiertas Kit, Level 1, Open Doors to Spanish

Puertas Abiertas Kit: Open Doors to Spanish. (J). 2006. per. 135.00 (978-0-9723341-2-9(2)) Heflin & Thrall Lang Pubns.

Puertas Abiertas Kit Level 1: Open Doors to Spanish. Jenifer Heflin. 2. (Running Time: 200 minutes). Orig. Title: Puertas Abiertas. (YA). 2003. pap. bk. 125.00 (978-0-9723341-0-5(6)) Heflin & Thrall Lang Pubns.
Designed to be used along with the workbook to practice what was presented on the videos.

Puertas Retorcidas: The Scariest Way in the World to Learn Spanish! Kathie S. Dior. Adapted by Kathie S. Dior. Tr. by Claudia Guerin & Cecilia Tenorio. Narrated by Gony Torres. Illus. by Krista Buuck & Andrew Edmonds. 1 CD. (Running Time: 1 hr 14 mins). Dramatization.Tr. of Twisted Doors. (SPA & ENG.). 2006. per. 34.95 (978-0-9710227-2-0(0)) Dior.

Puerto Rican Music in Hawaii: Kachi-Kachi Sound. Contrib. by Ted Solis. 1 cass. or CD. 1989. (0-9307-400140-9307-40014-2-4); audio compact disk (0-9307-40014-2-4) Smithsonian Folkways.
Artists include Charles Figueroa, Virginia Rodrigues, Glenn Ferreira, & others.

Puff & Other Family Classics. Peter Yarrow. 1 CD. (Running Time: 47 mins.). (ENG.). 2008. audio compact disk 9.95 (978-1-4027-5949-9(5)) Sterling.

Puffin Book of Five-Minute Stories. Read by Sophie Aldred & Christopher Timothy. 2 CDs. (ENG.). 2002. audio compact disk (978-0-14-180306-7(1)) Penguin Grp USA.

Puffin's Homecoming. Darice Bailer. 1 cass. (Running Time: 35 min.). (J). (gr. k-4). 2001. pap. bk. 16.95 (SP 3014C) Kimbo Educ.
Puffin & his mate raise their newborn chick in an underground burrow.

Puggle Hybrid: A Basic Guide to this Canine Hybrid. Karen Jean Matsko Hood. 2009. 29.95 (978-1-59808-856-4(4)); audio compact disk 24.95 (978-1-59808-857-1(2)) Whsprng Pine.

Puili-Hawaiian Rhythm Sticks. 1 cass. (Running Time: 1 hr.). (J). 2001. pap. bk. 10.95 (KIM 7046C); pap. bk. 14.95; pap. bk. & stu. ed. 11.95 (KIM 7046) Kimbo Educ.
Unusual rhythm stick activities combined with enchanting island music. Individual & partner routines. Hukilau, Enchanted Island, Lanakila & more. Includes manual.

Puja. 1 cass. (Running Time: 60 min.). bk. 15.00 (GP) Nada Prodns.
Ritual worship is a beautiful blend of Karma, Bhakti, Raja & Jnana Yoga. Devotees of God who feel divinely inspired can do puja as a sadhana with this booklet explaining the process, mantras & meaning, & with the tape one can easily learn the puja. Contains: Abhisheka; Alankara; Archana; Araati; Ganesh Mantras; Guru Stotras; Devi Mantras; Purusha Sukta; Narayana Sukta; Shanti Mantras; Sivananda Ashtottra; Sata Namavali; Arati & Invocation Chants.

Puja: Darsan Dena, Darsan Lena. unabr. ed. Julian C. Hollick. 1 cass. (Running Time: 60 min.). (Passages to India Ser.). 1991. 15.00 (978-1-56709-007-9(9), 1007) Indep Broadcast.
Hinduism is a bewildering mosaic of mythologies, rituals & gods. This program looks at Hinduism as worship in the daily lives of Indians.

***Pulgada, pie, yarda Audio CD.** April Barth. Adapted by Benchmark Education Co., LLC. (Content Connections Ser.). (SPA.). (J). 2010. audio compact disk 10.00 (978-1-61672-206-7(1)) Benchmark Educ.

Pulgarcita y Otros Cuentos Clasicos. abr. ed.Tr. of Little Thumb & Other Classic Tales. (SPA.). 2002. audio compact disk 13.00 (978-958-43-0138-3(1)) YoYoMusic.

Pulgarcito. Charles Perrault. 1 cass. (Running Time: 1 hr. 30 min.).Tr. of Tom Thumb. (SPA., (J). 2000. 12.95 (978-84-207-6729-1(8)) Pub: Grupo Anaya ESP. Dist(s): Distribks Inc

Pull of the Moon. unabr. ed. Elizabeth Berg. Narrated by Barbara Caruso. 4 cass. (Running Time: 4 hrs. 45 mins.). 1997. 35.00 (978-0-7887-1779-6(0), 95253E7) Recorded Bks.
As a woman impulsively drives away from her home, she begins to contemplate her relationships with her husband, her daughter, & her life.

Pull of the Moon. unabr. ed. Elizabeth Berg. Narrated by Barbara Caruso. 4 cass. (Running Time: 4 hrs. 45 mins.). 2002. 29.95 (978-0-7887-6228-4(1), RC453) Recorded Bks.
Can the middle age years still hold as much promise as the full moon of youth? Nan has no answer to that question, but she knows that the moon of her life is on the wane. As she drives away from home, turning the wheel toward an uncertain future, Nan begins to contemplate her relationships with her husband and her daughter. Slowly, over nights spent in highway motels, and meals eaten in booth-lined diners, she regains a focus in her life that she had given up for lost. Funny, poignant, and often dazzling, Elizabeth Berg's novel will instantly appeal to women of all ages.

***Pull up a Chair: The Vin Scully Story.** unabr. ed. Curt Smith. Read by Grover Gardner. (Running Time: 10 hrs. 0 mins.). 2010. 29.95 (978-1-4417-3243-9(8)); 59.95 (978-1-4417-3239-2(X)); audio compact disk 90.00 (978-1-4417-3240-8(3)) Blckstn Audio.

Pullet on the Midden, Set. unabr. ed. Rachel Knappett. Read by Lynne Verrall. 6 cass. (Running Time: 7 hr. 30 min.). (Reminiscence Ser.). (J). 1998. 54.95 (978-0-7531-0382-1(6), 980616) Pub: ISIS Lrg Prnt GBR. Dist(s): Ulverscroft US
Rachel Knappett was sent, as a land girl, to Bath Farm in South-West Lancashire. She was the only land girl & in fact, the only female attached to a group of highly experienced laborers who were unused to working side by side with women. Initially they were highly doubtful of her ability to do the job, but gradually she came not only to earn their respect but their friendship.

Pullett on the Midden. Rachel Knappett. Read by Lynne Verrall. 3 cass. (Running Time: 4 hrs. 30 mins.). 2001. 34.95 (980616) Pub: ISIS Audio GBR. Dist(s): Ulverscroft US

Pulling down Strongholds. Speeches. Joel Osteen. 1 Cass. (Running Time: 30 Mins.). (J). 2000. 6.00 (978-1-59349-061-4(5), JA0061) J Osteen.

Pulling down Strongholds, No. 1. Francis Frangipane. 1 cass. (Running Time: 90 mins.). (Pulling down Strongholds Ser.: Vol. 1). 2000. 5.00 (FF05-001) Morning NC.
Some of Francis' most famous life-changing messages are contained in this comprehensive 10-tape series.

Pulling down Strongholds, No. 2. Francis Frangipane. 1 cass. (Running Time: 90 mins.). (Pulling down Strongholds Ser.: Vol. 2). 2000. 5.00 (FF05-002) Morning NC.

Pulling down Strongholds Series. Francis Frangipane. 10 cass. (Running Time: 15 hrs.). 2000. 50.00 (FF05-000) Morning NC.

Pulling Princes: The Calypso Chronicles. unabr. ed. 5 CDs. (Running Time: 20700 sec.). (Calypso Chronicles). (YA). (gr. 7-13). 2005. audio compact disk 63.95 (978-1-74093-570-8(5)) Pub: Bolinda Pubng AUS. Dist(s): Bolinda Pub Inc

Pulling the Moves. unabr. ed. Margaret Clark. Read by Kate Hosking. 2 cass. (Running Time: 3 hrs. 25 mins.). 2002. (978-1-74030-252-4(4), 500956) Bolinda Pubng AUS.

Pulling Your Own Strings. abr. ed. Wayne W. Dyer. Read by Wayne W. Dyer. 1 cass. (Running Time: 1 hr. 30 min.). 1991. 18.00 (978-1-55994-433-5(1), CPN 1888) HarperCollins Pubs.

***Pulling Your Own Strings.** abr. ed. Wayne W. Dyer. Read by Wayne W. Dyer. (ENG.). 2005. (978-0-06-084567-4(8), Harper Audio); (978-0-06-084566-7(X), Harper Audio) HarperCollins Pubs.

Pulmonary Complications from Trauma or Sepsis. 1 cass. (General Sessions Ser.: C84-SP7A). 1984. 7.50 (8422) Am Coll Surgeons.

Pulp Physics: Astronomy: Humankind in Space & Time. unabr. ed. Scripts. Richard Berendzen. Read by Richard Berendzen. 6 cass. (Running Time: 9 hrs.). 2003. 29.95 (978-1-59007-355-1(X), N Millennium Audio) Pub: New Millenn Enter. Dist(s): PerseuPGW

Pulp Physics Set: Astronomy: Humankind in Space & Time. unabr. ed. Richard Berendzen. Read by Richard Berendzen. 6 cass. (Running Time: 9 hrs.). 2001. 29.95 (978-1-57511-034-9(2)) Pub Mills.
A comprehensive, yet easily understood, introduction to astronomy by one of our most prominent physicists.

Pulse. collector's unabr. ed. Edna Buchanan. Read by Anna Fields. 8 CDs. (Running Time: 8 hrs.). 2000. audio compact disk 64.00 (978-0-7366-5152-3(7)) Books on Tape.
If Daniel Alexander had not committed suicide, CPA Frank Douglas would have been dead before his forty-fifth birthday. Overcome with gratitude, Douglas sets out to track down the donor's family to offer personal thanks & find out all he can about his benefactor. What he finds, however, is a trail of corruption & murder that causes Frank to question the true dark nature of the heart that beats inside him.

Pulse. unabr. ed. Edna Buchanan. Narrated by Richard M. Davidson. 9 CDs. (Running Time: 10 hrs. 45 mins.). 1999. audio compact disk 83.00 (978-0-7887-3439-7(3), C1045E7) Recorded Bks.
Frank Douglas' heart transplant was a success, but something is driving him to find out who the organ donor was. His search wil take him deep into the labyrinth of another man's life, one filled with deception & danger.

Pulse, unabr. ed. Edna Buchanan. Narrated by Richard M. Davidson. 8 cass. (Running Time: 10 hrs. 45 mins.). 1998. 70.00 (978-0-7887-2599-9(8), 95535E7) Recorded Bks.

Pulse. unabr. collector's ed. Edna Buchanan. Read by Anna Fields. 6 cass. (Running Time: 9 hrs.). (Britt Montero Mystery Ser.). 1999. 48.00 (978-0-7366-4279-8(X), 4777) Books on Tape.
If Daniel Alexander had not committed suicide, CPA Frank Douglas would have been dead before his forty-fifth birthday. Overcome with gratitude, Douglas sets out to track down the donor's family to offer personal thanks & find out all he can about his benefactor. What he finds, however, is a trail of corruption & murder that causes Frank to question the true dark nature of the heart that beats inside him.

Pulse Audio- Adventure Volume 1. Short Stories. 1 CD. 2006. audio compact disk 4.95 (978-1-60245-068-4(4)) GDL Multimedia.

Pulse Audio- Comedy Volume 1. Short Stories. 1 CD. 2006. audio compact disk 4.95 (978-1-60245-069-1(2)) GDL Multimedia.

Pulse Audio- Kincaid the Strangeseeker Volume 3. Short Stories. 1 CD. 2006. audio compact disk 4.95 (978-1-60245-058-5(7)) GDL Multimedia.

Pulse Audio- Kincaid the Strangeseeker Volume 4. Short Stories. 1 CD. 2006. audio compact disk 4.95 (978-1-60245-059-2(5)) GDL Multimedia.

Pulse Audio- Kincaid the Strangeseeker Volume 5. Short Stories. 1 CD. 2006. audio compact disk 4.95 (978-1-60245-060-8(9)) GDL Multimedia.

Pulse Audio- Mr. Darnborough Investigates. Short Stories. 1 CD. 2006. audio compact disk 4.95 (978-1-60245-061-5(7)) GDL Multimedia.

Pulse Audio- Mysteries Volume 1. Short Stories. 1 CD. 2006. audio compact disk 4.95 (978-1-60245-070-7(6)) GDL Multimedia.

Pulse Audio- Old Time Radio Volume 1- Great Detectives. Scripts. 1 CD. 2006. audio compact disk 4.95 (978-1-60245-074-5(9)) GDL Multimedia.

Pulse Audio- Old Time Radio Volume 10- Radio Cowboys. 1 CD. 2006. audio compact disk 4.95 (978-1-60245-083-7(8)) GDL Multimedia.

Pulse Audio- Old Time Radio Volume 2 - Great Sleuths. Scripts. 1 CD. 2006. audio compact disk 4.95 (978-1-60245-075-2(7)) GDL Multimedia.

Pulse Audio- Old Time Radio Volume 3- Espionage. Scripts. 1 CD. 2006. audio compact disk 4.95 (978-1-60245-076-9(5)) GDL Multimedia.

Pulse Audio- Old Time Radio Volume 4- Famous Guest Stars. 1 CD. 2006. audio compact disk 4.95 (978-1-60245-077-6(3)) GDL Multimedia.

Pulse Audio- Old Time Radio Volume 5- Radio Comedy. 1 CD. 2006. audio compact disk 4.95 (978-1-60245-078-3(1)) GDL Multimedia.

Pulse Audio- Old Time Radio Volume 6- Comedy. 1 CD. 2006. audio compact disk 4.95 (978-1-60245-079-0(X)) GDL Multimedia.

Pulse Audio- Old Time Radio Volume 7- Science Fiction. 1 CD. 2006. audio compact disk 4.95 (978-1-60245-080-6(3)) GDL Multimedia.

Pulse Audio- Old Time Radio Volume 8- Radio Mystery. 1 CD. 2006. audio compact disk 4.95 (978-1-60245-081-3(1)) GDL Multimedia.

Pulse Audio- Old Time Radio Volume 9- Radio Westerns. 1 CD. 2006. audio compact disk 4.95 (978-1-60245-082-0(X)) GDL Multimedia.

Pulse Audio- Raffles Collection, Vol. 1. (ENG.). 2007. audio compact disk 13.95 (978-1-60245-025-7(0)) GDL Multimedia.

Pulse Audio- Raffles Volume 1. Short Stories. 1 CD. 2006. audio compact disk 4.95 (978-1-60245-055-4(2)) GDL Multimedia.

Pulse Audio- Raffles Volume 2. Short Stories. 1 CD. 2006. audio compact disk 4.95 (978-1-60245-056-1(0)) GDL Multimedia.

Pulse Audio- Raffles Volume 3. Short Stories. 1 CD. 2006. audio compact disk 4.95 (978-1-60245-057-8(9)) GDL Multimedia.

Pulse Audio- Sci-fi Volume 1. Short Stories. 1 CD. 2006. audio compact disk 4.95 (978-1-60245-071-4(4)) GDL Multimedia.

Pulse Audio- Suspense Volume 1. Short Stories. 1 CD. 2006. audio compact disk 4.95 (978-1-60245-072-1(2)) GDL Multimedia.

Pulse Audio- the Further Adventures of Sherlock Holmes Volume 1. Short Stories. 1 CD. 2006. audio compact disk 4.99 (978-1-60245-065-3(X)) GDL Multimedia.

Pulse Audio- the Further Adventures of Sherlock Holmes Volume 2. Short Stories. 1 CD. 2006. audio compact disk 4.99 (978-1-60245-066-0(8)) GDL Multimedia.

Pulse Audio- the Further Adventures of Sherlock Holmes Volume 3. Short Stories. 1 CD. 2006. audio compact disk 4.99 (978-1-60245-067-7(6)) GDL Multimedia.

Pulse Audio- the Hilary Caine Mysteries. Short Stories. 1 CD. 2006. audio compact disk 4.95 (978-1-60245-054-7(4)) GDL Multimedia.

Pulse Audio- the New Adventures of Harry Nile Volume 1. Short Stories. 1 CD. 2006. audio compact disk 4.99 (978-1-60245-062-2(5)) GDL Multimedia.

Pulse Audio- the New Adventures of Harry Nile Volume 2. Short Stories. 1 CD. 2006. audio compact disk 4.99 (978-1-60245-063-9(3)) GDL Multimedia.

Pulse Audio- the New Adventures of Harry Nile Volume 3. Short Stories. 1 CD. 2006. audio compact disk 4.99 (978-1-60245-064-6(1)) GDL Multimedia.

Pulse Audio- Thrillers Volume 1. Short Stories. 1 CD. 2006. audio compact disk 4.95 (978-1-60245-073-8(0)) GDL Multimedia.

Pulse Audio Complete Collection. (ENG.). 2007. audio compact disk 119.95 (978-1-60245-030-1(7)) GDL Multimedia.

Pulse of Danger. unabr. ed. Jon Cleary. Read by Christopher Scott. 10 cass. (Running Time: 15 hrs.). 2001. 84.95 (23965) Pub: Soundings Ltd GBR. Dist(s): Ulverscroft US

***Pulse: Stories.** Julian Barnes. Narrated by David Rintoul. (Running Time: 7 hrs. 0 mins. 0 sec.). (ENG.). 2011. audio compact disk 29.95 (978-1-60998-172-3(3)) Pub: AudioGO. Dist(s): Perseus Dist

Pumkids. unabr. ed. Rick Scott. 1 CD. (Running Time: 44 mins.). (J). (gr. k-5). 2007. audio compact disk 18.00 (978-0-9733515-4-5(3)) JSTR CAN.

Pump House Gang. unabr. ed. Tom Wolfe. Read by Harold N. Cropp. 7 cass. (Running Time: 10 hrs.). 1995. 49.95 (978-0-7861-0652-3(2), 1560) Blckstn Audio.
These exhilarating essays revive the Sixties with all their energy, their weirdness, their freaky vision, & their lurid legacy for life in the Eighties. Exposed are Ken Kesey & the Merry Pranksters, the rise of psychedelic lifestyle in America, & the founding of a bizarre new religion. In the midst of it all, many members of the redoubtable Pump House Gang become indoor sports - happily freaking out in pads rather than wiping out in the surf, but with the same unique Pump House Gang flair.

Pump House Gang. unabr. collector's ed. Tom Wolfe. Read by Michael Prichard. 6 cass. (Running Time: 9 hrs.). 1992. 48.00 (978-0-7366-2116-8(4), 2919) Books on Tape.
Tom Wolfe's second collection of essays about life in the 60s. Funny & irreverent.

***Pump Six & Other Stories.** unabr. ed. Paolo Bacigalupi. (Running Time: 13 hrs.). 2010. 24.99 (978-1-4418-9222-5(2), 9781441892225, Brilliance MP3) Brilliance Audio.

***Pump Six & Other Stories.** unabr. ed. Paolo Bacigalupi. Read by Jonathan Davis Stevens. (Running Time: 8 hrs.). 2010. 39.97 (978-1-4418-9224-9(9), 9781441892249, BADLE) Brilliance Audio.

***Pump Six & Other Stories.** unabr. ed. Paolo Bacigalupi. Read by Jonathan Davis Stevens & Eileen Stevens. (Running Time: 13 hrs.). 2010. 39.97 (978-1-4418-9223-2(0), 9781441892232, Brlnc Audio MP3 Lib) Brilliance Audio.

***Pump Six & Other Stories.** unabr. ed. Paolo Bacigalupi. Read by Jonathan Davis Stevens. (Running Time: 13 hrs.). 2010. audio compact disk 79.97 (978-1-4418-9221-8(4), 9781441892218, BriAudCD Unabrid) Brilliance Audio.

***Pump Six & Other Stories.** unabr. ed. Paolo Bacigalupi. Read by Jonathan Davis Stevens et al. (Running Time: 13 hrs.). 2010. audio compact disk 29.99 (978-1-4418-9220-1(6), 9781441892201, Bril Audio CD Unabri) Brilliance Audio.

Pumping Nylon: Easy to Early Intermediate Repertoire. Scott Tennant. (Pumping Nylon Ser.). (ENG.). 1998. audio compact disk 10.00 (978-0-7390-2613-7(5)) Alfred Pub.

Pumping Nylon: Intermediate to Advanced Repertoire. Scott Tennant. 1 CD. (Pumping Nylon Ser.). (ENG.). 1999. audio compact disk 10.00 (978-0-7390-0287-2(2), 18491) Alfred Pub.

***Pumping Piano Pieces - Boogie Woogie Blues & Ragtime Piano: The Jeremy Allen Intermediate Piano Library.** Jeremy Allen. (ENG.). 2010. pap. bk. 12.99 (978-1-4234-9755-4(4), 1423497554) H Leonard.

Pumpkin Book. Gail Gibbons. 11 vols. (Running Time: 15 mins.). (J). (ps-3). 2002. bk. 25.95 (978-0-87499-945-7(6)); pap. bk. & tchr.'s planning gde. ed. 37.95 (978-0-87499-946-4(4)) Live Oak Media.
Describes the pumpkin, how it's planted, grown, harvested, and its cultural significance.

Pumpkin Book. Gail Gibbons. Illus. by Gail Gibbons. 41 vols. (Running Time: 15 mins.). 2002. pap. bk. 39.95 (978-1-59112-673-7(8)); audio compact disk 12.95 (978-1-59112-671-3(1)) Live Oak Media.

Pumpkin Book. Gail Gibbons. Illus. by Gail Gibbons. (Running Time: 15 mins.). (J). (gr. k-3). 2002. 9.95 (978-0-87499-943-3(X)) Live Oak Media.

Pumpkin Book. unabr. ed. Gail Gibbons. 11 vols. (Running Time: 15 mins.). (J). 2002. pap. bk. 16.95 (978-0-87499-944-0(8)) Live Oak Media.
Takes a popular autumn symbol and explores its growth cycle from seed to table. The informative text, including instructions for young gardeners to grow and harvest their own pumpkins and to carve jack-o-lanterns, are clearly presented in this splendid resource with plenty of appeal for children.

Pumpkin Coach. Susan Sallis. 12 cass. (Running Time: 13 hrs. 30 mins.). (Soundings Ser.). (J). 2004. 94.95 (978-1-84283-889-1(X)); audio compact disk 99.95 (978-1-84283-919-5(5)) Pub: ISIS Lrg Prnt GBR. Dist(s): Ulverscroft US

***Pumpkin Eye.** Denise Fleming. 1 CD. (Running Time: 6 mins.). (J). (gr. k-2). 2009. bk. 29.95 (978-0-8045-4204-3(X)); bk. 27.95 (978-0-8045-6979-8(7)) Spoken Arts.

Pumpkin Rollers. Elmer Kelton. Narrated by George Guidall. 7 cass. (Running Time: 9 hrs. 15 mins.). 58.00 (978-0-7887-9443-8(4)) Recorded Bks.

Pumpkin Seed Massacre. unabr. ed. Susan Slater. Read by Christine Clayburg. 8 cass. (Running Time: 9 hrs. 30 min.). 2001. 49.95 (978-1-58116-043-7(7)) Books in Motion.
Ben Pecos has straddled Anglo and Native cultures. And now as a medical school graduate, Ben accepts an internship at one of New Mexico's Tewa Pueblos, where a plague-like epidemic is spreading among residents and tourists.

Pumpkins: The Unauthorized Biography of the Smashing Pumpkins. Martin Harper. (Maximum Ser.). (ENG.). 2001. audio compact disk 14.95 (978-1-84240-000-5(2)) Pub: Chrome Dreams GBR. Dist(s): IPG Chicago

Pumps & Pumping Equipment in Philippines: A Strategic Reference 2006. Compiled by Icon Group International, Inc. Staff. 2007. ring bd. 195.00 (978-0-497-82392-4(6)) Icon Grp.

Pumps & Valves in Mexico: A Strategic Reference 2006. Compiled by Icon Group International, Inc. Staff. 2007. ring bd. 195.00 (978-0-497-82358-0(6)) Icon Grp.

Pumps, Valves, & Compressors in Ecuador: A Strategic Reference 2007. Compiled by Icon Group International, Inc. Staff. 2007. ring bd. 195.00 (978-0-497-35927-0(8)) Icon Grp.

Punch: One Night, Two Lives, & the Fight That Changed Basketball Forever. unabr. ed. John Feinstein. Narrated by Richard M. Davidson. 9 cass. (Running Time: 12 hrs. 45 mins.). 2002. 78.00 (978-1-4025-3197-2(4)) Recorded Bks.

Punch: One Night, Two Lives, & the Fight That Changed Basketball Forever. unabr. ed. John Feinstein. 7 cass. (Running Time: 12 hrs.). 2002. 29.99 Recorded Bks.

Punch: One Night, Two Lives, & the Fight That Changed Basketball Forever. unabr. ed. John Feinstein. Narrated by Richard Davidson. 7 cass. (Running Time: 12 hrs. 45 mins.). 2004. 29.99 (978-1-4025-2484-4(6), 01734) Recorded Bks.

Punch, Brothers, Punch see Best of Mark Twain

Punch Line Rhyme. Jack Nussbaum. Read by Jack Nussbaum. 1 cass. (Running Time: 50 min.). 1995. (978-0-9636110-2-4(X)) Nut Tree Ent.
Presentation of humorous poetry. Live presentation.

Punch with Judy, unabr. ed. Avi. Narrated by Johnny Heller. 3 pieces. (Running Time: 4 hrs.). (gr. 6 up). 1998. 27.00 (978-0-7887-2069-7(4), 95422E7) Recorded Bks.
Punch, a young orpan boy, roams through the Old West with a traveling medicine show that stays just one step ahead of the law. But he doesn't mind the danger, as long as he is near Judy, the owner's beautiful daughter.

Punching Holes in the Darkness: Matthew 5:14-16. Ed Young. (J). 1979. 4.95 (978-0-7417-1046-8(3), A0048) Win Walk.

Punctuation: Syllabus. 2nd ed. Carl W. Salser & C. Theodore Yerian. (J). 1972. 56.20 (978-0-89420-178-3(6), 357500) Natl Book.

***Punctuation Takes a Vacation.** Robin Pulver. Narrated by John Beach. Illus. by Lynn Rowe Reed. (J). (gr. 1-3). 2009. bk. 28.95 (978-1-4301-0708-8(1)); pap. bk. 18.95 (978-1-4301-0707-1(3)) Live Oak Media.

Punish the Sinners. abr. ed. John Saul. Read by David Daoust. (Running Time: 6 hrs.). 2003. 62.25 (978-1-59086-833-1(1), 1590868331, BAudLibEd); audio compact disk 74.25 (978-1-59086-835-5(8), 1590868358, BACDLib Ed) Brilliance Audio.
Italy, 1252 Inquisition. Accusation. Fear. Torture. The guilty and the innocent dying for sins real and imagined, in the flames of the burning stake...

Neilsville, 1978 Peter Balsam has come to this sleepy desert town to teach its youth, and finds a mystery of mounting horror. Something is happening to the young girls of St. Francis Xavier High School- something evil. In bloodlet and terror a suicide contagion has swept the town...while a dark order of its holy men enacts a secret medieval ritual. Is hysteria manipulating these innocent children into violent self-destruction? Or has a supernatural force, a thirteenth-century madness, returned to...Punish the Sinners.

Punish the Sinners. abr. ed. John Saul. Read by David Daoust. (Running Time: 6 hrs.). 2005. audio compact disk 16.99 (978-1-59600-432-0(0), 9781596004320, BCD Value Price) Brilliance Audio.

Punish the Sinners. abr. ed. John Saul. Read by David Daoust. (Running Time: 6 hrs.). 2006. 39.25 (978-1-4233-0180-6(3), 9781423301806, BADLE); 24.95 (978-1-4233-0179-0(X), 9781423301790, BAD); 39.25 (978-1-4233-0178-3(1), 9781423301783, Brlnc Audio MP3 Lib); audio compact disk 24.95 (978-1-4233-0177-6(3), 9781423301776, Brilliance MP3) Brilliance Audio.

Punish the Sinners - Cry for the Strangers: And Comes the Blind Fury. abr. ed. John Saul. Narrated by David Daoust et al. (Running Time: 18 hrs.). 2005. 29.95 (978-1-59737-045-5(2), 9781597370455) Brilliance Audio.
Punish the Sinners (Narrator: David Daoust, Director: Laura Grafton, Engineer: Matthew Christilaw): Italy, 1252 Inquisition. Accusation. Fear. Torture. The guilty and the innocent dying for sins real and imagined, in the flames of the burning stake... Neilsville, 1978 Peter Balsam has come to this sleepy desert town to teach its youth, and finds a mystery of mounting horror. In bloodlet and terror a suicide contagion has swept the town...while a dark order of its holy men enacts a secret medieval ritual. Cry for the Strangers (Narrator: Mel Foster, Director: Laura Grafton, Engineer: Mikael Naramore): Clark's Harbor was the perfect coastal haven, jealously guarded against outsiders. But now strangers have come to settle there. And a small boy is suddenly free of a frenzy that had gripped him since birth... His sister is haunted by fearful visions... And one by one, in violent, mysterious ways the strangers are dying. Has a dark bargain been struck between the people of Clark's Harbor and some supernatural force? Or is it the sea itself calling out for human sacrifice? Comes the Blind Fury (Narrator: Tanya Eby, Director: Joyce Bean, Engineer: Mike Council): A century ago, a gentle blind girl walked the cliffs of Paradise Point. Then the children came - taunting, teasing - until she lost her footing and fell, shrieking her rage to the drowning sea... Now Michelle has come from Boston to live in the big house on Paradise Point. She is excited about her new life...until a hand reaches out of the swirling mists - the hand of a blind child. She is asking for friendship...seeking revenge...whispering her name.

***Punish the Sinners-ABR.** John Saul & Horror. 2010. audio compact disk 9.99 (978-1-4418-5666-1(8)) Brilliance Audio.

Punishment. unabr. ed. Crispin Sartwell. Read by Cliff Robertson. (Running Time: 10800 sec.). (Morality in Our Age Ser.). 2006. audio compact disk 25.95 (978-0-7861-6727-2(0)) Pub: Blckstn Audio. Dist(s): NetLibrary CO

Punishment. unabr. ed. Crispin Sartwell. Read by Cliff Robertson. Ed. by John Lachs & Mike Hassell. 2 cass. (Running Time: 3 hrs.). Dramatization. (Morality in Our Age Ser.). 1995. 17.95 Set. (978-1-56823-026-9(5), 10505) Knowledge Prod.
Punishment involves authority & the exercise of power by one or more humans over another - usually to preserve order & security. But power can be abused. What are the moral considerations involved in depriving others of their liberty (or even their life)? Is the purpose of incarceration to rehabilitate, to deter, or simply to punish? Is there a conflict between protecting society & seeing mitigating circumstances in every crime?.

Punishment of Virtue: Inside Afghanistan after the Taliban. unabr. ed. Sarah Chayes. Read by Renée Raudman. (Running Time: 15 hrs. 30 mins. 0 sec.). (ENG.). 2006. audio compact disk 37.99 (978-1-4001-0308-9(8)); audio compact disk 75.99 (978-1-4001-3308-6(4)); audio compact disk 24.99 (978-1-4001-5308-4(5)) Pub: Tantor Media. Dist(s): IngramPubServ

Punjab, Vol. 1. 1 cass. 1993. (F93033) Multi-Cultural Bks.

Punjab, Vol. 2. 1 cass. 1993. (F93034) Multi-Cultural Bks.

Punjabi Reader in the Arabic Script. Contrib. by Mumtaz Ahmad. 1992. 19.00 (978-0-931745-89-8(6)) Dunwoody Pr.

Punjabi Reader in the Arabic Script, Set. Mumtaz Ahmad. 2 cass. (Running Time: 1 hr. 30 min. per cass.). (ARA.). 1992. 19.00 (3082) Dunwoody Pr.
Fifty selections provide the intermediate student a wide variety of current newspaper stories with sufficent lexical & grammatical aids to facilitate their comprehension.

Punk Marketing: Get off Your A*s & Join the Revolution. abr. ed. Richard Laermer & Mark Simmons. 2008. audio compact disk 29.95 (978-1-60037-388-6(7)) Pub: Morgan James Pubng. Dist(s): IngramPubServ

Punk Rock. 1 CD. (Running Time: 1 hr.). 2000. audio compact disk (978-0-7601-3525-9(8)) Brentwood Music.
Songs include: "How I Feel," "Can't Stop Lov'n You," "Black Rain," "Cha-Cha-Cha," "Goodbye" & more.

***Punkzilla.** unabr. ed. Adam Rapp. (Running Time: 6 hrs.). 2010. 39.97 (978-1-4418-9300-0(8), 9781441893000, Candlewick Bril); 19.99 (978-1-4418-9299-7(0), 9781441892997, Candlewick Bril); audio compact disk 24.99 (978-1-4418-9295-9(8), 9781441892959, Candlewick Bril); audio compact disk 19.99 (978-1-4418-9297-3(4), 9781441892973, Candlewick Bril); audio compact disk 39.97 (978-1-4418-9298-0(2), 9781441892980, Candlewick Bril); audio compact disk 54.97 (978-1-4418-9296-6(6), 9781441892966, Candlewick Bril) Brilliance Audio.

***Punter's Turf.** unabr. ed. Peter Klein. Read by David Tredinnick. (Running Time: 11 hrs. 2 mins.). 2010. audio compact disk 93.95 (978-1-74214-641-6(4), 9781742146416) Pub: Bolinda Pubng AUS. Dist(s): Bolinda Pub Inc

***Punto Clave.** Malcolm Gladwell. Prod. by FonoLibro Inc. Narrated by Rafael Monsalve. (SPA.). 2010. 17.95 (978-1-61154-006-2(2)) Fonolibro Inc.

Punto Clave: Como los Pequenos Cambios Pueden Provocar Grandes Efectos. abr. ed. Malcolm Gladwell. Read by Rafael Monsalve.Tr. of Tipping Point. (SPA.). 2009. 59.99 (978-1-60775-712-2(5)) Find a World.

Punto Clave: Como los Pequenos Cambios Pueden Provocar Grandes Efectos. abr. ed. Malcolm Gladwell. 3. (Running Time: 12600 sec.).Tr. of Tipping Point. (SPA.). 2007. audio compact disk 24.95 (978-1-933499-09-3(5)) Fonolibro Inc.

Punto y Aparte. 2nd ed. Sharon W. Foerster & Anne Lambright. (SPA.). (J). (gr. 6-12). 2002. stu. ed. 48.44 (978-0-07-253809-0(0), 9780072538090) Pub: Glencoe. Dist(s): McGraw

Punto y Aparte. 3rd ed. Sharon W. Foerster. (C). 2005. pap. bk. 50.00 (978-0-07-321342-2(X), 9780073213422, Mc-H Human Soc) Pub: McGrw-H Hghr Educ. Dist(s): McGraw

Puntos de Partida Pt. 1: Student Program. 5th ed. Marty Knorre et al. 6 cass. (Running Time: 9 hrs.). (C). 1997. stu. ed. 40.00 (978-0-07-912990-1(0), Mc-H Human Soc) Pub: McGrw-H Hghr Educ. Dist(s): McGraw

Puntos de Partida Pt. II: Student Program. 5th ed. Marty Knorre. 6 cass. (Running Time: 9 hrs.). (C). 1997. stu. ed. 40.00 (978-0-07-912991-8(9), Mc-H Human Soc) Pub: McGrw-H Hghr Educ. Dist(s): McGraw

Punxsutawney Phil. unabr. ed. Julia Spencer Moutran. Perf. by Terry Bradshaw. 1 cass. (Running Time: 30 mins.). (J). 2000. bk. 59.98 (T 6334 S, Listening Lib) Random Audio Pubg.
Learn weather facts from this weather forecasting groundhog, a fact-filled book & cassette. Also includes a groundhog day video.

Punxsutawney Phil & His Weather Wisdom. unabr. ed. Julia F. Spencer. Perf. by Terry Bradshaw. 1 cass. (Running Time: 30 mins.). (J). 2000. bk. 16.98 (T6268SH, Listening Lib) Random Audio Pubg.
Children will learn weather facts from the famous forecasting groundhog.

Pupil. Audio Bk Con.

Pupil Edition. 7 cass. (Technology: Science Ser.). (gr. 3 up). 2000. (978-0-02-277524-7(2)) Macmillan McGraw-Hill Schl Div.

Pupil Edition. 14 cass. (Technology: Science Ser.). (gr. 4 up). 2000. (978-0-02-277525-4(0)) Macmillan McGraw-Hill Schl Div.

Pupil Edition. 21 cass. (Technology: Science Ser.). (gr. 5 up). 2000. (978-0-02-277526-1(9)) Macmillan McGraw-Hill Schl Div.

Pupil Edition. 28 cass. (Technology: Science Ser.). (gr. 6 up). 2000. (978-0-02-277527-8(7)) Macmillan McGraw-Hill Schl Div.

Puppermaster: The Secret Life of J. Edgar Hoover. unabr. ed. Richard Hack. 9 cass. 2004. 32.95 (978-1-59007-317-9(7)); audio compact disk 34.95 (978-1-59007-318-6(5)) Pub: New Millenn Enter. Dist(s): PerseuPGW

Puppermaster: The Secret Life of J. Edgar Hoover. unabr. ed. Richard Hack. Narrated by Dan Cashman. 9 cassettes. (Running Time: 13 hrs). 2005. 79.75 (978-1-4025-9076-4(8)); audio compact disk 109.75 (978-1-4025-9078-8(4)) Recorded Bks.

Puppet. unabr. ed. Joy Fielding. Read by Laura Hicks. 2 pieces. 2005. 49.95 (978-0-7927-3470-3(X), CMP 734); 79.95 (978-0-7927-3419-2(X), CSL 734); audio compact disk 99.95 (978-0-7927-3420-8(3), SLD 734) AudioGO.

Puppet Masters. unabr. ed. Robert A. Heinlein. Read by Lloyd James. 9 cass. (Running Time: 13 hrs. 30 min.). 1998. 62.95 (978-0-7861-1330-9(8), 2226) Blckstn Audio.
An invasion force is taking over communications, government, industry - & people's bodies! The nation is helpless to stop it because the invaders multiply far faster than they can be destroyed, controlling the mind of every unsuspecting person they encounter. Enter Sam Cavanaugh, a can-do intelligence officer for the United States most secret service. Cavanaugh is the only man who can stop the invaders but to do that he'll have to be invaded himself!.

Puppet Masters. unabr. ed. Robert A. Heinlein. Read by Lloyd James. (Running Time: 13 hrs.). 1998. 24.95 (978-0-7861-9270-0(4)); audio compact disk 81.00 (978-0-7861-8149-0(4)) Blckstn Audio.

Puppet Scripts for Use at Church. 1 cass. (Running Time: 1 hr.). 1979. 6.95 (978-0-8054-8372-7(1)) BH Pubng Grp.
Selected stories suitable for church puppet ministries, encouraging Bible study.

Puppet Scripts for Use at Church, Vol. 2. Everett Robertson. 1997. reel tape 27.99 (978-0-8054-7919-5(8)) BH Pubng Grp.

Puppet Scripts for Use in Church II. Ed. by Everett Robertson. 3 cass. (Running Time: 3 hr.). 1980. 19.95 (978-0-8054-8373-4(X)) BH Pubng Grp.
Contents covers approximately 100 scripts in the following areas: tithing, Bible study, visitation, Church Training, youth ministry, & other more general topics.

Puppet Uprising - Bread & Puppets. David Cayley. 4 CDs. (Running Time: 4 hrs.). 2005. audio compact disk 27.95 (978-0-660-19006-8(0)) Pub: Canadian Broadcasting CAN. Dist(s): Georgetown Term

Puppetry Clip Art. 2001. pap. bk. 25.00 (978-1-58302-184-2(1)) One Way St.

Puppets. Daniel Hecht. Read by Jason Collins. (Running Time: 54000 sec.). 2005. audio compact disk 99.00 (978-0-7861-7944-2(9)) Blckstn Audio.

Puppets. Daniel Hetch. Read by Jason Collins. (Running Time: 14 mins. 30 sec.). 2005. 85.95 (978-0-7861-3040-5(7)) Blckstn Audio.

Puppets. unabr. ed. Daniel Hecht. Read by Christopher Lane. 10 cass. (Running Time: 14 hrs. 30 mins.). 2005. 32.95 (978-0-7861-3436-6(4)); audio compact disk 34.95 (978-0-7861-7986-2(4)) Blckstn Audio.

Puppets. unabr. ed. Daniel Hecht. Read by Jason Collins. 13 vols. (Running Time: 54000 sec.). 2005. audio compact disk 29.95 (978-0-7861-8116-2(8)) Blckstn Audio.

Puppets & Nuclear War; Cogeneration & the Energy Crisis; Hong Kong Harbor; & Tigers in the World. Hosted by Nancy Pearlman. 1 cass. (Running Time: 28 min.). 10.00 (530) Educ Comm CA.

Puppets in Action. Scripts. Prod. by One Way Street Staff. (Running Time: 42 minutes). (Puppets in Action Ser.). 2002. audio compact disk Rental 18.00 (978-1-58302-207-8(4)) One Way St.
Six recorded Christmas puppet scripts ranging from 3 to 7 minutes in length, and using from 2 to 6 puppets. Titles are:The Good NewsWe Two Mice of Oberndorf AreAsk the AnimalsLet There be Peace on EarthThe Littlest AngelAn Old Testament Christmas Story.

Puppets in Action, No. 1. Prod. by Dale Liz VonSeggen. 2001. audio compact disk 15.00 (978-1-58302-167-5(1)) One Way St.
CD contains all six recorded puppet scripts.

Puppets in Action, No. 2. Prod. by Dale Liz VonSeggen. 2001. audio compact disk 15.00 (978-1-58302-168-2(X)) One Way St.
Contains all six recordings of the puppet scripts.

Puppets in Action, No. 3. Prod. by Dale Liz VonSeggen. 2001. audio compact disk 15.00 (978-1-58302-169-9(8)) One Way St.

Puppets in Action, No. 4. Prod. by Dale Liz VonSeggen. 2001. audio compact disk 15.00 (978-1-58302-170-5(1)) One Way St.
Contains all six prerecorded scripts.

Puppets in Action, No. 5. Prod. by Dale Liz VonSeggen. 2001. audio compact disk 15.00 (978-1-58302-171-2(X)) One Way St.
Contains all seven pre-recorded puppet scripts.

Puppets in Action, No. 6. Prod. by Dale Liz VonSeggen. 2001. audio compact disk 15.00 (978-1-58302-172-9(8)) One Way St.
Contains all seven pre-recorded scripts.

Puppets in Action - Easter. Scripts. 2002. audio compact disk 15.00 (978-1-58302-206-1(6)) One Way St.

Puppets in Action Christmas, Vol. 2. Scripts. Prod. by One Way Street Staff. (Running Time: 60 minutes). (Puppets in Action Ser.). 2002. audio compact disk Rental 18.00 (978-1-58302-208-5(2)) One Way St.
Six recorded Christmas puppet scripts ranging from 4 to 10 minutes in length, and using from 1 to 4 puppets. Titles are:The Jordean NewsPray, Little AngelThe Innkeeper'Twas the Night Before the ProgramA Reason to RejoiceMr. Pennypincher's First Christmas.

***Puppies, Dogs, & Blue Northers.** unabr. ed. Gary Paulsen. (Running Time: 3 hrs.). 2011. 12.99 (978-1-4558-0168-8(2), 9781455801688, BAD); 39.97 (978-1-4558-0169-5(0), 9781455801695, BADLE); 12.99 (978-1-4558-0166-4(6), 9781455801664, Brilliance MP3); 39.97 (978-1-4558-0167-1(4), 9781455801671, Brlnc Audio MP3 Lib); audio compact disk 12.99 (978-1-4558-0164-0(X), 9781455801640, Bril Audio CD Unabri); audio compact disk 39.97 (978-1-4558-0165-7(8), 9781455801657, BriAudCD Unabrid) Brilliance Audio.

***Puppies for Dummies.** abr. ed. Sarah Hodgson. Read by Brett Barry. (ENG.). 2008. (978-0-06-176481-3(7), Harper Audio); (978-0-06-176480-6(9), Harper Audio) HarperCollins Pubs.

Puppy Dogs Polka at the Kitty Cat Carnival. unabr. ed. Rhett Parrish. Perf. by Rhett Parrish. 2 cass. (Running Time: 1 hr. 01 min.). (J). (gr. k-2). 1991. 9.95 Set, incl. 48p. coloring bk. (978-0-9632433-0-0(6), P001) RPM Record.
A music gift set with a fun approach to learning written for preschool children. The 2 music tapes contain 22 original songs sung by Grammy nominated children's artist, Rhett Parrish. Each song helps teach concepts like telling time, the alphabet, counting, safety, etc. The coloring book has an attractive 4-color cover & is 48 pages long containing the complete lyrics plus a Parent's Guide for each song.

Puppy Fat. unabr. ed. Morris Gleitzman. Read by Morris Gleitzman. 2 cass. (Running Time: 3 hrs. 30 mins.). (J). 2003. 24.00 (978-1-74030-979-0(0)) Pub: Bolinda Pubng AUS. Dist(s): Bolinda Pub Inc

Puppy Fat. unabr. ed. Morris Gleitzman. Read by Morris Gleitzman. 2 CDs. (Running Time: 2 hrs. 30 mins.). (J). 2003. audio compact disk 43.95 (978-1-74093-127-4(0)) Pub: Bolinda Pubng AUS. Dist(s): Bolinda Pub Inc

Puppy for a Playmate. (J). 2005. audio compact disk (978-1-933796-17-8(0)) PC Treasures.

Puppy in a Puddle. unabr. ed. Lucy Daniels. Read by Clare Corbett. 3 CDs. (Running Time: 2 hrs. 45 mins.). (Animal Ark Ser.). (J). (gr. 4-6). 2008. audio compact disk 29.95 (978-1-4056-5815-7(0), Chivers Child Audio) AudioGO.

***Puppy in the Pulpit: Dixie had more than just a few lessons to teach her Master!** unabr. ed. Raelene Phillips. Narrated by Pam Ward. (ENG.). 2010. 10.98 (978-1-59644-949-7(7)); audio compact disk 16.98 (978-1-59644-948-0(9)) christianaud.

Puppy Who Wanted a Boy. unabr. ed. Jane Thayer. 1 cass. (Running Time: 6 min.). (J). (ps-2). 1993. pap. bk. 16.90 (978-0-8045-6690-2(9), 6690) Spoken Arts.
Reading Rainbow Review Book.

Puppyhood: How to Raise the Perfect Dog. abr. ed. Cesar Millan & Melissa Jo Peltier. Read by Cesar Millan. 2009. audio compact disk 30.00 (978-0-307-57735-1(X), Random AudioBks) Pub: Random Audio Pubg. Dist(s): Random

Puppy's First Steps: Raising a Happy, Healthy, Well-Behaved Dog. unabr. ed. Faculty of Cummings School of Veterinary Medicine, Tufts University et al. Read by James Boles. (YA). 2008. 59.99 (978-1-60514-500-6(9)) Find a World.

Puppy's First Steps: Teh Whole-Dog Approach to Raising a Happy, Healthy, Well-Behaved Puppy. unabr. ed. Read by James Boles. Ed. by Nicholas H. Dodman. 8 CDs. (Running Time: 10 hrs. 0 mins. 0 sec.). (ENG.). 2007. audio compact disk 69.99 (978-1-4001-3465-6(X)) Pub: Tantor Media. Dist(s): IngramPubServ

Puppy's First Steps: The Whole-Dog Approach to Raising a Happy, Healthy, Well-Behaved Puppy. unabr. ed. Read by James Boles. 8 CDs. (Running Time: 10 hrs. 0 mins. 0 sec.). (ENG.). 2007. audio compact disk 34.99 (978-1-4001-0465-9(3)) Pub: Tantor Media. Dist(s): IngramPubServ

Puppy's First Steps: The Whole-Dog Approach to Raising a Happy, Healthy, Well-Behaved Puppy. unabr. ed. Read by James Boles. Ed. by Nicholas H. Dodman. 1 MP3-CD. (Running Time: 10 hrs. 0 mins. 0 sec.). (ENG.). 2007. audio compact disk 24.99 (978-1-4001-5465-4(0)) Pub: Tantor Media. Dist(s): IngramPubServ

Puptents & Pebbles: A Nonsense ABC **see Twentieth-Century Poetry in English, No. 30, Recordings of Poets Reading Their Own Poetry**

Purchasing & Negotiations. Gary V. Whetstone. 6 cass. (Running Time: 9 hrs.). (Finance Ser.). 1996. 50.00 (978-1-58866-240-8(3), V1008A) Gary Whet Pub.
In the world, you don't get what you "deserve," you get what you negotiate. Learn how to save thousands of dollars annually & how to walk away with a win-win purchase.

Pure & Holy Passion. Perf. by Glad. 2002. audio compact disk Provident Mus Dist.

Pure As the Lily. unabr. collector's ed. Catherine Cookson. Read by Mary Woods. 7 cass. (Running Time: 10 hrs. 30 mins.). 1985. 56.00 (978-0-7366-0946-3(6), 1889) Books on Tape.
Life was not easy during the Depression. For young Mary Walton, there seemed to be no way out, her father chronically unemployed, her mother a whine, her brother irresponsible. Then Mary became housekeeper for a rich widower & life took on a happier hue.

Pure Attraction. Perf. by Kathy Troccoli. 1 cass. 1991. audio compact disk Brentwood Music.
Kathy's ground-breaking release features the top 5 mainstream radio hit, Everything Changes, as well as the No. 1 Christian radio singles, Love Was Never Meant to Die & Help Myself to You.

Pure Dead Brilliant. unabr. ed. 6 cass. (Running Time: 8 hrs. 30 min). 2003. 58.00 (978-1-4025-6529-8(1)) Recorded Bks.

Pure Dead Magic. unabr. ed. Debi Gliori. Narrated by Ron Keith. 4 pieces. (Running Time: 5 hrs. 30 mins.). (gr. 4 up). 2002. 37.00 (978-1-4025-1024-3(1)) Recorded Bks.
Signor Strega-Borgia is missing, and Signora Strega-Borgia is busy at witch school. The three Strega-Borgia children are in the care of a new too-perfect nanny. Before long, the two older children find themselves in more trouble than they can handle. The trouble begins when 10-year-old Pandora steals one of her mother's magic wands and accidentally shrinks baby Damp, who promptly gets sucked into and lost on the internet. Then they find that their missing father has been kidnapped by their evil uncle, and only the Strega-Borgia children can rescue him. That is, if they manage to avoid a gun-toting assassin in a bunny suit.

Pure Dead Magic. unabr. ed. Debi Gliori. Narrated by Ron Keith. 5 CDs. (Running Time: 5 hrs. 30 mins.). (gr. 4 up). 2002. audio compact disk 48.00 (978-1-4025-1957-4(5)) Recorded Bks.
Not another nanny! The three Strega-Borgia children enjoy having the run of the castle. With father kidnapped by the evil brother and mother taking night classes to become a better witch. Pandora, Titus, and Damp are left to their own wizardry. Well, another nanny can soon be easily dispatched. The moat alligator is still digesting the last one. But when baby Damp is zapped through the Internet by mistake and crazed assassins dressed as bunnies break in, it is the new capable nanny with magic up here sleeve who saves the night.

Pure Dead Wicked. Debi Gliori. Narrated by Ron Keith. 5 pieces. (Running Time: 7 hrs.). (gr. 4 up). 45.00 (978-1-4025-3126-2(5)) Recorded Bks.

Pure Drivel. abr. ed. Steve Martin. Read by Steve Martin. 2 cass. (Running Time: 2 hrs.). 1998. Rental 18.00; audio compact disk Rental 20.00 S&S Audio.
Commentary & hilarious observations by Steve Martin. Highly recommended.

Pure Drivel. unabr. ed. Steve Martin. Read by Steve Martin. 2006. 11.95 (978-0-7435-6381-9(6), Audioworks) Pub: S&S Audio. Dist(s): S and S Inc

Pure Drivel. unabr. ed. Steve Martin. Read by Steve Martin. (Running Time: 22 hrs. 0 mins. 0 sec.). 2007. audio compact disk 14.99 (978-0-7435-7153-1(3)) Pub: S&S Audio. Dist(s): S and S Inc

Pure Ella. Perf. by Ella Fitzgerald. 1 cass., 1 CD. 8.78 (VER 539206); audio compact disk 14.38 CD Jewel box. (VER 539206) NewSound.

***Pure Focus.** Kelly Howell. (ENG.). 2010. audio compact disk 14.95 (978-1-60568-062-0(1)) Brain Sync.

Pure Goldwater. unabr. ed. John W. Dean & Barry M. Goldwater, Jr. Read by Mel Foster. (Running Time: 14 hrs. 30 mins. 0 sec.). (ENG.). 2008. audio compact disk 39.99 (978-1-4001-0736-0(9)) Pub: Tantor Media. Dist(s): IngramPubServ

Pure Goldwater. unabr. ed. John W. Dean & Barry M. Goldwater, Jr. Read by Mel Foster. Narrated by Mel Foster. (Running Time: 14 hrs. 30 mins. 0 sec.). (ENG.). 2008. audio compact disk 29.99 (978-1-4001-5736-5(6)); audio compact disk 79.99 (978-1-4001-3736-7(5)) Pub: Tantor Media. Dist(s): IngramPubServ

Pure Heart, Enlightened Mind: The Zen Journals & Letters of Maura "Soshin" O'Halloran. abr. ed. Maura O'Halloran. Read by Mare Winningham. 2 cass. (Running Time: 3 hrs.). 1996. 17.95 (978-1-57453-048-3(8)) Audio Lit.
The first woman ever admitted to Toshoji Temple eloquently describes the rigors, hardships & ultimate joys of Zen training & temple life.

Pure in Heart. Neville Goddard. 1 cass. (Running Time: 62 min.). 1964. 8.00 (12) J & L Pubns.
Neville taught Imagination Creates Reality. He was a powerfully influential teacher of God as Consciousness.

Pure in Heart. Dallin H. Oaks. 4 cass. 1998. 14.95 Set. (978-1-57008-576-5(5), Bkcraft Inc) Deseret Bk.

Pure in Heart: Psalms 73. Ed Young. 1989. 4.95 (978-0-7417-1754-2(9), 754) Win Walk.

Pure Land. Alan Spence. (Isis Cassettes Ser.). 2007. 84.95 (978-0-7531-3683-6(X)) Pub: ISIS Lrg Prnt GBR. Dist(s): Ulverscroft US

Pure Land. Alan Spence. Read by Robbie Macnab. (Running Time: 43200 sec.). (Isis (CDs) Ser.). 2007. audio compact disk 99.95 (978-0-7531-2657-8(5)) Pub: ISIS Lrg Prnt GBR. Dist(s): Ulverscroft US

Pure Love. Thomas Merton. 1 cass. (Running Time: 60 min.). (St. Bernard Ser.). 8.95 (AA2136) Credence Commun.
Merton explains the great Cistercian mystic's rich & complex notion of pure love.

Pure Meditation. Pema Chödrön. 2 CDs. 2004. audio compact disk 19.95 (978-1-59179-262-8(2), AW00479D) Sounds True.
Listeners learn the art of "Pure Meditation" - the Tibetan path of deeper awareness and fully letting go. An authoritative guide to Tibetan Buddhism's fundamental practice.

Pure Nostalgia. Perf. by Joe Burke. 1 cass.; 9.98; audio compact disk 15.98 CD. Lifedance.
Mr. Burke's buttery-smooth voice & blue-eyed, familiar style recall the 30's & 40's with such songs as "Not for Me," "Call Me Irresponsible," "Corcovado," "Every Time We Say Goodbye," "A Foggy Day," "For All We Know," "Isn't This a Lovely Day," "Nearness of You," "Night & Day," "So Nice to Come Home to," "Someone to Watch over Me," "Stay As Sweet As You Are," "Teach Me Tonight," "They All Laughed" & "Wee Small Hours." Demo CD or cassette available.

Pure of Heart. 2007. audio compact disk (978-1-933919-07-2(8)) Catholic Answers.

***Pure Pleasure: Why Do Christians Feel So Bad about Feeling Good?** Gary L. Thomas. (Running Time: 6 hrs. 12 mins. 0 sec.). (ENG.). 2009. 14.99 (978-0-310-77336-8(9)) Zondervan.

Pure Relaxation. AudioVille Staff. Read by Emma Hignett. (Running Time: 0 hr. 30 mins.). 2005. 16.95 (978-1-59912-932-7(9)) Iofy Corp.

Pure Religion & Bad Company. Perf. by Gary Davis. Anno. by Bruce Bastin. 1 cass. (Running Time: 59 min.). 1991. (0-9307-400350-9307-40035-2-7); audio compact disk (0-9307-40035-2-7) Smithsonian Folkways.
Mixture of gospel vocals & deftly played blues & ragtime instrumentals from the guitar-playing evangelist. Includes "Hesitation Blues" & "Cocaine Blues".

Pure Senses: A Meditative Journey into Sounds & Vision. Edel Classics Staff. 2007. bk. 49.95 (978-3-937406-08-4(5)) Pub: edel CLASS DEU. Dist(s): Natl Bk Netwk

Pure Silence: Lessons in Living & Dying. Mark McCloskey. 2007. 12.75 (978-0-615-16419-9(6)) Puresilence.

***Pure Soapbox: A Cleansing Jolt of Perspective, Motivation, & Humor.** unabr. ed. Kimberlie Dykeman. (Running Time: 3 hrs.). (ENG.). 2010. 17.98 (978-1-59659-509-5(4), GildAudio) Pub: Gildan Media. Dist(s): HachBkGrp

Pure Suit of Happiness see May Swenson

Pure Worship: Refresh. Contrib. by Various Artists & Don Moen. (Pure Worship Ser.). 2008. audio compact disk 7.99 (978-5-557-46122-1(1)) Integrity Music.

Pure Worship: Renew. Contrib. by Various Artists & Don Moen. (Pure Worship Ser.). 2008. audio compact disk 7.99 (978-5-557-46120-7(5)) Integrity Music.

Pure Worship: Restore. Contrib. by Various Artists & Don Moen. (Pure Worship Ser.). 2008. audio compact disk 7.99 (978-5-557-46121-4(3)) Integrity Music.

PureLife: A Different Way of Living. Stephen Swisher & Kellie Copeland Swisher. (ENG.). 2009. audio compact disk 24.95 (978-1-60463-033-6(7)) K Copeland Pubns.

Purest Form of Love. Swami Amar Jyoti. 1 cass. 1980. 9.95 (K-29) Truth Consciousness.
What is love? Where should we start? Effects of pure Love. Revelation & Being. Beyond likes, dislikes & comparisons.

Pureza de la Iglesia: National Association of Evangelicals, 47th Annual Convention, Columbus, Ohio, March 7-9, 1989. Frank Fiorenza. 1 cass. (Workshops Ser.: No. 20-Wednesd). 1989. 4.25 ea. 1-8 tapes.; 4.00 ea. 9 tapes or more. Nat Assn Evan.

***Pureza, Pasion y Perseverancia en el Liderazgo.** Charles R. Swindoll.Tr. of Purity, Passion & Perseverance in Leadership. 2010. audio compact disk 30.00 (978-1-57972-877-9(4)) Insight Living.

Pureza Sexual en un Mundo de Perversion. Marco Barrientos. (SPA.). 2004. 25.00 (978-0-89985-434-2(6)) Christ for the Nations.

Purgatory see Five One Act Plays

Purgatory. Dante Alighieri. Read by Heathcote Williams. Tr. by Benedict Flynn. 3 cass. (Running Time: 4 hrs.). (Divine Comedy Ser.: Pt. 2). 1998. 17.98 (978-962-634-643-3(4), NA314314, Naxos AudioBooks) Naxos.
The second part of Dante's great epic trilogy, The Divine Comedy - ascent the terraces of the Mount of Purgatory to see the penance of the sinful.

Purgatory. abr. unabr. ed. Dante Alighieri. Read by Heathcote Williams. Tr. by Benedict Flynn. 3 CDs. (Running Time: 4 hrs.). (Divine Comedy Ser.: Pt. 2). 1998. audio compact disk 19.98 (978-962-634-143-8(2), NA314312, Naxos AudioBooks) Naxos.
The second part of Dante's great epic trilogy, The Diving Comedy - ascent the terraces of the Mount of Purgatory to see the penance of the sinful.

Purgatory. unabr. ed. Dante Alighieri. Read by Heathcote Williams. Tr. by Benedict Flynn. 4 CDs. audio compact disk 28.98 (978-962-634-316-6(8), NA431612) Naxos.

Purgatory: From the Divine Comedy. unabr. ed. Dante Alighieri. Read by Heathcote Williams. (YA). 2007. 34.99 (978-1-60252-539-9(0)) Find a World.

***Purgatory Hill.** pat mAcdonald & Melaniejane. (ENG.). (C). 2010. audio compact disk 10.00 (978-1-891609-11-4(4)) Pub: Home Brew Pr. Dist(s): Chicago Distribution Ctr

Purgatory River. unabr. ed. Frank Roderus. Read by Michael Taylor. 8 cass. (Running Time: 9 hrs. 18 min.). 2001. 49.95 (978-1-58116-046-8(1)) Books in Motion.
Amid the desolation of the American Southwest ran a river of hope, bringing pioneers to a forbidding land. The Eduardos, young Aaron Smithfield, and Talks-to-Ghosts, a native on a vision quest, all gather along the violent waters of the Purgatory.

Purging Polluted Relationships/NSM. George Bloomer. 2004. audio compact disk 14.95 (978-0-88368-446-7(2)) Whitaker Hse.

***Purging Your House, Pruning Your Family Tree: How to Rid Your Home & Family of Demonic Influence & Generational Depression.** unabr. ed. Perry Stone. Narrated by Jeffrey Kafer. (Running Time: 9 hrs. 30 mins. 0 sec.). (ENG.). 2011. audio compact disk 29.99 (978-1-59859-877-3(5)) Oasis Audio.

Purification Toward Enlightenment. Swami Amar Jyoti. 1 cass. 1995. 9.95 (P-61) Truth Consciousness.
Spiritual practices as part of our lifestyle. Being ready & receptive for God's working. Meditation on the Lotus of Light.

Purified. Contrib. by CeCe Winans et al. 2005. audio compact disk 17.98 (978-5-558-83396-6(3)) Pure SpringG.

Purifying Parental Programming. Michael P. Marshall. Read by Michael P. Marshall. Ed. by Jonathan C. Renaud. Music by Ted Crook. 1 cass. (Running Time: 52 min.). 1995. 9.00 (978-0-912403-03-8(9)) Prod Renaud.
A deep quest into understanding parents & the programs we may have taken on from them when we were children, ideas that may be hindering our full potential as adults. Includes a deep meditation that allows us to search our past for these no-longer-needed childhood programs.

Purifying the Heart. Swami Amar Jyoti. 2 cass. 1979. 12.95 (E-16) Truth Consciousness.
Swamiji's working with disciples. Human love & God's love. Being a genuine disciple. Results of purification.

Puritans & Situation Ethics. Gordon Clark. 1 cass. (Miscellaneous Lectures: No. 1). 5.00 Trinity Found.

Puritans vs. Witches. Paul Jehle. 1 CD. (Running Time: 1 hr. 4 mins.). 2001. audio compact disk 10.00 (978-1-929241-66-8(6)) Pub: Vsn Forum. Dist(s): STL Dist NA
Perhaps the most godly group of Christians to populate North America were the Puritans of New England. Yet no group has been more ruthlessly vilified by modern historians, and no subject more misrepresented than their famous Salem Witch Trials. In this brilliant, scholarly presentation, Dr. Paul Jehle goes beyond the popular rhetoric to expose the truth. He reveals both the wisdom and the failures associated with the Trials, and he makes the case that God used them to lay the foundation for the greatest revival in American history - the Great Awakening.

Puritans vs. Witches. Speeches. Paul Jehle. 1 cass. (Running Time: 1 hr. 4 mins.). 2001. 7.00 (978-1-929241-26-2(7)) Pub: Vsn Forum. Dist(s): STL Dist NA

Purity: Door to the Kingdom of God. Swami Amar Jyoti. 1 cass. 1991. 12.95 (M-84) Truth Consciousness.
Purification of body, mind, heart & soul - the process, stages & results. Crossing the ultimate barrier. On prayer.

Purity & the Dragon Lady. Based on a book by H. McCormick. Narrated by Ephraim/ L. McCormick. (YA). 2009. audio compact disk 15.00 (978-0-9818619-7-5(0)) TBT Pub.

Purity Code: Conversations with Youth Experts. Jim Burns. (Running Time: 2 hrs. 20 mins.). (Pure Foundations Ser.). 2008. audio compact disk 14.99 (978-0-7642-0547-7(1)) Pub: Bethany Hse. Dist(s): Baker Pub Grp

Purity in an Impure Age. 2003. 6.95 (978-1-932631-08-1(9)); audio compact disk 6.95 (978-1-932631-09-8(7)) Ascensn Pr.

Purity in Death. abr. ed. J. D. Robb, pseud. Read by Susan Ericksen. (Running Time: 6 hrs.). (In Death Ser.). 2007. audio compact disk 14.99 (978-1-4233-1752-4(1), 9781423317524, BCD Value Price) Brilliance Audio.

Purity in Death. abr. unabr. ed. J. D. Robb, pseud. Read by Susan Ericksen. 7 cass. (Running Time: 10 hrs.). (In Death Ser.:). 2002. 82.25 (978-1-58788-690-4(1), 1587886901, Unabridge Lib Edns) Brilliance Audio.

Purity in Death. unabr. ed. J. D. Robb, pseud. Read by Susan Ericksen. 7 cass. (Running Time: 10 hrs.). (In Death Ser.:). 2002. 30.95 (978-1-58788-689-8(8), 1587886898, BAU) Brilliance Audio.

Purity in Death. unabr. ed. J. D. Robb, pseud. Read by Susan Ericksen. (Running Time: 10 hrs.). (In Death Ser.). 2004. 39.25 (978-1-59335-434-3(7), 1593354347, Brlnc Audio MP3 Lib) Brilliance Audio.

Purity in Death. unabr. ed. J. D. Robb, pseud. Read by Susan Ericksen. (Running Time: 10 hrs.). (In Death Ser.). 2004. 39.25 (978-1-59710-614-6(3), 1597106143, BADLE); 24.95 (978-1-59710-615-3(1), 1597106151, BAD) Brilliance Audio.

Purity in Death. unabr. ed. J. D. Robb, pseud. Read by Susan Ericksen. (Running Time: 10 hrs.). (In Death Ser.). 2007. audio compact disk 36.95 (978-1-4233-1749-4(1), 9781423317494, Bril Audio CD Unabri); audio compact disk 97.25 (978-1-4233-1750-0(5), 9781423317500, BriAudCD Unabrid) Brilliance Audio.

Purity in Death. unabr. ed. J. D. Robb, pseud. Read by Susan Ericksen. (Running Time: 10 hrs.). (In Death Ser.). 2004. 24.95 (978-1-59335-122-9(4), 1593351224) Soulmate Audio Bks.
Louie Cogburn had spent three days holed up in his apartment, staring at his computer screen. His pounding headache was unbearable - like spikes drilling into his brain. And it was getting worse. Finally, when someone knocked at his door, Louie picked up a baseball bat, opened the door, and started swinging... The first cop on the scene fired his stunner twice and Louie died instantly. Detective Eve Dallas has taken over the investigation, but there's nothing to explain the man's sudden rage or death. The only clue is a bizarre message left on his computer screen: Absolute Purity Achieved. And when a second man dies under nearly identical circumstances, Dallas starts racking her brain for answers and for courage to face the impossible...that this might be a computer virus able to spread from machine to man.

Purity of Nature. Swami Jyotirmayananda. 1 cass. (Running Time: 1 hr.). 1990. 12.99 Yoga Res Foun.

Purity of Sound: An Acoustic Recording of Singing Bowls for Meditation. Perf. by Rainer Tillman. 1 cass. (Running Time: 69 min.). 10.00 (978-1-57863-061-5(4), Red) Red Wheel Weiser.
Tillman masterfully creates a continuous tapestry of sound on Tibetan singing bowls. This recording contains naturally occurring sound wave frequencies to relax brain activity. Along with singing bowls, other instruments included in this recording are bells, cymbals, sound plates, gongs, chimes & flutes. Great for meditation, yoga, massage, reading or any creative activity.

Purity of the Lotus. Swami Amar Jyoti. 1 cass. 1991. 9.95 (K-139) Truth Consciousness.
Purity, symbolized by the lotus, awakens love & devotion. Sublimity of purity. Meditation on the light filled lotus in the heart.

Purity, Passion & Perseverance in Leadership see Pureza, Pasion y Perseverancia en el Liderazgo

Purity Principle: God's Safeguards for Life's Dangerous Trails. unabr. ed. Randy C. Alcorn. Narrated by Lloyd James. 2 CDs. (Running Time: 2 hrs. 18 mins. 0 sec.). (ENG.). 2005. audio compact disk 15.98 (978-1-59644-232-0(8), Hovel Audio) christianaud.

***Purity Principle: God's Safeguards for Life's Dangerous Trails.** unabr. ed. Randy Alcorn. Narrated by Lloyd James. (ENG.). 2005. 9.98 (978-1-59644-233-7(6), Hovel Audio) christianaud.

Purloined Corn Popper. E. W. Hildick. Illus. by E. W. Hildick. 2000. 9.95 (978-0-87499-613-5(9)); 9.95 (978-0-87499-614-2(7)); 9.95 (978-0-87499-615-9(5)) Live Oak Media.

Purloined Corn Popper. unabr. ed. E. W. Hildick. Read by Carol Jordan Stewart. 3 cass. (Running Time: 4 hrs., 30 min.). (Felicity Snell Mystery Ser.). (J). (gr. 1-8). 1999. 23.95 (OAK 003, Chivers Child Audio) AudioGO.

Purloined Corn Popper. unabr. ed. E. W. Hildick. Read by Carol Jordan Stewart. 3 cass. (Running Time: 4 hrs. 11 mins.). (Felicity Snell Mystery Ser.: No. 1). (J). (gr. 4-7). 2000. 23.95 (978-0-87499-560-2(4), OAK003) Pub: Live Oak Media. Dist(s): AudioGO
In this first book in the series, Tim Kowalski & Freddie Fisher meet Felicity Snell, junior librarian & former private detective. Tim's mother's popcorn popper, where she kept her "tip money," is discovered missing. Under Felicity's wise direction, the boys learn the skills to solve the mystery & uncover the thief.

Purloined Corn Popper: A Felicity Snell Mystery. unabr. ed. E. W. Hildick. Read by Carol Jordan Stewart. 3 vols. (Running Time: 4 hrs. 11 mins.). (J). (gr. 4-7). 2000. bk. 38.95 (978-0-87499-558-9(2)) Live Oak Media.
Tim Kowalski & Freddie Fisher meet Felicity Snell, junior librarian & former private detective. Tim's mother's popcorn popper, where she kept her "tip money," is discovered missing. Under Felicity's wise direction, the boys learn the skills to solve the mystery & uncover the thief.

Purloined Letter see Classic Detective Stories, Vol. II, A Collection

Purloined Letter see Best of Edgar Allan Poe

Purloined Letter see Three Tales of Mystery

Purloined Letter. Edgar Allan Poe. 1977. (D-1) Jimcin Record.

Purloined Letter: Abridged. (ENG.). 2007. (978-1-60339-037-8(5)); cd-rom & audio compact disk (978-1-60339-038-5(3)) Listenr Digest.

Purloined Letter & Other Works. abr. ed. Edgar Allan Poe. Perf. by Anthony Quayle. 1 cass. Incl. Dream Within a Dream. (CPN 1288); Ulalume. (CPN 1288); Valley of Unrest. (CPN 1288); (J). 1984. 9.95 (978-1-55994-101-3(4), CPN 1288) HarperCollins Pubs.

Purple Cane Road. abr. ed. James Lee Burke. Read by Will Patton. (Dave Robicheaux Ser.). 2004. 15.95 (978-0-7435-4828-1(0)) Pub: S&S Audio. Dist(s): S and S Inc

Purple Cane Road. unabr. ed. James Lee Burke. Read by Nick Sullivan. 10 vols. (Running Time: 11 hrs. 40 min.). (Dave Robicheaux Ser.). 2000. bk. 84.95 (978-0-7927-2395-0(3), CSL 284, Chivers Sound Lib) AudioGO.
Dave Robicheaux has spent his life confronting the age-old adage that the sins of the father pass on to the son. Dead to him since his youth, his mother, Mae Guillory, has been shuttered away in the deep recess of Robicheaux's mind. Dave is stunned when a pimp looks at him & asks if he is the son of Mae Guillory, the whore a bunch of cops murdered thirty years ago.

Purple Cane Road. unabr. ed. James Lee Burke. Read by Nick Sullivan. 10 CDs. (Running Time: 15 hrs.). (Dave Robicheaux Ser.). 2001. audio compact disk 94.95 (978-0-7927-9909-2(7), SLD 060, Chivers Sound Lib) AudioGO.

Purple Climbing Days. unabr. ed. Patricia Reilly Giff. Read by Suzanne Toren. 1 cass. (Running Time: 1 hr. 2 mins.). (Follow the Reader Ser.). (J). (gr. 1-2). 1985. pap. bk. 17.00 incl. bk. & guide. (978-0-8072-0106-0(5), FTR108SP, Listening Lib) Random Audio Pubg.
Follow the kids of Ms. Rooney's second grade class as they learn & grow through an entire school year filled with fun & surprises. Corresponding Month: May.

Purple Cow: Transform Your Business by Being Remarkable. unabr. ed. Seth Godin. Read by Seth Godin. (Running Time: 3 hrs.). (ENG.). 2009. 9.98 (978-1-59659-391-6(1), GildAudio) Pub: Gildan Media. Dist(s): HachBkGrp

Purple Cow, Goops & More Goops. abr. ed. Gelett Burgess. Perf. by Carol Channing. 1 cass. (J). 1985. 8.98 (978-0-89845-151-1(5), CP 1656) HarperCollins Pubs.
Rhythm, music & humor perfect for developing listening skills.

Purple Decades. unabr. ed. Tom Wolfe. Read by Christopher Hurt. 11 cass. (Running Time: 16 hrs. 30 min.). 1988. 88.00 (978-0-7366-1428-3(1), 2314) Books on Tape.
Features the author's essays, articles & chapters from previous collections. From architecture to astronauts, from Upper West Side to Lower East Side, he identifies the trends of the recent past.

Purple Emperor. unabr. ed. Herbie Brennan. Narrated by Gerard Doyle. 11 CDs. (Running Time: 12 hrs. 25 mins.). (YA). 2005. audio compact disk 111.75 (978-1-4193-4711-5(X), C3356); 81.75 (978-1-4025-9529-5(8), 97780) Recorded Bks.
The emperor of the enchanted Faerie Realm has been murdered and now Pyrgus, his son, is the Emperor Elect. As Pyrgus contemplates his new responsibilities as emperor, his father's body is stolen! Hairstreak, evil leader of the Faeries of the Night, and his wicked henchmen have resurrected it as a zombie and plan to take control of the kingdom. Pyrgus and his courageous sister Holly Blue are banished from the realm and stripped of their magical powers. Herbie Brennan, author of more than 90 books, has been published in over 50 countries. This sequel to Faerie Wars (RB# 97634), a New York Times best-seller, is packed with demons and mystical creatures that will enthrall fantasy fans.

Purple Gorilla. unabr. ed. Richard D. Lansing, Jr.. Read by Richard D. Lansing, Jr. 1 cass. (Running Time: 21 min.). (J). 1997. pap. bk. 10.00 (978-0-9661844-2-6(4)); 6.00 (978-0-9661844-1-9(6)) Purple Gorilla.
A storyteller's car breaks down in the Okefenokee Swamp & is offered shelter in a home whose owner cautions storyteller, "Do not touch my purple gorilla".

Purple Pig, Vol. 1. Lyrics by Janet Smith Post. Voice by Jim Post. 1 C D. (J). 2000. audio compact disk 20.00 (978-0-9702826-1-3(3)) BTSBRBE.

Purple Place for Dying. unabr. collector's ed. John D. MacDonald. Read by Michael Prichard. 6 cass. (Running Time: 6 hrs.). (Travis McGee Ser.: Vol. 3). 1977. 36.00 (978-0-7366-0052-1(3), 1064) Books on Tape.
Travis McGee is a witness to a murder he can't prove & a kidnapping nobody believes. McGee becomes a pawn between a wealthy Southwestern patriarch, the law & a mysterious gang bent on insurance fraud.

Purple Socks & Other Toe Tingling Stories. unabr. ed. Short Stories. Perf. by Naomi Leithold. 1 cass. (Running Time: 50 mins.). (J). 1994. 10.00 (978-0-9701891-0-3(9)) Simply Storytelling.
Eight original, interactive stories for young children.

***Purple Testament.** 2010. audio compact disk (978-1-59171-234-3(3)) Falcon Picture.

***Purplicious.** unabr. ed. Victoria Kann & Elizabeth Kann. Read by Kathleen Mcinerney. Illus. by Victoria Kann. (ENG.). 2008. (978-0-06-172879-2(9)); (978-0-06-172959-1(0)) HarperCollins Pubs.

Purpose & Power in Retirement: New Opportunities for Meaning & Significance. Harold G. Koenig. 6 CDs. (Running Time: 7 hours). 2005. audio compact disk 14.95 (978-1-932031-87-4(1)) Pub: Templeton Pr. Dist(s): Chicago Distribution Ctr

Purpose by Design. Contrib. by Fred Hammond & Radical for Christ et al. Prod. by Fred Hammond & Paul Wright, III. 2007. 14.98 (978-5-557-92789-5(1), Verity) Brentwood Music.

Purpose-Driven Church: Growth Without Compromising Your Message & Mission. abr. ed. Rick Warren. (Running Time: 2 hrs. 25 mins. 0 sec.). (ENG.). 2003. 10.99 (978-0-310-26089-9(2)) Zondervan.

Purpose-Driven Church: Growth Without Compromising Your Message & Mission. unabr. ed. Rick Warren. 1999. 39.99 (978-0-310-22901-8(4)) Zondervan.

Purpose-Driven Church: Growth Without Compromising Your Message & Mission. unabr. ed. Rick Warren. (Running Time: 10 hrs. 12 mins. 0 sec.). (ENG.). 2003. 14.99 (978-0-310-26169-8(4)) Zondervan.

Purpose Driven Life. Rick Warren. 2005. 39.99 (978-1-59895-009-0(6)) Find a World.

Purpose Driven Life. Rick Warren. 2006. cd-rom 39.99 (978-1-59895-473-9(3)) Find a World.

Purpose Driven Life. unabr. ed. Rick Warren. Read by Rick Warren. (YA). 2005. 49.99 (978-1-59895-133-2(5)) Find a World.

Purpose Driven Life - For Commuters: What on Earth Am I Here For? abr. ed. Rick Warren. (Running Time: 9 hrs. 8 mins. 0 sec.). (ENG.). 2005. 11.99 (978-0-310-27069-0(3)) Zondervan.

Purpose Driven Life - For Commuters: What on Earth Am I Here For? abr. unabr. ed. Rick Warren. 4 CDs. (Running Time: 5 hrs. 0 mins. 0 sec.). (ENG.). 2005. audio compact disk 19.99 (978-0-310-25897-1(9)) Zondervan.

Purpose Driven Life - For Commuters: What on Earth Am I Here For? unabr. ed. Rick Warren. 7 CDs. (Running Time: 9 hrs. 8 mins. 0 sec.). (Purpose Driven Life Ser.). (ENG.). 2002. audio compact disk 34.99 (978-0-310-24788-3(8)) Zondervan.

Purpose Driven Life Commuter Audio Clip Strip - Levy. Zondervan Publishing Staff. 2005. audio compact disk 199.90 (978-0-310-60422-8(2)) Zondervan.

Purpose Driven Prayer CD. Karen Rebekah Sewell Bowen. (ENG.). 2005. audio compact disk 8.00 (978-0-9760730-0-0(5)) His Spt.

***Purpose DrivenÂ(r) Youth Ministry: 9 Essential Foundations for Healthy Growth.** unabr. ed. Doug Fields. (Running Time: 8 hrs. 21 mins. 0 sec.). (ENG.). 2009. 14.99 (978-0-310-30262-9(5)) Zondervan.

***Purpose-Filled Presentations: How Any Christian Can Communicate More Effectively to Anybody, Anytime, Anywhere.** unabr. ed. Tony Jeary. Narrated by Michael Koontz. (ENG.). 2009. 14.98 (978-1-59644-838-4(5)); audio compact disk 24.98 (978-1-59644-837-7(7)) christianaud.

Purpose for Man & Creation. Myles Munroe. 4 cass. 1992. 25.00 Set. (978-1-56043-909-7(2)) Destiny Image Pubs.

Purpose in Prayer. E. M. Bounds. Read by Scott Harrison. 3 cass. (Running Time: 5 hrs. 30 mins.). 1999. 23.95 (978-0-7861-1594-5(7), 2423) Blckstn Audio.

Purpose in Prayer. unabr. ed. E. M. Bounds. Read by Scott Harrison. (Running Time: 4 hrs. 0 mins.). 2008. 19.95 (978-1-4332-5032-3(2)); audio compact disk 40.00 (978-1-4332-5031-6(4)) Blckstn Audio.

***Purpose of Christmas.** unabr. ed. Rick Warren. Read by Rick Warren. 2 cass. (Running Time: 1 hr. 45 mins.). 2009. 25.75 (978-1-4407-2885-3(2)); audio compact disk 30.75 (978-1-4407-2886-0(0)) Recorded Bks.

Purpose of Christmas. unabr. ed. Rick Warren. Read by Rick Warren. 2 CDs. (Running Time: 2 hrs. 30 mins. 0 sec.). (ENG.). 2008. audio compact disk 19.99 (978-0-7435-8178-3(4)) Pub: S&S Audio. Dist(s): S and S Inc

***Purpose of Christmas.** unabr. collector's ed. Rick Warren. Read by Rick Warren. 2 CDs. (Running Time: 1 hr. 45 mins.). 2009. audio compact disk 22.95 (978-1-4407-2887-7(9)) Recorded Bks.

Purpose of Christmas Curriculum, Kit. Rick Warren. 2008. audio compact disk 19.99 (978-0-310-94212-2(8)) Zondervan.

Purpose of Evil. Jean Munzer. 2 cass. (Running Time: 2 hrs. 30 min.). 1992. 19.95 set. (978-1-57124-000-2(4)) Creat Seminars.
Understanding God's plan for humanity.

Purpose of His Coming: Why Jesus Christ was Born. Chuck Smith. (ENG.). 2000. audio compact disk 18.99 (978-1-932941-35-7(5)) Word For Today.

Purpose of Human Relationships. Asha Praver. 1 cass. (Running Time: 90 min.). (Relationships Ser.). 9.95 (AT-50) Crystal Clarity.
Explains: Why personal responsibility is the foundation for a spiritual approach to relationships; unconditional love as the main lesson of life; how human relationships reflect our relationship with God; using prayer to build relationships.

Purpose of Life According to World Renowned Psychic, Edgar Cayce. Stephen Hawley Martin. 2008. 2.95 (978-1-892538-26-0(1)) Pub: Oaklea Pr. Dist(s): Midpt Trade

Purpose of Life & Manner of Attaining It. Swami Jyotirmayananda. 1 cass. (Running Time: 1 hr.). 1990. 12.99 Yoga Res Foun.

Purpose of Meditation. Swami Amar Jyoti. 1 cass. 1980. 9.95 (I-14) Truth Consciousness.
Stages in meditation; where real meditation starts. Meditation is the key secret to realizing God.

Purpose of Prosperity. Speeches. Creflo A. Dollar. 4 cass. (Running Time: 5 hrs.). 2003. 20.00 (978-1-59089-800-0(1)); audio compact disk 28.00 (978-1-59089-801-7(X)) Creflo Dollar.

Purpose of the Church. Myles Munroe. 6 cass. 1993. 35.00 Set. (978-1-56043-913-4(0)) Destiny Image Pubs.

Purpose of the Church: Logos Feburary 22, 1998. Ben Young. 1998. 4.95 (978-0-7417-6074-6(6), B0074) Win Walk.

Purpose of the Female (Man) Myles Munroe. 10 cass. 1992. 48.00 Set. (978-1-56043-910-3(6)) Destiny Image Pubs.

Purpose of the Holy Spirit Series, Set. Elbert Willis. 4 cass. 13.00 Set. Fill the Gap.

Purpose of the Male (Man) Myles Munroe. 8 cass. 1992. 42.00 Set. (978-1-56043-911-0(4)) Destiny Image Pubs.

Purpose of the Past: Reflections on the Uses of History. unabr. ed. Gordon S. Wood. Read by Malcolm Hillgartner. (Running Time: 39600 sec.). 2008. 29.95 (978-1-4332-1005-1(3)); 65.95 (978-1-4332-1003-7(7)); audio compact disk 29.95 (978-1-4332-1006-8(1)); audio compact disk & audio compact disk 29.95 (978-1-4332-1007-5(X)); audio compact disk & audio compact disk 81.00 (978-1-4332-1004-4(5)) Blckstn Audio.

Purpose of the Past: Reflections on the Uses of History. unabr. ed. Gordon S. Wood. Read by Malcolm Hillgartner. (YA). 2008. 64.99 (978-1-60514-793-2(1)) Find a World.

Purposes of Prayer: Exploring the Purpose & Place of Prayer & Prophecy. Lynne Hammond. 2 CDs. 2006. audio compact disk 10.00 (978-1-57399-356-2(5)) Mac Hammond.

Purr... Fect Skills: Social Skills Keystage 1. rev. ed. Tina Rae. 2000. 55.95 (978-1-873942-18-5(4)) Pub: P Chapman GBR. Dist(s): SAGE

Purrfect Murder. Rita Mae Brown & Sneaky Pie Brown. Narrated by Kate Forbes. (Running Time: 30600 sec.). (Mrs. Murphy Mystery Ser.). 2008. audio compact disk 34.99 (978-1-4281-8090-1(7)) Recorded Bks.

Purrfect Murder. unabr. ed. Rita Mae Brown & Sneaky Pie Brown. Narrated by Kate Forbes. (Running Time: 8 hrs.). (Mrs. Murphy Mystery Ser.). 2008. 56.75 (978-1-4361-0248-3(0)); 72.75 (978-1-4281-8091-8(5)); audio compact disk 102.75 (978-1-4281-8093-2(1)) Recorded Bks.
This 16th entry in the wildly popular Mrs. Murphy mystery series finds Harry Haristeen and the peaceable residents of Crozet, Virginia, busily preparing their gardens and homes for winter. When wealthy Carla Paulson begins plotting her extravagant new home, she ruffles more than a few feathers. Soon Carla is stabbed to death, and standing over her with knife in hand is one of Harry's good friends.

Purse-onality CD. 1 cd. (Running Time: 79 mins). 2005. 14.99 (978-0-9776153-3-9(2)) Bluebonn Hills.

Pursued by Shadows. unabr. ed. Medora Sale. Read by Lynda Evans. (Inspector John Sanders Mystery Ser.). 2001. 49.95 (978-1-55686-918-1(5)) Books in Motion.
When the wife of a prosperous artist flees not only with his child, but also a valuable document, inspector John Sanders and Harriet Jeffries find themselves among people willing to kill.

Pursuing Excellence. unabr. ed. Perf. by Eknath Easwaran. 1 cass. (Running Time: 1 hr.). 1984. 7.95 (978-1-58638-595-8(X)) Nilgiri Pr.

Pursuing His Presence Series. Tommy Tenney. 3 cass. (Running Time: 4 hrs. 30 mins.). 1999. 19.99 (978-0-7684-0193-6(3)) Destiny Image Pubs.

Pursuing Love: Hos. 2:1-23. Ed Young. 1988. 4.95 (978-0-7417-1651-4(8), 651) Win Walk.

Pursuing Wisdom. Jack Deere. 1 cass. (Running Time: 90 mins.). (Proverbs Ser.: Vol. 8). 2000. 5.00 (JD08-008) Morning NC.
Practical wisdom for everyday living is brought to life in Jack's thorough exposition of this important book of the Bible.

Pursuit see Twentieth-Century Poetry in English, No. 4, Recordings of Poets Reading Their Own Poetry

Pursuit. abr. ed. Johanna Lindsey. Read by Michael Page. 5 CDs. (Running Time: 4 hrs.). (Sherring Cross Ser.). 2002. audio compact disk 61.25 (978-1-59086-018-2(7), 1590860187, CD Lib Edit) Brilliance Audio.
What was to be a grand adventure for Melissa MacGregor - an escape from the wilds of her Scottish home into the whirl of the London social scene - seems to pale before the promise in the passionate gaze of Lincoln Ross Burnett. Though they exchange but a few words before parting after a chance encounter on her grandfather's lands, Melissa instantly knows this bold stranger is her destiny, while Lincoln realizes his heart has been claimed forever and he will never be complete until Melissa MacGregor is his bride. But there are serious obstacles impeding the well-smitten Viscount Cambury's pursuit of glorious romance: sixteen of them - all big and brawny, six named Ian and all named MacFearson. The bane of Lincoln's youth, Melissa's stifling, disapproving uncles are now determined to rob him of his newfound happiness. Yet he is equally resolved to confront the peril - and to pursue his exquisite obsession all the way to London. . . and to the ends of the earth, if necessary.

Pursuit. abr. ed. Johanna Lindsey. Read by Michael Page. 4 CDs. (Running Time: 4 hrs.). (Sherring Cross Ser.). 2004. audio compact disk 14.99 (978-1-59355-667-9(5), 1593556675) Brilliance Audio.

Pursuit. abr. ed. Karen Robards. Read by Franette Liebow. 5 CDs. (Running Time: 6 hrs.). 2009. audio compact disk 26.99 (978-1-4233-6839-7(8), 9781423368397, BACD) Brilliance Audio.

Pursuit. abr. ed. Karen Robards. Read by Franette Liebow. (Running Time: 6 hrs.). 2010. audio compact disk 14.99 (978-1-4233-6850-2(9), 9781423368502, BCD Value Price) Brilliance Audio.

Pursuit. unabr. ed. Robert L. Fish. Read by Dan Lazar. 10 cass. (Running Time: 15 hrs.). 80.00 (978-0-7366-0438-3(3), 1407) Books on Tape.
The year is 1944. The German defense is collapsing. As the Allies cross into Poland, Colonel Helmut Von Schraeder, the "Monster" of the Miadanek death camp, uses plastic surgery to assume the identity of a Jewish prisoner & escape retribution.

Pursuit. unabr. ed. Johanna Lindsey. Read by Michael Page. 7 cass. (Running Time: 8 hrs.). (Sherring Cross Ser.). 2002. 29.95 (978-1-59086-014-4(4), 1590860144, BAU); 69.25 (978-1-59086-015-1(2), 1590860152, Unabridge Lib Edns) Brilliance Audio.
What was to be a grand adventure for Melissa MacGregor - an escape from the wilds of her Scottish home into the whirl of the London social scene - seems to pale before the promise in the passionate gaze of Lincoln Ross Burnett. Though they exchange but a few words before parting after a chance encounter on her grandfather's lands, Melissa instantly knows this bold stranger is her destiny, while Lincoln realizes his heart has been claimed forever and he will never be complete until Melissa MacGregor is his bride. But there are serious obstacles impeding the well-smitten Viscount Cambury's pursuit of glorious romance: sixteen of them - all big and brawny, six named Ian and all named MacFearson. The bane of Lincoln's youth, Melissa's stifling, disapproving uncles are now determined to rob him of his newfound happiness. Yet he is equally resolved to confront the peril - and to pursue his exquisite obsession all the way to London. . . and to the ends of the earth, if necessary.

Pursuit. unabr. ed. Johanna Lindsey. Read by Michael Page. (Running Time: 9 hrs.). (Sherring Cross Ser.). 2004. 39.25 (978-1-59335-402-2(9), 1593354029, Brinc Audio MP3 Lib) Brilliance Audio.

Pursuit. unabr. ed. Johanna Lindsey. Read by Michael Page. (Running Time: 8 hrs.). 2004. 39.25 (978-1-59710-617-7(8), 1597106178, BADLE); 24.95 (978-1-59710-616-0(X), 159710616X, BAD) Brilliance Audio.

Pursuit. unabr. ed. Johanna Lindsey. Read by Michael Page. (Running Time: 9 hrs.). (Sherring Cross Ser.). 2009. audio compact disk 92.97 (978-1-4233-6609-6(3), 9781423366096, BriAudCD Unabrid); audio compact disk 19.99 (978-1-4233-6608-9(5), 9781423366089, Bril Audio CD Unabri) Brilliance Audio.

Pursuit. unabr. ed. Johanna Lindsey. Read by Michael Page. (Running Time: 9 hrs.). (Sherring Cross Ser.). 2004. 24.95 (978-1-59335-147-2(X), 159335147X) Soulmate Audio Bks.

Pursuit. unabr. ed. Thomas Perry. Read by Tom Weiner. (Running Time: 45000 sec.). 2006. 72.95 (978-0-7861-4958-2(2)); audio compact disk 90.00 (978-0-7861-5835-5(2)); audio compact disk 29.95 (978-0-7861-6972-6(9)) Blckstn Audio.

Pursuit. unabr. ed. Karen Robards. Read by Franette Liebow. 1 MP3-CD. (Running Time: 12 hrs.). 2009. 39.97 (978-1-4233-6842-7(8), 9781423368427, Brinc Audio MP3 Lib); 39.97 (978-1-4233-6852-6(5), 9781423368526, BADLE); 24.99 (978-1-4233-6830-4(4), 9781423368304, Brilliance MP3); 24.99 (978-1-4233-6851-9(7), 9781423368519, BAD); audio compact disk 107.97 (978-1-4233-6841-0(X), 9781423368410, BriAudCD Unabrid); audio compact disk 38.99 (978-1-4233-6838-0(X), 9781423368380, Bril Audio CD Unabri) Brilliance Audio.

Pursuit: The Sinking of the Bismarck. unabr. ed. Ludovic Kennedy. Read by Ludovic Kennedy. 8 cass. (Running Time: 12 hrs.). 2002. 69.95 (978-0-7540-0754-8(5), CAB 2176) AudioGO.
In May 1941, the German battleship Bismarck headed out into the North Atlantic to raid Allied shipping. Found and shadowed by British cruisers, she was engaged by the Hood and the Prince of Wales. Within minutes she had sunk the former, the pride of the Royal Navy and damaged the latter. The Bismarck was attacked by Swordfish of the Fleet Air Arm, lost and then relocated, attacked once more and disabled. Now there was no choice for the pride of the Kriegsmarine but to run for safety and the French port of Brest. But then the battleships Rodney and King George V caught up with her.

***Pursuit: When Man Hunts Man.** Perf. by Tom DeCorsia & Ben Wright. 2010. audio compact disk 18.95 (978-1-57019-926-4(4)) Radio Spirits.

***Pursuit-ABR.** Johanna Lindsey & #3 Sherring Cross Series. 2010. audio compact disk 9.99 (978-1-4418-5641-8(2)) Brilliance Audio.

Pursuit & the Passion: The Joys of Living by Grace. 2004. 7.00 (978-1-57972-621-8(6)); audio compact disk 7.00 (978-1-57972-620-1(8)) Insight Living.

Pursuit of God: The Human Thirst for the Divine. unabr. ed. A. W. Tozer. 3 CDs. (Running Time: 3 hrs. 0 mins. 0 sec.). (ENG.). 2006. audio compact disk 21.98 (978-1-59644-421-8(5), Hovel Audio) christianaud.

***Pursuit of God: The Human Thirst for the Divine.** unabr. ed. A. w. Tozer. Narrated by Grover Gardner. (ENG.). 2006. 12.98 (978-1-59644-422-5(3), Hovel Audio) christianaud.

Pursuit of Happiness: And Other Sobering Thoughts. unabr. ed. George F. Will. Narrated by George F. Will. 2 cass. (Running Time: 2 hrs.). 1982. 18.00 (978-1-55690-428-8(2), 82047E7) Recorded Bks.
From presidents past to the Chicago Cubs, columnist George Will cuts to the quick every time. The opinions are provoking, the arguments never less than steel trap.

***Pursuit of Happyness.** abr. ed. Chris Gardner. Read by Andre Blake. (ENG.). 2006. (978-0-06-119058-2(6), Harper Audio); (978-0-06-119045-2(4), Harper Audio) HarperCollins Pubs.

Pursuit of Happyness. abr. ed. Chris Gardner. Read by Andre Blake. 5 CDs. (Running Time: 21600 sec.). 2006. audio compact disk 29.95 (978-0-06-089788-8(0), Harper Audio) HarperCollins Pubs.

***Pursuit of Holiness.** unabr. ed. Gerald Bridges & Jerry Bridges. Narrated by Arthur Morey. (Running Time: 4 hrs. 15 mins. 0 sec.). (ENG.). 2009. audio compact disk 15.98 (978-1-59644-841-4(5)) christianaud.

***Pursuit of Holiness.** unabr. ed. Jerry Bridges. Narrated by Arthur Morey. (ENG.). 2009. 9.98 (978-1-59644-842-1(3)) christianaud.

Pursuit of Honor. abr. ed. Vince Flynn. Read by Armand Schultz. (Running Time: 6 hrs. 0 mins. 0 sec.). 2009. audio compact disk 29.99 (978-0-7435-9681-7(1)) Pub: S&S Audio. Dist(s): S and S Inc

Pursuit of Honor. unabr. ed. Vince Flynn. Read by George Guidall. 11 CDs. (Running Time: 12 hrs. 0 mins. 0 sec.). 2009. audio compact disk 49.99 (978-0-7435-9683-1(8)) Pub: S&S Audio. Dist(s): S and S Inc

Pursuit of Intimacy Vol. 1: Exploring the Excellency of Knowing God. Mac Hammond. 5 cass. 2004. 25.00 (978-1-57399-145-2(7)); audio compact disk 25.00 (978-1-57399-144-5(9)) Mac Hammond.
Do you know God or do you just know about Him? Mac Hammond reveals truths about the intimacy that each one of us can pursue with our Creator. Leave religious ritual behind and start your journey toward a deeper relationship with your Heavenly Father by listening and applying the principles taught in this inspiring series of messages. It's time to begin your...pursuit of intimacy!.

Pursuit of Intimacy Vol. 2: Learning to Reflect the Heart of the Father. Mac Hammond. 5 cds. (Running Time: 5 hours). 2005. audio compact disk 25.00 (978-1-57399-195-7(3)) Mac Hammond.
Do you want the Word of God to come alive in your life? Do you want to alter your wrong behavior? Do you want to generate more hunger and affection for God? If you answered yes to any of these questions, this series is for you. In it, Mac Hammond examines the biblical example of pursuing intimacy that is found in the Song of Solomon, plus he illuminates the importance of understanding God's boundless love for each one of us.

Pursuit of Intimacy Volume 2: Learning to Reflect the Heart of the Father. Mac Hammond. 5 cass. (Running Time: 5 hours). 2005. 12.50 (978-1-57399-194-0(5)) Mac Hammond.

Pursuit of Justice. Willard Boyd Gardner. 3 cass. 2004. 14.95 (978-1-59156-155-2(8)); audio compact disk 14.95 (978-1-59156-166-8(3)) Covenant Comms.

***Pursuit of Justice.** unabr. ed. Mimi Latt. Read by Laural Merlington. (Running Time: 12 hrs.). 2010. 24.99 (978-1-4418-4157-5(1), 9781441841575, Brilliance MP3); 39.97 (978-1-4418-4158-2(X), 9781441841582, Brinc Audio MP3 Lib); 39.97 (978-1-4418-4160-5(1), 9781441841605, BADLE); 24.99 (978-1-4418-4159-9(8), 9781441841599, BAD) Brilliance Audio.

Pursuit of Knowledge: Prov. 2:3-6. Ed Young. 1992. 4.95 (978-0-7417-1905-8(3), 905) Win Walk.

Pursuit of Love. unabr. ed. Nancy Mitford. Read by Rosemary Davis. 8 cass. (Running Time: 9 hrs.). 2001. 69.95 (978-1-85089-837-5(5), 40891) Pub: ISIS Audio GBR. Dist(s): Ulverscroft US
Childhood at Alconleigh was scanty preparation for the realities of the outside world. And Linda, sweetest & most aimless of the Radletts, fell prey to a stuffy banker & a rabid communist before she found her ideal in a Frenchman.

***Pursuit of Meaning.** Featuring Ravi Zacharias. 1987. audio compact disk 9.00 (978-1-61256-029-8(6)) Ravi Zach.

Pursuit of Perfect. unabr. abr. ed. Tal Ben-Shahar. Read by Jeff Woodman. (Running Time: 16200 sec.). (ENG.). 2007. audio compact disk 26.95 (978-1-59887-512-6(4), 1598875124) Pub: HighBridge. Dist(s): Workman Pub

Pursuit of Perfect: To Stop Chasing & Start Living a Richer, Happier Life. unabr. ed. Tal Ben-Shahar. Read by Eric Conger. (ENG.). 2009. audio compact disk 29.95 (978-1-59887-899-8(9), 1598878999) Pub: HighBridge. Dist(s): Workman Pub

Pursuit of Pleasure. 4 cass. 45.00 set. (9919) MEA A Watts Cass.

Push & Pull. Sundance/Newbridge, LLC Staff. (Early Science Ser.). (gr. k-3). 2007. audio compact disk 12.00 (978-1-4007-6136-4(0)); audio compact disk 12.00 (978-1-4007-6138-8(7)); audio compact disk 12.00 (978-1-4007-6137-1(9)) Sund Newbrdge.

Push, Pull, Lift! Early Explorers Early Set B Audio CD. Sophie Petratos. Adapted by Benchmark Education Staff. (J). 2007. audio compact disk 10.00 (978-1-4108-8220-2(9)) Benchmark Educ.

Push through the Pain. 2003. 6.00 (978-1-58602-187-0(7)); audio compact disk 10.00 (978-1-58602-188-7(5)) E L Long.

Pushcart War. unabr. ed. Jean Merrill. Narrated by Mark Hammer. 4 pieces. (Running Time: 5 hrs.). (gr. 5 up). 1994. 35.00 (978-0-7887-0177-1(0), 94402E7) Recorded Bks.
The details of the war which raged between the lowly pushcart vendors & the mighty trucking firms in New York City.

Pusher. unabr. ed. Ed McBain, pseud. Read by Larry McKeever. 6 cass. (Running Time: 6 hrs.). (87th Precinct Ser.: Bk. 3). 1992. 36.00 (978-0-7366-2155-7(5), 2954) Books on Tape.
The boys of the 87th find themselves in a narcotics scam.

***Pushing Ice.** unabr. ed. Alastair Reynolds. Narrated by John Lee. (Running Time: 22 hrs. 30 mins. 0 sec.). 2010. 39.99 (978-1-4001-5960-4(1)); 25.99 (978-1-4001-7960-2(2)); audio compact disk 54.99 (978-1-4001-0960-9(4)) Pub: Tantor Media. Dist(s): IngramPubServ

***Pushing Ice (Library Edition)** unabr. ed. Alastair Reynolds. Narrated by John Lee. (Running Time: 22 hrs. 30 mins.). 2010. 54.99 (978-1-4001-2960-7(5)); audio compact disk 131.99 (978-1-4001-3960-6(0)) Pub: Tantor Media. Dist(s): IngramPubServ

Pushing the Bear: A Novel of the Trail of Tears. unabr. ed. Diane H. Glancy. 6 cass. (Running Time: 9 hrs.). 1999. 53.00 (978-0-7887-0850-3(3), 94996E7) Recorded Bks.
The horrible "relocation" trek of the Cherokee takes on new immediacy & meaning.

Pushkin & the Queen of Spades. unabr. ed. Alice Randall. Read by Pitts Lisa. 9 cass. (Running Time: 12 hrs. 30 mins.). 2004. 62.95 (978-0-7861-2691-0(4), 3254); audio compact disk 80.00 (978-0-7861-8685-3(2), 3254) Blckstn Audio.
Windsor Armstrong is a polished, Harvard-educated African-American professor of Russian literature. Her son, Pushkin X, is an exceedingly famous pro-football player, an achievement that impresses his mother not at all. Even more distressing, however, is that her beloved son has just become engaged to a gorgeous white Russian emigre who also happens to be a lap dancer.

Pushkin & the Queen of Spades: A Novel. unabr. ed. Alice Randall. Read by Pitts Lisa. (Running Time: 12 hrs. 30 mins.). 2004. audio compact disk 24.95 (978-0-7861-8610-5(0), 3254) Blckstn Audio.

Pushkin & the Queen of Spades: A Novel. unabr. ed. Alice Randall. Read by Lisa Pitts. 8 pieces. (Running Time: 11 hrs. 30 mins.). 2004. reel tape 32.95 (978-0-7861-2649-1(3)); audio compact disk 39.95 (978-0-7861-8725-6(5)) Blckstn Audio.

Puss in Boots see Storytime Favorites

Puss in Boots see Sleeping Beauty & Other Stories

Puss in Boots see Chat Botte

Puss in Boots see Gato con Botas

Puss in Boots see Chat Botte

***Puss in Boots.** Anonymous. 2009. (978-1-60136-530-9(6)) Audio Holding.

Puss in Boots. Pocketaudio. (J). 2002. pap. bk. 12.95 (978-2-89558-083-6(9)) Pub: Al Stanke CAN. Dist(s): Penton Overseas

Puss in Boots. l.t. ed. Short Stories. Illus. by Graham Percy. 1 CD. (Running Time: 10 mins.). Dramatization. (J). (ps-3). 2001. bk. 8.99 (978-84-8214-090-2(6)); bk. 8.99 (978-84-87650-24-6(4)) Pub: Peralt Mont ESP. Dist(s): imaJen

Puss in Boots. unabr. ed. Read by Julie Harris. 1 cass. (Running Time: 15 min.). (World of Words Ser.). (J). (gr. k-3). pap. bk. 10.00 (978-0-8045-6604-9(6), SAC 6500D) Spoken Arts.

Puss in Boots. unabr. ed. Narrated by Julie Harris. 1 cass., 10 bks. (Running Time: 15 min.). (World of Words Ser.). (J). (gr. k-3). 2001. pap. bk. 22.00 (978-0-8045-6704-6(2), 6500-D/10) Spoken Arts.

Puss in Boots. unabr. ed. Ed McBain, pseud. Read by Paul Shay. 6 cass. (Running Time: 9 hrs.). (Matthew Hope Mystery Ser.: No. 7). 1992. 48.00 (978-0-7366-2193-9(8), 2988) Books on Tape.
Carlton Markham is charged with his wife's murder. His attorney is Matthew Hope & Markham is Hope's second case as a lawyer (he lost his first). Markham is understandably nervous.

Puss in Boots & Other Fairy Tales from Around the World. abr. ed. Perf. by Ruby Dee. Ed. by Amabel Williams-Ellis & Clem A. Okafor. 1 cass. Incl. Baba Yaga. (J). (CDL5 1247); Biggoon & the Little Duck. (J). (CDL5 1247); Cockie Lockie, Henny Penny & Mr. Korbes the Fox. (J). (CDL5 1247); Hopi Turtle. (J). (CDL5 1247); Saturday, Sunday, Monday. (J). (CDL5 1247); (J). 1984. 9.95 (978-0-694-50676-7(1), CDL5 1247) HarperCollins Pubs.

Puss in Boots Collection. Anonymous. 2009. (978-1-60136-076-2(2)) Audio Holding.

Puss in Boots Collection. Narrated by Margot Kidder. (Running Time: 1 hr.). (J). 2006. 14.95 (978-1-60083-005-1(6)) Iofy Corp.

Puss 'n' Boots. 1 cass. (J). (ps-2). 1999. bk. 9.95 Incl. plastic case. Penton Overseas.

Puss 'n Boots. Read by Ian Finlay. Illus. by Annabel Malak. 1 cass. (Running Time: 15 mins.). (Classic Stories Ser.). (J). 2000. cass. & audio compact disk 9.95 (978-2-921997-85-0(1)) Coffragants CAN.
How can a cat help his master when he is wearing boots? Because Puss in Boots is loyal & more cunning than other cats.

Puss 'n Cahoots. Rita Mae Brown & Sneaky Pie Brown. Narrated by Kate Forbes. (Running Time: 32400 sec.). (Mrs. Murphy Mystery Ser.). 2007. audio compact disk 29.99 (978-1-4281-2483-7(7)) Recorded Bks.

Puss 'n Cahoots. unabr. ed. Rita Mae Brown & Sneaky Pie Brown. Read by Kate Forbes. 8 cass. (Running Time: 9 hrs.). (Mrs. Murphy Mystery Ser.). 2007. 77.75 (978-1-4281-2484-4(5)); audio compact disk 92.75 (978-1-4281-2486-8(1)) Recorded Bks.

Put on by Cunning. unabr. ed. Ruth Rendell. Read by Charles Kay. 6 cass. (Running Time: 9 hrs.). (Inspector Wexford Mystery Ser.: Bk. 11). 2000. 49.95 (978-0-7451-6597-4(4), CAB 1213) Pub: Chivers Audio Bks GBR. Dist(s): AudioGO
Sir Manuel Camargue, one of the great flutists of his time, was dead. An old man, ankle-deep in snow, he lost his foothold in the dark, slipping into water to be trapped under a lid of ice. There's nothing Chief Inspector Wexford likes better than an open-and-shut case. And yet there was the disturbing return of Camargue's daughter, now a considerable heiress, after an absence of 19 years.

Put on Your Crown: Life-Changing Moments on the Path to Queendom. unabr. ed. Queen Latifah. (Running Time: 4 hrs.). 2010. 19.98 (978-1-60788-197-1(7)); audio compact disk 22.98 (978-1-60788-196-4(9)) Pub: Hachet Audio. Dist(s): HachBkGrp

Put Out More Flags. unabr. collector's ed. Evelyn Waugh. Read by David Case. 8 cass. (Running Time: 8 hrs.). 1992. 48.00 (978-0-7366-2235-6(7), 3025) Books on Tape.
Evelyn Waugh uses his satirist's brush on WW II. Into this noble struggle he introduces Basil Seal. Basil has his own ideas about the war & how it can work for him.

Put Out the Fires. unabr. ed. Maureen Lee. Read by Maggie Ollerenshaw. 10 cass. (Running Time: 10 hrs.). 1998. 84.95 (978-0-7540-0223-9(3), CAB 1646) AudioGO.
Based on the lives of British civilians, as they struggle to survive after the war.

Put the Fun Back into Parenting: Stories That Teach. 2003. audio compact disk (978-1-930429-44-4(4)) Love Logic.

Put up or Shut Up: Luke 7:31-35. Ed Young. (J). 1981. 4.95 (978-0-7417-1199-1(0), A0199) Win Walk.

Put Your Dream to the Test: 10 Questions That Will Help You See It & Seize It. abr. ed. John C. Maxwell. 2009. audio compact disk 24.99 (978-1-4002-0227-0(2)) Nelson.

Put Your Finger in the Air. Perf. by William Janiak. 1 cass. (Running Time: 1 hr.). (J). 2001. pap. bk. 10.95 (KIM 70167C) Kimbo Educ.
Everything's Put Together, In the Barnyard, The Car Goes Beep, Clap Your Hands, I've Got Clothes On, We Are Counting the Numbers Today, This Way, Make a Circle, Expression Song, I'm Swinging My Arms & Legs. Includes guide.

Putt at the End of the World. Lee K. Abbott et al. 2001. 24.98 (978-1-58621-019-9(X)) Hachet Audio.

Putt at the End of the World. abr. ed. Lee K. Abbott et al. Read by Jeff Woodman. (ENG.). 2005. 14.98 (978-1-59483-462-2(8)) Pub: Hachet Audio. Dist(s): HachBkGrp

Puttin' on Ole Massa. unabr. ed. Gilbert Osofsky. Read by Michael Prichard. 8 cass. (Running Time: 12 hrs.). 1976. 64.00 (978-0-7366-0027-9(2), 1039) Books on Tape.
This is a compilation of slave narratives which have been verified by the editor for veracity. Stark & dramatic in their force, they tell of Man's unquenchable desire for freedom & the lengths he will go to in order to achieve it.

Puttin' on the Ritz. Perf. by Erich Kunzel & Cincinnati Pops Orchestra. 1 cass., 1 CD. 7.98 (TA 30366); audio compact disk 12.78 CD Jewel box. (TA 80366) NewSound.

Putting A Face on Grace. Richard Blackaby. 2008. audio compact disk 13.95 (978-0-615-22071-0(1)) Sapphire Dig.

Putting First Things First. Speeches. Taffi L. Dollar. 6 cass. (Running Time: 7 hrs.). 2004. 29.00 (978-1-59089-864-2(8)); audio compact disk 40.00 (978-1-59089-865-9(6)) Creflo Dollar.

Putting God First. Reed A. Benson. 1 cass. 7.98 (978-1-55503-757-4(7), 06004962) Covenant Comms.
With God in the forefront, all things are possible.

Putting It Together. Henry Niemann. 1 cass. 8.95 (253) Am Fed Astrologers.
Complete method for analyzing the chart.

Putting It Together: A Conversation Management Text. Kevin McClure. 2002. 21.85 (978-0-13-128190-5(9)) Longman.

Putting Like a Genius. Bob Rotella. 2004. 7.95 (978-0-7435-4181-7(2)) Pub: S&S Audio. Dist(s): S and S Inc

Putting Like a Genius. unabr. ed. Bob Rotella. 1 CD. (Running Time: 10 hrs. 0 mins. 0 sec.). (ENG.). 2002. audio compact disk 14.00 (978-0-7435-2634-0(1), Sound Ideas) Pub: S&S Audio. Dist(s): S and S Inc
Tells you how to tune out extraneous factors such as anger, fear and other emotional responses that often cause you to leave the ball short or run it by the hole. Tips feature a series of exercises and techniques that will help you visualize success on the green and gain more cofidence in our putting stroke.

Putting on the Full Armor of God. Rick Joyner. 1 cass. (Running Time: 90 mins.). (Combating Principalities Ser.: Vol. 2). 2000. 5.00 (RJ09-002) Morning NC.
"Principles of Spiritual Warfare" & "Putting on the Full Armor of God." These tapes highlight practical truths that lead to certain victory in spiritual warfare.

Putting Out of Your Mind. abr. ed. Robert J. Rotella. Read by Robert J. Rotella. 1 cass. (Running Time: 1 hr.). 1996. 12.00 (978-0-671-56796-5(9), 647403, Sound Ideas) S&S Audio.

Putting Out of Your Mind: 2005 Calendar. abr. ed. Bob Rotella & Bob Cullen. Read by Bob Rotella. 1 CD. (Running Time: 112 hrs. 0 mins. NaN sec.). (ENG., 2001. audio compact disk 14.00 (978-0-7435-0775-2(4), Sound Ideas) Pub: S&S Audio. Dist(s): S and S Inc

Putting Out the Fires. unabr. ed. Perf. by Eknath Easwaran. 1 cass. (Running Time: 1 hr.). 1986. 7.95 (978-1-58638-596-5(8)) Nilgiri Pr.

Putting Parents at Ease. 2004. audio compact disk (978-1-930429-52-9(5)) Love Logic.

Putting Parents at Ease: Nine Keys to Effective Parent-Teacher Conferences. unabr. ed. Jim Fay. Read by Jim Fay. Interview with Bert Gurule. 2 cass. (Running Time: 3 hrs.). 1998. 18.95 Set. (978-0-944634-97-4(4)) Love Logic.
Education expert Jim Fay shares nine elements that guarantee successful parent-teacher conferences. These easy-to-use techniques show teachers how to make parents comfortable in a school setting.

Putting Principles into Practice. Swami Amar Jyoti. 1 cass. (Running Time: 90 mins.). (Satsangs of Swami Amar Jyoti Ser.). 1999. 9.95 (978-0-933572-42-3(5), P-66) Truth Consciousness.
Twenty-four hour spiritual practice is possible in everyday life, leading us to awakening.

Putting Romance Back into Your Marriage. unabr. ed. Ronald Goldstein & Gertrude Di Francesco. 1 cass. (Running Time: 50 min.). 1983. 9.95 Newtown Psychological Ctr.
A candid view of ideas & techniques designed to enhance communication & sexual satisfaction in marriage.

Putting the Ark in the Middle of America: 1 Samuel 4:1-11. Ed Young. (J). 1987. 4.95 (978-0-7417-1614-9(3), 614) Win Walk.

Putting the One Minute Manager to Work. Kenneth V. F. Blanchard & Robert Lorber. Intro. by A. E. Whyte. 1 cass. (Running Time: 53 min.). (Listen & Learn U. S. A.! Ser.). 8.95 Listen USA.
Skills that will improve performance & productivity by making those principles work for you in every day business & personal situations.

Putting the One Minute Manager to Work. abr. ed. Kenneth V. F. Blanchard & Ken Blanchard. 1 CD. (Running Time: 10 hrs. 0 mins. 0 sec.). (ENG.). 2002. audio compact disk 14.00 (978-0-7435-2503-9(5), Nightgale) Pub: S&S Audio. Dist(s): S and S Inc
An indispensable success tool for any manager striving to get the most from his or her people. Relied on by the largest corporations in America for their ability to motivate emploees at every level, the strategies of One Minute Management can.

Putting the PRO in Your Program. Silvana Clark. 2 cass. (Running Time: 2 hrs.). 19.95 Set. (5011) Natl Inst Child Mgmt.
Many early childhood centers provide wonderful care for children but overlook factors such as proper telephone techniques, public speaking skills & making a positive first impression. Describes how to develop & maintain a professional image for your center.

Putting the Self Back into SELF Esteem. Interview. Betsy Haas. 1 CD. (Running Time: 58 mins). 2000. audio compact disk 10.95 (978-0-9776273-1-8(X)) Esteemed Human.
An audio journey through self awareness.

Putting Wings to Your Dreams: Ten Steps to Help You Overcome Life's Obstacles. unabr. ed. John W. Gibson. 1 cass. (Running Time: 1 hr.). (Personal Empowerment Library). 1996. 14.95 (978-0-9653656-0-4(3), GIB196) J W Gibson Prsntns.
Actualize your dreams by making plans, preparational, visualizing & expecting success through faith.

***Putting Your Best Book Forward: A Book Shepherd's Secrets to Producing Award Winning Books That Sell.** Authors Digital. Narrated by Authors Digital. (Running Time: 87). (ENG.). 2010. 4.99 (978-0-9827081-5-6(7), AuthDigit) AuthorsDig.

Putting Your Creative Genius to Work: How to Stir Your Imagination for Profitable Ideas. Michael J. Gelb. 6 cass. (Running Time: 6 hrs.). 1996. 59.95 Set, incl. wkbk. (14430A) Nightingale-Conant.

Putting Your Worries on A Shelf: Progressive Muscle & Sesory Awareness Relaxation with Marsha M. Linehan, Ph. D. , ABPP. Executive Producer Shree A. Vigil. Prod. by Behavioral Tech. 2005. audio compact disk 15.95 (978-0-9745002-9-4(1)) Behavioral Tech.

***Putumayo Yoga CD.** (ENG.). (J). 2010. audio compact disk 15.99 (978-1-58759-274-4(6)) BarefootBksMA.

Puzzled see Poetry of Langston Hughes

Puzzled see Poetry & Reflections

Puzzles & Activities for Children Ages 7-10: Year B. Marcia T. Lucey. (Catholic Corner Ser.). (J). (gr. 2-5). 2008. pap. bk. 14.95 (978-1-58459-374-4(1)) Wrld Lib Pubns.

Puzzling D. H. Lawrence: A Light & Enlightening Lecture, Featuring Elliot Engel. 2001. bk. 15.00 (978-1-890123-44-4(7)) Media Cnslts.

Pwr ACC Sys Sft P. A. S. S.-Acct. 21st ed. (C). 2004. audio compact disk 21.95 (978-0-324-20413-1(2)) Pub: South-West. Dist(s): CENGAGE Learn

Pwr ACC Sys Sftwr Netwks/Acct. 21st ed. (C). 2004. audio compact disk 452.95 (978-0-324-20412-4(4)) Pub: South-West. Dist(s): CENGAGE Learn

Pygmalion. George Bernard Shaw. Narrated by Flo Gibson. 2009. audio compact disk 16.95 (978-1-60646-132-7(X)) Audio Bk Con.

Pygmalion. George Bernard Shaw. Contrib. by Shannon Cochran & Nicholas Pennell. (Playaway Adult Fiction Ser.). (ENG.). 2009. 39.99 (978-1-60775-743-6(5)) Find a World.

Pygmalion. unabr. ed. George Bernard Shaw. Read by Flo Gibson. 2 cass. (Running Time: 3 hrs.). 1991. 14.95 (978-1-55685-217-6(7)) Audio Bk Con.
A cockney flower girl is transformed into a charming woman of the world by a Professor of Phonetics.

Pygmalion: A Romance in Five Acts. George Bernard Shaw. 2 cass. Dramatization. 16.95 Set. (12154FA) Filmic Archives.
A perceptive comedy of wit & grit about the unique relationship that develops between cockney flower girl, Eliza Doolittle, & her irascible speech professor, Henry Higgins. Live multi-cast radio performance.

Pygmalion: A Romance in Five Acts. George Bernard Shaw. 1 cass. (Running Time: 1 hr.). (Radiobook Ser.). 1987. 4.98 (978-0-929541-30-3(8)) Radiola Co.

Pygmalion: A Romance in Five Acts. abr. ed. George Bernard Shaw. Perf. by Michael Redgrave & Lynn Redgrave. 3 cass. Dramatization. 1984. 27.95 (978-0-694-50913-3(2), SWC 354) HarperCollins Pubs.
Cast includes: Michael Hordern, Donald Pleasence, Felicity Kendal, Pauline Jameson, Edward Hardwicke, Megs Jenkins, Ruth Dunning, Gaye Brown, Edward Atienza, Rosamund Greenwood, Frank Gatliff, James Mellor, Peter Armitage, & Robert Oates.

Pygmalion: A Romance in Five Acts. unabr. ed. George Bernard Shaw. Perf. by Shannon Cochran & Nicholas Pennell. 2 CDs. (Running Time: 1 hr. 39 mins.). Dramatization. (L. A. Theatre Works). 2000. audio compact disk 25.95 (978-1-58081-185-9(X), CDCTA32); 23.95 (978-1-58081-032-6(2), CTA32) L A Theatre.
A comedy of wit & grit about the unique relationship between a Cockney flower girl & her irascible speech professor. The Flower girl, Eliza Doolittle, teaches the egotistical phonetics professor, Henry Higgins, that to be a lady means more than just learning to speak like one.

Pygmalion: A Romance in Five Acts. unabr. ed. George Bernard Shaw. Perf. by Anton Lesser et al. 3 cass. (Running Time: 2 hrs. 75 mins.). 2002. 17.98 (978-962-634-768-3(6), Naxos AudioBooks) Naxos.
This remains one of the most popular stories, but mainly in the medium of the musical: the evergreen My Fair Lady. Yet much of the charm and wit comes from the words and timing in the original play.

Pygmalion: A Romance in Five Acts. unabr. ed. George Bernard Shaw. Perf. by Anton Lesser et al. Directed By John Tydeman. 3 CDs. (Running Time: 2 hrs. 40 mins.). 2002. audio compact disk 22.98 (978-962-634-268-8(4), Naxos AudioBooks) Naxos.

Pygmalion: A Romance in Five Acts. unabr. ed. George Bernard Shaw. Read by L. A. Theatre Works Cast. 2 cass. 1996. 16.95 Set, retail box. (978-0-8072-3556-0(3), Listening Lib) Random Audio Pubg.
A perceptive comedy of wit & grit about the unique relationship between cockney flower girl, Eliza Doolittle, & her irascible speech professor, Henry Higgins.

Pygmalion: A Romance in Five Acts. unabr. ed. George Bernard Shaw. Perf. by Michael Redgrave & Lynn Redgrave. 1 cass. 1999. 22.00 (21669L3) Recorded Bks.

Pygmies see Tanglewood Tales

Pygmy. unabr. ed. Chuck Palahniuk. (Running Time: 8.5 hrs. 0 mins.). 2009. 29.95 (978-1-4332-7726-9(3)); 54.95 (978-1-4332-7722-1(0)) Blckstn Audio.

Pygmy. unabr. ed. Chuck Palahniuk. Read by Paul Michael Garcia. (Running Time: 8 hrs. 30 mins.). 2009. audio compact disk 24.95 (978-1-4332-7725-2(5)); audio compact disk 70.00 (978-1-4332-7723-8(9)) Blckstn Audio.

Pylons see Twentieth-Century Poetry in English, No. 9, Recordings of Poets Reading Their Own Poetry

Pyotr Il'yich Tchaikovsky. Read by Jeremy Siepmann & Malcolm Sinclair. 4 CDs. (Running Time: 4 hrs. 10 min.). (Life & Works Ser.). 2003. pap. bk. 35.99 (978-1-84379-000-6(9)) Naxos.

Pyramid. unabr. ed. Henning Mankell. (Running Time: 12 hrs. 50 mins.). (Kurt Wallander Ser.). 2009. 29.95 (978-1-4332-8959-0(8)); 72.95 (978-1-4332-8955-2(5)); audio compact disk 105.00 (978-1-4332-8956-9(3)) Blckstn Audio.

Pyramid Acting. unabr. ed. Sally Atman. 1 cass. (Running Time: 1 hr. 50 min.). 1999. 10.95 (978-1-928843-01-6(8)) Ad Lib Res.
Acting method based on dramatic structure.

Pyramid Acting: Successful Character Building for the Serious Actor. Compiled by Sally Atman. 2006. audio compact disk 12.95 (978-1-928843-31-3(X)) Ad Lib Res.

***Pyramid of Doom: A Novel.** unabr. ed. Andy McDermott. Narrated by Gildart Jackson. (Running Time: 14 hrs. 30 mins. 0 sec.). (Nina Wilde/Eddie Chase Ser.). 2010. 29.99 (978-1-4526-5014-2(4)); 19.99 (978-1-4526-7014-0(5)); audio compact disk 39.99 (978-1-4526-0014-7(7)) Pub: Tantor Media. Dist(s): IngramPubServ

***Pyramid of Doom (Library Edition) A Novel.** unabr. ed. Andy McDermott. Narrated by Gildart Jackson. (Running Time: 14 hrs. 30 mins.). (Nina Wilde/Eddie Chase Ser.). 2010. 39.99 (978-1-4526-2014-5(8)); audio compact disk 95.99 (978-1-4526-3014-4(3)) Pub: Tantor Media. Dist(s): IngramPubServ

Pyramid of Success: Championship Philosophies & Techniques of Winning. Jim Herrick & John Wooden. 5 cass. (Running Time: 5 hrs.). 1995. 49.95 Set, incl. card. (12920AX) Nightingale-Conant.
You'll discover how to remain adaptable at all times & view adversity as a challenge - not an obstacle, & also how to identify & continually measure your progress toward your goals.

Pyramid Problem Solving: The New Way to Emotional Freedom. Created by Sally Atman. 2006. audio compact disk 12.95 (978-1-928843-33-7(6)) Ad Lib Res.

Pyramide Assassinee, Pt. 1. Christian Jacq. Read by Pierre Forest. 4 cass. (Juge d'Egypte Ser.). (FRE.). 1996. 39.95 (1797-TH) Olivia & Hill.
In ancient Egypt, Juge Pazair pursues his investigation of the mysterious death of two guards of the Sphinx. The reader discovers the secrets of medicine, justice & life in that ancient civilization.

Pyramide Assassinee, Pt. 2. Christian Jacq. Read by Pierre Forest. 4 cass. (Juge d'Egypte Ser.). (FRE.). 1996. 39.95 (1798-TH) Olivia & Hill.

Pyramide Assassinee, Pts. 1 & 2, set. Christian Jacq. Read by Pierre Forest. 8 cass. (Juge d'Egypte Ser.: Vol. 1). (FRE.). 1996. 69.95 (1797/98) Olivia & Hill.

Pyramids. Terry Pratchett. Read by Tony Robinson. (Discworld Ser.). (ENG.). 2005. audio compact disk 24.95 (978-0-552-15298-3(6)) Pub: Transworld GBR. Dist(s): IPG Chicago

Pyramids. unabr. ed. Terry Pratchett. Read by Nigel Planer. 8 cass. (Running Time: 11 hr.). (Discworld Ser.). (J). 2001. 69.95 (978-0-7531-0140-7(8), 970903) Pub: ISIS Lrg Prnt GBR. Dist(s): Ulverscroft US
It isn't easy being a teenage pharaoh. The Great Pyramid has just exploded because of paracosmic instability & then you've got to deal with all these assassins, sphinxes, huge wooden horses, mad high priests, philosophers, sacred crocodiles, gods, marching mummies, jobbing pyramid builders & Hat, the Vulture-Headed God of Unexpected Guests. And all you really wanted was the chance to do something for young people & the inner cities.

Pyramids. unabr. ed. Terry Pratchett. Read by Nigel Planer. 9 CDs. (Running Time: 33000 sec.). (Discworld Ser.). 2006. audio compact disk 84.95 (978-0-7531-1643-2(X)) Pub: ISIS Lrg Prnt GBR. Dist(s): Ulverscroft US

Pyramids of Light Healing Series, set Narrated by Meg Blackburn Losey. Composed by Barry Goldstein. 3 CDs. (Running Time: 178 mins.). 2004. audio compact disk 44.95 (978-0-9753223-1-4(1)) Spirit Light Res.
A series of CDs, with music by award winning composer and producer, Barry Goldstein and narrated and channeled by Dr. Meg Blackburn Losey, Author of "Pyramids of Light, Awakening to Multi-dimensional Realities". Each CD offers a healing expereince to the listener. CD one is a series of small journeys which explore powerful emotions and bring the listener full circle from self doubts to empowerment. CD two is Channeled and takes the listener through an interdimensional realization of harmonic attunement of all aspects of being so that they may operate as one focused being. CD three is an interdimensional healing journey through the energy fields and etheric bodies all the way to the soul self and back again.

Pyramids of Light Healing Series Set Two. Perf. by Barry Goldstein. Composed by Barry Goldstein. Narrated by Meg Blackburn Losey. Lyrics by Meg Blackburn Losey. 3 CDs. (Running Time: 3 hours, ten minutes). 2004. audio compact disk 44.95 (978-0-9753223-2-1(X)) Spirit Light Res.
3 CD set CD 1 - Opening the Heart? A most often question that the Masters receive is ?how do I open my heart space?? Gently, with Loving Passion, the Masters take the listener through easy revelations of self and heart and directly into the heart space. Music from Ambiology 1? The Heart.CD 2 - Language of Light, Language of Love?Haunting and beautifully melodic, the Language of Light is Channeled through Meg and interpreted by the Masters . Meg said that while recording this CD that she felt as if she was floating in pure love and that listening to it is like hearing messages from home. A fantastic journey of Being. Music is Barry?s new composition, ?Afloat in Love?.CD 3 - Opening the Third Eye? Led by the Masters through Meg, this guided journey teaches the listener to move into and connect to the third eye space. Brilliantly easy and gently guided, this CD provides safe methods for exploring other realities while connected with one's intuitive self. Music is ?Pulse of Life? written and performed by Barry Goldstein.

Pyramids of Mars. unabr. ed. Terrance Dicks. Narrated by Tom Baker. (Running Time: 6 hrs. 0 mins. 0 sec.). (Doctor Who Ser.). (ENG.). 2010. audio compact disk 39.95 (978-1-60283-823-9(2)) Pub: AudioGO. Dist(s): Perseus Dist

Pyruvate Carboxylase Deficiency - A Bibliography & Dictionary for Physicians, Patients, & Genome Researchers. Compiled by Icon Group International, Inc. Staff. 2007. ring bd. 28.95 (978-0-497-11284-4(1)) Icon Grp.

Pythagoras on the Therapeutic Value of Music. Instructed by Manly P. Hall. 8.95 (978-0-89314-231-5(X), C591018) Philos Res.

Pythagorean Theory of Number. Manly P. Hall. 5 cass. (Running Time: 150 min.). 1999. 40.00 Set. (978-0-89314-230-8(1)) Philos Res.
Includes: "Basic Philosophy of Numeration & Number;" "The Tetractys & the Motion of Number;" "The Fourth Pythagorean Proposition;" "The Human Soul & Archetypal Number;" & "The Symbolism of Number".

Pythons. Jody Sullivan Rake. Contrib. by Colleen Buckman. (African Animals Ser.). (ENG.). (gr. k-1). 2008. audio compact disk 14.65 (978-1-4296-3200-3(3)) CapstoneDig.

Pythons. unabr. rev. abr. ed. Michael Palin et al. 2 CDs. (Running Time: 2 hrs. 0 mins. 0 sec.). (ENG.). 2003. audio compact disk 16.95 (978-1-59397-400-8(0)) Pub: Macmill Audio. Dist(s): Macmillan

Q

Q: The Autobiography of Quincy Jones. abr. ed. Quincy Jones. 2000. 25.00 (978-0-553-52691-2(X), Random AudioBks); 29.95 (978-0-553-45670-7(9), Random AudioBks) Random Audio Pubg.

Q & A. Vikas Swarup. 2008. audio compact disk 27.95 (978-1-57270-879-2(4)) AudioGO.

Q & A. unabr. abr. ed. Vikas Swarup. Read by Kerry Shale. 5 cds. (Running Time: 6 hrs). (ENG.). 2008. audio compact disk 27.95 (978-1-57270-487-9(X)) Pub: AudioGO. Dist(s): Perseus Dist
Ram Mohammad Thomas may be in jail, but he is not a criminal. A penniless 18-year-old waiter from the slums of India, Ram appeared to be on the path to wealth when he correctly answered 12 questions on the TV show Who Wants to Win a Billion? The show's producers bribe the police to arrest him for cheating, and as Ram's lawyer rescues him from prison, he also extracts Ram's amazing life-story and a captivating portrait of 21st-century India.

Q & A Dialogue: Logos 03/21/99. Ben Young. 1999. 4.95 (978-0-7417-6125-5(4), B0125) Win Walk.

Q. Clearance. unabr. ed. Peter Benchley. Narrated by Jerry Farden. 9 cass. (Running Time: 13 hrs. 15 mins.). 1988. 78.00 (978-1-55690-429-5(0), 88999E5) Recorded Bks.
Timothy Burnham rises in the ranks of White House insiders & finds himself in jeopardy in this comic thriller.

Q Is for Quarry. Sue Grafton. Read by Judy Kaye. (Kinsey Millhone Mystery Ser.). 2002. audio compact disk 72.00 (978-0-7366-8836-9(6)) Books on Tape.

Q Is for Quarry. unabr. ed. Sue Grafton. 8 cass. (Running Time: 12 hrs.). (Kinsey Millhone Mystery Ser.). 2002. 48.00 (978-0-7366-8835-2(8)) Books on Tape.

Q Kids Sonnet. Ed. by Sholanda Sims. Lyrics by Mattie Simms. Music by Derrick Banks. (J). 2005. audio compact disk 12.00 (978-0-9772077-2-5(2)) Kan Inc.

QB VII. Leon Uris. Read by Dan Lazar. 10 cass. (Running Time: 15 hrs.). 1980. 80.00 (978-0-7366-0310-2(7), 1298) Books on Tape.
A legal battle over slander takes place in one of Britain's oldest law courts.

QBQ! The Question Behind the Question. unabr. ed. John G. Miller. 1 CD. (Running Time: 1 hr 10 min). (ENG.). (gr. 8). 2004. audio compact disk 14.95 (978-0-14-305709-3(X), PengAudBks) Penguin Grp USA.

QCD at 200 TeV. Ed. by L. Cifarelli & Y. Dokshitzer. (Ettore Majorana International Science Ser.: Vol. 60). (C). 1992. audio compact disk 205.00 (978-0-306-44222-3(1)) Spri.

***Qi Healing Kit: Energy Practices for Health & Vitality.** Lee Holden. (Running Time: 2:15:05). 2011. DVD, DVD, audio compact disk 29.95 (978-1-59179-738-8(1)) Sounds True.

QiGong: An Earth Cleansing. Bill Douglas. Read by Bill Douglas. 1 cass. (SMART Health & Mind Expansion Products Ser.). 1998. (978-1-893634-08-4(6)) Stress Mgm.
Relaxation therapy using ancient tools in modern language. Known to enhance health & creativity.

QiGong: Expanding Awareness. Bill Douglas. Read by Bill Douglas. 1 cass. (SMART Health & Mind Expansion Products Ser.). 1998. 12.00 (978-1-893634-07-7(8)) Stress Mgm.
Relaxation therapy using ancient methods in modern imagery known to enhance health & creativity.

Qigong: Qi Permeating Technique. unabr. ed. Wen-Ching Wu. Read by Wen-Ching Wu. 1 cass. (Running Time: 22 min.). 1994. 10.00 (978-1-889659-00-8(2), WDA001) Way of Dragon.
The instructor takes the listener through a guided visualization of a basic relaxation technique, Qi Permeating Qigong, & self massage.

Qigong & More Comfort, Inner Peace & Flexibility. Sue Michaelsen. Read by Sue Michaelsen. Contrib. by Maria A. Brazazgon et al. 8 cass. (Running Time: 8 hrs.). 2001. 35.00 (978-0-9701920-1-1(0)); audio compact disk 45.00 (978-0-9701920-4-2(5)) Michaelsen.
Companion text read by author to blind friends. Introduction to Traditional Chinese Medicine, Acupoints and blind-assisting instruction for practicing Qigong Gentle Exercise.

QiGong for Children's Health & Relaxation. Bill Douglas. Read by Bill Douglas. 1 cass. (SMART Health & Mind Expansion Products Ser.). (J). (gr. 2-8). 1998. 12.00 (978-1-893634-06-0(X)) Stress Mgm.
Relaxation therapy for children known to promote self esteem & outlook.

Qigong for Lifelong Health: Standing, Dissolving, & Opening the Energy Gates of Your Body. Bruce Frantzis. Narrated by Bruce Frantzis. (ENG.). 2009. audio compact disk 25.00 (978-1-55643-843-1(5)) Pub: North Atlantic. Dist(s): Random

Qigong Meditations. abr. ed. Ken Cohen. 1 CD. (Running Time: 3600 sec.). 2006. audio compact disk 14.95 (978-1-59179-435-6(8), AW00088D) Sounds True.

QiGong Relaxation Therapy. Bill Douglas. Read by Bill Douglas. 1 cass. (SMART Health & Mind Expansion Products Ser.). 1998. 12.00 (978-1-893634-05-3(1)) Stress Mgm.
Ancient techniques known to enhance health & creativity.

Quack, Gabble, Squawk & other Animal Tales. Adapted by Kirk/ E. Waller. (J). 2008. audio compact disk 14.95 (978-1-4276-3052-0(6)) AardGP.

Quack, Quack Quassical. Penton. 1 CD. (Running Time: 1 hr.). (J). 2001. audio compact disk 10.95 (978-0-9709490-3-5(0)) ZooKnowlogy.
Compilation of Mozart's music designed for babies & toddlers. Improves spatial intelligence & cognitive abilities & enhance a child's development.

Quail Cricket. Short Stories. (5122) Am Audio Prose.

Quaker Graveyard in Nantucket from "Lord Weary's Castle" see Twentieth-Century Poetry in English, No. 32-33, Recordings of Poets Reading Their Own Poetry

Quaker Lives: Almanina Barbour see Quaker Lives: Let Them Speak

Quaker Lives: Eric Johnson see Quaker Lives: Let Them Speak

Quaker Lives: John & Dorothy McCandless see Quaker Lives: Let Them Speak

Quaker Lives: Kenneth Boulding see Quaker Lives: Let Them Speak

Quaker Lives: Let Them Speak. 8 cass. Incl. Quaker Lives: Almanina Barbour. 1983.; Quaker Lives: Eric Johnson. 1983.; Quaker Lives: John & Dorothy McCandless. 1983.; Quaker Lives: Kenneth Boulding. 1983.; Quaker Lives: Nan Brown. 1983.; Quaker Lives: Ruth Bennett. 1983.; Quaker Lives: Stephen Cary. 1983.; Quaker Lives: Wallace Collett. 1983. 1983. 26.00 Set.; 4.50 ea. Pendle Hill.

Quaker Lives: Nan Brown see Quaker Lives: Let Them Speak

Quaker Lives: Ruth Bennett see Quaker Lives: Let Them Speak

Quaker Lives: Stephen Cary see Quaker Lives: Let Them Speak

Quaker Lives: Wallace Collett see Quaker Lives: Let Them Speak

Quakerism: Friends on the International Scene see Quakerism: Then and Now

Quakerism: Friends' Responsibility for Influencing Government see Quakerism: Then and Now

Quakerism: Friends' Service see Quakerism: Then and Now

Quakerism: John Woolman: A Play see Quakerism: Then and Now

Quakerism: The Candle of the Lord see Quakerism: Then and Now

Quakerism: The Changing Aspects of Quaker Testimonies see Quakerism: Then and Now

Quakerism: The Message of George Fox for Today see Quakerism: Then and Now

Quakerism: The Somehow Strangely Better see Quakerism: Then and Now

Quakerism: The Story of 1652: The Birth of Quakerism see Quakerism: Then and Now

Quakerism: Then & Now. 9 cass. Incl. Quakerism: Friends on the International Scene. Barrett Hollister. 1976.; Quakerism: Friends' Responsibility for Influencing Government. Raymond Wilson. 1976.; Quakerism: Friends' Service. John Sullivan. 1976.; Quakerism: John Woolman: A Play. Norman Bert. 1976.; Quakerism: The Candle of the Lord. Elfrida V. Foulds. 1976.; Quakerism: The Changing Aspects of Quaker Testimonies. Lyle Tatum. 1976.; Quakerism: The Message of George Fox for Today. John Curtis. 1976.; Quakerism: The Somehow Strangely Better. Elizabeth Watson. 1976.; Quakerism: The Story of 1652: The Birth of Quakerism. Eleanore S. Clarke. 1976.; 1976. 28.00 Set.; 4.50 ea. Pendle Hill.

Qualifications for Building God's House: 11 Samuel 7. Ed Young. (J). 1982. 4.95 (978-0-7417-1250-9(4), 250) Win Walk.

Qualifications for Successful Ministry, Pt. 1. Alfred D. Harvey, Jr. 10 cass. 2003. 50.00 (978-1-932508-38-3(4)) Doers Pub.

Qualifications for Successful Ministry, Pt. 3. Alfred D. Harvey, Jr. 10 cass. 2003. 50.00 (978-1-932508-40-6(6)) Doers Pub.

Qualifications of Successful Ministry, Pt. 2. Alfred D. Harvey, Jr. 10 cass. 2003. 50.00 (978-1-932508-39-0(2)) Doers Pub.

***Qualified Entente.** Kenneth Wapnick. 2010. 12.00 (978-1-59142-488-8(7)); audio compact disk 15.00 (978-1-59142-487-1(9)) Foun Miracles.

Qualified Plans: Coverage & Design Issues in 1989. unabr. ed. Ed. by James P. Klein. 1 cass. (Running Time: 25 min.). (Quarterly Employee Benefits Audio Reports). 1989. 55.00 series of 4. (T7-9237) PLI.
The Employee Benefits Reports, a quarterly Series of audiocassettes, is designed to keep practitioners & their clients informed of key litigation, legislation & regulatory actions. This audio series annually provides four twenty to thirty minute reports by experts on the most recent developments affecting employee benefits.

Qualified Plans, Professional Organizations, Health Care, & Welfare Benefits. 15 cass. (Running Time: 21 hrs.). 1999. 395.00 Set; incl. study guide 1188p. (MD53) Am Law Inst.
Advanced course is intended for lawyers & other professionals. Includes compensation, & other tax & non-tax problems of personal service & other closely-held businesses. As a bonus, the recording of all concurrently held sessions are included.

Qualities & Habits of Effective Leaders: Ecc. 10:12-20. Ed Young. 1994. 4.95 (978-0-7417-2005-4(1), 1005) Win Walk.

Qualities of a Karma Yogi. Swami Jyotirmayananda. Read by Swami Jyotirmayananda. 1 cass. (Running Time: 45 min.). 10.00 (830) Yoga Res Foun.

Qualities of a Sales Professional. Paul J. Meyer. 1 cass. (Running Time: 36 min.). 1988. 11.00 (978-0-89811-270-2(2), SP100073) Meyer Res Grp.
How to recognize the advantages you already have & how to develop new qualities for success in the exciting sales profession.

Qualities of a Sales Professional. Paul J. Meyer. 1 cass. 10.00 (SP100073) SMI Intl.
Professional selling is exciting & rewarding for those who reach success. Both relative newcomers & "old pros" will welcome this wealth of information. Master salesman Paul J. Meyer tells how to recognize the advantages you already have & how to develop new qualities for success in the exciting sales profession.

Qualities of a Successful Executive. 1980. audio compact disk (978-0-89811-291-7(5)) Meyer Res Grp.

Qualities of a Successful Executive. Paul J. Meyer. 1 cass. 10.00 (SP100036) SMI Intl.
What qualities are shared by successful executives? How can you develop those qualities? How can you seek those qualities in new members of your executive staff? Chairman of the Board of SMI International, Paul J. Meyer tells you what, how, & why.

Qualities of a Successful Executive. abr. ed. Paul J. Meyer. 1 cass. (Running Time: 39 min.). 11.00 (978-0-89811-151-4(X), 7193) Meyer Res Grp.
Chairman of the Board of SMI International tells you what qualities are shared by successful executives, how to develop them, & how to seek them in new members of your executive staff.

Qualities of a Successful Salesman. Paul J. Meyer. 1 cass. (Running Time: 35 min.). 11.00 (978-0-89811-020-3(3), 5157); Meyer Res Grp.
Salesman Paul J. Meyer tells how to recognize the advantages you already have & how to develop new qualities for success in the sales profession.

Qualities of an Excellent Servant. 6 cass. 19.95 (20156, HarperThor) HarpC GBR.

Qualities of God: Reassurance in Scripture & Song. Karla Carey. 1 cass. (Running Time: 30 min.). (Inspiration in Words & Music Ser.). 1988. 10.00 (978-1-55768-537-7(1)) LC Pub.

Qualities of Success. unabr. ed. Zig Ziglar. Narrated by Zig Ziglar. (Running Time: 2 hrs. 44 mins. 55 sec.). (ENG.). 2009. 13.99 (978-1-60814-649-9(9)); audio compact disk 19.99 (978-1-59859-706-6(X)) Oasis Audio.

Qualities of Success. unabr. ed. Zig Ziglar & Bert Newman. Read by Zig Ziglar. 6 cass. (Running Time: 6 hr.). (How to Stay Motivated Ser.: Vol. 1). 1993. 69.95 (978-1-56207-232-2(3)) Zig Ziglar Corp.
Developing the qualities of success demonstrates the three stages of becoming a winner - planning to win, preparing to win & expecting to win. Maintain a winning attitude by using a specific formula for success.

Qualities of Success: A Blueprint for Achievement. Zig Ziglar. Read by Zig Ziglar. 3 cass. (Running Time: 3 hrs.). 1990. bk. 40.00 (978-1-56207-210-0(2)); 30.00 (978-1-56207-209-4(9)) Zig Ziglar Corp.
Zig will encourage you to recognize & utilize the characteristics of success already within you. Motivate & increase your self-confidence with timeless stories & insights.

Qualities of Successful Sales Professionals. 1988. audio compact disk (978-0-89811-283-2(4)) Meyer Res Grp.

Quality Assurance & Outcomes Introduction: An Introduction to Quality & TQM Concepts in Healthcare for Health Personnel, Insurance

Companies, HMOs, Managed Care, Hospital Employees, Pharmaceutical & Medical Device Employees. Ed. by Daniel Farb. 2004. audio compact disk 49.95 (978-1-59491-102-6(9)) Pub: UnivofHealth. Dist(s): AtlasBooks
Anyone in healthcare needs to understand the basics of quality assurance and outcomes as they apply to medical and hospital practice. This multimedia introduction to the field will teach you the basic terminology and concepts as they apply to healthcare.

Quality Assurance for Pastoral Services. 1 cass. (Care Cassettes Ser.: Vol. 14, No. 1). 1987. 10.80 Assn Prof Chaplains.

Quality Assurance in the Nursing Home. unabr. ed. Charlotte Eliopoulos. Read by Charlotte Eliopoulos. 1 cass. (Running Time: 20 min.). 1991. 15.00 (978-1-882515-09-7(9)) Hlth Educ Netwk.
Describes quality assurance as a continuous process that permeates all aspects of nursing home's operations.

Quality in Continuing Education: Principles, Practices & Standards for Colleges & Universities. Leonard Freedman. (Higher & Adult Education Ser.). 1987. bk. 37.45 (978-1-55542-041-3(9), Jossey-Bass) Wiley US.

***Quality of Life: A Family & Caretaker's Guide to Elder Abuse Prevention.** Felton Wooten. 2009. audio compact disk 24.95 (978-1-61623-792-9(9)) Indep Pub IL.

***Quality of Mercy.** 2010. audio compact disk (978-1-59171-246-6(7)) Falcon Picture.

Quality of Mercy. Kenneth Wapnick. 4 CDs. 2005. audio compact disk 25.00 (978-1-59142-173-3(X), CD84) Foun Miracles.

Quality Plus II. Accreditation Council on Services for People with Disabilities Staff. Read by James Gardner & Tina Campanella. Prod. by Robert Sandidge. 6 cass. (Running Time: 5 hrs. 45 min.). 1996. 99.50 (978-1-57654-215-6(7)) Creat Core.
Explores how Outcome Based Performance Measures can enhance & expand organizational effectiveness for those providing services in the field of disabilities.

Quality Secret: The Right Way to Manage. William E. Conway. 2 cass. (Running Time: 3 hrs.). 1996. 18.95 (978-0-9631464-3-4(2)) Conway Qual.

Quality Without Tears. Philip B. Crosby. Read by Philip B. Crosby. 1 cass. (Running Time: 53 min.). 1989. 9.95 (978-0-07-014557-3(1)) McGraw.
Provides a solid base of comprehension for the individual who is genuinely interested in causing quality to happen & eliminating hassle in the process.

Quality Workforce Equals Higher Performance. 1 cass. (America's Supermarket Showcase '96 Ser.). 1996. 11.00 (NGA96-028) Sound Images.

Quant a Moi. Noblitt. (C). bk. & wbk. ed. 110.95 (978-0-8384-8438-8(7)) Heinle.

Quant a Moi. 2nd ed. Jeannette D. Bragger & Rice. 2000. bk. 48.50 (978-0-8384-1204-6(1)) Heinle.

Quant à Moi. 2nd ed. Jeannette D. Bragger & Rice. 1 CD. (Running Time: 90 mins). 2002. stu. ed. 17.50 (978-0-8384-0621-2(1)) Heinle.
Intermediate course that emphasize meaningful in-class communication and in-depth exploration of francophone cultures.

Quant a Moi. 2nd ed. Bragger & Rice. (C). bk. 69.95 (978-0-8384-8622-1(3)); bk. & stu. ed. 150.95 (978-0-8384-8726-6(2)) Heinle.

Quant a Moi. 4th ed. Jeannette D. Bragger & Rice. 6.75 (978-0-8384-1139-1(8)) Heinle.

Quantam Rose. Catherine Asaro. Read by Anna Fields. (Running Time: 14 hrs. 30 mins.). 2004. 69.95 (978-0-7861-2639-2(6)); audio compact disk 24.95 (978-0-7861-8623-5(2)) Blckstn Audio.

Quantam Rose. unabr. ed. Catherine Asaro. Read by Anna Fields. (Running Time: 14 hrs. 30 mins.). 2004. audio compact disk 88.00 (978-0-7861-8736-2(0)) Blckstn Audio.

Quantico Rules. unabr. ed. Gene Riehl. Read by David Colacci. (Running Time: 10 hrs.). (Puller Monk Ser.). 2004. 39.25 (978-1-59335-626-2(9), 1593356269, Brlnc Audio MP3 Lib) Brilliance Audio.
Puller Monk is a gambler. High stakes get his adrenaline flowing. But his dark side is about to catch up with him at a time when his life and the future of this nation hang in the balance. As an FBI agent in charge of a SPIN (Special Inquiries) Squad, Monk's job is to investigate the background of Judge Brenda Thompson, a presidential nominee to the U.S. Supreme Court and the first African-American woman to be nominated for this high office. When the judge is caught in a lie, Monk and agent Lisa Sands are set on a trail of corruption and murder that leads to the very top of the bureau - and a faceoff with a brutal killer who will stop at nothing to carry out his deadly mission.

Quantico Rules. unabr. ed. Gene Riehl. Read by David Colacci. (Running Time: 10 hrs.). (Puller Monk Ser.). 2004. 39.25 (978-1-59710-618-4(6), 1597106186, BADLE); 24.95 (978-1-59710-619-1(4), 1597106194, BAD) Brilliance Audio.

Quantico Rules. unabr. ed. Gene Riehl. Read by David Colacci. (Running Time: 10 hrs.). (Puller Monk Ser.). 2004. 24.95 (978-1-59335-215-8(8), 1593352158) Soulmate Audio Bks.

Quantico Rules: A Novel. unabr. ed. Gene Riehl. Read by David Colacci. 7 cass. (Running Time: 10 hrs.). (Puller Monk Ser.). 2003. 32.95 (978-1-59086-934-5(6), 1590869346, BAU); 82.25 (978-1-59086-935-2(4), 1590869354, Unabridge Lib Edns) Brilliance Audio.

Quantrill's War: The Life & Times of William Clarke Quantrill. unabr. ed. Duane Schultz. Narrated by Richard M. Davidson. 9 cass. (Running Time: 12 hrs. 30 mins.). 1997. 78.00 (978-0-7887-0644-8(6), 94821E7) Recorded Bks.
An account of an unscrupulous man who lied, cheated, tortured & murdered even before the Civil War provided him with justification.

Quants: How a New Breed of Math Whizzes Conquered Wall Street & Nearly Destroyed It. abr. ed. Scott Patterson. Read by Mike Chamberlain. 2010. 32.00 (978-0-7393-8506-7(2), Random AudioBks) Pub: Random Audio Pubg. Dist(s): Random

Quantum. Tom Grace. Read by Michael Kramer. 2000. 48.00 (978-0-7366-5917-8(X)); 48.00 Books on Tape.
With the discovery of a new power source, the global race is on between scientists & secret agents, American & Russians.

Quantum. abr. ed. Tom Grace. Read by Jerry O'Connell. (ENG.). 2005. 14.98 (978-1-59483-457-8(1)) Pub: Hachet Audio. Dist(s): HachBkGrp

Quantum. 2nd ed. Short Stories. G. Saul Snatsky. 1. (Running Time: 63 min.). Dramatization. 2004. audio compact disk (978-0-9761674-0-2(9)) Sauls Audio.

***Quantum: Einstein, Bohr, & the Great Debate about the Nature of Reality.** unabr. ed. Manjit Kumar. Read by Ray Porter. (Running Time: 14 hrs.). 2010. 29.95 (978-1-4417-6997-8(8)); 79.95 (978-1-4417-6994-7(3)); audio compact disk 32.95 (978-1-4417-6996-1(X)); audio compact disk 109.00 (978-1-4417-6995-4(1)) Blckstn Audio.

Quantum Flow Bioenergetics: Live Longer, Eliminate Stress, Mental Suffering & Physical Symptoms with Cutting Edge Energy Therapies - by Yourself!: Be Your Own Healer. Maryam Webster. 1 CD. (Running Time: 72 mins.). 2004. cd-rom & audio compact disk 60.00 (978-0-9761085-0-4(X), Quantum Flow) Quantum Flow Pubns.

Quantum Healing: Exploring the Frontiers of Mind Body Medicine. abr. ed. Deepak Chopra. Read by Deepak Chopra. (Running Time: 3600 sec.). (ENG.). 2007. audio compact disk 12.95 (978-0-7393-4396-8(3), Random AudioBks) Pub: Random Audio Pubg. Dist(s): Random

Quantum Imaging Mind Journey, No. 1. Don Paris & Ilona Selke. 2 cass. 1992. (978-1-884246-02-9(8)) Liv from Vis.

Quantum Imaging Mind Journey, No. 2. Don Paris & Ilona Selke. 2 cass. 1992. (978-1-884246-03-6(6)) Liv from Vis.

Quantum Leap Audible. Price Pritchett. Narrated by Eric Conger. (ENG.). 2007. 9.95 (978-0-944002-41-4(2)) Pritchett.

Quantum Leap in Consciousness. Swami Amar Jyoti. 1 cass. 1991. 9.95 (K-131) Truth Consciousness.
What is needed to bring a truly different consciousness & life for all on earth? Holocausts purify - are they avoidable?.

Quantum Leap Thinking: An Owner's Guide to the Mind. abr. ed. James Mapes. Perf. by James Mapes. 4 cass. (Running Time: 6 hrs.). 2004. 25.00 (978-1-59007-024-6(0)) Pub: New Millenn Enter. Dist(s): PerseuPGW
This user-friendly guide to mastering the mind will help you make quantum leaps in personal growth in terms of defining your vision and developing a personal road map. Strategies, insights and practical exercises will assist you in building a personal support system and developing high-performance teams.

***Quantum Man: Richard Feynman's Life in Science.** unabr. ed. Lawrence M. Krauss. (Running Time: 10 hrs. 5 mins.). (Great Discoveries Ser.). (ENG.). 2011. 29.95 (978-1-4417-8026-3(2)); audio compact disk 29.95 (978-1-4417-8025-6(4)) Blckstn Audio.

***Quantum Man: Richard Feynman's Life in Science.** unabr. ed. Lawrence M. Krauss. Read by To be Announced. (Running Time: 10 hrs. 5 mins.). (Great Discoveries Ser.). (ENG.). 2011. 65.95 (978-1-4417-8023-2(8)); audio compact disk 100.00 (978-1-4417-8024-9(6)) Blckstn Audio.

Quantum Mechanical View of Reality. Richard Phillips Feynman. 1 cass. 9.00 (A0220-83) Sound Photosyn.
From the first workshop that Richard conducted with Faustin & Brian at Esalen Institute.

Quantum Mechanical View of Reality. unabr. ed. Richard Phillips Feynman. 1 cass. (Running Time: 1 hr. 24 min.). 1983. 11.00 (13601) Big Sur Tapes.

Quantum Memory Power: Learn to Improve Your Memory with the World Memory Champion! unabr. ed. Dominic O'Brien & Dominic O'Brien. Read by Dominic O'Brien & Dominic O'Brien. Read by Dominic O'Brien. 5 cass. (Running Time: 63 hrs. 0 mins. 0 sec.). (ENG.). 2003. audio compact disk 35.00 (978-0-7435-2866-5(2), Nightgale) Pub: S&S Audio. Dist(s): S and S Inc

Quantum NLP: Thought into Manifestation. unabr. ed. Christiane Turner. (Running Time: 6 hrs.). (ENG.). 2008. 24.98 (978-1-59659-310-7(5), GildAudio) Pub: Gildan Media. Dist(s): HachBkGrp

Quantum NLP: Thought into Manifestation. unabr. rev. ed. Christiane Turner. Read by Christiane Turner. (Running Time: 8 hrs.). (ENG.). 2007. audio compact disk 29.98 (978-1-59659-082-3(3), GildAudio) Pub: Gildan Media. Dist(s): HachBkGrp

Quantum of Solace. unabr. ed. Ian Fleming. Read by Simon Vance. (Running Time: 8.5 hrs. NaN mins.). 2008. 29.95 (978-1-4332-4959-4(6)); audio compact disk 19.95 (978-1-4332-4958-7(8)); audio compact disk 70.00 (978-1-4332-7010-9(2)); audio compact disk 54.95 (978-1-4332-7009-3(9)) Blckstn Audio.

Quantum Psychology: Who Makes the Grass Green? Robert A. Wilson. 1 cass. 9.00 (A0777-90) Sound Photosyn.
Journeys into paradox by way of his inimitable strange loops. At the SJ New Age Renaissance Fair.

Quantum Rose. Catherine Asaro. Read by Anna Fields. (Running Time: 13 hrs. 30 mins.). 2004. 41.95 (978-1-59912-705-7(9)) Iofy Corp.

Quantum Spirituality. Swami Amar Jyoti. 1 cass. 1991. 9.96 (K-126) Truth Consciousness.
This crucial decade calls for drastic changes in our habitual patterns. Liberation from unconsciousness, the quantum leap.

Quantum Wellness: A Practical & Spiritual Guide to Health & Happiness. Kathy Freston. Frwd. by Mehmet C. Oz. (Running Time: 7 hrs. 30 mins.). (ENG.). 2008. audio compact disk 34.98 (978-1-60286-027-8(0), WeinsteinBks) Perseus Bks Grp.

Quantum Wellness: A Practical & Spiritual Guide to Health & Happiness. unabr. ed. Kathy Freston. 2008. 24.98 (978-1-60286-073-5(4), WeinsteinBks) Pub: Perseus Bks Grp. Dist(s): PerseuPGW

Quarante ans de Radio, Hosted by Bernadette Lafont. 2 cass. (Running Time: 3 hrs.). 1991. 26.95 (1463-RF) Olivia & Hill.
A tour of the last forty years of French radio.

Quarrel with the King: The Story of an English Family on the High Road to Civil War. unabr. ed. Adam Nicolson. Narrated by Simon Vance. (Running Time: 9 hrs. 0 mins. 0 sec.). (ENG.). 2008. audio compact disk 59.99 (978-1-4001-3876-0(0)); audio compact disk 19.99 (978-1-4001-5876-8(1)) Pub: Tantor Media. Dist(s): IngramPubServ

Quarrel with the King: The Story of an English Family on the High Road to Civil War. unabr. ed. Adam Nicolson. Read by Simon Vance. (Running Time: 9 hrs. 0 mins. 0 sec.). (ENG.). 2008. audio compact disk 29.99 (978-1-4001-0876-3(4)) Pub: Tantor Media. Dist(s): IngramPubServ

Quarry. Bill Pronzini. Read by Nick Sullivan. 5 cass. (Nameless Detective Mystery Ser.). 49.95 (978-0-7927-3401-7(7), CSL 728); audio compact disk 64.95 (978-0-7927-3402-4(5), SLD 728); audio compact disk 29.95 (978-0-7927-3403-1(3), CMP 728) AudioGO.

Quartered Safe Out Here: A Recollection of the War in Burma. unabr. ed. George MacDonald Fraser. Read by David Case. 7 cass. (Running Time: 10 hrs. 30 min.). 1996. 36.40 (978-0-913369-57-9(8), 4278) Books on Tape.
Sometimes funny, sometimes hair-raising account of the author's own life.

Quartermaine's Terms. Simon Gray. Perf. by Keene Curtis et al. 1 cass. (Running Time: 1 hr. 50 min.). 18.95 (TPT85) L A Theatre.
St. John Quartermaine, an amusingly dim but kindhearted teacher in Cambridge, is a man who has outlived his era.

Quartermaine's Terms. Simon Gray. Perf. by Holland Taylor. 2 cass. (Running Time: 1 hr. 50 mins.). 1998. 22.95 (978-1-58081-128-6(0), TPT85) L A Theatre.

Quartet Gospel. abr. ed. 1 cass. (Running Time: 1 hr.). 4.98 (978-1-57908-466-0(4), 5341); audio compact disk 5.98 (978-1-57908-465-3(6), 5341) Platinm Enter.

Quartet in Autumn. unabr. ed. Barbara Pym. Read by Elizabeth Stephan. 6 cass. (Running Time: 7 hrs.). (Isis Ser.). (J). 1995. 54.95 (978-1-85089-553-4(8), 91122) Pub: ISIS Lrg Prnt GBR. Dist(s): Ulverscroft US

Quartet in Heaven. Sheila Kaye-Smith. 6 cass. (Running Time: 6 hrs.). 24.95 (735) Ignatius Pr.
A look at St. Catherine of Genoa, St. Rose, St. Therese & Cornelia Connelly.

Quartet Legends. Perf. by Swanee Quintet et al. 1 CD. 1997. audio compact disk 15.98 (D2204) Diamante Music Grp.

Quartet of Cornish Cats. unabr. ed. A. L. Rowse. Read by Bill Kelsey. 5 cass. (Running Time: 5 hrs.). 1991. 30.00 (978-0-7366-1956-1(9), 2777) Books on Tape.
A.L. Rowse, the greatest living Shakespearean scholar & student of the Elizabethan Age, claims it is harder to write the biography of a cat than of a queen. He cites Virginia Woolf's biography of Mrs. Browning's dog Flush which inspired him to give us the story of Peter, the White Cat of Trennaren. It became a classic of animal literature & in this collection is companioned with stories about Peter's successors.

Quasars. 1 cass. (Running Time: 26 min.). 14.95 (23323) MMI Corp.
Discusses how quasars were discovered, radiation of quasars, significance & other characteristics.

Quayle. 1 cass. (Running Time: 1 hr.). 1998. 10.98 (978-0-7601-1833-7(7)); audio compact disk 15.98 (978-0-7601-1834-4(5)) Provident Mus Dist.

Quck Spanish for Housekeeping Mangers in Hotels. Carlos Sanchez. 1 cass. (Running Time: 1 hr. 30 mins.). 2001. 15.95 (978-1-891368-32-5(X), C10HH) Casa Ed KARISA.
Essential Spanish for housekeeping managers in hotels includes extensive vocabulary.

Que Desastre de Cuarto!, EDL Level 20. (Fonolibros Ser.: Vol. 18). (SPA.). 2003. 11.50 (978-0-7652-1040-1(1)) Modern Curr.

Que Es? (SPA.). (gr. k-1). 10.00 (978-0-7635-6271-7(8)) Rigby Educ.

Que Es Eso?, EDL Level 3. (Fonolibros Ser.: Vol. 26). (SPA.). 2003. 11.50 (978-0-7652-1015-9(0)) Modern Curr.

***Que es la Metafisica?** Conny Mendez. Narrated by FonoLibro Inc. & Isabel Varas.Tr. of What Is Metaphysics?. (SPA.). 2010. audio compact disk 12.95 (978-1-61154-003-1(8)) Fonolibro Inc.

Que Es Una Linea? Level 6, Vol. 3. (Fonolibros Ser.). 2003. 11.50 (978-0-7652-0989-4(6)) Modern Curr.

¿Qué está en el cobertizo? Audio CD. Benchmark Education Company. Based on a work by Brenda Parkes. (Shared Reading Classics Ser.). (J). (gr. k-2). 2009. audio compact disk 10.00 (978-1-60634-983-0(X)) Benchmark Educ.

Que Estas Pensando? Tr. of What Are You Thinking?. (SPA.). 2008. audio compact disk 21.00 (978-0-944129-20-3(X)) High Praise.

Que Gato!, EDL Level 16. (Fonolibros Ser.: Vol. 5). (SPA.). 2003. 11.50 (978-0-7652-1026-5(6)) Modern Curr.

Que Hacemos Con Estos Musicos? Marcos Witt. 1 cass.Tr. of What Shall We Do with These Musicians?. CanZion.
The life of a Christian musician.

***Que Hay Detras Del Nobre de Jesus?** Tr. of What Is Behind the Name of Jesus?. (SPA.). 2007. audio compact disk 6.00 (978-0-944129-41-8(2)) High Praise.

¿Qué hay en el bosque? Emergent Set A. Benchmark Education Staff. Ed. by Katherine Scraper. (Early Explorers Ser.). (J). 2008. audio compact disk 10.00 (978-1-60437-236-6(2)) Benchmark Educ.

Que Necesita Saber Sobre Tratamiento Medico. unabr. ed. John F. Taylor. Read by Timothy Taylor. 1 cass. (Running Time: 25 min.). (Answers to ADD Ser.). (SPA.). 1994. 9.95 (978-1-883963-18-7(4)) ADD Plus.
Exploding the medication myths, conquering the side effects, adjusting dosage level, gaining the child's cooperation, understanding the intended effects on behavior, explaining how medications work.

***¿Qué Necesitan Las Plantas? Audio Cd.** Debra Castor. Adapted by Benchmark Education Company, LLC. (Content Connections Ser.). (SPA.). (J). 2009. audio compact disk 10.00 (978-1-935472-74-2(7)) Benchmark Educ.

***¿Qué Necesitan Los Animales? Audio Cd.** Margaret Mcnamara. Adapted by Benchmark Education Company, LLC. (Content Connections Ser.). (SPA.). (J). 2009. audio compact disk 10.00 (978-1-935472-73-5(9)) Benchmark Educ.

Que Rica la Ronda. Poems. Alma Flor Ada & F. Isabel Campoy. 10 cassettes. (Running Time: 20 mins). Dramatization. (SPA.). (J). 1998. 11.95 (978-1-58186-010-8(2)) Del Sol Pub.

Que Se Dice, Nino? Tr. of What Do You Say, Dear?. (SPA.). 2004. 8.95 (978-0-7882-0269-8(3)) Weston Woods.

Que Si. 2nd ed. M. Victoria Garcia-Serrano. (C). bk. & wbk. ed. 75.95 (978-0-8384-7813-4(1)); bk. & wbk. ed. 78.95 (978-0-8384-8307-7(0)) Heinle.

Que Soy? Level 4, Vol. 9. 2003. 11.50 (978-0-7652-0996-2(9)) Modern Curr.

¿Que sucede despues de la Muerte? Mark Richards. 2007. audio compact disk 4.99 (978-1-933172-25-5(8)) Jayah Producc.

Que Tal? 5th ed. Thalia Dorwick. 1 CD. (Running Time: 1 hr.). (SPA.). (C). 1999. audio compact disk 7.50 (978-0-07-230770-2(6), Mc-H Human Soc) McGrw-H Hghr Educ.

¿Qué Tal? 5th ed. Thalia Dorwick et al. (C). 1998. 8.75 (978-0-07-013685-4(8), Mc-H Human Soc) Pub: McGrw-H Hghr Educ. Dist(s): McGraw

Que Tal? Pt. I: Listening Comprehension Component. unabr. ed. 1999. stu. ed. (978-0-07-229218-3(0), Mc-H Human Soc) McGrw-H Hghr Educ.
Manageable in length and communicative in approach, this brief introductory Spanish program is a favorite text for schools that have a limited number of contact hours per week and like to finish the entire book in the first year. The foundation of Qué tal? rests solidly on the development of the four skills (listening, speaking, reading and writing) with a nice selection of lively activities.

Que Tal? Pt. II: Listening Comprehension Component. unabr. ed. 1999. stu. ed. (978-0-07-229222-0(9), Mc-H Human Soc) McGrw-H Hghr Educ.

Que Tal? Adopter's Program. (SPA.). 1999. stu. ed. (978-0-07-229217-6(2)) McGrw-H Hghr Educ.

Que Tal? Audio Program: An Introductory Course. 7th ed. Maria Sablo-Yates. 2006. audio compact disk 52.81 (978-0-07-320944-9(9), 9780073209449, Mc-H Human Soc) Pub: McGrw-H Hghr Educ. Dist(s): McGraw

Qué Te Parece? James F. Lee. 6 cass. (Running Time: 9 hrs.). (SPA.). 1996. stu. ed. 33.40 (978-0-07-911093-0(2), Mc-H Human Soc) McGrw-H Hghr Educ.

Qué Te Parece? unabr. ed. James F. Lee. 6 cass. (Running Time: 9 hrs.). (SPA.). 1996. 33.40 (978-0-07-912180-6(2), Mc-H Human Soc) McGrw-H Hghr Educ.

Que Te Parece? 2nd ed. Created by McGraw-Hill Staff. 2002. audio compact disk 20.25 (978-0-07-237457-5(8)) McGraw.

Qué te Parece?, Vol. 2. 2nd ed. James F. Lee et al. 1 cass. (Running Time: 90 min.). (SPA.). (C). (gr. 6-12). 2000. stu. ed. 65.63 (978-0-07-231012-2(X), 9780072310122) Pub: Glencoe. Dist(s): McGraw

Queen & I. unabr. ed. Sue Townsend. Read by Angela Thorne. 8 cass. (Running Time: 12 hrs.). 2000. 59.95 (978-0-7451-4206-7(0), CAB 889) Pub: Chivers Audio Bks GBR. Dist(s): AudioGO
When the People's Republican Party achieves an unexpected election victory, their first act is to order the Royal Family out of Buckingham Palace! Their new home is Hell Close, and hell it is, as the Royals gird themselves for their new life living next door to the working class.

Queen & I. unabr. ed. Sue Townsend. Narrated by Barbara Rosenblat. 6 cass. (Running Time: 8 hrs.). 1993. 51.00 (978-1-55690-906-1(3), 93402E7) Recorded Bks.
A lighthearted fantasy in which the Royal Family of Great Britain is thrown out of their palaces by a new republican government & moved into welfare housing in a London slum to cope as best they can.

Queen-Ann's-Lace see Twentieth-Century Poetry in English, No. 4, Recordings of Poets Reading Their Own Poetry

Queen Fussy. Mister Tom. Illus. by Elvera Spivey. (J). (gr. 2-4). 1973. bk. (978-0-318-57347-2(4)) Oddo.

Queen Is in the Counting House. unabr. ed. Steven Thomas Oney. Photos by Ken Coleman & David Ellsworth. 1 CD. (Running Time: 1 hr. 12 min.). (Cape Cod Mystery Radio Theater Ser.: 27). (YA). 2002. audio compact disk 12.50 (978-0-9745668-3-2(7)) Cape Cod Radio.
The subject is baseball, the venue is Fenway Park as Captain Underhill and Doctor Scofield are enlisted to prevent the assassination of a star, Red Sox rookie.

Queen Isabella: Treachery, Adultery, & Murder in Medieval England. Alison Weir. Narrated by Lisette Lecat. (Running Time: 80100 sec.). 2005. audio compact disk 39.99 (978-1-4193-5480-9(9)) Recorded Bks.

Queen Isabella: Treachery, Adultery, & Murder in Medieval England. unabr. ed. Alison Weir. Read by Lisette Lecat. 18 CDs. (Running Time: 22 hrs.). 2005. audio compact disk 119.75 (978-1-4193-6306-1(9), C3453); 109.75 (978-1-4193-6304-7(2), 98210) Recorded Bks.
Popular historian Alison Weir has crafted best-selling biographies of such prominent icons as King Henry VIII and Queen Elizabeth I. A master at uncovering fascinating and little-known details, Weir brings these historical figures to life with a brilliant blend of entertainment and scholarship. No English queen has drawn more ire than the vilified Queen Isabella. Weir at long last delivers the definitive biography of one of the most controversial members of English royalty.

Queen Kat, Carmel & St Jude Get a Life. unabr. ed. Maureen McCarthy. 8 cass. (Running Time: 14 hrs. 35 mins.). 2002. (978-1-74030-456-6(X)) Bolinda Pubng AUS.

Queen Kat, Carmel & St Jude Get a Life. unabr. ed. Maureen McCarthy. Read by Kate Hood. (Running Time: 51600 sec.). (J). 2006. audio compact disk 108.95 (978-1-74093-892-1(5)) Pub: Bolinda Pubng AUS. Dist(s): Bolinda Pub Inc

Queen Kunti Series. 14 cass. (Running Time: 21 hrs.). 35.00 Bhaktivedanta.
The lectures on the Prayers of Queen Kunti from the 1st Canto of Srimad-Bhagavatam with one folder.

Queen Lucia. E. F. Benson. Narrated by Flo Gibson. (ENG.). 2007. audio compact disk 29.95 (978-1-55685-892-5(2)) Audio Bk Con.

Queen Lucia. abr. ed. E. F. Benson. Read by Geraldine McEwan. 2 cass. (Running Time: 3 hrs.). 1987. 15.95 (978-0-89845-590-8(1), CPN 2105) HarperCollins Pubs.
It was a time of peace for the very rich until amazing Lucia turned their world upside down.

Queen Lucia. unabr. ed. E. F. Benson. Read by Flo Gibson. 6 cass. (Running Time: 8 hrs.). 1998. 24.95 (978-1-55685-584-9(2)) Audio Bk Con.
The energetic, pretentious &, often malicious Lucia's reign as "Queen" over Riseholme's gentry is challenged by Olga, the dazzling diva. A fraudulent Guru & psychic & the exposure of her faulty Italian never quite puncture Lucia's inflated ego.

Queen Lucia. unabr. ed. E. F. Benson. Read by Geraldine McEwan. 8 cass. (Running Time: 9 hrs. 8 min.). 2001. 69.95 (978-1-85089-641-8(0), 91013) Pub: ISIS Audio GBR. Dist(s): Ulverscroft US
"Queen Lucia" is set in the garden-party world of the 1920s, a society ruthlessly dominated by the greatest arch-snob who has ever existed.

Queen Lucia. unabr. ed. E. F. Benson. Read by Geraldine McEwan. 9 CDs. (Running Time: 9 hrs. 8 mins.). (Isis Ser.). (J). 2002. audio compact disk 84.95 (978-0-7531-1478-0(X)) Pub: ISIS Lrg Prnt GBR. Dist(s): Ulverscroft US
Mrs. Emmeline lucas of Riseholm is a relentless social climber who rules her small English village with a calculating mind and an iron fist. She is attended at every turn by Peppino, who writes bad poetry, and her best fried, Georgie, with whom she plays Mozart duets and pretends to speak Italian. Lucia's position is shaken by a newcomer to Riseholm who absorbs Georgie into her own orbit and reveals Lucia's shallowness, vindictiveness, and ignorance of music and culture.

Queen Lucia Pt. 1: Make Way for Lucia. unabr. ed. E. F. Benson. Read by Nadia May. 6 cass. (Running Time: 8 hrs. 30 mins.). 1998. 44.95 (978-0-7861-1449-8(5), 2311) Blckstn Audio.
England, between the wars, was a paradise of utter calm & leisure for the very, very rich. But into this enclave is born Mrs. Emmeline Lucas - La Lucia, as she is known - a woman determined to lead a life quite different from the pomp & the subdued & hushed nature of her class.

Queen Mab Vol. III: Musical Verses. Rose Fyleman et al. 1 CD. (Running Time: 53 mins.). (YA). (gr. 4 up). 2007. audio compact disk 16.99 (978-976-41-0931-0(4)) U of the West JAM.

Queen Mab, Musical Verses Volume 3. Music by Ellen Kjelgaard Godula & Brian Godula. (J). 2007. audio compact disk 16.99 (978-0-9764109-3-5(1)) Pillar Rock.

Queen Margot. Alexandre Dumas. Read by Robert Whitfield. 13 cass. (Running Time: 19 hrs.).Tr. of Reine Margot. 2000. 85.95 (978-0-7861-1576-1(9), 2405) Blckstn Audio.
Begins in 1572 with the marriage of Marguerite de Valois to Henri de Navarre. Several important political events have led up to this marriage, including the mysterious murder of Henri de Navarre's mother, cleverly plotted by Catherine de Medici.

Queen Mother: The Official Biography. abr. ed. William Shawcross. Read by William Shawcross. (ENG.). 2009. audio compact disk 35.00 (978-0-307-57657-6(4), Random AudioBks) Pub: Random Audio Pubg. Dist(s): Random

Queen of a Distant Country. unabr. collector's ed. John Braine. Read by Stuart Courtney. 8 cass. (Running Time: 8 hrs.). 1985. 48.00 (978-0-7366-0496-3(0), 1470) Books on Tape.
The author probes the obsessive passion of a young man for a vital older woman & the painful ordeal which must follow - the exorcism of desire, the shattering of bonds, the shaking off of a profound & powerful influence.

Queen of Air & Darkness see Award Winning Science Fiction

Queen of Ambition. Fiona Buckley. Read by Josephine Bailey. 7 cass. (Running Time: 10.5 hrs.). 2002. 56.00 (978-0-7366-8577-1(4)) Books on Tape.

Queen of Angels. unabr. ed. Greg Bear. Narrated by George Guidall. 14 cass. (Running Time: 19 hrs. 45 mins.). 1991. 112.00 (978-1-55690-430-1(4), 91321E7) Recorded Bks.
Three people set out in pursuit of a murderer. Emanuel Goldsmith, a famous poet, murdered eight people, then disappeared.

Queen of Attolia. unabr. ed. Megan Whalen Turner. Narrated by Jeff Woodman. (Running Time: 9 hrs.). (YA). (gr. 6-10). 2008. 56.75 (978-1-4361-6552-5(0)); 61.75 (978-1-4281-5230-4(X)); audio compact disk 87.75 (978-1-4281-5235-9(0)) Recorded Bks.

Queen of Attolia. unabr. collector's ed. Megan Whalen Turner. Narrated by Jeff Woodman. 8 CDs. (Running Time: 9 hrs.). (YA). (gr. 6-10). 2008. audio compact disk 44.95 (978-1-4361-5074-3(4)) Recorded Bks.

Queen of Babble. abr. ed. Meg Cabot. Read by Kadushin Ilyana. 5 CDs. (Running Time: 21600 sec.). (Queen of Babble Ser.). 2006. audio compact disk 29.95 (978-0-06-112169-2(X), Harper Audio) HarperCollins Pubs.

***Queen of Babble.** abr. ed. Meg Cabot. Read by Kadushin Ilyana. (ENG.). 2006. (978-0-06-113526-2(7), Harper Audio); (978-0-06-113528-6(3), Harper Audio) HarperCollins Pubs.

Queen of Babble in the Big City. Meg Cabot. (Queen of Babble Ser.). 2007. audio compact disk 29.95 (978-0-06-111777-0(3), Harper Audio) HarperCollins Pubs.

Queen of Broken Hearts. abr. ed. Cassandra King. Read by Anne Twomey. (Running Time: 21600 sec.). 2007. audio compact disk 29.98 (978-1-4013-8489-0(7)) Pub: Hyperion. Dist(s): HarperCollins Pubs

Queen of Diamonds. 2001. audio compact disk 9.95 (978-1-930805-19-4(5)) XC Pubng.

Queen of Eene see Rolling Harvey down the Hill

Queen of Everything. unabr. ed. Deb Caletti. Read by Kate Rudd. (Running Time: 9 hrs.). 2010. 39.97 (978-1-4233-9638-3(3), 9781423396383, Brinc Audio MP3 Lib); 19.99 (978-1-4233-9637-6(5), 9781423396376, Brilliance MP3); 39.97 (978-1-4233-9640-6(5), 9781423396406, BADLE); 19.99 (978-1-4233-9639-0(1), 9781423396390, BAD); audio compact disk 19.99 (978-1-4233-9635-2(9), 9781423396352, Bril Audio CD Unabri); audio compact disk 54.97 (978-1-4233-9636-9(7), 9781423396369, BriAudCD Unabrid) Brilliance Audio.

Queen of Hearts, the; Sing a Song of Sixpence. 2004. 8.95 (978-1-56008-313-9(1)); cass. & flmstrp 30.00 (978-1-56008-751-9(X)) Weston Woods.

***Queen of Scots.** abr. ed. John Guy. Read by John Guy. (ENG.). 2004. (978-0-06-081367-3(9), Harper Audio) HarperCollins Pubs.

***Queen of Scots.** abr. ed. John Guy. Read by John Guy. (ENG.). 2004. (978-0-06-077854-5(7), Harper Audio) HarperCollins Pubs.

Queen of Scots: The Full Life of Mary Stuart. John Guy. 2004. 25.95 (978-0-06-058643-0(5)) HarperCollins Pubs.

Queen of Spades. Alexander Pushkin. 1986. (S-46) Jimcin Record.

***Queen of the Damned.** unabr. ed. Anne Rice. (ENG.). 2011. audio compact disk 25.00 (978-0-307-91408-8(9), Random AudioBks) Pub: Random Audio Pubg. Dist(s): Random

Queen of the Damned. unabr. ed. Anne Rice. Narrated by Frank Muller. 15 cass. (Running Time: 21 hrs. 45 mins.). (Vampire Chronicles: Bk. 3). 1995. 120.00 (978-0-7887-0100-9(2), 94341E7) Recorded Bks.
Akasha - the Queen of the Damned, mother of all vampires - has awakened from her 6,000 year sleep determined to become mankind's bloodthirsty savior.

Queen of the Elephants. unabr. ed. Mark Shand. Read by Paul Shelley. 6 cass. (Running Time: 9 hrs.). 2000. 49.95 (978-0-7451-6598-1(2), CAB 1214) Pub: Chivers Audio Bks GBR. Dist(s): AudioGO
Mark Shand sets out for India to take part in a film about the plight of the wild elephant herds in North-East India. He locates Parbati Barua, an expert with elephants, and they follow the elephants' ancient migratory route through the tea gardens of West Bengal. The feisty expert is given ample opportunity to exercise her skills on the journey, missing little of the beauty and eccentricity of all things Indian.

***Queen of the Night.** unabr. ed. J. A. Jance. Read by Greg Itzin. (ENG.). 2010. (978-0-06-204076-3(6), Harper Audio) HarperCollins Pubs.

Queen of the Night. unabr. ed. J. A. Jance. Read by Greg Itzin. (Brandon Walker Ser.: Bk. 4). 2010. audio compact disk 39.99 (978-0-06-198853-0(7), Harper Audio) HarperCollins Pubs.

***Queen of the Night: A Novel of Suspense.** unabr. ed. J. A. Jance. Read by Greg Itzin. (ENG.). 2010. (978-0-06-200994-4(X), Harper Audio) HarperCollins Pubs.

***Queen of the Nile.** 2010. audio compact disk (978-1-59171-212-1(2)) Falcon Picture.

Queen of This Realm. unabr. ed. Jean Plaidy. Read by Rosemary Davis. 16 cass. (Running Time: 27 hr. 15 min.). (Isis Ser.). (J). 1997. 104.95 (978-1-85695-207-1(X), 970310) Pub: ISIS Lrg Prnt GBR. Dist(s): Ulverscroft US

Queen Takes King. Gigi Levangie Grazer. Read by Phil Gigante & Tanya Eby. (ENG.). 2009. 64.99 (978-1-60847-933-7(1)) Find a World.

Queen Takes King. unabr. ed. Gigi Levangie Grazer. (Running Time: 11 hrs.). 2009. 39.97 (978-1-4233-2726-4(8), 9781423327264, BADLE) Brilliance Audio.

Queen Takes King. unabr. ed. Gigi Levangie Grazer. Read by Phil Gigante & Tanya Eby. (Running Time: 11 hrs.). 2009. 39.97 (978-1-4233-2724-0(1), 9781423327240, Brinc Audio MP3 Lib) Brilliance Audio.

Queen Takes King. unabr. ed. Gigi Levangie Grazer. Read by Phil Gigante. (Running Time: 11 hrs.). 2009. 24.99 (978-1-4233-2725-7(X), 9781423327257, BAD) Brilliance Audio.

Queen Takes King. unabr. ed. Gigi Levangie Grazer. Read by Phil Gigante & Tanya Eby. (Running Time: 11 hrs.). 2009. audio compact disk 89.97 (978-1-4233-2722-6(5), 9781423327226, BriAudCD Unabrid) Brilliance Audio.

***Queen Victoria.** Lytton Strachey. Read by Anais 9000. 2009. 27.95 (978-1-60112-231-5(4)) Babblebooks.

Queen Victoria. unabr. ed. E. F. Benson. Read by William Sutherland. 9 cass. (Running Time: 13 hrs.). 2000. 62.95 (978-0-7861-1741-3(9), 2546) Blckstn Audio.
Victoria was the daughter of Edward, Duke of Kent & Princess Mary Louise Victoria of Saxe-Coburg. In 1837, at the age of 18, she succeeded her uncle, William IV, to the throne of England. This was the first year of a reign that lasted an astonishing sixty-four years, until her death in 1901.

Queen Victoria. unabr. ed. Lytton Strachey. Read by Flo Gibson. 6 cass. (Running Time: 9 hrs.). 1998. bk. 24.95 (978-1-55685-522-1(2)) Audio Bk Con.
Portrait of England's long-reigning monarch, describing in fascinating detail her love for Prince Albert & her relations with King Leopold, Baroness Lehzen, Baron Stockmar & Lords Melbourne, Peel, Palmersten & Disraelil.

Queen Victoria. unabr. collector's ed. Lytton Strachey. Read by Donada Peters. 7 cass. (Running Time: 10 hrs. 30 mins.). 1988. 56.00 (978-0-7366-1276-0(9), 2185) Books on Tape.
Strachey, Victorian author of the scathing "Eminent Victorians", gives an oddly sympathetic biographical portrait of his monarch.

Queen Victoria: Born to Succeed. unabr. ed. Elizabeth Longford. Read by Donada Peters. 18 cass. (Running Time: 27 hrs.). 1992. 72.00 (978-0-7366-2302-5(7), 3086A) Books on Tape.
Queen Victoria notoriously liked to get her way. When asked how he dealt with her, Disraeli, her favorite prime minister, said: "I never argue; I never contradict. I sometimes forget.

Queen Victoria Pt. 2: Born to Succeed. unabr. ed. Elizabeth Longford. Read by Donada Peters. 9 cass. (Running Time: 13 hrs. 30 min.). 1992. 72.00 (3086B) Books on Tape.

Queen Victoria & the Victorian Novel: A Light & Enlightening Lecture for Middle School, Vol. 16. Featuring Elliot Engel. 2001. bk. 15.00 (978-1-890123-48-2(X)) Media Cnslts.

Queen Victoria's Little Wars. unabr. ed. Byron Farwell. Read by Bill Kelsey. 9 cass. (Running Time: 13 hrs. 30 min.). 1994. 72.00 (978-0-7366-2832-7(0), 3540) Books on Tape.
We meet the courageous, foolhardy & eccentric officers & men who fought Queen Victoria's small wars.

Queen Virtues. Elbert Willis. 1 cass. (Patience & Long-Suffering Ser.). 4.00 Fill the Gap.

Queen Zixi of Ix. unabr. ed. L. Frank Baum. Read by Flo Gibson. 3 cass. (Running Time: 4 hrs.). (J). 1995. 16.95 (978-1-55685-362-3(9)) Audio Bk Con.
Each wearer of the magic cloak has one wish granted with many surprising results. A King, a Queen & the Roly-Rogues parry & wage war in this exciting tale.

Queen Zixi of Ix: Or the Story of the Magic Cloak see Oz

Queenie Peavy. abr. ed. Robert Burch. 1 cass. (Running Time: 49 mins.). Dramatization. (J). (gr. 4-7). 1972. 9.95 (978-0-670-58425-3(8)) Live Oak Media.
Portrays the troubled existence of a thirteen-year-old girl living in Georgia.

Queenie Peavy. abr. ed. Robert Burch. 11 vols. (Running Time: 52 mins.). (J). (gr. 4-7). 1999. pap. bk. 15.95 (978-0-670-58427-7(4)) Live Oak Media.

Queens & Quarterbacks. Intro. by Janet Smith Post. Music by Jim Post. (J). 2000. audio compact disk 20.00 (978-0-9702826-4-4(8)) BTSBRBE.

Queen's Bastard. unabr. ed. Robin Maxwell. Narrated by Steven Crossley. 14 cass. (Running Time: 20 hrs. 30 mins.). 1999. 114.00 (978-0-7887-4387-0(2), 96122E7) Recorded Bks.
In the early years of Queen Elizabeth I's reign stories circulated that she had a child fathered by Robin Dudley, her beloved Master of the Horse. Years later, a man calling himself Arthur Dudley surfaced in Spain. From this, the author has seamlessly woven rumor & fact into a stunning piece of historical fiction that is equal parts romance & swash-buckling adventure.

Queen's Blue Velvet Dress - Universe. Steck-Vaughn Staff. 1 cass. (Running Time: 90 mins.). (J). 1999. (978-0-7398-0926-6(1)) SteckVau.

Queen's Confession: The Story of Marie Antoinette. unabr. ed. Victoria Holt. Read by Gabrielle Lloyd. 12 cass. (Running Time: 18 hrs.). 1999. 96.95 (978-0-7540-0312-0(4), CAB 1735) AudioGO.

Queen's Confession: The Story of Marie Antoinette. unabr. ed. Victoria Holt. Narrated by Davina Porter. 14 cass. (Running Time: 19 hrs.). 1998. 112.00 (978-0-7887-1925-7(4), 95346E7) Recorded Bks.
The unforgettable story of Marie Antoinette.

Queen's Confession: The Story of Marie Antoinette. unabr. collector's ed. Victoria Holt. Read by Donada Peters. 12 cass. (Running Time: 18 hrs.). 1995. 96.00 (978-0-7366-2988-1(2), 3677) Books on Tape.
Marie Antoinette comes to life in a story she might have written herself. From royalty to the Guillotine, a fascinating tale.

Queen's Gambit. unabr. ed. Walter Tevis. Narrated by Alexandra O'Karma. 7 cass. (Running Time: 10 hrs. 30 mins.). 1987. 60.00 (978-1-55690-431-8(2), 87870E7) Recorded Bks.
Beth was young, struggling for survival in a hostile, incomprehensible world when she found the elegant, deadly game of chess. It gave her strength & power, as long as she won.

Queen's Museum & Other Fanciful Tales. unabr. ed. Frank Richard Stockton. Read by Flo Gibson. 4 cass. (Running Time: 6 hrs.). (J). (gr. 2-5). 1989. 19.95 (978-1-55685-139-1(1)) Audio Bk Con.
Features "The Bee-Man of Orn," "The Christmas Truants," "The Griffin & the Minor Canon," "Old Pipes & the Dryad," "The Clocks of Rondaine," "The Fruit of the Fragile Palm," "Christmas Before Last," "Prince Hassak's March," "The Philopena" & "The Accommodating Circumstance".

Queen's Necklace see Extraordinary Adventures of Arsene Lupin

Queens of Country Music. 2006. audio compact disk 5.95 (978-1-59987-521-7(7)) Braun Media.

Queen's Pirate: Queen Elizabeth I & Sir Francis Drake. Short Stories. As told by Jim Weiss. 1 cass. (Running Time: 1 hr.). Dramatization. (J). 2002. 10.95 (978-1-882513-53-6(3)) Greathall Prods.

Queen's Pirate: Queen Elizabeth I & Sir Francis Drake. Short Stories. As told by Jim Weiss. 1 CD. (Running Time: 1 hr.). Dramatization. (YA). (gr. 2 up). 2002. audio compact disk 14.95 (978-1-882513-78-9(9)) Greathall Prods.

Queen's Ransom. Fiona Buckley. Read by Nadia May. 9 CDs. (Running Time: 41400 sec.). (Mystery at Queen Elizabeth I's Court Ser.). 2000. audio compact disk 72.00 (978-0-7861-9869-6(9), 2594) Blckstn Audio.
Lady-in-Waiting Ursula Blanchard has a mandate from the Secretary of State to spy on behalf of Queen Elizabeth I. Although she has already proven herself worthy of the Queen's gratitude, Ursula now must travel to France, where civil war may break out at any moment, to hand-carry a letter from Elizabeth to the Queen mother & Regent, Catherine. The mission to mediate peace between warring Protestant & Catholic French factions seems clear, but there are hidden forces at work.

Queen's Ransom: A Mystery at Queen Elizabeth I's Court Featuring Ursula Blanchard. unabr. ed. Fiona Buckley. Read by Nadia May. 7 cass. (Running Time: 10 hrs.). 2000. 49.95 (978-0-7861-1795-6(8), 2594) Blckstn Audio.

Queen's Secret. unabr. ed. Jean Plaidy. Read by Joan Walker. 8 cass. (Running Time: 12 hrs.). 2001. 69.95 (978-0-7531-0995-3(6), 001016) Pub: ISIS Audio GBR. Dist(s): Ulverscroft US

Queeny & Umber - Quality Friends. unabr. ed. Georgene Bradshaw & Charlene Wrighton. Lyrics by Carla Piper. Music by Carla Piper. Lyrics by Janne Bradshaw. Music by Janne Bradshaw. Illus. by Irene Clark. 1 cass. (Running Time: 17 min.). (J). 1999. 24.95 (978-1-886441-29-3(4), QCC4283) Zoo-phonics.
Story tells how Umber Umbrella Bird protects Queeny & her babies in a rainstorm. They become "quality" friends. Story & music reinforce learning of the phoneme "qu." Students can listen to the story as they read along with Level B3 Read-A-Long & they can sing along with the Lyric Booklet.

Queer Chair see Complete Ghost Stories

Queer Little Folks. Harriet Beecher Stowe. Read by Bobbie Frohman & Susan McCarthy. Engineer Scott Weiser. Music by David Thom.Tr. of 88. (ENG.). (J). 2008. audio compact disk 14.95 (978-0-9821853-0-8(8)) Alcazar AudioWorks.

Quelle Heure est-il Mickey? 1 cass. (Running Time: 1 hr. 30 mins.).Tr. of What Time Is It Mickey?. (FRE.). (J). (gr. 3 up). 1991. bk. 12.95 (1AD014) Olivia & Hill.

Quentin Corn. Mary Stolz. Narrated by Herb Duncan. 3 CDs. (Running Time: 3 hrs. 15 mins.). (gr. 5 up). audio compact disk 29.00 (978-1-4025-0474-7(8)) Recorded Bks.

Quentin Corn, unabr. ed. Mary Stolz. Narrated by Herb Duncan. 3 cass. (Running Time: 3 hrs. 15 mins.). (gr. 5 up). 1992. 27.00 (978-1-55690-584-1(X), 92121E7) Recorded Bks.
To save himself from becoming the main course at a barbecue, a pig disguises himself as a boy. It looks as if his daring trick will work until he meets young Emily, who is not fooled for a moment.

Quentin Crisp. Interview with Quentin Crisp. 1 cass. (Running Time: 30 min.). 1981. 12.95 (L015) TFR.
The naked civil servant, Crisp, talks about living in style.

Quentin Durward. unabr. ed. Walter Scott, Sr. Narrated by Flo Gibson. 12 cass. (Running Time: 18 hrs.). 2003. 39.95 (978-1-55685-667-9(9)) Audio Bk Con.
A brave youth in Louis XI's Scottish Guards fights to preserve the king's reign & woos the beautiful Countess of Croye.

Quentins. Maeve Binchy. Read by Terry Donnelly. 11 CDs. (Running Time: 16 hrs. 30 mins.). 2002. audio compact disk 99.95 (978-0-7927-2777-4(0), CCD 263); 79.95 (978-0-7927-2776-7(2)) Pub: Chivers Audio Bks GBR. Dist(s): AudioGO
Is it possible to tell the story of a generation, a city through the history of a restaurant? Ella Brady thinks so. She wants to film a documentary about Quentins that will capture the spirit of Dublin from the 1970s to the present day. And Quentin has a thousand stories to tell: tales of love, of betrayal, of revenge, of times when it looked ready for success, and of times when it seemed as if it must close in failure.

Quest. Laurie Blass. (C). 1999. 75.15 (978-0-07-913098-3(4), ESL/ELT) Pub: McGrw-H Hghr Educ. Dist(s): McGraw

Quest. Wilbur Smith & Wilbur Smith. Read by Clive Mantle. (Running Time: 6 hrs.). (ENG., 2007. 22.95 (978-0-230-01379-7(1)) Pub: Macmillan UK GBR. Dist(s): IPG Chicago

Quest. abr. ed. Wilbur Smith. Read by Clive Mantle. (Running Time: 25200 sec.). (ENG., 2007. audio compact disk 24.95 (978-0-230-01378-0(3)) Pub: Macmillan UK GBR. Dist(s): IPG Chicago

Quest, unabr. ed. Helen R. Hunt. Read by Flo Gibson. 8 cass. (Running Time: 11 hrs.). 1998. 26.95 (978-1-55685-540-5(0)) Audio Bk Con.
This semi-autobiographical feminist classic tells of Jean Winthrop's survival of her parents' unhappy marriage & her growth in searching for a meaningful life.

Quest. unabr. ed. Wilbur Smith. Narrated by Simon Vance. 2 MP3-CDs. (Running Time: 24 hrs.). 2007. 84.95 (978-0-7927-4901-1(4), Chivers Sound Lib); audio compact disk 134.95 (978-0-7927-4863-2(8), Chivers Sound Lib); 115.95 (978-0-7927-4925-7(1), Chivers Sound Lib) AudioGO.
Following River God, The Seventh Scroll, and Warlock, The Quest continues the epic story of the Warlock, Taita, wise in the lore of the ancient Gods and a master of magic and the supernatural. Egypt is struck by a series of terrible plagues that cripple the Kingdom, and then the ultimate disaster follows - the Nile fails. The waters that nourish and sustain the land dry up. Something catastrophic is taking place in the distant and totally unexplored depths of Africa from where the mighty river springs. In desperation Pharaoh sends for Taita, the only man who might be able to reach the source of the Nile and discover the cause of all their woes. But none have any idea of what a terrible enemy lies in ambush for The Warlock in those mysterious lands at the end of their world.

Quest. unabr. ed. Wilbur Smith. Read by Simon Vance. 19 CDs. (Running Time: 24 hrs. 0 mins. 0 sec.). (ENG.). 2007. audio compact disk 59.95 (978-1-4272-0133-1(1)) Pub: Macmill Audio. Dist(s): Macmillan

Quest, Vol.. I. unabr. ed. Jerry Ahern. Read by Charlie O'Dowd. 2 vols. No. 3. 2003. (978-1-58807-813-1(2)) Am Pubng Inc.

Quest, Vol. I. unabr. ed. Jerry Ahern. Read by Charlie O'Dowd. 2 cass. (Running Time: 3 hrs.). (Survivalist Ser.: No. 3). 2003. 18.00 (978-1-58807-304-4(1)) Am Pubng Inc.

Quest, Vol.. II. unabr. ed. Jerry Ahern. Read by Charlie O'Dowd. 2 vols. No. 3. 2003. (978-1-58807-814-8(0)) Am Pubng Inc.

Quest, Vol. II. unabr. ed. Jerry Ahern. Read by Charlie O'Dowd. 2 cass. (Running Time: 3 hrs.). (Survivalist Ser.: No. 3). 2003. 18.00 (978-1-58807-305-1(X)) Am Pubng Inc.

Quest: A Passion for Life. Simon and Schuster Staff. 1999. audio compact disk 12.00 (978-0-671-04772-6(8), Sound Ideas) S&S Audio.

Quest for a Lost World. Brian Blessed. 2001. (978-0-333-78245-3(3)) Macmillan UK GBR.

Quest for a Main Squeeze. 2001. audio compact disk 9.95 (978-1-930805-13-2(6)) XC Pubng.

Quest for a Soulmate: Powerful Insights for a Loving Relationship. unabr. ed. Liliane Fournier. (Running Time: 2 hrs.). (Quest Ser.). 2009. 19.99 (978-1-4233-8037-5(1), 9781423380375, Brilliance MP3) Brilliance Audio.

Quest for a Soulmate: Powerful Insights for a Loving Relationship. unabr. ed. Liliane Fournier. Read by Liliane Fournier. (Running Time: 2 hrs.). (Quest Ser.). 2009. 39.97 (978-1-4233-8038-2(X), 9781423380382, Brlnc Audio MP3 Lib); audio compact disk 55.97 (978-1-4233-8036-8(3), 9781423380368, BriAudCD Unabrid) Brilliance Audio.

Quest for a Wife: Mamiminbin, A Palawan Epic Sung by Masinu. Nicole Revel & Masinu Intaray. (ENG, FRE & PAL.). 2000. bk. 80.95 (978-92-3-003732-1(X)) Pub: UNESCO FRA. Dist(s): Renouf Publ

Quest for Alexis. Nancy Buckingham. Read by Judith Franklyn. 5 cass. (Running Time: 7 hrs. 30 mins.). 2001. 49.95 (978-1-85496-568-4(9), 65689) Pub: UlverLrgPrint GBR. Dist(s): Ulverscroft US

Quest for Camelot. 1 cass. (Running Time: 90 mins.). (J). 7.98 Blisterpack, incl. bklet., artwk. & certificate of Knighthood. (KID 72760); audio compact disk 12.78 Jewel box, incl. bklet. (KID 72761) NewSound.
Kayley & her friend Garrett, save the kingdom of Camelot from the evil Ruber.

Quest for Camelot. Perf. by Leann Rimes et al. 1 cass. (Running Time: 90 mins.). (J). 8.78 Soundtrack. (ATL 83097); audio compact disk 14.38 Jewel box, soundtrack. (ATL 83097) NewSound.
Kayley, must fulfill her family's obligation to protect the King & his magical sword, Excalibur, against the evil Knight Ruber & his wicked Griffin.

Quest for Cosmic Justice. unabr. collector's ed. Thomas Sowell. Read by Barrett Whitener. 5 cass. (Running Time: 7 hrs. 30 min.). 1999. 40.00 (978-0-7366-4864-6(X), 5194) Books on Tape.
The country's best-selling libertarian author gives a sweeping indictment of what he has dubbed "cosmic justice"-the new idea that the playing field must be tilted in order to be level.

Quest for Excellence. Marcus S. Robinson & Murray P. Kammer. 1993. 8.95 (978-0-9639703-2-9(1)) Wetware.

Quest for Excellence: A Pesonal Guide to High Performance. Lloyd Glauberman. 2 cass. (Hypno-Peripheral Processing Tapes Ser.). 34.95 Set. (851PA-1M) Nightingale-Conant.
This breakthrough psychotechnology program combines the methods of hypnotherapy with the latest teachings of Neuro-Linguistic Programming. Each high-impact tape gently overloads your conscious mind with messages on two channels at once, creating a synergistic whole that unleashes both hemispheres of your brain.

Quest for Freedom. Richard Delaney. Narrated by Richard Delaney. (ENG.). 2009. 29.95 (978-0-9706798-3-3(1)) Talahi Media.

Quest for Happiness, No. 1. Swami Jyotirmayananda. 1 cass. (Running Time: 45 min.). 1990. 10.00 Yoga Res Foun.

Quest for Happiness, No. 2. Swami Jyotirmayananda. 1 cass. (Running Time: 45 min.). 1990. 10.00 Yoga Res Foun.

Quest for Happiness, No. 3. Swami Jyotirmayananda. 1 cass. (Running Time: 45 min.). 1990. 10.00 Yoga Res Foun.

Quest for Happiness, No. 4. Swami Jyotirmayananda. 1 cass. (Running Time: 45 min.). 1990. 10.00 Yoga Res Foun.

Quest for Life. unabr. ed. Liliane Fournier & Gérard Fournier. Read by Liliane Fournier. (Running Time: 3 hrs.). (Quest Ser.). 2009. 39.97 (978-1-4233-8022-1(3), 9781423380221, Brlnc Audio MP3 Lib); 19.99 (978-1-4233-8021-4(5), 9781423380214, Brilliance MP3); audio compact disk 19.99 (978-1-4233-7825-9(3), 9781423378259, Bril Audio CD Unabri) Brilliance Audio.

Quest for Love. Swami Jyotirmayananda. 1 cass. (Running Time: 45 min.). 1990. 12.99 Yoga Res Foun.

Quest for Love & Passion: Breakthrough Views on Relationships. unabr. ed. Liliane Fournier. (Running Time: 2 hrs.). (Quest Ser.). 2009. 19.99 (978-1-4233-8033-7(9), 9781423380337, Brilliance MP3) Brilliance Audio.

Quest for Love & Passion: Breakthrough Views on Relationships. unabr. ed. Liliane Fournier. Read by Liliane Fournier. (Running Time: 2 hrs.). (Quest Ser.). 2009. 39.97 (978-1-4233-8034-4(7), 9781423380344, Brlnc Audio MP3 Lib); audio compact disk 55.97 (978-1-4233-8032-0(0), 9781423380320, BriAudCD Unabrid) Brilliance Audio.

Quest for Love Trilogy: Unleash Your Passion. John Gray et al. 3 cass. (Running Time: 180 min.). 2000. 29.95 (978-0-671-77182-9(5), Sound Ideas) S&S Audio.

Quest for Meaning, Vol. 1, Pts. I-II. Instructed by Robert Kane. 12 cass. (Running Time: 12 hrs.). 1999. 129.95 (978-1-56585-119-1(6)); audio compact disk 179.95 (978-1-56585-716-2(X)) Teaching Co.

Quest for Meaning Vol. 2: Values, Ethics, & the Modern Experience. Instructed by Robert Kane. 6 cass. (Running Time: 6 hrs.). 1999. 129.95 (978-1-56585-120-7(X)); audio compact disk 179.95 (978-1-56585-717-9(8)) Teaching Co.

Quest for Reality in Devotional Literature. Helen G. Hole. 5 cass. Incl. Quest for Reality in Devotional Literature: Love Calls Us to the Things of This World. 1978.; Quest for Reality in Devotional Literature: The Intersection of the Timeless with Time. 1978.; Quest for Reality in Devotional Literature: The Mind's Descent into the Heart. 1978.; Quest for Reality in Devotional Literature: The Modern Search for Wholeness. 1978.; Quest for Reality in Devotional Literature: The Way of Metaphor. 1978.; 1978. 17.50 Set.; 4.50 ea. Pendle Hill.

Quest for Reality in Devotional Literature: Love Calls Us to the Things of This World see Quest for Reality in Devotional Literature

Quest for Reality in Devotional Literature: The Intersection of the Timeless with Time see Quest for Reality in Devotional Literature

Quest for Reality in Devotional Literature: The Mind's Descent into the Heart see Quest for Reality in Devotional Literature

Quest for Reality in Devotional Literature: The Modern Search for Wholeness see Quest for Reality in Devotional Literature

Quest for Reality in Devotional Literature: The Way of Metaphor see Quest for Reality in Devotional Literature

Quest for Respect: A Healing Guide for Survivors of Rape. 3rd unabr. ed. Linda Braswell. 2 cass. (Running Time: 2 hrs.). 1991. 9.95 (978-0-934793-34-6(4)) Pathfinder AZ.
A guide to aid rape survivors in working toward the path to recovery.

Quest for Spiritual Teachers. Instructed by Manly P. Hall. 8.95 (978-0-89314-232-2(8), C850721) Philos Res.

Quest for Success: Powerful Secrets to Wealth, Happiness & a Deeply Meaningful Life. unabr. ed. Liliane Fournier & Gérard Fournier. Read by Liliane Fournier. (Running Time: 2 hrs.). (Quest Ser.). 2008. 39.97 (978-1-4233-8010-8(X), 9781423380108, Brlnc Audio MP3 Lib); 19.99 (978-1-4233-8009-2(6), 9781423380092, Brilliance MP3) Brilliance Audio.

Quest for Success: Powerful Secrets to Wealth, Happiness & a Deeply Meaningful Life. unabr. ed. Liliane Fournier & Gérard Fournier. (Running Time: 2 hrs.). (Quest Ser.). 2008. audio compact disk 19.99 (978-1-4233-7816-7(4), 9781423378167, Bril Audio CD Unabri) Brilliance Audio.

Quest for the Ancient Barometer see Weather Show

Quest for the Holy Grail. Richard Rohr. 8 cass. (Running Time: 9 hrs.). 64.95 Set in vinyl album. (AA2595); 17.95 bk. 191p. (GG2220) Credence Commun.
In an isolated New Mexico mountain setting, Father Richard Rohr led 100 men through a retreat they will not soon forget. It was intense. Primitive. Shot through with struggle, passion & radical gospel. Rohr used the most powerful myth in Western culture, the quest for the Holy Grail, to help men see, feel, hear & even touch the paschal mystery. He intends this retreat for men over 35. He assumes painful familiarity with men's personal demons; the tone & language are male. Men will find in Rohr's presentations a sure guide through the central dynamic myth of our culture. Women will see more deeply into the struggles men share with them.

Quest for the Holy Grail. Donald A. Tubesing. Read by Donald A. Tubesing. 1 cass. 1988. 11.95 (978-1-57025-008-8(1)) Whole Person.
Each of us has an inner "spiritual path." The metaphors of well-being in this presentation help you discover personal pathways to spiritual wellness.

Quest for the Lost City. unabr. collector's ed. Dana Lamb. Read by Jeanne Hopson. 10 cass. (Running Time: 15 hrs.). 1984. 80.00 (978-0-7366-0624-0(6), 1586) Books on Tape.
Lamb investigates the mysterious city of ancient palaces rumored to exist in the jungled interior.

Quest: Happy, Wealthy & Wise: Powerful Secrets to Achieving Authentic Success. unabr. ed. Liliane Fournier & Gérard Fournier. Read by Liliane Fournier. (Running Time: 2 hrs.). (Quest Ser.). 2008. 39.97 (978-1-4233-8014-6(2), 9781423380146, Brlnc Audio MP3 Lib); 19.99 (978-1-4233-8013-9(4), 9781423380139, Brilliance MP3); audio compact disk 55.97 (978-1-4233-8012-2(6), 9781423380122, BriAudCD Unabrid) Brilliance Audio.

Quest Listen/Speak 1 IM AC. Laurie Blass & Pamela Hartmann. (C). 2000. 19.51 (978-0-07-242806-3(6), ESL/ELT) Pub: McGrw-H Hghr Educ. Dist(s): McGraw

Quest Listen/Speak 2 IM AC. Laurie Blass. (C). 2000. 19.51 (978-0-07-242807-0(4), ESL/ELT) Pub: McGrw-H Hghr Educ. Dist(s): McGraw

Quest Listen/Speak 3 IM AC. Pamela Hartmann & Laurie Blass. (C). 2000. 19.51 (978-0-07-242808-7(2), ESL/ELT) Pub: McGrw-H Hghr Educ. Dist(s): McGraw

Quest Three: Energy Power. abr. ed. Bernie Siegal. Read by Bernie Siegal. 1 cass. (Running Time: 1 hr.). 1999. 16.85 (978-0-671-01098-0(0)) S and S Inc.
Provides new perspectives to help us make the most of our spiritual lives.

Question. Contrib. by Emery. Prod. by Aaron Sprinkle. 2005. audio compact disk 13.99 (978-5-558-92017-8(3)) Tooth & Nail.

Question. Contrib. by Emery. Prod. by Aaron Sprinkle & Matt Carter. 2006. 17.99 (978-5-558-10142-3(3)) Tooth & Nail.

Question of Attraction: A Novel. David Nicholls. Read by Eric Steele. 9 vols. 2004. bk. 79.95 (978-0-7927-3225-9(1), CSL 658, Chivers Sound Lib); bk. 99.95 (978-0-7927-3226-6(X), SLD 658, Chivers Sound Lib) AudioGO.

***Question of Belief.** unabr. ed. Donna Leon. Narrated by David Colacci. 8 CDs. (Running Time: 9 hrs. 0 mins. 0 sec.). (Commissario Guido Brunetti Mystery Ser.: Bk. 19). (ENG.). 2010. audio compact disk 29.95 (978-1-60283-917-5(4)) Pub: AudioGO. Dist(s): Perseus Dist

***Question of Belief.** unabr. ed. Donna Leon. Narrated by David Colacci. 1 Playaway. (Running Time: 9 hrs. 15 mi[illegible] 2010. 79.95 (978-0-7927-7206-4(7)); audio compa[illegible] 79.95 (978-0-7927-7144-9(3)) AudioGO.

Question of Birthtime. R. Ostrander. 1 cass. (Running Time: 90 min.). 1990. 8.95 (887) Am Fed Astrologers.

Question of Blood. abr. ed. Ian Rankin. Read by James MacPherson. (Running Time: 6 hrs.). (Inspector Rebus Ser.). 2007. audio compact disk 14.99 (978-1-4233-3356-2(X), 9781423333562, BCD Value Price) Brilliance Audio.

***Question of Blood.** abr. ed. Ian Rankin. Read by James Macpherson. (Running Time: 6 hrs.). 2010. audio compact disk 9.99 (978-1-4418-6700-1(7), 9781441867001, BCD Value Price) Brilliance Audio.

Question of Blood. unabr. ed. Ian Rankin. Read by Michael Page. 8 cass. (Running Time: 12 hrs.). (Inspector Rebus Novel Ser.). 2004. 34.95 (978-1-59086-489-0(1), 1590864891, BAU); 87.25 (978-1-59086-490-6(5), 1590864905, BrilAudUnabridg) Brilliance Audio.
When a former soldier and recluse murders two 17-year-old students at a posh Edinburgh boarding school, Rebus immediately suspects there is more to the case than meets the eye. Army investigators show up to snoop around the scene of the crime, and links between the killer and a local group of "Goths" (a morbid clique of black-clad teens who listen to heavy metal music) begin to surface. But just as Rebus finds himself in the thick of the murder inquiry, he's threatened with suspension from the police force: a man who had been menacing his partner and friend, Detective Sergeant Siobhan Clarke, dies in the same house fire that has left Rebus with horrible, painful burns. Rebus is immediately suspected of foul play. Now Rebus is faced with two harrowing missions: He must get to the root of the boarding school killing even as he tries to clear his own name.

Question of Blood. unabr. ed. Ian Rankin. Read by Michael Page. (Running Time: 12 hrs.). (Inspector Rebus Novel Ser.). 2004. 39.25 (978-1-59335-536-4(X), 159335536X, Brlnc Audio MP3 Lib); 24.95 (978-1-59335-273-8(5), 1593352735, Brilliance MP3) Brilliance Audio.

Question of Blood. unabr. ed. Ian Rankin. Read by Michael Page. (Running Time: 12 hrs.). (Inspector Rebus Ser.). 2004. 39.25 (978-1-59710-621-4(6), 1597106216, BADLE); 24.95 (978-1-59710-620-7(8), 1597106208, BAD) Brilliance Audio.

***Question of Blood.** unabr. ed. Ian Rankin. Read by Michael Page. (Running Time: 13 hrs.). (Inspector Rebus Ser.). 2010. audio compact disk 29.99 (978-1-4418-4083-7(4), 9781441840837, Bril Audio CD Unabri); audio compact disk 89.97 (978-1-4418-4084-4(2), 9781441840844, BriAudCD Unabrid) Brilliance Audio.

***question of Death.** Kerry Greenwood. Read by Stephanie Daniel. (Running Time: 5 hrs. 40 mins.). (Phryne Fisher Mystery: Ser.). 2009. 69.99 (978-1-74214-545-7(0), 9781742145457) Pub: Bolinda Pubng AUS. Dist(s): Bolinda Pub Inc

Question of Death. unabr. ed. Kerry Greenwood. Read by Stephanie Daniel. (Phryne Fisher Ser.). 2009. audio compact disk 77.95 (978-1-921415-85-2(1), 9781921415852) Pub: Bolinda Pubng AUS. Dist(s): Bolinda Pub Inc

Question of God. Armand M. Nicholi, Jr. Narrated by Robert Whitfield. (Running Time: 8 hrs. 30 mins.). (C). 2002. 27.95 (978-1-59912-706-4(7)) Iofy Corp.

Question of God. unabr. ed. Armand M. Nicholi, Jr. Read by Robert Whitfield. 6 pieces. 2004. reel tape 29.95 (978-0-7861-2525-8(X)); audio compact disk 35.95 (978-0-7861-9078-2(7)) Blckstn Audio.

Question of God: C. S. Lewis & Sigmund Freud Debate God, Love, Sex, & the Meaning of Life. unabr. ed. Armand M. Nicholi, Jr. Read by Robert Whitfield. 6 cass. (Running Time: 8 hrs. 30 mins.). 2002. 44.95 (978-0-7861-2173-1(4), 2924); audio compact disk 56.00 (978-0-7861-9546-6(0), 2924); audio compact disk 24.95 (978-0-7861-9251-9(8), 2924) Blckstn Audio.
Presents a fascinating comparison of the beliefs of Sigmund Freud and C. S. Lewis.

Question of Good & Bad. Swami Amar Jyoti. 1 cass. 1975. 9.95 (K-77) Truth Consciousness.
God's will is not bound by our dualistic notions of good & bad. Reading the open book of life. Guidelines for diet & Health.

Question of Guilt. unabr. ed. Frances Fyfield. Read by Rula Lenska. 8 cass. (Running Time: 8 hrs.). (Prosecutor Helen West Mysteries Ser.). 1993. 69.95 (978-0-7451-5972-0(9), CAB 602) AudioGO.

Question of Guilt. unabr. ed. Frances Fyfield. Read by Rula Lenska. 8 cass. (Running Time: 12 hrs.). (West & Bailey Mystery Ser.). 2000. 59.95 (CAB 602) Pub: Chivers Audio Bks GBR. Dist(s): AudioGO
When rich, middle-aged widow Eileen Cartwright becomes obsessed with Michael Bernard, her handsome solicitor, she plots the murder of his pretty wife. A Polish hospital porter is hired for the killing. Bumbling and remorseful, he is quickly caught. Prosecutor Helen West and Detective Geoffrey Bailey are assigned to the case. Only when Eileen Cartwright's extraordinary evil

reaches out even from behind prison bars, and her alliance with a young psychopath is revealed, are events brought to a tense and thrilling climax.

Question of Identity: Who Am I? Reed Hayes. 1 cass. 8.95 (149) Am Fed Astrologers.
Chart setup, angular houses, influence of planets on personality.

Question of Murder. Jessica Fletcher & Donald Bain. Read by Cynthia Darlow. 6 CDs. (Running Time: 24300 sec.). (Murder, She Wrote Ser.). 2006. audio compact disk 64.95 (978-0-7927-3943-2(4), SLD 923) AudioGO.

Question of Murder. Jessica Fletcher et al. Read by Cynthia Darlow. 5 cass. (Running Time: 24300 sec.). (Murder, She Wrote Ser.). 2006. 49.95 (978-0-7927-3942-5(6), CSL 923) AudioGO.

Question of Trust. Carole Thayne. 3 cass. 2004. 14.95 (978-1-59156-227-6(9)) Covenant Comms.

Question: Who Is Jesus? John 6:35-66;John 10:30. Ed Young. 1998. 4.45 (978-0-7417-2188-4(0), A1188) Win Walk.

Questioning Spirituality. David Steindl-Rast. 1 cass. 9.00 (OC2LW) Sound Horizons AV.

Questions along the Way. Swami Amar Jyoti. 1 cass. 1980. 9.95 (N-12) Truth Consciousness.
Difference between emotions & feelings, instincts & desires. The true meaning of love. Relationships with God.

Questions & Answers. Gordon Clark. 1 cass. (Miscellaneous Lectures: No. 5). 5.00 Trinity Found.

Questions & Answers. unabr. ed. Perf. by Eknath Easwaran. 1 cass. (Running Time: 1 hr.). 7.95 (978-1-58638-597-2(6)) Nilgiri Pr.

Questions & Answers, No. 1. J. Krishnamurti. 1 cass. (Running Time: 75 min.). (Saanen, Switzerland Talks - 1985 Ser.: No. 6). 8.50 (ASQ851) Krishnamurti.

Questions & Answers: At Open Gate. unabr. ed. Myrtle Smith. Prod. by David Keyston. 1 cass. (Running Time: 1 hrs. 14 min.). (Myrtle Smyth Audiotapes Ser.). 1998. (978-1-893107-10-6(8), M10, Cross & Crown) Healing Unltd.

Questions & Answers No. 1: Are You an Individual? J. Krishnamurti. 1 cass. (Running Time: 1 hr.). (Ojai Public Talks - 1984 Ser.: No. 5). 1999. 8.50 (AJQ841) Krishnamurti.
In the idyllic setting of the oak grove in Ojai, California, Krishnamurti began giving talks in 1922. Over the years, hundreds of thousands of people have heard Krishnamurti explore every aspect of our lives, his language & expression constantly changing, as he strove to communicate to each successive generation those profound truths which he had come upon & which he maintained were accessible to all.

Questions & Answers No. 1: God & Evil. J. Krishnamurti. 1 cass. (Running Time: 75 min.). (Brockwood Talks - 1984 Ser.: No. 5). 1999. 8.50 (ABQ841) Krishnamurti.
Krishnamurti addresses the timeless questions which mankind has always asked & he invites each one of us to suspend our beliefs & theories, to observe together, to walk together with the speakers as we inquire into the human condition.

Questions & Answers No. 1: Illusion Can Be a Fact. J. Krishnamurti. 1 cass. (Running Time: 75 min.). (Madras, India Talks 1985 Ser.: No. 5). 1999. 8.50 (AMQ851) Krishnamurti.
Krishnamurti addresses the timeless questions which mankind has always asked & he invites each one of us to suspend our beliefs & theories, to observe together, to walk together with the speaker as we inquire into the human condition.

Questions & Answers No. 1: To Be Psychologically Simple. J. Krishnamurti. 1 cass. (Running Time: 75 min.). (Brockwood Park Talks, 1985 Ser.). 1999. 8.50 (ABQ851) Krishnamurti.
Questions examined: How can we know if mystical & spiritual experiences are illusions unless we know reality? Is illness due simply to degeneration or abuse of the body, or does it have some other significance? What is my responsibility toward the present world crisis? Does asking for guidance necessarily prevent understanding, or can it be a means of discovering ourselves? If asking for guidance prevents understanding, what is the sense of listening to you, Krishnamurti? What is total vision? Is it an extension of our normal brain function or something totally different?.

Questions & Answers No. 1: Understanding Wholly Not Intellectually. J. Krishnamurti. 1 cass. (Running Time: 1 hr.). (Ojai Public Talks - 1983 Ser.: No. 5). 1999. 8.50 (AJQ831) Krishnamurti.
In the idyllic setting of the oak grove in Ojai, California, Krishnamurti began giving talks in 1922. Over the years, hundreds of thousands of people have heard Krishnamurti explore every aspect of our lives, his language & expression constantly changing, as he strove to communicate to each successive generation those profound truths which he had come upon & which he maintained were accessible to all.

Questions & Answers No. 1: Violence, Fear & Religious Division. J. Krishnamurti. 1 cass. (Running Time: 1 hr.). (Ojai Public Talks - 1982 Ser.: No. 1). 1999. 8.50 (AJQ821) Krishnamurti.

Questions & Answers No. 1: Why Escape from Fact? J. Krishnamurti. 1 cass. (Running Time: 75 min.). (Brockwood Park Talks, 1983 Ser.). 1999. 8.50 (ABQ831) Krishnamurti.
Questions examined: How do we know what you are saying is true? Is desire fundamental? Without desire could we function at all? Is there any solution to jealousy & mistrust other than isolating myself? When one understands intellectually what a habit is, how does one break free of habit?.

Questions & Answers No. 2: Awareness, Concentration & Attention. J. Krishnamurti. 1 cass. (Running Time: 1 hr.). (Ojai Public Talks - 1982 Ser.: No. 8). 8.50 (AJQ822) Krishnamurti.
In the idyllic setting of the oak grove in Ojai, California, Krishnamurti began giving talks in 1922. Over the years, hundreds of thousands of people have heard Krishnamurti explore every aspect of our lives, his language & expression constantly changing, as he strove to communicate to each successive generation those profound truths which he had come upon, & which he maintained were accessible to all.

Questions & Answers No. 2: Brain, Mind & Consciusness. J. Krishnamurti. 1 cass. (Running Time: 75 min.). (Brockwood Park Talks, 1983 Ser.). 1999. 8.50 (ABQ832) Krishnamurti.
Questions examined: Is awareness beyond time? What is the relationship between consciousness, mind, brain, & thought? Why don't you encourage people to hold group discussions? How is one to approach the problem of livelihood? You say very little about law. Why is that?.

Questions & Answers No. 2: Facts, Opinion, Justice & Sexuality? J. Krishnamurti. 1 cass. (Running Time: 1 hr.). (Ojai Public Talks - 1984 Ser.: No. 6). 1999. 8.50 (AJQ842) Krishnamurti.
In the idyllic setting of the oak grove in Ojai, California, Krishnamurti began giving talks in 1922. Over the years, hundreds of thousands of people have heard Krishnamurti explore every aspect of our lives, his language & expression constantly changing, as he strove to communicate to each successive generation those profound truths which he had come upon & which he maintained were accessible to all.

Questions & Answers No. 2: How Do We Waste Our Energy? J. Krishnamurti. 1 cass. (Running Time: 1 hr.). (Ojai Public Talks - 1983 Ser.: No. 6). 1999. 8.50 (AJQ832) Krishnamurti.

Questions & Answers No. 2: Is Action Based on Ideas? J. Krishnamurti. 1 cass. (Running Time: 75 min.). (Saanen, Switzerland Talks - 1985 Ser.: No. 7). 1999. 8.50 (ASQ852) Krishnamurti.

Questions & Answers No. 2: Living Vilnerably. J. Krishnamurti. 1 cass. (Running Time: 75 min.). (Brockwood Park Talks, 1985 Ser.). 1999. 8.50 (ABQ852) Krishnamurti.
Questions examined: Is there a faculty to see that there is no path to truth outside myself? What will give me the need, the energy to move in this direction? I am afraid to change. If I change, what will happen afterwards? How does one meet aggression & psychological attack from a close relative from whom one cannot escape? What do you say to people who pick part of what you say that fits their problems or interest & then discard the rest? There are many accounts of people following a particular discipline who come upon the immeasurable. Are they self-deluded?.

Questions & Answers No. 2: Observing Without Thought. J. Krishnamurti. 1 cass. (Running Time: 75 min.). (Madras, India Talks 1985 Ser.: No. 6). 1999. 8.50 (AMQ852) Krishnamurti.
Krishnamurti addresses the timeless questions which mankind has always asked & he invites each one of us to suspend our beliefs & theories, to observe together, to walk together with the speaker as we inquire into the human condition.

Questions & Answers No. 2: Why Do We Pray? J. Krishnamurti. 1 cass. (Running Time: 75 min.). (Brockwood Talks - 1984 Ser.: No. 2). 1999. 8.50 (ABQ842) Krishnamurti.
Krishnamurti addresses the timeless questions which mankind has always asked & he invites each one of us to suspend our beliefs & theories, to observe together, to walk together with the speakers as we inquire into the human condition.

Questions & Answers No. 3: Responsibility, Respectability & Self-Knowing. J. Krishnamurti. 1 cass. (Running Time: 1 hr.). (Ojai Public Talks - 1982 Ser.: No. 9). 1999. 8.50 (AJQ823) Krishnamurti.
In the idyllic setting of the oak grove in Ojai, California, Krishnamurti began giving talks in 1922. Over the years, hundreds of thousands of people have heard Krishnamurti explore every aspect of our lives, his language & expression constantly changing, as he strove to communicate to each successive generation those profound truths which he had come upon & which he maintained were accessible to all.

Questions & Answers No. 3: Time, Thought & Death. J. Krishnamurti. 1 cass. (Running Time: 75 min.). (Saanen, Switzerland Talks - 1985 Ser.: No. 8). 1999. 8.50 (ASQ853) Krishnamurti.

Questions & Answers No. 4: Negation of the "I" J. Krishnamurti. 1 cass. (Running Time: 1 hr.). (Ojai Public Talks - 1982 Ser.: No. 10). 1999. 8.50 (AJQ824) Krishnamurti.

Questions & Answers about Demons. Jack Deere. 1 cass. (Running Time: 90 mins.). (Demonic Inroads Ser.: Vol. 4). 2000. 5.00 (JD02-004) Morning NC.
First laying a foundation of insight into Satan's overall strategy, Jack then builds upon it with practical knowledge of the Christian's authority over demonic forces.

Questions & Answers about Tardive Dyskinesia. National Institute of Mental Health Staff. Read by Neva Duyndam. 1 cass. 1989. 9.95 (978-1-878159-07-6(0)) Duvall Media.
Tardive dyskinesia, a possible side effect of anti-psychotic drugs.

Questions & Answers; Bishop J. Timlin's Saturday Homily. Peter M. Stravinskas. 1 cass. (National Meeting of the Institute, 1994 Ser.). 4.00 (94N5) IRL Chicago.

Questions & Answers on Conversations with God, unabr. ed. Neale Donald Walsch. Read by Neale Donald Walsch. 4 cass. (Running Time: 6 hrs. 30 min.). 1999. 24.95 (978-1-57453-336-1(3)) Audio Lit.
Questions & answers are organized into a sequence that allows listeners to engage with the issues in a new way. By hearing how others have responded, listeners are invited to bring their own insights & thoughts to this material. Subjects covered range from the universal to the everyday, including relationships, health, sexuality, parenting & spiritual growth.

Questions & Answers on Relationship. 1 cass. (Running Time: 70 min.). (Relationship Ser.). 9.95 (QA-2) Crystal Clarity.
Discusses sex & celibacy, how to conceive a spiritual child; differences in male & female energies & approaches to life; Women's Lib examined; why women today are increasingly in the forefront of society; what to do when a spouse leaves the path.

Questions & Answers Session, Friday Night Homily. Jose Sanchez. 1 cass. (National Meeting of the Institute, 1994 Ser.). 4.00 (94N2) IRL Chicago.

Questions & Meanings of Intimate Relationship. 11 cass. (Running Time: 14 hrs.). 1992. 71.95 set. (978-0-7822-0399-8(X), INTIMATE) C G Jung IL.
This course explores the intimate human relationship in the light cast by analytical psychology & provides an orientation for coming to terms with oneself & with others as we enter the inevitable dance of being human.

Questions & Sermons from the Scriptures. Charles B. Beckert. 1 cass. 1996. 9.98 (978-1-57734-004-1(3), 06005322) Covenant Comms.
Creative ways to improve your knowledge & testimony of the scriptures.

Questions at the Foot of the Cross. Benedict J. Groeschel. 2 cass. (Running Time: 2 hrs. 8 min.). 1995. 17.95 Set. (TAH326) Alba Hse Comns.
We can't celebrate the resurrection without first dealing personally with the crucifixion & death of Jesus & our own sinfulness. This gives the answer to the final question: why are you seeking the living among the dead? Perfect reflection material for Lent & Good Friday.

Questions Christians Ask see Preguntas que Hacen los Cristianos

Questions for Success Vol. 1: Seven Categories of Questions That Bring Sales Success. unabr. ed. Karl Walinskas. 1 cass. (Running Time: 50 min.). 1998. bk. 12.95 (978-0-9667084-3-1(1)) Speaking Connect.
Learn the questions that give you the most valuable asset you'll ever have in making the sale - information!.

Questions for the Possibilites. Karen Proctor. 2007. audio compact disk 17.99 (978-1-60247-198-6(3)) Tate Pubng.

***Questions of a Man in Agony.** Featuring Ravi Zacharias. 2009. audio compact disk 9.00 (978-1-61256-014-4(8)) Ravi Zach.

Questions of Faith: What Do We Believe? abr. ed. Contrib. by Time Magazine. (Running Time: 35 mins.). (ENG.). 2006. 9.99 (978-1-59483-860-6(7)) Pub: Hachet Audio. Dist(s): HachBkGrp

Questions of Value, Vol. I-II. Instructed by Patrick Grim. 12 cass. (Running Time: 12 hrs). 2005. 129.95 (978-1-59803-092-1(2)); audio compact disk 69.95 (978-1-59803-094-5(9)) Teaching Co.

Questions on Archetypal Psychology. Read by Rafael Lopez-Pedraza. 1 cass. (Running Time: 1 hr.). 1984. 9.95 (978-0-7822-0150-5(4), ND7705) C G Jung IL.

Questions Rarely Asked. Riane Eisler. 1 cass. 9.00 (A0403-89) Sound Photosyn.
The partnership advocate is relaxed & personal as Faustin persues this rare interview with Brian recording.

Quests. Vada M. Gipson. 4 cass. 2003. 13.50 (978-0-9605014-2-7(8)) Levada.

Quete d'un Langue Parfaite dans l'Histoire de la Culture Europeenne. Umberto Eco. 1 cass. (Running Time: 60 mins.). (College de France Lectures). (FRE.). 1996. 21.95 (1856-LQP) Olivia & Hill.

Qui a Pique Mon Fromage? Spencer Johnson.Tr. of Who Moved My Cheese?. pap. bk. 18.95 (978-2-89558-006-5(5)) Pub: Coffragants CAN. Dist(s): Penton Overseas

Qui File Cecile? Boutegege & Longo. audio compact disk 12.95 (978-0-8219-3785-3(5)) EMC-Paradigm.

Quiche of Death. unabr. ed. M. C. Beaton, pseud. Read by Donald Peters. 6 CDs. (Running Time: 9 hrs.). (Agatha Raisin Mystery Ser.: Bk. 1). 2002. audio compact disk 48.00 (978-0-7366-8532-0(4)) Books on Tape.
The pretty Cotswold village of Carsely, where 20-year residents are called "incomers," is the retirement choice of fiftysomething p.r. career woman Agatha Raisin, fulfilling a lifelong dream. Gruff, tough, but not stupid, Agatha begins to soften her image - to the extent of entering a spinach quiche in Carsely's annual "best quiche" competition, buying one in London to pass off as her own. It doesn't win - but is taken home by Mr. Cummings-Browne, the judge and a noted philanderer. He eats it and dies, to be found next morning by his snobbish wife, Vera. The police pinpoint cowbane as the poison and call it an accident. But Agatha is sure there's murder afoot and nearly loses her own life before she proves it.

Quiche of Death, unabr. collector's ed. M. C. Beaton, pseud. Read by Donada Peters. 5 cass. (Running Time: 7 hrs. 30 mins.). (Agatha Raisin Mystery Ser.: Bk. 1). 1999. 40.00 (978-0-7366-4507-2(1), 4940) Books on Tape.
Newly retired & eager to make friends in her new home in the Cotswold village of Carsely, Agatha Raisin buys a quiche & enters it in the village quiche-making competition. It doesn't win but is taken home by Mr. Cummings-Browne, the judge & a noted philanderer. He eats it & dies, to be found next morning by his snobbish wife, Vera. The police pinpoint cowbane as the poison & call it an accident. But Agatha is sure there's murder afoot & nearly loses her own life before she proves it.

Quick & Easy Classroom Interventions. 3 CD set. (Running Time: 180 min). 2002. audio compact disk 21.95 (978-1-930429-31-4(2)) Pub: Love Logic. Dist(s): Penton Overseas

Quick & Easy Classroom Interventions: Twenty-Three Proven Tools for Increasing Student Cooperation. unabr. ed. Jim Fay. Interview with Bert Gurule. 2 cass. (Running Time: 2 hrs.). 1998. 18.95 (978-0-944634-53-0(2)) Pub: Love Logic. Dist(s): Penton Overseas
Classroom management techniques presented allow teachers to maintain classroom control with the most troublesome classroom behaviors.

Quick & Easy Learning: Echotech. Eldon Taylor. Read by Eldon Taylor. Ed. by Leslie Brice. 1 cass. (Running Time: 1 hr.). 1992. 19.95 (978-1-56705-003-5(4)) Gateways Inst.
Self improvement.

Quick & Easy Texas Hold'em: Learn to Play Poker's Most Popular Game. Neil Myers. 1 DVD. (ENG., 2005. pap. bk. 19.95 (978-0-8184-0653-9(4)) Pub: Kensgtn Pub Corp. Dist(s): Penguin Grp USA

Quick & Easy Way to Top Selling. unabr. ed. Robert L. Montgomery. Read by Robert L. Montgomery. 3 cass. (Running Time: 3 hrs.). 1985. pap. bk. & wbk. ed. 39.95 (978-1-55678-023-3(0), 1598, Lm Inc) Oasis Audio.
The key to closing 90% of calls, without lengthy meetings.

Quick & Simple ESL Arabic. Paul Pimsleur. (Running Time: 4 hrs.). 2001. 24.95 (978-1-60083-399-1(3), Audiofy Corp) Iofy Corp.

Quick & Simple ESL Chinese (Cantonese) Paul Pimsleur. (Running Time: 4 hrs.). 2001. 24.95 (978-1-60083-400-4(0), Audiofy Corp) Iofy Corp.

Quick & Simple ESL Chinese (Mandarin) Paul Pimsleur. (Running Time: 4 hrs.). 2001. 24.95 (978-1-60083-401-1(9), Audiofy Corp) Iofy Corp.

Quick & Simple ESL French. Paul Pimsleur. (Running Time: 4 hrs.). 2002. 24.95 (978-1-60083-402-8(7), Audiofy Corp) Iofy Corp.

Quick & Simple ESL German. Paul Pimsleur. (Running Time: 4 hrs.). 2001. 24.95 (978-1-60083-403-5(5), Audiofy Corp) Iofy Corp.

Quick & Simple ESL Haitian. Paul Pimsleur. (Running Time: 4 hrs.). 2004. 24.95 (978-1-60083-405-9(1), Audiofy Corp) Iofy Corp.

Quick & Simple ESL Hindi. Paul Pimsleur. (Running Time: 4 hrs.). 2001. 24.95 (978-1-60083-404-2(3), Audiofy Corp) Iofy Corp.

Quick & Simple ESL Italian. Paul Pimsleur. (Running Time: 4 hrs.). 2001. 24.95 (978-1-60083-406-6(X), Audiofy Corp) Iofy Corp.

Quick & Simple ESL Korean. Paul Pimsleur. (Running Time: 4 hrs.). 2001. 24.95 (978-1-60083-408-0(6), Audiofy Corp) Iofy Corp.

Quick & Simple ESL Portuguese (Brazilian) Paul Pimsleur. (Running Time: 4 hrs.). 2001. 24.95 (978-1-60083-409-7(4), Audiofy Corp) Iofy Corp.

Quick & Simple ESL Russian. Paul Pimsleur. (Running Time: 4 hrs.). 2000. 24.95 (978-1-60083-410-3(8), Audiofy Corp) Iofy Corp.

Quick & Simple ESL Spanish. Paul Pimsleur. (Running Time: 4 hrs.). 2000. 24.95 (978-1-60083-411-0(6), Audiofy Corp) Iofy Corp.

Quick & Simple ESL Vietnamese. Paul Pimsleur. (Running Time: 4 hrs.). 2003. 24.95 (978-1-60083-412-7(4), Audiofy Corp) Iofy Corp.

Quick & the Dead: A Novel, abr. ed. Jack Curtis. Read by Bruce McGill. Contrib. by Simon Moore. 2 cass. (Running Time: 3 hrs.). 1995. 17.00 (978-1-56876-035-3(3), 392830) Soundlines Ent.
With a six-gun Colt 44 on her hip, Ellen McKenzie, known as Lady Death, returns to the town of Redemption to do battle with the villainous mayor on the Quick Draw Jamboree, a twisted competition to prove who is the fastest draw. Without the help of a man called Cort, she'll have no chance against the mayor & his town thugs. A novelization of the movie.

***Quick Bite.** unabr. ed. Lynsay Sands. Read by Victoria Mcgee. (ENG.). 2009. (978-0-06-196163-2(9), Harper Audio); (978-0-06-195868-7(9), Harper Audio) HarperCollins Pubs.

Quick Cash Secrets. Ed. by Kris Solie-Johnson. 2007. audio compact disk 49.95 (978-0-939069-01-9(6)) Amer Inst Small Bus.

Quick Course in Miracles. Gary N. Arnold. (ENG.). 2008. audio compact disk 24.95i (978-1-57867-042-0(X)) Windhorse Corp.

Quick Draw! abr. ed. 1 cass. (Romper Room Sing & Read-Alongs Ser.). (J). 1986. 5.95 incl. bk. & sheet music. (978-0-89845-314-0(3), RRC 3143) HarperCollins Pubs.

Quick Fixes Vol. 1: Fifty-One Instant Solutions. unabr. ed. 1 cass. (978-1-891076-09-1(4)) Gemini Press.

Quick Look Electronic Drug Reference. Created by Lippincott Williams & Wilkins. (ENG.). 2009. audio compact disk 49.95 (978-0-7817-9718-4(7)) Lppncott W W.

Quick Phonics Assessment CD-ROM. Compiled by Benchmark Education Staff. 2005. audio compact disk 10.00 (978-1-4108-6370-6(0)) Benchmark Educ.

Quick Red Fox. unabr. collector's ed. John D. MacDonald. Read by Michael Prichard. 6 cass. (Running Time: 6 hrs.). (Travis McGee Ser.: Vol. 4). 1983. 36.00 (978-0-7366-0701-8(3), 1664) Books on Tape.
It was the standard blackmail scheme. For years, sultry Lysa Dean's name on a movie had meant a bonanza at the box office. Now a set of pictures could mean the end of her career. When first approached for help by lovely Dana Holtzer, Lysa's personal secretary, Travis McGee is thoroughly turned off by the tacky details. But being low on cash, & tenderly attracted by the star's intriguingly remote secretary, McGee sets out to locate his suspects - only to find that they start turning up dead!.

Quick Review of Civil Procedure. 3rd ed. Toby Miller & Friedenthal. (Quick Review Ser.). 1998. 23.00 (978-1-57793-050-1(9), 28394) Pub: Sum & Substance. Dist(s): West Pub

Quick Spanish for Environmental Service Managers in Hospitals. Carlos Sanchez. 1 cass. (Running Time: 1 hr. 30 mins.). 2002. 15.95 (978-1-891368-31-8(1), C10ES) Casa Ed KARISA.
Essential Spanish for directors of housekeeping in hospitals includes culture and leadership tips.

Quick Spanish for Food & Beverage Managers in Hotels. Carlos Sanchez. 1 cass. (Running Time: 1 hr. 30 mins.). 2001. 15.95 (978-1-891368-34-9(6), C120FB) Casa Ed KARISA.
Spanish for managers working in the food and beverage division in hotels. Complete vocabulary and repetition exercises.

Quick Spanish for Healthcare Professionals. Carlos A. Sanchez. 1 cass. (Running Time: 1 hr. 30 mins.). 1999. 15.95 (978-1-891368-29-5(X), C1OSH) Casa Ed KARISA.
Bare essential spanish for healthare providers includes 3 laminated cards for quick reference. Industry specific/basic spanish.

Quick Spanish for Human Resources Professionals. Carlos Sanchez. 1 cass. (Running Time: 1 hr. 30 mins.). 2001. 15.95 (978-1-891368-30-1(3)) Casa Ed KARISA.
All Human Resources functions are translated for easy communication with Spanish speakers.

Quick Spanish for Nutritional Service Managers in Hospitals. Carlos Sanchez. 1 cass. (Running Time: 1 hr. 30 mins.). 2002. 15.95 (978-1-891368-33-2(8), C1ONS) Casa Ed KARISA.
Essential Spanish for nutrition professionals in hospitals and healthcare. Includes culture and leadership.

Quick-Start Recruiter Training: Audio Boot Camp for Rookies. Bill Radin. 4 CDs. (Running Time: 3 hours). 2004. audio compact disk 149.00 (978-1-929836-11-6(2)) Innovative Consulting.

Quick Stress Busters. 1 cass. 12.95 (978-1-884305-66-5(0)) Changeworks.
This tape contains a number of brief trance experiences that can be easily included into the most hectic schedules. They are meant to be little "islands of peace" for times when you need fast relief in daily life.

Quick Work. Vicki Hollett. 2000. 17.50 (978-0-19-457295-8(1)) OUP.

Quick Work. Vicki Hollett. 2005. cd-rom, audio compact disk, audio compact disk 21.95 (978-0-19-457212-5(9)) OUP.

Quick Work Elementary. David Grant. 2003. audio compact disk 21.95 (978-0-19-457365-8(6)) OUP.

Quick Work Elementary. John Hughes et al. 2003. 17.50 (978-0-19-457291-0(9)) OUP.

Quick Work Intermediate. Vicki Hollett. 2001. 17.50 (978-0-19-457299-6(4)); audio compact disk 21.95 (978-0-19-457359-7(1)) OUP.

***QuickBooks: A 60-Minute Crash Course.** PUEI. 2009. audio compact disk 199.00 (978-1-935041-84-9(3), CareerTrack) P Univ E Inc.

Quickening. unabr. ed. Laura Catherine Brown. Read by Emily Schirner. 8 cass. (Running Time: 12 hrs.). 2000. 35.95 (978-1-58788-045-2(8), 1587880458, BAU) Brilliance Audio.
"Quickening" is the stage in pregnancy when a fetus shows signs of having a life of its own - a stage in the development that this first-time novelist likens to the equally dramatic step of a child moving away from home. Nineteen-year-old Mandy Boyle is leaving for college - full of ambition and anticipation, more than ready to sever ties with her blue-collar family and their backwater town. But then the sudden death of her father shatters her exciting new world and shows her that her connection with home is stronger than she thought. The first-person narrative of Quickening becomes compelling as Mandy, caught between her old and new lives, struggles to find a way through her increasingly turbulent world, where she's buffeted by problems she's too young and inexperienced to handle. During the six-month course of this novel, we observe the transformation - the quickening - of this young woman: No longer simply reacting to the people and circumstances around her, Mandy begins to choose, for the first time, a life for herself.

Quickening. unabr. ed. Laura Catherine Brown. Read by Emily Schirner. (Running Time: 12 hrs.). 2005. 39.25 (978-1-59600-550-1(5), 9781596005501, BADLE); 24.95 (978-1-59600-549-5(1), 9781596005495, BAD); 39.25 (978-1-59600-548-8(3), 9781596005488, Brinc Audio MP3 Lib); 24.95 (978-1-59600-547-1(5), 9781596005471, Brilliance MP3) Brilliance Audio.

***Quickening.** unabr. ed. Michelle Hoover. (Running Time: 9 hrs.). 2010. 29.95 (978-1-4417-6274-0(4)); 59.95 (978-1-4417-6271-9(X)); audio compact disk 29.95 (978-1-4417-6273-3(6)); audio compact disk 90.00 (978-1-4417-6272-6(8)) Blckstn Audio.

Quickening: Today's Trends, Tomorrow's World. Art Bell. Read by Ramona Bell. 4 cass. 1998. 24.95 Set. (978-1-879706-73-6(3)) Paper Chase.

Quickening Spirit of Radiance. unabr. ed. Kenneth G. Mills. 1 cass. (Running Time: 1 hr. 12 min.). 1990. pap. bk. 10.95 incl. transcription bklt. (978-0-919842-10-6(0), KGOC29) Ken Mills Found.
Cassette & transcription booklet of spontaneous philosophical lecture by Kenneth George Mills - "a message for the decade for all those who are attuned to the Wonders beyond the confines of this mental realm...".

Quickest Way to Enlightenment. unabr. ed. Sri H. W. L. Poonjaji. Read by Sri H. W. L. Poonjaji. 3 cass. (Running Time: 4 hrs. 50 min.). 1994. 24.00 (978-0-9632194-7-3(2)) The Gangaji Fnd.
Poonjaji reveals the secret for direct self-realization & ending egoic suffering.

Quickie. unabr. ed. James Patterson & Michael Ledwidge. 5 cass. (Running Time: 7 hrs. 30 mins.). 2007. 60.00 (978-1-4159-4203-1(X)) Books on Tape.

Quickie. unabr. ed. James Patterson & Michael Ledwidge. Read by Mary Stuart Masterson. 6 CDs. (Running Time: 7 hrs. 30 mins.). 2007. audio compact disk 60.00 (978-1-4159-4204-8(8)) Books on Tape.

Quickie. unabr. ed. James Patterson & Michael Ledwidge. Read by Mary Stuart Masterson. (Running Time: 6 hrs.). (ENG.). 2007. 14.98 (978-1-59483-927-6(1)) Pub: Hachet Audio. Dist(s): HachBkGrp

Quickie. unabr. ed. James Patterson & Michael Ledwidge. Read by Mary Stuart Masterson. (Running Time: 6 hrs.). (ENG.). 2008. audio compact disk 14.98 (978-1-60024-230-4(8)) Pub: Hachet Audio. Dist(s): HachBkGrp

QuickReads 2 Read Along. Prod. by Saddleback Educational Publishing. (YA). 2006. audio compact disk 44.95 (978-1-56254-792-9(5)) Saddleback Edu.

QuickReads 3 Read Along. Created by Saddleback Publishing. (Quickreads Ser.). (YA). 2005. audio compact disk 44.95 (978-1-56254-793-6(3)) Saddleback Edu.

Quicksand. Iris Johansen. Read by Jennifer Van Dyck. (Eve Duncan Ser.). 2009. 69.99 (978-1-60812-671-2(4)) Find a World.

Quicksand. abr. ed. Iris Johansen. Read by Jennifer Van Dyck. (Running Time: 6 hrs.). (Eve Duncan Ser.). 2008. audio compact disk 14.99 (978-1-4233-2913-8(9), 9781423329138, BCD Value Price) Brilliance Audio.

Quicksand. unabr. ed. Iris Johansen. Read by Jennifer Van Dyck. (Running Time: 9 hrs.). (Eve Duncan Ser.). 2008. 24.95 (978-1-4233-2910-7(4), 9781423329107, BAD); 39.25 (978-1-4233-2911-4(2), 9781423329114, BADLE); audio compact disk 24.95 (978-1-4233-2908-4(2), 9781423329084, Brilliance MP3); audio compact disk 34.95 (978-1-4233-2906-0(6), 9781423329060, Bril Audio CD Unabri); audio compact disk 87.25 (978-1-4233-2907-7(4), 9781423329077, BriAudCD Unabrid); audio compact disk 39.25 (978-1-4233-2909-1(0), 9781423329091, Brinc Audio MP3 Lib) Brilliance Audio.

***Quicksilver.** unabr. ed. Neal Stephenson. Read by Simon Prebble. (Running Time: 9 hrs.). (Baroque Cycle Ser.). 2010. 39.97 (978-1-4418-7500-6(X), 9781441875006, BADLE); 24.99 (978-1-4418-7498-6(4), 9781441874986, Brilliance MP3); 39.97 (978-1-4418-7499-3(2), 9781441874993, Brinc Audio MP3 Lib); audio compact disk 29.99 (978-1-4418-7496-2(8), 9781441874962, Bril Audio CD Unabri); audio compact disk 79.97 (978-1-4418-7497-9(6), 9781441874979, BriAudCD Unabrid) Brilliance Audio.

***Quicksilver: Volume One of the Baroque Cycle.** abr. ed. Neal Stephenson. Read by Simon Preble & Stina Nielsen. (ENG.). 2004. (978-0-06-081804-3(2), Harper Audio); (978-0-06-079805-5(X), Harper Audio) HarperCollins Pubs.

Quicksilver Kid. unabr. ed. Steve Hailes. Read by Maynard Villers. 4 cass. (Running Time: 5 hrs. 30 min.). 1996. 26.95 (978-1-55686-727-9(1)) Books in Motion.
Cliff Stone was a man mighty handy with a six-gun. He came to California in search of an uncle & rode smack into the middle of a vicious blood feud.

Quickstart English Audio. 2 CDs. 2006. audio compact disk 7.95 (978-1-60245-019-6(6)) GDL Multimedia.

Quickstart French Audio. 2 CDs. 2006. audio compact disk 7.99 (978-1-60245-020-2(X)) GDL Multimedia.

Quickstart German Audio. 2 CDs. 2006. audio compact disk 7.99 (978-1-60245-021-9(8)) GDL Multimedia.

Quickstart Italian Audio. 2 CDs. 2006. audio compact disk 7.99 (978-1-60245-022-6(6)) GDL Multimedia.

Quickstart Russian Audio. 2 CDs. 2006. audio compact disk 7.99 (978-1-60245-023-3(4)) GDL Multimedia.

Quickstart Spanish Audio. 2 CDs. 2006. audio compact disk 7.95 (978-1-60245-018-9(8)) GDL Multimedia.

Quickstrike. abr. ed. William W. Johnstone. 2 cass. (Running Time: 3 hrs.). (Code Name Ser.: No. 5). 2004. 18.00 (978-1-58807-432-4(3)) Am Pubng Inc.
Today, when bomb-throwing madmen rule nations and crime cartels strangle the globe, justice demands extreme measures. For twenty years, ex-CIA operations officer John Barrone fought his country's dirty back-alley wars. Now, he leads a secret strike force of former law enforcement, intelligence, and special operations professionals against America's enemies.Code Name: Quickstrike. When the first attacked rocked the United States, seven billionaires were in a new skyscraper with a group of murderous fanatics. So were four of the most dangerous covert warriors in the world. Now, as the country witnesses the devastation of coordinated terrorist strikes, John Barrone and his team are in the middle of the storm. Separating the killers from their targets, Barrone goes to battle. Because while the first counterstrike happens in Texas, the ultimate mission is halfway around the globe, where someone must cut out the heart of America's most deadly enemy.

Quickverse 50 Starter Edition. T. Parsons. 2004. audio compact disk 9.99 (978-1-57264-295-9(5)) Parsons Tech.

Quickverse 60 Expanded. T. Parsons. 2004. cd-rom & audio compact disk 99.95 (978-1-57264-315-4(3)) Parsons Tech.

Quickverse 60 Greek Edition C. T. Parsons. 2004. audio compact disk 99.95 (978-1-57264-319-2(6)) Parsons Tech.

Quickverse 8 Essentials. Findex Staff. 2004. audio compact disk 49.95 (978-1-930594-79-1(8)) Findex.

Quien esta en la Choza? (SPA.). (gr. k-1). 10.00 (978-0-7635-6272-4(6)) Rigby Educ.

Quien Nacera Aqui? see Who's Hatching Here?

Quien Nacera Aqui? Alma Flor Ada. (Libros Para Contar Ser.).Tr. of Who's Hatching Here?. (SPA., (J). (gr. k-3). 4.95 (978-1-58105-258-9(8)) Santillana.

Quien Se Ha Llevado Mi Queso? Spencer Johnson. 2008. audio compact disk 24.95 (978-1-933499-79-6(6)) Fonolibro Inc.

Quien Soy Yo. Contrib. by Casting Crowns. (Soundtraks Ser.). 2006. audio compact disk 8.99 (978-5-558-04309-9(1)) Christian Wrld.

Quien Subira? unabr. ed. Luis Mellado. (SPA.). 2000. 7.99 (978-0-8297-2594-0(6)) Pub: Vida Pubs. Dist(s): Zondervan

Quiera Su Cuerpo, Es Su Mejor Amigo Aprenda a Relajarse see Love Your Body Its Your Best Friend Learn to Relax

Quiero Adorar. unabr. ed. René González. (SPA.). 2000. 7.99 (978-0-8297-3284-9(5)) Pub: Vida Pubs. Dist(s): Zondervan

Quiero Adorar. unabr. ed. Rene Gonzalez. 2000. audio compact disk 11.99 (978-0-8297-3282-5(9)) Zondervan.

Quiero Alabarte. unabr. ed. Maranatha Singers. (SPA.). 2003. 9.99 (978-0-8297-3544-4(5)) Pub: Vida Pubs. Dist(s): Zondervan

Quiero Alabarte, Vol. 1. unabr. ed. 2000. audio compact disk 11.99 (978-0-8297-3301-3(9)) Zondervan.

Quiero Alabarte, Vol. 1. unabr. ed. Zondervan Publishing Staff. (SPA.). 2000. 7.99 (978-0-8297-3300-6(0)) Pub: Vida Pubs. Dist(s): Zondervan

Quiero Alabarte, Vol. 2. unabr. ed. 2000. audio compact disk 11.99 (978-0-8297-3306-8(X)) Zondervan.

Quiero Alabarte, Vol. 2. unabr. ed. Zondervan Publishing Staff. (SPA.). 2000. 7.99 (978-0-8297-3305-1(1)) Pub: Vida Pubs. Dist(s): Zondervan

Quiero Alabarte, Vol. 3. unabr. ed. 2000. audio compact disk 11.99 (978-0-8297-3311-2(6)) Zondervan.

Quiero Alabarte, Vol. 3. unabr. ed. Zondervan Publishing Staff. (SPA.). 2000. 7.99 (978-0-8297-3310-5(8)) Pub: Vida Pubs. Dist(s): Zondervan

Quiero Alabarte, Vol. 4. unabr. ed. 2000. audio compact disk 11.99 (978-0-8297-3316-7(7)) Zondervan.

Quiero Alabarte, Vol. 4. unabr. ed. Zondervan Publishing Staff. 1 cass. (Running Time: 1 hr.). (SPA.). 2000. 7.99 (978-0-8297-3315-0(9)) Zondervan.

Quiero Alabarte, Vol. 5. unabr. ed. 2000. audio compact disk 11.99 (978-0-8297-3321-1(3)) Zondervan.

Quiero Alabarte, Vol. 5. unabr. ed. Zondervan Publishing Staff. (SPA.). 2000. 7.99 (978-0-8297-3320-4(5)) Pub: Vida Pubs. Dist(s): Zondervan

Quiero Alabarte, Vol. 6. unabr. ed. 2000. audio compact disk 11.99 (978-0-8297-3326-6(4)) Zondervan.

Quiero Alabarte, Vol. 6. unabr. ed. Zondervan Publishing Staff. (SPA.). 2000. 7.99 (978-0-8297-3325-9(6)) Pub: Vida Pubs. Dist(s): Zondervan

Quiero Vivir. Mariano de Blas.Tr. of I want to Live. (SPA.). 2009. audio compact disk 25.00 (978-1-935405-15-3(2)) Hombre Nuevo.

***Quiet.** Paul Wilson. Read by Paul Wilson. (Running Time: 7 hrs. 45 mins.). 2010. 79.99 (978-1-74214-634-8(1), 9781742146348) Pub: Bolinda Pubng AUS. Dist(s): Bolinda Pub Inc

Quiet. unabr. ed. Paul Wilson. Read by Paul Wilson. (Running Time: 7 hrs. 45 mins.). 2009. audio compact disk 83.95 (978-1-921334-74-0(6), 9781921334740) Pub: Bolinda Pubng AUS. Dist(s): Bolinda Pub Inc

***Quiet.** unabr. ed. Paul Wilson. Read by Paul Wilson. (Running Time: 7 hrs. 45 mins.). 2010. 43.95 (978-1-921415-98-2(3), 9781921415982) Pub: Bolinda Pubng AUS. Dist(s): Bolinda Pub Inc

Quiet: The Power of Introverts in a World That Can't Stop Talking. abr. unabr. ed. Susan H. Cain. Read by Susan H. Cain. (ENG.). 2011. audio compact disk 35.00 (978-0-7393-4124-7(3), Random AudioBks) Pub: Random Audio Pubg. Dist(s): Random

Quiet American. unabr. ed. Graham Greene. Read by Joseph Porter. 5 cass. (Running Time: 7 hrs. 30 mins.). 2000. 39.95 (1371) Blckstn Audio.
A study of New World hope & innocence set in an Old World of violence. The scene is Saigon in the violent years when the French were desperately trying to hold their footing in the Far East. The principle characters are a skeptical British journalist, his attractive Vietnamese mistress & an eager young American sent out by Washington on a mysterious mission.

Quiet American. unabr. ed. Graham Greene. Read by Joseph Porter. 5 cass. (Running Time: 7 hrs.). 2001. 39.95 (978-0-7861-0419-2(8), 1371); audio compact disk 24.95 (978-0-7861-9005-8(1), 1371) Blckstn Audio.

Quiet American. unabr. ed. Graham Greene. Read by Joseph Porter. 6 CDs. (Running Time: 7 hrs 30 min.). 2004. audio compact disk 32.95 (978-0-7861-9331-8(X)); reel tape 29.95 (978-0-7861-2404-6(0)) Blckstn Audio.
The scene is Saigon in the violent years when the French were desperately trying to hold their footing in the Far East. The principal characters are a skeptical British journalist, his attractive Vietnamese mistress, and an eager young American sent out by Washington on a mysterious mission.

Quiet American. unabr. ed. Graham Greene. Read by Joseph Porter. 6 CDs. (Running Time: 7 hrs.). 2006. audio compact disk 48.00 (978-0-7861-9291-5(7), 1371) Blckstn Audio.

Quiet American. unabr. ed. Graham Greene. Read by Simon Cadell. 4 cass. (Running Time: 6 hrs.). 2000. 34.95 (CSL 066) Pub: Chivers Audio Bks GBR. Dist(s): AudioGO
Powerfully and accurately reflects the problems of war and the people embroiled in it.

Quiet Answer. Kenneth Wapnick. 4 CDs. 2006. audio compact disk 23.00 (978-1-59142-244-0(2), CD59) Foun Miracles.

Quiet Answer. Kenneth Wapnick. 1 CD. (Running Time: 3 hrs. 47 mins 47 secs.). 2006. 18.00 (978-1-59142-281-5(7), 3m59) Foun Miracles.

Quiet as a Nun. unabr. ed. Antonia Fraser. Read by Patricia Hodge. 6 cass. (Running Time: 9 hrs.). (Jemima Shore Mystery Ser.: Bk. 1). 2000. 49.95 (CAB 397) Pub: Chivers Audio Bks GBR. Dist(s): AudioGO
The newspaper item headed Nun Found Dead took T.V. reporter Jemima Shore by surprise. Sister Miriam of Blessed Eleanor's convent had apparently starved herself to death in a ruined tower adjoining the convent grounds. Memories came flooding back to Jemima of the days when she had been a schoolgirl at the convent, and a friend of Sister Miriam. Then came an appeal from the reverend Mother, "Jemima, something is terribly wrong...".

Quiet as a Nun. unabr. collector's ed. Antonia Fraser. Read by Wanda McCaddon. 7 cass. (Running Time: 7 hrs.). 1984. 42.00 (978-0-7366-0884-8(2), 1828) Books on Tape.
Jemima Shore, an addition to the list of investigators in the mystery genre, must solve a murder in the secluded tower at Blessed Eleanor's Convent in Sussex. The victim, an old school friend, left a puzzling note stating: "Jemima knows..." But Jemima doesn't.

Quiet Belief in Angels. unabr. ed. R. J. Ellory. Read by Mark Bramhall. (Running Time: 13 hrs. 30 mins.). 2009. 29.95 (978-1-4417-2245-4(9)); 79.95 (978-1-4417-2241-6(6)); audio compact disk 109.00 (978-1-4417-2242-3(4)) Blckstn Audio.

Quiet Center: Through Specialness to Love. Kenneth Wapnick. 1 CD. (Running Time: 11 hrs. 01 min. 34 secs). 2006. 53.00 (978-1-59142-250-1(7), 3m125); audio compact disk 59.00 (978-1-59142-249-5(3), CD125) Foun Miracles.

Quiet Christmas. David Miller. 2003. audio compact disk 15.95 (978-1-56589-781-6(1)) Pub: Crystal Clarity. Dist(s): Natl Bk Netwk

Quiet Companion: Peter Favre. Mary Purcell. 8 cass. 32.95 (744) Ignatius Pr.
Roommate of Francis Xavier who worked for reconciliation of Christians.

Quiet Confidence for a Woman's Heart. unabr. ed. Elizabeth George. Narrated by Elizabeth George. (Running Time: 4 hrs. 14 mins. 36 sec.). (ENG.). 2009. audio compact disk 19.99 (978-1-59859-552-9(0)) Oasis Audio.

***Quiet Confidence for a Woman's Heart.** unabr. ed. Elizabeth George. Narrated by Elizabeth George. (Running Time: 4 hrs. 14 mins. 36 sec.). (ENG.). 2009. 13.99 (978-1-60814-469-3(0)) Oasis Audio.

Quiet Desperation. unabr. ed. Rene Smeraglia. Read by Maynard Villers. 6 cass. (Running Time: 8 hrs. 24 min.). 1995. 36.95 Set. (978-1-55686-604-3(6)) Books in Motion.
Tuck Matson, ex-D.E.A. agent is drawn into a murder case when an ex-girlfriend calls for advice & is later found dead. Tuck discovers a maelstrom of industrial espionage & revenge.

Quiet Enemy. Short Stories. Cecil Dawkins. Read by Cecil Dawkins. 1 cass. (Running Time: 51 min.). 13.95 (978-1-55644-171-4(1), 3061) Am Audio Prose.

Quiet Escapes. Executive Producer Twin Sisters Productions Staff. 1 CD. (Running Time: 60 mins). (Growing Minds with Music Ser.). (J). 2003. audio compact disk 12.99 (978-1-57583-648-5(3)) Twin Sisters.
Escape to a garden in bloom, a walk along the beach, a cascading mountain stream, or a breathtaking vista with ten all new original instrumental compositions blended with the sounds of nature.

Quiet Game. abr. ed. Greg Iles. Read by Dick Hill. 4 cass. (Running Time: 6 hrs.). 2001. 53.25 (978-1-58788-408-5(9), 1587884089, Lib Edit) Brilliance Audio.
He seeks justice in a town where a thirty-year-old crime lies buried - and where everyone plays . . . The Quiet Game Penn Cage is no stranger to death. As a Houston prosecutor he sent sixteen men to death row, and watched seven of them die. But now, in the aftermath of his wife's death, the grief-stricken father packs up his four-year-old daughter, Annie, and returns

to his hometown in search of healing. But peace is not what he finds there. Natchez, Mississippi, is the jewel of the antebellum South, a city of old money and older sins, where passion, power, and racial tensions seethe beneath its elegant façade. After twenty years away, Penn is stunned to find his own family trapped in a web on intrigue and danger. Determined to save his father from a ruthless blackmailer, Penn stumbles over a link to the town's darkest secret: the thirty-year-old unsolved murder of a black Korean War veteran. But what drives him to act is the revelation that this haunting mystery is inextricably bound up in his own past. Under a blaze of national media attention, Penn reopens the case, only to find local records destroyed, the FBI file sealed, and the town closing ranks against him. Penn joins forces with Caitlin Masters, a beautiful young newspaper publisher, on a quest that will lead from the bayous of the South to the highest reaches of the U.S. government. His need to right a terrible wrong pits him against the FBI, the powerful judge who nearly destoyed his family, and his most dangerous adversary: a woman he loved more than twenty years before, and who haunts him still. His crusade for justice will ultimately lead him into a packed Mississippi courtroom, where he fighs a battle that could end a decades-old silence and force the truth to be spoken at last.

Quiet Game. abr. ed. Greg Iles. Read by Dick Hill. (Running Time: 6 hrs.). 2006. 39.25 (978-1-4233-0184-4(6), 9781423301844, BADLE); 24.95 (978-1-4233-0183-7(8), 9781423301837, BAD); audio compact disk 39.25 (978-1-4233-0182-0(X), 9781423301820, Brlnc Audio MP3 Lib); audio compact disk 24.95 (978-1-4233-0181-3(1), 9781423301813, Brilliance MP3) Brilliance Audio.

Quiet Game. abr. ed. Greg Iles. Read by Dick Hill. (Running Time: 21600 sec.). 2006. audio compact disk 16.99 (978-1-4233-2873-5(6), 9781423328735, BCD Value Price) Brilliance Audio.

***Quiet Game.** abr. ed. Greg Iles. Read by Dick Hill. (Running Time: 6 hrs.). 2010. audio compact disk 9.99 (978-1-4418-5684-5(6), 9781441856845, BCD Value Price) Brilliance Audio.

Quiet Game. unabr. ed. Greg Iles. Narrated by Tom Stechschulte. 14 cass. (Running Time: 21 hrs.). 2000. 119.00 (978-0-7887-4035-0(0), 96001E7) Recorded Bks.
Houston prosecutor Penn Cage returns to his childhood home in Natchez, Mississippi after his wife's death. Instead of finding peace, he stumbles upon shocking information about a decades-old murder steeped in racism.

Quiet Gentleman. Georgette Heyer. Read by Cornelius Garrett. 8 cass. (Running Time: 12 hrs.). 2002. 69.95 (978-0-7540-0836-1(3), CAB 2258) Pub: Chivers Pr GBR. Dist(s): AudioGO

Quiet Girl. unabr. ed. Peter Høeg. Read by James Gale. Tr. by Nadia Christensen. 12 CDs. (Running Time: 15 hrs. 0 mins. 0 sec.). Orig. Title: Den stille pige. (ENG.). 2007. audio compact disk 39.95 (978-1-4272-0216-1(8)) Pub: Macmill Audio. Dist(s): Macmillan

Quiet Heart Space: Meditations & Music for Children. June McIntyre. Read by June McIntyre. 1 CD. (Running Time: 56 min.). (J). (ps up). 1996. pap. bk. J McIntyre.
Spoken meditations (4) with instrumental music in background & 2 solo instrumental compositions. Purpose is to teach the child how to connect with higher self & for relaxation purposes.

Quiet Heart Space: Meditations & Music for Children. June McIntyre. Ed. by June McIntyre. Illus. by Coe Savage. Photos by Joseph Boyles. 1 cass. (Running Time: 56 mins.). (J). (ps up). 1996. pap. bk. 11.98 (978-1-889045-04-7(7)) J McIntyre.

Quiet Joy. Doc Childre. 1 cass. (Running Time: 1 hr. 30 mins.). 2001. 9.95 (978-1-879052-52-9(0)); audio compact disk 15.95 (978-1-879052-51-2(2)) HeartMath.
Compilation of of selections scientifically-designed releases of Heart Zones & Speed of Balance, features the more serene & peaceful side of Doc's musical style. A great backdrop for doing tai chi, yoga & massage. Calming, peaceful.

Quiet Lion Video: Author Reading. Read by Gina Anaya. Gina Anaya. Tammy West-Ruiz. 2009. DVD 1.99 (978-1-935315-02-5(1)) Red Ant.

Quiet Mind. 1 cass. (Running Time: 40 min.). (978-0-9667760-0-3(3)) Zebedee Res.
Clear your mind & relieve stress with this revolutionary breakthrough in meditative sound. The computer-generated sound frequencies on this tape are created to work with the harmonic arrangements that occur in the human body. Listen to these patterns of natural resonance & achieve a natural state of harmony & balance.

Quiet Mind: Imagery for Peaceful Living. Gerald G. Jampolsky & Diane Cirincione. Read by Gerald G. Jampolsky & Diane Cirincione. 6 cass. (Running Time: 6 hrs.). 49.95 (733AD) Nightingale-Conant.
You can live each day in a state of calm & serenity, accepting love & allowing yourself to be in harmony with the energies of the universe. The practical techniques you learn in this program will greatly enhance your creativity, allow you to relax at will, use the power of your mind to control your physical health...& achieve the peace of a Quiet Mind.

Quiet Mind: The Mystical Journey of a Tibetan Nomad. unabr. ed. Nawang Khechog. Read by Nawang Khechog. 1 CD. (Running Time: 55 min.). 1997. audio compact disk 16.98 (978-1-56455-550-2(X), MM00001D) Sounds True.
Reflects the far-reaching travels of this Tibetan flute master. With didgeridoo, Incan pan pipes, ocarina & more.

Quiet Moments. 1998. 14.99 (978-1-60689-167-4(7)) Pub: Youngheart Mus. Dist(s): Creat Teach Pr

Quiet Moments. Music by Greg Scelsa & Steve Millang. 1 LP. (Running Time: 60 mins.). (J). pupil's gde. ed. 10.95 (YM6) Kimbo Educ.
Resting songs with relaxation activities. Daydreams, Lotus Flower, Morning Mist, Tradewinds, Skyward & more. Includes lyric book.

Quiet Moments. Music by Greg Scelsa & Steve Millang. 1 cass. (Running Time: 1 hr.). (J). 2001. pap. bk. 10.95 (YM6C); pap. bk. 14.95 (YM6CD) Kimbo Educ.

Quiet Moments Kid's Relaxation Set: A Guide to the Tape Series for Parents & Teachers. Gary K. Mills. 1986. pap. bk. 20.00 (978-0-938669-12-8(5)) MediaHlth Pubns.

Quiet Moments with God. 2007. audio compact disk 15.99 (978-5-557-54314-9(7)) Kingsway Pubns GBR.

Quiet Moments with Greg & Steve. Music by Greg Scelsa & Steve Millang. 1 cass. (Running Time: 60 mins.). (J). (ps-3). 1984. 10.98 (978-0-945267-07-2(X), YR-006-CN); audio compact disk 13.98 (YM-006-CD) Youngheart Mus.
For resting & relaxation. Instrumental with some voice over.

Quiet Piano: The Music of Erie Chapman. 2003. audio compact disk 10.00 (978-0-9747366-5-5(1)) Erie Chapman.

Quiet Places. Perf. by Hap Palmer. 1 cass. (Running Time: 1 hr.). 2001. 9.95 (HP104); audio compact disk 14.95 (HP 104 CD) Hap-Pal Music.
A restful alternative to our fast-paced electronic age. Beautiful melodies comfort children during rest time. All original instrumental music with the natural sounds of a real orchestra. Familiarize children with sounds of the instruments while resting.

Quiet Places: Meditations along the Road to Inner Peace. 2003. audio compact disk 12.95 (978-0-9728293-3-5(4)) Capstone Institute.
Quiet Places is an original collection of relaxing and inspirational guided meditations designed to take you to that quiet place within, the doorway to hiher states of awareness and inner peace. Living from this calm and centered place will greatly enhance the quality of your life. Access your own personal kingdom, connect with your life purpose, awaken your highest creativity or simply take a much deserved vacation from your daily stresses. The introduction includes practical guidelines for daily meditation.

Quiet Places with Jesus. Isaias Powers. Read by Isaias Powers. Read by Andrea Star. 3 cass. (Running Time: 3 hrs. 10 min.). (YA). (gr. 9 up). 1985. 24.95 (978-0-89622-338-7(8)) Twenty-Third.
Reflections & meditations on scriptural references.

Quiet Places with Mary. Isaias Powers & Andrea Star. Read by Isaias Powers & Andrea Star. 3 cass. (Running Time: 3 hrs. 20 min.). (YA). (gr. 9 up). 1986. 24.95 (978-0-89622-340-0(X)) Twenty-Third.
Reflections & meditations on scriptural reference.

Quiet Please. unabr. collector's ed. Wyllis Cooper. Perf. by Ernest Chappell. 6 cass. (Running Time: 9 hrs.). 1998. bk. 34.98 (978-1-57019-171-8(9), 4177) Radio Spirits.
Surrealistic horror series. These 18 stories will grip you, stir your nerves and deliver a terrifying punch.

Quiet Please: Other Side of the Stars & Pavanne. Perf. by Ernest Chappell. 1 cass. (Running Time: 1 hr.). 2001. 6.98 (2268) Radio Spirits.

Quiet Please: The Evening & the Morning & The Hat, the Bed & John J. Catherine. Perf. by Ernest Chappell. 1 cass. (Running Time: 1 hr.). 2001. 6.98 (2205) Radio Spirits.

Quiet Please: The Think on the Fourble Board & Presto-Change-O, I'm Sure. Perf. by Ernest Chappell. 1 cass. (Running Time: 1 hr.). 2001. 6.98 (2165) Radio Spirits.

Quiet Revolution. Contrib. by Telecast. Prod. by Zach Hodges. 2008. audio compact disk 13.99 (978-5-557-47751-2(9)) BEC Recordings.

Quiet Room: A Journey Out of the Torment of Madness. abr. ed. Lori Schiller & Amanda Bennett. Read by Mary Beth Hurt. (ENG.). 2006. 14.98 (978-1-59483-758-6(9)) Pub: Hachet Audio. Dist(s): HachBkGrp

Quiet Sanctuaries in the City. Hosted by Nancy Pearlman. 1 cass. (Running Time: 29 min.). 10.00 (235) Educ Comm CA.

Quiet Strength. Read by Marguerite Gavin. Contrib. by Janette Oke. 1 CD. (Running Time: 6 hrs. 30 mins.). (Prairie Legacy Ser.: Bk. 3). 2000. audio compact disk 19.95 (2620) Blckstn Audio.
Surely a home of their own would satisfy the longings of her heart. Through the years, Virginia Simpson has learned that Grandma Marty's wisdom was right. When God allows something to be taken from you, He replaces it with something better. The long-awaited return of Jonathan and their renewed courtship, with a wedding soon to follow, are proof of God's loving ways. But the inner strength that God has been forming in Virginia's life through trials and disappointments is far from completion.

Quiet Strength. unabr. ed. Janette Oke. Read by Marguerite Gavin. 5 cass. (Running Time: 7 hrs.). (Prairie Legacy Ser.: Bk. 3). 2001. 39.95 (978-0-7861-2088-6(0), 2850) Blckstn Audio.

Quiet Strength. unabr. ed. Janette Oke. Read by Marguerite Gavin. (Running Time: 7 mins.). (Prairie Legacy Ser.: Bk. 3). 2005. 24.95 (978-0-7861-8663-1(1), 2850); audio compact disk 48.00 (978-0-7861-9683-8(1), 2850) Blckstn Audio.

Quiet Strength: The Faith, the Hope, & the Heart of a Woman Who Changed a Nation. Rosa Parks & Gregory J. Reed. Read by Deforia Lane. 1 cass. (Running Time: 60 min.). 1995. 12.99 (978-0-310-20002-4(4)) Zondervan.

***Quiet Strength: The Faith, the Hope & the Heart of a Woman Who Changed a Nation.** abr. ed. Rosa Parks. Told to Gregory J. Reed. (Running Time: 1 hr. 20 mins. 0 sec.). (ENG.). 2003. 7.99 (978-0-310-26090-5(6)) Zondervan.

Quiet Strength: The Principles, Practices, & Priorities of a Winning Life. abr. ed. Tony Dungy. Read by Tony Dungy. Told to Nathan Whitaker. (ENG.). 2007. audio compact disk 26.99 (978-1-4143-1803-5(0)) Tyndale Hse.

Quiet Strength: The Principles, Practices, & Priorities of a Winning Life. unabr. ed. Tony Dungy & Nathan Whitaker. Read by Peter Jay Fernandez. 9 cass. (Running Time: 10 hrs.). 2007. 72.75 (978-1-4281-9830-2(X)); audio compact disk 102.75 (978-1-4281-9832-6(6)) Recorded Bks.

Quiet Thoughts Celebrating the Light. Marti Eicholz. 1999. audio compact disk 10.95 (978-1-929518-08-1(0)) Inst for Transform.

Quiet Thunder: The Wisdom of Crazy Horse. Joseph Marshall. 6 CDs. (Running Time: 7 hrs. 30 mins.). 2005. audio compact disk 69.95 (978-1-59179-246-8(0), F894D) Sounds True.

Quiet Time. Richard Cobo. 1 cass. 1998. 9.95 (978-1-55961-486-3(2)); audio compact disk 14.95 (978-1-55961-485-6(4)) Relaxtn Co.

Quiet Time. Perf. by Rob Evans. (J). (ps-3). 1996. cass. & video 11.95 (978-84-7200-022-3(2)) Integrity Music.

Quiet Time: Very Pleasant Relaxation Training for Children. John F. Taylor. 1 cass. (Running Time: 29 min.). (J). (ps-6). 1993. 9.95 (978-1-883963-12-5(5)) ADD Plus.
Guided relaxation audio tape.

Quiet Time Songs. (Donut Man Ser.). (J). (ps-3). cass. & video 12.99 (09833) Vision Vid PA.

Quiet Times Series 1. Composed by L. A. Wendt. 1 cass. (Running Time: 45 min.). 1989. 9.98 (978-1-878328-04-5(2)); audio compact disk 13.98 (978-1-878328-05-2(0)) Realmusic.
Selections from Forest Song, Mountain Soliloquy & Embrace the Wind.

Quiet War of Rebecca Sheldon. unabr. ed. Kathleen Rowntree. Read by Patricia Gallimore. 10 cass. (Running Time: 15 hrs.). 2001. 84.95 (978-0-7531-1150-5(0), 010404) Pub: ISIS Audio GBR. Dist(s): ISIS Pub
When Rebecca Sheldon marries George Ludbury, she finds herself at war with his family as well as with the hypocrisy of the Edwardian society in which she lives. The story explores the insularity of Midlands country people between the years 1888 & 1923, vividly capturing the patriotic fervor of the pre-war years & the Home Front. Above all, though, we see Rebecca caught & controlled by circumstance, fighting her own battles, her own quiet war.

Quiet Wards. unabr. ed. Lucilla Andrews. Read by Margaret Holt. 4 cass. (Running Time: 6 hrs.). (Sound Ser.). 1988. 44.95 (978-1-85496-020-7(2), 60202) Pub: UlverLrgPrint GBR. Dist(s): Ulverscroft US

Quiet Water. Perf. by Paul Fitzgerald & Mark Flanagan. Created by Matthew Manning. Prod. by Stuart Wilde. 1 cass. 10.95 (CN618) White Dove NM.
Quiet Water is as soothing & refreshing as the name implies. Like water, acoustic guitars shimmer & ripple - sparkling, crystalline. Like water, waves of strings ebb & flow - darkly, deeply lapping & lulling. Side One is the sun breaking the surface & dancing back upward, reflections stretching into the distance, bright & warm. Side Two takes you beneath the surface, cool & mysterious, with the passing flow of myriad miniature water-life.

***Quiet World: Saving Alaska's Wilderness Kingdom, 1910-1960.** unabr. ed. Douglas Brinkley. (ENG.). 2011. (978-0-06-202718-4(2), Harper Audio) HarperCollins Pubs.

Quieting the Mind. Helen Palmer. Read by Helen Palmer. 3 cass. (Running Time: 3 hrs. 40 min.). 1992. 24.95 (978-7-900783-27-1(X), AA2550) Credence Commun.
Palmer guides us through the process of strengthening our inner observer.

Quietly in Their Sleep. unabr. ed. Donna Leon. Read by Anna Fields. 7 CDs. (Running Time: 10 hrs. 30 min.). (Commissario Guido Brunetti Mystery Ser.: Bk. 6). 2001. audio compact disk 56.00 (978-0-7861-9685-2(8), ZP2847) Blckstn Audio.
Commissario Guido Brunetti is kicking his heels, pondering the recent lack of crime in Venice, when a beautiful young woman appears at his office door. Now calling herself Maria Testa, his visitor is more familiar to Brunetti as Suor' Immacolata, the nun who once cared for his mother at the Casa di Cura in Dolo. But Maria has recently left her convent after the unexpected deaths of five patients. Brunetti offers to make some inquiries but finds no obvious cause for concern. Is Maria simply creating fears to justify abandoning her vocation? Or has she stumbled onto a deeply rooted, far more sinister scenario and put her own life in grave danger.

Quietly in Their Sleep. unabr. ed. Donna Leon. Read by Anna Fields. 6 cass. (Running Time: 8 hrs. 30 mins.). (Commissario Guido Brunetti Mystery Ser.: Bk. 6). 2001. 44.95 (978-0-7861-2086-4(X), 2847) Blckstn Audio.

Quietly in Their Sleep. unabr. ed. Donna Leon. Read by Bill Wallis. 8 cass. (Running Time: 12 hrs.). (Commissario Guido Brunetti Mystery Ser.: Bk. 6). 1998. 59.95 (978-0-7540-0156-0(3), CAB 1579) Pub: Chivers Audio Bks GBR. Dist(s): AudioGO
Commissario Guido Brunetti is pondering the recent lack of crime in Venice, when a woman arrives at his office. Her name is Maria Testa, a nun who once cared for his ailing mother. Maria has left her convent after the unexpected deaths of five patients. Brunetti believes that she may have stumbled on to something sinister.

Quijote de la Mancha. Miguel de Cervantes Saavedra. (SPA.). pap. bk. 20.95 (978-88-7754-892-4(4)) Pub: Cideb ITA. Dist(s): Distribks Inc

Qu'il y Ait Toujours le Soleil; Bonjour L'Hiver. Perf. by Charlotte Diamond. 1 cass. (Running Time: 1 hr.). (FRE.). (CD319) NewSound.

Quillan Games. unabr. ed. Read by William Dufris. (Running Time: 54000 sec.). (Pendragon Ser.: Bk. 7). (J). (gr. 5-9). 2006. 29.95 (978-1-59737-283-1(8), 9781597372831); audio compact disk 39.25 (978-1-59737-288-6(9), 9781597372886, Brinc Audio MP3 Lib); audio compact disk 24.95 (978-1-59737-287-9(0), 9781597372879, Brilliance MP3) Brilliance Audio.
Please enter a Synopsis.

Quillan Games. unabr. ed. D. J. MacHale. Read by William Dufris. (Running Time: 15 hrs.). (Pendragon Ser.: Bk. 7). 2006. 39.25 (978-1-59737-290-9(0), 9781597372909, BADLE); 24.95 (978-1-59737-289-3(7), 9781597372893, BAD) Brilliance Audio.

Quillan Games. unabr. ed. D. J. MacHale. Read by William Dufris. (Running Time: 15 hrs.). (Pendragon Ser.: Bk. 7). (J). (gr. 5-9). 2006. 92.25 (978-1-59737-284-8(6), 9781597372848, BrilAudUnabridg) Brilliance Audio.

Quillan Games. unabr. ed. D. J. MacHale. Read by William Dufris. (Running Time: 15 hrs.). (Pendragon Ser.: Bk. 7). 2009. audio compact disk 49.97 (978-1-4233-9908-7(0), 9781423399087, BriAudCD Unabrid); audio compact disk 19.99 (978-1-4233-9907-0(2), 9781423399070) Brilliance Audio.

Quiller: The 9TH Directive. unabr. collector's ed. Adam Hall. Read by David Case. 7 cass. (Running Time: 10 hrs. 30 min.). (Quiller Ser.). 1989. 56.00 (978-0-7366-1669-0(1), 2517) Books on Tape.
Quiller is back - still working without a gun, cover or contacts - behind the Iron Curtain, hiding in a city where there is no place to hide. Trusting in a woman who can't be trusted. Rescuing a man he would rather kill. Trying to save a world that is already heading over the brink.

Quiller Balalaika. unabr. ed. Adam Hall. 7 cass. (Running Time: 10 hrs. 30 mins.). 1998. 76.95 (978-1-85903-125-4(0)) Pub: Magna Story GBR. Dist(s): Ulverscroft US

Quiller Bamboo. unabr. ed. Adam Hall. Read by Simon Prebble. (Running Time: 10 hrs. 0 mins.). 2008. 29.95 (978-1-4332-5051-4(9)); 59.95 (978-1-4332-5048-4(9)); audio compact disk 80.00 (978-1-4332-5049-1(7)) Blckstn Audio.

Quiller Bamboo. unabr. collector's ed. Adam Hall. Read by David Case. 7 cass. (Running Time: 10 hrs. 30 min.). (Quiller Ser.). 1992. 56.00 (978-0-7366-2117-5(2), 2920) Books on Tape.
Quiller's mission: smuggle a Chinese dissident into Tibet. Two are dead already. Will three be a charm.

Quiller Barracuda. unabr. collector's ed. Adam Hall. Read by David Case. 7 cass. (Running Time: 10 hrs. 30 min.). (Quiller Ser.). 1991. 56.00 (978-0-7366-2023-9(0), 2838) Books on Tape.
In Miami, on the waterfront, a lont-time agent has been turned. Quiller gets the call to find out why. It looks like a simple job but with Quiller, nothing is ever simple. That's because he digs. he finds a gigantic conspiracy, one of global importance, with nothing less than the future of the White House at stake.

Quiller KGB. unabr. collector's ed. Adam Hall. Read by David Case. 7 cass. (Running Time: 10 hrs. 30 min.). (Quiller Ser.). 1991. 56.00 (978-0-7366-1989-9(5), 2805) Books on Tape.
Somebody wants to spoil German unification, kill it dead. Who can it be? Who can find out? Who better than Quiller. On site Quiller moves fast, tooo fast. He finds the target but gets targeted himself. He needs all of his luck, cunning & skill or this could be his last case.

Quiller Memorandum. unabr. ed. Adam Hall. Read by Simon Prebble. (Running Time: 27000 sec.). 2006. 54.95 (978-0-7861-4678-9(8)); audio compact disk 55.00 (978-0-7861-6728-9(9)); audio compact disk 29.95 (978-0-7861-7370-9(X)) Blckstn Audio.

Quiller Memorandum. unabr. collector's ed. Adam Hall. Read by Richard Green. 7 cass. (Running Time: 7 hrs.). (Quiller Ser.). 1979. 42.00 (978-0-7366-0143-6(0), 1145) Books on Tape.
This tale of espionage is set in West Berlin, 15 years after the end of World War II. British Agent Quiller, without gun, cover or contacts, has undertaken the mission of unearthing a neo-Nazi underground organization & its war-criminal leader. In the process, he discovers a complex & malevolent plot, more dangerous to the world than any crime committed during the war.

Quiller Meridian. unabr. collector's ed. Adam Hall. Read by David Case. 6 cass. (Running Time: 9 hrs.). (Quiller Ser.). 1994. 48.00 (978-0-7366-2641-5(7), 3379) Books on Tape.
One agent dead plus a Russian contact out in the cold equals a mess for Quiller. His mission: locate the contact before he (the contact) gets blown away. But no one anticipates an extremist coup. Suddenly the contact's in jeopardy & Quiller's caught in a murderous cross fire.

Quiller Salamander. unabr. ed. Adam Hall. Read by Simon Prebble. (Running Time: 28800 sec.). 2006. 59.95 (978-0-7861-4650-5(8)); audio compact disk

72.00 (978-0-7861-6786-9(6)); audio compact disk 29.95 (978-0-7861-7418-8(8)) Blckstn Audio.

Quiller Salamander. unabr. collector's ed. Adam Hall. Read by David Case. 6 cass. (Running Time: 9 hrs.). (Quiller Ser.). 1995. 48.00 (978-0-7366-2955-3(6), 3649) Books on Tape.
Quiller's most dangerous mission. He's in Cambodia to stop another Khmer Rouge bloodbath. Perilous & realistic.

Quiller Solitaire. unabr. ed. Adam Hall. Read by Simon Prebble. (Running Time: 8.5 hrs. 0 mins.). (ENG.). 2009. 29.95 (978-1-4332-9550-8(4)); 54.95 (978-1-4332-9546-1(6)); audio compact disk 76.00 (978-1-4332-9547-8(4)) Blckstn Audio.

Quiller Solitaire. unabr. collector's ed. Adam Hall. Read by David Case. 6 cass. (Running Time: 9 hrs.). (Quiller Ser.). 1992. 48.00 (978-0-7366-2304-9(3), 3087) Books on Tape.
German reunification has given Euroterrorists more room to roam. Quiller is sent in to pin down bomb threats.

Quiller's Run. unabr. collector's ed. Adam Hall. Read by David Case. 8 cass. (Running Time: 12 hrs.). (Quiller Ser.). 1991. 64.00 (978-0-7366-1901-1(1), 2727) Books on Tape.
Quiller as freelance is improbable, yet here he is probing the shadowed secrets of a devastating arms deal in Southast Asia. He finds the smuggler, a beautiful woman who seduces then kills any man who crosses her. Especially a man who knows too much - like Quiller.

Quilt. T. Davis Bunn. Narrated by Christina Moore. 2 cass. (Running Time: 2 hrs.). 1993. 19.00 (978-1-4025-4521-4(5)) Recorded Bks.

Quilter's Apprentice. unabr. ed. Jennifer Chiaverini. Narrated by Christina Moore. 6 cass. Lib. Ed. (Running Time: 8 hrs. 30 min.). (Elm Creek Quilts Ser.: No. 1). 2003. 59.75 (978-1-4025-6019-4(2), 97513) Recorded Bks.
Sarah McClure takes a job helping elderly Sylvia Compson prepare her family estate for sale. Sylvia, a master quilter, agrees to share the tricks of the trade with Sarah. As the two women grow close, Sylvia shares her family?s tragic past, compelling Sarah to look at her own life more closely.

Quilter's Homecoming. Jennifer Chiaverini. Read by Christina Moore. (Running Time: 36000 sec.). (Elm Creek Quilts Ser.: No. 10). 2007. audio compact disk 34.99 (978-1-4281-4781-2(0)) Recorded Bks.

Quin & Peep Play Hide & Seek. Momoko Kimoto. (J). 1913. bk. 10.95 (978-1-74126-041-0(8)) Pub: RICPub AUS. Dist(s): SCB Distributors

Quincunx or Inconjunct Aspect. Julie Baum. 1 cass. 8.95 (492) Am Fed Astrologers.
An AFA Convention workshop tape.

Quincy Troupe. unabr. ed. Quincy Troupe. Read by Quincy Troupe. 1 cass. (Running Time: 29 min.). 1990. 10.00 (020290) New Letters.
Troupe wrote the biography of Miles Davis that topped best-seller lists. Here, Troupe talks about the collaboration & reads from a new book of his own poetry, "Weather Reports".

Quincy Troupe Two. unabr. ed. Quincy Troupe. Ed. by James McKinley. Prod. by Rebeah Presson. 1 cass. (Running Time: 29 min.). (On the Air Ser.). 1992. 10.00 New Letters.
Troupe, co-author of best-selling Miles Davis autobiography, talks about shifting political agenda & writing.

Quinkins. 2004. bk. 24.95 (978-0-7882-0575-0(7)); pap. bk. 14.95 (978-0-7882-0637-5(0)); 8.95 (978-1-56008-314-6(X)); cass. & flmstrp 30.00 (978-1-56008-752-6(8)) Weston Woods.

Quinta Montana. Paulo Coelho. 2 cass. (Running Time: 2 hrs.). (SPA.). 2001. 29.00 (978-970-05-1298-3(3)) Pub: Grijalbo Edit MEX. Dist(s): Lectorum Pubns
From one of the world's most popular writers comes a retelling of the biblical story of Elijah that follows in the tradition of Paulo Coelho's international bestseller THE ALCHEMIST. Based on an event that awakened the author to the reality that tragedy is not punishment but challenge, LA QUINTA MONTANA teaches without being didactic, inspires without being sanctimonious.

Quintessential Guide to Conscious Creation: (3 volume set with 4 CDs) 2007. (978-0-9794279-0-9(8)) Jrny to Succes.

Quintile Methods. Jim Gross. 1 cass. 8.95 (135) Am Fed Astrologers.
Significance in degree symbol analysis & lunation cycle.

Quit: Read This Book & Stop Smoking. unabr. ed. Charles F. Wetherall. Read by Sean Pratt. (Running Time: 1 hr. 46 mins.). (ENG.). 2006. 9.98 (978-1-59659-117-2(X), GildAudio) Pub: Gildan Media. Dist(s): HachBkGrp

Quit Smoking. Patricia O'Malley. Perf. by Barry Weiss. 1 cass. (Running Time: 50 min.). 1998. (978-1-892450-11-1(9), 180) Promo Music.
Guided imagery.

Quit Smoking. Dorothy J. Papin-Griffith. 2005. audio compact disk 14.95 (978-0-9765935-3-9(X)) Gry L Prodns Inc.

Quit Smoking. unabr. ed. Richard Latham. (Running Time: 3240 sec.). (ENG.). 2006. audio compact disk 17.95 (978-0-9550584-1-7(4)) Meditainment Ltd GBR.

Quit Smoking: Release Smoking Forever. Stuart Wilde. 2 cass. (Running Time: 2 hrs.). (978-0-930603-32-8(X)); audio compact disk (978-0-930603-31-1(1)) White Dove NM.
To release smoking forever takes effort & courage. These subliminal affirmations will help you create a powerful inner feeling that you are in fact a non-smoker & that you can release smoking forever.

Quit Smoking Auto-Matically. Bob Griswold & Deirdre Griswold. (Running Time: 3480 sec.). (While-U-Drive Ser.). 2004. audio compact disk 15.98 (978-1-55848-712-3(3)) EffectiveMN.

Quit Smoking Auto-Matically. Robert E. Griswold & Deirdre Griswold. Read by Robert E. Griswold & Deirdre Griswold. 1 cass. (Running Time: 60 min.). (While-U-Drive Ser.). 1996. 11.98 (978-1-55848-906-6(1)) EffectiveMN.
Helps handle cravings & eventually totally eliminate any desire to smoke.

Quit Smoking Forever. abr. ed. Nina Mattikow. 3 cass. (Running Time: 3 hrs.). Dramatization. (Personal Achievement Ser.). 1992. 19.95 (978-1-55569-560-6(4), 43001) Great Am Audio.
From the American Lung Association, the most definitive stop smoking plan on the market today!.

Quit Smoking Now! Speeches. Edward Strachar. 1 cass. (Running Time: 55 mins.). 2002. 12.95 (978-0-9726941-1-7(0)); audio compact disk 14.95 (978-0-9726941-4-8(5)) InGenius Inc.

Quit Smoking Now: Reclaiming Your Personal Power. Carol Rios. 2007. audio compact disk 18.95 (978-1-4276-2336-2(8)) AardGP.

Quitamancha. Rescate VanPelt. 1 CD. (Running Time: 1 hr. 30 min.). (SPA.). 2003. audio compact disk 14.99 (978-0-8297-3842-1(8)) Pub: Vida Pubs. Dist(s): Zondervan

Quitamancha. Rescate VanPelt. 2002. 2.00 (978-0-8297-3845-2(2)); audio compact disk 3.60 (978-0-8297-3843-8(6)) Zondervan.

Quitamancha. unabr. ed. Rescate VanPelt. (SPA.). 2002. 9.99 (978-0-8297-3844-5(4)) Pub: Vida Pubs. Dist(s): Zondervan

Quite Early One Morning see Dylan Thomas

Quite Honestly. unabr. ed. John Mortimer. Narrated by Suzy Aitchison & Toby Longworth. 3 cass. (Running Time: 21420 sec.). 2006. 34.95 (978-0-7927-4547-1(7), CSL 1008) AudioGO.

Quite Honestly. unabr. abr. ed. John Mortimer. Narrated by Suzy Aitchison & Toby Longworth. 3 CDs. (Running Time: 21420 sec.). 2006. audio compact disk 39.95 (978-0-7927-4478-8(0), SLD 1008) AudioGO.

Quite Remarkable Adventures of the Owl & the Pussycat. abr. unabr. ed. Eric Idle. Read by Eric Idle. Composed by John Du Prez. 2 cass. (Running Time: 3 hrs.). 2004. 18.00 (978-1-59007-037-6(2)) Pub: New Millenn Enter. Dist(s): PerseuPGW
Owl and Pussycat undertake a journey to save the famed walking, talking Bong Tree.

Quite Ugly One Morning. unabr. ed. Christopher Brookmyre. Read by Kenny Blyth. 6 cass. (Isis Cassettes Ser.). (J). 2005. 54.95 (978-0-7531-1805-4(X)); audio compact disk 71.95 (978-0-7531-1847-4(5)) Pub: ISIS Lrg Prnt GBR. Dist(s): Ulverscroft US

Quitting for Good: A Day to Day Program to Stop Smoking. Robert P. Baker. 2 cass. 21.95 Self-Control Sys.
Day to day instructional material guiding the individual through the stop smoking process.

Quitting the Mob see Book You'll Actually Listen To (OT, NT, God, Church Leadership)

Quitting the Mob see Blood Covenant: The Michael Franzese Story

Quitting Time. unabr. ed. Robert J. Conley. Read by Ronald Wilcox. 4 cass. (Running Time: 6 hrs.). (Colfax Ser.). 1995. 25.00 (978-1-883268-24-4(9), 694299) Spellbinders.
Gunfighter, Oliver Colfax, is hired by a wealthy rancher to deal with cattle rustlers & murder is certain to change his life.

Quiver Full of Arrows. abr. ed. Jeffrey Archer. Read by Martin Jarvis. 2005. 8.95 (978-1-59397-796-2(4)) Pub: Macmill Audio. Dist(s): Macmillan

Quiver Full of Arrows. abr. ed. Jeffrey Archer. Read by Martin Jarvis. 3 CDs. (Running Time: 3 hrs. 0 mins. 0 sec.). (ENG.). 2006. audio compact disk 14.95 (978-1-59397-769-6(7)) Pub: Macmill Audio. Dist(s): Macmillan

Quiver Full of Arrows, Vol. 2. unabr. ed. Jeffrey Archer. Narrated by Martin Jarvis. 2 cass. (Running Time: 3 hrs.). 2000. 16.99 (978-0-00-104852-2(X)) Pub: HarpC GBR. Dist(s): Trafalgar
Two friends fall under the spell of a New York beauty with quite unexpected results. An offhand remark is taken seriously by a Chinese sculptor, and a British diplomat becomes the owner of a priceless work of art. An insurance claims advisor has a most surprising encounter on the train home to Sevenoaks.

Quiverings in the Net. Antonia P. Rabb. Read by Antonia P. Rabb. 1 cass. (Running Time: 30 min.). 1995. bk. 10.00; 10.00 (978-0-9644280-1-0(6)) A P Rabb.
Poetry with guitar.

Quizmaster. Compiled by Encyclopaedia Britannica, Inc. 2004. audio compact disk 19.95 (978-1-59339-109-6(9)) Ency Brit Inc.

Quo Vadis: A Narrative of the Time of Nero. unabr. ed. Henryk Sienkiewicz. Read by Frederick Davidson. 16 cass. (Running Time: 23 hrs. 30 mins.). 2000. 99.95 (978-0-7861-1732-1(X), 2537) Blckstn Audio.
Sienkiewicz continues his tradition of portraying great & decisive epochs in modern history by providing a picture of the opening scenes in the conflict of moral ideas within the Roman Empire, a conflict from which Christianity issued as the leading force in history.

Quo Vadis: A Narrative of the Time of Nero. unabr. ed. Henryk Sienkiewicz. Read by Frederick Davidson. (Running Time: 22 hrs. 0 mins.). (ENG.). 2009. 44.95 (978-1-4417-0393-4(4)); audio compact disk 123.00 (978-1-4417-0390-3(X)) Blckstn Audio.

Quo Vadis: Abridged. (ENG.). 2007. (978-1-60339-017-0(0)); cd-rom & audio compact disk (978-1-60339-018-7(9)) Listenr Digest.

Quo Vadis, America, Vol. I. unabr. ed. Fulton J. Sheen. 7 cass. (Running Time: 10 hrs. 30 mins.). (Life Is Worth Living Ser.: 0001). 1985. 29.95 F Sheen Comm.
The late Bishop Sheen speaks on the destiny of our country. Always illuminated by our inner sense of hope.

Quotations to Live By: The Wisdom & Wit of the Ages for Today. Created by Benjamin Williams. 1. (Running Time: 2 hrs.). Dramatization. 2006. audio compact disk 14.99 (978-0-9741868-8-7(0)) QuotationWorld.

Quote Master How to Ace Any Print Media Interview. Narrated by T. J. Walter. 2003. audio compact disk 39.00 (978-1-932642-19-3(6)) Media Training.

Qur'an: A Biography. unabr. ed. Bruce Lawrence. Narrated by Michael Prichard. (Running Time: 5 hrs. 0 mins. 0 sec.). (Books That Changed the World Ser.). (ENG.). 2007. audio compact disk 24.99 (978-1-4001-0387-4(8)); audio compact disk 19.99 (978-1-4001-5387-9(5)); audio compact disk 49.99 (978-1-4001-3387-1(4)) Pub: Tantor Media. Dist(s): IngramPubServ

Qur'an-E-Hakeem Learning Aid. Islamic Science Research Institute Staff. 5 cass. (Running Time: 450 min.). bk. 49.95 (978-0-86685-765-9(6)) Intl Bk Ctr.

Qwiklicks Blues & Funk Basics. Contrib. by Corey Christiansen. (Running Time: 2 hrs. 4 mins.). 2006. 24.95 (978-5-558-09167-0(3)) Mel Bay.

Qwizdom Q4 Elementary Presentation Curriculum. 2005. audio compact disk (978-0-9777346-3-4(3)) Qwizdom.

Qwizdom Q4 Middle School Presentation Curriculum. 2005. audio compact disk (978-0-9777346-4-1(1)) Qwizdom.

Qwizdom Q5 Elementary Presentation Curriculum. 2005. audio compact disk (978-0-9777346-0-3(9)) Qwizdom.

Qwizdom Q5 High School Presentation Curriculum. 2005. audio compact disk (978-0-9777346-2-7(5)); audio compact disk (978-0-9777346-5-8(X)) Qwizdom.

Qwizdom Q5 Middle School Presentation Curriculum. 2005. audio compact disk (978-0-9777346-1-0(7)) Qwizdom.

R

R. Buckminster Fuller. Interview with R. Buckminster Fuller & Norman Cousins. 1 cass. (Running Time: 1 hr.). 10.95 (F0440B090, HarperThor) HarpC GBR.

R. Crumb Handbook. R. Crumb et al. 2005. bk. 25.00 (978-1-84072-716-6(0), 487690 CBR) Pub: M Q Pubns GBR. Dist(s): IngramPubServ

***R. E. A. D. Y. for Inclusion Companion CD: R. E. A. D. Y. Form Templates & Handouts.** Kandis Lighthall. (ENG.). 2008. audio compact disk 10.00 (978-0-9761517-9-1(0)) ABTA Pubns.

R. F. K. Must Die! unabr. collector's ed. Robert Blair Kaiser. Read by Dan Lazar. 15 cass. (Running Time: 22 hrs. 30 min.). 1981. 120.00 (978-0-7366-0427-7(8), 1399) Books on Tape.
On the night of June 4,1968, Sirhan Bishara Sirhan shot & killed Senator Robert F. Kennedy in the steamy pantry of the Los Angeles Ambassador Hotel, Kennedy & his entourage had been celebrating his victory in the California primary for the Democratic nomination for President of the United States. The book begins on the night of Kennedy's assassination & moves forward chronologically to the end of Sirhan's trial.

R. H. Winnick. Interview with R. H. Winnick. 1 cass. (Running Time: 45 min.). 1978. 12.95 (L080) TFR.
Winnick talks on "Robert Frost: The Later Years," a disturbing account of a vicious & compulsively harmful old man who happened to be the best poet of his time. Includes excerpts from Frost's readings & a recording of his contribution to the 1961 presidential inauguration.

R Is for Ricochet. abr. ed. Sue Grafton. Read by Judy Kaye. 5 CDs. (Running Time: 6 hrs.). (Kinsey Millhone Mystery Ser.). (ENG.). 2005. audio compact disk 14.99 (978-0-7393-2086-0(6)) Pub: Random Audio Pubg. Dist(s): Random

R. U. R. unabr. ed. Karel Capek & British Broadcasting Corporation Staff. (Running Time: 1 hr. 30 mins. 0 sec.). (ENG.). 2010. audio compact disk 24.95 (978-1-60283-816-1(X)) Pub: AudioGO. Dist(s): Perseus Dist

R. V. Cassill. Interview. Interview with R. V. Cassill & Kay Bonetti. 1 cass. (Running Time: 57 min.). 13.95 (978-1-55644-002-1(2), 1012) Am Audio Prose.
Discussion of Cassill's use of Midwest roots in his short stories & unofficial censorship in the American literary establishment.

R. V. Cassill. unabr. ed. R. V. Cassill. Read by R. V. Cassill. 1 cass. (Running Time: 29 min.). 1990. 10.00 (051890) New Letters.
Author of 22 novels, & editor of both "The Norton Anthology of Short Fiction" & "The Norton Anthology of Contemporary Fiction" reads from his book "Collected Stories".

R. W. Schmbach Presents Greatest Hits, Vol. 1. 1 cass. 1995. 10.00 (978-1-888361-10-0(7)) Power Publns.

Ra Ma Da Sa: Healig Sound. 3rd ed. Joseph Michael Levry. 1 CD. 1999. audio compact disk 19.00 Root Light.

Ra ma da Sa: Healing Sound. Joseph Michael Levry. 1998. 19.00 (978-1-885562-11-1(X)) Root Light.

Rabbi Akiva & the Fall of Betar: Revolt! The Story of the Bar Kochba Rebellion - The Final Days of Rabbi Akiva. Shmuel Irons. Read by Shmuel Irons. 2 cass. (Running Time: 3 hrs.). 19.95 Set. (978-1-889648-16-3(7)) Jwish Her Fdtn.
A clear view of ancient history based on the Bible & Talmud & other ancient primary sources. A new way of looking at the past.

Rabbi Ben Ezra see Browning's Last Duchess

Rabbi Ben Ezra. 10.00 Esstee Audios.
A reading of one of Browning's best with analysis.

Rabbi Paul: An Intellectual Biography. unabr. ed. Bruce Chilton & Tom Weiner. (Running Time: 11 hrs. 5 mins.). 2008. 29.95 (978-1-4332-3081-3(X)); 72.95 (978-1-4332-3077-6(1)); audio compact disk 90.00 (978-1-4332-3078-3(X)) Blckstn Audio.

Rabbi vs. Chaplain: Is Jesus Israel's Promised Messiah? John McTernan & Tovia Singer. 2007. pap. bk. 11.95 (978-1-933641-27-0(4)) Bible Belt.

Rabbit & Bear & Why Hog's Tail Is Flat (Cherokee) unabr. ed. 1 cass. (Running Time: 30 mins.). 12.95 (C19202) J Norton Pubs.
Authentic Indian legends.

Rabbit & Rooster's Ride. Jill Eggleton. Illus. by Clive Taylor. (Sails Literacy Ser.). (gr. k up). 10.00 (978-0-7578-4040-1(X)) Rigby Educ.

***Rabbit & the Elephant: Why small Is the new Big for Today's Church.** unabr. ed. Tony Dale & George Barna. (ENG.). 2009. 14.98 (978-1-59644-736-3(2), christianSeed) christianaud.

Rabbit & the Elephant: Why small Is the new Big for Today's Church. unabr. ed. Tony Dale et al. Read by Tony Dale & Felicity Dale. (Running Time: 6 hrs. 19 mins. 48 sec.). (ENG.). 2009. audio compact disk 24.98 (978-1-59644-735-6(4), christianSeed) christianaud.

Rabbit at Rest. unabr. collector's ed. John Updike. Read by Michael Prichard. 13 cass. (Running Time: 19 hrs. 30 min.). (Rabbit Quartet: Bk. 4). 1990. 104.00 (978-0-7366-1867-0(8), 2698) Books on Tape.
John Updike's fourth & final novel about an ex- basketball player finds Harry "Rabbit" Angstrom with heart trouble, a Florida condo & a second grandchild. He searches for joy in the latter two events but finds little. Through the winter, spring & summer of 1989, as a debt-ridden, AIDS-plagued America looks the other way, Rabbit explores the bleak terrain of middle age, looking for reasons to live.

Rabbit Ears Beloved Bible Stories: The Creation; Noah & the Ark. unabr. ed. Listening Library. Read by Amy Grant & Kelly McGillis. (J). 2007. 34.99 (978-0-7393-7527-3(X)) Find a World.

Rabbit Ears Cherished Bible Stories: Parables that Jesus Told, the Savior Is Born. unabr. ed. Rabbit Ears. Read by Garrison Keillor & Morgan Freeman. (Rabbit Ears Ser.). (J). (gr. 1). 2007. audio compact disk 11.95 (978-0-7393-5606-7(2), Listening Lib) Pub: Random Audio Pubg. Dist(s): Random

Rabbit Ears Treasury of Animal Stories: How the Rhinoceros Got His Skin; How the Camel Got His Hump; How the Leopard Got His Spots; the Monkey People. unabr. ed. Listening Library. Read by Jack Nicholson et al. (J). 2007. 34.99 (978-0-7393-7531-0(8)) Find a World.

Rabbit Ears Treasury of Beatrix Potter: The Tale of Peter Rabbit; the Tale of Mr. Jeremy Fisher. unabr. ed. Beatrix Potter. Read by Meryl Streep. (J). 2007. 34.99 (978-0-7393-7533-4(4)) Find a World.

Rabbit Ears Treasury of Christmas Stories: Volume Two: Gingham Dog & Calico Cat, Lion & Lamb. unabr. ed. Rabbit Ears. Read by Amy Grant & Christopher Reeve. (Rabbit Ears Ser.). (ENG.). (J). (gr. 1). 2008. audio compact disk 11.95 (978-0-7393-5608-1(9), Listening Lib) Pub: Random Audio Pubg. Dist(s): Random

Rabbit Ears Treasury of Christmas Stories: Volume 1: A Gingerbread Christmas, the Steadfast Tin Soldier. unabr. ed. Rabbit Ears. Read by Jeremy Irons & Susan St. James. (Rabbit Ears Ser.). (ENG.). (J). (gr. 1). 2007. audio compact disk 11.95 (978-0-7393-5604-3(6), Listening Lib) Pub: Random Audio Pubg. Dist(s): Random

Rabbit Ears Treasury of Fables: The Three Little Pigs; the Three Billy Goats Gruff; Rumplestiltskin; the Tiger & the Brahmin; the Ugly Duckling. unabr. ed. Listening Library. Read by Holly Hunter et al. (J). 2007. 34.99 (978-0-7393-7535-8(0)) Find a World.

Rabbit Ears Treasury of Fairy Tales: Thumbelina; the Talking Eggs; the Fisherman & His Wife; the Emperor & the Nightingale. unabr. ed. Rabbit Ears. Read by Kelly McGillis et al. (J). 2007. 34.99 (978-0-7393-7537-2(7)) Find a World.

Rabbit Ears Treasury of Fairy Tales Vol. 2: King Midas & the Golden Touch; Jack & the Beanstalk. As told by Michael Caine. Music by Ellis Marsalis. Illus. by Rodica Prato. 1 cass. (Running Time: 1 hr.). 9.95 Weston Woods.
King Midas, granted his wish for the power to turn all things he touches to gold, learns that there are some things in life more precious than gold.

Rabbit Ears Treasury of Fairy Tales Vol. 2: King Midas & the Golden Touch; Jack & the Beanstalk. Narrated by Michael Caine. Composed by Ellis Marsalis. (Running Time: 30 mins.). (Rabbit Ears Collection). (J). (gr. k-4). 1998. 9.95 (PRE945AC) Weston Woods.

Rabbit Ears Treasury of Heroic Bible Stories: Jonah & the Whale; Jospeh & His Brothers. unabr. ed. Listening Library. Read by Jason Robards & Ruben Blades. (J). 2007. 34.99 (978-0-7393-7539-6(3)) Find a World.

Rabbit Ears Treasury of Heroines: Annie Oakley; the Song of Sacajawea; Finn Mccoul; Princess Scargo & the Birthday Pumpkin. unabr. ed. Listening Library. Read by Keith Carradine et al. (J). 2007. 34.99 (978-0-7393-7541-9(5)) Find a World.

Rabbit Ears Treasury of Storybook Classics: Puss in Boots; Brer Rabbit & the Wonderful Tar Baby; the Emperor's New Clothes; the Steadfast Tin Soldier. unabr. ed. Listening Library. Read by Tracey Ullman et al. (J). 2007. 34.99 (978-0-7393-7543-3(1)) Find a World.

Rabbit Ears Treasury of Tall Tales: Davy Crockett; Rip Van Winkle; Johnny Appleseed; Paul Bunyan. unabr. ed. Listening Library. Read by Nicolas Cage et al. (J). 2007. 34.99 (978-0-7393-7545-7(8)) Find a World.

Rabbit Ears Treasury of Tall Tales: Mose the Fireman; Stormalong; Pecos Bill; Brer Rabbit & Boss Lion. unabr. ed. Listening Library. Read by Michael Keaton et al. (J). 2007. 34.99 (978-0-7393-7547-1(4)) Find a World.

Rabbit Ears Treasury of World Tales: Fool & the Flying Ship; the Firebird; Pinocchio; the Boy Who Drew Cats. unabr. ed. Listening Library. Read by Robin Williams et al. (J). 2007. 34.99 (978-0-7393-7553-2(9)) Find a World.

Rabbit Ears Treasury of World Tales: Rumpelstiltskin; the Tiger & the Brahmin. unabr. ed. Listening Library. Read by Sigourney Weaver et al. (J). 2007. 34.99 (978-0-7393-7551-8(2)) Find a World.

Rabbit Factory. unabr. ed. Larry Brown. 9 cass. (Running Time: 12 hrs. 30 min.). 2003. 59.00 (978-1-4025-4818-5(4)) Recorded Bks.

Rabbit Factory: A Novel. unabr. ed. Larry Brown. Narrated by Tom Stechschulte. 7 cass. (Running Time: 12 hrs. 30 mins.). 2004. 29.99 (978-1-4025-4653-2(X), 03124) Recorded Bks.
Set in Memphis, Tennessee and northern Mississippi, The Rabbit Factory presents a wildly diverse cast of characters who are looking for love but not necessarily in all the right places. Helen is a sex-starved alcoholic who combs the local bars looking for the one thing her sugar daddy can't give her. Arthur, Helen's aging sugar daddy, is very wealthy, but suffers from severe self-confidence issues. Believing himself unloved, Eric is a runaway who oddly becomes Arthur's adopted son. Merlot is a college professor with plenty to give, but also a bizarre secret. And Anjalee is a hooker with a heart of gold who can barely stay one step ahead of big trouble.

***Rabbit Heart (Audio Book)** Colleen Hitchcock. (ENG.). 2011. 19.95 (978-0-9723441-2-8(8)) Leopard Spot.

Rabbit Hill. Robert Lawson. Narrated by Barbara Caruso. 3 CDs. (Running Time: 3 hrs.). (gr. 3 up). audio compact disk 29.00 (978-1-4025-0469-3(1)) Recorded Bks.

Rabbit Hill. abr. ed. Robert Lawson. 1 cass. (Running Time: 50 mins.). Dramatization. (J). (gr. 4-7). 1972. bk. 24.95 incl. bag. (978-0-670-58679-0(X)); pap. bk. 15.95 incl. bag. (978-0-670-58680-6(3)); 9.95 (978-0-670-58678-3(1)) Live Oak Media.
The adventures of the small animals who excitedly await the arrival of new folks.

Rabbit Hill, unabr. ed. Robert Lawson. Narrated by Barbara Caruso. 2 pieces. (Running Time: 3 hrs.). (gr. 3 up). 1997. 19.00 (978-0-7887-0384-3(6), 94574E7) Recorded Bks.
Filled with the innocence & charm of yesteryear, this whimsical classic is always a storytime favorite. When Little Georgie the Rabbit announces that new folks are moving into the big, empty house on Rabbit Hill, all the animals prepare for big changes.

Rabbit Is Rich. unabr. collector's ed. John Updike. Read by Michael Prichard. 12 cass. (Running Time: 18 hrs.). (Rabbit Quartet: Bk. 3). 1983. 96.00 (978-0-7366-0738-4(2), 1695) Books on Tape.
Rabbit, basically decent but not intellectual, is 10 years down the road from "Rabbit Redux." Now a middle-aged Toyota dealer, prosperous despite inflation & the energy crisis, he still seeks peace & contentment - items not standard in his life.

Rabbit Redux. unabr. collector's ed. John Updike. Read by Wolfram Kandinsky. 10 cass. (Running Time: 15 hrs.). (Rabbit Quartet: Bk. 2). 1981. 80.00 (978-0-7366-0293-8(3), 1281) Books on Tape.
A liberated Rabbit Angstrom loses his wife to a hotshot used car salesman dripping with Vitalis & acquires a menage that includes his son, a spaced-out white chick & an Evangelical black man. Rabbit lives a life that is bent, a normal life refracted in a funhouse mirror.

Rabbit, Run. unabr. ed. John Updike. Read by Wolfram Kandinsky. 8 cass. (Running Time: 12 hrs.). (Rabbit Quartet: Bk. 1). 2001. 29.95 (978-0-7366-6825-5(X)) Books on Tape.
Rabbit Angstom is 22 & a salesman in the local department store.

Rabbit, Run. unabr. collector's ed. John Updike. Read by Wolfram Kandinsky. 8 cass. (Running Time: 12 hrs.). (Rabbit Quartet: Bk. 1). 1980. 64.00 (978-0-7366-0292-1(5), 1280) Books on Tape.
In this story we meet Rabbit Angstrom, a 22-year-old salesman in a local department store. Married to the second best sweetheart of his high school years, he is the father of a preschool son & husband to an alcoholic wife. We are minded that there are such people & that salvation is a personal undertaking.

Rabbit-Tale of Mystery. Deborah Howe & James Howe. Read by Victor Garber. 2 cass. (Running Time: 2 hrs.). (Bunnicula Ser.). (J). (gr. 3-5). 2000. 18.00 (978-0-7366-9015-7(8)) Books on Tape.

Rabbit-Tale of Mystery. abr. ed. Deborah Howe & James Howe. Perf. by Lou Jacobi. 1 cass. (Running Time: 1 hr.). (Bunnicula Ser.). (J). (gr. 3-5). 1987. 11.95 (978-0-89845-750-6(5), CP 1700) HarperCollins Pubs.

Rabbit-Tale of Mystery. unabr. ed. Deborah Howe & James Howe. Read by Victor Garber. 2 vols. (Running Time: 1 hr. 42 mins.). (Bunnicula Ser.). (J). (gr. 3-7). 2004. pap. bk. 29.00 (978-0-8072-8204-5(9), YYA139SP, Listening Lib); 23.00 (978-0-8072-8203-8(0), LL0163, Listening Lib) Random Audio Pubg.
Before it's tool late, Harold the dog & chester the cat must find out the truth about the newest pet in the Monroe household, a suspicious-looking bunny with unusual habits & fangs!.

Rabbit Tales/Los Cuentos de Tio Conejo. Elida G. Bonet. Read by Elida G. Bonet. 1 cass. (Running Time: 1 hr. 13 min.). (J). 1998. 12.00 (978-0-9663662-0-4(4)) Under the Mango.
A collection of rabbit-as-trickster tales told in Latin America & contain influences from Africa, native American Indian & Spain.

Rabbit Tattoo. Susannah Brin. Narrated by Larry A. McKeever. (Fantasy Ser.). (J). 2001. 10.95 (978-1-58659-068-0(5)); audio compact disk 14.95 (978-1-58659-332-2(3)) Artesian.

***Rabhlail Ins an Leaba.** Na Shandies. (ENG.). 1990. 11.95 (978-0-8023-7035-8(7)) Pub: Clo Iar-Chonnachta IRL. Dist(s): Dufour

Rabin: our life, his Legacy: Our Life, His Legacy. Leah Rabin. Read by Claire Bloom. 2004. 10.95 (978-0-7435-4574-7(5)) Pub: S&S Audio. Dist(s): S and S Inc

Rabindranath Tagore; Nirad Chaudhuri; Hariprasad Chaurasia. unabr. ed. Julian C. Hollick. 1 cass. (Running Time: 60 min.). 1987. 15.00 (978-1-56709-038-3(9), 1077) Indep Broadcast.
"Rabindranath Tagore." A portrait of the first Asian to win the Nobel Prize for Literature. Tagore was a modern Renaissance man - writer, painter, poet, composer & humanitarian. "Nirad Chaudhuri." A self-portrait of the eccentric Bengali writer & chronicler of the twentieth century. "Hariprasad Chaurasia." A profile of the Pied Piper of Indian flute players.

Raboliot, Pts. 1-2. Maurice Genevoix. Read by Henri Virlogeux. 8 cass. (Running Time: 12 hrs.). (FRE.). 1995. 69.95 (1653/4-TH) Olivia & Hill.
The wellknown tale of the poacher, Raboliot & Bourrel, the lawman who tries to catch him. A fight without pity which leads Raboliot to hide in the forest. When Raboliot leaves the forest to see his family, tragedy awaits.

Raccoon, a Tradtional Passamaquoddy Story & Booklet. ed. 1 CD. (Running Time: 22 mins.). (MIS.). 2005. audio compact disk 14.95 (978-1-57970-343-1(7), SPS105D, Audio-For) J Norton Pubs.

Raccoon & a Possum: Stories & Songs 'Specially for Young Folks. Doug Elliott. Read by Doug Elliott. 1 cass. (Running Time: 60 min.). (J). (gr. 2 up). 1995. 14.95 (978-1-883206-11-6(1)) Native Ground.

Raccoon at Clear Creek Road. Carolyn B. Otto. Narrated by Alexi Komisar. Illus. by Cathy Trachok. 1 cass. (Smithsonian's Backyard Ser.). (J). (ps-2). 1995. 5.00 (978-1-56899-180-1(0), C5008) Soundprints.
In a willow tree behind the yellow house on Clear Creek Road, Raccoon nuzzles her newborn kits. Hungry, she soon leaves them to search for minnows at a nearby creek. But the rain-swollen water sweeps her away to the opposite bank, far from her kits. She finds food here - worms & beetles & berries! But when an owl swoops toward the willow, Raccoon must return to protect her kits. Can she recross the creek or will the owl get to the willow first?.

Raccoon at Clearcreek Road. 1 cass. (Running Time: 35 min.). (J). (gr. k-4). 2001. pap. bk. 19.95 (SP 5008C) Kimbo Educ.
Raccoon protects her young kits. Readalong.

Raccoon Hunting Questions. Tom Rakow. 1 cass. (Running Time: 60 mins.). 2001. 9.95 (978-1-891147-71-5(4)) Rock Dove.

Race. Richard North Patterson. Read by Michael Boatman. 8 cass. (Running Time: 13 hrs. 30 mins.). 2007. 74.95 (978-0-7927-5098-7(5)) AudioGO.

***Race.** Carl Sommer. (Quest for Success Ser.). (ENG.). (YA). 2009. bk. 19.95 (978-1-57537-331-7(9)); pap. bk. 11.95 (978-1-57537-380-5(7)) Advance Pub.

Race. abr. ed. Richard North Patterson. Read by Michael Boatman. 6 CDs. (Running Time: 7 hrs. 0 mins. 0 sec.). (ENG.). 2007. audio compact disk 29.95 (978-1-4272-0183-6(8)) Pub: Macmill Audio. Dist(s): Macmillan

Race. unabr. ed. Richard North Patterson. Narrated by Michael Boatman. 11 CDs. (Running Time: 13 hrs. 37 mins.). 2007. audio compact disk 99.95 (978-0-7927-5050-5(0)) AudioGO.

Race. unabr. ed. Richard North Patterson. Read by Michael Boatman. 1 MP3-CD. (Running Time: 13 hrs. 30 mins.). 2007. 59.95 (978-0-7927-5078-9(0)) AudioGO.

Race. unabr. ed. Richard North Patterson. Read by Michael Boatman. 11 CDs. (Running Time: 13 hrs. 30 mins. 0 sec.). (ENG.). 2007. audio compact disk 39.95 (978-1-4272-0181-2(1)) Pub: Macmill Audio. Dist(s): Macmillan

***Race / la Carrera.** ed. Carl Sommer. (Quest for Success Bilingual Ser.). (ENG & SPA.). (YA). 2009. bk. 21.95 (978-1-57537-430-7(7)) Advance Pub.

Race Across Europe: Armored Warfare, the Air War, Battle of the Bulge, Assault on Germany. unabr. ed. 4 CDs. (Running Time: 4 hrs.). (In Their Own Words Ser.: Vol. 2). 2002. audio compact disk 19.95 (978-0-9715690-1-0(0)) First Person.

Race Against Time. (Paws & Tales Ser.: Vol. 11). (J). 2001. 3.99 (978-1-57972-406-1(X)); audio compact disk 5.99 (978-1-57972-407-8(8)) Insight Living.

Race Against Time. Willard Boyd Gardner. 4 cass. 2004. 19.95 (978-1-57734-806-1(0)) Covenant Comms.

Race Against Time. Stephen Lewis. 5 CDs. (Running Time: 18000 sec.). (Massey Lecture 2005). 2005. audio compact disk 39.95 (978-0-660-19459-2(7)) Canadian Broadcasting CAN.

***Race & Culture: A World View.** unabr. ed. Thomas Sowell. (Running Time: 12 hrs.). 2010. 29.95 (978-1-4417-6183-5(7)); 72.95 (978-1-4417-6180-4(2)); audio compact disk 29.95 (978-1-4417-6182-8(9)); audio compact disk 105.00 (978-1-4417-6181-1(0)) Blckstn Audio.

Race & Culture: A World View. unabr. ed. Thomas Sowell. Read by Barrett Whitener. 9 cass. (Running Time: 13 hrs. 30 min.). 1997. 72.00 (978-0-7366-4065-7(7), 4576) Books on Tape.
From one of America's leading thinkers on race comes this trenchant analysis of why some groups succeed & others don't. After years of investigating world cultures, Thomas Sowell rejects the notion that politics, prejudice & genetics chiefly determine the socioeconomic fates of minorities, nations & civilizations. What matters most is "cultural capital", skills & values that distinguish one group's power from another's. Without developing this tool, Sowell argues, groups can never achieve true autonomy & strength, for which affirmative action & multi-culturalism are poor substitutes.

Race & Outcast Breed. abr. ed. Max Brand. Read by Barry Corbin. 2 cass. (Running Time: 3 hrs.). 2000. 7.95 (978-1-57815-090-8(6), 1058, Media Bks Audio) Media Bks NJ.
Captures the old West.

Race Based Questions & Biomedical Ethics. 1 cass. (Care Cassettes Ser.: Vol. 21, No. 4). 1994. 10.80 Assn Prof Chaplains.

Race Beat: The Press, the Civil Rights Struggle, & the Awakening of a Nation. Gene Roberts & Hank Klibanoff. Read by Richard Allen. (Playaway Adult Nonfiction Ser.). (ENG.). 2009. 99.99 (978-1-60812-501-2(7)) Find a World.

Race Beat: The Press, the Civil Rights Struggle, & the Awakening of a Nation. unabr. ed. Gene Roberts & Hank Klibanoff. (Running Time: 21 hrs.). 2007. 44.25 (978-1-4233-5141-2(X), 9781423351412, BADLE); 29.95 (978-1-4233-5140-5(1), 9781423351405, BAD) Brilliance Audio.

Race Beat: The Press, the Civil Rights Struggle, & the Awakening of a Nation. unabr. ed. Gene Roberts & Hank Klibanoff. Read by Richard Allen. 2 MP3-CDs. (Running Time: 21 hrs.). 2007. 44.25 (978-1-4233-5139-9(8), 9781423351399, Brinc Audio MP3 Lib); 29.95 (978-1-4233-5138-2(X), 9781423351382, Brilliance MP3); 132.25 (978-1-4233-5135-1(5), 9781423351351, BrilAudUnabridg); audio compact disk 142.25 (978-1-4233-5137-5(1), 9781423351375, BriAudCD Unabrid); audio compact disk 48.95 (978-1-4233-5136-8(3), 9781423351368, Bril Audio CD Unabri) Brilliance Audio.

Race Inside Me: The Story of Wilma Rudolph. Molly Jackel & Jerry Stemach. 2002. audio compact disk 200.00 (978-1-58702-861-8(1)) D Johnston Inc.

Race Inside Me: The Story of Wilma Rudolph. Molly Jackel & Jerry Stemach. Ed. by Jerry Stemach et al. Contrib. by Ted S. Hasselbring. (Start-to-Finish Books). (J). (gr. 4-5). 2002. 35.00 (978-1-58702-858-8(1)) D Johnston Inc.

Race Inside Me: The Story of Wilma Rudolph. Jerry Stemach. (Overcoming the Odds Sports Biographies Ser.). 2002. audio compact disk 18.95 (978-1-4105-0193-6(0)) D Johnston Inc.

Race Inside Me: The Story of Wilma Rudolph. unabr. ed. Molly Jackel & Jerry Stemach. Ed. by Jerry Stemach et al. Contrib. by Ted S. Hasselbring. 2 cass. (Start-to-Finish Books). (J). (gr. 4-5). 2002. (978-1-58702-843-4(3), H12) D Johnston Inc.
Wilma Rudolph became the first American woman to ever win three gold medals in a single Olympics. She accomplished that feat in Rome, Italy, in 1960. The roads to Rome, from Rome, and in Rome were filled with challenges and victories for this spunky black woman. Rudolph grew up in the 1940s and 50s in Clarkesville, Tennessee, a community divided by segregation and poverty.

Race Is a Nice Thing to Have: A Guide to Being a White Person or Understanding the White Persons in Your Life. Janet E. Helms. 1994. 11.95 (978-0-9633036-2-2(7)) Content Comms.

Race Marked Out for Us. Dan Comer. 1 cass. 3.00 (75) Evang Outreach.

Race Matters. unabr. ed. Ed. by Cornel West. 3 cass. (Running Time: 4 hrs.). 2004. 19.95 (978-0-945353-92-8(8), E30392u) Pub: Audio Partners. Dist(s): PerseuPGW
Profound reflections on race relations in the United States, encouraging appreciation of racial diversity & disavowing racial hatred & violence. Fusion of African American religious tradition with contemporary political wisdom & insight.

Race Rules: Navigating the Color Line. abr. ed. Michael Eric Dyson. Read by Michael Eric Dyson. 2 cass. (Running Time: 3 hrs. 20 min.). 2004. 17.95 (978-1-57270-032-1(7), E21032, Audio Editions) Pub: Audio Partners. Dist(s): PerseuPGW
A thoughtful evaluation of the pernicious influence of racial thinking across the broad canvas of American social & cultural life, from a leading African American.

Race to Disaster, unabr. ed. Peg Kehret. Narrated by Carine Montbertrand. 2 cass. (Running Time: 3 hrs.). (Frightmares Ser.: No. 7). (gr. 5 up). 1997. 19.00 (978-0-7887-0831-2(7), 94976E7) Recorded Bks.
Rosie & Kayo have a new Care Club project. They are taking Bone Breath, Rosie's dog, to the Oakwood Nursing Center to visit the residents. Old Mr. Winters is one of the girls' favorite people there. One night a murder occurs in the house opposite Oakwood. By the next day, Mr. Winters is missing & the two girls embark on a risky search for their white-haired friend.

Race to Disaster. unabr. ed. Peg Kehret. Read by Carine Montbertrand. 2 cass. (Running Time: 3 hrs.). (Frightmares Ser.: No. 7). (J). (gr. 4). 1997. pap. bk. 30.24 (978-0-7887-1261-6(6), 40507) Recorded Bks.

Race to the Finish: SoundTrax. Jay Althouse. Composed by Sally K. Albrecht. (ENG.). 2004. audio compact disk 39.95 (978-0-7390-3447-7(2)) Alfred Pub.

Race to the Pole. Ranulph Fiennes. Read by David Povall. 10 cass. 84.95 (978-0-7927-3386-7(X), CSL 721); audio compact disk 112.95 (978-0-7927-3387-4(8), SLD 721); audio compact disk 49.95 (978-0-7927-3388-1(6), CMP 721) AudioGO.

Race to the Pole by Hensen & Peary. Kenneth Bruce. 1 cass. (Running Time: 1 hr.). Dramatization. (Excursions in History Ser.). 12.50 Alpha Tape.

Rache des Computers. Bottcher. pap. bk. 21.95 (978-88-7754-762-0(6)) Pub: Cideb ITA. Dist(s): Distribks Inc

Rachel & Leah. Orson Scott Card. 2005. audio compact disk 29.95 (978-1-59038-502-9(0), Shadow Mount) Deseret Bk.

Rachel Carson: Voice for the Earth. unabr. ed. Ginger Wadsworth. Read by Melissa Hughes. 2 cass. (Running Time: 2 hrs.). (YA). (gr. 5 up). 1996. 17.95 (978-1-883332-21-1(4)) Audio Bkshelf.
Here is a chance to go behind the scenes of the writing of Silent Spring, the book that changed the world! & to learn about the woman who wrote it.

Rachel Fister's Blister. Amy MacDonald. Illus. by Marjorie Priceman. 1 cass. (Carry-Along Book & Cassette Favorites Ser.). (J). (gr. k-3). 1996. bk. 9.95 (978-0-395-77978-1(2), 491162) HM Harcourt.

Rachel Fister's Blister. Amy MacDonald. Illus. by Marjorie Priceman. (J). (ps-k). 2005. audio compact disk 6.00 (978-0-618-70899-4(5)) HM Harcourt.

***Rachel in Love.** Pat Murphy. 2009. (978-1-60136-492-0(X)) Audio Holding.

Rachel Ray. unabr. ed. Anthony Trollope. Read by Flo Gibson. 9 cass. (Running Time: 13 hrs. 30 min.). 1989. 28.95 (978-1-55685-142-1(1)) Audio Bk Con.
Politics, romance, & a battle over a Brewery cause ripples in the reflections of Lucas & Rachel.

Rachel's Fun Time. Rachel Sumner. 1 cass. (J). (ps-5). 1991. 9.98 (978-1-886673-01-4(2), Songs by Rachel) Rachels Recs.

Rachel's Fun Time Too! (ENG.). (J). 2007. audio compact disk 14.98 (978-1-886673-13-7(6), Songs by Rachel) Pub: Rachels Recs. Dist(s): Follet Higher Educ

Rachel's Fun Time Too! Rachel Sumner. 1 cass. (J). (ps-5). 1993. 9.98 (978-1-886673-02-1(0), Songs by Rachel) Rachels Recs.
Award-winning collection of lively, fun & educational songs & stories.

Rachel's Garden. abr. ed. Marta Perry. Read by Tanya Eby. (Running Time: 6 hrs.). (Pleasant Valley Ser.: Bk. 2). 2010. audio compact disk 14.99 (978-1-4418-0868-4(X), 9781441808684, BACD) Brilliance Audio.

Rachel's Garden. abr. ed. Marta Perry. Read by Tanya Eby. (Running Time: 3 hrs.). (Pleasant Valley Ser.: Bk. 2). 2011. audio compact disk 9.99 (978-1-4418-0869-1(8), 9781441808691, BCD Value Price) Brilliance Audio.

Rachel's Garden. unabr. ed. Marta Perry. Read by Tanya Eby. (Running Time: 9 hrs.). (Pleasant Valley Ser.: Bk. 2). 2010. 24.99 (978-1-4418-0864-6(7), 9781441808646, Brilliance MP3); 24.99 (978-1-4418-0866-0(3), 9781441808660, BAD); 39.97 (978-1-4418-0865-3(5), 9781441808653, Brinc Audio MP3 Lib); 39.97 (978-1-4418-0867-7(1), 9781441808677, BADLE); audio compact disk 29.99 (978-1-4418-0862-2(0), 9781441808622, Bril Audio CD Unabri); audio compact disk 79.97 (978-1-4418-0863-9(9), 9781441808639, BriAudCD Unabrid) Brilliance Audio.

Rachel's Holiday. unabr. ed. Marian Keyes. Read by Anne Flosnik. (Running Time: 12 hrs. 0 mins.). (ENG.). 2009. 29.95 (978-1-4332-4777-4(1)); 72.95 (978-1-4332-4774-3(7)); audio compact disk 90.00 (978-1-4332-4775-0(5)) Blckstn Audio.

Rachel's Holiday. unabr. ed. Marian Keyes. Narrated by Gerri Halligan. 12 cass. (Running Time: 16 hrs. 45 mins.). 2001. 102.00 (978-1-84197-244-2(4)) Recorded Bks.
The story of 27-year-old drug addict Rachel Walsh, who is sent to The Cloisters, an Irish Betty Ford Clinic, is hardly a holiday as keyes details virtually every moment of addiction, struggle and denial. Not that one expects quick cures, but the novel suffers from an agonizingly slow pace as

almost 60 chapters unwind before Rachel begins to acknowledge her problems. The romantic subplot with fellow addict Chris, battling her love-hate memories of New York City hunk Luke, is predictable. Rachel herself evokes little sympathy.

Rachel's Hope. Annette Pierce. 2 cass. (Running Time: 3 hrs.). 11.98 (978-1-55503-924-0(3), 07001339) Covenant Comms.

Rachel's Lullabies Old & New. Rachel Sumner. 1 cass. (J). (ps-3). 1990. 9.98 (978-1-886673-00-7(4), Songs by Rachel) Rachels Recs.

Rachel's Secret. Susan Sallis. 2009. 76.95 (978-1-4079-0606-5(2)); audio compact disk 84.95 (978-1-4079-0607-2(0)) Pub: Soundings Ltd GBR. Dist(s): Ulverscroft US

Rachmaninov - Sonata for Violoncello & Piano, Op. 19. Composed by Sergei Rachmaninoff. 2006. pap. bk. 29.98 (978-1-59615-415-5(2), 1596154152) Pub: Music Minus. Dist(s): H Leonard

Rachmaninov Six Scenes for Piano Duet. Composed by Sergei Rachmaninoff. 2006. pap. bk. 29.98 (978-1-59615-023-2(8), 1596150238) Pub: Music Minus. Dist(s): H Leonard

Racing Pigs & Giant Marrows. unabr. ed. Harry Pearson. Read by Harry Pearson. 6 cass. (Running Time: 6 hrs.). 1998. 54.95 (978-0-7540-0128-7(8), CAB1551) AudioGO.
A travelogue embracing a summer of shows & fairs in the northern counties of England. It includes picturesque descriptions of the landscapes, livestock & inhabitants of Cumbria, Durham, Northumberland & North Yorkshire. Tells of onions larger than human heads, the design faults of earwigs, & much more.

Racing September. unabr. ed. William DeSeta. Read by Kevin Foley. 8 cass. (Running Time: 9 hrs. 50 min.). 1996. 49.95 (978-1-55686-688-3(7)) Books in Motion.
New Jersey, summer, 1953, a 17 year-old whose parents are in Cuba on business strikes out for California, hitch-hiking. He races against time to get back before his parents return in September.

***Racing Toward Armageddon.** unabr. ed. Michael Baigent. Read by John Lee. (ENG.). 2009. (978-0-06-196165-6(5), Harper Audio); (978-0-06-196164-9(7), Harper Audio) HarperCollins Pubs.

Racing Toward Armageddon CD: The Three Great Religions & the Plot to End the World. unabr. ed. Michael Baigent. Read by John Lee. 2009. audio compact disk 39.99 (978-0-06-166238-6(0), Harper Audio) HarperCollins Pubs.

Racing Toward 2001: The Forces Shaping America's Religious Future. Russell Chandler. 2 cass. (Running Time: 2 hrs.). 1992. 14.99 (978-0-310-54138-7(7)) Zondervan.
Looks through the lens of religion at the major forces shaping our future & gives us windows through which to view the coming millennium.

Racist America: Roots, Current Realities, & Future Reparations. Joe R. Feagin. Narrated by Michael McFadden. 12 CDs. (Running Time: 15 hours). 2002. audio compact disk 59.95 (978-1-929011-25-4(3)) Scholarly Audio.
Despite the apparent advances since the civil rights era, America remains fundamentally racist, argues award-winning author Joe Feagin (former President of the American Sociological Association). Racism affects where we live, the clothes we wear, where we go to school, the people we marry, how we earn a living, how we raise our children, and other aspects of our lives.

Racist America: Roots, Current Realities, & Future Reparations. Joe R. Feagin. 1 CD. (Running Time: 15 hours). (C). 2002. audio compact disk 24.95 (978-0-9660180-8-0(7)) Scholarly Audio.

Rackets. unabr. ed. Thomas Kelly. Read by David Daoust. (Running Time: 50400 sec.). 2001. audio compact disk 24.95 (978-1-59600-543-3(2), 9781596005433, Brilliance MP3) Brilliance Audio.

Rackets: A Novel. unabr. ed. Thomas Kelly. Read by David Daoust. 9 cass. (Running Time: 14 hrs.). 2001. 37.95 (978-1-58788-550-1(6), 1587885506, BAU) Brilliance Audio.
Set in the union halls, taverns, and half built skyscrapers of midtown Manhattan and in the gritty uptown neighborhood of Inwood, The Rackets depicts every shade of New York Irish - as well as Italian mobsters, Russian killers, and a gun-running Gulf War veteran on disability. Our hero is Jimmy Dolan, who, after putting himself through college by working as a day laborer, goes to work for a smug Republican mayor. When he tries to settle an old dispute with his fists at a Gracie Mansion breakfast meeting, he finds himself out of a job - and sought out by Frankie Keefe, the corrupt union boss he knocked to the carpet. Jimmy's father Mike, a saintly widower, is running for president of the construction worker's union, but when he is brutally murdered, Jimmy has to decide whether to risk his life - and that of his girlfriend Tara, a bold New York City policewoman - in order to defend his father's honor and the interests of the rank and file.

Rackety Packety House & the Story of Prince Fairyfoot. unabr. ed. Frances Hodgson Burnett. Narrated by Flo Gibson. 2 cass. (Running Time: 2 hrs.). (J). (gr. 1-4). 2003. 14.95 (978-1-55685-717-1(9)) Audio Bk Con.
A doll's house and its ragged inhabitants survive many problems with the help of Peter Piper, Ridikilis, Gustibus and other colorful characters. In the second story the Prince's problem of too small feet is solved by two big feet.

Raconteur: Show Biz Stories from the Soul. As told by Jeff Wayne. 2001. 14.95 (978-1-929243-08-2(1)); audio compact disk 19.95 (978-1-929243-07-5(3)) Uproar Ent.

Racquetball. Barrie Konicov. 1 cass. 11.98 (978-0-87082-422-7(8), 104) Potentials.
The author, Barrie Konicov, reveals how to improve & upgrade your game of racquetball & be a potential winner.

Radcliffe's Christmas. Darren J. Butler. (ENG.). (J). 2002. audio compact disk 14.95 (978-0-9753367-2-4(X)) Onstage Pubng.

Radha Krishna Temple. 1 cass. (Running Time: 60 mins.). 4.95 (aa-6); audio compact disk 14.95 CD. (CD-6) Bhaktivedanta.

Radhe Govinda. Sivananda Radha. 1 cass. 1993. 9.95 (978-0-931454-43-1(3)) Timeless Bks.
Swami Radha chants traditional ancient Mantra. Effective in keeping the mind centered while working, or for meditation.

***Radiance.** unabr. ed. Alyson Noël & Kathleen McInerney. 3 CDs. (Running Time: 4 hrs.). (J). 2010. audio compact disk 14.99 (978-1-4272-1083-8(7)) Pub: Macmill Audio. Dist(s): Macmillan

Radiant Coat: Myths & Stories about the Crossing Between Life & Death. unabr. ed. Clarissa Pinkola Estes. 2 CDs. (Running Time: 5400 sec.). 2006. audio compact disk 19.95 (978-1-59179-438-7(2), AW00118D) Sounds True.

Radiant Fire of Purification. abr. ed. Swami Amar Jyoti. 1 cass. 1987. 9.95 (E-32) Truth Consciousness.
Comfort lovingness, the greatest obstacle. Maintaining balance. Clearing & purifying the subconscious. Slaps, hugs & austerities. Accepting the verdict of truth, being down to earth conscious.

Radiant Health: And A Strong Immune System. Dick Sutphen. 1 cass. (Running Time: 1 hr.). (RX17 Ser.). 1986. 14.98 (978-0-87554-307-9(3), RX116) Valley Sun.
Every day in every way, you become healthier & healthier. Radiant good health is your reality. Your immune system functions at optimum efficiency. Every day, your body's immune system becomes stronger. You eat a healthy diet & get adequate exercise & rest. You always think positively about your health. "Balance & harmony" are your key words for conditioned response.

Radiant Health: Guided Imagery for Well-Being. Catherine Sheen. 2 CDs. (Running Time: Depends on Track). 2005. audio compact disk 22.95 (978-0-9773381-7-7(7)) Reach In.
Radiant Health: Guided Meditation for Well-Being CDs focus on restoring your body to its natural state of radiant health by using imagery to release toxins and strengthen your DNA. These meditations can help you let go of stres and return to a natural feeling of well-being. The CDs include a Preparation for Meditation track.

Radiant Seas. unabr. ed. Catherine Asaro. Read by Anna Fields. (Running Time: 16 hrs.). 2000. audio compact disk 108.00 (978-0-7861-6635-0(5)); 76.95 (978-0-7861-1848-9(2), 2647) Blckstn Audio.
Sequel to "Primary Inversion" & continues the story of Sauscony & Jaibriol, each the heir to an interstellar empire. They are beginning to pick up what's left of their lives, in exile on a deserted planet with their children, when the fate of much of the known universe comes to rest on the shoulders of their young fragile family. Interstellar war erupts, Jaibriol is taken away to be an unwilling ruler. Sauscony must fight her way to rescue him from his own empire, without revealing that they are married.

Radiant Seas. unabr. ed. Catherine Asaro. Read by Anna Fields. (Running Time: 55800 sec.). (Saga of the Skolian Empire (Blackstone Audio) Ser.). 2006. audio compact disk 29.95 (978-0-7861-7352-5(1)) Blckstn Audio.

***Radiant Shadows.** unabr. ed. Melissa Marr. Read by Nick Landrum. (ENG.). 2010. (978-0-06-198399-3(3)); (978-0-06-199160-8(0)) HarperCollins Pubs.

Radiant Touch. abr. ed. Jim Oliver & Jorge Alfano. (Running Time: 2:00:00). 2007. audio compact disk 19.98 (978-1-55961-887-8(6)) Sounds True.

Radiation - Removing the Dross: Relax into Healing Series (Spoken Audio CD & Booklet) Nancy Hopps. (Relax Into Healing Ser.). 2007. pap. bk. 19.95 (978-0-9785985-2-5(0)) Pub: Syner Systs. Dist(s): Baker Taylor

Radiation & Your Survival. L. Ron Hubbard. 10 cass. (Running Time: 15 hrs.). 2002. pap. bk. 170.00 (978-1-57318-232-4(X)) Bridge Pubns Inc.

Radiation Therapy. Belleruth Naparstek. Composed by Steven M. Kohn. 1 cass. (Running Time: 32 min.). (Health Journeys Ser.). 1999. 12.98 (978-1-881405-22-1(2), 52) Hlth Jrnys.
Designed to help relax & prepare mind, body & spirit for radiation therapy, through a gentle but powerful technique called "guided imagery." Physician-endorsed & research-proven, this program consists of an imaginative narrative scored by soothing music.

***Radical.** unabr. ed. David Platt. (Running Time: 6 hrs. 24 mins. 0 sec.). (ENG.). 2010. audio compact disk 21.98 (978-1-59644-938-1(1)) christianaud.

***Radical: Taking Back Your Faith from the American Dream.** unabr. ed. David Platt. (ENG.). 2010. 12.98 (978-1-59644-939-8(X)) christianaud.

Radical Authenticity: Never Hide Again. Barry Neil Kaufman. (ENG.). 2007. audio compact disk 34.50 (978-0-9798105-6-5(6)) Option Inst.

Radical Career: Logos June 6, 1999. Ben Young. 1999. 4.95 (978-0-7417-6136-1(X), B0136) Win Walk.

Radical Cash Flow: Logos May 30, 1999. Ben Young. 1999. 4.95 (978-0-7417-6135-4(1), B0135) Win Walk.

Radical Chic & Mau-Mauing the Flak Catchers. unabr. ed. Tom Wolfe. Read by Harold N. Cropp. 3 cass. (Running Time: 4 hrs.). 1994. 23.95 (978-0-7861-0698-1(0), 1480) Blckstn Audio.
In "Radical Chic," Wolfe focuses primarily on one symbolic event: a gathering of the politically correct at Leonard Bernstein's duplex apartment on Park Avenue to meet spokesmen of the Black Panther Party. He re-creates the incongruous scene - & its astonishing repercussions - with high fidelity. In the companion essay, Wolfe travels west to San Francisco to survey another meeting-ground between militant minorities & the liberal white establishment. "Mau-Mauing the Flak Catchers" deals with the newly emerging art of confrontation, as practiced by San Francisco's militant minorities in response to a highly bureaucratized poverty program.

Radical Chic & Mau-Mauing the Flak Catchers. unabr. collector's ed. Tom Wolfe. Read by Michael Prichard. 7 cass. (Running Time: 7 hrs.). 1992. 42.00 (978-0-7366-2156-4(3), 2955) Books on Tape.
Tom Wolfe on the courting of the romantic radicals by the socially elite. Uproarious farce.

Radical Culture/Conservative Church. Paul Cain. 1 cass. (Running Time: 90 mins.). (Call to Radical Christianity Ser.: Vol.). 2000. 5.00 (PC01-001) Morning NC.
"Radical Culture/Conservative Church" & "The Rest of God." This is a call for the church to become a revolutionary power on the earth once again.

***Radical Forgiveness: A Revolutionary Five-Stage Process to Heal Relationships, Let Go of Anger & Blame, Find Peace in Any Situation.** Colin Tipping. (Running Time: 3:39:09). 2009. audio compact disk 24.95 (978-1-59179-767-8(5)) Sounds True.

***Radical Forgiveness: Experience the Power of True Freedom, Vol. 1.** Andy Andrews. (Running Time: 250). (ENG.). 2010. audio compact disk 150.00 (978-0-9827404-0-8(9)) Lightning Crown Pub.

Radical Forgiveness: Logos 04/25/99. Ben Young. 1999. 4.95 (978-0-7417-6130-9(0), B0130) Win Walk.

Radical Forgiveness - 5 CD Set: Making Room for the Miracle. abr. ed. Colin C. Tipping. Read by Colin C. Tipping. Read by JoAnna Tipping. 2006. audio compact disk 34.95 (978-0-9704814-6-7(2)) Global Thirteen.

Radical Hatred: Logos May 16, 1999. Ben Young. 1999. 4.95 (978-0-7417-6133-0(5), B0133) Win Walk.

Radical Hell: Logos 05/02/1999. Ben Young. 1999. 4.95 (978-0-7417-6131-6(9), B0131) Win Walk.

Radical Intolerance: Logos 04/18/1999. Ben Young. 1999. 4.95 (978-0-7417-6129-3(7), B0129) Win Walk.

Radical Love: Logos May 9, 1999. Ben Young. 1999. 4.95 (978-0-7417-6132-3(7), B0132) Win Walk.

Radical loving Care: Buildin. 5 CDs. 2006. audio compact disk 35.00 (978-0-9747366-8-6(6)) Erie Chapman.

Radical Manifestation - 4 CDs: The Fine Art of Creating the Life You Want. Colin C. Tipping. 2007. audio compact disk 29.99 (978-0-9786993-1-4(9)) Global Thirteen.

Radical Neo-Hermeticism. Peter L. Wilson. 2 cass. 1992. 18.00 set. (OC306-67) Sound Horizons AV.

Radical Niyazi Bey. Muzaffer Izgu. 2 cass. (Running Time: 2 hrs.). (YA). 2001. bk. 11.95 (978-1-84059-307-5(5)); bk. 11.95 (978-1-84059-306-8(7)) Pub: Milet Pub. Dist(s): Tuttle Pubng

Radical Passion: Logos 05/1999. Ben Young. 1999. 4.95 (978-0-7417-6134-7(3), B0134) Win Walk.

Radical Prayer. Matthew Fox. 2003. audio compact disk 69.95 (978-1-59179-119-5(7)) Sounds True.

Radical Prayer audio Book: Will you respond to the prayer of Jesus? Read by Derek Morris. (ENG.). 2008. audio compact disk 8.99 (978-0-9817124-1-3(X)) Trilogy Script.

Radical Prosperity: Inspirational Series with Ellen Grace O'Brian. Ellen Grace O'Brian. 3 cass. (Running Time: 4 hours). 2003. 21.95 (978-0-9660518-7-2(4), CSE Press); audio compact disk 21.95 (978-0-9660518-6-5(6), CSE Press) Ctr for Spirit.

Radical Recruiting: Increase Your Recruiting Efforts with This 5 Step Recruiting Process. Lisa Jimenez. Read by Lisa Jimenez. 6 CDs. (Running Time: 5 hrs. 42 min.). 2002. pap. bk. (978-0-9705807-3-3(8)) RX Success.

***Radical Reformission: Reaching Out without Selling Out.** Mark Driscoll. (Running Time: 5 hrs. 5 mins. 0 sec.). (ENG.). 2008. 14.99 (978-0-310-30500-2(4)) Zondervan.

Radical Self-Acceptance: A Buddhist Guide to Freeing Yourself from Shame. Tara Brach. 3 CDs. (Running Time: 011700 sec.). 2005. audio compact disk 24.95 (978-1-59179-321-2(1), AW00468D) Sounds True.

***Radical Self-Forgiveness Practices: Tools for Achieving True Self-Acceptance.** Colin Tipping. (Running Time: 2:00:00). 2010. audio compact disk 19.95 (978-1-60407-085-9(4)) Sounds True.

Radical Son: A Generational Odyssey. unabr. ed. David Horowitz. Read by Jeff Riggenbach. 14 cass. (Running Time: 20 hrs. 30 mins.). 1998. 89.95 (978-0-7861-1365-1(0), 2273) Blckstn Audio.
David Horowitz was one of the founders of the New Left & an editor of "Ramparts," the magazine that set the intellectual & revolutionary tone for the movement. From his vantage point at the center of the action, he provides vivid portraits of people who made the radical decade, while unmaking America at the same time. He was eventually transformed into an intellectual leader of conservatism & its most prominent activist in Hollywood.

Radical Sons. David Horowitz. 13 cass. (Running Time: 19.5 hrs.). 2001. 104.00 (978-0-7366-6364-9(9)) Books on Tape.

Radical Spirituality. 1 cass. (Condensed Books on Tape). 15.98 (978-0-87554-590-5(4), N120) Valley Sun.

Radical Surgery: Matthew 5:27-30. Ed Young. (J). 1979. 4.95 (978-0-7417-1052-9(8), A0053) Win Walk.

Radical Undoing: Overview, Vol. 1. Christopher S. Hyatt. Ed. by Nick Tharcher. Nick Tharcher. (ENG.). 2008. DVD & audio compact disk 49.99 (978-1-935150-09-1(X)) Orig Falcon.

Radical View of Addiction & Addictive Behavior. Andrew Weil. 2 cass. 18.00 (OC130) Sound Horizons AV.
Addiction is a universal process and problem, far more general than most people imagine. All addiction is psychological in origin, and the problem of addiction can only be solved on the psychic-spiritual level.

***Radically Simple Accounting Audio Book.** QC Computing. (Running Time: 4 hours). (ENG.). 2010. 40.00 (978-0-9639688-4-5(X)) QCComput.

Radicals & Visionairies: Entrepreneurs Who Revolutionized the 20th Century. Thaddeus Wawro. Read by Michael Drew Shaw. (Running Time: 17520 sec.). (ENG.). 2006. audio compact disk 24.95 (978-1-932531-85-5(8), 1932531858) Pub: Entrepreneur Pr. Dist(s): McGraw

Radio & Television Broadcasting & Communications Equipment in Philippines: A Strategic Reference 2006. Compiled by Icon Group International, Inc. Staff. 2007. ring bd. 195.00 (978-0-497-82393-1(4)) Icon Grp.

Radio & the Public Image. 10.00 (MC1002) Esstee Audios.
A historical panoply of the medium of radio from the 1920's onward. Discusses the individual images radio created, the composite picture of America through such soap operas as "Stella Dallas" & "My Gal Sunday".

Radio & World Evangelization: Proceedings of the 45th Annual Convention National Association of Evangelicals Buffalo, New York. Read by E. Brandt Gustavson. 1 cass. (Running Time: 60 min.). 1987. 4.00 (342) Nat Assn Evan.

Radio Broadcasts. 1 cass. (Running Time: 60 min.). 6.00 Once Upon Rad.

Radio Broadcasts from China, Vol. 1. 2 cass. (Running Time: 95 mins.). (CHI.). pap. bk. 49.50 (SCH100) J Norton Pubs.
Recordings of authentic news, music & cultural broadcasts (1979-1981) from the Peoples' Republic of China is designed for advanced learners to improve listening comprehension & reading ability. The accompanying texts provide a complete transcription of the recorded material in both traditional & simplified characters. Vol. 1: news, miscellaneous, from seeing roses to meteorologists at weather station.

Radio Broadcasts from China, Vol. 2. 1 cass. (Running Time: 80 mins.). (CHI.). pap. bk. 39.50 (SCH105) J Norton Pubs.
The trial of Lin Biao & Jiang Qing cliques.

Radio Caroline Story. Capital Radio. (Running Time: 0 hr. 45 mins.). 2005. 16.95 (978-1-59912-942-6(6)) Iofy Corp.

***Radio Christmas Spirits.** Perf. by Jack Benny & Phil Harris. 2010. audio compact disk 39.98 (978-1-57019-906-6(X)) Radio Spirits.

Radio Comedy Classics. 4 vols. (Running Time: 6 hrs.). (Radio Spirits Historical Collections). 2003. bk. 24.98 (978-1-57019-652-2(4), OTR50434) Pub: Radio Spirits. Dist(s): AudioGO

Radio Covers World War Two. unabr. ed. 6 cass. (Running Time: 6 hrs.). 29.95 (978-1-57816-006-8(5), RCW618) Audio File.
Selected radio news broadcasts providing an overview of radio's global coverage of the Second World War.

Radio Covers WW II. (Running Time: 6 hrs.). 2004. audio compact disk 29.95 (978-1-57816-193-5(2)) Audio File.

Radio Detective Classics. 6 vols. (Running Time: 6 hrs.). (Radio Spirits Historical Collections). bk. 34.98 (978-1-57019-655-3(9), OTR50442) Pub: Radio Spirits. Dist(s): AudioGO

Radio Detective Classics. 4 vols. (Running Time: 6 hrs.). (Radio Spirits Historical Collections). 2003. bk. 24.98 (978-1-57019-656-0(7), OTR50444) Pub: Radio Spirits. Dist(s): AudioGO

Radio Diaries: My So-Called Lungs. Prod. by Joe R. Richman. 1 CD. (Running Time: 23 mins.). 2002. audio compact disk 14.95 (978-0-9725782-4-0(2)) Radio Diaries.

Radio Diaries: New York Works. Prod. by Joe R. Richman. 1 CD. (Running Time: 1 hr.). 2002. audio compact disk 14.95 (978-0-9725782-3-3(4)) Radio Diaries.

Radio Diaries: Prison Diaries. Prod. by Joe R. Richman. 1 CD. (Running Time: 1 hr.). 2001. audio compact disk 14.95 (978-0-9725782-2-6(6)) Radio Diaries.

Radio Diaries: Teenage Diaries. Prod. by Joe R. Richman. 1 CD. (Running Time: 1 hr.). 2002. audio compact disk 14.95 (978-0-9725782-0-2(X)) Radio Diaries.

Radio Disney: Kid Jams. Prod. by Walter Elias Disney. 1 CD. (J). 1999. audio compact disk 10.98 (978-0-7634-0511-3(6)) W Disney Records.

Radio Disney: Kid Jams. Prod. by Walter Elias Disney. 1 cass. (J). (ps-3). 1999. 7.99 (978-0-7634-0512-0(4)) W Disney Records.

Radio Disney Jams, Vol. 2. 1 CD. (Running Time: 90 mins.). (J). (ps-3). 2000. audio compact disk 12.98 (978-0-7634-0619-6(8)); audio compact disk 12.98 (978-0-7634-0622-6(8)) W Disney Records.

Radio Favorites, Vol. 1. abr. collector's ed. 6 cass. (Running Time: 9 hrs.). 1998. bk. 17.49 (4003) Radio Spirits.
19 episodes include: "Amos 'n' Andy," "Damon Runyon Theatre," "Great Gildersleeve," "Fibber McGee and Molly," "Life of Riley," "Tom Mix," "Unsolved Mysteries," "Midnight," "Dangerous Assignment," "Suspense," "Lux Radio Theatre," "Mel Blanc Show," "Eddie Cantor Show," "Our Miss Brooks," "Have Gun, Will Travel," "The Jack Benny Program," "Escape," "Philip Marlowe" and "Philco Radio Time".

Radio Favorites, Vol. 2. collector's ed. 6 cass. (Running Time: 9 hrs.). 1998. bk. 17.49 (4004) Radio Spirits.
21 episodes include: "Academy Award Theatre," "The Whistler," "Life with Luigi," "Gunsmoke," "This Is Your F.B.I.," "Red Skelton Show," "Bulldog Drummond," "Bill Stern Sports Newsreel," "Strange Dr. Weird," "My Friend Irma," Mae West and Don Ameche's infamous Adam & Eve sketch, "Johnny Dollar," "My Favorite Husband," "Boston Blackie," "Bob and Ray," "Dimension X," "Screen Director's Playhouse," "Pat Novak for Hire," "The Six Shooter," "Murder at Midnight" and "Richard Diamond, Private Detective".

Radio France. E. A. Macaro. (J). (gr. 12). 1985. pap. bk. 16.96 (978-0-582-37684-7(X), 72581) Longman.

Radio Free Albemuth. unabr. ed. Philip K. Dick. Read by Tom Weiner. (Running Time: 8 hrs. 0 mins.). (ENG.). 2009. 29.95 (978-1-4332-9167-8(3)); 54.95 (978-1-4332-9163-0(0)); audio compact disk 76.00 (978-1-4332-9164-7(9)) Blckstn Audio.

Radio Frequency Identification Device (RFID) Technology in Hong Kong: A Strategic Reference 2006. Compiled by Icon Group International, Inc. Staff. 2007. ring bd. 195.00 (978-0-497-36001-6(2)) Icon Grp.

Radio Frequency Identification Device (RFID) Technology in New Zealand: A Strategic Reference 2007. Compiled by Icon Group International, Inc. Staff. 2007. ring bd. 195.00 (978-0-497-82371-9(3)) Icon Grp.

Radio Frequency Identification Device (RFID) Technology in United Kingdom: A Strategic Reference 2006. Compiled by Icon Group International, Inc. Staff. 2007. ring bd. 195.00 (978-0-497-82458-7(2)) Icon Grp.

Radio H-A-L-O. 1 cass. (Running Time: 90 mins.). 1997. 7.99 (978-0-7601-1249-6(5), C80004); audio compact disk 11.99 (978-0-7601-1261-8(4), CD80004) Pub: Brentwood Music. Dist(s): Provident Mus Dist
Hear an on location interview at the "Fiery Furnace" with Sandrach, Meshach & Abednego. Hear up to date news & traffic with "Eye in the Sky Guy Sly." In between weather with "Hunky Dorry" from Egypt, fashion with "Noah's Sons" from the Ark & sports with "Steel-Head Moore," you will hear hip & cool new "Bible Based" songs. Listen to the zany spoof commercials & comedy skits. Join DJ, Jacko Bonzo & his host of characters in a bazooloo broadcast that teaches kids that God is always with them.

Radio in That Wonderful Year 1948. Scripts. 2 Cassette. (Running Time: 2 hrs). Dramatization. 2004. 10.95 (978-1-57816-208-6(4)) Audio File.

Radio in That Wonderful Year 1949. 2 cass. (Running Time: 2 hrs). Dramatization. 2004. 10.95 (978-1-57816-203-1(3)) Audio File.

Radio Interview at Arlington, Virginia, Side B. Illus. by Morris Parloff & N. I. M. H. Staff. Rational Isl.

Radio Interview over KDCR. Garry De Young. 1 cass. 5.00 De Young Pr.

Radio Leicester Big Band: Millennium Big Band Jazz. 2nd ed. Prod. by Tim Nuzum. (Wildemuse Ser.). 2002. audio compact disk 10.00 (978-1-882204-41-0(7)) Wilde Pub.

Radio Mambo: Culture Clash Invades Miami. Culture Clash et al. Perf. by Culture Clash. 2 CDs. (Running Time: 1 hr. 25 mins.). 2002. audio compact disk 25.95 (978-1-58081-225-2(2), CDTPT157) Pub: L A Theatre. Dist(s): NetLibrary CO
The acclaimed comedy trio known as Culture Clash spent three months interviewing about 79 Miami residents for this mix of vignettes about urban renewal, crimes, hurricanes and immigration, as well as where to get a plate of arroz con pollo served by a six foot drag queen.

Radio Movie Classics: Cary Grant. adpt. ed. Perf. by Cary Grant. Intro. by Jeffrey Lyons. 2 cass. (Running Time: 3 hrs.). 1998. bk. 12.95 (978-1-57019-132-9(8), 6003) Radio Spirits.

Radio Mystery. Gertrude Chandler Warner. (Running Time: 5400 sec.). (Boxcar Children Ser.: No. 97). (J). 2005. audio compact disk 14.95 (978-0-7861-7483-6(8)) Blckstn Audio.

Radio Mystery. unabr. ed. Read by Aimee Lilly. Characters created by Gertrude Chandler Warner. 2 cass. (Boxcar Children Ser.: No. 97). (J). 2003. 12.99 (978-1-58926-290-4(5), Oasis Kids) Oasis Audio.

Radio Mystery. unabr. ed. Gertrude Chandler Warner. Narrated by Aimee Lilly. (Boxcar Children Ser.). (ENG.). (J). 2003. 10.49 (978-1-60814-090-9(3)) Oasis Audio.

Radio Now, Live! Firesign Live 1999. Perf. by Firesign Theatre. Text by Firesign Theatre. 2 CDs. (Running Time: 2 hrs. 1 min.). Dramatization. 2005. audio compact disk 15.95 (978-1-59938-023-0(4)) Lode Cat.
LIVE ON STAGE at the Alladin Theatre, Portland, in April 1999, The Firesign Theatre rocks, and the audience is rolling in the aisles! This live performance was recorded multitrack, and has been specially mixed and mastered for this Firesign Theatre Records release. Material from classic albums, including I Think We're All Bozos On This Bus, Don't Crush That Dwarf,and How Can You Be material from 1999's Give Me Immortality Or Give Me Death and a hilarious extended performance from Anythynge You Want To.

Radio Programs in Rhyme for Story Time. Alfreda C. Doyle. 2 cass. (Running Time: 1 hr. 45 min.). (J). (gr. 3-8). 1992. 39.00 set. (978-1-56820-090-3(0)) Story Time.
14 plus stories of rhyming entertainment. Stories include: A Zuetoo Mask Crew Go to the Gallery, Coats, Bean Sprouts, The House with the Big Eyes, & others.

Radio Public Service Announcement on Global Warming: Avoding an Imminent Threat to Human Quality-of-Survival. Ed. by H. Raymond Samuels, 2nd. 2006. 69.00 (978-1-897036-49-5(3)) Agora Pub Consort CAN.

Radio Public Service Announcement on Growing Violent Crime in Canadian Cities & Free Trade with the United States. H. Raymond Samuels, 2nd. 2006. 69.00 (978-1-897036-24-2(8)) Agora Pub Consort CAN.

Radio Reruns. Perf. by W. C. Fields et al. 16 cass. (Running Time: 8 hrs.). 63.66 Set. Moonbeam Pubns.

Radio Sessions: Junot Diaz with Mark Winegardner. Perf. by Mark Winegardner. Interview with Junot Diaz. 1 cass. (Running Time: 1 hr.). 1996. (978-0-9674703-1-3(5)) Hyena Prod.

Radio Sessions Vol. 2: Barry Hannah with Larry Brown & Brad Watson. Moderated by Barry Hannah. Interview with Brad Watson. 1 cass. (Running Time: 1 hr.). 1997. (978-0-9674703-0-6(7)) Hyena Prod.
Three masters of modern literature, spend an afternoon in Oxford, Mississippi discussing writing & life.

Radio WOOF Goes Back to School! Scripts. Featuring Bill Wellington. Bill Wellington. 1 CD. (Running Time: 49 min, 24 secs). Dramatization. (J). 2005. audio compact disk 12.00 (978-0-9777453-6-4(8)) Well In Tune.

Radioactive Accident on Navajo Lands, Pt. 1. Hosted by Nancy Pearlman. 1 cass. (Running Time: 28 min.). 10.00 (515) Educ Comm CA.

Radioactive Accident on Navajo Lands, Pt. 2. Hosted by Nancy Pearlman. 1 cass. (Running Time: 27 min.). 10.00 (516) Educ Comm CA.

Radiochemistry: An Increasingly Important Subject in Many Fields of Research. Instructed by Gregory R. Choppin & Patricia A. Baisden. 6 cass. (Running Time: 5 hrs. 18 min.). 180.00 incl. 332pp. manual. (40) Am Chemical.
Discusses general nuclear concepts, nuclear stability & radioactivity, & the interaction of radiation with matter.

Radiohead X-Posed. Chrome Dreams. (ENG., 2002. audio compact disk 14.95 (978-1-84240-154-5(8)) Pub: Chrome Dreams GBR. Dist(s): IPG Chicago

Radiology Without Films. Contrib. by Richard M. Heller et al. 1 cass. (American Academy of Pediatrics UPDATE: Vol. 18, No. 3). 1998. 20.00 Am Acad Pediat.

Radio's Best Kid's Shows, Vol. 1. 2 cass. (Running Time: 60 mins.). (J). 10.95 (978-1-57816-059-4(6), KS2401) Audio File.
Includes: "Jack Armstrong, the All American Boy" (1-29-41); "Terry & the Pirates" (2-9-42); "Straight Arrow" (3-24-49); "Don Winslow of the Navy" (1942); "Tennessee Jed" (5-26-47); "Silver Eagle" (7-20-54.

Radio's Best Kid's Shows, Vol. 2. 2 cass. (Running Time: 60 mins.). (J). 10.95 (978-1-57816-060-0(X), KS2402) Audio File.
Includes: "Tom Mix Straight Shooters" (8-10-45); "Little Orphan Annie" (10-22-35); "Bobby Benson & the B Bar B Riders" (8-15-50); "Buck Rogers in the 25th Century" (4-4-39); "Spy King" (7-31-47); "Adventures of Frank Merriwell" (11-13-48).

Radio's Best Kid's Shows, Vol. 3. 2 cass. (Running Time: 60 mins.). (J). 10.95 (978-1-57816-061-7(8), KS2043) Audio File.
Includes: "Adventures of Superman" (3-28-46); "Dick Tracy" (2-8-38); "Hop Harrigan" (10-4-44); "Jungle Jim" (1930s); "Mark Trail" (9-20-50); "Captain Midnight" (9-30-40).

Radio's Greatest Comedians. 5 cass. (Running Time: 5 hrs.). 19.95 (978-1-878427-22-9(9), XC1502); audio compact disk 19.95 (978-1-878427-21-2(0), XC1501) Cimino Pub Grp.

Radio's Greatest Comedies. 2002. 29.95 (978-0-7413-0172-7(5)) Radio Spirits.

Radio's Greatest Comedies. abr. ed. Nina Mattikow. 8 cass. (Running Time: 8 hrs.). Dramatization. (Eight Cassette Collector Packs Ser.). 1992. 29.95 Set. (978-1-55569-579-8(5), 48005) Great Am Audio.
Sixteen original broadcasts from radio's golden age.

Radio's Greatest Comedies. unabr. ed. Perf. by Jack Benny et al. 4 cass. (Running Time: 4 hrs.). (Crated Gift Cassettes Ser.). 1985. 16.95 (978-1-55569-073-1(4), 5770-01) Great Am Audio.
Includes Jack Benny, Amos n' Andy, Burns & Allen & Groucho Marx.

Radio's Greatest Crime Fighters. unabr. ed. 2 cass. (Running Time: 2 hrs.). (Double Value Pack Ser.). 1990. 9.95 (978-1-55569-373-2(3), 7106) Great Am Audio.
The Green Hornet, the F.B.I. in Peace & War, Gangbusters & Dragnet. Four complete shows.

Radio's Greatest Detectives. 5 cass. (Running Time: 5 hrs.). 19.95 (978-1-878427-24-3(5), XC1504); audio compact disk 19.95 (978-1-878427-23-6(7), XC1503) Cimino Pub Grp.

Radio's Greatest Detectives. Created by Radio Spirits. (Running Time: 10800 sec.). 2004. audio compact disk 9.98 (978-1-57019-728-4(8)) Radio Spirits.

Radio's Greatest Detectives. unabr. ed. 2 cass. (Running Time: 2 hrs.). (Double Value Pack Ser.). 1990. 9.95 (978-1-55569-366-4(0), 7099) Great Am Audio.
The Fat Man, The Thin Man, Mr. Keen & Bulldog Drummond. Four complete shows.

Radio's Greatest Moments. unabr. ed. 4 cass. (Running Time: 4 hrs.). (Crated Gift Cassettes Ser.). 16.95 (978-1-55569-075-5(0), 5770-03) Great Am Audio.
Includes greatest radio commercials, comedy, "This Was Radio", & Orson Welles' complete "War of the Worlds".

Radio's Greatest Mysteries. 2002. 29.95 (978-0-7413-0173-4(3)) Radio Spirits.

Radio's Greatest Mysteries. abr. ed. Nina Mattikow. 8 cass. (Running Time: 8 hrs.). Dramatization. (Eight Cassette Collector Packs Ser.). 1992. 29.95 Set. (978-1-55569-578-1(7), 48004) Great Am Audio.
Sixteen original broadcasts from radio's golden age.

Radio's Greatest Mysteries. abr. ed. Created by Radio Spirits. (Running Time: 10800 sec.). 2006. audio compact disk 9.98 (978-1-57019-820-5(9)) Radio Spirits.

Radio's Greatest Mysteries. unabr. ed. 4 cass. (Running Time: 4 hrs.). (Crated Gift Cassettes Ser.). 1985. 16.95 incl. wooden gift crate. (978-1-55569-074-8(2), 5770-02) Great Am Audio.
Includes "The Green Hornet," "Suspense," "Sherlock Holmes" & Humphrey Bogart as Sam Spade.

Radio's Greatest Shows. 2003. 29.95 (978-1-57019-654-6(0)) Radio Spirits.

Radio's Greatest Sitcoms. 5 cass. (Running Time: 5 hrs.). 19.95 (978-1-878427-26-7(1), XC1506); audio compact disk 19.95 (978-1-878427-25-0(3), XC1505) Cimino Pub Grp.

Radio's Greatest Westerns. 5 cass. (Running Time: 5 hrs.). 19.95 (978-1-878427-28-1(8), XC1508); audio compact disk 19.95 (978-1-878427-27-4(X), XC1507) Cimino Pub Grp.

Radio's Missing Masters. collector's ed. Perf. by Dick Powell et al. 20 cass. (Running Time: 30 hrs.). 1998. bk. & pap. bk. 59.98 (4019) Radio Spirits.
Many of the 60 selections are audition shows or premier episodes from popular series. Others are the only existing shows from a rare series. Includes: "Yours Truly, Johnny Dollar," "I Cover the Waterfront," "The Judge," "The Humphrey Bogart Theatre," "Safari," "Luigi," "Great Caesar's Ghost," "The Notorious Tariq," "The Clyde Beatty Show," "Tarzan, Lord of the Jungle," "Out of the Deep," "The Lone Ranger," "Boston Blackie," "Straight Arrow," "The Private Practice of Dr. Dana," "Escape," "Fibber McGee & Molly," "Emotion," "Mulligan's Travels," "That's Rich" and more. The booklet details each show & its history.

***Radio's Popular Vocalists.** RadioArchives.com. (Running Time: 600). (ENG.). 2006. audio compact disk 29.98 (978-1-61081-054-8(6)) Radio Arch.

Radio's Super Stars. Hosted by Fibber McGee and Molly. 1 cass. (Running Time: 60 min.). (Old Time Radio Classic Singles Ser.). 4.95 (978-1-57816-119-5(3), RS127) Audio File.
Fibber tunes in his old radio to sounds from the Golden Age of Radio. Includes many top stars from 1928 through the 40's.

Radio's Super Stars: Hosts-Fibber McGee & Molly. 1 cass. (Running Time: 60 min). 7.95 (DC-7960) Natl Recrd Co.
Fibber's Super-Hetrodyne Radio picks up sounds from radio's golden age. A truly great collection of nostalgic enjoyment, with recordings of performances by Amos N' Andy, Ruth Etting, Rudy Vallee, W. C. Fields, Jimmy Durante, Tallulla Bankhead, & more.

Radioscopie Series: Andre Malraux. Interview with Jacques Chancel. 1 cass. (FRE.). 1991. 18.95 (1024-RF) Olivia & Hill.
French author.

Radioscopie Series: Claude Levi-Strauss. Interview with Jacques Chancel. 1 cass. (FRE.). 1991. 18.95 (1335-RF) Olivia & Hill.
A rare interview with the noted ethnologist.

Radioscopie Series: Georges Brassens. Interview with Jacques Chancel. 1 cass. (FRE.). 1991. 16.95 (1020-RF) Olivia & Hill.
French balladier.

Radioscopie Series: Jacques Brel. Interview with Jacques Chancel. 1 cass. (FRE.). 1991. 16.95 (1021-RF) Olivia & Hill.
Belgian poet & songwriter.

Radioscopie Series: Jacques-Yves Cousteau. Interview with Jacques Chancel. 1 cass. (FRE.). 1991. 16.95 (1329-RF) Olivia & Hill.
"Prince" of the oceans.

Radioscopie Series: Joseph Kessel. Interview with Jacques Chancel. 1 cass. (FRE.). 1991. 16.95 (1173-RF) Olivia & Hill.
Writer.

Radioscopie Series: Marc Chagall. Interview with Jacques Chancel. 1 cass. (FRE.). 1991. 16.95 (1022-RF) Olivia & Hill.
Russian artist who lived in France.

Radioscopie Series: Marguerite Yourcenar. Interview with Jacques Chancel. 1 cass. (FRE.). 1991. 16.95 (1029-RF) Olivia & Hill.
Writer & first female member of the Academie Francaise.

Radioscopie Series: Raymond Aron. Interview with Jacques Chancel. 1 cass. (FRE.). 1991. 16.95 (1018-RF) Olivia & Hill.
French social & political thinker.

Radioscopie Series: Raymond Devos. Interview with Jacques Chancel. 1 cass. (FRE.). 1992. 16.95 (1534-RF) Olivia & Hill.
Popular French comedian.

Radioscopie Series: Raymond Gary. Interview with Jacques Chancel. 1 cass. 1992. 16.95 (1536-RF) Olivia & Hill.
Writer.

Radioscopie Series: Roland Barthes. Interview with Jacques Chancel. 1 cass. (FRE.). 1991. 16.95 (1019-RF) Olivia & Hill.
French writer & literary critic.

Radioscopie Series: Salvador Dali. Interview with Jacques Chancel. 1 cass. (FRE.). 1991. 16.95 (1023-RF) Olivia & Hill.
Spanish surrealist artist.

Radioscopie Series: Yves Montand. Interview with Jacques Chancel. 1 cass. (FRE.). 1991. 16.95 (1025-RF) Olivia & Hill.
French actor & singer.

Rafe Martin Tells His Children's Books. Short Stories. Rafe Martin. 1 cass. (Running Time: 60 min.). (J). 1994. 9.95 (978-0-938756-49-1(4)) Yellow Moon.
An accomplished storyteller as well as a writer, Martin does a star turn here with four of his best-known tales ("The Rough-Face Girl," "Foolish Rabbit's Big Mistake," "The Boy Who Lived with the Seals" & "The Boy Who Loved Mammoths").

Rafe Martin Tells His Children's Stories. (ENG.). 2008. audio compact disk 14.95 (978-0-938756-64-4(8)) Yellow Moon.

Raffi in Concert. Perf. by Raffi. 1 cass. (Running Time: 60 mins.). (J). 7.98 (RDR 8059); audio compact disk 12.78 Jewel box. (RDR 8059) NewSound.

Raffi in Concert: With the Rise & Shine Band. Perf. by Raffi. 1 cass. (Running Time: 41 mins.). (J). 1999. (978-1-886767-47-8(5)); (978-1-886767-73-7(4)); audio compact disk (978-1-886767-46-1(7)); audio compact disk (978-1-886767-72-0(6)) Rounder Records.
Listen, sing along & share in the excitement of a magical live performance, as Raffi brings his most popular tunes to a theater audience.

Raffi in Concert with the Rise & Shine Band. Raffi. 1 cass. (Running Time: 1 hr.). (J). 2001. 10.95 (KSR 0235C); audio compact disk 16.95 (KSR 0235CD) Kimbo Educ.
Recorded before a live audience! Day O, Apples & Bananas, Shake My Sillies Out, Knee Up Mother Brown, Time to Sing & more.

Raffi Radio. Raffi. 1 cass. (Running Time: 1 hr.). (J). 2001. 10.95 (KSR 11296C); audio compact disk 16.95 (KSr 11296CD) Kimbo Educ.
Kitchen Sing Sing, Sunflower, Sleido's Song, Coconut, Weather Report, Julia, Ripple of Love, Every Child & more.

Raffi Radio. Perf. by Raffi. 1 cass., 1 CD. (J). 7.98 (RDR 8063); audio compact disk 12.78 CD Jewel box. (RDR 8063) NewSound.

Raffi Radio. Perf. by Raffi. 1 cass. (J). 1999. (978-1-886767-55-3(6)) Rounder Records.
Songs & laughter, barks & banter...play radio! Join Raffi & his co-host Sleido JazzDog for this light-hearted & spirited radio broadcast from the magical land of Troubadouria, where imagination reigns. Filled with original & traditional music, silly interview, "berry nice" new reports & much more.

Raffi Radio. Perf. by Raffi. 1 cass. (J). 1999. (978-1-886767-81-2(5)); audio compact disk (978-1-886767-54-6(8)); audio compact disk (978-1-886767-80-5(7)) Rounder Records.

Raffi's Christmas Album. Raffi. 1 cass. (Running Time: 30 mins.). (J). 10.95 (KSR 8116C) Kimbo Educ.
Rudolph the Red-Nosed Reindeer, Frosty the Snowman, Must Be Santa, Jingle Bells, Silent Night & more.

Raffi's Christmas Album. Raffi. 1 LP. (Running Time: 30 mins.). (J). 2001. lp 10.95 (KSR 8116); audio compact disk 16.95 (KSR 8116CD) Kimbo Educ.

Raffi's Christmas Album. Perf. by Raffi. 1 CD. (Running Time: 31 mins.). (J). 1999. audio compact disk (978-1-886767-66-9(1)) Rounder Records.
Celebrate the Christmas holidays with old & new favorites, along with Raffi's inspiring "Every Little Wish.".

Raffi's Christmas Album. Perf. by Raffi. 1 cass. (Running Time: 31 mins.). (J). 1999. (978-1-886767-41-6(6)); (978-1-886767-67-6(X)); audio compact disk (978-1-886767-40-9(8)) Rounder Records.

Raffles. 1 cass. (Running Time: 90 mins.). pap. bk. 19.95 (S11125) J Norton Pubs.
Collection of singing stories by Hoagy Carmichael.

Raffles: A Thief in the Night. unabr. ed. E. W. Hornung. Read by Robin Browne. 7 cass. (Running Time: 7 hrs.). 1995. 61.95

(978-1-85089-716-3(6), 89096) Pub: ISIS Audio GBR. Dist(s): Ulverscroft US
The first "Gentleman Crook" appears in these entertaining short stories - Raffles is a man about town, an elegant & eligible bachelor with no apparent career but plenty of capital. Or is he? His ingenuous & loyal friend, Bunny, here recounts how they set about their nefarious life, as poor men in a world of wealth face with unbearable temptations to remove valuable items from unworthy possessors.

Raffles: Further Adventures of the Amateur Cracksman. E. W. Hornung. Read by Amy von Lecteur. 2009. 27.95 (978-1-60112-980-2(7)) Babblebooks.

Raffles, the Amateur Cracksman. unabr. ed. E. W. Hornung. Read by Walter Covell. 4 cass. (Running Time: 5 hrs. 30 mins.). 1992. audio compact disk 55.00 (978-0-7861-0632-5(8), 2122) Blckstn Audio.
Raffles, according to Ellery Queen, has been the inspiration for numerous fictional characters, including James Bond. Like Bond, Raffles is handsome & debonaire, with refined tastes, yet is swift, cunning, & utterly ruthless when the need arises. And just as Bond is a master of the gaming tables, so Raffles is undeniably "one of the best cricket players in the world." While Bond is on the side of law & order, Raffles makes his living by outwitting the law - pulling off some of the most daring burglaries imaginable. To the World he is a gentleman of leisure, living in the Albany, playing cricket for England & using his charm to gain entry to the fashionable houses he later robs.

Raffles, the Amateur Cracksman. unabr. ed. E. W. Hornung & Walter Covell. 6 cass. (Running Time: 5 hrs. 50 min.). 1989. 26.00 (C-199) Jimcin Record.
Stories of the most famous rogue in literature.

Raffles, the Amateur Cracksman. unabr. collector's ed. E. W. Hornung. Read by Walter Covell. 6 cass. (Running Time: 6 hrs.). 1989. 36.00 (978-0-7366-3953-8(5), 9199) Books on Tape.
Raffles is the greatest cracksman in the literature of roguery. He could have succeeded in any career, but he chose a life of crime. He intended his first robbery, forced on him by necessity, to be his last, but once he sampled the exhilaration of theft, he loved it. "Why settle down to some humdrum, uncongenial billet," he once asked Bunny Manders, his devoted companion, "when excitement, romance, danger & a decent living were all going begging together? Of course, it's very wrong, but we can't all be moralists, & the distribution of wealth is very wrong to begin with".

Raft. Robert Trumbell. Narrated by L. J. Ganser. 4 pieces. (Running Time: 5 hrs.). (gr. 7 up). 42.00 (978-1-4025-3129-3(X)) Recorded Bks.

Raft. unabr. ed. Robert Trumbell. Read by Tom Parker. 5 CDs. (Running Time: 5 hrs. 30 mins.). 2000. audio compact disk 40.00 (978-0-7861-9932-7(6), 1786) Blckstn Audio.
On January 16, 1942, three men boarded a TBD Devastator aircraft - a low-wing, single-engine torpedo-bomber - for an antisubmarine patrol flight. Although it was to be a relatively short flight, they became lost. When the fuel ran low, they decided to ditch into the Pacific. Before they would get their life raft to inflate, however, the plane sank beneath them, carrying most of the survival gear down with it. Thirty-four days later the raft landed on Puka Puka, a New Zealand governed atoll in the Danger Islands, having meandered 1,200 miles.

Raft. unabr. ed. Robert Trumbull. Read by Tom Parker. 4 cass. (Running Time: 5 hrs. 30 mins.). 1996. audio compact disk 32.95 (978-0-7861-1008-7(2), 1786) Blckstn Audio.

Rag, a Bone & a Hank of Hair. unabr. ed. Jonathan Gash. Narrated by Christopher Kay. 8 cass. (Running Time: 11 hrs. 15 mins.). 2000. 76.00 (978-1-84197-210-7(X), H1205L8) Recorded Bks.
Lovejoy has reluctantly agreed to visit some fellow antique dealers in London to investigate who has been selling them fake gemstones. He is not fond of London at the best of times, but this time he is in for a dreadful surprise.

Rag & Bone Shop. Robert Cormier. Narrated by Scott Shina. 3 CDs. (Running Time: 3 hrs.). (gr. 6 up). audio compact disk 32.00 (978-1-4025-1965-9(6)) Recorded Bks.

Rag & Bone Shop. unabr. ed. Robert Cormier. Narrated by Scott Shina. 2 pieces. (Running Time: 3 hrs.). (gr. 6 up). 2002. 19.00 (978-1-4025-1028-1(4)) Recorded Bks.
A seven-year-old girl has been bludgeoned to death and buried in a pile of leaves. Although the police have no leads, they are pressured to close the case as soon as possible. So they call in a master interrogator to question 12-year-old Jason, the victim's friend and the last person to see her alive. Although Jason is innocent, he is shy, insecure, and wants to give answers that will satisfy everyone. As the questioning becomes more subtle and probing, the interrogator's goal soon shifts from finding justice to gaining a quick confession from the boy.

Rag Bag Clan. unabr. ed. Richard A. Barth. Narrated by Roslyn Alexander. 4 cass. (Running Time: 5 hrs.). (Margaret Binton Mysteries Ser.). 1992. 35.00 (978-1-55690-720-3(6), 92232E7) Recorded Bks.
Margaret Binton goes undercover as a bag-lady to solve a friends murder.

Rag Nymph. unabr. ed. Catherine Cookson. Read by Susan Jameson. 8 cass. (Running Time: 12 hrs.). 2000. 59.95 (978-0-7451-4046-9(7), CAB 743) Pub: Chivers Audio Bks GBR. Dist(s): AudioGO
It is 1854, and "Raggie Annie" is peddling old clothes on the streets with her hand-cart. There she meets Millie Forester, a little girl who has been abandoned. What begins as an act of compassion, care of little Millie, and the young rag-nymph gives new meaning to Annie's life.

Rag Woman, Rich Woman. unabr. ed. Margaret Thomson Davis. Narrated by Jean Simmons. 10 cass. (Running Time: 14 hrs. 15 mins.). 1999. 89.00 (978-1-84197-018-9(2), H1018E7) Recorded Bks.
1920's, the slums of Glasgow, a girl growing up with a passionate desire to better herself. Rory dreams of marrying out of her background & becoming as much of a lady as her friend Victoria who has been brought up in middle class gentility. She believes she has found the answer to her prayers when she meets a handsome, restless intellectual called Matthew Drummond. When the betrayal comes, Rory is devastated & begins to sink back into the background she is determined to escape. After working in the market for a while, Rory begins to have ideas for a business of her own.

Raga from Music Today, Vol. 1. Music by Bismillah Khan. 1 cass. 1996. (A96005); audio compact disk (CD A96005) Multi-Cultural Bks.

Raga from Music Today, Vol. 2. Music by Mallikarjun Mansur. 1 cass. 1996. (A96006) Multi-Cultural Bks.

Raga from Music Today, Vol. 3. Music by Ravi Shankar. 1 cass. 1996. (A96007); audio compact disk (CD A96007) Multi-Cultural Bks.

Raga from Music Today, Vol. 4. Music by Kishori Amonkar. 1 cass. 1996. (A96008) Multi-Cultural Bks.

Raga of Omar Khayam. Agni Howard. 2002. audio compact disk 15.95 (978-1-56589-764-9(1)) Pub: Crystal Clarity. Dist(s): Natl Bk Netwk

Ragamuffin Gospel see Evangelio de Los Andrajosos

Rage. Jonathan Kellerman. (Alex Delaware Ser.: No. 19). 2005. 72.00 (978-1-4159-1996-5(8)); audio compact disk 96.00 (978-1-4159-2049-7(4)) Books on Tape.

Rage. Wilbur Smith. Read by Tim Pigott-Smith. 2 cass. (Running Time: 4 hrs.). (ENG., 2001. 16.99 (978-0-333-78163-0(5)) Pub: Macmillan UK GBR. Dist(s): Trafalgar
In the decades after World War II, South Africa struggles against the tribal violence at its hot heart. It is a conflict vividly mirrored by one family - the Courtneys - unified by a magnificent rage to live, shattered by a lust for power.

Rage. unabr. ed. Gwen Moffat. 5 cass. (Running Time: 7 hrs. 30 mins.). 1998. 63.95 (978-1-85903-147-6(1)) Pub: Magna Story GBR. Dist(s): Ulverscroft US

Rage, Pt. 1. unabr. collector's ed. Wilbur Smith. Read by Richard Brown. 11cass. (Running Time: 16 hrs. 30 min.). (Courtney Novels). 1988. 88.00 (978-0-7366-1294-4(7), 2202-A) Books on Tape.
Manfred & Shasa, ministers in the South African government, confront the ugly realities of Apartheid & a growing isolation in a hostile world.

Rage, Pt. 2. collector's ed. Wilbur Smith. Read by Richard Brown. 11 cass. (Running Time: 16 hrs. 30 min.). (Courtney Novels). 1988. 88.00 (978-0-7366-1295-1(5), 2202-B) Books on Tape.

Rage: The Unauthorized Biography of Rage Against the Machine. Harry Drysdale-Wood. (Maximum Ser.). (ENG.). 2001. audio compact disk 14.95 (978-1-84240-036-4(3)) Pub: Chrome Dreams GBR. Dist(s): IPG Chicago

***Rage Against God: How Atheism Led Me to Faith.** Zondervan. (Running Time: 4 hrs. 57 mins. 21 sec.). (ENG.). 2010. 22.99 (978-0-310-41260-1(9)) Zondervan.

Rage for Fame: The Ascent of Clare Boothe Luce. unabr. ed. Sylvia Jukes Morris. Read by Mary Peiffer. 12 cass. (Running Time: 18 hrs.). 1998. 96.00 (978-0-7366-4101-2(7), 4606) Books on Tape.
A biography of the social-climbing writer who married the publisher of LIFE Magazine.

Rage of Hercules. 2 cass. (Running Time: 1 hr. 40 mins.). Dramatization. (Odds Bodkin Musical Story Collection). 2001. 18.95 (978-1-882412-31-0(1)) Pub: Rivertree. Dist(s): Penton Overseas
The real Hercules was haunted by rages he could not control. He was the strongest adventurer in the world, yet in the end his towering ego was crushed by that very strength. Fully scored with virtuoso music on 12-string guitar.

Rage of Hercules. rev. ed. Odds Bodkin. 2 CDs. (Running Time: 1 hr. 40 mins.). Dramatization. (Odds Bodkin Musical Story Collection). 2001. audio compact disk 24.95 (978-1-882412-32-7(X)) Pub: Rivertree. Dist(s): Penton Overseas

Rage of Seventeen Ten: Baroque Favorites. 1 cass. (Vox - Turnabout Classical Ser.). 3.98 (CTX 4713); audio compact disk (ACD 8740) VOX Music Grp.

Rage Sleep. unabr. ed. C. W. Morton & Jack Mobley. Read by Stephen C. Perry. 7 cass. (Running Time: 10 hrs. 30 mins.). 1999. 49.95 (978-0-7861-1617-1(X), 2445) Blckstn Audio.
Anaex - doctors are stunned by the effectiveness of this new anesthetic. Patients go under in perfect form & recuperate in record time. General Thurmond S. Boothby, the most powerful American on the Korean peninsula, underwent a minor surgical procedure. The only problem was that the anesthesiologist used Anaex. It is only when an already tense situation in North Korea begins to escalate that Dr. Christopher Thorne starts to suspect that it may not be the medical miracle doctors had thought it was. As he discovers similarly violent behavior patterns in other patients who were given Anaex, he begins to think that perhaps it is the wonder drug that will push the United States to the brink of war.

Raggamuffin Hip Hop. 2004. audio compact disk 16.99 (978-5-554-23258-9(2)) Pub: Pt of Grace Ent. Dist(s): STL Dist NA

Ragged Dick. unabr. ed. Horatio Alger. Read by Flo Gibson. 4 cass. (Running Time: 5 hrs.). (J). (gr. 3-5). 1993. 19.95 (978-1-55685-275-6(4)) Audio Bk Con.
A rags-to-riches tale about an honest, ambitious, zesty & generous young bootblack in lower Manhattan in the late 1800's.

Ragged Plot. unabr. ed. Richard Barth. Narrated by Roslyn Alexander. 5 cass. (Running Time: 7 hrs.). (Margaret Binton Mysteries Ser.). 1992. 44.00 (978-1-55690-721-0(4), 92417E7) Recorded Bks.
Elderly sleuth Margaret Binton joins forces with the New York Police Department to solve the murder of a neighbor.

Ragged Trousered Philanthropists. Robert Tressell. Read by Tony Robinson & Stephen Twigg MP. (Running Time: 5 hrs. 0 mins. 0 sec.). (ENG.). 2009. audio compact disk 26.95 (978-1-934997-45-1(5)) Pub: CSAWord. Dist(s): PerseuPGW

Raggedy Andy Stories. unabr. ed. Johnny Gruelle. Read by Swoosie Kurtz. (J). 2005. audio compact disk 17.95 (978-0-06-058302-6(9), HarperChildAud) HarperCollins Pubs.

***Raggedy Andy Stories.** unabr. ed. Johnny Gruelle. Read by Swoosie Kurtz. (ENG.). 2005. (978-0-06-083900-0(7)); (978-0-06-083898-0(1)) HarperCollins Pubs.

Raggedy Ann & Andy: Day at the Fair. unabr. ed. Patricia Hall. Narrated by Christina Moore. 1 cass. (Running Time: 15 mins.). (ps up). 2000. 10.00 (978-1-4025-0206-4(0), 96869) Recorded Bks.
When sweet little Marcella and her Daddy go to the fair for the day, her toys are left at home - but Raggedy Ann and her brother Andy decide to have a fair of their own - with a slippery slide and everything! Listeners old and young alike will love this adorable tale about two of the most beloved toys of all time.

Raggedy Ann & Andy: Going to Grandma's. unabr. ed. Patricia Hall. Narrated by Christina Moore. 2 cass. (Running Time: 15 mins.). (ps up). 2002. 10.00 (978-1-4025-0204-0(4)) Recorded Bks.
When Marcella decides to visit her grandma, Raggedy Ann and Andy get to go along. That means they'll be flying in an airplane for the very first time! And they'll also get to explore the baggage hold area. Everybody's favorite rag dolls are sure to have the adventure of their lives.

Raggedy Ann & Andy: School Day Adventure. Patricia Hall. Narrated by Christina Moore. 1 cass. (Running Time: 15 mins.). (ps up). 2002. 10.00 (978-1-4025-0200-2(1)) Recorded Bks.
*Marcella's kindergarten class is having show-and-tell. When the students leave for lunch, Raggedy Ann * Andy join Mac the toy truck for a drive around the school. But they get lost, and lunch is almost over.*

Raggedy Ann & Andy Leaf Dance. Bobby Pearlman. Narrated by Christina Moore. (Running Time: 15 mins.). (ps up). 10.00 (978-1-4025-0202-6(8)) Recorded Bks.

Raggedy Ann & Raggedy Andy Stories. unabr. ed. Johnny Gruelle. Read by Kristen Underwood. 3 cass. (Running Time: 4 hrs.). 1996. 23.95 (978-0-7861-1019-3(8), 1797) Blckstn Audio.
Raggedy Ann has charmed millions of readers with her warm & optimistic outlook & unflappable approach to difficulties, while Raggedy Andy has pleased these same readers with his adventurous spirit & compassionate nature. As Gruelle's granddaughter said, "these stories contain nothing to cause fright, glorify mischief, excuse malice, or condone cruelty." All the original stories are included here, & all are guaranteed to delight & inspire.

Raggedy Ann Stories. abr. ed. Johnny Gruelle. Narrated by Marilyn King. 2 cass. (Running Time: 1 hr. 44 min.). (J). 12.95 (978-0-89926-162-1(0), 850) Audio Bk.

Raggedy Ann Stories. abr. ed. Johnny Gruelle. 1 cass. (Running Time: 1 hr. 30 mins.). 2004. 18.00 (978-0-06-058303-3(7)) HarperCollins Pubs.

***Raggedy Ann Stories.** unabr. ed. Johnny Gruelle. Read by Cecily Tyson. (ENG.). 2004. (978-0-06-078638-0(8)) HarperCollins Pubs.

***Raggedy Ann Stories.** unabr. ed. Johnny Gruelle. Read by Cecily Tyson. (ENG.). 2004. (978-0-06-081438-0(1)) HarperCollins Pubs.

Raggedy Ann the Birthday Party. 1 cass. (Running Time: 90 mins.). (J). 1987. bk. 19.94 (978-0-394-88871-2(5)) SRA McGraw.

Raging of the Rose see Savagery of Love: Brother Antoninus Reads His Poetry

Ragman: And Other Cries of Faith. abr. ed. Walter Wangerin, Jr.. Read by Walter Wangerin, Jr. 1 cass. (Running Time: 60 min.). 1989. 9.95 HarperCollins Pubs.

Ragopedia Vol. 1: Sample Chalans & Proper Technical Word Pronunciations. Shiv D. Batish & Ashwin Batish. 1 cass. (Running Time: 70 min.). 1991. 12.50 (978-1-882319-01-5(X), SR140044) Batish Pubns.
Music of India (educational).

Rags to Riches: You Don't Have to Be Poor. Tom Leding. Read by Gene Coleman. Frwd. by Pat Robertson. (ENG.). 2002. 39.99 (978-1-890915-09-4(2)) TLM Publ.

Ragtime. unabr. ed. E. L. Doctorow. Read by E. L. Doctorow. 4 cass. (Running Time: 6 hrs.). 1997. 24.95 (978-1-885608-27-7(6)) Airplay.
Brings us into the lives of three extraordinary different families whose own lives become remarkably entwined with Henry Ford, Harry Houdini, Emma Goldman, Sigmund Freud, & many others.

Ragtime: 15 Pieces for Piano Solo. Composed by John Kember. (ENG.). 2006. pap. bk. 14.95 (978-1-902455-34-1(7), 1902455347) Pub: Schott Music Corp. Dist(s): H Leonard

Ragtime, Blues & Jazz for Banjo. Fred Sokolow. 1983. bk. 16.95 (978-0-7866-0950-5(8), 93936P); 9.98 (978-1-56222-609-1(6), 93936C) Mel Bay.

Ragtime Feast Vol. 1: Forgotten Rags, 1. Charles Hunter & Tom Turpin. 2000. audio compact disk 16.95 Pro-Culture Eds.

Ragtime Fingerpicking Guitar: For Beginners. Brett Duncan. 2008. pap. bk. 24.95 (978-1-86469-377-5(0)) Kolala Music SGP.

***Ragtime Fool.** unabr. ed. Larry Karp. (Running Time: 13 hrs. 0 mins.). (Ragtime Mysteries Ser.). 2010. 29.95 (978-1-4417-3201-9(2)); 79.95 (978-1-4417-3197-5(0)); audio compact disk 109.00 (978-1-4417-3198-2(9)) Blckstn Audio.

Ragtime in Simla. Barbara Cleverly. Read by Terry Wale. 10 CDs. (Running Time: 11 hrs.). (Detective Joe Sandilands Ser.). (J). 2004. audio compact disk 89.95 (978-1-84283-785-6(0)) Pub: ISIS Lrg Prnt GBR. Dist(s): Ulverscroft US

Ragtime in Simla. unabr. ed. Barbara Cleverly. Read by Terry Wale. 8 cass. (Running Time: 12 hrs.). (Detective Joe Sandilands Ser.). (J). 2003. 69.95 (978-1-84283-461-9(4)) Pub: ISIS Lrg Prnt GBR. Dist(s): Ulverscroft US

Ragweed. Avi. Narrated by John McDonough. 4 CDs. (Running Time: 4 hrs. 45 mins.). (gr. 3 up). 1999. audio compact disk 39.00 (978-1-4025-1494-4(8), C1619) Recorded Bks.
Ragweed the mouse if four months old and anxious to see the world. So he says goodbye to his family and friends in the Woodlands and makes his way to the big city, where he comes face-to-face with Silversides, founder and president of F.E.A.R (Felines Enraged About Rodents).

Ragweed. Avi. Narrated by John McDonough. 4 pieces. (Running Time: 4 hrs. 45 mins.). (gr. 3 up). 2001. 36.00 (978-0-7887-4555-3(7), 96329E7) Recorded Bks.
Ragweed the mouse is four months old & anxious to see the world. So he says goodbye to his family & friends in the Woodlands & makes his way to the big city - where he comes face-to-face with Silversides, founder & president of F.E.A.R. (Felines Enraged About Rodents)!.

Raid on the Sun: Inside Israel's secret campaign that denied Saddam the Bomb. abr. ed. Rodger Claire. Read by Adam Grupper. 2004. 15.95 (978-0-7435-3936-4(2)) Pub: S&S Audio. Dist(s): S and S Inc

Raiders. unabr. ed. Harold Robbins. Read by Arthur Addison. 10 cass. (Running Time: 15 hrs.). 1996. 80.00 (978-0-7366-3232-4(8), 3893) Books on Tape.
Invades the sultry, seamy, sexy world of Hollywood where "The Carpetbaggers" left off 34 years ago. Dreams of his father's death still torment Jonas Cord, Jr. He mourns for the patriarchal approval he never received & vows that his illegitimate son will always know he loves him. But passion overtakes Jonas junior & threatens this promise. His billion-dollar enterprise moves to Las Vegas where Jonas takes on the Mob...with the "help" of his son. Ambition & desire drive father & son in a fierce battle in the boardroom & the bedroom.

***Raiders from the North: Empire of the Moghul.** unabr. ed. Alex Rutherford. Narrated by Simon Vance. (Running Time: 16 hrs. 0 mins.). 2010. 20.99 (978-1-4001-8750-8(8)) Tantor Media.

***Raiders from the North: Empire of the Moghul.** unabr. ed. Alex Rutherford. Narrated by Simon Vance. (Running Time: 14 hrs. 30 mins. 0 sec.). (ENG.). 2010. 29.99 (978-1-4001-6750-0(7)); audio compact disk 39.99 (978-1-4001-1750-5(X)); audio compact disk 95.99 (978-1-4001-4750-2(6)) Pub: Tantor Media. Dist(s): IngramPubServ

***Raiders' Ransom.** unabr. ed. Emily Diamand. Narrated by Charlotte Parry & James Clamp. 1 Playaway. (Running Time: 9 hrs.). (YA). (gr. 5-9). 2010. 59.75 (978-1-4407-6933-7(8)); 61.75 (978-1-4361-6293-7(9)); audio compact disk 87.75 (978-1-4361-6298-2(X)) Recorded Bks.

***Raiders' Ransom.** unabr. collector's ed. Emily Diamand. Narrated by Charlotte Parry & James Clamp. 8 CDs. (Running Time: 9 hrs.). (YA). (gr. 5-9). 2010. audio compact disk 44.95 (978-1-4361-6302-6(1)) Recorded Bks.

Raifteiri san Under-ground. Contrib. by Tadhg MacDhonnagain. (ENG.). 1993. audio compact disk 21.95 (978-0-8023-8094-4(8)) Pub: Clo Iar-Chonnachta IRL. Dist(s): Dufour

Raifteiri san Underground. Contrib. by Tadhg MacDhonnagain. (ENG.). 1993. 14.95 (978-0-8023-7094-5(2)) Pub: Clo Iar-Chonnachta IRL. Dist(s): Dufour

Rail Kings 3: The Wells Fargo Trail. Jim Walker. Narrated by Jack Garrett. 8 cass. (Running Time: 11 hrs. 30 mins.). 71.00 (978-0-7887-5276-6(6)) Recorded Bks.

Rail Warriors. unabr. ed. Gary McCarthy. Read by Gene Engene. 6 cass. (Running Time: 6 hrs.). (Derby Man Ser.: Bk. 9). 1995. 39.95 (978-1-55686-612-8(7)) Books in Motion.
Darby Buckingham charges into his most unbeatable challenge: helping the Union Pacific win the great railroad race across the continent.

Railroad & Churchyard. unabr. ed. Bjornstjerne Bjornson. Read by Walter Zimmerman. 1 cass. (Running Time: 1 hr. 26 mins.). 1980. 7.95 (N-50) Jimcin Record.
Two outstanding short stories by a Nobel Prize winner.

Railroad Equipment in Egypt: A Strategic Reference 2007. Compiled by Icon Group International, Inc. Staff. 2007. ring bd. 195.00 (978-0-497-35932-4(4)) Icon Grp.

Railroad Equipment in Uruguay: A Strategic Reference 2007. Compiled by Icon Group International, Inc. Staff. 2007. ring bd. 195.00 (978-0-497-82465-5(5)) Icon Grp.

Railroad Feast see Steve Heller

Railroad to Hell, No. 269. Jake Logan. 2 cass. (Running Time: 3 hrs.). 2001. 16.95 (978-1-890990-78-7(7)) Otis Audio.

Railroadin' Classics. 1 cass. or CD. (Running Time: 45 min.). NG-CD-920. (NG920) Native Ground.
Includes Tunes: "Wabash Cannonball," "Railroad Corral," "Paddy on the Railway," "The Lightning Express," "Casey Jones," "L&N Rag," "Freight Train," "New Lost Train," "Wreck of the Old 97," "In the Pines," "Kansas City Railroad Blues," "On the Dummy Line," "New River Train," "Reuben's Train," "Lost Train Blues," "Nine Hundred Miles." Performed on Banjo, Banjo-Guitar, Banjo-Mandolin, Fiddle, Mandolin, Dobro, Harmonica, Guitar, Jews Harp, Kazoo, Bones, Spoons, Washboard, Bass.

Railroadin' Classics. Wayne Erbsen. 9.95 (978-1-883206-29-1(4)); audio compact disk 14.95 (978-1-883206-27-7(8)) Native Ground.

Railway Builders. unabr. ed. Anthony Burton. Narrated by Anthony Burton. 5 cass. (Running Time: 7 hrs. 15 mins.). 2000. 48.00 (978-1-84197-227-5(4), H1195L8) Recorded Bks.
Concentrates on the people responsible for designing & actually building the railways, from the financiers, engineers & contractors to the gangers & navvies.

Railway Children. Edith Nesbit. Narrated by Flo Gibson. 4 cass. (Running Time: 6 hrs.). (J). 1985. 19.95 (978-1-55685-065-3(4)) Audio Bk Con.
Three children leave London with their mother, after their father mysteriously disappears, & go to live in a small house in the country near a railway station, where they find solace & adventure.

Railway Children. Edith Nesbit. Read by Eve Karpf et al. Adapted by Anna Britten. 2 cass. (Running Time: 2 hrs. 14 mins.). (J). 1996. 13.98 (978-962-634-585-6(3), NA208514, Naxos AudioBooks) Naxos.
When Roberta, Peter and Phyllis's father is arrested for a crime he did not commit and they have to start a new life in the country, they fear the happy times are gone forever. Little do they expect the exciting adventures and the new friends that await them.

Railway Children. abr. ed. Edith Nesbit. Read by Eve Karpf et al. Adapted by Anna Britten. 2 CDs. (Running Time: 2 hrs. 14 mins.). (J). (gr. 3-5). 1996. audio compact disk 17.98 (978-962-634-085-1(1), NA208512) Naxos.

Railway Children. unabr. ed. E. Nesbit. Narrated by Full Cast. (Running Time: 2 hrs. 0 mins. 0 sec.). (ENG.). 2010. audio compact disk 24.95 (978-1-60283-850-5(X)) Pub: AudioGO. Dist(s): Perseus Dist

Railway Children. unabr. ed. Edith Nesbit. Read by Johanna Ward. 5 cass. (Running Time: 7 hrs.). 1993. 39.95 (978-0-7861-0407-9(4), 1359) Blckstn Audio.
Roberta, Peter, & Phyllis were quite happy living in their ordinary red-brick house located in the suburbs. But when their father was called away, the children & their mother were compelled to move to a dark, shabby cottage in the country, & when this happened, their lives changed more than they ever could have imagined.

Railway Children. unabr. ed. Edith Nesbit. Read by Johanna Ward. (Running Time: 1 hr. 0 mins.). (ENG.). 2009. 29.95 (978-1-4417-0067-4(6)); audio compact disk 55.00 (978-1-4417-0064-3(1)) Blckstn Audio.

Railway Children. unabr. ed. Edith Nesbit. Read by Renée Raudman. (J). 2006. 49.99 (978-1-59895-680-1(9)) Find a World.

Railway Children. unabr. ed. Edith Nesbit. Narrated by Virginia Leishman. 5 pieces. (Running Time: 6 hrs. 45 mins.). (gr. 5 up). 2000. 44.00 (978-0-7887-3514-1(4), 95907E7) Recorded Bks.

Railway Children, unabr. ed. Edith Nesbit. Read by Virginia Leishman. 5 cass. (Running Time: 6 hrs. 45 mins.). (J). (gr. 5). 2000. pap. bk. 56.24 (978-0-7887-3652-0(3), 41017X4) Recorded Bks.

Railway Children. unabr. ed. Edith Nesbit. Narrated by Renée Raudman. (Running Time: 7 hrs. 0 mins. 0 sec.). (ENG.). (J). (gr. 4-7). 2008. 19.99 (978-1-4001-5882-9(6)); audio compact disk 55.99 (978-1-4001-3882-1(5)) Pub: Tantor Media. Dist(s): IngramPubServ

Railway Children. unabr. ed. Edith Nesbit. Read by Raudman Renée. (Running Time: 7 hrs. 0 mins. 0 sec.). (ENG.). (J). (gr. 4-7). 2008. audio compact disk 27.99 (978-1-4001-0882-4(9)) Pub: Tantor Media. Dist(s): IngramPubServ

Railway Children, Class Set. unabr. ed. Edith Nesbit. Read by Virginia Leishman. 5 cass. (Running Time: 6 hrs. 45 mins.). (J). 1999. 104.70 (978-0-7887-3680-3(9), 41017) Recorded Bks.
After their father mysteriously disappears, three children move to the English countryside with their mother. There they find adventure in their new home near a railway station.

Railway Man. unabr. ed. Eric Lomax. Read by Bill Paterson. 8 cass. (Running Time: 12 hrs.). 2000. 59.95 (978-0-7451-6669-8(5), CAB 1285) Pub: Chivers Audio Bks GBR. Dist(s): AudioGO
Eric Lomax was sent to Malaya in 1941 during World War II. Taken prisoner after the fall of Singapore, he was put to work on the Burma-Siam railway. There, he faced over two years of work and torture. Lomax never forgot his Japanese tormentor, and half a century later he found out he was still alive. This unforgettable story describes a life saved from bitterness by an extraordinary will to forgive.

Railwayman's Daughter. Dee Yates & Maggie Mash. 2008. 76.95 (978-1-84652-284-0(6)); audio compact disk 99.95 (978-1-84652-283-3(8)) Pub: Magna Story GBR. Dist(s): Ulverscroft US

Rain see Child's Garden of Verses

Rain. unabr. ed. V. C. Andrews. Read by Liza Ross. 10 cass. (Running Time: 11 hrs. 39 mins.). (Isis Ser.). (J). 2002. 84.95 (978-0-7531-1120-8(9)); audio compact disk 99.95 (978-0-7531-1197-0(7)) Pub: ISIS Lrg Prnt GBR. Dist(s): Ulverscroft US
Rain Arnold has fought to be the best daughter she can. She studies hard, helps her mother, and avoids the dangers of the city street. Then she overhears a heart-breaking revelation of a long-buried secret and everything Rain has known is left behind as she is sent to live with total strangers, the wealthy Hudson family. She finds refuge in the theatre, inside the walls of an exclusive private school. But will this be enough to fulfil her heart's desire: a place called home?.

Rain: What a Paperboy Learned about Business. unabr. ed. Jeffrey J. Fox. Read by Jeffrey J. Fox. 1 MP3-CD. (Running Time: 4 hrs.). 2009. 39.97 (978-1-4233-7625-5(0), 9781423376255, Brinc Audio MP3 Lib); 39.97 (978-1-4233-7627-9(7), 9781423376279, BADLE); 24.99 (978-1-4233-7626-2(9), 9781423376262, BAD); 24.99 (978-1-4233-7624-8(2), 9781423376248, Brilliance MP3); audio compact disk 62.97 (978-1-4233-7623-1(4), 9781423376231, BriAudCD Unabrid); audio compact disk 19.99 (978-1-4233-7622-4(6), 9781423376224, Bril Audio CD Unabri) Brilliance Audio.

Rain Came Down. David Shannon. (ENG.). (J). (ps-3). 2009. audio compact disk 18.95 (978-0-545-13857-4(4)) Scholastic Inc.

Rain Came Down. David Shannon. Narrated by Bruce Bailey Johnson. (ENG.). (J). (ps-3). 2009. audio compact disk 9.95 (978-0-545-13850-5(7)) Scholastic Inc.

Rain Dancer. Scott Huckabay. Prod. by Leonard G. Horowitz. 1. (Running Time: 60). 2007. audio compact disk 19.25 (978-0-923550-06-6(2)) Tetrahedron Pub.

Rain Drop Splash. 2004. 8.95 (978-1-56008-315-3(8)); cass. & flmstrp 30.00 (978-1-56008-753-3(6)) Weston Woods.

Rain Drop Splash; Josie & the Snow; Sun up; Happy Day, the; Where Does the Butterfly Go When in Rains? 2004. cass. & flmstrp (978-0-89719-729-8(1)) Weston Woods.

Rain Drop Splash; Josie & the Snow; Sun up; Happy Day, the; Where Does the Butterfly Go When It Rains? 2004. (978-0-89719-821-9(2)) Weston Woods.

Rain Drops see Gotas de Lluvia

Rain Forest. 1 cass. (Running Time: 1 hr.). 1992. 9.95 (978-1-55961-165-7(0)) Relaxtn Co.

Rain Forest. Sundance/Newbridge, LLC Staff. (Early Science Ser.). (gr. k-3). 2007. audio compact disk 12.00 (978-1-4007-6490-7(4)); audio compact disk 12.00 (978-1-4007-6489-1(0)); audio compact disk 12.00 (978-1-4007-6488-4(2)) Sund Newbrdge.

Rain Forest Adventure/Inside the Rain Forest. Steck-Vaughn Staff. (J). 1997. (978-0-8172-7370-5(0)) SteckVau.

Rain Forest Rhapsody. unabr. ed. Twin Sisters. Read by Twin Sisters. (YA). 2008. 44.99 (978-1-59922-320-9(1)) Find a World.

Rain Gods. abr. ed. James Lee Burke. Read by Will Patton. (Running Time: 7 hrs. 0 mins. 0 sec.). (ENG.). 2009. audio compact disk 29.99 (978-0-7435-8241-4(1)) Pub: S&S Audio. Dist(s): S and S Inc

Rain Gods. unabr. ed. James Lee Burke. Read by Will Patton. 13 CDs. (Running Time: 16 hrs. 0 mins. 0 sec.). 2009. audio compact disk 49.99 (978-0-7435-8243-8(8)) Pub: S&S Audio. Dist(s): S and S Inc

***Rain Gods: A Novel.** abr. ed. James Lee Burke. Read by Will Patton. (Running Time: 7 hrs. 0 mins. 0 sec.). (ENG.). 2011. audio compact disk 14.99 (978-1-4423-4075-6(4)) Pub: S&S Audio. Dist(s): S and S Inc

Rain God's Daughter & Other African Folktales. unabr. ed. Perf. by Ruby Dee. Ed. by Amabel Williams-Ellis. As told by Clem A. Okafor. 1 cass. (J). 1987. 9.95 (978-0-694-50688-0(5), CDL5 1329) HarperCollins Pubs.
These African folktales were told around the fire at night to a circle composed of both adults & children. In many such stories the audience acts as a chorus, repeating words or asking questions. Also includes " The Food Drum" & "Why the Tortoise Carries a Shell on His Back".

Rain Is Not My Indian Name. unabr. ed. Cynthia Leitich Smith. Read by Jenna Lamia. 2 cass. (Running Time: 3 hrs. 27 mins.). (J). (gr. 5-9). 2004. 23.00 (978-0-8072-0520-4(6), Listening Lib) Random Audio Pubg.
Tired of staying in seclusion since the death of her best friend, a fourteen-year-old Native American girl takes on a photographic assignment with her local newspaper to cover events at the Native American summer youth camp.

Rain of Gold, Pt. 1. unabr. collector's ed. Victor Villaseñor. Read by Michael Prichard. 9 cass. (Running Time: 13 hrs. 30 min.). 1996. 72.00 (978-0-7366-3482-3(7), 4123-A) Books on Tape.
A sweeping tableau of Latino family ties & cultural traditions.

Rain of Gold, Pt. 2. collector's ed. Victor Villaseñor. Read by Michael Prichard. 11 cass. (Running Time: 16 hrs. 30 min.). 1996. 88.00 (978-0-7366-3483-0(5), 4123-B) Books on Tape.

Rain of Roses see Rosario: Lluvia de Rosas

Rain on Us: Love & Truth Choir. David Scott. Perf. by Russ Harrington & Todd Tufts. 1 CD. 1999. audio compact disk (978-0-9675769-0-9(3)) Love & Truth.
Christian -based self interest w/music; devotional w/inspirational music - choir format.

Rain on Us: Love & Truth Choir. David Scott. Perf. by Russ Harrington. Illus. by Todd Tufts. 1 cass. 1999. (978-0-9675769-1-6(1)) Love & Truth.
Christian-based self interest w/music; devotional w/inspirational music - choir format.

Rain Rustlers. unabr. ed. Frank Roderus. Read by Kevin Foley. 6 cass. (Running Time: 6 hrs. 48 min.). (Heller Ser.: Bk. 2). 1991. 39.95 (978-1-55686-560-2(0)) Books in Motion.
Carl Heller is a self-appointed defender of victims of injustice who nonetheless favors a lazy lifestyle. As such, he works slowly but with a no-holds-barred approach. Heller wrecks a scam that threatens the entire San Luis Valley, thanks to the help of a lady pilot.

Rainbabies. 2004. 8.95 (978-0-7882-0094-6(1)); audio compact disk 12.95 (978-1-55592-946-6(X)) Weston Woods.

Rainbabies. Laura Krauss Melmed. Narrated by B. J. Ward. Music by John Jennings. Illus. by Jim LaMarche. 1 cass. (Running Time: 20 min.). (J). (ps-4). 2000. bk. 24.95 (QHRA382) Weston Woods.
The moon presents a childless couple with twelve tiny babies, each no bigger than a person's big toe. The new parents take care of the babies with tenderness & love, sometimes risking their own lives in the face of tremendous adversity to keep the babies safe. In the end they are rewarded with their heart's desire, a real child to cherish forever.

Rainbow. unabr. ed. Mark Kinkead-Weekes. Read by Maureen O'Brien. 8 cass. (Running Time: 8 hrs.). 2000. 119.95 (978-0-7540-0512-4(7), CAB1935) AudioGO.
Set in the rural midlands of England, this revolves around three generations of Brangwens, a family deeply involved with the land & noted for their strength & vigor. When Tom Brangwen marries a Polish widow, Lydia Lensky & adopts her daughter, Anna as his own, he is unprepared for the conflict & passion that erupts between them.

Rainbow. unabr. ed. D. h. Lawrence. Read by Flo Gibson. 14 cass. (Running Time: 19 hrs.). 1993. 42.95 (978-1-55685-284-8(3)) Audio Bk Con.
The physical passions & psychological needs of three generations of Brangwens, a family of farmers & craftsmen in Nottinghamshire, are explored in this intensely sensual, romantic & erotic novel. Although suppressed as obscene in 1915, the beauty & lyricism of the language make it uniquely palatable.

***Rainbow.** unabr. ed. D. h. Lawrence. Narrated by Wanda McCaddon. (Running Time: 20 hrs. 30 mins.). 2010. 23.99 (978-1-4526-7030-0(7)); 29.99 (978-1-4526-5030-2(6)); 39.99 (978-1-4526-0030-7(5)) Tantor Media.

Rainbow & the Rose. unabr. ed. Nevil Shute. Read by Robin Bailey. 8 cass. (Running Time: 8 hrs. 15 min.). 1990. 69.95 (978-0-7451-6282-9(7), CAB 489) AudioGO.
A small airplane on an errand of mercy has crashed in one of the most inaccessible parts of the world. Pilot Johnny Pascoe has a fractured skull & urgently needs medical care - but the only two passengers are a former flying pupil & an inexperienced young doctor.

Rainbow & the Rose. unabr. ed. Nevil Shute. Read by Robin Bailey. 8 cass. (Running Time: 12 hrs.). 2000. 59.95 (CAB 489) Pub: Chivers Audio Bks GBR. Dist(s): AudioGO
A small airplane on an errand of mercy has crashed in one of the most inaccessible districts in the world. The pilot, Johnnie Pascoe, has a fractured skull that needs urgent medical attention. Ronnie Scott, one of his former flying students, and a doctor, decide to attempt the dangerous mission as the past collides with the present.

Rainbow & the Throne: Rev. 4:3. Ed Young. (J). 1982. 4.95 (978-0-7417-1212-7(1), A0212) Win Walk.

Rainbow Butterfly. 1 cassette. (Running Time: 60 minutes, 57 seconds). 1979. 12.95 (978-1-55841-011-4(2)) Emmett E Miller.
Two relaxing, inspiring, deeply satisfying guided meditations. Dr. Miller is accompanied by the exquisite harp of Georgia Kelly. Side 1: Attuen to your essence, then gently break out of the cocoon of physical tension, spread your wings and fly. Side 2: A delightful journey through the color spectrum. Increases your sense of well-being and expands your consiousness and spirituality.

Rainbow Butterfly. 1 CD. 1979. audio compact disk 16.95 (978-1-55841-105-0(4)) Emmett E Miller.

Rainbow Cafe: A Ron Robinson Retrospective. Ron Robinson. 2007. audio compact disk 15.00 (978-0-931170-86-7(9)) Ctr Western Studies.

Rainbow Days. Josephine Cox. Read by Carole Boyd. 2003. audio compact disk 79.95 (978-0-7540-9455-5(3)) Pub: Chivers Audio Bks GBR. Dist(s): AudioGO

Rainbow Dreams Soundtrack. Created by Tracy Norrene Wilkinson. Based on a story by Tracy Norrene Wilkinson. 1 CD. 2006. audio compact disk 14.95 (978-0-9665918-1-1(X)) TNW Prod.
16 different styles of Original "feel good for everyone in the family" songs with good moral values. The kid in everyone will sing along with Rainbow Dreams.

Rainbow Fish. unabr. ed. Read by Blair Brown. 1 cass. (Running Time: 30 mins.).Tr. of Regenbogenfisch. (J). 2000. pap. bk. 12.98 (T 6504 SMH, Listening Lib) Random Audio Pubg.
Classic story about sharing.

Rainbow in the Clouds: The Story of Noah. Bert Polman. Ed. by Sandy Swartzentruber. (Running Time: 40 mins.). (Scripture Alive Ser.). 2001. 15.95 (978-1-56212-561-5(3), 415115) FaithAliveChr.

Rainbow in the Mist. Phyllis A. Whitney. Read by Anna Fields. 7 cass. (Running Time: 10 hrs.). 2000. 49.95 (978-0-7861-1573-0(4), 2402) Blckstn Audio.
Ulike her mother, a famous psychic, Christy Loren fears her unwanted legacy & the horrifying visions that always appear too late. Christy knows the blood-chilling dream that has haunted her will come to terrifying life.

Rainbow in the Mist. unabr. ed. Phyllis A. Whitney. Read by Anna Fields. 7 cass. (Running Time: 10 hrs. 30 mins.). 1999. 49.95 (FS9-51035) Highsmith.

Rainbow in the Morning. unabr. ed. Eileen Stafford. 10 cass. (Running Time: 15 hrs.). 1998. 98.95 (978-1-85903-100-1(5)) Pub: Magna Story GBR. Dist(s): Ulverscroft US

Rainbow in the Night: The Tumultuous Birth of South Africa. unabr. ed. Dominic Lapierre. Tr. by Kathryn Spink. (Running Time: 10 hrs. 5 mins.). 2009. audio compact disk 29.95 (978-1-4332-9158-6(4)) Blckstn Audio.

Rainbow in the Night: The Tumultuous Birth of South Africa. unabr. ed. Dominique Lapierre. (Running Time: 10 hrs. 50 mins.). (ENG.). 2009. 65.95 (978-1-4332-9155-5(X)) Blckstn Audio.

Rainbow in the Night: The Tumultuous Birth of South Africa. unabr. ed. Dominique Lapierre. Tr. by Kathryn Spink. Narrated by Simon Rudnicki. 8 CDs. (Running Time: 10 hrs. 50 mins.). 2009. audio compact disk 100.00 (978-1-4332-9156-2(8)) Blckstn Audio.

Rainbow in the Night: The Tumultuous Birth of South Africa. unabr. ed. Dominique Lapierre. (Running Time: 10 hrs. 50 mins.). (ENG.). 2009. 29.95 (978-1-4332-9159-3(2)) Blckstn Audio.

Rainbow Journey. abr. ed. Brenda Davies. Read by Brenda Davies. 2 cass. (Running Time: 2 hrs.). 1999. 16.85 Set. Ulvrscrft Audio.
A practical & inspirational guide to total well being through healing the body's major energy centers.

Rainbow Kingdom. (J). 1999. audio compact disk 14.95 (978-1-58467-000-1(2)) Gentle Wind.

Rainbow Kingdom. Paul Tracey. 1 cass. (Running Time: 40 min.). (J). (gr. k-3). 1985. 9.95 (978-0-939065-28-8(2), GW1032) Gentle Wind.
Songs with whimsical lyrics & catchy tunes.

***Rainbow (Library Edition)** unabr. ed. D. h. Lawrence. Narrated by Wanda McCaddon. (Running Time: 20 hrs. 30 mins.). 2010. 95.99 (978-1-4526-3030-4(5)); 39.99 (978-1-4526-2030-5(X)) Tantor Media.

Rainbow Magic: Ruby the Red Fairy & Amber the Orange Fairy. Daisy Meadows. Read by Kate Simses. (Playaway Children Ser.). (ENG.). (J). 2009. 34.99 (978-1-61545-636-9(8)) Find a World.

Rainbow Mars. collector's ed. Larry Niven. Read by Michael Prichard. 9 cass. (Running Time: 13 hrs. 30 min.). 2000. 72.00 (978-0-7366-4920-9(4), 5228) Books on Tape.
A groundbreaking new novel from the legendary New York Times best-selling author & five-time Hugo winner that weaves together time travel & fantasy to create an utterly unique view on the origin of Martian canals.

Rainbow Mars. collector's unabr. ed. Larry Niven. Read by Michael Prichard. 11 CDs. (Running Time: 13 hrs. 12 mins.). 2000. audio compact disk 88.00 (978-0-7366-5222-3(1)) Books on Tape.

Rainbow Mars, Pt. 1. collector's ed. Larry Niven. Read by Michael Prichard. 9 cass. (Running Time: 13 hrs. 30 min.). 2000. 72.00 (978-0-7366-4947-6(6)) Books on Tape.
Hanville Svetz must travel far back in time to figure out why the Martian canals have gone dry and what that means for Earth's future.

Rainbow Meditation. Michael P. Bovines. Read by Michael P. Bovines. 1 cass. (Running Time: 42 min.). (Healing Ser.). 1992. pap. bk. 9.98 (978-1-885768-00-1(1), M409) Circle of Light.
A beautiful guided journey through the end of a rainbow. This healing meditation balances & harmonizes your chakra energy system & promotes inner peace, good health & harmony.

Rainbow Meditation: Journey into Color Healing. Read by Michael P. Bovines. 1 CD. (Running Time: 41 mins.). (Healing Ser.). (C). 1993. audio compact disk 14.95 (978-1-885768-35-3(4)) Pub: Circle of Light. Dist(s): New Leaf Dist
You will be guided into a sacred journey of color healing to restore inner peace and self-love. This meditation will unlock your dormant creativity and awaken your inner power. A very magical meditation experience for beginners as well as the well seasoned meditator.

Rainbow Mewsik. Bill Bissett. Composed by Chris Meloche. 1 CD. (Running Time: 1 hr. 12 mins. 07 sec.). (Poetry Ser.). (ENG.). 2003. audio compact disk 9.95 (978-0-88995-231-7(0)) Pub: Red Deer CAN. Dist(s): IngramPubServ

Rainbow of My Own. Don Freeman. Illus. by Don Freeman. 11 vols. (Running Time: 6 mins.). 1982. pap. bk. 18.95 (978-1-59519-069-7(4)); pap. bk. 35.95 (978-1-59519-070-3(8)); 9.95 (978-1-59112-112-1(4)); audio compact disk 12.95 (978-1-59519-068-0(6)) Live Oak Media.

Rainbow of My Own. Don Freeman. Illus. by Don Freeman. Read by Linda Terheyden. 14 vols. (Running Time: 6 mins.). (J). 1982. pap. bk. & tchr. ed. 33.95 Reading Chest. (978-0-941078-19-1(1)) Live Oak Media.

Rainbow of My Own. unabr. ed. Don Freeman. 1 read-along cass. (Running Time: 6 min.). (J). 1982. 9.95 Live Oak Media.
A boy plays hide-&-go-seek & leapfrog in the rain with his imaginary friend - a rainbow. His friend disappears when the sun comes out, but when the boy goes home he finds a real rainbow of his very own.

Rainbow of My Own. unabr. ed. Don Freeman. Illus. by Don Freeman. Read by Linda Terheyden. 11 vols. (Running Time: 6 mins.). (J). (gr. k-3). 1982. pap. bk. 16.95 (978-0-941078-18-4(3)) Live Oak Media.

Rainbow of Songs. Bing Bingham. 1 cass. (Running Time: 36 min.). (J). (ps-3). 1988. pap. bk. 10.95 (978-0-937124-23-9(0), KIM 9112C); pap. bk. & pupil's gde. ed. 11.95 (KIM 9112) Kimbo Educ.
Songs of friendship, harmony & fun include Goober Peas, Primary Colors, Look at the World, The First Day of School, The Clapping Song, In Grandma's Garden & more. Includes guide.

Rainbow of the Sioux: Alone in Indian Country... Can a Ten-Year-Old Girl Survive? 1 CD. (Running Time: 3420 sec.). (J). (gr. k-6). 2006. audio compact disk 12.95 (978-1-933781-03-7(3)) TallTales Aud.

Rainbow Palace: Broadway Classics & More. Linda Arnold. 1 cass. (Running Time: 60 mins.). (J). (ps-3). 1996. 9.98 Incl. lyrics. (978-1-889212-04-3(0), CAAR4); audio compact disk 14.98 CD Incl. lyrics. (978-1-889212-03-6(2), CDAR4) Ariel Recs.
Children's sing alongs & Broadway classics performed by Linda Arnold & her daughter.

Rainbow Palace - Broadway Classics & More. Perf. by Linda Arnold. 1 cass. (Running Time: 60 mins.). (J). 10.98 (YM124-CN); audio compact disk 13.98 (YM124-CD) Youngheart Mus.
Songs include: "Overture"; "Rainbow Palace"; "Broadway Birthday Party"; "Happy Talk"; "Shenanigans"; "Top Hat, Bow Tie & Tails"; "I'd Do Anything"; "Daisey Bell on Broadway";"Do Re Mi"; "Heart"; "Broadway Banana" & more.

Rainbow People, unabr. ed. Short Stories. Laurence Yep. Narrated by George Guidall. 3 pieces. (Running Time: 4 hrs.). (gr. 6 up). 1993. 27.00 (978-1-55690-874-3(1), 93316E7) Recorded Bks.
A collection of twenty Chinese folktales that were passed on by word of mouth for generations, as told to the author by some old-timers newly settled in the United States. Listen & meet a butterfly man... a mouse with supernatural powers... the rainbow people... & many more unforgettable characters.

Rainbow Rehearsal. 1 cass. (Running Time: 1 hr. 30 mins.). 2000. 15.00 (978-0-929656-50-2(4)); audio compact disk 18.00 (978-0-929656-51-9(2)) Positive Prod.

Rainbow Serpent. 2004. pap. bk. 14.95 (978-0-7882-0630-6(3)); 8.95 (978-1-56008-316-0(6)); cass. & flmstrp 30.00 (978-1-56008-754-0(4)) Weston Woods.

Rainbow Sign. Perf. by Beausoleil et al. 1 cass. (Running Time: 59 min.). (Family Ser.). (J). 1992. 9.98 (8025); audio compact disk 14.98 (8025) Rounder Records.
A cross-cultural collection of children's songs, performed by an impressive roster of artists. The purpose of this recording is to foster understanding & improve relations between the diverse peoples of the world. Contributing artists include: Beausoleil, Flor de Cana, Ronnie Gilbert, John McCutcheon, Holly Near, Pete Seeger, Sweet Honey in the Rock, Arlo Guthrie, Yellowman, & the Horseflies.

Rainbow Six. abr. ed. Tom Clancy. Read by David Dukes. 4 cass. (Running Time: 6 hrs.). 1999. 25.95 (FS9-43195) Highsmith.

Rainbow Six. abr. ed. Tom Clancy. Read by David Dukes. 5 CDs. (Running Time: 6 hrs.). (Tom Clancy Ser.). (ENG.). 1998. audio compact disk 31.95 (978-0-375-40347-7(7)) Pub: Random Audio Pubg. Dist(s): Random

Rainbow Six, Pt. 1. Tom Clancy. Read by Michael Prichard. 13 cass. (Running Time: 19 hrs. 30 mins.). 1998. 104.00 (978-0-7366-4530-0(6), 4703-A) Books on Tape.
John Clark's back & he's stumbled on a band of terrorists bent on destroying the world.

Rainbow Six, Pt. 2. unabr. ed. Tom Clancy. Read by Michael Prichard. 12 cass. (Running Time: 18 hrs.). 1998. 96.00 (978-0-7366-4531-7(4), 4703-B) Books on Tape.
John Clark looks forward to a new mission. Opportunities come faster than expected: an incident at a Swiss bank, the kidnapping of an international trader in Germany, & a terrible raid on an amusement park in Spain.

Rainbow Tales. As told by Judith Black et al. 1 cass. (Running Time: 1 hr. 16 min.). (J). (gr. 3 up). 1997. 9.98 (978-1-57940-001-9(9)); audio compact disk 14.98 (978-1-57940-000-2(0)) Rounder Records.
Teachers, librarians, & parents who wish to introduce children & young adults to the world of storytelling will find this as a valuable resource in this collection.

Rainbow Tales, Too. As told by Melissa Barkin et al. 1 cass. (Running Time: 1 hr. 12 min.). (J). (gr. 3 up). 1997. 9.98 (978-1-57940-003-3(5)); audio compact disk 14.98 (978-1-57940-002-6(7)) Rounder Records.

Rainbow Trail. Zane Grey. Narrated by Jim Roberts. (Running Time: 10 hrs. 30 mins.). 1990. 30.95 (978-1-59912-816-0(0)) Iofy Corp.

Rainbow Trail. Zane Grey. Read by Michael Prichard. (Riders Ser.). (ENG.). 2004. audio compact disk 22.99 (978-1-4001-5109-7(0)) Pub: Tantor Media. Dist(s): IngramPubServ

Rainbow Trail. Zane Grey. Narrated by Michael Prichard. (Riders Ser.). (ENG.). 2005. audio compact disk 79.99 (978-1-4001-3109-9(X)) Pub: Tantor Media. Dist(s): IngramPubServ

Rainbow Trail. unabr. ed. Zane Grey. Read by Ian Esmo. 8 cass. (Running Time: 12 hrs.). 1999. 56.95 (1897) Blckstn Audio.
Three people fleeing Mormon persecution are held hostage in a canyon, Fay Larkin, John Shefford's fiancee, among them. The secret to the canyon lies in a hidden Mormon village of "sealed" wives, where the penalty for trespassing is death. Desperate to rescue his lady, the tenderfoot Shefford will have to fight his way to the canyon knowing that his efforts may end in bloody slaughter!.

Rainbow Trail. unabr. ed. Zane Grey. Read by Ian Esmo. 8 cass. (Running Time: 11 hrs. 30 mins.). 2006. 56.95 (978-0-7861-1132-9(1), 1897) Blckstn Audio.

Rainbow Trail. unabr. ed. Zane Grey. Read by Maynard Villers. 12 cass. (Running Time: 11 hrs. 12 min.). 1995. 64.95 (978-1-55686-601-2(1)) Books in Motion.
Here is an arm's length sequel to Riders of the Purple Sage. It answers the questions most often asked about what finally happened to Lassiter & Jane Withersteen.

Rainbow Trail. unabr. ed. Zane Grey. Read by Jim Roberts. 8 cass. (Running Time: 11 hrs. 30 min.). (YA). (gr. 9-12). 1991. 49.00 (C-223) Jimcin Record.
A tale of the wild west & the rush to find gold.

Rainbow Trail. unabr. ed. Zane Grey. Narrated by Michael Prichard. (Running Time: 12 hrs. 0 mins. 0 sec.). (Tantor Unabridged Classics Ser.). (ENG.). 2009. audio compact disk 22.99 (978-1-4001-5943-7(1)); audio compact disk 65.99 (978-1-4001-3943-9(0)); audio compact disk 32.99 (978-1-4001-0943-2(4)) Pub: Tantor Media. Dist(s): IngramPubServ

Rainbow Valley. L. M. Montgomery. Read by Grace Conlin. 8 CDs. (Running Time: 30600 sec.). (J). (gr. 4-7). 2005. audio compact disk 72.00 (978-0-7861-8181-0(8), 1704) Blckstn Audio.

Rainbow Valley. L. M. Montgomery. Narrated by Barbara Caruso. 8 CDs. (Running Time: 9 hrs.). (J). 1985. audio compact disk 78.75 (978-1-4193-1785-9(7)) Recorded Bks.

Rainbow Valley, unabr. ed. L. M. Montgomery. Read by Grace Conlin. 6 cass. (Running Time: 8 hrs. 30 mins.). (Avonlea Ser.: No. 6). (gr. 5-8). 1995. 44.95 (978-0-7861-0913-5(0), 1704) Blckstn Audio.
The winsome Anne Shirley is grown, has married her beloved Gilbert & is the mother of six frolicsome children. Anne & her family experience some unimaginable events when a strange family moves into a nearby mansion. The Meredith family is comprised of two boys & two girls, a minister father but no mother & a runaway girl named Mary Vance. The clever & mischievous Meredith kids join Anne's children in a private hideout to carry out plans to save Mary from the orphanage, to help the lonely minister find happiness, & to save a pet rooster from becoming a soup ingredient. The sun-dappled world of Rainbow Valley is always full of adventure & delight.

Rainbow Valley. unabr. ed. L. M. Montgomery. Read by Grace Conlin. 6 cass. (Running Time: 9 hrs.). (Avonlea Ser.: No. 6). (YA). (gr. 5-8). 1999. 44.95 (FS9-34201) Highsmith.

Rainbow Valley. unabr. ed. L. M. Montgomery. Read by Barbara Caruso. 6 cass. (Running Time: 9 hrs.). (J). 2004. 54.75 (978-1-4025-9924-8(2)) Recorded Bks.
Anne and Gilbert Blythe are married and have six mischievous children. Always seeking out new adventures and trying to help others, they're a rambunctious lot.

Rainbows & Rollercoasters. Poems. Glenn Hass. (Running Time: 30 min.). (J). 6.95 (978-0-9639615-1-8(9)) Life & Peace.

Rainbows & Waterfalls. J. Donald Walters. 2002. audio compact disk 15.95 (978-1-56589-750-2(1)) Pub: Crystal Clarity. Dist(s): Natl Bk Netwk

Rainbow's End. unabr. ed. Martha Grimes. Read by Donada Peters. 10 cass. (Running Time: 10 hrs.). (Richard Jury Novel Ser.). 1995. 80.00 (978-0-7366-3138-9(0), 3813) Books on Tape.
After three unrelated deaths occur, Richard Jury, Scotland Yard Chief Superintendent, finds a common thread that leads him to Santa Fe. With few clues & many distractions from the locals, Jury follows his insights to solve the crimes & head off another murder.

Rainbow's End. unabr. ed. Ellis Peters, pseud. Narrated by Simon Prebble. 5 cass. (Running Time: 7 hrs. 15 mins.). (Inspector George Felse Mystery Ser.: Vol. 13). 1991. 44.00 (978-1-55690-433-2(9), 91232E7) Recorded Bks.
Wealthy, talented Arthur Rainbow was a guaranteed success. But there was one place he hadn't expected to end up & that was beneath a church tower, his body smashed like a cracked walnut.

Rainbow's End: A Memoir of Childhood War & an African Farm. Lauren St John. Narrated by Bianca Amato. (Running Time: 40500 sec.). 2007. audio compact disk 34.99 (978-1-4281-4350-0(5)) Recorded Bks.

Rainbows of Intelligence: Raising Student Performance Through Multiple Intelligences. Perf. by Sue Teele. 2000. 99.95 (978-0-7619-7631-8(0), 86336) Pub: Corwin Pr. Dist(s): SAGE

Rainbows Promise-Music. 2007. audio compact disk 19.95 (978-1-56136-406-0(1)) Master Your Mind.

Rainbows, Stones & Dinosaur Bones. Perf. by Paul Strausman. 1 cass. (Running Time: 40 min.). (J). 9.95 (978-0-939065-25-7(8), GW1029) Gentle Wind.
Gentle & melodic songs perfect for singing, dancing & joining in.

Rainbows, Stones, & Dinosaur Bones. Paul Strausman. (J). 1999. audio compact disk 14.95 (978-0-939065-92-9(4)) Gentle Wind.

Rainer Maria Rilke. Stephen Spender. 1 cass. (Running Time: 51 min.). 1953. 11.95 (23016) J Norton Pubs.
As a visionary individualist, Rilke believed the poet's task to be that of transforming the outer world into his own inner invisibility.

Rainforest Adventure Director CD-ROM. Created by Augsburg Fortress Publishers. (Rainforest Adventures Ser.). 2007. audio compact disk 15.99 (978-0-8066-6159-9(3)) Augsburg Fortress.

Rainforest Adventure Sky High Storytelling. Created by Augsburg Fortress Publishers. (Running Time: 1800 sec.). (Rainforest Adventures Ser.). 2007. 19.99 (978-0-8066-6182-7(8)) Augsburg Fortress.

Rainforest Adventure Song. Created by Augsburg Fortress Publishers. (Rainforest Adventures Ser.). 2007. audio compact disk 25.99 (978-0-8066-6185-8(2)) Augsburg Fortress.

Rainforest Adventures Music Video. Created by Augsburg Fortress Publishers. (Rainforest Adventures Ser.). 2007. 19.99 (978-0-8066-6181-0(X)) Augsburg Fortress.

Rainforest & Ocean Waves. unabr. ed. Jeffrey Thompson. (Running Time: 2:00:00). 2009. audio compact disk 19.98 (978-1-55961-748-2(9)) Sounds True.

***Rainforest Requiem: Recordings of Wildlife in the Amazon Rainforest.** British Library Staff & Vrej Nersessian. (ENG.). 2010. audio compact disk 15.00 (978-0-7123-0513-6(0)) Pub: Britis Library GBR. Dist(s): Chicago Distribution Ctr

Raining Cats & Donkeys. Doreen Tovey. Read by Elizabeth Henry. 4 cass. (Running Time: 6 hrs.). 2001. 44.95 (23213) Pub: Soundings Ltd GBR. Dist(s): Ulverscroft US

Rainmaker. John Grisham. Read by Frank Muller. 1995. 96.00 (978-0-7366-8914-4(1)); audio compact disk 112.00 (978-0-7366-8908-3(7)) Books on Tape.

Rainmaker. N. Richard Nash. Featuring Jayne Atkinson et al. 2 cass. (Running Time: 1 hr. 50 mins.). 2001. 23.95 (978-1-58081-207-8(4), TPT152) L A Theatre.
Lizzie curry's father & two brothers are ore worried about her marital prospects than about the drought that's killing their cattle. When con man & dream-maker Bill Starbuck appears with a promise to bring rain, he becomes the vehicle for Lizzie's transformation.

Rainmaker. abr. ed. John Grisham. 4 cass. 22.95 Set. (47305) Books on Tape.
A young lawyer expects easy money on a routine lawsuit, but the case explodes into a war that could make him the biggest rainmaker in the land - or cost him his life.

Rainmaker. unabr. ed. John Grisham. Read by Frank Muller. 12 cass. (Running Time: 17 hrs.). 1999. 49.95 (FS9-34494) Highsmith.

Rainmaker. unabr. ed. N. Richard Nash. 2 cass. (Running Time: 2 hrs.). Dramatization. 2001. 22.95 L A Theatre.
A play that truly is a little miracle, so honest & touching in a way that almost anyone can relate to.

Rainmaker. unabr. ed. N. Richard Nash. 2 CDs. (Running Time: 1 hr. 50 mins.). 2001. audio compact disk 25.95 (978-1-58081-220-7(1), CDTPT152) L A Theatre.

Rainman. Lloyd Shelby. 2002. audio compact disk 15.00 (978-0-9721845-1-9(1)) PaintWORD.

Rainride see Twentieth-Century Poetry in English, No. 28, Recordings of Poets Reading Their Own Poetry

Rainsong. unabr. ed. Phyllis A. Whitney. Read by Anna Fields. 7 cass. (Running Time: 10 hrs.). 1998. 49.95 (978-0-7861-1512-9(2), 2362) Blckstn Audio.
Songwriter Hollis Sands's world collapses when her husband, legendary singer Ricky Sands, commits suicide. Wanting to escape the press & the pain, Hollis flees in anonymity to Windtop, the beautiful & imposing Long Island home of a family friend. The peaceful retreat soon turns nightmarish as small reminders of Ricky keep surfacing & a eerie version of Hollis's "Rainsong" echoes the house.

Rainsong. unabr. ed. Phyllis A. Whitney. Read by Anna Fields. 7 cass. (Running Time: 8 hrs.). 1999. 49.95 (FS9-50911) Highsmith.

***Rainsong.** unabr. ed. Phyllis A. Whitney. Read by Anna Fields. (Running Time: 10 hrs.). 2010. 29.95 (978-1-4417-0762-8(X)); audio compact disk 90.00 (978-1-4417-0759-8(X)) Blckstn Audio.

Rainstone Fall. Peter Helton & Andrew Wincott. 2009. 61.95 (978-1-84652-457-8(1)); audio compact disk 79.95 (978-1-84652-458-5(X)) Pub: Magna Story GBR. Dist(s): Ulverscroft US

Raintree County. unabr. ed. Ross Lockridge, Jr. Read by Lloyd James. (Running Time: 43 hrs. 5 mins.). 2008. 59.95 (978-1-4332-5794-0(7)); audio compact disk 130.00 (978-1-4332-5790-2(4)); audio compact disk 125.00 (978-1-4332-5791-9(2)) Blckstn Audio.

Raintree County, Pt. 1. unabr. collector's ed. Ross Lockridge, Jr. Read by Wolfram Kandinsky. 10 cass. (Running Time: 15 hrs.). 1982. 80.00 (978-0-7366-0367-6(0), 1351-A) Books on Tape.
The story of the 19th century in Raintree County, Indiana, particularly of the Civil War & its after-effects.

Raintree County, Pt. 2. unabr. collector's ed. Ross Lockridge, Jr. Read by Wolfram Kandinsky. 10 cass. (Running Time: 15 hrs.). 1982. 80.00 (978-0-7366-0368-3(9), 1351-B) Books on Tape.

Raintree County, Pt. 3. unabr. collector's ed. Ross Lockridge, Jr. Read by Wolfram Kandinsky. 11 cass. (Running Time: 16 hrs. 30 mins.). 1982. 88.00 (978-0-7366-0369-0(7), 1351-C) Books on Tape.

Raintree County Part A. unabr. ed. Ross Lockridge, Jr. Read by Lloyd James. (Running Time: 22 hrs. 0 mins.). 2008. audio compact disk 109.95 (978-1-4332-5788-9(2)) Blckstn Audio.

Raintree County Part B. unabr. ed. Ross Lockridge, Jr. Read by Lloyd James. (Running Time: 21 hrs. 5 mins.). 2008. audio compact disk 105.95 (978-1-4332-5789-6(0)) Blckstn Audio.

Rainwater. unabr. ed. Sandra Brown. Read by Victor Slezak. (Running Time: 7 hrs. 0 mins. 0 sec.). (ENG.). 2009. audio compact disk 29.99 (978-1-4423-0071-2(X)) Pub: S&S Audio. Dist(s): S and S Inc

Rainy City. unabr. ed. Earl Emerson. Narrated by George Reinholt. 6 cass. (Running Time: 9 hrs.). (Thomas Black Mystery Ser.: Vol. 1). 1992. 51.00 (978-1-55690-723-4(0), 92218E7) Recorded Bks.
Thomas Black, Seattle private eye, goes after a runaway wife.

Rainy Day: Early Explorers Emergent Set B Audio CD. Carrie Smith. Adapted by Benchmark Education Staff. (J). 2007. audio compact disk 10.00 (978-1-4108-8206-6(3)) Benchmark Educ.

Rainy Day for Sammy, Cassette Tape. Short Stories. 1 cassette. (Running Time: 14 mins). (J). 2006. 4.95 (978-1-57874-281-3(1)) Kaeden Corp.

Rainy Day for Sammy, CD. Short Stories. Kathleen Urmston & Grant Urmston. Narrated by Rick Sellers & Wesley McCraw. 1 CD. (Running Time: 23 mins.). (J). 2005. audio compact disk 7.95 (978-1-57874-104-5(1)) Kaeden Corp.

Rainy Day People. Susan C. Haley & Robert J. Delaney. Narrated by Sonja Lanzener. (ENG.). 2007. audio compact disk 39.95 (978-1-60031-016-4(8)) Spoken Books.

Rainy Day Rescue. Barbara Davoll & Dennis Hockerman. Illus. by Dennis Hockerman. 1 cass. (Christopher Churchmouse Ser.). (J). (ps-2). 1988. bk. 11.99 (978-0-89693-619-5(8), 3-1619) David C Cook.

Rainy Summer see Gathering of Great Poetry for Children

Rainy Weather. Read by Donald Davis. 1 cass. (Running Time: 50 min.). (gr. 3-7). 1994. 12.00 (978-0-87483-299-0(3)) Pub: August Hse. Dist(s): Natl Bk Netwk

Raise Da Roof. 1 cass. 4.98 (978-1-57908-426-4(5)); audio compact disk 5.98 (978-1-57908-421-9(4)) Platinm Enter.

Raise the Issues: An Integrated Approach to Critical Thinking. Carol Numrich. Contrib. by National Public Radio Staff. 1 cass. 1994. 37.95 (978-0-8013-1015-7(6)) Longman.
English as a second language.

Raise the Titanic! unabr. ed. Clive Cussler. Read by Larry McKeever. 9 cass. (Running Time: 13 hrs. 30 min.). (Dirk Pitt Ser.). 1991. 72.00 (978-0-7366-2024-6(9), 2839) Books on Tape.
The Sicilian Project is the defense plan of the decade. It creates a network that frees us from foreign attack. But there's a catch: the plan requires byzanium, that rarest element. The only byzanium in the world lies in the hold of the Titanic, 12,000 feet under the North Atlantic. What to do? Raise the Titanic.

Raise up a Mighty Generation: Portraits of Praise Live. Featuring Community Church of Sterling, VA. Members. 1 CD. 2000. audio compact disk 9.99 (978-0-7601-3421-4(9), SO33210) Pub: Brentwood Music. Dist(s): Provident Mus Dist
The Community Church, founded by Pastor Arlie Whitlow Jr., tries to reach with the reality of God's love. Songs included are "Welcome to Our Sanctuary," "It's Time," "Worship the Lord," "Second Chance" & more.

Raise Your Child's Creative IQ. Simone Bibeau. 1986. 99.00 (978-0-318-60221-9(0)) Perception Pubns.

Raise Your Child's Creative IQ: All Children Are Born Gifted. unabr. ed. Simone Bibeau. Read by Simone Bibeau. 4 cass. (Running Time: 5 hrs.). 1986. pap. bk. 99.00 incl. 4 bks. (978-0-940406-14-8(4), 014) Perception Pubns.
Over 100 activities that increase creativity. Parents learn: Why creativity is vital to your child's success; How to develop the proper home atmosphere to encourage creativity; How to improve your child's verbal & written skills which form the basis for personal, home & career success; How to stimulate your child's ability to find & solve problems, the foundation for our future inventors & scientists.

Raise Your Energy & Increase Your Motivation. Glenn Harrold. 1 cass. (Running Time: 1 hr. 30 mins.). 2002. 11.95 (978-1-901923-12-4(6)); audio compact disk 17.95 (978-1-901923-32-2(0)) Pub: Divinit Pubing GBR. Dist(s): Bookworld

Raise Your Hand If You're Sure: 11 Cor. 2:5-17. Ed Young. 1990. 4.95 (978-0-7417-1777-1(8), 777) Win Walk.

Raise Your Social I. Q. How to Do the Right Thing in Any Situation. unabr. ed. Michael K. Levine. Read by Mary Woods. 6 cass. (Running Time: 8 hrs. 30 mins.). 2000. 44.95 (978-0-7861-1688-1(9), 2511) Blckstn Audio.
Defines manners & etiquette for how we live today & shows readers how to keep their mouths foot-free.

Raised Catholic: Can You Tell? Perf. by Ed Stivender. 2 pieces. (Running Time: 1 hr. 51 mins.). (American Storytelling Ser.). 1993. 18.00 (978-0-87483-326-3(4)) Pub: August Hse. Dist(s): Natl Bk Netwk
Nostalgic, humorous stories about growing up Catholic.

***Raised on Fear - Audio.** Read by Jim Woodill. (ENG.). 2009. cd-rom 19.95 (978-0-9766135-4-1(9)) Eve Pub.

***Raised to Run.** Featuring Ravi Zacharias. 1989. audio compact disk 9.00 (978-1-61256-022-9(9)) Ravi Zach.

Raisin in the Sun. Lorraine Hansberry. 2 cass. (Running Time: 3 hrs.). 1999. 19.95 (CDL5-355) African Am Imag.

Raisin in the Sun. unabr. ed. Lorraine Hansberry. Read by Ossie Davis. Perf. by Ruby Dee. 2 cass. (Running Time: 2 hrs. 21 min.). Dramatization. (gr. 9-12). 1991. 18.95 (978-1-55994-378-9(5), CPN 355, Harper Audio) HarperCollins Pubs.

Raising a Family: Living on Planet Parenthood. abr. ed. Jeanne Elium & Don Elium. Read by Jeanne Elium & Don Elium. 2 cass. (Running Time: 3 hrs.). 1997. 17.95 (978-1-57453-217-3(0)) Audio Lit.
Provides new tools for building & maintaining a family in which all members feel safe, cared for & involved.

Raising a Giant Audo Cd. Read by Crisp Enterprises. 1999. audio compact disk 29.99 (978-1-892018-03-8(9)) R Crisp Ent.

Raising a Handicapped Child. unabr. collector's ed. Charlotte E. Thompson. Read by Ruth Stokesberry. 6 cass. (Running Time: 9 hrs.). 1988. 48.00 (978-0-7366-1337-8(4), 2240) Books on Tape.
Offers a guide to parents & others who care for physically disabled children & teenagers.

Raising a Magical Child. Joseph C. Pearce. Read by Joseph C. Pearce. 1 cass. (Running Time: 1 hr.). 1990. 10.95 (978-0-945093-20-6(9)) Enhanced Aud Systs.
Clear summary of Joseph Chilton Pearce, world renowned expert on the development of intelligence in children, featuring Phylicia Rashad of NBC's Cosby Show.

Raising a Thinking Child. abr. ed. Myrna B. Shure. 2 cass. (Running Time: 3 hrs.). 14.99 (47707) Books on Tape.
Parents can teach their children, as early as age four, to think critically & solve problems, explore consequences & consider others' feelings. Includes family role play & games & helps shy children assert themselves & impulsive ones cope.

Raising Abel. unabr. ed. Kathleen O'Neal Gear & W. Michael Gear. 13 cass. (Running Time: 19 hrs. 30 mins.). 2002. 104.00 (978-0-7366-8758-4(0)) Books on Tape.
When Veronica Tremain's brother is brutally murdered, both she and the FBI try to make sense of a bizarre conspiracy that seems to be targeting genetics professors. In search of secret papers her brother told her about in his last frantic phone call, Veronica meets three other people who are also on the run from his killers: two geneticists, Bryce and Rebecca, and Rebecca's son, Abel. Abel is an unusual but lovable little boy whom Rebecca would do anything to protect. When Rebecca is shot by a sniper, it is clear that Abel was the real target. Now, Veronica, Bryce and Abel are on the run, trying to figure out why one small boy is so important to a conspiracy of seemingly unstoppable killers.

Raising Boys. 2 CDs. 2005. audio compact disk 17.00 (978-1-933207-06-3(X)) Ransomed Heart.

Raising Children. unabr. ed. Read by Kelly Ryan Dolan. Narrated by Jill Shellabarger. (Running Time: 1 hr. 12 mins. 6 sec.). (What the Bible Says Ser.). 2008. audio compact disk 9.99 (978-1-59859-416-4(8)) Oasis Audio.

Raising Cooperative & Self-Confident Children: A Step-By-Step Guide for Conscious Parenting. Francine C. Beauvoir. Read by Francine C. Beauvoir. Read by Bruce Crapuchettes. 2 cass. (Running Time: 2 hrs.). 1998. (978-0-9667298-1-8(1)) Pasadena Pr.
A guide to parents to create & sustain connection with children which will prevent wounding.

Raising Dragons. Bryan Davis. Read by Peter Sandon. (Dragons in Our Midst Ser.). (ENG.). (YA). (gr. 7). 2009. 64.99 (978-1-60812-768-9(0)) Find a World.

Raising Dragons. unabr. ed. Bryan Davis. (Dragons in Our Midst Ser.). (ENG.). (YA). 2007. 10.49 (978-1-60814-350-4(3)) Oasis Audio.

Raising Dragons. unabr. ed. Bryan Davis. Narrated by Peter Sandon. (Running Time: 9 hrs. 46 mins. 20 sec.). (Dragons in Our Midst Ser.). (ENG.). (YA). 2009. audio compact disk 39.99 (978-1-59859-490-4(7)) Oasis Audio.

Raising Free & Happy Children. Peter Breggin. 1 cass. (Running Time: 1 hr. 1 min.). 11.95 (390) J Norton Pubs.
Peter Breggins outlines a revolutionary alternative to traditional views of parent-child relations. Suggesting neither regimentation nor permissiveness.

Raising Girls. 2 CDs. 2005. audio compact disk 17.00 (978-1-933207-07-0(8)) Ransomed Heart.

***Raising Girls.** unabr. ed. Melissa Trevathan & Sissy Goff. (Running Time: 8 hrs. 33 mins. 23 sec.). (ENG.). 2009. 12.99 (978-0-310-77189-0(7)) Zondervan.

Raising God's Children Alone. Rebecca Israel Tabb. (ENG.). 2006. audio compact disk 24.95 (978-0-9779771-0-9(2)) Ezekiel Pr VA.

Raising Good Kids. unabr. ed. Kenneth Livingston. Read by Kenneth Livingston. 1 cass. (Running Time: 1 hr. 30 min.). 1996. 14.95 (978-1-57724-008-2(1), Pmcpal Srce Audio) Objectivist Ctr.
Discussion about what parents & teachers can do to encourage the growth of virtue in children, even before children have acquired explicit moral concepts.

Raising Gorillas in Zoos. Hosted by Nancy Pearlman. 1 cass. (Running Time: 29 min.). 10.00 (1032) Educ Comm CA.

Raising Great Kids. unabr. ed. Henry Cloud & John Townsend. 1 cass. 1999. 17.99 (978-0-310-22572-0(8)) Zondervan.

Raising Great Kids: A Comprehensive Guide to Parenting with Grace & Truth. abr. ed. Henry Cloud & John Townsend. (Running Time: 1 hr. 0 mins. 0 sec.). (ENG.). 2003. 10.99 (978-0-310-26091-2(4)) Zondervan.

Raising Healthy Children in a Toxic World: Vol. 1. Speeches. Judit M. E. Rajhathy. Read by Judit M. E. Rajhathy. Ed. by Francis G. Mitchell & William Oulton. Des. by Francis G. Mitchell. Engineer William Oulton. Photos by Florian Kutchurean. 1. (Running Time: 90 mins.). Dramatization. 1999. 8.95 (978-1-895814-06-4(5), NWP113) NewWorld Pub CAN.

Raising Kids in Really Scary Times. abr. ed. Steve Bell & Valerie Bell. 1 cass. (Running Time: 1 hr.). 2003. audio compact disk 11.99 (978-1-58926-283-6(2), BE01-0216) Oasis Audio.

Raising Kids in Really Scary Times. unabr. ed. Steve Bell & Valerie Bell. 1 cass. (Running Time: 1 hr.). (Rapid Response Ser.). 2002. 8.99 (978-1-58926-059-7(7)) Oasis Audio.
Offers parents faith-based tools to help them teach their kids.

Raising Ourseves to the Bar Book on CD: Practical Advice & Encouragement for the Next Generation of Missionaries & Their Parents. Brad Wicox & Russell Wilcox. (YA). 2007. audio compact disk 15.95 (978-1-59038-833-4(X)) Deseret Bk.

Raising Positive Kids In a Negative World. Zig Ziglar. Read by Zig Ziglar. 6 cass. (Running Time: 9 hrs.). 1986. bk. 59.95 (978-1-56207-206-3(4)) Zig Ziglar Corp.
Zig offers practical pointers on how to help your child develop a healthy self-image & how to help your child avoid drugs.

Raising Sweetness. Diane Stanley. Illus. by G Brain Karas. (Running Time: 18 mins.). 2003. audio compact disk 12.95 (978-1-59112-493-1(X)) Live Oak Media.

Raising Sweetness. Diane Stanley. Illus. by G Brain Karas. (Running Time: 18 mins.). (J). 2003. 9.95 (978-1-59112-264-7(3)) Live Oak Media.

Raising Sweetness. Diane Stanley. Read by Tom Bodett. 11 vols. (Running Time: 18 mins.). (J). 2003. bk. 25.95 (978-1-59112-266-1(X)); bk. 28.95 (978-1-59112-516-7(2)); pap. bk. 16.95 (978-1-59112-265-4(1)) Pub: Live Oak Media. Dist(s): AudioGO

Raising Sweetness. Diane Stanley. Illus. by Diane Stanley. Read by Tom Bodett. 14 vols. (Running Time: 18 mins.). (J). 2003. pap. bk. 37.95 (978-1-59112-267-8(8)) Live Oak Media.

Raising the Bar. Mark Crow. 5 cass. (Running Time: 7 hrs. 30 mins.). 2002. (978-1-931537-31-5(3)) Vision Comm Creat.

Raising the Bar: Missionaries to Match the Message. Ed J. Pinegar. 2004. 9.95 (978-1-59156-242-9(2)); audio compact disk 11.95 (978-1-59156-243-6(0)) Covenant Comms.

***Raising the Dead: A Doctor Encounters the Miraculous.** unabr. ed. Chauncey W. Crandall, IV. Narrated by Chauncey W. Crandall, IV. Narrated by Wes Bleed. (Running Time: 5 hrs. 28 mins. 28 sec.). (ENG.). 2010. 16.09 (978-1-60814-752-6(5)); audio compact disk 22.99 (978-1-59859-775-2(2)) Oasis Audio.

Raising the Flag on Iwo Jima. As told by John Faber. (Running Time: 1 hr. 17 mins.). 2002. audio compact disk 19.95 (978-0-9714769-7-4(7)) Wizard Acdmy.
On July 1, 2002, a mysterious time capsule that had been launched from the past landed at Wizard Academy. I came to find out it had been launched on March 24, 1957, by John Faber, the National Press Photographers archivist, and Joe Rosenthal, the photographer who took the world's most celebrated photograph. Miraculously, the flat, round metal can contained an extremely fragile, reel-to-reel tape labeled, 'Iwo Jima Flag Raising - Joe Rosenthal interviewed by John Faber on 3-24-57 in Washington, DC.' You can imagine my excitement when my Audio Production Manager came back to me with a digitally remastered CD of the original recording that nobody had heard since the day it was recorded nearly half a century ago. The Battle of Iwo Jima raged for 36 days, yet Joe Rosenthal managed to capture it perfectly in a single moment of accidental magic. The Wizard's curiosity about that magical moment led to him finding a magical time capsule on his desktop. And because you share that same curiosity, he is delighted to share the "accidental magic" with you.

Raising the Odds for Responsible Behavior. 1 CD. (Running Time: 60 mins). 2002. audio compact disk 13.95 (978-1-930429-24-6(X)) Pub: Love Logic. Dist(s): Penton Overseas

Raising the Odds for Responsible Behavior. Jim Fay. Read by Jim Fay. 1 cass. (Running Time: 65 mins.). 1998. 11.95 (978-0-944634-36-3(2)) Pub: Love Logic. Dist(s): Penton Overseas
Shares practical, easy-to-use techniques to raise the odds that children will grow up to be independent, responsible decision-makers who believe they have the power to solve their own problems.

Raising the Peaceable Kingdom. Jeffrey Moussaieff Masson. Read by Tim Jerome. 3 cass. 29.95 (978-0-7927-3778-0(4), CSL 855); audio compact disk 49.95 (978-0-7927-3779-7(2), SLD 855) AudioGO.

Raising the Probability of Change: Susan Hite's Train Your Brain Series, Vol. 2. Susan Hite. 1 CD. (Running Time: 56). 2002. audio compact disk 15.00 (978-1-890123-55-0(2)) Media Cnslts.
Learn to be in control of your responses to things you can't change - and focus on what is in your control that can raise the probability of change in yourself and in others.

Raising up a Family to the Lord. Gene R. Cook. 2 CDs. 2004. audio compact disk 14.95 (978-1-59038-391-9(5)) Deseret Bk.
How can you teach your family with the Spirit of the Lord? How can you reach a wayward child? How can you hold more effective, enjoyable family home evenings? In Raising Up a Family to the Lord, Elder Cook teaches parents how to counter the destructive forces in the world we live in and explains how children can be taught to love the Lord.

Raising up Sons. Patricia Morgan. 1 cass. 6.00 (978-1-56043-373-6(6)) Destiny Image Pubs.

Raising Your Self-Esteem. Nathaniel Branden. 1 cass. (Running Time: 34 min.). 1989. 10.95 (857) J Norton Pubs.
Is lack of self-esteem keeping you from achieving your highest potential? Branden discusses raising your self-esteem. An innovative, extraordinarily powerful vehicle for personal growth.

Raising Your Self-Esteem. John Gray. 2 cass. (Running Time: 2 hrs.). 1996. 17.95 (978-1-886095-14-4(0)) Genesis Media Grp.

Raising Your Self-Esteem (audio CD) Nathaniel Branden. (ENG.). 2007. audio compact disk 12.95 (978-1-57970-468-1(9), Audio-For) J Norton Pubs.

***Raising Your Spirited Child.** abr. ed. Mary Sheedy Kurcinka. Read by Mary Sheedy Kurcinka. (ENG.). 2005. (978-0-06-112049-7(9), Harper Audio); (978-0-06-112048-0(0), Harper Audio) HarperCollins Pubs.

***Raisins & Almonds.** Kerry Greenwood. Read by Stephanie Daniel. (Running Time: 6 hrs. 55 mins.). (Phryne Fisher Mystery: Ser.). 2009. 69.99 (978-1-74214-559-4(0), 9781742145594) Pub: Bolinda Pubng AUS. Dist(s): Bolinda Pub Inc

Raisins & Almonds. unabr. ed. Kerry Greenwood. Read by Stephanie Daniel. (Running Time: 6 hrs. 55 mins.). (Phryne Fisher Ser.). 2009. audio compact disk 77.95 (978-1-74214-144-2(7), 9781742141442) Pub: Bolinda Pubng AUS. Dist(s): Bolinda Pub Inc

Raj. unabr. ed. Gita Mehta. Read by Nadia May. 12 cass. (Running Time: 17 hrs. 30 mins.). 2003. 83.95 (978-0-7861-1608-9(0), 2436) Blckstn Audio.
Remarkable story of a woman of royal birth coming of age during India's fight for independence. With rare grace & narrative flair, Mehta lays bare the complexities of Indian culture & tradition as few foreigners ever experience them.

Raj. unabr. ed. Gita Mehta. Read by Nadia May. (Running Time: 16 hrs. 30 mins.). 1999. 44.95 (978-0-7861-2222-6(6)) Blckstn Audio.

Raj. unabr. ed. Gita Mehta. Read by Nadia May. (Running Time: 59400 sec.). 2008. audio compact disk 44.95 (978-1-4332-4531-2(0)); audio compact disk & audio compact disk 110.00 (978-1-4332-4530-5(2)) Blckstn Audio.

Raja Yoga. (197) Yoga Res Foun.

Raja Yoga. Swami Jyotirmayananda. 1 cass. (Running Time: 1 hr.). 1990. 12.99 Yoga Res Foun.

Raja Yoga: Patanjalis Yoga Aphorisms. unabr. ed. Vivekananda. Read by Bidyut Bose. 4 cass. (Running Time: 4 hrs. 30 min.). 1993. 30.00 Set. (978-1-882915-00-2(3)) Vedanta Ctr Atlanta.
Yoga aphorisms of Patanjalis with commentary by Vivekananda. Patanjali, second century AD, covers psychology of mind & spiritual practice.

Raja Yoga & Prana Science. Swami Amar Jyoti. 1 cass. 1990. 9.95 (O-31) Truth Consciousness.
The mystic science of Prana (life force). The path of Raja Yoga, regulation & control of Prana.

Raja Yoga Retreat: A Four CD Set. Speeches. Swami Sridharananda. 4 cds. 2006. audio compact disk 29.95 (978-0-87481-371-5(9)) Vedanta Pr.

Raja Yoga, Science of the Self. Swami Amar Jyoti. 2 cass. 1987. 12.95 (P-50) Truth Consciousness.
Contemplation, concentration, meditation. Achieving balance & harmony. Mastery of self, control of destiny. No detail of life is insignificant. Purification of senses & emotions.

Rajah & the Big Blue Ball. Mosetta Penick Phillips-Cermak. Narrated by Stacy Stewart. Voice by Nina Glover. Music by Marc Gordon. (ENG.). (J). 2009. audio compact disk (978-0-9817777-5-7(9)) PM Moon Pubs.

Rajan & Sajan Mishra (Vocal), Vol. 1. Music by Rajan Mishra & Sajan Mishra. 1 cass. (Music Today Presents Ser.). 1992. (A92030) Multi-Cultural Bks.

Rajan & Sajan Mishra (Vocal), Vol. 2. Music by Rajan Mishra & Sajan Mishra. 1 cass. (Music Today Presents Ser.). 1992. (A92031) Multi-Cultural Bks.

Rajasthan, Vol. 1. Music by Langas & Manganiars. 1 cass. 1993. (F93001); audio compact disk (CD F93001) Multi-Cultural Bks.

Rajasthan, Vol. 2. Music by Langas & Manganiars. 1 cass. 1993. (F93002) Multi-Cultural Bks.

Raji Yoga: Two Lesson Course. (Running Time: 1 hr.). 12.99 (613) Yoga Res Foun.

Rake's Vow. Stephanie Laurens. Narrated by Simon Prebble. 10 cass. (Running Time: 14 hrs.). (Cynster Family Ser.: Bk. 2). 88.00 (978-0-7887-9605-0(4)) Recorded Bks.

Rakkety Tam. Brian Jacques. Narrated by Brian Jacques. 9 cass. (Running Time: 12 hrs.). (Redwall Ser.). (J). 2004. 79.75 (978-1-4193-0854-3(8)) Recorded Bks.

Rakkety Tam. unabr. ed. Brian Jacques. 11 CDs. (Running Time: 12 Hrs). (Redwall Ser.). (J). (gr. 3-6). 2004. audio compact disk 29.99 (978-1-4193-1243-4(X)) Recorded Bks.

Rakoff. abr. ed. David Fraud. 1 CD. (Running Time: 1 hr. 30 mins.). 2001. audio compact disk 21.95 (Random AudioBks) Random Audio Pubg.
"This American Life," clever parodies & other pieces created for Salon & new essays inspired by Rakoff's most recent adventures as a peripatetic reporter. The deep-seated belief that he is a fraud lends both a hilarious edge & a whimsical poignancy to Rakoff's writing.

Rally Cry. William R. Forstchen. Read by Patrick G. Lawlor. (Running Time: 55800 sec.). (Lost Regiment Ser.). 2006. 85.95 (978-0-7861-4505-8(6)); audio compact disk 99.00 (978-0-7861-7199-6(5)) Blckstn Audio.

Rally Cry. unabr. ed. William R. Forstchen. Read by Patrick G. Lawlor. (Running Time: 55800 sec.). (Lost Regiment Ser.). 2006. audio compact disk 29.95 (978-0-7861-7658-8(X)) Blckstn Audio.

Rallying Support for Success. Ratanjit. Contrib. by Raymond C Somich Sr. (Running Time: 3395 sec.). (Stress-Free Living Ser.). 2007. audio compact disk 17.90 (978-1-59076-250-9(9)) DscvrHlpPubng.

Ralph Carmichael & Friends Live. Perf. by Dave Boyer et al. 1997. (978-0-7601-1141-3(3), C50026) Brentwood Music.
Features big band gospel.

Ralph Richardson Reads Blake. Ralph Richardson. 1 cass. 10.95 (ECN 213) J Norton Pubs.
Richardson chose these poems himself & talks about each one, offering his views on their meaning & rich symbolism.

Ralph S Mouse. 3 CDs. 2004. audio compact disk 29.95 (978-0-7882-0983-3(3)) Weston Woods.

Ralph S. Mouse. Beverly Cleary. (Mouse & the Motorcycle Ser.). (J). 1985. 21.33 (978-0-676-30537-1(7)) SRA McGraw.

Ralph S. Mouse. unabr. ed. Beverly Cleary. Read by Stockard Channing. 2 cass. (Running Time: 3 hrs.). (Listening Library). (J). 1999. 17.95 (L178) Blckstn Audio.
When Ralph, the world's smartest mouse, learns that his old friend Matt - the bellhop at the Mountain View Inn - is about to lose his job because of mice in the hotel, he gets the housekeeper's son to take him to school with him.

Ralph S. Mouse. unabr. ed. Beverly Cleary. Read by William Roberts. 2 cass. (Running Time: 2 hrs. 5 mins.). (Mouse & the Motorcycle Ser.). (J). 2000. 18.00 (978-0-7366-9085-0(9)) Books on Tape.

***Ralph S. Mouse.** unabr. ed. Beverly Cleary. Read by B. D. Wong. (ENG.). 2007. (978-0-06-137379-4(6)); (978-0-06-137378-7(8)) HarperCollins Pubs.

Ralph S. Mouse. unabr. ed. Beverly Cleary. Read by B. D. Wong. (Running Time: 7200 sec.). (Mouse & the Motorcycle Ser.). (J). (gr. 4-7). 2007. audio compact disk 15.95 (978-0-06-128427-4(0), HarperChildAud) HarperCollins Pubs.

Ralph S. Mouse. unabr. ed. Beverly Cleary. Read by William Roberts. 2 cass. (Running Time: 2 hrs. 4 mins.). (Mouse & the Motorcycle Ser.). (J). (gr. 3-7). 1995. 23.00 (978-0-8072-7546-7(8), YA879CX, Listening Lib) Random Audio Pubg.
There are some amazing things happening at the Mountain View Inn, not the least of which is Ralph, driving a Laser XL7 sports car! Tune in as Ralph takes off on another exciting adventure!.

Ralph S. Mouse. unabr. ed. Beverly Cleary. Narrated by William Roberts. 2 vols. (Running Time: 2 hrs. 4 mins.). (Mouse & the Motorcycle Ser.). (J). (gr. 3-7). 1996. pap. bk. 29.00 (978-0-8072-7547-4(6), YA879SP, Listening Lib) Random Audio Pubg.

Ralph Salisbury. unabr. ed. Read by Ralph Salisbury. 1 cass. (Running Time: 29 min.). 1985. 10.00 New Letters.
Ralph Salisbury talks about his Native American Heritage & reads both poetry & fiction.

Ralph the Magic Rabbit. Adam Frost. Read by PH.D., Daniel Hill. (Running Time: 5280 sec.). (J). (gr. 1-4). 2007. audio compact disk 21.95 (978-1-4056-5607-8(7)) AudioGo GBR.

Ralph Vince: The New Role of Technical Analysis. Read by Ralph Vince. 1 cass. 30.00 Dow Jones Telerate.
Ralph will discuss money management by looking at the near future as a series of scenarios. These scenarios can then be mathematically processed

on a computer to dictate what the consequences of our actions are as they pertain to money management.

Ralph Waldo Emerson see Twentieth-Century Poetry in English, No. 2, Recordings of Poets Reading Their Own Poetry

Ralph Waldo Emerson: His Life Story. (DD8840) Natl Recrd Co.

Ralph Waldo Emerson: Idealist. Joseph Schiffman. 1 cass. (Running Time: 20 min.). (Six American Authors Ser.). 1968. 11.95 (23033) J Norton Pubs.
Describes the characteristic themes & style of expression of Emerson, his influence upon his contemporaries & his relevance to our time.

Ralph Waldo Emerson: Poems & Essays. Ralph Waldo Emerson. Read by Kenneth S. Lynn. 1 cass. Incl. American Scholar. (SAC 842); Concord Hymn. (SAC 842); Each & All. (SAC 842); Education & Politics. (SAC 842); Nature. (SAC 842); Rhodora. (SAC 842); Snow-Storm. (SAC 842); 10.95 (978-0-8045-0842-1(9), SAC 842) Spoken Arts.
Includes Each & All; The Rhodora; Concord Hymn; Snow-Storm; Nature.

Ralph Waldo Emerson: Selected Essays. unabr. ed. Ralph Waldo Emerson. Read by Jim Killavey. 7 cass. (Running Time: 10 hrs.). 1987. 49.95 (978-0-7861-0608-0(5), 2098) Blckstn Audio.
These essays are radiant with sensitivity & wonder.

Ralph Waldo Emerson: Selected Essays. unabr. ed. Ralph Waldo Emerson. Read by Jim Killavey. 7 cass. (Running Time: 10 hrs. 30 min.). 1989. 49.00 (C-185) Jimcin Record.
Emerson's most famous essays.

Ralph Waldo Emerson: Selected Essays. unabr. collector's ed. Ralph Waldo Emerson. Read by Jim Killavey. 7 cass. (Running Time: 10 hrs. 30 mins.). 1988. 56.00 (978-0-7366-3941-5(1), 9185) Books on Tape.
Argues that nature was God speaking to man; or that wisdom & knowledge flowed from an active, not just a contemplative life; or that society might be hostile to new ideas just out of cussedness rather than conviction.

Ralphie the Gopher. Rich Stim. 1 CD. (Running Time: 3540 sec.). (J). (gr. k-6). 2006. audio compact disk 12.95 (978-1-933781-05-1(X)) TallTales Aud.

***Ralph's Children.** Hilary Norman. 2010. 61.95 (978-1-4079-0687-4(9)); audio compact disk 71.95 (978-1-4079-0688-1(7)) Pub: Soundings Ltd GBR. Dist(s): Ulverscroft US

Ram Dass Audio Collection. Ram Dass. 2007. audio compact disk 39.95 (978-1-59179-512-4(5)) Sounds True.

Ram in the Well. June Knox-Mawer. Narrated by June Knox-Mawer. 6 cass. (Running Time: 6 hrs. 15 mins.). 56.00 (978-1-84197-421-7(8)) Recorded Bks.

Ram Rajya: In Search of Democracy. unabr. ed. Julian C. Hollick. 1 cass. (Running Time: 60 min.). (Passages to India Ser.). 1991. 15.00 (978-1-56709-021-5(4), 1021) Indep Broadcast.
Democracy in India would appear to be totally at odds with social rigidities & caste hierarchies, & democratic institutions have been subjected to severe abuse in recent years. Yet, against all odds, India remains a vibrant, if wounded, democracy.

Rama, unabr. ed. Jamake Highwater. Narrated by George Guidall. 4 cass. (Running Time: 5 hrs. 45 mins.). (YA). (gr. 7). 1997. 35.00 (94600E7) Recorded Bks.
With non-stop action, powerful superheroes & evil monsters, this is an exciting introduction to the richness of "The Ramayana." Highwater breathes new life into the ancient literary traditions of India.

Rama, Vol. 1. Music by Bhimsen Joshi et al. 1 cass. (Bhaktimala Ser.). 1992. (D92007); audio compact disk (CD D92007) Multi-Cultural Bks.

Rama, Vol. 2. Music by Rajan Mishra et al. 1 cass. (Bhaktimala Ser.). 1992. (D92008); audio compact disk (CD D92008) Multi-Cultural Bks.

Ramage Hawk. unabr. ed. John Pilkington. Read by Peter Wickham. 7 cass. 2008. 61.95 (978-1-84559-474-9(6)) Pub: Soundings Ltd GBR. Dist(s): Ulverscroft US

Ramayana. Sri Valmiki. Read by Amala-bhakta. 10 cass. (Running Time: 15 hrs.). 39.00 Incl. 1 vinyl album. Bhaktivedanta.
Portrays ideals - the ideal husband, wife, brother, friend & servant - under the most trying, if not overwhelming, circumstances.

Ramayana. abr. ed. Read by Ram Dass. Retold by William Buck. 3 cass. (Running Time: 4 hrs. 30 mi.). (Spiritual Classics on Cassette Ser.). 1991. 23.95 (978-0-944993-32-3(X)) Audio Lit.
This captivating Indian epic, created over 2000 years ago by the poet Valmiki, relates the eternal struggle between good and evil.

Ramayana of Valmiki. Tr. by N. Raghunathan. Prod. by Vedic Audio Knowledge (VAK). Voice by Michael Sternfeld. Directed By Michael Sternfeld. Voice by Richard Ross & Stephen White. (ENG.). 2007. (978-0-9822716-0-5(3)); (978-0-9822716-1-2(1)) Vedic Audio.

Ramayana of Valmiki, Vol. I. Tr. by N. Raghunathan. Prod. by Vedic Audio Knowledge (VAK). Voice by Michael Sternfeld. Directed By Michael Sternfeld. Voice by Richard Ross & Stephen White. (ENG.). 1998. 79.00 (978-0-9822716-2-9(X)) Vedic Audio.

Ramayana of Valmiki, Vol. II. Tr. by N. Raghunathan. Prod. by Vedic Audio Knowledge (VAK). Voice by Michael Sternfeld. Directed By Michael Sternfeld. Voice by Richard Ross & Stephen White. 2001. 79.00 (978-0-9822716-3-6(8)) Vedic Audio.

Ramayana of Valmiki, Vol. III. Tr. by N. Raghunathan. Prod. by Vedic Audio Knowledge (VAK). Voice by Michael Sternfeld. Directed By Michael Sternfeld. Voice by Richard Ross & Stephen White. (ENG.). 2003. 79.00 (978-0-9822716-4-3(6)) Vedic Audio.

Ramayana Within Us. Swami Amar Jyoti. 1 cass. 1987. 9.95 (K101) Truth Consciousness.
The Avatar & those he brings, parts of our being. The search for wholesomeness, integration. Rama Rajya, earth's hightest kingdom. Beauty of creation. The secret of darkness.

Ramble to Cashel-Celtic Fingerstyle Guitar Solos. Compiled by Stefan Grossman. 1999. pap. bk. 19.95 (978-0-7866-4494-0(X), 97241BCD) Mel Bay.

Ramblin' Perf. by Lucinda Williams. Anno. by John Morthland. Prod. by Tom Royals. 1 cass. (Running Time: 43 min.). 1991. (0-9307-400420-93); audio compact disk (0-9307) Smithsonian Folkways.

Rambling 'Round Brenham. Pamela G. McBride. 1 cass. (Running Time: 45 min.). 1994. 9.95 (978-0-9640993-1-9(4)) Miles to Go.
Travel.

Rambos Collection. Dottie Rambo. 1 cass. (Running Time: 30 mins.). 1998. 16.99 (978-0-7601-2120-7(6)); audio compact disk 19.99 (978-0-7601-2121-4(4)) Provident Mus Dist.

Ramhta, LOVE & RELATIONSHIPS see Ramtha, el AMOR Y LAS RELACIONES

Rammer. Short Stories. Larry Niven. Narrated by Pat Bottino. 1 CD. (Running Time: 77 mins). (Great Science Fiction Stories Ser.). 2004. audio compact disk 10.99 (978-1-884612-35-0(0)) AudioText.

Rammer. unabr. ed. Larry Niven. Read by Pat Bottino. Ed. by Allan Kaster. 1 cass. (Running Time: 1 hr. 20 min.). (Great Science Fiction Stories Ser.). 1997. 10.99 (978-1-884612-22-0(9)) AudioText.
A man wakes up 200 years after his death in a new body & finds himself serving a manipulative political State as he's training to become a starship pilot.

Rammer Jammer Yellow Hammer: A Journey into the Heart of Fan Mania. unabr. ed. Warren St. John. Read by Michael Kramer. 7 cass. (Running Time: 10 hrs. 30 mins.). 2004. 72.00 (978-1-4159-0341-4(7)) Books on Tape.
A native of Alabama returns to his roots to explore the realm of mania and fanaticism through the prism of the Alabama college football team.

Ramo. Phyllis Holly. 1 cass. (Running Time: 38 min). (Ramo the Elephant Ser.). (J). 1992. 10.95 (978-1-884877-01-8(X)) Creat Mats Lib.

Ramo Song Story Reading Book. Phyllis U. Hiller. Narrated by Phyllis U. Hiller. 1 cass. (Ramo the Elephant Ser.). (SPA.). 1995. 10.95 (978-1-884877-04-9(4)) Creat Mats Lib.
Four-star billboard magazine. Children's recording, "outstanding.".

Ramo the Elephant. 2nd ed. Phyllis U. Hiller. Illus. by Sandra Matasick. 2001. audio compact disk 14.95 (978-1-884877-16-2(8)) Creat Mats Lib.

Ramona. Helen Hunt Jackson. Read by Anais 9000. 2009. 33.95 (978-1-60112-242-1(X)) Babblebooks.

Ramona. unabr. ed. Helen Hunt Jackson. Read by Flo Gibson. 10 cass. (Running Time: 15 hrs.). 1992. 44.95 (978-1-55685-239-8(8)) Audio Bk Con.
An historical novel dealing with Spanish & Indian life in California & the plight of Ramona, who elopes with Alessandro, a Temecula Indian. Wherever they go, the United States government confiscates their land & the proud Alessandro comes to a tragic end.

Ramona: The Heart & Conscience of Early California. abr. ed. Helen Hunt Jackson. Read by Boots Martin. 4 cass. (Running Time: 6 hrs.). 2004. 19.95 (978-1-57270-007-9(6), M40007) Pub: Audio Partners. Dist(s): PerseuPGW
Now in its 112th year of continuous print publication, this extraordinarily popular novel weaves romance, history, & a passionate protest against the oppression of Native Americans in the 1800s.

Ramona & Her Father. Beverly Cleary. Read by Stockard Channing. 2 cass. (Running Time: 2 hrs. 10 mins.). (Ramona Quimby Ser.). (J). (gr. 3-5). 2000. 18.00 (978-0-7366-9143-7(X)) Books on Tape.

Ramona & Her Father. unabr. ed. Beverly Cleary. Read by Stockard Channing. 2 cass. (Running Time: 3 hrs.). (Ramona Quimby Ser.). (J). (gr. 3-5). 1999. 23.00 (LL 3192, Chivers Child Audio) AudioGO.

Ramona & Her Father. unabr. ed. Beverly Cleary. Read by Stockard Channing. 2 cass. (Running Time: 3 hrs.). (Ramona Quimby Ser.). (J). (gr. 3-5). 1999. 17.95 (L186) Blckstn Audio.
Things just aren't the same for Ramona since her father lost his job & her mother went to work all day at the doctor's office. Christmas is just around the corner, but with her mother working so late, who will make her costume for the annual church pageant?.

***Ramona & Her Father.** unabr. ed. Beverly Cleary. Read by Stockard Channing. (J). 2010. audio compact disk 14.99 (978-0-06-177407-2(3), HarperChildAud) HarperCollins Pubs.

***Ramona & Her Father.** unabr. ed. Beverly Cleary. Read by Stockard Channing. (ENG.). 2010. (978-0-06-204197-5(5)); (978-0-06-206017-4(1)) HarperCollins Pubs.

Ramona & Her Father. unabr. ed. Beverly Cleary. Read by William Roberts & Stockard Channing. 2 cass. (Running Time: 2 hrs. 7 mins.). (Ramona Quimby Ser.). (J). (gr. 3-7). 1990. 23.00 (978-0-8072-7274-9(4), YA 820 CX, Listening Lib) Random Audio Pubg.

Ramona & Her Mother. Beverly Cleary. Read by Stockard Channing. 2 cass. (Running Time: 2 hrs. 20 mins.). (Ramona Quimby Ser.). (J). (gr. 3-5). 2000. 18.00 (978-0-7366-9147-5(2)) Books on Tape.

Ramona & Her Mother. Beverly Cleary. (Ramona Quimby Ser.). (J). (gr. 3-5). 1979. 21.33 (978-0-394-66099-8(4)) SRA McGraw.

Ramona & Her Mother. unabr. ed. Beverly Cleary. Read by Stockard Channing. 2 cass. (Running Time: 3 hrs.). (Ramona Quimby Ser.). (J). (gr. 3-5). 1999. 23.00 (LL 3072, Chivers Child Audio) AudioGO.

Ramona & Her Mother. unabr. ed. Beverly Cleary. Read by Stockard Channing. 2 cass. (Running Time: 3 hrs.). (Ramona Quimby Ser.). (J). (gr. 3-5). 1999. 17.95 (L185) Blckstn Audio.
Too old to be given the special attention that her naughty little neighbor, Willa Jean, gets, & too young to be included with the adults like Beezus, Ramona doesn't know where she belongs.

***Ramona & Her Mother.** unabr. ed. Beverly Cleary. Read by Stockard Channing. (J). 2010. audio compact disk 14.99 (978-0-06-177409-6(X), HarperChildAud) HarperCollins Pubs.

***Ramona & Her Mother.** unabr. ed. Beverly Cleary. Read by Stockard Channing. (ENG.). 2010. (978-0-06-204198-2(3)); (978-0-06-206018-1(X)) HarperCollins Pubs.

Ramona & Her Mother. unabr. ed. Beverly Cleary. Read by Stockard Channing. 2 vols. (Running Time: 2 hrs. 18 mins.). (Ramona Quimby Ser.). (J). (gr. 3-7). 1989. pap. bk. 29.00 (978-0-8072-7319-7(8), YA815SP, Listening Lib) Random Audio Pubg.
Now that her father has found a job, Ramona hopes that her mother will stop working, & she won't have to stay with Howie's grandmother after school.

Ramona & Her Mother. unabr. ed. Beverly Cleary. Read by William Roberts. 2 cass. (Running Time: 2 hrs. 18 mins.). (Ramona Quimby Ser.). (J). (gr. 3-7). 1989. tchr.'s assessmt. gde. ed. 23.00 (978-0-8072-7259-6(0), YA 815 CX, Listening Lib) Random Audio Pubg.

Ramona & Her Mother. unabr. ed. Beverly Cleary. Read by Stockard Channing. 2 vols. (Running Time: 2 hrs. 7 mins.). (Ramona Quimby Ser.). (J). (gr. 3-7). 1990. pap. bk. 29.00 (978-0-8072-7314-2(7), YA 820 SP, Listening Lib) Random Audio Pubg.

Ramona & Her Mother. unabr. ed. Beverly Cleary. Read by Stockard Channing. (Running Time: 8280 sec.). (Ramona Quimby Ser.). (ENG.). (J). (gr. 2-7). 2007. audio compact disk 12.95 (978-0-7393-3895-7(1), Listening Lib) Pub: Random Audio Pubg. Dist(s): Random

Ramona Forever. unabr. ed. Beverly Cleary. Read by Stockard Channing. 2 cass. (Running Time: 2 hrs. 14 mins.). (Ramona Quimby Ser.). (J). (gr. 3-5). 1999. 23.00 (LL 3073, Chivers Child Audio) AudioGO.

Ramona Forever. unabr. ed. Beverly Cleary. Read by Stockard Channing. 2 cass. (Running Time: 2 hrs, 17 mins.). (Ramona Quimby Ser.). (J). (gr. 3-5). 1999. 17.95 (L184) Blckstn Audio.
For Ramona, it's hard being a grown-up third-grader. When her father worries about finding a teaching job, Ramona worries that she & her family may need to move away if he does. When Aunt Bea announces her wedding plans, Ramona jumps at the chance to be a bridesmaid. And the biggest surprise leads to a case of "siblingitis".

***Ramona Forever.** unabr. ed. Beverly Cleary. Read by Stockard Channing. (J). 2010. audio compact disk 14.99 (978-0-06-177410-2(3), HarperChildAud) HarperCollins Pubs.

***Ramona Forever.** unabr. ed. Beverly Cleary. Read by Stockard Channing. (ENG.). 2010. (978-0-06-206022-8(8)); (978-0-06-206219-2(0)) HarperCollins Pubs.

Ramona Forever. unabr. ed. Beverly Cleary. Read by Stockard Channing. 2 vols. (Running Time: 2 hrs. 14 mins.). (Ramona Quimby Ser.). (J). (gr. 3-7). 1988. pap. bk. 29.00 (978-0-8072-7318-0(X), YA817SP, Listening Lib) Random Audio Pubg.
Things are changing fast in the Quimbey house. For Ramona, it's hard enough being a grown-up third-grader. Her father is worried about finding a teaching job, & Ramona worries about where they'll move if he does find one.

Ramona Forever. unabr. ed. Beverly Cleary. Read by William Roberts. 2 cass. (Running Time: 2 hrs. 14 mins.). (Ramona Quimby Ser.). (J). (gr. 3-7). 1988. 23.00 (978-0-8072-7265-7(5), YA 817 CX, Listening Lib) Random Audio Pubg.

Ramona Quimby. Beverly Cleary. Read by Stockard Channing. 2 cass. (Running Time: 2 hrs. 5 mins.). (Ramona Quimby Ser.). (J). (gr. 3-5). 2000. 18.00 (978-0-7366-9082-9(4)) Books on Tape.

Ramona Quimby. unabr. ed. Beverly Cleary. Read by Stockard Channing. 2 cass. (Running Time: 3 hrs.). (Ramona Quimby Ser.). (J). (gr. 3-5). 1999. 17.95 (L182) Blckstn Audio.
Life is rough at the Quimby house, with Mrs. Quimby forced to work so that Mr. Quimby can go to college. But now that Ramona is eight, she can do many things she's never done before - like go to a new school with a new teacher & ride the bus, all by herself. In the end Ramona, & all the Quimbys, pull through the hard times.

***Ramona Quimby.** unabr. ed. Beverly Cleary. Read by Stockard Channing. (J). 2010. audio compact disk 14.99 (978-0-06-177417-1(0), HarperChildAud) HarperCollins Pubs.

Ramona Quimby. unabr. ed. Beverly Cleary. Read by Stockard Channing. 2 cass. (Running Time: 2 hrs. 5 min.). (Ramona Quimby Ser.). (J). (gr. 3-5). 1990. 15.95 (YA 816 CXR, Listening Lib) Random Audio Pubg.

Ramona Quimby. unabr. ed. Beverly Cleary. Read by William Roberts. 2 cass. (Running Time: 2 hrs. 5 mins.). (Ramona Quimby Ser.). (J). (gr. 3-7). 1990. 23.00 (978-0-8072-7262-6(0), YA 816 CX, Listening Lib) Random Audio Pubg.

Ramona Quimby. unabr. ed. Beverly Cleary. Read by Stockard Channing. 2 vols. (Running Time: 2 hrs. 5 mins.). (Ramona Quimby Ser.). (J). (gr. 3-7). 1989. pap. bk. 29.00 (978-0-8072-7320-3(1), YA816SP, Listening Lib) Random Audio Pubg.

Ramona Quimby. unabr. ed. Beverly Cleary. Read by Stockard Channing. 2 CDs. (Running Time: 2 hrs. 5 mins.). (Middle Grade Cassette Librariestm Ser.). (J). (gr. 3-7). 2004. audio compact disk 20.40 (978-0-8072-1613-2(5), S YA 816 CD, Listening Lib) Pub: Rand[illegible] Audio Pubg. Dist(s): NetLibrary CO

***Ramona Quimby, Age 8.** unabr. ed. Bev[illegible]eary. Read by Stockard Channing. (ENG.). 2010. (978-0-06-204[illegible]-9(1)); (978-0-06-206019-8(8)) HarperCollins Pubs.

Ramona Quimby Series. unabr. ed. Beverly Cleary. Read by Stockard Channing. 7 cass. (Running Time: 10 hrs. 30 min.). (J). (gr. 4-7). 1996. 45.00 (978-0-7366-3426-7(6), 4071) Books on Tape.
At age 8, Ramona can do a lot by herself: ride the bus, go to a new school - even babysit her little sister. It's a good thing, because her folks need her to pitch in; mother's gone to work. Can Ramona put up with a bratty four year-old, a taste of her own medicine?.

Ramona the Brave. unabr. ed. Beverly Cleary. Read by Stockard Channing. 2 cass. (Running Time: 2 hrs.). (Ramona Quimby Ser.). (J). (gr. 3-5). 1997. 23.00 (LL 3181, Chivers Child Audio) AudioGO.

Ramona the Brave. unabr. ed. Beverly Cleary. Read by Stockard Channing. 2 cass. (Running Time: 3 hrs.). (Ramona Quimby Ser.). (J). (gr. 3-5). 1999. 17.95 (L183) Blckstn Audio.
The Quimbys decide to build a new bedroom for Ramona & Mrs. Quimby takes a job to help pay for it. Ramona misses having her Mom, & her new room seems dark & scary. Then on her first day of school, the first-grade class laughs at her story about the house with the "chopped-out hole" & classmate Susan copies her special art project.

***Ramona the Brave.** unabr. ed. Beverly Cleary. Read by Stockard Channing. (J). 2010. audio compact disk 14.99 (978-0-06-177411-9(1), HarperChildAud) HarperCollins Pubs.

***Ramona the Brave.** unabr. ed. Beverly Cleary. Read by Stockard Channing. (ENG.). 2010. (978-0-06-204200-2(9)); (978-0-06-206020-4(1)) HarperCollins Pubs.

Ramona the Brave. unabr. ed. Beverly Cleary. Read by Stockard Channing. 2 vols. (Running Time: 2 hrs. 26 mins.). (Ramona Quimby Ser.). (J). (gr. 3-7). 1990. pap. bk. 29.00 (978-0-8072-7315-9(5), YA 821 SP, Listening Lib) Random Audio Pubg.

Ramona the Brave. unabr. ed. Beverly Cleary. Read by William Roberts. 2 cass. (Running Time: 2 hrs. 26 mins.). (Ramona Quimby Ser.). (J). (gr. 3-7). 1990. 23.00 (978-0-8072-7277-0(9), YA 821 CX, Listening Lib) Random Audio Pubg.

Ramona the Brave & Ramona Quimby, Age 8. unabr. ed. Beverly Cleary. Read by Stockard Channing. (Running Time: 4 hrs. 24 mins.). (Ramona Quimby Ser.). (ENG.). (J). (gr. 2-5). 2007. audio compact disk 19.95 (978-0-7393-4914-4(7), Listening Lib) Pub: Random Audio Pubg. Dist(s): Random

Ramona the Pest. Beverly Cleary. Read by Stockard Channing. 6 CDs. (Running Time: 2 hrs. 40 mins.). (Ramona Quimby Ser.). (J). (gr. 3-5). 2000. audio compact disk 32.00 (978-0-7366-9145-1(6)) Books on Tape.

Ramona the Pest. unabr. ed. Beverly Cleary. Read by Stockard Channing. 2 cass. (Running Time: 2 hrs.). (Ramona Quimby Ser.). (J). (gr. 3-5). 1997. 23.00 (LL 3152, Chivers Child Audio) AudioGO.

Ramona the Pest. unabr. ed. Beverly Cleary. Read by Stockard Channing. 2 cass. (Running Time: 3 hrs.). (Ramona Quimby Ser.). (J). (gr. 3-5). 1999. 17.95 (L180) Blckstn Audio.
This is the day Ramona starts kindergarten...the day she will learn to read & write & start to catch up with her older sister, Beezus. But little Susan - with the beautiful boing-boing curls - is just too bossy. When she calls Ramona a pest, it's more than Ramona can bear. It's almost enough to make her the world's first Kindergarten drop-out.

***Ramona the Pest.** unabr. ed. Beverly Cleary. Read by Stockard Channing. (J). 2010. audio compact disk 14.99 (978-0-06-177408-9(1), HarperChildAud) HarperCollins Pubs.

***Ramona the Pest.** unabr. ed. Beverly Cleary. Read by Stockard Channing. (ENG.). 2010. (978-0-06-206021-1(X)); (978-0-06-204201-9(7)) HarperCollins Pubs.

Ramona the Pest. unabr. ed. Beverly Cleary. Read by Stockard Channing. 2 cass. (Running Time: 2 hrs. 36 mins.). (Ramona Quimby Ser.). (J). (gr. 3-5). 1991. pap. bk. 28.00 (978-0-8072-7316-6(3), YA 819SP, Listening Lib) Random Audio Pubg.

Ramona the Pest - Ramona Forever. unabr. ed. Beverly Cleary. Read by Stockard Channing. (Running Time: 4 hrs. 50 mins.). (Ramona Quimby

Ser.). (ENG.). (J). (gr. 2-7). 2007. audio compact disk 19.95 (978-0-7393-3903-9(6), Listening Lib) Pub: Random Audio Pubg. Dist(s): Random

Ramona's World. Beverly Cleary. Read by Stockard Channing. 2 cass. (Running Time: 3 hrs.). (Ramona Quimby Ser.). (J). (gr. 3-5). 2000. 18.00 (5163) Books on Tape.
Now in the fourth grade, Ramona is adjusting to life as a big sister to baby Roberta, finding out what it means to have a best friend & experiencing the very first twinges of romance with her old buddy, Yard Ape.

Ramona's World. Beverly Cleary. 3 cass. (Running Time: 177 min.). (Ramona Quimby Ser.). (J). (gr. 3-5). 2001. audio compact disk 28.00 (978-0-8072-0509-9(5), Listening Lib) Random Audio Pubg.

Ramona's World. collector's ed. Beverly Cleary. Read by Stockard Channing. 2 cass. (Running Time: 3 hrs.). (Ramona Quimby Ser.). (J). (gr. 3-5). 1999. 18.00 (978-0-7366-9003-4(4)) Books on Tape.
Miss Quimby is back & she's as feisty as ever. Now in the fourth grade, Ramona is adjusting to life as a big sister to baby Roberta, finding out what it means to have a best friend & experiencing the very first twinges of romance with her old buddy, Yard Ape.

Ramona's World. unabr. ed. Beverly Cleary. Read by Stockard Channing. 2 cass. (Running Time: 3 hrs.). (Ramona Quimby Ser.). (J). (gr. 3-5). 1999. 23.00 (LL 0147, Chivers Child Audio) AudioGO.

***Ramona's World.** unabr. ed. Beverly Cleary. Read by Stockard Channing. (J). 2010. audio compact disk 14.99 (978-0-06-177412-6(X), HarperChildAud) HarperCollins Pubs.

***Ramona's World.** unabr. ed. Beverly Cleary. Read by Stockard Channing. (ENG.). 2010. (978-0-06-206015-0(5)); (978-0-06-206220-8(4)) HarperCollins Pubs.

Ramona's World. unabr. ed. Beverly Cleary. Read by Stockard Channing. 2 vols. (Running Time: 2 hrs. 57 mins.). (Ramona Quimby Ser.). (J). (gr. 3-7). 2004. pap. bk. 29.00 (978-0-8072-8169-7(7), Listening Lib) Random Audio Pubg.

Ramona's World. unabr. ed. Beverly Cleary. Read by William Roberts. 2 cass. (Running Time: 2 hrs. 57 mins.). (Ramona Quimby Ser.). (J). (gr. 3-7). 2004. 23.00 (978-0-8072-8168-0(9), YA123CX, Listening Lib) Random Audio Pubg.
This first new Ramona book in fifteen years stars the spunky nine-year-old, now in the fourth grade. She is struggling with her spelling, gleefully battling her old nemesis, Yard Ape, & joyfully making her first real girl friends. She's also dealing with life as a middle child - Beezus & Ramona have a baby sister, Roberta.

Ramona's World. unabr. ed. Beverly Cleary. Read by Stockard Channing. 3 CDs. (Running Time: 2 hrs. 59 mins.). (Ramona Quimby Ser.). (ENG.). (J). (gr. 3). 2005. audio compact disk 14.99 (978-1-4000-9911-5(0), Listening Lib) Pub: Random Audio Pubg. Dist(s): Random

Rampart Street. David Fulmer. Read by Dion Graham. 9 cass. (Running Time: 40500 sec.). (Valentin St. Cyr Mysteries Ser.). 2006. 79.95 (978-0-7927-3948-7(5), CSL 926); audio compact disk 99.95 (978-0-7927-3949-4(3), SLD 926) AudioGO.

Ramses Vol. 1: Son of the Light. Christian Jacq. Read by Martin Shaw. 2 cass. (Running Time: 3 hrs.). 1999. 16.85 (978-0-671-03359-0(X)) S and S Inc.
Tells of Ramses' training, through tests & traps, at the hands of his father, Seti, & of the dangerous intrigues which will decide who succeeds to the throne.

Ramses Vol. 2: The Temple of a Million Years. Christian Jacq. Read by Martin Shaw. 2 cass. (Running Time: 3 hrs.). 1999. 16.85 (978-0-671-03360-6(3)) S and S Inc.
He is abut to reach his coronation, & has all he should need to become a great pharaoah, but lurking in the shadows are new conspiracies against him.

Ramses Vol. 3. Christian Jacq. Read by Martin Shaw. 2 cass. (Running Time: 3 hrs.). 1999. 16.85 (978-0-671-03361-3(1)) S and S Inc.
To save Egypt from the Hittens, Ramses II must face the might of their powerful army. War seems inevitable & it is at Kadesh that the first major battle takes place. Will his father, now a celestial god, answer his pleas for help & guidance?.

Ramses Vol. 3. unabr. ed. Christian Jacq. Read by Stephen Thorne. 10 cass. (Running Time: 13 hrs.). (Isis Ser.). (J). 1999. 84.95 (978-0-7531-0591-7(8), 991106) Pub: ISIS Lrg Prnt GBR. Dist(s): Ulverscroft US
To save Egypt from the Hittites, Ramses II must face the might of a powerful army whose weapons are vastly superior to Egypt's own. War seems inevitable & it is at the impenetrable fortress of Kadesh that the first major battle is to take place. But the health of his beloved wife, Nefertari, is failing rapidly & a pro-Hittite underground network continues to grow. Ramses needs to travel South in search of the Stone Goddess, the last hope to save his dying Queen, but the imminent battle to save his entire civilization is to the North. Will Ramses father, now a celestial god, answer his desperate pleas for guidance?.

Ramses Vol. 5: Under the Western Acacia. Christian Jacq. Read by Martin Shaw. 2 cass. (Running Time: 3 hrs.). 1999. 16.85 (978-0-671-03363-7(8)) S and S Inc.
Ramses is now fifty; after bringing outstanding prosperity to Egypt, he could have hoped to enjoy serene old age, but soon he must sit in the shade of the Western Acacia to prepare for his final journey.

Ramses Vol. 5: Under the Western Acacia. unabr. ed. Christian Jacq. Read by Stephen Thorne. 8 cass. (Running Time: 12 hrs.). (Ramses Ser.: Vol. 5). (J). 2000. 69.95 (978-0-7531-0593-1(4), 000404) Pub: ISIS Lrg Prnt GBR. Dist(s): Ulverscroft US
Ramses is now fifty; in his old age, the time has come for Ramses to meet his final enemy in the shade of the Western Acacia.

Ramses Vol. 5: Under the Western Acacia. unabr. ed. Christian Jacq. Read by Stephen Thorne. 10 CDs. (Running Time: 10 hrs. 12 min.). (Isis Ser.). (J). 2001. audio compact disk 89.95 (978-0-7531-1325-7(2)) Pub: ISIS Lrg Prnt GBR. Dist(s): Ulverscroft US
Ramses is now fifty; after bringing outstanding prosperity to Egypt, he can hope to enjoy a serene old age. But as he strives to preserve peace, the Hittie Emperor exhorts him to wed his daughter under the threat of a new war, and the revengeful Libyans are rebelling... In his old age, the time has come for Ramses to meet his final enemy in the shade of Western Acacia.

Ramtha, a master's first Step see Ramtha, la claridad Mental: Un paso primordial para un Maestro

Ramtha; acceptance: the key to Magic see Ramtha, la Aceptacion: El secreto de la Magia

***Ramtha, amanecer de Pascua.** Des. by Pangraf Productions. (SPA.). 2010. audio compact disk 25.00 (978-1-935262-10-7(6)) Bel Shanai.

Ramtha, dinero y Manifestacion. Des. by Paulina Amador. (SPA., 2009. audio compact disk 16.50 (978-1-935262-05-3(X)) Bel Shanai.

***Ramtha, el AMOR Y LAS RELACIONES.** Tr. by Valeria Zimmermann.Tr. of Ramhta, LOVE & RELATIONSHIPS. (SPA.). (YA). 2009. audio compact disk 16.50 (978-1-935262-09-1(2)) Bel Shanai.

***Ramtha, el Descubrimiento del Alma y el Libro de la Vida.** Des. by Holo-Graphics. (SPA.). (YA). 2010. audio compact disk 25.00 (978-1-935262-13-8(0)) Bel Shanai.

Ramtha, la Aceptacion: El secreto de la Magia. Des. by Pangraf Productions.Tr. of Ramtha; acceptance: the key to Magic. (SPA., 2009. audio compact disk 16.50 (978-1-935262-04-6(1)) Bel Shanai.

Ramtha, la claridad Mental: Un paso primordial para un Maestro. Des. by Paulina Amador.Tr. of Ramtha, a master's first Step. (SPA., 2009. audio compact disk 25.00 (978-1-935262-01-5(7)) Bel Shanai.

Ramtha, la gran Obra: De la oruga a la Mariposa. Des. by Pangraf Productions.Tr. of Ramtha, the Great Work: from the Caterpillar to the Butterfly. (SPA., 2008. audio compact disk 25.00 (978-1-935262-02-2(5)) Bel Shanai.

Ramtha, la mariposa y el Alquimista. Des. by Paulina Amador. (SPA.). (YA). 2009. audio compact disk 16.50 (978-1-935262-06-0(8)) Bel Shanai.

Ramtha, LAS MEJORES COSAS SE LOGRAN con un CORAZON ALEGRE. Des. by Fizzo Pannosch. 2009. audio compact disk 33.33 (978-1-935262-07-7(6)) Bel Shanai.

Ramtha, los dias que ya Llegaron. Des. by Paulina Amador.Tr. of Ramtha,Miami -Change:the Days That are Here. (SPA., 2009. audio compact disk 25.00 (978-1-935262-00-8(9)) Bel Shanai.

***Ramtha, recordando el Futuro.** Engineer Pangraf Productions. 2009. 9.95 (978-1-935262-11-4(4)) Bel Shanai.

Ramtha, recupera tu Poder. Des. by Paulina Amador.Tr. of Ramtha, Taking back your Power. (SPA., 2008. audio compact disk 25.00 (978-1-935262-03-9(3)) Bel Shanai.

Ramtha, Taking back your Power see Ramtha, recupera tu Poder

Ramtha, the Great Work: from the Caterpillar to the Butterfly see Ramtha, la gran Obra: De la oruga a la Mariposa

Ramtha, una NAVIDAD MISTICA. Fizzo Pannosch. 2009. audio compact disk 16.50 (978-1-935262-08-4(4)) Bel Shanai.

Ramtha,Miami -Change:the Days That are Here see Ramtha, los dias que ya Llegaron

Rana Look. Sandra Brown. Read by Eliza Foss. 2002. audio compact disk 32.00 (978-0-7366-8855-0(2)) Books on Tape.

Rana Look. Sandra Brown. Read by Eliza Foss. 2002. 28.00 (978-0-7366-8854-3(4)) Books on Tape.

Rana, rema, rimas Canciones y Cuentos. Contrib. by Margarita Robleda. Illus. by Maribel Suarez. (Rana, Rema, Rimas Ser.). (SPA.). (J). (gr. k-3). bk. 7.95 (978-1-59437-822-5(3)) Santillana.

***Rana, rema, rimas. Canciones y Cuentos 2 (CD)** Margarita Robleda.Tr. of Rowing Rhyming Frog 2. (SPA.). (J). 2006. audio compact disk 9.95 (978-1-59820-522-0(6), Alfaguara) Santillana.

Ranch. Danielle Steel. Narrated by Ron McLarty. 12 CDs. (Running Time: 14 hrs. 30 mins.). 2001. audio compact disk 116.00 (978-0-7887-5178-3(6), C1340E7) Recorded Bks.
As three women - inseparable friends during college - reunite for a vacation at a Wyoming ranch, they share stories of their lives & spend scenic days together, helping each other discover ways to make their dreams come true.

Ranch. unabr. ed. Danielle Steel. Narrated by Ron McLarty. 10 cass. (Running Time: 14 hrs. 30 mins.). 1999. 90.00 (978-0-7887-0909-8(7), 95015E7) Recorded Bks.
As three women - inseparable friends during college - reunite for a vacation at Wyoming ranch, they share stories of their lives & spend scenic days together, helping each other discover ways to make their dreams come true.

Ranch Life & the Hunting-Trail. unabr. collector's ed. Theodore Roosevelt. Read by Larry McKeever. 8 cass. (Running Time: 8 hrs.). 1986. 48.00 (978-0-7366-0945-6(8), 1888) Books on Tape.
No American president has been closer to the working life of the West than Theodore Roosevelt. He met the unique characters of the Bad Lands - mountain men, buffalo hunters, Indians & cowboys & watched them change as the West filled up with people.

Rancon. l.t. ed. Paul Nothomb. (French Ser.). 2001. bk. 30.99 (978-2-84011-425-3(9)) Pub: UlverLrgPrint GBR. Dist(s): Ulverscroft US

Rand. unabr. ed. Loren Robinson. Read by Cameron Beierle. . (Hawk Adventure Ser.: Bk. 3). 2001. 64.95 (978-1-58116-066-6(6)) Books in Motion.
Lane Palmer is Hawk, a member of the anti-terrorist Counter Force of the FBI. A murder involving a cue-stick laser gun leads Palmer on the trail of a military man who may be secretly trying to get the United States into a war with China.

Randall Jarrell. Randall Jarrell. 1 cass. (Author Speaks Ser.). 1991. 14.95 J Norton Pubs.
Archival recordings of 20th-century authors.

Randall the Fastest Reindeer. Jim Harkey. Lyrics by Charles Seaton. (J). 2008. (978-1-59849-058-9(3)) P B Pubng.

Randa's Road Trips: To Monterey & Carmel with Map. Randa's Road Trips Staff. 1998. 15.95 (978-1-893402-00-3(2)) Randa Road.

RandB Guitar Method: Learn to Play Classic Rhythm & Blues Guitar with Step-by-Step Lessons & 31 Great Songs. Dave Rubin. 2007. pap. bk. 14.95 (978-0-634-07750-0(3), 0634077503) H Leonard.

R&B JamTrax for Guitar. Ralph Agresta. 1998. pap. bk. 39.95 (978-0-8256-1348-7(5), AM91045) Beekman Bks.

Randolph Caldecott: The Man behind the Medal. 2004. 8.95 (978-0-89719-925-4(1)); cass. & flmstrp 30.00 (978-0-89719-525-6(6)) Weston Woods.

Randolph Caldecott: the Man behind the Medal; Hey Diddle Diddle; Baby Bunting; Milkmaid. 2004. cass. & flmstrp 30.00 (978-1-56008-810-3(9)) Weston Woods.

Random Access. Ed. by Robert A. Monroe. 1 cass. (Running Time: 30 min.). (Meta Music Ser.). 1986. 12.95 (978-1-56102-221-2(7)) Inter Indus.
For the explorer with no preconceived destination in mind. A subtle piano & bass jazz influence, with a "peak" point late in the piece to encourage a profound meditative experience.

Random Acts of Grace: Dramatic Encounters with God's Love. abr. ed. Paul Johnson & Nicole Johnson. Read by Paul Johnson & Nicole Johnson. 2 cass. (Running Time: 2 hrs.). 1998. 15.99 (978-0-8054-1775-3(3)) BH Pubng Grp.

Random Acts of Kindness. unabr. ed. Conari Press Editors. Read by Ed Asner et al. 2 cass. (Running Time: 3 hrs.). 1995. 17.95 (978-1-57453-007-0(0)) Audio Lit.
Presents true stories of people who have been the givers or recipients of caring and compassionate acts.

Random Hearts. Warren Adler. Read by Michael Kramer. 1999. audio compact disk 64.00 (978-0-7366-5172-1(1)) Books on Tape.

Random Hearts. unabr. ed. Warren Adler. Read by Michael Kramer. 6 cass. (Running Time: 9 hrs.). 1999. 48.00 (978-0-7366-4498-3(9), 4934) Books on Tape.
Vivien Simpson was an ordinary wife & mother, happily married to a successful Washington lawyer. Edward Davis was just another ambitious, workaholic congressional aide, who much to his wife's dismay, thought an evening for two meant time spent with his typewriter. Total strangers to each other, a series of tragic & bizarre circumstances will bring them together. In the aftermath of one of the worst airplane disasters in Washington's history, two unidentified bodies are pulled from the wreckage. As a result, Vivien's & Edward's marriages are suddenly shattered & each will be forced to question the very nature of love itself.

Random Hearts. unabr. ed. Warren Adler. 8 CDs. (Running Time: 9 hrs. 25 mins.). 2001. audio compact disk 64.00 Books on Tape.
Vivien Simpson was an ordinary wife and mother, happily married to a successful Washington lawyer. Edward Davis was just another workaholic congressional aide who, much to his wife's dismay, thought a quiet evening for two meant time spent with his typewriter. There was no earthly reason why Vivien and Edward, total strangers, should have ever met. But the force of a passion beyond their comprehension brought them together under tragic and bizarre circumstances.

Random Island. unabr. ed. Alex Stuart. Read by Margaret Holt. 4 cass. (Running Time: 6 hrs.). 2001. 44.95 (978-1-85496-195-2(0), 61950) Pub: UlverLrgPrint GBR. Dist(s): Ulverscroft US

Random Passage. Bernice Morgan. Read by Marie McCarthy. 10 cass. (Running Time: 47700 sec.). (Storysound Ser.). 2003. 84.95 (978-1-85903-592-4(2)) Pub: Mgna Lrg Print GBR. Dist(s): Ulverscroft US

***Random Reminiscences of Men & Events.** John D. Rockefeller. Read by Anais 9000. 2009. 27.95 (978-1-60112-232-2(2)) Babblebooks.

Random Victim. unabr. ed. Michael A. Black. Narrated by Gene Engene. 1 MP3-CD. (Running Time: 11 hrs. 30 mins.). 2009. 24.95 (978-1-60548-217-0(X)); audio compact disk 57.95 (978-1-60548-216-3(1)) Books in Motion.

***Random Violence.** unabr. ed. Jassy Mackenzie. (Running Time: 11 hrs. 30 mins.). (Jade de Jong Investigations Ser.). 2011. 29.95 (978-1-4417-7116-2(6)); 65.95 (978-1-4417-7113-1(1)); audio compact disk 29.95 (978-1-4417-7115-5(8)); audio compact disk 100.00 (978-1-4417-7114-8(X)) Blckstn Audio.

Random Walk. Lawrence Block. Narrated by Norman Dietz. 8 cass. (Running Time: 11 hrs. 30 mins.). 76.00 (978-1-4025-0192-0(7)) Recorded Bks.

Random Walk down Wall Street: The Time-Tested Strategy for Successful Investing. unabr. ed. Burton G. Malkiel. Read by Kerin McCue. (Running Time: 15 hrs. 15 mins.). 2008. 61.75 (978-1-4361-6530-3(X)); audio compact disk 123.75 (978-1-4361-0527-9(7)) Recorded Bks.

Random Winds. unabr. collector's ed. Belva Plain. Read by Ruth Stokesberry. 13 cass. (Running Time: 19 hrs. 30 min.). 1987. 104.00 (978-0-7366-1158-9(4), 2083) Books on Tape.
Is an epochal saga about a family of physicians first Enoch, the dedicated country doctor; then Martin, his son, a brilliant neurosurgeon & Claire, his flamboyant, unconventional daughter.The story moves from a turn-of-the-century village in upstate New York to privileged estates outside London, from the bedsides of the rural poor to the frenetic emergency room of a New York hospital, from war-torn London to hideaways on the French Riviera. It tells of the trials & triumphs of a dynamic family struggling to hold its center & of love beyond anyone's power to deny.

***Randomity.** L. Ron Hubbard. (ENG.). 2002. audio compact disk 15.00 (978-1-4031-4216-0(5)) Bridge Pubns Inc.

Randy Stonehill: the Definitive Collection. Contrib. by Randy Stonehill. 2007. audio compact disk 7.97 (978-5-558-14537-3(4), Word Records) Word Enter.

Randy the Raindrop, Vol.1. Elaine Maxwell. (ENG.). (J). 2007. audio compact disk 19.99 (978-1-888564-01-3(6)) Studio Four TX.

Randy the Raindrop Vol. 1: Randy's New Friends; Randy's Big Adventure. Elaine Maxwell. Read by Elaine Maxwell. 1 cass. (Running Time: 30 min.). (MiMi's Bedtime Stories Ser.). (J). (ps-6). 1996. 9.00 (978-1-888564-00-6(8)) Studio Four TX.
Children's bedtime stories about a raindrop & his friends (both real & animated).

Raney. unabr. ed. Clyde Edgerton. Narrated by Ruth Ann Phimister. 5 cass. (Running Time: 6 hrs. 45 mins.). 1998. 46.00 (978-0-7887-1998-1(X), 95385 E7) Recorded Bks.
Raney has lived her whole life in her tiny southern home town. In the first few years of marriage, amidst family holidays, herds of well-meaning relatives & mounds of jello salads, their search for common ground begins.

Range Jester & Forgotten Treasure. abr. ed. Max Brand. Read by Barry Corbin. 2 cass. (Running Time: 3 hrs.). 2000. 7.95 (978-1-57815-087-8(6), 1055, Media Bks Audio) Media Bks NJ.
Captures the old West.

Range of Motion. unabr. ed. Elizabeth Berg. Read by Beth Fowler. 6 vols. (Running Time: 9 hrs.). 2001. bk. 54.95 (978-0-7927-2253-3(1), CSL 142, Chivers Sound Lib) AudioGO.
Jay Berman lingers in a coma as his wife Lainey waits for him to recover. She hopes to reach him with reminders of their life together: sweet-smelling flowers, his softly textured shirt, and spices from their kitchen. Through her ordeal, Lainey is sustained by her relationships with two very special women, each of whom teaches her about friendship and the power of hope.

Range of Motion. unabr. ed. Elizabeth Berg. Read by Beth Fowler. 6 CDs. (Running Time: 9 Hrs.). 2000. audio compact disk 64.95 (978-0-7927-9970-2(4), SLD 021, Chivers Sound Lib) AudioGO.

Range of Motion-Ao Asif Netral-O Method: Measurement & Documentation. C. Ryf & A. Weymann. 1999. bk. (978-3-13-116791-0(2)) G Thieme DEU.

***Ranger Rides to Town: Rain on a Mountain Fork - Down Sonora Way.** unabr. ed. Louis L'Amour. (ENG.). 2010. 14.99 (978-0-307-74878-2(2), Random AudioBks) Pub: Random Audio Pubg. Dist(s): Random

Ranger's Trail. unabr. ed. Elmer Kelton. Narrated by Jonathan Davis. 6 cass. (Running Time: 9 hrs.). (Texas Rangers Ser.: No. 4). 2002. 59.75 (978-1-4025-9347-5(3), W1015, Griot Aud); audio compact disk 89.75 (978-1-4025-9349-9(X), CW022, Griot Aud) Recorded Bks.

Rani in the Mermaid Lagoon/Fira & the Full Moon. unabr. ed. Lisa Papademetriou & Gail Herman. Read by Quincy Tyler & Debra Wiseman. (Running Time: 8520 sec.). (Disney Fairies Ser.). (ENG.). (J). (gr. 1). 2006. audio compact disk 19.99 (978-0-7393-3685-4(1), ImaginStudio) Pub: Random Audio Pubg. Dist(s): Random

Rank Devil Mountain. J. Gere. 2005. audio compact disk 16.95 (978-0-9762190-3-3(4)) J Gere.

Rank Obstinacy of Things. Paul Roche. Read by Paul Roche. 1 cass. (Running Time: 29 min.). 11.95 (23114) J Norton Pubs.
Roche talks about problems of translating Greek tragedy & reads in English & Greek. Includes selections from Agamemnon out of his translation of the Orestes plays by Aeschylus.

Ransom. Julie Garwood. Read by Jan Maxwell. 2004. 10.95 (978-0-7435-4575-4(3)) Pub: S&S Audio. Dist(s): S and S Inc

Ransom. abr. ed. Julie Garwood. Read by Jan Maxwell. 2 cass. (Running Time: 3 hrs.). 1999. 18.00 (FS9-43327) Highsmith.

Ransom. unabr. ed. Julie Garwood. Read by Paula Parker. 14 vols. (Running Time: 21 Hrs.). 2000. bk. 110.95 (978-0-7927-2413-1(5), CSL 302, Chivers Sound Lib) AudioGO.
Gillian finds the key to resolving her troubled past in handsome Scottish chieftans Ramsey Sinclair & Brodick Buchanan.

Ransom of Mercy Carter. unabr. ed. Caroline B. Cooney. Narrated by Christina Moore. 5 pieces. (Running Time: 6 hrs. 15 mins.). (gr. 7 up). 2001. 46.00 (978-0-7887-5263-6(4)) Recorded Bks.

Ransom of Paris. unabr. ed. Tom Nichols. Read by Maynard Villers. 8 cass. (Running Time: 9 hrs. 6 min.). 1996. 49.95 (978-1-55686-689-0(5)) Books in Motion.
During WWII Hitler ordered Paris to be destroyed by fire. The French government & the allies attempt to bribe the German general in charge with one million dollars to be paid after the war.

Ransom of Red Chief see O. Henry Favorites

Ransom of Red Chief see O. Henry Library

Ransom of Red Chief. O. Henry. Ed. by Walter Pauk & Raymond Harris. Illus. by Robert J. Pailthorpe. (Classics Ser.). (YA). (gr. 6-12). 1980. pap. bk. 17.96 (978-0-89061-190-6(4), 406) Jamestown.

Ransom of Red Chief. O. Henry. (J). 1984. Multi Media TX.

Ransom of Red Chief. O. Henry. Read by Rick Adamson. 1 cass. (Running Time: 35 mins.). (Creative Short Story Audio Library Ser.). (J). 1999. 11.00 (978-0-8072-6119-4(X), Y CS 906 CX, Listening Lib) Random Audio Pubg.

Ransom of Red Chief. rev. ed. O. Henry. Ed. by Don Kisner. Adapted by Don Kisner & Rick McVey. 1 cass. (Running Time: 35 mins.). (Read-Along Radio Dramas Ser.). (YA). (gr. 7 up). 1999. ring bd. 38.00 (978-1-878298-14-0(3)) Balance Pub.

Ransom of Red Chief. unabr. ed. O. Henry. 1 cass. (Running Time: 35 min.). (Creative Short Story Audio Library Ser.). (YA). (gr. 4-7). 1995. 9.98 (978-0-8072-6118-7(1), CS906CX, Listening Lib) Random Audio Pubg.

Ransom of Red Chief & Other Stories. O. Henry. (Reading & Training, Beginner Ser.). (J). (gr. 4-7). 2005. pap. bk. 21.95 (978-88-7754-928-0(9)) Cideb ITA.

Ransom of Red Chief & Other Stories. unabr. ed. O. Henry et al. Read by Jack Sondericker et al. 3 cass. (Running Time: 3 hrs. 30 min.). Dramatization. 1990. 21.95 (978-1-55686-089-8(7), 089) Books in Motion.
Three short stories: The Ransom of Red-Chief, Rip Van Winkle, Will Rogers.

Ransom Read Along. (Barclay Family Adventure Ser.). (YA). 2006. audio compact disk (978-1-56254-996-1(0)) Saddleback Edu.

Ransom Town. unabr. ed. Peter Alding. 5 cass. 1998. 63.95 Set. (978-1-85903-086-8(6)) Pub: Magna Story GBR. Dist(s): Ulverscroft US

Ransomed Femininity Live! Featuring Stasi Eldredge. 2003. audio compact disk 24.00 (978-1-933207-34-6(5)) Ransomed Heart.

Ranson's Folly. unabr. ed. Richard Harding Davis. Read by Jack Sondericker. 6 cass. (Running Time: 7 hrs.). Dramatization. 1990. 39.95 (978-1-55686-333-2(0), 333) Books in Motion.
Collection of Harding's most well known works. Included are two noveletts & three short stories; Ranson's Folly, The Bar Sinister, A Derelict, La Lettre D'Amour, In the Fog.

Rant: An Oral Biography of Buster Casey. Chuck Palahniuk. (Running Time: 36000 sec.). 2007. audio compact disk 34.99 (978-1-4281-4353-1(X)) Recorded Bks.

***Rant Zone.** abr. ed. Dennis Miller. Read by Dennis Miller. (ENG.). 2006. (978-0-06-113464-7(3), Harper Audio); (978-0-06-113463-0(5), Harper Audio) HarperCollins Pubs.

Rant Zone: An All-Out Blitz Against Soul-Sucking Jobs, Twisted Child Stars, Holistic Loons, & People Who Eat Their Dogs. abr. ed. Dennis Miller. Read by Dennis Miller. 3 CDs. (Running Time: 3 hrs.). 2001. 22.00 (978-0-694-52649-9(5)) HarperCollins Pubs.

Raoul Wallenberg. Harvey Rosenfeld. Read by Michael Kramer. (Running Time: 12 mins.). 2005. 65.95 (978-0-7861-3689-6(8)); audio compact disk 90.00 (978-0-7861-7676-2(8)) Blckstn Audio.

Raoul Wallenberg. unabr. ed. Harvey Rosenfeld. Read by Michael Kramer. (Running Time: 12 mins.). 2005. 29.95 (978-0-7861-7914-5(7)) Blckstn Audio.

Rap a Tap Tap: Here's Bojangles - Think of That! Leo Dillon & Diane Dillon. (J). 2005. bk. 28.95 (978-1-59519-369-8(3)) Pub: Live Oak Media. Dist(s): AudioGO

Rap City. 2 cass. (978-0-529-07001-2(4), WBC-32) Nelson.
Stands for Righteous & Pure; features some favorite passages of the Bible set to Rap.

Rap City. 2 CD. 1999. audio compact disk (978-0-529-07004-3(9), CD) Nelson.

Rap-Dancing into the Third Millenium. Featuring Terence McKenna. 1994. 9.95 (978-1-59157-021-9(2)) Assn for Cons.

Rap It Up. Mary Blakely. 1 cass. (Starbrights Ser.). Azuray Learn.
Multi-sensory education, workbooklet incl.

Rap 3R. 1 cass. (FRE.). 2001. pap. bk. 14.95 (JMPF01K) Jordan Music.
Hip sophisticated songs boost reading, writing & multiplication all at the same time. Side B allows for karaoke performances or creative writing.

Rap 3R (Multiplication) Sara Jordan. Rev. by Sara Jordan. Tr. by France Gauthier. Rev. by Martin LaCasse et al. 1 cass. (Running Time: 46 min.). (FRE., (J). 1991. pap. bk. 14.95 (978-1-895523-17-1(6), JMP F01K) Jordan Music.

Rap 3R (Multiplications) France Gauthier & Sara L. Jordan. 1 CD. (Running Time: 48 minutes). (FRE.). (J). 1991. audio compact disk 11.99 (978-1-894262-61-3(1), JMPF01CD) Jordan Music.
Hip sophisticated songs boost Multiplication skills. The English version of this album was nominated by the University of Louisville for the Grawemeyer Award in Education for "outstanding achievement with a potential for world-wide impact." This audio kit is especially designed for use in adolescent' academic upgrading. The songs would be a challenge for immersion students and are used primarily by francophones.

***Rapacia: The Second Circle of Heck.** unabr. ed. Dale E. Basye. Read by Bronson Pinchot. (Running Time: 10 hrs.). (Circles of Heck Ser.). 2011. 29.95 (978-1-4417-7144-5(1)); 59.95 (978-1-4417-7141-4(7)); audio compact disk 29.95 (978-1-4417-7143-8(3)); audio compact disk 90.00 (978-1-4417-7142-1(5)) Blckstn Audio.

Rapanese: The Musical Method of Learning Spanish. Robert D'Amours. 1 cass. (Running Time: 90 min.). 1994. (978-1-886447-08-0(X)) Rapanese.

Rapanese - Japanese, Vol. 1. Robert D'Amours. 2 cass. (Running Time: 2 hrs. 30 min.). 1993. (978-1-886447-04-2(7)) Rapanese.

Rapanese - Japanese Vol. 2: The Musical Method of Learning Japanese. Rapanese Staff & Robert D'Amours. 2 cass. (Running Time: 2 hrs.). 1995. (978-1-886447-10-3(1)) Rapanese.

Rapanese French Series 1: The Musical Method of Learning French. Robert D'Amours. Arranged by Rapanese Staff. 1 cass. (Running Time: 90 min.). 1996. (978-1-886447-06-6(3)) Rapanese.

Rapanese French Series 1 Vol. 1: The Musical Method of Learning French. Robert D'Amours. Ed. by Rapanese Staff. 1 CD. (Running Time: 72 MINS.). 1996. audio compact disk (978-1-886447-17-2(9)) Rapanese.
The musical method of learning French series 1 CD.

Rapanese French Series 2: The Musical Method of Learning French. Rapanese Staff & Robert D'Amours. 2 cass. (Running Time: 2 hrs. 30 min.). 2003. (978-1-886447-13-4(6)) Rapanese.

Rapanese Japanese Series. Robert D'Amours. 2004. audio compact disk (978-1-886447-20-2(9)) Rapanese.

Rapanese, Spanish Learning, Vol. 1. Robert D'Amours. (SPA.). 1994. audio compact disk (978-1-886447-15-8(2)) Rapanese.

Rapanese Spanish Series 1 & 2: The Musical Method of Learning Spanish. Rapanese Staff & Robert D'Amours. 2003. (978-1-886447-16-5(0)) Rapanese.

Rapanese Spanish Series 2: The Musical Method of Learning Spanish. Rapanese Staff & Robert D'Amours. 1996. audio compact disk (978-1-886447-18-9(7)) Rapanese.
RAPANESE The music and comedy method of learning Spanish series 2 CD.

Rapanese Spanish Series 2: The Musical Method of Learning Spanish. Rapanese Staff & Robert D'Amours. 2 cass. (Running Time: 2 hrs.). 1995. (978-1-886447-09-7(8)) Rapanese.

Rapanese Spanish Series 3: The Musical Method of Learning Spanish. Rapanese Staff & Robert D'Amours. 2 cass. (Running Time: 2 hrs. 30 min.). 1996. 16.95 (978-1-886447-12-7(8)); audio compact disk (978-1-886447-19-6(5)) Rapanese.
RAPANESE The music and comedy method of learning Spanish series 3.

Rape: The Work with Byron Katie. 2006. audio compact disk 15.00 (978-1-890246-38-9(7)) B Katie Int Inc.

***Rape of Lucrece & Other Poems.** abr. ed. William Shakespeare. (ENG.). 2006. (978-0-06-112636-9(5), Caedmon); (978-0-06-112635-2(7), Caedmon) HarperCollins Pubs.

Rape of Lucrece & Other Poems, unabr. ed. Poems. William Shakespeare. Perf. by Richard Burton et al. 2 cass. (Running Time: 3 hrs.). Incl. Passionate Pilgrim. (CPN 239); Phoenix & Turtle. (CPN 239); Sonnets to Sundry Notes of Music. (CPN 239); (J). 1984. 15.95 (978-1-55994-050-4(6), CPN 239) HarperCollins Pubs.

Rape of Nanking. unabr. ed. Iris Chang. Read by Anna Fields. (Running Time: 8 hrs. 30 mins.). 1998. audio compact disk 63.00 (978-0-7861-8093-6(5)) Blckstn Audio.

Rape of Nanking: The Forgotten Holocaust of World War II. unabr. ed. Iris Chang. Read by Anna Fields. 6 cass. (Running Time: 8 hrs. 30 mins.). 1998. bk. 44.95 (978-0-7861-1258-6(1), 2166) Blckstn Audio.
Tells how more than 300,000 Chinese civilians were systematically raped, tortured & murdered in December 1937 from three perspectives: that of the the Japanese soldiers who performed it; of the Chinese civilians who endured it; & finally of a group of Europeans & Americans who refused to abandon the city & were able to create a safety zone that saved almost 300,000 Chinese. It was Iris Chang who discovered the diaries of the German leader of this rescue effort, John Rabe, whom she calls the "Oskar Schindler of China".

Rape of Nanking: The Forgotten Holocaust of World War II. unabr. ed. Iris Chang. Read by Anna Fields. 7 CDs. (Running Time: 9 hrs.). 2004. audio compact disk 29.95 (978-0-7861-2942-3(5)); audio compact disk 24.95 (978-0-7861-2943-0(3)); reel tape 27.95 (978-0-7861-2941-6(7)) Blckstn Audio.
In December 1937, in the capital of china, one of the most brutal massacres in the long annals of wartime barbarity occurred. The Japanese army swept into the ancient city of Nanking and within weeks not only looted and burned the defenseless city but systematically raped, tortured, and murdered more than 300,000 Chinese civilians. Amazingly, the account of this atrocity was denied by the Japanese government. The Rape of Nanking tells the story from three perspectives: that of the Japanese soldiers who performed it, of the chinese civilians who endured it, and finally of a group of Europeans and Americans who refused to abandon the city and were able to create a safety zone that saved almost 300,000 Chinese. It was Iris Chang who discovered the diaries of the German leader of this rescue effort, John Rabe, whom she called the "Oskar Schindler of China," who worked tirelessly to save the innocent from slaughter.

Rape of Nanking: The Forgotten Holocaust of World War II. unabr. ed. Iris Chang. Read by Anna Fields. 6 cass. (Running Time: 9 hrs.). 2006. 29.95 (978-0-7861-1382-8(0)) Blckstn Audio.
In the Capital of China in December 1937, one of the most brutal massacres in the long annals of wartime barbarity occurred. Tells the story from three perspectives: that of the Japanese soldiers who performed it, of the Chinese civilians who endured it, & finally of a group of Europeans & Americans who created a safety zone that saved almost 300,000 Chinese.

Rape of the Fair Country. unabr. ed. Alexander Cordell. Read by Philip Madoc. 8 cass. (Running Time: 8 hrs.). 1993. bk. 69.95 (978-0-7451-5872-3(2)) AudioGO.

Raphael Affair. unabr. ed. Iain Pears. Read by Geoffrey Howard. 4 cass. (Running Time: 5 hrs. 30 mins.). (Jonathan Argyll Mystery Ser.: Bk. 1). 1997. 32.95 (978-0-7861-1093-3(7), 1859) Blckstn Audio.
Set in Rome, "The Raphael Affair" features the perpetually beset General Bottando of the Italian National Art Theft Squad; his glamorous assistant, Flavia di Stefano; & Jonathan Argyll, a British art historian. When Jonathan is arrested for breaking into an obscure church in Rome, he claims that it contains a long-lost Raphael hidden under a painting by Mantini. Further investigation reveals that the painting has disappeared.

Raphael Affair. unabr. ed. Iain Pears. 5 cass. (Jonathan Argyll Mystery Ser.: Bk. 1). (J). 2002. 49.95 (978-0-7531-1367-7(8)); audio compact disk 64.95 (978-0-7531-1421-6(6)) Pub: ISIS Lrg Prnt GBR. Dist(s): Ulverscroft US

Rapid Arabic, Vol. 1: 200+ Essential Words & Phrases Anchored into Your Long-Term Memory with Great Music. Created by Earworms. (Playaway Adult Nonfiction Ser.). (ARA & ENG.). 2009. 40.00 (978-1-60775-556-2(4)) Find a World.

Rapid Chinese. unabr. ed. earwormsLearning. Read by Earworms. (YA). 2008. 39.99 (978-1-60514-914-1(4)) Find a World.

Rapid Chinese: Mandarin. unabr. ed. earwormsLearning. Read by Earworms. (YA). 2007. 34.99 (978-1-60252-782-9(2)) Find a World.

Rapid French. unabr. ed. earwormsLearning. Read by Earworms. (YA). 2007. 39.99 (978-1-60252-922-9(1)) Find a World.

Rapid French. unabr. ed. earwormsLearning. Read by Earworms. (YA). 2008. 34.99 (978-1-60514-742-0(7)) Find a World.

Rapid German. unabr. ed. earwormsLearning. Read by Earworms. (YA). 2008. 39.99 (978-1-60514-743-7(5)) Find a World.

Rapid German. unabr. ed. earwormsLearning. Read by Earworms. (YA). 2008. 39.99 (978-1-60514-915-8(2)) Find a World.

Rapid Greek. unabr. ed. earwormsLearning. Read by Earworms. (YA). 2008. 39.99 (978-1-60514-744-4(3)) Find a World.

Rapid Greek. unabr. ed. earwormsLearning. Read by Earworms. (YA). 2008. 39.99 (978-1-60514-916-5(0)) Find a World.

Rapid Italian. unabr. ed. earwormsLearning. Read by Earworms. (YA). 2007. 34.99 (978-1-60252-857-4(8)) Find a World.

Rapid Italian. unabr. ed. earwormsLearning. Read by Earworms. (YA). 2008. 39.99 (978-1-60514-745-1(1)) Find a World.

Rapid Japanese. unabr. ed. earwormsLearning. Read by Earworms. (YA). 2007. 34.99 (978-1-60252-858-1(6)) Find a World.

Rapid Japanese. unabr. ed. earwormsLearning. Read by Earworms. (YA). 2008. 39.99 (978-1-60514-917-2(9)) Find a World.

Rapid Pain Control. 1 cass. (Running Time: 90 min.). 1995. 12.95 (978-1-884305-70-2(9)) Changeworks.
A comfortable drug-free alternative to all types of pain. From chronic pain that drugs can't touch to low level nagging aches to occasional trips to the dentist, this tape is a valuable resource.

Rapid Portuguese, Vol. 1: 200+ Essential Words & Phrases Anchored into Your Long-Term Memory with Great Music. Created by Earworms. (ENG & POR.). 2008. 39.99 (978-1-60514-746-8(X)) Find a World.

Rapid Recovery from Injury. Carol Ginandes. Perf. by Carol Ginandes. Music by Steven Mark Kohn. 3 CDs. (Running Time: 165 min.). (Health Journeys Ser.: 2602). 2004. audio compact disk 39.98 (978-1-881405-75-7(3)) Hlth Jrnys.
This comprehensive, 6-week, accelerated healing program provides a sequence of expert, self-hypnotic exercises, carefully designed to help diminish pain, soothe inflammation, rebuild healthy tissue, return strength & flexibiltiy and cultivate emotional well-being, for anyone who has sustained a recent fracture, soft tissue injury, burn or wound. The complete program consists of six, sequenced sessions, combining for a total of 165 minutes.

Rapid Review of Vowel & Prosodic Contexts. Joan Morley. (C). 1993. bk. 50.00 (978-0-472-00234-4(1), 00234) U of Mich Pr.

Rapid Russian. unabr. ed. earwormsLearning. Read by Earworms. (YA). 2008. 39.99 (978-1-60514-747-5(8)) Find a World.

Rapid Spanish. unabr. ed. earwormsLearning. Read by Earworms. (YA). 2007. 34.99 (978-1-60252-783-6(0)) Find a World.

Rapid Spanish. unabr. ed. earwormsLearning. Read by Earworms. (YA). 2008. 39.99 (978-1-60514-748-2(6)) Find a World.

Rapid Stress Reduction. Read by Mary Richards. 1 cass. (Running Time: 60 min.). (Energy Break Ser.). 2007. audio compact disk 19.95 (978-1-56136-150-2(X)) Master Your Mind.

Rapid Vocabulary Development Program. 4 cass. (Running Time: 4 hrs.). (YA). (gr. 8 up). 1987. stu. ed. 59.95 Communacad.
This well-thought-out program is more advanced than Wordcraft 3 & less difficult than The Bergen Evans Vocabulary Program. It is perfectly suited for individual, small group, or classroom use, & for High School & College Media Centers & Reading Labs. A total of 256 words are taught. Thirty-two lessons in all, with 8 words in each lesson. The 52 page Student Manual provides tests & exercises to aid involvement & retention. The cassette recordings insure correct pronunciation. This encourages the student to use the new words in conversation, & to make the words part of his/her everyday working vocabulary.

Rapidex English for Bangla Speakers. rev. ed. R.K. Gupta. 1998. pap. bk. 6.00 (978-81-223-0025-3(1)) P Mahal IND.

Rapidex English for Gujarati Speakers. rev. ed. R.K. Gupta. 1997. pap. bk. 6.00 (978-81-223-0021-5(9)) P Mahal IND.

Rapidex English for Gurmukhi Speakers. rev. ed. R.K. Gupta. 1990. pap. bk. 6.00 (978-81-223-0032-1(4)) P Mahal IND.

Rapidex English for Kannada Speakers. rev. ed. R.K. Gupta. 2008. pap. bk. 6.00 (978-81-223-0026-0(X)) P Mahal IND.

Rapidex English for Malayalam Speakers. rev. ed. R.K. Gupta. 2008. pap. bk. 6.00 (978-81-223-0028-4(6)) P Mahal IND.

Rapidex English for Marathi Speakers. rev. ed. R.K. Gupta. 2008. pap. bk. 6.00 (978-81-223-0024-6(3)) P Mahal IND.

Rapidex English for Oriya Speakers. rev. ed. R.K. Gupta. 1999. pap. bk. 6.00 (978-81-223-0031-4(6)) P Mahal IND.

Rapidex English for Tamil Speakers. rev. ed. R.K. Gupta. 2008. pap. bk. 6.00 (978-81-223-0023-9(5)) P Mahal IND.

Rapidex English for Telugu Speakers. rev. ed. R.K. Gupta. 1990. pap. bk. 6.00 (978-81-223-0022-2(7)) P Mahal IND.

Rapidex English for Urdu Speakers. rev. ed. R.K. Gupta. 1999. pap. bk. 6.00 (978-81-223-0030-7(8)) P Mahal IND.

Rapidex Office Secretary Course. Jayant Lal Neogy. 2009. audio compact disk 12.00 (978-81-223-1044-3(3)) P Mahal IND.

RAPmetic, the Arithmetic Rap. Gloria J. Musson & Cyril D. Musson. Illus. by Benjamin S. Miller. (J). (gr. 3 up). 1998. 6.50 (978-0-9619321-1-4(2)) Sq One Pubns.

Rappin' Heart Rhyme. (Song Box Ser.). (gr. 1-2). bk. 8.50 (978-0-322-00248-7(6)) Wright Group.

Rappin' Heart Rhyme: 1 Big Book, 6 Each of 1 Student Book, & 1 Cassette. (Song Box Ser.). (gr. 1-2). 68.95 (978-0-322-00274-6(5)) Wright Group.

***Rappin Mama Music Single - Shelley Sykes.** Shelley Shelley Sykes. (ENG.). (YA). 2010. 1.00 (978-0-9775258-8-1(0)) Beautiful AUS.

Rappin' Mother Goose: Nursery Rhymes. Gene Sicard et al. 5 cass. (Rappin' Mother Goose Fun-Rap Ser.). (J). (ps-3). 1991. bk. 11.95 (978-1-879755-00-0(9)) Recorded Pubns.
Rappin Mother Goose "Nursery Rhymes" audio cassette with exciting voices & fun sound effects in a "non-aggressive fun rap flavor.".

Rapscallion. James McGee & Andrew Wincott. 2009. 89.95 (978-1-84652-532-2(2)); audio compact disk 99.95 (978-1-84652-533-9(0)) Pub: Magna Story GBR. Dist(s): Ulverscroft US

Rapt: Attention & the Focused Life. unabr. ed. Winifred Gallagher. Read by Laural Merlington. 1 MP3-CD. (Running Time: 8 hrs.). 2009. 24.99 (978-1-4233-9322-1(8), 9781423393221, Brilliance MP3); 39.97 (978-1-4233-9323-8(6), 9781423393238, Brinc Audio MP3 Lib); 24.99 (978-1-4233-9324-5(4), 9781423393245, BAD); 39.97 (978-1-4233-9325-2(2), 9781423393252, BADLE); audio compact disk 82.97 (978-1-4233-9321-4(X), 9781423393214, BriAudCD Unabrid); audio compact disk 24.99 (978-1-4233-9320-7(1), 9781423393207) Brilliance Audio.

Raptor. unabr. ed. Paul Zindel. Read by L. J. Ganser. 3 cass. (Running Time: 4 hrs. 15 mins.). (J). 2000. pap. bk. & stu. ed. 42.24 (978-0-7887-4185-2(3), 41098) Recorded Bks.
Zack Norak's father, a paleontologist, has joined a dig for dinosaur bones in Utah. But when Zack finds a giant egg that hatches a baby raptor, soon he is face-to-face with its ferocious mother.

Raptor. unabr. ed. Paul Zindel. Narrated by L. J. Ganser. 3 pieces. (Running Time: 4 hrs. 15 mins.). (gr. 5 up). 2000. 29.00 (978-0-7887-4009-1(1), 96132E7) Recorded Bks.

Raptor, Class Set. unabr. ed. Paul Zindel. Read by L. J. Ganser. 3 cass. (Running Time: 4 hrs. 15 mins.). (J). 2000. 99.70 (978-0-7887-4186-9(1), 47091) Recorded Bks.

Raptor Red. Robert T. Bakker. 2004. 10.95 (978-0-7435-4576-1(1)) Pub: S&S Audio. Dist(s): S and S Inc

Raptor Red. unabr. ed. Robert T. Bakker. Narrated by Richard M. Davidson. 6 cass. (Running Time: 8 hrs. 30 mins.). 1995. 51.00 (978-0-7887-0455-0(9), 94647E7) Recorded Bks.
The dinosaur, Raptor Red, travels across the Utah floodpain, searching for a new mate & struggling to keep her species alive.

Raptor Zone. Gwen Moffat. Read by Patricia Gallimore. 6 cass. (Running Time: 7 hrs. 30 mins.). (Soundings Ser.). (J). 2004. 54.95 (978-1-84283-708-5(7)) Pub: ISIS Lrg Prnt GBR. Dist(s): Ulverscroft US

***Rapture.** Carol Ann Duffy. Read by Juliet Stevenson. (Running Time: 1 hr.). (ENG.). 2006. audio compact disk 19.95 (978-0-230-01438-1(0)) Pub: Macmillan UK GBR. Dist(s): IPG Chicago

Rapture: A Bible Prophecy Multimedia Study Kit. Perf. by Dave Reagan & Dennis Pollock. 1997. tchr. ed. 45.00 (978-0-945593-05-8(8)) Lamb Lion Minstrs.

Rapture: A Crowning Benefit of Redemption. Mac Hammond. 2 cass. (Running Time: 3 hrs.). 1999. cass. & video 19.95 (978-1-57399-081-3(7)) Mac Hammond.

Rapture: Christianity's Most Preposterous Belief. Chuck Missler. 2 CDs. (Running Time: 120 mins). (Briefing Packages by Chuck Missler). 2002. audio compact disk 19.95 (978-1-57821-198-2(0)) Koinonia Hse.
There continue to be many questions concerning the "Rapture" of the Church and its apparent contrast with the "Second Coming" of Jesus Christ. Where does this strange view come from? Is the term "rapture" even in the Bible? Clearly, the idea of the Rapture can be considered the most preposterous belief in Biblical Christianity. The situation regarding the doctrine of the Rapture is painfully similar to the famous quote by Dr. Richard Feynman, speaking of quantum physics: I think it is safe to say that no one understands quantum mechanics... in fact, it is often stated of all the theories proposed in this century, the silliest is quantum theory. Some say that the only thing that quantum theory has going for it, in fact, is that it is unquestionably correct.

Rapture: In the Twinkling of an Eye: Countdown to the Earth's Last Days. Tim LaHaye & Jerry B. Jenkins. Narrated by Richard Ferrone. (Running Time: 31500 sec.). 2006. 29.95 (978-1-4193-9669-4(2)) Recorded Bks.

Rapture: The Crowning Benefit of Redemption. Mac Hammond. 2 cass. (Running Time: 2 hrs.). 1999. Mac Hammond.
In this powerful pair of messages, Hammond brings fresh, biblical insight to this timely subject & deepens your appreciation for God's glorious plan of redemption.

Rapture: The Crowning Benefit of Redemption. Mac Hammond. 2008. audio compact disk 12.00 (978-1-57399-348-7(4)) Mac Hammond.

Rapture; Countdown to Earth's Last Days. Tim LaHaye & Jerry B. Jenkins. Read by Richard Ferrone. (Running Time: 31500 sec.). 2006. audio compact disk 39.99 (978-1-4193-9670-0(6)) Recorded Bks.

***Rapture in Death.** J. D. Robb, pseud. 2010. audio compact disk 9.99 (978-1-4418-5695-1(1)) Brilliance Audio.

Rapture in Death. abr. ed. J. D. Robb, pseud. Read by Susan Ericksen. (Running Time: 6 hrs.). (In Death Ser.:). 2001. 53.25 (978-1-58788-199-2(3), 1587881993, Lib Edit) Brilliance Audio.
Die and Experience the Pleasure. . . They died with smiles on their faces. Three apparent suicides: a brilliant engineer, an infamous lawyer, and a controversial politician. Three strangers with nothing in common - and no obvious reasons for killing themselves. Police lieutenant Eve Dallas found the deaths suspicious. And her instincts paid off when autopsies revealed small burns on the brains of the victims. Was it a genetic abnormality or a high-tech method of murder? Eve's investigation turned to the provocative world of virtual reality games - where the same techniques used to create joy and desire could also prompt the mind to become the weapon of its own destruction . .

Rapture in Death. abr. ed. J. D. Robb, pseud. Read by Susan Ericksen. (Running Time: 21600 sec.). (In Death Ser.). 2007. audio compact disk 14.99 (978-1-4233-1399-1(2), 9781423313991, BCD Value Price) Brilliance Audio.

Rapture in Death. unabr. ed. J. D. Robb, pseud. Read by Susan Ericksen. (Running Time: 9 hrs.). (In Death Ser.). 2006. 39.25 (978-1-4233-0188-2(9), 9781423301882, BADLE); 24.95 (978-1-4233-0187-5(0), 9781423301875, BAD); 39.25 (978-1-4233-0186-8(2), 9781423301868, Brlnc Audio MP3 Lib); audio compact disk 92.25 (978-1-4233-1353-3(4), 9781423313533, BriAudCD Unabrid); audio compact disk 36.95 (978-1-4233-1352-6(6), 9781423313526, Bril Audio CD Unabri); audio compact disk 24.95 (978-1-4233-0185-1(4), 9781423301851, Brilliance MP3) Brilliance Audio.
They died with smiles on their faces. Three apparent suicides: a brilliant engineer, an infamous lawyer, and a controversial politician. Three strangers with nothing in common - and no obvious reasons for killing themselves. Police lieutenant Eve Dallas found the deaths suspicious. And her instincts paid off when autopsies revealed small burns on the brains of the victims. Was it a genetic abnormality or a high-tech method of murder? Eve's investigation turned to the provocative world of virtual reality games - where the same techniques used to create joy and desire could also prompt the mind to become the weapon of its own destruction . .

Rapture in Death. unabr. ed. J. D. Robb, pseud. Read by Susan Ericksen. (Running Time: 32400 sec.). (In Death Ser.). 2007. 74.25 (978-1-4233-3724-9(7), 9781423337249, BrilAudUnabridg) Brilliance Audio.

Rapture-Music. 2007. audio compact disk 16.95 (978-1-56136-427-5(4)) Master Your Mind.

Rapture of Canaan. Sheri Reynolds. Read by Kathleen O'Malley. 6 cass. (Running Time: 9 hrs.). 1997. 48.00 (4383) Books on Tape.
When a young girl in a millenarian sect in South Carolina becomes pregnant, she must face public scorn & harsh punishment. This is the prelude to a tragedy that will transform the entire community.

Rapture of Canaan. Sheri Reynolds. Narrated by Alyssa Bresnahan. 8 CDs. (Running Time: 9 hrs. 15 mins.). 2001. audio compact disk 78.00 (978-0-7887-5205-6(7), C1362E7) Recorded Bks.
A portrait of a teenaged girl clashing with her controlled world. Growing up in a secluded religious community in the rural South, 15-year-old Ninah Huff has always been told what to think & how to act. But when handsome James becomes her prayer partner, she suddenly has emotions she doesn't understand.

Rapture of Canaan. unabr. ed. Sheri Reynolds. Read by Kathleen O'Malley. 6 cass. (Running Time: 9 hrs.). 1997. 48.00 (978-0-913369-87-6(X)) Books on Tape.

Rapture of Canaan. unabr. ed. Sheri Reynolds. Narrated by Alyssa Bresnahan. 6 cass. (Running Time: 9 hrs. 15 mins.). 1997. 51.00 (978-0-7887-1315-6(9), 95173E7) Recorded Bks.
Growing up in a secluded religious community in the rural South, 15-year old Ninah Huff has always been told what to think & how to act. But when handsome James becomes her prayer partner, she suddenly has emotions she doesn't understand.

Rapture of Freedom. 1 cass. 8.98 (KGOC22) Ken Mills Found.
Kenneth G. Mills conducts The Star-Scape Singers on tour in Europe. Original compositions by K. G. Mills, C. Dednick & J. Roede.

Rapture of the Church: Second Coming of Christ. Finis J. Dake, Sr. (J). (gr. k up). 5.95 (978-1-55829-035-8(4)) Dake Publishing.
Bible study.

Rapture Two Thousand - Party Over, Out of Time. Elvira Craig. 1 cass. (Running Time: 2 hrs.). 1997. Prophetess E C.
The length of the church age leading to the Rapture.

Rapunzel. 2004. pap. bk. 18.95 (978-1-55592-744-8(0)); pap. bk. 38.75 (978-1-55592-752-3(1)); pap. bk. 32.75 (978-0-7882-0246-9(4)); pap. bk. 14.95 (978-0-7882-0398-5(3)); audio compact disk 12.95 (978-1-55592-732-5(7)) Weston Woods.

Rapunzel. unabr. ed. 1 cass. (Running Time: 20 min.). Dramatization. (Magic Looking Glass Ser.). (J). (gr. 2-6). 1989. 9.95 (978-0-7810-0024-6(6), NIM-CW-127-3-C) NIMCO.
A folk story of German descent.

Rapunzel. unabr. ed. Paul O. Zelinsky. 1 cass. (Running Time: 15 min.). (J). (ps-4). 1998. bk. 8.95 (978-0-7882-0088-5(7), RAC379) Weston Woods.
The classic story of Rapunzel, the girl with the long, golden hair.

Rapunzel. unabr. ed. Read by Paul O. Zelinsky. 1 cass. (Running Time: 10 min.). (J). (ps-4). 1998. bk. 24.95 (978-0-7882-0684-9(2), HRA379) Weston Woods.

Rapunzel & Other Children's Favorites. (J). 2005. audio compact disk (978-1-933796-38-3(3)) PC Treasures.

***Rapunzel & Other Classics of Childhood.** unabr. ed. Read by Celebrity Narrators. (Running Time: 0.5 hr. NaN mins.). (Classics Read by Celebrities Ser.). (ENG.). 2010. 19.95 (978-1-4417-7815-4(2)); audio compact disk 9.95 (978-1-4417-7814-7(4)) Blckstn Audio.

***Rapunzel & Other Classics of Childhood.** unabr. ed. Various Authors. Read by Celebrity Narrators. (Running Time: 0.5 hr. NaN mins.). (Classics Read by Celebrities Ser.). (ENG.). 2010. 15.95 (978-1-4417-7812-3(8)); audio compact disk 20.00 (978-1-4417-7813-0(6)) Blckstn Audio.

Rapunzel & Other Tales by the Brothers Grimm. unabr. ed. Jacob W. Grimm & Wilhelm K. Grimm. 2 cass. (Running Time: 2 hrs.). (Classic Literature Ser.). 1997. 16.95 (978-1-55656-203-7(9)) Pub: Dercum Audio. Dist(s): APG
Visit the magic world of fairies, witches & goblins brought vividly to life by the masters of early nineteenth century folk tales, Jakob & Wilhelm Grimm. Includes "Rumplestiltskin," "Hansel & Gretel," "Rapunzel," "Little Red Riding Hood," "Snow White & the Seven Dwarfs," "The Sleeping Beauty in the Wood" & "Snow White & Rose Red".

Rare Beasts. Charles Ogden. Read by Ariadne Meyers. (Running Time: 7620 sec.). (Edgar & Ellen Ser.). (ENG.). (J). (gr. 4-7). 2007. audio compact disk 29.95 (978-0-439-02317-7(3)) Scholastic Inc.

Rare Beasts. unabr. ed. Charles Ogden. Read by Ariadne Meyers. (Edgar & Ellen Ser.). (J). 2007. 34.99 (978-1-60252-679-2(6)) Find a World.

Rare Beasts & Unique Adventures, Vol. 1. Richard Proulx. Perf. by Cathedral Singers. 1 cass. 1999. 10.95 (CS-467); 10.95 (CS-467); audio compact disk 15.95 (CD-467) GIA Pubns.

Rare Benedictine. unabr. ed. Ellis Peters, pseud. Read by Stephen Thorne. 3 cass. (Running Time: 3 hrs. 10 mins.). 2002. 19.95 (978-1-57270-266-0(4)) Pub: Audio Partners. Dist(s): PerseuPGW
Includes the classics "A Light on the Road to Woodstock," "The Price of Light." and "Eye Witness." These stories feature Peters's complex plots, mastery of language and deep understanding of human nature.

Rare Benedictine. unabr. ed. Ellis Peters, pseud. Read by Stephen Thorne. 3 cass. (Running Time: 4 hrs. 30 mins.). 2000. 31.95 (978-0-7451-4330-9(X), CAB 1013) Pub: Chivers Audio Bks GBR. Dist(s): AudioGO
Brother Cadfael is a cult figure of crime fiction. Yet the story of his entry into the monastery at Shrewsbury has been known hitherto only a few; now listeners can discover the chain of events that led him into the Benedictine Order.

Rare Coin Score. unabr. ed. Richard Stark, pseud. Read by Michael Kramer. 3 cass. (Running Time: 4 hrs. 30 mins.). 2001. 28.00 (978-0-7366-8383-8(6)) Books on Tape.
Parker has misgivings about this one: he's taken the job out of a need for excitement, he's let amateurs in on the job, & he's doing it to get close to a woman. Nonetheless, the prospect of ripping off an entire coin collectors' convention, and of two million dollars in small, easy-to-sell coins, is enough to get him motivated. Against the job, of course, there are the usual possibilities of death or prison. But keeping him on track is the new woman, Claire. Parker doesn't know from love, but there's something about her that makes her more than an entry in his bimbo parade.

Rare Elements. abr. ed. Ustad Sultan Khan. 1 CD. (Running Time: 3480 sec.). 2006. audio compact disk 16.98 (978-1-59179-470-7(6), MM01050D) Sounds True.
The yearning bow of Ustad Sultan Khan's sarangi and his timeless voice merge into one seamless instrument, borne here on the inspiring grooves of six leading remix artists. In late 2003, world-renowned sarangi master Ustad Sultan Khan recorded ten pieces in a New York studio with producer David Nichtern and an elite group of contemporary musicians. The result is Rare Elements: a pulsing spectrum that blends India's traditional sounds with a broad range of electronica and world beat. Joe Clausell opens the album with "Aja Maji," followed by Thievery Corporation's hypnotizing rendition of "Tarana" and Radar One's Sad Bachelor Remix of "Jana." Also featuring Ralph Rosario and Nickodemus & Osiris, Rare Elements offers a spellbinding fusion of Ustad Sultan Khan's instrumental force and vocal nuance, downtempo pulse lines, and moving rhythms for a unique listening experience that will rejuvenate mind, body, and soul.

Rare Meat. Kenward Elmslie. Read by Kenward Elmslie. 1 cass. (Running Time: 1 hr.). (Watershed Tapes of Contemporary Poetry). 1979. 11.95 (23620) J Norton Pubs.
A potpourri of poems, songs, speeches & chants.

Rare Ruby. unabr. ed. Dee Williams. Read by Kim Hicks. 10 cass. (Running Time: 15 hrs.). 2003. 84.95 (978-0-7540-0905-4(X), CAB 2327) AudioGO.

Rarely Heard Ragas. Music by Pandit Jasraj. 1 cass. 1997. (A97013); audio compact disk (CD A97013) Multi-Cultural Bks.

Rarely Heard Ragas. Music by Pandit B. Joshi. 1 cass. 1997. (A97011); audio compact disk (CD A97011) Multi-Cultural Bks.

Rarely Heard Ragas. Music by Asad A. Khan. 1 cass. 1997. (A97014); audio compact disk (CD A97014) Multi-Cultural Bks.

Rarely Heard Ragas, Vol. 4. Music by Vilayat Khan. 1 cass. 1997. (A97012); audio compact disk (CD A97012) Multi-Cultural Bks.

Rascal. Sterling North. Read by Jim Weiss. 3 cass. (Running Time: 4 hrs. 40 mins.). (J). 2000. 24.00 (978-0-7366-9166-6(9)) Books on Tape.
In this memoir, he recalls his year with Rascal, a very mischievous & resourceful raccoon. Real humor, a reverence for nature & joys of friendship.

Rascal. Sterling North & Jim Weiss. 3 cass. (Running Time: 4 hrs. 30 mins.). (J). 19.18 Blisterpack. (BYA 946) NewSound.
Rascal, a baby racoon is brought home by Sterling North to join his menagerie of animals.

Rascal. unabr. ed. Sterling North. Read by Jim Weiss. 3 cass. (Running Time: 4 hrs. 30 mins.). (J). (gr. 1-8). 1999. 30.00 (LL 0114, Chivers Child Audio) AudioGO.

Rascal. unabr. ed. Sterling North. Read by Jim Weiss. 3 cass. (Running Time: 4 hrs. 30 mins.). (YA). 1999. 23.98 (FS9-34626) Highsmith.

Rascal. unabr. ed. Sterling North. Read by Jim Weiss. 3 vols. (Running Time: 4 hrs. 41 mins.). (J). (gr. 4-7). 1998. pap. bk. 36.00 (978-0-8072-7897-0(1), 1124-AB, Listening Lib); 30.00 (978-0-8072-7896-3(3), 1124-AA, Listening Lib) Random Audio Pubg.
What more could an 11 year old boy ask for than a bike, woods to romp in, lots of freedom to do what he pleases & a baby raccoon!.

Rascal. unabr. ed. Sterling North. Narrated by Ed Sala. 3 pieces. (Running Time: 4 hrs. 15 mins.). (J). (gr. 5 up). 1998. 30.00 (978-0-7887-2219-6(0), 95518E7) Recorded Bks.
In 1918 Wisconsin, 11-year-old Sterling finds an abandoned, month-old raccoon. Taking the kit home, soon Sterling & his mischievous raccoon, Rascal, are enjoying one adventure after another.

Rascal. unabr. ed. Sterling North. Narrated by Ed Sala. 4 CDs. (Running Time: 4 hrs. 15 mins.). (gr. 5 up). 2000. audio compact disk 36.00 (978-0-7887-4212-5(4), C1151E7) Recorded Bks.

Rascal, Class Set. unabr. ed. Sterling North. Read by Ed Sala. 3 cass., 10 bks. (Running Time: 4 hrs. 30 min.). (YA). 1998. bk. 100.70 (978-0-7887-2541-8(6), 46711) Recorded Bks.
When 11-year-old Sterling brings an abandoned, month-old raccoon home, the two enjoy an unforgettable friendship.

Rascal, Homework Set. unabr. ed. Sterling North. Read by Ed Sala. 3 cass. (Running Time: 4 hrs. 30 min.). (YA). (gr. 7). 1998. bk. 43.24 (978-0-7887-2236-3(0), 40720) Recorded Bks.

Rascal in Trouble. unabr. ed. Paul Jennings & Paul Jennings. Read by Rebecca Macauley. (Running Time: 1200 sec.). (Rascal Ser.). (J). (ps-3). 2006. audio compact disk 39.95 (978-1-74093-540-1(3)) Pub: Bolinda Pubng AUS. Dist(s): Bolinda Pub Inc

Rascal Takes Off. unabr. ed. Paul Jennings. Read by Rebecca Macauley. (Running Time: 20 mins.). (Rascal Ser.). (J). 2005. audio compact disk 39.95 (978-1-74093-541-8(1)) Pub: Bolinda Pubng AUS. Dist(s): Bolinda Pub Inc

Rascal the Dragon. unabr. ed. Paul Jennings. Read by Rebecca Macauley. (Running Time: 20 mins.). (Rascal Ser.). (J). 2004. 18.00 (978-1-74093-338-4(9)); audio compact disk 39.95 (978-1-74093-515-9(2)) Pub: Bolinda Pubng AUS. Dist(s): Bolinda Pub Inc

Rascal the dragon Collection 2. Paul Jennings. Read by Rebecca Macauley. (Running Time: 17 mins.). (J). 2009. 39.99 (978-1-74214-396-5(2), 9781742143965) Pub: Bolinda Pubng AUS. Dist(s): Bolinda Pub Inc

Rascal the dragon Collection 2. unabr. ed. Paul Jennings. Read by Rebecca Macauley. (Running Time: 17 mins.). (Rascal Ser.). (J). 2007. audio compact disk 39.95 (978-1-74093-908-9(5)) Pub: Bolinda Pubng AUS. Dist(s): Bolinda Pub Inc

Rascals in Paradise. unabr. ed. James A. Michener & A. Grove Day. Read by Larry McKeever. 12 cass. (Running Time: 18 hrs.). 1995. 96.00 (978-0-7366-2897-6(5), 3597) Books on Tape.
Chronicle of the true adventures of ten men & one woman - each seeking solace & fulfillment in the broad Pacific.

Rascal's Trick. unabr. ed. Paul Jennings & Paul Jennings. Read by Rebecca Macauley. (Running Time: 1200 sec.). (Rascal Ser.). (J). (ps-1). 2006. audio compact disk 39.95 (978-1-74093-542-5(X)) Pub: Bolinda Pubng AUS. Dist(s): Bolinda Pub Inc

Rash. Pete Hautman. Read by Andy Paris. 6. (Running Time: 6 hrs. 50 mins.). 2006. 39.75 (978-1-4281-1098-4(4)); audio compact disk 66.75 (978-1-4281-1103-5(4)) Recorded Bks.

Rashmi Mayur Discusses the World's Dwindling Resources & Music Videos by Alabama & Santana. Hosted by Nancy Pearlman. 1 cass. (Running Time: 29 min.). 10.00 (1112) Educ Comm CA.

Raspberries! Jay O'Callahan. Perf. by Jay O'Callahan. Illus. by Will Moses. 1 cass. (Running Time: 46 min.). (J). (gr. 2 up). 1983. bk. 10.00 (978-1-877954-02-3(0)) Artana Prodns.
Magical berries! How can they change an unlucky farmer's life? A juicy and delicious story for the whole family.

Raspberries! Jay O'Callahan. Perf. by Jay O'Callahan. 1 CD. (Running Time: 46 min, 18 seconds). Dramatization. 2003. audio compact disk 15.00 (978-1-877954-40-5(3)) Pub: Artana Prodns. Dist(s): Yellow Moon
Magical berries! How can they change an unlucky farmer's life? A juicy and delicious story for the whole family. Winner of the Parent's Choice Gold Award.

Rasputin. unabr. ed. Harold Shukman. Read by Nigel Graham. 2 cass. (Running Time: 2 hrs.). (Pocket Biography Ser.). 1998. 24.98 (978-0-7531-0414-9(8), 980817) Pub: ISIS Audio GBR. Dist(s): Ulverscroft US
Gregory Rasputin is notorious in Russian history as a malign & destructive force, a man with unhealthy influence on the Empress Alexandra & undue power in Russian politics. An uneducated peasant, he left Siberia to become a wandering "holy man", soon acquiring a reputation as a healer. He was presented at court in 1905, when the Empress was desperately seeking a cure for her son. His positive effect on the heir's health made him indispensable. He was assassinated in 1916.

Rasputin: The Saint Who Sinned. unabr. ed. Brian Moynahan & John Gallagher. Narrated by Nelson Runger. 16 cass. (Running Time: 22 hrs. 30 mins.). 1998. 128.00 (978-0-7887-1759-8(6), 95237E7) Recorded Bks.
Born a coarse peasant & largely uneducated his entire life, Rasputin held sway in one of the greatest royal houses of Europe.

Rasputin's Daughter. Robert Alexander. Read by Josephine Bailey. (Playaway Adult Fiction Ser.). 2008. 59.99 (978-1-60640-986-2(7)) Find a World.

Rasputin's Daughter. unabr. ed. Robert Alexander. Narrated by Josephine Bailey. (Running Time: 8 hrs. 30 mins. 0 sec.). (ENG.). 2006. audio compact disk 29.99 (978-1-4001-0194-8(8)); audio compact disk 59.99 (978-1-4001-3194-5(4)); audio compact disk 19.99 (978-1-4001-5194-3(5)) Pub: Tantor Media. Dist(s): IngramPubServ

Rasselas, Prince of Abissinia. unabr. ed. Samuel Johnson. Read by Walter Zimmerman. 4 cass. (Running Time: 5 hrs.). 1984. 28.00 (C-101) Jimcin Record.
A tale of the mysterious East.

Rat Race. 2004. 8.95 (978-1-56008-317-7(4)); cass. & flmstrp 30.00 (978-1-56008-755-7(2)) Weston Woods.

Rat Race. unabr. ed. Dick Francis. Read by Ian Ogilvy. 4 cass. (Running Time: 6 hrs.). 2000. 34.95 (CAB 020) Pub: Chivers Audio Bks GBR. Dist(s): AudioGO
Matt Shore, flying for a small air-taxi charter firm, took five passengers on a routine flight to the races: two jockeys, a trainer, an owner and a friend. Awaiting them in the sky was a quick form of extinction, that was only avoided by luck. Matt guessed the sudden death had been aimed at one of his passengers, he didn't know which one, and he didn't particularly want to find out. But gradually he found himself caught in a dangerous web of deception, and action became necessary for survival.

Rat Run. unabr. ed. Gerald Seymour. Read by Crispin Redman. 12 cass. (Running Time: 17 hrs. 15 mins.). 2006. 109.75 (978-1-84505-621-6(3), Clipper Audio) Recorded Bks.

Ratastrophe Catastrophe. unabr. ed. David Lee Stone. Read by Robert Llewellyn. 3 cass. (Running Time: 4 hrs. 56 mins.). (Illmoor Chronicles: Bk. 1). (YA). 2004. 25.00 (978-0-8072-2079-5(5), Listening Lib) Random Audio Pubg.
The Duke of Dulwich is in distress - several reports are coming in that the city is beginning to be overrun by a plague of rats. Naturally he has killed off all witnesses, but daily the problem is becoming more obvious. His corrupt council, led by the hapless ex-wizard Tambor, has no solutions. He must send for mercenaries to rid his city of the rampant rodents. Heralds ride out from every gate, each hoping to bring back the savior of the city. Part-time herald, full-time thief, and grandson to Tambour, Jimmy Quickstint is the lucky man - falling haphazardly upon the skills of Diek Wustapha - a charmer - recently inhabited by magic and suddenly irresistible to girls, sheep - and rats. Diek fulfills his task and is promised $500 for his troubles. But once the rats have gone, the council reneges on their deal. Full of anger (and magic), Diek charms the children of Dulwich out of the city, playing on his mouth organ, where he disappears into the caves ad woodland of the surrounding area. The Duke is now in despair and has to resort to mercenaries to track him down. These include Groan Teethgrit (a man-mountain with more fingers than brain cells), Gordo Goldaxe (a dwarf who takes offence at people looking down on him) and Jimmy Quickstint (the only thief in history to go into a house with more than he came out with). It's not looking good.

Rate Yourself As a Manager. Roger Fritz. 1 cass. 8.95 (978-0-88684-084-6(8)) Listen USA.

Rater quick - oer Edition: U. S. Army Officer Evaluation Preparation Program. Compiled by Steven W. Moore & Mark S. Gerecht. 2007. audio compact disk 39.95 (978-1-886715-38-7(6)) Byrrd Ent Inc.

Rathcormick. Homan Potterton. 2008. 69.95 (978-1-84559-907-2(1)) Pub: Soundings Ltd GBR. Dist(s): Ulverscroft US

Rathcormick. Homan Potterton. Read by Gerry O'Brian. 2008. audio compact disk 79.95 (978-1-84559-908-9(X)) Pub: Soundings Ltd GBR. Dist(s): Ulverscroft US

***Ratification: The People Debate the Constitution, 1787-1788.** unabr. ed. Pauline Maier. (Running Time: 27 hrs. 0 mins. 0 sec.). 2010. 39.99 (978-1-4001-6965-8(8)); 28.99 (978-1-4001-8965-6(9)) Tantor Media.

***Ratification: The People Debate the Constitution, 1787-1788.** unabr. ed. Pauline Maier. Narrated by Johnny Heller. (Running Time: 27 hrs. 0 mins. 0 sec.). 2010. audio compact disk 59.99 (978-1-4001-1965-3(0)) Pub: Tantor Media. Dist(s): IngramPubServ

Ratification Debates: The U. S. Constitution. Wendy McElroy. Narrated by Walter Cronkite. (Running Time: 9000 sec.). (Audio Classics Ser.). 2006. audio compact disk 25.95 (978-0-7861-6977-1(X)) Pub: Blckstn Audio. Dist(s): NetLibrary CO

Ratification Debates: The U. S. Constitution. unabr. ed. Wendy McElroy. Perf. by Craig Deitschman et al. Ed. by George H. Smith. Narrated by Walter Cronkite. 2 cass. (Running Time: 75 min.). Dramatization. (U. S. Constitution Ser.). (YA). (gr. 10 up). 1987. 17.95 (978-0-938935-82-7(8), 390286) Knowledge Prod.
Performers also include Sam Tsoutsouvas & Robert Wynne. Some delegates to the Constitutional Convention had refused to sign the Constitution. Rhode Island had even refused to send representatives. Now the Constitution was being subjected to the harsh process of ratification by the states. Where, many asked, was a bill of rights? And from Virginia, the question resounded: What was the status of slavery?.

***Ratification (Library Edition) The People Debate the Constitution, 1787-1788.** unabr. ed. Pauline Maier. (Running Time: 27 hrs. 0 mins.). 2010. 59.99 (978-1-4001-9965-5(4)); audio compact disk 143.99 (978-1-4001-4965-0(7)) Pub: Tantor Media. Dist(s): IngramPubServ

Rational Curriculum. Leonard Peikoff. 1 cass. (Running Time: 90 min.). 1986. 10.95 (978-1-56114-058-9(9), LP05C) Second Renaissance.
Why the nature & purpose of education demand that only the "3 R's" & four additional subjects be taught to schoolchildren.

Rational Egoism in "The Fountainhead" Andrew Bernstein. 2 cass. (Running Time: 2 hrs. 20 min.). 1991. 19.95 Set. (978-1-56114-121-0(6), CB02D) Second Renaissance.

Rational Intuitive Mind. Robert Ornstein & David Galin. 10.95 (33031) J Norton Pubs.
Specific functions of the 2 sides of the brain.

Rational Living in an Irrational World. Albert Ellis. 1 cass. (Running Time: 57 min.). 9.95 (C020) A Ellis Institute.
Numerous techniques for living productively & non-miserably in a crazy world, while calmly trying to change what can be changed.

Rational Living in an Irrational World. Albert Ellis. 1 cass. (Running Time: 57 min.). 9.95 (C020) Inst Rational-Emotive.

Rational Mind. Hal Stone & Sidra Stone. 1 cass. (Running Time: 1 hrs.). (Mendocino Ser.: Vol. 14). 1997. 10.95 (978-1-56557-054-2(5), T14) Delos Inc.
Without a good mind, we are lost. But when this dominates our lives, we lose our energetic connection to the people around us &, in the deepest sense, to life itself. This tape shows how to separate from your mind & to reclaim your full birthright.

***Rational Optimist.** unabr. ed. Matt Ridley. Read by L. J. Ganser. (ENG.). 2010. (978-0-06-199766-2(8), Harper Audio) HarperCollins Pubs.

***Rational Optimist: How Prosperity Evolves.** unabr. ed. Matt Ridley. Read by L. J. Ganser. (ENG.). 2010. (978-0-06-199765-5(X), Harper Audio) HarperCollins Pubs.

Rational Optimist: How Prosperity Evolves. unabr. ed. Matt Ridley. Read by L. J. Ganser. 2010. audio compact disk 39.99 (978-0-06-199262-9(3), Harper Audio) HarperCollins Pubs.

Rational Parenting. Susan Crawford & Lynn C. Salsman. 4 cass. (Running Time: 3 hrs.). 1994. 39.95 Set. (978-1-56114-321-4(9), KK03D) Second Renaissance.
Techniques to assist parents in imparting a strong set of values, encouraging confidence & establishing rational methods of discipline.

Rationale of the Twitchell-Allen Three-Dimensional Personality Test (3-DPT) Doris T. Allen. 1 cass. (Running Time: 37 min.). 1966. (29236) J Norton Pubs.
A third dimension is added to projective test forms which thereby are sensed visually, tactually & proprioceptively. With increased involvement of the nervous system, spontaneity & expressiveness are typical & the subject characteristically responds from a depth of personality beyond his usual control.

Rationalism. Gordon Clark. 1 cass. (Lectures on Apologetics: No. 8). 5.00 Trinity Found.

Rationality of the Common Law. Arline Mann. 1 cass. (Running Time: 90 min.). 1991. 12.95 (978-1-56114-161-6(5), PM01C) Second Renaissance.

Ratking. unabr. ed. Michael Dibdin. Read by William Ganimara. 8 cass. (Running Time: 10 hrs. 40 min.). (Aurelio Zen Mystery Ser.). (J). 2001. 69.95 (978-1-85089-795-8(6), 8912X) Pub: ISIS Lrg Prnt GBR. Dist(s): Ulverscroft US

Raton Pass. unabr. collector's ed. Thomas W. Blackburn. Read by Christopher Lane. 8 cass. (Running Time: 8 hrs.). 1995. 48.00 (978-0-7366-2990-4(4), 3679) Books on Tape.
Greed drives the murderous schemes of men who lust after the Challon family's vast ranch. A temptress could topple the empire, too.

Rats. James Herbert & James Herbert. Read by Gareth Armstrong. 5 cass. (Running Time: 19500 sec.). (Isis Cassettes Ser.). 2005. 49.95 (978-0-7531-2145-0(X)) Pub: ISIS Lrg Prnt GBR. Dist(s): Ulverscroft US

Rats!, unabr. ed. Short Stories. Jane Cutler. Narrated by Johnny Heller. 2 pieces. (Running Time: 2 hrs. 15 mins.). (gr. 1 up). 1997. 19.00 (978-0-7887-0739-1(6), 94916E7) Recorded Bks.
In a hilarious sequel to "No Dogs Allowed," Jason & Edward Fraser encounter a new set of adventures. From girlfriends to Halloween ghouls, from baseball to baby rats, the brothers find surprises at every turn. This collection of five stories is full of fun & high spirits.

Rats. unabr. ed. James Herbert & James Herbert. Read by Gareth Armstrong. 6 CDs. (Running Time: 19500 sec.). (Isis (CDs) Ser.). 2005. audio compact disk 64.95 (978-0-7531-2455-0(6)) Pub: ISIS Lrg Prnt GBR. Dist(s): Ulverscroft US

Rats. unabr. ed. Paul Zindel. Narrated by L. J. Ganser. 4 pieces. (Running Time: 4 hrs. 45 mins.). (gr. 7 up). 2000. 37.00 (978-0-7887-4300-9(7), 96210E7) Recorded Bks.
Millions of huge, blood-thirsty rats are terrorizing Sarah Macafee's hometown & it will take all her brainpower & courage to save the neighborhood from being wiped out.

Rats. unabr. ed. Paul Zindel. Read by L. J. Ganser. 4 cass. (Running Time: 4 hrs. 45 mins.). (YA). 2000. pap. bk. & stu. ed. 59.99 (978-0-7887-4346-7(5), 41140) Recorded Bks.

Rats. unabr. ed. Paul Zindel. Narrated by L. J. Ganser. 4 CDs. (Running Time: 4 hrs. 45 mins.). (gr. 7 up). 2001. audio compact disk 39.00 (978-0-7887-5223-0(5), C1371E7) Recorded Bks.
Millions of huge, blood-thirsty rats are terrorizing Sarah Macafee's hometown, & it will take all her brainpower & courage to save the neighborhood from being wiped out.

Rats, Class Set. unabr. ed. Paul Zindel. Read by L. J. Ganser. 4 cass. (Running Time: 4 hrs. 45 mins.). (YA). 2000. 205.20 (978-0-7887-4446-4(1), 47137) Recorded Bks.
Millions of huge, blood-thirsty rats are terrorizing Sarah Macafee's hometown & it will take all her brainpower & courage to save the neighborhood from being wiped out.

Rats in the Walls. 1987. (A 2102) HarperCollins Pubs.

Rats in the Walls. abr. ed. H. P. Lovecraft. Perf. by H. P. McCallum. 1 cass. 1984. 12.95 (SWC 1347) HarperCollins Pubs.

Rats in the Walls. unabr. ed. H. P. Lovecraft. 1 cass. (Running Time: 90 min.). Dramatization. 2002. 12.95 (978-0-929483-07-8(3)) Centauri Express Co.

***Rats of Hamlintown.** Anonymous. 2009. (978-1-60136-534-7(9)) Audio Holding.

Rats Saw God: A Comic Emotionally Charged Tale, unabr. ed. Rob Thomas. Narrated by Johnny Heller. 5 pieces. (Running Time: 6 hrs. 30 mins.). (gr. 9 up). 1997. 44.00 (978-0-7887-0731-5(0), 94908E7) Recorded Bks.
Steve York is a brilliant but underachieving high school senior whose guidance counselor gives him one last chance to graduate. All he has to do is write a hundred-page essay on how he got where he is.

Rat's Tale. Tor Seidler. Read by Jason Katz. 3 cass. (Running Time: 3 hrs. 10 mins.). (J). 2000. 24.00 (978-0-7366-9167-3(7)) Books on Tape.
Montague Mad-Rat wants to impress Iisabel Moberly-Rat, but doesn't ' think he has a chance. But when the neighborhood pier may be turned into a parking lot, he learns that his efforts can be taken seriously & he does have a lot to offer.

Rat's Tale. Tor Seidler. 3 cass. (Running Time: 3 hrs. 18 mins.). (J). 19.18 Blisterpack. (BYA 947) NewSound.
Young Mantague Mad-Rat is feeling helpless & alone. He lives in an old sewer pipe under New York City & desperately wants to impress Isabel Moberly-Rat, but his only talent is for painting seashells.

Rat's Tale. unabr. ed. Tor Seidler. Read by Jim Weiss. 3 cass. (Running Time: 3 hrs. 18 mins.). (J). (gr. 1-8). 1999. 30.00 (LL 0111, Chivers Child Audio) AudioGO.

Rat's Tale. unabr. ed. Tor Seidler. Read by Jason Katz. 3 cass. (Running Time: 3 hrs. 18 mins.). (YA). 1999. 23.98 (FS9-34541) Highsmith.

Rat's Tale. unabr. ed. Tor Seidler. Read by Jason Katz. 3 cass. (Running Time: 3 hrs. 18 mins.). (J). (gr. 3-5). 1998. pap. bk. 35.00 (978-0-8072-7951-9(X), YA947SP, Listening Lib) Random Audio Pubg.
Rats rule in the streets, sewers, parks & wharves of New York City. Young Montague Mad-Rat leads a sheltered existence, until he meets beautiful & spunky Isabel Moberly-Rat. He discovers the greater rat class system & the politics & social norms therein, embarking on a bold adventure that includes romance, self-discovery & plenty of derring-do.

Rat's Tale. unabr. ed. Tor Seidler. Read by Jason Katz. 3 cass. (Running Time: 3 hr. 18 min.). (J). (gr. 3-7). 1998. 30.00 (978-0-8072-7950-2(1), YA947CX, Listening Lib) Random Audio Pubg.

Rats! the Story of the Pied Piper: Listening. Dave Perry & Jean Perry. (ENG.). 2003. audio compact disk 12.95 (978-0-7390-3083-7(3)) Alfred Pub.

Rats! the Story of the Pied Piper: SoundTrax. Dave Perry & Jean Perry. (ENG.). 2003. audio compact disk 59.95 (978-0-7390-3097-4(3)) Alfred Pub.

Rattapallax, No. 4. Ed. by George Dickerson et al. 2001. pap. bk. 7.95 (978-1-892494-28-3(0)) Pub: Rattapallax Pr. Dist(s): Ingram Bk Co

Rattler's Place. unabr. ed. Patricia Wrightson. (J). 2002. audio compact disk 39.95 (978-1-74030-845-8(X)) Pub: Bolinda Pubng AUS. Dist(s): Bolinda Pub Inc

Rattler's Place; The Sugar-Gum Tree; The Water Dragons. unabr. ed. Patricia Wrightson. Narrated by Stig Wemyss. 2 CDs. (Running Time: 1 hr. 30 mins.). (Great Aussie Bites Ser.: Vol. 4). (J). 2002. audio compact disk 43.95 (978-1-74030-852-6(2)) Pub: Bolinda Pubng AUS. Dist(s): Bolinda Pub Inc

Rattlesnake Crossing. abr. ed. J. A. Jance. Read by Yancy Butler. 4 cass. (Running Time: 5 hrs. 30 mins.). (Joanna Brady Mystery Ser.). 1999. 25.00 (FS9-43263) Highsmith.

Rattlesnake Crossing, unabr. ed. J. A. Jance. Read by Stephanie Brush. 8 cass. (Running Time: 11 hrs.). (Joanna Brady Mystery Ser.). 1999. 49.95 (978-1-55686-888-7(X)) Books in Motion.
A local gun dealer is found murdered & suspicion falls upon a rebellious newcomer.

***Rattlesnake Crossing.** unabr. ed. J. A. Jance. Read by C. J. Critt. (ENG.). 2010. (978-0-06-196724-5(6), Harper Audio) HarperCollins Pubs.

Rattlesnake Crossing. unabr. ed. J. A. Jance. Read by Sharon Williams. 6 cass. (Running Time: 9 hrs.). (Joanna Brady Mystery Ser.). 1999. 57.25 (FS9-43213) Highsmith.

***Rattlesnake Crossing: A Joanna Brady Mystery.** unabr. ed. J. A. Jance. Read by C. J. Critt. (ENG.). 2010. (978-0-06-195390-3(3), Harper Audio) HarperCollins Pubs.

Rauin into My Mirror Has Walked see Brian Patten Reading His Poetry

Rave On: The Biography of Buddy Holly. unabr. collector's ed. Philip Norman. Read by Rob McQuay. 9 cass. (Running Time: 13 hrs. 30 min.). 1997. 72.00 (978-0-7366-3645-2(5), 4307) Books on Tape.
The memory of the great Buddy Holly overshadows the American rock 'n' roll scene. He was only 22 when he died in a plane crash.

Ravel: An Introduction to Bolero & Ma Mere L'oye. Jeremy Siepmann. 2 CDs. (Running Time: 3 hrs.). (Classics Explained Ser.). 2003. pap. bk. (978-1-84379-093-8(9)) NaxMulti GBR.

Ravel - Debussy: The Greatest Hits. 1 cass. audio compact disk 10.98 CD. (978-1-57908-162-1(2), 3608) Platinm Enter.

Raveling. Peter Moore Smith. 2001. 24.98 (978-1-58621-122-6(6)) Hachet Audio.

Raveling. abr. ed. Peter Moore Smith. Read by Eric Stoltz. (ENG.). 2005. 14.98 (978-1-59483-458-5(X)) Pub: Hachet Audio. Dist(s): HachBkGrp

Ravelstein. abr. ed. Saul Bellow. 4 cass. (Running Time: 6 hrs.). 2000. 24.95 HighBridge.

Raven see Best of Edgar Allan Poe

Raven see Edgar Allan Poe, Set, Short Stories and Poems

Raven see Tales of Horror & Suspense

Raven see Edgar Allan Poe

Raven see Famous Story Poems

Raven. unabr. ed. V. C. Andrews. Read by Laurel Lefkow. 3 cass. (Running Time: 4 hrs. 30 min.). (Orphans Ser.). 2001. 34.95 (978-0-7531-0635-8(3), 991101) Pub: ISIS Audio GBR. Dist(s): ISIS Pub
Living with her drunken mother in a battered apartment hardly fit for humans, Raven often heard about how her birth twelve years ago was a big mistake. Then her mother was arrested & her Uncle Reuben took Raven to live with him, her aunt & two cousins. For the first time Raven had her own room in a clean, orderly household. But while she knew Uncle Reuben preferred not to have her there, Raven couldn't guess at the shocking secrets lurking beneath the family's ordinary facade... or anticipate the painful humiliation that would make her wish for her old life with Mama again.

Raven. unabr. ed. V. C. Andrews. Read by Laurel Lefkow. 4 CDs. (Running Time: 3 hrs. 45 min.). (Orphans Ser.: No. 4). (J). 2001. audio compact disk 51.95 (978-0-7531-1327-1(9)) Pub: ISIS Lrg Prnt GBR. Dist(s): Ulverscroft US
When her mother was arrested, her Uncle Reuben took Raven to live with him, her aunt and two cousins. Aunt Clara welcomed her warmly, and for the first time Raven had her own room in a clean, orderly household. But while she knew Uncle Reuben preferred not to have her there, Raven couldn't guess at the shocking secrets lurking beneath the family's ordinary facade.

Raven & Other Works. unabr. ed. Edgar Allan Poe. Perf. by Basil Rathbone. 1 cass. Incl. Alone. (CPN 1028); Annabel Lee. (CPN 1028); Black Cat. (CPN 1028); City in the Sea. (CPN 1028); Eldorado. (CPN 1028); Masque of the Red Death. (CPN 1028); To- (CPN 1028); 1984. 9.95 (CPN 1028) HarperCollins Pubs.

Raven & the Fox, Little Thumb & Many More Tales see Cuervo y la Zorra y Muchos Cuentos Mas

Raven & the Fox, Little Thumb & Many More Tales. (Running Time: 1 hr.). (J). 2001. 14.95 (978-1-60083-130-0(3), Audiofy Corp) Iofy Corp.

Raven & the Reaping. Contrib. by Famine. Prod. by Andres Magnusson. 2008. audio compact disk 13.99 (978-5-557-42229-1(3)) Solid State MO.

Raven in the Foregate. unabr. ed. Ellis Peters. Read by Vanessa Benjamin. 5 cass. (Running Time: 7 hrs.). 2000. 39.95 (978-0-7861-1337-8(5), 2232) Blckstn Audio.

Raven in the Foregate. unabr. ed. Ellis Peters, pseud. Read by Stephen Thorne. 6 cass. (Running Time: 6 hrs. 55 mins.). (Chronicles of Brother Cadfael Ser.: Vol. 12). 2000. 29.95 (978-1-57270-153-3(6), N61153u) Pub: Audio Partners. Dist(s): PerseuPGW
In 1141 A.D., a new priest arrives at Holy Cross, outside the Abbey of Saint Peter & Saint Paul. After the newcomer is found murdered, Brother Cadfael must sort out the complicated strands of innocence & guilt.

Raven in the Foregate. unabr. ed. Ellis Peters, pseud. Read by Vanessa Benjamin. 5 cass. (Running Time: 7 hrs. 30 mins.). (Chronicles of Brother Cadfael Ser.: Vol. 12). 1998. 39.95 (2232) Blckstn Audio.
Christmas, 1141 AD, Abbot Radulfus returns from London, bringing with him a priest for the vacant living of Holy Cross (known as the foregate). When he is found drowned in the millpond, suspicion is cast in many directions. Now Cadfael is left the task of sorting things out.

Raven in the Foregate. unabr. ed. Ellis Peters, pseud. Read by Stephen Thorne. 6 cass. (Running Time: 9 hrs.). (Chronicles of Brother Cadfael Ser.: Vol. 12). 2000. 49.95 (978-0-7451-4229-6(X), CAB 912) Pub: Chivers Audio Bks GBR. Dist(s): AudioGO
It's Christmas 1141 AD, and Abbot Radulfus returns from London with a priest for the vacant Foregate, a man of scholarship and discipline, but neither humility nor the common touch. When he is found drowned in the mill-pond, suspicion is cast in many directions and Brother Cadfael has the task of sorting it all out.

Raven in the Foregate. unabr. ed. Ellis Peters, pseud. Narrated by Patrick Tull. 6 cass. (Running Time: 8 hrs. 15 mins.). (Chronicles of Brother Cadfael Ser.: Vol. 12). 1995. 51.00 (978-0-7887-0163-4(0), 94388E7) Recorded Bks.
After years of studying with the Bishop, young Father Ailnoth has come to take over the parish of Holy Cross. But soon Ailnoth's true nature surfaces - harsh, cold-hearted & merciless. Someone lures him from his home & murders him. Who in Shrewsbury would kill a priest on Christmas Day?.

***Raven on the Wing.** Kay Hooper. Narrated by Susan Boyce. (Running Time: 5 hrs. 12 mins. 0 sec.). (ENG.). 2011. audio compact disk 19.95 (978-1-60998-143-3(X)) Pub: AudioGO. Dist(s): Perseus Dist

Raven Rise. unabr. ed. D. J. MacHale. Read by William Dufris. 1 MP3-CD. (Running Time: 61200 sec.). (Pendragon Ser.: Bk. 9). (J). 2008. audio

compact disk 39.25 (978-1-59737-304-3(4), 9781597373043, Brlnc Audio MP3 Lib) Brilliance Audio.
Please enter a Synopsis.

Raven Rise. unabr. ed. D. J. MacHale. Read by William Dufris. (Running Time: 17 hrs.). (Pendragon Ser.: Bk. 9). 2008. 39.25 (978-1-59737-306-7(0), 9781597373067, BADLE); 24.95 (978-1-59737-305-0(2), 9781597373050, BAD) Brilliance Audio.

Raven Rise. unabr. ed. D. J. MacHale. Read by William Dufris. 1 MP3-CD. (Running Time: 61200 sec.). (Pendragon Ser.: Bk. 9). (J). (gr. 5). 2008. audio compact disk 24.95 (978-1-59737-303-6(6), 9781597373036, Brilliance MP3) Brilliance Audio.

Raven Rise. unabr. ed. D. J. MacHale. Read by William Dufris. (Running Time: 17 hrs.). (Pendragon Ser.: Bk. 9). 2009. audio compact disk 19.99 (978-1-4233-9911-7(0), 9781423399117); audio compact disk 49.97 (978-1-4233-9912-4(9), 9781423399124, BriAudCD Unabrid) Brilliance Audio.

Raven, The Bells & Other Poems. unabr. ed. Edgar Allan Poe. Read by Hurd Hatfield. 1 cass. (J). 10.95 (978-0-8045-1023-3(7), SAC 1023) Spoken Arts.

Ravenmaster's Secret. unabr. ed. Elvira Woodruff. Read by Simon Vance. (J). 2007. 39.99 (978-1-59895-939-0(5)) Find a World.

Ravenmaster's Secret -Lib. Elvira Woodruff. Read by Kate Reading. 3 cass. (Running Time: 4 hrs.). 2005. 24.95 (978-0-7861-3023-8(7), 3432); audio compact disk 36.00 (978-0-7861-8090-5(0), 3432) Blckstn Audio.

Ravens. unabr. ed. George Dawes Green. Read by Robert Petkoff & Maggi-Meg Reed. (Running Time: 9 hrs.). (ENG.). 2009. 24.98 (978-1-60024-626-5(5)); audio compact disk 34.98 (978-1-60024-625-8(7)) Pub: Hachet Audio. Dist(s): HachBkGrp

***Raven's Flight.** Gav Thorpe. (ENG.). 2010. 17.00 (978-1-84416-857-6(3), Black Library) Pub: BL Pubng GBR. Dist(s): S and S Inc

Raven's Gate. unabr. ed. Anthony Horowitz. Read by Simon Prebble. 6 CDs. (Running Time: 7 hrs. 15 mins.). (Power of Five Ser.: Vol. 1). (YA). (gr. 5-9). 2005. audio compact disk 69.75 (978-1-4193-5553-0(8), C3402); 49.75 (978-1-4193-5049-8(8), 98111) Recorded Bks.
New York Times best-selling author Anthony Horowitz launches an exciting new fantasy series reminiscent of The Lord of the Rings but set in modern times. Punished for a crime he didn't commit, Matt is sent to a sinister town where, long ago, a great evil was banished. Now the evil is trying to return, and only Matt has the power to stop it.

Ravens in Winter. unabr. collector's ed. Bernd Heinrich. Read by Michael Russotto. 9 cass. (Running Time: 13 hrs. 30 min.). 1992. 72.00 (978-0-7366-2194-6(6), 2989) Books on Tape.
Heinrich watched ravens while they foraged, scaled cliffs to band fledglings, set up a giant aviary. What he found rivals a detective story in its complexity, false leads & finally, hard evidence.

Ravens of Avalon. Diana L. Paxson. Read by Lorna Raver. (Playaway Adult Fiction Ser.). 2008. 69.99 (978-1-60640-707-3(4)) Find a World.

Ravens of Avalon. unabr. ed. Diana L. Paxson. Narrated by Lorna Raver. (Running Time: 16 hrs. 0 mins. 0 sec.). (Avalon Ser.). (ENG.). 2007. audio compact disk 39.99 (978-1-4001-0496-3(3)); audio compact disk 29.99 (978-1-4001-5496-8(0)) Pub: Tantor Media. Dist(s): IngramPubServ

Ravens of Avalon. unabr. ed. Diana L. Paxson. Read by Lorna Raver. (Running Time: 16 hrs. 0 mins. 0 sec.). (Avalon Ser.). (ENG.). 2007. audio compact disk 79.99 (978-1-4001-3496-0(X)) Pub: Tantor Media. Dist(s): IngramPubServ

Ravenscar Dynasty. unabr. ed. Barbara Taylor Bradford. Read by Ric Jerrom. (Running Time: 17 hrs. 30 mins. 0 sec.). Bk. 1. (ENG.). 2006. audio compact disk 49.95 (978-1-4272-0043-3(2)) Pub: Macmill Audio. Dist(s): Macmillan

Ravensong: Cherokee Indian Poetry. unabr. ed. Poems. Raven Hail. Read by Raven Hail. 1 cass. (Running Time: 1 hr.). 1995. pap. bk. 12.00 (978-0-9617696-6-6(1)) Raven Hail.
Spoken poetry of Raven Hail, with chants, tom-tom & guitar accompaniment.

Ravensong: Cherokee Indian Poetry. unabr. ed. Poems. Raven Hail. Read by Raven Hail. 1 cass. (Running Time: 1 hr.). 1995. 8.00 Raven Hail.

Raving Fans: A Revolutionary Approach to Customer Service. abr. ed. Ken Blanchard & Sheldon Bowles. Read by Rick Adamson et al. (Running Time: 1 hr. 30 mins.). (ENG.). 2004. audio compact disk 15.00 (978-0-7393-0953-7(6)) Pub: Random Audio Pubg. Dist(s): Random

Ravished. unabr. ed. Amanda Quick, pseud. Read by Anne Flosnik. (Running Time: 12 hrs.). 2009. 39.97 (978-1-4233-8781-7(3), 9781423387817, Brlnc Audio MP3 Lib); 39.97 (978-1-4233-8783-1(X), 9781423387831, BADLE); 24.99 (978-1-4233-8780-0(5), 9781423387800, Brilliance MP3); 24.99 (978-1-4233-8782-4(1), 9781423387824, BAD); audio compact disk 82.97 (978-1-4233-8779-4(1), 9781423387794, BriAudCD Unabrid); audio compact disk 29.99 (978-1-4233-8778-7(3), 9781423387787, Bril Audio CD Unabri) Brilliance Audio.

***Ravished by a Highlander.** unabr. ed. Paula Quinn. Read by Carrington MacDuffie. (Running Time: 12 hrs. 5 mins.). (Children of the Mist Ser.). 2010. 29.95 (978-1-4417-7497-2(1)); 72.95 (978-1-4417-7494-1(7)); audio compact disk 105.00 (978-1-4417-7495-8(5)) Blckstn Audio.

Ravishing of Lol Stein. unabr. ed. Marguerite Duras. Tr. by Richard Seaver. Narrated by George Guidall. 4 cass. (Running Time: 5 hrs. 15 mins.). 1995. 35.00 (978-0-7887-0147-4(9), 94381E7) Recorded Bks.
Abandoned by her fiance during a dance at the Town Beach Casino, Lol froze the moment in her mind, replaying it obsessively over the next 10 years. Now she has returned to her hometown to confront her memories.

Raw Deal. unabr. ed. Les Standiford. Narrated by Ron McLarty. 8 cass. (Running Time: 10 hrs. 45 mins.). 1998. 70.00 (978-0-7887-1318-7(3), 95176E7) Recorded Bks.
The ambitious plans of a Cuban sugar baron are about to remove the sweet new taste of success from Johnny Deal's life. It's not just his business that's at stake; Johnny's wife & infant daughter are in danger, too.

Raw Material. unabr. collector's ed. Alan Sillitoe. Read by Richard Green. 6 cass. (Running Time: 6 hrs.). 1981. 36.00 (978-0-7366-0307-2(7), 1295) Books on Tape.
In "Raw Material," we meet Sillitoe's impoverished Midlands forebearers & learn why Sillitoe believes family relationships are the basis of all security, love & perhaps all truth. For him these relationships are the artistic "raw material" of his work, thus the family becomes not only the edifice of his life, but also grist for his mill.

Raw Materials. William Kupinse. (ENG.). 2008. audio compact disk 7.95i (978-0-9814854-2-3(1)) Hans O WA.

Raw Shark Texts. Steven Hall. 2007. audio compact disk (978-1-84767-156-1(X)) CanongateBooks GBR.

Raw Spirit: In Search of the Perfect Dram. unabr. ed. Iain Banks, pseud. Narrated by Tom Cotcher. 9 cass. (Running Time: 12 hrs. 30 mins.). 2004. 79.75 (978-1-84505-119-8(X), H1661MC, Clipper Audio) Recorded Bks.

***Rawhide Down.** unabr. ed. Del Quentin Wilber. (Running Time: 8 hrs. 30 mins. 0 sec.). (ENG.). 2011. audio compact disk 34.99 (978-1-4272-1183-5(3)) Pub: Macmill Audio. Dist(s): Macmillan

Ray Blackston Pack: Flabbergasted/A Delirious Summer/Lost in Rooville. Ray Blackston. (Running Time: 100800 sec.). 2005. audio compact disk 29.99 (978-1-59859-041-8(3)) Oasis Audio.

Ray Bradbury. Interview with Ray Bradbury. 1 cass. (Running Time: 30 min.). 1980. 12.95 (L011) TFR.
Bradbury talks about science fiction & fantasy, his obsessions with Dickens, Hemingway, George Bernard Shaw & other writers, his own library-centered method of self-education, & he reveals how his late father surprised him by re-appearing as a character in one of his books.

Ray Bradbury Tales of Fantasy. Read by Ray Bradbury. 2 cass. (Running Time: 3 hrs.). 15.95 (8148Q) Filmic Archives.
Includes: "The Illustrated Man"; "The Veldt"; "The Foghorn"; "The Smile"; "There Will Come Soft Rains"; "The Pedestrian".

Ray Centered Astrology. Joan Titsworth. 1 cass. 1992. 8.95 (1094) Am Fed Astrologers.

Ray Fisher: Willie's Lady. 1 cass. 9.98 (C-91) Folk-Legacy.
Strong singing of primarily traditional material from Scotland.

Ray Floyd: Golf. Read by Ray Floyd. 1 cass. 9.95 (978-0-89811-102-6(1), 7153) Lets Talk Assocs.
Ray Floyd talks about the people & events which influenced his career, & his own approach to his speciality.

Ray Gonzalez. unabr. ed. Read by Ray Gonzalez & Rebekah Presson. Ed. by James McKinley. 1 cass. (Running Time: 29 min.). (New Letters on the Air Ser.). 1992. 10.00 (101692); 18.00 2-sided cass. New Letters.
Gonzalez is interviewed by Rebekah Presson. Actors read parts of a book which Gonzalez edited, Without Discovery: A Native American Response to Columbus.

Ray Guy: Punter. Read by Ray Guy. 1 cass. 9.95 (978-0-89811-074-6(2), 7125) Lets Talk Assocs.
Ray Guy talks about the people & events which influenced his career, & his own approch to his speciality.

Ray Hicks Tells Four Traditional Jack Tales. 1 cass. 9.98 (C-14) Folk-Legacy.
Authentic folk tales from a North Carolina folksayer.

Ray of Sunshine. unabr. ed. Hilda McKenzie. Read by Julie Bevan. 8 cass. (Running Time: 10 hrs. 35 mins.). 1999. 83.95 (978-1-85903-268-8(0)) Pub: Magna Story GBR. Dist(s): Ulverscroft US
Emma Meredith, an orphan, is brought up by her kind grandmother, but when she dies, Emma is looked after by her three aunts, none of whom really want her. Eventually Emma finds work as a live-in maid to a wealthy family & the future looks even brighter when she befriends Daniel, the shy schoolmaster employed as tutor. When she is unfairly dismissed, Emma takes a position as housekeeper to a widow with two younger daughters. Emma knows she has at last found a purpose in life & is determined to give the girls all the love she has been denied.

Raymond Carver. Interview. Interview with Raymond Carver & Kay Bonetti. 1 cass. (Running Time: 1 hr.). 13.95 (978-1-55644-071-7(5), 3052) Am Audio Prose.
A discussion of Carver's life as a recovered alcoholic, the relationship between past family turmoil & his focus on the short story, & the happy effects of success on his work life.

Raymond Carver: The Hero's Journey. unabr. ed. Mark Richard. Perf. by John Mahoney & Kelly Nespor. 1 cass. (Running Time: 1 hr. 20 min.). 1992. 19.95 (978-1-58081-073-9(X)) L A Theatre.
Powerful & poignant evening of poetry & conversation from the work of Carver in the last year of his life.

Raymond Chandler's Goldfish. Raymond Chandler. Perf. by Harris Yulin & Harry Anderson. 1 CD. (Running Time: 90 min.). 2000. audio compact disk 15.95 Lodestone Catalog.
Chandler's gritty realism has never sounded better, with an outstanding cast.

Raymond Chandler's Goldfish. Raymond Chandler. Perf. by Harris Yulin & Harry Anderson. 1 cass. (Running Time: 60 min.). 1996. 12.95 (978-1-57677-057-3(5)) Lodestone Catalog.
Brings Philip Marlowe & his gritty world to life with superb performances, a fabulous audio-verite production in digital stereo, & a brilliant original blues score. "Goldfish" follows Marlowe in search of stolen pearls. The twists & turns to follow bring fully to life all of Chandler's realism, sardonic dialog & classic narrative style.

Raymond Chandler's 'Goldfish' Adapted by David Ossman. Directed By David Ossman. Raymond Chandler. 1 CD. (Running Time: 58 mins.). Dramatization. 2004. audio compact disk 15.95 (978-1-59938-042-1(0)) Lode Cat.

Raymond Johnson Promotes Flood Control Via Greenbelts Instead of by Channelization - Murrieta Creek in Riverside County, California, Boulder Creek in Colorado & Indian Bend Wash in Scottsdale, Arizona; School Wetlands. Hosted by Nancy Pearlman. 1 cass. (Running Time: 28 min.). 10.00 (1413) Educ Comm CA.

Rays of Calm: Relaxation for Teenagers. Christiane Kerr. (Calm for Kids Ser.). (J). (gr. 5-16). 2007. audio compact disk 17.95 (978-1-901923-92-6(4)) Divinit Pubing GBR.

Raza Spoken Here 2, Vol. 2. Poems. Perf. by Raul Salinas et al. Mario Torero. 1 CD. (Running Time: 66 min.). (SPA & ENG.). 2000. audio compact disk 15.00 (978-0-9660773-4-6(2)) Pub: Calaca Pr. Dist(s): SPD-Small Pr Dist

***Razones.** (SPA.). 2009. audio compact disk 14.99 (978-0-8297-6146-7(2)) Pub: CanZion. Dist(s): Zondervan

Razor Ramon. unabr. ed. Donald V. Allen. Read by Razor Ramon. 1 cass. (Running Time: 30 min.). Dramatization. (Official Audio Biography Series of the World Wrestling Federation). 5.99 (978-1-56703-042-6(4)) High-Top Sports.

Razor Sharp. abr. ed. Fern Michaels. Read by Laural Merlington. 4 CDs. (Running Time: 5 hrs.). (Sisterhood Ser.: No. 14). 2009. audio compact disk 14.99 (978-1-4418-0715-1(2), 9781441807151, BACD) Brilliance Audio.

Razor Sharp. abr. ed. Fern Michaels. Read by Laural Merlington. (Running Time: 5 hrs.). (Sisterhood Ser.: No. 14). 2010. audio compact disk 9.99 (978-1-4418-1687-0(9), 9781441816870, BCD Value Price) Brilliance Audio.

Razor Sharp. unabr. ed. Fern Michaels. Read by Laural Merlington. 1 MP3-CD. (Running Time: 7 hrs.). (Sisterhood Ser.: No. 14). 2009. 39.97 (978-1-4233-7980-5(2), 9781423379805, Brlnc Audio MP3 Lib); 24.99 (978-1-4233-7979-9(9), 9781423379799, Brilliance MP3); 24.99 (978-1-4233-7981-2(0), 9781423379812, BAD); 39.97 (978-1-4233-7982-9(9), 9781423379829, BADLE); audio compact disk 29.99 (978-1-4233-7977-5(2), 9781423379775, Bril Audio CD Unabri); audio compact disk 87.97 (978-1-4233-7978-2(0), 9781423379782, BriAudCD Unabrid) Brilliance Audio.

Razor's Edge **see Filo de la Navaja**

Razor's Edge. W. Somerset Maugham. Read by Pedro Montoya. (Running Time: 3 hrs.). 2002. 16.95 (978-1-60083-227-7(X), Audiofy Corp) Iofy Corp.

Razor's Edge. W. Somerset Maugham. Read by Frank Muller. 6 Cass. (Running Time: 10.5 Hrs). 19.95 (978-1-4025-2789-0(6)) Recorded Bks.

Razor's Edge. abr. ed. Dale Brown. Read by David McCallum. (Dale Brown's Dreamland Ser.). 2003. audio compact disk 29.95 (978-0-06-052262-9(3)) HarperCollins Pubs.

Razor's Edge. unabr. ed. W. Somerset Maugham. Read by Michael Page. 8 cass. (Running Time: 11 hrs.). (Bookcassette Classic Collection). 1994. 59.25 (978-1-56100-212-2(7), 1561002127, Unabridge Lib Edns) Brilliance Audio.
The Great War changed everything and the years following it were tumultuous - most of all for those who lived the war first-hand. Maugham himself is a character in this novel of self-discovery and search for meaning, but the protagonist is a character named Larry. Battered physically and spiritually by the war, Larry's physical wounds heal, but his spirit is changed almost beyond recognition. He leaves his betrothed, the beautiful and devoted Isabel. He studies philosophy and religion in Paris. He lives as a monk. He witnesses the exotic hardships of Spanish life. All of life that he can find - from an Indian Ashrama to labor in a coal mine - becomes Larry's spiritual experiment as he spurns the comfort and privilege of the Roaring '20's. Maugham's theme is the contrast of spiritual content between Larry and the growing materialism and sophistication of those he left behind - and the surprising irony of where both of those paths lead.

Razor's Edge. unabr. ed. W. Somerset Maugham. Read by Michael Page. 8 cass. (Running Time: 11 hrs.). 2003. 29.95 (978-1-59086-750-1(5), 1590867505, BAU) Brilliance Audio.

Razor's Edge. unabr. ed. W. Somerset Maugham. Read by Michael Page. (Running Time: 11 hrs.). 2004. 39.25 (978-1-59335-352-0(9), 1593353529, Brlnc Audio MP3 Lib) Brilliance Audio.

Razor's Edge. unabr. ed. W. Somerset Maugham. Read by Michael Page. (Running Time: 11 hrs.). 2004. 39.25 (978-1-59710-622-1(4), 1597106224, BADLE); 24.95 (978-1-59710-623-8(2), 1597106232, BAD) Brilliance Audio.

Razor's Edge. unabr. ed. W. Somerset Maugham. Read by Michael Page. (Running Time: 11 hrs.). 2005. audio compact disk 97.25 (978-1-59737-144-5(0), 9781597371445, BriAudCD Unabrid); audio compact disk 38.95 (978-1-59737-143-8(2), 9781597371438, Bril Audio CD Unabri) Brilliance Audio.

Razor's Edge. unabr. ed. W. Somerset Maugham. Narrated by Frank Muller. 7 cass. (Running Time: 10 hrs. 30 mins.). 1988. 60.00 (978-1-55690-434-9(7), 88410E7) Recorded Bks.
A young American abandons a life of privilege to seek spiritual comfort.

Razor's Edge. unabr. ed. W. Somerset Maugham. Read by Michael Page. (Running Time: 11 hrs.). 2004. 24.95 (978-1-59335-026-0(0), 1593350260) Soulmate Audio Bks.
The Great War changed everything and the years following it were tumultuous - most of all for those who lived the war first-hand. Maugham himself is a character in this novel of self-discovery and search for meaning, but the protagonist is a character named Larry. Battered physically and spiritually by the war, Larry's physical wounds heal, but his spirit is changed almost beyond recognition. He leaves his betrothed, the beautiful and devoted Isabel. He studies philosophy and religion in Paris. He lives as a monk. He witnesses the exotic hardships of Spanish life. All of life that he can find - from an Indian Ashrama to labor in a coal mine - becomes Larry's spiritual experiment as he spurns the comfort and privilege of the Roaring '20's. Maugham's theme is the contrast of spiritual content between Larry and the growing materialism and sophistication of those he left behind - and the surprising irony of where both of those paths lead.

Razor's Edge. unabr. collector's ed. W. Somerset Maugham. Read by Richard Green. 8 cass. (Running Time: 12 hrs.). 1977. 64.00 (978-0-7366-0077-4(9), 1087) Books on Tape.
Story of a young man in search of himself, set in Paris, the Riviera & Asia.

RBAAB: The Red-Blooded All-American Boy. Dick Jonas. 6 CDs. (Running Time: 6 hrs.). pap. bk. 17.00 EROSONIC.
The songbook companion to six albums of military aviation music. Includes "FSH": Vol. 1; "FSH": Vol. 2; "Two Sides of Dick Jonas," "Swamp Fox," "Nickel on the Grass," & "Itazuke Tower.".

RBAAB: The Red-Blooded All-American Boy. Dick Jonas. 6 CDs. (Running Time: 6 hrs.). 1997. pap. bk. 90.00 CD Set. (978-0-9657189-0-5(5)) EROSONIC.

RBRVS Plus 2. 6. 0: Updateable: An RBRVS-Based Fee Calculator. Created by Ingenix. (Ingenix Software Ser.). 2007. audio compact disk 299.95 (978-1-56337-956-7(2)) Ingenix Inc.

Re-Creating the World/Tough Mind, Tender Heart. Marianne Williamson. Read by Marianne Williamson. 1 cass. (Running Time: 90 mins.). (Lectures on a Course in Miracles). 1999. 10.00 (978-1-56170-451-4(2), M825) Hay House.

Re-Education & Reprogramming with Hypnotherapy for Everyone: A Manual for Mind Management: A Do-It-To Yourself: Self-Fulfilling Priceless - Programming. Joseph A. Ojeda & Tex Ojeda. 4 CDs. (Running Time: 6 hrs.). 2003. audio compact disk 29.95 (978-0-9740475-1-5(1)) T Ojeda.

Re-Empowering the Family. Carl Whitaker. 8 cass. (Running Time: 8 hrs.). 72.00 (A0368-88); cass. & video 175.00 (V0276-88) Sound Photosyn.
The world reknowned therapist offers a full workshop which includes in depth work with a distraught family.

Re-Entering. unabr. collector's ed. Eleanor Davidson Berman. Read by Wanda McCaddon. 8 cass. (Running Time: 8 hrs.). 1983. 48.00 (978-0-7366-0685-1(8), 1645) Books on Tape.
How one housewife tackled the back-to-work problem.

Re-Evaluating Your Life. Matt Dechsli. Read by Matt Dechsli. 6 cass. (Running Time: 6 hrs.). 1993. 59.95 Set. (609A) Nightingale-Conant.

Re-Evaluation Teacher, No. 1. 2 cass. 10.00 (978-1-893165-82-3(5)) Rational Isl.
For people interested in the theory & practice of teaching re-evaluation counseling.

Re-Evaluation Teacher, No. 2. 2 cass. 10.00 (978-1-893165-83-0(3)) Rational Isl.
For people interested in the thoery & practice of teaching re-evaluation counseling.

Re-Evaluation Teacher, No. 3. 3 cass. 10.00 (978-1-893165-84-7(1)) Rational Isl.
For people interested in the theory & practice of teaching re-evaluation counseling.

Re-Evaluation Teacher, No. 4. 2 cass. 10.00 (978-1-893165-85-4(X)) Rational Isl.

Re-Evaluation Teacher, No. 5. 2 cass. 10.00 (978-1-893165-86-1(8)) Rational Isl.

Re-Evaluation Teacher, No. 6. 1 cass. 10.00 (978-1-893165-87-8(6)) Rational Isl.

Re-evaluation Teacher, No. 8. 2 cass. 10.00 (978-1-893165-88-5(4)) Rational Isl.

Re-Evaluation Teacher, No. 11. 4 cass. 10.00 (978-1-893165-89-2(2)) Rational Isl.

Re-Evaluation Teacher, No. 12. 2 cass. 10.00 (978-1-893165-90-8(6)) Rational Isl.

Re-Evaluation Teacher, No. 15. 3 cass. 10.00 (978-1-893165-91-5(4)) Rational Isl.

Re-Evaluation Teacher, No. 17. 5 cass. 10.00 (978-1-893165-92-2(2)) Rational Isl.

Re-Evangelization of America. Fr. Hardon. 8 cass. (Running Time: 8 hrs.). 32.00 (92R) IRL Chicago.

Re-Forming the Past: History, the Fantastic, & the Postmodern Slave Narrative. A. Timothy Spaulding. 2005. audio compact disk 9.95 (978-0-8142-9084-2(1)) Pub: Ohio St U Pr. Dist(s): Chicago Distribution Ctr

***RE: Gabby: Three Weeks with God.** unabr. ed. Gabby Seviet & Megan Luetkenhoelter. 2011. audio compact disk 24.99 (978-0-8499-4944-9(0)) Nelson.

Re-Imagine! unabr. ed. Tom Peters. Read by Tom Peters. 7 CDs. (Running Time: 8 hrs. 30 mins.). 2004. audio compact disk 39.95 (978-1-59007-543-2(9)) Pub: New Millenn Enter. Dist(s): PerseuPGW

Re-Imagining the Anima: Eros or Animation? Read by Peter Mudd. 1 cass. (Running Time: 2 hrs.). 1988. 12.95 (978-0-7822-0211-3(X), 324) C G Jung IL.

Re-Parenting the Adult Child. 1991. stu. ed. 14.95 (978-0-9622150-1-8(5)) Aurora VA.

Re-Write Your Script. Read by Mary Richards. 1 cass. (Running Time: 90 mins.). 12.95 (209) Master Your Mind.
Eliminate old negative patterns of behavior & replace them with positive fulfilling ones.

Reach. Contrib. by Warren Barfield. Prod. by Marshall Altman. 2006. audio compact disk 11.97 (978-5-558-52385-0(9)) Essential Recs.

Reach! Finding Strength, Spirit, & Personal Power. abr. ed. Laila Ali & David Ritz. 2002. audio compact disk 26.95 (978-1-56511-657-3(7)) HighBridge.

Reach for the Sky: The Story of Douglas Bader D. S. O., D. F. C. unabr. ed. Paul Brickhill. Read by Robert Hardy. 12 cass. (Running Time: 53100 sec.). 1991. 101.95 (978-0-7451-5807-5(2)) AudioGO.

Reach for Tomorrow. Jessica Blair & Anne Dover. 2007. 94.95 (978-1-84652-135-5(1)); audio compact disk 99.95 (978-1-84652-136-2(X)) Pub: Magna Story GBR. Dist(s): Ulverscroft US

Reach Out. Sharon J. Swain & Biddi Kings. bk. 22.00 (978-0-281-05401-5(0)) Pub: SPCK Pubs GBR. Dist(s): Pilgrim OH

Reach Out & Teach. unabr. ed. Kay A. Ferrell. 8 cass. (Running Time: 8 hrs.). 225.00 (978-0-89128-130-6(4)) Am Foun Blind.
Gives parents information to raise their visually or multiply handicapped children.

Reach Out & Touch (Somebody's Hand) - ShowTrax. Arranged by Mac Huff. 1 CD. (Running Time: 5 mins.). 2000. audio compact disk 19.95 (08201242) H Leonard.
A hit for Diana Ross in 1970, this gospel-flavored SSA setting makes an excellent concert closer.

Reaching. Perf. by LaRue. 2002. audio compact disk Reunion Recs.

Reaching Cities Through Movements of Prayer for the World: Proceedings of the 45th Annual Convention National Association of Evangelicals Buffalo, New York. Read by David Bryant. 1 cass. (Running Time: 60 min.). 1987. 4.00 (341) Nat Assn Evan.

Reaching Colorado, Bk. 2. unabr. ed. Frank Roderus. Read by Kevin Foley. 4 cass. (Running Time: 5 hrs. 24 min.). 1995. 26.95 (978-1-55686-626-5(7)) Books in Motion.
Tenderfoot Harrison Wilke left Kansas & ended up in Colorado where he is confronted with the complex problem of how to steal money from those whom he believes stole it first.

Reaching for Glory: Lyndon Johnson's Secret White House Tapes, 1964-1965. abr. ed. Michael R. Beschloss. Read by Michael R. Beschloss. 2006. 17.95 (978-0-7435-6366-6(2), Audioworks) Pub: S&S Audio. Dist(s): S and S Inc

Reaching for the Invisible God: What Can We Expect to Find? abr. ed. Philip Yancey. Read by Philip Yancey. 2 cass. (Running Time: 2 hrs.). 2000. 16.99 Zondervan.
Author Philip Yancey asks the question How does a relationship with God work? & answers it with an investigation that turns up surprising and satisfying answers about: life and communication with an invisible God the Father & his Spirit, faith in the earthly realm where theology & experience often oppose each other, & growth as a Christian that comes from maturing into childlike faith.

Reaching for the Invisible God: What Can We Expect to Find? abr. ed. Philip Yancey. (Running Time: 3 hrs. 7 mins. 0 sec.). (ENG.). 2003. 10.99 (978-0-310-26092-9(2)) Zondervan.

Reaching for the Invisible God: What Can We Expect to Find? unabr. ed. Philip Yancey & Zondervan Publishing Staff. (Running Time: 8 hrs. 0 mins. 0 sec.). (ENG.). 2003. 14.99 (978-0-310-26172-8(4)) Zondervan.

Reaching for the Invisible God: What Can We Expect to Find? unabr. abr. ed. Philip Yancey. 2000. 17.99 (978-0-310-23955-0(9)) Zondervan.

Reaching for the Moon. Buzz Aldrin, Jr. Illus. by Wendell Minor. Narrated by Wendell Minor. (J). (gr. k-4). 2006. audio compact disk 12.95 (978-1-59519-580-7(7)) Live Oak Media.

Reaching for the Stars. Leslee Ann Michaels. (J). 1997. 10.95 (978-1-890059-67-5(6)) Happy Hrt Pr.

Reaching Learners Through Telecommunications: Management & Leadership Strategies for Higher Education. Becky Duning et al. (Higher & Adult Education Ser.). 1993. bk. 38.95 (978-1-55542-501-2(1), Jossey-Bass) Wiley US.

Reaching Out. Perf. by John Gerighty & Simeon Wood. 1 cass. (Running Time: 45 min.). 1997. 11.95 (978-0-86347-026-4(2), MoreHse Pubng) Church Pub Inc.
Pan pipes & classical guitar, preparation for & background for meditation. Played at Lee Abbey in England.

Reaching Out: Three Movements of the Spiritual Life. abr. ed. Henri J. M. Nouwen. Read by Murray Bodo. 4 CDs. (Running Time: 16200 sec.). 2006. audio compact disk 29.95 (978-0-86716-796-2(3)) St Anthony Mess Pr.

Reaching Out Through Religious Broadcasting: National Association of Evangelicals, 47th Annual Convention, Columbus, Ohio, March 7-9, 1989. Lloyd J. Ogilvie. 1 cass. (Luncheons Ser.: No. 114-Thursd). 1989. 4.00 ea. 1-8 tapes.; 4.25 ea. 9 tapes or more. Nat Assn Evan.

Reaching Out to Disenfranchised Catholic. 1 cass. (Care Cassettes Ser.: Vol. 15, No. 1). 1988. 10.80 Assn Prof Chaplains.

***Reaching People & Touching Lives Around the World: A Window of Opportunity for Global Outreach.** Tracy Sharpe & Linda V. Sharpe. (ENG.). 2010. 9.99 (978-1-936076-17-8(9)) Innovo Pub.

Reaching the Baby Boomers: Proceedings of the 45th Annual Convention National Association of Evangelicals Buffalo, New York. Read by Leith Anderson. 1 cass. (Running Time: 60 min.). 1987. 4.00 (308) Nat Assn Evan.

Reaching the Back Rows: National Association of Evangelicals, Columbus, Ohio, March 7-9, 1989. Paul B. Smith. 1 cass. (Luncheons Ser.: No. 105-Wednes). 1989. 4.25 ea. 1-8 tapes.; 4.00 ea. 9 tapes or more. Nat Assn Evan.

Reaching the Center Within. Swami Amar Jyoti. 1 cass. 1980. 9.95 (I-13) Truth Consciousness.
Stillness in meditation. Raising consciousness to the Supreme.

Reaching the Top see Pasos Hacia la Cumbre del Exito

Reaching to Heaven: A Spiritual Journey Through Life & Death. unabr. ed. James Van Praagh. Read by Jonathan Marosz. 4 cass. (Running Time: 6 hrs.). 1999. 32.00 (978-0-7366-4578-2(0), 4985) Books on Tape.
The author, a medium, provides readers with a practical guide to finding their own closer connection to the world beyond & richer success in their present life.

Reaching to Heaven: A Spiritual Journey Through Life & Death. unabr. ed. James Van Praagh. Read by Jonathan Marosz. 4 CDs. (Running Time: 4 hrs. 48 mins.). 2001. audio compact disk 32.00 Books on Tape.
Reveals how to chart a course for living as spiritual beings in a physical world. Sharing moving stories of after-death communication, showing us that even grievous emotional scars can be healed & that when we recondition ourselves properly we can discover our true spiritual natures & achieve self-awareness, self-worth & self-love.

Reaching Your Child's Heart. Sonya Shafer. (ENG.). 2008. 5.95 (978-1-61634-044-5(4)); audio compact disk 7.95 (978-1-61634-043-8(6)) Simply Char.

***Reaching Your Financial Destiny DVD.** Bryan E. Crute & Lee Jenkins. 2010. 14.95 (978-0-9827022-3-9(X)) Lifetogether.

Reaching Your Highest Potential in Life. Speeches. Joel Osteen. 1 Cass. (Running Time: 30 Mins.). (J). 2000. 6.00 (978-1-59349-072-0(0), JA0072) J Osteen.

Read-a-Rhyme: Creepers & Crawlers, Grades Preschool-First. Steven Traugh et al. Illus. by Catherine Yuh Rader & Kimberly Schamber. 2001. pap. bk. & tchr. ed. 17.99 (978-1-57471-707-5(3), 4303) Creat Teach Pr.

Read-a-Rhyme: Farm Fun, Grades Preschool-First. Steven Traugh & Sarah Fornara. Ed. by Cindy Truitt. Illus. by Catherine Yuh Rader & Kimberly Schamber. 2001. pap. bk. & tchr. ed. 17.99 (978-1-57471-705-1(7), 4301) Creat Teach Pr.

Read about China. Pao-Chen Lee. 2 cass. 1953. 8.95 ea. incl. suppl. materials. (978-0-88710-062-8(7)) Yale Far Eastern Pubns.

Read All about It. Lori Howard. 2000. 24.50 (978-0-19-436978-7(1)) OUP.

Read All about It, Bk. 1. Lori Howard. 1999. 24.50 (978-0-19-436977-0(3)) OUP.

Read All about It Starter. Susan Iannuzzi & Renee Weiss. 2005. audio compact disk 24.50 (978-0-19-438655-5(4)) OUP.

Read-Along Storybook & Audio Tape: Prince of Egypt. Jeff Goldblum. (Prince of Egypt Ser.). (J). (ps-3). 1998. bk. 7.99 (978-0-8499-5896-0(2)) Nelson.

Read-along with Sammy: Includes 1 of each 7 Sammy books, all 7 Sammy CD's, & a FREE Sammy plush Doll. Short Stories. 7 CD's. (Running Time: 14 mins each). (J). 2004. pap. bk. Rental 84.95 (978-1-57874-284-4(6)) Kaeden Corp.

Read-along with Sammy Cassette Tapes: Includes 1 of each 7 Sammy books, 1 of all 7 Sammy audio tapes & a FREE Sammy plush Doll. 7 cassettes. (J). 2006. pap. bk. Rental 65.95 (978-1-57874-285-1(4)) Kaeden Corp.

Read-Alongs Set 1. Created by Saddleback Publishing. (Quickreads Ser.). (J). 2005. audio compact disk (978-1-56254-791-2(7)) Saddleback Edu.

Read-Alongs Set 4. Created by Saddleback Publishing. (Quickreads Ser.). (J). 2005. audio compact disk (978-1-56254-794-3(1)) Saddleback Edu.

Read-Aloud Level A, Pack. (Metro Reading Ser.). (J). (gr. 12). 2000. 31.75 (978-1-58120-194-9(X)) Metro Teaching.

Read-Aloud Level B, 4 pack. (Metro Reading Ser.). (J). (gr. 12). 2000. 31.75 (978-1-58120-195-6(8)) Metro Teaching.

Read-Aloud Level C, 4 pack. (Metro Reading Ser.). (J). (gr. 12). 2000. 31.75 (978-1-58120-196-3(6)) Metro Teaching.

Read & Listen Cinderel. 1 cass. (J). 1994. 4.98 (978-0-88149-043-5(1)) Peter Pan.
Fairy tales & folklore.

Read & Listen Little Red Hen. 1 cass. (J). 1994. 4.98 (978-0-88149-045-9(8)) Peter Pan.

Read & Solve Math Problems, Vol. 1. Ann Edson & Allan A. Schwartz. 5 cass. (Running Time: 5 hrs.). (J). (gr. 2-4). act. bk. ed. & pupil's gde. ed. 79.00 Incl. 10 activity bks. . (978-0-89525-195-4(7), AKC 301) Ed Activities.
Introducing story problems, facts & questions, finding & writing number sentences for addition, subtraction, multiplication, more, fewer, less, using tables & graphs, more than one question, more than one step, too many facts, pre & post test.

Read & Solve Math Problems, Vol. 2. Ann Edson & Allan A. Schwartz. 5 cass. (J). (gr. 4-6). pap. bk., act. bk. ed., pupil's gde. ed. 79.00 Incl. 10 activity bks. . (978-0-89525-196-1(5), AKC 319) Ed Activities.
Word problem, writing equations, using maps, tables, & graphs, problems without numbers, hidden infromation, too much information, two-step problems.

Read Chinese, Bk. 1. exp. ed. Fred Wang. 4 cass. 1982. 8.95 ea. incl. suppl. materials. (978-0-88710-065-9(1)) Yale Far Eastern Pubns.

Read Chinese, Bk. 2. enl. ed. Richard Chang. 3 cass. 1983. 8.95 ea. incl. suppl. materials. (978-0-88710-067-3(8)) Yale Far Eastern Pubns.

Read Chinese, Bk. 3. Fred Wang & Richard Chang. 2 cass. 1963. 8.95 ea. incl. suppl. materials. (978-0-88710-069-7(4)) Yale Far Eastern Pubns.

Read Contracts. PUEI. audio compact disk 199.00 (978-1-934147-98-6(2), CareerTrack) P Univ E Inc.

***Read-it! Readers: Folklore set of 6 Audio - English & Spanish.** (Read-It! Readers Ser.). (MUL.). 2008. audio compact disk 55.62 (978-1-4048-4533-6(X)) CapstoneDig.

***Read-it! Readers: Gus the Hedgehog (set of 6 Audio - English & Spanish)** (Read-it! Readers en Español). (MUL.). 2008. audio compact disk 55.62 (978-1-4048-4530-5(5)) CapstoneDig.

***Read-it! Readers: the Life of Max set of 6 Audio - English & Spanish.** (Read-it! Readers en Español). (SPA.). 2008. audio compact disk 55.62 (978-1-4048-4531-2(3)) CapstoneDig.

Read My Heart: A Love Story in England's Age of Revolution. unabr. ed. Jane Dunn. (Running Time: 15 hrs. 30 mins. 0 sec.). (ENG.). 2008. audio compact disk 39.99 (978-1-4001-0967-8(1)); audio compact disk 79.99 (978-1-4001-3967-5(8)) Pub: Tantor Media. Dist(s): IngramPubServ

Read My Heart: A Love Story in England's Age of Revolution. unabr. ed. Jane Dunn. Narrated by Wanda McCaddon. (Running Time: 15 hrs. 30 mins. 0 sec.). (ENG.). 2008. audio compact disk 29.99 (978-1-4001-5967-3(9)) Pub: Tantor Media. Dist(s): IngramPubServ

Read Now! ed. Created by First Learning Programs. (J). 1992. act. bk. ed. 129.95 (978-0-9769312-0-1(6)) ReadNow.

Read-O-Mat: Syllabus. Alyce E. Faber. (J). 1976. 35.85 (978-0-89420-179-0(4), 114000) Natl Book.

Read on, Bk. 2. Nancy Nici Mare. (Read On Ser.). (ENG.). (C). 2003. 25.63 (978-0-07-282309-7(7), 0072823097, ESL/ELT) Pub: McGrw-H Hghr Educ. Dist(s): McGraw

Read on - Book 3 (Low Intermediate) - Audio CD (1) Nancy Mare. (Read On Ser.). (ENG.). (C). 2005. audio compact disk 25.63 (978-0-07-311286-2(0), 0073112860, ESL/ELT) Pub: McGrw-H Hghr Educ. Dist(s): McGraw

Read on - Book 3 (Low Intermediate) - Audiocassette (1) Nancy Mare. (Read On Ser.). (ENG.). (C). 2005. 25.63 (978-0-07-311285-5(2), 0073112852, ESL/ELT) Pub: McGrw-H Hghr Educ. Dist(s): McGraw

Read On! Two, Bk. 5. Artis Lee. Ed. by V. K. Lawson. Illus. by Jim Marks. Contrib. by Literacy Volunteers of America Staff. 1987. 10.00 (978-0-318-41218-4(7)) Lit Vol Am.

Read on 1. Nancy Nici Mare. (Read On Ser.). (ENG.). (C). 2003. 25.63 (978-0-07-282305-9(4), 0072823054, ESL/ELT) Pub: McGrw-H Hghr Educ. Dist(s): McGraw

Read on 2. Nancy Nici Mare. (Read On Ser.). (ENG.). (C). 2003. audio compact disk 25.63 (978-0-07-282310-3(0), 0072823100, ESL/ELT) Pub: McGrw-H Hghr Educ. Dist(s): McGraw

Read Read Read: Easy Ways to Teach Your Child to Read. 1 CD. (Running Time: 22 mins.). 2002. per. 19.95 (978-0-9722034-0-1(0)) T S Rudwick.
It has the alphabet sounds chant for learning the sounds of the alphabet in English.

***Read Test Trainer's Audio.** 2002. 2.50 (978-1-56853-345-2(4)) New Readers.

Read These Lips. abr. ed. Kate Clinton. Read by Kate Clinton. 1 CD. (Running Time: 1 hr. 30 mins.). 2001. audio compact disk 16.98 (978-1-929243-25-9(1)) Uproar Ent.

Read to Me. Vincent. Read by Vincent. 1 cass. (Running Time: 36 min.). (J). (gr. k-4). 1994. 9.98 (978-0-9634024-1-7(2), LR2002-4); audio compact disk 15.98 CD. (978-0-9634024-2-4(0), LR2002-2) Lighthse Recs.
Collection of 13 original songs featuring "Peace Like a River", "Read to Me", "Pen Pals", "Elvis Is King", "Ben Franklin" & the poetry of Edward Lear & Robert Louis Stevenson.

Read-Togethers Set I: Hairy Bear; The Hungry Giant; Yes Ma'am; Mrs. Wishy Washy; Smarty Pants; Sing A Song; Grandpa, Grandpa; Lazy Mary. 4 cass. (J). 1986. 44.00 (301AC) Wright Group.
Developed to make reading easy & fun. Read-Together stories devote each side of a cassette to one book & contain four steps: Child listens & follows story; Child participates in reading some of story; Teacher assists children in a variety of activities; Child reads alone.

Read-Togethers Set II: In a Dark Dark Wood; Three Little Ducks; The Big Toe; Boo-Hoo; Obadiah; One Cold Wet Night; Poor Old Polly; Woosh! 4 cass. (J). 1986. 44.00 (302AC) Wright Group.

Read-Togethers Set III: The Red Rose; Meanies; The Farm Concert; The Jigaree; Who Will Be My Mother; The Monster's Party; To Town; Dan, The Flying Man. 4 cass. (J). 1986. 44.00 (303AC) Wright Group.
Developed to make reading easy & fun. Read-Together stories devote each side of a cassette to one book & contain four steps: Child listens & follows story; Child participates in reading some parts of story; Teacher assists children in a variety of activities; Child reads alone.

Read, Write & Type Learning System: Site Licence. (J). 2000. audio compact disk 699.00 (978-0-9676349-5-1(4)) Talking Finger.

Read 100: Graded Readings for Today's World, 100-Word Reading Passages. Andrew E. Bennett. 1 CD. (Graded Readings for Today's World Ser.). (gr. 4-12). 2006. pap. bk. & stu. ed. 28.00 (978-0-86647-234-0(7)) Pro Lingua.

Read 100: 100-word reading passages. Andrew E. Bennett. 1 CD. 2006. audio compact disk Rental 18.00 (978-0-86647-233-3(9)) Pro Lingua.

Read 125: Graded Readings for Today's World, 125-Word Reading Passages. Andrew E. Bennett. 1 CD. (Graded Readings for Today's World Ser.). (gr. 4-12). 2006. pap. bk. & stu. ed. 28.00 (978-0-86647-237-1(1)) Pro Lingua.

Read 125: 125-word reading Passages. Andrew E. Bennett. 1 CD. 2006. audio compact disk 18.00 (978-0-86647-236-4(3)) Pro Lingua.

Read 50: Graded Readings for Today's World, 50-Word Reading Passages. Andrew E. Bennett. 1 CD. (Graded Readings Ser.). (gr. 4-12). 2006. pap. bk. & stu. ed. 28.00 (978-0-86647-228-9(2)) Pro Lingua.

Read 50: 50-word reading passages. Andrew E. Bennett. 1 CD. 2006. audio compact disk 18.00 (978-0-86647-227-2(4)) Pro Lingua.

Read 75: Graded Readings for Today's World, 75-Word Reading Passages. Andrew E. Bennett. 1 CD. (Graded Readings Ser.). (gr. 4-12). 2006. pap. bk. & stu. ed. 28.00 (978-0-86647-231-9(2)) Pro Lingua.

Read 75: 75-word reading passages. Andrew E. Bennett. 1 CD. 2006. audio compact disk 18.00 (978-0-86647-230-2(4)) Pro Lingua.

Reader. Bernhard Schlink. 2 cass.Tr. of Vorleser. 1998. 16.85 Set. (978-0-00-105540-7(2)) Ulvrscrft Audio.
Michael understands that her behaviour both now & in the past conceals a secret buried even deeper than her terrible crimes.

Reader. unabr. ed. Bernhard Schlink. Read by Campbell Scott. Tr. by Carol Janeway. 4 CDs. (Running Time: 4 hrs. 30 mins.).Tr. of Vorleser. (ENG.). 2008. audio compact disk 14.99 (978-0-7393-7595-2(4), Random AudioBks) Pub: Random Audio Pubg. Dist(s): Random

Reader. unabr. ed. Bernhard Schlink. Narrated by Campbell Scott. 1 cass. Tr. of Vorleser. 2000. 36.00 (21696) Recorded Bks.

Reader in Modern Literary Arabic. Farhat J. Ziadeh. 1 cass. (Running Time: 1 hr.). (ARA.). 1993. pap. bk. 110.00 (978-0-86685-749-9(4)) Intl Bk Ctr.

Readers & Writers. unabr. ed. Ray Bradbury et al. 3 CDs. (Running Time: 3 hrs. 0 mins. 0 sec.). (Selected Shorts: A Celebration of the Short Story Ser.). (ENG.). 2008. audio compact disk 28.00 (978-1-934033-08-1(1)) Pub: Symphony Space. Dist(s): IPG Chicago

Readers Are Leaders. Linda G. Gant. 1 cass. (J). (ps-3). (978-0-9673625-1-9(2)) Readers Are.
Depicts children in various reading formats. Each line of the song which each line has been illustrated. Extremely motivational for beginning readers & a foundation book for reading.

Reader's Guide Through the Wardrobe. unabr. ed. Marjorie Lamp Mead & Leland Ryken. Narrated by Simon Vance. 4 CDs. (Running Time: 4 hrs. 42 mins. 0 sec.). (ENG.). 2005. audio compact disk 21.98 (978-1-59644-216-0(6), Hovel Audio) christianaud.
Step inside the wardrobe!.You may be surprised at what you find. In this informative book, Lewis scholar Marjorie Lamp Mead and literary expert Leland Ryken unlock the door to The Lion, the Witch and the Wardrobe, inviting you to step inside-deeper and deeper, past the musty fur coats-and gaze in wide-eyed wonder once again at the magical wintry world Lucy first found.A Reader's Guide to the Wardrobe helps you examine the story from Lewis's point of view, shedding light on his imagination and use of literary forms. Even further, Mead and Ryken serve as guides through this first Narnian adventure, providing an inside look at characters, setting and

framework along with thoughtful questions for reflection and discussion. Here is a book that will help you see Narnia as Lucy did-with childlike wonder and anticipation for the adventure that lies ahead.

***Reader's Guide Through the Wardrobe: Exploring C. S. Lewis's Classic Story.** unabr. ed. Leland Ryken & Marjorie Mead. Narrated by Simon Vance. (ENG.). 2005. 12.98 (978-1-59644-217-7(4), Hovel Audio) christianaud.

Readers' Theater: Scripts for Young Readers. Read by Patrick Feehan. Retold by Heather McDonald. (J). 2009. 9.95 (978-1-60184-153-7(1)); 9.95 (978-1-60184-155-1(8)) Primry Concpts.

Readers' Theater: Scripts for Young Readers: the Peach Boy CD. Read by Patrick Feehan. (J). 2009. 9.95 (978-1-60184-157-5(4)) Primry Concpts.

Readers' Theater Stone Soup Audio CD: Scripts for Young Readers. Retold by Kelly Stewart. (J). 2008. audio compact disk 9.95 (978-1-60184-122-3(1)) Primry Concpts.

Readers' Theater the Emperor's New Clothes CD: Scripts for Young Readers: Retold by Joan Westley. (ENG., (J). 2008. audio compact disk 9.95 (978-1-60184-126-1(4)) Primry Concpts.

Readers' Theater the Magic Porridge Pot: Scripts for Young Readers: the Magic Porridge Pot CD. Retold by Kelly Stewart. (J). 2008. audio compact disk 9.95 (978-1-60184-118-6(3)) Primry Concpts.

Readers' Theater the Mitten Audio CD: Scripts for Young Readers. Retold by Kelly Stewart. (J). 2008. audio compact disk 9.95 (978-1-60184-124-7(8)) Primry Concpts.

Readers' Theater the Princess & the Pea Audio CD: Scripts for Young Readers. Retold by Kelly Stewart. (J). 2008. audio compact disk 9.95 (978-1-60184-116-2(7)) Primry Concpts.

Readers' Theater the Ugly Duckling Audio CD: Scripts for Young Readers. Retold by Joan Westley. (J). 2008. audio compact disk 9.95 (978-1-60184-120-9(5)) Primry Concpts.

Readers Theatre: Its Methods & Techniques. Marion Fairman. 1 cass. 1974. 5.95 incl. outline. (C32) Meriwether Pub.
This theatre form is a natural for schools with limited playing space & non-professional performers. Here on a single cassette is the "how, when, & why" for every type of Readers Theatre performance. The form's conventions are explained & described in detail. Suggestions for staging, lighting & interpretation are given together with techniques for the director. Play selection ideas included.

Readiness - I Am Thus - You Are Thus Too. unabr. ed. Tenshin R. Anderson. 1 cass. (Running Time: 1 hr. 13 min.). 1989. 11.00 (ZC001) Big Sur Tapes.
Anderson draws from literary & philosophical sources as well as from Zen tradition to address questions of identity & self, how to prepare for any situation with "readiness" & living gracefully with the unresolvable quandaries that abound in this life.

Readiness for Breakthrough. Swami Amar Jyoti. 1 cass. (Satsangs of Swami Amar Jyoti Ser.). (C). 1997. 9.95 (M-103) Truth Consciousness.
Breakthrough to the world of Spirit strikes at our most cherished beliefs & blocks. Masters eagerly give if we but allow.

Readiness for Change & Growth. Swami Amar Jyoti. 1 cass. 1989. 9.95 (M-76) Truth Consciousness.
Why does the one who seeks also hide? Ingredients for change. Loving harmony in all relationships.

Readiness for Enlightenment. Swami Amar Jyoti. 1 cass. 1976. 9.95 (M-64) Truth Consciousness.
Readiness of the disciple. Thorough inner renunciation. Childlike simplicity to see Divine Mother.

Reading a Horoscope Without Your Glasses. Sue Lovett. 1 cass. 8.95 (443) Am Fed Astrologers.
An AFA Convention workshop tape.

***Reading Advantage, Vol. 2.** 2nd ed. Casey Malarcher. (C). 2003. 37.95 (978-1-4130-0123-5(8)) Pub: Heinle. Dist(s): CENGAGE Learn

Reading & Discussion of the Gods in Every Man. Jean S. Bolen. 1 cass. 9.00 (A0233-89) Sound Photosyn.
At the Mill Valley Book Depot.

Reading & Improving Natural Abilities. Norman J. Caldwell. Read by Norman J. Caldwell. Arranged by Achieve Now Institute Staff. 1 cass. (Running Time: 20 min.). (Childrens' Self-Help Ser.). (J). 1988. 9.97 (978-1-56273-091-8(6)) My Mothers Pub.
Scanning the words more easily.

***Reading & Learning Strategies: Middle Grades Through High School Cd.** 3rd rev. ed. Lenski. (ENG.). 2010. audio compact disk 43.43 (978-0-7575-4208-4(5)) Kendall-Hunt.

Reading & Writing: How We Learn. 1 cass. (Running Time: 1 hr.). 10.95 (D0220B090, HarperThor) HarpC GBR.

Reading & Writing the Lakota Language: Lakota Iyapi un Wowapi Nahan Yawapi. Albert White Hat, Sr.. Read by Albert White Hat, Sr. Read by Duane Hollow Horn Bear & Neola Spotted Tail. (Running Time: 7982 sec.). 2007. audio compact disk 18.95 (978-0-87480-887-2(1)) Pub: U of Utah Pr. Dist(s): Chicago Distribution Ctr

Reading Aspects: Structures II. Bruno Huber. 1 cass. 8.95 (838) Am Fed Astrologers.

Reading at Cody's. Paul Auster. 1 cass. 9.00 (A0431-89) Sound Photosyn.
The popular modern novelist, "City of Glass," etc., dramatically reading his works in Berkeley.

Reading at Cody's in Berkeley. Robert Ornstein. 1 cass. 9.00 (A0697-90) Sound Photosyn.

Reading Between the Lines: A Christian Guide to Literature. unabr. ed. Gene Edward Veith, Jr. Read by Jeff Riggenbach. 8 cass. (Running Time: 12 hrs.). 1995. 56.95 (978-0-7861-0814-5(2), 1637) Blckstn Audio.
This is a guidebook for those who want to learn how to recognize books that are spiritually & aesthetically good.

Reading by the Colors: Overcoming Dyslexia & Other Reading Disabilities Through the Irlen Method. unabr. ed. Helen Irlen. Narrated by Barbara Caruso. 4 cass. (Running Time: 5 hrs.). 1999. 34.00 (978-0-7887-1593-8(3), 95212E7) Recorded Bks.
Expertly defines a major cause of reading difficulties & offers an easy-to-use solution for those who struggle every time they open a book.

Reading Chord Symbols in Classical & Popular Music. Duane Shinn. 1 cass. 19.95 (MR-6) Duane Shinn.
Discusses types of chord symbols. One type is an "absolute" symbol & is used mostly in popular music: Cm7, F9, G6, & so on; the other type is a "relative" symbol, in that it can be used in any key.

Reading Fluency Level F, Level F. Camille L. Z. Blachowicz. (ENG.). 2005. audio compact disk 43.96 (978-0-07-869122-5(2), 0078691222) Pub: Glencoe. Dist(s): McGraw

***Reading for Concepts Book A Cd.** Barbara R. Frey et al. (ENG.). 2008. audio compact disk 99.00 (978-0-7915-2139-7(7)) Phoenix Lrn.

***Reading for Concepts Book B Cd.** Barbara R. Frey et al. (ENG.). 2008. audio compact disk 99.00 (978-0-7915-2140-3(0)) Phoenix Lrn.

***Reading for Concepts Book C Cd.** Barbara R. Frey et al. (ENG.). 2008. audio compact disk 99.00 (978-0-7915-2141-0(9)) Phoenix Lrn.

***Reading for Concepts Book D Cd.** Barbara R. Frey et al. (ENG.). 2008. audio compact disk 99.00 (978-0-7915-2142-7(7)) Phoenix Lrn.

Reading Genius: The World's Most Advanced Reading System. Edward Strachar. 1995. (978-0-9717185-2-4(0)) InGenius Inc.

Reading Genius Tips. Speeches. Edward Strachar. 1 cass. (Running Time: 60 mins.). 2002. 14.95 (978-0-9719358-6-0(6)) InGenius Inc.

Reading Genius Tips. Speeches. Edward Strachar. 2 CDs. (Running Time: 90 mins.). 2002. audio compact disk 24.95 (978-0-9726941-5-5(3)) InGenius Inc.

Reading Georgian Grammar. rev. ed. Howard I. Aronson. 4 cass. (Running Time: 3 hrs. 30 min.). (J). (gr. 10-12). pap. bk. 99.50 (978-0-88432-704-2(3), SGG150) J Norton Pubs.
For beginners. Teaches how to read Georgian literature.

Reading Group. unabr. ed. Elizabeth Noble. Narrated by Gerri Halligan. 11 cass. (Running Time: 14 hrs. 45 mins.). 2005. 109.75 (978-1-84505-157-0(2), H1717) Recorded Bks.

Reading Her Poetry. Carolyn Kizer. Read by Carolyn Kizer. 1 cass. 9.00 (A0057-87) Sound Photosyn.
A strong performance by the Pulitzer Prize winner. Al Young is also here.

Reading His Poetry. unabr. ed. Alberto A. Rios. Read by Alberto A. Rios. 1 cass. 1987. 9.00 (978-1-56964-860-5(3), A0110-87) Sound Photosyn.
Poignant & socially conscious poetry. Ursula K. Leguin appears on this tape.

Reading His Poetry & Prose. Al Young. Read by Al Young. 1 cass. 9.00 (A0156-87) Sound Photosyn.
Al's rich voice finds the music in speech & image. Carolyn Kizer is also here.

Reading in the Dark. unabr. ed. Seamus Deane. Read by Stephen Rea. 6 CDs. (Running Time: 27000 sec.). 2001. audio compact disk 64.95 (978-0-7540-5445-0(4), CCD 136) AudioGO.
"Traces out a series of scenes of a boy's life in Derry, starting in February 1945, when the boy is quite young, and ending in July 1971, when the grown boy, now ten years out of college in Belfast, visits for a weekend. There are 47 scenes, all dated by month and year, with a strong concentration on the period 1948 to 1954. Two other dates are crucial to the book: 1922, the year of the shoot-out between the police and the IRA at the Derry distillery, the product of 'a last-minute protest at the founding of the new state'; and 1968, when 'the Troubles came'.

Reading in the Dark, unabr. ed. Seamus Deane. Narrated by Donal Donnelly. 7 cass. (Running Time: 9 hrs. 15 mins.). 1999. 60.00 (978-0-7887-2934-8(9), 95539E7) Recorded Bks.
Through the bittersweet story of a child growing up in post-war Northern Ireland, an intensely intimate view of this haunted, embattled land emerges.

Reading in the Dark. unabr. ed. Seamus Deane. Narrated by Donal Donnelly. 7 cass. (Running Time: 9 hrs. 15 mins.). 2002. 37.95 (978-0-7887-6705-0(4), RC491) Recorded Bks.
A powerful sense of truth rings through this achingly beautiful and brilliantly original story of a boy growing up in Northern Ireland in the 1950s. What is perhaps most remarkable about Deane's compelling debut novel, is his stunning use of language to faithfully convey the rhapsodic consciousness of childhood. The child's mind offers an intensely intimate perspective on the dangerous politically and religiously charged atmosphere of post-war Northern Ireland. The boy pieces together rumors, Church doctrine, and Celtic legends, all infused with deep emotional resonances. Family sorrows and political violence are transformed into poetry as he tries to uncover the terrible secrets of the adult world.

Reading Iran Reading Iranians. Michael C. Hillmann. (PER.). 1999. (3176) Dunwoody Pr.
Thirty-eight self-contained lesson modules aimed at improving reading proficiency in Persian, & arranged in order of increasing difficulty.

***Reading Jackie.** unabr. ed. William Kuhn. Read by Susan Denaker. (Running Time: 8 hrs.). (ENG.). 2010. audio compact disk 40.00 (978-0-307-91356-2(2)) Pub: Random Audio Pubg. Dist(s): Random

Reading Japanese. Eleanor H. Jorden. 17 cass. (Running Time: 15 hrs.). (JPN.). (J). (gr. 10-12). 1976. pap. bk. 275.00 (978-0-88432-096-8(0), AFJ450) J Norton Pubs.
25 lesson course is designed to introduce the adult foreigner to written Japanese. The Japanese material incorporated in the text includes samples of both printing & handwriting & of horizontal, Roman-style format as well as the traditional, vertical style of writing.

Reading Japanese. Eleanor Harz Jorden. 17 CDs. (Running Time: 15 hrs.). (JPN.). 2005. audio compact disk 275.00 (978-1-57970-262-5(7), AFJ450D, Audio-For) J Norton Pubs.
This 25-lesson course is designed to introduce non-Japanese leaners to written Japanese. The Japanese material incorporated in the text includes samples of both printing and handwriting and of horizontal, Roman-style format as well as the traditional, vertical style of writing. The first 8 lessons introduce kana, while each of the remaining lessons introduces 25 new kanzi characters. The audio CDs provide spoken transcriptions in Japanese of the printed exercises, and are essential to masery of the material.

Reading Jesus: A Writer's Encounter with the Gospels. unabr. ed. Mary Gordon. Narrated by Renée Raudman. (Running Time: 7 hrs. 0 mins. 0 sec.). (ENG.). 2009. 19.99 (978-1-4001-6501-8(6)); 14.99 (978-1-4001-8501-6(7)); audio compact disk 24.99 (978-1-4001-1501-3(9)); audio compact disk 49.99 (978-1-4001-4501-0(5)) Pub: Tantor Media. Dist(s): IngramPubServ

Reading Judas: The Gospel of Judas & the Shaping of Christianity. unabr. ed. Elaine Pagels & Karen L. King. 4 cass. (Running Time: 5 hrs. 30 mins.). 2007. audio compact disk 40.00 (978-1-4159-3926-0(8)) Random.

Reading Judas: The Gospel of Judas & the Shaping of Christianity. unabr. ed. Elaine Pagels & Karen L. King. 5 CDs. (Running Time: 5 hrs. 30 mins.). 2007. audio compact disk 60.00 (978-1-4159-3629-0(3), BksonTape) Pub: Random Audio Pubg. Dist(s): Random

Reading Lead Sheets for Keyboard. Jon Dryden. (ENG.). 2001. audio compact disk 10.00 (978-0-7390-1122-5(7)) Alfred Pub.

Reading Like a Writer: A Guide for People Who Love Books & for Those Who Want to Write Them. unabr. ed. Francine Prose. Read by Nanette Savard. 8 CDs. (Running Time: 32400 sec.). 2007. audio compact disk 34.95 (978-0-06-125656-1(0)) HarperCollins Pubs.

***Reading Like a Writer: A Guide for People Who Love Books & for Those Who Want to Write Them.** unabr. ed. Francine Prose. Read by Nanette Savard. (ENG.). 2007. (978-0-06-128738-1(5), Harper Audio); (978-0-06-128737-4(7), Harper Audio) HarperCollins Pubs.

***Reading Like a Writer: Chapter 1 - Close Reading.** abr. ed. Francine Prose. Read by Nanette Savard. (ENG.). 2006. (978-0-06-134070-3(7), Harper Audio) HarperCollins Pubs.

***Reading Like a Writer: Chapter 2 - Words.** abr. ed. Francine Prose. Read by Nanette Savard. (ENG.). 2006. (978-0-06-134094-9(4), Harper Audio) HarperCollins Pubs.

Reading-Listening Comprehension Skills, Level 3. Eunice Insel. 5 cass. (Running Time: 5 hrs.). (J). (gr. 2-6). pupil's gde. ed. 49.00 (978-0-89525-066-7(7), AC 18) Ed Activities.
Develops proficiency in following directions, arranging events in sequence, perceiving cause & effect, predicting outcomes, making inferences, discrimination between fact & opinion, main ideas & details.

Reading Lolita in Tehran: A Memoir in Books. Azar Nafisi. Narrated by Lisette Lecat. 13 cass. (Running Time: 18 hrs. 30 mins.). 2004. 109.75 (978-1-4025-9281-2(7)) Recorded Bks.
A harrowing yet poetic reflection on the transformative power of art and the determination of the human spirit. From 1995-97 in Iran, Azar Nafisi gathered with seven of her former students, all young women, to read and discuss forbidden works of Western literature. Reserved at first, the women soon learned to speak their minds and share their repressed dreams.

Reading Lolita in Tehran: A Memoir in Books. unabr. ed. Azar Nafisi. Narrated by Lisette Lecat. 15 CDs Library ed. (Running Time: 18 hrs. 30 min.). 2004. audio compact disk 109.75 (978-1-4025-9283-6(3)) Recorded Bks.

Reading Lolita in Tehran: A Memoir in Books. unabr. ed. Azar Nafisi. Narrated by Lisette Lecat. 16 CDs. (Running Time: 18 hrs. 30 mins.). 2004. audio compact disk 34.99 (978-1-4025-9084-9(9), 01672) Recorded Bks.
A #1 New York Times paperback nonfiction best-seller, Reading Lolita in Tehran is a harrowing yet poetic reflection on the transformative power of art and the determination of the human spirit. Hailed as a modern classic, this remarkable book appears on reading lists alongside such monumental works as The Great Gatsby and Pride and Prejudice. For the two years before she left Iran in 1997, Azar Nafisi gathered with seven of her former students, all young women, to read and discuss prohibited works of Western literature. Reserved at first, the women soon learned to speak their minds and share their forbidden dreams. From this utterly unique perspective emerged a celebration of the power of the written word and the triumph of the individual.

Reading Made Easy CD Version: 108 Lessons in printable PDF Files. Valerie Bendt. (ENG.). (J). 2007. 25.00 (978-1-885814-18-0(6)) Bendt Fmly.

Reading Magic: Why Reading Aloud to Our Children Will Change Their Lives. unabr. ed. Mem Fox. Narrated by Mem Fox. (Running Time: 3 hrs. 28 mins. 42 sec.). (ENG.). 2009. audio compact disk 15.99 (978-1-59859-481-2(8), SpringWater) Oasis Audio.

Reading Magic: Why Reading Aloud to Our Children Will Change Their Lives. unabr. ed. Mem Fox. Narrated by Mem Fox. (Running Time: 3 hrs. 28 mins. 42 sec.). (ENG.). 2009. 11.19 (978-1-60814-498-3(4), SpringWater) Oasis Audio.

Reading Maps, Globes, Charts, Graphs. Ann Edson & Eunice Insel. 2 cass. (Running Time: 3 hrs.). (J). (gr. 4-6). bk., stu. ed., instr.'s gde. ed. 39.00 incl. 8 activity bks. (978-0-89525-175-6(2), AKC 356) Ed Activities.
A hands-on approach to reading maps, charts, & other graphic materials that students will encounter in reference books, social studies texts, etc. Objectives include: understanding keys, vocabulary, & symbols, locating cardinal & intermediate directions, finding details in special maps (weather, road), using an atlas, reading a globe, locating places using latitude & longitude.

Reading Music Quickly Through Chord Analysis. Duane Shinn. 1 cass. 19.95 (MR-3) Duane Shinn.
Presents Bach's Prelude in C as an example & analyzes the chord structure measure by measure all the way through the piece.

Reading Myself see Robert Lowell: A Reading

Reading of Chogyam Trungpa, Rinpoche Poetry. Chogyam Trungpa. Read by David Rome. 1 cass. 1975. 12.50 (A099) Vajradhatu.
A selection of Rinpoche's poetry is read by David Rome.

Reading of Realities, Set. Robert F. Morneau. Read by Robert F. Morneau. 4 cass. (Running Time: 4 hrs.). 32.95 (TAH164) Alba Hse Comns.

Reading Out Loud to God. Alla R. Bozarth. 1 cass. (Running Time: 1 hr.). 1990. 10.00 Wisdom House.
This is a performance of forty-three poems including Belonging (Stars in Your Bones), Hymn to Gaea, Loving the Body, I Am & Celebration... many of which appear.

Reading Polish 1. Jerzy R. Krzyzanowski et al. 5 cass. (Running Time: 5 hrs.). 1984. 25.00 (978-0-87415-012-4(4), 11B) Foreign Lang.

Reading, Praying & Living the Psalms: An Audio Workshop to Help You under the Psalms. Speeches. Douglas Jacoby. 4 CDs. (Running Time: 4 Hours). 2005. audio compact disk 20.00 (978-0-9767583-8-9(5)) Illumination MA.

Reading Program 1 Audio Cards. Janie Haugen-McLane et al. 2008. 159.95 (978-1-58804-646-8(X)) PCI Educ.

Reading Program 2 Audio Cards. Janie Haugen-McLane et al. 2008. 159.95 (978-1-58804-647-5(8)) PCI Educ.

Reading Rhythm Patterns in Four-Four Time. Duane Shinn. 1 cass. 19.95 (MR-4) Duane Shinn.
Explains how to recognize & play rhythm patterns in 4/4 time.

Reading Rhythm Patterns in Three-Four Time. Duane Shinn. 1 cass. 19.95 (MR-5) Duane Shinn.
Explains how to recognize & play rhythm patterns with triple meter.

***Reading Room.** Ruth Hamilton. 2010. 84.95 (978-0-7531-3738-3(0)); audio compact disk 99.95 (978-0-7531-2729-2(6)) Pub: Isis Pubng Ltd GBR. Dist(s): Ulverscroft US

Reading Strategies Aa, Vols. 1-15. 1995. (978-1-56260-716-6(2)) Ed Developmental.

Reading Strategies As, Vols. 16-30. 1995. (978-1-56260-717-3(0)) Ed Developmental.

Reading Strategies Ba, Vols. 1-15. 1995. (978-1-56260-718-0(9)) Ed Developmental.

Reading Strategies Ba, Vols. 16-30. 1995. (978-1-56260-719-7(7)) Ed Developmental.

Reading Strategies Ca, Vols. 1-15. 1995. (978-1-56260-720-3(0)) Ed Developmental.

Reading Strategies Ca, Vols. 16-30. 1995. (978-1-56260-721-0(9)) Ed Developmental.

Reading Strategies Da, Vols. 1-30. 1995. (978-1-56260-722-7(7)) Ed Developmental.

Reading Strategies Ea, Vols. 1-30. 1995. (978-1-56260-723-4(5)) Ed Developmental.

Reading Strategies Fa, Vols. 1-30. 1995. (978-1-56260-724-1(3)) Ed Developmental.

Reading the I Ching. Michael P. Marshall. Read by Michael P. Marshall. Ed. by Jonathan C. Renaud. Music by Ted Crook. 1 cass. (Running Time: 52 min.). 1995. 9.00 (978-0-912403-11-3(X)) Prod Renaud.
Ancient Chinese divination through symbols, made meaningful for our world today.

Reading the Message of Sickness. Robert Reeves. 1986. 10.80 (0101) Assn Prof Chaplains.

***Reading the OED: One Man, One Year, 21,730 Pages.** unabr. ed. Ammon Shea. Read by William Dufris. (ENG.). 2008. (978-0-06-173588-2(4)); (978-0-06-174413-6(1)) HarperCollins Pubs.

Reading "The Shamanic Way in Ancient Egypt" by Charles Muses. Ruth-Inge Heinze. 1 cass. 9.00 (A0214-87) Sound Photosyn.
ICSS '87, also Stanley Krippner & Louis Mehl on tape.

Reading the Water: Adventures in Surf Fishing from Martha's Vineyard. Robert Post. 2008. audio compact disk 28.00 (978-1-933309-55-2(5)) Pub: A Media Intl. Dist(s): Natl Bk Netwk

Reading Thucydides. James V. Morrison. 2006. audio compact disk 9.95 (978-0-8142-9112-2(0)) Pub: Ohio St U Pr. Dist(s): Chicago Distribution Ctr

Reading, Writing & Revolution. 10.00 (HD415) Esstee Audios.

Reading Your Baby's Body Language. unabr. ed. Beverly Morgan. Read by Beverly Morgan. Read by Kathryn Nymoen. Contrib. by Lance Nottie. 1 cass. (Running Time: 1 hr.). (Breastfeeding Basics & Beyond Ser.: Vol. 1). 1998. 12.95 Norelco case. (978-1-891768-10-1(7)); 12.95 Library case. (978-1-891768-11-8(5)) Milky Way Pr.
Reveals the non-verbal language of infants with special attention to body language while breastfeeding. Landmark audio helps mothers develop the full relationship of breast feeding.

Reading 2000 Phonics Songs & Rhymes. 1 CD. (Running Time: 1 hr.). (gr. 2 up). 2004. audio compact disk 69.00 (978-0-673-62205-1(3)) Addson-Wesley Educ.
Original songs/rhymes help introduce each lesson's phonetic element and develop phonemic awareness. Also provides the instrumental track for all the songs.

Reading 2002 Selection Audiotape Package. (gr. 2 up). 2004. stu. ed. 45.95 (978-0-328-02516-9(X)) Addson-Wesley Educ.

Reading 8-pack Level M. Steck-Vaughn Staff. 2003. (978-0-7398-8002-9(0)) SteckVau.

Readings & Conversations: About the United States, Its People, Its History & Its Customs, No. 1. rev. ed. English Language Services Staff. (J). (gr. 9-12). 1976. 95.00 (978-0-87789-201-4(6), 1214) ELS Educ Servs.

Readings & Conversations: About the United States, Its People, Its History & Its Customs, No. 2. rev. ed. English Language Services Staff. (J). (gr. 9-12). 1976. 95.00 (978-0-87789-202-1(4), 1215) ELS Educ Servs.

Readings & Conversations in Polish: Intermediate Level. Maria Swiecicka-Ziemianek. 1 cass. (Running Time: 60 mins.). 1988. pap. bk. 29.50 (978-0-88432-252-8(1), AFP600) J Norton Pubs.
Intermediate-level listening/comprehension program. The readings are from contemporary Polish publications, while the conversations concern activities such as eating, getting around, birthdays & wedding receptions.

Readings from a Course in Miracles. Hosted by William N. Thetford. 1 cass. (Running Time: 1 hr.). 1980. 10.00 (978-1-883360-10-8(2), F-9) Found Inner Peace.

Readings from the People's Daily. 2 cass. 1985. 8.95 ea. incl. suppl. materials. (978-0-88710-136-6(4)) Yale Far Eastern Pubns.

Readings from the Sweeping Plain: No. 1 in the River Road Poetry Series. Michael Sharkey. Read by Michael Sharkey. Executive Producer Carol Jenkins. (ENG.). 2008. audio compact disk 18.00 (978-0-9804148-0-6(6)) RivRoad AUS.

Readings from Voices of a People's History of the United States. abr. ed. Anthony Arnove. Ed. by Howard Zinn. Contrib. by Josh Brolin et al. (ENG.). 2007. audio compact disk 14.95 (978-1-58322-752-7(0)) Pub: Seven Stories. Dist(s): Consort Bk Sales

Readings from "We Find Ourselves in Moonville" Jay Gummerman. 2 cass. (Running Time: 3 hrs.). 18.00 (A0661-83) Sound Photosyn.
Short stories.

Readings in a Manual of Modern Greek. 5 cass. (Running Time: 4 hrs. 18 min.). 75.00 (GRO420) J Norton Pubs.

Readings in Modern Dance, Vol. 2. Ed. by Michele J. Varon. (C). 1977. 15.00 (978-0-685-08571-4(6)) Dance Notation.

Readings in Sayable Chinese, No. 1. Yuen Ren Chao. (Spoken Language Ser.). 1985. 85.00 (978-0-87950-333-8(5)) Spoken Lang Serv.

Readings in Sayable Chinese, No. 2. Yuen Ren Chao. (Spoken Language Ser.). 1985. 65.00 (978-0-87950-334-5(3)) Spoken Lang Serv.

Readings in Sayable Chinese, No. 3. Yuen Ren Chao. (Spoken Language Ser.). 1985. 80.00 (978-0-87950-335-2(1)) Spoken Lang Serv.

Readings in the Greek New Testament. unabr. ed. Jonathan T. Pennington. (Running Time: 2 hrs. 0 mins. 0 sec.). (ENG.). 2003. 11.99 (978-0-310-26173-5(2)) Zondervan.

Reads Kid Sleepy see Poetry & Reflections

ReadSmart, Bk. 3. Pavlik. (Readsmart Ser.). (ENG.). (C). 2007. 67.81 (978-0-07-283899-2(X), 007283899X, ESL/ELT) Pub: McGrw-H Hghr Educ. Dist(s): McGraw

Ready, Fire, Aim: Zero to $100 Million in No Time Flat. unabr. ed. Michael Masterson. Read by Sean Pratt. (Running Time: 12 hrs.). (ENG.). 2008. 29.98 (978-1-59659-196-7(X), GildAudio) Pub: Gildan Media. Dist(s): HachBkGrp

Ready, Fire, Aim: Zero to $100 Million in No Time Flat. unabr. ed. Michael Masterson. Read by Sean Pratt. 6 CDs. (Running Time: 12 hrs.). (ENG.). 2008. audio compact disk 39.98 (978-1-59659-163-9(3), GildAudio) Pub: Gildan Media. Dist(s): HachBkGrp

Ready for Anything: 52 Productivity Principles for Work & Life. abr. ed. David Allen. 2004. 12.95 (978-0-7435-4783-3(7)) Pub: S&S Audio. Dist(s): S and S Inc

Ready for Anything: 52 Productivity Principles for Work & Life. abr. ed. David Allen & David Allen. Read by David Allen & David Allen. 3 CDs. (Running Time: 30 hrs. 0 mins. 0 sec.). (ENG.). 2003. audio compact disk 25.00 (978-0-7435-3530-4(8), Sound Ideas) Pub: S&S Audio. Dist(s): S and S Inc

Ready for Fall: Early Explorers Early Set A Audio CD. Benchmark Education Staff. (J). 2006. audio compact disk 10.00 (978-1-4108-7614-0(4)) Benchmark Educ.

Ready for Worship. Created by Lillenas Publishing Company. 2007. audio compact disk 99.99 (978-5-557-54392-7(9)); audio compact disk 99.99 (978-5-557-54391-0(0)) Lillenas.

Ready for Worship: 12 Complete Worship Sets with No Transpositions or Transitions Required. Contrib. by Carter Robertson. Created by Carter Robertson & Barny Robertson. Created by Barny Robertson. 2007. audio compact disk 16.00 (978-5-557-54395-8(3)) Lillenas.

Ready Freddy - Don't Sit on My Lunch & Shark Tooth Tale. unabr. ed. Abby Klein. Read by Fred Berman. (J). 2007. 34.99 (978-1-60252-785-0(7)) Find a World.

Ready Freddy - Help! A Vampire Is Coming & Halloween Fraidy-Cat. unabr. ed. Abby Klein. Read by Fred Berman. (J). 2008. 34.99 (978-1-60514-705-5(2)) Find a World.

Ready Freddy - Tooth Trouble & Homework Hassles. unabr. ed. Abby Klein. Read by Fred Berman. (J). 2007. 34.99 (978-1-60252-784-3(9)) Find a World.

***Ready, Freddy! 1: Tooth Trouble.** Weston Woods Staff. (J). audio compact disk 14.95 (978-0-545-05044-9(8)) Weston Woods.

***Ready, Freddy! 3: Homework Hassles.** Weston Woods Staff. (J). audio compact disk 14.95 (978-0-545-05043-2(X)) Weston Woods.

***Ready, Freddy! 4: Don't Sit on My Lunch!;** Weston Woods Staff. (J). audio compact disk 14.95 (978-0-545-05042-5(1)) Weston Woods.

Ready-Go Alphabet. Eunice Insel & Ann Edson. 7 cass. (Running Time: 7 hrs.). (J). (gr. k-1). 1986. tchr. ed. 89.00 incl. 10 activity bks. (978-0-89525-023-0(3), AKC 16) Ed Activities.
Individualized lessons, one for each letter of the alphabet, Each lesson contains about 10 minutes of recorded time plus activity time. A way for children to learn identification, naming, & forming the letters of the alphabet.

Ready-Go Math, Level 1. Ann Edson & Allan A. Schwartz. 8 cass. 89.95 incl. 8 activity bks., guide. (978-0-89525-030-8(6), AKC 60) Ed Activities.
Building readiness, one & two-digit numerals, telling time to the hour & half hour, using fractions, one half, using money, using ordinals, working with the number line, using place values, adding & subtracting, counting to 99.

Ready-Go...Begin to Learn. Eunice Insel & Ann Edson. 7 cass. (J). (gr. k-1). 1986. 98.00 incl. 10 activity bks., tchr's. guide. (978-0-89525-182-4(5), AKC 59) Ed Activities.
Includes: Recognizing Numbers-Numerals 1-9, 0, 10; recognizing shapes; sequencing: alphabet, story; using locational skills: up-down, in-out, left-right, over-under; discriminating size classicfication: same-different, opposite, big-little; introducing basic vocabulary.

Ready Heart: More Jane Yolen Stories. Perf. by Milbre Burch. As told by Milbre Burch. Based on a story by Jane Yolen. (ENG.). 2007. audio compact disk 20.00 (978-0-9795271-6-6(3)) Kind Crone.

Ready-Made Compliance Training: PowerPoint Presentations for Effective Education. Douglas S. Brown. 2007. audio compact disk 149.00 (978-1-60146-044-8(9)) Opus Communs.

Ready or Not. Chris Manby. 2008. audio compact disk 79.95 (978-0-7531-3080-3(7)) Pub: ISIS Audio GBR. Dist(s): Ulverscroft US

Ready or Not. unabr. ed. Meg Cabot. Read by Ariadne Meyers. 4 cass. (Running Time: 6 hrs. 27 mins.). (All American Girl Ser.: Vol. 2). (YA). 2005. 35.00 (978-0-307-24337-9(0), BksonTape); audio compact disk 42.50 (978-0-307-24614-1(0), BksonTape) Pub: Random Audio Pubg. Dist(s): NetLibrary CO

Ready or Not. unabr. ed. Chris Manby. 6 cass. (Running Time: 7 hrs. 30 mins.). 2008. 54.95 (978-0-7531-2174-0(3)) Pub: ISIS Audio GBR. Dist(s): Ulverscroft US

Ready or Not: Why Treating Children As Small Adults Endangers Their Future & Ours. unabr. ed. Kay S. Hymowitz. Narrated by Linda Stephens. 7 cass. (Running Time: 9 hrs. 30 min.). 2000. 61.00 (96321E7) Recorded Bks.
Experts have been telling us children know what is best for themselves. Yet many youngsters commit adult crimes or later have trouble taking on adult responsibilities. Scholar & journalist author reveals why so many children never seem to grow up.

***Ready, Set, Go!** unabr. ed. John Stadler. (ENG.). 2008. (978-0-06-169484-4(3)); (978-0-06-171341-5(4)) HarperCollins Pubs.

Ready, Set, Go! EFL for Native Speakers of Spanish, Levels 1-2. (Ready, Set, Go!). (J). (gr. 2-5). 2000. 8.99 (978-1-928882-90-9(0)) CCLS Pubg Hse.

Ready, Set, Go! EFL for Native Speakers of Spanish, Levels 3-4. (Ready, Set, Go!). (J). (gr. 2-5). 2000. 8.99 (978-1-928882-91-6(9)) CCLS Pubg Hse.

***Ready, Set, Go! Book 1 - CD De Áudio.** (ENG.). 2005. audio compact disk (978-0-7428-1737-1(7)) CCLS Pubg Hse.

***Ready, Set, Go! Book 2 - CD De Áudio.** (ENG.). 2005. audio compact disk (978-0-7428-1495-0(5)) CCLS Pubg Hse.

***Ready, Set, Go! Book 3 - CD De Áudio.** (ENG.). 2005. audio compact disk (978-0-7428-1496-7(3)) CCLS Pubg Hse.

***Ready, Set, Go! Book 4 - CD De Áudio.** (ENG.). 2005. audio compact disk (978-0-7428-1497-4(1)) CCLS Pubg Hse.

Ready, Set, Go! CD Bks. 1-4: English Language Teaching. 2005. audio compact disk (978-0-7428-1483-7(1)) CCLS Pubg Hse.
Ready, Set, Go! for native speakers of spanish/all-english versionBeginnersFollowing the success of Ready, Set, Go! for Spanish-speaking children and in response to requests from schools and teachers around the world, this easy-to-teach, easy-to-learn four-book series, specially designed for children in grades 1?4, is now also available in an all-English version.Both versions develop the four language skills through a gradual and carefully structured presentation of grammar and vocabulary and share the following features:Simple format for flexibility and liberty to choose teaching techniques Enjoyable, student-centered learning activitiesGradual introduction of written English, from recognition to production, to avoid interference with children?s native language learningAge-appropriate themes with lighthearted cartoon illustrations like the playful little characters that kids loveReady, Set, Go! for native speakers of Spanish has instructions and explanations in Spanish.Teacher?s resourcesTest/Picture Kit: includes suggestions for testing with correction key and answer keys for all exercisesPicture CardsAudiocassette: one tape for each two levels with lesson texts, reading texts and songsVideo (optional)Student?s materialStudent?s Books 1?4Audiocassette and video (optional).

Ready-Set-Read-Along. Eunice Insel. 3 cass. (J). (gr. k-1). 19.95 incl. 3 bks. & activity cards. (978-0-914296-40-9(X), AC 17) Ed Activities.
Bk. 1: "Do You See Sillies?"; Bk. 2: "Do You See Shapes?"; Bk. 3: "Do You See Numbers & Numeral?".

Ready... Set... Release: Music & Relaxation Exercises for Children. unabr. ed. Jeffry S. Allen et al. 1 cass. (Running Time: 74 mins.). (J). 2000. 10.95 Inner Coach.
Fun & calming exercises using music, breathing, muscle relaxation & active imagination to soothe & release tension.Researched & proven effective for children from pre-school to middle school.

Ready... Set... Release! Music & Relaxation Exercises for Children. unabr. ed. Roger J. Klein & Jeffrey S. Allen. 1 CD. (Running Time: 74 mins.). (ENG.). (J). (gr. 4-7). 1999. audio compact disk 15.95 (978-0-9636027-1-8(3)) Pub: Inner Coach. Dist(s): IPG Chicago

Ready, Set, Research! Compton's by Britannica. Compiled by Encyclopaedia Britannica, Inc. 2008. audio compact disk 24.95 Ency Brit Inc.

Ready, Set, Research! Compton's by Britannica. Compiled by Encyclopaedia Britannica, Inc. (gr. 3-5). 2008. audio compact disk 24.95 Ency Brit Inc.

Ready-Set-Sing Series. Penton Overseas, Inc. Staff. 4 CDs. (Running Time: 4 hrs.). (ReadySetSing! Ser.). (ENG.). (J). (ps-7). 2000. audio compact disk 19.49 (978-1-56015-971-1(5)) Penton Overseas.
A collection of over 120 all-time favorites.

Ready, Set, Succeed! How Successful Projects Triumph over Business as Usual. abr. ed. Read by Linda H. Schumacher. Abr. by Linda H. Schumacher. Intro. by Jay Speyerer. 2 CDs. (Running Time: 2 hrs. 7 mins). 2006. 18.95 (978-0-9754831-9-0(6)) Carscallen Pr.
Ready, Set, Succeed! is your guide to curing project paralysis ?an immobilizing condition that happens when you have so many projects, you don?t know which one to start first - - so you don?t start any of them. Or maybe your project paralysis is different ? it?s causing your important strategic business projects to continually get derailed by urgent day-to-day business emergencies.To meet or beat evolving customer needs and new market trends, your business needs the ability to develop and expand while conducting business as usual. Ready, Set, Succeed! gives you a simple, flexible roadmap for navigating your business through the complexities of a project ? from inception to successful conclusion. Maybe you need to - -? Add a new product or service? Introduce an innovative channel to deliver existing products or services? Move to a new business location or? Automate a business process with computers.Listening to this book will introduce you to tools and techniques for: ? Selecting the right project using a simple evaluation tool? Managing the scope, schedule, risks, and costs? Overcoming the stumbling blocks you?ll encounter during the project and ? Training your company to adopt the project mindset and do more projects.

Ready-to-Go Storytimes: Fingerplays, Scripts, Patterns, Music, & More. Gail Benton & Trisha Waichulaitis. 2003. audio compact disk 59.95 (978-1-55570-449-0(2)) Neal-Schuman.

Ready to Jump! Michael Shreave & B. C. Smith. 1 cass. (Running Time: 40 min.). (J). (ps-3). 1994. 7.95 (978-1-57061-001-1(0)) Sasquatch Bks.
Jump rope rhymes set to music.

Ready to Rock Kids, Vol. 1. unabr. ed. Mac & Friends. Composed by Don R. Macmannis. 1 CD. (Running Time: 52 mins.). (Ready to Rock Ser.). (ENG.). (J). (ps-4). 2007. audio compact disk 14.95 (978-1-57542-246-6(8)) Free Spirit Pub.

Ready to Rock Kids, Vol. 2. 2nd unabr. ed. Mac & Friends. Composed by Mac & Friends. 1 CD. (Running Time: 42 mins.). (Ready to Rock Ser.). (ENG.). (J). (ps-4). 2007. audio compact disk 14.95 (978-1-57542-247-3(6)) Free Spirit Pub.

Ready to Rock Kids, Vol. 3. 3rd ed. Mac and Friends & Mac & Friends. (Ready to Rock Ser.). (ENG.). (J). 2008. audio compact disk 14.95 (978-1-57542-305-0(7)) Free Spirit Pub.

Ready to Sing Again. Contrib. by Russell Mauldin. 1994. 11.98 (978-1-55897-136-3(X), 75602228) Pub: Brentwood Music. Dist(s): H Leonard

Ready to Sing Christmas. 1 CD. (Running Time: 1 hr.). audio compact disk (20196) Alfred Pub.

Ready to Sing... Christmas. Ed. by Jay Althouse. (Ready to Sing Ser.). (ENG.). 2001. audio compact disk 11.95 (978-0-7390-1975-7(9)) Alfred Pub.

Ready to Sing Contemporary. Contrib. by Russell Mauldin. 1995. 11.98 (978-0-7601-0023-3(3), 75602029) Pub: Brentwood Music. Dist(s): H Leonard

Ready to Sing Contemporary, Vol. 2. Contrib. by Russell Mauldin. 1996. 85.00 (978-0-7601-0875-8(7), 75606293); audio compact disk 85.00 (978-0-7601-0876-5(5), 75606294) Pub: Brentwood Music. Dist(s): H Leonard

Ready to Sing Contemporary, Vol. 2. Contrib. by Russell Mauldin. 1996. 11.98 (978-0-7601-0830-7(7), 75602070); 85.00 (978-0-7601-0874-1(9), 75606442); 4.00 (978-0-7601-0877-2(3), 75602069); 4.00 (978-0-7601-0878-9(1), 75602072); 4.00 (978-0-7601-0880-2(3), 75602071) Pub: Brentwood Music. Dist(s): H Leonard

Ready to Sing Contemporary, Vol. 3. Contrib. by Russell Mauldin. 1997. 11.98 (978-0-7601-1444-5(7), 75602101); audio compact disk 85.00 (978-0-7601-1447-6(1), 75606317) Pub: Brentwood Music. Dist(s): H Leonard

Ready to Sing Contemporary, Vol. 3. Contrib. by Russell Mauldin. 1997. 85.00 (978-0-7601-1445-2(5), 75606451); 85.00 (978-0-7601-1446-9(3), 75606316); 4.00 (978-0-7601-1448-3(X), 75602102); 4.00 (978-0-7601-1449-0(8), 75602099); 4.00 (978-0-7601-1450-6(1), 75602103); 4.00 (978-0-7601-1451-3(X), 75602100) Pub: Brentwood Music. Dist(s): H Leonard

Ready to Sing Contemporary - Volume 2. Contrib. by Russell Mauldin. 1996. 4.00 (978-0-7601-0879-6(X), 75602068) Pub: Brentwood Music. Dist(s): H Leonard

Ready to Sing Gospel Choir: Alto. Contrib. by Jonathan Crumpton & Russell Mauldin. Prod. by Russell Mauldin. (Ready to Sing Ser.). 2008. audio compact disk 5.00 (978-5-557-48009-3(9), Brentwood-Benson Music) Brentwood Music.

Ready to Sing Gospel Choir: Soprano. Contrib. by Jonathan Crumpton & Russell Mauldin. Prod. by Russell Mauldin. (Ready to Sing Ser.). 2008. audio compact disk 5.00 (978-5-557-48374-2(8), Brentwood-Benson Music) Brentwood Music.

Ready to Sing Gospel Choir: Tenor. Contrib. by Russell Mauldin. (Ready to Sing Ser.). 2008. audio compact disk 5.00 (978-5-557-48373-5(X), Brentwood-Benson Music) Brentwood Music.

Ready to Sing Southern Gospel, Volume 5. Contrib. by Johnathan Crumpton & Russell Mauldin. Prod. by Russell Mauldin. (Ready to Sing Ser.). (ENG.). 2008. audio compact disk 90.00 (978-5-557-42351-9(6), Brentwood-Benson Music) Brentwood Music.

Ready to Sing Southern Gospel, Volume 5. Contrib. by Russell Mauldin. (ENG.). 2008. audio compact disk 16.99 (978-5-557-42352-6(4), Brentwood-Benson Music); audio compact disk 10.00 (978-5-557-42350-2(8), Brentwood-Benson Music) Brentwood Music.

Ready to Sing Southern Gospel, Volume 5: Alto. Contrib. by Johnathan Crumpton & Russell Mauldin. Prod. by Russell Mauldin. (Ready to Sing Ser.). (ENG.). 2008. audio compact disk 5.00 (978-5-557-42348-9(6), Brentwood-Benson Music) Brentwood Music.

Ready to Sing Southern Gospel, Volume 5: Bass. Contrib. by Johnathan Crumpton & Russell Mauldin. Prod. by Russell Mauldin. (Ready to Sing Ser.). (ENG.). 2008. audio compact disk 5.00 (978-5-557-42346-5(X), Brentwood-Benson Music) Brentwood Music.

Ready to Sing Southern Gospel, Volume 5: Soprano. Contrib. by Johnathan Crumpton & Russell Mauldin. Prod. by Russell Mauldin. (ENG.). 2008. audio compact disk 5.00 (978-5-557-42349-6(4), Brentwood-Benson Music) Brentwood Music.

Ready to Sing Southern Gospel, Volume 5: Tenor. Contrib. by Johnathan Crumpton & Russell Mauldin. Prod. by Russell Mauldin. (Ready to Sing Ser.). (ENG.). 2008. audio compact disk 5.00 (978-5-557-42347-2(8), Brentwood-Benson Music) Brentwood Music.

Ready to Sing... Spirituals. Jay Althouse et al. 1 CD. (Running Time: 1 hr. 30 mins.). (Ready to Sing Ser.). (ENG.). 2000. audio compact disk 11.95 (978-0-7390-0924-6(9), 19810) Alfred Pub.

***Ready to Use Designs.** PUEI. 2008. audio compact disk 49.95 (978-1-935041-44-3(4), CareerTrack) P Univ E Inc.

Ready to Wed. unabr. ed. Melody Carlson. Narrated by Sherri Berger. (Running Time: 7 hrs. 12 mins. 8 sec.). (Grace Chapel Inn Ser.). (ENG.). 2009. 18.19 (978-1-60814-476-1(3)); audio compact disk 25.99 (978-1-59859-558-1(X)) Oasis Audio.

Reaffirming Our Spirit in Old Testament Light. Roland Murphy. 2 cass. (Running Time: 2 hrs. 45 min.). 1997. 18.95 (TAH380) St Pauls Alba.
Fr. Connor's reexamination of Deuteronomy, Jonah, Job, & the Song of Songs will help to develop an appreciative understanding of God in the story of salvation that can illuminate the course of contemporary spirituality.

Reagan: An American Story. collector's ed. Adriana Bosch. Read by Kate Reading. 7 cass. (Running Time: 10 hrs. 30 min.). 2000. 56.00 (978-0-7366-5063-2(6)) Books on Tape.
Over fifty exclusive interviews with Reagan's family, friends, advisors & adversaries. Following Reagan from his childhood with an alcoholic father through his Hollywood & political lives on to his battle with Alzheimer's disease, the only foe he could not defeat, readers of this book will learn of Reagan in the words of those who knew him best.

Reagan: The Hollywood Years. unabr. ed. Marc Eliot. Read by Marc Eliot. 12 CDs. (Running Time: 15 hrs. 0 mins. 0 sec.). (ENG.). 2008. audio compact disk 39.99 (978-1-4001-0778-0(4)); audio compact disk 79.99 (978-1-4001-3778-7(0)); audio compact disk 29.99 (978-1-4001-5778-5(1)) Pub: Tantor Media. Dist(s): IngramPubServ

Reagan Diaries. abr. ed. Ronald Reagan. Read by Eric Conger. (YA). 2008. 64.99 (978-1-60514-823-6(7)) Find a World.

Reagan Diaries. abr. ed. Ronald Reagan. Read by Eric Conger. Ed. by Douglas Brinkley. 3 CDs. (Running Time: 10800 sec.). 2007. audio compact disk 19.95 (978-0-06-128564-6(1), Harper Audio) HarperCollins Pubs.

Reagan Diaries: Extended Selections. abr. ed. Ronald Reagan. Read by Eric Conger. Ed. by Douglas Brinkley. (Running Time: 46800 sec.). 2007. audio compact disk 44.95 (978-0-06-123082-0(0)) HarperCollins Pubs.

***Reagan Diaries Extended Selections.** abr. ed. Ronald Reagan. Read by Eric Conger. (ENG.). 2007. (978-0-06-126267-8(6), Harper Audio); (978-0-06-126268-5(4), Harper Audio) HarperCollins Pubs.

***Reagan Diaries Selections.** abr. ed. Ronald Reagan. Read by Eric Conger. (ENG.). 2007. (978-0-06-146931-2(9), Harper Audio); (978-0-06-146930-5(0), Harper Audio) HarperCollins Pubs.

Reagan I Knew. unabr. ed. William F. Buckley, Jr. Read by Malcolm Hillgartner. 1 MP3-CD. (Running Time: 8 hrs. 30 mins.). 2009. 29.95 (978-1-4332-6282-1(7)); audio compact disk 70.00 (978-1-4332-6279-1(7)) Blckstn Audio.

Reagan I Knew. unabr. ed. William F. Buckley, Jr. Read by Malcolm Hillgartner. 5 CDs. (Running Time: 8 hrs. 30 mins.). 2009. audio compact disk 19.95 (978-1-4332-6281-4(9)) Blckstn Audio.

Reagan I Knew. unabr. ed. William F. Jr. Buckley. Read by Malcolm Hillgartner. (Running Time: 8.5 hrs. NaN mins.). 2009. audio compact disk 54.95 (978-1-4332-6278-4(9)) Blckstn Audio.

Reagan in His Own Voice. unabr. abr. ed. Kiron K. Skinner et al. 4 CDs. (Running Time: 60 hrs. 0 mins. 0 sec.). (ENG.). 2001. audio compact disk 30.00 (978-0-7435-0985-5(4), Audioworks) Pub: S&S Audio. Dist(s): S and S Inc

Reagan on Leadership: Executive Lessons from the Great Communicator. collector's ed. James M. Strock. Read by Michael Prichard. 6 cass. (Running Time: 9 hrs.). 2000. 48.00 (978-0-7366-5606-1(5)) Books on Tape.
When Ronald Reagan became President, he rejuvenated the country. How he turned it around is an inspiration for leaders everywhere. This book highlights the keys to his leadership skills & shows how they work in today's business world. His secrets include hiring the right people, negotiating from strength, motivating an audience, overcoming failure & perhaps most important, communicating an inspiring vision. Reagan was a leader of uncanny strength whose steely determination never flagged. He triumphed over challenges people in business face every day.

Reagan Psalms. A. D. Winans. Read by A. D. Winans. 1 cass. (Running Time: 60 min.). 1986. 5.75 (978-0-932593-15-3(1)) Black Bear.
A.D. Winans reads his own poetry.

Reaganomics Made Easy. Prod. by Robert Krulwich. 1 cass. (Running Time: 51 min.). 9.00 (L0040B090, HarperThor) HarpC GBR.

Reagans: A Political Portrait. collector's unabr. ed. Peter Hannaford. Read by Michael Prichard. 11 cass. (Running Time: 16 hrs. 30 mins.). 1984. 88.00 (978-0-7366-0958-6(X), 1901) Books on Tape.
Peter Hannaford gives shrewd insight into Reagan's management style & methods. The book thus becomes an important political reference work & an intimate portrait of Ronald & Nancy Reagan.

Real. Contrib. by Jake Smith et al. Prod. by Dan Strain. 2007. audio compact disk 11.99 (978-5-557-72624-5(1)) Rocket.

Real All Americans: The Team That Changed a Game, a People, a Nation. unabr. ed. Sally Jenkins. Read by Don Leslie. 11 CDs. (Running Time: 13 hrs.). 2007. audio compact disk 110.00 (978-1-4159-3868-3(7)) Random.

Real Alternative. Kenneth Wapnick. 4 CDs. 2005. audio compact disk 25.00 (978-1-59142-203-7(5), CD115) Foun Miracles.

***Real Alternative.** Kenneth Wapnick. 2009. 20.00 (978-1-59142-466-6(6)) Foun Miracles.

Real America: Messages from the Heart & Heartland. unabr. ed. Glenn Beck. 2004. 15.95 (978-0-7435-4829-8(9)) Pub: S&S Audio. Dist(s): S and S Inc

Real & Apparent Man. abr. ed. Vivekananda. Read by Bruce Robertson. 1 cass. (Running Time: 42 min.). 1987. 7.95 (978-1-882915-01-9(1)) Vedanta Ctr Atlanta.
Lecture by Swami Vivekananda discussing the real nature of humankind - spiritual.

Real Animal House: The Awesomely Depraved Saga of the Fraternity That Inspired the Movie. unabr. ed. Chris Miller. Narrated by Todd McLaren. (Running Time: 11 hrs. 0 mins. 0 sec.). (ENG.). 2006. audio compact disk 34.99 (978-1-4001-0337-9(1)); audio compact disk 24.99 (978-1-4001-5337-4(9)); audio compact disk 69.99 (978-1-4001-3337-6(8)) Pub: Tantor Media. Dist(s): IngramPubServ

Real Blues for Keyboard. Jeff Hammer. (Fast Forward Ser.). 1997. audio compact disk 15.95 (978-0-7119-4514-2(4)) Pub: Music Sales. Dist(s): H Leonard

Real Book of Real Estate: Real Experts, Real Advice, Real Success Stories. unabr. ed. Robert T. Kiyosaki. Read by Bruce Reizen. 2 MP3-CDs. (Running Time: 18 hrs.). 2009. 44.97 (978-1-4233-7304-9(9), 9781423373049, Brinc Audio MP3 Lib); 44.97 (978-1-4233-7306-3(5), 9781423373063, BADLE); 29.99 (978-1-4233-7305-6(7), 9781423373056, BAD); audio compact disk 97.97 (978-1-4233-7302-5(2), 9781423373025, BriAudCD Unabrid) Brilliance Audio.

Real Book of Real Estate: Real Experts, Real Advice, Real Success Stories. unabr. ed. Robert T. Kiyosaki. Read by Bruce Reizen et al. 2 MP3-CDs. (Running Time: 18 hrs.). 2009. 29.99 (978-1-4233-7303-2(0), 9781423373032, Brilliance MP3); audio compact disk 49.99 (978-1-4233-7301-8(4), 9781423373018, Bril Audio CD Unabri) Brilliance Audio.

Real Book Play-along - Volume 1 S-Z: 3-CD Set. Created by Hal Leonard Corporation Staff. 2008. pap. bk. 24.99 (978-1-4234-3365-1(3), 1423433653) H Leonard.

Real Boys: Rescuing Our Sons from the Myths of Boyhood. unabr. ed. William Pollack. Narrated by John McDonough. 15 cass. (Running Time: 21 hrs.). 2000. 120.00 (978-0-7887-3544-8(6), 95929E7) Recorded Bks.
Clinical psychologist William Pollack's research at Harvard Medical School confirms today's headlines: our sons are in trouble. As he examines the causes of this crisis, Dr. Pollack offers ways we can help boys grow up into healthy adults.

Real Change: From the World That Fails to the World That Works. unabr. ed. Newt Gingrich. Read by Callista Gingrich. 1 MP3-CD. (Running Time: 8 hrs. 0 mins. 0 sec.). (ENG.). 2008. audio compact disk 24.99 (978-1-4001-5656-6(4)); audio compact disk 34.99 (978-1-4001-0656-1(7)) Pub: Tantor Media. Dist(s): IngramPubServ

Real Change: From the World That Fails to the World That Works. unabr. ed. Newt Gingrich. Read by Calista Gingrich. 7 CDs. (Running Time: 8 hrs. 0 mins. 0 sec.). (ENG.). 2008. audio compact disk 69.99 (978-1-4001-3656-8(3)) Pub: Tantor Media. Dist(s): IngramPubServ

Real Comfort for Fearful Children: 2007 CCEF Annual Conference. Featuring Julie Smith-Lowe. (ENG.). 2007. audio compact disk 11.99 (978-1-934885-16-1(9)) New Growth Pr.

Real Conversations, No. 1. Cathcart & Vaughn. (J). 1992. 53.95 (978-0-8384-2250-2(0)) Heinle.

Real David Copperfield. unabr. collector's ed. Robert Graves. Read by David Case. 13 cass. (Running Time: 19 hrs. 30 min.). 1993. 104.00 (978-0-7366-2540-1(2), 3291) Books on Tape.

Real Deal: My Life in Business & Philanthropy. abr. ed. Sandy Weill & Judah S. Kraushaar. Read by Sandy Weill et al. (Running Time: 6 hrs.). (ENG.). 2006. 14.98 (978-1-59483-798-2(8)) Pub: Hachet Audio. Dist(s): HachBkGrp

Real Deal: My Life in Business & Philanthropy. abr. ed. Sandy Weill & Judah S. Kraushaar. Read by Sandy Weill et al. (Running Time: 6 hrs. 30 mins.). (ENG.). 2009. 44.98 (978-1-60788-271-8(X)) Pub: Hachet Audio. Dist(s): HachBkGrp

Real Diana. unabr. ed. Colin B. Campbell. Read by Roe Kendall. 10 cass. (Running Time: 14 hrs. 30 mins.). 1998. 69.95 (978-0-7861-1440-5(1), 2326) Blckstn Audio.
Reveals the reason the Campbell, author of "Diana In Private," knew so much about what went on behind palace gates: Diana herself was the source. Drawing upon these confidences, she brings us a most intimate & revealing portrait.

***Real Diana.** unabr. ed. Lady Colin Campbell. Read by Roe Kendall. (Running Time: 14 hrs. 30 mins.). 2010. 29.95 (978-1-4417-0769-7(7)); audio compact disk 118.00 (978-1-4417-0766-6(2)) Blckstn Audio.

Real Dr. Strangelove. Peter Goodchild. Contrib. by John de Lancie. (Running Time: 7320 sec.). 2006. audio compact disk 25.95 (978-1-58081-357-0(7)) Pub: L A Theatre. Dist(s): NetLibrary CO

Real Enemy. unabr. ed. Kathy Herman. Narrated by Tim Lundeen. (Running Time: 9 hrs. 10 mins. 26 sec.). (Sophie Trace Ser.). (ENG.). 2009. 20.99 (978-1-60814-506-5(9)) Oasis Audio.

Real Enemy. unabr. ed. Kathy Herman. Read by Aimee Lilly. Narrated by Tim Lundeen. (Running Time: 9 hrs. 10 mins. 26 sec.). (Sophie Trace Ser.). (ENG.). 2009. audio compact disk 29.99 (978-1-59859-512-3(1)) Oasis Audio.

Real Estate Gift: How Your Church Can Acquire Major Gifts Without Badgering Donors. 2006. (978-0-9769445-2-2(9), Am Charter Pr) Am Charter.

Real Estate Set: Mastering the Negotiation Process. Michael J. Lipsey et al. 6 cass. (Running Time: 9 hrs.). 1994. 69.95 (694AX) Nightingale-Conant.
Excel in the subtle art of real estate negotiations. Learn to get the terms you want, negotiate the contracts necessary, sign the listings & reach agreements.

Real Estate - Buyer, Side A; Real Estate - Seller, Side B. Frank L. Natter. 1 cass. (Running Time: 90 min.). (Type Law Tapes Ser.: No. 5). 1989. 10.00 (978-1-878287-60-1(5), ATA-5) Type & Temperament.
Implications & insights to understanding one's own personal legal & financial planning on the given subject.

Real Estate Accounting & Taxation. Deborah J. Levinson & Allan S. Kaufman. 6 cass. (Running Time: 6 hrs.). 1995. bk. 259.00 (978-0-88128-862-9(4), CPE0630) Bisk Educ.
Learn about new FASB Stmts, AcSec SOP's & other GAAP news; estate planning techniques, real estate investment trusts, gains & transfer tax changes, PAL changes, & how to structure foreign investment in U. S. real estate & much more.

Real Estate Agent's Guide to Making Money from 'No Equity' Properties & Expired Listings: How Agents Profit from 'Impossible' Situations with Little Work & No Financial Risk! Interview. Wes Weaver & Matthew Chan. 1 CD. (Running Time: 48 mins.). 2006. audio compact disk 12.00 (978-1-933723-05-1(X)) Ascend Beyond Pubng.

Real Estate & Collectibles. Narrated by Louis Rukeyser. 2 cass. (Running Time: 3 hrs.). (Secrets of the Great Investors Ser.: Vol. 9). 1996. 17.95 (978-1-56823-061-0(3)) Pub: Knowledge Prod. Dist(s): APG
Learn about the timeless strategies, tactics, judgments, & principles that have produced great wealth. Hear history's great figures & personalities - in their own words - describe their techniques & achievements in finance & investing. Now you can listen to these great lessons while commuting, traveling, walking...anytime your hands are busy, but your mind is not.

Real Estate & Collectibles. unabr. ed. Austin Lynas & Joanne Skousen. Read by Louis Rukeyser. (Running Time: 10800 sec.). (Secrets of the Great Investors Ser.). 2006. audio compact disk 25.95 (978-0-7861-6527-8(8)) Pub: Blckstn Audio. Dist(s): NetLibrary CO

Real Estate Appraising from A to Z - Complete Kit: Real Estate Appraiser, Homeowner, Home Buyer & Seller Survival Kit Series. 4th rev. ed. Guy Cozzi. 4 CDs. (Running Time: 10 hrs.). (Real Estate From A to Z Ser.). 2003. pap. bk. (978-1-887450-01-0(7)) Nemmar Real Est.

Real Estate Assessments. 1987. bk. 70.00; 45.00 PA Bar Inst.

Real Estate Broker Practice. Read by Martha Caron et al. (Running Time: 2 hrs. 45 min.). 1991. 89.00 Incl. 160p. tape materials. (RE-55220) Cont Ed Bar-CA.

Real Estate Cycles Nineteen Eighty-Six to Nineteen Eighty-Seven. Alice Q. Reichard. 1 cass. 8.95 (580) Am Fed Astrologers.
Current trends, changing markets, etc.

Real Estate Defaults, Workouts & Reorganizations. 11 cass. (Running Time: 16 hrs.). 1997. 315.00 Set; incl. study guide 688p. (MC37) Am Law Inst.
Practical, advanced course features discussions on restructuring the defaulted real estate loan & negotiation & documentation of a workout.

Real Estate Defaults, Workouts & Reorganizations. 11 cass. (Running Time: 16 hrs. 30 min.). 1999. stu. ed. 395.00 (AE33) Am Law Inst.

Real Estate Defaults, Workouts & Reorganizations. unabr. ed. 11 cass. (Running Time: 16 hrs.). 1997. 315.00 Incl. course materials. (MC37) Am Law Inst.
Intended for attorneys & other real estate professionals who represent real estate lenders, owners, tenants & others involved with nonperforming real estate loans. This practical course is developed against a background of the applicable law as it exists & continues to develop, the current bankruptcy court practice & recommendations of the National Bankruptcy Review Commission.

Real Estate Financing Documentation: Coping with the New Realities. 11 cass. (Running Time: 16 hrs.). 1998. 315.00 Set; incl. study guide. (MC42) Am Law Inst.
Advanced course examines in depth various aspects of real estate financing with commentary about future trends. Emphasizes the drafting & negotiating of loan documentation for new loans in light of the lessons learned from the climate of the early 1990s, as well as the trend toward use of corporate financing techniques.

Real Estate Forms Library. Ed. by Socrates Media Editors. 2005. audio compact disk 49.95 (978-1-59546-203-9(1)) Pub: Socrates Med LLC. Dist(s): Midpt Trade

Real Estate Funding Made Easy. Speeches. Mervin Evans. 3 CDs. (Running Time: 3-Hrs.). 2004. audio compact disk 39.99 (978-0-914391-87-6(9)) Comm People Pr.

Real Estate Gift Audio Book on CDs. 2006. audio compact disk 29.95 (978-0-9769445-1-5(0)) Am Charter.

***Real Estate Investing: Master Secrets to Getting Rich.** unabr. ed. Made for Success. Read by Donald Trump. (Running Time: 10 hrs.). (Made for Success Ser.). 2010. audio compact disk 39.95 (978-1-4417-6770-7(3)) Blckstn Audio.

***Real Estate Investing (Library Edition) Master Secrets to Getting Rich.** unabr. ed. Made for Success. Read by Donald Trump. (Running Time: 10 hrs.). (Made for Success Ser.). 2010. audio compact disk 123.00 (978-1-4417-6769-1(X)) Blckstn Audio.

Real Estate Investment: A Home-Study Course. William Nickerson. 6 cass. (Running Time: 4 hrs.). 75.00 (951-956) J Norton Pubs.
Nickerson outlines the secrets of financing, improving, operating & selling for maximum profits. This home-study course is a complete introduction for the beginning real estate investor.

Real Estate Investment Seminar. John M. Peckham et al. 3 cass. (Running Time: 5 hrs.). 39.95 (1071-1073) J Norton Pubs.
Master the secrets of real estate success from experts as they outline the profit opportunities in raw land & income property investment. The speakers give techniques & strategies on: How to use depreciation & leverage; Little known ways to minimize taxes; How to build an estate through property investment; Problems & how to avoid them.

Real Estate Law: Contract Breakers & Deal Makers. Prod. by Advantage Legal Seminars. (ENG.). 2008. 177.00 (978-0-9795737-2-9(6)) Anzman Publg.

Real Estate Opinion Letters. 4 cass. (Running Time: 5 hrs. 30 min.). bk. & instr.'s hndbk. ed. 55.00 (T6-9155) PLI.
This recording of the August 1990 program is intended for real estate lawyers who request & render legal opinion letters, particularly in loan transactions.

Real Estate Practice. 1988. bk. 95.00; 45.00 PA Bar Inst.

Real Estate Profit. 1 cass. (Running Time: 45 min.). (Success Ser.). 14.98 (978-1-55909-213-5(0), 80P) Randolph Tapes.
A winning upbeat attitude, following the strategies of millionaires. Subliminal messages are heard 3-5 minutes before becoming ocean sounds or music.

Real Estate Profits. 1 cass. (Specialized Sales Ser.). 19.98 (80) Randolph Tapes.
Big money makers have a winning upbeat attitude. You model your actions following the strategies of millionaires.

Real Estate Sales. Betty L. Randolph. Read by Betty L. Randolph. Read by Leonard Baron. Ed. by Success Education Institute International Staff. 1 cass. (Running Time: 60 min.). (Success Ser.). 1989. bk. 9.98 (978-1-55909-224-1(6), 150PM) Randolph Tapes.
Learn how to make good contacts & get more listings. Subliminal messages are heard 3-5 minutes before becoming ocean sounds or music.

Real Estate Transactions after Tax Reform. 1986. bk. 65.00; 35.00 PA Bar Inst.

Real Estate Transactions & Environmental Law. 1991. 65.00 (AC-638) PA Bar Inst.

Real Estate Workouts & Bankruptcies. 8 cass. (Running Time: 10 hrs.). 1991. 175.00 (T7-9330) PLI.

Real Faith. Featuring Bill Winston. 2. 2004. audio compact disk 16.00 (978-1-59544-020-4(8)) Pub: B Winston Min. Dist(s): Anchor Distributors
If you desire to have faith, know how faith works, increase in faith and see how faith can operate in your life then this seriesis for you.

Real Faith. Bill Winston. 2 cass. (Running Time: 1hr.10min.). (C). 2003. 10.00 (978-1-931289-83-2(2)) Pub: B Winston Min. Dist(s): Anchor Distributors

Real Help! For WordPerfect 6.0 for Windows. Tom McCaffrey & Rick Hall. Read by Tom McCaffrey & Marilyn Russell. 4 cass. (Running Time: 4 hrs. 30 min.). (Real Healp! Ser.). 1994. 43.95 set incl. practice data disk & reference card. (978-0-9639965-0-3(9)) Real Help Comm.
Training program for the WordPerfect 6.0 software for Windows. Training level is for Beginners: no prior word processing knowledge is required. Course materials cover most common word processing functions. Requires WordPerfect 6.0 for Windows software installed on customer's computer.

Real Home School. 1999. 12.95 (978-0-9672192-1-9(3)) Five Pnt Pubg.

Real Inspector Hound. Tom Stoppard. Perf. by Nigel Anthony & Roger Hammond. 1 cass. 10.95 (ECN 145) J Norton Pubs.
Two theatre critics, who are unwittingly caught up in the action of the thriller they are supposed to be reviewing.

Real Leadership: What Every Leader Needs to Know. abr. ed. John C. Maxwell. (Running Time: 4 hrs. 40 mins.). 2005. audio compact disk 29.99 (978-0-7852-6037-0(4)) Nelson.

Real Life: Preparing for the 7 Most Challenging Days of Your Life. abr. unabr. ed. Phil McGraw. Read by Phil McGraw. (Running Time: 10 hrs. 0 mins. 0 sec.). (ENG.). 2008. audio compact disk 39.99 (978-0-7435-7124-1(X)) Pub: S&S Audio. Dist(s): S and S Inc

Real Life Audio Lessons from the Bible: 24 Exciting Stories. 12 cass. (Filling Station Ser.). (J). 1995. 19.97 (978-1-58968-096-8(0)) Chrstn Dup Intl.

Real Life English. Steck-Vaughn Staff. (J). 1994. (978-0-8114-3635-9(7)) SteckVau.

Real Life English, Bk. 1, cass. 1. Steck-Vaughn Staff. 1993. 11.20 (978-0-8114-3634-2(9)) SteckVau.

Real Life English, Bk. 2, cass. 1. Steck-Vaughn Staff. 1993. 11.20 (978-0-8114-3636-6(5)) SteckVau.

Real Life English, Bk. 2, cass. 2. Steck-Vaughn Staff. 1993. 11.20 (978-0-8114-3637-3(3)) SteckVau.

Real Life English, Bk. 3, cass. 1. Steck-Vaughn Staff. 1993. 11.20 (978-0-8114-3638-0(1)) SteckVau.

Real Life English, Bk. 3, cass. 2. Steck-Vaughn Staff. 1993. 11.20 (978-0-8114-3639-7(X)) SteckVau.

Real Life English, Bk. 4, cass. 1. Steck-Vaughn Staff. 1993. 11.20 (978-0-8114-3640-3(3)) SteckVau.

Real Life English Pre-Lit. Steck-Vaughn Staff. 1994. 21.54 (978-0-8114-4565-8(8)) SteckVau.

Real Life English Pre-Lit 1. Steck-Vaughn Staff. 1994. (978-0-8114-3247-4(5)) SteckVau.

Real-Life English, Level 4: Units 7-10. Created by Steck-Vaughn Staff. (Real Life English Ser.). 1994. (978-0-8114-3641-0(1)) SteckVau.

Real-Life English, Literacy Level: Units 7-10. Created by Steck-Vaughn Staff. (Real Life English Ser.). 1994. (978-0-8114-3648-9(9)) SteckVau.

Real Life People, Real Life Stories. Ed Young. 5. 2001. 24.95 (978-0-7417-0034-6(4)) Win Walk.

Real Life People, Real Life Stories, Vol. 2. Ed Young. 5 cass. 2001. 24.95 (978-0-7417-0035-3(2)) Win Walk.

Real Life Selections 1-41: Spoken English Excerpts as Heard in America Daily Life, 125 Voices. Dee G. Davis. 4 cass. (Running Time: 4 hrs.). (YA). 1989. pap. bk. 10.00 (978-0-929350-34-9(0)) Am Spoken English.
Exact sounds are written phonetically with parallel columns in usual spelling. Extensive explanation of words, items not usually in small dictionaries.

Real Love. 1 cass. (Running Time: 1 hr.). 2003. 13.95 (978-1-932631-43-2(7)); audio compact disk 13.95 (978-1-932631-44-9(5)) Ascensn Pr.

Real Love. Greg Baer. (ENG.). 2004. audio compact disk 34.95 (978-1-892319-16-6(0)) Blue Rdge GA.

Real Love in Dating: The truth about finding the perfect Partner. Greg Baer. (ENG.). 2007. audio compact disk 27.95 (978-1-892319-33-3(0)) Blue Rdge GA.

Real Love in Marriage: The truth about finding genuine happiness now & Forever. Based on a book by Greg Baer. (ENG.). 2007. audio compact disk 32.95 (978-1-892319-34-0(9)) Blue Rdge GA.

Real Love in Parenting: Nine simple & powerfully effective principles for raising happy & responsible Children. Greg Baer. (ENG.). 2007. audio compact disk 44.95 (978-1-892319-35-7(7)) Blue Rdge GA.

***Real Magic.** abr. ed. Wayne W. Dyer. Read by Wayne W. Dyer. (ENG.). 2005. (978-0-06-084576-6(7), Harper Audio); (978-0-06-084574-2(0), Harper Audio) HarperCollins Pubs.

Real Magic: Creating Miracles in Everyday Life. Wayne W. Dyer. 6 cass. (Running Time: 6 hrs.). 1992. 59.95 set. (272A) Nightingale-Conant.

Real Malcolm X: An Intimate Portrait of the Man. Hosted by Dan Rather. Prod. by CBS News Staff. 1 cass. (Running Time: 60 min.). 1993. 19.98 Twntieth Cent Fox.

Real Man Inside. Verne Becker. 1 cass. 1992. 14.99 (978-0-310-54998-7(1)) Zondervan.

Real Meaning of Christmas. 2 cass. 7.95 (22-3, HarperThor) HarpC GBR.

Real Meaning of Christmas. Perf. by Cedarmont Kids. 1 cass. (Running Time: 30 mins.). 1997. 10.98; audio compact disk 15.98 CD. Provident Mus Dist.
The story of Christ's birth in story & in song.

Real Meaning of Christmas, Vol. 3. 1 cass. 1999. (978-0-7601-3074-2(4)); audio compact disk (978-0-7601-3073-5(6)) Brentwood Music.
Songs include: "Mary Did You Know?" - Helen Baylor; "Hark the Herald Angels Sing" - Virtue; "Christmas Is Here" - Daryl Coley; "Melody of Bethlehem" - Ben Tankard; "God's Greatest Gift" - Commissioned; "O Holy Night" - Colorado Mass Choir; "O Come, O Come Emmanuel" - Richard Smallwood; "We Sing Glory" - Fred Hammond & RFC; Untitled - John P. Kee; "The Christ of Christmas" - Hezekiah Walker & LFCC; "What a Night" - Tarralyn Ramsey.

Real Meaning of Christmas, Vol. 3. Prod. by Paul Wright. 1 CD. 1999. audio compact disk Brentwood Music.

Real Men Don't Apologize! abr. ed. James Belushi. Read by James Belushi. (Running Time: 14400 sec.). 2006. audio compact disk 39.25 (978-1-4233-2368-6(8), 9781423323686, Brlnc Audio MP3 Lib) Brilliance Audio.
Jim Belushi is a national celebrity who has starred in numerous movies as well as the current hit TV show airing on ABC, According to Jim. His "guy's guy" take on things has led to a huge following among both men and women who can't get enough of Jim and his irrepressible take on life. Now he's sharing his unique perspective with a funny new book about dating, marriage, and sex that is sure to hit home with every red-blooded American male and the women who love them. Any guy will relate to Belushi's self-discovered advice from the school of hard knocks. In character with his TV show, Belushi has strong opinions on how real men should act, and he relates his ideas with the trademark irreverent humor that has made him famous.

Real Men Don't Apologize! abr. ed. James Belushi. Read by James Belushi. (Running Time: 4 hrs.). 2006. 39.25 (978-1-4233-2370-9(X), 9781423323709, BADLE); 24.95 (978-1-4233-2369-3(6), 9781423323693, BAD) Brilliance Audio.

Real Men Don't Apologize! abr. ed. James Belushi. Read by James Belushi. (Running Time: 4 hrs.). 2007. audio compact disk 14.99 (978-1-4233-2371-6(8), 9781423323716, BCD Value Price) Brilliance Audio.

Real Men Don't Apologize! abr. ed. James Belushi. Read by James Belushi. (Running Time: 4 hrs.). 2010. audio compact disk 9.99 (978-1-4418-0824-0(8), 9781441808240, BCD Value Price) Brilliance Audio.

Real Men Don't Apologize! abr. ed. Jim Belushi. Read by Jim Belushi. (Running Time: 4 hrs.). 2006. audio compact disk 69.25 (978-1-4233-2366-2(1), 9781423323662, BACDLib Ed) Brilliance Audio.

Real Men Don't Apologize! unabr. abr. ed. James Belushi. Read by James Belushi. 1 MP3 CD. (Running Time: 14400 sec.). 2006. audio compact disk 24.95 (978-1-4233-2367-9(X), 9781423323679) Brilliance Audio.

Real Men Pray. God's Little Soldiers Staff. 2004. audio compact disk 16.98 (978-5-559-36862-7(8), 322-002) Pt of Grace Ent.

***Real Mermaids Don't Wear Toe Rings.** Helene Boudreau. (YA). 2010. 34.99 (978-1-61120-004-1(0)) Dreamscap OH.

Real Moments. unabr. ed. Barbara De Angelis. 2 cass. (Running Time: 3 hrs.). 1996. 16.99 (47292) Books on Tape.
Moments that make life matter, & how to have more of them. It is about experiencing fulfillment & meaning in your life now, not when you have more money, or find the right partner, or achieve your perfect weight, but in this & every moment.

Real Mother. abr. ed. Judith Michael. Read by Melissa Leo. 2005. audio compact disk 29.95 (978-0-06-072517-4(6)) HarperCollins Pubs.

***Real Mother.** abr. ed. Judith Michael. Read by Melissa Leo. (ENG.). 2005. (978-0-06-083882-5(5), Harper Audio); (978-0-06-083881-2(7), Harper Audio) HarperCollins Pubs.

Real Mother Goose. Read by Kathy Garver. Illus. by Blanche Fisher Wright. 4 cass. (Four-to-Go Ser.). (J). 11.98 Set. (978-1-55886-016-2(9)) Smarty Pants.

Real Mother Goose, Vol. 2. Read by Kathy Garver. Illus. by Blanche Fisher Wright. 4 cass. (Four-to-Go Ser.). (J). (ps-2). 11.98 (978-1-55886-017-9(7)) Smarty Pants.

Real Mother Goose: Banbury Cross & Other Favorites. Read by Kathy Garver. Illus. by Blanche Fisher Wright. 1 cass. (Playtape Ser.). (J). 3.98 (978-1-55886-007-0(X)) Smarty Pants.

Real Mother Goose: Hot Cross Buns & Other Favorites. Kathy Garver. Illus. by Blanche Fisher Wright. 1 cass. (Running Time: 1 hr.). Dramatization. (Poster & Cassette Ser.). (J). 3.98 (978-1-55886-011-7(8)) Smarty Pants.

Real Mother Goose: Humpty Dumpty & Other Favorites. Read by Kathy Garver. Illus. by Blanche Fisher Wright. 1 cass. (Running Time: 1 hr.). (Poster & Cassette Ser.). (J). 3.98 (978-1-55886-010-0(X)) Smarty Pants.

Real Mother Goose: If Wishes Were Horses & Other Favorites. Read by Kathy Garver. Illus. by Blanche Fisher Wright. 1 cass. (Running Time: 1 hr.). (Playtape). (J). 2.98 (978-1-55886-005-6(3)) Smarty Pants.

Real Mother Goose: Rain Rain & Other Favorites. Read by Kathy Garver. 1 cass. (Playtape Ser.). (J). 3.98 (978-1-55886-006-3(1)) Smarty Pants.

Real Mother Goose: The Cat & the Fiddle & Other Favorites. Read by Kathy Garver. Illus. by Blanche Fisher Wright. 1 cass. (Playtape Ser.). (J). 3.98 (978-1-55886-004-9(5)) Smarty Pants.

Real Mother Goose: The Tarts & Other Favorites. Read by Kathy Garver. Illus. by Blanche Fisher Wright. 1 cass. (Running Time: 1 hr.). (J). 3.98 (978-1-55886-008-7(8)) Smarty Pants.

Real Mother Goose Stories. Created by InAudio. (ENG.). (J). 2008. audio compact disk 24.00 (978-1-58472-630-2(X), In Aud) Sound Room.

***Real Murders.** unabr. ed. Charlaine Harris. Narrated by Therese Plummer. 1 Playaway. (Running Time: 6 hrs. 15 mins.). (Aurora Teagarden Mystery Ser.: Bk. 1). 2010. 59.75 (978-1-4407-4574-4(9)); 41.75 (978-1-4407-4571-3(4)); audio compact disk 56.75 (978-1-4407-4572-0(2)) Recorded Bks.

***Real Murders.** unabr. collector's ed. Charlaine Harris. Narrated by Therese Plummer. 5 CDs. (Running Time: 6 hrs. 15 mins.). (Aurora Teagarden Mystery Ser.: Bk. 1). 2010. audio compact disk 39.95 (978-1-4407-4573-7(0)) Recorded Bks.

Real People Real Challenges: Hope for the Suffering. Michael R. Emlet et al. 3 cass. (Running Time: 3 hrs.). 2003. audio compact disk 29.95 (978-1-930921-05-4(5)) Resources.

Real People Real Challenges: Hope for the Suffering. unabr. ed. Michael R. Emlet et al. 3 CDs. (Running Time: 3 hrs.). 2003. audio compact disk 29.95 (978-1-930921-30-6(6)) Resources.

Real Ponies Don't Go Oink! Patrick F. McManus. Narrated by Norman Dietz. 5 CDs. (Running Time: 6 hrs.). 2000. audio compact disk 40.00 (978-0-7887-4913-1(7), C1294E7) Recorded Bks.
Humorist Patrick McManus shares some of his vast store of anecdotes to guide you through the thornier patches of life. Join McManus & his friends, including Rancid & Crazy Eddie, as they venture into the great outdoors to face formidable foes like truck campers, tackle boxes & boat engines.

Real Ponies Don't Go Oink! unabr. ed. Patrick F. McManus. Narrated by Norman Dietz. 4 cass. (Running Time: 6 hrs.). 2000. 40.00 (978-0-7887-4316-0(3), 96036E7) Recorded Bks.

Real Power: Business Lessons from the Tao Te Ching. abr. ed. James A. Autry & Stephen Mitchell. Read by James A. Autry & Stephen Mitchell. 2 cass. (Running Time: 3 hrs.). 1998. bk. 17.95 (978-1-57453-283-8(9)) Audio Lit.
A unique management guide showing how its profound truths about the nature of real leadership can help transform the workplace into a source of immense satisfaction & fulfillment.

Real Property. Instructed by Julian C. Juergensmeyer. 6 cass. (Running Time: 8 hrs. 45 min.). (Outstanding Professors Ser.). 1999. 49.95 (978-0-940366-77-0(0)) Sum & Substance.
Lecture given by a prominent law school professor on the subjects of Civil Procedure, Contracts, Criminal, Real Property, Torts, & Exam Skills: Essay Writing.

Real Property. 2nd rev. ed. Julian C. Juergensmeyer. (Sum & Substance Ser.). 2002. 63.00 (978-0-314-24298-3(8), West Lglwrks) West.

Real Property Law Practice: Recent Developments (1992) Read by Stephen Cassidy et al. (Running Time: 4 hrs.). 1992. 115.00 Incl. 296p. tape materials. (RE-55252) Cont Ed Bar-CA.
Expert real property litigators examine & analyze the significant cases & legislation affecting real property law for the past year. They cover unlawful detainer in bankruptcy court, the Uniform Statutory Rule Against Perpetuities, toxic & hazardous waste issues, tax issues, Proposition 13, & rent control issues.

Real Property Purchase & Sale Agreements: Negotiating & Drafting in a Buyer's Market. Read by James Murad et al. (Running Time: 3 hrs.). 1991. 89.00 Incl. Ethics: 15 min., & 400p. tape materials & Action Guide. (RE-55215) Cont Ed Bar-CA.
Experts cover advantages & disadvantages of direct purchase & sale agreements over options & other acquisition vehicles. Covers the important clauses in purchase & sale agreements, including: parties to the sale; description of the property; terms of payment; conditions; representations & warranties; remedies clauses; escrow & closing provisions; & "miscellaneous" provisions.

Real Property 2002. 2nd rev. ed. Julian Conrad Juergensmeyer. (Sum & Substance Ser.). 2006. 74.00 (978-0-314-26492-3(2), West Lglwrks) West.

Real Property, 2005 ed. (Law School Legends Audio Series) 2005th rev. ed. Paula A. Franzese. 2005. 57.95 (978-0-314-16107-9(4), gilbert) West.

Real Property, 2005 ed. (Law School Legends Audio Series) 2005th rev. ed. Paula A. Franzese. (Law School Legends Audio Ser.). 2005. 58.00 (978-0-314-16108-6(2), gilbert) West.

***Real Questions, Real Answers about Sex: The Complete Guide to Intimacy as God Intended.** Louis McBurney & Melissa McBurney. (Running Time: 9 hrs. 31 mins. 0 sec.). (ENG.). 2009. 16.99 (978-0-310-30502-6(0)) Zondervan.

***Real Real.** unabr. ed. Emma Mclaughlin. Read by Mandy Siegfried. (ENG.). 2009. (978-0-06-178808-6(2)); (978-0-06-190204-8(7)) HarperCollins Pubs.

Real Responsibility. Stephen Gaskin. 1 cass. 9.00 (A0736-90) Sound Photosyn.
At the San Jose New Age Renaissance Faire, Stephen at his most intense, this time with some very welcomed topical political messages.

***Real Revolution Disc 10: What Is a Shallow Mind?** J. Krishnamurti. (Running Time: 1 hr.). 2009. audio compact disk 16.95 (978-1-888004-89-2(4)) Pub: K Publications GBR. Dist(s): SCB Distributors

***Real Revolution Disc 4: The Ideal of Non-Violence Is Not a Fact.** J. Krishnamurti. (Running Time: 1 hr.). 2009. audio compact disk 16.95 (978-1-888004-83-0(5)) Pub: K Publications GBR. Dist(s): SCB Distributors

***Real Revolution Disc 5: Passion Without Motive.** J. Krishnamurti. (Running Time: 1 hr.). 2009. audio compact disk 16.95 (978-1-888004-84-7(3)) Pub: K Publications GBR. Dist(s): SCB Distributors

***Real Revolution Disc 6: The End of Fear.** J. Krishnamurti. (Running Time: 1 hr.). 2009. audio compact disk 16.95 (978-1-888004-85-4(1)) Pub: K Publications GBR. Dist(s): SCB Distributors

***Real Revolution Disc 7: Most of Us Are Second Hand People.** J. Krishnamurti. (Running Time: 1 hr.). 2009. audio compact disk 16.95 (978-1-888004-86-1(X)) Pub: K Publications GBR. Dist(s): SCB Distributors

***Real Revolution Disc 8: Discipline Leads Dullness.** J. Krishnamurti. (Running Time: 1 hr.). 2009. audio compact disk 16.95 (978-1-888004-87-8(8)) Pub: K Publications GBR. Dist(s): SCB Distributors

***Real Revolution Disc 9: Why are we Discontent?** J. Krishnamurti. (Running Time: 1 hr.). 2009. audio compact disk 16.95 (978-1-888004-88-5(6)) Pub: K Publications GBR. Dist(s): SCB Distributors

Real Revolution, Ojai, California 1966: Fundamental Questions. J. Krishnamurti. (Running Time: 1 hr.). 2008. audio compact disk 16.95 (978-1-888004-80-9(0)) Pub: K Publications GBR. Dist(s): SCB Distributors

Real Revolution Ojai, California 1966: The Inner Urgency. J. Krishnamurti. (Running Time: 1 hr.). 2008. audio compact disk 16.95 (978-1-888004-81-6(9)) Pub: K Publications GBR. Dist(s): SCB Distributors

Real Revolution Ojai, California 1966: The Totality of Consciousness. J. Krishnamurti. (Running Time: 1 hr.). 2008. audio compact disk 16.95 (978-1-888004-82-3(7)) Pub: K Publications GBR. Dist(s): SCB Distributors

Real Rock Radio: Grade 1-6. 1 cass. (Running Time: 60 mins.). (Stereo Boom Box Ser.: Vol. 4). 1998. tchr. ed. & ring bd. 164.99 (978-1-57405-051-6(6)) CharismaLife Pub.

***Real Sex: The Naked Truth about Chastity.** unabr. ed. Lauren Winner. Narrated by Bernadett Dunne. (ENG.). 2006. 14.98 (978-1-59644-345-7(6), Hovel Audio) christianaud.

Real Sex: The Naked Truth about Chastity. unabr. ed. Lauren F. Winner. Read by Bernadette Dunn. 5 CDs. (Running Time: 5 hrs. 30 mins. 0 sec.). (ENG.). 2006. audio compact disk 23.98 (978-1-59644-344-0(8), Hovel Audio) christianaud.
In Real Sex: The Naked Truth about Chastity, Lauren Winner speaks candidly to single Christians about the difficulty - and the importance - of sexual chastity. With nuance and wit, she talks about her own sexual journey. Never dodging tough terms like "confession" and "sin," she grounds her discussion of chastity first and foremost in scripture. She confronts cultural lies about sex and challenges how we talk about sex in church (newsflash: however wrong it is, premarital sex can feel liberating and enjoyable!). Building on the thought of Wendell Berry, she argues that sex is communal rather than private, personal rather than public. Real Sex will be an essential read for single Christians grappling with chastity, for married Christians committed to monogamy, and for those who counsel them.

Real-Skin Rubber Monster Mask. unabr. ed. Miriam Cohen. 1 cass. (Running Time: 11 min.). (J). (gr. k-3). 1990. bk. 23.90 (978-0-8045-6589-9(9), 6589) Spoken Arts.

Real Solution. Swami Amar Jyoti. 1 cass. 1988. 9.95 (A-53) Truth Consciousness.
Evolution toward life Divine in New Zealand. How spiritual aspiration arises. Spirituality or social works - solving problems at the casual level. The need for transformation.

Real Solutions for Busy Moms. unabr. ed. Kathy Ireland. Narrated by Kathy Ireland. (Running Time: 6 hrs. 10 mins. 9 sec.). (ENG.). 2009. 16.09 (978-1-60814-543-0(3)) Oasis Audio.

Real Solutions for Busy Moms: Your Guide to Success & Sanity. unabr. ed. Kathy Ireland. Narrated by Kathy Ireland. 5 CDs. (Running Time: 6 hrs. 10 mins. 9 sec.). (ENG.). 2009. audio compact disk 22.99 (978-1-59859-534-5(2)) Oasis Audio.

Real Solutions to Weight Problems for Adults & Children: The Wellness Message Volume 1 - EMPOWER (Educate & Motivate People on Weight & Exercise Remedies) John Adler. 2 CDs. (Running Time: 1 hr. 33 mins.). 2003. audio compact disk 35.00 (978-0-9748112-0-8(3)) idea house.

Real Story of Christmas. unabr. ed. Read by James Earl Jones. 1 cass. (Running Time: 30 min.). 1996. 9.95 (978-1-888909-02-9(1)) Locke Grp.

Real Story of Easter. unabr. ed. Read by James Earl Jones. 2 cass. (Running Time: 2 hrs. 9 min.). 1996. 14.95 Set. (978-1-888909-01-2(3)) Locke Grp.
Comprised of the passages in the Bible which tell of the events leading to the crucifixion of Jesus, & his subsequent resurrection & ascension. The selections for this narration were taken primarily from the "Book of John," with additional selections from "Matthew," "Acts," "Hebrews" & "Romans".

Real Story of Jesus. unabr. ed. Read by James Earl Jones. 2 cass. (Running Time: 2 hrs. 22 min.). 1996. 14.95 (978-1-888909-03-6(X)) Locke Grp.

Real Story of Prophecy & the Apocalypse. unabr. ed. Read by James Earl Jones. 2 cass. (Running Time: 1 hr. 41 min.). 1996. 14.95 (978-1-888909-05-0(6)) Locke Grp.
The birth & life of Jesus, the time immediately after His death, His resurrection, when the first churches were formed & the promise of His return. The selections for this narration were taken from the "Book of Revelation," with additional selections from "Matthew" & "Luke," "1 Thessalonians," "2 Timothy," "2 Peter," & "1 John".

Real Story of the Early Church. unabr. ed. Read by James Earl Jones. 2 cass. (Running Time: 3 hrs. 12 min.). 1996. 14.95 (978-1-888909-04-3(8)) Locke Grp.

Real Talk. Lida R. Baker & Judith Tanka. 2006. audio compact disk (978-0-13-194547-0(5)) AddisonWesley.

Real Talk: Authentic English in Context. Lida R. Baker & Judith Tanka. 2006. audio compact disk (978-0-13-194094-9(5)) Pearson Educ.

Real Thief. unabr. ed. William Steig. Narrated by Barbara Caruso. 1 cass. (Running Time: 1 hr. 15 mins.). (gr. k up). 1995. 10.00 (978-0-7887-0173-3(8), 94398E7) Recorded Bks.
Gawaine Goose, the most honest citizen in the Kingdom & the most trusted guard of the King's Treasury, is accused of stealing some of the royal jewels.

Real Thing. (9520) Books on Tape.

***Real Thing.** unabr. ed. Barbara Delinsky. Read by Lauren Fortgang. (Running Time: 8 hrs.). 2011. 39.97 (978-1-4418-8521-0(8), 9781441885210, BADLE); 19.99 (978-1-4418-8519-7(6), 9781441885197, Brilliance MP3); 39.97 (978-1-4418-8520-3(X), 9781441885203, Brlnc Audio MP3 Lib); audio compact disk 19.99 (978-1-4418-8517-3(X), 9781441885173, Bril Audio CD Unabri); audio compact disk 69.97 (978-1-4418-8518-0(8), 9781441885180, BriAudCD Unabrid) Brilliance Audio.

***Real Thing.** unabr. ed. Tom Stoppard. Read by Andrea Bowen et al. 2 CDs. (Running Time: 1 hr. 30 mins.). 2009. audio compact disk 25.95 (978-1-58081-598-7(7)) L A Theatre.

Real-Time: A Two-Dimensional Electromagnetic Field Simulator. Huan-Shang Tsai. 1999. audio compact disk 129.95 (978-0-8493-2365-2(7)) Pub: CRC Pr. Dist(s): Taylor and Fran

***Real-Time Connections: Linking Your Job with God's Global Work.** unabr. ed. Bob Roberts Jr. (Running Time: 10 hrs. 1 mins. 17 sec.). (ENG.). 2010. 16.99 (978-0-310-78245-2(7)) Zondervan.

Real War. unabr. ed. Richard M. Nixon. Read by Wolfram Kandinsky. 9 cass. (Running Time: 13 hrs. 30 min.). 1980. 72.00 (978-0-7366-0578-6(9), 1548) Books on Tape.
As the 60s were an era when the nation's first priorities was to address problems within its boundaries, so in the 80s our agenda must start with security in this world.

Real War. unabr. collector's ed. Basil H. Liddell-Hart. Read by Rupert Keenlyside. 12 cass. (Running Time: 18 hrs.). 1985. 96.00 (978-0-7366-0478-9(2), 1453) Books on Tape.
This is a history of W. W. I. The origins of the war, the backroom agonies of the diplomats trying to avert it, the feelings of the generals who conducted it & details of the actual battles fill this authoritative study.

***Real Wifeys: On the Grind.** unabr. ed. Meesha Mink. (Running Time: 8 hrs. NaN mins.). (Real Wifeys Ser.). (ENG.). 2011. 29.95 (978-1-4417-7886-4(1)); audio compact disk 24.95 (978-1-4417-7885-7(3)) Blckstn Audio.

***Real Wifeys: On the Grind.** unabr. ed. Meesha Mink. Read by To be Announced. (Running Time: 8 hrs. NaN mins.). (Real Wifeys Ser.). (ENG.). 2011. 54.95 (978-1-4417-7883-3(7)); audio compact disk 76.00 (978-1-4417-7884-0(5)) Blckstn Audio.

Real World: Our Home Away from Home. Kenneth Wapnick. 10 CDs. 2006. audio compact disk 55.00 (978-1-59142-225-9(6), CD29) Foun Miracles.

Real World: Our Home Away from Home. Kenneth Wapnick. 2009. 49.00 (978-1-59142-451-2(8)) Foun Miracles.

Real World Audio Cards Set Of 10. Janie Haugen-McLane. 2006. 749.95 (978-1-58804-658-1(3)) PCI Educ.

***Real World English; Tuning in to Language & Culture: Audio Program 1.** Stuart Leigh & Rebecca Kalin. Prod. by Real World Productions, Inc. Staff. (Running Time: 9 hrs. 13 mins.). (Real World English; Tuning in to Language & Culture Ser.). 2005. stu. ed. 0.99 (978-1-60855-072-2(9)); stu. ed. 0.99 (978-1-60855-124-8(5)); stu. ed. 0.99 (978-1-60855-176-7(8)) Real Wrld Prod.

***Real World English; Tuning in to Language & Culture: Audio Program 1A.** Stuart Leigh & Rebecca Kalin. Prod. by Real World Productions, Inc. Staff. (Real World English; Tuning in to Language & Culture Ser.). 2005. stu. ed. 0.99 (978-1-60855-500-0(3)); stu. ed. 0.99 (978-1-60855-396-9(5)); stu. ed. 0.99 (978-1-60855-292-4(6)) Real Wrld Prod.

***Real World English; Tuning in to Language & Culture: Audio Program 1B.** Stuart Leigh & Rebecca Kalin. Prod. by Real World Productions, Inc. Staff. (Real World English; Tuning in to Language & Culture Ser.). 2005. stu. ed. 0.99 (978-1-60855-397-6(3)); stu. ed. 0.99 (978-1-60855-501-7(1)); stu. ed. 0.99 (978-1-60855-293-1(4)) Real Wrld Prod.

***Real World English; Tuning in to Language & Culture: Audio Program 10.** Stuart Leigh & Rebecca Kalin. Prod. by Real World Productions, Inc. Staff. (Real World English; Tuning in to Language & Culture Ser.). 2005. stu. ed. 0.99 (978-1-60855-185-9(7)); stu. ed. 0.99 (978-1-60855-081-4(8)); stu. ed. 0.99 (978-1-60855-133-0(4)) Real Wrld Prod.

***Real World English; Tuning in to Language & Culture: Audio Program 10A.** Stuart Leigh & Rebecca Kalin. Prod. by Real World Productions, Inc. Staff. (Real World English; Tuning in to Language & Culture Ser.). 2005. stu. ed. 0.99 (978-1-60855-414-0(7)); stu. ed. 0.99 (978-1-60855-310-5(8)); stu. ed. 0.99 (978-1-60855-518-5(6)) Real Wrld Prod.

***Real World English; Tuning in to Language & Culture: Audio Program 10B.** Stuart Leigh & Rebecca Kalin. Prod. by Real World Productions, Inc. Staff. (Real World English; Tuning in to Language & Culture Ser.). 2005. stu. ed. 0.99 (978-1-60855-415-7(5)); stu. ed. 0.99 (978-1-60855-519-2(4)); stu. ed. 0.99 (978-1-60855-311-2(6)) Real Wrld Prod.

***Real World English; Tuning in to Language & Culture: Audio Program 11.** Stuart Leigh & Rebecca Kalin. Prod. by Real World Productions, Inc. Staff. (Real World English; Tuning in to Language & Culture Ser.). 2005. stu. ed. 0.99 (978-1-60855-186-6(5)); stu. ed. 0.99 (978-1-60855-082-1(6)); stu. ed. 0.99 (978-1-60855-134-7(2)) Real Wrld Prod.

***Real World English; Tuning in to Language & Culture: Audio Program 11A.** Stuart Leigh & Rebecca Kalin. Prod. by Real World Productions, Inc. Staff. (Real World English; Tuning in to Language & Culture Ser.). 2005. stu. ed. 0.99 (978-1-60855-520-8(8)); stu. ed. 0.99 (978-1-60855-416-4(3)); stu. ed. 0.99 (978-1-60855-312-9(4)) Real Wrld Prod.

***Real World English; Tuning in to Language & Culture: Audio Program 11B.** Stuart Leigh & Rebecca Kalin. Prod. by Real World Productions, Inc. Staff. (Real World English; Tuning in to Language & Culture Ser.). 2005. stu. ed. 0.99 (978-1-60855-521-5(6)); stu. ed. 0.99 (978-1-60855-313-6(2)); stu. ed. 0.99 (978-1-60855-417-1(1)) Real Wrld Prod.

***Real World English; Tuning in to Language & Culture: Audio Program 12.** Stuart Leigh & Rebecca Kalin. Prod. by Real World Productions, Inc. Staff. (Real World English; Tuning in to Language & Culture Ser.). 2005. stu. ed. 0.99 (978-1-60855-135-4(0)); stu. ed. 0.99 (978-1-60855-187-3(3)); stu. ed. 0.99 (978-1-60855-083-8(4)) Real Wrld Prod.

***Real World English; Tuning in to Language & Culture: Audio Program 12A.** Stuart Leigh & Rebecca Kalin. Prod. by Real World Productions, Inc. Staff. (Real World English; Tuning in to Language & Culture Ser.). 2005. stu. ed. 0.99 (978-1-60855-418-8(X)); stu. ed. 0.99 (978-1-60855-522-2(4)); stu. ed. 0.99 (978-1-60855-314-3(0)) Real Wrld Prod.

***Real World English; Tuning in to Language & Culture: Audio Program 12B.** Stuart Leigh & Rebecca Kalin. Prod. by Real World Productions, Inc. Staff. (Real World English; Tuning in to Language & Culture Ser.). 2005. stu. ed. 0.99 (978-1-60855-523-9(2)); stu. ed. 0.99 (978-1-60855-315-0(9)); stu. ed. 0.99 (978-1-60855-419-5(8)) Real Wrld Prod.

***Real World English; Tuning in to Language & Culture: Audio Program 13.** Stuart Leigh & Rebecca Kalin. Prod. by Real World Productions, Inc. Staff. (Real World English; Tuning in to Language & Culture Ser.). 2005. stu. ed. 0.99 (978-1-60855-084-5(2)); stu. ed. 0.99 (978-1-60855-136-1(9)); stu. ed. 0.99 (978-1-60855-188-0(1)) Real Wrld Prod.

***Real World English; Tuning in to Language & Culture: Audio Program 13A.** Stuart Leigh & Rebecca Kalin. Prod. by Real World Productions, Inc. Staff. (Real World English; Tuning in to Language & Culture Ser.). 2005. stu. ed. 0.99 (978-1-60855-420-1(1)); stu. ed. 0.99 (978-1-60855-316-7(7)); stu. ed. 0.99 (978-1-60855-524-6(0)) Real Wrld Prod.

***Real World English; Tuning in to Language & Culture: Audio Program 13B.** Stuart Leigh & Rebecca Kalin. Prod. by Real World Productions, Inc. Staff. (Real World English; Tuning in to Language & Culture Ser.). 2005. stu. ed. 0.99 (978-1-60855-525-3(9)); stu. ed. 0.99 (978-1-60855-317-4(5)); stu. ed. 0.99 (978-1-60855-421-8(X)) Real Wrld Prod.

***Real World English; Tuning in to Language & Culture: Audio Program 14.** Stuart Leigh & Rebecca Kalin. Prod. by Real World Productions, Inc. Staff. (Real World English; Tuning in to Language & Culture Ser.). 2005. stu. ed. 0.99 (978-1-60855-189-7(X)); stu. ed. 0.99 (978-1-60855-085-2(0)); stu. ed. 0.99 (978-1-60855-137-8(7)) Real Wrld Prod.

***Real World English; Tuning in to Language & Culture: Audio Program 14A.** Stuart Leigh & Rebecca Kalin. Prod. by Real World Productions, Inc. Staff. (Real World English; Tuning in to Language & Culture Ser.). 2005. stu. ed. 0.99 (978-1-60855-318-1(3)); stu. ed. 0.99 (978-1-60855-526-0(7)); stu. ed. 0.99 (978-1-60855-422-5(8)) Real Wrld Prod.

***Real World English; Tuning in to Language & Culture: Audio Program 14B.** Stuart Leigh & Rebecca Kalin. Prod. by Real World Productions, Inc. Staff. (Real World English; Tuning in to Language & Culture Ser.). 2005. stu. ed. 0.99 (978-1-60855-527-7(5)); stu. ed. 0.99 (978-1-60855-319-8(1)); stu. ed. 0.99 (978-1-60855-423-2(6)) Real Wrld Prod.

***Real World English; Tuning in to Language & Culture: Audio Program 15.** Stuart Leigh & Rebecca Kalin. Prod. by Real World Productions, Inc. Staff. (Real World English; Tuning in to Language & Culture Ser.). 2005. stu. ed. 0.99 (978-1-60855-190-3(3)); stu. ed. 0.99 (978-1-60855-086-9(9)); stu. ed. 0.99 (978-1-60855-138-5(5)) Real Wrld Prod.

***Real World English; Tuning in to Language & Culture: Audio Program 15A.** Stuart Leigh & Rebecca Kalin. Prod. by Real World Productions, Inc. Staff. (Real World English; Tuning in to Language & Culture Ser.). 2005. stu. ed. 0.99 (978-1-60855-424-9(4)); stu. ed. 0.99 (978-1-60855-528-4(3)); stu. ed. 0.99 (978-1-60855-320-4(5)) Real Wrld Prod.

***Real World English; Tuning in to Language & Culture: Audio Program 15B.** Stuart Leigh & Rebecca Kalin. Prod. by Real World Productions, Inc. Staff. (Real World English; Tuning in to Language & Culture Ser.). 2005. stu. ed. 0.99 (978-1-60855-529-1(1)); stu. ed. 0.99 (978-1-60855-321-1(3)); stu. ed. 0.99 (978-1-60855-425-6(2)) Real Wrld Prod.

***Real World English; Tuning in to Language & Culture: Audio Program 16.** Stuart Leigh & Rebecca Kalin. Prod. by Real World Productions, Inc. Staff. (Real World English; Tuning in to Language & Culture Ser.). 2005. stu. ed. 0.99 (978-1-60855-139-2(3)); stu. ed. 0.99 (978-1-60855-191-0(1)); stu. ed. 0.99 (978-1-60855-087-6(7)) Real Wrld Prod.

***Real World English; Tuning in to Language & Culture: Audio Program 16A.** Stuart Leigh & Rebecca Kalin. Prod. by Real World Productions, Inc. Staff. (Real World English; Tuning in to Language & Culture Ser.). 2005. stu. ed. 0.99 (978-1-60855-322-8(1)); stu. ed. 0.99 (978-1-60855-426-3(0)); stu. ed. 0.99 (978-1-60855-530-7(5)) Real Wrld Prod.

***Real World English; Tuning in to Language & Culture: Audio Program 16B.** Stuart Leigh & Rebecca Kalin. Prod. by Real World Productions, Inc. Staff. (Real World English; Tuning in to Language & Culture Ser.). 2005. stu. ed. 0.99 (978-1-60855-531-4(3)); stu. ed. 0.99 (978-1-60855-427-0(9)); stu. ed. 0.99 (978-1-60855-323-5(X)) Real Wrld Prod.

***Real World English; Tuning in to Language & Culture: Audio Program 17.** Stuart Leigh & Rebecca Kalin. Prod. by Real World Productions, Inc. Staff. (Real World English; Tuning in to Language & Culture Ser.). 2005. stu. ed. 0.99 (978-1-60855-140-8(7)); stu. ed. 0.99 (978-1-60855-192-7(X)); stu. ed. 0.99 (978-1-60855-088-3(5)) Real Wrld Prod.

***Real World English; Tuning in to Language & Culture: Audio Program 17A.** Stuart Leigh & Rebecca Kalin. Prod. by Real World Productions, Inc. Staff. (Real World English; Tuning in to Language & Culture Ser.). 2005. stu. ed. 0.99 (978-1-60855-428-7(7)); stu. ed. 0.99 (978-1-60855-532-1(1)); stu. ed. 0.99 (978-1-60855-324-2(8)) Real Wrld Prod.

***Real World English; Tuning in to Language & Culture: Audio Program 17B.** Stuart Leigh & Rebecca Kalin. Prod. by Real World Productions, Inc. Staff. (Real World English; Tuning in to Language & Culture Ser.). 2005. stu. ed. 0.99 (978-1-60855-429-4(5)); stu. ed. 0.99 (978-1-60855-533-8(X)); stu. ed. 0.99 (978-1-60855-325-9(6)) Real Wrld Prod.

***Real World English; Tuning in to Language & Culture: Audio Program 18.** Stuart Leigh & Rebecca Kalin. Prod. by Real World Productions, Inc. Staff. (Real World English; Tuning in to Language & Culture Ser.). 2005. stu. ed. 0.99 (978-1-60855-089-0(3)); stu. ed. 0.99 (978-1-60855-141-5(5)); stu. ed. 0.99 (978-1-60855-193-4(8)) Real Wrld Prod.

***Real World English; Tuning in to Language & Culture: Audio Program 18A.** Stuart Leigh & Rebecca Kalin. Prod. by Real World Productions, Inc. Staff. (Real World English; Tuning in to Language & Culture Ser.). 2005. stu. ed. 0.99 (978-1-60855-430-0(9)); stu. ed. 0.99 (978-1-60855-326-6(4)); stu. ed. 0.99 (978-1-60855-534-5(8)) Real Wrld Prod.

***Real World English; Tuning in to Language & Culture: Audio Program 18B.** Stuart Leigh & Rebecca Kalin. Prod. by Real World Productions, Inc. Staff. (Real World English; Tuning in to Language & Culture Ser.). 2005. stu. ed. 0.99 (978-1-60855-327-3(2)); stu. ed. 0.99 (978-1-60855-535-2(6)); stu. ed. 0.99 (978-1-60855-431-7(7)) Real Wrld Prod.

***Real World English; Tuning in to Language & Culture: Audio Program 19.** Stuart Leigh & Rebecca Kalin. Prod. by Real World Productions, Inc. Staff. (Real World English; Tuning in to Language & Culture Ser.). 2005. stu. ed. 0.99 (978-1-60855-142-2(3)); stu. ed. 0.99 (978-1-60855-090-6(7)); stu. ed. 0.99 (978-1-60855-194-1(6)) Real Wrld Prod.

***Real World English; Tuning in to Language & Culture: Audio Program 19A.** Stuart Leigh & Rebecca Kalin. Prod. by Real World Productions, Inc. Staff. (Real World English; Tuning in to Language & Culture Ser.). 2005. stu. ed. 0.99 (978-1-60855-328-0(0)); stu. ed. 0.99 (978-1-60855-432-4(5)); stu. ed. 0.99 (978-1-60855-536-9(4)) Real Wrld Prod.

***Real World English; Tuning in to Language & Culture: Audio Program 19B.** Stuart Leigh & Rebecca Kalin. Prod. by Real World Productions, Inc. Staff. (Real World English; Tuning in to Language & Culture Ser.). 2005. stu. ed. 0.99 (978-1-60855-433-1(3)); stu. ed. 0.99 (978-1-60855-329-7(9)); stu. ed. 0.99 (978-1-60855-537-6(2)) Real Wrld Prod.

***Real World English; Tuning in to Language & Culture: Audio Program 2.** Stuart Leigh & Rebecca Kalin. Prod. by Real World Productions, Inc. Staff. (Real World English; Tuning in to Language & Culture Ser.). 2005. stu. ed. 0.99 (978-1-60855-125-5(3)); stu. ed. 0.99 (978-1-60855-177-4(6)); stu. ed. 0.99 (978-1-60855-073-9(7)) Real Wrld Prod.

***Real World English; Tuning in to Language & Culture: Audio Program 2A.** Stuart Leigh & Rebecca Kalin. Prod. by Real World Productions, Inc. Staff. (Real World English; Tuning in to Language & Culture Ser.). 2005. stu. ed. 0.99 (978-1-60855-294-8(2)); stu. ed. 0.99 (978-1-60855-398-3(1)); stu. ed. 0.99 (978-1-60855-502-4(X)) Real Wrld Prod.

***Real World English; Tuning in to Language & Culture: Audio Program 2B.** Stuart Leigh & Rebecca Kalin. Prod. by Real World Productions, Inc. Staff. (Real World English; Tuning in to Language & Culture Ser.). 2005. stu. ed. 0.99 (978-1-60855-503-1(8)); stu. ed. 0.99 (978-1-60855-295-5(0)); stu. ed. 0.99 (978-1-60855-399-0(X)) Real Wrld Prod.

***Real World English; Tuning in to Language & Culture: Audio Program 20.** Stuart Leigh & Rebecca Kalin. Prod. by Real World Productions, Inc. Staff. (Real World English; Tuning in to Language & Culture Ser.). 2005. stu. ed. 0.99 (978-1-60855-195-8(4)); stu. ed. 0.99 (978-1-60855-143-9(1)); stu. ed. 0.99 (978-1-60855-091-3(5)) Real Wrld Prod.

***Real World English; Tuning in to Language & Culture: Audio Program 20A.** Stuart Leigh & Rebecca Kalin. Prod. by Real World Productions, Inc. Staff. (Real World English; Tuning in to Language & Culture Ser.). 2005. stu. ed. 0.99 (978-1-60855-330-3(2)); stu. ed. 0.99 (978-1-60855-434-8(1)); stu. ed. 0.99 (978-1-60855-538-3(0)) Real Wrld Prod.

***Real World English; Tuning in to Language & Culture: Audio Program 20B.** Stuart Leigh & Rebecca Kalin. Prod. by Real World Productions, Inc. Staff. (Real World English; Tuning in to Language & Culture Ser.). 2005. stu. ed. 0.99 (978-1-60855-539-0(9)); stu. ed. 0.99 (978-1-60855-331-0(0)); stu. ed. 0.99 (978-1-60855-435-5(X)) Real Wrld Prod.

***Real World English; Tuning in to Language & Culture: Audio Program 21.** Stuart Leigh & Rebecca Kalin. Prod. by Real World Productions, Inc. Staff. (Real World English; Tuning in to Language & Culture Ser.). 2005. stu. ed. 0.99 (978-1-60855-144-6(X)); stu. ed. 0.99 (978-1-60855-196-5(2)); stu. ed. 0.99 (978-1-60855-092-0(3)) Real Wrld Prod.

***Real World English; Tuning in to Language & Culture: Audio Program 21A.** Stuart Leigh & Rebecca Kalin. Prod. by Real World Productions, Inc. Staff. (Real World English; Tuning in to Language & Culture Ser.). 2005. stu. ed. 0.99 (978-1-60855-540-6(2)); stu. ed. 0.99 (978-1-60855-436-2(8)); stu. ed. 0.99 (978-1-60855-332-7(9)) Real Wrld Prod.

***Real World English; Tuning in to Language & Culture: Audio Program 21B.** Stuart Leigh & Rebecca Kalin. Prod. by Real World Productions, Inc. Staff. (Real World English; Tuning in to Language & Culture Ser.). 2005. stu. ed. 0.99 (978-1-60855-541-3(0)); stu. ed. 0.99 (978-1-60855-437-9(6)); stu. ed. 0.99 (978-1-60855-333-4(7)) Real Wrld Prod.

***Real World English; Tuning in to Language & Culture: Audio Program 22.** Stuart Leigh & Rebecca Kalin. Prod. by Real World Productions, Inc. Staff. (Real World English; Tuning in to Language & Culture Ser.). 2005. stu. ed. 0.99 (978-1-60855-197-2(0)); stu. ed. 0.99 (978-1-60855-145-3(8)); stu. ed. 0.99 (978-1-60855-093-7(1)) Real Wrld Prod.

***Real World English; Tuning in to Language & Culture: Audio Program 22A.** Stuart Leigh & Rebecca Kalin. Prod. by Real World Productions, Inc. Staff. (Real World English; Tuning in to Language & Culture Ser.). 2005. stu. ed. 0.99 (978-1-60855-334-1(5)); stu. ed. 0.99 (978-1-60855-438-6(4)); stu. ed. 0.99 (978-1-60855-542-0(9)) Real Wrld Prod.

***Real World English; Tuning in to Language & Culture: Audio Program 22B.** Stuart Leigh & Rebecca Kalin. Prod. by Real World Productions, Inc. Staff. (Real World English; Tuning in to Language & Culture Ser.). 2005. stu. ed. 0.99 (978-1-60855-335-8(3)); stu. ed. 0.99 (978-1-60855-439-3(2)); stu. ed. 0.99 (978-1-60855-543-7(7)) Real Wrld Prod.

***Real World English; Tuning in to Language & Culture: Audio Program 23.** Stuart Leigh & Rebecca Kalin. Prod. by Real World Productions, Inc. Staff. (Real World English; Tuning in to Language & Culture Ser.). 2005. stu. ed. 0.99 (978-1-60855-146-0(6)); stu. ed. 0.99 (978-1-60855-094-4(X)); stu. ed. 0.99 (978-1-60855-198-9(9)) Real Wrld Prod.

***Real World English; Tuning in to Language & Culture: Audio Program 23A.** Stuart Leigh & Rebecca Kalin. Prod. by Real World Productions, Inc. Staff. (Real World English; Tuning in to Language & Culture Ser.). 2005. stu. ed. 0.99 (978-1-60855-544-4(5)); stu. ed. 0.99 (978-1-60855-336-5(1)); stu. ed. 0.99 (978-1-60855-440-9(6)) Real Wrld Prod.

***Real World English; Tuning in to Language & Culture: Audio Program 23B.** Stuart Leigh & Rebecca Kalin. Prod. by Real World Productions, Inc. Staff. (Real World English; Tuning in to Language & Culture Ser.). 2005. stu. ed. 0.99 (978-1-60855-441-6(4)); stu. ed. 0.99 (978-1-60855-337-2(X)); stu. ed. 0.99 (978-1-60855-545-1(3)) Real Wrld Prod.

***Real World English; Tuning in to Language & Culture: Audio Program 24.** Stuart Leigh & Rebecca Kalin. Prod. by Real World Productions, Inc. Staff. (Real World English; Tuning in to Language & Culture Ser.). 2005. stu. ed. 0.99 (978-1-60855-199-6(7)); stu. ed. 0.99 (978-1-60855-095-1(8)); stu. ed. 0.99 (978-1-60855-147-7(4)) Real Wrld Prod.

***Real World English; Tuning in to Language & Culture: Audio Program 24A.** Stuart Leigh & Rebecca Kalin. Prod. by Real World Productions, Inc. Staff. (Real World English; Tuning in to Language & Culture Ser.). 2005. stu. ed. 0.99 (978-1-60855-546-8(1)); stu. ed. 0.99 (978-1-60855-442-3(2)); stu. ed. 0.99 (978-1-60855-338-9(8)) Real Wrld Prod.

***Real World English; Tuning in to Language & Culture: Audio Program 24B.** Stuart Leigh & Rebecca Kalin. Prod. by Real World Productions, Inc. Staff. (Real World English; Tuning in to Language & Culture Ser.). 2005. stu. ed. 0.99 (978-1-60855-339-6(6)); stu. ed. 0.99 (978-1-60855-443-0(0)); stu. ed. 0.99 (978-1-60855-547-5(X)) Real Wrld Prod.

***Real World English; Tuning in to Language & Culture: Audio Program 25.** Stuart Leigh & Rebecca Kalin. Prod. by Real World Productions, Inc. Staff. (Real World English; Tuning in to Language & Culture Ser.). 2005. stu. ed. 0.99 (978-1-60855-148-4(2)); stu. ed. 0.99 (978-1-60855-096-8(6)); stu. ed. 0.99 (978-1-60855-200-9(4)) Real Wrld Prod.

***Real World English; Tuning in to Language & Culture: Audio Program 25A.** Stuart Leigh & Rebecca Kalin. Prod. by Real World Productions, Inc. Staff. (Real World English; Tuning in to Language & Culture Ser.). 2005. stu. ed. 0.99 (978-1-60855-340-2(X)); stu. ed. 0.99 (978-1-60855-444-7(9)); stu. ed. 0.99 (978-1-60855-548-2(8)) Real Wrld Prod.

***Real World English; Tuning in to Language & Culture: Audio Program 25B.** Stuart Leigh & Rebecca Kalin. Prod. by Real World Productions, Inc. Staff. (Real World English; Tuning in to Language & Culture Ser.). 2005. stu. ed. 0.99 (978-1-60855-341-9(8)); stu. ed. 0.99 (978-1-60855-549-9(6)); stu. ed. 0.99 (978-1-60855-445-4(7)) Real Wrld Prod.

***Real World English; Tuning in to Language & Culture: Audio Program 26.** Stuart Leigh & Rebecca Kalin. Prod. by Real World Productions, Inc. Staff. (Real World English; Tuning in to Language & Culture Ser.). 2005. stu. ed. 0.99 (978-1-60855-097-5(4)); stu. ed. 0.99 (978-1-60855-201-6(2)); stu. ed. 0.99 (978-1-60855-149-1(0)) Real Wrld Prod.

***Real World English; Tuning in to Language & Culture: Audio Program 26A.** Stuart Leigh & Rebecca Kalin. Prod. by Real World Productions, Inc. Staff. (Real World English; Tuning in to Language & Culture Ser.). 2005. stu. ed. 0.99 (978-1-60855-550-5(X)); stu. ed. 0.99 (978-1-60855-342-6(6)); stu. ed. 0.99 (978-1-60855-446-1(5)) Real Wrld Prod.

***Real World English; Tuning in to Language & Culture: Audio Program 26B.** Stuart Leigh & Rebecca Kalin. Prod. by Real World Productions, Inc. Staff. (Real World English; Tuning in to Language & Culture Ser.). 2005. stu. ed. 0.99 (978-1-60855-447-8(3)); stu. ed. 0.99 (978-1-60855-343-3(4)); stu. ed. 0.99 (978-1-60855-551-2(8)) Real Wrld Prod.

***Real World English; Tuning in to Language & Culture: Audio Program 27.** Stuart Leigh & Rebecca Kalin. Prod. by Real World Productions, Inc. Staff. (Real World English; Tuning in to Language & Culture Ser.). 2005. stu. ed. 0.99 (978-1-60855-202-3(0)); stu. ed. 0.99 (978-1-60855-098-2(2)); stu. ed. 0.99 (978-1-60855-150-7(4)) Real Wrld Prod.

***Real World English; Tuning in to Language & Culture: Audio Program 27A.** Stuart Leigh & Rebecca Kalin. Prod. by Real World Productions, Inc. Staff. (Real World English; Tuning in to Language & Culture Ser.). 2005. stu. ed. 0.99 (978-1-60855-344-0(2)); stu. ed. 0.99 (978-1-60855-448-5(1)); stu. ed. 0.99 (978-1-60855-552-9(6)) Real Wrld Prod.

***Real World English; Tuning in to Language & Culture: Audio Program 27B.** Stuart Leigh & Rebecca Kalin. Prod. by Real World Productions, Inc. Staff. (Real World English; Tuning in to Language & Culture Ser.). 2005. stu. ed. 0.99 (978-1-60855-553-6(4)); stu. ed. 0.99 (978-1-60855-345-7(0)); stu. ed. 0.99 (978-1-60855-449-2(X)) Real Wrld Prod.

***Real World English; Tuning in to Language & Culture: Audio Program 28.** Stuart Leigh & Rebecca Kalin. Prod. by Real World Productions, Inc. Staff. (Real World English; Tuning in to Language & Culture Ser.). 2005. stu. ed. 0.99 (978-1-60855-099-9(0)); stu. ed. 0.99 (978-1-60855-151-4(2)); stu. ed. 0.99 (978-1-60855-203-0(9)) Real Wrld Prod.

*Real World English; Tuning in to Language & Culture: Audio Program 28A. Stuart Leigh & Rebecca Kalin. Prod. by Real World Productions, Inc. Staff. (Real World English; Tuning in to Language & Culture Ser.). 2005. stu. ed. 0.99 (978-1-60855-554-3(2)); stu. ed. 0.99 (978-1-60855-450-8(3)); stu. ed. 0.99 (978-1-60855-346-4(9)) Real Wrld Prod.

*Real World English; Tuning in to Language & Culture: Audio Program 28B. Stuart Leigh & Rebecca Kalin. Prod. by Real World Productions, Inc. Staff. (Real World English; Tuning in to Language & Culture Ser.). 2005. stu. ed. 0.99 (978-1-60855-451-5(1)); stu. ed. 0.99 (978-1-60855-555-0(0)); stu. ed. 0.99 (978-1-60855-347-1(7)) Real Wrld Prod.

*Real World English; Tuning in to Language & Culture: Audio Program 29. Stuart Leigh & Rebecca Kalin. Prod. by Real World Productions, Inc. Staff. (Real World English; Tuning in to Language & Culture Ser.). 2005. stu. ed. 0.99 (978-1-60855-204-7(7)); stu. ed. 0.99 (978-1-60855-100-2(8)); stu. ed. 0.99 (978-1-60855-152-1(0)) Real Wrld Prod.

*Real World English; Tuning in to Language & Culture: Audio Program 29A. Stuart Leigh & Rebecca Kalin. Prod. by Real World Productions, Inc. Staff. (Real World English; Tuning in to Language & Culture Ser.). 2005. stu. ed. 0.99 (978-1-60855-556-7(9)); stu. ed. 0.99 (978-1-60855-452-2(X)); stu. ed. 0.99 (978-1-60855-348-8(5)) Real Wrld Prod.

*Real World English; Tuning in to Language & Culture: Audio Program 29B. Stuart Leigh & Rebecca Kalin. Prod. by Real World Productions, Inc. Staff. (Real World English; Tuning in to Language & Culture Ser.). 2005. stu. ed. 0.99 (978-1-60855-453-9(8)); stu. ed. 0.99 (978-1-60855-349-5(3)); stu. ed. 0.99 (978-1-60855-557-4(7)) Real Wrld Prod.

*Real World English; Tuning in to Language & Culture: Audio Program 3. Stuart Leigh & Rebecca Kalin. Prod. by Real World Productions, Inc. Staff. (Real World English; Tuning in to Language & Culture Ser.). 2005. stu. ed. 0.99 (978-1-60855-074-6(5)); stu. ed. 0.99 (978-1-60855-126-2(1)); stu. ed. 0.99 (978-1-60855-178-1(4)) Real Wrld Prod.

*Real World English; Tuning in to Language & Culture: Audio Program 3A. Stuart Leigh & Rebecca Kalin. Prod. by Real World Productions, Inc. Staff. (Real World English; Tuning in to Language & Culture Ser.). 2005. stu. ed. 0.99 (978-1-60855-400-3(7)); stu. ed. 0.99 (978-1-60855-504-8(6)); stu. ed. 0.99 (978-1-60855-296-2(9)) Real Wrld Prod.

*Real World English; Tuning in to Language & Culture: Audio Program 3B. Stuart Leigh & Rebecca Kalin. Prod. by Real World Productions, Inc. Staff. (Real World English; Tuning in to Language & Culture Ser.). 2005. stu. ed. 0.99 (978-1-60855-401-0(5)); stu. ed. 0.99 (978-1-60855-505-5(4)); stu. ed. 0.99 (978-1-60855-297-9(7)) Real Wrld Prod.

*Real World English; Tuning in to Language & Culture: Audio Program 30. Stuart Leigh & Rebecca Kalin. Prod. by Real World Productions, Inc. Staff. (Real World English; Tuning in to Language & Culture Ser.). 2005. stu. ed. 0.99 (978-1-60855-205-4(5)); stu. ed. 0.99 (978-1-60855-153-8(9)); stu. ed. 0.99 (978-1-60855-101-9(6)) Real Wrld Prod.

*Real World English; Tuning in to Language & Culture: Audio Program 30A. Stuart Leigh & Rebecca Kalin. Prod. by Real World Productions, Inc. Staff. (Real World English; Tuning in to Language & Culture Ser.). 2005. stu. ed. 0.99 (978-1-60855-558-1(5)); stu. ed. 0.99 (978-1-60855-350-1(7)); stu. ed. 0.99 (978-1-60855-454-6(6)) Real Wrld Prod.

*Real World English; Tuning in to Language & Culture: Audio Program 30B. Stuart Leigh & Rebecca Kalin. Prod. by Real World Productions, Inc. Staff. (Real World English; Tuning in to Language & Culture Ser.). 2005. stu. ed. 0.99 (978-1-60855-455-3(4)); stu. ed. 0.99 (978-1-60855-351-8(5)); stu. ed. 0.99 (978-1-60855-559-8(3)) Real Wrld Prod.

*Real World English; Tuning in to Language & Culture: Audio Program 31. Stuart Leigh & Rebecca Kalin. Prod. by Real World Productions, Inc. Staff. (Real World English; Tuning in to Language & Culture Ser.). 2005. stu. ed. 0.99 (978-1-60855-102-6(4)); stu. ed. 0.99 (978-1-60855-154-5(7)); stu. ed. 0.99 (978-1-60855-206-1(3)) Real Wrld Prod.

*Real World English; Tuning in to Language & Culture: Audio Program 31A. Stuart Leigh & Rebecca Kalin. Prod. by Real World Productions, Inc. Staff. (Real World English; Tuning in to Language & Culture Ser.). 2005. stu. ed. 0.99 (978-1-60855-560-4(7)); stu. ed. 0.99 (978-1-60855-456-0(2)); stu. ed. 0.99 (978-1-60855-352-5(3)) Real Wrld Prod.

*Real World English; Tuning in to Language & Culture: Audio Program 31B. Stuart Leigh & Rebecca Kalin. Prod. by Real World Productions, Inc. Staff. (Real World English; Tuning in to Language & Culture Ser.). 2005. stu. ed. 0.99 (978-1-60855-561-1(5)); stu. ed. 0.99 (978-1-60855-353-2(1)); stu. ed. 0.99 (978-1-60855-457-7(0)) Real Wrld Prod.

*Real World English; Tuning in to Language & Culture: Audio Program 32. Stuart Leigh & Rebecca Kalin. Prod. by Real World Productions, Inc. Staff. (Real World English; Tuning in to Language & Culture Ser.). 2005. stu. ed. 0.99 (978-1-60855-103-3(2)); stu. ed. 0.99 (978-1-60855-207-8(1)); stu. ed. 0.99 (978-1-60855-155-2(5)) Real Wrld Prod.

*Real World English; Tuning in to Language & Culture: Audio Program 32A. Stuart Leigh & Rebecca Kalin. Prod. by Real World Productions, Inc. Staff. (Real World English; Tuning in to Language & Culture Ser.). 2005. stu. ed. 0.99 (978-1-60855-562-8(3)); stu. ed. 0.99 (978-1-60855-458-4(9)); stu. ed. 0.99 (978-1-60855-354-9(X)) Real Wrld Prod.

*Real World English; Tuning in to Language & Culture: Audio Program 32B. Stuart Leigh & Rebecca Kalin. Prod. by Real World Productions, Inc. Staff. (Real World English; Tuning in to Language & Culture Ser.). 2005. stu. ed. 0.99 (978-1-60855-355-6(8)); stu. ed. 0.99 (978-1-60855-563-5(1)); stu. ed. 0.99 (978-1-60855-459-1(7)) Real Wrld Prod.

*Real World English; Tuning in to Language & Culture: Audio Program 33. Stuart Leigh & Rebecca Kalin. Prod. by Real World Productions, Inc. Staff. (Real World English; Tuning in to Language & Culture Ser.). 2005. stu. ed. 0.99 (978-1-60855-208-5(X)); stu. ed. 0.99 (978-1-60855-156-9(3)); stu. ed. 0.99 (978-1-60855-104-0(0)) Real Wrld Prod.

*Real World English; Tuning in to Language & Culture: Audio Program 33A. Stuart Leigh & Rebecca Kalin. Prod. by Real World Productions, Inc. Staff. (Real World English; Tuning in to Language & Culture Ser.). 2005. stu. ed. 0.99 (978-1-60855-356-3(6)); stu. ed. 0.99 (978-1-60855-564-2(X)); stu. ed. 0.99 (978-1-60855-460-7(0)) Real Wrld Prod.

*Real World English; Tuning in to Language & Culture: Audio Program 33B. Stuart Leigh & Rebecca Kalin. Prod. by Real World Productions, Inc. Staff. (Real World English; Tuning in to Language & Culture Ser.). 2005. stu. ed. 0.99 (978-1-60855-461-4(9)); stu. ed. 0.99 (978-1-60855-357-0(4)); stu. ed. 0.99 (978-1-60855-565-9(8)) Real Wrld Prod.

*Real World English; Tuning in to Language & Culture: Audio Program 34. Stuart Leigh & Rebecca Kalin. Prod. by Real World Productions, Inc. Staff. (Real World English; Tuning in to Language & Culture Ser.). 2005. stu. ed. 0.99 (978-1-60855-157-6(1)); stu. ed. 0.99 (978-1-60855-209-2(8)); stu. ed. 0.99 (978-1-60855-105-7(9)) Real Wrld Prod.

*Real World English; Tuning in to Language & Culture: Audio Program 34A. Stuart Leigh & Rebecca Kalin. Prod. by Real World Productions, Inc. Staff. (Real World English; Tuning in to Language & Culture Ser.). 2005. stu. ed. 0.99 (978-1-60855-462-1(7)); stu. ed. 0.99 (978-1-60855-358-7(2)); stu. ed. 0.99 (978-1-60855-566-6(6)) Real Wrld Prod.

*Real World English; Tuning in to Language & Culture: Audio Program 34B. Stuart Leigh & Rebecca Kalin. Prod. by Real World Productions, Inc. Staff. (Real World English; Tuning in to Language & Culture Ser.). 2005. stu. ed. 0.99 (978-1-60855-359-4(0)); stu. ed. 0.99 (978-1-60855-463-8(5)); stu. ed. 0.99 (978-1-60855-567-3(4)) Real Wrld Prod.

*Real World English; Tuning in to Language & Culture: Audio Program 35. Stuart Leigh & Rebecca Kalin. Prod. by Real World Productions, Inc. Staff. (Real World English; Tuning in to Language & Culture Ser.). 2005. stu. ed. 0.99 (978-1-60855-106-4(7)); stu. ed. 0.99 (978-1-60855-158-3(X)); stu. ed. 0.99 (978-1-60855-210-8(1)) Real Wrld Prod.

*Real World English; Tuning in to Language & Culture: Audio Program 35A. Stuart Leigh & Rebecca Kalin. Prod. by Real World Productions, Inc. Staff. (Real World English; Tuning in to Language & Culture Ser.). 2005. stu. ed. 0.99 (978-1-60855-464-5(3)); stu. ed. 0.99 (978-1-60855-568-0(2)); stu. ed. 0.99 (978-1-60855-360-0(4)) Real Wrld Prod.

*Real World English; Tuning in to Language & Culture: Audio Program 35B. Stuart Leigh & Rebecca Kalin. Prod. by Real World Productions, Inc. Staff. (Real World English; Tuning in to Language & Culture Ser.). 2005. stu. ed. 0.99 (978-1-60855-569-7(0)); stu. ed. 0.99 (978-1-60855-465-2(1)); stu. ed. 0.99 (978-1-60855-361-7(2)) Real Wrld Prod.

*Real World English; Tuning in to Language & Culture: Audio Program 36. Stuart Leigh & Rebecca Kalin. Prod. by Real World Productions, Inc. Staff. (Real World English; Tuning in to Language & Culture Ser.). 2005. stu. ed. 0.99 (978-1-60855-211-5(X)); stu. ed. 0.99 (978-1-60855-159-0(8)); stu. ed. 0.99 (978-1-60855-107-1(5)) Real Wrld Prod.

*Real World English; Tuning in to Language & Culture: Audio Program 36A. Stuart Leigh & Rebecca Kalin. Prod. by Real World Productions, Inc. Staff. (Real World English; Tuning in to Language & Culture Ser.). 2005. stu. ed. 0.99 (978-1-60855-362-4(0)); stu. ed. 0.99 (978-1-60855-466-9(X)); stu. ed. 0.99 (978-1-60855-570-3(4)) Real Wrld Prod.

*Real World English; Tuning in to Language & Culture: Audio Program 36B. Stuart Leigh & Rebecca Kalin. Prod. by Real World Productions, Inc. Staff. (Real World English; Tuning in to Language & Culture Ser.). 2005. stu. ed. 0.99 (978-1-60855-467-6(8)); stu. ed. 0.99 (978-1-60855-571-0(2)); stu. ed. 0.99 (978-1-60855-363-1(9)) Real Wrld Prod.

*Real World English; Tuning in to Language & Culture: Audio Program 37. Stuart Leigh & Rebecca Kalin. Prod. by Real World Productions, Inc. Staff. (Real World English; Tuning in to Language & Culture Ser.). 2005. stu. ed. 0.99 (978-1-60855-212-2(8)); stu. ed. 0.99 (978-1-60855-108-8(3)); stu. ed. 0.99 (978-1-60855-160-6(1)) Real Wrld Prod.

*Real World English; Tuning in to Language & Culture: Audio Program 37A. Stuart Leigh & Rebecca Kalin. Prod. by Real World Productions, Inc. Staff. (Real World English; Tuning in to Language & Culture Ser.). 2005. stu. ed. 0.99 (978-1-60855-572-7(0)); stu. ed. 0.99 (978-1-60855-468-3(6)); stu. ed. 0.99 (978-1-60855-364-8(7)) Real Wrld Prod.

*Real World English; Tuning in to Language & Culture: Audio Program 37B. Stuart Leigh & Rebecca Kalin. Prod. by Real World Productions, Inc. Staff. (Real World English; Tuning in to Language & Culture Ser.). 2005. stu. ed. 0.99 (978-1-60855-573-4(9)); stu. ed. 0.99 (978-1-60855-365-5(5)); stu. ed. 0.99 (978-1-60855-469-0(4)) Real Wrld Prod.

*Real World English; Tuning in to Language & Culture: Audio Program 38. Stuart Leigh & Rebecca Kalin. Prod. by Real World Productions, Inc. Staff. (Real World English; Tuning in to Language & Culture Ser.). 2005. stu. ed. 0.99 (978-1-60855-213-9(6)); stu. ed. 0.99 (978-1-60855-109-5(1)); stu. ed. 0.99 (978-1-60855-161-3(X)) Real Wrld Prod.

*Real World English; Tuning in to Language & Culture: Audio Program 38A. Stuart Leigh & Rebecca Kalin. Prod. by Real World Productions, Inc. Staff. (Real World English; Tuning in to Language & Culture Ser.). 2005. stu. ed. 0.99 (978-1-60855-470-6(8)); stu. ed. 0.99 (978-1-60855-574-1(7)); stu. ed. 0.99 (978-1-60855-366-2(3)) Real Wrld Prod.

*Real World English; Tuning in to Language & Culture: Audio Program 38B. Stuart Leigh & Rebecca Kalin. Prod. by Real World Productions, Inc. Staff. (Real World English; Tuning in to Language & Culture Ser.). 2005. stu. ed. 0.99 (978-1-60855-367-9(1)); stu. ed. 0.99 (978-1-60855-575-8(5)); stu. ed. 0.99 (978-1-60855-471-3(6)) Real Wrld Prod.

*Real World English; Tuning in to Language & Culture: Audio Program 39. Stuart Leigh & Rebecca Kalin. Prod. by Real World Productions, Inc. Staff. (Real World English; Tuning in to Language & Culture Ser.). 2005. stu. ed. 0.99 (978-1-60855-214-6(4)); stu. ed. 0.99 (978-1-60855-110-1(5)); stu. ed. 0.99 (978-1-60855-162-0(8)) Real Wrld Prod.

*Real World English; Tuning in to Language & Culture: Audio Program 39A. Stuart Leigh & Rebecca Kalin. Prod. by Real World Productions, Inc. Staff. (Real World English; Tuning in to Language & Culture Ser.). 2005. stu. ed. 0.99 (978-1-60855-368-6(X)); stu. ed. 0.99 (978-1-60855-472-0(4)); stu. ed. 0.99 (978-1-60855-576-5(3)) Real Wrld Prod.

*Real World English; Tuning in to Language & Culture: Audio Program 39B. Stuart Leigh & Rebecca Kalin. Prod. by Real World Productions, Inc. Staff. (Real World English; Tuning in to Language & Culture Ser.). 2005. stu. ed. 0.99 (978-1-60855-577-2(1)); stu. ed. 0.99 (978-1-60855-369-3(8)); stu. ed. 0.99 (978-1-60855-473-7(2)) Real Wrld Prod.

*Real World English; Tuning in to Language & Culture: Audio Program 4. Stuart Leigh & Rebecca Kalin. Prod. by Real World Productions, Inc. Staff. (Real World English; Tuning in to Language & Culture Ser.). 2005. stu. ed. 0.99 (978-1-60855-075-3(3)); stu. ed. 0.99 (978-1-60855-179-8(2)); stu. ed. 0.99 (978-1-60855-127-9(X)) Real Wrld Prod.

*Real World English; Tuning in to Language & Culture: Audio Program 4A. Stuart Leigh & Rebecca Kalin. Prod. by Real World Productions, Inc. Staff. (Real World English; Tuning in to Language & Culture Ser.). 2005. stu. ed. 0.99 (978-1-60855-298-6(5)); stu. ed. 0.99 (978-1-60855-506-2(2)); stu. ed. 0.99 (978-1-60855-402-7(3)) Real Wrld Prod.

*Real World English; Tuning in to Language & Culture: Audio Program 4B. Stuart Leigh & Rebecca Kalin. Prod. by Real World Productions, Inc. Staff. (Real World English; Tuning in to Language & Culture Ser.). 2005. stu. ed. 0.99 (978-1-60855-403-4(1)); stu. ed. 0.99 (978-1-60855-299-3(3)); stu. ed. 0.99 (978-1-60855-507-9(0)) Real Wrld Prod.

*Real World English; Tuning in to Language & Culture: Audio Program 40. Stuart Leigh & Rebecca Kalin. Prod. by Real World Productions, Inc. Staff. (Real World English; Tuning in to Language & Culture Ser.). 2005. stu. ed. 0.99 (978-1-60855-163-7(6)); stu. ed. 0.99 (978-1-60855-111-8(3)); stu. ed. 0.99 (978-1-60855-215-3(2)) Real Wrld Prod.

*Real World English; Tuning in to Language & Culture: Audio Program 40A. Stuart Leigh & Rebecca Kalin. Prod. by Real World Productions, Inc. Staff. (Real World English; Tuning in to Language & Culture Ser.). 2005. stu. ed. 0.99 (978-1-60855-370-9(1)); stu. ed. 0.99 (978-1-60855-474-4(0)); stu. ed. 0.99 (978-1-60855-578-9(X)) Real Wrld Prod.

*Real World English; Tuning in to Language & Culture: Audio Program 40B. Stuart Leigh & Rebecca Kalin. Prod. by Real World Productions, Inc. Staff. (Real World English; Tuning in to Language & Culture Ser.). 2005. stu. ed. 0.99 (978-1-60855-579-6(8)); stu. ed. 0.99 (978-1-60855-475-1(9)); stu. ed. 0.99 (978-1-60855-371-6(X)) Real Wrld Prod.

*Real World English; Tuning in to Language & Culture: Audio Program 41. Stuart Leigh & Rebecca Kalin. Prod. by Real World Productions, Inc. Staff. (Real World English; Tuning in to Language & Culture Ser.). 2005. stu. ed. 0.99 (978-1-60855-216-0(0)); stu. ed. 0.99 (978-1-60855-112-5(1)); stu. ed. 0.99 (978-1-60855-164-4(4)) Real Wrld Prod.

*Real World English; Tuning in to Language & Culture: Audio Program 41A. Stuart Leigh & Rebecca Kalin. Prod. by Real World Productions, Inc. Staff. (Real World English; Tuning in to Language & Culture Ser.). 2005. stu. ed. 0.99 (978-1-60855-476-8(7)); stu. ed. 0.99 (978-1-60855-372-3(8)); stu. ed. 0.99 (978-1-60855-580-2(1)) Real Wrld Prod.

*Real World English; Tuning in to Language & Culture: Audio Program 41B. Stuart Leigh & Rebecca Kalin. Prod. by Real World Productions, Inc. Staff. (Real World English; Tuning in to Language & Culture Ser.). 2005. stu. ed. 0.99 (978-1-60855-581-9(X)); stu. ed. 0.99 (978-1-60855-477-5(5)); stu. ed. 0.99 (978-1-60855-373-0(6)) Real Wrld Prod.

*Real World English; Tuning in to Language & Culture: Audio Program 42. Stuart Leigh & Rebecca Kalin. Prod. by Real World Productions, Inc. Staff. (Real World English; Tuning in to Language & Culture Ser.). 2005. stu. ed. 0.99 (978-1-60855-165-1(2)); stu. ed. 0.99 (978-1-60855-217-7(9)); stu. ed. 0.99 (978-1-60855-113-2(X)) Real Wrld Prod.

*Real World English; Tuning in to Language & Culture: Audio Program 42A. Stuart Leigh & Rebecca Kalin. Prod. by Real World Productions, Inc. Staff. (Real World English; Tuning in to Language & Culture Ser.). 2005. stu. ed. 0.99 (978-1-60855-478-2(3)); stu. ed. 0.99 (978-1-60855-582-6(8)); stu. ed. 0.99 (978-1-60855-374-7(4)) Real Wrld Prod.

*Real World English; Tuning in to Language & Culture: Audio Program 42B. Stuart Leigh & Rebecca Kalin. Prod. by Real World Productions, Inc. Staff. (Real World English; Tuning in to Language & Culture Ser.). 2005. stu. ed. 0.99 (978-1-60855-583-3(6)); stu. ed. 0.99 (978-1-60855-479-9(1)); stu. ed. 0.99 (978-1-60855-375-4(2)) Real Wrld Prod.

*Real World English; Tuning in to Language & Culture: Audio Program 43. Stuart Leigh & Rebecca Kalin. Prod. by Real World Productions, Inc. Staff. (Real World English; Tuning in to Language & Culture Ser.). 2005. stu. ed. 0.99 (978-1-60855-218-4(7)); stu. ed. 0.99 (978-1-60855-114-9(8)); stu. ed. 0.99 (978-1-60855-166-8(0)) Real Wrld Prod.

*Real World English; Tuning in to Language & Culture: Audio Program 43A. Stuart Leigh & Rebecca Kalin. Prod. by Real World Productions, Inc. Staff. (Real World English; Tuning in to Language & Culture Ser.). 2005. stu. ed. 0.99 (978-1-60855-376-1(0)); stu. ed. 0.99 (978-1-60855-480-5(5)); stu. ed. 0.99 (978-1-60855-584-0(4)) Real Wrld Prod.

*Real World English; Tuning in to Language & Culture: Audio Program 43B. Stuart Leigh & Rebecca Kalin. Prod. by Real World Productions, Inc. Staff. (Real World English; Tuning in to Language & Culture Ser.). 2005. stu. ed. 0.99 (978-1-60855-377-8(9)); stu. ed. 0.99 (978-1-60855-585-7(2)); stu. ed. 0.99 (978-1-60855-481-2(3)) Real Wrld Prod.

*Real World English; Tuning in to Language & Culture: Audio Program 44. Stuart Leigh & Rebecca Kalin. Prod. by Real World Productions, Inc. Staff. (Real World English; Tuning in to Language & Culture Ser.). 2005. stu. ed. 0.99 (978-1-60855-219-1(5)); stu. ed. 0.99 (978-1-60855-167-5(9)); stu. ed. 0.99 (978-1-60855-115-6(6)) Real Wrld Prod.

*Real World English; Tuning in to Language & Culture: Audio Program 44A. Stuart Leigh & Rebecca Kalin. Prod. by Real World Productions, Inc. Staff. (Real World English; Tuning in to Language & Culture Ser.). 2005. stu. ed. 0.99 (978-1-60855-586-4(0)); stu. ed. 0.99 (978-1-60855-482-9(1)); stu. ed. 0.99 (978-1-60855-378-5(7)) Real Wrld Prod.

*Real World English; Tuning in to Language & Culture: Audio Program 44B. Stuart Leigh & Rebecca Kalin. Prod. by Real World Productions, Inc. Staff. (Real World English; Tuning in to Language & Culture Ser.). 2005. stu. ed. 0.99 (978-1-60855-587-1(9)); stu. ed. 0.99 (978-1-60855-483-6(X)); stu. ed. 0.99 (978-1-60855-379-2(5)) Real Wrld Prod.

*Real World English; Tuning in to Language & Culture: Audio Program 45. Stuart Leigh & Rebecca Kalin. Prod. by Real World Productions, Inc. Staff. (Real World English; Tuning in to Language & Culture Ser.). 2005. stu. ed. 0.99 (978-1-60855-220-7(9)); stu. ed. 0.99 (978-1-60855-168-2(7)); stu. ed. 0.99 (978-1-60855-116-3(4)) Real Wrld Prod.

*Real World English; Tuning in to Language & Culture: Audio Program 45A. Stuart Leigh & Rebecca Kalin. Prod. by Real World Productions, Inc. Staff. (Real World English; Tuning in to Language & Culture Ser.). 2005. stu. ed. 0.99 (978-1-60855-380-8(9)); stu. ed. 0.99 (978-1-60855-588-8(7)); stu. ed. 0.99 (978-1-60855-484-3(8)) Real Wrld Prod.

*Real World English; Tuning in to Language & Culture: Audio Program 45B. Stuart Leigh & Rebecca Kalin. Prod. by Real World Productions, Inc. Staff. (Real World English; Tuning in to Language & Culture Ser.). 2005. stu. ed. 0.99 (978-1-60855-589-5(5)); stu. ed. 0.99 (978-1-60855-381-5(7)); stu. ed. 0.99 (978-1-60855-485-0(6)) Real Wrld Prod.

*Real World English; Tuning in to Language & Culture: Audio Program 46. Stuart Leigh & Rebecca Kalin. Prod. by Real World Productions, Inc. Staff. (Real World English; Tuning in to Language & Culture Ser.). 2005. stu. ed. 0.99 (978-1-60855-117-0(2)); stu. ed. 0.99 (978-1-60855-221-4(7)); stu. ed. 0.99 (978-1-60855-169-9(5)) Real Wrld Prod.

*Real World English; Tuning in to Language & Culture: Audio Program 46A. Stuart Leigh & Rebecca Kalin. Prod. by Real World Productions, Inc. Staff. (Real World English; Tuning in to Language & Culture Ser.). 2005. stu. ed. 0.99 (978-1-60855-590-1(9)); stu. ed. 0.99 (978-1-60855-486-7(4)); stu. ed. 0.99 (978-1-60855-382-2(5)) Real Wrld Prod.

*Real World English; Tuning in to Language & Culture: Audio Program 46B. Stuart Leigh & Rebecca Kalin. Prod. by Real World Productions, Inc. Staff. (Real World English; Tuning in to Language & Culture Ser.). 2005. stu. ed. 0.99 (978-1-60855-487-4(2)); stu. ed. 0.99 (978-1-60855-383-9(3)); stu. ed. 0.99 (978-1-60855-591-8(7)) Real Wrld Prod.

*Real World English; Tuning in to Language & Culture: Audio Program 47. Stuart Leigh & Rebecca Kalin. Prod. by Real World Productions, Inc. Staff. (Real World English; Tuning in to Language & Culture Ser.). 2005. stu. ed. 0.99 (978-1-60855-118-7(0)); stu. ed. 0.99 (978-1-60855-170-5(9)); stu. ed. 0.99 (978-1-60855-222-1(5)) Real Wrld Prod.

*Real World English; Tuning in to Language & Culture: Audio Program 47A. Stuart Leigh & Rebecca Kalin. Prod. by Real World Productions, Inc. Staff. (Real World English; Tuning in to Language & Culture Ser.). 2005. stu. ed. 0.99 (978-1-60855-384-6(1)); stu. ed. 0.99 (978-1-60855-592-5(5)); stu. ed. 0.99 (978-1-60855-488-1(0)) Real Wrld Prod.

*Real World English; Tuning in to Language & Culture: Audio Program 47B. Stuart Leigh & Rebecca Kalin. Prod. by Real World Productions, Inc. Staff. (Real World English; Tuning in to Language & Culture Ser.). 2005. stu. ed. 0.99 (978-1-60855-593-2(3)); stu. ed. 0.99 (978-1-60855-385-3(X)); stu. ed. 0.99 (978-1-60855-489-8(9)) Real Wrld Prod.

*Real World English; Tuning in to Language & Culture: Audio Program 48. Stuart Leigh & Rebecca Kalin. Prod. by Real World Productions, Inc. Staff. (Real World English; Tuning in to Language & Culture Ser.). 2005. stu. ed. 0.99 (978-1-60855-223-8(3)); stu. ed. 0.99 (978-1-60855-171-2(7)); stu. ed. 0.99 (978-1-60855-119-4(9)) Real Wrld Prod.

***Real World English; Tuning in to Language & Culture: Audio Program 48A.** Stuart Leigh & Rebecca Kalin. Prod. by Real World Productions, Inc. Staff. (Real World English; Tuning in to Language & Culture Ser.). 2005. stu. ed. 0.99 (978-1-60855-386-0(8)); stu. ed. 0.99 (978-1-60855-490-4(2)); stu. ed. 0.99 (978-1-60855-594-9(1)) Real Wrld Prod.

***Real World English; Tuning in to Language & Culture: Audio Program 48B.** Stuart Leigh & Rebecca Kalin. Prod. by Real World Productions, Inc. Staff. (Real World English; Tuning in to Language & Culture Ser.). 2005. stu. ed. 0.99 (978-1-60855-387-7(6)); stu. ed. 0.99 (978-1-60855-491-1(0)); stu. ed. 0.99 (978-1-60855-595-6(X)) Real Wrld Prod.

***Real World English; Tuning in to Language & Culture: Audio Program 49.** Stuart Leigh & Rebecca Kalin. Prod. by Real World Productions, Inc. Staff. (Real World English; Tuning in to Language & Culture Ser.). 2005. stu. ed. 0.99 (978-1-60855-120-0(2)); stu. ed. 0.99 (978-1-60855-172-9(5)); stu. ed. 0.99 (978-1-60855-224-5(1)) Real Wrld Prod.

***Real World English; Tuning in to Language & Culture: Audio Program 49A.** Stuart Leigh & Rebecca Kalin. Prod. by Real World Productions, Inc. Staff. (Real World English; Tuning in to Language & Culture Ser.). 2005. stu. ed. 0.99 (978-1-60855-596-3(8)); stu. ed. 0.99 (978-1-60855-492-8(9)); stu. ed. 0.99 (978-1-60855-388-4(4)) Real Wrld Prod.

***Real World English; Tuning in to Language & Culture: Audio Program 49B.** Stuart Leigh & Rebecca Kalin. Prod. by Real World Productions, Inc. Staff. (Real World English; Tuning in to Language & Culture Ser.). 2005. stu. ed. 0.99 (978-1-60855-389-1(2)); stu. ed. 0.99 (978-1-60855-597-0(6)); stu. ed. 0.99 (978-1-60855-493-5(7)) Real Wrld Prod.

***Real World English; Tuning in to Language & Culture: Audio Program 5.** Stuart Leigh & Rebecca Kalin. Prod. by Real World Productions, Inc. Staff. (Real World English; Tuning in to Language & Culture Ser.). 2005. stu. ed. 0.99 (978-1-60855-128-6(8)); stu. ed. 0.99 (978-1-60855-180-4(6)); stu. ed. 0.99 (978-1-60855-076-0(1)) Real Wrld Prod.

***Real World English; Tuning in to Language & Culture: Audio Program 5A.** Stuart Leigh & Rebecca Kalin. Prod. by Real World Productions, Inc. Staff. (Real World English; Tuning in to Language & Culture Ser.). 2005. stu. ed. 0.99 (978-1-60855-508-6(9)); stu. ed. 0.99 (978-1-60855-404-1(X)); stu. ed. 0.99 (978-1-60855-300-6(0)) Real Wrld Prod.

***Real World English; Tuning in to Language & Culture: Audio Program 5B.** Stuart Leigh & Rebecca Kalin. Prod. by Real World Productions, Inc. Staff. (Real World English; Tuning in to Language & Culture Ser.). 2005. stu. ed. 0.99 (978-1-60855-301-3(9)); stu. ed. 0.99 (978-1-60855-509-3(7)); stu. ed. 0.99 (978-1-60855-405-8(8)) Real Wrld Prod.

***Real World English; Tuning in to Language & Culture: Audio Program 50.** Stuart Leigh & Rebecca Kalin. Prod. by Real World Productions, Inc. Staff. (Real World English; Tuning in to Language & Culture Ser.). 2005. stu. ed. 0.99 (978-1-60855-121-7(0)); stu. ed. 0.99 (978-1-60855-173-6(3)); stu. ed. 0.99 (978-1-60855-225-2(X)) Real Wrld Prod.

***Real World English; Tuning in to Language & Culture: Audio Program 50A.** Stuart Leigh & Rebecca Kalin. Prod. by Real World Productions, Inc. Staff. (Real World English; Tuning in to Language & Culture Ser.). 2005. stu. ed. 0.99 (978-1-60855-494-2(5)); stu. ed. 0.99 (978-1-60855-390-7(6)); stu. ed. 0.99 (978-1-60855-598-7(4)) Real Wrld Prod.

***Real World English; Tuning in to Language & Culture: Audio Program 50B.** Stuart Leigh & Rebecca Kalin. Prod. by Real World Productions, Inc. Staff. (Real World English; Tuning in to Language & Culture Ser.). 2005. stu. ed. 0.99 (978-1-60855-599-4(2)); stu. ed. 0.99 (978-1-60855-391-4(4)); stu. ed. 0.99 (978-1-60855-495-9(3)) Real Wrld Prod.

***Real World English; Tuning in to Language & Culture: Audio Program 51.** Stuart Leigh & Rebecca Kalin. Prod. by Real World Productions, Inc. Staff. (Real World English; Tuning in to Language & Culture Ser.). 2005. stu. ed. 0.99 (978-1-60855-226-9(8)); stu. ed. 0.99 (978-1-60855-174-3(1)); stu. ed. 0.99 (978-1-60855-122-4(9)) Real Wrld Prod.

***Real World English; Tuning in to Language & Culture: Audio Program 51A.** Stuart Leigh & Rebecca Kalin. Prod. by Real World Productions, Inc. Staff. (Real World English; Tuning in to Language & Culture Ser.). 2005. stu. ed. 0.99 (978-1-60855-496-6(1)); stu. ed. 0.99 (978-1-60855-600-7(X)); stu. ed. 0.99 (978-1-60855-392-1(2)) Real Wrld Prod.

***Real World English; Tuning in to Language & Culture: Audio Program 51B.** Stuart Leigh & Rebecca Kalin. Prod. by Real World Productions, Inc. Staff. (Real World English; Tuning in to Language & Culture Ser.). 2005. stu. ed. 0.99 (978-1-60855-393-8(0)); stu. ed. 0.99 (978-1-60855-601-4(8)); stu. ed. 0.99 (978-1-60855-497-3(X)) Real Wrld Prod.

***Real World English; Tuning in to Language & Culture: Audio Program 52.** Stuart Leigh & Rebecca Kalin. Prod. by Real World Productions, Inc. Staff. (Real World English; Tuning in to Language & Culture Ser.). 2005. stu. ed. 0.99 (978-1-60855-175-0(X)); stu. ed. 0.99 (978-1-60855-123-1(7)); stu. ed. 0.99 (978-1-60855-227-6(6)) Real Wrld Prod.

***Real World English; Tuning in to Language & Culture: Audio Program 52A.** Stuart Leigh & Rebecca Kalin. Prod. by Real World Productions, Inc. Staff. (Real World English; Tuning in to Language & Culture Ser.). 2005. stu. ed. 0.99 (978-1-60855-602-1(6)); stu. ed. 0.99 (978-1-60855-394-5(9)); stu. ed. 0.99 (978-1-60855-498-0(8)) Real Wrld Prod.

***Real World English; Tuning in to Language & Culture: Audio Program 52B.** Stuart Leigh & Rebecca Kalin. Prod. by Real World Productions, Inc. Staff. (Real World English; Tuning in to Language & Culture Ser.). 2005. stu. ed. 0.99 (978-1-60855-395-2(7)); stu. ed. 0.99 (978-1-60855-603-8(4)); stu. ed. 0.99 (978-1-60855-499-7(6)) Real Wrld Prod.

***Real World English; Tuning in to Language & Culture: Audio Program 6.** Stuart Leigh & Rebecca Kalin. Prod. by Real World Productions, Inc. Staff. (Real World English; Tuning in to Language & Culture Ser.). 2005. stu. ed. 0.99 (978-1-60855-077-7(X)); stu. ed. 0.99 (978-1-60855-181-1(4)); stu. ed. 0.99 (978-1-60855-129-3(6)) Real Wrld Prod.

***Real World English; Tuning in to Language & Culture: Audio Program 6A.** Stuart Leigh & Rebecca Kalin. Prod. by Real World Productions, Inc. Staff. (Real World English; Tuning in to Language & Culture Ser.). 2005. stu. ed. 0.99 (978-1-60855-406-5(6)); stu. ed. 0.99 (978-1-60855-510-9(0)); stu. ed. 0.99 (978-1-60855-302-0(7)) Real Wrld Prod.

***Real World English; Tuning in to Language & Culture: Audio Program 6B.** Stuart Leigh & Rebecca Kalin. Prod. by Real World Productions, Inc. Staff. (Real World English; Tuning in to Language & Culture Ser.). 2005. stu. ed. 0.99 (978-1-60855-511-6(9)); stu. ed. 0.99 (978-1-60855-303-7(5)); stu. ed. 0.99 (978-1-60855-407-2(4)) Real Wrld Prod.

***Real World English; Tuning in to Language & Culture: Audio Program 7.** Stuart Leigh & Rebecca Kalin. Prod. by Real World Productions, Inc. Staff. (Real World English; Tuning in to Language & Culture Ser.). 2005. stu. ed. 0.99 (978-1-60855-130-9(X)); stu. ed. 0.99 (978-1-60855-182-8(2)); stu. ed. 0.99 (978-1-60855-078-4(8)) Real Wrld Prod.

***Real World English; Tuning in to Language & Culture: Audio Program 7A.** Stuart Leigh & Rebecca Kalin. Prod. by Real World Productions, Inc. Staff. (Real World English; Tuning in to Language & Culture Ser.). 2005. stu. ed. 0.99 (978-1-60855-408-9(2)); stu. ed. 0.99 (978-1-60855-304-4(3)); stu. ed. 0.99 (978-1-60855-512-3(7)) Real Wrld Prod.

***Real World English; Tuning in to Language & Culture: Audio Program 7B.** Stuart Leigh & Rebecca Kalin. Prod. by Real World Productions, Inc. Staff. (Real World English; Tuning in to Language & Culture Ser.). 2005. stu. ed. 0.99 (978-1-60855-513-0(5)); stu. ed. 0.99 (978-1-60855-409-6(0)); stu. ed. 0.99 (978-1-60855-305-1(1)) Real Wrld Prod.

***Real World English; Tuning in to Language & Culture: Audio Program 8.** Stuart Leigh & Rebecca Kalin. Prod. by Real World Productions, Inc. Staff. (Real World English; Tuning in to Language & Culture Ser.). 2005. stu. ed. 0.99 (978-1-60855-183-5(0)); stu. ed. 0.99 (978-1-60855-131-6(8)); stu. ed. 0.99 (978-1-60855-079-1(6)) Real Wrld Prod.

***Real World English; Tuning in to Language & Culture: Audio Program 8A.** Stuart Leigh & Rebecca Kalin. Prod. by Real World Productions, Inc. Staff. (Real World English; Tuning in to Language & Culture Ser.). 2005. stu. ed. 0.99 (978-1-60855-514-7(3)); stu. ed. 0.99 (978-1-60855-306-8(X)); stu. ed. 0.99 (978-1-60855-410-2(4)) Real Wrld Prod.

***Real World English; Tuning in to Language & Culture: Audio Program 8B.** Stuart Leigh & Rebecca Kalin. Prod. by Real World Productions, Inc. Staff. (Real World English; Tuning in to Language & Culture Ser.). 2005. stu. ed. 0.99 (978-1-60855-515-4(1)); stu. ed. 0.99 (978-1-60855-307-5(8)); stu. ed. 0.99 (978-1-60855-411-9(2)) Real Wrld Prod.

***Real World English; Tuning in to Language & Culture: Audio Program 9.** Stuart Leigh & Rebecca Kalin. Prod. by Real World Productions, Inc. Staff. (Real World English; Tuning in to Language & Culture Ser.). 2005. stu. ed. 0.99 (978-1-60855-080-7(X)); stu. ed. 0.99 (978-1-60855-132-3(6)); stu. ed. 0.99 (978-1-60855-184-2(9)) Real Wrld Prod.

***Real World English; Tuning in to Language & Culture: Audio Program 9A.** Stuart Leigh & Rebecca Kalin. Prod. by Real World Productions, Inc. Staff. (Real World English; Tuning in to Language & Culture Ser.). 2005. stu. ed. 0.99 (978-1-60855-412-6(0)); stu. ed. 0.99 (978-1-60855-516-1(X)); stu. ed. 0.99 (978-1-60855-308-2(6)) Real Wrld Prod.

***Real World English; Tuning in to Language & Culture: Audio Program 9B.** Stuart Leigh & Rebecca Kalin. Prod. by Real World Productions, Inc. Staff. (Real World English; Tuning in to Language & Culture Ser.). 2005. stu. ed. 0.99 (978-1-60855-413-3(9)); stu. ed. 0.99 (978-1-60855-517-8(8)); stu. ed. 0.99 (978-1-60855-309-9(4)) Real Wrld Prod.

***Real World English; Tuning in to Language & Culture: Audio Programs 1-13 (Level 1) 2 CDs.** Stuart Leigh & Rebecca Kalin. Prod. by Real World Productions, Inc. Staff. (Real World English; Tuning in to Language & Culture Ser.). 2005. stu. ed. 23.00 (978-1-60855-068-5(0)) Real Wrld Prod.

***Real World English; Tuning in to Language & Culture: Audio Programs 1-26 (Levels 1 & 2) 4 CDs.** Stuart Leigh & Rebecca Kalin. Prod. by Real World Productions, Inc. Staff. (Real World English; Tuning in to Language & Culture Ser.). 2005. stu. ed. 43.95 (978-1-60855-002-9(8)) Real Wrld Prod.

***Real World English; Tuning in to Language & Culture: Audio Programs 14-26 (Level 2) 2 CDs.** 2nd ed. Stuart Leigh & Rebecca Kalin. Prod. by Real World Productions, Inc. Staff. (Real World English; Tuning in to Language & Culture Ser.). 2005. stu. ed. 23.00 (978-1-60855-069-2(9)) Real Wrld Prod.

***Real World English; Tuning in to Language & Culture: Audio Programs 27-39 (Level 3) 2 CDs.** 3rd ed. Stuart Leigh & Rebecca Kalin. Prod. by Real World Productions, Inc. Staff. (Real World English; Tuning in to Language & Culture Ser.). 2005. stu. ed. 23.00 (978-1-60855-070-8(2)) Real Wrld Prod.

***Real World English; Tuning in to Language & Culture: Audio Programs 27-52 (Levels 1 & 2) 4 CDs.** Stuart Leigh & Rebecca Kalin. Prod. by Real World Productions, Inc. Staff. (Real World English; Tuning in to Language & Culture Ser.). 2005. stu. ed. 43.95 (978-1-60855-003-6(6)) Real Wrld Prod.

***Real World English; Tuning in to Language & Culture: Audio Programs 40-52 (Level 4) 2 CDs.** 4th ed. Stuart Leigh & Rebecca Kalin. Prod. by Real World Productions, Inc. Staff. (Real World English; Tuning in to Language & Culture Ser.). 2005. stu. ed. 23.00 (978-1-60855-071-5(0)) Real Wrld Prod.

Real World of the Writer. James Baldwin. 1 CD. (Running Time: 48 mins.). 2006. audio compact disk 12.95 (978-1-57970-401-8(8), C23029D, Audio-For) J Norton Pubs.

Real World of the Writer. William Saroyan. 1 cass. (Running Time: 48 min.). 1968. 11.95 (23067) J Norton Pubs.

This tape examines the sources of literary genius-the "reality" of such writers as Mark Twain, Whitman, Emerson, Thoreau, & Pope as "persons" - & analyzes the effect of geography & climate on the writer's style & productivity.

Real World, Real Heroes. Michael D. Christensen. 1 cass. 1997. 9.95 (978-1-57008-317-4(7), Bkcraft Inc) Deseret Bk.

***RealAge.** abr. ed. Michael F. Roizen. Read by Michael F. Roizen. (ENG.). 2005. (978-0-06-088906-7(3), Harper Audio); (978-0-06-113683-2(2), Harper Audio) HarperCollins Pubs.

RealAge: Are You As Young As You Can Be? abr. ed. Michael F. Roizen. Read by Michael F. Roizen. (Running Time: 10800 sec.). 2006. audio compact disk 14.95 (978-0-06-087727-9(8)) HarperCollins Pubs.

Realidades: Audio Program. audio compact disk 299.97 (978-0-13-035990-2(4)) PH School.

Realidades: Guided Practice Activities Teacher's Guide with Audio CDs. 2 CDs. tchr. ed. 32.97 (978-0-13-116538-0(0)) PH School.

Realidades 1: Audio Program. audio compact disk 299.97 (978-0-13-035993-3(9)) PH School.

Realidades 1: Guided Practice Activities. 2 CDs. audio compact disk 19.97 (978-0-13-116543-4(7)) PH School.

Realidades 1: Guided Practice Activities Teacher's Guide with Audio CDs. 2 CDs. tchr. ed. 32.97 (978-0-13-116539-7(9)) PH School.

Realidades 1: Placement Test: Realidades para Hispanohablantes W/Audio CD. 39.97 (978-0-13-116429-1(5)) PH School.

Realidades 2: Audio Program. audio compact disk 299.97 (978-0-13-035994-0(7)) PH School.

Realidades 2: Guided Practice Activities. 2 CDs. audio compact disk 19.97 (978-0-13-116544-1(5)) PH School.

Realidades 2: Guided Practice Activities Teacher's Guide with Audio CDs. 2 CDs. tchr. ed. 32.97 (978-0-13-116540-3(2)) PH School.

Realidades 3: Audio Program. audio compact disk 299.97 (978-0-13-035995-7(5)) PH School.

Realife. unabr. ed. Heather K. Bohr. Ed. by Thomas Unterseher & Thomas E. Unterseher. 4 cass. (Running Time: 4 hrs.). (JPN.). 1993. bk. & pap. bk. 89.99 (978-1-57237-045-6(9)); bk. & pap. bk. 89.99 Incl. 4 pap. bks. (978-1-57237-044-9(0)); bk. 89.99 (978-1-57237-046-3(7)); bk. & pap. bk. 89.99 Incl. 4 pap. bks. (978-1-57237-047-0(5)) Cultural Designs.

Mandarin.

Realife Business. unabr. ed. Heather K. Bohr. Ed. by Thomas Unterseher & Thomas E. Unterseher. 1 cass. (Running Time: 1 hr.). (SPA.). 1993. pap. bk. 22.99 (978-1-57237-026-5(2)); pap. bk. 22.99 (978-1-57237-030-2(0)); pap. bk. 22.99 (978-1-57237-042-5(4)); pap. bk. 22.99 (978-1-57237-034-0(3)); pap. bk. 22.99 (978-1-57237-038-8(6)) Cultural Designs.

Realife Business: With Cantonese CD. unabr. ed. Heather K. Bohr. Ed. by Thomas Unterseher & Thomas E. Unterseher. 1 CD. (Running Time: 1 hr.). 1993. pap. bk. 29.99 (978-1-57237-009-8(2)) Cultural Designs.

ESL.

Realife Business: With Japanese CD. unabr. ed. Heather K. Bohr. Ed. by Thomas Unterseher & Thomas E. Unterseher. 1 CD. (Running Time: 1 hr.). (JPN.). 1993. pap. bk. 29.99 (978-1-57237-005-0(X)) Cultural Designs.

Realife Business: With Korean CD. unabr. ed. Heather K. Bohr. Ed. by Thomas Unterseher & Thomas E. Unterseher. 1 CD. (Running Time: 1 hr.). (KOR.). 1993. pap. bk. 29.99 (978-1-57237-021-0(1)) Cultural Designs.

Teaching ESL to Korean speakers.

Realife Business: With Mandarin CD. unabr. ed. Heather K. Bohr. Ed. by Thomas Unterseher & Thomas E. Unterseher. 1 CD. (Running Time: 1 hr.). 1993. pap. bk. 29.99 (978-1-57237-013-5(0)) Cultural Designs.

ESL.

Realife Business: With Spanish CD. unabr. ed. Heather K. Bohr. Ed. by Thomas Unterseher & Thomas E. Unterseher. 1 CD. (Running Time: 1 hr.). (SPA.). 1993. pap. bk. 29.99 (978-1-57237-001-2(7)) Cultural Designs.

Realife Entertainment. unabr. ed. Heather K. Bohr. Ed. by Thomas Unterseher & Thomas E. Unterseher. 1 cass. (Running Time: 1 hr.). (SPA.). 1993. pap. bk. 22.99 (978-1-57237-025-8(4)); pap. bk. 22.99 (978-1-57237-029-6(7)); pap. bk. 22.99 (978-1-57237-041-8(6)); pap. bk. 22.99 (978-1-57237-033-3(5)); pap. bk. 22.99 (978-1-57237-037-1(8)) Cultural Designs.

Mandarin.

Realife Entertainment: With Cantonese CD. unabr. ed. Heather K. Bohr. Ed. by Thomas Unterseher & Thomas E. Unterseher. 1 CD. (Running Time: 1 hr.). 1993. pap. bk. 29.99 (978-1-57237-008-1(4)) Cultural Designs.

ESL.

Realife Entertainment: With Japanese CD. unabr. ed. Heather K. Bohr. Ed. by Thomas Unterseher & Thomas E. Unterseher. 1 CD. (Running Time: 1 hr.). (JPN.). 1993. pap. bk. 29.99 (978-1-57237-004-3(1)) Cultural Designs.

Realife Entertainment: With Korean CD. unabr. ed. Heather K. Bohr. Ed. by Thomas Unterseher & Thomas E. Unterseher. 1 CD. (Running Time: 1 hr.). (KOR.). 1993. pap. bk. 29.99 (978-1-57237-020-3(3)) Cultural Designs.

Teaching ESL to Korean speakers.

Realife Entertainment: With Mandarin CD. unabr. ed. Heather K. Bohr. Ed. by Thomas Unterseher & Thomas E. Unterseher. 1 CD. (Running Time: 1 hr.). 1993. pap. bk. 29.99 (978-1-57237-012-8(2)) Cultural Designs.

ESL.

Realife Entertainment: With Spanish CD. unabr. ed. Heather K. Bohr. Ed. by Thomas Unterseher & Thomas E. Unterseher. 1 CD. (Running Time: 1 hr.). (SPA.). 1993. pap. bk. 29.99 (978-1-57237-000-5(9)) Cultural Designs.

ESL teaching.

Realife Etiquette. unabr. ed. Heather K. Bohr. Ed. by Thomas Unterseher & Thomas E. Unterseher. 1 cass. (Running Time: 1 hr.). (SPA.). 1993. pap. bk. 22.99 (978-1-57237-027-2(0)); pap. bk. 22.99 (978-1-57237-031-9(9)); pap. bk. 22.99 (978-1-57237-048-7(3)); pap. bk. 22.99 (978-1-57237-035-7(1)); pap. bk. 22.99 (978-1-57237-039-5(4)) Cultural Designs.

Mandarin.

Realife Etiquette: With Cantonese CD. unabr. ed. Heather K. Bohr. Ed. by Thomas Unterseher & Thomas E. Unterseher. 1 CD. (Running Time: 1 hr.). 1993. pap. bk. 29.99 (978-1-57237-010-4(6)) Cultural Designs.

ESL.

Realife Etiquette: With Japanese CD. unabr. ed. Heather K. Bohr. Ed. by Thomas Unterseher & Thomas E. Unterseher. 1 CD. (Running Time: 1 hr.). (JPN.). 1993. pap. bk. 29.99 (978-1-57237-006-7(8)) Cultural Designs.

Realife Etiquette: With Korean CD. unabr. ed. Heather K. Bohr. Ed. by Thomas Unterseher & Thomas E. Unterseher. 1 CD. (Running Time: 1 hr.). (KOR.). 1993. pap. bk. 29.99 (978-1-57237-022-7(X)) Cultural Designs.

Teaching ESL to Korean speakers.

Realife Etiquette: With Mandarin CD. unabr. ed. Heather K. Bohr. Ed. by Thomas Unterseher & Thomas E. Unterseher. 1 CD. (Running Time: 1 hr.). 1993. pap. bk. 29.99 (978-1-57237-014-2(9)) Cultural Designs.

ESL.

Realife Etiquette: With Spanish CD. unabr. ed. Heather K. Bohr. Ed. by Thomas Unterseher & Thomas E. Unterseher. 1 CD. (Running Time: 1 hr.). (SPA.). 1993. pap. bk. 29.99 (978-1-57237-002-9(5)) Cultural Designs.

Realife Relationships. unabr. ed. Heather K. Bohr. Ed. by Thomas Unterseher & Thomas E. Unterseher. 1 cass. (Running Time: 1 hr.). (SPA.). 1993. pap. bk. 22.99 (978-1-57237-028-9(9)); pap. bk. 22.99 (978-1-57237-032-6(7)); pap. bk. 22.99 (978-1-57237-049-4(1)); pap. bk. 22.99 (978-1-57237-036-4(X)); pap. bk. 22.99 (978-1-57237-040-1(8)) Cultural Designs.

Mandarin.

Realife Relationships: With Cantonese CD. unabr. ed. Heather K. Bohr. Ed. by Thomas Unterseher & Thomas E. Unterseher. 1 CD. (Running Time: 1 hr.). 1993. pap. bk. 29.99 (978-1-57237-011-1(4)) Cultural Designs.

ESL.

Realife Relationships: With Japanese CD. unabr. ed. Heather K. Bohr. Ed. by Thomas Unterseher & Thomas E. Unterseher. 1 CD. (Running Time: 1 hr.). (JPN.). 1993. pap. bk. 29.99 (978-1-57237-007-4(6)) Cultural Designs.

Realife Relationships: With Korean CD. unabr. ed. Heather K. Bohr. Ed. by Thomas Unterseher & Thomas E. Unterseher. 1 CD. (Running Time: 1 hr.). (KOR.). 1993. pap. bk. 29.99 (978-1-57237-023-4(8)) Cultural Designs.

Teaching ESL to Korean speakers.

Realife Relationships: With Mandarin CD. unabr. ed. Heather K. Bohr. Ed. by Thomas Unterseher & Thomas E. Unterseher. 1 CD. (Running Time: 1 hr.). 1993. pap. bk. 29.99 (978-1-57237-015-9(7)) Cultural Designs.

ESL.

Realife Relationships: With Spanish CD. unabr. ed. Heather K. Bohr. Ed. by Thomas Unterseher & Thomas E. Unterseher. 1 CD. (Running Time: 1 hr.). (SPA.). 1993. pap. bk. 29.99 (978-1-57237-003-6(3)) Cultural Designs.

Realism in Literature. James T. Farrell. 1 cass. (Running Time: 29 min.). 1968. 11.95 (23008) J Norton Pubs.

A discussion of the significance of truth in life & literature.

Realism of Giovanni Verga: Multilingual Books Literature on Tape / Cd, Vol. 9. Ed. by Maurizio Falyhera & Cristina Giocometti. 1 cass. (Running Time: 90 mins.). (Audio Anthology of Italian Literature Ser.). (ITA.). 1999. spiral bd. 19.95 (978-1-58214-116-9(9)) Language Assocs.

Realism of Giovanni Verga: Multilingual Books Literature on Tape/CD. Ed. by Maurizio Falyhera & Cristina Giocometti. 1 CD. (Running Time: 90 mins.). (Audio Anthology of Italian Literature Ser.). (ITA.). 1999. spiral bd. 29.95 (978-1-58214-117-6(7)) Language Assocs.

Realism of Yoga. Swami Amar Jyoti. 1 cass. 1988. 9.95 (A-41) Truth Consciousness.

The Yogic way of life; human beings, not "human doings". How to reconcile "everything is God" & the reality we see. Aspiration, courage, patience - achievement.

Realistic Armor Finishing Techniques. Marcus Nicholls. 2007. audio compact disk 24.95 (978-1-905573-99-8(5)) Pub: Compendium GBR. Dist(s): Casemate Pubs

Realistic Visionary: A Portrait of George Washington. Peter R. Henriques. Read by George K. Wilson. (Running Time: 35100 sec.). 2006. audio compact disk 34.99 (978-1-4193-9611-3(0)) Recorded Bks.

Reality & Dreams, unabr. ed. Muriel Spark. Narrated by Jenny Sterlin. 4 cass. (Running Time: 4 hrs. 45 mins.). 1997. 35.00 (978-0-7887-1320-0(5), 95178E7) Recorded Bks.
After an accident lands film director Tom Richards in the hospital, he sinks into a comic, waking dream filled with demanding visitors. And when he recovers to find his replacement at the studio, his real world unfolds into a darkly funny sitcom.

Reality, Art, Illusion. 4 cass. (Running Time: 6 hrs.). 45.00 (211) MEA A Watts Cass.

Reality Bug. unabr. ed. Read by William Dufris. (Running Time: 36000 sec.). (Pendragon Ser.: Bk. 4). (J). (ps-7). 2005. 29.95 (978-1-59737-259-6(5), 9781597372596, BAU); cass., cass., DVD 82.25 (978-1-59737-260-2(9), 9781597372602, BrilAudUnabridg); DVD & audio compact disk 39.25 (978-1-59737-264-0(1), 9781597372640, Brinc Audio MP3 Lib); audio compact disk 19.99 (978-1-59737-263-3(3), 9781597372633, Brilliance MP3) Brilliance Audio.
The territory of Veelox has achieved perfect harmony. Fifteen-year-old Bobby Pendragon arrives on this territory in pursuit of the evil Saint Dane, but all is peaceful on Veelox - because it's deserted. The inhabitants have discovered a way to enter their own personal dream worlds, where they can be whomever they want, wherever they want. Their bodies lie in stasis while their minds escape to this dream realm. Fresh from his battle with Saint Dane on 1937 Earth, Bobby is confident that he can defeat whatever Saint Dane has planned for this world. But once Bobby enters the virtual world, will he be able to resist the lure of the ultimate in escapism?.

Reality Bug. unabr. ed. D. J. MacHale. Read by William Dufris. (Running Time: 10 hrs.). (Pendragon Ser.: Bk. 4). 2005. 39.25 (978-1-59737-266-4(8), 9781597372664, BADLE); 24.95 (978-1-59737-265-7(X), 9781597372657, BAD) Brilliance Audio.

Reality Bug. unabr. ed. D. J. MacHale. Read by William Dufris. (Running Time: 10 hrs.). (Pendragon Ser.: Bk. 4). 2009. audio compact disk 19.99 (978-1-4233-9901-8(3), 9781423399018); audio compact disk 49.97 (978-1-4233-9902-5(1), 9781423399025, BriAudCD Unabrid) Brilliance Audio.

***Reality Check.** unabr. ed. Peter Abrahams. Narrated by James Colby. 1 Playaway. (Running Time: 7 hrs. 30 mins.). (YA). (gr. 9 up). 2009. 59.75 (978-1-4407-4642-0(7)); 56.75 (978-1-4407-4633-8(8)); audio compact disk 77.75 (978-1-4407-4637-6(0)) Recorded Bks.

***Reality Check.** unabr. collector's ed. Peter Abrahams. Narrated by James Colby. 7 CDs. (Running Time: 7 hrs. 30 mins.). (YA). (gr. 9 up). 2009. audio compact disk 51.95 (978-1-4407-4641-3(9)) Recorded Bks.

Reality Check: The Irreverent Guide to Outsmarting, Outmanaging, & Outmarketing Your Competition. unabr. ed. Guy Kawasaki. Narrated by Paul Boehmer. (Running Time: 15 hrs. 0 mins. 0 sec.). (ENG.). 2008. audio compact disk 39.99 (978-1-4001-1064-3(5)); audio compact disk 29.99 (978-1-4001-6064-8(2)); audio compact disk 79.99 (978-1-4001-4064-0(1)) Pub: Tantor Media. Dist(s): IngramPubServ

Reality Course on Money: A One-Day Seminar. Read by G Edward Griffin. 4 cass. 35.00 (AC20) Am Media.
Focuses on the history of a small group of international financiers in their three-century quest for control over the world's money systems. Here is the story of the Rothschilds, the Warburgs, the Selligmans, the Morgans & the Rockefellers.

***Reality Is Broken: Why Games Make us Better & How They Can Change the World.** unabr. ed. Jane McGonigal. (Running Time: 12 hrs.). 2011. 39.97 (978-1-61106-430-8(9), 9781611064308, BADLE); 24.99 (978-1-61106-429-2(5), 9781611064292, BAD); 39.97 (978-1-61106-428-5(7), 9781611064285, Brinc Audio MP3 Lib); 24.99 (978-1-61106-427-8(9), 9781611064278, Brilliance MP3); audio compact disk 69.97 (978-1-61106-426-1(0), 9781611064261, BriAudCD Unabrid); audio compact disk 29.99 (978-1-61106-425-4(2), 9781611064254, Bril Audio CD Unabri) Brilliance Audio.

Reality Is Not What You Think. Adi Da Avatar Samraj. 1 cass. 1999. Dawn Horse Pr.

Reality of Christ. Rick Joyner. 1 cass. (Running Time: 90 mins.). (Walking in Truth Ser.: Vol. 4). 2000. 5.00 (RJ02-004) Morning NC.
Rick reinforces our calling to walk in truth & integrity while pursuing God's perfect will for our lives.

Reality of Good & Evil. Swami Amar Jyoti. 1 cass. 1987. 9.95 (F-14) Truth Consciousness.
Understanding how justice works. Universal ethics, the underlying unity. Correcting ourselves, forgiving others.

Reality of Heaven: 1 Corinthians 15:42-44. Ben Young. 2000. 4.95 (978-0-7417-6180-4(7), B0180) Win Walk.

Reality of Heaven (Easter) 1 Cor 15:42-44. Ed Young. 2000. 4.95 (978-0-7417-2253-9(4), 1253) Win Walk.

Reality of Redemption. Kenneth Copeland. 8 cass. (Running Time: 12 hrs.). 1983. stu. ed. 40.00 (978-0-88114-045-3(7)) K Copeland Pubns.
Indepth biblical study on redemption.

Reality of Redemption. Featuring B. I. II Winston. 3 cass. 2005. 15.00 (978-1-59544-114-0(X)) Pub: B Winston Min. Dist(s): Anchor Distributors

Reality of Redemption. Bill Winston. 3 cass. 2005. 15.00 (978-1-59544-116-4(6)) Pub: B Winston Min. Dist(s): Anchor Distributors

Reality of Redemption. Featuring Bill Winston. 3 CDs. 2005. audio compact disk 24.00 (978-1-59544-115-7(8)) Pub: B Winston Min. Dist(s): Anchor Distributors

Reality of Righteousness. Featuring Bill Winston. 6. 2004. audio compact disk 48.00 (978-1-59544-028-0(3)) Pub: B Winston Min. Dist(s): Anchor Distributors
In this powerful series, Pastor Winston reveals to the Believerthe importance of being in right standing with God so that yourprayers are heard and your faith increased. Learn to let go of the past so that you can have a better future.

Reality of Righteousness, Vol. 1. Featuring Bill Winston. 6 cass. (Running Time: 4hr.53min.). (C). 2003. 30.00 (978-1-931289-82-5(4)) Pub: B Winston Min. Dist(s): Anchor Distributors

Reality of Righteousness: The Righteous in Authority, Vol. 2. Bill Winston. 5 cass. (Running Time: 4hr.40min.). (C). 2003. 25.00 (978-1-931289-99-3(9)) Pub: B Winston Min. Dist(s): Anchor Distributors

Reality of Righteousness Vol. 3: The God-Class. Bill Winston. 6 cassettes. 2003. 15.00 (978-1-931289-03-0(4)) Pub: B Winston Min. Dist(s): Anchor Distributors

Reality of Righteousness Vol. 4: Freedom in Christ. Bill Winston. 3 cass. (C). 2003. 15.00 (978-1-931289-75-7(1)) Pub: B Winston Min. Dist(s): Anchor Distributors

Reality of the Archetype & the Spirit of Psychology. Charles Ponce. 1 cass. 9.00 (A0558-90) Sound Photosyn.
Redefining the concept of the archetype in the light of recent developments in philosophy & psychology.

Reality of the Holy Spirit, Vol. 1. Speeches. Creflo A. Dollar. 6 cass. (Running Time: 5 hrs.). 2005. audio compact disk 25.00 (978-1-59089-935-9(0)); audio compact disk 34.00 (978-1-59089-937-3(7)) Creflo Dollar.

Reality of the Supernatural World. Todd Bentley. Read by Charlie Glaize. (ENG.). 2008. 39.99 (978-1-4245-0865-5(7)) Tre Med Inc.

Reality of Utopia: Some Consequences of the Divergence Between Theory & Practice. Read by Paul Hollander. 1 cass. 3.00 (129) ISI Books.

Reality vs. Perception Pt. 1: Exodus 20:5. Ed Young. 1994. 4.95 (978-0-7417-1995-9(9), 995) Win Walk.

Reality vs. Perception Pt. 2: Ephesians 5;22- 6:4. Ed Young. 1994. 4.95 (978-0-7417-1996-6(7), 996) Win Walk.

Reality Zone. unabr. ed. Galexis. 2 cass. (Running Time: 3 hrs.). 1997. 19.95 (978-1-56089-057-7(6), G138) Visionary FL.
In creating realities, one must stay within the "zone." Galexis gives details on how to identify when you are outside the zone, & how to get back inside the zone so manifestation can occur. Includes questions & answers, & meditation.

Reality 2.0: Shamans, Psychedelics, & the Next Step in Evolution. unabr. ed. Daniel Pinchbeck. Read by Daniel Pinchbeck. 4 CDs. (Running Time: 4 hrs.). 2008. audio compact disk 29.95 (978-1-59179-666-4(0)) Sounds True.

Realizando Nuevos Descubrimientos. 2006. audio compact disk 30.00 (978-1-57972-708-6(5)) Insight Living.

Realization. Joseph Goldstein. 2 cass. (Running Time: 3 hrs.). 1992. 18.00 (OC282-62) Sound Horizons AV.

Realization. Swami Amar Jyoti. 1 cass. (Running Time: 90 mins.). 1977. 9.95 (R-9) Truth Consciousness.
Describing the glory of the indescribable. Openness & retention lead to realization. Taking God as Reality.

Realization of Being. unabr. ed. Eckhart Tolle. Read by Eckhart Tolle. 2 CDs. (Running Time: 2 hrs. 15 mins.). (Power of Now Teaching Ser.). 2001. audio compact disk 24.95 (978-1-56455-947-0(5), AW00587D) Sounds True.
This unique voice in contemporary spirituality explores our highest purpose in life, and how meditation can help us attain it.

Realize Your Goal: Enhance & Accelerate Goal Manifestation. Mark Bancroft. Read by Mark Bancroft. 1 cass., bklet. (Running Time: 1 hr.). (General Self-Development/Improvement Ser.). 1999. pupil's gde. ed. 12.95 (978-1-58522-007-6(8), 901, EnSpire Aud) EnSpire Pr.
Two complete sessions plus printed instruction manual/guidebook. With healing music soundtrack.

Realize Your Goal: Enhance & Accelerate Goal Manifestation. Mark Bancroft. Read by Mark Bancroft. 1 CD, bklet. (Running Time: 1 hr.). (General Self-Development/Improvement Ser.). 2006. audio compact disk 20.00 (978-1-58522-044-1(2)) EnSpire Pr.
Two complete sessions plus printed instructionmanual/guidebook. With healing music soundtrack.

Realize Your Potential. Robert J. McKain, Jr. 1 cass. 10.00 (SP100022) SMI Intl.
If your workday is boring & unfulfilling, listen to the cassette tape & learn how to change your situation & find complete fulfillment. Use these dynamic ideals to your own business or professional life. You can succeed! You can reach your goals!.

Realize Your Potential. abr. ed. Robert J. McKain, Jr. 1 cass. (Running Time: 59 min.). 11.00 (978-0-89811-047-0(5), 5194) Meyer Res Grp.
If your work day is boring & unfulfilling, this cassette will teach you to change your situation & find complete fulfillment.

Realizing Our Perfection. Swami Amar Jyoti. 2 cass. 1981. 12.95 (R-38) Truth Consciousness.
Why don't we see our perfection? Following cosmic laws. Easy to worship, difficult to face the living God.

Realizing Subjective Oneness. Swami Amar Jyoti. 1 cass. 1989. 9.95 (M-80) Truth Consciousness.
Our mission in this life. Solving the problem of unconsciousness. On faith, prayer, longing & meditation.

Realizing the Power of Now. Eckhart Tolle. 2003. audio compact disk 69.95 (978-1-59179-071-6(9)) Sounds True.

Realizing Your True Self. Ricki Rush. 1 cass. (Running Time: 1 hr.). (Inner Journeys for Inner Change Ser.: Vol. 1). 1995. 12.95 (978-0-9674292-0-5(X)) R Rush.
Two guided visualizations for achieving one's goals & dreams. Side A is "Releasing Self-Limitations". Side B is: Meeting Your Future Self".

Really Inconvenient Truths: Seven Environmental Catastrophes Liberals Don't Want You to Know about-Because They Helped Cause Them. unabr. ed. Iain Murray. (Running Time: 11 hrs. 0 mins.). 2008. 29.95 (978-1-4332-5105-4(1)); 65.95 (978-1-4332-5102-3(7)); audio compact disk 90.00 (978-1-4332-5103-0(5)) Blckstn Audio.

Really Rosie see Maurice Sendak

Really Rosie. Perf. by Carole King. Contrib. by Maurice Sendak. 1 cass. 1999. 5.98 (Sony Wonder); audio compact disk 11.98 Sony Music Ent.

Really Rosie. Maurice Sendak. Perf. by Carole King. 1 cass. (J). (ps up). 9.98 (294) MFLP CA.
This collaboration between an awesome author-illustrator & a great singer-songwriter produces magical tunes & images that will stay with you & your children for days.

Realm of Angels: Their Mission, Message & Ministry to You. Mac Hammond. 1 cass. 1996. 54.00 (978-1-57399-053-0(1)) Mac Hammond.

Realm of Angels: Their Mission, Message, & Ministry to You. Mac Hammond. (ENG.). 2007. audio compact disk 45.00 (978-1-57399-330-2(1)) Mac Hammond.

Realm of the Galaxies. 1 cass. (Running Time: 24 min.). 14.95 (8370) MMI Corp.
Discusses six men who changed the Universe: Ptolemy, Galileo, Newton, Herschel, Hubble & Einstein - their contributions to modern astronomical concepts.

Realm of the Panther: A Story of South Florida's Forests. Emily Costello. 1 cass. (Running Time: 35 min.). (J). (gr. k-4). 2001. 19.95 (SP 3020C) Kimbo Educ.
Two hungry young Florida panthers are on their own in the forest as their mother has left to find food. Includes read along book.

Realms of Gold: Letters & Poems of John Keats. abr. ed. John Keats. Read by Samuel West & Matthew Marsh. (Running Time: 9441 sec.). 2006. audio compact disk 17.98 (978-962-634-437-8(7), Naxos AudioBooks) Naxos.

Realms of Gold: The Classics in Christian Perspective. unabr. ed. Read by Ken Myers. 5 cass. (Running Time: 9 hrs. 3 mins.). 2001. 29.00 (978-0-9668411-6-9(6), AUBK-4) Mars Hill.

Realms of Gold: The Letters & Poems of John Keats. Poems. John Keats. Read by Samuel West & Matthew Marsh. Ed. by Perry Keenlyside. 2 cass. (Running Time: 2 hrs. 30 mins.). 1999. 13.98 (978-962-634-674-7(4), NA217414, Naxos AudioBooks) Naxos.
The letters of Keats between 1816 and 1821 are passionate, revealing and sensitive. It was within the context of these letters that many of his poems first appeared.

Realms of Gold: The Letters & Poems of John Keats. unabr. ed. Poems. John Keats. Read by Samuel West & Matthew Marsh. Ed. by Perry Keenlyside. 2 CDs. (Running Time: 2 hrs. 30 mins.). 1999. audio compact disk 15.98 (978-962-634-174-2(2), NA217412, Naxos AudioBooks) Naxos.

***Realms of the Gods.** Tamora Pierce. Read by Tamora Pierce. (ENG.). (YA). 2010. audio compact disk 55.00 (978-1-934180-27-3(0)) Full Cast Audio.

Realtime Machine Shorthand: Medical Terminology (MTERMI-11) unabr. ed. George P. Andrews & Beverly L. Ritter. 11 cass. (Running Time: 16 hrs. 30 min.). 1994. 80.00 (978-0-938643-53-1(3), 453) Stenotype Educ.
Dictation for Medical Terminology for Stenotypists (60-120 wpm).

Realtime Machine Shorthand Nos. 1-8: Ten Steps to Realtime Writing. unabr. ed. Beverly L. Ritter. 8 cass. (Running Time: 12 hrs.). 1993. 66.00 (978-0-938643-44-9(4), 152) Stenotype Educ.
Dictation for 10-Steps to Realtime Writing.

Realtime Machine Shorthand Vol. 1, Nos. 1-10: Theory. unabr. ed. Beverly L. Ritter. 10 cass. (Running Time: 10 hrs.). 1992. 45.00 (978-0-938643-38-8(X), 103B) Stenotype Educ.
Dictation for Volume I: Theory (Lessons 1-18).

Realtime Machine Shorthand Vol. 1, Nos. 11-20: Theory. unabr. ed. Beverly L. Ritter. 10 cass. (Running Time: 10 hrs.). 1992. 45.00 (978-0-938643-39-5(8), 103C) Stenotype Educ.
Dictation for Volume I: Theory (Lessons 18-28).

Realtime Machine Shorthand Vol. 1, Nos. 21-31: Theory. unabr. ed. Beverly L. Ritter. 11 cass. (Running Time: 11 hrs.). 1992. 49.50 (978-0-938643-40-1(1), 103D) Stenotype Educ.
Dictation for Volume I: Theory (Lessons 28-40).

Realtime Machine Shorthand Vol. 1, Nos. 32-40: Theory Review. unabr. ed. Beverly L. Ritter. 9 cass. (Running Time: 9 hrs.). 1992. 40.50 (978-0-938643-41-8(X), 103R) Stenotype Educ.
Dictation for Volume I: Theory (Reviews Selected Exercises, Lessons 13-40).

Realtime Machine Shorthand Vol. 1, Nos. 61-72: Speedbuilding. unabr. ed. Sally Floyd & Dot Mathias. 12 cass. (Running Time: 12 hrs.). 1990. 72.00 (978-0-938643-50-0(9), 403) Stenotype Educ.
Dictation for Speedbuilding for Court Reporting: Volume 1 (120-210 wpm).

Realtime Machine Shorthand Vol. 2, Nos. 31-40: Vocabulary Development. unabr. ed. Beverly L. Ritter. 10 cass. (Running Time: 10 hrs.). 1992. 60.00 (978-0-938643-46-3(0), 203) Stenotype Educ.
Dictation for Volume II: Vocabulary Development (covers all lessons).

Realtime Machine Shorthand Vol. 2, Nos. 73-83: Speedbuilding. unabr. ed. Sally Floyd & Dot Mathias. 11 cass. (Running Time: 11 hrs.). 1990. 66.00 (978-0-938643-51-7(7), 404) Stenotype Educ.
Dictation for Speedbuilding for Court Reporting: Volume 2 (130-225 wpm).

Realtime Machine Shorthand Vol. 3, Nos. 41-60: Reporter on the Job. unabr. ed. Beverly L. Ritter & Michael LaBorde. 20 cass. (Running Time: 20 hrs.). 1991. 120.00 (978-0-938643-48-7(7), 303B) Stenotype Educ.
Dictation for Volume III: Reporter on the Job (covers all lessons, 130-225 wpm).

Realtime Machine Shorthand Vol. 3, Nos 41A-50A: Reporter on the Job. unabr. ed. Beverly L. Ritter & Michael LaBorde. 10 cass. (Running Time: 10 hrs.). 1991. 60.00 (978-0-938643-47-0(9), 303A) Stenotype Educ.
Dictation for Volume III: Reporter on the Job (covers all lessons, 80-130 wpm).

Realtime Machine Shorthand Vol. 3, Nos. 41A-60: Reporter on the Job. unabr. ed. Beverly L. Ritter & Michael LaBorde. 30 cass. (Running Time: 30 hrs.). 1991. 180.00 (978-0-938643-49-4(5), 303) Stenotype Educ.
Dictation for Volume III: Reporter on the Job (all 30 cassettes).

Realtor & the Family. Richard Flint. 6 cass. 1980. 70.00 (978-0-937851-10-4(8)) Pendelton Lane.
The complexity of balancing a pressure-oriented career with a pressure-oriented home life is discussed. Topics are divided as follows: "Some Terms Defined," "The Major Problem Areas," "Pressures of the Real Estate Job," "Pressure of the Home," "Some Questions to Ponder" & "Some Rules to Live By".

Reap the Wind. abr. ed. Iris Johansen. Read by Sandra Burr. 4 cass. Library ed. (Running Time: 6 hrs.). 2002. 62.25 (978-1-59086-131-8(0), 1590861310, Lib Edit) Brilliance Audio.
Some would kill to know what Caitlin Vasaro knows. For the secrets she's kept hidden all her life are the kind the rich and powerful will do anything to possess. But not even Caitlin knows how much danger she is in - or how far someone will go to hunt her down. But she is about to find out when she enters a business deal with the mysterious and charismatic Alex Karazov and joins the hunt for one of the world's most coveted treasures, the Wind Dancer, an ancient statue of legendary beauty and power. But Karazov is a dangerous man who has an even more dangerous enemy and suddenly Caitlin is thrust into a shadowy world of intrigue and deception, unable to trust anyone, not even the one man who can help. Now she must outsmart the cleverest of killers, a psychopath obsessed with the Wind Dancer whose ruthless plan spans continents and whose lethal rampage won't stop at one death...or two...or even three - not until he finally gets what he wants: the secret Caitlin will die to keep.

Reap the Wind. abr. ed. Iris Johansen. Read by Sandra Burr. (Running Time: 6 hrs.). 2006. 39.25 (978-1-4233-0192-9(7), 9781423301929, BADLE); 24.95 (978-1-4233-0191-2(9), 9781423301912, BAD); audio compact disk 39.25 (978-1-4233-0190-5(0), 9781423301905, Brinc Audio MP3 Lib); audio compact disk 24.95 (978-1-4233-0189-9(7), 9781423301899, Brilliance MP3) Brilliance Audio.

Reap the Wind. abr. ed. Iris Johansen. Read by Sandra Burr. (Running Time: 6 hrs.). 2009. audio compact disk 9.99 (978-1-4418-0820-2(5), 9781441808202, BCD Value Price) Brilliance Audio.

Reap the Wind. unabr. ed. Iris Johansen. Read by Sandra Burr & Laural Merlington. (Running Time: 17 hrs.). 2009. 39.97 (978-1-4418-0134-0(0), 9781441801340, Brinc Audio MP3 Lib); 39.97 (978-1-4418-0136-4(7), 9781441801364, BADLE); 24.99 (978-1-4418-0135-7(9), 9781441801357, BAD); 24.99 (978-1-4418-0133-3(2), 9781441801333, Brilliance MP3); audio compact disk 87.97 (978-1-4418-0132-6(4), 9781441801326, BriAudCD Unabrid); audio compact disk 29.99 (978-1-4418-0131-9(6), 9781441801319, Bril Audio CD Unabri) Brilliance Audio.

***Reaper.** abr. ed. Ben Mezrich. Read by Stephen Lang. (ENG.). 2006. (978-0-06-114066-2(X), Harper Audio); (978-0-06-114067-9(8), Harper Audio) HarperCollins Pubs.

Reaper. unabr. ed. Ted Allbeury. Read by Steve Hodson. 6 cass. (Running Time: 9 hrs.). 2001. 49.95 (978-0-7451-4130-5(7), CAB 813) Pub: Chivers Audio Bks GBR. Dist(s): AudioGO
Anna Woltman seeks revenge for the senseless killing of her husband during World War II. She stalks the Nazi's one by one, who dare to still pay homage to Hitler, and then she kills them in cold blood. But when a secret Nazi organization starts to fight back, suddenly the hunter becomes the hunted.

Reaper. unabr. ed. Peter Lovesey. Read by Christopher Scott. 8 CDs. (Running Time: 7 hrs.30 mins.). (Sound Ser.). (J). 2002. audio compact disk 79.95 (978-1-86042-928-6(9)) Pub: ISIS Lrg Prnt GBR. Dist(s): Ulverscroft US

Reaper. unabr. ed. Peter Lovesey. Read by Christopher Scott. 8 cass. (Running Time: 12 hrs.). 2001. 84.95 (978-1-86042-870-8(3), 28703) Pub: Soundings Ltd GBR. Dist(s): Ulverscroft US
The bishop's body is found in a quarry. With him, a Bible underlined at the text "hath devoured thy living with harlots." His last phone call was to Madame Swish. Guilt? Or did someone help the bishop move closer to the Lord?.

Reaper Man. abr. ed. Terry Pratchett. Read by Tony Robinson. (Running Time: 3 hrs. 0 mins. 0 sec.). (Discworld Ser.). (ENG.). 2006. audio compact disk 24.95 (978-0-552-15301-0(X)) Pub: Transworld GBR. Dist(s): IPG Chicago

Reaper Man. unabr. ed. Terry Pratchett. Read by Nigel Planer. 6 cass. (Running Time: 7 hrs. 45 min.). (Discworld Ser.). (J). 2001. 54.95 (978-0-7531-0019-6(3), 951103) Pub: ISIS Lrg Prnt GBR. Dist(s): Ulverscroft US

Reaper Man. unabr. ed. Terry Pratchett. Read by Nigel Planer. 8 CDs. (Discworld Ser.). (J). 2007. audio compact disk 79.95 (978-0-7531-2212-9(X)) Pub: ISIS Lrg Prnt GBR. Dist(s): Ulverscroft US

***Reapers: A Botswana Mystery.** unabr. ed. Frederick Ramsay. Read by Ray Porter. (Running Time: 8 hrs. 30 mins.). (Botswana Mysteries Ser.). 2011. 29.95 (978-1-4417-6488-1(7)); 59.95 (978-1-4417-6485-0(2)) Blckstn Audio.

Reapers: A Thriller. abr. ed. John Connolly. Read by Jay O. Sanders. (Running Time: 6 hrs. 0 mins. 0 sec.). (ENG.). 2010. audio compact disk 14.99 (978-1-4423-0010-1(8)) Pub: S&S Audio. Dist(s): S and S Inc

***Reapers Are the Angels: A Novel.** unabr. ed. Alden Bell. Read by Tai Sammons. (Running Time: 8 hrs.). 2010. 29.95 (978-1-4417-6600-7(6)); 54.95 (978-1-4417-6597-0(2)); audio compact disk 76.00 (978-1-4417-6598-7(0)); audio compact disk 29.95 (978-1-4417-6599-4(9)) Blckstn Audio.

***Reapers (Library Edition) A Botswana Mystery.** unabr. ed. Frederick Ramsay. Read by Ray Porter. (Running Time: 8 hrs. 30 mins.). (Botswana Mysteries Ser.). 2011. audio compact disk 76.00 (978-1-4417-6486-7(0)) Blckstn Audio.

Reaping: Harvest Your Increase. Gary V. Whetstone. 4 cass. (Running Time: 6 hrs.). (Finance Ser.). 1993. pap. bk. 35.00 (978-1-58866-241-5(1), V1005A) Gary Whet Pub.
Are you tired of little harvests? Does it appear that you are missing the big harvests you deserve? Discover the revelation that "Jesus is Lord of the Harvest!".

Reaping the Whirlwind: A Trent Tyson Historical Mystery. Rosey Dow. Narrated by Ed Sala. 8 cass. (Running Time: 11 hrs.). 74.00 (978-1-4025-3662-5(3)) Recorded Bks.

Reappearance of the Christ. Alice A. Bailey. 5 cass. (Running Time: 7 hrs). (ENG.). 2000. 15.00 (978-0-85330-214-8(6)) Lucis.

***Reappearance of the Christ: Mp3.** Alice A. Bailey. (ENG.). 2009. audio compact disk Rental 18.00 (978-0-85330-298-8(7)) Lucis Pr GBR.

Reappraisals: Reflections on the Forgotten Twentieth Century. unabr. ed. Tony Judt. (Running Time: 14 hrs. 5 mins.). 2008. 32.95 (978-1-4332-1377-9(X)) Blckstn Audio.

Reappraisals: Reflections on the Forgotten Twentieth Century. unabr. ed. Tony Judt. Read by James Adams. (Running Time: 14 hrs. 50 mins.). 2008. 85.95 (978-1-4332-1375-5(3)); audio compact disk & audio compact disk 32.95 (978-1-4332-1378-6(8)); audio compact disk & audio compact disk 110.00 (978-1-4332-1376-2(1)) Blckstn Audio.

Reappraisals: Reflections on the Forgotten Twentieth Century. unabr. ed. Tony Judt & James Adams. 1 CD. (Running Time: 61200 sec.). 2008. audio compact disk 29.95 (978-1-4332-1379-3(6)) Blckstn Audio.

Reappraising Your Thirties & Reflecting on Your Forties. Nolan Brohaugh. Read by Nolan Brohaugh. Ed. by Ellen Harkins & Patricia Magerkurth. 1 cass. (Running Time: 24 min.). (Life Stages Ser.). 1990. 10.00 (978-1-56948-017-5(6)) Menninger Clinic.
Understanding the various issues that occur during the life cycle can help to put those events & stages in perspective. Nolan Brohaugh, MSW, explains the issues of concern both personally & professionally when people are in their 30's. He then reflects on the changes & transformation that occurs during a person's 40's.

Rearing African Children under American Occupation. Kwame R. Vanderhorst. 2 cass. (Running Time: 2 hrs. 20 min.). 1996. pap. bk. 12.00 (978-0-9652104-1-6(3)) Prep Our Youth.
Addresses the challenges & solutions of African American parents rearing African American children in the U.S.

Rearing Righteous Youth of Zion: Great News, Good News, Not-So-Good News. Brent L. Top & Bruce Chadwick. 2 cass. (Running Time: 3 hrs.). 1998. 14.95 (978-1-57008-414-0(9), Bkcraft Inc) Deseret Bk.

Rearmament see Poetry of Robinson Jeffers

Reason & Emotion. Nathaniel Branden. 2 cass. (Running Time: 1 hr. 19 min.). 19.90 (838-839) J Norton Pubs.
An examination of the relationship & problems that exist between reason & emotion; the conflict between social precepts & one's own desires; motivation as related to absence of emotion.

Reason & Emotion. Edwin Locke. 1 cass. (Running Time: 1 hrs. 35 min.). 1997. 12.95 (978-1-56114-410-5(X), IL46C) Second Renaissance.
Presentation of the view which integrates reason & emotion instead of putting them in conflict.

Reason & Emotion (2-CD Set) Nathaniel Branden. (ENG.). 2007. audio compact disk 19.90 (978-1-57970-485-8(9), Audio-For) J Norton Pubs.

Reason & Faith: Philosophy in the Middle Ages. Instructed by Thomas Williams. (ENG.). 2007. 129.95 (978-1-59803-338-0(7)); audio compact disk 69.95 (978-1-59803-339-7(5)) Teaching Co.

Reason & Intuition. Swami Jyotirmayananda. 1 cass. (Running Time: 45 min.). 1990. 10.00 Yoga Res Foun.

Reason & Virtue. Nathaniel Branden. 1 cass. (Running Time: 1 hr. 10 min.). (Basic Principles of Ojectivism Ser.). 11.95 (570) J Norton Pubs.
Independence, honesty, integrity, productiveness; their relation to survival & mental health.

Reason Enough. Perf. by Avalon Staff. 1 cass. 1999. 7.98 (978-0-7601-2804-6(9)) Brentwood Music.

Reason for a Flower. unabr. ed. Ruth Heller. 1 cass. (Running Time: 7 min.). (J). (gr. 1-4). 1989. pap. bk. 18.95 (6551-C) Spoken Arts.
Brilliantly shows the interdependency of plants and animals.

Reason for God: Belief in an Age of Skepticism. abr. ed. Timothy Keller. Read by Timothy Keller. (Running Time: 6 hrs.). (ENG.). (gr. 8 up). 2008. audio compact disk 34.95 (978-0-14-314294-2(1), PengAudBks) Penguin Grp USA.

Reason for Hope. abr. ed. Jane Goodall & Phillip Berman. (ENG.). 2005. 14.98 (978-1-59483-325-0(7)) Pub: Hachet Audio. Dist(s): HachBkGrp

Reason for Hope: A Spiritual Journey. Jane Goodall & Phillip Berman. 2001. 24.98 (978-1-57042-932-3(4)) Hachet Audio.

Reason for Hope: A Spiritual Journey. abr. ed. Jane Goodall & Phillip Berman. Read by Jane Goodall. (Running Time: 4 hrs. 30 mins.). (ENG.). 2009. 39.98 (978-1-60788-087-5(3)) Pub: Hachet Audio. Dist(s): HachBkGrp

Reason for Hope: A Spiritual Journey. unabr. ed. Jane Goodall & Phillip Berman. Read by Anna Fields. 6 cass. (Running Time: 9 hrs.). 1999. 48.00 (978-0-7366-4671-0(X), 5053) Books on Tape.
Explores her extraordinary life & personal spiritual odyssey. Blessed with faith, Goodall lived through the London blitz, postwar hardships, a terrorist attack in Africa & suffered through her husband's slow, agonizing death. At one with nature & challenged by man-made dangers of environmental destruction, inequality & genocide, Goodall offers insight into her perceptions of these threats & celebrates the people who are working for earth's renewal.

Reason for Hope: A Spiritual Journey. unabr. ed. Jane Goodall & Phillip Berman. Read by Anna Fields. 8 CDs. (Running Time: 9 hrs. 25 mins.). 2001. audio compact disk 64.00 Books on Tape.
Explores her extraordinary life & personal spiritual odyssey. A life blessed with faith, resolve & purpose, though not without its crises. Goodall lived through the London blitz, postwar hardships, a terrorist attack in Africa & suffered through her husband's slow, agonizing death. At one with nature & challenged by man-made dangers of environmental destruction, inequality & genocide, Goodall offers insight into her perceptions of these threats & celebrates the people who are working for earth's renewal.

Reason for My Hope. Charles F. Stanley. 1997. 15.99 (978-0-7852-7191-8(0)) Nelson.
Gives encouragement to those needing a touch of God's grace & love.

Reason I Like Chocolate & Other Children's Poems. Poems. 1 cass. (Running Time: 60 mins.). (J). (gr. 4-8). 1999. 12.95 (SFC-7775) African Am Imag.

Reason in Art. unabr. ed. George Santayana. Read by Bernard Mayes. 5 cass. (Running Time: 7 hrs.). 1994. 39.95 (978-0-7861-0447-5(3), 1399) Blckstn Audio.
Santayana explores the social & psychological origins of art. He examines its moral & ideal functions, its lapses into tastelessness, & the distinctive character of music, speech, poetry & prose. The Spanish-born philosopher develops a veiw of art as part of the broader human context, concluding that art prepares the world "to receive the soul & the soul to master the world." This is part of Santayana's five-volume masterpiece, "The Life of Reason," which established the Harvard professor as an eminent speculative philosopher, opposed to German idealism.

Reason in Common Sense. unabr. ed. George Santayana. Read by Robert L. Halvorson. 6 cass. (Running Time: 9 hrs.). 42.95 (53) Halvorson Assocs.

***Reason to Believe: Lessons from an Improbable Life.** unabr. ed. Deval Patrick. (ENG.). 2011. audio compact disk 35.00 (978-0-307-87808-3(2), Random AudioBks) Pub: Random Audio Pubg. Dist(s): Random

Reason to Boast: Romans 15:14-21. Ed Young. 1984. 4.95 (978-0-7417-1404-6(3), 404) Win Walk.

Reason to Boast: Romans 15:14-21. Ed Young. 1997. 4.95 (978-0-7417-2142-6(2), 1142) Win Walk.

Reason to Remember: 11 Peter 2:1-9. Ed Young. 1983. 4.95 (978-0-7417-1348-3(9), 348) Win Walk.

Reason to Strike: Matthew 20:1-16;19:27. Ed Young. (J). 1981. 4.95 (978-0-7417-1191-5(5), A0191) Win Walk.

Reason Why. R. A. Laidlaw. Read by Charlie Tremendous Jones. (Life-Changing Classics Ser.). (ENG.). 2007. audio compact disk 19.95 (978-1-933715-37-7(5)) Executive Bks.

Reason Why: The Story of the Fatal Charge of the Light Brigade. unabr. ed. Cecil Woodham-Smith. Narrated by Ian Stuart. 8 cass. (Running Time: 11 hrs. 15 mins.). 1994. 70.00 (978-0-7887-0051-4(0), 94250E7) Recorded Bks.
The infamous military disaster caused by two rival British commanders on a Crimcan battlefield in 1854 is recreated & analysed.

Reasonable doubts the O. J. simpson case & the criminal justice System. Alan M. Dershowitz. 2004. 10.95 (978-0-7435-4146-6(4)) Pub: S&S Audio. Dist(s): S and S Inc

Reasonable Faith the Scientific Case for Christianity. 2006. audio compact disk (978-1-932012-68-2(0)) Apologia Educ.

Reasons for Going it on Foot see William Pitt Root

Reasons People Fail to Receive Healing. Speeches. Creflo A. Dollar. 2 cass. (Running Time: 2 hrs. 45 mins.). 2006. 10.00 (978-1-59944-030-9(X)) Creflo Dollar.

***Reasons to Believe: How to Understand, Defend, & Explain the Catholic Faith.** unabr. ed. Scott Hahn. Narrated by Grover Gardner. (ENG.). 2010. 14.98 (978-1-59644-941-1(1), Hovel Audio); audio compact disk 24.98 (978-1-59644-940-4(3), Hovel Audio) christianaud.

Reaviva la Iglesia Senor! National Association of Evangelicals, 47th Annual Convention, Columbus, Ohio, March 7-9, 1989. Jose A. Reyes. 1 cass. (Luncheons Ser.: No. 107-Tuesda). 1989. 4.25 ea. 1-8 tapes.; 4.00 ea. 9 tapes or more. Nat Assn Evan.

Reb Moishe Babba. Isaac Bashevis Singer. Read by Isaac Bashevis Singer. 1 cass. (Running Time: 15 min.). 1961. 11.95 (23127) J Norton Pubs.
Singer reads an autobiographical prose fragment.

Rebecca. Daphne Du Maurier. Read by Emma Fielding. 4 cds. (Running Time: 5 hrs.). 2004. audio compact disk 28.98 (978-962-634-323-4(0), Naxos AudioBooks) Naxos.

Rebecca. Hollywood. 1 cass. (Running Time: 90 mins.). 1999. 13.10 (978-1-900912-81-5(3)) Pub: Mr Punch Prodns GBR. Dist(s): Ulverscroft US
Whilst holidaying in Monte Carlo, Maxim de Winter falls in love with a shy ladies companion. They get married & return to his beloved Manderley in Cornwell, where his new wife now meets the mysterious Mrs. Danvers & finds that Maxim's first wife, Rebecca, is not forgotten.

Rebecca. abr. ed. Daphne Du Maurier. Read by Emilia Fox. 2 cass. (Running Time: 3 hrs.). 1999. 13.95 (978-1-85998-644-8(7), HoddrStoughton) Pub: Hodder General GBR. Dist(s): Trafalgar
A novel of mystery and passion, a dark psychological tale of secrets and betrayal, dead loves and an estate called Manderley that is as much a presence as the humans who inhabit it: "when the leaves rustle, they sound very much like the stealthy movement of a woman in evening dress, and when they shiver suddenly and fall, and scatter away along the ground, they might be the pitter, patter of a woman's hurrying footsteps, and the mark in the gravel the imprint of a high-heeled satin.

Rebecca. abr. rev. ed. Daphne Du Maurier. Read by Jean Marsh. 4 cass. (Running Time: 6 hrs. 0 mins. 0 sec.). (ENG.). 1993. 24.95 (978-1-55927-261-2(9), 692908) Pub: Macmill Audio. Dist(s): Macmillan

Rebecca. adpt. ed. Daphne Du Maurier. Perf. by Diana Rigg et al. 4 cass. (Running Time: 3 hrs.). Dramatization. 1999. 24.95 (978-1-56938-316-2(2), AMP-3162) Acorn Inc.
Maxim de Winter's frightened naive second wife is haunted by the beautiful Rebecca, the late mistress of Manderly. She has unknowingly entered a labyrith of terror that could destroy her.

Rebecca. unabr. ed. Daphne Du Maurier. Read by Anna Massey. 11 cass. (Running Time: 14 hrs. 45 mins.). (gr. 9-12). 1999. 39.95 (978-1-57270-113-7(7), F91113u) Pub: Audio Partners. Dist(s): PerseuPGW
Max de Winter returns to his country estate with his young bride. But the unsettling presence of Rebecca (the first Mrs, de Winter) still lingers in the mansion & the persistent reminders from the grim housekeeper, Mrs. Danvers. The new Mrs. de Winter is nearly driven to despair by Mrs. Danvers' obsessive love of Rebecca, the socialite thought to have drowned at sea.

Rebecca. unabr. ed. Daphne Du Maurier. Narrated by Anna Massey. (ENG.). 2008. audio compact disk 39.95 (978-1-60283-500-9(4)) Pub: AudioGO. Dist(s): Perseus Dist

Rebecca. unabr. ed. Daphne Du Maurier. Read by Jane Bullen. 10 cass. (Running Time: 15 hrs.). 80.00 (978-0-7366-3650-6(1), 1296) Books on Tape.

Rebecca. unabr. ed. Daphne Du Maurier. Read by Anna Massey. (YA). 2007. 44.99 (978-1-60252-859-8(4)) Find a World.

Rebecca. unabr. ed. Daphne Du Maurier. Narrated by Alexandra O'Karma. 9 cass. (Running Time: 15.5 hrs.). 34.95 (978-1-4025-2788-3(8)) Recorded Bks.

Rebecca. unabr. ed. Daphne Du Maurier. Narrated by Alexandra O'Karma. 11 cass. (Running Time: 15 hrs. 30 mins.). 1988. 91.00 (978-1-55690-435-6(5), 88340E7) Recorded Bks.
A young, inexperienced woman runs headlong into the haunting memory of her husband's first wife when she marries & joins him at his country home, Manderly.

Rebecca. unabr. ed. Read by Anna Massey. (Running Time: 53100 sec.). (Cover to Cover Classics Ser.). 2006. audio compact disk 47.95 (978-1-57270-502-9(7)) Pub: Audio Partners. Dist(s): PerseuPGW
When the dashing Max de Winter finds a new wife while vacationing in Italy, he feels happy for the first time since Rebecca, his first wife, died. However, de Winter's grim housekeeper, Mrs. Danvers, is obsessively devoted to the first Mrs. de Winter and won't let the newlyweds forget Rebecca. As the tension escalates, Mrs. Danvers grows more desperate - and more deadly. Noted actor Anna Massey memorably narrates this tense title.

Rebecca of Sunnybrook Farm. abr. ed. Kate Douglas Wiggin. Read by Julie Harris. 1 cass. (J). 1984. 9.95 (978-0-89845-481-9(6), CDL5 1637) HarperCollins Pubs.

Rebecca of Sunnybrook Farm. abr. adpt. ed. Kate Douglas Wiggin. (Bring the Classics to Life: Level 1 Ser.). (ENG.). (gr. 4-7). 2008. audio compact disk 12.95 (978-1-55576-413-5(4)) EDCON Pubng.

Rebecca of Sunnybrook Farm. unabr. ed. Kate Douglas Wiggin. Read by Lorna Raver. (Running Time: 28800 sec.). (J). (gr. 4-7). 2007. 54.95 (978-1-4332-1066-2(5)) Blckstn Audio.

Rebecca of Sunnybrook Farm. unabr. ed. Kate Douglas Wiggin. Read by Lorna Raver. (Running Time: 28800 sec.). (J). (gr. 4-7). 2007. audio compact disk & audio compact disk 63.00 (978-1-4332-1067-9(3)) Blckstn Audio.

Rebecca of Sunnybrook Farm. unabr. ed. Kate Douglas Wiggin. Read by Shaela Connor. 6 cass. (Running Time: 8 hrs. 6 min.). Dramatization. 1993. 39.95 (978-1-55686-473-5(6), 473) Books in Motion.
Rebecca leaves Sunnybrook Farm & goes to live in a distant Main village with two maiden aunts. Rebecca meets with a cold reception & only her buoyant spirit enables her to bear the indignities put upon her.

Rebecca of Sunnybrook Farm, unabr. ed. Kate Douglas Wiggin. Narrated by Barbara Caruso. 6 cass. (Running Time: 8 hrs.). (gr. 5). 1997. 51.00 (978-0-7887-0888-6(0), 95026E7) Recorded Bks.
A free-spirited imp with sparkling eyes & insatiable curiosity, changes the lives of everyone she meets.

Rebecca of Sunnybrook Farm, unabr. ed. Kate Douglas Wiggin. Read by Flo Gibson. 5 cass. (Running Time: 7 hrs. 30 min.). (J). (gr. 3-5). 1991. 20.95 (978-1-55685-198-8(7)) Audio Bk Con.
Rebecca meets & copes with poverty & many difficulties with high spirit, a vivid imagination & a kind heart.

Rebecca of Sunnybrook Farm. unabr. ed. Kate Douglas Wiggin. Read by Lorna Raver. (Running Time: 28800 sec.). (J). (gr. 4-7). 2007. audio compact disk 29.95 (978-1-4332-1068-6(1)) Blckstn Audio.

Rebecca St. James. Contrib. by Rebecca St James & Steve Blair. (Early Years (EMI-Cmg) Ser.). 2006. audio compact disk 7.99 (978-5-558-24622-3(7)) FF Rcds.

Rebecca St. James: the Ultimate Collection. Contrib. by Rebecca St James. (Ultimate Collection). 2008. audio compact disk 18.99 (978-5-557-48829-7(4)) FF Rcds.

Rebecca to the Rescue. Read by Jake Warner. (J). (gr. k-6). 2008. audio compact disk 12.95 (978-1-933781-11-2(4)) TallTales Aud.

Rebecca West: A Life. collector's ed. Victoria Glendinning. Read by Donada Peters. 8 cass. (Running Time: 12 hrs.). 1999. 64.00 (978-0-7366-4644-4(2), 5025) Books on Tape.
Captures that life in its disturbing brilliance & pain.

Rebecca's Reward. abr. ed. Lauraine Snelling. Narrated by Renee Ertl. (Running Time: 7 hrs. 48 mins. 28 sec.). (Daughters of Blessing Ser.). (ENG.). 2008. 18.19 (978-1-60814-351-1(1)); audio compact disk 25.99 (978-1-59859-442-3(7)) Oasis Audio.

Rebecca's Tale. Sally Beauman. 1 cass. (Running Time: 90 min.). 2002. (978-0-00-714086-2(X)) Zondervan.
On the twentieth anniversary of the death of Rebecca, family friend Colonel Julyan receives an anonymous parcel in the post. A black notebook with two handwritten words on the title page, Rebecca's tale and two Pictures.

Rebecca's Tale. unabr. ed. Sally Beauman. 14 cass. (Running Time: 21 hrs. 15 mins.). 2002. 117.00 (978-0-7887-9563-3(5)) Recorded Bks.
Twenty years have passed since Rebecca died, and Manderley burned to the ground. In the small town nearby, an aged friend of the de Winters has received an anonymous package containing one of Rebecca's journals and two faded photographs. Aided by his daughter and a young scholar, he sets out to find out what really happened on Rebecca's last night.

Rebekah. Orson Scott Card. 2005. audio compact disk 29.95 (978-1-59038-501-2(2), Shadow Mount) Deseret Bk.

Rebel. Bernard Cornwell. Read by Tom Parker. 13 CDs. (Running Time: 16 hrs.). (Starbuck Chronicles: Vol. 1). 2001. audio compact disk 104.00 (978-0-7861-9785-9(4), 2704) Blckstn Audio.
A powerful & evocative story of the Civil War's first battle & the men who fought it.

***Rebel.** Carl Sommer. (Quest for Success Ser.). (ENG.). (YA). 2009. bk. 19.95 (978-1-57537-332-4(7)); pap. bk. 11.95 (978-1-57537-381-2(5)) Advance Pub.

Rebel. unabr. ed. Bernard Cornwell. Read by Tom Parker. 11 cass. (Running Time: 16 hrs.). (Starbuck Chronicles: Vol. 1). 2001. 76.95 (978-0-7861-1932-5(2), 2704) Blckstn Audio.

Rebel. unabr. ed. Bernard Cornwell. Read by David Case. 11 cass. (Running Time: 16 hrs. 30 mins.). (Starbuck Chronicles: Vol. 1). 2001. 88.00 (978-0-7366-8384-5(4)) Books on Tape.
Young Nate Starbuck has resolved to fight for the Confederacy, not out of any love of slavery but rather out of a wish to contradict his Boston parents, who have already practically disowned him after an affair he has had with an actress. He goes to Richmond, where he is rescued from a Yankee-hating mob by landowner Washington Faulconer. Nate is impressed by Faulconer, and he enlists Nate in his Legion, a militia that will take on the North. Nate thinks he is ready for battle, but he has never anticipated anything like the Battle of Manassas/First Bull Run. It is there that Nate realizes that he is a born soldier, and finally has a calling.

Rebel. unabr. ed. Bernard Cornwell. Read by Hayward Morse. 14 CDs. (Running Time: 21 hrs.). (Starbuck Chronicles: Vol. 1). 2001. audio compact disk 99.95 (978-0-7531-1083-6(0), 110830) Pub: ISIS Audio GBR. Dist(s): Ulverscroft US
Takes place during the War Between the States. Nathaniel Starbuck is the son of a well-known Boston abolitionist preacher. Starbuck finds himself stuck in Virginia in April 1861 & becomes a Rebel, but more out of rebellion against his father than out of belief in states' rights.

Rebel. unabr. ed. Bernard Cornwell. Read by Hayward Morse. 12 cass. (Running Time: 15 hrs.). (Starbuck Chronicles: Vol. 1). (J). 2004. 94.95 (978-1-85695-914-8(7), 960506) Pub: ISIS Lrg Prnt GBR. Dist(s): Ulverscroft US

Rebel, unabr. ed. Bernard Cornwell. Narrated by Ed Sala. 11 cass. (Running Time: 15 hrs.). (Starbuck Chronicles: Vol. 1). 1993. 91.00 (978-0-7887-3129-7(7), 95779E7) Recorded Bks.
When William Faulconer rescues Nate Starbuck from a Yankee-hating mob, he finds a willing recruit for Faulconer's Legion. But Nat discovers fighting against his native North is not easy.

Rebel. unabr. collector's ed. Heather Graham. Read by Mary Peiffer. 10 cass. (Running Time: 15 hrs.). 1998. 80.00 (978-0-7366-4350-4(8), 4810) Books on Tape.
As the Civil War turns brother against brother, Ian McKenzie receives an order to capture the South's most notorious spy: the Moccasin. She is beautiful, deadly - & she is his wife. Duty demands she hang, yet Ian's heart demands another choice..a magnificent rebellious love that can destroy or save them both.

***Rebel / el Rebelde.** ed. Carl Sommer. (Quest for Success Bilingual Ser.). (ENG & SPA.). (YA). 2009. bk. 21.95 (978-1-57537-431-4(5)) Advance Pub.

Rebel Angels. unabr. ed. Libba Bray. Read by Josephine Bailey. 12 CDs. (Running Time: 13 hrs. 30 mins.). (Gemma Doyle Trilogy: Bk. 2). 2005. audio compact disk 59.50 (978-0-307-28341-2(0), Listening Lib); 60.00 (978-0-307-28340-5(2), Listening Lib) Random Audio Pubg.
Ah, Christmas! Gemma Doyle is looking forward to a holiday from Spence Academy, spending time with her friends in the city, attending ritzy balls, and on a somber note, tending to her ailing father. As she prepares to ring in the New Year, 1896, a handsome young man, Lord Denby, has set his sights on Gemma, or so it seems. Yet amidst the distractions of London, Gemma’s visions intensify–visions of three girls dressed in white, to whom something horrific has happened, something only the realms can explain. . . . The lure is strong, and before long, Gemma, Felicity, and Ann are turning flowers into butterflies in the enchanted world of the realms that Gemma alone can bring them to. To the girls’ great joy, their beloved Pippa is there as well, eager to complete their circle of friendship. But all is not well in the realms–or out. The mysterious Kartik has reappeared, telling Gemma she must find the Temple and bind the magic, else great disaster will befall her. Gemma’s willing to do his intrusive bidding, despite the dangers it brings, for it means she will meet up with her mother’s greatest friend–and now her foe, Circe. Until Circe is destroyed, Gemma cannot live out her destiny. But finding Circe proves a most perilous task. From the Hardcover edition.

Rebel Angels. unabr. ed. Libba Bray. Read by Josephine Bailey. 7 CDs. (Running Time: 14 hrs. 6 mins.). (Gemma Doyle Trilogy: Bk. 2). (ENG.). (J). (gr. 7). 2005. audio compact disk 50.00 (978-0-307-28067-1(5), Listening Lib) Pub: Random Audio Pubg. Dist(s): Random

Rebel Angels. unabr. ed. Libba Bray. 5 cass. (Running Time: 8 hrs.). (Gemma Doyle Trilogy: Bk. 2). (J). (gr. 7). 2005. 28.00 (978-0-307-28066-4(7), Listening Lib) Pub: Random Audio Pubg. Dist(s): Random

Rebel Angels, unabr. ed. Robertson Davies. Read by Frederick Davidson. 9 cass. (Running Time: 13 hrs.). 1997. 62.95 (978-0-7861-1215-9(8), 2000) Blckstn Audio.
Weaves together the destinies of a remarkable cast of characters, creating a wise & witty portrait of love, murder, & scholarship at a modern university.

Rebel Angels: The Cornish Trilogy, Book 1. unabr. ed. Robertson Davies. Read by Frederick Davidson. (Running Time: 12 hrs. 0 mins.). 2010. 29.95 (978-1-4417-1874-7(5)); audio compact disk 105.00 (978-1-4417-1871-6(0)) Blckstn Audio.

Rebel Doctor. unabr. ed. Tom Nichols. Read by Maynard Villers. 6 cass. (Running Time: 7 hrs.). 1996. 39.95 (978-1-55686-679-1(8)) Books in Motion.
A Texas doctor & Confederate becomes a Union prisioner, escapes & has an adventurous return to Texas when he teams up with a female Confederate spy.

Rebel Guns. unabr. ed. Adam Rutledge. Read by Charlie O'Dowd. 6 vols. No. 2. 2002. (978-1-58807-564-2(8)) Am Pubng Inc.

Rebel Guns. unabr. ed. Adam Rutledge. Read by Charlie O'Dowd. 6 vols. (Running Time: 10 hrs.). (Patriots Ser.: No. 2). 2002. 30.00 (978-1-58807-086-9(7)) Am Pubng Inc.
In the British colonies of North America there arose a band of brave men and women who forged a free and independent nation. Their names live on today, as does their legacy, and we proudly call them Patriots. Fort Ticonderoga, 1775. Sure shots with their rifles, quick with their knives, and on fire with a passion for liberty, a ragtag band of patriots stands ready to attack the heavy cannons of the British - the mightiest armed force in the world. Mustering soldiers to capture British munitions, Virginia's own Daniel Reed must vanquish a madman in order to carry out his mission. At the same time, Quincy Reed, joining with the fearless Green Mountain Boys, is swept into a perilous raid on Fort Ticonderoga. But as they battle with guns, Daniel's sweetheart, the lovely Roxanne Darragh, fights for freedom with smiles and lies. She volunteers for a daring network of spies - America's first secret service. In the tumultuous days of war, these courageous men and women know their lives may be the price of victory; so, in the nights they seize their chance to love.

Rebel-in-Chief: Inside the Bold & Controversial Presidency of George W. Bush. unabr. ed. Fred Barnes. Read by Fred Barnes. 6 CDs. (Running Time: 5 hrs.). 2006. audio compact disk 45.90 (978-1-4159-2732-8(4)) Pub: Books on Tape. Dist(s): NetLibrary CO

Rebel-in-Chief: Inside the Bold & Controversial Presidency of George W. Bush. unabr. ed. Fred Barnes. Read by Fred Barnes. 3 cass. (Running Time: 5 hrs.). 2006. 45.00 (978-1-4159-2731-1(6), BksonTape) Pub: Random Audio Pubg. Dist(s): Random

Rebel of Bodie. unabr. ed. Gary McCarthy. Read by Gene Engene. 4 cass. (Running Time: 5 hrs. 36 min.). (Derby Man Ser.: Bk. 8). 1995. 26.95 (978-1-55686-589-3(9)) Books in Motion.
Darby Buckingham travels to the town of Bodie to lend aid to whiskey-soaked, ex-sheriff Rebel Morgan & help stem the bloody tide of violence in Bodie.

***Rebel Prince.** unabr. ed. Celine Kiernan. Read by Kate Rudd. (Running Time: 13 hrs.). (Moorehawke Trilogy). 2010. 39.97 (978-1-4418-9170-9(6), 9781441891709, Brinc Audio MP3 Lib); 24.99 (978-1-4418-9171-6(4), 9781441891716, BAD); 24.99 (978-1-4418-9169-3(2), 9781441891693, Brilliance MP3); 39.97 (978-1-4418-9172-3(2), 9781441891723, BADLE) Brilliance Audio.

***Rebel Prince.** unabr. ed. Celine Kiernan. Read by Ellen Grafton & Kate Rudd. (Running Time: 13 hrs.). (Moorehawke Trilogy). 2010. audio compact disk 34.99 (978-1-4418-9167-9(6), 9781441891679, Bril Audio CD Unabri); audio compact disk 89.97 (978-1-4418-9168-6(4), 9781441891686, BriAudCD Unabrid) Brilliance Audio.

Rebel Private, Front & Rear: Memoirs of a Confederate Soldier. unabr. collector's ed. William A. Fletcher. Read by Dick Estell. 8 cass. (Running Time: 8 hrs.). 1996. 48.00 (978-0-7366-3298-0(0), 3953) Books on Tape.
During the Civil War, William Fletcher, was a private in the Confederate army & served under Stonewall Jackson. He fought in many of the famous campaigns, was wounded, & after the war returned to Texas, where he operated a successful lumber business. He published his memoirs in the early 1900s, but with time & fortune, they were lost & forgotten.

Rebel Returns to the Faith CD. 2003. audio compact disk 6.95 (978-1-932631-65-4(8)) Ascensn Pr.

***Rebel Waltz.** unabr. ed. Kay Hooper. Narrated by Lyssa Browne. 4 CDs. (Running Time: 5 hrs.). 2009. audio compact disk 49.95 (978-0-7927-5970-6(2)) AudioGO.

Rebellion of Ronald Reagan: A History of the End of the Cold War. unabr. ed. James Mann. Narrated by Alan Sklar. 12 CDs. (Running Time: 14 hrs. 30 mins. 0 sec.). (ENG.). 2009. audio compact disk 39.99 (978-1-4001-1062-9(9)) Pub: Tantor Media. Dist(s): IngramPubServ

Rebellion of Ronald Reagan: A History of the End of the Cold War. unabr. ed. James Mann & Jim Mann. Narrated by Alan Sklar. 2 MP3-CDs. (Running Time: 14 hrs. 30 mins. 0 sec.). (ENG.). 2009. 29.99 (978-1-4001-6062-4(6)); audio compact disk 79.99 (978-1-4001-4062-6(5)) Pub: Tantor Media. Dist(s): IngramPubServ

Rebellious Desire. abr. ed. Julie Garwood. Read by Anne Flosnik & Elizabeth Swain. (Running Time: 6 hrs.). 2010. audio compact disk 14.99 (978-1-4418-1232-2(6), 9781441812322, BACD) Brilliance Audio.

***Rebellious Desire.** abr. ed. Julie Garwood. Read by Anne Flosnik. (Running Time: 6 hrs.). 2010. 9.99 (978-1-4418-9386-4(5), 9781441893864, BAD) Brilliance Audio.

Rebellious Desire. unabr. ed. Julie Garwood. (Running Time: 10 hrs.). 2010. 24.99 (978-1-4418-1230-8(X), 9781441812308, BAD); 39.97 (978-1-4418-1231-5(8), 9781441812315, BADLE) Brilliance Audio.

Rebellious Desire. unabr. ed. Julie Garwood. Read by Anne Flosnik. (Running Time: 10 hrs.). 2010. 24.99 (978-1-4418-1228-5(8), 9781441812285, Brilliance MP3); 39.97 (978-1-4418-1229-2(6), 9781441812292, Brinc Audio MP3 Lib); audio compact disk 29.99 (978-1-4418-1226-1(1), 9781441812261, Bril Audio CD Unabri); audio compact disk 87.97 (978-1-4418-1227-8(X), 9781441812278, BriAudCD Unabrid) Brilliance Audio.

Rebellious Teens: Proverbs 13:24. Ed Young. 1986. 4.95 (978-0-7417-1543-2(0), 543) Win Walk.

Rebels. abr. ed. John Jakes. Read by Bruce Watson. 4 cass. (Running Time: 6 hrs.). (Kent Family Chronicles: No. 2). 2000. 12.99 (978-1-57815-161-5(9), 4410, Media Bks Audio) Media Bks NJ.

Rebels. unabr. collector's ed. John Jakes. Read by Michael Kramer. 11 cass. (Running Time: 16 hrs. 30 min.). (Kent Family Chronicles: No. 2). 1993. 88.00 (978-0-7366-2398-8(1), 3167) Books on Tape.
The continuing adventures of Philip Kent during the American Revolution.

Rebels & Romantics: A Pot Pourri of 19th Century Verse. unabr. ed. Read by Peter Joyce & Helen Ambrose. 2 cass. 2000. 24.95 (978-1-86015-465-2(4)) Ulverscroft US.

Rebels in Vermont. Narrated by Tom Weakley. 1 CD. (Running Time: 58 mins.). 2002. audio compact disk 15.00 (978-0-9722021-0-7(2)) Highland VT.
The true story of the Northern most action of the American Civil/War. On Oct. 19, 1864 twenty confederate cavalry men raided the rail junction town of Stillbans, Vermont in an attempt to draw Union troops away from the South to guard the northern border. It was hoped by the confederacy that such a raid, originating in Canada, might draw the North into a conflict with England.

Rebels of Ireland: The Dublin Saga. abr. ed. Edward Rutherfurd. Read by John Keating. (Running Time: 32400 sec.). (ENG.). 2008. audio compact disk 19.99 (978-0-7393-6572-4(X), Random AudioBks) Pub: Random Audio Pubg. Dist(s): Random

Rebels of Ireland: The Dublin Saga. unabr. ed. Edward Rutherfurd. 20 cass. (Running Time: 30 hrs.). 2006. 129.00 (978-1-4159-2688-8(3)); audio compact disk 149.00 (978-1-4159-2689-5(1)) Books on Tape.

Rebels of the Heavenly Kingdom, unabr. ed. Katherine Paterson. Narrated by George Guidall. 5 pieces. (Running Time: 7 hrs. 15 mins.). (gr. 6 up). 1997. 44.00 (978-0-7887-0410-9(9), 94602E7) Recorded Bks.
In the midst of China's struggle to free itself from its dynastic rulers, two dedicated soldiers, a young man & woman, must choose between the idealism of cultural revolution & a growing love for each other.

Rebel's Reward. Steve Hill. 1 cass. 1996. 7.00 (978-0-7684-0018-2(X)) Destiny Image Pubs.

Rebirth see Classical Russian Poetry

Rebirth & Restoration. Benedict J. Groeschel. 1 cass. (National Meeting of the Institute, 1995 Ser.). 4.00 (95N7) IRL Chicago.

Rebirth of a Classic: Back to the Future in Sales. J. Douglas Edwards. Read by J. Douglas Edwards. Read by Tom Hopkins. 6 cass. (Running Time: 6 hrs.). 1993. 95.00 Set. (978-0-938636-33-5(2), 1385) T Hopkins Intl.
Selling strategies.

Rebirth of Kirk Franklin. Perf. by Kirk Franklin. 2002. audio compact disk 17.98 GospoCen.

Rebirth of Kirk Franklin. Perf. by Kirk Franklin. 2002. DVD Provident Mus Dist.

Rebirth Theme. unabr. ed. Richard Shelton et al. 1 cass. (Running Time: 29 min.). 1988. 10.00 (032588) New Letters.
A program of readings to coincide with the Easter Holiday.

Reborn. Perf. by Living Sacrifice. 1 cass. 1997. 9.99 12" vinyl. (R1083); audio compact disk 15.99 CD. (D1083) Diamante Music Grp.
Known as one of the industry's most recognizable hardcore/metal artists. Features: Reborn, Truth Solution, Awakening & more.

Reborn. Contrib. by Stryper. Prod. by Michael Sweet & Kenny Lee Lewis. Contrib. by Bill Edwards. 2005. audio compact disk 14.98 (978-5-558-90462-8(3)) Big3 Record.

***Rebound Rules.** unabr. ed. Rick Pitino & Pat Forde. Read by Holter Graham. (ENG.). 2008. (978-0-06-170745-2(7)); (978-0-06-170746-9(5)) HarperCollins Pubs.

Rebound Rules: The Art of Success 2. 0. unabr. ed. Rick Pitino & Pat Forde. Read by Holter Graham. 2008. audio compact disk 29.95 (978-0-06-166239-3(9), Harper Audio) HarperCollins Pubs.

Rebound to Better Health. unabr. ed. Bruce Fife. 1 cass. (Running Time: 60 mins.). (Health & Well-Being Ser.). (ENG.). (gr. 4-12). 2003. 9.95 (978-0-941599-45-0(0)) Piccadilly Bks.
Educational & instructional low-impact exercise program with proven significant advantages in fitness & physical therapy training.

REBT Home Study Program, 8 cass. & 4 videos. (Running Time: 8 hrs.). 1999. stu. ed. Incl. course outline. A Ellis Institute.

Rebuild the Church: Richard Rohr's Challenge for the New Millennium. Richard Rohr. 5 cass. (Running Time: 5 hrs.). 2001. vinyl bd. 39.95 (A6280) St Anthony Mess Pr.
Anguished by the fragmentation in the life of the Church today, Rohr invites us to join others and rebuild the Church in the twenty-first century.

Rebuilding a Culture of Virtuous Boyhood. Douglas W. Phillips. 1 cass. (Running Time: 1 hr. 14 mins.). 2001. 7.00 (978-1-929241-38-5(0)) Pub: Vsn Forum. Dist(s): STL Dist NA

Rebuilding a Culture of Virtuous Boyhood. Douglas W. Phillips. 1 CD. (Running Time: 1 hr. 14 mins.). 2001. audio compact disk 10.00 (978-1-929241-78-1(X)) Pub: Vsn Forum. Dist(s): STL Dist NA

Rebuilding the Indian: A Memoir. abr. ed. Fred Haefele. Read by George DelHoyo. 2 cass. (Running Time: 3 hrs.). 1998. 17.95 (978-1-57453-282-1(0)) Audio Lit.
After reaching midlife with many wrecks behind him: a divorce & tortured relationships with his father, son & daughter, Fred Haefele faces expectant fatherhood, he impulsively embarks on the quixotic project of rebuilding a 1941 Indian Chief motorcycle. The twists & turns of the project become the story of a man's rebuilding his life, redefining himself & taking a new chance on life.

Rebuilding the Real You. unabr. ed. Jack W. Hayford. Narrated by Greg Whalen. (Running Time: 6 hrs. 5 mins. 38 sec.). (ENG.). 2009. 16.09 (978-1-60814-549-2(2)) Oasis Audio.

Rebuilding the Real You. unabr. ed. Jack W. Hayford. Narrated by Greg Whalen. (Running Time: 6 hrs. 5 mins. 38 sec.). (ENG.). 2009. audio compact disk 22.99 (978-1-59859-545-1(8)) Oasis Audio.

Rebuilding your Self Esteem on a Rainy Day. Created by Gayle S. Rozantine. (ENG.). 2007. audio compact disk 15.95 (978-0-9797597-6-5(5)) G Rozantine.

Recall. abr. ed. Robert A. Monroe. Read by Robert A. Monroe. (Running Time: 30 min.). (Human Plus Ser.). 1989. 14.95 (978-1-56102-024-9(9)) Inter Indus.
Selectively retrieve information from conscious & nonconscious memory.

Recalled to Life. unabr. ed. Reginald Hill. Read by Brian Glover. 10 cass. (Running Time: 15 hrs.). (Dalziel & Pascoe Ser.). 2000. 69.95 (978-0-7451-4299-9(0), CAB 982) Pub: Chivers Audio Bks GBR. Dist(s): AudioGO
The year was 1963, the year of the Mickledore Hall Murder. The guests at the Hall that weekend included a CIA officer, a British diplomat with royal connections, and Cissy Kohler, a young American Nanny who had come to England for nearly thirty years, in jail, for murder.

Recap & Summary. Milton Diamond. 1 cass. (Running Time: 1 hr.). (Human Sexuality Ser.). 11.95 (34030) J Norton Pubs.

Recapture Youthful Vigor. Barrie Konicov. 1 cass. 11.98 (978-0-87082-355-8(8), 105) Potentials.
Jack Benny looked, acted & believed he was 39, even though his driver's license did not agree; he was able to tap the fountain of youth within his consciousness. You can do the same thing if you choose & according to the author, spread love & joy to those around you.

Recapturing the Jealousy of God. Paul Cain. 1 cass. (Running Time: 90 mins.). (Jealousy of God Ser.: Vol. 3). 2000. 5.00 (PC05-003) Morning NC.
Incl: Trembling at his Word," "Who Will Ascend to the Lord's Hill?" & "Recapturing the Jealousy of God." God is jealous for his people & Paul issues a prophetic call for believers to be equally jealous for God & his glory.

Recapturing Youth. Scripts. Eldon Taylor. 2 cass. (Running Time: 2 hours & 4 mins.). (Omniphonics Ser.). 29.95 (978-1-55978-814-4(3), 4015) Progress Aware Res.
3-D soundtrack with underlying subliminal affirmations, night & day versions.

Receive the Holy Spirit. Vincent M. Walsh. 5 cass. (Running Time: 5 hrs.). 1989. 20.00 (088) Key of David.
Features Monsignor Walsh & contains 4 talks, as well as a half-hour which summarizes a new booklet on Prayer Tongues.

Receive Your Healing Now! Read by Tim Greenwood. 1 cass. (Running Time: 60 mins.). 1999. (978-0-9666689-5-7(2)) TGMinist.

Receiving Answers to Prayer. Blaine Yorgason & Brenton Yorgason. Read by Marvin Payne. 1 cass. (Gospel Power Ser.). 6.95 (978-0-929985-43-5(5)) Jackman Pubng.
A father's letter to his son concerning recognizing various ways the Lord answers prayers.

Receiving Divine Healing. Speeches. Tim N. Enloe. 2 CDs. 2001. audio compact disk 17.99 (978-0-9749739-2-0(0)) E M Pubns.
Practical teaching on how to receive divine healing from Christ. Disc one contains, "Three Dimensions of Healing." Disc two contains, "Five Steps Toward Healing.".

Receiving Grace: Ephesians 2:1-10. Ed Young. 1983. 4.95 (978-0-7417-1301-8(2), 301) Win Walk.

Receiving Grace & Thanksgiving. Perf. by Zhiming Yuan. 1 cass. (Running Time: 90 mins.). (CHI.). (C). 2000. 5.00 (978-1-930490-11-6(9), 10B-204) CCM Pubs.
All good things are bestowed upon us by God as gifts to men. Men don't need to fully understand God to believe in Him. Even the renowned scientists acknowledge "the law of ignorance" as the highest law of science. To enjoy God's gift, one only needs to have a humble heart to receive His

An Asterisk (*) at the beginning of an entry indicates that the title is appearing for the first time.

grace. One who devotes himself to God is more thankful & receives more grace.

Receiving Love: Letting Yourself Be Loved Will Transform Your Relationship. abr. ed. Harville Hendrix & Helen Hunt. 2004. 15.95 (978-0-7435-3996-8(6)) Pub: S&S Audio. Dist(s): S and S Inc

Receiving Prosperity. Louise L. Hay. 1 CD. 2005. audio compact disk 10.95 (978-1-4019-0413-5(0)) Hay House.

Receiving Prosperity: How to Attract Wealth, Success & Love into Your Life! Louise L. Hay. Read by Louise L. Hay. 1 cass. (Running Time: 57 min.). (Conversations on Living Lecture Ser.). 1989. 10.00 Spanish ed., 55 mins. (217S) Hay House.
In this lecture, Ms. Hay explains how we can use the power of our thoughts to draw anything we want into our lives - money, fulfilling relationships, rewarding work, & much more. By elminating self-criticism & negative thought patterns, there is no limit to the good we can attract.

Receiving Prosperity: How to Attract Wealth, Success & Love into Your Life! Louise L. Hay. Read by Louise L. Hay. 1 cass. (Running Time: 57 min.). (Conversations on Living Lecture Ser.). 1989. 10.00 (978-0-937611-50-0(6), 217) Hay House.

Receiving Spiritual Gifts Series. Jack Deere. 4 cass. (Running Time: 6 hrs.). 2000. 20.00 (JD03-000) Morning NC.
This is a powerful debunking of aguments against the use of spiritual gifts & reveals major hindrances to believers walking in the power of God.

Receiving the Crown at Epiphany; The Dharma. Ann Ree Colton & Jonathan Murro. 1 cass. 10.00 (LivingLang) Random Info Grp.

Receiving the Energy of Connection. 2001. 20.00 (978-0-9714058-0-6(8)) Vanati.

Receiving the Light. Swami Amar Jyoti. 1 cass. 1991. 9.95 (M-85) Truth Consciousness.
In the ultimate climax of love, merging into Light. Preparation for sustaining the descent of Truth & Light.

Receiving Your Healing & Keeping It. unabr. ed. Keith A. Butler. 4 cass. (Running Time: 6 hrs.). 2001. 20.00 (A130) Word Faith Pubng.

Receiving Your Inheritance. Kenneth Copeland. 4 cass. (Running Time: 4 hrs.). 1984. stu. ed. 20.00 (978-0-88114-698-1(6)) K Copeland Pubns.
Biblical teaching on God's blessings.

Recent Advances in Infectious Diseases. Read by Marvin Turck. 1 cass. (Running Time: 9 min.). 1985. 12.00 (C8525) Amer Coll Phys.

Recent Advances in the Surgical Aspects of Gynecologic Oncology. (Postgraduate Programs Ser.). 85.00 (8516 (C85-PG6)) Am Coll Surgeons.
Covers some of the current surgical concepts for patients with gynecologic malignancies. 6 hours CME category 5 credits.

Recent Advances in the Treatment of Infertility. Galen et al. 1 cass. 1998. 25.00 (978-1-58111-076-0(6)) Contemporary Medical.

Recent Advances in the Treatment of Lymphoma. Read by George P. Canellos. 1 cass. (Running Time: 90 min.). 1985. 12.00 (C8553) Amer Coll Phys.

Recent Developments in Criminal Law. 1 cass. (Running Time: 1 hr.). 1988. 20.00 PA Bar Inst.

Recent Developments in the Tort of Outrage & Emotional Distress. Read by A. Roy DeCaro. 1 cass. 1988. 20.00 (AL-53) PA Bar Inst.

Recent Legislation in Employment Law. 2 cass. (Running Time: 2 hrs.). 1998. stu. ed. 25.00 (M215) Am Law Inst.
Will help the listener advise clients who need to stay updated on new employment laws.

Recent Trends in Pastoral Ministry to the Mentally Ill. Tom Summers. 1986. 10.80 (0907) Assn Prof Chaplains.

Receptivity. Swami Amar Jyoti. 1 cass. 1975. 9.95 (E-1) Truth Consciousness.
The Enlightened Being. Why we cannot see His full splendor & perfection. His working & our receptivity.

Recessional. unabr. ed. James A. Michener. Read by Larry McKeever. 17 cass. (Running Time: 25 hrs. 30 min.). 1995. 136.00 (978-0-7366-2956-0(4), 3650A/B) Books on Tape.
Florida retirement community residents & their young director battle fanatics who want to help the seniors by limiting their lifestyle choices. Real people & real issues.

Recessional, Pt. 1. James A. Michener. Read by Larry McKeever. 9 cass. (Running Time: 13 hrs. 30 min.). 1995. 72.00 (3650-A) Books on Tape.

Recessional, Pt. 2. James A. Michener. Read by Larry McKeever. 8 cass. (Running Time: 12 hrs.). 1995. 64.00 (3650-B) Books on Tape.

***Recessionistas: A Novel of the Once Rich & Powerful.** unabr. ed. Alexandra Lebenthal. (Running Time: 10 hrs. 0 mins.). 2010. 16.99 (978-1-4001-8842-0(3)); 24.99 (978-1-4001-6842-2(2)); audio compact disk 34.99 (978-1-4001-1842-7(5)); audio compact disk 83.99 (978-1-4001-4842-4(1)) Pub: Tantor Media. Dist(s): IngramPubServ

Recessive Multiple Epiphyseal Dysplasia - A Bibliography & Dictionary for Physicians, Patients, & Genome Researchers. Compiled by Icon Group International, Inc. Staff. 2007. ring bd. 28.95 (978-0-497-11285-1(X)) Icon Grp.

Recharge. abr. ed. Robert A. Monroe. Read by Robert A. Monroe. (Running Time: 30 min.). (Human Plus Ser.). 1989. 14.95 (978-1-56102-025-6(7)) Inter Indus.
Concentrated effects give equivalent of 90 minute nap.

Rechenka's Eggs. unabr. ed. Patricia Polacco. Narrated by Patricia Polacco. 1 cass. (Running Time: 11 min.). (J). (ps-4). 1993. pap. bk. 17.95 (978-0-8045-6586-8(4), 6586) Spoken Arts.
Babushka is preparing her beautifully painted Ukrainian eggs for the Easter Festival when she takes in Rechenka, an injured goose. One day, Rechenka breaks all of Babushka's lovingly crafted eggs.

Recipe for Murder. Don Druick. Perf. by Salvatore Migliore et al. 2 CDs. (Running Time: 3 hrs.). 2000. 22.50 (978-1-881137-65-8(1)) Canadian Broadcasting CAN.

Recipe for Murder. Don Druick. 2 cass. (Running Time: 2 hrs.). 2001. 17.00 (ZBSF037); audio compact disk 22.50 (ZBSF038) Lodestone Catalog.
Focuses on a different type of cuisine. "Sweet Death" deals not only with chocolates, but with all sorts of sweets. Also the competition between two teachers, a Japanese cuisine & Jewish cooking.

Recipe for Relationships Set: What a Healthy Relationship Looks Like. David Grudermeyer & Rebecca Grudermeyer. 2 cass. 18.95 INCL. HANDOUTS. (T-08) Willingness Wrks.

Recipes for Living & Loving. unabr. ed. Laura Huxley. 1 cass. (Running Time: 38 min.). 1961. 11.00 (06702) Big Sur Tapes.
Two meditations recorded to accompany the book "You Are Not the Target".

Recital Gems. Ed. by Carole Bigler. Contrib. by Valery Lloyd-Watts. (ENG.). 1997. audio compact disk 9.95 (978-0-7390-2780-6(8)) Alfred Pub.

Recital of Ancient Greek Poetry. 2nd exp. ed. Read by Stephen G. Daitz. Ed. by Stephen G. Daitz. 4 cass. (Running Time: 4 hrs.). (Living Voice of Greek & Latin Ser.). (GRE & ENG.). (YA). (gr. 10-12). 1978. pap. bk. 59.50 (978-0-88432-029-6(4), S23600) J Norton Pubs.
Includes selections from Homer, Sappho, Pindar, Euripides, Aristophanes, Timotheos & others. Each selection is read first in English translation & then in Greek.

Recital Winners. Ed. by Carole Bigler. Contrib. by Valery Lloyd-Watts. (ENG.). 1994. audio compact disk 10.95 (978-0-7390-3160-5(0)) Alfred Pub.

Recitation of the Rosary. 2 cass. (Running Time: 2 hrs.). 12.95 (978-0-8198-6424-6(2)) Pauline Bks.
Complete Set of Joyful, Sorrowful, & Glorious Mysteries & Litany of the Blessed Virgin Mary.

Reckless. Cecily von Ziegesar. Read by Joyce Bean. (It Girl Ser.: Bk. 3). (YA). (gr. 8-12). 2008. 54.99 (978-1-60640-603-8(5)) Find a World.

***Reckless.** unabr. ed. Cornelia Funke. Narrated by Elliott M. Hill. 6 CDs. (J). (gr. 3-6). 2010. audio compact disk 40.00 (978-0-307-58328-4(7), BksonTape) Pub: Random Audio Pubg. Dist(s): Random

***Reckless.** unabr. ed. Cornelia Funke. Read by Elliott M. Hill. (ENG.). (J). 2010. audio compact disk 40.00 (978-0-307-58326-0(0), Listening Lib) Pub: Random Audio Pubg. Dist(s): Random

***Reckless.** unabr. ed. Andrew Gross. Read by Christian Hoff. (ENG.). 2010. (978-0-06-199170-7(8), Harper Audio) HarperCollins Pubs.

Reckless. unabr. ed. Amanda Quick, pseud. Read by Anne Flosnik. (Running Time: 12 hrs.). 2010. 39.97 (978-1-4233-8787-9(2), 9781423387879, Brinc Audio MP3 Lib); 39.97 (978-1-4233-8789-3(9), 9781423387893, BADLE); 24.99 (978-1-4233-8786-2(4), 9781423387862, Brilliance MP3); 24.99 (978-1-4233-8788-6(0), 9781423387886, BAD); audio compact disk 82.97 (978-1-4233-8785-5(6), 9781423387855, BriAudCD Unabrid); audio compact disk 29.99 (978-1-4233-8784-8(8), 9781423387848, Bril Audio CD Unabri) Brilliance Audio.

Reckless. unabr. ed. Cecily von Ziegesar. (Running Time: 21600 sec.). (It Girl Ser.: Bk. 3). (YA). (gr. 8-12). 2006. audio compact disk 39.25 (978-1-4233-1718-0(1), 9781423317180, Brinc Audio MP3 Lib); audio compact disk 74.25 (978-1-4233-1716-6(5), 9781423317166, BriAudCD Unabrid); audio compact disk 24.95 (978-1-4233-1717-3(3), 9781423317173, Brilliance MP3) Brilliance Audio.
Please enter a Synopsis.

Reckless. unabr. ed. Cecily von Ziegesar. Read by Joyce Bean. (Running Time: 6 hrs.). (It Girl Ser.: Bk. 3). 2006. 39.25 (978-1-4233-1720-3(3), 9781423317203, BADLE); 24.95 (978-1-4233-1719-7(X), 9781423317197, BAD); audio compact disk 26.95 (978-1-4233-1715-9(7), 9781423317159, Bril Audio CD Unabri) Brilliance Audio.

***Reckless: A Novel.** unabr. ed. Andrew Gross. Read by Christian Hoff. (ENG.). 2010. (978-0-06-195369-9(5), Harper Audio) HarperCollins Pubs.

Reckless Abandon. unabr. ed. Stuart Woods. Read by Tony Roberts. (Running Time: 7 hrs.). (Stone Barrington Ser.: No. 10). 2004. audio compact disk 29.95 (978-1-59355-214-5(9), 1593552149, Bril Audio CD Unabri); 69.25 (978-1-59355-213-8(0), 1593552130, BrilAudUnabridg); 29.95 (978-1-59355-212-1(2), 1593552122, BAU); audio compact disk 82.25 (978-1-59355-215-2(7), 1593552157, BriAudCD Unabrid) Brilliance Audio.
Stone Barrington is, once again, right at home in New York City; but this time he is joined by the tenacious Holly Barker from Orchid Blues, the lady police chief of Orchid Island, Florida. In Reckless Abandon, Holly finally makes it to Manhattan, hot on the trail of an evil fugitive from her jurisdiction. Stone is, well, glad to see her, right up until the moment when her presence creates a great danger to both of them - and to their surprise, she becomes the pursued, not the pursuer.

Reckless Abandon. unabr. ed. Stuart Woods. Read by Tony Roberts. (Running Time: 7 hrs.). (Stone Barrington Ser.: No. 10). 2004. 39.25 (978-1-59335-650-7(1), 1593356501, Brinc Audio MP3 Lib); 24.95 (978-1-59335-286-8(7), 1593352867, Brilliance MP3) Brilliance Audio.

Reckless Abandon. unabr. ed. Stuart Woods. Read by Tony Roberts. (Running Time: 7 hrs.). (Stone Barrington Ser.: No. 10). 2004. 39.25 (978-1-59710-624-5(0), 1597106240, BADLE); 24.95 (978-1-59710-625-2(9), 1597106259, BAD) Brilliance Audio.

***Reckless Bride.** unabr. ed. Stephanie Laurens. Read by Simon Prebble. (Running Time: 13 hrs. 30 mins.). (Black Cobra Quartet Ser.). 2010. 29.95 (978-1-4417-5753-1(8)); 79.95 (978-1-4417-5749-4(X)); audio compact disk 109.00 (978-1-4417-5750-0(3)) Blckstn Audio.

***Reckless Bride.** unabr. ed. Stephanie Laurens. (ENG.). 2010. (978-0-06-200771-1(8), Harper Audio); (978-0-06-206805-7(9)) HarperCollins Pubs.

Reckless Endangerment. unabr. ed. Robert K. Tanenbaum. Read by Connor O'Brien. 11 cass. (Running Time: 16 hrs. 30 min.). (Butch Karp Mystery Ser.). 1999. 88.00 (978-0-7366-4351-1(6), 4828) Books on Tape.
Butch Karp & Marlene Ciampi discover themselves working on two sides of the same case when a set of homicides rocks downtown Manhattan. The Jewish community heads for a confrontation with the city's Arab population when an elderly shopkeeper is found slain beneath a mirror on which is scrawled a hate-filled message in Arabic. Butch Karp has his doubts about the handling of this case & another high-profile one, a cop killing. And in Brooklyn, a 16 year-old Arab runaway murderously defends herself against a malicious pimp & escapes into the helping hands of Marlene.

Reckless Endangerment. unabr. ed. Robert K. Tanenbaum. Read by James Daniels. (Running Time: 11 hrs.). 2010. 39.97 (978-1-4418-1870-6(7), 9781441818706, Brinc Audio MP3 Lib); 24.99 (978-1-4418-1869-0(3), 9781441818690, Brilliance MP3); 24.99 (978-1-4418-1871-3(5), 9781441818713, BAD); 39.97 (978-1-4418-1872-0(3), 9781441818720, BADLE) Brilliance Audio.

Reckless Eyeballin' A Starletta Duvall Mystery. Judith Smith-Levin. Narrated by Marc Johnson. 5 cass. (Running Time: 6 hrs. 45 mins.). 48.00 (978-1-4025-1228-5(7)) Recorded Bks.

***Reckless Faith: Let Go & Be Led.** Beth Guckenberger. (Running Time: 3 hrs. 26 mins. 0 sec.). (ENG.). 2008. 14.99 (978-0-310-30263-6(3)) Zondervan.

Reckless Love. unabr. ed. Elizabeth Lowell. Read by Laural Merlington. (Running Time: 11 hrs.). 2007. 39.25 (978-1-4233-1572-8(3), 9781423315728, BADLE); 24.95 (978-1-4233-1571-1(5), 9781423315711, BAD); audio compact disk 102.25 (978-1-4233-1558-2(8), 9781423315582, BriAudCD Unabrid); audio compact disk 39.25 (978-1-4233-1570-4(7), 9781423315704, Brinc Audio MP3 Lib); audio compact disk 38.95 (978-1-4233-1544-5(8), 9781423315445, Bril Audio CD Unabri); audio compact disk 24.95 (978-1-4233-1562-9(6), 9781423315629, Brilliance MP3) Brilliance Audio.

Reckless Personality: A Study of Mars. Annie Hershey. 1 cass. 8.95 (158) Am Fed Astrologers.
An AFA Convention workshop tape.

Reckoning. unabr. ed. Ted Allbeury. Read by Christian Rodska. 6 cass. (Running Time: 6 hrs.). 2000. 54.95 (978-0-7540-0504-9(6), CAB1927) AudioGO.
Katya Felinska is a beautiful & talented photo-journalist, committed to championing the rights of the oppressed. Max Inman is a brilliant & incisive political journalist. Max is also an undercover agent, one of M16's most important sources of Russian & German leaders in the tense months that led up to the fall of the Berlin Wall. Things go horribly wrong & Katya must use all her courage to save the man she loves.

***Reckoning.** unabr. ed. Kelley Armstrong. Read by Cassandra Morris. (ENG.). 2010. (978-0-06-199167-7(8)); (978-0-06-198396-2(9)) HarperCollins Pubs.

Reckoning. unabr. ed. Beverly Lewis. Read by Marguerite Gavin. 5 cass. (Running Time: 7 hrs.). (Heritage of Lancaster County Ser.: No. 3). 2006. 39.95 (978-0-7861-2603-3(5), 3199); audio compact disk 48.00 (978-0-7861-8935-9(5), 3199) Blckstn Audio.

Reckoning, unabr. ed. Beverly Lewis. Narrated by Barbara Caruso. 6 cass. (Running Time: 8 hrs.). (Heritage of Lancaster County Ser.: No. 3). 2000. 51.00 (978-0-7887-3080-1(0), 95501E7) Recorded Bks.
Katherine Mayfield has taken her rightful place as mistress of Mayfield Manor, but her thoughts keep returning to old friendships & the family that raised her.

Reckoning, Pt. 1. unabr. ed. David Halberstam. Read by Michael Anthony. 13 cass. (Running Time: 19 hrs. 30 mins.). 1993. 85.95 (978-0-7861-0289-1(6), 1254-A) Blckstn Audio.
Tackles the No. 1 subject for Americans today - our prosperity going down the drain...jobs flowing overseas...foreigners seizing our markets & beating us at our own game...the drastic change ahead for our economy. Halberstam chooses two companies, Ford & Nissan, each the embodiment of its society & tells their stories side by side, from the founders & owners right down to the men on the assembly line.

Reckoning, Pt. 1. unabr. collector's ed. David Halberstam. Read by Jonathan Marosz. 12 cass. (Running Time: 18 hrs.). 1997. 96.00 (978-0-7366-3798-5(2), 4470-A) Books on Tape.
History comes to life in the words of a 99-year-old Confederate war widow. Fascinating, poignant & beautifully written.

Reckoning, Pt. 2. unabr. ed. David Halberstam. Read by Michael Anthony. 11 cass. (Running Time: 16 hrs. 30 mins.). 1993. 76.95 (978-0-7861-0290-7(X), 1254-B) Blckstn Audio.
Tackles the No. 1 subject for Americans today - our prosperity going down the drain...jobs flowing overseas...foreigners seizing our markets & beating us at our own game...the drastic change ahead for our economy. Halberstam chooses two companies, Ford & Nissan, each the embodiment of its society & tells their stories side by side, from the founders & owners right down to the men on the assembly line.

Reckoning, Pt. 2. unabr. collector's ed. David Halberstam. Read by Jonathan Morosz. 11 cass. (Running Time: 16 hrs. 30 min.). 1997. 88.00 (978-0-7366-3799-2(0), 4470-B) Books on Tape.
Portrays the conflict between the culture of affluence & the culture of adversity.

Reclaim Your Energy. Lexa Finely. Tammy Chi. (ENG.). 2009. audio compact disk 14.95 (978-0-9822494-1-3(1)) Journey Spirit.

Reclaimed see Bible in Living Sound: Life and Times of the Old Testament; Life and Times of Jesus; Life and Times of Paul

Reclaiming Education: The Home-Schooling Alternative. unabr. ed. Lisa VanDamme. 1 cass. (Running Time: 1 hrs. 30 min.). 1998. 12.95 (978-1-56114-480-8(0), KV55C) Second Renaissance.
Experiences as a home-school teacher; discussing advantages of home-schooling & addressing common concerns.

Reclaiming Life after Any Loss. abr. ed. James Van Praagh. 2 cass. (Running Time: 3 hrs.). 2000. 18.95 (PengAudBks) Penguin Grp USA.
Grieving is a natural process. It is through our losses that we can transform ourselves & find new meaning to life. Author has illuminated the mysteries of death, the afterlife, & rebirth.

Reclaiming Nick. abr. ed. Susan May-Warren. Narrated by Brooke Sanford. (Noble Legacy Ser.). (ENG.). 2007. 16.09 (978-1-60814-352-8(X)) Oasis Audio.

Reclaiming Nick. abr. ed. Susan May Warren. Narrated by Brooke Sanford. (Running Time: 25560 sec.). (Noble Legacy Ser.). (ENG.). 2007. audio compact disk 22.99 (978-1-59859-209-2(2)) Oasis Audio.

Reclaiming of Power. 15 cass. 10.00 ea. (978-1-893165-93-9(0)) Rational Isl.
Theoretical & organizational advances re-evaluation counseling from 1981 to 1983. (Each chapter is complete within a single tape, hence parts of the set may be ordered independently. The table of contents is on the first tape).

Reclaiming Our Three Faces: Maiden, Mother, Crone. Read by Tesse Donnelly. 1 cass. (Running Time: 2 hrs.). 1988. 12.95 (978-0-7822-0056-0(7), 338) C G Jung IL.

Reclaiming the Goddess. Starhawk. 2 cass. 18.00 (OC120) Sound Horizons AV.

Reclaiming the Holidays Self Hypnosis Set. Dean A. Montalbano. (Hypnotic Sensory Response Audio Ser.). (J). 2000. 39.93 (978-0-9708772-7-7(7)) L Lizards Pub Co.

Reclaiming Your Lost Choice: Uncover Six Powerfil Choices to Transform Your Destiny. As told by Andy Andrews. 2005. audio compact disk 99.99 (978-0-9776246-4-5(1)) Lightning Crown Pub.

Reclaiming your Self Esteem by a Mountain Stream. Created by Gayle S. Rozantine. (ENG.). 2007. audio compact disk 15.95 (978-0-9797597-5-8(7)) G Rozantine.

Reclaiming Youth at Risk: Our Hope for the Future. abr. ed. Larry Brendtro et al. 2006. audio compact disk 29.95 (978-1-932127-92-8(5)) Solution Tree.

Recluse of Parma see Cartuja de Parma

Recognize the Voice of God Through His Word. Kenneth E. Hagin. (Developing the Human Spirit Ser.). 20.00 Faith Lib Pubns.

Recognizing Mental Status Problems in the Elderly. unabr. ed. Charlotte Eliopoulos. Read by Charlotte Eliopoulos. 1 cass. (Running Time: 25 min.). 1991. 15.00 (978-1-882515-13-4(7)) Hlth Educ Netwk.
Reviews normal & abnormal mental function in older adults.

Recognizing Roadblocks to Healing. Kenneth E. Hagin. 4 cass. 16.00 (30H) Faith Lib Pubns.

Recognizing Techniques of Deception in Anti-Mormon Literature. Duane S. Crowther. Read by Duane S. Crowther. 1 cass. (Running Time: 90 min.). 1984. 13.98 (978-0-88290-247-0(4), 1811) Horizon Utah.
Presents an examination of many literary techniques commonly used in anti-Mormon literature. It identifies 24 methods frequently used to deceive, distort and slander.

Recognizing the Opportunity in Stress. Gary Applegate. 1 cass. 1986. 10.00 Berringer Pub.
Skill Development's founder, Dr. Gary Applegate, presents the unique Skill Development approach to successful change.

Recognizing What Is in Your Surroundings see Reconociendo lo Que Esta A Tu Alrededor

Recollections & Observations. David Brinkley. 1 cass. (Running Time: 1 hr. 18 mins.). 2001. 12.95 Smithson Assocs.

Recollections of Abraham Maslow. Abraham H. Maslow. Contrib. by Rollo May et al. 1 cass. (Running Time: 90 min.). 1971. 11.00 (01405) Big Sur Tapes.
Moving speeches by Rollo May, Denis O'Donovan, & Anthony Sutich about Abraham Maslow & the influence he had on their personal lives & work as well as on the broader human potential movement.

Recollections of Reagan: A Portrait of Ronald Reagan. collector's ed. Read by Michael Prichard. Ed. by Peter Hannaford. 6 cass. (Running Time: 9 hrs.). 1999. 48.00 (978-0-7366-4626-0(4), 5011) Books on Tape.
These reminiscences about Ronald Reagan from more than fifty of his friends & colleagues include the thoughts of such dignitaries as Margaret Thatcher, Helmut Kohl, George Bush, Pete Wilson, George Shultz & Mike Wallace. Filled with anecdotes, both poignant & humorous, there are also fascinating bits of history, from Reagan's early days in film to his appointment as Governor of California, to his unsuccessful bid for the White House in 1976, to his two-term presidency.

Reconcilable Differences (Divorce & Remarriage) Mark 10:1-9, 1104. Ed Young. 1996. 4.95 (978-0-7417-2104-4(X)) Win Walk.

Reconciliation see Ship That Died of Shame

Reconciliation. Neville Goddard. 1 cass. (Running Time: 62 min.). 1965. 8.00 (91) J & L Pubns.
Neville taught Imagination Creates Reality. He was a powerfully influential teacher of God as Consciousness.

Reconciliation: I Must Confess. Jeff Cavins. (ENG.). 2007. audio compact disk 9.95 (978-1-934567-07-4(8)) Excorde Inc.

***Reconciliation: Islam, Democracy, & the West.** unabr. ed. Benazir Bhutto. Read by Rita Wolf. (ENG.). 2008. (978-0-06-167262-0(9)); (978-0-06-167263-7(7)) HarperCollins Pubs.

Reconciliation: Islam, Democracy, & the West. unabr. ed. Benazir Bhutto. Read by Rita Wolf. 8 cass. (Running Time: 12 hrs.). 2008. 110.00 (978-1-4159-5616-8(2), BksonTape); audio compact disk 110.00 (978-1-4159-5604-5(9), BksonTape) Pub: Random Audio Pubg. Dist(s): Random

Reconciliation: 11 Cor. 5:20;6:2. Ed Young. 1990. 4.95 (978-0-7417-1788-7(3), 788) Win Walk.

Reconnecting: A Self-Coaching Solution to Revive Your Love Life. unabr. ed. Joseph J. Luciani. Read by Joseph J. Luciani. 8 CDs. (Running Time: 9 hrs.). (ENG.). 2009. audio compact disk 29.95 (978-1-60283-574-0(8)) Pub: AudioGO. Dist(s): Perseus Dist

Reconociendo lo Que Esta A Tu Alrededor. Tr. of Recognizing What Is in Your Surroundings. (SPA.). 2008. audio compact disk 14.00 (978-0-944129-13-5(7)) High Praise.

Reconsidering Christianity in the Light of Buddhism. Donald Swearer. 5 cass. Incl. Reconsidering Christianity in the Light of Buddhism: Community & Future Hope. 1976.; Reconsidering Christianity in the Light of Buddhism: Eschatology & Impermanence. 1976.; Reconsidering Christianity in the Light of Buddhism: Prayer & Meditation. 1976.; Reconsidering Christianity in the Light of Buddhism: Requisites for a Theology of Dialogue. 1976.; Reconsidering Christianity in the Light of Buddhism: Selflessness & No-self. 1976.; 1976. 17.50 Set.; 4.50 ea. Pendle Hill.

Reconsidering Christianity in the Light of Buddhism: Community & Future Hope see Reconsidering Christianity in the Light of Buddhism

Reconsidering Christianity in the Light of Buddhism: Eschatology & Impermanence see Reconsidering Christianity in the Light of Buddhism

Reconsidering Christianity in the Light of Buddhism: Prayer & Meditiation see Reconsidering Christianity in the Light of Buddhism

Reconsidering Christianity in the Light of Buddhism: Requisites for a Theology of Dialogue see Reconsidering Christianity in the Light of Buddhism

Reconsidering Christianity in the Light of Buddhism: Selflessness & No-self see Reconsidering Christianity in the Light of Buddhism

Reconstructed Corpse. unabr. ed. Simon Brett. Narrated by Simon Prebble. 5 cass. (Running Time: 6 hrs. 15 mins.). (Charles Paris Mystery Ser.). 1994. 44.00 (978-0-7887-0110-8(X), 94351E7) Recorded Bks.
Charles Paris is cast as a missing & presumed dead public figure on a television true crime reenactment program & finds himself in the path of a killer.

Reconstruction. Mick Herron. 2008. 84.95 (978-0-7531-3273-9(7)); audio compact disk 99.95 (978-0-7531-3274-6(5)) Pub: Isis Pubng Ltd GBR. Dist(s): Ulverscroft US

Reconstruction Pt. 2: America's Unfinished Revolution, 1863-1877. unabr. ed. Eric Foner. Read by Don Norman. 13 cass. (Running Time: 38 hrs.). 1990. 85.95 (978-0-7861-0212-9(8), 1187A,B); 62.95 (978-0-7861-0213-6(6), 1187A,B) Blckstn Audio.
The period following the Civil War was one of the most controversial eras in American history. This landmark book captures the drama of these turbuelent years that played such an important role in shaping modern America.

Reconstruction of the Ano-Genital Region. 2 cass. (Plastic & Maxillofacial Surgery Ser.: C85-PL1). 1985. 15.00 (8580) Am Coll Surgeons.

Reconstructionist. unabr. ed. Josephine Hart. Read by John Lee. 5 cass. (Running Time: 7 hrs. 30 mins.). 2001. 40.00 (978-0-7366-8502-3(2)) Books on Tape.
Jack is a psychiatrist whose special ability is to reconstruct the hidden family lives of his patients. He would do better to apply his talents to himself, for there is trauma and terror at the heart of his own family romance. His relationship with his sister Kate, a "miraculous beauty," does not just involve being supportive of her own traumas and neuroses, but also involves dancing naked with her. When the family's estate in Ireland is about to be sold, he takes possession, and tries to come to grips with the rvents that he has repressed so well and which have marked them both; the disintegration of their parents' marriage and their probable death.

Record Keeping for Business: Syllabus. Marvin W. Hempel. (J). 1977. 139.80 (978-0-89420-180-6(8), 359000) Natl Book.

Record Keeping for Personal Finance: Syllabus. Marvin W. Hempel. (J). 1976. 124.25 (978-0-89420-181-3(6), 358000) Natl Book.

Record Setting Sales: How to Hit Sales Goals Higher Than You Ever Thought Possible. Dale Ledbetter. 1 cass. (Running Time: 5 hrs.). 79.95 (V50208) CareerTrack Pubns.
In this lively program, Dale shares his exclusive strategies that can catapult your own sales. No theories. No preaching. No hollow exhortations. Just solid hands-on training in practical, proven sales skills you can use immediately.

Recordando. unabr. ed. Marcos Witt.Tr. of Remembering. (SPA.). 2003. 9.99 (978-0-8297-4404-0(5)) Pub: Vida Pubs. Dist(s): Zondervan

Recordando Otra Vez. unabr. ed. Marcos Witt. 2004. audio compact disk 14.99 (978-0-8297-4582-5(3)) Pub: Vida Pubs. Dist(s): Zondervan

Recorder. Peter Gelling. (Progressive Ser.). 2004. pap. bk. 19.95 (978-1-86469-223-5(5), 256-152) Kolala Music SGP.

Recorder Express (Soprano Recorder Method for Classroom or Individual Use) Soprano Recorder Method for Classroom or Individual Use. Artie Almeida. (ENG.). 2003. audio compact disk 12.95 (978-0-7579-1108-8(0)) Alfred Pub.

Recorder for Beginners. Ed. by Alfred Publishing. (ENG.). 2001. audio compact disk 10.00 (978-0-7390-1102-7(2)) Alfred Pub.

Recorder Frolics (Book/CD) Easy Recorder Pieces for Soprano Recorder. Robert a. Amchin. Ed. by Holl Karen. Holl Brent. Holl Brent. Reikes Robin. Nichols Michael. (ENG., (J). 2008. pap. bk. 15.95 (978-0-9797522-9-2(9)) Beatin Path.

***Recorder from the Beginning, Bk. 1.** John Pitts. 2004. bk. 11.95 (978-1-84449-518-4(3), 1844495183) Pub: Music Sales. Dist(s): H Leonard

Recorder Music for Children. Jerry Silverman. 1990. bk. 15.95 (978-0-7866-1020-4(4), 94381P) Mel Bay.

Recorder Music for Children. Jerry Silverman. 1990. 9.98 (978-0-87166-975-9(7), 94381C) Mel Bay.

Recorder Music of French Composers. 1 cass. 11.95 (C11222) J Norton Pubs.
Includes seven different kinds of recorders, percussion, harpsichord, & viola da gamba.

Recorder School: Alto. Marion Verbruggen et al. (ENG.). 1996. audio compact disk 15.95 (978-0-87487-570-6(6), Warner Bro) Alfred Pub.

Recorder School: Soprano. Marion Verbruggen et al. (ENG.). 1996. audio compact disk 15.95 (978-0-87487-568-3(4), Warner Bro); audio compact disk 15.95 (978-0-87487-566-9(8), Warner Bro) Alfred Pub.

Recorder School Vol. 3: Alto. Marion Verbruggen et al. (ENG.). 1996. audio compact disk 15.95 (978-0-87487-572-0(2), Warner Bro) Alfred Pub.

Recorder Wizard. Emma Coulthard. 2005. pap. bk. 8.95 (978-0-8256-3338-6(9), CH68575, Chester Music) Pub: Music Sales. Dist(s): H Leonard

RecorderWorld. Composed by Pam Wedgwood. (Faber Edition: RecorderWorld Ser.). (ENG.). 2005. audio compact disk 7.95 (978-0-571-52290-3(4)) Pub: Faber Mus Ltd GBR. Dist(s): Alfred Pub

Recording Machine. J. Krishnamurti. 1 cass. (Running Time: 1 hr.). (Ojai Public Talks - 1983 Ser.: No. 3). 8.50 (AJT833) Krishnamurti.
In the idyllic setting of the oak grove in Ojai, California, Krishnamurti began giving talks in 1922. Over the years, hundreds of thousands of people have heard Krishnamurti explore every aspect of our lives, his language & expression constantly changing, as he strove to communicate to each successive generation those profound truths which he had come upon, & which he maintained were accessible to all.

Recordkeeping: HR Executive Answers. (ENG.). 2009. audio compact disk 497.00 (978-1-60029-055-8(8)) M Lee Smith.

Records: I. A Dream; II. A Vision see Twentieth-Century Poetry in English, No. 2, Recordings of Poets Reading Their Own Poetry

Recover Your Health. Zoilita Grant. 2001. audio compact disk 15.95 (978-1-890575-32-8(1)) Zoilita Grant.

Recovering Charles. Jason F. Wright. 2008. audio compact disk 25.95 (978-1-59038-980-5(8), Shadow Mount) Deseret Bk.

Recovering from Alcoholism. Steven Halpern. Read by Steven Halpern. 1 cass. (Running Time: 60 min.). (Soundwave 2000 AudioActive Subliminal Ser.). 1990. 9.98 (978-1-878625-12-0(8), SRXB 2022) Inner Peace Mus.
Relaxing, beautiful music with subliminal affirmations to support individuals in recovery.

Recovering from Co-Dependency. Steven Halpern. Read by Steven Halpern. 1 cass. (Running Time: 60 min.). (Soundwave 2000 AudioActive Subliminal Ser.). 1990. 9.98 (978-1-878625-11-3(X), SRXB 2021) Inner Peace Mus.

Recovering from Crack & Cocaine Addiction. Directed By Gerald T. Rogers. Contrib. by Dennis C. Daley. (Living Sober Ser.: Segment H). 1994. pap. bk. 89.00 NTSC. (978-1-56215-064-8(2), Jossey-Bass) Wiley US.

Recovering from Illness or Injury. Jane Pernotto Ehrman. Read by Jane Pernotto Ehrman. (Playaway Adult Nonfiction Ser.). (ENG.). 2009. 39.99 (978-1-60812-740-5(0)) Find a World.

Recovering from Spiritual Blindness. David T. Demola. 12 cass. 48.00 (S-1072) Faith Fellow Min.

Recovering from Trauma: Violent Crime, Car Accidents & Disasters. Karen Dorfman. 1 cass. (Running Time: 1 hr. 30 mins.). 2000. 15.00 (978-0-9703997-0-0(7)) K Dorfman.

Recovering Our Tradition: What Is Our Vision of the Church? Joan Chittister. 1 cass. (Running Time: 1 hr.). 1995. 29.95 (AA8383) Credence Commun.
Sister Chittister asks, quite traditionally, whether the Catholic church is really "One, Holy, Catholic & Apostolic." Then she insists that tradition & vision be united with integrity. As she probes the history & contemporary practice of the church, she discovers that those four familiar adjectives are betrayed on every side. Given at the 1994 Call to Action Conference, her speech was interrupted by frequent, spontaneous applause & concluded with the longest standing ovation Credence has ever heard, much less pusblished. This would be a superb place to start with your discussion groups.

Recovering Self-Esteem & Change - Not Chance. 1 cass. (Recovery - The New Life Ser.). 1979. 8.95 (1596G) Hazelden.

Recovering Stolen Dreams. unabr. ed. Ahlam Shalhout. 1 cass. (Running Time: 40 min.). (J). 1999. 12.95 (978-0-9668179-0-4(7)) Expressions Woven.
Reveals the path of self-discovery of one man.

Recovering the Apostolic Gospel. Rick Joyner. 1 cass. (Running Time: 90 mins.). (Church History & the Coming Move of God Ser.: Vol. 4). 2000. 5.00 (RJ11-004) Morning NC.
Church history is brought to life with practical applications & insights into how the enemy uses the same strategy against every new move of God.

Recovering the Lost Tools of Learning AudioBook. Douglas Wilson. Read by Gentry Rench. (ENG.). 2008. audio compact disk 20.00 (978-1-59128-403-1(1)) Canon Pr ID.

Recovering the Soul: A Scientific & Spiritual Search. Larry Dossey. 1 cass. (Running Time: 58 min.). 1990. bk. 10.95 (978-1-56176-152-4(4)) Mystic Fire.
Larry Dossey, M.D., explores the crossroads of mysticism & healing, religion & physics.

Recovery, Tape 3. abr. ed. Robert A. Monroe. Read by Robert A. Monroe. 6 cass. (Emergency Ser.). 1983. 69.00 (978-1-56102-702-6(2)); Inner Indus.
Play immediately after surgery.

Recovery: The Peace that Heals. Thomas D. Oates, Jr. (Running Time: 2 hrs.). 1998. 12.95 (978-0-9665122-1-2(9)) Sacred Earth Film.
Recovery, The Peace That Heals is a true story of hope healing & full recovery from chronic Fatigue Immune Dysfunction Syndrome (CFIDS), & the twelve things that engage the unlimited healing power of divine spirit.

Recovery & Re-Emergence, No. 1. 2 cass. 10.00 ea. (978-1-893165-94-6(9)) Rational Isl.
Shared experiences of mental health system survivors, about being survivors of the mental health system, & about using re-evaluation counseling.

Recovery & Re-Emergence, No. 2. 2 cass. 10.00 ea. (978-1-893165-95-3(7)) Rational Isl.

Recovery & Re-Emergence, No. 3. 6 cass. 10.00 ea. (978-1-893165-96-0(5)) Rational Isl.

Recovery Continues. 1 cass. 1990. 20.00 (978-0-9622887-3-9(X)) SA Literature.
Essays on principles crucial to continued recovery of sex addiction.

***Recovery from Death & Divorce.** 2010. audio compact disk (978-0-9826360-0-8(8)) Mid A Bks & Tapes.

Recovery from Schizophrenia. Richard Warner. 2 cass. 18.00 (OC147) Sound Horizons AV.

***Recovery Now TRAUMA: Self-Help Trauma Therapy.** Traumatology Institute. Created by Traumatology Institute. Prod. by Psych Ink Resources; Traumatology Institute. (Running Time: 105). (ENG.). 2010. 37.95 (978-0-615-40199-7(6)) PsychRes.

Recovery of Factory Wastes, Consumer Recycling & Military Bombing Debris. Hosted by Nancy Pearlman. 1 cass. (Running Time: 29 min.). 10.00 (903) Educ Comm CA.

Recovery of the Sacred, Pt. 1. Read by Richard J. Neuhaus. (139) ISI Books.

Recovery of the Sacred, Pt. 2. Read by Richard J. Neuhaus. 1 cass. 3.00 (140) ISI Books.
Includes discussion.

Recreated Human Spirit. Kenneth Copeland. 1 cass. 1983. 5.00 (978-0-88114-737-7(0)) K Copeland Pubns.
Biblical teaching on the human spirit.

Recreating the World: Feminist Art in the '80s. 1 cass. (Running Time: 30 min.). 9.95 (B0160B090, HarperThor) HarpC GBR.

Recreating Your Self. unabr. ed. Nancy J. Napier. Read by Nancy J. Napier. 8 cass. (Running Time: 8 hrs.). 1996. 89.95 (978-0-9658191-0-7(8)) Lotus Blossom.
Self-hypnosis guided visualizations & exercises.

Recreation. (205) Yoga Res Foun.

Recreation. Swami Jyotirmayananda. 1 cass. (Running Time: 1 hr.). 1990. 12.99 Yoga Res Foun.

Recreation & Leisure Modern Society. 6th ed. Richard Kraus. (C). 2001. audio compact disk 124.99 (978-0-7637-1791-9(6), 1791-6) Jones Bartlett.

Recreation in the Santa Monica Mountains & Rim of the Valley Corridor. Hosted by Nancy Pearlman. 1 cass. (Running Time: 28 min.). 10.00 (401) Educ Comm CA.

Recreational Boats & Equipment in Croatia: A Strategic Reference 2006. Compiled by Icon Group International, Inc. Staff. 2007. ring bd. 195.00 (978-0-497-35901-0(4)) Icon Grp.

Recreational Vehicles in France: A Strategic Reference 2006. Compiled by Icon Group International, Inc. Staff. 2007. ring bd. 195.00 (978-0-497-35957-7(X)) Icon Grp.

Recruit, Interview & Hire. PUEI. 2007. audio compact disk 199.00 (978-1-934147-12-2(5), CareerTrack) P Univ E Inc.

Recruit to Win. Dave Johnson. (Dave Johnson Educational Library). 65.00 D Johnson.
Shows how to get your recruit prospect to sell You on why You should let them into your business.

Recruiter, Pt. 1. Prod. by Big Sonny Entertainment Staff. (Running Time: 30 min.). 2004. audio compact disk 16.98 (978-5-559-49507-1(7)) Pub: Pt of Grace Ent. Dist(s): STL Dist NA

Recruiting & the Art of Control: How to Fill More Jobs in a Candidate-Driven Market. Read by Bill Radin. 6 CDs. (Running Time: 5 hours). 2002. audio compact disk 195.00 (978-1-929836-08-6(2)) Innovative Consulting.
Sales training and skill development for recruiters.

Recruiting & the Art of Control: How to Fill More Jobs in a Candidate-Driven Market. Bill Radin. Read by Bill Radin. 1 cass. (Running Time: 5 hrs.). 1997. wbk. ed. & vinyl bd. 195.00 (978-0-9626147-5-0(0)) Innovative Consulting.
Sales & performance improvement training for recruiters.

Recruiting in a Soft Economy: Seven Ways to Beat a Recession. Read by Bill Radin. 2001. audio compact disk 79.95 (978-1-929836-03-1(1)) Innovative Consulting.

Recruiting Local Government Executives: Practical Insights for Hiring Authorities & Candidates. David N. Ammons & James J. Glass. (Public Administration Ser.). 1989. bk. 48.00 (978-1-55542-190-8(3), Jossey-Bass) Wiley US.

Recruiting Starts with Sharing & Caring, Vol. 1. unabr. ed. Ilene L. Meckley. 1 cass. (Running Time: 55 min.). 1997. 12.00 (978-1-892464-01-9(2)) Meckley Pubng Co.
How to successfuly recruit for network marketing by sharing & caring.

Recruiting 101: Building A Big Network Fast. Randy Gage. (ENG.). 2004. audio compact disk 77.00 (978-0-9744363-4-0(8)) Prime Concepts Grp.

Recruiting 2000. Mark Sangerman. Read by Mark Sangerman. 6 cass. (Running Time: 6 hrs.). 1998. 79.00 (978-0-9676932-0-0(9)) M Sangerman.
Step by step instructions how to establish & sustain a profitable homebased recruiting (employment) business.

Rectal & Abdominal Approaches to Procidentia. 2 cass. (Colon & Rectal Surgery Ser.: C84-CR2). 1984. 15.00 (8429) Am Coll Surgeons.

Rectification, Pt. 1. Henry Niemann. 1 cass. 8.95 (254) Am Fed Astrologers.
Find the correct ASC-MC for recorded birthtimes.

Rectification, Pt. 2. Henry Niemann. 1 cass. 8.95 (255) Am Fed Astrologers.

Rectification of the Lyric see Twentieth-Century Poetry in English, No. 28, Recordings of Poets Reading Their Own Poetry

Rectification Success. Doe Koppana. 1 cass. 8.95 (203) Am Fed Astrologers.
Reagan's rectified chart with method.

Rectifications. Thomas Seers. Read by Thomas Seers. 1 cass. (Running Time: 90 min.). 1994. 8.95 (1133) Am Fed Astrologers.
Rectifying the horoscope (finding time of birth from events).

Rector of Justin: A Novel. unabr. ed. Louis Auchincloss. Read by Dan Lazar. 7 cass. (Running Time: 10 hrs. 30 mins.). 1976. 56.00 (978-0-7366-0039-2(6), 1050) Books on Tape.
The Rector of a New England Episcopal private school for boys, 80-year-old Dr. Frank Prescott, is seen through the eyes of those lives he has touched.

Rector's Wife. unabr. ed. Joanna Trollope. Read by Nadia May. 7 cass. (Running Time: 10 hrs.). 1995. 49.95 (978-0-7861-0768-1(5), 1617) Blckstn Audio.
For twenty years, Anna Bouverie has been the dutiful wife of a village rector, scraping by on his pitiful salary, making cakes for the church bake sales, ironing (badly) her husband's surplices, & clothing herself & her children in

parishioners' hand-me-downs. But when an expected promotion to archdeacon falls through, her husband retreats into bitterness. Anna, faced by isolation, the lost hope of a better life, & the bullying of her daughter at school, finally rebels. She takes a job in a supermarket, earning money, a sense of her own worth, the disapproval of the parish, & the icy fury of her husband. At the same time she is observed with passionate interest by three men, each of whom plays a role in the part-tragic, part-triumphant blossoming of her life.

Recuerda las reglas Audio CD: Emergent Set A. Benchmark Education Staff. Ed. by Katherine Scraper. (Early Explorers Ser.). (J). 2008. audio compact disk 10.00 (978-1-60437-245-8(1)) Benchmark Educ.

Recuperation, Tape 4. Robert A. Monroe. Read by Robert A. Monroe. 6 cass. (Emergency Ser.). 1983. 69.00 (978-1-56102-703-3(0)); Inter Indus.
Play during recuperation stages as often as possible.

Recycled. unabr. ed. Chief Little Summer et al. (Recycled). (YA). (gr. 6-12). 1999. audio compact disk 15.95 CD. (978-1-880440-16-2(4)) Piqua Pr.
Pets reincarnate several times throughout our life time.

Recycled Citizen. Charlotte MacLeod. 2001. 40.00 (978-0-7366-7051-7(3)) Books on Tape.
The Kelling family is planning a charity auction when dead bodies start showing up and the finger of suspicion points to them.

Recycled Metal Materials in China. Compiled by Icon Group International, Inc. Staff. 2007. ring bd. 195.00 (978-0-497-35891-4(3)) Icon Grp.

Recycled Plastics in China: A Strategic Reference 2006. Compiled by Icon Group International, Inc. Staff. 2007. ring bd. 195.00 (978-0-497-35892-1(1)) Icon Grp.

Recycling - Stories about Recycling. unabr. ed. Alfreda C. Doyle. Read by Alfreda C. Doyle. 1 cass. (Running Time: 30 min.). (J). 1996. ring bd. 9.95 (978-1-56820-156-6(7)) Story Time.
Stories that give ideas on recycling & how to recycle.

Recycling Dialogue. Alfreda C. Doyle. Read by Sell Out Recordings Staff. 1 cass. (Running Time: 1 hr.). 1991. 25.00 (S.O.R. 4004) Sell Out Recordings.
Where to find or locate recyclables, business recycling & other possibilities.

Recycling Equipment in Bulgaria: A Strategic Reference 2007. Compiled by Icon Group International, Inc. Staff. 2007. ring bd. 195.00 (978-0-497-35849-5(2)) Icon Grp.

Recycling Equipment in Finland: A Strategic Reference 2006. Compiled by Icon Group International, Inc. Staff. 2007. ring bd. 195.00 (978-0-497-35939-3(1)) Icon Grp.

Recycling Equipment in Germany: A Strategic Reference 2006. Compiled by Icon Group International, Inc. Staff. 2007. ring bd. 195.00 (978-0-497-35984-3(7)) Icon Grp.

Recycling Household & Business Waste. Hosted by Nancy Pearlman. 1 cass. (Running Time: 27 min.). 10.00 (406) Educ Comm CA.

***Red.** Jack Ketchum. (Running Time: 7 mins.). 2009. 19.95 (978-1-897331-25-5(8), AudioRealms); audio compact disk 31.95 (978-1-897304-69-3(2), AudioRealms) Dorch Pub Co.

Red: A Baseball Life. Red Schoendienst. Narrated by Bob Carpenter. (Running Time: 3 hrs.). 1998. 19.95 (978-1-57167-240-7(0)) Pub: Sports Pub. Dist(s): IngramPubServ
The life story of St. Louis Cardinals Hall of Famer Red Schoendienst.

Red: A Baseball Life. Red Schoendienst. Read by Bob Carpenter. 1 cass. 1998. 19.95 Sports Pub.
The life story of a St. Louis Cardinals Hall of Famer.

Red: The Heroic Rescue. Ted Dekker. Read by Rob Lamont. 8 cass. (Running Time: 12 hrs.). (Books of History Chronicles: Bk. 2). 32.99 (978-1-58926-597-4(1), Oasis Kids) Oasis Audio.

Red: The Heroic Rescue. unabr. ed. Ted Dekker. Read by Rob Lamont. 12 CDs. (Running Time: 14 hrs.). (Books of History Chronicles: Bk. 2). 2004. audio compact disk 96.00 (978-0-7861-8486-6(8), 3334) Blckstn Audio.

Red: The Heroic Rescue. unabr. ed. Ted Dekker. Narrated by Rob Lamont. (Books of History Chronicles: Bk. 2). (ENG.). 2004. 25.19 (978-1-60814-353-5(8)); audio compact disk 35.99 (978-1-58926-599-8(8), Oasis Kids) Oasis Audio.

***Red & Me.** unabr. ed. Bill Russell. Read by Peter Jay Fernandez. (ENG.). 2009. (978-0-06-190100-3(8), Harper Audio); (978-0-06-190101-0(6), Harper Audio) HarperCollins Pubs.

Red & Me: My Coach, My Lifelong Friend. Bill Russell. Read by Peter Jay Fernandez. Told to Alan Steinberg. (Playaway Adult Nonfiction Ser.). (ENG.). 2009. 59.99 (978-1-60847-928-3(5)) Find a World.

Red & Me: My Coach, My Lifelong Friend. abr. unabr. ed. Bill Russell. Read by Peter Jay Fernandez. 2009. audio compact disk 29.99 (978-0-06-177890-2(7), Harper Audio) HarperCollins Pubs.

Red & Red. unabr. ed. Carol Ann Nelson. Perf. by R C F Kids Staff. Illus. by Costain. 1 cass. (Running Time: 24 mins.). (J). (ps-k). 1998. 7.00 (978-1-893886-01-8(8)) Harmonic Computing.
Ten songs that sing text called Red & Red & song activities to ask questions about book text. Highlights over 30 foundation skills for preschoolers from social, language, reading & math. Side A, vocals & instrumentals. Side B, instrumentals only.

Red & the Black. Stendhal. Read by Fabio Camero. (Running Time: 3 hrs.). 2002. 16.95 (978-1-60083-195-9(8), Audiofy Corp) Iofy Corp.

Red & the Black. abr. ed. Stendhal. 3 CDs. (Running Time: 4 Hrs. 30 Mins.). 2004. audio compact disk 9.99 (978-1-57050-047-3(9)) Multilingua.

***Red & the Black.** unabr. ed. Stendhal. Read by David Case. (Running Time: 18 hrs. 30 mins.). 2010. 44.95 (978-1-4332-1993-1(X)); 95.95 (978-1-4332-1989-4(1)); audio compact disk 123.00 (978-1-4332-1990-0(5)) Blckstn Audio.

Red & the Black: A Chronicle of 1830. unabr. ed. Stendhal. Narrated by Davina Porter. 15 cass. (Running Time: 20 hrs.). 1988. 120.00 (978-1-55690-436-3(3), 88900E7) Recorded Bks.
Julien Sorel is the handsome young tutor to the mayor's children, penniless but driven by ambition. Madame de Renal, 30, is a tender, virtuous & loyal wife with the nature of an angel. Between them a passion plunges them from the heights to the depths.

Red & the Black: A Chronicle of 1830. unabr. collector's ed. Stendhal. Read by David Case. 13 cass. (Running Time: 19 hrs. 30 mins.). 1990. 104.00 (978-0-7366-1813-7(9), 2649) Books on Tape.
In December of 1827, Marie Henri Beyle read an account of the trial of a man charged with attempted murder. With this as inspiration, Beyle - under the pen name of Stendhal - set about writing one of the great psychological novels of all time. Set in a provincial French town, & in Paris, it is the story of Julien Sorel, a handsome young tutor who is both hero & villain. Cold, opportunistic, he seeks to fulfill his lust for power & wealth, uncompromising even with his influential mistress. Yet he is victimized by his own romantic soul & by the military & strong religious forces.

Red Arc: A Call for Liberacion Con Salsa y Cool. Raul Salinas & Fred Ho. Perf. by Raul Salinas. 1. (ENG.). 2005. audio compact disk 16.00 (978-0-916727-19-2(X)) Pub: Wings Pr. Dist(s): IPG Chicago
What we have here is a poetic fusion that defies categorization: It is Zen, but it is angry; it is Indian and Chicano, but its rhythms are those of Charlie Parker and Thelonius Monk; it is regional in its setting and imagery, hemispheric in its vision. In short, it is raúlrsalinas ? one long enjambed bop calling for liberación con salsa y cool. Salinas performs his poems to the accompaniment of Fred Ho's jazz baritone sax.

***Red Bade of Courage: Bring the Classics to Life.** adpt. ed. Stephen Crane. (Bring the Classics to Life Ser.). 2008. pap. bk. 21.95 (978-1-55576-502-6(5)) EDCON Pubng.

Red Badge of Courage. Stephen Crane. Read by Michael Kramer. 4 cass. (Running Time: 5 hrs. 30 min.). 1995. 19.95 (978-1-55685-357-9(2)) Audio Bk Con.
A stunning study of a young man's psychological reactions to combat. This is a realistic picture of a youth's emotional journey from greenhorn to bloodied veteran of the American Civil War.

Red Badge of Courage. Stephen Crane. Narrated by Michael Kramer. (ENG.). 2008. audio compact disk 24.95 (978-1-60646-061-0(7)) Audio Bk Con.

Red Badge of Courage. Stephen Crane. 4 cass. (Running Time: 6 hrs.). 2002. 32.00 (978-0-7366-8623-5(1)) Books on Tape.
A Union soldier deserts his regiment in battle, and must clear his conscience through valor.

Red Badge of Courage. Stephen Crane. (Reading & Training, Elementary Ser.). (J). (gr. 4-7). 2005. pap. bk. 21.95 (978-88-7754-907-5(6)) Cideb ITA.

Red Badge of Courage. Stephen Crane. 2 cass. (Running Time: 3 hrs.). 19.95 set. (8112Q) Filmic Archives.
This is an American classic & one of the first realistic treatments of modern warfare. Set against the background of the Civil War, a young Union solider learns the meaning of cowardice & true heroism. A stunning psychological portrait.

Red Badge of Courage. Stephen Crane. (ENG.). 2008. audio compact disk 9.95 (978-1-60245-180-3(X)) GDL Multimedia.

Red Badge of Courage. Stephen Crane. Read by Sean Pratt. (Running Time: 5 hrs.). 2002. 22.95 (978-1-59912-108-6(5), Audiofy Corp) Iofy Corp.

Red Badge of Courage. Stephen Crane. Read by Walter Lewis. 4 cass. (Running Time: 5 hrs. 15 mins.). 2000. 22.98 (978-962-634-708-9(2), NA420814); audio compact disk 26.98 (978-962-634-208-4(0), NA420812, Naxos AudioBooks) Naxos.
Tired of farm life, Henry Fleming seeks excitement & the thrill of battle during the Civil War. The young union soldier's illusions are soon brutally shattered.

Red Badge of Courage. Stephen Crane. 1 cass. (Running Time: 1 hr.). (Radiobook Ser.). 1987. 4.98 (978-0-929541-23-5(5)) Radiola Co.

Red Badge of Courage. Stephen Crane. Read by Sean Pratt. (Running Time: 17820 sec.). (Unabridged Classics in MP3 Ser.). (ENG.). 2008. audio compact disk 24.00 (978-1-58472-552-7(4), In Aud) Sound Room.

Red Badge of Courage. Stephen Crane & John Matern. Ed. by Jerry Stemach et al. Illus. by Jack Nichols. Contrib. by Ed Smaron & Ted S. Hasselbring. (Start-to-Finish Books: Vol. 2). 2000. 35.00 (978-1-58702-432-0(2)) D Johnston Inc.

Red Badge of Courage. Retold by John Matern. Stephen Crane. (Classic Adventures Ser.). 1999. audio compact disk 18.95 (978-1-4105-0132-5(9)) D Johnston Inc.

Red Badge of Courage. Narrated by Mike Vendetti. (ENG.). 2009. audio compact disk 9.99 (978-1-934814-08-6(3)) Red Planet Au.

Red Badge of Courage. abr. ed. Stephen Crane. Read by Walter Lewis. (Running Time: 18961 sec.). 2006. audio compact disk 28.98 (978-962-634-391-3(5), Naxos AudioBooks) Naxos.

Red Badge of Courage. abr. ed. Stephen Crane. Read by Richard Thomas. 2 cass. (Running Time: 3 hrs.). 2004. 18.00 (978-1-59007-133-5(6)) Pub: New Millenn Enter. Dist(s): PerseuPGW
The experiences of Henry Fleming, a soldier in the Civil War, restores words and phrases omitted in the 1895 publication by D. Appleton of New York. The missing Chapter XII is also restored. "In an essay, 'The Red Badge of Courage Nobody Knows,' included in the volume, Binder describes his editorial procedures and discusses the 'new novel' that is the result. He provides an introduction and textual notes.

Red Badge of Courage. abr. adpt. ed. Stephen Crane. (Bring the Classics to Life: Level 3 Ser.). 2008. audio compact disk 12.95 (978-1-55576-447-0(9)) EDCON Pubng.

Red Badge of Courage. unabr. ed. Stephen Crane. Read by Robert Ryan. 4 cass. (Running Time: 6 hrs.). 23.80 (E-419) Audio Bk.
Novel of an individual soldier's stress during the civil war.

Red Badge of Courage. unabr. ed. Stephen Crane. Read by Anthony Heald. (Running Time: 5 hrs. 0 mins.). 2008. 29.95 (978-1-4332-1504-9(7)); 34.95 (978-1-4332-1502-5(0)); audio compact disk 40.00 (978-1-4332-1503-2(9)) Blckstn Audio.

Red Badge of Courage. unabr. ed. Stephen Crane. Read by Gene Engene. 3 cass. (Running Time: 4 hrs. 15 min.). 21.95 (978-1-55686-111-6(7), 111) Books in Motion.
A raw recruit experiences unexpected emotions when thrown into the ferocity and horror of battle.

Red Badge of Courage. unabr. ed. Stephen Crane. 5 CDs. (Running Time: 6 hrs.). 2002. audio compact disk 40.00 (978-0-7366-8690-7(8)) Books on Tape.

Red Badge of Courage. unabr. ed. Stephen Crane. Read by Roger Dressler. 4 CDs. (Running Time: 5 hrs.). (Classic Collection). 2001. audio compact disk 29.95 (978-1-58788-606-5(5), 1587886065, CD Unabridged); audio compact disk 69.25 (978-1-58788-607-2(3), 1587886073, CD Unabrid Lib Ed) Brilliance Audio.
Bored with farm life, and anxious for some excitement, Henry Fleming sets off to join the Union troops fighting the Civil War. An inexperienced fighter, he is anxious to get into battle to prove his patriotism and courage. He swaggers to keep up his spirits waiting for battle, but when suddenly thrust into the slaughter he is overcome with blind fear and runs from the field of battle. He is ashamed when he joins the wounded, for he has not earned their "red badge of courage" and becomes enraged when he witnesses the death of his terribly maimed friend. In a confused struggle with his own army's retreating soldiers, he is wounded but not by enemy gunfire. In an effort to redeem himself in his own eyes, he begins to fight frantically and, in the heat of battle, automatically seizes the regiment's colors in a daring charge that proves him truly courageous. The unnamed battle in the novel has been identified as that as Chancellorsville. While considered one of the most compelling stories of warfare of all time, Stephen Crane had never seen a battle when he wrote The Red Badge of Courage in 1895.

Red Badge of Courage. unabr. ed. Stephen Crane. Read by Roger Dressler. 4 cass. (Running Time: 5 hrs.). 2002. 19.95 (978-1-59086-296-4(1), 1590862961, BAU) Brilliance Audio.

Red Badge of Courage. unabr. ed. Stephen Crane. Read by Roger Dressler. (Running Time: 5 hrs.). 2004. 39.25 (978-1-59335-338-4(3), 1593353383, Brlnc Audio MP3 Lib) Brilliance Audio.

Red Badge of Courage. unabr. ed. Stephen Crane. Read by Roger Dressler. (Running Time: 5 hrs.). 2004. 39.25 (978-1-59710-626-9(7), 1597106267, BADLE); 24.95 (978-1-59710-627-6(5), 1597106275, BAD) Brilliance Audio.

Red Badge of Courage. unabr. ed. Stephen Crane. Read by Sean Pratt. (YA). 2006. 49.99 (978-1-59895-178-3(5)) Find a World.

Red Badge of Courage. unabr. ed. Stephen Crane. Read by Robert L. Halvorson. 4 cass. (Running Time: 6 hrs.). (J). 28.95 (55) Halvorson Assocs.

Red Badge of Courage. unabr. ed. Stephen Crane. Read by Jim Killavey & Jim Roberts. 4 cass. (Running Time: 5 hrs.). 1980. 24.00 incl. album. (C-15) Jimcin Record.
Crane's famous story of war & interior struggle.

Red Badge of Courage, unabr. ed. Stephen Crane. Narrated by Frank Muller. 3 cass. (Running Time: 4 hrs. 30 mins.). 1981. 26.00 (978-1-55690-437-0(1), 81240E7) Recorded Bks.
A young man's trial by fire in the greatest fictional re-creation of America's Civil War.

Red Badge of Courage. unabr. ed. Stephen Crane. Read by Roger Dressler. (Running Time: 5 hrs.). 2004. 24.95 (978-1-59335-022-2(8), 1593350228) Soulmate Audio Bks.
Bored with farm life, and anxious for some excitement, Henry Fleming sets off to join the Union troops fighting the Civil War. An inexperienced fighter, he is anxious to get into battle to prove his patriotism and courage. He swaggers to keep up his spirits waiting for battle, but when suddenly thrust into the slaughter he is overcome with blind fear and runs from the field of battle. He is ashamed when he joins the wounded, for he has not earned their "red badge of courage" and becomes enraged when he witnesses the death of his terribly maimed friend. In a confused struggle with his own army's retreating soldiers, he is wounded but not by enemy gunfire. In an effort to redeem himself in his own eyes, he begins to fight frantically and, in the heat of battle, automatically seizes the regiment's colors in a daring charge that proves him truly courageous. The unnamed battle in the novel has been identified as that as Chancellorsville. While considered one of the most compelling stories of warfare of all time, Stephen Crane had never seen a battle when he wrote The Red Badge of Courage in 1895.

Red Badge of Courage. unabr. ed. Stephen Crane. Read by Sky Vogel. 5 cds. (Running Time: 4 hrs 56 mins). (YA). 2002. pap. bk. (978-1-58472-313-4(0), In Aud) Sound Room.
A powerful portrayal of the reality of war.

Red Badge of Courage. unabr. ed. Stephen Crane. Read by Sky Vogel. 5 cds. (Running Time: 4 hrs 57 mins). (YA). 2002. audio compact disk 29.95 (978-1-58472-311-0(4), 078, In Aud) Pub: Sound Room. Dist(s): Baker Taylor

Red Badge of Courage. unabr. ed. Stephen Crane. Read by Sky Vogel. 1 cd. (Running Time: 4 hrs 57 mins). (YA). 2002. audio compact disk 18.95 (978-1-58472-395-0(5), In Aud) Pub: Sound Room. Dist(s): Baker Taylor
MP3 format.

Red Badge of Courage. unabr. ed. Stephen Crane. Narrated by William Dufris. (Running Time: 5 hrs. 0 mins. 0 sec.). (Tantor Unabridged Classics Ser.). (ENG.). 2008. audio compact disk 19.99 (978-1-4001-1038-4(6)); audio compact disk 19.99 (978-1-4001-6038-9(3)); audio compact disk 39.99 (978-1-4001-4038-1(2)) Pub: Tantor Media. Dist(s): IngramPubServ

Red Badge of Courage. unabr. ed. Stephen Crane & John Matern. Ed. by Jerry Stemach et al. Illus. by Jack Nichols. Contrib. by Ted S. Hasselbring. 1 cass. (Running Time: 1 hr.). (Start-to-Finish Books: Vol. 1). 2000. 7.00 (978-1-893376-10-6(9), F05) D Johnston Inc.
The realistic Civil War novel probes the mind of a youth named Henry in his first few days of battle. A Union infantryman, Henry rides a roller coaster of doubt, exhilaration, terror, and other emotions. Fleering in panic from a skirmish that his regiment was winning, Henry wanders among the dead and dying with their "red badges of courage".

Red Badge of Courage, Set. unabr. ed. Stephen Crane. Read by Pat Bottino. 4 cass. 1999. 32.95 (FS9-51108) Highsmith.

Red Badge of Courage: Abridged. (ENG.). 2007. (978-1-60339-035-4(9)); cd-rom & audio compact disk (978-1-60339-036-1(7)) Listenr Digest.

Red Badge of Courage: An Episode of the American Civil War. Stephen Crane. audio compact disk (978-1-4025-2332-8(7)) Recorded Bks.

Red Badge of Courage: Classic Collection. unabr. ed. Stephen Crane. (Running Time: 6 hrs. 0 mins.). 2008. audio compact disk 19.95 (978-1-4332-1505-6(5)) Blckstn Audio.

Red Badge of Courage: The Hero as Myth & Symbol. John E. Hart. 1 cass. (Running Time: 28 min.). 1968. 11.95 (23042) J Norton Pubs.
A study of the mythical pattern of heroic achievement as seen in this classic work.

Red Badge of Courage & Other Stories. unabr. ed. Stephen Crane. Read by Jack Dahlby. 6 cass. (Running Time: 9 hrs.). (J). (gr. 1-8). 1999. 40.00 (LL 0033, Chivers Child Audio) AudioGO.

Red Badge of Courage & Other Stories. unabr. ed. Stephen Crane. Read by Jack Dahlby. 6 cass. (Running Time: 6 hrs. 39 min.). Incl. Bride Comes to Yellow Sky. 1976. (CXL 523CX); Mystery of Heroism. 1976. (CXL 523CX); Open Boat. 1976. (CXL 523CX); 1976. 44.98 (978-0-8072-2998-9(9), CXL 523CX, Listening Lib) Random Audio Pubg.
Henry Fleming, the young Union soldier in "The Red Badge of Courage", has his romantic illusions about war too brutally shattered by the reality of war's confusion, bloodshed, & the horrors it unleashes. This story & the other three included in this collection are some of the most skillfully crafted stories in the English language.

Red Badge of Courage & Other Stories. unabr. collector's ed. Stephen Crane. Read by Michael Prichard. 8 cass. (Running Time: 8 hrs.). Incl. Blue Hotel. 1984. (1108); Bride Comes to Yellow Sky. 1984. (1108); Open Boat. 1984. (1108); (J). 1978. 48.00 (978-0-7366-0100-9(7), 1108) Books on Tape.
The setting is the Civil War, the hero is Henry Flemming, who, swept up in the current of events, joins the Union Army. He plunges heedlessly into battle, at first loses his courage, then later regains it for the crucial confrontation. One of the most realistic war stories ever written & a striking depiction of how soldiers behave under fire.

Red Badge of Courage & Other Stories, Set. unabr. ed. Stephen Crane. Read by Jack Dahlby. 6 cass. 1999. 44.98 (LL 0033) AudioGO.

Red Barber: Play-by-Play Pioneer. janell hughes. (ENG.). 2009. audio compact disk 16.00 (978-0-9818365-5-3(0)) Baseball Voice.

Red Bat at Sleep Hollow Lane. Janet Halfmann. Illus. by Daniel Stegos. (ENG.). (J). (ps-2). 2005. 8.95 (978-1-59249-344-9(0), SC5027) Soundprints.

***Red Blade East: Gonji V1.** T. C. Rypel. (Running Time: 9 mins.). 2009. 19.95 (978-1-897331-15-6(0), AudioRealms) Dorch Pub Co.

Red Blade from the East. T. C. Rypel. (Running Time: 9 mins.). 2009. audio compact disk 34.95 (978-1-897304-54-9(4)) Dorch Pub Co.

Red Blazer Girls. unabr. ed. Michael D. Beil. Read by Tai Alexandra Ricci. (ENG.). (J). (gr. 3). 2009. audio compact disk 34.00 (978-0-7393-7958-5(5), Listening Lib) Pub: Random Audio Pubg. Dist(s): Random

Red Blazer Girls: The Vanishing Violin. unabr. ed. Michael D. Beil. Read by Tai Alexandra Ricci. (J). 2010. 34.00 (978-0-307-71052-9(1), Listening Lib) Pub: Random Audio Pubg. Dist(s): Random

***Red Blazer Girls: the Mistaken Masterpiece.** unabr. ed. Michael D. Beil. (ENG.). (J). 2011. audio compact disk 37.00 (978-0-307-91579-5(4), Listening Lib) Pub: Random Audio Pubg. Dist(s): Random

Red Box. unabr. ed. Rex Stout. Read by Michael Prichard. 6 cass. (Running Time: 8 hrs.). (Nero Wolfe Ser.). 2004. 29.95 (978-1-57270-053-6(X), N61053u) Pub: Audio Partners. Dist(s): PerseuPGW
Archie tells the story of a beautiful model's untimely death from a chocolate candy, which leads to the supreme insult of Nero Wolfe's career. When another murder occurs in his own home, he must solve the case to save his pride.

Red Box. unabr. ed. Rex Stout. Narrated by Michael Prichard. (Running Time: 28800 sec.). (Nero Wolfe Ser.). (ENG.). 2008. audio compact disk 29.95 (978-1-60283-350-0(8)) Pub: AudioGO. Dist(s): Perseus Dist

Red Box. unabr. collector's ed. Rex Stout. Read by Michael Prichard. 6 cass. (Running Time: 9 hrs.). (Nero Wolfe Ser.). 1994. 48.00 (978-0-7366-2697-2(2), 3431) Books on Tape.
Lovely woman turns up dead. Before anyone else does, Nero Wolfe must solve the mystery of a box of cyanide-laced candy.

Red Calvary see Konaya Armiya

Red Cap. unabr. ed. Philip McCutchan. 8 cass. (Commander Shaw Ser.). (J). 1998. 69.95 (978-1-872672-41-0(8)) Pub: Mgna Lrg Print GBR. Dist(s): Ulverscroft US

Red Cap. unabr. ed. G. Clifton Wisler. Read by Johnny Heller. 3 cass. (Running Time: 4 hrs. 30 mins.). (YA). 1999. 98.70 (978-0-7887-3630-8(2), 46985) Recorded Bks.
When 13-year-old Ransom Powell hears a Union division needs a drummer, he lies about his age & enlists. Soon he discovers the Civil War is more horrible than exciting. And when his regiment is captured & taken to a Confederate prison ravaged by disease, he wonders if he will ever see home again.

Red Cap, unabr. ed. G. Clifton Wisler. Narrated by Johnny Heller. 3 pieces. (Running Time: 4 hrs. 30 mins.). (gr. 7 up). 2000. 28.00 (978-0-7887-3531-8(4), 95920E7a) Recorded Bks.

Red Cap, unabr. ed. G. Clifton Wisler. Read by Johnny Heller. 3 cass. (Running Time: 4 hrs. 30 mins.). (YA). 2000. pap. bk. & stu. ed. 41.24 (978-0-7887-3629-2(9), 41018X4) Recorded Bks.

Red Carpet see Alfombra Roja

Red Carpet. 2004. bk. 24.95 (978-1-56008-228-6(3)); 8.95 (978-1-56008-318-4(2)); cass. & flmstrp 30.00 (978-1-56008-756-4(0)) Weston Woods.

Red Carpets & Other Banana Skins: The Autobiography. abr. ed. Rupert Everett. (Running Time: 4 hrs. 30 mins.). (ENG.). 2007. 14.98 (978-1-59483-622-0(1)) Pub: Hachet Audio. Dist(s): HachBkGrp

Red Carpets & Other Banana Skins: The Autobiography. abr. ed. Rupert Everett. (Running Time: 4 hrs. 30 mins.). (ENG.). 2009. 44.98 (978-1-60788-294-7(9)) Pub: Hachet Audio. Dist(s): HachBkGrp

Red Cell. Richard Marcinko. Based on a work by John Weisman. (Rogue Warrior Ser.: Bk. 2). 2004. 10.95 (978-0-7435-4589-1(3)) Pub: S&S Audio. Dist(s): S and S Inc

Red Chameleon. unabr. ed. Stuart M. Kaminsky. Narrated by Mark Hammer. 6 cass. (Running Time: 8 hrs. 45 mins.). (Inspector Porfiry Rostnikov Mystery Ser.: No. 3). 1992. 51.00 (978-1-55690-725-8(7), 92107E7) Recorded Bks.
Inspector Rostinikovof of the Moscow police investigates a bloody murder.

Red Chief. unabr. ed. Ion L. Idriess. Read by James Condon. 9 cass. (Running Time: 13 hrs. 30 mins.). 2001. (978-1-86442-319-8(6), 581156) Bolinda Pubng AUS.
The true story of the young warrior Red Kangaroo, who became chief of his tribe - the revered & powerful Red Chief of the Gunne-dah district. A tale handed down from generation by generation & given by the last survivor, "King" Bungaree, to the white settlers of the district.

***Red Chief.** unabr. ed. Ion L. Idriess. Read by James Condon. (Running Time: 10 hrs.). 2010. audio compact disk 87.95 (978-1-74214-674-4(0), 9781742146744) Pub: Bolinda Pubng AUS. Dist(s): Bolinda Pub Inc

Red Circle: A Sherlock Holmes Adventure. (ENG.). 2007. (978-1-60339-069-9(3)); cd-rom & audio compact disk (978-1-60339-070-5(7)) Listenr Digest.

Red Cross: Early Explorers Fluent Set B Audio CD. Mary Clare Goller. Adapted by Benchmark Education Staff. (J). 2007. audio compact disk 10.00 (978-1-4108-8249-3(7)) Benchmark Educ.

Red Crystal. Clare Francis. 2 cass. (Running Time: 3 hrs.). (ENG., 2001. (978-0-333-90345-2(5)) Macmillan UK GBR.

Red Crystal. unabr. ed. Clare Francis. Read by Steven Pacey. 12 cass. (Running Time: 18 hrs.). 2000. 79.95 (978-0-7451-6619-3(9), CAB 1235) Pub: Chivers Audio Bks GBR. Dist(s): AudioGO
It's the 1960's and the most sinister of terrorist groups is born. Secretly funded by Moscow and trained in Italy, the crystal Faction came to England to wage war. For Nick Ryder of Special Branch, infiltrating the cell presented a daunting challenge. But he is soon drawn into a tangled web of sex, drugs and murder. At the center is Gabriele Schroeder, leader of the Crystal Faction, a ruthless woman for whom killing has become a pleasure.

Red Death: Featuring an Original Easy Rawlins Short Story Silver Lining. unabr. ed. Walter Mosley. Read by Stanley Bennett Clay. 6 cass. (Running Time: 9 hrs.). (Easy Rawlins Mystery Ser.). 1994. 48.00 (978-0-7366-2833-4(9), 3541) Books on Tape.
It's L.A., early 1950s. Easy Rawlins, a black P.I., wants the LAPD off his back. That's simple, compared to his love life!.

Red Detachment of Women. Chi-Yu Ho. 1 cass. 7.95 incl. script. (978-0-88710-150-2(X)) Yale Far Eastern Pubns.

Red Dog. Rudyard Kipling. 1 cass. 1989. 8.95 (S-79) Jimcin Record.
Mowgli's greatest challenge.

***Red Dog: A Story from the Jungle Books.** Rudyard Kipling. 2009. (978-1-60136-511-8(X)) Audio Holding.

***Red Door.** unabr. ed. Charles Todd. Narrated by Simon Prebble. 9 CDs. (Running Time: 10 hrs. 45 mins.). (Inspector Ian Rutledge Mystery Ser.: Bk. 12). 2010. audio compact disk 94.95 (978-0-7927-6867-8(1)) AudioGO.

***Red Door: An Inspector Ian Rutledge Mystery.** Charles Todd. Narrated by Simon Prebble. (Running Time: 10 hrs. 45 mins. 0 sec.). (ENG.). 2011. audio compact disk 29.95 (978-1-60998-160-0(X)) Pub: AudioGO. Dist(s): Perseus Dist

Red Door Sessions: Chloe Brisson. Chloe Brisson. (ENG.). 2008. 14.99 (978-1-892424-31-0(2)) abba dabba prods.

Red Dragon. abr. ed. Thomas Harris. 2004. 10.95 (978-0-7435-4577-8(X)) Pub: S&S Audio. Dist(s): S and S Inc

Red Dragon. unabr. ed. Thomas Harris. Read by Alan Sklar. 10 vols. (Running Time: 15 hrs.). 2002. bk. 84.95 (978-0-7927-2532-9(8), CSL 421, Chivers Sound Lib) AudioGO.
Exploring both the nature of human evil and the nerveracking anatomy of a forensic investigation. A frightening vision of the dark side of our well-lighted world. Introduced again, Dr. Hannibal Lecter and Will Graham, the FBI man who hunted Lecter down, risks his sanity and his life to a dual killer called the Red Dragon.

Red Egg & Ginger. (Greetings Ser.: Vol. 1). (gr. 2-3). 10.00 (978-0-7635-5864-2(8)) Rigby Educ.

Red Flags & Referrals: Gaming Employee Training on Problem Gambling. Elizabeth M. George & Lorraine D. Grymala. 1998. ring bd. 3999.00 (978-1-930467-10-1(9)) N AM MN Coun Gambling.

***Red Garden.** unabr. ed. Alice Hoffman. Read by Nancy Travis. (Running Time: 8 hrs. 30 mins.). (ENG.). 2011. audio compact disk 35.00 (978-0-307-87775-8(2), Random AudioBks) Pub: Random Audio Pubg. Dist(s): Random

***Red Glass.** unabr. ed. Laura Resau. Read by Emma Bering. 7 CDs. (Running Time: 7 hrs. 56 mins.). (YA). (gr. 7-10). 2009. audio compact disk 50.00 (978-0-7393-7978-3(X), Listening Lib) Pub: Random Audio Pubg. Dist(s): Random

Red Glass. unabr. ed. Laura Resau. (ENG.). (J). (gr. 5). 2009. audio compact disk 45.00 (978-0-7393-7976-9(3), Listening Lib) Pub: Random Audio Pubg. Dist(s): Random

***Red Glove.** unabr. ed. Holly Black. (Curse Workers Ser.: Bk. 2). (J). 2011. audio compact disk 40.00 (978-0-307-71185-4(4), Listening Lib) Pub: Random Audio Pubg. Dist(s): Random

Red Gold. Alan Furst. Read by Richard Matthews. 2002. 40.00 (978-0-7366-8925-0(7)) Books on Tape.

Red Grammer's Favorite Sing Along Songs. Perf. by Red Grammer. 1 cass. (J). (ps-6). 1993. 10.00 (978-1-886146-04-4(7)); audio compact disk 15.00 CD. (978-1-886146-09-9(8)) Red Note Recs.

Red-Haired Brat. Joanna Dessau. Read by Anna Bentinck. 8 cass. (Running Time: 10 hrs.). (Soundings Ser.). (J). 2004. 69.95 (978-1-84283-746-7(X)) Pub: ISIS Lrg Prnt GBR. Dist(s): Ulverscroft US

Red Harvest. unabr. ed. Dashiell Hammett. Read by Michael Prichard. 7 cass. (Running Time: 7 hrs.). 1996. 42.00 (978-0-7366-3442-7(8), 4086) Books on Tape.

Red Harvest. unabr. ed. Dashiell Hammett. Read by William Dufris. 6 cass. (Running Time: 9 hrs.). (Isis Ser.). (J). 1994. 54.95 (978-1-85695-707-6(1), 940903) Pub: ISIS Lrg Prnt GBR. Dist(s): Ulverscroft US

Red Harvest. unabr. ed. Dashiell Hammett. Read by William Dufris. 6 CDs. (Running Time: 6 hrs. 45 min.). (Isis Ser.). (J). 2000. audio compact disk 64.95 (978-0-7531-0705-8(8), 107058) Pub: ISIS Lrg Prnt GBR. Dist(s): Ulverscroft US

Red Hat: Adventure Tales for Young Listeners. Katie Green. 1 CD. (Running Time: 67 min.). (J). 2003. audio compact disk 15.00 (978-0-9722032-1-0(4)) Oak Stars.
Parents? Choice Recommended Award, 2003; Parents? Guide to Children?s Media Award, 2003; Children?s Music Web Award Winner 2003.The Red Hat: Adventure Tales for Young Listeners and Their Friends is a collections of stories, with songs and activities for children ages 4 to 9. Katie Green is a speech /language pathologist, educator, and National Storytelling Association Award winner (1998). On this recording, she combines her interests and talents. It includes seven stories, many of which include environmental sounds and special effects that are further enhanced when listened to with earphones or well separated speakers.

Red Hat Club Rides Again. Haywood Smith. Read by Cynthia Darlow. 2005. 20.95 (978-1-59397-663-7(1)) Pub: Macmill Audio. Dist(s): Macmillan

Red Hat Club Rides Again. abr. ed. Haywood Smith. Read by Cynthia Darlow. 2005. 14.95 (978-1-59397-662-0(3)) Pub: Macmill Audio. Dist(s): Macmillan

Red Hat Club Rides Again. unabr. ed. Haywood Smith. 2005. 29.95 (978-0-7927-3518-2(8), CMP 772); 54.95 (978-0-7927-3516-8(1), CSL 772); audio compact disk 79.95 (978-0-7927-3517-5(X), SLD 772) AudioGO.

Red Hat Society (TM) Fun & Friendship after Fifty. abr. ed. Sue Ellen Cooper. (ENG.). 2005. 14.98 (978-1-59483-164-5(5)) Pub: Hachet Audio. Dist(s): HachBkGrp

Red Hat Society(TM) Fun & Friendship after Fifty. abr. ed. Sue Ellen Cooper. (Running Time: 3 hrs.). (ENG.). 2009. 29.98 (978-1-60788-038-7(5)) Pub: Hachet Audio. Dist(s): HachBkGrp

Red-Headed League see Adventures of Sherlock Holmes

Red-Headed League see Classic Detective Stories, Vol. II, A Collection

Red-Headed League see Adventures of Sherlock Holmes

Red-Headed League see Sherlock Holmes: Selected Stories

Red-Headed League see Selections from the Adventures of Sherlock Holmes

Red-Headed League. unabr. ed. Arthur Conan Doyle. 1 cass. (Running Time: 67 min.). (Creative Short Story Audio Library Ser.). (YA). (gr. 7-12). 1995. 11.00 (978-0-8072-6109-5(2), CS903CX, Listening Lib) Random Audio Pubg.

***Red-Headed Stepchild.** unabr. ed. Jaye Wells. Narrated by Cynthia Holloway. (Running Time: 9 hrs. 0 mins. 0 sec.). (Sabina Kane Ser.). (ENG.). 2010. 24.99 (978-1-4001-6902-3(X)); audio compact disk 34.99 (978-1-4001-1902-8(2)) Pub: Tantor Media. Dist(s): IngramPubServ

***Red-Headed Stepchild.** unabr. ed. Jaye Wells. Narrated by Cynthia Holloway. (Running Time: 9 hrs. 30 mins.). (Sabina Kane Ser.). 2010. 16.99 (978-1-4001-8902-1(0)) Tantor Media.

***Red-Headed Stepchild (Library Edition)** unabr. ed. Jaye Wells. Narrated by Cynthia Holloway. (Running Time: 9 hrs. 0 mins. 0 sec.). (Sabina Kane Ser.). (ENG.). 2010. audio compact disk 83.99 (978-1-4001-4902-5(9)) Pub: Tantor Media. Dist(s): IngramPubServ

***Red-Headed Stepchild (Library Edition)** unabr. ed. Jaye Wells. Narrated by Cynthia Holloway. (Running Time: 9 hrs. 30 mins.). (Sabina Kane Ser.). 2010. 34.99 (978-1-4001-9902-0(6)) Tantor Media.

Red Helmet. unabr. ed. Homer Hickam. Narrated by Kirsten Potter. (Running Time: 12 hrs. 5 mins. 0 sec.). (ENG.). 2008. 27.99 (978-1-60814-354-2(6)) Oasis Audio.

Red Helmet. unabr. ed. Homer Hickam. Narrated by Kirsten Potter. 10 CDs. (Running Time: 12 hrs. 5 mins. 0 sec.). (ENG.). 2008. audio compact disk 39.99 (978-1-59859-426-3(5)) Oasis Audio.

***Red Herring: A Joe Gunther Novel.** Archer Mayor. Narrated by William Dufris. (Running Time: 8 hrs. 52 mins. 0 sec.). (ENG.). 2010. audio compact disk 29.95 (978-1-60998-100-6(6)) Pub: AudioGO. Dist(s): Perseus Dist

***Red Herring Without Mustard: A Flavia de Luce Mystery.** unabr. ed. Alan Bradley. (ENG.). 2011. audio compact disk & audio compact disk 35.00 (978-0-307-57643-9(4), Random AudioBks) Pub: Random Audio Pubg. Dist(s): Random

Red Hook Road. unabr. ed. Ayelet Waldman. Read by Kimberly Farr. (ENG.). 2010. audio compact disk 40.00 (978-0-307-73539-3(7), Random AudioBks) Pub: Random Audio Pubg. Dist(s): Random

Red Horizons. unabr. ed. Ion M. Pacepa. Read by Phillip J. Sawtelle. 11 cass. (Running Time: 16 hrs.). 1988. 76.95 (978-0-7861-0014-9(1), 1014) Blckstn Audio.
Exposes the corruption of the Communist regime of Romania's President Nicolae Ceausescu & reveals Ceausescu's active role in international terrorism & intelligence gathering.

Red Horseman. unabr. ed. Stephen Coonts. Read by Michael Prichard. 10 cass. (Running Time: 15 hrs.). (Jake Grafton Novel Ser.: Vol. 5). 1993. 80.00 (978-0-7366-2541-8(0), 3292) Books on Tape.
Jake Grafton, now a rear admiral, is in Moscow to verify that Soviet nuclear weapons will be dismantled. The former USSR is a place of shifting loyalties & Grafton soon finds he's a target for assassination.

Red Hot Lies: How Global Warming Alarmists Use Threats, Fraud, & Deception to Keep You Misinformed. unabr. ed. Christopher Horner. (Running Time: 8 hrs. NaN mins.). (ENG.). 2008. 29.95 (978-1-4332-1510-0(1)); 24.95 (978-1-4332-1508-7(X)); audio compact disk 24.95 (978-1-4332-1509-4(8)) Blckstn Audio.

Red Hot Lies: How Global Warming Alarmists Use Threats, Fraud, & Deception to Keep You Misinformed. unabr. ed. Christopher C. Horner. (Running Time: 8 hrs. NaN mins.). 2008. 54.95 (978-1-4332-1506-3(3)); audio compact disk 70.00 (978-1-4332-1507-0(1)) Blckstn Audio.

Red-Hot Rattoons. unabr. ed. Elizabeth Winthrop. 4 cass. (Running Time: 5 hours). (J). 2003. 29.00 (978-1-932076-46-2(8)) Full Cast Audio.
Tap dancing rats! A secret animal city underneath New York! Delightful animal fantasy from the bestselling author of THE CASTLE IN THE ATTIC!Armed with a boom box, a stage wardrobe, and a tube of city maps, five tap-dancing country rats, who call themselves the Rattoons, set off to seek their fame in Rat Hollow-the rat community that pulses with a life all its own beneath the streets of New York City. But when Rat Hollow turns its back on them, the Rattoons break the law and take their act aboveground to dance for humans in front of the Metropolitan Museum, only to find that danger assails them from every direction. So the Rattoons turn to Oliver String Bean Bailey, the legendary human impresario who knows rat speak. Will he help them achieve their dancing dream?.

Red Hot Rattoons. unabr. ed. Elizabeth Winthrop. Read by Full Cast Production Staff. (J). 2007. 39.99 (978-1-60252-513-9(7)) Find a World.

Red House Mystery. A. A. Milne. Read by Amy von Lecteur. 2009. 27.95 (978-1-60112-983-3(1)) Babblebooks.

Red House Mystery. unabr. ed. A. A. Milne. Read by Flo Gibson. 4 cass. (Running Time: 5 hrs. 30 mins.). 1998. 19.95 (978-1-55685-614-3(8)) Audio Bk Con.
Amateur detective Antony Gillingham & Gill, his "Watson," investigate a mysterious shooting & the disappearance of their host during a house party in the English countryside. A clever plot with witty dialogue & intriguing characters.

Red House Mystery. unabr. ed. A. A. Milne. Read by William Sutherland. 5 cass. (Running Time: 7 hrs. 30 mins.). 1999. 39.95 (2440) Blckstn Audio.
Mark Ablett's stately mansion, the Red House, is filled with very proper guests when his most improper brother returns from Australia. In the study, the brother dies...rather suddenly, with a bullet between his eyes. The study is locked from the inside & Mark is missing!.

Red House Mystery. unabr. ed. A. A. Milne. Read by William Sutherland. 5 cass. (Running Time: 7 hrs.). 2006. 39.95 (978-0-7861-1612-6(9), 2440) Blckstn Audio.

Red Is Beautiful Audio CD. Roberta John. Illus. by Jason David. Narrated by Jessie Ruffenach & Maybelle Little. (Running Time: 30 mins). (NAV & ENG.). 2005. audio compact disk 10.95 (978-1-893354-51-7(2)) Pub: Salina Bkshelf. Dist(s): Natl Bk Netwk
Audio narration of Red Is Beautiful. Nashasha is teased unmercifully by her classmates. Called Chiizhii, ?the girl with the rough skin,? she dreads having to go to school and counts the days until summer will arrive and school will end. She wants to be free from the laughter and unkind remarks that makes school so unpleasant for her.However, Nashasha has much to be thankful for. Her grandmother is a kind, wise woman who teaches her the many things about life that cannot be learned at school. One evening, Grandmother tells Nashasha about the uses of chiih. By practicing what she learns, Nashasha discovers a way to stop the teasing.With troubles familiar to all school children, Nashasha?s story will hearten those facing peer pressure, teasing, and discrimination.

Red Knife. unabr. ed. William Kent Krueger. Read by Buck Schirner. 1 MP3-CD. (Running Time: 9 hrs.). (Cork O'Connor Ser.). 2008. 24.95 (978-1-4233-4177-2(5), 9781423341772, Brilliance MP3); 39.25 (978-1-4233-4180-2(5), 9781423341802, BADLE); 39.25 (978-1-4233-4178-9(3), 9781423341789, Brlnc Audio MP3 Lib); 24.95 (978-1-4233-4179-6(1), 9781423341796, BAD); audio compact disk 34.95 (978-1-4233-4175-8(9), 9781423341758, Bril Audio CD Unabri); audio compact disk 92.25 (978-1-4233-4176-5(7), 9781423341765, BriAudCD Unabrid) Brilliance Audio.

Red Land, Black Land: Daily Life in Ancient Egypt. Barbara Mertz. Read by Lorna Raver. (Playaway Adult Nonfiction Ser.). (ENG.). 2009. 70.00 (978-1-60775-625-5(0)) Find a World.

Red Land, Black Land: Daily Life in Ancient Egypt. unabr. ed. Barbara Mertz. Narrated by Lorna Raver. (Running Time: 15 hrs. 0 mins. 0 sec.). (ENG.). 2008. audio compact disk 39.99 (978-1-4001-0575-5(7)); audio compact disk 29.99 (978-1-4001-5575-0(4)); audio compact disk 79.99 (978-1-4001-3575-2(3)) Pub: Tantor Media. Dist(s): IngramPubServ

Red Leaves. unabr. ed. Perf. by Belva Plain. 9 CDs. (Running Time: 13 hrs.). 2005. 81.00 (978-1-4159-0774-0(9)); 63.00 (978-1-4159-0369-8(7)) Books on Tape.

Red Leaves. unabr. ed. Paullina Simons. Read by Sandra Burr. (Running Time: 15 hrs.). 2008. 39.25 (978-1-4233-5876-3(7), 9781423358763, Brlnc Audio MP3 Lib); 39.25 (978-1-4233-5878-7(3), 9781423358787, BADLE); 24.95 (978-1-4233-5875-6(9), 9781423358756, Brilliance MP3); 24.95 (978-1-4233-5877-0(5), 9781423358770, BAD) Brilliance Audio.

Red Letters Project. Velocity Entertainment Staff. Prod. by Symbionic Entertainment Staff. (Running Time: 3.5 hrs.). (ENG.). 2010. audio compact disk 29.99 (978-1-4143-1729-8(8)) Tyndale Hse.

Red Level Audiocassettes. (Individual Components Ser.). 100.00 (978-0-8092-9463-3(X)) M-H Contemporary.

Red Light. T. Jefferson Parker. Read by Anna Fields. 2000. audio compact disk 72.00 (978-0-7366-6069-3(0)) Books on Tape.

Red Light. abr. ed. T. Jefferson Parker. Read by Tavia Gilbert. (Running Time: 5 hrs.). (Merci Rayborn Ser.). 2010. audio compact disk 14.99 (978-1-4418-2543-8(6), 9781441825438, BACD) Brilliance Audio.

Red Light. abr. ed. T. Jefferson Parker. Read by Tavia Gilbert. (Running Time: 5 hrs.). (Merci Rayborn Ser.). 2010. audio compact disk 9.99 (978-1-4418-2545-2(2), 9781441825452, BCD Value Price) Brilliance Audio.

Red Light. unabr. ed. T. Jefferson Parker. Read by Anna Fields. 8 cass. (Running Time: 12 hrs.). 2000. 64.00 (978-0-7366-5070-0(9)) Books on Tape.
Investigating the death of two prostitutes, Merci Rayborn finds that the evidence points to the two cops she loves the most.

Red Light. unabr. ed. T. Jefferson Parker. Read by Anna Fields. 9 CDs. (Running Time: 10 hrs. 36 mins.). 2001. audio compact disk 72.00 Books on Tape.

Red Light. unabr. ed. T. Jefferson Parker. Read by Tavia Gilbert. (Running Time: 12 hrs.). (Merci Rayborn Ser.). 2010. 39.97 (978-1-4233-5577-9(6), 9781423355779, Brlnc Audio MP3 Lib); 24.99 (978-1-4233-5576-2(8), 9781423355762, Brilliance MP3); 24.99 (978-1-4233-5578-6(4), 9781423355786, BAD); audio compact disk 97.97 (978-1-4233-5575-5(X), 9781423355755, BriAudCD Unabrid); audio compact disk 29.99 (978-1-4233-5574-8(1), 9781423355748, Bril Audio CD Unabri) Brilliance Audio.

***Red Light.** unabr. ed. T. Jefferson Parker. Read by Tavia Gilbert. (Running Time: 12 hrs.). (Merci Rayborn Ser.). 2010. 39.97 (978-1-4233-5579-3(2), 9781423355793, BADLE) Brilliance Audio.

Red Lily see William Carlos Williams Reads His Poetry

Red Lily. Nora Roberts. Read by Susie Breck. (In the Garden Trilogy: Bk. 3). 2009. 69.99 (978-1-60775-692-7(7)) Find a World.

Red Lily. abr. ed. Nora Roberts. Read by Susie Breck. (Running Time: 21600 sec.). (In the Garden Trilogy: Bk. 3). 2006. audio compact disk 16.99 (978-1-59737-358-6(3), 9781597373586, BCD Value Price) Brilliance Audio.
A Harper has always lived at Harper House, the centuries-old mansion just outside of Memphis. And for as long as anyone alive remembers, the ghostly Harper Bride has walked the halls, singing lullabies at night... Hayley Phillips came to Memphis hoping for a new start, for herself and her unborn child. She wasn't looking for a handout from her distant cousin Roz, just a job at her thriving In the Garden nursery. What she found was a home surrounded by beauty and the best friends she's ever had - including Roz's son Harper. To Hayley's delight, her new daughter Lily has really taken to him. To Hayley's chagrin, she has begun to dream about Harper - as much more than a friend... If Hayley gives in to her desire, she's afraid the foundation she's built with Harper will come tumbling down. Especially since she's begun to suspect that her feelings are no longer completely her own. Flashes of the past and erratic behavior make Hayley believe that the Harper Bride has found a way inside of her mind and body. It's time to put the Bride to rest once and for all, so Hayley can know her own heart again - and whether she's willing to risk it.

***Red Lily.** abr. ed. Nora Roberts & #3 In The Garden Series. 2010. audio compact disk 9.99 (978-1-4418-5664-7(1)) Brilliance Audio.

Red Lily. abr. ed. Nora Roberts. Read by Susie Breck. (Running Time: 36000 sec.). (In the Garden Trilogy: Bk. 3). 2005. audio compact disk 97.25 (978-1-59355-623-5(3), 9781593556235, BACDLib Ed) Brilliance Audio.
Please enter a Synopsis.

Red Lily. unabr. ed. Anatole France. Read by Flo Gibson. 6 cass. (Running Time: 9 hrs.). (YA). (gr. 9 up). 1991. 24.95 (978-1-55685-210-7(X)) Audio Bk Con.
Wife of one man, mistress of another, Therese meets & falls in love with the sculptor Dechartre. This torrid love affair is doomed by jealousy.

Red Lily. unabr. ed. Nora Roberts. Read by Susie Breck. (Running Time: 10 hrs.). (In the Garden Trilogy: Bk. 3). 2005. 39.25 (978-1-59710-629-0(1), 9781597106290, BADLE); 24.95 (978-1-59710-628-3(3), 9781597106283, BAD); 87.25 (978-1-59355-620-4(9), 9781593556204, BrilAudUnabridg); audio compact disk 36.95 (978-1-59600-823-6(7), 9781596008236, Bril Audio CD Unabri); audio compact disk 24.95 (978-1-59335-746-7(X), 9781593357467, Brilliance MP3); audio compact disk 39.25 (978-1-59335-880-8(6), 9781593358808, Brlnc Audio MP3 Lib) Brilliance Audio.
Please enter a Synopsis.

Red Limit: The Search for the Edge of the Universe. abr. unabr. ed. Timothy Ferris. Read by Timothy Ferris. 4 cass. (Running Time: 6 hrs.). 2004. 25.00 (978-1-931056-16-8(1), N Millennium Audio) New Millenn Enter.
Tumultuous tale of groundbreaking discoveries by a group of scientists whose rivalries & emotions played as important a part as their intellectual brilliance.

Red Mars. unabr. ed. Kim Stanley Robinson. Narrated by Richard Ferrone. 17 cass. (Running Time: 24 hrs.). 1993. 109.75 (978-0-7887-4084-8(9), 96112E7) Recorded Bks.
For centuries, the red planet has enticed the people of Earth. Now an intrepid group has colonized Mars. This is the remarkable story of the world they create & the powers that struggle to control it. Based on years of research, this is an astonishing vision of our galactic future.

Red Monarch: Scenes from the Life of Stalin. unabr. collector's ed. Yuri Krotkov. Read by Justin Hecht. 7 cass. (Running Time: 7 hrs.). 1982. 42.00 (978-0-7366-0440-6(5), 1409) Books on Tape.
Stalin is drawn as a classical Gemini: a mixture of good & evil. What power does to the behavior of those who are manipulated by it is shown in scenes which take us from the Russia of Pre-World War II through Stalin's death.

Red Moon at Sharpsburg. unabr. ed. Rosemary Wells. Narrated by Julia Gibson. 6 cass. (Running Time: 7 hrs.). (YA). 2007. 39.95 (978-1-4281-8335-3(3)) Recorded Bks.

Red Moon at Sharpsburg. unabr. ed. Rosemary Wells. Narrated by Julia Gibson. 6 cass. (Running Time: 7 hrs.). (YA). (gr. 5-8). 2007. 51.75 (978-1-4281-8334-6(5)); audio compact disk 66.75 (978-1-4281-8339-1(6)) Recorded Bks.

Red Moon Rising: Sputnik & the Hidden Rivalries That Ignited the Space Age. unabr. ed. Matthew Brzezinski. Narrated by Charles Stransky. (ENG.). 2007. audio compact disk 36.95 (978-1-59887-523-2(X), 159887523X) Pub: HighBridge. Dist(s): Workman Pub

Red Moon Rising: Sputnik & the Hidden Rivals That Ignited the Space Age. unabr. ed. Matthew Brzezinski. Read by Charles Stransky. (YA). 2008. 59.99 (978-1-60514-749-9(4)) Find a World.

Red Moon's Raid. abr. ed. Matthew S. Hart. Read by Paul Nixon. Abr. by Odin Westgaard. 2 cass. (Running Time: 3 hrs.). (Cody's Law Ser.: No. 11). 2004. 18.00 (978-1-58807-145-3(6)) Am Pubng Inc.
He rides alone for a breed that stands apart. He wears the badge of the Texas Rangers and a pair of silver spurs. He is the servant of a fiercely held code of right and wrong. His name is Cody. The Rangers made Texas a land of law. Men like Cody made the Rangers a legend. Lieutenant Oliver Whitcomb is a strict believer in law and order. So is Sam Cody. They don't always see eye to eye on how to enforce it, but they are both Texas Rangers. When an outlaw gang led by renegade Comanche Red Moon kidnaps Whitcomb's nineteen-year-old daughter, it's Cody who rides at the lieutenant's side. They will follow Red Moon into the badlands of West Texas and from there to death itself, if that's what it takes. What they don't know is that the cruel and cunning Red Moon plans to exact a price more terrible than death, not only from his two pursuers but from Whitcomb's innocent daughter as well.

Red Mutiny: Eleven Fateful Days on the Battleship Potemkin. Neal Bascomb. Narrated by John McDonough. (Running Time: 54000 sec.). 2007. audio compact disk 39.99 (978-1-4281-3728-8(9)) Recorded Bks.

Red Necklace. unabr. ed. Sally Gardner. Read by Carrington MacDuffie. 8 CDs. (Running Time: 9 hrs. 46 mins.). (YA). (gr. 7-10). 2008. audio compact disk 50.00 (978-0-7393-6231-0(3), Listening Lib) Pub: Random Audio Pubg. Dist(s): Random
The winds of change are blowing through Paris in the winter of 1789, both for France and for our hero, a striking and mysterious Gypsy boy named Yann Margoza. He was born with a gift for knowing what people are thinking and an uncanny ability to throw his voice, and he has been using those skills while working for a rather foolish magician. That work will soon end, however, and on the night of the magician's final performance, Yann's life will truly begin. That's the night he meets shy Sido, an heiress with a cold-hearted father, a young girl who has only known loneliness until now. Though they have the shortest of conversations, an attachment is born that will influence both their paths. And what paths those will be! While Revolution is afoot in France, Sido is being used as the pawn of a fearful villain who goes by the name Count Kalliovski. Some have instead called him the devil, and only Yann, for Sido's sake, will dare to oppose him.

Red Necklace: A Novel of the French Revolution. unabr. ed. Sally Gardner. Read by Carrington MacDuffie. (Running Time: 35160 sec.). (ENG.). (J). (gr. 5). 2008. audio compact disk 50.00 (978-0-7393-5648-7(8), Listening Lib) Pub: Random Audio Pubg. Dist(s): Random

***Red November: Inside the Secret U. S. - Soviet Submarine War.** unabr. ed. W. Craig Reed. Read by Tom Weiner. (Running Time: 14 hrs. 0 mins.). 2010. 29.95 (978-1-4417-5267-3(6)); audio compact disk 32.95 (978-1-4417-5266-6(8)) Blckstn Audio.

***Red November: Inside the Secret U. S. -Soviet Submarine War.** unabr. ed. Craig W. Reed. (Running Time: 14 hrs. 0 mins.). 2010. 79.95 (978-1-4417-5263-5(3)); audio compact disk 118.00 (978-1-4417-5264-2(1)) Blckstn Audio.

***Red on Red: A Novel.** unabr. ed. Edward Conlon. (ENG.). 2011. audio compact disk 35.00 (978-0-307-87609-6(8), Random AudioBks) Pub: Random Audio Pubg. Dist(s): Random

Red Orchestra: The Story of the Berlin Underground & the Circle of Friends Who Resisted Hitler. unabr. ed. Anne Nelson. (Running Time: 14 hrs. 0 mins. 0 sec.). (ENG.). 2009. audio compact disk 37.99 (978-1-4001-1017-9(3)); audio compact disk 24.99 (978-1-4001-6017-4(0)) Pub: Tantor Media. Dist(s): IngramPubServ

Red Orchestra: The Story of the Berlin Underground & the Circle of Friends Who Resisted Hitler. unabr. ed. Anne Nelson. Read by Anne Nelson. (Running Time: 14 hrs. 0 mins. 0 sec.). (ENG.). 2009. audio compact disk 75.99 (978-1-4001-4017-6(X)) Pub: Tantor Media. Dist(s): IngramPubServ

Red Pavilion. unabr. ed. Robert H. Van Gulik. Narrated by Frank Muller. 4 cass. (Running Time: 5 hrs.). (Judge Dee Mysteries Ser.). 1986. 35.00 (978-1-55690-438-7(X), 86550E7) Recorded Bks.
Investigating three deaths on Paradise Island, Judge Dee becomes enmeshed in the seductive life of a beguiling courtesan.

Red Phoenix. abr. ed. Larry Bond. Read by J. Charles. (Running Time: 21600 sec.). 2007. audio compact disk 14.99 (978-1-4233-2112-5(X), 9781423321125, BCD Value Price) Brilliance Audio.

Red Phoenix. unabr. ed. Larry Bond. Read by Michael Prichard. 8 cass. (Running Time: 12 hrs.). 1990. 64.00 (2541-B) Books on Tape.
The Second Korean War has just begun & the Third World War may not be far behind. It looks like Vietnam all over again, only on a world scale. A masterful techno-thriller that shows our men & women in their most vulnerable, but finest hour... as they shape events that will profoundly alter, perhaps devastate, the world as they know it.

Red Phoenix. unabr. ed. Larry Bond. Read by Michael Prichard. 9 cass. (Running Time: 13 hrs. 30 mins.). 1990. 72.00 (978-0-7366-1694-2(2), 2541-A) Books on Tape.
The Second Korean War has just begun & the Third World War may not be far behind. Conflict threatens on all fronts & the growing tension draws in not only Washington, Moscow & Beijing, but Europe, Japan & all of Southeast Asia as well. It looks like Vietnam all over again, only on a world scale. Red Phoenix is a stunning debut by a craftsman who collaborated with Tom Clancy on Red Storm Rising. He does more than construct a masterful techno-thriller...he gives us men & women in their most vulnerable but finest hour...as they shape events that will profoundly alter, perhaps devastate, the world as they know it.

Red Phoenix. unabr. ed. Larry Bond. Read by J. Charles. (Running Time: 24 hrs.). 2006. 44.25 (978-1-4233-1224-6(4), 9781423312246, BADLE); 29.95 (978-1-4233-1223-9(6), 9781423312239, BAD); audio compact disk 112.25 (978-1-4233-1220-8(1), 9781423312208, BriAudCD Unabrid); audio compact disk 44.25 (978-1-4233-1222-2(8), 9781423312222, Brlnc Audio MP3 Lib); audio compact disk 44.95 (978-1-4233-1219-2(8), 9781423312192, Bril Audio CD Unabri); audio compact disk 29.95 (978-1-4233-1221-5(X), 9781423312215, Brilliance MP3) Brilliance Audio.
From the author who collaborated with Tom Clancy on Red Storm Rising, this is the book that dares to show us the military hardware, global upheavals, and raw combat a second Korean War would unleash. How F-16s would last across the 38th Parallel. How ultra-modern submarines would vie for the seas. And how two armies would turn the snowfields of Asia red with blood. A thundering geopolitical thriller of vast scope, this is Red Phoenix - and a new standard for military/political suspense fiction. "A big, big book...A superb storyteller...Larry Bond seems to know everything about warfare, from the grunt in a foxhole to the fighter pilots far above the earth...Red Phoenix is wonderfully entertaining and deserves to be the bestseller it is." - New York Times Book Review "Gripping...masterfully accurate...Mr. Bond is in complete command." - Baltimore Sun "Harrowingly real and persuasive." - Newsday "A direct hit! The techno-thriller has a new ace, and his name is Larry Bond." - Tom Clancy.

Red Planet. unabr. ed. Robert A. Heinlein. Narrated by William Dufris. 6 CDs. (Running Time: 7 hrs.). 2008. audio compact disk 45.00 (978-1-934180-26-6(2)) Full Cast Audio.

Red Pottage. Mary Cholmondeley. Read by Anais 9000. 2008. 27.95 (978-1-60112-205-6(5)) Babblebooks.

Red Prophet. Orson Scott Card. Read by Stephen Hoye et al. (Running Time: 43200 sec.). (Tales of Alvin Maker Ser.). 2007. 72.95 (978-1-4332-0137-0(2)); audio compact disk 90.00 (978-1-4332-0138-7(0)); audio compact disk 29.95 (978-1-4332-0139-4(9)) Blckstn Audio.

Red Prophet. Orson Scott Card. Read by Ray Verna. 7 cass. (Running Time: 10 hrs.). (Tales of Alvin Maker Ser.: No. 2). 1993. 53.20 (978-1-56544-048-7(X), 550004); Rental 10.10 30 day rental Set. (550004) Literate Ear.
Alvin sets out into an America that could have been, to become a blacksmith's apprentice. Caught up in the battles with the Unmaker, the ultimate force of evil, & wars between Red men & White, Alvin's destiny begins to take shape.

***Red Pyramid.** unabr. ed. Rick Riordan. Read by Kevin R. Free & Katherine Kellgren. 1 MP3-CD. (Running Time: 15 hrs.). (Kane Chronicles: Bk. 1). 2010. 24.99 (978-1-4418-5097-3(X), 9781441850973, Brilliance MP3); 39.97 (978-1-4418-5099-7(6), 9781441850997, Brlnc Audio MP3 Lib) Brilliance Audio.

***Red Pyramid.** unabr. ed. Rick Riordan. Read by Kevin R. Free and Katherine Kellgren. (Running Time: 14 hrs.). (Kane Chronicles: Bk. 1). 2010. 24.99 (978-1-4418-5100-0(3), 9781441851000, BAD); 39.97 (978-1-4418-5101-7(1), 9781441851017, BADLE) Brilliance Audio.

***Red Pyramid.** unabr. ed. Rick Riordan. Read by Kevin R. Free & Katherine Kellgren. 12 CDs. (Running Time: 15 hrs.). (Kane Chronicles: Bk. 1). 2010. audio compact disk 29.99 (978-1-4418-5095-9(3), 9781441850959, Bril Audio CD Unabri); audio compact disk 72.97 (978-1-4418-5096-6(1), 9781441850966, BriAudCD Unabrid) Brilliance Audio.

Red Queen. abr. ed. Philippa Gregory. Read by Bianca Amato. (Running Time: 6 hrs. 30 mins. 0 sec.). Bk. 2. (ENG.). 2010. audio compact disk 29.99 (978-1-4423-0439-0(1)) Pub: S&S Audio. Dist(s): S and S Inc

Red Queen. unabr. ed. Philippa Gregory. Read by Bianca Amato. 11 CDs. (Running Time: 13 hrs. 0 mins. 0 sec.). Bk. 2. 2010. audio compact disk 39.99 (978-1-4423-0488-8(X)) Pub: S&S Audio. Dist(s): S and S Inc

Red Rabbit. Tom Clancy. Read by Scott Brick. 2002. 199.00 (978-0-7366-8887-1(0)) Books on Tape.
It is very early in Jack Ryan's career - so early that he has not yet even become an analyst for the CIA. But a series of nasty encounters with an IRA splinter group has brought Ryan to the attention of the CIA's Deputy Director and his British counterpart.

Red Rabbit. abr. ed. Tom Clancy. Read by Dennis Boutsikaris. 5 CDs. (Running Time: 6 hrs.). (Tom Clancy Ser.). (ENG.). 2002. audio compact disk 31.95 (978-0-553-71310-7(8)) Pub: Random Audio Pubg. Dist(s): Random

Red Rabbit. unabr. ed. Tom Clancy. Read by Scott Brick. 11 cass. (Running Time: 13 hrs. 30 mins.). 2002. 149.00 (978-0-7366-8884-0(6)) Books on Tape.

Red Reding Hood; Aunt Nina & Her Nephews & Nieces; Ernest & Celestine's Picnic; What's under My Bed? 2004. (978-0-89719-855-4(7)) Weston Woods.

Red Riding Hood. 2004. bk. 24.95 (978-1-56008-209-5(7)); pap. bk. 14.95 (978-0-7882-0649-8(4)); pap. bk. 32.75 (978-1-55592-301-3(1)); pap. bk. 32.75 (978-1-55592-302-0(X)); pap. bk. 14.95 (978-1-56008-087-9(6)); pap. bk. 14.95 (978-0-7882-0399-2(1)); 8.95 (978-1-56008-319-1(0)); 8.95 (978-1-56008-320-7(4)); 8.95 (978-1-56008-425-9(1)); cass. & flmstrp 30.00 (978-0-89719-635-2(X)); cass. & flmstrp 30.00 (978-1-56008-757-1(9)) Weston Woods.

Red Riding Hood. Read by Famous Theater Company Staff. 1 cass. (J). (ps-2). 3.98 (978-1-55886-030-8(4)) Smarty Pants.
A children's fairy tale about a young girl & a big bad wolf.

Red Riding Hood. Read by Hollywood Studio Orchestra Staff. 1 cass. (J). (ps-2). 3.98 (978-1-55886-038-4(X)) Smarty Pants.

Red Riding Hood. James Marshall. 1 cass., 5 bks. (Running Time: 8 min.). (J). pap. bk. 32.75 Weston Woods.
On her way to Granny's house, Red Riding Hood is tricked by the bad wolf.

Red Riding Hood. James Marshall. 1 cass. (Running Time: 8 min.). (J). (ps-3). bk. 24.95; pap. bk. 12.95 (RAC345); pap. bk. 12.95 (PRA345) Weston Woods.
On her way to Granny's house, Red Riding Hood is tricked by the bad wolf. From the book by James Marshall.

Red Riding Hood; Aunt Nina & Her Nephews & Nieces; Ernest & Celestine's Picnic; What's under by Bed? 2004. cass. & flmstrp (978-0-89719-755-7(0)) Weston Woods.

Red River. abr. ed. Lalita Tademy. Read by Tim Cain & Gammy Singer. (Running Time: 6 hrs.). (ENG.). 2007. 14.98 (978-1-59483-547-6(0)) Pub: Hachet Audio. Dist(s): HachBkGrp

Red River. abr. ed. Lalita Tademy. Read by Tim Cain & Gammy Singer. (Running Time: 6 hrs.). (ENG.). 2009. 44.98 (978-1-60788-291-6(4)) Pub: Hachet Audio. Dist(s): HachBkGrp

Red River. unabr. ed. Lalita Tademy. 10 cass. (Running Time: 15 hrs.). 2007. 100.00 (978-1-4159-3708-2(7)); audio compact disk 120.00 (978-1-4159-3621-4(8)) Books on Tape.

Red River Haint. Arlie Garrett & Debby Garrett. (J). 1995. pap. bk. 4.95 (978-0-87129-613-9(6), R58) Dramatic Pub.

Red River to Appomattox. unabr. ed. Shelby Foote. Read by Grover Gardner. 3 pieces. (Running Time: 183600 sec.). (Civil War: A Narrative Ser.). 2008. audio compact disk 54.95 (978-0-7861-9101-7(5), 1104A,B) Blckstn Audio.

Red River to Appomattox, Vol. 3. unabr. ed. Shelby Foote. Read by Grover Gardner. 14 cass. (Running Time: 41 hrs.). 1997. 89.95 (978-0-7861-0116-0(4), 1104A,B) Blckstn Audio.
In the third - & last - volume of this vivid history, Shelby Foote brings to a close the story of four years of turmoil & strife which altered American life forever. Here, told in vivid narrative & as seen from both sides, are those climactic struggles, great & small, on & off the field of battle, which finally decided the fate of this nation.

Red River to Appomattox, Part 1. unabr. ed. Shelby Foote. Read by Grover Gardner. (Running Time: 88200 sec.). (Civil War: A Narrative Ser.). 2008. audio compact disk 130.00 (978-1-4332-3412-5(2)) Blckstn Audio.

Red Road: Native American Paths to Recovery. Dick Brooks & Peggy Berryhill. 1 cass. (Running Time: 60 min.). 10.00 (978-0-89486-723-1(7), 5634A) Hazelden.
Native Americans discuss using native spirituality in their recovery.

Red Rock Mysteries. ed. Jerry B. Jenkins & Chris Fabry. (Running Time: 4 hrs. 30 mins. 0 sec.). (Red Rock Mysteries Ser.). (ENG.). 2009. audio compact disk 19.99 (978-1-59859-600-7(4)) Oasis Audio.

Red Room see Star & Other Stories

Red Room. unabr. ed. Nicci French. Read by Jane Markham. 12 cass. (Running Time: 12 hrs. 20 min.). 2001. (978-0-7531-1258-8(2)) ISIS Audio GBR.
Kit Quinn is a young woman who inhabits dangerous worlds: crime scenes, interrogations, hospitals for the criminally insane. Horribly wounded in a brutal attack, she must return to the site of her worst fears. She is asked by the police to advise them on a simple murder inquiry. A young runaway has been found dead near a London canal and the chief suspect is the man who wounded her.

Red Room & Other Stories see Classic Ghost Stories, Vol. 1, A Collection

Red Scare. 10.00 (HT400) Esstee Audios.

Red Scare in Court. unabr. collector's ed. Arthur J. Sabin. Read by Dick Estell. 12 cass. (Running Time: 18 hrs.). 1993. 96.00 (978-0-7366-2439-8(2), 3204) Books on Tape.
Recounts 1950s "red scare" trial where low-cost insurance provider, with Communist Party ties, was liquidated.

Red Scarf Girl: A Memoir of the Cultural Revolution. Ji-Li Jiang. Narrated by Christina Moore. 5 pieces. (Running Time: 6 hrs. 15 mins.). (gr. 4 up). 1999. 46.00 (978-0-7887-2637-8(4)) Recorded Bks.

Red Scarf Girl: A Memoir of the Cultural Revolution, unabr. ed. Ji-Li Jiang. Narrated by Christina Moore. 5 cass. (Running Time: 6 hrs.15 mins.). (J). (gr. 4). 46.00 (978-0-7887-2975-1(6), 95638E7) Recorded Bks.
The true story of a family's courage in one of the most terrifying eras of modern history. Twelve-year-old Ji-li Jiang has brains, friends & a bright future, until Mao Zedong launches China's infamous Cultural Revolution. Available to libraries only.

Red Scarf Girl: A Memoir of the Cultural Revolution. unabr. ed. Ji-Li Jiang. Read by Christina Moore. 1999. pap. bk. & stu. ed. 59.20 (978-0-7887-3005-4(3), 40827) Recorded Bks.

Red Scarf Girl: A Memoir of the Cultural Revolution, Class Set. unabr. ed. Ji-Li Jiang. Read by Christina Moore. 5 cass. (Running Time: 6 hrs. 15 mins.). (J). 1999. 116.30 (978-0-7887-3035-1(5), 46759) Recorded Bks.

Red Scream. unabr. ed. Mary Willis Walker. Read by Anna Fields. 8 cass. (Running Time: 12 hrs.). 1996. 64.00 (978-0-7366-3381-9(2), 4031) Books on Tape.
Molly Cates, crime reporter for the "Lone Star Monthly" & true daughter of Texas, plans to witness Louie Bronk's execution (Bronk is a serial killer). But suddenly, her boss doesn't want her there & neither does the husband of Bronk's most famous victim. Why should they care.

Red Scream, unabr. ed. Mary Willis Walker. Narrated by C. J. Critt. 10 cass. (Running Time: 14 hrs. 45 mins.). 1996. 85.00 (978-0-7887-0468-0(0), 94661E7) Recorded Bks.
Shortly after reporter Molly Cates agrees to attend the execution of a serial killer, she receives an anonymous message that forces her to question the true indentity of the Texas Scalper.

Red Seas under Red Skies. unabr. ed. Scott Lynch. Narrated by Michael Page. (Running Time: 25 hrs. 30 mins. 0 sec.). (Gentlemen Bastards Ser.). (ENG.). 2009. audio compact disk 54.99 (978-1-4001-1052-0(1)); audio compact disk 109.99 (978-1-4001-4052-7(8)); audio compact disk 39.99 (978-1-4001-6052-5(9)) Pub: Tantor Media. Dist(s): IngramPubServ

Red Shoe Diaries. 1 cass. (Running Time: 1 hr. 30 mins.). 2003. 13.99 (978-1-931669-42-9(2)) Showtime Net Inc.
Contains the music of Salman Kings Red Shoe Diaries.

Red Shoes see Little Match Girl & Other Tales

Red Shoes. Jeff Beal. (Advanced Ser.). (ENG.). 2005. audio compact disk 19.95 (978-0-7579-3136-9(7), ENS00306, Warner Bro) Alfred Pub.

Red Shoes: On Torment & the Recovery of Soul Life. unabr. abr. ed. Clarissa Pinkola Estes. 1 CD. (Running Time: 4500 sec.). 2006. audio compact disk 14.95 (978-1-59179-439-4(0), AW00202D) Sounds True.

Red Skelton. (Running Time: 10 min.). 10.95 (753) J Norton Pubs.
On side one, Deadeye has struck it rich in oil, & is sharing his wealth with Red's rich cast of character. Side two has Red at the airport, cavorting with characters Willy Lump-Lump & Junior.

Red Skelton. Perf. by Rod O'Connor & Verna Felton. 1 cass. (Running Time: 60 min.). 7.95 (CM-4105) Natl Recrd Co.
Red Skelton skit presents comedy in the great Skelton tradition as Deadeye looks for Bowlegged Bullroose. In "Big Town," Steve Wilson, Managing Editor of the "Illustrated Press," & his assistant track down a hit & run killer.

Red Skelton. Created by Radio Spirits. (Running Time: 10800 sec.). 2004. audio compact disk 9.98 (978-1-57019-552-5(8)) Radio Spirits.

Red Skelton. Featuring Red Skelton. 1950. audio compact disk 12.95 (978-1-57970-507-7(3), Audio-For) J Norton Pubs.

Red Skelton: Character Troubles. Perf. by Red Skelton et al. (ENG.). 2008. audio compact disk 31.95 (978-1-57019-868-7(3)) Radio Spirits.

***Red Skelton: I Dood It.** Perf. by Red Skelton & Harriet Hilliard. 2010. audio compact disk 27.95 (978-1-57019-916-5(7)) Radio Spirits.

Red Skelton: Scrapbook of Satire. Perf. by Verna Felton & Rod O'Connor. 1 cass. (Running Time: 60 min.). 7.95 (CC-8440) Natl Recrd Co.
"The Warehouse Elevator" contains great Red Skelton comedy with his famous characters, Clem Kiddlehopper & Junior. "Careless Driving" is a funny skit between Red, his grandmom & a policeman.

Red Skelton Christmas Show of 1951. 1953. (CC-8070) Natl Recrd Co.

Red Skelton, No. 2: Looking for Trouble & April Fool's Day. unabr. ed. 1 cass. (Running Time: 60 min.). Dramatization. 7.95 Norelco box. (CC-9805) Natl Recrd Co.
Looking for Trouble: Red Skelton appears as Deadeye in "The Man Who Stole My Gal," as Clem Kadiddlehopper in "I've Been Insulted," & as Junior, the Mean Little Kid, in "Time to Go to Bed, Kiddies." With Verna Felton, Rod O'Connor, Gigi Pearson & Singing star Anita Ellis. Raleigh Cigarette, 1946. April Fool's Day: Red stars as Willy Lump-Lump, making an appearance in Traffic Court. Once again he is the Mean Little Kid in "The Great Pie Mystery"...a big bite has been taken from Grandma's freshly baked pie. With Verna Felton, Rod O'Connor, & Anita Ellis. Raleigh Cigarettes, 1947.

Red Skelton Show. Perf. by Red Skelton & Jack Benny. 6 cass. (Running Time: 9 hrs.). 2002. 34.98 (4700) Radio Spirits.
Red Skelton started his career on river boats and in vaudeville, and looked to clowns as the inspiration for his hilarious characters. Vol. 1 features Red as Junior ("I dood it again"), the singing cab driver Clem Kadiddlehopper and Sheriff Deadeye ("The fastest gun in the West") in episodes from 1941 and 1942.

Red Skelton Show, Vol. 1. Perf. by Red Skelton. 6 cass. (Running Time: 9 hrs.). 2002. 34.98 (4691) Radio Spirits.

Red Skelton Show: A Three Cent Stamp & The Big Business Venture. Perf. by Red Skelton. 1 cass. (Running Time: 1 hr.). 2001. 6.98 (1593) Radio Spirits.

Red Skelton Show: Has Anybody Here Seen Willie? & Neighborhood Theatre. Perf. by Red Skelton. 1 cass. (Running Time: 1 hr.). 2001. 6.98 (1564) Radio Spirits.

Red Skelton Show: Helter Shelter & The Big Scare. Perf. by Red Skelton. 1 cass. (Running Time: 1 hr.). 2001. 6.98 (1790) Radio Spirits.

Red Skelton Show: How to Make Enemies & Public Speeches. Perf. by Red Skelton. 1 cass. (Running Time: 1 hr.). 2001. 6.98 (1591) Radio Spirits.

Red Skelton Show: Junior's Horse & Red Buys a Prizefighter. Perf. by Red Skelton. 1 cass. (Running Time: 1 hr.). 2001. 6.98 (1876) Radio Spirits.

Red Skelton Show: People Who Brag & Sunday Dinner. Perf. by Red Skelton. 1 cass. (Running Time: 1 hr.). 2001. 6.98 (1523) Radio Spirits.

Red Skelton Show: Red Gives a Party & Red Goes to the Fights. Perf. by Red Skelton. 1 cass. (Running Time: 1 hr.). 2001. 6.98 (2624) Radio Spirits.

Red Skelton Show: Skunk Patrol's Benefit Show & A New Year's Puzzle. Perf. by Red Skelton. 1 cass. (Running Time: 1 hr.). 2001. 6.98 (1592) Radio Spirits.

Red Skelton Show: The Hamburger Stand & Old Man Winter. Perf. by Red Skelton. 1 cass. (Running Time: 1 hr.). 2001. 6.98 (2429) Radio Spirits.

Red Skelton Show: The Little Christmas Tree & The Day After Christmas. Perf. by Red Skelton. 1 cass. (Running Time: 1 hr.). 2001. 6.98 (1524) Radio Spirits.

Red Skelton Show: Things to Be Thankful For & People Who Owe Money. Perf. by Red Skelton. 1 cass. (Running Time: 1 hr.). 2001. 6.98 (1522) Radio Spirits.

Red Skelton Show: Women Are Ruling the World & Fear. Perf. by Red Skelton. 1 cass. (Running Time: 1 hr.). 2001. 6.98 (1590) Radio Spirits.

Red Skelton Show Pt. 1 & Pt. 2: I Caught the Devil. Perf. by Red Skelton. 1 cass. (Running Time: 1 hr.). 2001. 6.98 (1594) Radio Spirits.

Red Sky at Morning. unabr. ed. Richard Bradford. Read by Dan Lazar. 7 cass. (Running Time: 7 hrs.). 1976. 42.00 (978-0-7366-0021-7(3), 1032) Books on Tape.
This novel takes us back in time to World War II. When his father goes to war, the hero, Josh Arnold & his mother leave Mobile to settle in a small New Mexico town for the duration.

Red Sky at Morning. unabr. ed. Richard Bradford. Narrated by Norman Dietz. 6 cass. (Running Time: 7 hrs. 45 mins.). 1987. 51.00 (978-1-55690-439-4(8), 87890E7) Recorded Bks.
The year is 1944, Josh's beloved father goes off to join the Navy. Josh & his wilting Southern-belle mother, Miss Anne, go off to New Mexico. Miss Anne & her permanent houseguest, Jimbob Buel, triple sherry, play bridge & wilt some more. Josh, meanwhile, comes resoundingly of age.

Red Sky at Night, unabr. ed. James W. Hall. Narrated by Frank Muller. 8 cass. (Running Time: 10 hrs. 30 mins.). (Thorn Ser.). 1997. 75.00 (978-0-7887-1294-4(2), 95128E7) Recorded Bks.
Thorn, a fiercely independent fishing guide from Key Largo, fights for his life against obsessive revenge & brilliance gone mad.

Red Sky in Morning: A Novel of World War II. unabr. ed. Patrick Culhane. Read by Joe Barrett. (Running Time: 10 hrs. 0 mins.). 2008. 29.95 (978-1-4332-3137-7(9)); 65.95 (978-1-4332-3133-9(6)); audio compact disk 80.00 (978-1-4332-3134-6(4)) Blckstn Audio.

Red Sky in Mourning: A Helen Bradley Mystery. Patricia H. Rushford. Narrated by Cristine McMurdo-Wallis. 6 cass. (Running Time: 8 hrs. 15 mins.). 54.00 (978-0-7887-5114-1(X)) Recorded Bks.

Red Sky in Mourning: The True Story of a Woman's Courage & Survival at Sea. Tami Oldham Ashcraft. 2004. 15.95 (978-0-7435-4830-4(2)) Pub: S&S Audio. Dist(s): S and S Inc

Red Square, unabr. ed. Martin Cruz Smith. Narrated by Frank Muller. 10 cass. (Running Time: 14 hrs. 30 mins.). (Arkady Renko Ser.: No. 3). 1993. 85.00 (978-1-55690-896-5(2), 93338E7) Recorded Bks.
Arkady Renko has returned from exile & is back on the homicide squad in a newly democratic Moscow. When his informant & his underworld bank on wheels are consumed in a ball of fire, Arcady finds himself in an investigation that points to the heart of Russia's decaying infrastructure.

Red Square. unabr. collector's ed. Martin Cruz Smith. Read by Wolfram Kandinsky. 12 cass. (Running Time: 18 hrs.). (Arkady Renko Ser.: No. 3). 1993. 96.00 (978-0-7366-2593-7(3), 3338) Books on Tape.
Inspector Arkady Renko is back from exile & on the job in the new, free, democratic Russia. Renko launches an investigation when a car bomb demolishes an informer. He's then led to Moscow's Mafia chiefs & ironically, back to the love of his life, Irena Asanova.

***Red Star over Hollywood: The Film Colony's Long Romance with the Left.** unabr. ed. Ronald Rodosh. Read by Stefan Rudnicki. (Running Time: 10 hrs. 30 mins.). 2010. 29.95 (978-1-4332-1929-0(8)); 65.95 (978-1-4332-1925-2(5)); audio compact disk 100.00 (978-1-4332-1926-9(3)) Blckstn Audio.

Red Star Rogue: The Untold Story of a Soviet Submarine's Nuclear Strike Attempt on the U. S. 2005. 65.95 (978-0-7861-4417-4(3)); audio compact disk 81.00 (978-0-7861-7394-5(7)) Blckstn Audio.

Red Star Rogue: The Untold Story of A Soviet Submarine's Nuclear Strike Attempt on the US. unabr. ed. Kenneth Sewell. Read by Kyle Prue. Told to Clint Richmond. 9 cass. (Running Time: 11 hrs.). (YA). 2005. 29.95 (978-0-7861-4414-3(9)) Blckstn Audio.

Red Star Rogue: The Untold Story of a Soviet Submarine's Nuclear Strike Attempt on the US. unabr. ed. Kenneth Sewell. Read by Brian Emerson. 10 CDs. (Running Time: 39600 sec.). 2005. audio compact disk 29.95 (978-0-7861-7397-6(1)) Blckstn Audio.

***Red State Uprising: How to Take Back America.** unabr. ed. Erick Erickson & Lewis K. Uhler. (Running Time: 8 hrs. 30 mins.). 2010. 29.95 (978-1-4417-6267-2(1)); 54.95 (978-1-4417-6264-1(7)); audio compact disk 29.95 (978-1-4417-6266-5(3)); audio compact disk 76.00 (978-1-4417-6265-8(5)) Blckstn Audio.

Red Storm Rising. Tom Clancy. Read by Michael Prichard.Tr. of Tormenta Roja. 2002. 184.00 (978-0-7366-9122-2(7)) Books on Tape.

Red Storm Rising. unabr. ed. Tom Clancy. Read by Michael Prichard. 10 cass. (Running Time: 15 hrs.).Tr. of Tormenta Roja. 1986. 80.00 (978-0-7366-1097-1(9), 2024-A); 80.00 (978-0-7366-1098-8(7), 2024-B) Books on Tape.
When Moslem fanatics sabotage the Russian oil supply, the Soviets plan a takeover of the Persian Gulf. Will it lead to WW III? When Soviet tanks begin to roll, the West is caught off guard. What looks like a thrust turns into an all-out-shooting war, possibly the climatic battle for control of the globe.

Red Suit Diaries: A Real-Life Santa on Hopes, Dreams, & Childlike Faith. abr. ed. Ed Butchart. Read by Ed Butchart. 2 cass. (Running Time: 3 hrs.). 2003. 17.95 (978-1-59355-238-1(6), 1593552386); 44.25 (978-1-59355-239-8(4), 1593552394); audio compact disk 62.25 (978-1-59355-241-1(6), 1593552416) Brilliance Audio.
Tom Brokaw said it best about the author: This Santa "can only be described as the real thing." With warmth, humor, and wonder, Ed Butchart shares his stories as a professional Santa Claus in The Red Suit Diaries. Deftly combining his Santa persona with his passion for God, Butchart reveals himself as a once-hardened Marine who found Jesus and began to serve others in unusual ways. Listeners will be enthralled by The Red Suit Diaries - from Santa's day job refurbishing medical equipment for the disabled, to the sweetest of secrets whispered in Santa's ear and written in letters, to the story of how he unknowingly found "Mrs. Claus." Woven throughout is a faith and a joy of giving that energizes Butchart's mission to spread love to all kinds of children and adults.

Red Suit Diaries: A Real-Life Santa on Hopes, Dreams, & Childlike Faith. abr. ed. Ed Butchart. Read by Ed Butchart. (Running Time: 3 hrs.). 2004. 24.95 (978-1-59335-269-1(7), 1593352697, Brilliance MP3); 39.25 (978-1-59335-490-9(8), 1593354908, Brinc Audio MP3 Lib) Brilliance Audio.

Red Suit Diaries: A Real-Life Santa on Hopes, Dreams, & Childlike Faith. abr. ed. Ed Butchart. Read by Ed Butchart. (Running Time: 3 hrs.). 2005. 39.25 (978-1-59600-829-8(6), 9781596008298, BADLE); 24.95 (978-1-59710-630-6(5), 9781597106306, BAD) Brilliance Audio.

Red Tape Murder & Other Stories. unabr. ed. Short Stories. Robert H. Van Gulik. Narrated by Frank Muller. 2 cass. (Running Time: 2 hrs. 30 mins.). (Judge Dee Mysteries Ser.). 1986. 18.00 (978-1-55690-440-0(1), 86160E7) Recorded Bks.
Three mysteries investigated by Seventh-Century Chinese magistrate, Judge Dee include the title story; "Five Auspicious Clouds" & "He Came with the Rain.".

Red Tent. Anita Diamant. Narrated by Carol Bilger. 10 CDs. (Running Time: 12 hrs.). audio compact disk 97.00 (978-0-7887-6187-4(0)) Recorded Bks.

Red Tent. Anita Diamant. Narrated by Carol Bilger. 8 cass. (Running Time: 12 hrs.). 1997. 88.00 (978-0-7887-8923-6(6), 96750) Recorded Bks.
Dinah is mentioned only briefly in the Book of Genesis; his father, Jacob, and his sons are given more attention. The author draws on her sense of history and her remarkable literary talent to shift the focus and let Dinah speak of her family and her life.

Red Tent. unabr. rev. ed. Anita Diamant. Read by Carol Bilger. 10 CDs. (Running Time: 12 hrs. 0 mins. 0 sec.). (ENG.). 2002. audio compact disk 49.95 (978-1-55927-709-9(2)) Pub: Macmill Audio. Dist(s): Macmillan

***Red Thread: A Novel.** unabr. ed. Ann Hood. (Running Time: 8 hrs. 0 mins.). 2010. 29.95 (978-1-4417-3501-0(1)); 54.95 (978-1-4417-3497-6(X)); audio compact disk 29.95 (978-1-4417-3500-3(3)); audio compact disk 76.00 (978-1-4417-3498-3(8)) Blckstn Audio.

***Red Thread of Desire.** Featuring Adyashanti. (ENG.). 2010. audio compact disk 16.00 (978-1-933986-81-4(6)) Open Gate Pub.

Red to Black. unabr. ed. Alex Dryden. Narrated by Anne Flosnik. (Running Time: 13 hrs. 30 mins. 0 sec.). (ENG.). 2009. 24.99 (978-1-4001-6373-1(0)); audio compact disk 75.99 (978-1-4001-4373-3(X)); audio compact disk 37.99 (978-1-4001-1373-6(3)) Pub: Tantor Media. Dist(s): IngramPubServ

***Red to Black.** unabr. ed. Alex Dryden. Narrated by Anne Flosnik. (Running Time: 13 hrs. 30 mins.). 2009. 18.99 (978-1-4001-8373-9(1)) Tantor Media.

Red Trailer Mystery. unabr. collector's ed. Julie Campbell. Read by Ariadne Meyers. 3 cass. (Running Time: 5 hrs. 18 mins.). (Trixie Belden Ser.: No. 2). (J). (gr. 4-7). 2005. 30.00 (978-1-4000-9003-7(2), BksonTape) Random Audio Pubg.
Trixie and Honey's friend Jim has run away from Sleepyside - before anyone could tell him that he is the only heir to the huge Frayne fortune. The girls set out across upstate New York in a trailer to track him down... and stumble onto another mystery along the way!.

Red Victory: A History of the Russian Civil War.unabr. ed. W. Bruce Lincoln. Read by Grover Gardner. 15 cass. (Running Time: 22 hrs. 30 min.). 1990. 112.00 (978-0-7366-1836-6(8), 2670) Books on Tape.
The Russian Civil War was one of the pivotal events of our century. It shattered the status quo in Europe, the important balance of power between nations, cost seven million dead & lasted three disastrous years (1918-1921).

Red Wallet: To Feed the Famished. Jonathan Murro & Ann Ree Colton. 1 cass. 7.95 A R Colton Fnd.
Discusses the goal of God-Realization.

Red, White & Blue. abr. ed. Susan Isaacs. Read by John Shea. 4 cass. (Running Time: 6 hrs.). 1999. 25.00 (FS9-43296) Highsmith.

Red, White & Blue. unabr. ed. Susan Isaacs. Read by Susan O'Malley. 12 cass. (Running Time: 17 hrs. 30 mins.). 1999. 83.95 (978-0-7861-1519-8(X), 2369) Blckstn Audio.
FBI special agent Charlie Blair of Wyoming & journalist Lauren Miller of New York are drawn together by an appalling hate crime & by their mutual passion for justice. They are not only simply kindred spirits, but actual kin, descendants of immigrants who met on a boat on their way to America. Charlie is about to risk his life, infiltrating an armed group of white supremacists called Wrath. Lauren's job is to investigate a bombing that Wrath supposedly masterminded.

Red, White & Blue. unabr. ed. Susan Isaacs. (Running Time: 63000 sec.). 2007. audio compact disk 120.00 (978-0-7861-5802-7(6)); audio compact disk 44.95 (978-0-7861-5803-4(4)) Blckstn Audio.

Red, White & Blue Murder. Jeanne M. Dams. Read by Kate Reading. (Hilda Johansson Mystery Ser.: Bk. 2). 2000. audio compact disk 40.00 (978-0-7366-7134-7(X)) Books on Tape.

Red, White & Blue Murder. collector's ed. Jeanne M. Dams. Read by Kate Reading. 5 cass. (Running Time: 7 hrs. 30 min.). (Hilda Johansson Mystery Ser.: Bk. 2). 2000. 40.00 (978-0-7366-5592-7(1)) Books on Tape.
The Studebaker household is in turmoil; the news that President McKinley has been assassinated is more than anyone can stand. South Bend, Indiana, is not a hotbed of anarchist activity, but something is clearly going on. When McKinley's death is blamed on foreign born anarchists, Hilda Johansson, a recent immigrant, is concerned that fellow immigrants might be swept up in a wave of xenophobia. Despite orders to mind her own business, she sets out to discover exactly what is happening, no matter what it might cost her.

***Red, White & Liberal.** abr. ed. Alan Colmes. Read by Alan Colmes. (ENG.). 2004. (978-0-06-075491-4(5), Harper Audio); (978-0-06-081340-6(7), Harper Audio) HarperCollins Pubs.

Red, White & Liberal: How Left Is Right & Right Is Wrong. abr. ed. Alan Colmes. Read by Alan Colmes. 5 CDs. (Running Time: 6 hrs.). 2003. audio compact disk 29.95 (978-0-06-057224-2(8)) HarperCollins Pubs.

Red Wind. unabr. abr. ed. Raymond Chandler. Read by Elliott Gould. 2 CDs. (Running Time: 1.5 hrs.). 2004. audio compact disk 21.95 (978-1-59007-108-3(5)); 15.00 (978-1-59007-107-6(7)) Pub: New Millenn Enter. Dist(s): PerseuPGW
In the four long stories in this collection, Marlowe is hired to protect a rich old guy from a gold digger, runs afoul of crooked politicos, gets a line on some stolen jewels with a reward attached, and stumbles across a murder victim who may have been an extortionist.

Red Wings of Christmas. abr. ed. Narrated by Wesley Eure. Illus. by Ronald G. Paolillo. 2 cass. (Running Time: 2 hrs. 40 min.). (ENG.). (J). (gr. 3-7). 1993. 14.95 (978-0-88289-998-5(8)) Pelican.
A magical & lively audio performance of this Christmastime favorite by soap opera & children's television star Wesley Eure.

Red Wolf Conspiracy. unabr. ed. Robert V. S. Redick. Narrated by Michael Page. (Running Time: 19 hrs. 0 mins. 0 sec.). (Chathrand Voyage Ser.). (ENG.). 2009. audio compact disk 49.99 (978-1-4001-1294-4(X)); audio compact disk 34.99 (978-1-4001-6294-9(7)); audio compact disk 99.99 (978-1-4001-4294-1(6)) Pub: Tantor Media. Dist(s): IngramPubServ

Red Zone. abr. ed. Tim Green. 2 cass. (Running Time: 3 hrs.). 1998. 17.98 (978-1-57042-594-3(9)) Hachet Audio.

Redback. unabr. ed. Howard Jacobson. Read by Raymond Sawyer. 12 cass. (Running Time: 18 hrs.). (Isis Ser.). (J). 2004. 94.95 (978-1-85089-797-2(2), 89101) Pub: ISIS Lrg Prnt GBR. Dist(s): Ulverscroft US

Redbird Christmas: A Novel. unabr. ed. Fannie Flagg. 4 cass. (Running Time: 6 hrs.). 2004. 36.00 (978-1-4159-0359-9(X)); audio compact disk 45.00 (978-1-4159-0497-8(9)) Books on Tape.
The beloved author of Fried Green Tomatoes and other bestsellers gives us an audiobook about a remote small town, where something unusual happens one Christmas morning that changes a family and a town, forever. Like John Grisham's Skipping Christmas and David Baldacci's The Christmas Train, this novel is perfect for the holiday season, or anytime, and it is made even more special because the story is one that is close to Fannie Flagg's heart.

Redcap. Brian Callison. 2007. 69.95 (978-1-84559-626-2(9)); audio compact disk 84.95 (978-1-84559-692-7(7)) Pub: ISIS Audio GBR. Dist(s): Ulverscroft US

Redcoat. collector's ed. Bernard Cornwell. Read by David Case. 11 cass. (Running Time: 16 hrs. 30 min.). 2000. 88.00 (978-0-7366-5448-7(8)) Books on Tape.
Across the fields of ice & blood in a place called Valley Forge, history will be written & will change in ways they cannot imagine the lives of these men & women, participants & bystanders alike.

Redcoat. unabr. ed. Bernard Cornwell. Read by Hayward Morse. 14 CDs. (Running Time: 15 hrs. 40 min.). (Isis Ser.). (J). 2003. audio compact disk 104.95 (978-0-7531-1838-2(6)); 94.95 (978-0-7531-1780-4(0)) Pub: ISIS Lrg Prnt GBR. Dist(s): Ulverscroft US
When Britain and America went to war, it was as if brother fought against brother. At the Forefront of the battle, between roaring enemy guns and the backstabbing of their open politicians, stood the Redcoats. To the British, a Redcoat was the brave suppressor of upstart Yankee rebellion. To American Patriots, the "Bloodybacks" were the thieves of their freedom and plunderers of their birthright.

Redcoat. unabr. ed. Will McCann. Read by Maynard Villers. 7 cass. (Running Time: 6 hrs.). 1996. 39.95 (978-1-55686-733-0(6)) Books in Motion.
Two ex-Texas Rangers join forces with the Canadian Mounted Police to catch American smugglers supplying whiskey & guns to Indians in Canada & hopefully avert an Indian war.

Redcoats & Rebels: The War for America 1770-1781. collector's ed. Christopher Hibbert. Read by David Case. 10 cass. (Running Time: 15 hrs.). 2000. 80.00 (978-0-7366-5634-4(0)) Books on Tape.
For far too long, America's epic struggle for independence from British rule has been shrouded in a haze of legend & invention. In this stirring & colorful account of a Revolution from the perspective of a vanquished. here the fabled heroes & villains on both sides of the conflict come to life in a remarkably compelling work that truly reveals, for perhaps the first time, not only how the colonists won the war, but why the British lost it.

Redeemed. Bill Winston. 6 cass. (Running Time: 5hr.47min.). (C). 1999. 25.00 (978-1-931289-17-7(4)) Pub: B Winston Min. Dist(s): Anchor Distributors

***Redeemed: By Catherine Mae.** Created by Catherine Clifford. (Running Time: 48 minutes). (ENG.). 2009. audio compact disk 16.99 (978-0-615-33612-1(4)) Pure Pearl.

Redeemed from Death. Featuring Bill Winston. 4 cass. 2006. audio compact disk 20.00 (978-1-59544-185-0(9)); audio compact disk 32.00 (978-1-59544-186-7(7)) Pub: B Winston Min. Dist(s): Anchor Distributors

Redeemed from Poverty. Featuring Bill Winston. 4 cass. 2005. 20.00 (978-1-59544-118-8(2)); audio compact disk 32.00 (978-1-59544-119-5(0)) Pub: B Winston Min. Dist(s): Anchor Distributors

Redeemed from Poverty. Featuring Bill Winston. 4 CDs. 2006. audio compact disk 32.00 (978-1-59544-183-6(2)) Pub: B Winston Min. Dist(s): Anchor Distributors

Redeemed from Poverty, 2. Featuring Bill Winston. 4 cass. 2005. 20.00 (978-1-59544-121-8(2)); audio compact disk 32.00 (978-1-59544-122-5(0)) Pub: B Winston Min. Dist(s): Anchor Distributors

Redeemed from Poverty, 4. Featuring Bill Winston. 4 cass. 2006. 20.00 (978-1-59544-182-9(4)) Pub: B Winston Min. Dist(s): Anchor Distributors

Redeemed from Sickness. Featuring Bill Winston. 4 cass. 2006. 20.00 (978-1-59544-171-3(9)); 20.00 (978-1-59544-175-1(1)); audio compact disk 32.00 (978-1-59544-172-0(7)) Pub: B Winston Min. Dist(s): Anchor Distributors

Redeemed from the Curse of the Law. Kenneth E. Hagin. 3 cass. 12.00 (49H) Faith Lib Pubns.

Redeemed Israel (Audio) Reunited & Restored. Batya Ruth Wootten. Voice by Ran Alan Ricard. (ENG.). 2009. 24.95 (978-1-886987-34-0(3)) KeyofDavid.

Redeemer. Perf. by Darren Bridgett & Anna Bullard. Based on a play by Cybèle May. Directed By Norman Kern. Prod. by Aifen Wang. Score by G. D. French & Norman Kern. Engineer Norman Kern. (ENG.). 2008. audio compact disk 24.95 (978-0-9820969-0-1(9)) Crazy Dreams.

Redeemer of the Nations, Come. Composed by J. Michael Thompson. 2001. audio compact disk 16.00 (978-1-58459-087-3(4)) Wrld Lib Pubns.

Redeeming Love. Francine Rivers. Narrated by Kate Forbes. 15 CDs. (Running Time: 17 hrs. 15 mins.). audio compact disk 142.00 (978-0-7887-8969-4(4)) Recorded Bks.

Redeeming Love. unabr. ed. Francine Rivers. Narrated by Kate Forbes. 12 cass. (Running Time: 17 hrs. 15 mins.). 2001. 103.00 (978-0-7887-5011-3(9), K0031E7) Recorded Bks.
A Biblical story of Hosea, setting in the 1850s amidst California's gold country.

Redefining Beautiful: What God Sees When God Sees You. unabr. ed. Jenna Lucado & Max Lucado. (Running Time: 4 hrs. 2 mins. 5 sec.). (ENG.). 2009. 13.99 (978-1-60814-607-9(3)); audio compact disk 19.99 (978-1-59859-659-5(4)) Oasis Audio.

Redefining Third-World Development in the Post-Cold War Era. Hazel Henderson et al. 1 cass. 9.00 (A0331-89) Sound Photosyn.
Setting new practical priorities to meet our needs & ideals.

Redemption. Debra Lee. 1 CD. (Running Time: 60 mins.). 2002. audio compact disk 3.99 (978-1-58608-064-8(4)) New Concepts.

Redemption. Candace Long. Read by Candace Long. 2006. audio compact disk 8.95 (978-0-9788322-0-9(5)) auDEO Media.

Redemption. abr. ed. Karen Kingsbury & Gary Smalley. Read by Sandra Burr. (Running Time: 4 hrs.). (Redemption Ser.). 2005. 49.25 (978-1-59355-882-6(1), 9781593558826, BAudLibEd); 19.95 (978-1-59355-881-9(3), 9781593558819); audio compact disk 21.95 (978-1-59355-883-3(X), 9781593558833, BACD); audio compact disk 69.25 (978-1-59355-884-0(8), 9781593558840, BACDLib Ed) Brilliance Audio.
When Laura Baxter Jacobs finds out that her husband is involved in an adulterous relationship and wants a divorce, she decides she will love him and remain faithful to her marriage at all costs. This book shows how God can redeem seemingly hopeless relationships, and it illustrates one of Gary Smalley's key messages: Love is a decision.

Redemption. abr. ed. Karen Kingsbury & Gary Smalley. Read by Sandra Burr. (Running Time: 4 hrs.). (Redemption Ser.). 2006. 39.25 (978-1-4233-0284-1(2), 9781423302841, BADLE); 9.99 (978-1-4233-0283-4(4), 9781423302834, BAD); 39.25 (978-1-4233-0282-7(6), 9781423302827, Brlnc Audio MP3 Lib); audio compact disk 9.99 (978-1-4233-0281-0(8), 9781423302810, Brilliance MP3) Brilliance Audio.
A Betrayal Kari Baxter Jacobs is furious, hurt, and confused. Her husband, Tim, a respected professor of journalism, is having an affair with a student. Stunned, Kari returns home to the Baxter family to sort things out. But when an old flame shows up, she is more confused than ever. A Decision How can Kari forgive her husband? And what about her own revived feelings for Ryan, a man she knows she should avoid? What remedy could possibly ease the pain? A Hope The gifted writing team of Gary Smalley and Karen Kingsbury brings us a profound story of redemption. A betrayal. A broken marriage. Will Kari ever love again? A story of love at all costs.

***Redemption.** abr. ed. Karen Kingsbury & Gary Smalley. Read by Sandra Burr. (Running Time: 4 hrs.). (Redemption Ser.). 2010. audio compact disk 9.99 (978-1-4418-7831-1(9), 9781441878311, BCD Value Price) Brilliance Audio.

Redemption. abr. ed. Leon Uris. Read by Charles Keating. 4 cass. (Running Time: 6 hrs.). 1999. 25.00 (978-0-694-51551-6(5), 692949) HarperCollins Pubs.
Continues to explore the saga of the long-frustrated Irish people & the growing momentum of their heroic journey toward independence, weaving together unforgettable new characters as well as those the world came to know so well in "Trinity".

***Redemption.** abr. ed. Leon Uris. Read by Charles Keating. (ENG.). 2005. (978-0-06-085601-4(7), Harper Audio); (978-0-06-085602-1(5), Harper Audio) HarperCollins Pubs.

Redemption, Pt. 1. unabr. ed. Leon Uris. Read by Michael Mitchell. 11 cass. (Running Time: 16 hrs. 30 min.). 1996. 88.00 (978-0-7366-3427-4(4), 4072-A) Books on Tape.
Violence grips Ireland after its long-held hopes for home rule are dashed by England's more urgent matters: fighting for its own existence in the catastrophic First World War.

Redemption: Cd Album. Created by Andrew Wommack. (ENG.). 2008. audio compact disk 30.00 (978-1-59548-118-4(4)) A Wommack.

Redemption: God's Grand Design. 3rd rev. ed. 13.00 (978-1-57924-558-0(7)); audio compact disk 15.50 (978-1-57924-559-7(5)) BJUPr.

Redemption: The Last Battle of the Civil War. unabr. ed. Nicholas Lemann. Read by Michael Prichard. (YA). 2007. 39.99 (978-1-59895-881-2(X)) Find a World.

Redemption: The Last Battle of the Civil War. unabr. ed. Nicholas Lemann. Narrated by Michael Prichard. (Running Time: 9 hrs. 0 mins. 0 sec.). (ENG.). 2006. audio compact disk 29.99 (978-1-4001-0283-9(9)); audio compact disk 59.99 (978-1-4001-3283-6(5)) Pub: Tantor Media. Dist(s): IngramPubServ

Redemption: The Last Battle of the Civil War. unabr. ed. Nicholas Lemann. Read by Michael Prichard. (Running Time: 9 hrs. 0 mins. 0 sec.). (ENG.). 2006. audio compact disk 19.99 (978-1-4001-5283-4(6)) Pub: Tantor Media. Dist(s): IngramPubServ

Redemption Ark. unabr. ed. Alastair Reynolds. Narrated by John Lee. (Running Time: 27 hrs. 30 mins. 0 sec.). (Revelation Space Ser.). (ENG.). 2009. audio compact disk 64.99 (978-1-4001-0957-9(4)); audio compact disk 129.99 (978-1-4001-3957-6(0)); audio compact disk 44.99 (978-1-4001-5957-4(1)) Pub: Tantor Media. Dist(s): IngramPubServ

Redemption at Dry Creek. Cynthia Haselhoff. (Running Time: 0 hr. 36 mins.). 1998. 10.95 (978-1-60083-465-3(5)) Iofy Corp.

***Redemption at Dry Creek.** Cynthia Haseloff. 2009. (978-1-60136-457-9(1)) Audio Holding.

Redemption Falls. unabr. ed. Joseph O'Connor. Narrated by Peter Marinker. (Running Time: 68400 sec.). (ENG.). 2007. audio compact disk 49.95 (978-1-60283-305-0(2)) Pub: AudioGO. Dist(s): Perseus Dist

Redemption of Sarah Cain. Beverly Lewis. Narrated by Barbara Caruso. 6 cass. (Running Time: 8 hrs. 30 mins.). 54.00 (978-0-7887-9613-5(5)) Recorded Bks.

Redemption of Sarah Cain. Beverly Lewis. Narrated by Steven Crossley. 7 CDs. (Running Time: 8 hrs. 30 mins.). 2000. audio compact disk 69.00 (978-1-4025-3812-4(X)) Recorded Bks.

Redemption Through Grace. Manly P. Hall. 1 cass. 8.95 (978-0-89314-233-9(6), C900930) Philos Res.

***Redesign Your Thought Box: Embrace Your Greatness.** Debra Hollinrake. Ed. by Debra Hollinrake. Illus. by Joseph Cerna. Engineer Joseph Cerna. (Running Time: 38). (ENG.). 2010. audio compact disk 12.95 (978-0-615-35936-6(1)) Intentional Pow.

Red/Every Cat. Created by Steck-Vaughn Staff. (Running Time: 362 sec.). (Primary Take-Me-Home Books Level A Ser.). 1998. 9.80 (978-0-8172-8657-6(8)) SteckVau.

Redfin. E. J. Gold. Read by Menlo Macfarlane & Robbert Trice. 1 cass. Dramatization. 15.00 (MT122) Union Label.
He is only a goldfish living in a glass bowl, but gradually Redfin awakens to the reality of his situation, & what he can do about it. This play is a chilling analogy to our own condition.

Redheaded League see Sherlock Holmes: Selected Stories

Redheaded League see Famous Cases of Sherlock Holmes

Redheaded League see Stories of Sherlock Holmes

Redhill Rococo. Shena Mackay. Read by Julia Franklin. 5 CDs. (Running Time: 5 hrs. 42 mins.). (Isis (CDs) Ser.). (J). 2004. audio compact disk 59.95 (978-0-7531-2281-5(2)) Pub: ISIS Lrg Prnt GBR. Dist(s): Ulverscroft US

Redhill Rococo. unabr. ed. Shena Mackay. Read by Julia Franklin. 4 cass. (Running Time: 6 hrs.). 2001. 44.95 (978-0-7531-0817-8(8), 010113) Pub: ISIS Audio GBR. Dist(s): Ulverscroft US

Redhunter: A Novel Based on the Life & Times of Senator Joe McCarthy. William F. Buckley, Jr. 10 cass. (Running Time: 15 hrs.). 1999. 80.00 (4997) Books on Tape.
Senator Joseph McCarthy rose & fell in just four years, yet he gave a name to an era. In 1952 he was the most lionized & the most hated man in America but little was known about him. McCarthy's personal charm & single-minded determination took him from Washington, D.C., as the youngest United States senator but it wasn't until 1950, in Wheeling West Virginia, that McCarthy bewitched the nation & unleashed a crusade, with his claim that Communists had infiltrated the United States government.

Redhunter: A Novel Based on the Life & Times of Senator Joe McCarthy. abr. ed. William F. Buckley, Jr.. Contrib. by William F. Buckley, Jr. (ENG.). 2006. 14.98 (978-1-59483-744-9(9)) Pub: Hachet Audio. Dist(s): HachBkGrp

Redhunter: A Novel Based on the Life & Times of Senator Joe McCarthy. unabr. ed. William F. Buckley, Jr. Read by Jonathan Marosz. 10 cass. (Running Time: 15 hrs.). 1999. 80.00 Books on Tape.
Senator Joseph McCarthy rose & fell in just four years, yet he gave a name to an era. In 1952 he was the most lionized & the most hated man in America. But little was known about him. McCarthy's personal charm & single-minded determination took him from Wisconsin & his indigent life as a chicken farmer to Washington, D.C., as the youngest United States senator. But it wasn't until 1950, in Wheeling, West Virginia, that McCarthy bewitched the nation & unleashed a crusade with his claim that Communists had infiltrated the United States government.

Redhunter: A Novel Based on the Life & Times of Senator Joe McCarthy. unabr. ed. William F. Buckley, Jr. Read by Jonathan Marosz. 9 cass. (Running Time: 13 hrs. 30 mins.). 1999. 39.98 (FS9-43900) Highsmith.

Rediscovering Church: The Story & Vision of Willow Creek Community Church. abr. ed. Lynne Hybels & Bill Hybels. (Running Time: 2 hrs. 0 mins. 0 sec.). (ENG.). 2003. 9.99 (978-0-310-26093-6(0)) Zondervan.

Rediscovering God in America: Reflections on the Role of Faith in Our Nation's History & Future. unabr. ed. Newt Gingrich. Narrated by Newt Gingrich. Narrated by Callista Gingrich. (ENG.). 2006. 10.49 (978-1-60814-357-3(0)); audio compact disk 14.99 (978-1-59859-175-0(4)) Oasis Audio.

Rediscovering Holiness: Know the fullness of life with God. unabr. ed. J. I. Packer. (Running Time: 11 hrs. 15 mins. 0 sec.). (ENG.). 2009. audio compact disk 26.98 (978-1-59644-757-8(5), Hovel Audio) christianaud.

***Rediscovering Holiness: Know the fullness of life with God.** unabr. ed. J. I. Packer. Narrated by James Adams. (ENG.). 2009. 16.98 (978-1-59644-758-5(3), Hovel Audio) christianaud.

Rediscovering Masculine Potentials. Read by Robert Moore. 4 cass. (Running Time: 5 hrs. 20 min.). 1987. 32.00 (978-0-7822-0176-5(8), 232) C G Jung IL.
The popular tape set of Moore's groundbreaking work on four archetypes of the male psyche: King, Warrior, Magician & Lover. He describes the mature masculine potential imaged by each of these archetypes & the shadow manifestations that occur when these images remain unconscious & acted out.

Rediscovering Our True Self. Swami Amar Jyoti. 1 cass. 1979. 9.95 (M-17) Truth Consciousness.
The highest purpose & Goal in life is the rediscovery within. Forgetting our own True Self & God, nothig else ever fully satisfies.

Rediscovering the Kingdom. Myles Munroe. (Running Time: 2 hrs. 38 mins.). 2007. 19.99 (978-1-4245-0692-7(1)) Tre Med Inc.

Rediscovering the Kingdom: Ancient Hope for Our 21st Century World. abr. ed. Myles Munroe. (Running Time: 9480 sec.). 2006. audio compact disk 19.99 (978-0-7684-0245-2(X)) Destiny Image Pubs.

Rediscovering the Kingdom Volume 1. abr. ed. Myles Munroe. (Running Time: 15540 sec.). 2006. audio compact disk 24.99 (978-0-7684-0251-3(4)) Destiny Image Pubs.

Rediscovering the Kingdom Volume 3. abr. ed. Myles Munroe. (Running Time: 13140 sec.). 2006. audio compact disk 24.99 (978-0-7684-0253-7(0)) Destiny Image Pubs.

Rediscovering the Kingdom Volume 4. abr. ed. Myles Munroe. (Running Time: 16620 sec.). 2006. audio compact disk 24.99 (978-0-7684-0254-4(9)) Destiny Image Pubs.

Rediscovering the Kingdom Volume 5. abr. ed. Myles Munroe. (Running Time: 20280 sec.). 2006. audio compact disk 24.99 (978-0-7684-0255-1(7)) Destiny Image Pubs.

Rediscovering the Mature Masculine: Resources from Archetypal Psychology. Read by Robert Moore. 3 cass. (Running Time: 4 hrs.). 1990. 24.95 (978-0-7822-0205-2(5), 423) C G Jung IL.

Rediscovering the Navajo Language see Dine Bizaad Binahoo'aah: Rediscovering the Navajo Language Workbook

Rediscovering Values: On Wall Street, Main Street, & Your Street. unabr. ed. Jim Wallis. Read by Jim Wallis. (Running Time: 7 hrs. 30 mins. 0 sec.). (ENG.). 2010. audio compact disk 29.99 (978-1-4423-0509-0(6)) Pub: S&S Audio. Dist(s): S and S Inc

Redneck Christmas Carol. E. J. Sullivan. Illus. by Ernie Eldredge. 2003. bk. 9.95 (978-1-58173-266-5(X)) Sweetwtr Pr AL.

Redneck Night Before Christmas. E. J. Sullivan. Illus. by Ernie Eldredge. (Night Before Christmas Ser.). 2003. bk. 9.95 (978-1-58173-265-8(1)) Sweetwtr Pr AL.

Redneck Riviera. unabr. ed. Sophie Dunbar. Read by Lynda Evans. 6 cass. (Running Time: 8 hrs.). (Claire & Dan Claiborne Eclaire Mystery Ser.: Bk. 2). 2001. 39.95 (978-1-55686-814-6(6)) Books in Motion.
While vacationing at the site of a gulf coast beauty pageant, Claire and husband Dan find deadly manipulation as contestants are found murdered.

Reduce Equipment Maintenance Costs Through a Fully Insured Maintenance Program. 1 cass. (America's Supermarket Showcase '96 Ser.). 1996. 11.00 (NGA96-015) Sound Images.

Reduce Shakespeare Company Radio Show, Vol. 3. unabr. ed. Edward J. Renehan, Jr. 2004. 16.98 (978-1-929243-63-1(4)) Uproar Ent.

Reduce Stress. Betty L. Randolph. 1 cass. (Running Time: 45 mins.). (Self-Hypnosis Ser.). 9.98 (978-1-55909-144-2(4), 803) Randolph Tapes.
Progressive Relaxation. Bio-feedback training, also for corporate seminars on stress management. For PMS. Music background & spoken word.

Reduce Stress & Anxiety: Hypnotic & Sublimnial Learning. David Illig. 2000. audio compact disk 19.95 (978-0-86580-010-6(3)) Success World.

Reduce Stress For Children. 1 cass. (Running Time: 45 min.). (I Can Ser.). 9.98 (978-1-55909-089-6(8), 74S) Randolph Tapes.
Enables children to let-go of stress on a conscious & subconscious level. Subliminal messages are heard 3-5 minutes before becoming ocean sounds or music.

Reduced Shakespeare Christmas. abr. ed. Adam Long et al. 1 cass. (Running Time: 50 mins.). 2004. 12.95 (978-1-57270-069-7(6), C11069a); audio compact disk 15.95 (978-1-57270-075-8(0), C11075a, Audio Editions) Pub: Audio Partners. Dist(s): PerseuPGW
A silly, sly & slapstick take on the holiest of seasons! Listen as these wacky guys chase those Yuletide blues away with this hilarious spoof of Hanukkah, Kwanzaa & an obscure little holiday called Christmas.

Reduced Shakespeare Company Christmas. 1 cass. (Running Time: 50 mins.). 2001. 12.95 (RSCP002) Lodestone Catalog.

Reduced Shakespeare Company Radio Show. Perf. by BBC Production Staff. 2 cass. (Running Time: 3 hrs.). 2001. 19.95 (RSCP001) Lodestone Catalog.
This presentation is not just for Shakespearian scholars, but for everyone. The three zanies at RSC present literary fact, opinion, slander & satire at such a headlong pace that they get through all of the Bard's plays.

Reduced Shakespeare Company Radio Show, Vol. 1. unabr. ed. Edward J. Renehan, Jr. 2004. 16.95 (978-1-929243-61-7(8)) Uproar Ent.

Reduced Shakespeare Company Radio Show, Vol. 2. unabr. ed. Edward J. Renehan, Jr. 11 cassettes. (Running Time: 14.5 hrs). 2004. 16.98 (978-1-929243-62-4(6)) Uproar Ent.

Reduced Shakespeare Radio Show. unabr. ed. Adam Long et al. 2 cass. (Running Time: 3 hrs.). 2004. 17.95 (978-1-57270-059-8(9), C21059a) Pub: Audio Partners. Dist(s): PerseuPGW
With music & sound effects, the actors "reenact" the complete works of Shakespeare: "Romeo & Juliet," "Hamlet," "The Histories," "The Tragedies," "The Comedies," & "Shakespeare's Little Known Trip to America".

Reducing Alcohol Consumption. Michael P. Kelly. 1 cass. 1992. 14.95 (978-1-883700-14-0(0)) ThoughtForms.
Self help.

Reducing High Blood Pressure. Matthew Manning. Music by Paul Rumsey. 1 cass. (Running Time: 90 min.). 1991. 11.95 (MM-112) White Dove NM.
The medical profession acknowledges that relaxation is ultimately more effective than medication in reducing & controlling hypertension. This tape explores the role of diet & exercise in reducing high blood pressure, & also covers published work by doctors in the areas of relaxation & biofeedback.

Relax deeply with the guided imagery & music by Paul Rumsey on Side Two.

Reducing Stress. Shad Helmstetter. 1 cass. (Self-Talk Cassettes Ser.). 10.95 (978-0-937065-20-4(X)) Grindle Pr.

Redwall. Brian Jacques. Read by Brian Jacques. 8 cass. (Running Time: 12 hrs.). (Redwall Ser.). (J). (gr. 4-8). 2000. 50.00 (978-0-7366-9097-3(2)) Books on Tape.
Tale of danger, laughter, hairbreadth escapes, tragedy, mystery, touch of wonder, a truly despicable villain & a hero: Matthias, a young mouse who must rise above his fears & failures to save his friends at Redwall Abbey.

Redwall. Brian Jacques. 9 cass. (Running Time: 643 min.). (Redwall Ser.). (J). (gr. 4-8). 2001. audio compact disk 55.00 (978-0-8072-8610-4(9), Listening Lib) Random Audio Pubg.

Redwall. Brian Jacques & Bruce Coville. Perf. by Brian Jacques & Bruce Coville. 9 CDs. (Running Time: 10 hrs. 43 mins.). (Redwall Ser.). (J). (gr. 4-7). 2004. audio compact disk 55.25 (978-0-8072-2017-7(5), Listening Lib) Pub: Random Audio Pubg. Dist(s): NetLibrary CO

Redwall. unabr. ed. Brian Jacques. Read by Brian Jacques. 8 cass. (Running Time: 10 hrs. 43 mins.). (Redwall Ser.). (J). (gr. 4-7). 1997. 50.00 (978-0-8072-7878-9(5), YA940CX, Listening Lib) Random Audio Pubg.
Is jam-packed with the things we long for in a great adventure; danger, laughter, hairbreadth escapes, tragedy, mystery, a touch of wonder, a truly despicable villain & a hero: Mathias, a young mouse who must rise above his fears & failures to save his friends at Redwall Abbey.

Redwall. unabr. ed. Brian Jacques. Read by Brian Jacques. Read by Full Cast Production Staff. 9 CDs. (Running Time: 38580 sec.). (Redwall Ser.). (ENG.). (J). (gr. 7). 2005. audio compact disk 40.00 (978-0-307-28174-6(4), Listening Lib) Pub: Random Audio Pubg. Dist(s): Random

Redwall. unabr. ed. Brian Jacques. Narrated by Ron Keith. 9 cass. (Running Time: 13 hrs. 15 mins.). (Redwall Ser.). (J). (gr. 4-8). 1997. 77.00 (978-0-7887-0382-9(X), 94573E7) Recorded Bks.
Set in Medieval times & drawing on the King Arthur legend, this is the tale of one shy member of a religious order of mice who leads the abbey's defense against a villainous rat's savagery.

Redwall: The Quest. unabr. ed. Brian Jacques. Read by Brian Jacques. Read by BBC Cast Staff. 3 cass. (Running Time: 3 hrs. 5 min.). (Redwall Ser.: Bk. 2). (J). (gr. 4-8). 1998. 19.95 (978-0-8072-7965-6(X), YA943CXR, Listening Lib) Random Audio Pubg.
The adventures of Matthias & his peace-loving mice continues.

Redwall: The Wall. unabr. ed. Brian Jacques. Read by Brian Jacques. 3 cass. (Running Time: 3 hrs. 10 mins.). (Redwall Radio Play Ser.: Bk. 1). (J). (gr. 4-8). 1997. 19.95 (978-0-8072-7840-6(8), 495624, Listening Lib) Random Audio Pubg.
Recounts the exploits of the peace-loving mice who must defend their home against Cluny, the Scourge & his army of rats.

Redwall: The Wall; The Quest; The Warrior. unabr. ed. Brian Jacques. 8 cass. (Running Time: 12 hrs.). (Redwall Radio Play Ser.: Bks. 1, 2, 3). (J). (gr. 4-8). 1998. 56.95 (L192) Blckstn Audio.
The mice in the village of Redwall are under siege - the evil rat Cluny & his gang have conquering on their minds, & it's up to the sweet, timid mouse friar Matthias to come up with a scheme to outwit "The Scourge".

Redwall: The Wall; The Quest; The Warrior. unabr. ed. Brian Jacques. Read by Brian Jacques. 8 cass. (Running Time: 12 hrs.). (Redwall Ser.: Bks. 1-3). (J). (gr. 4-8). 1999. 52.00 (978-0-7366-4489-1(X), 4928) Books on Tape.
This hero is Matthias, a young mouse who must rise above his fears & failures to save his friends at Redwall Abbey. The villain is Cluny the Scourge, one of the most deliciously despicable rats of all time. The unforgettable cast of supporting characters includes the stalwart badger Constance, the irrepressible Basil Stag Hare & the elderly wisemouse Brother Methuselah. But most of all there is Matthias, seeking his true destiny in a journey that will lead him through danger & despair to true wisdom.

Redwall: The Warrior. unabr. ed. Brian Jacques. Read by Brian Jacques. Perf. by BBC Cast Staff. 2 cass. (Running Time: 2 hrs.). (Redwall Radio Play Ser.: Bk. 3). (J). (gr. 4-8). 1998. 15.95 (978-0-8072-7968-7(4), 395746, Listening Lib) Random Audio Pubg.
Final installment of the mouse epic. The good-hearted defenders of Redwall Abbey have stood against the wrath of Cluny the Scourge & his horde of rats. Now Cluny has a new scheme & his minions are digging a tunnel under the thick walls of the Abbey. As they do, the stalwart Matthias remains missing. Will Redwall stand? Will Matthias return?.

Redwall Bk. 1: The Wall. Brian Jacques. 3 cass. (Running Time: 5 hrs.). (Redwall Ser.). (J). (gr. 4-8). 1999. 15.98 blisterpack. (BYA 931) NewSound.

Redwall Bk. 2: The Quest. Brian Jacques. 3 cass. (Running Time: 5 hrs.). (Redwall Ser.). (J). (gr. 4-8). 1999. 15.98 blisterpack. (BYA943) NewSound.
Matthias the mouse's adventures & exploits.

Redwall Bk. 3: The Warrior. Brian Jacques. 2 cass. (Redwall Ser.). (J). (gr. 4-8). 12.78 blisterpack. (BYA 951) NewSound.
Wraps up the adventures of the peace loving mice who love, honor & defend their Redwall.

Redwall Bks. 1, 2, 3: The Wall; The Quest; The Warrior. unabr. ed. Brian Jacques. 8 cass. (Running Time: 12 hrs.). (Redwall Ser.). (J). (gr. 4-8). 1999. 59.98 (FS9-34622) Highsmith.

Redwall Bks. 1, 2, 3: The Wall; The Quest; The Warrior. unabr. ed. Brian Jacques. 8 vols. (Running Time: 10 hrs. 43 mins.). (Redwall Radio Play Ser.: Bks. 1-3). (J). (gr. 4-7). 1997. pap. bk. 58.00 (978-0-8072-7879-6(3), YA940SP, Listening Lib) Random Audio Pubg.
Is jam-packed with the things we long for in a great adventure; danger, laughter, hairbreadth escapes, tragedy, mystery, a touch of wonder, a truly despicable villain & a hero: Mathias, a young mouse who must rise above his fears & failures to save his friends at Redwall Abbey.

Redwood Summer Demonstration & the California Conservation Corps. Hosted by Nancy Pearlman. 1 cass. (Running Time: 28 min.). 10.00 (809) Educ Comm CA.

Reed of God. abr. ed. Caryll Houselander. (Running Time: 19800 sec.). (ENG.). 2007. audio compact disk 28.95 (978-0-86716-870-9(6)) St Anthony Mess Pr.

Reed Whittemore. unabr. ed. Poems. Reed Whittemore. Read by Reed Whittemore. 1 cass. (Running Time: 29 min.). 1988. 10.00 (012988) New Letters.
Reads his famous poem "Ode to New York" & talks about his life & work.

Reed's Commuter Tune-Ups Vol. 2, set: Taking the High Road. Thomas D. Reed. 4 cass. (Running Time: 4 hrs.). 1998. 19.95 (978-0-9668366-1-5(8)) Nevada Fellowship Found.

Reef. Di Morrissey. Read by Kate Hood. (Running Time: 14 hrs. 50 mins.). 2009. 99.99 (978-1-74214-267-8(2), 9781742142678) Pub: Bolinda Pubng AUS. Dist(s): Bolinda Pub Inc

Reef. abr. ed. Nora Roberts. Read by Sandra Burr. 3 CDs. (Running Time: 3 hrs.). 2003. audio compact disk 14.99 (978-1-59086-532-3(4), 1590865324, BAU); audio compact disk 62.25 (978-1-59086-566-8(9), 1590865669, BAU) Brilliance Audio.
The Reef is the story of Tate Beaumont, a beautiful young student of marine archeology - and of Matthew Lassiter, a sea-scarred young man who shares her dream of finding Anguelique's Curse, the jeweled amulet surrounded by legend and said to be long lost at the bottom of the sea. Forced into a reluctant partnership with Matthew and his uncle, Tate soon learns that her arrogant but attractive fellow diver holds as many secrets as the sea itself. And when the truth emerges about the mysterious death of Matthew's father eight years earlier, desire - and danger - begin to rise to the surface. True to form, Nora Roberts offers a story of grand passion and gripping adventure, bringing her devoted fans to the hidden undersea world - and to the deepest parts of the human heart.

Reef. abr. ed. Nora Roberts. Read by Sandra Burr. (Running Time: 3 hrs.). 2009. audio compact disk 9.99 (978-1-4418-0118-0(9), 9781441801180, BCD Value Price) Brilliance Audio.

Reef. unabr. ed. Di Morrissey. Read by Kate Hood. (Running Time: 53400 sec.). 2006. audio compact disk 108.95 (978-1-74093-732-0(5)) Pub: Bolinda Pubng AUS. Dist(s): Bolinda Pub Inc

Reef. unabr. ed. Di Morrissey. Read by Kate Hood. (Running Time: 14 hrs. 50 mins.). 2009. 43.95 (978-1-74214-438-2(1), 9781742144382) Pub: Bolinda Pubng AUS. Dist(s): Bolinda Pub Inc

Reef. unabr. ed. Nora Roberts. Read by Sandra Burr. 8 cass. (Running Time: 13 hrs.). 1998. 39.95 (978-1-56740-405-0(7), 1567404057, BAU) Brilliance Audio.

Reef. unabr. ed. Nora Roberts. Read by Sandra Burr. (Running Time: 13 hrs.). 2005. 39.25 (978-1-59600-771-0(0), 9781596007710, BADLE); 24.95 (978-1-59600-770-3(2), 9781596007703, BAD); audio compact disk 24.95 (978-1-59600-768-0(0), 9781596007680, Brilliance MP3); audio compact disk 39.25 (978-1-59600-769-7(9), 9781596007697, Brlnc Audio MP3 Lib) Brilliance Audio.

Reef. unabr. ed. Nora Roberts. Read by Sandra Burr. (Running Time: 46800 sec.). 2008. audio compact disk 102.25 (978-1-4233-5620-2(9), 9781423356202, BriAudCD Unabrid) Brilliance Audio.

Reef. unabr. ed. Nora Roberts. Read by Sandra Burr. (Running Time: 13 hrs.). 2009. audio compact disk 29.99 (978-1-4418-0117-3(0), 9781441801173, Bril Audio CD Unabri) Brilliance Audio.

Reef. unabr. ed. Nora Roberts. Read by Sandra Burr. 8 cass. 1999. 73.25 (FS9-43357) Highsmith.

Reef. unabr. ed. Edith Wharton. Read by Flo Gibson. 7 cass. (Running Time: 10 hrs.). (Classic Books on Cassettes Ser.). 1988. 25.95 (978-1-55685-105-6(7)) Audio Bk Con.
Will the love of George Darrow & Anna Leath survive the gradual disclosure of a previous love affair? Set against the dignified background & tradition of an old French chateau, we watch the characters grapple with their fate.

Reef. unabr. ed. Edith Wharton. Read by Eleanor Bron. 8 cass. (Running Time: 12 hrs.). 2000. 69.95 (978-0-7540-0471-4(6), CAB 1894) AudioGO.
When Anna Leath, a young American widow, has a chance encounter in London with George Darrow, her first love, she feels disturbed. She returns to her country chateau in France to await her future. But it turns out that Anna's future & the very foundation of her life, is fragile where it appears most strong.

Reef. unabr. ed. Edith Wharton. Read by Kristen Underwood. 8 cass. (Running Time: 11 hrs. 30 mins.). 1996. 56.95 (978-0-7861-0981-4(5), 1758) Blckstn Audio.
Anna Leath, an American widow living in France, has engaged in a love affair with George Darrow, a diplomat. However, when Darrow is on his way to consolidate marriage plans at Anna's beautiful French chateau, he encounters Sophy Viner, a beauty who is as sprightly & spontaneous as Anna is restrained & demur. Soon after, Anna's affair with Darrow becomes the reef on which the lives of four people are in danger of foundering.

Reef. unabr. ed. Edith Wharton. Read by Kristen Underwood. (Running Time: 37800 sec.). 2007. audio compact disk 29.95 (978-0-7861-6209-3(0)); audio compact disk & audio compact disk 81.00 (978-0-7861-6208-6(2)) Blckstn Audio.

Reef of Death. unabr. ed. Paul Zindel. Narrated by Jeff Woodman. 3 pieces. (Running Time: 3 hrs. 30 mins.). (gr. 7 up). 1998. 27.00 (978-0-7887-2073-4(2), 95426E7) Recorded Bks.
While visiting his uncle in Cairns, Australia, 17-year-old PC McPhee helps an Aboriginal girl hunt for sacred treasure. But they aren't the only ones searching & soon PC is involved in a deadly game of hide-&-seek, far beneath the ocean's surface.

Reefer Madness: Sex, Drugs, & Cheap Labor in the American Black Market. unabr. ed. Eric Schlosser. 2004. 21.95 (978-0-7435-4960-8(0)) Pub: S&S Audio. Dist(s): S and S Inc

Reel & Rock. Perf. by David Holt et al. 1 cass. (Running Time: 30 min.). 1992. 9.98 (978-0-942303-28-5(8)) Pub: High Windy Audio. Dist(s): August Hse
Twelve traditional & original old-time songs, including "Free Little Bird," "Sail Away," "Dixie Darlin'," & "Forked Deer." (One of Merle Watson's last projects.) Can be used for sheer entertainment or for the serious study of traditional music. Naird award winner.

Reel Justice! Power Passion & Persuasion in the Modern Courtroom. Dominic J. Gianna. 6 cass. (Running Time: 6 hrs.). 2001. pap. bk. 185.00 (978-0-943380-67-4(7)) PEG MN.

Reel Justice! Power Passion & Persuasion in the Modern Courtroom. Dominic J. Gianna. Instructed by Dominic J. Gianna. 6 CDs. (Running Time: 6 hrs.). 2002. pap. bk. 205.00 (978-0-943380-68-1(5)) PEG MN.

***Reel Stuff.** Ed. by Martin Greenberg. 2009. (978-1-60136-500-2(4)) Audio Holding.

Reeled In: 3 Big Whoppers from God's Word. Created by Group Publishing. (Simply Junior High Ser.). 2007. DVD & audio compact disk 30.00 (978-5-557-54489-4(5)) Group Pub.

***Reelin' in Tradition.** Louise Mulcahy. Mick Mulcahy. (ENG.). 2009. audio compact disk 25.95 (978-0-8023-8180-4(4)) Pub: Clo Iar-Chonnachta IRL. Dist(s): Dufour

***Reenchantment of everyday Life.** abr. ed. Thomas Moore. Read by Thomas Moore. (ENG.). 2005. (978-0-06-089367-5(2), Harper Audio); (978-0-06-089368-2(0), Harper Audio) HarperCollins Pubs.

Reengineering Case Studies for Local Government. 4 cass. (Running Time: 6 hrs.). 29.95 (978-1-882403-14-1(2)) Alliance Innov.

***Reengineering the Corporation.** abr. ed. Michael Hammer & James Champy. Read by Michael Hammer & James Champy. (ENG.). 2005. (978-0-06-088418-5(5), Harper Audio); (978-0-06-088417-8(7), Harper Audio) HarperCollins Pubs.

Reengineering Yourself: Using Tomorrow's Success Tools to Excel Today. Daniel Burrus. 6 cass. (Running Time: 6 hrs.). 1995. 59.95 wkbk. (10360AT) Nightingale-Conant.
Describes how to establish customer relationships that span time, costs & competition. Also, why current successes may plant the seeds of future failures.

Refelctions on the Serenity Prayer. Edd Anthony. 1 CD. (Running Time: 1 hr. 5 min.). 2003. audio compact disk 16.95 (978-1-881586-09-8(X)) Canticle Cass.

***Referral Engine: Teaching Your Business to Market Itself.** unabr. ed. John Jantsch. (Running Time: 7 hrs.). (ENG.). 2010. 27.98 (978-1-59659-582-8(5), GildAudio) Pub: Gildan Media. Dist(s): HachBkGrp

ReFIRED, not Retired... reignite your zest for Life. Phyllis May. 2006. audio compact disk 11.95 (978-0-9758997-2-4(4)) P May.

Reflecting the Sky. unabr. ed. S. J. Rozan. Read by Kathy Hsieh. 8 vols. (Running Time: 12 hrs.). 2001. bk. 69.95 (978-0-7927-2488-9(7), CSL 377, Chivers Sound Lib) AudioGO.
Lydia Chin is hired by Grandfather Gao, one of the most respected figures in Chinatown, for what appears to be a simple task. Lydia, along with her professional partner Bill Smith, is to fly to Hong Kong to deliver a family heirloom to the young grandson of a recently deceased colleague of Grandfather Gao. But before they can deliver the heirloom, the grandson is kidnapped & two separate ransom demands are made. Lydia & Bill must quickly learn their way around a place where the rules are different, the stakes are high & the cost of failure is too dire to imagine.

Reflection. (704) Yoga Res Foun.

Reflection. unabr. ed. Joe Bright. Read by Ron Varela. 8 cass. (Running Time: 9 hrs. 12 min.). 2001. 49.95 (978-1-55686-753-8(0)) Books in Motion.
Bren Stevens is mystified when he is willed a million English pounds and an old mansion from a murder victim he had never met. Could the mansion's mirror be a portal for time travel?.

Reflection on Brahman, No. 1. Swami Jyotirmayananda. Read by Swami Jyotirmayananda. 1 cass. (Running Time: 45 min.). 10.00 (805) Yoga Res Foun.

Reflection on Brahman, No. 2. Swami Jyotirmayananda. 1 cass. (Running Time: 45 min.). 1990. 10.00 Yoga Res Foun.

Reflection on the Serenity Prayer. Edd Anthony. Read by Edd Anthony. Read by Tony Heim. 1 cass. (Running Time: 60 min.). 1992. 8.95 (978-1-881586-00-5(6), FC-5) Canticle Cass.
Spoken word meditation & music.

Reflections. Contrib. by Jason Champion. 2008. audio compact disk 13.99 (978-5-557-47100-8(6)) Pt of Grace Ent.

Reflections. Gabriela Diana Kaplan. 2006. audio compact disk (978-1-4276-0323-4(5)) AardGP.

***Reflections.** unabr. ed. Nora Roberts. Read by Angela Dawe. (Running Time: 6 hrs.). (Davidov Ser.). 2010. 24.99 (978-1-4418-5715-6(X), 9781441857156, Brilliance MP3); 39.97 (978-1-4418-5716-3(8), 9781441857163, Brlnc Audio MP3 Lib); 39.97 (978-1-4418-5717-0(6), 9781441857170, BADLE); audio compact disk 24.99 (978-1-4418-5713-2(3), 9781441857132, Bril Audio CD Unabri); audio compact disk 79.97 (978-1-4418-5714-9(1), 9781441857149, BriAudCD Unabrid) Brilliance Audio.

Reflections. unabr. ed. Idries Shah. Read by David Wade. 2 vols. (Running Time: 3 hrs.). 1997. bk. 17.00 (978-1-883536-09-1(X), REFL2, Hoopoe Books) ISHK.
Author's own observations, fables, comments & aphorisms.

Reflections, No. II. Poems. Wayne H. Ross. 1 cass. (Running Time: 45 min.). 1995. pap. bk. 30.00; 12.00 W H Ross.
Book of poetry.

Reflections: A Piano Sampler. Windham Hill Staff. 1 cass. 1998. 15.00 (978-1-56170-562-7(4)) Hay House.

Reflections: Indian Stories. Read by Tsonakwa. 1 cass. (J). (gr. k up). 9.98 (327) MFLP CA.
An excellent collection of ancient stories, myths & legends told in the traditional way by an Abenaki tribesman.

Reflections: Life after the White House. Barbara Bush. 2004. 15.95 (978-0-7435-4831-1(0)) Pub: S&S Audio. Dist(s): S and S Inc

Reflections & Peace-Music. 2007. audio compact disk 16.95 (978-1-56136-432-9(0)) Master Your Mind.

Reflections at Sixty-Five. Hal Stone & Sidra Stone. 1 cass. (Running Time: 1 hr.). (Mendocino Ser.). 1994. 10.95 (97[illegible]6557-012-2(X), T36) Delos Inc.
Hal Stone, a major consciousness tea[illegible] psychospiritual innovator, has had a rich & full 65 years. In this very pe[illegible]al interview by his wife, Sidra, he reflects on his life, his philosophy & his transformational journey.

Reflections for Adoptive Parents. 2005. 29.95 (978-1-59649-652-1(5)); audio compact disk 24.95 (978-1-59649-650-7(9)) Whsprng Pine.

Reflections for Catholic Feminists. 2005. 29.95 (978-1-59649-768-9(8)) Whsprng Pine.

Reflections for Catholic Women. 2005. 29.95 (978-1-59649-805-1(6)); audio compact disk 24.95 (978-1-59649-801-3(3)) Whsprng Pine.

Reflections for Catholics. 2005. 29.95 (978-1-59649-758-0(0)); audio compact disk 24.95 (978-1-59649-757-3(2)) Whsprng Pine.

Reflections for Fathers. 2005. 29.95 (978-1-59649-688-0(6)); audio compact disk 24.95 (978-1-59649-687-3(8)) Whsprng Pine.

Reflections for Foster Parents. 2005. 29.95 (978-1-59649-700-9(9)); audio compact disk 24.95 (978-1-59649-699-6(1)) Whsprng Pine.

Reflections for Graduates. 2005. 29.95 (978-1-59649-709-2(2)); audio compact disk 24.95 (978-1-59649-708-5(4)) Whsprng Pine.

Reflections for Highly Effective People. abr. ed. Stephen R. Covey. 1 cass. 9.95 (67190) Books on Tape.
Dr. Covey has taken some of his most powerful ideas & observations from his bestselling "The 7 Habits of Highly Effective People" that provides an inspirational recharge that will bring you closer to a sense of personal effectiveness & purpose.

Reflections for Lent. 2005. 29.95 (978-1-59808-010-0(5)); audio compact disk 24.95 (978-1-59808-009-4(1)) Whsprng Pine.

Reflections for Mothers. 2005. 29.95 (978-1-59649-724-5(6)); audio compact disk 24.95 (978-1-59649-723-8(8)) Whsprng Pine.

Reflections for Today see Reflexiones de Hoy

Reflections for Women: A Collection of Inspirational Poetry, Prayers, & Bible Verses for Daily Reflection. Karen Jean Matsko Hood. 2003. 24.95 (978-1-59210-005-7(8)); audio compact disk 29.95 (978-1-59210-159-7(3)) Whsprng Pine.

Reflections II, Content see Twentieth-Century Poetry in English, No. 26, Recordings of Poets Reading Their Own Poetry

Reflections in Black History: African American Women. Margaret W. Kemp. Read by Margaret W. Kemp. Read by Delores Lefall & Jacqueline Olive. 30 cass. (Running Time: 30 hrs.). (Great African Americans Known & Unknown Ser.). 1996. 375.00 (978-1-891102-00-4(1)) Reflect Black Hist.

Reflections in Black History: Great African Americans Known & Unknown. Margaret W. Kemp. Read by Margaret W. Kemp. Read by Floyd Wilson & Edwin Jones. 10 cass. (Running Time: 10 hrs.). (Abolitionists Ser.: Vol. 1). 1996. 12.95 (978-1-891102-01-1(X)) Reflect Black Hist.
Biographical sketches of great African Americans in all walks of life.

Reflections in Black History Vol. 1: African American Women. Margaret W. Kemp. Read by Jacqueline Boykins. 1 cass. (Running Time: 60 min.). 1998. 12.95 (978-1-891102-47-9(8)) Reflect Black Hist.
Biographical sketches.

Reflections in Black History Vol. 1: Great African Americans Known & Unknown. Margaret W. Kemp. Read by Margaret W. Kemp. Read by Jackie Olive & Leah Williamson. 10 cass. 1996. 129.00 (978-1-891102-31-8(1)) Reflect Black Hist.

Reflections in Black History Vol. 1: Great African Americans Known & Unknown. Margaret W. Kemp. Read by Margaret W. Kemp. Read by Keith Holmes & Darien Campbell, Sr. 10 cass. (Abolitionists Ser.: Vol. 1). 1996. 12.95 (978-1-891102-21-9(4)) Reflect Black Hist.

Reflections in Black History Vol. 1: Great African Americans Known & Unknown. unabr. ed. Margaret W. Kemp. Read by Margaret W. Kemp. Read by Bus Howard & Clemmie Solomon. 10 cass. (Civil Rights Ser. 2: Vol. 1). 1996. 12.95 (978-1-891102-11-0(7)) Reflect Black Hist.

Reflections in Black History Vol. 2: African American Women. Margaret W. Kemp. Contrib. by Gloria Thornton. 1 cass. (Running Time: 60 min.). 1998. 12.95 (978-1-891102-49-3(4)) Reflect Black Hist.

Reflections in Black History Vol. 2: Great African Americans Known & Unknown. Margaret W. Kemp. Read by Margaret W. Kemp. Read by Delores Lefall & Jacqueline Olive. 10 cass. (Great African Americans Known & Unknown Ser.). 1996. 129.00 (978-1-891102-32-5(X)) Reflect Black Hist.

Reflections in Black History Vol. 2: Great African Americans Known & Unknown. Margaret W. Kemp. Read by Margaret W. Kemp. Read by Jacqueline Boykins & Keith Holmes. 10 cass. (Running Time: 1 hrs.). (Abolitionists Ser.: Vol. 2). 1996. 12.95 (978-1-891102-02-8(8)) Reflect Black Hist.

Reflections in Black History Vol. 2: Great African Americans Known & Unknown. Margaret W. Kemp. Read by Margaret W. Kemp. Read by Floyd Wilson et al. 1 cass. (Running Time: 1 hr.). (Education Ser. 3: Vol. 2). 1996. 12.95 (978-1-891102-22-6(2)) Reflect Black Hist.

Reflections in Black History Vol. 2: Great African Americans Known & Unknown. unabr. ed. Margaret W. Kemp. Read by Margaret W. Kemp. Read by Delores Lefall et al. 10 cass. (Entertainment Music Ser. 2: Vol. 2). 1996. 12.95 (978-1-891102-12-7(5)) Reflect Black Hist.

Reflections in Black History Vol. 3: African American Women. unabr. ed. Margaret W. Kemp. Contrib. by Bus Howard. 1 cass. (Running Time: 60 min.). 1998. 12.95 (978-1-891102-50-9(8)) Reflect Black Hist.

Reflections in Black History Vol. 3: Great African Americans Known & Unknown. Margaret W. Kemp. Read by Margaret W. Kemp. Read by Delores Lefall & Jacqueline Boykins. 10 cass. (Great African Americans Known & Unknown Ser.). 1996. 10.95 (978-1-891102-33-2(8)) Reflect Black Hist.

Reflections in Black History Vol. 3: Great African Americans Known & Unknown. Margaret W. Kemp. Read by Margaret W. Kemp. Read by Lonnie E. Kemp, Jr. et al. 1 cass. (Running Time: 1 hr.). (Abolitionists Ser.: Vol. 3). 1996. 12.95 (978-1-891102-03-5(6)) Reflect Black Hist.

Reflections in Black History Vol. 3: Great African Americans Known & Unknown. Margaret W. Kemp. Read by Margaret W. Kemp. Read by Leah Williamson et al. 1 cass. (Running Time: 1 hr.). (Education Ser.: Vol. 3). 1996. 12.95 (978-1-891102-23-3(0)) Reflect Black Hist.

Reflections in Black History Vol. 4: Great African Americans Known & Unknown. Margaret W. Kemp. Read by Margaret W. Kemp. Read by Keith Holmes & Bus Howard. 1 cass. (Running Time: 1 hr.). (Art Ser.: Vol. 1). 1996. 12.95 (978-1-891102-04-2(4)) Reflect Black Hist.

Reflections in Black History Vol. 4: Great African Americans Known & Unknown. Margaret W. Kemp. Read by Margaret W. Kemp. Read by Delores Lefall & Bus Howard. 1 cass. (Running Time: 1 hr.). (Entertainment Music Ser. 2: Vol. 4). 1996. 12.95 (978-1-891102-14-1(1)) Reflect Black Hist.

Reflections in Black History Vol. 4: Great African Americans Known & Unknown. Margaret W. Kemp. Read by Margaret W. Kemp. Read by Jacqueline Boykin & Greg Bardgeman. 10 cass. (Literature-Journalism Ser. 3: Vol. 4). 1996. 12.95 (978-1-891102-24-0(9)) Reflect Black Hist.

Reflections in Black History Vol. 5: Great African Americans Known & Unknown. Margaret W. Kemp. Read by Margaret W. Kemp. 1 cass. (Running Time: 1 hr.). (Literature-Journalism Ser. 2: Vol. 5). 1996. 12.95 (978-1-891102-15-8(X)) Reflect Black Hist.

Reflections in Black History Vol. 5: Great African Americans Known & Unknown. Margaret W. Kemp. Read by Margaret W. Kemp. Read by Clemmie Solomon & Bus Howard. 1 cass. (Running Time: 1 hr.). (Military Ser. 3: Vol. 5). 1996. 12.95 (978-1-891102-25-7(7)) Reflect Black Hist.

Reflections in Black History Vol. 5: Great African Americans Known & Unknown. Margaret W. Kemp. Read by Margaret W. Kemp. Read by Jacqueline Boykins & E. Augustus Jones. 1 cass. (Running Time: 1 hr.). (Black West Ser.: Vol. 5). 1996. 12.95 (978-1-891102-05-9(2)) Reflect Black Hist.

Reflections in Black History Vol. 6: Great African Americans Known & Unknown. Margaret W. Kemp. Read by Margaret W. Kemp. Read by Jacqueline Olive & Bus Howard. 1 cass. (Running Time: 1 hr.). (Business Ser. 1: Vol. 6). 1996. 12.95 (978-1-891102-06-6(0)) Reflect Black Hist.

Reflections in Black History Vol. 6: Great African Americans Known & Unknown. Margaret W. Kemp. Read by Margaret W. Kemp. Read by Jacqueline Boykin & Bus Howard. 1 cass. (Running Time: 1 hr.). (Literature-Journalism Ser. 2: Vol. 6). 1996. 12.95 (978-1-891102-16-5(8)) Reflect Black Hist.

Reflections in Black History Vol. 6: Great African Americans Known & Unknown. Margaret W. Kemp. Read by Margaret W. Kemp. Read by Sharon Solomon & Bus Howard. 1 cass. (Running Time: 1 hr.). (Politicians Ser. 3: Vol. 6). 1996. 12.95 (978-1-891102-26-4(5)) Reflect Black Hist.

Reflections in Black History Vol. 7: Great African Americans Known & Unknown. Margaret W. Kemp. Read by Margaret W. Kemp. Read by Anthony Jackson & Leah Williamson. 1 cass. (Running Time: 1 hr.). (Politicians Ser. 2: Vol. 2). 1996. 12.95 (978-1-891102-17-2(6)) Reflect Black Hist.

Reflections in Black History Vol. 7: Great African Americans Known & Unknown. Margaret W. Kemp. Read by Margaret W. Kemp. Read by Lonnie E. Kemp, Jr. & Sharon Solomon. 1 cass. (Running Time: 1 hr.). (Science Ser. 3: Vol. 7). 1996. 12.95 (978-1-891102-27-1(3)) Reflect Black Hist.

Reflections in Black History Vol. 7: Great African Americans Known & Unknown. Margaret W. Kemp. Read by Margaret W. Kemp. Read by Jacqueline Boykins et al. 1 cass. (Running Time: 1 hr.). (Business Ser. 1: Vol. 7). 1996. 12.95 (978-1-891102-07-3(9)) Reflect Black Hist.

Reflections in Black History Vol. 8: Great African Americans Known & Unknown. Margaret W. Kemp. Read by Margaret W. Kemp. Read by Lonnie E. Kemp, Jr. & Jacqueline Olive. 1 cass. (Running Time: 1 hr.). (Science Ser. 3: No. 8). 1996. 12.95 (978-1-891102-28-8(1)) Reflect Black Hist.

Reflections in Black History Vol. 8: Great African Americans Known & Unknown. Margaret W. Kemp. Read by Margaret W. Kemp. Read by Leah Williams & Bus Howard. 1 cass. (Running Time: 1 hr.). (Civil Rights Ser. 1: Vol. 8). 1996. 12.95 (978-1-891102-08-0(7)) Reflect Black Hist.

Reflections in Black History Vol. 8: Great African Americans Known & Unknown. Margaret W. Kemp. Read by Margaret W. Kemp. Read by Lonnie E. Kemp, Jr. & Gloria Thornton. 1 cass. (Running Time: 1 hr.). (Politicians Ser. 2: Vol. 8). 1996. 12.95 (978-1-891102-18-9(4)) Reflect Black Hist.

Reflections in Black History Vol. 9: Great African Americans Known & Unknown. Margaret W. Kemp. Read by Margaret W. Kemp. Read by Lonnie E. Kemp, Jr. & Bus Howard. 10 cass. (Sports Ser.: Vol. 3). 1996. 10.95 (978-1-891102-29-5(X)) Reflect Black Hist.

Reflections in Black History Vol. 9: Great African Americans Known & Unknown. Margaret W. Kemp. Read by Margaret W. Kemp. Read by Jacqueline Boykin & E. Augustus Jones. 1 cass. (Running Time: 1 hr.). (Civil Rights Ser. 1: Vol. 9). 1996. 12.95 (978-1-891102-09-7(5)) Reflect Black Hist.

Reflections in Black History Vol. 9: Great African Americans Known & Unknown. Margaret W. Kemp. Read by Margaret W. Kemp. Read by Darien Campbell, Sr. & Jacqueline Boykins. 1 cass. (Running Time: 1 hr.). (Religion Ser. 2: Vol. 9). 1996. 12.95 (978-1-891102-19-6(2)) Reflect Black Hist.

Reflections in Black History Vol. 10: Great African Americans Known & Unknown. Margaret W. Kemp. Read by Margaret W. Kemp. Read by Leah Williamson & E. Augustus Jones. 10 cass. (Education Ser. 1: Vol. 1). 1996. 12.95 (978-1-891102-10-3(9)) Reflect Black Hist.

Reflections in Black History Vol. 10: Great African Americans Known & Unknown. Margaret W. Kemp. Read by Margaret W. Kemp. Read by Darien Campbell, Sr. & Leah Williamson. 1 cass. (Running Time: 1 hr.). (Religion Ser. 2: Vol. 10). 1996. 12.95 (978-1-891102-20-2(6)) Reflect Black Hist.

Reflections in Black History Vol. 10: Great African Americans Known & Unknown. Margaret W. Kemp. Read by Margaret W. Kemp. Read by Keith Holmes & Lonnie E. Kemp, Jr. 1 cass. (Running Time: 1 hr.). (Sports Ser. 3: Vol. 10). 1996. 12.95 (978-1-891102-30-1(3)) Reflect Black Hist.

***Reflections in Pink Fundraiser: A Collection of Bible Verses, Prayers, & Inspirational Poetry for Reflection & Healing.** Karen Jean Matsko Hood. 2011. audio compact disk 24.95 (978-1-59434-589-0(9)) Whsprng Pine.

Reflections in Turquoise. abr. ed. Beatrixe Coty. Read by Mary M. Lewis. 1 cass. (Running Time: 90 min.). (Listen to Love Ser.). 3.98 (903R) Audio Bk.
From Boston to New Mexico, a love is pursued & is at last fulfilled.

Reflections of a Family Man. Calvin Trillin. 1 cass. (Running Time: 1 hr. 19 mins.). 2001. 12.95 Smithson Assocs.

Reflections of a Neoconservative. unabr. ed. Irving Kristol. Read by Tory Hanson. 10 cass. (Running Time: 14 hrs. 30 mins.). 1993. vinyl bd. 69.95 (978-0-7861-0059-0(1), 1056) Blckstn Audio.
This important work, by the "godfather" of neoconservatism, is more or less a political autobiography which shows the development of the neoconservative mind.

Reflections of an Adolescent. Poems. SeKeithia Johnson. (Running Time: 50 mins.). (YA). 2006. audio compact disk 10.00 (978-0-9776740-1-5(0)) Dep Rotz.

Reflections of an Englishwoman Abroad. unabr. ed. Barbara Robinson. Read by Barbara Robinson. 1 cass. (Reflections Ser.). 1999. 12.00 (978-0-9669477-0-0(3)) B Robinson.
Inspirational verse with a backdrop of music.

***Reflections of Bethlehem.** Charles R. Swindoll. 2009. audio compact disk 9.99 (978-1-57972-822-9(7)) Insight Living.

Reflections of Christ. Compiled by Richard D. Serpa Jr. 2008. audio compact disk 6.99 (978-5-557-48001-7(3)) Pt of Grace Ent.

Reflections on a Nation at Risk **see Discussion on Purpose of Education**

Reflections on a Wicked World. abr. ed. Ogden Nash. Perf. by Ogden Nash. 1 cass. 1984. 12.95 (978-0-694-50206-6(5), SWC 1307) HarperCollins Pubs.

Reflections on Adam's Rib: The Feminine in the Androgyne. Read by Charles Ponce. 1 cass. (Running Time: 2 hrs.). 1976. 12.95 (978-0-7822-0228-1(4), 026) C G Jung IL.

Reflections on Dante's Divine Comedy: Purgatorio & Paradiso. Gil Bailie. 12 cass. (Running Time: 12 hrs.). vinyl bd. 79.95 (AA2734) Credence Commun.
Perhaps no one can do justice to explaining the meaning & majesty of this towering genius, but Bailie comes brilliantly close. When you finish listening to his fascinating lectures, you feel you know Dante, you're glad you know, & you are humble that you don't know more.

Reflections on Dante's Divine Comedy: The Inferno. Gil Bailie. 12 cass. (Running Time: 12 hrs.). vinyl bd. 79.95 (AA2733) Credence Commun.

Reflections on Esoteric Christianity. Instructed by Manly P. Hall. 8.95 (978-0-89314-235-3(2), C811220) Philos Res.

Reflections on Facing Cancer. E. Ronal Mudd. 1986. 10.80 (0808B) Assn Prof Chaplains.

Reflections on Intimacy & Sexuality: Biblical & Spiritual Insights. Mary G. Durkin. 4 cass. (Running Time: 4 hrs.). 32.95 incl. shelf-case. (TAH085) Alba Hse Comns.
A present vision of intimacy & human sexuality. Includes the pastoral implications from a spiritual & biblical perspective based on the theology of the body as articulated by John Paul II in his recent weekly audience.

Reflections on John's Gospel. Gil Bailie. 12 cass. (Running Time: 12 hrs.). vinyl bd. 79.95 (AA2732) Credence Commun.
Perhaps you've read John's gospel as mystical theology, or a moral summons or a sacramental treasure, but have you ever looked at this gospel as the passing of an entire culture - a culture based on the temple & its sacrifice? Bailie, using the profound new findings by anthropologist Rene Girard, sees all the old meanings, but adds a new level: the level of cultural revolution. When you interpret John this way, details, patterns, sayings, symbolic actions & reactions take on meanings that are profound & dawn-fresh.

Reflections on the Artist's Way. Julia Cameron. 3 CDs. (Running Time: 2 Hrs 30 Mins). 2005. audio compact disk 24.95 (978-1-59179-318-2(1), AW00230D) Sounds True.
Unblock your natural creativity with help from Reflections on the Artist's Way, Julia Cameron's groundbreaking audiotape on unleashing your inner artist (formerly released as The Artist's Way). Her unique system helps instill the creativity "habit," while yielding powerful results. God's greatest gift to you, she teaches, is your creativity. It is a divine expression, which can be repaid only through another creative act. Discussing creativity's unlimited capacity for transformation, Julia Cameron offers her step-by-step methods for getting started. Are we all born creative? How can you overcome the "I'm not talented enough" conditioning stifling your dreams? An award-winning writer, poet, filmmaker, and musician, Cameron examines these questions with cutting wit and a helpful heart. Includes informative live lecture, exercises, and studio question and answer session.

Reflections on the Empty Tomb: 1 John 3:1-2. Ed Young. (J). 1983. 4.95 (978-0-7417-1293-6(8), 293) Win Walk.

Reflections on the Fatima Children. John De Marchi. 1 cass. 1989. 2.50 (978-1-56036-067-4(4)) AMI Pr.

***Reflections on the Lord's Prayer.** Susan Brower. (Running Time: 2 hrs. 5 mins. 0 sec.). (ENG.). 2009. 14.99 (978-0-310-30264-3(1)) Zondervan.

Reflections on the Psalms. 2005. 24.95 (978-0-7861-4357-3(6)); audio compact disk 27.00 (978-0-7861-7496-6(X)) Blckstn Audio.

Reflections on the Psalms. unabr. ed. C. S. Lewis. Read by Ralph Cosham. 2005. 29.95 (978-0-7861-7811-7(6)) Blckstn Audio.

Reflections on the Revolution in France. unabr. ed. Edmund Burke. Read by Bernard Mayes. 8 cass. (Running Time: 11 hrs. 30 mins.). 1990. 56.95 (978-0-7861-0111-5(3), 1101) Blckstn Audio.
This began as a letter to a young French friend who asked Burke's opinion whether France's new ruling class would succeed in creating a better order. Doubtless he expected a favorable reply, but Burke was suspicious of various tendencies of the revolution from the start & perceived that the revolutionaries were actually subverting the true "social order.".

Reflections on the Revolution in France/Rights of Man. Edmund Burke et al. Read by Craig Deitschmann. (Running Time: 10800 sec.). (Giants of Political Thought Ser.). 2006. audio compact disk 25.95 (978-0-7861-6982-5(6)) Pub: Blckstn Audio. Dist(s): NetLibrary CO

Reflections on Thirty Years in Academia. unabr. ed. Edwin Locke. 1 cass. (Running Time: 1 hrs. 30 min.). 1997. 12.95 (978-1-56114-521-8(1), KL51C) Second Renaissance.
A discussion of such issues as the tenure system, the "diversity" movement, & recent changes in the intellectual climate.

Reflections on Toscanini. unabr. collector's ed. Harvey Sachs. Read by Barrett Whitener. 8 cass. (Running Time: 8 hrs.). 1997. 48.00 (978-0-7366-3667-4(6), 4342) Books on Tape.
A story about the most famous operatic & symphonic conductor in history.

Reflections Poetry by Ruth Ann Turner. Ruth Ann Turner. 2006. audio compact disk Rental 15.00 (978-0-9792270-1-1(1)) Musicians Guild.

Reflective Therapist. Jeffrey A. Kottler. Read by Jeffrey A. Kottler. 2 cass. (Running Time: 2 hrs.). 1991. bk. 32.00 (978-1-55542-395-7(7), Jossey-Bass) Wiley US.
The author describes what it means to be a psychotherapist. Candid conversations with a panel of practicing therapists.

Reflex. Stephen Jay Gould. Narrated by Christine Marshall & William Dufris. 1 CD. (Running Time: 14 Hrs. 13 Mins.). 2004. audio compact disk 29.45 (978-1-58439-004-6(2)) Pbk Dig Inc.
Davy thinks he's alone...what if he isn't?When Davy was a young teen, he discovered that he was capable of teleportation. At first, it was only when he was terrified and in horrible danger. Later, he learned to control his ability, and went to work for a secret government agency.Now, a mysterious group of people has taken Davy captive. They don't want to hire him, and they don't have any hope of appealing to him to help them. What they want is to own him. They want to use his abilities for their own purposes, whether Davy agrees to it or not. And so they set about brainwashing him and conditioning him, and they have found a way to keep a teleport captive.But there's one thing that they don't know. No one knows it, not even Davy.The secret is that experiencing teleportation, over and over again, can teach a person how to do it. Davy's wife Millie is the only person on Earth who has teleported nearly as often as he has. She discovered her new talent the same way Davy did - in mortal danger, facing imminent death, she suddenly found herself in her own apartment.Now, if she can learn to control this ability, and fast, she may be able to rescue Davy. ------------------ -This MP3-CD Audiobook can only be played on an MP3 compatible CD player or an MP3 device like an Apple iPod. Please make sure that you CD player is MP3 compatible before you purchase this audiobook.

Reflex. unabr. ed. Dick Francis. Read by Tony Britton. 8 cass. (Running Time: 8 hrs. 30 mins.). 2000. 34.95 (978-1-57270-135-9(8), N81135u) Pub: Audio Partners. Dist(s): PerseuPGW
Jockey Philip Nore sets out to discover the truth about the murder of George Millace, a track photographer. Slowly, Nore unravels secrets of corruption, blackmail & murder & unwittingly sets himself up as the killer's next target.

Reflex. unabr. ed. Dick Francis. Read by Tony Britton. 8 cass. (Running Time: 12 hrs.). 2000. 59.95 (978-0-7451-6831-9(0), CAB 546) Pub: Chivers Audio Bks GBR. Dist(s): AudioGO
Philip Nore is nearing the end as a jockey. George Millace is finished in photography. The difference is, Millace is dead, and Nore has discovered Millace's secret: a set of files that could blow the top off the racing world! Soon, Nore has uncovered corruption on a scale he had never imagined.

Reflex. unabr. ed. Dick Francis. Narrated by Simon Prebble. 7 cass. (Running Time: 9 hrs.). 2000. 60.00 (978-0-7887-3128-0(9), 95767E7) Recorded Bks.
This fast-paced story of a jockey's courageous murder investigation exposes the politics & corruption at the heart of the British racing world.

Reflex Sympathetic Dystrophy - Pain Free: Technique One. Arranged by Teri Gore. 1. (Running Time: 47 min). 2005. audio compact disk (978-1-59971-089-1(7)) AardGP.
Reflex Sympathetic Dystrophy is a horrible, painful, life altering disease. You can live pain free. Dr. Gore will lead you through some wonderful experiences of relaxation, that will ease your discomfort. You will feel better, function better, and create a new life for yourself. Dr. Gore's soothing relazing voice will help you relax into a fabulous feeling of healing and comfort. Experience today the relief that you have been seeking.

Reflex Sympathetic Dystrophy & Causalgia. Marilee Schuchard. 1 cass. (Running Time: 40 min.). 1997. bk. 15.00 (978-1-58111-002-9(2)) Contemporary Medical.
General understanding & pathophysiology of reflex (pain) sympathetic dystrophy & causalgia; medical & surgical interventions, presents rehab treatment.

Reflexiones de Hoy. Mariano de Blas.Tr. of Reflections for Today. (SPA.). 2009. 24.95 (978-1-935405-03-0(9)) Hombre Nuevo.

Reflexology, Vol. 9. Jonathan Parker. 2 cass. (Running Time: 2 hrs.). 1998. 17.00 (978-1-58400-008-2(2)) QuantumQuests Intl.

Reflowering of the Goddess in Art & Literature. Gloria Orenstein. 1 cass. 9.00 (A0335-88) Sound Photosyn.
A professor addressing, with slides, the subject of her expertise & newly published book, from Embodying the Spiritual in the Art of the Future Symposium.

REFlux: Poetic Spirit & Spoken Soul. Poems. Perf. by Marc Lacy. Prod. by Charles Owens. 1 CD. 2004. audio compact disk 14.00 (978-0-9749712-1-6(9)) AVO Pubng.

Reformation. Stephen Mansfield. 1 cass. (Running Time: 90 mins.). (Basic Church History Ser.: Vol. 4). 2000. 5.00 (SM01-004) Morning NC.
Stephen does a masterful job of making church history come to life. This is an overview starting from pentecost & continuing through the 20th century.

Reformation, Pt. 2. unabr. ed. Will Durant & Ariel Durant. Read by Alexander Adams. 10 cass. (Running Time: 15 hrs.). (Story of Civilization Ser.). 1997. 80.00 (978-0-7366-3620-9(X), 4279-B) Books on Tape.
At the beginning of the sixteenth century, a movement began to sweep through Western Europe, shaking the stability of every state & institution in its path - the Reformation.

Reformation, Pt. 3. unabr. collector's ed. Will Durant & Ariel Durant. Read by Alexander Adams. 12 cass. (Running Time: 18 hrs.). (Story of Civilization Ser.). 1997. 96.00 (978-0-7366-3619-3(6), 4279) Books on Tape.

Reformation Biographies (2002) 2002. 24.00 (978-1-59128-374-4(4)); 30.00 (978-1-59128-376-8(0)) Canon Pr ID.

***Reformation for Armchair Theologians.** unabr. ed. Glen Sunshine. Narrated by Kate Reading. (ENG.). 2005. 14.98 (978-1-59644-205-4(0), Hovel Audio) christianaud.

Reformation for Armchair Theologians. unabr. ed. Glen S. Sunshine. Narrated by Kate Reading. 5 CDs. (Running Time: 6 hrs. 30 mins. 0 sec.). (ENG.). 2005. audio compact disk 23.98 (978-1-59644-204-7(2), Hovel Audio) christianaud.

Reformation to the Great Awakening. Stephen Mansfield. 1 cass. (Running Time: 90 mins.). (Basic Church History Ser.: Vol. 5). 2000. 5.00 (SM01-005) Morning NC.
Stephen does a masterful job of making church history come to life. This is an overview starting from pentecost & continuing through the 20th century.

Reformed Is Not Enough: Basic Categories. Read by Douglas Wilson. 6. 2002. 14.00 (978-1-59128-467-3(8)); 18.00 (978-1-59128-469-7(4)) Canon Pr ID.

Reformed Is Not Enough: Saints & Sinners. Read by Douglas Wilson. 8. 2002. 22.00 (978-1-59128-470-3(8)); 28.00 (978-1-59128-472-7(4)) Canon Pr ID.

Reformed Is Not Enough: The Declarations of God. Read by Douglas Wilson. 8. 2002. Rental 22.00 (978-1-59128-473-4(2)); 28.00 (978-1-59128-475-8(9)) Canon Pr ID.

***Reformed Pastor.** unabr. ed. Richard Baxter. Narrated by Simon Vance. (ENG.). 2007. 16.98 (978-1-59644-443-0(6), Hovel Audio) christianaud.

Reformed Pastor: A Pattern for Personal Growth & Ministry. unabr. ed. Richard Baxter. Read by Simon Vance. (Running Time: 8 hrs. 24 mins. 0 sec.). (ENG.). 2007. audio compact disk 26.98 (978-1-59644-442-3(8)) christianaud.

***Reformed Vampire Support Group.** unabr. ed. Catherine Jinks. Read by Caroline Lee. 9 CDs. (Running Time: 11 hrs. 32 mins.). (YA). (gr. 8 up). 2009. audio compact disk 65.00 (978-0-7393-8530-2(5), Listening Lib) Pub: Random Audio Pubg. Dist(s): Random

Reformer: The Power of the Enneagram Individual Type Audio Recording. Scripts. Based on a work by Enneagram Institute Staff. 1 CD. (Running Time: 60 mins.). 2004. audio compact disk 10.00 (978-0-9755222-0-2(5)) Enneagr.
Type One Individual Type Audio Recording (ITAR) in CD format from the audio tapeset The Power of the Enneagram. Includes a 25 minute introduction to the system as a whole, as well as a 35 minute exposition on Type One. An excellent way for therapists or business consultants to introduce the Enneagram to clients, or to work with the Enneagram in ongoing situations.

Reforming Marriage. Read by Gene Helsel. 5 cass. 1997. 20.00 (978-1-59128-541-0(0)) Canon Pr ID.

Reforming Marriage AudioBook. Douglas Wilson. Read by Gene Helsel. 5 CDs. (ENG.). 1997. audio compact disk 20.00 (978-1-59128-540-3(2)) Canon Pr ID.

Reforming Marriage Conference (2004) 7 cass. 2004. 22.00 (978-1-59128-247-1(0)) Canon Pr ID.

Reforming Marriage Conference (2004) Read by Doug and Nancy Wilson. 2004. 18.00 (978-1-59128-245-7(4)) Canon Pr ID.

Reforming Marriage Conference (2004) Read by Douglas Wilson. 2004. 18.00 (978-1-59128-242-6(X)) Canon Pr ID.

Reforming the Church in the 21st Century. Prod. by Generations Radio. 2008. audio compact disk 9.95 (978-0-9801910-4-2(1)) Gen With Vis.

Reforming the Nations: An Example from the Life of Noah Webster. Instructed by Stephen McDowell. 2000. 5.95 (978-1-887456-26-5(0)) Providence Found.

Reforms of Vatican II: How Have We Done? Where Are We Going? Kenneth Untener. 2 cass. (Running Time: 2 hrs.). 2001. 18.95 (A6680) St Anthony Mess Pr.
Examines Church past, present and future against the backdrop of the Second Vatican Council held 30 years ago.

Refractory Anemia: Prelukemia Syndrome. Read by Stephen H. Robinson. 1 cass. (Running Time: 90 min.). 1985. 12.00 (C8562) Amer Coll Phys.

Refresh Your Spirit. abr. ed. Matthew McKay & Patrick Fanning. Read by Jerry Landis. 1 cass. (Running Time: 20 min.). (Daily Relaxer Audio Ser.). (ENG.). 1998. reel tape 7.95 (978-1-57224-097-1(0)) New Harbinger.

Refreshed Heart. John Eldredge. 2009. audio compact disk 9.99 (978-1-4002-0264-5(7)) Nelson.

Refreshing Journeys. Julie Lusk. Perf. by Steven Zdenek Eckels. 1 cass. (Running Time: 54 min.). 1995. 11.95 (978-1-57025-068-2(5)) Whole Person.
This imagery sampler provides a powerful introduction to guided imagery & its potential for stress management & enhancing well-being.

Refuge. unabr. ed. Gillian White. Read by Jilly Bond. 8 cass. (Running Time: 10 hrs.). (Isis Ser.). (J). 2002. 69.95 (978-0-7531-1462-9(3)) Pub: ISIS Lrg Prnt GBR. Dist(s): Ulverscroft US
A chilling depiction of revenge and the forces of evil Shelley, mother of various children by different fathers, loves all her kids with a fierce passion. She has always defended Joey, her eldest, when he seemed out of control. But an eight-week-old baby set alight in its pram by some rowdy youths - surely her Joey couldn't have been involved in that? In her heart she knows that he was there, although he protests his innocence. And when the police arrive and take him away for questioning, she has to endure the primitive hostility of a neighbourhood outraged by the death of an innocent little child.

Refuge: An Unnatural History of Family & Place. Ed. by Terry Tempest Williams. Music by David Darling. 2 cass. (Running Time: 2 hrs.). 1994. 16.95 (978-0-939643-46-2(4), 3554, NrthWrd Bks) TandN Child.
Refuge tells two parallel stories of death and life while exploring the delicate bonds that hold an ecosystem and a family together.

Refuge & Strength: Selections from the Psalter of the Book of Common Prayer. The Choir of the Church of St. Luke in the Fields. (ENG.). audio compact disk 18.00 (978-0-89869-354-6(3)) Church Pub Inc.

Refuge in Stillness. Swami Amar Jyoti. 1 dolby cass. 1984. 9.95 (M-51) Truth Consciousness.
Taking refuge through the process of stilling, clearing & unburdening the mind. Seeing as it is.

Refugee Blues see Twentieth-Century Poetry in English, No. 1, Recordings of Poets Reading Their Own Poetry

Refugee in America see Poetry of Langston Hughes

Refugees see Caedmon Treasury of Modern Poets Reading Their Own Poetry

Refunding - An Introduction. Update Publicare Staff. 1 cass. (Running Time: 1 hr.). 1992. 11.95 (37SOR302CT) Sell Out Recordings.
An educational session on refunding, approaches, short cuts, & other how to's.

Refusal to Mourn the Death, by Fire, of a Child in London see Dylan Thomas Reading: And Death Shall Have No Dominion and Other Poems

Refusal to Mourn the Death, by Fire, of a Child in London see Dylan Thomas Reading His Poetry

Refusal to Mourn the Death, by Fire, of a Child in London see Caedmon Treasury of Modern Poets Reading Their Own Poetry

Reg D Made Easy: Reg D Rule 504 Made Easy: How to Prepare & Present Your Funding Request to Raise $1M Private Capital. Mervin L. Evans. 3 Audiocassettes. (Running Time: 4 Hour). 2003. 99.99 (978-0-914391-53-1(4)) Comm People Pr.

Reg d Rule 504 Made Easy: Finding Your Private Investors. Speeches. Mervin Evans. 1 CD or Audiocassett. (Running Time: 60m). 2002. 19.99 (978-0-914391-24-1(0)) Comm People Pr.
How to locate Private Capital !.

Regalo de Arrullos para Ninos. Perf. by J. Aaron Brown. Ed. by J. Aaron Brown. Tr. by Sysy Pineda. Illus. by Jim Vienneau. 1 cass. (Running Time: 60 min.). (SPA.). (J). (ps). 1988. bk. 12.95 (978-0-927945-02-8(9)) Someday Baby.
Children's lullabies in Spanish.

Regalo de Navidad. unabr. ed. Richard Paul Evans. Read by Angel Pineda.Tr. of Christmas Box. 2004. 9.95 (978-0-7435-4668-3(7)) Pub: S&S Audio. Dist(s): S and S Inc

Regalo del Tiempo: Cartas A MIS Hijos. Jorge Ramos. Read by Jorge Ramos. (SPA.). 2009. 59.99 (978-1-61545-564-5(7)) Find a World.

Regalo del Tiempo: Cartas A Mis Hijos. abr. ed. Jorge Ramos. Read by Jorge Ramos. 5 cds. (Running Time: 21600 sec.). (SPA.). 2007. audio compact disk 24.95 (978-1-933499-53-6(2)) Fonolibro Inc.

Regan Bauman Bull Roast. Contrib. by Ronald Gov Reagan. 1976. audio compact disk 12.95 (978-1-57970-498-8(0), Audio-For) J Norton Pubs.

Regathering of Israel. Derek Prince. 1 cass. (Running Time: 90 min.). 1998. 5.95 (4343) Derek Prince.
Regathered Israel is God's banner to the nations, warning that the present age is near its end. How should we respond?.

Regatta. unabr. ed. Libby Purves. Read by Belinda Lang. 8 cass. (Running Time: 8 hrs.). 2000. 69.95 (978-0-7540-0513-1(5), CAB1936) AudioGO.
Anasi, child of council & parental carelessness, is cast up for the summer in a Suffolk town. Her host's complacency & her own demons drive her to torpedo its peace with a well-timed revelation about what she has seen. The results are comic & catastrophic for Anasi, for cozy Sheila & her peevish husband Simon, for this lover & the whole summer community around them.

Regenbogenfisch see Rainbow Fish

Regency Buck. Georgette Heyer. 9 cass. (Running Time: 13 hrs. 30 min.). 2000. 72.00 Audio Bk Con.
A lovely, vivacious & daring heroine meets her match in her guardian. A witty & entertaining historical novel reminiscent of Jane Austen.

Regency Buck. unabr. collector's ed. Georgette Heyer. Read by Flo Gibson. 9 cass. (Running Time: 13 hrs. 30 mins.). 1983. 72.00 (978-0-7366-0643-1(2), 1601) Books on Tape.
The heroine, Judith Taverner, is lovely, vivacious & daring. But she meets her match in her guardian, the lofty & self-consequential Lord Worth. True to her own sense of self-value, Judith challenges him in a duel of wits.

Regency Etiquette. A Lady of Distinction. Ed. by Nadia May. 4 CDs. (Running Time: 4 hrs.). 2004. audio compact disk 32.00 (978-0-7861-8334-0(9), 3395) Blckstn Audio.

Regency Etiquette. A Lady of Distinction. Narrated by Nadia May. (Running Time: 4 hrs.). (C). 2004. 22.95 (978-1-59912-580-0(3)) Iofy Corp.

Regency Etiquette Library Edition: The Mirror of Graces. unabr. ed. A Lady of Distinction. Ed. by Nadia May. 3 cass. (Running Time: 4 hrs.). 2004. 23.95 (978-0-7861-2841-9(0), 3395) Blckstn Audio.
This book, written by a woman who wished to remain anonymous, covers the social customs and manners of her time, the late eighteenth and early nineteenth centuries, the times of Jane Austen and of Napoleon. It is devoted in large part to the ¿English lady¿s costume¿ but also covers deportment, movement, the correct dances, propriety, and aids to beauty and health.

Regenerate. abr. ed. Robert A. Monroe. Read by Robert A. Monroe. (Running Time: 30 min.). (Human Plus Ser.). 1989. 14.95 (978-1-56102-026-3(5)) Inter Indus.
Aid in the physical healing of body areas.

Regeneration. Gordon Clark. 1 cass. (Lectures on the Holy Spirit: No. 3). 5.00 Trinity Found.

Regeneration. unabr. ed. Pat Barker. Narrated by Steven Crossley. 7 cass. (Running Time: 10 hrs. 15 mins.). 1996. 60.00 (978-0-7887-0658-5(6), 94835E7) Recorded Bks.
Barker's inspiring novel brilliantly recreates the high idealism & unimaginable carnage of "the war to end all wars.".

Regeneration Not Rehabilitation. Elbert Willis. 1 cass. (Purpose of the Holy Spirit Ser.). 4.00 Fill the Gap.

***Regent.** Arnold Bennett. Read by Alfred von Lecteur. 2010. 27.95 (978-1-60112-960-4(2)) Babblebooks.

Reggae on the River, No. 1. 10th ed. 1 cass. 1994. 9.98 (978-1-56628-029-7(X), EB2981/WB42549-4) MFLP CA.
Recorded live at the 10th annual Reggae on the River in Humboldt County, California by world-famous Reggae artists.

Reggae on the River, No. 2. 10th ed. 1 cass. 1994. 9.98 (978-1-56628-031-0(1), EB2982/WB42550-4) MFLP CA.

Reggae Worship, Vol. 2. 1 CD. 1999. audio compact disk 16.98 (KMGD9472) Provident Mus Dist.

Reggae Worship, Vol. 3. 1 CD. 1999. audio compact disk 16.95 (KMGD9542) Provident Mus Dist.

***Reggie: You Can't Change Your Past, but You Can Change Your Future.** unabr. ed. Reggie Dabbs & John Driver. (ENG.). 2011. 12.98 (978-1-61045-105-5(8)); audio compact disk 21.98 (978-1-61045-104-8(X)) christianaud.

Regime: Evil Advances / Before They Were Left Behind. Jerry B. Jenkins & Tim LaHaye. Narrated by Richard Ferrone. (Running Time: 35100 sec.). (Before They Were Left Behind Ser.). 2005. 29.95 (978-1-4193-5338-3(1)) Recorded Bks.

Regime: Evil Advances / Before They Were Left Behind. abr. ed. Tim LaHaye & Jerry B. Jenkins. 2 CDs. (Running Time: 10800 sec.). (Before They Were Left Behind Ser.). (ENG.). 2005. audio compact disk 19.99 (978-1-4143-0575-2(3), TynFic) Tyndale Hse.

Regime: Evil Advances Before They Were Left Behind. Jerry B. Jenkins & Tim LaHaye. Narrated by Richard Ferrone. (Running Time: 35100 sec.). 2005. audio compact disk 34.95 (978-1-4193-5339-0(X)) Recorded Bks.

Regimental Affair. unabr. ed. Allan Mallinson. Narrated by Erick Graham. 10 cass. (Running Time: 13 hrs. 30 mins.). 2001. 92.00 (978-1-84197-196-4(0), H1183E7) Recorded Bks.
It is 1817, & Captain Matthew Hervey has returned from his bloody battles in India to find England in political & economic disorder. Despite the chaos surrounding him, Hervey develops a passionate relationship that will alter his life & future dramatically.

Reginald Gibbons. unabr. ed. Reginald Gibbons. Read by Reginald Gibbons. 1 cass. (Running Time: 29 min.). Incl. Ruined Motel; Saints; 1987. 10.00 New Letters.
The editor of the Tri-Quarterly reads poems from two of his books.

Regional Accents of France. 3 cass., 3 bks. (Running Time: 3 hrs.). bk. 59.95 (SFR215) J Norton Pubs.
Authentic monologs on culture, customs, & daily life in different regions of France assist the development of oral comprehension.

Regional Correlations of Earthquakes with Planetary Positions. Judith Hill. 1 cass. 9.00 (A0042-86) Sound Photosyn.
Informative & generous with astrological details & dates to be aware of.

Regional Interstate Banking. 1987. bk. 80.00 incl. book.; 45.00 cass. only.; 35.00 book only. PA Bar Inst.

Regional Parks East of San Francisco Bay. Hosted by Nancy Pearlman. 1 cass. (Running Time: 28 min.). 10.00 (609) Educ Comm CA.

Regions of the U. S. Series: World Events over Time Collection. Eugene Lieber. (ENG.). 2006. audio compact disk 160.00 (978-1-935069-18-8(7)) IAB Inc.

Regions of the United States Audio CD Theme Set: Set of 6 Set A. Adapted by Benchmark Education Staff. (English Explorers Ser.). (J). (gr. 3-6). 2007. audio compact disk 60.00 (978-1-4108-9842-5(3)) Benchmark Educ.

Regions of the United States Audio CD Theme Set: Set of 6 Set B. Adapted by Benchmark Education Staff. (English Explorers Ser.). (J). (gr. 3-6). 2007. audio compact disk 60.00 (978-1-4108-9821-0(0)) Benchmark Educ.

Regions of the World Series: World Events over Time Collection. Eugene Lieber. (ENG.). 2006. audio compact disk 120.00 (978-1-935069-23-2(3)) IAB Inc.

Regions of U. S. A. Steck-Vaughn Staff. 1 cass. (Running Time: 90 mins.). 2002. (978-0-7398-6221-6(9)) SteckVau.

Regreso de Ricitos de Oro. Steck-Vaughn Staff. 1 cass. (Running Time: 1 hr. 30 min.). (SPA.). 1999. (978-0-7398-0744-6(7)) SteckVau.

Regressing Chart into Parent's Past. Lynne Koiner. 1 cass. 8.95 (547) Am Fed Astrologers.
Events before birth reveal current mind-set.

Regression into Space. 1 cass. 15.00 (#103) Aletheia Psycho.
A rebirthing guided reverie with a choice of two musical themes as background.

Regression Through the Mirrors of Time. Brian L. Weiss. 2008. audio compact disk 15.00 (978-1-4019-2235-1(X)) Hay House.

Regression to Times & Places. abr. ed. Brian L. Weiss. 2008. audio compact disk 15.00 (978-1-4019-2233-7(3)) Hay House.

Regret see Great French & Russian Stories, Vol. 1, A Collection

Regret-Free Living: Hope for Past Mistakes & Freedom from Unhealthy Patterns. unabr. ed. Stephen Arterburn & John Shore. Narrated by Stephen Arterburn. (Running Time: 6 hrs. 9 mins. 16 sec.). (ENG.). 2009. 18.19 (978-1-60814-578-2(6)); audio compact disk 25.99 (978-1-59859-625-0(X)) Oasis Audio.

Regular Guy. Sarah Weeks. Narrated by Johnny Heller. 2 CDs. (Running Time: 1 hr. 45 mins.). (gr. 3 up). audio compact disk 22.00 (978-0-7887-9525-1(2)) Recorded Bks.

Regular Guy. unabr. ed. Sarah Weeks. Read by Johnny Heller. (J). 2000. pap. bk. & stu. ed. 44.20 (978-0-7887-4187-6(X), 41095) Recorded Bks.
How could "Wuckums" & Lorraine Strang possibly be Guy's parents, when he is so normal & they are so strange? Bob-o Smith, the nerdiest boy in school, was born on the same day in the same hospital Guy was. Obviously the boys were switched at birth. So Guy hatches an ingenious plan. A wacky modern take on a classic theme: the search for identity.

Regular Guy. unabr. ed. Sarah Weeks. Narrated by Johnny Heller. 2 pieces. (Running Time: 1 hr. 45 mins.). (gr. 3 up). 2000. 21.00 (978-0-7887-4006-0(7), 95947E7) Recorded Bks.

Regular Guy, Class Set. unabr. ed. Sarah Weeks. Read by Johnny Heller. 2 cass. (Running Time: 1 hr. 45 mins.). (YA). 2000. 178.80 (978-0-7887-4188-3(8), 47088) Recorded Bks.

Regulation D Offerings & Private Placements: Thursday - Saturday, March 12-14, 1998, Scottsdale, (Phoenix) Doubletree La Posada Resort. 7 cass. (Running Time: 10 hrs.). 1998. 215.00 Inc. course materials. (MC61) Am Law Inst.
Examines the current developments, including amendments, interpretations, no-action letters, & enforcement initiatives in Regulation D & other non-public offerings, with an eye on the problems faced by practitioners in meeting changing client & industry demands. Special emphasis is placed on the new wave of state & federal enforcement actions & private litigation & planning to avoid liability.

Regulation of Health: Case Studies of Sweden & Switzerland. Peter Zweifel et al. (Developments in Health Economics & Public Policy Ser.). (C). 1998. 166.00 (978-0-7923-8342-0(7)) Spri.

Regulators. Stephen King. Read by Kate Nelligan. (Running Time: 9 hrs.). (ENG.). (gr. 12 up). 2009. audio compact disk 39.95 (978-0-14-314391-8(3), PengAudBks) Penguin Grp USA.

Regulators. unabr. ed. Richard Bachman, pseud. Narrated by Frank Muller. 9 cass. (Running Time: 12 hrs. 15 mins.). 1997. 80.00 (978-0-7887-1163-3(6), 95006E7) Recorded Bks.
Bachman enjoyed huge success with "The Bachman Books" & "Thinner." Then, in 1985, his true identity was inadvertently revealed & his alter ego inflicted him with a terminal case of cancer. His fans know the gory details of his demise. Novices will understand when they compare this novel to its companion piece, "Desperation" by Stephen King.

Reharge Your Spirit: Quantum Leap Meditations. (ENG.). 2008. audio compact disk 15.00 (978-0-9778706-2-2(6)) J Stefaniak.

Rehnquist Choice: The Untold Story of the Nixon Appointment That Redefined the Supreme Court. unabr. ed. John W. Dean. Read by Michael Rafkin. 8 vols. (Running Time: 12 hrs.). 2002. bk. 69.95 (978-0-7927-2537-4(9), CSL 426, Chivers Sound Lib); audio compact disk 94.95 (978-0-7927-9869-9(4), SLD 120, Chivers Sound Lib) AudioGO.
Watergate figure John Dean blows the whistle on his old boss, former president Richard Nixon, and his efforts to pack the Supreme Court through forced resignations of sitting justices, a plan cooked up before he was even inaugurated. This is the explosive, never-before-revealed story of how William Rehnquist became a Supreme Court Justice, told by the man responsible for his candidacy.

Reigate Squires see Memoirs of Sherlock Holmes

Reigning as Kings. Bill Winston. 2 cass. (Running Time: 1hr.28min.). (C). 1995. 10.00 (978-1-931289-72-6(7)) Pub: B Winston Min. Dist(s): Anchor Distributors

Reigning in Life Through Diligence. Speeches. Creflo A. Dollar. 4 cass. (Running Time: 5 hrs.). 2002. 20.00 (978-1-59089-216-9(X)); audio compact disk 28.00 (978-1-59089-217-6(8)) Creflo Dollar.

Reigning Mercy. 1 cass. (Running Time: 1 hr.). 2000. 10.98 (978-0-7786-1332-9(1)); audio compact disk 17.98 (978-0-7786-1331-2(3)) Pub: Madacy Ent Grp CAN. Dist(s): New Day Christian

Reigning Now with Christ. Derek Prince. 6 cass. 29.95 (I-RC1) Derek Prince.

Reiki: Healing Yourself. abr. ed. Marsha Jean Burack. 2 CDs. 2003. audio compact disk 29.95 (978-1-880441-62-6(4)) Reiki Heal.

Reiki Class. William L. Rand. 3 cass. (Running Time: 3 hrs.). 1994. pap. bk. Set. (978-1-886785-01-4(5)) Vision Pub.
Instruction in Reiki Training - Laying-on-Hands Healing.

Reiki Healing Yourself: A Guided Hands-On Self Treatment for the Novice or the Reiki Practitioner - Hard of Hearing Version. unabr. ed. Marsha Burack. Read by Marsha Burack. 2 cass. (Running Time: 66 min. per cass.). 1990. 22.50 Set. (978-1-880441-42-8(X), 104); 12.95 Words & music. (978-1-880441-40-4(3), 101); 9.95 Music only. (978-1-880441-46-6(2), 103); 12.95 (978-1-880441-41-1(1), 102) Reiki Heal.
For the hard of hearing. Teaches the listener hands-on healing.

Reiki Meditations for Self-Healing: Traditional Japanese Practices for Your Energy & Vitality. Bronwen Stiene. 2008. audio compact disk 19.95 (978-1-59179-670-1(9)) Sounds True.

Reiki Space of Peace & Love. Music by Merlin's Magic. Featuring Frank Arjava Petter. (Running Time: 60 mins.). 2003. audio compact disk 16.95 (978-0-910261-25-8(3), Inner Worlds Mus) Lotus Pr.
This is the most meditative Merlin's Magic production up to now, with compositions that unite in the "silent eye" of Reiki. The sounds of the Far Eastern spheres unfold in virtual deep stillness, led by the rhythm of the heart.

Reiki Symposium: An Extraordinary Journey into the Heart of Reiki. Speeches. Laura Ellen Gifford et al. Ed. by David Edward Rothstein. Prod. by Spiritsync Publishing Staff. 4 CDs. 2004. audio compact disk 29.99 (978-0-9749082-0-5(7), ssp-0401) Spiritsync Pub.
The Reiki Symposium is a comprehensive resource by master teachers, practitioners and pioneers in the field of Reiki from across the United States who came to New York City to share a wealth of insightful information recorded live and presented now as a powerful four CD set. The wide breadth of scope may serve as a well-rounded introduction to Reiki, while offering deep insights to experienced Reiki practitioners and teachers who will welcome this series as a treasured addition to their Reiki library.Topics include:The definition of ReikiConnecting with the roots of Reiki The benefits of using healing touch and life force energyAn international search for the original source of Reiki Comparison of the original Japanese Reiki ideals with the Reiki of todayLogistics of teaching Reiki in a college environmentUsing Reiki through archetypal imagesHow Reiki teachers are creating harmony within their communitiesReiki compared with other healing modalitiesThe mind-body-spirit connection within the architecture of Western medicineThe impact of the National Institute of Health's alternative medicine divisionHow Reiki relieves anxiety and augments the immune systemUsing Reiki in conjunction with hypnosis, aromatherapy and acupressureTreating trauma, cancer and Raynaud's disease with ReikiUsing Reiki with pets, racehorses and other animalsComparison between the various lineages of ReikiThe proposed Reiki teaching standardsHow hospitals are teaching Reiki to their staffsThe use of Reiki within the business and corporate communitiesScientific experiments validating the healing energy of ReikiHow Reiki is bridging the gap between spirituality and scienceHow the medical and dental professions are using Reiki with their patientsand much more...This comprehensive series of lectures and discussion will provide a context for learning and enlightenment that will be cherished for years to come.

***Reilly's Luck.** unabr. ed. Louis L'Amour. (ENG.). 2011. audio compact disk 30.00 (978-0-307-91484-2(4), Random AudioBks) Pub: Random Audio Pubg. Dist(s): Random

***Reilly's Return.** unabr. ed. Tami Hoag. Narrated by Susan Boyce. 5 CDs. (Running Time: 6 hrs. 0 mins. 0 sec.). (ENG.). 2010. audio compact disk 19.95 (978-1-60283-920-5(4)) Pub: AudioGO. Dist(s): Perseus Dist

***Reilly's Return.** unabr. ed. Tami Hoag. Narrated by Susan Boyce. 1 Playaway. (Running Time: 6 hrs. 5 mins.). 2010. 59.95 (978-0-7927-7229-3(6)); audio compact disk 59.95 (978-0-7927-7182-1(6)) AudioGO.

Reimagining Church: Pursuing the Dream of Organic Christianity. unabr. ed. Frank Viola. (Running Time: 10 hrs. 30 mins. 0 sec.). (ENG.). 2009. audio compact disk 26.98 (978-1-59644-722-6(2), Hovel Audio) christianaud.

***Reimagining Church: Pursuing the Dream of Organic Christianity.** unabr. ed. Frank Viola. Narrated by Lloyd James. (ENG.). 2009. 16.98 (978-1-59644-723-3(0), Hovel Audio) christianaud.

Reimagining Reading: A Literacy Institute. unabr. ed. Janet Allen. 4 cass. (Running Time: 6 hrs.). (YA). 2002. 99.00 (978-1-57110-339-0(2)) Stenhsa Pubs.

Reimagining Reading: A Literacy Institute. unabr. ed. Janet Allen. 5 CDs. (Running Time: 6 hrs.). (ENG.). (C). (gr. 4-12). 2001. audio compact disk 55.00 (978-1-57110-347-5(3)) Stenhsa Pubs.

Reimbursement for Surgical Services: Who Decides? 2 cass. (General Sessions Ser.: C84-SP3). 1984. 15.00 (8418) Am Coll Surgeons.

Reimer - Gordon Debate on Music Learning: Complementary or Contradictory Views? Contrib. by Bennett Reimer & Edwin Gordon. 1 cass. (Running Time: 90 min.). 1994. 13.50 (978-1-56545-052-3(3)) MENC.

Reincarnation. Eldon Taylor. 1 cass. (Running Time: 62 min.). (Inner Talk Ser.). 16.95 incl. script. (978-1-55978-001-8(0), 5401C) Progress Aware Res.
Soundtrack - Musical Themes with underlying subliminal affirmations.

Reincarnation: Babbling Brook. Eldon Taylor. 1 cass. 16.95 (978-1-55978-761-1(9), 5401F) Progress Aware Res.

Reincarnation: Claiming Your Past, Creating Your Future. abr. ed. Lynn Ewell Sparrow. Read by Kitt Weagant. 1 cass. (Running Time: 60 min.). 1988. 9.95 HarperCollins Pubs.

Reincarnation & the Nation; Scriptural Necessities: Jewel in the Lotus. Jonathan Murro. 1 cass. 7.95 A R Colton Fnd.

Reincarnation in the Natal Chart. A. Bratt. 1 cass. (Running Time: 90 min.). 1984. 8.95 (038) Am Fed Astrologers.

Reincarnation, Karma & Resurrection. Jack Boland. 3 cass. 1977. 27.95 (978-0-88152-009-5(8)) Master Mind.
A revelation of the master plan of life. Participate in the unfolding of your own spiritual destiny.

Reincarnation of King Bharata (A); Lord Krsna fights Banasura (B) 1 cass. (Spiritual Stories Ser.). 5.00 Bhaktivedanta.

Reincarnationist. unabr. ed. M. J. Rose. Read by Phil Gigante. (Running Time: 12 hrs.). (Reincarnationist Ser.). 2009. 24.99 (978-1-4233-9830-1(0), 9781423398301, Brilliance MP3); 39.97 (978-1-4233-9831-8(9), 9781423398318, Brlnc Audio MP3 Lib); audio compact disk 34.99 (978-1-4233-9828-8(9), 9781423398288); audio compact disk 89.97 (978-1-4233-9829-5(7), 9781423398295, BriAudCD Unabrid) Brilliance Audio.

Reindeer Jive - ShowTrax. John Jacobson & Roger Emerson. 1 CD. 2000. audio compact disk 19.95 (09970203) H Leonard.
There will be swing dancing on the rooftop with this great showstopper in the popular SongKit Single format.

Reindeer Moon. unabr. ed. Elizabeth Marshall Thomas. Narrated by Alyssa Bresnahan. 12 cass. (Running Time: 17 hrs. 15 mins.). 1996. 97.00 (978-0-7887-0298-3(X), 94491E7) Recorded Bks.
Yanan lived over 20 thousand years ago on the ice-swept tundra of Siberia. Her people are hunters, living in kinship with tigers & wolves, struggling through harsh winters with little meat & wood & rejoicing in brief, glorious summers.

Reindeer Spirit: Following the Rhythms of Nature As a Way to Soul. Linda Leonard. 1 cass. (Running Time: 1 hr. 21 min.). 1995. 10.95 (978-0-7822-0505-3(4), 580) C G Jung IL.
To research her book "Creation's Heartbeat: Following the Reindeer Spirit", Jungian analyst Linda Leonard traveled to the Arctic regions of Eurasia, where the "shamanic" peoples who live in accord with the rhythms of nature regard reindeer as spiritual messengers. Leonard's presentation explores the challenges of reviving the "Reindeer Spirit," a metaphor for an ancient, feminine, instinctual rhythm of soul that offers a path to the ecological & creative living needed by the modern world.

reine des Eaux. unabr. ed. Kai Meyer. Read by Odile Cohen. (YA). 2007. 79.99 (978-2-35569-007-5(3)) Find a World.

Reine Margot see Queen Margot

Reinforcement of Gregg Symbols & Theory: Series 90 Format. rev. ed. Donald J. Macksoud. Ed. by Elizabeth Gray. 12 cass. 1989. 158.50 (978-0-937901-06-9(7)) Reinforcement Lrn.
Twenty-four audio reinforcement lessons designed to develop an automatic response on all Gregg shorthand theory using a response conditioning learning methodology.

Reinhart in Love. unabr. collector's ed. Thomas Berger. Read by Michael Russotto. 12 cass. (Running Time: 18 hrs.). 1991. 96.00 (978-0-7366-1990-5(9), 2806) Books on Tape.
Carlo Reinhart returns home from service in occupied Germany & finds the postwar U.S. a different world: housing developments, gadget technology, a physical & spiritual malaise that boom times evoke. Good-hearted & intelligent, sympathetic but cynical, Reinhart is a participant who nevertheless remains a spectator.

Reinhart's Women. unabr. collector's ed. Thomas Berger. Read by Christopher Hurt. 8 cass. (Running Time: 12 hrs.). (Reinhart Ser.). 1989. 64.00 (978-0-7366-1552-5(0), 2421) Books on Tape.
Carl Reinhart, fascinated with women ever since having been born by one, finds himself at close quarters & cross purposes with a variety of female persons. But Reinhart has a trick or two left in him.

Reino del Dragón de Oro see Kingdom of the Golden Dragon

Reinterpreting New England Indians & the Colonial Experience. Colin G. Calloway. Ed. by Neal Salisbury. 2009. 25.00 (978-0-9794662-5-0(3)) U Pr of Va.

Reintroduction of Paddlefish in Texas. Hosted by Nancy Pearlman. 1 cass. (Running Time: 29 mins.). 1999. 10.00 (1506) Educ Comm CA.
Award-winning actor Ed Begley, Jr. Explains his Ecological Lifestyle.

Reinvent Your Life. unabr. ed. Alvin Slaughter. Narrated by Alvin Slaughter. (Running Time: 4 hrs. 18 mins. 21 sec.). (ENG.). 2010. 13.99 (978-1-60814-626-0(X)); audio compact disk 19.99 (978-1-59859-680-9(2)) Oasis Audio.

Reinvent Yourself: Earn Big Money Without Competition by Doing What you Love!: Wealth & Creativity. (ENG.). 2009. audio compact disk 29.95 (978-0-9774811-2-5(3)) C Allman.

Reinventando el Amor. abr. ed. Contrib. by Jorge Rivera. 2006. audio compact disk 17.00 (978-1-58459-318-8(0)) Wrld Lib Pubns.

Reinventing the Body, Resurrecting the Soul: How to Create a New You. unabr. ed. Deepak Chopra. Read by Deepak Chopra. (ENG.). 2009. audio compact disk 35.00 (978-0-7393-8198-4(9), Random AudioBks) Pub: Random Audio Pubg. Dist(s): Random

Reinventing Yourself. 1 cass. 12.98 (978-0-87554-503-5(3), 1101) Valley Sun.
A program to support the primary qualities of self-renewing adults. You're encouraged to accept & adapt to change, establish priorities, decide what you what, pursue your best options, become committed to values & goals, communicate, seek intimacy, learn from the past, make decisions with enthusiasm, distinguish essentials, focus time & energy, master your skills, gather information & more.

Reinventing Yourself: How to Become the Person You've Always Wanted to Be. abr. unabr. ed. Steve Chandler. 3 CDs. (Running Time: 3 hrs.). (ENG.). 2000. audio compact disk 24.95 (978-1-56511-419-7(1), 1565114191) Pub: HighBridge. Dist(s): Workman Pub

Reinvention: How to Make the Rest of Your Life the Best of Your Life. unabr. ed. Brian Tracy. Read by Brian Tracy. (Running Time: 4 hrs. 30 mins.). (ENG.). 2009. 24.98 (978-1-59659-387-9(3), GildAudio); audio compact disk 29.98 (978-1-59659-271-1(0)) Pub: Gildan Media. Dist(s): HachBkGrp

Reinvention: Turning the Tide of Change (Audio Workshop) Created by Wendy Y. Bailey. 1 CD. (Running Time: 60 minutes). 2004. audio compact disk 19.00 (978-0-9749914-4-3(5)) Brilliance In Action.
Reinvention: Turning the Tide of ChangeDo you feel that your life is in a constant state of transition? Is this transition paralyzing you or preventing you from accomplishing what you really want in life and business? Change is a definite and certain thing. Knowing what you can do in these challenging times is the key. Listen and discover the seven steps for reinvention. Transition doesn't have to be difficult when you prepare yourself for the journey. Reinvention is the way! Includes detailed TeleClass notes and challenge assignments.

Reir de Nuevo. 2007. audio compact disk 36.00 (978-1-57972-742-0(5)) Insight Living.

Reivers, unabr. ed. William Faulkner. Narrated by Mark Hammer. 9 cass. (Running Time: 12 hrs. 15 mins.). 1996. 78.00 (978-0-7887-0611-0(X), 94791E7) Recorded Bks.
The unforgettable odyssey of an eleven-year-old boy & his family's black handyman. They steal the grandfather's car & journey through the Mississippi countryside.

Rejected Overtures of God: Matthew 21:33-45. Ed Young. (J). 1981. 4.95 (978-0-7417-1207-3(5), A0207) Win Walk.

Rejection: Cause & Cure. Derek Prince. 1 cass. 5.95 (042) Derek Prince.
Rejection is perhaps the deepest wound ever suffered by the human spirit, but God has provided the healing remedy.

Rejection Pt. I: Romans 10:1-13. Ed Young. 1984. 4.95 (978-0-7417-1390-2(X), 390) Win Walk.

Rejection Pt. II: Romans 10:14-21. Ed Young. 1984. 4.95 (978-0-7417-1391-9(8), 391) Win Walk.

Rejection/Taking People for Granted. Marianne Williamson. Read by Marianne Williamson. 1 cass. (Running Time: 90 mins.). (Lectures on a Course in Miracles). 1999. 10.00 (978-1-56170-258-9(7), M761) Hay House.

***Rejoice.** Prod. by Women of Faith. 2011. audio compact disk 13.99 (978-1-4261-1045-0(6)) Nelson.

Rejoice. abr. ed. Karen Kingsbury & Gary Smalley. Read by Sandra Burr. 3 cass. (Running Time: 4 hrs.). (Redemption Ser.). 2004. 19.95 (978-1-59355-845-1(7), 1593558457); 49.25 (978-1-59355-846-8(5), 1593558465); audio compact disk 21.95 (978-1-59355-847-5(3), 1593558473); audio compact disk 69.25 (978-1-59355-848-2(1), 1593558481) Brilliance Audio.
A Terrible Tragedy Brooke and Peter are struggling in their marriage when they are faced with the single worst moment ever. What was supposed to be a pool party for their two daughters and a handful of children ends in disaster. As three-year-old Hayley fights for her life, the Baxter family draws together, not even sure how to pray. A Shattered Life Peter is devastated by Hayley's accident. Unable to see past his own guilt, he distances himself from Brooke and their girls and finds other ways to ease his pain. Illegal ways. Peter's choices send him spiraling into a cavernous abyss that threatens to destroy not only his relationship with Brooke but his life. A Reason to Rejoice Against the backdrop of great pain and loss, a Baxter wedding takes place in New York City, a wedding that gives all of them a reason to smile again. Now, what will it take for Brooke and the Baxters to move forward, and how will the sudden loss of one special woman change them all?.

Rejoice. abr. ed. Karen Kingsbury & Gary Smalley. Read by Sandra Burr. (Running Time: 4 hrs.). (Redemption Ser.). 2006. 39.25 (978-1-4233-0312-1(1), 9781423303121, BADLE); 9.99 (978-1-4233-0311-4(3), 9781423303114, BAD); 39.25 (978-1-4233-0310-7(5), 9781423303107, Brlnc Audio MP3 Lib); audio compact disk 9.99 (978-1-4233-0309-1(1), 9781423303091, Brilliance MP3) Brilliance Audio.

***Rejoice.** abr. ed. Karen Kingsbury & Gary Smalley. Read by Sandra Burr. (Running Time: 4 hrs.). (Redemption Ser.). 2010. audio compact disk 9.99 (978-1-4418-7834-2(3), 9781441878342, BCD Value Price) Brilliance Audio.

Rejoice: Richard Smallwood. Perf. by Richard Smallwood. 1 cass., 1 CD. 1998. 10.98; audio compact disk 15.98 CD. Provident Mus Dist.
The right blend of traditional & contemporary gospel.

Rejoice: Romans 5:3-11. Ed Young. 1984. 4.95 (978-0-7417-1363-6(2), 363) Win Walk.

Rejoice! Hymns to the Virgin Mary. Directed By Kevin Smith. (ENG.). 2008. audio compact disk 18.00 (978-0-88141-336-6(4)) St Vladimirs.

Rejoice in Hope. FSP Staff & Kurt. 1993. audio compact disk 14.95 (978-0-8198-6453-6(6), 332-304) Pauline Bks.

Rejoice in the Lord. Created by Standard Publishing. (God Rocks! Bibletoons Ser.). (J). 2007. 39.99 (978-0-7847-1980-0(2)) Standard Pub.

Rejoice, O Virgin. 1 cass., 1 CD. (ENG.). 12.00 (000279); audio compact disk 18.00 CD. (000282) Conciliar Pr.
Featuring hymns to the Mother of God which express her role in our salvation & the Church's love for her. Music is drawn from various traditions & includes several new Byzantine arrangements.

Rejoice, the Lord Is King. 1 cass. 8.98 (1000934) Covenant Comms.
A selection of choice hymns.

Rejoice, Unwedded Bride. 1 CD. (Running Time: 1 hr. 5 mins.). 2005. audio compact disk 16.95 (978-0-8146-7893-0(9)) Liturgical Pr.

Rejoice with Good Christians All Rejoice. Contrib. by Richard Kingsmore. (ENG.). 2008. audio compact disk 24.99 (978-5-557-43525-3(5)) Allegis.

***Rejoicing with Joyce.** Joyce Webster. Perf. by Joyce Webster. (ENG., 2010. audio compact disk (978-0-9826781-2-1(6)) Etcetera USA.

Rejuvenate: Music for Healing. Windham Hill Staff. 1 cass. 1998. 15.00 (978-1-56170-555-9(1)) Hay House.

Rejuvenation with Julie Russell. Julie Russell. 1 cass. 1994. 12.00 (978-1-886673-99-1(3), Songs by Rachel) Rachels Recs.
A series of yoga poses with techniques & relaxation.

Rekindle the Romance: Spice. Barrie Konicov. 1 cass. 11.98 (978-0-87082-366-4(3), 106) Potentials.
Explores ways to spice up your relationship, rekindle the fires of passion, joy, happiness, love & bring that excitement back into your relationship.

Rekindling the Priesthood. Andrew Cusack. 5 cass. (Running Time: 6 hrs. 21 min.). 1994. 40.95 (TAH307) Alba Hse Comns.
This dynamic & pastorally touching retreat is absolutely "must listening" for any priest searching for a holistic & realistic approach for living the priesthood in the present crisis-ridden world. It is an excellent source of comfort & strength in aiding you in rekindling the spirit of your priesthood.

Relajamiento: (Relaxation) Carlos González. Read by Carlos González. Ed. by Dina Gonzalez. 1 cass. (Running Time: 32 min.). (SPA.). 1990. 10.00 (978-1-56491-017-2(2)) Imagine Pubs.
In Spanish. Mental drill that enables the person to relax.

Relajamiento en el Caos: Seis Pasos Faciles para Apreender a Relajarse. Tr. by Alejandro Godoy. 1 CD. (Running Time: 1 hr. 30 mins.). 2000. audio compact disk 15.95 (978-1-893238-09-1(1)) Doc Borrie.

Relapse. David L. Ohlms. Read by David L. Ohlms. Ed. by JoAnn Moore. 1 cass. (Running Time: 1 hr.). 1994. 10.95 (978-1-56168-003-0(6), A9404) GWC Inc.
Ohlms explains how relapse begins when an addict loses conscious contact with memory of the pain of their addiction. Ohlms details the signs of relapse that follow this loss of memory which include overconfidence, resentments, cross-drug dependancy.

Relapse Prevention with REBT. F. Michler Bishop. 1 cass. 1999. bk. & wbk. ed. 22.95 (C050) A Ellis Institute.
Learn to identify your most dangerous triggers & respond adaptively to them; how to avoid future relapse; how to achieve greater short & long-term pleasure.

Relating to Others in Love: A Study of Romans 12-16. 1998. 39.95 (978-1-57972-261-6(X)) Insight Living.

Relations Between the Ego & the Unconscious. Read by Peter Mudd. 3 cass. (Running Time: 3 hrs. 30 min.). 1987. 24.95 (978-0-7822-0210-6(1), 267) C G Jung IL.

Relationship. Stephanie Clement. 1 cass. 8.95 (772) Am Fed Astrologers.

Relationship. Osho Oshos. Read by Osho Oshos. 1 cass. (Running Time: 90 min.). 10.95 (DCM-0005) Oshos.
Answers Questions such as "When should we preserve with a partner & when should we abandon a relationship as hopeless or even destructive?" & "Why am I afraid of other people?".

Relationship: A Myth for Our Time. Read by Murray Stein. 1 cass. (Running Time: 1 hr.). 1989. 9.95 (978-0-7822-0296-0(9), 397) C G Jung IL.

Relationship: A Myth for Our Time. unabr. ed. Murray Stein. 1 cass. (Running Time: 45 min.). 1991. 11.00 (11902) Big Sur Tapes.
Explores one of the primary obsessions of our culture, linking it to an absence of kinship & community, & the impersonal nature of "society." Relationship becomes a myth in the sense of "a concept that is larger than logic allows - it exceeds the human dimension & the human capacity for fulfillment, & it implies the religious".

Relationship - A Spiritual Approach. 1 cass. (Running Time: 90 min.). (Relationship Ser.). 9.95 (ST-12S) Crystal Clarity.
Topics include: What it means to "spiritualize" a relationship; how to attract true friends; overcoming self-consciousness; how friends speed our spirtual progress; why marriages go stale; the importance of commitment; the place of sex in a spiritual marriage.

Relationship Age: The coming relationship age 2006-2016 & how you can profit from It. Speeches. 4. (Running Time: 4 hrs 11 min). 2006. cd-rom 45.00 (978-0-9787285-0-2(5), 0-9787285-0-5) LightBolt.
The Coming Relationship Age 2006-2016... and How You Can Profit From It.Why the Information Age is OVER!How to tell which stocks will grow 2006-2016.Be Ready for the next economic BOOM.When America moved from the agricultural age to the industrial age, there were winners and loser. When America moved from the industrial age to the information age, many were caught off-guard. The information age ended in 1992 when more information was produced in digital format than in traditional non-digital forms. Yet, many people today think we are still in the information age. ... But we are NOT!A new age is upon us, the relationship age.Each age moves a little faster. Each age offers profit and pitfalls. Within each are there are winners and losers ? which will you be?The Relationship age takes the listener through a series of talks about: What defines an age?* What companies will profit from the coming age?* How will the coming age affect your career?.*

Relationship & the Composite Chart. Terry Warneke. 1 cass. (Running Time: 90 min.). 1990. 8.95 (721) Am Fed Astrologers.

Relationship As a Spiritual Path. P Ferrini. audio compact disk 16.95 (978-1-879159-55-6(4)) Heartways Pr.

Relationship as a Spiritual Path. unabr. ed. Paul Ferrini. Read by Paul Ferrini. 2 cass. (Running Time: 2 hrs. 40 min.). (Christ Mind Talks & Workshops Ser.). 1997. audio compact disk 16.95 Set. (978-1-879159-29-7(5)) Heartways Pr.
A workshop given at the Agape International Center of Truth in May 1997.

Relationship-Based Care: A Model for Transforming Practice. Read by Mary Koloroutis et al. 2008. 39.95 (978-1-886624-82-5(8)) Creative Hlth Care.

Relationship Between Me & Truth. J. Krishnamurti. 1 cass. (Running Time: 75 min.). (Krishnamurti & Professor David Bohm - 1980 Ser.: No. 5). 8.50 (ABD805) Krishnamurti.
Krishnamurti & Prof. Bohm offer penetrating, in-depth dialogues which shed light on the fundamental issues of existence.

Relationship Dance. unabr. ed. Helaine Z. Harris. Read by Helaine Z. Harris. 2 cass. (Running Time: 1 hr. 40 min.). 1991. 18.50 (978-0-9652343-0-6(4)) An Awakening Encino.
Designed to assist with releasing dysfunctional & or addictive patterns that prevent having the kind of relationship that is wanted.

Relationship Delineation. Jeanne D. Lawlor. 1 cass. 8.95 (737) Am Fed Astrologers.

Relationship Excellence Secrets: Self-Responsibility, Vulnerability, Synchronizing. David Grudermeyer & Rebecca Grudermeyer. 2 cass. 18.95 Including Handouts. (T-57) Willingness Wrks.

Relationship Healing: Generate Awareness & Healing for Relationships. Mark Bancroft. Read by Mark Bancroft. 1 cass., bklet. (Running Time: 1 hr.). (Relationships/Family/Parenting Ser.). 1999. wbk. ed. 12.95 (978-1-58522-026-7(4)) EnSpire Pr.
Two complete sessions plus printed instructionmanual/guidebook. With healing music soundtrack.

Relationship Healing: Generate Awareness & Healing for Relationships. Mark Bancroft. Read by Mark Bancroft. 1 CD, 1 bklet. (Running Time: 1 hr.). (Relationships/Family/Parenting Ser.). 2006. audio compact disk 20.00 (978-1-58522-047-2(7)) EnSpire Pr.

Relationship Improvement. Dick Sutphen. 1 cass. (Running Time: 1 hr.). (Probe Seven Ser.). 14.98 (978-0-87554-367-3(7), P103) Valley Sun.
"Your relationship gets better & better. Yes, it does. You let the little things go. Accept this...".

Relationship Management, Vol. 4. Mac Hammond. 1 cass. (Simplify Your Life Ser.: Vol. 4). 1997. 30.00 (978-1-57399-056-1(6)) Mac Hammond.
How to properly manage your relationships to be mutually fulfilling & free of contention & strife.

Relationship of Freedom to Self-Interest. J. Krishnamurti. 1 cass. (Running Time: 75 min.). (Brockwood Park Talks, 1985 Ser.: No. 3). 8.50 (ABT853) Krishnamurti.
Subjects examined: Do we realize how little freedom we have? Are pleasure, fear, self-interest, time, thought, all one movement? Does change imply a movement in time? If we understand that all time is now, then is change meaningless? Why has man suffered from time immemorial? Is there an end to sorrow? Is love a continuation & remembrance of pleasure? Or is love entirely beyond thought & time? What relationship has love to sorrow, to compassion? Where there is love, there is absolute freedom. Can we live our daily life with that perfume?.

Relationship of Time & Thought to Fear. J. Krishnamurti. 1 cass. (Running Time: 75 min.). (Brockwood Park Talks, 1985 Ser.: No. 2). 8.50 (ABT852) Krishnamurti.
Subjects examined: What is the nature of beauty? What is its relationship to thought, time, & love? Can memory apprehend that which is beautiful? Time is the movement of memory, knowledge, experience. Can this movement ever end? What is the connection between thought & time? Can thinking in the deepest valley of the brain ever stop? Is relationship the closeness, the feeling for each other, based on thought? Is it possible to end fear now so completely that you are free?.

Relationship of Zoning to State Environmental Regulation. 1 cass. 1990. 45.00 (AC-580) PA Bar Inst.

***Relationship Principles of Jesus.** unabr. ed. Tom Holladay. (Running Time: 6 hrs. 33 mins. 0 sec.). (ENG.). 2008. 21.99 (978-0-310-30934-5(4)) Zondervan.

Relationship Readiness. 2005. audio compact disk (978-1-932086-23-2(4)) L Lizards Pub Co.

Relationship Readiness Self Hypnotic Set. Dean A. Montalbano. (Hypnotic Sensory Response Audio Ser.). 2000. 39.95 (978-0-9708772-5-3(0)) L Lizards Pub Co.

Relationship Release. Created by Ellen Chernoff Simon. 1 CD. (Running Time: 70 min.). 2004. audio compact disk 18.00 (978-0-9765587-7-4(7)) Imadulation.
his audio program is designed to assist you in healing from the emotional pain of a relationship breakup. the ending of hte relationshipis framed in the context of higher learning and the life lessons it offers. The bigger picture and the eternal nature of love is explored as well as the importance of the most significant love of all, self-love, which acknowledges the divine within.

Relationship Reprogramming. Barrie Konicov. 1 cass. 11.98 (978-0-87082-356-5(6), 107) Potentials.
Use this cassette to reprogram relationships with husband or wife, parents, children, brothers & sisters. You will no longer hurt those closer to you or be hurt by them.

Relationship Reprogramming. Barrie Konicov. 1 CD. 2004. audio compact disk 19.98 (978-1-56001-689-2(2)) Potentials.
We always seem to hurt those closest to us, or are hurt by them. Take this situation in hand - with or without the other person. Use this program to reframe your relationships with husband or wife, parents, children, brothers or sisters.You will find the self-hypnosis on track 1 and the subliminal on track 2. The easy-listening music of the subliminal, together with the self-hypnosis, is the original format which most people love and with which they are most familiar.

Relationship Rescue: A Seven Step Strategy for Reconnecting with Your Partner. abr. ed. Phil McGraw. 4 CDs. (Running Time: 50 hrs. 0 mins. 0 sec.). (ENG.). 2000. audio compact disk 32.00 (978-0-7435-0046-3(6), Sound Ideas) Pub: S&S Audio. Dist(s): S and S Inc

Relationship Series. Elbert Willis. 4 cass. 13.00 Fill the Gap.

Relationship Spread (Tarot Class) Robert Michael Place. Perf. by Robert Michael Place. Ed. by Leisa ReFalo. Prod. by Leisa ReFalo. (ENG., 2009. 25.00 (978-1-935194-04-0(6), Hermes Pubns) Tarot Connect.

Relationship Strategies. Jim Cathcart & Tony Alessandra. Read by Jim Cathcart & Tony Alessandra. 6 cass. 59.95 (1431A) Nightingale-Conant.

Relationship to Locality. Carolyn Dodson. 1 cass. 8.95 (092) Am Fed Astrologers.

Relationship with God. Derek Prince. 1 cass. 5.95 (002) Derek Prince.
The New Covenant is an invitation to fellowship with God through the sacrifice of Jesus.

Relationship with God's People. Derek Prince. 1 cass. 5.95 (003) Derek Prince.
Covenant relationship with God brings us into true communion also with the people of God.

Relationships. 1981. Archae Edns.

Relationships. 1 cass. (Running Time: 45 min.). (Relationship Ser.). 9.98 (978-1-55909-005-6(7), 23S); 9.98 90 min. extended length stereo music. (978-1-55909-006-3(5), 23X) Randolph Tapes.
Helps develop inter-personal communication skills thus enabling one to better get along with others. Subliminal messages are heard 3-5 minutes before becoming ocean sounds or music.

Relationships. John E. Bradshaw. (Running Time: 14400 sec.). 2008. audio compact disk 100.00 (978-1-57388-280-4(1)) J B Media.

Relationships. Dean Sherman. 1999. 30.00 (978-0-935779-07-3(8)) Crown Min.
Focuses on the proper relationship principles for relating to the opposite sex, & explores the hows & whys.

Relationships. Eldon Taylor. Interview with Progress Aware Staff. 1 cass. (Running Time: 62 min.). (Inner Talk Ser.). 16.95 (978-1-55978-311-8(7), 5355A) Progress Aware Res.
Soundtrack - Tropical Lagoon with underlying subliminal affirmations.

Relationships. unabr. ed. Read by Kelly Ryan Dolan. Narrated by Jill Shellabarger. (Running Time: 1 hr. 9 mins. 40 sec.). (What the Bible Says Ser.). 2008. audio compact disk 9.99 (978-1-59859-417-1(6)) Oasis Audio.

Relationships. unabr. ed. Beverly J. Farrell. (Running Time: 90 min.). 1988. 8.95 (730) Am Fed Astrologers.
Features a tool for using Comparison Charts in various types of relationships.

Relationships. unabr. ed. Paul R. Scheele. 1 cass. (Running Time: 34 min.). (Paraliminal Tapes Ser.). 1993. 24.95 (978-0-925480-22-4(3)) Learn Strategies.
Discover the secret of solving people problems. Resolve personal conflicts with others. Improve the quality of your relationships. Heal interpersonal wounds. Attract loving, supportive individuals.

Relationships: An Open & Honest Guide to Making Bad Relationships Better & Good Relationships Great. Les Parrott & Leslie Parrott. 2 cass. (Running Time: 60 min. per cass.). 1998. 16.99 (978-0-310-22435-8(7)) Zondervan.
"Relationships" Describes who we are and what we bring to our relationships; how our families of origin shape the way we relate to others; how to bridge the gender gap and learn the language of the opposite sex; tips for building friendships that last; secrets to finding the love we long for and to handling sexual issues; how to handle failed friendships and breakups without falling apart; how to relate to God without feeling phony.

Relationships: Changing Past Patterns. unabr. ed. Paul Ferrini. Read by Paul Ferrini. 2 cass. (Running Time: 2 hrs.). (Christ Mind Talks & Workshops Ser.). 1997. audio compact disk 16.95 Set. (978-1-879159-32-7(5)) Heartways Pr.
A talk given at Redondo Beach Church of Religious Science in November 1997.

Relationships: Instruments of Grace. Stephen R. Schwartz. 6 cass. 54.00 Set. Riverrun Piermont.

Relationships: (Mystery of Sex) Excerpts. Laurel Elizabeth Keyes. Voice by Laurel Elizabeth Keyes. 1 CD. (Running Time: 90 mins.). 2006. audio compact disk 10.00 (978-0-9791360-6-1(7)) Gentle Living.
Laurel Keyes giving a workshop from her book Mystery of Sex. She discusses the challenges of understanding the differences of males and females and how to "give birth to the best in each other." This tape is a great addition to her book also.

Relationships: Program from the Award Winning Public Radio Series: the Best of the Infinite Mind. Interview. Hosted by Fred Goodwin. 1 CD. (Running Time: 1 hr.). 2003. audio compact disk 21.95 (978-1-932479-86-7(4), LCM 270) Lichtenstein Creat.
The bar scene, a blind date: Does it matter where you find love? How about in an arranged marriage? And what goes on in the brain when you meet someone special? In this program we delve into our archives to bring you some of the best of The Infinite Mind on Relationships.

Relationships: Real & Archetypal. Read by Lois Khan. 7 cass. (Running Time: 10 hrs. 30 min.). 1988. 51.95 (978-0-7822-0117-8(2), 309S) C G Jung IL.
Explores the unique dimensions of several basic human relationships: father-daughter, husband-wife, brother-sister, sister-sister, brother-brother, grandparent-grandchild, & mother-son.

Relationships: The Path to Self-Discovery. unabr. ed. Carol Howe. 3 cass. (Running Time: 4 hrs. 30 min.). 1995. 24.95 (978-1-889642-03-1(7)); 79.95 NTSC. (978-1-889642-19-2(3)) C Howe.
The "SOB's" will save you! This widely-acclaimed workshop reveals exactly how our most difficult relationships become our greatest gifts. Learn how we create our hurtful or boring relationships & how to heal them. This set identifies: How & why we are in our relationships - personal, professional, & casual; the perfect way they can reflect to us our own "unfinished business"; Specific steps in the healing & liberating process, leading inevitably to peace of mind.

Relationships: Your Ruin or Rejoicing. Gary V. Whetstone. 6 cass. (Running Time: 9 hrs.). (Family & Relationships Ser.). 1995. bk. 50.00 (978-1-58866-230-9(6), VA004A) Gary Whet Pub.
It is critical that you understand how to develop right relationships in your life. You will learn how to screen test relationships, what to look for in a man or woman.

Relationships & a Course in Miracles, Set. Speeches. Jerry F. Stefaniak. 3 CDs. (Running Time: 4 hrs 30 mins). 2006. audio compact disk 20.00 (978-0-9778706-1-5(8)) J Stefaniak.
Relationships are seen in A Course in Miracles as one of the most powerful tools that can transform our lives. Within each person we meet, we have the opportunity to either extend and grow, or judge and withdraw. And in intimate relationships, the chances to grow are unlimited.If you are interested in learning more about A Course in Miracles, there is no better way of understanding the concepts than by attending Jerry Stefaniak's classes. The next best thing is listening to his talks on tape or CD.This three CD series is an excellent resource for anyone who wants to better their relationships. Reverend Stefaniak uses humor, real down-to-earth, day-to-day examples and his own life to help the listener understand these wonderful and powerful teachings. Altogether these talks total over 4 hours of spiritual and practical support. This series also includes his powerful meditations.Topics covered are:- The Trap of Special Relationships-Creating a Holy Relationship- Keeping Your Relationship Holy.

Relationships & Communication. abr. ed. John L. Lund. 4 cass. (Running Time: 5 hrs. 24 min.). 1997. bk. 19.95 (978-1-891114-26-7(3)) Pub: Commun Co. Dist(s): Granite UT
Owning our words & behavior, learning the love language of others, ten articles of commitment, apologies & forgiveness.

Relationships & Recovery. Pia Mellody. Read by Pia Mellody. 4 cass. pap. bk. 35.00 Set. (A13) Featuka Enter Inc.
Provides information regarding how important relationships are affected by recovery & how to negotiate problem areas that are provoked by the recovery process.

Relationships & Spirituality: How to Use Your Relationship as a Spiritual Path, Set. David Grudermeyer & Rebecca Grudermeyer. 2 cass. 18.95 INCL. HANDOUTS. (T-02) Willingness Wrks.

Relationships & Togetherness. Sylvia Sherman. 1 cass. 8.95 (315) Am Fed Astrologers.
Planetary comparision's are fun to explore.

Relationships as Mirrors. Shakti Gawain. 1 cass. (Running Time: 1 hr. 30 min.). 1991. 11.95 (978-0-931432-71-2(5)) Nataraj Pub.
Shakti Gawain focuses on what makes relationships of all kinds work. Her unique & powerful perspective will certainly help people improve the quality of their lives.

Relationships by Design: God's Blueprint for Intimacy. abr. ed. Chuck Bomar. (Relationships by Design Super-Ser.). 2008. audio compact disk 33.00 (978-5-557-43771-4(1)) Group Pub.

Relationships, Gifts of the Spirit: How to view challenging relationships as opportunities for Growth. Julie Hutslar. (ENG.). 2008. audio compact disk 28.00 (978-0-9753000-6-0(7)) Luminous Epinoia.

Relationships in Conflict: Innovations for Working with Couples, Teenagers & Their Parents, Co-Workers & Friends & Other Individuals in Challenging Relationships. David Wexler. 11 cass. (Running Time: 12 hrs.). 2004. 129.00 (978-0-9755159-0-7(X)) IAHB.

Relationships in Conflict: New Perspectives & Innovations for Working with: Couples, Teenagers & Their Parents, Co-Workers & Friends, & Other Individuals in Challenging Relationships. David Wexler. 11 cass. (Running Time: 12 hours). 2004. audio compact disk 129.00 (978-0-9755159-5-2(0)) IAHB.

Relationships in Spiritual Life. Contrib. by Tsering Everest. 2 cass. (Running Time: 2 hrs.). 14.00 (978-1-881847-21-2(7)) Padma Pub CA.
Lama Tsering Everest offers her unique & fresh viewpoint on how relationships can be integrated into spiritual life.

Relationships of Grace. abr. ed. Chris Karcher. (Running Time: 1 hr.). 2004. 9.99 (978-1-932356-21-2(5)); audio compact disk 9.99 (978-1-932356-20-5(7)) Pub: AdamsKing Pubng. Dist(s): STL Dist NA

Relationships Series. 6 cass. 44.95 incl. vinyl storage album. (LS-7) Crystal Clarity.
Presents: Relationships - A Spiritual Approach; How to Spiritualize Marriage; Questions & Answers on Relationships; How to Work with People (by Asha Praver, Anada minister & teacher); Men, Women, Marriage, & Sex (by Asha Praver, Ananda minister & teacher).

Relationships: Starting, Maintaining, & Ending: Starting, Maintaining, & Ending. Gary Applegate. 2 cass. 1986. 20.00 Berringer Pub.
Skill Development's founder, Dr. Gary Applegate, presents the unique Skill Development approach to successful change.

Relationships Workshop. Marianne Williamson. 2 cass. 1992. 18.00 (SH15) Sound Horizons AV.

Relationships/Forgiving Our Parents. Marianne Williamson. Read by Marianne Williamson. 1 cass. (Running Time: 90 mins.). (Lectures on a Course in Miracles). 1999. 10.00 (978-1-56170-673-0(6), M871) Hay House.

Relative Danger. Charles Benoit. Read by Patrick G. Lawlor. (Running Time: 30600 sec.). 2006. 59.95 (978-0-7861-4758-8(X)) Blckstn Audio.

Relative Danger. unabr. ed. Charles Benoit. Read by Patrick G. Lawlor. (Running Time: 30600 sec.). 2006. audio compact disk 72.00 (978-0-7861-6342-7(9)); audio compact disk 29.95 (978-0-7861-7261-0(4)) Blckstn Audio.

Relative Pitch Ear Training SuperCourse. David Lucas Burge. 21 Audio Cassettes. (Running Time: 31 hours, 20 minutes). 1986. 399.00 (978-0-942542-30-1(4)) EarTraining.
Learn the language of music pitch. How to compose all chords & identify them by ear! Gain a "lightning fast ear" to play by ear, improvise, compose, sight-sing, transpose & appreciate music.

Relative Pitch Ear Training SuperCourse. David Lucas Burge. 4 cass. 1986. 95.00 (978-0-942542-82-0(7)); 95.00 (978-0-942542-83-7(5)); 95.00 (978-0-942542-84-4(3)); 95.00 (978-0-942542-85-1(1)) EarTraining.
Learn the language of music - pitch - how to compose all chords & identify them by ear! Gain a "lightning fast ear" to play by ear, improvise, compose, sight-sing, transpose & appreciate music.

Relative Pitch Ear Training SuperCourse, David Lucas Burge. 6 cass. 1986. 95.00 (978-0-942542-81-3(9)) EarTraining.

Relative Pitch Ear Training SuperCourse, Level 1. David Lucas Burge. 9 CDs. 1999. audio compact disk 95.00 (978-0-942542-31-8(2)) EarTraining.
Learn the language of music - pitch. How to compose all chords & identify them by ear! Gain a "lightning fast ear" to play by ear, improvise, compose, sight-sing, transpose & appreciate music.

Relative Pitch Ear Training SuperCourse, Level 2. David Lucas Burge. 8 CDs. 1999. audio compact disk 95.00 (978-0-942542-32-5(0)) EarTraining.
Learn the language of music - pitch. How to compose all chords & identify them by ear! Gain a "lightning fast ear" to play by ear, improvise, compose, sight-sign, transpose & appreciate music.

Relative Pitch Ear Training SuperCourse, Level 3. David Lucas Burge. 8 CDs. 1999. audio compact disk 95.00 (978-0-942542-33-2(9)) EarTraining.
Learn the language of music - pitch. How to compose all chords & identify them by ear! Gain a "lightning fast ear" to play by ear, improvise, compose, sight-sing, transpose & appreciate music.

Relative Pitch Ear Training SuperCourse, Level 4. David Lucas Burge. 8 CDs. 1999. audio compact disk 95.00 (978-0-942542-34-9(7)) EarTraining.

Relative Pitch Ear Training SuperCourse, Level 5. David Lucas Burge. 8 CDs. 1999. audio compact disk 95.00 (978-0-942542-35-6(5)) EarTraining.

Relative Pitch Ear Training SuperCourse, Vol. 15. David Lucas Burge. 41 Audio CDs. (Running Time: 31 hrs. 20 mins.). 1999. audio compact disk 399.00 (978-0-942542-80-6(0)) EarTraining.
Learn the language of music - pitch. How to compose all chords - and identify them by ear! Gain a "lightning fast ear" to play by ear, improvise, compose, sight-sing, transpose and appreciate music.

Relative Pitch Ear Training SuperCourse, Sample Lesson, Vol. 1. David Lucas Burge. 1 cass. 1986. 14.95 (978-0-942542-87-5(8)); audio compact disk 14.95 (978-0-942542-37-0(1)) EarTraining.
Learn the language of music - pitch. How to compose all chords & identify them by ear! Gain a "lightning fast ear" to play by ear, improvise, compose, sight-sing, transpose & appreciate music.

Relatives Came. 9.95 (978-1-59112-288-3(0)) Live Oak Media.

Relatives Came. Cynthia Rylant. Read by Bonnie Kelly-Young. Illus. by Stephen Gammell. 1 cass. (J). 2000. pap. bk. 19.97 (978-0-7366-9212-0(6)) Books on Tape.
A lively, homespun lot who seem to multiply as the pages turn, overflowing the house & instigating their own brand of fun.

Relatives Came. Cynthia Rylant. 1 cass. (Running Time: 35 min.). (J). (gr. k-4). 2001. bk. 15.95 (VX-532C) Kimbo Educ.
A young girl is sent to live with her uncle Jim in the city. Includes book.

Relatives Came. Cynthia Rylant. Illus. by Stephen Gammell. 11 vols. (Running Time: 7 mins.). 1999. bk. 28.95 (978-1-59112-546-4(4)); pap. bk. 39.95 (978-1-59112-545-7(6)) Live Oak Media.

Relatives Came. Cynthia Rylant. Read by Bonnie Kelly-Young. Illus. by Stephen Gammell. 14 vols. (Running Time: 7 mins.). (J). (gr. k-3). 1999. pap. bk. & tchr. ed. 37.95 Reading Chest. (978-0-87499-534-3(5)) Live Oak Media.
An hilarious account of a family's summer visit with their relatives from Virginia combined with complementary musical compositions.

Relatives Came. Cynthia Rylant. Illus. by Stephen Gammell. (Running Time: 7 mins.). (J). (gr. k-3). 1999. 9.95 (978-0-87499-535-0(3)); audio compact disk 12.95 (978-1-59112-323-1(2)) Live Oak Media.

Relatives Came. Cynthia Rylant. (J). 1985. bk. 40.43 (978-0-07-511736-0(3)) SRA McGraw.

Relatives Came. Cynthia Rylant & Distribution Media Staff. (J). 1986. bk. 14.00 (978-0-676-31727-5(8)) Random.

Relatives Came. unabr. ed. Cynthia Rylant. Read by Bonnie Kelly-Young. Illus. by Stephen Gammell. 7 vols. (Running Time: 7 mins.). (J). (gr. k-3). 1999. pap. bk. 16.95 (978-0-87499-532-9(9)) AudioGO.

Relatives Came. unabr. ed. Cynthia Rylant. Read by Bonnie Kelly-Young. Illus. by Stephen Gammell. 11 vols. (Running Time: 7 mins.). (J). (gr. k-3). 1999. bk. 25.95 (978-0-87499-533-6(7)) Live Oak Media.

Relativism: Feet Firmly Planted in Mid-Air. unabr. ed. Instructed by Gregory Koukl. 2 cass. (Running Time: 4 hrs.). 1999. 12.95 (978-0-9673584-3-7(4)) Stand to Reason.
Today's most pressing apologetic issue is moral relativism. The myth of moral neutrality is exposed, as well as the idea that evolution can explain morality.

Relativity: The Special & General Theory. abr. ed. Albert Einstein & Albert Einstein. Read by Julian Lopez-Morillas. 2 CDs. (Running Time: 2 hrs. 30 mins.). (ENG.). 2001. audio compact disk 22.95 (978-1-56511-511-8(2), 1565115112) Pub: HighBridge. Dist(s): Workman Pub

Relativity & the Absolute. Swami Amar Jyoti. 1 cass. 1986. 9.95 (R-86) Truth Consciousness.
A full understanding of the link between Absolute & relativity. Nondualism & the personal God. The future dream of Oneness.

Relax. Dorothy J. Papin-Griffith. 2005. audio compact disk 14.95 (978-0-9765935-1-5(3)) Gry L Prodns Inc.

Relax. Uma Silbey. Read by Uma Silbey. 1 cass. (Running Time: 45 min.). 10.00 UMA.
Guided spoken meditation with sound background.

Relax. Windham Hill Staff. 1 cass. 1998. 15.00 (978-1-56170-554-2(3)) Hay House.

Relax. abr. ed. David Ison. (Running Time: 1 hr. 0 mins. 0 sec.). 2011. audio compact disk 9.98 (978-1-60297-023-6(8)) Sounds True.

Relax. abr. ed. Robert A. Monroe. Read by Robert A. Monroe. (Running Time: 30 min.). (Human Plus Ser.). 1989. 14.95 (978-1-56102-027-0(3)) Inter Indus.
Gain instant relief from tensions while staying alert.

Relax: Meditations for Flute. Donald Walters. 2003. audio compact disk 15.95 (978-1-56589-777-9(3)) Pub: Crystal Clarity. Dist(s): Natl Bk Netwk

Relax: Meditations for Piano. Donald Walters. 2001. audio compact disk 15.95 (978-1-56589-774-8(9)) Pub: Crystal Clarity. Dist(s): Natl Bk Netwk

Relax! You Only Live Once. Loretta LaRoche. Read by Loretta LaRoche. 2 cass. (Running Time: 1 hr. 18 mins.). (Wgbh Specials Ser.). (gr. 7 up). 2004. 14.95 (978-1-57807-216-3(6), WG817) WGBH Boston.
Reveals how to lose your worries by finding your sense of humor in the most unlikely situations. Offers solutions to life's little challenges, like "making food your friend" and respecting your inner wisdom. Includes a relaxation session led by Loretta herself.

Relax: Your Life Depends on It. Created by Kathryn Seifert. 1 CD. (Running Time: 1 hr). 2007. cd-rom (978-0-9763972-8-1(5)) S Pub Co.

Relax - Quick! (Cassette) Simple, Effective Relaxation Processes You Can Do in Moments... Anytime, Anywhere. Nancy Hopps. Read by Nancy Hopps. 1 cass. (Running Time: 1 hr.). (ENG.). 1994. 11.00 (978-0-9663069-2-7(9)) Pub: Syner Systs. Dist(s): Baker Taylor

Relax - Quick! (CD) Simple, Effective Relaxation Processes You Can Do in Moments... Anytime, Anywhere. Nancy Hopps. Read by Nancy Hopps. 1 CD. (Running Time: 1 hr.). 1995. audio compact disk 16.00 (978-0-9663069-3-4(7)) Pub: Syner Systs. Dist(s): Baker Taylor

Relax & Breathe Vol. 1: Enhanced Multi-Media. Created by Kate Harding. Prod. by Tool Studios. 2002. cd-rom & audio compact disk 14.95 (978-0-9740420-0-8(5)) Kate Co.

Relax & De-Stress: Rest, Re-balance, & Replenish with Classical Music for Healing. Andrew Weil & Joshua Leeds. (Running Time: 1 hr. 14 mins.). 2006. audio compact disk 17.98 (978-1-59179-540-7(0), M1099D) Sounds True.

Relax & Eliminate Stress. Dick Sutphen. 1 cass. (Running Time: 1 hr.). (Only Subliminals Ser.). 1990. 12.98 (978-0-87554-442-7(8), T202) Valley Sun.
One hour of soothing, digitally mastered stereo music with positive subliminal suggestions phrased for maximum acceptance by your subconscious mind.

Relax & Enjoy Your Baby. Sylvia K. Olkin. 2 cass. (Running Time: 2 hrs.). (Relax & Enjoy Your Baby Ser.: Vol. 1). 1996. bk. 16.95 (978-1-55961-346-0(7), BP7506) Relaxtn Co.

Relax & Let Go (Autogenic) Read by Mary Richards. 1 cass. (Running Time: 45 min.). (Energy Break Ser.). 2007. audio compact disk 19.95 (978-1-56136-152-6(6)) Master Your Mind.

Relax & Let Go of Tension. Scott Sulak. 1998. 15.00 (978-1-932659-06-1(4)) Change For Gd.

Relax & Release Life's Daily Demands. Lea Blumberg. 1 CD. 2002. audio compact disk 19.95 (978-0-9747487-0-2(6)) L Blumberg.
Hypnosis CD for Stress Reduction.

Relax Awhile. Narrated by Dick Lutz. 1 cass. (Running Time: 24 min.). 1984. 7.95 (978-0-931625-14-5(9), 14) DIMI Pr.
Lengthy & detailed with a beneficial relaxation narration. Reversible.

Relax, Daydream & Draw. Don Campbell. 1 cass., 1 CD. (Mozart Effect Ser.: Vol. 2). (J). 7.18 (CG 84292); audio compact disk 12.78 CD Jewel box. (CG 84292) NewSound.

Relax, Energize, Discover: Guided Imagery & Relaxation Journeys. unabr. ed. Roxanne E. Daleo. Read by Roxanne E. Daleo. 1 cass. (Running Time: 31 min.). (MindWorks for Children Ser.). (YA). (gr. 8 up). 1987. 12.95 (978-1-889447-09-4(9)) Mindwrks Chldrn.
This guided imagery relaxation program combines the classic technique of progressive muscle relaxation with guided imagery of a beautiful natural spring found in the woodlands to promote deep rest & calm.

Relax for a Healthier Mind & Body. unabr. ed. Gloria Pincu. Read by Gloria Pincu. 1 cass. (Running Time: 15 min.). 1994. 10.00 (978-0-9658173-3-2(4)) BLS Pub.
Relaxation exercise - guided images.

Relax from Head to Toe. Read by Paul Fair. 1 cass. (Running Time: 45 min.). (Relaxation Ser.). 1996. 12.95 (978-1-889896-06-9(3), S4047) Strs Les Inc.
Stress reduction.

Relax... Let Go... Relax. 1 cass. (Running Time: 55 min.). (Sensational Relaxation Ser.: No. 1). 11.95 (978-0-938586-94-4(7), RLX) Whole Person.
Mentally scan your body for tension - then discharge that tension through breathing & releasing. Let comforting relaxation spread throughout, & store this peaceful sense for "instant replay" later. Side A: Revitalization. Images of warmth & calm encourage progressive muscle relaxation in this "any time of the day" revitalization experience. Side B: Relaxation. With a sequential reflection on the day, gradually surrender accumulated tension in this "end of the day" relaxer.

Relax Mind & Body. unabr. ed. Krs Edstrom. Read by Krs Edstrom. 1 cass. (Running Time: 40 min.). (Inner Mastery Ser.). 1994. 12.95 Bk. box size. (978-1-886198-00-5(4), IMS01) Soft Stone Pub.
Teaches you how to internalize the "art of relaxation" and is ideal as a daily relaxation tune-up. You will discover deeper relaxation and learn how to resource it throughout the day. Your energy will rise as you unblock conscious and unconscious tension. KRS uses her own unique blend of "body-talk" skills such as meditation, breathing and visualization techniques combined with age-old ones that not only delivers immediate results, but also imparts new skills to draw on for a lifetime. Music designed to calm as you cultivate awareness. Endorsed by hospitals, airlines and psychologists. Too often we "go through the motions" of life, not tuned in to what is happening internally - how our mind and body interrelate and how the outside world and our inside world interrelate. The purpose of these tapes is not only that you feel results after each listen, but that you develop increasingly deeper skills to serve you in all of life's challenges and excursions. Commonly considered negatives such as pain, stress and insomnia are experienced in a new, non-judgmental way that invites insight and is both growth-promoting and freeing. Once perceived enemies turn into welcome teachers. Similarly, positive and everyday events such as watching a bird soar, hitting a ball or conducting business are experienced in a more complete way; a way that enriches your relationship to self and thus the outside world.

Relax Mind & Body: Meditations to Soothe & Center. unabr. ed. Krs Edstrom. 1 CD. (Running Time: 37 mins.). (Inner Mastery Ser.). 2007. audio compact disk 16.95 (978-1-886198-15-9(2)) Pub: Soft Stone Pub. Dist(s): Ingram Bk Co

Relax Now. Eldon Taylor. Read by Eldon Taylor. Ed. by Leslie Brice. 1 cass. (Running Time: 1 hr.). 1992. 12.95 (978-1-56705-024-0(7)) Gateways Inst.
Self improvement.

Relax Now. Eldon Taylor. Read by Eldon Taylor. Interview with XProgress Aware Staff. 1 cass. (Running Time: 1 hr. 30 min.). (Power Imaging Ser.). 16.95 incl. script. (978-1-55978-178-7(5), 8006) Progress Aware Res.
Hypnosis & soundtrack with underlying subliminal affirmations.

Relax Now! Removing Stress from Your Life. Sheila Hayward. 1998. bk. 19.95 (978-0-8069-6309-9(3)) Sterling.

Relax on the Beach & Relax in a Meadow. Narrated by Dick Lutz. 1 cass. (Running Time: 15 min.). 1984. 7.95 (978-0-931625-15-2(7), 15) DIMI Pr.
Imagine yourself on the beach on side A or in a meadow on side B. Detailed narration helps you visualize the scene with appropriate background sounds.

Relax, Re-New & Re-Energize. Adele Greenfield. 2 cass. (Running Time: 1 hr. 44 min.). 29.95 CareerTrack Pubns.
Contains exercises for relaxation to re-energize mind, body & spirit.

Relax, Renew & Energize: A Powerful 7 Step Guide for Reclaiming Your Life! Jennifer Yessler & Hug Audio. Read by Diane Burket. Ed. by Dave Bolick & Tracy Dodson. Lisa Pavlock & Dewulf Kristen. (ENG.). 2008. audio compact disk 9.99 (978-0-9820704-1-3(1)) HUG.

Relax Rx: A Self-Hypnosis Program for Health & Well-Being. Steven Gurgevich. 2008. audio compact disk 19.95 (978-1-59179-962-7(7)) Sounds True.

Relax Two. Read by Paul Fair. 1 cass. (Running Time: 45 min.). (Relaxation Ser.). 1996. 12.95 (978-1-889896-01-4(2), S4034) Strs Les Inc.
Stress reduction.

Relax Without Drugs. Virgil B. Smith. 1 cass. (Running Time: 15 min.). 1979. 5.95 (978-1-878507-03-7(6), 26C) Human Grwth Services.
Use of narration & music to teach relaxation on physical & conscious thought levels; also progressive desensitization toward stimuli which the listener has had excessive reactions about.

Relax Your Way to a Richer Life. Guy Finley. (ENG.). 2006. 7.49 (978-1-929320-60-8(4)) Life of Learn.

Relax Your Way to Thin: Hypnosis Weight Loss Motivation. Trevor Scott. 2003. audio compact disk 19.95 (978-0-9763138-2-3(0)) Beverly Hills CA.

Relax Your Way to Thin - Low Carb: Hypnosis Weight Loss Motivation. Trevor H. Scott. 2003. audio compact disk 19.95 (978-0-9763138-3-0(9)) Beverly Hills CA.

Relaxation. 1 cass. 10.00 (978-1-58506-009-2(7), 15) New Life Inst OR.
Become peaceful & calm in body & mind. Experience the joy of total relaxation whenever you want.

Relaxation. 1 cass. (Running Time: 60 min.). 10.95 (015) Psych Res Inst.
Deep relaxation techniques.

Relaxation. 1 cass. (Running Time: 45 min.). (Health Ser.). 9.98 (978-1-55909-026-1(X), 34S); 9.98 90 min. extended length stereo music. (978-1-55909-027-8(8), 34X) Randolph Tapes.
Relaxation for a healthy mind & body! Subliminal messages are heard 3-5 minutes before becoming ocean sounds or music.

Relaxation. Rick Brown. Read by Rick Brown. Ed. by John Quatro. 1 cass. (Running Time: 30 min.). (Subliminal - Soft Sounds Ser.). 1993. 10.95 (978-1-57100-072-9(0), S103); 10.95 (978-1-57100-096-5(8), W103); 10.95 (978-1-57100-120-7(4), H103) Sublime Sftware.
Transports user to a warm, soothing bath tub.

Relaxation. Pat Carroll. Read by Pat Carroll. Narrated by Tony Carroll. 1 cass. (Running Time: 30 min.). 10.00 Inner-Mind Concepts.
Explains how to relax the entire body - experiencing peace & freedom.

Relaxation. Richard Jafolla & Mary-Alice Jafolla. Read by Richard Jafolla & Mary-Alice Jafolla. (Health & Healing Ser.). 1986. 12.95 (270) Stppng Stones.
Motivational tapes that work on the subconscious mind (subliminal) & conscious mind to bring about self-improvement.

Relaxation. Barrie Konicov. 1 cass. (Video-Audio System Ser.). cass. & video 24.98 (978-0-87082-449-4(X), SYS 108); 16.98 (978-1-56001-300-6(1), SCII 108) Potentials.
xperience peace & calm, joy & relaxation & how to relax without stress or strain.

Relaxation. Barrie Konicov. 1 CD. 2003. audio compact disk 16.98 (978-0-87082-962-8(9)) Potentials.
We always seem to hurt those closest to us, or are hurt by them. Take this situation in hand - with or without the other person. Use this program to reframe your relationships with husband or wife, parents, children, brothers or sisters.You will find the self-hypnosis on track 1 and the subliminal on track 2. The easy-listening music of the subliminal, together with the self-hypnosis, is the original format which most people love and with which they are most familiar.

Relaxation. Barrie Konicov. 2 CDs. 2003. audio compact disk 27.98 (978-1-56001-986-2(7)) Potentials.
Learning to relax can eliminate high blood pressure, headaches, and stomach problems. You can reduce the effects of stress. Enjoy peace, tranquility, and deep relaxation with this program.This 2-CD program from our Super Consciousness series is our newest, most powerful format. On the self-hypnosis CD, SC programs have the Subliminal Persuasion soundtrack added under Barrie?s voice. And the 17th Century Baroque music on the Subliminal CD has the same beat as your body's natural rhythm, thereby allowing the suggestions to enter deeply and effortlessly.

Relaxation. Sivananda Radha. 1 cass. (GER.). 1974. 7.95 (978-0-931454-30-1(1)) Timeless Bks.
Introduces the principles of Yogic teachings to lead the listener through a thorough relaxation. This tape is helpful for stress reduction.

Relaxation. Sivananda Radha. 2002. 15.95 (978-0-931454-96-7(4)) Pub: Timeless Bks. Dist(s): Baker Taylor

Relaxation. Betty L. Randolph. 1 stereo cass. (Running Time: 45 min.). (Self-Hypnosis Ser.). 9.98 (978-1-55909-161-9(4), 103) Randolph Tapes.
A relaxation training program. Music background & spoken word.

***Relaxation.** Swami Sivananda Radha. (ENG.). 2002. audio compact disk 15.95 (978-1-932018-26-4(3)) Pub: Timeless Bks. Dist(s): Baker Taylor

Relaxation. Eldon Taylor. 1 cass. (Running Time: 62 min.). (Neurophonics Ser.). 16.95 (978-1-55978-652-2(3), 1003) Progress Aware Res.
Sound patterns for Altered States of Consciousness with underlying subliminal affirmations & frequency response signals. Use with headphones only.

Relaxation. Barry Tesar. 1 cass. (Running Time: 1 hr.). (Subliminal Inspiration Ser.). 1992. 9.98 (978-1-56470-007-0(0)) Success Cass.
Subliminal program.

Relaxation. unabr. ed. Hugh Fraser. (Running Time: 1 hr. 0 mins. 0 sec.). (HarperCollinsAudioBooks Ser.). (ENG., 2005. audio compact disk 14.95 (978-0-00-719561-9(3)) Pub: HarpC GBR. Dist(s): IPG Chicago
This recording offers a guided development towards a state of deep relaxation and calm. It will provide a means of unlocking and freeing habitual muscular tension and pacifying the autonomic nervous system.

Relaxation, No. E103. Rick Brown. Read by Rick Brown. Ed. by John Quatro. 1 cass. (Running Time: 30 min.). (Subliminal - Easy Listening Ser.). 1993. 10.95 (978-1-57100-000-2(3)) Sublime Sftware.
"Relaxation" transports user to a warm, soothing bath tub.

Relaxation, No. J103. Rick Brown. Read by Rick Brown. Ed. by John Quatro. 1 cass. (Running Time: 30 min.). (Subliminal - Easy Listening Ser.). 1993. 10.95 (978-1-57100-024-8(0)) Sublime Sftware.
"Relaxation" - transports user to a warm, soothing bath tub.

Relaxation, No. N103. Rick Brown. Read by Rick Brown. Ed. by John Quatro. 1 cass. (Running Time: 30 min.). (Subliminal - New Age Ser.). 1993. 10.95 (978-1-57100-048-4(8)) Sublime Sftware.

Relaxation: Classic. Eldon Taylor. Read by Eldon Taylor. Ed. by Leslie Brice. 1 cass. (Running Time: 1 hr.). 1992. 16.95 (978-1-56705-181-0(2)) Gateways Inst.
Self improvement.

Relaxation: Easy. Eldon Taylor. Read by Eldon Taylor. Ed. by Leslie Brice. 1 cass. (Running Time: 1 hr.). 1992. 16.95 (978-1-56705-182-7(0)) Gateways Inst.

Relaxation: Four Guided Journeys to Peace & Serenity. Michael Hayes Samuelson. 2001. 19.95 (978-0-9710216-3-1(5)) Green Glass Prod.

Relaxation: Harmonies. Eldon Taylor. Read by Eldon Taylor. Ed. by Leslie Brice. 1 cass. (Running Time: 1 hr.). 1992. 16.95 (978-1-56705-183-4(9)) Gateways Inst.

Relaxation: Instructions for Chanting Mantras. Sivananda Radha. Narrated by Sivananda Radha. 1 CD. (Running Time: 37 mins.). 2002. audio compact disk 15.95 (978-0-931454-90-5(5)) Pub: Timeless Bks. Dist(s): Baker Taylor
Introduces the principle of yogic teaching to lead the listener through a thorough relaxation. This tape is helpful for stress reduction.

Relaxation: La Relajacion. Barrie Konicov. 1 cass. (Running Time: 1 hr. 08 min.). (Spanish-Language Audios Ser.). (SPA.). 1995. 11.98 (978-0-87082-804-1(5), 108) Potentials.
Begin to experience peace & calm, joy & relaxation. In turn you will learn to relax, diminish headaches, stress & that uncomfortable, uptight feeling in your stomach. Your blood pressure may even return to normal!.

Relaxation: Ocean. Eldon Taylor. Read by Eldon Taylor. Ed. by Leslie Brice. 1 cass. (Running Time: 1 hr.). 1992. 16.95 (978-1-56705-184-1(7)) Gateways Inst.
Self improvement.

Relaxation: Stream. Eldon Taylor. Read by Eldon Taylor. Ed. by Leslie Brice. 1 cass. (Running Time: 1 hr.). 1992. 16.95 (978-1-56705-185-8(5)) Gateways Inst.

Relaxation & De-Sensitization Training, Set-RD. Russell E. Mason. Read by Russell E. Mason. 6 cass. (Running Time: 5 hrs. 54 min.). (Train-Ascendance Cassettes Ser.). 1975. pap. bk. 45.00 (978-0-89533-006-2(7), 55.GT-RD) F I Comm.
Orientation & practice both for de-sensitization to solve problems & for purposeful or meditative relaxation.

Relaxation & Deep Meditation. Swami Amar Jyoti. 1 dolby cass. 1976. 9.95 (P-49) Truth Consciousness.
Postures for relaxation & deep meditation. Regulation of Prana for body & mind. Intense practices. The only true purpose of life.

Relaxation & Esteem Building: The Geometry of Being - Geometry in Motion. Eldon Taylor. Directed By Eldon Taylor. 1 cass. (Running Time: 30 min.). (Sacred Geometry Ser.). 1997. cass. & video 29.95 (978-1-55978-697-3(3), V104) Progress Aware Res.
Geometry in motion developing from fractals, forming mandalas, absolutely mesmerizing with tones & frequencies.

Relaxation & Inspiration. 1 cassette. 1985. 12.95 (978-1-55841-102-9(X)) Emmett E Miller.
Simple, comforting, and invigorating. After relaxing into a deep meditation, you gain inspiration from the deeper levels of your being. Your meditative experience continues over beautiful classical music.

Relaxation & Inspiration. 1 CD. 1985. audio compact disk 16.95 (978-1-55841-129-6(1)) Emmett E Miller.
Simple, comforting and invigorating. After relaxing into a deep meditation, you gain inspiration from the deeper levels of your being. Your meditative experience continues over beautiful classical music.

Relaxation & Meditation. unabr. ed. Twin Sisters Productions. Read by Twin Sisters Productions. (YA). 2007. 59.99 (978-1-60252-700-3(8)) Find a World.

Relaxation & Mindfulness: Demystifying Stress. Daniel Goleman et al. 2 cass. (Running Time: 2 hrs.). 1996. 16.95 (978-1-879323-49-0(4)) Sound Horizons AV.
Combining deep relaxation with awareness training, this program extends the effects of relaxation sessions into the day as a stress buffer, so people can cope with worries & anxieties on their own without medication. Developed at Harvard & the University of Massachusetts Medical Schools, it has been found effective for the physical symptoms of stress, including high blood pressure, neck & back pain, gastrointestinal problems & chronic headache. Those who are already experiencing the physical or mental effects of stress, or those who simply want to be able to relax more effectively, will learn the techniques they need.

Relaxation & Stress Management Program. Edward A. Charlesworth. 3 cass. (Running Time: 1 hr. 48 min.). Incl. Relaxation & Stress Management Program: Autogenic Relaxation: Arms & Hands; Relaxation & Stress Management Program: Autogenic Relaxation: Legs & Feet; Relaxation & Stress Management Program: Progressive Relaxation & Deep Muscle Relaxation; Relaxation & Stress Management Program: Visual Imagery Relaxation & Image Rehearsal Practice; 1986. 34.95 Set.; 12.95 ea. Stress Mgmt Res.
Learn to relax without tranquilizers, alcohol, or cigarette. Increase your physical & mental relaxation skills.

Relaxation & Stress Management Program: Autogenic Relaxation: Arms & Hands see Relaxation & Stress Management Program

Relaxation & Stress Management Program: Autogenic Relaxation: Legs & Feet see Relaxation & Stress Management Program

Relaxation & Stress Management Program: Progressive Relaxation & Deep Muscle Relaxation see Relaxation & Stress Management Program

Relaxation & Stress Management Program: Visual Imagery Relaxation & Image Rehearsal Practice see Relaxation & Stress Management Program

Relaxation & Stress Reduction: Letting Go of Stress - Learning to Relax. Diana Keck. Read by Diana Keck. 1 cass. 9.95 (978-0-929653-00-6(9), TAPE 100) Mntn Spirit Tapes.

Relaxation & Stress Reduction: Relaxing Into the Self - Sleep Induction. Diana Keck. Read by Diana Keck. 1 cass. 9.95 (978-0-929653-01-3(7), TAPE 101) Mntn Spirit Tapes.

Relaxation & Stress Relief, Vol. 6. Jonathan Parker. Read by Jonathan Parker. 1 CD. (Running Time: 1 hr.). (Subliminal Ser.: Vol. 4). 1999. audio compact disk (978-1-58400-047-1(3)) QuantumQuests Intl.
Subliminal affirmations with gentle woodwinds music on compact disc.

Relaxation Basics: A Doctor's Prescription for Stress Relief. unabr. ed. Mary Pullig Schatz. 1 CD. (Running Time: 0 hr. 57 mins. 43 sec.). (ENG.). 2008. audio compact disk 13.95 (978-1-930485-22-8(0)) Pub: Rodmell Pr. Dist(s): PerseuPGW

Relaxation Collection. 6 cass. (Running Time: 6 hrs.). 29.95 (978-1-55961-423-8(4)) Relaxtn Co.

Relaxation Company's Healing Music Project Collection: Experience the Healing Power of Music. abr. ed. Created by Relaxation Company Sleep Center. (Running Time: 3 hrs. 0 mins. 0 sec.). (ENG.). 2006. audio compact disk 24.98 (978-1-55961-725-3(X)) Pub: Relaxtn Co. Dist(s): S and S Inc

Relaxation: Deep Muscle: Breathing Instructions for Hyperventilation. unabr. ed. John Marquis. (Running Time: 45 min.). 1986. 10.00 Self Mgmt Schls.

Relaxation Exercise & Energy Movement & Focusing Exercise. 1 cass. (Running Time: 1 hr.). 2004. 8.95 (978-0-9617713-4-8(8), WT-101) Perelandra Ltd.

Relaxation Experience. Susan Quiring. 2 cass. (Running Time: 3 hrs.). 1996. 15.95 (978-1-55977-441-3(X)) CareerTrack Pubns.

Relaxation Experience: Reduce Stress Through Imagery & Music. 2 cass. (Running Time: 1 hr. 22 min.). 1996. 15.95 Set. (Q10202) CareerTrack Pubns.
Relieve the effects of stress quickly & easily...whenever & wherever you need to. Through guided imagery & specially selected music, these tapes will help you achieve a state of calm & relaxation at a moment's notice. You'll be able to release tensions & replenish your energy. You'll find it easier to face the daily challenges life throws your way.

Relaxation for Expectant Mothers: Spoken Audio CD. Narrated by Hopps Nancy. (ENG.). 2002. audio compact disk 16.00 (978-0-9663069-8-9(8)) Syner Systs.

Relaxation for Weight Loss: Start Each Meal with a 5-Minute Relaxation Program & Break the Stress-Fat Connection. Gael Chiarella. 1 CD. (Running Time: 1 hr.). 2001. audio compact disk 12.00 (93-0278) Relaxtn Co.
Reduce weight by using relaxation to decrease stress. In response to stress, our bodies produce cortisol, which stimulates appetite particularly for carbohydrates. Studies prove that cortisol levels can be reduced by learning simple skills of relaxation. Follow the author's soothing voice for three 5-minute guided meditations that teach you to focus on breath, visualize tranquil imagery and create a sensation of deep relaxation.

Relaxation Gift Set: 2 Best-Selling Guided Imagery Cassettes. gif. ed. Nancy Hopps. 2 cass. (Running Time: 3 hrs.). (ENG.). 2000. pap. bk. 19.95 (978-0-9663069-4-1(5)) Pub: Syner Systs. Dist(s): Baker Taylor
Relaxations & affirmation techniques.

Relaxation Healing. Peggy Huddleston. 2005. audio compact disk 19.95 (978-0-9645757-5-2(2)) NID Pub.

Relaxation Methods for Coping. Gail C. Feldman. 1 cass. (Running Time: 50 min.). (Adult Coping Ser.). 1985. 11.95 (978-0-945054-08-5(4)) Speaking Health.

Relaxation Procedures in Cancer Treatment. William Redd & Thomas Burish. 2 cass. (Running Time: 60 min.). 25.00 Leo Media.
The passive induction procedure involves focusing the patien attention on the sensations in various muscle groups & shifting attention to scenes to maintain the relaxed state & distract the patient from the treatment procedure. The active relaxation induction involves tensing & relaxing several muscle groups.

Relaxation... Pure & Simple. Marilyn Winfield. Read by Marilyn Winfield. 1 cass. (Running Time: 20 mins.). 2000. (978-0-9679210-6-8(6)) Pathwy Heal.
Guided visualization techniques.

***Relaxation Revolution: Enhancing Your Personal Health Through the Science & Genetics of Mind Body Healing.** unabr. ed. Herbert Benson & William Proctor. (Running Time: 8 hrs. 30 mins.). 2010. 15.99 (978-1-4001-8746-1(X)) Tantor Media.

***Relaxation Revolution: Enhancing Your Personal Health Through the Science & Genetics of Mind Body Healing.** unabr. ed. Herbert Benson & William Proctor. Narrated by Gerry Gartenberg. (Running Time: 7 hrs. 30 mins. 0 sec.). (ENG.). 2010. 19.99 (978-1-4001-6746-3(9)); audio compact disk 71.99 (978-1-4001-4746-5(8)); audio compact disk 29.99 (978-1-4001-1746-8(1)) Pub: Tantor Media. Dist(s): IngramPubServ

Relaxation Techniques. Martha Bramhall. 1986. 9.75 (978-0-932491-26-8(X)) Res Appl Inc.
A guide to relaxation using guided imagery & imagination.

Relaxation Techniques: Reduce Stress & Anxiety & Enhance Well-Being. Scripts. Katerina Volny & Lillian Nejad. 1CD. (Running Time: 3600 sec.). 2008. audio compact disk 14.95 (978-1-84590-078-6(2)) Crown Hse GBR.

Relaxation Techniques for Ministry. Robert Potter. 1986. 10.80 (0707B) Assn Prof Chaplains.

Relaxation Techniques with Anastasia. Anastasia. Narrated by Anastasia. (ENG.). 2009. audio compact disk 14.99 (978-0-9840992-1-0(0)) BayView Ent.

Relaxation Through CHAANGE. Ann Seagrave & Faison Covington. Read by Ann Seagrave & Faison Covington. (Anxiety Treatment Ser.). 12.50 CHAANGE.
Features muscle relaxation on one side & relaxation through imagery on the reverse.

Relaxation Training at a Mountain Lodge. Created by Gayle S. Rozantine. (ENG.). 2006. audio compact disk 15.95 (978-0-9797597-2-7(2)) G Rozantine.

Relaxation Training by the Mountain Stream. Created by Gayle S. Rozantine. (ENG.). 2006. audio compact disk 15.95 (978-0-9797597-3-4(0)) G Rozantine.

Relaxation Training by the Sea. Created by Gayle S. Rozantine. (ENG.). 2006. audio compact disk 15.95 (978-0-9797597-0-3(6)) G Rozantine.

Relaxation Training on a Rainy Day. Created by Gayle S. Rozantine. (ENG.). 2006. audio compact disk 15.95 (978-0-9797597-1-0(4)) G Rozantine.

Relaxation/Affirmation Techniques (Cassette) Spoken Audio Cassette. Nancy Hopps. Read by Nancy Hopps. 1 cass. (Running Time: 1 hr.). (ENG.). 1989. 11.00 (978-0-9663069-0-3(2)) Pub: Syner Systs. Dist(s): Baker Taylor

Relaxation/Affirmation Techniques (CD) Spoken Audio CD. Nancy Hopps. Read by Nancy Hopps. 1 CD. (Running Time: 1 hr.). (ENG.). 1995. audio compact disk 16.00 (978-0-9663069-1-0(0)) Pub: Syner Systs. Dist(s): Baker Taylor

Relaxations, Vol. 3. unabr. ed. Rama Berch. 3 cass. (Running Time: 2 hrs. 30 min.). 1992. (978-1-930559-06-6(2)) STC Inc.
Compilation of "Life's Breath", "Cultivating Awareness" & "Meditation Music", designed to facilitate deep meditation & relaxation.

Relaxations, Vol. 3, set. unabr. ed. Rama Berch. 3 CDs. (Running Time: 2 hrs. 30 min.). 1992. audio compact disk (978-1-930559-07-3(0)) STC Inc.

Relaxed & Stress-Free Childbirth, Vol. 119. 2000. 24.95 (978-1-58557-028-7(1)) Dynamic Growth.

Relaxed Attention. David Barber. 1986. 10.95 Spectra Pub Co.
Explains the relationship between concentration & relaxation in attaining high productivity. The program focuses attention on the task to be done, using only those muscles that are really necessary for that task. This permits maximum concentration without distraction. In this condition an individual can work, think & solve problems more effectively & efficiently.

Relaxed Flight. Michael P. Kelly. 1 cass. 1992. 14.95 (978-1-883700-06-5(X)) ThoughtForms.
Self help.

Relaxed Home Schooling Workshop Vol. C: Materials & Methods for Elementary Grades. unabr. ed. Mary Hood. 4 cass. (Running Time: 6 hrs.). (Relaxed Home Schooling Workshop Tapes: Vol. C). 2002. 19.95 (978-0-9707597-4-0(6)) Ambleside Educ.
Elementary grades methods and materials, math, science, social studies, children's literature and arts.

Relaxed Home Schooling Workshop Vol. D: Working with Teens. unabr. ed. Mary Hood. 4 cass. (Running Time: 6 hrs.). (Relaxed Home Schooling Workshop Tapes: Vol. D). 2002. 19.95 (978-0-9707597-5-7(4)) Ambleside Educ.
Planning and carrying through plans for middle school, high school, and college entrance.

Relaxed Home Schooling Workshop Vol. A: Overview of Relaxed Home Schooling. 8th unabr. ed. Mary Hood. 4 cass. (Running Time: 6 hrs.). (Relaxed Home Schooling Workshop Tapes: Vol. A). 2002. 19.95 (978-0-9707597-2-6(X)) Ambleside Educ.

Relaxed Home Schooling Workshop Vol. B: Working With Young Children. unabr. ed. Mary Hood. 4 cass. (Running Time: 6 hrs.). (Relaxed Home Schooling Workshop Tapes: Vol. B). 2002. 19.95 (978-0-9707597-3-3(8)) Ambleside Educ.
Discusses development from preschool through elementary years.

Relaxed Homeschooling Workshop Series. As told by Mary Hood. 2007. audio compact disk 49.95 (978-0-9707597-8-8(9)) Ambleside Educ.

Relaxercise: Ten Effortless Techniques for a More Flexible, Energetic, Pain-Free, Stress-Free Body. David Zemach-Bersin & Mark Reese. Read by David Zemach-Bersin & Mark Reese. 6 cass. (Running Time: 5 hrs.). 1987. 70.00 (978-1-55552-031-1(6)) Metamorphous Pr.
Relaxercise is a series of easy exercises for relaxed self control & tension free movement. They consist of gentle movements practiced for short periods of time - suitable for any age or physical ability.

Relaxing. Ed. by Peter Samuels. (Running Time: 60 mins.). 2002. audio compact disk 15.99 (978-1-904451-26-6(8)) Global Jrny GBR GBR.

Relaxing at High Speed. Jeff Davidson. 1998. 8.95 (978-1-60729-360-6(9)) Breath Space Inst.

Relaxing at the Dentist with Guided Meditation. abr. ed. Paisha Rochlin. Read by Paisha Rochlin. Perf. by Mimi Dye. 1 cass. (C). 1999. (978-0-9675925-2-7(6)) Program for Well.
Guided mediation with viola background to help dental patients relax during treatment. Helps listeners relax and use the power of imagination to create comfort & manage pain, relaxation, meditation & pain management.

Relaxing in the Lord. C. S. Lovett. Read by C. S. Lovett. 1 cass. (Running Time: 60 min.). 6.95 (545) Prsnl Christianity.
Relaxes your body so that your body's computer system can respond to the "New Image." To be used with the "Help Lord" book.

Relaxing into ADHD Anxiety & Fear: Attentional Guided Imagery Specifically Developed for Those with ADD/ADHD. Twila L. Gates. Perf. by Twila L. Gates. Prod. by Molly O'Neill & PowerSystems. (ENG.). 2007. 9.99 (978-1-935277-05-7(7)); audio compact disk 14.99 (978-1-935277-04-0(9)) PowerSystems.

Relaxing into ADHD Perfectionism: Attentional Guided Imagery Specifically Developed for Those with ADD/ADHD. Twila L. Gates. Perf. by Twila L. Gates. Prod. by Molly O'Neill & PowerSystems. (ENG.). 2008. audio compact disk 14.99 (978-1-935277-09-5(X)) PowerSystems.

Relaxing into ADHD Shame: Attentional Guided Imagery Specifically Developed for Those with ADD/ADHD. Twila L. Gates. Perf. by Twila L. Gates. Prod. by Molly O'Neill & PowerSystems. (ENG.). 2007. 9.99 (978-1-935277-07-1(3)); audio compact disk 14.99 (978-1-935277-06-4(5)) PowerSystems.

Relaxing into Sleep. Read by Mary Richards. 12.95 (304) Master Your Mind.
Discusses how to put the day to rest, releasing all tension in your body, giving your body & mind the signal to let go & relax.

Relaxing Journey in Meditation. 1 CD. (Running Time: 41 min.). 2003. audio compact disk 15.99 (978-0-9744909-4-6(6)) Real Life Less.
Anyone can meditate with this relaxing combination of soothing words and music. Release stress, quiet your mind and sit back to enjoy your own personal journey. In this half-hour meditation CD, Debbie Gisonni begins with guided imagery, followed by quiet music and sounds of nature by Shauneen of BitterSweetNow.

Relaxing sound of Ocean Waves: Ambient audio for gentle relaxation, meditation, deep sleep, yoga, spa & Lounge. Max Bollinger. (ENG.). 2009. cd-rom 24.00 (978-0-9561165-1-2(5)) Max Bollinger GBR.

Relay Beginner Class: Italian Language in Use. Adrian Doff & Christopher Jones. (Running Time: 1 hr. 21 mins.). 2001. 21.00 (978-88-8433-303-2(2)) Cambridge U Pr.

Relay KET Exam Practice: Italian Language in Use. University of Cambridge Local Examinations Syndication Staff. (Language in Use Ser.). 2001. (978-88-8433-318-6(0)) Cambridge U Pr.

Relay PET Exam Practice: Italian Language in Use. University of Cambridge Local Examinations Syndication Staff. (Running Time: 1 hr. 20 mins.). (Language in Use Ser.). 2001. (978-88-8433-320-9(2)) Cambridge U Pr.

Relay Pre-Intermediate Class Set: Italian Language in Use. Adrian Doff & Christopher Jones. (Running Time: 41 mins.). 2001. 20.00 (978-88-8433-308-7(3)) Cambridge U Pr.

Relazione di un Viaggio a Constantinopoli. Giambattista Casti. Read by Elsa Proverbio. 1 cass. (Running Time: 1 hrs.). (Letterati, Memorialisti E Viaggiatori Del 700 Ser.). (ITA.). 1996. pap. bk. 19.50 (978-1-58085-463-4(X)) Interlingua VA.

Release. abr. ed. Robert A. Monroe. Read by Robert A. Monroe. (Running Time: 30 min.). (Human Plus Ser.). 1989. 14.95 (978-1-56102-028-7(1)) Inter Indus.
Use to turn off particular function when purpose has been accomplished.

Release & Freedom from Closed-In Places. Norman J. Caldwell. Read by Norman J. Caldwell. Ed. by Achieve Now Institute Staff. 1 cass. (Running Time: 20 min.). (Fear No More Ser.). 1988. 9.97 (978-1-56273-098-7(3)) My Mothers Pub.
Explore your inner feelings.

Release & Recharge. unabr. ed. Robert A. Monroe. Read by Robert A. Monroe. (Running Time: 45 min.). (Gateway Experience - Discovery Ser.). 1981. 14.95 (978-1-56113-253-9(5)) Monroe Institute.
Release your fears & emotions.

Release & Relax (the Ultimate Healer Subliminal Series, 2 Of 6) Break through barriers & relieve Stress. Kyrah Malan. 1 CD. (Running Time: 27 mins). 2006. audio compact disk 39.95 (978-0-9787324-2-4(1), SPS2) K Malan.
The ultimate in subliminal affirmations! Music, messages and binaural beats are specifically designed to work together to assist you in removing obstacles. Let go of negative situations, relationships, and beliefs. Feel calm and peaceful. Excellent for stress relief. What you hear is beautiful music that has been proven in university studies or harmonize and organize your energy field, putting you in a calm, receptive state quickly and easily.What your subconscious hears are specially designed affirmations and suggestions, designed to rewrite subconscious beliefs and change behavior faster and more effectively than any subliminal program available today.The Foundation set is designed to be used in order, each CD building on the effects of the previous CDs, and includes Love Your Life, Release & Relax, Energy & Power, Manifest & Magnetize, Live Your Life, and Spirit & Soul. Can be used independently.Unlike typical subliminal programs which recommend you listen to them for at least 30 days, Ultimate healer CDs help create positive results in only 17 days; some people report results in as little

as 2 or 3 days!You can play them during everyday activities, while driving, reading, or at work, or listen to them with headphones. You have freedom and flexibility with The Ultimate Healer Subliminal Series.

Release Anger. Lexa Finley. 2009. audio compact disk 14.95 (978-0-9822494-5-1(4)) Journey Spirit.

Release Anger, Resentment & Frustration: With the EOL Facilitated Self-Healing Process. unabr. ed. Sue Singleton & Aaron Singleton. 1 cass. (Running Time: 1 hr. 30 min.). 2000. 18.00 (978-1-931075-05-3(0)) Way to Balnce.
A facilitating self-healing process, featuring music & sound harmonics conducive to healing.

Release Back Pain. Michael Reed Gach. (Running Time: 1 hr. 15 mins.). 2006. audio compact disk 15.95 (978-1-59179-087-7(5), W720D) Sounds True.

Release Discomfort. Read by Mary Richards. (Subliminal Impact Ser.). 12.95 (409) Master Your Mind.
Presents two pain control techniques that assist in either letting go of discomfort or reducing it to a more comfortable level.

Release Fear. Lexa Finley. Tammy Chi. 2009. audio compact disk 14.95 (978-0-9822494-3-7(8)) Journey Spirit.

Release Fear, Doubt, Worry. Michael P. Bovines. Read by Michael P. Bovines. Ed. by Christian Flint. 1 cass. (Running Time: 30 min.). (Healing Ser.). 1993. pap. bk. 9.98 (978-1-885768-08-7(7), M411) Circle of Light.
A beautiful guided meditation to help assist you in releasing the negative emotions which keep us from fulfilling our potential for success & happiness. Great tape to get un-stuck.

Release Fear, Panic & Anxiety: With the EOL Facilitated Self-Healing Process. unabr. ed. Sue Singleton & Aaron Singleton. 1 cass. (Running Time: 1 hr. 30 mins.). 2000. 18.00 (978-1-931075-03-9(4)) Way to Balnce.
A facilitating self-healing process, featuring music & sound harmonics conducive to healing.

Release from Addictions. Matthew Manning. Music by Ben Horne. 1 cass. 11.95 (MM-111) White Dove NM.
This tape is designed to help the person who has become over-dependent upon non-prescription drugs, cigarettes, alcohol, gambling or even sugar. A three-stage withdrawal program is outlined to be as painless & effective as possible. Side Two is a self-healing exercise with music by Ben Horne.

Release from Phobias. Matthew Manning. Read by Matthew Manning. Music by Paul Fitzgerald & Mark Flanagan. 1 cass. 11.95 (MM-116) White Dove NM.
The link between fear & relaxation is explored. Matthew describes how many fears & phobias originate, & gives treatments & techniques for releasing phobias. Side Two is an exercise designed to deeply relax the listener & work with positive self-suggestions to overcome a phobia.

Release from the Curse. Derek Prince. 2 cass. 1990. 5.95 ea. Derek Prince.
Are you frustrated? Bewildered? Defeated? Never fully satisfied? You can pass from the dark shadow of a curse into the sunlight of God's blessing!.

Release Guilt. Lexa Finley. 2009. audio compact disk 12.95 (978-0-9822494-6-8(2)) Journey Spirit.

Release Guilt. Kelly Howell. 1 cass. (Running Time: 1 hr.). (Brain Wave Subliminal Ser.). 1996. 9.95 (978-1-881451-37-2(2)) Brain Sync.
Subliminal messages designed specifically to release guilt and self-sabotaging thoughts are easily absorbed by your subconscious mind. The music, messages and frequencies break the chains of fear and worry and allow you to live truly guilt-free.

Release Loss, Grief of Sadness: With the EOL Facilitated Self-Healing Process. unabr. ed. Sue Singleton & Aaron Singleton. 1 cass. (Running Time: 1 hr. 30 mins.). 2000. 18.00 (978-1-931075-07-7(7)) Way to Balnce.
A facilitating self-healing process, featuring music & sound harmonics conducive to healing.

Release of the Spirit. unabr. ed. Watchman Nee. 3 CDs. (Running Time: 3 hrs. 42 mins. 0 sec.). (ENG.). 2005. audio compact disk 18.98 (978-1-59644-127-9(5), Hovel Audio) christianaud.
Nee exhorts believers that through the breaking of the outward man there comes a release of the inward Spirit. By means of our brokenness the Spirit rejuvenates our faith and makes us fit for service.

***Release of the Spirit.** unabr. ed. Watchman Nee. Narrated by Lloyd James. (ENG.). 2005. 10.98 (978-1-59644-125-5(9), Hovel Audio) christianaud.

Release Stress - Live Harmony. unabr. ed. Dick Sutphen. Read by Dick Sutphen. 1 cass. (Running Time: 1 hr.). (Spirit Guide Meditations). 1999. 14.98 (978-0-87554-635-3(8), SG108) Valley Sun.
A guide can help you learn to detach & retreat into a calm inner space. Be physically relaxed & emotionally at ease.

Release the Past. Ivy Preston. Read by Jacqueline King. 4 cass. (Running Time: 6 hrs.). 1999. 44.95 (65913) Pub: Soundings Ltd GBR. Dist(s): Ulverscroft US

Release Through Settlement. Swami Amar Jyoti. 1 cass. 1979. 9.95 (R-27) Truth Consciousness.
The struggle of the seeker. Settling down & coming to the main business. Realizing the Oneness.

Release to God's Ultimate. Derek Prince. 1 cass. (I-4088) Derek Prince.

Release Your Anointing: Tapping the Power of the Holy Spirit in You. T. D. Jakes. (Running Time: 16488 sec.). 2008. audio compact disk 29.99 (978-0-7684-2656-4(1)) Destiny Image Pubs.

Release Your Anointing: Tapping the Power of the Holy Spirit in You. T. D. Jakes. (ENG.). 2008. 19.99 (978-1-4245-0813-6(4)) Tre Med Inc.

Release Your E. S. P. 1 cass. 10.00 (978-1-58506-041-2(0), 81) New Life Inst OR.
Release your own psychic powers-develop your ESP to the maximum.

Release Yourself from Drugs. Norman J. Caldwell. Read by Norman J. Caldwell. Ed. by Achieve Now Institute Staff. 1 cass. (Running Time: 20 min.). (Better Health Ser.). 1988. 9.97 (978-1-56273-053-6(3)) My Mothers Pub.
Yes, you can! Take back control of your body, mind & life. Feel your natural high!.

Release Yourself from Guilt. 4 cass. 79.95 (C10125) CareerTrack Pubns.
Guilt means you have a conscience. That's good. But there's a big difference between having a conscience & letting guilt rule your life. In this program, you'll listen in as a real women's support group discusses the issues of guilt in their lives.

Releasing: Waving Goodbye, Leaving & Smiling. Stuart Wilde. 1 cass. (Running Time: 1 hr.). 11.95 (978-0-930603-42-7(7)) White Dove NM.
Releasing situations can be hard because the mind tends to hold on. Use this tape to get over the people, places, jobs & old energies that you feel you need to "step beyond." Give the past "the boot." Step into a new, happier & more prosperous life. There is no talking or introduction on this tape, just a full hour of energy-creating messages laid under inspirational new age music.

Releasing a Love. Rick Brown. Read by Rick Brown. Ed. by John Quatro. 1 cass. (Running Time: 30 min.). (Subliminal - Soft Sounds Ser.). 1993. 10.95 (978-1-57100-082-8(8), S127); 10.95 (978-1-57100-106-1(9), W127); 10.95 (978-1-57100-130-6(1), H127) Sublime Sftware.
I love you, release you & let go.

Releasing a Love, No. E127. Rick Brown. Read by Rick Brown. Ed. by John Quatro. 1 cass. (Running Time: 30 min.). (Subliminal - Easy Listening Ser.). 1993. 10.95 (978-1-57100-010-1(0)) Sublime Sftware.
"Releasing a Love" - I love you, release you & let go.

Releasing a Love, No. J127. Rick Brown. Read by Rick Brown. Ed. by John Quatro. 1 cass. (Running Time: 30 min.). (Subliminal - Jazz Ser.). 1993. 10.95 (978-1-57100-034-7(8)) Sublime Sftware.

Releasing a Love, No. N127. Rick Brown. Read by Rick Brown. Ed. by John Quatro. 1 cass. (Running Time: 30 min.). (Subliminal - New Age Ser.). 1993. 10.95 (978-1-57100-058-3(5)) Sublime Sftware.

Releasing Addiction. Read by Mary Richards. (Subliminal Impact Ser.). 12.95 (636) Master Your Mind.
Presents suggestions to take control of one's life & reinforce the decision to be free.

Releasing & Letting Go. Read by Mary Richards. (Subliminal Impact Ser.). 12.95 Master Your Mind.
Gives the inner strength & wisdom to retain the best from every experience.

Releasing Anger. Eldon Taylor. 1 cass. (Running Time: 62 min.). (Inner Talk Ser.). 16.95 incl. script. (978-1-55978-302-6(8), 5353A) Progress Aware Res.
Soundtrack - Tropical Lagoon with underlying subliminal affirmations.

Releasing Anger: Music Theme. Eldon Taylor. 1 cass. 16.95 (978-1-55978-125-1(4), 5353C) Progress Aware Res.

Releasing Anger & Resentment: Free Yourself from the Past, Create a Positive Future. Joyce Levine. Read by Joyce Levine. 1 cass. (Running Time: 1 hr.). 1994. 11.95 (978-1-885856-02-9(4)) Vizualizations.
"Releasing Anger & Resentment" - Side 1, why - importance of release, exercises; Side 2 - guided meditation.

Releasing Anxiety & Insomnia: Creative Visualizations for Creating a New Reality. Created by Stanley Haluska. 1 CD. (Running Time: 70 mins). 2004. audio compact disk 15.00 (978-0-9668872-8-0(X), AP113) Awakening Pubns Inc.

Releasing Anxiety & Insomnia: Creative Visualizations into Self Empowerment & Spiritual Identity. (ENG.). 2009. 15.95 (978-0-9758866-8-7(1)) Awakening Pubns Inc.

Releasing Co-Dependent Patterns: Easy. Eldon Taylor. Read by Eldon Taylor. Ed. by Leslie Brice. 1 cass. (Running Time: 1 hr.). 1992. 16.95 (978-1-56705-191-9(X)) Gateways Inst.
Self improvement.

Releasing Co-Dependent Patterns: Ocean. Eldon Taylor. Read by Eldon Taylor. Ed. by Leslie Brice. 1 cass. (Running Time: 1 hr.). 1992. 16.95 (978-1-56705-192-6(8)) Gateways Inst.

Releasing Co-Dependent Patterns: Stream. Eldon Taylor. Read by Eldon Taylor. Ed. by Leslie Brice. 1 cass. (Running Time: 1 hr.). 1992. 16.95 (978-1-56705-193-3(6)) Gateways Inst.

Releasing Co-Dependent Patterns: Whisper. Eldon Taylor. Read by Eldon Taylor. Ed. by Leslie Brice. 1 cass. (Running Time: 1 hr.). 1992. 16.95 (978-1-56705-198-8(7)) Gateways Inst.

Releasing Codependent Patterns. Eldon Taylor. 1 cass. (Running Time: 62 min.). (Inner Talk Ser.). 16.95 (978-1-55978-312-5(5), 53861A) Progress Aware Res.
Soundtrack - Tropical Lagoon with underlying subliminal affirmations.

Releasing Codependent Patterns: Babbling Brook. Eldon Taylor. 1 cass. 16.95 (978-1-55978-531-0(4), 53861F) Progress Aware Res.

Releasing Codependent Patterns: Music Theme. Eldon Taylor. 1 cass. 16.95 (978-0-940699-57-1(5), 53861D) Progress Aware Res.

Releasing Endorphines for Pain Release. Patricia O'Malley. Perf. by Barry Weiss. 1 cass. (Running Time: 50 min.). 1998. (978-1-892450-23-4(2), 121) Promo Music.
Guided imagery.

Releasing Fear & Anxiety. John Gray. 2 cass. (Running Time: 2 hrs.). 1996. 17.95 (978-1-886095-15-1(9)) Genesis Media Grp.

Releasing Our Consciousness. Swami Amar Jyoti. 2 cass. 1979. 12.95 (K-36) Truth Consciousness.
The flight of consciousness, raising ourselves from gross earth consciousness for evolution's sake. The Foundation of conduct before knowledge can be taught.

Releasing Physical Pain. Patricia O'Malley. Perf. by Barry Weiss. 1 cass. (Running Time: 50 min.). 1998. (978-1-892450-22-7(4), 120) Promo Music.
Guided imagery.

Releasing Silicone Toxicity - Starlight Journey into Healing. 1 cass. (303) Mntn Spirit Tapes.
"Releasing Silicone Toxicity" (side 1): A tape for women with toxicity resulting from breast implant leakage. Images focus on the healing power of the breath as a cleansing for the body. "Starlight Journey into Healing" (side 2): Utilizing the healing power of color, the immune system is strengthened & the mind cleansed of negative emotion.

Releasing Silicone Toxicity & Starlight Journey into Healing. Diana E. Keck. Read by Diana Keck. 1 cass. (Running Time: 54 min.). (Healing Ser.). 1992. 9.95 (978-0-929653-20-4(3)) Mntn Spirit Tapes.
A tape for women with toxicity resulting from breast implant leakage. Images focus on the healing power of the breath as cleansing for the body.

Releasing Stress. Eldon Taylor. 2 cass. (Running Time: 62 min. per cass.). (Omniphonics Ser.). 29.95 incl. script . (978-1-55978-809-0(7), 4010) Progress Aware Res.
3-D soundtrack with underlying subliminal affirmations, night & day versions.

Releasing Stress, Vol. 106. 1998. 24.95 (978-1-58557-022-5(2)) Dynamic Growth.

Releasing Stress: Echotech. Eldon Taylor. Read by Eldon Taylor. Ed. by Leslie Brice. 1 cass. (Running Time: 1 hr.). 1992. 16.95 (978-1-56705-005-9(0)) Gateways Inst.
Self improvement.

Releasing the Anointing. 2009. audio compact disk 5.00 (978-0-9819971-4-8(7)) TSEA.

Releasing the Fear of Rejection. Eldon Taylor. 1 cass. (Running Time: 62 min.). (Inner Talk Ser.). 16.95 incl. script. (978-1-55978-529-7(2), 53814F) Progress Aware Res.
Soundtrack - Babbling Brook with underlying subliminal affirmations.

Releasing the Fear of Rejection: Music Theme. Eldon Taylor. 1 cass. 16.95 (978-1-55978-584-6(5), 53814M) Progress Aware Res.

Releasing the Power of Faith. Kenneth Copeland. 1 cass. (Running Time: 1 hr.). 1973. 5.00 (978-0-88114-812-1(1), 02-0025) K Copeland Pubns.

Releasing the Power of Faith. Kenneth Copeland. 1 cass. (Faith Ser.: No. 3). 1982. 5.00 (978-0-938458-69-2(8)) K Copeland Pubns.
Indepth biblical study on faith.

Releasing the Pressure: Reducing Hypertension for Greater Health & Well Being. Nick Kemp & Tina Taylor. 2006. audio compact disk 27.95 (978-0-9551104-1-2(6)) Transforming Pr.

Releasing Worries & Concerns. Patricia O'Malley. Perf. by Barry Weiss. 1 cass. (Running Time: 50 min.). 1998. (978-1-892450-02-9(X), 103) Promo Music.
Guided imagery.

Releasing Worry, Anxiety & Stress: Through Positive Imaging, Positive Faith & Relaxation Techniques. 1995. 12.00 (978-0-9703223-0-2(5)) Church of Creator Incarnate.

Releasing You from Fear CD. Stephen Richards. (ENG.). 2009. 7.99 (978-1-902578-51-4(1)) Pub: Mirage Pub UK GBR. Dist(s): Gardners Bks

Releasing Your Creative Energy. Ray DiGiuseppe. 1 cass. (Running Time: 69 min.). 9.95 (C044) A Ellis Institute.
Learn how to remove your blocks to creativity, & apply new techniques & solutions to your work-related & personal problems.

Releasing Your Creative Energy. Ray DiGiuseppe. 1 cass. (Running Time: 69 min.). 9.95 (C044) Inst Rational-Emotive.

Releasing Your Destiny. John Chacha. 2006. audio compact disk 29.99 (978-1-59933-015-0(6)) Pub: Morning NC. Dist(s): Destiny Image Pubs

Releasing Your Destiny. John Chacha. 2007. 29.99 (978-1-4245-0687-3(5)) Tre Med Inc.

Releasing Your Inner Slave Driver: Finding New Self Love, Peace & Joy. unabr. ed. Galexis. 2 cass. (Running Time: 3 hrs.). 1996. 19.95 (G120) Visionary FL.
Practical living of spiritual principles workshop. Ending the internal pressure nightmare to find the true, loving, fun self to have ease & joy. Meditation included.

Releasing Your Potential: Exposing the Hidden You. Myles Munroe. 10 cass. 1992. 48.00 (978-1-56043-906-6(8)) Destiny Image Pubs.

Releasing Your True Glory see Liberando Tu Gloria Verdadera

Relentless. Clair Poulson. 3 cass. 2004. 14.95 (978-1-57734-978-5(4)); audio compact disk 14.95 (978-1-57734-979-2(2)) Covenant Comms.

Relentless. unabr. ed. Dean Koontz. Read by Dan John Miller. (Running Time: 9 hrs.). 2009. 39.97 (978-1-4233-5700-1(0), 9781423357001, BADLE); 24.99 (978-1-4233-5699-8(3), 9781423356998, BAD); 24.99 (978-1-4233-5697-4(7), 9781423356974, Brilliance MP3); 39.97 (978-1-4233-5698-1(5), 9781423356981, Brlnc Audio MP3 Lib); audio compact disk 97.97 (978-1-4233-5696-7(9), 9781423356967, BriAudCD Unabrid); audio compact disk 40.99 (978-1-4233-5695-0(0), 9781423356950) Brilliance Audio.

Relentless Faith. John Bevere. 2009. audio compact disk 14.99 (978-1-933185-54-5(5)) Messengr Intl.

Relentless Faith. Creflo A. Dollar. 2009. audio compact disk 14.00 (978-1-59944-757-5(6)) Creflo Dollar.

***Relentless Faith Life Message Series.** John Bevere. 2010. audio compact disk 0.00 (978-1-933185-63-7(5)) Messengr Intl.

Relentless Pursuit. unabr. ed. Alexander Kent, pseud. Narrated by Steven Crossley. 9 cass. (Running Time: 13 hrs. 15 mins.). (Richard Bolitho Ser.: Bk. 25). 2001. 85.00 (978-1-4025-1806-5(4)) Recorded Bks.

Relevance of Easter: Matt. 28:6-10. 1994. 4.95 (978-0-7417-2007-8(8), 1007) Win Walk.

Relevance of Literature to Science. Robert Oppenheimer. 1 cass. (Running Time: 19 min.). 9.95 J Norton Pubs.

Relevance of Literature to Science CD. Speeches. J. Robert Oppenheimer. 1 CD. (Running Time: 19 mins.). 2006. audio compact disk 12.95 (978-1-57970-410-0(7), C33010D, Audio-For) J Norton Pubs.
The nuclear scientist and author gives a brief talk on the relevance of literary culture to scientists.

Relevance of the New Cat. for Religious Life; Arch. Cacciavillan Sunday Homily. Ellen Curran. 1 cass. (National Meeting of the Institute, 1994 Ser.). 4.00 (94N9) IRL Chicago.

Relfections in Black History Vol. 3: Great African Americans Known & Unknown. Margaret W. Kemp. Read by Margaret W. Kemp. Read by Keith Holmes. 1 cass. (Running Time: 1 hr.). (Entertainment Music Ser. 2: Vol. 3). 1996. 12.95 (978-1-891102-13-4(3)) Reflect Black Hist.

Reliability of the Bible, I. Dan Comer. 1 cass. 3.00 (76) Evang Outreach.

Reliability of the Bible, II. Dan Comer. 1 cass. 3.00 (77) Evang Outreach.

***Reliable Wife.** unabr. ed. Robert Goolrick. 2010. audio compact disk 34.99 (978-1-4407-2172-4(6)) Recorded Bks.

Relic see Twentieth-Century Poetry in English, No. 25, Recordings of Poets Reading Their Own Poetry

Relic. abr. ed. Douglas Preston & Lincoln Child. Read by David Colacci. 3 CDs, Library ed. (Running Time: 3 hrs.). (Pendergast Ser.: No. 1). 2003. audio compact disk 62.25 (978-1-59086-570-5(7), 1590865707, BAU) Brilliance Audio.
Just days before a massive exhibition opens at the popular New York Museum of Natural History, visitors are being savagely murdered in the museum's dark hallways and secret rooms. Autopsies indicate that the killer cannot be human... But the museum's directors plan to go ahead with a big bash to celebrate the new exhibition, in spite of the murders. Museum researcher Margo Green must find out who - or what - is doing the killing. But can she do it in time to stop the massacre?.

Relic. unabr. ed. Douglas Preston & Lincoln Child. Read by David Colacci. (Running Time: 12 hrs.). (Pendergast Ser.: No. 1). 2007. 39.25 (978-1-4233-3044-8(7), 9781423330448, BADLE); 24.95 (978-1-4233-3043-1(9), 9781423330431, BAD); audio compact disk 39.25 (978-1-4233-3042-4(0), 9781423330424, Brlnc Audio MP3 Lib); audio compact disk 24.95 (978-1-4233-3041-7(2), 9781423330417, Brilliance MP3) Brilliance Audio.

Relic. unabr. ed. Douglas Preston & Lincoln Child. Read by David Colacci. (Running Time: 13 hrs.). 2010. audio compact disk 89.97 (978-1-4418-3590-1(3), 9781441835901, BriAudCD Unabrid); audio compact disk 29.99 (978-1-4418-3589-5(X), 9781441835895, Bril Audio CD Unabri) Brilliance Audio.

Relic Quest. unabr. ed. Robert Cornuke. Narrated by Robert Cornuke. (ENG.). 2005. 18.89 (978-1-60814-358-0(9)); audio compact disk 26.99 (978-1-59859-021-0(9)) Oasis Audio.

Relics. Michael Jan Friedman. Read by James Doohan. (Running Time: 2 hrs.). 2003. 19.95 (978-1-60083-428-8(0), Audiofy Corp) Iofy Corp.

***Relics of Time.** Paul Magrs. Narrated by Tom Baker & Full Cast. 1 CDs. (Running Time: 1 hr. 0 mins. 0 sec.). (Doctor Who Ser.). (ENG.). 2010. audio compact disk 24.95 (978-1-4084-6667-4(8)) Pub: AudioGO. Dist(s): Perseus Dist

Relief from Allergies, 2 cass. (Running Time: 2 hrs.). 2001. 24.95 (978-1-58557-035-5(4)) Dynamic Growth.

Relief from Arthritis, 2 cass. (Running Time: 3 hrs.). 2001. 24.95 (978-1-58557-036-2(2)) Dynamic Growth.

Relief from Arthritis: Harmonies. Eldon Taylor. Read by Eldon Taylor. Ed. by Leslie Brice. 1 cass. (Running Time: 1 hr.). 1992. 16.95 (978-1-56705-162-9(6)) Gateways Inst.
Self improvement.

Relief from Arthritis: Ocean. Eldon Taylor. Read by Eldon Taylor. Ed. by Leslie Brice. 1 cass. (Running Time: 1 hr.). 1992. 16.95 (978-1-56705-163-6(4)) Gateways Inst.

Relief from Arthritis: Stream. Eldon Taylor. Read by Eldon Taylor. Ed. by Leslie Brice. 1 cass. (Running Time: 1 hr.). 1992. 16.95 (978-1-56705-164-3(2)) Gateways Inst.

Relief from Back-Pain, 2 cass. (Running Time: 2 hrs.). 2001. 24.95 (978-1-58557-037-9(0)) Dynamic Growth.

Relief from Insomnia. Matthew Manning. Music by Nick Arkle. 1 cass. 11.95 (MM-114) White Dove NM.
With so many people living anxious, hurried lives, out of harmony with themselves & the rhythms of nature, insomnia has become a problem of our modern times. This tape outlines how to be aware of nature's rhythms in order to sleep more easily. Side Two includes not only 6 pre-sleep exercises but also a meditation & guided imagery for deeper sleep.

Relief from Pain. Norman J. Caldwell. Read by Norman J. Caldwell. Ed. by Achieve Now Institute Staff. 1 cass. (Running Time: 20 min.). (Health-Imaging Ser.). 1988. 9.97 (978-1-56273-075-8(4)) My Mothers Pub.
Natural forces are yours to release.

Relief from Pain. Matthew Manning. Music by Paul Fitzgerald & Mark Flanagan. 1 cass. 11.95 (MM-115) White Dove NM.
Sometimes pain is not just a warning but a disease in itself. Whatever form of physical pain one suffers, this tape is intended to help. Side One outlines methods of pain control. Side Two helps transport the listener away from pain through a lengthy relaxation exercise.

Relief from the Automatic Stay: Creditors' Rights in Bankruptcy. 1 cass. 1989. bk. 45.00 (AC-515) PA Bar Inst.

Relief of Back Pain. Barrie Konicov. 1 cass. 11.98 (978-0-87082-358-9(2), 109) Potentials.
Professional hypnotist Barrie Konicov directs you through a hypnotic process which could relieve back pain, & then uses a relaxation method to lessen the tension in your back. It is reinforced with strong positive suggestions directed to your mind.

Relieve Anxiety. Betty L. Randolph. 1 stereo cass. (Running Time: 45 min.). (Self-Hypnosis Ser.). 9.98 (978-1-55909-154-1(1), 816) Randolph Tapes.
Used to dispel unhappy, worried feelings. Music background & spoken word.

Relieve Anxiety with Medical Hypnosis. Steven Gurgevich. Read by Steven Gurgevich. (Playaway Adult Nonfiction Ser.). (ENG.). 2009. 39.99 (978-1-60812-776-4(1)) Find a World.

Relieve Jet Lag: Relax, Sleep & Refresh with Sound Therapy. Kelly Howell. 2004. audio compact disk 16.95 (978-1-881451-54-9(2)) Brain Sync.

Relieve Pain. (Running Time: 45 min.). (Health Ser.). 9.98 (978-1-55909-131-2(2), 107S) Randolph Tapes.
Helps alleviate pain. Good for migraines-neck-back-any pain.

Relieve Stress. Mary Lee LaBay. 2006. audio compact disk 5.95 (978-1-934705-15-5(2)) Awareness Engin.

Relieve Stress. Lee Pulos. Read by Lee Pulos. 1 cass. (Running Time: 60 min.). 9.95 (978-1-55569-428-9(4), 4014) Great Am Audio.
Subliminal self-help.

Relieve Stress. Betty L. Randolph. Read by Betty L. Randolph. Read by Leonard Baron. Ed. by Success Education Institute International. 1 cass. (Running Time: 60 min.). (Health Ser.). 1989. 9.98 (978-1-55909-184-8(3), 25S) Randolph Tapes.
Relaxation messages guide you into letting go of stress, including PMS. Subliminal messages are heard 3-5 minutes before becoming ocean sounds or music.

Relieve Stress: Subliminal. Lee Pulos. Read by Lee Pulos. 3 cass. (Running Time: 3 hrs.). 19.95 (978-1-55569-404-3(7), 7158) Great Am Audio.
Contains: Learn to Relax, Relieve Stress & Anxiety & Master Self-Hypnosis.

Relieve Stress & Anxiety. Barrie Konicov. 1 cass. (Video-Audio System Ser.). cass. & video 24.98 (978-0-87082-450-0(3), SYS 110); 14.98 (978-0-87082-359-6(0), 110); 16.98 (978-1-56001-301-3(X), SCII 110) Potentials.
Learn to tell your feelings how to feel, rather than having them tell you how to feel, & how to feel good all the time.

Relieve Stress & Anxiety. Barrie Konicov. 1 CD. 2003. audio compact disk 16.98 (978-0-87082-954-3(8)) Potentials.
Test results show that stress, illness, and disease are all interrelated. For a happier, healthier life, you must learn to control your feelings. Barrie Konicov can teach you how. You will find the self-hypnosis on track 1 and the subliminal on track 2. The easy-listening music of the subliminal, together with the self-hypnosis, is the original format which most people love and with which they are most familiar.

Relieve Stress & Anxiety. Barrie Konicov. 2 CDs. 2003. audio compact disk 27.98 (978-1-56001-987-9(5)) Potentials.

Relieve Stress & Anxiety. Lee Pulos. 2 cass. (Running Time: 60 min. per cass.). (Self Hypnosis & Subliminal Reinforcement Ser.). 14.95 (978-1-55569-228-5(1), SUB-8004) Great Am Audio.
Presents tools for positive self-change.

Relieve Stress & Anxiety. Barry Tesar. 1 cass. (Running Time: 1 hr.). (Subliminal Inspiration Ser.). 1992. 9.98 (978-1-56470-019-3(4)) Success Cass.
Subliminal program.

Relieve Stress & Anxiety. Barry Tesar. 2 cass. 1998. 14.95 Set. (978-1-889800-17-2(1)) TNT Media Grp.

Relieve Stress & Anxiety: Alivie Su Tension y Ansiedad. Barrie Konicov. 1 cass. (Running Time: 1 hr. 30 min.). (Spanish-Language Audios Ser.). (SPA.). 1995. 11.98 (978-0-87082-802-7(9), 110) Potentials.
Unhappy feelings can really get to you. Learn to tell your feelings how to feel, instead of having them tell you. Learn how to feel good all the time.

Relieve Stress & Tension. 1 cass. 10.00 (20) New Life Inst OR.
Learn to release anxiety & stress. Become more relaxed, confident & happy.

Relieve Stress by Meditation. Read by James Fadiman. 1 cass. (Running Time: 60 min.). 9.95 (978-1-55569-380-0(6), PSG-2003) Great Am Audio.

Relieve Stress in Seconds: Mike Cohen's Instant Relaxation Experience. Created by Mike Cohen. 1 CD. (Running Time: 37 mins). 2004. audio compact disk 16.98 (978-0-9675050-3-9(8)) Audio Educ.
Audio CD provides instant stress relief. Relieve Stress in Seconds with Mike Cohen's Instant Relaxation Experience.

Relieve Stress in Ten Days. Herbert Fensterheim. 1 cass. (Running Time: 60 min.). (Self-Improvement Through Self-Help Ser.). (978-1-55569-195-0(1), SFH-6200) Great Am Audio.
Presents a program that teaches how to control disturbing symptoms & turn them into productive energy.

***Relieve Stress with Medical Hypnosis.** Steven Gurgevich. (Running Time: 2:00:00). 2010. audio compact disk 19.95 (978-1-59179-782-1(9)) Sounds True.

Relieve Tension & Anxiety. abr. ed. Harold H. Bloomfield & Sirah Vettese. Read by Harold H. Bloomfield & Sirah Vettese. 1 cass. (Self-Hypnosis Ser.). 1986. 9.95 (978-0-88749-039-2(5), TDM 0395) HarperCollins Pubs.
A detailed dialogue with valuable insights, information & strategies to help the listener understand & cope with the problem are an indispensable part of the break-through process. Also contains a unique series of self-hypnosis & visualization exercises to be practiced daily to release the listener's built-in ability to change his or her own life.

Relieving Osteoarthritis. Matthew Manning. Music by Ben Horne. 1 cass. 11.95 (MM-117) White Dove NM.
The tape explains the close relationship that often exists between emotional stress & arthritis. By changing a negative attitude to a positive approach to life, many find relief from symptoms. Side Two is a relaxation & visualization exercise written especially for osteoarthritis.

Relieving Pre-Menstrual Tension. Matthew Manning. Narrated by Liz Gebhardt. Music by Mike Rowland. 1 cass. 11.95 (MM-120) White Dove NM.
The tape, narrated by actress Liz Gebhardt, explores the role of diet & benefits of natural therapies like oil of evening primrose in tackling PMT. There is an insightful section on changing negative attitudes about masculinity & femininity which can adversely affect PMT. Side Two has a deep relaxation exercise including a number of positive affirmations.

Religieuse. Denis Diderot. Read by E. Amiell & J. Carle. 6 cass. (FRE.). 1992. 56.95 (1551-52) Olivia & Hill.
Diderot's famous novel of a young woman forced to become a nun by her impoverished parents. It describes her sufferings & punishment in the convent, her escape & subsequent misfortunes.

Religieuse. Denis Diderot. 3 cass. (FRE.). 1995. 31.95 (1522-VSL) Olivia & Hill.

Religieuse, Pt. 1. Denis Diderot. Read by E. Amiell & J. Carle. 3 cass. 1992. 31.95 (1551-VSL) Olivia & Hill.

Religion. Osho Oshos. 1 cass. 9.00 (A0652-89) Sound Photosyn.

Religion. unabr. ed. Tim Willocks. Narrated by Simon Vance. 21 CDs. (Running Time: 25 hrs. 19 mins.). 2007. audio compact disk 139.95 (978-0-7927-4861-8(1)) AudioGO.

Religion - An Internal Experience/Receiving the Spirit. Marianne Williamson. Read by Marianne Williamson. 1 cass. (Running Time: 90 mins.). (Lectures on a Course in Miracles). 1999. 10.00 (978-1-56170-259-6(5), M762) Hay House.

Religion & Astrology. ACT Staff. 1 cass. 8.95 (483) Am Fed Astrologers.

Religion & Authority, No. 1. J. Krishnamurti. 1 cass. (Running Time: 1 hr.). (Krishnamurti with Dr. Allan W. Anderson Ser.: No. 15). 8.50 (APA7415) Krishnamurti.
These 1974 dialogues cover the entire spectrum of Krishnamurti's teaching in a series highly regarded for its depth of inquiry into each particular subject.

Religion & Authority, No. 2. J. Krishnamurti. 1 cass. (Running Time: 1 hr.). (Krishnamurti with Dr. Allan W. Anderson Ser.: No. 16). 8.50 (APA7416) Krishnamurti.

Religion & Morality: Indispensable Supports. unabr. ed. David Barton. Read by David Barton. 1 cass. (Running Time: 1 hr.). 1994. 4.95 (978-0-925279-38-5(2), A14) Wallbuilders.
Exmaines the statements of Founding Fathers who agreed with George Washington that "religion & morality are the indispensable supports" for American society. A great tool for introducing the beliefs of the Founders.

Religion & Nationalism. 4 cass. Incl. Religion & Nationalism: Liberation by Violence: A Dilemma for Pacifists. . Lyle Tatum. 1976.; Religion & Nationalism: Quakers & the American Revolution. . William Frost. 1976.; Religion & Nationalism: Religion & Revolution: An Overview. 4 cass. Steven Piker. 1976.; Religion & Nationalism: Whose Tea Party This Time? 4 cass. George Lakey. 1976.; 1976. 15.00; 4.50 Pendle Hill.

Religion & Nationalism: Liberation by Violence: A Dilemma for Pacifists see Religion & Nationalism

Religion & Nationalism: Quakers & the American Revolution see Religion & Nationalism

Religion & Nationalism: Religion & Revolution: An Overview see Religion & Nationalism

Religion & Nationalism: Whose Tea Party This Time? see Religion & Nationalism

Religion & Personality in Aging Process. Paul Moyer. 1986. 10.80 (0211) Assn Prof Chaplains.

Religion & Science. abr. ed. Bertrand Russell. Read by David Case. 2 CDs. (Running Time: 2 hrs.). (ENG.). 2001. audio compact disk 24.95 (978-1-56511-519-4(8), 1565115198) Pub: HighBridge. Dist(s): Workman Pub

Religion & Sexuality. 4 cass. 45.00 (811) MEA A Watts Cass.

Religion & the Renewal of America's Public Life. Parker J. Palmer. 4 cass. Incl. Religion & the Renewal of America's Public Life: A Spirituality of Public Life: The Stranger As Spiritual Guide. 1982.; Religion & the Renewal of America's Public Life: Private, Public, & Political: The Vital Links. 1982.; Religion & the Renewal of America's Public Life: The Nature of Public Life: Toward a New-Old Vision. 1982.; Religion & the Renewal of America's Public Life: What Meetings & Churches Can Do to Renew Our Public Life. 1982.; 1982. 15.00 Set.; 4.50 ea. Pendle Hill.

Religion & the Renewal of America's Public Life: A Spirituality of Public Life: The Stranger As Spiritual Guide see Religion & the Renewal of America's Public Life

Religion & the Renewal of America's Public Life: Private, Public, & Political: The Vital Links see Religion & the Renewal of America's Public Life

Religion & the Renewal of America's Public Life: The Nature of Public Life: Toward a New-Old Vision see Religion & the Renewal of America's Public Life

Religion & the Renewal of America's Public Life: What Meetings & Churches Can Do to Renew Our Public Life see Religion & the Renewal of America's Public Life

Religion As a Way of Life. Swami Amar Jyoti. 1 cass. 1989. 9.95 (Q-23) Truth Consciousness.
Religion, the right way of living, puts us in touch with ourselves. Coming back on the path, seeing the way clearly.

Religion for the Hell of It. Featuring Robert Anton Wilson. 1986. 9.95 (978-1-59157-012-7(3)) Assn for Cons.

Religion for the Hell of It. unabr. ed. Robert Anton Wilson. 2 cass. 1987. 18.00 (978-1-56964-805-6(0), A0263-87) Sound Photosyn.
Live at a comedy club in San Francisco, RAW is wickedly rollicking as he tears apart established religions & establishes some new ones in a confetti of jokes & information.

Religion in the Ancient Mediterranean World, Vol. I-IV. Instructed by Glenn S. Holland. 24 cass. (Running Time: 24 hrs.). bk. 99.95 (978-1-59803-032-7(9), 6340) Teaching Co.

Religion in the Ancient Mediterranean World, Vol. I-IV. Instructed by Glenn S. Holland. 24 CDs. (Running Time: 24 hrs.). 2005. bk. 129.95 (978-1-59803-034-1(5), 6340) Teaching Co.

Religion of Our Enemies: II Chron. 25:2. Ed Young. 1987. 4.95 (978-0-7417-1602-6(X), 602) Win Walk.

Religion of Small Societies. unabr. ed. Ninian Smart. Read by Ben Kingsley. (Running Time: 10800 sec.). (Religion, Scriptures, & Spirituality Ser.). 2006. audio compact disk 25.95 (978-0-7861-6379-3(8)) Pub: Blckstn Audio. Dist(s): NetLibrary CO

Religion of Small Societies. unabr. ed. Ninian Smart. Read by Ben Kingsley. Ed. by Walter Harrelson & Mike Hassell. 2 cass. (Running Time: 3 hrs.). Dramatization. (Religion, Scriptures & Spirituality Ser.). 1994. 17.95 (978-1-56823-016-0(8), 10459) Knowledge Prod.
"Primitive" religious practices & understandings - those without a surviving sacred literature - are recognized by many to be in no way inferior to other religious beliefs. The non-literate religions here are compared to each other & to more literate religions; they also are analyzed based on geographical concentration, historical development, & the type of religious concepts they embrace.

Religion Saves: And Nine Other Misconceptions. Mark Driscoll. Read by Mark Driscoll. (Running Time: 11 hrs. 30 mins.). (Re:Lit Ser.). 2009. audio compact disk 34.99 (978-1-4335-1279-7(3), Crossway Audio) CrosswayIL.

Religion vs. America. Leonard Peikoff. Read by Leonard Peikoff. 1 cass. (Running Time: 90 min.). 1986. 12.95 (978-1-56114-062-6(7), LP09C) Second Renaissance.
The profound irreconcilability between religion & the pro-reason philosophy upon which the United States was founded.

Religion vs. Man. John Ridpath. 2 cass. (Running Time: 3 hrs.). 1989. 24.95 (978-1-56114-126-5(7), CR03D) Second Renaissance.

Religion What Does It Mean? William O'Malley. 3 cass. (Running Time: 3 hrs. 28 min.). 1999. 29.95 (TAH418) Alba Hse Comns.
A study of the potential of the human soul as it seeks the presence of God.

Religion Without Labels. unabr. ed. Swami Amar Jyoti. 1 cass. (Satsangs of Swami Amar Jyoti Ser.). 1997. 9.95 (978-0-933572-22-5(0), Q-24) Truth Consciousness.
Respecting differences & variety in the foundation stone of peace. There is One behind all multiplicity. Trust God, follow Dharma.

Religions of the Axial Age: An Approach to the World¿s Religions. Instructed by Mark W. Muesse. 12 CDs. (Running Time: 12 hrs.). 2007. 69.95 (978-1-59803-281-9(X)); 129.95 (978-1-59803-280-2(1)) Teaching Co.

Religions of the World. Gerry Porath. 12 cass. 29.95 set, incl. tote. (978-1-55503-239-5(7), 0500151) Covenant Comms.
A capsule look at over 30 different faiths. Comes in a convenient tote.

Religious Addiction. John Bradshaw. (Running Time: 10800 sec.). 2008. audio compact disk 100.00 (978-1-57388-204-0(6)) J B Media.

***Religious Affections: How Man's Will Affects His Character Before God.** unabr. ed. Jonathan Edwards. Narrated by Simon Vance. (ENG.). 2007. 19.98 (978-1-59644-439-3(8), Hovel Audio) christianaud.

Religious Affections: How Man's Will Affects His Character Before God. unabr. ed. Jonathan Edwards. Narrated by Simon Vance. (Running Time: 15 hrs. 24 mins. 0 sec.). (ENG.). 2007. lp 24.98 (978-1-59644-438-6(X)) christianaud.

Religious Affections: How Man's Will Affects His Character Before God. unabr. ed. Jonathan Edwards. Read by Simon Vance. (Running Time: 15 hrs. 24 mins. 0 sec.). (ENG.). 2007. audio compact disk 34.98 (978-1-59644-437-9(1)) christianaud.

Religious Body: The First C. D. Sloan Mystery. unabr. ed. Catherine Aird. Read by Robin Baily. 4 cass. (Running Time: 5 hrs. 20 mins.). (C. D. Sloan Mystery Ser.). 2000. 24.95 (978-1-57270-149-6(8), N41149u) Pub: Audio Partners. Dist(s): PerseuPGW
Sister Anne has been murdered. Inspector C. D. Sloan has been called in by the convent to solve the case. But if the Sister was killed just after dinnertime on Wednesday, why was she seen participating at vespers later that same evening.

Religious Comes Alive Series Album 5: 12 CD Dramatized Audio Stories. 2006. 45.00 (978-1-60079-027-0(5)) YourStory.

Religious Dimension of Family Life. John Shea. 1 cass. (Running Time: 1 hr.). 1988. 8.95 (978-0-914070-60-3(6), 335) ACTA Pubns.
Demonstrates how people discover God amid the joy & suffering of family life. Using biblical passages & stories & legends from a variety of cultures.

Religious Dimensions of Rehabilitation. Richard Horst & Herbert Grulke. 1986. 10.80 (0510) Assn Prof Chaplains.

Religious Experience. Vincent M. Walsh. 1 cass. 1986. 4.00 Key of David.
Personal stories & examples told to promote a full understanding of the basic powers of the Renewal. Includes "Understanding the Spirit".

Religious Experimentation & Irrationalism. Gordon Clark. 1 cass. (Lectures on Apologetics: No. 9). 5.00 Trinity Found.

Religious Function of the Self. Read by June Singer. 2 cass. (Running Time: 2 hrs.). 1980. 16.95 (978-0-7822-0259-5(4), 075) C G Jung IL.

Religious Functions of the Psyche. Read by Lionel Corbett. 9 cass. (Running Time: 12 hrs. 20 min.). 1986. 61.95 (978-0-7822-0039-3(7), 220S) C G Jung IL.
A seminar reviewing recent developments in self psychology from the point of view of the relationship between the transpersonal self & the personal self.

Religious Functions of the Psyche: Manifestations of the Self. Read by Lionel Corbett. 2 cass. (Running Time: 3 hrs. 30 min.). 1987. 21.95 Set. (978-0-7822-0041-6(9), 272) C G Jung IL.

Religious Influences in the Public School. Beckham et al. 1 cass. (Running Time: 50 min.). 1985. 7.95 Ed Law Assn.

Religious Intuition. Thomas Merton. 1 cass. 8.95 (AA2374) Credence Commun.

Religious Life As a Force for Re-Evangelization. James C. Hickey. 1 cass. (National Meeting of the Institute, 1990 Ser.). 4.00 (90N1) IRL Chicago.

Religious Life, 1969. J. Krishnamurti. Read by J. Krishnamurti. 1 cass. (Running Time: 60 min.). 8.50 (ARL69) Krishnamurti.

***Religious Literacy: What Every American Needs to Know - and Doesn't.** unabr. ed. Stephen R. Prothero. Read by Stephen R. Prothero. 2007. (978-0-06-126257-9(9), Harper Audio); (978-0-06-126258-6(7), Harper Audio) HarperCollins Pubs.

Religious Live, Teach & Strengthen the Culture of Life. Jack Gallagher. 1 cass. 4.00 (96A1) IRL Chicago.

Religious Meaning of Chastity. Thomas Merton. 1 cass. (Running Time: 60 min.). (Chastity Ser.). 4.50 (AA2129) Credence Commun.
Discussions on the positive, symbolic dimension of chastity.

Religious Principles of Greek Tragedy. Thomas Merton. 1 cass. 8.95 Credence Commun.

Religious Problem in a Multi-Cultural Society. Read by Joseph Henderson. 1 cass. (Running Time: 90 min.). 1983. 10.95 (978-0-7822-0088-1(5), 047) C G Jung IL.

Religious Professional's Contribution to Health Care: A History. 1 cass. (Care Cassettes Ser.: Vol. 10, No. 6). 1983. 10.80 Assn Prof Chaplains.

Religious Symptomatology & Mental Illness. Wayne Oates. 1986. 10.80 (0109) Assn Prof Chaplains.

Reliquary. unabr. ed. Douglas Preston & Lincoln Child. Read by Dick Hill. (Running Time: 14 hrs.). (Pendergast Ser.: No. 2). 2008. 39.25 (978-1-4233-5638-7(1), 9781423356387, BADLE); 24.95 (978-1-4233-5637-0(3), 9781423356370, BAD); audio compact disk 39.25 (978-1-4233-5636-3(5), 9781423356363, Brlnc Audio MP3 Lib); audio compact disk 112.25 (978-1-4233-5634-9(9), 9781423356349, BriAudCD Unabrid); audio compact disk 38.95 (978-1-4233-5633-2(0), 9781423356332, Bril Audio CD Unabri); audio compact disk 24.95 (978-1-4233-5635-6(7), 9781423356356, Brilliance MP3) Brilliance Audio.

Relique see Love Poems of John Donne

Reliving the Passion: Meditations on the Suffering, Death & Resurrection of Jesus as Recorded in Mark. Walter Wangerin, Jr. 2 cass. (Running Time: 3 hrs.). 1992. 14.99 (978-0-310-75538-8(7)) Zondervan.

Relocation & Key West Florida Experience, Pts. 1 & 2. Carol Hemingway. 1 cass. 8.95 (419) Am Fed Astrologers.

Relocation Astrology. ACT Staff. Read by ACT Staff. 1 cass. (Running Time: 90 min.). 1984. 8.95 (011) Am Fed Astrologers.

Reluctance see Robert Frost Reads

Reluctance see Twentieth-Century Poetry in English, No. 6, Recordings of Poets Reading Their Own Poetry

Reluctant Dragon. Kenneth Grahame. (Running Time: 5400 sec.). (J). (ps-7). 2005. audio compact disk 29.95 (978-0-7861-8213-8(X)) Blckstn Audio.

Reluctant Dragon. Kenneth Grahame. Read by John Dildine & Ginny Dildine. 1 cass. (Running Time: 52 min.). (J). (gr. k-6). 1988. 9.95 (978-0-939065-43-1(6), GW 1047) Gentle Wind.
Everyone knows that since a dragon is a dragon & St. George is St. George, there will have to be a fight. Everyone that is except the dragon. He'd rather write poetry.

Reluctant Dragon. Kenneth Grahame. (Running Time: 1 hr.). 2005. 17.95 (978-1-59912-707-1(5)) Iofy Corp.

Reluctant Dragon. Kenneth Grahame. Read by John Dildine et al. Perf. by Linda Schrade. (J). 1999. audio compact disk 14.95 (978-0-939065-88-2(6)) Gentle Wind.

Reluctant Dragon. Kenneth Grahame. Read by Steven McLaughlin. (Running Time: 0 hr. 57 mins. 0 sec.). (PlainTales Classics Ser.). (ENG.). (J). (gr. k-2). 2009. audio compact disk 12.95 (978-0-9819032-2-4(3)) Pub: PlainTales. Dist(s): IPG Chicago

Reluctant Dragon. abr. ed. Kenneth Grahame. (Running Time: 1 hr.). (J). 2005. 15.95 (978-0-7861-3024-5(5)) Blckstn Audio.

Reluctant Dragon. unabr. ed. Kenneth Grahame. Perf. by Boris Karloff. 1 cass. (J). 1984. 9.95 (978-0-694-50794-8(6), CDL5 1074) HarperCollins Pubs.
This story tells how a dragon who was introverted & poetical made friends with a little boy who had very much the same personality.

Reluctant Dragon. unabr. ed. Kenneth Grahame. (Running Time: 1 hr.). (J). 2005. audio compact disk 17.00 (978-0-7861-8091-2(9)) Blckstn Audio.

Reluctant Fundamentalist. unabr. ed. Mohsin Hamid. 4 CDs. (Running Time: 4 hrs. 43 mns.). 2007. audio compact disk 49.95 (978-0-7927-4688-1(0)) AudioGO.

Reluctant Fundamentalist. unabr. ed. Mohsin Hamid. Read by Satya Bhabha. 4 CDs. (Running Time: 16980 sec.). (ENG.). 2007. audio compact disk 29.95 (978-1-60283-177-3(7)) Pub: AudioGO. Dist(s): Perseus Dist

Reluctant Mage. unabr. ed. Karen Miller. Read by Geisslinger Nell. (Running Time: 16 hrs.). (Fisherman's Children Ser.). (ENG.). 2010. 29.98 (978-1-60788-246-6(9)) Pub: Hachet Audio. Dist(s): HachBkGrp

Reluctant Metrosexual. Peter Hyman. Narrated by Peter Hyman. (Running Time: 10 hrs.). (C). 2004. 30.95 (978-1-59912-708-8(3)) Iofy Corp.

Reluctant Metrosexual: Dispatches from an Almost Hip Life. Peter Hyman. 5 cass. (Running Time: 7 hrs.). 2004. 49.95 (978-0-7861-2749-8(X), 3296); audio compact disk 64.00 (978-0-7861-8539-9(2), 3296) Blckstn Audio.

Reluctant Metrosexual: Dispatches from an Almost Hip Life. unabr. ed. Peter Hyman. Read by Peter Hyman. 5 cass. (Running Time: 7 hrs. 30 mins.). 2005. 29.95 (978-0-7861-2727-6(9), E3296) Blckstn Audio.

Reluctant Mr. Darwin: An Intimate Portrait of Charles Darwin & the Making of His Theory of Evolution. unabr. ed. David Quammen. Narrated by Grover Gardner. 6 CDs. (Running Time: 28020 sec.). (Great Discoveries Ser.). (ENG.). 2006. audio compact disk 29.95 (978-1-57270-569-2(8)) Pub: AudioGO. Dist(s): Perseus Dist

Reluctant Mr. Darwin: An Intimate Portrait of Charles Darwin & the Making of His Theory of Evolution. unabr. ed. David Quammen. Narrated by Grover Gardner. 6 CDs. (Running Time: 28020 sec.). (Sound Library). 2006. audio compact disk 79.95 (978-0-7927-4072-8(6), SLD 979) AudioGO.

***Reluctant Prophet: A Novel.** unabr. ed. Nancy Rue. Narrated by Kirsten Potter. (Running Time: 13 hrs. 0 mins. 39 sec.). (ENG.). 2010. 25.89 (978-1-60814-764-9(9)) Oasis Audio.

***Reluctant Prophet: A Novel.** unabr. ed. Nancy Rue & Stephen Arterburn. Narrated by Stephen Arterburn & Kirsten Potter. (Running Time: 13 hrs. 0 mins. 39 sec.). (ENG.). 2010. audio compact disk 36.99 (978-1-59859-782-0(5)) Oasis Audio.

Reluctant Queen: The Story of Anne of York. Jean Plaidy. Read by Kate Binchy. 10 CDs. (Running Time: 15 hrs.). 2001. audio compact disk 89.95 (978-0-7531-1060-7(1), 110601) Pub: ISIS Audio GBR. Dist(s): Ulverscroft US

Reluctant Queen: The Story of Anne of York. unabr. ed. Jean Plaidy. Read by Kate Binchy. 8 cass. (Running Time: 11 hrs.). 1994. 69.95 (978-1-85695-830-1(2), 940908) Pub: ISIS Audio GBR. Dist(s): Ulverscroft US

***Reluctant Spy: My Secret Life in the CIA's War on Terror.** unabr. ed. John Kiriakou & Michael Ruby. Narrated by Arthur Morey. (Running Time: 7 hrs. 0 mins.). 2010. 14.99 (978-1-4001-8598-6(X)); 29.99 (978-1-4001-9598-5(5)); 19.99 (978-1-4001-6598-8(9)); audio compact disk 59.99 (978-1-4001-4598-0(8)) Pub: Tantor Media. Dist(s): IngramPubServ

***Reluctant Spy: My Secret Life in the CIA's War on Terror.** unabr. ed. John Kiriakou & Michael G. Ruby. Narrated by Arthur Morey. (Running Time: 7 hrs. 0 mins. 0 sec.). (ENG.). 2010. audio compact disk 29.99 (978-1-4001-1598-3(1)) Pub: Tantor Media. Dist(s): IngramPubServ

Reluctant Suitor. Kathleen E. Woodiwiss. Read by Lynn Redgrave. 1975. 9.99 (978-0-06-074385-7(9)); audio compact disk 9.99 (978-0-06-074377-2(8)) HarperCollins Pubs.

***Reluctant Suitor.** abr. ed. Kathleen E. Woodiwiss. Read by Lynn Redgrave. (ENG.). 2005. (978-0-06-088422-2(3), Harper Audio); (978-0-06-088421-5(5), Harper Audio) HarperCollins Pubs.

Reluctant Widow. unabr. ed. Georgette Heyer. Read by Cornelius Garrett. 8 cass. (Running Time: 12 hrs.). 2002. 59.95 (CAB 1525) AudioGO.
Elinor Rochdale is rather surprised that her new employer is quite rich, and more so at the decayed grandeur of the house to which she is transported. Realizing that there has been a case of mistaken identity, she nevertheless agrees to an audacious plan and is swept into a dangerous adventure. overnight, Elinor becomes mistress of a ruined estate. By midnight she is a bride, by dawn a widow.

Reluctant Widow. unabr. ed. Georgette Heyer. Read by Cornelius Garrett. 8 cass. (Running Time: 12 hrs.). 2000. 59.95 (978-0-7540-0102-7(4), CAB 1525) Pub: Chivers Audio Bks GBR. Dist(s): AudioGO

Remain Disease Free. unabr. ed. Dick Sutphen. Read by Dick Sutphen. 1 cass. (Running Time: 1 hr.). (Spirit Guide Meditations). 1999. 14.98 (978-0-87554-630-8(7), SG103) Valley Sun.
A spiritual meditation in which one visualizes the arteries clear, the cells healthy, a balanced immune system, healthy metabolism, & fully functioning liver.

***Remainder.** unabr. ed. Tom McCarthy. Narrated by James Langton. (Running Time: 9 hrs. 30 mins.). 2010. 34.99 (978-1-4526-2010-7(5)); audio compact disk 83.99 (978-1-4526-3010-6(0)) Pub: Tantor Media. Dist(s): IngramPubServ

***Remainder: A Novel.** unabr. ed. Tom McCarthy. Narrated by James Langton. (Running Time: 9 hrs. 30 mins.). 2010. 16.99 (978-1-4526-7010-2(2)); 24.99 (978-1-4526-5010-4(1)); audio compact disk 34.99 (978-1-4526-0010-9(4)) Pub: Tantor Media. Dist(s): IngramPubServ

Remains of an Altar. Phil Rickman. (Merrily Watkins Ser.). 2007. 89.95 (978-0-7531-3750-5(X)); audio compact disk 99.95 (978-0-7531-2718-6(0)) Pub: ISIS Audio GBR. Dist(s): Ulverscroft US

Remains of an Altar. Phil Rickman. Read by Julie Maisey. (Running Time: 5 hrs. 33 mins. 0 sec.). (Merrily Watkins Ser.). (ENG., 2007. audio compact disk 29.95 (978-1-84724-319-5(3)) Pub: Quercus GBR. Dist(s): IPG Chicago

Remains of Company D: A Story of the Great War. unabr. ed. James Carl Nelson. (Running Time: 13 hrs. 0 mins.). 2010. 29.95 (978-1-4417-2748-0(5)); 79.95 (978-1-4417-2744-2(2)); audio compact disk 109.00 (978-1-4417-2745-9(0)) Blckstn Audio.

Remains of Tom Lehrer. 3 CDs. (Running Time: 4 hrs. 30 mins.). 2001. bk. 49.98 (R2 79831) Rhino Enter.

Remains Silent. Michael Baden & Linda Kenney Baden. 10 cds. 2005. audio compact disk 38.25 (978-1-4159-2508-9(9)) Pub: Books on Tape. Dist(s): NetLibrary CO

Remains Silent. unabr. ed. Michael Baden & Linda Kenney Baden. 6 cass. (Running Time: 9 hrs.). 2005. 54.00 (978-1-4159-2507-2(0)) Books on Tape.

Remains to Be Seen. J. M. Gregson & Jonathan Keeble. 2009. 54.95 (978-1-84652-479-0(2)) Pub: Magna Story GBR. Dist(s): Ulverscroft US

Remaking of Modern Armies & The Revolution in Warfare. unabr. collector's ed. Basil H. Liddell-Hart. Read by Bill Kelsey. 8 cass. (Running Time: 12 hrs.). 1989. 64.00 (978-0-7366-1545-7(8), 2414) Books on Tape.
Examines the change in warfare introduced by atomic weapons.

Remarkable Ben. 10.00 Esstee Audios.
Explains how Ben Franklin tried to end the Revolutionary War & saved lives by meeting with General Howe.

Remarkable Creatures. unabr. ed. Tracy Chevalier. Read by Susan Lyons & Charlotte Parry. 8 CDs. (Running Time: 10 hrs.). (ENG.). (gr. 12 up). 2010. audio compact disk 39.95 (978-0-14-314530-1(4), PenAudBks) Pub: Pnguin Bks Ltd GBR. Dist(s): Penguin Grp USA

***Remarkable Creatures.** unabr. ed. Tracy Chevalier. Narrated by Charlotte Parry & Susan Lyons. 1 Playaway. (Running Time: 10 hrs. 15 mins.). 2010. 59.75 (978-1-4407-7176-7(6)); 67.75 (978-1-4407-7173-6(1)); audio compact disk 92.75 (978-1-4407-7174-3(X)) Recorded Bks.

***Remarkable Creatures.** unabr. collector's ed. Tracy Chevalier. Narrated by Charlotte Parry & Susan Lyons. 8 CDs. (Running Time: 10 hrs. 15 mins.). 2010. audio compact disk 44.95 (978-1-4407-7175-0(8)) Recorded Bks.

Remarkable Creatures: Epic Adventures in the Search for the Origins of Species. unabr. ed. Sean B. Carroll. Read by Jim Bond. 1 MP3-CD. (Running Time: 9 hrs.). 2009. 39.97 (978-1-4233-7807-5(5), 9781423378075, Brlnc Audio MP3 Lib); 39.97 (978-1-4233-7809-9(1), 9781423378099, BADLE); 24.99 (978-1-4233-7808-2(3), 9781423378082, BAD); 24.99 (978-1-4233-7806-8(7), 9781423378068, Brilliance MP3); audio compact disk 92.97 (978-1-4233-7805-1(9), 9781423378051, BriAudCD Unabrid); audio compact disk 29.99 (978-1-4233-7804-4(0), 9781423378044, Bril Audio CD Unabri) Brilliance Audio.

Remarkable Healing. Michael P. Marshall. Read by Michael P. Marshall. Ed. by Jonathan C. Renaud. Music by Ted Crook. 1 cass. (Running Time: 52 min.). 1995. 9.00 (978-0-912403-20-5(9)) Prod Renaud.
The mystery of emotions & physical pain are all signals to help us rebalance our lives & move with the flow.

Remarkable Journey of Prince Jen. unabr. ed. Lloyd Alexander. Narrated by Steven Crossley. 6 pieces. (Running Time: 8 hrs.). (gr. 6 up). 1991. 54.00 (978-0-7887-2636-1(6), 95508E7) Recorded Bks.
The Prince begins his quest for a kingdom of legendary renown bearing only humble gifts & enormous pride. He marches headlong into misfortune, miscreants & endearing characters.

Remarkable Recovery. Caryle Hirshberg & Marc I. Barasch. Read by Caryle Hirshberg & Marc I. Barasch. 2 cass. (Running Time: 3 hrs.). 1995. 17.00 (978-1-57042-230-0(3), 4-522303) Hachet Audio.
This collaboration between research scientist Caryle Hirshberg & author/editor Marc Ian Barasch breaks through years of scientific skepticism about the importance of the mind-body-spirit connection in the healing process & provides a new & powerful hope for recovery.

Remarkable Rocket see Favorite Children's Stories: A Collection

Remarkable Rocket see Happy Prince & Other Stories

Remarkable Women Collection. David A. Adler. Illus. by Karen Ritz & Robert Casilla. 33 vols. (Running Time: 35 mins.). 1997. pap. bk. 51.95 (978-1-59112-846-5(3)) Live Oak Media.

Rembrandt Affair. abr. ed. Daniel Silva. Read by Phil Gigante. 5 CDs. (Running Time: 6 hrs.). (Gabriel Allon Ser.: No. 10). 2010. audio compact disk 26.99 (978-1-4233-2821-6(3), 9781423328216, BACD) Brilliance Audio.

Rembrandt Affair. abr. ed. Daniel Silva. (Running Time: 6 hrs.). (Gabriel Allon Ser.: No. 10). 2011. audio compact disk 14.99 (978-1-4233-2822-3(1), 9781423328223, BCD Value Price) Brilliance Audio.

***Rembrandt Affair.** unabr. ed. Daniel Silva. Read by Phil Gigante. 1 Playaway. (Running Time: 12 hrs.). 2010. 39.99 (978-1-4418-7369-9(4)) Brilliance Audio.

Rembrandt Affair. unabr. ed. Daniel Silva. Read by Phil Gigante. 1 MP3-CD. (Running Time: 11 hrs.). (Gabriel Allon Ser.: No. 10). 2010. 24.99 (978-1-4233-2817-9(5), 9781423328179, Brilliance MP3); audio compact disk 36.99 (978-1-4233-2815-5(9), 9781423328155, Bril Audio CD Unabri) Brilliance Audio.

***Rembrandt Affair.** unabr. ed. Daniel Silva. Read by Phil Gigante. 1 MP3-CD. (Running Time: 11 hrs.). (Gabriel Allon Ser.: No. 10). 2010. 39.97 (978-1-4233-2818-6(3), 9781423328186, Brlnc Audio MP3 Lib); 24.99 (978-1-4233-2819-3(1), 9781423328193, BAD); 39.97 (978-1-4233-2820-9(5), 9781423328209, BADLE); audio compact disk 97.97 (978-1-4233-2816-2(7), 9781423328162, BriAudCD Unabrid) Brilliance Audio.

Rembrandt Tape. E. J. Gold. 1 cass. (Running Time: 50 min.). 1988. 9.98 (TP170) Union Label.
Uses Rembrandt's studio & art production approach as a model for transformational work.

Rembrandt's Beret. unabr. ed. John Alcorn. 1 cass. (Running Time: 14 min.). (J). (gr. 3-6). 1993. bk. 24.90 (978-0-8045-6675-9(5), 6675) Spoken Arts.

Remediation Engineering Design Concepts: CRCnetBASE 1999. Suthan S. Sutherson. 1999. audio compact disk 199.95 (978-0-8493-2168-9(9), 2168) Pub: CRC Pr. Dist(s): Taylor and Fran

Remediation of Chlorinated & Recalcitrant Compounds, 2002: Proceedings - Conference (3d: 2002: Monterey, Calif.) Ed. by A. R. Gavaskar & A. S. C. Chen. 2002. audio compact disk 295.00 (978-1-57477-132-9(9)) Battelle.

Remedies Bar Review: Audio CDs & Outlines. 2005. audio compact disk (978-0-9743923-1-8(6), GCC Pubs) Lib Soldiers.

Remedies for Deppresion see Remedios para la Depresion

Remedies, 2005 ed. (Law School Legends Audio Series) (Law School Legends Audio Ser.). 2006. 52.00 (978-0-314-16110-9(4), gilbert); 51.95 (978-0-314-16109-3(0), gilbert) West.

***Remedios para la Depresion.** Guadalupe Venegas.Tr. of Remedies for Deppresion. (SPA.). 2010. audio compact disk 15.00 (978-0-9825744-8-5(7)) Hombre Nuevo.

Remedy. Contrib. by David Crowder Band et al. 2007. audio compact disk 13.99 (978-5-557-60488-8(X)) Pt of Grace Ent.

Remedy. Contrib. by David Crowder Band et al. 2008. audio compact disk 14.99 (978-5-557-44621-1(4)) Pt of Grace Ent.

***Remedy: The Five-Week Power Plan to Detox Your System, Combat the Fat, & Rebuild Your Mind & Body.** unabr. ed. Supa Nova Slom. (Running Time: 7 hrs. 30 mins.). 2010. 29.95 (978-1-4417-3477-8(5)); 54.95 (978-1-4417-3473-0(2)); audio compact disk 29.95 (978-1-4417-3476-1(7)); audio compact disk 69.00 (978-1-4417-3474-7(0)) Blckstn Audio.

Remember. abr. ed. Karen Kingsbury. Read by Sandra Burr. Told to Gary Smalley. (Running Time: 14400 sec.). (Redemption Ser.). 2005. 19.95 (978-1-59355-886-4(4), 9781593558864); audio compact disk 21.95 (978-1-59355-888-8(0), 9781593558888, BACD); audio compact disk 69.25 (978-1-59355-889-5(9), 9781593558895, BACDLib Ed) Brilliance Audio.
She has locked up her heart, convinced that no one - including God - could love her. Four unlikely people - Alzheimer's patients - find the cracks in Ashley's heart and slowly help her remember. Then comes the nightmare of September 11, which forever changes the lives of the Baxter family, causing them to remember what is important and leading them to make decisions that are both heartbreaking and hope-filled. Landon Blake, who has loved Ashley since he was a teenager, tries to dull the pain of her rejection by immersing himself in the rescue efforts at Ground Zero. Tragedy and healing. Hurt and forgiveness. Redemption. And powerful lessons about remembering. Novelist Karen Kingsbury and relationship expert Gary Smalley have teamed up to bring you an inspiring series of stories that explore the relationship principles Gary has been teaching for more than thirty years.

Remember. abr. ed. Karen Kingsbury & Gary Smalley. Read by Sandra Burr. (Running Time: 4 hrs.). (Redemption Ser.). 2005. 39.25 (978-1-59737-972-4(7), 9781597379724, BADLE); 9.99 (978-1-59737-971-7(9), 9781597379717, BAD); 39.25 (978-1-59737-970-0(0), 9781597379700, Brlnc Audio MP3 Lib); 9.99 (978-1-59737-969-4(7), 9781597379694, Brilliance MP3); 49.25 (978-1-59355-887-1(2), 9781593558871, BAudLibEd) Brilliance Audio.

***Remember.** abr. ed. Karen Kingsbury & Gary Smalley. Read by Sandra Burr. (Running Time: 4 hrs.). (Redemption Ser.). 2010. audio compact disk 9.99 (978-1-4418-7832-8(7), 9781441878328, BCD Value Price) Brilliance Audio.

Remember. unabr. ed. Barbara Taylor Bradford. Read by Lorelei King. 10 cass. (Running Time: 12 hr. 30 min.). (Isis Ser.). (J). 1994. 84.95 (978-1-85695-875-2(2), 941002) Pub: ISIS Lrg Prnt GBR. Dist(s): Ulverscroft US
Nicky Wells, television war correspondent loses the only man she truly loved, dashing English aristocrat Charles Devereaux. Nicky seeks solace in her work & friendship with the photographer Cleeland Donovan. She thinks she might fall in love again. But she is forced to remember Charles when confronted by evidence that he led a secret double life.

Remember. unabr. ed. Barbara Taylor Bradford. Read by Lorelei King. 10 CDs. (Running Time: 12 hrs. 15 min.). (Isis Ser.). (J). 2000. audio compact disk 89.95 (978-0-7531-0702-7(3), 107007) Pub: ISIS Lrg Prnt GBR. Dist(s): Ulverscroft US

Remember: II Timothy 1:5. Ed Young. 1984. 4.95 (978-0-7417-1383-4(7), 383) Win Walk.

Remember & Perish Not. Anita Canfield. 2 cass. 1998. 14.95 Set. (978-1-57008-421-8(1), Bkcraft Inc) Deseret Bk.

Remember August. Perf. by Remember August. 1 CD. 1999. audio compact disk 16.98 (978-1-57908-485-1(0)) Platinm Enter.

Remember Him. Virgil B. Smith. Read by Bruce Seely. 1 cass. (Running Time: 12 min.). 1972. 5.95 (978-1-878507-06-8(0), 36C) Human Grwth Services.
Examination of the contributions of Jesus Christ to Jews & all mankind, & the resulting potential for human progress, as taught in the King James Bible & other scriptures.

***Remember Me.** Margaret Thornton & Maggie Mash. 2010. 84.95 (978-1-84652-489-9(X)); audio compact disk 99.95 (978-1-84652-490-5(3)) Pub: Magna Story GBR. Dist(s): Ulverscroft US

Remember Me? abr. ed. Sophie Kinsella, pseud. Read by Charlotte Parry. (ENG.). 2008. audio compact disk 14.99 (978-0-7393-8236-3(5)) Pub: Random Audio Pubg. Dist(s): Random

Remember Me. unabr. ed. Trezza Azzopardi. Read by Corrie James. (Running Time: 8 hrs.). 2004. 74.25 (978-1-59355-439-2(7), 1593554397, BrilAudUnabridg); 29.95 (978-1-59355-438-5(9), 1593554389, BAU); audio compact disk 31.95 (978-1-59355-440-8(0), 1593554400, Bril Audio CD Unabri); audio compact disk 87.25 (978-1-59355-441-5(9), 1593554419, BriAudCD Unabrid) Brilliance Audio.
Seventy-two-year-old, red-haired Winnie - homeless and abandoned time and again by those she's trusted - would say she's no trouble. She is content to let the days go by, minding her own business, bothering no one. Winnie would rather not recall the past, and at her age, doesn't see much point in thinking about the future. But she is catapulted out of her exile when a young girl robs her of her suitcase and her wig - her only material possessions. Winnie then embarks on a journey to find the thief, and what begins as a search for stolen belongings becomes the rediscovery of a stolen life. Forced to take stock of how events long buried have brought her to a derelict house on the edge of nowhere, she relives the secrets of a past

she had disowned. As she pieces together the fragments of her life, Winnie recognizes that she is no longer simply on a hunt for stolen goods. After all these years, she has not escaped from her life at all: she has been circling it, and now must come to terms with it. ALSO AVAILABLE AS A GROVE PRESS HARDCOVER.

Remember Me. unabr. ed. Trezza Azzopardi. Read by Corrie James. (Running Time: 8 hrs.). 2004. 39.25 (978-1-59335-530-2(0), 1593355300, Brlnc Audio MP3 Lib); 24.95 (978-1-59335-276-9(X), 159335276X, Brilliance MP3) Brilliance Audio.

Remember Me. unabr. ed. Trezza Azzopardi. Read by Corrie James. (Running Time: 8 hrs.). 2004. 39.25 (978-1-59710-634-4(8), 1597106348, BADLE); 24.95 (978-1-59710-635-1(6), 1597106356, BAD) Brilliance Audio.

Remember Me. unabr. ed. Mary Higgins Clark. Read by Mary Peiffer. 7 cass. (Running Time: 10 hrs. 30 min.). 1995. 56.00 (978-0-7366-2920-1(3), 3618) Books on Tape.
Menley Nichols finally could stop blaming herself for her young son's accidental death after the birth of her daughter. Determined to start over, the family is blissfully unaware that someone in their midst has a different agenda.

Remember Me? unabr. ed. Sophie Kinsella, pseud. Narrated by Rosalyn Landor. 10 CDs. (Running Time: 12 hrs. 45 mins.). 2008. audio compact disk 110.00 (978-1-4159-4387-8(7)) Random.

Remember Me to Harold Square. unabr. ed. Paula Danziger. Read by Paula Danziger. 2 cass. (YA). 1999. 16.98 (FS9-26769) Highsmith.

Remember Me to Harold Square. unabr. ed. Paula Danziger. Read by Paula Danziger. 2 cass. (Running Time: 3 hrs. 4 mins.). (J). (gr. 7 up). 1995. pap. bk. 23.00 (978-0-8072-7526-9(3), YA874SP, Listening Lib); 18.00 (978-0-8072-7525-2(5), YA874CX, Listening Lib) Random Audio Pubg.

Remember Not To Forget: Luke 17:11-19. Ed Young. (J). 1978. 4.95 (978-0-7417-1023-9(4), A0023) Win Walk.

Remember Summer. abr. ed. Elizabeth Lowell. Read by Laural Merlington. 2 cass. 1999. 17.95 (FS9-50989) Highsmith.

Remember Summer. unabr. ed. Elizabeth Lowell. Read by Laural Merlington. (Running Time: 9 hrs.). 2006. 39.25 (978-1-4233-1451-6(4), 9781423314516, BADLE); 24.95 (978-1-4233-1450-9(6), 9781423314509, BAD); 39.25 (978-1-4233-1449-3(2), 9781423314493, Brlnc Audio MP3 Lib); 24.95 (978-1-4233-1448-6(4), 9781423314486, Brilliance MP3); audio compact disk 92.25 (978-1-4233-1447-9(6), 9781423314479, BriAudCD Unabrid); audio compact disk 34.95 (978-1-4233-1446-2(8), 9781423314462, Bril Audio CD Unabri) Brilliance Audio.
The most grueling challenge of Raine Smith's equestrian career looms before her - the Olympic Games. Little does she realize that she's about to face greater perils in the arms of a stranger than she's ever found on the back of her horse. Cord Elliott is a man trained to deflect disaster, and his mission is to ensure that Raine Smith remains untouched by sudden gunfire at the Summer Games. Yet from the moment Raines meets Cord's ice-blue glance, she knows he's more hazardous to her heart than a sniper's bullet. Falling for a man who answers to the call of intrigue and holds secrets that can never be shared is to endure the broken promises, unexplained absences, and constant danger that comes with his profession. But in the fiery passion of irresistible love, a summer to remember seems worth every risk.

Remember Summer. unabr. ed. Elizabeth Lowell. Read by Laural Merlington. 6 cass. 1999. 57.25 (FS9-51048) Highsmith.

Remember the Forgotten. unabr. ed. Joe Moriarty & Yoka Moriarty. Read by Joe Moriarty et al. Read by David Allen et al. 1 cass. (Running Time: 1 hr.). 1985. 10.00 Crtv Source.
Music mixed with voices to create dramatization for spiritual understanding & personal growth.

Remember the Rules: Early Explorers Emergent Set A Audio CD. Benchmark Education Staff. (J). 2006. audio compact disk 10.00 (978-1-4108-7596-9(2)) Benchmark Educ.

Remember the Sabbath: Exodus 20:8-11, 1221. Ed Young. 1999. 4.95 (978-0-7417-2221-8(6), 1221) Win Walk.

Remember Tomorrow. Poems. Nigel Jenkins. 1 cass. 1997. pap. bk. 22.00 (978-1-85902-434-8(3)) Pub: Gomer Pr GBR. Dist(s): St Mut
Selections are from previous publications & from author's new book "Ambush".

Remember When. abr. ed. Read by Susan Ericksen. 5. (Running Time: 21600 sec.). (In Death Ser.). 2007. audio compact disk 14.99 (978-1-4233-3204-6(0), 9781423332046, BCD Value Price) Brilliance Audio.

Remember When. abr. ed. Judith McNaught. 2 cass. (Running Time: 4 hrs.). 1997. 14.40 (978-0-671-57739-1(5), 908769, Audioworks) S&S Audio.

Remember When. abr. ed. Nora Roberts & J. D. Robb. Read by Susan Ericksen. (Running Time: 6 hrs.). 2009. audio compact disk 9.99 (978-1-4418-0834-9(5), 9781441808349, BCD Value Price) Brilliance Audio.

Remember When. unabr. ed. Nora Roberts & J. D. Robb. Read by Susan Ericksen. (Running Time: 16 hrs.). 2003. 97.25 (978-1-59355-185-8(1), 1593551851, BrilAudUnabridg); audio compact disk 39.95 (978-1-59355-187-2(8), 1593551878, Bril Audio CD Unabri); audio compact disk 112.25 (978-1-59355-188-9(6), 1593551886, BriAudCD Unabrid) Brilliance Audio.

Remember When. unabr. ed. Nora Roberts & J. D. Robb. Read by Susan Ericksen. (Running Time: 16 hrs.). 2004. 39.25 (978-1-59335-628-6(5), 1593356285, Brlnc Audio MP3 Lib) Brilliance Audio.

Remember When. unabr. ed. Nora Roberts & J. D. Robb. Read by Susan Ericksen. (Running Time: 16 hrs.). 2004. 39.25 (978-1-59710-637-5(2), 1597106372, BADLE); 24.95 (978-1-59710-636-8(4), 1597106364, BAD) Brilliance Audio.

Remember When. unabr. ed. Nora Roberts & J. D. Robb. Read by Susan Ericksen. (Running Time: 16 hrs.). 2004. 24.95 (978-1-59335-234-9(4), 1593352344) Soulmate Audio Bks.

***Remember Who You Are: The Story Behind the Song.** Angelica Ganea-Mileto. Perf. by Angelica Ganea-Mileto. (ENG.). 2010. pap. bk. 21.99 (978-0-9784940-0-1(8)) StreamEnt CAN.

Remembered. Tamera Alexander. Read by Barbara McCulloh. 14 cass. (Running Time: 16 hrs. 75 mins.). (Fountain Creek Chronicles: Bk. 3). 2007. 113.75 (978-1-4281-6034-7(5)) Recorded Bks.

Remembered by God: Gen. 41:1-40. Ed Young. 1988. 4.95 (978-0-7417-1681-1(X), 681) Win Walk.

Remembered Melody-Music. 2007. audio compact disk 16.95 (978-1-56136-408-4(8)) Master Your Mind.

Remembered Morning see Twentieth-Century Poetry in English, No. 12, Recordings of Poets Reading Their Own Poetry

Remembering see Recordando

Remembering. Art Fettig. 1 cass. 5.95 (CH-T6) Growth Unltd.
Both children & parents can benefit from this remarkable memory system.

Remembering. Eldon Taylor. 1 cass. (Running Time: 62 min.). (Neurophonics Ser.). 16.95 (978-1-55978-655-3(8), 1006) Progress Aware Res.
Sound patterns for Altered States of Consciousness with underlying subliminal affirmations & frequency response signals. Use with headphones only.

Remembering. unabr. ed. Wendell Berry. (Running Time: 4 hrs. 15 mins. 0 sec.). (ENG.). 2009. audio compact disk 21.98 (978-1-59644-779-0(6), christaudio) christianaud.

***Remembering: A Novel (Port William)** unabr. ed. Wendell Berry. Narrated by Michael Kramer. (ENG.). 2009. 12.98 (978-1-59644-780-6(X), christaudio) christianaud.

Remembering Blue. abr. ed. Connie May Fowler. Read by Connie May Fowler. 4 cass. (Running Time: 6 hrs.). 2000. 24.95 (978-1-57453-337-8(1)) Audio Lit.
Mattie Fiona Blue, recently widowed & filled with grief, spins a tale of her beloved husband, Nick, his birth, his death, his love of the sea, his gnawing fear of a family legend of drowning & their unflagging devotion to each other. While mourning Nick, Mattie tells of her own life as she journeys from the loneliness of a broken home & disapproving mother to the chaotic sphere of Nick Blue & his sprawling Greek-American fishing family, whose ties to the sea extend across generations, continents & time.

Remembering Denny. collector's ed. Calvin Trillin. Read by Barrett Whitener. 5 cass. (Running Time: 7 hrs. 30 min.). 1999. 40.00 (978-0-7366-4880-6(1), 5103) Books on Tape.
Everybody idolized Denny Hansen. He was a varsity swimmer & a Rhodes Scholar whose million dollar smile & bright future made him the subject of a feature in Life magazine. A clean cut college hero filled with limitless promise, Denny symbolized everything thought of a good in 1950s America. But life worked out differently for Denny. By middle age he was alone & unfulfilled, he committed suicide at fifty-five.

Remembering Dreams. Pat Carroll. Read by Pat Carroll. Ed. by Tony Carroll. 1 cass. (Running Time: 30 min.). 10.00 Inner-Mind Concepts.
Presents suggestions to expand consciousness by remembering dreams & understanding their meaning.

Remembering Grandma Moses. Beth Moses Hickok. Read by Beth Moses Hickok. 1 cass. (Running Time: 1 hr. 05 min.). 1997. pap. bk. 22.00 (978-1-884592-07-2(4)); cass. & audio compact disk 12.00 (978-1-884592-06-5(6)) Images from the Past.
The author, an octogenarian herself, reads the complete text of her book with additional stories about GM's childhood & her artistry in the kitchen. Also the story of Christmastime 1934 when the author was 23 & considering marriage into the Moses family.

Remembering Marcel. Compiled by Stephen B. Rekas. 2001. spiral bd. 24.95 (978-0-7866-6165-7(8)) Mel Bay.

Remembering Mog. unabr. ed. Colby Rodowsky. Narrated by Julie Dretzin. 3 pieces. (Running Time: 4 hrs.). (gr. 7 up). 2002. 28.00 (978-1-4025-1436-4(0)) Recorded Bks.
Annie always admired her older sister Mog. Two years ago, Mog was killed by a robber the night before her graduation. As her own graduation approaches, Annie finds herself torn between excitement for her future and guilt that she will now move into a life her sister never had a chance to know. Since Mog's death, Annie's family has refused to deal with their loss. Her father is sad but keeps it to himself. Annie's mother has removed every family photo of Mog and keeps Mog's locked room exactly the way it was the last time she was there. No mention is ever made of Mog at all. Gradually, Annie realizes that she must find of way of remembering her sister and letting her go at the same time.

Remembering Names & Faces. Alan Butkowsky. Read by Alan Butkowsky. 2 cass. 20.00 Set. (219A) Nightingale-Conant.

***Remembering Peter Sellers: An Audio Portrait from the BBC Archives.** Compiled by Broadcasting Corp. British. Narrated by Phill Jupitus. (Running Time: 2 hrs. 0 mins. 0 sec.). (ENG.). 2010. audio compact disk 24.95 (978-1-4084-6654-4(6)) Pub: AudioGO. Dist(s): Perseus Dist

Remembering Polio. Created by Canadian Broadcasting Corporation. (Running Time: 7200 sec.). (ENG.). 2007. audio compact disk 19.95 (978-0-660-19736-4(7)) Canadian Broadcasting CAN.

***Remembering Spike Milligan: An Audio Portrait from the BBC Archives.** Compiled by Broadcasting Corp. British. (Running Time: 2 hrs. 0 mins. 0 sec.). (ENG.). 2010. audio compact disk 24.95 (978-1-4084-6653-7(8)) Pub: AudioGO. Dist(s): Perseus Dist

Remembering Steve (W. T.) abr. ed. Terri Irwin. (ENG.). 2007. audio compact disk 29.95 (978-0-7435-7002-2(2)) Pub: S&S Audio. Dist(s): S and S Inc

Remembering Sweetness: Walter Payton & the Bears. D. Johnston Inc. Staff. 2002. audio compact disk 200.00 (978-1-58702-860-1(3)) D Johnston Inc.

Remembering Sweetness: Walter Payton & the Bears. Alan Venable. (Overcoming the Odds Sports Biographies Ser.). 2002. audio compact disk 18.95 (978-1-4105-0192-9(2)) D Johnston Inc.

Remembering Sweetness: Walter Payton & the Bears. Alan Venable. Ed. by Jerry Stemach et al. Contrib. by Ted S. Hasselbring. 2 cass. (Running Time: 3 hrs.). (Start-to-Finish Books). (J). (gr. 4-5). 2002. 35.00 (978-1-58702-857-1(3)) D Johnston Inc.

Remembering Sweetness: Walter Payton & the Bears. unabr. ed. Alan Venable. Ed. by Jerry Stemach et al. Contrib. by Ted S. Hasselbring. 2 cass. (Running Time: 3 hrs.). (Start-to-Finish Books). (J). (gr. 2-3). 2002. (978-1-58702-842-7(5), H11) D Johnston Inc.
In thirteen years as a running back for the NFL Chicago Bears, Walter Payton (1954-1999) established himself as possibly the greatest football player ever. Even though he was a small man as pro football players go, he made himself into a dazzling and ferocious runner that no defender wanted to tackle. In the course of his career, Walter not only broke almost every record for a football running back, he also became one of the most loved and admired players in the game.

Remembering the Future: Thoughts on Faith & History. Glenn Thomas Carson. Voice by Glenn Thomas Carson. (ENG.). 2009. audio compact disk 5.00 (978-0-9801966-2-7(0)) Pola Str Pr.

Remembering the Good Times. unabr. ed. Richard Peck. Read by Richard Peck. (Running Time: 60 min.). (YA). (gr. 7 up). 1987. bk. 15.98 incl. guide. (978-0-8072-1848-8(0), JRH126SP, Listening Lib) Random Audio Pubg.
Three best friends. They didn't seem to need anyone else. But when one of the trio commits suicide, the other two can only wonder, "How well did we know our best friend?".

Remembering the Holy Spirit. Elizabeth Johnson. 2 cass. (Running Time: 2 hrs.). 2001. vinyl bd. 17.95 (A6260) St Anthony Mess Pr.
Takes a dynamic and profound look at the Christian mystery of the Holy Spirit.

Remembering the Purpose. Swami Amar Jyoti. 1 cass. 1977. 9.95 (K-10) Truth Consciousness.
The Source sustains us, nothing else. Missing the Purpose, we miss everything. Definition of spirituality. Raising our consciousness, solving our problems.

Remembering You: Faith on the Home Front Trilogy. Penelope J. Stokes. Narrated by Ruth Ann Phimister. 12 cass. (Running Time: 17 hrs.). 98.00 (978-1-4025-3805-6(7)) Recorded Bks.

Remembrance. 1 cass. (Running Time: 30 min.). 9.95 (I0880B090, HarperThor) HarpC GBR.

Remembrance. Jude Deveraux. Read by J. Smith-Cameron. 2004. 10.95 (978-0-7435-4578-5(8)) Pub: S&S Audio. Dist(s): S and S Inc

Remembrance & Mourning: An Expanded View of Post-Traumatic Stress Disorder. Cardwell C. Nuckols. Read by Cardwell C. Nuckols. Ed. by Dick Ulett & JoAnn Moore. 4 cass. (Running Time: 1 hr.). 1995. 34.95 (978-1-56168-005-4(2), A9406) GWC Inc.
Early life & repeated trauma cause a complicated clinical picture. Exploration of the treatment of Post-Traumatic Stress Disorder.

Remembrance & Realization. Swami Amar Jyoti. 1 cass. 1976. 9.95 (R-70) Truth Consciousness.
The nutshell message of all Satsangs & scriptures. Realizing what we believe. At any cost, avoiding forgetfulness. Love teaches us to be One.

Remembrance of God. Swami Jyotirmayananda. Read by Swami Jyotirmayananda. 1 cass. (Running Time: 60 min.). 12.99 (736) Yoga Res Foun.

Remembrance of God. Swami Jyotirmayananda. 1 cass. (Running Time: 45 min.). 1990. 10.00 Yoga Res Foun.

Remembrance of the Golden Light. unabr. ed. Carolyn Ann O'Riley. 1 cass. (Running Time: 45 mins.). 2000. audio compact disk 12.50 (978-1-891870-16-3(5)) Archangels Pen.
Archangel Michael divinely inspired meditation tape. Side A: "Remembrance of the Golden Light"; Side B: "Connecting with Your Solar Angel.".

Remembrance of the Light. unabr. ed. Swami Amar Jyoti. 1 cass. (Running Time: 1 hr.). (Satsangs of Swami Amar Jyoti Ser.). 2000. 9.95 (978-0-933572-57-7(3), P-68) Truth Consciousness.
maintaining focus on Light, God, throughout all activities. Aids to remembrance and inspiration. A light-full life.

Remembrance of Things Past. Marcel Proust. Read by Neville Jason. 39 CDs. (Running Time: 50 hrs.). 2004. audio compact disk 239.98 (978-962-634-253-4(6), Naxos AudioBooks) Naxos.

Remembrances of The Guru, Paramahansa Yogananda. Brother Mokshananda. 1984. 6.50 (2510) Self Realization.
The late author explains practical ways by which every seeker can tune in with the divine help that flows through a true guru. He shares many beautiful stories that show how the guru works in our everyday lives.

Remind Me Who I Am Again. unabr. ed. Linda Grant. Narrated by Patricia Gallimore. 8 cass. (Running Time: 10 hrs. 30 mins.). 2000. 71.00 (978-1-84197-073-8(5), H1068E7) Recorded Bks.
This book tells two stories, the trauma of total memory loss & the lack of identity felt by second generation Anglo-Jews, whose parents effectively erased their past. MID, a disease eating away her mother's mind, is shown from Linda's view. Rose can't recall where she lives, what she has said or done, but she can pretend. She can answer rationally & seem normal. Linda struggled just to prove Rose had a problem. For the author, MID erases the past. Rose knew two worlds, that of her parents, immigrants from rural Ukraine & the Western world of opportunity. With the loss of Rose's memory, Grant's last link to that unknown world is slowly fading away.

Reminder: 1 Cor. 16:13-14. Ed Young. 1986. 4.95 (978-0-7417-1526-5(0), 526) Win Walk.

Reminiscences & Future Projections. Laura Huxley. 2 cass. 18.00 (A0730-90) Sound Photosyn.
Listen to this charming woman tell of her exploits in the years since the death of her husband Aldous.

Reminiscences of a Dancing Man see Poetry of Thomas Hardy

Reminiscences of a Stock Operator. abr. ed. Based on a book by Edwin Lefevre. 2 cass. (Running Time: 2 hrs. 24 mins.). 2004. 18.00 (978-1-59280-195-4(1), Marketplc Aud) Marketplace Bks.
??I learned early that there is nothing new in Wall Street. There can't be because speculation is as old as the hills. Whatever happens in the stock market today has happened before and will happen again. I've never forgotten? The fact that I remember that way is my way of capitalizing experience.?-from Reminiscences of a Stock OperatorFirst published in 1923, Reminiscences of a Stock Operator is the fictionalized biography of Jesse Livermore, one of the greatest speculators who ever lived. Now, more than 70 years later, Reminiscences remains the most widely read, highly recommended investment book ever written. Generations of investors have found that it has more to teach them about themselves and other investors than years of experience in the market. They have also discovered that its trading advice and keen analyses of market price movements ring as true today as in 1923.Jesse Livermore won and lost tens of millions of dollars playing the stock and commodities markets during the early 1900's ? at one point making the then-astronomical amount of ten million dollars in just one month of trading. So potent a market force was he in his day that, in 1929, he was widely believed to be the man responsible for causing the Crash. He was forced into seclusion and had to hire a bodyguard.Originally reviewed in The New York Times as a nonfiction book, Reminiscences of a Stock Operator vividly recounts Livermore's mastery of the markets from the age of 14. Always good at figures, he learns, early on, that he can predict which way the numbers will go. Starting out with an investment of five dollars, he amasses a fortune by his early twenties and establishes himself as a major player on the Street. He makes his first killing in 1906, selling short on Union Pacific. He goes on to corner the cotton market, and has a million-dollar day. Bullish in bear markets, and bearish among bulls, he claims that only suckers gamble on the market. The trick, he advises, is to protect yourself by balancing your investments, and selling big on the way down. Livermore goes broke three times, but he comes back each time feeling richer for the learning experience.Offering profound insights into the motivations, attitudes, and feelings shared by every investor, Reminiscences of a Stock Operator is a timeless instructional tale that will enrich the lives ? and the portfolios ? of today's traders as it has those of generations past.

Reminiscences of a Stock Operator. abr. ed. Edwin Lefevre. 2 CDs. (Running Time: 8640 sec.). 2004. audio compact disk 24.00 (978-1-59280-194-7(3), Marketplc Aud) Marketplace Bks.

Reminiscences of Childhood see Dylan Thomas Reading

Reminiscences of My Life in Camp see Black Pioneers in American History, Vol. 1, 19th Century

Reminiscences of Reich's Life. Eva Reich et al. 2 cass. (Running Time: 2 hrs.). 1974. 18.00 (07702) Big Sur Tapes.
Eva Reich begins the session with instructions on how to build & use an orgone accumulator. The next three panelists then describe their personal interactions with Wilhelm Reich & describe his earthy & dynamic personality. David Boadella ends the session with some general remarks about key concepts in orgonomy.

Reminiscences of Sherlock Holmes (His Last Bow) The Adventure of Wisteria Lodge & Other Stories. unabr. ed. Arthur Conan Doyle. Read by David Timson. 6 CDs. (Running Time: 24082 sec.). (Classic Literature with

Classical Music Ser.). 2006. audio compact disk 41.98 (978-962-634-407-1(5), Naxos AudioBooks) Naxos.

***Reminiscences of the Cuban Revolutionary War.** abr. ed. Ernesto Che Guevara. Read by Bruno Gerardo. (ENG.). 2009. (978-0-06-188259-3(3), Harper Audio); (978-0-06-180748-0(6), Harper Audio) HarperCollins Pubs.

Reminscence. Elijah Jackson. 1 cass. (Running Time: 1 hr.). 2000. 11.99 (978-0-9706112-6-0(9), Sarah Jean Recs); audio compact disk 17.99 (978-0-9706112-7-7(7), Sarah Jean Recs) Pub: Pt of Grace Ent. Dist(s): STL Dist NA

Remnant. Keith C. Terry. 2 cass. 1997. 11.98 (978-1-57734-077-5(9), 07001479) Covenant Comms.
An exciting sequel to best-selling novels "Out of Darkness" & "Into the Light".

Remnant: On the Brink of Armageddon. Tim LaHaye & Jerry B. Jenkins. Narrated by Richard Ferrone. 7 cass. (Running Time: 10 hrs. 30 mins.). (Left Behind Ser.: Bk. 10). 70.00 (978-1-4025-2390-8(4)); audio compact disk 89.00 (978-1-4025-3649-6(6)) Recorded Bks.

Remnant: On the Brink of Armageddon. Tim LaHaye & Jerry B. Jenkins. 8 CDs. (Left Behind Ser.: Bk. 10). 2002. audio compact disk 39.95 (978-1-4025-1819-5(6), 00322) Recorded Bks.

Remnant: On the Brink of Armageddon. unabr. ed. Tim LaHaye & Jerry B. Jenkins. Narrated by Richard Ferrone. 6 cass. (Running Time: 10 hrs. 30 mins.). (Left Behind Ser.: Bk. 10). 2004. 29.95 (978-1-4025-1860-7(9), 01384); audio compact disk 39.95 (978-1-4025-1861-4(7), 00332) Recorded Bks.
As the battered earth reels under judgements from heaven, Global Community leader Nicolae Carpathia tightens the screws on anyone who refuses to proclaim total allegiance to him. He has a million of his enemies just where he wants them massed at Petra and within striking distance of devastating firepower.

Remnants. Poems. Seaon Ducote. Narrated by Seaon Ducote. e.g., 1 cd. (Running Time: e.g., 45 min.). Dramatization. 2006. audio compact disk 12.95 (978-0-9787597-3-5(7)) PureLight Pubns.
Poet/Artist, and metaphysician, Seaon Ducote, narrates her writings of prose and poetry into a descriptive celebration of reminders and awakenings of who we are, and are not, in this beautiful patchwork of people, places, and emotional threads of life.

Remodeling Your Home: Proverbs 24:3-4. Ed Young. (J). 1981. 4.95 (978-0-7417-1156-4(7), A0156) Win Walk.

Remorseful Day. 3rd abr. ed. Colin Dexter. Read by Kevin Whately. 3 CDs. (Running Time: 3 hrs.). (ENG., 2001. audio compact disk (978-0-333-90718-4(3)) Macmillan UK GBR.

***Remote Bliss.** M. Cheryl Green. Read by Dan Gold. (Running Time: 55). (ENG.). 2008. 2.99 (978-1-61114-001-9(3)) Mind Wings Aud.

Remote Control. abr. ed. Stephen White. Read by Dick Hill. 4 cass. Library ed. (Running Time: 6 hrs.). (Dr. Alan Gregory Ser.). 2003. 62.25 (978-1-59086-484-5(0), 1590864840, Lib Edit); audio compact disk 74.25 (978-1-59086-881-2(1), 1590868811, BACDLib Ed) Brilliance Audio.
Emma Spire is the daughter of the assassinated Surgeon General of the United States. She has been on the cover of every national magazine. Her beauty, her brains, her bravery - all are public property. Everyone wants a piece of her - and she must escape the feeding frenzy at all costs. But she cannot, and the consequences are deadly. Thus the stage is set for Dr. Alan Gregory's most stunning, brainteasing crisis yet. The Colorado-based psychologist-sleuth must solve a case of twisted desire and terror to save not only a golden girl pursued by the furies of fame but also his wife, Boulder County D.A. Lauren Crowder, imprisoned on suspicion of murder. For it was Lauren who took Emma under her wing, and it was Lauren who pulled the trigger on the mysterious stalker who menaced Emma's safety and sanity. Step by step, amid accelerating acts of terror, Alan Gregory suspects he may be dealing not with a sick mind fixated on a fantasy of female perfection but with deadly greed fueled by a high-tech prize that may be worth billions. Meanwhile, his investigation is turned into a desperate race against time as a medical emergency threatens to turn his wife's incarceration into a death sentence.

Remote Control. abr. ed. Stephen White. Read by Dick Hill. (Running Time: 21600 sec.). (Dr. Alan Gregory Ser.). 2005. audio compact disk 16.99 (978-1-59600-400-9(2), 9781596004009, BCD Value Price) Brilliance Audio.

Remote Control. abr. ed. Stephen White. Read by Dick Hill. (Running Time: 6 hrs.). (Dr. Alan Gregory Ser.). 2006. 39.25 (978-1-4233-0194-3(3), 9781423301943, Brinc Audio MP3 Lib); 24.95 (978-1-4233-0193-6(5), 9781423301936, Brilliance MP3); 39.25 (978-1-4233-0196-7(X), 9781423301967, BADLE); 24.95 (978-1-4233-0195-0(1), 9781423301950, BAD) Brilliance Audio.

***Remote Control.** abr. ed. Stephen White. (Dr. Alan Gregory Ser.). 2010. audio compact disk 9.99 (978-1-4418-5662-3(5)) Brilliance Audio.

Remote Control. unabr. ed. Andy McNab. Read by Ric Jerrom. 12 cass. 1998. 96.95 Dolby Sound. (978-0-7540-0175-1(X), CAB 1598) AudioGO.
Nick Stone left the Special Air Service in 1993, five years after being involved in the shooting of IRA terrorists in Gibraltar. Now with British Intelligence, he discovers the senseless murders of fellow SAS soldier Kev Brown & his family in Washington, D.C. Only Kelly, just seven years old, has survived. Immediately, the two of them are on the run for their lives.

Remote Control. unabr. ed. Andy McNab. Read by Ric Jerrom. 12 CDs. (Running Time: 18 hrs.). 2002. audio compact disk 110.95 (978-0-7540-5496-2(9), CCD 187) AudioGO.

Remote Control. unabr. ed. Stephen White. Read by Michael Kramer. 8 cass. (Running Time: 12 hrs.). (Dr. Alan Gregory Ser.). 1997. 64.00 (978-0-7366-3769-5(9), 4442) Books on Tape.
In his most complex & personal case yet, psychologist Alan Gregory must work quickly to save his wife, attorney Lauren Crowder, who is under arrest for apparently shooting her best friend's blackmailer.

Remote Viewing. Keith Harary. 1 cass. 9.00 (A0034-86) Sound Photosyn.
A psychic endeavor available to everyone.

Remote Viewing. unabr. ed. Robert A. Monroe. Read by Robert A. Monroe. (Running Time: 45 min.). (Gateway Experience - Freedom Ser.). 1983. 14.95 (978-1-56113-263-8(2)) Monroe Institute.
Utilize your energy tools for remote perception.

Remote Viewing: An Introduction to Coordinate Remote Viewing. David Morehouse. 5 CDs. (Running Time: 6 hrs.). 2006. audio compact disk 29.95 (978-1-59179-240-6(1), AW00888D) Sounds True.
David Morehouse has become recognized as a leading authority on the phenomenon of Remote Viewing-the ability we all possess to tap into the universal consciousness and look across vast distances of time and space. Now this renowned expert, who will be hosting the Sci-Fi Channel's(tm) new psychic reality show The Gift, presents an introductory program perfect for those who want to get their first taste of their limitless potential. Remote Viewing: An Audio Introduction includes an overview of the science and history of Remote Viewing; four guided viewing sessions to demonstrate your innate psychic ability, and much more.

Remote Viewing (Astral Projection) Babbling Brook. Eldon Taylor. 1 cass. 16.95 (978-1-55978-545-7(4), 5402F); 16.95 incl. script. (978-1-55978-002-5(9), 5402D) Progress Aware Res.
Soundtrack - Synthesized moments with underlying subliminal affirmations.

Removal of Warts. Barrie Konicov. 1 cass. (YA). 11.98 (978-0-87082-360-2(4), 111) Potentials.
Professional hypnotist Barrie Konicov reveals how to remove warts through self-hypnosis.

Remove: UFO Implants, vol. 1. August Stahr. Read by August Stahr. 1 cass. (Running Time: 1 hr. 30 min.). (Planetary Issues Ser.). (ENG.). 1993. 44.00 (978-1-884686-03-0(6)) Celestl Guardn.
Guided meditation.

Remove Mental Stress, No. 1. Swami Jyotirmayananda. 1 cass. (Running Time: 1 hr.). 1990. 12.99 Yoga Res Foun.

Remove Mental Stress, No. 2. Swami Jyotirmayananda. 1 cass. (Running Time: 1 hr.). 1990. 12.99 Yoga Res Foun.

Remove Road Rage. Mary Lee LaBay. 2003. audio compact disk 19.95 (978-1-934705-03-2(9)) Awareness Engin.

Remove Road Rage. Mary Lee LaBay. 2003. audio compact disk 19.95 (978-1-934705-19-3(5)) Awareness Engin.

Remove the Earth. Contrib. by Advent. Prod. by Mitchell Marlow & Al Jacob. 2008. audio compact disk 13.99 (978-5-557-50311-2(0)) Solid State MO.

Removing All Sorrow & Suffering: An Informal Talk by Paramahansa Yogananda. Read by Paramhansa Yogananda. (Collector's Ser.: 9). 2007. audio compact disk 14.00 (978-0-87612-509-0(7)) Self Realization.

Removing Blocks to Change: Why People Don't Change & What to Do about It. David Grudermeyer & Rebecca Grudermeyer. 2 cass. 18.95 (T-45) Willingness Wrks.

Removing Body Idea. Swami Jyotirmayananda. 1 cass. (Running Time: 45 min.). 1990. 10.00 Yoga Res Foun.

Removing the Blocks. abr. ed. Leo J. Fishbeck. Read by Leo J. Fishbeck. 3 cass. (Running Time: 3 hrs. 6 min.). 1993. 30.00 (978-1-883373-00-9(X)) R S Outreach.
Mental & spiritual strategies for removing unconscious resistance patterns.

Removing the High Places. Derek Prince. 1 cass. (I-4172) Derek Prince.

Removing the Rock/In the Name of the Father. Marianne Williamson. Read by Marianne Williamson. 1 cass. (Running Time: 90 mins.). (Lectures on a Course in Miracles). 1999. 10.00 (978-1-56170-462-0(8), M845) Hay House.

Removing the Sense of Separation. Swami Amar Jyoti. 1 cass. 1982. 9.95 (P-44) Truth Consciousness.
How to realize the Oneness that is already there? The real cause of separation. Expanding our consciousness boldly.

Renaissance. 1 cass., 1 CD. 8.78 (WH 11216); audio compact disk 13.58 CD Jewel box. (WH 11216) NewSound.

Renaissance. Paul Johnson. Read by Geoffrey Howard. 2000. audio compact disk 40.00 (978-0-7366-6302-1(9)) Books on Tape.

Renaissance. unabr. ed. Paul Johnson. Read by Geoffrey Howard. 4 cass. (Running Time: 6 hrs.). 2000. 32.00 (978-0-7366-5652-8(9), 5451) Books on Tape.
The Renaissance holds an undying place in the human imagination and its great heroes remain our own. Perhaps no era in history has been more revolutionary or more romanticized. But what was the Renaissance? In this compact book, Paul Johnson tackles that question with the towering erudition that is his trademark. He begins by painting the economic, technological and social background before focusing on the individuals who made the era so memorable. Finally, he examines the spread and decline of the Renaissance and its abiding legacy.

Renaissance. unabr. ed. Paul Johnson. Read by Geoffrey Howard. 4 cass. (Running Time: 6 hrs.). 2001. 24.95 (978-0-7366-5693-1(6)); audio compact disk 29.95 (978-0-7366-5710-5(X)) Books on Tape.
Holds an undying place in the human imagination & its great heroes remain our own. This period of profound evolution in European thought transformed the West from medieval to modern & produced the most astonishing outpouring of artistic creation the world has ever known. Perhaps no era has been more revolutionary or more romanticized. But what was the Renaissance?.

Renaissance: Machiavelli. Joseph Mazzeo. 1 CD. (Running Time: 50 mins.). 2006. audio compact disk 12.95 (978-1-57970-361-5(5), C19020D, Audio-For) J Norton Pubs.
Consideration of Machiavelli's contributions to ethical and political thought. Recorded at the YM-YWHA Poetry Center in New York city.

Renaissance: Studies in Art & Poetry see Cambridge Treasury of English Prose: Dickens to Butler

Renaissance: Studies in Art & Poetry. unabr. ed. Walter Pater. Read by Nadia May. 5 cass. (Running Time: 7 hrs.). 1995. 39.95 (978-0-7861-0895-4(9), 1673) Blckstn Audio.
A compendium of Walter Pater's early writings in which he extends the chronology of the Renaissance from the Middle Ages to the 18th century. The essays discuss the work of Pico della Mirandola, Botticelli, Leonardo, Michelangelo, & others. However, it is the conclusion which gained for Pater the reputation as a daring modern philosopher, a "demoralizing moralizer." His cry of "art for art's sake" became the manifesto of the Aesthetic Movement.

Renaissance: Studies in Art & Poetry. unabr. collector's ed. Walter Pater. Read by David Case. 7 cass. (Running Time: 7 hrs.). 1991. 42.00 (978-0-7366-1932-5(1), 2754) Books on Tape.
It is impossible to measure but difficult to underestimate the impact this book has had on thought, sensibility & artistic achievements of the last hundred years. Pater's writing influenced not only aesthetes & artists who worked in the visual maedia, but also authors in the forefront of modernism, James Joyce, Marcel Proust, Virginia Woolf & W. B. Yeats.

Renaissance & Early Music for Banjo. Kyle Datesman. (ENG.). 2009. lib. bdg. 19.99 (978-0-7866-2782-0(4)) Mel Bay.

Renaissance Duets. Composed by Nathaniel Gunod. (Play-along Library for Classical Guitar Ser.). (ENG.). 1996. audio compact disk 9.95 (978-0-7390-2617-5(8)) Alfred Pub.

Renaissance in England. Compiled by Benchmark Education Staff. 2006. audio compact disk 10.00 (978-1-4108-6655-4(6)) Benchmark Educ.

Renaissance in Italy. Compiled by Benchmark Education Staff. 2006. audio compact disk 10.00 (978-1-4108-6654-7(8)) Benchmark Educ.

Renaissance Man. unabr. ed. Harriet Greenberg. Read by Ed Begley, Jr. 2 cass. (Running Time: 3 hrs.). 1994. 16.95 (978-1-56876-027-8(2)) Soundlines Ent.
A one time hot-shot advertising executive is forced to take a job teaching a group of undisciplined Army recruits some basic academic skills. A heartwarming drama with plenty of laughs.

Renaissance of Consciousness. Swami Amar Jyoti. 1 dolby cass. 1986. 9.95 (O-28) Truth Consciousness.
A concise history of the human search: realism, idealism & beyond. The dawn of the New Age, the present imperative for conscious seeking.

Renaissance of Grace. Perf. by Aurora Juliana Ariel & Bruce BecVar. Des. by Aurora Juliana Ariel. Prod. by Bruce BecVar. (ENG.). 2008. 16.95 (978-0-9816501-2-8(0)) Aeos Inc.

Renaissance of the American Indian. unabr. ed. Stan Steiner. 1 cass. (Running Time: 35 mins.). 12.95 (19010) J Norton Pubs.
Describes the Renaissance of the American Indian, the social barriers he has had to face, his experience in various careers & the anachronistic traditions of Indian culture that confuse his progress.

Renaissance, the Audio CD Theme Set: Set of 6 Set B. Adapted by Benchmark Education Staff. (English Explorers Ser.). (J). (gr. 3-6). 2007. audio compact disk 60.00 (978-1-4108-9830-2(X)) Benchmark Educ.

Renaissance, the Reformation, & the Rise of Nations, I-IV. Instructed by Andrew C. Fix. 24 cass. (Running Time: 24 hrs.). 99.95 (978-1-59803-037-2(X), 3940) Teaching Co.

Renaissance, the Reformation, & the Rise of Nations, I-IV. Instructed by Andrew C. Fix. 24 CDs. (Running Time: 24 hrs.). 2005. audio compact disk 129.95 (978-1-59803-039-6(6), 3940) Teaching Co.

Renaissance 2003 Winter Catalog. Audio Renaissance Staff. 0.01 (978-1-55927-859-1(5)) Pub: Macmill Audio. Dist(s): Macmillan

Renal Tubular Acidoses. Read by Vardaman M. Buckalew, Jr. 1 cass. (Running Time: 9 min.). 1985. 12.00 (C8527) Amer Coll Phys.

Renascence see Poetry of Edna St. Vincent Millay

Renato's Luck. unabr. ed. Jeff Shapiro. Read by Edward Lewis. 9 cass. (Running Time: 12 hrs.). 2001. 34.95 (978-0-7366-4952-0(2)) Books on Tape.
Renato Tizzoni rediscovers his zest for life through a trip to Rome that saves his marriage, his family and his village.

Rencontre avec vous - 5 exercices de Sophrologie. unabr. ed. Danièle Gouyon. Read by Danièle Gouyon. (YA). 2007. 69.99 (978-2-35569-097-6(9)); 69.99 (978-2-35569-095-2(2)) Find a World.

***Render unto Caesar: Serving the Nation by Living our Catholic Beliefs in Political Life.** Archbishop Charles Chaput. Read by Jeff Blackwell. (ENG.). 2009. audio compact disk 24.95 (978-1-936231-13-3(1)) Cath Audio.

***Render unto Rome: The Secret Life of Money in the Catholic Church.** unabr. ed. Jason Berry. (ENG.). 2011. audio compact disk 35.00 (978-0-307-87742-0(6), Random AudioBks) Pub: Random Audio Pubg. Dist(s): Random

Rendevous with Destiny. 10.00 (HD422) Esstee Audios.

Rendez-Vous: An Invitation to French. 3rd ed. Judith A. Muyskens et al. 1990. tchr. ed. 23.75 (978-0-07-540877-2(5)) McGraw.

Rendez-Vous: An Invitation to French. 5th ed. Judith A. Muyskens & Alice C. Omaggio Hadley. 1 cass. (Running Time: 1 hr.). (FRE & ENG.). (C). 1998. 8.75 (978-0-07-044437-9(4), Mc-H Human Soc) Pub: McGrw-H Hghr Educ. Dist(s): McGraw

Rendez-Vous: An Invitation to French, Pt. A. 5th ed. Judith A. Muyskens & Alice C. Omaggio Hadley. 1 cass. (Running Time: 90 min.). (FRE.). (C). 1998. 47.18 (978-0-07-913638-1(9), Mc-H Human Soc) Pub: McGrw-H Hghr Educ. Dist(s): McGraw

Rendez-Vous: An Invitation to French, Pt. B. 5th ed. Judith A. Muyskens & Alice C. Omaggio Hadley. 1 cass. (Running Time: 90 min.). (C). 1998. stu. ed. 47.18 (978-0-07-913639-8(7), Mc-H Human Soc) Pub: McGrw-H Hghr Educ. Dist(s): McGraw

Rendez-Vous Pt. 1: An Invitation to French. 6th ed. Judith A. Muyskens & Alice C. Omaggio Hadley. (ENG.). (C). 2002. stu. ed. 53.75 (978-0-07-249807-3(2), 0072498072, Mc-H Human Soc) Pub: McGrw-H Hghr Educ. Dist(s): McGraw

Rendezvous. unabr. ed. Amanda Quick, pseud. Read by Anne Flosnik. (Running Time: 12 hrs.). 2009. 39.97 (978-1-4233-8775-6(9), 9781423387756, Brlnc Audio MP3 Lib); 39.97 (978-1-4233-8777-0(5), 9781423387770, BADLE); 24.99 (978-1-4233-8774-9(0), 9781423387749, Brilliance MP3); 24.99 (978-1-4233-8776-3(7), 9781423387763, BAD); audio compact disk 82.97 (978-1-4233-8773-2(2), 9781423387732, BriAudCD Unabrid); audio compact disk 29.99 (978-1-4233-8772-5(4), 9781423387725, Bril Audio CD Unabri) Brilliance Audio.

Rendezvous & Other Stories. unabr. ed. Daphne Du Maurier. Read by Edward De Souza. 8 cass. (Running Time: 12 hrs.). 2000. 59.95 (CAB 341) Pub: Chivers Audio Bks GBR. Dist(s): AudioGO
A happily married woman commits suicide for no apparent reason; a con artist plays the same bold game too often; and a novelist embarks on a romantic adventure but is woefully disappointed. In all of these stories and more, glimpses of personal lives and human emotions are vividly portrayed.

Rendezvous & Other Stories. unabr. ed. Patrick O'Brian. Read by David Case. 7 cass. (Running Time: 10 hrs. 30 min.). 1995. 56.00 (978-0-7366-3106-8(2), 3782) Books on Tape.
Few readers know that O'Brian, best known for his Aubrey/Maturin series (the British navy's exploits during Napoleonic wars), earned his reputation as a writer of short stories.

Rendezvous in Majorca. Scripts. Ian Feldman. 4 cass. (Running Time: 5hrs. 50mins.). 2007. 29.95 (978-1-932623-01-7(9), 1); audio compact disk 29.95 (978-1-932623-00-0(0), 1-932623-00-0) SSI.
Trixey Haygood, a beautiful young operative concealed by British MI6 and SIS officials for years on the Isle of Majorca in the Mediterranean, reveals a shocking truth from her past to a man searching for the final pieces of a mysterious puzzle from the Second World War:What actually happened to the remnants of Nazi Germany?s ultra-secret project to build the world's first Hydrogen Bomb?Threatened by the newly formed CIA and the Soviet?s battle hardened KGB, the heroine tells her tale of the past; of being caught in a dangerous struggle between her idealism to expose the truth and protecting an ex-Nazi who holds the critical key to assembling nuclear weapons components stolen by the Soviet Union from the Nazi?s at war?s end. Realizing that time is running out while being viciously pursued by both CIA and KGB operatives, they attempt to divulge part of that secret conspiracy to the world before two innocent Americans are electrocuted as the Spies falsely accused of giving America?s nuclear secrets to the Soviets. . . .Racing across Europe, its high-energy plot exposes the true evils of Cold War politics during the anti-Communism purges of Joseph McCarthy, while pitting American, British and Soviet agents against each other in a life and death struggle of power and intrigue. The dark tale unravels the truth of how known Nazi?s and their clandestine secrets were used to strengthen each Nation?s grip on world domination in the early 1950?s, while fearless men and extravagantly beautiful women rendezvous and scheme in mysterious locales beginning in the post-war aftermath of Nazi Germany. Finally, as the world?s press is about to be told of the conspiracy, even the British are forced to hide it as their own leaders are blackmailed by the vindictive Director of the CIA bringing the Allied alliance to the brink of disaster.Now without British protection herself and no refuge to hide within, the heroine becomes the Soviet?s prime target, and only they know that she and her Nazi ally have the final component that must be obtained to achieve their undeniable goal; detonation of the Soviet Union?s first Hydrogen Bomb. . .

Rendezvous in Majorca. I.t. ed. Ian Feldman. (ENG., 2007. 9.95 (978-0-9743673-8-5(9), 0-9743673-8-9) SSI.

Rendezvous with Rama. unabr. ed. Arthur C. Clarke. Read by Peter Ganim. (Running Time: 9 hrs.). 2009. 24.99 (978-1-4233-9500-3(X), 9781423395003, Brilliance MP3) Brilliance Audio.

Rendezvous with Rama. unabr. ed. Arthur C. Clarke. Read by Peter Ganim & Robert J. Sawyer. (Running Time: 9 hrs.). 2009. 39.97 (978-1-4233-9501-0(8), 9781423395010, Brlnc Audio MP3 Lib) Brilliance Audio.

Rendezvous with Rama. unabr. ed. Arthur C. Clarke. Read by Peter Ganim. (Running Time: 9 hrs.). 2009. 39.97 (978-1-4233-9502-7(6), 9781423395027, BADLE) Brilliance Audio.

Rendezvous with Rama. unabr. ed. Arthur C. Clarke. Read by Peter Ganim & Robert J. Sawyer. (Running Time: 9 hrs.). 2009. audio compact disk 92.97 (978-1-4233-9499-0(2), 9781423394990, BriAudCD Unabrid) Brilliance Audio.

Rendezvous with Rama. unabr. ed. Arthur C. Clarke. Read by Peter Ganim. (Running Time: 9 hrs.). 2009. audio compact disk 29.99 (978-1-4233-9498-3(4), 9781423394983, Bril Audio CD Unabri) Brilliance Audio.

Rendezvous with Rama. unabr. ed. Arthur C. Clarke. Read by Hayward Morse. 8 cass. (Running Time: 12 hrs.). 2000. 59.95 (978-0-7451-6739-8(X), CAB 1355) Pub: Chivers Audio Bks GBR. Dist(s): AudioGO

In the year 2077, thousands of tons of rock and metal traveling at 50 miles per second impacted the earth. Over 50,000 people died. While new age dawned, mankind deemed that no other catastrophe would ever be allowed to breach the defenses of the Earth again. So began Project Spaceguard. Years later, in a way no one could have predicted, it justified its existence.

Rendezvous with Rama. unabr. collector's ed. Arthur C. Clarke. Read by Dan Lazar. 8 cass. (Running Time: 8 hrs.). 1980. 48.00 (978-0-7366-0258-7(5), 1253) Books on Tape.

In 2130, a new celestial body is discovered heading toward the Sun. Earthlings name this object "Rama" - a vast cylinder, about 31 miles long & 12 miles across, with a mass of at least ten trillion tons. The spaceship "Endeavor," directed by Commander Bill Norton, lands on Rama & has 3 weeks to explore its hollow interior. Inside the vessel they discover a completely self-contained world - a world that has been cruising through space for perhaps more than a million years.

Rene see Treasury of French Prose

Rene. Rene De Chateaubriand. 1 cass. 1991. 16.95 (1408-LV) Olivia & Hill.

When Amelie realizes that her feelings for her brother Rene include desire, she retires to a convent. Rene, who has come to typify the Romantic hero, takes refuge in the wilds of North America.

Rene Gonzalez "The Hummingbird" Perf. by René Gonzálex. 1 cass. (Running Time: 38 min.). 1999. audio compact disk 19.95 (978-1-879542-75-4(7), EFMRG1); audio compact disk 19.95 Ellis Family Mus.

Virtuoso classical guitarist Rene Gonzalez performs classical pieces on the solo guitar. Pieces are from the Renaissance through the late 19th century & include works by Scarlatti, Albeniz, Sor, Coste, Pujol & Sagreras. Great listening & educational tool.

***Rene y el Pigmeo en la Selva.** Emma Romeu. (J). 2008. 9.95 (978-1-61658-339-2(8)) Indep Pub IL.

Renegade. abr. ed. Donald Clayton Porter. Read by Lloyd James. 4 vols. No. 2. 2003. 25.00 (978-1-58807-218-4(5)); (978-1-58807-749-3(7)); audio compact disk 30.00 (978-1-58807-402-7(1)); audio compact disk (978-1-58807-841-4(8)) Am Pubng Inc.

Renegade. unabr. ed. Ted Dekker. Narrated by Adam Verner. (Books of History Chronicles: Bk. 3). (ENG.). 2008. 13.99 (978-1-60814-360-3(0)); audio compact disk 19.99 (978-1-59859-346-4(3)) Oasis Audio.

Renegade. unabr. ed. M. Lehman. Read by Gene Engene. 4 cass. (Running Time: 5 hrs.). Dramatization. 1991. 26.95 (978-1-55686-367-7(5), 367) Books in Motion.

Sequel to the popular Texans on the Powder. This action packed western traces the fate of a young man gone bad despite himself.

Renegade: The Making of a President. unabr. ed. Richard Wolffe. Read by Richard Wolffe. (ENG.). 2009. audio compact disk 30.00 (978-0-7393-8526-5(7), Random AudioBks) Pub: Random Audio Pubg. Dist(s): Random

***Renegade History of the United States.** unabr. ed. Thaddeus Russell. (Running Time: 12 hrs. 0 mins.). 2010. 34.99 (978-1-4001-9851-1(8)); 24.99 (978-1-4001-6851-4(1)); 17.99 (978-1-4001-8851-2(2)); audio compact disk 83.99 (978-1-4001-4851-6(0)); audio compact disk 34.99 (978-1-4001-1851-9(4)) Pub: Tantor Media. Dist(s): IngramPubServ

***Renegade Hunter: A Rogue Hunter Novel.** unabr. ed. Lynsay Sands. Read by Kirby Heyborne. (ENG.). 2010. (978-0-06-201590-7(7), Harper Audio); (978-0-06-199889-8(3), Harper Audio) HarperCollins Pubs.

Renegade Trail. abr. ed. Matthew S. Hart. Read by Charlton Griffin. Abr. by Odin Westgaard. 2 vols. No. 6. 2003. 18.00 (978-1-58807-248-1(7)); (978-1-58807-743-1(8)) Am Pubng Inc.

Renegades. abr. ed. T. Jefferson Parker. Read by David Colacci. (Running Time: 6 hrs.). (Charlie Hood Novel Ser.: Bk. 2). 2010. audio compact disk 14.99 (978-1-4233-4592-3(4), 9781423345923, BCD Value Price) Brilliance Audio.

Renegades. unabr. ed. T. Jefferson Parker. Read by David Colacci. (Running Time: 11 hrs.). (Charlie Hood Novel Ser.: Bk. 2). 2009. 39.97 (978-1-4233-4590-9(8), 9781423345909, BADLE); 39.97 (978-1-4233-4588-6(6), 9781423345886, Brlnc Audio MP3 Lib); 24.99 (978-1-4233-4587-9(8), 9781423345879, Brilliance MP3); 24.99 (978-1-4233-4589-3(4), 9781423345893, BAD); audio compact disk 92.97 (978-1-4233-4586-2(X), 9781423345862, BriAudCD Unabrid); audio compact disk 34.99 (978-1-4233-4585-5(1), 9781423345855, Bril Audio CD Unabri) Brilliance Audio.

Renegades of Pern. unabr. ed. Anne McCaffrey. Read by Dick Hill. 8 cass. (Running Time: 12 hrs.). (Dragonriders of Pern Ser.). 1993. 73.25 (978-1-56100-134-7(1), 1561001341, Unabridge Lib Edns) Brilliance Audio.

Renegades of Pern. unabr. ed. Anne McCaffrey. Read by Dick Hill. (Running Time: 12 hrs.). (Dragonriders of Pern Ser.). 2005. 39.25 (978-1-59737-032-5(0), 9781597370325, BADLE); 24.95 (978-1-59737-031-8(2), 9781597370318, BAD); audio compact disk 39.25 (978-1-59737-030-1(4), 9781597370301, Brlnc Audio MP3 Lib); audio compact disk 24.95 (978-1-59737-029-5(0), 9781597370295, Brilliance MP3); audio compact disk 107.25 (978-1-59737-028-8(2), 9781597370288, BriAudCD Unabrid); audio compact disk 37.95 (978-1-59737-027-1(4), 9781597370271, Bril Audio CD Unabri) Brilliance Audio.

As long as the people of Pern could remember, the Holds had protected them from Thread, the deadly silver strands that fell from the sky and ravaged the land. In exchange for sanctuary in the huge stone fortresses, the people tithed to their lord Holders, who in turn supported the Weyrs, whose dragons were Pern's greatest weapon against Thread. But not everyone on Pern was part of that system of mutual care and protection, particularly those who had been rendered holdless as punishment for wrongdoing. And there were some, like Jayge's trader clan, who simply preferred the freedom of the roads to the security of a hold. Others, like Aramina's family, had lost their holds through injustice and cruelty. For all the holdless, life was a constant struggle for survival. Then, from the ranks of the criminals and the disaffected, rose a band of renegades, led by the Lady Thella. No one was safe from Thella's depredations, and now her quarry was Aramina, reputed to have a telepathic link with dragons. But when Thella mistakenly vented her rage on Jayge's family, she made a dangerous enemy. For Jayge was bent on revenge - and he would never let her have the girl who heard dragons!.

Renew & Recharge Wellness Program: For the Mind, Body, & Spirit. (Running Time: 60 mins.). 2001. (978-0-9711674-2-1(7)) Fresco Enterp.

Renew Me. Contrib. by Malcolm Williams & the Voices of Faith & Gregory Payton. Prod. by Malcolm Williams. (Running Time: 1 hr.). 2003. audio compact disk 16.98 (978-5-552-41385-0(7)) Pub: Pt of Grace Ent. Dist(s): STL Dist NA

Renew Your Life with Yoga. Instructed by Mataji-Indra Devi. 2 cass. 19.95 (978-0-88432-235-1(1), S31020) J Norton Pubs.

Learn the ancient secrets to a healthy body & a peaceful mind. Provides step-by-step instructions for breathing and all the fundamental yoga exercises.

Renew Your Life with Yoga (2-CD Set) Indra Devi. (ENG.). 2007. audio compact disk 19.95 (978-1-57970-479-7(4), Audio-For) J Norton Pubs.

Renew your Mind. 4 cass. 2004. 19.99 (978-1-58602-222-8(9)) E L Long.

Renew Your Mind. Kenneth Copeland. 1 cass. 1989. 5.00 (978-0-88114-815-2(6)) K Copeland Pubns.

Biblical teaching on renewing your mind.

Renewable Energy Equipment & Services in Bulgaria: A Strategic Reference 2007. Compiled by Icon Group International, Inc. Staff. 2007. ring bd. 195.00 (978-0-497-35850-1(6)) Icon Grp.

Renewable Energy Equipment & Services in Denmark: A Strategic Reference 2007. Compiled by Icon Group International, Inc. Staff. 2007. ring bd. 195.00 (978-0-497-35913-3(8)) Icon Grp.

Renewable Energy Equipment & Services in Dominican Republic: A Strategic Reference 2007. Compiled by Icon Group International, Inc. Staff. 2007. ring bd. 195.00 (978-0-497-35916-4(2)) Icon Grp.

Renewable Energy Equipment & Services in India: A Strategic Reference 2006. Compiled by Icon Group International, Inc. Staff. 2007. ring bd. 195.00 (978-0-497-36020-7(9)) Icon Grp.

Renewable Energy Equipment & Services in Slovakia: A Strategic Reference 2007. Compiled by Icon Group International, Inc. Staff. 2007. ring bd. 195.00 (978-0-497-35873-0(5)) Icon Grp.

Renewable Energy Equipment & Services in United Kingdom: A Strategic Reference 2007. Compiled by Icon Group International, Inc. Staff. 2007. ring bd. 195.00 (978-0-497-82459-4(0)) Icon Grp.

Renewable Energy Equipment in Poland: A Strategic Reference 2007. Compiled by Icon Group International, Inc. Staff. 2007. ring bd. 195.00 (978-0-497-82395-5(0)) Icon Grp.

Renewable Energy Projects in Estonia: A Strategic Reference 2006. Compiled by Icon Group International, Inc. Staff. 2007. ring bd. 195.00 (978-0-497-35934-8(0)) Icon Grp.

Renewal. Russell Shaw. Read by Al Covaia. 7 cass. (Running Time: 10 hrs. 30 min.). 1987. 28.95 (320) Ignatius Pr.

A novel which gives the insider's look at the conflicts between the liberal & conservative elements in the American Catholic Church & the common faith which unites them.

Renewal of Spirit. Debbie Friedman. Ed. by Randee Friedman. Tr. by Randee Friedman. 1 cass., 1 CD. (Running Time: 49 min.). 1995. 9.95 (978-1-890161-21-7(7)); audio compact disk 15.95 (978-1-890161-22-4(5)) Sounds Write.

Debbie's adult recording of 13 original songs from her powerful healing service.

Renewal of the Human Brain. J. Krishnamurti. 1 cass. (Running Time: 75 min.). (Krishnamurti & Professor David Bohm - 1980 Ser.: No. 9). 8.50 (ABD809) Krishnamurti.

Krishnamurti & Prof. Bohm offer penetrating, in-depth dialogues which shed light on the fundamental issues of existence.

Renewal of Youth: Psalm 103. Ed Young. 1989. 4.95 (978-0-7417-1763-4(8), 763) Win Walk.

Renewal of Youth Pt. 1: Psalm 103. Ed Young. 1989. 4.95 (978-0-7417-1762-7(X), 762) Win Walk.

Renewing of the Mind, Vol. 5. Featuring Bill Winston. 6. 2004. audio compact disk 48.00 (978-1-59544-025-9(9)) Pub: B Winston Min. Dist(s): Anchor Distributors

Learn profound Bibical truths that prove you are a Heir ofthe world.

Renewing of the Mind, Vol. 6. Featuring Bill Winston. 2. 2004. audio compact disk 16.00 (978-1-59544-026-6(7)) Pub: B Winston Min. Dist(s): Anchor Distributors

Take back what is rightfully yours by skillfully using the Word of God.

Renewing the Mind, Vol. 1. Featuring Bill Winston. 3. 2004. audio compact disk 24.00 (978-1-59544-021-1(6)) Pub: B Winston Min. Dist(s): Anchor Distributors

Identify the steps to renew your mind to the Word of God.

Renewing the Mind, Vol. 1. Bill Winston. 3 cass. (Running Time: 2hr.47min.). (C). 2001. 15.00 (978-1-931289-21-4(2)) Pub: B Winston Min. Dist(s): Anchor Distributors

Renewing the Mind, Vol. 2. Featuring Bill Winston. 4. 2004. audio compact disk 32.00 (978-1-59544-022-8(4)) Pub: B Winston Min. Dist(s): Anchor Distributors

Transform your belief system through the Law of Meditation.

Renewing the Mind, Vol. 3. Featuring Bill Winston. 6. 2004. audio compact disk 48.00 (978-1-59544-023-5(2)) Pub: B Winston Min. Dist(s): Anchor Distributors

Learn how to destroy old thought patterns and negativeself images.

Renewing the Mind, Vol. 4. Featuring Bill Winston. 5. 2004. audio compact disk 40.00 (978-1-59544-024-2(0)) Pub: B Winston Min. Dist(s): Anchor Distributors

Establish a "Kingdom Mentality" and experience days of Heavean on Earth.

Renewing the Mind Vol. 2: The Law of Meditation. Bill Winston. 4 cass. (Running Time: 3hr.41min.). (C). 2001. 20.00 (978-1-931289-22-1(0)) Pub: B Winston Min. Dist(s): Anchor Distributors

Renewing the Mind Vol. 3: As A Man Thinketh. Bill Winston. 6 cassettes. 2001. 30.00 (978-1-931289-23-8(9)) Pub: B Winston Min. Dist(s): Anchor Distributors

Renewing the Mind Vol. 4: Days of Heaven on Earth. Bill Winston. 5 cass. (Running Time: 4hr.27min.). (C). 2002. 25.00 (978-1-931289-24-5(7)) Pub: B Winston Min. Dist(s): Anchor Distributors

Renewing the Mind Vol. 5: Heirs of the World. Bill Winston. 6 cass. (Running Time: 4hr.03min.). (C). 2002. 30.00 (978-1-931289-25-2(5)) Pub: B Winston Min. Dist(s): Anchor Distributors

Renewing the Mind Vol. 6: Spiritually-Minded. Bill Winston. 2 cass. (Running Time: 1hr.20min.). (C). 2002. 10.00 (978-1-931289-26-9(3)) Pub: B Winston Min. Dist(s): Anchor Distributors

Renewing the Mind Power Pack. Featuring Bill Winston. 6. 2001. audio compact disk 48.00 (978-1-59544-069-3(0)) Pub: B Winston Min. Dist(s): Anchor Distributors

This premium packed teaching is the culmination of the bestof the six volumes of the "Renewing of the Mind" series thataddresses the mind renewal process. Change your thinkingand you will change your life!.

Renewing the Mind Power Pack. Bill Winston. 6 cass. (Running Time: hhr.mmmin.). 2002. 30.00 (978-1-931289-13-9(1)) B Winston Min.

Renewing Your Marriage at Midlife. abr. ed. Steve Brody & Cathy Brody. 2 cass. (Running Time: 3 hrs.). 2001. 18.00 (978-1-59040-082-1(8), Phoenix Audio) Pub: Amer Intl Pub. Dist(s): PerseuPGW

Renewing Your Mind Vol. 1: Learning to Change. Creflo A. Dollar. 3 cass. (Running Time: 4 hrs. 30 mins.). 2000. 15.00 (978-1-931172-50-9(1), TS259, Kidz Faith) Pub: Creflo Dollar. Dist(s): STL Dist NA

Renewing Your Mind Vol. 2: Benefits of Renewing Your Mind. Creflo A. Dollar & Taffi L. Dollar. 4 cass. (Running Time: 6 hrs.). 2000. 20.00 (978-1-931172-52-3(8), TS262, Kidz Faith) Pub: Creflo Dollar. Dist(s): STL Dist NA

Renewing Your Mind Vol. 3: Mind Is the Control Center for Life. Creflo A. Dollar & Taffi L. Dollar. 4 cass. (Running Time: 6 hrs.). 2000. 20.00 (978-1-931172-54-7(4), TS263, Kidz Faith) Pub: Creflo Dollar. Dist(s): STL Dist NA

Renno. abr. ed. Donald Clayton Porter. Read by Lloyd James. 4 vols. No. 5. 2003. 25.00 (978-1-58807-221-4(5)); (978-1-58807-752-3(7)) Am Pubng Inc.

Renno. abr. ed. Donald Clayton Porter. Read by Lloyd James. 5 vols. No. 5. 2004. audio compact disk 30.00 (978-1-58807-405-8(6)); audio compact disk (978-1-58807-844-5(2)) Am Pubng Inc.

Renouncing Our Bondage. Swami Amar Jyoti. 1 dolby cass. 1985. 9.95 (K-70) Truth Consciousness.

Applying fresh thinking to the habitual mechanisms of life; giving up the unnatural & unneedful.

Renovación Matrimonial. P. Miguel Carmena. (SPA.). (YA). 2005. audio compact disk 16.95 (978-0-9674222-2-0(1)) Hombre Nuevo.

Renovation of the Heart: Putting on the Character of Christ. unabr. ed. Dallas Willard. Read by Dallas Willard. (Running Time: 46800 sec.). 2006. audio compact disk 99.00 (978-0-7861-6339-7(9)) Blckstn Audio.

***Renovation of the Heart: Putting on the Character of Christ.** unabr. ed. Dallas Willard. (ENG.). 2005. 16.98 (978-1-59644-150-7(X), Hovel Audio) christianaud.

Renovation of the Heart: Putting on the Character of Christ. unabr. ed. Dallas Willard. 1 MP3 CD. (Running Time: 12 hrs. 0 mins. 0 sec.). (ENG.). 2005. lp 19.98 (978-1-59644-151-4(8), Hovel Audio) christianaud.

Renovation of the Heart lays a foundation for understanding the ruin and restoration of humanity by discussing human nature and its components, how they operate, and how they are renewed. It outlines the general pattern of personal transformation - not as a formula, but as a systematic process.

Renovation of the Heart: Putting on the Character of Christ. unabr. ed. Dallas Willard. Narrated by Dallas Willard. 10 CDs. (Running Time: 12 hrs. 0 mins. 0 sec.). (ENG.). 2005. audio compact disk 28.98 (978-1-59644-152-1(6), Hovel Audio) christianaud.

Rentfree Guaranteed (CD) Jim Anderson. 2009. audio compact disk 20.00 (978-0-932574-20-6(3)) Brun Pr.

Renunciation. (710) Yoga Res Foun.

Renunciation: The Purpose of Letting Go. Sivananda Radha. 1 cass. 1974. 7.95 (978-0-931454-64-6(6)) Timeless Bks.

Shows the way to overcome possessiveness, self-pity, fantasies & desires.

Renunciation & Contemplation. Thomas Merton. 1 cass. (Running Time: 60 min.). (Origins of Prayer Ser.). 8.95 (AA2073) Credence Commun.

Merton at his richest, sharing the best of monastic contemplation.

Renunciation of Desire & Will. Thomas Merton. 1 cass. (Running Time: 60 min.). (Origins of Prayer Ser.). 8.95 (AA2074) Credence Commun.

Renunciation of Selfish Actions. (703) Yoga Res Foun.

Renunciation of Selfish Actions. Swami Jyotirmayananda. 1 cass. (Running Time: 1 hr.). 1990. 12.99 Yoga Res Foun.

Renunciation of Thought. Swami Amar Jyoti. 1 dolby cass. 1986. 9.95 (J-52) Truth Consciousness.

The calm waters of awareness. Our thought creates the world of matter; the transformation within will create a new world.

Renunciation, Service & Tranquility. Swami Amar Jyoti. 1 cass. 1975. 9.95 (N-15) Truth Consciousness.

A practical discourse on subjects that t[illegible] our lives day to day including renunciation, service, anger, dealing with children.

Reorganization Problems in Depth. 1987. bk. 125.00 incl. book.; 80.00 cass. only.; 45.00 book only. PA Bar Inst.

Repacking Your Bags: Lighten Your Load for the Rest of Your Life. abr. ed. Richard J. Leider & David A. Shapiro. Read by Michael Toms. 2 cass. (Running Time: 3 hrs.). 1996. 17.95 (978-1-57453-027-8(5), 330096) Audio Lit.

Repair to Her Grave. Sarah Graves. Read by Lindsay Ellison. 8 CDs. (Home Repair Is Homicide Mystery Ser.). 2004. audio compact disk 39.95 (978-0-7927-3278-5(2), SLD 677, Chivers Sound Lib) AudioGO.

Repeating God's Name. Swami Amar Jyoti. 1 cass. 1977. 9.95 (H-5) Truth Consciousness.

Incessant Prayer. Taking God's Name with every breath, inherent power awakens, miracles happen, ego dissolves, Reality shines.

Repentance. Derek Prince. 1 cass. (B-2011); 5.95 (055) Derek Prince.

No one ever placed a greater emphasis than Jesus Himself on repentance as the only door to true faith.

Repentance: A Creative, Life-Giving Power. Mother Basilea Schlink. 1 cass. (Running Time: 30 min.). 1985. (0212) Evang Sisterhood Mary.

Reveals an open door for those who are seeking true joy & wish to attain the love of Jesus for their personal lives. Includes " Love for Jesus - A Gift Beyond Compare".

Repentance, True & False. Michael Pearl. (ENG.). 2008. audio compact disk (978-1-934794-24-1(4)) No Greater Joy.

Repenting from Sins of the Fathers. Rick Joyner. 1 cass. (Running Time: 90 mins.). (Church History & the Coming Move of God Ser.: Vol. 5). 2000. 5.00 (RJ11-005) Morning NC.

Church history is brought to life with practical applications & insights into how the enemy uses the same strategy against every new move of God.

Repercussions. Timothy Barcomb. (ENG.). 2008. pap. bk. 45.00 (978-0-9821242-2-2(8)) Plowboy VT.

Repetition of Mantra. (708); (714) Yoga Res Foun.

Repetition of Mantra. Swami Jyotirmayananda. 1 cass. (Running Time: 1 hr.). 1990. 12.99 Yoga Res Foun.

Repetitive Heart, Part IX see Twentieth-Century Poetry in English, No. 9, Recordings of Poets Reading Their Own Poetry

Repetitive Motion Syndrome. (Running Time: 49 hrs. 56 min.). 1989. 11.95 (WA890304, HarperThor) HarpC GBR.

Repetitive Strain Injuries. Linda J. Johnson. 1 cass. (Running Time: 81 min.). 1997. bk. 20.00 (978-1-58111-001-2(4)) Contemporary Medical.
Repetitive strain injury - what is it? How does it occur? Successful treatment & mental/rehab management of RSI.

Repetitive Trauma Injuries in Workers' Compensation Cases. 1995. bk. 99.00 (ACS-968) PA Bar Inst.
A host of repetitive trauma injuries can afflict today's employee, from degenerative arthritis to carpal tunnel syndrome to stress fractures. In such cases, you must be prepared to deal with a complex combination of medical & legal issues. Regardless of which side you represent, you must know what casehandling strategies exist & when to employ them.

Replace. Karen Jean Matsko Hood. 2005. 24.95 (978-1-59210-011-8(2)); audio compact disk 29.95 (978-1-59210-161-0(5)) Whsprng Pine.

***Replacement.** unabr. ed. Brenna Yovanoff. Read by Kevin T. Collins. (Running Time: 9 hrs.). 2010. 24.99 (978-1-4418-8848-8(9), 9781441888488, BAD); 39.97 (978-1-4418-8849-5(7), 9781441888495, BADLE) Brilliance Audio.

***Replacement.** unabr. ed. Brenna Yovanoff. Read by Kevin T. Collins. 1 MP3-CD. (Running Time: 11 hrs.). (YA). 2010. 24.99 (978-1-4418-8846-4(2), 9781441888464, Brilliance MP3); 39.97 (978-1-4418-8847-1(0), 9781441888471, Brlnc Audio MP3 Lib); audio compact disk 24.99 (978-1-4418-8844-0(6), 9781441888440, Bril Audio CD Unabri); audio compact disk 69.97 (978-1-4418-8845-7(4), 9781441888457, BriAudCD Unabrid) Brilliance Audio.

Replacement Audio CD Album with Labels. Created by Candyce Ihnot. 1991. audio compact disk 15.00 (978-1-59621-315-9(9)) Read Naturally.

Replacement Audio CD Album without Labels. Created by Candyce Ihnot. 1991. audio compact disk 10.00 (978-1-59621-317-3(5)) Read Naturally.

Replacement Cassette Album with Labels. Created by Candyce Ihnot. 1991. 14.00 (978-1-59621-314-2(0)) Read Naturally.

Replacement Cassette Album without Labels. Created by Candyce Ihnot. 1991. 9.00 (978-1-59621-316-6(7)) Read Naturally.

***Replacement Cd: Np on Computer Concepts, 8/E, Comprehensive.** 8th ed. (C). 2005. audio compact disk 44.95 (978-1-4188-3939-0(6)) Pub: Course Tech. Dist(s): CENGAGE Learn

Replaces 0965838072 (book) And 0965838056 (CD) see Peer-Reviewed Journal: A Comprehensive Guide Through the Editorial Process - Book & CD

Replay. unabr. ed. Sharon Creech. Read by Christopher Burns. 3 cds. (Running Time: 2.5 hrs). (J). 2005. audio compact disk 17.95 (978-0-06-082074-9(8), HarperChildAud) HarperCollins Pubs.

Replay. unabr. ed. Sharon Creech. 3 CDs. (Running Time: 3 hrs. 45 mins.). 2005. audio compact disk 29.75 (978-1-4193-6674-1(2), C3489); 29.75 (978-1-4193-6669-7(6), 98237) Recorded Bks.
The first to win both the Carnegie and Newbery medals, best-selling author Sharon Creech tells the story of a 12-year-old daydreamer who replays his life as an intrepid young hero. Surrounded by his siblings, Leonardo scarcely makes a ripple in his large, boisterous family until he lands a part in his school play and finds a mysterious trunk in his attic. Soon fantasy and reality converge. But how do the secrets of that attic trunk change Leo's view of his father and himself?.

***Replay.** unabr. ed. Sharon Creech. Read by Christopher Burns. (ENG.). 2005. (978-0-06-089379-8(6)); (978-0-06-089380-4(X)) HarperCollins Pubs.

Replay. unabr. ed. Ken Grimwood. Narrated by William Dufris. (Running Time: 11 hrs. 30 mins. 0 sec.). (ENG.). 2008. audio compact disk 69.99 (978-1-4001-4010-7(2)) Pub: Tantor Media. Dist(s): IngramPubServ

Replay. unabr. ed. Ken Grimwood. Read by William Dufris. (Running Time: 11 hrs. 30 mins. 0 sec.). (ENG.). 2008. audio compact disk 34.99 (978-1-4001-1010-0(6)); audio compact disk 24.99 (978-1-4001-6010-5(3)) Pub: Tantor Media. Dist(s): IngramPubServ

Reply to a Begging Letter see Great American Essays: A Collection

Report Card. unabr. ed. Andrew Clements. Read by Dina Sherman. 2 CDs. (Running Time: 3 hrs. 21 mins.). (YA). 2005. audio compact disk 30.00 (978-0-307-20751-7(X), Listening Lib); 23.00 (978-0-307-20750-0(1), Listening Lib) Random Audio Pubg.
Nora Rose is a genius, who is trying to convince her teachers, parents and principal that tests are a stupid way to measure intelligence.

Report from a UFO Abductee. Arthur Young & Bill Woodard. 1 cass. 9.00 (A0696-90) Sound Photosyn.
An up to date report of one man's current UFO involvement.

Report from Chile: Oscar Ichazo & the School. unabr. ed. Claudio Naranjo. 1 cass. (Running Time: 59 min.). 1970. 11.00 (04204) Big Sur Tapes.
Reports his personal impressions of Sufi master Ichazo at Ichazo's school in the Chilean town of Arica in 1970, & of the mysteries of the extraordinary & ecstatic states of consciousness to which he & others were taken by the school's discipline.

Report from Ground Zero: The Story of the Rescue Efforts at the World Trade Center. unabr. ed. Dennis Smith. Read by Scott Brick. 12 cass. (Running Time: 18 hrs.). 2002. 96.00 (978-0-7366-8436-1(0)); audio compact disk 112.00 (978-0-7366-8443-9(3)) Books on Tape.
September 11, 2001 changed the world forever. For firefighter and writer Dennis Smith, the reality of that change was brought home to him when he volunteered for duty at Ground Zero, the site of the destroyed World Trade Center. For weeks, he combed through the still-smoldering rubble, looking for victims and helping the devastated firemen and policemen mourn their own dead.

Report from Rio. 2 cass. (Running Time: 3 hrs.). 1992. 18.00 set. (OC295-65) Sound Horizons AV.

Report of Ministries in Specialized Settings. 1 cass. (Running Time: 90 min). (Care Cassettes Ser.: Vol. 11, No. 1). 1984. 10.80 Assn Prof Chaplains.

Reporter Series: Jury Charge 1. National Shorthand Reporters Association. 1 cass. 9.00 (CT-33) Natl Ct Report.
Designed for practicing reporters between the RPR & CM speeds. Five-minute selections of jury charge - 5 at 200 wpm, 5 at 210 wpm.

Reporter Series: Jury Charge 2. National Shorthand Reporters Association. 9.00 (CT-34) Natl Ct Report.
Designed for practicing reporters between the RPR & CM speeds. Five-minute selections of jury charge - 5 at 220 wpm. 5 at 230.

Reporter Series: Jury Charge 3. National Shorthand Reporters Association. 9.00 (CT-35) Natl Ct Report.
Designed for practicing reporters between the RPR & CM speeds. Five-minute selections of jury charge - 5 at 230 wpm. 5 at 240.

Reporter Series: Literary-1. National Shorthand Reporters Association. 1 cass. 9.00 (CT_36) Natl Ct Report.
Designed for practicing reporters between the RPR & CM speeds. Five-minute selections of literary dictation - 5 at 170 wpm, 5 at 180 wpm.

Reporter Series: Literary-2. National Shorthand Reporters Association. 1 cass. 9.00 (CT-37) Natl Ct Report.
Designed for practicing reporters between the RPR & CM speeds. Five-minute selections of literary dictation - 5 at 180 wpm, 5 at 190 wpm.

Reporter Series: Literary-3. National Shorthand Reporters Association. 1 cass. 9.00 (CT-38) Natl Ct Report.
Designed for practicing reporters between the RPR & CM speeds. Five-minute selections of literary dictation - 5 at 190 wpm, 5 at 200 wpm.

Reporter Series: Testimony 1. National Shorthand Reporters Association. 1 cass. 9.00 (CT-30) Natl Ct Report.

Reporter Series: Testimony 2. National Shorthand Reporters Association. 1 cass. 9.00 (CT-31) Natl Ct Report.

Reporter Series: Testimony 3. National Shorthand Reporters Association. 1 9.00 (CT-32) Natl Ct Report.
Designed for practicing reporters between the RPR & CM speeds. Five minute selections of testimony dictation - 5 at 230 wpm, 5 at 240 wpm.

Reporter's Life. unabr. collector's ed. Walter Cronkite. Read by Barrett Whitener. 11 cass. (Running Time: 16 hrs. 30 mins.). 1997. 88.00 (978-0-913369-84-5(5), 135443) Books on Tape.

Reporting Live. Lesley Stahl. 2004. 15.95 (978-0-7435-4847-2(7)) Pub: S&S Audio. Dist(s): S and S Inc

Reposition Yourself: Living Life Without Limits. abr. ed. T. D. Jakes. Read by T. D. Jakes. 5 CDs. (Running Time: 6 hrs. 0 mins. 0 sec.). (ENG.). 2007. audio compact disk 29.95 (978-0-7435-6728-2(5)) Pub: S&S Audio. Dist(s): S and S Inc

***Representative Men.** Ralph Waldo Emerson. Read by Anais 9000. 2009. 27.95 (978-1-60112-240-7(3)) Babblebooks.

Representing a Buyer of a "Lemon" Auto. Henry J. Sommer & Dennis H. Replansky. 1 cass. (Running Time: 1 hr.). 1986. 20.00 PA Bar Inst.

Representing an Individual Entering a Nursing Home. 1997. bk. 99.00 (ACS-1421) PA Bar Inst.
According to a recent study, at age 65 an individual has a 43% chance of spending some time in a nursing home his or her life. This likelihood of needing nursing home care increases for persons over age 65. In Pennsylvania, there are 2.4 million people over age 60. Nearly every family has at least one member who is at risk of needing nursing home care. The average cost of nursing home care in Pennsylvania is more than $4,400 per month. Few people have insurance that covers this cost. Most nursing home residents will need help from Medicaid, but a new federal law makes lawyers criminally liable for providing some kinds of planning advice to clients who apply for Medicaid.

Representing Clients in Countywide Reassessments. 1997. bk. 99.00 (ACS-1318); bk. 99.00 (ACS-1318) PA Bar Inst.
Real estate tax reassessments are taking place (or expected to take place) in a number of counties across the Commonwealth over the next few years. Designed for both plaintiffs' & defense attorneys, this includes a discussion of the law in the areas of ordering & conducting a reassessment as well as the mechanics of representing a client throughout the revaluation process.

Representing Divorce Clients in a Bad Economy. 1 cass. 1991. bk. 45.00 (AC-642) PA Bar Inst.

Representing Estate & Trust Beneficiaries & Fiduciaries. 8 cass. (Running Time: 12 hrs.). 1999. 345.00 Set; incl. study guide 298p. (AD84) Am Law Inst.
Advanced course examines specific areas in which attorneys are shown new techniques, & explores new areas of litigation, such as class action suits.

Representing Justice: Stories of Law & Literature. Instructed by Susan Sage Heinzelman. 12 cass. 54.95 (978-1-59803-140-9(6)); audio compact disk 69.95 (978-1-59803-142-3(2)) Teaching Co.

Representing Long-Term Care Providers. 1998. bk. 99.00 (ACS-2131) PA Bar Inst.
As someone who represents long-term care providers, you know that the long-term care continuum has expanded dramatically in recent years through nursing homes, assisted living facilities, continuing care retirement communities, & home health agencies. In this you explore the legal topics affecting your long-term care clients' businesses.

Representing Long Term Care Providers in Pennsylvania. 1986. bk. 140.00; 85.00 PA Bar Inst.

Representing Parties in the Sale of a Business. Read by James Topinka et al. (Running Time: 5 hrs. 30 min.). 1991. 97.00 Incl. 292p. tape materials. (BU-54143) Cont Ed Bar-CA.

Representing Residential Landlords & Tenants. 1987. bk. 80.00; 45.00 PA Bar Inst.

Representing Residential Landlords & Tenants. 1998. bk. 99.00 (ACS-1411); bk. 99.00 (ACS-1411) PA Bar Inst.
Gives you the tools to be a powerful advocate for your landlord or tenant client. The authors give solutions to problems. They focus on lease preparation & negotiation from both the landlord's & tenant's perspectives, landlord's remedies, & tenant's defenses & remedies.

Representing Start-Up & High-Tech Companies. 1985. bk. 70.00 incl. book.; 45.00 cass. only.; 25.00 book only. PA Bar Inst.

Representing Tax-Exempt Organizations. 1985. bk. 55.00 incl. book.; 35.00 cass. only.; 20.00 book only. PA Bar Inst.

Representing Tax-Exempt Organizations. 1990. 45.00 (AC-592) PA Bar Inst.

Representing the Borrower in a Real Property Foreclosure or Workout. Read by Louis Weller et al. (Running Time: 3 hrs. 30 min.). 1992. 115.00 Incl. 125p. tape materials. (RE-55232) Cont Ed Bar-CA.
Experienced attorneys provide an overview of the real estate foreclosure & workout process, from the perspective of borrower's counsel. They cover injunctions; lender liability & anti-deficiency issues; judicial & trustee sale foreclosures; loan workouts (restructuring alternatives); the effect of bankruptcy filings; & tax consequences.

Representing the Discharged Employee. Contrib. by Margaret M. Hayden & Craig H. Livingston. (Running Time: 4 hrs.). 1983. 80.00 incl. program handbook. NJ Inst CLE.
Previews the current status of the employment at will doctrine, analyzes all federal & state law governing the employment relationship, pinpoints contracted remedies, outlines all judicial & administrative remedies.

Representing the Elderly Client. Contrib. by Barbara J. Collins & William A. Dombi. 6 cass. (Running Time: 7 hrs. 30 min.). 1990. 75.00 set. (T7-9289) PLI.

Representing the Faces of the Future. Don C. Keenan. (ENG.). 2007. audio compact disk 185.00 (978-0-9743248-8-3(4)) Trial Guides.

Representing the Growing Business: Tax, Corporate, Securities & Accounting Issues. 12 cass. (Running Time: 17 hrs. 30 min.). 1999. stu. ed. 345.00 (MD59) Am Law Inst.
Enables practitioners to acquire a feel for the broad range of tax, business, & accounting problems that affect smaller & medium-sized businesses & offers creative solutions, planning strategies, & techniques for dealing with every stage of the company's growth.

Representing the Liquor Licensee. 1988. bk. 105.00 incl. book.; 55.00 cass. only.; 50.00 book only. PA Bar Inst.

Representing Your Audited Client Before the IRS. Richard M. Feldheim. 3 cass. bk. 159.00 set, incl. textbk. & quizzer. (CPE4350) Bisk Educ.
Get helpful advice on interviewing audited clients, gathering & presenting information, appealing adverse audits to the Appeals Division, & litigating tax controversies.

Reprinted Pieces. Charles Dickens. Read by Anais 9000. 2009. 27.95 (978-1-60112-210-0(1)) Babblebooks.

Reproducing Our Ministry. Rick Joyner. 1 cass. (Running Time: 90 mins.). (Vision Ser.: Vol. 7). 2000. 5.00 (RJ16-007) Morning NC.
This tape series will help to impart new vision or restore lost vision in the church.

Reproduction Is the Flaw of Love. unabr. ed. Lauren Grodstein. Read by Ernie Schwartz. (Running Time: 21600 sec.). 2006. audio compact disk 63.95 (978-1-74093-657-6(4)) Pub: Bolinda Pubng AUS. Dist(s): Bolinda Pub Inc

Reprogramming the Overweight Mind. Kelly T. Burris. Read by Kelly T. Burris. 1 CD. (Running Time: 55 mins.). 2000. pap. bk. 19.95 (978-0-9644241-0-4(X)) Illumine Studios.

Reproof Deserved see Sir John Betjeman Reading His Poetry

Reptile Room: Or, Murder! Lemony Snicket, pseud. Read by Curry Tim. (Series of Unfortunate Events Ser.: Bk. 2). (J). 2006. 22.00 (978-0-06-085269-6(0), HarperChildAud) HarperCollins Pubs.

Reptile Room: Or, Murder! unabr. ed. Lemony Snicket, pseud. Read by Tim Curry. 3 CDs. (Running Time: 3 hrs. 11 mins.). (Series of Unfortunate Events Ser.: Bk. 2). (ENG.). (J). (gr. 5-8). 2003. audio compact disk 14.99 (978-0-8072-1991-1(6), Listening Lib) Pub: Random Audio Pubg. Dist(s): Random

Reptile Room: Or, Murder!, Vol. 2. unabr. ed. Lemony Snicket, pseud. Read by Tim Curry. 3 CDs. (Running Time: 3 hrs. 11 mins.). (Series of Unfortunate Events Ser.: Bk. 2). (J). (gr. 4-7). 2004. audio compact disk 30.00 (978-0-8072-1711-5(5), S YA 284 CD, Listening Lib); 23.00 (978-0-8072-8868-9(3), LL0218, Listening Lib) Random Audio Pubg.
After narrowly escaping the clutches of the dastardly Count Olaf, who tried to make away with their fortune, the three Baudelaire orphans are taken in by a kindly herpetologist with whom they live happily for an all-too-brief time.

Reptiles. Bev Harvey. 1 cass. Dramatization. (J). pap. bk. 6.95 (978-0-86545-101-8(X)) Spizzirri.
Scientific facts about turtles, snakes & lizards.

Reptiles of all Kinds. Bobbie Kalman & Kelley MacAulay. (What Kind of Animal Is It? Ser.). (ENG.). (J). 2005. audio compact disk 10.00 (978-0-7787-7598-0(4)) CrabtreePubCo CAN.

Republic. Plato. Read by Bruce Alexander. 4 cass. (Running Time: 5 hrs.). 2000. 22.98 (978-962-634-695-2(7), NA419514); audio compact disk 28.98 (978-962-634-195-7(5), NA419512, Naxos AudioBooks) Naxos.
Tackles the big issues of the state and the individual: how the state should be ruled, and by whom; and the way the individual should lead his life - and why.

Republic. unabr. ed. Plato. Read by Pat Bottino. Tr. by B. Jowett. 9 cass. (Running Time: 13 hrs.). 1995. 62.95 (978-0-7861-0712-4(X), 1589) Blckstn Audio.
Perhaps the greatest single treatise written on political philosophy, it has influenced strongly the thought of Western man concerning the questions of justice, rule, obedience & the good life. This is true whether one agrees with Plato's answer or, if dissatisfied, seeks a different solution. The work is also undoubtedly the best introduction to Plato's philosophy in general. Not only does it contain his ideas on the state & man, but also his famous theory of forms, his theory of knowledge & his view on the role of music & poetry in society.

***Republic.** unabr. ed. Plato. Read by Pat Bottino. (Running Time: 12 hrs. 30 mins.). 2010. 29.95 (978-1-4417-4072-4(4)); audio compact disk 105.00 (978-1-4417-4069-4(4)) Blckstn Audio.

***Republic.** unabr. ed. null Plato. Narrated by James Langton. (Running Time: 13 hrs. 30 mins.). 2010. 18.99 (978-1-4001-8616-7(1)); 29.99 (978-1-4001-6616-9(0)); audio compact disk 79.99 (978-1-4001-4616-1(X)); audio compact disk 39.99 (978-1-4001-1616-4(3)) Pub: Tantor Media. Dist(s): IngramPubServ

Republic & Its Inheritance. 1 cass. (Running Time: 30 min.). (Gilbert Highet Ser.). 11.95 (23305) J Norton Pubs.
Some of the ideals that inspired the Founding Fathers & the experiences of immigrants to America over the last hundred years, as told by themselves. Includes "The Immigrants".

Republic & Its Inheritance & the Immigrants (audio CD) Gilbert Highet. (ENG.). 2006. audio compact disk 9.95 (978-1-57970-439-1(5), Audio-For) J Norton Pubs.

Republican Gomorrah: Inside the Movement That Shattered the Party. unabr. ed. Max Blumenthal. Read by William Hughes. (Running Time: 11 hrs.). 2009. audio compact disk 34.95 (978-1-4417-2843-2(0)) Blckstn Audio.

Republican Gomorrah: Inside the Movement That Shattered the Party. unabr. ed. Max Blumenthal. Read by William Hughes. (Running Time: 11 hrs. 0 mins.). 2009. 29.95 (978-1-4417-2844-9(9)); 65.95 (978-1-4417-2840-1(6)); audio compact disk 100.00 (978-1-4417-2841-8(4)) Blckstn Audio.

Republican Noise Machine: Right-Wing Media & How It Corrupts Democracy. unabr. ed. David Brock. Read by Michael Kramer. 10 cass. (Running Time: 15 hrs.). 2004. 81.00 (978-0-7366-9770-5(5)) Books on Tape.
A former-right wing journalist David Brock argues that conservative media has skewed American politics noticeably to the right.

Republican Party Reptile: The Confessions, Adventures, Essays & (Other) Outrages of P. J. O'Rourke. unabr. ed. P. J. O'Rourke. Read by Christopher Hurt. 5 cass. (Running Time: 7 hrs.). 1992. 39.95 (978-0-7861-0288-4(8), 1253) Blckstn Audio.
What is the Republican Party Reptile? It is neoconservatism with its pants down around its ankles, the Rehnquist Supreme Court on drugs, a disco Hobbes living without shame or federally mandated safety regulations. The Republican Party Reptile supports a strong defense policy but sees no reason to conduct it whilst sober. The RPR believes in minimum governmental interference in private affairs - unless the government brings over extra girls & some ice. In short, the RPR is the new label that our political spectrum has been crying out for - the conservative with a sense of humor.

Reputations Ten Years After. unabr. collector's ed. Basil H. Liddell-Hart. Read by Bill Kelsey. 8 cass. (Running Time: 8 hrs.). 1988. 48.00 (978-0-7366-1296-8(3), 2203) Books on Tape.
Presents an examination of ten leading figures of W. W. I, "the war to end all wars," ten years after the armistice. The author revisits generals on both sides, including Joffre, Foch, Petain, Ludendorff & Pershing.

Requiem at the Refuge. Sister Carol Anne O'Marie. Narrated by Marguerite Gavin. (Running Time: 8 hrs. 30 mins.). (C). 2002. 27.95 (978-1-59912-581-7(1)) Iofy Corp.

Requiem at the Refuge. unabr. ed. Carol Anne O'Marie. Read by Marguerite Gavin. 7 CDs. (Running Time: 8 hrs. 30 mins.). 2002. audio compact disk 56.00 (978-0-7861-9390-5(5), 3020); 44.95 (978-0-7861-2361-2(3), 3020) Blckstn Audio.
In Sister Mary Helen's latest venture as an inadvertent detective, the elderly nun must make do without her even more elderly sidekick, Sister Eileen. Eileen has gone back to Ireland to be with her dying sister, so Mary Helen has no one with whom to share her fears when the head of St. Francis College dies suddenly and is replaced by the coldly efficient Sister Patricia. Surely, Mary Helen feels, she will be swept aside as too old in the "clean sweep" that Sister Patricia is famous for in the order. To her rescue comes young Sister Anne, who runs the Refuge. When a woman from the Refuge is found murdered in the alley, Sister Mary Helen goes to work searching for clues.

Requiem for a Dream. Hubert Selby, Jr.. Read by Hubert Selby, Jr. 1 cass. (Running Time: 30 min.). 8.95 (AMF-14) Am Audio Prose.
A short interview with Selby, & he reads from his novel "Requiem for a Dream".

Requiem for a Mezzo. Carola Dunn. Read by Bernadette Dunne. (Running Time: 23400 sec.). (Daisy Dalrymple Mystery Ser.). 2006. 44.95 (978-0-7861-4596-6(X)); audio compact disk 55.00 (978-0-7861-6992-4(3)) Blckstn Audio.

Requiem for a Mezzo. unabr. ed. Carola Dunn. Read by Bernadette Dunne. (Running Time: 23400 sec.). (Daisy Dalrymple Mystery Ser.). 2006. audio compact disk 29.95 (978-0-7861-7508-6(7)) Blckstn Audio.

Requiem for an Assassin. Barry Eisler. Read by Scott Brick. (Running Time: 13 hrs.). Bk. 6. (ENG.). (gr. 8). 2007. audio compact disk 29.95 (978-0-14-314203-4(8), PengAudBks) Penguin Grp USA.

Requiem for Moses. William X. Kienzle. (Father Koesler Mystery Ser.: No. 18). 2001. 56.00 (978-0-7366-6844-6(6)) Books on Tape.

Requiem for the Plantagenet Kings see Poetry of Geoffrey

Requiem Mass: And Office for the Dead. Monks of Solesmes Staff. 1 CD. 1985. audio compact disk 16.95 (978-1-55725-104-6(5), 930-073) Paraclete MA.

Requiem Shark. unabr. ed. Nicholas Griffin. Narrated by Patrick Tull. 10 cass. (Running Time: 13 hrs. 45 mins.). 2001. 88.00 (978-0-7887-5004-5(6), 96368E7) Recorded Bks.
The apprentice to slaver turned pirate Bartholomew Roberts, young Williams is charged with writing the biography of the captain & entertaining the crew with his fiddle playing. Their adventures are in search of a mythical ship filled with gold.

Required Reading & Other Dangerous Subjects. unabr. ed. Amy Tan. Read by Amy Tan. Perf. by David Phillips. Prod. by Kathi Kamen Goldmark. 1 cass. (Running Time: 48 min.). Dramatization. 1996. 7.99 (978-1-893803-02-2(3), DQYDJ-0004) Dont Quit.
Writing & the pitfalls of being placed on the best-seller lists.

Requirements for Greatness: Justice, Mercy & Humility. unabr. ed. Lori Wilke. Read by Tom Wilke. 2 cass. (Running Time: 3 hrs.). 1998. 12.98 Set. (978-1-891916-04-5(1)) Spirit To Spirit.
Learn the three requirements to a life of greatness in God's kingdom.

Rescripting the Child Within. Eldon Taylor. 1 cass. (Running Time: 62 min.). (Inner Talk Ser.). 16.95 incl. script. (978-1-55978-135-0(1), 5350C) Progress Aware Res.
Soundtrack - Musical Themes with underlying subliminal affirmations.

Rescripting the Child Within: Babbling Brook. Eldon Taylor. 1 cass. 16.95 (978-1-55978-481-8(4), 5350F) Progress Aware Res.

Rescripting the Child Within: Harmonies. Eldon Taylor. Read by Eldon Taylor. Ed. by Leslie Brice. 1 cass. (Running Time: 1 hr.). 1992. 16.95 (978-1-56705-347-0(5)) Gateways Inst.
Self improvement.

Rescripting the Child Within: Ocean. Eldon Taylor. Read by Eldon Taylor. Ed. by Leslie Brice. 1 cass. (Running Time: 1 hr.). 1992. 16.95 (978-1-56705-348-7(3)) Gateways Inst.

Rescue see Gathering of Great Poetry for Children

Rescue see Tom McGuane Reads Three Untitled Short Stories from Work in Progress

Rescue. Joseph Conrad. Read by Anais 9000. 2008. 27.95 (978-1-60112-151-6(2)) Babblebooks.

Rescue. Gordon Korman. (Kidnapped Ser.). (ENG.). (J). (gr. 4-7). 2010. audio compact disk 39.95 (978-0-545-02750-2(0)) Scholastic Inc.

Rescue. Kathryn Lasky. Read by Pamela Garelick. (Running Time: 18000 sec.). (Guardians of Ga'Hoole Ser.: Bk. 3). (J). (gr. 3-7). 2007. 34.95 (978-1-4332-0107-3(0)); audio compact disk 36.00 (978-1-4332-0108-0(9)) Blckstn Audio.

***Rescue.** Anita Shreve. Read by Dennis Holland. (Running Time: 9 hrs.). (ENG.). 2011. audio compact disk & audio compact disk 19.98 (978-1-60941-372-9(5)) Pub: Hachet Audio. Dist(s): HachBkGrp

Rescue. abr. ed. Nicholas Sparks. Read by Mary Beth Hurt & John Bedford Lloyd. 5 CDs. (Running Time: 6 hrs.). Date not set. audio compact disk 14.98 (978-1-59483-108-9(4)) Hachet Audio.

Rescue. abr. ed. Nicholas Sparks. Read by Mary Beth Hurt & John Bedford Lloyd. (ENG.). 2005. 14.98 (978-1-59483-455-4(5)) Pub: Hachet Audio. Dist(s): HachBkGrp

Rescue. collector's ed. Nicholas Sparks. Read by Johnny Heller. 7 cass. (Running Time: 10 hrs. 30 min.). 2000. 35.95 (978-0-7366-5658-0(8)) Books on Tape.

***Rescue.** unabr. ed. Kathryn Lasky. Read by Pamela Garelick. (Running Time: 5 hrs.). (Guardians of Ga'Hoole Ser.: Bk. 3). 2010. audio compact disk 19.95 (978-1-4417-5540-7(3)) Blckstn Audio.

Rescue. unabr. ed. Kathryn Lasky. Read by Pamela Garelick. (Running Time: 5 hrs.). (Guardians of Ga'Hoole Ser.: Bk. 3). (gr. 3-7). 2010. audio compact disk 19.95 (978-1-4332-0109-7(7)) Blckstn Audio.

***Rescue.** unabr. ed. Anita Shreve. Read by Dennis Holland. (Running Time: 7 hrs. 30 mins.). (ENG.). 2010. 24.98 (978-1-60788-673-0(1)); audio compact disk 29.98 (978-1-60788-672-3(3)) Pub: Hachet Audio. Dist(s): HachBkGrp

Rescue. unabr. ed. Nicholas Sparks. Read by Johnny Heller. 8 vols. (Running Time: 12 hrs.). 2000. bk. 69.95 (978-0-7927-2441-4(0), CSL 330, Chivers Sound Lib); audio compact disk 94.95 (978-0-7927-9980-1(1), SLD 031, Chivers Sound Lib) AudioGO.
When confronted by raging fires or deadly accidents, volunteer fireman Taylor McAden feels compelled to take terrifying risks. But there is one leap of faith Taylor can't bring himself to make: He can't fall in love.

Rescue. unabr. ed. Nicholas Sparks. Read by Johnny Heller. (ENG.). 2005. 16.98 (978-1-59483-454-7(7)) Pub: Hachet Audio. Dist(s): HachBkGrp

Rescue. unabr. ed. Nicholas Sparks. Read by Mary Beth Hurt & John Bedford Lloyd. (Running Time: 10 hrs.). (ENG.). 2009. 70.98 (978-1-60788-102-5(0)) Pub: Hachet Audio. Dist(s): HachBkGrp

Rescue: A Romance of the Shallows. unabr. collector's ed. Joseph Conrad. Read by Wolfram Kandinsky. 12 cass. (Running Time: 18 hrs.). 1992. 96.00 (978-0-7366-2263-9(2), 3051) Books on Tape.
Civil War rages between the native tribes of the Malay straits. Captain Tim Wingard sides with the Rajah Hassim. But as is the case with so much in the East, nothing is quite straightforward & events unfold by indirection.

Rescue: Stories of Survival from Land & Sea. unabr. ed. Short Stories. Pete Sinclair et al. Ed. by Clint Willis. 4 cass. (Running Time: 6 hrs.). (Adrenaline Ser.). 2001. 24.95 (978-1-885408-58-7(7), LL050) Listen & Live.
A team of professional readers bring to life some amazing true adventures of people plucked from danger in a variety of settings. Includes stories about an accident-plagued canoe trip, mountain-climbing stories & other scenes of out-door action & emotion.

Rescue Dogs: A Basic Guide to These Canine Pets. Karen Jean Matsko Hood. 2006. 29.95 (978-1-59808-834-2(3)); audio compact disk 24.95 (978-1-59808-835-9(1)) Whsprng Pine.

Rescue Ink: How Ten Guys Saved Countless Dogs & Cats, Twelve Horses, Five Pigs, One Duck, & a Few Turtles. unabr. ed. Denise Flaim. (Running Time: 1 hr. 0 mins.). 2009. 29.95 (978-1-4332-9688-8(8)) Blckstn Audio.

Rescue Ink: How Ten Guys Saved Countless Dogs & Cats, Twelve Horses, Five Pigs, One Duck, & a Few Turtles. unabr. ed. Rescue Ink. (Running Time: 9.5 hrs. NaN mins.). (ENG.). 2009. audio compact disk & audio compact disk 34.95 (978-1-4332-9687-1(X)) Blckstn Audio.

Rescue Ink: How Ten Guys Saved Countless Dogs & Cats, Twelve Horses, Five Pigs, One Duck, & a Few Turtles. unabr. ed. Denise Rescue Ink with Flaim. (Running Time: 7 hrs. 0 mins.). (ENG.). 2009. 59.95 (978-1-4332-9684-0(5)); audio compact disk 90.00 (978-1-4332-9685-7(3)) Blckstn Audio.

Rescue Josh McGuire, unabr. ed. Ben Mikaelsen. Narrated by Ed Sala. 6 cass. (Running Time: 8 hrs.). (J). (gr. 4). 1997. 51.00 (978-0-7887-0559-5(8), 94735E7) Recorded Bks.
Thirteen-year-old Josh McGuire runs away with an orphaned bear cub, vowing to protect it until hunting laws are changed. But the Montana wilderness is a dangerous place & saving the cub's life may cost Josh his own.

Rescue: Live Worship. Contrib. by Newsong. Prod. by Paul Mills. Contrib. by Don Moen & Chris Thomason. 2005. audio compact disk 13.99 (978-5-559-01500-2(8)) Pt of Grace Ent.

Rescue Swine One-One: True Stories & Poems about Life at an Animal Sanctuary. abr. ed. Steve Lawrence. Read by Steve Lawrence. Ed. by Jay Wrolstad & Emily Johnson. 1 cass. (Running Time: 1 hr.). (J). (gr. 2-9). 1996. 7.95 (978-0-9650379-1-4(6)) Msty Valley NY.

Rescue Your Financial Life: 11 Things You Can Do Now to Get Back on Track. Kimberly Lankford. 4 cass. (Running Time: 6 hrs.). 2004. 24.00 (978-1-932378-40-5(5)); audio compact disk 28.00 (978-1-932378-41-2(3)) Pub: A Media Intl. Dist(s): Natl Bk Netwk

Rescue Your Love Life: Changing Those Dumb Attitudes & Behaviors That Will Sink Your Marriage. Henry Cloud & John Townsend. Read by Henry Cloud & John Townsend. (Running Time: 27000 sec.). 2005. audio compact disk 55.00 (978-0-7861-7579-6(6)) Blckstn Audio.

Rescue Your Love Life: Changing Those Dumb Attitudes & Behaviors That Will Sink Your Marriage. Henry Cloud & John Townsend. 2005. 19.99 (978-1-59859-006-7(5)) Oasis Audio.

Rescue Your Love Life: Changing Those Dumb Attitudes & Behaviors That Will Sink Your Marriage. unabr. ed. Henry Cloud & John Townsend. Narrated by Henry Cloud & John Townsend. (ENG.). 2005. 16.09 (978-1-60814-361-0(9)); audio compact disk 22.99 (978-1-59859-005-0(7)) Oasis Audio.

Rescued. John Bevere & Mark Andrew Olsen. Read by Roma Downey et al. (Running Time: 2 hrs.). 2007. audio compact disk 19.99 (978-0-7642-0457-9(2)) Pub: Bethany Hse. Dist(s): Baker Pub Grp

Rescued see Bible in Living Sound: Life and Times of the Old Testament; Life and Times of Jesus; Life and Times of Paul

Rescued Audio Theatre. John Bevere. 2007. audio compact disk 19.99 (978-1-933185-09-5(0)) Messengr Intl.

Rescuers, unabr. ed. Margery Sharp. Narrated by Davina Porter. 3 cass. (Running Time: 3 hrs. 30 mins.). (Rescuers Ser.). (gr. 2 up). 1995. 27.00 (978-0-7887-0208-2(4), 94433E7) Recorded Bks.
A young poet is cruelly locked away in the dungeons of the forbidding Black Castle & the Prisoners Aid Society, a venerable mouse institution dedicated to helping the captives of the world is sending a team to rescue him. Brings the lively adventures of Miss Bianca, Nils the Sailor Mouse & Bernard to a new generation of children.

Rescuers. unabr. ed. Margery Sharp. Narrated by Davina Porter. 3 CDs. (Running Time: 3 hrs. 30 mins.). (Rescuers Ser.). (gr. 2 up). 2000. audio compact disk 27.00 (978-0-7887-4211-8(6), C1150E7) Recorded Bks.

***Rescuing Seneca Crane.** unabr. ed. Susan Runholt. Narrated by Krista Sutton. 6 CDs. (Running Time: 6 hrs. 35 mins.). (YA). (gr. 5-8). 2009. audio compact disk 50.00 (978-0-307-57977-5(8), Listening Lib) Pub: Random Audio Pubg. Dist(s): Random

Research: Final Aspects. Gary Duncan. 1 cass. 8.95 (103) Am Fed Astrologers.
An AFA Convention workshop tape.

Research & Statistics Update. ACT Staff. 1 cass. 8.95 (484) Am Fed Astrologers.
What works, what doesn't?.

Research Challenge: Beat Computers. J. Urban-Lurian & M. Urban-Lurian. 1 cass. 8.95 (353) Am Fed Astrologers.
Alcoholism research.

Research for Truth. Kyriacos Markides. 1 cass. 1993. 9.00 (OC321-69) Sound Horizons AV.

Research on the Internet Video with Teacher's Manual. Holt, Rinehart and Winston Staff. 1998. 62.20 (978-0-03-052243-7(9)) Holt McDoug.

Researching & Writing the Historical Novel. Brenda Wilbee. 1 cass. (Running Time: 45 min.). (How to Write Best-Selling Romance Ser.: Tape 5). 1988. 7.95 (978-0-943777-12-2(7)) byBrenda.
Explains how to write historical novels.

Researching Legislative Histories: Capitol Learning Audio Course. Robert Gee. Prod. by TheCapitol.Net. (ENG.). 2008. 47.00 (978-1-58733-082-7(2)); 47.00 (978-1-58733-080-3(6)) TheCapitol.

Researching Legislative Histories: Finding Legislative Intent in Bills & Committee & Conference Reports. Ed. by TheCapitol.Net. 2006. 107.00 (978-1-58733-033-9(4)) TheCapitol.

Researching Pennsylvania Statutes. 1 cass. 1987. 20.00 PA Bar Inst.

Resentment & Forgiveness. John Bradshaw. (Running Time: 21600 sec.). 2008. audio compact disk 175.00 (978-1-57388-256-9(9)) J B Media.

Reservation Road. abr. ed. John Burnham Schwartz. Read by Stanley Tucci et al. (Running Time: 10800 sec.). (ENG.). 2007. audio compact disk 14.99 (978-0-7393-5812-2(X), Random AudioBks) Pub: Random Audio Pubg. Dist(s): Random

Reservations Required. John MacArthur, Jr. 2 cass. 7.95 (22-25, HarperThor) HarpC GBR.

***Reserve.** unabr. ed. Russell Banks. Read by Tom Stechschulte. (ENG.). 2008. (978-0-06-162938-9(3)); (978-0-06-162940-2(5)) HarperCollins Pubs.

Reserve. unabr. ed. Russell Banks. Read by Tom Stechschulte. (Running Time: 34200 sec.). 2008. audio compact disk 39.95 (978-0-06-145751-7(5), Harper Audio) HarperCollins Pubs.

Reset. abr. ed. Robert A. Monroe. Read by Robert A. Monroe. (Running Time: 30 min.). (Human Plus Ser.). 1989. 14.95 (978-1-56102-029-4(X)) Inter Indus.
Immediately restore high energy levels.

Reset: How This Crisis Can Restore Our Values & Renew America. unabr. ed. Kurt Andersen. Read by Kurt Andersen. (ENG.). 2009. audio compact disk 15.00 (978-0-307-70500-6(5), Random AudioBks) Pub: Random Audio Pubg. Dist(s): Random

***Reset: Iran, Turkey, & America's Future.** unabr. ed. Stephen Kinzer. (Running Time: 10 hrs. 0 mins.). 2010. 34.99 (978-1-4001-9701-9(5)); 16.99 (978-1-4001-8701-0(X)) Tantor Media.

***Reset: Iran, Turkey, & America's Future.** unabr. ed. Stephen Kinzer. Narrated by Alan Sklar. (Running Time: 9 hrs. 0 mins. 0 sec.). 2010. 24.99 (978-1-4001-6701-2(9)); audio compact disk 69.99 (978-1-4001-4701-4(8)); audio compact disk 34.99 (978-1-4001-1701-7(1)) Pub: Tantor Media. Dist(s): IngramPubServ

Reshith Binah: A Hebrew Primer. Sidney M. Fish. 1 cass. 1976. 7.00 (978-0-685-42013-3(2)) Bloch.

Resident Alien. unabr. collector's ed. Ian Whitcomb. Read by Ian Whitcomb. 9 cass. (Running Time: 13 hrs. 30 min.). 1991. 72.00 (978-0-7366-1902-8(X), 2728) Books on Tape.
Resident Alien, a semi-autobiographical novel, is the work of Ian Whitcomb, an Englishman educated at Trinity College, Dublin, & a former pop star turned writer & entertainer who has spent the last 25 years in Los Angeles. Combining an affectionate, impressionistic evocation-cum-history of his chosen city with a lurid & funny account of his efforts to set up house, Whitcomb details the tribulations endured at the hands of assorted lodgers, spongers, over-sexed women & dubious-sounding friends.

Resident Patient see Memoirs of Sherlock Holmes

Residential Property Management. Ed. by Socrates Media Editors. 2005. audio compact disk 29.95 (978-1-59546-204-6(X)) Pub: Socrates Med LLC. Dist(s): Midpt Trade

Residential Real Estate. 1986. bk. 65.00; 35.00 PA Bar Inst.

Residential Real Estate Documents. 1998. bk. 99.00 (ACS-1439) PA Bar Inst.
This is a basic, nuts & bolts real estate book that focuses on helping attorneys better understand the various documents involved in residential real estate transactions.

Residential Real Estate Documents. 1999. bk. 99.00 (ACS-2225) PA Bar Inst.
The experienced authors bring you up-to-date on the fundamental documents & procedures, & provide with plenty of practice tips & helpful information.

Residential Transactions. Joseph E. Goeters. 2002. audio compact disk 20.95 (978-0-324-14380-5(X)) Pub: South-West. Dist(s): CENGAGE Learn

Residential Transactions: A Guide to Real Estate. Joseph E. Goeters. 2002. audio compact disk 7.95 (978-0-324-18868-4(4)) South-West.

Residential Wood-Framed Housing in France: A Strategic Reference 2006. Compiled by Icon Group International, Inc. Staff. 2007. ring bd. 195.00 (978-0-497-35958-4(8)) Icon Grp.

Residing unto Divine Mother. Swami Amar Jyoti. 1 cass. 1991. 9.95 (K-136) Truth Consciousness.
Divine Mother is all this. She is pervadedness. She wills & becomes. Right conviction & focus on Oneness.

***Residue: The Distinguishing Factor in Christianity.** Lynne Hammond. 2010. audio compact disk 6.00 (978-1-57399-468-2(5)) Mac Hammond.

Resilience: Program from the Award Winning Public Radio Series. Hosted by John Goodwin. Comment by John Hockenberyy. 1 CD. (Running Time: 1 hr.). 2005. audio compact disk 21.95 (978-1-932479-87-4(2)) Lichtenstein Creat.
How is it that adversity can defeat some people, and bring out the best in others? In the shadow of the recent terrorist attacks on the United States, many Americans have risen to new challenge with courage and grace. This show explores what lets some people not only "bounce back" from disaster, but even gain in strength through adversity. The show includes interviews with psychologist Dr. Al Siebert, author of The Survivor Personality; and Dr. Karen Reivich, Co-Director of the Penn Resiliency Project at the University of Pennsylvania. One of the world's best known neuro-biologists, Dr. Robert Sapolsky, discusses how stress harms us... and helps us. And storyteller Laura Simms shares an Arabic story that reveals how even in grief we are not alone. Plus, John Hockenberry contributes a moving, insightful commentary on volcanos, SCUD missiles, terrorism, and resiliency.

Resilience: Reflections on the Burdens & Gifts of Facing Life's Adversities. unabr. ed. Elizabeth Edwards. Read by Elizabeth Edwards. (ENG.). 2009. audio compact disk 25.00 (978-0-307-57719-1(8), Random AudioBks) Pub: Random Audio Pubg. Dist(s): Random

Resist Peer Pressure! 1 cass. (Educational Ser.). 12.98 (85) Randolph Tapes.
A helpful aid in resisting CO-DEPENDENCY. Also strengthens your resolve to "Say No" when "NO" is the right answer. This tape works for all ages!.

Resist the Devil: Draw Near to God. Read by Mother Basilea Schlink. 1 cass. (Running Time: 30 min.). 1985. (0214) Evang Sisterhood Mary.
Explores the consequences of sin & the way out & a biblical answer to this exciting question. Includes: "Who Is Ready to Come to the Marriage Supper of the Lamb?".

***Resistance.** John Kucak. (ENG.). (YA). 2009. 4.99 (978-1-936076-09-3(8)) Innovo Pub.

Resistance. unabr. collector's ed. Anita Shreve. Read by Frances Cassidy. 6 cass. (Running Time: 9 hrs.). 1995. 48.00 (978-0-7366-3121-1(6), 3797) Books on Tape.
December, 1943 - the last war-time winter. In a small village, a young Belgian woman & an American lieutenant meet by chance. She's locked into a joyless marriage, works for the resistance, waits for the war to end.

Resistance: A Frenchwoman's Journal of the War. unabr. ed. Agnes Humbert & Barbara Mellor. Read by Joyce Bean. 10 CDs. (Running Time: 12 hrs. 0 mins. 0 sec.). (ENG.). 2008. audio compact disk 34.99 (978-1-4001-0833-6(0)); audio compact disk 24.99 (978-1-4001-5833-1(8)); audio compact disk 69.99 (978-1-4001-3833-3(7)) Pub: Tantor Media. Dist(s): IngramPubServ

Resistance: The Warsaw Ghetto Uprising. unabr. ed. Israel Gutman. Read by Michael Prichard. 8 cass. (Running Time: 12 hrs.). 1995. 64.00 (978-0-7366-3107-5(0), 3783) Books on Tape.
Hundreds of dwellers won't crumble, their spirit expressed in their slogan: All are ready to die as human beings.

Resistance, Ses Chants, Ses Poetes. Poems. 2 CDs. (FRE.). 1995. audio compact disk 38.95 (1359-AD) Olivia & Hill.
Written with blood & tears, these songs & poems of the Resistance are very moving: "Le chant des Marais," "Le chant des partisans" & many more of the songs composed by some of France's leading poets.

***Resisters.** unabr. ed. Eric Nylund. (Running Time: 6 hrs.). (Resisters Ser.). 2011. 39.97 (978-1-61106-961-7(0), 9781611069617, BADLE); 19.99 (978-1-61106-958-7(0), 9781611069587, Brilliance MP3); 39.97 (978-1-61106-959-4(9), 9781611069594, Brlnc Audio MP3 Lib); audio compact disk 19.99 (978-1-61106-956-3(4), 9781611069563, Bril Audio CD Unabri); audio compact disk 59.97 (978-1-61106-957-0(2), 9781611069570, BriAudCD Unabrid) Brilliance Audio.

Resisting Allergies. Matthew Manning. Music by Nick Arkle. 1 cass. 11.95 (MM-109) White Dove NM.
Resisting Allergies explores the links between stress & development of allergies. It explains how the allergy sufferer often craves the very thing that causes them to react. Side Two is a relaxation & visualization exercise intended to fight allergies.

Resolution. Denise Mina. Read by Katy Anderson. 12 CDs. (Running Time: 14 hrs. 20 mins.). (Isis (CDs) Ser.). (J). 2005. audio compact disk 99.95 (978-0-7531-2427-7(0)) Pub: ISIS Lrg Prnt GBR. Dist(s): Ulverscroft US

Resolution. unabr. ed. Denise Mina. 10 cass. (Running Time: 14 hrs. 20 mins.). (Isis Cassettes Ser.). (J). 2005. 84.95 (978-0-7531-2014-9(3)) Pub: ISIS Lrg Prnt GBR. Dist(s): Ulverscroft US

Resolution. unabr. ed. Robert B. Parker. Read by Titus Welliver. (Running Time: 16200 sec.). (ENG.). 2008. audio compact disk 29.95 (978-0-7393-6613-4(0), Random AudioBks) Pub: Random Audio Pubg. Dist(s): Random

***Resolution.** unabr. ed. Robert B. Parker. Read by Titus Welliver. (ENG.). 2010. 14.99 (978-0-307-75089-1(2), Random AudioBks) Pub: Random Audio Pubg. Dist(s): Random

Resolution of Construction Claims. 1987. bk. 115.00; 70.00 PA Bar Inst.

Resolutions. unabr. ed. 1 cass. (Running Time: 29 min.). 1988. 10.00 New Letters.
Poems about the New Year's holiday are mixed with bits of holiday folklore.

Resolutions of a Yoga. 1 cass. 12.99 (204) Yoga Res Foun.
Includes: "How to Overcome Hatred".

Resolutions of a Yogi, No. 3. Swami Jyotirmayananda. 1 cass. (Running Time: 1 hr.). 1990. 12.99 Yoga Res Foun.

Resolutions of the New Year. (138) Yoga Res Foun.

Resolutions of the New Year, No. 1. Swami Jyotirmayananda. 1 cass. (Running Time: 1 hr.). 1990. 12.99 Yoga Res Foun.

Resolve. Contrib. by Last Tuesday. Prod. by Matthew Thiessen & Joe Marlett. 2005. audio compact disk 13.98 (978-5-559-05720-0(7)) Mono Vs Ster.

Resolve in God. Speeches. 1 CD. 2003. audio compact disk 14.95 (978-1-930612-17-4(6)) Sentinel Grp.

Resolve Your Anger: With Optimal Thinking. unabr. ed. Rosalene Glickman. (Running Time: 30 mins.). (ENG.). 2009. 6.95 (978-1-59659-484-5(5), GildAudio) Pub: Gildan Media. Dist(s): HachBkGrp

Resolved: A Novel. abr. ed. Robert K. Tanenbaum. Read by Lee Sellars. 2004. 15.95 (978-0-7435-4846-5(9)) Pub: S&S Audio. Dist(s): S and S Inc

Resolves for the New Year. 1 cass. 12.99 (707) Yoga Res Foun.
Topics include: "Mental & Physical Purity," "Contentment" & "Austerity".

Resolving Anger. 1998. 24.95 (978-1-58557-008-9(7)) Dynamic Growth.

Resolving Conflict in Close Corporations. 1 cass. (Running Time: 50 min.). 1994. 95.00 Incl. study guide. (Y608) Am Law Inst.
Examines the kinds of disputes that arise & the contract provisions, oppression statutes, & litigation strategies that lawyers use to resolve them.

Resolving Conflict in Marriage. 1 cass. 1994. 10.95 (978-0-88432-725-7(6), C29501) J Norton Pubs.

Resolving Conflict Once & for All: A Practical How-To Guide to Mediating Disputes. unabr. ed. Dennis J. Ernst & Mark Stein. Read by Mark Stein. 3 cass. (Running Time: 3 hrs.). 1997. 19.95 (978-0-9656429-1-0(7)) Mediation First.
Applying the skills of mediation in the workplace, school, organization, community & professional practice.

Resolving Conflict (War & Peace) Psalm 141:3; Proverbs 15:1. Ed Young. 1991. 4.95 (978-0-7417-1865-5(0), 865) Win Walk.

Resolving Conflicts in the Workplace. 3 cass. (Running Time: 3 hrs. 30 min.). 1994. 155.00 Set; incl. study guide 389p. (M129) Am Law Inst.
Candidly examines the various "assisted" & "unassisted" alternatives to lawsuits with emphasis reducing transactional costs.

***Resolving Everyday Conflict.** unabr. ed. Ken Sande & Kevin Johnson. (ENG.). 2011. 9.98 (978-1-61045-103-1(1), Hovel Audio); audio compact disk 15.98 (978-1-61045-102-4(3), Hovel Audio) christianaud.

Resolving Infertility: Understanding the Options & Choosing Solutions When You Want to Have a Baby. Diane Aronson. 2 cass. (Running Time: 3 hrs.). 1999. 18.00 (978-0-694-52219-4(8), Harper Audio) HarperCollins Pubs.
Explores every possible outcome of the infertility journey, whether it leads to conception & childbirth, adoption, surrogacy, or resolving without children.

Resolving Interpersonal Conflict. Mac Hammond. 2008. audio compact disk 6.00 (978-1-57399-380-7(8)) Mac Hammond.

Resolving Problems. Betty L. Randolph. Read by Betty L. Randolph. Read by Leonard Baron. Ed. by Success Education Institute International Staff. 1 cass. (Running Time: 60 min.). (Success Ser.). 1989. bk. 14.98 Ocean Format. (978-1-55909-259-3(9), 470P) Randolph Tapes.
Features 60,000 messages with left-right brain. Male-female voice tracks with Megafonic Subliminals. Ocean (P).

Resolving Problems & Emergencies: English That Manages Unexpected Challenges. Scripts. Natasha Cooper. 4 CDs. (Running Time: 4 hrs. 15 mins.). 2004. pap. bk. 79.99 (978-1-932521-09-2(7)) Cooper Learn Syst.
Business English Conversation. ESL levels: intermediate- advanced. Packaged in a multimedia vinyl album with an accompanying book.

Resolving Problems & Emergencies: English That Manages Unexpected Challenges. Natasha Cooper. 4. (Running Time: 4 hrs. 15 mins.). (ENG & RUS.). 2003. pap. bk. 69.99 (978-1-932521-03-0(8)); pap. bk. 79.99 (978-1-932521-04-7(6)) Cooper Learn Syst.

Resolving Problems & Emergencies: English That Manages Unexpected Challenges. Scripts. Natasha Cooper. 4 cass. Dramatization. 2003. pap. bk. 69.99 (978-1-932521-08-5(9)) Cooper Learn Syst.

Resolving Problems & Emergencies: Power English: WHAT to Say, & HOW to Say It, 4. Scripts. Natasha Cooper. 4 cass. (Running Time: 4 hrs. 30 mins.). Dramatization. 2003. 49.99 (978-1-932521-01-6(1)) Cooper Learn Syst.
Cassettes in soft poly cases. Phrases, scripts and dialogues for solving problems and emergencies. Corresponding book - "Resolving Problems and Emergencies", ISBN 1-932521-00-3.

Resolving Problems & Emergencies Vol. 4. Scripts. Natasha Cooper. 4 CDs. (Running Time: 4 hrs. 30 mins.). Dramatization. 2003. audio compact disk 59.99 (978-1-932521-02-3(X)) Cooper Learn Syst.
Cd's in soft poly cases. Phrases, scripts, and dialogues for resolving problems and emergencies. Accompanying book "Resolving Problems and Emergencies", ISBN 1-932521-07-0.

Resolving Traumatic Memories: Metaphors & Symbols in Psychotherapy. David J. Grove & B. I. Panzer. 1991. pap. bk. 52.95 (978-0-8290-2417-3(4)) Irvington.

Resolving Your Past. Ray DiGiuseppe. 1 cass. 1999. 9.95 (C070) A Ellis Institute.
Discusses the latest research on how early events impact us & shows how to heal from hurts & grievances & move on.

Resonance. A. J. Scudiere. Prod. by Skyboat Road Company. Directed By Skyboat Road Company. (ENG.). 2009. 39.99 (978-0-9799510-3-9(8)) Ink Gr.

Resonance. unabr. ed. A. J. Scudiere. 15 CDs. (Running Time: 16 hrs. 30 mins.). 2008. 49.99 (978-0-9799510-2-2(X)) Ink Gr.

Resonance & the Myths of Nations. unabr. ed. Rubert Sheldrake. 1 cass. (Running Time: 1 hr. 23 min.). 1988. 11.00 (02302) Big Sur Tapes.
According to Sheldrake, through the morphic resonance of ritual, followers of the path are helped & connected with all past followers to come into resonance with the entire tradition.

Resonant Fields of Heart & Brain. unabr. ed. Joseph C. Pearce & Rupert Sheldrake. 1 cass. (Running Time: 90 min.). 1993. 11.00 (02305) Big Sur Tapes.
Explains how the habits of nature influence us, & vice versa; & about the profound role the heart plays - biologically as well as metaphorically - in our emotional & cognitive systems.

Resonant Tuning. abr. ed. Robert A. Monroe. Read by Robert A. Monroe. (Mind Food Ser.). 1981. 14.95 (978-1-56102-413-1(9)) Inter Indus.
Breathing exercises to change & vitalize the system.

Resonet in Laudibus - ShowTrax. Arranged by John Leavitt. 1 CD. (Running Time: 5 mins.). 2000. audio compact disk 19.95 (08703276) H Leonard.
This 14th century German carol text sparkles in a joyful John Leavitt setting. Opt. percussion.

Resort Real Estate & Clubs: Formation, Operation & Documentation. 10 cass. (Running Time: 15 hrs.). 1994. 360.00 Set; incl. study guide_ 951p. (M143) Am Law Inst.
Advanced course considers legal aspects of the planning, financing, development, management, & operation of resort & club properties. Designed for attorneys with general real estate experience who seek an in-depth exposure to the law & techniques particular to resort real estate.

Resort Real Estate & Clubs: Formation, Operation & Documentation. 8 cass. (Running Time: 12 hrs. 30 min.). 1999. stu. ed. 345.00 (AE16) Am Law Inst.

Resort to Murder. Carolyn G. Hart. Read by Kate Reading. (Henrie O Mystery Ser.). 2001. audio compact disk 64.00 (978-0-7366-7906-0(5)) Books on Tape.

Resort to Murder. unabr. ed. Carolyn G. Hart. 7 cass. (Running Time: 10 hrs. 30 min.). (Henrie O Mystery Ser.). 2001. 56.00 (978-0-7366-6851-4(9)) Books on Tape.
Henrie O joins a wedding party in Bermuda only to discover that death is an uninvited guest.

Resort to Murder: Thirteen Tales of Mystery by Minnesota's Premier Writers. unabr. ed. William Kent Krueger et al. 5 CDs. (Running Time: 5 hrs. 45 mins.). 2008. audio compact disk 29.95 (978-0-9817491-1-2(9)) Pub: Holton Hse. Dist(s): Adventure Pubns

Resource Sharing: Libraries Beyond Walls. 3 cass. 1990. 24.00 set. Recorded Res.

Resources for the Journey: A Profile of Mennonite Church USA. 2007. DVD & audio compact disk 19.99 (978-0-8361-9376-3(8)) Herald Press.

Respect. AIO Team Staff. Created by Tyndale House Publishers Staff. (Running Time: 1 hr. 10 mins. 0 sec.). (Adventures in Odyssey Life Lessons Ser.). (ENG.). (J). (gr. 1-7). 2006. audio compact disk 5.99 (978-1-58997-375-6(5), Tyndale Ent) Tyndale Hse.

Respect. Linda Eyre & Richard Eyre. 2 cass. (Running Time: 3 hrs.). (Teaching Your Children Values Ser.). (J). (ps-7). 2000. pap. bk. 16.95 (978-1-56015-787-8(9)) Penton Overseas.
Tape 1: a coaching, "how-to" program for parents; Tape 2: "Alexander's Amazing Adventures" program featuring stories, songs, sound effects & background music, that helps children ages 4-12 to develop social skills, communication skills & life skills. Includes activity cards.

Respect: Yourself, the Savior & Others. Troy Dunn. 1 CD. audio compact disk 10.98 (978-1-57734-085-0(X), 2500752) Covenant Comms.
From dating tips to spiritual slugs, Troy Dunn teaches keys to respect.

Respect: Yourself, the Savior & Others. Troy Dunn. 1 cass. 1997. 9.98 (978-1-57734-083-6(3), 06005438) Covenant Comms.
From dating tips to "spiritual slugs," Troy Dunn teaches keys to respect.

Respect & Good Manners. Eldon Taylor. 1 CD. (Running Time: 52 min.). (Whole Brain Innertalk Ser.). 1998. audio compact disk (978-1-55978-852-6(6)) Progress Aware Res.

Respect & Good Manners. Eldon Taylor. 1 CD. (Running Time: 52 min.). (Whole Brain Innertalk Ser.). 1999. audio compact disk (978-1-55978-920-2(4)) Progress Aware Res.

Respect for Students. unabr. ed. Daniel Greenberg. 1 cass. (Running Time: 1 hr.). 1991. 10.00 (978-1-888947-55-7(1)) Sudbury Valley.
A seminar on a key concept in self-directed education.

Respect Others: Exodus 20:13-15. Ed Young. 1999. 4.95 (978-0-7417-2223-2(2), 1223) Win Walk.

***Respectable Sins: Confronting the Sins We Tolerate.** unabr. ed. Jerry Bridges. Narrated by John Haag. (ENG.). 2009. 10.98 (978-1-59644-844-5(X), christianSeed); audio compact disk 18.98 (978-1-59644-843-8(1), christianSeed) christianaud.

Respectable Trade. unabr. ed. Philippa Gregory. Read by Diana Bishop. 12 cass. (Running Time: 18 hrs.). (Isis Ser.). (J). 1999. 94.95 (978-0-7531-0478-1(4), 981113) Pub: ISIS Lrg Prnt GBR. Dist(s): Ulverscroft US
Bristol in 1787 is a booming city where power & wealth beckon those who dare to take risks. Josiah Cole, a small dockside trader, is prepared to gamble everything to join the big players of the city, but needs cash & a well-connected wife. Marriage to Frances Scott provides a mutually convenient solution. Trading her social contacts for Josiah's protection, Frances finds her life & fortune dependent on the respectable trade of sugar, rum & slaves.

Respiratory Failure & Sepsis. Moderated by Roger C. Bone. Contrib. by Elizabeth Jacobs et al. 1 cass. (Running Time: 90 min.). 1985. 12.00 (A8506) Amer Coll Phys.
This topic is discussed by a moderator & experts who offer differing opinions.

Respiratory System. Compiled by Benchmark Education Staff. 2006. audio compact disk 10.00 (978-1-4108-6703-2(X)) Benchmark Educ.

Respiratory Tract. D. Hastings-Nield. (Anatomy Project). 1997. audio compact disk 199.95 (978-1-85070-825-4(8), Parthenon Pbng) Pub: CRC Pr. Dist(s): Taylor and Fran

Response & Size-up DVD. International Association of Fire Chiefs Staff & National Fire Protection Association. 2005. 315.95 (978-0-7637-3606-4(6)) Jones Bartlett.

Response of a Creature. Thomas Merton. 1 cass. 8.95 (AA2261) Credence Commun.

Response to Intervention: Implementing Powerful & Practical Strategies to Identify & Serve Students with Learning Challenges. Hosted by Kelly Harmon. 4 CDs. (Running Time: 4 hrs 4 mins). 2008. audio compact disk 95.00 (978-1-886397-90-3(2)) Bureau of Educ.

Response to the Challenge. unabr. ed. Read by Bob Richards. 1 cass. (Running Time: 30 min.). 15.00 B R Motivational.
A recorded live speech by Bob Richards on meeting our challenges of creativity to benefit mankind, of health in an age of softness, of brotherhood in an age of prejudice.

Responsibility. AIO Team Staff. Created by Tyndale House Publishers Staff. (Running Time: 1 hr. 10 mins. 0 sec.). (Adventures in Odyssey Ser.). (ENG.). (J). (gr. 1-7). 2006. audio compact disk 5.99 (978-1-58997-376-3(3), Tyndale Ent) Tyndale Hse.

Responsibility. J. Krishnamurti. 1 cass. (Running Time: 1 hr.). (Krishnamurti with Dr. Allan W. Anderson Ser.: No. 3). 8.50 (APA743) Krishnamurti.
These 1974 dialogues cover the entire spectrum of Krishnamurti's teaching in a series highly regarded for its depth of inquiry into each particular subject.

Responsibility: A Key to Excellence. G. Michael Durst. Read by G. Michael Durst. 1 cass. (Running Time: 45 min.). 18.00 textbook. Train Sys.

***Responsibility: How to Create a Third Dynamic.** L. Ron Hubbard. (ENG.). 2002. audio compact disk 15.00 (978-1-4031-1516-4(8)) Bridge Pubns Inc.

Responsibility for Self. unabr. ed. Robert A. Monroe. Read by Robert A. Monroe. (Running Time: 54 min.). (Explorer Ser.). 1983. 12.95 (978-1-56113-010-8(9), 11) Monroe Institute.
The five levels of Human Consciousness.

Responsibility for the World. J. Krishnamurti. 1 cass. (Running Time: 1 hr.). (Ojai Public Talks - 1983 Ser.: No. 1). 8.50 (AJT831) Krishnamurti.
In the idyllic setting of the oak grove in Ojai, California, Krishnamurti began giving talks in 1922. Over the years, hundreds of thousands of people have heard Krishnamurti explore every aspect of our lives, his language & expression constantly changing, as he strove to communicate to each successive generation those profound truths which he had come upon, & which he maintained were accessible to all.

Responsibility in a Chaotic World. J. Krishnamurti. Read by J. Krishnamurti. 1 cass. (Running Time: 90 min.). (Ojai Public Talks - 1985 Ser.). 1985. 8.50 (978-1-55994-325-3(4), AJT851) Krishnamurti.

Responsibility in a Chaotic World. abr. ed. J. Krishnamurti. Read by J. Krishnamurti. 1 cass. (Running Time: 60 min.). (Ojai Talks Ser.). 1988. bk. 9.95 (978-0-06-250475-3(4)) HarperCollins Pubs.
In an intimate dialogue with his audience, Krishnamurti explores the many aspects of disorder - power politics, violence, world chaos - that result in personal & sexual ambition, & he considers the exploitation that results from pure self-interest.

Responsibility of the Corporate Parent for the Activities of a Subsidiary. Contrib. by Thomas J. Heiden. 8 cass. (Running Time: 10 hrs. 30 min.). 1990. 175.00 (T7-9297) PLI.

Responsibility to Self. Roy W. Menninger. Read by Roy W. Menninger. 1 cass. (Running Time: 51 min.). (Executive Seminar Ser.). 1987. 10.00 (978-1-56948-007-6(9)) Menninger Clinic.
Roy W. Menninger, MD, reaffirms one premise of the seminar programs: increased self-understanding & self-acceptance expand our capacity to be productive & responsible.

Responsible Oneness. Swami Amar Jyoti. 1 cass. 1978. 9.95 (R-16) Truth Consciousness.
How to merge ego in responsible Oneness. Becoming what we truly are & finding fulfillment.

Responsible Parenting. Eknath Easwaran. 1 cass. (Running Time: 59 min.). 1990. 7.95 (978-1-58638-598-9(4), RP) Nilgiri Pr.
Whether or not we have children of our own, each of us has a responsibility to the next generation. Responding to a recent report on the state of our nation's children, this talk considers how we can protect & inspire them.

Responsible Tourism Around the World. Hosted by Nancy Pearlman. 1 cass. (Running Time: 29 min.). 10.00 (1015) Educ Comm CA.

Responsibility & Relationship. J. Krishnamurti. 1 cass. (Running Time: 1 hr.). (Krishnamurti with Dr. Allan W. Anderson Ser.: No. 4). 8.50 (APA744) Krishnamurti.
These 1974 dialogues cover the entire spectrum of Krishnamurti's teaching in a series highly regarded for its depth of inquiry into each particular subject.

Respuestas al Sindrome DDA Se Acabaron las Rabietas Forma Efectiva de Controlar el Enojo. unabr. ed. John F. Taylor. Read by Marisela Rizik. 1 cass. (Running Time: 37 min.). (Answers to ADD Ser.). (SPA.). 1994. 9.95 (978-1-883963-19-4(2)) ADD Plus.
Teaching negotiation skills, sidestepping power struggles, safe anger venting, three constructive uses of anger, discovering the hurts behind the anger, facilitating healthy expression of anger.

Respuestas Claras para una Iglesia Confundida. 2006. audio compact disk 50.00 (978-1-57972-711-6(5)) Insight Living.

***Rest: Living in Sabbath Simplicity.** Keri Wyatt Kent. (Running Time: 7 hrs. 16 mins. 0 sec.). (ENG.). 2009. 14.99 (978-0-310-77316-0(4)) Zondervan.

Rest Area. unabr. ed. Clay McLeod Chapman. Read by Clay McLeod Chapman. (YA). 2008. 54.99 (978-1-60514-501-3(7)) Find a World.

Rest Assured. John Sears. 1 cass. (Running Time: 57 min.). 10.95 (765) J Norton Pubs.
This tape employs a combination of relaxing music & psychological suggestions to gently lull you to sleep. Cure your insomnia, fatigue, tension, & wake up fully rested.

Rest Assured. unabr. ed. Nicholas Rhea. 7 CDs. (Running Time: 28800 sec.). (Story Sound CD Ser.). 2006. audio compact disk 71.95 (978-1-85903-939-7(1)) Pub: Mgna Lrg Print GBR. Dist(s): Ulverscroft US

Rest Assured. unabr. ed. Nicholas Rhea. Read by Graham Padden. 6 cass. (Story Sound Ser.). (J). 2006. 54.95 (978-1-85903-893-2(X)) Pub: Mgna Lrg Print GBR. Dist(s): Ulverscroft US

Rest for the Mind, Body, & Spirit: Quiet Meditation. Concept by Vicky Thurlow. (ENG.). 2008. audio compact disk 14.95 (978-0-9817055-7-6(X)) DVT Invest.

Rest Is Noise: Listening to the Twentieth Century. Alex Ross. Read by Grover Gardner. (Playaway Adult Nonfiction Ser.). 2008. 109.99 (978-1-60640-767-7(8)) Find a World.

Rest Is Noise: Listening to the Twentieth Century. unabr. ed. Alex Ross. Read by Grover Gardner. (Running Time: 82800 sec.). 2007. 34.95 (978-1-4332-0792-1(3)); 95.95 (978-1-4332-0795-2(8)); audio compact disk 44.95 (978-1-4332-0794-5(X)) Blckstn Audio.

Rest Is Noise: Listening to the Twentieth Century. unabr. ed. Alex Ross. Read by Grover Gardner. (Running Time: 82800 sec.). 2007. audio compact disk 34.95 (978-1-4332-0793-8(1)) Blckstn Audio.

Rest Is Noise: Listening to the Twentieth Century. unabr. ed. Alex Ross & Grover Gardner. (Running Time: 82800 sec.). 2007. audio compact disk 120.00 (978-1-4332-0796-9(6)) Blckstn Audio.

Rest Is Silence. Keith Mccarthy. 2008. 76.95 (978-0-7531-2898-5(5)); audio compact disk 99.95 (978-0-7531-2899-2(3)) Pub: ISIS Audio GBR. Dist(s): Ulverscroft US

Rest of God. Paul Cain. 1 cass. (Running Time: 90 mins.). (Call to Radical Christianity Ser.: Vol. 2). 2000. 5.00 (PC01-002) Morning NC.
"Radical Culture/Conservative Church" & "The Rest of God." This is a call for the church to become a revolutionary power on the earth once again.

Rest of Her Life. unabr. ed. Laura Moriarty. Read by Julia Gibson. 10 CDs. (Running Time: 39600 sec.). 2007. audio compact disk 39.95 (978-0-06-136927-8(6), Harper Audio) HarperCollins Pubs.

Rest of Our Lives. Harvey Jackins. 12 cass. 10.00 ea. (978-1-893165-97-7(3)) Rational Isl.
Advances in counseling theory & practice 1983-1985.

Rest of the Story: Matthew 1:1-17. Ed Young. 1991. 4.95 (978-0-7417-1897-6(9), 897) Win Walk.

Rest of Us: The Rise of America's Eastern European Jews. unabr. collector's ed. Stephen Birmingham. Read by Jonathan Reese. 11 cass. (Running Time: 16 hrs. 30 min.). 1993. 88.00 (978-0-7366-2399-5(X), 3168) Books on Tape.
Story of Eastern European Jews who thronged into New York to escape czarist Russia between 1882 & 1915.

***Resta números de dos dígitos Audio CD.** April Barth. Adapted by Benchmark Education Co., LLC. (Content Connections Ser.). (SPA.). (J). 2010. audio compact disk 10.00 (978-1-61672-207-4(X)) Benchmark Educ.

Restaurando los Muros. Carlos Ortiz. 6 cass. (SPA.). 2003. 29.99 (978-0-89985-415-1(X)); audio compact disk 35.00 (978-0-89985-414-4(1)) Christ for the Nations.

Restaurant at the End of the Universe. unabr. ed. Douglas Adams. Read by Douglas Adams. 4 cass. (Running Time: 6 hrs.). 2004. 25.00 (978-1-59007-262-2(6)); audio compact disk 39.95 (978-1-59007-263-9(4)) Pub: New Millenn Enter. Dist(s): PerseuPGW

Restaurant at the End of the Universe. unabr. ed. Douglas Adams. Read by Martin Freeman. (Running Time: 20760 sec.). (ENG.). 2006. audio compact disk 29.95 (978-0-7393-3207-8(4), Random AudioBks) Pub: Random Audio Pubg. Dist(s): Random

Restaurant Spanish. 2003. ring bd. (978-0-9744783-6-4(9)) Spanish Acad Cu Inst.

Restful, Revitalizing Sleep. Read by Robert E. Griswold. 1 cass. 1992. 10.95 (978-1-55848-039-1(0)) EffectiveMN.
You don't have to have insomnia to benefit from this tape. It can help you enjoy a peaceful night's sleep & wake up feeling better than ever.

***Restful, Revitalizing Sleep + Overcoming Worry.** Bob Griswold. (Running Time: 53). 2010. 14.95 (978-1-55848-112-1(5)) EffectiveMN.

Restful Sleep. 1 cass. (Running Time: 45 min.). (Health Ser.). 9.98 (978-1-55909-004-9(9), 22S); 15.98 90 min. extended length stereo music. (978-1-55909-179-4(7), 22X) Randolph Tapes.
Promotes restful sleep. Subliminal messages are heard 3-5 minutes before becoming ocean sounds or music.

Restful Sleep. Mary Lee LaBay. 2006. audio compact disk 7.95 (978-1-934705-17-9(9)) Awareness Engin.

Restful Sleep. Barry Tesar. 1 cass. (Running Time: 1 hr.). (Subliminal Inspiration Ser.). 1992. 9.98 (978-1-56470-008-7(9)) Success Cass.
Subliminal program.

Restful Sleep: A Step-by-Step Program for Learning to Relax Instantly. Created by David Bresler. (ENG.). 2007. audio compact disk 19.95 (978-1-887211-05-5(5), Imag Res) AlphaBks CA.

Restful Sleep: Feeling Safe, Secure & Loved. Carol Rios. 2007. audio compact disk 19.99 (978-1-4276-2335-5(X)) AardGP.

Resting in God's Care: Coping with Fear, Anxiety & Stress. Word Consultants Staff. 1 cass. (Running Time: 60 mins.). 1999. 9.95 (T9375) Liguori Pubns.
Features biblical affirmations set to music. Designed to help increase trust in God & reduce fears, anxieties & stress.

Resting in Righteous. Creflo A. Dollar. 20.00 (978-1-59089-010-3(8)) Pub: Creflo Dollar. Dist(s): STL Dist NA

Resting in Stillness: Integrative Restoration - iRest Yoga Nidra. Richard Miller. Richard Miller. 2009. 15.00 (978-1-893099-09-8(1)) Pub: Anahata Pr. Dist(s): Ctr of Timeless

Resting in the Lord: 1 Cor.1:30. Ed Young. 1983. 4.95 (978-0-7417-1302-5(0), 302) Win Walk.

***Resting on Faithful & True.** Created by Laura Davis. Prod. by Laura Davis. (ENG.). 2009. audio compact disk 15.00 (978-0-9843234-1-8(4)) Imm Suc Enter.

Restitution: Luke 19:1-10. Ed Young. 1982. 4.95 (978-0-7417-1239-4(3), 239) Win Walk.

Restless. unabr. ed. William Boyd. Narrated by Rosamund Pike. 10 CDs. (Running Time: 38880 sec.). 2006. audio compact disk 94.95 (978-0-7927-4371-2(7), SLD 995); audio compact disk 59.95 (978-0-7927-4563-1(9), CMP 995) AudioGO.

Restless. unabr. ed. William Boyd. Read by Rosamund Pike. (Running Time: 10 hrs. 0 mins. 0 sec.). (ENG.). 2006. audio compact disk 39.95 (978-1-4272-0021-1(1)) Pub: Macmill Audio. Dist(s): Macmillan

Restless Heart. unabr. ed. Jessica Blair. Read by Trudy Harris. 9 cass. (Running Time: 12 hrs.). (Storysound Ser.). (J). 2003. 76.95 (978-1-85903-600-6(7)) Pub: Mgna Lrg Print GBR. Dist(s): Ulverscroft US

Restless Is the Heart. Contrib. by Bernadette Farrell. 2005. audio compact disk 17.00 (978-5-559-48769-4(4)) OR Catholic.

Restless Peace. Barbara Murphy. 6 cass. (Running Time: 8 hrs.). (Story Sound Ser.). (J). 2004. 54.95 (978-1-85903-693-8(7)) Pub: Mgna Lrg Print GBR. Dist(s): Ulverscroft US

Restless Sleep: Inside New York City's Cold Case Squad. unabr. ed. Stacy Horn. Read by Eliza Foss. 8 cass. (Running Time: 11 hrs. 30 mins.). 2006. 79.75 (978-1-4193-4941-6(4)) Recorded Bks.
In this enticing narrative The Restless Sleep, the author sheds light on the dark world of the NYPD's real-life Cold Case Squad - a special command of detectives who take on the homicide cases that remain unsolved after their initial period of investigation. Those who comprise its ranks are often characterized as misfits and lone wolves - but brilliant ones, to be sure. Here, their fascinating and deeply troubling stories of cases closed - and others that remain open - are conveyed in chilling detail.

Restoration. Derek Prince. 3 cass. 14.95 (011-012-013) Derek Prince.
Restoration is the single, all-encompassing word that sums up God's purposes for His two covenant peoples - both Israel & Church - at this time.

Restoration: A Novel of Seventeenth-Century England. unabr. ed. Rose Tremain. Narrated by John Franklyn-Robbins. 10 cass. (Running Time: 14 hrs. 45 mins.). 1992. 85.00 (978-1-55690-765-4(6), 92418E7) Recorded Bks.
The story of Robert Merivel, 17th Century doctor to the Royal dogs & member of the King's Court until he is cast out & has to fend for himself.

Restoration: Romans 11:12-26. Ben Young. 1997. 4.95 (978-0-7417-6031-9(2)) Win Walk.

Restoration Pt. I: Romans 11:12-26. Ed Young. 1984. 4.95 (978-0-7417-1392-6(6), 392) Win Walk.

Restoration Pt. II: Romans 11:12-26. Ed Young. 1984. 4.95 (978-0-7417-1393-3(4), 393) Win Walk.

Restoration Pt. III: Romans 11:26-36. Ed Young. 1984. 4.95 (978-0-7417-1394-0(2), 394) Win Walk.

Restoration is Hard Work. Rick Joyner. 1 cass. (Running Time: 90 mins.). (Heart of David Ser.: Vol. 2). 2000. 5.00 (RJ13-002) Morning NC.
"Restoring the Tabernacle of David," "Restoration is Hard Work" & "the Kingdom is Here - Dwell in it." These tapes not only address the need for a foundation of truth; they impart the essential devotion of having a love for the truth.

Restorative Sleep. abr. ed. Robert A. Monroe. Read by Robert A. Monroe. (Running Time: 30 min.). (Human Plus Ser.). 1989. 14.95 (978-1-56102-030-0(3)) Inter Indus.
Learn to enhance recuperation from illness, injury or surgery.

Restore My Heart CD. Glenn. 2009. audio compact disk 19.99 (978-1-932960-09-9(0)) Kardo Intl Min.

***Restoring America CD.** Peter J. Marshall. 2005. audio compact disk (978-0-9771811-2-4(X)) Pet Mars Mini.

Restoring Apostolic Leadership. Paul Cain. 1 cass. (Running Time: 90 min.). (New Kind of Leader Ser.: Vol. 1). 2000. 5.00 (PC03-001) Morning NC.
Incl: "Restoring Apostolic Leadership" & "World Evangelization." This series addresses the characteristics of the coming apostolic leadership.

Restoring Broken Things. unabr. ed. Stephen Curtis Chapman. 2005. 27.99 (978-1-58926-842-5(3), 6842) Pub: Oasis Audio. Dist(s): TNT Media Grp

Restoring Broken Things. unabr. ed. Steven Curtis Chapman & Scotty Smith. Read by Steven Curtis Chapman & Scotty Smith. (Running Time: 21600 sec.). 2005. audio compact disk 29.99 (978-1-58926-843-2(1), 6843) Pub: Oasis Audio. Dist(s): TNT Media Grp

Restoring Broken Things. unabr. ed. Steven Curtis Chapman & Scotty Smith. (ENG.). 2006. 20.99 (978-1-60814-362-7(7)) Oasis Audio.

Restoring Economic Order. E. C. Harwood. 1 cass. (Running Time: 58 min.). 10.95 (290) J Norton Pubs.

Restoring Faith: America's Religious Leaders Answer Terror with Hope. abr. ed. Read by Forrest Church. Ed. by Forrest Church. 2 cass. (Running Time: 3 hrs.). 2001. 15.95 (978-1-57270-272-1(9), L21272) Pub: Audio Partners. Dist(s): PerseuPGW
These live recordings of profound and inspiring sermons delivered in many congregations immediately after September 11, 2001, challenge listeners to learn and understand with their heads and their hearts and provide an enduring testament to the power of religious freedom in action.

Restoring Faith: America's Religious Leaders Answer Terror with Hope. abr. ed. Read by Forrest Church. Ed. by Forrest Church. 2 CDs. (Running Time: 2 hrs. 20 mins.). (Audio Editions Ser.). (ENG.). 2001. audio compact disk 15.95 (978-1-57270-273-8(7)) Pub: AudioGO. Dist(s): Perseus Dist
The shock and sadness felt during the week following the September 11 attacks drew Americans to houses of worship in record numbers. Regardless of creed, they asked the same questions: Where is God amidst the devastation? How to answer hate with love? Is there hope for peace.

Restoring Godly Families. Creflo A. Dollar. 2009. audio compact disk 50.00 (978-1-59944-755-1(X)) Creflo Dollar.

Restoring Hope in a Woman's Heart. 2 CDs. 2006. audio compact disk 11.00 (978-1-933207-20-9(5)) Ransomed Heart.

Restoring New Testament Christianity, Adron Doran. Read by Adron Doran. 6 cass. (Restoring New Testament Christianity Ser.). 24.99 (978-0-89098-160-3(4)) Twent Cent Christ.
Dr. Doran puts more than sixty years of ministry experience & wisdom into this series. He leads us back to the New Testament church by way of the Restoration Movement, its plea, its problems & its personalities.

Restoring Restful & Healing Sleep - Ending Insomnia. Scott Sulak. 1998. 15.00 (978-1-932659-08-5(0)) Change For Gd.

Restoring the Tabernacle of David. Rick Joyner. 1 cass. (Running Time: 90 mins.). (Heart of David Ser.: Vol. 1). 2000. 5.00 (RJ13-001) Morning NC.
"Restoring the Tabernacle of David," "Restoration is Hard Work" & "the Kingdom is Here - Dwell in it." These tapes not only address the need for a foundation of truth; they impart the essential devotion of having a love for the truth.

Restoring the Temple: A Celebration of the Feminine Spirit Panel Discussion. 1 cass. (Running Time: 1 hrs. 40 min.). 10.95 (978-0-7822-0528-2(3), 594) C G Jung IL.

Restoring your Self Esteem by the Sea. Created by Gayle S. Rozantine. (ENG.). 2007. audio compact disk 15.95 (978-0-9797597-4-1(9)) G Rozantine.

Restraint of Beasts. abr. ed. Magnus Mills. Read by Peter Capaldi. 2 cass. (Running Time: 3 hrs.). 1999. 16.85 (978-0-00-105567-4(4)) Ulvrscrft Audio.
Meet Tam & Ritchie: two dour Scots laborers. Overly fond of denim, workshy, permanently discontented, intent on getting to the pub every night - in short, just your average workmen. A tale of the perils of teamwork & timidity.

Restraint of Beasts. unabr. ed. Magnus Mills. Read by Greg Wagland. 6 cass. (Running Time: 9 hrs.). 2000. 54.95 (978-0-7531-0771-3(6), 000116) Pub: ISIS Audio GBR. Dist(s): Ulverscroft US
Tam & Ritchie are two dour Scots laborers, fond of denim, work-shy, permanently discontented, intent on getting to the pub every night come hell or high water, until their new supervisor dispatches them to a farmsite in England. Who exactly are the Hall brothers & what do they keep on their farm?.

Restricting Immunity under the Recreational Use Act after Walsh. 1 cass. (Running Time: 45 min.). 1991. 25.00 (AL-121) PA Bar Inst.

Restrictive Covenants in Individual Employment Contracts. 1 cass. 1989. bk. 45.00 (AC-540) PA Bar Inst.

Restructured Thrift Industry after FIRREA: A Guide for the Practitioner. unabr. ed. Contrib. by Eric Luse. 4 cass. (Running Time: 5 hrs. 30 min.). 1989. 50.00 course handbk. (T7-9266) PLI.
This recording of PLI's December 1989 satellite program is designed to provide practitioners with a guide to the major provisions of FIRREA, its impact on short- & long-term planning & activities, how it will affect the regulation of the savings industry & the obligations it imposes - & opportunities it offers.

Restructuring of America: How to Survive & Profit. unabr. ed. A. David Coles. Read by David Curry. Ed. by Brunswick Press Staff. Illus. by BJ Graphics Staff. 2 cass. (Running Time: 2 hrs. 45 min.). 1989. bk. 29.95 set, incl. charts, graphs, & vinyl bklt. cover. (978-0-9622444-0-7(6)) Equidata VA.
A handbook of survival in the coming global economic & financial collapse. It will show you how to avoid the panic in the streets as the U. S. dollar becomes worthless while making profits from the upheaval.

Resultados del Programa de Comparación Internacional para América del Sur. United Nations. (Cuadernos Estadísticos de la CEPAL Ser.). (SPA.). 2008. audio compact disk 20.00 (978-92-1-323147-0(4)) Untd Nat Pubns.

Results of Karma Yoga. Swami Amar Jyoti. 1 cass. 1979. 9.95 (G-11) Truth Consciousness.
Finding our proper places. Definition of true Karma Yoga. Importance of attitude.

Results That Last: Hardwiring Behaviors That Will Take Your Company to the Top. (ENG.). 2008. 24.95 (978-0-9749986-6-4(4)) Fire St Pubng.

Resumes & Cover Letters: Your Tickets for Admission. Joe Hodowanes. Read by Joe Hodowanes. 1 cass. (Running Time: 90 min.). 1998. 14.95 (978-0-9664427-0-0(9)) J M Wanes.
Resume mistakes to avoid, formatting of resume. Avoid major mistakes on cover letters, & four principles for effective cover letters.

Resurfacing Audio Workshop: Techniques for Exploring Consciousness. unabr. ed. Harry Palmer. 6 cass. (Running Time: 4 hrs.). 1997. 59.95 incl. manual. (978-0-9626874-7-1(2)) Stars Edge.
A participatory workshop that helps one gain control of one's life.

Resurgence of the Ku Klux Klan. 1 cass. (Running Time: 30 min.). 9.95 (NJ-81-02-23, HarperThor) HarpC GBR.

Resurrected Gangsta. Perf. by God's Original Gangstaz. 1 cass. 1997. audio compact disk 15.99 CD. (D7520) Diamante Music Grp.
From the mean streets of South Central Los Angeles, these ministers of the Gospel have risen to boldly go where few men have gone before. Reaching from the ghettos to the suburbs, they bring the message of hope to a wicked & perverse generation.

Resurrecting Midnight. unabr. ed. Eric Jerome Dickey. Read by Dion Graham. (Running Time: 15 hrs.). (Gideon Ser.). 2009. 24.99 (978-1-4233-4569-5(X), 9781423345695, Brilliance MP3); 39.97 (978-1-4233-4572-5(X), 9781423345725, BADLE); audio compact disk 97.97 (978-1-4233-4568-8(1), 9781423345688, BriAudCD Unabrid); audio compact disk 36.99 (978-1-4233-4567-1(3), 9781423345671, Bril Audio CD Unabri) Brilliance Audio.

Resurrecting Midnight, No. 2. unabr. ed. Eric Jerome Dickey. Read by Dion Graham. (Running Time: 15 hrs.). (Gideon Ser.). 2009. 39.97 (978-1-4233-4570-1(3), 9781423345701, Brinc Audio MP3 Lib); 24.99 (978-1-4233-4571-8(1), 9781423345718, BAD) Brilliance Audio.

Resurrection. Duane S. Crowther. Read by Duane S. Crowther. 1 cass. (Running Time: 90 min.). 1990. 13.98 (978-0-88290-403-0(5), 1809) Horizon Utah.
A discussion of Latter-day Saint doctrines of the resurrection, beginning with the resurrection of Jesus Christ & showing that it is the pattern for all mankind. The author also discusses the nature of a resurrected body & shows from the scriptures that it will conform to the heavenly kingdom which the recipient is to inherit.

Resurrection. Sandra Frazier. 1 CD. 1999. audio compact disk 15.95 (978-1-884039-16-4(2)) Mystic-Art Media.

Resurrection. Derek Prince. 2 cass. 11.90 (108-109) Derek Prince.
This single most important event that has ever occurred in human history also foreshadows the great & final climax.

Resurrection. unabr. ed. Nancy Holder & Debbie Viguié. Read by Cassandra Morris. (Running Time: 7 hrs.). (Wicked Ser.). 2009. 39.97 (978-1-4418-0711-3(X), 9781441807113, BADLE) Brilliance Audio.

Resurrection. unabr. ed. Leo Tolstoy. Narrated by Simon Vance. 14 CDs. (Running Time: 16 hrs. 54 mins. 0 sec.). (ENG.). 2005. audio compact disk 34.98 (978-1-59644-134-7(8), Hovel Audio) christianaud.

Resurrection. unabr. ed. Leo Tolstoy. Tr. by Louise Maude from RUS. Narrated by Simon Vance. 2 MP3CDs. (Running Time: 16 hrs. 54 mins. 0 sec.). (ENG.). 2005. lp 29.98 (978-1-59644-135-4(6), Hovel Audio) christianaud.
Leo Tolstoy stands tall among the great Russian novelists of the nineteenth century. Tolstoy based Resurrection, the last of his novels, on a true story of a philanderer whose misuse of a beautiful young orphan girl leads to her ruin. Fate brings the two together many years later and the meeting awakens the mana??s moral conscience. Anger, intimacy, forgiveness and grace result. While the situation of Tolstoya??s plot is alien to most people, his nuanced treatment of mortal life is familiar to all. Later in his life Tolstoy confessed that he earlier had seduced two young girls for his pleasure. Perhaps his own deeds and their horrible consequences motivated him to write this novel with special passion. It is a particularly moving tale. Tolstoya??s Resurrection is marvelous in the fullest sense of the word a?? a story so improbable that it must be a miraculous achievement.

***Resurrection.** unabr. ed. Leo Tolstoy. Narrated by Simon Vance. (ENG.). 2005. 19.98 (978-1-59644-137-8(2), Hovel Audio) christianaud.

Resurrection. unabr. ed. Debbie Viguié. Read by Cassandra Morris. Created by Nancy Holder. Illus. by Nancy Holder. (Running Time: 10 hrs.). (Wicked Ser.). 2009. 24.99 (978-1-4418-0708-3(X), 9781441807083, Brilliance MP3); 39.97 (978-1-4418-0709-0(8), 9781441807090, Brinc Audio MP3 Lib); 24.99 (978-1-4418-0710-6(1), 9781441807106, BAD); audio compact disk 24.99 (978-1-4418-0706-9(3), 9781441807069, Bril Audio CD Unabri); audio compact disk 54.97 (978-1-4418-0707-6(1), 9781441807076, BriAudCD Unabrid) Brilliance Audio.

Resurrection: Logos April 12, 1998. Ben Young. 1998. 4.95 (978-0-7417-6079-1(7), B0079) Win Walk.

Resurrection: The Message. Eugene H. Peterson. Read by Kelly Ryan Dolan. (Running Time: 7200 sec.). 2006. audio compact disk 17.99 (978-1-59859-123-1(1)) Oasis Audio.

Resurrection Day. unabr. ed. Brendan DuBois. Read by Jeremy Gage. 12 vols. (Running Time: 17 hrs.). 2000. bk. 96.95 (978-0-7927-2328-8(7), CSL 217, Chivers Sound Lib) AudioGO.
It's 1972, ten years since the Cuban missile crisis triggered a nuclear war. Russia has been decimated & the United States is a shell of its former self. President John F. Kennedy, believed killed during the war, is reviled. In Boston, Glove arrives at a murder scene. A friendless man & veteran of the '62 war has been shot to death. Carl learns that the man knew the truth about the war's origins & the secrets of JFK's final hours. Joined by Sandy Price, a reporter from the London Times, the two search for the truth about the veteran & his killers.

Resurrection Faith. Richard Fragomeni. 1 cass. (Running Time: 59 mins.). 2001. 8.95 (A8031) St Anthony Mess Pr.
Resurrection faith is more than as assent to an idea. It is living in the presence of the risen Christ.

***Resurrection in May.** unabr. ed. Lisa Samson. Narrated by Pam Ward. (Running Time: 10 hrs. 26 mins. 44 sec.). (ENG.). 2010. 19.59 (978-1-60814-680-2(4)); audio compact disk 27.99 (978-1-59859-729-5(9)) Oasis Audio.

Resurrection Life. Gloria Copeland. 6 cass. 1986. stu. ed. 30.00 (978-0-88114-749-0(4)) K Copeland Pubns.
Biblical teaching on restoration & revival.

Resurrection Life. Gloria Copeland. 6 cass. 1986. 30.00 (978-1-57562-108-1(8)) K Copeland Pubns.
Biblical teaching on the Resurrection.

Resurrection Living. Elbert Willis. 4 cass. 13.00 Fill the Gap.

Resurrection Man. Charlotte MacLeod. 6 cass. (Running Time: 9 hrs.). 2001. 48.00 (978-0-7366-6359-5(2)) Books on Tape.
The Countess Ouspenska, expert forger of Byzantine icons, tells Max Bittersohn that an old acquaintance, Bartolo Arbalest - the "Resurrection Man" - has set up an exclusive art restoration business. Meanwhile, valuable objets d'arts are stolen from the homes of Boston's wealthiest citizens...shortly after their owners have them restored.

***Resurrection Men.** abr. ed. Ian Rankin. Read by James MacPherson. (Running Time: 6 hrs.). (Inspector Rebus Ser.). 2010. audio compact disk 9.99 (978-1-4418-6783-4(X), 9781441867834, BCD Value Price) Brilliance Audio.

Resurrection Men. unabr. ed. Ian Rankin. Read by Joe Dunlop. 12 cass. (Running Time: 17 hrs.). (Inspector Rebus Novel Ser.: Vol. 14). 2003. 36.95 (978-1-59086-485-2(9), 1590864859, BAU); 97.25 (978-1-59086-486-9(7), 1590864867, CD Unabrid Lib Ed) Brilliance Audio.
Inspector John Rebus has messed up badly this time, so badly that he is sent to a kind of reform school for damaged cops. While there among the last-chancers known as "resurrection men," he joins a covert mission to gain evidence of a drug heist orchestrated by three of his classmates. But the group has been assigned an unsolved murder that may have resulted from Rebus's own mistake. Now Rebus can't determine if he's been set up for a fall or if his disgraced classmates are as ruthless as he suspects. When Detective Sergeant Siobhan Clarke discovers her investigation of an art dealer's murder is tied to Rebus's inquiry, the two - protege and mentor - join forces. Soon they find themselves in the midst of an even bigger scandal than they imagined - a plot with conspirators in every corner of Scotland and deadly implications about their colleagues.

Resurrection Men. unabr. ed. Ian Rankin. Read by Joe Dunlop. (Running Time: 17 hrs.). (Inspector Rebus Novel Ser.). 2004. 39.25 (978-1-59335-601-9(3), 1593356013, Brlnc Audio MP3 Lib) Brilliance Audio.

Resurrection Men. unabr. ed. Ian Rankin. Read by Joe Dunlop. (Running Time: 17 hrs.). (Inspector Rebus Ser.). 2004. 39.25 (978-1-59710-639-9(9), 1597106399, BADLE); 24.95 (978-1-59710-638-2(0), 1597106380, BAD) Brilliance Audio.

***Resurrection Men.** unabr. ed. Ian Rankin. Read by Joe Dunlop. (Running Time: 16 hrs.). (Inspector Rebus Ser.). 2010. audio compact disk 29.99 (978-1-4418-4018-9(4), 9781441840189); audio compact disk 89.97 (978-1-4418-4019-6(2), 9781441840196, BriAudCD Unabrid) Brilliance Audio.

Resurrection Men. unabr. ed. Ian Rankin. Read by Joe Dunlop. (Running Time: 17 hrs.). (Inspector Rebus Ser.). 2004. 24.95 (978-1-59335-139-7(9), 1593351399) Soulmate Audio Bks.

Resurrection Men: An Inspector Rebus Novel. abr. ed. Ian Rankin. Read by James MacPherson. (Running Time: 21600 sec.). (Inspector Rebus Ser.). 2007. audio compact disk 14.99 (978-1-4233-3355-5(1), 9781423333555, BCD Value Price) Brilliance Audio.

Resurrection Mystery. Instructed by Manly P. Hall. 8.95 (978-0-89314-237-7(9), C840422) Philos Res.

Resurrection Narratives. Mary Thompson. 2 cass. (Running Time: 1 hr. 47 min.). 1994. 17.95 (TAH315) Alba Hse Comns.
Sr. Mary reviews & compares the synoptic gospels (Matthew, Mark, & Luke) & the gospel of St. John - drawing interesting, fascinating & spiritually rewarding images associated with the death & resurrection of Christ. Excellent for adult religious education classes & other groups.

Resurrection Power. Contrib. by Dale Mathews & Michael Frazier. 1996. 24.95 (978-0-7601-0682-2(7), 75600265) Pub: Brentwood Music. Dist(s): H Leonard

Resurrection Power: Understanding & Accessing the Resurrection Power of God. Lynne Hammond. 2008. audio compact disk 12.00 (978-1-57399-405-7(7)) Mac Hammond.

Resurrection Report: A Journalist Investigates the Most Debated Event in History. William Proctor. 1998. 15.99 (978-0-8054-1151-5(8)) BH Pubng Grp.

Resurrection Revisited: 1 Cor. 15:12-19. Ed Young. 1986. 4.95 (978-0-7417-1518-0(X), 518) Win Walk.

Resurrection Row. Anne Perry. Narrated by Davina Porter. 7 CDs. (Running Time: 8 hrs. 15 mins.). (Thomas Pitt Ser.). audio compact disk 71.00 (978-0-7887-9873-3(1)) Recorded Bks.

Resurrection Row. unabr. ed. Anne Perry. Narrated by Davina Porter. 6 cass. (Running Time: 8 hrs. 15 mins.). (Thomas Pitt Ser.). 1981. 58.00 (978-0-7887-6088-4(2), H1219L8) Recorded Bks.
After a wonderful night at the theater, Thomas & Charlotte find themselves confronted with a corpse in the driver's seat of a hansom cab. Even more shocking - it is the body of a peer of the realm who was recently buried the week before. Determined to get to the bottom of things, Inspector Pitt begins his investigation within the proper channels while his intrepid wife Charlotte renews a tie from her past to get inside Lord Fitzroy-Hammond's world.

Resurrection: the Message. unabr. ed. Eugene H. Peterson. Narrated by Kelly Ryan Dolan. (ENG.). 2006. 12.59 (978-1-60814-363-4(5)) Oasis Audio.

Resurrection Truth. Kenneth Copeland. 2 cass. 1988. 10.00 (978-0-88114-919-7(5)) K Copeland Pubns.
Biblical teaching on powerful.

Resurrectionist. Jack O'Connell. Read by Holter Graham. (Playaway Adult Fiction Ser.). 2008. 54.99 (978-1-60640-523-9(3)) Find a World.

Resurrectionist. unabr. ed. Jack O'Connell. Read by Holter Graham. 9 CDs. (Running Time: 11 hrs. 30 mins.). (ENG., 2008. audio compact disk 34.95 (978-1-59887-594-2(9), 1598875949) Pub: HighBridge. Dist(s): Workman Pub

Resurrectionist: A Novel. abr. ed. Thomas F. Monteleone. 4 cass. (Running Time: 6 hrs.). 1995. 22.95 (978-1-56876-050-6(7), 693295) Soundlines Ent.
GOP presidential candidate Thomas Flanagan & his campaign manager should both be dead after their jet crashes. Instead, Flanagan emerges unscathed - & after touching his fatally wounded friend, discovers that he now has the power to heal the dying...& resurrect the dead. Though at first many are convinced Flanagan is the new messiah, the dark side of his "gift" eventually surfaces, revealing a horrible truth far worse than death.

RET & Assertiveness Training. Albert Ellis. 1 cass. (Running Time: 82 min.). 9.95 (C019) A Ellis Institute.
Distinguishes assertive from aggressive behavior & helps you overcome emotional blocks to communicating more effectively.

RET & Assertiveness Training. Albert Ellis. 1 cass. (Running Time: 82 min.). 9.95 (C019) Inst Rational-Emotive.
Distinguish assertive from aggressive behavior. Learn how to overcome emotional blocks to assertiveness, & how to do assertiveness training within a REBT framework.

Retablissement. unabr. ed. Robert A. Monroe. Read by Roland Simon. 1 cass. (Running Time: 30 min.). (Human Plus Ser.). (FRE.). 1993. 14.95 (978-1-56102-103-1(2)) Inter Indus.
Learn to adjust, balance or maintain any part of physical body.

Retail in Indonesia: A Strategic Reference 2007. Compiled by Icon Group International, Inc. Staff. 2007. ring bd. 195.00 (978-0-497-36032-0(2)) Icon Grp.

Retailing Equipment & Services in India: A Strategic Reference 2007. Compiled by Icon Group International, Inc. Staff. 2007. ring bd. 195.00 (978-0-497-36021-4(7)) Icon Grp.

Retailing in the New Millennium. Jay Diamond & Sheri Litt. audio compact disk (978-1-56367-304-7(5)) Fairchild.

Retain Recall Release. abr. ed. Robert A. Monroe. Read by Robert A. Monroe. (Mind Food Ser.). 1988. 14.95 (978-1-56102-414-8(7)) Inter Indus.
Incorporates encoding cues to assist in memory process.

Rethinking America. abr. ed. Hedrick Smith. Read by Michael Hansen. 4 cass. (Running Time: 6 hrs.). 1995. 24.95 (978-1-879371-98-9(7), 20390) Pub Mills.
A provocative inside portrait of America at a crucial crossroads. Smith leads us into the schools & businesses of America to show how our traditional approach to commerce & education is obsolete for the new global economy - & how our innovators are succeeding by rethinking America. Measuring this country against its major competitors, Smith shows how global competition has radically altered the way people work, what schools need to teach, & the nature of power & people's relationships on the job. He discloses how differently decisions are made & power is wielded in the corporate boardrooms of America, Germany, & Japan. Education is where the race begins. Smith contrasts what American school teachers emphasize, compared with skills & values taught elsewhere.

Rethinking Education: Educating Hearts & Minds. Contrib. by Daniel Goleman & George Lucas. 2007. audio compact disk 14.95 (978-1-934441-03-9(1)) More Than Snd.

Rethinking Reason: With So Many Different Faiths, Does Someone Have to Be Wrong for Someone to Be Right? R. Craig Strickland. (Running Time: 9540 sec.). 2007. audio compact disk 19.99 (978-1-60462-763-3(8)) Tate Pubng.

Rethinking Thin: The New Science of Weight Loss - -and the Myths & Realities of Dieting. unabr. ed. Gina Kolata. Read by Ellen Archer. 7 CDs. (Running Time: 8 hrs. 30 mins. 0 sec.). (ENG.). 2007. audio compact disk 69.99 (978-1-4001-3450-2(1)); audio compact disk 24.99 (978-1-4001-5450-0(2)) Pub: Tantor Media. Dist(s): IngramPubServ

Rethinking Thin: The New Science of Weight Loss - And the Myths & Realities of Dieting. unabr. ed. Gina Kolata. Read by Ellen Archer. 7 CDs. (Running Time: 8 hrs. 30 mins. 0 sec.). (ENG.). 2007. audio compact disk 34.99 (978-1-4001-0450-5(5)) Pub: Tantor Media. Dist(s): IngramPubServ

Rethinking Thin: The New Science of Weight Loss - and the Myths & Realities of Dieting. unabr. ed. Gina Kolata. Read by Ellen Archer. (YA). 2007. 54.99 (978-1-60252-923-6(X)) Find a World.

Retinal Manifestations of Systemic Disease. 3 cass. (Ophthalmic Surgery Ser.: C85-OP1). 1985. 22.50 (8569) Am Coll Surgeons.

Retinoblastoma - A Bibliography & Dictionary for Physicians, Patients, & Genome Researchers. Compiled by Icon Group International, Inc. Staff. 2007. ring bd. 28.95 (978-0-497-11286-8(8)) Icon Grp.

Retire Happy: What You Can Do Now to Guarantee a Great Retirement. rev. ed. Ralph Warner & Richard Stim. (ENG.). 2009. audio compact disk 19.99 (978-1-4133-0960-7(7)) Nolo.

Retired Colonel see Poetry & Voice of Ted Hughes

Retiree Medical Liabilities, FAS 106, & Cost Containment: New Approaches to Redesign, Prefunding, & Disclosure. Cynthia M. Combe & Harold Dankner. (Tax Law & Estate Planning Course Handbook Ser.). 1992. pap. bk. 40.00 (978-0-685-69488-6(7)) PLI.

Retirement: Opportunity or Threat? Granger Westburg. 1986. 10.80 (0905B) Assn Prof Chaplains.

Retirement: Opportunity or Threat? Carroll Wise. 1986. 10.80 (0906) Assn Prof Chaplains.

***Retirement Day.** Peter Dawson. 2009. (978-1-60136-458-6(X)) Audio Holding.

Retirement Day. Peter Dawson. (Running Time: 0 hr. 42 mins.). 1998. 10.95 (978-1-60083-472-1(8)) Iofy Corp.

Retirement Options Coach's Training Audiotapes. Speeches. Conducted by Richard P. Johnson. 8 cass. (Running Time: 12 hrs.). 2003. 34.95 (978-0-9743623-1-1(X)) Retirement Opt.

Retirement Planning after TRA '86. James B. Findley. (Running Time: 40 min.). 25.00 Am Soc Chart.
Examines the effect of the Tax Reform Act on 401(k) plans, IRAs, & other elective deferral plans.

Retirement Planning for Everyone. unabr. ed. David K. Luhman. Read by David K. Luhman. 1 cass. (Running Time: 1 hr. 30 min.). (Personal Finance for Everyone Ser.: Vol. 2). 1996. 9.00 (978-1-889297-12-5(7)) Numen Lumen.
The retirement challenge, Social Security, compounding & the time value of money, retirement plan basics, defined benefit plans, defined contribution & savings plans, 401(k) plans, Keogh plans, SEPs, IRAs, managing money in your retirement account.

Retirement Planning in Changing Times: A Practitioner's Guide to Strategies & Distributions. Sidney Kess & Barbara Weltman. 3 cass. (Running Time: 3 hrs.). 1997. stu. ed. 150.00 (09101) Toolkit Media.
Addresses important retirement planning issues, including: sources of retirement planning income, retirement savings goals, charitable giving, qualified plan & IRA strategies & much more. Recommended for twelve house of CPE credit.

Retirement Plans & IRAs for Small Businesses & Professional Organizations. 1998. bk. 99.00 (ACS-2110) PA Bar Inst.
Planning for retirement is increasingly on the minds of business & individual clients as they prepare for life after work. With many new options available come a host of complex questions & decisions in choosing the right plan to meet the client's needs. This examines the fundamentals of retirement plans & IRA's, state & federal income & estate taxes, plan design & how to provide the client with a plan at the lowest possible cost.

Retiring: An Easy, Smart Guide to an Enjoyable Retirement. Hope Egan & Barbara Wagner. (B & N Basics Ser.). 2003. audio compact disk 9.98 (978-0-7607-3772-9(X), Silver Lini) M Friedman Pub Grp Inc.

Retracing Our Steps Back Home. Swami Amar Jyoti. 1 dolby cass. 1985. 9.95 (M-62) Truth Consciousness.
Faith keeps us in touch with our True Self. Crumbling the wall of resistance & separation. Help from the angels. Myth of polytheism.

Retrato de Dorian Gray. unabr. ed. Oscar Wilde. Read by Fabio Camero. 3 CDs.Tr. of Portrait of Dorian Gray. (SPA.). 2002. audio compact disk 17.00 (978-958-9494-97-4(8)) YoYoMusic.

Retrato del Artista Joven. abr. ed. James Joyce. Read by Hernando Iván Cano. 3 CDs.Tr. of Portray of the Artist as a Young Man. (SPA.). 2002. audio compact disk 17.00 (978-958-8161-26-6(6)) YoYoMusic.

Retrato en Sepia see Portrait in Sepia

Retread Tires - As Good As New. Hosted by Nancy Pearlman. 1 cass. (Running Time: 29 min.). 10.00 (1110) Educ Comm CA.

Retreat for Beginners. unabr. ed. Ronald Knox. Read by Jim Lewis. 6 cass. 1988. 24.95 (943) Ignatius Pr.
This is a collection of talks originally given to schoolboys, but the simple tone in no way masks the erudition. He preached at Oxford & at boarding schools, to priests & to the laity, always touching & delighting his listeners.

Retreat for Lay People. Ronald Knox. Read by Cynthia Splatt. 7 cass. (Running Time: 10 hrs. 30 min.). 1987. 28.95 (933) Ignatius Pr.
Collection of talks, for treatments of all ages.

Retreat for Men: The Creed of the Catechism of the Catholic Church. Fr. Hardon. 13 cass. 52.00 incl. notes. (94C) IRL Chicago.

Retreat, Hell! unabr. ed. W. E. B. Griffin. Read by Dick Hill & Susie Breck. (Running Time: 18 hrs.). (Corps Ser.: Bk. 10). 2004. 36.95 (978-1-59355-298-5(X), 159355298X, BAU) Brilliance Audio.
It is the fall of 1950. The Marines have made a pivotal breakthrough at Inchon, but a roller coaster awaits them. The bit in his teeth, Douglas MacArthur is intent on surging across the 38th parallel toward the Yalu River, where he is certain no Chinese are waiting for him, while Major Ken McCoy, operating undercover, hears a different story entirely, and is just as intent on nailing down the truth before it is too late. Meanwhile, Brigadier General Fleming Pickering, shuttling between two continents, works desperately to mediate the escalating battle between MacArthur and President Harry Truman, while trying to keep his mind from the cold fact that somewhere out there, his own daredevil pilot son, Pick, is lost behind enemy lines - and may be lost forever. Before Retreat, Hell! is finished, all their fates will be determined - and for some of them, it will be a bitter pill indeed.

Retreat, Hell! unabr. ed. W. E. B. Griffin. Read by Dick Hill. (Running Time: 18 hrs.). (Corps Ser.: Bk. 10). 2004. 107.25 (978-1-59355-299-2(8), 1593552998, BrilAudUnabridg) Brilliance Audio.

Retreat, Hell! unabr. ed. W. E. B. Griffin. Read by Dick Hill & Susie Breck. (Running Time: 18 hrs.). (Corps Ser.: Bk. 10). 2004. audio compact disk 44.95 (978-1-59355-300-5(5), 1593553005, Bril Audio CD Unabri) Brilliance Audio.

Retreat, Hell! unabr. ed. W. E. B. Griffin. Read by Dick Hill & Susie Breck. (Running Time: 18 hrs.). (Corps Ser.: Bk.10). 2004. audio compact disk 127.25 (978-1-59355-301-2(3), 1593553013, BriAudCD Unabrid) Brilliance Audio.

Retreat, Hell! unabr. ed. W. E. B. Griffin. Read by Dick Hill & Susie Breck. (Running Time: 18 hrs.). (Corps Ser.: Bk. 10). 2004. 44.25 (978-1-59335-641-5(2), 1593356412, Brlnc Audio MP3 Lib) Brilliance Audio.

Retreat, Hell! unabr. ed. W. E. B. Griffin. Read by Dick Hill & Susie Breck. (Running Time: 18 hrs.). (Corps Ser.: Bk. 10). 2004. 44.25 (978-1-59710-641-2(0), 1597106410, BADLE) Brilliance Audio.

Retreat, Hell! unabr. ed. W. E. B. Griffin. Read by Dick Hill. (Running Time: 18 hrs.). (Corps Ser.: Bk. 10). 2004. 29.95 (978-1-59710-640-5(2), 1597106402, BAD) Brilliance Audio.

Retreat, Hell! unabr. ed. W. E. B. Griffin. Read by Dick Hill & Susie Breck. (Running Time: 18 hrs.). (Corps Ser.: Bk. 10). 2004. 29.95 (978-1-59335-264-6(6), 1593352646) Soulmate Audio Bks.

Retreat on the Lord's Prayer. Chester P. Michael. 1985. 28.00 (978-0-940136-16-8(3)) Open Door Inc.

Retreat Talks, Vol. 1. Speeches. Featuring Adyashanti. 2 Cassettes. (Running Time: 3 hrs.). 2004. 20.00 (978-0-9717036-7-4(1), 2RTA-1) Pub: Open Gate Pub. Dist(s): New Leaf Dist
"Retreat Talks" highlights the powerful and uniquely engaging talks Adyashanti gives at retreats, with dialogs removed. This distilled presentation of teachings offers five talks recorded in April 2004: "Welcome to Retreat," "Life Is," "Ego Is Not a Problem," "Getting to Nothing," and "Beyond Tradition." Adyashanti invites us into the depth of the retreat experience; clarifies that ego is not something that needs to be dismantled, dissolved, thrown away, or raised into a higher state; and reveals what it takes to move beyond the teachings that have been stepping stones on our spiritual journey.

Retreat Talks: Volume 3. Featuring Adyashanti. 3 CDs. (Running Time: 3.5 hours). (ENG.). 2006. audio compact disk 29.00 (978-1-933986-16-6(6)) Open Gate Pub.

Retreat Talks - Volume Two: Audio Satsangs with Adyashanti - Excepts from Retreats in June 2004, May 2005 & June 2005. Featuring Adyashanti. 3 CDs. (Running Time: 3 hrs., 30 min.). 2005. audio compact disk 29.00 (978-0-9763788-7-7(6), 2RTA-2) Open Gate Pub.
The ?Retreat Talks? series highlights the powerful and uniquely engaging talks Adyashanti gives at retreats?with dialogues removed. Volume 2 features nine insightful talks selected from silent retreats in June 2004, May 2005, and June 2005. This distilled presentation of teachings invites the listener to engage in a journey of insight and self-discovery as Adyashanti explores the following topics: The Most Powerful Illusion, Destination Unknown, The Commentator, The Collapse of Fantasy, Knowledge is Dead, Letting Go of Control, Surrender Happens, Trust, and Innocence.

Retreat Talks, Vol. 4. Featuring Adyashanti. (ENG.). 2008. audio compact disk 29.00 (978-1-933986-41-8(X)) Open Gate Pub.

Retreat with the Psalms: Directions for a Priest's Life & Ministry. Carroll Stuhlmueller. 6 cass. (Running Time: 7 hrs. 37 min.). 1993. 40.95 (TAH286) Alba Hse Comns.
The eleven outstanding talks contain much new material to stimulate a renewal of their attitude to the Breviary, to the Psalms & to their ministry.

And the Laity will notice the difference too; homilies will have a new tone & more substantial content.

Retreat with the Psalms: Directions for a Priest's Life & Ministry. unabr. ed. Carroll Stuhlmueller. 6 cass. (Running Time: 7 hrs. 37 min.). 1993. 40.95 (TAH286) Alba Hse Comns.
These eleven outstanding talks contain much new material to stimulate a renewal of their attitude to the Breviary, to the Psalms & to their ministry. The laity will notice the difference also; homilies will have a new tone & more substantial content.

Retribution. abr. ed. Dale Brown et al. Read by Christopher Lane. (Running Time: 6 hrs.). (Dale Brown's Dreamland Ser.). 2008. audio compact disk 14.99 (978-1-4233-1305-2(4), 9781423313052, BCD Value Price) Brilliance Audio.

Retribution. unabr. ed. Dale Brown & Jim DeFelice. Read by Christopher Lane. (Running Time: 12 hrs.). (Dale Brown's Dreamland Ser.). 2007. 39.25 (978-1-4233-1303-8(8), 9781423313038, BADLE); 24.95 (978-1-4233-1302-1(X), 9781423313021, BAD); 82.25 (978-1-4233-1297-0(X), 9781423312970, BrilAudUnabridg); audio compact disk 36.95 (978-1-4233-1298-7(8), 9781423312987, Bril Audio CD Unabri); audio compact disk 24.95 (978-1-4233-1300-7(3), 9781423313007, Brilliance MP3); audio compact disk 97.25 (978-1-4233-1299-4(6), 9781423312994, BriAudCD Unabrid); audio compact disk 39.25 (978-1-4233-1301-4(1), 9781423313014, Brinc Audio MP3 Lib) Brilliance Audio.

Retribution. unabr. ed. Stuart M. Kaminsky. Read by Scott Brick. 6 cass. (Running Time: 9 hrs.). (Lew Fonesca Mystery Ser.: Vol. 2). 2001. 48.00 (978-0-7366-8485-9(9)) Books on Tape.
Lew Fonesca, depressed freelance process server, has two more cases to solve.

Retribution. unabr. ed. R. J. Pineiro. Read by Barrett Whitener. 13 cass. (Running Time: 19 hrs.). 1995. 85.95 (978-0-7861-0901-2(7), 1709) Blckstn Audio.
A year ago, in the sky over Iraq, a hero was forged in the heat of battle when Navy Lt. Kevin Dalton destroyed Saddam Hussein's secret arsenal of nuclear missiles. Dalton now works for the CIA. As Saddam prepares to strike at the heart of the United States, Dalton finds himself facing the ultimate horror; nuclear weapons acquired from the Russian Mafia through an infamous international arms dealer smuggled into the U.S. They are Saddam's revenge for his defeats at the hands of America. Reunited with the beautiful Mossad agent Khalela, Dalton must untangle a web of conspiracy that leads from Jersey City mosques to the backwoods of Virginia, from Atlantic City casinos to the bayous of Louisiana. Only he & Khalela can prevent the weapons from reaching their separate targets.

Retrieved Reformation see O. Henry Favorites

Retrieved Reformation see Best of O. Henry

Retro. unabr. ed. Loren D. Estleman. Read by Mel Foster. (Running Time: 7 hrs.). (Amos Walker Ser.). 2004. 27.95 (978-1-59355-406-4(0), 1593554060, BAU); 69.25 (978-1-59355-407-1(9), 1593554079, BrilAudUnabridg) Brilliance Audio.
Amos Walker has made a lot of friends - and a few enemies - in his years as a detective in Detroit, but he has never had to deal with quite the trouble he finds when he agrees to grant the deathbed wish of Beryl Garnet. Beryl was a madam with a long, successful career. She's got no regrets about that, but she does about her son. She hasn't seen him in a long time and would like him to know his mother never forgot him. So she asks Walker to make sure that her son gets her ashes when she's gone. He obliges her, finding her son, who has been in Canada since the 1960s, evading the law since he was a Vietnam War protester. A simple favor, melancholy, but benign. Except that before he can get settled back in Detroit, Garnet's son is dead, and Walker is the prime suspect. He has little choice but to find out who might have done the deed and tried to pin the blame on him...and in the process he discovers another murder, of a prizefighter from the 1940s. Curtis Smallwood was the father of Beryl Garnet's son. And if that wasn't bad enough, the two murders, fifty-three years apart, were committed with the same gun.

Retro. unabr. ed. Loren D. Estleman. Read by Mel Foster. (Running Time: 7 hrs.). (Amos Walker Ser.). 2004. 24.95 (978-1-59335-310-0(3), 1593353103, Brilliance MP3); 39.25 (978-1-59335-469-5(X), 159335469X, Brinc Audio MP3 Lib) Brilliance Audio.

Retro. unabr. ed. Loren D. Estleman. Read by Mel Foster. (Running Time: 7 hrs.). (Amos Walker Ser.). 2004. 39.25 (978-1-59710-642-9(9), 1597106429, BADLE); 24.95 (978-1-59710-643-6(7), 1597106437, BAD) Brilliance Audio.

Retro-Sensuals. unabr. ed. Vera Mann et al. Read by J. P. Linton & Paula Jean Ewin. 1 cass. (Running Time: 1 hr. 20 min.). (Love Story Classics Ser.). (J). (gr. 8 up). 1995. 11.95 (978-0-9637488-5-0(8)) Love Story Class.
The fourth volume of an unabridged anthology on the theme of love - two rare romance novelettes from the early 1950's.

Retro-Sensuals 2. unabr. ed. Doris Knight & J. P. Linton. Read by J. P. Linton & Michelle Gay. 1 cass. (Running Time: 1 hr.). (Love Story Classics Ser.). (J). (gr. 8 up). 1996. 7.95 (978-0-9637488-6-7(6)) Love Story Class.
The fifth volume of an unabridged anthology on the theme of love - one rare romance novelette from the early 1950's & one original short story inspired by the genre.

Retrograde Planet Update. Carol Ruth. 1 cass. 8.95 (709) Am Fed Astrologers.
An AFA Convention workshop tape.

Retrograde Planets. Joanne Wickenburg. Read by Joanne Wickenburg. 1 cass. (Running Time: 90 min.). 1994. 8.95 (1170) Am Fed Astrologers.

Retrogrades. Mohan Koparkar. 1 cass. 8.95 (202) Am Fed Astrologers.
Natal, progressed & transit with mundane & karmic application.

Retrogrades. Mohan Koparkar. Read by Mohan Koparkar. 1 cass. (Running Time: 90 min.). 1994. 8.95 (1136) Am Fed Astrologers.
Retrograde planets - what they mean.

Retrospective. William Meredith. Read by William Meredith. 1 cass. (Running Time: 41 min.). (Watershed Tapes of Contemporary Poetry). 1976. 10.95 (23632) J Norton Pubs.
A reading recorded at the Folger Shakespeare Library.

Rett Syndrome: Solving the Puzzle. Marlene Johnson. Read by Darrel Favrhow. Ed. by Neva Duyndam. 1 cass. (Running Time: 46 min.). 1991. 9.95 (978-1-878159-16-8(X)) Duvall Media.
Through Kristamae's story, tells the facts about Rett Syndrome (symptoms & treatment), its effect on the family, & sources of support.

Rett Syndrome - A Bibliography & Dictionary for Physicians, Patients, & Genome Researchers. Compiled by Icon Group International, Inc. Staff. 2007. ring bd. 28.95 (978-0-497-11287-5(6)) Icon Grp.

Return see Tales of Unrest

Return see Twentieth-Century Poetry in English, No. 24, Recordings of Poets Reading Their Own Poetry

Return. William Shatner. Read by William Shatner. (Star Trek Ser.). 2004. 10.95 (978-0-7435-1953-3(1)) Pub: S&S Audio. Dist(s): S and S Inc

Return. William Shatner et al. Read by William Shatner. (Running Time: 4 hrs.). 2005. 19.95 (978-1-60083-435-6(3), Audiofy Corp) Iofy Corp.

Return. Winans, The. 1 cass., 1 CD. 7.98 (26161-4); audio compact disk 11.98 CD. (26161-2) Warner Christian.

Return. abr. ed. Karen Kingsbury. Read by Sandra Burr. (Running Time: 14400 sec.). (Redemption Ser.). 2005. 19.95 (978-1-59355-891-8(0), 9781593558918); audio compact disk 21.95 (978-1-59355-893-2(7), 9781593558932, BACD) Brilliance Audio.
A Shattered Relationship Luke, golden boy and the Baxter family's only son, has walked away from everything that mattered most to him: his faith, his family, and Reagan, his only love. Devastated by the events of September 11, 2001, Luke decides that life is random, faith a fraud, and God a fantasy. A Secret A baby is about to be born, but with Reagan a thousand miles away in New York City, Luke has no idea he's the father. Now, though, someone in his family learns the truth. The problem? She has a secret of her own, one that will change the Baxters' lives forever. A Revelation What will it take for Luke to return to the family who loves and aches for him? And what extremes will a certain young firefighter take to help bring the Baxters together again, and in the process, find his place in the family? A story of tenacious love and longing for a lost son.

Return. abr. ed. Karen Kingsbury & Gary Smalley. Read by Sandra Burr. (Running Time: 4 hrs.). (Redemption Ser.). 2005. 39.25 (978-1-59737-976-2(X), 9781597379762, BADLE); 9.99 (978-1-59737-975-5(1), 9781597379755, BAD); 49.25 (978-1-59355-892-5(9), 9781593558925, BAudLibEd); audio compact disk 69.25 (978-1-59355-894-9(5), 9781593558949, BACDLib Ed); audio compact disk 9.99 (978-1-59737-973-1(5), 9781597379731, Brilliance MP3); audio compact disk 39.25 (978-1-59737-974-8(3), 9781597379748, Brinc Audio MP3 Lib) Brilliance Audio.

***Return.** abr. ed. Karen Kingsbury & Gary Smalley. Read by Sandra Burr. (Running Time: 4 hrs.). (Redemption Ser.). 2010. audio compact disk 9.99 (978-1-4418-7833-5(5), 9781441878335, BCD Value Price) Brilliance Audio.

Return. collector's ed. Buzz Aldrin, Jr. & John Barnes. Read by Scott Brick. 7 cass. (Running Time: 10 hrs. 30 min.). 2000. 56.00 (978-0-7366-5456-2(9)) Books on Tape.
A former astronaut deals with a Shuttle accident that's no accident & a nuclear war that threatens an international space crew.

Return. unabr. ed. Buzz Aldrin, Jr. 6 cass. (Running Time: 9 hrs.). 2000. 24.95 (978-0-7366-5488-3(7)) Books on Tape.

Return. unabr. ed. Buzz Aldrin, Jr. & John Barnes. Read by Scott Brick. 8 CDs. (Running Time: 9 hrs.). 2000. audio compact disk 34.95 (978-0-7366-5491-3(7)) Books on Tape.

***Return: Book IV of Voyagers.** unabr. ed. Ben Bova. Read by Stefan Rudnicki. (Running Time: 15 hrs. 30 mins.). 2010. 29.95 (978-1-4332-7773-3(5)); 85.95 (978-1-4332-7769-6(7)); audio compact disk 118.00 (978-1-4332-7770-2(0)) Blckstn Audio.

Return & Reign of Jesus Christ. John MacArthur, Jr. (John MacArthur's Bible Studies). 24.75 (HarperThor) HarpC GBR.

Return Chart of Saturn: Life Styles of Mid-Adulthood. James Lale. 1 cass. (Running Time: 90 min.). 1988. 8.95 (626) Am Fed Astrologers.

Return from the Inferno. abr. ed. Mack Maloney. 2 cass. (Running Time: 3 hrs.). (Wingman Ser.: Vol. 9). 2002. 9.95 (978-1-931953-01-6(5)) Listen & Live.

Return Journey. unabr. ed. Ruby M. Ayres. Read by Rosemary Davis. 8 cass. (Running Time: 8 hrs. 15 min.). 1993. 69.95 (978-1-85089-682-1(8), 21091) Pub: ISIS Audio GBR. Dist(s): Ulverscroft US
A sea trip to Port Said is suddenly enlivened when the sparkling Rocky joins the ship at Toulon. She makes an enormous impact on the rest of the passengers who find themselves warming to her delightful charm & friendly ways. Relationships form & emotions are stirred at sea, & Rocky plays a hand in the excitements of the voyage.

Return Journey. unabr. ed. Maeve Binchy. Read by Fionnula Flanagan. 4 cass. (Running Time: 6 hrs.). 2001. 29.95; audio compact disk 26.00 Books on Tape.
A collection of 14 short stories of life, love & learning that reveal Binchy's unrivaled understanding of matters of the heart.

Return of a Private see Great American Short Stories

Return of a Private. unabr. ed. Hamlin Garland. Read by Donald White. (Running Time: 80 min.). Dramatization. 1981. 7.95 (N-62) Jimcin Record.
Reflections of the rise of realism.

Return of Bert & I. Narrated by Marshall Dodge & Robert Bryan. (Running Time: 31 min.). 8.95 (978-0-9607546-5-6(2), 9) Bert and I Inc.
Comic tales from DownEast.

Return of Bert & I - Bert & I Stem Inflation. Marshall Dodge & Bob Bryan. 1 cass. audio compact disk 13.95 CD. (978-0-9607546-2-5(8)) Bert and I Inc.
More of favorite Downeast stories fun for the whole family.

Return of Buddy Bush. unabr. ed. Shelia P. Moses. Read by Cherise Booth. 3 CDs. (Running Time: 2 hrs. 45 mins.). (YA). 2006. audio compact disk 29.75 (978-1-4193-5319-2(5), C3386); 19.75 (978-1-4193-5314-7(4), 98160) Recorded Bks.
A Coretta Scott King Honor Book Award recipient for The Legend of Buddy Bush, Shelia P. Moses pens a sequel that reveals what really happened to Buddy. In rural 1947 North Carolina, Buddy¿s Northern notions of equal opportunity soon enrage local Klansmen. When Buddy - jailed for a crime he didn¿t commit - disappears, niece Pattie Mae is concerned. Clues lead to Harlem, where she observes blacks working and running businesses just as white folks do. But can anyone there secretly help her find Buddy and prove his innocence?.

Return of Deathwind. unabr. ed. G. M. Farley. Read by Jack Sondericker. 3 cass. (Running Time: 3 hrs.). 1995. 21.95 (978-1-55686-585-5(6)) Books in Motion.
Lewis Wetzel is Deathwind, named & feared by the Indians of the Ohio valley frontier. Wetzel volunteers to rescue the daughter of a colonist captured by Indians.

Return of Depression Economics & the Crisis of 2008. unabr. ed. Paul Krugman. Read by Don Leslie. (ENG.). 2008. audio compact disk 31.95 (978-0-7393-8472-5(4), Random AudioBks) Pub: Random Audio Pubg. Dist(s): Random

Return of Dr. Fu-Manchu. Sax Rohmer, pseud. Read by Amy von Lecteur. 2009. 27.95 (978-1-60112-990-1(4)) Babblebooks.

Return of Dr. Fu-Manchu. Sax Rohmer, pseud. Read by John Bolen. (Running Time: 7 hrs. 45 mins.). (Fu-Manchu Ser.: Vol. 2). 2002. 27.95 (978-1-60083-620-6(8), Audiofy Corp) Iofy Corp.

Return of Dr. Fu-Manchu. unabr. ed. Sax Rohmer, pseud. Narrated by John Bolen. 7 CDs. (Running Time: 7 hrs. 43 mins.). (Fu-Manchu Ser.: Vol. 2). (ENG.). 2002. audio compact disk 39.00 (978-1-4001-0051-4(8)); audio compact disk 20.00 (978-1-4001-5051-9(5)) Pub: Tantor Media. Dist(s): IngramPubServ

Return of Dr. Fu Manchu. unabr. ed. Sax Rohmer, pseud. Read by John Bolen. (Fu-Manchu Ser.: Vol. 2). (ENG.). 2002. audio compact disk 78.00 (978-1-4001-3051-1(4)) Pub: Tantor Media. Dist(s): IngramPubServ

Return of Dr. Fu-Manchu, with EBook. unabr. ed. Sax Rohmer, pseud. Narrated by John Bolen. (Running Time: 7 hrs. 30 mins. 0 sec.). (Fu-Manchu Ser.). (ENG.). 2009. 19.99 (978-1-4001-6112-6(6)); 7.02 (978-1-4001-8112-4(7)); audio compact disk 27.99 (978-1-4001-1112-1(9)) Pub: Tantor Media. Dist(s): IngramPubServ

Return of Dr. Fu-Manchu, with eBook. unabr. ed. Sax Rohmer, pseud. Narrated by John Bolen. (Running Time: 7 hrs. 30 mins.). (Fu-Manchu Ser.). 2009. 27.99 (978-1-4001-9112-3(2)); audio compact disk 55.99 (978-1-4001-4112-8(5)) Pub: Tantor Media. Dist(s): IngramPubServ

Return of Hickey Vol. 2. Short Stories. Perf. by Zach Galligan et al. Directed By Allan A. Goldstein. 3 cass. (Running Time: 60 min.). (YA). (gr. 8 up). 1988. 24.95 (30410, Monterey SoundWorks) Monterey Media Inc.
Hickey returns to the Lawrenceville school after a semester's suspension only to find that his place as kingpin has been usurped by a newcomer, " The Tennessee Shad." Their ensuing battle of wits makes for more merriment, culminating in a raucous political campaign.

Return of History & the End of Dreams. unabr. ed. Robert Kagan. Narrated by Holter Graham. (Running Time: 11220 sec.). (ENG.). 2008. audio compact disk 19.95 (978-1-60283-432-3(6)) Pub: AudioGO. Dist(s): Perseus Dist

Return of Little Big Man. collector's ed. Thomas Berger. Read by Michael Russotto. 13 cass. (Running Time: 19 hrs. 30 min.). 1999. 104.00 (978-0-7366-4561-4(6), 4968) Books on Tape.
Jack Crabb, the only white survivor of Custer's Last Stand, dies at age 111, cutting short his tale. Jack gives a blow by blow eyewitness account of the assassination of Wild Bill Hickock & that it really happened at the OK Corral. He also meets, shoots, drinks & rides with Bat Masterson, Annie Oakley & Doc Holliday. Jack even travels with Buffalo Bill Cody in his Wild West show where he is embraced by Queen Victoria & the Prince of Wales & Jack witnesses the murder of one of America's greatest heroes, Sitting Bull.

Return of Little Big Man. unabr. ed. Thomas Berger. Read by Stuart Milligan. 16 cass. (Running Time: 24 hrs.). (Isis Ser.). (J). 2001. 104.95 (978-0-7531-0864-2(X), 000807) Pub: ISIS Lrg Prnt GBR. Dist(s): Ulverscroft US

Return of Little Big Man. unabr. ed. Thomas Berger. Read by Stuart Milligan. 18 CDs. (Running Time: 19 hrs.). (Isis Ser.). (J). 2002. audio compact disk 116.95 (978-0-7531-1581-7(6)) Pub: ISIS Lrg Prnt GBR. Dist(s): Ulverscroft US
Jack Crabb was one hundred and eleven years old when he originally dictated his memoirs. His supposed death cut short his tale just as he had finished recounting how he was the last white survivor of Custer's Last Stand. A newly discovered manuscript, however, reveals that Jack faked his death to get out of his publishing contract. Now he completes the story of his extraordinary life in this long-awaited sequel to the best-selling literary classic. As Jack writes about the gunfight at the Ok Corral and the assassination of Wild Bill Hickok, we meet, shoot, drink and ride with dozens of ranchers, bar girls, saloon owners and gunslingers.

***return of Rathalorn.** Dave Luckett. Read by Stanley McGeagh. (Running Time: 4 hrs.). (School of Magic Ser.). (J). 2010. 59.99 (978-1-74214-638-6(4), 9781742146386) Pub: Bolinda Pubng AUS. Dist(s): Bolinda Pub Inc

return of Rathalorn. unabr. ed. Dave Luckett. Read by Stanley McGeagh. (Running Time: 4 hrs.). (School of Magic Ser.). (J). 2009. audio compact disk 57.95 (978-1-74214-132-9(3), 9781742141329) Pub: Bolinda Pubng AUS. Dist(s): Bolinda Pub Inc

Return of Sherlock Holmes. Arthur Conan Doyle. Read by David Timson. 2004. pap. bk. 17.98 (978-962-634-824-6(0), Naxos AudioBooks) Naxos.

Return of Sherlock Holmes. unabr. ed. Arthur Conan Doyle. Read by Walter Covell. 8 cass. (Running Time: 11 hrs. 30 mins.). 1983. 56.95 (978-0-7861-0592-2(5), 2081) Blckstn Audio.
Trapped in mortal combat with the dastardly Professor Moriarty, Holmes & his opponent plunged to their deaths in the Reichenback Falls. For ten long years Baker Street was without its most revered resident. Then in 1903, Doyle took pity on his readers & brought the sagacious sleuth back to life.

***Return of Sherlock Holmes.** unabr. ed. Arthur Conan Doyle. Read by Ralph Cosham. (Running Time: 6.5 hrs. NaN mins.). (ENG.). 2011. 29.95 (978-1-4417-2381-9(1)); 44.95 (978-1-4417-2377-2(3)); audio compact disk 24.95 (978-1-4417-2380-2(3)); audio compact disk 69.00 (978-1-4417-2378-9(1)) Blckstn Audio.

Return of Sherlock Holmes. unabr. ed. Arthur Conan Doyle. Read by Walter Covell. 8 cass. 1999. 56.95 (FS9-34270) Highsmith.

Return of Sherlock Holmes. unabr. ed. Arthur Conan Doyle. Read by Walter Covell. 8 cass. (Running Time: 12 hrs.). Incl. Abbey Grange. 1981. (C-51); Adventure of Black Peter. Arthur Conan Doyle. 1981. (C-51); Adventure of Charles Augustus Milverton. Arthur Conan Doyle. 1981. (C-51); Adventure of the Six Napoleons. Arthur Conan Doyle. 1981. (C-51); Dancing Men. 1981. (C-51); Empty House. 1981. (C-51); Golden Pince-Nez. 1981. (C-51); Missing Three-Quarter. Arthur Conan Doyle. 1981. (C-51); Norwood Builder. Arthur Conan Doyle. 1981. (C-51); Priory School. 1981. (C-51); Second Stain. 1981. (C-51); Solitary Cyclist. 1981. (C-51); Three Students. 1981. (C-51); 1981. 49.00 (C-51) Jimcin Record.
Thirteen exciting Sherlock Holmes adventures.

Return of Sherlock Holmes. unabr. ed. Arthur Conan Doyle. Read by David Timson. 2004. 22.98 (978-962-634-324-1(9), Naxos AudioBooks) Naxos.

Return of Sherlock Holmes. unabr. ed. Arthur Conan Doyle. Read by David Timson. 10 CDs. (Classic Literature with Classical Music Ser.). 2006. audio compact disk 62.98 (978-962-634-398-2(2), Naxos AudioBooks) Naxos.

***Return of Sherlock Holmes.** unabr. ed. Arthur Conan Doyle. Narrated by Simon Prebble. (Running Time: 12 hrs. 0 mins.). 2010. 17.99 (978-1-4001-8519-1(X)) Tantor Media.

***Return of Sherlock Holmes.** unabr. ed. Arthur Conan Doyle. Narrated by Simon Prebble. (Running Time: 10 hrs. 30 mins. 0 sec.). (ENG.). 2010. 24.99 (978-1-4001-6519-3(9)); audio compact disk 32.99 (978-1-4001-1519-8(1)); audio compact disk 65.99 (978-1-4001-4519-5(8)) Pub: Tantor Media. Dist(s): IngramPubServ

Return of Sherlock Holmes. unabr. ed. Arthur Conan Doyle. Read by David Timson. 3 CDs. audio compact disk 22.98 (978-962-634-301-2(X), NA330112) Naxos.

Return of Sherlock Holmes. unabr. collector's ed. Arthur Conan Doyle. Read by Walter Covell. 8 cass. (Running Time: 12 hrs.). (J). 1982. 64.00 (978-0-7366-3854-8(7), 9051) Books on Tape.
Includes the adventures of: "The Empty House," "The Norwood Builder," "The Dancing Men," "The Solitary Cyclist," "The Prory School," "Black Peter," "Charles Augustus Milverton," "The Golden Pince-Nez," "The Missing Three-Quarter," "The Abbey Grange" & "The Second Stain".

Return of Sherlock Holmes: The Adventure of the Dancing Men. Arthur Conan Doyle. Narrated by Edward Raleigh. (Running Time: 2 hrs. 30 mins.). 2006. 14.95 (978-1-60083-049-5(8)) Iofy Corp.

Return of Sherlock Holmes: The Adventure of the Empty House. Arthur Conan Doyle. Narrated by Edward Raleigh. (Running Time: 3 hrs.). 2006. 14.95 (978-1-59912-997-6(3)) Iofy Corp.

Return of Sherlock Holmes III: The Adventure of Black Peter & Other Stories. unabr. abr. ed. Arthur Conan Doyle. Read by David Timson. 4 CDs. (Running Time: 16476 sec.). (Classic Fiction Ser.). 2005. audio compact disk 28.98 (978-962-634-346-3(X)) Naxos UK GBR.

Return of Sky Ghost. abr. ed. Mack Maloney. 2 cass. (Running Time: 3 hrs.). (Wingman Ser.: Vol. 15). 2002. 9.95 (978-1-931953-07-8(4)) Listen & Live.

Return of Tarzan. Edgar Rice Burroughs. Read by Shelly Frasier. (Tarzan Ser.). (ENG.). 2001. audio compact disk 84.00 (978-1-4001-3002-3(6)) Pub: Tantor Media. Dist(s): IngramPubServ

Return of Tarzan. abr. ed. Edgar Rice Burroughs. Narrated by Stan Winiarski. 2 cass. (Running Time: 3 hrs.). 2001. 16.95 (978-0-929071-82-4(4)) B-B Audio.
In this second book, Tarzan decided to give up Jane, leave civilization and return to the African Jungle. There he first heard of Opar, the city of gold, left over from fabled Atlantis.It was a city of hideous men and of beautiful savage women, over wh.

Return of Tarzan. unabr. ed. Edgar Rice Burroughs. Read by Robert Whitfield. 6 cass. (Running Time: 9 hrs.). 2000. 44.95 (978-0-7861-1728-4(1), 2531) Blckstn Audio.
Tarzan has renounced his right to the woman he loves & civilization holds no pleasure for him. After a brief & harrowing period among men, he turns back to the African jungle where he grew to manhood. It is there he first heard of Opar, the city of gold, left over from fabled Atlantis. It is a city of hideous men & of beautiful, savage women, over whom reigns La, high priestess of the Flaming God.

Return of Tarzan. unabr. ed. Edgar Rice Burroughs. Read by Shelly Frazier. 8 CDs. (Running Time: 12 hrs.). 2001. audio compact disk 63.00; audio compact disk 25.00 Books on Tape.
Tarzan must lead a tribe of primitive warriors through the ancient crypts if he wants to escape the grip of Opar!.

Return of Tarzan. unabr. ed. Edgar Rice Burroughs. Read by Shelly Frasier. (Tarzan Ser.). (J). 2007. 49.99 (978-1-59895-940-6(9)) Find a World.

Return of Tarzan. unabr. ed. Edgar Rice Burroughs. Narrated by Shelly Frasier. 8 CDs. (Running Time: 8 hrs. 52 mins.). (Martian Ser.: Vol. 2). (ENG.). 2001. audio compact disk 42.00 (978-1-4001-0002-6(X)) Pub: Tantor Media. Dist(s): IngramPubServ
Tarzan, after valiantly giving up Jane to another man, is sent on a special assignment to North Africa. While escaping a new Russian enemy he discovers Opar, the city of gold, buried in the midst of the jungle. Beneath its tranquil façade, he encounters La, the high priestess of the Flaming God, brutal men, savage women and a blood stained altar of sacrifice. Tarzan must lead a tribe of primitive warriors through the ancient crypts to escape! This is the second book in the Tarzan series.

Return of Tarzan. unabr. ed. Edgar Rice Burroughs. Narrated by Shelly Frasier. (Running Time: 9 hrs. 0 mins. 0 sec.). (Tarzan Ser.). (ENG.). 2009. audio compact disk 32.99 (978-1-4001-0933-3(7)) Pub: Tantor Media. Dist(s): IngramPubServ

Return of Tarzan. unabr. ed. Edgar Rice Burroughs. Read by Shelly Frasier. Narrated by Shelly Frasier. (Running Time: 9 hrs. 0 mins. 0 sec.). (Tarzan Ser.). (ENG.). 2009. 22.99 (978-1-4001-5933-8(4)); audio compact disk 65.99 (978-1-4001-3933-0(3)) Pub: Tantor Media. Dist(s): IngramPubServ

Return of Tarzan Bk. 2. unabr. ed. Edgar Rice Burroughs. Read by David Sharp. 6 cass. (Running Time: 9 hrs.). Dramatization. 1993. 39.95 (978-1-55686-479-7(5), 479) Books in Motion.
While returning from England to Africa, Tarzan has a shipboard altercation with evil Nickolas Rokoff who swears vengeance. But Tarzan has greater concerns on his mind as he leaves modern civilization behind to discover an ancient decrepit civilization.

Return of the Angels. Philip Chapman. 1 cass. 10.95 (LA010); audio compact disk 15.95 compact disc. (LA010D) Lghtwrks Aud & Vid.
A light-filled, emotionally joyful, classical New Age album that stirs the heart. A peaceful composition of lush strings & synthesizer that creates a non-intrusive ambiance for relaxation or quiet activity. We loved it so much we used it in the beginning title sequence of the video "Opening to Angels".

Return of the Ark: Psalm 24. Ed Young. 1989. 4.95 (978-0-7417-1747-4(6), 747) Win Walk.

Return of the Dancing Master. unabr. ed. Henning Mankell & Dick Hill. Tr. by Laurie Thompson. (Running Time: 13 hrs. NaN mins.). 2008. 29.95 (978-1-4332-2577-2(8)); 79.95 (978-1-4332-2573-4(5)); audio compact disk 99.00 (978-1-4332-2574-1(3)) Blckstn Audio.

Return of the Divine Feminine. Andrew Harvey. 2 cass. 1995. 19.95 (978-1-879323-41-4(9)) Sound Horizons AV.
Noted mystical writer Andrew Harvey explains the change we must undergo in order to live in accordance with the new divine feminine energy on the planet. Provided are historical & current views on the Goddess' emergence in human consciousness, as well as exercises & meditations from the acclaimed author of "Journey in Ladakh," "The Hidden Journey," & "The Way of Passion".

Return of the Dove Set: Empowerment to Ascension Is Written in Your Heart. Diadra Price. 1995. 15.95 (978-1-887884-01-3(7)) Wings of Spirit.

Return of the Eagle. Paul Buchanan. Narrated by Larry A. McKeever. (Mystery Ser.). (J). 2000. audio compact disk 14.95 (978-1-58659-276-9(9)) Artesian.

Return of the Eagle. unabr. ed. Paul Buchanan. Narrated by Larry A. McKeever. 1 cass. (Running Time: 40 min.). (Mystery Ser.). (J). 2000. 10.95 (978-1-58659-007-9(3), 54102) Artesian.

Return of the Eagles. unabr. ed. James Follett. Read by Glen McCready. 6 cass. (Running Time: 28800 sec.). (Story Sound Ser.). 2007. 54.95 (978-1-85903-984-7(7)); audio compact disk 71.95 (978-1-84652-095-2(9)) Pub: Mgna Lrg Print GBR. Dist(s): Ulverscroft US

Return of the Godess. 2007. audio compact disk 19.95 (978-1-56136-405-3(3)) Master Your Mind.

Return of the Gypsy. unabr. ed. Philippa Carr. Read by Liz Holliss. 10 cass. (Running Time: 15 hrs.). (Philippa Carr's Saga Ser.). 2001. 84.95 (978-0-7531-0994-6(8), 010209) Pub: ISIS Audio GBR. Dist(s): Ulverscroft US
From childhood, Jessica has been fascinated with the wandering gypsies who occassionally stay on her father's estate. It is the mysterious Jake who travels with their band who captures her imagination. Jessica's determination to save him from the gallows leads her into a meeting that changes the course of her life & will seemingly remove Jake from it forever. But the gypsy's unexpected return shatters her tranquil world & puts her into mortal danger.

Return of the Indian. Lynne Reid Banks. Read by Lynne Reid Banks. 3 cass. (Running Time: 2 hrs. 30 mins.). (Indian in the Cupboard Ser.: No. 2). (J). (gr. 4-7). 2000. 24.00 (978-0-7366-9076-8(X)) Books on Tape.
Omri & Patrick are in for some close encounters when they once again venture into the magical cupboard.

Return of the Indian. l.t. unabr. ed. Lynne Reid Banks. 3 cass. (Running Time: 3 hrs. 30 min.). (Indian in the Cupboard Ser.: No. 2). (J). (gr. 4-7). 1989. bk. 22.95 (978-0-8161-9284-7(7), Macmillan Ref) Gale.
Omri & Patrick are in for some close encounters when their curiosity gets the best of them & they venture once again into the magical cupboard.

Return of the Indian. unabr. ed. Lynne Reid Banks. Read by Lynne Reid Banks. 3 vols. (Running Time: 3 hrs. 38 mins.). (Indian in the Cupboard Ser.: No. 2). (J). (gr. 3-7). 1990. pap. bk. 36.00 (978-0-8072-7309-8(0), YA810SP, Listening Lib); 30.00 (978-0-8072-7241-1(8), YA810CX, Listening Lib) Random Audio Pubg.

Return of the Jedi. Ed. by Disney Staff. Based on a story by George Lucas. 1 cass. (Read Along Star Wars Ser.). (J). bk. 7.99 (978-0-7634-0193-1(5)); bk. 14.99 (978-0-7634-0196-2(X)) W Disney Records.

Return of the Jedi: The Original Radio Drama. unabr. abr. ed. George Lucas & Lucasfilm Ltd. Staff. Perf. by Anthony Daniels & John Lithgow. Contrib. by Full Cast Production Staff. 3 CDs. (Running Time: 3 hrs.). Dramatization. (ENG.). 1996. audio compact disk 34.95 (978-1-56511-158-5(3), 1565111583) Pub: HighBridge. Dist(s): Workman Pub

Return of the King. J. R. R. Tolkien. Narrated by Rob Inglis. 16 CDs. (Running Time: 15 hrs. 30 mins.). (Lord of the Rings Ser.: Bk. 3). 2000. audio compact disk 158.00 (978-0-7887-3959-0(X), C1114) Recorded Bks.
Frodo & Sam make a terrible journey to the heart of the land of the Shadow in a final reckoning with the power of Sauron.

Return of the King. unabr. ed. J. R. R. Tolkien. Narrated by Rob Inglis. 11 cass. (Running Time: 15 hrs. 30 mins.). (Lord of the Rings Ser.: Bk. 3). 1997. 91.00 (978-1-55690-320-5(0), 90016E7) Recorded Bks.
Frodo & Sam make a terrible journey to the heart of the land of the Shadow in final reckoning with the power of Sauron.

Return of the King. unabr. ed. J. R. R. Tolkien. Read by Rob Inglis. 11 cass. (Running Time: 15 hrs.). (Lord of the Rings Ser.: Bk. 3). (gr. 9-12). 2004. 34.99 (978-0-7887-8955-7(4), 00394); audio compact disk 49.99 (978-0-7887-8984-7(8), 00242) Recorded Bks.
Frodo and Sam make a terrible journey to the heart of the Land of the Shadow in a final reckoning with the power of Sauron.

Return of the King. unabr. ed. J. R. R. Tolkien. (Lord of the Rings Ser.: Bk. 3). 2002. pap. bk. (978-0-00-764610-4(0)) Zondervan.
The little hobbit and his trusty companions make a terrible journey to the heart of the land of the Shadow in a final reckoning with thepower of Sauron.

Return of the King. unabr. abr. ed. J. R. R. Tolkien. 3 CDs. (Running Time: 3 hrs. 30 mins.). Bk. 3. (ENG.). 2002. audio compact disk 19.95 (978-1-56511-669-6(0), 1565116690) Pub: HighBridge. Dist(s): Workman Pub

Return of the Mother. abr. ed. Andrew Harvey. Read by Andrew Harvey. 2 cass. (Running Time: 3 hrs.). 1995. 17.95 (978-1-57453-019-3(4)) Audio Lit.
Unearths traces of the sacred feminine in major world religions & calls for a spiritual revolution "in the name of & for the love of the Divine Mother".

Return of the Native. Thomas Hardy. Read by Flo Gibson. 9 cass. (Running Time: 13 hrs. 30 min.). 1995. 28.95 (978-1-55685-348-7(3)) Audio Bk Con.
Eustacia Vye, sensuous & as wild as the moors of Egdon Heath, brings doom to her lovers, Damon Wildeve & Clym Yeobright. This contrasted with the kindness & faithfulness of Thomasin, Diggory Venn & the local furze cutters, forms a gripping tale.

Return of the Native. Thomas Hardy. Read by Alan Rickman. 12 cass. (Running Time: 15 hrs. 45 min.). 69.95 (CC-017) C to C Cassettes.
Clym Yeobright plans to return to Egdon Heath for a simple life. Eustacia Vye however sees in her marriage to the cosmopolitan Clym her only possibility of liberation & happiness.

Return of the Native. Thomas Hardy. 1 cass. (Running Time: 1 hr.). (Radiobook Ser.). 1987. 4.98 (978-0-929541-24-2(3)) Radiola Co.

Return of the Native. Thomas Hardy. Narrated by Patrick Tull. 12 cass. (Running Time: 16 hrs. 30 mins.). 98.00 (978-0-7887-4379-5(1)) Recorded Bks.

Return of the Native. unabr. ed. Thomas Hardy. Read by Alan Rickman. 12 cass. (Running Time: 15 hrs. 45 mins.). (J). (gr. 9-12). 2004. 44.95 (978-1-57270-090-1(4), F91090u) Audio Partners.
Set in pastoral England, Clym Yeobright returns home to open a school in Egdon Heath. He falls in love with Eustacia Vye & their turbulent marriage smolders & explodes in violent tragedy.

Return of the Native. unabr. ed. Thomas Hardy. Narrated by Alan Rickman. (Running Time: 56700 sec.). (Cover to Cover Classics Ser.). (ENG.). 2007. audio compact disk 39.95 (978-1-57270-570-8(1)) Pub: AudioGO. Dist(s): Perseus Dist

Return of the Native. unabr. ed. Thomas Hardy. Read by Nadia May. 10 cass. (Running Time: 14 hrs. 30 mins.). 1995. 69.95 (978-0-7861-0705-6(7), 1582) Blckstn Audio.
Set in Egdon Heath, a wild tract of country in the south-west of England, this is a masterpiece of dramatic tension. Clym Yeobright, a diamond merchant in Paris, returns to his home in Egdon where he falls passionately in love with the sensuous, free-spirited Eustacia Vye. She, while in a brief state of infatuation, marries him, hoping he will take her away to the more exciting life in Paris. But Eustacia's dreams of escape are not be realized. Clym Yeobright, the returning native, cannot bring her salvation.

Return of the Native. unabr. ed. Thomas Hardy. Read by Nadia May. (Running Time: 50400 sec.). 2007. audio compact disk 29.95 (978-0-7861-5824-9(7)); audio compact disk 99.00 (978-0-7861-5823-2(9)) Blckstn Audio.

Return of the Native. unabr. ed. Thomas Hardy. Read by Nadia May. (YA). 2008. 84.99 (978-1-60514-750-5(8)) Find a World.

Return of the Native. unabr. ed. Thomas Hardy. Narrated by Simon Vance. (Running Time: 13 hrs. 30 mins.). 2010. 18.99 (978-1-4001-8507-8(6)); 27.99 (978-1-4001-6507-0(5)); audio compact disk 35.99 (978-1-4001-1507-5(8)); audio compact disk 72.99 (978-1-4001-4507-2(4)) Pub: Tantor Media. Dist(s): IngramPubServ

Return of the Native. unabr. collector's ed. Thomas Hardy. Read by Jill Masters. 11 cass. (Running Time: 16 hrs. 30 mins.). 1983. 88.00 (978-0-7366-3976-7(4), 9524) Books on Tape.
Set in pastoral England, the story concerns a sophisticated diamond merchant who throws away his career to become a schoolteacher. He learns the hard way that "you can't go home again".

Return of the Nephilim: What's Behind the UFO's? Chuck Missler. 2 CDs. (Running Time: 2 hours). (Briefing Packages by Chuck Missler). 2003. audio compact disk 19.95 (978-1-57821-209-5(X)) Koinonia Hse.
What's behind the UFO's? Are they real? Where are they from?Are they the Nephilim of ages past? What does the Bible say about them? What's their agenda for Planet Earth?This subject has not gone away. On the contrary, much new evidence has surfaced with global implications. Chuck explores the Biblical relevance and disturbing agenda of the apparent extraterrestrial life forms that have been forcing themselves into our global consciousness and reveals their most disturbing agenda.

***Return of the Primitive: The Anti-Industrial Revolution.** unabr. ed. Ayn Rand. Read by Bernadette Dunne. (Running Time: 13 hrs. NaN mins.). (ENG.). 2011. audio compact disk 29.95 (978-1-4332-2680-9(4)) Blckstn Audio.

Return of the Primitive: The Anti-Industrial Revolution. unabr. ed. Rand Ayn. Read by Bernadette Dunne. (Running Time: 13 hrs. 0 mins.). 2009. 72.95 (978-1-4332-2677-9(4)); audio compact disk 109.00 (978-1-4332-2678-6(2)) Blckstn Audio.

Return of the Primitive: The Anti-Industrial Revolution. unabr. ed. Ayn Rand. Read by Bernadette Dunne. (Running Time: 13 hrs. NaN mins.). (ENG.). 2011. 29.95 (978-1-4332-2681-6(2)) Blckstn Audio.

Return of the Prodigal Son: A Story of Homecoming. Henri J. M. Nouwen. Read by Dan Anderson. 4 cass. (Running Time: 2 hrs.). 2005. 32.95 (978-0-86716-739-9(4)) St Anthony Mess Pr.
This powerful meditation illuminates the parable of the prodigal son found in Luke?s Gospel. Nouwen discovers anew the reality that God?s love is unconditional and shares his own spiritual journey with us.In this audiobook, Nouwen shares his own experience as the wayward son as well as the vengeful older brother and the compassionate father. He speaks to all who have known loneliness, dejection, jealousy or anger, and invites us to homecoming, affirmation and reconciliation.

Return of the Rancher. unabr. ed. Max Brand. Read by Bill Weideman. (Running Time: 7 hrs.). 2007. 39.25 (978-1-4233-3494-1(9), 9781423334941, BADLE); 24.95 (978-1-4233-3493-4(0), 9781423334934, BAD); audio compact disk 24.95 (978-1-4233-3491-0(4), 9781423334910, Brilliance MP3); audio compact disk 39.25 (978-1-4233-3492-7(2), 9781423334927, Brlnc Audio MP3 Lib) Brilliance Audio.

Return of the Rancher. unabr. ed. Max Brand. Read by Bill Weideman. (Running Time: 8 hrs.). 2009. audio compact disk 19.99 (978-1-4418-0463-1(3), 9781441804631, Bril Audio CD Unabri); audio compact disk 59.97 (978-1-4418-0464-8(1), 9781441804648, BriAudCD Unabrid) Brilliance Audio.

Return of the Rishi: A Doctor's Story of Spiritual Transformation & Ayurvedic Healing. abr. ed. Deepak Chopra. Read by Deepak Chopra. 2 cass. (Running Time: 2 hrs. 8 mins.). (Chopra, Deepak Ser.). (ENG.). 1995. reel tape 16.95 (978-1-878424-12-9(2)) Amber-Allen Pub.
A physician's story of spiritual transformation & Ayurvedic healing. Dr. Chopra utilizes colorful anecdotes that reveal the missing link in Western medicine: recognition of the knower inside, or the "rishi".

***Return of the Soldier.** Rebecca West. Read by Amy von Lecteur. 2009. 27.95 (978-1-60112-971-0(8)) Babblebooks.

Return of the Soldier. unabr. ed. Rebecca West. Read by Flo Gibson. 2 cass. (Running Time: 3 hrs.). 1998. 14.95 (978-1-55685-516-0(8)) Audio Bk Con.
Chris' "shell-shock" or amnesia blocks out fifteen years as he returns home to his wife's decorative genius only to remember & revisit Margaret, the earlier love of his life.

Return of the Soldier. unabr. ed. Rebecca West. Read by Nadia May. 3 cass. (Running Time: 4 hrs.). 1997. 23.95 (978-0-7861-1174-9(7), 1963) Blckstn Audio.
In this story of a wounded man & the three concerned women who seek to heal him, West explores the complexity of the mind & its subtle strategies for coping with life's realities.

Return of the Spirit: C. G. Jung's Psychological Foundation for Twelve Step Programs. Ronald P. Lavin. Read by Thomas P. Lavin. 7 cass. (Running Time: 7 hrs.). 1996. 51.95 (978-0-7822-0520-6(8), 588) C G Jung IL.
Discusses Jung's understanding of the many forms of spirit & the ways in which Twelve Step Programs can support the re-discovery of the creative spirit. Also discussed is the shadow of Twelve Step Programs which can snuff out the spirit which thirsts for wholeness.

***Return Policy.** Michael Snyder. (Running Time: 11 hrs. 38 mins. 0 sec.). (ENG.). 2009. 14.99 (978-0-310-30266-7(8)) Zondervan.

Return to Akenfield. Craig Taylor. 2007. 54.95 (978-1-84559-662-0(5)) Pub: Soundings Ltd GBR. Dist(s): Ulverscroft US

Return to Akenfield: Portrait of an English Village in the 21st Century. Craig Taylor. Read by Stephen Thorne. (Running Time: 25200 sec.). 2007. audio compact disk 64.95 (978-1-84559-687-3(0)) Pub: Soundings Ltd GBR. Dist(s): Ulverscroft US

Return to Apostolic Ministry. Rick Joyner. 1 cass. (Running Time: 90 mins.). (Vision Ser.: Vol. 8). 2000. 5.00 (RJ16-008) Morning NC.
This tape series will help to impart new vision or restore lost vision in the church.

Return to Connecticut see Twentieth-Century Poetry in English, No. 24, Recordings of Poets Reading Their Own Poetry

Return to Gallows Hill. Anne Schraff. Narrated by Larry A. McKeever. (Horror Ser.). (J). 2004. 10.95 (978-1-58659-080-2(4)); audio compact disk 14.95 (978-1-58659-338-4(2)) Artesian.

Return to Glory. Joel Freeman & Don Griffin. 2004. audio compact disk 29.99 (978-0-7684-0225-4(5)) Destiny Image Pubs.

Return to Gone-Away. unabr. ed. Elizabeth Enright. Read by Colleen Delaney. (J). 2007. 34.99 (978-1-59895-986-4(7)) Find a World.

Return to Gone-Away Lake. Elizabeth Enright. Read by Colleen Delaney. (Running Time: 5 hrs.). 2005. 19.95 (978-1-59912-904-4(3)) Iofy Corp.

Return to Gone-Away Lake. Elizabeth Enright. Narrated by Pamela Dillman. 4 CDs. (Running Time: 5 Hrs.). (J). 2004. audio compact disk 27.95 (978-1-59316-030-2(5)) Listen & Live.
Enjoy the follow-up adventures of Portia, Foster, and cousin Julian engaged in more than the usual summer pastimes of sun, fun and games. The three intrepid children soon discover a fascinating abandoned summer resort, consisting of deserted crumbling Victorian summer homes surrounding a vanished lake, which is now a swamp.

Return to Harken House. unabr. ed. Joan Aiken. Narrated by Jill Tanner. 3 cass. (Running Time: 3 hrs. 45 mins.). (gr. 6 up). 1992. 27.00 (978-1-55690-608-4(0), 92301E7) Recorded Bks.
As the dark spectre of World War Two hangs over England, young Julia returns to the funny old house in which she was born & a three hundred year old mystery comes alive again to haunt her.

Return to Harmony. unabr. ed. Janette Oke & T. Davis Bunn. Narrated by Christina Moore. 5 cass. (Running Time: 6 hrs.). 1996. 43.00 (978-0-7887-5110-3(7), K0024L8) Recorded Bks.
Though Jodie Harland & Bethan Keefe are about as different as two young women can be, they have developed a strong bond of friendship in the quiet town of Harmony, North Carolina. But as the World plunges into war & sorrow, their friendship is tested when Jodie's dreams of a grand future come in conflict with Bethan's quiet desire to follow God's will for her.

Return to Howliday Inn. unabr. ed. James Howe. Read by Victor Garber. 2 vols. (Running Time: 2 hrs. 27 mins.). (Bunnicula Ser.). (J). (gr. 3-7). 2004. pap. bk. 29.00 (978-0-8072-8416-2(5), YA192SP, Listening Lib); 23.00 (978-0-8072-8415-5(7), YA192CX, Listening Lib) Random Audio Pubg.
Chester, who has been reading avidly about the paranormal, predicts that they will soon be traveling someplace & chances are they are not going to like it. Indeed they are not, as the very next day, the Monroes leave for their vacation, dropping Chester, Harold & Howie off at the scene of some

previous harrowing experiences - Chateau Bow-Wow, the boarding kennel that Chester so aptly has dubbed "Howliday Inn." And this visit promises to be no less harrowing than the last.

Return to Life: The Process of Post-Abortion Healing. 1 cass. (Running Time: 1 hr.). 2003. 13.95 (978-1-932631-31-9(3)); audio compact disk 13.95 (978-1-932631-32-6(1)) Ascensn Pr.

Return to Love. Anita Stansfield. 2 cass. 1999. 11.98 (978-1-57734-145-1(7), 07001525) Covenant Comms.
Can true love be found & lost & found again?.

***Return to Love.** abr. ed. Marianne Williamson. Read by Marianne Williamson. (ENG.). 2005. (978-0-06-079806-2(8), Harper Audio); (978-0-06-084800-2(6), Harper Audio) HarperCollins Pubs.

Return to Love. unabr. abr. ed. Marianne Williamson. Read by Marianne Williamson. 2 cass. (Running Time: 3 hrs.). 2004. audio compact disk 22.95 (978-0-06-076510-1(0)) HarperCollins Pubs.

Return to Mars. unabr. ed. Ben Bova. Read by Stefan Rudnicki. (Running Time: 16 hrs. 0 mins.). (ENG.). 2009. 29.95 (978-1-4332-6382-8(3)); 89.95 (978-1-4332-6378-1(5)); audio compact disk 110.00 (978-1-4332-6379-8(3)) Blckstn Audio.

***Return to Marshall's Bayou: Dassas Cormier Mystery Series Book 1.** Prod. by Siren Audio Studios. Adapted by S. H. Baker. Based on a novel by S. H. Baker. (ENG.). 2010. audio compact disk 25.99 (978-0-9844180-4-6(0)) Siiren Audio.

***Return to Me.** Robin Lee Hatcher. (Running Time: 7 hrs. 19 mins. 0 sec.). (ENG.). 2009. 14.99 (978-0-310-30503-3(9)) Zondervan.

Return to Paradise. unabr. ed. James A. Michener. Read by Larry McKeever. 15 cass. (Running Time: 22 hrs. 30 min.). 1995. 120.00 (978-0-7366-3030-6(9), 3712) Books on Tape.
The exotic South Pacific fills the senses in this landmark Michener novel. Drama & adventure, Polynesian style.

***Return to Prosperity: How America Can Regain Its Economic Superpower Status.** unabr. ed. Arthur B. Laffer & Stephen Moore. Narrated by Dick Hill. (Running Time: 12 hrs. 0 mins.). 2010. 17.99 (978-1-4001-8617-4(X)) Tantor Media.

***Return to Prosperity: How America Can Regain Its Economic Superpower Status.** unabr. ed. Arthur B. Laffer & Stephen Moore. Narrated by Dick Hill. (Running Time: 9 hrs. 0 mins. 0 sec.). (ENG.). 2010. 24.99 (978-1-4001-6617-6(9)); audio compact disk 34.99 (978-1-4001-1617-1(1)); audio compact disk 69.99 (978-1-4001-4617-8(8)) Pub: Tantor Media. Dist(s): IngramPubServ

Return to Rhanna. unabr. ed. Christine M. Fraser. Read by Vivien Heilbron. 10 cass. (Running Time: 10 hrs.). 1993. 84.95 (978-0-7451-4199-2(4), CAB 882) AudioGO.
At first, their return to Rhanna from the mainland seemed perfect to Shona & Niall McLachlan. The friendly spirit of the islanders was stronger than ever! However, tragedy strikes & Shona stands to lose everything & everyone that she has ever cared for.

Return to Ritual see Twentieth-Century Poetry in English, No. 1, Recordings of Poets Reading Their Own Poetry

Return to Rome. unabr. ed. Francis J. Beckwith. (ENG.). 2008. 16.98 (978-1-59644-648-9(X), Hovel Audio) christianaud.

***Return to Rome: Confessions of an Evangelical Catholic.** unabr. ed. Francis J. Beckwith. Narrated by Grover Gardner. (ENG.). 2009. 12.98 (978-1-59644-685-4(4), Hovel Audio) christianaud.

Return to Rome: Confessions of an Evangelical Catholic. unabr. ed. Francis J. Beckwith. Narrated by Grover Gardner. 4 CDs. (Running Time: 5 hrs. 0 mins. 0 sec.). (ENG.). 2009. audio compact disk 21.98 (978-1-59644-684-7(6), Hovel Audio) christianaud.

Return to Sender see Devolver al Remitente

Return to Sender. Zoe Barnes. 2009. 69.95 (978-0-7531-3362-0(8)); audio compact disk 84.95 (978-0-7531-3363-7(6)) Pub: Isis Pubng Ltd GBR. Dist(s): Ulverscroft US

Return to Sender. abr. ed. Fern Michaels. Read by Angela Dawe. 4 CDs. (Running Time: 5 hrs.). 2010. audio compact disk 26.99 (978-1-4233-4618-0(1), 9781423346180, BACD) Brilliance Audio.

***Return to Sender.** abr. ed. Fern Michaels. Read by Angela Dawe. (Running Time: 5 hrs.). 2010. 9.99 (978-1-4418-9357-4(1), 9781441893574, BAD) Brilliance Audio.

Return to Sender. abr. ed. Fern Michaels. Read by Angela Dawe. (Running Time: 6 hrs.). 2010. audio compact disk 14.99 (978-1-4233-4619-7(X), 9781423346197, BCD Value Price) Brilliance Audio.

***Return to Sender.** unabr. ed. Julia Alvarez. Read by Olivia Preciado & Ozzie Rodriguez. (ENG.). (J). 2010. audio compact disk 39.00 (978-0-307-70730-7(X), Listening Lib) Pub: Random Audio Pubg. Dist(s): Random

***Return to Sender.** unabr. ed. Julia Alvarez. Narrated by Ozzie Rodriguez & Olivia Preciado. 6 CDs. (J). (gr. 3-6). 2010. audio compact disk 39.00 (978-0-307-70764-2(4), Listening Lib) Pub: Random Audio Pubg. Dist(s): Random

Return to Sender. unabr. ed. Fern Michaels. Read by Angela Dawe. 1 MP3-CD. (Running Time: 9 hrs.). 2010. 24.99 (978-1-4233-4614-2(9), 9781423346142, Brilliance MP3); 24.99 (978-1-4233-4616-6(5), 9781423346166, BAD); 39.97 (978-1-4233-4615-9(7), 9781423346159, Brinc Audio MP3 Lib); 39.97 (978-1-4233-4617-3(3), 9781423346173, BADLE); audio compact disk 36.99 (978-1-4233-4612-8(2), 9781423346128, Bril Audio CD Unabri); audio compact disk 97.97 (978-1-4233-4613-5(0), 9781423346135, BriAudCD Unabrid) Brilliance Audio.

Return to Sodom & Gomorrah: Bible Stories from Archaeologists, unabr. ed. Charles R. Pellegrino. Narrated by Richard M. Davidson. 12 cass. (Running Time: 16 hrs. 45 mins.). 97.00 (978-0-7887-0303-4(X), 94496E7) Recorded Bks.
Often called the real Indiana Jones, Pellegrino - acclaimed author, scientist & adventurer - takes the listener on an extraordinary tour of Old Testament archaeological sites from the Nile to the Jordan & Tigris-Euphrates rivers. Available to libraries only.

Return to Stonemoor. Kay Stephens. Read by Julia Franklyn & Julia Franklin. 6 cass. (Storysound Ser.). (J). 1999. 54.95 (978-1-85903-296-1(6)) Pub: Mgna Lrg Print GBR. Dist(s): Ulverscroft US

***Return to Sullivans Island.** unabr. ed. Dorothea Benton Frank. Read by Robin Miles. (ENG.). 2009. (978-0-06-190244-4(6), Harper Audio); (978-0-06-190245-1(4), Harper Audio) HarperCollins Pubs.

Return to Sullivans Island. unabr. ed. Dorothea Benton Frank. Read by Robin Miles. (Lowcountry Tales Ser.). 2009. audio compact disk 39.99 (978-0-06-177448-5(0), Harper Audio) HarperCollins Pubs.

Return to the Center. Bede Griffiths. 4 cass. (Running Time: 5 hrs. 34 min.). 1983. 36.00 set. (03305) Big Sur Tapes.
In a large canvas yurt meeting room at Ojai Foundation in California, Father Bede Griffiths addresses his audience to the accompaniment of crickets & nearness to nature. This gathering completes his 1983 lecture tour in America.

Return to the Center. Richard Rohr. Read by Richard Rohr. 4 cass. (Running Time: 3 hrs. 30 min.). 1991. 29.95 Set. (978-7-900782-98-4(2), AA2444) Credence Commun.
Rohn discusses the search for, the retreat from, & the experience of contemplation.

Return to the Garden/Your Ministry. Marianne Williamson. Read by Marianne Williamson. 1 cass. (Running Time: 90 mins.). (Lectures on a Course in Miracles). 1999. 10.00 (978-1-56170-637-2(X), M867) Hay House.

Return to the Hundred Acre Wood. unabr. ed. David Benedictus. Illus. by Mark Burgess. (Running Time: 3 hrs.). (ENG.). (ps up). 2009. audio compact disk 19.95 (978-0-14-314507-3(X), PengAudBks) Penguin Grp USA.

Return to the Sacred. Richard Rohr. 1 cass. (Running Time: 55 min.). 8.95 (AA2852) Credence Commun.
There are not two worlds - a sacred & a profane. There are two ways of seeing the same world. If we can let go of who we think we are, we can see who we really are. And when we do, we will see the sacred for ourselves.

Return to the Stable: An Imaginary Gathering 20 Years Later. Stephen P. Steenwyk. (Running Time: 1 hr. 15 mins.). (Noel Ser.). 2000. 15.95 (978-1-56212-562-2(1), 416104) FaithAliveChr.

Return to Thrush Green. Miss Read. Read by June Barrie. 6 vols. (Running Time: 9 hrs.). 2003. audio compact disk 64.95 (978-0-7540-5591-4(4)) Pub: Chivers Audio Bks GBR. Dist(s): AudioGO

Return to Thrush Green. unabr. ed. Miss Read. Read by June Barrie. 6 cass. (Running Time: 9 hrs.). 2003. 54.95 (978-0-7540-0984-9(X), CAB 2367) AudioGO.

Return to Tibet. unabr. collector's ed. Heinrich Harrer. Read by Grover Gardner. 7 cass. (Running Time: 7 hrs.). 1987. 42.00 (978-0-7366-1139-8(8), 2064) Books on Tape.
Shows us the present-day regime under Chinese rule & compares it with the freedom of the past, when religion & faith were central to life.

Return to Unity. Derek Prince. 1 cass. 1991. 5.95 (I-4331) Derek Prince.
In the sight of Jesus there is only one Church on earth: His Bride. The Church began in unity - how can we return to it?.

Return to Vienna. unabr. ed. Nancy Buckingham. Read by Anne Cater. 5 cass. (Running Time: 7 hrs. 30 min.). (Sound Ser.). 2004. 49.95 (978-1-85496-703-9(7), 67037) Pub: UlverLrgPrint GBR. Dist(s): Ulverscroft US
Vienna meant happiness then heartbreak for Jessica Varley. She had spent the brief days of her idyllic marriage there, before the seemingly senseless accident that killed her dashing husband. Now she had returned, to discover what had really happened, to resist the attraction of a cynical, mocking man who claimed he loved her ... & to follow a dangerous trail through deception & violence to a terrifying end.

Return to Virtue. unabr. ed. John Bradshaw. 2 cass. (Running Time: 2 hrs. 20 min.). 1996. 16.00 (978-1-57388-024-4(8)) J B Media.
Ground-breaking new material which combines ancient wisdom with modern brain research to offer positive new approaches for re-educating yourself & practical guidelines for educating children.

Return to Virtue: An Ancient Key to Developing Emotional Intelligence. John Bradshaw. (Running Time: 8400 sec.). 2008. audio compact disk 100.00 (978-1-57388-025-1(6)) J B Media.

Return to Warbow. unabr. collector's ed. Les Savage, Jr. Read by Jonathan Marosz. 5 cass. (Running Time: 5 hrs.). 1995. 30.00 (978-0-7366-2985-0(8), 3675) Books on Tape.
An ex-con, wrongly-convicted, returns to Warbow to reconcile with his son. But not before taking 13 of his hard years out of the real culprit's hide.

Return to Zion. Bodie Thoene & Brock Thoene. Narrated by Suzanne Toren. 11 cass. (Running Time: 15 hrs. 45 mins.). (Zion Chronicles: Bk. 3). 94.00 (978-0-7887-5148-6(4)) Recorded Bks.

Return to Zion. unabr. ed. Bodie Thoene & Brock Thoene. Read by Susan O'Malley. 13 CDs. (Running Time: 16 hrs.). (Zion Chronicles: Bk. 3). 2001. audio compact disk 104.00 (978-0-7861-9750-7(1), 2746) Blckstn Audio.
The Jewish people, gazing down the vista of time, have longed for the rebirth of their nation. Out of the ashes of the Holocaust, thousands of Jews have returned to Israel only to be caught in the life-and-death struggle of the nation. Now in the final weeks of British occupation in Palestine, can they endure the coming fury? With Moshe the target of a dangerous conspiracy and Rachel imprisoned behind the walls of the Old City, David and Ellie marshall efforts in the last attempts of the Jewish Agency to arm its people against the onslaught that will surely come on the day the British pull out.

Return to Zion. unabr. ed. Bodie Thoene & Brock Thoene. Read by Susan O'Malley. 11 cass. (Running Time: 16 hrs.). (Zion Chronicles: Bk. 3). 2001. 76.95 (978-0-7861-1976-9(4), 2746) Blckstn Audio.

Return with Honor. Bernell Christensen. 1 CD. audio compact disk 10.98 (978-1-57734-115-4(5), 2500795) Covenant Comms.
Inspirational stories & thoughts on returning home to God.

Return with Honor. Bernell Christensen. 1 cass. 1997. 9.98 (978-1-57734-007-2(8), 06005357) Covenant Comms.

Return Ye Children of Men; The Three Heavens. Ann Ree Colton & Jonathan Murro. 1 cass. 7.95 A R Colton Fnd.

Returned to Frisco, Nineteen Forty-Six see Twentieth-Century Poetry in English, No. 27, Recordings of Poets Reading Their Own Poetry

Returning: A Spiritual Journey. abr. ed. Dan Wakefield. Read by Dan Wakefield. 2 cass. (Running Time: 3 hrs.). 1998. 17.95 (978-1-57453-137-4(9)) Audio Lit.
A thoughtful & thoroughly modern man's renewal of his spiritual quest with the support of the community of the church.

Returning Home. Swami Amar Jyoti. 1 cass. 1978. 9.95 (R-10) Truth Consciousness.
We come from God & go back to God; in between we go round & round & call it progress. The science of Oneness.

Returning Home. Kenneth Wapnick. 4 CDs. 2005. audio compact disk 21.00 (978-1-59142-202-0(7), CD80) Foun Miracles.

Returning to Earth. unabr. ed. Jim Harrison. (Running Time: 7 mins. 30 sec.). (YA). 2007. audio compact disk 55.00 (978-0-7861-5875-1(1)) Blckstn Audio.

Returning to Earth. unabr. ed. Jim Harrison. Read by Traci Svendsgaard et al. (Running Time: 944000 sec.). 2007. 24.95 (978-0-7861-4679-6(6)); 54.95 (978-0-7861-4945-2(0)); audio compact disk 24.95 (978-0-7861-6677-0(0)); audio compact disk 29.95 (978-0-7861-7361-7(0)) Blckstn Audio.

Returning to Our First Love. Rick Joyner. 1 cass. (Running Time: 90 mins.). (Church History & the Coming Move of God Ser.: Vol. 3). 2000. 5.00 (RJ11-003) Morning NC.
Church history is brought to life with practical applications & insights into how the enemy uses the same strategy against every new move of God.

Reunion. Perf. by Deliverance. 1 cass. 10.98 (978-1-57908-226-0(2), 1339); audio compact disk 15.98 CD. (978-1-57908-225-3(4)) Platinm Enter.

Reunion. abr. ed. Karen Kingsbury & Gary Smalley. Read by Sandra Burr. 4 CDs. (Running Time: 4 hrs.). (Redemption Ser.). 2004. audio compact disk 69.25 (978-1-59355-853-6(8), 1593558538); 19.95 (978-1-59355-850-5(3), 1593558503); 49.25 (978-1-59355-851-2(1), 1593558511); audio compact disk 21.95 (978-1-59355-852-9(X), 159355852X) Brilliance Audio.
A Deadly Diagnosis In the fifth and final book in the Redemption series, plans are being made for a family reunion. Nearly all the adult Baxter children have a reason to celebrate - except one. As the preparations get under way, a deadly diagnosis sends shock waves through the Baxter family and threatens to tear them apart. A Heartbreaking Secret The reality of what might lie ahead brings each of the Baxters to a place of faith and honesty. In the process, Elizabeth and John come to grips with a secret they haven't shared with anyone, a secret they rarely admit even to themselves. At the same time, a young man is making his rise in Hollywood and wondering about his place in life. A Glorious Celebration Amidst the threat of sorrow, the Baxters share in their most wonderful celebration of all - a moment to remember that love always wins out, no matter how long the struggle, a reminder that God reigns even in the darkest night. A story of God's grace and redemption, his victory even in the most difficult times.

Reunion. abr. ed. Karen Kingsbury & Gary Smalley. Read by Sandra Burr. (Running Time: 4 hrs.). (Redemption Ser.). 2006. 39.25 (978-1-4233-0298-8(2), 9781423302988, Brinc Audio MP3 Lib); 9.99 (978-1-4233-0297-1(4), 9781423302971, Brilliance MP3); 39.25 (978-1-4233-0300-8(8), 9781423303008, BADLE); 9.99 (978-1-4233-0299-5(0), 9781423302995, BAD) Brilliance Audio.

***Reunion.** abr. ed. Karen Kingsbury & Gary Smalley. Read by Sandra Burr. (Running Time: 4 hrs.). (Redemption Ser.). 2010. audio compact disk 9.99 (978-1-4418-7835-9(1), 9781441878359, BCD Value Price) Brilliance Audio.

Reunion. unabr. ed. Alan Lightman. 4 cass. (Running Time: 6 hrs.). 2003. 56.00 (978-0-7366-9467-4(6)) Books on Tape.
In reliving memories of a passionate affair during his college years, a mild-mannered professor considers the nature of memory.

Reunion: A flowing session of guided Hatha Yoga. Marcia Galleher. Read by Marcia Galleher. Perf. by Marcia Galleher. 2004. audio compact disk (978-0-9676459-2-6(1)) Mobius Prods.

Reunion in Death. abr. ed. J. D. Robb, pseud. Read by Susan Ericksen. (Running Time: 6 hrs.). (In Death Ser.). 2007. audio compact disk 14.99 (978-1-4233-1748-7(3), 9781423317487, BCD Value Price) Brilliance Audio.

Reunion in Death. unabr. ed. J. D. Robb, pseud. Read by Susan Ericksen. 7 cass. (Running Time: 10 hrs.). (In Death Ser.). 2002. 30.95 (978-1-58788-685-0(5), 1587886855, BAU) Brilliance Audio.

Reunion in Death. unabr. ed. J. D. Robb, pseud. Read by Susan Ericksen. 7 cass. (Running Time: 10 hrs.). (In Death Ser.:). 2002. 78.25 (978-1-58788-686-7(3), 1587886863, Unabridge Lib Edns) Brilliance Audio.

Reunion in Death. unabr. ed. J. D. Robb, pseud. Read by Susan Ericksen. (Running Time: 10 hrs.). (In Death Ser.). 2004. 39.25 (978-1-59335-587-6(4), 1593355874, Brlnc Audio MP3 Lib) Brilliance Audio.

Reunion in Death. unabr. ed. J. D. Robb, pseud. Read by Susan Ericksen. (Running Time: 10 hrs.). (In Death Ser.). 2004. 39.25 (978-1-59710-645-0(3), 1597106453, BADLE); 24.95 (978-1-59710-644-3(5), 1597106445, BAD) Brilliance Audio.

Reunion in Death. unabr. ed. J. D. Robb, pseud. Read by Susan Ericksen. (Running Time: 10 hrs.). (In Death Ser.). 2007. audio compact disk 36.95 (978-1-4233-1745-6(9), 9781423317456, Bril Audio CD Unabri); audio compact disk 97.25 (978-1-4233-1746-3(7), 9781423317463, BriAudCD Unabrid) Brilliance Audio.

Reunion in Death. unabr. ed. J. D. Robb, pseud. Read by Susan Ericksen. (Running Time: 10 hrs.). (In Death Ser.). 2004. 24.95 (978-1-59335-140-3(2), 1593351402) Soulmate Audio Bks.
At exactly 7:30 p.m., Walter Pettibone arrived home to over a hundred friends and family shouting, "surprise!" It was his birthday. Although he had known about the planned event for weeks, the real surprise was yet to come. At 8:45 p.m., a woman with emerald eyes and red hair handed him a glass of champagne. One sip of birthday bubbly, and he was dead. The woman's name is Julie Dockport. No one at the party knew who she was. But Detective Eve Dallas remembers her all too well. Eve was personally responsible for her incarceration nearly ten years ago. And now, let out on good behavior, she still has nothing but bad intentions. It appears she wants to meet Dallas again - in a reunion neither will forget... "Edgy [and] sexy."-Publishers Weekly.

Reunions: Till We Meet Again. (Running Time: 30 min.). 10.95 (G0660B090, HarperThor) HarpC GBR.

***Rev. Dr. Mark Grawehr.** Mark Grawehr. 2008. 17.00 (978-1-61658-506-8(4)) Indep Pub IL.

***Rev. Gary Davis: The Video Collection.** Contrib. by Gary Davis. (ENG.). 2008. 24.95 (978-1-57940-869-5(9)) Rounder Records.

Rev. Ivan Stang Live at Starwood. Featuring Ivan Stang. 2001. audio compact disk 12.95 (978-1-59157-005-9(0)) Assn for Cons.

Rev. Jesse Jackson: "Our Time Has Come" Read by Jesse Jackson. 1 cass. (Running Time: 50 min.). 1984. 8.98 (MCA-5530) U Studios Home Vid.
Rev. Jackson speech delivered at the 1984 Democratic National Convention, advancing the argument for equal rights for the elderly, women, poor, underprivileged & other minority groups.

Reva Blue. James Lawrence. Read by Marilyn Langbehn. 4 cass. (Running Time: 5 hrs.). 1989. 26.95 (978-1-55686-302-8(0), 302) Books in Motion.
A young Indian woman's life becomes entwined with two fearless partners fighting against great odds to build a freight company in the old West.

Reveal: Dream Big Never Quit, Vol. 1. As told by Rudy Ruettiger et al. (ENG.). 2009. mass mkt. 15.98 (978-0-9820802-1-4(2)) Nikko.

Revealed. Tamera Alexander. Read by Barbara McCulloh. 12 cass. (Running Time: 14 hrs.). (Fountain Creek Chronicles: Bk. 2). 2007. 98.75 (978-1-4281-3530-7(8)) Recorded Bks.

Revealed Knowledge. Kenneth Copeland. 6 cass. 1987. stu. ed. 30.00 (978-0-88114-756-8(7)) K Copeland Pubns.
Receiving knowledge from the Holy Spirit.

Reveille in Washington: 1860-1865. unabr. ed. Margaret Leech. Read by Grace Conlin. 15 cass. (Running Time: 22 hrs.). 1995. 95.95 (978-0-7861-0812-1(6), 1635) Blckstn Audio.
Margaret Leech's Pulitzer Prize-winning history paints a wonderfully vivid & lively picture of Washington D. C. during the Civil War. In addition to the major events & figures such as Lincoln, Leech uses relling anecdotes & draws upon cameo players such as Louisa May Alcott, Walt Whitman, Andrew Carnegie & a Confederate lady spy to create a living portrait of a sleepy, unfinished city as it struggles to become the strong capital of a united nation.

Revelacion Divina del Infierno. abr. ed. Mary K. Baxter. 1 cass. (Running Time: 58 mins.).Tr. of Divine Revelation of Hell. (SPA.). 1998. 7.99 (978-0-88368-346-0(6)) Whitaker Hse.

Revelacion Divina del Infierno. unabr. ed. Mary K. Baxter. 2 cass. (Running Time: 2 hrs. 54 min.).Tr. of Divine Revelation of Hell. (SPA.). 1998. 14.99 (978-0-88368-347-7(4)) Whitaker Hse.
Over a period of 40 days, God gave Mary Baxter visions of hell & commissioned her to tell all to choose life. Here is an account of the place & beings of hell contrasted with the glories of heaven.

Revelaciones. Deepak Chopra. 1 cass. (Running Time: 1 hr.).Tr. of Revelations: Journey into Healing. (SPA.). 2002. (978-968-5163-08-8(1)) Taller del Exito.
A journey into healing.

Revelation. (LifeLight Bible Studies: Course 15). 13.95 (20-2318) Concordia.

Revelation. Randall C. Bird. 1 cass. 9.95 (978-1-57734-263-2(1), 06005705) Covenant Comms.
Receiving the mind & will of the Lord.

Revelation. Read by Roscoe L. Browne. 1 cass. 1.99 (978-0-529-07154-5(1), WBC-18) Nelson.

Revelation. Neville Goddard. 1 cass. (Running Time: 62 min.). 1963. 8.00 (101) J & L Pubns.
Neville taught Imagination Creates Reality. He was a powerfully influential teacher of God as Consciousness.

Revelation. Lester Sumrall. 12 cass. (Running Time: 18 hrs.). 1999. 48.00 (978-1-58568-113-6(X)) Sumrall Pubng.

Revelation. abr. ed. Karen Traviss. Read by Mark Thompson. (Running Time: 21600 sec.). (Star Wars Ser.). (ENG.). 2008. audio compact disk 29.95 (978-0-7393-2401-1(2), Random AudioBks) Pub: Random Audio Pubg. Dist(s): Random

Revelation. deluxe ed. Chuck Missler. 24 cass. (Running Time: 36 hrs.). (Heirloom Edition Ser.). 1996. im. lthr. 89.95 (978-1-880532-00-3(X)) Koinonia Hse.
The Book of Revelation consists of 404 verses that contain over 800 allusions to the Old Testament. These are detailed, along with Chuck's analysis of the design and structure of this fascinating book. Learn about the past, present and future of the Church and our ultimate destiny. This is an ideal "first study" and foundational for every Christian.

***Revelation.** unabr. ed. Kate Brian, pseud. Narrated by Cassandra Campbell. (Running Time: 7 hrs. 0 mins.). (Private Ser.). 2010. 14.99 (978-1-4001-8238-1(7)); audio compact disk 29.99 (978-1-4001-1238-8(9)) Pub: Tantor Media. Dist(s): IngramPubServ

***Revelation.** unabr. ed. Kate Brian, pseud. Narrated by Cassandra Campbell. (Running Time: 7 hrs. 0 mins. 0 sec.). (Private Ser.). 2011. 19.99 (978-1-4001-6238-3(6)) Pub: Tantor Media. Dist(s): IngramPubServ

Revelation. unabr. ed. Drew Karpyshyn. Narrated by David Colacci. (Running Time: 9 hrs. 0 mins. 0 sec.). (Mass Effect Ser.). (ENG.). 2008. audio compact disk 34.99 (978-1-4001-1005-6(X)); audio compact disk 24.99 (978-1-4001-6005-1(7)); audio compact disk 69.99 (978-1-4001-4005-3(6)) Pub: Tantor Media. Dist(s): IngramPubServ

Revelation: A Biblical Interpretation. Concept by Ermance Rejebian. (ENG.). 2007. 5.99 (978-1-60339-141-2(X)); audio compact disk 5.99 (978-1-60339-142-9(8)) Listenr Digest.

Revelation ... Unveiling the End, Act 1: The Heavenly Stage. 2006. audio compact disk 46.00 (978-1-57972-717-8(4)) Insight Living.

Revelation ... Unveiling the End, Act 2: The Earthly Drama. 2006. audio compact disk 46.00 (978-1-57972-728-4(X)) Insight Living.

Revelation & Daniel Prophecy Vol. 2. Speeches. Ronald G. Fanter. 16 cass. (Running Time: 90 mins.). 2003. 80.00 (978-1-931215-40-4(5)) Cut Edge Min.
Tapes Included In This VolumePreach To All CreationThe Catching AwaySecond Advent of ChristThe Throne RoomClothed In GloryEnoch's Heavenly ScrollThe Sealed ScrollLoosing The Seven SealsOlivet DiscourseProphecies of DanielRam And HegoatAntiochus EpiphanesThe Fourth KingdomThe Roman EmpireSpirit of FearThe Dark Ages.

Revelation & Praise. 3 cass. 9.99 (978-0-529-07122-4(3), WBC-34) Nelson.

Revelation Comes Alive. 1 cass. (Running Time: 30 min.). 1985. (0287) Evang Sisterhood Mary.
When God Asks Us; Under the Banner of the Lamb; Prepared for the Great Moments; Overcomers in the City of God.

Revelation Commentary. Chuck Missler. 24 audio CDs. (Running Time: 28 hours). (Chuck Missler Commentaries). 2006. audio compact disk 89.95 (978-1-57821-315-3(0)) Koinonia Hse.
The Book of Revelation is the only book of the Bible with a Promise to the reader! Why? What makes this book so special? Revelation is a "lens" that puts the entire Bible into focus. The lens is focused on the person of Jesus Christ, and his destiny is imminent. This is a book of victory: We are overcomers! We are the ultimate winners in the game of life! (I read the ending: we win!) One of the reasons this book strikes us as strange is because of our lack of understanding concerning the Old Testament. The Book of Revelation consists of 404 verses that contain over 800 allusions to the Old Testament. These are detailed, along with Chuck's analysis of the design and structure of this fascinating book. Learn about the past, present and future of the Church and our ultimate destiny. This is an ideal "first study" and foundational for every Christian.This collection of 24 individual audio CD's contains more than 24 hours of Verse-by-Verse commentary on the book of Revelation coupled with extensive study notes. Plus, as an added bonus, this package also includes the fully automated MP3 2 CD-ROM set for a total of 26 CD's.

Revelation Gifts of the Spirit. Kenneth E. Hagin. 4 cass. 16.00 (09H) Faith Lib Pubns.

***Revelation (Library Edition)** unabr. ed. Kate Brian, pseud. Narrated by Cassandra Campbell. (Running Time: 7 hrs. 0 mins.). (Private Ser.). 2010. 29.99 (978-1-4001-9238-0(2)); audio compact disk 71.99 (978-1-4001-4238-5(5)) Pub: Tantor Media. Dist(s): IngramPubServ

***Revelation of God Through Us.** Featuring Ravi Zacharias. 2006. audio compact disk 9.00 (978-1-61256-064-9(4)) Ravi Zach.

Revelation of Humility. Elbert Willis. 1 cass. (Humility of Heaven Ser.). 4.00 Fill the Gap.

Revelation of Redemption. Kenneth Copeland. 6 cass. 2006. (978-1-57562-680-2(2)) K Copeland Pubns.

Revelation of Redemption. Kenneth Copeland. 6 cass. 1982. stu. ed. 30.00 Set incl. study guide. (978-0-938458-50-0(7)) K Copeland Pubns.
Understanding God's redemption.

Revelation of Ruchiradam. 2001. audio compact disk 24.95 (978-1-57097-126-6(9)) Dawn Horse Pr.

Revelation of St. John the Divine. Read by Heathcote Williams. 1 cass. (Running Time: 1 hr. 30 mins.). 2000. 9.98 (978-962-634-686-0(8), NA118614, Naxos AudioBooks) Naxos.
The theme is the apocalypse: the end of the world and the coming of Christ in Judgement. His is the work of a prophet, uniquely in The New Testament, and it bears vivid witness to the sense of an apocalyptic atmosphere, possessing a terrible beauty.

Revelation of St. John the Divine. abr. ed. Read by Heathcote Williams. 1 CD. (Running Time: 1 hr. 30 mins.). 2000. audio compact disk 11.98 (978-962-634-186-5(6), NA118612, Naxos AudioBooks) Naxos.

***Revelation of the Magi: The Lost Tale of the Wise Men's Journey to Bethlehem.** unabr. ed. Brent Landau. Narrated by Maurice England & Roger Mueller. (Running Time: 1 hr. 18 mins. 20 sec.). (ENG.). 2010. 13.99 (978-1-60814-784-7(3)); audio compact disk 19.99 (978-1-59859-833-9(3)) Oasis Audio.

Revelation Revealed. 10 cass. 30.00 set. (CRR) J Van Impe.
A verse-by-verse commentary on the book of Revelation in the Bible.

Revelation Revealed. Jack Van Impe. Read by Jack Van Impe. 8 cass. (Running Time: 8 hrs.). 30.00 J V I Minist.
Verse-by-verse commentary on the book of Revelation in the Bible.

Revelation Space. unabr. ed. Alastair Reynolds. Narrated by John Lee. (Running Time: 22 hrs. 0 mins. 0 sec.). (Revelation Space Ser.). (ENG.). 2009. audio compact disk 54.99 (978-1-4001-0955-5(8)); audio compact disk 109.99 (978-1-4001-3955-2(4)); audio compact disk 39.99 (978-1-4001-5955-0(5)) Pub: Tantor Media. Dist(s): IngramPubServ

***Revelation Unveiled.** ed. Zondervan. (Running Time: 16 hrs. 38 mins. 54 sec.). (ENG.). 2010. 14.99 (978-0-310-86982-5(X)) Zondervan.

Revelation Unveiling the End, Act 1: Unveiling the End see Apocalipsis Revelando el Fin, Primer Acto: El Escenario Celestial

Revelation Unveiling the End, Act 2: the Earthly Drama see Apocalipsis Revelando el Fin, Segundo Acto: El Drama Terrenal

Revelation... Unveiling the End, Act 3. 2007. audio compact disk 50.00 (978-1-57972-754-3(9)) Insight Living.

Revelations: Journey into Healing see Revelaciones

Revelations of Divine Love. unabr. ed. Julian of Norwich. Read by Pam Ward. (Running Time: 6 hrs. 0 mins. 0 sec.). (ENG.). 2009. audio compact disk 24.98 (978-1-59644-680-9(3), Hovel Audio) christianaud.

***Revelations of Divine Love.** unabr. ed. Julian of Norwich. Narrated by Pam Ward. (ENG.). 2009. 14.98 (978-1-59644-681-6(1), Hovel Audio) christianaud.

Revenge. Ellen Gilchrist. Read by Ellen Gilchrist. 1 cass. 1986. 13.95 (978-1-55644-157-8(6), 6061) Am Audio Prose.
The author reads "Revenge" from "In the Land of Dreamy Dreams.".

Revenge: A Story of Hope. abr. ed. Laura Blumenfeld. 2004. 15.95 (978-0-7435-4845-8(0)) Pub: S&S Audio. Dist(s): S and S Inc

Revenge in Paradise. Terrye Robins. Read by Terrye Robins. (Running Time: 33660 sec.). 2008. audio compact disk 40.99 (978-1-60247-788-9(4)) Tate Pubng.

Revenge, love, & Forgiveness see Venganza, amor y Perdon

Revenge of Innocents. abr. ed. Nancy Taylor Rosenberg. Read by Sandra Burr. (Running Time: 21600 sec.). (Carolyn Sullivan Ser.). 2008. audio compact disk 14.99 (978-1-4233-0710-5(0), 9781423307105, BCD Value Price) Brilliance Audio.

Revenge of Innocents. unabr. ed. Nancy Taylor Rosenberg. 1. (Running Time: 13 hrs.). (Carolyn Sullivan Ser.). 2007. 24.95 (978-1-4233-0705-1(4), 9781423307051, Brilliance MP3) Brilliance Audio.

Revenge of Innocents. unabr. ed. Nancy Taylor Rosenberg. Read by Sandra Burr. (Running Time: 13 hrs.). (Carolyn Sullivan Ser.). 2007. 39.25 (978-1-4233-0708-2(9), 9781423307082, BADLE); 24.95 (978-1-4233-0707-5(0), 9781423307075, BAD); 92.25 (978-1-4233-0737-2(2), 9781423307372, BrilAudUnabridg); audio compact disk 36.95 (978-1-4233-0703-7(8), 9781423307037, Bril Audio CD Unabri); audio compact disk 39.25 (978-1-4233-0706-8(2), 9781423307068, Brinc Audio MP3 Lib); audio compact disk 107.25 (978-1-4233-0704-4(6), 9781423307044, BriAudCD Unabrid) Brilliance Audio.

Revenge of the Dinosaurs. unabr. ed. Tom B. Stone. Narrated by Jeff Woodman. 2 cass. (Running Time: 2 hrs. 30 mins.). (Graveyard School Ser.: No. 5). (gr. 3-7). 2001. 19.00 (978-0-7887-0708-7(6), 94883E7) Recorded Bks.
An adventure of spooky danger & grisly humor centers around a school so weird that its students are dying to go to class.

Revenge of the Fiend. unabr. ed. Sheila Lavelle. Read by Judy Bennett. 2 cass. (Running Time: 2 hrs.). (Adventures with the Fiend Ser.). (YA). 1997. 18.95 (CCA 3366, Chivers Child Audio) AudioGO.

Revenge of the Kudzu Debutantes: A Novel. unabr. ed. Cathy Holton. Read by Marguerite Gavin. (Running Time: 9 hrs. NaN mins.). 2009. 29.95 (978-1-4332-3473-6(4)); audio compact disk 80.00 (978-1-4332-3470-5(X)); audio compact disk 59.95 (978-1-4332-3469-9(6)) Blckstn Audio.

Revenge of the Lawn Gnomes. R. L. Stine. (Goosebumps Ser.: No. 34). (J). (gr. 3-7). 1996. 7.98 (978-0-7634-0085-9(8)) W Disney Records.

Revenge of the Living Dummy. unabr. ed. R. L. Stine. Read by Alissa Hunnicutt. (Goosebumps HorrorLand Ser.: No. 1). (J). 2008. 34.99 (978-1-60514-570-9(X)) Find a World.

Revenge of the Mountain Man. abr. ed. William W. Johnstone. Read by Doug van Liew. (Mountain Man Ser.: No. 4). 2002. 25.00 (978-1-59183-002-3(8)) Pub: Otis Audio. Dist(s): Lndmrk Audiobks

Revenge of the Mountain Man. abr. ed. William W. Johnstone. Read by Doug van Liew. 4 cass. (Running Time: 6 hrs.). (Mountain Man Ser.: No. 4). 2002. 24.95 (978-1-890990-99-2(X), 99099) Otis Audio.
Western with sound effects.

Revenge of the Shadow King. Derek Benz. Read by Erik Steele. (Grey Griffins Ser.). (J). (gr. 4-7). 2006. 84.95 (978-0-439-87913-2(2)) Scholastic Inc.

Revenge of the Shadow King. unabr. ed. Derek Benz. Read by Erik Steele. 9 CDs. (Running Time: 10 hrs.). (Grey Griffins Ser.). (ENG.). (J). 2006. audio compact disk 39.95 (978-0-439-87592-9(7), Scholastic) Scholastic Inc.

Revenge of the Shadow King. unabr. ed. Derek Benz & J. S. Lewis. Read by Erik Steele. (J). 2007. 59.99 (978-1-60252-656-3(7)) Find a World.

Revenge of the Sith Episode III. unabr. ed. Matthew Stover. 6 cass. (Running Time: 9 hrs.). 2005. 54.00 (978-1-4159-1589-9(X)); audio compact disk 72.00 (978-1-4159-1673-5(X)) Books on Tape.

Revenge of the Sith Episode III, Vol. 3. unabr. ed. Matthew Stover. Read by Jonathan Davis. (Running Time: 14 hrs.). (Star Wars Ser.). (ENG.). 2005. audio compact disk 49.95 (978-0-7393-1833-1(0)) Pub: Random Audio Pubg. Dist(s): Random

Revenge of the Whale: The True Story of the Whaleship Essex. unabr. ed. 4 cass. (Running Time: 5:30 hrs.). (YA). 2004. 34.95 (978-0-9741711-9-7(0)) Audio Bkshelf.

Revenge of the Whale: The True Story of the Whaleship Essex. unabr. ed. Nathaniel Philbrick. Read by Taylor Mali. 5 CDs. (Running Time: 5 hrs. 30 mins.). (YA). 2005. audio compact disk 44.95 (978-0-9761932-0-3(5)) Audio Bkshelf.

Revenge of the Whale: The True Story of the Whaleship Essex. unabr. ed. Nathaniel Philbrick. Read by Taylor Mali. (YA). 2008. 64.99 (978-1-60514-604-1(8)) Find a World.

Revenge of the Witch. unabr. ed. Joseph Delaney. Read by Christopher Evan Welch. 5 CDs. (Running Time: 5 hrs. 15 mins.). (Last Apprentice Ser.: Bk. 1). (J). (gr. 5-8). 2005. audio compact disk 25.95 (978-0-06-082402-0(6), HarperChildAud) HarperCollins Pubs.

Revenge of the Witch. unabr. ed. Joseph Delaney. Read by Christopher Evan Welch. 5 cass. (Running Time: 5 hrs. 15 mins.). (Last Apprentice Ser.: Bk. 1). (YA). (gr. 5-8). 2006. 49.75 (978-1-4193-8441-7(4)); audio compact disk 49.75 (978-1-4193-8446-2(5)) Recorded Bks.

Revenue Act of Nineteen Ninety-Five. Editorial Resource Group Staff. 2 cass. (Running Time: 8 hrs.). 119.00 set, incl. wkbk. (751915EZ) Am Inst CPA.
Like previous AICPA courses on new tax laws, our forthcoming course will alert you to new tax-saving opportunities besides the obvious ones, steer you away from pitfalls, & contain down-to-earth examples, checklists, sample forms, & other practice aids.

Revenue Reconciliation Act of 1993. Gregory B. McKeen. 2 cass. 1994. 119.00 incl. wkbk. (751912VC) Am Inst CPA.
This best-selling course thoroughly clarifies those provisions of the new law that have the biggest impact on your clients or your employer & contains scores of practical tax-saving suggestions & practice aids. Included with the course materials at no extra charge is the Research Institute's 756-page paperback, Revenue Reconciliation Act of 1993 - Complete Analysis of the Law with Code Provisions As Amended & Committee Reports.

Reverberator. unabr. ed. Henry James. Read by Flo Gibson. 5 cass. (Running Time: 6 hrs. 30 mins.). 1998. 20.95 (978-1-55685-585-6(0)) Audio Bk Con.
Account of the impact of American journalism & scandal on a family in Parisian society.

REVERE: Reversing the Effects of Violence by Engaging Reciprocal Esteem. Gary F. Hutchison. 3 cass. (Running Time: 4 hrs. 30 mins.). 1994. 21.50 (978-1-885631-01-5(4)) G F Hutchison.
A self-help program to eliminate anger & violent reactions, & replace them with a problem solving approach & compassion.

Reverence: Music for Choir-Led Worship. Contrib. by Chris Barron. Created by Eon Endicott Trotman & Stan Endicott. 2007. audio compact disk 16.99 (978-5-557-69961-7(9)) Lillenas.

Reverence: Music for Choir-Led Worship. Contrib. by Chris Barron. Created by Stan Endicott & Eon Trotman. 2007. audio compact disk 12.00 (978-5-557-69963-1(5)) Lillenas.

Reverence: Music for Choir-Led Worship. Created by Eon Trotman & Stan Endicott. 2007. audio compact disk 90.00 (978-5-557-69965-5(1)) Lillenas.

Reverence God: Exodus 20:7-11. Ed Young. 1999. 4.95 (978-0-7417-2220-1(8), 1220) Win Walk.

Reverence Human Life: Exodus 20:13. Ed Young. 1985. 4.95 (978-0-7417-1433-6(7), 433) Win Walk.

Reverend Mark Twain: Theological Burlesque, Form, & Content. Joe B. Fulton. 2006. audio compact disk 9.95 (978-0-8142-9101-6(5)) Pub: Ohio St U Pr. Dist(s): Chicago Distribution Ctr

Reverend Martin Luther King, Jr., Level 1. 2 cass. (Running Time: 3 hrs.). (SmartReader Ser.). (J). 1999. pap. bk. & tchr. ed. 19.95 (978-0-7887-0760-5(4), 79347T3) Recorded Bks.
During the struggle for civil rights, Doctor King became a powerful spokesman for nonviolent resistance. Learn about his eloquent path to this position.

Reverend Martin Luther King, Jr., Level 2. 2 cass. (Running Time: 3 hrs.). (SmartReader Ser.). (J). 1999. pap. bk. & tchr. ed. 19.95 (978-0-7887-0122-1(3), 79310T3) Recorded Bks.

Reverend William Brewster: Gospel Music Composer. 1 cass. (Running Time: 30 min.). 9.95 (C060DB090, HarperThor) HarpC GBR.

Reverie of Poor Susan see Treasury of William Wordsworth

Reveries du Promeneur Solitaire. Jean-Jacques Rousseau. Read by G. Bejean. 3 cass. (Running Time: 4 hrs. 30 mins.). (FRE.). 1991. 31.95 (1482-VSL) Olivia & Hill.
Ten meditations on various phases of his life written in Rousseau's last years.

***Reversal.** abr. ed. Michael Connelly. Read by Peter Giles. (Running Time: 6 hrs. 30 mins.). (Mickey Haller Ser.). (ENG.). 2010. 19.98 (978-1-60788-649-5(9)); audio compact disk 29.98 (978-1-60788-648-8(0)) Pub: Hachet Audio. Dist(s): HachBkGrp

***Reversal.** unabr. ed. Michael Connelly. Read by Peter Giles. (Running Time: 11 hrs. 30 mins.). (Mickey Haller Ser.). 2010. 26.98 (978-1-60788-647-1(2)); audio compact disk 39.98 (978-1-60024-725-5(3)) Pub: Hachet Audio. Dist(s): HachBkGrp

Reverse Aging: A Self-Fulfilling Self-Concept. Scripts. Created by Michael Brickey. 1 CD. (Running Time: 30 mins.). 2003. audio compact disk 14.95 (978-0-9701555-8-0(1)) New Resour.
CD helps you relax, go into a trance, and effortlessly absorb the Attitudes, Beliefs and Coping Skills (Anti-aging ABCs) that foster vitality, longevity, and good health. The suggestions are enhanced by the original 4-track keyboard music of John David Jones. They let you effortlessly absorb ageless concepts, profoundly relax, and help relieve insomnia.

Reverse Aging: Hypnotic Journeys to Ageless Lifestyles. Scripts. Created by Michael Brickey. 6 CDs. (Running Time: 3 hrs.). 2003. audio compact disk 79.95 (978-0-9701555-2-8(2)) New Resour.
These six CDs help you relax, go into a trance, and effortlessly absorb the Attitudes, Beliefs and Coping Skills (Anti-aging ABCs) that foster vitality, longevity, and good health. The suggestions are enhanced by the original 4-track keyboard music of John David Jones. They let you effortlessly absorb ageless concepts, profoundly relax, and help relieve insomnia.

Reverse Aging: #1 the Beattitudes: Hypnotic Journeys to Ageless Lifestyles. Scripts. Created by Michael Brickey. 1 CD. (Running Time: 30 mins.). 2003. audio compact disk 14.95 (978-0-9701555-3-5(0)) New Resour.
CD helps you relax, go into a trance, and effortlessly absorb the Attitudes, Beliefs and Coping Skills (Anti-aging ABCs) that foster vitality, longevity, and good health. The suggestions are enhanced by the original 4-track keyboard music of John David Jones. They let you effortlessly absorb ageless concepts, profoundly relax, and help relieve insomnia.

Reverse Aging: #2 Getting Better All the Time: Hypnotic Journeys to Ageless Lifestyles. Scripts. Created by Michael Brickey. 1 CD. (Running Time: 30 mins.). 2003. audio compact disk 14.95 (978-0-9701555-4-2(9)) New Resour.

Reverse Aging: #3 Seeing Yourself with Perspective Lenses. Scripts. Created by Michael Brickey. 1 CD. (Running Time: 30 mins.). 2003. audio compact disk 14.95 (978-0-9701555-5-9(7)) New Resour.

Reverse Aging: #4 Remissioning & Living on Purpose. Scripts. Created by Michael Brickey. 1 CD. (Running Time: 30 mins.). 2003. audio compact disk 14.95 (978-0-9701555-6-6(5)) New Resour.

Reverse Aging: #5 Resilient Coping Skills. Scripts. Created by Michael Brickey. 1 CD. (Running Time: 30 mins.). 2003. audio compact disk 14.95 (978-0-9701555-7-3(3)) New Resour.

Reverse of the Medal. Patrick O'Brian. Read by Simon Vance. (Running Time: 32400 sec.). (Aubrey-Maturin Ser.). 2006. 59.95 (978-0-7861-4369-6(X)); audio compact disk 63.00 (978-0-7861-7533-8(8)) Blckstn Audio.

Reverse of the Medal. Patrick O'Brian. Narrated by Patrick Tull. 9 CDs. (Running Time: 10.5 hrs.). (Aubrey-Maturin Ser.). audio compact disk 39.95 (978-1-4025-7071-1(6)) Recorded Bks.

Reverse of the Medal. Patrick O'Brian. Read by Robert Hardy. 2 cass. (Running Time: 3 hrs.). (Aubrey-Maturin Ser.). 1999. 16.85 (978-0-00-105546-9(1)) Ulvrscrft Audio.
Jack returns from his duties protecting whalers off South America & is persuaded by a casual acquaintance to make investments in the city.

Reverse of the Medal. abr. unabr. ed. Patrick O'Brian. Read by Simon Vance. (Running Time: 32400 sec.). (Aubrey-Maturin Ser.). 2006. audio compact disk 29.95 (978-0-7861-7818-6(3)) Blckstn Audio.

Reverse of the Medal. abr. unabr. ed. Patrick O'Brian. Read by Simon Vance. 8 cass. (Running Time: 32400 sec.). (Aubrey-Maturin Ser.). 2006. 29.95 (978-0-7861-4473-0(4)) Blckstn Audio.

Reverse of the Medal. abr. unabr. ed. Patrick O'Brian & Simon Vance. 9 CDs. (Running Time: 32400 sec.). (Aubrey-Maturin Ser.). 2006. audio compact disk 29.95 (978-0-7861-7280-1(0)) Blckstn Audio.

Reverse of the Medal. unabr. ed. Patrick O'Brian. Read by Richard Brown. 8 cass. (Running Time: 12 hrs.). (Aubrey-Maturin Ser.). 1993. 64.00 (978-0-7366-2400-8(7), 3169) Books on Tape.
Stephen Maturin steps in to save Aubrey's reputation, ruined as the result of a deliberate plot. Eleventh in series.

Reverse of the Medal. unabr. ed. Patrick O'Brian. Narrated by Patrick Tull. 7 cass. (Running Time: 10 hrs. 15 mins.). (Aubrey-Maturin Ser.). 1994. 60.00 (978-0-7887-0145-0(2), 94252E7) Recorded Bks.
Captain Jack Aubrey, home in London, unwittingly invests his prize money in illegal activities & winds up in jail.

Reverse Speech: The Voice of Truth. David John Oates. Narrated by David John Oates. 4 cass. (Running Time: 3 hrs.). 1996. 29.95 (978-1-882899-05-0(9), RSDJOAT01) J Johnston Seminars.
This 4-tape set demonstrates one of the most important discoveries in human history: a heretofore unknown, subliminal channel of human speech that always reveals the truth of the speaker's thoughts, no matter what that speaker is saying! Hard-to-believe and frequently controversial, the methodology demonstrated in this 4-tape set has nevertheless been used successfully in criminal investigations, corporate- and private investor consultation, to provide unmatched insights for personal growth, for providing otherwise inaccessible insights into the emotional correlates of disease including cancer, etc. The 4-tape set includes lectures by Reverse Speech discoverer David John Oates, accompanied by examples drawn from the lyrics of popular music, statements of politicians, celebrities, children, etc. You will be able to hear these voices from the subconscious with your own ears!.

***Reversibility... YtilibisreveR.** Created by Uncommon Sensing LLC. (ENG.). 2005. audio compact disk 60.00 (978-0-9826724-6-4(2)) Uncommon Sens.

Reversible Error. unabr. ed. Robert K. Tanenbaum. Read by Connor O'Brien. 7 cass. (Running Time: 10 hrs. 30 min.). (Butch Karp Mystery Ser.). 1997. 56.00 (978-0-7366-3686-5(2), 4365) Books on Tape.
A killer is at work on the New York streets & no one seems to want to catch him.

Reversible Errors. Scott Turow. 2002. audio compact disk 96.00 (978-0-7366-8881-9(1)) Books on Tape.

Reversible Errors. abr. ed. Scott Turow. Read by David Birney. 5 CDs. (Running Time: 21600 sec.). (ENG.). 2005. audio compact disk 14.99 (978-0-7393-2263-5(X), Random AudioBks) Pub: Random Audio Pubg. Dist(s): Random

Reversible Errors. unabr. ed. Scott Turow. 9 cass. (Running Time: 13 hrs. 30 mins.). 2002. 64.00 (978-0-7366-8839-0(0)) Books on Tape.

Reversing Hurry Sickness: Getting Off the Fastrack. Bruce A. Baldwin. Read by Bruce A. Baldwin. (Running Time: 60 min.). 1983. 8.95 (978-0-933583-06-1(0), PDC834) Direction Dynamics.
Book on Tape: Chapter from "It's All in Your Head." Discusses how to slow down.

Reversing Hypertension: A Vital New Program to Prevent, Treat, & Reduce High Blood Pressure. abr. ed. Julian M. Whitaker. Narrated by Michael Prichard. (Running Time: 10800 sec.). 2006. audio compact disk 22.95 (978-1-933310-07-7(3)) STI Certified.

Reversing the Aging Process Naturally: A Practical Guide for the Prevention of Pre-Mature Aging. abr. ed. Gary Null. Read by Gary Null. 2 cass. (Running Time: 3 hrs.). 1996. bk. 16.95 Set. (978-0-9644002-0-7(0)) Common Mode Hrmnic Wave.
Naturally reversing the aging process.

Reves et Complices (Dreams & Accomplices) Nicole Gratton. Illus. by Julie Tessier. 1 cass. (Coffragants Ser.). (FRE.). (J). 1998. bk. 16.95 Plastic case, incl. text bklet. (978-2-921997-03-4(7)) Penton Overseas.

Review & Drafting of Employee Benefits Plans. Jerry Fellows. 2006. audio compact disk 49.95 (978-1-59701-089-4(8)) Aspatore Bks.

Review for National Board Exam, Pt. 1. Steven C. Eggleston & Inez Freedman. 12 cass. (Running Time: 18 hrs.). 1986. 39.95 SCE Prod & List & Lrn.
Review material in core sciences for students taking the chiropractic national boards.

Review for National Board Exam, Pt. 2. Steven C. Eggleston & Inez Freedman. 16 cass. 1987. 39.95 SCE Prod & List & Lrn.
Review material for chiropractic national board exam covering clinical areas.

Review for the ASVAB. Comex Systems Staff. 2004. audio compact disk 400.00 (978-1-56030-211-7(9)) Comex Systs.

Review of Divine Healing. Elbert Willis. 4 cass. 13.00 Fill the Gap.

Review of Meet the Superkids. 1 CD. (J). 2005. audio compact disk (978-1-59833-989-5(3)) Rowland Reading.

Review of Superkids' Club. 1 CD. (J). 2005. audio compact disk (978-1-59833-990-1(7)) Rowland Reading.

Review on Spiritual Warfare, Pt. 5. Rick Joyner. 1 cass. (Running Time: 90 mins.). (Spiritual Warfare Ser.: Vol. 5). 2000. 5.00 (RJ15-005) Morning NC.
God has designed spiritual weapons of warfare for Christians to use & the insightful teaching in this five-part series will encourage, strengthen & prepare you to wage war against the enemy.

Review Pack: Adobe Flash CS4, Illustrated. Sherry Bishop. (C). 2009. audio compact disk 8.95 (978-1-4390-4080-5(X)) Pub: Course Tech. Dist(s): CENGAGE Learn

Review Pack: Spotlight on Computer Applications. Jennifer Gipp & Course Technology Staff. (C). 2005. audio compact disk 9.95 (978-1-4188-6509-2(5)) Pub: Course Tech. Dist(s): CENGAGE Learn

Review Question on Stock Markets. Sam Crawford. 1 cass. 8.95 (505) Am Fed Astrologers.

Reviewing Basic Nursing Assistant Content: Basic Restorative Services. Patricia Hoefler. 1991. (978-1-56533-153-2(2)) MEDS Pubng.

Reviewing Basic Nursing Assistant Content: Personal Care/Resident Rights. Patricia Hoefler. 1991. (978-1-56533-154-9(0)) MEDS Pubng.

Reviewing Basic Nursing Assistant Content: Preparing for the Exam. Patricia Hoefler. 1991. (978-1-56533-150-1(8)) MEDS Pubng.

Reviewing Basic Nursing Assistant Content Pt. 1: Basic Nursing Skills. Patricia Hoefler. 1991. (978-1-56533-151-8(6)) MEDS Pubng.

Reviewing Basic Nursing Assistant Content Pt. 2: Basic Nursing Skills. Patricia Hoefler. 1991. (978-1-56533-152-5(4)) MEDS Pubng.

***Revise Us Again: Living from a Renewed Christian Script.** unabr. ed. Frank Viola. (Running Time: 6 hrs. 0 mins. 0 sec.). (ENG.). 2011. audio compact disk 21.98 (978-1-61045-032-4(9)) christianaud.

Revised St. Alban Hymnal: Hymn Tunes from the St. Alban Hymnal. Perf. by Carmen Synnes. 3 CDs. (Running Time: 2 hrs.). 2002. audio compact disk 75.00 (978-0-935461-93-0(0)) St Alban Pr CA.
All of the hymn tunes from the Revised St. Alban Hymnal. Sold only as set with three Compact Disc and a looseleaf Organ-Edition Hymnal.

Revisiting the 10 Commandments: A Contemporary Update to Irving Younger's Classic Credibility & Cross-examination. Stephen D. Easton. 2003. stu. ed. 185.00 (978-0-943380-50-6(2)) PEG MN.

Revisiting the 10 Commandments: A Contemporary Update to Irving Younger's Classic Credibility & Cross-examination. Speeches. Stephen D. Easton. Perf. by Stephen D. Easton. Based on a work by Irving Younger. 6 CDs. (Running Time: 6 hrs.). 2003. pap. bk. 205.00 (978-0-943380-75-9(8)) PEG MN.

Revitalizing Human Communities - "Africa 2000" & Habitat Specialist Eric Carlson on United Nations Development Programme's Projects. Hosted by Nancy Pearlman. 1 cass. (Running Time: 29 min.). 10.00 (1021) Educ Comm CA.

***Revival: The Struggle for Survival Inside the Obama White House.** unabr. ed. Richard Wolffe. Read by Richard Wolffe. (Running Time: 9 hrs.). (ENG.). 2010. audio compact disk 40.00 (978-0-307-74989-5(4), Random AudioBks) Pub: Random Audio Pubg. Dist(s): Random

Revival at Brownsville. Mark Powell. 1 cass. 1996. 10.99 (978-0-7684-0027-4(9)); audio compact disk 15.99 CD. (978-0-7684-0026-7(0)) Destiny Image Pubs.

Revival Fire. Michael Brown. 3 cass. (Running Time: 4 hrs. 30 mins.). 1996. 17.99 (978-1-56043-747-5(2)) Destiny Image Pubs.

Revival in the Catholic Church. unabr. ed. Vincent M. Walsh. 1 cass. (Running Time: 1 hr.). 1996. 10.00 (978-0-943374-26-0(X)) Key of David.

Revival in the Scottish Hebrides. abr. ed. Duncan B. Campbell. 3 CDs. (Running Time: 3 hrs.). 2000. 19.99 (978-0-7684-0198-1(4)) Destiny Image Pubs.

Revive Our Hearts Conference. Nancy Leigh DeMoss. 2003. (978-0-940110-46-5(6)) Life Action Publishing.

Revive the Stones Cass. 2004. 20.00 (978-1-57855-624-3(4)) T D Jakes.

Revive Us Again. Carl MaultsBy and the Rejoicensemble. 1. 2005. audio compact disk 18.00 (978-0-89869-490-1(6)) Church Pub Inc.
This album is a beautifully recorded "follow-up" to Carl MaultsBy's Playing Gospel Piano: The Basics, published in late 2003. Carl and the Ensemble, together with instrumentalists, offer spirited renditions of African-American gospel favorites in the jazz improvisation tradition. Carl sings and, of course, presides at the piano.

Revive Us Oh Lord, Vol 1: A Stirring Study of Revival in These Last Days. 2008. audio compact disk 36.00 (978-1-57399-342-5(5)) Mac Hammond.

Revive Us Oh Lord, Vol 2: Cultivating Spiritual Hunger. Mac Hammond. 2008. audio compact disk 30.00 (978-1-57399-343-2(3)) Mac Hammond.

Revive Us Oh Lord, Vol 3: Inviting the Holy Spirit¿s Operations into Your Life. Mac Hammond. 2008. audio compact disk 24.00 (978-1-57399-344-9(1)) Mac Hammond.

Revived. World Wide Message Tribe. 1 cass., 1 CD. 8.98 (46581-4); audio compact disk 13.98 (46581-2) Warner Christian.

Revived by His Word. Donna Christian. 2006. audio compact disk 10.00 (978-0-9672804-5-5(1)) Family Harvest.

Reviving Ophelia: Saving the Selves of Adolescent Girls. abr. ed. Mary Pipher. 2 cass. 14.95 (47964) Books on Tape.
A look-obsessed, sexist society is destroying the self-esteem of our daughters, which can lead to addictions & suicide. Dr. Pipher tells parents how to help.

Reviving Ophelia: Saving the Selves of Adolescent Girls, unabr. ed. Mary Pipher. Narrated by Linda Stephens. 10 cass. (Running Time: 13 hrs. 30 mins.). 1996. 85.00 (978-0-7887-0519-9(9), 94714E7) Recorded Bks.
Sessions with adolescent girls have prompted this clinical psychologist to wonder why more girls are falling prey to depression, eating problems, etc.

Reviving Sanctification. Creflo A. Dollar. 2008. audio compact disk 34.00 (978-1-59944-742-1(8)) Creflo Dollar.

Reviving the Lifeless. Drew Weber. (YA). 2006. audio compact disk 10.00 (978-1-4276-0417-0(7)) AardGP.

***Revolt.** Carl Sommer. (Quest for Success Ser.). (ENG.). (YA). 2009. bk. 19.95 (978-1-57537-333-1(5)); pap. bk. 11.95 (978-1-57537-382-9(3)) Advance Pub.

***Revolt / la Revuelta.** ed. Carl Sommer. (Quest for Success Bilingual Ser.). (ENG & SPA.). (YA). 2009. bk. 21.95 (978-1-57537-432-1(3)) Advance Pub.

Revolt of Islam. Bernard Lewis. 1 CD. (Running Time: 1 hr. 30 mins.). 2005. audio compact disk 12.95 (978-0-660-18970-3(4)) Pub: Canadian Broadcasting CAN. Dist(s): Georgetown Term

Revolt of Mother see Women in Literature, the Short Story: A Collection

Revolt of Mother. unabr. ed. Mary E. Wilkins Freeman. 1 cass. (Running Time: 58 min.). Dramatization. 1977. 7.95 (D-5) Jimcin Record.
Women's lib in the 1800's.

Revolt of the Highbrows. 10.00 (HT408) Esstee Audios.

Revolt of the Masses. unabr. ed. José Ortega y Gasset. Read by Michael Edwards. 5 cass. (Running Time: 7 hrs.). 1988. 39.95 (978-0-7861-0011-8(7), 1010) Blckstn Audio.
Who are the masses? Ortega saw them as the group of people disposed to mediocrity, opposed to excellence & inclined towards conformed thinking. Agglomerated, they wield a frightful amount of power which we see today as they assertively lay claim to a myriad of demands & "rights.".

Revolt of the Teddy Bears. abr. ed. James P. Duffy. Perf. by Peggy Cass. 1 cass. (Running Time: 61 min.). (J). (gr. k-4). 1986. 8.98 (978-0-89845-633-2(9), CP1791) HarperCollins Pubs.
Paris is in turmoil. Teddy bears are rioting in the streets. It's up to the newly retired Chief of police May Gray - a French poodle - to solve the case & end the revolt.

Revoltes de la Bounty. abr. ed. Jules Verne. Read by Nathalie Adam. 1 cass. (FRE.). 1995. 19.95 (1754-KFP) Olivia & Hill.
Due to the brutality on his ship of Captain Bligh, the crew mutinies & puts him & eighteen seamen who remain faithful to him on a barge & sets them out to sea. The Bounty & the mutineers head towards Polynesia & there begins their adventure.

Revolting Rhymes & Dirty Beasts. unabr. ed. Roald Dahl. Read by Alan Cumming. 1 cass. (Running Time: 1 hr.). (J). (gr. 3-5). 2002. 12.00 (978-0-06-009127-9(4)) HarperCollins Pubs.

***Revolting Rhymes & Dirty Beasts.** unabr. ed. Roald Dahl. Read by Alan Cumming. (ENG.). 2004. (978-0-06-078949-7(2)); (978-0-06-081497-7(7)) HarperCollins Pubs.

Revolting Rhymes & Dirty Beasts. unabr. ed. Roald Dahl. Read by Alan Cumming. 2 CDs. (Running Time: 3 hrs.). (J). 2004. audio compact disk 13.95 (978-0-06-074055-9(8), HarperChildAud) HarperCollins Pubs.

Revolution. abr. ed. Dale Brown et al. Read by Phil Gigante. (Running Time: 5 hrs.). (Dale Brown's Dreamland Ser.). 2009. audio compact disk 14.99 (978-1-4233-1314-4(3), 9781423313144, BCD Value Price) Brilliance Audio.

Revolution. unabr. ed. Dale Brown & Jim DeFelice. Read by Christopher A. Lane. (Running Time: 12 hrs.). (Dale Brown's Dreamland Ser.). 2008. 24.95 (978-1-4233-1311-3(9), 9781423313113, BAD) Brilliance Audio.

Revolution. unabr. ed. Dale Brown & Jim DeFelice. Read by Christopher Lane. 1 MP3-CD. (Running Time: 12 hrs.). (Dale Brown's Dreamland Ser.). 2008. 39.25 (978-1-4233-1310-6(0), 9781423313106, Brinc Audio MP3 Lib); 39.25 (978-1-4233-1312-0(7), 9781423313120, BADLE); audio compact disk 97.25 (978-1-4233-1308-3(9), 9781423313083, BriAudCD Unabrid) Brilliance Audio.

***Revolution.** unabr. ed. Jennifer Donnelly. Narrated by Emily Janice Card & Emma Bering. 12 CDs. (YA). (gr. 7-12). 2010. audio compact disk 54.00 (978-0-307-74629-0(1), Listening Lib) Pub: Random Audio Pubg. Dist(s): Random

***Revolution.** unabr. ed. Jennifer Donnelly. Read by Emma Bering & Emily Janice Card. (Running Time: 15 hrs. 4 mins.). (ENG.). (J). 2010. audio compact disk 54.00 (978-0-307-74621-4(6), Listening Lib) Pub: Random Audio Pubg. Dist(s): Random

Revolution. unabr. ed. Loren Robinson. Read by Ron Varela. 6 cass. (Running Time: 6 hrs. 24 min.). (American Blend Ser.: Bk. 1). 2001. 39.95 (978-1-55686-746-0(8)) Books in Motion.
The saga of two immigrant families following their movements through 200 years. The migration west brings these two families together.

Revolution: A Manifesto. unabr. ed. Ron Paul. Read by Bob Craig. (Running Time: 5 hrs. 30 mins.). (ENG.). 2008. 16.98 (978-1-60024-356-1(8)); audio compact disk 24.98 (978-1-60024-355-4(X)) Pub: Hachet Audio. Dist(s): HachBkGrp

Revolution: Key West & Castro. Patrick Lennon. Read by Andrew Hodas. (ENG.). 2007. audio compact disk 24.95 (978-0-9796752-2-5(7)) Fiction Pub.

***Revolution: The Lost Beatles Interviews.** Geoffrey Giuliano. 2009. (978-1-60136-529-3(2)) Audio Holding.

Revolution Bk. 2. unabr. ed. Dale Brown & Jim DeFelice. Read by Christopher Lane. 1 MP3-CD. (Running Time: 12 hrs.). (Dale Brown's Dreamland Ser.). 2008. 24.95 (978-1-4233-1309-0(7), 9781423313090, Brilliance MP3); audio compact disk 36.99 (978-1-4233-1307-6(0), 9781423313076, Bril Audio CD Unabri) Brilliance Audio.

Revolution & Evolution in Public Contracting. 1997. bk. 99.00 (ACS-1268) PA Bar Inst.
Designed to inform you of the latest developments & trends in public contracting. Many of these are revolutionary & quickly evolving issues from better value & more effective use of information technology in the procurement process by states & local governments, to the privatization of many government operations, litigation involving union-only project labor agreements on public construction projects, to current employment law issues such as the relationship between the Right to Know Act & the Prevailing Wage Act, to the modified total case approach for proving damages against the Commonwealth.

Revolution & Modernity (2004) 2004. 28.00 (978-1-59128-398-0(1)); 35.00 (978-1-59128-400-0(7)) Canon Pr ID.

Revolution in Astrological Capability. Hai Halevi. 1 cass. 8.95 (540) Am Fed Astrologers.

Revolution in World Missions. K. P. Yohannan. 4 cass. (Running Time: 6 hrs.). 1999. 15.99 (978-1-56599-993-0(2)) ACW Pr.

Revolution Is Not a Dinner Party. unabr. ed. Ying Chang Compestine. Read by Jodi Long. 4 CDs. (Running Time: 4 hrs. 45 mins.). (YA). (gr. 5 up). 2007. audio compact disk 38.00 (978-0-7393-6161-0(9), Listening Lib) Pub: Random Audio Pubg. Dist(s): Random
Nine-year-old Ling is very comfortable with her life; her parents are both dedicated doctors in the best hospital in Wuhan. But when Comrade Li, one of Mao's political officers, moves into a room in their apartment, Ling begins to witness the gradual disintegration of her world. In an atmosphere of increasing mistrust, Ling fears for the safety of her neighbors, and soon for herself and family. Over the course of four years, Ling manages to blossom, even as she suffers more horrors than many people face in a lifetime.

Revolution of Love. David Glen Hatch. 1 cass. 1997. 9.98 (978-1-57734-099-7(X), 06005527) Covenant Comms.
A fireside of inspiring words & music.

***Revolutionaries: A New History of the Invention of America.** unabr. ed. Jack Rakove. Read by Bronson Pinchot. (Running Time: 15 hrs.). 2010. 29.95 (978-1-4417-7343-2(6)); 85.95 (978-1-4417-7340-1(1)); audio compact disk 34.95 (978-1-4417-7342-5(8)); audio compact disk 118.00 (978-1-4417-7341-8(X)) Blckstn Audio.

Revolutionary Architect: Frank Lloyd Wright. Louis Untermeyer. 1 cass. (Running Time: 18 min.). (Makers of the Modern World Ser.). 1968. 11.95 (11010) J Norton Pubs.
The story of Frank Lloyd Wright & of his choice between honest arrogance & hypocritical humility.

Revolutionary Parenting. unabr. ed. George Barna. Narrated by Scott Dente. (ENG.). 2007. 12.59 (978-1-60814-364-1(3)) Oasis Audio.

Revolutionary Parenting. unabr. ed. George Barna. Read by Christine Dente. Narrated by Scott Dente. (Running Time: 18000 sec.). (ENG.). 2007. audio compact disk 17.99 (978-1-59859-213-9(0)) Oasis Audio.

Revolutionary Road. unabr. ed. Richard Yates. Read by Mark Bramhall. 9 CDs. (Running Time: 11 hrs. 30 mins.). (ENG.). 2008. audio compact disk 29.95 (978-0-7393-5937-2(1), Random AudioBks) Pub: Random Audio Pubg. Dist(s): Random

Revolutionary Speeches & Poems of Ireland. Read by Michael MacLiammoir. 1 cass. 10.95 (SAC 749) Spoken Arts.

Revolutionary Theme Muzik. Contrib. by R-Swift. 2007. audio compact disk 13.99 (978-5-557-70347-5(0)) C Mason Res.

Revolutionary War on Wednesday. unabr. ed. Mary Pope Osborne. Read by Mary Pope Osborne. (Running Time: 35 mins.). (Magic Tree House Ser.: No. 22). (J). (gr. k-3). 2004. pap. bk. 17.00 (978-0-8072-0931-8(7), S FTR 254 SP, Listening Lib) Random Audio Pubg.

Revolutionary Wealth. abr. ed. Alvin Toffler & Heidi Toffler. Read by Laura Dean & Kevin Gray. (Running Time: 34200 sec.). (ENG.). 2006. audio compact disk 39.95 (978-0-7393-3374-7(7), Random AudioBks) Pub: Random Audio Pubg. Dist(s): Random

Revolutionary Wealth: How it Will Be Created & How it Will Change Our Lives. unabr. ed. Alvin Toffler & Heidi Toffler. 13 cass. (Running Time: 19 hrs.). 2006. 104.00 (978-1-4159-2993-3(9)); audio compact disk 128.00 (978-1-4159-2994-0(7)) Books on Tape.

Revolutions, Set. Eugene Kamenda. 4 cass. 47.50 (S19700) J Norton Pubs.
Concepts, Chinese, French & Russian Revolutions.

Revolutions Series: World Events over Time Collection. Eugene Lieber. (ENG.). 2006. audio compact disk 140.00 (978-1-935069-16-4(0)) IAB Inc.

Revolutions That Never Were (1996) 1996. 16.00 (978-1-59128-272-3(1)); 20.00 (978-1-59128-274-7(8)) Canon Pr ID.

Revolve Tour: Inside Out: 10 Smash Hits from Chicks That Rock. 2007. audio compact disk 9.99 (978-5-557-59875-0(8), Word Records) Word Enter.

***Revolver.** unabr. ed. Marcus Sedgwick. Read by Peter Berkrot. (Running Time: 4 hrs.). 2010. 19.99 (978-1-4418-4568-9(2), 9781441845689, BAD); 39.97 (978-1-4418-4560-3(7), 9781441845603, Brinc Audio MP3 Lib); 39.97 (978-1-4418-4576-4(3), 9781441845764, BADLE); 19.99 (978-1-4418-4552-8(6), 9781441845528, Brilliance MP3); audio compact disk 62.97 (978-1-4418-4544-3(5), 9781441845443, BriAudCD Unabrid); audio compact disk 19.99 (978-1-4418-4536-8(4), 9781441845368) Brilliance Audio.

Reward. unabr. ed. Peter Corris. Read by Peter Hosking. 8 cass. (Running Time: 5 hrs. 30 mins.). 2004. 64.00 (978-1-86442-314-3(5), 581259) Pub: Bolinda Pubng AUS. Dist(s): Lndmrk Audiobks
Cliff Hardy is reluctantly drawn into a scheme to claim the reward on a 17-year-old abduction case. He is distracted by a hot new lover, but when one of the schemers turns up dead, the case gets his full attention. Who paid the cops to suppress the ransom note & how come they're always one jump ahead of Hardy?.

Reward - A Hundredfold. 1985. (0245) Evang Sisterhood Mary.

Reward Employees. PUEI. 2007. audio compact disk 199.00 (978-1-934147-62-7(1), CareerTrack) P Univ E Inc.

Rewards & Fairies. unabr. ed. Rudyard Kipling. Read by Flo Gibson. 5 cass. (Running Time: 7 hrs. 30 min.). (J). (gr. 2 up). 1994. 20.95 (978-1-55685-328-9(9)) Audio Bk Con.
This sequel to "Puck of Pook's Hill" is full of historical adventures & fun. "Cold Iron", "Gloriana", "The Wrong Thing", "Marklake Witches", "The Knife & Naked Chalk", "Brother Square-Toes", "A Priest in Spite of Himself", "The Conversion of Sir Wilfred", "A Doctor of Medicine", "Simple Simon", & "The Tree of Justice" are the titles of these imaginative tales.

Rewards at the Judgment Seat: How the Fear of the Lord Produces a Life That Pleases God. Mac Hammond. 4 cass. (Running Time: 4 hrs.). (Last Millennium Ser.: Vol. 2). 1999. (978-1-57399-089-9(2)) Mac Hammond.
The Judgement Seat of God. The very name has a tendency to send a sobering chill through the heart of many Christians. But is this the attitude a believer should hold?.

Rewards of a Renewed Soul. As told by Frank Damazio. 6. 2002. 59.99 (978-1-886849-88-4(9)) CityChristian.

Rewiring the Brain: Program from the Award Winning Public Radio Series. Hosted by Fred Goodwin. Comment by John Hockenberry. Contrib. by Edward Taub et al. 1 cass. (Running Time: 1 hr.). (Infinite Mind Ser.). 1998. audio compact disk 21.95 (978-1-888064-35-3(8), LCM 27) Lichtenstein Creat.
People recovering from stroke and traumatic brain injury demonstrate that the ability of the brain to rewire and reprogram itself is much greater than previously thought. New methods of rehabilitation are changing lives, and the way neuroscientists think about the human brain.

Rework: Change the Way You Work Forever. abr. unabr. ed. Jason Fried & David Heinemeier Hansson. Read by Mike Chamberlain. (ENG.). 2010. audio compact disk 24.00 (978-0-307-70451-1(3), Random AudioBks) Pub: Random Audio Pubg. Dist(s): Random

Rewritable - Write-Once Multifunctional Disk: Overview of Optical Storage Market Developments. 1 cass. 1990. 8.50 Recorded Res.

Rewritable Optical Storage Devices: Developing Media for Worm - Rewritable Optical Disk Drives. 1 cass. 1990. 8.50 Recorded Res.

Rewrites a Memoir. Neil Simon. 2004. 15.95 (978-0-7435-4844-1(2)) Pub: S&S Audio. Dist(s): S and S Inc

Rex Allen: Sixteen Golden Hits. Prod. by Walt Disney Records Staff. 1 cass. 1998. 22.50 (978-0-7634-0400-0(4)) W Disney Records.

REXExtreme Fluency Audio. Benchmark Education Staff. 2004. audio compact disk 10.00 (978-1-4108-2547-6(7)) Benchmark Educ.

Rey de los Pleitos. abr. ed. Scripts. John Grisham. 6 CDs. (Running Time: 25200 sec.).Tr. of King of Torts. (SPA.). 2006. audio compact disk 29.95 (978-1-933499-20-8(6)) Fonolibro Inc.
FonoLibro les trae el audiolibro en espa?ol del bestseller "El Rey de Los Pleitos" de John Grisham, uno de los mas famosos escritores internacionales de novelas en la actualidad y autor de los bestsellers "La Firma", "El Informe Pelicano", "Tiempo para Matar", "El Intermediario," "El Cliente" y otros exitos llevados al cine. ?El Rey de los Pleitos,? llega a usted en una magnifica produccion, con la calidad reconocida de Fonolibro, lider de audiolibros en espa?ol. A pesar de su juventud, Clay Carter ve su futuro con cierto cinismo. Hace a?os que ejerce de abogado publico de oficio y la situacion no parece que vaya a cambiar. De ahi su resignacion al abordar un nuevo caso que promete ser como tantos otros: debe defender a un adolescente acusado de asesinato, un hecho corriente en la ciudad de Washington. Sin embargo, cuando Clay empieza a indagar en el pasado de su cliente, se entera de que este se hallaba bajos los efectos de un farmaco en fase de experimentacion cuando cometio el crimen. El laboratorio creador del producto, ansioso de que el suceso no salga a la luz, le propone a Clay un pacto. Para cumplirlo, el joven abogado debera estar dispuesto a jugar sucio. A pesar de sus reticencias iniciales, Clay acabara aceptando, al entender que esta puede ser la oportunidad de su vida: la compa?ia es una de las empresas farmaceuticas mas importantes del pais. La mision promete ser dura por el complejo entramado de poder e intereses en juego, pero la tentacion es demasiado grande: de la noche a la ma?ana, Clay podria convertirse en el nuevo rey de los pleitos.En su nuevo thriller de corte legal, John Grisham pone al descubierto el enorme poder que poseen ciertos bufetes de abogados, a la vez que analiza las consecuencias que puede tener una ambicion desmesurada.El Intermediario de John Grisham, tambien disponible en audiolibro de FonoLibro.

Reynolds Price. unabr. ed. Reynolds Price. Read by Reynolds Price. 1 cass. (Running Time: 29 min.). 1988. 10.00 New Letters.
Price reads from his novel Good Hearts & is interviewed.

Reynolds Price: Interview. Interview. Interview with Reynolds Price & Kay Bonetti. 1 cass. (Running Time: 1 hr.). 13.95 (978-1-55644-052-6(9), 2102) Am Audio Prose.
Talk covers Price's views on the novel as a Christian form, Flannery O'Connor, letters as a form of truth telling, & Tolstoy, Hemingway, Auden, & other writers he calls "examples.".

RE680X Roald Dahl CD Read-Alongs - Complete Set. Lakeshore Learning Materials Staff. (J). 2008. pap. bk. 179.00 (978-1-60666-680-7(0)) Lkeshore Learn Mats.

RE686 James & the Giant Peach CD Read-along Kit. Lakeshore Learning Materials Staff. (J). 2008. pap. bk. 42.50 (978-1-60666-681-4(9)) Lkeshore Learn Mats.

RE687 Matilda CD Read-along Kit. Lakeshore Learning Materials Staff. (J). 2008. pap. bk. 54.50 (978-1-60666-682-1(7)) Lkeshore Learn Mats.

RE688 Charlie & the Chocolate Factory CD Read-along Kit. Lakeshore Learning Materials Staff. (J). 2008. pap. bk. 53.50 (978-1-60666-683-8(5)) Lkeshore Learn Mats.

RE689 the Giraffe & the Pelly & Me CD Read-along Kit. Lakeshore Learning Materials Staff. (J). 2008. pap. bk. 37.50 (978-1-60666-684-5(3)) Lkeshore Learn Mats.

RE725X Favorite Picture Book CD Read-Alongs - Set 1. Lakeshore Learning Materials Staff. (J). 2008. pap. bk. 179.00 (978-1-60666-685-2(1)) Lkeshore Learn Mats.

RE731 Anansi & the Moss-Covered Rock CD Read-along Kit. Lakeshore Learning Materials Staff. (J). 2008. pap. bk. 40.50 (978-1-60666-686-9(X)) Lkeshore Learn Mats.

RE732 Stone Soup CD Read-along Kit. Lakeshore Learning Materials Staff. (J). 2008. pap. bk. 39.50 (978-1-60666-687-6(8)) Lkeshore Learn Mats.

RE733 Caps for Sale CD Read-along Kit. Lakeshore Learning Materials Staff. (J). 2008. pap. bk. 39.50 (978-1-60666-688-3(6)) Lkeshore Learn Mats.

RE740X Favorite Chapter Book CD Read-Alongs - Set 1 - Complete Set. Lakeshore Learning Materials Staff. (J). 2008. pap. bk. 155.00 (978-1-60666-689-0(4)) Lkeshore Learn Mats.

RFK: A Candid Biography of Robert F. Kennedy. abr. ed. C. David Heymann. 2 cass. (Running Time: 3 hrs.). 1998. 17.95 (978-1-55935-290-1(6), 290-60K) Soundelux.
Never-before-released information on Robert Kennedy's loves, friends, enemies & secrets, by the award winning author of "A Woman Named Jackie.".

RFK: A Candid Biography of Robert F. Kennedy. unabr. ed. C. David Heymann. Read by Connor O'Brien. 7 cass. (Running Time: 10 hrs. 30 mins.). 1999. 152.00 (978-0-7366-4544-7(6)) Books on Tape.
Exposes Kennedy's inner contradictions, the machination of his political career, his private liaison, his enemies & his lovers.

RFK: A Candid Biography of Robert F. Kennedy. unabr. ed. C. David Heymann. Read by John Edwardson. 9 cass. (Running Time: 13 hrs. 30 mins.). 1999. 96.00 (4952-A) Books on Tape.

RFP (Request for Proposal) 2 cass. 1990. 16.00 Recorded Res.

Rhacsyn a'r Goeden Hud. Sain. 2005. 6.99 (978-88-88020-20-4(9)); audio compact disk 10.99 (978-88-88020-19-8(5)) De Falco ITA.

Rhagor o Ganeuon Tecwyn y Tractor. Myrddin Ap Dafydd et al. 2005. 3.49 (978-0-00-077400-2(6)) Zondervan.

Rhanna Mystery. unabr. ed. Christine M. Fraser. Read by Vivien Heilbron. 8 cass. (Running Time: 8 hrs.). 1998. 69.95 (978-0-7540-0225-3(X), CAB 1648) AudioGO.
After twenty years of marriage, Fergus & Kirsteen are going to be apart for the first time. Their marriage is in jeopardy when a beautiful young woman appears in their life.

Rhanna Mystery. unabr. ed. Christine M. Fraser. Read by Vivien Heilbron. 8 cass. 1999. 69.95 (CAB 1648) AudioGO.

Rhapsody in Blue Concerto in F Major. Perf. by George Gershwin et al. 1 cass., 1 CD. 7.98 (TA 30166); audio compact disk 12.78 Jewel box. (TA 80166) NewSound.

Rhapsody of Song. 1 cass. 8.98 (KGOC23) Ken Mills Found.
Kenneth G. Mills conducts The Star-Scape Singers on tour in Europe. Original compositions.

Rheingold: Psychological Implications of Wagner's Ring. Josip Pasic. Read by Josip Pasic. 2 cass. (Running Time: 1 hr. 45 min.). 1993. 16.95 (978-0-7822-0435-3(X), 514) C G Jung IL.
Josip Pasic's presentation addresses not only the opera's myth, but also the more subtle musical structures, exploring the "terra incognita," that twilight zone of our lives where all the categories of the mind begin to dissolve in order for the more nascent, authentic life to emerge.

Rhema Favorites. Kenneth W. Hagin, Jr. 4 cass. 16.00 (18J) Faith Lib Pubns.

Rhetoric, Poetics & Logic. unabr. ed. Aristotle. Read by Frederick Davidson. 10 cass. (Running Time: 14 hrs. 30 mins.). 1992. 69.95 (978-0-7861-0301-0(9), 1265) Blckstn Audio.
All effective debaters, whether they know it or not, employ Aristotle's three basic principles of effective argument, which form the spine of Rehetoric: "ethos," the impact of the speaker's character upon the audience; "pathos," the arousing of the emotions; & "logos," the advancement of pertinent arguments. Aristotle discusses several aspects of epic poetry, lyric poetry, & comedy & he draws a dramatic distinction between poetry & history. Logic includes: classification into 10 categories, proposition, syllogism & inductive & deductive reasoning.

***Rhetoric, Poetics, & Logic.** unabr. ed. Aristotle. Read by Frederick Davidson. (Running Time: 14 hrs. 30 mins.). 2010. 29.95 (978-1-4417-4511-8(4)); audio compact disk 118.00 (978-1-4417-4508-8(4)) Blckstn Audio.

Rhett Butler's People. unabr. ed. Donald McCaig. Narrated by John Bedford Lloyd. 14 CDs. (Running Time: 18 hrs. 1 min.). 2007. audio compact disk 115.95 (978-0-7927-5194-6(9)) AudioGO.

Rhett Butler's People. unabr. ed. Donald McCaig & John Bedford Lloyd. Read by John Bedford Lloyd. (Running Time: 18 hrs. 0 mins. 0 sec.). (ENG.). 2007. audio compact disk 49.95 (978-1-4272-0327-4(X)) Pub: Macmill Audio. Dist(s): Macmillan

***Rhialto the Marvellous.** unabr. ed. Jack Vance. (Running Time: 7 hrs.). (Tales of the Dying Earth Ser.). 2010. 24.99 (978-1-4418-1477-7(9), 9781441814777, BAD); 39.97 (978-1-4418-1478-4(7), 9781441814784, BADLE) Brilliance Audio.

***Rhialto the Marvellous.** unabr. ed. Jack Vance. Read by Arthur Morey. (Running Time: 7 hrs.). (Tales of the Dying Earth Ser.). 2010. 39.97 (978-1-4418-1476-0(0), 9781441814760, Brinc Audio MP3 Lib); 24.99 (978-1-4418-1475-3(2), 9781441814753, Brilliance MP3); audio compact disk 79.97 (978-1-4418-1474-6(4), 9781441814746, BriAudCD Unabrid); audio compact disk 29.99 (978-1-4418-1473-9(6), 9781441814739, Bril Audio CD Unabri) Brilliance Audio.

Rhianna & the Castle of Avalon. unabr. ed. Dave Luckett. Read by Mikaela Martin. (Running Time: 13500 sec.). (Rhianna Ser.). (J). (gr. 3-11). 2006. audio compact disk 54.95 (978-1-74093-735-1(X)) Pub: Bolinda Pubng AUS. Dist(s): Bolinda Pub Inc

Rhianna & the Dogs of Iron. unabr. ed. Dave Luckett. Read by Mikaela Martin. 3 vols. (Running Time: 11700 sec.). (Rhianna Ser.). (J). (gr. 3-8). 2005. audio compact disk 54.95 (978-1-74093-627-9(2)) Pub: Bolinda Pubng AUS. Dist(s): Bolinda Pub Inc

Rhianna & the Wild Magic (The Girl, the Dragon, & the Wild Magic) unabr. ed. Dave Luckett. Read by Mikaela Martin. 3 CDs. (Running Time: 3 hrs. 15 mins.). (Rhianna Ser.). (J). 2005. audio compact disk 54.95 (978-1-74093-141-0(6)) Pub: Bolinda Pubng AUS. Dist(s): Bolinda Pub Inc

Rhinegold: The Quest for Power & Its Psychological Cost. Jean S. Bolen. Read by Jean Shinoda Bolen. 1 cass. (Running Time: 90 min.). 1993. 10.95 (978-0-7822-0420-9(1), 506-1) C G Jung IL.
Part one of the set The Ring of Power: A Jungian Understanding of Wagner's Ring Cycle.

Rhineland Inheritance. unabr. ed. T. Davis Bunn. Read by Ron Varela. 4 cass. (Running Time: 5 hrs. 48 min.). (Destiny Ser.: Bk. 1). 2001. 26.95 (978-1-55686-955-6(X)) Books in Motion.
Jake Burnes, a war-weary American captain, faces a nation in ruins and a daunting assignment on the border between Germany and France during the close of WWII.

Rhinemann Exchange. unabr. ed. Robert Ludlum. Read by Michael Prichard. 11 cass. (Running Time: 16 hrs. 30 mins.). 1984. 88.00 (1754) Books on Tape.
David Spaulding was a top secret American agent on a mission that he himself barely understood. Jean Cameron was a beautiful young widow who had been betrayed by the havoc of war & was determined never to let herself be hurt in that way again. They came together in Buenos Aires, a wartime city of violence & intrigue where representatives of America & Nazi Germany played a deadly game with the fate of the world in perilous balance.

Rhinemann Exchange. unabr. collector's ed. Robert Ludlum. Read by Michael Prichard. 11 cass. (Running Time: 16 hrs. 30 mins.). 1984. 88.00 (978-0-7366-0804-6(4)) Books on Tape.
David Spaulding is a top-secret American agent on a mission that he himself does not fully understand. Jean Cameron is a beautiful young widow who has been betrayed once by the havoc of war & is determined never to let herself be hurt that way again. They come together in Buenos Aires, a wartime city of violence & intrigue where representatives of America and Nazi Germany play a deadly games with the fate of the world in perilous balance.

Rhinoceros. abr. ed. Eugène Ionesco. Perf. by Zero Mostel & Gene Wilder. 2 cass. Dramatization. 1984. 17.96 (CDL5 364) HarperCollins Pubs.
Cast includes: Karen Black, Robert Weil, Joe Silver, Marilyn Chris, Robert Fields, Melody Santangelo, Lou Cutell, Don Calfa, Kathryn Harkin, Lorna Thayer, Howard Morton, & Percy Rodrigues.

Rhinoplasty - Complications & How to Avoid Them. 2 cass. (Otorhinolaryngology Ser.: C85-OT2). 1985. 15.00 (8574) Am Coll Surgeons.

Rhode Island: Newport. 1 cass. (Running Time: 90 min.). (Guided Auto Tape Tour). 12.95 (E4); Comp Comms Inc.

Rhode Island Blues. unabr. ed. Fay Weldon. Read by Jan Francis. 10 cass. (Running Time: 15 hrs.). 2001. 84.95 (978-0-7540-0685-5(9), CAB 2107) Pub: Chivers Audio Bks GBR. Dist(s): AudioGO

Rhodora see Poetry of Ralph Waldo Emerson

Rhodora see Ralph Waldo Emerson: Poems and Essays

Rhubarb. unabr. ed. Garrison Keillor. Contrib. by Garrison Keillor. (ENG., 2008. audio compact disk 13.95 (978-1-59887-733-5(X), 159887733X) Pub: HighBridge. Dist(s): Workman Pub

Rhubarb. unabr. ed. Craig Silvey. Read by Humphrey Bower. (Running Time: 10 hrs. 10 mins.). 2007. audio compact disk 87.95 (978-1-74093-958-4(1), 9781740939584) Pub: Bolinda Pubng AUS. Dist(s): Bolinda Pub Inc

Rhyme & Reason with Animals: For the Love of Animals. Poems. Craig Gosling. 1 CD. (Running Time: 75 mins.). 2005. audio compact disk 12.00 (978-0-9746705-5-3(3)) Mentzer Prtng Ink.

Rhyme of the Remittance Man see Poetry of Robert W. Service

Rhyme Time: A Beginner's Collection of Nursery Rhymes Translated into French. 2nd ed. Marilyn Simundson-Olson. Read by Marilyn Simundson-Olson. Illus. by Dolores H. Tschudi. 1 cass. (Running Time: 21 min.). (Children's Edition Ser.: Vol. 1). (ENG & FRE.). (J). (ps-12). 1996. pap. bk. (978-1-888228-30-4(X)) Global Rhyme Time.
Rhymes taught you English, Rhyme Time will teach you French. Cassette is sold only in conjunction with book & includes all rhymes/songs. Let's Go-Rhyme en francais!.

Rhyme Time: French. 1 cass. (Running Time: 21 mins.). spiral bd. 22.95 (SFR560) J Norton Pubs.
Beginner's level program translates well-known English nursery rhymes into French in a fast, fun way. French rhythm, pronunciation, accent, vocabulary & grammar are learned effortlessly as students memorize & recite amusing nursery rhymes.

Rhyme Time: Spanish. deluxe ed. 1 cass., bklet. (Running Time: 26 mins.). (SPA & ENG., (J). 2001. pap. bk. 22.95 (SSP670) J Norton Pubs.
Beginner's level program translates well-known English nursery rhymes into Spanish in a fast, fun way. Spanish rhythm, pronunciation, accent, vocabulary & grammar are learned effortlessly as students memorize & recite amusing rhymes such as "Little Bo-Peep" or "Baa, Baa Black Sheep" to a rousing rap rhythm.

Rhyme Time Vol. 2: A Global Approach to Enhance the Learning of French. Marilyn Simundson-Olson. Read by Marilyn Simundson-Olson. 1 cass. (Running Time: 19 min.). (J). 1995. bk. 22.00 Tchr's. ed., incl. transparencies. (978-1-888228-11-3(3)) Global Rhyme Time.
Rhymes taught you English, Rhyme Time will teach you French. Cassette is sold only in conjunction with boo & includes all rhymes/songs. Let's Go-Rhyme en francais!.

Rhyme Time Vol. 2: A Global Approach to Enhance the Learning of French, Vol. 3. Marilyn Simundson-Olson. Read by Marilyn Simundson-Olson. Illus. by Dolores H. Tschudi. 1 cass. (Running Time: 22 min.). (ENG & FRE.). 1997. bk. & tchr. ed. 22.00 (978-1-888228-15-1(6)) Global Rhyme Time.

Rhymes & Rhythms Package: For the ESL Classroom. Lisa Tenuta. 2001. pap. bk. 27.00 (978-0-86647-163-3(4)) Pro Lingua.

Rhymes 'N Rhythms: For the ESL Classroom. Lisa Tenuta. (gr. 5-12). 2003. pap. bk. & stu. ed. 28.00 (978-0-86647-179-4(0)); audio compact disk 18.00 (978-0-86647-176-3(6)) Pro Lingua.

Rhymes on Parade. Hap Palmer. (J). 1989. 11.95 Ed Activities.

Rhymes'N Rhythms: For the ESL Classroom. Told to Lisa Tenuta. 1 cass. 2001. 15.00 (978-0-86647-138-1(3)) Pro Lingua.

Rhymetown. abr. ed. 1 cass. (Romper Room Sing & Read-Alongs Ser.). (J). 1986. 5.95 incl. bk. & music sheet. (978-0-89845-317-1(8), RRC 3178) HarperCollins Pubs.

Rhyming Simon Says: Name the Animals. (J). 1990. 5.95 (978-1-878427-04-5(0)) Cimino Pub Grp.

Rhyming Words. 1 cass. (Running Time: 1 hr.). (J). (ps-2). 2001. 10.95 (RAP 1591C) Kimbo Educ.
Kids learn phonics by singing along with wholesome, fun rap music. It's the easiest teaching aid ever. Includes lyrics & teaching guide.

Rhythm All Around: 10 Rhythmic Songs for Singing & Learning. Composed by Sally K. Albrecht & Jay Althouse. (ENG.). 2007. audio compact disk 39.95 (978-0-7390-4644-9(6)) Alfred Pub.

***Rhythm & Dance Cd.** rev. ed. Johnson/Davis. (ENG.). 2010. audio compact disk 41.51 (978-0-7575-0998-8(3)) Kendall-Hunt.

***Rhythm & Dues: Companion CD.** Lindamichelle Baron. (Running Time: 34 mins.). 2001. audio compact disk 10.00 (978-0-940938-07-6(3)) Harlin Jacque.

Rhythm & Game Songs for the Little Ones. Perf. by Ella Jenkins. 1 cass. (Running Time: 25 min.). (J). (ps). 1990. (0-9307-45027-4-7) Smithsonian Folkways.
Guides nursery school children through simple, engaging rhythm exercises, encouraging them to vary lyrics, tunes & activities. Includes "Hop, Skip, Jump to My Lou," "Teddy Bear" & "Jack & Jill".

Rhythm & Rhymes. Perf. by Josh Greenberg et al. Arranged by Josh Greenberg & Bill Vitek. (J). 2001. audio compact disk 14.95 (978-0-939065-80-6(0)) Gentle Wind.

Rhythm & Rhymes. Josh Greenberg & Bil Vitek. Perf. by Josh Greenberg & Mother Goose Mother Goose Jazz Band. 1 cass. (Running Time: 26 min.). (J). (ps-2). 1982. 9.95 (978-0-939065-08-0(8), GW 1008) Gentle Wind.
Don't be deceived by these familiar titles. This jazzy recording is not just for younger children. Older children (of all ages) will be dancing to the sophisticated & rhythmic jazz arrangements. An exciting introduction to the sounds of many different instruments & vocal styles. Includes: "Brother John," "Do You Know the Muffin Man," "Three Blind Mice," "Starlight," "Starbright," "Boggie Woogie Ghost," "Mad Man Polka," "Long Bridge," "Simple Simon" & more.

Rhythm & Role Play. Carolyn Graham et al. 1 cass. (YA). (gr. 5-12). 1991. 14.95 (978-0-943327-09-9(1)) JAG Pubns.
Contains all the plays, in chanting, rhythmic style, for pronunciation & cadence of informal American English.

Rhythm Band for Little People. 1 cass. (Running Time: 1 hr.). (J). 2001. pap. bk. 32.95 incl. manual, ditto master & 16 posters. (KIM 0840C); pap. bk. 33.95 (KIM 0840); pap. bk. 34.95 (KIM 0840CD) Kimbo Educ.
A rhythmic treat guaranteed to fascinate your little ones. From the tap of the tambourine to the beat of the drum, children enjoy playing their instruments as they follow symbols on easy-to-read charts. Includes slow & fast tempos. Also offers piano accompaniment for simple performances & parent programs. Includes Ditto Master & sixteen (18" X 24") posters.

Rhythm Bible. Daniel Fox. (ENG.). 2002. audio compact disk 10.00 (978-0-7390-2678-6(X)) Alfred Pub.

Rhythm Guitar Encyclopedia. Jody Fisher. (ENG.). 1996. audio compact disk 16.50 (978-0-7390-2621-2(6)) Alfred Pub.

Rhythm in My Shoes. Jessica Harper. 1 cass. (Running Time: 40 mins.). (J). 2000. 9.98 (978-1-57940-047-7(7)); audio compact disk 14.98 (978-1-57940-046-0(9)) Rounder Records.
Presents the world as a child knows it, encouraging a sense of self-confidence & self-worth.

Rhythm in Poetry, Pt. A. Gilbert Highet. 1 cass. (Gilbert Highet Ser.). 10.95 (23320) J Norton Pubs.
Poetry is like music: it says many things through its rhythms & poetry, like music, conveys many meanings through its sounds.

Rhythm in Poetry & Melody in Poetry (audio CD) Gilbert Highet. (ENG.). 2007. audio compact disk 9.95 (978-1-57970-449-0(2), Audio-For) J Norton Pubs.

Rhythm of Closeness. John Lee. 2 cass. (Running Time: 1 hr. 50 min.). 1999. 16.95 (978-1-56889-025-8(7), A5695); 33.90 Incl. public performance rights for schools & libraries. Lghtwrks Aud & Vid.
From one of America's leading authorities in the field of personal growth comes a program for learning to create joyous, loving, caring relationships with the people you love.

Rhythm of Creation - The Voice of Africa. Perf. by Mooi River Zulu Mambaso Worship Staff. 1 cass. 10.98 (C70002); audio compact disk 15.98 (CD 70002) Pub: Brentwood Music. Dist(s): Provident Mus Dist
Ancient rhythms are blended with songs of praise to God through an ambient mix of sounds & textures.

Rhythm of Life. 1 cass. (Running Time: 1 hr.). 1990. 8.95 (978-0-8356-1916-5(8)) Theos Pub Hse.
Examines culture & the changing face of God.

Rhythm of Life: Living Every Day with Passion & Purpose. abr. ed. Matthew Kelly. 2004. 17.95 (978-0-7435-4495-5(1)) Pub: S&S Audio. Dist(s): S and S Inc

Rhythm of Superconciousness. 1 cass. (Opening Up the Superconciousness Ser.). 9.95 (84T) Crystal Clarity.
Talks about the inner side of spirituality; the law of magnetic attraction - how it affects us; opening up to the superconscious flow.

Rhythm of the Pridelands. 1 cass. (Classic Collections). (J). 10.99 (978-1-55723-699-9(2)); 10.99 Norelco. (978-1-55723-700-2(X)); audio compact disk 16.99 CD. (978-1-55723-701-9(8)); audio compact disk 16.99 (978-1-55723-702-6(6)) W Disney Records.

Rhythm of the Rocks. 1 cass. (Running Time: 35 min.). (J). (ps-6). 1993. 9.95 (978-1-885430-00-7(0), FS106) Frnds St Music.
Traditional & original multi-cultural songs.

Rhythm of the Saints. Perf. by Paul Simon. 1 cass. (J). 9.98 (2563); audio compact disk 17.98 (D2563) MFLP CA.
Paul Simon embarks on a journey to Brazil, land of fantastic rhythmic diversity.

Rhythm of Which a Chief Walks Gracefully. Perf. by Obo Addy. 1 cass. (Running Time: 52 min.). 1994. 9.98 Norelco. (978-1-56628-049-5(4), EB 2550/WB 4EB D2550/WB 42561-2); audio compact disk 15.98 CD. (978-1-56628-048-8(6), EB D2550/WB 42561-2) MFLP CA.
African percussion by Ghanian drum master.

Rhythm Party. Composed by Sandy Feldstein & David Feldstein. 2004. audio compact disk 9.95 (978-1-932895-13-1(2)) PlayinTime Prdtns.

Rhythm Piano. Duane Shinn. 1 cass. 1988. 39.95 (978-0-912732-61-9(X)) Duane Shinn.

Rhythm Sticks for Kids. 1 cass. (Running Time: 1 hr.). (J). 2001. pap. bk. 10.95 (KIM 2014C); pap. bk. 11.95 (KIM 2014); pap. bk. 14.95 (KIM 2014CD) Kimbo Educ.
These activities are loaded with rhythmic fun. The activities are simple & repetitive & are set to popular theme music with a contemporary sound, making it easier for children to memorize & tap out simple routines. Perfect for home or school. Electric Sticks, Sing a Happy Song, Happy Sticks, Tap Together, Be a Tapper & more. Includes guide.

Rhythm to the Rescue! 10 Unison Songs in 10 Different Rhythmic Styles. Composed by Sally K. Albrecht. (ENG.). 1997. audio compact disk 29.95 (978-0-7390-2125-5(7)) Alfred Pub.

Rhythmic Aerobex see Prime Time Aerobics

***Rhythmic Aerobics, Volume 2: Drumming for Rhythms of Shuffle, Swing, 6/8 & Odd Time Signatures.** Jim Ryan. (ENG.). 2008. pap. bk. 22.95 (978-0-7866-8014-6(8)) Mel Bay.

Rhythmic Chants for Learning Spoken Chinese. Wendy Da & Steven Da. (Eazychin Series for Learning Chinese Ser.). (CHI & ENG.). 2005. pap. bk. 24.95 (978-7-5619-1461-8(X), RHCHLE) Pub: Beijing Lang CHN. Dist(s): China Bks

Rhythmic Chants for Learning Spoken Chinese, Vol. 2. Wendy Da & Steven Da. (Eazy Chinese Series for Learning Chinese Ser.). (CHI & ENG.). 2005. audio compact disk 25.95 (978-7-5619-1510-3(1), RHCHLE2) Pub: Beijing Lang CHN. Dist(s): China Bks

***Rhythmic Chants for Learning Spoken Chinese 2 CD-ROM.** (CHI.). 2006. audio compact disk 19.95 (978-7-900689-23-8(0)) Pub: Beijing Lang CHN. Dist(s): China Bks

Rhythmic Flow into the Unknown. Swami Amar Jyoti. 1 dolby cass. 1984. 9.95 (R-61) Truth Consciousness.
Returning to the cosmic flow, the basis of all living; inperceptibly, through unassuming unfoldment, it leads us to the Source. The sublime voice of Justice.

Rhythmic Group Singing. Perf. by Ella Jenkins. 1 cass. (Running Time: 60 mins.). (J). (ps-3). 1999. 12.95 (SF-45030) African Am Imag.

Rhythmic Parachute Play. 2 CDs. (Running Time: 2 hrs.). (YA). (gr. 2 up). 2001. audio compact disk 24.95 (KEA6020CD) Kimbo Educ.
Everyone's favorite for years. Do the umbrella, mountain & mushroom while developing motor skills. Note: This album has been used with success from grade schools to geriatric centers. Includes instructional manual.

Rhythmic Parachute Play. Created by JoAnn Seker & George Jones. 2 cass. (Running Time: 2 hrs.). (YA). (gr. 2 up). 2001. pap. bk. 18.95 (KEA 6020C); pap. bk. 20.95 (KEA 6020) Kimbo Educ.

Rhythmic Reading with Rap. Vincent Taylor. Illus. by Tennille Herron. (YA). (gr. 2 up). 2000. pap. bk. & wbk. ed. 12.99 (978-0-9704512-1-7(0)) TriEclipse.

***Rhythmic Twist: Triplet Concepts for Drumset.** Jeff Salem. (ENG.). 2010. pap. bk. 14.99 (978-1-4234-9634-2(5), 1423496345) Pub: Hudson Music. Dist(s): H Leonard

Rhythmic Vocabulary: A Musician's Guide to Understanding & Improvising with Rhythm. Alan Dworsky & Betsy Sansby. 1997. bk. 29.95 (978-0-9638801-2-3(8)) Pub: Dancing Hands. Dist(s): SCB Distributors

Rhythmic Vocabulary: A Musician's Guide to Understanding & Improvising with Rhythm. Alan Dworsky & Betsy Sansby. Illus. by Robert Jackson. 1997. pap. bk. 29.95 (978-0-7866-3613-6(0)) Dancing Hands.

Rhythmically Moving 1. Perf. by Gemini. 1 cass. 10.95 (978-0-931114-64-9(0), M2001-C); 10.95 (978-0-931114-53-3(5), M2001) High-Scope.
Music with a well-defined beat, intended for music lovers, parents, & teachers of music, physical education, early childhood education, special education, folk dance, recreation, & fitness. Melodies include: All the Way to Galway, Sliding, Happy Feet, Oh How Lovely, Gaelic Waltz, Southwind, Arkansas Traveler/Sailor's Hompipe/Turkey in the Straw, O'Keefe Slide/Kerry Slide, & more!.

Rhythmically Moving 1. Perf. by Gemini. Directed By Phyllis S. Weikart. 1 CD. (Running Time: 1 hr. 20 mins.). 1983. audio compact disk 15.95 (978-0-929816-13-5(7), M2201) High-Scope.

Rhythmically Moving 2. Perf. by Gemini. 1 cass. 10.95 (978-0-931114-65-6(9), M2002-C) High-Scope.

Rhythmically Moving 2. Perf. by Gemini. Directed By Phyllis S. Weikart. 1 CD. (Running Time: 90 mins.). 1983. audio compact disk 15.95 (978-0-929816-14-2(5), M2202) High-Scope.
Music with a well-defined beat, intended for music lovers, parents & teachers of music, physical education, early childhood education, special education, folk dance, recreation & fitness. Melodies include: Rakes of Mallow, Seven Jumps, Haya Ze Basadeh, Djurdjevka Kolo, Limbo Rock, Blackberry Quadrille, Fjaskern, Yankee Doodle & more.

Rhythmically Moving 3. Perf. by Gemini. 1 cass. (Running Time: 90 mins.). 10.95 (978-0-931114-66-3(7), M2003-C) High-Scope.

Rhythmically Moving 3. Perf. by Gemini. Directed By Phyllis S. Weikart. 1 CD. (Running Time: 90 mins.). 1983. audio compact disk 15.95 (978-0-929816-15-9(3), M2003) High-Scope.

Rhythmically Moving 4. Perf. by Gemini. 1 cass. (Running Time: 90 mins.). 10.95 (978-0-931114-67-0(5), M2004-C) High-Scope.

Rhythmically Moving 4. Perf. by Gemini. 1 CD. (Running Time: 90 mins.). 1984. audio compact disk 15.95 (978-0-929816-16-6(1), M2204) High-Scope.

Rhythmically Moving 5. Perf. by Gemini. 1 cass. (Running Time: 90 mins.). 10.95 (978-0-931114-68-7(3), M2005-C); 10.95 record. (978-0-931114-57-1(8), M2005) High-Scope.
Music with a well-defined beat, intended for music lovers, parents, & teachers of music, physical education, early childhood education, special education, folk dance, recreation, & fitness. Melodies include: Jamaican Holiday, Twelfth Street Rag, Corrido, The Entertainer, Carnavalito, Ajde Noga Za Nogama, Hora Hassidit, Kendime, plus more!.

Rhythmically Moving 5. Perf. by Gemini. Directed By Phyllis S. Weikart. 1 CD. (Running Time: 90 mins.). 1984. audio compact disk 15.95 (978-0-929816-29-6(3), M2205) High-Scope.
Music with a well-defined beat, intended for music lovers, parents & teachers of music, physical education, early childhood education, special education, folk dance, recreation & fitness. Melodies include: Jamaican Holiday, Twelfth Street Rag, Corrido, The Entertainer, Carnavalito, Ajde Noga Za Nogama, Hora Hassidit, Kendime plus more!.

Rhythmically Moving 6. Perf. by Gemini. 1 cass. (Running Time: 90 mins.). 10.95 (978-0-931114-69-4(1), M2006-C); 10.95 record. (978-0-931114-58-8(6), M2006) High-Scope.

Rhythmically Moving 6. Perf. by Gemini. Directed By Phyllis S. Weikart. 1 CD. (Running Time: 90 mins.). 1984. audio compact disk 15.95 (978-0-929816-30-2(7), M2206) High-Scope.

Rhythmically Moving 7. Perf. by Gemini. 1 cass. (Running Time: 90 mins.). 10.95 (978-0-931114-70-0(5), M2007-C); 10.95 record. (978-0-931114-59-5(4), M2007) High-Scope.

Rhythmically Moving 7. Perf. by Gemini. Directed By Phyllis S. Weikart. 1 CD. (Running Time: 90 mins.). 1985. audio compact disk 15.95 (978-0-929816-31-9(5), M2207) High-Scope.

Rhythmically Moving 8. Perf. by Gemini. 1 cass. (Running Time: 90 mins.). 10.95 (978-0-931114-71-7(3), M2008-C); 10.95 record. (978-0-931114-60-1(8), M2008) High-Scope.

Rhythmically Moving 8. Perf. by Gemini. Directed By Phyllis S. Weikart. 1 CD. (Running Time: 90 mins.). 1985. audio compact disk 15.95 (978-0-929816-32-6(3), M2208) High-Scope.

Rhythmically Moving 9. Perf. by Gemini. 1 cass. (Running Time: 90 mins.). 10.95 record. (978-0-931114-61-8(6), M2009); 10.95 (978-0-931114-72-4(1), M2009-C) High-Scope.

Rhythmically Moving 9. Perf. by Gemini. Directed By Phyllis S. Weikart. 1 CD. (Running Time: 90 mins.). 1985. audio compact disk 15.95 (978-0-929816-33-3(1), M2209) High-Scope.

Rhythmically Walking. 2 cass. (Running Time: 2 hrs. 40 min.). 1989. 15.95 (978-0-929816-06-7(4), M4800) High-Scope.
If your'e looking for a way to turn your daily stroll into an enjoyable, invigorating workout, this audio tape can help. This tape leads you through two separate walking programs - you choose the one best suited to your current fitness level. Learn to pace yourself & monitor your heart rate.

Rhythms for Basic Motor Skills. 1 cass. (Running Time: 1 hr.). (J). 2001. pap. bk. 10.95 (KIM 9074C) Kimbo Educ.
Methods & music that really work to help children learn tempos & basic skips, gallops & hops. Positive stops between bands. Includes guide.

Rhythms of Awakening. Glen Velez. (Running Time: 1 hr.). 2005. audio compact disk 16.98 (978-1-59179-276-5(2), M923D) Sounds True.

Rhythms of Childhood. Perf. by Ella Jenkins. 1 cass. (Running Time: 40 min.). (J). (ps-4). 1989. (0-9307-450080-9307-45008-2-8); audio compact disk (0-9307-45008-2-8) Smithsonian Folkways.
Emphasizes rhythms found in nature, dance & traditional African chants, using vocals, guitar, banjo, baritone ukulele, harmonica & drums. Includes "Pretty Trees around the World," "The Cuckoo," "Michael Row Your Boat Ashore," "All Will Be Dancing" & "Kum Ba Ya".

Rhythms of Peace. unabr. ed. Nawang Khechog. 1 CD. (Running Time: 58 min.). 1996. audio compact disk 16.98 (978-1-56455-411-6(2), MM00294D) Sounds True.
An otherworldly masterpiece that uses soothing melodic textures to explore the inner stillness that is the essence of peace. Each composition is an evocative, textured meditation that suggests the vast spaces & sacred serenity of Khechog's beloved Himalayas. With bamboo flute, didgeridoo, gongs, bells, & drums, Nawang develops a mystical sense of the rhythms of peace that reach from Tibet into the heart of the world.

Rhythms of Polynesia. (Luau Celebration Ser.: 2). 2001. audio compact disk 16.95 (978-1-58513-094-8(X)) Dance Fantasy.
Selections include Tiki, Pate Ko'e, Tamure Sheila, Inu, Francais Danielle, Tahitian Fire, Tahua, Afata, Soke, Kokino Mambo, Pua Mana, Hip Hop Hula, Samoan Slap Dance, and Kahiko Tutu.

Rhythms of Polynesia Vol. 2. (Luau Celebration Ser.: 2). 2001. 14.95 (978-1-58513-083-2(4)) Dance Fantasy.

Rhythms of Rapture: Sacred Musics of Haitian Vodou. Prod. by Elizabeth McCaulister. Anno. by Gage Averill et al. 1 cass. or CD. 1995. (0-9307-404640-9307-40464-2-5); audio compact disk (0-9307-40464-2-5) Smithsonian Folkways.

Rhythms of the Chakras. unabr. ed. Perf. by Glen Velez. 1 CD. (Running Time: 52 mins.). 2000. stu. ed. 16.98 (978-1-56455-593-9(3), M006D) Sounds True.
Evoke spontaneous movements & sensations that help focus mental energy - & healing - on all of the chakras. Chant along with vocalizations based on specific vowel sounds designed to increase healing power.

Rhythms of the Chakras: Drumming for the Body's Energy Center. Perf. by Glen Velez. 1 cass., 1 CD. 7.98 (STA 6); audio compact disk 12.78 CD Jewel box. (STA 6) NewSound.

Rhythms of the Goddess. Raul J. Canigares. 1 cass. (Running Time: 1 hr.). 1994. 9.95 (978-0-89281-507-4(8), Heal Arts VT) Inner Tradit.

Rhythms on Parade. Perf. by Hap Palmer. 1 cass. (Running Time: 1 hr.). (J). 2001. 9.95 (HP 102); audio compact disk 14.95 (HP 102) Hap-Pal Music.
Twenty-four lively songs introduce the joy of rhythm. Child basic musical concepts as they move & sing. They also improve skills in language, math, fine & gross motor coordination. Songs contain a variety of playful images which stimulate children's creative & imaginative powers. For extra fun, children can use rhythm instruments such as wood blocks, sticks, bells, tamborines & maracas.

Rhythms on Parade. Hap Palmer. 1 read-along cass. (J). 11.95 (EA 633C) Kimbo Educ.
Children learn basic musical concepts through rhythmic tunes & clever lyrics.

Rhytidectomy - Complications & How to Avoid Them. 2 cass. (Otorhinolaryngology Ser.: C85-OT1). 1985. 15.00 (8573) Am Coll Surgeons.

RH033 Linux Essentials Training Course. Created by K-Alliance Staff. 2007. 995.00 (978-1-60540-018-1(1)) K Alliance.

Ribaudie et Repentanche: Old French Comic Fabliaux & Moral Tales. Brian Levy et al. Created by Chaucer Studio. 2004. pap. bk. 17.00 (978-0-8425-2590-9(4), BYU Press) Brigham.

Ribbentrop: A Biography. unabr. ed. Michael Bloch. Read by David Case. 9 cass. (Running Time: 13 hrs. 30 mins.). 1994. 72.00 (3390-A); 64.00 (3380-B) Books on Tape.
People joked about Joachim von Ribbentrop, Hitler's Foreign Minister. But when he negotiated a nonaggression pact with Stalin, they quit laughing. It guaranteed war.

Ribbentrop: A Biography. unabr. ed. Michael Bloch. Read by David Case. 17 cass. (Running Time: 25 hrs. 30 min.). 1994. 136.00 (978-0-7366-2642-2(5), 3380A/B) Books on Tape.

Ribbon Breath Meditation: A Fifteen-Minute Healing. 1. (Running Time: 15 min). 2004. audio compact disk 18.95 (978-0-9752561-0-7(6)) T Agri.

Ribbon of Moonlight. Margaret Kaine & Julia Franklin. 2009. 84.95 (978-1-84652-483-7(0)); audio compact disk 99.95 (978-1-84652-484-4(9)) Pub: Magna Story GBR. Dist(s): Ulverscroft US

Ribbons: The Gulf War - A Poem. William Heyen. 1991. 12.95 (978-1-877770-47-0(7)) Time Being Bks.

Ribs of Death. Joan Aiken. Read by Angela Down. 6 cass. 1999. 54.95 (65832) Pub: Soundings Ltd GBR. Dist(s): Ulverscroft US

***Ribsy.** unabr. ed. Beverly Cleary. Read by Neil Patrick Harris. (ENG.). 2004. (978-0-06-081435-9(7)); (978-0-06-079046-2(6)) HarperCollins Pubs.

Ribsy. unabr. ed. Beverly Cleary. Read by Neil Patrick Harris. (Running Time: 010800 sec.). (Henry Huggins Ser.). (J). [illegible]-7). 2005. audio compact disk 22.00 (978-0-06-081607-0(4), Harper[illegible]d) HarperCollins Pubs.

Ribsy, unabr. ed. Beverly Cleary. Narrate[illegible] [illegible]arbara Caruso. 3 pieces. (Running Time: 3 hrs. 45 mins.). (Henry Huggins Ser.). (gr. 3 up). 1994. 27.00 (978-0-7887-0021-7(9), 94220E7) Recorded Bks.
When Ribsy gets separated from his family at a shopping mall, he jumps into the wrong car - a car filled with five children with plans to give him a bubble bath.

Ribsy. unabr. ed. Beverly Cleary. Narrated by Barbara Caruso. 4 CDs. (Running Time: 3 hrs. 45 mins.). (Henry Huggins Ser.). (gr. 3 up). 2001. audio compact disk 39.00 (978-0-7887-4963-6(3), C1308E7) Recorded Bks.
When Ribsy gets separated from his family at a shopping mall, he jumps into the wrong car - a car filled with five children with plans to give him a bubble bath.

Rice Without Rain, unabr. ed. Minfong Ho. Narrated by Christina Moore. 5 pieces. (Running Time: 6 hrs.). (gr. 9 up). 1997. 44.00 (978-0-7887-1222-7(5), 95125E7) Recorded Bks.
In the village in Thailand where 17-year-old Jinda lives, drought has shriveled the rice crop. The farmers fear that after paying half of it to the landowner for rent, they won't have enough to feed their families. When she meets a group of university students, she begins to see ways to break the centuries-old tradition that is starving her people. Based on the conditions leading to the student uprising at Thammasart University in Bangkok in 1976, incorporates images of Mingfong Ho's own childhood in Thailand.

Rice Without Rain. unabr. ed. Minfong Ho. Read by Christina Moore. 5 cass. (Running Time: 6 hrs. 00 min.). (YA). (gr. 2). 1997. Rental 13.50; bk. 64.75 (978-0-7887-1253-1(5), 40499) Recorded Bks.

***Rich: A Dyamonde Daniel Book.** Nikki Grimes. Read by Nikki Grimes. (ENG.). (J). 2010. audio compact disk 20.00 (978-1-936223-36-7(8)) Full Cast Audio.

Rich Are Different. Susan Howatch. Narrated by Nadia May. (Running Time: 30 hrs. 30 mins.). 2001. 66.95 (978-1-59912-709-5(1)) Iofy Corp.

Rich Are Different. unabr. ed. Susan Howatch. Read by Nadia May. 2 pieces. (Running Time: 63000 sec.). 2001. audio compact disk 34.95 (978-0-7861-9403-2(0), 2875A, B) Blckstn Audio.

Rich Are Different. unabr. ed. Susan Howatch. Narrated by Nadia May. 12 cass. (Running Time: 30 hrs. 30 mins.). 2001. 83.95 (978-0-7861-2114-4(9), 2875A, B); 62.95 (978-0-7861-2115-1(7), 2875A, B) Blckstn Audio.

Rich Are Different. unabr. ed. Susan Howatch. Read by Nadia May. (Running Time: 104400 sec.). 2007. audio compact disk 160.00 (978-0-7861-5865-2(4)) Blckstn Audio.

Rich Brother & Coming Attractions. Tobias Wolff. Read by Tobias Wolff. 1 cass. (Running Time: 61 min.). 1985. 13.95 (978-1-55644-138-7(X), 5091) Am Audio Prose.

Rich Brother, Rich Sister: Two Different Paths to God, Money & Happiness. unabr. ed. Robert T. Kiyosaki & Emi Kiyosaki. (Running Time: 12 hrs.). 2009. 24.95 (978-1-4233-7289-9(1), 9781423372899, Brilliance MP3) Brilliance Audio.

Rich Brother, Rich Sister: Two Different Paths to God, Money & Happiness. unabr. ed. Robert T. Kiyosaki & Emi Kiyosaki. Read by Sandra Burr. 1 MP3-CD. (Running Time: 12 hrs.). 2009. 39.25 (978-1-4233-7290-5(5), 9781423372905, Brlnc Audio MP3 Lib) Brilliance Audio.

Rich Brother, Rich Sister: Two Different Paths to God, Money & Happiness. unabr. ed. Robert T. Kiyosaki & Emi Kiyosaki. Read by Sandra Burr & Jim Bond. (Running Time: 12 hrs.). 2009. 39.25 (978-1-4233-7292-9(1), 9781423372929, BADLE); 24.95 (978-1-4233-7291-2(3), 9781423372912, BAD); audio compact disk 87.25 (978-1-4233-7288-2(3), 9781423372882, BriAudCD Unabrid) Brilliance Audio.

Rich Brother, Rich Sister: Two Different Paths to God, Money & Happiness. unabr. ed. Robert T. Kiyosaki & Emi Kiyosaki. Read by Sandra Burr & Sandra Jim Bond. (Running Time: 12 hrs.). 2009. audio compact disk 29.99 (978-1-4233-7287-5(5), 9781423372875, Bril Audio CD Unabri) Brilliance Audio.

***Rich Christians in an Age of Hunger: Moving from Affluence to Generosity.** unabr. ed. Ron Sider. Narrated by David Cochran Heath. (ENG.). 2010. 16.98 (978-1-59644-384-6(7)); audio compact disk 26.98 (978-1-59644-383-9(9)) christianaud.

Rich Dad Advisor's: ABC's of Getting Out of Debt: Turn Bad Debt into Good Debt & Bad Credit into Good Credit. abr. ed. Garrett Sutton. (ENG.). 2005. 14.98 (978-1-59483-138-6(6)) Pub: Hachet Audio. Dist(s): HachBkGrp

Rich Dad Advisor's: Own Your Own Corporation: Why the Rich Own Their Own Companies & Everyone Else Works for Them. abr. ed. Garrett Sutton. (ENG.). 2005. 14.98 (978-1-59483-279-6(X)) Pub: Hachet Audio. Dist(s): HachBkGrp

Rich Dad, Poor Dad / Rich Dad Prophecy (Bundle) Robert T. Kiyosaki. 2005. 44.99 (978-1-59895-019-9(3)) Find a World.

Rich Dad, Poor Dad & the Rich Dad Prophecy. unabr. ed. Robert T. Kiyosaki & Sharon L. Lechter. Read by Robert T. Kiyosaki & Sharon L. Lechter. (YA). 2005. 54.99 (978-1-59895-138-7(6)) Find a World.

Rich Dad Secrets: Secrets to Money, Business & Investing & How You Can Profit From Them. unabr. ed. Robert T. Kiyosaki. 6 cass. (Running Time: 9 hrs.). 1999. wbk. ed. 59.95 (978-1-55525-006-5(8), 21090a) Nightingale-Conant.
The rich follow a different set of rules for making & keeping money. In fact, the rich live in a world most of us know nothing about.They pay less in taxes & set up their lives in such a way that money constantly.

Rich Dad's Advisors, Vol. 1, Set. abr. ed. Blair Singer & Garrett Sutton. Read by Jim Ward et al. (Running Time: 9 hrs.). (ENG.). 2007. audio compact disk 39.98 (978-1-60024-119-2(0)) Pub: Hachet Audio. Dist(s): HachBkGrp

Rich Dad's Advisors: Turn Bad Debt into Good Debt & Bad Credit into Good Credit. abr. ed. Garrett Sutton. 3 CDs. (Running Time: 3 hrs.). (ENG., 2004. audio compact disk 24.98 (978-1-58621-736-5(4)) Pub: Hachet Audio. Dist(s): HachBkGrp

Rich Dad's Advisors: Box Set. abr. ed. Blair Singer & Garrett Sutton. Read by Jim Ward & Bill Ratner. (Running Time: 9 hrs.). (ENG.). 2007. 26.98 (978-1-60024-120-8(4)) Pub: Hachet Audio. Dist(s): HachBkGrp

Rich Dad's Advisor's: Sales Dogs: You Do Not Have to Be an Attach Dog to Be Successful in Sales. abr. ed. Blair Singer. Read by Bill Ratner. (ENG.). 2005. 14.98 (978-1-59483-185-0(8)) Pub: Hachet Audio. Dist(s): HachBkGrp

Rich Dad's AdvisorsÂ(r): the ABC's of Building a Business Team That Wins: The Invisible Code of Honor That Takes Ordinary People & Turns them into a Championship Team. abr. ed. Blair Singer. Read by Jim Ward. (Running Time: 3 hrs.). (ENG.). 2009. 39.98 (978-1-60788-110-0(1)) Pub: Hachet Audio. Dist(s): HachBkGrp

Rich Dad's AdvisorsÂ(r): the ABC's of Getting Out of Debt: Turn Bad Debt into Good Debt & Bad Credit into Good Credit. abr. ed. Garrett Sutton. (Running Time: 3 hrs.). (ENG.). 2009. 39.98 (978-1-60024-905-1(1)) Pub: Hachet Audio. Dist(s): HachBkGrp

Rich Dad's AdvisorsÂ(r): the ABC's of Real Estate Investing: The Secrets of Finding Hidden Profits Most Investors Miss. abr. ed. Ken McElroy. (Running Time: 3 hrs.). (ENG.). 2009. 39.98 (978-1-60024-637-1(0)) Pub: Hachet Audio. Dist(s): HachBkGrp

Rich Dad's Advisors(R): the ABCs of Real Estate Investing: The Secrets of Finding Hidden Profits Most Investors Miss. abr. ed. Ken McElroy. (ENG.). 2005. 14.98 (978-1-59483-186-7(6)) Pub: Hachet Audio. Dist(s): HachBkGrp

Rich Dad's Before You Quit Your Job: 10 Real-Life Lessons Every Entrepreneur Should Know about Building a Multimillion-Dollar Business. abr. ed. Robert T. Kiyosaki. Read by Deanna Hurst & Jim Ward. Told to Sharon L. Lechter. 3 CDs. (Running Time: 4 hrs.). (ENG.). 2005. audio compact disk 24.98 (978-1-59483-077-8(0)) Pub: Hachet Audio. Dist(s): HachBkGrp

Rich Dad's Before You Quit Your Job: 10 Real-Life Lessons Every Entrepreneur Should Know about Building a Multimillion-Dollar Business. abr. ed. Robert T. Kiyosaki & Sharon L. Lechter. Read by Jim Ward & Deanna Hurst. (Running Time: 4 hrs.). (ENG.). 2009. 39.98 (978-1-60788-060-8(1)) Pub: Hachet Audio. Dist(s): HachBkGrp

Rich Dad's Cash Flow. Robert T. Kiyosaki & Sharon L. Lechter. 2002. 24.98 (978-1-58621-244-5(3)) Hachet Audio.

Rich Dad's Cashflow Quadrant: Employee, Self-Employed, Business Owner, or Investor... Which Is the Best Quadrant for You? abr. ed. Robert T. Kiyosaki & Sharon L. Lechter. Read by Robert T. Kiyosaki & Jim Ward. 3 CDs. (Running Time: 3 hrs.). (ENG.). 2001. audio compact disk 24.98 (978-1-58621-093-9(9)) Pub: Hachet Audio. Dist(s): HachBkGrp

Rich Dad's Cashflow Quadrant: Employee, Self-Employed, Business Owner, or Investor... Which Is the Best Quadrant for You? abr. ed. Robert T. Kiyosaki & Sharon L. Lechter. Read by Jim Ward. (ENG.). 2005. 14.98 (978-1-59483-445-5(8)) Pub: Hachet Audio. Dist(s): HachBkGrp

Rich Dad's Cashflow Quadrant: Employee, Self-Employed, Business Owner, or Investor... Which Is the Best Quadrant for You? abr. ed. Robert T. Kiyosaki & Sharon L. Lechter. Read by Robert T. Kiyosaki & Jim Ward. (Running Time: 3 hrs.). (ENG.). 2009. 39.98 (978-1-60788-076-9(8)) Pub: Hachet Audio. Dist(s): HachBkGrp

Rich Dad's Cashflow Quadrant: Rich Dad's Guide to Financial Freedom. Robert T. Kiyosaki & Sharon L. Lechter. Narrated by Richard M. Davidson. 7 cass. (Running Time: 9 hrs.). 62.00 (978-0-7887-5260-5(X)) Recorded Bks.

Rich Dad's Classics. abr. ed. Robert T. Kiyosaki & Sharon L. Lechter. 9 CDs. (Running Time: 9 hrs.). (ENG.). 2005. audio compact disk 39.98 (978-1-59483-089-1(4)) Pub: Hachet Audio. Dist(s): HachBkGrp

Rich Dad's Conspiracy of the Rich: The 8 New Rules of Money. unabr. ed. Robert T. Kiyosaki. Read by Dave Mallow. (Running Time: 9 hrs.). (ENG.). 2009. 15.98 (978-1-60024-899-3(3)); audio compact disk 22.98 (978-1-60024-898-6(5)) Pub: Hachet Audio. Dist(s): HachBkGrp

Rich Dad's Guide to Investing: What the Rich Invest in, That the Poor & Middle Class Do Not! Robert T. Kiyosaki & Sharon L. Lechter. 2002. 24.98 (978-1-58621-245-2(1)) Hachet Audio.

Rich Dad's Guide to Investing: What the Rich Invest in, That the Poor & Middle Class Do Not! abr. ed. Robert T. Kiyosaki & Sharon L. Lechter. Read by Robert T. Kiyosaki & Jim Ward. 3 CDs. (Running Time: 3 hrs.). (ENG.). 2001. audio compact disk 24.98 (978-1-58621-092-2(0)) Pub: Hachet Audio. Dist(s): HachBkGrp

Rich Dad's Guide to Investing: What the Rich Invest in, That the Poor & Middle Class Do Not! abr. ed. Robert T. Kiyosaki & Sharon L. Lechter. Read by Jim Ward. (ENG.). 2005. 14.98 (978-1-59483-444-8(X)) Pub: Hachet Audio. Dist(s): HachBkGrp

Rich Dad's Guide to Investing: What the Rich Invest in, That the Poor & Middle Class Do Not! abr. ed. Robert T. Kiyosaki & Sharon L. Lechter. Read by Robert T. Kiyosaki & Jim Ward. (Running Time: 3 hrs.). (ENG.). 2009. 39.98 (978-1-60788-081-3(4)) Pub: Hachet Audio. Dist(s): HachBkGrp

Rich Dad's Guide to Raising Your Child's Financial I. Q. Robert T. Kiyosaki & Sharon L. Lechter. (ENG.). 1999. pap. bk. (978-0-9643856-4-1(3)) TechPress.

Rich Dad's Increase Your Financial IQ: Get Smarter with Your Money. abr. ed. Robert T. Kiyosaki. Read by Dave Mallow. (Running Time: 3 hrs. 30 mins.). (ENG.). 2008. 19.98 (978-1-60024-261-8(8)); audio compact disk 24.98 (978-1-60024-260-1(X)) Pub: Hachet Audio. Dist(s): HachBkGrp

Rich Dad's Prophecy: Why the Biggest Stock Market Crash in History Is Still Coming... & How You Can Prepare Yourself & Profit from It! abr. ed. Robert T. Kiyosaki & Sharon L. Lechter. Read by Robert T. Kiyosaki & Jim Ward. 3 CDs. (Running Time: 3 hrs.). (ENG.). (YA). 2002. audio compact disk 24.98 (978-1-58621-436-4(5)) Pub: Hachet Audio. Dist(s): HachBkGrp

Rich Dad's Prophecy: Why the Biggest Stock Market Crash in History Is Still Coming... & How You Can Prepare Yourself & Profit from It! abr. ed. Robert T. Kiyosaki & Sharon L. Lechter. Read by Jim Ward. (ENG.). 2005. 14.98 (978-1-59483-357-1(5)) Pub: Hachet Audio. Dist(s): HachBkGrp

Rich Dad's Prophecy: Why the Biggest Stock Market Crash in History Is Still Coming... & How You Can Prepare Yourself & Profit from It! abr. ed. Robert T. Kiyosaki & Sharon L. Lechter. Read by Robert T. Kiyosaki & Jim Ward. (Running Time: 8 hrs.). (ENG.). 2009. 39.98 (978-1-60788-086-8(5)) Pub: Hachet Audio. Dist(s): HachBkGrp

Rich Dad's Real Estate Advantages: Tax & Legal Secrets of Successful Real Estate Investors. abr. ed. Sharon L. Lechter & Garrett Sutton. Read by Sharon L. Lechter & Garrett Sutton. Read by Robert T. Kiyosaki. (Running Time: 3 hrs.). (ENG.). 2006. 14.98 (978-1-59483-965-8(4)) Pub: Hachet Audio. Dist(s): HachBkGrp

Rich Dad's Real Estate Advantages: Tax & Legal Secrets of Successful Real Estate Investors. abr. ed. Sharon L. Lechter & Garrett Sutton. Read by Sharon L. Lechter & Garrett Sutton. Read by Robert T. Kiyosaki. (Running Time: 3 hrs.). (ENG.). 2009. 39.98 (978-1-60788-285-5(X)) Pub: Hachet Audio. Dist(s): HachBkGrp

Rich Dad's Retire Young, Retire Rich. abr. ed. Robert T. Kiyosaki & Sharon L. Lechter. Read by Jim Ward. (ENG.). 2005. 14.98 (978-1-59483-380-9(X)) Pub: Hachet Audio. Dist(s): HachBkGrp

Rich Dad's Retire Young, Retire Rich: How to Get Rich Quickly & Stay Rich Forever! abr. ed. Robert T. Kiyosaki & Sharon L. Lechter. Read by Robert T. Kiyosaki & Jim Ward. 3 CDs. (Running Time: 3 hrs.). (ENG.). 2002. audio compact disk 24.98 (978-1-58621-256-8(7)) Pub: Hachet Audio. Dist(s): HachBkGrp

Rich Dad's Retire Young, Retire Rich: How to Get Rich Quickly & Stay Rich Forever! abr. ed. Robert T. Kiyosaki & Sharon L. Lechter. Read by Robert T. Kiyosaki & Jim Ward. (Running Time: 3 hrs.). (ENG.). 2009. 39.98 (978-1-60788-088-2(1)) Pub: Hachet Audio. Dist(s): HachBkGrp

Rich Dad's Rich Kid, Smart Kid: Giving Your Child a Financial Head Start. Robert T. Kiyosaki & Sharon L. Lechter. Narrated by Richard M. Davidson. 8 cass. (Running Time: 10 hrs. 30 mins.). 88.00 (978-0-7887-9791-0(3)) Recorded Bks.

Rich Dad's Rich Kid, Smart Kid: Giving Your Child a Financial Head Start. abr. ed. Robert T. Kiyosaki & Sharon L. Lechter. Read by Jim Ward. (ENG.). 2005. 14.98 (978-1-59483-435-6(0)) Pub: Hachet Audio. Dist(s): HachBkGrp

Rich Dad's Rich Kid, Smart Kid: Giving Your Child a Financial Head Start. abr. ed. Robert T. Kiyosaki & Sharon L. Lechter. Read by Robert T. Kiyosaki & Sharon L. Lechter. Read by Jim Ward. (Running Time: 3 hrs.). (ENG.). 2009. 39.98 (978-1-60788-089-9(X)) Pub: Hachet Audio. Dist(s): HachBkGrp

Rich Dad's Success Stories: Real Life Success Stories from Real Life People Who Followed the Rich Dad Lessons. abr. ed. Robert T. Kiyosaki & Sharon L. Lechter. Read by Melody Butiu et al. 5 CDs. (Running Time: 6 hrs.). (ENG.). 2003. audio compact disk 31.98 (978-1-58621-572-9(8)) Pub: Hachet Audio. Dist(s): HachBkGrp

Rich Dad's Success Stories: Real Life Success Stories from Real Life People Who Followed the Rich Dad Lessons. abr. ed. Robert T. Kiyosaki & Sharon L. Lechter. Read by Melody Butiu et al. (ENG.). 2005. 14.98 (978-1-59483-184-3(X)) Pub: Hachet Audio. Dist(s): HachBkGrp

Rich Dad's Success Stories: Real Life Success Stories from Real Life People Who Followed the Rich Dad Lessons. abr. ed. Robert T. Kiyosaki & Sharon L. Lechter. Read by Robert T. Kiyosaki et al. (Running Time: 6 hrs.). (ENG.). 2009. 49.98 (978-1-60024-989-1(2)) Pub: Hachet Audio. Dist(s): HachBkGrp

Rich Fools of Houston: Luke 12:13-21. Ed Young. (J). 1982. 4.95 (978-0-7417-1217-2(2), A0217) Win Walk.

***Rich Inside & Out: A Handbook for Life.** unabr. ed. Russell Simmons & Chris Morrow. (ENG.). 2011. audio compact disk 29.95 (978-0-14-242832-0(9), PengAudBks) Penguin Grp USA.

Rich Is a Religion: Breaking the Timeless Code to Wealth. unabr. ed. Mark Stevens. Read by Mark Stevens. (Running Time: 4 hrs.). (ENG.). 2008. 24.98 (978-1-59659-294-0(X), GildAudio) Pub: Gildan Media. Dist(s): HachBkGrp

Rich Kid, Smart Kid: Giving Your Children a Financial Head Start. Robert T. Kiyosaki & Sharon L. Lechter. 2002. 24.98 (978-1-58621-246-9(X)); 17.98 (978-1-58621-242-1(7)) Hachet Audio.
For parents who value education and want to give their child a financial and academic head start in life. A good education is more important than ever. But the current educational system may not be providing for all of your child's needs.

Rich Lessons Poor Parenting(Joseph: Gen. 37:1-11. Ed Young. 1988. 4.95 (978-0-7417-1677-4(1), 677) Win Walk.

Rich Like Them: My Door-to-Door Search for the Secrets of Wealth in America's Richest Neighborhoods. unabr. ed. Ryan D'Agostino. Narrated by Patrick G. Lawlor. (Running Time: 8 hrs. 0 mins. 0 sec.). (ENG.). 2009. audio compact disk 19.99 (978-1-4001-5994-9(6)); audio compact disk 59.99 (978-1-4001-3994-1(5)); audio compact disk 29.99 (978-1-4001-0994-4(9)) Pub: Tantor Media. Dist(s): IngramPubServ

Rich Man & Lazarus. Reinhard Bonnke. (Running Time: Approx: 50 min.). (ENG.). 2001. audio compact disk 7.00 (978-0-9758789-9-6(9)) E-R-Productions.
Through this classic Bible story, Reinhard Bonnke paints a vivid, step-by-step picture of why some people go to hell, yet through Jesus Christ, they experience hope, and a new outlook on life instead.

Rich Man & the Shoe-Maker, the; Brian Wildsmith's Wild Animals; Patrick; Mr Gumpy's Outing; May I Bring a Friend? 2004. (978-0-89719-834-9(4)); cass. & flmstrp (978-0-89719-742-7(9)) Weston Woods.

Rich Man & the Shoemaker. 2004. pap. bk. 14.95 (978-0-7882-0625-2(7)) Weston Woods.

Rich Man & the Shoemaker, the; Brian Wildsmith's Wild Animals. 2004. 8.95 (978-1-56008-851-6(6)); cass. & flmstrp 30.00 (978-0-89719-661-1(9)) Weston Woods.

Rich Mullins. Perf. by Rich Mullins & Amy Grant. Prod. by Reed Arvin. 1 cass. 1986. audio compact disk Brentwood Music.
After writing Amy Grant's 1983 smash hit, Sing Your Praise to the Lord, Mullins recorded his first album. Features Amy Grant on background vocals.

Rich Mullins Songs 2. Prod. by Reed Arvin & Rich Mullins. Compiled by Dean Diehl. 1 CD. 1999. audio compact disk Brentwood Music.

Rich Woman: A Book on Investing for Women. unabr. ed. Kim Kiyosaki. Read by Kim Kiyosaki. (Running Time: 7 hrs.). 2008. 39.25 (978-1-4233-7297-4(2), 9781423372974, Brlnc Audio MP3 Lib); 39.25 (978-1-4233-7299-8(9), 9781423372998, BADLE); 24.95 (978-1-4233-7296-7(4), 9781423372967, Brilliance MP3); 24.95 (978-1-4233-7298-1(0), 9781423372981, BAD); audio compact disk 82.25 (978-1-4233-7295-0(6), 9781423372950, BriAudCD Unabrid); audio compact disk 29.99 (978-1-4233-7294-3(8), 9781423372943, Bril Audio CD Unabri) Brilliance Audio.

***Rich Woman: A Book on Investing for Women.** unabr. ed. Kim Kiyosaki. Read by Kim Kiyosaki. (Running Time: 7 hrs.). 2010. audio compact disk 14.99 (978-1-61106-443-8(0), 9781611064438, BCD Value Price) Brilliance Audio.

Rich Young Ruler. Perf. by Rich Young Ruler & Gene Eugene. 1 cass., 1 Cd. 1998. 10.98 (978-0-7601-1854-2(X)); audio compact disk 16.98 CD. (978-0-7601-1855-9(8)) Provident Mus Dist.
Features 13 hypnotic songs.

Richard Adams. Interview with Richard Adams. 1 cass. (Running Time: 25 min.). 1975. 11.95 (L001) TFR.
Adams talks on "Watership Down" & "Shardik," stories he invented for his children.

Richard Bausch. unabr. ed. Richard Bausch. Read by Richard Bausch. 1 cass. (Running Time: 29 min.). 1988. 10.00 New Letters.
Bausch reads from the short story "Ancient History" & is interviewed.

Richard Blade Collector's Series I. abr. ed. Jeffrey Lord. Read by Lloyd James. 6 cass. (Running Time: 9 hrs.). (Richard Blade Collector's Ser.: No. 1). 2004. 35.00 (978-1-58807-484-3(6)) Am Pubng Inc.
This special Collector's Edition includes the first three novels in Jeffrey Lord's 'Richard Blade' series, covering the exploits of British secret agent Blade as he is thrust into parallel dimensions to explore and exploit. In The Bronze Axe, Blade is propelled into an unknown time and place where he finds himself helping a beautiful princess. While they run for their lives from a savage rival faction, Blade must endure unimaginable trials. In The Jade Warrior, Blade finds himself in Dimension X and in mortal danger. The land is in peril. The Mongs, a cruel people, attack the aristocratic Caths. Into this maelstrom comes Blade, the man who can help change the outcome. But only if he can trust someone to help him and time doesn't run out first. In Jewel of Tharn, Blade must fight to survive in a world of stagnation, brutal oppression, and violent intrigue. Finding himself in a position to overthrow the oppressors and restore a civilization, he must find the strength, skill, wit, and patience to strike at the right place and time while manipulating those who would use him for their own ends.

Richard Blade Collector's Series II. abr. ed. Jeffrey Lord. Read by Carol Eason. 6 cass. (Running Time: 9 hrs.). (Richard Blade Collector's Ser.: No. 2). 2004. 35.00 (978-1-58807-485-0(4)) Am Pubng Inc.

Richard Blade Collector's Series III. abr. ed. Jeffrey Lord. Read by Carol Eason. 6 cass. (Running Time: 9 hrs.). (Richard Blade Collector's Ser.: No. 3). 2004. 35.00 (978-1-58807-486-7(2)) Am Pubng Inc.

Richard Brinsley Sheridan: The School for Scandal. Richard Brinsley Sheridan. Perf. by Alec McCowen et al. 2 cass. 15.95 (SCN 101) J Norton Pubs.
Satirises the mannered & heartless society of 18th-century London, where reputation rather than truth holds sway & the appearance of virtue is much more important than its possession.

Richard Burton Anthology of Classic Poetry. Read by Richard Burton. 1 cass. 19.95 (8022Q) Filmic Archives.
A varied & satisfying selection of poems, including the complete "Rime of the Ancient Mariner" by Samuel Coleridge, "Fern Hill" by Dylan Thomas, "The Passionate Shepherd to His Love" by Christopher Marlowe, "Death Be not Proud" by John Donne, Prospero's speech, "Our Revels Now Are Ended" from Shakespeare's "The Tempest" & many more.

Richard C. Wald: Senior Vice President, News, ABC-TV see Scene Behind the Screen: The Business Realities of the TV Industry

Richard Chase Tells Jack Tales. 1 cass. 9.98 (C-6) Folk-Legacy.
Traditional tales told in a one-room schoolhouse in Tennessee.

Richard Condon's the Manchurian Candidate. Richard Condon. Read by Robert Vaughn. 2 read-along cass. bk. 34.95 (S23910) J Norton Pubs.

Richard Diamond. Perf. by Dick Powell. (ENG.). 2008. audio compact disk 31.95 (978-1-57019-851-9(9)) Radio Spirits.

***Richard Diamond: Trouble.** Perf. by Dick Powell & Virginia Gregg. 2009. audio compact disk 18.95 (978-1-57019-907-3(8)) Radio Spirits.

***Richard Diamond, Private Detective.** RadioArchives.com. (Running Time: 600). (ENG.). 2005. audio compact disk 29.98 (978-1-61081-039-5(2)) Radio Arch.

Richard Diamond, Private Detective, Vol. 3. 6 cass. (Running Time: 9 hrs.). 2002. 34.98 (4689) Radio Spirits.

Richard Diamond, Private Detective: A Christmas Carol & The Thomas Jason Case. Perf. by Dick Powell. 1 cass. (Running Time: 1 hr.). 2001. 6.98 (2107) Radio Spirits.

Richard Diamond, Private Detective: Blackmail by Carrier Pigeon & Lieutenant Levinson Kidnapped. Perf. by Dick Powell. 1 cass. (Running Time: 1 hr.). 2001. 6.98 (2148) Radio Spirits.

Richard Diamond, Private Detective: Chapel Hill Police Officer Symposium Speech & Mona Lisa Murder. Perf. by Dick Powell. 1 cass. (Running Time: 1 hr.). 2001. 6.98 (2625) Radio Spirits.

Richard Diamond, Private Detective: Harry Baker Kills His Voice & The Professor Leonardo Case. Perf. by Dick Powell. 1 cass. (Running Time: 1 hr.). 2001. 6.98 (1525) Radio Spirits.

Richard Diamond, Private Detective: Lady in Distress & Red Rose. Perf. by Dick Powell. 1 cass. (Running Time: 1 hr.). 2001. 6.98 (1696) Radio Spirits.

Richard Diamond, Private Detective: Private Eye Test & Photographer's Card. Perf. by Dick Powell. 1 cass. (Running Time: 1 hr.). 2001. 6.98 (1988) Radio Spirits.

Richard Diamond, Private Detective: The Butcher Shop & Monsieur Beauchand. Perf. by Dick Powell. 1 cass. (Running Time: 1 hr.). 2001. 6.98 (2126) Radio Spirits.

Richard Diamond, Private Detective: The Cop Killer & Marilyn Connors Case. Perf. by Dick Powell. 1 cass. (Running Time: 1 hr.). 2001. 6.98 (2404) Radio Spirits.

Richard Diamond, Private Detective: The Gibson Murder Case & Newspaper Boy & the Ring. Perf. by Dick Powell. 1 cass. (Running Time: 1 hr.). 2001. 6.98 (2587) Radio Spirits.

Richard Diamond, Private Detective: The Jewel Thief. 6 cass. (Running Time: 6 hrs.). 1999. 19.98 (AB238) Radio Spirits.

Richard Diamond, Private Detective: Tom Waxman Murdered & George Watkins Framed. Perf. by Dick Powell. 1 cass. (Running Time: 1 hr.). 2001. 6.98 (2206) Radio Spirits.

Richard Diamond, Private Detective Vol. 1. collector's ed. Perf. by Dick Powell. Created by Blake Edwards. 6 cass. (Running Time: 9 hrs.). 1998. bk. 34.98 (4392) Radio Spirits.
Lighthearted detective Richard Diamond is fast on his feet and even faster with a quip. Heavy when he needs to be, Diamond still enjoys having a little fun on the job. The end of each show usually finds him at his girlfriend's Park Avenue penthouse singing a number on her baby grand. 18 episodes including, The Statue of Kali, Ralph Baxter Escapes from Jail, Cross State Trucking, The Woman Who Cried Wolf, Carnival Killer, Hat Pin Case, Big Foot Grafton, Wrong Laundry Tag and 10 more.

Richard Diamond, Private Detective Vol. 2. collector's ed. Perf. by Dick Powell et al. 6 cass. (Running Time: 9 hrs.). 1999. bk. 34.98 (4191) Radio Spirits.

Richard Dooling. unabr. ed. Read by Richard Dooling & Rebekah Presson. Ed. by James McKinley. 1 cass. (Running Time: 29 min.). (New Letters on the Air Ser.). 1994. 10.00 (091294); 18.00 2-sided cass. New Letters.
Dooling is interviewed by Rebekah Presson & reads from his second book.

Richard Eberhart. Interview with Richard Eberhart. 1 cass. (Running Time: 25 min.). 1979. 10.95 (L020) TFR.
The author talks about his poetry & his famous joie de vivre. He advises struggling young poets to go into the business world.

Richard Eberhart. unabr. ed. Read by Richard Eberhart. 1 cass. (Running Time: 29 min.). 1985. 10.00 New Letters.
The Pulitzer Prize winning poet reads from Florida Poems & talks about his work.

Richard Eberhart Reading His Poetry. abr. ed. Poems. Richard Eberhart. Perf. by Richard Eberhart. 1 cass. Incl. Cancer Cells. (SWC 1243); For a Lamb. (SWC 1243); Fury of Aerial Bombardment. (SWC 1243); Go to the Shrine That's on a Tree. (SWC 1243); Groundhog. (SWC 1243); Horse Chestnut Tree. (SWC 1243); I Walked out to the Graveyard to See the Dead. (SWC 1243); If I Could Only Live at the Pitch That Is Near Madness. (SWC 1243); Meditation. (SWC 1243); New Hampshire, February. (SWC 1243); Nothing but Change. (SWC 1243); On a Squirrel Crossing the Road in Autumn. (SWC 1243); Rumination. (SWC 1243); Sea-Hawk. (SWC 1243); Seals, Terns, Time. (SWC 1243); 1984. 12.95 (978-0-694-50175-5(1), SWC 1243) HarperCollins Pubs.

Richard Eberhart Reading His Poetry. unabr. ed. Poems. Richard Eberhart. Perf. by Richard Eberhart. 1 cass. Incl. Am I My Neighbor's Keeper? (SWC 1430); Crosse at Ninety Miles an Hour. (SWC 1430); Explorer on Main Street. (SWC 1430); Hardening into Print. (SWC 1430); Ides of March. (SWC 1430); Illusion of Eternity. (SWC 1430); Incomparable Light. (SWC 1430); Maine Roustabout. (SWC 1430); Marrakech. (SWC 1430); Mastery. (SWC 1430); New England Bachelor. (SWC 1430); On Returning to a Lake in Spring. (SWC 1430); Place. (SWC 1430); Sea Burial from the Cruiser Reve. (SWC 1430); Wedding on Cape Rosier. (SWC 1430); 1985. 12.95 (SWC 1430) HarperCollins Pubs.

Richard Flint Live. Richard Flint. 6 cass. 1982. 70.00 (978-0-937851-08-1(6)) Pendelton Lane.
These cassettes are all designed for a quick pick-up. Each tape contains a different subject which is very humorous & pointed in its information. Many of the tapes are about what happens to a life when one discovers self-confidence. Titles include: "Are You Archie Bunker's Cousin," "Levels of Flight," "How Do You Kill s Salesperson," "That's One Giant Step," "Falsely Accused" & "You've Got the Power".

Richard Flint Requested. Richard Flint. 5 cass. 1983. 70.00 (978-0-937851-11-1(6)) Pendelton Lane.
Cassette album offering the author's discussions of two topics. "I Ain't Gonna Quit" deals with the psychology of change, why people fear it, & what it takes for human lives to accept change. "Crashing Through Your Road Blocks" is a research project done with sales people in order to discover the common threads of struggle that they experience.

Richard Ford Interview with Kay Bonetti. Interview. Interview with Richard Ford & Kay Bonetti. 1 cass. 1986. 13.95 (978-1-55644-152-3(5), 6032) Am Audio Prose.
Ford reveals himself to be a man deeply committed to the religion of art, but never at the expense of a rich & rewarding personal life with his wife & friends which he believes is the necessary foundation for everything he does.

Richard Gilewitz: Live at Charlotte's Web. Contrib. by Richard Gilewitz. 2007. 24.95 (978-5-557-47317-0(3)) Mel Bay.

Richard Harteis: Marathon. unabr. ed. Richard Harteis. Read by Richard Harteis. 1 cass. (Running Time: 29 min.). 1990. 10.00 (011990) New Letters.
Harteis reads from his book, "Marathon" & talks about his life with Pulitzer Prize-winning poet William Meredith.

Richard Harvey's Blackjack PowerPrep Session. 2nd ed. Richard Harvey. 1 CD. (Running Time: 70 mins.). Orig. Title: Preparing YOU to WIN. 2004. audio compact disk 14.95 (978-0-9672182-6-7(8)) Mystic Ridge Bks.
This compact disc audio book provides blackjack players with their essential practice session just before each trip to the casino. Based upon the material introduced in the author's ground-breaking bestseller, Blackjack The SMART Way, Richard Harvey's PowerPrep reminds players of everything they need to know to win - from picking a good casino and a good table, to advanced strategy (using the author's leading-edge methods).

Richard Howard. unabr. ed. Richard Howard. Read by Richard Howard. 1 cass. (Running Time: 29 min.). 1989. 10.00 New Letters.
Howard reads poetry form No Traveller & is interviewed.

Richard Hugo. unabr. ed. Read by Richard Hugo. 1 cass. (Running Time: 29 min.). 1985. 10.00 New Letters.
The widely known poet here reads from White Center.

Richard Hugo Memorial. unabr. ed. 1 cass. (Running Time: 29 min.). 1985. 10.00 New Letters.
A reading by Hugo, & also excerpts from Hugo's "Remarks" read by William Stafford & David Ray.

Richard II. William Shakespeare. 2009. (978-1-60136-063-2(0)) Audio Holding.

Richard II. Derek Traversi. 1 cass. (Running Time: 40 min.). (Shakespeare's Critics Speak Ser.). 1965. 11.95 (23098) J Norton Pubs.
This royal tragedy is approached as an acute & personal reading of historical events.

Richard III see Richard III

Richard III. William Shakespeare. Perf. by Folio Theatre Players. 1 cass. Dramatization.Tr. of Richard III. 10.95 (978-0-8045-0891-9(7), SAC 7117) Spoken Arts.

Richard III. unabr. ed. William Shakespeare. Narrated by Flo Gibson. (Running Time: 3 hrs. 58 mins.).Tr. of Richard III. 2004. 16.95 (978-1-55685-759-1(4)) Audio Bk Con.

Richard III. unabr. ed. William Shakespeare. Read by Arkangel Cast Staff. Narrated by David Troughton et al. (Arkangel Shakespeare Ser.).Tr. of Richard III. (ENG.). 2005. audio compact disk 24.95 (978-1-932219-29-6(3)) Pub: AudioGO. Dist(s): Perseus Dist
The Yorkists have emerged victorious from the civil wars and Edward IV wears the English crown. Edward's brother, Richard, harbors his own kingly ambitions and will stop at nothing to achieve the throne. Manipulative and entirely amoral, the hero-villain Richard is one of Shakespeare's greatest roles. Performed by David Troughton, Philip Voss, and the Arkangel cast.

Richard III. unabr. ed. William Shakespeare. Read by Audio Partners Staff. 2 cass. (Running Time: 3 hrs. 34 mins.). (Arkangel Shakespeare Ser.).Tr. of Richard III. 2004. 17.95 (978-1-932219-69-2(2), Atlntc Mnthly) Pub: Grove-Atltic. Dist(s): PerseuPGW

Richard Jeni's Greatest Bits. Perf. by Richard Jeni. 2000. audio compact disk 16.98 (978-1-929243-13-6(8)) Uproar Ent.

Richard Kennedy: Collected Stories. unabr. ed. Read by Christopher King. 2 cass. Dramatization. (J). (gr. 5-8). 1992. 16.98 set. (978-0-8072-7373-9(2), YA 840 CX, Listening Lib) Random Audio Pubg.

Richard Kern, Action. Ed. by Dian Hanson. (ENG., 2007. 39.99 (978-3-8228-5649-9(5)) Pub: Taschen DEU. Dist(s): IngramPubServ

Richard M. Nixon: The Nixon Tapes. Speechworks Jerden. 1 cass. (Running Time: 44 min.). 1994. audio compact disk 10.98 (978-1-885959-10-2(9), JRCS 7035) Jerden Recs.
Excerpted highlights from 8 major speeches given by President Richard M. Nixon, from his "Checkers" speech in 1952 to his resignation in 1974.

Richard McCall: The Misogi Challenge. Read by Richard McCall. 1 cass. 30.00 Dow Jones Telerate.
In this seminar, you will learn how to analyze the Samurai's Shinjutsu (unstoppable action-oriented mentality) using Richard's warrior A.C.T.I.O.N. plan. Accept all possible losses before entering the battle, Center yourself, mind, body & spirit, Trust your subconscious abilities & warrior intuition, Imagine a successful mission, Only live in the present moment, Never stop once you have begun.

Richard Milhous Nixon. Roger Morris. Read by Walter Hawn. 26 cass. (Running Time: 38 hrs.). 1993. 151.20 (978-1-56544-010-4(2), 150004); Rental 26.00 30 day rental Set. (150004) Literate Ear.
The initial work in a projected three-volume biography of perhaps this century's most controversial President. The color & detail help us understand his development as a politician & as a person.

Richard Murphy. unabr. ed. Read by Richard Murphy. 1 cass. (Running Time: 29 min.). 1985. 10.00 New Letters.
The Irish poet reads from High Island.

Richard Nixon: Future of the G.O.P. see Buckley's Firing Line

Richard Price. Interview. Interview with Richard Price & Kay Bonetti. 1 cass. (Running Time: 53 min.). 1984. 13.95 (978-1-55644-054-0(5), 2112) Am Audio Prose.
Discussion of major influences on Price's style & subject matter.

Richard Pryor... And It's Deep Too! The Complete Warner Bros. Recordings (1968-1992) Richard Pryor. 9 CDs. (Running Time: 13 hrs. 30 mins.). 2001. bk. 79.98 (R2 76655) Rhino Enter.

Richard Rhodes. unabr. ed. Read by Richard Rhodes. Ed. by James McKinley. 1 cass. (Running Time: 29 min.). (New Letters on the Air Ser.). 1980. 10.00 (022580); 18.00 2-sided cass. New Letters.
Rhodes reads excerpts from his books The Ungodly, Holy Secrets, & The Last Safari & from a Playboy essay on cocaine.

Richard Rhodes. unabr. ed. Richard Rhodes. Read by Richard Rhodes. 1 cass. (Running Time: 29 min.). Incl. Making of the Atomic Bomb. 1987. (21); 1987. 10.00 (21) New Letters.
Rhodes reads & talks about the Manhattan Project.

Richard Shaver - Reality of the Inner Earth. collector's ed. Ed. by Tim Swartz. 1 CD. (Running Time: 1 hr.). 2005. bk. 22.95 (978-1-892062-92-5(5)) Inner Light.
This book exposes the reality of underground races, lost civilizations, subsurface kingdoms and forgotten inhabitants of a hidden world. Richard Shaver caused a wave of controversy when he claimed to have gone into the hidden caverns and battled a race of underground dwellers known as the Dero. Here are some of his previously unpublished works as well as final proof of the existence of the Titans, the Demented Dero, the Atlantean Root Race and other bizarre creatures of the mysterious deep. The reader will learn the identities of evil collaborators who use deception to keep the existence of the underworld a deep dark, secret. This is your opportunity to return to the caves with Richard S. Shaver.

Richard Shelton. Read by Richard Shelton. 1 cass. (Running Time: 29 min.). 1985. 10.00 New Letters.
Richard Shelton reads poems about the Sonora Desert & its preservation.

Richard Smallwood: Rejoice. Perf. by Richard Smallwood. 1 cass. 1999. (978-0-7601-1745-3(4)); audio compact disk (978-0-7601-1746-0(2)) Brentwood Music.

Richard Smallwood: The Definitive Gospel Collection. Contrib. by Richard Smallwood. (Definitive Gospel Collection). 2008. audio compact disk 7.99 (978-5-557-49738-1(2), Word Records) Word Enter.

Richard Smallwood Live in Atlanta, Adoration: With Vision. Perf. by Richard Smallwood. 1 cass. (V 50015) Brentwood Music.
At the forefront of Gospel music, Smallwood delivers an extraordinary performance in this live recording. Includes: Bless the Lord, Everything That Has Breath, Thank You & I Will Sing Praise.

Richard Smallwood with Vision: Healing - Live in Detroit. Perf. by Richard Smallwood. 1 cass., 1 CD. 1998. 10.98 (978-0-7601-2584-7(8)); audio compact disk 16.98 (978-0-7601-2585-4(6)) Provident Music.
From whispered praises to unrestrained & heartfelt cries to God.

Richard Temple. Narrated by Graeme Malcolm. 7 cass. (Running Time: 36780 sec.). (Sound Library). 2006. 59.95 (978-0-7927-4226-5(5), CSL 958); audio compact disk 89.95 (978-0-7927-4052-0(1), SLD 958) AudioGO.

Richard Thompson Teaches Traditional Guitar Instrumentals. 1998. audio compact disk 19.95 (978-0-7935-6256-5(2)) Pub: Homespun Video. Dist(s): H Leonard

Richard Wilbur. Richard Wilbur. Read by Richard Wilbur. Interview with Robert Stewart. Prod. by Rebekah Presson. 1 cass. (Running Time: 29 min.). 1990. 10.00 (101290) New Letters.
The former Poet Laureate of the United States reads from his Collected Poems, for which he won his second Pulitzer Prize.

Richard Wilbur Readings. unabr. ed. Poems. Richard Wilbur. Read by Richard Wilbur. 1 cass. Incl. Advice to a Prophet. (SWC 1248); Aspen & the Stream. (SWC 1248); Complaint. (SWC 1248); Grasshopper. (SWC 1248); Lilacs. (SWC 1248); On the Marginal Way. (SWC 1248); Running. (SWC 1248); Seed Leaves. (SWC 1248); Shame. (SWC 1248); She. (SWC 1248); Someone Talking to Himself. (SWC 1248); Two Voices in a Meadow. (SWC 1248); Undead. (SWC 1248); Under Cygnus. (SWC 1248); Villon: Ballade of the Ladies of Time Past. (SWC 1248); Walking to Sleep. (SWC 1248); Wood. (SWC 1248); 1972. 14.00 (978-0-694-50177-9(8), SWC 1248) HarperCollins Pubs.

Riches & Honor! unabr. ed. Edwene Gaines. (ENG.). 2006. 14.98 (978-1-59659-106-6(4), GildAudio) Pub: Gildan Media. Dist(s): HachBkGrp

Riches from the East. Bede Griffiths. Perf. by Bede Griffiths. 5 cass. (Running Time: 4 hrs. 30 min.). 1996. pap. bk. (AA3026) Credence Commun.
Explains the growing importance of eastern religions, how they can help enrich your spirituality, & how they are bringing the church to a new vitality.

Riches Untold: Chronicles of the Golden Frontier. abr. ed. Gilbert Morris. 2 cass. (Running Time: 3 hrs.). 2001. 14.99 (978-1-58926-009-2(0)) Oasis Audio.
Jennifer DeSpain's life used to be quiet & dull, but that was before a whirlwind romance & marriage & before a tragedy that leaves her with only a defunct newspaper to her name. With hopes for a fresh start, Jennifer & her two children move to Nevada where she will have to resolve the challenges of poverty, newspaper publishing, a reversal in fortune & matters of the heart, all with the help of some colorful friends & God.

Riches Within Your Reach! abr. ed. Robert Collier. Contrib. by Joel Fotinos. (Running Time: 6 hrs.). (ENG.). (gr. 12 up). 2010. audio compact disk 29.95 (978-0-14-314556-1(8), PengAudBks) Penguin Grp USA.

Richest Man in Babylon. George S. Clason. 1 cass. (Running Time: 34 min.). 11.00 (978-0-89811-029-6(7), 5172); Meyer Res Grp.
The 3 principles of financial success that worked in ancient Babylon will work for you today.

Richest Man in Babylon. George S. Clason. 2005. audio compact disk 13.99 (978-1-4193-4999-7(6)) Recorded Bks.

Richest Man in Babylon: The Laws of Financial Success Are the Same Today As They Were over 6000 Years Ago. George S. Clason. Read by Billy Nash. 6 cass. (Running Time: 5 hrs.). 39.95 (978-1-57949-006-5(9)) Destination Success.
Timeless advice sheds light on today's stock market boom, debt, credit cards, bankruptcies & early retirement. Learn invaluable lessons, digested from hundreds of thousands of clay tablets & entire libraries discovered within the ruins of Babylon.

Richest Man in Babylon: The Laws of Financial Success Are the Same Today As They Were over 6000 Years Ago. George S. Clason. Narrated by Billy Nash. 6 cass. (Running Time: 5 hrs.). 1997. 39.95 F Fell Pubs Inc.
Learn how to seek wealth & financial security. Go back almost 6,000 years to Babylon where the principles of wealth accumulation were founded. Sheds light on today's stock market boom, debt & credit cards, bankruptcies & early retirement.

Richest Man in Babylon - Book & Audiobook. George Clason. 2007. per. 24.99 (978-956-291-456-7(9)) Edit Benei CHL.

Richest Man in Babylon & the Magic Story: Two Classic Allegorical Dramatizations about Building Wealth & Achieving Personal Success. unabr. ed. Selected by Napoleon Hill Motivational Theatre Staff. 1 CD. (Running Time: 1 hr. 0 mins. 0 sec.). (ENG.). 2002. audio compact disk 14.00 (978-1-55927-692-4(4)) Pub: Highroads Media. Dist(s): Macmillan

Richest Man in Babylon; As a Man Thinketh. George S. Clason & James Allen. 1 cass. 10.00 (SP100014) SMI Intl.
The three principles of financial success that worked in ancient Babylon will work for you today. These two inspirational messages provide you with winning attitudes & winning strategies.

Richest Man in the World. 1 cass. 10.00 Esstee Audios.
The story of how Andrew Carnegie rose from poverty to being the tycoon dominating finance.

Richest Man in Town: The Twelve Commandments of Wealth. abr. ed. Randall Jones. Read by Randall Jones. (Running Time: 5 hrs.). (ENG.). 2009. 18.98 (978-1-60024-580-0(3)); audio compact disk 26.98 (978-1-60024-579-4(X)) Pub: Hachet Audio. Dist(s): HachBkGrp

***Richest Poor Kid / el niño Pobre Más Rico Del Mundo/ with CD.** ed. Carl Sommer. Illus. by Jorge Martinez. (Another Sommer-Time Story Bilingual Ser.). (ENG & SPA.). (J). 2009. bk. 26.95 (978-1-57537-190-0(1)) Advance Pub.

Richest Season. Maryann McFadden. Read by Cassandra Campbell. (Playaway Adult Fiction Ser.). (ENG.). 2009. 64.99 (978-1-60812-804-4(0)) Find a World.

Richest Season. unabr. ed. Maryann McFadden. Narrated by Cassandra Campbell. (Running Time: 12 hrs. 0 mins. 0 sec.). (ENG.). 2008. audio compact disk 69.99 (978-1-4001-3808-1(6)); audio compact disk 24.99 (978-1-4001-5808-9(7)) Pub: Tantor Media. Dist(s): IngramPubServ

Richest Season. unabr. ed. Maryann McFadden. Narrated by Cassandra Campbell. (Running Time: 12 hrs. 0 mins. 0 sec.). (ENG.). 2008. audio compact disk 34.99 (978-1-4001-0808-4(X)) Pub: Tantor Media. Dist(s): IngramPubServ

Richistan: A Journey Through the American Wealth Boom & the Lives of the New Rich. unabr. ed. Robert Frank. Read by Dick Hill. (YA). 2008. 54.99 (978-1-60514-795-6(8)) Find a World.

Richistan: A Journey Through the American Wealth Boom & the Lives of the New Rich. unabr. ed. Robert Frank. Narrated by Dick Hill. 6 CDs. (Running Time: 7 hrs. 30 mins. 0 sec.). (ENG.). 2007. audio compact disk 29.99 (978-1-4001-0445-1(9)) Pub: Tantor Media. Dist(s): IngramPubServ

Richistan: A Journey Through the American Wealth Boom & the Lives of the New Rich. unabr. ed. Robert Frank. Read by Dick Hill. 1 MP3-CD. (Running Time: 7 hrs. 30 mins. 0 sec.). (ENG.). 2007. 19.99 (978-1-4001-5445-6(6)); audio compact disk 59.99 (978-1-4001-3445-8(5)) Pub: Tantor Media. Dist(s): IngramPubServ

Richman & the Shoemaker. Brian Wildsmith. 1 cass. (Running Time: 1 hr.). (J). (ps-2). 2000. pap. bk. 12.95 Weston Woods.
Familiar beasts in their natural habitats will surprise & delight elementary school children.

Richmond Electronic Dictionary, 2000: Spanish-English Bilingual Electronic Dictionary. VV Staff. (SPA & ENG.). (J). (gr. k-12). audio compact disk 34.95 (978-84-294-9508-9(8), Richmond) Santillana.

Richness & Poverty. unabr. ed. Chogyam Trungpa & S. Rinpoche. 1 cass. (Running Time: 1 hr. 32 min.). 1970. 11.00 (13001) Big Sur Tapes.
Trungpa believes that spirituality is something applicable to everyday life, applying the metaphor of richness & poverty to the process of spiritual seeking.

Rick Altizer: Blue Plate Special. Perf. by Rick Altizer. 1 cass. 1999. 10.98 (KMGC 8645); audio compact disk 16.98 (KMGD 8645) Provident Mus Dist.

Rick & Lorraine Lee: Living in the Trees. 1 cass. 9.98 (C-55) Folk-Legacy.
Some old, more new songs, many with dulcimer.

Rick Blair: Always by My Side. Perf. by Rick Blair. 1 cass. 1999. 10.98 (KMGC 864149); audio compact disk 16.98 (KMGD 9711) Provident Mus Dist.

Rick Fielding: Lifeline. 1 cass., 1 CD. 9.98 (C-123); audio compact disk 14.98 CD. (CD-123) Folk-Legacy.
A very talented Canadian singer & songmaker & multi-instrumentalist.

Rick Foster's Eternal Guitar. Rick Foster. 1 CD. (Running Time: 90 mins.). 1995. bk. 22.95 (978-0-7866-1448-6(X), 95665BCD) Mel Bay.

Rick Foster's Favorite Hymns for Acoustic Guitar. Rick Foster. 1 cass. pap. bk. 19.95 (95438P); 10.98 stereo. (95438C) Mel Bay.
Fourteen guitar solos on hymns & sacred songs transcribed exactly as played by recording artist Rick Foster. Selections include: "Jesu, Joy of Man's Desiring," "Morning Has Broken;" "Be Still My Soul;" "A Mighty Fortress Is Our God;" "Amazing Grace;" & more.

Rick O. Shea Mysteries. R. Shea. 1 cass. (Running Time: 1 hr.). 2001. 12.95 (SMPD004) Lodestone Catalog.
With gun in hand & tongue in cheek, Rick O. Shea leads you through suspense & laughter. Trouble in Black Silk & it smells like murder.

Rick O. Shea Mysteries. R. Shea. 1 cass. (Running Time: 1 hr.). 2002. 12.95 (978-1-896617-02-2(6), SMA-003) Stuffed Moose CAN.
His name's Rick. Rick O. Shea. He's a private eye....... sometimes. The government cut his job retraining program. Rick knows the two inescapable things in life are death and bureaucrats. Hey, who d'ya think invented taxes?.

Ricker Compilation of Vital Records of Early Connecticut: Based on the Barbour Collection of Connecticut Town Vital Records & Other Statistical Sources. Jacquelyn Ladd Ricker. 2006. audio compact disk 59.99 (978-0-8063-9879-2(5)) Genealog Pub.

Ricks Licks: Intermediate Level. Rick Gratton. 1996. pap. bk. 15.95 (978-0-7866-1854-5(X), 95436BCD) Mel Bay.

Ricky: The Unauthorized Biography of Ricky Martin. Harry Drysdale-Wood & Gillian Adams. (Maximum Ser.). (ENG.). 2001. audio compact disk 14.95 (978-1-84240-026-5(6)) Pub: Chrome Dreams GBR. Dist(s): IPG Chicago

Ricky Gervais Presents: the World of Karl Pilkington. abr. ed. Karl Pilkington et al. 2006. 24.98 (978-1-4013-8732-7(2)) Pub: Hyperion. Dist(s): HarperCollins Pubs

Ricky Martin: Red-Hot & on the Rise! abr. ed. Kathleen Tracy. Read by Christian Noble & Karesa McElheny. 2 cass. (Running Time: 3 hrs.). 1999. 9.95 (978-0-7366-4598-0(5), 4992) Books on Tape.
Ricky Martin's life from his boyhood in Puerto Rico to his rise to superstardom.

Ricky Martin: Red-Hot & on the Rise! abr. ed. Kathleen Tracy. Read by Karesa McElheny & C. Noble. 2 CDs. (Running Time: 2 hrs.). 1999. audio compact disk 11.95 (978-0-7366-4599-7(3)) Books on Tape.
At 27, Ricky Martin, the sizzling Latin heartthrob, has electrified audiences for decades. Now, with his first English-language album, which has the hit single Livin' La Vida Loca, racing up the charts, he is poised on the brink of superstardom. With his smoldering dark eyes & seductive good looks, he's captured the attention & hearts of women around the globe. this timely profile of Martin's life starts with his childhood in Puerto Rico & chronicles his rise to popularity as a Latin singer, an actor on television & stages.

Ricky Martin: Red-Hot & on the Rise! abr. ed. Kathleen Tracy. Read by Christian Nobel & Karesa McElheny. 2 cass. (Running Time: 3 hrs.). (SPA.). 1999. 9.95 (978-0-7366-4601-7(9), 4992-CS) Books on Tape.

Ricky Martin: Red-Hot & on the Rise! abr. ed. Kathleen Tracy. Read by Christian Noble & Karesa McElheny. 2 CDs. (Running Time: 2 hrs.). (SPA.). 1999. audio compact disk 11.95 (978-0-7366-4637-6(X), 4992-S) Books on Tape.
Ricky Martin's life from his boyhood in Puerto Rico to his rise to superstardom.

Ricky Martin: Red-Hot & on the Rise! collector's ed. Kathleen Tracy. Read by Karesa McElheny & C. Noble. 2 cass. (Running Time: 3 hrs.). 1999. 9.95 (978-0-7366-4602-4(7)) Books on Tape.
At 27, Ricky Martin, the sizzling Latin heartthrob, has electrified audiences for decades. Now, with his first English-language album, which has the hit single Livin' La Vida Loca, racing up the charts, he is poised on the brink of superstardom. With his smoldering dark eyes & seductive good looks, he's captured the attention & hearts of women around the globe. this timely profile of Martin's life starts with his childhood in Puerto Rico & chronicles his rise to popularity as a Latin singer, an actor on television & stages.

Ricky Martin: Red-Hot & on the Rise! collector's unabr. ed. Kathleen Tracy. Read by Christian Noble & Karesa McElheny. 2 CDs. (Running Time: 2 hrs.). 2000. audio compact disk 12.95 (978-0-7366-5189-9(6)) Books on Tape.

Ricky with the Tuft see Sleeping Beauty & Other Stories

RICO Litigation. Moderated by Jed S. Rakoff & John R. Wing. 7 cass. (Running Time: 11 hrs.). 1991. 197.50 NY Law Pub.
Topics include the background & elements of RICO; substantive applications of civil & criminal RICO; special problems of civil & criminal RICO cases; parallel proceedings & collateral consequences; techniques for representing plaintiffs & defendants in civil RICO actions; & the future of civil RICO.

Ricochet. Paula Gosling. 7 cass. (Sound Ser.). (J). 2003. 61.95 (978-1-84283-413-8(4)) Pub: ISIS Lrg Prnt GBR. Dist(s): Ulverscroft US

Ricochet. abr. ed. Sandra Brown. Read by Dennis Boutsikaris. 2006. 17.95 (978-0-7435-6181-5(3)) Pub: S&S Audio. Dist(s): S and S Inc

Ricochet. abr. ed. Sandra Brown. Read by Dennis Boutsikaris. (Running Time: 6 hrs. 0 mins. 0 sec.). (ENG.). 2008. audio compact disk 14.99 (978-0-7435-7620-8(9)) Pub: S&S Audio. Dist(s): S and S Inc

Ricochet. unabr. ed. Sandra Brown. Read by Dennis Boutsikaris. 11 CDs. (Running Time: 13 hrs.). 2006. audio compact disk 119.75 (978-1-4281-0635-2(9)); 89.75 (978-1-4281-0633-8(2)) Recorded Bks.
Ricochet tells the story of Detective Sergeant Duncan Hatcher, whose attraction to a judge's wife threatens to undermine an already dangerous case.

Ricochet. unabr. ed. Sandra Brown. Read by Dennis Boutsikaris. 2006. 29.95 (978-0-7435-6182-2(1)) Pub: S&S Audio. Dist(s): S and S Inc

Ricochet. unabr. ed. Sandra Brown. Read by Dennis Boutsikaris. (Running Time: 13 hrs. 0 mins. 0 sec.). 2008. audio compact disk 21.99 (978-0-7435-8164-6(4)) Pub: S&S Audio. Dist(s): S and S Inc

Rico's Hawk. Randy Houk. Read by Tom Chapin. Illus. by Nancy Lane. Narrated by Tom Chapin. 1 cass. (Running Time: 13 min.). (Humane Society of the United States Animal Tales Ser.). (J). (gr. 1-4). 1998. pap. bk. 9.95 (978-1-58021-033-1(3)); pap. bk. 19.95 (978-1-58021-031-7(7)) Benefactory.
Did the boy heal the hawk, or did the hawk heal the boy? (Answer: yes!) A troubled inner-city child develops hope & self-esteem working with animals at Green Chimneys, a working farm & school.

Riddle: Where Ideas Come from & How to Have Better Ones. abr. ed. Andrew Razeghi. Read by Jim Bond. 1 MP3-CD. (Running Time: 8 hrs.). 2008. 39.25 (978-1-4233-5990-6(9), 9781423359906, Brinc Audio MP3 Lib); 24.95 (978-1-4233-5989-0(5), 9781423359890, Brilliance MP3); audio compact disk 87.25 (978-1-4233-5988-3(7), 9781423359883, BriAudCD Unabrid); audio compact disk 29.95 (978-1-4233-5987-6(9), 9781423359876, Bril Audio CD Unabri) Brilliance Audio.

Riddle: Where Ideas Come from & How to Have Better Ones. unabr. abr. ed. Andrew Razeghi. (Running Time: 8 hrs.). 2008. 24.95 (978-1-4233-5991-3(7), 9781423359913, BAD) Brilliance Audio.

Riddle: Where Ideas Come from & How to Have Better Ones. unabr. abr. ed. Andrew Razeghi. Read by Jim Bond. (Running Time: 8 hrs.). 2008. 39.25 (978-1-4233-5992-0(5), 9781423359920, BADLE) Brilliance Audio.

Riddle & the Rune. unabr. ed. Grace Chetwin. Narrated by Grace Chetwin. 8 cass. (Running Time: 11 hrs.). (gr. 5). 1992. 72.00 (978-1-55690-605-3(6), 92210E7) Recorded Bks.
In this sequel to "Gom on Windy Mountain," Gom sets out to find his mother, Harga - a mysterious woman rumored to be the greatest wizard in the world.

***riddle of Green.** Isobelle Carmody. Read by Isobelle Carmody. (Running Time: 5 hrs. 5 mins.). (Legend of Little Fur Ser.). (J). 2009. 39.99 (978-1-74214-161-9(7), 9781742141619) Pub: Bolinda Pubng AUS. Dist(s): Bolinda Pub Inc

Riddle of Green. unabr. ed. Isobelle Carmody. Read by Isobelle Carmody. (Running Time: 5 hrs. 5 mins.). (Legend of Little Fur Ser.). (J). 2008. audio compact disk 57.95 (978-1-74214-077-3(7), 9781742140773) Pub: Bolinda Pubng AUS. Dist(s): Bolinda Pub Inc

Riddle of the Prairie Bride. unabr. ed. Kathryn Reiss. 4 CDs. (Running Time: 4 hrs. 30 mins.). (American Girl History Mysteries Ser.). 2005. audio compact disk 39.95 (978-1-4193-3832-8(3), C3273); 31.75 (978-1-4193-3543-3(X), 98009) Recorded Bks.
The beloved American Girl History Mysteries features intrepid girls faced with intriguing situations. The author of this installment, Kathryn Reiss, has received the ALA Best Book for Young Adults Award. In Riddle of the Prairie Bride, it's 1878 and Ida Deming and her papa are looking forward to meeting his mail-order bride. But is this woman really who she claims to be?.

Riddle of the Red Purse. unabr. ed. Patricia Reilly Giff. 1 read-along cass. (Polka Dot Private Eye Ser.). (J). (gr. 1-2). 1989. bk. 15.98 (978-0-8072-0166-4(9), FTR 135 SP, Listening Lib) Random Audio Pubg.
Dawn's chance to solve another mystery. The red purse she finds in the school yard contains a shopping list, some sandy, gritty material & 17 cents. Three people say the purse in theirs, but whose is it really?.

Riddle of the River. Catherine Shaw. 2008. 84.95 (978-1-4079-0172-5(9)); audio compact disk 89.95 (978-1-4079-0173-2(7)) Pub: Soundings Ltd GBR. Dist(s): Ulverscroft US

Riddle of the Sands. Erskine Childers. Read by Dermot Kerrigan. (Running Time: 9209 sec.). 2006. audio compact disk 17.98 (978-962-634-385-2(0), Naxos AudioBooks) Naxos.

Riddle of the Sands. unabr. ed. Erskine Childers. Read by David Fendig. 8 cass. (Running Time: 12 hrs.). 1997. 26.95 (978-1-55685-509-2(5), 509-5) Audio Bk Con.
This book is widely regarded as the first classic spy novel. Two unlikely sailing companions stumble into intrigue off the North Sea coast of pre-World War Germany.

Riddle of the Sands. unabr. ed. Erskine Childers. Read by Anton Lesser. 8 cass. (Running Time: 9 hrs. 50 min.). 1999. 34.95 (978-1-57270-103-8(X), F81103u) Pub: Audio Partners. Dist(s): PerseuPGW
While exploring the Frisian Coast in a yacht, two men are terrified to discover a carefully laid plan for the invasion of England.

Riddle of the Sands. unabr. ed. Erskine Childers. Read by Robert Whitfield. 8 cass. (Running Time: 11 hrs. 30 mins.). 1997. 56.95 (978-0-7861-1082-7(1), 1901) Blckstn Audio.
The tale of two Englishmen who discover German preparations for an invasion of England. Its richly authentic background of inshore sailing, its vivid evocation of the late 1890s, & its romantic tension, all combine with edge-of-the-seat suspense to make this a remarkably absorbing story.

Riddle of the Sands. unabr. ed. Erskine Childers. Read by Richard Heffer. 9 cass. (Running Time: 10 hrs. 20 mins.). (Isis Cassettes Ser.). (J). 2004. 76.95 (978-0-7531-1824-5(6)) Pub: ISIS Lrg Prnt GBR. Dist(s): Ulverscroft US

Riddle of the Sands. unabr. ed. Erskine Childers. Read by Walter Zimmerman & Jim Killavey. 7 cass. (Running Time: 11 hrs.). 1989. 36.00 incl. album. (C-49) Jimcin Record.
This story reflects the tensions & the sense of imminent danger that grew ever stronger as Europe moved toward World War I. Two Englishmen cruising among the Frisian Islands near the German coast uncover a carefully laid plan for the invasion of England.

Riddle of the Sands. unabr. ed. Erskine Childers. Narrated by Patrick Tull. 9 cass. (Running Time: 12 hrs.). 1989. 78.00 (978-1-55690-442-4(8), 89180E7) Recorded Bks.
The first spy thriller. It is 1903 & two men discover a secret invasion plot while sailing in the Baltic.

Riddle of the Sands. unabr. collector's ed. Erskine Childers. Read by Walter Zimmerman & J. Roberts. 8 cass. (Running Time: 12 hrs.). 1981. 64.00 (978-0-7366-3853-1(9), 9049) Books on Tape.
The book, written in 1902, reflects the tensions & the sense of imminent danger that grew stronger as Europe moved toward World War I. Two Englishmen cruising among the Frisian Islands near the German coast uncover a carefully laid plan for the invasion of England.

Riddle of the Sands: A Record of Secret Service. unabr. ed. Erskine Childers. Read by Simon Vance. (Running Time: 10 hrs. 5 mins.). 2009. 29.95 (978-1-4332-6770-3(5)); audio compact disk 90.00 (978-1-4332-6767-3(5)) Blckstn Audio.

Riddle of the Third Mile. unabr. ed. Colin Dexter. Read by Michael Pennington. 6 cass. (Running Time: 9 hrs.). (Inspector Morse Mystery Ser.: Bk. 6). 2000. 49.95 (978-0-7451-5895-2(1), CAB 672) Pub: Chivers Audio Bks GBR. Dist(s): AudioGO
When a dismembered torso is pulled from the Oxford Canal, Inspector Morse has to identify the body. His only clue is a shredded letter. But the letter soon leads Morse to the battle of El Alamein and two revengeful brothers, a seedy Soho bar, a mysterious woman, and an unmistakable murder.

Ride a Purple Pelican. unabr. ed. Jack Prelutsky. Read by Jack Prelutsky. 1 cass. (Running Time: 45 mins.). (J). (ps-3). 1988. 11.00 (978-0-8072-0158-9(8), FTR 131 CX, Listening Lib) Random Audio Pubg.
A delightful collection of crowd pleasing songs, performed by the poet himself & accompanied by Michael Isaacson.

Ride Away on Your Horses: Music, Now I'm One! John M. Feierabend & Luann Saunders. 1 cass. (First Steps in Music Ser.). (ENG., (J). (ps). 2000. 9.95 (978-1-57999-088-6(6)); audio compact disk 12.95 (978-1-57999-084-8(3)) Pub: GIA Pubns. Dist(s): IPG Chicago
The 67 songs & rhymes that are recorded on this CD come from all five of the books in the First Steps in Music series. These songs & rhymes are designed specifically for one-year-old children & include bounces such as "Ride Away on Your Horses," wiggles & tickles like "This Is the Father," simple songs like "Ring Around the Rosey," lullabies like "Go to Sleep, Go to Sleepy" & tapping & clapping favorites like "Higgley Piggley Pop".

Ride down Mount Morgan. unabr. ed. Arthur Miller. Read by Brian Cox et al. 2 CDs. (Running Time: 1 hr. 40 mins.). 2006. audio compact disk 25.95 (978-1-58081-335-8(6), LA 068) Pub: L A Theatre. Dist(s): NetLibrary CO

Ride for the Brand: The Poetry & Songs of Red Steagall. Red Steagall. 1 cass. 1994. 12.95 (978-0-87565-136-1(4)) Tex Christian.

Ride into Town see Your Own World

Ride of A Lifetime: Doing Business the Orange County Choppers Way. unabr. ed. Paul Teutul. Read by Walter Dixon. (Running Time: 4 hrs.). (ENG.). 2009. 24.98 (978-1-59659-383-1(0), GildAudio) Pub: Gildan Media. Dist(s): HachBkGrp

Ride of A Lifetime: Doing Business the Orange County Choppers Way. unabr. ed. Paul Teutul. Read by Matt Reis & Walter Dixon. (Running Time: 4 hrs. 30 mins.). (ENG.). 2009. audio compact disk 29.98 (978-1-59659-338-1(5), GildAudio) Pub: Gildan Media. Dist(s): HachBkGrp

Ride of Our Lives: Roadside Lessons of an American Family. unabr. ed. Mike Leonard. Narrated by Marc Cashman. 7 CDs. (Running Time: 7 hrs. 45 mins.). 2006. audio compact disk 53.55 (978-1-4159-2722-9(7)) Pub: Books on Tape. Dist(s): NetLibrary CO

Ride of Our Lives: Roadside Lessons of an American Family. unabr. ed. Mike Leonard. Narrated by Marc Cashman. 6 cass. (Running Time: 7 hrs. 45 mins.). 2006. 54.00 (978-1-4159-2721-2(9), BksonTape) Pub: Random Audio Pubg. Dist(s): Random

Ride or Die Chick: The Story of Treacherous & Teflon. unabr. ed. J. M. Benjamin. Read by Hassan Johnson. (Running Time: 5 hrs. 30 mins.). 2009. 29.95 (978-1-4417-2089-4(8)); 34.95 (978-1-4417-2085-6(5)); audio compact disk 29.95 (978-1-4417-2088-7(X)); audio compact disk 55.00 (978-1-4417-2086-3(3)) Blckstn Audio.

Ride the Dark Trail. unabr. ed. Louis L'Amour. Read by Terrence Mann. (Running Time: 21600 sec.). (Sacketts Ser.: No. 18). (ENG.). 2008. audio compact disk 25.95 (978-0-7393-4220-6(7), Random AudioBks) Pub: Random Audio Pubg. Dist(s): Random

Ride the Red Sun Down. unabr. ed. Tom Nichols. Read by Maynard Villers. 6 cass. (Running Time: 9 hrs.). 1996. 39.95 (978-1-55686-678-4(X)) Books in Motion.
Marty Keller, ex-Texas Ranger turned bounty hunter, is on the vengeance trail to find the three men who murdered his family.

***Ride the Red Trail.** Wayne D. Overholser. 2009. (978-1-60136-340-4(0)) Audio Holding.

Ride the River. unabr. ed. Louis L'Amour. Read by Jamie Rose. 5 CDs. (Running Time: 18000 sec.). (Sacketts Ser.: No. 5). (ENG.). 2006. audio compact disk 25.95 (978-0-7393-1903-1(5)) Pub: Random Audio Pubg. Dist(s): Random

Ride Through the Solar System. Perf. by Michele Stein & Bryan Smith. 1 cass. (J). (ps-5). 9.98 (288) MFLP CA.
Fasten your helmets tight to your heads & hold on tightly to your beds for a whoosh journey to outer space in this action-packed adventure story with lively songs loaded with facts about the planets.

Ride with Custer. unabr. ed. Tom Nichols. Read by Rusty Nelson. 8 cass. (Running Time: 10 hrs. 30 min.). (John Whyte Ser.: Bk. 2). 2001. 49.95 (978-1-55686-912-9(6)) Books in Motion.
Whyte serves in the Union forces at Gettysburg, with young General Custer. As the war continues, John Whyte is taken prisoner.

Ride with Me: The Florida Keys. unabr. ed. Barney Hicks et al. Read by Grover Gardner & Kimberly Schraf. 1 cass. (Running Time: 1 hrs. 50 min.). (Ride with Me Ser.). 1998. bk. 10.95 (978-0-942649-41-3(9)) RWM Assocs.
Original work - describes both the history of & current attractions in the Florida Keys.

Ride with Me - America, Vol. 1. Robert W. Magee. Read by Robert W. Magee. 1 cass. (Running Time: 90 min.). (Ride with Me Ser.). 1992. 10.95 (978-0-942649-23-9(0)) RWM Assocs.
Anecdotal discussion of American history, geography, legends & trivia. Stories taken from "Ride with Me" series.

Ride with Me - Atlanta Story. Robert W. Magee. Read by Kimberly Shraf & Michael Russotto. 1 cass. (Running Time: 90 min.). (Ride with Me Ser.). 1994. 17.95 (978-0-942649-27-7(3)) RWM Assocs.
Anecdotal discussion of the development & history of the city of Atlanta, Georgia.

Ride with Me - Boston - New Haven (I-95) Roderick I. Sweet & Sheilah Sweet. Read by John MacDonald & Flo Gibson. Ed. by Robert W. Magee. 1

cass. (Running Time: 1 hr. 30 min.). 1990. 10.95 (978-0-942649-11-6(7)) RWM Assocs.
Narrative on Rhode Island & Connecticut history - geography - legends - trivia keyed to highway markers on Interstate-95. Original work.

Ride with Me - Chincoteague & Assateague, Islands of Virginia. Robert W. Magee. Read by Kimberly Shraf & Michael Russotto. 1 cass. (Running Time: 1 hr. 30 mins.). (Ride with Me Ser.). 1995. 10.95 (978-0-942649-32-1(X)) RWM Assocs.
Anecdotal discussion of the development & history of the Chincoteague & Assateague islands.

Ride with Me - Connecticut (I-95 - I-91) Joanna Foster. Read by John MacDonald & Patricia Hicks. Ed. by Robert W. Magee. 1 cass. (Running Time: 1 hr. 20 min.). 1989. 10.95 (978-0-942649-10-9(9)) RWM Assocs.
Narrative on Connecticut history - geography - legends - trivia keyed to highway markers on Interstate-95. Original work.

Ride with Me - Delaware. Robert W. Magee. Read by Grover Gardner & Flo Gibson. 1 cass. (Running Time: 1 hr. 30 min.). 1989. 10.95 (978-0-942649-06-2(0)) RWM Assocs.
Narrative on history & development of the state of Delaware. Original work.

Ride with Me - East Texas (I-10) Doc Ball & Helen Ball. Read by Helen Ball & Grover Gardner. Ed. by Robert W. Magee. 1 cass. (Running Time: 1 hr. 30 min.). 1989. 10.95 (978-0-942649-09-3(5)) RWM Assocs.
Narrative on history & development of East Texas between Houston & San Antonio keyed to milepost markers on I-10. Original work.

Ride with Me - Georgia (I-95) Charles A. Briggs. Read by John MacDonald & Barnabas B. Hicks. Ed. by Robert W. Magee. 1 cass. (Running Time: 1 hr. 15 min.). 1989. 10.95 (978-0-942649-08-6(7)) RWM Assocs.
Narrative on Georgia history - geography - legends - trivia keyed to highway markers on Interstate-95. Original work.

Ride with Me - Hoosier State. Richard H. Magee & Mary Magee. Read by Michael Rusotto & Kimberly Schraf. Ed. by Robert W. Magee. 2 cass. (Running Time: 2 hrs. 20 min.). (Ride with Me Ser.). 1994. 17.95 Set. (978-0-942649-28-4(1)) RWM Assocs.
Anecdotal discussion of Indiana history, geography, legends & trivia keyed to milepost markers along Interstate-65 north to south.

Ride with Me - Indiana (I-80) Richard H. Magee & Mary Magee. Read by John MacDonald. Ed. by Robert W. Magee. 1 cass. (Running Time: 1 hr. 30 min.). 1991. 10.95 (978-0-942649-18-5(4)) RWM Assocs.
Narrative on history - geography - legends of Indiana keyed to milepost markers on I-80. Original work.

Ride with Me - Kentucky (I-75) John Durrell. Read by Grover Gardner. Ed. by Robert W. Magee. 2 cass. (Running Time: 2 hrs. 5 min.). (Ride with Me Ser.). 1992. 17.95 (978-0-942649-19-2(2)) RWM Assocs.
Anecdotal discussion of Kentucky history, geography, legends & trivia keyed to milepost markers along Interstate-75 north to south.

Ride with Me - Mount Vernon Story. Deborah Powers & Robert W. Magee. Read by John MacDonald et al. 1 cass. (Running Time: 90 min.). (Ride with Me Ser.). 1993. 10.95 (978-0-942649-24-6(9)) RWM Assocs.
Anecdotal discussion of history of Mount Vernon & of the Mount Vernon Ladies Association. North to south.

Ride with Me - North Florida (I-95) Barnabas B. Hicks. Read by Barnabas B. Hicks. Read by Grover Gardner. Ed. by Robert W. Magee. 1 cass. (Running Time: 1 hr. 30 min.). 1989. 10.95 (978-0-942649-07-9(9)) RWM Assocs.
Narrative on Florida history - geography - legends - trivia keyed to highway markers on Interstate-95. Original work.

Ride with Me - Ohio (I-80) Melinda M. Davies. Read by John MacDonald. Ed. by Robert W. Magee. 2 cass. (Running Time: 3 hrs.). 1991. 17.95 (978-0-942649-17-8(6)) RWM Assocs.
Narrative on history - geography - legends of Ohio keyed to milepost markers on I-80. Original work.

Ride with Me - Pennsylvania (I-81) Roberta S. Knapp. Read by John MacDonald. Ed. by Robert W. Magee. 1 cass. (Running Time: 1 hr. 30 min.). 1990. 10.95 (978-0-942649-14-7(1)) RWM Assocs.
Narrative on history & development of Pennsylvania Paso keyed to milepost markers on I-81. Original work.

Ride with Me - Shenandoah Valley (I-81) Charles A. Briggs. Read by Grover Gardner. Ed. by Robert W. Magee. 2 cass. (Running Time: 2 hrs.). 1991. 17.95 (978-0-942649-15-4(X)) RWM Assocs.
Narrative on history - geography - legends of Virginia's Shenandoah Valley keyed to milepost markers on I-81. Original work.

Ride with Me - Tennessee (I-75) Matthew Magee & Barbara Magee. Read by Grover Gardner. Ed. by Robert W. Magee. 1 cass. (Running Time: 90 min.). (Ride with Me Ser.). 1992. 10.95 (978-0-942649-20-8(6)) RWM Assocs.
Anecdotal discussion of Tennessee history, geography, legends & trivia keyed to milepost markers along Interstate-75 north to south.

Ride with Me - the Keystone State. Roberta S. Knapp. Read by John MacDonald. Ed. by Robert W. Magee. 2 cass. (Running Time: 2 hrs.). 1991. 17.95 (978-0-942649-16-1(8)) RWM Assocs.
Narrative on history - geography - legends of Pennsylvania keyed to milepost markers on I-80. Original work.

Ride with Me - the Peach State. Amy Durrell. Read by Grover Gardner. Ed. by Robert W. Magee. 2 cass. (Running Time: 1 hr. 15 min.). (Ride with Me Ser.). 1992. 17.95 (978-0-942649-21-5(4)) RWM Assocs.
Anecdotal discussion of Georgia history, geography, legends & trivia keyed to milepost markers along Interstate-75 north to south.

Ride with Me - the Pennsylvania Turnpike. Roberta S Knapp & Robert W. Magee. Read by Grover Gardner & Michael Russotto. 1 cass. (Running Time: 90 min.). (Ride with Me Ser.). 1992. 10.95 (978-0-942649-25-3(7)) RWM Assocs.
Anecdotal discussion of the development of the Pennsylvania Turnpike.

Ride with Me - West Texas (I-10) Doc Ball & Helen Ball. Read by Helen Ball & Gary DuPriest. Ed. by Robert W. Magee. 2 cass. (Running Time: 3 hrs.). 1990. 17.95 (978-0-942649-13-0(3)) RWM Assocs.
Narrative on history & development of West Texas between San Antonio & El Paso keyed to milepost markers on I-10. Original work.

Ride with Me - Williamsburg. Hal E. Gieseking. Read by Grover Gardner. Ed. by Robert W. Magee. 1 cass. (Running Time: 1 hr. 30 min.). 1990. 10.95 (978-0-942649-12-3(5)) RWM Assocs.
Narrative on history & development of Colonial Williamsburg. Original work.

Ride with Me, Mariah Montana. unabr. collector's ed. Ivan Doig. Read by Paul Shay. 10 cass. (Running Time: 15 hrs.). 1990. 80.00 (978-0-7366-1868-7(6), 2699) Books on Tape.
Spurred by the 1989 centennial of Montana's statehood & the recent loss of his wife. Jick McCaskill criss-crosses the state in a Winnebago with his photographer daughter, the strong-willed Mariah & her ex-husband Riley, an eccentric journalist. While Riley writes on-the-scene dispatches & Mariah takes photos of the places they visit. Jick recounts Montana's, as well as his family's good & bad times.

Ride with Olympy see World of James Thurber

Ride, You Tonto Raiders! Louis L'Amour. 2009. (978-1-60136-050-2(9)) Audio Holding.

Ride, You Tonto Raiders! Louis L'Amour. Narrated by John Randolph Jones. (Running Time: 2 hrs. 30 mins.). 2006. 12.95 (978-1-60083-058-7(7)) Iofy Corp.

Ride, You Tonto Raiders! unabr. ed. Louis L'Amour. Read by John Malloy. 1 cass. (Running Time: 1 hr. 30 min.). Dramatization. 1993. 7.95 (978-1-882071-28-9(X), 030) B-B Audio.
Matt Sabre was no trouble hunter, but when Billy Curtin called him a liar and went for his gun, Matt had to draw and fire. With his last dying breath, Curtin asked Matt to take $5000 to his wife Jenny on the Pivotrock... Jennys in trouble.

Rider from Lost Creek. unabr. ed. Louis L'Amour. 3 cass. (Running Time: 4 hrs. 30 mins.). (YA). 2006. 19.95 (978-0-7861-4399-3(1)); audio compact disk 19.95 (978-0-7861-7439-3(0)) Blckstn Audio.

Rider of Lost Creek. Louis L'Amour. Read by Jim Gough. (Running Time: 16200 sec.). 2006. 34.95 (978-0-7861-4563-8(3)); audio compact disk 36.00 (978-0-7861-7076-0(X)) Blckstn Audio.

Rider of the Ruby Hills. (Running Time: 16200 sec.). 2005. 34.95 (978-0-7861-3042-9(3)); audio compact disk 36.00 (978-0-7861-7946-6(5)) Blckstn Audio.

Rider of the Ruby Hills. unabr. ed. Read by Jim Gough. 5 CDs. (Running Time: 16200 sec.). 2005. audio compact disk 19.95 (978-0-7861-7988-6(0)); audio compact disk 29.95 (978-0-7861-8114-8(1)) Blckstn Audio.

Rider of the Ruby Hills. unabr. ed. Read by Jim Gough. 4 cass. (Running Time: 16200 sec.). 2005. 19.95 (978-0-7861-3438-0(0)) Blckstn Audio.

Rider of the Ruby Hills & Showdown Trail. unabr. ed. Read by Jim Gough. (Running Time: 32400 sec.). 2006. cass. & cass. 24.95 (978-0-7861-4681-9(8)); audio compact disk 25.95 (978-0-7861-6679-4(7)); audio compact disk & audio compact disk 29.95 (978-0-7861-7363-1(7)) Blckstn Audio.

***Riders.** Tim Winton & Tim Winton. Read by Stanley McGeagh. (Running Time: 10 hrs.). 2009. 84.99 (978-1-74214-295-1(8), 9781742142951) Pub: Bolinda Pubng AUS. Dist(s): Bolinda Pub Inc

Riders. unabr. ed. Tim Winton. Read by Stanley McGeagh. 9 CDs. (Running Time: 10 hrs.). 2001. audio compact disk 93.95 (978-1-74030-383-5(0)) Pub: Bolinda Pubng AUS. Dist(s): Bolinda Pub Inc

Riders. unabr. ed. Tim Winton. Read by Stanley McGeagh. 8 cass. (Running Time: 10 hrs.). 2004. 64.00 (978-1-86340-607-9(7), 551206) Bolinda Pubng AUS.
Fred Scully waits at the arrival gate of an international airport for his wife & seven-year-old daughter. After two years in Europe they are finally settling down, in the cottage in the Irish countryside that he's renovated by hand. Then the flight lands, the glass doors hiss open, & Scully's life begins to go down in flames.

Riders. unabr. ed. Tim Winton. Read by Stanley McGeagh. (Running Time: 10 hrs.). 2008. 43.95 (978-1-74214-023-0(8), 9781742140230) Pub: Bolinda Pubng AUS. Dist(s): Bolinda Pub Inc

Riders, Vol. 1. unabr. ed. Jilly Cooper. Read by Belinda Lang. 12 cass. (Running Time: 12 hrs.). 1995. 96.95 (978-0-7451-4292-0(3), CAB 975) AudioGO.
Set against the glamorous background of international showjumping, Riders charts the lives & loves of a tight-knit circle of star riders. The characters include: Rupert Campbell-Black, the attractive darling of the show ring; Jake Lovell, a half-gypsy, in whose hands the most difficult horse, or woman, becomes biddable; & brilliant Fenella Maxwell, the Bardot of the horse boxes. The settings include Wembley, Dublin, Rome & the Los Angeles Olympics.

Riders, Vol. 2. unabr. ed. Jilly Cooper. Read by Belinda Lang. 12 cass. (Running Time: 12 hrs.). 1995. 96.95 (978-0-7451-6523-3(0), CAB 1139) AudioGO.
The multi-stranded love story continues as the tight-knit circle of riders unite through raging ambition, bitter rivalry & the terror of failure. Billy Lloyd-Foxe is the best friend of Rupert Campbell-Black. Will Billy's rocky marriage survive while he's too busy competing? And what of Dino Ferranti, America's Golden Boy, whose obsessive desire with Fenella Maxwell in no way softens his determination to rob her of the gold medal.

Riders of Judgment. Ralph Compton. 4 cass. (Running Time: 6 hrs.). 2001. 24.95 (978-1-890990-79-4(5)) Otis Audio.
Danielle Strange & her brothers track the last of the men who killed her father into Mexico. But the murderer turns out to be a wealthy cattleman & he's hired every lowlife in the territory to put the Strange family in Boot Hill.

Riders of the Dawn. unabr. ed. Read by Jim Gough. 3 cass. (Running Time: 16200 sec.). 2006. 19.95 (978-0-7861-4550-8(1)); audio compact disk 19.95 (978-0-7861-7128-6(6)); audio compact disk 29.95 (978-0-7861-7568-0(0)) Blckstn Audio.

Riders of the Dawn. unabr. ed. Read by Jim Gough. (Running Time: 16200 sec.). 2006. 34.95 (978-0-7861-4644-4(3)); audio compact disk 36.00 (978-0-7861-6596-4(0)) Blckstn Audio.

***Riders of the Purple Sage.** Zane Grey. Read by Amy von Lecteur. 2009. 27.95 (978-1-60112-966-6(1)) Babblebooks.

Riders of the Purple Sage. Zane Grey. Narrated by Jim Roberts. (Running Time: 11 hrs.). 1991. 30.95 (978-1-59912-149-9(2)) Iofy Corp.

Riders of the Purple Sage. Zane Grey. Read by John Bolen. (Running Time: 11 hrs.). 2003. 29.95 (978-1-60083-631-2(3), Audiofy Corp) Iofy Corp.

Riders of the Purple Sage. Zane Grey. Read by John Hitchcock. (Running Time: 11 hrs. 13 mins.). 2003. 34.95 (978-1-59912-109-3(3), Audiofy Corp) Iofy Corp.

Riders of the Purple Sage. Zane Grey. Narrated by John Lescault. (Running Time: 40440 sec.). (Unabridged Classics in MP3 Ser.). (ENG.). 2008. audio compact disk 26.00 (978-1-58472-536-7(2), In Aud) Sound Room.

Riders of the Purple Sage. Zane Grey. Read by John Bolen. (Riders Ser.). (ENG.). 2003. audio compact disk 96.00 (978-1-4001-3062-7(X)) Pub: Tantor Media. Dist(s): IngramPubServ

Riders of the Purple Sage. abr. ed. Zane Grey. Perf. by St. Charles Players. 2 cass. (Running Time: 1 hr. 40 mins.). 2000. 16.95 (978-1-56994-519-3(5), 338314) Monterey Media Inc.
A lazy evening wind bends the sage as it passes. A lone coyote greets the dusk with a plaintive howl. Suddenly, the nearby canyon rings with the sound of echoing gunfire. There's been trouble for some time now. Beliefs & passion become intertwined with betrayal & violence.

Riders of the Purple Sage. unabr. ed. Zane Grey. Read by Pat Bottino. 9 cass. (Running Time: 13 hrs.). 1997. 62.95 (978-0-7861-1122-0(4), 1872) Blckstn Audio.
The setting is in Utah, in the year 1871. Jane Withersteen, a wealthy & contented rancher, befriends Bernie Venters, who happens to be a non-Mormon. This angers several Elders who pressure her to break with Bernie & then decree that she must marry the grim, arrogant Elder Tull. Jane resists & Tull & his band try to break her will by the use of more violent methods. Enter Lassiter, al loner from the North, who has a fearsome reputation as a deadly hand with a gun.

Riders of the Purple Sage. unabr. ed. Zane Grey. Read by Gene Engene. 12 cass. (Running Time: 12 hrs. 30 min.). 1989. 64.95 (978-1-55686-309-7(8), 309) Books in Motion.
Lassiter sides with the beautiful & gentle Jane Withersteen to help her protect her ranch from cattle rustlers & greedy men.

Riders of the Purple Sage. unabr. ed. Zane Grey. Read by John Bolen. (YA). 2007. 69.99 (978-1-59895-802-7(X)) Find a World.

Riders of the Purple Sage. unabr. ed. Zane Grey. Read by Jim Roberts. 9 cass. (Running Time: 13 hrs. 30 mins.). 1999. 62.95 (FS9-34272) Highsmith.

Riders of the Purple Sage. unabr. ed. Zane Grey. Read by Jim Roberts. 8 cass. (Running Time: 11 hrs. 55 min.). (YA). (gr. 9-12). 1991. 49.00 (C-222) Jimcin Record.
Zane Grey still ranks as the all-time best-selling author of westerns & this thrilling adventure is the most popular of his tales.

Riders of the Purple Sage. unabr. ed. Zane Grey. Narrated by Donald Buka. 9 cass. (Running Time: 12 hrs. 30 mins.). 1990. 78.00 (978-1-55690-443-1(6), 90076E7) Recorded Bks.
A woman's Utah ranch is threatened by a vengeful Mormon Elder. Jane Withersteen is a wealthy, contented rancher in the Mormon village of Cottonwoods, until the churchmen decree she must marry the arrogant Elder Tull. When she refuses, Tull & his band turn nasty using the valley's water as his leverage. That's when Lassiter rides into town, determined to teach Tull & his mob a lesson.

Riders of the Purple Sage. unabr. ed. Zane Grey. Read by John Hitchcock. 1 cd. (Running Time: 8 hrs 49 mins). 2002. audio compact disk 18.95 (978-1-58472-396-7(3), In Aud) Pub: Sound Room. Dist(s): Baker Taylor
MP3 format.

Riders of the Purple Sage. unabr. ed. Zane Grey. Narrated by John Bolen. 1 MP3 CD. (Running Time: 11 hrs. 18 mins.). (Riders Ser.). (ENG.). 2003. audio compact disk 23.00 (978-1-4001-5062-5(0)) Pub: Tantor Media. Dist(s): IngramPubServ
A gentile sage-rider is about to be whipped by the Mormans to coerce the rich and beautiful Jane Withersteen to marry against her will. In desperation Jane whispers the prayer, "whence cometh my help!" Just then an unlikely hero, the infamous gunfighter, Lassiter routs the persecutors and is drawn into this conflict on the Utah-Arizona border.The mysterious loner hires on to Jane's ranch. Through battles with gun slinging cattle-rustlers, cut-throats and the calculating Mormans, Lassiter unveils his tale of an endless search for a woman abducted long ago. Grey unfolds his story of seduction, secrecy, captivity and escape on the dust swept purple plains.Judged by critics to be Zane Grey's best novel, Riders of the Purple Sage changed the western genre when it was first published in 1912. This novel shows the gritty as well the gallant in a more candid portrayal of the west than had come before.

Riders of the Purple Sage. unabr. ed. Zane Grey. Narrated by John Bolen. (Running Time: 11 hrs. 30 mins. 0 sec.). (ENG.). 2009. 22.99 (978-1-4001-5917-8(2)); audio compact disk 32.99 (978-1-4001-0917-3(5)); audio compact disk 65.99 (978-1-4001-3917-0(1)) Pub: Tantor Media. Dist(s): IngramPubServ

Riders of the Purple Sage. unabr. collector's ed. Zane Grey. Read by Dan Lazar. 7 cass. (Running Time: 10 hrs. 30 mins.). 1981. 56.00 (978-0-7366-0475-8(8), 1450) Books on Tape.
A picturesque romance set in the unspoiled grandeur of Utah when Mormon authority ruled unchallenged. Jane Withersteen befriends a young rider on her range, Bernie Venters, a non-Mormon. Angered Elders resent this alliance, & put pressure on Jane to break with Bernie.

Riders of the Purple Sage: Abridged. (ENG.). 2007. (978-1-60339-059-0(6)); cd-rom & audio compact disk (978-1-60339-060-6(X)) Listenr Digest.

***Riders of the Purple Sage: The Restored Edition.** unabr. ed. Zane Grey. Read by Mark Bramhall. (Running Time: 12 hrs. 30 mins.). 2010. 29.95 (978-1-4417-7011-0(9)); 72.95 (978-1-4417-7008-0(9)); audio compact disk 105.00 (978-1-4417-7009-7(7)) Blckstn Audio.

Riders of the Silences. unabr. ed. Max Brand. Read by Dick Hill. (Running Time: 7 hrs.). 2007. 39.25 (978-1-4233-3478-1(7), 9781423334781, BADLE); 24.95 (978-1-4233-3477-4(9), 9781423334774, BAD) Brilliance Audio.

Riders of the Silences. unabr. ed. Max Brand. Read by Dick Hill. (Running Time: 7 hrs.). 2007. 39.25 (978-1-4233-3476-7(0), 9781423334767, Brinc Audio MP3 Lib); 24.95 (978-1-4233-3475-0(2), 9781423334750, Brilliance MP3) Brilliance Audio.

Riders of the Silences. unabr. ed. Max Brand. Read by Dick Hill. (Running Time: 7 hrs.). 2009. audio compact disk 19.99 (978-1-4418-0457-0(9), 9781441804570, Bril Audio CD Unabri); audio compact disk 59.97 (978-1-4418-0458-7(7), 9781441804587, BriAudCD Unabrid) Brilliance Audio.

Riders of the Three-Toed Horse: A RadioPlay. Garrett W. Vance & Birke R. Duncan. Based on a story by Garrett W. Vance. Narrated by Michael J. Leonard. Garrett W. Vance. (ENG.). 2009. audio compact disk 11.50 (978-0-9710582-4-8(5)) NW Folklore.

Riders on the Storm. unabr. ed. John Densmore. Read by John Densmore. 8 cass. (Running Time: 11 hrs. 40 mins.). 32.00 (978-0-9627387-9-1(4)) Seven Wolves.
The former drummer for the Doors traces his musical career & his partner's, the late Jim Morrison.

Riders to the Sea. John Millington Synge. 1 cass. Dramatization. 10.95 (SAC 8046) Spoken Arts.

Riders to the Sea & In the Shadow of the Glen. unabr. ed. John Millington Synge. Perf. by Radio Eirann Players. 10.95 (978-0-8045-0743-1(0), SAC 8046) Spoken Arts.

***Rides a Dread Legion: Book One of the Demonwar Saga.** unabr. ed. Raymond E. Feist. Read by John Meagher. (ENG.). 2010. (978-0-06-204295-8(5), Harper Audio); (978-0-06-206238-3(7), Harper Audio) HarperCollins Pubs.

Ridesharing Plans & Commuting Alternatives. Hosted by Nancy Pearlman. 1 cass. (Running Time: 30 min.). 10.00 (603) Educ Comm CA.

***Ridge.** unabr. ed. Michael Koryta. (Running Time: 10 hrs.). (ENG.). 2011. 29.98 (978-1-60941-234-0(6)) Pub: Hachet Audio. Dist(s): HachBkGrp

Ridgerunner. unabr. ed. Richard Ripley. Read by Gene Engene. 6 cass. (Running Time: 6 hrs. 30 min.). Dramatization. 1991. 39.95 (978-1-55686-358-5(6), 358) Books in Motion.
A highly publicized & mysterious hermit living in the inhospitable Selway-Bitterroot wilderness in central Idaho is chased & finally caught by the forest service.

***Ridiculous Bliss: Being Happy All the Time.** unabr. ed. Made for Success. Read by Matthew Ferry. (Made for Success Ser.). 2010. audio compact disk 34.95 (978-1-4417-6805-6(X)) Blckstn Audio.

***Ridiculous Bliss (Library Edition) Being Happy All the Time.** unabr. ed. Made for Success. Read by Matthew Ferry. (Running Time: 7 hrs. 30 mins.). (Made for Success Ser.). 2010. audio compact disk 105.00 (978-1-4417-6804-9(1)) Blckstn Audio.

Riding for the Brand. unabr. ed. Louis L'Amour. Read by Mark Murphey & Jill Fine. 2 cass. (Running Time: 3 hrs.). 1986. 14.95 (978-0-931969-19-5(0), 019) Book of the Rd.
Colorful & sweeping stories of cattle roundups, Indian war parties attacking wagon trains, discoveries of gold & robberies by armed gangs of outlaws. These are the yarns that were told around the campfires by cowhands, drifters, prospectors & bandits.

Riding for the Brand; McQueen of the Tumbling K; Law of the Desert Born. abr. ed. Louis L'Amour. 2 cass. (Running Time: 3 hrs.). (Louis L'Amour Collector Ser.:). 2000. 7.95 (978-1-57815-096-0(5), 1067, Media Bks Audio) Media Bks NJ.

Riding for the Brand; McQueen of the Tumbling K; Law of the Desert Born; Man Riding West. abr. ed. Louis L'Amour. 3 cass. (Running Time: 5 hrs.). (Great Mysteries - Louis L'Amour Ser.). 2001. audio compact disk 11.99 (978-1-57815-526-2(6), Media Bks Audio) Media Bks NJ.

Riding Freedom. unabr. ed. Pam Muñoz Ryan. Narrated by Melissa Hughes. 2 CDs. (Running Time: 2 hrs. 30 mins.). (J). (gr. 4-6). 2009. audio compact disk 34.95 (978-0-9814890-4-9(4)) Audio Bkshelf.

Riding in Cars with Boys: Confessions of a Bad Girl Who Makes Good. Beverly Donofrio. Narrated by Christina Moore. 6 CDs. (Running Time: 5 hrs. 30 mins.). audio compact disk 48.00 (978-1-4025-3497-3(3)) Recorded Bks.

Riding in Cars with Boys: Confessions of a Bad Girl Who Makes Good. Beverly Donofrio. 4 cass. (Running Time: 5 hrs. 45 mins.). 2004. 24.99 (978-0-7887-8963-2(5), 00474) Recorded Bks.

Riding in Cars with Boys: Confessions of a Bad Girl Who Makes Good. unabr. ed. Beverly Donofrio. Narrated by Christina Moore. 5 cass. (Running Time: 5 hrs. 30 mins.). 2001. 48.00 (978-0-7887-8853-6(1)) Recorded Bks.
Once her strict family told her she couldn't go to college, Beverly lost interest in everything except smoking, drinking and rebelling against authority. Learn how Beverly eventually turned her life around.

Riding Lessons. unabr. ed. Sara Gruen. Read by Maggi-Meg Reed. (YA). 2008. 54.99 (978-1-60514-826-7(1)) Find a World.

Riding Lessons. unabr. ed. Sara Gruen. Read by Maggi-Meg Reed & Maggie-Meg Reed. 9 CDs. (Running Time: 10 hrs. 30 mins.). (ENG., 2008. audio compact disk 34.95 (978-1-59887-648-2(1), 1598876481) Pub: HighBridge. Dist(s): Workman Pub

Riding Out of Your Mind. unabr. ed. Robert J. Rotella & Chrystine Jones. 3 Cass. (Running Time: 120 min.). 1985. 39.95 incl. bk. Creative Mgmt.
For dedicated equestrians who wish to reach the heights of riding excellence through mental discipline. Rotella says "Competitive riding makes enormous demands on the mind & emotions. The key to competing at your best is to maintain confidence, concentration & composure". Chrystine Jones, an international, rider emphasizes, "The mental aspect of riding is an integral part of the successful competitor & for all who want to excel".

Riding the Bomb. unabr. ed. Charles R. Grizzle. Read by Maynard Villers. 8 cass. (Running Time: 8 hrs. 42 min.). 1995. 49.95 (978-1-55686-634-0(8)) Books in Motion.
Experiences of people overtaken by war are not just war stories, instead they are adventures of courage, endurance & amazing survival. Here are a few stories of those who survived terror.

Riding the Bullet. unabr. ed. Stephen King. Read by Josh Hamilton. 2 CDs. (Running Time: 20 hrs. 0 mins. 0 sec.). (ENG.). 2002. audio compact disk 20.00 (978-0-7435-2587-9(6)) Pub: S&S Audio. Dist(s): S and S Inc
A college student's mother is dying in a Maine hospital. When he hitches a ride to see her, the driver is not who he appears to be.

Riding the Bullet. unabr. ed. Stephen King. Read by Josh Hamilton. 2006. 11.95 (978-0-7435-6338-3(7), Audioworks) Pub: S&S Audio. Dist(s): S and S Inc

Riding the Iron Rooster: By Train Through China. unabr. collector's ed. Paul Theroux. Read by Michael Prichard. 12 cass. (Running Time: 18 hrs.). 1989. 96.00 (978-0-7366-1619-5(5), 2479) Books on Tape.
In Riding the Iron Rooster, Theroux's practiced eye, adventurous spirit & rich prose produce a vivid memoir, full of people & talk - warm, outspoken conversations about the private life of China today, the Cultural Revolution & Mao; about writing novels, growing fruit & the details of everyday life; about discontent, patriotism & the possibility of a better life in America.

Riding the Rap. unabr. ed. Elmore Leonard. Read by Alexander Adams. 7 cass. (Running Time: 10 hrs. 30 min.). 1995. 42.00 (978-0-7366-2973-7(4), 3664) Books on Tape.
An oft-missing bookie disappears again & a no-nonsense U.S. Marshal must track him down. Witty, punchy dialogue.

***Riding the Rap.** unabr. ed. Elmore Leonard. Read by Frank Muller. 2010. (978-0-06-199385-5(9), Harper Audio); (978-0-06-199767-9(6), Harper Audio) HarperCollins Pubs.

Riding the Rap. unabr. ed. Elmore Leonard. Narrated by Frank Muller. 5 cass. (Running Time: 7 hrs.). 1995. 44.00 (978-0-7887-0334-8(X), 94526E7) Recorded Bks.
Supercool Chip Ganz has concocted the crime of the century: take rich men hostage & hold them chained & blindfolded until they are willing to pay for their release. But before he gets away with the money, he'll have to match wits & guns with coal miner-turned-federal marshal Raylan Givens.

Riding the Tiger of Change. Hazel Henderson. 3 cass. 24.00 (OC146) Sound Horizons AV.

Riding the Wild One Home: The Journey of Spiritual Awakening. Ellen Grace O'Brian. 5 cassettes. (Running Time: 4 hours). 2003. 21.95 (978-0-9660518-5-8(8), CSE Press); audio compact disk 21.95 (978-0-9660518-8-9(2), CSE Press) Ctr for Spirit.

Riding the Winds of Change. F. G. Rodgers. 1 cass. 8.95 (978-0-88684-077-8(5)) Listen USA.

Riding to the Tigris. unabr. collector's ed. Freya Stark. Read by Donada Peters. 6 cass. (Running Time: 6 hrs.). 1991. 36.00 (978-0-7366-1991-2(7), 2807) Books on Tape.
Journey on horseback through Turkey with this insightful & gifted travel writer.

Riding Trees: Denny & I. unabr. ed. Interview with Mike Anderson. 1 cass. (Running Time: 42 min.). (J). (gr. 2-12). 1996. 10.00 (978-1-929050-01-7(1)) MW Prods.
Stories of growing up in a small town in Illinois. Four stories & one song.

Ridley Pearson: The Art of Deception, the Body of David Hayes, Cut & Run. abr. ed. Ridley Pearson. Read by Dick Hill. (Running Time: 18 hrs.). 2007. audio compact disk 34.95 (978-1-4233-2321-1(1), 9781423323211, BACD) Brilliance Audio.

Ridley Pearson: The Pied Piper, the First Victim, Parallel Lies. abr. ed. Ridley Pearson. Read by Dale Hull et al. (Running Time: 12 hrs.). 2006. audio compact disk 34.95 (978-1-59737-718-8(X), 9781597377188, BACD) Brilliance Audio.
The Pied Piper: In Seattle, they're calling him The Pied Piper - someone who comes in the night and takes children away. To newly promoted police lieutenant Lou Boldt and police psychologist Daphne Matthews, it's clear this isn't about a single lunatic or random kidnappings: these crimes are well orchestrated, well executed, and, most chilling of all, occurring in cities across the country. The First Victim: A shipping container washed ashore leads Seattle television news anchor Stevie McNeal and reporter friend Melissa on the trail of a scam involving the importation of illegal aliens. A career stepping-stone for McNeal, the investigation puts her at cross-purposes with the Seattle Police Department's Lou Boldt and Sergeant John LaMoia. When Melissa disappears, perhaps at the hands of the Chinese Triad, McNeal turns from foe to ally and teams up with the detectives on an investigation that takes them from Seattle's docklands to the offices of the INS. Parallel Lies: A grieving man is on a mission to bring down the railroad company he blames for his wife and children's deaths - no matter who else dies in the process. Tyler, the ex-cop who is looking to redeem himself after being suspended from the force, will stop at nothing to catch the perpetrator.

Ridley Pearson Three Books in One Collection: Middle of Nowhere/the Art of Deception/Parallel Lies. abr. ed. (Running Time: 64800 sec.). 2005. 29.95 (978-1-59737-050-9(9), 9781597370509) Brilliance Audio.
Middle of Nowhere (Narrator: Ridley Pearson, Engineer: Mountain Beach): The "blue flu" has struck the Seattle Police Force and the majority of officers are on an unofficial strike. When a string of robberies and the brutal near-murder of a female cop descend on the city, the pressure of being a nearly one-man operation threatens Lou Boldt's psyche and his marriage. With the help of Daphne Matthews and Sergeant John LaMoia, Boldt comes to realize that the robberies, assaults, and strike are somehow connected - and that his life is now in very real danger. The Art of Deception (Narrator: Dick Hill, Engineer: Mike Council): A troubled Mary Ann Walker takes a nosedive off a bridge. Seattle's police department macho man John LaMoia takes the call, along with the beauteous cop psychologist Daphne Matthews. They suspect her boyfriend, known to beat Mary Ann. But the case somehow becomes too slippery to close. Lou Boldt, the supervising officer, is entangled in a conundrum of his own: two women have disappeared and a road crew worker's death may have a connection to the missing women. Parallel Lies (Narrator: Dick Hill, Engineer: Mike Council): A grieving man is on a mission to bring down the railroad company he blames for his wife and children's deaths - no matter who else dies in the process. Tyler, the ex-cop who is looking to redeem himself after being suspended from the force, will stop at nothing to catch the perpetrator.

***Rieding - Concerto in B Minor for Violin & Orchestra Op. 35.** Composed by Oscar Rieding. (ENG.). 2006. pap. bk. 19.95 (978-3-905477-40-5(8), 3905477408) Pub: Dowani Intl LIE. Dist(s): H Leonard

***Rieding: Concerto in G Major, Op. 24: For Violin & Piano.** Ed. by Herbert Scherz. Composed by Oskar Rieding. (ENG.). 2008. pap. bk. 19.95 (978-3-905477-74-0(2), 3905477742) Pub: Dowani Intl LIE. Dist(s): H Leonard

Rife Microscope on Something's Happening! Bud Curtis. 2 cass. (Roy Tuckman Interview Ser.). 18.00 set. (A0495-89) Sound Photosyn.
Bud Curtis talks with Roy of the breakthrough medical & scientific inventions of Royal Raymond Rife whose suppressed work includes a 50,000 power optical natural light microscope & virus killing "ray".

Rife Ray Update. Bud Curtis. 1 cass. (Roy Tuckman Interview Ser.). 9.00 (A0469-89) Sound Photosyn.

Riffs of the Magi: A Jazzplay Christmas. Hosted by John Boutte. 1 CD. (Running Time: 1 hr.). 2001. audio compact disk 15.95 (EXIT004) Lodestone Catalog.
It's Christmas Eve & this night an aging jazz singer tells her daughter about her beginnings the jams & juke joints & rent parties that set her on the path of jazz.

Rifle. unabr. ed. Gary Paulsen. Narrated by Norman Dietz. 2 pieces. (Running Time: 2 hrs.). (gr. 6 up). 1997. 19.00 (978-0-7887-0529-8(6), 94724E7) Recorded Bks.
In this wonderfully crafted novel, a rifle, not the people who come to own it, is the main character. Follows the rifle from its creation in 1768 to a shattering event as it roars back to life in 1994.

Rifles for Watie. unabr. ed. Harold Keith. Narrated by Tom Stechschulte. 9 pieces. (Running Time: 12 hrs. 15 mins.). (gr. 8 up). 1999. 81.00 (978-0-7887-3209-6(9), 95754E7) Recorded Bks.
Sixteen-year-old Jefferson Davis Bussey can hardly wait to leave his Kansas farm & join the Union forces. As his friends die in battle, however, he discovers there is little glory in war. And when he infiltrates the enemy as a spy, he wonders if he will be able to betray his new rebel companion.

Rifles for Watie. unabr. ed. Harold Keith. Read by Tom Stechschulte. 9 cass. (Running Time: 12 hrs. 15 mins.). (YA). (gr. 8). 2000. pap. bk. & stu. ed. 94.20 (978-0-7887-3192-1(0), 40927X4) Recorded Bks.

Rifles for Watie. unabr. ed. Harold Keith. Narrated by Tom Stechschulte. 11 CDs. (Running Time: 12 hrs. 15 mins.). (gr. 8 up). 2000. audio compact disk 94.00 (978-0-7887-3732-9(5), C1103E7) Recorded Bks.

Rifles for Watie, Class Set. unabr. ed. Harold Keith. Read by Tom Stechschulte. 9 cass. (Running Time: 12 hrs. 15 mins.). (YA). 1999. 151.30 (978-0-7887-3238-6(2), 46894) Recorded Bks.

Rifts, Runs & Embellishments. unabr. ed. Jeannie Deva. 1 cass. (Running Time: 1 hr.). (Deva Method Advanced Vocal Exercises Ser.: Vol. 4). 1996. 12.00 (978-1-882224-18-0(3)) Jeannie Deva.
Fourth of a series of advanced vocal exercise tapes that complement "The Contemporary Vocalist Improvement Course".

Rigby PM Plus Software Green Level. Created by Rigby. (Pm Plus Ser.). (J). (gr. k-1). 2002. audio compact disk 49.00 (978-0-7578-5975-5(5)) Rigby Educ.

Rigby PM Shared: A Kitten for the King, Level Green 3 in 1 Package. Brenda Parkes. Illus. by Phillip Webb. 2006. pap. bk. 115.07 (978-1-4189-4652-4(4)) Rigby Educ.

Rigby PM Shared: Bears, Level Blue 3 in 1 Package. Brenda Parkes. 2006. pap. bk. 115.07 (978-1-4189-4651-7(6)) Rigby Educ.

Rigby PM Shared: Counting Clues, Level Red 3 in 1 Package. Brenda Parkes. 2006. pap. bk. 115.07 (978-1-4189-4647-0(8)) Rigby Educ.

Rigby PM Shared Fiction: Kitten for the King, Level Green. Created by Rigby. 2006. audio compact disk 13.33 (978-1-4189-4642-5(7)) Rigby Educ.

Rigby PM Shared Fiction: Yumbo Gumbo, Level Blue. Created by Rigby. 2006. audio compact disk 13.33 (978-1-4189-4640-1(0)) Rigby Educ.

Rigby PM Shared Fiction: Zoom Zap!, Level Magenta. Created by Rigby. 2006. audio compact disk 13.33 (978-1-4189-4634-0(6)) Rigby Educ.

Rigby PM Shared: Going to Grandma's, Level Yellow 3 in 1 Package. Brenda Parkes. 2006. pap. bk. 115.07 (978-1-4189-4649-4(4)) Rigby Educ.

Rigby PM Shared: How Frogs Grow, Level Magenta 3 in 1 Package. Brenda Parkes. 2006. pap. bk. 115.07 (978-1-4189-4645-6(1)) Rigby Educ.

Rigby PM Shared: Incredible Insects, Level Green 3 in 1 Package. Brenda Parkes. 2006. pap. bk. 115.07 (978-1-4189-4653-1(2)) Rigby Educ.

Rigby PM Shared Readers: Going to Grandma's. Created by Rigby. 2006. audio compact disk 13.33 (978-1-4189-4639-5(7)) Rigby Educ.

Rigby PM Shared Readers: How Frogs Grow. Created by Rigby. 2006. audio compact disk 13.33 (978-1-4189-4635-7(4)) Rigby Educ.

Rigby PM Shared Readers: When Barney Went to the Vet. Created by Rigby. 2006. audio compact disk 13.33 (978-1-4189-4638-8(9)) Rigby Educ.

Rigby PM Shared: the No Goat Zone, Level Red 3 in 1 Package. Brenda Parkes. Illus. by Judith Rossell. 2006. pap. bk. 115.07 (978-1-4189-4646-3(X)) Rigby Educ.

Rigby PM Shared: When Barney Went to the Vet, Level Yellow 3 in 1 Package. Brenda Parkes. Illus. by Rae Dale. 2006. pap. bk. 115.07 (978-1-4189-4648-7(6)) Rigby Educ.

Rigby PM Shared: Yumbo Gumbo, Level Blue 3 in 1 Package. Brenda Parkes. Illus. by Jane Wallace-Mitchell. 2006. pap. bk. 115.07 (978-1-4189-4650-0(8)) Rigby Educ.

Rigby PM Shared: Zoon Zap!, Level Magenta 3 in 1 Package. Brenda Parkes. Illus. by Roberto Fino. 2006. pap. bk. 115.07 (978-1-4189-4644-9(3)) Rigby Educ.

***Rigged.** unabr. ed. Ben Mezrich. Read by Ben Mezrich. (ENG.). 2007. (978-0-06-155519-0(3)); (978-0-06-155523-7(1)) HarperCollins Pubs.

Rigged: The True Story of an Ivy League Kid Who Changed the World of Oil, from Wall Street to Dubai. unabr. ed. Ben Mezrich. Read by Ben Mezrich. (YA). 2007. 49.99 (978-1-60252-813-0(6)) Find a World.

Rigged: The True Story of an Ivy League Kid Who Changed the World of Oil, from Wall Street to Dubai. unabr. ed. Ben Mezrich. Read by Ben Mezrich. 2007. audio compact disk 34.95 (978-0-06-136359-7(6), Harper Audio) HarperCollins Pubs.

Rigged: The True Story of an Ivy League Kid Who Changed the World of Oil, from Wall Street to Dubai. unabr. ed. Ben Mezrich. Read by Ben Mezrich. 2008. audio compact disk 19.95 (978-0-06-167288-0(2), Harper Audio) HarperCollins Pubs.

Riggin' up the Lights. Contrib. by Johnathan Crumpton et al. Prod. by Craig Adams. (ENG.). 2004. audio compact disk 24.99 (978-5-559-41388-4(7), Brentwood-Benson Music) Brentwood Music.

Right & Wrong Spelled Out: Exodus 19. Ed Young. 1985. 4.95 (978-0-7417-1427-5(2), 427) Win Walk.

Right & Wrong Thinking Series. Kenneth E. Hagin. 3 cass. 1994. 12.00 Set. (70H) Faith Lib Pubns.

Right Approach. Swami Amar Jyoti. 1 dolby cass. 1980. 9.95 (K-30) Truth Consciousness.
Humility, the scientific basis for receiving. Learning how to let go. Seriousness about the Goal. Finding our center & being there.

Right Attitude. Swami Amar Jyoti. 1 dolby cass. 1986. 9.95 (M-66) Truth Consciousness.
The pure & proper tuned-in perspective, a must for receiving. Nonexistence of darkness. Coming out of the veil of ignorance.

Right Attitude about Healing. Mac Hammond. 1 cass. (Running Time: 1 hr.). 2005. 5.00 (978-1-57399-211-4(9)); audio compact disk 5.00 (978-1-57399-260-2(7)) Mac Hammond.

Right Attitude to Rain. Alexander McCall Smith. Narrated by Davina Porter. (Running Time: 32400 sec.). (Isabel Dalhousie Ser.: No. 3). 2006. 24.99 (978-1-4281-0850-9(5)) Recorded Bks.

Right Attitude to Rain. Alexander McCall Smith. Read by Davina Porter. (Running Time: 32400 sec.). (Isabel Dalhousie Ser.: No. 3). 2006. audio compact disk 29.99 (978-1-4281-0548-5(4)) Recorded Bks.

Right Brain Healing: the Jesus Nature. John E. Bradshaw. (Running Time: 10800 sec.). 2008. audio compact disk 100.00 (978-1-57388-217-0(8)) J B Media.

Right Brained Guide to a Left Brained Industry: Marketing & Buying Fine Art Online. Marques Vickers. 2002. cd-rom & audio compact disk 19.95 (978-0-9706530-2-4(6)) Marquis Pubng.

Right Call. unabr. ed. Kathy Herman. Narrated by Tim Lundeen. (Running Time: 9 hrs. 58 mins. 47 sec.). (Sophie Trace Ser.). (ENG.). 2010. 20.99 (978-1-60814-619-2(7)); audio compact disk 29.99 (978-1-59859-673-1(X)) Oasis Audio.

Right Conduct & How to Promote It. 1 cass. (Running Time: 1 hr.). 12.99 (180) Yoga Res Foun.

Right Eye of the Commander see Luck of Roaring Camp & Other Stories

***Right Fight: How Great Leaders Use Healthy Conflict to Drive Performance, Innovation, & Value.** unabr. ed. Saj-nicole Joni & Damon Beyer. Narrated by Laural Merlington. (Running Time: 6 hrs. 0 mins.). 2010. 13.99 (978-1-4001-8468-2(1)); 24.99 (978-1-4001-6468-4(0)); audio compact disk 34.99 (978-1-4001-1468-9(3)); audio compact disk 69.99 (978-1-4001-4468-6(X)) Pub: Tantor Media. Dist(s): IngramPubServ

Right from the Beginning. unabr. ed. Patrick J. Buchanan. Read by Michael Wells. 10 cass. (Running Time: 15 hrs.). 1991. 69.95 (978-0-7861-0215-0(2), 1189) Blckstn Audio.
"Right from the Beginning" is the personal memoir of Pat Buchanan, the story of how the most controversial conservative in America got where he is today & how he came to believe as he does.

Right Hand Arranging Techniques. 1 cass. 19.95 Incl. right-hand style sheet. (V-3) Duane Shinn.
Arranging techniques for your right-hand - Melodrama; off-beat arps; cross-hands; reversed register; stuffed octaves; color-tone undernotes; octave-6ths; chord note undernotes; octave-3rds. If you've ever envied the pianist who can switch from one style to another effortlessly, this will show you how.

Right Hand of Evil. abr. ed. John Saul. Read by Lee Meriwether. 3 cass. 1999. 24.00 (FS9-50897) Highsmith.

Right Hand of Evil. unabr. ed. John Saul. Read by Bill Weideman. 7 cass. (Running Time: 11 hrs.). 1999. 39.95 (978-1-56740-419-7(7), 1567404197, BAU); 73.25 (978-1-56740-645-0(9), 1567406459, Unabridge Lib Edns) Brilliance Audio.
Just as their troubled marriage is reaching the breaking point, Ted and Janet Conway inherit a home that has been in the family for more than a century. Eager to make a new beginning, the Conways and their three children head for the promise of a better life in the small Louisiana town of St. Albans. But within the long-abandoned, sprawling Victorian manse lies the dark history of the Conway name - a grim bloodline poisoned by suicide, strange disappearances, voodoo rituals, and rumors of murder. The Conways know nothing of the soul-shattering secrets that, once revealed, will threaten to consume every living soul in their fiery wake. For with each generation of the Conway name comes a hellish day of reckoning.

Right Hand of Evil. unabr. ed. John Saul. Read by Bill Weideman. (Running Time: 11 hrs.). 2006. 39.25 (978-1-4233-1370-0(4), 9781423313700, BADLE); 24.95 (978-1-4233-1369-4(0), 9781423313694, BAD); 39.25 (978-1-4233-1368-7(2), 9781423313687, Brinc Audio MP3 Lib); 24.95 (978-1-4233-1367-0(4), 9781423313670, Brilliance MP3); audio compact disk 102.25 (978-1-4233-1366-3(6), 9781423313663, BriAudCD Unabrid); audio compact disk 38.95 (978-1-4233-1365-6(8), 9781423313656, Bril Audio CD Unabri) Brilliance Audio.

Right Hand of Evil. unabr. ed. John Saul. Read by Bill Weideman. 7 cass. 1999. 39.95 (FS9-43908) Highsmith.

Right Ho, Jeeves. P. G. Wodehouse. Contrib. by Michael Hordern & Richard Briers. 3 CDs. (Running Time: 3 hrs. 20 mins.). (Jeeves & Wooster Ser.).

2006. audio compact disk 39.95 (978-0-7927-3994-4(9), BBCD 145) AudioGO.

***Right Ho, Jeeves.** P. G. Wodehouse. Narrated by Richard Briers & Michael Hordern. (Running Time: 3 hrs. 22 mins. 0 sec.). (ENG., 2010. audio compact disk 29.95 (978-0-563-52799-2(4)) Pub: AudioGO. Dist(s): Perseus Dist

***Right Ho, Jeeves.** P. G. Wodehouse. Read by Alfred 9000. 2009. 27.95 (978-1-60112-968-0(8)) Babblebooks.

Right Ho, Jeeves. abr. ed. P. G. Wodehouse. Narrated by Martin Jarvis. 4 CDs. (Running Time: 5 hrs. 7 mins. 10 sec.). (ENG.). 2009. audio compact disk 26.95 (978-1-934997-35-2(8)) Pub: CSAWord. Dist(s): PerseuPGW

Right Ho, Jeeves. unabr. ed. P. G. Wodehouse. Read by Ian Carmichael. 5 cass. (Running Time: 6 hrs. 54 mins.). (Jeeves & Wooster Ser.). 2004. 27.95 (978-1-57270-422-0(5)) Pub: Audio Partners. Dist(s): PerseuPGW
When Jeeves suggests dreamy, soulful Gussie Fink-Nottle don scarlet tights and false beard to win over soppy Madeline Bassett, Bertie Wooster doubts this is the way to get his friend hitched. Meanwhile, Bertie's eccentric Aunt Dahlia asks him to hand out prizes at the Market Snodsbury Grammar School, which he's sure he would have to get drunk to do. Complicating maters, Madeline invites Gussie to stay at her friend's house in the country. The friend turns out to be Bertie's cousin Angela and the house - Aunt Dahlia's. Thinking things have definitely gotten out of hand, Bertie takes Jeeves off the case, acting on his own plan to bring Gussie and Madeline together. But when things go disastrously wrong, who can Bertie turn to but Jeeves? Acclaimed actor Ian Carmichael brings comic flair to this rollicking tale by the man The Times (London) called a "brilliantly funny writer.".

Right Ho, Jeeves. unabr. ed. P. G. Wodehouse. Read by Ian Carmichael. Narrated by Jonathan Cecil. 6 CDs. (Jeeves & Wooster Ser.). (ENG.). 2004. audio compact disk 29.95 (978-1-57270-423-7(3)) Pub: AudioGO. Dist(s): Perseus Dist

Right Ho, Jeeves. unabr. ed. P. G. Wodehouse. Read by Frederick Davidson. 6 cass. (Running Time: 8 hrs. 30 mins.). (Jeeves & Wooster Ser.). 1992. 44.95 (978-0-7861-0363-8(9), 1320) Blckstn Audio.
This is a complex case fo the Wooster intellect. Gussie Fink-Nottle (he of the newtspotting disposition) falls in love with Madeline (the-stars-are-God's-daisy-chain) Bassett & has lost his chump. Cousin Angela falls out of love with Tuppy Glossop & gives a passable imitation of a woman scorned. Aunt Dahlia is in a stew over the acckers, & worst of all, Jeeves has passed sentence of death on Bertie's tout ce qui'il est chic white mess jacket.

Right Ho, Jeeves, unabr. ed. P. G. Wodehouse. Narrated by Alexander Spencer. 5 cass. (Running Time: 6 hrs.). (Jeeves & Wooster Ser.). 1988. 44.00 (978-1-55690-444-8(4), 88070E7) Recorded Bks.
Bertie Wooster tries unsuccessfully to solve the romantic entanglements of his friends.

Right Is Wrong: How the Lunatic Fringe Hijacked America, Shredded the Constitution, & Made Us All Less Safe (And What You Need to Know to End the Madness) abr. ed. Arianna S. Huffington. Read by Arianna S. Huffington. 5 CDs. (Running Time: 6 hrs. 30 mins.). (ENG.). 2008. audio compact disk 29.95 (978-0-7393-6987-6(3), Random AudioBks) Pub: Random Audio Pubg. Dist(s): Random

Right Livelihood: Stewardship, Managing by Values, & Leadership & the New Science. Peter Block et al. Read by Peter Block et al. 6 cass. (Running Time: 9 hrs.). 1998. bk. 49.95 (978-1-57453-286-9(3)) Audio Lit.
Three different titles concerning livelihood.

Right Livelihood on the Path of Soul Purpose. Christopher Love. Read by Christopher Love. 1 cass. (Running Time: 30 min.). 10.95 (978-1-891820-09-0(5)) World Sangha Pubg.
Self-hypnosis meditation for healing, self-improvement & realizing our full & powerful potential as spiritual beings.

Right Man: The Surprise Presidency of George W. Bush - An Inside Account. unabr. ed. David Frum. Read by Dan Cashman. 8 cass. (Running Time: 12 hrs.). 2004. 34.95 (978-1-59007-411-4(4)) Pub: New Millenn Enter. Dist(s): PerseuPGW

Right Motive - the Right Power. George King. 2007. audio compact disk (978-0-937249-48-2(3)) Aetherius Soc.

Right Next Door: The Courtship of Carol Sommars; Father's Day. unabr. ed. Debbie Macomber. Read by Angela Dawe. (Running Time: 11 hrs.). 2010. audio compact disk 29.99 (978-1-4418-1969-7(X), 9781441819697, Bril Audio CD Unabri) Brilliance Audio.

***Right Next Door: The Courtship of Carol Sommars; Father's Day.** unabr. ed. Debbie Macomber. Read by Angela Dawe. (Running Time: 11 hrs.). 2010. 24.99 (978-1-4418-1971-0(1), 9781441819710, Brilliance MP3); 39.97 (978-1-4418-1972-7(X), 9781441819727, Brlnc Audio MP3 Lib); 24.99 (978-1-4418-1973-4(8), 9781441819734, BAD); 39.97 (978-1-4418-1974-1(6), 9781441819741, BADLE); audio compact disk 87.97 (978-1-4418-1970-3(3), 9781441819703, BriAudCD Unabrid) Brilliance Audio.

Right Now: A 12-Step Program for Defeating the Obama Agenda. unabr. ed. Michael Steele. Narrated by Richard Allen. (Running Time: 6 hrs. 30 mins. 0 sec.). (ENG.). 2010. audio compact disk 34.99 (978-1-4001-1483-2(7)) Pub: Tantor Media. Dist(s): IngramPubServ

***Right Now: A 12-Step Program for Defeating the Obama Agenda.** unabr. ed. Michael Steele. Narrated by Richard Allen. (Running Time: 6 hrs. 30 mins.). 2010. 14.99 (978-1-4001-8483-5(5)) Tantor Media.

Right Now: A 12-Step Program to Restore America's Future. unabr. ed. Michael Steele. Narrated by Richard Allen. (Running Time: 6 hrs. 30 mins. 0 sec.). (ENG.). 2010. 24.99 (978-1-4001-6483-7(4)); audio compact disk 69.99 (978-1-4001-4483-9(3)) Pub: Tantor Media. Dist(s): IngramPubServ

Right Now Praise. Contrib. by Jonathan Nelson et al. 2008. audio compact disk 13.99 (978-5-557-51560-3(7)) Integrity Music.

Right Occupation. Read by Eknath Easwaran. 1 cass. (Running Time: 1 hr.). 1986. 7.95 (978-1-58638-599-6(2)) Nilgiri Pr.
Discusses how one's choice of occupation is very important.

Right on Time: The Complete Guide for Time-Pressured Managers. Lester R. Bittel. 1 cass. (Running Time: 1 hr.). 1991. 9.95 (978-0-07-005586-5(6)) McGraw.
A hands-on guide to one of the most vital of management skills - effective time management.

***Right Path.** Nora Roberts. 2011. audio compact disk 24.99 (978-1-4418-5718-7(4)) Brilliance Audio.

Right Place at the Right Time. unabr. collector's ed. Robert MacNeil. Read by Robert MacNeil. 8 cass. (Running Time: 12 hrs.). 1986. 64.00 (978-0-7366-0952-4(0), 1896) Books on Tape.
In this candid memoir, MacNeil reveals his off-camera personality as he recalls some of the highlights of his career.

Right Question. Charles D. Brennan, Jr. 6 cass. (Running Time: 9 hrs.). (New Think Selling Ser.). 1999. wbk. ed. 99.00 (978-1-928821-02-1(2), 110) Brennan Sales Inst.
"Breakthrough" advanced questioning & listening techniques.

Right Relationship to Thought. 2 cass. (Running Time: 2 hrs. 34 min.). (Bodhgaya Ser.: Vol. 3). 1996. 16.00 (978-1-883929-11-4(3)) Moksha Pr.
Reveals that the right relationship to thought can only be found when the fundamental truth of no limitation guides us through the endless complexity of life.

Right-Side-Up Stories for Upside-Down-People. Melea J. Brock. Read by Melea J. Brock. 2 cass. (Running Time: 3 hrs.). (YA). 2001. pap. bk. 14.98 (978-0-9667455-8-0(2)) Right-Side-Up.

Right Side-Up Stories for Upside-Down-People, No. 3. Melea J. Brock. 1 cass. (Running Time: 1 hr. 15 mins.). Dramatization. 1993. pap. bk. 10.00 (978-0-9667455-2-8(3)) Right-Side-Up.
Four original stories written & told by Melea J. Brock. All allegorical about issues involving all ages from adolescent to senior adult.

Right-Side-Up Stories for Upside-Down-People Vols. 3-4: Listen with Your Heart. Melea J. Brock. (Running Time: 100 mins.). (YA). (gr. 2 up). 2001. bk. 10.98 (978-0-9667455-9-7(0)) Right-Side-Up.

Right-Standing with God. Kenneth Copeland. 12 cass. (Running Time: 12 hrs.). 1983. bk. & stu. ed. 60.00 (978-0-938458-36-4(1)) K Copeland Pubns.
Biblical teaching on living before God.

Right Stuff. unabr. collector's ed. Tom Wolfe. Read by Michael Prichard. 11 cass. (Running Time: 16 hrs. 30 min.). 1989. 88.00 (978-0-7366-1555-6(5), 2423) Books on Tape.
Tom Wolfe's celebrated narrative of the U. S. space program & the people who were a part of it.

Right Thing. unabr. ed. Judy Astley. Read by Diana Bishop. 6 cass. (Running Time: 8 hrs.). (Isis Ser.). (J). 1999. 54.95 (978-0-7531-0618-1(3), 990713) Pub: ISIS Lrg Prnt GBR. Dist(s): Ulverscroft US
Funerals are strange things. Kitty didn't really want to go to his one, an old school friend she hadn't seen for years, & she didn't bargain for the way it made her think of the past. It reminded her of the baby she had given up for adoption when she was eighteen. Reminded her how cruelly short life can be. She decides she has to see the baby she gave up to make sure she had done the right thing but Kitty is unprepared for the upheaval which follows for her and her family.

Right Thought, Speech & Action. Swami Amar Jyoti. 1 cass. 1976. 9.95 (F-12) Truth Consciousness.
Right thought, speech & action - the meaning of perfection. Symptoms of wrong thinking. Faith in the justice of God.

Right to Abortion. Andrew Bernstein. 1 cass. (Running Time: 90 min.). 1994. 12.95 (978-1-56114-385-6(5), CB08C) Second Renaissance.

Right to Die. unabr. ed. Rex Stout. Read by Michael Prichard. 4 cass. (Running Time: 6 hrs.). (Nero Wolfe Ser.). 2003. 24.95 (978-1-57270-314-8(8)) Pub: Audio Partners. Dist(s): PerseuPGW
A client presents Wolfe with a difficult job: to find something unsavory about his son's fiancee in order to stop their interracial marriage. The withe girl's record comes up clean but she comes up dead, with her black fiance accused. Nero and Archie set out to prove his innocence.

Right to Die. unabr. ed. Rex Stout. Narrated by Michael Prichard. (Nero Wolfe Ser.). (ENG.). 2003. audio compact disk 27.95 (978-1-57270-315-5(6)) Pub: AudioGO. Dist(s): Perseus Dist

Right to Die. unabr. collector's ed. Rex Stout. Read by Michael Prichard. 6 cass. (Running Time: 6 hrs.). (Nero Wolfe Ser.). 1997. 48.00 (978-0-7366-3531-8(9), 4170) Books on Tape.
When a beautiful Caucasian heiress turns up dead, all clues point to her African-American fiance - who goes straight to Nero Wolfe for help.

Right to Die: Decision Making & Documentation. 1 cass. (Running Time: 50 min.). (CLE TV: The Lawyers' Video Magazine Ser.). 1992. stu. ed. 95.00 (Y501) Am Law Inst.
Covers issues to be raised, decisions to be made, & their conversion to legally sound provisions in living wills & related documents.

Right to Life. Charles E. Rice & Mildred Jefferson. 1 cass. (Running Time: 50 min.). 10.95 (328) J Norton Pubs.

Right to Write: An Invitation & Initiation into the Writing Life. abr. ed. Julia Cameron. Read by Julia Cameron. 2 cass. 16.95 Set. Macmill Audio.

Right Understanding. unabr. ed. Perf. by Eknath Easwaran. 1 cass. (Running Time: 1 hr.). 1980. 7.95 (978-1-58638-600-9(X)) Nilgiri Pr.

Right Use of Our Senses. Swami Amar Jyoti. 1 cass. 1977. 9.95 (O-3) Truth Consciousness.
On the senses, their creation & use, control & purification, Knowledge of the body. The perfect science of Raja Yoga, Reading from "Chandogya Upanishad".

Right Use of Power. unabr. ed. Peter Block. 3 CDs. (Running Time: 3 hrs.). 2002. audio compact disk 29.95 (978-1-56455-903-6(3), AW00569D) Sounds True.
Management consultant fast forwards us to the business model of the future: a self-governing, accountable organization where power is shared equally, and work has meaning far beyond conventional measures. Join this business visionary as he explores: The "community" of workers, and how faith, service, and communication redefine success; How to retain the best co-workers, and why it has little to do with money, & more.

Right Way to Terminate an Employee. Dora C. Fowler. 1 cass. (Running Time: 60 min.). 9.95 (978-1-57323-021-6(9)) Natl Inst Child Mgmt.
Child care management training materials.

Right-Weight Mind. Gary Applegate. 1 cass. 1986. 10.00 Berringer Pub.
Skill Development's founder, Dr. Gary Applegate, presents the unique Skill Development approach to successful change.

Right Words at the Right Time. Marlo Thomas. 2002. audio compact disk 20.00 (978-0-7435-2768-2(2), Audioworks) S&S Audio.

Right Words at the Right Time. abr. ed. Marlo Thomas. 2 cass. (Running Time: 22 hrs. 0 mins. 0 sec.). (ENG.). 2002. 18.00 (978-0-7435-2470-4(5), Audioworks); audio compact disk 20.00 (978-0-7435-2471-1(3), Audioworks) Pub: S&S Audio. Dist(s): S and S Inc

Righteous Gentiles. 10.00 (HE832) Esstee Audios.
The fight for decency by the Christian world & its civilized leaders.

Righteous in Authority. Featuring Bill Winston. 5. 2004. audio compact disk 40.00 (978-1-59544-029-7(1)) Pub: B Winston Min. Dist(s): Anchor Distributors
Give voice to the Word of God and exercise the authority God has given you as born-again Beliver in this earth. When the righteous are in authority, the people rejoice.

***Righteous Indignation: Excuse Me While I Save the World.** unabr. ed. Andrew Breitbart. (Running Time: 8 hrs.). (ENG.). 2011. 26.98 (978-1-60788-695-2(2)); audio compact disk & audio compact disk 29.98 (978-1-60788-694-5(4)) Pub: Hachet Audio. Dist(s): HachBkGrp

Righteous Men. abr. ed. Sam Bourne. Read by Dennis Boutsikaris. 2006. 17.95 (978-0-7435-6528-8(2), Audioworks) Pub: S&S Audio. Dist(s): S and S Inc

Righteous Pop Music, Vol. 1. Mark Bradford. 1 CD. (Running Time: 1 hr.). Dramatization. 1996. pap. bk. 15.00 (978-1-58302-128-6(0), DRP-01) One Way St.
Collection of ten religious musical performance pieces created for use with puppetry.

Righteous Pop Music, Vol. 2. Mark Bradford. 1 CD. (Running Time: 1 hr.). Dramatization. 1996. pap. bk. 15.00 (978-1-58302-130-9(2), DRP-02) One Way St.

Righteous Pop Music, Vol. 3. 1999. audio compact disk 15.00 (978-1-58302-145-3(0)) One Way St.
A religious collection of parodies of old and new tunes.

Righteous Pop Music, Vol. 4. 1999. audio compact disk 15.00 (978-1-58302-147-7(7)) One Way St.
Great for puppet performing, youth lip synch groups or just plain listening pleasure. This collection of christian musical parodies are songs from the 90's.

Righteous Pop Music, Vol. 5. 2001. audio compact disk 15.00 (978-1-58302-202-3(3)) One Way St.
A religious collection of parodies of old and new tunes.

Righteous Pop Music, Vol. 6. 2002. audio compact disk 15.00 (978-1-58302-205-4(8)) One Way St.
Various Christian parodies of old and new tunes.

Righteous Requirement of the Law. Derek Prince. 1 cass. (I-4146) Derek Prince.

Righteous Trio. Dan Corner. 1 cass. 3.00 (78) Evang Outreach.

Righteousness. Michael Pearl. 4 CDs. 2003. audio compact disk (978-1-892112-50-7(7)) No Greater Joy.

Righteousness & Wealth. Creflo A. Dollar. 20.00 (978-1-59089-200-8(3)) Pub: Creflo Dollar. Dist(s): STL Dist NA

Righteousness of God by Faith, Vol. 1. Speeches. Creflo A. Dollar. 6 CDs. (Running Time: 5 hrs.). 2001. audio compact disk 28.00 (978-1-59089-895-6(8)) Creflo Dollar.

Righteousness, Purity & Perfection. Swami Amar Jyoti. 1 cass. 1988. 9.95 (Q-21) Truth Consciousness.
Religion means going the right way, coming to right terms with ourselves. Using our God-given faculties.

Righteousness, Temperance, Judgement. Michael Pearl. (ENG.). 2008. audio compact disk (978-1-934794-23-4(6)) No Greater Joy.

Rightfully Mine, Pt. 1. unabr. ed. Doris Mortman. Read by Frances Cassidy. 11 cass. (Running Time: 16 hrs. 30 min.). 1996. 88.00 (978-0-7366-3397-0(9), 4045A) Books on Tape.
"Intriguing, fun & romantic." (The New York Times).

Rightfully Mine, Pt. 2. Doris Mortman. Read by Frances Cassidy. 9 cass. (Running Time: 13 hrs. 30 min.). 1996. 72.00 (4045-B) Books on Tape.

Rightist Militias. 1 cass. (Leonard Peikoff Show Ser.). 1996. 12.95 (LPXXC3) Second Renaissance.

Rightly Dividing the Word. Rick Joyner. 1 cass. (Running Time: 90 mins.). (Foundation Ser.: Vol. 3). 2000. 5.00 (RJ04-003) Morning NC.
Firmly establishing basic Christian principles, these messages also illuminate some of the primary enemies of truth, such as legalism & the control spirit.

Rightness Addiction: If I'm Right, How Come I'm Unhappy? David Grudermeyer & Rebecca Grudermeyer. 2 cass. 18.95 (T-06) Willingness Wrks.

Rightness of God by Faith. Creflo A. Dollar. 20.00 (978-1-59089-012-7(4)) Pub: Creflo Dollar. Dist(s): STL Dist NA

Rights & Privileges of Sonship. David T. Demola. 16 cass. 64.00 (S-1079) Faith Fellow Min.

Rights & Responsibilities: Reading & Communication for Civics: Chapters 1-16. Created by McGraw-Hill Staff. 2004. 23.13 (978-0-07-286351-2(X), 9780072863512, ESL/ELT) Pub: McGrw-H Hghr Educ. Dist(s): McGraw

Rights & the Courts. Thomas A. Bowden et al. 4 cass. (Running Time: 4 hrs.). 1995. 39.95 (978-1-56114-402-0(9), PB01D) Second Renaissance.
Roe vs. Wade; the right of self defense; criminal violations of rights.

Rights of Children. unabr. ed. Hosted by John Holt. 1 cass. (Famous Authorities Talk about Children Ser.). 10.95 (C40067) J Norton Pubs.

Rights of Man. unabr. ed. Thomas Paine. Read by Bernard Mayes. 7 cass. (Running Time: 10 hrs.). 1990. 49.95 (978-0-7861-0218-1(7), 1192) Blckstn Audio.
Unquestionably one of the great classics on the subject of democracy. Paine created a language of modern politics which brought important issues to the common man & the working classes. Employing direct, vehement prose, Paine defends popular rights, national independence, revolutionary war & economic growth - all of which were considered, at the time, to be dangerous & even seditious issues.

Rights of Man: Great Thinkers & Great Movements. Instructed by Paul Gordon Lauren. 2008. 129.95 (978-1-59803-495-0(2)); audio compact disk 69.95 (978-1-59803-496-7(0)) Teaching Co.

Rights of War & Peace. abr. ed. Hugo Grotius. Read by Robert L. Halvorson. 6 cass. (Running Time: 5 hrs. 40 mins). 42.95 (46) Halvorson Assocs.

Rigoletto: An Introduction to Verdi's Opera. Thomson Smillie. Read by David Timson. 1 CD. (Running Time: 1 hr. 30 min.). (Opera Explained Ser.). 2003. audio compact disk 8.99 (978-1-84379-038-9(6)) NaxMulti GBR.

Rigoletto Verdi. Perf. by Leonard Warren et al. Conducted by Walter Herbert. 2 CDs. audio compact disk 33.95 VAI Audio.
The legendary baritone Leonard Warren stars in this thrilling live 1952 performance from the New Orleans Opera.

Rigorists see Twentieth-Century Poetry in English, No. 2, Recordings of Poets Reading Their Own Poetry

Rigueza - Wealth. Carlos González. Ed. by Dina Gonzalez. 4 cass. (Running Time: 2 hrs. 13 min.). (SPA.). 1993. 50.00 set. (978-1-56491-058-5(X)) Imagine Pubs.
This course helps you become wealthier - some selling techniques included.

Rikki Tikki Tavi. 2004. bk. 24.95 (978-1-56008-648-2(3)); 8.95 (978-0-7882-0098-4(4)); audio compact disk 12.95 (978-1-55592-731-8(9)) Weston Woods.

Rikki-Tikki-Tavi. Rudyard Kipling. (J). 1979. (N-28) Jimcin Record.

Rikki-Tikki-Tavi. Rudyard Kipling. Narrated by Michael York. Illus. by Jerry Pinkney. Music by Ernest Troost. 1 cass. (Running Time: 30 min.). (J). (gr. 1-5). 2000. bk. 24.95 (QHRA385) Weston Woods.
A courageous mongoose becomes the loyal pet of a small boy named Teddy & protects him & his family from two evil cobras who live in their garden.

Rikki-Tikki Tavi - Paddy's Christmas - Hansel & Gretel. EDCON Publishing Group Staff. (ENG.). 2008. audio compact disk 12.95 (978-0-8481-0419-1(6)) EDCON Pubng.

Rikki Tikki Tavi & Other Children's Favorites. (J). 2005. audio compact disk (978-1-933796-27-7(8)) PC Treasures.

Rikki-Tikki-Tavi & Other Classic Tales. Rudyard Kipling et al. Narrated by Samuel L. Jackson et al. (Playaway Children Ser.). (ENG.). (J). (ps-5). 2009. 44.99 (978-1-60812-594-4(7)) Find a World.

Rikki-Tikki-Tavi & Other Stories. Rudyard Kipling. Read by Madhav P. Sharma. 2 cass. (Running Time: 2 hrs. 33 mins.). (J). 1995. 13.98 (978-962-634-552-8(7), NA205214, Naxos AudioBooks) Naxos.

Rikki-Tikki-Tavi & Other Stories. abr. ed. Rudyard Kipling. Read by Madhav P. Sharma. 2 CDs. (Running Time: 2 hrs. 33 mins.). (J). 1995. audio compact disk 17.98 (978-962-634-052-3(5), NA205212, Naxos AudioBooks) Naxos.

Rikki-Tikki-Tavi & Toomai of the Elephants. Rudyard Kipling. 1 CD. (Running Time: 1 hr. 10 mins.). (J). (gr. 2-5). 2002. pap. bk. 32.00 (978-1-58472-316-5(5), In Aud) Sound Room.

Rikki-Tikki-Tavi & Toomai of the Elephants. Rudyard Kipling. Read by Ralph Cosham. (Unabridged Classics (in Audio) Ser.). (J). 2008. pap. bk. 36.00 (978-1-58472-431-5(5), In Aud) Sound Room.

Rikki-Tikki-Tavi & Toomai of the Elephants. unabr. ed. Rudyard Kipling. Read by Ralph Cosham. 1 CD. (Running Time: 1 hr. 10 mins.). (J). 2000. audio compact disk 16.00 (978-1-58472-107-9(3), Commuters Library) Sound Room.

Rikki-Tikki-Tavi & Toomai of the Elephants. unabr. ed. Short Stories. Rudyard Kipling. Read by Ralph Cosham. 1 cd. (Running Time: 1 hr 9 mins). (J). 2002. audio compact disk 16.95 (978-1-58472-314-1(9), 020, In Aud) Pub: Sound Room. Dist(s): Baker Taylor
The story of a mongoose combatting cobras in the garden of his adopted family. Also includes the story of Toomai, an Indian boy who rode elephants.

Riley. unabr. ed. Catherine Cookson. Read by Elizabeth Henry. 16 CDs. (Running Time: 17.5 hrs.). (Sound Ser.). 2002. audio compact disk 109.95 (978-1-86042-946-0(7)) Pub: Mgna Lrg Print GBR. Dist(s): Ulverscroft US
There were many who said of Riley (as he was almost always known) that in his early life he appeared to be older than his years. With a harsh childhood behind him, he left school with little in the way of knowledge but brimful of optimism and secure in the knowledge that one of his teachers, Fred Beardsley, had faith in his future. While on honeymoon in Paris, Fred Beardsley ran into Riley, who said he'd won first prize in a talent competition and had been offered a 'position' at The Little Palace Theatre in Felburn Fred and his wife were amazed when it became clear that Riley had actually been appointed assistant stage-manager. And then he further surprised them by forming a close friendship with the leading lady, thirty-something Nyrene Forbes-Mason. What Riley hadn't told them, however, was that he had great hopes of the relationship developing into something more than a friendship... Riley's relationship with Nyrene did indeed develop, although its outcome was not quite as he had planned. In a career that.

Riley. unabr. ed. Catherine Cookson. Read by Elizabeth Henry. 15 cass. (Running Time: 22 hrs.). 2000. 104.95 (978-1-86042-501-1(1), 25011) Pub: Soundings Ltd GBR. Dist(s): Ulverscroft US
With a harsh childhood behind him, Riley left school with little in the way of knowledge but a brimful of optimism & secure in the understanding that one of his teachers, Fred Beardsley, had faith in his future. When the two meet up in Paris, they find they have both taken positions at The Little Palace Theatre in Fellburn.

Rilke: Selected Poems. unabr. ed. Poems. Read by Stephen Mitchell. Tr. by Stephen Mitchell. 2 cass. (Running Time: 2 hrs.). (Unabridged Ser.). 1995. 16.95 (978-0-944993-02-6(8)) Audio Lit.

Rilke - Poet of Inwardness: Lyric Poetry. Thomas Merton. 1 cass. 8.95 (AA2460) Credence Commun.

Rilla of Ingleside. L. M. Montgomery. Narrated by Barbara Caruso. 8 cass. (Running Time: 11 hrs.). (YA). 1921. 71.75 (978-1-4193-0839-0(4)) Recorded Bks.

Rilla of Ingleside. unabr. ed. L. M. Montgomery. Read by Anna Fields. 8 cass. (Running Time: 11 hrs. 30 mins.). (Avonlea Ser.: No. 8). (gr. 5-8). 1998. 56.95 (978-0-7861-1275-3(1), 2172) Blckstn Audio.
Anne's children are almost grown up, except for pretty, high-spirited Rilla. No one can resist her bright hazel eyes & dazzling smile. Rilla, almost fifteen, can't think any further ahead than going to her very first dance at the Four Winds lighthouse & getting her first kiss from handsome Kenneth Ford. But undreamed-of challenges await the irrepressible Rilla when the world of Ingleside becomes endangered by a far-off war. She is swept into a drama that tests her courage & leaves her changed forever.

***Rilla of Ingleside.** unabr. ed. L. M. Montgomery. Read by Anna Fields. (Running Time: 15 hrs.). 2010. 29.95 (978-1-4417-6733-2(9)); audio compact disk 100.00 (978-1-4417-6731-8(2)) Blckstn Audio.

Rimas y Canciones de Fonetica. 1 cass. (Running Time: 1 hr.).Tr. of Phonics Songs & Rhymes. (SPA.). (gr. k up). 2000. 44.08 (978-0-673-64862-4(1)); audio compact disk 77.28 (978-0-673-64451-0(0)) Addson-Wesley Educ.
All the songs and rhymes for the program, plus the instrumental track, are included in these tapes and CDs.

Rimas y Canciones de Fonetica. 1 cass. (Running Time: 1 hr.).Tr. of Phonics Songs & Rhymes. (SPA.). (gr. 1 up). 2000. 44.08 (978-0-673-64863-1(X)); audio compact disk 77.28 (978-0-673-64452-7(9)) Addson-Wesley Educ.

Rimas y Canciones de Fonetica. 1 cass. (Running Time: 1 hr.).Tr. of Phonics Songs & Rhymes. (SPA.). (gr. 2 up). 2000. 44.08 (978-0-673-64864-8(8)); audio compact disk 77.28 (978-0-673-64453-4(7)) Addson-Wesley Educ.

Rimas y Canciones de Fonetica. 1 cass. (Running Time: 1 hr.).Tr. of Phonics Songs & Rhymes. (SPA.). (gr. 3 up). 2000. 44.08 (978-0-673-64865-5(6)); audio compact disk 77.28 (978-0-673-64454-1(5)) Addson-Wesley Educ.

Rimas y Leyendas. unabr. ed. Gustavo Adolfo Becquer. (SPA.). 2007. audio compact disk 17.00 (978-958-8218-98-4(5)) YoYoMusic.

Rimas y Risas, Green Tape. 2 cass. (SPA.). (J). (gr. k-3). 1991. 21.00 (978-1-56334-012-3(7)) Hampton-Brown.
Stories in the Rimas y Risas (Green) Big Books consist of Los seis deseos de la jirafa, Sale el oso, El chivo en la huerta & La gallinita, & gallo y el frijol.

Rimas y Risas Red Tape Set. 2 cass. (SPA.). (J). (gr. k-3). 1990. 21.00 Hampton-Brown.
Stories include Veo, veo & Una semilla nada mas, Pinta, pinta, Gregorita, Pan, pan, gran pan.

Rimbaud. Poems. Arthur Rimbaud. Read by Laurent Terzieff. Contrib. by Alain Borer. 2 cass. (FRE.). 1991. 26.95 (1278-RF) Olivia & Hill.
Recounts the life of Arthur Rinnbaud with extracts from his poems.

Rime di Petrarca. Francesco Petrarch. Read by Antonio Baldini. 1 cass. (Running Time: 1 hrs.). (ITA.). 1997. pap. bk. 19.50 (978-1-58085-466-5(4)) Interlingua VA.

Rime of the Ancient Mariner see Poetry of Coleridge

Rime of the Ancient Mariner see Classics of English Poetry for the Elementary Curriculum

Rime of the Ancient Mariner see Don Juan

Rime of the Ancient Mariner. Samuel Taylor Coleridge. 1 cass. Incl. Frost at Midnight. (SAC 7016); Kubla Khan. (SAC 7016); Youth & Age. (SAC 7016); 10.95 (SAC 7016) Spoken Arts.

Rime of the Ancient Mariner. unabr. ed. Samuel Taylor Coleridge. Perf. by James Mason. 1 CD. (Running Time: 1 hr.). 2001. audio compact disk 12.95 (978-1-57511-100-1(4)) Pub Mills.
A sailor who offends nature by killing a seabird, takes the listener on a macabre odyssey that includes brushes with monsters, a ship manned by zombies & a game of dice with Death.

Rime of the Ancient Mariner. unabr. ed. Samuel Taylor Coleridge. Perf. by James Mason. 1 cass. (Running Time: 1 hr.). 2002. 12.00 (978-1-57511-093-6(8)) Pub: Pub Mills. Dist(s): TransVend
About a sailor who offends nature by killing a seabird takes the listener on a macabre odyssey that includes brushes with sea monsters, a ship manned by zombies, and a game of dice with Death.

Rime of the Ancient Mariner & Other Great Poems. unabr. ed. Samuel Taylor Coleridge et al. Read by Christopher Plummer & Bramwell Fletcher. 2 cass. (Cassette Bookshelf Ser.). 1987. 15.98 (978-0-8072-3472-3(9), CB112CX, Listening Lib) Random Audio Pubg.
Poems include "Kubla Kahn", "The Tyger", "The Daffodils", "To a Skylark", "She Walks in Beauty", "Ode to a Grecian Urn", "Bright Star" & more.

Rinconete y Cortadillo. Miguel de Cervantes Saavedra. (Leer en Espanol: Level 2 Ser.). 2008. pap. bk. 13.99 (978-84-9713-062-2(6)) Santillana Univ de Salamanca ESP.

Rinconete Y Cortadillo. Miguel de Cervantes Saavedra. Read by Santiago Munevar. (Running Time: 1 hr.). 2002. 14.95 (978-1-60083-144-7(3), Audiofy Corp) Iofy Corp.

Rinconete y Cortadillo. unabr. ed. Miguel de Cervantes. Read by Santiago Munevar. (SPA.). 2002. audio compact disk 13.00 (978-958-43-0135-2(7)) YoYoMusic.

Rindiendo Honor y Gloria. 33 DC. (SPA.). (gr. 13). 2007. audio compact disk 14.99 (978-0-8297-5250-2(1)) Zondervan.

Ring: The Story of a Frontier Dog. Walter McCaleb. Read by Jody Wright. 4 CDs. (Running Time: 4 hrs. 40 mins.). 2003. audio compact disk 29.95 (978-0-9722299-5-1(7)) WSG Gallery.
Join in a story of a frontier dog . . . told from the dog's point of view! The author, Walter McCaleb, wrote this book in 1921 from Carrizo Springs, Texas. Take a peek back in time when the frontier was not a memory, but alive and well. Ring, the frontier dog, describes his unending quest to protect both his master and family. He tussles with coyotes, and hunts civit cats, opossums, bobcats, raccoons and more.Abridged & edited by AudioVision Books.

***Ring-A-Ding Girl.** 2010. audio compact disk (978-1-59171-243-5(2)) Falcon Picture.

Ring & Die. Stella Whitelaw. 2008. 54.95 (978-1-84559-898-3(9)); audio compact disk 71.95 (978-1-84559-899-0(7)) Pub: Soundings Ltd GBR. Dist(s): Ulverscroft US

Ring Around a Rainbow: A Health & Safety Adventure. unabr. ed. Sandra Robbins. 1 cass. (Running Time: 32 min.). Dramatization. (See-More Ser.). (J). (gr. k-5). 2001. 5.50 (978-1-882601-13-4(0)) See-Mores Wrkshop.
Created for children based on Shadow Box Theatre's Production.

Ring Around a Rainbow: A Healthy & Safety Story. Sandra Robbins. Music by Iku Olmsted. 1 CD. (Running Time: 32 mins). (See-More's Stories Ser.). (J). 2001. pap. bk. 16.95 (978-1-882601-42-4(4)) See-Mores Wrkshop.

Ring for Jeeves. abr. ed. P. G. Wodehouse. Read by Simon Callow. 2 cass. (Jeeves & Wooster Ser.). 2002. (978-0-14-180365-4(7)) Pnguin Bks Ltd GBR.
'It might possibly assist your lordship if I were to bring a small bottle of champagne to the library.''You think of everything, Jeeves.'It was some minutes later, as Jeeves was passing through the living room with the brain-restorer on a small tray that Destiny came in through the french window .

Ring for Jeeves. unabr. ed. P. G. Wodehouse. Read by Nigel Lambert. 6 cass. (Running Time: 9 hrs.). (Jeeves & Wooster Ser.). 2000. 49.95 (978-0-7451-6611-7(3), CAB 1227) Pub: Chivers Audio Bks GBR. Dist(s): AudioGO
Bill Rowcester was well and truly in the gumbo, but setting himself up as a bookie might not have been his smartest move. Particularly when it threatens his oncoming nuptials with Jill Wyvern! Lucky for Bill, he had a land-lease on Jeeves whose formidable genius was at liberty to save the day!.

Ring Lardner: Best Short Stories. unabr. collector's ed. Ring Lardner. Read by Daniel Grace. 8 cass. (Running Time: 12 hrs.). (J). 1977. 64.00 (978-0-913369-99-9(3), 1009) Books on Tape.
For a whole generation of readers who have grown to maturity without reading Ring Lardner, this book will introduce one of the great American storytellers. Larnder was a heavyweight author who dealt with lightweight themes. His style, sardonic & irreverent, made it difficult for him to be taken seriously by the literary establishment but in reality, Lardner was one of the foremost experimental writers of his time & his talent shines in these stories.

Ring Lardner Selection. Ed. by Gary Gabriel. 6 cass. (Running Time: 6 hrs.). (Audio Drama 101 Ser.: Vol. 4). 1998. 14.95 (978-1-892077-03-5(5)) Lend-A-Hand Soc.

Ring Lardner Short Stories. Ring Lardner. 1987. 18.00 (978-0-8072-3457-0(5), Listening Lib) Random Audio Pubg.

Ring of Clay. Margaret Kaine. Read by Julia Franklin. 7 cass. (Running Time: 9 hrs. 15 mins.). (Story Sound Ser.). (J). 2004. 61.95 (978-1-85903-711-9(9)); audio compact disk 79.95 (978-1-85903-739-3(9)) Pub: Mgna Lrg Print GBR. Dist(s): Ulverscroft US

***Ring of Fire.** unabr. ed. Pierdomenico Baccalario. Read by Carrington MacDuffie. 7 CDs. (Running Time: 8 hrs. 18 mins.). (Century Ser.: Bk. 1). (J). (gr. 5-7). 2009. audio compact disk 50.00 (978-0-307-58246-1(9), Listening Lib) Pub: Random Audio Pubg. Dist(s): Random

Ring of Fire, Bk. 1. unabr. ed. Pierdomenico Baccalario. Read by Carrington MacDuffie. (ENG.). (J). (gr. 5). 2009. audio compact disk 37.00 (978-0-307-58243-0(4), Listening Lib) Pub: Random Audio Pubg. Dist(s): Random

Ring of Power: A Jungian Understanding of Wagner's Ring Cycle. Jean S. Bolen. Read by Jean Shinoda Bolen. 4 cass. (Running Time: 4 hrs. 50 min.). 1993. 31.95 (978-0-7822-0419-3(8), 506S) C G Jung IL.
Jean Shinoda Bolen takes the listener into the archetypal story of the dysfunctional family in The Ring of the Niebelung, Richard Wagner's four-part opera cycle comprised of The Rheingold, The Valkyrie, Siegfried, & Twilight of the Gods. Through the storytelling commentary, we learn how archetypal psychology, dysfunctional relationship psychology with its insights into narcissism & co-dependency, & patriarchy, come together in the Ring Cycle - & in our own lives.

***Ring of Rocamadour.** unabr. ed. Michael D. Beil. Read by Tai Alexandra Ricci. 6 CDs. (Running Time: 6 hrs. 55 mins.). (J). (gr. 4-7). 2009. audio compact disk 50.00 (978-0-7393-7960-8(7), Listening Lib) Pub: Random Audio Pubg. Dist(s): Random

***Ring of Solomon.** unabr. ed. Jonathan Stroud. Read by Simon Jones. (ENG.). (J). 2010. audio compact disk 48.00 (978-0-307-73861-5(2), Listening Lib) Pub: Random Audio Pubg. Dist(s): Random

Ring of the King: A Story from Nelson Mandela's Favorite African Folktales. Read by Alan Rickman. Compiled by Nelson Mandela. (Running Time: 12 mins.). (ENG.). 2009. 1.99 (978-1-60024-779-8(2)) Pub: Hachet Audio. Dist(s): HachBkGrp

Ring of Thoth. Arthur Conan Doyle. Read by John Bolen. (Running Time: 8 hrs.). 2002. 27.95 (978-1-60083-614-5(3), Audiofy Corp) Iofy Corp.

Ring of Thoth & Other Tales see Tales of the Supernatural

Ring of Thoth & Other Tales. Arthur Conan Doyle. Contrib. by John Bolen. (Playaway Young Adult Ser.). (ENG.). 2009. 69.99 (978-1-60775-790-0(7)) Find a World.

Ring of Thoth & Other Tales. Arthur Conan Doyle. Read by John Bolen. (ENG.). 2005. audio compact disk 78.00 (978-1-4001-3043-6(3)) Pub: Tantor Media. Dist(s): IngramPubServ

Ring of Thoth & Other Tales. unabr. ed. Arthur Conan Doyle. Narrated by John Bolen. 7 CDs. (Running Time: 6 hrs. 24 mins.). (ENG.). 2002. audio compact disk 39.00 (978-1-4001-0043-9(7)); audio compact disk 20.00 (978-1-4001-5043-4(4)) Pub: Tantor Media. Dist(s): IngramPubServ

Ring of Thoth & Other Tales. unabr. ed. Arthur Conan Doyle. Narrated by John Bolen. (Running Time: 8 hrs. 0 mins. 0 sec.). (ENG.). 2009. audio compact disk 27.99 (978-1-4001-1088-9(2)); audio compact disk 55.99 (978-1-4001-4088-6(9)); audio compact disk 19.99 (978-1-4001-6088-4(X)) Pub: Tantor Media. Dist(s): IngramPubServ

Ring the Bell Backwards. Sybil Marshall. 16 cass. (Running Time: 19 hrs. 30 mins.). (Soundings Ser.). (J). 2005. 104.95 (978-1-84283-878-5(4)) Pub: ISIS Lrg Prnt GBR. Dist(s): Ulverscroft US

Ring the Bell Backwards. unabr. ed. Sybil Marshall. 17 CDs. (Running Time: 19 hrs. 30 mins.). (Soundings (CDs) Ser.). (J). 2005. audio compact disk 109.95 (978-1-84283-930-0(6)) Pub: ISIS Lrg Prnt GBR. Dist(s): Ulverscroft US

Ring up Phone Sales. Dan Coen. (Ring Up Phone Sales: Vol. 1). 2002. 24.95i (978-0-9660436-3-1(4)) DCD Pub.

Ringing up Sales. Art Sobczak. Read by Art Sobczak. 6 cass. (Running Time: 5 hrs. 30 min.). 1989. 79.95 Set, incl. action guide. (2008) Dartnell Corp.
A comprehensive telephone sales rep training program.

Ringo Starr. abr. ed. Alan Clayson. Read by Mike Read. 3 CDs. (Running Time: 3 hrs. 36 mins.). 2003. audio compact disk (978-1-86074-538-6(5)) Sanctuary Pubng GBR.
Ringo's replacement of Pete Best as the Beatles' drummer changed musical history, adding the final perfect touch to what would become the world's reigning rock band. But Starr had his own personality and talents that shone through the group, creating memorable tunes, carving out a successful solo career, and infusing the group with his distinctively droll brand of humor. This book covers the life and career of Ringo, with plenty of fun trivia and little-known facts.

Ringworld. unabr. ed. Larry Niven. Read by Patrick Cullen. 8 cass. (Running Time: 11 hrs. 30 mins.). 1996. 56.95 (978-0-7861-0977-7(7), 1754) Blckstn Audio.
A modern science-fiction classic, "Ringworld" won the Hugo & Nebula Awards for best novel in 1970. "I myself have dreamed up an intermediate step between Dyson Spheres & planets. Build a ring 93 million miles in radius one Earth orbit which would make it 600 million miles long. If we have the mass of Jupiter to work with, & if we make it a million miles wide, we get a thickness of about a thousand meters. The Ringworld would thus be much sturdier than a Dyson sphere.".

Ringworld. unabr. collector's ed. Larry Niven. Read by Connor O'Brien. 8 cass. (Running Time: 12 hrs.). 1997. 64.00 (978-0-7366-3770-1(2), 4443) Books on Tape.
A huge architectural ring is constructed in outer space. In time it will house the inhabitants of the dying Earth. A whole new world is emerging, a world of huge dimensions, encompassing an area three million times the area of the Earth. Ringworld has a gravitational field & high walls to preserve its atmosphere. Its proximity to the sun maintains the new planet's climate. With those kinds of resources at its disposal, humankind can begin anew, but not without meeting the disquieting challenges of a brave new world.

Ringworld Engineers. unabr. collector's ed. Larry Niven. Read by Connor O'Brien. 8 cass. (Running Time: 12 hrs.). 1998. 64.00 (978-0-7366-3992-7(6), 4280) Books on Tape.

Ringworld Throne. unabr. collector's ed. Larry Niven. Read by Connor O'Brien. 9 cass. (Running Time: 13 hrs. 30 min.). 1996. 72.00 (978-0-7366-4321-4(4), 4800) Books on Tape.
Odd events are happening once again on Ringworld. Incoming spacecraft are being destroyed, the humanoids known as vampires are breeding in alarming numbers & the Ringworld Protectors, who normally stick to their own kind, are at war with their own species. Someone must take control of the Ringworld to ensure its survival. The prime candidate: Louis Wu, the 200-year-old human scientist, who first discovered Ringworld.

Ringworld's Children. Larry Niven. Read by Barrett Whitener. (Running Time: 9 hrs. 30 mins.). (J). 2004. 30.95 (978-1-59912-582-4(X)) Iofy Corp.

Ringworld's Children. unabr. ed. Larry Niven. Read by Barrett Whitener. (Running Time: 9 hrs. 30 mins.). 2005. audio compact disk 24.95 (978-0-7861-8524-5(4), 3295); audio compact disk 34.95 (978-0-7861-8589-4(9), ZE3295) Blckstn Audio.

Ringworld's Children. unabr. ed. Read by Barrett Whitener. 7 cass. (Running Time: 9 hrs. 30 mins.). 2004. 49.95 (978-0-7861-2748-1(1), 3295); audio compact disk 64.00 (978-0-7861-8538-2(4), 3295) Blckstn Audio.

Ringworld's Children. unabr. ed. Read by Barrett Whitener. 7 cass. (Running Time: 10 hrs.). 2005. reel tape 29.95 (978-0-7861-2726-9(0), E3295) Blckstn Audio.

Rinn na NGael. Contrib. by Nioclas Toibin. (ENG.). 1994. 13.95 (978-0-8023-7104-1(3)) Pub: Clo Iar-Chonnachta IRL. Dist(s): Dufour

Rinn na NGael. Contrib. by Nioclas Toibin. (ENG.). 1999. audio compact disk 20.95 (978-0-8023-8104-0(9)) Pub: Clo Iar-Chonnachta IRL. Dist(s): Dufour

Rinse & Dry: Huge Thunderstorm & Big Blow. Created by Thomas W. Gustin. 1 CD. (Running Time: 1 hr, 19 mins, 52 secs). 2004. audio compact disk 8.00 (978-0-9761848-4-3(2), EC4) Gustech.
Features 2 extremely high quality recordings made 10 Aug 03 & 11 May 03 here at the Emerald Cave. Escape to nature while She cleans & rebalances all of her local energy in this huge thunderstorm. Then settle down & enjoy the drying breezes in your ears as She dries out the earth once again.

Rio Crece, EDL Level 16. (Fonolibros Ser.). (SPA.). 2003. 11.50 (978-0-7652-1021-0(5)) Modern Curr.

***Riot.** unabr. ed. Walter Dean Myers. 3 CDs. (Running Time: 2 hrs. 36 mins.). (YA). (gr. 6-8). 2009. audio compact disk 30.00 (978-0-307-58340-6(6), BksonTape) Pub: Random Audio Pubg. Dist(s): Random

Riot. unabr. ed. Walter Dean Myers. (J). (gr. 7). 2009. 25.00 (978-0-307-58338-3(4), Listening Lib) Pub: Random Audio Pubg. Dist(s): Random

Riotous Assembly. unabr. ed. Tom Sharpe. Read by David Case. 6 cass. (Running Time: 9 hrs.). 1991. 48.00 (978-0-7366-1933-2(X), 2755) Books on Tape.
When Miss Hazelstone kills her Zulu cook in a crime of passion, the South African police are quick on the scene, & what a crew they are! Commandant van Heerden, whose secret longing for the heart of an English gentleman leads to the most memorable transplant operation yet recorded; Lieutenant Verkramp, ever active in his search for Communist sympathizers; & Constable Els, with his penchant for shooting first & thinking later. However Miss Hazelstone is their equal, as the Commandant learns when she makes him captive in her remarkable rubber room. Not a political novel in any previously imagined sense, Riotous Assembly provides a completely fresh approach to the incongruities of South Africa, & Tom Sharpe is the perfect author for it.

Rip Roarin' Paul Bunyan Tales. abr. ed. Odds Bodkin & Master Talesman. 1 cass. (Running Time: 45 mins.). (Odds Bodkin Musical Story Collection). (gr. k-3). 2003. bk. 9.95 (978-1-882412-16-7(8)) Pub: Rivertree. Dist(s): Penton Overseas
Two new Paul Bunyan Stories & " the Bedcats," a traditional bunyan story.

***Rip-Roaring Wealth.** unabr. ed. Made for Success. Read by Mark Victor Hansen. (Running Time: 5 hrs.). (Made for Success Ser.). 2010. audio compact disk 29.95 (978-1-4417-6350-1(3)) Blckstn Audio.

***Rip-Roaring Wealth (Library Edition)** unabr. ed. Made for Success. Read by Mark Victor Hansen. (Running Time: 5 hrs.). (Made for Success Ser.). 2010. audio compact disk 105.00 (978-1-4417-6349-5(X)) Blckstn Audio.

Rip Van Christmas: A Christmas Musical for Young Voices. Dennis Allen & Nan Allen. 1 cass. (Running Time: 1 hr.). (J). 1991. 12.99 (MU-9134C); audio compact disk 80.00 (MU-9134T) Lillenas.
Based on the classic story, this fun-filled musical begins in the 1890s & takes us into the 1990s to bring a new impact to the "peace & goodwill" message of Christmas. Great songs written in unison/optional 2-part, with plenty of humorous dialogue. Enjoyable to perform, easy to state & suitable for kids of all ages. Side 1, stereo trax; Side 2, split-channel.

Rip Van Winkle see Great American Short Stories

Rip Van Winkle see Ten All Time Favorite Stories

Rip Van Winkle see Childhood Legends

Rip Van Winkle. Granowsky. (J). 1993. (978-0-8114-2224-6(0)) SteckVau.

Rip Van Winkle. As told by Anjelica Huston. Music by Jay Unger & Molly Mason. Illus. by Rick Meyerowitz. 1 cass. (Running Time: 1 hr.). 9.95 Weston Woods.
Haunting tale follows Rip Van Winkle into the mysterious Catskill Mountains where he falls into a deep sleep for 20 years after sharing a strange brew with a band of odd fellows.

Rip Van Winkle. Washington Irving. Read by Hurd Hatfield. 1 cass. (J). 10.95 (978-0-8045-0997-8(2), SAC 7023) Spoken Arts.

Rip Van Winkle. Read by Jim Weiss. 1 cass. (Running Time: 1 hr.). (J). (GHP11) NewSound.

Rip Van Winkle. abr. ed. Washington Irving. Narrated by Elinor G. Hoffman. 2 cass. (Running Time: 50 min.). (J). 12.95 (978-0-89926-131-7(0), 819) Audio Bk.

Rip Van Winkle. abr. adpt. ed. Washington Irving. (Bring the Classics to Life: Level 1 Ser.). (ENG.). (gr. 1-16). 2008. audio compact disk 12.95 (978-1-55576-417-3(7)) EDCON Pubng.

Rip Van Winkle. unabr. ed. Washington Irving. Read by Donada Peters. (J). 2006. 39.99 (978-1-59895-676-4(0)) Find a World.

Rip Van Winkle & Other Stories. Washington Irving. Read by Donada Peters. (ENG.). 2004. audio compact disk 19.99 (978-1-4001-5118-9(X)); audio compact disk 24.99 (978-1-4001-0118-4(2)) Pub: Tantor Media. Dist(s): IngramPubServ

Rip Van Winkle & Other Stories. Washington Irving. Read by Donada Peters. (ENG.). 2005. audio compact disk 49.99 (978-1-4001-3118-1(9)) Pub: Tantor Media. Dist(s): IngramPubServ

Rip Van Winkle & Other Stories. unabr. ed. Washington Irving. Narrated by Donada Peters. (Running Time: 4 hrs. 30 mins. 0 sec.). (ENG.). 2008. 19.99 (978-1-4001-5892-8(3)); audio compact disk 19.99 (978-1-4001-0892-3(6)); audio compact disk 39.99 (978-1-4001-3892-0(2)) Pub: Tantor Media. Dist(s): IngramPubServ

Rip Van Winkle & Other Stories. unabr. collector's ed. Short Stories. Washington Irving. Read by Donada Peters. 5 cass. (Running Time: 5 hrs.). (YA). 1993. 30.00 (978-0-7366-2352-0(3), 3129) Books on Tape.
Collection of short stories including "Rip Van Winkle," "The Legend of Sleepy Hollow" plus seven others.

Rip Van Winkle & the Devil & Tom Walker. Washington Irving. Narrated by Stephen McLaughlin. 1 CD. (Running Time: 1 hr. 10 mins. 0 sec.). (PlainTales Classics Ser.). (ENG.). (J). (gr. 2-4). 2009. audio compact disk 12.95 (978-0-9819032-7-9(4)) Pub: PlainTales. Dist(s): IPG Chicago

Rip Van Winkle & the Legend of Sleepy Hollow. Washington Irving. Narrated by John MacDonald. (ENG.). 2007. audio compact disk 16.95 (978-1-60646-031-3(5)) Audio Bk Con.

Rip Van Winkle & the Legend of Sleepy Hollow. Washington Irving. Narrated by John MacDonald. (J). 2008. audio compact disk 22.95 (978-1-60646-024-5(2)) Audio Bk Con.

Rip Van Winkle & the Legend of Sleepy Hollow. Washington Irving. 1 cass. (Running Time: 1 hr.). (Radiobook Ser.). 1987. 4.98 (978-0-929541-25-9(1)) Radiola Co.

Rip Van Winkle & the Legend of Sleepy Hollow. unabr. ed. Washington Irving. Narrated by John MacDonald. 2 cass. (Running Time: 2 hrs. 30 min.). (J). 1986. 14.95 (978-1-55685-066-0(2)) Audio Bk Con.
Rip Van Winkle returns to a strange world after a long sleep.

Rip Van Winkle & the Legend of Sleepy Hollow. unabr. ed. Washington Irving. Read by Jim Beach. 2 cass. (Running Time: 3 hrs.). (J). 1990. 17.95 (978-0-7861-0204-4(7), 1179) Blckstn Audio.
Washington Irving was the first American writer to kindle worldwide interest through his intoxicating tales. With Rip Van Winkle, Ichabod Crane, & Diedrich Knickerbocker, Irving created three lasting folklore characters worthy to be compared with Huckleberry Finn & Captain Ahab.

Rip Van Winkle & the Legend of Sleepy Hollow, unabr. ed. Washington Irving. Narrated by George Guidall. 2 pieces. (Running Time: 2 hrs.). (gr. 4 up). 1999. 18.00 (978-1-55690-915-3(2), 93411E7) Recorded Bks.
Two classic tales from America's past about a man who returns to his village after a long sleep & a run-in with a ghostly rival. Hear Rip Van Winkle, the man who slept for 20 years; Ichabod Crane, the strict schoolmaster & the horrifying Headless Horseman.

***Rip Van Winkle Caper.** 2010. audio compact disk (978-1-59171-175-9(4)) Falcon Picture.

Rip Van Winkle/Gulliver's Travels. Short Stories. As told by Jim Weiss. 1 CD. (Running Time: 1 hr.). Dramatization. (Storyteller's Version Ser.). (J). (gr. k up). 1999. audio compact disk 14.95 (978-1-882513-36-9(3), 1124-011) Greathall Prods.
Three classics in one! The sly humor of Rip Van Winkle, Gulliver's adventures among the tiny Lilliputians and the wisdom of a Jewish folk tale.

Rip Van Winkle/Gulliver's Travels. Short Stories. As told by Jim Weiss. 1 cass. (Running Time: 1 hr.). Dramatization. (Storyteller's Version Ser.). (J). (gr. k up). 1992. 10.95 (978-1-882513-11-6(8), 1124-10) Greathall Prods.

Rip Wan Winkle. Washington Irving. 10.00 (LSS1100) Esstee Audios.

Ripen. Contrib. by Shawn McDonald. Prod. by Christopher Stevens & Will Hunt. 2006. audio compact disk 13.99 (978-5-558-55060-3(0)) Pt of Grace Ent.

Ripening Rubies. Max Pemberton. 1 cass. 1989. 7.95 (S-48) Jimcin Record.
Mysterious jewel robberies in high society.

Ripley under Ground. unabr. ed. Patricia Highsmith. Read by Nigel Lambert. 8 cass. (Running Time: 9 hrs. 5 min.). (Mr. Ripley Ser.). 1993. 69.95 (978-1-85089-853-6(1), 91094) Eye Ear.
To avoid charges of forgery the Buckmaster Gallery must produce the British artist Derwatt. But he, inconveniently, is dead. Tom Ripley is the only man who can perform the miraculous - but Tom cannot afford another scandal, & will stop at nothing, including murder, to avoid discovery.

Ripley under Ground. unabr. ed. Nigel Lambert & Patricia Highsmith. Read by Georgette Heyer. 8 cass. (Running Time: 12 hrs.). (Isis Ser.). (J). 2004. 69.95 (978-1-85089-853-5(7), 91094) Pub: ISIS Lrg Prnt GBR. Dist(s): Ulverscroft US

Ripley under Water. unabr. ed. Patricia Highsmith. Read by Geoffrey Matthews. 8 cass. (Running Time: 11 hrs. 20 min.). (Mr. Ripley Ser.). (J). 2004. 69.95 (978-1-85089-888-7(X), 92061) Pub: ISIS Lrg Prnt GBR. Dist(s): Ulverscroft US

Ripley's Believe It or Not! Created by Radio Spirits. (Running Time: 10800 sec.). 2004. 9.98 (978-1-57019-740-6(7)); audio compact disk 9.98 (978-1-57019-739-0(3)) Radio Spirits.

Ripped Seminar, Tape 1. Clarence Bass. Read by Clarence Bass. Interview with Bill Reynolds. 1 cass. (Running Time: 60 min.). 1980. 12.95 Clarence Bass.
Begins with Clarence's background & then details the training regimen he used to achieve 2.4 percent bodyfat & win his class in the Past-40 Mr. America & Mr. USA bodybuilding competitions.

Ripped Seminar, Tape 4. Clarence Bass. Read by Clarence Bass. Interview with David Prokop. 1 cass. (Running Time: 60 min.). 1990. 14.95 Clarence Bass.
Clarence focuses on periodization for bodybuilders, the aerobics problem/solution, the Cooper Clinic medical & fitness evaluations, turning 50, new developments in bodyfat tests & lifestyle for success.

Ripped Seminar, Tape 5. Clarence Bass. Read by Clarence Bass. 1 cass. (Running Time: 1 hr.). 1994. 14.95 Clarence Bass.
New cassette on motivation. Traces how Clarence Bass has kept training for over 40 years & how you can follow in his footsteps.

Ripped Seminar, Tapes 1, 4 & 5. Clarence Bass. 3 cass. 29.95 Clarence Bass.
Question & answers format which trace the development of Clarence Bass Ripped diet & training philosophy, including a fascinating new cassette (#5) on motivation.

***Rippin' It Old School.** unabr. ed. Raymond Bean. Read by Nick Podehl. (Running Time: 2 hrs.). (Sweet Farts Ser.). 2010. 9.99 (978-1-4418-8375-9(4), 9781441883759, Brilliance MP3); 39.97 (978-1-4418-8376-6(2), 9781441883766, Brlnc Audio MP3 Lib); 9.99 (978-1-4418-8377-3(0), 9781441883773, BAD); 39.97 (978-1-4418-8378-0(9), 9781441883780, BADLE); audio compact disk 39.97 (978-1-4418-8374-2(6), 9781441883742, BriAudCD Unabrid) Brilliance Audio.

***Rippin' It Old School.** unabr. ed. Raymond Bean. Read by Nick Podehl. (Running Time: 2 hrs.). (Sweet Farts Ser.). (YA). 2010. audio compact disk 9.99 (978-1-4418-8373-5(8), 9781441883735, Bril Audio CD Unabri) Brilliance Audio.

***Ripple Effect.** Zondervan Publishing Staff. (Running Time: 5 hrs. 11 mins. 22 sec.). (Time Thriller Trilogy). (YA). 2010. 9.99 (978-0-310-86966-5(8)) Zondervan.

Ripple Effect: Our Harvest. Betty J. Eadie. Read by Betty J. Eadie. 8 cass. (Running Time: 6 hrs.). 1999. 34.95 (978-1-892714-01-5(9)) Pub: Onjinjinkta. Dist(s): Natl Bk Netwk
In-depth answers to the most frequently asked questions about life and death, from the author of Embraced by the Light.

Ripple Effect: Our Harvest. Read by Betty J. Eadie. 1999. 20.00 Onjinjinkta.
Inspirational.

Riptide. 1999. (978-1-57042-785-5(2)) Hachet Audio.

Riptide. abr. ed. Douglas Preston & Lincoln Child. Read by David Birney. (ENG.). 2006. 14.98 (978-1-59483-820-0(8)) Pub: Hachet Audio. Dist(s): HachBkGrp

Riptide. abr. ed. Douglas Preston & Lincoln Child. Read by David Birney. (Running Time: 4 hrs. 30 mins.). (ENG.). 2009. 39.98 (978-1-60788-156-8(X)) Pub: Hachet Audio. Dist(s): HachBkGrp

Riptide. unabr. ed. Catherine Coulter. Read by Laural Merlington. 8 cass. (Running Time: 11 hrs.). (FBI Thriller Ser.: No. 5). 2000. 35.95 (978-1-56740-363-3(8), 1567403638, BAU) Brilliance Audio.
With four back-to-back bestselling suspense thrillers to her credit, Catherine Coulter has earned an ever-growing following thanks to her vivid characters and satisfyingly unpredictable plots. Now Coulter delivers a novel predicated on a baffling threat, fueled by a hatred dating back a generation. Political speechwriter Becca Matlock is at the top of her professional game, working for the re-election campaign of New York's popular governor, when she receives the first phone call: "Stop sleeping with the governor or I'll kill him." Although Becca isn't sleeping with the governor, the menacing ultimatums persist. The police suddenly stop believing her, even after the stalker murders an innocent person to prove his point. When the governor is shot in the neck, Becca flees for the safety of coastal Maine, choosing to hide not only from the stalker but also from the authorities. For sanctuary, she goes to Riptide, the home of a college friend - where she soon finds herself at even greater risk. .

Riptide. unabr. ed. Catherine Coulter. Read by Laural Merlington. (Running Time: 11 hrs.). (FBI Thriller Ser.: No. 5). 2005. 39.25 (978-1-59600-586-0(6), 9781596005860, BADLE); 24.95 (978-1-59600-585-3(8), 9781596005853, BAD); audio compact disk 39.25 (978-1-59600-584-6(X), 9781596005846, Brlnc Audio MP3 Lib); audio compact disk 24.95 (978-1-59600-583-9(1), 9781596005839, Brilliance MP3) Brilliance Audio.

Riptide. unabr. ed. Catherine Coulter. Read by Laural Merlington. (Running Time: 11 hrs.). (FBI Thriller Ser.: No. 5). 2009. audio compact disk 29.99 (978-1-4233-9050-3(4), 9781423390503, Bril Audio CD Unabri); audio compact disk 99.97 (978-1-4233-9051-0(2), 9781423390510, BriAudCD Unabrid) Brilliance Audio.

Riptide. unabr. ed. Douglas Preston & Lincoln Child. Read by Scott Brick. (Running Time: 15 hrs. 30 mins.). (ENG.). 2010. 24.98 (978-1-60788-472-9(0)) Pub: Hachet Audio. Dist(s): HachBkGrp

Risas y Sonrisas: Cognate Folder. Concept by Leticia Smith.Tr. of Laughter & Smiles. (SPA., (J). 2009. audio compact disk 7.99 (978-0-9760147-0-6(X)) Risas Y Sonris.

Rise Above: God Can Set You Free from Your Weight Problems Forever. Gwen Shamblin. 2000. 15.99 (978-0-7852-6893-2(6)) Nelson.

Rise above Depression - Feel Free Again. Scott Sulak. 2 cass. (Running Time: 2 hrs.). 1998. 15.00 (978-1-932659-01-6(3)) Change For Gd.

***Rise above Unfair Treatment.** John Bevere. (ENG.). 2010. audio compact disk 14.99 (978-1-933185-55-2(4)) Messengr Intl.

Rise above Your Problems. Jennifer Crow. 2 cass. (Running Time: 2 hrs.). 2001. (978-1-931537-14-8(3)) Vision Comm Creat.

Rise & Fall of Adolf Hitler. unabr. collector's ed. William L. Shirer. Read by Larry McKeever. 4 cass. (Running Time: 4 hrs.). 1986. 24.00 (978-0-7366-0947-0(4), 1890) Books on Tape.
As an American correspondent in Berlin, William Shirer had met Hitler, listened to his fiery speeches, & observed him firsthand. This is based on what Shirer saw & on his later research of the massive files captured by the Allies.

Rise & Fall of Alexandria: Birthplace of the Modern Mind. unabr. ed. Justin Pollard & Howard Reid. Narrated by Simon Vance. (Running Time: 12 hrs. 0 mins. 0 sec.). (ENG.). 2006. audio compact disk 24.99 (978-1-4001-5277-3(1)); audio compact disk 75.99 (978-1-4001-3277-5(0)); audio compact disk 37.99 (978-1-4001-0277-8(4)) Pub: Tantor Media. Dist(s): IngramPubServ

Rise & Fall of Ego. Swami Jyotirmayananda. 1 cass. (Running Time: 45 min.). 1990. 10.00 Yoga Res Foun.

Rise & Fall of F. Scott Fitzgerald: A Light & Enlightening Lecture. Featuring Elliot Engel. 2000. bk. 15.00 (978-1-890123-26-0(9)) Media Cnslts.

Rise & Fall of Jesse James. abr. ed. Robertus Love. Read by Michael Martin Murphey. 2 cass. (Running Time: 3 hrs.). 1997. 17.95 (978-1-57453-175-6(1)) Audio Lit.
Newspaperman Robertus Love knew Frank James & pieced together the incredible history of Jesse's rise to fame on the wrong side of the law & his eventual death at the hands of Robert Ford, a member of his own gang.

Rise & Fall of Michael Eisner. unabr. ed. Scripts. Richard Hack. 6 cass. (Running Time: 9 hrs.). 2004. 29.95 (978-1-59007-400-8(9)); audio compact disk 49.95 (978-1-59007-401-5(7)) Pub: New Millenn Enter. Dist(s): PerseuPGW

Rise & Fall of Soviet Communism Pts. I-II, Vol. 1: A History of Twentieth-Century Russia. Instructed by Gary Hamburg. 8 cass. (Running Time: 12 hrs.). 1996. 129.95 (978-1-56585-242-6(7)) Teaching Co.

Rise & Fall of Soviet Communism Vol. 2: A History of Twentieth-Century Russia. Instructed by Gary Hamburg. 4 cass. (Running Time: 6 hrs.). 1996. 129.95 (978-1-56585-243-3(5)) Teaching Co.

Rise & Fall of the British Empire. Instructed by Patrick N. Allitt. 2009. 199.95 (978-1-59803-583-4(5)); audio compact disk 269.95 (978-1-59803-584-1(3)) Teaching Co.

Rise & Fall of the Old Testament Church. Scott Hahn. 4 cass. 22.95 (5284-C) Ignatius Pr.
Continuing his systematic overview of Old Testament history & theology, Professor Hahn shows you what happened when Israel turned its' back on God's covenant & tried to become "like the other nations". Studying the books of Joshua I & 2 Kings through the Prophets & the Book of Daniel, Hahn shows how the history of Israel prepares the way for the New Covenant in Christ.

Rise & Fall of the Soviet Union, Set. Cerebellum Academic Team Staff. Executive Producer Ronald M. Miller. (Running Time: 2 hrs.). (Just the Facts Ser.). 2010. 39.95 (978-1-59163-602-1(7)) Cerebellum.

Rise & Fall of the Third Reich. William L. Shirer. Read by Larry McKeever. 1987. 96.00 (978-0-7366-1112-1(6)); 96.00 (978-0-7366-1113-8(4)); 64.00 (978-0-7366-1114-5(2)) Books on Tape.

Rise & Fall of the Third Reich, Pt. 2. William L. Shirer. Read by Larry McKeever. 12 cass. (Running Time: 18 hrs.). 1987. 96.00 (2037-B) Books on Tape.

Rise & Fall of the Third Reich, Pt. 3. William L. Shirer. Read by Larry McKeever. 12 cass. (Running Time: 18 hrs.). 1987. 96.00 (2037-C) Books on Tape.

Rise & Fall of the Third Reich, Pt. 4. William L. Shirer. Read by Larry McKeever. 8 cass. (Running Time: 12 hrs.). 1987. 64.00 (2037-D) Books on Tape.

***Rise & Fall of the Third Reich: A History of Nazi Germany.** unabr. ed. William L. Shirer. Read by Grover Gardner. (Running Time: 46 hrs. 0 mins.). 2010. audio compact disk 125.00 (978-1-4417-3418-1(X)) Blckstn Audio.

***Rise & Fall of the Third Reich: A History of Nazi Germany.** unabr. ed. William L. Shirer. Read by Grover Gardner. (Running Time: 57 hrs. 30 mins.). 2010. 59.95 (978-1-4417-3421-1(X)); audio compact disk 59.95 (978-1-4417-3420-4(1)) Blckstn Audio.

***Rise & Fall of the Third Reich: A History of Nazi Germany (Part 1 Of 3)** unabr. ed. William L. Shirer. Read by Grover Gardner. (Running Time: 15 hrs. 30 mins.). 2010. 42.95 (978-1-4417-3417-4(1)) Blckstn Audio.

***Rise & Fall of the Third Reich: A History of Nazi Germany (Part 2 Of 3)** unabr. ed. William L. Shirer. Read by Grover Gardner. (Running Time: 15 hrs. 30 mins.). 2010. 42.95 (978-1-4417-5229-1(3)) Blckstn Audio.

***Rise & Fall of the Third Reich: A History of Nazi Germany (Part 3 Of 3)** unabr. ed. William L. Shirer. Read by Grover Gardner. (Running Time: 15 hrs. 0 mins.). 2010. 42.95 (978-1-4417-5230-7(7)) Blckstn Audio.

Rise & Fall of the Third Reich Pt. 1: A History of Nazi Germany. unabr. ed. William L. Shirer. Read by Larry McKeever. 12 cass. (Running Time: 18 hrs.). 1987. 96.00 (978-0-7366-1111-4(8), 2037-A) Books on Tape.
Historical account of Hitler's empire, compiled from documents seized by the Allies after World War II. Part 1 of 4.

Rise & Shine. Raffi. 1 cass . (Running Time: 1 hr.). (J). 2001. 10.95 (KSR8111C); lp 10.95 (KSR 8111); audio compact disk 16.95 (KSR 8111CD) Kimbo Educ.
Includes Rise & Shine, Walk, Walk, Walk, The Numbers Rhumba, Thumbelina, Big Beautiful Planet, He's Got the Whole World, Row, Row, Row Your Boat, The Wheels on the Bus, Five Little Ducks.

Rise & Shine. Perf. by Raffi. 1 cass. (J). (ps-6). 10.98 (289) MFLP CA.
Incredible music of this pied piper of children's music. Songs include: "Daniel," "Rhumba," "Thumbeline," "Rise & Shine," "Ducks Like Rain," "I'm in the Mood," & many more.

Rise & Shine. Perf. by Raffi. 1 cass., 1 CD. (J). 7.98 (RDR 8055); audio compact disk 12.78 CD Jewel box. (RDR 8055) NewSound.

Rise & Shine. Perf. by Raffi. 1 cass. (Running Time: 34 mins.). (J). 1999. (978-1-886767-39-3(4)); (978-1-886767-65-2(3)); audio compact disk

(978-1-886767-38-6(6)); audio compact disk (978-1-886767-64-5(5)) Rounder Records.
Spirited & full of life, the songs here range from Raffi's joyous "Rise & Shine" to his inspiring rendition of "This Little Light of Mine.".

Rise & Shine: A Novel. Anna Quindlen. Narrated by Carol Monda. (Running Time: 39600 sec.). 2006. audio compact disk 34.99 (978-1-4193-8725-8(1)) Recorded Bks.

Rise & Shine: A Novel. unabr. ed. Read by Carol Monda. Ed. by Anna Quindlen. 9 CDs. (Running Time: 11 hrs.). 2006. audio compact disk 99.75 (978-1-4193-8893-4(2), C3684); 79.75 (978-1-4193-8891-0(6), 98334) Recorded Bks.
It's Monday morning when Meghan Fitzmaurice blows her perfect life to bits. The host of "Rise and Shine," the country's highest rated morning talk show, Meghan cuts to a commercial break, but not before she mutters two forbidden words into her open mike. It's the end of an era, not only for Meghan, a household face who is not equipped to deal with disgrace, but for her younger sister Bridget, a social worker in the Bronx who has lived always in Meghan's long shadow. The effect of Meghan's on-air profanity - and truth telling - is felt by her son, her husband, her friends, her fans and even the city of New York, the capitol of appearance over reality. But above all it transforms the sister with whom she's shared everything, even the mixed blessings of fame. What follows is a story about a city big enough to hold prep school rappers, rich poseurs, familiar strangers, and autograph seekers in the ladies room at black tie balls. But ultimately it's about how, in very different ways, the Fitzmaurice girls whip the place into shape. Meghan and Bridget, Bridget and Meghan. They share smart mouths, a fractured childhood, and a powerful connection that even the worst tragedy can't rupture.

Rise & Shine: A Parents Guide for Redirecting Everyday Power Struggles. Tim Jordan. Read by Tim Jordan. 1 cass. (Running Time: 40 mins.). 1996. 10.00 (978-0-9705335-2-4(7)); audio compact disk 10.00 (978-0-9705335-7-9(8)) Child & Families.
Helps parents learn about behavioral stages, behind the power struggles: how to redirect everyday power struggles, learn cooperation at home.

Rise, Let Us Be on Our Way. unabr. ed. John Paul II, pseud. Read by Kristoffer Tabori. (ENG.). 2005. 14.98 (978-1-59483-147-8(5)) Pub: Hachet Audio. Dist(s): HachBkGrp

Rise, Let Us Be on Our Way. unabr. ed. Pope John Paul II. Read by Kristoffer Tabori. Tr. by Walter Ziemba. (Running Time: 5 hrs.). (ENG.). 2009. 34.98 (978-1-60024-879-5(9)) Pub: Hachet Audio. Dist(s): HachBkGrp

Rise of Adolph Hitler. 10.00 (HE809) Esstee Audios.
The story of the evolution of the madman who made genocide & hatred the norm for an entire continent & generation.

Rise of Ancient Israel, Set. Moderated by Hershel Shanks et al. 4 cass. 1992. 32.95 (978-1-880317-28-0(1), 7HC2) Biblical Arch Soc.
Biblical archaeology & biblical studies.

Rise of Big Business: The Failure of Trusts & Cartels. Murray Newton Rothbard. 2 cass. (Running Time: 1 hr. 50 min.). 19.95 (212) J Norton Pubs.
Shows how the existence of monopolies can only be maintained for short periods without the interventionist support of the State; how these failures in the late 1800's led to Big Business support of much "progressive" legislation.

Rise of David Levinsky. Abraham Cahan. Read by Anais 9000. 2008. 33.95 (978-1-60112-130-1(X)) Babblebooks.

Rise of Dispensationalism: Logos 02/1999. Ben Young. 1999. 4.95 (978-0-7417-6121-7(1), B0121) Win Walk.

Rise of Endymion. unabr. ed. Dan Simmons. Read by Victor Bevine. (Running Time: 20 hrs.). (Hyperion Cantos Ser.). 2009. 44.97 (978-1-4233-8170-9(X), 9781423381709, Brinc Audio MP3 Lib); 44.97 (978-1-4233-8171-6(8), 9781423381716, BADLE); 29.99 (978-1-4233-8169-3(6), 9781423381693, Brilliance MP3); audio compact disk 49.99 (978-1-4233-8167-9(X), 9781423381679, Bril Audio CD Unabri); audio compact disk 99.97 (978-1-4233-8168-6(8), 9781423381686, BriAudCD Unabrid) Brilliance Audio.

Rise of Fascism: Nazi Germany. Kenneth Bruce. 1 cass. (Running Time: 1 hr.). Dramatization. (Excursions in History Ser.). 12.50 Alpha Tape.

Rise of Hasidism. 10.00 Esstee Audios.
A look at a movement which should be of interest to Christians & Jews alike.

Rise of Nuclear Iran: How Tehran Continues to Defy the West. unabr. ed. Dore Gold. (Running Time: 8.5 hrs. NaN mins.). (ENG.). 2009. audio compact disk 29.95 (978-1-4332-9198-2(3)) Blckstn Audio.

Rise of Nuclear Iran: How Tehran Continues to Defy the West. unabr. ed. Dore Gold. (Running Time: 8.5 hrs. 0 mins.). (ENG.). 2009. 29.95 (978-1-4332-9199-9(1)) Blckstn Audio.

Rise of Nuclear Iran: How Tehran Defied the West. unabr. ed. Dore Gold. (Running Time: 8.5 hrs. 0 mins.). (ENG.). 2009. 54.95 (978-1-4332-9195-1(9)); audio compact disk 76.00 (978-1-4332-9196-8(7)) Blckstn Audio.

Rise of Sectionalism & the Monroe Doctrine. Kenneth Bruce. 1 cass. (Running Time: 1 hr. 16 min.). Dramatization. (Excursions in History Ser.). 12.50 Alpha Tape.

Rise of Silas Lapham. William Dean Howells. Read by Flo Gibson. 8 cass. (Running Time: 12 hrs.). 1990. 26.95 (978-1-55685-168-1(5)) Audio Bk Con.
Silas Lapham's rise from poverty to paint tycoon & his plunge to bankruptcy do not alter his common decency. Still, his family is a puzzlement to the aristocratic Coreys, whose son is wooing one of Lapham's daughters.

Rise of Silas Lapham. rev. ed. William Dean Howells. Ed. by Robert James Dixson. (American Classics: No. 8). 1988. 65.00 (978-0-13-024761-2(8), 58231) Prentice ESL.

Rise of Silas Lapham. unabr. ed. William Dean Howells. Read by Jonathan Reese. 9 cass. (Running Time: 13 hrs. 30 mins.). 2001. 72.00 (978-0-7366-8266-4(X)) Books on Tape.
Silas Lapham has cornered the mineral paint market, and is now a tycoon by anyone's standards. Still, his family is having difficulty integrating itself into the high society of Gilded Age Boston. It is the conflict between old money and new money . An old-money suitor, Tom Corey, is in love with one of Lapham's daughters, and his own parents are horrified at the prospect of such a match. Financial and ethical ruin overtake Lapham, as he loses his money in stocks and acknowledges he cheated a business partner to get his start, but his "rise" is a moral one: he accepts bankruptcy rather than unethical success.

Rise of Silas Lapham. unabr. ed. William Dean Howells. Read by Jim Killavey. 10 cass. (Running Time: 15 hrs.). 1993. 49.00 Incl. vinyl album. Jimcin Record.
The realistic story of the rise & redemptive fall of an American tycoon. Considered the author's best novel.

Rise of the American Republic. unabr. ed. John R. Alden. Read by John MacDonald. 16 cass. (Running Time: 23 hrs. 30 mins.). 1989. 99.95 set. (978-0-7861-0153-5(9), 1138) Blckstn Audio.
Recommended listening for all Americans (as well as foreigners seeking to gain historical wisdom & insight), this magisterial & lucid history of America, from the beginning to the present, is written with a lighter touch by a respected historian.

***Rise of the Darklings.** unabr. ed. Paul Crilley. Read by Katherine Kellgren. 6 CDs. (Running Time: 7 hrs.). (Invisible Order Trilogy: Bk. 1). 2010. audio compact disk 54.97 (978-1-4418-8866-2(7), 9781441888662, BriAudCD Unabrid) Brilliance Audio.

***Rise of the Darklings.** unabr. ed. Paul Crilley. Read by Katherine Kellgren. 1 MP3-CD. (Running Time: 7 hrs.). (Invisible Order Trilogy: Bk. 1). (YA). 2010. 24.99 (978-1-4418-8867-9(5), 9781441888679, Brilliance MP3); audio compact disk 24.99 (978-1-4418-8865-5(9), 9781441888655, Bril Audio CD Unabri) Brilliance Audio.

Rise of the Evening Star. Brandon Mull. Contrib. by E. B. Stevens. (Running Time: 43200 sec.). (Fablehaven Ser.: Bk. 2). (J). (gr. 3-7). 2007. audio compact disk 39.95 (978-1-59038-764-1(3), Shadow Mount) Deseret Bk.

Rise of the Fourth Reich: The Secret Societies That Threaten to Take over America. unabr. ed. Jim Marrs. Read by J. Paul Boehmer. (Running Time: 16 hrs. 0 mins. 0 sec.). (ENG.). 2008. audio compact disk 39.99 (978-1-4001-0816-9(0)); audio compact disk 79.99 (978-1-4001-3816-6(7)); audio compact disk 29.99 (978-1-4001-5816-4(8)) Pub: Tantor Media. Dist(s): IngramPubServ

Rise of the Greeks. unabr. ed. Michael Grant. Read by Nadia May. 10 cass. (Running Time: 14 hrs. 30 mins.). 1990. 69.95 (978-0-7861-0175-7(X), 1156) Blckstn Audio.
The everyday life of the citizens & the policies & government of these states are focal points of the book, as are the lives of the leading personalities of the age.

***Rise of the Wyrm Lord: The Door Within Trilogy - Book Two.** unabr. ed. Wayne Thomas Batson. Narrated by Wayne Thomas Batson. (Running Time: 10 hrs. 51 mins. 37 sec.). (Door Within Ser.). 2010. 19.59 (978-1-60814-789-2(4)); audio compact disk 29.99 (978-1-59859-845-2(7)) Oasis Audio.

Rise of Theodore Roosevelt. Edmund Morris. Read by John MacDonald. 1991. 80.00 (978-0-7366-2078-9(8)) Books on Tape.

Rise of Theodore Roosevelt. abr. ed. Edmund Morris. Read by Harry Chase. 8 CDs. (Running Time: 9 hrs.). (ENG.). 2002. audio compact disk 37.95 (978-0-7393-0182-1(9)) Pub: Random Audio Pubg. Dist(s): Random

***Rise of Theodore Roosevelt.** abr. ed. Edmund Morris. Read by Harry Chase. (ENG.). 2010. audio compact disk 19.99 (978-0-307-87819-9(8), Random AudioBks) Pub: Random Audio Pubg. Dist(s): Random

Rise of Theodore Roosevelt. unabr. ed. Edmund Morris. Read by John MacDonald. 20 cass. (Running Time: 30 hrs.). 1991. 80.00 (978-0-7366-2077-2(X), 2883-A/B) Books on Tape.
The hard-riding adventure story that was the life of Teddy Roosevelt.

Rise of Theodore Roosevelt, Pt. 1. unabr. ed. Edmund Morris. Read by Grover Gardner. 10 cass. (Running Time: 15 hrs.). 2003. 69.95 (978-0-7861-0070-5(2), 1066-A) Blckstn Audio.
This is the story of seven men - a naturalist, a writer, a lover, a hunter, a cowboy, a soldier & the politician - who merged at the age of forty-two to become the youngest President in history.

Rise of Theodore Roosevelt, Pt. 1. unabr. ed. Edmund Morris. Read by John MacDonald. 10 cass. (Running Time: 15 hrs.). 1991. 80.00 (2883-A) Books on Tape.
A sweeping narrative of the man & his legend. It is told as a hard-riding adventure story, spanning the years from Roosevelt's birth in 1858 to President McKinley's death & TR's assumption of office in 1901.

Rise of Theodore Roosevelt, Pt. 2. unabr. ed. Edmund Morris. Read by Grover Gardner. 10 cass. (Running Time: 15 hrs.). 2003. 69.95 (978-0-7861-0071-2(0), 1066-B) Blckstn Audio.
This is the story of seven men - a naturalist, a writer, a lover, a hunter, a cowboy, a soldier & the politician - who merged at the age of forty-two to become the youngest President in history.

Rise of Theodore Roosevelt, Pt. 2. unabr. ed. Edmund Morris. Read by John MacDonald. 10 cass. (Running Time: 15 hrs.). 1991. 80.00 (2883-B) Books on Tape.
The hard-riding adventure story that was the life of Teddy Roosevelt.

Rise to Rebellion: A Novel of the American Revolution. Jeff Shaara. Narrated by George Guidall. 18 CDs. (Running Time: 20 hrs. 45 mins.). audio compact disk 166.00 (978-1-4025-1550-7(2)) Recorded Bks.

Rise to Rebellion: A Novel of the American Revolution. Jeff Shaara. Narrated by George Guidall. 15 cass. (Running Time: 20 hrs. 45 mins.). 2001. 125.00 (978-1-4025-0688-8(0), 96923) Recorded Bks.
A stirring tale of the American Revolution featuring many figures who have become legends, John and Abigail Adams, George Washington, Ben Franklin, Thomas Jefferson, and more. Reconstructing the Boston Massacre, the Boston Tea party, Bunker Hill and Concord. it vividly chronicles the events that led a scattered group of colonies to declare independence.

Rise up & Enter In. Gloria Copeland. 5 cass. 1986. stu. ed. 25.00 (978-0-88114-743-8(5)) K Copeland Pubns.
Biblical teaching on resting in God.

***Rise up & Sing!** Created by Lillenas Publishing Company. (ENG.). 2008. audio compact disk 12.00 (978-5-557-37033-2(1)) Lillenas.

Rise up & Walk! Plugging in to the Power of Grace. 2003. 13.95 (978-1-932631-59-3(3)); audio compact disk 13.95 (978-1-932631-60-9(7)) Ascensn Pr.

Rise up My People. John Angotti. 1 cass. 11.00 (978-1-58459-060-6(2)); 16.00 (978-1-58459-061-3(0)) Wrld Lib Pubns.
Parish contemporary collection of text & music.

Rise up Shepherd & Follow - ShowTrax. Arranged by Larry Farrow. 1 CD. (Running Time: 5 mins.). 2000. audio compact disk 19.95 (08742396) H Leonard.
The richness of this wonderful African American spiritual is preserved in this brilliant contemporary setting.

Rise Vision Comin. Haki R. Madhubuti. 2003. audio compact disk 15.00 (978-0-88378-258-3(8)) Pub: Third World. Dist(s): Chicago Distribution Ctr

Risen: A Worship Sequence for Easter Sunday. 1 cass. 1994. 19.99 Lillenas.

Risen Lord: 1 Cor. 15:1-11. Ed Young. 1986. 4.95 (978-0-7417-1513-5(9), 513) Win Walk.

Rising. Brian Keene. Read by Peter Delloro. 8 CDs. (Running Time: 9 mins.). 2009. audio compact disk 34.95 (978-1-897304-44-0(7)) Dorch Pub Co.

***Rising.** Brian Keene. Read by Peter Delloro. 1 MP3-CD. (Running Time: 9 mins.). 2009. 19.95 (978-1-897331-22-4(3), AudioRealms) Dorch Pub Co.

Rising: Antichrist Is Born - Before They Were Left Behind. unabr. ed. Tim LaHaye & Jerry B. Jenkins. 7 cass. (Left Behind Ser.). 69.75 (978-1-4193-2054-5(8)); audio compact disk 89.75 (978-1-4193-2056-9(4)) Recorded Bks.

Rising: Antichrist Is Born - Before They Were Left Behind. unabr. ed. Tim LaHaye & Jerry B. Jenkins. (Left Behind Ser.). 2005. 29.95 (978-1-4193-3297-5(X)); audio compact disk 39.95 (978-1-4193-3298-2(8)) Recorded Bks.

Rising: Edge of War. unabr. ed. Peter Biskind et al. Read by Luke Daniels. (Running Time: 12 hrs.). (Red Dragon Ser.). 2010. 36.99 (978-1-4233-7018-5(X), 9781423370185, Brilliance MP3) Brilliance Audio.

Rising: Shadows of War. unabr. ed. Larry Bond & Jim DeFelice. Read by Luke Daniels. (Running Time: 15 hrs.). (Red Dragon Ser.). 2009. 19.99 (978-1-4233-7011-6(2), 9781423370116, Brilliance MP3); 39.97 (978-1-4233-7012-3(0), 9781423370123, Brinc Audio MP3 Lib); 19.99 (978-1-4233-7013-0(9), 9781423370130, BAD); 39.97 (978-1-4233-7014-7(7), 9781423370147, BADLE); audio compact disk 69.97 (978-1-4233-7010-9(4), 9781423370109, BriAudCD Unabrid) Brilliance Audio.

***Rising above Disappointment.** Mason Betha. (ENG.). 2010. 24.99 (978-1-60989-000-1(0)) Born To Succee.

Rising above Irritations. Swami Amar Jyoti. 1 cass. 1978. 9.95 (P-21) Truth Consciousness.
How to have peace while flowing in the river of life. Learning to swim over the waves, not drowning in them. Golden opportunities for growth.

Rising above Mediocrity: Raising Your Level of Expectancy. Speeches. Told to Joel Osteen. 1 Cass. (Running Time: 30 Mins.). 2001. Rental 6.00 (978-1-59349-115-4(8), JA0115) J Osteen.

Rising above Your Failures. Short Stories. Joel Osteen. 1 Cass. (Running Time: 30 Mins.). (J). 2000. 6.00 (978-1-59349-070-6(4), JA0070) J Osteen.

Rising from the Plains. unabr. ed. John McPhee. Read by Walter Zimmerman. 7 cass. (Running Time: 7 hrs.). 1991. 42.00 (978-0-7366-1934-9(8), 2756) Books on Tape.
It is said of geologists that they reflect in their professional styles the sort of country in which they grew up. David Love is an example. Born shortly after the turn of the century, he was raised on an isolated Wyoming ranch & nurtured by the outdoors. He grew familiar with the composition of the high-country the way someone raised on a ship gets familiar with the sea. So when John McPhee began his exploration of Rocky Mountain geology, he sought out Love, now pre-eminent in this field. With McPhee asking questions & interpreting answers, it's like the country talking about itself.

Rising from the Plains: From Annals of the Former World. unabr. ed. John McPhee. Narrated by Nelson Runger. 5 cass. (Running Time: 7 hrs. 30 mins.). (Annals of the Former World Ser.: No. 3). 2000. 48.00 (978-0-7887-4313-9(9), 96022E7) Recorded Bks.
The author's Pulitzer Prize-winning collection takes him to the high country of Utah along the Continental Divide in this volume. His guide is David Love "the grand old man of Rocky Mountain geology." As he helps McPhee see the changes that have shaped this region, Love also traces his own family's history in the oil-rich, windswept land.

Rising Phoenix. Kyle Mills. Read by Michael Kramer. 1998. audio compact disk 88.00 (978-0-7366-8535-1(9)) Books on Tape.

Rising Phoenix. unabr. ed. Kyle Mills. Read by Michael Kramer. 9 cass. (Running Time: 13 hrs. 30 mins). 1998. 72.00 (978-0-7366-4119-7(X), 4623) Books on Tape.
A deadly plague strikes America's cities. Someone has taken the war on drugs into his own hands & poisoned the narcotics supply. And the majority of Americans approve!.

Rising Signs. Carolyn Dodson. 1 cass. 8.95 (093) Am Fed Astrologers.
What to look for in others, descriptions of the signs.

Rising Sun see Love Poems of John Donne

Rising Sun Pt. 3: The Decline & Fall of the Japanese Empire. collector's ed. John Toland. Read by John MacDonald. 9 cass. (Running Time: 13 hrs. 30 min.). 1988. 72.00 (978-0-7366-1430-6(3), 2315-B); 80.00 (978-0-7366-1431-3(1), 2315-C) Books on Tape.
A saga of people caught up in the flood of war, told as it happened - muddled, ennobling, disgraceful, frustrating, full of contradiction & paradox.

Rising Sun Pt. 3: The Decline & Fall of the Japanese Empire. unabr. collector's ed. John Toland. Read by John MacDonald. 9 cass. (Running Time: 13 hrs. 30 min.). 1988. 72.00 (978-0-7366-1429-0(X), 2315-A) Books on Tape.

Rising Thunder: From Lincoln's Election to the Battle of Bull Run: An Eyewitness History. unabr. collector's ed. Richard Wheeler. Read by Dick Estell. 9 cass. (Running Time: 13 hrs. 30 min.). 1995. 72.00 (978-0-7366-3139-6(9), 3814) Books on Tape.
You could hear the thunder of conflict by the 1850s. In Boston drawing rooms, Abolitionists vowed to preserve the Union...at all costs. To South Carolina plantation owners, property & states' rights were sacred...they pledged their honor & their lives. Political parties jockeyed furiously to find the candidate that would push their agendas. When Lincoln entered the White House, both sides had reached their boiling points. When a final compromise failed, shots rang out at Fort Sumter. And in the first major battle at Bull Run, relates Wheeler, the slaughter shattered all hope of a quick, easy war.

Rising Tide. abr. ed. Jeff Shaara. Read by Larry Pine. (Running Time: 21600 sec.). (ENG.). 2006. audio compact disk 29.95 (978-0-7393-3463-8(8), Random AudioBks) Pub: Random Audio Pubg. Dist(s): Random

Rising Tide. unabr. ed. Jeff Shaara. 16 cass. (Running Time: 24 hrs.). 2006. 128.00 (978-1-4159-3326-8(X)); audio compact disk 126.65 (978-1-4159-3327-5(8)) Pub: Books on Tape. Dist(s): NetLibrary CO

Rising Tide: The Great Mississippi Flood of 1927 & How It Changed America. John M. Barry. 1 cass. 1998. (Audioworks) S&S Audio.

Rising Tide: The Great Mississippi Flood of 1927 & How It Changed America. abr. ed. John M. Barry. Read by George Grizzard. 2004. 15.95 (978-0-7435-4843-4(4)) Pub: S&S Audio. Dist(s): S and S Inc

Rising Tide: Why Tax Cuts Are the Key to Prosperity & Freedom. abr. ed. Lawrence Kudlow. 4 CDs. (Running Time: 6 hrs.). 2004. audio compact disk 29.95 (978-0-06-072345-3(9)) HarperCollins Pubs.

Rising Tides. Nora Roberts. Read by David Stuart. (Chesapeake Bay Ser.: Bk. 2). 2008. 69.99 (978-1-60640-805-6(4)) Find a World.

Rising Tides. abr. ed. Nora Roberts. Read by David Stuart. (Running Time: 3 hrs.). (Chesapeake Bay Ser.: Bk. 2). 2005. audio compact disk 62.25 (978-1-59600-091-9(0), 9781596000919, BACDLib Ed) Brilliance Audio.
New York Times bestselling author Nora Roberts presents the second novel in a dramatic trilogy of three men who return home to honor their father's last wish - to care for Seth, a troubled boy in need of a family. Coming home has taught the brothers more than they ever dreamed about the meaning of family and responsibility. Now it is time to learn the meaning of acceptance and love. Of three brothers, it was Ethan who shared his father's passion for the Maryland shore. And now with his father gone, Ethan is determined to make the family boatbuilding business a success. But amidst his achievements lie the most important challenges of his life. There is young Seth, who needs him more than ever. And a woman he has always loved but never believed he could have. But beneath Ethan's seemingly still waters is a dark and painful past. He must learn to see around the shadows to accept who he is. Because through Ethan's past lies the future - and his

one chance at happiness. Look for the other titles in this series: Book One: Sea Swept and Book Three: Inner Harbor.

Rising Tides. abr. rev. ed. Nora Roberts. Read by David Stuart. (Running Time: 3 hrs.). (Chesapeake Bay Ser.: Bk. 2). 2005. audio compact disk 14.99 (978-1-59600-090-2(2), 9781596000902) Brilliance Audio.

Rising Tides. unabr. ed. Nora Roberts. Read by David Stuart. (Running Time: 10 hrs.). (Chesapeake Bay Ser.: Bk. 2). 2005. 39.25 (978-1-59710-647-4(X), 9781597106474, BADLE); 24.95 (978-1-59710-646-7(1), 9781597106467, BAD); 24.95 (978-1-59335-793-1(1), 9781593357931, Brilliance MP3); 39.25 (978-1-59335-927-0(6), 9781593359270, Brlnc Audio MP3 Lib); 29.95 (978-1-59600-089-6(9), 9781596000896, BAU) Brilliance Audio.

Rising Tides. unabr. ed. Nora Roberts. Read by David Stuart. (Running Time: 10 hrs.). (Chesapeake Bay Ser.: Bk. 2). 2008. audio compact disk 97.25 (978-1-4233-5648-6(9), 9781423356486, BriAudCD Unabrid); audio compact disk 36.95 (978-1-4233-5647-9(0), 9781423356479, Bril Audio CD Unabri) Brilliance Audio.

Rising Tides. unabr. ed. Nora Roberts. Read by David Stuart. 8 cass. (Chesapeake Bay Ser.: Bk. 2). 1999. 73.25 (FS9-43215) Highsmith.

Risk. Dick Francis. 2 cass. (Running Time: 3 hrs.). 1990. 15.95 HarperCollins Pubs.

Risk. abr. ed. Dick Francis. Read by Sheila Hart. 2 cass. (Running Time: 3 hrs.). 2000. 7.95 (978-1-57815-048-9(5), 1020, Media Bks Audio) Media Bks NJ.
Roland Britten, an accountant by profession, but an amateur jockey by preference, awakens to find he cannot move nor see & is tied in the dark near a generator. But why & by whom?.

Risk. unabr. ed. Dick Francis. Read by Geoffrey Howard. 5 cass. (Running Time: 7 hrs.). 1999. 39.95 (978-0-7861-1482-5(7), 2334) Blckstn Audio.
Roland Britten, an amateur jockey & accountant by profession, awakens one morning to find he is lying in the dark, tied to a generator. But why? And where? And by whom? And what will happen next?.

Risk. unabr. ed. Dick Francis. Read by Geoffrey Howard. 5 CDs. (Running Time: 25200 sec.). 2000. audio compact disk 40.00 (978-0-7861-8782-9(4), 2334) Blckstn Audio.

Risk. unabr. ed. Dick Francis. Read by Geoffrey Howard. (Running Time: 25200 sec.). 2007. audio compact disk 29.95 (978-0-7861-6174-4(4)) Blckstn Audio.

Risk. unabr. ed. Dick Francis. Read by David Case. 8 cass. (Running Time: 8 hrs.). 1994. 64.00 (978-0-7366-2834-1(7), 3542) Books on Tape.
Roland Britten is caught in a deadly game of cat-&-mouse. But who is out to get the accountant & champion steeplechase jockey?.

Risk. unabr. ed. Dick Francis. Read by Tony Britton. 6 cass. (Running Time: 9 hrs.). 2000. 49.95 (978-0-7451-5955-3(9), CAB 660) Pub: Chivers Audio Bks GBR. Dist(s): AudioGO
An amateur rider can hope for little more than a chance to ride in the Gold Cup. So when Roland Britton, an accountant, rides and wins, he is overjoyed. His final reward, however, is to be kidnapped and held in a dark hole for several days.

Risk. unabr. ed. Dick Francis. Narrated by Simon Prebble. 6 cass. (Running Time: 8 hrs. 15 mins.). 2000. 51.00 (978-0-7887-0356-0(0), 94548E7) Recorded Bks.
One morning Roland Britten, an amateur jockey & an accountant, awakes to find himself stiff, cold, & tied to a generator.

Risk, Set. unabr. ed. Dick Francis. Read by Geoffrey Howard. 5 cass. 1999. 39.95 (FS9-43389) Highsmith.

Risk: An Adventure to Live. Featuring John Eldredge. (ESP.). 2009. audio compact disk 12.99 (978-1-933207-39-1(6)) Ransomed Heart.

Risk: Are You Willing to Trust God with Everything? Kenny Luck. (God's Man Ser.). (ENG.). 2008. audio compact disk 24.99 (978-1-934384-20-6(8)) Pub: Treasure Pub. Dist(s): STL Dist NA

Risk Assessment & Risk Management in Environmental Law: Thursday-Friday, October 8-9, 1998 - Madison Hotel, Washington D. C. Optional Introductory Session, Wednesday Evening, October 7. 9 cass. (Running Time: 13 hrs. 30 min.). 345.00 Incl. course materials. (MD37) Am Law Inst.
Wednesday: Designed to familiarize lawyers & managers with the risk concepts that they need to know in order to effectively practice environmental law; Thursday: Examines how changes in risk assessment & risk management translate into decisions that affect the practice of law; Friday: Concentrates on administrative & regulatory practice issues.

Risk It! & How to Become a More Loving Person. Jack Marshall. 1 cass. 2004. 7.98 (978-1-55503-395-8(4), 06004482) Covenant Comms.
Youth talk - Giving a no-fail formula for making life work.

Risk Management in Obstetrics & Gynecology. Contrib. by Albert L. Strunk et al. 1 cass. (American College of Obstetrics & Gynecologists UPDATE: Vol. 23, No. 3). 1998. 20.00 Am Coll Obstetric.

Risk of Being Heroes - Ethical Decision-Making. Larry Ulrich. 1986. 10.80 (0205) Assn Prof Chaplains.

Risk of Creativity: A Dialogs in Amsterdam. Steven Harrison. (Running Time: 25200 sec.). 2008. audio compact disk 39.95 (978-1-59181-067-4(1)) Pub: Sentient Pubns. Dist(s): Natl Bk Netwk

Risk Pool. unabr. ed. Richard Russo. (Running Time: 19 hrs. 58 mins.). 2005. 112.00 (978-1-74093-651-4(5)) Pub: Bolinda Pubng AUS. Dist(s): Bolinda Pub Inc

Risk Pool. unabr. ed. Ed. by Richard Russo. (Running Time: 19 hrs. 58 mins.). 2005. 44.25 (978-1-74093-652-1(3)) Pub: Bolinda Pubng AUS. Dist(s): Bolinda Pub Inc

Risk Proofing Families in a World Gone Crazy: National Association of Evangelicals, 47th Annual Convention, Columbus, Ohio, March 7-9, 1989. Donald M. Joy. 1 cass. (Luncheons Ser.: No. 108-Tuesda). 1989. 4.25 ea. 1-8 tapes.; 4.00 9 tapes or more. Nat Assn Evan.

Risk Worth Taking. abr. rev. ed. Robin Pilcher. Read by Gerard Doyle. 3 CDs. (Running Time: 3 hrs. 30 mins. 0 sec.). (ENG.). 2004. audio compact disk 19.95 (978-1-59397-363-6(2)) Pub: Macmill Audio. Dist(s): Macmillan

Riskin & Doxsee's Dispute Resolution for Lawyers Video Tapes: Tape 1-Dispute Negotiation - the Thompson V. Decker Medical Malpractice Claim (American Casebook Seriesreg;) Leonard L. Riskin & Deborah J. Doxsee. 2005. 123.00 (978-0-314-00420-8(3), West Lglwrks) West.

Riskin & Doxsee's Dispute Resolution for Lawyers Video Tapes: Tape 2-Transaction Negotiation - the Carton Contract (American Casebook Seriesreg;) Leonard L. Riskin & Deborah J. Doxsee. 2005. 123.00 (978-0-314-00421-5(1), West Lglwrks) West.

Riskin & Doxsee's Dispute Resolution for Lawyers Video Tapes: Tape 3-Mediation - the Red Devil Dog Lease (American Casebook Series) Leonard L. Riskin & Deborah J. Doxsee. 1991. 123.00 (978-0-314-00422-2(X), West Lglwrks) West.

Riskin & Doxsee's Dispute Resolution for Lawyers Video Tapes: Tape 4-ADR Overview - the Roark V. Daily Bugle Libel Claim - the Thompson V. Decker Medical Malpractice Claim (American Casebook Seriesreg;) Leonard L. Riskin & Deborah J. Doxsee. 2005. 123.00 (978-0-314-00423-9(8), West Lglwrks) West.

Risking. David S. Viscott. 1 cass. 10.00 (SP100030) SMI Intl.
Unless you risk failure, you cannot enjoy success. Knowing how to risk, what to risk, & when to risk maximizes odds for personal victory. Listen & learn to make good decisions, to avoid fool-hardy risks, & to take the creative risks that lead to success.

Risking: Art of Being More Fully Alive. Jonathan Robinson. Read by Jonathan Robinson. 1 cass. (Running Time: 90 min.). 1990. 9.95 (978-1-57328-792-0(X)) Focal Pt Calif.
For most adults, life takes on a routine or ordinary flavor after awhile. Unfortunately, this tendency dulls our passion for life, & undermines our ability to reach our deepest dreams. This audio tape will inspire & inform you in how to make your day to day life more adventurous & joyful once again. In the tape, the five laws of successful risktaking are presented, & practical ways to make use of them are discussed. Topics & exercises include risktaking in relationships, career goals, leisure time pursuits, spirituality, & personal growth.

Risking It All. unabr. ed. Ann Granger. Read by Kim Hicks. 8 cass. (Running Time: 12 hrs.). 2002. 96.95 (978-0-7540-0827-9(4), CAB 2249) Pub: Chivers Pr GBR. Dist(s): AudioGO

Risks & Rewards, Vol. 24. AIO Team Staff. Prod. by Focus on the Family Staff. 4 CDs. (Running Time: 6 hrs.). (Adventures in Odyssey Ser.: No. 24). (ENG.). (J). (gr. 3-7). 1996. audio compact disk 24.99 (978-1-56179-455-3(4)) Pub: Focus Family. Dist(s): Tyndale Hse

Risks, Liabilities & Trends in Community Association Law. Moderated by Wendell A. Smith. Contrib. by Wayne S. Hyatt. (Running Time: 4 hrs.). 1985. 85.00 incl. program handbook. NJ Inst CLE.
Analyzes such issues as standing to sue, developers' liability, fiduciary obligations of community association board members, enforcement of community association rules & regulations.

Risky Bizness. Based on a novel by Oak Summers. 2007. audio compact disk 12.95i (978-1-4276-1909-9(3)) AardGP.

Risky Business. unabr. ed. Nora Roberts. Read by Gabra Zackman. (Running Time: 7 hrs.). 2010. 24.99 (978-1-4418-3016-6(2), 9781441830166, Brilliance MP3); 39.97 (978-1-4418-3017-3(0), 9781441830173, Brlnc Audio MP3 Lib); 39.97 (978-1-4418-3018-0(9), 9781441830180, BADLE); audio compact disk 24.99 (978-1-4418-3014-2(6), 9781441830142, Bril Audio CD Unabri); audio compact disk 79.97 (978-1-4418-3015-9(4), 9781441830159, BriAudCD Unabrid) Brilliance Audio.

***Rita Ann Higgins: Reads 52 of Her Poems.** Rita Ann Higgins. (ENG.). 1994. 11.95 (978-0-8023-0024-9(3)) Pub: Clo Iar-Chonnachta IRL. Dist(s): Dufour

Rita Dove. Rita Dove. Read by Rita Dove. 1 cass. (Running Time: 29 min.). 1991. 10.00 (080985) New Letters.
Rita Dove reads from her Pulitzer Prize-winning book," Thomas & Beulah" & talks with Rebekah Presson.

Rita Dove, Vol. II. unabr. ed. Ed. by Jim McKinley. Prod. by Rebekah Presson. 1 cass. (Running Time: 29 min.). (New Letters on the Air Ser.). 1994. 10.00 (050793) New Letters.
The Pulitzer Prize winning poet is also America's first Africa-American Poet Laureate. Dove reads poetry & prose & talks about her development as an artist, as well as about the pitfalls of being a black woman trained in the classics.

Rita Hayworth & Shawshank Redemption, unabr. ed. Stephen King. Narrated by Frank Muller. 3 cass. (Running Time: 4 hrs. 30 mins.). 1984. 26.00 (978-1-55690-432-5(0), 84063E7) Recorded Bks.
Wrongly-convicted Andy Dufresne finds a way out of the state prison but leaves a gift of hope behind. The inspiration for the movie.

Rite: The Making of a Modern Exorcist. Matt Baglio. 6 CDs. (Running Time: 7 hrs. 30 mins.). 2009. audio compact disk 34.95 (978-0-86716-933-1(8)) St Anthony Mess Pr.

Rite Brain 2004. Created by Church Publishing. 1. 2001. audio compact disk 101.00 (978-0-89869-411-6(6)) Church Pub Inc.
This major upgrade of the popular CD-ROM includes "Lesser Feasts and Fasts 2003;" the updated "Book of Occasional Services 2003" with church planting liturgies in English, Spanish, and French; and "The Book of Common Prayer" in Spanish. Use "The Rite Brain" to create custom bulletins, produce annotated materials for study groups, or search through the liturgical resources of the Episcopal Church.

Rite of Passage: A Paradigm for Hospital Ministry. 1 cass. (Care Cassettes Ser.: Vol. 16, No. 9). 1989. 10.80 Assn Prof Chaplains.

Rite Song: Version 2. 0. 2004. audio compact disk 296.00 (978-0-89869-392-8(6)) Church Pub Inc.
This new version of our useful music resource has been expanded to include text, graphic files, and listening reference MID fies for "Voices Found," "Enriching Our Music I and II," and the Appendix from "The Hymnal 1982 Accompaniment Edition (S289-S448). It also contains "The Hymnal 1982," "Wonder, Love and Praise;" and "Lift Every Voice and Sing II." - Downloadalbe to bulletins- Fully searchable- Listening reference- Exportable copyright forms.

Rite Word 2004: Revised Standard Version & New Revised Standard Version. Created by Church Publishing. 2001. audio compact disk 150.00 (978-0-89869-463-5(9)) Church Pub Inc.

Rites of Autumn, Cliff Schimmels. 2 cass. (Running Time: 3 hrs.). 1995. 17.99 (978-1-886463-13-4(1)) Oasis Audio.

Rites of Passage. unabr. ed. William Golding. Read by William Golding. 8 cass. (Running Time: 9 hrs. 50 min.). 2001. 69.95 (978-1-85089-700-2(X), 90033) Pub: ISIS Audio GBR. Dist(s): Ulverscroft US
This is book one in the sea trilogy, To the Ends of the Earth.

Rites of Passage: Program from the Award Winning Public Radio Serie. Interview. Hosted by John Goodwin. 1 CD. (Running Time: 1 hr.). 2001. audio compact disk 21.95 (978-1-932479-88-1(0), LCM 164) Lichtenstein Creat.
Whether it's a birth or a bar mitzvah, a wedding or a funeral, we mark the stages of our lives with rituals and celebrations. Why are these occasions so important? This program explores the psychological and social implications of rites of passage. Guests include Dr. Ronald Grimes, a professor of religion and culture at Wilfrid Laurier University in Ontario, Canada; Karen Karbo writer of Generation Ex: Tales From the Second Wives Club; Dr. Stephen Balfour, who teaches courses on Contemporary American Rites of Passage at Texas A & M University; and Thomas Lynch, a poet, writer and undertaker.

Ritm: an Accelerated Course in Russian: An Accelerated Course in Russian. Robin Aizlewood. (Routledge Intensive Language Courses Ser.). 2006. bk. 110.00 (978-0-415-22301-0(6), RU016) Pub: Routledge. Dist(s): Taylor and Fran

Ritmo de la Vida. Contrib. by Julissa. 2007. audio compact disk 14.98 (978-5-557-63535-6(1)) Integrity Music.

Ritmos de Ecuador. Compiled by Vicki Corona. Gustavo Ayala. 1985. audio compact disk 16.95 (978-1-58513-172-3(5)) Dance Fantasy.

Ritual. Perf. by Roth, Gabrielle, and the Mirrors. 1 cass. 9.95 (MT046) White Dove NM.
Soft, sensual trance music with a ritual beat - a grounding remembrance for Mother Earth.

***Ritual Bath.** unabr. ed. Faye Kellerman. Read by Mitchell Greenberg. (ENG.). 2007. (978-0-06-157303-5(3)); (978-0-06-157304-0(3)) HarperCollins Pubs.

Ritual Bath. unabr. ed. Faye Kellerman. Read by Mitchell Greenberg. 7 CDs. (Running Time: 8 hrs.). (Peter Decker & Rina Lazarus Novel Ser.). 2008. audio compact disk 19.95 (978-0-06-144181-3(3), Harper Audio) HarperCollins Pubs.

Ritual Ceremonies: The Reality of the Psyche Enacted. Read by Barry Williams. 1 cass. (Running Time: 90 min.). (Patterns of Divinity Ser.: No. 1). 1988. 10.95 (978-0-7822-0328-8(0), 301) C G Jung IL.

Ritual Conga Drumming. Antonio C. Silva. 1 cass. 7.00 (A0134-86) Sound Photosyn.
At Shaman Conference '86.

Ritual Death. unabr. ed. Brad Reynolds. Read by Kevin Foley. 8 cass. (Running Time: 9 hrs. 24 min.). (Father Mark Townsend Mystery Ser.). 2001. 49.95 (978-1-55686-985-3(1)) Books in Motion.
During a peaceful visit with his grandparents on Puget Sound, Father Mark becomes involved in the murder investigation of his grandfather's best friend, a boatsman possibly involved with international smuggling.

Ritual Drumming: Evoking the Sacred Through Rhythms of the Spirit. 2nd ed. Compiled by Mishlen Linden & Louis Martinie. (Running Time: 1 hr.). 2005. bk. 12.95 (978-1-59477-072-2(7), Destiny Recs) Inner Tradit.

Ritual in Death. J. D. Robb, pseud. Read by Susan Ericksen. (In Death Ser.). (ENG.). 2009. 34.99 (978-1-60812-651-4(X)) Find a World.

Ritual in Death. unabr. ed. J. D. Robb, pseud. Read by Susan Ericksen. (Running Time: 3 hrs.). (In Death Ser.). 2008. 25.25 (978-1-4233-6196-1(2), 9781423361961, Brlnc Audio MP3 Lib); 25.25 (978-1-4233-6198-5(9), 9781423361985, BADLE); 19.95 (978-1-4233-6195-4(4), 9781423361954, Brilliance MP3); 19.95 (978-1-4233-6197-8(0), 9781423361978, BAD); audio compact disk 44.25 (978-1-4233-6194-7(6), 9781423361947, BriAudCD Unabrid); audio compact disk 19.99 (978-1-4233-6193-0(8), 9781423361930, Bril Audio CD Unabri) Brilliance Audio.

Ritual, Initiation, & Contemporary Religion. Read by Robert Moore. 1 cass. (Running Time: 90 min.). 1985. 10.95 (978-0-7822-0173-4(3), 172) C G Jung IL.

Rituals of Religion. Madalyn M. O'Hair. 1 cass. (Running Time: 27 min.). 10.95 (31010) J Norton Pubs.
A thorough discussion on religious ritual, a tracing of initial forms to present day expressions. What is done & why; primary components of a rite; & qualifications for performance or initiation of a ritualistic action.

Rituals of the Season. unabr. ed. Margaret Maron. Narrated by C. J. Critt. 7 cass. (Running Time: 9 hrs.). (Deborah Knott Mystery Ser.: No. 11). 2005. 69.75 (978-1-4193-2868-8(9), 97964); audio compact disk 89.75 (978-1-4193-2870-1(0), C3208) Recorded Bks.

***Rival Rails: The Race to Build America's Greatest Transcontinental Railroad.** unabr. ed. Walter R. Borneman. (Running Time: 15 hrs. 0 mins. 0 sec.). 2010. 24.99 (978-1-4001-6768-5(X)); 18.99 (978-1-4001-8768-3(0)); audio compact disk 37.99 (978-1-4001-1768-0(2)); audio compact disk 90.99 (978-1-4001-4768-7(9)) Pub: Tantor Media. Dist(s): IngramPubServ

Rivalry. unabr. ed. Norman Corwin. Perf. by Paul Giamatti et al. 2 CDs. (Running Time: 1 hr. 44 mins.). 2009. audio compact disk 25.95 (978-1-58081-569-7(3)) L A Theatre.

***Rivalry: Mystery at the Army-Navy Game.** unabr. ed. John Feinstein. Read by John Feinstein. (ENG.). (J). 2010. audio compact disk 35.00 (978-0-307-74585-9(6), Listening Lib) Pub: Random Audio Pubg. Dist(s): Random

Rivals. Richard Brinsley Sheridan. 2 cass. (Running Time: 2 hrs.). Dramatization. 10.95 (SAC 8049/8050) Spoken Arts.

***Rivals.** unabr. ed. Tim Green. Read by Tim Green. (ENG.). 2010. (978-0-06-198629-1(1)) HarperCollins Pubs.

Rivals. unabr. ed. Richard Sheridan. Narrated by Flo Gibson. 2003. 16.95 (978-1-55685-720-1(9)) Audio Bk Con.
Ensign Beverly (alias Captain Absolute) and Bob Acres contend for the hand of Lydia Languish. Among the many delightful characters is Mrs. Malaprop.

***Rivals: A Baseball Great Novel.** unabr. ed. Tim Green. Read by Tim Green. (ENG.). 2010. (978-0-06-193825-2(4)) HarperCollins Pubs.

***Rivals: How the Power Struggle between China, India & Japan Will Shape Our Next Decade.** unabr. ed. Bill Emmott. (Running Time: 11 hrs. 5 mins.). (ENG.). 2010. 29.95 (978-1-4417-7697-6(4)); audio compact disk 32.95 (978-1-4417-7696-9(6)) Blckstn Audio.

***Rivals: How the Power Struggle between China, India & Japan Will Shape Our Next Decade.** unabr. ed. Bill Emmott. Read by To be Announced. (Running Time: 11 hrs. 5 mins.). (ENG.). 2010. 72.95 (978-1-4417-7694-5(X)); audio compact disk 105.00 (978-1-4417-7695-2(8)) Blckstn Audio.

Rivals of Spring. Cliff Schimmels. 2 cass. (Running Time: 2 hrs.). 1995. 17.99 (978-1-886463-11-0(5)) Oasis Audio.

Riven Kingdom. unabr. ed. Karen Miller. Narrated by Josephine Bailey. (Running Time: 21 hrs. 0 mins. 0 sec.). (Godspeaker Ser.). (ENG.). 2009. 34.99 (978-1-4001-6317-5(X)); audio compact disk 99.99 (978-1-4001-4317-7(9)); audio compact disk 49.99 (978-1-4001-1317-0(2)) Pub: Tantor Media. Dist(s): IngramPubServ

***Riven Kingdom.** unabr. ed. Karen Miller. Narrated by Josephine Bailey. (Running Time: 21 hrs. 0 mins.). (Godspeaker Ser.). 2009. 24.99 (978-1-4001-8317-3(0)); 49.99 (978-1-4001-9317-2(6)) Tantor Media.

Riven Rock. unabr. ed. T. C. Boyle. Read by Michael Russotto. 14 cass. (Running Time: 21 hrs.). 1999. 112.00 (978-0-7366-4316-0(8), 4772) Books on Tape.
In 1905, Stanley McCormick, heir to millions, is most definitely mad. Diagnosed a schizophrenic maniac after a disastrous honeymoon, he is forbidden contact with all women including his wife & cosseted in "Riven Rock," a family estate. Katherine McCormick never divorces her husband & returns to Riven Rock year after year, ever hopeful one of the psychiatrists she enlists will return Stanley to her, free of demons, a yearned for lover.

River. Gary Paulsen. Read by Peter Coyote. 2 cass. (Running Time: 2 hrs. 45 mins.). (YA). 2000. 18.00 (978-0-7366-9052-2(2)) Books on Tape.
Sequel to "Hatched, The River," pits a boy against nature for the second time in his life. When a freak storm leaves his companion grievously injured, Brian Robeson is on his own with only his wits to pull him through.

River. Tricia Wastvedt. Narrated by Bernadette Dunne. (Running Time: 10 hrs.). 2005. 30.95 (978-1-59912-710-1(5)) Iofy Corp.

River. Tricia Wastvedt. Read by Kate Reading. (Running Time: 36000 sec.). 2005. cass., cass., DVD 59.95 (978-0-7861-3030-6(X)); DVD, audio compact disk, audio compact disk 72.00 (978-0-7861-7935-0(X)) Blckstn Audio.

River. unabr. ed. Gary Paulsen. Read by Peter Coyote. 2 vols. (Running Time: 2 hrs. 31 mins.). (Middle Grade Cassette Librariestm Ser.). (J). (gr. 5-9). 2004. pap. bk. 29.00 (978-0-8072-8704-0(0), S YA 241 SP, Listening Lib); 23.00 (978-0-8072-8703-3(2), YA241CX, Listening Lib) Random Audio Pubg.

River. unabr. ed. Gary Paulsen. Read by Peter Coyote. 3 CDs. (Running Time: 2 hrs. 31 mins.). (ENG.). (J). (gr. 3). 2005. audio compact disk 14.99 (978-1-4000-9917-7(X), Listening Lib) Pub: Random Audio Pubg. Dist(s): Random

River. unabr. ed. Tricia Wastvedt. Read by Kate Reading. 9 cass. (Running Time: 36000 sec.). 2005. 29.95 (978-0-7861-3046-7(6)); DVD & audio compact disk 29.95 (978-0-7861-8151-3(6)); audio compact disk 32.95 (978-0-7861-7998-5(8)) Blckstn Audio.

River: One Man's Journey down the Colorado, Source to Sea. collector's ed. Colin Fletcher. Read by Arthur Addison. 12 cass. (Running Time: 18 hrs.). 2000. 96.00 (978-0-7366-4849-3(6)) Books on Tape.
At the age sixty-seven, backpack guru Colin Fletcher decided to make a six-month, single-handed, foot & raft expedition down the full length of the Colorado River.

River at Green Knowe. L. M. Boston. Read by Simon Vance. (Running Time: 18000 sec.). (Green Knowe Chronicles). (J). (ps-7). 2005. audio compact disk 27.95 (978-1-59316-062-3(3)) Listen & Live.

River at Green Knowe. unabr. ed. L. M. Boston. Read by Simon Vance. (J). 2007. 39.99 (978-1-60252-860-4(8)) Find a World.

River Between Us. Richard Peck. Read by Lina Patel. 4 cass. (Running Time: 5 hrs. 25 mins.). (J). (gr. 7 up). 2004. 32.00 (978-1-4000-8626-9(4), Listening Lib); audio compact disk 32.30 (978-1-4000-8982-6(4), Listening Lib) Pub: Random Audio Pubg. Dist(s): NetLibrary CO

River Between Us. unabr. ed. Richard Peck. Read by Lina Patel & Daniel Passer. (Running Time: 14040 sec.). (ENG.). (J). (gr. 3-7). 2005. audio compact disk 30.00 (978-0-307-28250-7(3), Listening Lib) Pub: Random Audio Pubg. Dist(s): Random

River Boy. unabr. ed. Tim Bowler. Read by Emilia Fox. 4 CDs. (Running Time: 6 hrs.). (J). 2002. audio compact disk 34.95 (978-0-7540-6503-6(0), CHCD 003, Chivers Child Audio) AudioGO.

River Boy. unabr. ed. Tim Bowler. Narrated by Christina Moore. 3 pieces. (Running Time: 4 hrs. 15 mins.). (gr. 9 up). 1997. 28.00 (978-1-4025-0198-2(6), 96865) Recorded Bks.
Jess and her parents have brought Grandpa back to his boyhood home by the river. He wants to finish one last painting before he dies. Jess is training to be a long distance swimmer, so when Grandpa is napping, she practices in the river. But soon she starts seeing a presence there - one that is also affecting Grandpa's painting. Who is the boyish figure Jess sees in the river? What does he want her to do? Tim Bowler grew up in a house overlooking an estuary of the Thames. A scholar, translator and writer, he wanted to create a book that would use the river as a spiritual metaphor for the course of life and death.

River Folk. unabr. ed. Margaret Dickinson. Read by Patricia Gallimore. 12 cass. (Running Time: 16 hrs. 30 mins.). (Sound Ser.). (J). 2002. 94.95 (978-1-84283-094-9(5)) Pub: ISIS Lrg Prnt GBR. Dist(s): Ulverscroft US

River God. abr. ed. Wilbur Smith. Read by Dick Hill. 3 CDs. (Running Time: 3 hrs.). 2003. audio compact disk 14.99 (978-1-59086-521-7(9), 1590865219, BAU); audio compact disk 62.25 (978-1-59086-559-0(6), 1590865596, BAU) Brilliance Audio.
Ancient Egypt. Land of the Pharaohs. A kingdom built on gold. A legend shattered by greed.... Now the Valley of Kings lies ravaged by war, drained of its lifeblood, as weak men inherit the cherished crown. For Tanus, the fair-haired young lion of a warrior, the gods have decreed that he will lead Egypt's army in a bold attempt to reunite the Kingdom's shattered halves. But Tanus will have to defy the same gods to attain the reward they have forbidden him, an object more prized than battle's glory: possession of the Lady Lostris, a rare beauty with skin the color of oiled cedar - destined for the adoration of a nation, and the love of one extraordinary man.

River God. abr. ed. Wilbur Smith. Read by Dick Hill. 2 cass. (Running Time: 3 hrs.). 2000. 7.95 (978-1-57815-021-2(3), 1044, Media Bks Audio) Media Bks NJ.
Exploding with all the passion & rage of the ancient heartland of the Nile Kings, the Land of the Pharaohs lies ravaged by war, drained of its lifeblood as weak men inherit the cherished crown.

River God. unabr. ed. Wilbur Smith. Read by Dick Hill. (Running Time: 24 hrs.). 2006. 44.25 (978-1-4233-2875-9(2), 9781423328759, Brinc Audio MP3 Lib); 29.95 (978-1-4233-2874-2(4), 9781423328742, Brilliance MP3); 49.97 (978-1-4233-2877-3(9), 9781423328773, BADLE) Brilliance Audio.

River God. unabr. ed. Wilbur Smith. Read by Dick Hill. (Running Time: 24 hrs.). 2006. 29.95 (978-1-4233-2876-6(0), 9781423328766, BAD) Brilliance Audio.

River God, Pt. 1. unabr. ed. Wilbur Smith. Read by David Case. 9 cass. (Running Time: 13 hrs. 30 min.). (Courtney Novels). 1995. 72.00 sale to libraries only. (978-0-7366-3123-5(2), 3799A) Books on Tape.
Ancient Egypt, the land of the pharaohs, a kingdom built on gold - it all lies ravaged by civil war. But the gods have decreed that Tanus, a fair-haired warrior, will lead Egypt's army in a bold attempt to reunite the kingdom's shattered halves.

River God, Pt. 2. unabr. ed. Wilbur Smith. Read by David Case. 9 cass. (Running Time: 13 hrs. 30 min.). (Courtney Novels). 1995. 72.00 sale to libraries only. (3799-B) Books on Tape.

River God from "Notebook" see Twentieth-Century Poetry in English, No. 32-33, Recordings of Poets Reading Their Own Poetry

River Home: An Angler's Explorations. unabr. ed. Jerry Dennis. Narrated by Ed Sala. 5 cass. (Running Time: 7 hrs.). 1998. 44.00 (978-0-7887-2190-8(9), 95486E7) Recorded Bks.
Tales of fishing, friendship & family are your passport to wonderful woods & rivers. The genius of the acclaimed nature writer is that he celebrates the ordinary while conveying uncommon wisdom.

River Horse: A Voyage Across America. William Least Heat-Moon. Read by Barrett Whitener. 14 cass. (Running Time: 20 hrs.). 2001. 34.95 (978-0-7366-4955-1(7)) Books on Tape.
The author's journey across America, from New York to Oregon, in a small boat.

River Horse: A Voyage Across America. William Least Heat-Moon. Read by Jay O. Sanders. 2004. 15.95 (978-0-7435-1936-6(1)) Pub: S&S Audio. Dist(s): S and S Inc

River Horse: A Voyage Across America. collector's ed. William Least Heat-Moon. Read by Barrett Whitener. 14 cass. (Running Time: 20 hrs.). 2000. 112.00 (978-0-7366-4753-3(8), 5091) Books on Tape.

***River in the Sky.** unabr. ed. Elizabeth Peters. Read by Barbara Rosenblat. (ENG.). 2010. (978-0-06-198809-7(X), Harper Audio) HarperCollins Pubs.

***River in the Sky: A Novel.** unabr. ed. Elizabeth Peters. Read by Barbara Rosenblat. (ENG.). 2010. (978-0-06-195367-5(9), Harper Audio) HarperCollins Pubs.

River Instrumental: Knowing You. Eagles' Wings Ministries. 2007. audio compact disk 16.00 (978-5-558-72598-8(2)) Pub: Sigma F RUS. Dist(s): Destiny Image Pubs

River Killings. unabr. ed. Merry Bloch Jones. Read by Marguerite Gavin. (Running Time: 34200 sec.). 2006. 59.95 (978-0-7861-4763-2(6)); audio compact disk 72.00 (978-0-7861-6347-2(X)); audio compact disk 29.95 (978-0-7861-7266-5(5)) Blckstn Audio.

***River King.** Alice Hoffman. Read by Laural Merlington. (Playaway Adult Fiction Ser.). (ENG.). 2009. 64.99 (978-1-4418-2297-0(6)) Find a World.

River King. abr. ed. Alice Hoffman. Read by Laural Merlington. (Running Time: 6 hrs.). 2009. audio compact disk 14.99 (978-1-4418-1265-0(2), 9781441812650, BCD Value Price) Brilliance Audio.

River King. unabr. ed. Alice Hoffman. Read by Laural Merlington. 7 cass. (Running Time: 10 hrs.). 2000. 32.95 (978-1-56740-378-7(6), 1567403786, BAU); 73.25 (978-1-56740-745-7(5), 1567407455, Unabridge Lib Edns) Brilliance Audio.
For more than a century, the small town of Haddan, Massachusetts, has been divided, as if by a line drawn down the center of Main Street, separating those born and bred in the village from those who attend the prestigious Haddan School. But one October night the two worlds are thrust together due to an inexplicable death, and the town's divided history is revealed in all its complexity. The lives of everyone involved are unraveled: from Carlin Leander, the fifteen-year-old girl who is as loyal as she is proud, to Betsy Chase, a woman running from her own destiny; from August Pierce, a boy who unexpectedly finds courage in his darkest hour, to Abel Grey, the police officer who refuses to let unspeakable actions - both past and present - slide by without notice. Entertainment Weekly has declared that Alice Hoffman's worlds are "replete with miracles" and The Boston Globe has praised her "iridescent prose, taut narrative suspense, and alluring atmosphere." Now she brings us a novel as compelling as it is daring, an exploration of forgiveness and hope, a wondrous tale of innocence and evil, and of the secrets we keep.

River King. unabr. ed. Alice Hoffman. Read by Laural Merlington. (Running Time: 10 hrs.). 2005. 39.25 (978-1-59600-534-1(3), 9781596005341, BADLE); 24.95 (978-1-59600-533-4(5), 9781596005334, BAD); 39.25 (978-1-59600-532-7(7), 9781596005327, Brinc Audio MP3 Lib); 24.95 (978-1-59600-531-0(9), 9781596005310, Brilliance MP3) Brilliance Audio.

River King. unabr. ed. Alice Hoffman. Read by Laural Merlington. (Running Time: 10 hrs.). 2009. audio compact disk 29.99 (978-1-4418-1263-6(6), 9781441812636, Bril Audio CD Unabri); audio compact disk 87.97 (978-1-4418-1264-3(4), 9781441812643, BriAudCD Unabrid) Brilliance Audio.

***River Kings' Road: A Novel of Ithelas.** unabr. ed. Liane Merciel. (Running Time: 13 hrs. 30 mins.). (Ithelas Ser.). 2010. 29.95 (978-1-4417-5923-8(9)); 79.95 (978-1-4417-5919-1(0)); audio compact disk 32.95 (978-1-4417-5922-1(0)); audio compact disk 109.00 (978-1-4417-5920-7(4)) Blckstn Audio.

River Knows. Amanda Quick, pseud. Read by Katherine Kellgren. (Playaway Adult Fiction Ser.). 2008. 64.99 (978-1-60640-901-5(8)) Find a World.

River Knows. abr. ed. Amanda Quick, pseud. Read by Katherine Kellgren. (Running Time: 14400 sec.). 2008. audio compact disk 14.99 (978-1-4233-1493-6(X), 9781423314936, BCD Value Price) Brilliance Audio.

River Knows. unabr. ed. Amanda Quick, pseud. (Running Time: 9 hrs.). 2007. audio compact disk 92.25 (978-1-4233-1487-5(5), 9781423314875, BriAudCD Unabrid) Brilliance Audio.

River Knows. unabr. ed. Amanda Quick, pseud. Read by Katherine Kellgren. (Running Time: 9 hrs.). 2007. 39.25 (978-1-4233-1491-2(3), 9781423314912, BADLE); 24.95 (978-1-4233-1490-5(5), 9781423314905, BAD); 74.25 (978-1-4233-1485-1(9), 9781423314851, BrilAudUnabridg); audio compact disk 34.95 (978-1-4233-1486-8(7), 9781423314868, Bril Audio CD Unabri); audio compact disk 24.95 (978-1-4233-1488-2(3), 9781423314882, Brilliance MP3); audio compact disk 39.25 (978-1-4233-1489-9(1), 9781423314899, Brinc Audio MP3 Lib) Brilliance Audio.

River Love Audio Book. Margaret Van Damm. Based on a book by Margaret Van Damm. (ENG.). 2007. audio compact disk 29.95 (978-1-932278-34-7(6)) Pub: Mayhaven Pub. Dist(s): Baker Taylor

***river not yet Tamed.** unabr. ed. Nancy Cato. Read by Kate Hosking. (Running Time: 6 hrs. 12 mins.). (All the Rivers Run Ser.). 2010. audio compact disk 63.95 (978-1-74214-645-4(7), 9781742146454) Pub: Bolinda Pubng AUS. Dist(s): Bolinda Pub Inc

River Notes. Barry Lopez. Read by Barry Lopez. Music by David Darling. 1 cass. (Running Time: 1 hr.). 1994. 10.95 (978-0-939643-13-4(8), 3534, NrthWrd Bks) TandN Child.
John Burroughs, award-winning author, explores the subtle threads that connect us to the landscape and explores seasonal cycles of the river.

River of Darkness. Rennie Airth. Narrated by Christopher Kay. 12 CDs. (Running Time: 14 hrs.). (John Madden Mystery Ser.: Bk. 1). 1999. audio compact disk 120.00 (978-1-4025-4046-2(9)) Recorded Bks.

River of Darkness. Airth Rennie. 2 cass. (Running Time: 3 hrs.). (ENG., 2001. (978-0-333-90495-4(8)) Macmillan UK GBR.

River of Darkness. unabr. ed. Rennie Airth. Narrated by Christopher Kay. 10 cass. (Running Time: 14 hrs.). (John Madden Mystery Ser.: Bk. 1). 2002. 92.00 (978-1-84197-383-8(1)) Recorded Bks.
In 1921, the bloodied bodies of Colonel Fletcher, his wife and two staff are found in a manor house in Surrey. The police have put the murders down to a violent robbery, but Detective Inspector Madden from Scotland Yard has his own suspicions. In the meantime the killer is plotting his second strike.

River of Darkness. unabr. ed. Rennie Airth. Narrated by Christopher Kay. 10 cass. (Running Time: 14 hrs.). (John Madden Mystery Ser.: Bk. 1). 2002. 44.95 (978-1-4025-1836-2(6), RF906) Recorded Bks.

River of Death. Alistair MacLean. Read by Gordon Griffin. 4 cass. (Running Time: 4 hrs.). 1999. 44.95 (62256) Pub: Soundings Ltd GBR. Dist(s): Ulverscroft US

River of Death. unabr. ed. Alistair MacLean. 4 cass. (Sound Ser.). 2004. 44.95 (978-1-85496-225-6(6)) Pub: UlverLrgPrint GBR. Dist(s): Ulverscroft US

River of Doubt: Theodore Roosevelt's Darkest Journey. abr. ed. Candice Millard. Read by Richard Ferrone. (Running Time: 21600 sec.). (ENG.). 2006. audio compact disk 19.99 (978-0-7393-4050-9(6), Random AudioBks) Pub: Random Audio Pubg. Dist(s): Random

River of Grace. Composed by Matthew Baute. 2008. audio compact disk 17.00 (978-1-58459-413-0(6)) Wrld Lib Pubns.

River of Hope: My Journey with Kathy in Search of Healing from Lou Gehrig's Disease. unabr. ed. Read by David Tank. (ENG.). 2009. 17.95 (978-0-9815064-1-8(0)) Planert Creek.

River of Love, Power & Vision. 2000. 69.00 (978-1-893027-36-7(8)) Path of Light.

River of Ruin. unabr. ed. Jack Du Brul. Read by J. Charles. 11 cass. (Running Time: 16 hrs.). (Philip Mercer Ser.). 2002. 34.95 (978-1-59086-357-2(7), 1590863577, BAU); 102.25 (978-1-59086-358-9(5), 1590863585) Brilliance Audio.
In the heart of Panama, a volcanic lake feeds a serpentine river - its stone banks laid by the Incas, who took back the gold and jewels plundered from them by the conquistadors. Legend has it that the Twice-Stolen Treasure has been buried for centuries in the Panamanian jungle. Discovering it means surviving the black waters of the River of Ruin... It begins at a Paris auction house, with a favor granted by an old high school friend to geologist Philip Mercer: the opportunity to buy a rare diary written during the French attempt at digging the Panama Canal. But Mercer isn't the only one who wants it. Three Chinese assassins have been dispatched to get it, forcing Mercer into a subterranean game of cat and mouse that takes him from the hellish maze of l'empire de la mort and through the sewers of Paris. Mercer realizes he has uncovered an intricate Chinese plot to trigger a deadly shift in the world's balance of power. At stake is control of the canal, recently handed over to the government of Panama by the United States. Only Philip Mercer - with help from beautiful U.S. Army officer Lauren Vanik, a cell of French Foreign Legion commandos, and a crusty eighty-year-old retired sea captain named Harry White - can stop them.

River of Ruin. unabr. ed. Jack Du Brul. Read by J. Charles. (Running Time: 57600 sec.). (Philip Mercer Ser.). 2004. audio compact disk 39.25 (978-1-59335-287-5(5), 1593352875, Brinc Audio MP3 Lib) Brilliance Audio.

River of Ruin. unabr. ed. Jack Du Brul. Read by J. Charles. (Running Time: 16 hrs.). (Philip Mercer Ser.). 2004. 39.25 (978-1-59710-648-1(8), 1597106488, BADLE); 24.95 (978-1-59710-649-8(6), 1597106496, BAD) Brilliance Audio.

River of Ruin. unabr. ed. Jack Du Brul. Read by J. Charles. (Running Time: 16 hrs.). (Philip Mercer Ser.). 2004. 24.95 (978-1-59335-014-7(7), 1593350147) Soulmate Audio Bks.

***River of Shadows.** unabr. ed. Robert V. S. Redick. (Running Time: 18 hrs. 0 mins. 0 sec.). (Chathrand Voyage Ser.). 2011. 34.99 (978-1-4001-6682-4(9)); 22.99 (978-1-4001-8682-2(X)); audio compact disk 49.99 (978-1-4001-1682-9(1)) Pub: Tantor Media. Dist(s): IngramPubServ

***River of Shadows (Library Edition)** unabr. ed. Robert V. S. Redick. (Running Time: 18 hrs. 0 mins.). (Chathrand Voyage Ser.). 2011. 49.99 (978-1-4001-9682-1(5)); audio compact disk 119.99 (978-1-4001-4682-6(8)) Pub: Tantor Media. Dist(s): IngramPubServ

River of Stars. Read by Marcia Lane. (J). 1999. audio compact disk 14.95 (978-0-939065-67-7(3)) Gentle Wind.

River of Stars. Read by Marcia Lane. 1 cass. (Running Time: 55 min.). (J). (gr. 1-5). 1993. 9.95 (978-0-939065-53-0(3), GW1057) Gentle Wind.
Songs & stories from around the world - includes The Pied Piper & The Emperor's New Clothes.

River of the Sun. unabr. collector's ed. James Ramsey Ullman. Read by Michael Prichard. 9 cass. (Running Time: 13 hrs. 30 min.). 1976. 72.00 (978-0-7366-0001-9(9), 1011) Books on Tape.
The story is set in the Amazon River Basin during the days following World War II. The characters are a group of men & women on an expedition searching for a legendary river. This tributary of the Amazon is in an area reported to be rich in oil. The plot encompasses a mystery, a love affair & a hair-raising escape.

River Rising. Athol Dickson. Read by Dion Graham. 2007. audio compact disk (978-1-4281-0076-3(8)) Recorded Bks.

River Road (Audio Book) A Novel in Stories. Tricia Currans-Sheehan. 2009. audio compact disk 35.95 (978-0-89823-249-3(X)) Pub: New Rivers Pr. Dist(s): Consort Bk Sales

River Running West Pt. 2: The Life of John Wesley Powell. unabr. ed. Donald Worster. 10 cass. (Running Time: 15 hrs.). 2001. 80.00 (978-0-7366-6829-3(2)); 80.00 (978-0-7366-7139-2(0)) Books on Tape.

River Runs Through It & Other Stories. Norman F. Maclean. Read by Norman F. Maclean. 1 cass. (Running Time: 77 min.). 1985. 13.95 (978-1-55644-126-4(6), 5031) Am Audio Prose.

River Runs Through It & Other Stories. Norman F. Maclean. Read by Ivan Doig. 3 cass. (Running Time: 4 hrs.). 1994. 24.95 (978-0-939643-41-7(3), 3570, NrthWrd Bks) TandN Child.
Life in Missoula, Montana, in 1937 centered around family, fly fishing and the Big Blackfoot River.

River Runs Through It & Other Stories. abr. ed. Norman MacLean. Read by Norman F. Maclean. 4 CDs. (Running Time: 17100 sec.). (ENG.). 2006. audio compact disk 24.95 (978-1-59887-033-6(5), 1598870335) Pub: HighBridge. Dist(s): Workman Pub

River Runs Through It & Other Stories. abr. ed. Norman F. Maclean. Read by Ivan Doig. (YA). 2006. 39.99 (978-1-59895-205-6(6)) Find a World.

***River Runs Through It & Other Stories.** unabr. ed. Norman F. Maclean. (ENG.). 2010. audio compact disk 26.95 (978-1-61573-112-1(1), 1615731121) Pub: HighBridge. Dist(s): Workman Pub

River Runs Through It & Other Stories. unabr. ed. Short Stories. Norman F. Maclean. Narrated by Joel Fabiani. 6 cass. (Running Time: 8 hrs. 30 mins.). 1993. 51.00 (978-1-55690-822-4(9), 93122E7) Recorded Bks.
Three stories set in the Montana wilderness of the 1920's & 1930's, told in semi-autobiographical style by one of the last remaining frontiersmen born & raised there.

River Secrets. unabr. ed. Shannon Hale. Narrated by Mark Holt. 8 CDs. (Running Time: 7 hrs. 30 mins.). (Books of Bayern Ser.: Bk. 3). (YA). (gr. 5-10). 2009. audio compact disk 55.00 (978-1-934180-21-1(1)) Full Cast Audio.

River Sorrow, unabr. ed. Craig Holden. Narrated by Richard Ferrone. 9 cass. (Running Time: 12 hrs. 45 mins.). 1995. 78.00 (978-0-7887-0152-8(5), 94374E7) Recorded Bks.
When Dr. Adrian Lancaster walks into the neglected & ransacked house, he finds one of the boys he was trying to help - naked & lifeless, hanging from the ceiling. Minutes later when the police arrive, Adrian is thrust into a nightmare that will hurtle him back into the violent & obsessive world of his past.

River Thunder, unabr. ed. William Hobbs. Narrated by Christina Moore. 4 pieces. (Running Time: 5 hrs. 15 mins.). (gr. 7 up). 1997. 35.00 (978-0-7887-2786-3(9), 95672E7) Recorded Bks.
In the companion to "Downriver," Jessie & her troubled teenage companions have returned to the Grand Canyon to run the big rapids. Their adventure is both exciting & therapeutic, allowing them to work through their anger & restlessness.

River to River Trail: The Hike Through Shawnee National Forest in Southern Illinois: A Collection of Piano Solos. 2000. 11.99 (978-0-9708613-1-3(1)) Really Big.

River Town: Two Years on the Yangtze. unabr. ed. Peter Hessler. 11 cass. (Running Time: 16 hrs. 30 mins.). 2002. 88.00 (978-0-7366-8659-4(2)) Books on Tape.
Peter Hessler, a 26-year-old Peace Corps volunteer, bridged cultures and made friends during his two year residency in Fuling. Great story.

River War: An Historical Account of the Reconquest of the Soudan. unabr. collector's ed. Winston L. S. Churchill. Read by David Case. 10 cass. (Running Time: 15 hrs.). 1991. 80.00 (978-0-7366-1957-8(7), 2778) Books on Tape.
Nearly 100 years ago - in 1898 - the British sent an expeditionary force under General Kitchener to the Sudan to avenge General Gordon & put down a rebellion led by the Khalifa Abdullah. Kitchener's army closed with Abdullah at Omdurman; the results were an early version of Desert Storm. Riding in Kitchener's calvary was a young subaltern, Winston Churchill, who had come to write as well as fight. Even at a young age Churchill exuded authority, & this book, which made him famous, has become a classic.

River Why. David James Duncan. Read by Dick Hill. (Running Time: 55800 sec.). 2006. 85.95 (978-0-7861-4611-6(7)); audio compact disk 108.00 (978-0-7861-6883-5(8)) Blckstn Audio.

River Why. unabr. ed. David James Duncan. Read by Dick Hill. 13 CDs. (Running Time: 55800 sec.). 2006. audio compact disk 34.95 (978-0-7861-6880-4(3)) Blckstn Audio.

River Why. unabr. ed. David James Duncan. Read by Dick Hill. (Running Time: 55800 sec.). 2006. audio compact disk 29.95 (978-0-7861-7466-9(8)) Blckstn Audio.

River 1: King in the Land. Eagles' Wings Ministries. 2007. audio compact disk 16.00 (978-5-558-72528-5(1)) Pub: Sigma F RUS. Dist(s): Destiny Image Pubs

River 2: Undiscovered Country. Eagles' Wings Ministries. 2007. audio compact disk 16.00 (978-5-558-72502-5(8)) Pub: Sigma F RUS. Dist(s): Destiny Image Pubs

River 3: Lament for the Poor. Eagles' Wings Ministries. 2007. audio compact disk 16.00 (978-5-558-72479-0(X)) Pub: Sigma F RUS. Dist(s): Destiny Image Pubs

River 3 Lament for the Poor. Robert Stearns. (Running Time: 1 hr.07 mins. 23 sec.). 1998. audio compact disk 16.00 (978-2-03-674050-1(2)) Pub: Kairos Pubg. Dist(s): STL Dist NA

River 4: Prepare the Way. Eagles' Wings Ministries. 2007. audio compact disk 16.00 (978-5-558-72469-1(2)) Pub: Sigma F RUS. Dist(s): Destiny Image Pubs

River 5: Dance with Me. Eagles' Wings Ministries. 2007. audio compact disk 16.00 (978-5-558-72474-5(9)) Pub: Sigma F RUS. Dist(s): Destiny Image Pubs

River 6: Freedom's Fire. Eagles' Wings Ministries. 2007. audio compact disk 16.00 (978-5-558-63214-9(3)) Pub: Sigma F RUS. Dist(s): Destiny Image Pubs

Riverboat. unabr. ed. Douglas Hirt. Read by Rusty Nelson. 8 cass. (Running Time: 9 hrs. 12 min.). (Riverboat Ser.: Bk. 1). 1999. 49.95 (978-1-55686-880-1(4)) Books in Motion.
A talt of the old Mississippi.

River's Daughter. unabr. ed. Vella Munn. Read by Stephanie Brush. 8 cass. (Running Time: 11 hrs. 48 min.). (Women of the West Ser.). 1996. 49.95 (978-1-55686-659-3(3)) Books in Motion.
Barr Conner, a loner, & Dark Water, the keeper of her tribe's history, work together to bring peace & harmony between settlers & the Rogue Indian Tribe in the lush Oregon Territory.

***River's Edge.** Terri Blackstock. (Running Time: 9 hrs. 40 mins. 0 sec.). (Cape Refuge Ser.). (ENG.). 2008. 14.99 (978-0-310-30430-2(X)) Zondervan.

River's End. abr. ed. Nora Roberts. Read by Sandra Burr. (Running Time: 10800 sec.). 2006. audio compact disk 14.99 (978-1-4233-2969-5(4), 9781423329695, BCD Value Price) Brilliance Audio.

River's End. abr. ed. Nora Roberts. Read by Sandra Burr. 2 cass. (Running Time: 2 hrs.). 1999. 17.95 (FS9-43367) Highsmith.

River's End. unabr. ed. Nora Roberts. Read by Sandra Burr. 9 cass. (Running Time: 14 hrs.). 1999. 39.95 (978-1-56740-412-8(X), 156740412X, BAU) Brilliance Audio.
The #1 New York Times bestselling author presents her most seductively suspenseful novel yet. Olivia's parents had been one of Hollywood's glittering golden couples . . . until the night the monster came. The monster who destroyed their beautiful home and took her mother away from her forever. The monster with the face of her father . . . Now a young woman, Olivia finds her memory of that night has faded. Her mother's grieving family spared no effort to keep Olivia safe from the publicity, taking her to grow up in the beautiful natural splendor of the Pacific Northwest. But, despite the terror and the years that have passed, a part of her still yearns to recall those horrifying events, to know the truth about her childhood. With the help of a young writer named Noah Brady, she could have the chance. The son of the police officer who found four-year-old Olivia cowering in her bedroom closet so many years ago, Noah wants to reconstruct that infamous night - and tell the story that has become part of Hollywood legend. With Noah, Olivia has a chance to confront her tragic past - and the longings of her own lonely heart. But before she can confront her past, she must safeguard her future. For in this forest haven, this remote corner of the country, the monster walks again . .

River's End. unabr. ed. Nora Roberts. Read by Sandra Burr. (Running Time: 14 hrs.). 2006. 39.25 (978-1-4233-1407-3(7), 9781423314073, BADLE); 24.95 (978-1-4233-1406-6(9), 9781423314066, BAD); audio compact disk 39.25 (978-1-4233-1405-9(0), 9781423314059, Brlnc Audio MP3 Lib); audio compact disk 107.25 (978-1-4233-1403-5(4), 9781423314035, BriAudCD Unabrid); audio compact disk 40.95 (978-1-4233-1402-8(6), 9781423314028, Bril Audio CD Unabri); audio compact disk 24.95 (978-1-4233-1404-2(2), 9781423314042, Brilliance MP3) Brilliance Audio.

River's End. unabr. ed. Nora Roberts. Read by Sandra Burr. 9 cass. (Running Time: 9 hrs.). 1999. 39.95 (FS9-43307) Highsmith.

Rivers of Fire. Patrick Carman. Narrated by Jonathan Davis. (Running Time: 27060 sec.). (Atherton Ser.: No. 2). (ENG.). (J). (gr. 4-7). 2008. audio compact disk 29.95 (978-0-545-07623-4(4)) Scholastic Inc.

Rivers of Fire. unabr. ed. Patrick Carman. Read by Jonathan Davis. (Atherton Ser.: Bk. 2). (J). 2008. 54.99 (978-1-60252-985-4(X)) Find a World.

Rivers of Fire. unabr. ed. Patrick Carman. Read by Jonathan Davis. 6 CDs. (Running Time: 7 hrs. 31 mins.). (Atherton Ser.: No. 2). (ENG.). (J). (gr. 4-7). 2008. audio compact disk 64.95 (978-0-545-07624-1(2)) Scholastic Inc.

Rivers of Life: What Lies Behind the Modern Religions of Mankind. Instructed by Manly P. Hall. 1 cass. (Running Time: 1 hr.). 8.95 (978-0-89314-238-4(7), C610706) Philos Res.

Rivers of the Heart. unabr. ed. Audrey Howard. Read by Carole Boyd. 12 cass. (Running Time: 15 hrs.). 2001. 45.95 (978-0-7540-0595-7(X), CAB2018) Pub: Chivers Audio Bks GBR. Dist(s): AudioGO
Kitty Hayes has only loved one man. From the moment she met him, she believed with all her heart that her adopted brother, Freddy, would one day be her husband, but he chooses to marry her pretty, feminine, despised sister instead, it breaks more than her heart. Torn between fury & sorrow, Kitty sets out to show them all she doesn't care & makes her own brilliant match.

Rivers of Zadaa. unabr. ed. D. J. MacHale. Read by William Dufris. (Running Time: 13 hrs.). (Pendragon Ser.: Bk. 6). 2005. 39.25 (978-1-59737-282-4(X), 9781597372824, BADLE); 24.95 (978-1-59737-281-7(1), 9781597372817, BAD) Brilliance Audio.

Rivers of Zadaa. unabr. ed. D. J. MacHale. Read by William Dufris. (Running Time: 46800 sec.). (Pendragon Ser.: Bk. 6). (J). (gr. 5-9). 2005. 92.25 (978-1-59737-276-3(5), 9781597372763, BrilAudUnabridg); audio compact disk 39.25 (978-1-59737-280-0(3), 9781597372800, Brlnc Audio MP3 Lib); audio compact disk 24.95 (978-1-59737-279-4(X), 9781597372794, Brilliance MP3) Brilliance Audio.
Please enter a Synopsis.

Rivers of Zadaa. unabr. ed. D. J. MacHale. Read by William Dufris. (Running Time: 13 hrs.). (Pendragon Ser.: Bk. 6). 2009. audio compact disk 19.99 (978-1-4233-9905-6(6), 9781423399056); audio compact disk 49.97 (978-1-4233-9906-3(4), 9781423399063, BriAudCD Unabrid) Brilliance Audio.

Riverside Villas Murder. unabr. collector's ed. Kingsley Amis. Read by Richard Green. 6 cass. (Running Time: 6 hrs.). 1981. 36.00 (978-0-7366-0234-1(8), 1230) Books on Tape.
Its hero is a 14-year-old boy, Peter Furneaux. Like all 14-year-olds, he is hovering hopefully on the brink between sexual inexperience & initiation, & in this book Peter suddenly becomes an adult. A crime is committed by an unknown & almost unidentifiable assailant. Only Peter begins to guess at the truth which leads to the river bank by moonlight.

Rizzo's War. unabr. ed. Lou Manfredo. Read by Bobby Cannavale. (Running Time: 10 hrs. 0 mins. 0 sec.). (ENG.). 2009. audio compact disk 39.99 (978-1-4272-0784-5(4)) Pub: Macmill Audio. Dist(s): Macmillan

RL's Dream. Walter Mosley. Read by Michael Kramer. 6 cass. (Running Time: 9 hrs.). 48.00 (978-0-7366-3231-7(X)) Books on Tape.
A young southern girl befriends a dying blues musician whose tale strikes a note in her soul. Will she risk it all for him?.

RL's Dream. unabr. ed. Walter Mosley. Read by Michael Kramer. 6 cass. (Running Time: 9 hrs.). 1996. 48.00 (3892) Books on Tape.
Soupspoon Wise, a great musician in his time, played a thousand bars & clubs. But the music of one night lingers in his mind: the night he played with Robert "RL" Johnson, the reigning genius of country blues. It's a memory that obsesses him. Old now & ill, Soupspoon tells his story to Kiki Waters, a young white woman who has taken him in. Her feeling for him is lyrical, & like a great ballad, stays with us long after the music ends.

RMX.Extended Play. Marilla Alexander. 2003. bk. 20.00 (978-3-931126-74-2(9)) Pub: Die Gestalten DEU. Dist(s): Prestel Pub NY

Roach Approach, Noah's Journey of Faith: Read along. (J). 2003. audio compact disk 12.99 (978-0-9742997-1-6(5)) Wacky World.

Road. Cormac McCarthy. Read by Rupert Degas. (Playaway Adult Fiction Ser.). 2009. 59.99 (978-1-60775-751-1(6)) Find a World.

Road. abr. ed. Cormac McCarthy. Read by Rupert Degas. 4 CDs. (Running Time: 5 hrs. 9 mins.). 2009. audio compact disk 28.98 (978-962-634-971-7(9)) Naxos.

Road. movie tie-in ed. Cormac McCarthy. 2008. audio compact disk 29.99 (978-1-4361-7439-8(2)) Recorded Bks.

Road. unabr. ed. Cormac McCarthy. Read by Tom Stechschulte. 6 cass. (Running Time: 6 hrs. 75 mins.). 2006. 51.75 (978-1-4281-0549-2(2)); audio compact disk 77.75 (978-1-4281-0551-5(4)) Recorded Bks.

Road. unabr. ed. Cormac McCarthy. Narrated by Tom Stechschulte. 6 CDs. (Running Time: 6 hrs. 45 mins.). 2008. audio compact disk 56.75 (978-1-4361-1303-8(2)) Pub: Recorded Bks. Dist(s): NetLibrary CO

Road. unabr. ed. Cormac McCarthy. 6 CDs. (Running Time: 24300 sec.). 2006. audio compact disk 29.99 (978-1-4281-1278-0(2)) Recorded Bks.

Road Ahead. Kriyananda, pseud. 1 cass. (Running Time: 60 min.). 9.95 (SS-26) Crystal Clarity.
Reviews & updates his booklet analyzing Paramhansa Yogananda's predictions of late 20th century catastrophes.

Road Ahead. abr. ed. Bill Gates. Read by Rick Adamson. 2 cass. (Running Time: 3 hrs.). 1999. (3994132) Penguin-HghBrdg.
The Microsoft co-founder takes us back to the days when he dropped out of Harvard to start his own software company. Convinced that personal computers would one day be on every desktop & in every home, he resolved to make software easier & more enjoyable to use. This vision helped shape the entire software industry. Here, he explores new territory on the information highway & describes the future digital age.

Road Ahead. unabr. ed. Christabel Bielenberg. Read by Sheila Mitchell. 6 cass. (Running Time: 6 hrs. 54 min.). 2001. 54.95 (978-1-85695-561-4(3), 93062) Pub: ISIS Audio GBR. Dist(s): Ulverscroft US
Following the success of The Past Is Myself, Christabel Bielenberg received thousands of letters begging her to describe what happened next. The Road Ahead takes up her story with the outbreak of peace.

Road Ahead. unabr. ed. Bill Gates. Read by Alexander Adams. 7 cass. (Running Time: 10 hrs. 30 min.). 1996. 56.00 (978-0-7366-3261-4(1), 3918) Books on Tape.
The man who led the way on the information highway now forecasts what lies ahead. Who better than Bill Gates to tell how the coming age of technology will transform our lives?

Road Ahead, unabr. ed. Bill Gates. Narrated by Richard M. Davidson. 9 cass. (Running Time: 12 hrs. 30 mins.). 1996. 78.00 (978-0-7887-0458-1(3), 94651E7) Recorded Bks.
The founder of Microsoft personally guides listeners through a preview of the amazing possibilities on the information superhighway. Those listeners who know little about computers will enjoy Gates' clear explanations, mercifully free of technical jargon. Those who are already knowledgeable about computers will be enticed by his description of what the growing universe of computer technology will offer in the future.

Road Back to Paris. unabr. ed. A. J. Liebling. Read by Walter Zimmerman. 9 cass. (Running Time: 13 hrs. 30 min.). 1989. 72.00 (978-0-7366-1510-5(5), 2382) Books on Tape.
A. J. Liebling earned his reputation at the New Yorker, where he covered sporting events, "low life," & then World War II. Liebling was in his element as a war correspondent. He had a natural affinity for the scruffy private soldiers, & reported their war in a singular & reflective way.

Road Builders, Audiocassette. B. G. Hennessy. (Metro Reading Ser.). (J). (gr. k). 2000. 8.46 (978-1-58120-989-1(4)) Metro Teaching.

***Road Dogs.** unabr. ed. Elmore Leonard. Read by Peter Francis James. (ENG.). 2009. (978-0-06-190180-5(6), Harper Audio); (978-0-06-190178-2(4), Harper Audio) HarperCollins Pubs.

***Road Dogs.** unabr. ed. Elmore Leonard. Read by Peter Francis James. 2010. audio compact disk 19.99 (978-0-06-201090-2(5), Harper Audio) HarperCollins Pubs.

Road from Connemara: Songs & Stories told & sung to Ewan MacColl. Contrib. by Joe Heaney. (ENG.). 2001. audio compact disk 32.95 (978-0-8023-8143-9(X)) Pub: Clo Iar-Chonnachta IRL. Dist(s): Dufour

Road from Coorain. unabr. ed. Jill Ker Conway. Narrated by Barbara Caruso. 7 cass. (Running Time: 9 hrs. 15 mins.). 1993. 60.00 (978-1-55690-859-0(8), 93301E7) Recorded Bks.
Memoir of her childhood in the Australian outback during World War II, her school days in Sydney in the 50's & her adulthood in America as an historian & the first woman president of Smith College.

Road from Coorain. unabr. ed. Jill Ker Conway. Narrated by Barbara Caruso. 7 cass. (Running Time: 9 hrs. 25 min.). 1999. 58.00 (93301) Recorded Bks.
Caruso's lightly accented voice proves the perfect choice for Conway's account of growing up in Australia in the 1930s & 40s.

***Road from Home.** unabr. ed. David Kherdian. Read by Adriana Sevan. (ENG.). 2009. (978-0-06-180537-0(8), GreenwillowBks); (978-0-06-176235-2(0), GreenwillowBks) HarperCollins Pubs.

Road Home. abr. ed. Tommy Tenney. Narrated by Aimee Lilly. (ENG.). 2007. 13.99 (978-1-60814-365-8(1)) Oasis Audio.

Road Home. abr. ed. Tommy Tenney & Mark Andrew Olsen. Narrated by Aimee Lilly. (Running Time: 21600 sec.). (ENG.). 2007. audio compact disk 19.99 (978-1-59859-246-7(7)) Oasis Audio.

Road Home. abr. ed. Rose Tremain. Read by Juliet Stevenson. 6 CDs. (Running Time: 8 hrs.). 2009. audio compact disk 34.98 (978-962-634-946-5(8), Naxos AudioBooks) Naxos.

Road Is Still the Road. Andy Wilkinson. 1 cass. (Running Time: 1 hr.). 1996. 10.00 (978-1-888609-03-5(6)); audio compact disk 15.00 (978-1-888609-02-8(8)) Grey Hrse Pr.

Road Kill. Kinky Friedman. 4 cass. (Running Time: 6 hrs.). 1998. 32.00 (4633) Books on Tape.
The incorrigible Kinky Friedman, private detective & public nuisance, takes to the road with his old friend, the legendary singer Willie Nelson. Aboard Willie's bus, Kinky discovers that something is bothering his old pal. It turns out that on a barren stretch of Arizona highway, the singer's bus struck an intoxicated Indian. The result was mincemeat & an apparently unshakable Indian curse. When someone shoots one of Nelson's crew, mistaking him for the singer, Kinky makes a quick deduction: Whether it's a dead Indian's curse or a live gunman's bullet, Willie is indeed in danger. Sleuthing from his lower Manhattan loft, Kinky is in for a classic misadventure.

Road Kill. unabr. ed. Kinky Friedman. Read by Edward Lewis. 4 cass. (Running Time: 6 hrs.). 1998. 32.00 (978-0-7366-4130-2(0), 4633) Books on Tape.
The incorrigible private detective & public nuisance takes to the road with Willie Nelson & battles an Indian curse.

Road Less Traveled: Further along the Road Less Traveled: Togetherness & Separateness in Marriage & the Family. abr. ed. M. Scott Peck. 1 cass. (Running Time: 1 hr.). 1987. 9.95 S&S Audio.

Road Less Traveled Set: A New Psychology of Love, Traditional Values, & Spritual Growth. Michael Scott Peck. 6 cass. (Running Time: 6 hrs.). 49.95 (461AD) Nightingale-Conant.
If you want to achieve greater self-understanding, nurture deeper relationships, & experience the most profound sense of what being human means, then you must learn to face & solve life's problems with the timeless psychological & spiritual tools that Dr. Peck shows you how to keep & use. As you progress, you'll rediscover such traditional values as honesty, trust, commitment & self-reliance.

Road Less Traveled Set: A New Psychology of Love, Traditional Values, & Spritual Growth. abr. ed. Michael Scott Peck. 6 cass. (Running Time: 6 hrs.). 1986. 59.95 Set. (978-0-671-63467-4(4)) S&S Audio.

Road Less Traveled Set: A New Psychology of Love, Traditional Values, & Spritual Growth. gif. ed. Michael Scott Peck. 3 cass. (Running Time: 270 min.). 1999. 29.95 (978-0-671-75890-5(X), Audioworks) S&S Audio.

Road Less Traveled Set: A New Psychology of Love, Traditional Values, & Spritual Growth. unabr. ed. Michael Scott Peck. 6 cass. (Running Time: 6 hrs.). 53.95 (SS0003) Books on Tape.
M. Scott Peck's compelling fusion of spiritual & psychological insight made "The Road Less Traveled" a publishing landmark - the longest running title on "The New York Times" best-seller list ever.

Road Less Traveled Set: A New Psychology of Love, Traditional Values, & Spritual Growth. 25th unabr. abr. ed. M. Scott Peck. Read by M. Scott Peck. 4 CDs. (Running Time: 43 hrs. 0 mins. 0 sec.). (ENG.). 2002. audio compact disk 30.00 (978-0-7435-2730-9(5), Audioworks) Pub: S&S Audio. Dist(s): S and S Inc

Road Map to Healing: The Seven Stages of Personal Healing, Set. David Grudermeyer & Rebecca Grudermeyer. 2 cass. (Running Time: 2 hrs.). 18.95 INCL. HANDOUTS. (T-30) Willingness Wrks.

Road of Lost Innocence. Somaly Mam. Read by Tanya Eby Sirois. (Playaway Adult Nonfiction Ser.). (ENG.). 2009. 54.99 (978-1-60775-863-1(6)) Find a World.

Road of Lost Innocence: The True Story of a Cambodian Heroine. unabr. ed. Somaly Mam. Read by Tanya Eby Sirois. 1 MP3-CD. (Running Time: 5 hrs.). 2008. 24.95 (978-1-4233-7346-9(4), 9781423373469, Brilliance MP3); 39.25 (978-1-4233-7349-0(9), 9781423373490, BADLE); 39.25 (978-1-4233-7347-6(2), 9781423373476, Brlnc Audio MP3 Lib); 24.95 (978-1-4233-7348-3(0), 9781423373483, BAD); audio compact disk 74.25 (978-1-4233-7345-2(6), 9781423373452, BriAudCD Unabrid); audio compact disk 26.95 (978-1-4233-7344-5(8), 9781423373445, Bril Audio CD Unabri) Brilliance Audio.

Road of the Dead. unabr. ed. Kevin Brooks. Narrated by Paul Thornley. 8 CDs. (Running Time: 11 hrs. 45 mins.). (YA). (gr. 9 up). 2007. audio compact disk 108.75 (978-1-4281-6451-2(0)); 78.75 (978-1-4281-6446-8(4)) Recorded Bks.
Carnegie Medal and ALA Book of the Year winner Kevin Brooks delivers unnerving suspense and righteous revenge in The Road of the Dead. When his sister Rachel is brutally raped and murdered on the desolate English moors, 14-year-old psychic Ruben sees it - feels it - happen, though he is many miles away in London. And as soon as his hotheaded, gun-packing older brother Cole learns of what has befallen their sister, the two bereaved teenagers begin a vengeful journey north.

Road of the Patriarch. abr. ed. Read by David Colacci. (Running Time: 21600 sec.). (Sellswords Ser.: Bk. 3). 2007. audio compact disk 14.99 (978-1-4233-1647-3(9), 9781423316473, BCD Value Price) Brilliance Audio.

Road of the Patriarch. unabr. ed. Read by David Colacci. (Running Time: 46800 sec.). (Forgotten Realms Ser.). [illegible] 92.25 (978-1-4233-1639-8(8), 9781423316398, BrilAudUnabridg); audio compact disk 107.25 (978-1-4233-1641-1(X), 9781423316411, BriAudCD Unabrid); audio compact disk 39.25 (978-1-4233-1643-5(6), 9781423316435, Brlnc Audio MP3 Lib) Brilliance Audio.
Please enter a Synopsis.

Road of the Patriarch. unabr. ed. R. A. Salvatore. Read by David Colacci. (Running Time: 13 hrs.). (Forgotten Realms Ser.). 2006. audio compact disk 38.95 (978-1-4233-1640-4(1), 9781423316404, Bril Audio CD Unabri) Brilliance Audio.

Road of the Patriarch. unabr. ed. R. A. Salvatore. Read by David Colacci. (Running Time: 13 hrs.). (Sellswords Ser.: Bk. 3). 2006. 39.25

(978-1-4233-1645-9(2), 9781423316459, BADLE); 24.95 (978-1-4233-1644-2(4), 9781423316442, BAD); 24.95 (978-1-4233-1642-8(8), 9781423316428, Brilliance MP3) Brilliance Audio.

***Road Rage.** unabr. ed. Joe Hill et al. Read by Stephen Lang. (ENG.). 2009. (978-0-06-176872-9(3), Harper Audio); (978-0-06-176873-6(1), Harper Audio) HarperCollins Pubs.

Road Rage. unabr. ed. Ruth Rendell. Narrated by Davina Porter. 9 cass. (Running Time: 12 hrs. 30 mins.). (Inspector Wexford Mystery Ser.: Bk. 17). 1998. 83.00 (978-0-7887-1867-0(3), 95289K8) Recorded Bks.
A group of protestors take drastic measures, including the taking of five hostages, to halt construction on a proposed highway through the forest near Kingsmarkham. When Inspector Wexford learns that one of the hostages is his wife Dora, he is caught in a spiral of frustration & fear.

Road Rage: Includes 'Duel & Throttle. unabr. ed. Joe Hill et al. Read by Stephen Lang. 2 CDs. (Running Time: 2 hrs. 30 mins.). 2009. audio compact disk 19.99 (978-0-06-172635-4(4), Harper Audio) HarperCollins Pubs.

Road Rage Relaxation. 2005. audio compact disk (978-1-932086-28-7(5)) L Lizards Pub Co.

Road Rage Relaxation: A Hypnosis Tape. Narrated by Dean A. Montalbano. (Hypnotic Sensory Response Audio Ser.). 2000. 39.95 (978-0-9708772-2-2(6)) L Lizards Pub Co.

Road Sage: Mindfulness Techniques for Drivers. Sylvia Boorstein. 1 CD. (Running Time: 4500 sec.). 2006. audio compact disk 14.95 (978-1-59179-491-2(9), AW00419D) Sounds True.
Take the Stress Out of Driving with Simple Mindfulness Meditation Practices. On Road Sage, you take a seat next to meditation teacher Sylvia Boorstein for the driver's education course you never heard in school: the essential techniques of mindfulness meditation, presented especially for anyone who drives a car. With simple exercises, real-life stories "on the road," and an occasional pop quiz, Boorstein teaches you how to work with the physical sensations and mind-states that grip every driver: anxiety, impatience, frustration, and even anger. You learn to see your morning commute as an opportunity to practice the calm, alert, and balanced state of mind and body that is the centerpiece of mindful living. There can be "beautiful dharma" in that traffic jam ahead, once we learn to awaken to it through these powerful practices and teachings. So stop fuming about the car in front of you and reach your destination relaxed and aware of the magic in each moment of life - even while stuck in traffic - with America's "Road Sage" - Sylvia Boorstein.

Road Scholar Board Game: French - English. Des. by Donald S. Rivera. 1 cass. (Running Time: 1 hr. 30 min.). (FRE & ENG.). (J). (gr. 2 up). 1999. 19.95 Incl. game board, die & playing pieces, bilingual language cards & instructions. (978-1-56015-691-8(0)) Penton Overseas.
Players learn an amazing number of words & phrases as they navigate exciting twists & turns along the way to reaching the ancient ruins.

Road Song: A Memoir. unabr. ed. Natalie Kusz. Narrated by Barbara Caruso. 7 cass. (Running Time: 10 hrs.). 1992. 60.00 (978-1-55690-643-5(9), 92350E7) Recorded Bks.
Autobiographical memoir of growing up in Alaska in the 1960s. In 1969 her family abandoned the city, packed up the car & headed to Alaska. They ended up a hundred miles from Fairbanks in a dilapidated house surrounded by 258 acres of spruce, birch & willow & no road. When the first winter came with Mr. Kusz working in Prudhoe Bay, money running out & tempatures 60 below, the Kusz family was living so close to disaster that the question was not when it would strike but whom.

Road South. Shelley Stewart. Narrated by Dion Graham. 7 cass. (Running Time: 10 hrs. 15 mins.). 61.00 (978-1-4025-3678-6(X)) Recorded Bks.

Road That Carried Me Here. 1 cass. (Running Time: 1 hr. 10 mins.). 10.00 (VCRM401) Lodestone Catalog.

Road That Carried Me Here, Vol. 1. abr. ed. Poems. Ray McNiece. Read by Ray McNiece. 1 cass. (Running Time: 1 hr.). 1997. bk. 9.95 (978-0-933087-56-9(X)) Bottom Dog Pr.
Selection of McNiece's best poems.

Road to Appomattox. Robert Hendrickson. Narrated by Nelson Runger. 8 CDs. (Running Time: 9 hrs.). audio compact disk 78.00 (978-1-4025-3499-7(X)) Recorded Bks.

Road to Appomattox. unabr. ed. Robert Hendrickson. Narrated by Nelson Runger. 7 cass. (Running Time: 9 hrs.). 1999. 60.00 (978-0-7887-2930-0(6), 95716E7) Recorded Bks.
Putting down their arms & flags, Lee's Confederate troops made a formal surrender at Appomattox on April 12, 1865. Join the author as he traces the path of the bloody engagements that ended the Civil War. Combining passages from diaries, military reports, & newspapers, he provides vivid, first-hand accounts of both Northern & Southern fighting men & officers.

Road to Armageddon. Charles R. Swindoll & John Walvoord. 1 cass. (Running Time: 60 mins.). 1999. cass. & video 39.99 (978-0-8499-8785-4(7)) Nelson.

Road to Armageddon. unabr. ed. Larry Collins. Read by Scott Brick. 11 cass. (Running Time: 16 hrs. 30 min.). 2004. 38.95 (978-1-59007-455-8(6)); audio compact disk 79.95 (978-1-59007-456-5(4)) New Millenn Enter.

Road to Armageddon: Wars in the Gulf. Grant R. Jeffrey. 2 cass. (Running Time: 2 hrs.). 14.95 set. (978-1-879840-00-3(6)) Global AZ.
The mid-east crises in Iraq & how the Gulf War fits into Biblical prophecy & what is next.

Road to Berry Edge. unabr. ed. Elizabeth Gill. Read by Janet Dale. 8 cass. (Running Time: 8 hrs.). 1998. 69.95 Set. (978-0-7540-0068-6(0), CAB1491) AudioGO.
It is 1903, ten years after his brother's death, when Rob Berkeley comes home to Berry Edge, bringing with him memories that Faith Norman would rather forget. His return also brings hope to the small town, for Rob is determined to bring the floundering steelworks back to full strength. But every time Rob looks at his dead brother's fiancee, he is reminded of the part he played in her bereavement; while Rob's resemblance to his brother is intolerable for Faith. But soon the likeness becomes more welcome than painful.

Road to Bethlehem. Dennis Allen. 2001. 75.00 (978-0-633-01649-4(7)); 11.98 (978-0-633-01647-0(0)); audio compact disk 85.00 (978-0-633-01650-0(0)); audio compact disk 16.98 (978-0-633-01648-7(9)) LifeWay Christian.

Road to Christmas. (Paws & Tales Ser.: No. 43). 2002. 3.99 (978-1-57972-504-4(X)); audio compact disk 5.99 (978-1-57972-505-1(8)) Insight Living.

Road to Conversion. 2004. 24.95 (978-1-888992-62-5(X)); audio compact disk 27.95 (978-1-888992-63-2(8)) Catholic Answers.

Road to Creativity. unabr. ed. Billy J. Johnston. Read by Billy J. Johnston. 1 cass. (Running Time: 90 min.). 1991. 5.95 (RRC911B) Johnston Mus Grp.
The author tells you how to become the person everyone says is "The most creative person I know." How to make yourself a highly creative problem-solver in any business or hobby. Specific steps to creative ideas, as well as exercises to keep yourself sharp, open-minded & inventive.

Road to Devine Destiny Cass. 2004. 20.00 (978-1-57855-614-4(7)) T D Jakes.

Road to Dune. Brian Herbert et al. Read by Scott Brick. 2005. 23.95 (978-1-59397-805-1(7)) Pub: Macmill Audio. Dist(s): Macmillan

Road to Dune. unabr. ed. Brian Herbert et al. Read by Scott Brick. 12 CDs. (Running Time: 14 hrs. 0 mins. 0 sec.). (Dune Ser.). (ENG.). 2005. audio compact disk 49.95 (978-1-59397-776-4(X)) Pub: Macmill Audio. Dist(s): Macmillan

Road to Dune. unabr. ed. Frank Herbert et al. Read by Scott Brick. 10 cass. (Running Time: 15 hrs.). 2005. 104.00 (978-1-4159-2567-6(4)); audio compact disk 128.00 (978-1-4159-2568-3(2)) Books on Tape.

Road to Everlasting Change. Musin Valeriy and victoria. 2009. audio compact disk (978-1-60743-924-0(7)) Indep Pub IL.

Road to Gandolfo. unabr. collector's ed. Robert Ludlum. Read by Michael Prichard. 7 cass. (Running Time: 10 hrs. 30 mins.). 1984. 56.00 (978-0-7366-0805-3(2), 1755) Books on Tape.
This story combines a motley cast-characters all-with the U. S. Army's latest fall guy in a mad plot to kidnap the most beloved pontiff since John XXIII. The ransom: one American dollar for every Catholic in the world. The problem: Pope Francesco I says: "Gentle Souls, why not?".

Road to Hana. Kirsten Whatley. 2004. audio compact disk 4.95 (978-1-57306-184-1(0)) Bess Pr.

Road to Healthy Living. Sharon L. Cavusgil. (Alliance: the Michigan State University Textbook Series of Theme-Based Content Instruction for ESL/EFL). (C). 1996. 15.00 (978-0-472-00254-2(6), 00254) U of Mich Pr.

***Road to Hell.** Sheila Quigley. Read by Julia Franklin. 2010. audio compact disk 71.95 (978-1-84652-923-8(9)) Pub: Magna Story GBR. Dist(s): Ulverscroft US

***Road to Hell.** Sheila Quigley & Julia Franklin. 2010. 64.95 (978-1-84652-922-1(0)) Pub: Magna Story GBR. Dist(s): Ulverscroft US

Road to Jerusalem. Contrib. by Yochanan Ben Yehuda. 2005. audio compact disk 16.98 (978-5-559-01468-5(0)) Pt of Grace Ent.

Road to Life. John H. Ricard. 1 cass. (Running Time: 1 hr.). (Inspiring Presentations from the National Rosary Congress Ser.). 2.50 (978-1-56036-098-8(4)) AMI Pr.

Road to Mars: A Post-Modem Novel. abr. ed. Eric Idle. Read by Eric Idle. 2 cass. (Running Time: 3 hrs.). 1999. 17.95 Set. (978-1-55935-318-2(X)) Soundelux.
Science-fiction thriller about life on the interpanetary comedy circuit.

Road to Mecca. Athol Fugard. Contrib. by Julie Harris et al. Directed By Steve Albrezzi. Contrib. by Raymond Guarna et al. 2 CDs. (Running Time: 7740 sec.). 2007. audio compact disk 25.95 (978-1-58081-302-0(X)) L A Theatre.

Road to Mecca. unabr. ed. Athol Fugard. Perf. by Julie Harris et al. 2 cass. (Running Time: 2 hrs. 10 mins.). 1996. 23.95 (978-1-58081-015-9(2), TPT86) L A Theatre.
When her husband dies, aging Miss Helen begins to fill her home in the remote South African bush with strange sculptures made of beer cans & old headlights. A local clergyman & a young woman visitor try to decide whether Miss Helen's peculiar art is outpouring of creativity or mandness.

Road to Memphis, unabr. ed. Mildred D. Taylor. Narrated by Lynne Thigpen. 7 pieces. (Running Time: 9 hrs. 45 mins.). (Logan Family Saga Ser.: Pt. 3). (gr. 6 up). 1997. 60.00 (978-0-7887-0426-0(5), 94618E7) Recorded Bks.
In 1941, 17-year-old Cassie Logan is dreaming of college & law school. But she is about to find out how fragile plans can be for African Americans in the deep South.

Road to Morocco. Perf. by Bob Hope & Bing Crosby. 1 cass. (Running Time: 60 min.). Dramatization. (Lux Radio Theater Ser.). 1943. 6.00 Once Upon Rad.
Radio broadcasts - humor.

Road to Nab End: An Extraordinary Northern Childhood. unabr. ed. William Woodruff. Read by Sam Kelly. 10 vols. (Running Time: 14 hrs.). 2003. 84.95 (978-0-7540-0970-2(X), CAB 2392, Chivers Sound Lib); audio compact disk 94.95 (978-0-7540-5585-3(X), CCD 276, Chivers Sound Lib) AudioGO.

Road to Nowhere. abr. ed. Paul Robertson. Narrated by Greg Whalen. (ENG.). 2008. 16.09 (978-1-60814-366-5(X)); audio compact disk 22.99 (978-1-59859-379-2(X)) Oasis Audio.

Road to Omaha. unabr. collector's ed. Robert Ludlum. Read by Michael Prichard. 12 cass. (Running Time: 18 hrs.). 1992. 96.00 (978-0-7366-2195-3(4), 2990) Books on Tape.
General MacKenzie Hawkins & Sam Deveraux are back. Can they get revenge against the powers-that-be? Can they take Nebraska?.

Road to Oz. unabr. ed. L. Frank Baum. Read by Flo Gibson. 3 cass. (Running Time: 4 hrs. 30 min.). (Oz Ser.). (YA). (gr. 5-8). 1982. 16.95 (978-1-55685-545-0(1)) Audio Bk Con.
When Dorothy & Toto become lost, they seek the Land of Oz & meet the Shagey Man, Polychrome, The Rainbow's Daughter, Button Bright. The Scoodlers, Donkeys, Foxes & all the characters we have learned to love, who assembled for Princess Ozma's birthday celebration.

Road to Paradise. unabr. ed. Max Allan Collins. (Running Time: 9.5 hrs. NaN mins.). 2008. 29.95 (978-1-4332-2273-3(6)); 59.95 (978-1-4332-2269-6(8)); audio compact disk 80.00 (978-1-4332-2270-2(1)) Blckstn Audio.

Road to Paradise Island. unabr. ed. Victoria Holt. Read by Susan Jameson. 10 cass. (Running Time: 15 hrs.). 2000. 69.95 (978-0-7451-6837-1(X), CAB 329) Pub: Chivers Audio Bks GBR. Dist(s): AudioGO
Unexpectedly coming upon a neglected grave whose name bears an uncanny resemblance to her own, Annalice Mallory longs to know more of its occupant. When a journal and an old map of an island once inhabited by the ancestries are found, Annalice is intrigued. Soon, Annalice finds herself drawn into a web of danger, where she can trust no one but herself, and where the past is inextricably entwined with the present.

Road to Paris. unabr. ed. Nikki Grimes. Read by Myra Lucretia Taylor. 3 cass. (Running Time: 3 hrs.). (J). (gr. 5-7). 2007. 30.75 (978-1-4281-6311-9(5)); audio compact disk 30.75 (978-1-4281-6316-4(6)) Recorded Bks.

Road to Purgatory. unabr. ed. Max Allan Collins. Read by Stanley Tucci. (Running Time: 9 hrs.). 2004. 39.25 (978-1-59710-651-1(8), 1597106518, BADLE); 24.95 (978-1-59710-650-4(X), 159710650X, BAD); 24.95 (978-1-59335-773-3(7), 1593357737, Brilliance MP3); 39.25 (978-1-59335-907-2(1), 1593359071, Brinc Audio MP3 Lib); 74.25 (978-1-59355-953-3(4), 1593559534, BAudLibEd); 29.95 (978-1-59355-952-6(6), 1593559526, BrilAudUnabridg); audio compact disk 31.95 (978-1-59355-954-0(2), 1593559542, Bril Audio CD Unabri); audio compact disk 87.25 (978-1-59355-955-7(0), 1593559550, BriAudCD Unabrid) Brilliance Audio.
It's 1942, and Michael O'Sullivan, the young boy who accompanied his gangster father on the road, has grown to manhood. A battle-scarred veteran of the Bataan jungles at 22, he returns to Chicago and his old war against the Capone mob. As Michael "Satariano," he must risk his life and soul, becoming a trusted aid to Frank Nitti himself. Interwoven is the parallel tale, set in 1922, of Michael's father, chief enforcer to Irish godfather John Looney. Ultimately, these two Michael O'Sullivans will reach similar crossroads as their fates converge in the purgatory of good men trapped in bad lives.

Road to Reading: Phonics Program-Language Skills. unabr. ed. 33 cass. (Running Time: 20 min. per cass.). (J). 10.95 ea. incl. duplicating master & tchr's. guide. (SAC 4002); 299.00 (978-0-8045-4002-5(0)) Spoken Arts.
Contains 33 lessons that goes through all the sounds of the alphabet. Road to Reading is designed to complement any existing reading program. The program is flexibly designed for individual, remedial or enrichment work.

Road to Reality: Coming Home to Jesus from the Unreal World. K. P. Yohannan. 4 cass. (Running Time: 6 hrs.). 1999. 15.99 (978-1-56599-988-6(6)) Yahshua Pub.

Road to Recovery. David Freudberg. 1 cass. (Running Time: 1 hr.). (Thinking about Drinking Ser.). 1987. 10.95 (978-1-886373-01-3(9)) Human Media.
Side A - 1st person accounts by 3 alcoholics who battled their way to a life of stable sobriety. Side B - AA's history, philosophy, traditions & healing magic.

Road to Recovery. unabr. ed. Rick Warren & John Baker. 8 cass. (Running Time: 12 hrs.). 1998. 24.99 Sermons, set of 8. (978-0-310-22263-7(X)) Zondervan.

Road to Recovery, the/Coming Clean. unabr. ed. Zondervan Publishing Staff. 1998. audio compact disk 3.13 (978-0-310-22120-3(X)) Zondervan.

Road to Recovery, the/Letting Go. unabr. ed. Zondervan Publishing Staff. 1998. audio compact disk 3.13 (978-0-310-22119-7(6)) Zondervan.

Road to Recovery, the/Maintaining Momentum. unabr. ed. Zondervan Publishing Staff. 1998. audio compact disk 3.14 (978-0-310-22125-8(0)) Zondervan.

Road to Recovery, the/Making Changes. unabr. ed. Zondervan Publishing Staff. 1998. audio compact disk 3.14 (978-0-310-22123-4(4)) Zondervan.

Road to Recovery, the/Repairing Relationships. unabr. ed. Zondervan Publishing Staff. 1998. audio compact disk 3.14 (978-0-310-22124-1(2)) Zondervan.

Road to Recovery, the/Where to Get Help When You Hurt. unabr. ed. Zondervan Publishing Staff. 1998. audio compact disk 3.13 (978-0-310-22118-0(8)) Zondervan.

Road to Rowanbrae. unabr. ed. Doris Davidson. Read by Pamela Donald. 9 cass. (Running Time: 12 hrs.). 1999. 90.95 (978-1-85903-260-2(5)) UlverLrgPrint GBR.
Sold by a drunken father for thirty pounds at age sixteen, Mysie was forced to scrap a living for herself - but was finally given the chance to leave her tragic past behind & enjoy true happiness.

Road to Ruin. Donald E. Westlake. Read by William Dufris. 6 vols. (Dortmunder Ser.). 2004. bk. 54.95 (978-0-7927-3215-0(4), CSL 654, Chivers Sound Lib); bk. 69.95 (978-0-7927-3216-7(2), SLD 654, Chivers Sound Lib); bk. 29.95 (978-0-7927-3217-4(0), CMP 654, Chivers Sound Lib) AudioGO.

Road to Ruin. unabr. ed. Donald E. Westlake. Read by William Durfris. 6 cass. (Running Time: 9 hrs.). (Dortmunder Ser.). 2004. 29.95 (978-1-57270-402-2(0)) Pub: Audio Partners. Dist(s): PerseuPGW

Road to Ruin. unabr. ed. Donald E. Westlake. Read by William Durfris. 8 CDs. (Dortmunder Ser.). (ENG.). 2004. audio compact disk 34.95 (978-1-57270-403-9(9)) Pub: AudioGO. Dist(s): Perseus Dist

Road to Samarcand. unabr. ed. Read by Simon Vance. (Running Time: 28800 sec.). 2008. 29.95 (978-1-4332-0654-2(4)); 44.95 (978-1-4332-0652-8(8)); audio compact disk 29.95 (978-1-4332-0655-9(2)); audio compact disk & audio compact disk 29.95 (978-1-4332-0656-6(0)); audio compact disk & audio compact disk 55.00 (978-1-4332-0653-5(6)) Blckstn Audio.

Road to Self-Mastery: Shaman Techniques from Hawaii. Serge Kahili King. 2 cass. (Running Time: 2 hrs.). 1994. 10.95 (978-0-8356-1909-7(5), Quest) Pub: Theos Pub Hse. Dist(s): Natl Bk Netwk

***Road to Serfdom.** unabr. ed. Friedrich A. Hayek. Read by William Hughes. (Running Time: 9 hrs. 30 mins.). 2010. 29.95 (978-1-4417-5387-8(7)); 79.95 (978-1-4417-5383-0(4)); audio compact disk 32.95 (978-1-4417-5386-1(9)); audio compact disk 109.00 (978-1-4417-5384-7(2)) Blckstn Audio.

Road to Serfdom: A Classic Warning Against the Dangers to Freedom. collector's ed. Friedrich A. Hayek. Read by David Case. 7 cass. (Running Time: 10 hrs. 30 min.). 2000. 56.00 (978-0-7366-5106-6(3)) Books on Tape.
Originally published in 1944, when Eleanor Roosevelt supported the efforts of Stalin & Albert Einstein subscribed to the socialist program, it was seen as heretical for its warning against state control over the means of production. For Hayek, the collectivist idea of giving government more economic control led not to Utopia but to Nazi Germany & fascist Italy. Since then, it has established itself alongside the works of de Tocqueville, Mill & Orwell for its warning on the tradeoff between individual liberty & government authority.

Road to Success Vol. 1: What You Must Know to Be a Successful Entrepreneur! Hosted by Mitch Schlimer. Contrib. by Mark Victor Hansen & Wally Amos. 6 cass. (Running Time: 6 hrs.). (Motivators Ser.). 1997. 59.95 (978-1-891720-00-0(7), RTS1) Lets Talk.
Created from the most valuable interviews on "Let's Talk Business Radio," & includes Wally Amos, Les Brown, Wilson Harrell, Harvey Mackay, Terri Lonier, Mark Victor Hansen, Fred DeLuca, Brian Tracy & others.

Road to Success & How to Improve the Quality of Life see Camino del Éxito y Cómo Mejorar la Calidad de Vida

Road to Success & How to Improve the Quality of Life. Hugo Tapias. Read by Pedro Montoya. (Running Time: 3 hrs.). 2001. 16.95 (978-1-60083-263-5(6), Audiofy Corp) Iofy Corp.

Road to the Right. Featuring John Costigan. (ENG.). 2009. audio compact disk (978-0-9755891-4-4(8)) Jack Ryan Assocs.

***Road to Truth.** L. Ron Hubbard. (ENG.). 2002. audio compact disk 15.00 (978-1-4031-1224-8(X)) Bridge Pubns Inc.

Road to Ubar: Finding the Atlantis of the Sands. collector's ed. Nicholas Clapp. Read by Edward Lewis. 6 cass. (Running Time: 9 hrs.). 1999. 48.00 (978-0-7366-4631-4(0), 5016) Books on Tape.
The most fabled city in ancient Arabia was Ubar. Buried in the desert without a trace, it became the Atlantis of the Sands.

Road to Venture Capital: How to Raise $$ for Your Business. Speeches. Mervin L. Evans. 4 Audiocassette. (Running Time: 330 Minutes). 2002. 99.99 (978-0-914391-23-4(2)) Comm People Pr.

Road to Victory: The Voices of World War II. (Running Time: 1 hr.). 2004. audio compact disk 16.99 (978-1-894003-36-0(5)) Pub: Scenario Prods CAN. Dist(s): PerseuPGW

Road to Wealth. Robert G. Allen. 6 cass. (Running Time: 6 hrs.). 1995. 59.95 (12180AM) Nightingale-Conant.
Equipped with the facts & tips in this wealth-building program, you'll know how to tap the incredible power of "info-preneuring" & lower your annual spending by 20 percent without sacrifice. You'll even discover the 12 keys to total financial freedom...the can't-fail way to get an instant 30 percent return on your investment...& the seven best-kept secrets of the exceedingly wealthy.

Road to Wealth: A Comprehensive Guide to Your Money, Everything You Need to Know in Good & Bad Times. abr. ed. Suze Orman. Read by Suze Orman. 5 CDs. (Running Time: 6 hrs.). (ENG.). 2001. audio compact disk 29.95 (978-0-553-52838-1(6)) Pub: Random Audio Pubg. Dist(s): Random

Road to Wealth & Wisdom. unabr. ed. Gary Arnold & Van Musso. Ed. by Earl Partlow. 1 cass. (Running Time: 1 hr.). 1997. pap. bk. 12.95 (978-1-57867-146-5(9)) Windhorse Corp.
Learn a set of proven techniques designed to filter out purity conciousness & develop wealth consciousness.

Road to Wellville. unabr. ed. T. C. Boyle. Read by Jonathan Reese. 14 cass. (Running Time: 21 hrs.). 1993. 112.00 (978-0-7366-2594-4(1), 3339) Books on Tape.
Visitors flock to Dr. Kellogg in search of the magic pill to prolong life...or the profit from its manufacture.

Road to Wigan Pier. unabr. ed. George Orwell. Read by Frederick Davidson. 6 cass. (Running Time: 8 hrs. 30 mins.). (gr. 9-12). 1993. 44.95 (978-0-7861-0304-1(3), 1268) Blckstn Audio.
The first part of this book is the searing yet beautiful account of what Orwell found "on the road to Wigan Pier." In the second part he asks why Socialism, which alone in his opinion could conserve human values from the ravages of industrialism, had so little appeal.

Road to Wigan Pier. unabr. ed. George Orwell. Read by Frederick Davidson. (Running Time: 8 hrs. NaN mins.). 2009. 29.95 (978-1-4332-6504-4(4)); audio compact disk 70.00 (978-1-4332-6501-3(X)) Blckstn Audio.

Road to Wigan Pier, unabr. ed. George Orwell. Narrated by Patrick Tull. 6 cass. (Running Time: 7 hrs. 30 mins.). 1988. 51.00 (978-1-55690-446-2(0), 88730E7) Recorded Bks.
A portrait of life in the coal mines of the North of England during the Depression.

Road to Wigan Pier. unabr. collector's ed. George Orwell. Read by Richard Green. 7 cass. (Running Time: 7 hrs.). 1981. 42.00 (978-0-7366-0555-7(X), 1528) Books on Tape.
Times were hard for English workers in the 1930s when George Orwell dramatized their plight in the documentary expose of the underclasses.

Road Towards Return. Marques Vickers. 2003. cd-rom & audio compact disk 19.95 (978-0-9706530-8-6(5)) Marquis Pubng.

Road Unseen. unabr. ed. Peter Jenkins & Barbara Jenkins. Read by Paul Shay & Jeanne Hopson. 6 cass. (Running Time: 9 hrs.). 1987. Rental 11.95 (2072) Books on Tape.
The Jenkin's walk across America, although an exhilarating adventure, is also an exhausting test of their physical & spiritual endurance. It became a crucible for their Christian faith.

Road Virus Heads North. unabr. ed. Stephen King. Read by Jay O. Sanders. 2006. 10.95 (978-0-7435-6386-4(7), Audioworks) Pub: S&S Audio. Dist(s): S and S Inc

Road Warrior: How to Keep Your Faith, Relationships, & Integrity When Away from Home. unabr. ed. Stephen Arterburn & Sam Gallucci. (Everyman Ser.). (ENG.). 2008. 13.99 (978-1-60814-367-2(8)) Oasis Audio.

Road Warrior: How to Keep Your Faith, Relationships, & Integrity When Away from Home. unabr. ed. Stephen Arterburn & Sam Gallucci. Read by Stephen Arterburn. (Running Time: 21600 sec.). (Everyman Ser.). (ENG.). 2008. audio compact disk 19.99 (978-1-59859-327-3(7)) Oasis Audio.

Road Without Turning: A Classic Adventure Story. Malcolm Wheeler-Nicholson. Read by Douglas Wheeler-Nicholson. Intro. by Caleb Carr. Adapted by Nicky Brown. 2008. audio compact disk 12.00 (978-0-9818091-1-3(1)) BMA Studios.

Roadblocks to Health & Healing. Bill Winston. 4 cass. (C). 1994. 20.00 (978-1-931289-73-3(5)) Pub: B Winston Min. Dist(s): Anchor Distributors

***Roadkill on the Highway to Heaven.** Chonda Pierce. (Running Time: 4 hrs. 43 mins. 0 sec.). (ENG.). 2009. 14.99 (978-0-310-30504-0(7)) Zondervan.

Roadmaps & Revelations. Contrib. by Parachute Band. (Worshiptools Ser.). 2007. pap. bk. 29.95 (978-5-557-57357-3(7)) Integrity Music.

Roads of Destiny see O. Henry Favorites

Roads to Quoz: An American Mosey. unabr. ed. William Least Heat-Moon. Read by Sherman Howard. (Running Time: 20 hrs.). (ENG.). 2008. 26.98 (978-1-60024-490-2(4)) Pub: Hachet Audio. Dist(s): HachBkGrp

Roadside Attractions: Stories That Take You Away. unabr. ed. N.P.R-National Public Radio Staff. Read by Noah Adams. 1 CD. (Running Time: 1 hr.). (ENG.). 2009. audio compact disk 14.95 (978-1-59887-855-4(7), 1598878557) Pub: HighBridge. Dist(s): Workman Pub

Roadside Crosses. abr. ed. Jeffery Deaver. Read by Michele Pawk. (Running Time: 6 hrs. 0 mins. 0 sec.). (ENG.). 2009. audio compact disk 29.99 (978-0-7435-8213-1(6)) Pub: S&S Audio. Dist(s): S and S Inc

Roadside Crosses. unabr. ed. Jeffery Deaver. Read by Michele Pawk. 14 CDs. (Running Time: 16 hrs. 0 mins. 0 sec.). (ENG.). 2009. audio compact disk 49.99 (978-0-7435-8215-5(2)) Pub: S&S Audio. Dist(s): S and S Inc

***Roadside Crosses: A Kathryn Dance Novel.** abr. ed. Jeffery Deaver. Read by Michele Pawk. (Running Time: 6 hrs. 0 mins. 0 sec.). (ENG.). 2011. audio compact disk 14.99 (978-1-4423-4073-2(8)) Pub: S&S Audio. Dist(s): S and S Inc

Roadside Photographs. Music by Joshua Williams. 2001. audio compact disk 12.95 (978-1-57921-435-7(5)) Pub: WinePress Pub. Dist(s): Spring Arbor Dist

Roadside Turf Management. 2006. audio compact disk 40.00 (978-0-89118-560-4(7)) Am Soc Agron.

***Roadwork.** unabr. ed. Stephen King. (Running Time: 10 hrs. 30 mins.). 2010. 29.95 (978-1-4417-3311-5(6)); 65.95 (978-1-4417-3307-8(8)); audio compact disk 60.00 (978-1-4417-3308-5(6)) Blckstn Audio.

Roadwork. unabr. ed. Stephen King. (Running Time: 10 hrs.). (ENG.). 2010. audio compact disk 29.95 (978-0-14-242786-6(1), PengAudBks) Penguin Grp USA.

Roald Dahl. Roald Dahl. 4 cass. (J). 1985. HarperCollins Pubs.

Roald Dahl. Roald Dahl. 4 cass. (Running Time: 4 hrs.). Incl. Charlie & the Chocolate Factory. Roald Dahl. (J). (SBC 122); Enormous Crocodile. Roald Dahl. (J). (SBC 122); Fantastic Mr. Fox. Roald Dahl. Read by Roald Dahl. (J). (SBC 122); James & the Giant Peach. Roald Dahl. Read by Roald Dahl. (J). (SBC 122); Magic Finger. Roald Dahl. (J). (SBC 122); (J). 1980. 29.95 (978-0-89845-026-2(8), SBC 122) HarperCollins Pubs.

Roald Dahl Collection: Charlie, James - Peach, Fantastic Mr. Fox, Enormous Crocodile, Magic Finger. abr. ed. Roald Dahl. Read by Roald Dahl. (Running Time: 12600 sec.). (J). (gr. 4-7). 2007. audio compact disk 27.50 (978-0-06-121496-7(5), HarperChildAud) HarperCollins Pubs.

Roald Hoffman. Roald Hoffmann. Read by Roald Hoffmann. Interview with Rebekah Presson. 1 cass. (Running Time: 29 min.). 1991. 10.00 (053191) New Letters.
Hoffman is a Nobel Laureate - in chemistry! Although he still practices & teaches chemistry at Cornell University, Hoffman has a great love of poetry & has published two volumes of verse.

Roane's Rules: How to Make the Right Impression - Working the Room, or One-on-One, What to Say & How to Say It. unabr. rev. ed. Susan RoAne. Read by Susan RoAne. 3 CDs. (Running Time: 3 hrs. 0 mins. 0 sec.). (ENG., 2003. audio compact disk 19.95 (978-1-55927-850-8(1)) Pub: Macmill Audio. Dist(s): Macmillan

***Roar.** Carl Sommer. (Quest for Success Ser.). (ENG.). (YA). 2009. bk. 19.95 (978-1-57537-334-8(3)); pap. bk. 11.95 (978-1-57537-383-6(1)) Advance Pub.

***Roar.** unabr. ed. Emma Clayton. Narrated by Jane Collingwood. 1 Playaway. (Running Time: 12 hrs. 15 mins.). (YA). (gr. 5-8). 2009. 64.75 (978-1-4407-4265-1(0)); 67.75 (978-1-4407-4256-9(1)); audio compact disk 108.75 (978-1-4407-4260-6(X)) Recorded Bks.

***Roar.** unabr. collector's ed. Emma Clayton. Narrated by Jane Collingwood. 10 CDs. (Running Time: 12 hrs. 15 mins.). (YA). (gr. 5-8). 2009. audio compact disk 51.95 (978-1-4407-4264-4(2)) Recorded Bks.

***Roar / el Rugido.** ed. Carl Sommer. (Quest for Success Bilingual Ser.). (ENG & SPA.). (YA). 2009. bk. 21.95 (978-1-57537-433-8(1)) Advance Pub.

Roar of Silence. Don Campbell. Read by Don Campbell. 2 cass. (Running Time: 2 hrs. 40 min.). 1995. 10.95 (978-0-8356-2099-4(9), Quest) Pub: Theos Pub Hse. Dist(s): Natl Bk Netwk

***Roaring Lambs: A Gentle Plan to Radically Change Your World.** Robert Briner. (Running Time: 4 hrs. 15 mins. 0 sec.). (ENG.). 2009. 14.99 (978-0-310-30505-7(5)) Zondervan.

Roaring Twenties: The Harding Years; From Harding to Coolidge; The Flight of the Spirit of St. Louis; And What Else Happened in 1920; The Crash of the Bull Market; The Saga of Herbert Hoover. Kenneth Bruce. 6 cass. in album. (Running Time: 6 hrs. 38 min.). (Excursions in History Ser.). 25.50 Set. Alpha Tape.

Roaring 2000's Investor: Building the Wealth & Lifestyle You Desire in the Greatest Boom in History. Harry S. Dent, Jr.. Read by Harry S. Dent, Jr. 2004. 10.95 (978-0-7435-1937-3(X)) Pub: S&S Audio. Dist(s): S and S Inc

Roaring 2000s Investor: Strategies for the Life You Want. Harry S. Dent, Jr.. Read by Harry S. Dent, Jr. 2004. 10.95 (978-0-7435-1938-0(8)) Pub: S&S Audio. Dist(s): S and S Inc

Rob Roy. unabr. ed. Walter Scott, Sr. Read by Frederick Davidson. 14 cass. (Running Time: 20 hrs. 30 mins.). 1995. 89.95 (978-0-7861-0767-4(7), 1616) Blckstn Audio.
Strong plot & superb detail combine to make "Rob Roy" a captivating tale - & an extraordinary portrait of the haunted highlands & the glorious Scottish past.

Rob Roy. unabr. ed. Walter Scott, Sr. Read by Frederick Davidson. (Running Time: 68400 sec.). 2007. audio compact disk 120.00 (978-0-7861-6059-4(4)) Blckstn Audio.

Rob Roy. unabr. ed. Walter Scott, Sr. & Frederick Davidson. (Running Time: 68400 sec.). 2007. audio compact disk 44.95 (978-0-7861-6060-0(8)) Blckstn Audio.

Robb Forman Dew. Interview. Interview with Robb Forman Dew & Kay Bonetti. 1 cass. (Running Time: 58 min.). 13.95 (978-1-55644-098-4(7), 4042) Am Audio Prose.
Robb Dew discusses her Southern roots & the effect of her family life, background & the "sense of place" on her career & work.

Robbed a Bank. Lilian Jackson Braun. Narrated by George Guidall. 5 CDs. (Running Time: 6 hrs.). (Cat Who... Ser.). 2000. audio compact disk 48.00 (978-0-7887-4746-5(0), C1232E7) Recorded Bks.
After a mysterious death at Pickax's newly opened hotel, Jim Qwilleran & his sagacious Siamese cats Koko & Yum Yum set out to get to the bottom of it all.

Robbed a Bank. unabr. ed. Lilian Jackson Braun. Narrated by George Guidall. 4 cass. (Running Time: 6 hrs.). (Cat Who... Ser.). 1999. 40.00 (978-0-7887-4032-9(6), 96010) Recorded Bks.

Robber-Barons. Ayn Rand. 1 cass. (Running Time: 30 min.). 1990. 12.95 (978-1-56114-111-1(9), AR26C) Second Renaissance.

Robber Bride. unabr. ed. Margaret Atwood. Narrated by Barbara Caruso. 15 cass. (Running Time: 21 hrs. 30 mins.). 1994. 120.00 (978-1-55690-964-1(0), 94107E7) Recorded Bks.
Tony is a military historian who speaks backwards & looks like a newly hatched bird. The waifish Charis works in a store that sells crystals & New Age drivel. Roz is a successful financier who drives a BMW & hired a private detective to snoop on her husband. The three of them, it would seem, have nothing in common. But an iron thread binds them together: Zenia, a woman who stole all their men, a woman who changes personae as often as some people change shoes, a woman whose ashes they believe lie buried in a metal canister at Mount Pleasant cemetery. But Zenia is back.

Robber Fox: Audiocassette. Jill Eggleton. (Sails Literacy Ser.). (gr. 1 up). 10.00 (978-0-7578-4044-9(2)) Rigby Educ.

Robbie: The Unauthorized Biography of Robbie Williams. Tim Footman. (Maximum Ser.). (ENG.). 2001. audio compact disk 14.95 (978-1-84240-017-3(7)) Pub: Chrome Dreams GBR. Dist(s): IPG Chicago

Robbie Solomon: A Solo Collection. 2007. pap. bk. 24.95 (978-0-8074-0994-7(4), 993289) URJ Pr.

Robe. unabr. ed. Lloyd C. Douglas. Read by Stuart Langston. 16 cass. (Running Time: 23 hrs. 30 mins.). 2002. 99.95 (978-0-7861-2328-5(1), 3036) Blckstn Audio.

Robe, Pt. 1. unabr. ed. Lloyd C. Douglas. Read by Bob Erickson. 8 cass. (Running Time: 12 hrs.). 1984. 64.00 (978-0-7366-0377-5(8), 1356-A) Books on Tape.
A novel based on the life of the young Roman soldier, Marcellus, who was in charge of the cruxifiction of Christ & who won His robe when the garments were gambled for.

Robe, Pt. 2. unabr. ed. Lloyd C. Douglas. Read by Bob Erickson. 16 cass. (Running Time: 1 hr. 30 min. per cass.). 1984. 64.00 (1356-B) Books on Tape.

Robe: The Enduring Classic of One Man's Quest for Faith & Truth. unabr. ed. Lloyd C. Douglas. (Running Time: 79200 sec.). 2007. audio compact disk 120.00 (978-0-7861-5960-4(X)) Blckstn Audio.

Robe: The Enduring Classic of One Man's Quest for Faith & Truth. unabr. ed. Lloyd C. Douglas. Read by Stuart Langton. 2 pieces. (Running Time: 81000 sec.). 2007. audio compact disk 39.95 (978-0-7861-9107-9(4), 3036) Blckstn Audio.

***Robe of Skulls.** unabr. ed. Vivian French. (Running Time: 4 hrs.). (First Tale from the Five Kingdoms Ser.). 2010. 39.97 (978-1-4418-9029-0(7), 9781441890290, Candlewick Bril); 14.99 (978-1-4418-9028-3(9), 9781441890283, Candlewick Bril); audio compact disk 14.99 (978-1-4418-9024-5(6), 9781441890245, Candlewick Bril); audio compact disk 14.99 (978-1-4418-9026-9(2), 9781441890269, Candlewick Bril); audio compact disk 39.97 (978-1-4418-9027-6(0), 9781441890276, Candlewick Bril); audio compact disk 44.97 (978-1-4418-9025-2(4), 9781441890252, Candlewick Bril) Brilliance Audio.

Robe of Skulls - AUDIO. Vivian French. 2009. audio compact disk (978-0-7636-4373-7(4)) Candlewick Pr.

Robe, Ring & Shoes: Luke 15:22. Ed Young. 1985. 4.95 (978-0-7417-1462-6(0), 462) Win Walk.

Robert A. Cook's Teaching Set. Robert A. Cook. 12 cass. (Running Time: 18 hrs). 2000. 24.99 (978-7-902031-69-1(0)) Chrstn Dup Intl.

Robert Altman see Movie Makers Speak: Directors

Robert Altman: An Oral Biography. abr. ed. Mitchell Zuckoff. (ENG.). 2009. audio compact disk 30.00 (978-0-307-57661-3(2), Random AudioBks) Pub: Random Audio Pubg. Dist(s): Random

***Robert Altman: The Oral Biography.** unabr. ed. Mitchell Zuckoff. 15 CDs. (Running Time: 18 hrs.). 2009. audio compact disk 100.00 (978-1-4159-6648-8(6), BksonTape) Pub: Random Audio Pubg. Dist(s): Random

Robert & Elizabeth Barrett Browning: A Light & Enlightening Lecture. Featuring Elliot Engel. 2000. bk. 15.00 (978-1-890123-31-4(5)) Media Cnslts.

Robert & Elizabeth Barrett Browning: Best Loved Poems. abr. ed. Robert Browning & Elizabeth Barrett Browning. Read by Joanna David. 2 CDs. (Running Time: 2 hrs. 24 mins.). 2001. audio compact disk 17.96 Books on Tape.
A unique weaving of poetry performed in a biographical context, offering a rare glimpse into the artistic, passionate nature of genius.

Robert & Elizabeth Barrett Browning: Best Loved Poems. unabr. ed. Poems. Robert Browning & Elizabeth Barrett Browning. Read by Sean Barrett et al. Ed. by Madge Manfred. Narrated by Joanna David & Steven Pacey. 2 CDs. (Running Time: 2 hr. 30 mins.). (ENG.). (gr. 9-12). 2004. 19.95 (978-1-57270-044-4(0), D21044) Pub: AudioGO. Dist(s): Perseus Dist
Includes 70 complete poems with biographical background.

Robert & Elizabeth Barrett Browning: How Do I Love Thee? unabr. ed. Poems. Robert Browning & Elizabeth Barrett Browning. Read by Sean Barrett et al. Ed. by Madge Manfred. 2 cass. (Running Time: 3 hrs.). (Robert & Elizabeth Barrett Browning Ser.). (J). (gr. 9-12). 2004. 17.95 (978-1-57270-034-5(3), D21034a) Pub: Audio Partners. Dist(s): PerseuPGW
This is a biographical introduction to the poetry of Elizabeth Barrett & Robert Browning, followed by a complete reading from "Sonnets from the Portuguese".

Robert Anton Wilson: Neophobes & Neophiles: The Futurist Dialect. 1 cass. (Running Time: 1 hr.). (Cypress College). 1980. 9.00 (F104) Freeland Pr.
The author explains the title of his talk, & from there he explores the ramifications of the rate of change on our current attitudes.

Robert Anton Wilson Explains Everything: (or Old Bob Exposes His Ignorance) Robert Anton Wilson. 5 CDs. (Running Time: 6 Hrs). 2005. audio compact disk 34.95 (978-1-59179-375-5(0), AW00574D) Sounds True.
From the author of the legendary underground bestseller The Illuminatus! Trilogy and more than thirty other books comes a long-awaited audio event: Robert Anton Wilson Explains Everything. This once-in-a-lifetime, 12-session recording captures one of the most unconventional and brilliant writers of this century in conversation, and makes available to Wilson's legion of fans a refreshing insider's view of this enigmatic (and often misunderstood) author. Robert Anton Wilson discusses such topics as futurist psychology, the paranormal, God, conspiracies real and imagined, James Joyce, "guerrilla ontology" - plus rare personal reflections on his extraordinary life.

Robert Bly. Read by Robert Bly. 1 cass. (Running Time: 29 min.). 1985. 10.00 New Letters.
The charismatic American poet accompanies his poetry reading with the dulcimer.

Robert Bly II. Robert Bly. 1 cass. (Running Time: 29 min.). (New Letters on the Air Ser.). 1992. 10.00 (120691) New Letters.
This program includes an interview about Bly's best-selling book, "Iron John," & poems from his "Selected Poems.".

Robert Boissiere. Robert Boissiere. Read by Robert Boissiere. 1 cass. (Running Time: 29 min.). 1990. 10.00 (042790) New Letters.
Boissiere lived with Hopi Indians in the 1940's, was made father to a Hopi girl & later married a Hopi woman. He reads from, "Meditations with the Hopi," & talks about his experiences & beliefs.

Robert Browning: Poems. abr. unabr. ed. Robert Browning. Read by Derek Jacobi et al. 2 CDs. (Running Time: 8700 sec.). (ENG.). 2006. audio compact disk 16.95 (978-1-59887-041-1(6), 1598870416, HighBridge Classics) Pub: HighBridge. Dist(s): Workman Pub
Selections spanning the poet's career, read by leading actors of the British stage and screen: Douglas Hodge, David Horovitch, Derek Jacobi, Jeremy Northam, Diana Quick, Prunella Scales, and Sian Thomas.

Robert Browning: Selected Poems. unabr. ed. Robert Browning. Read by Frederick Davidson. 4 cass. (Running Time: 5 hrs. 30 mins.). 2000. 32.95 (978-0-7861-0406-2(6), 1358) Blckstn Audio.

Robert Browning: Selected Poems. unabr. ed. Poems. Read by Frederick Davidson. 4 cass. (Running Time: 6 hrs.). 1999. 32.95 (1358) Blckstn Audio.
Includes: "Johannes Agricola in Meditation," "The Pied Piper of Hamelin," "Fra Lippo Lippi," "A Toccata of Galuppi's," "The Lost Leader," "The Statue & the Bust," "How it Strikes a Contemporary," "The Patriot," "Memorabilia," "James Lee's Wife," "Confessions," "Youth & Art," "A Likeness," "Mr. Sludge," "The Medium," "House," "St. Martin's Summer," "The Names," "Beatrice Signorini," & "Spring Song".

Robert Burns: Fiddle Duets. 2004. audio compact disk 19.95 (978-1-871931-97-6(5)) Pub: Taigh Teud GBR. Dist(s): Music Sales

Robert Coover. Interview. Interview with Robert Coover & Kay Bonetti. 1 cass. (Running Time: 52 min.). 13.95 (978-1-55644-009-0(X), 1052) Am Audio Prose.
Contains material on the threat of libel in relation to the history of the publication of "The Public Burning".

Robert Crais: The Monkey's Raincoat, Stalking the Angel, Lullaby Town. abr. ed. Robert Crais. Read by David Stuart & James Daniels. (Running Time: 18 hrs.). (Elvis Cole Ser.). 2006. audio compact disk 34.95 (978-1-4233-1682-4(7), 9781423316824, BACD) Brilliance Audio.

Robert Crais: Voodoo River, Sunset Express, Indigo Slam. abr. ed. Robert Crais. Narrated by Patrick G. Lawlor & David Stuart. (Running Time: 12 hrs.). (Elvis Cole Ser.). 2007. audio compact disk 34.95 (978-1-4233-2320-4(3), 9781423323204, BACD) Brilliance Audio.

Robert Creeley. Read by Robert Creeley. 1 cass. (Running Time: 29 min.). 1985. 10.00 New Letters.
One of a weekly half-hour radio program with authors talking & presenting their own works.

Robert Creeley, No. II. Robert Creeley. Read by Robert Creeley. 1 cass. (Running Time: 29 min.). 1988. 10.00 (041588) New Letters.
Interview with poet, & poet reads from his book "Mirrors".

Robert Crews. unabr. collector's ed. Thomas Berger. Read by Grover Gardener. 5 cass. (Running Time: 7 hrs. 30 min.). 1994. 40.00 (978-0-7366-2835-8(5), 3543) Books on Tape.
Robert Crews plays Robinson Crusoe when his buddies die in a plane crash. He's all alone, except for "Friday", a real sweetheart on the run.

Robert Dana. Read by Robert Dana. 1 cass. (Running Time: 29 min.). 1985. 10.00 New Letters.
Iowa poet Robert Dana reads from "In Fugitive Season" & others.

Robert Day. Read by Robert Day. 1 cass. (Running Time: 29 min.). 1987. 10.00 New Letters.
Author reads a humorous novel about how his modern cowboy novel "The Last Cattle Drive" did not get made into a movie.

Robert Day II: The Last Cattle Drive. unabr. ed. Robert Day. Read by Robert Day. Prod. by Rebekah Presson. 1 cass. (Running Time: 29 min.). 1987. 10.00 (010987) New Letters.
The author of the popular cowboy novel "The Last Cattle Drive" tells of his experiences with Hollywood.

Robert E. Howard's People of the Dark. Robert E. Howard. 2007. audio compact disk 29.95 (978-0-8095-7171-0(4)) Diamond Book Dists.

Robert E. Howard's Red Nails. Robert E. Howard. 2007. audio compact disk 27.95 (978-0-8095-7197-0(8)) Diamond Book Dists.

Robert E. Howard's the Hour of the Dragon. Robert E. Howard. 2007. audio compact disk 37.95 (978-0-8095-7194-9(3)) Diamond Book Dists.

Robert E. Lee. unabr. ed. Robert Hogrogian. 1 cass. (Running Time: 16 min.). (People to Remember Ser.). (J). (gr. 4-7). 1979. bk. 16.99 (978-0-934898-34-8(0)); pap. bk. 9.95 (978-0-934898-04-1(9)) Jan Prods.
This is the story of the man who led the South in a Nation Divided.

Robert E. Lee. unabr. ed. Emory M. Thomas. Narrated by Richard M. Davidson. 16 cass. (Running Time: 22 hrs. 30 mins.). 1996. 128.00 (978-0-7887-0569-4(5), 94746E7) Recorded Bks.
Personal biography reveals Lee's desire to return honor to his family name, his struggles in a "proper" marriage & his life as an engineer on the Mississippi.

***Robert E. Lee.** unabr. ed. Noah Andre Trudeau. Read by Tom Weiner. (Running Time: 8 hrs. 30 mins.). 2010. 29.95 (978-1-4417-5036-5(3)); 54.95 (978-1-4417-5032-7(0)); audio compact disk 76.00 (978-1-4417-5033-4(9)) Blckstn Audio.

Robert E. Lee: Young Confederate. unabr. ed. Helen Albee Monsell. Read by Lloyd James. 4 cass. (Running Time: 5 hrs. 30 mins.). (Childhood of Famous Americans Ser.). (gr. 1-3). 2001. pap. bk. 35.95 (978-0-7861-2027-7(4), K2794) Blckstn Audio.
Lee's childhood in the South as a member of a slave-owning family follows the course of his life up until his surrender at Appomatox. Children will gain an understanding of the causes & events leading to the Civil War, focusing on the man who turned down the field command of the United States Army & became the leader of the Confederate Army.

Robert E. Lee & His High Command, Parts I-II. Instructed by Gary W. Gallagher. 12 cass. (Running Time: 12 hrs.). bk. 54.95 (978-1-56585-848-0(4), 8557) Teaching Co.

Robert E. Lee & His High Command, Parts I-II. Instructed by Gary W. Gallagher. 12 CDs. (Running Time: 12 hrs.). 2004. bk. 69.95 (978-1-56585-850-3(6), 8557) Teaching Co.

Robert E. Lee's Civil War. unabr. collector's ed. Bevin Alexander. Read by Dick Estell. 8 cass. (Running Time: 12 hrs.). 1999. 64.00 (978-0-7366-4502-7(0), 4937) Books on Tape.
The author, military strategist & historian, presents a provocative re-examination of the military genius Robert E. Lee, & a critical re-evaluation of the performance of the generals who led the armies of both South & North as they struggled to adapt traditional strategies to a new era of warfare. Robert E. Lee - the South's most revered military leader - receives full credit for both his outstanding defensive maneuvers & for his remarkable achievement in holding together a disorganized & often under-equipped Confederate army for three grueling years. Demonstrates how Lee's rigid belief in launching large-scale attacks on Union armies led inevitably to the Confederacy's defeat.

Robert E. Mckee - MASTER BUILDER: Audio production of the published book - 6 CD Set. Leon Claire Metz. Narrated by Jeffrey M. Goldberg Ballyhoo! Studios. Created by Louis B. McKee Robert E. & Evelyn McKee Foundation. (ENG.). 2006. audio compact disk 59.95 (978-0-9646793-5-1(3)) R E McKee Fnd.

Robert Evans see Movie Makers Speak: Producers

Robert F. Kennedy & His Times (audio CD) ed. Interview. Arthur M. Schlesinger, Jr. Interview with Heywood Hale Broun. 1 CD. (Running Time: 55 mins.). 2007. audio compact disk 12.95 (978-1-57970-455-1(7), C40349D, Audio-For) J Norton Pubs.

Robert F. Williams: Self Respect, Self Defense & Self Determination. Ed. by The Freedom Archives. (AK Press Audio Ser.). (ENG., 2005. audio compact disk 14.98 (978-1-904859-31-4(3)) Pub: AK Pr GBR. Dist(s): Consort Bk Sales

Robert Frost see Robert Lowell: A Reading

Robert Frost. Robert Frost. 1 cass. (Running Time: 1 hr.). (Author Speaks Ser.). 1991. 14.95 J Norton Pubs.
Archival recordings of 20th-century authors.

Robert Frost. Contrib. by Unapix Inner Dimension Staff. 1 cass. 1997. 10.95 (978-1-57523-170-9(0)) Unapix Enter.

Robert Frost. unabr. collector's ed. Jeffrey Meyers. Read by Jonathan Reese. 11 cass. (Running Time: 16 hrs. 30 mins.). 1997. 88.00 (978-0-7366-3738-1(9), 4415) Books on Tape.
Tells of his early & middle years that were marked by tragedy: the loss of two children in infancy, the death of another in childbirth, the suicide & insanity of two other children, & the death of his wife.

Robert Frost: Fire & Ice. Poems. 1 cass. (Running Time: 63 min.). 14.95 (8117Q) Filmic Archives.
America's favorite poet laureate is brought to life in this superb dramatic portrayal. Includes 14 best-loved poems, woven into the narrative.

Robert Frost in Recital. unabr. abr. ed. Robert Frost. Read by Robert Frost. 1 cass. (Running Time: 51 min.). Incl. Aim Was Song. (CPN 1523); America Is Hard to See. (CPN 1523); Cabin in the Clearing. (CPN 1523); Case for Jefferson. (CPN 1523); Closed for Good. (CPN 1523); Come In. (CPN 1523); Desert Places. (CPN 1523); Does No One at All Ever Feel This Way in the Least. (CPN 1523); Drumlin Woodchuck. (CPN 1523); Fire & Ice. (CPN 1523); Gift Outright. (CPN 1523); Hardship of Accounting. (CPN 1523); It Is Almost the Year Two Thousand. (CPN 1523); Masque of Reason. (CPN 1523); Need of Being Versed in Country Things. (CPN 1523); Not Quite Social. (CPN 1523); Old Man's Winter Night. (CPN 1523); On Looking up by Chance at the Constellations. (CPN 1523); Once by the Pacific. (CPN 1523); Oven Bird. (CPN 1523); Runaway. (CPN 1523); Secret Sits. (CPN 1523); Soldier. (CPN 1523); Spring Pools. (CPN 1523); Stopping by Woods on a Snowy Evening. (CPN 1523); Two Tramps in Mud Time. (CPN 1523); (gr. 9-12). 1993. 12.00 (978-0-89845-593-9(6), CPN 1523) HarperCollins Pubs.

Robert Frost, On. Robert Pack. 1 cass. (Running Time: 1 hr. 4 min.). 1963. 11.95 (23198) J Norton Pubs.
The public, cherished image of Frost has confused many readers, who tend to read incorrectly into his poems. Pack contends that he is a terrifying poet whose work contains hidden, impending violence. He reads some of Frost's work to illustrate his point.

Robert Frost Reads. Robert Frost. Read by Robert Frost. 1 cass. (Running Time: 55 min.). 1965. 11.95 (23066) J Norton Pubs.
The poet reads & discusses his poems & his special view of the world, including the "free symbols of poetry".

Robert Frost Reads. abr. ed. Robert Frost. Read by Robert Frost. 1 cass. (Running Time: 60 min.). (Poet Anniversary Ser.). 1987. 8.98 HarperCollins Pubs.

Robert Frost Reads. unabr. ed. Poems. Robert Frost. Read by Robert Frost. 2 cass. (Running Time: 5 hrs. 51 min.). 17.95 (H115) Blckstn Audio.
Includes "The Road Not Taken," "The Pasture," "Birches," "Death of a Hired Man," "Mending Wall" & more.

Robert Frost Reads. unabr. abr. ed. Poems. Robert Frost. Read by Robert Frost. 1 cass. (Running Time: 1 hr.). Incl. Acquainted with the Night. (CPN 1060); After Apple-Picking. (CPN 1060); Birches. (CPN 1060); Choose Something Like a Star. (CPN 1060); Considerable Speck. (CPN 1060); Death of a Hired Man. (CPN 1060); Departmental. (CPN 1060); Etherealizing. (CPN 1060); Happiness Makes up in Height. (CPN 1060); Mending Wall. (CPN 1060); Mowing. (CPN 1060); My November Guest. (CPN 1060); One More Brevity. (CPN 1060); One Step Backward Taken. (CPN 1060); Pasture. (CPN 1060); Provide, Provide. (CPN 1060); Reluctance. (CPN 1060); Reluctance. (CPN 1060); Tree at My Window. (CPN 1060); Tuft of Flowers. (CPN 1060); West-Running Brook. Robert Frost. (CPN 1060); Why Wait for Science. (CPN 1060); Witch of Coos. (CPN 1060); 1993. 12.00 (978-0-89845-804-6(8), CPN 1060) HarperCollins Pubs.

Robert Frost Reads His Poems. Poems. Robert Frost. 1 CD. (Running Time: 54 MINS.). 2005. audio compact disk 12.95 (978-1-57970-222-9(8), C23066D) J Norton Pubs.

Robert G. Lee Live at the Arrowhead Bowl. Perf. by Robert G. Lee. Prod. by Randy Ray. 1 cass. (Running Time: 50 min.). 1993. 9.98 (978-1-57919-077-4(4)) Randolf Prod.
Stand up comedy routines.

Robert Graves Reads from His Poetry & the White Goddess. abr. ed. Robert Graves. Read by Robert Graves. 1 cass. (Running Time: 1 hr.). Incl. Blue-Fly. (V 1066); Cat-Goddesses. (V 1066); Death Room. (V 1066); Fallen Tower of Siloam. (V 1066); Foreboding. (V 1066); Leaving the Rest Unsaid. (V 1066); Like Snow. (V 1066); Love Story. (V 1066); My Name & I. (V 1066); Ogres & Pygmies. (V 1066); Sirocco at Deya. (V 1066); Survivor. (V 1066); Theseus & Ariadne. (V 1066); Time. (V 1066); To Bring the Dead to Life. (V 1066); To Juan at the Winter Solstice. (V 1066); (J). 1985. 11.95 (978-1-55994-081-8(6), V 1066) HarperCollins Pubs.

Robert Graves Reads from His Poetry & the White Goddess. unabr. ed. Poems. Robert Graves. Read by Robert Graves. 1 cass. (Running Time: 47 mins.). 11.95 (H157) Blckstn Audio.
Includes "The Haunted House," "The Hills of May," "The Cool Web" & "Jealous Man." Also a selection from his novel, "The White Goddess.".

Robert Graves Reads the Rubaiyat of Omar Khayyam. unabr. ed. Read by Robert Graves. Tr. by Omar Ali-Shah. 1 cass. (Running Time: 1 hr.). 10.95 (978-0-8045-1010-3(5), SAC 1010) Spoken Arts.

Robert Half on Hiring. Robert Half. Read by Rex Trailer. 4 cass. (Running Time: 4 hrs.). 1990. 40.00 incl. outline. (978-0-942563-06-1(9)); Rental 13.00 incl. outline. (978-0-942563-09-2(3)) CareerTapes.
Features a how-to guide for selecting employees. It covers such topics as deciding what you need, recruiting the best candidates, evaluating resumes, screening, interviewing, reading the candidate, checking references, making a decision, landing the candidate you want & firing.

Robert Hayden. Interview with Robert E. Hayden. 1 cass. (Running Time: 30 min.). 1978. 11.95 (L034) TFR.
The first black to hold the position of Consultant in Poetry to the Library of Congress, Hayden describes his feelings about poetry & color, & he reads excerpts from his poems.

Robert Heinlein. Robert A. Heinlein. 1 cass. (Running Time: 1 hr.). (Author Speaks Ser.). 1991. 14.95 J Norton Pubs.
Archival recordings of 20th-century authors.

Robert Heinlein Addresses the U. S. Naval Academy (audio CD) Robert Heinlein. (ENG.). 2007. audio compact disk 12.95 (978-1-57970-470-4(0), Audio-For) J Norton Pubs.

Robert J. Conley. unabr. ed. Ed. by Jim McKinley. Prod. by Rebekah Presson. 1 cass. (Running Time: 29 min.). (New Letters on the Air Ser.). 1994. 10.00 (041194) New Letters.
Conley is the author of many mass-market books about Native Americans but his best novel on the subject was deemed "too literary" for his New York publishers. In "Mountain Windsong: A Novel of the Trail of Tears," about the relocation of Cherokee Indians from North Carolina to Oklahoma in the 1830s. Conley structures his own story around an old Native myth & incorporates actual Indian treaty documents into the narrative.

Robert Kennedy: His Life. unabr. ed. Evan Thomas. Read by Ray Porter. (Running Time: 73800 sec.). 2006. 29.95 (978-0-7861-4792-2(X)); audio compact disk 29.95 (978-0-7861-6247-5(3)) Blckstn Audio.

Robert Kennedy: His Life. unabr. ed. Evan Thomas. Read by Ray Porter. (Running Time: 73800 sec.). 2006. 99.95 (978-0-7861-4795-3(4)); audio compact disk 44.95 (978-0-7861-7205-4(3)); audio compact disk 120.00 (978-0-7861-6242-0(2)) Blckstn Audio.

Robert Kerlan, M.D. Exercise Without Fear. Read by Robert Kerlan. 1 cass. (Running Time: 1 hr.). 9.95 (978-0-89811-088-3(2), 7139) Lets Talk Assocs.
Robert Kerlan talks about his approach to his speciality.

Robert Klein: Child of the '50s. 1 CD. (Running Time: 1 hr. 30 mins.). 2001. audio compact disk 9.98 (R2 70769) Rhino Enter.

Robert Klein: Mind over Matter. 1 CD. (Running Time: 1 hr. 30 mins.). 2001. audio compact disk 9.98 (R2 70768) Rhino Enter.

Robert Krausz: Symmetrics - the Dynamic Symmetry of the Markets. Read by Robert Krausz. 1 cass. (Running Time: 1 hr.). 30.00 Dow Jones Telerate.
A stand alone system, this new methodology can dovetail with other valid methods of technical analysis. Symmetrics when used with any other method will display data in time & price. For example, Symmetrics will give you moving average points, correct not only in price but also in time. Symmetrics provides forecasting ability in any time period. It allows trading & analysis to come together in one package, without requiring separate analysis for the decision making process & generating solid rules that can be back-tracked & validated.

Robert LeFevre: Banquet. 1 cass. (Running Time: 90 min.). (Cypress College). 1980. 10.00 (F106) Freeland Pr.
On hand to share their experiences, favorite anecdotes, & fond recollections of a much-loved figure, are Richard & Caroline Deyo. Harry Hoiles, & others.

Robert LeFevre: Do You Really Want a Free Society? 1 cass. (Running Time: 60 min.). (Cal State Univ., Long Beach). 1984. 9.00 (F163) Freeland Pr.
Government abolishment is not the immediate answer, says the author.

Robert LeFevre: The Anatomy of the State. 6 cass. (Running Time: 6 hrs.). (Remanent Tapes). 1983. 60.00 (R270ABCDEF) Freeland Pr.
Reveals the nature of government, how it was created & its preception through the centuries.

Robert LeFevre: The Nature of Money. 6 cass. (Running Time: 7 hrs.). (Remanent Tapes). 1982. 69.00 (R275ABCDEF) Freeland Pr.
What is money? How did it evolve? The author gives a historical view of private & public money, inflation-deflation, & the concept of "subjective value." Also an example where an English king attempted to substitue junk metal for silver in the kingdoms' coins & what resulted.

Robert LeFevre: We Did It Before. 1 cass. (Running Time: 1 hr. 30 min.). (Freeland Ser.). 1983. 10.00 (FL4) Freeland Pr.
On side one LeFevre recounts his experiences in such efforts as developing the Freedom School in Colorado, & offers advice based on them. On side two Foster presents several reasons for the demise of the effort to establish a libertarian society in a Third World nation.

Robert LeFevre Pt. 1: Justice. 1 cass. (Running Time: 60 min.). (Cypress College). 1980. 9.00 (F115) Freeland Pr.
A workshop based on the opening statement that "Justice is the arrangement that ensues in a relationship between persons in which the argreement that was voluntarily entered into by all the parties is kept in all respects, & not violated; & that is the only justice that there is.".

Robert LeFevre Pt. 2: Justice. 1 cass. (Running Time: 1 hr.). (Cypress College). 1980. 9.00 (F116) Freeland Pr.
The author discribes, in this second part of the Justice Workshop, the ramifications of contracts, killings, etc.

Robert Louis Stevenson: A Light & Englightening Literary Program by Professor Elliot Engel, Vol. 29. Elliot Engel. 1 CD. (Running Time: 49 mins.). (J). 2001. audio compact disk 15.00 (978-1-890123-58-1(7)) Media Cnslts.
Dr Engel reviews the endearing children's works created by this great Scottish author and his other startling accomplishments in life and literature.

Robert Louis Stevenson: His Poetry, Prose & the Story of His Life. unabr. ed. Poems. Robert Louis Stevenson. Read by George Rose. 1 cass. (Running Time: 1 hr.). Incl. Home Is the Sailor, Home from the Sea. Robert Louis Stevenson. (SWC 1448); It Is Good to Have Been Young in Youth. Robert Louis Stevenson. (SWC 1448); There Never Was a Child but Has Hunted Gold & Been a Pirate. Robert Louis Stevenson. (SWC 1448); Wealth I Seek Not, Hope Nor Love. Robert Louis Stevenson. (SWC 1448); 1984. 12.95 (978-0-694-50263-9(4), SWC 1448) HarperCollins Pubs.

Robert Louis Stevenson: Kidnapped. abr. ed. Robert Louis Stevenson. Read by John Samson. Contrib. by Elizabeth Bradbury. 2 cass. (Running Time: 2 hrs.). 15.95 (SCN 187) J Norton Pubs.
Balfour is caught up in the troubles following the events of 1745 when Jacobite Scots rebelled against the English Crown & sought to restore 'Bonnie Prince Charlie' to the Scottish throne.

Robert Lowell. Robert Lowell. 1 cass. (Running Time: 1 hr.). (Author Speaks Ser.). 1991. 14.95 J Norton Pubs.
Archival recordings of 20th-century authors.

Robert Lowell: A Reading. unabr. ed. Robert Lowell. Perf. by Robert Lowell. 1 cass. (Running Time: 1 hr.). Incl. Epilogue A. (SWC 1569); Exile's Return. (SWC 1569); Eye & Tooth. (SWC 1569); Homecoming. (SWC 1569); Jean Stafford: A Letter. (SWC 1569); Marriage. (SWC 1569); Memories of West Street & Lepke. (SWC 1569); Mermaid: Fifth Section. (SWC 1569); Old Flame. (SWC 1569); Reading Myself. (SWC 1569); Robert Frost. (SWC 1569); Skunk Hour. (SWC 1569); Stalin. (SWC 1569); William Carlos Williams. (SWC 1569); 1984. 11.95 (978-1-55994-094-8(8), SWC 1569) HarperCollins Pubs.
Tapes of Lowell's final recital of December 8, 1976 at the Poetry Center.

Robert Ludlum Value Collection: The Bourne Identity, the Bourne Supremacy, the Bourne Ultimatum. abr. ed. Robert Ludlum. Read by Darren McGavin. 8 CDs. (Running Time: 9 hrs.). (ENG.). 2005. audio compact disk 34.95 (978-0-7393-1737-2(7), Random AudioBks) Pub: Random Audio Pubg. Dist(s): Random

Robert Mapplethorpe: An Overview: Jewel Case. Robb Lazarus et al. 1995. audio compact disk 49.95 (978-1-886664-31-9(5)); audio compact disk 49.95 (978-1-886664-32-6(3)) Digital Collect.

Robert Mapplethorpe: The Controversy: Jewel Case. Robb Lazarus et al. 1995. audio compact disk 79.95 (978-1-886664-39-5(0)); audio compact disk 79.95 (978-1-886664-40-1(4)) Digital Collect.

Robert Monroe: Early Childhood. Robert A. Monroe. 1 cass. (Running Time: 1 hr.). (Mobius Track Ser.). 1989. 12.95 (978-1-56102-600-5(X)) Inter Indus.
Monroe discusses the early formative years of his life.

Robert Monroe: Laboratory Procedures. unabr. ed. Robert A. Monroe. Read by Robert A. Monroe. 1 cass. (Running Time: 45 min.). (Explorer Ser.). 1983. 12.95 (978-1-56113-023-8(0), 24) Monroe Institute.
Robert Monroe describes his laboratory procedures.

Robert Monroe: Later Childhood. Robert A. Monroe. 1 cass. (Running Time: 1 hr.). (Mobius Track Ser.). 1989. 12.95 (978-1-56102-601-2(8)) Inter Indus.
Monroe discusses the later formative years of his life.

Robert Monroe: Life As Wave Forms. unabr. ed. Robert A. Monroe. Read by Robert A. Monroe. 1 cass. (Running Time: 45 min.). (Explorer Ser.). 1983. 12.95 (978-1-56113-022-1(2), 23) Monroe Institute.
A review of 10 years of Robert Monroe's work.

Robert Olen Butler. unabr. ed. Ed. by Jim McKinley. Prod. by Rebekah Presson. 1 cass. (Running Time: 29 min.). (New Letters on the Air Ser.). 1994. 10.00 (032194) New Letters.
The winner of the 1993 Pulitzer Prize for Fiction reads from his new, erotic novel, "They Whisper." Butler says that artists aren't intellectuals, they're sensualists, thus his protagonist in the new book learns about himself by recalling the details of his sexual relationships with the many women in his life.

Robert Penn Warren Reads Selected Poems. abr. ed. Robert Penn Warren. Perf. by Robert Penn Warren. 1 cass. (Running Time: 1 hr.). Incl. American Portrait: Old Style. (SWC 1654); Bearded Oaks. (SWC 1654); Child Next Door. (SWC 1654); Folly on Royal Street. (SWC 1654); Function of Blizzard. (SWC 1654); Heart of Autumn. (SWC 1654); Leaf. (SWC 1654); Little Boy & Lost Shoe. (SWC 1654); Love Recognized. (SWC 1654); Mediterranean Beach. (SWC 1654); Midnight Outcry. (SWC 1654); Mortmain. (SWC 1654); Pondy Woods. (SWC 1654); Sirocco. (SWC 1654); Vision. (SWC 1654); 1984. 12.95 (978-0-694-50342-1(8), SWC 1654) HarperCollins Pubs.

Robert Peters. unabr. ed. Read by Robert Peters. 1 cass. (Running Time: 29 min.). 1985. 10.00 New Letters.
California poet reads from "Songs for Son" & a dramatic sequence from "Picnic in the Snow: Ludwig II of Bavaria".

Robert Pinsky. Read by Robert Pinsky. 1 cass. (Running Time: 29 min.). 1985. 10.00 New Letters.
The California poet reads from "History of My Heart".

Robert Poole: A New Approach to National Defense. 1 cass. (Running Time: 60 min.). (Long Beach City College). 1983. 9.00 (F147) Freeland Pr.
The author's knowlege of the latest in arms technology is one of the highlights of this program.

Robert Poole: Unconventional Approaches to Property Rights. 1 cass. (Running Time: 60 min.). (Cal State Univ., Long Beach Ser.). 1981. 9.00 (F122) Freeland Pr.
Discusses the problems of obscure property, (i.e., who owns the airwaves?) & offers solutions to such questions.

Robert Preston see Movie Makers Speak: Actors

Robert Stewart. Read by Robert Stewart. 1 cass. (Running Time: 29 min.). 1985. 10.00 New Letters.
Kansas City poet Robert Stewart reads plumbing poems & others.

Robert Stone. Interview. Interview with Robert Stone & Kay Bonetti. 1 cass. (Running Time: 1 hr. 30 min.). 13.95 (978-1-55644-060-1(X), 2142) Am Audio Prose.
Discusses Stone's central thematic concerns, both religious & political, plus his ideas about the place of craft, vision & plot in fiction. "The interview is thoroughgoing, insightful, & a cogent exploration of Stone's writings, his background, & working habits".

Robert Stone. unabr. ed. Robert Stone. Read by Robert Stone. 1 cass. (Running Time: 29 min.). 1989. 10.00 New Letters.
Stone reads from his novel Children of Light & is interviewed.

Robert Sward. Read by Robert Sward. 1 cass. (Running Time: 29 min.). 1985. 10.00 New Letters.
Robert Sward's books include "Kissing Dancer" & "Thousand Year Old Fiancee".

Robert Taylor Jr. unabr. ed. Robert Taylor, Jr.. Read by Robert Taylor, Jr. 1 cass. (Running Time: 29 min.). Incl. Fiddle & Bow; 1987. 10.00 New Letters.
Reads from his unusual novel & plays fiddle music.

Robert Vavra's Horses of the Wind. 2001. audio compact disk 19.99 (978-0-9711329-9-3(2)) Equivision.

Roberto the Insect Architect. (J). 2005. bk. 24.95 (978-0-439-80450-9(7)); bk. 29.95 (978-0-439-80455-4(8)) Weston Woods.
A termite named Roberto pursues his dream of becoming an architect and travels to the big city where he hopes to find success. This funny and inspirational story will encourage viewers of any age to build their dreams.

Roberts & Barrand: Dark Ships in the Forest. 1 cass. (Running Time: 1 hr.). 9.98 (C-65); audio compact disk 14.98 (CD-65) Folk-Legacy.
Ballads of the Supernatural.

Roberts Ridge: A Story of Courage & Sacrifice on Takur Ghar Mountain, Afghanistan. unabr. ed. Malcolm MacPherson. Read by Joe Barrett. (Running Time: 30600 sec.). 2008. 59.95 (978-1-4332-4539-8(6)); cass. & audio compact disk 80.00 (978-1-4332-4540-4(X)); audio compact disk 29.95 (978-1-4332-4541-1(8)) Blckstn Audio.

Robert's Rules of Order. abr. ed. Henry M. Robert. Perf. by Aaron Meza. 5 CDs. 2004. audio compact disk 34.95 (978-1-59007-480-0(7)) New Millenn Enter.

Robert's Rules of Order. abr. ed. Henry M. Robert. 4 cass. (Running Time: 6 hrs.). 2001. 24.95 (978-1-57511-057-8(1)) Pub Mills.
Guide to running any meeting in an orderly fashion.

Robert's Rules of Order. 10th abr. ed. Scripts. Henry Roberts. Read by Aaron Meza. 4 cass. (Running Time: 6 hrs.). 2004. 24.95 (978-1-59007-357-5(6)) Pub: New Millenn Enter. Dist(s): PerseuPGW

Robespierre. Henri Guillemin. 1 cass. (Running Time: 1 hr.). (FRE.). 1991. 16.95 (1512-RF) Olivia & Hill.
Guillemin recounts on France-Culture the downfall of Robespierre, the Revolutionary hero known as "l'Incorruptible.".

Robespierre & His Time. 1 cass. (Running Time: 1 hr.). 10.00 Esstee Audios.
The world's foremost terrorist & his life & influence.

Robin at Hickory Street. Dana Meachen Rau. Narrated by Alexi Komisar. Illus. by Joel Snyder. 1 cass. (Running Time: 1 hr.). (Smithsonian's Backyard Ser.). (J). (ps-2). 1995. 5.00 (978-1-56899-173-3(8), C5007) Soundprints.
Spring has arrived! Brown yards have turned green & daffodils burst with color. Soon Robin will arrive, too. Robin & his flock fly north from their southern winter swampland. Each bird searches for his own home. But there are no vacant yards for Robin. They are all taken by older robins who warn him to stay away. Behind the bluestone house on Hickory Street, the yard looks clear. Has he finally found a home?.

Robin at Hickory Street. Dana Meachen Rau. Illus. by Joel Snyder. Narrated by Alexi Komisar. 1 cass. (Running Time: 1 hr.). (Smithsonian's Backyard Ser.). (ENG.). (J). (ps-3). 1995. 19.95 (978-1-56899-172-6(X), BC5007) Soundprints.

Robin Behn. Robin Behn. Read by Robin Behn. 1 cass. (Running Time: 29 min.). 1990. 10.00 (051190) New Letters.
Poet reads from & discusses her book "Paper Bird".

Robin des Bois Junior. 1 cass. (Running Time: 1 hr.). (Children's Collection). (FRE.). (J). 1995. bk. 14.95 (1AD080) Olivia & Hill.

***Robin Hood.** Tr. by Sara Tobon. Illus. by Jennifer Tanner. Retold by Aaron Shepard & Anne L. Watson. (Classic Fiction Ser.). (SPA.). 2010. audio compact disk 14.60 (978-1-4342-2576-4(3)) CapstoneDig.

***Robin Hood.** abr. ed. 2007. audio compact disk 13.00 (978-958-8318-07-3(6)) Pub: Yoyo Music COL. Dist(s): YoYoMusic

Robin Hood. unabr. ed. Imogen Christie. Read by Robert Glenister. 2 cass. (Running Time: 2 hrs.). (J). (gr. 1-8). 1999. 18.95 (CTC 775, Chivers Child Audio) AudioGO.

***Robin Hood.** unabr. ed. David B. Coe. (Running Time: 11 hrs. 0 mins.). 2010. 65.95 (978-1-4417-5593-3(4)); audio compact disk 100.00 (978-1-4417-5594-0(2)) Blckstn Audio.

***Robin Hood.** unabr. ed. David B. Coe. Read by Robin Sachs. (Running Time: 11 hrs. 0 mins.). 2010. 29.95 (978-1-4417-5597-1(7)); audio compact disk 19.95 (978-1-4417-5596-4(9)) Blckstn Audio.

Robin Hood. unabr. ed. Benedict Flynn. Read by John McAndrew. (J). 2006. 34.99 (978-1-59895-343-5(5)) Find a World.

Robin Hood. unabr. ed. Howard Pyle. Read by John Chatty. 8 cass. (Running Time: 8 hrs.). (J). 1980. 56.00 (C-44) Jimcin Record.
Robin, Friar Tuck, Little John, & the rest of the merry men cavort in Sherwood Forest & make life miserable for the Sheriff of Nottingham & Prince John.

***Robin Hood.** unabr. ed. Howard Pyle. Narrated by Simon Vance. (Running Time: 11 hrs. 30 mins.). 2010. 17.99 (978-1-4001-8705-8(2)); 22.99 (978-1-4001-6705-0(1)); 29.99 (978-1-4001-9705-7(8)); audio compact disk 29.99 (978-1-4001-1705-5(4)); audio compact disk 65.99 (978-1-4001-4705-2(0)) Pub: Tantor Media. Dist(s): IngramPubServ

Robin Hood. unabr. ed. Louis Rhead. Read by Flo Gibson. 5 cass. (Running Time: 7 hrs.). (J). (gr. 5-8). 1991. 20.95 (978-1-55685-216-9(9)) Audio Bk Con.
Bold Robin Hood, skilled archer, huntsman, robber of the rich & champion of the poor & downtrodden, has many adventures in Sherwood forest. Friar Tuck, Little John, Maid Marion & Will Scarlet are part of his merry band of benevolent outlaws.

Robin Hood - Silver Arrow. unabr. ed. 1 cass. (Running Time: 20 min.). Dramatization. (Magic Looking Glass Ser.). (J). (gr. 2-6). 1989. 9.95 (978-0-7810-0050-5(5), NIM-CW-131-1-C) NIMCO.
A folk tale of English descent.

Robin Hood - The Sheriff Speaks. Alvin Granowsky. 1 cass. (Point of View Stories Ser.). (J). (gr. 4-7). 1993. 8.49 (978-0-8114-2221-5(6)) SteckVau.
Two versions of the traditional story & a retelling from the viewpoint of a story character motivate students to read & analyze literature through critical thinking. Flip-book presentation emphasizes the difference in the two story versions & encourages students to complete both & compare.

Robin Hood Read Along. 1 cass. (Running Time: 90 mins.). (J). (ps-3). 1999. pap. bk. 6.98 (978-0-7634-0590-8(6)) W Disney Records.

Robin Minard. Ed. by Ulrich Krempel. (ENG & GER., pap. bk. 15.00 (978-3-7757-9000-0(4)) Pub: Hatje Cantz DEU. Dist(s): Dist Art Pubs

Robin, the Outlaw. Tim Winkey. Read by Michael Bernstein. 2 cass. (Running Time: 1 hr. 48 min.). 1993. 14.88 set. (978-1-881903-00-0(1)) DW Artworks.
A new version of Robin Hood, based on the stories of Howard Pyle: how Robin becomes an outlaw, his true relationship with Lady Marian & the Sheriff of Nottingham, & how the outlaws of Sherwood Forest actually rob the rich & the greedy. For general audiences.

Robin Who Showed the Way see Secret Garden: A Young Reader's Edition of the Classic Story

Robinson: A History of Rome. unabr. ed. 12 cass. (Running Time: 18 hrs.). 2002. 88.00 (978-1-929718-08-5(X), 9002-4) Audio Conn.
This is the story of a tiny market town on the Tiber, its rise to world domination, and then its slow, terrible plunge to utter ruin. The rise and all fo Rome is the single greatest drama in all human history.

Robinson Crusoe. Narrated by Daniel Defoe et al. (ENG.). 2007. 12.95 (978-0-9801087-0-5(5)) Alpha DVD.

Robinson Crusoe. Daniel Defoe. Narrated by John Lescault. (Running Time: 43800 sec.). (Unabridged Classics in MP3 Ser.). (ENG.). 2008. audio compact disk 26.00 (978-1-58472-538-1(9), In Aud) Sound Room.

Robinson Crusoe. William Defoe. Read by Frederick Davidson. (Running Time: 11 hrs.). 1989. 34.95 (978-1-59912-583-1(8)) Iofy Corp.

Robinson Crusoe. Daniel Defore. 2005. cd-rom 34.95 (978-1-4193-6526-3(6)) Record Bks.

***Robinson Crusoe.** abr. ed. Daniel Defoe. Read by Santiago Munevar. 2008. audio compact disk 17.00 (978-958-8318-31-8(9)) Pub: Yoyo Music COL. Dist(s): YoYoMusic

Robinson Crusoe. abr. adpt. ed. Daniel Defoe. (Bring the Classics to Life: Level 3 Ser.). (ENG.). 2008. audio compact disk 12.95 (978-1-55576-446-3(0)) EDCON Pubng.

Robinson Crusoe. unabr. ed. Daniel Defoe. Read by John Lee. (Running Time: 11 hrs. 0 mins.). 2008. audio compact disk 29.95 (978-1-4332-5145-0(0)); audio compact disk 65.95 (978-1-4332-5142-9(6)); audio compact disk 90.00 (978-1-4332-5143-6(4)) Blckstn Audio.

Robinson Crusoe. unabr. ed. Daniel Defoe. Read by Tom Casaletto. (Running Time: 11 hrs.). 2004. 24.95 (978-1-59710-653-5(4), 1597106534, BAD) Brilliance Audio.

Robinson Crusoe. unabr. ed. Daniel Defoe. Read by John Lescault. (YA). 2006. 84.99 (978-1-59895-177-6(7)) Find a World.

Robinson Crusoe. unabr. ed. Daniel Defoe. Narrated by Simon Vance. (Running Time: 10 hrs. 30 mins. 0 sec.). (ENG.). 2008. audio compact disk 22.99 (978-1-4001-5692-4(0)) Pub: Tantor Media. Dist(s): IngramPubServ

Robinson Crusoe. unabr. ed. Daniel Defoe. Read by Simon Vance. (Running Time: 10 hrs. 30 mins. 0 sec.). (ENG.). 2008. audio compact disk 32.99 (978-1-4001-0692-9(3)) Pub: Tantor Media. Dist(s): IngramPubServ

Robinson Crusoe. unabr. ed. Daniel Defoe. Read by Simon Vance. Narrated by Simon Vance. (Running Time: 10 hrs. 30 mins. 0 sec.). (Tantor Unabridged Classics Ser.). (ENG.). 2008. audio compact disk 65.99 (978-1-4001-3692-6(X)) Pub: Tantor Media. Dist(s): IngramPubServ

***Robinson Crusoe.** unabr. ed. Daniel Defoe. Compiled by James Baldwin. Narrated by Simon Vance. (ENG.). 2010. 10.98 (978-1-59644-980-0(2), MissionAud); audio compact disk 12.98 (978-1-59644-979-4(9), MissionAud) christianaud.

Robinson Crusoe. unabr. ed. Read by John Lee. Narrated by Daniel Defoe & Daniel Defoe. (Running Time: 11 hrs. 0 mins.). 2008. audio compact disk & audio compact disk 19.95 (978-1-4332-5144-3(2)) Blckstn Audio.

Robinson Crusoe: A BBC Radio Full-Cast Dramatization. Daniel Defoe. (Running Time: 2 hrs. 0 mins. 0 sec.). (ENG.). 2009. audio compact disk 24.95 (978-1-60283-758-4(9)) Pub: AudioGO. Dist(s): Perseus Dist

Robinson Crusoe: An A+ Audio Study Guide. unabr. ed. Philip Clarke. (Running Time: 1 hr.). (ENG.). 2006. 5.98 (978-1-59483-722-7(8)) Pub: Hachet Audio. Dist(s): HachBkGrp

Robinson Crusoe: As Told in One-Syllable Words. unabr. ed. Daniel Defoe. Read by Richard Brown. 2 cass. (Running Time: 3 hrs.). (J). (gr. 4 up). 1990. 14.95 (978-1-55685-164-3(2)) Audio Bk Con.
A compelling tale of adventure, courage & ingenuity & the eternal urge to find a distant land where the perfect life can be built from nothing. The enduring partnership of Crusoe & his man Friday warms the heart.

***Robinson Crusoe: Bring the Classics to Life.** adpt. ed. Daniel Defoe. (Bring the Classics to Life Ser.). 2008. pap. bk. 21.95 (978-1-55576-501-9(7)) EDCON Pubng.

Robinson Crusoe: The Complete Story of Robinson Crusoe see Great English Literature of the 18th Century

Robinson Crusoe: The Complete Story of Robinson Crusoe. Daniel Defoe. Contrib. by Roy Marsden. 2 CDs. (Running Time: 1 hr. 52 mins.). (J). 2006. audio compact disk 29.95 (978-0-7927-4336-1(9), BBCD 163) AudioGO.

Robinson Crusoe: The Complete Story of Robinson Crusoe. Daniel Defoe. (Running Time: 11 hrs. 30 mins.). 2005. audio compact disk 81.00 (978-0-7861-7878-0(7)) Blckstn Audio.

Robinson Crusoe: The Complete Story of Robinson Crusoe. Daniel Defoe. Read by Jim Weiss. 2002. audio compact disk 72.00 (978-0-7366-9121-5(9)) Books on Tape.

Robinson Crusoe: The Complete Story of Robinson Crusoe. Daniel Defoe. Read by Jim Weiss. (J). 2002. 64.00 (978-0-7366-8953-3(2)) Books on Tape.

Robinson Crusoe: The Complete Story of Robinson Crusoe. Daniel Defoe. 2001. 16.99 (978-0-00-105242-0(X)) Pub: HarpC GBR. Dist(s): Trafalgar

Robinson Crusoe: The Complete Story of Robinson Crusoe. Daniel Defoe. Read by John Lescault. (Running Time: 12 hrs. 15 mins.). 2002. 33.95 (978-1-59912-111-6(5), Audiofy Corp) Iofy Corp.

Robinson Crusoe: The Complete Story of Robinson Crusoe. Daniel Defoe. Read by Ron Keith. 8 Cass. (Running Time: 13.5 Hrs). 19.95 (978-1-4025-3322-8(5)) Recorded Bks.

Robinson Crusoe: The Complete Story of Robinson Crusoe. abr. ed. Daniel Defoe. 1 cass. (Running Time: 50 min.). Dramatization. 5.95 (978-0-89926-195-9(7), 1005); Audio Bk.
Full cast.

Robinson Crusoe: The Complete Story of Robinson Crusoe. abr. ed. Daniel Defoe. Read by Anton Rodgers. 2 cass. (Running Time: 3 hrs.). 2000. 7.95 (978-1-57815-124-0(4), 1086, Media Bks Audio) Media Bks NJ.
A young man from England finds himself shipwrecked on a desert island. After twenty-four years, he discovers a footprint in the sand & encounters exotic happenings.

Robinson Crusoe: The Complete Story of Robinson Crusoe. abr. ed. Daniel Defoe. Read by Nigel Anthony. 3 CDs. (Running Time: 3 hrs. 15 mins.). 1995. audio compact disk 22.98 (978-962-634-065-3(7), NA306512, Naxos AudioBooks) Naxos.

Robinson Crusoe: The Complete Story of Robinson Crusoe. unabr. ed. Daniel Defoe. Read by Frederick Davidson. 8 cass. (Running Time: 11 hrs. 30 mins.). (YA). (gr. 9-12). 1989. 56.95 (978-0-7861-0056-9(7), 1053) Blckstn Audio.
The marvel of this timeless tale of adventure & utility verges on the inexpressible. Beginning with the restless longings of young Robinson Crusoe for travel & adventure & climaxes with the ultimate fusion of man's resourcefulness with the agents of nature.The remarkably realistic account of the marooned Crusoe's ability to make himself an endurable existence in his solitude bespeaks Defoe's genius for life-like fiction. Its message argues a strong case for the concept of individualism.

Robinson Crusoe: The Complete Story of Robinson Crusoe. unabr. ed. Daniel Defoe. Read by Frederick Davidson. 8 cass. (Running Time: 41400 sec.). 2005. 27.95 (978-0-7861-3461-8(5), E1053); audio compact disk 27.95 (978-0-7861-8038-7(2), ZE1053); audio compact disk 29.95 (978-0-7861-8165-0(6), ZM1053) Blckstn Audio.

Robinson Crusoe: The Complete Story of Robinson Crusoe. unabr. ed. Daniel Defoe. Read by Tim Behrens. 6 cass. (Running Time: 8 hrs. 30 min.). 39.95 (978-1-55686-107-9(9), 107) Books in Motion.
Robinson Crusoe, sole survivor from a shipwreck, crawls upon the beach of a deserted island north of Brazil. His courage & ingenuity are put to the test as he fights to survive alone under primitive conditions.

Robinson Crusoe: The Complete Story of Robinson Crusoe. unabr. ed. Daniel Defoe. Read by Tom Casaletto. 8 cass. (Running Time: 11 hrs.). (Bookcassette Classic Collection). 1995. 59.25 (978-1-56100-259-7(3), 1561002593, Unabridge Lib Edns) Brilliance Audio.
Son of a middle-class Englishman, Robinson Crusoe takes to the sea to find adventure. And find it he does when on one of his voyages he is shipwrecked on a deserted South American island for thirty-five years. After scavenging his broken ship for useful items, he had only his skills and ingenuity to keep him alive as there was to be no one else on the island for the next twenty-four years. In the middle of that twenty-fourth year he rescued a native about to be eaten by cannibals who were using his island for a place of feasting. Crusoe named this man Friday, after the day of his rescue. Friday became his faithful servant and friend, even returning with him to England after their deliverance by an English ship. Listeners will enjoy Crusoe's determination for survival against all odds and admire the spirituality that gave him the strength to survive. A hero through the ages, he richly deserves the admiration that has endured over three centuries.

Robinson Crusoe: The Complete Story of Robinson Crusoe. unabr. ed. Daniel Defoe. Read by Tom Casaletto. 8 cass. (Running Time: 11 hrs.). 2002. 29.95 (978-1-59086-280-3(5), 1590862805, BAU) Brilliance Audio.

Robinson Crusoe: The Complete Story of Robinson Crusoe. unabr. ed. Daniel Defoe. Read by Tom Casaletto. (Running Time: 11 hrs.). 2004. 39.25 (978-1-59335-427-5(4), 1593354274, Brlnc Audio MP3 Lib) Brilliance Audio.

Robinson Crusoe: The Complete Story of Robinson Crusoe. unabr. ed. Daniel Defoe. Read by Tom Casaletto. (Running Time: 11 hrs.). 2004. 39.25 (978-1-59710-652-8(6), 1597106526, BADLE) Brilliance Audio.

Robinson Crusoe: The Complete Story of Robinson Crusoe. unabr. ed. Daniel Defoe. Read by Tom Casaletto. (Running Time: 39600 sec.). (Classic Collection). 2005. audio compact disk 97.25 (978-1-59737-146-9(7), 9781597371469, BriAudCD Unabrid); audio compact disk 36.95 (978-1-59737-145-2(9), 9781597371452, Bril Audio CD Unabri) Brilliance Audio.

Robinson Crusoe: The Complete Story of Robinson Crusoe. unabr. ed. Daniel Defoe. Read by Robert L. Halvorson. 7 cass. (Running Time: 630 min.). 35.95 (96) Halvorson Assocs.

Robinson Crusoe: The Complete Story of Robinson Crusoe. unabr. ed. Daniel Defoe. Read by Frederick Davidson. 8 cass. (Running Time: 8 hrs.). 1999. 56.95 (FS9-51096) Highsmith.

Robinson Crusoe: The Complete Story of Robinson Crusoe, unabr. ed. Daniel Defoe. Narrated by Ron Keith. 9 cass. (Running Time: 13 hrs. 30 mins.). 1991. 78.00 (978-1-55690-447-9(9), 91407E) Recorded Bks.
A shipwrecked sailor struggles to survive on a deserted island.

Robinson Crusoe: The Complete Story of Robinson Crusoe. unabr. ed. Daniel Defoe. Read by Tom Casaletto. (Running Time: 11 hrs.). 2004. 24.95 (978-1-59335-195-3(X), 159335195X) Soulmate Audio Bks.
Son of a middle-class Englishman, Robinson Crusoe takes to the sea to find adventure. And find it he does when on one of his voyages he is shipwrecked on a deserted South American island for thirty-five years. After scavenging his broken ship for useful items, he had only his skills and ingenuity to keep him alive as there was to be no one else on the island for the next twenty-four years. In the middle of that twenty-fourth year he rescued a native about to be eaten by cannibals who were using his island for a place of feasting. Crusoe named this man Friday, after the day of his rescue. Friday became his faithful servant and friend, even returning with him to England after their deliverance by an English ship. Listeners will enjoy Crusoe's determination for survival against all odds and admire the spirituality that gave him the strength to survive. A hero through the ages, he richly deserves the admiration that has endured over three centuries.

Robinson Crusoe: The Complete Story of Robinson Crusoe. unabr. ed. Daniel Defoe. Read by John Lescault. 1 cd. (Running Time: 10 hrs 45 mins). (YA). 2002. audio compact disk 18.95 (978-1-58472-397-4(1), In Aud) Pub: Sound Room. Dist(s): Baker Taylor
MP3 format.

Robinson Crusoe: The Complete Story of Robinson Crusoe. unabr. ed. Daniel Defoe. 1 cass. (Running Time: 1 hr.). Dramatization. 10.95 (SAC 1018) Spoken Arts.

Robinson Crusoe: The Complete Story of Robinson Crusoe. unabr. collector's ed. Daniel Defoe. Read by Dan Lazar. 8 cass. (Running Time: 12 hrs.). (J). 1977. 64.00 (978-0-7366-0007-1(8), 1017) Books on Tape.
Based on the true story of Alexander Selkirk who was cast away on an island & created a wealth of imaginative detail.

Robley Wilson. unabr. ed. Robley Wilson. 1 cass. (Running Time: 29 min.). (New Letters on the Air Ser.). 1992. 10.00 (031392) New Letters.
Wilson reads from his novel, "The Victim's Daughter," & talks about the perils of trying to make a living as a serious author.

***Robopocalypse: A Novel.** unabr. ed. Daniel Wilson. (ENG.). 2011. audio compact disk 35.00 (978-0-307-91390-6(2), Random AudioBks) Pub: Random Audio Pubg. Dist(s): Random

Robot City Vol. 1: Odyssey. abr. ed. Isaac Asimov. Perf. by Peter MacNicol et al. 1 cass. (Running Time: 60 min.). Dramatization. 1988. 9.95 (978-0-89845-797-1(1), CPN 1837) HarperCollins Pubs.

Robot Club. abr. ed. Prod. by Greg Clayman. 1 cass. (Running Time: 1 hr.). 1997. 19.95 (978-1-57304-908-5(5)) Hachet Audio.

Robot Rampage: A Buzz Beaker Brainstorm. Scott Nickel. Illus. by Andy J. Smith. (Buzz Beaker Brainstorm Ser.). (gr. 1-3). 2008. audio compact disk 14.60 (978-1-4342-0581-0(9)) CapstoneDig.

Robot Series MP3 Boxed Set. unabr. ed. Isaac Asimov & Isaac Asimov. Narrated by William Dufris. (Running Time: 30 hrs. 30 mins. 0 sec.). (ENG.). 2009. audio compact disk 29.95 (978-1-4001-2029-1(2)) Pub: Tantor Media. Dist(s): IngramPubServ

Robotics in Mexico: A Strategic Reference 2006. Compiled by Icon Group International, Inc. Staff. 2007. ring bd. 195.00 (978-0-497-82359-7(4)) Icon Grp.

Robots of Dawn. unabr. ed. Isaac Asimov. Read by William Dufris. (Running Time: 15 hrs. 30 mins. 0 sec.). (Robot Ser.). (ENG.). 2007. audio compact disk 39.99 (978-1-4001-0423-9(8)); audio compact disk 79.99 (978-1-4001-3423-6(4)); audio compact disk 29.99 (978-1-4001-5423-4(5)) Pub: Tantor Media. Dist(s): IngramPubServ

Rocannon's World. Ursula K. Le Guin. (Hainish Ser.). 2005. 22.00 (978-1-57453-575-4(7)) Audio Lit.
A world shared by three native humanoid races - the cavern-dwelling Gdemiar, elvish Fiia, and warrior clan, Liuar - is suddenly invaded and conquered by a fleet of ships from the stars. Earth scientist Rocannon is on that world, and he sees his friends murdered and his spaceship destroyed. Marooned among alien peoples, he leads the battle to free this new world - and finds that legends grow around him even as he fights.

Rocannon's World. unabr. ed. Ursula K. Le Guin. Read by Stefan Rudnicki. (Running Time: 18000 sec.). 2007. 34.95 (978-1-4332-1081-5(9)); audio compact disk 29.95 (978-1-4332-1083-9(5)) Blckstn Audio.

Rocannon's World. unabr. ed. Ursula K. Le Guin & Stefan Rudnicki. (Running Time: 18000 sec.). 2007. audio compact disk 45.00 (978-1-4332-1082-2(7)) Blckstn Audio.

Rocannon's World. unabr. abr. ed. Ursula K. Le Guin. 5 CDs. (Running Time: 6 hrs.). (Hainish Ser.). 2005. audio compact disk 25.95 (978-1-57453-574-7(9)) Audio Lit.

Rock. Christine Sinclair. 1 CD. (Running Time: 1 hr.). 1993. pap. bk. 22.95 (978-1-85626-108-1(5)) Pub: Kyle Cathie GBR. Dist(s): Trafalgar

Rock: Romans 9:19-33. Ed Young. 1984. 4.95 (978-0-7417-1389-6(6), 389) Win Walk.

Rock: The Unauthorized Biography of Kid Rock. Michael Thomson. (Maximum Ser.). (ENG., 2001. audio compact disk 14.95 (978-1-84240-035-7(5)) Pub: Chrome Dreams GBR. Dist(s): IPG Chicago

Rock-a-Bye. 1 cass. (Classic Collections). (J). 10.99 (978-0-7634-0027-9(0)); audio compact disk 10.99 (978-0-7634-0026-2(2)); audio compact disk 16.99 (978-0-7634-0029-3(7)) W Disney Records.

Rock-a-Bye. 1 CD. (Running Time: 1 hr.). (Classic Collections). (J). (ps-k). 1996. audio compact disk 16.99 (978-0-7634-0028-6(9)) W Disney Records.

Rock-a-Bye Baby. 4 cass. (Running Time: 4 hrs.). (Wood Cassette Toys Ser.). (J). 1991. 19.95 (978-1-55569-483-8(7), CWP-8315) Great Am Audio.
Contains: Nursery rhymes, lullabies, relaxing ocean waves with lullaby theme & playtime music.

Rock-a-Bye Baby. 1 cass. (Running Time: 1 hr.). 1995. 26.95 (978-1-55569-704-4(6)) Great Am Audio.

Rock-a-Bye Baby. Penton. 1 CD. (Running Time: 1 hr. 30 mins). (Relaxation Ser.). (ENG.). (J). 2003. audio compact disk 7.95 (978-1-59125-333-4(0)) Penton Overseas.

Rock-a-Bye Collection, Vol. 1. Created by J. Aaron Brown & Hal Leonard Corporation Staff. 1 cass. (Child's Gift of Lullabyes Ser.). 1990. pap. bk. 12.95 (978-0-7935-3076-2(8), 0793530768) H Leonard.

Rock-a-Bye Collection, Vol. 2. Ed. by J. Aaron Brown. Illus. by Jim Vienneau. 1 cass. (J). (ps). 1990. bk. 12.95 (978-0-927945-04-2(5)) Someday Baby.
A collection of original lullabies. This fully orchestrated collection is a Grammy Award Finalist. Side One is with vocals & Side Two is instrumental only so that the parent can sing along. Includes a full color lyric book.

Rock-a-Bye Horse. 1 cass. (Running Time: 1 hr.). (J). 1995. pap. bk. 11.95 (978-1-55569-697-9(X)) Great Am Audio.

Rock-a-Bye-Moon/The Man in the Moon. Steck-Vaughn Staff. 1996. (978-0-8172-6464-2(7)) SteckVau.

Rock-a-Bye Songbook. 1 cass., 1 CD. (Running Time: 1 hr.). (Kidzup Ser.). (J). 2001. pap. bk. 12.99 (978-1-894281-79-9(9)) Pub: Kidzup CAN. Dist(s): Penton Overseas
A classic collection of all time favorite lullabies.

Rock-a-Tot. Kidzup Productions Staff. 1 cass. (Running Time: 90 mins.). (Kidzup Toddler Ser.). (J). 1999. 8.99 (978-1-894281-13-3(6)); audio compact disk 12.99 (978-1-894281-14-0(4)) Pub: Kidzup CAN. Dist(s): Penton Overseas
Fourteen great original, fun songs for toddlers. Easy to sing melodies.

Rock & Blues Play-along Trax: Improvisational Concepts for Guitar. Dave Uhrich. 2002. bk. 14.95 (978-0-7866-6459-7(2), 99228CDB) Mel Bay.

Rock & Hawk see Poetry of Robinson Jeffers

Rock & Roll: An Unruly History. unabr. ed. Robert Palmer. Read by Joe McCargar. (Running Time: 11 hrs.). 2008. 39.25 (978-1-4233-5800-8(7), 9781423358008, Brlnc Audio MP3 Lib); 39.25 (978-1-4233-5802-2(3), 9781423358022, BADLE); 24.95 (978-1-4233-5799-5(X), 9781423357995, Brilliance MP3); 24.95 (978-1-4233-5801-5(5), 9781423358015, BAD) Brilliance Audio.

Rock & Roll Diner: Popular American Cooking, Classic Rock & Roll Music. Sharon O'Connor. 1 cass. (Running Time: 1 hr.). (Sharon O'Connor's Menus & Music Ser.). 1996. bk. 24.95 (978-1-883914-12-7(4)) Menus & Music.

Rock & Royalty: Reality Fiction. Nicole Richie. 2005. audio compact disk 29.95 (978-0-06-082616-1(9)) HarperCollins Pubs.

***Rock & the River.** unabr. ed. Kekla Magoon. Read by Dion Graham. 1 MP3-CD. (Running Time: 7 hrs.). 2010. 24.99 (978-1-4418-5866-5(0), 9781441858665, Brilliance MP3); 39.97 (978-1-4418-5867-2(9), 9781441858672, Brlnc Audio MP3 Lib); 24.99 (978-1-4418-5868-9(7), 9781441858689, BAD); 39.97 (978-1-4418-5869-6(5), 9781441858696, BADLE); audio compact disk 29.99 (978-1-4418-5864-1(4), 9781441858641, Bril Audio CD Unabri); audio compact disk 69.97 (978-1-4418-5865-8(2), 9781441858658, BriAudCD Unabrid) Brilliance Audio.

Rock Around the Mouse. 1 cass. (Running Time: 1 hr.). (Retro Mickey Ser.). (J). 7.99 Norelco. (978-1-55723-941-9(X)); audio compact disk 13.99 (978-1-55723-942-6(8)) W Disney Records.

Rock Band: Flute Play-along Pack. Created by Hal Leonard Corporation Staff. 2008. pap. bk. 12.99 (978-1-4234-7254-4(3), 1423472543) H Leonard.

Rock Bass: Rock, Blues, Reggae, Funk, Jazz, Etc. Jacky Reznicek. 2002. pap. bk. 26.95 (978-3-932587-98-6(7)) AMA Verlag DEU.

***Rock-Bound Honesty.** Ernest Haycox. 2009. (978-1-60136-459-3(8)) Audio Holding.

Rock-Bound Honesty. Ernest Haycox. (Running Time: 0 hr. 30 mins.). 2000. 10.95 (978-1-60083-539-1(2)) Iofy Corp.

Rock Chops for Guitar. Ed. by Alfred Publishing. (ENG.). 2001. audio compact disk 10.95 (978-1-929395-39-2(6)) Pub: Workshop Arts. Dist(s): Alfred Pub

Rock-Cito. Kidzup Productions Staff. 1 cass. (Running Time: 90 mins.). (Kidzup Foreign Language Ser.). (SPA.). (J). 1999. 8.99 (978-1-894281-29-4(2)) Pub: Kidzup CAN. Dist(s): Penton Overseas
Fourteen great original, fun songs for toddlers.

Rock Climbing: Making it to the Top. (High Five Reading - Blue Ser.). (ENG.). (gr. 1-2). 2007. audio compact disk 5.95 (978-1-4296-1412-2(9)) CapstoneDig.

Rock Climbing: Making It to the Top. Cynthia A. Dean. (High Five Reading Ser.). (ENG., (gr. 4-5). 2005. audio compact disk 5.95 (978-0-7368-5755-0(9)) CapstoneDig.

Rock Cycle. Compiled by Benchmark Education Staff. 2006. audio compact disk 10.00 (978-1-4108-6685-1(8)) Benchmark Educ.

Rock Drumming. Steven Sher. 1 cass. (Running Time: 1 hr.). 1997. pap. bk. 19.95 (978-1-875726-51-6(9), 256-108) Kolala Music SGP.

Rock Drums for Beginners. Workshop Arts Staff. (ENG.). 1998. audio compact disk 10.00 (978-0-7390-1830-9(2), 18404) Alfred Pub.

Rock Guitar for Adults: The Grown-Up Approach to Playing Guitar. Tobias Hurwitz. 1 CD. (Running Time: 1 hr.). (ENG.). 1999. audio compact disk 10.95 (978-1-929395-08-8(6)) Pub: Workshop Arts. Dist(s): Alfred Pub

Rock Guitar for Beginners. Joe Bouchard. (ENG.). 1997. audio compact disk 9.95 (978-0-7390-2637-3(2)) Alfred Pub.

Rock Guitar Handbook. Mark Lonergan. 1997. bk. 9.95 (978-0-7866-2705-9(0), 94173BCD) Mel Bay.

Rock Guitar Made Easy. Corey Christiansen. (ENG.). 2005. bk. 14.95 (978-0-7866-4461-2(3), 21043BCD) Mel Bay.

***Rock Guitar Secrets.** Peter Fischer. (ENG., 2000. pap. bk. (978-3-927190-62-7(4)) Alfred Pub.

Rock Guitar Solos, Vol. 2. Brett Duncan. (Progressive Ser.). 2004. pap. bk. 19.95 (978-1-86469-257-0(X), 256-156) Kolala Music SGP.

Rock Guitar Tab: Sheet Music. 2003. audio compact disk 19.95 (978-0-634-05350-4(7)) H Leonard.

Rock in the Lake of America: Romans 2:14-15. Ed Young. 1987. 4.95 (978-0-7417-1605-7(4), 605) Win Walk.

Rock Jam Trax for Bass. Ralph Agresta. 1993. pap. bk. 11.95 (978-0-8256-1355-5(8), AM91048) Beekman Bks.

Rock JamTrax for Guitar. Ralph Agresta. 1 CD. (Running Time: 1 hr.). 1997. audio compact disk 12.95 (978-0-8256-1607-5(7)) Pub: Music Sales. Dist(s): H Leonard

Rock Jockeys. unabr. ed. Gary Paulsen. Narrated by Jeff Woodman. 1 cass. (Running Time: 1 hr.). (Gary Paulsen's World of Adventure Ser.: Bk. 4). (gr. 4 up). 1997. 10.00 (978-0-7887-0953-1(4), 95079E7) Recorded Bks.
Rick, J.D. & Spud are the Rock Jockeys, ready to tackle the sheer mountain face known as Devil's Wall. But on that mountain, they will discover a gruesome secret that has lain hidden for years.

Rock Keyboard for Beginners. Workshop Arts Staff. (ENG.). 1998. audio compact disk 10.00 (978-0-7390-1831-6(0), 18413) Alfred Pub.

Rock Keyboard Method. Peter Gelling. 1 cass. (Running Time: 1 hr.). (Progressive Ser.). 1998. pap. bk. 19.95 (978-1-875690-60-2(3), 256-158) Kolala Music SGP.

Rock Keyboard Styles. Dick Grove & Larry Muhoberac. 1985. pap. bk. 17.95 (978-0-7390-1832-3(9), 2710) Alfred Pub.

Rock Licks Encyclopedia. Tomas Cataldo. (ENG.). 2001. audio compact disk 10.00 (978-0-7390-1111-9(1)) Alfred Pub.

Rock Licks for Bass. Jeff Dedrick. 1996. bk. 9.95 (978-0-7866-2690-8(9), 96545BCD) Mel Bay.

Rock Masterclass with Rick Wakeman. Capital Radio. Read by Rick Wakeman & Tony Hale. (Running Time: 1 hr.). 2005. 16.95 (978-1-59912-933-4(7)) Iofy Corp.

Rock n' Blues Harmonica. rev. ed. Jon Gindick. 2004. audio compact disk 24.95 (978-0-930948-10-8(6), CS10116) Cross Harp.

Rock n' Learn Phonics. 2 cass. (Running Time: 1 hr. 40 min.). (J). (gr. k-6). 2001. pap. bk. 16.95 (RL 900C) Kimbo Educ.
Learn beginning sounds, letter combinations, silent consonants, "rule breakers" & more. Presents concepts in rock & rap songs followed by practice reading words. Book included.

Rock 'n Learn Phonics. 2 cass. and 2 CDs. (Running Time: 50 min.). (J). (gr. 1-4). 2001. pap. bk. & tchr. ed. 19.99 (978-1-878489-01-2(1)) Rock N Learn.
Rules are presented in song or rhyme, followed by practice reading words. Teaches short vowels, long vowels, silent e, blends, digraphs, diphthongs, words with syllables etc.

Rock n' Learn Phonics. Illus. by Anthony Guerra & Bart Harlan. 3 CDs. (Running Time: 3 hrs.). (J). (gr. 1 up). 1997. bk., pap. bk., wbk. ed. 34.95 (978-1-878489-61-6(5), RL961) Rock N Learn.

Rock 'n Roll. 2001. bk. 13.95 (978-1-85909-974-2(2), Warner Bro) Alfred Pub.

Rock 'n' Roll Era. 1 CD. (Running Time: 1 hr.). 1999. audio compact disk 9.99 Time-Life.

Rock n' Roll Fitness Fun. Georgiana Stewart. 1 cass. (Running Time: 1 hr.). (J). 2001. pap. bk. 10.95 (KIM9115C); pap. bk. 11.95 (KIM9115); pap. bk. 14.95 (KIM9115CD) Kimbo Educ.
Will get kids of all ages exercising to the "oldies but goodies" of the 50's & 60's. Rock Around the Clock, Let the Good Times Roll, At the Hop & more. Includes instructional guide.

Rock 'n Roll Songs That Teach. 1 cass. (Running Time: 1 hr.). (J). 2001. 10.95 (KUB 6000C); audio compact disk 14.95 (KUB 6000CD) Kimbo Educ.
Kids learn new skills! You'll find dances, songs, circle games, activities all set to a rock & roll beat, Read a Book, Opposites, Rhyming Song, Green Eggs & Ham, Button Factory & more.

Rock 'n Roll Teddy Bear. Gary Rosen & Bill Shontz. Perf. by Gary Rosen & Bill Shontz. 1 cass. (Running Time: 38 min.). (Rosenshontz Ser.). (J). (ps-6). 1992. 8.98 (978-1-879496-50-7(X)); 8.98 Incl. Long Box. (978-1-879496-51-4(8)); audio compact disk 13.98 (978-1-56896-041-8(7)) Lightyear Entrtnmnt.
A two-man group singing delightful children's songs.

Rock n' Together. Perf. by Craig Taubman. Music by Craig Taubman. Prod. by Michael Turner. 1 cass. (Running Time: 38 min.). 1998. 9.98; 14.98 Craig n Co.
This 1998 NAPPA Gold award recordings is a favorite of both parents & children. It includes from the rock anthem, "One" to the doo-wop harmonies in "Seven Wonders" to the jamming beat of the classic "Haircut".

Rock Odyssey, Pt. 1. unabr. collector's ed. Ian Whitcomb. Read by Ian Whitcomb. 7 cass. (Running Time: 10 hrs. 30 min.). 1986. 56.00 (978-0-7366-0990-6(3), 1928-A) Books on Tape.
In 1965 Ian Whitcomb's novelty rocker "You Turn Me On" was number eight on the national charts. In 1966 he was nowheresville! A certified rock 'n roll flash in the pan. Whitcomb tells his story with a survivor's humor.

Rock Odyssey, Pt. 2. collector's ed. Ian Whitcomb. Read by Ian Whitcomb. 6 cass. (Running Time: 9 hrs.). 1986. 48.00 (978-0-7366-0991-3(1), 1928-B) Books on Tape.
In 1965 Ian Whitcomb's novelty rocker "You Turn Me On" was number eight on the national charts. In 1966 he was nowheresville! A certified rock 'n roll flash in the pan. Whitcomb tells his story with a survivor's humor.

Rock of Ages. Contrib. by Bill & Gloria Gaither and Their Homecoming Friends et al. Prod. by Bill Gaither. 2008. 19.99 (978-5-557-47756-7(X)) Gaither Music Co.

Rock of Ages: Exclusive Interviews. 16 cass. (Running Time: 16 hrs.). 1997. 19.99 Set. (978-0-9668267-0-8(1), A1148) Delta Music Inc.

Rock of Kiever. unabr. ed. Max Brand. Read by William Dufris. 6 cass. (Running Time: 9 hrs.). (Sagebrush Western Ser.). (J). 2005. 54.95 (978-1-57490-315-7(2)) Pub: ISIS Lrg Prnt GBR. Dist(s): Ulverscroft US

Rock On! The Rock 'n' Roll Greats. Colin King. 2004. audio compact disk 14.99 (978-1-84067-473-6(3)) Pub: Caxton Editions GBR. Dist(s): Bk Sales Inc

Rock Orchard. unabr. ed. Paula Wall. (Running Time: 6 hrs.). 2005. audio compact disk 29.95 (978-1-59600-080-3(5), 9781596000803, Bril Audio CD Unabri) Brilliance Audio.
Please enter a Synopsis.

Rock Orchard. unabr. ed. Paula Wall. Read by Susan Ericksen. (Running Time: 6 hrs.). 2005. 39.25 (978-1-59710-655-9(0), 9781597106559, BADLE); 24.95 (978-1-59710-654-2(2), 9781597106542, BAD); 24.95 (978-1-59335-796-2(6), 9781593357962, Brilliance MP3); 39.25 (978-1-59335-930-0(6), 9781593359300, Brlnc Audio MP3 Lib) Brilliance Audio.
"Some women barter their bodies like whores with wedding bands. Some use sex like a sword. But some women can touch a man and heal like Jesus. The man who sees sunrise from a Belle woman's bed will swear he's been born again." So begins Paula Wall's funny, poignant, and sexy novel, The Rock Orchard. Musette Belle could lay her hand on a baby's heart and see his life as if he'd already lived it. Even in death, she continues to shock the good citizens of Leaper's Fork, Tennessee, and her descendents are doing their best to carry on her legacy. Angela Belle, a haunting and beautiful siren, lures every man she meets into greatness, while her illegitimate and very independent daughter, Dixie, serves tea and vanilla wafers to the statue of the Confederate soldier she believes is her father. But when Charlotte Belle, a woman who would rather spend the night with Jack Daniels than any man she knows, seduces a stranger in the cemetery, it not only transforms the two people involved, but the entire town.

Rock Orchard. unabr. ed. Paula Wall. Read by Susan Eriksen. (Running Time: 6 hrs.). 2005. 29.95 (978-1-59600-078-0(3), 9781596000780, BAU) Brilliance Audio.
Please enter a Synopsis.

Rock Orchard. unabr. ed. Paula Wall. Read by Susan Ericksen. (Running Time: 6 hrs.). 2005. 69.25 (978-1-59600-079-7(1), 9781596000797, BrilAudUnabridg); audio compact disk 82.25 (978-1-59600-081-0(3), 9781596000810, BriAudCD Unabrid) Brilliance Audio.

Rock Piano for Beginning to Advanced Students. Andrew Scott. 1 CD. (Running Time: 1 hr.). (Progressive Ser.). 1997. pap. bk. 24.95 (978-1-875726-28-8(4), 256-160) Kolala Music SGP.

Rock Poetry - Four Piece Band. Perf. by Mystery Hound. Music by Fred Dawson. 1 cass. (Running Time: 1 hr.). 9.00 (A0318-88) Sound Photosyn.

Rock Rats. unabr. ed. Ben Bova et al. Read by Ira Claffey. 9 CDs. (Running Time: 10 hrs. 0 mins. 0 sec.). (Grand Tour; also Asteroid Wars Ser.). (ENG.). 2005. audio compact disk 39.95 (978-1-59397-492-3(2)) Pub: Macmill Audio. Dist(s): Macmillan

Rock Saxophone Method. Peter Gelling. (Progressive Ser.). 2004. pap. bk. 19.95 (978-1-86469-130-6(1), 256-161) Kolala Music SGP.

Rock, Slap & Funk Bass. Dan Gutt. 1995. bk. 14.95 (978-0-87166-857-8(2), 94346BCD) Mel Bay.

Rock-Solid Choice: Acts 1:15-26. Ed Young. 1997. 4.95 (978-0-7417-2149-5(X), 1149) Win Walk.

Rock Solid Drum Patterns. Dave Zubraski. (Fast Forward Ser.). 1997. bk. 15.95 (978-0-7119-4799-3(6)) Pub: Music Sales. Dist(s): H Leonard

Rock Solid Early/ Middle Elementary Annual CD 2008-2009. 2008. audio compact disk 19.99 (978-0-687-64866-5(1), Cokebury) Abingdon.

Rock Solid Preschool Annual CD 2008-2009. 2008. audio compact disk 19.99 (978-0-687-64802-3(5), Cokebury) Abingdon.

Rock Springs. Short Stories. 1 cass. (Running Time: 1 hr.). 1985. (6031) Am Audio Prose.

Rock Steady Bass Styles. Phil Mulford. (Fast Forward Ser.). 1997. audio compact disk 15.95 (978-0-7119-4501-2(2)) Pub: Music Sales. Dist(s): H Leonard

Rock Studies for Bass: The Bottom Line. Jeff Dedrick. 1996. bk. 9.95 (978-0-7866-2691-5(7), 94534BCD) Mel Bay.

Rock That Could Steal Our Fold. David Benoit. 1 cass. (Running Time: 1 hr.). (YA). (gr. 7 up). 6.00 (978-0-923105-07-5(7)) Glory Ministries.
A factually documented seminar dealing with the deception of contemporary Christian music.

Rock the Baby. Perf. by Mr. AL. 1 cass. (Running Time: 1 hr.). (J). (ps). 10.95 (MHC-97); audio compact disk 13.95 (MHD-97) Child Like.
Designed to ease infants & toddlers through the transitions of their day. Includes rock, ballads, jazz & even an adult/child tango. Includes: "Point to Someone You Love," "Bouncin' on My Knee," "Diaper Changing Time," "Lap Time," "I Like My Bath," "Peek-A-Boo," "Dream Baby," & "I'm So Glad to See You.".

Rock-Tout-Petit. Kidzup Productions Staff. 1 cass. (Running Time: 90 mins.). (Kidzup Foreign Language Ser.). (FRE.). (J). 1999. 8.99 (978-1-894281-37-9(3)); audio compact disk 12.99 (978-1-894281-38-6(1)) Pub: Kidzup CAN. Dist(s): Penton Overseas
Fourteen great original, fun songs for toddlers. Easy to sing melodies.

Rock Types. Compiled by Benchmark Education Staff. 2006. audio compact disk 10.00 (978-1-4108-6686-8(6)) Benchmark Educ.

Rockabilly. Tim Frew. (CD Ser.). 2001. bk. 16.98 (978-1-56799-307-3(9), Friedman-Fairfax) M Friedman Pub Grp Inc.

Rockbound. abr. ed. Frank Parker Day. Narrated by Richard Donat. 3 CDs. (Running Time: 3 1/2 hrs.). (ENG.). 2005. audio compact disk 24.95 (978-0-86492-396-7(1)) Pub: BTC Audiobks CAN. Dist(s): U Toronto Pr
When 18-year-old David Jung arrives on the windswept island of Rockbound to claim his modest inheritance, he has nothing but the rags on his back and a fisherman¿s determination to survive. Battling the unpredictable sea and steering his way between Rockbound¿s two warring clans, the friendless orphan gradually builds a life for himself. He marries and has a son, finds a soulmate in lighthouse keeper Gershom Born, and falls deeply (and secretly) in love with Mary, the island schoolteacher. But he does not reckon on the wicked cunning of his great-uncle Uriah, self-proclaimed king of Rockbound and David¿s one true enemy.

Rockefeller Family Portrait: From John D. to Nelson. unabr. collector's ed. William Manchester. Read by Christopher Hurt. 5 cass. (Running Time: 5 hrs.). 1984. 30.00 (978-0-7366-0714-8(5), 1677) Books on Tape.
This American portrait focuses on 3 generations, John D., his son Junior & his grandson Nelson. Manchester traces John D.'s influences on his family: his philanthropy, his Fundamentalist religion, his hard-headed business sense & his dislike of publicity. He also examines the family's change of image from robber-barons to social humanitarians.

Rockefellers, Pt. 1. unabr. ed. Peter Collier & David Horowitz. Read by Michael Anthony. 11 cass. (Running Time: 32 hrs.). 1994. 76.95 (978-0-7861-0361-4(2), 1318A, B) Blckstn Audio.
Against a richly detailed backdrop of history, the story of this unique American family unfolds. It begins with Senior, who amassed a fortune amid the muck & disorder of the Pennsylvania oil fields & left his son, Mr. Junior, to deal with the public outcry. It follows Junior as he built the charities & foundations that made the name a public institution. It also tracks the lives of Junior's sons the five Rockefeller Brothers. Here then is Laurance, clever & charming as a youth, burnt out & cynical by middle age; Winthrop, shy, awkward, the black sheep who finally made a mark for himself in the eyes of everyone but his family; JDR3, introverted & anxious even after years of proving himself; David, a man on the move who took the nation's front-ranking bank & made it number three; & Nelson, ambitious, aggressive, the brother who broke the unwritten family code.

Rockefellers, Pt. 2. unabr. ed. Peter Collier & David Horowitz. Read by Michael Anthony. 11 cass. (Running Time: 32 hrs.). 1994. 76.95 (978-0-7861-0680-6(8), 1318A, B) Blckstn Audio.
Against a richly detailed backdrop of history, the story of this unique American family unfolds. The senior Rockefeller amassed a fortune amid the muck & disorder of the Pennsylvania oil fields; his son was left to deal with the public orations that made the family name a public institution. Also follows Junior's five sons, very different men with different fates: Winthrop, the shy black sheep who made a mark for himself in the eyes of everyone but his family; David, a man who took the nation's front-ranking bank & made it number three; & ambitious, aggressive Nelson, who broke the unwritten family code.

Rockefellers: An American Dynasty. unabr. ed. Peter Collier & David Horowitz. Read by Grover Gardner. 18 cass. (Running Time: 27 hrs.). 144.00 (978-0-7366-1511-2(3), 2383-A/B) Books on Tape.
This is the story of the most powerful family in America. It starts with John D., the remarkable man who created Standard Oil, & concludes with the most recent generation, large in number, various in quality.

Rockefellers: An American Dynasty. unabr. ed. Peter Collier & David Horowitz. Read by Grover Gardner. 9 cass. (Running Time: 13 hrs. 30 mins.). 1989. 72.00 (2383-A); 72.00 (2383-B) Books on Tape.
John D. created Standard Oil, also created one of the most powerful families in America.

Rockefellers: An American Dynasty (Part One) Peter Collier and David Horowitz. Narrated by Michael Anthony. (Running Time: 16 hrs.). (C). 1993. 72.95 (978-1-59912-711-8(3)) Iofy Corp.

Rockefellers: An American Dynasty (Part Two) Peter Collier and David Horowitz. Narrated by Michael Anthony. (Running Time: 16 hrs. NaN mins.). 1993. 63.95 (978-1-59912-712-5(1)) Iofy Corp.

Rocket Baby - Shake, Rattle & Rhyme. Pref. by Rocket Baby Records Staff. Prod. by Ronnie Silos. Composed by Ronnie Silos. Lyrics by Alma Albancio-Silos. Music by Alma Albancio-Silos. Prod. by Thom Steinhoff. (J). 2002. audio compact disk 14.95 (978-0-9722524-0-9(1)) Rocket Baby Inc.

Rocket Baby - Shake, Rattle & Rhyme, Vol. II. Prod. by Ronnie Silos et al. 1. (J). 2004. audio compact disk 14.95 (978-0-9722524-1-6(X)) Rocket Baby Inc.

Rocket Boys: A Memoir. Homer Hickam. 2004. 15.95 (978-0-7435-4848-9(5)) Pub: S&S Audio. Dist(s): S and S Inc

Rocket Boys: A Memoir. Homer H. Hickam, Jr. 2000. 15.99 (978-0-7435-0567-3(0), Audioworks) S&S Audio.

Rocket Boys: A Memoir. abr. ed. Homer H. Hickam & Homer Hickam. Read by Beau Bridges. (Running Time: 4 hrs. 30 mins. 0 sec.). (ENG.). 2006. audio compact disk 14.95 (978-0-7435-6506-6(1), S&S Encore) Pub: S&S Audio. Dist(s): S and S Inc

Rocket City. unabr. ed. Cathryn Alpert. Read by Cathryn Alpert. 2 cass. (Running Time: 2 hrs.). (Authors Reading Ser.). 1995. 13.95 set. (978-1-55644-408-1(7), 15011) Am Audio Prose.
Author reads unabridged excerpts from novel.

Rocket Men. John DeChancie. 1 cass. (Running Time: 1 hr.). 2001. 22.95 (HHIR005) Lodestone Catalog.

Rocket Men: The Epic Story of the First Men on the Moon. unabr. ed. Craig Nelson. Contrib. by Richard McGonagle. 14 CDs. (Running Time: 17 hrs.). (ENG.). (gr. 12 up). 2009. audio compact disk 39.95 (978-0-14-314479-3(0), PengAudBks) Penguin Grp USA.

Rocket Ship Galileo. unabr. ed. Robert A. Heinlein. Read by Spider Robinson. (Running Time: 19800 sec.). 2007. 19.95 (978-0-7861-4789-2(X)); 34.95 (978-0-7861-4783-0(0)); audio compact disk 19.95 (978-0-7861-6282-6(1)); audio compact disk 29.95 (978-0-7861-7209-2(6)); audio compact disk 45.00 (978-0-7861-6276-5(7)) Blckstn Audio.

Rocketeer Read-Along. 1 cass. (Running Time: 15 min.). (J). bk. 5.98 Disney Prod.

Rocketeer 3-D Comic Book with 3-D Sound. 1 cass. (Running Time: 1 hr.). (J). pap. bk. 7.98 Disney Prod.

Rocketman. 1 cass. (Running Time: 1 hr.). (J). 1997. W Disney Records.
Soundtrack to the feature film comedy about a man's dream of space travel.

Rockets. unabr. ed. Peter M. Spizzirri. Read by Charles Fuller. Ed. by Linda Spizzirri. 1 cass. (Running Time: 15 min.). Dramatization. (Educational Coloring Book & Cassette Ser.). (J). (gr. 1-8). pap. bk. 6.95 (978-0-86545-114-8(1)) Spizzirri.
Describe how rockets were invented and how they were used in the past or used today.

Rockin' & Rollin' with Mrs B. Carri Blake-Brekke. 2004. audio compact disk 15.95 (978-0-9720549-4-2(4)) Moms Pride.

Rockin' down the Road. 1998. 14.99 (978-1-60689-168-1(5)) Pub: Youngheart Mus. Dist(s): Creat Teach Pr

Rockin' down the Road. Greg Scelsa. 1 cass. (Running Time: 1 hr.). (J). 2001. pap. bk. 10.95 (YM 015C); pap. bk. 14.95 (YM 015CD) Kimbo Educ.
Rockin' the USA, Yellow Submarine, I Can't Sit Still, Dancin' Machine, Three Billy Goats Gruff & more. Includes guide.

Rockin' down the Road. Music by Greg Scelsa & Steve Millang. 1 cass. (Running Time: 1 hr.). (J). 1996. 10.98 (978-0-945267-14-0(2), YM015-CN); lp 12.98 (978-0-945267-16-4(9), YM015-R); audio compact disk 13.98 (978-0-945267-12-6(6), YM015-CD) Youngheart Mus.
Songs include: "Rockin' the U.S.A."; "Sunshine Medley"; "Yellow Submarine"; Three Billy Goats Gruff"; "Riding in My Car"; "Snowflake"; "Can't Sit Still"; "This Land Is Your Land"; "Dancin' Machine"; "Long Tall Texan"; "Green Grass Grew All Around" & "Home on the Range.".

Rock'in in Time: A Social History of Rock-and-Roll. 6th ed. David P. Szatmary. 2006. pap. bk. 56.67 (978-0-13-175588-8(9)) Pearson Educ CAN CAN.

Rockin' on a Christmas Eve - ShowTrax. Music by Roger Emerson & John Jacobson. 1 CD. (Running Time: 50 mins.). 2000. audio compact disk 19.95 (08742334) H Leonard.
There will be rockin' on the rooftops with this '50s style holiday original. Super choreography showcase!.

Rockin' Readers. John Archambault & David Plummer. Read by Carla Hamaguchi. 1 CD. (Running Time: 1 hr.). (J). (gr. k-3). 2001. audio compact disk 13.99 (CTP 2787) Creat Teach Pr.
Contains narrated & musical versions of the 12 Rockin Reader books. Titles include: I'm a Can-Do Kid; Grandmother's Garden; Magical Miracle Me; Counting Kittens; Electric Car; Rhythm, Rhythm; Rickety Rock around the Clock; Anthills & Apartments; I Paint Blue; Baseball Cards & Piggy Banks; The Fox & the Chicken & I Love the Mountains.

Rockin' Readers, Vol. 2787. Ed. by Carla Hammaguchi. Prod. by John Archambault & David Plummer. Illus. by Kathi Ember. (Rockin' Readers Ser.). (J). 2001. audio compact disk 13.98 (978-1-57471-780-8(4)) Creat Teach Pr.
A recording containing narrated and musical versions of the 12 Rockin' Reader books. Titles include: I'm a Can-Do Kid; Grandmother's Garden; Magical, Miracle Me; Counting Kittens; Electric Car; Rhythm, Rhythm; Rickety Rock around the Clock; Anthills and Apartments; I Paint Blue; Baseball Cards and Piggy Banks; The Fox and the Chicken; and I Love the Mountains.

Rockin' Readers, Vol. 2788. John Archambault & David Plummer. Read by Carla Hamaguchi. Illus. by Kathi Ember. 1 cass. (Running Time: 1 hr.). (Rockin' Readers Ser.). (J). (gr. k-3). 2001. 10.99 (978-1-57471-779-2(0), CTP 2788) Creat Teach Pr.
Contains narrated & musical versions of the 12 Rockin Reader books. Titles include: I'm a Can-Do Kid; Grandmother's Garden; Magical Miracle Me; Counting Kittens; Electric Car; Rhythm, Rhythm; Rickety Rock around the Clock; Anthills & Apartments; I Paint Blue; Baseball Cards & Piggy Banks; The Fox & the Chicken & I Love the Mountains.

Rockin' Red: Sing along with Your Favorite Christian Hits. Contrib. by Jen King. Prod. by Brian Green. (Kids Sing-along Songs Ser.). (J). (gr. 4-7). 2004. audio compact disk 9.99 (978-5-559-68513-7(5), Brentwood Records) Brentwood Music.

Rockin' Rhythms & Rhymes: Musical Chants, Rhythms & Rhymes for the E. S. L. Classroom. Lonnie DiZovi. Illus. by Jeremiah Hazelton. 1996. pap. bk. 28.50 (978-0-935301-71-7(2)) Vibrante Pr.

Rockin' the Alphabet. Perf. by Mr. AL. 1 cass. (Running Time: 1 hr.). (YA). (ps up). 10.95 (CRP-DO2); audio compact disk 13.95 Child Like.
All new original tunes geared toward language development (with a little "shakin'" thrown in). Try his "Funky Backwards Alphabet," his fun counting song, or learn long & short vowel sounds. Plenty of just moving too, with "Fancy Dancing," "Shake It Up," or "Show Me Your Shoes," & more. .

Rocking Chair. Joshua S. Mauney. 2007. audio compact disk 24.99 (978-1-60247-442-0(7)) Tate Pubng.

Rocking Chair Classics: Heart-warming Stories from One of America's Foremost Storytellers. As told by Andy Andrews. 2005. audio compact disk 19.99 (978-0-9776246-3-8(3)) Lightning Crown Pub.

Rocking Chair Love. unabr. ed. Kathleen Gibson. Read by Kathleen Gibson. Illus. by Jo Dose. 1 cass. (Running Time: 20 min.). (Rainbow Readers Ser.). (J). (ps-3). 1996. pap. bk. 12.50 (978-1-888862-02-7(5), RR6202) Rainbow Rdrs.
An endearing tale of the precious legacy of shared moments of tenderness. Early reader includes musical read along cassette & traditional lullabies, activities encouraging family togetherness, communication, feelings & creativity.

Rocking in a Free World. Mark Allen Gray. 1. 2007. audio compact disk 9.95 (978-0-9761095-5-6(7)) Gray Technolgies.

Rock/Jazz Solos for Bass. Earl Gately. 1982. bk. 9.95 (978-0-7866-2689-2(5), MB96544BCD) Mel Bay.

Rockoon. Perf. by Tangerine Dream. 1 cass. (Running Time: 1 hr.). 9.98 (MPC2802); audio compact disk 14.98 CD. Miramar Images.
This album marks the launch of TD's multi-album contract with Miramar. Noted for a prolific string of layered synthesizer recordings, Rockoon exemplifies the band's foray into a decidedly rock-tinged groove.

Rocks & Minerals. Dorling Kindersley Publishing Staff. Contrib. by Martin Sheen. (DK Eyewitness Bks.). (ENG.). (J). 2006. 12.99 (978-0-7566-2368-5(5)) DK Pub Inc.

Rocks & Minerals. Steck-Vaughn Staff. (J). 2002. 9.00 (978-0-7398-6207-0(3)) SteckVau.

Rocks & Minerals Audio CD Theme Set: Set of 6 Set B. Adapted by Benchmark Education Staff. (English Explorers Ser.). (J). (gr. 3-6). 2007. audio compact disk 60.00 (978-1-4108-9816-6(4)) Benchmark Educ.

Rocks & Soil. Sundance/Newbridge, LLC Staff. (Early Science Ser.). (gr. k-3). 2007. audio compact disk 12.00 (978-1-4007-6444-0(0)); audio compact disk 12.00 (978-1-4007-6445-7(9)); audio compact disk 12.00 (978-1-4007-6443-3(2)) Sund Newbrdge.

Rocks & Stones: The Discoveries of Geology. Kingsley Dunham. 1 cass. (Running Time: 1 hr.). 1990. 12.95 (ECN180) J Norton Pubs.

Rock's Hidden Persuaders. unabr. ed. Dan Peters & Steve Peters. Read by Dan Peters & Steve Peters. 1 cass. (Running Time: 1 hr. 11 min.). 1985. 7.99 (280055) Bethany Hse.
The authors of the bestseller "Why Knock Rock?" explain backmasking, presenting new evidence concerning subliminal messages & their effect on listeners.

Rocksburg Railroad Murders. unabr. ed. K. C. Constantine. Read by Lloyd James. 5 cass. (Running Time: 7 hrs. 30 min.). (Mario Balzic Ser.: Vol. 1). 1997. 40.00 (978-0-7366-3622-3(6), 4281) Books on Tape.
When someone bludgeons a prominent citizen & leaves his body at the Rocksburg railroad station, Mario Balzic suspects the man's stepson.

Rocks/Las Rocas: Hard, Soft, Smooth, & Rough/Duras, Blandas, Lisas y Asperas. abr. ed. Natalie M. Rosinsky. Tr. by Sol Robledo. Illus. by Matthew John. (Amazing Science Ser.). (SPA.). (gr. k). 2008. audio compact disk 14.60 (978-1-4048-4475-9(9)) CapstoneDig.

Rocky Fortune, collector's ed. Perf. by Frank Sinatra. 6 cass. (Running Time: 9 hrs.). 1998. bk. 34.98 (4052) Radio Spirits.
18 episodes about a footloose and fancy-free drifter who jumps from one adventurous job to another, finding danger at every turn.

Rocky Fortune: Social Director & Let's Find a Murderer. Perf. by Frank Sinatra. 1 cass. (Running Time: 1 hr.). 2001. 6.98 (2088) Radio Spirits.

Rocky Fortune: The Little Voice of Murder & Rocket to the Morgue. Perf. by Frank Sinatra. 1 cass. (Running Time: 1 hr.). 2001. 6.98 (2405) Radio Spirits.

Rocky Jordan. Contrib. by Jack Moyles. (Running Time: 10800 sec.). 2004. 9.98 (978-1-57019-582-2(X)); audio compact disk 9.98 (978-1-57019-583-9(8)) Radio Spirits.

Rocky Jordan: Black Ball & The Strange Death of Van Dorn. 1 cass. (Running Time: 1 hr.). 2001. 6.98 (2545) Radio Spirits.

Rocky Jordan: The Big Heist & Trail of the Assassin. 1 cass. (Running Time: 1 hr.). 2001. 6.98 (2626) Radio Spirits.

Rocky Jordan: The Case of the Sleepy Camel & Bockseich Boy. 2001. 6.98 (1558) Radio Spirits.

Rocky Jordan: The Genakos Affair & Man in the Nile. 1 cass. (Running Time: 1 hr.). 2001. 6.98 (2564) Radio Spirits.

Rocky Jordan Secrets of the Tambourine. Perf. by Jay Novello et al. 2008. audio compact disk 31.95 (978-1-57019-876-2(4)) Radio Spirits.

***Rocky Jordan, Volume 1.** RadioArchives.com. (Running Time: 600). (ENG.). 2003. audio compact disk 29.98 (978-1-61081-013-5(9)) Radio Arch.

***Rocky Jordan, Volume 2.** RadioArchives.com. (Running Time: 600). (ENG.). 2006. audio compact disk 29.98 (978-1-61081-046-3(5)) Radio Arch.

Rocky Mountain High: A Tribute to John Denver. Perf. by John Denver. 1 cass. (Running Time: 1 hr.). 7.98 (CMH 8026); audio compact disk 11.18 (CMH 8026) NewSound.

Rocky Mountain Moving Picture Association. Loren D. Estleman. Narrated by George Guidall. 6 CDs. (Running Time: 7 hrs.). 2001. audio compact disk 58.00 (978-0-7887-5199-8(9), C1356E7) Recorded Bks.
In 1913, Dimitri Pulski sets out to investigate a strange company. Arriving in the booming Hollywood area, it isn't long before Dmitri is writing his own movie scenarios for The Rocky Mountain Moving Picture Association, while the company fights off Thomas Edison.

Rocky Mountain Moving Picture Association, unabr. ed. Loren D. Estleman. Narrated by George Guidall. 5 cass. (Running Time: 7 hrs.). 2000. 45.00 (978-0-7887-3776-3(7), 95993E7) Recorded Bks.
In 1913, Dmitri Pulski sets out to investigate a strange company. Arriving in the booming Hollywood area, it isn't long before Dmitri is writing his own movie scenarios for The Rocky Mountain Moving Picture Association, while the company fights off Thomas Edison.

Rocky Mountain National Park: Estes Park to Grand Lake. 1 cass. (Running Time: 90 min.). (Guided Auto Tape Tour). 12.95 (P3); Comp Comms Inc.

***Rocky Road to Romance.** unabr. ed. Janet Evanovich. Read by C. J. Critt. (ENG.). 2004. (978-0-06-078641-0(8), Harper Audio); (978-0-06-081476-2(4), Harper Audio) HarperCollins Pubs.

Rocky Road to Romance. unabr. ed. Janet Evanovich. Read by C. J. Critt. 6 CDs. (Running Time: 9 hrs.). 2004. audio compact disk 14.95 (978-0-06-073825-9(1)) HarperCollins Pubs.

Rococo. unabr. ed. Adriana Trigiani. 2005. 63.00 (978-1-4159-2011-4(7)); audio compact disk 81.00 (978-1-4159-2135-7(0)) Books on Tape.

Rod Carew: Hitting. Read by Rod Carew. 1 cass. (Running Time: 1 hr.). 9.95 (978-0-89811-063-0(7), 7114) Lets Talk Assocs.
Rod Carew talks about the people & events which influenced his career, & his own approach to his speciality.

Rod Kessler. unabr. ed. Rod Kessler. Read by Rod Kessler. 1 cass. (Running Time: 29 min.). 1986. 10.00 New Letters.
Three short stories from the collection, "Off in Zimbabwe".

Rod Morgenstein: Double-Bass Drumming. Rod Morgenstein. 2 cass. (Running Time: 2 hrs.). pap. bk. 24.95 (BD037) DCI Music Video.
Learn numerous drum techniques, concepts, beats & fills through a combination of two audio cassettes & a book. Contains double-bass drum shuffle, double-bass beats & fills, 6-note groupings, "awkward" fills, cymbal "smashing" & bass drum aerobics.

Rod Morgenstein: Grooving in Styles - Filling in the Holes. Rod Morgenstein. 2 cass. (Running Time: 2 hrs.). pap. bk. 24.95 (BD036) DCI Music Video.
Learn numerous drum techniques, concepts, beats & fills through a combination of two cassettes & a book. Contains a highly diversified selection of beats stressing feel & groove & in-depth look at ghost strokes, linear beats, hi-hat tricks & more.

Rod Morgenstein: Odd Time. Rod Morgenstein. 2 cass. (Running Time: 2 hrs.). pap. bk. 24.95 (BD035) DCI Music Video.
Learn numerous drum techniques, concepts, beats & fills through a combination of two audio cassettes & a book. Contains a wide range of "Odd Time" topics including beats in different time signatures, soloing ideas, odd note groupings, jamming & much more.

Rod of God. Derek Prince. 1 cass. (Running Time: 60 min.). 5.95 (I-4261) Derek Prince.

Rodeo Ranch. Max Brand. (Running Time: 1 hr. 48 mins.). 1999. 10.95 (978-1-60083-489-9(2)) Iofy Corp.

***Rodeo Ranch.** Max Brand. 2009. (978-1-60136-401-2(6)) Audio Holding.

Rodeo Revival: John 3:1-8. Ed Young. 1985. 4.95 (978-0-7417-1472-5(8), 472) Win Walk.

Rodeo Revival: Luke 12. Ed Young. 1985. 4.95 (978-0-7417-1473-2(6), 473) Win Walk.

Rodeo Revival - Friday: Joh 3:16. Ed Young. 1984. 4.95 (978-0-7417-1412-1(4), 412) Win Walk.

Rodeo Revival - Saturday: Luke 12:16-21. Ed Young. 1984. 4.95 (978-0-7417-1413-8(2), 413) Win Walk.

Rodeo Revival - Sunday: Acts 24: 24-25. Ed Young. 1984. 4.95 (978-0-7417-1415-2(9), 415) Win Walk.

Roderick Hudson. unabr. ed. Henry James. Read by Flo Gibson. 9 cass. (Running Time: 12 hrs. 30 min.). 1998. 28.95 (978-1-55685-506-1(0)) Audio Bk Con.
A talented young American sculptor goes to study in Rome under the protection of a wealthy benefactor. A disastrous love affair & disillusionment about his art causes his utter demoralization.

Rodin, Pt. 1. unabr. ed. Frederic V. Grunfeld. Read by Simon Vance. 10 cass. (Running Time: 29 hrs.). 1996. 69.95 (978-0-7861-1016-2(3), 1794A, B) Blckstn Audio.
Auguste Rodin was not only the greatest sculptor but also one of the most remarkable personalities of modern times. Documents a lifetime of both artistic & personal struggle - against poverty, against the conservative Salon & against an art establishment that for years denied him recognition. Rodin's crucial love affair with his pupil, Camille Claudel, emerges here in all its tragic complexity, as do his relationships with the British painter Gwen John & the American-born duchess Claire de Choiseul. Grunfeld also sheds new

light on Rodin's friendships with some of the most gifted writers & artists of the day.

Rodin, Pt. 2. unabr. ed. Frederic V. Grunfeld. Read by Simon Vance. 9 cass. (Running Time: 29 hrs.). 1996. 62.95 (978-0-7861-1022-3(8), 1794A, B) Blckstn Audio.

Rodney Marsh: Striker. Read by Rodney Marsh. 1 cass. (Running Time: 1 hr.). 9.95 (978-0-89811-096-8(3), 7147) Lets Talk Assocs.
Rodney Marsh talks about the people & events which influenced his career, & his approach to his speciality.

Rodney Stone. Arthur Conan Doyle. Read by Peter Joyce. 6 cass. 2000. 54.95 (978-1-86015-464-5(6)) Ulverscroft US.

Rodomonte's Revenge. unabr. ed. Gary Paulsen. Narrated by Jeff Woodman. 1 cass. (Running Time: 1 hr.). (Gary Paulsen's World of Adventure Ser.: BK. 2). (gr. 4 up). 2001. 10.00 (978-0-7887-1122-0(9), 95116E7) Recorded Bks.
Brett & Tom are crazy about video games. Now they're ready to take on the best one of all - "Rodomonte's Revenge." But when the game begins to take over Brett & Tom's minds, they find that they might become a permanent part of the action.

***Rodrick Rules.** unabr. ed. Jeff Kinney. Narrated by Ramon de Ocampo. 1 Playaway. (Running Time: 2 hrs. 15 mins.). (J). (gr. 4-8). 2009. 51.75 (978-1-4407-0419-2(8)) Recorded Bks.

***Rodrick Rules.** unabr. ed. Jeff Kinney. Narrated by Ramon de Ocampo. 2 cass. (Running Time: 2 hrs. 15 mins.). (Diary of a Wimpy Kid Ser.: Bk. 2). (J). (gr. 4-8). 2009. 25.75 (978-1-4361-3867-3(1)); audio compact disk 25.75 (978-1-4361-3866-6(3)) Recorded Bks.

Rodrick Rules. unabr. ed. Jeff Kinney. Narrated by Ramon de Ocampo. 2 CDs. (Running Time: 2 hrs. 15 mins.). (Diary of a Wimpy Kid Ser.: Bk. 2). (J). (gr. 4-8). 2009. audio compact disk 14.99 (978-1-4361-9632-1(9)) Recorded Bks.

Rodrigo - Concierto de Aranjuez: Guitar Play-along 2-CD Set. Composed by Joaquin Rodrigo. 2007. pap. bk. 39.98 (978-1-4234-3654-6(7), 1423436547) Pub: Music Minus. Dist(s): H Leonard

Rodrigo - Fantasia para un Gentilhombre: Guitar Play-along 2-CD Set. Composed by Joaquin Rodrigo. 2007. pap. bk. 49.98 (978-1-59615-386-8(5), 1596153865) Pub: Music Minus. Dist(s): H Leonard

Rodriguez. unabr. ed. Ed. by James McKinley. Prod. by Rebeah Presson. 1 cass. (Running Time: 29 min.). (On the Air Ser.). 1993. 10.00 New Letters.
Rodriguez, Chicano poet, editor, & former gang member, reads from The Concrete River & talks about trying to save his own son from gang life.

Rodriguez Affair. James Pattinson & James Pattinson. 2008. 44.95 (978-1-84559-719-1(2)); audio compact disk 51.95 (978-1-84559-720-7(6)) Pub: Soundings Ltd GBR. Dist(s): Ulverscroft US

Rodzina see Rodzina

Rodzina. unabr. ed. Karen Cushman. 4 CDs. (Running Time: 4 hrs. 47 mins.).Tr. of Rodzina. (J). (gr. 5 up). 2004. audio compact disk 45.00 (978-0-8072-1616-3(X), S YA 442 CD, Listening Lib) Random Audio Pubg.

Roger Aplon. Read by Roger Aplon. 1 cass. (Running Time: 29 min.). 1985. 10.00 New Letters.
San Francisco poet Roger Alpon reads from "Stiletto" & "From Dawn's Early Light at 120 Miles Per Hour".

Roger Dawson's Power Negotiating for Salespeople. Roger Dawson. 6 cass. (Running Time: 6 hrs.). 59.95 (11750AM) Nightingale-Conant.
This breakthrough program - the ultimate weapon for selling in today's fiercely competitive business climate - shows you how to get anything you want from the buyer...& still have them believing they won. Learn why you should never, ever say yes to the first offer or counteroffer. Discover why it pays to negotiate in dollars instead of percentages. And find out how to counter the "good guy/bad guy" gambit...close the sale against lower-priced competition...even get a buyer to accept your initial offer without countering at a lower price. Guaranteed to increase your income by thousands of dollars every year, this revolutionary program will give you real power over buyers - power you can use to increase your sales without conceding discounts or incentives.

Roger Kahn. Interview with Roger Kahn. 1 cass. (Running Time: 50 min.). 1980. 12.95 (L040) TFR.
The author of "The Boys of Summer" gives his views on a variety of sports, including how baseball is a father & son game.

Roger Kilgore Public Defender: The Case of Don Winthrope & The Case of Eddie Lewis. 1 cass. (Running Time: 1 hr.). 2001. 6.98 (1697) Radio Spirits.

Roger Love's Vocal Power: Speaking with Authority, Clarity & Conviction. unabr. ed. Roger Love. Read by Roger Love. 7 CDs. (Running Time: 7 hrs.). (ENG.). 2005. audio compact disk 29.98 (978-1-59659-011-3(4), GildAudio) Pub: Gildan Media. Dist(s): HachBkGrp

Roger Maris: A Title to Fame. unabr. ed. Harvey Rosenfeld. Read by Ian Esmo. 10 cass. (Running Time: 14 hrs. 30 mins.). 1999. 69.95 (978-0-7861-1595-2(5), 2424) Blckstn Audio.
Rosenfeld argues that treatment by the press was both shabby & tragic: Maris, one of baseball's most misunderstood heroes, still has not received his rightful place in the game's history - membership in the Baseball Hall of Fame. He makes a forceful case for at least according to him his overdue "title to fame." Recounts the slugger's life including his post-baseball years until his death from cancer in 1985.

Roger Rabbit. 1 cass. (Running Time: 1 hr.). (FRE.). (J). (gr. 3 up). 1991. bk. 14.95 (1AD038) Olivia & Hill.

Rogers Hornsby. unabr. ed. Charles C. Alexander. Read by Ian Esmo. 9 cass. (Running Time: 13 hrs.). 1998. 62.95 (978-0-7861-1379-8(0), 2263) Blckstn Audio.
The study of one of baseball's most important & most enigmatic figures. He was a seven-time National League batting champion, & his 1924 average remains the major-league high for this century.

Rogers' Rules for Success. Henry Rogers. 1 cass. (Running Time: 55 min.). 8.95 (978-0-88684-044-0(9)) Listen USA.
Rogers gives what he believes to be the standard rules for success.

Roger's Version. unabr. collector's ed. John Updike. Read by Michael Prichard. 8 cass. (Running Time: 12 hrs.). 1988. 64.00 (978-0-7366-1297-5(1), 2204) Books on Tape.
When God spoke to Moses, the words got carved in stone. When he talked to Dale Kohler, they were tapped into a terminal. Nevertheless, the young technician believes, & he takes his story to Roger Lambert, professor of divine studies at a fashionable Ivy League school. Then the man of religion talks the convert out of his faith.

Rogue. Danielle Steel. Read by Brian Keith Lewis. (Playaway Adult Fiction Ser.). 2008. 89.99 (978-1-60640-907-7(7)) Find a World.

Rogue. abr. ed. Fabio. Read by Deborah McLiam. 1 cass. (Running Time: 90 min.). 1994. 5.99 (978-1-57096-010-9(0), RAZ 911) Romance Alive Audio.
In superstar Fabio's second novel, English heiress Natalie Desmond resists handsome & swaggering Ryder Remington, until he assists in a search for her missing aunt, & together they discover an all consuming love.

Rogue. abr. ed. Danielle Steel. Read by Brian Keith Lewis. (Running Time: 6 hrs.). 2009. audio compact disk 14.99 (978-1-4233-2037-1(9), 9781423320371, BCD Value Price) Brilliance Audio.

Rogue. unabr. ed. Danielle Steel. Read by Brian Keith Lewis. (Running Time: 10 hrs.). 2008. 24.95 (978-1-4233-2032-6(8), 9781423320326, Brilliance MP3); 39.25 (978-1-4233-2033-3(6), 9781423320333, Brinc Audio MP3 Lib); 39.25 (978-1-4233-2035-7(2), 9781423320357, BADLE); 24.95 (978-1-4233-2034-0(4), 9781423320340, BAD); audio compact disk 36.95 (978-1-4233-2030-2(1), 9781423320302, Bril Audio CD Unabri); audio compact disk 97.25 (978-1-4233-2031-9(X), 9781423320319, BriAudCD Unabrid) Brilliance Audio.

Rogue Angel: The spiritual journey of one of the FBI's Ten Most Wanted. Jodi Werhanowicz. Read by Naomi Rhode. 8 CDs. 2005. audio compact disk 29.95 (978-0-9774294-1-7(5)) Ezekiel.
The story of the woman who saved Christmas for over ten million children. By the time she was twenty-seven, Mary Kay Beard was on the FBI Ten Most Wanted List, with a mafia contract out on her and warrants in four states. In 1972 she was capture, tried and sentenced for armed robbery. In solitary confinement in an Alabama jail, she experienced a profound spiritual transformation. Ten years later she founded Angel Tree which has provided Christmas gifts to the children of inmates all over the world. This is a dramatic and inspiring story of a life redeemed from crime and one woman's journey to purpose and wholeness. Foreword by Charles Colson.

Rogue Angel 1: Destiny. 2007. audio compact disk 19.99 (978-1-59950-205-2(4)) GraphicAudio.

Rogue Angel 1-5: MP3 CD Long Haul Boxset. Based on a book by Alex Archer. (ENG.). 2007. 59.95 (978-1-59950-486-5(3)) GraphicAudio.

Rogue Angel 10: Serpent's Kiss. Based on a novel by Alex Archer. 2008. audio compact disk 19.99 (978-1-59950-445-2(6)) GraphicAudio.

Rogue Angel 11: Provenance. Based on a novel by Alex Archer. 2008. audio compact disk 19.99 (978-1-59950-466-7(9)) GraphicAudio.

Rogue Angel 12: The Soul Stealer. Alex Archer. 2008. audio compact disk 19.99 (978-1-59950-505-3(3)) GraphicAudio.

Rogue Angel 13: Gabriel's Horn. Alex Archer. 2008. audio compact disk 19.99 (978-1-59950-509-1(6)) GraphicAudio.

Rogue Angel 14: Swordsman's Legacy. Alex Archer. 2009. audio compact disk 19.99 (978-1-59950-527-5(4)) GraphicAudio.

Rogue Angel 15: Swordman's Legacy. Alex Archer. 2009. audio compact disk 19.99 (978-1-59950-572-5(X)) GraphicAudio.

Rogue Angel 16: Polar Quest. Alex Archer. 2009. audio compact disk 19.99 (978-1-59950-584-8(3)) GraphicAudio.

Rogue Angel 17: Eternal Journey. Based on a novel by Alex Archer. 2009. audio compact disk 19.99 (978-1-59950-612-8(2)) GraphicAudio.

Rogue Angel 18: Sacrifice. Based on a novel by Alex Archer. 2009. audio compact disk 19.99 (978-1-59950-620-3(3)) GraphicAudio.

Rogue Angel 19: Seeker's Curse. Based on a novel by Alex Archer. 2010. audio compact disk 19.99 (978-1-59950-636-4(X)) GraphicAudio.

Rogue Angel 20: Footprints. Based on a novel by A;ex Archer. 2010. audio compact disk 19.99 (978-1-59950-627-2(0)) GraphicAudio.

***Rogue Angel 21: Paradox.** Alex Archer. 2010. audio compact disk 19.99 (978-1-59950-654-8(8)) GraphicAudio.

***Rogue Angel 22: The Spirit Banner.** Alex Archer. 2010. audio compact disk 19.99 (978-1-59950-714-9(5)) GraphicAudio.

***Rogue Angel 23: Sacred Ground.** Alex Archer. 2011. audio compact disk (978-1-59950-735-4(8)) GraphicAudio.

***Rogue Angel 24: The Bone Conjurer.** Alex Archer. 2011. audio compact disk 19.99 (978-1-59950-745-3(5)) GraphicAudio.

Rogue Angel 3: The Spider Stone. 2007. audio compact disk 19.99 (978-1-59950-318-9(2)) GraphicAudio.

Rogue Angel 4: The Chosen. Alex Archer. Contrib. by Nanette Savard et al. Directed By Nanette Savard. Contrib. by Colleen Delany et al. (Running Time: 21600 sec.). (Rogue Angel Ser.). 2007. audio compact disk 19.99 (978-1-59950-334-9(4)) GraphicAudio.

Rogue Angel 5: Forbidden City. Alex Archer. Contrib. by Nanette Savard et al. Directed By Nanette Savard. Contrib. by Colleen Delany et al. (Running Time: 21600 sec.). (Rogue Angel Ser.). 2007. audio compact disk 19.99 (978-1-59950-344-8(1)) GraphicAudio.

Rogue Angel 6: The Lost Scrolls. Created by Graphic Audio. (Running Time: 18000 sec.). (Rogue Angel Ser.). 2007. audio compact disk 19.99 (978-1-59950-362-2(X)) GraphicAudio.

Rogue Angel 7: God of Thunder. Alex Archer. (Running Time: 18000 sec.). (Rogue Angel Ser.). 2007. audio compact disk 19.99 (978-1-59950-380-6(8)) GraphicAudio.

Rogue Angel 8: Secret of the Slaves. Alex Archer. (Running Time: 18000 sec.). (Rogue Angel Ser.). 2007. audio compact disk 19.99 (978-1-59950-393-6(X)) GraphicAudio.

Rogue Angel 9: Warrior Spirit. Created by GraphicAudio. (Running Time: 21600 sec.). (Rogue Angel Ser.). 2008. audio compact disk 19.99 (978-1-59950-413-1(8)) GraphicAudio.

Rogue Berserker. unabr. ed. Fred Saberhagen. Read by Paul Michael Garcia. (Running Time: 10 hrs. 0 mins.). 2009. 29.95 (978-1-4332-1713-5(9)); 85.95 (978-1-4332-1709-8(0)); audio compact disk 118.00 (978-1-4332-1710-4(4)) Blckstn Audio.

Rogue Cop. William P. McGivern. Read by Grover Gardner. (Running Time: 5 hrs. 30 mins.). 2004. 24.95 (978-1-59912-584-8(6)) Iofy Corp.

Rogue Cop. unabr. ed. William P. McGivern. Read by Christopher Lane. 5 CDs. (Running Time: 5 hrs. 30 mins.). 2004. audio compact disk 40.00 (978-0-7861-8734-8(4), 3243); 32.95 (978-0-7861-2637-8(X), 3243) Blckstn Audio.
From the station-houses to the joy-houses, they knew about Mike Carmody. He was the best cop money could buy. And when the Syndicate boys said jump, Carmody knew just how high. But they couldn't buy Carmody's kid brother Eddie. And when Eddie turned against them, the Mob snuffed him out like a nickel cigar.

***Rogue Forces.** unabr. ed. Dale Brown. Read by William Dufris. (ENG.). 2009. (978-0-06-180604-9(8), Harper Audio); (978-0-06-180603-2(X), Harper Audio) HarperCollins Pubs.

Rogue Forces. unabr. ed. Dale Brown. Read by William Dufris. 9 CDs. (Running Time: 10 hrs.). 2009. audio compact disk 39.99 (978-0-06-162950-1(2), Harper Audio) HarperCollins Pubs.

***Rogue Hunter.** unabr. ed. Lynsay Sands. Read by Rick Robertson. (ENG.). 2010. (978-0-06-195870-0(0), Harper Audio); (978-0-06-196725-2(4), Harper Audio) HarperCollins Pubs.

***Rogue Island: A Novel.** unabr. ed. Bruce DeSilva. Narrated by Paul Boehmer. (Running Time: 8 hrs. 30 mins.). 2010. 15.99 (978-1-4526-7001-0(3)); 19.99 (978-1-4526-5001-2(2)); 29.99 (978-1-4526-0001-7(5)) Tantor Media.

***Rogue Island (Library Edition) A Novel.** unabr. ed. Bruce DeSilva. Narrated by Paul Boehmer. (Running Time: 8 hrs. 30 mins.). 2010. 71.99 (978-1-4526-3001-4(1)); 29.99 (978-1-4526-2001-5(6)) Tantor Media.

Rogue Male. unabr. ed. Geoffrey Household. 4 cass. (Running Time: 4 hrs.). 1998. 57.95 (978-1-872672-86-1(8)) Pub: Magna Story GBR. Dist(s): Ulverscroft US

Rogue Nation. unabr. ed. Stephen R. Lawhead & Ross Lawhead. 8 CDs. 2004. audio compact disk 29.99 (978-1-57683-575-3(8)) NavPress.

Rogue of My Own. abr. ed. Johanna Lindsey. Read by Rosalyn Landor. (Running Time: 4 hrs.). (Reid Family Ser.). 2010. audio compact disk 14.99 (978-1-4418-2540-7(1), 9781441825407, BACD) Brilliance Audio.

***Rogue of My Own.** abr. ed. Johanna Lindsey. Read by Rosalyn Landor. (Running Time: 4 hrs.). (Reid Family Ser.). 2010. 9.99 (978-1-4418-9355-0(5), 9781441893550, BAD) Brilliance Audio.

Rogue of My Own. unabr. ed. Johanna Lindsey. Read by Rosalyn Landor. 1 MP3-CD. (Running Time: 9 hrs.). (Reid Family Ser.). 2009. 39.97 (978-1-4233-7661-3(7), 9781423376613, Brinc Audio MP3 Lib); 39.97 (978-1-4233-7663-7(3), 9781423376637, BADLE); 24.99 (978-1-4233-7660-6(9), 9781423376606, Brilliance MP3); 24.99 (978-1-4233-7662-0(5), 9781423376620, BAD); audio compact disk 97.97 (978-1-4233-7659-0(5), 9781423376590, BriAudCD Unabrid); audio compact disk 36.99 (978-1-4233-7658-3(7), 9781423376583, Bril Audio CD Unabri) Brilliance Audio.

Rogue Officer. Garry Douglas Kilworth. 2009. 61.95 (978-1-4079-0380-4(2)); audio compact disk 79.95 (978-1-4079-0381-1(0)) Pub: Soundings Ltd GBR. Dist(s): Ulverscroft US

Rogue Warrior: Seize the Day. Richard Marcinko. 2004. 10.95 (978-0-7435-4581-5(8)) Pub: S&S Audio. Dist(s): S and S Inc

Rogues' Gallery. John Malcolm. (Soundings Ser.). 2006. 61.95 (978-1-84559-346-9(4)) Pub: ISIS Lrg Prnt GBR. Dist(s): Ulverscroft US

Rogue's Gallery: An Interest in Unalive Bodies. Perf. by Dick Powell & Gerald Mohr. (ENG.). 2008. audio compact disk 18.95 (978-1-57019-867-0(5)) Radio Spirits.

Rogue's Gallery: Little Drops of Rain & The House of Fear. Perf. by Dick Powell. 1 cass. (Running Time: 1 hr.). 2001. 6.98 (1698) Radio Spirits.

Rogue's Gallery: McDonald Murder Case & Murder with Muriel. Perf. by Dick Powell. 1 cass. (Running Time: 1 hr.). 2001. 6.98 (2525) Radio Spirits.

Rogue's Gallery: Star of Savoy & Lady with a Gun. Perf. by Dick Powell. 1 cass. (Running Time: 1 hr.). 2001. 6.98 (2166) Radio Spirits.

Rogue's Gallery: The Ski Lodge & Blondes Prefer Gentlemen. Perf. by Dick Powell. 1 cass. (Running Time: 1 hr.). 2001. 6.98 (1857) Radio Spirits.

Rogues in Music. (YA). 1994. 17.00 (978-0-89898-809-3(8), BMR05096, Warner Bro) Alfred Pub.

Rogue's Life. Wilkie Collins. Read by Anais 9000. 2009. 27.95 (978-1-60112-230-8(6)) Babblebooks.

Rogue's Life. Wilkie Collins. 4 cass. (Running Time: 6 hrs.). 2000. 32.95 (978-0-7861-1863-2(6), 2662) Blckstn Audio.
Mr. Frank Softly was sent to one of the most fashionable & famous public school. He ran away three times & was flogged three times. He made four aristocratic connections, learnt (his word) to play at cricket, to hate rich people, to cure warts & few other strange things. It was the setting for a life of adventure & roguery to follow, from prison cell to even worse disasters.

Rogue's Life. Wilkie Collins. Read by Bernard Mayes. 4 cass. (Running Time: 6 hrs.). 2000. 32.95 (2662) Blckstn Audio.
Mr. Frank Softly was sent to one of the most fashionable & famous of the great public schools. I will not mention it by name, because I don't think the masters would be proud of my connection with it. I ran away three times & was flogged three times. I made four aristocratic connections, I learn to play at cricket, to hate rich people, to cure wart, to write Latin verses, to swim, to recite speeches, to cook kidneys on toast, to draw caricatures of the masters, to construe Greek plays, to black boots & to receive kicks & serious advice resignedly. Who will say that the fashionable public school was of no use after that?.

Rogue's Life. unabr. ed. Wilkie Collins. Read by Bernard Mayes. (Running Time: 5.5 hrs. 0 mins.). 2008. 29.95 (978-1-4332-4584-8(1)) Blckstn Audio.

Rogue's Life. unabr. ed. Wilkie Collins. Read by Bernary Mayes. (Running Time: 19800 sec.). 2008. audio compact disk & audio compact disk 50.00 (978-1-4332-4583-1(3)) Blckstn Audio.

Rogue's Proposal. Stephanie Laurens. Narrated by Simon Prebble. 10 cass. (Running Time: 14 hrs.). (Cynster Family Ser.: Bk. 4). 88.00 (978-0-7887-9640-1(2)) Recorded Bks.

Roi Arthur et Autres Rois. 1 cass. (Running Time: 1 hr., 30 mins.). (Musicontes Ser.).Tr. of King Arthur & Other Kings. (FRE.). (J). 2000. bk. 24.95 (978-2-09-230490-7(9)) Pub: F Nathan FRA. Dist(s): Distribks Inc

Roi Arthur et les Chavaliers. Claude Louvet. pap. bk. 21.95 (978-88-7754-782-8(0)) Pub: Cideb ITA. Dist(s): Distribks Inc

Roi Babar see Babar the King

Roi Se Meurt. Eugène Ionesco. Perf. by Michel Aumont & Michel Duchaussoy. 2 cass. (Running Time: 2 hrs.). (FRE.). 1991. 26.95 (1062-RF) Olivia & Hill.
In Ionesco's classic of the theater of the absurd we witness the countdown to the King's death.

Roi-Soliel Se le Aussi. l.t. ed. Philippe Beaussant. (French Ser.). 2001. bk. 30.99 (978-2-84011-409-3(7)) Pub: UlverLrgPrint GBR. Dist(s): Ulverscroft US

Rojo. Zondervan Publishing Staff. 2003. audio compact disk 14.99 (978-0-8297-4412-5(6)) Zondervan.
RED is a fresh album, different and experimental; it is a great production by Emmanuel Epinosa, one of the youngest, most creative producers, who above all, is connected with God's purpose.This is an album with strong lyrics; it is pop-rock with some influence from reggae, industrial music and acoustic rock.The intention of this project is to have a multi-textural expression, where we mix guitars, base with synthesizers and energetic singers."We wanted to have a recording that would have lots of diversity but not change the context" says Oswaldo, guitarist of the band. What we intended to do is to have the honest, intimate song of a normal person with a supernatural God.

Rojo. unabr. ed. Zondervan Publishing Staff. (SPA.). 2003. 9.99 (978-0-8297-4414-9(2)) Pub: Vida Pubs. Dist(s): Zondervan

Rojo y Negro. abr. ed. Stendhal. Read by Fabio Camero. 3 CDs. (SPA.). 2002. audio compact disk 17.00 (978-958-8161-02-0(9)) YoYoMusic.

Roland Flint. unabr. ed. Read by Roland Flint. 1 cass. (Running Time: 29 min.). 1985. 10.00 New Letters.
Widely published poet Roland Flint here reads from Resuming Green.

Roland the Minstrel Pig & Other Stories. unabr. ed. William Steig. Perf. by Carol Channing. 1 cass. (Running Time: 1 hr.). Incl. "B" Book. Phyllis McGinley. (J). (CDL5 1305); Loudmouse. Richard Wilbur. (J). (CDL5 1305); Tom, Sue & the Clock. Conrad Aiken. (J). (CDL5 1305); (J). 1984. 9.95 (978-0-694-50694-1(X), CDL5 1305) HarperCollins Pubs.

Role & Opportunity of Adjunctive Ministry. Joe Abbott. 1 cass. (Running Time: 1 hr.). 1986. 10.80 (0305B) Assn Prof Chaplains.

***Role Models.** unabr. ed. John Waters. (Running Time: 8 hrs. 0 mins.). 2010. 15.99 (978-1-4001-8703-4(6)); 29.99 (978-1-4001-9703-3(1)) Tantor Media.

***Role Models.** unabr. ed. John Waters. (Running Time: 7 hrs. 30 mins. 0 sec.). (ENG.). 2010. 19.99 (978-1-4001-6703-6(5)); audio compact disk 59.99 (978-1-4001-4703-8(4)); audio compact disk 29.99 (978-1-4001-1703-1(8)) Pub: Tantor Media. Dist(s): IngramPubServ

Role of a CFO in a Venture Capital Backed Company: Top Chief Financial Officers on Best Practices for Working with VCs, Management Compensation Structures & Financial Management Best Practices. Ed. by ReedLogic Staff. 2006. audio compact disk 499.95 (978-1-59701-078-8(2)) Aspatore Bks.

***Role of a Lifetime: Reflections on Faith, Family, & Significant Living.** unabr. ed. James Brown. Read by James Brown. Told to Nathan Whitaker. Frwd. by Tony Dungy. (Running Time: 2 hrs.). (ENG.). 2010. 16.98 (978-1-60788-715-7(0)) Pub: Hachet Audio. Dist(s): HachBkGrp

Role of Academic Advising in Student Persistence: NACADA Webinar No. 26. Featuring Susan Campbell & Charlie Nutt. (ENG.). 2009. audio compact disk 140.00 (978-1-935140-68-9(X)) Nat Acad Adv.

Role of Children in the Meeting of the Church. Douglas W. Phillips. 1 cass. (Running Time: 1 hr.). 2000. 7.00 (978-1-929241-07-1(0)) Pub: Vsn Forum. Dist(s): STL Dist NA

Role of Children in the Meeting of the Church. Douglas W. Phillips. 1 CD. (Running Time: 1 hr.). 2000. audio compact disk 10.00 (978-1-929241-77-4(1)) Pub: Vsn Forum. Dist(s): STL Dist NA
The biblical example is that entire families are present for corporate worship. Age-segregated worship is rooted in evolutionary humanism, not biblical Christianity. "Suffer the little children" to be in the presence of God and begin to experience the true blessing of family-centered worship.

Role of Electronic Marketing in Independent Supermarkets. 1 cass. (Running Time: 1 hr.). (America's Supermarket Showcase '96 Ser.). 1996. 11.00 (NGA96-007) Sound Images.

Role of Faculty Advisors in Student Success: NACADA Webinar No. 32. Featuring Kathy Stockwell & Maura Reynolds. (ENG.). 2010. audio compact disk 140.00 (978-1-935140-74-0(4)) Nat Acad Adv.

Role of Government in Our Society. M. Stanton Evans & George S. McGovern. 1 cass. (Running Time: 1 hr. 5 min.). 11.95 (228) J Norton Pubs.

Role of government in our Society. Milton Friedman & Joseph Clark. 1 CD. (Running Time: 1 HR). 2005. audio compact disk 12.95 (978-1-57970-220-5(1), AF0152D) J Norton Pubs.

Role of Government in Your Life: Romans 13:1-17. Ben Young. 1997. 4.95 (978-0-7417-6034-0(7), B0034) Win Walk.

***Role of HR in Communicating Sensitive Issues.** PUEI. 2009. audio compact disk 199.00 (978-1-935041-49-8(5), CareerTrack) P Univ E Inc.

Role of Jesus Christ in Modern Society: Proceedings of the 45th Annual Convention National Association of Evangelicals Buffalo, New York. Read by Pat Robertson. 1 cass. (Running Time: 60 min.). 1987. 4.00 (346) Nat Assn Evan.

Role of Men & Women. 1 cass. (Running Time: 1 hr.). 10.00 (RJ129) Esstee Audios.

Role of Negativity. Swami Amar Jyoti. 1 cass. (Running Time: 1 hr.). 1977. 9.95 (O-8) Truth Consciousness.
Negativity as a balancing force of creation. The play of Maya - the drama & our roles. The dynamism of relativity, the great dream of God.

Role of Personality in Science. C. P. Snow. 1 cass. (Running Time: 44 min.). 1970. 11.95 (33011) J Norton Pubs.

Role of Philosophy. Nathaniel Branden. 1 cass. (Running Time: 1 hr. 25 min.). (Basic Principles of Objectivism Ser.). 11.95 (561) J Norton Pubs.
What is philosophy? The historical role of reason; the bankruptcy of today's culture; objectivism; objectivism vs. subjectivism.

Role of Philosophy & Psychology in History. Leonard Peikoff. 1 cass. (Running Time: 90 min.). 1984. 12.95 (978-1-56114-055-8(4), LP04C) Second Renaissance.
How philosophy is the fundamental influence shaping the course of human history.

Role of Prostaglandins & Thromboxane in the Control of Blood Pressure & Renal Function. Read by Michael J. Dunn. 1 cass. (Running Time: 90 min.). 1985. 12.00 (C8532) Amer Coll Phys.

Role of Religion. Howard B. Lyman. 1 cass. (Running Time: 24 min.). (Single Again Ser.). 10.95 (35025) J Norton Pubs.

Role of Religious in the Evangelization of the Americas. Torres Bishop. 1 cass. (Running Time: 1 hr.). (National Meeting of the Institute, 1992 Ser.). 4.00 (92N1) IRL Chicago.

Role of Research in Industry. Crawford H. Greenewalt. 1 cass. (Running Time: 22 min.). 10.95 (13011) J Norton Pubs.
A discussion of the importance & value of scientific research in industry.

Role of the Advocate. William F. Buckley, Jr. & F. Lee Bailey. 1 CD. (Running Time: 55 mins.). 2005. audio compact disk 12.95 (978-1-57970-256-4(2), C32044D, Audio-For) J Norton Pubs.

Role of the Clergy in Innovative Concepts in Wholistic Health Care. Granger Westburg & Douglas Turvey. 1 cass. (Running Time: 1 hr.). 1986. 10.80 (0506) Assn Prof Chaplains.

Role of the Critic. Rex A. Barnett. 1 cass. (Running Time: 55 min.). (YA). 16.99 (978-0-924198-05-2(2)) Hist Video.

Role of the Director in a Hostile Takeover. 1 cass. (Running Time: 1 hr.). 1988. 35.00 PA Bar Inst.

Role of the Parent: Ephesians 6:4. Ed Young. 1986. 4.95 (978-0-7417-1540-1(6), 540) Win Walk.

Role of the Pastor. Rick Joyner. 1 cass. (Running Time: 90 mins.). (Vision Ser.: Vol. 4). 2000. 5.00 (RJ16-004) Morning NC.
This tape series will help to impart new vision or restore lost vision in the church.

Role of the Rabbi. 1 cass. (Running Time: 1 hr.). 10.00 (RJ128) Esstee Audios.

Role of the Speech-Language Pathologist in Facilitating Emergent Literacy Skills. Barbara J. Ehren. 1 cass. (Running Time: 1 hr.). 2000. pap. bk. 79.00 (978-1-58041-048-9(0), 0112254) Am Speech Lang Hearing.
FAQ's asked by SLP's will be answered.

Role of Violence. Gil Bailie. 1 cass. (Running Time: 90 min.). 8.95 incl. study guide. (AA2809) Credence Commun.
In this introductory lecture, Bailie uses the seminal thought of Rene Girard, a brilliant anthropologist, to explain John's Gospel. Bailie shows how the role of violence in religion & culture is completely recast by John. Bailie shows you vividly how revolutionary the violence of the crucifixion is in John's vision & how it really changed the history of the world. Bailie is a consummate teacher, clear & thorough; but the thought is radical so it will require close attention.

Role of Vision Questing among North American Shamans. William Lyon. 1 cass. (Running Time: 1 hr.). 9.00 (A0079-86) Sound Photosyn.
ICSS '86.

Role of Women in Ministry. Mac Hammond. 1 cass. (Running Time: 1 hr.). 2005. 5.00 (978-1-57399-209-1(7)); audio compact disk 5.00 (978-1-57399-263-3(1)) Mac Hammond.

Role of Worship. Swami Amar Jyoti. 1 cass. (Running Time: 1 hr.). 1978. 9.95 (P-13) Truth Consciousness.
The science of worship, & its purpose. Avoiding mechanical repetition. Surrendering the results to God. What is impurity?.

Role of Yoga in the Modern Age. Kriyananda, pseud. 1 cass. (Running Time: 1 hr.). 9.95 (ST-71) Crystal Clarity.
Topics include: What is "the modern age;" the popularization of society; causes of the world's present turmoil; how even small groups practicing yoga can bring about change.

Rolf Dieter Brinkmann. unabr. ed. Read by Rolf D. Brinkmann & Rebekah Presson. Ed. by James McKinley. 1 cass. (Running Time: 29 min.). (New Letters on the Air Ser.). 1978. 10.00 (030478); 18.00 2-sided cass. New Letters.
This memorial program features Brinkmann's readings as well as translations presented by his friends.

Rolfing in Motion: A Guide to Balancing Your Body. 2nd ed. Mary Bond. Read by Mary Bond. (Running Time: 1 hr. 30 mins.). 2005. bk. 14.95 (978-1-59477-074-6(3), Destiny Audio Edits) Inner Tradit.

Roll of Thunder, Hear My Cry. Mildred D. Taylor. 1 cass. (Running Time: 1 hr.). (J). 1978. 21.33 (978-0-394-66791-1(3)) SRA McGraw.

Roll of Thunder, Hear My Cry. unabr. ed. Mildred D. Taylor. Read by Lynne Thigpen. 6 vols. (Running Time: 7 hrs. 26 mins.). (J). (gr. 5-9). 2004. pap. bk. 48.00 (978-0-8072-0678-2(4), Listening Lib); audio compact disk 42.50 (978-0-8072-1608-8(9), S YA 342 CD, Listening Lib) Pub: Random Audio Pubg. Dist(s): NetLibrary CO

Roll of Thunder, Hear My Cry. unabr. ed. Mildred D. Taylor. Read by Lynne Thigpen. 7 CDs. (Running Time: 26760 sec.). (ENG.). (J). (gr. 7-7). 2005. audio compact disk 34.00 (978-0-307-28172-2(8), Listening Lib) Pub: Random Audio Pubg. Dist(s): Random

Roll of Thunder, Hear My Cry. unabr. ed. Mildred D. Taylor. Narrated by Lynne Thigpen. 6 cass. (Running Time: 8 hrs.). (Logan Family Saga Ser.: Pt. 1). (J). (gr. 6). 1994. 51.00 (978-0-7887-0018-7(9), 94217E7) Recorded Bks.
An authentic portrait of African American life in 1930s Mississippi. Meet the Logans, a close-knit family whose loving bonds give them the spirit to defy rural Southern racism.

Roll of Thunder, Hear My Cry. unabr. ed. Mildred D. Taylor. Narrated by Lynne Thigpen. 7 CDs. (Running Time: 8 hrs.). (J). (gr. 6). 2000. audio compact disk 69.00 (978-0-7887-4646-8(4), C1195E7) Recorded Bks.
An authentic portrait of African American life in 1930s Mississippi.

Roll of Thunder, Hear My Cry. unabr. ed. Mildred D. Taylor. Read by Lynne Thigpen. 6 cass. (Running Time: 7 hrs. 26 mins.). (J). (gr. 5-9). 2004. 40.00 (978-0-8072-0622-5(9), Listening Lib) Random Audio Pubg.
Why is the land so important to Cassie's family? It takes the events of one turbulent year - the year of the night riders and the burnings, the year a white girl humiliates Cassie in public simply because she is black - to show Cassie that having a place of their own is the Logan family's lifeblood. It is the land that gives the Logans their courage and pride, for no matter how others may degrade them, the Logans possess something no one can take away.

***Rollback: The Battleplan Against Big Government.** unabr. ed. Thomas E. Woods. (Running Time: 8 hrs. 0 mins.). 2011. 19.99 (978-1-4001-6918-4(6)); 29.99 (978-1-4001-1918-9(9)); 71.99 (978-1-4001-4918-6(5)) Tantor Media.

***Rollback: The Battleplan Against Big Government.** unabr. ed. Thomas E. Woods, Jr. (Running Time: 8 hrs. 0 mins.). 2011. 15.99 (978-1-4001-8918-2(7)) Tantor Media.

***Rollback (Library Edition) The Battleplan Against Big Government.** unabr. ed. Thomas E. Woods, Jr. (Running Time: 8 hrs. 0 mins.). 2011. 29.99 (978-1-4001-9918-1(2)) Tantor Media.

Roller-Coaster. unabr. ed. Michael Gilbert. Read by Nigel Graham. 8 cass. (Running Time: 7 hrs. 30 min.). (Isis Ser.). (J). 1994. 69.95 (978-1-85695-848-6(5), 941007) Pub: ISIS Lrg Prnt GBR. Dist(s): Ulverscroft US

Roller Coaster of Life. Troy Dunn. 1 cass. (Running Time: 1 hr.). 2004. 7.98 (978-1-55503-399-6(7), 06004490) Covenant Comms.
Youth talk about the excitement of life's ups & downs.

Roller Skates. Ruth Sawyer. Narrated by Kate Forbes. 4 pieces. (Running Time: 5 hrs. 30 mins.). (gr. 4 up). 2001. 38.00 (978-0-7887-5032-8(1)) Recorded Bks.

Rolling Back the Carpet of Time. Kenneth Wapnick. 2008. 12.00 (978-1-59142-360-7(0)); audio compact disk 14.00 (978-1-59142-359-1(7)) Foun Miracles.

Rolling Back the Welfare State. unabr. ed. Stephen Moses. Read by Stephen Moses. 1 cass. (Running Time: 1 hr. 30 min.). 1996. 14.95 (978-1-57724-007-5(3), Prncpal Srce Audio) Objectivist Ctr.
The author explains how the objectivist ethics gives us the tools to dismantle it & rebuild on solid ground, replacing welfare programs with private insurance. He discusses concrete strategies for successful political change.

Rolling Harvey down the Hill. unabr. ed. Jack Prelutsky. Read by Jack Prelutsky. 1 cass. (Running Time: 1 hr.). Incl. Gopher in the Garden. Jack Prelutsky. (J). (CPN 1699); Pack Rat's Day & Other Poems. Jack Prelutsky. (J). (CPN 1699); Queen of Eene. Jack Prelutsky. (J). (CPN 1699); Snopp on the Sidewalk & Other Poems. Jack Prelutsky. (J). (CPN 1699); Toucans Two & Other Poems. Jack Prelutsky. (J). (CPN 1699); Rolling Harvey down the Hill. Jack Prelutsky. (J). (CPN 1699); (J). 1984. 9.95 (978-0-89845-152-8(3), CPN 1699) HarperCollins Pubs.
A collection of animal, character, & monster rhymes.

Rolling Harvey down the Hill. unabr. ed. Jack Prelutsky. Read by Boychoir of Ann Arbor. 1 cass. (Running Time: 31 mins.). (J). (gr. 1-3). 1993. 11.00 (978-0-8072-0217-3(7), FTR167CX, Listening Lib) Random Audio Pubg.
Are you & the kids on your block like Harvey & his friends? If you are one of you has just eaten a worm! Sales from this title benefit the Make-a-Wish Foundation.

Rolling Nowhere. unabr. ed. Ted Conover. Read by Ted Conover. 7 cass. (Running Time: 10 hrs.). 2001. 32.95 (978-1-58788-675-1(8), 1587886758, BAU); 78.25 (978-1-58788-676-8(6), 1587886766, CD Unabrid Lib Ed) Brilliance Audio.
"I crouched quietly in the patch of tall weeds. Around me fell the shadow of the viaduct that carried a highway over the railroad yards. From the edge of the yards, I squinted as I watched the railroad cars being switched from track to track. Cars and trucks were rolling over the viaduct, but what occupied my attention was the dark, cool corridor underneath it, where I hoped to intercept my train." Riding the rails, Ted Conover tasted the life of a tramp with companions like Pistol Pete, BB, and Sheba Sheila Sheils. From them he learned survival skills - how to "read" a freight train, scavenge for food and clothing, avoid the railroad "bulls." He was initiated into the customs of their unique, shadowy society - men and women bound together by a mutual bond of failure, camaraderie, and distrust. Sixty-five freight trains, 12,000 miles, and fifteen states later, Conover chronicles his impressions of their lives in this fascinating piece of first-hand reporting that becomes a thoughtful story of self-discovery.

Rolling Nowhere. unabr. ed. Ted Conover. Read by Ted Conover. (Running Time: 10 hrs.). 2005. 39.25 (978-1-59600-606-5(4), 9781596006065, BADLE); 24.95 (978-1-59600-605-8(6), 9781596006058, BAD) Brilliance Audio.

Rolling Nowhere: Riding the Rails with America's Hoboes. unabr. ed. Ted Conover. Read by Ted Conover. (Running Time: 36000 sec.). 2005. audio compact disk 24.95 (978-1-59600-603-4(X), 9781596006034, Brilliance MP3) Brilliance Audio.

Rolling Nowhere: Riding the Rails with America's Hobos. unabr. ed. Ted Conover. Read by Ted Conover. (Running Time: 36000 sec.). 2005. audio compact disk 39.25 (978-1-59600-604-1(8), 9781596006041, Brlnc Audio MP3 Lib) Brilliance Audio.

Rolling Stones. Robert A. Heinlein. Read by David Baker. (Running Time: 8 hrs.). 2005. 34.95 (978-1-60083-554-4(6)) Iofy Corp.

Rolling Stones. unabr. ed. Robert A. Heinlein. Read by Full Cast Production Staff. (J). 2007. 49.99 (978-1-60252-575-7(7)) Find a World.

Rolling Stones: As It Happened. Chrome Dreams. 4 CDs. (Running Time: 4 hrs.). (ENG., 2001. audio compact disk 32.50 (978-1-84240-131-6(9)) Pub: Chrome Dreams GBR. Dist(s): IPG Chicago
A unique 4-CD collection of classic interviews with The Rolling Stones, spanning the whole of the band's turbulent existence from the early 1960's to the present day. Each disc concentrates on a particular decade and features rare recordings of the complete Stones' membership - Mick Jagger, Keith Richards, Charlie Watts, Brian Jones, Bill Wyman, Mick Taylor and Ronnie Wood - as well as those who worked, loved and lived through it all with them.

Rollo & Tweedy & the Ghost at Dougal Castle Book & Tape. abr. ed. Laura J. Allen. Illus. by Laura J. Allen. Prod. by Chuck Lewkowicz. 1 cass. (Running Time: 1 hr.). (I Can Read Bks.). (J). (gr. k-3). 1996. 8.99 (978-0-694-70053-0(3)) HarperCollins Pubs.

Roly-Poly Pudding. Read by Frances Sternhagen. 1 cass. (Running Time: 1 hr.). (Beatrix Potter Ser.). (J). pap. bk. 13.45 (SAC 6532) Spoken Arts.

ROM Dance: Seated Version & Body Awareness & Breathing. Patricia Yu & Diane Harlowe. Read by Patricia Yu. 1 cass. (Running Time: 22 min.). 1993. 9.95 (978-1-877950-13-1(0)) Uncharted Ctry Pub.
Side A - The ROM Dance adapted for those with difficulty standing or who use wheelchairs. Uses images of sunlight, warm water, & friendship. Side B - Body awareness, breathing, & relaxation program.

ROM Dance in Moonlight & Soothing Meditation. Patricia Yu & Diane Harlowe. Read by Patricia Yu. 1 cass. (Running Time: 22 min.). 1993. 9.95 (978-1-877950-12-4(2)) Uncharted Ctry Pub.
Side A - The Moonlight version of the ROM Dance - has been adapted for people with sunlight sensitivity, uses images of moonlight, water, & friendship. Side B - Soothing relaxation & meditation experience.

ROM Dance in Sunlight & Body Awareness & Breathing. Patricia Yu & Diane Harlowe. Read by Patricia Yu. 1 cass. (Running Time: 22 min.). 1993. 9.95 (978-1-877950-11-7(4)) Uncharted Ctry Pub.
Side A - Original version of the ROM Dance, using images of sunlight, warm water, & friendship. Side B - Soothing relaxation & body awareness.

ROM Dance, Tape One: Side A - The ROM Dance Verse; Side B - Relaxation - Body Awareness. Diane Harlowe & Patricia Yu. 1 cass. (Running Time: 30 min.). 1984. 9.95 Uncharted Ctry Pub.
ROM dance verse & music for arthritis patients, relaxation methods & body awareness on second side.

ROM Dance, Tape Two: Side C - Relaxation - Imagined Environment; Side D - Releasing Stress or Pain. Diane Harlowe & Patricia Yu. 1 cass. (Running Time: 1 hr.). 1984. 9.95 Uncharted Ctry Pub.
Features relaxation methods to assist in releasing stress & dealing with pain. Music is included.

Roma Downey Healing Angel. Perf. by Roma Downey. Music by Phil Coulter. 1 cass. (Running Time: 1 hr.). 1998. (978-0-7601-3180-0(5)); audio compact disk (978-0-7601-3179-4(1)) Brentwood Music.
Delivers a sense of spiritual well-being through the universal themes of family, love & loss. Roma's soft accent & serene delivery add a timely & human touch that inspires meditations of life.

Roman Blood. unabr. ed. Steven Saylor. Read by Scott Harrison. 11 cass. (Running Time: 16 hrs.). 1996. 76.95 (978-0-7861-1058-2(9), 1829) Blckstn Audio.
In Rome, 80 B.C., on a warm spring morning, Gordianus the Finder receives a summons to the house of a then-unknown young advocate and orator, Cicero. Ambitious and brilliant, the twenty-six-year-old Cicero is about to argue his first important case. His client is a wealthy farmer, one Sextus Roscius of the town of Ameria, who stands accused of the most unforgivable act in Ancient Rome: the murder of his father. Hired by Cicero to investigate the charges, Gordianus sets out to discover the truth in a case and a society - rife with deceit, betrayal and conspiracy.

Roman Blood: A Novel of Ancient Rome. unabr. ed. Steven Saylor. Read by Scott Harrison. (Running Time: 15 hrs. 0 mins.). 2010. 29.95 (978-1-4417-1294-3(1)); audio compact disk 118.00 (978-1-4417-1291-2(7)) Blckstn Audio.

Roman Catholic Gospel. Dan Corner. 1 cass. (Running Time: 1 hr.). 3.00 (79) Evang Outreach.

Roman de la Momie: Level 2. T. F. Gautier. (FRE.). bk. 14.95 (978-2-09-032927-8(0), CL9270E) Pub: Cle Intl FRA. Dist(s): Continental Bk

Roman de Renart. Read by C. Deis et al. 3 cass. (Running Time: 3 hrs.). (FRE.). 1991. 31.95 (1392-VSL) Olivia & Hill.
These versified tales of the 12th century present human society under the guise of animals.

Roman Fever: Domesticity & Nationalism in Nineteenth-Century American Womens Writing. Annamaria Formichella Elsden. 2004. audio compact disk 9.95 (978-0-8142-9030-9(2)) Pub: Ohio St U Pr. Dist(s): Chicago Distribution Ctr

***Roman Games: A Plinius Secundus Mystery.** unabr. ed. Bruce Macbain. (Running Time: 8 hrs. 30 mins.). 2010. 29.95 (978-1-4417-6495-9(X)); 54.95 (978-1-4417-6492-8(5)); audio compact disk 76.00 (978-1-4417-6493-5(3)) Blckstn Audio.

Roman Lives: A Selection of Eight Lives. Plutarch. Read by Nicholas Farrell. 2004. pap. bk. 41.98 (978-962-634-302-9(8)) Naxos.

Roman Road: Romans 1:1-17. Ed Young. 1996. 4.95 (978-0-7417-2105-1(8), 1105) Win Walk.

Roman Ruins. Decipher Inc. Staff. 1 cass. (Running Time: 1 hr.). (How to Host a Murder Ser.: Vol. 11). 1996. pap. bk. 16.00 (978-1-878875-91-4(4)) Decipher Inc.

Roman Way. unabr. ed. Edith Hamilton. Read by Nadia May. 5 cass. (Running Time: 7 hrs.). 1994. 39.95 (978-0-7861-0686-8(7), 1471) Blckstn Audio.
Edith Hamilton shows us Rome through the eyes of the Romans. Plautus & Terence, Cicero & Caesar, Catullus, Horace, Virgil, & Augustus come to life in their ambitions, their work, their loves & hates. "The Roman Way" makes vividly interesting the contrast between Roman & Greek culture. Moreover, it reveals how surprisingly similar was Roman civilization to that of modern America - in respects ranging from an interest in good roads & good

plumbing, to the popular veneration of home & mother. Our heritage from Rome includes everything from moral laws to stock characters in the drama. Skillful, witty, subtle in understanding, this book shows us what the Romans were like, how they lived, what they thought & accomplished.

Romance. Barbour Books Staff. 1 CD. (Running Time: 1 hr.). 1999. bk. 9.97 (978-1-57748-582-7(3)) Barbour Pub.

Romance. Windham Hill Staff. 1 cass. (Running Time: 1 hr.). 1998. 15.00 (978-1-56170-563-4(2)) Hay House.

Romance. abr. ed. David Mamet. Contrib. by Ed Begley, Jr. & Gordon Clapp. (Running Time: 4440 sec.). 2007. audio compact disk 25.95 (978-1-58081-354-9(2)) Pub: L A Theatre. Dist(s): NetLibrary CO

Romance. unabr. ed. Joseph Conrad & Ford Madox Ford. Narrated by Flo Gibson. 12 cass. (Running Time: 17 hrs. 30 mins.). 2003. 39.95 (978-1-55685-741-6(1)) Audio Bk Con.

Romance. unabr. ed. Ed McBain, pseud. Read by Arthur Addison. 6 cass. (Running Time: 9 hrs.). (87th Precinct Ser.: Bk. 47). 1995. 48.00 (978-0-7366-3122-8(4), 3798) Books on Tape.
McBain torques up the intrigue & satire, weaving romantic dialogue into the investigation while taking potshots at various dramatis personae of the theater world.

Romance: Program from the Award Winning Public Radio Series. Hosted by Fred Goodwin. Comment by John Hockenberry. Contrib. by Helen Fisher et al. 1 cass. (Running Time: 1 hr.). (Infinite Mind Ser.). 1998. audio compact disk 15.00 (978-1-888064-26-1(9), LCM 38) Lichtenstein Creat.
Is there one true love for everyone, a soul mate waiting to be found? Or, is true love something that develops over time? Just in time for Valentine?s Day, we repeat this program exploring approaches to romance from differing perspectives, both ancient (arranged marriages) and technological (Internet relationships). With commentary by John Hockenberry and Anne Beatts, one of Saturday Night Live?s original writers.

Romance - Releasing Our Stuff/When Form Changes. Marianne Williamson. Read by Marianne Williamson. 1 cass. (Running Time: 90 mins.). (Lectures on a Course in Miracles). 1999. 10.00 (978-1-56170-260-2(9), M763) Hay House.

Romance & Horary Astrology. Gilbert Navarro & S. Simonea. Read by Gilbert Navarro & S. Simonea. 1 cass. (Running Time: 90 min.). 1994. 8.95 (1113) Am Fed Astrologers.
Horary astrology questions concerning romance.

Romance Angels: How to Work with the Angels to Manifest Great Love. Doreen Virtue. 1 cass. (Running Time: 1 hr.). 2000. 10.95 (978-1-56170-714-0(7), 4031) Hay House.
Side A teaches how to call upon the romance angels & receive their help in every facet of your live. Gives specific examples of how the angelic kingdom can intervene in Cupid-like fashion. Side B takes you through a relaxing meditation that allows the angels to clear away blocks that could be interfering with your love life.

Romance Angels: How to Work with the Angels to Manifest Great Love. Doreen Virtue. Music by Steven Halpern. 1 CD. 2005. audio compact disk 10.95 (978-1-4019-0414-2(9)) Hay House.

Romance de la Luna, Luna see Poesia y Drama de Garcia Lorca

Romance de la Pena Negra see Poesia y Drama de Garcia Lorca

Romance del Emplazado see Poesia y Drama de Garcia Lorca

Romance Double Feature. 1 cass. (Running Time: 1 hr.). Incl. Romance Double Feature: Heart's Delight. (878); Romance Double Feature: To Catch a Rainbow. (878); 10.95 (878) Audio Bk.
Two modern stories with passionate plots & exotic settings.

Romance Double Feature: Heart's Delight see Romance Double Feature

Romance Double Feature: To Catch a Rainbow see Romance Double Feature

Romance Espiritual. unabr. ed. Santiago. (SPA.). 2004. 9.99 (978-0-8297-3644-1(1)) Vida Pubs.

Romance in Marriage: Spicing It Up! Brenton Yorgason & Margaret Yorgason. 1 cass. (Running Time: 1 hr.). 7.98 (978-1-55503-734-5(8), 069405) Covenant Comms.
Finding fulfillment.

Romance in Spanish (Pasion sin Fronteras) Advanced-Level. 1 cass. (Running Time: 60 min.). 16.95 (CSP320) J Norton Pubs.

Romance in the Stars. unabr. ed. Sue Lovett. Read by Sue Lovett. (Running Time: 90 min.). 1986. 8.95 (555) Am Fed Astrologers.
Discusses which Planets & Transits have the potential fo Love.

Romance Mild to Wild: L-Book. Rrrose Carbinela. Sheri. 2008. 14.95 (978-1-934889-17-6(2)) Lbook Pub.

Romance of a Busy Broker see Favorite Stories by O. Henry

Romance of Atlantis. unabr. collector's ed. Taylor Caldwell. Read by Roses Prichard. 7 cass. (Running Time: 10 hrs. 30 mins.). 1981. 56.00 (978-0-7366-0458-1(8), 1430) Books on Tape.
Atlantis is threatened by powerful neighboring states. Tension increases when the ruler of an adjacent kingdom bids to marry the empress. If she marries him, Atlantis would be safe from invasion. Yet such a marriage contradicts the deepest feelilngs of her heart, the secret wisdom of her lineage & her sacred trust as queen.

***Romance of Redemption.** Chuck Missler. (ENG.). 2009. audio compact disk 19.95 (978-1-57821-448-8(3)) Koinonia Hse.

Romance of Redemption: Book of Ruth. Chuck Missler. 2 cass. (Running Time: 3 hrs.). (Briefing Packages by Chuck Missler). 1993. vinyl bd. 14.95 (978-1-880532-83-6(2)) Koinonia Hse.
What does this famous love story from the Old Testament have to do with the Feast of Pentecost? What critical element in Messianic genealogy is found in the Book of Ruth?The law shut out this Gentile Moabitess but grace took her in. Discover God's love for Israel, the Church and yourself through this beautiful love story of redemption.This key book of Bible prophecy highlights the role of the Goel, the kinsman-redeemer.Find out why the Book of Ruth is an essential study to understand the Book of Revelation!.

Romance of Satan. Steve Hill. 1 cass. (Running Time: 1 hr.). 1996. 7.00 (978-0-7684-0017-5(1)) Destiny Image Pubs.

Romance of the Harem. Anna Leonowens & Susan P. Morgan. Ed. by Susan P. Morgan. (Victorian Literature & Culture Ser.). 1991. 18.50 (978-0-8139-1328-5(4)) U Pr of Va.

Romance Reader. unabr. ed. Pearl Abraham. Narrated by Suzanne Toren. 6 cass. (Running Time: 9 hrs.). 1997. 51.00 (978-0-7887-1230-2(6), 95154E7) Recorded Bks.
Unveils the mysterious lifestyle of a Chassidic Jewish community in New York state. As the rabbi's oldest child, Rachel must set a proper example, but when she's alone she reads forbidden books about romance & modern women. Soon her search for the life she reads about in those pages clashes with the restrictive world she knows only too well.

Romance Sonambula see Poesia y Drama de Garcia Lorca

Romance Without Regret. (YA). 2004. 16.95 (978-1-888992-56-4(5)); audio compact disk 21.95 (978-1-888992-58-8(1)); audio compact disk 10.95 (978-1-888992-59-5(X)) Catholic Answers.

Romance Without Regret (Secular) (YA). 2004. 8.95 (978-1-888992-57-1(3)) Catholic Answers.

Romances. 4 cass. (Running Time: 5 hrs.). 2001. 36.95 (RMNC124) Lodestone Catalog.
A Year & a Day; Breathless; Crooked Hearts & the Hoyden.

Romancing a Dream. Perf. by William Julien. Arranged by William Julien. 1. 2001. audio compact disk 12.00 (978-0-9773731-0-9(X)) MaestroMedia Pr.

***Romancing Mister Bridgerton: the Epilogue II.** unabr. ed. Julia Quinn. Read by Kevan Brighting. (ENG.). 2007. (978-0-06-147266-4(2), Harper Audio); (978-0-06-153701-1(2), Harper Audio) HarperCollins Pubs.

Romancing the Flow: Allowing Ease. unabr. ed. Galexis. 2 cass. (Running Time: 3 hrs.). 1995. 19.95 Set. (978-1-56089-039-3(8), G117) Visionary FL.
Practical living of spiritual principles workshop. How to create a momentum of joy in one's daily life. Meditation included.

Romancing the Home. Ed Young. 1999. 4.95 (978-0-7417-2208-9(9), 1208) Win Walk.

Romancing the Nephites. abr. ed. Becky Paget. 1 cass. (Running Time: 60 min.). (YA). (gr. 6-12). 1993. 9.98 (978-1-55503-593-8(0), 0700924) Covenant Comms.
Youth fiction.

Romancing the shadow: illuminating the dark side of the Soul: Illuminating the Dark Side of the Soul. Connie Zweig & wolf. 2004. 10.95 (978-0-7435-4591-4(5)) Pub: S&S Audio. Dist(s): S and S Inc

Romancing the Stone: Song of Sol. 1:8-17. Ed Young. 1991. 4.95 (978-0-7417-1867-9(7), 867) Win Walk.

Romane: the Gypsy Sound in Nashville. Created by Mel Bay Publications Inc. (Running Time: 1 hr. 4 mins.). 2006. 24.95 (978-5-558-09015-4(4)) Mel Bay.

Romanian. 2 cass. (Running Time: 80 min.). (Language - Thirty Library). bk. 16.95 Moonbeam Pubns.
Using the proven method based on the famous U.S. Military accelerated language learning program, Language/30 courses stress conversationally useful words & phrases.

Romanian. Ed. by Charles Berlitz. 2 cass. (Running Time: 1 hr. 30 mins.). (Language/30 Brief Course Ser.). 2001. pap. bk. 21.95 (AF1063) J Norton Pubs.
Quick, highly condensed introduction to the words & phrases you'll need to communicate effectively in the country you're visiting. Cassettes & phrase guide book are in a vinyl album.

Romanian. unabr. ed. Pimsleur Staff. 5 CDs. (Running Time: 50 hrs. 0 mins. 0 sec.). (Compact Ser.). (RUM & ENG.). 2005. audio compact disk 49.95 (978-0-7435-5053-6(6), Pimsleur) Pub: S&S Audio. Dist(s): S and S Inc

Romanian: Language/30. rev. ed. Educational Services Corporation Staff. 2 cass. (Running Time: 1 hr. 30 min.). (ROM.). 1995. pap. bk. 21.95 incl. phrase bk. (978-0-910542-88-3(0)) Educ Svcs DC.
Guided practice including greetings, introduction, & questions at hotels, restaurants, places of business & entertainment. Phrases spoken in target language & English, so tapes can be used while driving or exercising. Ideal for the business traveler, tourist, or as a refresher course.

Romanian: Learn to Speak & Understand Romanian with Pimsleur Language Program. unabr. ed. Pimsleur Staff & Pimsleur. (Running Time: 8 hrs. 0 mins. 0 sec.). (Conversational Ser.). (ENG.). 2008. audio compact disk 49.95 (978-0-7435-6622-3(X), Pimsleur) Pub: S&S Audio. Dist(s): S and S Inc

Romanian: Learn to Speak & Understand Romanian with Pimsleur Language Programs. Pimsleur Staff & Pimsleur. (Running Time: 500 hrs. 0 mins. NaN sec.). (Compact Ser.). (ENG.). 2003. audio compact disk 115.00 (978-0-7435-0021-0(0), Pimsleur) Pub: S&S Audio. Dist(s): S and S Inc

Romanian: Learn to Speak & Understand Romanian with Pimsleur Language Programs. unabr. ed. Pimsleur. (Running Time: 16 hrs. 0 mins. 0 sec.). (Comprehensive Ser.). (ENG.). 2008. audio compact disk 345.00 (978-0-7435-6623-0(8), Pimsleur) Pub: S&S Audio. Dist(s): S and S Inc

Romanian: Learn to Speak & Understand Romanian with Pimsleur Language Programs. unabr. ed. Pimsleur Staff. (Running Time: 5 hrs. 0 mins. 0 sec.). (Basic Ser.). (ENG.). 2008. audio compact disk 24.95 (978-0-7435-6621-6(1), Pimsleur) Pub: S&S Audio. Dist(s): S and S Inc

Romanian Bible. Contrib. by Christian Duplications International Staff. 12 cass. (Running Time: 12 hrs.). (RUM.). 1991. 39.98 Set. (978-7-902033-57-2(X)) Chrstn Dup Intl.

Romanian Bible - New Testament: Cornilescu Version. Read by Alexandru Sorin Farc. 1994. 39.97 (978-1-58968-055-5(3)) Chrstn Dup Intl.

Romanian Bible - Old Testament: Cornilescu Version. Read by Alexandru Sorin Farc. 1994. 119.97 (978-1-58968-056-2(1)) Chrstn Dup Intl.

Romanian Folk Music. 1 cass. (Running Time: 1 hr.). 1994. 12.95 (978-0-88432-356-3(0), C11146) J Norton Pubs.

Romanian New Testament. Narrated by Alexandru S. Farc. 15 cass. (Running Time: 15 hrs.). 39.98 (7101A) Chrstn Dup Intl.

Romanian Old Testament. Contrib. by A. Farc. 48 cass. (Running Time: 72 hrs.). (RUM.). 1994. 119.98 (978-7-902033-50-3(2)) Chrstn Dup Intl.
Bible.

Romanism & the Westminster Confession. James Bordwine. 1 cass. (Running Time: 1 hr.). (Conference on Christianity & Roman Catholicism Ser.: No. 9). 5.00 Trinity Found.

Romanism in Romans. Scott Hahn. 13 cass. (Running Time: 13 hrs.). 1995. 59.95 (5145-C) Ignatius Pr.
In one of his most fascinating tape series, Hahn invites you to a detailed chapter by chapter study of the Book of Romans - perhaps the single most disputed Scriptural book dividing Catholics & Protestants. Hahn shows how many Protestants overlook the explicitly Catholic aspects of the Book of Romans & dramatically misinterpret what Paul said about justification by faith.

Romano-Ward Syndrome - A Bibliography & Dictionary for Physicians, Patients, & Genome Researchers. Compiled by Icon Group International, Inc. Staff. 2007. ring bd. 28.95 (978-0-497-11288-2(4)) Icon Grp.

Romanov Bride. unabr. ed. Robert Alexander. Read by Stefan Rudnicki & Gabrielle De Cuir. (Running Time: 34200 sec.). 2008. 29.95 (978-1-4332-1402-8(4)); 59.95 (978-1-4332-1400-4(8)); audio compact disk 29.95 (978-1-4332-1404-2(0)); audio compact disk & audio compact disk 29.95 (978-1-4332-1403-5(2)); audio compact disk & audio compact disk 80.00 (978-1-4332-1401-1(6)) Blckstn Audio.

Romanov Prophecy. abr. ed. Steve Berry. Read by L. J. Ganser. 5 CDs. (Running Time: 20700 sec.). (ENG.). 2006. audio compact disk 14.99 (978-0-7393-2085-3(8)) Pub: Random Audio Pubg. Dist(s): Random

Romanov Ransom. unabr. ed. Anne A. Thompson. Read by Wanda McCaddon. 8 cass. (Running Time: 12 hrs.). 1983. 64.00 (978-0-7366-0597-7(5), 1564) Books on Tape.
Ward Grant is a hard-luck CIA hand, bad enough to be in East Germany, worse to have his cover blown, but unthinkable to be caught & shipped to Lubyanka for interrogation. Even as American officials demand Grant's release, Russian agents announce the price: a dozen long-vanished jeweled Faberge Easter eggs made for Czar Nicholas. Enter Henryk Kessel, CIA ace, who skillfully manipulates KGB, Russian emigres, & art dealers in a high-stakes gamble to keep Lubyanka from becoming Grant's tomb.

Romanovs: The Final Chapter. unabr. collector's ed. Robert K. Massie. Read by Geoffrey Howard. 7 cass. (Running Time: 10 hrs. 30 mins.). 1998. 56.00 (978-0-7366-4098-5(3), 4603) Books on Tape.
This non-fiction account follows scientific attempts to identify the skeletons of Russia's royal family.

Romans. Chuck Missler. 24 audio CDs. (Running Time: 24 hours aprox). (Chuck Missler Commentaries). 2007. audio compact disk 89.95 (978-1-57821-359-7(2)) Koinonia Hse.
The Grace of God Revealed: His righteousness, Our iniquity and His Remedy through grace. The book of Romans, Paul's definitive teaching on Christian doctrine, is addressed to the saints - to believers. It is regarded by many as the most comprehensive and profound book in the New Testament. This book will delight the greatest logician, hold the attention of the wisest of men, and bring the most prideful soul to tears of repentance at the feet of the Savior.

Romans. Michael Pearl. (ENG.). 2007. (978-1-934794-26-5(0)) No Greater Joy.

Romans, Pt. 1. (LifeLight Ser.). 2001. audio compact disk 15.00 (978-0-570-07870-8(9), 20-3336) Concordia.

Romans, Pt. 2. (LifeLight Ser.). 2001. audio compact disk 15.00 (978-0-570-07886-9(5), 20-3342) Concordia.

Romans, A Courtroom Drama. Tom Westwood. 2008. audio compact disk 42.95 (978-1-4276-2942-5(0)) AardGP.

Romans Completed Pt. 1: The Destiny of Israel & the Church (Romans, Chapters 9-11) Derek Prince. 4 cass. 1990. 19.95 (I-RP3) Derek Prince.
We can never fully appreciate our place in God's family until we understand His dealings with Israel. This systematic study of Romans 9-11 uncovers a mystery long ignored by the Church.

Romans Completed Pt. 2: Walking Out Your Faith under Pressure (Romans, Chapters 12-16) Derek Prince. 4 cass. 1990. 19.95 (I-RP4) Derek Prince.
Chapters 12-16 of the book of Romans are the "nitty-gritty" down-to-earth truths on how to live what you believe. They are nothing less than the key to survival!.

Romans I. 1 cass. (Running Time: 1 hr.). (LifeLight Bible Studies: Course 5). 13.95 (20-2265) Concordia.

Romans II. 1 cass. (Running Time: 1 hr.). (LifeLight Bible Studies: Course 6). 13.95 (20-2270) Concordia.

Romans One to Five, Album 1. Derek Prince. 6 cass. (Running Time: 60 min.). (Roman Pilgrimage Ser.). 29.95 (A-RP1) Derek Prince.

Romans Q & A Dr. Young & Ben Young. Ed Young. 1997. 4.95 (978-0-7417-2145-7(7), 1145) Win Walk.

Romans Six to Eight, Album 2. Derek Prince. 6 cass. (Running Time: 6 hrs.). (Roman Pilgrimage Ser.). 29.95 (A-RP2) Derek Prince.

Romantic Addictions/Perceptions vs. Behavior. Marianne Williamson. Read by Marianne Williamson. 1 cass. (Running Time: 90 mins.). (Lectures on a Course in Miracles). 1999. 10.00 (978-1-56170-261-9(7), M764) Hay House.

Romantic Brass. Perf. by Empire Brass Quintet. 1 cass. (Running Time: 1 hr.). 7.98 (TA 30301); audio compact disk 12.78 (TA 80301) NewSound.

Romantic Era. Abr. by iSummaries Staff. 2007. audio compact disk 39.95 (978-1-934488-28-7(3)) L England.

Romantic Impressions, Bks. 1 & 3. Scott Price & Martha Mier. 1 CD. (Running Time: 1 hr. 30 mins.). (ENG.). 2000. audio compact disk 10.95 (978-0-7390-1720-3(9), 16458) Alfred Pub.

Romantic Journey. Nancy Buckingham. Read by Katherine Hunt. 4 cass. (Running Time: 4 hrs.). 1999. 44.95 (65387) Pub: Soundings Ltd GBR. Dist(s): ISIS Pub

Romantic Journey. abr. ed. Nancy Buckingham. Read by Katherine Hunt. 4 cass. (Running Time: 6 hrs.). 2001. 44.95 (978-1-85496-538-7(7), 65387) Pub: UlverLrgPrint GBR. Dist(s): Ulverscroft US

Romantic Love - Boon or Menace? Albert Ellis. 1 cass. (Running Time: 47 min.). 9.95 (C021) Inst Rational-Emotive.
Provides a comprehensive list of the pros & cons of romantic love, & shows you how to better achieve it (along with other kinds of love); & how to be happy - with or without romance!.

Romantic Love & Sexuality. Nathaniel Branden. 6 cass. (Running Time: 6 hrs.). 49.50 (978-0-88432-188-0(6), S00865) J Norton Pubs.
In love & want to stay that way? Want to establish a new romantic relationship? Exactly waht is romantic love anyhow & why is it so difficult to achieve? Branden's penetrating analysis of romantic love helps to provide answers to these questions & much more.

Romantic Love & Sexuality CD Set. Nathaniel Branden. 11 CDs. (Running Time: 9 hrs.). 2005. audio compact disk 49.50 (978-1-57970-267-0(8), S00865D, Audio-For) J Norton Pubs.
In love and want to stay that way? Or want to establish a new romantic relationship? Exactly what is romantic love anyhow, and why is it so difficult to achieve? And once achieved, why is it as difficult to sustain? Nathaniel Branden's penetrating analysis of romantic love helps provide answers to these and other questions. You will share his insights into such subjects as the evolution of romantic love, healthy versus neurotic love, love and sex, goals of a relationship, dealing with emotional repression, communicating dissatisfactions, and the concept of marriage.

Romantic Love, Bodily Sex & Freedom. Peter Breggin. 1 cass. (Running Time: 51 min.). 10.95 (979) J Norton Pubs.

Romantic Manifesto: A Philosophy of Literature. unabr. ed. Ayn Rand. Read by Bernadette Dunne. (Running Time: 7.5 hrs. 0 mins.). 2008. 29.95 (978-1-4332-2673-1(1)); 54.95 (978-1-4332-2669-4(3)); audio compact disk 60.00 (978-1-4332-2670-0(7)) Blckstn Audio.

***Romantic Manifesto: A Philosophy of Literature.** unabr. ed. Ayn Rand. Read by Bernadette Dunne. (Running Time: 7 hrs. 15 mins.). 2010. audio compact disk 19.95 (978-1-4332-2672-4(3)) Blckstn Audio.

Romantic Piano Anthology. Ed. by Nils Franke. Created by Hal Leonard Corporation Staff. 2008. pap. bk. 12.95 (978-1-902455-92-1(4), 1902455924) Pub: Schott Music Corp. Dist(s): H Leonard

Romantic Poets. Stephen Bygrave. 1997. 41.95 (978-0-415-14662-3(3)) Pub: Routledge. Dist(s): Taylor and Fran

Romantic Poets. unabr. ed. William Blake. (Running Time: 10 hrs.). (ENG.). 2005. audio compact disk 29.95 (978-1-56511-986-4(X), 156511986X) Pub: Penguin-HghBrdg. Dist(s): Penguin Grp USA

Romantic Poets: Astrobiography. Robert Powell. 1 cass. (Running Time: 1 hr.). 8.95 (579) Am Fed Astrologers.
Studied in light of Hermetic Astrology.

Romantic Raga. Music by Amjad A. Khan et al. 1 cass. (Running Time: 1 hr.). 1995. (A95031); audio compact disk (CD A95031) Multi-Cultural Bks.

Romantic Raga, Vol. 1. Music by Hariprasad Chaurasia et al. 1 cass. (Running Time: 1 hr.). 1994. (A94009); audio compact disk (CD A94009) Multi-Cultural Bks.

Romantic Raga, Vol. 2. Music by Bismillah Khan et al. 1 cass. (Running Time: 1 hr.). 1994. (A94010) Multi-Cultural Bks.

Romantic Relationships. Marianne Williamson. 4 cass. (Running Time: 4 hrs.). 1997. 30.00 (978-1-56170-273-2(0), M776) Hay House.
Lectures based on "A Course in Miracles" includes Tape 1: "Romantic Tyranny; More on Relationships"; Tape 2: "Romance: Releasing Our Stuff; When Form Changes"; Tape 3: "Obessive Relationships; I Need Do Nothing"; & Tape 4: "Freedom in Romance; Release in Relationships".

Romantic Relationships. Marianne Williamson. 4 CDs. 2004. audio compact disk 23.95 (978-1-4019-0400-5(9)) Hay House.

Romantic Round-Ups. unabr. ed. Contrib. by Susan Musleh. 1 cass. (Running Time: 3 min.). (Susan's Romantic Adventures - A Secret Admirer's Kit Ser.). (C). 1998. 24.95 (978-1-893494-03-9(9), RR-400) Susans Romantic Adv.

Romantic Tyranny/Honest Emotion. Marianne Williamson. Read by Marianne Williamson. 1 cass. (Running Time: 90 mins.). (Lectures on a Course in Miracles). 1999. 10.00 (978-1-56170-262-6(5), M765) Hay House.

Romanticism, Naturalism & the Novels of Ayn Rand. Nathaniel Branden. Read by Nathaniel Branden. 1 cass. (Running Time: 2 hrs.). 18.00 (577-578) J Norton Pubs.
These tapes deal with Rand's literary method. Branden discusses naturalism & fatalism; romanticism & fatalism; romanticism & free will as they exist in her works.

Romanticism, Naturalism & the Novels of Ayn Rand, Pt. I. Nathaniel Branden. 1 cass. (Running Time: 1 hr. 4 min.). (Basic Principles of Objectivism Ser.). 11.95 (577) J Norton Pubs.
Naturalism & fatalism; Romaticism & fatalism; Romanticism & free will; The literary method of Ayn Rand.

Romanticism, Naturalism & the Novels of Ayn Rand, Pt. II. Nathaniel Branden. 1 cass. (Running Time: 56 min.). (Basic Principles of Objectivism Ser.). 10.95 (578) J Norton Pubs.

Romany & Raq. George Bramwell Evens. Read by Terry Waite. 4 cass. (Running Time: 4 hrs. 30 mins.). (Soundings Ser.). (J). 2004. 44.95 (978-1-84283-505-0(X)) Pub: ISIS Lrg Prnt GBR. Dist(s): Ulverscroft US

Romany in the Country. unabr. ed. George Bramwell Evens. Read by Terry Waite. 4 cass. (Running Time: 5 hrs.). (Sound Ser.). (J). 2003. 44.95 (978-1-84283-297-4(2)) Pub: ISIS Lrg Prnt GBR. Dist(s): Ulverscroft US

Romanza. Perf. by Andrea Bocelli. 1 cass. (Running Time: 1 hr.). 8.78 (PHI 539207); audio compact disk 13.58 CD Jewel box. (PHI 539207) NewSound.
Collection of soul-stirring, original Italian love songs.

Romanza (A Spanish Romance) Arranged by Aaron Stang. (Warner Bros. Publications 21st Century Guitar Ensemble Ser.). (ENG.). 2002. audio compact disk 19.95 (978-0-7579-9558-3(6), Warner Bro) Alfred Pub.

Rome: The Biography of a City. unabr. ed. Christopher Hibbert. Read by Grover Gardner. 6 cass. (Running Time: 9 hrs.). (Cassette Library). 1987. 44.98 (978-0-8072-3040-4(5), CXL529CX, Listening Lib) Random Audio Pubg.
The author charts an unforgettable journey from Rome's mythical inception through today.

Rome & the Barbarians, I-III. Instructed by Kenneth Harl. 18 cass. (Running Time: 18 hrs.). bk. 79.95 (978-1-56585-899-2(9), 3460) Teaching Co.

Rome & the Barbarians, I-III. Instructed by Kenneth Harl. 18 CDs. (Running Time: 18 hrs.). 2004. bk. 99.95 (978-1-56585-901-2(4), 3460) Teaching Co.

Rome Audio Guide. unabr. ed. Olivier Maisonneuve & Marlène Duroux. Read by Kate Gibbens & Ron Morris. (YA). 2007. 69.99 (978-2-35569-021-1(9)) Find a World.

Rome Long Ago. Compiled by Benchmark Education Staff. 2005. audio compact disk 10.00 (978-1-4108-5511-4(2)) Benchmark Educ.

Rome on the Euphrates. unabr. collector's ed. Freya Stark. Read by Donada Peters. 10 cass. (Running Time: 15 hrs.). 1991. 80.00 (978-0-7366-1958-5(5), 2779) Books on Tape.
The history of the long frontier of the Euphrates through eight centuries of Roman warfare. When Roman legions marched into Asia Minor 200 years before Christ, their plan was to secure a buffer zone between the Mediterranean, which they virtually owned & the area beyond, which they sought to isolate rather than control.

Rome Sweet Home. Based on a book by Scott Hahn & Kimberly Hahn. 4 cass. (Running Time: 5 hrs.). 2001. 22.95 (978-1-57058-316-2(1), rc03) St Joseph Communs.
For over a decade, Scott and Kimberly Hahn have been speaking around the country?even circling the globe?sharing with thousands the story of their conversion to the Catholic Church and the truth and splendor of Catholicism.Their conversion story is fast becoming legendary, and has inspired others to reflect deeply on their own faith. Now you can listen to the complete story of this outstanding Catholic couple as they expound on the fascinating yet intimate details of their personal pilgrimage into the fullness of the Faith. Rome Sweet Home recounts the Hahn?s incredible journey into the Catholic Church. It will deepen your own understanding and appreciation of the Faith.

Rome Tapes. Narrated by Juliet Stevenson. 2 cass. (Running Time: 2 hrs.). 1998. 16.95 Set, incl. map. (978-1-900652-00-1(5)) Capital VA.
Travel back in time to experience the sights, sounds & events of Rome's past at sixteen historic sites. In Rome, be a spectator in the colosseum as gladiators fight to the death, hear Puccini's Tosca plunge to her death at Castel Sant'Angelo, meet Michelangelo planning the building of St. Peters.

***Rome Wasn't Burnt in a Day.** abr. ed. Joe Scarborough. Read by Joe Scarborough. (ENG.). 2004. (978-0-06-078651-9(5), Harper Audio) HarperCollins Pubs.

Rome Wasn't Burnt in a Day: The Real Deal on How Politicians, Bureaucrats, & Other Washington Barbarians Are Bankrupting America. abr. ed. Joe Scarborough. 2004. audio compact disk 29.95 (978-0-06-075147-0(9)) HarperCollins Pubs.

Rome 1960: The Olympics That Changed the World. unabr. ed. David Maraniss. Narrated by L. J. Ganser. (Running Time: 16 hrs. 15 mins.). 2008. 61.75 (978-1-4361-6521-1(0)); audio compact disk 123.75 (978-1-4361-2373-0(9)) Recorded Bks.

Rome '44. unabr. ed. Raleigh Trevelyan. Read by David Case. 11 cass. (Running Time: 16 hrs. 30 min.). 1999. 88.00 (978-0-7366-4285-9(4), 4783) Books on Tape.
The 1944 Allied drive for the liberation of Rome, from the January landings at Anzio to the entrance into the Holy City on June 5, is one of the great epics of World War II. Now in a masterwork of narrative history, the full story is set down by that rarest of all authorities, a distinguished historian who was also a participant in the events.

Romeo & Juliet see Shakespeare

Romeo & Juliet. (Audio BookNotes Guide). (C). 2002. audio compact disk 9.95 (978-1-929011-07-0(5)) Scholarly Audio.

Romeo & Juliet. William Shakespeare. Ed. by Jerry Stemach. Retold by Gail Portnuff Venable. Narrated by Nick Sandys. 2000. audio compact disk 200.00 (978-1-58702-482-5(9)) D Johnston Inc.

Romeo & Juliet. William Shakespeare. Perf. by Michael Sheen & Kate Beckinsale. 3 cass. (Running Time: 2 hrs. 51 mins.). Dramatization. (Plays of William Shakespeare Ser.). 1997. 17.98 (978-962-634-625-9(6), NA312514, Naxos AudioBooks); audio compact disk 22.98 (978-962-634-125-4(4), NA312512, Naxos AudioBooks) Naxos.
The "star-crossed" lovers of this great romantic tragedy, fascinates audiences year after year. This version uses the text of The New Cambridge Shakespeare, used by the Royal Shakespeare Company and educational institutions across the world.

Romeo & Juliet. William Shakespeare. Perf. by Swan Theatre Players. 1 cass. (Running Time: 1 hr.). Dramatization. 10.95 (SAC 812) Spoken Arts.

Romeo & Juliet. William Shakespeare & Cedric Watts. 2001. audio compact disk 21.45 (978-1-903342-16-9(3)) Wordsworth Educ GBR.

Romeo & Juliet. Jerry Stemach. William Shakespeare. (Classic Literature Ser.). 2000. audio compact disk 18.95 (978-1-4105-0152-3(3)) D Johnston Inc.

Romeo & Juliet. Prod. by Barbara Worthy. Hosted by William Shakespeare. 3 CDs. (Running Time: 3 hrs.). 2005. audio compact disk 24.95 (978-0-660-19037-2(0)) Pub: Canadian Broadcasting CAN. Dist(s): Georgetown Term
Originally a tragedy by William Shakespeare published in quarto in 1957, the characters of Romeo and Juliet have been depicted in literature, music, dance, and theatre. The appeal of the young hero and heroine - whose families the Montagues and Capulet, respectively, are implacable enemies -is such that they have become, to the popular imagination, the representative type of star-crossed lovers.

Romeo & Juliet. abr. ed. William Shakespeare. Ed. by Jerry Stemach et al. Illus. by Bob Stotts. Narrated by Nick Sandys. Contrib. by Ted S. Hasselbring. 1 cass. (Running Time: 1 hr.). (Start-to-Finish Books). (J). 2000. 7.00 (978-1-58702-322-4(9), F25K2) D Johnston Inc.
This may be the most famous love story in the world. With its timeless themes of young love and teenage rebellion, the story holds as much relevance for people today as it did for people in shakespeare's time. In recent times, it has been reinterpreted in many screen adaptations, and also as the hit Broadway musical, West Side Story. In spite of their warning families, Romeo Montague and Juliet Capulet fall in love. Their love is an act of rebellion with tragedy.

***Romeo & Juliet.** abr. ed. William Shakespeare. Read by Claire Bloom & Albert Finney. (ENG.). 2003. (978-0-06-074325-3(5), Caedmon) HarperCollins Pubs.

***Romeo & Juliet.** abr. ed. William Shakespeare. Read by Claire Bloom & Albert Finney. (ENG.). 2004. (978-0-06-081471-7(3), Caedmon) HarperCollins Pubs.

Romeo & Juliet. unabr. ed. William Shakespeare. Read by Flo Gibson. 3 cass. (Running Time: 4 hrs.). 1992. 16.95 (978-1-55685-235-0(5)) Audio Bk Con.
The deadly feud between the Montagues & the Capulets forces Romeo & Juliet to wed in secret. After a fatal street quarrel, Romeo is banished from Verona & Juliet takes a sleeping potion to bring on the semblance of death to prevent her marriage to Paris. There are tragic consequences for these ill-starred lovers.

Romeo & Juliet. unabr. ed. William Shakespeare. Narrated by Joseph Fiennes et al. (Arkangel Shakespeare Ser.). (ENG.). 2005. audio compact disk 24.95 (978-1-932219-30-2(7)) Pub: AudioGO. Dist(s): Perseus Dist
The noble Veronese houses of Montague and Capulet are locked in a bitter feud. When Romeo, a Montague, and Juliet, a Capulet, fall in love, they are swept up in a series of violent events and cruel twists of fortune. Their secret meetings propel them inexorably to a tragic fate. A true masterpiece, this unforgettable work contains some of the Bard's most beautiful poetry. Performed by Joseph Fiennes, Maria Miles, and the Arkangel cast.

Romeo & Juliet. unabr. ed. William Shakespeare. Perf. by Claire Bloom & Albert Finney. 2 cass. (Running Time: 3 hrs.). Dramatization. 17.95 (H134) Blckstn Audio.
Simple but dramatic cautionary tale about the blindness that both love & hate engender.

Romeo & Juliet. unabr. ed. William Shakespeare. Read by Full Ensemble Cast. (YA). 2006. 39.99 (978-1-59895-341-1(9)) Find a World.

Romeo & Juliet. unabr. ed. William Shakespeare. Read by Audio Partners Staff. 2 cass. (Running Time: 3 hrs. 3 mins.). 2004. 17.95 (978-1-932219-70-8(6), Atlntc Mnthly) Pub: Grove-Atltic. Dist(s): PerseuPGW
Romeo and Juliet are desperately in love, but their families are locked in a bitter feud. Their secret meetings propel them inexorably to a tragic fate. A true masterpiece, this unforgettable work contains some of the Bard's most beautiful poetry. Performed by Joseph Fiennes, Maria Miles, and the Arkangel cast.

Romeo & Juliet. unabr. ed. William Shakespeare. Perf. by Claire Bloom & Albert Finney. 2 cass. (Running Time: 2 hrs.). Dramatization. 2000. 28.00 (21519E5); 40.20 (40751E5) Recorded Bks.

Romeo & Juliet, Set. unabr. ed. William Shakespeare. Contrib. by Naxos Audiobooks Staff. 3 CDs. (Running Time: 2 hrs. 51 mins.). (New Cambridge Shakespeare Audio Ser.). (ENG.). 1997. audio compact disk 28.99 (978-0-521-62562-3(9)) Cambridge U Pr.

Romeo & Juliet, Set. unabr. ed. William Shakespeare. 2 cass. (Running Time: 2 hrs.). 1999. 18.00 (FS9-51063) Highsmith.

Romeo & Juliet, Vol. 2. William Shakespeare. Ed. by Jerry Stemach et al. Illus. by Bob Stotts. Narrated by Nick Sandys. Contrib. by Ted S. Hasselbring. (Start-to-Finish Books). 2000. 35.00 (978-1-58702-483-2(7)) D Johnston Inc.

Romeo & Juliet, Vol. 2. William Shakespeare. Ed. by Jerry Stemach et al. Illus. by Bob Stotts. Narrated by Nick Sandys. Contrib. by Ted S. Hasselbring. (Start-to-Finish Books). 2002. 100.00 (978-1-58702-964-6(2)) D Johnston Inc.

Romeo & Juliet: As Told by Jim Weiss. Short Stories. Retold by Jim Weiss. 1 CD. (Running Time: 62 mins.). Dramatization. (Storyteller's Version Ser.: 037). (J). 2005. 14.95 (978-1-882513-85-7(1), 1124-037) Greathall Prods.

Romeo & Juliet: BBC Radio. unabr. ed. William Shakespeare. Read by Kenneth Branagh. 3 CDs. (Running Time: 3 hrs. 36 mins.). 2001. audio compact disk 25.20 Books on Tape.
The renowned Renaissance Theatre Company presents an uncut performance of the most romantic tragedy of all time.

***Romeo & Juliet & Vampires.** unabr. ed. William Shakespeare. Read by Stina Nielsen. (ENG.). 2010. (978-0-06-201206-7(1)); (978-0-06-204138-8(X)) HarperCollins Pubs.

Romeo & Juliet-Audio Book CD: Shakespeare Series-Level 2. abr. ed. William Shakespeare. (Easy Reading Shakespeare Ser.). (ENG.). (J). 2008. audio compact disk 12.95 (978-1-55576-665-8(X)) EDCON Pubng.

Romeo & Juliet, the 1-Hour Guidebook: An Illustrated Guidebook Featuring the Play. 2004. per. 21.95 (978-0-9749506-3-1(7)) Bermond Pr.

Romeo & Juliet Together (and Alive!) at Last. unabr. ed. Avi. Narrated by Jeff Woodman. 2 pieces. (Running Time: 2 hrs. 30 mins.). (gr. 5 up). 1997. 19.00 (978-0-7887-1589-1(5), 95201E7) Recorded Bks.
Take two love-struck but shy eighth graders, cast them in the lead roles of a school production & wait for the scene where they have to kiss each other.

Romewalks. unabr. ed. Anya Shetherly. Prod. by Carol Shapiro. Narrated by Maria Tucci. 2 cass. (Running Time: 3 hrs.). 1999. 18.00 (978-1-890489-03-8(4)) Pub: Sound Trvl FRA. Dist(s): Penton Overseas
With this audio guide you can keep your eyes on some of the most remarkable cultural treasures & extraordinary monuments of Western Civilization while you listen to the history, scandal & triumphs of this magnificent city. Maps included.

Romiette & Julio. unabr. ed. 7 cass. (Running Time: 9 hrs. 30 mins.). 2003. 61.00 (978-1-4025-0891-2(3)) Recorded Bks.

Rommel: Gunner Who? unabr. ed. Spike Milligan. Read by Spike Milligan. 6 cass. (Running Time: 7 hrs.). 1993. 54.95 (978-1-85089-829-0(4), 88061) Pub: ISIS Audio GBR. Dist(s): Ulverscroft US
Britain's looniest war hero & his comrades forge into Tunis, cocksure & carefree. This is the second book in an autobiographical series.

Rommel Papers, Pt. 1. unabr. ed. Basil H. Liddell-Hart. Read by Wolfram Kandinsky. 9 cass. (Running Time: 13 hrs. 30 min.). 1978. 72.00 (978-0-7366-0083-5(3), 1093-A) Books on Tape.
World War II produced military heroes by the drove, but none more richly deserved the title than Field Marshall Erwin Rommel, "the Desert Fox." His Career reached from the sands of Africa to Normandy's beaches. His audacious campaigns drove his staff to despair & stupefied the opposition.

Rommel Papers, Pt. 2. Basil H. Liddell-Hart. Read by Wolfram Kandinsky. 10 cass. (Running Time: 15 hrs.). 1978. 80.00 (1093-B) Books on Tape.

Rommel Plot, unabr. ed. John Tarrant & Clive Egleton. Narrated by Alexander Spencer. 6 cass. (Running Time: 8 hrs.). 1981. 51.00 (978-1-55690-448-6(7), 81250E7) Recorded Bks.
A special agent is dispatched on a solo mission to assassinate Germany's top general, but a sudden change of events puts him beyond everyone's control.

Romola. unabr. ed. George Eliot. Read by Flo Gibson. 15 cass. (Running Time: 21 hrs. 30 mins.). 1997. 43.95 (978-1-55685-453-8(6), 453-6) Audio Bk Con.
An historical novel about a valiant Florentine woman in the 15th century who marries a hedonistic Greek. She later falls under the influence of Savonarola, the Italian reformist, who shows her the way to peace through faith & caring for the needy. The plague, vengeance, the Inquisition, bigamy, torture & execution are part of this great saga.

Romola, unabr. ed. George Eliot. Read by Nadia May. 16 cass. (Running Time: 23 hrs. 30 mins.). 1999. 99.95 (978-0-7861-1287-6(5), 2186) Blckstn Audio.
Recreation of the upheavals of fifteenth-century Florence: the time of the expulsion of the Medici, the invasion by Charles VIII of France & the ascendancy & fall of Savonarola. Living in the city-state at this time is the noble & courageous Romola, who finds herself increasingly disillusioned by Savonarola's career & repelled by her unscrupulous & self-indulgent husband, Tito Melema.

Romola. unabr. ed. George Eliot. Read by Nadia May. (Running Time: 79200 sec.). 2008. audio compact disk 44.95 (978-0-7861-6219-2(8)); audio compact disk & audio compact disk 120.00 (978-0-7861-6218-5(X)) Blckstn Audio.

Rompiendo el Silencio: Relatos de Nuevas Escritoras Colombianas. 3 cass. (Running Time: 4 hrs 30 min.). (SPA.). 29.75 (978-1-4025-6318-8(3)) Recorded Bks.

Rompiendo los Limites. unabr. ed. Edwin Santiago. (SPA.). 2006. audio compact disk 14.99 (978-0-8297-4870-3(9)) Pub: Vida Pubs. Dist(s): Zondervan

Romping. 1 cass. (Running Time: 51 min.). (J). (ps-3). 1985. 10.00 (978-1-879846-06-7(3)) Cloudstone NY.
A joyous collection of silly & touching stories for ages 2 to 6 & parents who drive car pools. Parents' Choice.

Romping. 2nd unabr. ed. Arnold Lobel & M. B. Goffstein. Read by Diane Wolkstein. Music by Shirley Keller. 1 CD. (Running Time: 1 hr.). (J). (gr. k-4). 2001. audio compact disk 15.00 (978-1-879846-15-9(2)) Cloudstone NY.
Hannukah at the time of the year when there is the least amount of outer light. At the time, when the inner light of faith becomes the outer light of action, miracles happen.

Romy's Walk. Peggy Stoks. Narrated by Christina Moore. 6 cass. (Running Time: 8 hrs. 30 mins.). (Abounding Love Ser.: Vol. 2). 54.00 (978-0-7887-9021-8(8)) Recorded Bks.

Ron Brown: Future of the Democrats. 1 cass. (Running Time: 60 min.). 1989. 11.95 (K0740B090, HarperThor) HarpC GBR.

Ron Jeremy: The Hardest (Working) Man in Show Business. Ron Jeremy. 2007. audio compact disk 29.95 (978-0-06-123021-9(9)) HarperCollins Pubs.

Ronald Morgan Goes to Camp. unabr. ed. Patricia Reilly Giff. Read by Jeff Woodman. 1 cass. (Running Time: 30 mins.). (J). 1999. 80.70 (978-0-7887-3689-6(2), 46993) Recorded Bks.
When summer comes & there's nothing to do, Ronald Morgan's friends want him to go to camp with them. But Ronald doesn't want to go. His friends are excited about all the medals they will win, but poor Ronald is afraid he isn't good enough to win a medal.

Ronald Morgan Goes to Camp. unabr. ed. Patricia Reilly Giff. Narrated by Jeff Woodman. 1 cass. (Running Time: 15 mins.). (gr. k up). 2000. 10.00 (978-0-7887-3622-3(1), 95978E7) Recorded Bks.

Ronald Morgan Goes to Camp. unabr. ed. Patricia Reilly Giff. Read by Jeff Woodman. 1 cass. (Running Time: 30 mins.). (J). 2000. pap. bk. & stu. ed. 23.24 (978-0-7887-3660-5(4), 41026X4) Recorded Bks.

Ronald Reagan. unabr. collector's ed. Dinesh D'Souza. Read by Michael Prichard. 9 cass. (Running Time: 13 hrs. 30 min.). 1998. 72.00 (978-0-7366-4089-3(4), 4597) Books on Tape.
This controversial appraisal of Ronald Reagan argues for his enduring political legacy.

Ronald Reagan: Fate, Freedom & the Making of History. John P. Diggins. Read by Ray Porter. (Running Time: 61200 sec.). 2007. 89.95 (978-0-7861-4818-9(7)); audio compact disk 108.00 (978-0-7861-6184-3(1)) Blckstn Audio.

Ronald Reagan: Fate, Freedom & the Making of History. unabr. ed. John P. Diggins. Read by Ray Porter. (Running Time: 61200 sec.). 2007. 32.95 (978-0-7861-4817-2(9)); audio compact disk 34.95 (978-0-7861-6183-6(3)); audio compact disk 44.95 (978-0-7861-7169-9(3)) Blckstn Audio.

Ronald Reagan: State Governorship see Buckley's Firing Line

Ronald Reagan & Margaret Thatcher: A Political Marriage. unabr. ed. Nicholas Wapshott. Read by Simon Vance. (YA). 2008. 59.99 (978-1-60514-966-0(7)) Find a World.

Ronald Reagan & Margaret Thatcher: A Political Marriage. unabr. ed. Nicholas Wapshott. Narrated by Simon Vance. (Running Time: 11 hrs. 0

mins. 0 sec.). (ENG.). 2007. audio compact disk 24.99 (978-1-4001-5590-3(8)) Pub: Tantor Media. Dist(s): IngramPubServ

Ronald Reagan & Margaret Thatcher: A Political Marriage. unabr. ed. Nicholas Wapshott. Read by Simon Vance. (Running Time: 11 hrs. 0 mins. 0 sec.). (ENG.). 2007. audio compact disk 34.99 (978-1-4001-0590-8(0)); audio compact disk 69.99 (978-1-4001-3590-5(7)) Pub: Tantor Media. Dist(s): IngramPubServ

Ronald Reagan: the Great Speeches: Volume 2. abr. ed. Ronald Reagan. 1 CD. (Running Time: 3938 sec.). (Ronald Reagan: the Great Speeches Ser.). 1999. audio compact disk 15.98 (978-1-885959-23-2(0), JRCD 7050) Jerden Recs.
More speeches from "The Great Communicator." Features highlights of famous speeches, including "Star Wars," Candidacy for Re-Election, "Iran-Contra Controversy," "Disarmament" & "Farewell to the Nation.".

Ronald Reagan's Greatest Laughs. 2 cass. (Running Time: 3 hrs.). 2003. 24.95 (978-0-9716807-8-4(7)); audio compact disk 24.95 (978-0-9716807-7-7(9)) NewsMax Media.

Rond Point: Une Perspective Actionnelle. Catherine Flumian et al. 2006. audio compact disk 20.60 (978-0-13-225450-2(6)) Pearson Educ CAN CAN.

Rond Point Workbook/Lab Manual: Edition Nord-Americaine. Catherine Flumian et al. 2006. audio compact disk 27.60 (978-0-13-232675-9(2)) Pearson Educ CAN CAN.

Ronda del Alfabeto. 1 cass. (Running Time: 1 hr.). cass. & flmstrp 9.00 (Natl Textbk Co) M-H Contemporary.

Ronicky Doone. unabr. ed. Max Brand. Read by Roger Dressler. (Running Time: 7 hrs.). (Doone Ser.). 2007. 39.25 (978-1-4233-3490-3(6), 9781423334903, BADLE); 24.95 (978-1-4233-3489-7(2), 9781423334897, BAD); audio compact disk 24.95 (978-1-4233-3487-3(6), 9781423334873, Brilliance MP3); audio compact disk 39.25 (978-1-4233-3488-0(4), 9781423334880, Brlnc Audio MP3 Lib) Brilliance Audio.

Ronicky Doone. unabr. ed. Max Brand. Read by Roger Dressler. (Running Time: 6 hrs.). (Doone Ser.). 2009. audio compact disk 19.99 (978-1-4418-0475-4(7), 9781441804754, Bril Audio CD Unabri); audio compact disk 59.97 (978-1-4418-0476-1(5), 9781441804761, BriAudCD Unabrid) Brilliance Audio.

Ronicky Doone's Reward. unabr. ed. Max Brand. Read by Roger Dressler. (Running Time: 7 hrs.). (Doone Ser.). 2007. 39.25 (978-1-4233-3514-6(7), 9781423335146, BADLE); 24.95 (978-1-4233-3513-9(9), 9781423335139, BAD) Brilliance Audio.

Ronicky Doone's Reward. unabr. ed. Max Brand. Read by Roger Dressler. (Running Time: 25200 sec.). (Doone Ser.). 2007. audio compact disk 24.95 (978-1-4233-3511-5(2), 9781423335115, Brilliance MP3); audio compact disk 39.25 (978-1-4233-3512-2(0), 9781423335122, Brlnc Audio MP3 Lib) Brilliance Audio.

Ronicky Doone's Reward. unabr. ed. Max Brand. Read by Roger Dressler. (Running Time: 8 hrs.). (Doone Ser.). 2009. audio compact disk 19.99 (978-1-4418-0481-5(1), 9781441804815, Bril Audio CD Unabri); audio compact disk 59.97 (978-1-4418-0482-2(X), 9781441804822, BriAudCD Unabrid) Brilliance Audio.

Ronicky Doone's Treasure. unabr. ed. Max Brand. Read by Roger Dressler. (Running Time: 6 hrs.). (Doone Ser.). 2007. 39.25 (978-1-4233-3526-9(0), 9781423335269, BADLE); 24.95 (978-1-4233-3525-2(2), 9781423335252, BAD) Brilliance Audio.

Ronicky Doone's Treasure. unabr. ed. Max Brand. Read by Roger Dressler. (Running Time: 21600 sec.). (Doone Ser.). 2007. audio compact disk 24.95 (978-1-4233-3523-8(6), 9781423335238, Brilliance MP3); audio compact disk 39.25 (978-1-4233-3524-5(4), 9781423335245, Brlnc Audio MP3 Lib) Brilliance Audio.

Ronicky Doone's Treasure. unabr. ed. Max Brand. Read by Roger Dressler. (Running Time: 6 hrs.). (Doone Ser.). 2009. audio compact disk 19.99 (978-1-4418-0487-7(0), 9781441804877) Brilliance Audio.

***Ronicky Doone's Treasure.** unabr. ed. Max Brand. Read by Roger Dressler. (Running Time: 6 hrs.). 2009. audio compact disk 59.97 (978-1-4418-0488-4(9), 9781441804884, BriAudCD Unabrid) Brilliance Audio.

Ronnie & Nancy: Their Path to the White House - 1911 To 1980. abr. ed. Bob Colacello. Read by Harry Chase. (ENG.). 2005. 14.98 (978-1-59483-146-1(7)) Pub: Hachet Audio. Dist(s): HachBkGrp

Ronnie & Nancy: Their Path to the White House - 1911 To 1980. abr. ed. Bob Colacello. Read by Harry Chase. (Running Time: 6 hrs.). (ENG.). 2009. 49.98 (978-1-60024-883-2(7)) Pub: Hachet Audio. Dist(s): HachBkGrp

Ronnie & Rosey. unabr. ed. Judie Angell. 1 cass. (Running Time: 1 hr.). (YA). (gr. 7 up). 1999. pap. bk. 15.98 (978-0-8072-1842-6(1), JJRH123SP, Listening Lib) Random Audio Pubg.
A story of high school intrigue that will captivate young people everywhere. Narrated word-for-word up to an exciting point in the story. When the narrator stops, listeners finish reading the story on their own.

Ronnie Wathen, Pts. I & II. unabr. ed. Read by Ronnie Wathen. 2 cass. (Running Time: 1 hr.). 1985. 10.00; 18.00 New Letters.
English born "Troubadour" Ronnie Wathen recites Irish poetry as well as his original works & plays the Irish pipes.

Rooftop Affair: II Samuel 11:1-4. Ed Young. 1986. 4.95 (978-0-7417-1537-1(6), 537) Win Walk.

Rookery Blues. abr. ed. Jon Hassler. Read by Jon Hassler. Contrib. by Chuck Dewey & George Maurer. 1 cass. (Running Time: 1 hr.). 24.95 (978-0-9650850-0-7(7), PCAB-3500) Pine Curtain.

***Rookie Dad: Thoughts on First-Time Fatherhood.** David Jacobsen. (Running Time: 3 hrs. 39 mins. 0 sec.). (ENG.). 2009. 12.99 (978-0-310-77224-8(9)) Zondervan.

Rookie of the Year. unabr. ed. Sam Harper. Read by Dan Hedaya. 1 cass. (Running Time: 1 hr. 30 min.). 1993. 12.95 (978-1-56876-008-7(6)) Soundlines Ent.
When little leaguer, Henry Rowengartner breaks his arm, he thinks his baseball career comes to a halt for good. But when his cast is removed, he finds he can throw a baseball over 100 miles an hour. The Cubs, with a last ditch effort, sign Henry to the team, in the hopes they'll win the pennant. But what they get is a far more valuable lesson.

***Room: A Novel.** unabr. ed. Emma Donoghue. Read by Ellen Archer et al. (Running Time: 11 hrs.). (ENG.). 2010. 24.98 (978-1-60788-628-0(6)) Pub: Hachet Audio. Dist(s): HachBkGrp

***Room: A Novel.** unabr. ed. Emma Donoghue. Read by Michal Friedman et al. 9 CDs. (Running Time: 11 hrs.). 2010. audio compact disk 29.98 (978-1-60788-627-3(8)) Pub: Hachet Audio. Dist(s): HachBkGrp

Room at the Top. unabr. ed. John Braine. Read by Paul McGann. 8 cass. (Running Time: 8 hrs.). 1999. 69.95 (978-0-7540-0306-9(X), CAB1729) AudioGO.

Room for Doubt? Borrower Doubt Series. Ben Young. 2000. 4.95 (978-0-7417-6202-3(1)) Win Walk.

Room Full of Mirrors. abr. unabr. ed. Charles R. Cross. Read by Lloyd James. 9 cass. (Running Time: 50400 sec.). 2006. 72.95 (978-0-7861-4541-6(2)); audio compact disk 25.95 (978-0-7861-7137-8(5)) Blckstn Audio.

Room Full of Mirrors: A Biography of Jimi Hendrix. unabr. ed. Charles R. Cross. Read by Lloyd James. (Running Time: 48600 sec.). 2006. 72.95 (978-0-7861-4707-6(5)); audio compact disk 29.95 (978-0-7861-7601-4(6)); audio compact disk 99.00 (978-0-7861-6586-5(3)) Blckstn Audio.

Room in the Inn. M. Blankenship & R. Courtney. 1994. 75.00 (978-0-7673-0685-0(6)); 11.98 (978-0-7673-0652-2(X)); audio compact disk 85.00 (978-0-7673-0716-1(X)) LifeWay Christian.

Room of My Own. Read by Donald Davis. 1 CD. (Running Time: 57 mins.). 2002. audio compact disk 14.95 (978-0-87483-689-9(1)) Pub: August Hse. Dist(s): Natl Bk Netwk
Sibling rivalry. Sometimes, a kid just isn't ready for some little squirt to come along and invade his space, his own room. So what if there's an extra ben in the room, isn't that were the stuffed animals are supposed to sleep? How could a couple of otherwise sensible parents just bring a new kid home without even consulting their very own son? Still, a younger sibling can be in need of a big brother's guidance. And a big brother, even if not so very big, can have a lot of offer, once he gets used to the idea.

Room of My Own. unabr. ed. Donald Davis. Read by Donald Davis. (J). 2007. 34.99 (978-1-60252-576-4(5)) Find a World.

Room of My Own. unabr. ed. Ann Tatlock. Narrated by Kate Forbes. 9 cass. (Running Time: 13 hrs.). 1999. 78.00 (978-0-7887-2939-3(X), 95720E7) Recorded Bks.
This charming old-fashioned story of a girl growing up during the depression will convince you that anything is possible. After she confronts hardship for the first time in a hobo village, 13-year-old Virginia Eade discovers the true source of happiness.

Room of One's Own. abr. ed. Virginia Woolf. Read by Claire Bloom. 1 cass. (Running Time: 1 hr.). (J). (gr. 9-12). 1984. 11.95 (978-0-89845-802-2(1), CPN 1718) HarperCollins Pubs.

Room of One's Own. unabr. ed. Virginia Woolf. Read by Flo Gibson. 3 cass. (Running Time: 3 hrs. 6 mins.). 2002. vinyl bd. 24.95 (978-1-55685-521-4(4)) Audio Bk Con.
With fancy, wit & logic, Virginia Woolf stresses the need of a fixed income & a room of one's own for the spiritual & intellectual freedom to become a writer.

Room of One's Own. unabr. ed. Virginia Woolf. Read by Penelope Dellaporta. 5 cass. (Running Time: 5 hrs.). 2001. 24.95 (978-0-7366-6809-5(8)) Books on Tape.
For an author to be succesful, particularly a woman, she needs her own identity... a room of her own.

Room of One's Own. unabr. collector's ed. Virginia Woolf. Read by Penelope Dellaporta. 5 cass. (Running Time: 5 hrs.). 1979. 40.00 (978-0-7366-0159-7(7), 1159) Books on Tape.
This is an investigation of the woman artist as writer. Speculating on the imaginary life of Shakespeare's equally talented sister, Woolf posits the necessity of a room of one's own for the writer to pursue her craft.

Room on Lorelei Street. unabr. ed. Mary E. Pearson. Read by Natalie Ross. (Running Time: 7 hrs.). 2010. audio compact disk 24.99 (978-1-4418-0522-5(2), 9781441805225, Bril Audio CD Unabri) Brilliance Audio.

***Room on Lorelei Street.** unabr. ed. Mary E. Pearson. Read by Natalie Ross. (Running Time: 7 hrs.). 2010. 24.99 (978-1-4418-0524-9(9), 9781441805249, Brilliance MP3); 39.97 (978-1-4418-0525-6(7), 9781441805256, Brlnc Audio MP3 Lib); 39.97 (978-1-4418-0527-0(3), 9781441805270, BADLE); 24.99 (978-1-4418-0526-3(5), 9781441805263, BAD); audio compact disk 54.97 (978-1-4418-0523-2(0), 9781441805232, BriAudCD Unabrid) Brilliance Audio.

Room One: A Mystery or Two. unabr. ed. Andrew Clements. Read by Keith Nobbs. 3 CDs. (Running Time: 3 hrs.). (J). 2006. audio compact disk 29.75 (978-1-4281-0892-9(0), C3828); 29.75 (978-1-4281-0887-5(4), 98462) Recorded Bks.
Ted Hammond loves a good mystery, and in the spring of his fifth-grade year, he's working on a big one. How can his school in the little town of Plattsford stay open next year if there are going to be only five students? Out here on the Great Plains in western Nebraska, everyone understands that if you lose the school, you lose the town. But the mystery that has Ted's full attention at the moment is about that face, the face he sees in the upper window of the Andersons' house as he rides past on his paper route. The Andersons moved away two years ago, and their old farmhouse is empty, boarded up tight. At least it's supposed to be. A shrinking school in a dying town. A face in the window of an empty house. At first these facts don't seem to be related. But Ted Hammond learns that in a very small town, there's no such thing as an isolated event. And the solution of one mystery is often the beginning of another.

Room One: A Mystery or Two. unabr. ed. Andrew Clements. Read by Keith Nobbs. (J). 2006. 11.95 (978-0-7435-6426-7(X)) Pub: S&S Audio. Dist(s): S and S Inc

Room One: A Mystery or Two. unabr. ed. Andrew Clements. Read by Keith Nobbs. 3 CDs. (Running Time: 3 hrs. 0 mins. 0 sec.). (ENG.). (J). (gr. 3-7). 2006. audio compact disk 19.95 (978-0-7435-5560-9(0)) Pub: SandS Childrens. Dist(s): S and S Inc

Room Service. unabr. ed. Beverly Brandt. (Running Time: 11 hrs. 30 mins.). 2010. 29.95 (978-1-4332-9183-8(5)); 65.95 (978-1-4332-9179-1(7)); audio compact disk 100.00 (978-1-4332-9180-7(0)) Blckstn Audio.

Room to Grow: An Appetite for Life. unabr. ed. Tracey Gold. Read by Tracey Gold. 2 cass. (Running Time: 3 hrs.). 2004. 25.00 (978-1-59007-255-4(3)) Pub: New Millenn Enter. Dist(s): PerseuPGW
Tracey Gold was well known to television audiences in the 80s as the wholesome teenage sister on the long-running series Growing Pains. She co-starred for seven years alongside Kirk Cameron as brainy sister Carol Seaver in a picture-perfect American family. A working actress since the age of 4, she was a pretty and professional young star with a limitless future. But behind the smiles Tracey was fighting the battle of her life.

Room to Move: Women's Workplace Design. 1 cass. (Running Time: 30 min.). 9.95 (B0200B090, HarperThor) HarpC GBR.

Room with a View. E. M. Forster. Read by Frederick Davidson. (Running Time: 7 hrs. 30 mins.). 1992. 27.95 (978-1-59912-397-4(5)) Iofy Corp.

Room with a View. E. M. Forster. Read by Wanda Mccaddon. (Running Time: 7 hrs. 30 mins.). 2002. 26.95 (978-1-59912-112-3(3), Audiofy Corp) Iofy Corp.

Room with a View. E. M. Forster. Narrated by Wanda McCaddon. (Running Time: 27060 sec.). (Unabridged Classics in MP3 Ser.). (ENG.). 2008. audio compact disk 24.00 (978-1-58472-451-3(X), In Aud) Sound Room.

Room with A View. E. M. Forster. Narrated by Flo Gibson. 2009. audio compact disk 27.95 (978-1-60646-116-7(8)) Audio Bk Con.

Room with a View. abr. ed. E. M. Forster. Read by Juliet Stevenson. Abr. by Katrin Williams. (Running Time: 5 hrs. 0 mins. 0 sec.). (ENG.). 2008. audio compact disk 26.95 (978-1-934997-07-9(2)) Pub: CSAWord. Dist(s): PerseuPGW

Room with a View. unabr. ed. E. M. Forster. Read by Flo Gibson. 5 cass. (Running Time: 7 hrs.). 1992. 20.95 (978-1-55685-266-4(5)) Audio Bk Con.
Breathtakingly beautiful scenes of Italy & Hertfordshire are the backdrop of this charming & often comical romance. Your narrator expresses a special joy in sharing this gem.

Room with a View. unabr. ed. E. M. Forster. Read by Joanna David. 6 cass. (Running Time: 7 hrs. 15 mins.). 2003. 29.95 (978-1-57270-345-2(8)) Pub: Audio Partners. Dist(s): PerseuPGW

Room with a View. unabr. ed. E. M. Forster. Narrated by Joanna David. 6 CDs. (Running Time: 7 hrs. 15 mins.). (ENG.). 2003. audio compact disk 29.95 (978-1-57270-346-9(6)) Pub: AudioGO. Dist(s): Perseus Dist

Room with a View. unabr. ed. E. M. Forster. Read by Frederick Davidson. 5 cass. (Running Time: 7 hrs.). 1992. 39.95 (978-0-7861-0324-9(8), 1285) Blckstn Audio.
Portrays the love of a British woman for an expatriate living in Italy, a country which to Forster represents the forces of true passion. Caught up in a world of social snobbery, Lucy Honeychurch, finds herself constrained by the claustrophobic influence of her British guardians, who encourage her to take up with a well-connected boor. When she regrets that her hotel room has no view, a member of the lower class offers to trade rooms with her. Lucy becomes caught in a struggle between her own emotions & social conventions. In the end, however, Lucy finds love with a man whose free spirit reminds her of a "room with a view.".

Room with a View. unabr. ed. E. M. Forster. Read by Frederick Davidson. 7 CDs. (Running Time: 7 hrs.). 2000. audio compact disk 56.00 (978-0-7861-9926-6(1), 1285) Blckstn Audio.

Room with a View. unabr. ed. E. M. Forster. Read by Frederick Davidson. 1 CD. (Running Time: 7 hrs. 30 mins.). 2001. audio compact disk 19.95 (zm1285) Blckstn Audio.
The love of a British woman for an expatriate living in Italy, a country which to Forster represents the forces of true passion. Caught up in a world of social snobbery, Lucy Honeychurch finds herself constrained by the claustrophobic influence of her British guardians, who encourage her to take up with a well-connected boor. When she regrets that her hotel room has no view, a member of the lower class offers to trade rooms with her. Lucy becomes caught in a struggle between her own emotions & social conventions. In the end, however, Lucy finds love with a man whose free spirit reminds her of a "room with a view".

Room with a View. unabr. ed. E. M. Forster. Read by Jill Masters. 6 cass. (Running Time: 9 hrs.). 2001. 29.95 (978-0-7366-6766-1(0)) Books on Tape.
A young Victorian Englishwoman runs from love in Florence but returns to England where she must be taught how to listen to her heart.

Room with a View. unabr. ed. E. M. Forster. Read by Joanna David. 6 cass. (Running Time: 9 hrs.). 2000. 49.95 (978-0-7451-5943-0(5), CAB 545) Pub: Chivers Audio Bks GBR. Dist(s): AudioGO
Lucy Honeychurch, a British citizen abroad in Florence, is portrayed with great sympathy. In her relationships with her dismal cousin Charlotte, the unconventional Emerson's and her supercilious fiance, Lucy is torn between lingering Victorian social properties and the spontaneous prompting of her own underdeveloped heart.

Room with a View. unabr. ed. E. M. Forster. Read by Wanda Mccaddon. (YA). 2007. 59.99 (978-1-59895-866-9(6)) Find a World.

Room with a View, unabr. ed. E. M. Forster. Narrated by John Franklyn-Robbins. 6 cass. (Running Time: 8 hrs. 15 mins.). 1993. 51.00 (978-1-55690-835-4(0), 93203E7) Recorded Bks.
When her family & friends promote a proper but passionless marriage, a young woman must choose between doing what is expected of her & following her heart.

Room with a View. unabr. ed. E. M. Forster. Read by Wanda McCaddon. 6 cds. (Running Time: 7 hrs 31 mins). 2002. audio compact disk 33.95 (978-1-58472-317-2(3), 096, In Aud) Pub: Sound Room. Dist(s): Baker Taylor
The romantic story of Lucy Honeychurch set in Italy and England.

Room with a View. unabr. ed. E. M. Forster. Read by Wanda McCaddon. 1 cd. (Running Time: 7 hrs 31 mins). 2002. audio compact disk 18.95 (978-1-58472-398-1(X), In Aud) Pub: Sound Room. Dist(s): Baker Taylor
MP3 format.

***Room with a View.** unabr. ed. E. M. Forster. Narrated by Steven Crossley. (Running Time: 8 hrs. 0 mins.). 2010. 15.99 (978-1-4001-8609-9(9)) Tantor Media.

***Room with a View.** unabr. ed. E. M. Forster. Narrated by Steven Crossley. (Running Time: 8 hrs. 0 mins. 0 sec.). (ENG.). 2010. 19.99 (978-1-4001-6609-1(8)); audio compact disk 55.99 (978-1-4001-4609-3(7)); audio compact disk 27.99 (978-1-4001-1609-6(0)) Pub: Tantor Media. Dist(s): IngramPubServ

Room with a View. unabr. collector's ed. E. M. Forster. Read by Jill Masters. 6 cass. (Running Time: 9 hrs.). (J). 1993. 48.00 (978-0-7366-2401-5(5), 3170) Books on Tape.
Victorian Englishwoman is faced with choosing between convention & the call of her heart.

Room with a View. 2nd ed. E. M. Forster. 2 CDs. (Running Time: 7 hrs. 11 mins.). 2005. audio compact disk 19.95 (978-0-9748692-0-9(1)) Access Dig Des.
This Audio Book is a live performanc by Nita Moyer, is provided on a single Compact Disk in "MP3" format. It contains more than 7 hours of unabridged audio of the original text. The book can be played on most MP3 players (most CD/DVD players, Mobile audio devices, PDAs, Pocket PCs and PC CD-ROMs). A bonus CD includes the complete and accessible E-texts of 18 Victorian authors.

Room with a View: Classic Collection. unabr. ed. E. M. Forster. Read by Frederick Davidson. (Running Time: 8 hrs. 0 mins.). 2009. audio compact disk 19.95 (978-1-4332-8785-5(4)) Blckstn Audio.

Roomful of Hovings: And Other Profiles. unabr. ed. John McPhee. Read by Walter Zimmerman. 7 cass. (Running Time: 10 hrs. 30 min.). 1989. 56.00 (978-0-7366-1575-4(X), 2442) Books on Tape.
A Roomful of Hovings is a collection of biographical miniatures. The profiles include Thomas Hovings, the renowned art historian who slips in & out of politics, also the late Euell Gibbons, a forager, America's most knowledgeable expert on edible wild plants, & author of Stalking the Wild Asparagus. The sketches continue with Carroll Brewster of M. I. T.-in-Africa; Robert Twynam, the man who grew the grass at Wimbledon; & finally Temple Fielding, the mercurial & influential author of the most popular guides to Europe.

Roominghouse, Winter see Poetry & Voice of Margaret Atwood

***Rooms: A Novel.** unabr. ed. James L. Rubart. Read by James L. Rubart. (Running Time: 11 hrs.). 2010. 39.97 (978-1-4418-8817-4(9), 9781441888174, Brlnc Audio MP3 Lib); 24.99 (978-1-4418-8816-7(0), 9781441888167, Brilliance MP3); 24.99 (978-1-4418-8818-1(7), 9781441888181, BAD); 39.97 (978-1-4418-8819-8(5), 9781441888198, BADLE); audio compact disk 69.97 (978-1-4418-8814-3(4), 9781441888143, BriAudCD Unabrid); audio compact disk 24.99

(978-1-4418-8812-9(8), 9781441888129, Bril Audio CD Unabri) Brilliance Audio.

Rooney. unabr. ed. Catherine Cookson. Read by John Woodvine. 6 cass. (Running Time: 6 hrs.). 1993. bk. 54.95 (978-0-7451-5866-2(8), CAB 163) AudioGO.

Rooney 'Roo see Let's Read Together

Rooney Roo Read along CD: Vowel Teams Phonics. Barbara DeRubertis. (J). 1998. audio compact disk 4.25 (978-1-57565-182-8(3)) Pub: Kane Pr. Dist(s): Lerner Pub

Roosevelt & Churchill: Men of Secrets. unabr. ed. David Stafford. Read by Richard McGonagle. 8 cass. (Running Time: 12 hrs.). 2001. 34.95 (978-1-57270-227-1(3), E81227u, Audio Editions) Pub: Audio Partners. Dist(s): PerseuPGW

Recently released wartime files provide an intriguing look behind the congenial facade of two world leaders, revealing how each guarded knowledge from the other in pursuit of separate national interests.

Roosevelt & Churchill: Men of Secrets. unabr. ed. David Stafford. Narrated by Richard McGonagle. (Running Time: 41760 sec.). (ENG.). 2007. audio compact disk 37.95 (978-1-57270-857-0(3)) Pub: AudioGO. Dist(s): Perseus Dist

Roosevelt & Hopkins. unabr. collector's ed. Robert E. Sherwood. Read by E. H. Jones. 9 cass. (Running Time: 13 hrs. 30 min.). 2001. 72.00 Books on Tape.

The classic account of President Roosevelt's foreign policy during WWII and Harry Hopkins' role in it.

Roosevelt & Hopkins, Pt. A. unabr. collector's ed. Robert E. Sherwood. Read by E. H. Jones. 11 cass. (Running Time: 16 hrs. 30 min.). 2001. 88.00 Books on Tape.

Roosevelt & Hopkins, Pt. B. unabr. collector's ed. Robert E. Sherwood. Read by E. H. Jones. 12 cass. (Running Time: 18 hrs.). 2001. 96.00 Books on Tape.

Roosevelt & Stalin: The Failed Courtship. unabr. ed. Robert A. Nisbet. Read by Michael Wells. 3 cass. (Running Time: 4 hrs.). 1990. 23.95 (978-0-7861-0211-2(X), 1186) Blckstn Audio.

In this book Robert Nisbet tells the story of one of the most remarkable diplomatic courtships in modern history: the courtship of Stalin during World War II by President Roosevelt.

Roosevelts. unabr. ed. Peter Collier & David Horowitz. Read by Jeff Riggenbach. 14 cass. (Running Time: 20 hrs. 30 mins.). 1994. 89.95 (978-0-7861-0747-6(2), 1500) Blckstn Audio.

In this riveting book we see Teddy, the flamboyant politican & Rough Rider, who was also a "Papa Bear," passing on an ethos of sacrifice & achievement to his "cubs." Filled with drama & anecdote, presenting familiar characters in penetrating new light. "The Roosevelts" is a soaring tale of triumph over heartbreak & frailty. But it is also a daunting story of the vanity of human wishes.

Roosevelts: An American Saga. unabr. ed. Peter Collier & David Horowitz. Read by Jeff Riggenbach. (Running Time: 20 hrs. 5 mins.). 2008. 44.95 (978-1-4332-5842-8(0)); audio compact disk 120.00 (978-1-4332-5839-8(0)) Blckstn Audio.

Roosevelts: An American Saga. unabr. ed. Peter Collier & David Horowitz. Read by Michael Kramer. 14 cass. (Running Time: 21 hrs.). 1995. 112.00 (978-0-7366-3021-4(X), 3704) Books on Tape.

This great biography shows how the two Roosevelt clans competed for family legacy. Which side won?.

***Root & Branch: Charles Hamilton Houston, Thurgood Marshall, & the Struggle to End Segregation.** unabr. ed. Rawn James, Jr. Narrated by Dominic Hoffman. 8 CDs. (Running Time: 10 hrs.). 2010. audio compact disk 80.00 (978-0-307-71489-3(6), BksonTape) Pub: Random Audio Pubg. Dist(s): Random

Root & Wings. Puja Thomson. Music by Richard Shulman. 1 CD. (Running Time: 60 min.). 1999. wbk. ed. 16.00; wbk. ed. 12.00 Hlth Jrnys.

Root of All Evil: How to Rightly Relate to Money, Wealth & Power. Mac Hammond. 2 cass. (Running Time: 2 hrs.). 1994. (978-1-57399-083-7(3)) Mac Hammond.

The Bible doesn't say money is the root of all evil. It says the love of money is. In this liberating series, Mac helps you develop a healthy, biblical view of money.

Root of All Evil: How to Rightly Relate to Money, Wealth, & Power. Mac Hammond. 2008. audio compact disk 12.00 (978-1-57399-377-7(8)) Mac Hammond.

Root of Bitterness: Hebrews 12:12-17. Ed Young. 1992. 4.95 (978-0-7417-1938-6(X), 938) Win Walk.

Rootabaga Stories. Carl Sandburg. Read by Flo Gibson. 2 cass. (Running Time: 3 hrs.). (J). 1996. 14.95 (978-1-55685-405-7(6)) Audio Bk Con.

Lively, imaginative & full of play on words & unusual characters such as the Gold Buckskin Wincher, the Potato Face Blind Man, Rags Habakuk, the Flongboos, Slipfoot, Hatrack the Horse, Rag Bag Mammy & more.

Rootabaga Stories. Carl Sandburg. Narrated by Flo Gibson. (J). 2007. audio compact disk 16.95 (978-1-55685-977-9(5)) Audio Bk Con.

***Rooted: Reflections on the Gardens in Scripture.** Murray Andrew Pura. (Running Time: 4 hrs. 18 mins. 29 sec.). (ENG.). 2010. 13.99 (978-0-310-39579-9(8)) Zondervan.

Roots. Contrib. by Shawn McDonald. Prod. by Christopher Stevens. 2008. audio compact disk 13.99 (978-5-557-59465-3(5)) Pt of Grace Ent.

Roots: The Saga of an American Family. unabr. ed. Alex Haley. Read by Avery Brooks. 3 MP3-CDs. (Running Time: 30 hrs.). 2007. 84.95 (978-0-7927-4906-6(5)); audio compact disk 147.95 (978-0-7927-4928-8(6)); audio compact disk 139.95 (978-0-7927-4852-6(2)) AudioGO.

Roots: The Saga of an American Family. unabr. ed. Alex Haley. Intro. by Michael Eric Dyson. Narrated by Avery Brooks. (Running Time: 108000 sec.). (ENG.). 2007. audio compact disk 39.95 (978-1-60283-289-3(7)); audio compact disk 59.95 (978-1-60283-197-1(1)) Pub: AudioGO. Dist(s): Perseus Dist

Roots: The Saga of an American Family. 30th abr. ed. Alex Haley. Narrated by Avery Brooks. Intro. by Michael Eric Dyson. (Running Time: 53700 sec.). (ENG.). 2008. audio compact disk 19.95 (978-1-60283-386-9(9)) Pub: AudioGO. Dist(s): Perseus Dist

Roots - the Saga of an American Family. unabr. ed. Alex Haley. Read by Avery Brooks. (YA). 2007. 99.99 (978-1-60252-788-1(1)) Find a World.

Roots & Blues Fingerstyle Guitar: Acoustic Guitar Private Lessons. Steve James. 1999. pap. bk. 19.95 (978-1-4234-4579-1(1), 1423445791) Pub: String Letter. Dist(s): H Leonard

Roots & Wings: Guided Imagery & Meditations to Transform Your Life. Puja Thomson. Read by Puja Thomson. Perf. by Richard Shulman. 1 cass. (Running Time: 58 min.). 1995. pap. bk. 11.95 (978-1-928663-02-7(8)); pap. bk. & wbk. ed. 24.99 (978-1-928663-04-1(4)); pap. bk. & wbk. ed. 29.95 (978-1-928663-03-4(6)); audio compact disk 15.95 (978-1-928663-01-0(X)) Roots & Wings NY.

A journey with Puja Thomson's clear, resonant voice & Richard Shulman's inspired music into your life's story: discover the power of roots & wings to transform past, present & future; honor & strengthen spiritual roots & wings to rekindle trust in inner guidance, appreciate blessings & manifest dreams.

Roots of Buddhist Psychology. Jack Kornfield. 2005. audio compact disk 69.95 (978-1-59179-432-5(3)) Sounds True.

Roots of Character. Wendell Smith. 6 cass. (Running Time: 6 hrs.). 2001. 29.99 (978-1-886849-66-2(8)) CityChristian.

Roots of Codependence. Pia Mellody. Read by Pia Mellody. 1 cass. (Running Time: 1 hr.). 10.00 (A8) Featuka Enter Inc.

How codependence develops & why.

Roots of Human Behavior. 6 cass. (Running Time: 6 hrs.). 29.95 (978-1-56585-009-5(2)) Teaching Co.

Roots of Human Behavior. Instructed by Barbara King. 6 CDs. (Running Time: 6 hrs.). audio compact disk 39.95 (978-1-56585-282-2(6)) Teaching Co.

Roots of Jesus' Spirituality: Our Old Testament Heritage. unabr. ed. Stephen Doyle. 5 cass. (Running Time: 6 hrs. 55 min.). 1993. 40.95 Set. (TAH289) Alba Hse Comns.

In these ten outstanding lectures, Fr. Doyle introduces us to Jesus the Jew, the Priest, the Messiah, the Prophet, the Redeemer, & the Goal of Creation. An enriching study & spiritual tool.

Roots of Modern Masculinity. Robert A. Johnson. 1 cass. (Running Time: 1 hr.). 1990. 11.00 (01201) Big Sur Tapes.

***Roots of Obama's Rage.** unabr. ed. Dinesh D'Souza. (Running Time: 8 hrs. 30 mins.). 2010. 29.95 (978-1-4417-6169-9(1)); audio compact disk 29.95 (978-1-4417-6168-2(3)) Blckstn Audio.

***Roots of Obama's Rage (Library Edition)** unabr. ed. Dinesh D'Souza. (Running Time: 8 hrs. 30 mins.). 2010. 54.95 (978-1-4417-6166-8(7)); audio compact disk 76.00 (978-1-4417-6167-5(5)) Blckstn Audio.

Roots of Our Impoverishment. Swami Amar Jyoti. 1 cass. (Running Time: 1 hr.). 1992. 9.95 (B-17) Truth Consciousness.

God's plan was for paradise. How we lost our golden heritage & what keeps us from finding it again.

Roots of Resistance: Selected Highlights from the Freedom Archives. Speeches. 1 CD. (Running Time: 72 mins.). (YA). 2002. audio compact disk 10.00 (978-0-9727422-0-7(4)) Freedom Archives.

In 71 carefully selected minutes, you will hear:Ho Chi Minh speaking in English to the U.S. anti-war movement Fannie Lou Hamer leading the singing of Go Tell It On the Mountain and much, much more.Topics include civil rights and Black liberation, Vietnam victory, the prison movement, Puerto Rico, Chile, Native American movements, women's liberation, the International Hotel.Among other voices you will hear are: Assata Shakur, Amilcar Cabral, Lolita Lebron, Winnie Mandela, Nelson Mandela, Maya Angelou, Ruchell Magee, Angela Davis, Fred Hampton, Mario Savio, Bernardine Dohrn, Kathy Boudin, Jane Fonda, Ramsey Clark, Salvador Allende, Fidel Castro, Cesar Chavez - and the list goes on. The CD also features poetry recited by June Jordan, Judy Grahn, Marge Piercy, and Meridel LeSueur, with music by Joan Baez, Victor Jara, Sweet Honey in the Rock, and others.The voices and sounds on this CD are but a tiny fraction of a wondrous multiplicity of recorded sound, with in-depth analysis, live coverage, incisive interviews, highly-produced documentaries, poetry, music, and raw materials on many topics - all found in The Freedom Archives. There's no way we can convey the entire collection on just one CD - that's why we call it Volume 1!.

Roots of Robert Johnson. Stefan Grossman & Woody Mann. 1997. bk. 22.95 (978-0-7866-2776-9(X), 95074BCD) Mel Bay.

Roots of Satisfaction. Ariel Kane & Shya Kane. Contrib. by Helene DeLillo. 1 cass. (Running Time: 1 hrs. 22 min.). (Being in the Moment Ser.). 1995. (978-1-888043-01-3(6)) ASK Prodns.

Reveals to the listener how to recognize & bypass the common misconceptions & obstacles to self-fulfillment so they can access a profound sense of satisfaction.

Roots of the Messiah: Outcasts, Kings, & Carpenters. unabr. ed. Narrated by Kailey Bell & Todd Busteed. (Running Time: 0 hr. 58 mins. 50 sec.). (Kidz Rock Ser.). (ENG.). (J). 2009. 6.29 (978-1-60814-546-1(8)); audio compact disk 8.99 (978-1-59859-602-1(0)) Oasis Audio.

Roots of Tomorrow. Manly P. Hall. 1 cass. (Running Time: 1 hr.). 8.95 (978-0-89314-239-1(5), C870920) Philos Res.

Deals with psychology & self-help.

Roots of War: Profiling the Middle East. Chuck Missler. 1 CD and 1 CD-ROM. (Running Time: 2 hrs). (Briefing Packages by Chuck Missler). 2002. audio compact disk 19.95 (978-1-57821-186-9(7)) Koinonia Hse.

As diligent Bible students, most of us are familiar with the emergence of the empires that were profiled in Daniel 2 and Daniel 7; the Babylonian, Persian, Greek and Roman empires. However, many of us are probably a little hazy about the tide of events subsequent to that period.Find out what is really going on in the Middle East.In this comprehensive overview of India, Pakistan, Iraq, Iran, Saudi Arabia, Egypt, Jordan, Turkey and Israel, Chuck covers the background of each country as well as their military strengths, political agendas, historical roots, religious affiliations and what role they each play in Bible prophecy.

Roots Run Deep. Contrib. by Jadon Lavik. Prod. by Zach Hodges et al. 2008. audio compact disk 13.99 (978-5-557-47028-5(X)) BEC Recordings.

Rooum see Widdershins: The First Book of Ghost Stories

***Ropa Vieja.** unabr. ed. Laura Lippman. Read by Linda Emond & Francois Battiste. (ENG.). 2008. (978-0-06-176316-8(0), Harper Audio); (978-0-06-176313-7(6), Harper Audio) HarperCollins Pubs.

Rope - In Case. unabr. ed. Lillian Beckwith. Read by Hannah Gordon. 6 cass. (Running Time: 6 hrs.). 1998. 54.95 (978-0-7540-0193-5(8), CAB 1616) AudioGO.

Based on life in the Hebrides & the importance of having a rope.

Rope Walk. unabr. ed. Carrie Brown. Narrated by Elaina Erika Davis. (Running Time: 39300 sec.). (ENG.). 2007. audio compact disk 39.95 (978-1-60283-054-7(1)) Pub: AudioGO. Dist(s): Perseus Dist

Ropes & Knots DVD. International Association of Fire Chiefs Staff & National Fire Protection Association. 2005. 315.95 (978-0-7637-3607-1(4)) Jones Bartlett.

Rory's Little Broadway. Rory. Perf. by Rory. 1 cass. (Running Time: 30 min.). (J). 1992. 8.98 (978-1-56406-546-9(4)); 8.98 (978-1-56406-575-9(8)); audio compact disk 13.98 (978-1-56406-562-9(6)) Sony Music Ent.

Ten showtunes for kids & parents.

Rosa. Nikki Giovanni. Illus. by Bryan Collier. 1 CD. (Running Time: 14 mins.). (J). (gr. 2-5). 2007. bk. 29.95 (978-0-545-04261-1(5)); bk. 24.95 (978-0-545-04262-8(3)) Weston Woods.

On December 1, 1955, Rosa Parks boarded a Montgomery, Alabama city bus and refused to give up her seat to a white man, an act that ignited a movement that changed modern history.

Rosa. unabr. ed. Jonathan Rabb. Narrated by Simon Prebble. (Running Time: 16 hrs. 0 mins. 0 sec.). (ENG.). 2009. audio compact disk 79.99 (978-1-4001-4250-7(4)); audio compact disk 39.99 (978-1-4001-1250-0(8)); audio compact disk 29.99 (978-1-4001-6250-5(5)) Pub: Tantor Media. Dist(s): IngramPubServ

Rosa, Vols. I & II. Cynthia Ozick. Read by Cynthia Ozick. Contrib. by Arthur L. Klein & Christopher King. 2 cass. (Running Time: 1 hr. 21 min.). 1986. 10.95 ea. Spoken Arts.

Ozick reads her prize winning story 'Rosa'.

Rosa Alada. Alma Flor Ada. (Cuentos Para Todo el Ano Ser.). (SPA., (J). (gr. k-3). 4.95 (978-1-58105-252-7(9)) Santillana.

Rosa Parks. Douglas Brinkley. Read by Karen White. 2000. audio compact disk 56.00 (978-0-7366-6865-1(9)) Books on Tape.

Rosa Parks. unabr. ed. Douglas Brinkley. Read by Karen White. 5 cass. (Running Time: 7 hrs.). 2000. 24.95 (978-0-7366-5738-9(X)) Books on Tape.

The woman whose simple yet heroic act sounded the death knell for Jim Crow & the times she helped to change.

Rosa Parks. unabr. ed. Douglas Brinkley. Read by Karen White. 7 CDs. (Running Time: 10 hrs. 30 mins.). 2001. audio compact disk 56.00 Books on Tape.

Rosa Parks. unabr. collector's ed. Douglas Brinkley. Read by Karen White. 5 cass. (Running Time: 7 hrs. 30 min.). 2000. 40.00 (978-0-7366-5440-1(2)) Books on Tape.

The woman whose simple yet heroic act sounded the death knell for Jim Crow and the times she helped to change.

Rosa Parks: Freedom Fighter. (Step into History Ser.). 2000. audio compact disk 18.95 (978-1-4105-0137-0(X)) D Johnston Inc.

Rosa Parks: Freedom Fighter. Devorah Major. Ed. by Jerry Stemach. Narrated by Denise Jordan Walker. 2000. audio compact disk 200.00 (978-1-58702-446-7(2)) D Johnston Inc.

Rosa Parks: Not Giving In with Buffalo Bill & Farley's Raiders. James Collins. Illus. by Brian T. Cox. (Time Traveler's Adventure Ser.). (J). 2006. bk. 13.50 (978-1-932332-17-9(0)) Toy Box Prods.

Rosa Parks: The Complete Memorial Service for the Mother of the Modern Civil Rights Movement. unabr. ed. Rosa & Raymond Parks Institute. (Running Time: 8 hrs.). 2010. 24.99 (978-1-4233-9308-5(2), 9781423393085, BAD); 39.97 (978-1-4233-9304-7(X), 9781423393047, BADLE) Brilliance Audio.

Rosa Parks: Freedom Fighter. Ed. by Jerry Stemach et al. Contrib. by Devorah Major. Illus. by Jeff Ham. Narrated by Denise Jordan Walker. Contrib. by Ted S. Hasselbring. (Start-to-Finish Books: Vol. 3). (J). (gr. 2-3). 2000. 35.00 (978-1-58702-447-4(0)) D Johnston Inc.

Rosa Parks: Freedom Fighter. unabr. ed. Devorah Major. Ed. by Jerry Stemach et al. Illus. by Jeff Ham. Narrated by Denise Jordan Walker. Contrib. by Ted S. Hasselbring. 1 cass. (Running Time: 1 hr.). (Start-to-Finish Books: Vol. 3). (J). (gr. 2-3). 2000. (978-1-893376-49-6(4), F10S) D Johnston Inc.

People say that Rosa Parks refused to yield her seat to a white man on a segregated Montgomery, Alabama, bus in 1955 because she was "tired." This book explains what that "tiredness" of segregation! Rosa is called the "mother of Civil Rights" for that action in Montgomery, but her activism began long before. Her grandfather was a black Alabaman who would sit up all night with a shotgun in his lap to ward off the KKK.

Rosa Parks Mother of Civil Rights. Cerebellum Academic Team. (Running Time: 30 mins.). (Just the Facts Ser.). 2005. 24.95 (978-1-59163-529-1(2)) Cerebellum.

Rosalie Sorrels: If I Could Be the Rain. 1 cass. (Running Time: 1 hr.). 9.98 (C-31) Folk-Legacy.

A wonderful early recording of an important artist.

Rosario: Lluvia de Rosas. Mariano de Blas.Tr. of Rain of Roses. (SPA.). 2009. audio compact disk 50.00 (978-1-935405-12-2(8)) Hombre Nuevo.

Rosario: Lluvia de Rosas. P. Mariano de Blas. (SPA.). (YA). 2005. audio compact disk 49.99 (978-1-935405-96-2(9)) Hombre Nuevo.

Rosary. Narrated by Owen F. Campion. 2003. 9.95 (978-1-59276-029-9(5)); audio compact disk 14.95 (978-1-59276-011-4(2)) Our Sunday Visitor.

Let the soothing voice and reverent tone of Monsignor Owen F. Campion accompany you through the Joyful, Sorrowful, Luminous, and Glorious Mysteries of the Rosary.

Rosary. Created by Sheldon Cohen & J. Mazza. 1 cass. (Running Time: 1 hr. 20 min.). Dramatization. 1983. 9.95 (978-0-914070-31-3(2), 303); audio compact disk 14.95 (978-0-87946-072-3(5), 401) ACTA Pubns.

Bestselling rendition of all 15 mysteries with original music & meditations.

Rosary: (Including the Mysteries of Light) Arranged by Sheldon Cohen. 1 cass. (Running Time: 92). 2004. 9.95 (978-0-87946-241-3(8), 316); audio compact disk 14.95 (978-0-87946-240-6(X), 410) ACTA Pubns.

Rosary for the Millennium. unabr. ed. Perf. by Benedictine Sisters of Erie Staff. Contrib. by Joan Chittister. 3 cass. (Running Time: 1 hr. 30 min.). 1998. 20.00 (978-1-890890-34-6(0), A218) Benetvision.

Contemporary & creative presentation of the rosary includes meditations & musical accompaniments, with inspiring & challenging meditations from the booklet. Music includes piano, oboe, mode chant, rounds & sung hymns.

Rosary! It's a Catholic Thing! Jo-Ann Minvielle & Carol Camp Twork. Composed by R. Cody Twork. Voice by R. Cody Twork. 2 CDs. (Running Time: 97 mins). (YA). 2003. audio compact disk 12.99 (978-0-9707979-5-7(8)) Contemp Com.

Recitation of "Rosary! It's a Catholic Thing!" with a background of techno pop and rock music, appeals to teens and adults as well.

Rosary Murders. unabr. collector's ed. William X. Kienzle. Read by Edward Holland. 7 cass. (Running Time: 10 hrs. 30 min.). (Father Koesler Mystery Ser.: No. 1). 1997. 56.00 (978-0-7366-3721-3(4), 4402) Books on Tape.

A serial murderer preys on the nuns & priests of Detroit & the ever-resourceful priest investigates.

Rosary Novenas to Our Lady. Based on a work by Charles V. Lacey. Music by Sheldon Cohen. 1 cassette. (Running Time: 70 minutes). 2002. 9.95 (978-0-87946-229-1(9), 306) ACTA Pubns.

Rosary of Light. Vinny Flynn & Still Waters. 1 cass. (Running Time: 58 mins.). 2003. 10.00 (978-1-884479-17-5(0)) Spirit Song.

Two renditions of the rosary, each recited with meditations on the luminous mysteries, and instrumental background music. 35 minute rosary with dramatic readings from the Gospel; and 23 minute rosary with brief readings from the Gospel.

Rosary of Light. Illus. by Vinny Flynn & Still Waters. 1 CD. (Running Time: 58 mins.). 2003. audio compact disk 14.00 (978-1-884479-18-2(9)) Spirit Song.

Two renditions of the Rosary, each recited with meditation on the luminous mysteries and instrumental background music. 35 minute rosary with dramatic readings from the Gospel; and 23 minute rosary with brief readings from the Gospel.

Rosary on Tape. Owen F. Campion. 1 cass. (Running Time: 1 hr. 30 min.). 1990. bk. 7.95 (978-0-87973-188-5(5), 188) Our Sunday Visitor.
A unique way to pray the Rosary. Each of the Joyful, Sorrowful, & Glorious mysteries are introduced with an original meditation by Father Campion. Following along with Rosary beads is not necessary, so the Rosary can be said anywhere. Tape is ideal for shut-ins & busy people.

Rosary with the Pope. Narrated by John Paul II, pseud. 1 cass. (Running Time: 1 hr.). 1994. 14.95 (345); audio compact disk 19.95 (345) GIA Pubns.

Rosa's Island. unabr. ed. Valerie Wood. Read by Phyllida Nash. 8 cass. (Running Time: 12 hrs.). 2003. 69.95 (978-0-7540-0906-1(8), CAB 2338) AudioGO.

Rose. unabr. ed. V. C. Andrews. Read by Laurel Lefkow. 5 CDs. (Running Time: 5 hrs.). (Isis Ser.). (J). 2002. audio compact disk 59.95 (978-0-7531-1587-9(5)) Pub: ISIS Lrg Prnt GBR. Dist(s): Ulverscroft US
Rose never imagined her entire life would change in a heartbeat. Beautiful and talented, Rose was the apple of her father's eye. But when he is tragically taken from her, his carefully hidden secrets destroy the only life Rose has ever known - and lead her into a world of luxury unlike any she has imagined.

Rose. unabr. ed. V. C. Andrews. Read by Laurel Lefkow. 4 cass. (Running Time: 5 hrs.). (Shooting Star Ser.: No. 3). (J). 2002. 44.95 (978-0-7531-1558-9(1)) Pub: ISIS Lrg Prnt GBR. Dist(s): Ulverscroft US

Rose. unabr. ed. Martin Cruz Smith. Narrated by Steven Crossley. 10 cass. (Running Time: 14 hrs. 30 mins.). 1997. 85.00 (978-0-7887-0918-0(6), 95058E7) Recorded Bks.
Jonathan Blair, a destitute adventurer & explorer, has been hired to locate a missing young cleric in the northern England mining town of Wigan. Carries you deep into the layers of mystery, passion & power that Blair encounters above & below ground in the coal-veiled town.

Rose. unabr. collector's ed. Martin Cruz Smith. Read by Edward Lewis. 8 cass. (Running Time: 12 hrs.). 1997. 64.00 (978-0-913369-68-5(3), 4319) Books on Tape.

Rose & Crown: Ship in Full Sail see Sean O'Casey Reading I Knock at the Door & Other Works

Rose & the Body of the Rose see Twentieth-Century Poetry in English, No. 28, Recordings of Poets Reading Their Own Poetry

Rose & the Lily. Frances Parkinson Keyes. 7 cass. (Running Time: 7 hrs.). 28.95 (751) Ignatius Pr.
Lives of St. Rose of Lima & St. Marian of Quito.

Rose & the Ring. unabr. ed. William Makepeace Thackeray. Read by Flo Gibson. 2 cass. (Running Time: 3 hrs.). (Classic Books on Cassettes Ser.). (J). 1988. 14.95 (978-1-55685-108-7(1)) Audio Bk Con.
A magic rose & ring bring instant beauty & charm to each of their possessors causing strange & romantic antics.

Rose Arch. unabr. ed. Linda Sole. Read by Trudy Harris. 6 cass. (Running Time: 8 hrs.). (Story Sound Ser.). (J). 2004. 54.95 (978-1-85903-672-3(4)) Pub: Mgna Lrg Print GBR. Dist(s): Ulverscroft US

***Rose by any other Name.** Maureen McCarthy. Read by Rebecca Macauley. (Running Time: 10 hrs. 10 mins.). (YA). 2010. 79.99 (978-1-74214-601-0(5), 9781742146010) Pub: Bolinda Pubng AUS. Dist(s): Bolinda Pub Inc

Rose by Any Other Name. unabr. ed. Maureen McCarthy. Read by Rebecca Macauley. (Running Time: 10 hrs. 10 mins.). (YA). 2009. audio compact disk 87.95 (978-1-74093-969-0(7), 9781740939690) Pub: Bolinda Pubng AUS. Dist(s): Bolinda Pub Inc

Rose Called Moonlight. Elizabeth Daish. 5 cass. (Running Time: 6 hrs. 35 mins.). (Story Sound Ser.). (J). 2004. 49.95 (978-1-85903-704-1(6)) Pub: Mgna Lrg Print GBR. Dist(s): Ulverscroft US

Rose Cottage. Mary Stewart. Read by Jan Francis. 2 cass. (Running Time: 2 hrs. 56 mins.). 1997. mass mkt. 16.95 (978-1-85998-876-3(8), HoddrStoughton) Pub: Hodder General GBR. Dist(s): Trafalgar

Rose Cottage. abr. ed. Mary Stewart. Read by Samantha Eggar. 2 cass. (Running Time: 3 hrs.). 2001. 18.00 (978-1-59040-071-5(2)) Pub: Amer Intl Pub. Dist(s): PerseuPGW

***Rose Cottage Chronicles: Civil War Letters of the Bryant-Stephens Families of North Florida.** unabr. ed. Various Authors. Read by Christopher Walker. (Running Time: 19 hrs. NaN mins.). (ENG.). 2011. 44.95 (978-1-4417-8541-1(8)); audio compact disk 123.00 (978-1-4417-8539-8(6)) Blckstn Audio.

Rose Cottage Chronicles: Civil War Letters of the Bryant-Stephens Families of North Florida. unabr. ed. Read by Chris Walker. Ed. by Arch Frederic Blakely et al. 13 cass. (Running Time: 19 hrs.). 2000. 85.95 (978-0-7861-1784-0(2), 2583) Blckstn Audio.

Rose for Ana Maria. unabr. ed. Frank Yerby. Read by Michael Prichard. 8 cass. (Running Time: 8 hrs.). 1977. 48.00 (978-0-7366-0093-4(0), 1101) Books on Tape.
Meet Diego, a young Spanish revolutionary living in Paris, who has killed the Spanish consul as a protest against the Spanish government. Diego must flee, so he throws in with another revolutionary, a provocative young woman named Ana Maria. In exchange for help in fleeing France, they agree to assassinate a high-ranking Spanish official.

Rose for Emily & Wash. abr. ed. William Faulkner. Read by Tammy Grimes. 1 cass. (Running Time: 1 hr.). 1984. 12.95 (978-0-694-50337-7(1), SWC 1638) HarperCollins Pubs.

Rose for Every Month. unabr. ed. Sally Stewart. Read by Anne Dover. 12 cass. (Running Time: 16 hrs. 30 mins.). (Sound Ser.). 2002. 94.95 (978-1-85496-819-7(X)) Pub: UlverLrgPrint GBR. Dist(s): Ulverscroft US
James Rushton planned that his daughter, Jane, should marry her cousin William. However, plain, quiet Jane wanted more than William's obedient acquiescence, for she had loved her handsome cousin for a long time. Discovering a shameless betrayal, Jane took the most daring decision of her life, to go and live and work in Italy. It was the beginning of a long, passionate, and overwhelming involvement with the aristocratic, impoverished Buonaventura family, whose lives she was to revolutionize.

Rose for Pingerton. (J). 2004. cass. & flmstrp 30.00 (978-0-89719-520-1(5)) Weston Woods.

Rose for Pinkerton. (J). 2004. bk. 24.95 (978-0-7882-0644-3(3)); pap. bk. 14.95 (978-0-7882-0643-6(5)); 8.95 (978-0-89719-920-9(0)) Weston Woods.

Rose for Pinkerton. Steven Kellogg. 1 cass. (Running Time: 6 min.). (J). (ps-3). 1999. pap. bk. 12.95 (QPRA125) Weston Woods.
When Pinkerton's family decides that he's lonely, they get him a kitten named Rose.

Rose in Bloom. unabr. ed. Louisa May Alcott. Read by Flo Gibson. 6 cass. (Running Time: 9 hrs.). (YA). (gr. 6-9). 1991. 24.95 (978-1-55685-201-5(0)) Audio Bk Con.
Rose Campbell returns from two years travel in Europe vowing to shun romance until she has proved herself a capable person in her own right. However, she manages to combine her philanthropic endeavours with a whirlwind of parties & is soon surrounded by many admirers. Who will win her loving heart?.

Rose in Bloom. unabr. ed. Louisa May Alcott. Read by C. M. Herbert. 6 cass. (Running Time: 9 hrs.). (YA). 1998. 44.95 (1911) Blckstn Audio.
The charming account of the adventures of Rose Campbell as she grows into young womanhood.

Rose in Bloom. unabr. ed. Louisa May Alcott. Read by C. M. Hebert. 6 cass. (Running Time: 8 hrs. 30 mins.). 2000. 44.95 (978-0-7861-1139-8(9), 1911) Blckstn Audio.

Rose in Bloom. unabr. ed. Louisa May Alcott. Narrated by Barbara Caruso. 7 pieces. (Running Time: 10 hrs.). (gr. 7 up). 2002. 61.00 (978-1-4025-2725-8(X)) Recorded Bks.
Returning to the "Aunt Hill" from a two-year trip around the world, 20-year-old Rose Campbell suddenly finds herself surrounded by male admirers, all expecting her to marry them! Rose is rich and pretty, and she suspects many of these suitors are more interested in her wealth than her dreams. But she is determined to live her own life and find her own love, despite the many plans of aunts, uncles, and cousins.

Rose Labyrinth. unabr. ed. Titania Hardie. Read by Carolyn Seymour. (Running Time: 13 hrs. 0 mins.). 2008. 29.95 (978-1-4332-5558-8(8)); audio compact disk 99.00 (978-1-4332-5556-4(1)); audio compact disk 79.95 (978-1-4332-5555-7(3)) Blckstn Audio.

Rose Labyrinth. unabr. ed. Titania Hardie. (Running Time: 13 hrs. 0 mins.). 2008. audio compact disk 32.95 (978-1-4332-5557-1(X)) Blckstn Audio.

Rose Madder. Stephen King. Contrib. by Stephen King. Contrib. by Blair Brown. (Running Time: 18 hrs.). (ENG.). (gr. 12 up). 2009. audio compact disk 49.95 (978-0-14-314394-9(8), PengAudBks) Penguin Grp USA.

Rose of Ruby Street. unabr. ed. Carol Rivers. Read by Tanya Myers. 11 cass. (Story Sound Ser.). (J). 2006. 89.95 (978-1-85903-829-1(8)) Pub: Mgna Lrg Print GBR. Dist(s): Ulverscroft US

Rose of Ruby Street. unabr. ed. Carol Rivers & Tanya Myers. Read by Tanya Myers. 13 CDs. (Running Time: 14 hrs. 35 mins.). (Story Sound CD Ser.). (J). 2006. audio compact disk 99.95 (978-1-85903-942-7(1)) Pub: Mgna Lrg Print GBR. Dist(s): Ulverscroft US

Rose of Sebastopol. unabr. ed. Katharine McMahon. Narrated by Josephine Bailey. 10 CDs. (Running Time: 12 hrs. 30 mins. 0 sec.). (ENG.). 2009. audio compact disk 79.99 (978-1-4001-4142-5(7)) Pub: Tantor Media. Dist(s): IngramPubServ

Rose of Sebastopol. unabr. ed. Katharine McMahon. Narrated by Josephine Bailey. 10 CDs. (Running Time: 12 hrs. 30 mins. 0 sec.). (ENG.). (gr. 8). 2009. audio compact disk 39.99 (978-1-4001-1142-8(0)) Pub: Tantor Media. Dist(s): IngramPubServ

Rose of Sebastopol. unabr. ed. Katharine McMahon. Read by Josephine Bailey. 2 MP3-CDs. (Running Time: 12 hrs. 30 mins. 0 sec.). (ENG.). (gr. 8). 2009. audio compact disk 29.99 (978-1-4001-6142-3(8)) Pub: Tantor Media. Dist(s): IngramPubServ

Rose of Sharon: Advent Reflections. Edward Hays. 1 cass. (Running Time: 60 min.). 9.95 (For Peace Pubng) Ave Maria Pr.
Two advent conferences to help you prepare for the birth of Christ by reflecting on the gift of the Advent Rose blooming in the midst of Christmastide & an insight into Mary, the Rainbow Mother of God, in her twin Advent feasts of Our Lady of Guadalupe & the Immaculate Conception.

Rose of Solitude see Savagery of Love: Brother Antoninus Reads His Poetry

Rose of Solitude: The Way of Life & the Way of Death see Savagery of Love: Brother Antoninus Reads His Poetry

Rose of Tibet. unabr. collector's ed. Lionel Davidson. Read by Rupert Keenlyside. 8 cass. (Running Time: 12 hrs.). 1982. 64.00 (978-0-7366-0341-6(7), 1327) Books on Tape.
When his brother is mysteriously lost in Tibet, Charles Houston leaves his teaching job in London to find him. His search takes him to India & Sikkim, through a succesion of exotic locales & finally to Tibet where Houston falls in love with Mei-Hua, the abbess of the monastery of Yamdring.

Rose Petal Soup. Sarah Harrison. 2009. 69.95 (978-0-7531-4203-5(1)); audio compact disk 84.95 (978-0-7531-4204-2(X)) Pub: Isis Pubng Ltd GBR. Dist(s): Ulverscroft US

Rose Rent, unabr. ed. Ellis Peters. Read by Nadia May. 5 cass. (Running Time: 7 hrs.). (Chronicles of Brother Cadfael Ser.: Vol. 13). 1990. 39.95 (978-0-7861-0100-9(8), 1093) Blckstn Audio.
In this work, wealthy young widow Judith Perle rents her house to the Abbey at Shrewsbury for the price of a single rose per year. The monk charged with delivering the flower is murdered, the rose tree destroyed & Judith vanishes. All in all, it makes for a thorny case for Brother Cadfael to solve.

Rose Rent. unabr. ed. Ellis Peters, pseud. Narrated by Patrick Tull. 6 cass. (Running Time: 8 hrs. 30 mins.). (Chronicles of Brother Cadfael Ser.: Vol. 13). 1995. 51.00 (978-0-7887-0223-5(8), 94448E7) Recorded Bks.
A wealthy widow rents her house to the Abbey for the price of a single rose. Shortly before the rent is due, the rosebush is destroyed & the widow kidnapped. Brother Cadfael must discover who stands to gain from these peculiar crimes.

Rose Revived. unabr. ed. Katie Fforde. Read by Eve Matheson. 10 cass. (Running Time: 10 hrs.). 1996. 84.95 (978-0-7451-6656-8(3), CAB 1272) AudioGO.
Joining a cleaning company wouldn't be everyone's choice for a career move, but May, Harriet & Sally all desperately need money to keep themselves afloat while they look for something meaningful to do with their lives. This hilarious & poignant tale follows their attempts to make ends meet while mopping up their love lives & polishing their dreams!.

Rose Rosse per Il. Regina Assini. pap. bk. 20.95 (978-88-7754-904-4(1)) Pub: Cideb ITA. Dist(s): Distribks Inc

Rose with Wings. Alma Flor Ada. (Stories for the Year 'Round Ser.). (J). (gr. k-3). 4.95 (978-1-58105-319-7(3)) Santillana.

Rose Without a Thorn. unabr. ed. Jean Plaidy. Read by Lucy Scott & Frances Jeater. 8 cass. (Running Time: 12 hrs.). (Queens of England Ser.: Vol. 11). 2001. 69.95 (978-0-7531-0998-4(0), 010416) Pub: ISIS Audio GBR. Dist(s): ISIS Pub
Henry VIII's fifth wife was innocent in all but the art of love. If Katherine Howard had not been born both poor & beautiful, or had she not been adopted by the Dowager Duchess of Norfolk, she might indeed have wed her childhood playmate, Thomas Culpepper. But left to run wild, Katherine is introduced to secret pleasures. As she grows up she is made to serve the political ambitions of her powerful uncle, the Duke of Norfolk. When the aging King Henry VIII choses Katherine as his fifth wife, her tragic destiny is sealed.

Roseanna. Maj Sjöwall & Per Wahlöö. (Martin Beck Police Mystery Ser.: No. 1). 2008. audio compact disk 19.95 (978-1-4332-4906-8(5)) Blckstn Audio.

Roseanna. unabr. ed. Maj Sjöwall & Per Wahlöö. Tr. by Lois Roth & Tom Weiner. (Running Time: 7 hrs. NaN mins.). (Martin Beck Police Mystery Ser.: No. 1). 2008. 29.95 (978-1-4332-4907-5(3)); 44.95 (978-1-4332-4904-4(9)); audio compact disk 60.00 (978-1-4332-4905-1(7)) Blckstn Audio.

Rosebuds. Margaret Mayhew. Read by Ruth Sillers. 6 cass. (Running Time: 8 hrs.). 2005. 54.95 (978-1-85903-839-0(5)); audio compact disk 71.95 (978-1-85903-889-5(1)) Pub: UlverLrgPrint GBR. Dist(s): Ulverscroft US

Rosellen Brown. Interview. Interview with Rosellen Brown & Kay Bonetti. 1 cass. (Running Time: 1 hr. 24 min.). 1982. 13.95 (978-1-55644-039-7(1), 2032) Am Audio Prose.
This interview contains thoughts on Brown's central themes, the women's movement, "Tender Mercies," & the elusive process of creating a world out of words.

Rosemary. Margaret Kaine. 10 cass. (Running Time: 13 hrs. 15 mins.). (Story Sound Ser.). (J). 2004. 84.95 (978-1-85903-712-6(7)); audio compact disk 99.95 (978-1-85903-771-3(2)) Pub: Mgna Lrg Print GBR. Dist(s): Ulverscroft US

***Rosemary & Rue: An October Daye Novel.** unabr. ed. Seanan McGuire. Read by Mary Robinette Kowal. (Running Time: 11 hrs.). (October Daye Ser.). 2010. 39.97 (978-1-4418-6172-6(6), 9781441861726, Brlnc Audio MP3 Lib); 14.99 (978-1-4418-6171-9(8), 9781441861719, Brilliance MP3); 39.97 (978-1-4418-6174-0(2), 9781441861740, BADLE); 24.99 (978-1-4418-6173-3(4), 9781441861733, BAD); audio compact disk 89.97 (978-1-4418-6170-2(X), 9781441861702, BriAudCD Unabrid); audio compact disk 29.99 (978-1-4418-6169-6(6), 9781441861696, Bril Audio CD Unabri) Brilliance Audio.

Rosemary for Remembrance. unabr. ed. Susan Sallis. Read by Jacqueline King. 10 cass. (Running Time: 6 hrs. 30 mins.). (Sound Ser.). 2002. 84.95 (978-1-85496-897-5(1)) Pub: UlverLrgPrint GBR. Dist(s): Ulverscroft US
Concluding the story of the Rising Family. As World War II breaks out, the Risings try to hold down the secrets of the past. March is separated from her son; discovering the truth about his bight, he tries to drown hi bitterness in fighting the Luftwaffe. April's shy daughter, Davina, cannot understand why Albert has left her. Victor, the talented, ebullient soldier son of May, watches the two cousins and trusts that the strength of the family will pull them through.

Rosemary Tree. unabr. collector's ed. Elizabeth Goudge. Read by Donada Peters. 9 cass. (Running Time: 13 hrs. 30 mins.). 1989. 72.00 (978-0-7366-1513-6(X), 2384) Books on Tape.
Michael Stone was once a famous author. That was before he went to prison. Now, just released, he needs to get back his bearings. In the village of Belmaray he finds much to muse on...a former sweetheart married to a kindly vicar, a young schoolmistress, shopkeepers, children, animals & nature.

***Rosemary's Baby.** unabr. ed. Ira Levin. Read by Mia Farrow. (ENG.). 2005. (978-0-06-089810-6(0), Harper Audio); (978-0-06-089811-3(9), Harper Audio) HarperCollins Pubs.

Rosemary's Baby. unabr. ed. Ira Levin. Read by Mia Farrow. 6 CDs. (Running Time: 6.5 hrs). 2005. audio compact disk 34.95 (978-0-06-082815-8(3)) HarperCollins Pubs.

Rosencrantz & Guildenstern Are Dead. Tom Stoppard. Perf. by Edward Petherbridge et al. 2 cass. (Running Time: 2 hrs.). 15.95 (SCN 124) J Norton Pubs.
In this play, two of the background characters in Shakespeare's Hamlet become the central figures.

***Roses.** unabr. ed. Leila Meacham. Read by Coleen Marlo. (ENG.). 2010. audio compact disk 40.00 (978-0-307-75083-9(3), Random AudioBks) Pub: Random Audio Pubg. Dist(s): Random

Roses Are Pink, Your Feet Really Stink. Diane deGroat. Read by Jason Harris & Peter Pamela Rose. 1 CD. (Running Time: 10 mins.). (Gilbert Ser.). (J). (gr. k-3). 2009. pap. bk. 18.95 (978-1-4301-0700-2(6)) Live Oak Media.

Roses Are Red. abr. ed. James Patterson. (Alex Cross Ser.: No. 6). 2001. 32.98 (978-1-58621-072-4(6)) Hachet Audio.

Roses Are Red. abr. ed. James Patterson. Read by Keith David & Jason Culp. (Alex Cross Ser.: No. 6). (ENG.). 2005. 14.98 (978-1-59483-451-6(2)) Pub: Hachet Audio. Dist(s): HachBkGrp

Roses Are Red. collector's ed. James Patterson. Read by Peter Jay Fernandez. 6 cass. (Running Time: 9 hrs.). (Alex Cross Ser.: No. 6). 2000. 26.95 (978-0-7366-5644-3(8)) Books on Tape.

Roses Are Red. unabr. ed. James Patterson. Read by Peter Jay Fernandez. (Alex Cross Ser.: No. 6). (ENG.). 2005. 16.98 (978-1-59483-450-9(4)) Pub: Hachet Audio. Dist(s): HachBkGrp

Roses Are Red. unabr. ed. James Patterson. Read by Peter Jay Fernandez. (Running Time: 8 hrs.). (Alex Cross Ser.: No. 6). (ENG.). 2009. 49.98 (978-1-60788-090-5(3)) Pub: Hachet Audio. Dist(s): HachBkGrp

Roses Are Red. unabr. ed. James Patterson. Read by Paul Birchard. 6 cass. (Running Time: 9 hrs.). (Alex Cross Ser.: No. 6). 2001. (978-0-7531-1074-4(1)) ISIS Audio GBR.
A series of meticulously planned bank robberies ends in murder, and Alex Cross must pit his wits against the bizarre and sadistic mastermind behind the crimes. Although torn between dedication to his job and commitment to his family, Cross cannot ignore the case, despite the risks he knows will come with hunting down a killer and the heartbreaking cost.

Rose's Garden. unabr. ed. Carrie Brown. Read by Jeremy Gage. 8 vols. (Running Time: 12 hrs.). 2000. bk. 69.95 (978-0-7927-2268-7(X), CSL 157, Chivers Sound Lib) AudioGO.
Conrad and Rose had been married over fifty years. It's now four months since Rose's death and Conrad finds himself horribly alone, rejecting offers of consolation and neglecting Rose's garden. It isn't Rose though, but the visitation is so startling that Conrad feels compelled to reach out to others in the small New Hampshire town he lives in.

Roses of Light. Ted Andrews. Read by Ted Andrews. 1 cass. (Running Time: 43 min.). 1994. 10.00 (978-1-888767-00-1(6)) Life Magic Ent.
Music & meditation to relax & heal the body, mind & spirit. Contains tones & images to relieve stress & renew health.

Roses Red as Blood. Anne Schraff. (Running Time: 4159 sec.). (Pageturners Ser.). (J). 2004. 10.95 (978-1-56254-713-4(5), SP7135) Saddleback Edu.

Roses Round the Door. unabr. ed. Christine M. Fraser. 8 cass. (Running Time: 8 hrs.). 1998. 83.95 (978-1-872672-32-8(9)) Pub: Magna Story GBR. Dist(s): Ulverscroft US

Roses Round the Door. unabr. ed. Doreen Tovey. Read by Anne Cater. 5 cass. (Running Time: 6 hrs.). 1999. 49.95 (978-1-86042-640-7(9), 26409) Pub: Soundings Ltd GBR. Dist(s): Ulverscroft US
Uses her own experiences of Somerset to provide us with lively & eccentric, sometimes outrageous characters, including the long-suffering Aunt Louisa, a cantankerous landlord & feuding neighbors which she & her husband are obliged to tolerate. An interesting, at times hilarious, account of parochial life which is universal in its ability to entertain.

***Rosetta Key.** unabr. ed. William Dietrich. Read by Jeff Woodman. (ENG.). 2008. (978-0-06-163242-6(2)); (978-0-06-163243-3(0)) HarperCollins Pubs.

Rosetta Key. unabr. ed. William Dietrich. Read by Jeff Woodman. 2009. audio compact disk 19.99 (978-0-06-172759-7(8), Harper Audio) HarperCollins Pubs.

Rosetta Stone. Stephen Sloan. Narrated by Larry A. McKeever. (Ancient Egyptian Mystery Ser.). (J). 2004. 10.95 (978-1-58659-125-0(8)); audio compact disk 14.95 (978-1-58659-359-9(5)) Artesian.

***Rosetta Stone(r) Version 3: French Level 1,2,3,4 & 5 Set with Audio Companiontrade;** Rosetta Stone. 2009. 699.00 (978-1-60829-696-5(2)) RosettaStone.

***Rosetta Stone(r) Version 3: French Level 4 with Audio Companiontrade;** Rosetta Stone. 2009. 299.00 (978-1-60829-695-8(4)) RosettaStone.

***Rosetta Stone(r) Version 3: French Level 5 with Audio Companiontrade;** Rosetta Stone. 2009. 299.00 (978-1-60829-778-8(0)) RosettaStone.

***Rosetta Stone(r) Version 3: German Level 1,2,3,4 & 5 Set with Audio Companiontrade;** Rosetta Stone. 2009. 699.00 (978-1-60829-700-9(4)) RosettaStone.

***Rosetta Stone(r) Version 3: German Level 4 with Audio Companiontrade;** Rosetta Stone. 2009. 299.00 (978-1-60829-699-6(7)) RosettaStone.

***Rosetta Stone(r) Version 3: German Level 5 with Audio Companiontrade;** Rosetta Stone. 2009. 299.00 (978-1-60829-780-1(2)) RosettaStone.

***Rosetta Stone(r) Version 3: Italian Level 1,2,3,4 & 5 Set with Audio Companiontrade;** Rosetta Stone. 2009. 699.00 (978-1-60829-698-9(9)) RosettaStone.

***Rosetta Stone(r) Version 3: Italian Level 4 with Audio Companiontrade;** Rosetta Stone. 2009. 299.00 (978-1-60829-697-2(0)) RosettaStone.

***Rosetta Stone(r) Version 3: Italian Level 5 with Audio Companiontrade;** Rosetta Stone. 2009. 299.00 (978-1-60829-779-5(9)) RosettaStone.

***Rosetta Stone(r) Version 3: Spanish (Spain) Level 1,2,3,4 & 5 Set with Audio Companiontrade;** Rosetta Stone. 2009. 699.00 (978-1-60829-702-3(0)) RosettaStone.

***Rosetta Stone(r) Version 3: Spanish (Spain) Level 4 with Audio Companiontrade;** Rosetta Stone. 2009. 299.00 (978-1-60829-701-6(2)) RosettaStone.

***Rosetta Stone(r) Version 3: Spanish (Spain) Level 5 with Audio Companiontrade;** Rosetta Stone. 2009. 299.00 (978-1-60829-781-8(0)) RosettaStone.

Rosewood Casket. Sharyn McCrumb. Narrated by C.M. Hébert. (Running Time: 10 hrs. 30 mins.). (Ballad Ser.: No. 4). 1996. 30.95 (978-1-59912-713-2(X)) Iofy Corp.

Rosewood Casket. unabr. ed. Sharyn McCrumb. Read by C. M. Herbert. 7 cass. (Running Time: 10 hrs.). (Ballad Ser.: No. 4). 2003. 49.95 (978-0-7861-0994-4(7), 1771) Blckstn Audio.
Randall Stargill's four sons have gathered at their mountain farm to build a coffin for their dying father. His passing causes a dilemma for his sons, who must come to terms with their dysfunctional family & also decide what to do with the farm, which has been Stargill land since 1790. Only Clayt, the youngest, a naturalist & Daniel Boone reenactor, who loves the land like a later-day pioneer, wants to save the farm from a real estate developer bent on despoiling the mountain.

Rosewood Casket. unabr. ed. Sharyn McCrumb. Read by C. M. Herbert. 9 CDs. (Running Time: 10 hrs.). (Ballad Ser.: No. 4). 1996. audio compact disk 72.00 (978-0-7861-9844-3(3), 1771) Blckstn Audio.

Rosewood Casket. unabr. ed. Sharyn McCrumb. Read by C. M. Herbert. 1 CD. (Running Time: 10 hrs. 30 mins.). (Ballad Ser.: No. 4). 2001. audio compact disk 19.95 (zm1771) Blckstn Audio.

Rosewood Casket. unabr. ed. Sharyn McCrumb. Narrated by Sally Darling. 9 cass. (Running Time: 12 hrs.). (Ballad Ser.: No. 4). 1996. 78.00 (978-0-7887-0522-9(9), 94717E7) Recorded Bks.
A local wise woman arrives as Randall Stargill lies dying. She has a small box containing the bones of a small child she wants buried with Randall.

Rosie & Jim's Christmas. abr. ed. 1 cass. (Running Time: 1 hr.). (J). 1999. 7.50 (978-1-86117-178-8(1)) Ulvrscrft Audio.

Rosie & Jim's Music Party. abr. ed. 1 cass. (Running Time: 1 hr.). (J). 1999. 7.50 (978-1-86117-145-0(5)) Ulvrscrft Audio.
Traditional ragdolls that have been left on a hired boat. They come alive & have many exciting adventures along the canal.

Rosie Dunne. abr. ed. Cecelia Ahern. Read by Russell Copley et al. 5 CDs. (Running Time: 6 hrs.). 2005. audio compact disk 29.98 (978-1-4013-8225-4(8), Hyperion Audio) Pub: Hyperion. Dist(s): HarperCollins Pubs

Rosie Dunne. unabr. ed. Cecelia Ahern. Read by Anna Fields. 6 cass. 2005. 54.95 (978-0-7927-3479-6(3), CSL 757); audio compact disk 79.95 (978-0-7927-3480-2(7), SLD 757) AudioGO.

Rosie Meadows Regrets. Catherine Alliott. Read by Jan Francis. 14 vols. 2003. 110.95 (978-0-7540-0959-7(9), CAB 2381, Chivers Sound Lib) AudioGO.

Rosie of the River. Catherine Cookson. Read by Susan Jameson. 6 CDs. (Running Time: 9 hrs.). 2001. audio compact disk 64.95 (978-0-7540-5421-4(7), CCD 112) Pub: Chivers Audio Bks GBR. Dist(s): AudioGO
Fred and Sally plan a boating holiday to the Norfolk Broads but Sally is filled with trepidation. They set off, but her misgivings are soon justified as a series of disasters threaten to ruin their holiday... until they meet Rosie.

Rosie of the River. unabr. ed. Catherine Cookson. Read by Susan Jameson. 6 cass. (Running Time: 6 hrs.). 2001. 54.95 (978-0-7540-0633-6(6), CAB2055) Pub: Chivers Audio Bks GBR. Dist(s): AudioGO
When Fred Carpenter suggests to his wife, Sally, that they should take a boating holiday on the Norfolk Broads, she is filled with trepidation. Nevertheless, she summons her courage & they set off, with Fred at the helm. Sally's misgivings are soon justified as a series of disasters threaten to ruin their holiday. Then everything changes when they encounter the fifteen-year-old Rosie.

Rosie's Big City Ballet. unabr. ed. Patricia Reilly Giff. Read by Christina Moore. 1 cass. (Running Time: 1 hr.). (Ballet Slippers Ser.). (J). 1999. 70.70 (978-0-7887-3221-8(8), 46877) Recorded Bks.
After Rosie watches the big city ballet, she wants to dance on stage someday, too. But when she tries to practice, either her best friend or her mother always has something for her to do. How will she find time for everything?.

Rosie's Big City Ballet. unabr. ed. Patricia Reilly Giff. Narrated by Christina Moore. 1 cass. (Running Time: 1 hr.). (Ballet Slippers Ser.). (gr. 1 up). 2000. 10.00 (978-0-7887-3156-3(4), 95829E7) Recorded Bks.

Rosie's Big City Ballet. unabr. ed. Patricia Reilly Giff. Read by Christina Moore. 1 cass. (Running Time: 1 hr.). (Ballet Slippers Ser.). (J). 2000. pap. bk. & stu. ed. 22.24 (978-0-7887-3175-4(0), 40910X4) Recorded Bks.

Rosie's Walk see Paseo de Rosita

Rosie's Walk. 2004. bk. 24.95 (978-0-89719-685-7(6)); pap. bk. 18.95 (978-1-55592-884-1(6)); pap. bk. 18.95 (978-1-55592-880-3(3)); pap. bk. 38.75 (978-1-55592-882-7(X)); pap. bk. 38.75 (978-1-55592-881-0(1)); pap. bk. 32.75 (978-1-55592-303-7(8)); pap. bk. 32.75 (978-1-55592-304-4(6)); pap. bk. 14.95 (978-0-7882-0073-2(6)); pap. bk. 14.95 (978-1-55592-669-4(X)); 8.95 (978-1-56008-321-4(2)); 8.95 (978-0-7882-0285-8(5)); 8.95 (978-1-56008-426-6(X)); cass. & flmstrp 30.00 (978-0-89719-550-8(7)); audio compact disk 12.95 (978-1-55592-885-8(4)) Weston Woods.

Rosie's Walk. Pat Hitchins. 1 cass. (Running Time: 3 min.). (J). (ps-2). pap. bk. 12.95 (RAC125) Weston Woods.
Against the strains of a catchy barnyard tune, a single-minded fox stalks an unsuspecting hen.

Rosie's Walk. Pat Hutchins. 1 cass., 5 bks. (Running Time: 5 min.). (J). pap. bk. 32.75 Weston Woods.
A single minded fox stalks an unsuspecting chicken.

Rosie's Walk. Pat Hutchins. 1 cass. (Running Time: 5 min.). (J). (ps-3). bk. 24.95; pap. bk. 12.95 (PRA125) Weston Woods.
A single minded fox stalks an unsuspecting chicken. From the book by Pat Hutchins.

Rosie's Walk; One Monday Morning; Last Free Bird, the; Selfish Giant. 2004. (978-0-89719-829-5(8)); cass. & flmstrp (978-0-89719-737-3(2)) Weston Woods.

Ross Poldark. Winston Graham. Read by Micheal Maloney. 3 cass. (Running Time: 4 hrs. 5 mins.). 18.00 (978-1-4050-0621-7(8)) Pub: Macmillan UK GBR. Dist(s): Trafalgar

Ross Poldark. unabr. ed. Winston Graham. Read by Tony Britton. 10 cass. (Running Time: 15 hrs.). (Poldark Ser.: Bk. 1). 2000. 69.95 (CAB 732) Pub: Chivers Audio Bks GBR. Dist(s): AudioGO
It is Cornwall in the 1780's. After the grim war in America, Ross Poldark returns to his land and family. But the joyful homecoming is soured, for his father is dead, his estate is derelict, and the woman he loves is engaged to his cousin. But when he rescues a half-starved street girl from a fairground brawl, his life will be changed forever.

Rosseau & the Enlightenment. Kenneth Bruce. 1 cass. (Running Time: 1 hr.). Dramatization. (Excursions in History Ser.). 12.50 Alpha Tape.
Explores Rosseau's impact on his times.

Rossetti: His Life & Works. unabr. collector's ed. Evelyn Waugh. Read by David Case. 6 cass. (Running Time: 9 hrs.). 2001. 48.00 Books on Tape.
An essential part of the Waugh canon displaying perhaps an unexpected talent for art criticism.

Rossini's Ghost. Composed by Gioachino Rossini. (Composer's Specials Ser.). 1998. audio compact disk 12.95 (978-0-634-00890-0(0), 0634008900) H Leonard.

Rossini's Ghost - ShowTrax. 1 CD. (Running Time: 1 hr.). 2000. audio compact disk 12.95 (00841334) H Leonard.

Rossinver Braes. Tony O'Connell. Ben Lennon. (ENG.). 2008. audio compact disk 25.95 (978-0-8023-8174-3(X)) Pub: Clo Iar-Chonnachta IRL. Dist(s): Dufour

Rostnikov's Vacation. unabr. ed. Stuart M. Kaminsky. Narrated by Mark Hammer. 6 cass. (Running Time: 8 hrs. 30 mins.). (Inspector Porfiry Rostnikov Mystery Ser.: No. 6). 1993. 51.00 (978-1-55690-840-8(7), 93208E7) Recorded Bks.
A Russian homicide investigator suspects murder when an old friend dies in the Black Sea resort of Yalta.

Rosy Is My Relative. unabr. ed. Gerald Durrell. Read by Jamie Glover. 6 cass. (Running Time: 9 hrs.). 2000. 49.95 (978-0-7451-6666-7(0), CAB 1282) Pub: Chivers Audio Bks GBR. Dist(s): AudioGO
What does a young man bequeathed five hundred pounds and an elephant with a taste for liquor do? Adrian Rockwhistle thought he had the answer, he'd give her to the circus. But it wasn't so easy. Together Adrian and Rosy cut a path of destruction through the peaceful countryside of Southern England... Until her hapless victims invoke a law against her.

Rotarian Socialism. Frank Chodorov. 1 cass. (Running Time: 57 min.). 10.95 (198) J Norton Pubs.

Roth to Riches: The Ordinary to Roth IRA Handbook. unabr. ed. John D. Bledsoe. Read by John D. Bledsoe. 2 cass. (Running Time: 2 hrs. 28 min.). 1998. 24.95 Set. (978-0-9629114-2-2(9)) Legacy TX.
Describes how to maximize your IRA; explains the how, when, why & how much of Roth conversions.

Rothschilds. unabr. ed. Frederic Morton. Read by Frederick Davidson. 7 cass. (Running Time: 10 hrs.). 2000. 49.95 (978-0-7861-0478-9(3), 1430) Blckstn Audio.

Rothschilds. unabr. ed. Frederick Morton. Read by Frederick Davidson. 7 cass. (Running Time: 10 hrs. 30 min.). 1993. 49.95 (1430) Blckstn Audio.
Morton brings that elusive clan to flesh-and-blood life and now, the drama, elegance, humor and extraordinary characters are unforgettable. Luxuriates in the social andhuman details of what happened once the Rothschilds had financed England, bailed out the returning French Bourbons, helped Austria intervene in Italy and lent millions to the Holy See itself.

Rothstein. David Pietrusza. Read by Grover Gardner. (Running Time: 14 hrs. 30 mins.). 2003. 41.95 (978-1-59912-585-5(4)) Iofy Corp.

Rothstein. David Pietrusza & Grover Gardner. 10 cass. (Running Time: 14 hrs. 30 mins.). 2002. 69.95 (978-0-7861-2581-4(0), 3167) Blckstn Audio.

Rothstein: The Life, Times, & Murder of the Criminal Genius Who Fixed the 1919 World Series. unabr. ed. David Pietrusza. Read by Grover Gardner. 13 CDs. (Running Time: 14 hrs. 30 mins.). 2006. audio compact disk 104.00 (978-0-7861-8983-0(5), 3167) Blckstn Audio.

Rotten Ralph Feels Rotten. Jack Gantos. Illus. by Nicole Rubel. 1 cass. (Running Time: 12 mins.). (J). (gr. k-3). 2007. bk. 29.95 (978-1-4301-0095-9(8)) Live Oak Media.

Rotten Ralph Feels Rotten. Jack Gantos. Read by Jack Gantos. Illus. by Nicole Rubel. 1 CD. (Running Time: 12 mins.). (Rotten Ralph Ser.). (J). (ps-3). 2007. bk. 28.95 (978-1-4301-0098-0(2)) Live Oak Media.

***Rotten School #1 And #2.** unabr. ed. R. L. Stine. Read by Michael Mckean. (ENG.). 2005. (978-0-06-085462-1(6)); (978-0-06-085461-4(8)) HarperCollins Pubs.

Rottweiler. unabr. ed. Ruth Rendell. Read by Jennifer McMahon. 9 cass. (Running Time: 13 hrs. 30 min.). 2004. 72.00 (978-1-4159-0157-1(0)); audio compact disk 90.00 (978-1-4159-0765-8(X)) Books on Tape.
When the first victim is discovered, the bite mark on her neck prompts the media to name the killer "the Rottweiler". But as the death toll rises, it becomes clear that that which distinguishes this killer is not bite marks but his taking a small trinket.

Rouge et le Noir see Treasury of French Prose

Rouge et le Noir. Stendhal. audio compact disk 12.95 (978-0-8219-3763-1(4)) EMC-Paradigm.

Rouge et le Noir. Stendhal. 3 cass. (Running Time: 3 hrs.). (FRE.). 1996. pap. bk. 39.50 set. (978-1-58085-354-5(4)) Interlingua VA.
Includes first 8 chapters, French text. The combination of written text & clarity & pace of diction will open the door for intermediate & advanced students to genuine comprehension & the use of literary texts for advancement in rapid understanding of written & oral language materials. The audio text plus written text concept makes foreign languages accessible to a much wider range of students than books alone.

Rouge et le Noir. Stendhal. 5 cass. (Running Time: 5 hrs.). Dramatization. (FRE.). 1991. 46.95 (1126-RF) Olivia & Hill.
Traces the story of Julien Sorel during the Restoration in France.

Rough Cider. unabr. ed. Peter Lovesey. Read by Stephen Thorne. 6 cass. (Running Time: 6 hrs. 21 min.). (Isis Ser.). (J). 2001. 54.95 (978-1-85089-785-9(9), 88022) Pub: ISIS Lrg Prnt GBR. Dist(s): Ulverscroft US

Rough Country. abr. ed. John Sandford, pseud. Read by Eric Conger. (Running Time: 6 hrs.). No. 3. (gr. 12 up). 2009. audio compact disk 29.95 (978-0-14-314485-4(5)) Penguin Grp USA.

Rough Country. unabr. ed. John Sandford, pseud. Read by Eric Conger. 8 CDs. (Running Time: 10 hrs.). No. 3. (gr. 12 up). 2009. audio compact disk 39.95 (978-0-14-314484-7(7), PengAudBks) Penguin Grp USA.

***Rough Crossings: Britain, the Slaves, & the American Re.** abr. ed. Simon Schama. Read by Simon Schama. (ENG.). 2006. (978-0-06-117152-9(2), Harper Audio); (978-0-06-117154-3(9), Harper Audio) HarperCollins Pubs.

Rough Crossings: Britain, the Slaves, & the American Revolution. abr. ed. Simon Schama. Read by Simon Schama. 10 CDs. (Running Time: 41400 sec.). 2006. audio compact disk 39.95 (978-0-06-113702-0(2)) HarperCollins Pubs.

Rough Draft. unabr. ed. James W. Hall. Read by Sandra Burr. (Running Time: 12 hrs.). 2007. 39.25 (978-1-4233-3614-3(3), 9781423336143, BADLE); 24.95 (978-1-4233-3613-6(5), 9781423336136, BAD) Brilliance Audio.

Rough Draft. unabr. ed. James W. Hall. Read by Sandra Burr. (Running Time: 43200 sec.). 2007. audio compact disk 24.95 (978-1-4233-3611-2(9), 9781423336112, Brilliance MP3); audio compact disk 39.25 (978-1-4233-3612-9(7), 9781423336129, Brlnc Audio MP3 Lib) Brilliance Audio.

Rough Guide to African Blues. Compiled by Phil Stanton. 2008. audio compact disk 14.98 (978-1-906063-08-5(7)) Pub: Rough Guides GBR. Dist(s): PerseuPGW

Rough Guide to African Street Party. Compiled by John Armstrong. 2008. audio compact disk 14.95 (978-1-906063-24-5(9)) Pub: Rough Guides GBR. Dist(s): PerseuPGW

Rough Guide to Australian Aboriginal Music. Compiled by Bruce Elder. (Music Rough Guides). 2008. audio compact disk 14.95 (978-1-906063-31-3(1)) Rough Guides GBR.

Rough Guide to Bellydance Cafe. Compiled by Nili Belkind. 2008. audio compact disk 14.98 (978-1-906063-07-8(9)) Pub: Rough Guides GBR. Dist(s): PerseuPGW

Rough Guide to Bollywood Gold. Compiled by DJ Ritu. 2008. audio compact disk 14.95 (978-1-906063-04-7(4)) Pub: Rough Guides GBR. Dist(s): PerseuPGW

Rough Guide to Brazilian Street Party. Compiled by John Armstrong. (Music Rough Guides). 2008. audio compact disk 14.95 (978-1-906063-30-6(3)) Rough Guides GBR.

Rough Guide to Congo Gold. Compiled by Martin Sinnock. 2008. audio compact disk 14.95 (978-1-906063-21-4(4)) Pub: Rough Guides GBR. Dist(s): PerseuPGW

Rough Guide to Cuban Street Party. Compiled by Pablo Yglesiasstrong. (Music Rough Guides). 2008. audio compact disk 14.95 (978-1-906063-22-1(2)) Rough Guides GBR.

Rough Guide to Flamenco. 2nd ed. Compiled by Jan Fairley. 2008. audio compact disk 14.98 (978-1-906063-11-5(7)) Pub: Rough Guides GBR. Dist(s): PerseuPGW

Rough Guide to Hungarian Gypsy. Compiled by Dan Rosenberg. 2008. audio compact disk 14.95 (978-1-906063-23-8(0)) Pub: Rough Guides GBR. Dist(s): PerseuPGW

Rough Guide to Indian Lounge. Compiled by DJ Ritu. 2008. audio compact disk 14.98 (978-1-906063-14-6(1)) Pub: Rough Guides GBR. Dist(s): PerseuPGW

Rough Guide to Klezmer Revival. Compiled by Dan Rosenberg. 2008. audio compact disk 14.95 (978-1-906063-27-6(3)) Pub: Rough Guides GBR. Dist(s): PerseuPGW

Rough Guide to Latin Funk. Compiled by Pablo Yglesias. 2008. audio compact disk 14.95 (978-1-906063-18-4(4)) Pub: Rough Guides GBR. Dist(s): PerseuPGW

Rough Guide to Latino Nuevo. Compiled by Pablo Yglesias. 2008. audio compact disk 14.95 (978-1-906063-12-2(5)) Pub: Rough Guides GBR. Dist(s): PerseuPGW

Rough Guide to North African Cafe. Compiled by John Armstrong. 2008. audio compact disk 14.98 (978-1-906063-09-2(5)) Pub: Rough Guides GBR. Dist(s): PerseuPGW

Rough Guide to Salsa. 2nd ed. Compiled by Pablo Yglesias. 2008. audio compact disk 14.95 (978-1-906063-06-1(0)) Pub: Rough Guides GBR. Dist(s): PerseuPGW

Rough Guide to Salsa Clandestina. Compiled by Pablo Yglesias. 2008. audio compact disk 14.98 (978-1-906063-13-9(3)) Pub: Rough Guides GBR. Dist(s): PerseuPGW

Rough Guide to Salsa Dura. 2008. audio compact disk 14.98 (978-1-906063-00-9(1)) Pub: Rough Guides GBR. Dist(s): PerseuPGW

Rough Guide to the Music of Brazil. 2nd ed. Compiled by John Armstrong. 2008. audio compact disk 14.95 (978-1-906063-10-8(9)) Pub: Rough Guides GBR. Dist(s): PerseuPGW

Rough Guide to the Music of Paris. Compiled by Guillaume Veillet. 2008. audio compact disk 14.98 (978-1-906063-16-0(8)) Pub: Rough Guides GBR. Dist(s): PerseuPGW

Rough Guide to Vietnam. Compiled by Paul Fisher. 2008. audio compact disk 14.95 (978-1-906063-05-4(2)) Pub: Rough Guides GBR. Dist(s): PerseuPGW

Rough Justice. Jack Higgins. Read by Michael Page. (Sean Dillon Ser.). 2009. 64.99 (978-1-60775-683-5(8)) Find a World.

Rough Justice. abr. ed. Jack Higgins. Read by Michael Page. (Running Time: 5 hrs.). (Sean Dillon Ser.). 2009. audio compact disk 14.99 (978-1-4233-6813-7(4), 9781423368137) Brilliance Audio.

Rough Justice. unabr. ed. Jack Higgins. Read by Michael Page. (Running Time: 11 hrs.). (Sean Dillon Ser.). 2008. 39.25 (978-1-4233-7000-0(7), 9781423370000, BADLE); 39.25 (978-1-4233-6998-1(X), 9781423369981, Brlnc Audio MP3 Lib); 24.95 (978-1-4233-6999-8(8), 9781423369998, BAD); 24.95 (978-1-4233-6997-4(1), 9781423369974, Brilliance MP3); audio compact disk 87.25 (978-1-4233-6996-7(3), 9781423369967, BriAudCD Unabrid); audio compact disk 34.95 (978-1-4233-6995-0(5), 9781423369950, Bril Audio CD Unabri) Brilliance Audio.

Rough Justice, unabr. ed. Lisa Scottoline. Narrated by Barbara Rosenblat. 8 cass. (Running Time: 11 hrs. 30 mins.). 1999. 75.00 (978-0-7887-1760-4(X), 95238E7) Recorded Bks.
The murder trial is near its end & defense attorney Marta Richter's client, millionaire businessman Elliot Steere, is sure to be acquitted. But when he inadvertently admits his guilt to her, Richter is faced with a chilling choice: remain silent, or begin looking for new evidence - this time to convict him.

***Rough Justice: The Rise & Fall of Eliot Spitzer.** unabr. ed. Peter Elkind. Narrated by Arthur Morey. (Running Time: 13 hrs. 30 mins.). 2010. 18.99 (978-1-4001-8735-5(4)); 24.99 (978-1-4001-6735-7(3)); 37.99 (978-1-4001-9735-4(X)); audio compact disk 90.99 (978-1-4001-4735-9(2));

audio compact disk 37.99 (978-1-4001-1735-2(6)) Pub: Tantor Media. Dist(s): IngramPubServ

*Rough Justice Low Price. abr. ed. Lisa Scottoline. Read by Kate Burton. (ENG.). 2005. (978-0-06-088720-9(6), Harper Audio); (978-0-06-088721-6(4), Harper Audio) HarperCollins Pubs.

Rough Riders. unabr. ed. Theodore Roosevelt. Narrated by John Randolph Jones. 4 cass. (Running Time: 5 hrs. 30 mins.). 1993. 35.00 (978-1-55690-914-6(4), 93410E7) Recorded Bks.
Theodore Roosevelt's account of the Spanish American War as seen by his regiment, the 1st U.S. Volunteer Cavalry, known to the American public as the Rough Riders.

Rough Riders. unabr. collector's ed. Theodore Roosevelt. Read by Jonathan Reese. 6 cass. (Running Time: 6 hrs.). 1993. 36.00 (978-0-7366-2440-4(6), 3205) Books on Tape.
Roosevelt was Assistant Secretary of the Navy in 1898 when war broke out in Cuba. He was fervent in urging that we "...drive the Spaniard from the Western World".

Rough Start, Great Finish. John Bytheway. (YA). 2007. audio compact disk 14.95 (978-1-59038-832-7(1)) Deseret Bk.

Rough Water: Stories of Survival from the Sea. 2009. audio compact disk 24.95 (978-1-59316-451-5(3)) Listen & Live.

Rough Weather. unabr. ed. Robert B. Parker. Read by Joe Mantegna. 5 CDs. (Running Time: 5 hrs. 30 mins.). (Spenser Ser.). (ENG.). 2008. audio compact disk 29.95 (978-0-7393-3998-5(2), Random AudioBks) Pub: Random Audio Pubg. Dist(s): Random

Roughing It. Mark Twain. 2007. 33.95 (978-1-60112-015-1(X)) Babblebooks.

Roughing It, unabr. ed. Mark Twain. Narrated by Norman Dietz. 11 cass. (Running Time: 16 hrs.). 1987. 91.00 (978-1-55690-449-3(5), 87480E7) Recorded Bks.
An account of the author's seven-year "pleasure trip" to the silver mines of Nevada.

***Roughing It.** unabr. ed. Mark Twain. Narrated by Peter Berkrot. (Running Time: 19 hrs. 0 mins.). 2010. 22.99 (978-1-4526-7045-4(5)); 29.99 (978-1-4526-5045-6(4)); audio compact disk 39.99 (978-1-4526-0045-1(7)) Pub: Tantor Media. Dist(s): IngramPubServ

***Roughing It.** unabr. ed. Mark Twain. Narrated by Robin Field. (ENG.). 2010. 34.98 (978-1-59644-982-4(9), MissionAud); audio compact disk 39.98 (978-1-59644-981-7(0), MissionAud) christianaud.

Roughing It. unabr. collector's ed. Mark Twain. Read by Michael Prichard. 12 cass. (Running Time: 18 hrs.). 1986. 96.00 (978-0-7366-1071-1(5), 1998) Books on Tape.
In his youth Mark Twain drifted through the West. He worked as a civil servant, gold prospector, reporter & lecturer. This is Twain's record - fact & impression - of those early years.

Roughing It & Life in the Mississippi. Mark Twain. 1 cass. (Running Time: 1 hr.). (Radiobook Ser.). 1987. 4.98 (978-0-929541-19-8(7)) Radiola Co.
Two complete stories.

***Roughing It (Library Edition)** unabr. ed. Mark Twain. Narrated by Peter Berkrot. (Running Time: 19 hrs. 0 mins.). 2010. 39.99 (978-1-4526-2045-9(8)); audio compact disk 95.99 (978-1-4526-3045-8(3)) Pub: Tantor Media. Dist(s): IngramPubServ

Roughneck Nine-One: The Extraordinary Story of a Special Forces A-Team at War. unabr. ed. Frank Antenori & Hans Halberstadt. Read by Patrick G. Lawlor. (Running Time: 10 hrs. 0 mins. 0 sec.). (ENG.). 2006. audio compact disk 69.99 (978-1-4001-3260-7(6)); audio compact disk 24.99 (978-1-4001-5260-5(7)); audio compact disk 34.99 (978-1-4001-0260-0(X)) Pub: Tantor Media. Dist(s): IngramPubServ

Roughneck Nine-One: The Extraordinary Story of a Special Forces A-Team at War. unabr. ed. S. F. C. Frank Antenori & Hans Halberstadt. Read by Patrick G. Lawlor. (YA). 2007. 59.99 (978-1-60252-924-3(8)) Find a World.

Roumain sans Peine. 1 cass. (Running Time: 1 hr. 30 min.). (FRE & RUM.). 2000. bk. 75.00 (978-2-7005-1317-2(7)) Pub: Assimil FRA. Dist(s): Distribks Inc

Round & Round the Garden. unabr. ed. Alan Ayckbourn. Read by Rosalind Ayers et al. 1 cass. (Running Time: 1 hr. 26 mins.). 2001. 20.95 (978-1-58081-158-3(2), TPT83) L A Theatre.

'Round & 'Round the Garden: Music in My First Year! John M. Feierabend & Luann Saunders. 1 CD. (Running Time: 1 hr. 0 mins. 0 sec.). (First Steps in Music Ser.). (ENG., (J). (ps). 2000. audio compact disk 12.95 (978-1-57999-083-1(5)) Pub: GIA Pubns. Dist(s): IPG Chicago
Derived from the First Steps in Music books, the 61 recordings are best suited for use with children in their first year of life. These include such favorites as "To Market, To Market," "This Little Piggy," "Rain, Rain, Go Away," "Ally Bally" & "Hot Cross Buns.".

Round & Round the Garden: Music in My First Year! John M. Feierabend & Luann Saunders. 1 cass. (Running Time: 1 hr. 0 mins. 0 sec.). (First Steps in Music Ser.). (ENG., (J). (ps). 2000. 9.95 (978-1-57999-087-9(8)) Pub: GIA Pubns. Dist(s): IPG Chicago

Round Dance Tonight! Perf. by Black Lodge Singers Staff. 1 cass. (Running Time: 1 hr.). 7.98 (CANR 6278); audio compact disk 11.98 (CANR 6278) NewSound.

Round Ireland with a Fridge. Tony Hawks. Read by Tony Hawks. 2 cass. (Running Time: 3 hrs.). 1999. 16.85 Set. (978-1-85686-512-8(6)) Ulvrscrft Audio.

Round Midnight. Perf. by Tyscot. 1 cass. (Running Time: 1 hr.). 10.98 (978-1-57908-267-3(X), 1351); audio compact disk 15.98 (978-1-57908-266-6(1), 1351) Platinm Enter.

Round Rock. unabr. ed. Michelle Huneven. Read by Tim Jerome. 10 vols. (Running Time: 15 hrs.). 2000. bk. 84.95 (978-0-7927-2250-2(7), CSL 139, Chivers Sound Lib) AudioGO.
In a small town in the Santa Bernita Valley, Red Ray, a lawyer whose alcoholism has destroyed his marriage, establishes Round Rock, a drunk farm. The farm houses Libby Daw, whose husband has run off to Los Angeles; and Lewis Fletcher, a sometimes graduate student, who finds his keen intelligence sorely tested by Ray at Round Rock. As these people and others begin to discover their destinies, each of them struggles for equilibrium.

Round the Bend. unabr. ed. Nevil Shute. Read by John Telfer. 12 cass. (Running Time: 18 hrs.). 2002. 69.95 (CAB 2137) AudioGO.
Running a polyglot airline n the persian Gulf was hard work, even for a man like Tom Cutter. His old friend Connie, Eurasian mystic and first-class engineer, was just the help he needed, especially when he arrived with his beautiful sister as company. Fate was taking a hand, and the three destinies interlocked as events moved swiftly towards a compelling climax.

Round the Bend. unabr. collector's ed. Nevil Shute. Read by Christopher Hurt. 9 cass. (Running Time: 13 hrs. 30 min.). 1985. 72.00 (978-0-7366-0827-5(3), 1777) Books on Tape.
Tom Cutter is in love with airplanes & he organizes an independent flying service on the Persian Gulf. He sees opportunities everywhere, also dangers.

Round the Fire Stories. unabr. ed. Arthur Conan Doyle. Read by Alexander John. 7 cass. (Running Time: 18 hrs.). 2001. 61.95 (978-1-85695-749-6(7), 940409) Pub: ISIS Audio GBR. Dist(s): Ulverscroft US
Seventeen stories of murder, madness, ghosts, unsolved crimes, diabolical traps & inexplicable disappearances.

Round the Horne. Kenneth Horne. 2 cass. (Running Time: 2 hrs.). Dramatization. (BBC Humor Ser.). 1991. 14.95 Minds Eye.
Dramatizations produced by the BBC.

***Round the Horne Vol. 2: The Very Best Episodes.** Narrated by Kenneth Horne. Lyn Took. (Running Time: 2 hrs. 0 mins. 0 sec.). (ENG., 2010. audio compact disk 24.95 (978-1-84607-001-3(5)) Pub: AudioGO. Dist(s): Perseus Dist

Round the Horne: Very Best Episodes: The BBC Radio Comedy Series. Created by Broadcasting Corp. British. (Running Time: 2 hrs. 0 mins. 0 sec.). (ENG.). 2009. audio compact disk 24.95 (978-1-60283-748-5(1)) Pub: AudioGO. Dist(s): Perseus Dist

Round the World on a Wheel. unabr. collector's ed. John F. Fraser. Read by Michael Prichard. 10 cass. (Running Time: 15 hrs.). 1985. 80.00 (978-0-7366-0820-6(6), 1769) Books on Tape.
Fraser, accompanied by two friends cycled for 19,237 miles, through seventeen countries & across three continents, returning to London after two years & two months.

Round Trip. Ann Jonas. Read by Linda Terheyden. (Live Oak Readalong Ser.). pap. bk. 18.95 (978-1-59519-345-2(6)) Pub: Live Oak Media. Dist(s): AudioGO

Round Trip. Ann Jonas. Illus. by Ann Jonas. (Running Time: 5 mins.). 1992. 9.95 (978-1-59112-113-8(2)) Live Oak Media.

Round Trip. unabr. ed. Ann Jonas. Illus. by Ann Jonas. Read by Linda Terheyden. 11 vols. (Running Time: 5 mins.). (J). (gr. k-3). 1992. bk. 25.95 (978-0-87499-269-4(9)); pap. bk. 16.95 (978-0-87499-268-7(0)); pap. bk. & tchr. ed. 33.95 (978-0-87499-270-0(2)) Live Oak Media.
This trip from a small town to the city & back again is accomplished by turning the book upside down & viewing the illustrations from a different perspective.

Round Trip. unabr. ed. Ann Jonas. 1 cass. (Running Time: 5 min.). (J). (gr. k-4). 1992. 9.95 Live Oak Media.

Round-Up: Favorite Western Themes. Perf. by Erich Kunzel & Cincinnati Pops Orchestra. 1 cass. (Running Time: 1 hr.). 7.98 (TA 30141); audio compact disk 12.78 (TA 80141) NewSound.

Round up the Sin Gang Tape. Patricia Holland. 1 cass. (Running Time: 50 min.). Dramatization. (J). 1993. incl. script. Let Us Tch Kids.
Skits for drama/puppets for religious/Bible.

Rounder: Cowboy Tales & Poems. As told by Tex Carroll. (ENG.). 2007. audio compact disk 15.95 (978-0-9802014-6-3(3)) Four T Two.

Rounders 3. abr. ed. Max Evans. Read by Brian Keith. 4 cass. (Running Time: 6 hrs.). 2003. 25.00 (978-1-59040-216-0(2)) Brilliance Audio.
Contains The Rounders, The Great Wedding and The Orange County Cowboys.

Rounding the Mark. unabr. ed. Andrea Camilleri. Read by Grover Gardner. (Running Time: 6 hrs. 0 mins.). (Inspector Montalbano Mystery Ser.). 2010. 29.95 (978-1-4417-2181-5(9)); 44.95 (978-1-4417-2177-8(0)); audio compact disk 55.00 (978-1-4417-2178-5(9)) Blckstn Audio.

Rounds Galore. 1 cass. (Running Time: 1 hr.). bk. 14.95 (C-700); audio compact disk 14.95 (CD-700) Folk-Legacy.
Thirty-two examples from Sol Weber's published collection of 340 rounds.

Roundtable: The Future of Religion. 1 cass. (Running Time: 90 min.). 1985. 10.95 (978-0-7822-0322-6(1), 170) C G Jung IL.

Roundtable Discussion: Session 1. 1 cass. 1990. 8.50 Recorded Res.

Roundtable Discussion: Session 10. 1 cass. 1990. 8.50 Recorded Res.

Roundtable Discussion: Session 2. 1 cass. 1990. 8.50 Recorded Res.

Roundtable Discussion: Session 3. 1 cass. 1990. 8.50 Recorded Res.

Roundtable Discussion: Session 5. 1 cass. 1990. 8.50 Recorded Res.

Roundtable Discussion: Session 6. 1 cass. 1990. 8.50 Recorded Res.

Roundtable Discussion: Session 7. 1 cass. 1990. 8.50 Recorded Res.

Roundtable Discussion: Session 8. 1 cass. 1990. 8.50 Recorded Res.

Roundtable Discussion: Session 9. 1 cass. 1990. 8.50 Recorded Res.

Roundtable Discussion on Advanced Discovery. 1995. bk. 99.00 (ACS-1033) PA Bar Inst.
In this advanced level look at some of the stickiest discovery issues, the Honorable R. Stanton Wettick elicits candid, thoughtful responses from a panel leading litigators about how to conduct truly effective discovery. Using a series of hypothetical situations, Judge Wettick & his panel discuss everyday, recurring problems & provide insight into discovery techniques & strategies.

Rousseau. Henri Guillemin. 1 cass. (FRE.). 1991. 22.95 (1213-VSL) Olivia & Hill.

Rousseau & Revolution, Pt. 2. collector's ed. Will Durant & Ariel Durant. Read by Alexander Adams. 13 cass. (Running Time: 19 hrs. 30 min.). (Story of Civilization Ser.). 1999. 104.00 (978-0-7366-4757-1(0), 5079-B) Books on Tape.
A history of Europe during much of the eighteenth century that concentrates on the French Revolution & the beginnings of the Romantic movement.

Rousseau & Revolution, Pt. 3. collector's ed. Will Durant & Ariel Durant. Read by Alexander Adams. 12 cass. (Running Time: 18 hrs.). (Story of Civilization Ser.). 1999. 96.00 (978-0-7366-4758-8(9), 5079-C) Books on Tape.

Rousseau in 90 Minutes. Paul Strathern. Read by Robert Whitfield. (Running Time: 1 hr. 30 mins.). 2004. 15.95 (978-0-7861-2781-8(3), 3314); audio compact disk 17.00 (978-0-7861-8535-1(X), 3314) Blckstn Audio.

Rousseau in 90 Minutes. unabr. ed. Paul Strathern. Read by Robert Whitfield. (Running Time: 1 hr. 30 mins.). (Philosophers in 90 Minutes Ser.). 2004. reel tape 14.95 (978-0-7861-2786-3(4)); audio compact disk 14.95 (978-0-7861-8534-4(1)) Blckstn Audio.

Route des Flandres, Set. Claude Simon. Read by Antoine Vitez. 6 cass. (FRE.). 1991. 47.95 (1122-AV) Olivia & Hill.
The narrator of the novel tells the story of contemporary Flanders devastated by war in 1940 & of Flanders of the Convention era when the narrator's ancestor Reixach also experienced defeat on the battlefield.

Route Sixty-Six: America's Main Street. unabr. ed. Jimmy Gray. Read by Dennis Stone. 1 cass. (Running Time: 60 min.). (Americana Ser.). 1995. 9.95 (978-1-887262-02-6(4), AudioMagazine) Natl Tape & Disc.
For two generations, Route 66 was the main street of America. It was the mother road & there was never another like it. With narrative & character voices with background music.

Route Sixty-Six: The Mother Road. abr. ed. Michael Wallis. Read by Michael Wallis. Read by Michael Martin Murphey. 2 cass. (Running Time: 3 hrs.). 1995. 17.95 (978-0-944993-96-5(6)) Audio Lit.
Stories, songs & fables, funny, heartwarming & magical celebrate this legendary roadway. Wallis & Murphey will take you down one of the world's most famous roads the road of dreamers, ramblers & drifters like John Steinbeck, Woody Guthrie & Jack Kerouac where you will meet the people & places that helped make Route 66 an American legend.

Route to Miracles. Elbert Willis. 1 cass. (Miracle Land Ser.). 4.00 Fill the Gap.

Route 66: America's Main Street. unabr. ed. Jimmy Gray. Narrated by Dennis Stone. Prod. by Joe Loesch. 1 cass. (Running Time: 1 hr.). (Americana Ser.). 1999. 12.95 (978-1-887729-68-0(2)) Toy Box Prods.
For three generations, this was the highway that linked America together. The stories of the tourists, the Okies, the wartime GI's & the people who ran the tourist courts & cafes.

Route 66: The Mother Road. Prod. by Kitchen Sisters Kitchen Sisters. 1 cass. (Running Time: 64 min.). 11.95 (G0110B090, HarperThor) HarpC GBR.

***Routes & Radishes: And Other Things to Talk about at the Evangelical Crossroads.** unabr. ed. Mark L. Russell et al. (Running Time: 6 hrs. 43 mins. 53 sec.). (ENG.). 2010. 22.99 (978-0-310-57601-3(6)) Zondervan.

Routes 'n Roots: An Explorer's Guide to America. (Running Time: 30 min.). (YA). (gr. 9 up). BackPax Int.
Exciting audio journey for kids, parents, & even teachers.

***Routes of Man: How Roads Are Changing the World & the Way We Live Today.** unabr. ed. Ted Conover. Read by Dick Hill. (Running Time: 13 hrs.). 2010. 24.99 (978-1-4418-5929-7(2), 9781441859297, Brilliance MP3); 24.99 (978-1-4418-5931-0(4), 9781441859310, BAD) Brilliance Audio.

***Routes of Man: How Roads Are Changing the World & the Way We Live Today.** unabr. ed. Ted Conover. Read by Dick Hill. (Running Time: 13 hrs.). 2010. 39.97 (978-1-4418-5930-3(6), 9781441859303, Brinc Audio MP3 Lib); 39.97 (978-1-4418-5932-7(2), 9781441859327, BADLE); audio compact disk 29.99 (978-1-4418-5927-3(6), 9781441859273, Bril Audio CD Unabri); audio compact disk 92.97 (978-1-4418-5928-0(4), 9781441859280, BriAudCD Unabrid) Brilliance Audio.

Routledge German Dictionary of Business, Commerce & Finance: German-English/English-German Deutsch-Englisch/Englisch-Deutsch. 2nd rev. ed. Routledge Staff.Tr. of Worterbuch fur Wirtschaft, Handel und Finanzen Englisch. 2004. audio compact disk 360.00 (978-0-415-30237-1(4)) Pub: Routledge. Dist(s): Taylor and Fran

Routledge German Dictionary of Environmental Technology /Worterbuch Umwelttechnologie: English-German/German-English. Amy Newland. (Routledge Bilingual Specialist Dictionaries Ser.). 1998. cd-rom 440.00 (978-0-415-14271-7(7)) Pub: Routledge. Dist(s): Taylor and Fran

Routledge German Dictionary of Information Technology/Worterbuch Informationstechnologie: English-German/German-English. Ed. by U. Seeburger. (Bilingual Specialist Dictionaries Ser.). (ENG & GER.). 1998. cd-rom 440.00 (978-0-415-13963-2(5), D1995) Pub: Routledge. Dist(s): Taylor and Fran

Routledge Intensive Dutch Course. Dennis Strik et al. (Routledge Intensive Language Courses Ser.). (ENG & DUT., 2006. audio compact disk 89.95 (978-0-415-26192-0(9), RU42125) Pub: Routledge. Dist(s): Taylor and Fran

Routledge Intensive German Course. Paul Hartley. (Routledge Intensive Language Courses Ser.). (ENG & GER., (C). 2006. audio compact disk 90.00 (978-0-415-25347-5(0)) Pub: Routledge. Dist(s): Taylor and Fran

Routledge Intensive Italian Course. Anna Proudfoot et al. Contrib. by Stefania Bochicchio. 2004. 87.95 (978-0-415-24081-9(6)) Pub: Routledge. Dist(s): Taylor and Fran

Roux Morgue. unabr. ed. Claire M. Johnson. Read by Christine Williams. (Running Time: 27000 sec.). 2008. 59.95 (978-1-4332-1166-9(1)); audio compact disk 29.95 (978-1-4332-1168-3(8)); audio compact disk & audio compact disk 80.00 (978-1-4332-1167-6(X)) Blckstn Audio.

Rover. Joseph Conrad. 2008. 27.95 (978-1-60112-157-8(1)) Babblebooks.

Rover. unabr. collector's ed. Joseph Conrad. Read by Wolfram Kandinsky. 7 cass. (Running Time: 10 hrs. 30 min.). 1992. 56.00 (978-0-7366-2305-6(1), 3088) Books on Tape.
It is the age of Napoleon. France & England are at war & Peyrol, a retired naval gunner living in the countryside beyond Toulon, distrusts all landsmen & their slogans.

***Rover Rob's Tales: The Life of Pirate Dog with Grace O'Malle, the Irish Sea Queen.** Yaelle Byrd. 2008. (978-1-61584-902-4(5)) Indep Pub IL.

Roverandom. J. R. R. Tolkien. Read by Derek Jacobi. 2 cass. (Running Time: 3 hrs.). (J). 1998. 14.95 (978-0-00-105535-3(6)) Zondervan.
A real dog, Rover, is turned into a toy by a wizard.

Rover's Tales. unabr. ed. Short Stories. Michael Z. Lewin. Read by Michael Z. Lewin. 4 cass. (Running Time: 6 hrs.). 1999. 32.95 (2354) Blckstn Audio.
Rover looks at a dog's life from his own point of view, offering ground-level perspectives on human life as he combats the injustices committed against his fellow canines.

Rover's Tales. unabr. ed. Michael Z. Lewin. 4 cass. (Running Time: 5 hrs. 30 mins.). 2000. 32.95 (978-0-7861-1503-7(3), 2354) Blckstn Audio.

Row 22, Seats A & B - Audiobook. Short Stories. Frederick Waterman. Read by Scott Brick. 6 CD's. (Running Time: 2 hrs. 30 min.). 2006. audio compact disk 29.95 (978-0-9726770-1-1(1)) Canfield Mackenize.

Rowan. unabr. ed. Anne McCaffrey. Read by Jean Reed Bahle. 8 cass. (Running Time: 12 hrs.). (Rowan Ser.). 1990. 73.25 (978-1-56100-062-3(0), 1561000620, Unabridge Lib Edns) Brilliance Audio.
Told in the timeless style of Anne McCaffrey, "The Rowan" is the first installment in a new and wonderful trilogy. This is sci-fi at its best: a contemporary love story as well as an engrossing view of our world in the future. The kinetically gifted, trained in mind/machine gestalt, are the most valued citizens of the Nine Star League. Using mental powers alone, these few Prime Talents transport ships, cargo and people between Earth's Moon, Mars' Demos and Jupiter's Callisto. An orphaned young girl, simply called The Rowan, is discovered to have superior telepathic potential and is trained to become Prime Talent on Callisto. After years of self-sacrificing dedication to her position, The Rowan intercepts an urgent mental call from Jeff Raven, a young Prime Talent on distant Deneb. She convinces the other Primes to merge their powers with hers to help fight off an attack by invading aliens. Her growing relationship with Jeff gives her the courage to break her status-imposed isolation, and choose the more rewarding world of love and family.

Rowan. unabr. ed. Anne McCaffrey. Read by Jean Reed-Bahle. (Running Time: 12 hrs.). (Rowan/Damia Ser.). 2007. 39.25 (978-1-4233-3032-5(3), 9781423330325, BADLE) Brilliance Audio.

Rowan. unabr. ed. Anne McCaffrey. Read by Jean Reed Bahle. (Running Time: 12 hrs.). (Rowan/Damia Ser.). 2007. 24.95 (978-1-4233-3031-8(5), 9781423330318, BAD) Brilliance Audio.

Rowan. unabr. ed. Anne McCaffrey. Read by Jean Reed-Bahle. (Running Time: 43200 sec.). (Rowan/Damia Ser.). 2007. audio compact disk 39.25 (978-1-4233-3030-1(7), 9781423330301, Brinc Audio MP3 Lib); audio compact disk 24.95 (978-1-4233-3029-5(3), 9781423330295, Brilliance MP3) Brilliance Audio.

***Rowan.** unabr. ed. Anne McCaffrey. Read by Jean Reed Bahle. (Running Time: 10 hrs.). (Rowan/Damia Ser.). 2010. audio compact disk 29.99 (978-1-4418-4067-7(2), 9781441840677, Bril Audio CD Unabri); audio compact disk 89.97 (978-1-4418-4068-4(0), 9781441840684, BriAudCD Unabrid) Brilliance Audio.

Rowan & the Ice Creepers. unabr. ed. Emily Rodda. Read by Steven Crossley. 5 cass. (Running Time: 6 hrs. 45 mins.). (J). 2004. 45.75 (978-1-4025-6394-2(9)) Recorded Bks.
Rowan and his two friends climb an icy mountain to discover the origin of all the frigid weather. What they find is amazing enormous Ice Creepers!.

Rowan & the Keeper of the Crystal. Emily Rodda. Narrated by Steven Crossley. 3 pieces. (Running Time: 4 hrs. 30 mins.). (gr. 2 up). 28.00 (978-0-7887-9985-3(1)) Recorded Bks.

Rowan & the Travelers. Emily Rodda. Narrated by Steven Crossley. 3 pieces. (Running Time: 4 hrs.). (gr. 2 up). 2002. 28.00 (978-0-7887-9989-1(4)) Recorded Bks.
The Travelers usually come to Rin every few years. So it seems strange when they decide to visit two years ina row. After they arrive, a mysterious spell begins trapping the people of Rin in a deep sleep. Rowan must figure out what's happening.

Rowan & the Zebak. Emily Rodda. Narrated by Steven Crossley. 4 pieces. (Running Time: 4 hrs. 45 mins.). (gr. 2 up). 37.00 (978-0-7887-9987-7(8)) Recorded Bks.

***Rowan Atkinson's the Atkinson People: Classic BBC Radio Comedy Series.** Created by Rowan Atkinson & Richard Curtis. (Running Time: 2 hrs. 0 mins. 0 sec.). (ENG.). 2010. audio compact disk 24.95 (978-1-4084-6716-9(X)) Pub: AudioGO. Dist(s): Perseus Dist

Rowan Hood: Outlaw Girl of Sherwood Forest. unabr. ed. Nancy Springer. Narrated by Emily Gray. 3 pieces. (Running Time: 4 hrs.). (Tales of Rowan Hood Ser.: No. 1). (gr. 6 up). 2002. 29.00 (978-1-4025-0646-8(5)) Recorded Bks.

Rowan Hood Returns: The Final Chapter. abr. ed. Nancy Springer. Read by Emily Gray. 3 cass. (Running Time: 4 hrs.). (Tales of Rowan Hood Ser.: No. 5). (J). 2005. 28.75 (978-1-4193-4981-2(3), 98105) Recorded Bks.
Rowan Hood has been searching for the men who murdered her mother for two long years. Now she knows their names, and with her band of friends from Sherwood Forest, she sets out for revenge.

Rowan of Rin. unabr. ed. Emily Rodda. Narrated by Steven Crossley. 3 pieces. (Running Time: 4 hrs.). (gr. 2 up). 2002. 28.00 (978-0-7887-9983-9(5)) Recorded Bks.
One day the people of Rin wake to discover their mountain stream has stopped flowing. In order to save their village, six of the strongest and bravest men and women of Rin decide to climb the forbidden mountain to figure out why the stream has dried up. But only the young boy Rowan can read the secret map that shows the way up the mountain. Rowan is the least courageous person in the village. He is terrified of the legend that says a fierce dragon lives atop the mountain, but he tries not to think of that. He simply worries about surviving the dangerous quest.

Rowing in Eden. collector's unabr. ed. Barbara Rogan. Read by Anna Fields. 9 CDs. (Running Time: 10 hrs. 36 mins.). 2000. audio compact disk 36.00 (978-0-7366-5213-1(2)) Books on Tape.
The small town of Old Wickham is awakened in a tangle of troubled lives & unsettled new relationships.

Rowing in Eden. unabr. collector's ed. Barbara Rogan. Read by Anna Fields. 8 cass. (Running Time: 12 hrs.). 1999. 16.00 (978-0-7366-4829-5(1), 5175) Books on Tape.

Rowing Rhyming Frog: Stories & Songs. Contrib. by Margarita Robleda. Illus. by Maribel Suarez. (Rowing Frog's Rhymes Ser.). (J). (gr. k-3). 2004. pap. bk. 7.95 (978-1-59437-307-7(8)) Santillana.

Rowing Rhyming Frog 2 see Rana, rema, rimas. Canciones y Cuentos 2 (CD)

Rowland Perkins: Talent Agent see Scene Behind the Screen: The Business Realities of the TV Industry

Roxaboxen. unabr. ed. Alice McLerran. 1 cass. (Running Time: 9 min.). (J). (gr. k-4). 1992. pap. bk. 16.95 (978-0-8045-6676-6(3), 6676) Spoken Arts.
Roxaboxen may look like any ordinary rocky hill, but Marian and her friends all knew it was a sparkling world of jeweled homes and two ice cream shops.

Roxana. Daniel Defoe. Read by Anais 9000. 2008. 27.95 (978-1-60112-155-4(5)) Babblebooks.

Roxanne & George the Green Genie: Audiobook. Narrated by Sherry Cutrer. Based on a book by Sherry Cutrer & Kristen Laviolette. Music by Brian Gorman. (ENG.). (J). 2010. audio compact disk 11.95 (978-0-9795095-5-1(6)) From Me To.

Roxanne & Ruby the Rug: Audiobook. Narrated by Sherry Cutrer. Based on a book by Sherry Cutrer. Music by Brian Gorman. (ENG.). (J). 2010. audio compact disk 11.95 (978-0-9795095-4-4(8)) From Me To.

Roxanne Daleo's. (J). 1999. Hlth Jrnys.

Roxanne with Cleo, Pat, & Ray: Audiobook. Sherry M. Cutrer. Illus. by Sherry M. Cutrer. Illus. by Kristen Laviolette. Voice by Kristen Laviolette et al. Music by Brian Gorman. (ENG.). (J). 2010. audio compact disk 11.95 (978-0-9795095-3-7(X)) From Me To.

Roxey's Choice. Virginia Havens. 2 cass. 9.98 set. (978-1-55503-721-5(6), 079442) Covenant Comms.
Will a young beauty compromise her values?.

Roy Blount, Jr. Roy Blount, Jr.. Read by Roy Blount, Jr. 1 cass. (Running Time: 29 min.). 1989. 10.00 New Letters.
Blount reads comic essays from Now, Where Were We & is interviewed.

Roy Blount, Jr. Interview. Interview with Roy Blount, Jr. & Kay Bonetti. 1 cass. (Running Time: 1 hr. 15 min.). 1983. 13.95 (978-1-55644-067-0(7), 3032) Am Audio Prose.
A discussion of tradition of American humor, "making it" in the free-lance market, & Blount's place in the Southern renaissance in parajournalism.

Roy Cohn et al: McCarthyism see Buckley's Firing Line

Roy Emerson: Tennis. Read by Roy Emerson. 1 cass. 9.95 (978-0-89811-086-9(6), 7137) Lets Talk Assocs.
Roy Emerson talks about the people & events which influenced his career, & his own approach to his speciality.

Roy Rogers Show. unabr. ed. 2 cass. (Running Time: 2 hrs.). 10.95 Set. (978-1-57816-004-4(9), RR2401) Audio File.
Four broadcasts of the radio show.

Roy Smalley: Father, Son, Baseball. Read by Roy Smalley. 1 cass. 9.95 (978-0-89811-138-5(2), 7182) Lets Talk Assocs.
Roy Smalley talks about the people & events which influenced his career, & his own approach to his specialties.

Roy Stuart, Vol. 5. Roy Stuart. (FRE, GER & ENG., 2008. 39.99 (978-3-8228-4501-1(9)) Pub: Taschen DEU. Dist(s): IngramPubServ

Roy Stuart: The Fourth Body. Roy Stuart & Dian Hanson. (ENG, FRE & GER., 2004. 39.99 (978-3-8228-2557-0(3)) Pub: Taschen DEU. Dist(s): IngramPubServ

Roy Tuckman Interview. Timothy Leary. 2 cass. (Roy Tuckman Interview Ser.). 18.00 Set. (A0192-83) Sound Photosyn.

Roy Tuckman Interview. Dennis J. McKenna. 2 cass. (Roy Tuckman Interview Ser.). 18.00 set. (A0026-84) Sound Photosyn.
Dennis & Terence McKenna co-authored "The Invisible Landscape." Dennis has gone on to achieve his doctorate in ethnopharmacology.

Roy Tuckman Interview. Robert A. Wilson. 2 cass. (Roy Tuckman Interview Ser.). 18.00 Set. (A0153-87) Sound Photosyn.

***Royal Assassin.** unabr. ed. Robin Hobb. Narrated by Paul Boehmer. (Running Time: 30 hrs. 0 mins. 0 sec.). (Farseer Ser.). (ENG.). 2010. audio compact disk 109.99 (978-1-4001-4435-8(3)) Pub: Tantor Media. Dist(s): IngramPubServ

Royal Brass. Perf. by Empire Brass Quintet. 1 cass., 1 CD. 7.98 (TA 30257); audio compact disk 12.78 CD Jewel box. (TA 80257) NewSound.

Royal Breed. Judith Saxton. Read by Lindsay Sandison. 14 cass. (Running Time: 21 hrs.). 2001. 99.95 (990109) Pub: ISIS Audio GBR. Dist(s): Ulverscroft US

Royal Bride. Joan Wolf. Narrated by Jill Tanner. 8 cass. (Running Time: 11 hrs. 30 mins.). 71.00 (978-0-7887-8925-0(2)) Recorded Bks.

Royal Court Music of Thailand. Perf. by Bangkok College of Dramatic Arts Fine Arts Dept. Musicians Staff. Contrib. by M. R. Chitrabongs. 1 cass. 1994. (0-9307-404130-9307-40413-2-1); audio compact disk (0-9307-40413-2-1) Smithsonian Folkways.
Contains four cherished & exquisite compositions performed with an enchanting mix of xylophones, gongs, cymbals, fiddles, guitars & breathtaking vocals.

Royal Escape. unabr. ed. Georgette Heyer. Read by Cornelius Garrett. 10 CDs. (Running Time: 15 hrs.). 2002. audio compact disk 94.95 (978-0-7540-5448-1(9), CCD 139) AudioGO.

Royal Escape. unabr. ed. Georgette Heyer. Read by Cornelius Garrett. 10 cass. (Running Time: 12 hrs.). 2001. 84.95 (978-0-7540-0694-7(8)) Pub: Chivers Audio Bks GBR. Dist(s): AudioGO

Royal Flash. unabr. ed. George MacDonald Fraser. Read by David Case. 7 cass. (Running Time: 10 hrs. 30 min.). (Flashman Ser.). 1994. 56.00 (978-0-7366-2696-5(4), 3430) Books on Tape.
Harry Flashman, England's No. 1 scoundrel, tries to stay a jump ahead of death in tumultuous 1848. Second in series.

Royal Highness. unabr. ed. Thomas Mann. Read by Robert Whitfield. 8 cass. (Running Time: 12 hrs.). 1997. 56.95 (978-0-7861-1191-6(7), 1948) Blckstn Audio.
Careful depiction (personified by Klaus Heinrich) of a decaying, stratified society rejuvenated by modern forces illustrates in fable what he regarded as a universal truth - that ripeness & death are necessary conditions for rebirth.

Royal Palm see Poetry of Hart Crane

Royal Power of Faith. 1 cass. (Running Time: 30 min.). 1985. (0241) Evang Sisterhood Mary.
A key that can open every door; The answer to impossible situations. Includes: "Waiting Is Worth It".

Royal Road to Sonship. Mark Chironna. 1 cass. 1992. 7.00 (978-1-56043-925-7(4)) Destiny Image Pubs.

Royal Web. unabr. collector's ed. Ladislas Farago & Andrew Sinclair. Read by John McDonald. 7 cass. (Running Time: 10 hrs. 30 mins.). 1986. 56.00 (978-0-7366-0753-7(6), 1706) Books on Tape.
Against the clash of dynasties & rattling sabers that forged modern Europe, the story of Victoria of England & her husband Frederick of Prussia, emerges as a tragic love story while opening a spy hole into the secret history of the nineteenth century.

Royals. Kitty Kelley. 4 cass. 1998. 7.99 Set. (978-0-671-58264-7(X), Audioworks) S&S Audio.
Historical - British.

Royals. abr. ed. Kitty Kelley. 2 cass. (Running Time: 3 hrs.). 1997. 17.98 (978-1-57042-527-1(2)) Hachet Audio.

Royalty Patrenia Turner Authors Poems from an Ex-Queen of England. 3rd ed. Royalty Patrenia Turner. 2007. (978-0-9793803-1-0(6)) Royalty Turner.

***Rp Access 2003 Illust Brief.** (C). 2004. audio compact disk 6.95 (978-0-619-18771-2(9)) Pub: Course Tech. Dist(s): CENGAGE Learn

***Rp Access 2003 Illust Complt.** (C). 2004. audio compact disk 6.95 (978-0-619-18773-6(5)) Pub: Course Tech. Dist(s): CENGAGE Learn

***Rp Access 2003 Illust Intro.** (C). 2004. audio compact disk 6.95 (978-0-619-18772-9(7)) Pub: Course Tech. Dist(s): CENGAGE Learn

***Rp Adobe Illustrator 11 Dsgn.** (C). 2004. audio compact disk 6.95 (978-0-619-27313-2(5)) Pub: Course Tech. Dist(s): CENGAGE Learn

***Rp Adobe In-Design 3.0 Dp.** (C). 2004. audio compact disk 6.95 (978-0-619-05783-1(1)) Pub: Course Tech. Dist(s): CENGAGE Learn

***Rp Adobe Photoshop 8.0 Dsgn.** (C). 2004. audio compact disk 6.95 (978-0-619-27309-5(7)) Pub: Course Tech. Dist(s): CENGAGE Learn

***Rp Dreamweaver Mx 2004 Illus.** (C). 2004. audio compact disk 6.95 (978-0-619-05788-6(2)) Pub: Course Tech. Dist(s): CENGAGE Learn

***Rp Excel 2003-Illust Brief.** (C). 2004. audio compact disk 6.95 (978-0-619-18797-2(2)) Pub: Course Tech. Dist(s): CENGAGE Learn

***Rp Excel 2003-Illust Complte.** (C). 2004. audio compact disk 6.95 (978-0-619-18799-6(9)) Pub: Course Tech. Dist(s): CENGAGE Learn

***Rp Frontpage 2003-Illust Brf.** (C). 2004. audio compact disk 6.95 (978-0-619-05780-0(7)) Pub: Course Tech. Dist(s): CENGAGE Learn

***Rp Frontpage 2003-Illust Cmp.** (C). 2004. audio compact disk 6.95 (978-0-619-05782-4(3)) Pub: Course Tech. Dist(s): CENGAGE Learn

***Rp, Mac Intro Graphics, Dp.** (C). 2005. audio compact disk 6.95 (978-1-4188-4306-9(7)) Pub: Course Tech. Dist(s): CENGAGE Learn

***Rp Macromed Dreamweavr Mx 04.** (C). 2004. audio compact disk 6.95 (978-0-619-05785-5(8)) Pub: Course Tech. Dist(s): CENGAGE Learn

***Rp Macromedia Director Mx 04.** 2nd ed. (C). 2004. audio compact disk 6.95 (978-0-619-27317-0(8)) Pub: Course Tech. Dist(s): CENGAGE Learn

***Rp Macromedia Mx 2004 Web Co.** (C). 2004. audio compact disk 6.95 (978-0-619-27311-8(9)) Pub: Course Tech. Dist(s): CENGAGE Learn

***Rp Mastering Applications.** (C). 2004. audio compact disk 6.95 (978-0-619-26750-6(X)) Pub: Course Tech. Dist(s): CENGAGE Learn

***Rp MS Word 2003-Illust Brief.** (C). 2004. audio compact disk 6.95 (978-0-619-18822-1(7)) Pub: Course Tech. Dist(s): CENGAGE Learn

***Rp Multimedia for Web-Reveal.** (C). 2005. audio compact disk 6.95 (978-1-4188-3957-4(4)) Pub: Course Tech. Dist(s): CENGAGE Learn

***Rp Np Excel 2003.** 2nd ed. (C). 2005. audio compact disk 6.95 (978-0-619-26816-9(6)) Pub: Course Tech. Dist(s): CENGAGE Learn

***Rp Np HTML, Xhtml, & Dhtml.** 3rd ed. (C). 2005. audio compact disk 6.95 (978-0-619-26757-5(7)) Pub: Course Tech. Dist(s): CENGAGE Learn

***Rp Np Internetcompr 05.** 5th ed. (C). 2005. audio compact disk 6.95 (978-0-619-26814-5(X)) Pub: Course Tech. Dist(s): CENGAGE Learn

***Rp Np MS Excel 2003 Vba-Adv.** (C). 2004. audio compact disk 6.95 (978-0-619-21433-3(3)) Pub: Course Tech. Dist(s): CENGAGE Learn

***Rp Np on HTML & Xhtml, Compr.** (C). 2004. audio compact disk 6.95 (978-0-619-26755-1(0)) Pub: Course Tech. Dist(s): CENGAGE Learn

***Rp Np on HTML & Xhtml, Intro.** (C). 2004. audio compact disk 6.95 (978-0-619-26753-7(4)) Pub: Course Tech. Dist(s): CENGAGE Learn

***Rp Office 2003-Illust 2nd Cs.** (C). 2004. audio compact disk 6.95 (978-0-619-18848-1(0)) Pub: Course Tech. Dist(s): CENGAGE Learn

***Rp Perform W/Office 2003 Intr.** (C). 2004. audio compact disk 6.95 (978-0-619-18368-4(3)) Pub: Course Tech. Dist(s): CENGAGE Learn

***Rp Powerpoint 2003 Brief.** (C). 2004. audio compact disk 6.95 (978-0-619-05750-3(5)) Pub: Course Tech. Dist(s): CENGAGE Learn

***Rp Powerpoint 2003 Illust.** (C). 2004. audio compact disk 6.95 (978-0-619-05775-6(0)) Pub: Course Tech. Dist(s): CENGAGE Learn

***Rp Publisher 2003 Illust Int.** (C). 2004. audio compact disk 6.95 (978-0-619-27319-4(4)) Pub: Course Tech. Dist(s): CENGAGE Learn

***Rp Succeed W/Ms Access 2003.** (C). 2005. audio compact disk 6.95 (978-0-619-26822-0(0)) Pub: Course Tech. Dist(s): CENGAGE Learn

RPL Audio Books Series. Michael A. Rome et al. 6 cass. 85.00 Set. Recorded Pubns.
Includes: "Protect Your Life Savings," Plan Your Estate Right," "New Tax Saving Ideas," "Tax Mistakes & Genius of the Rich & Famous," "Tax Aspects of Divorce & Separation," "Keep Every Last Dime".

RPM - Christmas: Secular Tunes-Sacred Truths. (YA). 2003. audio compact disk 15.00 (978-1-58302-246-7(5)) One Way St.
Parody writer, Mark Bradford has written Christian (Christmas) lyrics to 10 songs of the past. You'll hear "Born in Bethlehem" to the tune of Bruce Springsteen's "Born in the USA" song and "Sleepin' on a Bed of Hay" to the tune of "Sitting on the Dock of the Bay." These songs will be a great hit among puppet groups as they look for performance pieces for this upcoming Christmas season. Familiar tunes are listed after title when title differs.Titles include:-Get This Season Started/Get This Party Started-I'm Gettin' Something Good/I'm into Something Good-Manger Zone/Danger Zone-Mary/Sherry-Sleeping on a Bed of Hay/Sitting on the Dock of the Bay-Wise Man Soul Man-Time of the Season-Born in Bethlehem/Born in the USA-I've Got to Hide These Gifts Away/I've Got to Hide Your Love Away-Gloria.

RS&B: A Collection of Favorites. 1 cass. (Running Time: 1 hr.). 2002. 8.98 (MS16C); audio compact disk 12.98 (MS16CD) Faith Lib Pubns.

RSC Sonnets. abr. ed. William Shakespeare. 2 cass. (Running Time: 2 hrs.). 1999. (978-1-84032-193-7(8), HoddrStoughton) Hodder General GBR.
In a unique collaboration between the Royal Shakespeare Company & Hodder Headlines Audiobooks, ten of the RSC's greatest voices perform all one hundred & fifty four of Shakespeare's sonnets.

RTG Bills: Legal Time & Billing. 1996. audio compact disk 95.00 (978-0-918103-07-9(X)) RTG Data.

RTIQLation: Spoken Essence of Music. Perf. by Marc Lacy. 2008. audio compact disk 14.00 (978-0-9749712-2-3(7)) AVO Pubng.

Ruach 5765 Songbook: New Jewish Tunes Israel. 2005. pap. bk. 19.95 (978-0-8074-0958-9(8), 993249) URJ Pr.

Ruah Hadashah, No. 1. 3 cass. 10.00 (978-1-893165-98-4(1)) Rational Isl.
Shared experiences of Jews & others interested in Jewish liberation & about Jews using re-evaluation counseling.

Ruah Hadashah, No. 2. 4 cass. 10.00 (978-1-893165-99-1(X)) Rational Isl.

Ruah Hadashah, No. 3. 6 cass. 10.00 ea. (978-1-58429-000-1(5)) Rational Isl.

Ruah Hadashah, No. 4. 5 cass. 10.00 ea. (978-1-58429-001-8(3)) Rational Isl.

Ruah Hadashah, No. 5. 6 cass. 10.00 ea. (978-1-58429-002-5(1)) Rational Isl.

Ruah Hadashah, No. 6. 7 cass. 10.00 ea. (978-1-58429-003-2(X)) Rational Isl.

Rubaiyat of Omar Khayyam. Omar Khayyam. 10.00 Esstee Audios.
Presents background material along with a reading.

Rubaiyat of Omar Khayyam Explained Audiobook, Set. unabr. ed. Poems. Paramhansa Yogananda. Read by J. Donald Walters. 4 cass. (Running Time: 6 hrs. 27 min.). 2003. 29.95 (978-1-56589-127-2(9)) Pub: Crystal Clarity. Dist(s): Natl Bk Netwk

Rubber Band. Rex Stout. Read by Michael Prichard. (Running Time: 8 hrs.). (Nero Wolfe Ser.). 2005. 27.95 (978-1-59912-388-2(6)) Iofy Corp.

Rubber Band. unabr. ed. Rex Stout. Read by Michael Prichard. 6 cass. (Running Time: 8 hrs.). (Nero Wolfe Ser.). 2004. 29.95 (978-1-57270-052-9(1), N61052u) Pub: Audio Partners. Dist(s): PerseuPGW
What do a wild-west lynching & a respected English nobleman have in common? Nero Wolfe solves a questionable homicide amidst a corporate high finance scandal.

Rubber Band. unabr. ed. Rex Stout. Read by Michael Prichard. (Running Time: 28800 sec.). (Nero Wolfe Ser.). (ENG.). 2006. audio compact disk 29.95 (978-1-57270-527-2(2)) Pub: AudioGO. Dist(s): Perseus Dist
Out of all of Rex Stout's Nero Wolfe mysteries, Rubber Band stands out as one of the most intricate. The normally unflappable detective is brought on to investigate what appears to be a clean case of larceny, but soon it turns into a quagmire of blackmail and broken promises. Crossing eras and oceans, Wolfe and his trusty assistant Archie Goodwin must find the link between a lynching and a respected British peer. At stake is the life of Wolfe's beautiful young client and a million dollars.

Rubber Band. unabr. collector's ed. Rex Stout. Read by Michael Prichard. 6 cass. (Running Time: 9 hrs.). (Nero Wolfe Ser.). 1994. 48.00 (978-0-7366-2695-8(6), 3429) Books on Tape.
That which began as a simple case of larceny has quickly turned into a messy case of blackmail, international scandal & murder. Go along with Nero Wolfe & his assistant, Archie Goodwin, as they bridge eras & oceans to find the link which solves this engaging mystery.

Rubber Biscuits & Rama Lama Ding Dongs: Doo-Wop for Kids! 1 CD. (Running Time: 1 hr. 30 mins.). (J). 2001. audio compact disk 11.98 (R2 75584); 7.98 (R4 75583) Rhino Enter.
Grown-ups love doo-wop and now kids can too with this lighthearted collection of the gene's silliest hits. Also includes liner notes by Dr. Demento.

Rubber Houses. unabr. ed. Ellen Yeomans. Narrated by Chelsea Mixon. 2 CDs. (Running Time: 1 hr. 45 mins.). (YA). (gr. 7 up). 2009. audio compact disk 29.00 (978-1-934180-50-1(5)) Full Cast Audio.

Rubber Legs & White Tail-Hairs. unabr. ed. Patrick F. McManus. Narrated by Norman Dietz. 5 cass. (Running Time: 6 hrs. 15 mins.). 2000. 45.00 (978-0-7887-4386-3(4), 96101E7) Recorded Bks.
Hilarious sportsman returns with this collection of insights about youth, the great outdoors & the philosophy of fileting fish.

Rubbings of Maya Sculpture. Merle G. Robertson. 1998. audio compact disk 425.00 (978-0-8061-9946-7(6)) U of Okla Pr.

Rubens: Music of His Time. Hugh G. Griffin. 1 CD. (Running Time: 1 hr. 30 min.). (Art & Music Ser.). 2003. audio compact disk (Naxos AudioBooks) Naxos.

Rubies & Rebels. Lynn Gardner. 3 cass. 2004. 14.95 (978-1-59156-258-0(9)); audio compact disk 15.95 (978-1-59156-317-4(8)) Covenant Comms.

Rubies in the Orchard: How to Uncover the Hidden Gems in Your Business. unabr. ed. Francis Wilkinson & Lynda Resnick. Read by Lynda Resnick. (ENG.). 2009. audio compact disk 29.95 (978-0-7393-8317-9(5), Random AudioBks) Pub: Random Audio Pubg. Dist(s): Random

An Asterisk (*) at the beginning of an entry indicates that the title is appearing for the first time.

Rubinstein: A Life. unabr. collector's ed. Harvey Sachs. Read by Alexander Adams. 15 cass. (Running Time: 22 hrs. 30 min.). 1998. 120.00 (978-0-7366-4122-7(X), 4626) Books on Tape.
Examines the life & music of the great modern pianist, Artur Rubinstein, consummate musical genius, philanderer, narcissist.

Rubinstein-Taybi Syndrome - A Bibliography & Dictionary for Physicians, Patients, & Genome Researchers. Compiled by Icon Group International, Inc. Staff. 2007. ring bd. 28.95 (978-0-497-11289-9(2)) Icon Grp.

Rubout. abr. ed. Elaine Viets. 4 cass. (Running Time: 360 min.). (Francesca Vierling Mystery Ser.: No. 2). 2000. 25.00 (978-1-58807-053-1(0)) Am Pubng Inc.

Ruby. Read by Laura Esterman & Tom Stewart. Music by Tim Clark. 4 cass. (Running Time: 3 hrs. 30 min.). 25.00 set. (RS) ZBS Ind.
Sound effects by Tim Clark.

Ruby. collector's ed. Ann Hood. Read by Kimberly Schraf. 6 cass. (Running Time: 9 hrs.). 1999. 48.00 (978-0-7366-4805-9(4), 5156) Books on Tape.
After the tragic death of her husband of barely one year, Olivia, a milliner from New York City, finds herself unable to surmount her grief...until she meets Ruby. Young, pregnant, delinquent & abandoned by her family, Ruby has no home. With her eye on the possible adoption of the newborn, Olivia offers the rebellious teen a place to stay. An unlikely friendship is forged as Olivia nurtures Ruby & her unborn child & experiences the daily challenges presented by a wayward teen who may or may not teach Olivia how to life again.

Ruby. unabr. ed. V. C. Andrews. Narrated by Barbara Rosenblat. 12 cass. (Running Time: 16 hrs. 30 mins.). (Landry Ser.: Vol. 1). 1997. 97.00 (978-0-7887-1088-9(5), 94981E7) Recorded Bks.
Ruby Landry's early years & family are a mystery. But her past is waiting to overshadow her as she develops into a beautiful young artist.

Ruby: A Galactic Gumshoe. unabr. ed. Meatball Fulton. Read by Laura Esterman et al. 4 cass. (Running Time: 3 hrs. 30 min.). Dramatization. (J). (gr. 4 up). 1982. 25.00 set. (978-1-881137-06-1(6)) ZBS Found.
Ruby, the radio series heard on over 600 stations in the U. S., is a comic cosmic saga, a zany blend of science fiction, hard-boiled dialogue & hot electronic music. Other readers include Count Stovall, Elaine Graham, Cara Duff-McCormick, Chris McCaan & Dave Herman.

Ruby: A Galactic Gumshoe, Set. unabr. ed. Meatball Fulton. Read by Laura Esterman et al. 8 CDs. (Running Time: 3 hr. 30 min.). Dramatization. (J). (gr. 4 up). 1982. audio compact disk 59.95 (978-1-881137-92-4(9), ZBSF008) ZBS Found.

Ruby Five: The Land of Zoots, Vol. 1. unabr. ed. Thomas M. Lopez. 1 cass. (Running Time: 1 hr. 10 min.). Dramatization. (Ruby Ser.: Vol. 5). 1998. 10.00 (978-1-881137-50-4(3), ZBSF023) ZBS Found.
The inhabitants of the Awakening Archipelago are changing their environment based on a mythical children's story, "The Land of the Zoots." Ruby is hired to find out who created the story in the first place.

Ruby Five Vol. 1: The Land of Zoots. unabr. ed. Thomas M. Lopez. 1 CD. (Running Time: 1 hr. 10 min.). Dramatization. (Ruby Ser.: Vol. 5). 1998. audio compact disk 12.50 (978-1-881137-51-1(1), ZBSF024) ZBS Found.

Ruby Five Vol. 2: The Land of Zoots. unabr. ed. Thomas M. Lopez. 1 cass.; 1 CD. (Running Time: 1 hr. 10 min.). Dramatization. (Ruby Ser.: Vol. 5). 1998. 10.00 (978-1-881137-56-6(2), R5B); audio compact disk 12.50 CD. (978-1-881137-53-5(8), R5BCD) ZBS Found.
Ruby's search for the creator of the mythical Land of Zoots continues.

Ruby Five Vol. 3: The Land of Zoots. unabr. ed. Thomas M. Lopez. 1 cass. (Running Time: 1 hr. 10 min.). Dramatization. (Ruby Ser.: Vol. 5). 1998. 10.00 (978-1-881137-54-2(6), R5C); audio compact disk 12.50 (978-1-881137-55-9(4), R5CCD) ZBS Found.
Conclusion of Ruby's quest to find the creator of the Land of Zoot.

Ruby Four, Set. Meatball Fulton. Prod. by Thomas M. Lopez. 8 cass. 45.00 (ZBSF007) ZBS Ind.

Ruby Four Pt. 1: The Moon Coins of Sonto Lore. unabr. ed. Thomas M. Lopez. Read by Blanche Blackwell et al. 2 cass. (Running Time: 2 hrs.). Dramatization. (J). (gr. 4 up). 1994. 15.00 Set. (978-1-881137-38-2(4), R4S 1/2); audio compact disk 20.00 (978-1-881137-94-8(5), R4S 1/2CD) ZBS Found.
Ruby is hired to find the moon coins of Sonto Lore, the mythical fourth moon of Summa Nulla that some believe still orbits & influences the planet.

Ruby Four Pt. 2: The Turban of El Morya. unabr. ed. Thomas M. Lopez. 2 cass. (Running Time: 2 hrs.). Dramatization. (J). (gr. 4 up). 1994. 15.00 set. (978-1-881137-39-9(2), R4S 3/4); audio compact disk 20.00 (R4S 3/4CD) ZBS Found.
The planet of Summa Nulla is evolving. The vibrations are rising, time is speeding up while everything else is falling apart. Ruby has found the second coin on a Reptoid planet. The Reptoids are now looking for her.

Ruby Four Pt. 3: Dark Night of the Reptoids. unabr. ed. Thomas M. Lopez. 2 cass. (Running Time: 2 hrs.). Dramatization. 1995. 15.00 set. (978-1-881137-40-5(6), R4S5/6); audio compact disk 20.00 CD. (978-1-881137-99-3(6), R4S5/6CD) ZBS Found.
Ruby must cross dimensions to reach the Reptoid planet in search of Teru. She arrives during a bizarre carnival called "Dark Night of the Reptoids." Meanwhile, Teru & Francois escape the city.

Ruby Four Pt. 4: Man Moon for Rubina. unabr. ed. Thomas M. Lopez. 2 cass. (Running Time: 2 hr.). 1995. 15.00 (978-1-881137-41-2(4), R4S7/8); audio compact disk 20.00 CD. (978-1-881137-98-6(8), R4S7/8CD) ZBS Found.
The conclusion of the Ruby Four series. And/Or & Nikola Tesla orchestrate the birth of a new planet Summa Nulla into the fifth dimension.

Ruby Holler. Sharon Creech. Narrated by Suzanne Toren. 4 pieces. (Running Time: 5 hrs. 30 mins.). (gr. 3 up). 42.00 (978-1-4025-1713-6(0)) Recorded Bks.

***Ruby Holler.** abr. ed. Sharon Creech. Read by Donna Murphy. (ENG.). 2005. (978-0-06-084842-2(1)); (978-0-06-084841-5(3)) HarperCollins Pubs.

Ruby Holler. unabr. ed. Sharon Creech. Read by Donna Murphy. (J). 2008. 44.99 (978-1-60514-657-7(9)) Find a World.

Ruby I: The Adventures of a Galactic Gumshoe. 3 CDs. (Running Time: 3 hrs.). 2001. audio compact disk 35.00 (ZBSF002) Lodestone Catalog.

Ruby I: The Adventures of a Galactic Gumshoe. Meatball Fulton. Prod. by Tom Lopez. 4 cass. (Running Time: 3 hrs.). 1996. 25.00 (978-1-57677-063-4(X), ZBSF001) Lodestone Catalog.
This sassy cosmic saga is a zany blend of sci-fi, hard-boiled mystery & hot electronic music. It's fast, funny & Meatball Fulton's most popular story ever. Sprinkled with satirical songs from the swinging Android Sisters, this snappy-paced story follows Ruby on the quest for Truth & the Intergalactic Way, as she tries to track down the malefactors who are manipulating the media. Along the way you'll meet some of the weird inhabitants of the planet Summa Nulla: the Tookah, oddball archaeologist T. J. Teru, a Frankie named Angel Lips, technowitches Onoffon & Offonoff & many more fabulous characters.

Ruby II: The Adventures of a Galactic Gumshoe. 4 cass. (Running Time: 4 hrs.). 2001. 25.00 (ZBSF003); audio compact disk 29.95 (ZBSF004) Lodestone Catalog.

Ruby III: The Adventures of a Galactic Gumshoe. 8 cass. (Running Time: 10 hrs.). 2001. 49.95 (ZBSF005); audio compact disk 55.00 (ZBSF006) Lodestone Catalog.

Ruby in the Smoke. Philip Pullman. Read by Anton Lesser. 2 vols. (Running Time: 6 hrs. 26 mins.). (Sally Lockhart Ser.: Bk. 1). (J). (gr. 7 up). 2004. pap. bk. 38.00 (978-1-4000-9015-0(6), Listening Lib); 35.00 (978-1-4000-8512-5(8), Listening Lib) Random Audio Pubg.

Ruby in the Smoke. unabr. ed. Philip Pullman. Read by Anton Lesser. (Sally Lockhart Ser.: Bk. 1). (ENG.). (J). (gr. 7). 2008. audio compact disk 39.00 (978-0-7393-6781-0(1), Listening Lib) Pub: Random Audio Pubg. Dist(s): Random

Ruby IV: The Adventures of a Galactic Gumshoe. 8 cass. (Running Time: 8 hrs.). 2001. 45.00 (ZBSF007); audio compact disk 59.95 (ZBSF008) Lodestone Catalog.

Ruby Joe: Hot Rod Deluxe. Perf. by Ruby Joe. Prod. by Billy Zoom. 1 cass., 1 CD. 1999. 10.98 (978-0-7601-2782-7(4)); audio compact disk 16.98 CD. (978-0-7601-2781-0(6)) Provident Mus Dist.
Cruise the high road through tunes taken directly from scripture, or that relay clear analogies for Christian living.

Ruby Mccollum. Ron Milner. Contrib. by Shirley Knight et al. 2 CDs. (Running Time: 7140 sec.). 1997. audio compact disk 25.95 (978-1-58081-327-3(5)) L A Theatre.

Ruby Red Album. Perf. by Jewels and the Gems Staff. Prod. by Julia W. Blagden & Joe Francis. Contrib. by Margrit Eichler. Illus. by Laura Brock. 1 cass. (J). (ps-4). 1997. 9.95 (978-0-9659511-0-4(3), GEM 0001-4); audio compact disk 11.95 CD. (978-0-9659511-1-1(1), GEM 0001-2) Multifaceted.
Orchestrated folk songs for children & parents.

***Ruby Slippers: How the Soul of a Woman Brings Her Home.** unabr. ed. Jonalyn Grace Fincher. (Running Time: 7 hrs. 14 mins. 0 sec.). (ENG.). 2008. 14.99 (978-0-310-30933-8(6)) Zondervan.

Ruby Sunrise. Rinne Groff. Read by Full Cast Production Staff. Directed By Brendon Fox. Contrib. by Elizabeth Moss. Des. by Mark Holden. (Running Time: 6540 sec.). (L. A. Theatre Works Audio Theatre Collections). 2007. audio compact disk 25.95 (978-1-58081-371-6(2)) Pub: L A Theatre. Dist(s): NetLibrary CO

Ruby Three, Set. Meatball Fulton. Prod. by Thomas M. Lopez. 10 cass. (ZBSF005) ZBS Ind.

Ruby Three B: The Invisible World, Set. unabr. ed. Meatball Fulton. Read by Laura Esterman et al. 4 cass. (Running Time: 5 hr.). Dramatization. (J). (gr. 4 up). 1993. 25.00 (978-1-881137-05-4(8)); audio compact disk 29.95 (978-1-881137-84-9(8)) ZBS Found.
Ruby & friends encounter the Astral Bar & Grill, a movable restaurant which changes its decor like a chameleon to adapt to its new patrons, & the shifting city of Zumzammin where all is not as it seems.

Ruby Two. unabr. ed. Meatball Fulton. Read by Laura Esterman et al. 4 cass. (Running Time: 4 hrs.). Dramatization. (J). (gr. 4 up). 1985. 25.00 set. (978-1-881137-07-8(4)) ZBS Found.
Ruby 2, winds its way through even more bizarre & exotic locations in the galaxy. Strange "windows" have been appearing in the minds of the Bulldada, & Ruby must discover if an alien presence is behind this phenomena.

Ruby Two, Set. Meatball Fulton. Read by Tom Stewart & Gregorio Rosenblum. Music by Tim Clark. 4 cass. (Running Time: 4 hrs.). 25.00 (ZBSF003) ZBS Ind.
Special effects by Tim Clark.

Ruby Two, Set. unabr. ed. Meatball Fulton. Read by Laura Esterman et al. 4 CDs. (Running Time: 4 hr.). Dramatization. (J). (gr. 4 up). 1985. audio compact disk 29.95 (978-1-881137-87-0(2), ZBSF004) ZBS Found.
Ruby 2, winds its way through even more bizarre & exotic locations in the galaxy. Strange "windows" have been appearing in the minds of the Bulldada, & Ruby must discover if an alien presence is behind this phenomena.

Ruby V: The Adventure of a Galactic Gumshoe. 3 CDs. (Running Time: 3 hrs.). 2001. audio compact disk 29.95 (ZBSF024) Lodestone Catalog.

Ruby V: The Adventures of a Galactic Gumshoe. 3 cass. (Running Time: 3 hrs.). 2001. 25.00 (ZBS023) Lodestone Catalog.

Ruby 3 Set: The Underworld. unabr. ed. Meatball Fulton. Read by Laura Esterman et al. 4 cass. (Running Time: 5 hrs.). Dramatization. (J). (gr. 4 up). 1993. 25.00 (978-1-881137-15-3(5)); audio compact disk 55.00 (978-1-881137-85-6(6), ZBSF006) ZBS Found.
Ruby is investigating an invisible force that's causing a buying frenzy at Magnifico, City of Malls.

***Ruby's Spoon: A Novel.** unabr. ed. Anna Lawrence Pietroni. Read by Bernadette Dunne. (Running Time: 13 hrs. 0 mins.). 2010. 29.95 (978-1-4417-3609-3(3)); 79.95 (978-1-4417-3605-5(0)); audio compact disk 109.00 (978-1-4417-3606-2(9)) Blckstn Audio.

***Ruddy Gore.** Kerry Greenwood. Read by Stephanie Daniel. (Running Time: 7 hrs.). (Phryne Fisher Mystery: Ser.). 2009. 49.99 (978-1-74214-238-8(9), 9781742142388) Pub: Bolinda Pubng AUS. Dist(s): Bolinda Pub Inc

Ruddy Gore. unabr. ed. Kerry Greenwood. Read by Stephanie Daniel. (Running Time: 7 hrs.). (Phryne Fisher Ser.). 2006. audio compact disk 77.95 (978-1-74093-818-1(6)) Pub: Bolinda Pubng AUS. Dist(s): Bolinda Pub Inc

Ruddy Gore. unabr. ed. Kerry Greenwood. Read by Stephanie Daniel. (Running Time: 7 hrs.). (Phryne Fisher Mystery: Ser.). 2009. 43.95 (978-1-74214-159-6(5), 9781742141596) Pub: Bolinda Pubng AUS. Dist(s): Bolinda Pub Inc

Rude Awakening. unabr. ed. Rand D. Johnson. Read by Ron Varela. 6 cass. (Running Time: 8 hrs. 12 min.). 2001. 39.95 (978-1-55686-810-8(3)) Books in Motion.
Awakening in an alcoholic haze, Ray Ganz discovers a well-dressed corpse sharing his room. Is the dead man's beautiful wife involved, now surviving her second murdered husband?.

Rude Awakenings of a Jane Austen Addict. unabr. ed. Laurie Viera Rigler. Narrated by Kate Reading. 1 MP3-CD. (Running Time: 9 hrs. 30 mins. 0 sec.). (ENG.). 2009. 24.99 (978-1-4001-6249-9(1)); audio compact disk 69.99 (978-1-4001-4249-1(0)); audio compact disk 34.99 (978-1-4001-1249-4(4)) Pub: Tantor Media. Dist(s): IngramPubServ

Rudimental Drumset Solos for the Musical Drummer. Rob Leytham. 2002. bk. 14.95 (978-0-7866-4980-8(1), 98415BCD) Mel Bay.

Rudolfo Anaya. Interview. Interview with Rudolfo A. Anaya & Kay Bonetti. 1 cass. (Running Time: 53 min.). 1982. 13.95 (978-1-55644-035-9(9), 2012) Am Audio Prose.
A discussion of Anaya's place in Chicano tradition, the small press success story surrounding publication of "Bless Me Ultima," which has sold over 100,000 copies, & mix of linear & mythic time in his novels.

Rudolfo Anaya. unabr. ed. Read by Rudolfo A. Anaya & Rebekah Presson. Ed. by James McKinley. 1 cass. (Running Time: 29 min.). (New Letters on the Air Ser.). 1994. 10.00 (091994); 18.00 2-sided cass. New Letters.
Anaya is interviewed by Rebekah Presson & reads from his novel, Alburquerque.

Rudolfo Anaya Interview. 20.97 (978-0-13-090507-9(0)) P-H.

Rudolph, Frosty & Friends Favorite Christmas Songs. Perf. by Burl Ives et al. 1 cass. (Running Time: 30 mins.). 2000. 9.98 (Sony Wonder); audio compact disk 13.98 Sony Music Ent.
Original music from the beloved holiday television classics "Rudolph the Red-Nosed Reindeer," "Frosty the Snowman," "Santa Claus Is Coming to Town" & "The Little Drummer Boy".

Rudolph the Red-Nosed Reindeer. Robert L. May. (ENG.). (J). 2004. (978-1-55709-137-6(4)) Applewood.

Rudy, Set. abr. ed. James Ellison. Read by Sean Astin. 2 cass. (Running Time: 3 hrs.). 1993. 16.95 (978-1-56876-019-3(1)) Soundlines Ent.
Rudy Ruettiger had a dream to go to college & play on the football team at Notre Dame. Undaunted by the skepticism of his family, he pursues his dream, from hitting the books to toughing it out on the field, Rudy proves anyone can attain their dream with hard work & perserverance.

Rudyard Kipling. unabr. ed. Andrew Lycett. Read by Frederick Davidson. (Running Time: 19 hrs. 50 mins.). 2008. 44.95 (978-1-4332-4580-0(9)); audio compact disk & audio compact disk 160.00 (978-1-4332-4579-4(5)) Blckstn Audio.

Rudyard Kipling. unabr. collector's ed. Lord Cohen Of Birkenhead. Read by Richard Green. 11 cass. (Running Time: 16 hrs. 30 min.). 1979. 88.00 (978-0-7366-0385-0(9), 1362) Books on Tape.
Birkenhead's book takes us back to the late 1800's, when England ruled the world & her last frontier was India.

Rudyard Kipling, Pt. 1. Andrew Lycett. Read by Frederick Davidson. 11 cass. (Running Time: 32 hrs.). 2000. 76.95 (978-0-7861-1823-6(7), 2622A,B) Blckstn Audio.
This gripping biography calls on a wealth of unpublished material to unravel the intricate story of the misunderstood genius who wrote "Kim," "The Jungle Books" & "If" (only recently voted Britain's favorite poem). Mixing intimate detail with a thorough understanding of the social, intellectual, artistic & political climate of the time, it shows Kipling at the center of a high-achieving clan. Recently discovered letters shed light on Kipling's most intimate relationships & help explain how India influenced his personal, political & literary development.

Rudyard Kipling, Pt. 2. Andrew Lycett. Read by Frederick Davidson. 11 cass. (Running Time: 32 hrs.). 2000. 76.95 (978-0-7861-1890-8(3), 2622A,B) Blckstn Audio.

Rudyard Kipling: Barrack Room Ballads. Rudyard Kipling. 1 cass. 10.95 (ECN208) J Norton Pubs.
These ballads, which depict the lot of "Tommy Atkins," the soubriquet given to the common British soldier, were among the first non-traditional verses to use the accent & idioms of ordinary people & not the language of the educated upper classes. Actors from Britain's National Theatre company sing a selection, including "Mandalay" & "Gentleman-Rankers," famous for its chorus, "We're poor little lambs.".

Rudyard Kipling in Vermont: Birthplace of the Jungle Books. unabr. collector's ed. Stuart Murray. Read by Stuart Langton. 4 cass. (Running Time: 6 hrs.). 1999. 32.00 (978-0-7366-4379-5(6), 4843) Books on Tape.
After marrying an American woman, Rudyard Kipling built a spacious home in Vermont where he wrote "The Jungle Books".

Rudyard Kipling's Plain Tales from the Hills. Read by Martin Jarvis. Based on a story by Rudyard Kipling. 1 cass. 12.00 (978-1-878427-16-8(4), XC401) Cimino Pub Grp.

Rue Morgue Redux. Edgar Allan Poe. 2 CDs. (Running Time: 2 hrs.). 2005. audio compact disk 15.95 (978-0-660-19384-7(1)) Canadian Broadcasting CAN.

Ruffian on the Stair. unabr. ed. Nina Bawden. Read by Bill Wallis. 6 cass. (Running Time: 9 hrs.). 2002. 54.95 (978-0-7540-0778-4(2), CAB 2200) AudioGO.

Ruffle, Coo & Hoo Doo. Randy Houk. Illus. by Randy Houk. Read by Tom Chapin. Narrated by Tom Chapin. 1 cass. (Running Time: 13 min.). (Humane Society of the United States Animal Tales Ser.). (J). (gr. 1-5). 1993. pap. bk. 9.95 (978-1-882728-48-0(3)) Benefactory.
What on earth are emerald green parrots doing in Connecticut? Neighbors chuckle in amazement as the parrots bound for pet stores escape & make stick nests in a huge fir, along with a family of great horned owls.

Ruffle, Coo & Hoo Doo, Incl. plush animal. Randy Houk. Illus. by Randy Houk. Read by Tom Chapin. Narrated by Tom Chapin. 1 cass. (Running Time: 13 min.). (Humane Society of the United States Animal Tales Ser.). (J). (gr. 1-5). 1993. bk. 34.95 (978-1-882728-17-6(3)) Benefactory.

Ruffle, Coo & Hoo Doo, Incl. plush animal. Randy Houk. Illus. by Randy Houk. Read by Tom Chapin. Narrated by Tom Chapin. 1 cass. (Running Time: 13 min.). (Humane Society of the United States Animal Tales Ser.). (J). (gr. 1-5). 1996. pap. bk. 19.95 (978-1-882728-38-1(6)) Benefactory.

Ruffler's Child. John Pilkington. Read by Michael Tudor Barnes. 6 cass. (Running Time: 25200 sec.). (Soundings Ser.). 2007. 54.95 (978-1-84559-242-4(5)) Pub: ISIS Lrg Prnt GBR. Dist(s): Ulverscroft US

Rufus & Christopher & the Magic Bubble. Eileen Hastings. (Rufus & Christopher Ser.). (J). (gr. k-2). 1974. pap. bk. 7.94 (978-0-87783-197-6(1)) Oddo.

Rufus & Christopher in the Land of Lies. Eileen Hastings. (Rufus & Christopher Ser.). (J). (gr. 2-4). 1972. pap. bk. 7.94 (978-0-87783-198-3(X)) Oddo.

Rufus & Christopher Series, Set. Eileen Hastings. (J). (gr. 2-4). pap. bk. 23.82 (978-0-87783-234-8(X)) Oddo.

Rufus M. Eleanor Estes. Narrated by Christina Moore. 4 cass. (Running Time: 5 hrs.). (J). 2001. 37.75 (978-1-4025-9578-3(6)) Recorded Bks.

Rugby Chapel see Treasury of Matthew Arnold

Rugg on the Radio, No. 2. Frederick E. Rugg. 1 cass. (Running Time: 25 min.). 1997. 10.00 (978-1-883062-16-3(0)) Ruggs Recommend.
A consumer-oriented presentation on selecting an undergraduate college.

Rugrats: A Live Adventure. Perf. by Mark Mothersbaugh. 1 cass., 1 CD. (Rugrats Ser.). (J). (ps-2). 8.78 (UNI 90190); audio compact disk 14.98 CD Jewel box. (UNI 90190) NewSound.
Includes: "The Movers' Rap," "Rugrats Theme," "Nothing to Be a-Scared of" & more.

Rugrats: In Search of the Might Reptar. 1 cass. (Running Time: 1 hr. 30 mins.). (J). 2001. 9.98 (R4 72980); audio compact disk 13.98 (R2 72981) Rhino Enter.

Rugrats: In Search of The Mighty Reptar. (J). 2002. 6.98 (978-1-56826-866-8(1), 72980); audio compact disk 9.98 (978-1-56826-867-5(X), 72981) Rhino Enter.
Kid Rhino teams up with Nickelodeon to bring kids two original Rugrats stories. Those adorable babies, Tommy and Chuckie, along with Reptar, will

win your children over with their crazy adventures. Features the Reptar On Ice song.

Rugrats Sing-Along. 1 cass. (Rugrats Ser.). (J). (ps-2). 1998. Lyric bk. incl. (978-1-893143-00-5(7)) Playground Enter Mktg.
Soundtrack includes 5 songs with lyric book that contains words for songs & graphics.

Ruin of the Roman Empire: A New History. unabr. ed. James J. O'Donnell. Read by Mel Foster. (Running Time: 19 hrs. 0 mins. 0 sec.). (ENG.). 2008. audio compact disk 29.99 (978-1-4001-5874-4(5)); audio compact disk 79.99 (978-1-4001-3874-6(4)) Pub: Tantor Media. Dist(s): IngramPubServ

Ruin of the Roman Empire: A New History. unabr. ed. James J. O'Donnell. Read by Mel Foster. (Running Time: 19 hrs. 0 mins. 0 sec.). (ENG.). 2008. audio compact disk 39.99 (978-1-4001-0874-9(8)) Pub: Tantor Media. Dist(s): IngramPubServ

Ruin, Romance, & Redemption: The Story of Ruth for Every Woman. Speeches. Victoria Jacoby. 4 CDS. (Running Time: 4 hours). 2005. audio compact disk 20.00 (978-0-9767583-0-3(X)) Illumination MA.

Ruina de la Casa de los Ushers y Otros Cuentos Terrorificos. unabr. ed. Edgar Allan Poe. 3 CDs.Tr. of Horror Tales. (SPA.). 2002. audio compact disk 17.00 (978-958-9494-62-2(5)) YoYoMusic.

Ruined Castle of Manorbier see Twentieth-Century Poetry in English, No. 25, Recordings of Poets Reading Their Own Poetry

Ruined Maid see Evening with Dylan Thomas

Ruined Motel see Reginald Gibbons

Ruins. abr. ed. Scott Smith. Read by Patrick Wilson. 2006. 17.95 (978-0-7435-6344-4(1), Audioworks) Pub: S&S Audio. Dist(s): S and S Inc

Ruins. abr. movie tie-in ed. Scott Smith. Read by Patrick Wilson. (Running Time: 6 hrs. 0 mins. 0 sec.). (ENG.). 2008. audio compact disk 14.99 (978-0-7435-7217-0(3)) Pub: S&S Audio. Dist(s): S and S Inc

Ruins. unabr. ed. Scott Smith. Read by Patrick Wilson. 2006. 29.95 (978-0-7435-6345-1(X), Audioworks) Pub: S&S Audio. Dist(s): S and S Inc

Ruins of Gorlan. unabr. ed. John Flanagan. Read by John Keating. 7 CDs. (Running Time: 7 hrs. 45 mins.). (Ranger's Apprentice Ser.: Bk. 1). (J). (gr. 4-8). 2006. audio compact disk 74.75 (978-1-4193-9399-0(5), C3736); 59.75 (978-1-4193-9394-5(4)) Recorded Bks.
Will is an orphan and a ward of the castle. He hopes to someday become a great hero. But he is a small boy and only the biggest and toughest are selected as warriors. He has other talents though, and they catch the attention of the mysterious Ranger Halt. Will soon masters stealth and accuracy with the bow. His life depends on his keen intelligence and quick reflexes because evil is lurking - the Great Enemy, Morgarath is plotting her revenge and return to power.

Ruiseñor y la Rosa - El Cumpleaños de la Infanta. unabr. ed. Oscar Wilde. Read by Carlos Zambrano.Tr. of Nightingale & the Rose. (SPA.). 2002. audio compact disk 13.00 (978-958-43-0137-6(3)) YoYoMusic.

Rule Against Murder. unabr. ed. Louise Penny. Read by Ralph Cosham. (Running Time: 10 hrs. 0 mins.). (Chief Inspector Armand Gamache Ser.: Bk. 4). 2009. 29.95 (978-1-4332-5130-6(2)); audio compact disk 29.95 (978-1-4332-5129-0(9)); audio compact disk 80.00 (978-1-4332-5128-3(0)); audio compact disk 59.95 (978-1-4332-5127-6(2)) Blckstn Audio.

Rule & Exercises of Holy Dying see Cambridge Treasy Burton

Rule Britannia. unabr. ed. Daphne Du Maurier. Read by Jane Bullen. 8 cass. (Running Time: 8 hrs.). 64.00 (1205) Books on Tape.
A satire that looks to the future - to that moment in history when Britain's last hope for survival is a union with the U. S. Driven by a failing economy & a hopelessly divided population, Britain accepts the idea of the formation of USUK as a saving solution. But when marriage begins to look like a military take-over, the Brits rebel.

Rule Britannia. unabr. ed. Daphne Du Maurier. Read by Donada Peters. 7 cass. (Running Time: 10 hrs. 30 mins.). 1997. 56.00 (978-0-7366-3651-3(X), 4316) Books on Tape.
A combined United States United Kingdom looked good to the politicians but not to the Brits.

Rule Eleven Sanctions of the Federal Rules of Civil Procedure. Read by Louis C. Bechtle. 1 cass. 1989. 20.00 (AL-73) PA Bar Inst.

Rule of Four. abr. ed. Ian Caldwell & Dustin Thomason. Read by Josh Hamilton. 2004. 15.95 (978-0-7435-3938-8(9)) Pub: S&S Audio. Dist(s): S and S Inc

Rule of Four. unabr. ed. Ian Caldwell & Dustin Thomason. Narrated by Jeff Woodman. 9 cass. (Running Time: 13 hrs.). 2004. 79.75 (978-1-4193-0927-4(7), 97890MC) Recorded Bks.

Rule of Four. unabr. ed. Ian Caldwell & Dustin Thomason. Read by Jeff Woodman. 2004. 29.95 (978-0-7435-4321-7(1)) Pub: S&S Audio. Dist(s): S and S Inc

***Rule of Nine.** Steve Martini. Narrated by Dan Woren. 1 Playaway. (Running Time: 11 hrs. 9 mins.). 2010. 94.95 (978-0-7927-7216-3(4)) AudioGO.

***Rule of Nine.** unabr. ed. Steve Martini. Narrated by Dan Woren. 1 MP3-CD. (Running Time: 11 hrs. 9 mins.). 2010. 59.95 (978-0-7927-7215-6(6)); audio compact disk 94.95 (978-0-7927-7154-8(0)) AudioGO.

***Rule of Nine.** unabr. ed. Steve Martini. Read by Dan Woren. (ENG.). 2010. (978-0-06-199768-6(4), Harper Audio) HarperCollins Pubs.

***Rule of Nine.** unabr. ed. Steve Martini. Read by Dan Woren. (Paul Madriani Ser.: Bk. 11). 2010. audio compact disk 39.99 (978-0-06-200853-4(6), Harper Audio) HarperCollins Pubs.

***Rule of Nine: A Paul Madriani Novel.** unabr. ed. Steve Martini. Read by Dan Woren. (ENG.). 2010. (978-0-06-198878-3(2), Harper Audio) HarperCollins Pubs.

Rule #1: The Simple Strategy for Successful Investing in Only 15 Minutes a Week! abr. ed. Phil Town. Read by Phil Town. 4 CDs. (Running Time: 16200 sec.). (ENG.). 2006. audio compact disk 27.95 (978-0-7393-2464-6(0), Random AudioBks) Pub: Random Audio Pubg. Dist(s): Random

Ruler of the World. (23307-A) J Norton Pubs.

Rules. unabr. ed. Cynthia Lord. Narrated by Jessica Almasy. 4 cass. (Running Time: 4 hrs.). (J). (gr. 4-7). 2007. 33.75 (978-1-4281-5206-9(7)); audio compact disk 46.75 (978-1-4281-5211-3(3)) Recorded Bks.

Rules: Time-Tested Secrets for Capturing the Heart of Mr. Right. abr. ed. Ellen Fein & Sherrie Schneider. (ENG.). 2006. 5.98 (978-1-59483-746-3(5)) Pub: Hachet Audio. Dist(s): HachBkGrp

Rules at My House. unabr. ed. Betty Gouge. 1 cass. (Running Time: 20 min.). Dramatization. (KidSkills Interpersonal Skill Ser.). (J). (ps-1). 1986. 11.95 (978-0-934275-25-5(4)); Fam Skills.
"Why not?" "Why can't I?" These are questions every young child asks. Understanding & accepting the answers takes skill which this story imparts.

Rules at School: Early Explorers Emergent Set A Audio CD. Benchmark Education Staff. (J). 2006. audio compact disk 10.00 (978-1-4108-7595-2(4)) Benchmark Educ.

Rules Change: Job 2. Ed Young. 1983. 4.95 (978-0-7417-1315-5(2), 315) Win Walk.

Rules for Decision. Kenneth Wapnick. 10 CDs. 2006. audio compact disk 60.00 (978-1-59142-234-1(5), CD40) Foun Miracles.

Rules for Decision. Kenneth Wapnick. 1 CD. (Running Time: 11 hrs, 3 mins. 24 secs.). 2006. 53.00 (978-1-59142-248-8(5), 3m40) Foun Miracles.

Rules for Marriage: Time-Tested Secrets for Making Your Marriage Work. abr. ed. Ellen Fein & Sherrie Schneider. 2 cass. (Running Time: 3 hrs.). 2001. 18.00 (978-1-55935-357-1(0)) Soundelux.

***Rules for Radical Conservatives: Beating the Left at Its Own Game to Take Back America.** unabr. ed. David Kahane. (Running Time: 9 hrs. 30 mins.). 2010. 34.99 (978-1-4001-9860-3(7)); 24.99 (978-1-4001-6860-6(0)); 16.99 (978-1-4001-8860-4(1)); audio compact disk 83.99 (978-1-4001-4860-8(X)); audio compact disk 34.99 (978-1-4001-1860-1(3)) Pub: Tantor Media. Dist(s): IngramPubServ

Rules for Renegades: How to Make More Money, Rock Your Career, & Revel in Your Individuality. unabr. ed. Christine Comaford-Lynch. Read by Christine Comaford-Lynch. (Running Time: 6 hrs. 30 mins.). (ENG.). 2008. 24.98 (978-1-59659-256-8(7), GildAudio) Pub: Gildan Media. Dist(s): HachBkGrp

Rules for the New MLMer Audio. Created by Kim Klaver. 2 cass. 2001. 14.95 (978-1-891493-08-9(6)) Max Out Prodns.
The '5 worst things you can say to a good prospect' and tips to market on the internet.For people in Direct Sales and Network Marketing.

Rules for Visionary Leaders: Simple Solutions to Lead Organizations Through Complex Times. abr. ed. 3 cass. (Running Time: 3 hrs.). 2002. 19.95 (978-0-9671010-7-1(7)) Lifestrides Pubg.

Rules of Attraction. Christina Dodd. Narrated by Anne Flosnik. 8 cass. (Running Time: 11 hrs.). (Governess Brides Ser.: Bk. 3). 71.00 (978-1-4025-0250-7(8)) Recorded Bks.

***Rules of Attraction.** unabr. ed. Simone Elkeles. (Running Time: 8 hrs.). (YA). 2010. 24.99 (978-1-61106-065-2(6), 9781611060652, Brilliance MP3); audio compact disk 24.99 (978-1-61106-063-8(X), 9781611060638, Bril Audio CD Unabri) Brilliance Audio.

***Rules of Attraction.** unabr. ed. Simone Elkeles. Read by Blas Kisic & Roxanne Hernandez. (Running Time: 9 hrs.). (YA). 2010. 39.97 (978-1-61106-067-6(2), 9781611060676, BADLE) Brilliance Audio.

***Rules of Attraction.** unabr. ed. Simone Elkeles. Read by Roxanne Hernandez & Blas Kisic Hernandez. (Running Time: 8 hrs.). (YA). 2010. 39.97 (978-1-61106-066-9(4), 9781611060669, Brlnc Audio MP3 Lib); audio compact disk 54.97 (978-1-61106-064-5(8), 9781611060645, BriAudCD Unabrid) Brilliance Audio.

Rules of Attraction. unabr. ed. Bret Easton Ellis. Read by Lauren Fortgang, Davis & Jonathan Danny Gerard. (Running Time: 10 hrs.). 2009. audio compact disk 99.97 (978-1-4418-0620-8(2), 9781441806208, BriAudCD Unabrid) Brilliance Audio.

Rules of Attraction. unabr. ed. Bret Easton Ellis. Read by Lauren Fortgang et al. (Running Time: 13 hrs.). 2009. 24.99 (978-1-4418-0621-5(0), 9781441806215, Brilliance MP3) Brilliance Audio.

Rules of Attraction. unabr. ed. Bret Easton Ellis. Read by Jonathan Davis et al. (Running Time: 13 hrs.). 2009. 39.97 (978-1-4418-0622-2(9), 9781441806222, Brlnc Audio MP3 Lib); 39.97 (978-1-4418-0623-9(7), 9781441806239, BADLE); audio compact disk 29.99 (978-1-4418-0619-2(9), 9781441806192, Bril Audio CD Unabri) Brilliance Audio.

Rules of Betrayal. unabr. ed. Christopher Reich. Read by Paul Michael. 10 CDs. (Running Time: 12 hrs.). 2010. audio compact disk 40.00 (978-0-7393-8498-5(8), Random AudioBks) Pub: Random Audio Pubg. Dist(s): Random

Rules of Deception. unabr. ed. Christopher Reich. Read by Paul Michael. (YA). 2008. 84.99 (978-1-60514-997-4(7)) Find a World.

Rules of Deception. unabr. ed. Christopher Reich & Jonathan M. Reich. Read by Paul Michael. 12 CDs. (Running Time: 14 hrs.). (ENG.). 2008. audio compact disk 39.95 (978-0-7393-5800-9(6), Random AudioBks) Pub: Random Audio Pubg. Dist(s): Random

Rules of Engagement. abr. ed. Catherine Bush. Narrated by Wendy Van Riesen. 4 CDs. (Running Time: 4 hrs.). (ENG.). 2004. audio compact disk 29.95 (978-0-86492-361-5(9)) Pub: BTC Audiobks CAN. Dist(s): U Toronto Pr

Rules of Engagement. unabr. ed. Graham Hurley. Read by Peter Wickham. 12 cass. (Running Time: 18 hrs.). 2001. 94.95 (978-0-7531-1093-5(8), 010407) Pub: ISIS Audio GBR. Dist(s): ISIS Pub
The world is in crisis. The superpowers are on the edge of a nuclear abyss. In Britain, the government acts to safeguard its interests. One key city is sealed off & civil rights are suspended. Supreme power is handed over to one man. The Controller. The Controller is above the law. The Controller is all powerful. The Controller must be obeyed. Gillespie knows otherwise.

Rules of Engagement: Finding Faith & Purpose in a Disconnected World. unabr. ed. Chad Hennings & Michael Levin. Narrated by Chad Hennings. (Running Time: 4 hrs. 51 mins. 20 sec.). (ENG.). 2010. 16.09 (978-1-60814-620-8(0)); audio compact disk 22.99 (978-1-59859-674-8(8)) Oasis Audio.

Rules of Engagement Part 1. Elizabeth Moon. 2009. audio compact disk 19.99 (978-1-59950-532-9(0)) GraphicAudio.

Rules of Engagement Part 2. Based on a novel by Elizabeth Moon. (Serrano Legacy Ser.: Bk. 5). 2009. audio compact disk 19.99 (978-1-59950-552-7(5)) GraphicAudio.

Rules of Engagement Vol. 15: The Art of Strategic Prayers & Spiritual Warfare. Speeches. Narrated by N. Cindy Trimm. 1 CD. (Running Time: 45 mins.). 2001. audio compact disk 15.00 (978-1-931635-05-9(6)) Kingdom Life.

Rules of Life. Richard Templar. 2006. audio compact disk 39.50 (978-0-273-70863-6(5), FT Pren) Pearson EducLt GBR.

Rules of Management. Richard Templar. 2005. audio compact disk 39.50 (978-0-273-70797-4(3), FT Pren) Pearson EducLt GBR.

Rules of Prey. John Sandford, pseud. (Prey Ser.). 2005. audio compact disk 29.99 (978-1-4193-6363-4(8)) Recorded Bks.

Rules of Sex: Social & Legal Guidelines for those who have Never Been Told. Nora Baladerian. (YA). 2006. spiral bd. 29.96 (978-0-9773405-1-4(1)) Ment Heal Consul.

Rules of Silence. abr. ed. David Lindsey. Read by Lou Diamond Phillips. (ENG.). 2005. 14.98 (978-1-59483-348-9(6)) Pub: Hachet Audio. Dist(s): HachBkGrp

Rules of Survival. unabr. ed. Nancy Werlin. Read by Daniel Passer. 5 CDs. (Running Time: 6 hrs.). (YA). (gr. 8 up). 2007. audio compact disk 38.00 (978-0-7393-5115-4(X)) Pub: Random Audio Pubg. Dist(s): Random

Rules of Survival. unabr. ed. Nancy Werlin. Read by Daniel Passer. (Running Time: 22080 sec.). (ENG.). (J). (gr. 7-12). 2007. audio compact disk 30.00 (978-0-7393-4908-3(2), Listening Lib) Pub: Random Audio Pubg. Dist(s): Random

Rules of the Game: The ABC's of Relationships, Vol. 1. unabr. ed. Stephen R. Jeffrey. Read by Stephen R. Jeffrey. 1 cass. (Running Time: 75 min.). (YA). (gr. 7 up). 1999. 11.95 (978-1-893455-02-3(5)) Aloha Pubg & Mktg.

Rules of the Hunt. unabr. ed. O et al. Read by Michael Page. (Running Time: 16 hrs.). 2009. 24.99 (978-1-4233-9120-3(9), 9781423391203, Brilliance MP3); 39.97 (978-1-4233-9121-0(7), 9781423391210, Brlnc Audio MP3 Lib) Brilliance Audio.

Rules of the Hunt. unabr. ed. Victor O'Reilly. Read by Michael Page. (Running Time: 15 hrs.). 2009. 24.99 (978-1-4233-9122-7(5), 9781423391227, BAD); 39.97 (978-1-4233-9123-4(3), 9781423391234, BADLE) Brilliance Audio.

Rules of the Road: A Plaintiff Lawyer's Guide to Proving Liability. Rick Friedman & Patrick Malone. (ENG.). 2007. audio compact disk 115.00 (978-0-9743248-7-6(6)) Trial Guides.

***Rules of Thumb.** unabr. ed. Alan M. Webber. Read by Alan M. Webber. (ENG.). 2009. (978-0-06-180605-6(6), Harper Audio); (978-0-06-177649-6(1), Harper Audio) HarperCollins Pubs.

Rules of Vengeance. unabr. ed. Christopher Reich. Read by Paul Michael. (ENG.). 2009. audio compact disk 39.95 (978-0-7393-5802-3(2), Random AudioBks) Pub: Random Audio Pubg. Dist(s): Random

Rules of Victory: How to Transform Chaos & Conflict - Strategies from the Art of War. abr. ed. James Gimian & Barry Boyce. Read by James Gimian & Barry Boyce. (Running Time: 21600 sec.). (ENG.). 2008. audio compact disk 29.95 (978-1-59030-512-6(4)) Pub: Shambhala Pubns. Dist(s): Random

Rules of Victory: How to Transform Chaos & Conflict-Strategies from the Art of War. abr. ed. James Gimian et al. Read by James Gimian et al. (YA). 2008. 54.99 (978-1-60514-856-4(3)) Find a World.

Rules of Wealth. Richard Templar. 2006. audio compact disk 54.00 (978-0-273-71105-6(9), FT Pren) Pub: Pearson EducLt GBR. Dist(s): Trans-Atl Phila

Rules to Break & Laws to Follow: How Your Business Can Beat the Crisis of Short-Termism. unabr. ed. Don Peppers & Martha Rogers. (Running Time: 7 hrs.). 2008. 39.25 (978-1-4233-5999-9(2), 9781423359999, BADLE) Brilliance Audio.

Rules to Break & Laws to Follow: How Your Business Can Beat the Crisis of Short-Termism. unabr. ed. Don Peppers & Martha Rogers. Read by Don Peppers & Martha Rogers. 1 MP3-CD. (Running Time: 7 hrs.). 2008. 39.25 (978-1-4233-5997-5(6), 9781423359975, Brlnc Audio MP3 Lib) Brilliance Audio.

Rules to Break & Laws to Follow: How Your Business Can Beat the Crisis of Short-Termism. unabr. ed. Don Peppers & Martha Rogers. (Running Time: 7 hrs.). 2008. 24.95 (978-1-4233-5998-2(4), 9781423359982, BAD) Brilliance Audio.

Rules to Break & Laws to Follow: How Your Business Can Beat the Crisis of Short-Termism. unabr. ed. Don Peppers & Martha Rogers. Read by Don Peppers & Martha Rogers. 1 MP3-CD. (Running Time: 7 hrs.). 2008. 24.95 (978-1-4233-5996-8(8), 9781423359968, Brilliance MP3); audio compact disk 82.25 (978-1-4233-5995-1(X), 9781423359951, BriAudCD Unabrid); audio compact disk 29.95 (978-1-4233-5994-4(1), 9781423359944, Bril Audio CD Unabri) Brilliance Audio.

Rules(TM) II: More Rules to Live & Love By. abr. ed. Ellen Fein & Sherrie Schneider. (ENG.). 2006. 9.99 (978-1-59483-745-6(7)) Pub: Hachet Audio. Dist(s): HachBkGrp

Ruling by Prayer. Derek Prince. 1 cass. 5.95 (020) Derek Prince.
God has destined us to rule with Him, but the scepter He offers us is prayer.

Ruling in Babylon: Effective Christian Influence in Godless Environments. unabr. ed. Doug Giles. (YA). 2001. bk. 19.95 (978-0-9667501-3-3(6)) Clash Ministries.

Ruling in Righteousness, Vol. 2. Creflo A. Dollar. 20.00 (978-1-59089-014-1(0)) Pub: Creflo Dollar. Dist(s): STL Dist NA

Ruling in Righteousness, Vol. 2. Speeches. Creflo A. Dollar. 7 CDs. (Running Time: 5 hrs.). 2001. audio compact disk 28.00 (978-1-59089-898-7(2)) Creflo Dollar.

Ruling Passion. unabr. ed. Reginald Hill. Read by Brian Glover. 8 cass. (Running Time: 12 hrs.). (Dalziel & Pascoe Ser.). 2000. 69.95 (978-0-7540-0042-6(7), CAB 1465) Pub: Chivers Audio Bks GBR. Dist(s): AudioGO
Peter Pascoe is in shock: A weekend in the country with old friends turns into a nightmare when he finds three of them dead and the missing fourth a prime suspect with the local police. They want his cooperation, and Superintendent Andy Dalziel wants him back in Yorkshire where a string of unsolved burglaries is getting out of hand.

***Ruling Sea.** unabr. ed. Robert V. S. Redick. Narrated by Michael Page. (Running Time: 27 hrs. 30 mins.). (Chathrand Voyage Ser.). 2010. 59.99 (978-1-4001-9295-3(1)); 28.99 (978-1-4001-8295-4(6)) Tantor Media.

***Ruling Sea.** unabr. ed. Robert V. S. Redick. Narrated by Michael Page. (Running Time: 27 hrs. 30 mins. 0 sec.). (Chathrand Voyage Ser.). (ENG.). 2010. 39.99 (978-1-4001-6295-6(5)); audio compact disk 119.99 (978-1-4001-4295-8(4)); audio compact disk 59.99 (978-1-4001-1295-1(8)) Pub: Tantor Media. Dist(s): IngramPubServ

Ruling Your World: Ancient Strategies for Modern Life. Sakyong Mipham. (Running Time: 9000 sec.). (ENG.). 2007. audio compact disk 24.95 (978-1-59030-515-7(9), Shamb Audio) Pub: Shambhala Pubns. Dist(s): Random

Rum Diary: A Novel. Hunter S. Thompson. 2006. 44.95 (978-0-7861-4435-8(1)); audio compact disk 55.00 (978-0-7861-7375-4(0)) Blckstn Audio.

Rum Diary: A Novel. Hunter S. Thompson. Read by Johnny Depp. 4 cass. (Running Time: 4 hrs.). 1999. 24.35 (978-0-671-03352-1(2)) S and S Inc.

Rum Diary: A Novel. Hunter S. Thompson. 2000. audio compact disk 15.99 (978-0-7435-0556-7(5), Audioworks) S&S Audio.

Rum Diary: A Novel. Hunter S. Thompson. Read by Campbell Scott. 2004. 15.95 (978-0-7435-4849-6(3)) Pub: S&S Audio. Dist(s): S and S Inc

Rum Diary: A Novel. unabr. ed. Hunter S. Thompson. 2006. 29.95 (978-0-7861-7750-9(0)) Blckstn Audio.

Rum Punch. unabr. ed. Elmore Leonard. Read by Alexander Adams. 8 cass. (Running Time: 8 hrs.). 1992. 64.00 (978-0-7366-2306-3(X), 3089) Books on Tape.
Ordell Robbie, a vicious Palm Beach gunrunner, looks to retire with a million in the bank. Louis Gara, an antsy ex-con, wants nothing more than to keep his nose clean. Max Cherry, bail bondsman, aches for something like action. And Jackie Burke, a stewardess cum smuggler's mule, schemes to keep her fine-at-forty tail out of jail.

Rumble & a Grumble. (Sails Literacy Ser.). (gr. 1 up). 10.00 (978-0-7578-2663-4(6)) Rigby Educ.

Rumble Fish. abr. ed. S. E. Hinton. 1 cass. (Running Time: 54 mins.). Dramatization. (J). (gr. 4-7). 1977. 9.95 (978-0-670-61045-7(3)) Live Oak Media.

Rumble Fish, unabr. ed. S. E. Hinton. Narrated by Tom Stechschulte. 3 pieces. (Running Time: 3 hrs.). (gr. 6 up). 1995. 27.00 (978-0-7887-0376-8(5), 94567E7) Recorded Bks.
An easy way to begin discussing the provocative issues of teenage violence & gangs. Story of a fourteen year old who idolizes his big brother, the toughest streetfighter in the city. Powerful images & poignant insights.

Rumble Fish, Set. abr. ed. S. E. Hinton. 11 vols. (Running Time: 54 mins.). Dramatization. (J). (gr. 4-7). 1977. bk. 24.95 incl. cloth bk. in bag. (978-0-670-61042-6(9)); pap. bk. 15.95 incl. pap. bk. in bag. (978-0-670-61046-4(1)) Live Oak Media.

Rumble Fish, Set. unabr. ed. S. E. Hinton. Read by Tom Stechschulte. 3 cass. (Running Time: 3 hrs.). (YA). (gr. 9). 1995. pap. bk. 38.75 Homework pack. (978-0-7887-1854-0(1), 40226); 26.00 Steady reader. (978-0-7887-2353-7(7), 79666); 37.75 Steady reader homework pack. (978-0-7887-2363-6(4), 40768); 91.80 Class pack. (978-0-7887-1696-6(4), 46053) Recorded Bks.

Rumble Tumble. unabr. ed. Joe R. Lansdale. Read by Phil Gigante. (Running Time: 7 hrs.). (Hap & Leonard Ser.). 2009. 39.97 (978-1-4233-8447-2(4), 9781423384472, Brinc Audio MP3 Lib); 39.97 (978-1-4233-8449-6(0), 9781423384496, BADLE); 24.99 (978-1-4233-8446-5(6), 9781423384465, Brilliance MP3); 24.99 (978-1-4233-8448-9(2), 9781423384489, BAD); audio compact disk 87.97 (978-1-4233-8445-8(8), 9781423384458, BriAudCD Unabrid); audio compact disk 29.99 (978-1-4233-8444-1(X), 9781423384441, Bril Audio CD Unabri) Brilliance Audio.

Rumer Godden: A Storyteller's Life. unabr. ed. Anne Chisholm. Narrated by Carole Boyd. 9 cass. (Running Time: 12 hrs.). 1998. 78.00 (978-0-7887-3898-2(4), 96078E7) Recorded Bks.
Portrays Rumer Godden's years in India, where she defied rigid social expectations & was poisoned by a servant - & her new life in England.

Rumi. Coleman Barks. Prod. by Coleman Barks. (Running Time: 1 hr.). 2005. audio compact disk 15.95 (978-0-660-19370-0(1)) Canadian Broadcasting CAN.

Rumi: Lament of the Reed. Perf. by Seyyed Hossein Nasr & Suleyman Erguner. 1 cass. (Running Time: 1 hr. 8 mins.). 2000. 8.95 (978-1-931445-10-8(9)); audio compact disk 16.95 (978-1-931445-09-2(5)) A S R Media.
Poems in Persian & in English by a well known muslim scholar & music is directed by one of the most outstanding sufi musician of the present time.

Rumi: Voice of Longing. unabr. ed. Jalal al-Din Rumi. 2 CDs. (Running Time: 2 hrs. 30 mins.). 2001. audio compact disk 24.95 (978-1-56455-832-9(0)) Sounds True.
Translated and performed by the Rumi scholar Coleman Barks, these works echo with a spiritual complexity that defies their outward simplicity. As Sufism acknowledges the truth of other religions, so does Rumi's poetry reflect universal themes: the search for the highest truth, the mystery of surrender, the longing to overcome ego imprisonment.

Rumi, the Friend of God. unabr. ed. Stephan Hoeller. 1 cass. (Running Time: 1 hr. 30 min.). 1995. 11.00 (40021) Big Sur Tapes.
The life & work of Sufi poet Jalaluddin Rumi dramatically manifests what mystics consider our basic purpose in this world: to journey from outward to inward. For some mystics, another human being becomes the inspiration of the journey. In each of the three major periods of Rumi's life, a different friend embodied Rumi's genius, leading him to the mystical fulfillment that brought forth his unequaled expressions of Divine love.

Rumination see Richard Eberhart Reading His Poetry

Rummy Affair of Old Biffy, unabr. ed. Short Stories. P. G. Wodehouse. Narrated by Alexander Spencer. 2 cass. (Running Time: 3 hrs.). 1984. 18.00 (978-1-55690-450-9(9), 84069E7) Recorded Bks.
Bertie Wooster's friend, Charles Edward Biffen, finds himself in a jam that only Jeeves can unjam. Also includes "Fixing it for Freddie"; "Clustering Round Young Bingo" & "Bertie Changes His Mind".

***Rumo & His Miraculous Adventures: A Novel in Two Books.** unabr. ed. Walter Moers. (Running Time: 19 hrs. 30 mins.). 2010. 44.95 (978-1-4417-5801-9(1)); 99.95 (978-1-4417-5797-5(X)); audio compact disk 123.00 (978-1-4417-5798-2(8)) Blckstn Audio.

Rumor Has It. Tami Hoag. Read by Lyssa Browne. (ENG.). 2009. audio compact disk 19.95 (978-1-60283-552-8(7)) Pub: AudioGO. Dist(s): Perseus Dist

Rumor of War. unabr. ed. Philip Caputo. Read by Barry Cooper. 8 cass. Dramatization. 47.60 (A-116) Audio Bk.
Vietnam war story, through the Eyes of a Marine Officer.

Rumor of War. unabr. ed. Philip Caputo. Read by Wolfram Kandinsky. 9 cass. (Running Time: 13 hrs. 30 min.). 1978. 72.00 (978-0-7366-0115-3(5), 1122) Books on Tape.
Caputo's narrative helps us understand the psychology of modern half-wars, where friend & foe are almost indistiguishable & every step, in jungle or city, may lead to terror or ambush. In 1965 as a Marine Corps officer, the author landed at Danang & for 16 unforgettable months battled heat, fatigue, disease & Viet Cong in a contest that admitted no rules.

Rumor or Truth: Acts 28:11-30. Ed Young. 2000. 4.95 (978-0-7417-2258-4(5), 1258) Win Walk.

Rumors. E. Jean Beres. Read by Don Hagen. (ENG.). 2009. audio compact disk 5.49 (978-0-9825278-1-8(0)) Mind Wings Aud.

***Rumors.** E. Jean Beres. Read by Don Hagen. (Running Time: 56). (ENG.). 2009. 2.99 (978-1-61114-011-8(0)) Mind Wings Aud.

***Rumors: a luxe Novel.** unabr. ed. Anna Godbersen. Read by Nina Siemaszko. (ENG.). 2008. (978-0-06-170961-6(1)); (978-0-06-171010-0(5)) HarperCollins Pubs.

Rumors of Another World: What on Earth Are We Missing? unabr. ed. Philip Yancey & Zondervan Publishing Staff. (Running Time: 10 hrs. 0 mins. 0 sec.). (ENG.). 2003. 22.99 (978-0-310-26174-2(0)) Zondervan.

Rumors of Peace. Gary E. Parker. Narrated by Pete Bradbury. 9 cass. (Running Time: 13 hrs.). 81.00 (978-1-4025-1174-5(4)); audio compact disk 116.00 (978-1-4025-3471-3(X)) Recorded Bks.

Rumors UV Hurricane. Bill Bissett & Bill Roberts. (Running Time: 1 hr. 10 mins.). (ENG.). 2003. audio compact disk 12.95 (978-0-88995-276-8(0)) Pub: Red Deer CAN. Dist(s): IngramPubServ

Rumour Has It. Jill Mansell. 2009. 76.95 (978-0-7531-4170-0(1)); audio compact disk 99.95 (978-0-7531-4171-7(X)) Pub: Isis Pubng Ltd GBR. Dist(s): Ulverscroft US

Rumours & Borders. David Milligan. 2005. audio compact disk 19.95 (978-0-660-19284-0(5)) Canadian Broadcasting CAN.

Rumpelstiltskin see Stories Children Love to Hear

Rumpelstiltskin see Grimms' Fairy Tales

Rumpelstiltskin. (J). 1980. bk. 25.00 (978-0-07-487075-4(0)) McGraw.

Rumpelstiltskin. unabr. ed. Doris N. Dixon. Narrated by Robert Guillaume. Music by Michael Carpenter. 1 cass. (Running Time: 15 min.). Dramatization. (J). 1993. pap. bk. 9.95 (978-1-882179-16-9(1)) Confetti Ent.
The Confetti Company, a cast of multi-ethnic children, reenact the classic fairytale told in a modern, upbeat tempo.

Rumpelstiltskin. unabr. ed. Narrated by Julie Harris. 1 cass. (Running Time: 15 min.). (J). (gr. k-3). 2001. pap. bk. 10.00 (978-0-8045-6606-3(2), 6500-F); pap. bk. 22.00 (978-0-8045-6706-0(9), 6500-F/10) Spoken Arts.

Rumpelstiltskin. unabr. ed. Ed McBain, pseud. Read by Michael Prichard. 8 cass. (Running Time: 8 hrs.). (Matthew Hope Mystery Ser.: No. 2). 1986. 48.00 (978-0-7366-1033-9(2), 1963) Books on Tape.
She's a rock star of the 60s, hungry for a come-back. He's a divorced lawyer working to put his life back together. Their one-night stand is brief but torrid. When she is found the next day, brutally murdered & her six-year-old daughter turns up missing, Matthew Hope inherits love's toughest labor-hunting down a culprit who kidnaps & kills.

Rumpelstiltskin - A Deal Is a Deal. Alvin Granowsky. 1 cass. (Point of View Stories Ser.). (J). (gr. 4-6). 1993. 8.49 (978-0-8114-2215-4(1)) SteckVau.
Two versions of the traditional story & a retelling from the viewpoint of a story character motivate students to read & analyze literature through critical thinking. Flip-book presentation emphasizes the difference in the two story versions & encourages students to complete both & compare.

***Rumplestiltskin.** Anonymous. 2009. (978-1-60136-538-5(1)) Audio Holding.

Rumplestiltskin & Other Children's Favorites. (J). 2005. audio compact disk (978-1-933796-39-0(1)) PC Treasures.

Rumplestiltskin Collection. Anonymous. 2009. (978-1-60136-077-9(0)) Audio Holding.

Rumplestiltskin Collection. Narrated by Catherine O'Hara. (Running Time: 0 hr. 30 mins.). (J). 2006. 14.95 (978-1-60083-006-8(4)) Iofy Corp.

Rumpole à la Carte. unabr. ed. John Mortimer. Read by Frederick Davidson. 7 cass. (Running Time: 10 hrs.). 1992. 49.95 (978-0-7861-0351-5(5), 1308) Blckstn Audio.
Here are six delightful tales featuring everyone's favorite barrister for the defense. Horace Rumpole, disheveled, polemical, & immensely fond of cigars, Wordsworth, & Chateau Thames Embankment, once again takes center stage. Delicious characters such as his wife, Hilda, otherwise known as She Who Must Be Obeyed, & his philandering colleague Claude Erskine-Brown are back as Rumpole visits a snooty restaurant where he engages in a battle of wills over his adored mashed spuds, takes the unaccustomed role of prosecutor, & ventures - unwillingly - onto a ship where he confronts, of all things, a detective novelist.

Rumpole & the Age of Miracles. John Mortimer. Narrated by Patrick Tull. 8 CDs. (Running Time: 9 hrs. 15 mins.). 2001. audio compact disk 82.00 (978-0-7887-5191-2(3), C1348E7) Recorded Bks.
Rumpole of the Bailey fortifies himself with a nip of claret, then approaches his cases with razor-sharp wit & the flourish of a Shakespearean actor. It will take all of his cunning to keep these clients out of prison: a man of the cloth who refuses to defend himself, a husband accused of trying to drown his spouse while they share a bath, a young wife charged with eliminating her elderly mate & others. In fact, to get them off the hook demands a miracle. Includes: Rumpole & the Bubble Reputation, Rumpole & the Barrow Boy, Rumpole & the Age of Miracles, Rumpole & the Tap End, Rumpole & the Chambers Party, Rumpole & Portia & Rumpole & the Quality of Life.

Rumpole & the Age of Miracles. unabr. ed. John Mortimer. Narrated by Patrick Tull. 7 cass. (Running Time: 9 hrs. 15 mins.). 1988. 62.00 (978-0-7887-3483-0(0), 95892E7) Recorded Bks.
Rumple needs his razor-sharp wit & a miracle to solve these cases: "Rumpole & the Bubble Reputation" "Rumpole & the Barrow Boy," "Rumpole & the Age of Miracles," "Rumpole & the Tap End," "Rumpole & the Chambers Party" "Rumpole & Portia & Rumpole & the Quality of Life.

Rumpole & the Angel of Death. unabr. ed. John Mortimer. Read by Frederick Davidson & Nadia May. 7 cass. (Running Time: 10 hrs.). 1996. 49.95 (978-0-7861-0974-6(2), 1751) Blckstn Audio.
Collection of six tales of the "barrister (who's) as much a detective as Sherlock Holmes or Hercule Poirot." The comic, courageous, & corpulent "great defender of muddled & sinful humanity" is joined by a winning cast of villains & victims in tales whose wry humor & sparkling wit deftly send up the British legal system.

Rumpole & the Angel of Death. unabr. ed. John Mortimer. Narrated by Patrick Tull & Jill Tanner. 8 cass. (Running Time: 10 hrs. 45 mins.). (Rumpole of the Bailey Ser.: Vol. 7). 1996. 70.00 (978-0-7887-0514-4(8), 94708E7) Recorded Bks.
For the first time, Hilda, Rumpole's wife, tells a story of her own.

Rumpole & the Golden Thread. John Mortimer. Read by Bill Wallis. 8 cass. (Running Time: 9 hrs.). 2003. 69.95 (978-0-7540-0907-8(6), CAB 2329) AudioGO.

Rumpole & the Golden Thread. unabr. ed. John Mortimer. Read by Bill Wallis. 8 CDs. (Running Time: 12 hrs.). 2003. audio compact disk 79.95 (978-0-7540-5553-2(1), CCD 244) AudioGO.

Rumpole & the Golden Thread. unabr. ed. John Mortimer. Read by Frederick Davidson. 7 cass. (Running Time: 10 hrs.). 2003. 49.95 (978-0-7861-0855-8(X), 1653) Blckstn Audio.
In this engaging collection of stories, Rumpole continues to juggle deftly the vagaries of law, the ambiguities of crime, & the contradictions of the human heart in his death-defying performances on behalf of justice.

Rumpole & the Golden Thread. unabr. ed. John Mortimer. Narrated by Patrick Tull. 7 cass. (Running Time: 10 hrs. 30 mins.). (Rumpole of the Bailey Ser.: Vol. 5). 1991. 60.00 (978-1-55690-451-6(7), 91211E7) Recorded Bks.
Back in the harness after his abortive retirement to Florida, Rumpole glories in the mushroom pie, rainy day life of the Old Bailey. Here he spars with some old familiars like the venomous Judge Bullingham & makes the acquaintance of some fresh foes The comic adventures of an English trial attorney & six others.

Rumpole & the Penge Bungalow Murders. unabr. ed. John Mortimer. Read by Bill Wallis. (Running Time: 21420 sec.). 2005. 27.95 (978-1-57270-473-2(X)) Pub: Audio Partners. Dist(s): PerseuPGW
One of the most enduring and endearing literary characters ever to come out of Britain, Horace Rumpole has often alluded to the Penge Bungalow murders in the many stories of his cases, but fans have never before been privy to the tantalizing details. With trademark wit, Rumpole recalls memoir-style the case that established his reputation, and at the same time clears up mysteries about his early days - most significantly, how his wife Hilda ("She Who Must Be Obeyed") first came to darken his door. In the case itself, occurring some years after World War II, a young man has been accused of murdering his father and his father's friend, both ex-RAF pilots. At first a mere junior on the case, young Rumpole risks ruffling feathers with his dogged determination to secure justice - and ends up defending the accused on his own. Accomplished performer Bill Wallis gives voice to this treat for Rumpoleans and mystery fans alike.

Rumpole & the Penge Bungalow Murders. unabr. ed. John Mortimer. Read by William Wallis. 5 cass. 2005. 39.95 (978-0-7927-3437-6(8), CSL 743); audio compact disk 59.95 (978-0-7927-3438-3(6), SLD 743) AudioGO.

Rumpole & the Penge Bungalow Murders. unabr. ed. John Mortimer. Read by Bill Wallis. (Running Time: 21420 sec.). (Audio Editions Mystery Masters Ser.). (ENG.). 2005. audio compact disk 27.95 (978-1-57270-474-9(8)) Pub: AudioGO. Dist(s): Perseus Dist

Rumpole & the Primrose Path. John Mortimer. Read by Bill Wallis. 6 vols. (Running Time: 9 hrs.). 2003. 54.95 (978-0-7540-8356-6(X)) Pub: Chivers Audio Bks GBR. Dist(s): AudioGO

Rumpole Christmas: Stories. John Mortimer. (Running Time: 4 hrs. 30 mins. 0 sec.). (ENG.). 2009. audio compact disk 24.95 (978-1-60283-799-7(6)) Pub: AudioGO. Dist(s): Perseus Dist

Rumpole for the Defence. unabr. ed. John Mortimer. Read by Bill Wallis. 6 cass. (Running Time: 9 hrs.). 2003. 54.95 (978-0-7540-0967-2(X), CAB 2389); audio compact disk 64.95 (978-0-7540-5581-5(7), CCD 272) AudioGO.

Rumpole for the Defence. unabr. ed. John Mortimer. Read by Frederick Davidson. 5 cass. (Running Time: 7 hrs.). 1991. 39.95 (978-0-7861-0236-5(5), 1206) Blckstn Audio.
In this delightful collection of stories, Rumpole straightens everyone out in the shocking case of a "bent copper," gallantly teaches a Professor of Moral Philosophy about blackmail, consults with the dear departed when a will is contested, traces the path of true love when a doctor is accused of murder, & (in the name of duty, of course) drinks to excess with a teetotaling member of the prosecution.

Rumpole for the Defence. unabr. ed. John Mortimer. Narrated by Patrick Tull. 6 cass. (Running Time: 7 hrs. 45 mins.). (Rumpole of the Bailey Ser.: Vol. 4). 1991. 51.00 (978-1-55690-452-3(5), 91108E7) Recorded Bks.
Horace Rumpole, English barrister, pits wits against the minds of crime.

Rumpole Misbehaves. unabr. ed. John Mortimer & John Mortimer. Narrated by Bill Wallis. (Running Time: 12600 sec.). (ENG.). 2007. audio compact disk 19.95 (978-1-60283-303-6(6)) Pub: AudioGO. Dist(s): Perseus Dist

Rumpole of the Bailey. unabr. ed. John Mortimer. Read by Robert Hardy. 6 cass. (Running Time: 9 hrs.). 2002. 54.95 (978-0-7540-0787-6(1), CAB 2209) AudioGO.

Rumpole of the Bailey. unabr. ed. John Mortimer. Read by Robert Hardy. 6 cass. (Running Time: 9 hrs.). 2002. 49.95 (978-0-7540-5493-1(4), CCD 184, Chivers Sound Lib) AudioGO.
Of incisive with and a nose that cuts swathes through the judicial system, Horace Rumpole features in these short stories.

Rumpole of the Bailey, unabr. ed. John Mortimer. Read by Frederick Davidson. 6 cass. (Running Time: 8 hrs. 30 mins.). 1991. 44.95 (978-0-7861-0255-6(1), 1223) Blckstn Audio.
Indeed Rumpole, the irreverent, iconoclastic, claret-swilling, poetry-spouting barrister at law, is so peculiarly compelling that he has frequently been compared with Jeeves, Bertie Wooster & Sherlock Holmes - the most loved of all eccentric English characters.

Rumpole of the Bailey. unabr. ed. John Mortimer. Narrated by Patrick Tull. 6 cass. (Running Time: 8 hrs. 30 mins.). (Rumpole of the Bailey Ser.: Vol. 1). 1993. 51.00 (978-1-55690-920-7(9), 93416E7) Recorded Bks.
The first collection of stories in the series featuring the irrasible Horace Rumpole, English barrister.

Rumpole on Trial. unabr. ed. John Mortimer. Read by Timothy West. 6 cass. (Running Time: 8 hr. 8 mins.). 2002. 29.95 (978-1-57270-267-7(2)) Pub: Audio Partners. Dist(s): PerseuPGW

Rumpole on Trial. unabr. ed. John Mortimer. Read by Timothy West. 8 cass. (Running Time: 8 hrs.). 1995. 69.95 (978-0-7451-4289-0(3), CAB 972) AudioGO.
Horace Rumpole returns with seven new cases. Winding his way from the courthouse to the bar, Rumpole defends an eight-year-old against the threats of local authority, is wooed by a violinist & is brought before the Disciplinary Tribunal & Bar Council. Who will be for & against Rumpole, & will he live to fight another day?.

Rumpole on Trial. unabr. ed. John Mortimer. Read by Timothy West. 8 CDs. 2000. audio compact disk 79.95 (978-0-7540-5361-3(X), CCD 052) Pub: Chivers Audio Bks GBR. Dist(s): AudioGO

Rumpole Rests His Case. John Mortimer. Read by Tony Britton. 6 cass. (Running Time: 9 hrs.). 2003. 54.95 (978-0-7540-0872-9(X), CAB 3294); audio compact disk 64.95 (978-0-7540-5532-7(9), CCD 223) AudioGO.

Rumpole Rests His Case. unabr. ed. John Mortimer. Read by Tony Britton. 6 cass. (Running Time: 9 hrs.). 2002. 29.95 (978-1-57270-281-3(8), Audio Editions) Pub: Audio Partners. Dist(s): PerseuPGW
Horace Rumpole is one of the most enduring and endearing characters to come out of Britain. Cynical and devious yet immensely honest and determined to secure justice, the barrister triumphs over prejudice and pomposity.

Rumpole's Last Case. John Mortimer. Read by Bill Wallis. 8 vols. (Running Time: 12 hrs.). 2003. 69.95 (978-0-7540-8385-6(3)); audio compact disk 74.95 (978-0-7540-8778-6(6)) Pub: Chivers Audio Bks GBR. Dist(s): AudioGO

Rumpole's Last Case. unabr. ed. John Mortimer. Read by Frederick Davidson. 6 cass. (Running Time: 8 hrs. 30 mins.). 1995. 44.95 (978-0-7861-0801-5(0), 1625) Blckstn Audio.
Rumpole is on the job again, with his taste for claret, his penchant for poetry & his reputation for a good story. This time, several interesting cases of murder & suspicious doings pass through chambers. Rumpole uses the refined taste of a garage mechanic to discover the reasons for the robbery of a case of wine; indulges his knowledge of bloodstains & typewriters; & recalls three delightful battles with his arch-enemy, the Mad Bull (Judge Roger Bullingham).

Rumpole's Last Case. unabr. ed. John Mortimer. Read by Frederick Davidson. (Running Time: 30600 sec.). (Rumpole Ser.). 2006. audio compact disk 63.00 (978-0-7861-5940-6(5)); audio compact disk 29.95 (978-0-7861-7068-5(9)) Blckstn Audio.

Rumpole's Last Case. unabr. ed. John Mortimer. Narrated by Patrick Tull. 7 cass. (Running Time: 9 hrs. 45 mins.). (Rumpole of the Bailey Ser.: Vol. 6). 1994. 60.00 (978-0-7887-0057-6(X), 94256E7) Recorded Bks.
Seven stories in which the beloved barrister spars with his arch-foe, the Mad Bull (aka Judge Roger Bullingham).

Rumpole's Return. unabr. ed. John Mortimer. Read by Robert Hardy. 4 cass. (Running Time: 6 hrs.). 2002. 39.95 (978-0-7540-0831-6(2), CAB 2253); audio compact disk 64.95 (978-0-7540-5513-6(2), CCD 204) Pub: Chivers Pr GBR. Dist(s): AudioGO

Rumpole's Return. unabr. ed. John Mortimer. Narrated by Patrick Tull. 4 cass. (Running Time: 6 hrs.). (Rumpole of the Bailey Ser.: Vol. 3). 1991. 35.00 (978-1-55690-453-0(3), 91102E7) Recorded Bks.
Horace Rumpole abandons the delights of sunny Florida for the dusty corridors of the Old Bailey.

Rumpus in the Rain Forest. Scripts. 1 cass. or 1 CD. (Running Time: 25 mins.). (J). (gr. 1-5). 2000. pap. bk. & tchr. ed. 29.95 Bad Wolf Pr.
A Frog in the rain forest desperately wants to get off the jungle floor & see the sky, but who will help him climb above the canopy? The Jaguar loves the jungle floor, the Sloth family keeps falling asleep & the Howler Monkeys have gone nuts. The Boas offer to slither up a tree, but can you really ever trust a boa? Meanwhile, two bungling Explorers stumble by in search of the Lost Ancient City of Chocolate. No wonder the jungle is going crazy. And have you ever seen so many ants? A musical tour of the various levels of the jungle that reinforces in fun fashion the importance of the rain forests. Sheet music available.

Rumsfeld Way. Jeffrey A. Krames. Narrated by George Wilson. 5 CDs. (Running Time: 5 hrs. 45 mins.). audio compact disk 48.00 (978-1-4025-3722-6(0)) Recorded Bks.

Rumsfeld Way: The Leadership Wisdom of a Battle-Hardened Maverick. abr. ed. Jeffrey A. Krames. 3 cass. (Running Time: 4 hrs. 30 mins.). (McGraw Hill Audiobks.). 2003. 24.00 (978-0-9724462-1-1(4)); audio compact disk 28.00 (978-0-9724462-9-7(X)) Pub: A Media Intl. Dist(s): Natl Bk Netwk

This book examines Rumsfeld's many career challenges, details what he did to quickly and clearheadedly deal with each, and reveals how he has engineered some of twentieth century America's most stunning victories.

Rumsfeld's War: The Untold Story of America's Anti-Terrorist Commander. unabr. ed. Rowan Scarborough. Narrated by Alan Sklar. 5 CDs. (Running Time: 6 hrs. 30 mins. 0 sec.). (ENG.). 2004. audio compact disk 24.99 (978-1-4001-0115-3(8)); audio compact disk 49.99 (978-1-4001-3115-0(4)); audio compact disk 19.99 (978-1-4001-5115-8(5)) Pub: Tantor Media. Dist(s): IngramPubServ

Run. Stuart Woods. Narrated by John Bedford Lloyd & Frank Muller. 7 CDs. (Running Time: 8 hrs. 30 mins.). (Will Lee Ser.: No. 5). 2000. audio compact disk 69.00 (978-0-7887-4890-5(4), C1265E7) Recorded Bks.

Mississippi Senator Lee is in the spotlight. In strictest confidence, the Vice President has told Lee he will not run for President. he urges Lee to announce his candidacy but when the President is felled by a stroke, the Vice President takes over. Now, uncertain of the Vice President's plans, Lee is in a perilous political position. Everywhere he turns, he sees layers of conspiracy building that threaten to derail his campaign.

Run, abr. ed. Johnny Quarles. Read by Jeff Curran. 4 cass. (Running Time: 6 hrs.). 1998. 24.95 (978-1-890990-14-5(0), 692424) Otis Audio.

In a heart warming story of America's last land run for six million acres of the Cherokee Outlet, following the trials & tribulations of gold diggers, orphans, cowhands & immigrants, Quales leads his people to their destiny with twists at every turn while they strive to fulfill the dream of owning their own land.

***Run.** abr. ed. Stuart Woods. Read by Ken Howard. (ENG.). 2005. (978-0-06-084203-1(2), Harper Audio); (978-0-06-084202-4(4), Harper Audio) HarperCollins Pubs.

Run. abr. ed. Stuart Woods. Read by Ken Howard. (Will Lee Ser.: No. 5). 2005. audio compact disk 14.95 (978-0-06-079106-3(3)) HarperCollins Pubs.

***Run.** unabr. ed. Ann Patchett. Read by Peter Francis James. (ENG.). 2007. (978-0-06-155446-9(4)); (978-0-06-155447-6(2)) HarperCollins Pubs.

Run. unabr. ed. Ann Patchett. Read by Peter Francis James. 2008. audio compact disk 19.99 (978-0-06-167289-7(0), Harper Audio) HarperCollins Pubs.

Run. unabr. ed. Stuart Woods. Read by Jonathan Marosz. 6 cass. (Running Time: 9 hrs.). (Will Lee Ser.: No. 5). 2000. 48.00 (978-0-7366-5451-7(8), 5322) Books on Tape.

Will Lee has finally established himself at the heart of American government as the respected senator from his home state of Georgia. Forced to announce his candidacy for the presidency sooner than originally planned, the road to the White House becomes more treacherous & deadly.

***Run.** unabr. ed. Stuart Woods. Read by Jonathan Marosz. (ENG.). 2007. (978-0-06-084188-1(5), Harper Audio); (978-0-06-084189-8(3), Harper Audio) HarperCollins Pubs.

Run. unabr. ed. Stuart Woods. Narrated by Frank Muller. 6 cass. (Running Time: 8 hrs. 30 mins.). (Will Lee Ser.: No. 5). 2000. 54.00 (978-0-7887-4302-3(3), 96219E7) Recorded Bks.

As a Mississippi senator declares his candidacy, he steps into a world of ruthless power struggles & hidden agendas.

Run. unabr. collector's ed. Stuart Woods. Read by Jonathan Marosz. 7 CDs. (Running Time: 8 hrs. 12 mins.). (Will Lee Ser.: No. 5). 2000. audio compact disk 56.00 (978-0-7366-6072-3(0)) Books on Tape.

Will Lee has finally established himself at the heart of American government as the respected senator from his home state of Georgia. Forced to announce his candidacy for the presidency sooner than originally planned, the road to the White House becomes more treacherous & deadly.

Run Away Home. abr. ed. Jennie L. Hansen. 2 cass. 9.98 set. (978-1-55503-636-2(8), 0700940) Covenant Comms.

Run Away Home, Set. Jennie L. Hansen. 2 cass. 11.98 (978-1-57734-209-0(7), 07001622) Covenant Comms.

Run for Your Life. unabr. ed. James Patterson & Michael Ledwidge. Read by Bobby Cannavale & Dallas Roberts. (Running Time: 7 hrs.). (Michael Bennett Ser.: No. 2). (ENG.). 2009. 19.98 (978-1-60024-439-1(4)) Pub: Hachet Audio. Dist(s): HachBkGrp

Run for Your Life. unabr. ed. James Patterson & Michael Ledwidge. Read by Dallas Roberts & Bobby Cannavale. (Running Time: 7 hrs.). (ENG.). 2009. audio compact disk 19.98 (978-1-60024-829-0(2)) Pub: Hachet Audio. Dist(s): HachBkGrp

Run for Your Life. unabr. ed. James Patterson & Michael Ledwidge. Read by Bobby Cannavale & Dallas Roberts. 6 CDs. 2008. audio compact disk 120.00 (978-1-4159-6107-0(7), BksonTape) Pub: Random Audio Pubg. Dist(s): Random

Run If You Dare. unabr. ed. Randy Powell. Narrated by Johnny Heller. 3 pieces. (Running Time: 4 hrs.). (gr. 9 up). 2001. 28.00 (978-0-7887-9375-2(6)) Recorded Bks.

Run Jump Skip & Sing. Perf. by Barney Staff. 1 CD. (J). (ps-3). 1997. audio compact disk 14.98 (978-1-57064-210-4(9)) Lyrick Studios.

Run, Jump, Skip & Sing. Barney Staff. (J). (ps-3). 1997. audio compact disk 14.98 (978-1-57064-211-1(7)) Lyrick Studios.

Run Ma Run. Lois H. Dick. 1 cass. 1991. 10.75 (978-0-00-147497-0(9)) BJUPr.

Run, Ma, Run. Lois Hoadley Dick. 2 cass. (Running Time: 102 min.). (YA). (gr. 7 up). 2000. 10.95 (978-0-89084-911-8(0), 051177) BJUPr.

Run, Rasputin Run! Jennifer Miller. Narrated by Pat Fraley. (ENG.). 2008. audio compact disk 27.95 (978-1-60031-034-8(6)) Spoken Books.

Run, River, Run. Ann Zwinger. Read by Ann Zwinger. 2 cass. (Running Time: 3 hrs.). 1994. 16.95 (978-0-939643-38-7(3), 3518, NrthWrd Bks) TandN Child.

Combines first-hand experience with scientific insight to paint a picture of some of America's wildest lands.

Run Silent Run Deep. unabr. ed. Edward L. Beach, Jr. Read by Wolfram Kandinsky. 11 cass. (Running Time: 16 hrs. 30 mins.). 1989. 88.00 (978-0-7366-1514-3(8), 2385) Books on Tape.

Commander Edward Richardson & his exec, Jim Bledoe, are bound together by wartime duty, & divided by jealousy, pride & love for one beautiful woman. Their home is the submarine, the U.S.S. Walrus, part of the "silent service," its mission to destroy the Japanese navy in the dark days of World War II.

Run the Blockade. unabr. ed. G. Clifton Wisler. Narrated by Gerard Doyle. 3 pieces. (Running Time: 3 hrs. 30 mins.). (gr. 5 up). 2002. 28.00 (978-1-4025-1333-6(X)) Recorded Bks.

When his father dies at sea, Henry Severn must move from Ireland to Liverpool to help his family survive. Only 14 years old, Henry takes a post as ship's boy and lookout on Banshee, a British steam-powered blockade runner during the American Civil War. Huge profits are available to any craft able to break through the line of Union warships and reach Wilmington, North Carolina. The Banshee is fast, and Henry is an eagle-eyed lookout, but with each run through the line, the danger of being captured or blasted to bits increases.

Run the Risk. unabr. ed. Scott Frost. (Running Time: 9 hrs. 4 mins. 48 sec.). (ENG.). 2005. audio compact disk 22.99 (978-1-4001-5152-3(X)); audio compact disk 69.99 (978-1-4001-3152-5(9)) Pub: Tantor Media. Dist(s): IngramPubServ

Run the Risk. unabr. ed. Scott Frost. Read by Shelly Frasier. 8 CDs. (Running Time: 9 hrs. 4 mins. 48 sec.). (ENG.). 2005. audio compact disk 34.99 (978-1-4001-0152-8(2)) Pub: Tantor Media. Dist(s): IngramPubServ

***Run to Overcome: The Inspiring Story of an American Champion's Long-Distance Quest to Achieve a Big Dream.** unabr. ed. Meb Keflezighi. Contrib. by Dick Patrick. Narrated by Jon Gauger. (Running Time: 6 hrs. 5 mins. 53 sec.). (ENG.). 2010. 17.49 (978-1-60814-779-3(7)) Oasis Audio.

***Run to Overcome: The Inspiring Story of an American Champion's Long-Distance Quest to Achieve a Big Dream.** unabr. ed. Meb Keflezighi. Narrated by Jon Gauger. Contrib. by Dick Patrick. (Running Time: 6 hrs. 5 mins. 53 sec.). (ENG.). 2010. audio compact disk 24.99 (978-1-59859-839-1(2)) Oasis Audio.

Run to the Mountain: The Journals of Thomas Merton, 1939-1941: The Story of a Vocation. abr. ed. Thomas Merton. Read by Michael Toms. 2 cass. (Running Time: 3 hrs.). (Journals of Thomas Merton: Vol. 1). 1997. 17.95 (978-1-57453-102-2(6)) Audio Lit.

An intimate glimpse at the inner life of a young, pre-monastic Merton & the yearning for God that eventually led him to his true vocation.

Run to Win. 1 cassette. 1980. 12.95 (978-1-55841-028-2(7)) Emmett E Miller.

The techniques presented on this cassette have been proved effective by world champions. Deep relaxation helps you gain access to your full potential. Mental focusing and image rehearsal, known as "The Master Skill" to professional and world class performers will help you self-program the highest levels of achievement you desire.

Run to Win. 1 CD. 1985. audio compact disk 16.95 (978-1-55841-116-6(X)) Emmett E Miller.

Whatever your sport - marathon, basketball, tennis, golf - this tape can show you how to focus energy and achieve your goal. Access your inner strength through deep relaxation, then use mental image rehearsal to self-program success.

Run with the Horses: The Quest for Life at Its Best. unabr. ed. Eugene H. Peterson. 1 MP3CD. (Running Time: 6 hrs. 0 mins. 0 sec.). (ENG.). 2005. lp 19.98 (978-1-59644-117-0(8), Hovel Audio) christianaud.

***Run with the Horses: The Quest for Life at its Best.** unabr. ed. Eugene H. Peterson. Narrated by Lloyd James. (ENG.). 2005. 14.98 (978-1-59644-116-3(X), Hovel Audio) christianaud.

Run with the Horses: The Quest for Life at its Best. unabr. ed. Eugene H. Peterson. Narrated by Lloyd James. 5 CDs. (Running Time: 6 hrs. 0 mins. 0 sec.). (ENG.). 2005. audio compact disk 23.98 (978-1-59644-118-7(6), Hovel Audio) christianaud.

"If you have raced with men on foot, and they have wearied you, how will you compete with horses?" Jeremiah 12:5. We all long to live life at its best-to fuse freedom and spontaneity with purpose and meaning. Why then do we often find our lives so humdrum, so unadventuresome, so routine? Or else so frantic, so full of activity, but still devoid of fulfillment? How do we learn to risk, to trust, to pursue wholeness and excellence-to run with the horses in the jungle of life? In a series of profound reflections on the life of Jeremiah the prophet, Eugene Peterson explores the heart of what it means to be fully and genuinely human. His writing is filled with humor and self-reflection, insight and wisdom, helping to set a course for others in the quest for life at its best.

Run with the Hunted. abr. ed. Charles Bukowski. Read by Charles Bukowski. Ed. by John Martin. 1 cass. (Running Time: 90 min.). 1993. 12.00 (978-1-55994-769-5(1), CPN 2372) HarperCollins Pubs.

Run with the Winners: Developing a Championship Lifestyle from Hebrews 11. Warren W. Wiersbe. Read by Warren W. Wiersbe. 4 cass. 18.95 (978-0-8474-2224-1(0)) Back to Bible.

In these 20 messages on Hebrews 11, he traces the lives of some Old Testament heroes of the faith-& helps today's believers make some pertinent applications to their own lives.

Run Your Business So It Doesn't Run You. Linda Leigh Francis. Orig. Title: How to Run Your Business So It Doesn't Run You. 2001. 34.50 (978-0-9657879-2-5(3)) Borah Pr.

Runaway see Robert Frost in Recital

Runaway see Twentieth-Century Poetry in English, No. 6, Recordings of Poets Reading Their Own Poetry

***Runaway.** Carl Sommer. (Quest for Success Ser.). (ENG.). (YA). 2009. bk. 19.95 (978-1-57537-335-5(1)); pap. bk. 11.95 (978-1-57537-384-3(X)) Advance Pub.

***Runaway.** Grace Thompson. 2010. 69.95 (978-1-4079-0861-8(8)); audio compact disk 84.95 (978-1-4079-0862-5(6)) Pub: Soundings Ltd GBR. Dist(s): Ulverscroft US

Runaway. abr. ed. Heather Graham. Read by Juliet Mills. 2 cass. (Running Time: 3 hrs.). 1994. 16.95 Set. (978-1-879371-83-5(9), 40300) Pub Mills.

Set against the backdrop of one of this country's bloodiest confrontations, this historical novel brings to life a breathtakingly passionate love story. Tara Bent, framed for a crime she did not commit, escapes to New Orleans where she meets Jarrett McKenzie, a grieving widower on his journey home to his Florida farmland. Torn between his loyalty for his Seminole half brother & his own way of life, Jarrett is drawn to Tara hoping she might fill the empty spaces in his life. Tara cautiously surrenders her fear of Indians, joining Jarrett in his resistance of President Jackson's bloody persecution of the Seminoles, until, in one shattering moment, Tara's past catches up with her.

Runaway. unabr. ed. Read by Kymberly Dakin. 7 cass. 59.95 (978-0-7927-3366-9(5), CSL712); audio compact disk 89.95 (978-0-7927-3367-6(3), SLD712) AudioGO.

Runaway. unabr. ed. Terry Kay. Read by Dick Hill. (Running Time: 15 hrs.). 2008. 39.25 (978-1-4233-5346-1(3), 9781423353461, BADLE); 24.95 (978-1-4233-5345-4(5), 9781423353454, BAD) Brilliance Audio.

Runaway. unabr. ed. Terry Kay. Read by Dick Hill. Directed By J. C. Howe. Contrib. by Paul A. Torres. (Running Time: 54000 sec.). 2008. audio compact disk 39.25 (978-1-4233-5344-7(7), 9781423353447, Brlnc Audio MP3 Lib); audio compact disk 24.95 (978-1-4233-5343-0(9), 9781423353430, Brilliance MP3) Brilliance Audio.

Runaway. unabr. ed. Alice Munro. Narrated by Kymberly Dakin. 5 CDs. (Running Time: 39780 sec.). (Audio Editions Ser.). (ENG.). 2004. audio compact disk 37.95 (978-1-57270-446-6(2)) Pub: AudioGO. Dist(s): Perseus Dist

Captivating readers with astounding insights into humanity, Alice Munro delivers some of her finest prose in this stunning collection of short stories. In "Runaway," a neighbor helps a wife escape from her husband; in "Passion," alcoholism disrupts a young woman's first love affair; in "Trespasses," 14-year old Lauren learns a disturbing secret about her birth; and in "Tricks," a woman falls for a stranger and agrees to meet him in the same place the following year. The trilogy "Chance," "Soon," and "Silence" depicts a young teacher, Juliet, who meets her lover on a train and then, by terrible chance, visits his home on the day after his wife's funeral. The concluding story, "Powers," spans 50 years, several towns, and four characters including Tessa, whose psychic powers take her on the vaudeville circuit.

***Runaway / la Escapada.** ed. Carl Sommer. (Quest for Success Bilingual Ser.). (ENG & SPA.). (YA). 2009. bk. 21.95 (978-1-57537-434-5(X)) Advance Pub.

Runaway Asteroid: A David Foster Starman Adventure. abr. ed. Michael D. Cooper. Abr. by Michael D. Cooper. Read by Charlie O'Dowd. 2 cass. (Running Time: 180 mins.). (Starman Ser.: No. 2). 2004. 18.00 (978-1-58807-475-1(7)); (978-1-58807-792-9(6)) Am Pubng Inc.

By the middle of the 21st Century, a severe, global depression set in, unprecedented in scope. Governments fell and the infrastructure of the Earth decayed, initiating the worst period in human history. The age became known as the Collapse, and was characterized by worldwide violence, terrorism, and unrestrained criminal opportunism. But the century ended with a glimmer of hope. The concepts of stewardship, accountability, and mutual responsibility revived. Starlight Enterprise was founded in 2089, committed to rebuilding the Earth and its culture. It quickly became known for high ideals, philanthropy, and interplanetary ventures. In the early 22nd Century, Starlight Enterprise produced its first Starmen. The Starmen were the gifted and highly trained venturers of Starlight Enterprise. With their exploits, a new age of exploration and discovery began. Earth had not seen such a time for more than six centuries. In the course of their adventures, the Starmen gradually learned the amazing history of the Solar System - a history is far different from what Earth had long believed. Finally, they discovered the opportunity and responsibility of the people of Earth to defend and preserve their home ? now understood not to be a country or even a planet, but the entire system of worlds circling our star. The Starman series follows the adventures of three new Starmen and chronicles the saga of the Solar System in the glorious middle years of the 22nd Century.The Runaway Asteroid: Starman #2.The Starmen are hot on the trail of an escaping pirate named Lurton Zimbardo. Starlight Enterprise discovered that the pirates had a secret base in the Asteroid Belt - an ancient base, built by aliens millennia before but abandoned and hidden in the Asteroid Belt for some unknown reason. Starlight Enterprise sends the three Starmen on a quick mission to locate the hidden base, but the mission becomes highly complex when Zimbardo shows himself time and again one step ahead of the forces of light. Zimbardo has discovered that the black asteroid his base is on has a shield around it that hides the base from radar, making it all but impossible to detect. His plan for revenge is simple: He simply activates the amazing atomic drive of the asteroid and sends the rock heading on a collision course with Earth at a speed of 300,000 mph. Zimbardo's ultimatum to Earth is simple as well: Surrender, or your planet will become pulverized by an invisible, unstoppable rock! Starmen David Foster, Mark Seaton and Joe Taylor work with odd characters and limited resources to to escape Zimbardo's clutches and divert the asteroid before it smashes into Earth. Will they be able to locate the asteroid in time, or will Zimbardo have one last trick up his sleeve that will spell the ultimate defeat for Earth?.

Runaway Bride (Songs from the Motion Picture) - ShowTrax. Arranged by Roger Emerson. 1 CD. (Running Time: 5 mins.). 2000. audio compact disk 30.00 (08201128) H Leonard.

The hit soundtrack fo Julia Roberts' summer blockbuster features this irresistible line-up of tunes: "I Love You" (Martina McBride), "Ready to Run" (Dixie Chicks) & "You Can't Hurry Love" (Dixie Chicks).

Runaway Bunny. 1 cass. (J). (ps-4). 15.95 (VX-73C) Kimbo Educ.

In an imaginary game of hide-and-seek, a young bunny keeps running away from his mother who lovingly finds her child every time.

Runaway Bunny. Margaret Wise Brown. Illus. by Clement Hurd. 9.95 (978-1-59112-499-3(9)) Live Oak Media.

Runaway Bunny. Margaret Wise Brown. Illus. by Clement Hurd. 11 vols. (Running Time: 7 mins.). 1985. bk. 28.95 (978-1-59519-074-1(0)); pap. bk. 18.95 (978-1-59519-072-7(4)); pap. bk. 35.95 (978-1-59519-073-4(2)); 9.95 (978-1-59112-114-5(0)); audio compact disk 12.95 (978-1-59519-071-0(6)) Live Oak Media.

Runaway Bunny. abr. ed. Margaret Wise Brown. Illus. by Clement Hurd. (Share a Story Ser.). (J). (ps-1). 2007. 9.99 (978-0-06-114271-0(9), HarperFestival) HarperCollins Pubs.

Runaway Bunny. unabr. ed. Margaret Wise Brown. Read by Linda Terheyden. Illus. by Clement Hurd. 11 vols. (Running Time: 7 mins.). (J). (gr. k-3). 1985. bk. 25.95 (978-0-941078-78-8(7)); pap. bk. 16.95 (978-0-941078-76-4(0)); pap. bk. & tchr. ed. 33.95 Reading Chest. (978-0-941078-77-1(9)) Live Oak Media.

In an imaginative & imaginary game of verbal hide-&-seek, a young bunny keeps running away from his mother who lovingly finds her child every time.

Runaway Bunny. unabr. ed. Margaret Wise Brown. 1 read-along cass. (Running Time: 7 min.). (J). (ps-4). 1985. 9.95 Live Oak Media.

Runaway Bunny. unabr. abr. ed. Margaret Wise Brown. Perf. by Si Hanh. Illus. by Clement Hurd. 1 cass. (Share a Story Ser.). (J). (ps up). 1998. 9.99 (978-0-694-70095-0(9)) HarperCollins Pubs.

Runaway Dolls. unabr. ed. Ann M. Martin & Laura Godwin. Read by Lynn Redgrave. (ENG.). (J). (gr. 3). 2008. audio compact disk 30.00 (978-0-7393-7179-4(7), Listening Lib) Pub: Random Audio Pubg. Dist(s): Random

Runaway Dolls. unabr. ed. Ann M. Martin & Laura Godwin. Read by Lynn Redgrave. 4 CDs. (Running Time: 4 hrs. 57 mins.). (J). (gr. 4-7). 2008. audio compact disk 38.00 (978-0-7393-7181-7(9), Listening Lib) Pub: Random Audio Pubg. Dist(s): Random

***Runaway Heart.** Zondervan. (Running Time: 8 hrs. 3 mins. 49 sec.). (Westward Dreams Ser.). (ENG.). 2010. 9.99 (978-0-310-86940-5(4)) Zondervan.

Runaway Horses, Chickens & Other Upset People. unabr. ed. Julian Padowicz. Read by Julian Padowicz. 1 cass. (Running Time: 25 min.). (J). (gr. 4 up). 1997. 9.95 Incl. discussion guide. (978-1-881288-17-6(X), BFI AudioBooks) BusnFilm Intl.

Four characters learn from each other how to take control of conflict by being sensitive to the other person's feelings.

Runaway Jury. John Grisham. Read by Frank Muller. 1997. audio compact disk 96.00 (978-0-7366-8913-7(3)) Books on Tape.

Runaway Jury. unabr. ed. John Grisham. Read by Frank Muller. 10 cass. (Running Time: 15 hrs.). 1997. 80.00 (978-0-913369-34-0(9), 4198) Books on Tape.

They're in the middle of a multi-million dollar legal hurricane: twelve men & women who've been investigated, watched, manipulated & harassed by high-priced lawyers who'll stop at nothing to secure a verdict.

Runaway Jury. unabr. ed. John Grisham. Narrated by Frank Muller. 12 cass. (Running Time: 14 hrs. 30 mins.). 1997. 97.00 (978-0-7887-0724-7(8), 94901E7) Recorded Bks.
In a case against Pynex, one of the nation's most powerful tobacco companies, someone is controlling the jury & millions of dollars hang in the balance.

Runaway Ralph. unabr. ed. Beverly Cleary. Read by William Roberts. 2 cass. (Running Time: 3 hrs. 25 mins.). (Mouse & the Motorcycle Ser.). (J). 2000. 18.00 (978-0-7366-9086-7(7)) Books on Tape.
About a mouse named Ralph.

***Runaway Ralph.** unabr. ed. Beverly Cleary. Read by B. D. Wong. (ENG.). 2007. (978-0-06-137380-0(X)); (978-0-06-137381-7(8)) HarperCollins Pubs.

Runaway Ralph. unabr. ed. Beverly Cleary. Read by B. D. Wong. (Running Time: 7200 sec.). (Mouse & the Motorcycle Ser.). (J). (gr. 4-7). 2007. audio compact disk 15.95 (978-0-06-128428-1(9), HarperChildAud) HarperCollins Pubs.

Runaway Ralph. unabr. ed. Beverly Cleary. 1 read-along cass. (Running Time: 48 min.). (Mouse & the Motorcycle Ser.). (J). (gr. 3-5). 1983. 15.98 incl. bk. & guide. (978-0-8072-1084-0(6), SWR 22 SP, Listening Lib) Random Audio Pubg.
Ralph, an energetic mouse, hops in his motorcycle to search for adventure. But home starts to look pretty good after a few fur-raising escapades.

Runaway Ralph. unabr. ed. Beverly Cleary. Read by William Roberts. 2 vols. (Running Time: 2 hrs. 35 mins.). (Mouse & the Motorcycle Ser.). (J). (gr. 3-7). 1995. pap. bk. 29.00 (978-0-8072-7539-9(5), YA880SP, Listening Lib); 23.00 (978-0-8072-7537-5(9), YA880CX, Listening Lib) Random Audio Pubg.
Even mice must get away from their pestering siblings. And Ralph is no different, because he is tired of his mother telling him what to do, & tired of his pesky little brothers & sisters. But is he prepared for the vast & scary world he'll find once he takes off on his motorcycle?.

Runaway Ralph, Set. unabr. ed. Beverly Cleary. Read by William Roberts. 2 cass. (Running Time: 1 hr. 30 mins. per cass.). (Listening Library). (J). 1999. 17.95 (L181) Blckstn Audio.
Ralph is determined to grow up & live a life of speed, danger & excitement - he is going to run away. When he speeds off down the open road on his red motorcycle, he has no idea he's headed for adventure beyond his wildest dreams.

Runaways. abr. ed. V. C. Andrews. Read by Fran Tunno. 2 cass. (Orphans Ser.). 1999. 17.95 Set. (978-1-55935-295-6(7)) Soundelux.
Conclusion of the "Orphan Series." Brings the orphans Butterfly, Crystal, Brooke, & Raven together for a suspense-packed conclusion.

Runaways. unabr. ed. V. C. Andrews. Read by Laurel Lefkow. 8 cass. (Running Time: 9 hrs. 09 min.). (Orphans Ser.: No. 5). (J). 2001. 69.95 (978-0-7531-0636-5(1)) Pub: ISIS Lrg Prnt GBR. Dist(s): Ulverscroft US
In the grim foster home for orphans, Brooke, Crystal, Raven and Butterfly have each other. Then they discover a secret that shatters their fragile hopes of a better life and escape as runaways in a borrowed car. Raven hopes to be a singer, Butterfly a dancer, Crystal plans for college and Brooke wants to find her mother. However, soon they are penniless and as vulnerable as ever. They have only each other to ask if they should give up their dreams.

Runaways. unabr. ed. V. C. Andrews. Read by Laurel Lefkow. 8 CDs. (Running Time: 9 hrs. 4 min.). (Isis Ser.). (J). 2001. audio compact disk 79.95 (978-0-7531-0803-1(8)) Pub: ISIS Lrg Prnt GBR. Dist(s): Ulverscroft US
In the grim foster home for orphans, Brook, Crystal, Raven and Butterfly have each other. They discover a secret that shatters their fragile hopes of a better life and escape as runaways in a borrowed car. Raven hopes to be a singer, Butterfly a dancer, Crystal plans for college and Brooke wants to find her mother. However, soon they are penniless and as vulnerable as ever. They have only each other to ask if they should give up their dreams.

Rune see Poetry & Voice of Muriel Rukeyser

Runemarks. unabr. ed. Joanne Harris. Read by Sile Bermingham. 14 CDs. (Running Time: 17 hrs. 1 min.). (YA). (gr. 7-10). 2008. audio compact disk 65.00 (978-0-7393-6286-0(0), Listening Lib) Pub: Random Audio Pubg. Dist(s): Random
Not that anyone would admit it was goblins. In Maddy Smith's world, Order rules. Chaos, old gods, Faëries, goblins, magic, glamours - all of these were supposedly vanquished centuries ago. But Maddy knows that a small bit of magic has survived. The "ruinmark" she was born with on her palm proves it - and makes the other villagers fearful that she is a witch (though she's helpful in dealing with the goblins-in-the-cellar problem). But the mysterious traveler One-Eye sees Maddy's mark not as a defect but as a destiny. And Maddy will need every scrap that One-Eye can teach her about runes, cantrips, and glamours - every ounce of magic she can command - if she is to survive that destiny.

Runemarks. unabr. ed. Joanne Harris. Read by Sile Bermingham. (ENG.). (J). (gr. 5). 2008. audio compact disk 50.00 (978-0-7393-6284-6(4), Listening Lib) Pub: Random Audio Pubg. Dist(s): Random

Runenberg. Archim Seiffarth. pap. bk. 21.95 (978-88-7754-806-1(1)) Pub: Cideb ITA. Dist(s): Distribks Inc

***RuneWarriors.** collector's unabr. ed. James Jennewein & Tom S. Parker. Narrated by Richard Poe. 7 CDs. (Running Time: 8 hrs. 30 mins.). (YA). (gr. 6-10). 2009. audio compact disk 41.95 (978-1-4361-5176-4(7)) Recorded Bks.

***RuneWarriors.** unabr. ed. James Jennewein & Tom S. Parker. Narrated by Richard Poe. 1 Playaway. (Running Time: 8 hrs. 30 mins.). (YA). (gr. 6-10). 2009. 56.75 (978-1-4407-0377-5(9)); 61.75 (978-1-4361-5167-2(8)); audio compact disk 87.75 (978-1-4361-5172-6(4)) Recorded Bks.

Runner. Christopher Reich. Narrated by George Guidall. 11 cass. (Running Time: 16 hrs. 15 mins.). 2001. 99.00 (978-0-7887-4031-2(8), 96150E7) Recorded Bks.
Plunges you into the chaos of 1945 postwar Germany, where enemies often appear as allies. American lawyer & former police detective Judge Devlin is in Europe sifting through evidence of Nazi atrocities. He is part of the International Military tribunal, but his agenda is personal. He hopes to convict SS member & former Olympic sprinter Eric Seyss, the man responsible for his brother's death. When he learns that Eric has just escaped from an American POW camp, he is set for a desperate race for vengeance.

Runner. Christopher Reich. Narrated by George Guidall. 14 CDs. (Running Time: 16 hrs. 15 mins.). 2001. audio compact disk 134.00 (978-0-7887-5161-5(1), C1324E7) Recorded Bks.

Runner. unabr. ed. Peter May. Read by Simon Vance. (Running Time: 13 hrs. 0 mins.). 2010. 29.95 (978-1-4417-2558-5(X)); 79.95 (978-1-4417-2554-7(7)); audio compact disk 109.00 (978-1-4417-2555-4(5)) Blckstn Audio.

Runner. unabr. ed. Thomas Perry. Narrated by Joyce Bean. 11 CDs. (Running Time: 15 hrs. 30 mins. 0 sec.). (Jane Whitefield Novels Ser.). (ENG.). 2009. audio compact disk 79.99 (978-1-4001-4018-3(8)) Pub: Tantor Media. Dist(s): IngramPubServ

Runner. unabr. ed. Thomas Perry. Read by Joyce Bean. 11 CDs. (Running Time: 15 hrs. 30 mins. 0 sec.). (Jane Whitefield Novels Ser.). (ENG.). 2009. audio compact disk 39.99 (978-1-4001-1018-6(1)); audio compact disk 29.99 (978-1-4001-6018-1(9)) Pub: Tantor Media. Dist(s): IngramPubServ

Runner with the Lots see Twentieth-Century Poetry in English, No. 12, Recordings of Poets Reading Their Own Poetry

***Runners: 101 Inspirational Stories of Energy, Endurance, & Endorphins.** unabr. ed. Jack L. Canfield et al. Read by Christina Traister & Dan John Miller. 1 MP3-CD. (Running Time: 11 hrs.). (Chicken Soup for the Soul (Audio Health Communications) Ser.). 2010. 14.99 (978-1-4418-7795-6(9)); 39.97 (978-1-4418-8201-1(4)); 39.99 (978-1-4418-8203-5(0)) Brilliance Audio.

Running see Richard Wilbur Readings

Running. Eldon Taylor. 1 cass. (Running Time: 62 min.). (Inner Talk Ser.). 16.95 incl. script. (978-1-55978-525-9(X), 53810F) Progress Aware Res.
Soundtrack - Babbling Brook with underlying subliminal affirmations.

Running: Contemporary Moments. Eldon Taylor. 1 cass. 16.95 (978-1-55978-609-6(4), 53810N) Progress Aware Res.

Running: Rhythm. Eldon Taylor. Read by Eldon Taylor. Ed. by Leslie Brice. 1 cass. (Running Time: 1 hr.). 1992. 16.95 (978-1-56705-258-9(4)) Gateways Inst.
Self improvement.

Running: Stream. Eldon Taylor. Read by Eldon Taylor. Ed. by Leslie Brice. 1 cass. (Running Time: 1 hr.). 1992. 16.95 (978-1-56705-259-6(2)) Gateways Inst.

Running - Brisk Walking - Improve & Win. Norman J. Caldwell. Read by Norman J. Caldwell. Ed. by Achieve Now Institute Staff. 1 cass. (Running Time: 20 min.). (Sports Achievement Ser.). 1988. 9.97 (978-1-56273-086-4(X)) My Mothers Pub.
Running or brisk walking is now your choice.

Running - Walking. 1 cass. (Running Time: 60 min.). 10.95 (SP6) Psych Res Inst.
Mental sprots conditioning.

Running a Hotel on the Roof of the World. unabr. ed. Alec LeSueur. Read by Christopher Scott. 7 cass. (Running Time: 10 hrs. 30 min.). (Sound Ser.). 2001. 61.95 (978-1-86042-696-4(4), 26964) Pub: UlverLrgPrint GBR. Dist(s): Ulverscroft US

Running & Jogging. Barrie Konicov. 1 cass. 11.98 (978-0-87082-423-4(6), 112) Potentials.
Learn how to mentally release the chemicals in your brain which stimulates creativity, logical thinking, & brings on a beautiful, natural high.

Running Away: Psalm 139. Ed Young. 1983. 4.95 (978-0-7417-1300-1(4), 300) Win Walk.

Running Blind. Lee Child. Read by Dick Hill. (Jack Reacher Ser.). 2008. 74.99 (978-1-60640-806-3(2)) Find a World.

Running Blind. abr. ed. Lee Child. Read by Dick Hill. (Running Time: 21600 sec.). (Jack Reacher Ser.). 2006. audio compact disk 16.99 (978-1-4233-1950-4(8), 9781423319504, BCD Value Price) Brilliance Audio.

Running Blind. unabr. ed. Lee Child. Read by Dick Hill. 8 cass. (Running Time: 12 hrs.). (Jack Reacher Ser.). 2000. 32.95 (978-1-56740-362-6(X), 156740362X) Brilliance Audio.
People say that knowledge is power. The more knowledge, the more power. Suppose you knew the winning numbers in the lottery? What would you do? You would run to the store. You would mark the numbers on the play card. And you would win. Same for the stock market. Same for basketball or the horses or anything. Same for killing people. Women are dying. Women who have nothing in common except the fact that they once worked for the military. And they knew Jack Reacher. How and why these women are in danger completely baffles the elite FBI team working the case. There is no trace evidence. There are no links between victims. Their bodies have no fatal wounds. And the killer entered their homes and exited again like a summer breeze. Are these perfect crimes? There is only one certainty: there is a new kind of killer out there, one so calm, cautious, and careful that even the brilliant Reacher is left running blind.

Running Blind. unabr. ed. Lee Child. Read by Dick Hill. (Running Time: 12 hrs.). (Jack Reacher Ser.). 2004. 39.25 (978-1-59600-494-8(0), 1596004940, BADLE); 24.95 (978-1-59600-493-1(2), 1596004932, BAD); 39.25 (978-1-59600-492-4(4), 1596004924, Brinc Audio MP3 Lib); 24.95 (978-1-59600-491-7(6), 1596004916, Brilliance MP3) Brilliance Audio.

Running Blind. unabr. ed. Lee Child. Read by Dick Hill. (Running Time: 43200 sec.). (Jack Reacher Ser.). 2007. audio compact disk 102.25 (978-1-4233-3831-4(6), 9781423338314, BriAudCD Unabrid); audio compact disk 38.95 (978-1-4233-3830-7(8), 9781423338307, Bril Audio CD Unabri) Brilliance Audio.

***Running Dream.** unabr. ed. Wendelin Van Draanen. (ENG.). (J). 2011. audio compact disk 34.00 (978-0-307-74798-3(0), Listening Lib) Pub: Random Audio Pubg. Dist(s): Random

Running from God: Jonah 1:1-3. Ed Young. 1997. 4.95 (978-0-7417-2144-0(9), 1144) Win Walk.

Running from the Law. unabr. ed. Lisa Scottoline. Narrated by Barbara Rosenblat. 5 cass. (Running Time: 7 hrs. 15 mins.). 44.00 (978-0-7887-0648-6(9), 94825E7) Recorded Bks.
As a fast-talking wisecracking rebel with a cause, Rita Morrone makes one tough poker player & an even tougher trial lawyer. When Morrone defends a federal judge, the action turns deadly & she finds herself in the middle of a frightening game. Available to libraries only.

***Running from the Law Low Price.** abr. ed. Lisa Scottoline. Read by Karen Allen. (ENG.). 2005. (978-0-06-088660-8(9), Harper Audio); (978-0-06-088658-5(7), Harper Audio) HarperCollins Pubs.

Running Hot. Jayne Ann Krentz. Read by Sandra Burr. (Playaway Adult Fiction Ser.). (ENG.). 2009. 64.99 (978-1-60812-667-5(6)) Find a World.

Running Hot. abr. ed. Jayne Ann Krentz. Read by Sandra Burr. (Running Time: 6 hrs.). (Arcane Society Ser.). 2009. audio compact disk 14.99 (978-1-4233-2641-0(5), 9781423326410, BCD Value Price) Brilliance Audio.

Running Hot. unabr. ed. Jayne Ann Krentz. Read by Sandra Burr. 1 MP3-CD. (Running Time: 10 hrs.). (Arcane Society Ser.). 2008. 24.95 (978-1-4233-2636-6(9), 9781423326366, Brilliance MP3); 39.25 (978-1-4233-2639-7(3), 9781423326397, BADLE); 24.95 (978-1-4233-2638-0(5), 9781423326380, BAD); 39.25 (978-1-4233-2637-3(7), 9781423326373, Brinc Audio MP3 Lib); audio compact disk 34.99 (978-1-4233-2634-2(2), 9781423326342, Bril Audio CD Unabri); audio compact disk 92.25 (978-1-4233-2635-9(0), 9781423326359, BriAudCD Unabrid) Brilliance Audio.

Running in the Family. abr. ed. Michael Ondaatje. Read by Michael Ondaatje. (Running Time: 9000 sec.). 2006. audio compact disk 24.00 (978-0-7861-7043-2(3)) Blckstn Audio.

Running in the Family. unabr. ed. Michael Ondaatje. Read by Michael Ondaatje. (Running Time: 9000 sec.). 2006. audio compact disk 19.95 (978-0-7861-7557-4(5)) Blckstn Audio.

***Running Man.** unabr. ed. Stephen King. (Running Time: 10 hrs. 0 mins.). 2010. 29.95 (978-1-4417-3279-8(9)); 59.95 (978-1-4417-3275-0(6)); audio compact disk 60.00 (978-1-4417-3276-7(4)) Blckstn Audio.

Running Man. unabr. ed. Stephen King. (Running Time: 8 hrs.). (ENG.). 2010. audio compact disk 29.95 (978-0-14-242821-4(3), PengAudBks) Penguin Grp USA.

Running Meditation: Connect with Power & Energy. Kelly Howell. 1 CD. (Running Time: 60 mins.). (ENG.). 2004. audio compact disk 14.95 (978-1-881451-88-4(7)) Brain Sync.
Just slip on your headphones and start your workout. Within minutes you will experience an exhilarating upsurge of energy that will boost you into the "Zone." You'll feel the limitless energy of the universe flow through your body, igniting personal power and strengthening endurance. The cumulative training benefits are astonishing and positively life-changing.

Running Meditation: Connect with Power & Energy. unabr. ed. Read by Kelly Howell. 1 cass. (Running Time: 60 mins.). 1995. 11.95 (978-1-881451-27-3(5)) Brain Sync.
Experience a tremendous surge of power & enthusiasm created by the fusion of modern musical forms. Let the music & special audio frequencies balance the brain & push the mind into the peak performance brain state known as the Zone. This transcendent state of consciousness is marked by moments of exhilaration, relaxed concentration & timelessness, which ignites personal power & strengthens endurance. Woven into the music is guided imagery that invokes modern mythological archetypes which serve to ground & transform the running experience into a truly self-empowering meditation.

***Running Out of Dog.** unabr. ed. Dennis Lehane. (ENG.). 2007. (978-0-06-136930-8(6), Harper Audio) HarperCollins Pubs.

Running Out of Time. Margaret Peterson Haddix. Read by Kimberly Schraf. 4 cass. (Running Time: 5 hrs. 45 mins.). (J). 2000. 30.00 (978-0-7366-9178-9(2)) Books on Tape.
Jessie is sent on a journey outside of the only world she knows to save the children of 1840 Clifton, only to realize it is really 1996 & the life she has known is a reconstructed tourist site.

Running Out of Time. unabr. ed. Margaret Peterson Haddix. Read by Kimberly Schraf. 4 cass. (Running Time: 6 hrs.). (J). (gr. 1-8). 1999. 29.98 (LL 0128, Chivers Child Audio) AudioGO.

Running Out of Time. unabr. ed. Margaret Peterson Haddix. Read by Kimberly Schraf. 4 vols. (Running Time: 5 hrs. 23 mins.). (J). (gr. 5-9). 1998. pap. bk. 38.00 (978-0-8072-8032-4(1), YA972SP, Listening Lib); 32.00 (978-0-8072-8031-7(3), YA972CX, Listening Lib) Random Audio Pubg.
Jesse makes a dangerous & daring journey to save the children of 1840 Clifton. It is then that Jesse realizes it is really 1996.

Running Out of Time, Set. unabr. ed. Margaret Peterson Haddix. Read by Kimberly Schraf. 4 cass. (YA). 1999. 29.98 (FS9-43238) Highsmith.

Running Right. (Running Time: 45 min.). 9.98 (978-1-55909-125-1(8), 102S) Randolph Tapes.

***Running Scared.** abr. ed. Elizabeth Lowell. Read by Maria Tucci. (ENG.). 2004. (978-0-06-081499-1(3), Harper Audio) HarperCollins Pubs.

Running Scared. unabr. ed. Ann Granger. Read by Nicole Arumugam. 8 cass. (Running Time: 12 hrs.). 2002. 69.95 (978-0-7540-0738-8(3), CAB 2160) AudioGO.
Aspiring actress and part-time private investigator Fran Varady knew there would be maximum disruption when her friend Ganesh decided to modernize his uncle's newsagents, starting with the washroom. But she isn't prepared for the nightmare that begins when an agitated passer-by asks to use it: hours later he's found stabbed to death, leaving a message for Fran to meet him, and a mysterious role of film hidden behind the old pipes.

***Running Scared Low Price.** abr. ed. Elizabeth Lowell. Read by Maria Tucci. (ENG.). 2004. (978-0-06-078326-6(5), Harper Audio) HarperCollins Pubs.

Running Scared 2007: Fear, Worry & the God of Rest. CCEF Faculty Staff. (ENG.). 2007. 150.00 (978-1-934885-01-7(0)) New Growth Pr.

Running Scared 2007: Fear, Worry & the God of Rest. Featuring CCEF Faculty Staff. (ENG.). 2007. audio compact disk 175.00 (978-1-934885-00-0(2)) New Growth Pr.

Running the Amazon. unabr. collector's ed. Joe Kane. Read by Michael Russotto. 9 cass. (Running Time: 13 hrs. 30 mins.). 1992. 72.00 (978-0-7366-2118-2(0), 2921) Books on Tape.
A firsthand account of the only expedition ever to travel the entire 42,000 mile Amazon River.

Running the Christian Race. Bill Winston. 4 cass. (Running Time: 2hr.48min.). (C). 2001. 20.00 (978-1-931289-74-0(3)) Pub: B Winston Min. Dist(s): Anchor Distributors

Running the Race. ldr.'s ed. (J). (gr. 1-6). 2001. audio compact disk 69.95 (978-0-633-00770-6(6)) LifeWay Christian.

Running Waters: Where Angler, Fish & Fly Are Destined to Meet. abr. ed. Datus Proper. Narrated by Lloyd James. (Running Time: 16200 sec.). 2008. audio compact disk 28.00 (978-1-933309-21-7(0)) Pub: A Media Intl. Dist(s): Natl Bk Netwk

Running with Scissors: A Memoir. Augusten Burroughs. Read by Augusten Burroughs. audio compact disk 29.95 (978-0-7927-3849-7(7), CMP 870) AudioGO.

Running with Scissors: A Memoir. Augusten Burroughs. 2005. audio compact disk 74.95 (978-0-7927-3809-1(8)) AudioGO.

Running with Scissors: A Memoir. movie tie-in unabr. ed. Augusten Burroughs. 7 CDs. (Running Time: 32400 sec.). (ENG.). 2006. audio compact disk 29.95 (978-1-59397-781-8(6)) Pub: Macmill Audio. Dist(s): Macmillan

Running with Scissors: A Memoir. unabr. rev. ed. Augusten Burroughs. Read by Augusten Burroughs. (Running Time: 32400 sec.). (ENG.). 2006. audio compact disk 29.95 (978-1-4272-0071-6(8)) Pub: Macmill Audio. Dist(s): Macmillan

Running with the Bulls: My Years with the Hemingways. abr. ed. Valerie Hemingway. Read by Anne Flosnik. (Running Time: 6 hrs.). 2004. audio compact disk 74.25 (978-1-59600-065-0(1), 1596000651, BACDLib Ed) Brilliance Audio.
A chance encounter in Spain in 1959 brought young Irish reporter Valerie Danby-Smith face-to-face with Ernest Hemingway. The interview was awkward and brief, but before it ended something had clicked into place. For the next two years, Valerie devoted her life to Hemingway and his wife, Mary, traveling with them through beloved old haunts in Spain and France and living with them during the tumultuous final months in Cuba. In name a personal secretary, but in reality a confidante and sharer of the great man's secrets and sorrows, Valerie literally came of age in the company of one of the greatest literary lions of the twentieth century. Five years after his death, Valerie became a Hemingway herself when she married the writer's estranged son Gregory. Now, at last, she tells the story of the incredible years she spent with this extravagantly talented and tragically doomed family. In prose of brilliant clarity and stinging candor, Valerie evokes the magic and the pathos of Papa Hemingway's last years. Swept up in the wild revelry that always exploded around Hemingway, Valerie found herself

dancing in the streets of Pamplona, cheering bullfighters at Valencia, careening around hairpin turns in Provence, and savoring the panorama of Paris from her attic room in the Ritz. But it was only when Hemingway threatened to commit suicide if she left that she realized how troubled the aging writer was - and how dependent he had become on her. In Cuba, Valerie spent idyllic days and nights typing the final draft of A Movable Feast, even as Castro's revolution closed in. After Hemingway shot himself, Valerie returned to Cuba with his widow, Mary, to sort through thousands of manuscript pages and smuggle out priceless works of art. It was at Ernest's funeral that Valerie, then a researcher for Newsweek, met Hemingway's son Gregory - and again a chance encounter drastically altered the course of her life. Their twenty-one-year marriage finally unraveled as Valerie helplessly watched her husband succumb to the demons that had plagued him since childhood. Valerie Hemingway played an intimate, indispensable role in the lives of two generations of Hemingways. This memoir, by turns luminous, enthralling, and devastating, is the account of what she enjoyed, and what she endured, during her astonishing years of living as a Hemingway.

Running with the Bulls: My Years with the Hemingways. unabr. ed. Valerie Hemingway. Read by Anne Flosnik. (Running Time: 12 hrs.). 2004. 39.25 (978-1-59710-656-9), 1597106569, BADLE); 24.95 (978-1-59710-657-3(7), 1597106577, BAD); 39.25 (978-1-59335-923-2(3), 1593359233, Brlnc Audio MP3 Lib); 24.95 (978-1-59335-789-4(3), 1593357893, Brilliance MP3); 32.95 (978-1-59600-062-9(7), 1596000627); 87.25 (978-1-59600-063-6(5), 1596000635, BrilAudUnabridg) Brilliance Audio.

Running with the Demon. unabr. ed. Terry Brooks. Narrated by George Wilson. 12 cass. (Running Time: 16 hrs. 30 mins.). (Word & the Void Ser.: Bk. 1). 1998. 97.00 (978-0-7887-2168-7(2), 95464E7) Recorded Bks.
Two strangers appear in Hopewell, Illinois in the middle of a steel strike. One is a demon of the void & the other a knight of the word.

Running with the Giants: What the Old Testament Heroes Want You to Know about Life & Leadership. unabr. ed. John C. Maxwell. (ENG.). 2005. 9.99 (978-1-59483-362-5(1)) Pub: Hachet Audio. Dist(s): HachBkGrp

Running with the Whole Body¿: Your Guide to Running Faster & Farther ¿ Based on the work of Dr. Moshe Feldenkrais. Scripts. Jack Heggie. 4 CDs. 2005. audio compact disk 49.95 (978-1-884605-18-5(4)) Genesis II.
If you run, walk, hike or play sports, this is the program for you! You will learn a series of exercises based on the teachings of Dr. Moshe Feldenkrais that will enable you to make dynamic improvements in your running and walking. In addition, your overall movements will become smoother and more powerful. You will discover a secret that Jack calls the ?drive point? in your arms and shoulders and learn how to use your whole body to run faster with less effort and pain.What are the Benefits??Faster walking and running ?Greater power?Reduced risk of injury?Improved coordination?Improved sports performance?Reduced pain?Increased distance?Less effort in walking and running?Greater endurance.

Running with the Whole Body: Your Guide to Running Faster & Farther with Less Pain. Jack Meggie. 5 cass. (Running Time: 5 hrs.). 2000. 39.95 (978-1-884605-14-7(1)) Genesis II.
Lessons to help you run & walk faster & farther with less effort. Based on book with same title.

***Runny Babbit.** unabr. ed. Shel Silverstein. Read by Dennis Locorriere. (ENG.). 2005. (978-0-06-088980-7(2)); (978-0-06-088979-1(9)) HarperCollins Pubs.

Runny Babbit: A Billy Sook. unabr. ed. Shel Silverstein. Read by Dennis Locorriere. 1 CD. (Running Time: 23 mins.). (J). (gr. 2-8). 2005. 13.95 (978-0-06-082396-2(8), HarperChildAud) HarperCollins Pubs.

Runt the Brave. Daniel Schwabauer. (Running Time: 6 hrs.). (J). 2005. audio compact disk 26.99 (978-0-9742972-2-4(4)) Pub: Clear W Pr. Dist(s): STL Dist NA

Rupert Brooke: His Life & Poetry. Rupert Brooke. Read by Douglas Hodge. Adapted by Mike Read. Narrated by Mike Read. 2008. audio compact disk 25.69 (978-1-906147-28-0(0)) CSA Telltapes GBR.

Rupert of Hentzau. Anthony Hope-Hawkins. Read by Alfred von Lecteur. 2009. 27.95 (978-1-60112-987-1(4)) Babblebooks.

Rupert of Hentzau. unabr. ed. Anthony Hope-Hawkins. Read by Richard Brown. 7 cass. (Running Time: 10 hrs. 30 mins.). 1989. 25.95 (978-1-55685-137-7(5)) Audio Bk Con.
A single rose, a love letter & the honor of a queen fall into the hands of a charming debonair rogue.

Rural Communities: Early Explorers Early Set B Audio CD. Christina Riska. Adapted by Benchmark Education Staff. (J). 2007. audio compact disk 10.00 (978-1-4108-8230-1(6)) Benchmark Educ.

RUS' A Comprehensive Course in Russian. Sarah Smyth & Elena V. Crosbie. 4 cass. (Running Time: 5 hrs. 28 mins.). (RUS & ENG., (C). 2002. 28.99 (978-0-521-01074-0(8)) Cambridge U Pr.

Rush Home Road. abr. ed. Lori Lansens. Read by Ruby Dee. (ENG.). 2005. 14.98 (978-1-59483-370-0(2)) Pub: Hachet Audio. Dist(s): HachBkGrp

Rush Hour. Catherine Hunter. Music by Weakerthans. 1 CD. (Running Time: 1 hr. 17 mins.). 2004. audio compact disk 12.95 (978-1-894177-08-5(8)) Pub: Cyclops Pr CAN. Dist(s): Literary Pr Gp
A riveting collection of spoken word poems written and performed by one of North America's most powerful new literary voices. Includes a "bonus track" recording of the title poem with music accompaniment by the smash hit band The Weakerthans.

Rush Hour Brazilian Portuguese with Book. Contrib. by Berlitz Editors. 2 cass. (Running Time: 2 hrs.). (Berlitz Rush Hour All-Audio Ser.). 2001. pap. bk. 19.95 (978-2-8315-7720-3(9)) Pub: Berlitz Intl Inc. Dist(s): Globe Pequot

Rush Hour Portuguese. Berlitz Editors. (POR & ENG.). 2002. pap. bk. 21.95 (978-2-8315-7758-6(6)) Pub: Berlitz Intl Inc. Dist(s): Globe Pequot

Rush Hour Refresher. Michael R. Gach. 1 cass. (Running Time: 30 min.). (Greater Energy Ser.). 1987. 9.95 (978-0-945093-01-5(2)) Enhanced Aud Systs.
Explains how acupressure relieves tension & energize the body.

Rush Hour Relaxation. Dick Sutphen. 1 cass. (Running Time: 60 min.). 1989. 9.95 (978-1-55569-335-0(0), RHR-7027) Great Am Audio.

Rush Limbaugh: An Army of One. unabr. ed. Zev Chafets. Read by Erik Synnestvedt. (Running Time: 8 hrs.). (ENG.). 2010. audio compact disk 29.98 (978-1-59659-460-9(8), GildAudio) Pub: Gildan Media. Dist(s): HachBkGrp

***Rush Limbaugh: An Army of One.** unabr. ed. Zev Chafets. Read by Erik Synnestvedt. (Running Time: 8 hrs.). (ENG.). 2010. 29.98 (978-1-59659-578-1(7), GildAudio) Pub: Gildan Media. Dist(s): HachBkGrp

Rush Limbaugh Is a Big Fat Idiot: And Other Observations. abr. ed. Al Franken. 2 cass. 15.95 Set. (09738) Books on Tape.
Al Franken tackles Rush Limbaugh (no small task), the politicians & the issues in ways few have dared. Don't miss his informative discussions with the man who has "America's easiest job," Limbaugh's fact-checker.

Rush of Wings. unabr. ed. Kristen Heitzmann. 12 cass. (Running Time: 17 hrs.). 2004. 99.75 (978-1-4025-6967-8(X)) Recorded Bks.

Rush to the Hospital: The Bugville Critters. unabr. ed. Robert Stanek, pseud. Narrated by Victoria Charters. (Running Time: 19 mins.). (ENG.). (J). 2008. 5.95 (978-1-57545-357-6(6), RP Audio Pubng) Pub: Reagent Press. Dist(s): OverDrive Inc

Rushing to Paradise. unabr. ed. J. G. Ballard. Read by Jonathon Oliver. 8 cass. (Running Time: 9 hrs. 15 min.). (Isis Ser.). (J). 1995. 69.95 (978-1-85695-849-3(3), 950604) Pub: ISIS Lrg Prnt GBR. Dist(s): Ulverscroft US

Russell Baker. Interview with Russell Baker. 1 cass. (Running Time: 35 min.). 1973. 11.95 (L006) TFR.
Baker gives some bizarre hints on how to function in a grotesque world - our own, & Buchwald observes some of the craziness during the Nixon & Reagan periods.

Russell Baker's Book of American Humor. abr. ed. Read by Tony Randall. 4 cass. (Running Time: 240 min.). 1994. 21.95 Set. (978-1-55935-151-5(9)) Soundelux.
A collection of American humor writings.

Russell Banks. Interview. Interview with Russell Banks & Kay Bonetti. 1 cass. 1986. 13.95 (978-1-55644-148-6(7), 6012) Am Audio Prose.
Thorough & Wide-ranging discussion of Banks' social and aesthetic visions and the relationship between the two, plus central questions of craft in the work of this highly gifted writer.

Russell Banks. unabr. ed. Russell Banks. Read by Russell Banks. 1 cass. (Running Time: 29 min.). Incl. Gully; 1987. 10.00 New Letters.
Reads from "Success Stories," a political fable of vigilantes in a Third World ghetto.

Russell Flint see Sir John Betjeman Reading His Poetry

Russell Sands: How the "Turtles" Were Taught Trend Following Techniques. Read by Russell Sands. 1 cass. 30.00 Dow Jones Telerate.
Russ will explain why trend following works & why it will continue to work in the future. He will point out what he feels are the dangers & shortcomings of other types of trading methodologies, all from the viewpoint of statistical analysis & standard probability theory. Russ will show you how the Turtles were taught to define & exploit trends in the Futures markets through the use of both classical & proprietary technical analysis & he will give you some ground rules on how to devise your own customized trading system, including how to interpret computer testing results & how to avoid the dangers of optimization or curve fitting in the attempt to create a profitable & workable system.

Russia see Classical Russian Poetry

Russia & the Soviet Union. unabr. ed. Ralph Raico. Read by Harry Reasoner et al. 2 cass. (Running Time: 3 hrs.). (World's Political Hot Spots Ser.). 1991. 17.95 Set. (978-0-938935-93-3(3), 10358) Knowledge Prod.
The Soviet Union never was a monolith; it was a collection of nationalities, many with serious objections to union. The demise of communism holds great promise & danger not only for former Soviets, but for everyone.

Russia & the Soviet Union: Knowledge Products. unabr. ed. Raico Ralph. Read by Reasoner Harry. 2006. audio compact disk 25.95 (978-0-7861-6692-3(4)) Pub: Blckstn Audio. Dist(s): NetLibrary CO

Russia Between the World Wars. 10.00 (HE815) Esstee Audios.
Stalin's triumph over Trotsky & how he shaped the USSR in his own image.

Russia House. unabr. collector's ed. John le Carré. Read by David Case. 10 cass. (Running Time: 15 hrs.). (George Smiley Novels Ser.). 1989. 80.00 (978-0-7366-2162-5(8), 2961) Books on Tape.
In Moscow, at a small British trade fair, documents change hands: military secrets that can alter the course of events in the age of Glasnost & Perestroika. It can destroy the people it touches - particularly Barley Blair. A drinker, a saxophonist, a derelict publisher, Blair is perplexed to find the papers addressed to him & reluctant to front for British Intelligence. Their invitation to heroism lacks appeal. What does appeal is Katya Orlova, the lovely intermediary who offers Blair this "gift of trust".

Russia Smarts by Dancing Beetle. Eugene Ely et al. 1 cass. (Running Time: 88 min.). (J). 1994. 10.00 Erthviibz.
Russian science, myth, ecology & nature sounds come together when Ms. Swan & the spunky musical humans read & sing with Dancing Beetle.

Russia under the Bolshevik Regime, Pt. 1. unabr. collector's ed. Richard Pipes. Read by Geoffrey Howard. 9 cass. (Running Time: 13 hrs. 30 min.). 1996. 72.00 (978-0-7366-3329-1(4), 3981-A) Books on Tape.
"Bolshevism", says Pipes, "was the most audacious attempt in history to subject the entire life of a country to a master plan." Perhaps that's why Lenin, Stalin & Trotsky pulled it off. Their practices remained in place for decades following the establishment of the Bolshevik regime in 1917. (Hitler & Mussolini adapted similar practices for their own purposes).

Russia under the Bolshevik Regime, Pt. 2. unabr. ed. Richard Pipes. Read by Geoffrey Howard. 7 cass. (Running Time: 10 hrs. 30 min.). 1996. 56.00 (978-0-7366-3330-7(8), 3981-B) Books on Tape.

Russia under the Old Regime. unabr. collector's ed. Richard Pipes. Read by Wolfram Kandinsky. 14 cass. (Running Time: 21 hrs.). 1994. 112.00 (978-0-7366-2644-6(1), 3381) Books on Tape.
One wants to talk about the evolution of the Russian state, but that's the problem: there virtually was none, from the Middle Ages to WW I. Then the communists added 60 more years in the deep freeze. Only today is progress a possibility. From his vantage point at Harvard, Professor Richard Pipes sees in Russian history a sweeping epic that helps us better understand the Russia of today.

Russia, World War Three & Armageddon. 1 cass. 7.00 (978-1-884137-77-8(6)) J Van Impe.

Russia, World War Three, & Armageddon. Jack Van Impe. Read by Jack Van Impe. 1 cass. (Running Time: 62 min.). 7.00 J V I Minist.
In-depth study of Bible eschatology, especially the role of Russia in endtime events leading to Christ's return.

Russia, World War Three, & Armageddon. Jack Van Impe. 1989. 7.00 (978-0-934803-19-9(6)) J Van Impe.
Sermon cassette in which the author discusses Gog, Meshech, Tubal, Rosh & Tarshish & outlines Daniel's Seventy Weeks.

Russian see Acting with an Accent

Russian. Ed. by Charles Berlitz. 2 cass. (Running Time: 1 hr. 30 mins.). (Language/30 Brief Course Ser.). pap. bk. 21.95 (AF1029) J Norton Pubs.
Quick, highly condensed introduction to the words & phrases you'll need to communicate effectively in the country you're visiting. Cassettes & phrase guide book are in a vinyl album.

Russian. Sandra Costinett. 10 cass. (RUS.). 150.00 Set. (Natl Textbk Co) M-H Contemporary.
20 lesson program motivates students toward rapid & effective mastery of Russian.

Russian. Penton Overseas, Inc. Staff. 2 cass. (Running Time: 80 min.). (Language - Thirty Library). bk. 16.95 set in vinyl album. Moonbeam Pubns.
Using the proven method based on the famous U.S. Military accelerated language learning program, Language/30 courses stress conversationally useful words & phrases.

Russian. Harold Stearns. 4 cass. (Running Time: 6 hrs.). (Accent English Ser.). (RUS & ENG.). 1991. bk. 89.50 set, incl. visual aids cards. J Norton Pubs.
English as a second language instructional program.

Russian. Holger Von Rauch. Tr. by Kathleen Luft from GER. 1 cass. (Running Time: 1 hrs. 30 min.). (TravelWise Ser.). (ENG & RUS., 1998. pap. bk. 16.95 (978-0-7641-7113-0(5)) Barron.
Designed especially for international travelers, provides introductions to foreign destinations.

Russian. Daphne West. 1 cass. (Running Time: 60 min.). (Language Complete Course Packs Ser.). 1993. 19.95 (Passport Bks) McGraw-Hill Trade.

Russian. abr. ed. Created by Berlitz. (Berlitz Phrase Books & CD Ser.). (RUS & ENG., 2008. audio compact disk 14.95 (978-981-268-403-5(4)) Pub: Berlitz Pubng. Dist(s): Langenscheidt

Russian. unabr. ed. Gary McCarthy. Read by Maynard Villers. 8 cass. (Running Time: 10 hrs. 36 min.). (Rivers West Ser.: Bk. 4). 1996. 49.95 (978-1-55686-717-0(4)) Books in Motion.
The Russians build an outpost on the California coast, but Anton Rostov discovers a mecca inland where game & grizzly thrive along the Russian River.

Russian, Vol. I. Penton Overseas, Inc. Staff. 255.00 (1977, Lm Inc) Oasis Audio.
Features methods in learning a second language.

Russian: Language 30. Educational Services Corporation Staff. 2004. audio compact disk 21.95 (978-1-931850-08-7(9)) Educ Svcs DC.

Russian: Language/30. rev. ed. Educational Services Corporation Staff. Intro. by Charles Berlitz. 2 cass. (RUS.). 1995. pap. bk. 21.95 (978-0-910542-86-9(4)) Educ Svcs DC.
Russian self-teaching language course.

Russian: Learn to Speak & Understand Russian with Pimsleur Language Programs. 3rd unabr. ed. Pimsleur. Created by Pimsleur. 5 CDs. (Running Time: 50 hrs. 0 mins. 0 sec.). (Basic Ser.). (RUS & ENG.). 2005. audio compact disk 24.95 (978-0-7435-5076-5(5), Touchstone) Pub: S and S. Dist(s): S and S Inc

Russian: Learn to Speak & Understand Russian with Pimsleur Language Programs. 3rd unabr. ed. Pimsleur Staff. 8 CDs. (Running Time: 80 hrs. 0 mins. 0 sec.). (Instant Conversation Ser.). (RUS & ENG.). 2005. audio compact disk 49.95 (978-0-7435-5050-5(1), Pimsleur) Pub: S&S Audio. Dist(s): S and S Inc

Russian: Mir Russkikh. ACTR Staff. 3 cass. 1997. 79.95 Set, incl. bklet. Kendall-Hunt.

Russian No. 1: Learn to Speak & Understand Russian with Pimsleur Language Programs. Pimsleur Staff. (Running Time: 11 hrs. 50 mins. 0 sec.). (Express Ser.). (ENG.). 2003. audio compact disk 11.95 (978-0-7435-3389-8(5), Pimsleur) Pub: S&S Audio. Dist(s): S and S Inc

Russian No. 1: Learn to Speak & Understand Russian with Pimsleur Language Programs. 3rd rev. ed. Pimsleur Staff. 16 CDs. (Running Time: 160 hrs. 0 mins. 0 sec.). (Pimsleur Language Program Ser.). (ENG.). 2001. audio compact disk 345.00 (978-0-7435-0620-5(0), Pimsleur) Pub: S&S Audio. Dist(s): S and S Inc

Russian Audio Book of Proverbs. Poems. Narrated by E. Poysti. 1 cass. (RUS.). 1998. 9.95 (978-1-885024-26-8(6)) Slavic Christian.

Russian Audio Book of Psalms. Poems. Narrated by E. Poysti. 1 cass. (RUS.). 1997. 14.95 (978-1-885024-25-1(8)) Slavic Christian.

Russian Audio New Testament (Synodal Version) Poems. Narrated by E. Poysti. 1 cass. (RUS.). 1998. 29.95 (978-1-885024-27-5(4)) Slavic Christian.

Russian Bible - New Testament (Spoken Word) Synodal Version. Read by Earl Poysti. 12 cass,. 1994. 29.97 (978-1-58968-059-3(6), 8002A) Chrstn Dup Intl.

Russian Culture Keys. Klara K. Lewis. 1 cass. (Running Time: 90 min.). 1995. 12.95 (978-1-886821-30-9(5)) Pavleen.
This one of a kind presentation of Russian culture covers hundreds of culture keys related to these topics: meeting people, Russian hospitality & passion for party, shopping, eating out, & do's & don'ts in Russia.

Russian Culture Keys. 2nd ed. Klara K. Lewis. (In the Shoes of the Traveler Ser.). 1995. pap. bk. 14.95 (978-1-886821-13-2(5)) Pavleen.

Russian Dance see Christmas with Ogden Nash

Russian Debutante's Handbook. unabr. ed. Gary Shteyngart. Read by Rider Strong. (YA). 2008. 64.99 (978-1-60514-843-4(1)) Find a World.

Russian Declensions & Conjugations Handbook. Oscar E. Swan. 1 cass. (RUS.). 14.95 (BRU111) J Norton Pubs.
Aid for beginning or advanced students of Russian grammar.

Russian Enigma. unabr. ed. Clive Egleton. Narrated by Frank Muller. 5 cass. (Running Time: 6 hrs. 30 mins.). 1985. 44.00 (978-1-55690-454-7(1), 85160E7) Recorded Bks.
Sequel to "The Eisenhower Deception." The canvas shoe clamped in the St. Bernard's jaws was fairly new & bone dry. The other shoe was wetter & still on its owner's foot. The rest of George Deakin's body lay face down in the surf. Double agents, defectors & deceit lead Winter, the head of the British SIS, through a maze of CIA & KGB plots & counterplots.

Russian Feminism: Twenty Years Forward. Beth Holmgren & Igor Sopronenko. (ENG.). 2009. 21.95 (978-0-253-35431-0(5)) Ind U Pr.

Russian for Speakers of English 1. 2nd ed. 16 cass. (Running Time: 15 hrs.). (Pimsleur Tapes Ser.). (RUS.). 1995. 345.00 set. (18603, Pimsleur) S&S Audio.
Spoken foreign-language proficiency training. Thirty, half-hour, intensive, spoken-language lesson units to be completed at the rate of one lesson per day for 30 days. By achieving eighty-percent correct answers to the questions in each unit, the Pimsleur Spoken Language Programmed Instructional Method will enable the learner to achieve the ACTFL Intermediate-Low Spoken Proficiency Level.

Russian for Speakers of English 2. unabr. ed. 16 cass. (Running Time: 15 hrs.). (Pimsleur Tapes Ser.). (RUS.). 1996. 345.00 set. (18601, Pimsleur) S&S Audio.
An additional thirty-lesson unit program, accomplished at the same rate as a Pimsleur I. Will enable the learner to achieve the ACTFL Intermediate-Mid Spoken Proficiency Level.

Russian for Speakers of English 3. unabr. ed. 16 cass. (Running Time: 15 hrs.). (Pimsleur Tapes Ser.). (RUS & ENG.). 1997. 345.00 Set. (18602, Pimsleur) S&S Audio.
An additional thirty-lesson-unit program, for a total of ninety lesson units. Will allow the learner to achieve the ACTFL Intermediate-High Spoken Proficiency Level.

Russian Girl. unabr. collector's ed. Kingsley Amis. Read by David Case. 8 cass. (Running Time: 12 hrs.). 1993. 64.00 (978-0-7366-2542-5(9), 3293) Books on Tape.
London professor's integrity is put to the test by a Russian poetess seeking his endorsement.

Russian Hide & Seek. unabr. collector's ed. Kingsley Amis. Read by David Case. 7 cass. (Running Time: 10 hrs. 30 mins.). 1988. 56.00 (978-0-7366-1363-7(3), 2262) Books on Tape.
The scene is England 50 years after its conquest by the Soviets.

Russian Hill Murders. Shirley Tallman. Read by Anna Fields. (Running Time: 7 hrs.). (Sarah Woolstone Mystery Ser.: Bk. 2). 2005. audio compact disk 55.00 (978-0-7861-7945-9(7)) Blckstn Audio.

Russian Hill Murders. Shirley Tallman. Read by Anna Fields. (Running Time: 28800 sec.). (Sarah Woolstone Mystery Ser.: Bk. 2). 2005. 44.95 (978-0-7861-3041-2(5)) Blckstn Audio.

Russian Hill Murders. unabr. ed. Shirley Tallman. Read by Shirley Tallman. 13 vols. (Running Time: 7 hrs.). (Sarah Woolstone Mystery Ser.: Bk. 2). 2005. audio compact disk 29.95 (978-0-7861-8115-5(X)) Blckstn Audio.

Russian Hill Murders. unabr. ed. Shirley Tallman. Read by Anna Fields. 6 CDs. (Running Time: 28800 sec.). (Sarah Woolstone Mystery Ser.: Bk. 2). 2005. audio compact disk 29.95 (978-0-7861-7987-9(2)) Blckstn Audio.

Russian Hill Murders. unabr. ed. Shirley Tallman. Read by Anna Fields. 5 cass. (Running Time: 28800 sec.). (Sarah Woolstone Mystery Ser.: Bk. 2). 2005. 29.95 (978-0-7861-3437-3(2)) Blckstn Audio.

Russian Hill Storm Year: Winter Rain. Poems. Elihu Blotnick. 1 CD. (Running Time: 30 min.). 2005. audio compact disk 11.00 (978-0-915090-85-3(6)) Firefall.
RUSSIAN HILL Storm Year presents Elihu Blotnick from Russian Hill, in poetry in his own voice. The CD is a gift of mood and place, of company for a cold wet night, and explores the inner and outer weather, of the San Francisco hill life."When the sun sets, I live in a Chinese lantern", the first poem on the CD, rode BART, the San Francisco subway, for four years, as part of the poetry-in-transit series, commuting daily throughout the Bay Area as ten 20x21 posters.Journalist Sandra Ann Harris has reviewed the CD in advance. "Blotnick's soft deep voice is as evocative as the fog that swirls around the hill, shrouding panoramic views with a veil of white and turning the hill in on itself. The poems start by looking outward, but as they are read the listener is taken deeper into Russian Hill's tiny byways, its history, its rumbling and grumbling cable car tracks and, ultimately, deep into the poet's mind. As he says in the cover notes, 'The view outward opens each mind to itself, then the hill becomes an ark of inward exploration.?".

Russian I. 3rd rev. ed. Pimsleur Staff. 4 CDs. (Running Time: 400 hrs. 0 mins. NaN sec.). (Pimsleur Language Program Ser.). (ENG.). 2001. audio compact disk 19.95 (978-0-7435-0618-2(9), Pimsleur) Pub: S&S Audio. Dist(s): S and S Inc

Russian I, Set. 1995th ed. Paul Pimsleur. 16 cass. (Pimsleur Language Learning Ser.). 1995. pap. bk. & stu. ed. 345.00 SyberVision.

Russian I Basic. Paul Pimsleur. 8 lessons on 4 cass. (Pimsleur Language Learning Ser.). 1995. 29.95 (52166-1) SyberVision.

Russian II, Set. 1996th ed. Paul Pimsleur. 16 cass. (Pimsleur Language Learning Ser.). 1996. pap. bk. & stu. ed. 345.00 (0671-57075-7) SyberVision.

Russian II: Learn to Speak & Understand Russian with Pimsleur Language Programs. 2nd ed. Pimsleur Staff & Pimsleur. (Running Time: 160 hrs. 0 mins. 0 sec.). (Comprehensive Ser.). (ENG.). 2003. audio compact disk 345.00 (978-0-7435-2598-5(1), Pimsleur) Pub: S&S Audio. Dist(s): S and S Inc

Russian III, Set. 1998th ed. Paul Pimsleur. 16 cass. (Pimsleur Language Learning Ser.). 1998. pap. bk. & stu. ed. 345.00 (0671-57963-0) SyberVision.

Russian III: Learn to Speak & Understand Russian with Pimsleur Language Programs. 2nd ed. Pimsleur Staff. (Running Time: 160 hrs. 0 mins. 0 sec.). (Comprehensive Ser.). (ENG.). 2004. audio compact disk 345.00 (978-0-7435-2891-7(3), Pimsleur) Pub: S&S Audio. Dist(s): S and S Inc

Russian in a Minute. 1 cass. (Language in a Minute Cassette Ser.). 5.95 (978-0-943351-27-8(8), XC1011) Cimino Pub Grp.
Feel at home in any foreign country with these 101 esssential words & phrases. Hear each word introduced in English, hear them pronounced by a Voice of America instructor. Practice at your own pace, you can check yourself with the wallet sized dictionary included.

Russian in 60 Minutes. Created by Berlitz. (Berlitz in 60 Minutes Ser.). (RUS & ENG., 2008. audio compact disk 9.95 (978-981-268-392-2(5)) Pub: Berlitz Pubng. Dist(s): Langenscheidt

Russian Intermediate Reader. unabr. ed. Igor Michalchenko. 8 cass. (RUS.). 175.00 (978-0-8442-4266-8(7), Natl Textbk Co) M-H Contemporary.
Outstanding collection of 19th & 20th century literature for intermediate classes. Selections range from Pushkin to Solzhenitsyn.

Russian Legends & Fairy Tales. Lucy Maxym. Perf. by Ron Foster et al. Music by Walter Raim. 2 cass. 15.00 Set. Crnrs of the Wrld.
A group of highly accomplished actors, actresses, musicians & technicians, with impressive backgrounds in theater, films, TV & public radio, have joined together to bring these relatively unknown stories to life in English. The actors perform as a repertory group. Thus the hero of one story is the villain in another; a heroine in one story is a fish in another, & narrators change from story to story. The sound effects are delightful. The music is either composed specifically for these cassettes or adapted from the wealth of gorgeous music written by Russian composers who used many of these stories as librettos for their operas & ballets.

Russian Listening Comprehension Three. Maria D. Lekic. 3 cass. 1995. 15.00 (978-0-87415-192-3(9), 75C) Foreign Lang.
Audio tapes of video-taped talk show, "Tema" to be used with the Russian Listening Comprehension III student manual.

Russian Literature, Classics Of. Ernest J. Simmons. 4 cass. (Running Time: 3 hrs. 22 min.). 42.00 Set. (S114) J Norton Pubs.
Covers such famous writers as Pushkin, Tolstoy, Dostoevsky & Chekhov.

Russian New Testament. Contrib. by Christian Duplications International Staff. 12 cass. (RUS.). 1991. 24.98 Set. (978-7-902033-71-8(5)) Chrstn Dup Intl. Bible.

Russian New Testament. Narrated by Earl Poysti. 12 cass. (Running Time: 18 hrs.). (RUS.). 1994. 29.99 (978-7-902033-64-0(2)) Chrstn Dup Intl.

Russian New Testament: Holy Synod Version. (RUS.). 2002. 26.00 (978-1-57449-116-6(4), 107714) Pub: Hosanna NM. Dist(s): Am Bible

Russian Oboe Music of the 20th Century. Marc Fink. Contrib. by Dmitri Novgorodsky & Russian Folk Orchestra of the University of Wisconsin-Madison; Victor Gorod. 2008. audio compact disk 15.00 (978-1-931569-15-6(0)) Pub: U of Wis Pr. Dist(s): Chicago Distribution Ctr

Russian on Location. Eli Hinkel. 1 cass. (Languages on Location Ser.). (RUS., 1994. bk. 10.95 (978-0-8120-8149-7(8)) Barron.

Russian on the Go, Level 2. Thomas R. Beyer, Jr. 2 cass. (Languages on the Go Ser.). (ENG & RUS.). 1995. pap. bk. 12.95 (978-0-8120-8211-1(7)) Barron.

Russian Revolution. 1 cass. 13.95 (C19703) J Norton Pubs.

Russian Revolution. 10.00 (HE805) Esstee Audios.
A view of what happened in Russia after 1917.

Russian Revolution. Kenneth Bruce. 3 cass. (Excursions in History Ser.). 16.50 Set. Alpha Tape.

Russian Revolution. unabr. ed. Alan Moorehead. Narrated by Nelson Runger. 9 cass. (Running Time: 12 hrs. 30 mins.). 1989. 78.00 (978-1-55690-455-4(X), 89430E7) Recorded Bks.
In 1917 Russia explodes in a revolution by the Bolsheviks against the powerful Czar Nicholas, & the rise of Lenin.

Russian Revolution. unabr. collector's ed. Alan Moorehead. Read by Bill Kelsey. 8 cass. (Running Time: 12 hrs.). 1987. 64.00 (978-0-7366-1121-3(5), 2044) Books on Tape.
World War II's abrupt end brought us many gifts, none stranger than the papers of the German State. These were captured virtually complete & to this day give up secrets not dreamed of. One that emerges from Moorehead's research is the extent to which Germany was involved in the Russian Revolution. The ironic result of this clandestine maneuver was Germany's sure defeat on the Eastern front.

Russian Revolution, Pt. 1. unabr. collector's ed. Richard Pipes. Read by Wolfram Kandinsky. 15 cass. (Running Time: 22 hrs. 30 min.). 1993. 120.00 (978-0-7366-2353-7(1), 3130-A) Books on Tape.
An illuminating & authoritative history of the political & military struggle for power.

Russian Revolution, Pt. 2. unabr. collector's ed. Richard Pipes. Read by Wolfram Kandinsky. 11 cass. (Running Time: 16 hrs. 30 min.). 1993. 88.00 (978-0-7366-2354-4(X), 3130-B) Books on Tape.

Russian Revolution, Pt. 3. unabr. collector's ed. Richard Pipes. Read by Wolfram Kandinsky. 10 cass. (Running Time: 15 hrs.). 1993. 80.00 (978-0-7366-2355-1(8), 3130-C) Books on Tape.

***Russian Revolution: From Tsarism to Bolshevism.** unabr. ed. Jonathan D. Smele. 7 CDs. (Running Time: 8 hrs. 15 mins.). 2009. audio compact disk 98.75 (978-1-4407-3462-5(3)) Recorded Bks.

Russian Scripts. 1 cass. Dramatization. (RUS.). 1993. 15.00 incl. script. (978-1-58302-135-4(3), STP-17) One Way St.
Four puppet programs with English scripts, ranging from three to eight minutes each, using two or three puppets.

Russian Scripts. Tr. by Sherry Ifft. (Running Time: 32 minutes). (RUS.). 2002. audio compact disk 20.00 (978-1-58302-213-9(9)) One Way St.
The script/CD book includes four scripts recorded in Russian on CD. The book contains the English print this CD contains the Russian pre-recorded plays.Titles are:The Book of LifeThe Light of the WorldOne Way to HeavenWaiting for the Love Letter.

Russian Stage One: Live from Moscow: Student-Licensed Version, Vol. 2. ACTR. (C). 1998. cd-rom & audio compact disk 37.50 (978-0-7872-4678-5(6), 0787246786) Kendall-Hunt.

***Russian Winter.** unabr. ed. Daphne Kalotay. Read by Kathleen Gati. 2010. (978-0-06-206236-9(0), Harper Audio) HarperCollins Pubs.

***Russian Winter: A Novel.** unabr. ed. Daphne Kalotay. Read by Kathleen Gati. (ENG.). 2010. (978-0-06-201237-1(1), Harper Audio) HarperCollins Pubs.

Russian with Ease see Nuevo Ruso sin Esfuerzo

Russian with Ease see Russisch ohne Muhe Heute

Russian 2. 24 cass. (Running Time: 28 hrs. 30 min.). J Norton Pubs.

Russians, Pt. 1. unabr. collector's ed. Hedrick Smith. Read by Wolfram Kandinsky. 10 cass. (Running Time: 15 hrs.). 1979. 80.00 (978-0-7366-0125-2(2), 1132-A) Books on Tape.

Russians, Pt. 2. collector's ed. Hedrick Smith. Read by Wolfram Kandinsky. 9 cass. (Running Time: 13 hrs. 30 min.). 1979. 72.00 (978-0-7366-0126-9(0), 1132-B) Books on Tape.
How Russia looked in pre-Glasnost days. Written by New York Times Moscow Bureau Chief.

Russia's Quest for American Empire: The Lost Frontier on the Last Frontier. Tim Hostiuck. Read by Tim Hostiuck. 1 cass. (Running Time: 40 min.). 1993. 12.00 (978-1-928952-04-6(6)) Misty Peaks.
Prince Rezanov's dream of empire in Washington, Oregon & California was launched in 1806 from his capital New Archangel (Sitka, Alaska) into a sea of romances, disasters & triumphs, to be swamped under a wave of American adventurers by 1867.

Russia's War: Blood upon the Snow. collector's ed. Richard Overy. Read by David Case. 10 cass. (Running Time: 15 hrs.). 1999. 80.00 (978-0-7366-4616-1(7)) Books on Tape.
Fifty years after the end of World War II, historians now are coming to the consensus that Russia played the decisive role in the defeat of Hitler. At least 25 million Soviet soldiers & civilians perished at home & on the battlefield in the bloodiest struggle of our century.

Russisch ohne Muhe Heute. 1 cass. (Running Time: 1 hr. 30 min.).Tr. of Russian with Ease. (GER & RUS., 1997. pap. bk. 75.00 (978-2-7005-1005-8(4)) Pub: Assimil FRA. Dist(s): Distribks Inc

Russka, Pt. 1. unabr. ed. Edward Rutherfurd. Read by Nadia May. 15 cass. (Running Time: 42 hrs. 30 mins.). 1994. 95.95 (978-0-7861-0684-4(0), 1469A,B) Blckstn Audio.
Russka is the story of four families who are divided by ethnicity but united in shaping the destiny of Russia. From a single riverside village situated at one of the country's geographic crossroads, Russia's Slav peasant origins are influenced by the Greco-Iranian, Kazar, Jewish, & Mongol invasions. Unified by this one place, the many cultures blend to form a rich & varied tapestry. Edward Rutherford transforms the epic history of a great civilization into a human story of flesh & blood, boldness & action, & firmly establishes his position as today's foremost novelist of great & ancient cultures.

Russka, Pt. 2. unabr. ed. Edward Rutherfurd. Read by Nadia May. 14 cass. (Running Time: 42 hrs. 30 mins.). 1994. 89.95 (978-0-7861-0685-1(9), 1469A,B) Blckstn Audio.

Russka, Pt. A. unabr. collector's ed. Edward Rutherfurd. Read by David Case. 15 cass. (Running Time: 22 hrs. 30 min.). 1998. 120.00 (978-0-7366-4165-4(3), 4668-A) Books on Tape.
Spanning eighteen hundred years, this novel explores the dramatic unfolding of Russian history.

Russka, Pt. B. unabr. collector's ed. Edward Rutherfurd. Read by David Case. 13 cass. (Running Time: 19 hrs. 30 min.). 1998. 106.00 (978-0-7366-4166-1(1), 4668-B) Books on Tape.

Rust Bucket. abr. ed. Atk Butterfly. Read by Carol Eason. Abr. by Odin Westgaard. 2 cass. (Running Time: 3 hrs.). (Rust Bucket Ser.). 2004. 18.00 (978-1-58807-445-4(5)) Am Pubng Inc.
Rust Bucket opens a new and novel science fiction adventure series. Just as intelligent alien life is discovered by the Union of Planets, Dave Oden is dismissed from the Space Academy. He may be seventh in his class, but when budget cuts hit, his family is not wealthy enough or connected enough to save his Navy career. But all he wants is to get into space, and there are people around him who recognize his talent. He gets into space as a garbageman - and gunner - on a private gunship protecting freighters against pirates. The rest, as they say, is future history. This is modern space opera, and Right goes all out against Might.

Rustlers of Pecos County. Zane Grey. Read by Jim Gough. (Running Time: 28800 sec.). 2006. 54.95 (978-0-7861-4528-7(5)); audio compact disk 63.00 (978-0-7861-7176-7(6)) Blckstn Audio.

Rustlers of Pecos County. unabr. ed. Zane Grey. Read by Jim Gough. (Running Time: 28800 sec.). 2006. audio compact disk 29.95 (978-0-7861-7610-6(5)) Blckstn Audio.

Rustlers on the Frying Pan. unabr. ed. M. Lehman. Read by Gene Engene. 4 cass. (Running Time: 5 hrs. 24 min.). 2001. 26.95 (978-1-55686-791-0(3)) Books in Motion.
Posing as a cowhand to find the men who killed his father, Todd Lang faces discovery when the owner of the Frying Pan Ranch disappears.

Rusty. Perf. by Slick Shoes. 1 cass. 1997. audio compact disk 15.99 CD. (D1088) Diamante Music Grp.
A young & highly-regarded Southern California band with a 14-year old lead singer brings you fun, catchy songs such as Feeble, Cliche, Regrets, Prove Me Wrong & more.

Rusty Goodman-the Essential Collection. Contrib. by Rusty Goodman. (Gospel Legacy Ser.). 2005. audio compact disk 13.99 (978-5-558-93091-7(8)) Pt of Grace Ent.

Rusty Nail. J. A. Konrath. Read by Susie Breck & Dick Hill. (Playaway Adult Fiction Ser.). 2008. 79.99 (978-1-60640-899-5(2)) Find a World.

Rusty Nail. abr. ed. J. A. Konrath. Read by Dick Hill & Susie Breck. (Running Time: 14400 sec.). (Jacqueline "Jack" Daniels Mystery Ser.). 2007. audio compact disk 14.99 (978-1-4233-1238-3(4), 9781423312383, BCD Value Price) Brilliance Audio.

Rusty Nail. unabr. ed. J. A. Konrath. Read by Susie Breck & Dick Hill. (Running Time: 8 hrs.). (Jacqueline "Jack" Daniels Mystery Ser.). 2006. 39.25 (978-1-59710-658-0(5), 9781597106580, BADLE); 24.95 (978-1-59710-659-7(3), 9781597106597, BAD) Brilliance Audio.

Rusty Nail. unabr. ed. J. A. Konrath. Read by Dick Hill & Susie Breck. (Running Time: 8 hrs.). (Jacqueline "Jack" Daniels Mystery Ser.). 2006. 69.25 (978-1-59355-495-8(8), 9781593554958, BrilAudUnabridg) Brilliance Audio.
Please enter a Synopsis.

Rusty Nail. unabr. ed. J. A. Konrath. Read by Susie Breck & Dick Hill. 7 cds. (Running Time: 28800 sec.). (Jacqueline "Jack" Daniels Mystery Ser.). 2006. audio compact disk 32.95 (978-1-59355-496-5(6), 9781593554965, Bril Audio CD Unabri); audio compact disk 87.25 (978-1-59355-497-2(4), 9781593554972, BriAudCD Unabrid); audio compact disk 24.95 (978-1-59335-733-7(8), 9781593357337, Brilliance MP3) Brilliance Audio.

Rusty Nail. unabr. ed. J. A. Konrath. Read by Dick Hill & Susie Breck. (Running Time: 28800 sec.). (Jacqueline "Jack" Daniels Mystery Ser.). 2006. audio compact disk 39.25 (978-1-59335-867-9(9), 9781593358679, Brinc Audio MP3 Lib) Brilliance Audio.

Rusty Raccoon: Moon-Star Stories. Sandi Johnson. Perf. by Van Buchanan. Narrated by Sybrina Durant. 1 cass. (J). (ps-6). 1988. 4.99 (978-1-929063-49-9(0), 148); audio compact disk 9.99 (978-1-929063-44-4(X), 145) Moons & Stars.
The baby raccoon comes out of the woods to visit a family & a little boy who adores him. A cat & dog can't stand his manners.

Rut: Una historia de amor: Serie Heroes de la fe. 2000. (978-1-57697-843-6(5)) Untd Bible Amrcas Svce.

Ruth. Elizabeth Gaskell. Read by Eve Matheson. 14 vols. (Running Time: 21 hrs.). 2003. audio compact disk 115.95 (978-0-7540-5587-7(6)) Pub: Chivers Audio Bks GBR. Dist(s): AudioGO

Ruth. unabr. ed. Elizabeth Gaskell. Read by Flo Gibson. 10 cass. (Running Time: 14 hrs. 30 min.). 1995. 44.95 (978-1-55685-376-0(9)) Audio Bk Con.
Dealing compassionately with unmarried motherhood, this book was suppressed in its time. Ruth, a young orphan, is seduced & deserted by Henry Bellingham. Left to raise her son, she meets with cruelty & kindness & grows through her trials to become a truly remarkable woman.

Ruth, Set. unabr. ed. Elizabeth Gaskell. Read by Eve Matheson. 14 cass. 2000. 110.95 (978-0-7540-0381-6(7), CAB 1804) AudioGO.
Portrays the nature & sensibility of a fallen woman. Orphaned heroine Ruth, apprenticed to a dressmaker, is seduced & abandoned by a wealthy young man. Shamed in the eyes of society by her illegitimate son, Ruth finds a path that affirms we are not bound to repeat our mistakes.

Ruth: The Message of Redemption & Revival in the Book of Ruth. Nancy Leigh DeMoss. (ENG.). 2007. audio compact disk 27.99 (978-0-940110-73-1(3)) Life Action Publishing.

***Ruth & Esther Commentary.** Chuck Missler. 2009. audio compact disk 44.95 (978-1-57821-432-7(7)) Koinonia Hse.

Ruth Appleby. Elvi Rhodes. Read by Anne Dover. 9 cass. (Running Time: 13 hrs. 30 min.). 1999. 79.95 (67959) Pub: Soundings Ltd GBR. Dist(s): Ulverscroft US

Ruth Appleby. unabr. ed. Elvi Rhodes. Read by Anne Dover. 9 cass. (Sound Ser.). 2004. 76.95 (978-1-85496-795-4(9)) Pub: UlverLrgPrint GBR. Dist(s): Ulverscroft US

Ruth Bell Graham: Celebrating an Extraordinary Life. abr. ed. Narrated by Walter Cronkite. Contrib. by Barbara Bush et al. (Running Time: 12600 sec.). 2007. audio compact disk 24.99 (978-0-8499-9156-1(0)) Nelson.

Ruth Hill: Ayn Rand Meets Hiawatha. (Running Time: 60 min.). (Cal State Univ., Long Beach). 1984. 9.00 (F167) Freeland Pr.
The author tells of her experiences with Ms. Rand, of her dealings with the media & academia & their reception of her best-selling, epic novel, "Hanta Yo.".

Ruth Moore: Cold As a Dog & the Wind Northeast. 1 cass. bk. 14.98 (BK-502) Folk-Legacy.
Wonderful ballads of the Maine Coast with Gordon reciting several of his own favorites, combining humor & drama.

Ruth Whitman. Ruth Whitman. Read by Ruth Whitman. 1 cass. (Running Time: 29 min.). Incl. Tamsen Donner: A Woman's Journey; Testing of Hanna Senesh; 1987. 10.00 New Letters.

Ruth Whitman. unabr. ed. Read by Ruth Whitman & Judy Ray. Ed. by James McKinley. 1 cass. (Running Time: 29 min.). (New Letters on the Air Ser.). 1986. 10.00 (120586); 18.00 2-sided cass. New Letters.
Whitman is interviewed by Judy Ray & reads poems from her books Tamsen Donner: A Woman's Journey & the Testing of Hannah Senesh.

***Ruthless Game Unabridged CDs.** Christine Feehan. (Running Time: 14 hrs.). (ENG.). 2010. audio compact disk 39.95 (978-0-14-242887-0(6), PengAudBks) Penguin Grp USA.

Ruthless Need. unabr. ed. Catherine Cookson. Read by Gordon Griffin. 9 cass. (Running Time: 13 hrs. 30 mins.). 1999. 75.95 (20184) Pub: Soundings Ltd GBR. Dist(s): Ulverscroft US

Ruthless Trust: The Ragamuffin's Path to God. abr. ed. Brennan Manning. Read by Brennan Manning. 2 cass. (Running Time: 3 hrs.). 2004. 18.95 (978-0-06-058486-3(6)) HarperCollins Pubs.

Ruthless.com. Read by Jay Sanders. Created by Tom Clancy & Martin Greenberg. 3 CDs. (Running Time: 3 hrs.). (Tom Clancy's Power Plays Ser.:

No. 2). 2003. audio compact disk 23.50 (978-0-7435-0425-6(9), Audioworks) S&S Audio.

Ruthless.com, abr. ed. Read by Jay Sanders. Created by Tom Clancy & Martin Greenberg. 2 cass. (Tom Clancy's Power Plays Ser.: No. 2). 1999. 18.00 (FS9-40113) Highsmith.

Rutles. Neil Innes & Eric Idle. 1 CD. (Running Time: 1 hr. 30 mins). 2001. audio compact disk 16.98 (R2 75760) Rhino Enter.

Rw Audio Cards Basic Vocabulary 1. Janie Haugen-McLane. 2006. 79.95 (978-1-58804-563-8(3)) PCI Educ.

Rw Audio Cards Basic Vocabulary 2. Janie Haugen-McLane. 2006. 79.95 (978-1-58804-564-5(1)) PCI Educ.

Rw Audio Cards Comminuty Helpers, Places & Vehicles. Janie Haugen-McLane. 2006. 79.95 (978-1-58804-565-2(X)) PCI Educ.

Rw Audio Cards Sight Words 1. Janie Haugen-McLane. 2006. 79.95 (978-1-58804-566-9(8)) PCI Educ.

Rw Audio Cards Telling Time Words. Janie Haugen-McLane. 2006. 79.95 (978-1-58804-567-6(6)) PCI Educ.

Rx for Murder. unabr. ed. Dorothy R. Kliewer. Read by Laurie Klein. 6 cass. (Running Time: 7 hrs.). 1995. 39.95 (978-1-55686-576-3(7)) Books in Motion.
The medical community is suspicious of Dr. Howard's controversial new treatment involving drugs & hypnosis. A young novelist learns Howard's clinic is a perfect place for murder.

Rx for Stress. George J. Pratt. Narrated by George J. Pratt. (ENG.). 2009. audio compact disk 25.00 (978-1-934726-02-0(8)) P C Pr.

***RX: Freedom to Travel Language Series: French.** Narrated by Katheryn Hill & Edgard Yemelong. (ENG.). 2010. audio compact disk 19.95 (978-1-934814-15-4(6)) Red Planet Au.

***RX: Freedom to Travel Language Series: German.** Narrated by Kathryn Hill & David Reggi. (ENG & GER.). 2009. audio compact disk 19.95 (978-1-934814-14-7(8)) Red Planet Au.

***RX: Freedom to Travel Language Series: Greek.** Narrated by Kathryn Hill & Ria Bithos. (ENG & GRE.). 2009. audio compact disk 19.95 (978-1-934814-17-8(2)) Red Planet Au.

***RX: Freedom to Travel Language Series: Mandarin.** Narrated by Katheryn Hill & Anji Yuan. (ENG.). 2010. audio compact disk 19.95 (978-1-934814-21-5(0)) Red Planet Au.

***RX: Freedom to Travel Language Series: Swedish.** Narrated by Katheryn Hill & Elisabeth Kihlberg. (ENG.). 2010. audio compact disk 19.95 (978-1-934814-20-8(2)) Red Planet Au.

***Ryan & Robbie's Bike Ride Adventure: And Lao Lao's Chinese Secrets.** Roger Hackett. Illus. by Jared Beckstrand. Narrated by Liu Quinjia. 1 CD. (Running Time: 18 mins.). (J). (gr. 4). 2009. lib. bdg. 15.95 (978-0-9820254-6-8(7)) Ryan n Rob.

Rykers. unabr. ed. K. E. Soderberg. Read by Gene Engene. 6 cass. (Running Time: 8 hrs. 30 min.). 1996. 39.95 (978-1-55686-715-6(8)) Books in Motion.
This is the story of Tobias & Zack Ryker, wilderness men, courageous men, men who hired out as scouts, guiding settlers to the fertile valleys of the California frontier.

Ryland's Footsteps. Sally Prue. 6 CDs. 2005. audio compact disk 59.95 (978-0-7540-6705-4(X), Chivers Child Audio) AudioGO.

Ryoko Character CD. Perf. by Natsuko Kuwatani. (YA). 2007. 9.98 (978-1-59409-850-5(6)) Bandai Ent.

S

S. A. S. S. Y. 1 cass. 1997. 20.00 (978-1-57855-009-8(2)) T D Jakes.

S. A. T. Masters. 3 cass. (Running Time: 30 min. per cass.). 29.95 Set, incl. 2 wkbks. (LF109) OptimaLearning.
Effective in both home & school, providing valuable strategies to teenagers about to take the S.A.T.

S & C Paton: I've Got a Song. 1 cass. (J). 9.98 (C-52) Folk-Legacy.
A collection of songs for kids. Songs to sing & songs to DO.

S Corporations. Gregory B. McKeen. 1 cass. 129.00 incl. wkbk. & template. (752758KQ); 119.00 incl. cass. & wkbk. (752759KQ) Am Inst CPA.
This course has been revised & updated to reflect The Revenue Reconciliation Act of 1989 & recent IRS rulings & regulations.

S Corporations & Their Increased Importance after Tax Reform. 1987. bk. 70.00 incl. book.; 55.00 cass. only.; 15.00 book only. PA Bar Inst.

S Is for Silence. abr. ed. Sue Grafton. Read by Judy Kaye. 5 CDs. (Running Time: 21600 sec.). (Kinsey Millhone Mystery Ser.). (ENG.). 2006. audio compact disk 14.99 (978-0-7393-4185-8(5), Random AudioBks) Pub: Random Audio Pubg. Dist(s): Random

S Is for Silence. unabr. ed. Sue Grafton. Read by Judy Kaye. 7 cass. (Kinsey Millhone Mystery Ser.). 2005. 63.00 (978-1-4159-2483-9(X)); audio compact disk 76.50 (978-1-4159-2484-6(8)) Pub: Books on Tape. Dist(s): NetLibrary CO

S Is for Silence. unabr. ed. Sue Grafton. Read by Judy Kaye. 10 CDs. (Running Time: 43200 sec.). (Kinsey Millhone Mystery Ser.). (ENG.). 2005. audio compact disk 44.95 (978-0-7393-2309-0(1), Random AudioBks) Pub: Random Audio Pubg. Dist(s): Random

S Is for Stories Grade 3. Created by Rigby Staff. (Rigby Literacy Ser.). (J). (gr. 3 up). 2002. audio compact disk 25.00 (978-0-7578-2273-5(8)) Rigby Educ.

S. J. Perelman. S. J. Perelman. Read by S. J. Perelman. 1 cass. 10.95 (978-0-8045-0705-9(8), SAC 43-2) Spoken Arts.

S. J. Perelman. Interview with S. J. Perelman. 1 cass. (Running Time: 25 min.). 1978. 12.95 (L063) TFR.
The only man who was ever born in Brooklyn, N. Y. & Providence, R. I. talks about writing Marx Brother's movies, his oscar for "Around the World in Eighty Days," & why the British talk Yiddish.

S. J. Perelman, A Conversation With. Interview with Heywood Hale Broun & S. J. Perelman. 1 cass. (Running Time: 56 min.). (Broun Radio Ser.). 11.95 (40098) J Norton Pubs.
The legendary humorist & author recalls anecdotes behind the funny acerbic stories he has written about his travels for the "New Yorker" magazine.

S. O. R. Losers. unabr. ed. Avi. Narrated by Jeff Woodman. 2 cass. (Running Time: 2 hrs.). 1996. 18.00 Set. (94570) Recorded Bks.

S. O. R. Losers, unabr. ed. Avi. Narrated by Jeff Woodman. 2 pieces. (Running Time: 2 hrs.). (gr. 4 up). 1997. 19.00 (978-0-7887-0379-9(X), 94570E7) Recorded Bks.
The story of the wackiest bunch of losers since the Bad News Bears. A rib-tickling romp across the middle school soccer fields that's guaranteed to have children & teachers laughing out loud.

S. O. S. Contrib. by Krystal Meyers. (Mastertrax Ser.). 2008. audio compact disk 9.98 (978-5-557-36648-9(2)) Pt of Grace Ent.

S. O. S. Songs of the Sea. Lynn Kleiner. (ENG.). 2008. audio compact disk 14.95 (978-0-7390-5351-5(5)) Alfred Pub.

S. S. Bathtub. David Louis LaMotte. Illus. by Carrie Patterson. 1 CD. (J). 2005. bk. 20.00 (978-0-9772893-0-1(3)) Lower Dryad Music.

S-T-R-E-T-C-H Your Rewards Budget: Maximize the Return on your Employee Recognition Investment. Speeches. Kevin Aguanno. 1 CD. (Running Time: 40 minutes). 2005. audio compact disk 14.87 (978-1-895186-37-6(4)) Multi-Media ON CAN.
Running out of funds? This recording tells you how you can stretch your rewards budget by spending it more effectively, leveraging your investment to maximize the performance of your team... and your organization.Reading an excerpt from his book 101 Ways to Reward Team Members for $20 (or Less!), the author teaches you how to:- Improve employee morale - Improve team motivation and employee motivation - Improve departmental and cross-organizational teaming - Maximize the benefits of rewards and recognition programmes - Avoid the common rewarding mistakes - Choose a reward that suits the recipient - Choose a reward that suits the accomplishment - Tie a reward to a specific accomplishment - Give rewards in a timely fashion.

Sabbath. Wayne Muller. 2007. audio compact disk 24.95 (978-1-59179-595-7(8)) Sounds True.

Sabbath: The Unauthorized Biography of Black Sabbath. Mark Crampton. (Maximum Ser.). (ENG.). 2001. audio compact disk 14.95 (978-1-84240-082-1(7)) Pub: Chrome Dreams GBR. Dist(s): IPG Chicago

Sabbath Gate: Enter with Jubilee. James Hansen. Read by James Hansen. Dramatization. 1999. audio compact disk 15.95 (10985) OR Catholic.
Stories, prayers and songs to celebrate the jubilee.

Sabbath History Seminars. Arranged by James W. Wood. (ENG.). 2006. audio compact disk 59.95 (978-1-930920-31-6(8)) L L T Prods.

Sabbath Morn. unabr. ed. John William Wainwright. Narrated by Christopher Kay. 5 cass. (Running Time: 6 hrs.). 1999. 46.00 (978-1-84197-015-8(8), H1015E7) Recorded Bks.
Rogate-on-Sands is a seaside town whose population consists mainly of the retired & whose economy is heavily reliant on the annual influx of summer visitors. The small local police force copes efficiently with petty crime which comes its way. Sunday, July 7th, drastically alters that situation. The day dawns hazily, holding the promise of sunshine & soaring temperatures but within an hour a police constable has been murdered & a siege has developed, a situation which threatens to get out of hand. Then, with the small force already at full stretch, there is a rash of arson attacks in the town.

Sabbath Morn. unabr. ed. John William Wainwright. Narrated by Christopher Kay. 5 CDs. (Running Time: 6 hrs.). 1999. audio compact disk 46.00 (978-1-84197-096-7(4), C1125E7) Recorded Bks.

Sabbath Rest. Michael Pearl. 1 CD. 2003. audio compact disk (978-1-892112-44-6(2)) No Greater Joy.

Sabbath's Theater. unabr. ed. Philip Roth. Read by David Dukes. (YA). 2008. 64.99 (978-1-60514-844-1(X)) Find a World.

Sabbatical: A Romance. John Barth. Read by John Barth. 1 cass. (Running Time: 30 min.). 1984. 8.95 (AMF-2) Am Audio Prose.
Barth reads from "Sabbatical" & talks about the CIA, academia & storytelling.

Sabian Astrology. Constance DeMarco. 1 cass. 8.95 (082) Am Fed Astrologers.
Marc Edmund Jones 500 - -interpretation of a chart at random.

Sabian Astrology Chart Interpretation. Constance DeMarco. 1 cass. 8.95 (083) Am Fed Astrologers.
Examples using Marc Edmund Jones' technique.

Sabian Method of Chart Comparison. Ron Boyce. 1 cass. 8.95 (032) Am Fed Astrologers.
Systematic analysis of compatibility using Sabian method.

Sabian Temperament Types. Del O'Connor. 1 cass. 8.95 (264) Am Fed Astrologers.

Sabine's Notebook: In Which the Extraordinary Correspondence of Griffin & Sabine Continues. Nick Bantock. Read by Maxwell Caufield & Marina Sirtis. 1 cass. (Running Time: 90 min.). Dramatization. 1992. 10.95 (978-1-879371-41-5(3), 30010) Pub Mills.
The end of Griffin & Sabine, the surprise best-seller of 1991, left readers on the edge of a precipice. With Sabine's notebook, they begin, with Griffin, they fall. Faced with the terrifying prospect of meeting his own fictional character, Griffin runs.

Sable Doughboys. unabr. collector's ed. Tom Willard. Read by Dick Estell. 8 cass. (Running Time: 8 hrs.). 1997. 48.00 (978-0-7366-3672-8(2), 4349) Books on Tape.
Adrian & David Sharps become officer candidates in the army's first Negro officer training program located in Des Moines, Iowa.

Sabor del Pueblo. 1 cass. (Running Time: 1 hr.). Incl. Pt. 1. Sabor del Pueblo: Lydia Mendoza. Interview with Lydia Mendoza. (A063AB090); Pt. 2. Sabor del Pueblo: Narciso Martinez. Interview with Narciso Martines. (A063AB090); (ENG & SPA.). 10.95 (A063AB090, HarperThor); 10.95 (A063BB090, HarperThor); 10.95 (A063CB090, HarperThor); 10.95 (A063DB090, HarperThor); 10.95 (A063EB090, HarperThor) HarpC GBR.

Sabor del Pueblo: Contemporary Chicano Music see Sabor del Pueblo

Sabor del Pueblo: Corridos see Sabor del Pueblo

Sabor del Pueblo: Curandero (Folk Healers) see Sabor del Pueblo

Sabor del Pueblo: El Vaquero (the Cowboy) see Sabor del Pueblo

Sabor del Pueblo: Jovita Gonzalez see Sabor del Pueblo

Sabor del Pueblo: Lydia Mendoza see Sabor del Pueblo

Sabor del Pueblo: Mariachi Music see Sabor del Pueblo

Sabor del Pueblo: Narciso Martinez see Sabor del Pueblo

Sabor del Pueblo: Santiago & Flaco Jimenez see Sabor del Pueblo

Sabor del Pueblo: Tales of the Supernatural see Sabor del Pueblo

Sabotage: America's Enemies Within the CIA. unabr. ed. Rowan Scarborough. Read by Tom Weiner. (Running Time: 23400 sec.). 2007. 29.95 (978-1-4332-0062-5(7)); audio compact disk 29.95 (978-1-4332-0063-2(5)); audio compact disk 29.95 (978-1-4332-0064-9(3)) Blckstn Audio.

Sabotage: America's Enemies Within the CIA. unabr. ed. Rowan Scarborough. (Running Time: 23400 sec.). 2007. 54.95 (978-1-4332-0060-1(0)); audio compact disk 63.00 (978-1-4332-0061-8(9)) Blckstn Audio.

Sabotage: Torments & Vices. ltd. ed. Robert Jelinek & Christoph Steinegger. 2003. bk. 35.00 (978-3-931126-97-1(8)) Pub: Die Gestalten DEU. Dist(s): Prestel Pub NY

Sabotage in the Sky. L. Ron Hubbard. Read by Jim Meskimen et al. Narrated by R. F. Daley. (Stories from the Golden Age Ser.). 2009. audio compact disk 9.95 (978-1-59212-279-0(5)) Gala Pr LLC.

Saboteurs. unabr. ed. W. E. B. Griffin. Read by David Colacci. (Running Time: 11 hrs.). (Men at War Ser.). 2006. 24.95 (978-1-4233-1968-9(0), 9781423319689, BAD) Brilliance Audio.

***Saboteurs: A Men at War Novel.** W. E. B. Griffin & William E. Butterworth, IV. Read by David Colacci. (Playaway Adult Fiction Ser.). 2010. 79.99 (978-1-4418-3807-0(4)) Find a World.

Saboteurs: A Men at War Novel. unabr. ed. William E. Butterworth, IV. Read by David Colacci. (Running Time: 11 hrs.). (Men at War Ser.). 2006. 39.25 (978-1-4233-1969-6(9), 9781423319696, BADLE) Brilliance Audio.

Saboteurs: A Men at War Novel. unabr. ed. William E. Butterworth, IV & W. E. B. Griffin. Read by David Colacci. (Running Time: 39600 sec.). (Men at War Ser.). 2006. 87.25 (978-1-4233-1963-4(X), 9781423319634, BrilAudUnabridg); audio compact disk 102.25 (978-1-4233-1965-8(6), 9781423319658, BriAudCD Unabrid); audio compact disk 39.95 (978-1-4233-1964-1(8), 9781423319641, Bril Audio CD Unabri) Brilliance Audio.
Please enter a Synopsis.

Saboteurs: A Men at War Novel. unabr. ed. W. E. B. Griffin. Read by David Colacci. (Running Time: 39600 sec.). (Men at War Ser.). 2006. 34.95 (978-1-4233-1962-7(1), 9781423319627, BAU); audio compact disk 39.25 (978-1-4233-1967-2(2), 9781423319672, Brinc Audio MP3 Lib); audio compact disk 24.95 (978-1-4233-1966-5(4), 9781423319665, Brilliance MP3) Brilliance Audio.

Sabriel. unabr. ed. Garth Nix. 7 cass. (Running Time: 10 hrs. 50 mins.). (Old Kingdom Ser.: No. 1). (J). (gr. 7 up). 2004. 46.00 (978-0-8072-0563-1(X), S YA 351 CX, Listening Lib) Random Audio Pubg.

Sabriel. unabr. ed. Garth Nix. Read by Tim Curry. 10 CDs. (Running Time: 10 hrs. 50 mins.). (Old Kingdom Ser.: No. 1). (J). (gr. 7 up). 2004. audio compact disk 59.50 (978-0-8072-1605-7(4), S YA 351 CD, Listening Lib); pap. bk. 54.00 (978-0-8072-0794-9(2), S YA 351 SP, Listening Lib) Random Audio Pubg.
"Since childhood, Sabriel has lived outside the walls of the Old Kingdom, away from the random power of Free Magic, and away from the Dead who refuse to stay dead. But now her father, the Charter-Mage Abhorsen, is missing, and to find him Sabriel must travel deep into the Old Kingdom, where she confronts an evil that threatens much more than her life-and comes face-to-face with her own hidden destiny.".

Sabriel. unabr. ed. Garth Nix. Read by Tim Curry. (Old Kingdom Ser.: No. 1). (ENG.). (J). (gr. 7). 2008. audio compact disk 60.00 (978-0-7393-6825-1(7), Listening Lib) Pub: Random Audio Pubg. Dist(s): Random

Sabrina. unabr. ed. Lori Wick. Narrated by Jill Shellabarger. (Running Time: 8 hrs. 22 mins. 27 sec.). (Big Sky Dreams Ser.). (ENG.). 2008. 19.59 (978-1-60814-369-6(4)); audio compact disk 27.99 (978-1-59859-431-7(1)) Oasis Audio.

Sacagawea: The Trip to the West. Alan Venable. (Step into History Ser.). 2001. audio compact disk 18.95 (978-1-4105-0171-4(X)) D Johnston Inc.

Sacagawea: The Trip to the West, Vol. 11. Alan Venable. Ed. by Jerry Stemach et al. Illus. by Jeff Ham. Narrated by Barbara Jersey. Contrib. by Ted S. Hasselbring. (Start-to-Finish Books). (J). (gr. 2-3). 2001. 35.00 (978-1-58702-732-1(1)) D Johnston Inc.

Sacagawea: The Trip to the West, Vol. 11. unabr. ed. Alan Venable. Ed. by Jerry Stemach et al. Illus. by Jeff Ham. Narrated by Barbara Jersey. Contrib. by Ted S. Hasselbring. 1 cass. (Running Time: 1 hr.). (Start-to-Finish Books). (J). (gr. 2-3). 2001. (978-1-58702-679-9(1), F44) D Johnston Inc.
In 1803, U.S. President Thomas Jefferson commissioned army officers Meriwether Lewis and William Clark to find a suitable route of travel from the Mississippi River settlement of St. Louis westward to the Pacific Ocean. Sacagawea (sometimes spelled Sacajawea) was a young Shoshoni Indian woman who accompanied the expedition on its journey. Kidnapped in the Rockies as a young girl by an Indian raiding party. Sacagawea had been transported to an Indian settlement.

Sacajawea. Joseph Bruchac. 2003. audio compact disk 44.95 (978-1-883332-94-5(X)) Audio Bkshelf.

Sacajawea. Joseph Bruchac. (YA). 2003. 34.95 (978-1-883332-88-4(5)) Audio Bkshelf.

Sacajawea. unabr. ed. Robert Hogrogian. 1 cass. (Running Time: 20 min.). (People to Remember Ser.: Set II). (J). (gr. 4-7). 1979. bk. 16.99 (978-0-934898-59-1(6)); pap. bk. 9.95 (978-0-934898-14-0(6)) Jan Prods.
The appealing story of the woman who accompanied Lewis & Clark on the history-making expedition.

Sacajawea, Pt. 1. unabr. collector's ed. Anna Lee Waldo. Read by Kate Reading. 12 cass. (Running Time: 18 hrs.). 1994. 96.00 (978-0-7366-2750-4(2), 3475-A) Books on Tape.
Daughter of a Shoshoni chief & the only woman on Lewis & Clark's expedition, Sacajawea confronts America's turbulent growth.

Sacajawea, Pt. 2. unabr. collector's ed. Anna Lee Waldo. Read by Kate Reading. 10 cass. (Running Time: 15 hrs.). 1994. 80.00 (978-0-7366-2751-1(0), 3745-B) Books on Tape.
Clad in a doeskin, alone but unafraid, she stands straight & proud before the onrushing forces of America's turbulent growth: Sacajawea, daughter of a Shoshoni chief, lone woman on Lewis & Clark's expedition.

Sacajawea, Pt. 3. unabr. collector's ed. Anna Lee Waldo. Read by Kate Reading. 14 cass. (Running Time: 21 hrs.). 1994. 112.00 (978-0-7366-2752-8(9), 3475-C) Books on Tape.

Sacco Writes to His Son see Dylan Thomas Reading

Sachem. abr. ed. Donald Clayton Porter. Read by Lloyd James. 4 vols. No. 4. 2003. 25.00 (978-1-58807-220-7(7)); (978-1-58807-751-6(9)); audio compact disk 30.00 (978-1-58807-404-1(8)); audio compact disk (978-1-58807-843-8(4)) Am Pubng Inc.

Sack of Panama: Sir Henry Morgan's Adventures on the Spanish Main. unabr. ed. Peter Earle. Narrated by Walt MacPherson. 7 cass. (Running Time: 10 hrs.). 1983. 60.00 (978-1-55690-456-1(8), 83057E7) Recorded Bks.
Henry Morgan, licensed pirate, was encouraged by the English king to prey on the treasure routes of Imperial Spain.

Sackett. unabr. ed. Louis L'Amour. Read by David Strathairn. 4 CDs. (Running Time: 14400 sec.). (Sacketts Ser.). (ENG.). 2006. audio compact disk 30.00 (978-0-7393-2113-3(7), Random AudioBks) Pub: Random Audio Pubg. Dist(s): Random
William Tell Sackett had followed a different path from his younger brothers, but his name, like theirs, was spoken with respect and just a little fear. Where Orrin had brought law and order from New Mexico to the plains of Montana, backed up by the gunfighting talents of his brother Tye, Tell Sackett's destiny drew him to Texas after he had to kill a man. There, in the high, lonesome country, he came upon a vein of pure gold. All he'd wanted was enough to buy a ranch, but he soon learned that gold had ways of its own with men. From the Paperback edition.

Sackett Brand. unabr. ed. Louis L'Amour. Read by David Strathairn. (Running Time: 14400 sec.). (Sacketts Ser.: No. 12). (ENG.). 2008. audio compact disk 25.95 (978-0-7393-4221-3(5)) Pub: Random Audio Pubg. Dist(s): Random

Sackett's Land. unabr. ed. Louis L'Amour. Read by John Curless. 4 cass. (Running Time: 4 hrs.). (Sacketts Ser.: No. 1). 1999. 24.95 (FS9-43266) Highsmith.

Sackett's Land. unabr. ed. Louis L'Amour. Read by John Curless. 5 CDs. (Running Time: 6 hrs.). (Sacketts Ser.: No. 1). (ENG.). 2005. audio compact disk 25.95 (978-0-7393-1795-2(4), Random AudioBks) Pub: Random Audio Pubg. Dist(s): Random

Saco Invisible de Morris. Tr. of Morris's Disappearing Bag. (SPA.). 2004. 8.95 (978-0-7882-0301-5(0)) Weston Woods.

Sacrament. deluxe unabr. ed. Michael J. Vines. 6 cass. (Running Time: 7 hrs. 30 min.). (YA). 2001. lib. bdg. 35.00 (978-0-932079-17-6(2), 79172) TimeFare AudioBks.

Sacrament. unabr. ed. Clive Barker. Narrated by Ron Keith. 14 cass. (Running Time: 19 hrs. 45 mins.). 112.00 (978-0-7887-0632-5(2), 94807E7) Recorded Bks.

Sacrament: An Ordinance of Redeeming Power. abr. ed. David A. Christensen. 2006. audio compact disk 12.95 (978-1-59038-202-8(1)) Deseret Bk.

Sacrament - Matrimony. Fr. Hardon. 9 cass. (Running Time: 13 hrs.). 36.00 (93G) IRL Chicago.

Sacrament of Abortion. Interview with Ginette Paris & James Hillman. 1 cass. (Running Time: 1 hr.). pap. bk. 12.95 (978-1-879816-04-6(0)) Pub: Spring Pubns. Dist(s): Natl Bk Netwk
Controversial interview of psychologist-feminist Ginette Paris on pro-abortion.

Sacrament of Acceptance. Read by Wayne Monbleau. 3 cass. (Running Time: 3 hrs.). 1993. 15.00 (978-0-944648-28-5(2), LGT-1217) Loving Grace Pubns.
Religious.

Sacrament of Reconciliation: Door to Forgiveness & Healing. Kenan Osborne. 3 cass. (Running Time: 3 hrs.). 2001. 24.95 (A7050) St Anthony Mess Pr.
A guide to understanding the new rituals as doors to healing grace and a more authentic faith.

Sacramento. unabr. ed. Barbara Francis. Read by Jean DeBarbieris. 6 cass. (Running Time: 8 hrs.). Dramatization. 1990. 39.95 (978-1-55686-336-3(5), 336) Books in Motion.
MaryAnn Poole discovers she is about to marry her half-brother. Shocked & broken-hearted she leaves home & finds employment with the kindly proprietor of a mercantile store in Sacramento. While on a trip to San Francisco, the great earthquake strikes, & MaryAnn's life is changed forever.

Sacramentos. Contrib. by Jaime Cortez & Kevin Walsh. 2005. audio compact disk 15.95 (978-5-558-85321-6(2)) OR Catholic.

Sacraments: Actions of the Holy Spirit. 1 CD. (Running Time: 60 mins). 2007. audio compact disk 9.95 (978-0-9717687-9-6(X)) Excorde Inc.

Sacraments & the Holy Eucharist. Peter M. Stravinskas. 1 cass. (National Meeting of the Institute, 1994 Ser.). 4.00 (94N4) IRL Chicago.

Sacraments Explained. Interview with Mother Angelica. Contrib. by Mitch Pacwa. 1 cass. (Running Time: 60 min.). (Mother Angelica Live Ser.). 10.00 (978-1-55794-064-3(9)) Eternal Wrd TV.

Sacraments for the Third Millennium. Kenan Osborne. 1 cass. (Running Time: 1 hr.). 2001. 8.95 (A6971) St Anthony Mess Pr.
What legacy of the sacraments does this century give to the next millennium?.

***Sacred & Profane.** unabr. ed. Faye Kellerman. Read by Mitchell Greenberg. (ENG.). 2008. (978-0-06-162920-4(0)); (978-0-06-162921-1(9)) HarperCollins Pubs.

Sacred & Profane. unabr. ed. Faye Kellerman. Read by Mitchell Greenberg. 8 CDs. (Running Time: 9 hrs. 30 mins.). (Peter Decker & Rina Lazarus Novel Ser.). 2008. audio compact disk 19.95 (978-0-06-144180-6(5), Harper Audio) HarperCollins Pubs.

Sacred Art of Dying: Living with Hope. Richard Groves. 2 cass. (Running Time: 2 hrs.). 2001. 16.95 (A8080) St Anthony Mess Pr.
A thousand years ago monks at the Abbey of Cluny in France were recognized for their care of the dying. Groves shares an ancient book from the Cluny monastic library and teaches about the sacred art of dying.

Sacred Art of Stealing. Christopher Brookmyre. Read by Terry Wale & Lesley Mackie. 10 CDs. (Running Time: 12 hrs. 24 mins.). (Isis (CDs) Ser.). (J). 2004. audio compact disk 89.95 (978-0-7531-2328-7(2)) Pub: ISIS Lrg Prnt GBR. Dist(s): Ulverscroft US

Sacred Art of Stealing. unabr. ed. Christopher Brookmyre. Read by Lesley Mackie & Terry Wale. 9 cass. (Running Time: 12 hrs. 24 mins.). (Isis Cassettes Ser.). (J). 2004. 76.95 (978-0-7531-1745-3(2)) Pub: ISIS Lrg Prnt GBR. Dist(s): Ulverscroft US

Sacred Balance. David T. Suzuki. (Running Time: 3600 sec.). 2005. audio compact disk 15.95 (978-0-660-19471-4(6)) Canadian Broadcasting CAN.

Sacred Body. Kelly Howell. 2004. audio compact disk 14.95 (978-1-881451-94-5(1)) Brain Sync.

Sacred Book of the Werewolf. unabr. ed. Victor Pelevin. (Running Time: 7 hrs. NaN mins.). 2008. 54.95 (978-1-4332-4675-3(9)); audio compact disk 60.00 (978-1-4332-4676-0(7)) Blckstn Audio.

Sacred Book of the Werewolf. unabr. ed. Victor Pelevin. (Running Time: 7 hrs. NaN mins.). 2008. 29.95 (978-1-4332-4678-4(3)) Blckstn Audio.

Sacred Book of the Werewolf. unabr. ed. Victor Previn. (Running Time: 7 hrs. 0 mins.). 2008. audio compact disk & audio compact disk 29.95 (978-1-4332-4677-7(5)) Blckstn Audio.

Sacred Chants from a Tibetan Chant Master. Perf. by Monks of Sed-Gyued Datsang Tantric College. 1 CD. (TIB.). 1999. audio compact disk 17.00 (978-0-9668588-1-5(6)) Healing Buddha.

Sacred Choices for People Undergoing Chemotherapy. unabr. ed. Narrated by Judie A. Chiappone. Prod. by Judie A. Chiappone. 1 cass. (Running Time: 42 mins.). 2000. 12.00 (978-0-9700654-2-1(6)) Holistic Reflect.

Sacred Clowns. unabr. ed. Tony Hillerman. Read by Jonathan Marosz. 8 cass. (Running Time: 8 hrs.). (Joe Leaphorn & Jim Chee Novel Ser.). 1994. 64.00 (978-0-7366-2645-3(X), 3382) Books on Tape.
A routine truancy case leads Navajo policemen Joe Leaphorn & Jim Chee to the scene of two grisly murders. Their investigation leads to a team of lobbyists intent on putting a toxic waste dump on the reservation.

Sacred Clowns. unabr. ed. Tony Hillerman. Narrated by George Guidall. 6 cass. (Running Time: 8 hrs.). (Joe Leaphorn & Jim Chee Novel Ser.). 1993. 51.00 (978-1-55690-910-8(1), 93406E7) Recorded Bks.
Two Navajo Tribal Policemen struggle with the seemingly unrelated murders of a Reservation high school teacher & a Tano Pueblo religious leader.

Sacred Clowns. unabr. ed. Tony Hillerman. Read by Gil Silverbird. 1 CD. (Running Time: 1 hr. 30 min.). (Joe Leaphorn & Jim Chee Novel Ser.). 2005. audio compact disk 14.95 (978-0-06-081506-6(X)) HarperCollins Pubs.

Sacred Contract of America: Fulfilling the Vision of Our Mystic Founders. Caroline Myss. 4 CDs. (Running Time: 17100 sec.). 2007. audio compact disk 29.95 (978-1-59179-606-0(7), AW01170D) Sounds True.

Sacred Contracts: Awakening Your Divine Potential. unabr. ed. Caroline Myss. Read by Caroline Myss. 5 CDs. (Running Time: 6 hrs.). 2001. audio compact disk 34.95 (978-1-56455-936-4(X), AW00576D) Sounds True.
Dr. Myss helps listeners take the next step in their personal evolutions, through the use of archetypes as tools for self-transformation. First identified by the legendary psychiatrist and author C.G. Jung, archetypes are symbols for unconscious energies and potentials held in common by all of humanity. Dr. Myss identifies a tool box of 12 major archetypal patterns, and explains their roles in the alchemy of spirituality. Listeners join this respected medical intuitive as she explores how we can identify our personal archetypes, uncover their higher purpose, and then work with them for self-understanding and spiritual development. Shared with her hallmark humor, honesty, and intelligence.

Sacred Country. unabr. ed. Rose Tremain. Read by Selina Cadell. 10 cass. (Running Time: 13 hrs.). 1994. 84.95 (978-1-85695-732-8(2), 940414) Pub: ISIS Audio GBR. Dist(s): Ulverscroft US
On the day of the funeral of King George VI in 1952, Mary Ward has a revelation. She realizes she isn't a girl at all-she's a boy; & she isn't Mary; but someone else. A mistake has been made. In time the mistake will be remedied - in time she will grow up to be a boy. The ineradicable tragic belief alters the course of her life in ways that are unimaginable to the rest of humanity, safe within their fixed genders & identities.

Sacred Cows - An Ecological Solution. Hosted by Nancy Pearlman. 1 cass. (Running Time: 30 min.). 10.00 (520) Educ Comm CA.

Sacred Disk. abr. ed. Charles West. 2 cass. (Running Time: 3 hrs.). 2004. 18.00 (978-1-58807-340-2(8)) Am Pubng Inc.
Winner of the first annual Salvo Press Mystery Novel Award, The Sacred Disc is a story of an accidental private investigator who inherits a detective agency in California's San Joaquin Valley. For his first major case, Bob Fisher is hired by the leaders of the Eternal Truth Temple, a religious cult nestled into the Sierras near Yosemite National Park, to find a missing computer disc containing the cult's sacred text. The prime suspects are former cult members who have formed a committee to expose the cult as a fraud. After asking only a few questions, the murders begin. Fisher must not only overcome his own shady past, but confront zealots who will stop at nothing to keep outsiders away from their real cause.

Sacred Drumming. Ed. by Steven Ash & Renata Ash. 2001. audio compact disk (978-1-84181-092-8(4), Godsfield Pr) Octopus Pub Grp GBR.

Sacred Earth Drums. Perf. by David Gordon & Steve Gordon. 1 cass., 1 CD. 7.98 (SQR 811); audio compact disk 11.98 CD Jewel box. (SQR 811) NewSound.
Celebrate the sacredness of life & reverence for the Earth.

***Sacred Echo.** Margaret Feinberg. (Running Time: 3 hrs. 29 mins. 0 sec.). (ENG.). 2008. 16.99 (978-0-310-30268-1(4)) Zondervan.

Sacred Elephant. unabr. ed. Poems. Heathcote Williams. Read by Heathcote Williams. Read by Caroline Webster et al. 2 CDs. (Running Time: 1 hr. 58 mins.). 1996. audio compact disk 15.98 (978-962-634-097-4(5), NA209712, Naxos AudioBooks) Naxos.
Poem exploring the life of elephants in their natural habitat, in captivity and details their relentless destruction at the hands of man. Also includes a compilation of facts and figures from elephant history.

Sacred Elephant. unabr. ed. Poems. Heathcote Williams. Read by Heathcote Williams. Read by Caroline Webster et al. 2 cass. (Running Time: 1 hr. 58 mins.). 1996. 13.98 (978-962-634-597-9(7), NA209714, Naxos AudioBooks) Naxos.

Sacred Elephant. unabr. ed. Heathcote Williams. Read by Heathcote Williams. Read by Caroline Webster & Harry Burton. (Running Time: 7101 sec.). 2007. audio compact disk 17.98 (978-962-634-453-8(9), Naxos AudioBooks) Naxos.

Sacred Flute Soloist: 10 Solos Arranged for Flute & Keyboard (Acc. /Performance) Jay Althouse et al. Ed. by Jean Anne Shafferman. (ENG.). 2000. audio compact disk 12.95 (978-0-7390-0977-2(X), 19845) Alfred Pub.

Sacred Fount. Henry James. 5 cass. (Running Time: 7 hrs.). 2000. 20.95 (978-1-55685-605-1(9)) Audio Bk Con.
At a house party in England, the narrator investigates relationships that drain, invigorate or inspire.

Sacred Games: A Novel. unabr. ed. Vikram Chandra. Read by Ismail Bashey. (Running Time: 35 hrs. 50 mins.). (ENG.). 2009. 59.95 (978-1-4332-4955-6(3)); 105.95 (978-1-4332-4952-5(9)); 85.95 (978-1-4332-9083-1(9)); audio compact disk 169.00 (978-1-4332-4953-2(7)) Blckstn Audio.

Sacred Ground. Perf. by Sweet Honey in the Rock. 1 cass. 1998. 10.98 (978-1-56628-070-9(2), 42580); audio compact disk 15.98 CD. (978-1-56628-069-3(9), 42580D) MFLP CA.

Sacred Ground: Music & Window Frequencies for Meditation. Kelly Howell. 2 CDs. (Running Time: 120 mins.). (ENG.). 2002. audio compact disk 16.95 (978-1-881451-89-1(5)) Brain Sync.
Vivid imagery sparkles before your mind's eye. You feel exalted as your soul soars to the higher ethers of universal knowledge. In blissful states you experience untold depths of inner peace. This comprehensive 2 CD audio program takes you into the elusive Theta State. Over a 4-week period, your brain's electro-magnetic energy is progressively balanced, organized - amplified. You enter the precise state of meditation essential to empower visualization and accelerate manifestation.

Sacred Ground: Open the Window to the Core of Your Being. Prod. by Kelly Howell. 4 cass. (Running Time: 4 hrs.). 1997. 34.95 (978-1-881451-61-7(5)) Brain Sync.
Allows you to quickly reach depths of meditation that would otherwise take years of practise to attain. Exquisite music is combined with pure & precisely tuned sound waves that fit through narrow biological windows to directly affect your cells.

Sacred Heart & the French Revolution. Perf. by John Vennari. 1 cass. (Running Time: 90 mins.). 7.00 (20200) Cath Treas.
Explains the history & definition of the devotion & demonstrates that obedience to the request of the Sacred Heart could have prevented one of the greatest catastrophes of modern times... the French Revolution.

Sacred Heart of Jesus & Divine Mercy. Benjamin B. Reese. 1 cass. (Inspiring Presentations from the National Rosary Congress Ser.). 2.50 (978-1-56036-100-8(X)) AMI Pr.

Sacred Hearts. unabr. ed. Sarah Dunant. (ENG.). 2009. audio compact disk 40.00 (978-0-7393-2508-7(6), Random AudioBks) Pub: Random Audio Pubg. Dist(s): Random

Sacred Higher Sex. Christopher Love. Read by Christopher Love. 1 cass. (Running Time: 30 min.). 1997. 10.95 (978-1-891820-23-6(0)) World Sangha Pubg.
Self-hypnosis meditation for healing, self-improvement & realizing our full & powerful potential as spiritual beings.

Sacred Hoops Spiritual Lessons of A Hardwood Warrior: Spiritual Lessons of A Hardwood Warrior. Phil Jackson. 2004. 10.95 (978-0-7435-4592-1(3)) Pub: S&S Audio. Dist(s): S and S Inc

Sacred Hymns for Sunday Afternoon & Sacred Music for Sunday Afternoon. 2 cass. 10.98 (10001204) Covenant Comms.
Thirty-eight uplifting, hymns & music.

Sacred Hymns in the Cherokee Language. Tr. by Prentice Robinson. Contrib. by Prentice Robinson. Contrib. by Willena Robinson. Photos by Willena Robinson. 2005. audio compact disk 21.95 (978-1-882182-19-0(7)) Cherokee Lang & Cult.

Sacred Images: Visible Representations of Divine Principles. Instructed by Manly P. Hall. 8.95 (978-0-89314-242-1(5), C820808) Philos Res.

Sacred Instrumental Duets: Accompaniment/Performance. Ed. by Jean Anne Shafferman. (ENG.). 2003. audio compact disk 12.95 (978-0-7390-3211-4(9)) Alfred Pub.

Sacred Island. Perf. by Taj Mahal & Hula Blues Band. 1 cass., 1 CD. 8.78 (PM 82165); audio compact disk 13.58 CD Jewel box. (PM 82165) NewSound.

Sacred Journey. Sam Keen. 6 cass. (Running Time: 6 hrs.). 1995. 59.95 (11950AM) Nightingale-Conant.
Like a novelist constructing a character, you'll piece together the details of your life to discover your personal truths, your destiny & your spiritual path. You'll reflect on your hopes & fears...recover lost dreams...unravel the myths that shape your life...even uncover spiritual gems hidden in your autobiography.

Sacred Journey of Childbirth. Lea Blumberg. 1 CD. 2003. audio compact disk 19.95 (978-0-9747487-1-9(4)) L Blumberg.
Hypnosis for childbirth preparation to relax through pregnancy and birth.

***Sacred Journeys: Christian Authors Reveal How the Bible Impacts Their Lives.** unabr. ed. Oasis Audio Staff. Narrated by Wayne Shepherd. (Running Time: 0 hr. 56 mins. 19 sec.). (ENG.). 2010. 9.09 (978-1-60814-770-0(3)); audio compact disk 12.99 (978-1-59859-804-9(X)) Oasis Audio.

Sacred Landscapes. John Michele. 5 cass. 45.00 (OC78) Sound Horizons AV.

Sacred Landscapes, Earth Mysteries. John Michele. 1 cass. 9.00 (OC54L) Sound Horizons AV.

***Sacred Marriage: What If God Designed Marriage to Make Us Holy More Than to Make Us Happy?** Gary L. Thomas. (Running Time: 8 hrs. 14 mins. 0 sec.). (ENG.). 2008. 14.99 (978-0-310-29259-3(X)) Zondervan.

Sacred Meditations. 1 CD. (Running Time: 9 hrs.). 2003. audio compact disk 10.00 (978-0-9745431-0-9(1)) scholia.
These 51 meditations were written in 1606 by Johann Gerhard at the age of 22. This audiobook is in MP3 format and is devotional. Music and voice are added between the individual mediations.Go to http://www.scholia.net for a full description of the contents of "Sacred Meditations.".

Sacred Music of William Ferris. Voice by William Ferris. 1998. audio compact disk 16.00 (978-0-937690-64-2(3), 3528) Wrld Lib Pubns.

Sacred Mysteries of the Human Body. Manly P. Hall. 1 cass. 8.95 (978-0-89314-243-8(3)) Philos Res.

***Sacred Parenting: How Raising Children Shapes Our Souls.** Gary L. Thomas. (Running Time: 7 hrs. 16 mins. 0 sec.). (ENG.). 2009. 14.99 (978-0-310-30506-4(3)) Zondervan.

***Sacred Pathways: Discover Your Soul's Path to God.** unabr. ed. Gary L. Thomas. (Running Time: 6 hrs. 14 mins. 0 sec.). (ENG.). 2009. 14.99 (978-0-310-29969-1(1)) Zondervan.

Sacred Piano Literature: A Comprehensive Survey for the Church Musician. Compiled by Anna Leppert-Largent. 1. 2004. audio compact disk 34.00 (978-0-89869-396-6(9)) Church Pub Inc.
What keyboard music does a church musician use to play a service when an organ is not available? The answer may be found in this comprehensive listing of more than 3,000 selections for piano appropriate for sacred services. Listings include the publication source, hymn tune used, level of difficulty, and in most cases, a brief description of the style, on a fully searchable CD-ROM for Windows and Mac.

Sacred Place. Contrib. by Rufino Zaragoza. 2005. 17.00 (978-5-558-59264-1(8)) OR Catholic.

Sacred Poetry: The Enlightened Heart, Poems of Rumi & Poems of Kabir. unabr. ed. Poems. Read by Coleman Barks. Ed. by Stephen Mitchell & Jacob Needleman. Tr. by Robert Bly. 6 cass. (Running Time: 9 hrs.). 1998. bk. 49.95 (978-1-57453-278-4(2)) Audio Lit.
Includes "The Enlightened Heart," & "Poems of Rumi," & "Poems of Kabir".

Sacred Pool. Carolyn Conger. Read by Carolyn Conger. 1 cass. (Running Time: 65 min.). 1988. 10.00 (CC1002) Tigers Nest Aud.
Two visualizations with music allow the listener to relax, balance, body energies, tap inner wisdom & self-healing.

Sacred Practices for Conscious Living. unabr. ed. Nancy J. Napier. Read by Nancy J. Napier. 1 cass. 1997. 45.95 (978-0-9658191-2-1(4)) Lotus Blossom.
Guided meditations & exercises.

Sacred Pranic Breathing. Sai Maa Lakshmi Devi. 2002. audio compact disk 16.00 (978-1-933488-11-0(5)) HIU Pr.
In this powerful CD, Sai Maa Lakshmi Devi leads us in two pranic breathing exercises where we bring cosmic energy into ourblood to fill our consciousness with Light. Sai Maa concludes by leading using 16 repetitions of OM, the ancient primordial mantra, or sound, from which the universe springs. When we listen to or repeat this Sanskrit mantra we can experience the God Presence within.Includes: Breathing the Light; Magnifying the Light; 16 Repetitions of OMSan Rafael, California 2002.

Sacred Quest, Vol. 5. Chris Heimerdinger. 4 cass. (Tennis Shoes Adventure Ser.). 2004. 19.95 (978-1-57734-492-6(8)); audio compact disk 21.95 (978-1-59156-305-1(4)) Covenant Comms.

Sacred Revolution: Live Frome Oneday03. Contrib. by Passion et al. (Running Time: 3 hrs. 20 mins.). 2003. 19.98 (978-5-550-26116-3(2)) Pt of Grace Ent.

Sacred Rites of the Seasons. Ted Andrews. 2 cass. (Running Time: 48 min.). 2000. 17.95 (978-1-888767-08-7(1)) Life Magic Ent.
Based on exercises from "The Occult Christ: Angelic Mysteries & the Divine Feminine".

Sacred Roles in Marriage: Keys to Creating Fantastic Relationships. William G. DeFoore. (ENG.). 2004. audio compact disk 29.99 (978-0-9814740-5-2(5)) Halcyon Life.

Sacred Romance. John Eldredge. 2005. audio compact disk 19.99 (978-1-59859-098-2(7)) Oasis Audio.

Sacred Romance: Drawing Closer to the Heart of God. unabr. ed. John Eldredge & Brent Curtis. (ENG.). 2004. 23.09 (978-1-60814-370-2(8)) Oasis Audio.

Sacred Romance: Drawing Closer to the Heart of God. unabr. ed. John Eldredge & Kelly Ryan Dolan. 6 cass. (Running Time: 8 hrs.). 2004. 27.99 (978-1-58926-664-3(1)) Oasis Audio.

Sacred Romance: Drawing Closer to the Heart of God. unabr. ed. John Eldredge et al. 7 CDs. (Running Time: 8 hrs.). (ENG.). 2004. audio compact disk 32.99 (978-1-58926-665-0(X)) Oasis Audio.

Sacred Romance Live! Drawing Closer to the Heart of God. Featuring John Eldredge & Brent Curtis. 2002. audio compact disk 39.99 (978-1-933207-30-8(2)) Ransomed Heart.

Sacred Self: Guided Meditation to Contact & Experience the True Self Within. Mark Bancroft. Read by Mark Bancroft. 1 cass., bklet. (Running Time: 90 mins.). (Spirituality & Consciousness Ser.). 1999. instr.'s gde. ed. 12.95 (978-1-58522-010-6(8), 714, EnSpire Aud) EnSpire Pr.
Two complete sessions plus printed instruction manual/guidebook. With healing music soundtrack.

Sacred Self: Guided Meditation to Contact & Experience the True Self Within. Read by Mark Bancroft. 1 CD, 1 bklet. (Running Time: 1 hr.). (Spirituality & Consciousness Ser.). 2006. audio compact disk 20.00 (978-1-58522-066-3(3)) EnSpire Pr.
Two complete sessions plus printed instructionmanual/guidebook. With healing music soundtrack.

Sacred Self: Reclaiming Soul Energy for Healing & Maintaining a Healthy Body, Mind & Spirit. unabr. ed. Meredith L. Young-Sowers. 3 cass. (Running Time: 2 hrs. 30 min.). 1997. pap. bk. 35.00 (978-1-883478-08-7(1)) Stillpoint.
Explores the nature of soul & spirit, & the relationship soul has to your life, to your physical body & to your thinking body. You'll learn that you have a spiritual DNA that holds your life purpose & your own fullest potential for this lifetime, & how to use & expand Divine Love, the energy of spirit, to live your life most effectively.

Sacred Self Workshop. Marianne Williamson. Music by David Ison. 2 cass. 1995. 19.95 (978-1-879323-25-4(7)) Sound Horizons AV.
This program includes gorgeous meditations, interactive processes, soul stirring lectures & transformative music. Recorded "live" at The Esalen Institute in Big Sur, CA. In this program, Marianne tells us that the purpose of our lives is to become the sacred, enlightened self which already exists in each of us. We are all coded for brilliance; by infusing our lives with spirit we can release the dysfunctional patterns that keep us from living our lives with passion. The 'Sacred Self' is the part of us that is serene & indestructible. By committing with heart to a new path we can begin to live our lives as an endless prayer. Marianne's dynamic style & meditations help us open ourselves to greater love, abundance & joy in our lives.

Sacred Sexuality: Healing & Enhancing Body, Mind & Spirit for the Art of Making Love. William G. DeFoore. (ENG.). 2006. audio compact disk 29.99 (978-0-9785244-7-0(0)) Halcyon Life.

Sacred Shore. Janette Oke & T. Davis Bunn. Narrated by Suzanne Toren. 6 cass. (Running Time: 8 hrs.). (Song of Acadia Ser.: Vol. 2). 54.00 (978-1-4025-1751-8(3)) Recorded Bks.

Sacred Silence. unabr. ed. Perf. by Eknath Easwaran. 1 cass. (Running Time: 1 hr.). 1987. 7.95 (978-1-58638-601-6(8)) Nilgiri Pr.

Sacred Solos for All Seasons: Medium High Voice. Composed by Jay Althouse. (ENG.). 2002. audio compact disk 12.95 (978-0-7390-2397-6(7)) Alfred Pub.

Sacred Solos for All Seasons: Medium Low Voice. Composed by Jay Althouse. (ENG.). 2002. audio compact disk 12.95 (978-0-7390-2400-3(0)) Alfred Pub.

Sacred Solos for Flute, Vol. I. Dona Gilliam & Mizzy McCaskill. 1 cass. 10.98 stereo. (94014C); audio compact disk 15.98 CD. (95557CD) Mel Bay.
An outstanding collection of flute solos, ideal for use in church celebrations. Selections include "Chorale from Cantata No. 147" by J. S. Bach, "Canon" by Pachelbel, "Sarabande" by Corelli, "Aire from The Messiah" by Handel, "Ave Maria" by Schubert, "Meditation from Thais" by Massenet, & more.

Sacred Solos for the Flute, Vol. 1. Mizzy McCaskill. 1984. pap. bk. 23.95 (978-0-7866-1390-8(4), 94014CDP) Mel Bay.

Sacred Solos for the Flute, Vol. 2. Mizzy McCaskill. 1989. pap. bk. 23.95 (978-0-7866-1391-5(2), 94246CDP) Mel Bay.

Sacred Songs of Russia. Gloriae Dei Cantores. 1 CD. (Running Time: 90 mins.). 1999. audio compact disk 16.95 (978-1-55725-224-1(6), GDCD100) Paraclete MA.

Sacred Sounds. Jorge Alfano. 1 cass. (Running Time: 1 hr.). 1996. 9.95 (978-1-55961-359-0(9)); audio compact disk 14.95 (978-1-55961-358-3(0)) Relaxtn Co.

Sacred Sounds of Santeria: Rhythms of the Orishas. Contrib. by Raul J. Canizares. (Running Time: 60 mins.). 2004. audio compact disk 12.95 (978-1-59477-002-9(6)); audio compact disk 12.95 (978-1-59477-003-6(4)) Inner Tradit.

Sacred Sounds of the Female Orishas: Rhythms of the Goddess. 2nd ed. Compiled by Raul Canizares. (Running Time: 1 hr.). 2005. bk. 12.95 (978-1-59477-071-5(9), Destiny Recs) Inner Tradit.

Sacred Spaces. Perf. by Steve Amerson. 2005. audio compact disk 15.98 (978-5-559-33764-7(1)) Pub: Pt of Grace Ent. Dist(s): STL Dist NA

Sacred Spaces Tracks. Perf. by Steve Amerson. 2005. audio compact disk 29.95 (978-5-559-33763-0(3)) Pub: Pt of Grace Ent. Dist(s): STL Dist NA

Sacred Stone. abr. ed. Clive Cussler & Craig Dirgo. Read by J. Charles. (Running Time: 21600 sec.). (Oregon Files Ser.: No. 2). 2004. audio compact disk 16.99 (978-1-59600-423-8(1), 9781596004238, BCD Value Price) Brilliance Audio.

Sacred Stone. unabr. ed. Clive Cussler & Craig Dirgo. Read by J. Charles. (Running Time: 11 hrs.). (Oregon Files Ser.: No. 2). 2004. 39.25 (978-1-59710-660-3(7), 1597106607, BADLE); 24.95 (978-1-59710-661-0(5), 1597106615, BAD); 24.95 (978-1-59335-709-2(5), 1593357095, Brilliance MP3); 39.25 (978-1-59335-843-3(1), 1593358431, Brlnc Audio MP3 Lib); 32.95 (978-1-59355-206-0(8), 1593552068, BAU); 87.25 (978-1-59355-207-7(6), 1593552076, BrilAudUnabridg); audio compact disk 36.95 (978-1-59355-209-1(2), 1593552092, Bril Audio CD Unabri); audio compact disk 102.25 (978-1-59355-210-7(6), 1593552106, BriAudCD Unabrid) Brilliance Audio.
Clive Cussler debuted his new series, The Oregon Files, with the incredible adventure of Golden Buddha. Now he follows that triumph with Sacred Stone, a rollicking new tale featuring the enigmatic captain of The Oregon, Juan Cabrillo. In the remote wastelands of Greenland, an ancient artifact possessing catastrophic radioactive power is unearthed. But the astounding find puts the world at risk. Caught between two militant factions bent on wholesale slaughter, Juan Cabrillo and his network of spies known as The Corporation must fight to protect the stone - and prevent the outbreak of World War III.

Sacred Stories of the Medicine Wheel. unabr. ed. Dinawa. Read by Dinawa. Ed. by Tomi Keitten. 1 cass. (Running Time: 59 min.). 1994. 10.95 (978-0-9630485-6-1(2)) In Print.
This is the first of 4 Native American oral teachings preserved from one generation to another. It is a participatory connection revealing the practical principal of the medicine life of native culture, relevant to our lives.

Sacred Storytelling. Midge Miles. 2 cass. (Running Time: 1 hr. 46 min.). 1993. 17.95 (AA2644) Credence Commun.
Miles tells stories & she tells about stories - how they capture, entertain or redeem, depending on our skills & intents.

Sacred the Earth: A Spirituality of Creation. Elizabeth Johnson. 1 cass. (Running Time: 1 hr. 30 mins.). 2001. 9.95 (A8011) St Anthony Mess Pr.
Embrace the ascetic, contemplative and prophetic dimensions of life.

Sacred Theology & Morality. Interview with Mother Angelica et al. 1 cass. (Running Time: 60 min.). (Mother Angelica Live Ser.). 1988. 10.00 (978-1-55794-103-9(3), T54) Eternal Wrd TV.

Sacred Time: A Novel. unabr. ed. Ursula Hegi. Read by Annabella Sciorra et al. 2004. 23.95 (978-0-7435-4962-2(7)) Pub: S&S Audio. Dist(s): S and S Inc

Sacred Treasures: Choral Masterworks from Russia. 1 cass., 1 CD. 7.98 (HOS 11109); audio compact disk 12.78 CD Jewel box. (HOS 11109) NewSound.

Sacred Twins & Spider Woman. unabr. ed. Narrated by Geri Keams. 1 cass. (Running Time: 1 hr.). 1995. 12.95 (C11319) J Norton Pubs.
Storytellers hold a special place of honor in the Navajo tribal circle because they carry tradition & custom from one generation to another. They also teach about the knowledge of "the great circle of life" & "the beauty way." These two creation stories told in English & accompanied by drums & song, Keams, (Streak-of-Black-Forest Navajo Clan), brings the listener into the circle & beauty way.

Sacred Twins & Spider Woman: And Other Navajo Creation Stories. unabr. ed. Perf. by Geri Keams. 1 cass. (Running Time: 1 hr.). (Native American Storytime Ser.). 2001. 11.95 Parabola Bks.
As a child on the reservation, Geri Keams listened as her grandmother passed down these tales. Now she too has taken on the role of storyteller, and from the richness of the Navajo tradition she brings us these timeless creation stories. Includes "Coyote Brings Fire" and "Hunter Boy Meets Rabbit Man".

Sacred Verses, Healing Sounds Vol. 1&2: The Bhagavad Gita & Hymns of the Rig Veda. unabr. ed. Deepak Chopra. 3 CDs. (Running Time: 3 hrs.). (Chopra, Deepak Ser.). (ENG.). 2004. audio compact disk 21.95 (978-1-878424-78-5(5)) Amber-Allen Pub.
Deepak Chopra explores the therapeutic power of sound through language and music. In each volume he reads a selection of sacred verses from ancient Sanskrit hymns and prayers that reveal eternal truths about the nature of life and the universe.

***Sacred Way: Spiritual Practices for Everyday Life.** Zondervan. (Running Time: 7 hrs. 6 mins. 31 sec.). (ENG.). 2010. 14.99 (978-0-310-86988-7(9)) Zondervan.

Sacred Way of Life. Galexis. 2 cass. (Running Time: 3 hrs.). 1995. 17.95 (978-1-56089-037-9(1)) Visionary FL.
Learn to develop a life of inner knowing; exquisite, elegant, & profoundly meaningful. Includes meditation on Side 4.

Sacred Yes Vol. 1: Letters from the Infinite. abr. ed. Deborah G. Johnson. (Running Time: 17100 sec.). 2006. audio compact disk 29.95 (978-1-59179-479-0(X)) Sounds True.

***Sacredness of Questioning Everything.** David Dark. (Running Time: 7 hrs. 22 mins. 0 sec.). (ENG.). 2009. 15.99 (978-0-310-30269-8(2)) Zondervan.

Sacrifice. Ed. by Bill Cuomo. Contrib. by Lamb & Yochanan Ben Yehuda. Prod. by Yochanan Ben Yehuda & Jerry Marcellino. 2005. audio compact disk 16.98 (978-5-558-78714-6(7)) Pt of Grace Ent.

Sacrifice. abr. ed. Mitchell Smith. Read by Jay O. Sanders. 4 cass. (Running Time: 6 hrs.). 1997. 24.95 (978-1-57511-022-6(9)) Pub Mills.
Florida is being terrorized by the Sweetwater killer, whose pattern is to slash the throats of women wearing uniforms.

Sacrifice. abr. ed. Karen Traviss. Read by Marc Thompson. (Running Time: 23400 sec.). (Star Wars Ser.). (ENG.). 2007. audio compact disk 29.95 (978-0-7393-4274-9(6), Random AudioBks) Pub: Random Audio Pubg. Dist(s): Random

Sacrifice. abr. ed. Robert Whitlow. Read by Robert Whitlow. 2 cass. (Running Time: 150 mins.). 2002. 22.99 (978-1-58926-030-6(9)); audio compact disk 19.99 (978-1-58926-031-3(7)) Oasis Audio.
Attorney Scott Ellis has returned home to Catawba, North Carolina and agreed to defend Lester Garrison, a racist teenager, charged in a shooting. Scott has also agreed to advise a mock trial team at Catawba High School. Both situations hold surprise, challenge and unexpected sacrifice.

Sacrifice. unabr. ed. William X. Kienzle. 7 cass. (Running Time: 10 hrs. 30 min.). (Father Koesler Mystery Ser.: No. 23). 2001. 56.00 (978-0-7366-6850-7(0)) Books on Tape.
Father Koesler is left with a murder mystery when an Anglican priest converts to the Roman Catholic priesthood.

Sacrifice. unabr. ed. Andrew Vachss. Read by Phil Gigante. (Running Time: 9 hrs.). (Burke Ser.). 2010. audio compact disk 29.99 (978-1-4418-2127-0(9), 9781441821270, Bril Audio CD Unabri) Brilliance Audio.

***Sacrifice.** unabr. ed. Andrew Vachss. Read by Phil Gigante. (Running Time: 9 hrs.). (Burke Ser.). 2010. 39.97 (978-1-4418-2130-0(9), 9781441821300, Brlnc Audio MP3 Lib); 24.99 (978-1-4418-2129-4(5), 9781441821294, Brilliance MP3); 24.99 (978-1-4418-2131-7(7), 9781441821317, BAD); 39.97 (978-1-4418-2132-4(5), 9781441821324, BADLE); audio compact disk 79.97 (978-1-4418-2128-7(7), 9781441821287, BriAudCD Unabrid) Brilliance Audio.

Sacrifice & Obligation, Freedom & Human Rights. Robert LeFevre. 1 cass. (Running Time: 1 hr. 52 min.). 12.50 (1002) J Norton Pubs.
Where does one's obligations lie? & who is responsible? the individual or the group?.

Sacrifice of Isaac. Neil Gordon. 2004. 15.95 (978-0-7435-4051-3(4)) Pub: S&S Audio. Dist(s): S and S Inc

Sacrifice of Praise. Contrib. by Geron Davis et al. 1997. 11.98 (978-0-00-513544-0(3), 75608604) Pub: Brentwood Music. Dist(s): H Leonard

Sacrificial Ground. unabr. ed. Thomas H. Cook. Narrated by George Guidall. 7 cass. (Running Time: 9 hrs. 15 mins.). (Frank Clemons Mystery Ser.: Vol. 1). 1993. 60.00 (978-1-55690-828-6(8), 93140E7) Recorded Bks.
An Atlanta cop becomes personally involved in a murder investigation.

Sad Cypress. unabr. ed. Agatha Christie. Read by David Suchet. 4 cass. (Running Time: 6 hrs.). 2002. 25.95 (978-1-57270-268-4(0)) Pub: Audio Partners. Dist(s): PerseuPGW
Elinor Carlisle once had money, happiness, and a wonderful fiance, but now she's on trial for murder. Hercules Poirot is called in to sift through clues and red herrings, searching for the complex truth hidden within a maze of deceit.

Sad Cypress. unabr. ed. Agatha Christie. Narrated by David Suchet. (Running Time: 21900 sec.). (Hercule Poirot Mystery Ser.). (ENG.). 2005. audio compact disk 27.95 (978-1-57270-476-3(4)) Pub: AudioGO. Dist(s): Perseus Dist
Elinor Carlisle is accused of killing two people in a jealous rage to secure the wavering affections of her distant cousin and fiancé Welman. Hired to investigate, Hercule Poirot discovers that the evidence overwhelmingly fingers Elinor. When he finds himself agreeing she is the murderer, the skeptical sleuth characteristically looks for reasons why she must be innocent. Assumed identities, an exhumed body, a possible killer nurse, morphine, and a riveting courtroom setting make this a favorite among Christie-ites. David Duchet reads this exciting whodunit with panache.

Sad Memories of a Lost Opportunity. T. D. Jakes. 1 cass. 1999. 6.00 (978-1-57855-450-8(0)) T D Jakes.

Sad Shepherd: A Christmas Story. Based on a story by Henry Van Dyke. (ENG.). 2007. 5.00 (978-1-60339-107-8(X)); audio compact disk 5.00 (978-1-60339-108-5(8)) Listenr Digest.

***Sad Tale of the Brothers Grossbart.** unabr. ed. Jesse Bullington. (Running Time: 14 hrs.). 2010. 24.99 (978-1-4418-6829-9(1), 9781441868299, Brilliance MP3); 39.97 (978-1-4418-6830-5(5), 9781441868305, Brlnc Audio MP3 Lib); 24.99 (978-1-4418-6831-2(3), 9781441868312, BAD); 39.97 (978-1-4418-6832-9(1), 9781441868329, BADLE) Brilliance Audio.

***Sad Tale of the Brothers Grossbart.** unabr. ed. Jesse Bullington. Read by Christopher Lane. (Running Time: 15 hrs.). 2010. audio compact disk 29.99 (978-1-4418-6827-5(5), 9781441868275, Bril Audio CD Unabri); audio compact disk 99.97 (978-1-4418-6828-2(3), 9781441868282, BriAudCD Unabrid) Brilliance Audio.

Sad Truth about Happiness. abr. ed. Anne Giardini. 3 CDs. (Running Time: 12600 sec.). (ENG.). 2006. audio compact disk 24.95 (978-0-86492-402-5(X)) Pub: Goose Ln Eds CAN. Dist(s): U Toronto Pr

Sadako & the Thousand Paper Cranes. Eleanor Coerr. Narrated by Christina Moore. (Running Time: 1 hr.). (gr. 2 up). audio compact disk 19.00 (978-1-4025-2333-5(5)) Recorded Bks.

Sadako & the Thousand Paper Cranes. unabr. ed. Eleanor Coerr. Narrated by Christina Moore. 1 cass. (Running Time: 1 hr.). (gr. 2 up). 2002. 12.00 (978-1-4025-1984-0(2)) Recorded Bks.
Sadako is born in Hiroshima shortly before the atomic bomb is dropped. She grows into a wonderful, high-spirited girl with dreams of becoming the fastest runner in her school. One day at school, she has a dizzy spell and collapses. At the hospital, Sadako and her family learn that the atomic bomb sickness has begun to affect her. To pass the time during her hospital stay, she begins to build origami cranes.

Sadako & the Thousand Paper Cranes. unabr. ed. Read by Corinne Orr. Eleanor Coerr. 1 cass. (Running Time: 47 mins.). (Follow the Reader Ser.). (J). (gr. 3-7). 1986. pap. bk. 17.00 (978-0-8072-0118-3(9), FTR114SP, Listening Lib) Random Audio Pubg.
The true story of Sadako Sasaki, who discovers she has the horrible atomic bomb sickness leukemia. Her valiant struggle with death has made her a symbol of peace among the children of her native Japan.

Saddam's Bombmaker: The Daring Escape of the Man Who Built Iraq's Secret Weapon. unabr. ed. Khidhir Hamza. Read by Robert Whitfield. Told to Jeff Stein. 9 CDs. (Running Time: 41400 sec.). 2002. audio compact disk 49.95 (978-0-7861-9095-9(7)) Blckstn Audio.

Saddam's Bombmaker: The Daring Escape of the Man Who Built Iraq's Secret Weapon. unabr. ed. Khidhir Hamza & Jeff Stein. Read by Robert Whitfield. 9 pieces. (Running Time: 13 hrs. 30 min.). 2004. reel tape 39.95 (978-0-7861-2403-9(2)) Blckstn Audio.

Saddam's Bombmaker: The Terrifying Inside Story of the Iraqi Nuclear & Biological Weapons Agenda. unabr. ed. Khidhir Hamza & Jeff Stein. Read by Robert Whitfield. 1 MP3. (Running Time: 13 hrs.). 2002. audio compact disk 24.95 (978-0-7861-9114-7(7), 3030); 62.95 (978-0-7861-2372-8(9), 3030); audio compact disk 80.00 (978-0-7861-9388-2(3), 3030) Blckstn Audio.
Hamza, the Iraqi scientist who designed Baghdad's nuclear bomb, tells how he secretly developed the bomb with the cynical help of U.S., French, German, and British suppliers and experts and kept it hidden from U.N. inspectors after the Gulf War.

Saddle Pals. Perf. by Riders in the Sky. 1 cass. (Running Time: 32 min.). (Family Ser.). (J). 1987. 9.98 (8011); audio compact disk 14.98 (8011) Rounder Records.
The Riders are joined by their kids & a host of Nashville's best musicians.

***Saddlebum's Bondage.** D. B. Newton. 2009. (978-1-60136-460-9(1)) Audio Holding.

Saddlebum's Bondage. Dwight Newton. (Running Time: 0 hr. 24 mins.). 1998. 10.95 (978-1-60083-455-4(8)) Iofy Corp.

***Saddled: How a Spirited Horse Reined Me in & Set Me Free.** unabr. ed. Susan Richards. (Running Time: 7 hrs. 0 mins.). 2010. 14.99 (978-1-4001-8576-4(9)) Tantor Media.

***Saddled: How a Spirited Horse Reined Me in & Set Me Free.** unabr. ed. Susan Richards. Narrated by Karen White. (Running Time: 8 hrs. 0 mins. 0 sec.). (ENG.). 2010. 19.99 (978-1-4001-6576-6(8)); audio compact disk 59.99 (978-1-4001-4576-8(7)); audio compact disk 29.99 (978-1-4001-1576-1(0)) Pub: Tantor Media. Dist(s): IngramPubServ

Sadhana. Swami Amar Jyoti. 1 cass. 1987. 9.95 (P-62) Truth Consciousness.
Doing spiritual practices with love, faith & devotion to the Goal. Initiation, the linking within with the Master, One who knows. On grace & true religion. Overcoming our resistance.

Sadhana: An Ethno-Ambient Journey into Oneness. abr. ed. Maneesh De Moor. (Running Time: 3780 sec.). 2006. audio compact disk 16.98 (978-1-59179-477-6(3)) Sounds True.

Sadhana Vol. 1: The Daily Practice of Yoga. 1 CD. (Running Time: 1 hr. 30 mins.). 1997. audio compact disk 16.95 (978-0-9661286-0-4(5)) Peace of Mind.

Sadhana Vol. 2: The Daily Practice of Yoga. 1 CD. (Running Time: 1 hr. 30 mins.). 1999. audio compact disk 16.95 (978-0-9661286-1-1(3)) Peace of Mind.

Sadhana the Daily Practice of Meditation. 2000. audio compact disk 16.95 (978-0-9661286-2-8(1)) Peace of Mind.

Sadie Was a Lady. unabr. ed. Joan Jonker. Read by Clare Higgins. 12 cass. (Running Time: 12 hrs.). 1999. 96.95 (978-0-7540-0257-4(8), CAB1680) AudioGO.
Sadie Wilson, the eldest of six children has suffered abuse from her parents all of her life. When she meets Mary Ann & her friends, she finds the love & warmth she has never known & is able to escape her parents. But her thoughts are never far from her brothers & sisters.

Sadie When She Died. unabr. ed. Ed McBain, pseud. Read by Jonathan Marosz. 5 cass. (Running Time: 5 hrs.). (87th Precinct Ser.: Bk. 26). 1998. 30.00 (978-0-7366-3993-4(4), 4356) Books on Tape.
A woman is dead & her husband is glad. What will her little black book tell the boys at 87th Precinct about her nocturnal adventures?.

Safar Nameh i Shahbanou. Excerpts. 8. (Running Time: 12 hrs). (PER.). 1995. 50.00 (978-0-9633129-9-0(5)) Mehriran Pubg.
Mansoreh Pirnia and Empress Farah eloquently recount their 25 years of travel throughout Iran.

Safari Jeff & Shannon Visit Africa. Shannon Kavanagh & Rob Davie. (Great Green Adventure Ser.). 2004. bk. 14.95 (978-0-9734409-0-4(2)) Pub: Croctalk CAN. Dist(s): Hushion Hse

Safari Songs. 1 cass. (Sing-Along Ser.). (J). (ps-3). 1998. bk. 11.99 (978-0-7634-0414-7(4)) W Disney Records.

Safarini in Transit: Music of African Immigrants. Perf. by Frank Ulwenya et al. 1 CD. (Running Time: 67 mins.). (AFR.). 2000. audio compact disk 15.00 (SFW 40457) Smithsonian Folkways.
Cultural profile of African immigrants in the U.S.

***Safe at Home.** Mike Lupica. Contrib. by Keith Nobbs. (Running Time: 3 hrs.). (Comeback Kids Ser.). (ENG.). (J). 2010. audio compact disk 19.95 (978-0-14-314574-5(6), PengAudBks) Penguin Grp USA.

Safe at Home with Teddy Ruxpin. Michelle Baron. Illus. by Julie Armstrong. 1 cass. (Teddy Ruxpin Safe 'n' Sound Ser.). (J). 1988. (978-0-934323-70-3(4)) Alchemy Comms.

Safe Bet. unabr. ed. John Francome. Read by Nigel Carrington. 8 cass. (Running Time: 8 hrs.). 1999. 69.95 (978-0-7531-0567-2(5), 990612) Pub: ISIS Audio GBR. Dist(s): Ulverscroft US
Jockey Mike Powell has just got divorced & he's lost a fortune buying & selling horses. Then he is killed in a car crash. When his ex-brother-in-law Jed Harvard discovers that Mike's estate has been left to a stranger, he decides to look into Mike's shady past where all is not what it seems.

Safe Bet. unabr. ed. John Francome. Read by Nigel Carrington. 8 CDs. (Running Time: 8 hrs.). 2000. audio compact disk 79.95 (107953) Pub: ISIS Audio GBR. Dist(s): Ulverscroft US
Jockey Mike Powell has just gotten divorced & he's lost a fortune buying & selling horses. Then he is killed in a car crash. When his ex-brother-in-law Jed Harvard discovers that Mike's estate has been left to a stranger, he decides to look into Mike's shady past, where all is not what it seems. A compelling novel of suspense from a front runner in the racing thriller stakes.

Safe Driving. Steven Halpern. 1 cass. (Soundwave Two Thousand, the Audio Active Subliminal Ser.). 1990. (2005) Inner Peace Mus.
Relaxing, beautiful music with subliminal affirmations.

Safe Driving. Betty L. Randolph. Read by Betty L. Randolph. Read by Leonard Baron. Ed. by Success Education Institute International. 1 cass. (Running Time: 45 min.). (Health Ser.). 1989. bk. 9.98 (978-1-55909-196-1(7), 63M) Randolph Tapes.
Designed to promote stressless safe driving, with more energy, concentration, & confidence. Subliminal messages are heard 3-5 minutes before becoming ocean sounds or music.

Safe Driving. Eldon Taylor. 1 CD. (Running Time: 52 min.). (Whole Brain Innertalk Ser.). 1998. audio compact disk (978-1-55978-859-5(3)) Progress Aware Res.

Safe Driving: Effective Affirmations to Help You Drive Alertly & Stress-Free. Louise L. Hay. Read by Louise L. Hay. Music by Jerry Florence. Contrib. by Jeffrey Thompson. 1 cass. (Running Time: 60 min.). (Subliminal Mastery Ser.). 1990. 10.95 (978-0-937611-73-9(5), 704) Hay House.
Transform the everyday driving routine from an ordeal into a safe & peaceful experience by listening to these affirmations designed to help us drive with more care & less stress. The lively, yet calming music will help make driving time pleasurable.

Safe Flying with Kitty Hawk's Chart. Vince Ploscik. 1 cass. 1992. 8.95 (1083) Am Fed Astrologers.

Safe Harbor. abr. ed. Luanne Rice. 2004. 15.95 (978-0-7435-4850-2(7)) Pub: S&S Audio. Dist(s): S and S Inc

***Safe Harbor: A Drake Sisters Novel.** Christine Feehan. Narrated by Alyssa Breshnahan. (Running Time: 13 hrs. 50 mins. 0 sec.). (ENG.). 2011. audio compact disk 29.95 (978-1-60998-142-6(1)) Pub: AudioGO. Dist(s): Perseus Dist

Safe Harbour. unabr. ed. Danielle Steel. Read by Kyf Brewer. 7 cass. (Running Time: 10 hrs. 30 min.). 2003. 57.60 (978-0-7366-9442-1(0)); audio compact disk 72.00 (978-0-7366-9554-1(0)) Books on Tape.

***Safe Haven.** Nicholas Sparks. Read by Rebecca Lowman. (Running Time: 7 hrs.). (ENG.). 2011. audio compact disk & audio compact disk 14.98 (978-1-60941-392-7(X)) Pub: Hachet Audio. Dist(s): HachBkGrp

***Safe Haven.** abr. ed. Nicholas Sparks. Read by Rebecca Lowman. (Running Time: 7 hrs.). (ENG.). 2010. 15.98 (978-1-60788-618-1(9)); audio compact disk 22.98 (978-1-60788-617-4(0)) Pub: Hachet Audio. Dist(s): HachBkGrp

***Safe Haven.** unabr. ed. Nicholas Sparks. Read by Rebecca Lowman. (Running Time: 11 hrs.). (ENG.). 2010. 24.98 (978-1-60788-620-4(0)); audio compact disk 34.98 (978-1-60788-619-8(7)) Pub: Hachet Audio. Dist(s): HachBkGrp

Safe, Healthy, Empowered She. abr. ed. Rebecca St. James & Lynda Hunter-Bjorklund. Read by Rebecca St. James. 4 cass. (Running Time: 6 hrs.). 25.99 (978-1-58926-733-6(8)) Oasis Audio.

Safe, Healthy, Empowered She. abr. ed. Rebecca St. James & Lynda Hunter-Bjorklund. Read by Rebecca St. James. 5 CDs. (Running Time: 6 hrs.). 2004. audio compact disk 27.99 (978-1-58926-734-3(6)) Oasis Audio.

Safe House. unabr. ed. Jon Cleary. Read by Gordon Griffin. 11 cass. (Running Time: 16 hrs. 30 mins.). (Sound Ser.). 2001. 89.95 (978-1-86042-208-9(X), 2208x) Pub: UlverLrgPrint GBR. Dist(s): Ulverscroft US
Occupied Germany, 1945. Die Spinne ("The Spider") is all that is left of Nazi Europe, but it is a ruthlessly efficient, secret organization helping war criminals to escape. Among them is Dr. Karl Besser, once the "butcher" of Auchwitz, fleeing to South America with his wife & two sons. Thousands of holocaust survivors are on the move too. Besser comes face to face with a beautiful Jewess whose mother he sent to the gas chamber.

Safe House. unabr. ed. Nicci French. Read by Julian Franklyn. 8 cass. (Running Time: 10 hrs.). 2000. 69.95 (978-0-7531-0652-5(3), 991211) Pub: ISIS Audio GBR. Dist(s): Ulverscroft US
When Dr. Sam Laschen, expert in post-traumatic stress, agrees against her better judgement to provide a haven for the survivor of a horrific assault, she thinks she's helping out. Not putting herself & her child, Elsie, at risk. But as Fiona finds her way into the hearts of her hosts, nowhere & nobody is safe any longer.

Safe House. unabr. ed. Nicci French. Read by Judith Franklin. 10 CDs. (Running Time: 10 hrs. 59 min.). (Isis Ser.). (J). 2003. audio compact disk 89.95 (978-0-7531-2247-1(2)) Pub: ISIS Lrg Prnt GBR. Dist(s): Ulverscroft US

Safe House. unabr. ed. Andrew Vachss. Read by Phil Gigante. (Running Time: 10 hrs.). (Burke Ser.). 2010. audio compact disk 79.97 (978-1-4418-2158-4(9), 9781441821584, BriAudCD Unabrid); audio compact disk 29.99 (978-1-4418-2157-7(0), 9781441821577, Bril Audio CD Unabri) Brilliance Audio.

***Safe House.** unabr. ed. Andrew Vachss. Read by Phil Gigante. (Running Time: 10 hrs.). (Burke Ser.). 2010. 24.99 (978-1-4418-2402-8(2), 9781441824028, BAD); 39.97 (978-1-4418-2403-5(0), 9781441824035, BADLE); 39.97 (978-1-4418-2160-7(0), 9781441821607, Brlnc Audio MP3 Lib); 24.99 (978-1-4418-2159-1(7), 9781441821591, Brilliance MP3) Brilliance Audio.

Safe in the Spotlight. unabr. ed. Elaine Scott. Narrated by Nelson Runger. 1 cass. (Running Time: 1 hr.). (gr. 2 up). 1997. 10.00 (978-0-7887-0747-6(7), 94924E5) Recorded Bks.
The Dawn Animal Agency, which hires out healthy animals for work in television & movies, funds the Sanctuary for Animals, which provides housing & care for animals too old or sick to work themselves.

Safe in Their Alabaster Chambers see **Poems & Letters of Emily Dickinson**

Safe Medication Use in the Nursing Home. unabr. ed. Charlotte Eliopoulos. Read by Charlotte Eliopoulos. 1 cass. (Running Time: 25 min.). 1991. 15.00 (978-1-882515-10-3(2)) Hlth Educ Netwk.
Reviews effects of aging on drug administration, metabolism, & excretion, & describes practices to assure regulatory compliance.

Safe Money in Tough Times: Everything You Need to Know to Survive the Financial Crisis. unabr. ed. Jonathan Pond. Narrated by Dick Hill. 1 MP3-CD. (Running Time: 6 hrs. 30 mins. 0 sec.). (ENG.). 2009. audio compact disk 19.99 (978-1-4001-6165-2(7)); audio compact disk 49.99 (978-1-4001-4165-4(6)) Pub: Tantor Media. Dist(s): IngramPubServ

Safe Money in Tough Times: Everything You Need to Know to Survive the Financial Crisis. unabr. ed. Jonathan Pond. Read by Dick Hill. 6 CDs. (Running Time: 6 hrs. 30 mins. 0 sec.). (ENG.). 2009. audio compact disk 24.99 (978-1-4001-1165-7(X)) Pub: Tantor Media. Dist(s): IngramPubServ

Safe People. Henry Cloud. 1 cass. 1995. 16.99 (978-0-310-59568-7(1)) Zondervan.

Safe People: How to Find Relationships That Are Good for You & Avoid Those That Aren't. abr. ed. Henry Cloud & John Townsend. (Running Time: 2 hrs. 0 mins. 0 sec.). (ENG.). 2003. 9.99 (978-0-310-26094-3(9)) Zondervan.

Safe People Unabr Download. unabr. ed. Henry Cloud & John Townsend. (Running Time: 8 hrs. 0 mins. 0 sec.). (ENG.). 2003. 12.99 (978-0-310-26237-4(2)) Zondervan.

Safe Return Home. Elizabeth Waite. 2009. 54.95 (978-1-4079-0260-9(1)); audio compact disk 64.95 (978-1-4079-0261-6(X)) Pub: Soundings Ltd GBR. Dist(s): Ulverscroft US

Safe Sex - Myth or Reality. Speeches. Created by Mike Goss. 1. (Running Time: 73 mins.). 2005. audio compact disk 15.95 (978-0-9746884-1-1(X)) Ab Amer.

Safe Strategies for Financial Freedom. abr. ed. Van K. Tharp et al. Read by John Lescault. (Running Time: 14580 sec.). 2005. audio compact disk 28.00 (978-1-932378-66-5(9)) Pub: A Media Intl. Dist(s): Natl Bk Netwk

Safe Thus Far: 1 Cor. 10:12-13. Ed Young. 1988. 4.95 (978-0-7417-1668-2(2), 668) Win Walk.

Safecracker Suite: Drumming & Storytelling. Ed. by Ralph Leighton. As told by Richard Phillips Feynman. 1988. audio compact disk 15.00 (978-1-58490-019-1(9)) Scientific Consulting.

Safeguarding Your Teenager from the Dragons of Life. abr. ed. Bettie B. Youngs. Read by Bettie B. Youngs. 1 cass. (Running Time: 90 min.). 1992. 9.95 (978-1-55874-267-3(0)) Health Comm.
Self-esteem expert, Bettie Youngs provides a blueprint for raising teenagers who are competent to deal with life.

Safely Home. abr. ed. Randy C. Alcorn. Narrated by Steve Sever. (Running Time: 5 hrs. 45 mins. 30 sec.). (ENG.). 2007. audio compact disk 24.99 (978-1-59859-309-9(9)) Oasis Audio.

Safer: A Novel of Suspense. unabr. ed. Sean Doolittle. Read by Patrick G. Lawlor. (Running Time: 9 hrs.). 2009. 39.97 (978-1-4233-7749-8(4), 9781423377498, BADLE); 39.97 (978-1-4233-7747-4(8), 9781423377474, Brlnc Audio MP3 Lib); 24.99 (978-1-4233-7748-1(6), 9781423377481, BAD); 24.99 (978-1-4233-7746-7(X), 9781423377467, Brilliance MP3); audio compact disk 89.97 (978-1-4233-7745-0(1), 9781423377450, BriAudCD Unabrid); audio compact disk 34.99 (978-1-4233-7744-3(3), 9781423377443, Bril Audio CD Unabri) Brilliance Audio.

Safer Driving. 1 cass. (Health Ser.). 12.98 (63) Randolph Tapes.
Use this tape for stressless safe driving. Good for more energy, concentration, confidence.

Safety, Set. 2004. act. bk. ed. 13.99 (978-1-57583-327-9(1)) Twin Sisters.

Safety & Health Factors in Welding & Cutting. pap. bk. & tchr. ed. 125.00 (AVA18463VNB1AIF) Natl Tech Info.

Safety & Security Begins at the Front Desk. PUEI. 2007. audio compact disk 199.00 (978-1-934147-63-4(X), Fred Pryor) P Univ E Inc.

Safety & Security Begins at the Front Desk. PUEI. 2008. audio compact disk 199.00 (978-1-934147-85-6(0), CareerTrack) P Univ E Inc.

Safety & Security Equipment & Services in Czech Republic: A Strategic Reference 2007. Compiled by Icon Group International, Inc. Staff. 2007. ring bd. 195.00 (978-0-497-35907-2(3)) Icon Grp.

Safety & Security Equipment & Services in Turkey: A Strategic Reference 2007. Compiled by Icon Group International, Inc. Staff. 2007. ring bd. 195.00 (978-0-497-82445-7(0)) Icon Grp.

Safety Kids Vol. 3: Protect Their Minds. Janeen J. Brady. Illus. by Evan Twede. (J). (gr. k-6). 1992. pap. bk. 12.95 (978-0-944803-77-6(6)) Brite Music.

Safety Kids Personal Safety, Vol. 1. Janeen Brady. Tr. by Oscar Underwood. (SPA.). (J). (gr. k-6). 1984. bk. 12.95 (978-0-944803-17-2(2)) Brite Music.

Safety Kids Personal Safety: Dialogue Book. Janeen Brady. Tr. by Oscar Underwood. (SPA.). (J). (gr. k-6). 1984. 4.95 (978-0-944803-18-9(0)) Brite Music.

Safety of the Cyclone's Center. unabr. ed. John Lilly. 2 cass. (Running Time: 1 hr. 59 min.). 1970. 16.00 Set. (03905) Big Sur Tapes.
Drawing from his book "The Center of the Cyclone" Lilly shares advise for navigators in unknown spaces. He draws from his personal life history, his involvement in scientific projects, the development of his values & the things he has learned from his own experience with inner space travel.

Safety on Wheels. Richard G. Boyer. (Safety Ser.). (J). (gr. k-5). 1974. pap. bk. 7.94 (978-0-87783-199-0(8)) Oddo.

Safety Rock. (J). 2003. audio compact disk 15.00 (978-1-58302-234-4(1)) One Way St.
The songs address topics that will help teach lifetime values to young people. Titles/message are:-Don't Go Out Alone Now/Safety in groups-Mr. Policeman/Thanks to policemen-Call 911/In emergencies, call 911-Stop, Drop, and Roll/Steps for fire safety-Don't Talk to Strangers/Don't talk to people you do not know-Don't Be Cruel/Anti-bullying, and more.

Safety Theme Audio CD. ed. (J). 2004. audio compact disk (978-1-4108-1831-7(4)) Benchmark Educ.

Saffron's Army. Frederick E. Smith. 8 cass. (Running Time: 10 hrs. 35 mins.). (Story Sound Ser.). (J). 2005. 69.95 (978-1-85903-755-3(0)) Pub: Mgna Lrg Print GBR. Dist(s): Ulverscroft US

Saffron's War. Frederick Smith. (Story Sound Ser.). (J). 2005. 54.95 (978-1-85903-754-6(2)) Pub: Mgna Lrg Print GBR. Dist(s): Ulverscroft US

Saffy's Angel. Hilary McKay. Read by Julia Sawalha. 3 vols. (Running Time: 4 hrs. 43 mins.). (Casson Family Ser.: Bk. 1). (J). (gr. 4-7). 2004. pap. bk. 36.00 (978-0-8072-2098-6(1), Listening Lib); audio compact disk 35.00 (978-1-4000-8986-4(7), Listening Lib) Random Audio Pubg.

Saffy's Angel. unabr. ed. Hilary McKay. 3 cass. (Running Time: 4 hrs. 43 mins.). (Casson Family Ser.: Bk. 1). (J). (gr. 4-7). 2004. 30.00 (978-0-8072-0824-3(8), LYA 372 CX, Listening Lib) Random Audio Pubg.
Saffron's two sisters, Cadmium and Rose, and her brother Indigo were named after colors found on a color chart. When Saffron, known as Saffy, learns that her name is not on the chart, it soon leads to the discovery that she has been adopted. Though Saffy's siblings assure her that it makes no difference at all, she sets out on an adventurous and sometimes hilarious search for her angel, who is her key to the past. How Saffy discovers what her angel is, lies at the heart of this enchanted tale.

Sag Harbor: A Novel. unabr. ed. Colson Whitehead. Read by Mirron Willis. (ENG.). 2009. audio compact disk 39.95 (978-0-7393-8190-8(3), Random AudioBks) Pub: Random Audio Pubg. Dist(s): Random

Saga & Contemporary Romance. Brenda Wilbee. 1 cass. (Running Time: 45 min.). (How to Write Best-Selling Romance Ser.: Tape 6). 7.95 (978-0-943777-13-9(5)) byBrenda.

Saga of a Wayward Sailor. unabr. collector's ed. Tristan Jones. Read by Richard Brown. 7 cass. (Running Time: 10 hrs. 30 mins.). 1990. 56.00 (978-0-7366-1869-4(4), 2700) Books on Tape.
Tristan Jones was born in the South Atlantic aboard a British ship off one of the most remote islands in the world, Tristan da Cunha. It was a fitting birthplace for a man who would one day hold nine world sailing records. He left school at the age of 13, signed on a sailing barge & has been at sea ever since. Saga of a Wayward Sailor tells of his experiences in Norway & the Baltic Sea, the canals & rivers of Western Europe, the English Channel, the Bay of Biscay & the Atlantic Ocean.

Saga of Cimba: A Journey from Nova Scotia to the South Seas. unabr. collector's ed. Richard Maury. Read by Christopher Hurt. 6 cass. (Running Time: 6 hrs.). 1987. 36.00 (978-0-7366-1134-3(7), 2057) Books on Tape.
This journey by a young American through big seas in a small ship has become a classic of adventure.

Sagan of Science. John Robbins. 1 cass. (Christianity & Science Ser.: No. 2). 5.00 Trinity Found.

Sage of Monticello. unabr. ed. Dumas Malone. Read by Anna Fields. (Running Time: 66600 sec.). (Jefferson & His Time Ser.). 2007. audio compact disk 120.00 (978-0-7861-6172-0(8)); audio compact disk 44.95 (978-0-7861-6173-7(6)) Blckstn Audio.

Sagebrush Cinderella. Max Brand. Read by Richard Rohan. (Running Time: 1 hr. 42 mins.). 1998. 10.95 (978-1-60083-457-8(4)) Iofy Corp.

Sagebrush Trilogy. unabr. ed. Idah M. Strobridge. Read by Flo Gibson. 8 cass. (Running Time: 11 hrs.). 1996. 26.95 (978-1-55685-442-2(0)) Audio Bk Con.
"In Miners' Mirage Land," "The Loom of the Desert," & "The Land of Purple Shadows" contain vivid & beautiful descriptions of deserts & mountains in Nevada & California as well as tales of the plights & perils of early settlers & miners during the Gold Rush.

Sages: Warren Buffett, George Soros, Paul Volcker, & the Maelstrom of Markets. unabr. ed. Charles R. Morris. Read by Sean Runnette. 5 CDs. (Running Time: 5 hrs. 30 mins.). (ENG.). 2009. audio compact disk 24.95 (978-1-59887-912-4(X), 159887912X) Pub: HighBridge. Dist(s): Workman Pub

Sagesse. Paul Verlaine. Read by A. Deviegue & G. Bejean. 1 cass. (FRE.). 1991. 22.95 (1489-VSL) Olivia & Hill.
This collection, published in 1881 when Verlaine turned to religion & was received into the Roman Catholic church, contains some of his finest work.

Sagittarius. Narrated by Patricia G. Finlayson. Music by Mike Cantwell. Contrib. by Marie De Seta & TMY Communications Staff. 1 cass. (Running Time: 30 min.). (Astrologer's Guide to the Personality Ser.: Vol. 9). 1994. 7.99 (978-1-878535-20-7(X)) De Seta-Finlayson.
Astrological description of the sign of Sagittarius; individually customized, covering love, money, career, relationships & more.

Sagittarius: November Twenty-Two - December Twenty-One. Barrie Konicov. 1 cass. (Hypno-Astrology Ser.). 11.98 (978-0-87082-097-7(4), 113) Potentials.
The author, Barrie Konicov, explains how each sign of the Zodiac has its positive & negative aspects, & that as individuals, in order to master our own destiny, we must enhance our positive traits.

Sagittarius: Unleash the Power of Your True Self. 1 cass. (Running Time: 1 hr.). 1999. 9.99 (978-1-928996-08-8(6)) MonAge.

Sagittarius: Your Relationship with the Energy of the Universe. Loy Young. 1993. 9.95 (978-1-882888-21-4(9)) Aquarius Hse.

Sagittarius Rising. unabr. collector's ed. Cecil Lewis. Read by Donald MacKechnie. 8 cass. (Running Time: 12 hrs.). 1989. 64.00 (978-0-7366-1515-0(6), 2386) Books on Tape.
Features memoirs of a combat pilot in England's Royal Flying Corps during W. W. I.

Sagittarius Surviving. unabr. collector's ed. Cecil Lewis. Read by Thomas Whitworth. 5 cass. (Running Time: 5 hrs.). 1992. 30.00 (978-0-7366-2307-0(8), 3090) Books on Tape.
Cecil Lewis joined the RAF during WW I when he was 17. After ten hours of instruction he went overseas. He flew combat missions until the war ended, then went off to Peking to teach the Chinese to fly.

Saguna Upasana, No. 1. Swami Jyotirmayananda. 1 cass. (Running Time: 1 hr.). 1990. 12.99 Yoga Res Foun.

Saguna Upasana, No. 2. Swami Jyotirmayananda. Read by Swami Jyotirmayananda. 1 cass. (Running Time: 60 min.). 12.99 (722) Yoga Res Foun.

Saguna Upasana, No. 3. Swami Jyotirmayananda. 1 cass. (Running Time: 1 hr.). 1990. 12.99 Yoga Res Foun.

Sahaja - Being Natural. Swami Amar Jyoti. 1 cass. 1987. 9.95 (K-91) Truth Consciousness.
Natural, conscious living. Bringing out our potential, letting go the unwanted. Being unnatural is to suffer. The birth of humility & wisdom.

Sahara. Michael Palin. 8 CDs. (Running Time: 12 hrs.). 2003. audio compact disk 79.95 (978-0-7540-8743-4(3), CCD 295) Pub: Chivers Audio Bks GBR. Dist(s): AudioGO

Sahara. abr. ed. Clive Cussler. Read by Tom Wopat. 2 cass. (Running Time: 3 hrs.). (Dirk Pitt Ser.). 1999. (978-0-671-57764-3(6), 391506, Audioworks) S&S Audio.
A toxic compound in the African desert is killing thousands of people & threatening to extinguish marine life in the world's seas. As Dirk Pitt crosses the desert to uncover a deadly conspiracy, he stumbles across astonishing secrets.

Sahara. unabr. ed. Clive Cussler. Read by Michael Prichard. 13 cass. (Running Time: 19 hrs. 30 min.). (Dirk Pitt Ser.). 1992. 104.00 (978-0-7366-2264-6(0), 3052) Books on Tape.

Sahara. unabr. ed. Michael Palin. Narrated by Michael Palin. (Running Time: 6 hrs. 0 mins. 0 sec.). (ENG.). 2010. audio compact disk 49.95 (978-1-60283-835-2(6)) Pub: AudioGO. Dist(s): Perseus Dist

Sahara. unabr. ed. Read by Michael Palin. 8 cass. (Running Time: 12 hrs.). 2003. 69.95 (978-0-7540-8314-6(4), CAB 2436) Pub: Chivers Audio Bks GBR. Dist(s): AudioGO

Sahara Crosswind. unabr. ed. T. Davis Bunn. Read by Ron Varela. 4 cass. (Running Time: 4 hrs.). (Destiny Ser.: Bk. 3). 2001. 26.95 (978-1-55686-970-9(3)) Books in Motion.

Sai Yoga. Indra Devi. 1 cass. (Running Time: 50 min.). 10.95 (31022) J Norton Pubs.
Explains advanced asanas based on the teachings of Sai Baba; provides instruction in this new advanced approach to Yoga.

Sail. abr. ed. James Patterson & Howard Roughan. Read by Jennifer Van Dyck & Dylan Baker. (Running Time: 6 hrs.). (ENG.). 2008. 14.98 (978-1-60024-203-8(0)) Pub: Hachet Audio. Dist(s): HachBkGrp

Sail. abr. ed. Howard Roughan & James Patterson. Read by Dylan Baker & Jennifer Van Dyck. (Running Time: 6 hrs.). (ENG.). 2009. audio compact disk 14.98 (978-1-60024-588-6(9)) Pub: Hachet Audio. Dist(s): HachBkGrp

Sail. unabr. ed. James Patterson & Howard Roughan. Read by Jennifer Van Dyck & Dylan Baker. (Running Time: 8 hrs.). (ENG.). 2008. 26.98 (978-1-60024-205-2(7)); audio compact disk 39.98 (978-1-60024-206-9(5)) Pub: Hachet Audio. Dist(s): HachBkGrp

Sail. unabr. ed. James Patterson & Howard Roughan. Read by Jennifer Van Dyck & Dylan Baker. 5 cass. 2008. 80.00 (978-1-4159-5613-7(8), BksonTape); audio compact disk 80.00 (978-1-4159-5427-0(5), BksonTape) Pub: Random Audio Pubg. Dist(s): Random
Set sail. Barely out of sight of land, the Dunne family finds its summer getaway to paradise already turning into the trip from hell. Carrie, the eldest, has thrown herself off the side of the boat in a bid for attention. Sixteen-year-old Mark is getting high belowdecks. And Ernie, their ten-year-old brother, is nearly catatonic. It's shaping up to be the worst vacation ever. Soak up the sun. Katherine Dunne had hoped this trip would bring back the togetherness they'd lost when her husband died four years earlier. Maybe if her new husband, a high-powered Manhattan attorney, had been able to postpone his trial and join them it would all have been okay.... Prepare to die. Suddenly, a disaster hits - and it's perfect. Faced with real danger, the Dunnes rediscover the meaning of family and pull together in a way they haven't in a long time. But this catastrophe is just a tiny taste of the danger that lurks ahead: someone wants to make sure that the Dunne family never makes it out of paradise alive.

Sailing. Perf. by Erich Kunzel & Cincinnati Pops Orchestra. 1 cass., 1 CD. 7.98 (TA 30292); audio compact disk 12.78 CD Jewel box. (TA 80292) NewSound.

Sailing above the Clouds of Thought. Swami Amar Jyoti. 1 dolby cass. 1985. 9.95 (J-49) Truth Consciousness.
Why we have ups & downs. Our Center of Identity, common to all, is beyond thoughts. Self-victimization of mind. A simple, natural approach.

Sailing Alone Around the World. Joshua Slocum. Read by Alan Sklar. (Playaway Adult Nonfiction Ser.). (ENG.). 2009. 69.99 (978-1-60812-811-2(3)) Find a World.

Sailing Alone Around the World. Joshua Slocum. Read by Alan Sklar. (Running Time: 7 hrs. 48 mins.). 2003. 27.95 (978-1-60083-643-5(7), Audiofy Corp) Iofy Corp.

Sailing Alone Around the World. Joshua Slocum. Narrated by Alan Sklar. (Running Time: 28200 sec.). (ENG.). 2003. audio compact disk 20.00 (978-1-4001-5075-5(2)) Pub: Tantor Media. Dist(s): IngramPubServ

Sailing Alone Around the World. Joshua Slocum. Narrated by Alan Sklar. (ENG.). 2005. audio compact disk 78.00 (978-1-4001-3075-7(1)) Pub: Tantor Media. Dist(s): IngramPubServ

Sailing Alone Around the World, unabr. ed. Joshua Slocum. Read by Bernard Mayes. 6 cass. (Running Time: 8 hrs. 30 mins.). 1993. 44.95 (978-0-7861-0368-3(X), 1325) Blckstn Audio.
Challenged by an expert who said it couldn't be done, Joshua Slocum, a fearless New England sea captain, set out in April of 1895 to prove that a man could sail alone around the world. 46,000 miles & a little over 3 years later, the proof was complete. Captain Slocum had accomplished the incredible feat single-handedly in a trusty 34-foot sloop called the "Spray." This is Slocum's own account of his remarkable adventures during the historic voyage.

Sailing Alone Around the World, unabr. ed. Joshua Slocum. Narrated by Nelson Runger. 5 cass. (Running Time: 6 hrs. 30 mins.). 1988. 44.00 (978-1-55690-457-8(6), 88700E7) Recorded Bks.
Joshua Slocum was the first man ever to sail around the world single-handedly. He completed his voyage in 1895, without radio & modern technology, when native pirates roamed the seas. It makes for an exciting tale, all 46,000 miles & three years of it.

Sailing Alone Around the World. unabr. ed. Joshua Slocum. Narrated by Alan Sklar. (Running Time: 8 hrs. 0 mins. 0 sec.). (Tantor Unabridged Classics Ser.). (ENG.). 2009. 19.99 (978-1-4001-5935-2(0)); audio compact disk 27.99 (978-1-4001-0935-7(3)) Pub: Tantor Media. Dist(s): IngramPubServ

Sailing Alone Around the World. unabr. ed. Joshua Slocum. Read by Alan Sklar. (Running Time: 8 hrs. 0 mins. 0 sec.). (ENG.). 2009. audio compact disk 55.99 (978-1-4001-3935-4(X)) Pub: Tantor Media. Dist(s): IngramPubServ

Sailing Alone Around the World. unabr. collector's ed. Joshua Slocum. Read by Jonathan Reese. 7 cass. (Running Time: 7 hrs.). 1976. 42.00 (978-0-7366-0002-6(7), 752378) Books on Tape.
Written before the turn of the century. Slocum was 51 when he circled the globe in a 36-foot craft of his own construction. His story is a classic tale of the sea.

Sailing Elysium. Narrated by Helen Olson. (ENG.). 2008. audio compact disk 39.95 (978-1-935061-00-7(3)) Dog Audio.

Sailing from Byzantium. unabr. ed. Colin Wells. Read by Lloyd James. (Running Time: 9 hrs. 0 mins. 0 sec.). (ENG.). 2006. audio compact disk 34.99 (978-1-4001-0285-3(5)) Pub: Tantor Media. Dist(s): IngramPubServ

Sailing from Byzantium: How a Lost Empire Shaped the World. unabr. ed. Colin Wells. Read by Lloyd James. (Running Time: 9 hrs. 0 mins. 0 sec.). (ENG.). 2006. audio compact disk 24.99 (978-1-4001-5285-8(2)) Pub: Tantor Media. Dist(s): IngramPubServ

Sailing from Byzantium: How a Lost Empire Shaped the World. unabr. ed. Colin Wells. Read by Sean Pratt & Lloyd James. (Running Time: 9 hrs. 0 mins. 0 sec.). (ENG.). 2006. audio compact disk 69.99 (978-1-4001-3285-0(1)) Pub: Tantor Media. Dist(s): IngramPubServ

Sailing into san Diego. 2005. audio compact disk (978-0-9769796-1-6(6)) C C Lee.

***Sailing the Big Flush Audio Book.** Intro. by Daniel MacNaughton. (Running Time: 1230). (ENG.). 2010. audio compact disk 39.99 (978-0-9830915-0-9(1)) Eastport Prod.

Sailing the Flying Ship: Stories & Thoughts on Navigating Life. Mary Hamilton. 1 cass. (Running Time: 53 min.). 1998. 10.00 (978-1-885556-05-9(5)) Hidden Sprng.
A weaving of folktales & personal stories along with thoughts on navigating life with stories as a guide.

Sailing the Wine-Dark Sea: Why the Greeks Matter. abr. ed. Thomas Cahill. Read by Olympia Dukakis. (Running Time: 6 hrs.). (ENG.). 2003. audio compact disk 29.95 (978-0-7393-0687-1(1)) Pub: Random Audio Pubg. Dist(s): Random

Sailing to Byzantium see Poetry of William Butler Yeats

Sailing to Byzantium. unabr. ed. Robert A. Silverberg. Read by Tom Parker. 2 cass. (Running Time: 7 hrs.). 2000. 17.95 (978-0-7861-1736-9(2), 2541); audio compact disk 24.00 (978-0-7861-9905-1(9), 2541) Blckstn Audio.
Their hotel was beautifully situated, high on the northern slope of the huge artficial mound knows as the paneium that was sacred to the goat-footed god. From here thay had a total view of the city. There were ghosts & chimeras & phastasies everywhere about. A burly thick-thighed swordsman appeared on the porch of the temple of poseidon holding a Gorgon's severed head & waxed it in a wide arc, grinning broadly. In the street below the hotel gate three small pink sphinxes, no bigger than housecats, stretched & yawned & began to prowl the curbside. A larger one, lion-sized, watched warily from an alleyway: their mother, surely. Even at this distance he could hear her loud purring.

Sailing to Capri. Elizabeth A. Adler. Narrated by Carrington MacDuffie. 7 cass. (Sound Library). 2006. 59.95 (978-0-7927-3856-5(X), CSL 881); audio compact disk 89.95 (978-0-7927-3857-2(8), SLD 881); audio compact disk 29.95 (978-0-7927-4247-0(8), CMP 881) AudioGO.

Sailing to Cythera: And Other Anatole Stories. unabr. ed. Nancy Willard. Narrated by Barbara Rosenblat. 2 cass. (Running Time: 2 hrs.). (gr. 4). 1992. 19.00 (978-1-55690-589-6(0), 92120E7) Recorded Bks.
Meet Anatole, the lovable little boy whose magical adventures lead him into the wallpaper... on the back of a winged horse & to a highly unusual game of checkers with the evil wizard, Arcimboldo the Marvelous.

Sailor Historian: The Best of Samuel Eliot Morison. unabr. ed. Samuel Eliot Morison. Read by Richard Brown. 15 cass. (Running Time: 22 hrs. 30 mins.). 1991. 120.00 (978-0-7366-1935-6(6), 2757) Books on Tape.
From her distinguished father's lifetime work, Emily Morison Beck, the historian's daughter & frequent companion, has chosen the excerpts & articles that appear in Sailor Historian. Consequently this collection may claim to be the best representation of Morison's writing extant, capturing him in all his scope, depth & vigor. Morison possessed not only a first-rate mind but also a soaring imagination. This latter quality distinguished him from most other professors, & freed him from lecture halls & libraries. He sailed his own ships in the wake of his heroes - Columbus, Magellan & Drake - & he shares his voyages with us.

Sailor Moon: Songs from the Hit TV Series. 1 cass. (Running Time: 1 hr.). (J). 2002. 10.98 (978-1-56826-641-1(3), 72267); audio compact disk 16.98 (978-1-56826-640-4(5), 72267) Rhino Enter.
Sailor Moon fights evil by moonlight. This hop soundtrack to the internationally successful television series (originally from Japan) is chock full of upbeat pop tunes.

Sailor Moon: Songs from the Hit TV Series. Rhino Records Staff. 1 cass. (Running Time: 1 hr.). (J). 1998. 10.98 (978-1-56826-639-8(1), 72266) Rhino Enter.

Sailor Moon: Songs from the Hit TV Series with Other. Rhino Records Staff. 1 CD. (Running Time: 1 hr.). (J). (ps-3). 1998. audio compact disk 16.98 (978-1-56826-638-1(3), 72267) Rhino Enter.

Sailor Moon: Unnatural Phenomena. Rhino Records Staff. 1 cass. (J). (ps-3). 1998. 7.99 (978-1-56826-628-2(6)) Rhino Enter.

Sailor Moon & the Scouts Lunarock. 1 CD. (Running Time: 1 hr.). (J). 2002. audio compact disk 17.98 (978-0-7379-0042-2(3), 75654) Rhino Enter.

Sailor on Horseback: The Biography. unabr. ed. Irving Stone. Read by Wolfram Kandinsky. 9 cass. (Running Time: 13 hrs. 30 mins..). 1977. 72.00 (978-0-7366-0074-3(4), 1084) Books on Tape.
Irving Stone's narrative gives us an insight into the development of the forces integral to London's life & career.

***Sailor on Seas of Fate.** Michael Moorcock. (Running Time: 6 mins.). 2009. 19.95 (978-1-897331-33-0(9), AudioRealms) Dorch Pub Co.

Sailor on the Seas of Fate. Michael Moorcock. (Running Time: 6 mins.). 2009. audio compact disk 29.95 (978-1-897304-02-0(1)) Dorch Pub Co.

Sailor on the Seas of Fate. abr. ed. Michael Moorcock. Read by Jeffrey West. (Running Time: 18000 sec.). 2006. audio compact disk 29.95 (978-0-8095-6246-6(4)) Pub: Wildside. Dist(s): Diamond Book Dists

Sailor on the Seas of Fate. abr. ed. Michael Moorcock. Read by Jeffrey West. Directed By Fred Godsmark. (Running Time: 18000 sec.). (Elric Ser.: Vol. 2). 2007. audio compact disk 19.95 (978-0-8095-6245-9(6)) Pub: Wildside. Dist(s): Diamond Book Dists

Sailorboy's Tale see Winter's Tales

Sailors Blue. Perf. by Abbott and Costello & Rudy Vallee. (Running Time: 57 min). 10.95 (#487) J Norton Pubs.
Lou decides to become a sailor & ends up an admiral. Rudy Vallee is the guest. He manages to get in a few songs between arguements with Lou.

Sailors Blue/Rudy Vallee Guest Appearance. Featuring Abbott/Costello. 1950. audio compact disk 12.95 (978-1-57970-501-5(4), Audio-For) J Norton Pubs.

***Sails Literacy Poetry: Grasshopper Stew: Grade 2.** Created by Rigby Reading. (Sails Ser.). 2003. audio compact disk 15.47 (978-0-7578-8436-8(9)) Rigby Educ.

***Sails Literacy Poetry: Shark Snacks: Grade K.** Created by Rigby Reading. (Sails Ser.). 2003. audio compact disk 15.47 (978-0-7578-8434-4(2)) Rigby Educ.

S'aimer sans Tabac. unabr. ed. Khalatbari. Read by Khalatbari. Read by Thierry Aveline. 2007. 69.99 (978-2-35569-065-5(0)) Find a World.

Saint. Read by Vincent Price. (Running Time: 3 hrs.). 2004. 9.98 (978-1-57019-693-5(1)) Radio Spirits.

***Saint.** abr. ed. Ted Dekker. Read by Kevin King. (Running Time: 5 hrs.). (Books of History Chronicles: Bk. 2). 2010. audio compact disk 9.99 (978-1-4418-7815-1(7), 9781441878151, BCD Value Price) Brilliance Audio.

Saint. collector's ed. Perf. by Vincent Price & Tom Conway. 6 cass. (Running Time: 9 hrs.). 1998. bk. 34.98 (4396) Radio Spirits.
Freelance sleuth Simon Templar, the debonair "Robin Hood of modern crime," known to friend & foe alike as...The Saint, in 18 detective adventures.

Saint. unabr. ed. Ted Dekker. Read by Kevin King. (Running Time: 10 hrs.). (Books of History Chronicles: Bk. 2). 2006. 39.25 (978-1-4233-2684-7(9), 9781423326847, BADLE); 24.95 (978-1-4233-2683-0(0), 9781423326830, BAD); 82.25 (978-1-4233-2678-6(4), 9781423326786, BrilAudUnabridg); audio compact disk 97.25 (978-1-4233-2680-9(6), 9781423326809, BriAudCD Unabrid); audio compact disk 39.25 (978-1-4233-2682-3(2), 9781423326823, Brinc Audio MP3 Lib); audio compact disk 36.95 (978-1-4233-2679-3(2), 9781423326793, Bril Audio CD Unabri); audio compact disk 24.95 (978-1-4233-2681-6(4), 9781423326816, Brilliance MP3) Brilliance Audio.
Carl Strople is an assassin with unusual telekinetic gifts. He's been kidnapped, taken into hiding, and had his memory wiped out over a ten-month period of intense training and torture. With a new set of memories and developing skills, he is being molded into a killer for an extraordinary mission. Saint...he's not who you think. Or perhaps who he even thinks he is.

***Saint.** unabr. ed. Ted Dekker. Read by Kevin King. (Running Time: 10 hrs.). (Books of History Chronicles: Bk. 2). 2010. audio compact disk 19.99 (978-1-4418-7839-7(4), 9781441878397, Bril Audio CD Unabri) Brilliance Audio.

Saint, Vol. 1. 6 cass. 24.98 Moonbeam Pubns.

Saint, Vol. 2. 6 cass. 24.98 Moonbeam Pubns.

Saint: Big Swindle. Featuring Vincent Price. 6 cass. (Running Time: 6 hrs.). 1999. 19.98 (AB191) Radio Spirits.

Saint: Fishes Gotta Eat & A Real Gone Guy. Perf. by Vincent Price. 1 cass. (Running Time: 1 hr.). 2001. 6.98 (1796) Radio Spirits.

Saint: Follow the Leader & The Frightened Author. Perf. by Vincent Price. 1 cass. (Running Time: 1 hr.). 2001. 6.98 (1792) Radio Spirits.

Saint: Santa Claus Is No Saint & Ladies Never Lie-Much. Perf. by Vincent Price. 1 cass. (Running Time: 1 hr.). 2001. 6.98 (1877) Radio Spirits.

Saint: Simon Carries the Ivy & The Ghosts Who Came to Dinner. Perf. by Vincent Price. 1 cass. (Running Time: 1 hr.). 2001. 6.98 (1795) Radio Spirits.

Saint: The Bakery. Perf. by Vincent Price. (MM-0602) Natl Recrd Co.

Saint: The Carnival Murder & The Bride Who Lost Her Groom. Perf. by Vincent Price. 1 cass. (Running Time: 1 hr.). 2001. 6.98 (1794) Radio Spirits.

Saint: The Case of the Previewed Crime & A Sonata for Slayers. Perf. by Vincent Price. 1 cass. (Running Time: 1 hr.). 2001. 6.98 (1793) Radio Spirits.

Saint: The Corpse Said Ouch & Cupid & the Corpse. Perf. by Vincent Price. 1 cass. (Running Time: 1 hr.). 2001. 6.98 (1589) Radio Spirits.

Saint: The Problem of the Peculiar Payoff & Chiseling Chimpanzee. Perf. by Vincent Price. 1 cass. (Running Time: 1 hr.). 2001. 6.98 (1965) Radio Spirits.

Saint: The Terrible Tintype & Marvin Hickerson, Private Eye. Perf. by Vincent Price. 1 cass. (Running Time: 1 hr.). 2001. 6.98 (2023) Radio Spirits.

Saint: The What-Not What Got Hot & Button, Button. Perf. by Vincent Price. 1 cass. (Running Time: 1 hr.). 2001. 6.98 (1588) Radio Spirits.

Saint Aloysius Gonzaga. 2000. audio compact disk 8.00 (978-1-58002-607-9(9)) Journeys Faith.

Saint Alphonsus Ligouri. 2000. audio compact disk 8.00 (978-1-58002-605-5(2)) Journeys Faith.

Saint & Mr. Teal. unabr. ed. Leslie Charteris. Read by David Case. 8 cass. (Running Time: 8 hrs.). (Saint Ser.). 1991. 48.00 (978-0-7366-1992-9(5), 2808) Books on Tape.
The Saint knows more than he should about a Paris murder & the murderer wants the Saint silenced.

Saint Angela Merici. 2000. audio compact disk 8.00 (978-1-58002-602-4(8)) Journeys Faith.

Saint Anthony of Padua. 2000. audio compact disk 8.00 (978-1-58002-604-8(4)) Journeys Faith.

Saint Augustine. 2000. audio compact disk 8.00 (978-1-58002-606-2(0)) Journeys Faith.

Saint Augustine. Garry Wills. Read by Alexander Adams. 2000. audio compact disk 32.00 (978-0-7366-5210-0(8)) Books on Tape.

Saint Augustine. collector's ed. Garry Wills. Read by Alexander Adams. 4 cass. (Running Time: 6 hrs.). 1999. 32.00 (978-0-7366-4822-6(4)) Books on Tape.
Gary Wills examines this famed fourth-century bishop & seminal thinker whose grounding in classical philosophy formed his interpretation of Christian doctrine. Saint Augustine explores Augustine's thought as well as the everyday man who set pen to parchment. It challenges many misconceptions, including those regarding his early sexual excesses. It portrays Augustine as being "peripheral in his day, a provincial on the margins of classical culture" who didn't even know Greek.

Saint Augustine. unabr. ed. Perf. by Eknath Easwaran. 1 cass. (Running Time: 1 hr.). 1992. 7.95 (978-1-58638-631-3(X)) Nilgiri Pr.

Saint Augustine. unabr. ed. Garry Wills. Read by Alexander Adams. 4 CDs. (Running Time: 4 hrs. 48 mins.). 2001. audio compact disk 16.00 Books on Tape.
Examines this famed fourth-century bishop & seminal thinker whose grounding in classical philosophy formed his interpretation of Christian doctrine. Saint Augustine explores Augustine's thought as well as the everyday man who set pen to parchment. It challenges many misconceptions, including those regarding his early sexual excesses. It portrays Augustine as being "peripheral in his day, a provincial on the margins of classical culture" who didn't even know Greek.

Saint Augustine. unabr. ed. Garry Wills. Read by Alexander Adams. 4 cass. (Running Time: 6 hrs.). 2000. 24.95 (978-0-7366-4942-1(5)) Books on Tape.

Saint Benedict. 2000. audio compact disk 8.00 (978-1-58002-608-6(7)) Journeys Faith.

Saint Benedict. Solesmes. audio compact disk 16.95 (978-1-55725-098-8(7)) Paraclete MA.

Saint Bernadette. 2000. audio compact disk 8.00 (978-1-58002-609-3(5)) Journeys Faith.

Saint Bernardine of Siena. 2000. audio compact disk 8.00 (978-1-58002-610-9(9)) Journeys Faith.

Saint Bonaventure. 2000. audio compact disk 8.00 (978-1-58002-611-6(7)) Journeys Faith.

Saint Catherine de Ricci. 2000. audio compact disk 8.00 (978-1-58002-612-3(5)) Journeys Faith.

Saint Catherine of Bologna. 2000. audio compact disk 8.00 (978-1-58002-613-0(3)) Journeys Faith.

Saint Catherine of Genoa. 2000. audio compact disk 8.00 (978-1-58002-614-7(1)) Journeys Faith.

Saint Catherine of Siena. 2000. audio compact disk 8.00 (978-1-58002-615-4(X)) Journeys Faith.

Saint Charles Borromeo. 2000. audio compact disk 8.00 (978-1-58002-616-1(8)) Journeys Faith.

Saint Clare of Assisi. 2000. audio compact disk 8.00 (978-1-58002-617-8(6)) Journeys Faith.

Saint Clare of Montefalco. 2000. audio compact disk 8.00 (978-1-58002-618-5(4)) Journeys Faith.

Saint Dominic. 2000. audio compact disk 8.00 (978-1-58002-619-2(2)) Journeys Faith.

Saint Dominic Savio. 2000. audio compact disk 8.00 (978-1-58002-620-8(6)) Journeys Faith.

Saint Edith Stein. 2000. audio compact disk 8.00 (978-1-58002-621-5(4)) Journeys Faith.

Saint Edmund Campion: Priest & Martyr. Evelyn Waugh. 7 cass. 28.95 (737) Ignatius Pr.
A martyr during the reign of Elizabeth I of England written by the great English writer.

Saint Fraces Cabrini. 2000. audio compact disk 8.00 (978-1-58002-622-2(2)) Journeys Faith.

Saint Francis of Assisi. 2000. audio compact disk 8.00 (978-1-58002-623-9(0)) Journeys Faith.

Saint Francis of Assisi. unabr. ed. Perf. by Eknath Easwaran. 1 cass. (Running Time: 1 hr.). 1992. 7.95 (978-1-58638-602-3(6)) Nilgiri Pr.

Saint Gabriel of Sorrows. 2000. audio compact disk 8.00 (978-1-58002-650-5(8)) Journeys Faith.

Saint Gemma Galgani. 2000. audio compact disk 8.00 (978-1-58002-651-2(6)) Journeys Faith.

Saint Gerard Majella. 2000. audio compact disk 8.00 (978-1-58002-652-9(4)) Journeys Faith.

Saint Iggy. K. L. Going. Read by Stephen Hoye. 5. (Running Time: 5 hrs. 28 mins.). (J). 2006. audio compact disk 32.30 (978-0-7393-3782-0(3)) Pub: Books on Tape. Dist(s): NetLibrary CO

Saint Ignatius Loyola. 2000. audio compact disk 8.00 (978-1-58002-653-6(2)) Journeys Faith.

Saint in the Slave Trade. Arnold Lunn. Read by Wayne Jordan. 4 cass. (Running Time: 4 hrs.). 1987. 18.95 (747) Ignatius Pr.
Life & work of St. Peter Claver.

***Saint Is Heard.** Perf. by Vincent Price & Larry Dobkin. 2010. audio compact disk 39.98 (978-1-57019-943-1(4)) Radio Spirits.

Saint Joan, unabr. ed. George Bernard Shaw. Read by Flo Gibson. 3 cass. (Running Time: 4 hrs. 30 min.). 1998. 16.95 (978-1-55685-280-0(0)) Audio Bk Con.
A naive country maid from Domremy obeys voices from God & charms her way to the head of the French army & the coronation of the Dauphin. Her simplicity confounds a world unready to accept her & is condemned for heresy.

Saint Joan: A Chronicle Play in Six Scenes & an Epilogue. unabr. ed. George Bernard Shaw. (Running Time: 3 hrs. 30 mins.). 2010. 29.95 (978-1-4417-2780-0(9)); 34.95 (978-1-4417-2776-3(0)); audio compact disk 49.00 (978-1-4417-2777-0(9)) Blckstn Audio.

Saint Joan of Arc. 2000. audio compact disk 8.00 (978-1-58002-654-3(0)) Journeys Faith.

Saint Joan of Arc. collector's unabr. ed. Jeremy Roberts. Read by Karen White. 2 CDs. (Running Time: 2 hrs. 24 mins.). 2000. audio compact disk 12.95 (978-0-7366-5234-6(5)) Books on Tape.
A poor peasant girl, Jehanette D'Arc became one of the best known figures in French world history. Later known as Saint Joan of Arc, she began to hear the voices of saints & angels when she was thirteen years old. In 1429, these voices guided her into battle & eventually helped her lead the French army to victory over England. Saint Joan of Arc led men into battle & was martyred for her religious beliefs when she was just a teenager. In this compelling look at the mysterious & spiritual events that surrounded her life & death, discover the honesty, devotion & courage of a girl who inspired an army, a king & eventually a country.

Saint Joan of Arc. unabr. ed. Jeremy Roberts. Read by Karen White. 1 cass. (Running Time: 90 mins.). (Biography Ser.). (YA). (gr. 5-12). 2000. 9.95 (5272) Books on Tape.
Looks at the mysterious & spiritual events that surrounded Joan's life & death, discover the honesty, devotion & courage of a girl who inspired an army, a king & eventually a country.

Saint Joan of Arc. unabr. ed. Jeremy Roberts. Read by Karen White. 1 CD. (Running Time: 90 mins.). (Biography Ser.). (YA). 2000. audio compact disk 18.00 (5272-CD) Books on Tape.

Saint Joan of Arc. unabr. ed. Jeremy Roberts. Read by Karen White. 1 cass. (Running Time: 1 hr. 30 mins.). 2000. 9.95 (978-0-7366-4706-9(6)); 9.95 (978-0-7366-5058-8(X)) Books on Tape.
A poor peasant girl, Jehanette D'Arc became one of the best known figures in French world history. Later known as Saint Joan of Arc, she began to hear the voices of saints & angels when she was thirteen years old. In 1429, these voices guided her into battle & eventually helped her lead the French army to victory over England. Saint Joan of Arc led men into battle & was martyred for her religious beliefs when she was just a teenager. In this compelling look at the mysterious & spiritual events that surrounded her life & death, discover the honesty, devotion & courage of a girl who inspired an army, a king & eventually a country.

Saint John Bosco. 2000. audio compact disk 8.00 (978-1-58002-656-7(7)) Journeys Faith.

Saint John of the Cross. 2000. audio compact disk 8.00 (978-1-58002-655-0(9)) Journeys Faith.

Saint John Vianney. 2000. audio compact disk 8.00 (978-1-58002-657-4(5)) Journeys Faith.

Saint Joseph of Cupertino. 2000. audio compact disk 8.00 (978-1-58002-658-1(3)) Journeys Faith.

Saint Judas see Poetry & Voice of James Wright

Saint Leibowitz & the Wild Horse Woman. unabr. collector's ed. Walter M. Miller, Jr. Read by Jonathan Marosz. 13 cass. (Running Time: 19 hrs. 30 min.). 1998. 104.00 (978-0-7366-4268-2(4), 4767) Books on Tape.
Millennia have passed since the Flame Deluge with pockets of civilization still besieged by barbarians.

Saint Leopold Mandic. 2000. audio compact disk 8.00 (978-1-58002-660-4(5)) Journeys Faith.

Saint Louis Marie de Montfort. 2000. audio compact disk 8.00 (978-1-58002-661-1(3)) Journeys Faith.

Saint Margaret Mary Alacoque. 2000. audio compact disk 8.00 (978-1-58002-662-8(1)) Journeys Faith.

Saint Maria Goretti. 2000. audio compact disk 8.00 (978-1-58002-664-2(8)) Journeys Faith.

Saint Maxmilian Kolbe. 2000. audio compact disk 8.00 (978-1-58002-665-9(6)) Journeys Faith.

Saint Maybe. unabr. ed. Anne Tyler. Read by Mary Peiffer. 8 cass. (Running Time: 12 hrs.). 1993. 64.00 (978-0-7366-2441-1(4), 3206) Books on Tape.
Family's youngest son blames himself for the sudden death of his older brother & seeks forgiveness.

Saint Maybe. unabr. ed. Anne Tyler. Narrated by George Guidall. 9 cass. (Running Time: 13 hrs.). 1992. 78.00 (978-1-55690-711-1(7), 92402E7) Recorded Bks.
In 1965, seventeen-year-old Ian Bedloe meddles in his older brother's life, after which nothing can ever be the same. Ian's drawn to the Church of the Second Chance for personal salvation.

Saint Meets His Match. unabr. ed. Leslie Charteris. Read by David Case. 8 cass. (Running Time: 8 hrs.). (Saint Ser.). 1991. 48.00 (978-0-7366-1993-6(3), 2809) Books on Tape.
The Saint joins Scotland Yard as a special agent but soon finds himself on the wrong side of the Commissioner.

Saint Meets the Tiger. unabr. ed. Leslie Charteris. Read by David Case. 8 cass. (Running Time: 8 hrs.). (Saint Ser.). 1990. 48.00 (978-0-7366-1870-0(8), 2701) Books on Tape.
"If there were to be any Saint books at all, obviously there had to be a first, & this is it. And I still think it was a good thing to have started. And that the fiction world today needs a Saint more than it ever did...Even now, half a century later, I still cling to the belief that there will always be a public for the old-style hero, who had a clear idea of justice, & more than a technical appeal to love, & the ability to have some fun in his crusades".

Saint Michael the Archangel. 2000. audio compact disk 8.00 (978-1-58002-668-0(0)) Journeys Faith.

Saint Mudd, abr. ed. Steve Thayer. Read by Frank Muller. 2 cass. (Running Time: 3 hrs.). 1995. 16.95 (978-1-879371-95-8(2), 393487) Pub Mills.
All the legendary gangsters of the era come together in St. Paul to play & loot & kill. And they roam free in a city full of corrupt cops, crooked politicians, graft, bootleg liquor, & opium dreams, amid a few failed saints. The prime would-be saint of the novel is Grover Mudd, a St. Paul newspaper reporter who was gassed in the Great War & is now a consumptive, disillusioned by what is happening to his town & at the same time suicidally idealistic. One other potential saint is Stormy Day, a gentle black woman whom Grover Mudd has come to love. But he is also attracted to the beautiful blond moll Roxanne Schultz.

Saint Nicholas of Tolentino. 2000. audio compact disk 8.00 (978-1-58002-669-7(9)) Journeys Faith.

***Saint on Death Row: The Story of Dominique Green.** unabr. ed. Thomas Cahill. Read by Thomas Cahill. 3 CDs. (Running Time: 3 hrs. 45 mins.). 2009. audio compact disk 40.00 (978-1-4159-6379-1(7), BksonTape) Pub: Random Audio Pubg. Dist(s): Random

Saint on Death Row: The Story of Dominique Green. unabr. ed. Thomas Cahill. Read by Thomas Cahill. 2009. audio compact disk 25.00 (978-0-7393-8374-2(4), Random AudioBks) Pub: Random Audio Pubg. Dist(s): Random

Saint Padre Pio. 2000. audio compact disk 8.00 (978-1-58002-670-3(2)) Journeys Faith.

Saint Paschal Baylon. 2000. audio compact disk 8.00 (978-1-58002-671-0(0)) Journeys Faith.

Saint Patrick of Ireland. unabr. ed. Philip Freeman. Narrated by Alan Sklar. (Running Time: 6 hrs. 6 mins. 0 sec.). (ENG.). 2004. audio compact disk 55.99 (978-1-4001-3111-2(1)) Pub: Tantor Media. Dist(s): IngramPubServ

Saint Patrick Was a Cajun. L. E. McCullough. 1998. audio compact disk 24.95 (978-1-900428-46-0(6), OS10512) Pub: Ossian IRL. Dist(s): H Leonard

Saint Patrick's Battalion. unabr. ed. James Alexander Thom. Narrated by William Dufris. (Running Time: 10 hrs. 30 mins. 0 sec.). (ENG.). 2006. audio compact disk 34.99 (978-1-4001-0303-4(7)) Pub: Tantor Media. Dist(s): IngramPubServ

Saint Patrick's Battalion. unabr. ed. James Alexander Thom. Read by William Dufris. (Running Time: 10 hrs. 30 mins. 0 sec.). (ENG.). 2006. audio compact disk 24.99 (978-1-4001-5303-9(4)); audio compact disk 69.99 (978-1-4001-3303-1(3)) Pub: Tantor Media. Dist(s): IngramPubServ

Saint Paul. 2000. audio compact disk 8.00 (978-1-58002-672-7(9)) Journeys Faith.

***Saint Paul.** Benedict XVI, pseud. (ENG.). 2010. audio compact disk Rental 18.95 (978-1-936231-21-8(2)) Cath Audio.

Saint Paul: His Life, Faith & Legacy. Ronald D. Witherup. 2008. audio compact disk 59.95 (978-0-9795255-6-8(X)) Now You Know.

Saint Paul's Most Notorious. Erik Rivenes. 2005. audio compact disk (978-0-615-12585-5(9)) Tommy Gun.

Saint Peregrine. 2000. audio compact disk 8.00 (978-1-58002-673-4(7)) Journeys Faith.

Saint Philomena. 2000. audio compact disk 8.00 (978-1-58002-625-3(7)) Journeys Faith.

Saint Rita of Cascia. 2000. audio compact disk 8.00 (978-1-58002-626-0(5)) Journeys Faith.

Saint Robert Bellarmine. 2000. audio compact disk 8.00 (978-1-58002-627-7(3)) Journeys Faith.

Saint Rose of Viterbo. 2000. audio compact disk 8.00 (978-1-58002-628-4(1)) Journeys Faith.

***Saint: Saint Overboard & the Saint Plays with Fire: Two BBC Radio Crimes Full-Cast Dramatizations.** Charteris Leslie. Narrated by Paul Rhys & Full Cast. (Running Time: 2 hrs. 0 mins. 0 sec.). (ENG.). 2010. audio compact disk 24.95 (978-1-4084-6697-1(X)) Pub: AudioGO. Dist(s): Perseus Dist

Saint, Signs & Symbols: Clip Art. W. Ellwood Post. 2004. cd-rom & audio compact disk 39.95 (978-0-8192-2142-1(2), MoreHse Pubng) Church Pub Inc.

Saint Stanislaus Kostka. 2000. audio compact disk 8.00 (978-1-58002-629-1(X)) Journeys Faith.

Saint Teresa of Avila. 2000. audio compact disk 8.00 (978-1-58002-630-7(3)) Journeys Faith.

Saint Therese of Lisieux. 2000. audio compact disk 8.00 (978-1-58002-631-4(1)) Journeys Faith.

Saint Thomas More's Utopia. abr. ed. Thomas More. Read by Denis Clarke. Tr. by Gilbert Burnet. 2 cass. (Running Time: 3 hrs.). 1998. 15.95 (978-0-940147-46-1(7)) Source Bks CA.
The classic of political philosophy written in the 16th century.

Saint Valentine's Day Murders. unabr. ed. Ruth Dudley Edwards. Read by Bill Wallis. 6 cass. (Running Time: 9 hrs.). 2001. 54.95 (978-0-7540-0607-7(7), CAB2030) Pub: Chivers Audio Bks GBR. Dist(s): AudioGO
Robert Amiss, still in the Civil Service, is seconded to the wasteland of the newley privatized British Conservation Corporation. He is soon rocked by the malice & envy he finds among the filing cabinets. The pettiness & practical jokes, however, soon lead to murder.

Saint Valentine's Day Murders. unabr. ed. Ruth Dudley Edwards. Read by Bill Wallis. 6 CDs. (Running Time: 23820 sec.). (Jack Crossman Adventures Ser.). 2001. audio compact disk 64.95 (978-0-7540-5413-9(6), CCD 104) Pub: Chivers Audio Bks GBR. Dist(s): AudioGO

Saint Vincent de Paul. 2000. audio compact disk 8.00 (978-1-58002-632-1(X)) Journeys Faith.

Saint vs. Scotland Yard. unabr. ed. Leslie Charteris. Read by David Case. 7 cass. (Running Time: 7 hrs.). (Saint Ser.). 1991. 42.00 (978-0-7366-1959-2(3), 2780) Books on Tape.
That debonair rogue of criminal detection, Simon Templar - alias The Saint - returns to continued battle with Claude Augustus Teal, the gum-chewing Chief Inspector of Scotland Yard. But Teal is not The Saint's target - Scorpion is. The Yard wants Scorpion too, but can't catch him. Which makes the game all the more attractive to The Saint, particularly given the stakes - blackmail, theft, assassination, mayhem & murder.

Saint Watching. Phyllis McGinley. 9 cass. 36.95 (702) Ignatius Pr.
The human side of holiness: Bernard, Philip Neri, Teresa of Avila & others.

sainte folie du Couple. unabr. ed. Paule Salomon. Read by Paule Salomon. (YA). 2007. 69.99 (978-2-35569-089-1(8)) Find a World.

Saintly Powers at Easter; The Baptism of Jesus. Ann Ree Colton & Jonathan Murro. 1 cass. 7.95 A R Colton Fnd.

Saints see Reginald Gibbons

Saints. 6 cass. (Running Time: 6 hrs.). 19.95 (978-0-8198-6899-2(X)) Pauline Bks.
Meet 24 Christian Heroes.

Saints. Perf. by Jane M. deVyver. 4 cass. (Running Time: 4 hrs. 25 min.). (Treasury of Orthodox Christian Prayers Ser.: Vol. 2). 1998. 24.95 (978-1-881211-50-1(9)) Firebird Videos.
Includes a reading of "The Life of St. Mary" & six Akathists (extended hymns) chanted to Saints: St. Xenia of St. Petersburg & St. Seraphim of Sarov; St. Herman of Alaska & St. Metropolitan Innocent; St. John the Theologian & St. Nicholas of Myra.

***Saints.** unabr. ed. Orson Scott Card. (Running Time: 24 hrs. 30 mins.). 2011. 44.95 (978-1-4417-3354-2(X)) Blckstn Audio.

Saints Always Belong to the Present. unabr. ed. John J. Wright. Read by Al Covaia. 4 cass. (Running Time: 6 hrs.). 18.95 (745) Ignatius Pr.
Reflections on seventeen saints including Elizabeth Ann Seton, the first American-born saint.

Saints & Other Sinners. Milbre Burch. Perf. by Milbre Burch. (ENG.). 2005. audio compact disk 20.00 (978-0-9795271-0-4(4)) Kind Crone.

Saints & Ourselves Series. 23 cass. 32.95 8 cass. (738); 32.95 8 cass. (739); 28.95 7 cass. (740) Ignatius Pr.
This series portrays various saints in whom we can see ourselves.

Saints & Scoundrels (2001) 2001. 22.00 (978-1-59128-362-1(0)); 28.00 (978-1-59128-364-5(7)) Canon Pr ID.

Saints & Sinners. Perf. by Jeff Conaway & Vikki Lizzi. Lyrics by Vikki & Kenickie. Vikki & Kenickie. Lyrics by Cheston Vincent. Stardust Comics. (ENG.). 2008. audio compact disk 16.99 (978-0-9816699-5-3(6)) Helen D.

Saints & Villains. unabr. ed. Denise Giardina. (Running Time: 73800 sec.). 2007. audio compact disk 120.00 (978-0-7861-6005-1(5)) Blckstn Audio.

Saints & Villains. unabr. ed. Denise Giardina. Read by Susan O'Malley. (Running Time: 73800 sec.). 2007. audio compact disk 44.95 (978-0-7861-6006-8(3)) Blckstn Audio.

Saints & Villains: A Novel. unabr. ed. Denise Giardina. Read by Susan O'Malley. 14 cass. (Running Time: 21 hrs.). 1998. 89.95 (2292) Blckstn Audio.
Dietrich Bonhoeffer, the German theologian & Nazi resister risked his life - & finally lost it - through his participation in a failed plot to assassinate Hitler & topple his regime. Here is Bonhoeffer experiencing the awakening of his social conscience while witnessing racism in the United States during his studies at Union Theological Seminary. Confronts the painful dilemmas that beset righteous men in times of great evil, when sin & necessity seem entwined.

Saints & Villians. Denise Giardina & Susan O'Malley. 14 cass. (Running Time: 20 hrs. 30 mins.). 2002. 89.95 (978-0-7861-1416-0(9), 2292) Blckstn Audio.

Saints at War. Robert Freeman & Dennis Wright. 2 cass. 2004. 14.95 (978-1-57734-990-7(3)) Covenant Comms.

Saints for Our Times. Theodore Maynard. 9 cass. 36.95 (743) Ignatius Pr.
The facts & legends of 18 saints from the 12th to the 20th century.

Saint's Getaway. unabr. ed. Leslie Charteris. Read by David Case. 7 cass. (Running Time: 7 hrs.). (Saint Ser.). 1991. 42.00 (978-0-7366-1960-8(7), 2781) Books on Tape.
The Saint, bitten by an improbable contrition, makes a singular & difficult vow to two of his best friends: No more trouble. While the three of them are on vacation together in Austria, enjoying a relaxing walk along the river, they come on a fight. With iron self-control The Saint holds back...for 90 seconds before launching into the battle. Had he known that before the night was out he would find a corpse in his bed, cross swords with Prince Rudolf & get involved in the theft of the crown jewels, he might have hesitated longer.

Saints in Combat. 2003. (978-1-59024-118-9(5)); audio compact disk (978-1-59024-119-6(3)) B Hinn Min.

Saints in Praise: Their Very Best. Contrib. by West Angeles Church of God in Christ Mass Choir. 1996. audio compact disk 6.99 (978-7-474-03747-3(5)) Pt of Grace Ent.

***Saints (Library Edition)** unabr. ed. Orson Scott Card. (Running Time: 24 hrs. 30 mins.). 2011. audio compact disk 140.00 (978-1-4417-3351-1(5)) Blckstn Audio.

Saints of SLAM! Perf. by Hari Sky Campbell et al. Prod. by Kevin McCameron & Daniel Brewster. 1 cass. (Running Time: 90 mins.). 2000. 14.95 (978-0-9666484-9-2(8)) Dimby Co Inc.
Stand up.

Saint's Paradise: Trombone Shout Bands from the United House of Prayer. Nick Spitzer. Perf. by Madison's Lively Stones Staff et al. 1 CD. (Running Time: 65 min.). 1999. 14.00 Smithsonian Folkways.
Includes history of United House of Prayer bands & photos.

***Saints (Part 1 of 2 Parts)** unabr. ed. Orson Scott Card. (Running Time: 12 hrs. 30 mins.). 2011. 72.95 (978-1-4417-3350-4(7)) Blckstn Audio.

***Saints (Part 2 of 2 Parts)** unabr. ed. Orson Scott Card. (Running Time: 12 hrs.). 2011. 72.95 (978-1-4417-4446-3(0)) Blckstn Audio.

Saints, Sinners & Lovers. T. Glover-Sedgewick. 1 cass. 8.95 (526) Am Fed Astrologers.
An AFA Convention workshop tape.

Saints Who Made History. Maisie Ward. 12 cass. 47.95 (731) Ignatius Pr.
Tells of those who brought the early centuries of the Church to life.

Saints Who Made History. unabr. ed. Maisie Ward. Read by William Nelson. 12 cass. (Running Time: 18 hrs.). 1989. audio compact disk 55.00 (978-0-7861-0130-6(X), 1116) Blckstn Audio.
Maisie Ward provides us with some momentous & living history of the Catholic Church by focusing on several of its great Saints. Included are accounts of Athanasius, Irenaeus & of course, Augustine. She makes history come to life & anyone interested in Catholic Church history will find this to be invaluable listening.

Saison en Enfer. Poems. Arthur Rimbaud. 1 cass. (Running Time: 90 min.). (FRE.). 2000. pap. bk. 29.50 Incl. dual language bk. & transcript. (978-1-58085-372-9(2)) Interlingua VA.
French poetry.

Saison en Enfer. Arthur Rimbaud. Read by Bruno Sermonne. 1 cass. (FRE.). audio compact disk 32.95 CD. (1608-RF) Olivia & Hill.
Rimbaud's famous collection of poetry & prose read by Bruno Sermonne on French National Radio.

Saison en Enfer. Arthur Rimbaud. Read by Bruno Sermonne. 1 cass. (FRE.). 1992. 16.95 (1607-RF) Olivia & Hill.
Rimbaud's famous collection of poetry & prose read on French National Radio.

Saison en Enfer. Read by Frederique Roberge. 1 cass. (Running Time: 90 min.). (FRE.). bk. 24.50 Incl. transcript. Interlingua VA.
French poetry.

Saki: Selected Short Stories. unabr. collector's ed. Saki. Read by Hugh Burden. 6 cass. (Running Time: 6 hrs.). (J). 1983. 36.00 (978-0-7366-3987-3(X), 9901) Books on Tape.
Short Stories Include: "Sredni Vashtar," "The Storyteller," "Morlvera," "The She-Wolf," "The Open Window," "The Music on the Hill," "Mrs. Packletide's Tiger," "The Story of St. Vespaluus," "Tobermory," "The Schartz Metterklume Method," "The Hounds of Fate," "The Mouse," "The Brogue," etc.

Saki: Strange Tales. unabr. ed. Saki. Read by Patrick Horgan. 2 cass. (Running Time: 1 hr. 39 min.). Incl. Lumber Room. 1987. (CB 111CX); Open Window. 1987. (CB 111CX); Sredni Vashtar. 1987. (CB 111CX); (Cassette Bookshelf Ser.). 1987. 15.98 (978-0-8072-3433-4(8), CB 111CX, Listening Lib) Random Audio Pubg.
Includes ten of Saki's best.

Saki: The Playboy of the Weekend World. Saki. Read by Emlyn Williams. 1 cass. 10.95 (ECN 080) J Norton Pubs.
Includes ten stories which all display the characteristic humor & slightly sinister undertones associated with this author.

Sakunaka, the Handsome Young Man: A Story from Nelson Mandela's Favorite African Folktales. Read by LaTanya Richardson Jackson. Compiled by Nelson Mandela. Composed by Vusi Mahlasela. (Running Time: 7 mins.). (ENG.). 2009. 1.99 (978-1-60024-826-9(8)) Pub: Hachet Audio. Dist(s): HachBkGrp

Sal y Pimienta: Spanish Learning CD for Children. Susy Dorn. 1 CD. (SPA.). (J). 2005. audio compact disk Rental 16.00 (978-0-9764010-2-5(9)) Susy Dorn Prodns.
Sal y Pimienta or Salt and Pepper is a music CD with twenty short easy to learn songs in Spanish composed by Susy Dorn. This CD expands on ¡Cantemos En Español! with songs that teach about: the names of insects, the hours of the day, emotions, the magic words of "Please and Thank you" and many more. SONG TITLES AND DESCRIPTIONS: 1. Sal y Pimienta (Salt and Pepper) 2. ¿Qué comen los animales? (What do animals eat?) 3. Las Emociones (The Emotions) 4. Rimas 1 (Rhymes 1, Animals playing instruments.) 5. El Reloj (The Clock) 6. Los Animales del Mar (Animals of the Sea) 7. Buenos Hábitos (Good Habits; Wash hands, brush teeth, etc...) 8. Rimas 2 (Rhymes 2; Animals looking at objects) 9. La Casa Loca (The Crazy House; "La señora vacuums, sweeps, makes toast, etc...) 10. Los Vegetales (The Vegetables) 11. Mi Amiga Pancha (My Friend Pancha; A song about spots) 12. Cuatro Palabras Mágicas (The Four Magic Words) 13. Pelotas (Balls; A song about Basketballs, soccer balls, volley balls, tennis balls, etc...) 14. La Naturaleza (Nature; A song about the sun, moon, rain, stars, wind, etc...) 15. Los Sonidos de los Animales (The Sounds Animals Make) 16. La Mano y los Dedos (The Hand and the Fingers) 17. Los Utiles Escolares (School Supplies) 18. Los Insectos (The Insects) 19. El Espacio (The Space; A song about the solar system) 20. Cantemos en Español (Let's Sing in Spanish) MORE ABOUT THE ARTIST: Besides a singer, author and song writer for children, Susy Dorn is a Spanish Immersion teacher in the Silicon Valley and Bay Area, California. With a bachelor's degree in early childhood development, Susy has managed to develop Spanish Immersion materials that are fun and effective such as books, music CDs, and DVDs for her students to supplement the learning of Spanish in her program.

Salaat: The Islamic Prayer from A to Z. 2nd rev. ed. Mamdouh N. Mohamed. 2005. pap. bk. 29.95 (978-0-9652877-2-2(6)) B 200.

Saladin in His Time. unabr. ed. P. H. Newby. Narrated by Kerin McCue. 7 cass. (Running Time: 9 hrs. 45 mins.). 1995. 60.00 (978-0-7887-0169-6(X), 94394E7) Recorded Bks.
Biography of the great Kurdish general, renowned for his courage & magnanimity, who became Sultan of Egypt & Syria & Campaigned against the Crusading armies to drive the Christians from Palestine.

Salaire de la peur, Set. Georges Arnaud. 3 cass. (FRE.). 1991. 34.95 (1404-LV) Olivia & Hill.
The suspenseful story of truck drivers maneuvering over mountain passes & racing against time to bring their cargoes of nitroglycerin to the site of a raging oilwell fire.

Salamandastron. Brian Jacques. (Running Time: 12 hrs.). (Redwall Ser.). 2004. audio compact disk 29.99 (978-1-4193-0045-5(8), 01872) Recorded Bks.

Salambo. Gustave Flaubert. Read by Laura Garcia. (Running Time: 3 hrs.). 2002. 16.95 (978-1-60083-199-7(0), Audiofy Corp) Iofy Corp.

Salambo. abr. ed. Gustave Flaubert. Read by Laura Garcia. 3 CDs. (SPA.). 2002. audio compact disk 17.00 (978-958-9494-86-8(2)) YoYoMusic.

Salambo: High Priestess of Ancient Carthage. unabr. ed. Gustave Flaubert. Read by Fred Williams. (Running Time: 12 hrs. 0 mins.). 2009. 29.95 (978-1-4417-0610-2(0)); audio compact disk 105.00 (978-1-4417-0607-2(0)) Blckstn Audio.

Salami see Philip Levine

Salammbo. unabr. ed. Gustave Flaubert. Read by Fred Williams. 9 cass. (Running Time: 13 hrs.). 2000. 62.95 (978-0-7861-1827-4(X), 2626) Blckstn Audio.
First published in 1862, Flaubert's account of the historical struggle between Rome & Carthage is rich with detail of the lives & rites of two ancient kingdoms moved by their allegiance to very different gods. Beyond the gardens of Hamilcar's palace, beyond the walls of Carthage stood the Roman hordes, waiting to annihilate the noblest city of ancient Africa. Within the city all was madness. The veil of the goddess Tanit had fallen to Matho, Roman soldier-of-fortune. But when Salambo, the exquisite daughter of Hamilcar, rode into the Roman camp, to exchange her beauty for the veil of Carthage, he threw away victory, his abandoned army, his nation, his soul, for the price of her body.

Salar the Salmon. unabr. collector's ed. Henry Williamson. Read by Donada Peters. 8 cass. (Running Time: 8 hrs.). (J). 1985. 48.00 (978-0-7366-0907-4(5), 1850) Books on Tape.
Salar is a 5-year-old salmon returning to the stream of his birth. He faces great dangers-cruising lampreys, poachers with their cruel nets & spears, sharp-eyed otters, cascading falls-all between Salar & his goal in the spawning sands.

Salary Negotiation: How to Make $1000 a Minute. Jack Chapman. 2 cass. (Running Time: 3 hrs.). 1995. 15.95 (978-0-943066-68-4(9)) CareerTrack Pubns.

Sale & Lease of Goods. Douglas J. Whaley. 3 cass. (Running Time: 4 hrs. 40 mins.). (Outstanding Professors Ser.). 1995. 50.00 (978-0-940366-68-8(1), 28425) Pub: Sum & Substance. Dist(s): West Pub
Scope of U.C.C.: Article 2 (Sales), Article 2A (Leases); U. N. Treaty on the Sale of Goods; Offer & Acceptance; Warranties; Magnusson-Moss Warranty Act; Warranties for Leases & International Transactions; Terms of the Contract; Unconscionability; Identification; Risk of Loss (no breach); Perfect Tender Rule; Cure; Acceptance; Rejection; Revocation of Acceptance; Risk of Loss (breach); Impossibility; Remedies; Anticipatory Repudiation; Remedies in Leases & International Transactions; Statute of Limitations; Letters of Credit.

Sale & Lease of Goods, 2005 ed. (Law School Legends Audio Series) 2005th rev. ed. Michael I. Spak. (Law School Legends Audio Ser.). 2005. 52.00 (978-0-314-16112-3(0), gilbert); 47.95 (978-0-314-16111-6(2), gilbert) West.

Salem Falls. unabr. ed. Jodi Picoult. Narrated by Julia Gibson. 16 cass. (Running Time: 19 hrs.). 2008. 69.95 (978-1-4193-9034-0(1)); 113.75 (978-1-4193-9033-3(3)); audio compact disk 72.95 (978-1-4193-9036-4(8)); audio compact disk 123.75 (978-1-4193-9035-7(X)) Recorded Bks.

Salem's Lot. unabr. ed. Stephen King. Read by Ron McLarty. (Running Time: 173 hrs. 0 mins. 0 sec.). (ENG.). 2004. audio compact disk 59.95 (978-0-7435-3696-7(7), Audioworks) Pub: S&S Audio. Dist(s): S and S Inc

'Salem's Lot. unabr. ed. Stephen King. Read by Ron McLarty. 2004. 29.95 (978-0-7435-3924-1(9)) Pub: S&S Audio. Dist(s): S and S Inc

Sales Advantage: How to Get It, Keep It, & Sell More Than Ever. abr. ed. Dale Carnegie et al. Read by John Dossett. 3 CDs. (Running Time: 30 hrs. 0 mins. 0 sec.). (ENG.). 2003. audio compact disk 24.95 (978-0-7435-2479-7(9), Sound Ideas) Pub: S&S Audio. Dist(s): S and S Inc

Sales & Marketing. Incl. Sales & Marketing: Iris: Sales - Record Manufacturer; Sales & Marketing: John: Sales - Video Tape Production; Sales & Marketing: Tom: Sales - Cable TV; Sales & Marketing: Vicki: Sales - Radio & TV Syndicates; (Selections from the Career Strategy Cassette Library). 11.95 per cass. J Norton Pubs.
In-depth interviews with young men & women with 5 - 10 years job experience. Guides to career planning for college students in making intelligent decisions about their future careers.

Sales & Marketing. unabr. ed. Michael A. Kamins. Narrated by Grover Gardner. 2 CDs. (Running Time: 2 hrs. 30 mins.). (New York Times Pocket MBA Ser.). 2003. audio compact disk 19.95 (978-1-885408-96-9(X)) Listen & Live.

Sales & Marketing: Iris: Sales - Record Manufacturer see Sales & Marketing

Sales & Marketing: John: Sales - Video Tape Production see Sales & Marketing

Sales & Marketing: Tom: Sales - Cable TV see Sales & Marketing

Sales & Marketing: Vicki: Sales - Radio & TV Syndicates see Sales & Marketing

Sales & Marketing: 25 Keys to Selling Your Products. unabr. ed. Michael A. Kamins. Read by Grover Gardner. 2 cass. (Running Time: 2 hrs. 30 mins.). (New York Times Pocket MBA Ser.). 2000. 16.95 (978-1-885408-42-6(0), LL035) Listen & Live.
Learn the 25 keys to build brand awareness, understand the secrets of advertising & pricing strategies, & integrate the four Ps of marketing.

Sales Bible: The Ultimate Sales Resource. unabr. ed. Jeffrey Gitomer. Read by Jeffrey Gitomer. (Running Time: 8 hrs. 0 mins. 0 sec.). (ENG.). 2008. audio compact disk 39.95 (978-0-7435-7266-8(1)) Pub: S&S Audio. Dist(s): S and S Inc

Sales Bible: The Ultimate Sales Resource. unabr. ed. Jeffrey Gitomer. Read by Jeffrey Gitomer. CDs 16. (Running Time: 8 hrs. 0 mins. 0 sec.). (ENG.). 2008. 59.99 (978-0-7435-7378-8(1)) Pub: S&S Audio. Dist(s): S and S Inc

Sales Body Language Manual: Sales Skills Development Using Techniques from Dramatics & Psychology for All Levels of Salespeople. Daniel Farb & Bruce Gordon. 2004. audio compact disk 59.95 (978-1-59491-010-4(3)) Pub: UnivofHealth. Dist(s): AtlasBooks

Sales Closing for Dummies. unabr. abr. ed. Tom Hopkins. Read by Tom Hopkins. 1 cass. (Running Time: 090 min.). (For Dummies Ser.). 1998. 13.00 (978-0-694-51920-0(0), CPN10148) HarperCollins Pubs.

Sales Closing Power. J. Douglas Edwards. 1987. 99.95 (978-0-942645-03-3(0)) LJR Group.

Sales Dogs: You Do Not Have to Be an Attack Dog to Be Successful in Sales. abr. ed. Blair Singer & Robert T. Kiyosaki. Read by Blair Singer & Robert T. Kiyosaki. Read by Bill Ratner. 3 CDs. (Running Time: 3 hrs.). (ENG.). 2003. audio compact disk 24.98 (978-1-58621-464-7(0)) Pub: Hachet Audio. Dist(s): HachBkGrp

Sales Dogs: You Do Not Have to Be an Attack Dog to Be Successful in Sales. abr. ed. Blair Singer & Robert T. Kiyosaki. Read by Blair Singer & Robert T. Kiyosaki. Read by Bill Ratner. (Running Time: 3 hrs.). (ENG.). 2009. 39.98 (978-1-60024-950-1(7)) Pub: Hachet Audio. Dist(s): HachBkGrp

***Sales Guy's 7 Rules for Outselling the Recession.** Jeb Blount. (ENG.). 2009. 5.95 (978-1-4272-0821-7(2)) Pub: Macmill Audio. Dist(s): Macmillan

Sales Humor Delivery Skills 1: Sales Skills Development Using Techniques from Dramatics for All Levels of Salespeople. Daniel Farb & Bruce Gordon. 2004. audio compact disk 74.95 (978-1-932634-43-3(6)) Pub: UnivofHealth. Dist(s): AtlasBooks

Sales Humor Writing Skills 1 Manual: Sales Skills Development Using Techniques from Dramatics & Joke Writing for All Levels of Salespeople. Daniel Farb & Bruce Gordon. 2004. audio compact disk 84.95 (978-1-59491-012-8(X)) Pub: UnivofHealth. Dist(s): AtlasBooks

Sales Leap. Paul R. Scheele. 1 cass. (Paraliminal Tapes Ser.). 1988. 24.95 (978-0-925480-01-9(0)) Learn Strategies.
Develop the skills, thought processes & integrity of the super-sales professional.

Sales Magic. Kerry L. Johnson. 6 cass. bk. 72.95 (G4261X); 59.95 (4261AX) Nightingale-Conant.
Double your sales volume in 21 days! Kerry Johnson shows you how by introducing you to an entirely different system of selling, one based on trust. He teaches you to literally "read" clients & communicate with them subconsciously, so you can predict how - & when - they'll buy. Learn why it's more important to listen to customers rather than pitch them. Discover how to improve rapport through matching, mirroring, calibrating & reframing techniques. And find out how to detect a prospect's nonverbal buying signals.

Sales Magic: The Seven Principles of Sales Mastery. unabr. ed. Linda Cline Chandler. Read by Linda Cline Chandler. 6 cass. (Running Time: 7 hrs.). (Sales Mastery Ser.). 1997. 129.95 (978-0-9639400-4-9(X), L2A3) Lrning Two-Thousand.
Outstanding, comprehensive sales training audio tape album. Covers the fundamentals of selling & the 21 habits of sales masters. Motivational, original & empowering.

Sales Management One. J. Douglas Edwards. Read by J. Douglas Edwards. 2 cass. (Running Time: 2 hrs.). 1993. 30.00 (978-0-938636-32-8(4), 5010) T Hopkins Intl.
Sales managers ideas & methods for building a successful sales team.

***Sales Mastery Academy: Professional Selling Skills in the 21st Century ndash; Prospecting to Closing.** Made for Success. Read by Zig Ziglar et al. (Running Time: 7 hrs. NaN mins.). (Made for Success Ser.). (ENG.). 2011. audio compact disk 29.95 (978-1-4417-7503-0(X)); audio compact disk 105.00 (978-1-4417-7502-3(1)) Blckstn Audio.

Sales Motivation. 1998. 24.95 (978-1-58557-021-8(4)) Dynamic Growth.

Sales Motivation (Hypnosis), Vol. 14. Jayne Helle. 1 cass. (Running Time: 28 min.). 1997. 15.00 (978-1-891826-13-9(1)) Introspect.
Be a natural self-starter, overcome the fear of rejection & earn financial success. Increase your confidence.

Sales Power. 1 cass. 10.00 (978-1-58506-040-5(2), 72) New Life Inst OR.
Become an irresistible selling personality.

Sales Power. Richard Jafolla & Mary-Alice Jafolla. Read by Richard Jafolla & Mary-Alice Jafolla. (Career Ser.). 1986. 12.95 (230) Stppng Stones.
Motivational tapes that work on the subconscious mind (subliminal) & conscious mind to bring about self-improvement.

Sales Power. Betty L. Randolph. Read by Betty L. Randolph. Read by Leonard Baron. Ed. by Success Education Institute International. 1 cass. (Running Time: 60 min.). (Success Ser.). 1989. bk. 14.98 Ocean Format. (978-1-55909-240-1(8), 300P); bk. 14.98 Music Format. (978-1-55909-241-8(6), 300PM) Randolph Tapes.
60,000 messages left-right brain. Male-female voice tracks with Megafonic Subliminals. Ocean (P) & Music (PM).

Sales Professional's 4 CD Series. Jeff Davidson. 4 CDs. (Running Time: 120 min.). 2006. audio compact disk 48.95 (978-0-9771296-0-7(8)) Breath Space Inst.

Sales Professional's 4 CD Series. Jeff Davidson. 2005. 43.95 (978-1-60729-231-9(9)) Breath Space Inst.

Sales Professional's 4CD Series. Jeff Davidson. 2005. audio compact disk (978-1-60729-570-9(9)) Breath Space Inst.

Sales Questions That Close the Sale. Charles D. Brennan, Jr. 6 cass. (Running Time: 6 hrs.). 1996. wbk. ed. 99.00 (978-1-928821-00-7(6), 440) Brennan Sales Inst.
Presents advanced selling & communication skills to develop stronger relationships & differentiate oneself from competition.

Sales Rep Navigator: How to Find the Perfect Sales Rep or Distributor for Your Business. William G. Radin. Read by Bill Radin. Ed. by Betsy Smith. 1 cass. (Running Time: 5 hrs.). 1996. bk. & wbk. ed. 59.95 (978-0-9626147-6-7(9)) Innovative Consulting.
Sales & performance improvement training for recruiters.

Sales, Success & Prosperity. Norman J. Caldwell. Read by Norman J. Caldwell. Ed. by Achieve Now Institute Staff. 1 cass. (Running Time: 20 min.). (Success Now Ser.). 1988. 9.97 (978-1-56273-064-2(9)) My Mothers Pub.
Your earning power is unlimited!.

Sales Velocity Seminar Series Live. Based on a book by Matthew Ferry. 6 Cds. 2005. audio compact disk 59.95 (978-0-9761929-2-3(6)) Spirit Pub CA.

Salesmanship: Syllabus. 2nd ed. Marvin W. Hempel. (YA). 1980. 244.55 (978-0-89420-182-0(4), 130800) Natl Book.

Sali de Paseo. 1 cass. (Running Time: 35 min.).Tr. of I Went Walking. (SPA.). (J). 2001. 15.95 (VXS-42C) Kimbo Educ.

Sali de Paseo. Sue Williams. Illus. by Julie Vigas. 14 vols. (Running Time: 4 mins.). 1996. pap. bk. 39.95 (978-1-59519-188-5(7)) Live Oak Media.

Sali de Paseo. Sue Williams. Illus. by Julie Vivas. (Running Time: 4 mins.). 1996. 9.95 (978-1-59112-115-2(9)); 9.95 (978-1-59112-181-7(7)) Live Oak Media.

Sali de Paseo. Sue Williams. Illus. by Julie Vigas. (Running Time: 4 mins.). 1996. audio compact disk 12.95 (978-1-59519-186-1(0)) Live Oak Media.

Sali de Paseo. Sue Williams. Illus. by Julie Vigas. 11 vols. (Running Time: 4 mins.). (SPA.). (J). 1996. pap. bk. 18.95 (978-1-59519-187-8(9)) Pub: Live Oak Media. Dist(s): AudioGO

Sali de Paseo. unabr. ed. Sue Williams. Read by Susan Rybin. Illus. by Julie Vigas. 11 vols. (Running Time: 4 mins.). (SPA.). (J). (gr. k-3). 1996. pap. bk. 16.95 (978-0-87499-365-3(2), LK1422) Pub: Live Oak Media. Dist(s): AudioGO
A young child goes for a walk and discovers a colorful parade of animals along the way.

Sali de Paseo, Grades K-3. unabr. ed. Sue Williams. Read by Susan Rybin. Illus. by Julie Vigas. 14 vols. (Running Time: 4 mins.).Tr. of I Went Walking. (SPA.). 1996. pap. bk. & tchr. ed. 37.95 Reading Chest. (978-0-87499-366-0(0)) Live Oak Media.
A young child goes for a walk & discovers a colorful parade of animals along the way.

Salish, Beginning. 2 cass. (Running Time: 2 hrs. 10 min.). bk. 39.95 (AFSA10) J Norton Pubs.
Course for beginners.

Sallie Robbin or a Lighted Candle in Her Heart. Mary M. Slappey. 1985. bk. (978-0-318-60153-3(2)) Interspace Bks.

Sally Hemings - An American Scandal: The Struggle to Tell the Controversial True Story. abr. ed. Tina Andrews. Read by Tina Andrews. 5 CDs. (Running Time: 6 hrs). 2001. audio compact disk 24.95 (978-0-9701295-7-4(2)) Malibu.

Sally the Swinging Snake. Hap Palmer. (J). 1987. 11.95 (978-1-55737-826-2(6)) Ed Activities.

Sally the Swinging Snake. Hap Palmer. 1 CD. (Running Time: 1 hr.). (J). 2001. pap. bk. 14.95 (EA 617CD) Kimbo Educ.
Everything Has a Shape - Percival the Parrot - Muddy Water Puddle - On the Count of Five & more. Includes guide.

Sally the Swinging Snake. Perf. by Hap Palmer. 1 cass. (Running Time: 1 hr.). (J). 2001. pap. bk. 11.95 (EA 617C); pap. bk. 11.95 (EA 617) Kimbo Educ.

Salmon for Simon. Betty Waterton. Illus. by Ann Blades. (J). 2004. 8.95 (978-1-56008-322-1(0)); cass. & flmstrp 30.00 (978-1-56008-758-8(7)) Weston Woods.

Salmon of Doubt: Hitchhiking the Galaxy One Last Time. Douglas Adams. 6 cass. (Running Time: 8 hrs.). 2002. 58.00 (978-1-4025-2860-6(4)) Recorded Bks.

Salmon of Doubt: Hitchhiking the Galaxy One Last Time. unabr. ed. Douglas Adams. Read by Simon Jones et al. 6 cass. (Running Time: 8 hrs.). 2004. 34.95 (978-1-59007-150-2(6)); audio compact disk 39.95 (978-1-59007-151-9(4)) Pub: New Millenn Enter. Dist(s): PerseuPGW

Salmon of Doubt: Special Edition. abr. ed. Douglas Adams. Read by Simon Jones. 2004. 18.00 (978-1-59007-586-9(2)) Pub: New Millenn Enter. Dist(s): PerseuPGW

Salmon of Doubt: Special Edition. abr. ed. Douglas Adams. Read by Simon Jones. 2 CDs. (Running Time: 2 hrs.). 2004. audio compact disk 21.95 (978-1-59007-561-6(7)) Pub: New Millenn Enter. Dist(s): PerseuPGW

Salmos del Rey David: Primera Parte - Salmos 1 al 87. unabr. ed. Read by Pedro Montoya. 3 CDs.Tr. of Psalms of King David part One. (SPA.). 2002. audio compact disk 17.00 (978-958-9494-81-3(1)) YoYoMusic.

Salmos del Rey David - Segunda Parte - Salmos 88 Al 150. unabr. ed. Read by Pedro Montoya. 3 CDs.Tr. of Psalms of King David part Two. (SPA.). 2002. audio compact disk 17.00 (978-958-9494-82-0(X)) YoYoMusic.

Salmos y proverbios de el Puma. (NVI Biblia Audio Ser.). 2007. audio compact disk 22.99 (978-0-8297-5260-1(9)) Zondervan.

Salome. Oscar Wilde & Insomniac Press Staff. 1 CD. (Running Time: 30 min.). 2004. audio compact disk 15.99 (978-1-895837-98-8(7)) Pub: Insomniac CAN. Dist(s): Consort Bk Sales

Salome. Oscar Wilde & Insomniac Press Staff. 1 cass. (Running Time: 30 min.). 2004. reel tape 9.99 (978-1-895837-76-6(6)) Pub: Insomniac CAN. Dist(s): Consort Bk Sales

Salomon. Charles R. Swindoll.Tr. of Solomon. 2009. audio compact disk 27.00 (978-1-57972-841-0(3)) Insight Living.

Salomy Jane's Kiss see Luck of Roaring Camp & Other Stories

Salon Biz: Tips for Success. Geri Mataya. 1 cass. (SalonOvations Ser.). 1995. 10.95 (978-1-56253-301-4(0), Milady) Pub: Delmar. Dist(s): CENGAGE Learn

Salon Business. Milady Publishing Company Staff. 1 cass. (Standard Ser.: Chapter 26). 1995. 14.95 (978-1-56253-298-7(7), Milady) Pub: Delmar. Dist(s): CENGAGE Learn

Salon for the Soul. Created by Adam Gainsburg. Instructed by Adam Gainsburg. (ENG.). 2007. audio compact disk 13.95 (978-0-9788535-3-2(9)) Soulsign.

Salon Solutions: Answers to Common Salon Problems. Cotter. 1 cass. (SalonOvations Ser.). 1996. 16.95 (978-1-56253-343-4(6), Milady) Pub: Delmar. Dist(s): CENGAGE Learn

Salsa! The Rhythm of Latin Music. Charley Gerard & Marty Sheller. Ed. by Lawrence Aynesmith. (Performance in World Music Ser.: No. 9). 1998. pap. bk. 24.95 (978-0-941677-35-6(4)) White Cliffs Media.

Salsa & Pepper. Paul T. Smith. 2003. bk. 19.95 (978-0-7866-5419-2(8), 98712BCD) Mel Bay.

Salsa Session. Birger Sulsbruck et al. 1988. 19.95 (978-0-685-69139-7(X), TV29999) Shawnee Pr.

Salsa, Soul & Swing: Dances for Kids. 1 CD. (Running Time: 35 mins.). (J). 2000. pap. bk. 14.95 (KIM 9159CD) Kimbo Educ.
Little ones will be inspired to cut a rug when they hear this groovin' collection of songs from the 1940s to the present. Lyrics & choreographed instructions included.

Salsa, Soul & Swing: Dances for Kids. 1 cass. (Running Time: 35 mins.). (J). (gr. k up). 2000. pap. bk. 10.95 (KIM 9159C) Kimbo Educ.

Salt. 2004. 8.95 (978-1-56008-323-8(9)); cass. & flmstrp 30.00 (978-1-56008-759-5(5)) Weston Woods.

Salt: A World History. unabr. ed. Mark Kurlansky. Read by Scott Brick. 10 cass. (Running Time: 14 hrs.). 2004. 39.95 (978-1-59007-247-9(2)); audio compact disk 49.95 (978-1-59007-246-2(4)) Pub: New Millenn Enter. Dist(s): PerseuPGW
About the history of salt and the importance of salt as not only our only edible rock, but as a currency, a necessary mineral, a preservative, a curative and a huge part of our vocabulary.

Salt & Blood. unabr. ed. Peter Corris. Read by Peter Hosking. (Running Time: 5 hrs. 40 mins.). (Cliff Hardy Mysteries). 2007. audio compact disk 63.95 (978-1-74093-930-0(1), 9781740939300) Pub: Bolinda Pubng AUS. Dist(s): Bolinda Pub Inc

Salt of the Earth. Salt of the Earth Staff. 2004. audio compact disk 16.98 (978-5-559-37563-2(2), 322-001) Pt of Grace Ent.

***Salt Reaper: Selected Poems from the Flats.** Lasana M. Sekou. 2008. audio compact disk 15.00 (978-0-913441-75-6(9)) Pub: Hse of Nehesi ANT. Dist(s): SPD-Small Pr Dist

Salt Stone Selected Poems see John Woods

Salta, Oscar: Level 1, Vol. 5. 2003. 11.50 (978-0-7652-0992-4(6)) Modern Curr.

Salta, Ranita, Salta! see Jump, Frog, Jump!

Salta Ranita Salta. 9.95 (978-1-59112-182-4(5)) Live Oak Media.

Salta, Ranita, Salta! Robert Kalan. Illus. by Byron Barton. 14 vols. (Running Time: 6 mins.). 1996. pap. bk. 39.95 (978-1-59519-191-5(7)); 9.95 (978-1-59112-116-9(7)); audio compact disk 12.95 (978-1-59519-189-2(5)) Live Oak Media.

Salta, Ranita, Salta! Robert Kalan. Illus. by Byron Barton. 11 vols. (Running Time: 6 mins.). (SPA.). (J). 1996. pap. bk. 18.95 (978-1-59519-190-8(9)) Pub: Live Oak Media. Dist(s): AudioGO

¡Salta, Ranita, Salta! unabr. ed. Robert Kalan. Read by Susan Rybin. Illus. by Byron Barton. 11 vols. (Running Time: 6 mins.). (SPA.). (J). (gr. k-3). 1996. pap. bk. 16.95 (978-0-87499-367-7(9), LK1626) Pub: Live Oak Media. Dist(s): AudioGO
A rollicking, cumulative tale of a frog who tries to catch a fly without getting caught itself. Even the youngest listener will be able to figure out how the frog gets away.

Salta, Ranita, Salta!, Grades K-3. unabr. ed. Robert Kalan. Read by Susan Rybin. Illus. by Byron Barton. 14 vols. (Running Time: 6 mins.).Tr. of Jump, Frog, Jump!. (SPA.). 1996. pap. bk. & tchr. ed. 37.95 Reading Chest. (978-0-87499-369-1(5)) Live Oak Media.

Salta, Ranita, Salta! (Jump, Frog, Jump!) unabr. ed. Robert Kalan. Read by Susan Rybin. Illus. by Byron Barton. 1 cass. (Running Time: 5 mins.). (SPA.). (J). (gr. k-3). 1996. bk. 24.95 (978-0-87499-368-4(7)) Live Oak Media.

Salty Piece of Land. abr. ed. Jimmy Buffett. Read by John David Souther. (ENG.). 2005. 14.98 (978-1-59483-136-2(X)) Pub: Hachet Audio. Dist(s): HachBkGrp

Salty Piece of Land. abr. ed. Jimmy Buffett. Read by Jimmy Buffett. Read by John David Souther & Hank Jacobs. (Running Time: 9 hrs.). (ENG.). 2009. 59.98 (978-1-60024-913-6(2)) Pub: Hachet Audio. Dist(s): HachBkGrp

Salty Tang. Ed Young. (J). 1979. 4.95 (978-0-7417-1047-5(1), A0047) Win Walk.

Saludar y a Celebrar, EDL Level 4. (Fonolibros Ser.: Vol. 23). (SPA.). 2003. 11.50 (978-0-7652-1012-8(6)) Modern Curr.

Saludos. Ozete. (C). bk. 86.95 (978-0-8384-8119-6(1)); bk. 89.95 (978-0-8384-8237-7(6)); bk. 90.95 (978-0-8384-8298-8(8)) Heinle.

Salut Au Monde! see Twentieth-Century Poetry in English, No. 16, Walt Whitman Speaks for Himself

Salute to American POW's. Pat O'Brien. (ENG.). 2008. audio compact disk 12.95 (978-1-57970-496-4(4), Audio-For) J Norton Pubs.

Salvadoro the Ant. unabr. ed. Paul Coleman. Read by Paul Coleman. 1 cass. (Running Time: 1 hr.). Dramatization. (J). (gr. k-6). 1995. 10.00 (978-1-884115-04-2(7)) Tims Tunes.
Fairy-tales for children written & narrated by the author, who walks thousands of miles for peace & the environment.

Salvage & Overhaul DVD. International Association of Fire Chiefs Staff & National Fire Protection Association. 2005. 315.95 (978-0-7637-3612-5(0)) Jones Bartlett.

Salvaje, de Corazon: Descubramos el Secreto del Alma Masculina. unabr. abr. ed. John Eldredge. Read by Toni Pujols. Tr. by Ricardo Acosta. (Running Time: 12600 sec.). 2007. audio compact disk 27.00 (978-1-4332-1139-3(4)) Blckstn Audio.

Salvaje de Corazon: Wild at Heart. abr. ed. John Eldredge. Narrated by Toni Pujos. (SPA.). 2006. 10.49 (978-1-60814-371-9(6)); audio compact disk 14.99 (978-1-59859-035-7(9)) Oasis Audio.

Salvation. Swami Amar Jyoti. 1 cass. 1992. 9.95 (R-108) Truth Consciousness.
The greatest salvation: all is Perfection, Divine. All else is fiction, a dream. Ending the spell of Maya, illusion.

Salvation Affirmations: Book of John. Raymond L. Cramblit. (Running Time: 22 mins.). 2002. audio compact disk 5.00 (978-0-9722989-3-3(2)) R Cramblit.

Salvation Affirmations: New Testament Version. Raymond L. Cramblit. Read by Raymond L. Cramblit. 1 CD. (Running Time: 70 mins.). 2002. audio compact disk 15.00 (978-0-9722989-1-9(6)) R Cramblit.

***Salvation City.** unabr. ed. Sigrid Nunez. (Running Time: 10 hrs. 0 mins.). 2010. 34.99 (978-1-4001-9853-5(4)); 16.99 (978-1-4001-8853-6(9)); 24.99 (978-1-4001-6853-8(8)); audio compact disk 83.99 (978-1-4001-4853-0(7)); audio compact disk 34.99 (978-1-4001-1853-3(0)) Pub: Tantor Media. Dist(s): IngramPubServ

Salvation Gotta Have It. 1 CD. (Running Time: 32 mins.). 2002. audio compact disk 6.99 (978-1-57583-535-8(5), 3004CD) Twin Sisters.
You cannot earn your way to heaven; it is truly a gift. Whoever calls upon the name of the Lord will be saved! With a contemporary pop music sound, these new songs will be loved by kids and adults who want to celebrate the unconditional love and marvelous grace of God.

Salvation in Death. J. D. Robb, pseud. Read by Susan Ericksen. (In Death Ser.). 2009. 104.99 (978-1-60812-694-1(3)) Find a World.

Salvation in Death. abr. ed. J. D. Robb, pseud. Read by Susan Ericksen. 5 CDs. (Running Time: 6 hrs.). (In Death Ser.). 2008. audio compact disk 19.99 (978-1-4233-3763-8(8), 9781423337638, BACD) Brilliance Audio.

Salvation in Death. abr. ed. J. D. Robb, pseud. Read by Susan Ericksen. (Running Time: 6 hrs.). (In Death Ser.). 2009. audio compact disk 14.99 (978-1-4233-3764-5(6), 9781423337645, BCD Value Price) Brilliance Audio.

Salvation in Death. unabr. ed. J. D. Robb, pseud. Read by Susan Ericksen. (Running Time: 13 hrs.). (In Death Ser.). 2008. 39.25 (978-1-4233-3762-1(X), 9781423337621, BADLE); 39.25 (978-1-4233-3760-7(3), 9781423337607, Brinc Audio MP3 Lib); 24.95 (978-1-4233-3761-4(1), 9781423337614, BAD); 24.95 (978-1-4233-3759-1(X), 9781423337591, Brilliance MP3); audio compact disk 102.25 (978-1-4233-3758-4(1), 9781423337584, BriAudCD Unabrid); audio compact disk 38.99 (978-1-4233-3757-7(3), 9781423337577, Bril Audio CD Unabri) Brilliance Audio.

Salvation in Lights. Contrib. by Mike Farris. 2007. audio compact disk 13.99 (978-5-557-70345-1(4)) INO Rec.

***Salvation Is from the Jews.** Roy Schoeman. 2009. audio compact disk 34.95 (978-1-58617-350-0(2)) Pub: Ignatius Pr. Dist(s): Midpt Trade

Salvation of a Forsyte & More. unabr. ed. John Galsworthy. Read by Flo Gibson. 4 cass. (Running Time: 6 hrs.). (Forsyte Saga Ser.). 1992. 19.95 (978-1-55685-224-4(X)) Audio Bk Con.
Apart from the title story, this moving collection includes: "A Portrait," "The Choice," "The Apple Tree," "The Consummation," "Defeat," "The Juryman," "Peace Meeting," & "Two Looks.".

Salvation of Your Loved Ones. 2003. (978-1-59024-099-1(5)); audio compact disk (978-1-59024-098-4(7)) B Hinn Min.

Sam & George. Ed. by Robert A. Monroe. 1 cass. (Running Time: 30 min.). (Meta Music Ser.). 1985. 12.95 (978-1-56102-222-9(5)) Inter Indus.
A conversation between two very unlikely friends in musical form, in reduced tempo to allow the emotional philosophy engendered to be more easily experienced.

Sam & the Lucky Money. 2004. bk. 24.95 (978-0-7882-0698-6(2)); pap. bk. 18.95 (978-1-55592-113-2(2)); pap. bk. 38.75 (978-1-55592-641-0(X)); pap. bk. 32.75 (978-1-55592-305-1(4)); pap. bk. 14.95 (978-0-7882-0699-3(0)); 8.95 (978-0-7882-0093-9(3)); audio compact disk 12.95 (978-1-55592-945-9(1)) Weston Woods.

Sam & the Lucky Money. Karen Chinn. Illus. by Cornelius Van Wright & Ying-Hwa Hu. Narrated by Ming-Na Wen. 1 cass., 5 bks. (Running Time: 11 min.). (J). pap. bk. 32.75 Weston Woods.
It's the Chinese New Year & Sam is finally old enough to choose how his lucky money will be spent. After exploring several options, Sam meets a stranger who helps him make the perfect decision.

Sam & the Lucky Money. Karen Chinn. Illus. by Cornelius Van Wright & Ying-Hwa Hu. Narrated by Ming-Na Wen. 1 cass. (Running Time: 11 min.). (J). (ps-3). bk. 24.95 Weston Woods.

Sam & the Lucky Money. Karen Chinn. Narrated by Ming-Na Wen. Music by Bruce Zimmerman. Illus. by Cornelius Van Wright & Ying-Hwa Hu. 1 cass. (Running Time: 11 min.). (J). (ps-3). 2000. pap. bk. 12.95 (QPRA381) Weston Woods.

Sam Bangs & Moonshine. Evaline Ness. (J). 1985. 14.00 (978-0-394-76652-2(0)) SRA McGraw.

Sam Finds the Way: Early Explorers Early Set A Audio CD. Benchmark Education Staff. (J). 2006. audio compact disk 10.00 (978-1-4108-7618-8(7)) Benchmark Educ.

Sam Hamill. unabr. ed. Sam Hamill. 1 cass. (Running Time: 29 min.). (New Letters on the Air Ser.). 1992. 10.00 (052292) New Letters.
Hamill reads from his book "Mandala" & says interesting things about poets & his life.

Sam Hawkins Pirate Detective & the Pointy Head Lighthouse. Ian Billings. 4 CDs. 2005. audio compact disk 34.95 (978-0-7540-6707-8(6), Chivers Child Audio) AudioGO.

Sam Houston, unabr. ed. John H. Williams. Read by Jeff Riggenbach. 8 cass. (Running Time: 11 hrs. 30 mins.). 1993. 56.95 (978-0-7861-0425-3(2), 1377) Blckstn Audio.
Sam Houston was one of the most colorful & legendary figures of American history. During his life he held an astonishing range of high positions: governor of two states (Tennessee & Texas), congressman (Tennessee), senator (Texas), & President of the Republic of Texas for most of its period of independence. He was an ardent expansionist who helped to make "manifest destiny" a reality, & more than any other individual, he was responsible for Texas's entry into the United States.

***Sam Houston.** unabr. ed. Walter M. Woodward. Read by Benjamin Becker. (Running Time: 2 hrs.). 2011. audio compact disk 24.99 (978-1-61106-484-1(8), 9781611064841, Bril Audio CD Unabri); audio compact disk 29.97 (978-1-61106-489-6(9), 9781611064896, BriAudCD Unabrid) Brilliance Audio.

***Sam Krupnik Series: All about Sam; Attaboy, Sam!; See You Around, Sam!; Zooman Sam.** unabr. ed. Lois Lowry. Read by Bryan Kennedy. (Running Time: 11 hrs.). (Sam Krupnik Ser.). 2010. 24.99 (978-1-4418-5905-1(5), 9781441859051, Brilliance MP3); 39.97 (978-1-4418-5906-8(3), 9781441859068, Brinc Audio MP3 Lib); 39.97 (978-1-4418-5907-5(1), 9781441859075, BADLE); audio compact disk 24.99 (978-1-4418-5903-7(9), 9781441859037, Bril Audio CD Unabri); audio compact disk 79.97 (978-1-4418-5904-4(7), 9781441859044, BriAudCD Unabrid) Brilliance Audio.

Sam Pig & His Fiddle. unabr. ed. Alison Uttley. 1 cass. (Running Time: 6 min.). (J). (gr. 2-5). 1987. bk. 16.95 (978-0-8045-6576-9(7), 6576) Spoken Arts.

Sam Pig & the Dragon. unabr. ed. Alison Uttley. 1 cass. (Running Time: 6 min.). (J). (gr. 2-5). 1987. bk. 16.95 (978-0-8045-6574-5(0), 6574) Spoken Arts.

Sam Pig & the Hurdy-Gurdy Man. unabr. ed. Alison Uttley. 1 cass. (Running Time: 6 min.). (J). (gr. 2-5). 1987. bk. 16.95 (978-0-8045-6575-2(9), 6575) Spoken Arts.

Sam Pig & the Wind. unabr. ed. Alison Uttley. 1 cass. (Running Time: 6 min.). (J). (gr. 2-5). 1987. bk. 16.95 (978-0-8045-6577-6(5), 6577) Spoken Arts.

Sam Pig's Trousers. unabr. ed. Alison Uttley. 1 cass. (Running Time: 6 min.). (J). (gr. 2-5). 1987. bk. 16.95 (978-0-8045-6581-3(3), 6581) Spoken Arts.

Sam Spade. 6 cass. 24.98 Moonbeam Pubns.

Sam Spade. Perf. by Howard Duff & Steven Dunne. 2 cass. (Running Time: 2 hrs.). vinyl bd. 10.95 (978-1-57816-077-8(4), SP2401) Audio File.
Includes: "Apple of Eve Caper" (6-19-49); "Flopsy, Mopsy & Cottontail Caper" (1949); "The 25/1235679 Caper" (12-15-50); "Prodigal Panda Caper" (12-29-50).

Sam Spade: Capers. Perf. by Howard Duff & Lurene Tuttle. 2009. audio compact disk 18.95 (978-1-57019-896-0(9)) Radio Spirits.

***Sam Spade: The Final Capers.** Perf. by Steven Dunne & Lurene Tuttle. 2010. audio compact disk 31.95 (978-1-57019-942-4(6)) Radio Spirits.

Sam Spade: The Kandy Tooth. unabr. ed. Perf. by Howard Duff et al. Hosted by Robert Montgomery. 1 cass. (Running Time: 60 min.). Dramatization. 1948. 7.95 Norelco box. (MM-8130) Natl Recrd Co.
This intriguing detective story is just like re-opening the case of the Maltese Falcon. Casper Gutman, the fat man, returns to the scene after seven years absence, but this time he is looking for a tooth...a very special tooth...that is in the bridgework of a man's mouth. Lovely Hope Lavergne hires Sam, & so do several others, & then the plot thickens & the fun begins.

Sam Spade, Detective. Directed By William Spier. 6 cass. (Running Time: 6 hrs.). 1999. 19.98 (AB117) Radio Spirits.

Sam Tan - Ffynnon y Parc a Storiau Eraill. Sain. 2005. 5.99 (978-0-00-077082-0(5)) Zondervan.

Sam the Minuteman Book & Tape. abr. ed. Nathaniel Benchley. Illus. by Arnold Lobel. 1 cass. (I Can Read Bks.). (J). (gr. k-3). 1991. 8.99 (978-1-55994-354-3(8), TBC 3548) HarperCollins Pubs.

Sam Walton: Made in America. Sam Walton. Read by Philip Franklin. 2000. 56.00 (978-0-7366-5659-7(6)); audio compact disk 64.00 (978-0-7366-8293-0(7)) Books on Tape.

Samadhi. Swami Jyotirmayananda. 1 cass. (Running Time: 1 hr.). 1990. 12.99 Yoga Res Foun.

Samadhi (Superconsciousness) (714) Yoga Res Foun.

Samanske Bubny see Shamanic Drum: A Guide to Sacred Drumming

Samanta y Estrellita see Samantha & Starlight Audio Story with Finger Puppet in Spanish

Samantha: A Soap Opera & Vocabulary Book for Students of English As a Second Language. Meryl R. Becker. (C). 2001. 25.00 (978-0-472-00308-2(9)) U of Mich Pr.

Samantha & Starlight Audio Story: Samantha & Starlight Compact Disc. Short Stories. Joy Frost. 1 Compact Disc. (Running Time: 20 min). (J). 2003. audio compact disk 14.00 (978-0-9716991-8-2(6)) Pub: Joy Stories. Dist(s): Baker Taylor
"Samantha and Starlight" is the story of a young girl with great confidence, determination and a strong belief in how to take charge of a situation. She works towards the positive outcome of what she desires. Samantha?s belief in herself and her love for Starlight, a beautiful, chocolate-brown foal, models for children the power of their own inner strength.

Samantha & Starlight Audio Story in Spanish. Short Stories. Joy Frost. 1 CD. (Running Time: 20 Min.). (SPA.). (J). 2004. audio compact disk 14.00 (978-0-9745977-4-4(0)) Joy Stories.
Exciting new audio stories by Joy B. Frost are original, metaphorical audio bedtime stories that are aimed at raising self-esteem. These stories are filled with positive messages with that are based on the principles of confidence building. These stories have won 7 awards in the past two years. "Samantha and Starlight" is the story of a young girl with great confidence, determination and a strong belief in how to take charge of a situation. She works towards the positive outcome of what she desires. Samantha's belief in herself and her love for Starlight, a beautiful, chocolate-brown foal, models for children the power of their own inner strength. Suggested age 4-9 years old.

Samantha & Starlight Audio Story with Finger Puppet: Samantha & Starlight Compact Disc with Finger Puppet. Short Stories. Joy Frost. 1 Compact Disc. (Running Time: 20 min). (J). 2003. audio compact disk 20.00 (978-0-9716991-9-9(4)) Pub: Joy Stories. Dist(s): Baker Taylor
"Samantha and Starlight" is the story of a young girl with great confidence, determination and a strong belief in how to take charge of a situation. She works towards the positive outcome of what she desires. Samantha's belief in herself and her love for Starlight, a beautiful, chocolate-brown foal, models for children the power of their own inner strength.

Samantha & Starlight Audio Story with Finger Puppet in Spanish. Short Stories. Joy Frost. 1 CD with Finger Pup. (Running Time: 20 Min.). Orig. Title: Samanta y Estrellita. (SPA.). (J). 2004. audio compact disk 20.00 (978-0-9745977-6-8(7)) Joy Stories.
Exciting new audio stories by Joy B. Frost are original, metaphorical audio bedtime stories that are aimed at raising self-esteem. These stories are filled with positive messages with that are based on the principles of confidence building. These stories have won 7 awards in the past two years. "Samantha and Starlight" is the story of a young girl with great confidence, determination and a strong belief in how to take charge of a situation. She works towards the positive outcome of what she desires. Samantha's belief in herself and her love for Starlight, a beautiful, chocolate-brown foal, models for children the power of their own inner strength. Suggested age 4-9 years old.

Samantha Saves the Stream: Early Explorers Fluent Set A Audio CD. Benchmark Education Staff. (J). 2006. audio compact disk 10.00 (978-1-4108-7636-2(5)) Benchmark Educ.

Samantha the Duck. (J). 2002. audio compact disk 15.00 (978-0-9708635-8-4(6)) ePress-online.

Samarpana (Soul Offering) Perf. by Charugita R. Shukla. 1 cass. (Running Time: 45 min.). 9.95 (SP) Nada Prodns.
Inspiring & soul stirring Bhajans of Gujerat. Gaeye Ganapat; Nina Jhukayi; Mana Maru Eka Ja De China Gari; Raghupati Raya; Pathika Tare; Mangal Mandir; Hushu Janu, Kemare Visare; Prarthu Aaje.

Same Game New Rules. Bill Caskey. 1. (Running Time: 1:08). 2003. audio compact disk 17.95 (978-0-9722587-0-8(1)) Caskey Ach Strat.

Same Game New Rules: 23 Timeless Principles for Selling & Negotiating. 2nd ed. Bill Caskey. 2 CD's and 1 book. Orig. Title: Same Game New Rules: Contemporary Insights for the Advanced Sales Professional. 2004. pap. bk. 49.95 (978-0-9758510-5-0(5)); audio compact disk 39.95 (978-0-9758510-4-3(7)) Caskey Ach Strat.
23 INSIGHTS THAT WILL RADICALLYCHANGE YOUR APPROACH ANDPROFOUNDLY CHANGE YOUR RESULTSFinally, a book that teaches you how to thinkSame Game, New Rules provokes a deeper level of thought aboutselling and achievement in business. As the rules of selling change,thinking must change as well. For the sales professional, antiquatedthinking will lead to way too much work for way too little money.This book raises the professional seller to a new level of awarenessabout selling and achievement. it does it by giving the readernew ways to think about the old game of selling.

Same Game New Rules: Contemporary Insights for the Advanced Sales Professional see Same Game New Rules: 23 Timeless Principles for Selling & Negotiating

Same Kind of Different As Me: A Modern-Day Slave, an International Art Dealer, & the Unlikely Woman Who Bound Them Together. abr. unabr. ed. Ron Hall & Denver Moore. Read by Dan Butler & Barry Scott. Told to Lynn Vincent. (Running Time: 3 hrs. 30 mins.). 2007. audio compact disk 16.99 (978-0-8499-6395-7(8)) Nelson.

Same-Sex Love: Some Archetypal Reflections. Read by Karin Lofthus Carrington. 1 cass. (Running Time: 90 min.). 1991. 10.95 (978-0-7822-0033-1(8), 434) C G Jung IL.
Drawing on the work of C. G. Jung & others, San Francisco therapist & author Carrington discusses the individual & archetypal significance of homoerotic & homosexual relationships, & how a deeper understanding of such bonds informs the collective consciousness at this moment in history.

Same Soul, Many Bodies: Discover the Healing Power of Future Lives through Progression Therapy. abr. ed. Brian L. Weiss. Read by Brian L. Weiss. 4 cass. (Running Time: 43 hrs. 0 mins. 0 sec.). (ENG.). 2004. audio compact disk 29.95 (978-0-7435-3833-6(1), Sound Ideas) Pub: S&S Audio. Dist(s): S and S Inc

Same Soul, Many Bodies: Discover the Healing Power of Future Lives through Progression Therapy. abr. ed. Brian L. Weiss. 2004. 15.95 (978-0-7435-5112-0(5)) Pub: S&S Audio. Dist(s): S and S Inc

Same Stuff as Stars. unabr. ed. 5 cass. (Running Time: 6 hrs. 45 min.). (J). 2004. 46.00 (978-1-4025-7356-9(1)) Recorded Bks.

Same Sweet Girls. Cassandra King. 2 CDs. (Running Time: 60240 sec.). (Captain Richard Bolitho Adventures Ser.). 2005. audio compact disk 49.95 (978-0-7927-3467-3(X), CMP 735) AudioGO.

Same Sweet Girls. abr. ed. Cassandra King. Read by Patricia Kalember. (Running Time: 21600 sec.). 2007. audio compact disk 14.98 (978-1-4013-8490-6(0)) Pub: Hyperion. Dist(s): HarperCollins Pubs

Same Sweet Girls. unabr. ed. Cassandra King. Read by Laura Hicks. 1 MP3-CD. 2005. 29.95 (978-0-7927-3441-3(6), CMP 735); 84.95 (978-0-7927-3421-5(1), CSL 735); audio compact disk 110.95 (978-0-7927-3422-2(X), SLD 735) AudioGO.

Same Sweet Girls. unabr. abr. ed. Cassandra King. Read by Patricia Kalember. 4 cass. (Running Time: 6 hrs.). 2005. 25.98 (978-1-4013-9960-3(6)) Pub: Hyperion. Dist(s): HarperCollins Pubs

Samhain (Halloween) Zsuzsanna E. Budapest. 1 cass. 9.00 (A0705-90) Sound Photosyn.
Filled with recipes for rituals & enchantments. Witchcraft at its best. Faustin interviews, Brian records.

Sami Shamanism. Erich Kasten. 1 cass. 9.00 (A0202-87) Sound Photosyn.
From the 1987 ICSS, with Licuaco.

***Samii Legkii Sposob Ponimaniya Ho'oponopono: Yasnie Otveti na Chasto Zadavayemiye Voprosi - Tom I, Vol. 1.** Mabel Katz. (RUS.). 2009. 19.95 (978-0-9825910-2-4(0)) Your Business.

Samit & the Dragon. (J). (ps-4). 1985. bk. (978-0-318-59509-2(5)) Listen USA.

Samit & the Dragon. Joseph Currier. 1 read-along cass. (Running Time: 14 min.). (WellinWorld Ser.: 2-9). (J). (ps-4). 1985. bk. 8.95 incl. bk. (978-0-88684-177-5(1), TC:114578) Listen USA.
A Wellin story about healing yourself when you're feeling ill.

***Sammy & His Behavior Problems: Stories & Strategies from a Teacher's Year.** Caltha Crowe. Read by Caltha Crowe. 2010. audio compact disk 29.95 (978-1-892989-36-9(0)) NE Found Child.

Sammy & Juliana in Hollywood. unabr. ed. Benjamin Alire Sáenz. Read by Robert Ramirez. 6 cass. (Running Time: 9 hrs. 7 mins.). (J). (gr. 4-7). 2006. 45.00 (978-0-307-28591-1(X), Listening Lib); audio compact disk 60.00 (978-0-307-28592-8(8), Listening Lib) Pub: Random Audio Pubg. Dist(s): Random

Sammy at the Farm, Cassette. Short Stories. 1 cassette. (Running Time: 14 mins). (J). 2006. 4.95 (978-1-57874-276-9(5)) Kaeden Corp.

Sammy at the Farm, CD. Short Stories. Kathleen Urmston & Karen Evans. Narrated by Rick Sellers & Wesley McCraw. 1 CD. (Running Time: 13 mins). (J). 2004. audio compact disk 7.95 (978-1-57874-098-7(3)) Kaeden Corp.

Sammy Cassette Tapes: 1 of each 7 Tapes. Short Stories. 7 cassettes. (Running Time: 14 mins. each). (J). 2006. 29.95 (978-1-57874-283-7(8)) Kaeden Corp.

Sammy CD's: 1 of each 7 CD's. Short Stories. 7 CD's. (Running Time: 14 mins. each). (J). 2004. audio compact disk 48.95 (978-1-57874-282-0(X)) Kaeden Corp.

Sammy Gets a Ride, Cassette Tape. Short Stories. 1 cassette. (Running Time: 14 mins). (J). 2006. 4.95 (978-1-57874-279-0(X)) Kaeden Corp.

Sammy Keyes & the Art of Deception. Wendelin Van Draanen. Illus. by Wendelin Van Draanen. 2004. 9.95 (978-1-59112-991-2(5)); 9.95 (978-1-59112-992-9(3)); 9.95 (978-1-59112-993-6(1)); audio compact disk 12.95 (978-1-59112-994-3(X)); audio compact disk 12.95 (978-1-59112-995-0(8)); audio compact disk 12.95 (978-1-59112-996-7(6)); audio compact disk 12.95 (978-1-59112-997-4(4)); audio compact disk 12.95 (978-1-59112-998-1(2)); audio compact disk 12.95 (978-1-59112-999-8(0)) Live Oak Media.

Sammy Keyes & the Art of Deception. Wendelin Van Draanen. Illus. by Wendelin Van Draanen. (J). 2004. 9.95 (978-1-59112-990-5(7)) Live Oak Media.

Sammy Keyes & the Art of Deception. Wendelin Van Draanen. Illus. by Wendelin Van Draanen. 41 vols. (Running Time: 7 hrs. 10 mins.). (Sammy Keyes Ser.: Bk. 8). 2004. pap. bk. 36.95 (978-1-59519-001-7(5)); pap. bk. 54.95 (978-1-59519-003-1(1)); audio compact disk 49.95 (978-1-59519-002-4(3)) Live Oak Media.

Sammy Keyes & the Art of Deception. Wendelin Van Draanen. Illus. by Wendelin Van Draanen. 4 cass. (Running Time: 7 hrs. 10 mins.). (Sammy Keyes Ser.: Bk. 8). (J). 2005. 31.95 (978-1-59519-000-0(7)) Pub: Live Oak Media. Dist(s): AudioGO

Sammy Keyes & the Curse of Moustache Mary. Wendelin Van Draanen. Illus. by Wendelin Van Draanen. 2001. 9.95 (978-0-87499-789-7(5)); 9.95 (978-0-87499-790-3(9)); 9.95 (978-0-87499-843-6(3)); audio compact disk 12.95 (978-0-87499-844-3(1)); audio compact disk 12.95 (978-0-87499-845-0(X)); audio compact disk 12.95 (978-0-87499-846-7(8)); audio compact disk 12.95 (978-0-87499-847-4(6)); audio compact disk 12.95 (978-0-87499-848-1(4)) Live Oak Media.

Sammy Keyes & the Curse of Moustache Mary. Wendelin Van Draanen. Illus. by Wendelin Van Draanen. 11 vols. (Running Time: 6 hrs. 15 mins.). (Sammy Keyes Ser.: Bk. 5). 2001. pap. bk. 36.95 (978-0-87499-793-4(3)); pap. bk. 49.95 (978-0-87499-850-4(6)); 9.95 (978-0-87499-791-0(7)) Live Oak Media.

Sammy Keyes & the Curse of Moustache Mary. unabr. ed. Wendelin Van Draanen. Read by Tara Sands. 4 cass. (Running Time: 6 hrs. 15 mins.). (Sammy Keyes Ser.: Bk. 5). (J). (gr. 3-7). 2001. 29.95 (978-0-87499-792-7(5), OAK010); audio compact disk 44.95 (978-0-87499-849-8(2)) Live Oak Media.
The normally unflappable heroine encounters a corpse, an arsonist & an irate policeman, as well as her first real experience with adolescent angst. Sammy & her friends meet Lucinda Huntley & her 200-pound pig & become involved in a centuries old family feud involving Lucinda's great grandma, Moustache Mary.

Sammy Keyes & the Dead Giveaway. unabr. ed. Wendelin Van Draanen. Narrated by Tara Sands. 4 cass. (Running Time: 7 hrs. 6 mins.). (Sammy Keyes Ser.: Bk. 10). (J). (gr. 5-7). 2006. pap. bk. 36.95 (978-1-59519-770-2(2)) Live Oak Media.

Sammy Keyes & the Dead Giveaway. unabr. ed. Wendelin Van Draanen. 4 cass. (Running Time: 25560 sec.). (Sammy Keyes Ser.: Bk. 10). (J). (gr. 5-8). 2006. 31.95 (978-1-59519-768-9(0)) Live Oak Media.
The tenth mystery in the popular Sammy Keyes series offers more spirit and adventure than ever! Sammy accidentally makes a deadly mistake, but all clues point to her nemesis Heather, and she gets blamed. As Sammy struggles with her conscience she gets distracted helping an ailing senior citizen in her fight against urban renewal.

Sammy Keyes & the Hollywood Mummy. Wendelin Van Draanen. 11 vols. (Running Time: 6 hrs. 45 mins.). (Sammy Keyes Ser.: Bk. 6). 2001. pap. bk. 36.95 (978-0-87499-800-9(X)) Live Oak Media.

Sammy Keyes & the Hollywood Mummy. Wendelin Van Draanen. Read by Tara Sands. 6 CDs. (Running Time: 6 hrs. 45 mins.). (Sammy Keyes Ser.: Bk. 6). (J). 2001. audio compact disk 49.95 (978-0-87499-867-2(0)) Live Oak Media.
When Sammy's mom dumped her with Grams to go to Hollywood & become a star, Sammy dealt with it. But when Sammy discovers that Lady Lana has changed her name, dyed her hair & shaved ten years off her age, she hops a bus to Hollywood & finds her mom in deeper trouble than she expected. One of Lana's biggest competitors is found dead in the room next door. Is Sammy's mother the next likely victim... or the prime suspect?.

Sammy Keyes & the Hollywood Mummy. Wendelin Van Draanen. Illus. by Wendelin Van Draanen. 2 cass. 2001. 9.95 (978-0-87499-797-2(6)); 9.95 (978-0-87499-861-0(1)); audio compact disk 12.95 (978-0-87499-863-4(8)); audio compact disk 12.95 (978-0-87499-866-5(2)) Live Oak Media.

Sammy Keyes & the Hollywood Mummy. Wendelin Van Draanen. Illus. by Wendelin Van Draanen. 11 vols. (Running Time: 6 hrs. 45 mins.). (Sammy Keyes Ser.: Bk. 6). 2001. pap. bk. 54.95 (978-0-87499-868-9(9)); 9.95 (978-0-87499-796-5(8)); 9.95 (978-0-87499-798-9(4)); audio compact disk 12.95 (978-0-87499-862-7(X)); audio compact disk 12.95 (978-0-87499-864-1(6)); audio compact disk 12.95 (978-0-87499-865-8(4)); audio compact disk 12.95 (978-0-87499-991-4(X)) Live Oak Media.

Sammy Keyes & the Hollywood Mummy. unabr. ed. Wendelin Van Draanen. Read by Tara Sands. 4 cass. (Running Time: 6 hrs. 45 mins.). (Sammy Keyes Ser.: Bk. 6). (J). 2001. 23.95 (978-0-87499-799-6(2), OAK011) Pub: Live Oak Media. Dist(s): AudioGO

Sammy Keyes & the Hotel Thief. Wendelin Van Draanen. Read by Tara Sands. 4 CDs. (Running Time: 4 hrs.). (Sammy Keyes Ser.: Bk. 1). (J). 2000. audio compact disk 34.95 (978-0-87499-875-7(1), OAK 012) Live Oak Media.
Sammy Keyes spots a man pawing through a purse and because the police won't believe her, she investigates the crime herself.

Sammy Keyes & the Hotel Thief. Wendelin Van Draanen. Illus. by Wendelin Van Draanen. 2000. 9.95 (978-0-87499-689-0(9)); audio compact disk 12.95 (978-0-87499-871-9(9)); audio compact disk 12.95 (978-0-87499-874-0(3)) Live Oak Media.

Sammy Keyes & the Hotel Thief. Wendelin Van Draanen. Illus. by Wendelin Van Draanen. 11 vols. (Running Time: 4 hrs.). (Sammy Keyes Ser.: Bk. 1). 2000. pap. bk. 39.95 (978-0-87499-876-4(X)); 9.95 (978-0-87499-690-6(2)); 9.95 (978-0-87499-691-3(0)); audio compact disk 12.95 (978-0-87499-872-6(7)); audio compact disk 12.95 (978-0-87499-873-3(5)) Live Oak Media.

Sammy Keyes & the Hotel Thief. unabr. ed. Wendelin Van Draanen. 3 vols. (Running Time: 4 hrs.). (Sammy Keyes Ser.: Bk. 1). (J). (gr. 4-7). 2000. bk. 38.95 (978-0-87499-694-4(5)) Live Oak Media.

Sammy Keyes & the Hotel Thief. unabr. ed. Wendelin Van Draanen. Read by Tara Sands. 11 vols. (Running Time: 4 hrs.). (Sammy Keyes Ser.: Bk. 1). (J). (gr. 4-7). 2000. pap. bk. 30.95 (978-0-87499-693-7(7)); 25.95 (978-0-87499-692-0(9), OAK006) Live Oak Media.
Although she's a girl detective starring in a new series, Sammy is not Nancy Drew. She's smart-mouthed & hard-hitting, unpopular at school & on the outs with the law. Readers follow the sleuth through her saucy first-person narrative as she tries to find a burglar who's made a number of hits in her neighborhood, one of which she witnessed while spying on her neighbors with binoculars. The solution will likely come as a surprise & the sleuth delights from start to finish. Although this young gumshoe is not yet a professional herself, she's well on her way & certainly worth watching. Keep your binoculars trained on Sammy Keyes.

Sammy Keyes & the Hotel Thief, unabr. ed. Wendelin Van Draanen. Read by Tara Sands. 34 vols. (Running Time: 4 hrs.). (Sammy Keyes Ser.: Bk. 1). (J). 2000. pap. bk. & tchr. ed. 43.95 Reading Chest. (978-0-87499-695-1(3)) Live Oak Media.

Sammy Keyes & the Psycho Kitty Queen. Wendelin Van Draanen. Read by Tara Sands. 4. (Running Time: 25200 sec.). (Sammy Keyes Ser.: Bk. 9). (YA). (gr. 8). 2006. 31.95 (978-1-59519-772-6(9)); audio compact disk 49.95 (978-1-59519-773-3(7)) Live Oak Media.

Sammy Keyes & the Runaway Elf. Wendelin Van Draanen. Illus. by Wendelin Van Draanen. 2001. 9.95 (978-0-87499-731-6(3)); 9.95 (978-0-87499-732-3(1)); 9.95 (978-0-87499-733-0(X)); audio compact disk 12.95 (978-0-87499-853-5(0)); audio compact disk 12.95 (978-0-87499-854-2(9)); audio compact disk 12.95 (978-0-87499-855-9(7)) Live Oak Media.

Sammy Keyes & the Runaway Elf. Wendelin Van Draanen. Illus. by Wendelin Van Draanen. 11 vols. (Running Time: 5 hrs.). (Sammy Keyes Ser.: Bk. 4). 2001. pap. bk. 39.95 (978-0-87499-858-0(1)); audio compact disk 12.95 (978-0-87499-856-6(5)) Live Oak Media.

Sammy Keyes & the Runaway Elf. unabr. ed. Wendelin Van Draanen. Read by Tara Sands. 4 CDs. (Running Time: 5 hrs.). (Sammy Keyes Ser.: Bk. 4). (J). 2001. audio compact disk 34.95 (978-0-87499-857-3(3), OAK 015) Live Oak Media.
In this Christmas season story, several strange things are happening and Sammy is called upon to help out.

Sammy Keyes & the Runaway Elf. unabr. ed. Wendelin Van Draanen. Read by Tara Sands. 3 vols. (Running Time: 5 hrs.). (Sammy Keyes Ser.: Bk. 4). (J). (gr. 4-7). 2001. bk. 38.95 (978-0-87499-736-1(4)); 23.95 (978-0-87499-734-7(8), OAK009) Pub: Live Oak Media. Dist(s): AudioGO
Rich Mrs. Landvogt's dog has been kidnapped, little Elyssa Keltner keeps running away from home, Grams' unpleasant neighbor has disappeared & Sam's obnoxious classmate is up to her old tricks.

Sammy Keyes & the Sammy Keys Skeleton Man. Wendelin Van Draanen. Illus. by Wendelin Van Draanen. 2000. 9.95 (978-0-87499-696-8(1)); 9.95 (978-0-87499-697-5(X)); 9.95 (978-0-87499-698-2(8)); audio compact disk 12.95 (978-0-87499-879-5(4)); audio compact disk 12.95 (978-0-87499-880-1(8)); audio compact disk 12.95 (978-0-87499-881-8(6)); audio compact disk 12.95 (978-0-87499-882-5(4)) Live Oak Media.

Sammy Keyes & the Search for Snake Eyes. Wendelin Van Draanen. Illus. by Wendelin Van Draanen. 2003. 9.95 (978-1-59112-268-5(6)); 9.95 (978-1-59112-269-2(4)); 9.95 (978-1-59112-270-8(8)); 9.95 (978-1-59112-271-5(6)); audio compact disk 12.95 (978-1-59112-476-4(X)); audio compact disk 12.95 (978-1-59112-477-1(8)); audio compact disk 12.95 (978-1-59112-478-8(6)); audio compact disk 12.95 (978-1-59112-479-5(4)) Live Oak Media.

Sammy Keyes & the Search for Snake Eyes. Wendelin Van Draanen. Illus. by Wendelin Van Draanen. 11 vols. (Running Time: 6 hrs.). (Sammy Keyes Ser.: Bk. 7). 2003. pap. bk. 36.95 (978-1-59112-273-9(2)); pap. bk. 54.95 (978-1-59112-281-4(3)); audio compact disk 12.95 (978-1-59112-474-0(3)); audio compact disk 12.95 (978-1-59112-475-7(1)) Live Oak Media.

Sammy Keyes & the Search for Snake Eyes. unabr. ed. Wendelin Van Draanen. Read by Tara Sands. 6 CDs. (Running Time: 6 hrs.). (Sammy Keyes Ser.: Bk. 7). (J). 2003. audio compact disk 59.95 (978-1-59112-280-7(5)) Pub: Live Oak Media. Dist(s): AudioGO

Sammy Keyes & the Search for Snake Eyes. unabr. ed. Wendelin Van Draanen. Read by Tara Sands. 4 cass. (Running Time: 6 hrs.). (Sammy Keyes Ser.: Bk. 7). (J). 2005. 31.95 (978-1-59112-272-2(4)) Pub: Live Oak Media. Dist(s): AudioGO

Sammy Keyes & the Sisters of Mercy. Wendelin Van Draanen. Read by Tara Sands. 5 CDs. (Running Time: 5 hrs. 14 mins.). (Sammy Keyes Ser.: Bk. 3). (J). 2001. audio compact disk 44.95 (978-0-87499-837-5(9), OAK 014) Live Oak Media.
Sammy is serving detention time by helping out at St. Mary's church when a valuable cross is stolen. She soon uncovers a heist of enormous proportion.

Sammy Keyes & the Sisters of Mercy. Wendelin Van Draanen. Illus. by Wendelin Van Draanen. 2001. 9.95 (978-0-87499-724-8(0)); 9.95 (978-0-87499-726-2(7)); audio compact disk 12.95 (978-0-87499-836-8(0)) Live Oak Media.

Sammy Keyes & the Sisters of Mercy. Wendelin Van Draanen. Illus. by Wendelin Van Draanen. 11 vols. (Running Time: 5 hrs. 14 mins.). (Sammy Keyes Ser.: Bk. 3). 2001. pap. bk. 49.95 (978-0-87499-838-2(7)); 9.95 (978-0-87499-725-5(9)); 9.95 (978-0-87499-841-2(7)); audio compact disk 12.95 (978-0-87499-833-7(6)); audio compact disk 12.95 (978-0-87499-834-4(4)); audio compact disk 12.95 (978-0-87499-835-1(2)); audio compact disk 12.95 (978-0-87499-842-9(5)) Live Oak Media.

Sammy Keyes & the Sisters of Mercy. unabr. ed. Wendelin Van Draanen. 4 vols. (Running Time: 5 hrs. 14 mins.). (Sammy Keyes Ser.: Bk. 3). 2001. bk. 44.95 (978-0-87499-729-3(1)) Live Oak Media.

Sammy Keyes & the Sisters of Mercy. unabr. ed. Wendelin Van Draanen. 11 vols. (Running Time: 5 hrs. 14 mins.). (Sammy Keyes Ser.: Bk. 3). (J). 2001. pap. bk. 36.95 (978-0-87499-728-6(3)) Live Oak Media.

Sammy Keyes & the Sisters of Mercy. unabr. ed. Wendelin Van Draanen. Read by Tara Sands. 4 cass. (Running Time: 5 hrs. 14 mins.). (Sammy Keyes Ser.: Bk. 3). (J). (gr. 4-7). 2001. 29.95 (978-0-87499-727-9(5), OAK008) Pub: Live Oak Media. Dist(s): AudioGO
Junior-high sleuth Sammy returns for a third adventure. This time out, she's serving detention time by helping out at St. Mary's church when Father Mayhew's valuable ivory cross is stolen. Sammy cuts through the disguises to uncover a heist of enormous proportion.

Sammy Keyes & the Sisters of Mercy, Set. unabr. ed. Wendelin Van Draanen. 4 vols. (Running Time: 5 hrs. 14 mins.). (Sammy Keyes Ser.: Bk. 3). 2001. pap. bk. 49.95 (978-0-87499-730-9(5)) Live Oak Media.

Sammy Keyes & the Skeleton Man. Wendelin Van Draanen. Read by Tara Sands. 4 CDs. (Running Time: 4 hrs. 32 mins.). (Sammy Keyes Ser.: Bk. 2). (J). 2000. audio compact disk 34.95 (978-0-87499-883-2(2), OAK 013) Live Oak Media.
Weird things are happening this Halloween night, Frankenstein is tied to a chair with his head twisted around and Sammy Keyes collides with a skeleton.

Sammy Keyes & the Skeleton Man. Wendelin Van Draanen. Illus. by Wendelin Van Draanen. 11 vols. (Running Time: 4 hrs. 32 mins.). (Sammy Keyes Ser.: Bk. 2). 2000. pap. bk. 39.95 (978-0-87499-884-9(0)) Live Oak Media.

Sammy Keyes & the Skeleton Man, unabr. ed. Wendelin Van Draanen. 14 vols. (Sammy Keyes Ser.: Bk. 2). (J). 2000. pap. bk. & tchr. ed. 43.95 Reading Chest. (978-0-87499-702-6(X)) Live Oak Media.
The live-wire young sleuth catapults into another headlong caper after scotching a murder attempt on Halloween. Nerving themselves to approach a spooky house while out trick-or-treating, Sammy & her friends find the door open, a fire set on the floor & reclusive old Chauncey LeBard tied to a chair. A robbery, it seems, but what's missing? Sammy commences to pry with a will, it's not as if Sammy's life isn't already complicated. She lives illegally with her grandmother in modest seniors-only housing while her mother is pursuing Hollywood dreams, has to fend off a suspicious neighbor & keep up with her school work in the face of multiple distractions.

Sammy Keyes & the Skeleton Man, unabr. ed. Wendelin Van Draanen. 3 vols. (Sammy Keyes Ser.: Bk. 2). (J). (gr. 4-7). 2000. bk. 38.95 (978-0-87499-701-9(1)); pap. bk. 30.95 (978-0-87499-700-2(3)) Live Oak Media.

Sammy Keyes & the Skeleton Man, unabr. ed. Wendelin Van Draanen. Read by Tara Sands. 3 cass. (Running Time: 4 hrs. 32 mins.). (Sammy Keyes Ser.: Bk. 2). (J). (gr. 4-7). 2000. 25.95 (978-0-87499-699-9(6), OAK007) Live Oak Media.

***Sammy Keyes & the Wild Things.** unabr. ed. Wendelin Van Draanen. Narrated by Tara Sands. 6 CDs. (Running Time: 7 hrs. 11 mins.). (YA). (gr. 5-8). 2009. audio compact disk 49.95 (978-1-4301-0732-3(4)) Live Oak Media.

***Sammy Keyes & the Wild Things.** unabr. ed. Wendelin Van Draanen. Narrated by Tara Sands. 6 CDs. (Running Time: 7 hrs. 11 mins.). (Sammy Keyes Ser.: Bk. 11). (YA). (gr. 5-8). 2009. pap. bk. 54.95 (978-1-4301-0733-0(2)) Live Oak Media.

Sammy Keyes Mystery Series. Wendelin Van Draanen. 2 vols. (Sammy Keyes Ser.). (J). (gr. 4-7). 2000. pap. bk. 44.95 (978-0-87499-710-1(0)) Live Oak Media.

Sammy Keyes Series. Wendelin Van Draanen. Illus. by Wendelin Van Draanen. 29 cass. (Running Time: 31 hrs. 46 mins.). 2004. 213.95 (978-0-87499-988-4(X)); audio compact disk 310.95 (978-0-87499-999-0(5)) Live Oak Media.

Sammy Sosa: An Autobiography. Sammy Sosa & Marcos Breton. 5 cass. (Running Time: 7 hrs.). 54.00 (978-1-4025-0380-1(6)) Recorded Bks.

Sammy Sosa: An Autobiography. abr. ed. Sammy Sosa et al. (ENG.). 2005. 14.98 (978-1-59483-465-3(2)) Pub: Hachet Audio. Dist(s): HachBkGrp

Sammy the Seal. abr. ed. Syd Hoff. Illus. by Syd Hoff. (I Can Read Bks.). (J). (ps-3). 2007. 9.99 (978-0-06-133540-2(1), HarperFestival) HarperCollins Pubs.

Sammy the Seal. unabr. ed. Syd Hoff. Narrated by Johnny Heller. 1 cass. (Running Time: 15 mins.). (gr. k up). 2000. 11.00 (978-0-7887-4233-0(7), 96209M5) Recorded Bks.
Tongue-in-cheek humor to capture fresh young imaginations.

Sammy the Seal. unabr. ed. Syd Hoff. Read by Johnny Heller. 1 cass. (Running Time: 15 mins.). (J). 2000. pap. bk. & stu. ed. 32.95 (978-0-7887-4347-4(3), 47138) Recorded Bks.

Sammy the Seal. unabr. ed. Syd Hoff. Illus. by Syd Hoff. (I Can Read Bks.). (J). (ps-3). 2001. 8.99 (978-0-694-70109-4(2)) HarperCollins Pubs.

Sammy the Seal, Class Set. unabr. ed. Syd Hoff. Read by Johnny Heller. 1 cass., 10 bks. (Running Time: 15 mins.). (J). 2000. pap. bk. 168.80 (978-0-7887-4447-1(X), 47138) Recorded Bks.

Sammy's Hamburger Caper, Cassette. Short Stories. 1 cassette. (Running Time: 14 mins). (J). 2006. 4.95 (978-1-57874-277-6(3)) Kaeden Corp.

Sammy's Hamburger Caper, CD. Short Stories. Kathleen Urmston & Craig Urmston. Narrated by Rick Sellers & Wesley McCraw. (Running Time: 24 mins). (J). 2005. audio compact disk 7.95 (978-1-57874-100-7(9)) Kaeden Corp.

Sammy's House. unabr. ed. Kristin Gore. Read by Kirsten Potter. 11 CDs. (Running Time: 13 hrs. 30 mins.). 2008. audio compact disk 120.00 (978-1-4159-4154-6(8)) Random.

Sammy's Moving, Cassette. Short Stories. 1 cassette. (Running Time: 14 mins). (J). 2006. 4.95 (978-1-57874-278-3(1)) Kaeden Corp.

Sammy's Moving, CD. Short Stories. Kathleen Urmston & Karen Evans. Narrated by Rick Sellers & Wesley McCraw. 1 CD. (Running Time: 19 mins.). (J). 2005. audio compact disk 7.95 (978-1-57874-101-4(7)) Kaeden Corp.

Sammy's Slippery Day, Cassette. Short Stories. 1 cassette. (Running Time: 14 mins). (J). 2006. 4.95 (978-1-57874-280-6(3)) Kaeden Corp.

Sammy's Slippery Day, CD. Short Stories. Kathleen Urmston & Craig Urmston. Narrated by Rick Sellers & Wesley McCraw. 1 CD. (Running Time: 22 mins.). (J). 2005. audio compact disk 7.95 (978-1-57874-103-8(3)) Kaeden Corp.

Samoan - English Mini-Book Set with Audio. Claudia Schwalm. 1999. pap. bk. 21.95 (978-1-57371-036-7(9)) Cultural Cnnect.

Sample Forms CD. Prod. by California Association of REALTORS(r). 2007. audio compact disk (978-1-934858-03-5(X)) Real Estate Bus.

Sample Safety Plans, Vol. 9. rev. ed. Ed. by Asper Publishers Staff. 2005. audio compact disk 174.50 (978-0-7355-5554-9(0), Aspen) WoltersKlu.

Sample Safety Plans Cd 8 0, Vol. 8. rev. ed. Kirk. 2004. audio compact disk 174.50 (978-0-7355-5079-7(4), Aspen) WoltersKlu.

Sampler. 1 cass. (Running Time: 1 hr.). 5.00 (SAM) ZBS Ind.
Scenes from Fourth Tower, Moon, Incredible Adventures, Stars & Stuff.

Sampler: Elements of Literature. Holt, Rinehart and Winston Staff. 1997. 11.33 (978-0-03-050844-8(4)) Holt McDoug.

Sampler Five. 1 cass. (Running Time: 36 min.). (J). 9.95 (978-0-939065-45-5(2), GW1049) Gentle Wind.
Songs & stories for children.

Sampler Four. 1 cass. (Running Time: 39 min.). (J). 9.95 (978-0-939065-35-6(5), GW1039) Gentle Wind.

Sampler of American Humor. Narrated by Flo Gibson et al. 2007. audio compact disk 16.95 (978-1-55685-914-4(7)) Audio Bk Con.

Sampler of American Humor. unabr. ed. Mark Twain et al. Read by Grover Gardner et al. 2 cass. (Running Time: 3 hrs.). Incl. Carrie's Comedy. Alden.; How I Killed a Bear. Warner.; Nothing to Wear. W. A. Butler.; Oon Criteek de Bernhardt. Field.; Pelican. Wharton.; Pigs is Pigs. E. P. Butler.; Story of Speech. Mark Twain.; Story of the Old Ram. Mark Twain.; 2007. 14.95 (978-1-55685-028-8(X)) Audio Bk Con.
These rib-ticklers inclusde Twain's "The Story of the Old Ram" & "The Story of a Speech", E.P. Butler's "Pigs is Pigs", W.A. butler's "Nothing to Wear", Warner's "How I Killed a Bear", Field's "Oon Criteek de Bernhardt", Alden's "Carrie's Comedy", & Wharton's "The Pelican".

Sampler '89. 1 cass. (Running Time: 48 min.). 1989. 9.98 Windham Hill.

Sam's Letters to Jennifer. unabr. ed. James Patterson. Read by Anne Heche & Jane Alexander. (ENG.). 2005. 14.98 (978-1-59483-235-2(8)) Pub: Hachet Audio. Dist(s): HachBkGrp

Sam's Letters to Jennifer. unabr. ed. James Patterson. Read by Anne Heche & Jane Alexander. (Running Time: 4 hrs.). (Replay Edition Ser.). (ENG.). 2007. audio compact disk 14.98 (978-1-60024-109-3(3)) Pub: Hachet Audio. Dist(s): HachBkGrp

Sam's Quest for the Crimson Crystal. Ben Furman. Narrated by Pat Heiss. (J). 2007. audio compact disk 28.95 (978-0-9778731-1-1(0)) Black Hawk Pr.

Sam's Seasons/Seasons. Steck-Vaughn Staff. 1996. (978-0-8172-6462-8(0)) SteckVau.

Sam's Song. Reggie Simon & Eva Schossleitner. 2 cass. (Running Time: 0.140). 2003. audio compact disk 20.00 (978-0-9724906-1-0(2)) Softy Paw.

Samson Agonistes see Poetry of John Milton

Samuel: Moroni's Young Warrior, abr. ed. Clair Poulson. 2 cass. (Running Time: 2 hrs.). (gr. 6-12). 1993. 11.98 (978-1-55503-596-9(5), 0700894) Covenant Comms.
Youth fiction.

Samuel: Thunder in Paradise. Clair Poulson. 2 cass. 1996. 11.98 Set. (978-1-55503-922-6(7), 07001363) Covenant Comms.
An exciting book of Mormon adventure.

Samuel Adams. Ira Stoll. Read by Paul Boehmer. (Playaway Adult Nonfiction Ser.). (ENG.). 2009. 64.99 (978-1-60812-548-7(3)) Find a World.

Samuel Adams: A Life. unabr. ed. Ira Stoll. Narrated by Paul Boehmer. 9 CDs. (Running Time: 10 hrs. 30 mins. 0 sec.). (ENG.). 2008. audio compact disk 69.99 (978-1-4001-3978-1(3)) Pub: Tantor Media. Dist(s): IngramPubServ

Samuel Adams: A Life. unabr. ed. Ira Stoll. Read by Paul Boehmer. 1 MP3-CD. (Running Time: 10 hrs. 30 mins. 0 sec.). (ENG.). 2008. 24.99 (978-1-4001-5978-9(4)); audio compact disk 34.99 (978-1-4001-0978-4(7)) Pub: Tantor Media. Dist(s): IngramPubServ

Samuel Adams - Father of the American Revolution. Annette Francis. Prod. by Nigel Matthews. 1 cass. (Running Time: 45 min.). 1996. pap. bk. 14.95 (978-1-889086-05-7(3), SA-201); 9.95 (978-1-889086-04-0(5), SA-202) Pan Mass.
A biography of Boston's fiery patriot & master propagandist, Samuel Adams, set against the turbulence of his time...plus recitations of his most famous speeches & writings.

Samuel & the Butterflies. unabr. ed. Perf. by Mike Anderson. 1 cass. (Running Time: 47 min.). (J). (gr. k-6). 1997. 10.00 (978-1-929050-07-9(0)) MW Prods.
Original stories & traditional songs for children.

Samuel Blink & the Forbidden Forest. Matt Haig. Read by Simon Vance. (Running Time: 24780 sec.). (J). (gr. 4-7). 2007. audio compact disk 34.95 (978-0-545-00524-1(8)) Scholastic Inc.

Samuel Blink & the Forbidden Forest. unabr. ed. Matt Haig. Read by Simon Vance. (J). 2007. 49.99 (978-1-60252-789-8(X)) Find a World.

Samuel Blink & the Forbidden Forest. 2nd ed. Matt Haig. Read by Simon Vance. (Running Time: 24780 sec.). (ENG.). (J). (gr. 4-7). 2007. audio compact disk 64.95 (978-0-545-00528-9(0)) Scholastic Inc.

Samuel de Champlain: Explorer of the Great Lakes Region & Founder of Quebec. unabr. ed. Josepha Sherman. Read by Eileen Stevens. (Running Time: 2 hrs.). (Library of Explorers & Exploration Ser.). 2009. 39.97 (978-1-4233-8197-6(1), 9781423381976, BADLE); 39.97 (978-1-4233-8196-9(3), 9781423381969, Brlnc Audio MP3 Lib); 19.99 (978-1-4233-8195-2(5), 9781423381952, Brilliance MP3); audio compact disk 39.97 (978-1-4233-8194-5(7), 9781423381945, BriAudCD Unabrid); audio compact disk 19.99 (978-1-4233-8193-8(9), 9781423381938, Bril Audio CD Unabri) Brilliance Audio.

Samuel de Champlain: Father of New France. unabr. ed. Samuel Eliot Morison. Read by Richard Brown. 5 cass. (Running Time: 7 hrs. 30 mins.). 1990. 40.00 (978-0-7366-1776-5(0), 2615) Books on Tape.
Samuel de Champlain is today one of the least known explorers of the New World, but in his day he was a great force in North America. He charted the Atlantic coast from Newfoundland to the tip of Cape Cod & explored routes to the west. He founded Quebec & established peaceful relations with the Algonquin & Huron Indians. For 30 years he did everything he could to make French settlements in Canada permanent & self-sufficient. He was also an artist, a mapmaker so accurate that his charts can still be used today, & a noted writer. But most of all, Champlain was a leader, a man who inspired loyalty. Had France perservered in Canada, Champlain would be the Canadian national father figure. He is well worth remembering.

Samuel, Gadianton's Foe. Clair Poulson. 2 cass. 11.98 (978-1-55503-662-1(7), 0700967) Covenant Comms.
An exciting, fast-paced adventure.

Samuel I & II Commentary: Through the Bible with Chuck Missler. Chuck Missler. 1 MP3 CD-ROM. (Running Time: 16 hours). (Chuck Missler Commentaries). 2003. cd-rom 39.95 (978-1-57821-211-8(1)) Koinonia Hse.
*"And all this assembly shall know that the LORD saveth not with sword and spear: for the battle [is] the LORD'S, and he will give you into our hands." And it came to pass, when the Philistine arose, and came and drew nigh to meet David, that David hasted, and ran toward the army to meet the Philistine..." -1 Samuel 17:47-48This MP3 is compatible with both Windows and Macintosh operating systems and includes: * Over 10 hours of Verse-by-Verse audio teaching through the books of I & II Samuel as MP3 files.* Extensive searchable study notes as PDF files.*

Samuel Konkin III: Counter Economics. 2 cass. (Running Time: 2 hrs.). (Remanent Tapes). 18.00 (R303A & B) Freeland Pr.
Covers libertarian strategies vs politics, gradulism principle, statism vs counter-economics.

Samuel Morse & the Telegraph. David Seidman et al. Illus. by Rod Whigham. (Inventions & Discovery Ser.). (ENG.). (gr. 3-4). 2007. audio compact disk 6.95 (978-1-4296-1119-0(7)) CapstoneDig.

Samuel Morse & the Telegraph (INK Audiocassette) (Inventions & Discovery Ser.). (ENG.). 2007. audio compact disk 5.95 (978-0-7368-7989-7(7)) CapstoneDig.

Samuel Skinner: The World's Transportation Needs. (Running Time: 1 hr.). 1989. 11.95 (K0700B090, HarperThor) HarpC GBR.

Samuel Taylor Coleridge: The Rime of the Ancient Mariner. Samuel Taylor Coleridge. Read by Douglas Leach. 1 cass. 10.95 (ECN 179) J Norton Pubs.
Coleridge explores one of the favourite themes of his earlier discursive poems & manages to achieve the tone of a genuine folkballad.

Samurai. Barry Sadler. Read by Charlton Griffin. Abr. by Odin Westgaard. 2 vols. (Casca Ser.: No. 19). 2004. (978-1-58807-559-8(1)); audio compact disk (978-1-58807-724-0(1)) Am Pubng Inc.

Samurai. abr. ed. Barry Sadler. Read by Charlton Griffin. Abr. by Odin Westgaard. 2 vols. (Casca Ser.: No. 19). 2004. audio compact disk 25.00 (978-1-58807-293-1(2)) Am Pubng Inc.

Samurai. abr. ed. Barry Sadler. Read by Carol Eason. Abr. by Odin Westgaard. 2 vols. (Casca Ser.: No. 19). 2004. 18.00 (978-1-58807-119-4(7)) Am Pubng Inc.

***Samurai.** unabr. ed. Shusaku Endo. Narrated by David Holt. (Running Time: 12 hrs. 17 mins. 18 sec.). (ENG.). 2010. audio compact disk 36.99 (978-1-59859-743-1(4), SpringWater) Oasis Audio.

Samurai Audiopack - Bushido , the Book of 5 Rings , & Zen Mind Control. Inazo Nitobe et al. Tr. by Urara Tsukamoto. Narrated by Urara Tsukamoto & Ross M. Armetta. 5 CDs. (Running Time: 5 hrs. 30 Mins. Approx.). 2005. audio compact disk 25.99 (978-1-59733-204-0(6), Martial Strat) InfoFount.
Learn the theory and discipline of martial arts ? KNOW HOW TO WIN ! Martial Strategist?s Samurai Pack (5CD) set is a combination of popular Japanese Martial Strategy and Spiritual titles combined in a discounted packageBushido ?The Soul of Japan (3CD) outlines the fundamentals of Oriental marital training, virtue, and philosophy. This audiobook explains the discipline, physical, and moral training of the Japanese warrior and its integration into Japanese culture. It can help you create successful, honorable, and respectable, actions and campaigns.Starting at 13 years old, Musashi Miyamoto fought over 60 life and death battles - never losing! Gorin No Sho - The Book of 5 Rings (1CD) describes the fundamentals of Kendo and marital training as proven successful in actual combat by Japan's Greatest Samurai - Musashi Miyamoto. Learn about black spots, rhythms, positioning, psyching your opponent out and much more - you?ll know winning strategies.This audiobook explains practical combat theories, training, and execution. It is an original translation and absolutely unique - IT IS ACCURATELY AND MINIMALLY INTERPRETED! This is the only truly unabridged audiobook CD version available of this classic master work. Zen Mind Control (1CD) is chapter 8 (Zen Mind Training) from Zen, The Religion of the Samurai. It is a straightforward, non dogmatic and practical study of Zen Buddhism that is accessible and USEFUL. This audiobook can change your life. Martial Strategists are strategy specialists. They obtain, translate, and make the most useful military and strategy editions - unequaled for practical application, and value.Contents (partial) Bushido as an Ethical System; Sources of Bushido; Rectitude or Justice; Courage, the Spirit of Daring and Bearing; Benevolence, the Feeling of Distress; Politeness; Veracity or Truthfulness; Honor; The Duty of Loyalty; Education and Training of a Samurai; Self-Control; The Institutions of Suicide and Redress; The Sword, the Soul of the Samurai; The Training and Position of Woman. The Book of 5 Rings includes The Ground Chapter, The Water Chapter, The Fire Chapter, The Wind Chapter, The Ku / Sky Chapter. Zen Mind Control includes The First Step in the Mental Training; The Next Step in the Mental Training; The Third Step in the Mental Training; Zazen, or the Sitting in Meditation; The Breathing Exercise of the Yogi; Calmness of Mind; Zazen and the Forgetting of Self; Zen and Supernatural Power; True Dhyana; Let Go of Your Idle Thoughts; 'The Five Ranks of Merit'.More information on the individual titles and complete audiobook sets is available at www.InfoFount.com.

***Samurai Kids #1: White Crane: White Crane.** unabr. ed. Sandy Fussell. (Running Time: 5 hrs.). (Samurai Kids Ser.). 2011. 19.99 (978-1-4558-0103-9(8), 9781455801039, Candlewick Bril); 39.97 (978-1-4558-0104-6(6), 9781455801046, Candlewick Bril); 19.99 (978-1-4558-0100-8(3), 9781455801008, Candlewick Bril); 39.97 (978-1-4558-0101-5(1), 9781455801015, Candlewick Bril); audio compact disk 19.99 (978-1-4558-0098-8(8), 9781455800988, Candlewick Bril); audio compact disk 49.97 (978-1-4558-0099-5(6), 9781455800995, Candlewick Bril) Brilliance Audio.

***Samurai Kids #2: Owl Ninja: Owl Ninja.** unabr. ed. Sandy Fussell. (Running Time: 6 hrs.). (Samurai Kids Ser.). 2011. 19.99 (978-1-4558-0110-7(0), 9781455801107, Candlewick Bril); 39.97 (978-1-4558-0111-4(9), 9781455801114, Candlewick Bril); 19.99 (978-1-4558-0107-7(0), 9781455801077, Candlewick Bril); 39.97 (978-1-4558-0108-4(9), 9781455801084, Candlewick Bril); audio compact disk 19.99 (978-1-4558-0105-3(4), 9781455801053, Candlewick Bril); audio compact disk 49.97 (978-1-4558-0106-0(2), 9781455801060, Candlewick Bril) Brilliance Audio.

Samurai Shortstop. unabr. ed. Alan Gratz. Read by Arthur Morey. 6 CDs. (Running Time: 7 hrs. 21 mins.). (YA). (gr. 7 up). 2006. audio compact disk 50.00 (978-0-7393-3624-3(X), Listening Lib); 40.00 (978-0-7393-3629-8(0), Listening Lib) Pub: Random Audio Pubg. Dist(s): Random
From his first day at boarding school, Toyo Shimada sees how upperclassmen make a sport out of terrorizing the first-years. Still, he's taken aback when the seniors keep him from trying out for the baseball team - especially after he sees their current shortstop. Toyo isn't afraid to prove himself; He's more troubled by his uncle's recent suicide. Although Uncle Koji's defiant death was supposedly heroic, it has made Toyo question many things about his family's samurai background. And worse, Toyo fears that his father may be next. It all has something to do with - the way of the warrior - but Toyo doesn't understand even after his father agrees to teach it to him. As the gulf between them grows wider, Toyo searches desperately for a way to prove there is a place for his family's samurai values in modern Japan. Baseball might just be the answer, but will his father ever accept a "Western" game that stands for everything he despises?.

Samurai Shortstop. unabr. ed. Alan Gratz. Read by Arthur Morey. (Running Time: 26460 sec.). (ENG.). (J). (gr. 7-12). 2006. audio compact disk 39.00 (978-0-7393-3639-7(8), Listening Lib) Pub: Random Audio Pubg. Dist(s): Random

Samvarga Upasana. Swami Jyotirmayananda. 1 cass. (Running Time: 1 hr.). 1990. 12.99 Yoga Res Foun.

San Andreas. unabr. ed. Alistair MacLean. Read by Alistair Maydon. 8 cass. (Running Time: 10 hrs.). 2001. 69.95 (978-1-85089-752-1(2), 90073) Pub: ISIS Audio GBR. Dist(s): Ulverscroft US
Without warning the lights aboard the ship, the San Andreas, died. This is no ordinary power cut, however. Somebody aboard is intent on sabotage.

San Antonio. Scripts. Hank Mitchum. 5 CDs. (Running Time: 6 hrs). (Stagecoach Ser.: No. 25). 2005. 14.99 (978-1-58807-869-8(8)) Am Pubng Inc.
Only a hard case like Wolf Bixler could lead the children of President Tejada across the savage wilderness to safety in San Antonio. If he succeeded he'd collect a fortune in gold. But rebels and road agents stood in his way as did U.S. Marshall Stu Jarrell who had sworn to capture Bixler dead or alive.

San Antonio. unabr. ed. Hank Mitchum. Read by Charlie O'Dowd. 4 cass. (Running Time: 5 hrs. 20 mins.). (Stagecoach Ser.: No. 25). 2001. 25.00 (978-1-58807-081-4(6)) Am Pubng Inc.
As Mexico seethed with turmoil, American convict, Wolf Bixler, awaited the hangman's noose in a stinking prison south of the border. Then, unexpectedly, he was offered a chance to escape with his life. Only a hard case like Bixler could lead the children of President Tejada across hundreds of miles of savage wilderness to safety in San Antonio. If he succeeded, he'd collect a fortune in gold. But rebels and road agents stood in his way, as did U.S. Marshall Stu Jarrell, who had sworn to capture Bixler alive if possible, dead if necessary. And even if Bixler did make it to San Antonio with his charges, gun trouble awaited him there - more than even he, a man who lived by and for violence, had ever bargained for.

San Antonio Riverwalk Royalty Free Images. Marques Vickers. 2003. audio compact disk 29.95 (978-0-9706530-6-2(9), 1) Marquis Pubng.

San Francisco: Tower to Tower - Square to Square. unabr. ed. Andrew Flack. Read by Barbara Duff & Denis J. Sullivan. 1 cass. (Running Time: 1 hr.). (Day Ranger Walking Adventures on Audio Cassette Ser.). 1990. 19.95 (978-1-877894-04-6(4)) Day Ranger.
Scripted dialogue & music to accompany an original walking route of different neighborhoods of San Francisco. Uses first hand accounts, eyewitness stories & brief excerpts of identified literature. Detailed maps included.

San Francisco - I Love It! Pace International Research, Inc. Staff. 1984. 3.25 (978-0-89209-077-8(4)) Pace Grp Intl.

San Francisco Earthquake & Fire. Kenneth Bruce. 1 cass. (Running Time: 1 hr.). Dramatization. (Excursions in History Ser.). 12.50 Alpha Tape.

San Francisco Is Burning: The Untold Story of the 1906 Earthquake & Fires. unabr. ed. Dennis Smith. Narrated by Alan Sklar. (Running Time: 12 hrs. 30 mins. 0 sec.). (ENG.). 2005. audio compact disk 34.99 (978-1-4001-0179-5(4)); audio compact disk 22.99 (978-1-4001-5179-0(1)); audio compact disk 69.99 (978-1-4001-3179-2(0)) Pub: Tantor Media. Dist(s): IngramPubServ

San Francisco Selections, '86. 12 cass. (Running Time: 90 min. per cass.). 1986. 120.00 incl. vinyl storage binder. Amer Coll Phys.
Includes Aggressive Management of Acute Myocardial Infarction; Prevention & Management of Stroke; New Developments in Management & Treatment of Diabetes; Fluid & Electrolyte Disturbances in the Critically Ill Patient; Thyroid Disease; Management of Severe & Refractory Hypertension; & more.

San Joaquin Freshwater Marsh Reserve. Hosted by Nancy Pearlman. 1 cass. (Running Time: 28 min.). 10.00 (220) Educ Comm CA.

San Juan, Suite II. Perf. by Michael Gettel. 1 cass. 9.98; audio compact disk 15.98 Lifedance.
Piano, bass & some vocals. Uses impressionistic tone poems to capture the essence of the misty San Juan Islands in Washington State. Demo CD or cassette available.

San Juan Suite. Perf. by Michael Gettel. 1 cass. 9.98 (MPC2701); audio compact disk 14.98 CD. Miramar Images.
Inspired by the beauty of the Pacific Northwest's San Juan Islands. Gettel uses the piano as a photographer would use a camera, gently mixing in the natural sounds of the Puget Sound.

San Juan Suite. Perf. by Michael Gettel. 1 cass., 1 CD. 7.98 (NAR 45596); audio compact disk 12.78 CD Jewel box. (NAR 45596) NewSound.

San Marco, 1527-1740. Gloriae Dei Cantores. 2 CDs. (Running Time: 90 mins.). 1995. audio compact disk 33.95 (978-1-55725-093-3(6), GDCD014) Paraclete MA.

San Patracio Battalion. 1 cass. 10.00 Esstee Audios.
The story of American deserters in the Mexican War.

San Pedro Ring. unabr. ed. Elliot Conway. Read by Steven Crossley. 3 cass. (Running Time: 4 hrs.). 2000. 34.95 (978-1-86042-544-8(5), 25445) Pub: Soundings Ltd GBR. Dist(s): Ulverscroft US

Sana Nuestra Tierra. unabr. ed. Marcos Witt. (SPA.). 2003. 9.99 (978-0-8297-4424-8(X)) Pub: Vida Pubs. Dist(s): Zondervan

Sanando las Heridas Del Alma: Conozca La Clave Para Fortalecer Su Autoestima Y Experimentar Paz Interior. Rafael Ayala. 2003. (978-1-931059-36-7(5)) Taller del Exito.

Sanando las Heridas del Alma. Rafael Ayala. 2 cass. (Running Time: 2 hrs.).Tr. of Healing the Soul. (SPA.). 2002. 20.00 (978-958-95949-9-5(9)) Taller del Exito.
Helps you develop a stronger self-esteem.

Sanatana Dharma. unabr. ed. Swami Amar Jyoti. 1 cass. (Satsangs of Swami Amar Jyoti). 1997. 9.95 (978-0-933572-25-6(5), Q-25) Truth Consciousness.
Man in relationship to God is Sanatana Dharma, the universal, eternal religion. Stages of spiritual practice.

Sanate a ti Mismo. Betty L. Randolph. 1 cass. (Health Ser.). (SPA.). 1989. bk. 9.98 (978-1-55909-189-3(4), 27E) Randolph Tapes.
Presents a program in spanish. Features male-female voice tracks with the right-left brain.

Sanctification. Gordon Clark. 1 cass. (Lectures on the Holy Spirit: No. 4). 5.00 Trinity Found.

Sanctification. Michael Pearl. 3 CDs. 2003. audio compact disk (978-1-892112-48-4(5)) No Greater Joy.

Sanctification of Time in the Third Millennium, Morning & Evening Prayer, with Night Prayer. Music by Evensong Vocal Ensemble Staff. 2001. audio compact disk 14.95 (978-0-9715123-5-1(3)) Watchmaker Pr.

Sanctification/Sin No More. Michael Pearl. 1 cd. (Running Time: 10 hrs, 45 mins). 2002. (978-1-892112-94-1(9)) No Greater Joy.

Sanction of the Victims. Ayn Rand. Read by Leonard Peikoff. 1 cass. (Running Time: 90 min.). 1981. 12.95 (978-1-56114-057-2(0), LP06C) Second Renaissance.
The talk Ayn Rand was scheduled to deliver before she died, presented movingly in her stead - & in tribute to her - by Leonard Peikoff. In it she tells businessmen that by financing the universities which preach the destruction of capitalism, they are paying the bill for their own enslavement.

Sanction of the Victims. Ayn Rand. Read by Ayn Rand. 1 cass., 1 video. (Running Time: 52 min.). 1981. 17.95 (978-1-56114-115-9(1), AR34C); cass. & video 39.95 (R35G) Second Renaissance.

Sanctity. Thomas Merton. 1 cass. 8.95 (AA2459) Credence Commun.

Sanctity of Life. 2004. audio compact disk 14.00 (978-1-57972-666-9(6)) Insight Living.

Sanctity of Life: The Inescapable Issue, Charles R. Swindoll. 2 cass. 1998. 11.95 (978-1-57972-146-6(X)) Insight Living.

Sanctuary see Selected Short Stories by Edith Wharton

Sanctuary. Beverly Lewis & David Lewis. 2 cass. (Running Time: 180 min.). 2001. 15.99 (978-0-7642-2512-3(X)) Bethany Hse.

Sanctuary. abr. ed. Faye Kellerman. Read by Buck Schirner. 2 cass. (Running Time: 3 hrs.). (Peter Decker & Rina Lazarus Novel Ser.). 2000. 7.95 (978-1-57815-022-9(1), 1006, Media Bks Audio) Media Bks NJ.
The intrigue of the international diamond trade challenge a Jewish family.

***Sanctuary.** abr. ed. Beverly Lewis. Narrated by Aimee Lilly. (Amish Country Crossroads Ser.). (ENG.). 2010. 12.98 (978-1-59644-142-2(9), christaudio) christianaud.

Sanctuary. unabr. ed. Faye Kellerman. Read by Bernadette Dunne. 9 cass. (Running Time: 13 hrs. 30 min.). (Peter Decker & Rina Lazarus Novel Ser.). 1996. 72.00 sale to libraries only. (978-0-7366-3355-0(3), 4006) Books on Tape.
When a successful Los Angeles diamond dealer & his family disappear, everyone wants to make it look like they've run out on their past. But business is solid & profitable. For detective Peter Decker, the facts don't add up. Why run if the present is so good? Decker is stumped, because the family left their valuables, too. Then another diamond dealer turns up dead in New York. Decker & his wife Rina follow a maze of intrigue that leads them around the world...& dumps them off dangerously close to their own backyard.

Sanctuary. unabr. ed. Raymond Khoury. Read by Richard Ferrone. 12 CDs. (Running Time: 16 hrs.). (ENG.). (gr. 8 up). 2007. audio compact disk 39.95 (978-0-14-314233-1(X), PengAudBks) Penguin Grp USA.

Sanctuary. unabr. ed. Nora Roberts. Read by Sandra Burr. (Running Time: 15 hrs.). 2008. 39.25 (978-1-4233-7899-0(7), 9781423378990, Brlnc Audio MP3 Lib); 39.25 (978-1-4233-7901-0(2), 9781423379010, BADLE); 24.95 (978-1-4233-7898-3(9), 9781423378983, Brilliance MP3); 24.95 (978-1-4233-7900-3(4), 9781423379003, BAD); audio compact disk 117.25 (978-1-4233-7897-6(0), 9781423378976, BriAudCD Unabrid); audio compact disk 34.95 (978-1-4233-7896-9(2), 9781423378969, Bril Audio CD Unabri) Brilliance Audio.

Sanctuary Sparrow. Ellis Peters, pseud. Perf. by Derek Jacobi & Sean Pertwee. 1 cass. (Running Time: 1 hr. 20 min.). Dramatization. (Chronicles of Brother Cadfael Ser.: Vol. 7). 1999. 9.95 (978-1-56938-268-4(9), AMP-2689) Acorn Inc.
Cadfael is back on the trail of treachery & murder when the town's goldsmith is robbed & left for dead, & the townspeople launch a witch hunt.

Sanctuary Sparrow. unabr. ed. Ellis Peters. Read by Vanessa Benjamin. 6 cass. (Running Time: 8 hrs. 30 mins.). (Chronicles of Brother Cadfael Ser.: Vol. 7). 1998. 44.95 (978-0-7861-1269-2(7), 2205) Blckstn Audio.
In the gentle Shrewsbury spring of 1140, the midnight matins at the Benedictine abbey suddenly reverberate with an unholy sound - a hunt in full cry. Pursued by a drunken mob, the quarry is running for its life. When the frantic creature bursts into the nave to claim sanctuary, Brother Cadfael finds himself fighting off armed townsmen to save a terrified young man.

Sanctuary Sparrow. unabr. ed. Ellis Peters, pseud. Narrated by Patrick Tull. 7 cass. (Running Time: 9 hrs. 30 mins.). (Chronicles of Brother Cadfael Ser.: Vol. 7). 1993. 60.00 (978-1-55690-806-4(7), 93115E7) Recorded Bks.
In the middle of the abbey's evening services, an angry mob pursues a young boy into the sacred peace of the sanctuary. Terrified & in tatters, he clutches at the altar-cloth, grasping for mercy in the only place he might find it.

***Sanctuary Sparrow: The Seventh Chronicle of Brother Cadfael.** unabr. ed. Ellis Peters. Read by Vanessa Benjamin. (Running Time: 8 hrs. 30 mins.). (Chronicles of Brother Cadfael Ser.). 2010. 29.95 (978-1-4417-5167-6(X)); audio compact disk 76.00 (978-1-4417-5165-2(3)) Blckstn Audio.

Sanctus. Jerry Barnes. 1995. audio compact disk 14.95 (978-0-8198-6986-9(4), 332-326) Pauline Bks.

Sand. unabr. collector's ed. Will James. Read by Connor O'Brien. 7 cass. (Running Time: 10 hrs. 30 mins.). 1999. 48.00 (978-0-7366-4402-0(4), 4863) Books on Tape.
This is the story about "sand" the gumption it takes to tackle the challenges of life. Set in the Great Plains, the characters are cowboys & horses. The heroine is the daughter of an old rancher & all the cowboys dream of leading the conquered black stallion to her. And the heart of the story is the hero's long duel with the horse & how "the little grain of sand within him" starts to grow.

Sand Against the Tide, Bk. 2. unabr. ed. Paul Bishop. Read by Maynard Villers. 8 cass. (Running Time: 10 hrs. 30 min.). 1996. 49.95 (978-1-55686-699-9(2)) Books in Motion.
This is the sequel to Citadel Run, the story of the L.A.P.D. & Calico Jack Walker. He retires & goes into the fishing charter business, a decision that later becomes a nightmare.

Sand Castle. Rita Mae Brown. Read by Marguerite Gavin. (Playaway Adult Fiction Ser.). (ENG.). 2009. 39.99 (978-1-60812-529-6(7)) Find a World.

Sand Castle. unabr. ed. Rita Mae Brown. Narrated by Marguerite Gavin. (Running Time: 1 hr. 30 mins. 0 sec.). (ENG.). 2008. audio compact disk 19.99 (978-1-4001-5821-8(4)); audio compact disk 39.99 (978-1-4001-3821-0(3)) Pub: Tantor Media. Dist(s): IngramPubServ

Sand Castle. unabr. ed. Rita Mae Brown. Read by Marguerite Gavin. 2 CDs. (Running Time: 1 hr. 30 mins. 0 sec.). (ENG.). 2008. audio compact disk 19.99 (978-1-4001-0821-3(7)) Pub: Tantor Media. Dist(s): IngramPubServ

Sand Castle Contest. Steck-Vaughn Staff. 1996. (978-0-8172-6465-9(5)) SteckVau.

Sand County Almanac. Aldo Leopold. Read by Stewart L. Udall. 2 cass. (Running Time: 3 hrs.). 1988. 16.95 (978-0-939643-11-0(1), NrthWrd Bks) TandN Child.
Classic collection of essays by the father of the land.

Sand County Almanac. abr. ed. Aldo Leopold & Aldo Leopold. Read by Stewart L. Udall. (Running Time: 9900 sec.). (ENG.). 2006. audio compact disk 24.95 (978-1-59887-073-2(4), 1598870734) Pub: HighBridge. Dist(s): Workman Pub

Sand Creek Massacre. 10.00 Esstee Audios.
Col Chivington's brutal murders - why, how, where, are all explored.

Sand Daughter. Sarah Bryant. 2008. 99.95 (978-1-4079-0072-8(2)); audio compact disk 109.95 (978-1-4079-0073-5(0)) Pub: Soundings Ltd GBR. Dist(s): Ulverscroft US

Sand Pebbles, Pt. 1. unabr. collector's ed. Richard McKenna. Read by Wolfram Kandinsky. 9 cass. (Running Time: 13 hrs. 30 min.). 1986. 72.00 (978-0-7366-0552-6(5), 1526-A) Books on Tape.
It helps to remember that China was a basket case in 1900. Disease, famine, opium, pirates, pestilence, warlords, rickshaws, Tongs, slaves - they really existed. Western nations found no law there, so they made their own. Enter Jake Holman, crewman on Sao Pablo, a gunboat far up the Yangtze. Jake is navy through & through - but with a difference. He loves China & its people & that is where the conflict starts.

Sand Pebbles, Pt. 2. unabr. collector's ed. Richard McKenna. Read by Wolfram Kandinsky. 7 cass. (Running Time: 10 hrs. 30 min.). 1986. 56.00 (978-0-7366-0553-3(3), 1526-B) Books on Tape.
China was a basket case in 1900 - disease, famine, opium, pirates, warlords, slaves - & the American Navy organized patrols deep into China. Enter Jake Holamn, crewman on "San Pablo," a gunboat far up th Yangtze. Jake is Navy through & through - but with a difference. He loves China & its people & that is where the conflict starts.

***Sand Sharks.** unabr. ed. Margaret Maron. Narrated by C. J. Critt. 8 cass. (Running Time: 9 hrs.). 2009. 72.75 (978-1-4407-2006-2(1)) Recorded Bks.

***Sand Sharks.** unabr. ed. Margaret Maron. Narrated by C. J. Critt. 1 Playaway. (Running Time: 9 hrs.). (Deborah Knott Mystery Ser.: Bk. 15). 2009. 59.75 (978-1-4407-2009-3(6)) Recorded Bks.

***Sand Sharks.** unabr. ed. Margaret Maron. Narrated by C. J. Critt. 8 CDs. (Running Time: 9 hrs.). (Deborah Knott Mystery Ser.: Bk. 15). 2009. audio compact disk 92.75 (978-1-4407-2007-9(X)) Recorded Bks.

***Sand Sharks.** unabr. collector's ed. Margaret Maron. Narrated by C. J. Critt. 8 CDs. (Running Time: 9 hrs.). (Deborah Knott Mystery Ser.: Bk. 15). 2009. audio compact disk 51.95 (978-1-4407-2008-6(8)) Recorded Bks.

Sandals: Ephesians 6:15, 646. Ed Young. 1988. 4.95 (978-0-7417-1646-0(1), 646) Win Walk.

Sandburg Out Loud: A Selection of Carl Sandburg's Rotabaga Stories, Poetry, & Folksongs Collected in the Amercan Songbag. As told by Carol Birch et al. Music by David Holt. (Running Time: 1 hr. 5 mins.). 2002. 12.00 (978-0-87483-677-6(8)); audio compact disk 16.95 (978-0-87483-676-9(X)) Pub: August Hse. Dist(s): Natl Bk Netwk

Sandcastles. unabr. ed. Luanne Rice. 8 cass. (Running Time: 12 hrs.). 2006. 72.00 (978-1-4159-3071-7(6)); audio compact disk 90.00 (978-1-4159-3072-4(4)) Books on Tape.

Sandfloor Cathedral. Contrib. by Lee Johnson. 2007. DVD & audio compact disk 19.99 (978-5-557-57974-2(5)) Vision Vid PA.

Sandhoff Disease - A Bibliography & Dictionary for Physicians, Patients, & Genome Researchers. Compiled by Icon Group International, Inc. Staff. 2007. ring bd. 28.95 (978-0-497-11290-5(6)) Icon Grp.

sandia gigantesca Audio CD. Benchmark Education Company. Based on a work by Brenda Parkes. (Shared Reading Classics Ser.). (J). (gr. k-2). 2009. audio compact disk 10.00 (978-1-60634-978-6(3)) Benchmark Educ.

sandia grandotota y Enorme. (SPA.). (gr. k-1). 10.00 (978-0-7635-6273-1(4)) Rigby Educ.

Sanditon. unabr. ed. Jane Austen. Read by Flo Gibson. 2 cass. (Running Time: 3 hrs.). 1999. 14.95 (978-1-55685-029-5(8)) Audio Bk Con.
This hilarious seaside segment of a novel was begun as Jane Austen was dying & leaves off after the tenth chapter. Excerpts from each of her six completed novels are also included.

Sandman Express. Chris Patella & Eileen Oddo. Read by Chris Patella & Eileen Oddo. Read by George Rabbai. (Running Time: 30 min.). (J). (ps-3). 1989. 9.95 Musical Munchkins.
Features songs, dramatics plays, games & activities designed for children.

Sandman Sleep. unabr. ed. Robert A. Monroe. Read by Robert A. Monroe. 1 cass. (Running Time: 30 min.). (TimeOut Ser.). 1990. 14.95 (978-1-56102-806-1(1)) Inter Indus.
Fall asleep laughing with this affectionate spoof on sleep tape narratives.

Sandman Slim. unabr. ed. Richard Kadrey. Read by MacLeod Andrews. (Running Time: 10 hrs.). 2009. 24.99 (978-1-4418-0041-1(7), 9781441800411, Brilliance MP3); 39.97 (978-1-4418-0042-8(5), 9781441800428, Brlnc Audio MP3 Lib); 24.99 (978-1-4418-0043-5(3), 9781441800435, BAD); 39.97 (978-1-4418-0044-2(1), 9781441800442, BADLE); audio compact disk 34.99 (978-1-4418-0039-8(5), 9781441800398); audio compact disk 89.97 (978-1-4418-0040-4(9), 9781441800404, BriAudCD Unabrid) Brilliance Audio.

Sandmann. E. T. A. Hoffmann. pap. bk. 21.95 (978-88-7754-791-0(X)) Pub: Cideb ITA. Dist(s): Distribks Inc

Sandra Alcosser. unabr. ed. Sandra Alcosser. Read by Sandra Alcosser. 1 cass. (Running Time: 29 min.). 1986. 10.00 New Letters.
Sandra Alcosser, a nature poet, reads from "A Fish to Feed All Hunger".

Sandra Benitez. unabr. ed. Ed. by Jim McKinley. Prod. by Rebekah Presson. 1 cass. (Running Time: 29 min.). (New Letters on the Air Ser.). 1994. 10.00 (111593) New Letters.
At age 52, Benitez, who is of Puerto Rican heritage, has published her first novel. Set in Mexico, "A Place Where the Sea Remembers" tells its story through vignettes about a village & its inhabitants. "I'm confident that the reader will feel the emotional grip of a splendid new storyteller" writes one reviewer of Benitez's tales.

Sandra Brown Suspense Collection. gif. ed. Sandra Brown. Read by Jan Maxwell et al. 15 CDs. 2003. audio compact disk 49.95 (978-0-7435-3524-3(0), Audioworks) Pub: S&S Audio. Dist(s): S and S Inc
From the #1 New York Times bestselling author Sandra Brown, comes three riveting audiobooks in one special package. THE SWITCH Read by Jan Maxwell Gillian Lloyd switches places with her identical twin sister, Melina. The next morning Gillain is found brutally butchered in her own bed. Determined to avenge the murder, Melina vows to stop at nothing to learn the truth. But soon she is on the run from police, the FBI, and the mastermind whose evil plot to engineer the perfect "switch" could result in disastrous consequences on a global scale. ENVY Read by Victor Slezak Book editor Maris Matherly-Reed receives a tantalizing partial manuscript submitted by a writer identified only as P.M.E. Curiosity compels her to track down the author, Parker Evans, and work with him to complete the novel. But as the story unfolds, Maris becomes convinced it is more than just fiction. When someone close to her dies, the presence of evil looms even closer... THE CRUSH Read by Tom Wopat While serving as a juror on a high-profile murder trial, Dr. Rennie Newton finds herself defending the inalienable rights of the accused - even though there is considerable evidence of his guilt. When she arrives home, five dozen roses ominously await her. As she becomes the obsession of Lozada - the accused murderer she helped acquit - Rennie is drawn into a ferocious endgame with an embittered cop who wants Lozada - by any means necessary.

Sandra Jackson's 35 Tips for Caregivers, A Boomer's Guide to Caring for a Loved One: Good hints peppered with common Sense. (ENG.). 2008. audio compact disk 18.95 (978-0-9675873-6-3(0)) P J Pub.

Sandra Nichols Found Dead. unabr. ed. George V. Higgins. Read by Ian Esmo. 7 cass. (Running Time: 10 hrs.). 1996. 49.95 (978-0-7861-1010-0(4), 1787) Blckstn Audio.
A dead body, discovered by a hapless plant thief blithely trespassing in a rural Massachusetts wetland, turns out to belong to a woman with a past, name of Sandra Nichols. Wrongful death? Murder one? We'll leave that to Jerry Kennedy. Inasmuch as Sandra Nichols was murdered several months before her body was found, alibis are fairly easy to come by, even for Peter Wade, Sandra's ex, who is the most likely suspect. On the criminal side of the law, if the defendant isn't caught in the act, there are three things a prosecutor must prove, all of which Wade has in spades: motive, means, & opportunity. The evidence is too elusive to establish Wade's guilt beyond a reasonable doubt; wrongful death is easier: all Jerry Kennedy needs to do is make Wade's part in Sandra's death 51 percent certain.

Sandra Nichols Found Dead. unabr. ed. George V. Higgins. Read by Michael Kramer. 7 cass. (Running Time: 10 hrs. 30 min.). 1996. 56.00 (978-0-7366-3429-8(0), 4073) Books on Tape.
In this latest & possibly most intriguing outing with Jerry Kennedy, Higgins' great counsel for the defense, Kennedy switches sides. He's on the attack now, more dangerous than ever.

Sandra Nichols Found Dead. unabr. ed. George V. Higgins. Narrated by George Guidall. 7 cass. (Running Time: 9 hrs. 15 mins.). 1996. 60.00 (978-0-7887-0618-9(7), 94789E7) Recorded Bks.
When the wife of a wealthy businessman is found dead in a Massachusetts wetland, a respected criminal defense attorney becomes her children's legal guardian.

Sandry's Book. unabr. ed. Tamora Pierce. Read by Full Cast Production Staff. (Circle of Magic Ser.: No. 1). (YA). 2006. 39.99 (978-1-59895-503-3(9)) Find a World.

Sandry's Book. var. ed. Full Cast Production Staff. Featuring Full Cast Production Staff. 4 cass. (Running Time: 6 hrs.). (Circle of Magic Ser.: No. 1). (YA). (gr. 6-9). 2002. lib. bdg. 29.00 (978-0-9717540-9-6(8), 02004L) Full Cast Audio.
No sex, no violence, no aliens, no monsters. Yet, I liked it. A musical detective fantasy for children, this winsome audio play concerns a little orphan with a musical gift who is sent to an orphanage in Venice, where composer Antonio Vivaldi conducts a girls' orchestra. The kindly ex-priest shows her a rare Stradivarius tied to the mysterious disappearance of a nobly born infant.

Sands at Seventy see Twentieth-Century Poetry in English, No. 17, Walt Whitman Speaks for Himself

Sands of Sakkara. Glenn Meade. Read by David Case. 13 cass. (Running Time: 19 hrs. 30 min.). 1999. 104.00 (4999) Books on Tape.
November 1943: Adolf Hitler sanctioned his most audacious mission ever, to kill U.S. President Franklin D. Roosevelt & Prime Minister Winston Churchill as they visit Cairo for a secret conference to plan the Allied invasion of Europe. This really happened & is the basis for Glenn Meade's spectacular new novel. Major Johann Halder, one of the Abwehr's most brilliant, daring agents, accompanied by an expert undercover team & a young & beautiful Egyptologist, Rachel Stern, must race against time, across a hostile desert, to reach Cairo & successfully carry out the assignment. To fail will spell death for both Halder & his young son.

Sands of Sakkara. unabr. ed. Glenn Meade. Read by David Case. 13 cass. (Running Time: 19 hrs. 30 mins.). 1998. 104.00 (978-0-7366-4613-0(2), 4734) Books on Tape.
Sara Tate takes a new job as a New York City prosecutor and is assigned to a third-rate burglary. Meanwhile, her attorney-husband, Jared Lynch's services are solicited by the small time hoodlum accused of the same burglary Sara is prosecuting. Jut one catch: if he loses the case, they'll kill his wife. Sara has been similarly warned: win the case or your husband

dies. In court and at home, husband and wife go head to head while harboring the terrible secret of their motives. And no matter who wins, one of them will lose everything.

Sands of Time. unabr. ed. Connie Monk. Read by Julia Sands. 10 cass. (Running Time: 13 hrs. 15 mins.). (Story Sound Ser.). (J). 2004. 84.95 (978-1-85903-642-6(2)) Pub: Mgna Lrg Print GBR. Dist(s): Ulverscroft US

Sands of Time: A Hermux Tantamog Adventure. Michael Hoeye. Read by Campbell Scott. 4 cass. (Running Time: 5 hrs. 57 mins.). (J). (gr. 5-9). 2004. 29.75 (978-0-8072-0884-7(1), Listening Lib) Pub: Random Audio Pubg. Dist(s): NetLibrary CO
Hermux Tantamoq is out to discover the royal library of an ancient kingdom of cats.

Sands of Time: A Hermux Tantamoq AdventureTM. Michael Hoeye. Read by Campbell Scott. 4 vols. (Running Time: 5 hrs. 57 mins.). (J). (gr. 5-9). 2004. pap. bk. 40.00 (978-1-4000-9016-7(4), Listening Lib) Random Audio Pubg.

Sands of Windee. unabr. ed. Arthur W. Upfield. Narrated by Nigel Graham. 7 cass. (Running Time: 10 hrs.). (Inspector Napoleon Bonaparte Mystery Ser.). 1994. 58.00 (978-1-55690-983-2(7), 94122) Recorded Bks.
When Luke Marks disappears near Windee station, the local authorities write it off as an act of nature, but Bony, examining a photo of the scene of Marks disappearance, leaps at the chance to investigate. For in the background of the photograph, unseen by the white constables is a blackman's sign - a bundle of sticks with a sheepbone through it - that proclaims - "a white man was murdered here.".

Sandstorm. abr. ed. James Rollins. Read by Dennis Boutsikaris. (Sigma Force Ser.: Bk. 1). 2005. audio compact disk 14.95 (978-0-06-087469-8(4)) HarperCollins Pubs.

***Sandstorm.** abr. ed. James Rollins. Read by Dennis Boutsikaris. (ENG.). 2004. (978-0-06-077909-2(8), Harper Audio); (978-0-06-081384-0(9), Harper Audio) HarperCollins Pubs.

Sandstorm. unabr. ed. June Knox-Mawer. Read by Sian Thomas. 12 cass. (Running Time: 12 hrs.). 1998. 96.95 (978-0-7540-0141-6(5), CAB1564) AudioGO.
It was the summer of 1913 & 18-year old Rose was embarking on a new life as the bride of the dashing Captain Geoffrey Chetwynd. Far from home & stuck with this man she barely knew, Rose felt unsure: Geoffrey was becoming an enigma to her & the charm that wooed her changed to vicious neglect.

***Sandstorm.** unabr. ed. James Rollins. Read by John Meagher. (ENG.). 2010. (978-0-06-195861-8(1), Harper Audio); (978-0-06-196024-6(1), Harper Audio) HarperCollins Pubs.

SandWitch: A Halloween Fable. Jim Schisgall. 1 cass. (Running Time: 13 mins.). 1997. pap. bk. 6.95 (978-1-890997-00-7(5)) Hardy Hill Ent.
Gentle, slightly scary story, a girl rescues a stranded witch, & herself, from an isolated island.

Sandworms of Dune see Dune Trilogy

Sandworms of Dune. abr. ed. Frank Herbert. 1 cass. (Running Time: 90 mins.). 1984. 12.95 (978-0-694-50306-3(1), SWC 1565) HarperCollins Pubs.

Sandworms of Dune. rev. unabr. ed. Brian Herbert et al. Read by Scott Brick. 16 CDs. (Running Time: 70200 sec.). (Dune Ser.). (ENG.). 2007. audio compact disk 59.95 (978-1-4272-0112-6(9)) Pub: Macmill Audio. Dist(s): Macmillan

Sandy & Caroline Paton: Folksongs & Ballads. 1 cass. 9.98 (C-30) Folk-Legacy.
Really good songs, pleasantly presented.

Sandy & Caroline Paton: New Harmony. 1 cass. 9.98 (C-100) Folk-Legacy.
Fine songs, good singing, excellent backing.

Sandy & Caroline Paton: When the Spirit Says Sing. Sandy Paton & Caroline Paton. Illus. by Joyce Richardson. Intro. by Chip Wood. 1 cass. (J). (gr. k-8). 1989. pap. bk. 9.98 (978-0-938702-06-1(8), C1002) Folk-Legacy.
Songs for youngsters, sung with kids.

Sandy & Jeanie Darlington. 1 cass. 9.98 (C-28) Folk-Legacy.
Old & new songs from two young interpreters.

***Sandy Koufax: A Lefty's Legacy.** abr. ed. Jane Leavy. Read by Jane Leavy. Read by Robert Pinsky. (ENG.). 2009. (978-0-06-195641-6(4), Harper Audio); (978-0-06-195884-7(0), Harper Audio) HarperCollins Pubs.

***Sandy Koufax: A Lefty's Legacy.** unabr. ed. Jane Leavy. Read by Charley Steiner. (ENG.). 2009. (978-0-06-195642-3(2), Harper Audio); (978-0-06-195883-0(2), Harper Audio) HarperCollins Pubs.

Sandy Shaw: Life Extension, Intelligence Increase & The Effects of Government Intervention. (Running Time: 60 min.). (Cypress College). 1980. 7.00 (F114) Freeland Pr.
Discusses the reasons why lifespans are increasing for humans & animals; includes up-to-date information on how to raise one's I.Q.

Sandy the Tinker see Weird Stories

Sandy's World Sing & Read Alongs: Clean up Your Room Rag. Rose Blue. Read by Barbara Barrie. 1 cass. (Running Time: 12 min.). (J). 1986. 9.95 incl. bk. (978-0-89845-499-4(9), TBC 4999) HarperCollins Pubs.

Sandy's World Sing & Read Alongs: Happy Birthday & All That Jazz. unabr. ed. Rose Blue & Janet Gari. Read by Barbara Barrie. 1 cass. (Running Time: 12 min.). (J). (ps-1). 1986. 9.95 incl. bk. (978-0-89845-496-3(4), TBC 4964) HarperCollins Pubs.

Sandy's World Sing & Read Alongs: Rock-a-New Baby Rock. unabr. ed. Rose Blue. Read by Barbara Barrie. 1 cass. (Running Time: 12 min.). (J). (ps-1). 1986. 9.95 incl. bk. (978-0-89845-498-7(0), TBC 4980) HarperCollins Pubs.

Sandy's World Sing & Read Alongs: Starting School Blues. abr. ed. Rose Blue. Read by Barbara Barrie. 1 cass. (Running Time: 12 min.). (J). (ps-1). 1986. 9.95 incl. bk. (978-0-89845-497-0(2), TBC 4972) HarperCollins Pubs.

Sane Advice. Perf. by La Wanda Page. 2001. audio compact disk 16.98 (978-1-929243-29-7(4)) Uproar Ent.

Sang Spell. Phyllis Reynolds Naylor. Read by Ron Rifkin. 3 cass. (Running Time: 4 hrs. 45 mins.). (J). 2000. 24.00 (978-0-7366-9010-2(7)) Books on Tape.
When his mother is killed, Josh hitchhikes across country only to find himself trapped in a mysterious village in the Appalachian Mountains. There he discovers not only who he is, but the true powers of the human mind.

Sang Spell. unabr. ed. Phyllis Reynolds Naylor. Read by Ron Rifkin. 3 cass. (Running Time: 4 hrs. 42 mins.). (YA). (gr. 5 up). 2000. pap. bk. 35.00 (978-0-8072-8293-9(6), YYA153SP, Listening Lib) Random Audio Pubg.

Sang Spell. unabr. ed. Phyllis Reynolds Naylor. Read by Ron Rifkin. 3 cass. (Running Time: 4 hrs. 42 mins.). (YA). (gr. 7-12). 2000. 30.00 (978-0-8072-8292-2(8), LL0183, Listening Lib) Random Audio Pubg.

Sangeet Ka Anand, Vol. 1. 1 cass. 1993. (A93015) Multi-Cultural Bks.

Sangeet Ka Anand, Vol. 2. 1 cass. 1993. (A93016) Multi-Cultural Bks.

Sangeet Ka Anand, Vol. 3. 1 cass. 1993. (A93017) Multi-Cultural Bks.

Sangre. Benny Hinn. (SPA.). 1999. 10.99 (978-0-88113-218-2(7)) Grupo Nelson.

***Sanibel Flats.** unabr. ed. Randy Wayne White. Narrated by Dick Hill. (Running Time: 12 hrs. 0 mins. 0 sec.). (Doc Ford Ser.). (ENG.). 2010. 24.99 (978-1-4001-6668-8(3)); 17.99 (978-1-4001-8668-6(4)); audio compact disk 69.99 (978-1-4001-4668-0(2)); audio compact disk 34.99 (978-1-4001-1668-3(6)) Pub: Tantor Media. Dist(s): IngramPubServ

***Sanity Savers.** abr. ed. Dale Vicky Atkins & Barbara Scala. (ENG.). 2006. (978-0-06-135550-9(X), Harper Audio) HarperCollins Pubs.

Sannie Langtand & the Visitor: A Story from Nelson Mandela's Favorite African Folktales. Read by C. C. H. Pounder. Compiled by Nelson Mandela. (Running Time: 23 mins.). (ENG.). 2009. 1.99 (978-1-60024-839-9(X)) Pub: Hachet Audio. Dist(s): HachBkGrp

Sans Frontieres: The Basal Program. 3 cass. (Running Time: 3 hrs.). (FRE.). 45.00 (Natl Textbk Co) M-H Contemporary.
Expose students to nature accents, authentic dialogues, paused drills & guided pronunciation work.

Sanskrit, Vol. I. Des. by Vyaas Houston. 8 cass. (Running Time: 8 hrs.). (YA). 1991. ring bd. 235.00 (978-1-57970-015-7(2), AFSK10) J Norton Pubs.
Contains 11 full-page illustrations of the mouth positions essential for learning to pronounce Sanskrit. Also includes pages which are color-coded to allow you to see the symmetry of the language & facilitate memorization.

Sanskrit, Vol. II. Des. by Vyaas Houston. 4 cass. (Running Time: 6 hrs.). (YA). 1991. ring bd. 155.00 (978-1-57970-016-4(0), AFSK20) J Norton Pubs.
Includes pages which are color-coded to allow you to see the symmetry of the language & facilitate memorization.

Sanskrit Pronunciation: Booklet & Audio. Bruce Cameron Hall & Bruce C. Hall. Read by Bruce Cameron Hall. 1 cass. (Running Time: 45 min.). (ENG.). 1992. 15.00 (978-1-55700-021-7(2)) Theos U Pr.
Includes instructions for pronouncing Sanskrit letters & words, & over 160 Sanskrit terms pronounced & defined.

Santa & Pete: A Novel of Christmas Present & Past. Christopher Moore & Pamela Johnson. 2004. 7.95 (978-0-7435-4223-4(1)) Pub: S&S Audio. Dist(s): S and S Inc

Santa Biblia Reina Valera. Narrated by Juan Ovalle. (SPA.). 2008. audio compact disk 99.99 (978-1-930034-51-8(2)) Casscomm.

Santa Bowed at Christmas. Contrib. by Herb Owen. 1995. 11.98 (978-0-7601-0155-1(8), 75602043) Pub: Brentwood Music. Dist(s): H Leonard

Santa Claus Sits Down see Great Christmas Comedy: Selected Sketches

Santa Clawed. unabr. ed. Rita Mae Brown & Sneaky Pie Brown. Read by Kate Forbes. 6 CDs. (Running Time: 6 hrs. 30 mins.). (Mrs. Murphy Mystery Ser.). 2008. audio compact disk 34.99 (978-1-4361-7236-3(5)) Recorded Bks.

Santa Cruise: A Holiday Mystery at Sea. unabr. ed. Mary Higgins Clark & Carol Higgins Clark. Read by Carol Higgins Clark. (Regan Reilly Mystery Ser.). 2006. 17.95 (978-0-7435-6268-3(2)); audio compact disk 29.95 (978-0-7435-6391-8(3), Audioworks) Pub: S&S Audio. Dist(s): S and S Inc

Santa Evita. unabr. collector's ed. Tomas E. Martinez. Read by Mary Peiffer. 10 cass. (Running Time: 15 hrs.). 1998. 80.00 (978-0-7366-4005-3(3), 4503) Books on Tape.
The preserved corpse of Eva Peron became an important symbol of power in Argentina. This blackly comic novel recounts its "adventures".

Santa Fe. unabr. ed. Hank Mitchum. Read by Charlie O'Dowd. 4 cass. (Running Time: 5 hrs. 20 mins.). (Stagecoach Ser.: No. 6). 2001. 25.00 (978-1-58807-079-1(4)) Am Pubng Inc.
When he led the westbound stage out of Kansas, Clay Reiner, chief field agent of the Hanlon Stage Line, had no idea how severely this trip would test his skills as a troubleshooter. During the grueling four and a half day run to Santa Fe, Reiner must lead the passengers through savage mountain weather, Indian warriors, and scavenger outlaws. However, one of the passengers is being stalked by a menace that is even deadlier because it comes from an unexpected source.

Santa Fe. unabr. ed. Hank Mitchum. Read by Charlie O'Dowd. 4 vols. 2003. (978-1-58807-590-1(7)) Am Pubng Inc.

Santa Fe Dead. unabr. ed. Stuart Woods. Read by Michael Kramer. 7 CDs. (Running Time: 8 hrs.). (ENG.). (gr. 8). 2008. audio compact disk 29.95 (978-0-14-314318-5(2), PengAudBks) Penguin Grp USA.

***Santa Fe Edge.** unabr. ed. Stuart Woods. Contrib. by Michael Kramer. (Running Time: 8 hrs.). (ENG.). 2010. audio compact disk 29.95 (978-0-14-242880-1(9), PengAudBks) Penguin Grp USA.

***Santa Fe Rules.** abr. ed. Stuart Woods. Read by Tony Roberts. (ENG.). 2005. (978-0-06-084198-0(2), Harper Audio); (978-0-06-084197-3(4), Harper Audio) HarperCollins Pubs.

Santa Fe-Taos. unabr. ed. Roadrunner Audio Staff. 1 cass. (Running Time: 1 hr. 15 min.). (Listen As You Drive Ser.). 1988. 12.95 (978-0-944857-02-1(7), 11002) Matthew Media.
Designed for use in car between Santa Fe, New Mexico, & the mountain art colony & ski resort of Taos. Covers History, Geology, culture, & Biology.

Santa Fe Trail. abr. ed. Ralph Compton. Read by Jim Gough. 4 cass. (Running Time: 6 hrs.). (Trail Drive Ser.: Bk. 10). 1999. 24.95 (978-1-890990-09-1(4)) Otis Audio.
An extraordinary saga of trail-blazing cowboys who made their fortune driving cattle from Texas to the Great Frontier. He's a wealthy Englishman with two beautiful daughters. They're five dusty Texans & a gambling man. Together, they are all on the ride for their lives.

Santa Fe Trail. unabr. ed. Cliff Hatton. Read by Tom Hunsinger. 2 cass. (Running Time: 3 hrs.). 2001. 24.95 (978-1-85496-115-0(2), 61152) Pub: Soundings Ltd GBR. Dist(s): Ulverscroft US

Santa Fe Trail Revisited. Gregory M. Franzwa. Read by Gregory M. Franzwa. 4 cass. (Running Time: 4 hrs.). 1989. pap. bk. 14.95 incl. bklt. (978-0-935284-91-1(5)) Patrice Pr.

Santa Lucia Secrets. unabr. ed. Steve Hailes. Read by Maynard Villers. 8 cass. (Running Time: 9 hrs. 12 min.). 2001. 49.95 (978-1-55686-878-8(2)) Books in Motion.
Former California miner Bob Alcott had struck it rich. When learning his body has been taken over by consumption, Alcott is drawn to the Santa Lucia Mountains, where he discovers life's secrets.

Santa Monica Mountains. Hosted by Nancy Pearlman. 1 cass. (Running Time: 29 min.). 10.00 (201) Educ Comm CA.

Santa Monica Mountains Conservancy. Hosted by Nancy Pearlman. 1 cass. (Running Time: 28 min.). 10.00 (403) Educ Comm CA.

Santa Olivia. unabr. ed. Jacqueline Carey. Narrated by Susan Ericksen. (Running Time: 13 hrs. 30 mins. 0 sec.). (ENG.). 2009. audio compact disk 24.99 (978-1-4001-6252-9(1)); audio compact disk 34.99 (978-1-4001-1252-4(4)); audio compact disk 69.99 (978-1-4001-4252-1(0)) Pub: Tantor Media. Dist(s): IngramPubServ

Santa Time. 1 cass. (Running Time: 30 min.). (J). (gr. k-3). 2001. bk. 6.95 (736) Happy Kids Prods.
Five original holiday songs and seven traditional Christmas carols.

Santa, You've Got Mail (Musical) - ShowTrax. John Jacobson & Kirby Shaw. 1 CD. 2000. audio compact disk 59.95 (09970186) H Leonard.
Mr. Walker, the beleaguered postman, finds no joy in the bustling holiday season until he discovers how each of his deliveries makes someone's holiday celebration possible. A wonderful approach to learning about all the December holidays.

***Santaroga Barrier.** unabr. ed. Frank Herbert. Narrated by Scott Brick. (Running Time: 9 hrs. 0 mins.). 2010. 15.99 (978-1-4001-8486-6(X)); 24.99 (978-1-4001-6486-8(9)); audio compact disk 34.99 (978-1-4001-1486-3(1)) Pub: Tantor Media. Dist(s): IngramPubServ

***Santaroga Barrier (Library Edition)** unabr. ed. Frank Herbert. Narrated by Scott Brick. (Running Time: 9 hrs. 0 mins.). 2010. 34.99 (978-1-4001-9486-5(5)); audio compact disk 83.99 (978-1-4001-4486-0(8)) Pub: Tantor Media. Dist(s): IngramPubServ

Santa's Coming. unabr. ed. Twin Sisters Productions. Read by Twin Sisters. (J). 2007. 44.99 (978-1-60252-640-2(0)) Find a World.

Santa's Flight Test: A Comedy Satire. unabr. ed. Barry Friedman & Greg Knowles. Perf. by Tony Owen et al. 1 cass. (Running Time: 40 min.). Dramatization. (J). 1992. 10.95 (978-1-882320-00-4(X)) Helion Audio.
Santa has been flying his sleigh without a license long enough, according to Mrs. Santa. At her insistence, the old wide-bellied guy terrorizes the flight instructor & eventually pulls a snow-job on the FAA to pass his licensing exam with flying colors. This hilarious farce satirizes the plight of pilots everywhere who try to navigate through overcrowded airspace.

Santa's Key. deluxe ed. Patricia Louise Sedgwick. 2004. bk. 12.95 (978-0-9688190-1-2(X)) Pub: FDD1 CAN. Dist(s): Hushion Hse

Santa's Rockin' Christmas Eve (A Rock 'n Roll Evening at the North Pole for Unison & 2-Part Voices) Listening. Jay Althouse. Composed by Sally K. Albrecht. (ENG.). 2003. audio compact disk 12.95 (978-0-7390-3189-6(9)) Alfred Pub.

Santa's Rockin' Christmas Eve (A Rock 'n Roll Evening at the North Pole for Unison & 2-Part Voices) SoundTrax. Jay Althouse. Composed by Sally K. Albrecht. (ENG.). 2003. audio compact disk 59.95 (978-0-7390-3188-9(0)) Alfred Pub.

Santa's Sack of Christmas Songs. 1 cass. (Running Time: 30 min.). (J). (gr. k-6). 1987. bk. 10.95 (978-0-937124-03-1(6), KIM9105C) Kimbo Educ.
Santa's sack is brimming with merry music. A shiny Christmas package of all new & old favorite songs, such as: Rudolph the Red-Nosed Reindeer, Up on the Housetop, Silent Night, Winter Wonderland, Country Christmas, Frosty the Snowman, Santa Clause is Coming to Town, Jingle Bells & more. Includes guide.

Santa's Sack of Christmas Songs. 1 LP. (Running Time: 1 hr.). (J). 2001. pap. bk. 11.95 (KIM 9105) Kimbo Educ.

Santa's Secret. unabr. ed. Sandi N. Ebert. Read by Edward Nugent, Sr. 1 cass. (Running Time: 7 hrs. 30 min.). (J). (ps-4). 1997. pap. bk. 4.95 (978-0-9660336-1-8(2)) Santas Secret.

Santa's Sub: Moon-Star Records. Sandi Johnson. Narrated by Van Buchanan. 1 cass., 1 CD. (J). (ps-6). 1998. 6.99 (978-1-929063-21-5(0), 121); audio compact disk 12.99 CD. (978-1-929063-22-2(9), 122) Moons & Stars.
The children of Atlantis have never seen Santa. A mermaid helps them send a letter in a bottle, & Santa's submarine is off to the rescue. Includes song.

Santidad de la Vida. 2003. audio compact disk 12.00 (978-1-57972-555-6(4)) Insight Living.

Santo Rosario. Created by Sheldon Cohen & J. Mazza. 1 cass. (Running Time: 1 hr. 20 min.). (SPA.). 1993. 9.95 (978-0-914070-33-7(9), 315) ACTA Pubns.
Bestselling rendition of all 15 mysteries with original music & meditations in Spanish.

Santo Rosario: Con Los Misterios Luminosos. Arranged by Sheldon Cohen. 2 CDs. (Running Time: 100 mins.). 2004. audio compact disk 14.95 (978-0-87946-254-3(X), 412) ACTA Pubns.
This Spanish-language version of the bestselling version of the Rosary includes the Joyful, Sorrowful and Glorious Mysteries, as well as the new Mysteries of Light.

Santos & Santos. unabr. ed. Octavio Solis. Perf. by Anthony Diaz-Perez et al. 1 cass. (Running Time: 1 hr. 53 min.). 1997. 22.95 (978-1-58081-040-1(3)) L A Theatre.
A story centered around a morally ambivalent Mexican-American law firm that subsidizes its well meaning political battles with drug money. A chain reaction of tragedy ensues when the youngest & well meaning "good brother" betrays his brother.

Santos de Agua Mansa, California. unabr. ed. Alex Espinoza. Read by Cony Madera. Tr. by Liliana Valenzuela. (Running Time: 36000 sec.). 2007. 54.95 (978-1-4332-1098-3(3)); audio compact disk 29.95 (978-1-4332-1141-6(6)); audio compact disk 63.00 (978-1-4332-1099-0(1)) Blckstn Audio.

Sanuk Sanuk: Thai Language, Stages 1-2. National Thai Language Curriculum Project Staff. 1 cass. (Running Time: 34 mins.). EducServs AUS.

Sapelo: Time Is Winding Up. Short Stories. Created by Diane Ferlatte. Contrib. by Beverlee Patton-Miller. 1 cassette. (YA). 1991. 10.00 (978-0-9760432-0-1(3)) D Ferlatte.

***Sapphique.** unabr. ed. Catherine Fisher. Narrated by Kim Mai Guest. 10 CDs. (YA). (gr. 7-12). 2010. audio compact disk 48.00 (978-0-307-70713-0(X), Listening Lib) Pub: Random Audio Pubg. Dist(s): Random

***Sapphique.** unabr. ed. Catherine Fisher. Read by Kim Mai Guest. (ENG.). (J). 2010. audio compact disk 48.00 (978-0-307-70711-6(3), Listening Lib) Pub: Random Audio Pubg. Dist(s): Random

Sapphire Blue Birthday Album. Julia W. Blagden et al. Perf. by Jewels and the Gems Staff. Illus. by Laura Brock. Contrib. by Nicholas Perry. (J). 2000. bk. 14.00 (978-0-9659511-3-5(8)) Pub: Multifaceted. Dist(s): Sparkling Recs

Sapphire Blue Birthday Album. Julia W. Blagden et al. Perf. by Jewels and the Gems Staff. Illus. by Laura Brock. Contrib. by Nicholas Perry. (J). (ps-4). 2000. 12.00 (978-0-9659511-2-8(X)) Pub: Multifaceted. Dist(s): Sparkling Recs

Sapphire Dreams. Perf. by Mars Lasar. 1 cass., 1 CD. 7.98 (RM 44); audio compact disk 14.38 CD Jewel box. (RM 44) NewSound.

Sapphire Skies & Dancing Clouds. abr. ed. Relaxation Company Staff & Jeffrey Thompson. Created by Mick Rossi. (Running Time: 2:00:00). 2007. audio compact disk 19.98 (978-1-55961-843-4(4)) Sounds True.

Sapphires & Smugglers. Lynn Gardner. 2 cass. 1999. 13.95 (978-1-57734-435-3(9), 07002017) Covenant Comms.
Romantic sequel to "Turquoise & Terrorists.".

Sappho's Leap. unabr. ed. Erica Jong. Narrated by Erica Jong. 2004. 37.95 (978-1-4025-7787-1(7), RH071) Recorded Bks.
Takes listeners into the world of Sappho, a love poet of ancient Greece. Sappho reveals a world of fantastic adventure full of dramatic, passionate, and fiery characters. The author?s sensual and vivid narration perfectly captures the awe-inspiring spirit of this unforgettable heroine.

Sappho's Leap. unabr. ed. Narrated by Erica Jong. 9 cass. (Running Time: 13 hrs.). 2004. 79.75 (978-1-4025-7786-4(9), 97672) Recorded Bks.

Sara Cleveland of Brant Lake, NY. 1 cass. 9.98 (C-33) Folk-Legacy.
Traditional ballads from the Upper Hudson Valley.

Sara Grey: Songs & Ballads. Contrib. by Ed Trickett. 1 cass. 9.98 (C-38) Folk-Legacy.
One of the finest singers of the folksong revival.

Sara Paretsky CD Collection: Total Recall, Blacklist, Fire Sale. abr. ed. Sara Paretsky. Read by Sandra Burr. (Running Time: 18 hrs.). 2009. audio compact disk 34.99 (978-1-4233-9726-7(6), 9781423397267, BACD) Brilliance Audio.

Saraband for Two Sisters. unabr. ed. Philippa Carr. Read by Lindsay Sandison. 10 cass. (Running Time: 15 hrs.). (Isis Ser.). (J). 2001. 84.95 (978-1-85695-278-1(9), 960406) Pub: ISIS Lrg Prnt GBR. Dist(s): Ulverscroft US

Sarabel to the Rescue. Narrated by Lani Minella. (Running Time: 3600 sec.). (J). (gr. k-6). 2007. audio compact disk 12.95 (978-1-933781-08-2(4)) TallTales Aud.

Sarah: How a Hockey Mom Turned Alaska's Political Establishment Upside Down. Kaylene Johnson. 2008. audio compact disk 19.95 (978-1-4332-6786-4(1)) Blckstn Audio.

Sarah: How a Hockey Mom Turned Alaska's Political Establishment Upside Down. unabr. ed. Kaylene Johnson. Read by Cassandra Campbell. (Running Time: 3 hrs. NaN mins.). 2008. 29.95 (978-1-4332-6787-1(X)); audio compact disk 22.95 (978-1-4332-6783-3(7)); audio compact disk 33.00 (978-1-4332-6784-0(5)) Blckstn Audio.

Sarah -Lib. (Running Time: 12 hrs. 0 mins.). 2005. 72.95 (978-0-7861-3022-1(9)); audio compact disk 90.00 (978-0-7861-8089-9(7)) Blckstn Audio.

Sarah -Lib: Mp3. (Running Time: 12 hrs. 0 mins.). 2005. audio compact disk 29.95 (978-0-7861-8211-4(3)) Blckstn Audio.

Sarah Bishop, unabr. ed. Scott O'Dell. Narrated by Cheryl Haas. 4 pieces. (Running Time: 5 hrs. 30 mins.). (gr. 6 up). 1997. 35.00 (978-0-7887-0594-6(6), 94771E7) Recorded Bks.
Fifteen-year-old Sarah Bishop's father is a Tory. As the Revolution blazes through the New York countryside, patriots murder her father & burn down their farm before her eyes. Fleeing alone into the wilderness, the frightened survivor wonders if there is any safe place left for her.

Sarah Brady: To Own a Gun. Sarah Brady. Read by Sarah Brady. 1 cass. (Running Time: 1 hr.). 10.95 (K0430B090, HarperThor) HarpC GBR.

Sarah Conley: A Novel. unabr. collector's ed. Ellen Gilchrist. Read by Mary Peiffer. 6 cass. (Running Time: 9 hrs.). 1998. 48.00 (978-0-7366-4132-6(7), 896037) Books on Tape.
A woman gets a second chance at the love of her life, but discovers strange things about her former lover's past.

Sarah Foster: Why the New Hebrides Experiment Failed. 1983. (FL4) Freeland Pr.

Sarah Groves: Just Showed up for My Own Life. Directed By Chip Johnson. Contrib. by Sara Groves & Troy Groves. (Running Time: 1 hr. 2 mins.). (Nomad (Video) Ser.). 2006. 14.98 (978-5-558-26035-9(1)) INO Rec.

***Sarah Jane Adventures: Deadly Download: An Audio Exclusive Adventure.** Jason Arnopp. Narrated by Elisabeth Sladen. (Running Time: 1 hr. 0 mins. 0 sec.). (ENG.). 2011. audio compact disk 24.95 (978-1-4084-6664-3(3)) Pub: AudioGO. Dist(s): Perseus Dist

***Sarah Jane Adventures: Wraith World: An Audio Exclusive Adventure.** Cavan Scott & Mark Wright. Narrated by Elisabeth Sladen. (Running Time: 1 hr. 0 mins. 0 sec.). (ENG.). 2011. audio compact disk 24.95 (978-1-4084-6663-6(5)) Pub: AudioGO. Dist(s): Perseus Dist

Sarah Laughed. unab. abr. ed. Vanessa L. Ochs. Read by Carrington MacDuffie. (Running Time: 16200 sec.). 2005. audio compact disk 28.00 (978-1-932378-84-9(7)) Pub: A Media Intl. Dist(s): Natl Bk Netwk
In this vivid collection, the Biblical matriarchs are brought to new life and revealed to be inspiring role models for women today.

Sarah Learns Not to Be Afraid. Flemons. (ENG.). (J). 2009. audio compact disk 6.99 (978-0-9767612-2-8(X)) Chosen Intl.

Sarah Ogan Gunning: Girl of Constant Sorrow. 1 cass. 9.98 (C-26) Folk-Legacy.
Traditional singer & songmaker from Kentucky.

Sarah Orne Jewett's Best Short Stories. Sarah Orne Jewett. Narrated by Flo Gibson. (ENG.). 2007. audio compact disk 16.95 (978-1-55685-921-2(X)) Audio Bk Con.

Sarah Orne Jewett's Best Short Stories, unabr. ed. Short Stories. Sarah Orne Jewett. Read by Flo Gibson. 2 cass. (Running Time: 3 hrs.). 1994. 14.95 (978-1-55685-318-0(1)) Audio Bk Con.
"A White Heron", "The Dulham Ladies", "The Guests of Mrs. Timms", "Miss Peck's Promotion", "Miss Tempy's Watchers", & "The Town Poor" comprise this gentle & often comic collection.

***Sarah Palin: A New Kind of Leader.** unabr. ed. Joe Hilley. (Running Time: 3 hrs. 0 mins. 0 sec.). (ENG.). 2008. 14.99 (978-0-310-29633-1(1)) Zondervan.

Sarah, Plain & Tall. Patricia MacLachlan. 3 cass. (Running Time: 3 hrs. 30 min.). (J). 2001. audio compact disk 25.00 (HarperChildAud) HarperCollins Pubs.
Includes "Skylark" and "Caleb's Story".

Sarah, Plain & Tall. Patricia MacLachlan. 1 cass. 1987. 7.45 (978-0-440-85117-2(3), Random AudioBks) Random Audio Pubg.

Sarah, Plain & Tall. unabr. ed. Patricia MacLachlan. Read by Glenn Close. (J). 2007. 34.99 (978-1-60252-790-4(3)) Find a World.

Sarah, Plain & Tall. unabr. ed. Patricia MacLachlan. Read by Glenn Close. (J). (ps-2). 2001. audio compact disk 25.95 (978-0-694-52602-4(9)) HarperCollins Pubs.

Sarah, Plain & Tall. unabr. ed. Patricia MacLachlan. 1 cass. (Running Time: 1 hr. 30 mins.). 2003. 7.99 (978-0-06-058463-4(7)) HarperCollins Pubs.

***Sarah, Plain & Tall.** unabr. ed. Patricia Maclachlan. Read by Glenn Close. (ENG.). 2008. (978-0-06-180216-4(6), KTegenBooks); (978-0-06-180215-7(8), KTegenBooks) HarperCollins Pubs.

***Sarah, Plain & Tall Collection.** unabr. ed. Patricia Maclachlan. Read by Glenn Close. (ENG.). 2004. (978-0-06-081830-2(1), KTegenBooks); (978-0-06-081829-6(8), KTegenBooks) HarperCollins Pubs.

Sarah Sadler. Perf. by Sarah Sadler. 2002. audio compact disk Essential Recs.

Sarah Simpson's Rules for Living. Rebecca Rupp. Read by Emily Durante. (Playaway Children Ser.). (J). 2008. 34.99 (978-1-60640-889-6(5)) Find a World.

Sarah Simpson's Rules for Living. unabr. ed. Rebecca Rupp. Read by Emily Durante. 1 MP3-CD. (Running Time: 1 hr.). 2008. 31.97 (978-1-4233-6907-3(6), 9781423369073, Brinc Audio MP3 Lib); 14.95 (978-1-4233-6908-0(4), 9781423369080, BAD); 31.97 (978-1-4233-6909-7(2), 9781423369097, BADLE); 14.95 (978-1-4233-6906-6(8), 9781423369066, Brilliance MP3); audio compact disk 14.95 (978-1-4233-6904-2(1), 9781423369042, Bril Audio CD Unabri) Brilliance Audio.

Sarah Simpson's Rules for Living. unabr. ed. Rebecca Rupp. Read by Emily Durante. 1 CD. (Running Time: 1 hr.). (J). (gr. 3-6). 2008. audio compact disk 31.97 (978-1-4233-6905-9(X), 9781423369059, BriAudCD Unabrid) Brilliance Audio.

Sarah Whitman. Diane Pearson. (Soundings Ser.). (J). 2010. 84.95 (978-1-84559-245-5(X)) Pub: ISIS Lrg Prnt GBR. Dist(s): Ulverscroft US

Saraha Special. Esmé Raji Codell. Read by Phylicia Rashad. 3 CDs. (Running Time: 3 hrs. 20 mins.). (J). (gr. 3-7). 2004. audio compact disk 25.50 (978-1-4000-8991-8(3), Listening Lib) Pub: Random Audio Pubg. Dist(s): NetLibrary CO

***Sarah's Choice.** unabr. ed. Wanda Brunstetter. Narrated by Jaimee Draper. (Running Time: 6 hrs. 0 mins. 0 sec.). (Brides of Lehigh Canal Ser.). (ENG.). 2010. 16.09 (978-1-60814-790-8(8)) Oasis Audio.

***Sarah's Choice.** unabr. ed. Wanda E. Brunstetter. Narrated by Jaimee Draper. (Running Time: 6 hrs. 0 mins. 0 sec.). (Brides of Lehigh Canal Ser.). (ENG.). 2010. audio compact disk 22.99 (978-1-59859-811-7(2)) Oasis Audio.

***Sarah's Garden.** unabr. ed. Kelly Long. Read by To be Announced. (Running Time: 10 hrs. 5 mins.). (Patch of Heaven Novels Ser.). (ENG.). 2010. 29.95 (978-1-4417-7738-6(5)); 65.95 (978-1-4417-7735-5(0)); audio compact disk 100.00 (978-1-4417-7736-2(9)) Blckstn Audio.

Sarah's Key. unabr. ed. Tatiana de Rosnay. Read by Polly Stone. 8 CDs. (Running Time: 10 hrs. 0 mins. 0 sec.). (ENG.). 2009. audio compact disk 29.95 (978-1-4272-0847-7(6)) Pub: Macmill Audio. Dist(s): Macmillan

Sarah's Quilt: The Continuing Story of Sarah Agnes Prine 1906. unabr. ed. Nancy E. Turner. Read by Valerie Leonard. 12 cass. (Running Time: 60720 sec.). 2005. 96.95 (978-0-7927-3639-4(7), CSL 803); DVD, audio compact disk, audio compact disk 117.95 (978-0-7927-3640-0(0), SLD 803) AudioGO.

Sarah's Song. unabr. ed. Karen Kingsbury. Narrated by Alexandra O'Karma. 3 cass. (Running Time: 3 hrs. 45 mins.). 2004. 29.75 (978-1-4193-1856-6(X), K1126) Recorded Bks.

Saranagati & Gitavali. Srila B. Thakura. 3 cass. 15.00 Set, incl. 1 vinyl album. Bhaktivedanta.
Devotional poems about the process of surrendering one's heart at the feet of Lord Krsna. It shows how to serve the Lord, obtain His protection, depend on Him, develop loyalty to Him & act humbly before Him. Expressions of the highest flights of bhakti-yoga, they soar with ecstatic love for Lord Krsna & His companions & help increase the listener's faith, appreciation & devotion.

Sara's Song. unabr. ed. Fern Michaels. Read by Jennifer Wydra. 8 vols. (Running Time: 12 hrs.). 2000. bk. 69.95 (978-0-7927-2251-9(5), CSL 140, Chivers Sound Lib) AudioGO.
A brilliant career and loving friends weren't enough to heal Dr. Sara Killian's aching heart. For a brief moment world famous rock star, Dallas Lord, was part of her life until he disappeared. Dallas had given Sara a priceless gift: a love song written just for her. The legacy brings Sara intrigue, betrayal and danger. And when she meets Adam Lord, Dallas's older brother, she finds herself torn between Adam, the most handsome man she's ever known, and Dallas, the man her heart won't let her forget.

Sara's Song. unabr. ed. Fern Michaels. Read by Jennifer Wydra. 12 CDs. (Running Time: 18 hrs.). 2000. audio compact disk 110.95 (978-0-7927-9975-7(5), SLD 026, Chivers Sound Lib) AudioGO.
A brilliant career & loving friends weren't enough to heal Sara's broken heart & when she meets rock star Dallas Lord, their legacy brings Sara intrique, betrayal & danger.

Saratoga Backtalk: A Charlie Bradshaw Mystery. unabr. collector's ed. Stephen Dobyns. Read by Jonathan Marosz. 6 cass. (Running Time: 6 hrs.). 1995. 36.00 (978-0-7366-2969-0(6), 3660) Books on Tape.
Charlie Bradshaw's pushy sidekick turns up leads galore after wealthy horseowner's suspicious death.

Saratoga Bestiary. unabr. collector's ed. Stephen Dobyns. Read by Jonathan Marosz. 7 cass. (Running Time: 7 hrs.). 1994. 42.00 (978-0-7366-2792-4(8), 3507) Books on Tape.
A gambling party at the Saratoga Springs hotel, a stolen painting, a dead grocer - that's Super Bowl Sunday for Charlie Bradshaw.

Saratoga Fleshpot. unabr. collector's ed. Stephen Dobyns. Read by Jonathan Marosz. 6 cass. (Running Time: 6 hrs.). 1996. 36.00 (978-0-7366-3356-7(1), 4007) Books on Tape.
It's a real downer for Victor Plotz, Charlie Bradshaw's sidekick, when his stock market tips don't pan out & he has to work security to pay the bills. He hires on for the annual Saratoga Springs horse auction, a real stuffy affair. But Vic knows how to have fun...& it gets him in trouble. When Fleshpot, a renegade colt, sells for a half million then suddenly minds its manners, Vic calls foul. Was there a switch? Officials ignore him, & it takes three murders to get their attention.

Saratoga Haunting. unabr. collector's ed. Stephen Dobyns. Read by Jonathan Marosz. 6 cass. (Running Time: 6 hrs.). 1994. 36.00 (978-0-7366-2836-5(3), 3544) Books on Tape.
In which Charlie Bradshaw learns from an unearthed skeleton that secrets from an old case don't always stay buried.

Saratoga Headhunter. unabr. collector's ed. Stephen Dobyns. Read by Jonathan Marosz. 6 cass. (Running Time: 6 hrs.). 1994. 36.00 (978-0-7366-2754-2(5), 3477) Books on Tape.
A former jockey hiding out in Charlie Bradshaw's house literally loses his head. Charlie tracks down the killer.

Saratoga Hexameter. unabr. collector's ed. Stephen Dobyns. Read by Jonathan Marosz. 8 cass. (Running Time: 8 hrs.). 1994. 48.00 (978-0-7366-2890-7(8), 3590) Books on Tape.
Colleague's murder leads Charlie Bradshaw to a poetic clue in a series of mysterious deaths.

Saratoga Longshot. unabr. collector's ed. Stephen Dobyns. Read by Jonathan Marosz. 6 cass. (Running Time: 6 hrs.). 1994. 36.00 (978-0-7366-2698-9(0), 3432) Books on Tape.
Looking for a missing teenager in New York City, small-town cop Charlie Bradshaw finds nothing but trouble.

Saratoga Snapper. unabr. collector's ed. Stephen Dobyns. Read by Jonathan Marosz. 7 cass. (Running Time: 7 hrs.). 1994. 42.00 (978-0-7366-2793-1(6), 3508) Books on Tape.
When his partner snaps pictures of tourists, ex-cop Charlie Bradshaw gets more excitement than he bargained for.

Saratoga Springs. unabr. ed. Meatball Fulton. Read by Bill Raymond et al. 5 cass. (Running Time: 6 hrs.). Dramatization. (J). (gr. 4 up). 1989. 29.95 Set. (978-1-881137-13-9(9)) ZBS Found.
Life in Small Town America can be witty, charming & sometimes even touching. Author Meatball Fulton has filled this quaint upstate New York village with bizarre & loveable characters.

Saratoga Strongbox. unabr. collector's ed. Stephen Dobyns. Read by Jonathan Marosz. 4 cass. (Running Time: 6 hrs.). 1999. 32.00 (978-0-7366-4295-8(1), 4788) Books on Tape.
Vic Plotz, Charlie Bradshaw's shameless sidekick, can't resist the opportunity to collect a cool $2,000 just for picking up a suspicious suitcase in Montreal. Problem is Vic can't do it but he knows someone who can & will for only $1,000, leaving Vic with $1,000 for doing nothing. This little scam, however, sets off a chain of events that will lead Victor & Charlie on a disastrous course that leads from sin to dirty money to murder.

Saratoga Swimmer. unabr. collector's ed. Stephen Dobyns. Read by Jonathan Marosz. 6 cass. (Running Time: 6 hrs.). 1994. 36.00 (978-0-7366-2753-5(7), 3476) Books on Tape.
The plot behind the murder of his boss at a Saratoga stable may cost ex-cop Charlie Bradshaw his life.

Sarek. A. C. Crispin. (Star Trek Ser.). 2004. 10.95 (978-0-7435-4665-2(2)) Pub: S&S Audio. Dist(s): S and S Inc

Sarek: A Star Trek Adventure. unabr. ed. A. C. Crispin. Read by Nick Sullivan. 10 vols. (Running Time: 15 hrs.). 2001. bk. 84.95 (978-0-7927-2471-1(2), CSL 360, Chivers Sound Lib) AudioGO.
Spock's mother, Amanda Grayson, is dying & Spock returns to the planet Vulcan where he & Sarek enjoy a rare moment of rapprochement. But just as his wife's illness grows worse, duty calls Sarek away, once again sowing seeds of conflict between father & son. Yet soon, Sarek & Spock must put aside their differences & work together to foil a far reaching plot to destroy the Federation, a plot that Sarek has seen for nearly his entire career.

Sarny: A Life Remembered, unabr. ed. Gary Paulsen. Narrated by Lynne Thigpen. 3 pieces. (Running Time: 4 hrs. 15 mins.). (gr. 7 up). 1998. 27.00 (978-0-7887-2082-6(1), 95435E7) Recorded Bks.
In this sequel to "Nightjohn," Sarny plans how she will run away from the plantation where she is a slave, while the Civil War rages around her. The master has sold her young son & daughter. Can she find the strength & courage to find them?.

Sartoris, unabr. ed. William Faulkner. Narrated by George Guidall. 9 cass. (Running Time: 12 hrs. 45 mins.). 1993. 78.00 (978-1-55690-897-2(0), 93339E7) Recorded Bks.
After fighting in World War I, Bayard Sartoris returns to Jefferson, Mississippi consumed with guilt over the death of his brother John & driven by a haunting desire for self-destruction.

Sartre in 90 Minutes. unabr. ed. Paul Strathern. Read by Robert Whitfield. (Running Time: 5400 sec.). (Philosophers in 90 Minutes Ser.). 2007. 22.95 (978-0-7861-3685-8(5)); audio compact disk 24.00 (978-0-7861-4365-8(7)) Blckstn Audio.

Sarum: The Novel of England. unabr. ed. Edward Rutherfurd & Nadia May. Illus. by Edward Rutherfurd. (Running Time: 46 hrs. 5 mins.). 2008. 59.95 (978-1-4332-5471-0(9)); audio compact disk 130.00 (978-1-4332-5470-3(0)); audio compact disk 130.00 (978-1-4332-5469-7(7)) Blckstn Audio.

Sarum: The Novel of England, Pt. 2. unabr. collector's ed. Edward Rutherfurd. Read by David Case. 12 cass. (Running Time: 18 hrs.). 1998. 96.00 (978-0-7366-4242-2(0), 4742-B) Books on Tape.
The whole sweep of British history & civilization unfolds through the story of one place, Salisbury, from before recorded time to the present day.

Sarum Pt. 1: The Novel of England. unabr. ed. Edward Rutherfurd. Read by Nadia May. 10 cass. (Running Time: 46 hrs. 30 mins.). 1994. 69.95 (978-0-7861-0748-3(0), 1499A,B,C) Blckstn Audio.
Sarum is a meticulously researched, authoritative account of the entire sweep of English civilization: the life of the early hunters & farmers, the creation of Stonehenge, the dawn of Christianity & the building of Salisbury Cathedral, the Black Death, the Wars of the Roses, the Reformation, the wars in America, the Industrial Age, Victorian social reforms, the World War II invasion of Normandy, & the modern-day concerns of a once-preeminent empire. And its story is one that Americans claim as part of their own legacy.

Sarum Pt. 1: The Novel of England. unabr. collector's ed. Edward Rutherfurd. Read by David Case. 12 cass. (Running Time: 18 hrs.). 1998. 96.00 (978-0-7366-4241-5(2), 4742-A) Books on Tape.
Sarum follows the turbulent story of the entire course of English history from the Ice Age to the present day.

Sarum Pt. 2: The Novel of England. unabr. ed. Edward Rutherfurd. Read by Nadia May. 11 cass. (Running Time: 46 hrs. 30 mins.). 1994. 76.95 (978-0-7861-0839-8(8), 1499A,B,C) Blckstn Audio.

Sarum Pt. 3: The Novel of England. unabr. ed. Edward Rutherfurd. Read by Nadia May. 11 cass. (Running Time: 46 hrs. 30 mins.). 1994. 76.95 (978-0-7861-0840-4(1), 1499A,B,C) Blckstn Audio.

Sarum Pt. 3: The Novel of England. unabr. collector's ed. Edward Rutherfurd. Read by David Case. 8 cass. (Running Time: 12 hrs.). 1998. 64.00 (978-0-7366-4243-9(9), 4742-C) Books on Tape.
The whole sweep of British history & civilization unfolds through the story of one place, Salisbury, from before recorded time to the present day.

SAS Fifty-Five: Evaluation of Internal Control Structures. Dave Dennis. 6 cass. 129.00 set, incl. textbk. & quizzer. (978-0-88128-351-8(7), CPE2070) Bisk Educ.
Gain a complete understanding of the new internal control structure requirements that help you to more effectively plan, implement, & document audits.

Sash Cord see Black Museum

***Sasha & Malia Obama: Historic First Kids CD.** Sarah Tieck. (Big Buddy Biographies CD Ser.). 2010. cd-rom 27.07 (978-1-61613-074-9(1)) ABDO Pub Co.

***Sasha & Malia Obama: Historic First Kids Site CD.** Sarah Tieck. (Big Buddy Biographies Site CD Ser.). 2010. cd-rom 57.07 (978-1-61613-254-5(X)) ABDO Pub Co.

Sasha's Tail: Lessons from a Life with Cats. unabr. collector's ed. Jacqueline Damian. Read by Mary Peiffer. 6 cass. (Running Time: 6 hrs.). 1995. 36.00 (978-0-7366-3184-6(4), 3852) Books on Tape.
What do cats think about their owners? How do cats relate to each other & the dreaded canine? Entertaining "tails".

Sashenka. unabr. ed. Simon Montefiore. Narrated by Anne Flosnik. 16 CDs. (Running Time: 20 hrs. 30 mins. 0 sec.). (ENG.). 2008. audio compact disk 49.99 (978-1-4001-1007-0(6)) Pub: Tantor Media. Dist(s): IngramPubServ

Sashenka. unabr. ed. Simon Montefiore. Read by Josephine Bailey. (Running Time: 20 hrs. 30 mins. 0 sec.). (ENG.). 2008. audio compact disk 99.99 (978-1-4001-4007-7(2)); audio compact disk 34.99 (978-1-4001-6007-5(3)) Pub: Tantor Media. Dist(s): IngramPubServ

***Sassafrass, Cypress & Indigo: A Novel.** unabr. ed. Ntozake Shange. (Running Time: 8 hrs.). 2010. 29.95 (978-1-4417-6558-1(1)); 54.95 (978-1-4417-6555-0(7)); audio compact disk 76.00 (978-1-4417-6556-7(5)); audio compact disk 29.95 (978-1-4417-6557-4(3)) Blckstn Audio.

***SAT ACT PSAT 2010 Platinum Edition.** Topics Entertai Staff. 2010. audio compact disk 49.99 (978-1-60077-591-8(8)) TOPICS Ent.

SAT AudioLearn. 5 CDs. (Running Time: 4.2 hrs). 2008. stu. ed. 99.99 (978-1-59262-024-1(8)) AudioLearn.

SAT Comprehensive Program 2009. unabr. ed. Richard Paul Evans. Read by Campbell Scott. 2005. 17.95 (978-0-7435-5250-9(4)) Pub: S&S Audio. Dist(s): S and S Inc

SAT Master. Eric Jensen. 3 cass. (Running Time: 3 hrs.). (Success Ser.). (YA). (gr. 8-12). 1987. 24.95 Incl. wkbk. (978-0-945525-09-7(5)) Learning Forum.
Features strategies to improve performance on the SAT.

SAT Vocabulary AudioLearn. 2 CDs. (Running Time: 2 Hours). 2008. audio compact disk 39.99 (978-1-59262-022-7(1)) AudioLearn.

SAT Vocabulary Builder. unabr. ed. Ewald Neumann. Read by James Davis & Heidi Davis-Spargo. 3 cass. (Running Time: 4 hrs. 30 min.). (Vocabulary Builder Ser.). (C). (gr. 11-12). 1992. pap. bk. 24.95 Set. (978-0-9625001-2-1(7)) Spargo Comns.
A study aid for the verbal portion of the SAT Exam including a 64 page book, 3 (90 minute) cassettes & 200 flash cards.

SAT Words to Go: Vocabulary Building for Super Busy Students. unabr. ed. Kaplan Publishing Staff. (Running Time: 23 hrs. 0 mins. 0 sec.). 2004. audio compact disk 19.95 (978-0-7435-3843-5(9), Sound Ideas) Pub: S&S Audio. Dist(s): S and S Inc

SAT Words to Go: Vocabulary Building for Super Busy Students. unabr. ed. Kaplan Publishing Staff. 2005. 11.95 (978-0-7435-5200-4(8)) Pub: S&S Audio. Dist(s): S and S Inc

Satan & His Host. Blaine Yorgason & Brenton Yorgason. Read by Marvin Payne. 1 cass. (Gospel Power Ser.). 6.95 (978-0-929985-45-9(1)) Jackman Pubng.
A father's letter to his son on how to deal with unseen spirits.

Satanism: Attack on Youth. Greg Reid. 2 cass. (Running Time: 3 hrs.). 1991. 20.00 Set. (SAOY) Amer Focus Pub.
Greg Reid, a former victim of Satanic cults & a former occult practitioner, offers practical answers & a plea from the heart. He reveals the open secret about the only escape from Satanism & the occult - the "only" way out.

Satanism: The Devil's Snare. David Di Canio. 2 cass. (Running Time: 3 hrs.). 1990. 20.00 Set. (STDS) Amer Focus Pub.
The escalation of Satanism & satanic involvement by America's children, teens & adults is literally becoming the norm. David DiCanio lights the path to guide those with the greatest need to the Way of Salvation.

Satanism in Prisons Story. As told by Frank M. Brim. Told to Alan H. Peterson. (American Focus on Satanic Crime Ser.: Vol. 30). 1992. 34.95 (978-1-877858-22-2(6), TSIPT) Amer Focus Pub.

Satan's Circus: Murder, Vice, Police Corruption, & New York's Trial of the Century. abr. ed. Mike Dash. Read by David Ackroyd. (Running Time: 21600 sec.). (ENG.). 2007. audio compact disk 29.95 (978-0-7393-4288-6(6), Random AudioBks) Pub: Random Audio Pubg. Dist(s): Random

Satan's Counterfeit Strategy. Jack Deere. 1 cass. (Running Time: 90 mins.). (Loving God & Hating Evil Ser.: Vol. 1). 2000. 5.00 (JD05-001) Morning NC.
The teaching contained in this miniseries can change your life & strengthen your relationship with God.

***Satan's Deputy.** T. T. Flynn. 2009. (978-1-60136-402-9(4)) Audio Holding.

Satan's Deputy. T. T. Flynn. (Running Time: 2 hrs. 6 mins.). 2000. 10.95 (978-1-60083-522-3(8)) Iofy Corp.

Satan's Goal (Tree) Chron.21:1-8, Zech. 3, 640. Ed Young. 1987. 4.95 (978-0-7417-1640-8(2), 640) Win Walk.

Satan's Primary Strategy. Jack Deere. 1 cass. (Running Time: 90 mins.). (Demonic Inroads Ser.: Vol. 1). 2000. 5.00 (JD02-001) Morning NC.
First laying a foundation of insight into Satan's overall strategy, Jack then builds upon it with practical knowledge of the Christian's authority over demonic forces.

***Satan's School for Scandal: A Harry Landers Episode.** Jack Bates. Read by Bruce Reizen. (ENG.). 2010. 2.99 (978-1-61114-022-4(6)); 2.99 (978-0-9827919-3-6(3)) Mind Wings Aud.

Satan's Servants. Dan Corner. 1 cass. 3.00 (80) Evang Outreach.

Satan's Silence. unabr. ed. Alex Matthews. Read by Lynda Evans. 8 cass. (Running Time: 10 hrs. 30 min.). (Cassidy McCabe Mystery Ser.). 2001. 49.95 (978-1-55686-752-1(2)) Books in Motion.
Psychotherapist Cassidy McCabe gains a strange new client, following her patient's terrifying flashback of Satanic rituals. Is it still happening 20 years later?.

Satan's Snaps, Traps & Snares. Jack Marshall. 1 cass. 2004. 9.95 (978-1-57734-226-7(7), 06005713) Covenant Comms.
A super effective, entertaining youth talk.

Satan's Snaps, Traps & Snares & The Foolishness of Going One on One with the Devil. Jack Marshall. 1 cass. 6.98 (978-1-55503-360-6(1), 061984) Covenant Comms.
Two super-effective, entertaining youth talks.

Satan's Strategy: Logos January 16, 2000. Ben Young. 2000. 4.95 (978-0-7417-6165-1(3), B0165) Win Walk.

Satan's Tail. Dale Brown. (Dale Brown's Dreamland Ser.). 2005. 25.95 (978-0-06-052038-0(8)) HarperCollins Pubs.

Satan's Tail. abr. ed. Dale Brown. Read by Larry Pressman. 5 CDs. (Running Time: 6 hrs.). (Dale Brown's Dreamland Ser.). 2005. audio compact disk 14.95 (978-0-06-052267-4(4)) HarperCollins Pubs.

Satan's Target: Genesis 3:1-7, 639. Ed Young. 1987. 4.95 (978-0-7417-1639-2(9), 639) Win Walk.

***Satanta's Woman.** Cynthia Haseloff. 2009. (978-1-60136-522-4(5)) Audio Holding.

Satchmo: The Louis Armstrong Story. R. Porter. 2 Cds. (Running Time: 3 hrs.). 2005. audio compact disk 19.95 (978-0-660-18559-0(8)) Pub: Canadian Broadcasting CAN. Dist(s): Georgetown Term

Satchmo's Blues. unabr. ed. Allan Schroeder. Narrated by Peter Francis James. 1 cass. (Running Time: 30 mins.). (gr. 1 up). 1997. 10.00 (978-0-7887-0699-8(3), 94873E7) Recorded Bks.
Fictionalized account of Louis Armstrong's early childhood. Young Satchmo's determination will capture listeners' hearts & their imaginations will soar along with the dream of this extraordinary young man.

Satellite Down. unabr. ed. Rob Thomas. Narrated by Johnny Heller. 5 pieces. (Running Time: 7 hrs. 15 mins.). (gr. 11 up). 1998. 46.00 (978-0-7887-2703-0(6), 95643E7) Recorded Bks.
Seventeen-year-old Patrick Sheridan becomes a television reporter on "Classroom Direct." As he becomes a celebrity, he enjoys the money & fame, but grows less sure of who he is, or wants to be.

Satellite Pastoral Care Programs in the Small Community: Hospital Resource. 1 cass. (Care Cassettes Ser.: Vol. 11, No. 3). 1984. 10.80 Assn Prof Chaplains.

Satellite Sisters' Uncommon Senses. unabr. ed. Lian Dolan et al. 8 cass. (Running Time: 12 hrs.). 2002. 64.00 (978-0-7366-8633-4(9)) Books on Tape.
The Satellite Sisters, five real-life sisters, gather on radio from all over the country and the world to discuss their divergent lives.

Satguru & the Modern Mind. unabr. ed. Swami Amar Jyoti. 1 cass. (Satsangs of Swami Amar Jyoti Ser.). 1996. 9.95 (E-35) Truth Consciousness.
Why does Satguru come to help us? Learning to trust. Ills of the modern mind. True intelligence & intuitive life.

Satin Dolls. Friedman-Fairfax and Sony Music Staff. 1 cass. (CD Ser.). 1994. pap. bk. 15.98 (978-1-56799-125-3(4), Friedman-Fairfax) M Friedman Pub Grp Inc.

Satirical Journalism. Read by Heywood Hale Broun et al. 1 cass. (Running Time: 56 min). (Broun Radio Ser.). 11.95 (40090) J Norton Pubs.
With Herblock ("Herblock: Special Report") & David Levine.

Satisfaction: Program from the Award Winning Public Radio Serie. Interview. Hosted by Fred Goodwin. Comment by John Hockenberry. 1 CD. (Running Time: 1 hr.). 2004. audio compact disk 21.95 (978-1-932479-89-8(9), LCM 320) Lichtenstein Creat.
Turns out the Danes are the most satisfied people in the world. Who knew? We'll look at the biology of satisfaction and its role in the human experience, and learn why too much choice can leave us DIS-satisfied. Plus, a sneak preview as jazz artist and philosopher diva Nora York performs her new single "What I Want," and commentary from the rarely satisfied John Hockenberry.

Satisfaction & Happiness. Dick Sutphen. 1 cass. (Running Time: 1 hr.). (RX17 Ser.). 1986. 14.98 (978-0-87554-301-7(4), RX110) Valley Sun.
You now create the space for satisfaction & happiness in your life. You do what you need to do to attain satisfaction & happiness. You accept what you cannot change, & change what you can. Satisfaction & happiness are your divine right & you open to accept what is rightfully yours.

Satisfaction Guaranteed see Science Fiction Favorites of Isaac Asimov

Satisfaction Guaranteed see Isaac Asimov Library

Satisfied Customers Tell Three Friends, Angry Customers Tell 3,000. Pete Blackshaw. Read by Lloyd James. (Playaway Adult Nonfiction Ser.). 2008. 39.99 (978-1-60640-692-2(2)) Find a World.

Satisfied Customers Tell Three Friends, Angry Customers Tell 3,000: Running a Business in Today's Consumer-Driven World. unabr. ed. Pete Blackshaw. Narrated by Lloyd James. (Running Time: 5 hrs. 30 mins. 0 sec.). (ENG.). 2008. audio compact disk 49.99 (978-1-4001-3731-2(4)); audio compact disk 19.99 (978-1-4001-5731-0(5)) Pub: Tantor Media. Dist(s): IngramPubServ

Satisfied Customers Tell Three Friends, Angry Customers Tell 3,000: Running a Business in Today's Consumer-Driven World. unabr. ed. Pete Blackshaw. Read by Lloyd James. (Running Time: 5 hrs. 30 mins. 0 sec.). (ENG.). 2008. audio compact disk 24.99 (978-1-4001-0731-5(8)) Pub: Tantor Media. Dist(s): IngramPubServ

***Satori.** unabr. ed. Don Winslow. (Running Time: 10 hrs.). (ENG.). 2011. 25.98 (978-1-60788-693-8(6)); audio compact disk 29.98 (978-1-60788-692-1(8)) Pub: Hachet Audio. Dist(s): HachBkGrp

Satrange Case of Dr. Jekyll & Mr. Hyde see Extraño Caso Del Dr. Jekyll y Mr Hyde

Satsang 1. 1 cass. (Running Time: 1 hr.). 9.95 (SS1) Nada Prodns.
Chanting, kirtan & prayers as done in all the Sivananda Ashrams & by devotees around the world. Includes: Jai Ganesh (Mantras); Prema Mudita; Adi Divya Jyoti Maha; Brahma Murari; Nama Ramayana; Sri Ram Jai Ram (Mantra); Arati; Jai Jagadish Hare; Hey Prabu & prayers.

Satsang 2. 1 cass. (Running Time: 1 hr.). 9.95 (SS2) Nada Prodns.
Ragas, Mantras & Prayers: Raga Yaman Kalyan - Vandana Hai Sharaday; Raga Bhairavi - Prema Mudita; Raga Yaman - Dhana Lakshmi; Deity Shlokas; Shantih Mantras & Prayers.

Satsang 3. 1 cass. (Running Time: 1 hr.). 9.95 (SS3) Nada Prodns.
Simple chants arranged in beautiful Ragas to create peace & joy in the heart: Hari Narayana Govinda; Rama Chandra; Bolay Natha; Narayana; Govinda Jai Jai; Nataraj; Hari Hari Bol; Bansuri.

Saturday. unabr. ed. Ian McEwan. Read by Steven Crossley. 9 CDs. (Running Time: 11 Hrs). 2005. audio compact disk 34.99 (978-1-4193-3287-6(2)) Recorded Bks.

Saturday Night at the Blue Note. Perf. by Oscar Peterson. 1 cass., 1 CD. 7.98 (TA 33306); audio compact disk 12.78 CD Jewel box. (TA 83306) NewSound.

Saturday Night at the Pahala Theatre. Lois-Ann Yamanaka. 1 cass. 1993. pap. bk.; 8.00 Selections from pap bk. (978-0-910043-32-8(9)) Bamboo Ridge Pr.

Saturday Night Fish Fry - ShowTrax. Arranged by Kirby Shaw. 1 CD. (Running Time: 5 mins.). 2000. audio compact disk 19.95 (08742177) H Leonard.
From the '40s big band era, this sassy arrangement is a great change of pace for jazz & show groups. Lots of fun!.

Saturday Night Poets: A Reading with Memories of the Twenties. Malcolm Cowley. Read by Malcolm Cowley. 1 cass. (Running Time: 1 hr. 7 min.). 1968. 11.95 (23048) J Norton Pubs.

Saturday, Sunday, Monday see Puss in Boots & Other Fairy Tales from Around the World

Saturday Sweeping see Philip Levine

Saturday the Rabbi Went Hungry. unabr. ed. Harry Kemelman. Narrated by George Guidall. 5 cass. (Running Time: 7 hrs. 15 mins.). (Rabbi Small Mystery Ser.). 1997. 44.00 (978-0-7887-1761-1(8), 95239E7) Recorded Bks.
As the Jewish community at Barnard's Crossing prepares for Yom Kippur, a missing member of the temple congregation turns up dead in his own garage.

Saturdays. Elizabeth Enright. Read by Pamela Dillman. (Running Time: 5 hrs.). 2006. 19.95 (978-1-59912-899-3(3)) Iofy Corp.

Saturdays. unabr. ed. Elizabeth Enright. Read by Pamela Dillman. (J). 2007. 34.99 (978-1-59895-941-3(7)) Find a World.

Saturdays. unabr. ed. Elizabeth Enright. 4 CDs. (Running Time: 5 hrs.). (What's New Ser.). (J). 2004. audio compact disk 27.95 (978-1-59316-020-3(8), LL112) Listen & Live.

Saturdays & Teacakes. Lester L. Laminack. Perf. by Lester L. Laminack. Illus. by Chris K. Soentpiet. (Running Time: 35 mins.). (ENG.). (J). 2009. audio compact disk 6.95 (978-1-56145-514-0(8)) Peachtree Pubs.

Saturday's Child see Poetry of Countee Cullen

Saturdays with Stella: How My Dog Taught Me to Sit, Stay & Come When God Calls. Allison Pittman. (ENG.). 2009. audio compact disk 19.99 (978-1-934384-24-4(0)) Pub: Treasure Pub. Dist(s): STL Dist NA

Saturn: A Novel of the Ringed Planet. Ben Bova. Read by Amanda Karr & Stefan Rudnicki. 2004. 26.95 (978-1-59397-495-4(7)) Pub: Macmill Audio. Dist(s): Macmillan

Saturn: A Novel of the Ringed Planet. unabr. rev. ed. Ben Bova & Ben Bova. Read by Amanda Karr & Stefan Rudnicki. Ed. by Patrick Hayden Nielsen. 11 CDs. (Running Time: 13 hrs. 30 mins. 0 sec.). (Grand Tour Ser.). (ENG.). 2004. audio compact disk 44.95 (978-1-59397-494-7(9)) Pub: Macmill Audio. Dist(s): Macmillan

Saturn: Handling Your Responsibility. Joyce Levine. Read by Joyce Levine. 1 cass. (Running Time: 45 min.). (Integrating Astrological Cycles Ser.). 1994. 9.95 (978-1-885856-03-6(2)) Vizualizations.
Side 1 - Integrating Saturn cycles - information & exercises. Side 2 - guided meditation.

Saturn: Our Point of Stability. Karen McCoy. 1 cass. (Running Time: 90 min.). 1988. 8.95 (699) Am Fed Astrologers.

Saturn: Planet of Grief & Mourning. Joan Kellogg. 1 cass. 8.95 (684) Am Fed Astrologers.
An AFA Convention workshop tape.

Saturn: The Greatest Benefit. Annie Hershey. 1 cass. 8.95 (157) Am Fed Astrologers.

Saturn - Chiron: Guided Visualizations. Luisa De La Lama. Narrated by Leila Gomez Bear & Jaques Bourquin. Music by Summa. 6 cass. (Running Time: 30 min.). (Power Planets Inner Jounreys Ser.). 1994. 11.95 set. (978-1-883381-03-5(7)) White Dragon.
Guided visualizations to contact the archetypal powers of Saturn & Chiron using Greek mythological figures. Theme narrated from the book "Power Planets".

Saturn - Truth or Trouble. Henrietta Cramton. 1 cass. 8.95 (847) Am Fed Astrologers.

Saturn & Mars in Synastry. Mary Jo Putney. 1 cass. 8.95 (286) Am Fed Astrologers.
Examine tie that binds & bond that burns.

Saturn & the Landmark Ages. Dorothy Santangelo. 1 cass. 8.95 (459) Am Fed Astrologers.

Saturn & Uranus. Joanne Wickenburg. 1 cass. 8.95 (599) Am Fed Astrologers.
Influence natally & by transit.

Saturn in Pisces. Laura Des Jardins. Read by Laura Des Jardins. 1 cass. (Running Time: 90 min.). 1994. 8.95 (1167) Am Fed Astrologers.

Saturn in Sagittarius. Gladys M. Hall. 1 cass. 8.95 (532) Am Fed Astrologers.
Relate to energies & know what to expect.

Saturn Karma. Louise Fimlaid. 1 cass. 8.95 (786) Am Fed Astrologers.

Saturn Observations. Clara Darr. 1 cass. 8.95 (775) Am Fed Astrologers.

Saturn-Pluto Square. Shirley Chenoweth. 1 cass. (Running Time: 60 min.). 1992. 8.95 (1020) Am Fed Astrologers.

Saturn the Spiritual Side. Harold Hason. 1 cass. 8.95 (415) Am Fed Astrologers.
Determine incarnational timing.

Saturn, the Taskmaster. Carol Ruth. 1 cass. 8.95 (300) Am Fed Astrologers.
Interpret & use Saturn cycles for personal benefit.

Saturn Through the Houses & Signs. Henrietta Cramton. 1 cass. 8.95 (068) Am Fed Astrologers.
What Saturn does in his 2 1/2 year stay in your chart.

Saturnalia. unabr. ed. Lindsey Davis. Narrated by Christian Rodska. 1 MP3-CD. (Running Time: 12 hrs. 14 mins.). (Marcus Didius Falco Ser.). 2007. 54.95 (978-0-7927-4902-8(2), Chivers Sound Lib); audio compact disk 89.95 (978-0-7927-4845-8(X), Chivers Sound Lib); 74.95 (978-0-7927-4926-4(X), Chivers Sound Lib) AudioGO.
It is the Roman holiday of Saturnalia. The days are short, the nights are for wild parties. A general has captured a famous enemy of Rome, and brings her home to adorn his Triumph as a ritual sacrifice. The logistics go wrong; she acquires a mystery illness - then a young man is horrendously murdered and she escapes from house arrest. Marcus Didius Falco is pitted against his old rival, the Chief Spy Anacrites, in a race to find the fugitive before her presence angers the public and makes the government look stupid. Falco has other priorities, for Helena's brother Justinus has also vanished, perhaps fatally involved once more with the great lost love of his youth. Against the riotous backdrop of the season of misrule, the search seems impossible and only Falco seems to notice that some dark agency is bringing death to the city streets.

***Saturnalia: A Marcus Didius Falco Novel.** Lindsey Davis. Narrated by Christian Rodska. (Running Time: 10 hrs. 0 mins. 0 sec.). (ENG.). 2011. audio compact disk 34.95 (978-1-4084-6801-2(8)) Pub: AudioGO. Dist(s): Perseus Dist

Saturn's Race. Larry Niven & Steven Barnes. Read by Scott Brick. 2000. audio compact disk 96.00 (978-0-7366-7136-1(6)) Books on Tape.

Saturn's Race. collector's unabr. ed. Larry Niven & Steven Barnes. Read by Scott Brick. 10 cass. (Running Time: 15 hrs.). 2000. 80.00 (978-0-7366-5937-6(4)) Books on Tape.
Chaz Koto is a citizen of Xanadu, a near future perfect society hosting the wealthiest men & women on Earth. Along with his fellow citizens, he bears the burden of a dark secret that the outside world would be shocked to hear. Lenore Myles is a student who travels to Xanadu & becomes involved with Koto. When Koto unwittingly lends her his access codes, Lenore stumbles upon the grisly truth behind Xanadu's glittering facade. Lenore is soon on the run, hunted down by Saturn, a mysterious entity that moves aggressively to contain the security breach. With the interests of the world's wealthiest people at stake & powerful technology at Saturn's fingertips, Lenore is in a race for her life against a truly formidable foe.

Satyajit Ray Returns; Crisis in the Bombay Film Industry. unabr. ed. Julian C. Hollick. 1 cass. (Running Time: 30 min.). 1989. 12.50 (978-1-56709-037-6(0), 1075) Indep Broadcast.
"Satyajit Ray Returns." A retrospective of the career of the great Bengali filmmaker. "Crisis in the Bombay Film Industry." Wet sari nights in Bombay.

Saucer. unabr. ed. Stephen Coonts. Read by Dick Hill. 6 cass. (Running Time: 9 hrs.). (Saucer Ser.: No. 1). 2002. 29.95 (978-1-59086-078-6(0), 1590860780, BAU); 69.25 (978-1-59086-079-3(9), 1590860799, Unabridge Lib Edns) Brilliance Audio.
When Rip Cantrell, a seismic survey worker in the Sahara, spots a glint of reflected light in the distance - he investigates and finds a piece of metal apparently entombed in the sandstone. Before long, Rip and his colleagues uncover a flying saucer that has been resting there for 140,000 years. Their discovery doesn't remain a secret for long. The U.S. Air Force sends a UFO investigation team, which arrives just minutes before a team sent by an Australian billionaire to steal the saucer's secrets. Before either side can outwit the other, the Libyan military arrives. Meanwhile, Rip has been checking out the saucer. With the help of a beautiful ex-Air Force test pilot, Charley Pine, Rip flies the saucer away, embarking on a fantastic journey into space and around the world, keeping just ahead of those who want the saucer for themselves.

Saucer. unabr. ed. Stephen Coonts. Read by Dick Hill. (Running Time: 9 hrs.). (Saucer Ser.: No. 1). 2004. 39.25 (978-1-59335-592-0(0), 1593355920, Brinc Audio MP3 Lib) Brilliance Audio.

Saucer. unabr. ed. Stephen Coonts. Read by Dick Hill. (Running Time: 9 hrs.). (Saucer Ser.: No. 1). 2004. 39.25 (978-1-59710-662-7(3), 1597106623, BADLE); 24.95 (978-1-59710-663-4(1), 1597106631, BAD) Brilliance Audio.

Saucer. unabr. ed. Stephen Coonts. Read by Dick Hill. (Running Time: 9 hrs.). (Saucer Ser.: No. 1). 2004. 24.95 (978-1-59335-141-0(0), 1593351410) Soulmate Audio Bks.

Saucer Full of Secrets. Keith Rodway. (Running Time: 1 hr. 13 mins. 0 sec.). (ENG., 2000. audio compact disk 15.95 (978-1-84240-080-7(0)) Pub: Chrome Dreams GBR. Dist(s): IPG Chicago

***Saucer: the Conquest.** Stephen Coonts. Contrib. by Dick Hill. (Playaway Adult Fiction Ser.). (ENG.). 2010. 69.99 (978-1-4418-5601-2(3)) Find a World.

Saudi Arabic: Modern. 185.00 (1967, Lrn Inc) Oasis Audio.
Presents methods in learning a second language.

Saudi Arabic Basic Course FSI CDs & Text. 19 CDs. (Running Time: 9 hrs). (ARA.). 2005. audio compact disk 225.00 (978-1-57970-106-2(X), AFA234D) J Norton Pubs.

Saudi Bombing Inquiry Dropped. Leonard Peikoff. 1 cass. (Philosophy: Who Needs It? Ser.). 1998. 12.95 (LPXXC62) Second Renaissance.

Saudis, unabr. ed. Sandra Mackey. Read by Nadia May. 13 cass. (Running Time: 19 hrs.). (ENG.). 1990. 85.95 (978-0-7861-0276-1(4), 1242) Blckstn Audio.
This remarkable book gets to the heart of Saudi society & government, & provides an in-depth chronicle of the "oil boom" years, as the medieval nomadic society clashes with the intrusion of foreigners, wealth, & technology, & struggles for a vital place of power in the modern world.

Saul & Patsy. Charles Baxter. Contrib. by John Rubinstein. (Playaway Adult Fiction Ser.). (ENG.). 2008. 59.99 (978-1-60640-677-9(9)) Find a World.

Saul & Patsy. unabr. ed. Charles Baxter. Read by John Rubinstein. 8 cass. (Running Time: 12 hrs.). 2004. 34.95 (978-1-59007-472-5(6)); audio compact disk 59.95 (978-1-59007-473-2(4)) Pub: New Millenn Enter. Dist(s): PerseuPGW

Saul Bellow. Interview with Saul Bellow. 1 cass. (Running Time: 20 min.). 1972. 10.95 (L009) TFR.
Bellow explains how he managed to keep writing during the depression, he expresses resentment at being grouped as "a Jewish writer" & he says there is no such thing.

Saul Steinberg. Read by Saul Steinberg. 1978. (L045) TFR.

Savage Beauty Pt. A: The Life of Edna St. Vincent Millay. unabr. ed. Nancy Milford. Read by Kimberly Schraf. 9 cass. (Running Time: 13 hrs. 30 mins.). 2002. 72.00 (978-0-7366-8492-7(1)) Books on Tape.
For those who believe America's bohemianism began in the 1960s, this biography of Edna St. Vincent Millay serves as a powerful corrective. Possessed of an electric personality and a highly original poetic voice, Millay burst on the bohemian scene in 1917 with her poem "Renascence," went to Vassar on the financial support of her poetry's admirers, and made another grand entrance into bohemia upon her arrival in Greenwich Village. Her sexuality was as incandescent as her poetry. She was known for her ardent bisexuality and for the extraordinary number of sexual partners she took. She left such figures as Edmund Wilson begging for her favors. Nancy Milford has gotten unprecedented access to Millay's letters and journals, and this is the first authorized and authoritative Millay biography.

Savage Beauty Pt. B: The Life of Edna St. Vincent Millay. unabr. ed. Nancy Milford. Read by Kimberly Schraf. 9 cass. (Running Time: 13 hrs. 30 mins.). 2002. 72.00 (978-0-7366-8509-2(X)) Books on Tape.

***Savage City.** unabr. ed. T. J. English. (ENG.). 2011. (978-0-06-202747-4(6), Harper Audio) HarperCollins Pubs.

***Savage Day.** unabr. ed. Jack Higgins. Read by Michael Page. (Running Time: 6 hrs.). (Simon Vaughn Ser.). 2010. audio compact disk 87.97 (978-1-4418-4422-4(8), 9781441844224, BriAudCD Unabrid); audio compact disk 29.99 (978-1-4418-4421-7(X), 9781441844217, Bril Audio CD Unabri) Brilliance Audio.

***Savage Day.** unabr. ed. Jack Higgins. Read by Michael Page. (Running Time: 6 hrs.). (Simon Vaughn Ser.). 2010. 24.99 (978-1-4418-4426-2(0), 9781441844262, BAD) Brilliance Audio.

Savage Day. unabr. collector's ed. Jack Higgins. Read by Larry McKeever. 5 cass. (Running Time: 5 hrs.). 1985. 30.00 (978-0-7366-0506-9(1), 1480) Books on Tape.
Simon Vaughn, a British officer turned gun runner, is sprung from a Greek prison by the British on condition that he pose as an undercover arms dealer in Northern Ireland. He gets more than he bargained for-$500,000 in hijacked gold, a smuggling operation in Ulster & a murderous manhunt.

Savage Detectives. unabr. ed. Roberto Bolaño. (Running Time: 25 hrs. 50 mins.).Tr. of Detectives Salvajes. 2009. 44.95 (978-1-4332-9265-1(3)) Blckstn Audio.

Savage Detectives. unabr. ed. Roberto Bolaño. Read by Armando Duran. (Running Time: 24 hrs. 5 mins.).Tr. of Detectives Salvajes. 2009. audio compact disk & audio compact disk 44.95 (978-1-4332-9264-4(5)) Blckstn Audio.

Savage Detectives: A Novel. unabr. ed. Roberto Bolaño. (Running Time: 15 hrs. 0 mins.). (ENG.). 2009. 85.95 (978-1-4332-9261-3(0)); 65.95 (978-1-4332-9331-3(5)) Blckstn Audio.

Savage Detectives: A Novel. unabr. ed. Roberto Bolaño. Tr. by Natasha Wimmer from SPA. Narrated by Eddie Lopez & Armando Duran. 24 CDs. (Running Time: 25 hrs. 50 mins.). 2009. audio compact disk 140.00 (978-1-4332-9262-0(9)) Blckstn Audio.

Savage Garden. abr. ed. Mark Mills. Read by Ian Stuart. (Running Time: 6 hrs.). 2008. audio compact disk 14.99 (978-1-4233-3800-0(6), 9781423338000, BCD Value Price) Brilliance Audio.

Savage Garden. unabr. ed. Mark Mills. Read by Ian Stuart. (Running Time: 9 hrs.). 2007. 39.25 (978-1-4233-3798-0(0), 9781423337980, BADLE); 24.95 (978-1-4233-3797-3(2), 9781423337973, BAD); 74.25 (978-1-4233-3792-8(1), 9781423337928, BriAudUnabridg); audio compact disk 92.25 (978-1-4233-3794-2(8), 9781423337942, BriAudCD Unabrid); audio compact disk 39.25 (978-1-4233-3796-6(4), 9781423337966, Brinc Audio MP3 Lib); audio compact disk 24.95 (978-1-4233-3795-9(6), 9781423337959, Brilliance MP3); audio compact disk 34.95 (978-1-4233-3793-5(X), 9781423337935, Bril Audio CD Unabri) Brilliance Audio.

Savage Horde, Vol.. I. Jerry Ahern. Read by Charlie O'Dowd. 2 vols. No. 6. 2004. (978-1-58807-819-3(1)) Am Pubng Inc.

Savage Horde, Vol. I. unabr. ed. Jerry Ahern. Read by Charlie O'Dowd. 2 cass. (Running Time: 3 hrs.). (Survivalist Ser.: No. 6). 2004. 18.00 (978-1-58807-310-5(6)) Am Pubng Inc.

Savage Horde, Vol.. II. Jerry Ahern. Read by Charlie O'Dowd. 2 vols. No. 6. 2004. (978-1-58807-820-9(5)) Am Pubng Inc.

Savage Horde, Vol.. II. unabr. ed. Jerry Ahern. Read by Charlie O'Dowd. 2 cass. (Running Time: 3 hrs.). (Survivalist Ser.: No. 6). 2004. 18.00 (978-1-58807-311-2(4)) Am Pubng Inc.

***Savage Inequalities: Children in America's Schools.** unabr. ed. Jonathan Kozol. Read by Mark Winston. 1 CD MP3. (Running Time: 9 hrs.). 2010. 24.99 (978-1-4418-4161-2(X), 9781441841612, Brilliance MP3); 39.97 (978-1-4418-4162-9(8), 9781441841629, Brinc Audio MP3 Lib) Brilliance Audio.

Savage Kingdom. unabr. collector's ed. Zane Grey. Read by Dan Lazar. 5 cass. (Running Time: 5 hrs.). 1998. 30.00 (978-0-7366-0327-0(1), 1313) Books on Tape.
Nature closely observed by leading sportsman & author.

Savage Kingdom: The True Story of Jamestown, 1607, & the Settlement of America. unabr. ed. Benjamin Woolley. Read by David Drummond. (YA). 2007. 59.99 (978-1-60252-926-7(4)) Find a World.

Savage Kingdom: The True Story of Jamestown, 1607, & the Settlement of America. unabr. ed. Benjamin Woolley. Read by David Drummond. (Running Time: 14 hrs. 0 mins. 0 sec.). (ENG.). 2007. audio compact disk 39.99 (978-1-4001-0470-3(X)); audio compact disk 29.99 (978-1-4001-5470-8(7)); audio compact disk 79.99 (978-1-4001-3470-0(6)) Pub: Tantor Media. Dist(s): IngramPubServ

Savage My Kinsman. Elisabeth Elliot. Read by Elisabeth Elliot. 4 cass. (Running Time: 4 hrs.). 1989. 18.95 (978-0-8474-2006-3(X)) Back to Bible.
The Author shares her experiences of living with an Indian tribe & explains how one can know the joy of committed Christian living.

Savage Place. unabr. collector's ed. Robert B. Parker. Read by Michael Prichard. 5 cass. (Running Time: 5 hrs.). (Spenser Ser.). 1989. 40.00 (978-0-7366-1621-8(7), 2481) Books on Tape.
TV reporter Candy Sloan has eyes the color of cornflowers & legs that stretch all the way to heaven. She also has somebody threatening to rearrange her lovely face if she keeps on snooping into charges of Hollywood racketeering. Spenser's job is to keep Candy healthy until she breaks the biggest story of her career. But her star witness has just bowed out with three bullets in his chest, two tough guys have doubled up to test Spenser's skill with his fists, & Candy is about to use her own sweet body as live bait in a deadly romantic game - a game that may cost Spenser his life.

Savage Season. unabr. ed. Joe R. Lansdale. Read by Phil Gigante. (Running Time: 5 hrs.). (Hap & Leonard Ser.). 2009. 39.97 (978-1-4233-8387-1(7), 9781423383871, Brinc Audio MP3 Lib); 24.99 (978-1-4233-8386-4(9), 9781423383864, Brilliance MP3) Brilliance Audio.

Savage Season. unabr. ed. Joe R. Lansdale. Read by Philippe Gigantes. (Running Time: 5 hrs.). (Hap & Leonard Ser.). 2009. 39.97 (978-1-4233-8389-5(3), 9781423383895, BADLE) Brilliance Audio.

Savage Season. unabr. ed. Joe R. Lansdale. Read by Phil Gigante. (Running Time: 5 hrs.). (Hap & Leonard Ser.). 2009. 24.99 (978-1-4233-8388-8(5), 9781423383888, BAD); audio compact disk 29.99 (978-1-4233-8384-0(2), 9781423383840); audio compact disk 87.97 (978-1-4233-8385-7(0), 9781423383857, BriAudCD Unabrid) Brilliance Audio.

Savage Tales of Solomon Kane. unabr. ed. Robert E. Howard. Narrated by Paul Boehmer. (Running Time: 12 hrs. 30 mins. 0 sec.). (ENG.). 2010. 24.99 (978-1-4001-6228-4(9)); 18.99 (978-1-4001-8228-2(X)); audio compact disk 69.99 (978-1-4001-4228-6(8)); audio compact disk 34.99 (978-1-4001-1228-9(1)) Pub: Tantor Media. Dist(s): IngramPubServ

***Savage Thunder: Antietam & the Bloody Road to Freedom.** unabr. ed. Jim Murphy. Narrated by Kevin Orton. 1 Playaway. (Running Time: 3 hrs.). (J). (gr. 4-8). 2009. 54.75 (978-1-4407-1413-9(4)); 30.75 (978-1-4407-1405-4(3)); audio compact disk 30.75 (978-1-4407-1409-2(6)) Recorded Bks.

***Savage Thunder: Antietam & the Bloody Road to Freedom.** unabr. collector's ed. Jim Murphy. Narrated by Kevin Orton. 3 CDs. (Running Time: 3 hrs.). (J). (gr. 4-8). 2009. audio compact disk 25.95 (978-1-4407-3590-5(5)) Recorded Bks.

Savage Truth on Money. abr. ed. Terry Savage. 4 cass. (Running Time: 4 hrs.). 2000. 25.00 (978-0-929071-66-4(2)) B-B Audio.
Does the thought of saving for retirement, coping with debt, or paying for college leave you fearful and frazzled? Are you confused and intimidated by expert financial advice you cant understand? Do you want to invest in stocks and mutual funds but can.

Savage Truth on Money. unabr. ed. Terry Savage. Read by Anna Fields. 9 cass. (Running Time: 11 hrs. 30 mins.). 2000. 62.95 (978-0-7861-1818-2(0), 2617); audio compact disk 88.00 (978-0-7861-9853-5(2), 2617) Blckstn Audio.
The candid & up-front advice is aimed at your mind, your heart & your balance sheet. Whether you're just starting out or well on your way, Terry Savage will empower you to make informed money decisions & evaluate the advice that the financial industry sends your way. From her experience as a stock trader, stockbroker, investment advisor, television commentator & bestselling personal finance author, she will enable you to manage your money by freeing yourself from debt, creating a budget you can live with & investing wisely.

Savage War of Peace: Algeria 1954-1962. collector's ed. Alistair Horne. Read by Bill Kelsey. 10 cass. (Running Time: 15 hrs.). 2000. 80.00 (978-0-7366-5099-1(7)); 96.00 (978-0-7366-5100-4(4)) Books on Tape.
The Algerian war was at once the last of the old style colonial wars & the archetype of horribly savage new conflicts, undeclared wars between old & new worlds, waged successfully by urban terrorists & country based guerrillas against crack modern armies. In eight years, more than a million Algerians died & an equal number of Europeans lost their homes. It was a tragedy rife with lessons Americans had to learn all over again in Vietnam. As the Third World continues to make it aspirations felt & established political powers continue to maintain an order they must struggle to impose, the story of Algeria's fight for independence stand as mode & prophecy.

Savage War of Peace: Algeria 1954-1962. unabr. ed. Alistair Horne. Read by James Adams. (Running Time: 108000 sec.). 2008. audio compact disk 44.95 (978-1-4332-0887-4(3)); audio compact disk 44.95 (978-1-4332-0888-1(1)); audio compact disk & audio compact disk 140.00 (978-1-4332-0885-0(7)) Blckstn Audio.

Savage Wilderness. unabr. ed. Harold Coyle. Read by Geoffrey Howard. 11 cass. (Running Time: 16 hrs.). 1998. 76.95 (978-0-7861-1304-0(9), 2215) Blckstn Audio.
Takes us back to a time when America's vast riches were up for grabs, & British forces, joined by the American colonial militias, & the French aided by their Indian allies, were locked in battle over the great territories of the Ohio valley.

***Savage Wilderness.** unabr. ed. Harold Coyle. Read by Geoffrey Howard. (Running Time: 16 hrs. 0 mins.). 2010. 29.95 (978-1-4417-1908-9(3)); audio compact disk 118.00 (978-1-4417-1905-8(9)) Blckstn Audio.

Savagery of Love: Brother Antoninus Reads His Poetry. unabr. ed. Brother Antoninus. Perf. by Brother Antoninus. 1 cass. Incl. Afterglow of the Rose. (SWC 1260); Face I Know. (SWC 1260); From the Rock Untombed. (SWC 1260); Immortal Strangeness. (SWC 1260); Raging of the Rose. (SWC 1260); Rose of Solitude. (SWC 1260); Rose of Solitude: The Way of Life & the Way of Death. (SWC 1260); 1984. 12.95 (978-0-694-50184-7(0), SWC 1260) HarperCollins Pubs.

Savages. unabr. ed. Bill Pronzini. Read by Nick Sullivan. 6 CDs. (Running Time: 7 hrs. 13 mins.). (Nameless Detective Mystery Ser.). 2007. audio compact disk 64.95 (978-0-7927-4857-1(3)) AudioGO.

***Savages.** unabr. ed. Don Winslow. (Running Time: 11 hrs. 0 mins.). 2010. 34.99 (978-1-4001-9766-8(X)); 17.99 (978-1-4001-8766-9(4)) Tantor Media.

***Savages.** unabr. ed. Don Winslow. Narrated by Michael Kramer. 1 MP3-CD. (Running Time: 7 hrs. 30 mins. 0 sec.). 2010. 24.99 (978-1-4001-6766-1(3)); audio compact disk 83.99 (978-1-4001-4766-3(2)); audio compact disk 34.99 (978-1-4001-1766-6(6)) Pub: Tantor Media. Dist(s): IngramPubServ

Savages. unabr. collector's ed. Joe Kane. Read by Michael Russotto. 8 cass. (Running Time: 12 hrs.). 1999. 64.00 (9[illegible]-7366-4303-0(6), 4794) Books on Tape.
The author returns to the river to search [illegible] the Huaorani, a nation of 1,300 nomadic Indians so isolated they speak a language unrelated to any other on earth, so fierce that for millennia they had defended a territory the size of Massachusetts against all comers. But theirs is a territory rich in oil & now the Huaorani find themselves besieged by a wave of hell-bent oil companies, dogged missionaries all claiming to represent their best interests.

Savannah. James Reasoner. Read by Lloyd James. (Running Time: 34200 sec.). (Civil War Battle Ser.). 2006. 59.95 (978-0-7861-4506-5(4)); audio compact disk 72.00 (978-0-7861-7198-9(7)) Blckstn Audio.

Savannah. unabr. ed. James Reasoner. Read by Lloyd James. (Running Time: 34200 sec.). (Civil War Battle Ser.: Bk. 9). 2006. audio compact disk 29.95 (978-0-7861-7657-1(1)) Blckstn Audio.

Savannah: Or, A Gift for Mr. Lincoln. unabr. ed. John Jakes. Narrated by Ed Sala. 6 cass. (Running Time: 8 hrs. 45 mins.). 2004. 59.75 (978-1-4193-0931-1(5), 97891MC) Recorded Bks.

Savannah Blues. abr. ed. Mary Kay Andrews. Read by Susan Ericksen. (Running Time: 21600 sec.). 2007. audio compact disk 14.99 (978-1-4233-2332-7(7), 9781423323327, BCD Value Price) Brilliance Audio.

Savannah Blues. unabr. ed. Mary Kay Andrews. Read by Susan Ericksen. 9 cass. (Running Time: 13 hrs.). 2002. 34.95 (978-1-58788-790-1(8), 1587887908, BAU); 96.25 (978-1-58788-791-8(6), 1587887916, Unabridge Lib Edns) Brilliance Audio.
Eloise Foley, known to her friends as Weezie, has been through the divorce from hell. Her ex-husband Tal (aka Talmadge Evans III) was awarded their house in Savannah's historic district, the house that Weezie had spent years painstakingly restoring to its original splendor. Weezie was awarded the two-bedroom carriage house on the same property. Each was sure the other would sell. But Tal has taken up residence in the main house with his new girlfriend Caroline DeSantos (who never seems to perspire or have a hair out of place during the wilting Savannah summer), Weezie is running her antiques business out back, and neither will budge. She's also got a few loony relatives and a hunky former boyfriend to contend with, and if that's not enough, dirty deals aplenty wherever she turns. In this town, where everybody knows everybody's business, something's got to give, and something does.

Savannah Blues. unabr. ed. Mary Kay Andrews. Read by Susan Ericksen. (Running Time: 13 hrs.). 2004. 39.25 (978-1-59335-403-9(7), 1593354037, Brinc Audio MP3 Lib) Brilliance Audio.

Savannah Blues. unabr. ed. Mary Kay Andrews. Read by Susan Ericksen. (Running Time: 13 hrs.). 2004. 39.25 (978-1-59710-665-8(8), 1597106658, BADLE); 24.95 (978-1-59710-664-1(X), 159710664X, BAD) Brilliance Audio.

Savannah Blues. unabr. ed. Mary Kay Andrews. Read by Susan Ericksen. (Running Time: 46800 sec.). 2006. audio compact disk 107.25 (978-1-4233-2330-3(0), 9781423323303, BriAudCD Unabrid); audio compact disk 36.95 (978-1-4233-2329-7(7), 9781423323297, Bril Audio CD Unabri) Brilliance Audio.

Savannah Blues. unabr. ed. Mary Kay Andrews. Read by Susan Ericksen. (Running Time: 13 hrs.). 2004. 24.95 (978-1-59335-148-9(8), 1593351488) Soulmate Audio Bks.

Savannah Breeze. abr. ed. Mary Kay Andrews. Read by Isabel Keating. 5 CDs. (Running Time: 21600 sec.). 2006. audio compact disk 29.95 (978-0-06-085285-6(2)) HarperCollins Pubs.

***Savannah Breeze.** abr. ed. Mary Kay Andrews. Read by Isabel Keating. (ENG.). 2006. (978-0-06-113494-4(5), Harper Audio); (978-0-06-113495-1(3), Harper Audio) HarperCollins Pubs.

Savannah Breeze. unabr. ed. Mary Kay Andrews. Read by Moira Driscoll. 10 cass. (Running Time: 51780 sec.). 2006. 84.95 (978-0-7927-3926-5(4), Chivers Sound Lib); audio compact disk 110.95 (978-0-7927-3927-2(2), Chivers Sound Lib); audio compact disk 29.95 (978-0-7927-3971-5(X), Chivers Sound Lib) AudioGO.

Savannah {or} a Gift for Mr. Lincoln. abr. ed. John Jakes. Read by Dylan Baker. 2006. 17.95 (978-0-7435-6167-9(8)) Pub: S&S Audio. Dist(s): S and S Inc

Savannah Purchase, Set unabr. ed. Jane Aiken Hodge. Read by Diana Bishop. 6 cass. 1999. 54.95 (CAB 1601) AudioGO.

Savannas of Africa Audio CD. Adapted by Benchmark Education Company Staff. Based on a work by Katherine Scraper. (Early Explorers Set C Ser.). (J). (gr. 1). 2008. audio compact disk 10.00 (978-1-60437-537-4(X)) Benchmark Educ.

Save a Tree for Me: 1 Big Book, 6 Each of 1 Student Book, & 1 Cassette. (Song Box Ser.). (gr. 1-2). bk. 68.95 (978-0-7802-3206-8(2)) Wright Group.

Save in the Cross. Richard Kingsmore. 1999. 75.00 (978-0-633-00536-8(3)); audio compact disk 16.98 (978-0-633-00524-5(X)) LifeWay Christian.

Save in the Cross Choral Cassette. Richard Kingsmore. 1999. 11.98 (978-0-633-00532-0(0)) LifeWay Christian.

Save in the Cross Split Acc Cd. Richard Kingsmore. 1999. audio compact disk 85.00 (978-0-633-00528-3(2)) LifeWay Christian.

Save Me. Perf. by Lori Wilke. 1 cass. (Running Time: 5 min.). 1998. 9.98 Sound track. (978-1-891916-33-5(5)) Spirit To Spirit.

***Save Me.** unabr. ed. Lisa Scottoline. (Running Time: 10 hrs. 0 mins. 0 sec.). (ENG.). 2011. audio compact disk 39.99 (978-1-4272-1132-3(9)) Pub: Macmill Audio. Dist(s): Macmillan

Save Our Earth. pap. bk. (978-0-9649986-3-6(7)) Iguana Prodns.

Save the Animals, Save the Earth: Songs about Endangered Animals & the Earth. Lois Skiera-Zucek. 1 cass. (Running Time: 35 min.). (J). (ps-4). 2001. pap. bk. 10.95 (KIM 9124C); pap. bk. 11.95 (KIM 9124) Kimbo Educ.
Starring many of our animal friends from around the world! Original songs for kids about the importance of protecting the earth's animals & their habitats. An exciting variety of musical styles, including rap, rock, calypso & more, make this a fun way for children to learn. Song guide included.

Save the River!/Take Care of Earth. Steck-Vaughn Staff. 1997. (978-0-8172-7387-3(5)) SteckVau.

Save the World. 1 cass. (Club Baby Ser.). (J). 7.98 (NRR 3) NewSound.

Save Time & Energy: NACADA Webinar Series 17. Featuring Leigh Cunningham & Marsha A. Miller. (ENG.). 2008. audio compact disk 140.00 (978-1-935140-59-7(0)) Nat Acad Adv.

Save Your Heart for Me. Gwen Shamblin. (ENG.). 2008. audio compact disk (978-1-892729-02-6(4)) Weigh Down Work.

"Save Yourself from This Perverse Generation" Modernism & the Old Covenant. Perf. by John Vennari. 1 cass. (Running Time: 90 mins.). 2000. 7.00 (20227) Cath Treas.
Many Churchmen in high places are awash in the old modernist error that today's "religion of the Old Covenant" (that rejects Christ) is a legitimate means of salvation. This error is having disastrous repercussions throughout the Church worldwide. Learn of the project presently underway by the United States bishops to re-write the lectionary, in collaboration with Jewish

rabbis to remove anything from it deemed to be "anti-Jewish." This amounts to a complete betrayal of Jesus Christ & the destruction of the Gospel. This error is refuted by citing the work of the eminent theologian, the late Msgr. Joseph Clifford Fenton.

Saved see Bible in Living Sound: Life and Times of the Old Testament; Life and Times of Jesus; Life and Times of Paul

Saved a Wretch Like Me: Eph. 2:8-9. Ed Young. 1988. 4.95 (978-0-7417-1665-1(8), 665) Win Walk.

Saved & Sanctified. Bill Winston. 6 cass. (Running Time: 4hr.54min.). (C). 1996. 25.00 (978-1-931289-59-7(X)) Pub: B Winston Min. Dist(s): Anchor Distributors

Saved by Grace. Gloria Copeland. 2 cass. 1990. 10.00 (978-0-88114-903-6(9)) K Copeland Pubns.
Biblical teaching on grace.

Saved by the Bell. Barbara Davoll & Dennis Hockerman. Illus. by Dennis Hockerman. 1 cass. (Christopher Churchmouse Ser.). (J). (ps-2). 1988. bk. 11.99 (978-0-89693-614-0(7), 3-1614) David C Cook.

Saved by the Bell: Sountrack to the Original Hit TV Series. Perf. by Michael Damian. 1 CD. (Running Time: 1 hr.). (J). 2002. audio compact disk 16.98 (978-1-56826-504-9(2), 71880) Rhino Enter.

Saved by the Light Seminar: An Evening with Dannion Brinkley. Dannion Brinkley. 2 cass. 1995. 16.95 (978-1-879323-39-1(7)) Sound Horizons AV.
The question "What happens after death?" is now answered by the best-selling author of "Saved by the Light." Dannion Brinkley describes his two near-death experiences, including the 117 insights revealed to him by 13 beings of light, & how what he experienced on "the other side" changed his life & can change yours.

Saved by the Lion King: Daniel 6:7-28. Ed Young. 1995. 4.95 (978-0-7417-2074-0(4), 1074) Win Walk.

***Saved from What?** unabr. ed. R. C. Sproul. Narrated by Lloyd James. (ENG.). 2010. 10.98 (978-1-59644-989-3(6)) christianaud.

***Saved from What?** unabr. ed. R. c. Sproul & R. C. Sproul. Narrated by Lloyd James. (Running Time: 3 hrs. 30 mins. 0 sec.). (ENG.). 2010. audio compact disk 15.98 (978-1-59644-988-6(8)) christianaud.

Saved, Healed & Delivered. Bernita Conway. 1 cass. (Running Time: 90 mins.). (He Still Heals Ser.: Vol. 5). 2000. 5.00 (SAO1-005) Morning NC.
Learn about the healing power of God that is available to believers today.

Saved, Sealed, Delivered. Perf. by Chicago Mass Choir. 1 cass. 10.98 (978-1-57908-446-2(X)); audio compact disk 16.98 (978-1-57908-445-5(1)) Platinm Enter.

Saved the Day. Contrib. by Phillips Craig & Dean. (Praise Hymn Soundtracks Ser.). 2007. audio compact disk 8.98 (978-5-557-63291-1(3)) Pt of Grace Ent.

Saveurs du Savoir. Roland Barthes. Read by Roland Barthes. 4 cass. (FRE.). 1995. 39.95 (1743-RF) Olivia & Hill.
The French critic reads from some of his most famous works. With testimonials by Antoine Campagnon & Julia Kristeva, among others.

Saving a Life: How We Found Courage When Death Rescued Our Son. unabr. ed. Charles Morris & Janet Morris. Narrated by Charles Morris & Janet Morris. (Running Time: 3 hrs. 38 mins. 0 sec.). (ENG.). 2008. audio compact disk 16.99 (978-1-59859-359-4(5)) Oasis Audio.

Saving A Life: How We Found Courage When Death Rescued Our Son. unabr. ed. Charles Morris & Janet Morris. Narrated by Charles Morris & Janet Morris. (Running Time: 3 hrs. 38 mins. 0 sec.). (ENG.). 2008. 11.89 (978-1-60814-372-6(4)) Oasis Audio.

Saving Agnes: A Novel. unabr. ed. Rachel Cusk. Narrated by Jenny Sterlin. 6 cass. (Running Time: 8 hrs. 45 mins.). 1998. 51.00 (978-0-7887-2111-3(9), 95436E7) Recorded Bks.
With flowing, poetic prose, the author weaves an engrossing story of a young woman's search for her own identity. Although her desperate attempts to forget the lover who jilted her culminate in a series of one-night-stands & in an affair with a mysterious heroin addict, Agnes' sparkling sense of humor affirms her resilience.

Saving Cascadia. abr. ed. John J. Nance. Read by John J. Nance. (Running Time: 6 hrs.). 2005. audio compact disk 74.25 (978-1-59355-966-3(6), 9781593559663, BACDLib Ed) Brilliance Audio.
A few hundred years ago, Cascadia Island didn't even exist. Like the Washington seacoast, it was rock submerged beneath the Pacific. A massive earthquake changed that, exploding the rock upward, making it land - unstable land, according to seismologist Dr. Doug Lam. Lam has spent years researching the Cascadia Subduction Zone. He published a theory that the unrelieved tectonic strain beneath the idyllic landscape of Cascadia Island could be triggered with modern construction processes - with catastrophic results. The paper was disregarded, even ridiculed, by his peers and by mega wealthy developer Mick Walker, who stands to earn millions from the construction of a luxury resort on Cascadia. The elegant casino, hotel, and convention center will reap millions for him even if the tiny island only lasts for a short time... When a series of earthquakes begins to shake the Northwest Corridor, Doug's worst fears are confirmed. In an attempt to convince Walker to evacuate Cascadia immediately, Doug hurries to join guests arriving for the resort's grand opening. As the tremors wreak havoc across the Northwest coastal area, the military is left with too few resources to assist the people on Cascadia. Convinced that the island will be in ruins within hours, Doug reluctantly calls upon his girlfriend, Jennifer Lindstrom, president of Nightingale Aviation - a major medical transport helicopter company - for help. With snow falling, visibility dropping, and winds increasing, Doug embarks on an impossible mission with Jennifer and Nightingale's helicopters to evacuate over three hundred people, while smaller earthquakes continue to herald the approach of a catastrophic tsunami. John J. Nance hurtles readers along a nail-biting quest to rescue hundreds of stranded vacationers and resort staff. Meticulously researched, and with the signature authenticity only a veteran pilot could provide, Saving Cascadia is a hair-raising thriller of awesome magnitude.

Saving Cascadia. abr. ed. John J. Nance. Read by John J. Nance. (Running Time: 21600 sec.). 2006. audio compact disk 16.99 (978-1-59737-336-4(2), 9781597373364, BCD Value Price) Brilliance Audio.
A few hundred years ago, Cascadia Island didn't even exist. Like the Washington seacoast, it was rock submerged beneath the Pacific. A massive earthquake changed that, exploding the rock upward, making it land - unstable land, according to seismologist Dr. Doug Lam. Lam has spent years researching the Cascadia Subduction Zone. He published a theory that the unrelieved tectonic strain beneath the idyllic landscape of Cascadia Island could be triggered with modern construction processes - with catastrophic results. The paper was disregarded, even ridiculed, by his peers and by mega wealthy developer Mick Walker, who stands to earn millions from the construction of a luxury resort on Cascadia. The elegant casino, hotel, and convention center will reap millions for him even if the tiny island only lasts for a short time... When a series of earthquakes begins to shake the Northwest Corridor, Doug's worst fears are confirmed. In an attempt to convince Walker to evacuate Cascadia immediately, Doug hurries to join guests arriving for the resort's grand opening. As the tremors wreak havoc across the Northwest coastal area, the military is left with too few resources to assist the people on Cascadia. Convinced that the island will be in ruins within hours, Doug reluctantly calls upon his girlfriend, Jennifer Lindstrom, president of Nightingale Aviation - a major medical transport helicopter company - for help. With snow falling, visibility dropping, and winds increasing, Doug embarks on an impossible mission with Jennifer and Nightingale's helicopters to evacuate over three hundred people, while smaller earthquakes continue to herald the approach of a catastrophic tsunami. John J. Nance hurtles readers along a nail-biting quest to rescue hundreds of stranded vacationers and resort staff. Meticulously researched, and with the signature authenticity only a veteran pilot could provide, Saving Cascadia is a hair-raising thriller of awesome magnitude.

Saving Cascadia. unabr. ed. John J. Nance. Read by John J. Nance. (Running Time: 13 hrs.). 2005. 39.25 (978-1-59710-666-5(6), 9781597106665, BADLE); 39.25 (978-1-59335-816-7(4), 9781593358167, Brinc Audio MP3 Lib); 24.95 (978-1-59335-682-8(X), 9781593356828, Brilliance MP3); 34.95 (978-1-59086-761-7(0), 9781590867617, BAU); 92.25 (978-1-59086-762-4(9), 9781590867624, BrilAudUnabridg) Brilliance Audio.
Please enter a Synopsis.

Saving Cascadia. unabr. ed. John J. Nance. Read by John J. Nance. (Running Time: 13 hrs.). 2005. 24.95 (978-1-59710-667-2(4), 9781597106672, BAD) Brilliance Audio.

Saving CeeCee Honeycutt. Beth Hoffman. Contrib. by Jenna Lamia. (Running Time: 10 hrs.). (ENG.). (gr. 12 up). 2010. audio compact disk 39.95 (978-0-14-314554-7(1), PenAudBks) Pub: Pnguin Bks Ltd GBR. Dist(s): Penguin Grp USA

***Saving CeeCee Honeycutt.** unabr. ed. Beth Hoffman. Read by Jenna Lamia. 8 CDs. 2010. audio compact disk 80.00 (978-0-307-71217-2(6), BksonTape) Pub: Random Audio Pubg. Dist(s): Random

Saving Cinnamon: The Amazing True Story of a Missing Military Puppy & the Desperate Mission to Bring Her Home. unabr. ed. Christine Sullivan. Narrated by Laural Merlington. (Running Time: 8 hrs. 0 mins.). 2009. 15.99 (978-1-4001-8480-4(0)); 24.99 (978-1-4001-6480-6(X)); audio compact disk 34.99 (978-1-4001-1480-1(2)); audio compact disk 69.99 (978-1-4001-4480-8(9)) Pub: Tantor Media. Dist(s): IngramPubServ

Saving Elijah. unabr. ed. Fran Dorf. Narrated by Suzanne Toren. 11 cass. (Running Time: 13 hrs. 45 mins.). 2001. 88.00 (978-0-7887-4996-4(X), 96370E7) Recorded Bks.
Dinah Galligans youngest child is in the life-threatening coma & she would do anything to save him. Then she meets a taunting, seductive spirit that helps her to make a desperate choice.

Saving Energy in Religious Structures & Buildings for Non-Profit Organizations. Hosted by Nancy Pearlman. 1 cass. (Running Time: 29 min.). 10.00 (1104) Educ Comm CA.

Saving Faith. David Baldacci. Read by Michael Kramer. 1999. audio compact disk 88.00 (978-0-7366-6068-6(2)) Books on Tape.

Saving Faith. David Baldacci. Read by Michael Kramer. 9 cass. (Running Time: 13 hrs.). 2000. 72.00 (978-0-7366-4791-5(0), 5138) Books on Tape.
Both the FBI & a killer search for the same two people in a tale of power gone mad in Washington.

Saving Faith. abr. ed. David Baldacci. (Running Time: 4 hrs. 30 mins.). (ENG.). 2006. 14.98 (978-1-59483-770-8(8)) Pub: Hachet Audio. Dist(s): HachBkGrp

Saving Faith. abr. ed. David Baldacci. 4 cass. 1999. 25.98 (FS9-51087) Highsmith.

Saving Faith. unabr. ed. David Baldacci. Read by Michael Kramer. 11 CDs. (Running Time: 13 hrs. 24 mins.). 2001. audio compact disk 44.00 Books on Tape.
Both the FBI & a killer search for the same two people in a tale of power gone mad in Washington D.C.

Saving Fish from Drowning. unabr. ed. Amy Tan. Read by Amy Tan. (Running Time: 18 hrs.). 2005. 44.25 (978-1-59737-736-2(8), 9781597377362, BADLE); 29.95 (978-1-59737-735-5(X), 9781597377355, BAD); 39.95 (978-1-59737-729-4(5), 9781597377294, BAU); 97.25 (978-1-59737-730-0(9), 9781597377300, BrilAudUnabridg); audio compact disk 39.95 (978-1-59737-731-7(7), 9781597377317, Bril Audio CD Unabri); audio compact disk 29.95 (978-1-59737-733-1(3), 9781597377331, Brilliance MP3); audio compact disk 44.25 (978-1-59737-734-8(1), 9781597377348, Brinc Audio MP3 Lib); audio compact disk 112.25 (978-1-59737-732-4(5), 9781597377324, BriAudCD Unabrid) Brilliance Audio.
A pious man explained to his followers: "It is evil to take lives and noble to save them. Each day I pledge to save a hundred lives. I drop my net in the lake and scoop out a hundred fishes. I place the fishes on the bank, where they flop and twirl. 'Don't be scared,' I tell those fishes. 'I am saving you from drowning.' Soon enough, the fishes grow calm and lie still. Yet, sad to say, I am always too late. The fishes expire. And because it is evil to waste anything, I take those dead fishes to market and I sell them for a good price. With the money I receive, I buy more nets so I can save more fishes." - Anonymous Twelve American tourists join an art expedition that begins in the Himalayan foothills of China - dubbed the true Shangri-La - and heads south into the jungles of Burma. But after the mysterious death of their tour leader, the carefully laid plans fall apart, and disharmony breaks out among the pleasure-seekers as they come to discover that the Burma Road is paved with less-than-honorable intentions, questionable food, and tribal curses. And then, on Christmas morning, eleven of the travelers boat across a misty lake for a sunrise cruise - and disappear. Drawing from the current political reality in Burma and woven with pure confabulation, Amy Tan's picaresque novel poses the question: How can we discern what is real and what is fiction, in everything we see? How do we know what to believe? Saving Fish from Drowning finds sly truth in the absurd: a reality TV show called Darwin's Fittest, a repressive regime known as SLORC, two cheroot-smoking twin children hailed as divinities, and a ragtag tribe hiding in the jungle - where the sprites of disaster known as Nats lurk, as do the specters of the fabled Younger White Brother and a British illusionist who was not who he was worshipped to be. With her signature "idiosyncratic, sympathetic characters, haunting images, historical complexity, significant contemporary themes, and suspenseful mystery" (Los Angeles Times), Amy Tan spins a provocative and mesmerizing tale about the mind and the heart of the individual, the actions we choose, the moral questions we might ask ourselves, and above all, the deeply personal answers we seek when happy endings are seemingly impossible.

Saving Francesca. Melina Marchetta. Read by Rebecca Macauley. (Running Time: 6 hrs. 30 mins.). (YA). 2009. 69.99 (978-1-74214-332-3(6), 9781742143323) Pub: Bolinda Pubng AUS. Dist(s): Bolinda Pub Inc

Saving Francesca. unabr. ed. Melina Marchetta. Read by Rebecca Macauley. 5 cass. (Running Time: 6 hrs. 15 mins.). (YA). 2004. 40.00 (978-1-74093-002-4(9)); audio compact disk 77.95 (978-1-74093-114-4(9)) Pub: Bolinda Pubng AUS. Dist(s): Bolinda Pub Inc

***Saving Francesca.** unabr. ed. Melina Marchetta. Read by Rebecca Macauley. (Running Time: 6 hrs. 30 mins.). (YA). 2010. 43.95 (978-1-74214-752-9(6), 9781742147529) Pub: Bolinda Pubng AUS. Dist(s): Bolinda Pub Inc

Saving Freedom: We Can Stop America's Slide into Socialism. unabr. ed. Jim DeMint. Read by J. Charles. (Running Time: 9 hrs.). 2009. 24.99 (978-1-4418-1162-2(1), 9781441811622, BAD); 49.97 (978-1-4418-1163-9(X), 9781441811639, BADLE) Brilliance Audio.

Saving Freedom: We Can Stop America's Slide into Socialism. unabr. ed. Jim DeMint. Read by J. Charles. (Running Time: 10 hrs.). 2009. 24.99 (978-1-4418-1160-8(5), 9781441811608, Brilliance MP3); 39.97 (978-1-4418-1161-5(3), 9781441811615, Brinc Audio MP3 Lib); audio compact disk 29.99 (978-1-4418-1158-5(3), 9781441811585, Bril Audio CD Unabri); audio compact disk 92.97 (978-1-4418-1159-2(1), 9781441811592, BriAudCD Unabrid) Brilliance Audio.

Saving Grace. Julie Garwood. 2004. 10.95 (978-0-7435-4593-8(1)) Pub: S&S Audio. Dist(s): S and S Inc

Saving Grace. Gerald Hammond. 4 cass. (Running Time: 5 hrs. 35 mins.). (Story Sound Ser.). (J). 2005. 44.95 (978-1-85903-765-2(8)) Pub: Mgna Lrg Print GBR. Dist(s): Ulverscroft US

Saving Grace. collector's ed. Barbara Rogan. Read by Anna Fields. 9 cass. (Running Time: 13 hrs. 30 mins.). 2000. 72.00 (978-0-7366-5574-3(3)) Books on Tape.
Jonathan Fleishman has always been perceived as a rare politician, powerful, successful, idealistic & genuinely committed to the good of the people. When his beloved daughter, Grace, holds him to standards politically impossible to maintain & when his spotless record is challenged by rumors of corruption by a ruthless young journalist with whom Grace is romantically entangled, Jonathan's good life is abruptly shattered & Grace, faced with what she believes is the betrayal of a lover who used her to get at her father, comes to realize that neither man is what he seems, even to himself.

Saving Grace. unabr. ed. Lee Smith. Narrated by Christina Moore. 7 cass. (Running Time: 9 hrs. 45 mins.). 2000. 65.00 (978-0-7887-4385-6(6), 96250E7) Recorded Bks.
The daughter of a snake-handling preacher who ignores the needs of his family, Florida Grace doesn't think much of Jesus. In fact, he's the reason for the trouble in her life.

Saving Graces. Patricia Gaffney. Read by Judith Ivey. (Running Time: 5 hrs.). 2000. 24.00 (Random AudioBks) Random Audio Pubg.

Saving Graces, unabr. ed. Patricia Gaffney. Read by Beth Fowler. 10 vols. (Running Time: 15 hrs.). 2000. bk. 84.95 (978-0-7927-2344-8(9), CSL 233, Chivers Sound Lib) AudioGO.
For ten years, Emma, Rudy, Lee & Isabel have shared a deep affection that has helped them deal with the ups & downs in life. Calling themselves the Saving Graces, the quartet is united by understanding, honesty & acceptance - a connection that has grown stronger over the years. Emma is sharp-tongued & soft-hearted; Rudy is a beauty with an extraordinary gift for love; Lee longs for motherhood in her idyllic marriage; Isabel, the oldest, is a survivor. However, they will not be prepared for a crisis of astounding proportions that is yet to come.

Saving Graces. unabr. ed. Patricia Gaffney. Read by Beth Fowler. 14 CDs. (Running Time: 21 hrs.). 2002. audio compact disk 115.95 (SLD 105) AudioGO.
For ten years, Emma,Rudy, Lee and Isabel have shared a deep affection that has helped them deal with the ebb and flow of expectations and disappointments common to us all. Calling themselves the Saving Graces, the quartet is united by understanding, honesty and acceptance. Though these sisters of the heart and soul have seen it all, they will not be prepared for a crisis of astounding proportions that will put their love and courage to the ultimate test.

Saving Milly: Love, Politics, & Parkinson's Disease. Morton Kondracke. Read by Michael Prichard. 2002. 48.00 (978-0-7366-8788-1(2)) Books on Tape.

Saving Money: An Easy, Smart Guide to Saving Money. Barbara Loos. (B & N Basics Ser.). 2003. audio compact disk 9.98 (978-0-7607-3801-6(7), Silver Lini) M Friedman Pub Grp Inc.

Saving Mountain Lions & Recycling Trash. Hosted by Nancy Pearlman. 1 cass. (Running Time: 30 min.). 10.00 (522) Educ Comm CA.

Saving Oregon, Idaho & Washington's Hells Canyon Country. Hosted by Nancy Pearlman. 1 cass. (Running Time: 29 min.). 10.00 (910) Educ Comm CA.

Saving Our Cities. Francis Frangipane. 1 cass. (Running Time: 90 mins.). (Basics of Spiritual Warfare Ser.: Vol. 4). 2000. 5.00 (FF02-004) Morning NC.
Francis combines years of practical experience with a soundbiblical perspective in this popular & important series.

Saving Our Seas. unabr. ed. Perf. by Eknath Easwaran. 1 cass. (Running Time: 1 hr.). 1989. 7.95 (978-1-58638-603-0(4)) Nilgiri Pr.

Saving Sarah Cain. 2008. audio compact disk 13.99 (978-5-557-49745-9(5), Word Records) Word Enter.

Saving Shiloh. Phyllis Reynolds Naylor. Read by Henry Leyva. 2 cass. (Running Time: 3 hrs. 10 mins.). (Shiloh Ser.: No. 3). (J). (gr. 4-7). 2000. 38.25 (978-0-7366-9048-5(4)) Pub: Books on Tape. Dist(s): NetLibrary CO
Marty tries to help Judd change his mean ways, treating him with respect & trusting him, even while rumors persist in the community that he has murdered a man.

Saving Shiloh. unabr. ed. Phyllis Reynolds Naylor. Read by Henry Leyva. 2 vols. (Running Time: 3 hrs. 10 mins.). (J). (gr. 3-7). 2004. pap. bk. 29.00 (978-0-8072-0456-6(0), Listening Lib); 20.40 (978-0-8072-0455-9(2), Listening Lib) Pub: Random Audio Pubg. Dist(s): NetLibrary CO

Saving Sweetness. Read by Tom Bodett. 11 vols. (Running Time: 13 mins.). (Live Oak Readalong Ser.). (J). 2005. pap. bk. 16.95 (978-0-87499-898-6(0)) AudioGO.
A resourceful little orphan convinces the sheriff to rescue her from mean Mrs. Sump and adopt her in this tale.

Saving Sweetness. Read by Tom Bodett. 41 vols. (Running Time: 13 mins.). (J). 2002. pap. bk. & tchr.'s planning gde. ed. 37.95 (978-0-87499-900-6(6)) Live Oak Media.

Saving Sweetness. Read by Tom Bodett. 11 vols. (Running Time: 13 mins.). (J). (ps-4). 2002. bk. 25.95 (978-0-87499-899-3(9)) Live Oak Media.

Saving Sweetness. Diane Stanley. Illus. by G. Brian Karas. 11 vols. (Running Time: 13 mins.). 2002. bk. 28.95 (978-1-59112-548-0(0)); pap. bk. 39.95 (978-1-59112-547-1(2)) Live Oak Media.

Saving Sweetness. Diane Stanley. Illus. by G. Brian Karas. (Running Time: 13 mins.). 2002. 9.95 (978-0-87499-897-9(2)); audio compact disk 12.95 (978-1-59112-329-3(1)) Live Oak Media.

Saving Tax Dollars with Extensions on Federal Estate & Pennsylvania Inheritance Taxes. 1 cass. 1988. 35.00 (AC-452) PA Bar Inst.

Saving the Badlands Adventure: With Buffalo Biff & Farley's Raiders. unabr. ed. Joe Loesch. Ed. by Cheryl J. Hutchinson. Illus. by Ott Denney. 1 cass. (Running Time: 1 hr. 03 min.). (Backyard Adventure Ser.: Vol. 2). (J).

(gr. 1-5). 1995. pap. bk. 14.95 (978-1-887729-02-4(X)); pap. bk. 16.95 INCL. PAPERBK. (978-1-887729-03-1(8)) Toy Box Prods.
The Raiders set out to save the old Indian burial grounds from greedy land developers.

Saving the Endangered Hunting & Gathering Kalahari Desert Bushmen in Africa's Botswana & Namibia. Hosted by Nancy Pearlman. 1 cass. (Running Time: 29 min.). 10.00 (1101) Educ Comm CA.

Saving the Future. Lance Auburn Everette. Read by Sherri Barth. 2 cass. (Running Time: 3 hrs.). 2005. 15.99 (978-1-58943-271-0(1)) Am Pubng Inc.
This is the third book in a truly unique series of historical action-adventure novels: Michael. Sometimes, in history, things worked out for the best against all odds. Maybe Somebody intervened on the side of the correct path - even when we didn't know what that path was. But to intervene in the affairs of human beings without disrupting civilization completely is to wield human tools - and human weapons. So when the Archangels arrive to Change Things, watch out! The Inquisition in Spain was out to destroy libraries containing thousands of years of human knowledge, including the last known copies of the works of ancient scholars, playwrights, and poets, and the scientific advances in Spain under the Moors. But many of these "heathen" books survived. Did Somebody help? Published for the first time ever by Americana Publishing. Michael: Spirituality - with an edge.

Saving the Future. Lance Auburn Everette. Read by Marguerite Gavin. 3 CDs. (Running Time: 3 hrs.). 2005. audio compact disk 9.99 (978-1-58943-484-4(6)) Am Pubng Inc.

Saving the Queen. unabr. ed. William F. Buckley, Jr. Read by James Buschmann. 8 CDs. (Running Time: 10 hrs.). (Blackford Oakes Mystery Ser.). 2000. audio compact disk 64.00 (978-0-7861-8641-9(0), 3273) Blckstn Audio.

Saving the Queen. unabr. ed. William F. Buckley, Jr. Read by James Buschmann. 7 cass. (Running Time: 10 hrs.). (Blackford Oakes Mystery Ser.). 2001. 49.95 (978-0-7861-2713-9(9), 3273) Blckstn Audio.

Saving the Queen. unabr. collector's ed. William F. Buckley, Jr.. Read by William F. Buckley, Jr. 7 cass. (Running Time: 10 hrs. 30 mins.). (Blackford Oakes Mystery Ser.). 1980. 56.00 (978-0-7366-0336-2(0)) Books on Tape.
Blackford Oakes plays the international counter-intelligence game for all it's worth.

Saving the Seals from Extinction. Kenneth Bruce. 1 cass. (Running Time: 1 hr.). Dramatization. (Excursions in History Ser.). 12.50 Alpha Tape.

Saving the World. Julia Alvarez. Narrated by Blanca Camacho. (Running Time: 59400 sec.). 2006. audio compact disk 39.99 (978-1-4193-7794-5(9)) Recorded Bks.

Saving the World. abr. ed. James Patterson. Read by Valentina de Angelis. 4 CDs. (Running Time: 5 hrs.). (Maximum Ride Ser.: No. 3). (ENG.). 2009. audio compact disk 9.98 (978-1-60024-444-5(0)) Pub: Hachet Audio. Dist(s): HachBkGrp

Saving the World. abr. unabr. ed. James Patterson. Read by Jill Apple. (Running Time: 6 hrs.). (Maximum Ride Ser.: No. 5). (ENG.). 2009. 16.98 (978-1-60024-447-6(5)) Pub: Hachet Audio. Dist(s): HachBkGrp

Saving the World. unabr. ed. Julia Alvarez. Read by Blanca Camacho. 14 CDs. (Running Time: 16 hrs.). 2006. audio compact disk 119.75 (978-1-4193-8916-0(5), C3690); 109.75 (978-1-4193-8914-6(9), 98339) Recorded Bks.
In Saving the World, the author weaves the stories of two courageous women - separated by two centuries - into a breathtaking novel of love and idealism in an increasingly troubled world. A best-selling, Latin-American author living in Vermont, Alma stays behind when her husband travels to the Dominican Republic to help fight AIDS. She needs the time to work on her latest book, but she has terrible writer's block. Soon, her focus is diverted to an entirely new story, that of the early 19th-century anti-smallpox expedition of Dr. Francisco Balmis. Accompanying Dr. Balmis was Doña Isabel, who cared for the orphan boys serving as living carriers of the smallpox vaccine. It is the narrative of the courageous Doña Isabel that provides hope and inspiration when Alma's husband is taken captive. Mesmerizing and poetic, Saving the World is a visionary tale that raises profound questions about the world we live in - and whether or not it is beyond redemption.

Saving the World. unabr. ed. James Patterson. Read by Jill Apple. (Running Time: 6 hrs.). (ENG.). 2010. audio compact disk 9.98 (978-1-60024-833-7(0)) Pub: Hachet Audio. Dist(s): HachBkGrp

Saving the World. unabr. ed. James Patterson. Read by Nancy Wu. 8 cass. (Running Time: 9 hrs. 25 mins.). (Maximum Ride Ser.: Bk. 3). (YA). (gr. 6-10). 2007. 67.75 (978-1-4281-4830-7(2)); audio compact disk 87.75 (978-1-4281-4835-2(3)) Recorded Bks.

Saving the World at Work: What Companies & Individuals Can Do to Go Beyond Making a Profit to Making a Difference. abr. unabr. ed. Tim Sanders. Read by Tim Sanders. (ENG.). 2008. audio compact disk 29.95 (978-0-7393-7040-7(5), Random AudioBks) Pub: Random Audio Pubg. Dist(s): Random

Saving the Zog. 2002. (978-0-7398-5124-1(1)) SteckVau.

Saving the Zog Level 2. (J). 2002. audio compact disk (978-0-7398-5334-4(1)) SteckVau.

Saving Your Marriage Before It Starts: Seven Questions to Ask Before & after You Marry. Les Parrott & Leslie Parrott. 2 cass. (Running Time: 2 hrs.). 1995. 16.99 (978-0-310-49248-1(3)) Zondervan.
Focuses on love & marriage.

Saving Your Marriage Before It Starts: Seven Questions to Ask Before-and after-You Marry. unabr. ed. Les Parrott, III & Leslie Parrott. (Running Time: 4 hrs. 8 mins. 0 sec.). (ENG.). 2006. 8.99 (978-0-310-26754-6(4)) Zondervan.

***Saving Your Second Marriage Before It Starts: Nine Questions to Ask Before (and after) You Remarry.** . Les and Leslie Parrott. (Running Time: 6 hrs. 24 mins. 0 sec.). (ENG.). 2009. 17.99 (978-0-310-30509-5(8)) Zondervan.

Saving Your Second Marriage Before It Starts: Nine Questions to Ask Before (and after) You Remarry. abr. ed. Les Parrott, III & Leslie Parrott. (Running Time: 2 hrs. 20 mins. 0 sec.). (ENG.). 2003. 8.99 (978-0-310-26095-0(7)) Zondervan.

Saving Your Second Marriage Before It Starts: Nine Questions to Ask Before (and after) You Remarry. unabr. ed. Les Parrott, III & Leslie Parrott. 2001. 17.99 (978-0-310-24066-2(2)) Zondervan.

***Saving Zasha.** unabr. ed. Randi G. Barrow. Narrated by Roger Mueller. (Running Time: 5 hrs. 0 mins. 0 sec.). (ENG.). 2011. audio compact disk 19.99 (978-1-59859-886-5(4)) Oasis Audio.

Savior-Centered Marriage. George Pace. 1 cass. 9.95 (978-1-57734-284-7(4), 06005810) Covenant Comms.
Keys to building an eternal marriage.

Savior Heals without a Scar. Read by Sheri Dew & Wendy Nelson. 2007. audio compact disk 13.95 (978-1-59038-836-5(4)) Deseret Bk.

Savior Is Born-Christmas First Service: Luke 2. Ed Young. 1995. 4.95 (978-0-7417-2082-5(5), 1082) Win Walk.

Savior of Her People: The Story of Esther. Bert Polman. (Running Time: 40 mins.). (Scripture Alive Ser.). 2000. 15.95 (978-1-56212-430-4(7), 415110) FaithAliveChr.

Savior of the World. Mormon Youth Chorus and Symphony. 1 cass. 8.95 (10001360); audio compact disk 12.95 (28001001) Covenant Comms.
A sacred cantata of word & music.

Savior of the World: A Sacred Cantata. Janice K. Perry & Joy S. Lundberg. 1 cass. 7.98 (1000217) Covenant Comms.

Savior's Prophecies: The from the Fall of Jerusalem to the Second Coming. Richard D. Draper. 4 cass. 2004. 19.95 (978-1-57734-866-5(4)) Covenant Comms.

Savior's Teachings on Service: How Much Is Enough? Jack Marshall. 1 cass. (Running Time: 50 min.). 1996. 7.98 Digital. (978-1-55503-907-3(3), 06005195) Covenant Comms.
Advice on developing a "Good Samaritan" attitude. Brother Marshall breaks down the different attitudes exhibited by each individual in the parable: the Levite & priest, the innkeeper, & the Samaritan. He teaches the importance of service & how much the Lord requires of us.

Saviour King. Contrib. by Hillsong. 2007. 19.98 (978-5-557-60948-7(2)) Hillsong Pubng AUS.

Saviour King. Contrib. by Hillsong. 2007. audio compact disk 17.98 (978-5-557-60949-4(0)); audio compact disk 29.98 (978-5-557-60946-3(6)); audio compact disk 19.95 (978-5-557-60947-0(4)) Hillsong Pubng AUS.

Saviour's Gate, unabr. ed. Tim Sebastian. Narrated by Simon Prebble. 7 cass. (Running Time: 10 hrs. 15 mins.). 1992. 60.00 (978-1-55690-727-2(3), 92336E7) Recorded Bks.
International intrigue involving Russian, British & American secret agents & the collapse of the Soviet Union.

Savitri Saves Her Husband from Death (A); Cyavana regains His Youth (B) 1 cass. (Spiritual Stories Ser.). 5.00 Bhaktivedanta.

Savoir Dire: Cours de Phonetique Et de Prononciation. Diane M. Dansereau. (FRE.). (C). 1990. pap. bk. 39.56 (978-0-669-20998-3(8)) HM Harcourt.

Savoir Faire. Mosele & Dalmolin. 2005. audio compact disk (978-0-8384-1102-5(9)) Heinle.

Savoir-Faire: An Advanced French Course - Cassettes. Catrine Carpenter & Elspeth Broady. 2001. bk. 89.95 (978-0-415-15312-6(3)) Pub: Routledge. Dist(s): Taylor and Fran

Savor the Moment. abr. ed. Nora Roberts. Read by Angela Dawe. (Running Time: 5 hrs.). (Bride Quartet Ser.: Bk. 3). 2010. audio compact disk 14.99 (978-1-4233-6893-9(2), 9781423368939, BACD) Brilliance Audio.

Savor the Moment. abr. ed. Nora Roberts. (Running Time: 6 hrs.). (Bride Quartet Ser.: Bk. 3). 2011. audio compact disk 9.99 (978-1-4233-6894-6(0), 9781423368946, BCD Value Price) Brilliance Audio.

Savor the Moment. unabr. ed. Nora Roberts. Read by Angela Dawe. (Running Time: 9 hrs.). (Bride Quartet Ser.: Bk. 3). 2010. 39.97 (978-1-4233-6890-8(8), 9781423368908, Brinc Audio MP3 Lib); 39.97 (978-1-4233-6892-2(4), 9781423368922, BADLE); 24.99 (978-1-4233-6889-2(4), 9781423368892, Brilliance MP3); 24.99 (978-1-4233-6891-5(6), 9781423368915, BAD); audio compact disk 92.97 (978-1-4233-6888-5(6), 9781423368885, BriAudCD Unabrid); audio compact disk 34.99 (978-1-4233-6887-8(8), 9781423368878, Bril Audio CD Unabri) Brilliance Audio.

Savvy. Ingrid Law. (Running Time: 7 hrs.). (ENG.). (gr. 12 up). 2008. audio compact disk 29.95 (978-0-14-314348-2(4), PengAudBks) Penguin Grp USA.

Savvy Networker. unabr. abr. ed. Contrib. by Caryl Krannich & Ron Krannich. 2 cass. (Running Time: 3 hrs.). 2002. 16.95 (978-1-885408-77-8(3)) Listen & Live.

Savvy Networking. (ENG.). 2009. audio compact disk 29.99 (978-0-9819877-0-5(2)) Nierenberg.

Savvy Traveler - French. 6 cass. (Running Time: 5 hrs. 15 mins.). (FRE.). 59.95 (SFR600) J Norton Pubs.
You will learn important words & phrases for dining, shopping, travel & doing business that will help start you on your way conversationally in a wide range of situations.

Savvy Traveler - French: Business. unabr. ed. Ed. by Janis M. Yates. 2 cass. (Running Time: 3 hrs.). (FRE.). 1996. 21.95 (978-0-88432-906-0(2), SFR575) J Norton Pubs.
Useful vocabulary & phrases for doing business in countries where French is spoken, or with French business people.

Savvy Traveler - French: Dining. unabr. ed. Ed. by Janis M. Yates. 2 cass. (Running Time: 3 hrs.). (FRE.). 1996. 21.95 (978-0-88432-907-0(0), SFR580) J Norton Pubs.
Useful vocabulary for dining in France & in French restaurants.

Savvy Traveler - French: Shopping. unabr. ed. Ed. by Janis M. Yates. 1 cass. (Running Time: 30 min.). (FRE.). 1996. 14.95 (978-0-88432-908-4(9), SFR585) J Norton Pubs.
Useful vocabulary & phrases for shopping in countries where French is spoken.

Savvy Traveler - French: Travel. unabr. ed. Ed. by Janis M. Yates. 1 cass. (Running Time: 30 min.). (FRE.). 1996. 12.95 (978-0-88432-909-1(7), SFR590) J Norton Pubs.
Useful vocabulary & phrases for traveling in countries where French is spoken.

Savvy Traveler - German: Dining. unabr. ed. Ed. by Janis M. Yates. 2 cass., bklet. (Running Time: 1 hr. 39 mins.). (GER.). 1997. pap. bk. 21.95 (978-0-88432-944-2(5), SGE580) J Norton Pubs.
Useful vocabulary for dining in German & in German restaurants.

Savvy Traveler - Italian: Dining. unabr. ed. Ed. by Janis M. Yates. 2 cass., bklet. (Running Time: 1 hr. 30 mins.). (Savvy Traveler Ser.). (ITA.). 1997. pap. bk. 21.95 (978-0-88432-958-9(5), SIT580) J Norton Pubs.
Useful vocabulary for dining in Italy & in Italian restaurants.

Savvy Traveler - Spanish: Shopping. Ed. by Janis M. Yates. 1 cass. (Running Time: 1 hr. 6 mins.). (Savvy Traveler Ser.). 1996. bk. 14.95 (978-0-88432-916-9(X), SSP585) J Norton Pubs.
Learn important words & phrases that will help start you on your way conversationally in a wide range of situations. Example sentences give practice in using the appropriate vocabulary in basic sentence constructions. Printed word lists are included for all words & phrases recorded.

Savvy Traveler - Spanish: Travel. Ed. by Janis M. Yates. 1 cass. (Running Time: 60 min.). (Savvy Traveler Ser.). (SPA.). 1996. bk. 14.95 (978-0-88432-917-6(8), SSP590) J Norton Pubs.

Savvy Traveler - Spanish Set: Business. Ed. by Janis M. Yates. 2 cass. (Running Time: 1 hr. 50 mins.). (Savvy Traveler Ser.). 1996. bk. 21.95 (978-0-88432-914-5(3), SSP575) J Norton Pubs.

Savvy Traveler - Spanish Set: Food & Dining. Ed. by Janis M. Yates. 2 cass. (Running Time: 1 hr. 39 mins.). (Savvy Traveler Ser.). 1996. bk. 21.95 (978-0-88432-915-2(1), SSP580) J Norton Pubs.

Savvy Traveler Series. Janis M. Yates. 6 cass. (Running Time: 5 hrs. 15 mins.). (SPA.). 2001. 59.95 (SSP600) J Norton Pubs.

Saxaphone JamTrax. rev. ed. Ralph Agresta. 1 CD. (Running Time: 1 hr.). 1998. pap. bk. 9.95 (978-0-8256-1647-1(6), AM945626) Music Sales.

***Saxon Algebra 1.** Created by Saxon Publishers. (ENG.). 2008. audio compact disk 91.00 (978-1-60277-491-9(9)) Saxon Pubs.

***Saxon Algebra 2.** Created by Saxon Publishers. (ENG.). 2008. audio compact disk 96.60 (978-1-60277-518-3(4)) Saxon Pubs.

***Saxon Geometry.** Created by Saxon Publishers. (ENG.). 2009. audio compact disk 93.80 (978-1-60277-554-1(0)) Saxon Pubs.

***Saxon Matematicas, Intermedias 3.** Created by Saxon Publishers. (SPA.). 2007. audio compact disk 88.93 (978-1-60032-422-2(3)) Saxon Pubs.

***Saxon Matematicas, Intermedias 3.** Created by Saxon Publishers. (ENG.). 2008. audio compact disk 268.80 (978-1-60277-596-1(6)) Saxon Pubs.

***Saxon Matematicas Intermedias 4.** Stephen Hake. (ENG.). 2008. audio compact disk 268.80 (978-1-60277-595-4(8)) Saxon Pubs.

***Saxon Matematicas, Intermedias 4.** Created by Saxon Publishers. (SPA.). 2007. audio compact disk 89.60 (978-1-60032-428-4(2)) Saxon Pubs.

***Saxon Matematicas, Intermedias 5.** Created by Saxon Publishers. (SPA.). 2007. audio compact disk 89.60 (978-1-60032-434-5(7)) Saxon Pubs.

***Saxon Matematicas, Intermedias 5.** Created by Saxon Publishers. (SPA.). 2008. audio compact disk 268.80 (978-1-60277-594-7(X)) Saxon Pubs.

***Saxon Matematicas 1.** Created by Saxon Publishers. (SPA.). 2007. audio compact disk 186.67 (978-1-60032-817-6(2)) Saxon Pubs.

***Saxon Math, Course 2.** Created by Saxon Publishers. 2006. audio compact disk 55.45 (978-1-59141-841-2(0)) Saxon Pubs.

***Saxon Math, Course 3.** Created by Saxon Publishers. 2006. audio compact disk 56.20 (978-1-59141-890-0(9)) Saxon Pubs.

***Saxon Math, Intermediate 3.** Created by Saxon Publishers. (ENG.). 2007. audio compact disk 75.60 (978-1-60032-421-5(5)) Saxon Pubs.

***Saxon Math, Intermediate 4.** Created by Saxon Publishers. (ENG.). 2007. audio compact disk 75.60 (978-1-60032-427-7(4)) Saxon Pubs.

***Saxon Math, Intermediate 5.** Created by Saxon Publishers. (ENG.). 2007. audio compact disk 75.60 (978-1-60032-432-1(0)) Saxon Pubs.

***Saxon Math, Math 5/4.** Created by Saxon Publishers. (ENG.). 2007. audio compact disk 7.63 (978-1-60032-208-2(5)) Saxon Pubs.

***Saxon Math, Math 6/5.** Created by Saxon Publishers. (ENG.). 2007. audio compact disk 7.63 (978-1-60032-209-9(3)) Saxon Pubs.

Saxons, Vikings, & Celts: The Genetic Roots of Britain & Ireland. unabr. ed. Bryan Sykes. Read by Dick Hill. (Running Time: 10 hrs. 0 mins. 0 sec.). (ENG.). 2006. audio compact disk 69.99 (978-1-4001-3335-2(1)); audio compact disk 24.99 (978-1-4001-5335-0(2)); audio compact disk 34.99 (978-1-4001-0335-5(5)) Pub: Tantor Media. Dist(s): IngramPubServ
Saxons, Vikings, and Celts is the most illuminating book yet to be written about the genetic history of Britain and Ireland. Through a systematic, ten-year DNA survey of more than 10,000 volunteers, Bryan Sykes has traced the true genetic makeup of British Islanders and their descendants. This historical travelogue and genetic tour of the fabled isles, which includes accounts of the Roman invasions and Norman conquests, takes readers from the Pontnewydd cave in North Wales, where a 300,000-year-old tooth was discovered, to the resting place of "The Red Lady" of Paviland, whose anatomically modern body was dyed with ochre by her grieving relatives nearly 29,000 years ago. A perfect work for anyone interested in the genealogy of England, Scotland, or Ireland, Saxons, Vikings, and Celts features a chapter specifically addressing the genetic makeup of those people in the United States who have descended from the British Isles.

Saxophone. Peter Gelling. (Progressive Ser.). 2004. pap. bk. 19.95 (978-1-86469-222-8(7), 256-166) Kolala Music SGP.

Saxophone Method, Bk. 1. Andrew Scott. 1 CD. (Running Time: 90 mins.). (Progressive Ser.). 1997. pap. bk. (978-0-947183-04-2(3)) Kolala Music SGP.

Say & Do(r) Social Scenes Combo CD-ROM. (J). 2005. audio compact disk (978-1-58650-503-5(3)) Super Duper.

Say "Cheese" unabr. ed. Patricia Reilly Giff. 1 cass. (Running Time: 55 mins.). (Follow the Reader Ser.). (J). (gr. 1-2). 1985. pap. bk. 17.00 incl. bk. & guide. (978-0-8072-0108-4(1), FTR109SP, Listening Lib) Random Audio Pubg.
Follow the kids in Ms. Rooney's second-grade class as they learn & grow through the entire school year filled with fun & surprises. Corresponding Month: June.

Say Cheese - And Die Screaming! R. L. Stine. (Running Time: 2 hrs. 30 mins.). (Goosebumps HorrorLand Ser.: No. 8). (J). (gr. 4-7). 2009. 34.99 (978-1-60775-988-1(8)) Find a World.

Say Cheese - And Die Screaming! R. L. Stine. (Goosebumps HorrorLand Ser.: No. 8). (ENG.). (J). (gr. 4-7). 2009. audio compact disk 9.95 (978-0-545-11258-1(3)); audio compact disk 29.95 (978-0-545-11942-9(1)) Scholastic Inc.

Say Cheese - & Die Screaming! R. L. Stine. Read by Meredith Zeitlin. (Goosebumps HorrorLand Ser.: No. 8). (J). (gr. k). 2009. 34.99 (978-1-60812-520-3(3)) Find a World.

Say Good-bye to Anxiety: How to Stop Worrying & Enjoy Your Life. David Grudermeyer & Rebecca Grudermeyer. 2 cass. 18.95 Incl handouts. (T-37) Willingness Wrks.

Say Goodbye. abr. ed. Lisa Gardner. Read by Ann Marie Lee & Lincoln Hoppe. (ENG.). 2008. audio compact disk 29.95 (978-0-7393-2158-4(7)) Pub: Random Audio Pubg. Dist(s): Random

Say Goodbye. unabr. ed. Lisa Gardner. Read by Ann Marie Lee & Lincoln Hoppe. (YA). 2008. 74.99 (978-0-7393-7581-5(4)) Find a World.

Say Goodbye. unabr. ed. Lisa Gardner. Read by Ann Marie Lee & Lincoln Hoppe. 8 cass. 2008. 90.00 (978-1-4159-5634-2(0), BksonTape); audio compact disk 90.00 (978-1-4159-4382-3(6), BksonTape) Pub: Random Audio Pubg. Dist(s): Random
For Kimberly Quincy, FBI Special Agent, it all starts with a pregnant hooker. The story Delilah Rose tells Kimberly about her johns is too horrifying to be true - but prostitutes are disappearing, one by one, with no explanation, and no one but Kimberly seems to care. Said the spider to the fly . . . As a member of the Evidence Response Team, dead hookers aren't exactly Kimberly's specialty. The young agent is five months pregnant - she has other things to worry about than an alleged lunatic who uses spiders to do his dirty work. But Kimberly's own mother and sister were victims of a serial killer. And now, without any bodies and with precious few clues, it's all too clear that a serial killer has found the key to the perfect murder . . . or Kimberly is chasing a crime that never happened. imberly's caught in a web more lethal than any spider's, and the more she fights for answers, the more tightly she's trapped. What she doesn't know is that she's close - too close - to a psychopath who makes women's nightmares come alive, and if he has his twisted way, it won't be long before it's time for Kimberly to.

Say Goodbye. unabr. ed. Lisa Gardner. Read by Ann Marie Lee & Lincoln Hoppe. (Running Time: 11 hrs.). (ENG.). 2008. audio compact disk 39.95 (978-0-7393-2157-7(9)) Pub: Random Audio Pubg. Dist(s): Random

Say Goodbye. unabr. ed. Lewis Shiner. Read by Lewis Shiner. 2001. 25.00 (978-1-59040-140-8(9), Phoenix Audio) Pub: Amer Intl Pub. Dist(s): PerseuPGW

Say Goodbye to... Surgery Anxiety. Jacqueline Sidman. 2005. audio compact disk 24.95 (978-0-9727033-1-4(4)) Anton Pubng.

Say It. Roland Flint. Read by Roland Flint. 1 cass. (Watershed Tapes of Contemporary Poetry). 1978. 10.95 (23622) J Norton Pubs.
Joint release with the book from Dryad Press.

Say It Before You Get It. Alfred D. Harvey, Jr. 1 Cass. 2003. 5.00 (978-1-932508-29-1(5)) Doers Pub.

Say it Easily. Wang Xiaoning. (CHI & ENG.). 2004. pap. bk. 14.95 (978-7-80187-406-1(4), SAIT1) China Bks.

Say it Easily, Vol. 2. Wang Xiaoning. (CHI & ENG.). 2004. pap. bk. 14.95 (978-7-80187-407-8(2), SAIT2) China Bks.

Say it Easily, Vol. 3. Wang Xiaoning. (CHI & ENG.). 2004. pap. bk. 14.95 (978-7-80187-408-5(0), SAIT3) China Bks.

Say It Fast & Easy in Spanish: Answer Keys & Transcript. Mark Frobose. (SPA.). 2002. per. 71.00 (978-1-893564-76-3(2)); per. 24.99 (978-1-893564-77-0(0)) Macmill Audio.

Say It in Tibetan. Norbu Chophel. 2001. pap. bk. 25.00 (978-81-86230-01-5(7)) Laurier Bks CAN.

Say-It Language Card for Landscaping. Prod. by Language Arts Press LLC. (ENG & SPA.). 2007. audio compact disk 15.95 (978-0-9791699-1-5(7)) Lang Arts Pr.

Say-It Language Cards: The Construction Trades. Prod. by Language Arts Press LLC. (ENG & SPA.). 2007. audio compact disk 15.95 (978-0-9791699-0-8(9)) Lang Arts Pr.

Say It Right! Elsie E. Bock. 2 cass. (Running Time: 2 hrs.). vinyl bd. 24.95 (978-0-88432-439-3(7), SO3070) J Norton Pubs.
Socialy & on the job, you are judged by the way you speak. An easy-to-follow audio teach to help you use grammar correctly & effectively. Uses dramatized situations, memory pegs & clear examples to make learning easy & fun. Tells you how to identify everyday errors & once you learn to spot mistakes, you'll stop making them.

Say It Right! Bock Elsie. 2 CDs. (Running Time: 2 hrs.). 2005. audio compact disk 24.95 (978-1-57970-139-0(6), S03070D) J Norton Pubs.

Say It Rite the pronunciation of the top prescribed medications Vol. 1: Medication Pronunciation. Prod. by Zachery Post CPhT. Voice by Tony Ryan RPh. (ENG.). 2007. audio compact disk 9.99 (978-0-9820215-0-7(X)) Say It Rite.

Say It Straight-Learn by Doing. Abe Wagner. 1 cass. Date not set. pap. bk. & wbk. ed. (978-0-926632-04-2(3)) A Wagner & Assocs.
Provides questions & offers experiential opportunities through its exercises. Can be used independently or with organizational training programs for communication.

Say It Straight Or You'll Show It Crooked. Abe Wagner. 3 cass. (Running Time: 55 min.). 29.95 (978-0-926632-02-8(7), 1-800-283-8023) A Wagner & Assocs.
Explains fourteen say it straight principles.

Say It Well! The Expressive Voice Audio Coach. 4 cass. 59.95 (978-0-9668621-0-2(4)) Comwell Pr.
Voice improvement program including vocal warm-ups & workouts.

Say It with Poison, unabr. ed. Ann Granger. Narrated by Judith Boyd. 6 cass. (Running Time: 6 hrs.). 1999. 53.00 (H1011K4, Clipper Audio) Recorded Bks.

Say It with Poison: A Mitchell & Markby Mystery. unabr. ed. Ann Granger. Narrated by Judith Boyd. 6 cass. (Running Time: 9 hrs.). (Mitchell & Markby Mystery Ser.). 1999. 53.00 (978-1-84197-011-0(5), H1011E7) Recorded Bks.
When Meredith Mitchell agreed to stay with her actress cousin Eve in the run up to Eve's daughter's wedding she anticipated a degree to drama but she can hardly have expected it to include murder, blackmail & unrequited love or to involve a certain Chief Inspector Markby, a middle-aged divorcee. A material witness to the only case of murder the Cotswold village of Westerfield has ever seen Meredith soon becomes involved in the case & with helping Chief Inspector Markby. Meredith is a career diplomat & soon needs her considerable skills when steering a path between her duty to the police & loyalty to her cousin's family.

Say It with Poison: A Mitchell & Markby Mystery. unabr. ed. Ann Granger. Narrated by Judith Boyd. 7 CDs. (Running Time: 9 hrs.). (Mitchell & Markby Mystery Ser.). 2000. audio compact disk 73.00 (978-1-84197-116-2(2), C1206E7) Recorded Bks.

Say No More. Contrib. by House of Heroes. Prod. by Oran Thornton. 2006. audio compact disk 13.99 (978-5-558-40903-1(7)) Mono Vs Ster.

Say "No to Drugs" 1 cass. (Running Time: 1 hrs.). (Young People Ser.). (J). 1991. 12.98 (62) Randolph Tapes.
Say "NO" to drugs & say "YES" to a brighter future-this tape can help you do it.

Say No to Murder. unabr. ed. Nancy Pickard. Read by Samantha Shea. 6 vols. (Running Time: 9 hrs.). (Jenny Cain Mystery Ser.). 2000. bk. 54.95 (978-0-7927-2214-4(0), CSL 103, Chivers Sound Lib) AudioGO.
Jenny Cain is thrilled about the Liberty Harbor Restoration: a picturesque collection of shops, museums and restaurants. When a runaway truck barrels into the project committee, it seems someone in Port Frederick is out to sink Liberty Harbor. Detective Geof Bushfield reels in a prime suspect, unfortunately it's the first person Jenny is desperate to prove innocent! Fishing for a ruthless killer, Jenny has to bait her trap fast, before the cold New England waters close in over her own head!.

Say, Sing & Sign the Music. Ann Perkoski. 2 CDs. (Running Time: 1 hr. 10 mins.). (American Sign Language Ser.). (J). (gr. k-6). 1999. audio compact disk 14.95 (978-1-887120-21-0(1)) Prodn Assocs.
A compilation of the music presented in the series.

Say the Magic Words: How to Get What You Want from the People Who Have What You Need. abr. ed. Lynette Padwa. Read by Matilda Novak. 3 CDs. (Running Time: 10800 sec.). 2005. audio compact disk 23.95 (978-1-59316-059-3(3), LL151) Listen & Live.
It takes more than good social skills to get what you want from your child's teacher, your hairdresser, mechanic, hotel reservation agent and more. Encounters that were once simple are now like mini-excursions to a foreign land. Say The Magic Word is your passport to mastering these daily encounters. You'll find the most effective way to get what you want and need - and know what not to say and do. The insights and information come directly from the pros, people who have spent years in their particular line of work - and their advice is entertaining and unnervingly candid.

Say What? 911 Call Taking. 1 CD. (Running Time: 1 hr.). wbk. ed. 49.00 Prof Pride.
911 What are you reporting? Ten 911 calls-made by a professional comedian to an actual Call Taker. Very funny.

Say What? 911 Call Taking. 1 cass. 2000. 24.95 Prof Pride.
Ten 911 calls made by a professional comedian to an actual Call Taker.

Say When: A Novel. unabr. ed. Elizabeth Berg. Read by David Colacci. 5 cass. (Running Time: 7 hrs.). 2003. 29.95 (978-1-59086-751-8(3), 1590867513, BAU); 74.25 (978-1-59086-752-5(1), 1590867521); audio compact disk 29.95 (978-1-59086-753-2(X), 159086753X, CD); audio compact disk 82.25 (978-1-59086-754-9(8), 1590867548, CD Unabrid Lib Ed) Brilliance Audio.
Griffin is a happy man. Settled comfortably in a Chicago suburb, he adores his eight-year-old daughter, Zoe, and his wife, Ellen - shy, bookish Ellen, who is as dependable as she is dependent on him for his stability and his talent for gently controlling the world they inhabit. But when he wakes one morning to hear of his wife's love affair with another man and her request for a divorce, Griffin's view of life is irrevocably altered. Overnight he goes from being Ellen's husband to being her roommate, from a lover to a man denied passion and companionship. Now he must either move on or fight for his marriage, forgive his wife or condemn her for her betrayal, deny or face up to his part in the sudden undoing of his seemingly perfect life. From the New York Times bestselling author of Open House and True to Form comes a brilliant novel that charts the days and nights of a family whose normalcy has been shattered. With startling clarity and a trademark blend of humor and poignancy, Say When follows a man on an emotional journey to redefine his notions about love and happiness and asks questions relevant to any contemporary couple: when is a relationship worth saving and when is it better to let it go? Might a man and a woman define betrayal differently? How honest are we with those to whom we are ostensibly closest?.

Say When: A Novel. unabr. ed. Elizabeth Berg. Read by David Colacci. (Running Time: 7 hrs.). 2004. 39.25 (978-1-59335-355-1(3), 1593353553, Brlnc Audio MP3 Lib) Brilliance Audio.

Say When: A Novel. unabr. ed. Elizabeth Berg. Read by David Colacci. (Running Time: 7 hrs.). 2004. 39.25 (978-1-59710-669-6(0), 1597106690, BADLE); 24.95 (978-1-59710-668-9(2), 1597106682, BAD) Brilliance Audio.

Say When: A Novel. unabr. ed. Elizabeth Berg. Read by David Colacci. (Running Time: 7 hrs.). 2004. 24.95 (978-1-59335-025-3(2), 1593350252) Soulmate Audio Bks.

Say Yes. unabr. ed. Audrey Couloumbis. 3 cass. (Running Time: 4 hrs. 45 mins.). (J). (gr. 5-9). 2004. 30.00 (978-0-8072-0818-2(3), LYA 375 CX, Listening Lib) Random Audio Pubg.
The unforgettable story of a preteen on her own, bravely making choices for the first time in her life. When twelve-year-old Casey's sole guardian, her stepmother Sylvia, doesn't come home one night, Casey believes she's run off with her boyfriend. The question is will Sylvia come back? And even more urgent, how will Casey fend for herself in their New York City apartment? Paulie, the landlord's teenage foster son, offers to forge Sylvia's signature on the rent check, but his help comes at a price. And if Casey says yes to his proposition, she'll be breaking the law. And if she says no, foster care.

***Say Yes to God: A Call to Courageous Surrender.** Kay Warren. (Running Time: 6 hrs. 11 mins. 30 sec.). (ENG.). 2010. 14.99 (978-0-310-33223-7(0)) Zondervan.

Say You Love Me. abr. ed. Johanna Lindsey. Read by Michael Page. (Running Time: 3 hrs.). (Malory Ser.). 2008. audio compact disk 14.99 (978-1-4233-6600-3(X), 9781423366003, BCD Value Price) Brilliance Audio.

Say You Love Me. unabr. ed. Johanna Lindsey. Read by Michael Page. (Running Time: 9 hrs.). (Malory Ser.). 2008. 39.25 (978-1-4233-6599-0(2), 9781423365990, BADLE); 39.25 (978-1-4233-6597-6(6), 9781423365976, Brlnc Audio MP3 Lib); 24.95 (978-1-4233-6596-9(8), 9781423365969, Brilliance MP3); 24.95 (978-1-4233-6598-3(4), 9781423365983, BAD); audio compact disk 92.25 (978-1-4233-6595-2(X), 9781423365952, BriAudCD Unabrid); audio compact disk 29.95 (978-1-4233-6594-5(1), 9781423365945, Bril Audio CD Unabri) Brilliance Audio.

Say Your Prayers. Bridgestone Staff. 2004. cd-rom & audio compact disk 9.95 (978-1-56371-729-1(8)) Brdgstn Multimed Grp.

Say You're One of Them. abr. ed. Uwem Akpan. Read by Dion Graham & Robin Miles. (Running Time: 2 hrs. 20 mins.). (ENG.). 2008. 9.98 (978-1-60024-300-4(2)) Pub: Hachet Audio. Dist(s): HachBkGrp

Say You're One of Them. unabr. ed. Uwem Akpan. Read by Robin Miles & Dion Graham. 3 CDs. (Running Time: 2 hrs. 45 mins.). (Oprah's Book Club Ser.: No. 63). (ENG.). 2009. audio compact disk 18.98 (978-1-60788-341-8(4)) Pub: Hachet Audio. Dist(s): HachBkGrp

***Say You're One of Them.** unabr. ed. Uwem Akpan. Read by Robin Miles & Don Graham. 10 CDs. (Running Time: 11 hrs.). 2009. audio compact disk 110.99 (978-1-60788-366-1(X)) Pub: Hachet Audio. Dist(s): HachBkGrp

Say You're One of Them. unabr. ed. Uwem Akpan. Read by Kevin Free et al. (Running Time: 13 hrs.). (ENG.). 2009. 26.98 (978-1-60788-446-0(1)) Pub: Hachet Audio. Dist(s): HachBkGrp

Say You're One of Them. unabr. ed. Uwem Akpan. Read by Dion Graham et al. 2 MP3-CDs. (Running Time: 13 hrs.). (ENG.). 2009. audio compact disk 69.99 (978-1-60788-367-8(8)) Pub: Hachet Audio. Dist(s): HachBkGrp

Sayable Chinese. Yuen Ren Chao. 15 dual track cass. (Spoken Language Ser.). 1985. 230.00 (978-0-87950-336-9(X)) Spoken Lang Serv.

Saying No to the One You Love. Read by Peter Schellenbaum-Scheel. 1 cass. (Running Time: 90 min.). 1988. 10.95 (978-0-7822-0247-2(0), 352) C G Jung IL.

***Saying Yes! to Christ Call, CD.** Charles R. Swindoll. 2010. audio compact disk 7.99 (978-1-57972-885-4(5)) Insight Living.

Sayings of the Buddha: The Dhammapada. unabr. ed. Dhammapada. Read by Jacob Needleman. Tr. by Thomas Byrom. 1 cass. (Running Time: 1 hr. 30 min.). 1995. 10.95 (978-0-944993-83-5(4)) Audio Lit.
Tradition tells us that these words come directly from the mouth of the Buddha. This sacred text has guided the lives of countless people in their struggle for inner transformation.

Sayonara & the Bridges at Toko-Ri. unabr. ed. James A. Michener. Read by Larry McKeever. 9 cass. (Running Time: 13 hrs. 30 min.). 1995. 72.00 (978-0-7366-3069-6(4), 3751) Books on Tape.
These early Michener masterpieces explore, with care & compassion, the love for a woman, for a family & for duty in war.

SCA Tape. Bruce F. Elving. Read by Carol Elving. 1 cass. (Running Time: 30 min.). 1986. 4.00 F M Atlas.
Gives samples of programming received on the medium of FM-SCA, or radio subcarriers (background music, talking book for the blind, data noise, telemetry, foreign language broadcasts).

***Scab for Treasurer?** Trudi Strain Trueit. (Secrets of A Lab Rat Ser.). (ENG.). 2011. audio compact disk 29.99 (978-0-545-26766-3(8)) Scholastic Inc.

***Scab for Treasurer?** Trudi Strain Trueit. Narrated by Oliver Wyman. (Secrets of A Lab Rat Ser.). (ENG.). 2011. audio compact disk 19.99 (978-0-545-16978-3(X)) Scholastic Inc.

Scaffolding: New & Selected Poems see Jane Cooper

Scale Down: Live It Up. Danna Demetre. (Running Time: 26640 sec.). 2006. audio compact disk 24.99 (978-0-8007-4431-1(4)) Pub: Revell. Dist(s): Baker Pub Grp

Scales & Arpeggios (from the Aristocats) - ShowTrax. Arranged by Audrey Snyder. 1 CD. 2000. audio compact disk 19.95 H Leonard.
This charming song from Walt Disney's "The Aristocrats" is set in a quasi classical style that can't miss. Includes a delightful solfege countermelody & even a little of Beethoven's "Ode to Joy" theme.

Scales & Modes for Guitar. Peter Gelling. (Progressive Ser.). 2004. pap. bk. 24.95 (978-1-86469-058-3(5), 256-165) Kolala Music SGP.

Scales Don't Lie: Daniel 4:1-37. Ed Young. 1995. 4.95 (978-0-7417-2072-6(8), 1071) Win Walk.

Scales, Modes & Improvising for Guitar Manual: Complete Learn to Play Instructions. Peter Gelling. 2007. pap. bk. 29.95 (978-1-86469-386-7(X)) Kolala Music SGP.

Scales of Justice. Ngaio Marsh. Read by Benedict Cumberbatch. (Running Time: 3 hrs. 44 mins. 0 sec.). (ENG.). 2008. audio compact disk 28.95 (978-1-4055-0508-6(7)) Pub: Little BrownUK GBR. Dist(s): IPG Chicago

***Scales of Justice.** Ngaio Marsh. 2010. 54.95 (978-0-7531-4449-7(2)); audio compact disk 71.95 (978-0-7531-4450-3(6)) Pub: Isis Pubng Ltd GBR. Dist(s): Ulverscroft US

Scales of Justice, unabr. ed. Ngaio Marsh. Read by Nadia May. 6 cass. (Running Time: 8 hrs. 30 mins.). 1996. 44.95 (978-0-7861-0927-2(0), 1682) Blckstn Audio.
The quiet village of Swevenings seemed an English pastoral paradise, until the savagely beaten body of a lord was found near a tranquil stream. Suddenly, the playground of British blue-bloods has been soiled by murder & the lowest sort of intrigue. But if anyone can clean it up, it's the famous Inspector Roderick Alleyn of Scotland Yard.

Scales of Justice. unabr. ed. Ngaio Marsh. Read by James Saxon. 6 cass. (Running Time: 9 hrs.). (Inspector Alleyn Mystery Ser.). 2000. 49.95 (978-0-7451-6144-0(8), CAB 252) Pub: Chivers Audio Bks GBR. Dist(s): AudioGO
The people of Swevenings are disrupted only by a fierce competition to catch a monster trout, the Old Un, who lives in a stream called the Chyne. But a neighbor is found brutally murdered, and near the corpse lies the monster trout., freshly killed. Inspector Roderick Alleyn is called to the crime scene.

***Scales of Justice: A Roderick Alleyn Mystery.** unabr. ed. Ngaio Marsh. Read by Nadia May. (Running Time: 8 hrs. 30 mins.). 2010. 29.95 (978-1-4417-4701-3(X)); audio compact disk 76.00 (978-1-4417-4698-6(6)) Blckstn Audio.

Scalper's Trail. unabr. ed. Will C. Knott. Read by Maynard Villers. 4 cass. (Running Time: 4 hrs. 6 min.). (Golden Hawk Ser.: Bk. 6). 1996. 26.95 (978-1-55686-687-6(9)) Books in Motion.
Golden Hawk hires out to lead a band of tenderfeet through a maze of mountains & dead-end gullies ruled by the proud Blackfoot Nation.

Scaly Blood Squirters & Other Extreme Reptiles. June Preszler. Contrib. by Patrick Olson & Charity Jones. (Extreme Life Ser.). (ENG.). (gr. 3-4). 2008. audio compact disk 12.99 (978-1-4296-3214-0(3)) CapstoneDig.

***Scandal.** unabr. ed. Kate Brian, pseud. Narrated by Cassandra Campbell. (Running Time: 6 hrs. 0 mins. 0 sec.). (Private Ser.). 2011. 19.99 (978-1-4001-6302-1(1)); 13.99 (978-1-4001-8302-9(2)); audio compact disk 24.99 (978-1-4001-1302-6(4)) Pub: Tantor Media. Dist(s): IngramPubServ

Scandal. unabr. ed. Amanda Quick, pseud. Read by Anne Flosnik. (Running Time: 12 hrs.). 2009. 39.97 (978-1-4233-8769-5(4), 9781423387695, Brlnc Audio MP3 Lib); 39.97 (978-1-4233-8771-8(6), 9781423387718, BADLE); 24.99 (978-1-4233-8768-8(6), 9781423387688, Brilliance MP3); 24.99 (978-1-4233-8770-1(8), 9781423387701, BAD); audio compact disk 82.97 (978-1-4233-8767-1(8), 9781423387671, BriAudCD Unabrid); audio compact disk 29.99 (978-1-4233-8766-4(X), 9781423387664, Bril Audio CD Unabri) Brilliance Audio.

Scandal in Belgravia. unabr. ed. Robert Barnard. Read by Michael Tudor-Barnes. 6 cass. (Running Time: 9 hrs.). 2001. 54.95 (978-1-84283-077-2(5)) Pub: Soundings Ltd GBR. Dist(s): Ulverscroft US

Scandal in Belgravia, unabr. ed. Robert Barnard. Read by Frederick Davidson. 5 cass. (Running Time: 7 hrs.). 1993. 89.95 (978-0-7861-0464-2(3), 1416) Blckstn Audio.
The personal, deeply moving story of two men, Peter Proctor, recently retired as a senior British cabinet minister & Timothy Wycliffe, a young aristocrat who was bludgeoned to death more than thirty years ago. Only now, over three decades later, does Wycliffe's brutal death become Proctor's obsession. Relieved of his official post after a long & distinguished career, Proctor decides to write his memoirs. But beyond a banal chapter on his youth, nothing will come. Memories of Timothy Wycliffe take over his mind, pushing aside all other thoughts. It is only in probing the past, in tracking down the people who knew Wycliffe, in discovering the shocking truth of his murder, that Peter Proctor will find peace.

Scandal in Bohemia see Adventures of Sherlock Holmes

Scandal in Bohemia see Sherlock Holmes: Selected Stories

Scandal in Bohemia see Famous Cases of Sherlock Holmes

Scandal in Bohemia see Selections from the Adventures of Sherlock Holmes

Scandal in Bohemia. Retold by John Bergez. Arthur Conan Doyle. (Sherlock Holmes Mysteries Ser.). 2000. audio compact disk 18.95 (978-1-4105-0157-8(4)) D Johnston Inc.

Scandal in Bohemia. Arthur Conan Doyle. Ed. by Jerry Stemach. Retold by John Bergez. Narrated by Nick Sandys. 2000. audio compact disk 200.00 (978-1-58702-497-9(7)) D Johnston Inc.

Scandal in Bohemia. Arthur Conan Doyle. Ed. by Jerry Stemach et al. Retold by John Bergez. Illus. by Michael Letwenko & Edward Letwenko. Narrated by Nick Sandys. Contrib. by Ted S. Hasselbring. (Start-to-Finish Books). (J). (gr. 2-3). 2000. 35.00 (978-1-58702-498-6(5)) D Johnston Inc.
Sherlock HOlmes was the greatest detective in England. But there was one woman who had outsmarted him. Years ago, the King of Bohemia had an affair with a beautiful American opera singer name Irene Adler. Now the King is getting married and he's worried that the bride's family will call off the wedding if they find out about his past indiscretions.

Scandal in Bohemia. abr. ed. Arthur Conan Doyle. Ed. by Jerry Stemach et al. Retold by John Bergez. Illus. by Michael Letwenko & Edward Letwenko. Narrated by Nick Sandys. Contrib. by Ted S. Hasselbring. 1 cass. (Running Time: 1 hr.). (J). (gr. 2-3). 2000. (978-1-58702-325-5(3), F30K2) D Johnston Inc.
Sherlock Holmes was the greatest detective in England. But there was one woman who had outsmarted him. Years ago, the King of Bohemia had an affair with a beautiful American opera singer named Irene Adler. Now the King is getting married and he's worried that the bride's family will call off the wedding if they find out about his past indiscretions.

Scandal in Bohemia. unabr. ed. Arthur Conan Doyle. 1 cass. (Running Time: 52 min.). Dramatization. 1977. 7.95 (D-11) Jimcin Record.
Sherlock Holmes meets his match in "The Woman".

Scandal in Bohemia, Vol. 3. Arthur Conan Doyle. Ed. by Jerry Stemach et al. Retold by John Bergez. Illus. by Michael Letwenko & Edward Letwenko.

Narrated by Nick Sandys. Contrib. by Ted S. Hasselbring. (Start-to-Finish Books). (J). (gr. 2-3). 2002. 100.00 (978-1-58702-987-5(1)) D Johnston Inc.

Scandal in Fair Haven. unabr. ed. Carolyn G. Hart. Read by Kate Reading. 7 cass. (Running Time: 10 hrs. 30 min.). (Henrie O Mystery Ser.). 1998. 56.00 (978-0-7366-4144-9(0), 4648) Books on Tape.
Henrie O, an ex-journalist turned sleuth, is looking forward to a quiet holiday at a wealthy friend's mountain cabin in Tennessee. Instead she finds herself in the middle of another murder mystery, this time in the well-heeled neighborhood of Fair Haven.

***Scandal in Spring.** unabr. ed. Lisa Kleypas. Read by Rosalyn Landor. (Running Time: 9 hrs.). (Wallflower Ser.: Bk. 4). 2010. 24.99 (978-1-4418-5197-0(6), 9781441851970, Brilliance MP3); 39.97 (978-1-4418-5198-7(4), 9781441851987, Brlnc Audio MP3 Lib); 24.99 (978-1-4418-5199-4(2), 9781441851994, BAD); 39.97 (978-1-4418-5200-7(X), 9781441852007, BADLE); audio compact disk 29.99 (978-1-4418-5195-6(X), 9781441851956, Bril Audio CD Unabri); audio compact disk 79.97 (978-1-4418-5196-3(8), 9781441851963, BriAudCD Unabrid) Brilliance Audio.

***Scandal (Library Edition)** unabr. ed. Kate Brian, pseud. Narrated by Cassandra Campbell. (Running Time: 6 hrs. 0 mins.). (Private Ser.). 2011. 24.99 (978-1-4001-9302-8(8)); audio compact disk 59.99 (978-1-4001-4302-3(0)) Pub: Tantor Media. Dist(s): IngramPubServ

Scandal Monger see Selected European Short Stories

Scandal of Father Brown. unabr. ed. G. K. Chesterton. Read by John Graham. 4 cass. (Running Time: 5 hrs. 30 mins.). 2001. 24.95 (978-1-57270-181-6(1), N41181u) Pub: Audio Partners. Dist(s): PerseuPGW
Father Brown uses his distinctive style of deduction to solve the seemingly unsolvable. His cherubic face, his dull eyes behind thick glasses, & his air of outward confusion disguise an amazing perspicacity.

Scandal of Father Brown. unabr. ed. G. K. Chesterton. Read by Michael Pocaro. 4 cass. (Running Time: 5 hrs. 30 mins.). (Father Brown Mystery Ser.). 1988. 32.95 (978-0-7861-0058-3(3), 1055) Blckstn Audio.
Father Brown's powers of detection allow him to sit beside the immortal Holmes but he is also, to quote Rufus King, "in all senses a most pleasantly fascinating human being".

Scandal of Father Brown. unabr. collector's ed. G. K. Chesterton. Read by David Case. 6 cass. (Running Time: 6 hrs.). (Father Brown Mystery Ser.). 1994. 36.00 (978-0-7366-2756-6(1), 3479) Books on Tape.
Mystery stories featuring the priest-detective Father Brown.

Scandal of the Season. Sophie Gee. Read by Cameron Stewart. (Playaway Adult Fiction Ser.). 2008. 44.99 (978-1-60640-524-6(1)) Find a World.

Scandal of the Season. unabr. ed. Sophie Gee. Read by Cameron Stewart. 8 CDs. (Running Time: 10 hrs.). (ENG.). 2007. audio compact disk 34.95 (978-1-59887-529-4(9), 1598875299) Pub: HighBridge. Dist(s): Workman Pub

***Scandal on Rincon Hill: A Sarah Woolson Mystery.** unabr. ed. Shirley Tallman. Read by Carrington MacDuffie. (Running Time: 12 hrs. NaN mins.). (Sarah Woolson Mysteries Ser.). 2010. 29.95 (978-1-4417-7322-7(3)); 72.95 (978-1-4417-7319-7(3)); audio compact disk 105.00 (978-1-4417-7320-3(7)) Blckstn Audio.

Scandal Takes a Holiday. unabr. ed. Lindsey Davis. Read by Jamie Glover. 7 cass. (Running Time: 35940 sec.). (Marcus Didius Falco Ser.). 2005. 59.95 (978-0-7927-3551-9(X), CSL 789); audio compact disk 79.95 (978-0-7927-3552-6(8), SLD 789) AudioGO.

Scandalmonger. William Safire. Narrated by Paul Hecht. 15 CDs. (Running Time: 17 hrs.). 2001. audio compact disk 142.00 (978-0-7887-5166-0(2), C1328E7) Recorded Bks.
The Secretary of the Treasury may be involved in shady financial dealings & certainly has a mistress. The Vice President - a political rival - enlists a reporter to help discredit the secretary, but the Vice President has skeletons in his own closet, which are exposed by the reporter he entrusts. This may sound like modern times, but the characters are Alexander Hamilton, Thomas Jefferson & the notorious James Callender.

Scandalmonger. unabr. ed. William Safire. Read by Larry McKeever. 13 cass. (Running Time: 19 hrs.). 2000. 85.95 (978-0-7861-1746-8(X), 2550) Blckstn Audio.
Exploding any notion that the political sex scandal is a recent phenomenon, our press-hounded founding fathers star in an outrageous & fact-based novel. Safire unveils the story behind the nation's first great political scandals. With dialogue drawn from letters & historical records & notes that scrupulously separate fact from fiction, Safire's novel is studded with masterly portraits of George Washington, John Adams & Aaron Burr. He demonstrates how media intrusiveness into private lives & politicians' manipulation of the press are as old as the Constitution.

Scandalmonger. unabr. ed. William Safire. Narrated by Paul Hecht. 12 cass. (Running Time: 17 hrs.). 2000. 101.00 (978-0-7887-4364-1(3), 96258E7) Recorded Bks.
The Vice President & Treasury Secretary are embroiled in a scandal involving secret love affairs & shady financial dealings. But the men in question are two of America's most-beloved Founding Fathers: Thomas Jefferson & Alexander Hamilton.

***Scandalous.** unabr. ed. Karen Robards. (Running Time: 11 hrs.). (Banning Sisters Ser.). 2010. 24.99 (978-1-4418-6433-8(4), 9781441864338, BAD); 39.97 (978-1-4418-6434-5(2), 9781441864345, BADLE) Brilliance Audio.

***Scandalous.** unabr. ed. Karen Robards. Read by Justine Eyre. (Running Time: 10 hrs.). (Banning Sisters Ser.). 2010. 24.99 (978-1-4418-6431-4(8), 9781441864314, Brilliance MP3); 39.97 (978-1-4418-6432-1(6), 9781441864321, Brlnc Audio MP3 Lib); audio compact disk 29.99 (978-1-4418-6429-1(6), 9781441864291, Bril Audio CD Unabri); audio compact disk 89.97 (978-1-4418-6430-7(X), 9781441864307, BriAudCD Unabrid) Brilliance Audio.

***Scandalous: The Cross & the Resurrection of Jesus.** unabr. ed. D. A. Carson. Narrated by John Haag. (ENG.). 2010. 12.98 (978-1-59644-889-6(X), Hovel Audio); audio compact disk 21.98 (978-1-59644-888-9(1), Hovel Audio) christianaud.

***Scandalous Again.** unabr. ed. Christina Dodd. Read by Justine Eyre. (Running Time: 9 hrs.). (Switching Places Ser.: No. 1). 2010. 24.99 (978-1-4418-2584-1(3), 9781441825841, BAD); 39.97 (978-1-4418-2583-4(5), 9781441825834, Brlnc Audio MP3 Lib); 39.97 (978-1-4418-2585-8(1), 9781441825858, BADLE); 24.99 (978-1-4418-2582-7(7), 9781441825827, Brilliance MP3); audio compact disk 89.97 (978-1-4418-2581-0(9), 9781441825810, BriAudCD Unabrid); audio compact disk 29.99 (978-1-4418-2580-3(0), 9781441825803, Bril Audio CD Unabri) Brilliance Audio.

Scandalous Gospel of Jesus: What's So Good about the Good News? Peter J. Gomes. Read by Patrick G. Lawlor. (Playaway Adult Nonfiction Ser.). (ENG.). 2008. 59.99 (978-1-60640-987-9(5)) Find a World.

Scandalous Gospel of Jesus: What's So Good about the Good News? unabr. ed. Peter J. Gomes. Read by Patrick G. Lawlor. 7 CDs. (Running Time: 8 hrs. 0 mins. 0 sec.). (ENG.). 2007. audio compact disk 29.99 (978-1-4001-0499-4(8)); audio compact disk 19.99 (978-1-4001-5499-9(5)); audio compact disk 59.99 (978-1-4001-3499-1(4)) Pub: Tantor Media. Dist(s): IngramPubServ

Scandalous Lady Wright. unabr. ed. Marion Chesney. Read by Jenny Quayle. 4 cass. (Running Time: 6 hrs.). 1999. 44.95 (978-0-7531-0504-7(7), 990106) Pub: ISIS Audio GBR. Dist(s): Ulverscroft US
Fashionable society regarded Sir Benjamin Wright with utmost honor & respect, but his wife, Lady Emma, knew him to be a drunken, jealous brute, & now she is accused of her husband's murder. It becomes apparent to Emma that her late husband had secrets...& enemies. When the practical Comte Saint-Juste offered his services, Lady Emma was about to discover what the French dedication to l'amour really meant.

Scandalous Marriage. unabr. ed. Cathy Maxwell. Narrated by Virginia Leishman. 8 CDs Lib. Ed. (Running Time: 9 hrs. 50 min.). 2004. audio compact disk 89.75 (978-1-4025-2916-0(3), C1828) Recorded Bks.
Just as a beautiful debutante enters London society, dishonor drives her to the isolated countryside. While in hiding, Leah Carrollton encounters the dashing and noble Devon Marshall. They once felt a passionate spark for one another, and now it seems their feelings might rekindle. But the cruel truth is that they are from rival families. Leah's brother once challenged Devon to a duel, and there are rumors that her father is responsible for a terrible accident that killed Devon's father.

Scandalous Marriage. unabr. collector's ed. Cathy Maxwell. Narrated by Virginia Leishman. 7 cass. (Running Time: 9 hrs. 30 mins.). 2004. 69.75 (978-0-7887-9500-8(7), L1014) Recorded Bks.

Scandal's Bride. Stephanie Laurens. Narrated by Simon Prebble. 10 cass. (Running Time: 14 hrs.). (Cynster Family Ser.: Bk. 3). 88.00 (978-0-7887-9639-5(9)) Recorded Bks.

Scandaroon. unabr. collector's ed. Henry Williamson. Read by Donada Peters. 4 cass. (Running Time: 4 hrs.). 1986. 24.00 (978-0-7366-0909-8(1), 1852) Books on Tape.
Scandaroons are a variety of homing pigeon. The story is set in rural Devon shortly after W. W. I. During that war pigeons carried messages from outposts to their home base. They probably looked for a peaceful retirement, but their ancient enemies, the hawks, had other ideas. Thus the story is about conflicts within nature & their reverberations in man.

Scanning Relaxation: Self-Relaxation. Scripts. Edward A. Charlesworth. 1 CD-ROM. (Running Time: 13 mins.). 2004. audio compact disk 16.95 (978-0-87822-437-1(8), 5164) Res Press.
Accompanies "Stress Management for Adolescents: A Cognitive-Behavioral Approach, " by Diane de Anda, 0-87822-444-0 (Program Guide), 0-87822-436-X (Student Manual).

Scapegoat. unabr. ed. Daphne Du Maurier. Read by Paul Shelley. 10 cass. (Running Time: 10 hrs.). 1996. 84.95 (978-0-7451-4132-9(3), CAB815) AudioGO.

Scar Saloon. Sholeh Wolpe. 2005. 22.00 (978-1-59709-066-7(2)) Red Hen Press.

Scaramouche. Rafael Sabatini. Read by Anais 9000. 2008. 27.95 (978-1-60112-183-7(0)) Babblebooks.

Scaramouche. unabr. ed. Rafael Sabatini. Narrated by Flo Gibson. 9 cass. (Running Time: 13 hrs. 30 mins.). 2003. 28.95 (978-1-55685-688-4(1),) Audio Bk Con.
This romance of the French revolution tells of Andre-Louis' remarkable career as a lawyer, a politician, the remarkable actor (and rabble-rouser for the downtrodden), Saramouche. His love life and the amazing revelation of his parenthood are part of this exciting tale.

Scaramouche. unabr. ed. Rafael Sabatini. Read by Robert Whitfield. 9 cass. (Running Time: 13 hrs. 30 mins.). 1998. 62.95 (1820) Blckstn Audio.
Drama about a daring hero of 18th century France.

Scaramouche. unabr. ed. Rafael Sabatini. Read by Robert Whitfield. 9 cass. (Running Time: 13 hrs.). 2001. 62.95 (978-0-7861-1090-2(2), 1820) Blckstn Audio.

Scaramouche. unabr. ed. Rafael Sabatini. (Running Time: 43200 sec.). 2007. audio compact disk 90.00 (978-0-7861-6227-7(9)) Blckstn Audio.

Scaramouche. unabr. ed. Rafael Sabatini. Read by Robert Whitfield. (Running Time: 43200 sec.). 2007. audio compact disk 29.95 (978-0-7861-7212-2(6)) Blckstn Audio.

Scaramouche. unabr. collector's ed. Rafael Sabatini. Read by Doug Brown. 10 cass. (Running Time: 15 hrs.). (J). 1983. 80.00 (978-0-7366-0365-2(4), 1349) Books on Tape.
"Scaramouche" is a story of intrigue & romance in the early days of the French Revolution.

Scarborough Fair. Scott Wilson. 4 cass. (Running Time: 6 hrs.). 2001. 25.00 (978-1-58807-068-5(9)) Am Pubng Inc.
Born John Paul in 1747 in Arbigland, Scotland, he put to sea at age 13 and by 21 was master of John, trading between Scotland and the West Indies. After changing his name to John Paul Jones to escape detection after killing a mutineer in self-defense, in 1775, on the outbreak of the War of Independence, he volunteered for America's infant Navy. Off Flamborough Head 4 years later, just south of Scarborough on the Yorkshire coast, John Paul Jones became America's first Naval hero. This is the story of his epic victory.

Scarecrow. Matthew Reilly. Read by Sean Mangan. (Running Time: 12 hrs. 50 mins.). 2009. 94.99 (978-1-74214-277-7(X), 9781742142777) Pub: Bolinda Pubng AUS. Dist(s): Bolinda Pub Inc

Scarecrow. abr. ed. Michael Connelly. Read by Peter Giles. (Running Time: 6 hrs.). (Jack McEvoy Ser.: No. 2). (ENG.). 2009. 14.98 (978-1-60024-572-5(2)) Pub: Hachet Audio. Dist(s): HachBkGrp

Scarecrow. abr. ed. Michael Connelly. Read by Peter Giles. (Running Time: 6 hrs.). (Jack McEvoy Ser.: No. 2). (ENG.). 2010. audio compact disk 14.98 (978-1-60024-832-0(2)) Pub: Hachet Audio. Dist(s): HachBkGrp

Scarecrow. abr. rev. ed. Matthew Reilly. Read by Scott Sowers. 4 CDs. (Running Time: 5 hrs. 0 mins. 0 sec.). (ENG.). 2004. audio compact disk 24.95 (978-1-55927-988-8(5)) Pub: Macmill Audio. Dist(s): Macmillan

Scarecrow. unabr. ed. Michael Connelly. Read by Peter Giles. (Running Time: 11 hrs.). (Jack McEvoy Ser.: No. 2). (ENG.). 2009. 26.98 (978-1-60024-575-6(7)); audio compact disk 39.98 (978-1-60024-574-9(9)) Pub: Hachet Audio. Dist(s): HachBkGrp

***Scarecrow.** unabr. ed. Michael Connelly. Read by Peter Giles. 10 CDs. (Running Time: 11 hrs. 15 mins.). 2009. audio compact disk 100.00 (978-1-4159-6459-0(9), BksonTape) Pub: Random Audio Pubg. Dist(s): Random

Scarecrow. unabr. ed. Matthew Reilly. Read by Sean Mangan. 1 MP3-CD. (Running Time: 12 hrs. 50 mins.). 2007. 39.25 (978-1-74201-111-0(X)) Pub: Bolinda Pubng AUS. Dist(s): Bolinda Pub Inc

Scarecrow. unabr. ed. Matthew Reilly. Read by Sean Mangan. 11 CDs. (Running Time: 12 hrs. 50 mins.). 2004. audio compact disk 103.95 (978-1-74093-375-9(3)) Pub: Bolinda Pubng AUS. Dist(s): Bolinda Pub Inc

Scarecrow. unabr. ed. Matthew Reilly. Read by Sean Mangan. 9 cass. (Running Time: 12 hrs. 50 mins.). 2004. 72.00 (978-1-74093-228-8(5)) Pub: Bolinda Pubng AUS. Dist(s): Bolinda Pub Inc

Scarecrow. unabr. ed. Matthew Reilly. Read by Sean Mangan. (Running Time: 46200 sec.). 2007. audio compact disk 43.95 (978-1-921334-36-8(3), 9781921334368) Pub: Bolinda Pubng AUS. Dist(s): Bolinda Pub Inc

Scarecrow & His Servant. collector's unabr. ed. Philip Pullman. Read by Graeme Malcolm. 3 cass. (Running Time: 4 hrs. 30 mins.). (J). (gr. 4-7). 2005. 30.00 (978-0-307-28380-1(1), Listening Lib); audio compact disk 32.30 (978-0-307-28381-8(X), Listening Lib) Pub: Random Audio Pubg. Dist(s): NetLibrary CO

Scarecrow & His Servant. unabr. ed. Philip Pullman. Read by Graeme Malcolm. 4 CDs. (Running Time: 13920 sec.). (ENG.). (J). (gr. 3-7). 2005. audio compact disk 30.00 (978-0-307-28074-9(8), Listening Lib) Pub: Random Audio Pubg. Dist(s): Random

Scarecrow & the Snowman see Ellery Queen

Scarecrows: Matthew 12:14-29. Ed Young. 1984. 4.95 (978-0-7417-1368-1(3), 368) Win Walk.

Scared Stiff: Fast, Effective Treatment for Anxiety Disorders. David Burns. 9 cass. (Running Time: 90 mins.). 2004. 149.00 (978-0-9755159-1-4(8)); audio compact disk 149.00 (978-0-9755159-6-9(9)) IAHB.

Scaredy Cats. unabr. ed. Allan Zullo. Read by John Ratzenberger. 2008. 1.37 (978-1-4233-8077-1(0), 9781423380771, BAD) Brilliance Audio.

Scaredy Cats & The Princess & the Dragon. unabr. ed. Don Wood & Audrey Wood. Read by Andrew Belling. 1 cass. (Running Time: 20 min.). (Theatre Ser.). (ENG., (J). (ps-3). 1989. 4.99 (978-0-85953-372-0(7)) Childs Play GBR.
Stories, songs, & kitten & dragon talk that go along with the popular series by Don & Audrey Wood.

Scariest Shows Ever! unabr. ed. Radio Spirits Staff & Alfred Hitchcock. 10 CDs. (Running Time: 10 hrs.). 2006. audio compact disk 39.98 (978-1-57019-785-7(7), 43712) Radio Spirits.
Chills will fall over you as darkly as the oncoming night. No matter what you are afraid of, you'll find it here. 10 relentless hours of Alfred Hitchcock, Lucille Fletcher, Vincent Price, Edgar Allen Poe and more will trap you in terror!.

Scaring Crows. unabr. ed. Priscilla Masters. Narrated by Briony Sykes. 7 cass. (Running Time: 9 hrs.). 2000. 62.00 (978-1-84197-047-9(6), H1052E7) Recorded Bks.
Two bodies are discovered inside a farmhouse, that of Farmer Sommers & his son Jack. The fatal wounds look to be from the family shotgun, found lying by the door of the scene. The obvious explanation is murder followed by suicide, except that forensic evidence doesn't support this view. Complications abound as Joanna tries to uncover the murderer's identity. In addition, she discovers that Farmer Sommer's daughter Ruthie has mysteriously disappeared. A massive police hunt is launched in a desperate bid to uncover some trace of her, or anything she might have known.

Scarlatti Inheritance. unabr. collector's ed. Robert Ludlum. Read by Michael Prichard. 8 cass. (Running Time: 12 hrs.). 1984. 64.00 (978-0-7366-0801-5(X), 1751) Books on Tape.
An elite member of the Nazi high command is ready to defect, bringing with him information vital to the allied cause. He will deal Army Intelligence Major Matther Canfield, one of the few people in the world who knows what the file contains.

Scarlet. unabr. ed. Stephen R. Lawhead. Narrated by Adam Verner. (Running Time: 12 hrs. 8 mins. 0 sec.). (King Raven Trilogy: Bk. 2). (ENG.). 2007. audio compact disk 34.99 (978-1-59859-299-3(8)) Oasis Audio.

Scarlet. unabr. ed. Stephen R. Lawhead. Narrated by Adam Verner. (King Raven Trilogy). (ENG.). 2007. 24.49 (978-1-60814-373-3(2)) Oasis Audio.

Scarlet Angel. unabr. ed. Peggy Graham. Read by Julia Franklin. 10 cass. (Running Time: 14 hrs.). (Sound Ser.). (J). 2003. 84.95 (978-1-84283-468-8(1)) Pub: ISIS Lrg Prnt GBR. Dist(s): Ulverscroft US

Scarlet Brigade & the Virtue of Obedience. Fulton J. Sheen. 1 cass. 4.00 (78A) IRL Chicago.

***Scarlet Contessa: A Novel of the Italian Renaissance.** unabr. ed. Jeanne Kalogridis. (Running Time: 18 hrs. 0 mins.). 2010. 22.99 (978-1-4001-8753-9(2)); audio compact disk 119.99 (978-1-4001-4753-3(0)) Pub: Tantor Media. Dist(s): IngramPubServ

***Scarlet Contessa: A Novel of the Italian Renaissance.** unabr. ed. Jeanne Kalogridis. Narrated by Wanda McCaddon. (Running Time: 16 hrs. 30 mins. 0 sec.). 2010. 34.99 (978-1-4001-6753-1(1)); audio compact disk 49.99 (978-1-4001-1753-6(4)) Pub: Tantor Media. Dist(s): IngramPubServ

Scarlet Feather. Maeve Binchy. Narrated by Barbara Caruso. 17 CDs. (Running Time: 20 hrs. 15 mins.). audio compact disk 160.00 (978-0-7887-9849-8(9)) Recorded Bks.

Scarlet Feather. unabr. ed. Maeve Binchy. Narrated by Barbara Caruso. 14 cass. (Running Time: 20 hrs. 15 mins.). 2001. 119.00 (978-0-7887-5461-6(0), 96596K8) Recorded Bks.
Follows a year in the life, with all its heartaches & triumphs, of two friends from a cooking school as they work to realize their dream of having the best catering business in Dublin.

Scarlet Feather. unabr. ed. Maeve Binchy. Read by Barbara Caruso. 11 cass. (Running Time: 20 hrs.). 2004. 39.95 (978-0-7887-5427-2(0), 00114) Recorded Bks.

Scarlet Letter see Letra Escarlata

Scarlet Letter. (Audio BookNotes Guide). 2002. audio compact disk 9.95 (978-1-929011-08-7(3)) Scholarly Audio.

Scarlet Letter. Nathaniel Hawthorne. Narrated by Pat Bottino. (ENG.). 2008. 12.95 (978-0-9801087-6-7(4)) Alpha DVD.

Scarlet Letter. Nathaniel Hawthorne. Read by Michael Learned. 2 cass. (Running Time: 2 hrs. 10 min.). 19.95 set. (8019Q) Filmic Archives.
The four-time Emmy Award-winning actress brings to life this masterpiece of American Literature that probes the darker side of human nature against the background of Puritan New England. A practical treat for English teachers & lovers of English literature.

Scarlet Letter. Nathaniel Hawthorne. Read by Hernando Iván Cano. (Running Time: 3 hrs.). 2002. 16.95 (978-1-60083-222-2(9), Audiofy Corp) Iofy Corp.

Scarlet Letter. Nathaniel Hawthorne. Read by Shelly Frasier. (Running Time: 9 hrs.). 2003. 27.95 (978-1-60083-629-9(1), Audiofy Corp) Iofy Corp.

Scarlet Letter. Nathaniel Hawthorne. Read by Allison Green. 6 cass. (Running Time: 8 hrs. 30 min.). 1993. 43.80 (978-1-56544-005-0(6), 350029) Literate Ear.
Hester Pryne, convicted of adultery, must wear a scarlet "A" upon the breast of her gray Puritan dresses. With her sin thus in public view, she struggles to achieve reconciliation with God & self.

Scarlet Letter. Nathaniel Hawthorne. Read by Katinka Wolf. (Running Time: 9384 sec.). (Classic Literature with Classical Music Ser.). 2006. audio compact disk 17.98 (978-962-634-392-0(3), Naxos AudioBooks) Naxos.

Scarlet Letter. Nathaniel Hawthorne. (Saddleback's Illustrated Classics Ser.). (YA). 2005. audio compact disk (978-1-56254-937-4(5)) Saddleback Edu.

Scarlet Letter. Nathaniel Hawthorne. Narrated by Annie Wauters. (Running Time: 34320 sec.). (Unabridged Classics in MP3 Ser.). (ENG.). 2008. audio compact disk 24.00 (978-1-58472-539-8(7), In Aud) Sound Room.

Scarlet Letter. Nathaniel Hawthorne. Read by Shelly Frasier. (ENG.). 2003. audio compact disk 84.00 (978-1-4001-3060-3(3)) Pub: Tantor Media. Dist(s): IngramPubServ

***Scarlet Letter.** Ed. by Oxford University Press Staff. (Oxford Bookworms ELT Ser.). 2008. audio compact disk 18.95 (978-0-19-479153-3(X)) Pub: OUP-CN CAN. Dist(s): OUP

Scarlet Letter. abr. ed. Nathaniel Hawthorne. Perf. by Basil Rathbone. 1 cass. (Virginia Practice Ser.: Vol. 2). 1984. 12.95 (SWC 1197) HarperCollins Pubs.

Scarlet Letter. abr. ed. Nathaniel Hawthorne. Read by Jane Seymour. 3 vols. (Classics Collection). (YA). 1987. audio compact disk 11.99 (978-1-57815-522-4(3), Media Bks Audio) Media Bks NJ.

Scarlet Letter. abr. ed. Nathaniel Hawthorne. Read by Jane Seymour. 2 cass. (Running Time: 3 hrs.). 2000. 7.95 (978-1-57815-113-4(9), 1075, Media Bks Audio) Media Bks NJ.
An English scholar sends his young wife to Boston in the 17th century. He discovers his wife's illegitimate child & banished from the city wearing a scarlet "A".

Scarlet Letter. abr. ed. Nathaniel Hawthorne. Read by Katinka Wolf. 2 CDs. (Running Time: 2 hrs. 30 mins.). (Classic Fiction Ser.). 1994. audio compact disk 15.98 (978-962-634-013-4(4), NA201312, Naxos AudioBooks) Naxos.
The plight of Hester Prynne, an independent-minded woman who after giving birth to a child after an illicit affair, refuses to name the father and is forced to wear the letter A for adulteress embroidered on her dress.

Scarlet Letter. abr. ed. Nathaniel Hawthorne. Read by Katinka Wolf. 2 cass. (Running Time: 2 hrs. 30 mins.). (Classic Fiction Ser.). 1994. 14.98 (978-962-634-513-9(6), NA201314, Naxos AudioBooks) Naxos.

Scarlet Letter. abr. ed. Nathaniel Hawthorne. Perf. by Lesley Ann Warren. 3 CDs. (Running Time: 6 hrs.). 2004. audio compact disk 25.00 (978-1-59007-135-9(2)) Pub: New Millenn Enter. Dist(s): PerseuPGW
An English scholar sends his young wife to Boston in the 17th century. He discovers his wife's illegitimate child, and banished from the city wearing a scarlet "A".

Scarlet Letter. collector's unabr. ed. Nathaniel Hawthorne. Read by Donada Peters. 6 cass. (Running Time: 6 hrs.). 2000. 48.00 (978-0-7366-5132-5(2)) Books on Tape.
Because Hester Prynne commits adultery & refuses to name her lover, she must wear a scarlet "A" on her breast of her gown for the rest of her life.

Scarlet Letter, unabr. ed. Nathaniel Hawthorne. Read by Flo Gibson. 6 cass. (Running Time: 8 hrs. 30 min.). 1994. 24.95 (978-1-55685-341-8(6)) Audio Bk Con.
The social consequences of adultery in Puritan Boston are vividly drawn when Hester Prynne is forced to wear a scarlet "A" on her bosom & faces the tortured conscience of the Reverend Dimmesdale & the viscious jealousy of Roger Collingworth.

Scarlet Letter, unabr. ed. Nathaniel Hawthorne. Read by Kristen Underwood. 7 cass. (Running Time: 10 hrs.). (gr. 9-12). 1994. 49.95 (978-0-7861-0876-3(2), 1538) Blckstn Audio.
Convicted & imprisoned because she was unwilling to name her partner in adultery, Hester Prynne is forced to wear a scarlet "A" on the breast of her gown for the remainder of her life.

Scarlet Letter. unabr. ed. Nathaniel Hawthorne. Read by Kristen Underwood. (Running Time: 9 hrs. 30 mins.). 2008. 19.95 (978-1-4332-1261-1(7)); audio compact disk 19.95 (978-1-4332-1262-8(5)) Blckstn Audio.

Scarlet Letter. unabr. ed. Nathaniel Hawthorne. Read by Gene Engene. 6 cass. (Running Time: 7 hrs. 30 min.). 39.95 (978-1-55686-104-8(4), 104) Books in Motion.
American classic. Beautiful Hester Prynne gives birth to an illegitimate child. Persecuted by the puritanical townspeople & the church, she is forced to a lifetime of public ridicule because she will not name the father of her child.

Scarlet Letter. unabr. ed. Nathaniel Hawthorne. Read by Gene Engene. 7 CDs. (Running Time: 7 hrs. 30 min.). 2001. audio compact disk 45.50 (978-1-58116-194-6(8)) Books in Motion.
Hester Prynne gives birth to an illegitimate child. The Puritanical townspeople and the church demand to know who the father is.

Scarlet Letter. unabr. ed. Nathaniel Hawthorne. Read by Dick Hill. 8 CDs. (Running Time: 9 hrs.). (Classic Collection). 2001. audio compact disk 37.95 (978-1-58788-610-2(3), 1587886103, CD Unabridged); audio compact disk 96.25 (978-1-58788-611-9(1), 1587886111, CD Unabrid Lib Ed) Brilliance Audio.
The classic American story of Hester Prynne, accused of adultery, ostracized by her Puritan community & abandoned by both her lover & her husband Perhaps the first American novel to explore the ambiguities of morality, love & public judgement. The Scarlet Letter rightfully deserves its respected reputation.

Scarlet Letter. unabr. ed. Nathaniel Hawthorne. Read by Dick Hill. (Running Time: 9 hrs.). 2004. 39.25 (978-1-59335-388-9(X), 159335388X, Brlnc Audio MP3 Lib) Brilliance Audio.

Scarlet Letter. unabr. ed. Nathaniel Hawthorne. Read by Dick Hill. (Running Time: 9 hrs.). 2004. 49.97 (978-1-59710-671-9(2), 1597106712, BADLE); 24.95 (978-1-59710-670-2(4), 1597106704, BAD) Brilliance Audio.

Scarlet Letter. unabr. ed. Nathaniel Hawthorne. Read by Kristen Underwood. 7 cass. (Running Time: 10 hrs. 30 mins.). 1999. 49.95 (FS9-34238) Highsmith.

Scarlet Letter. unabr. ed. Nathaniel Hawthorne. Read by John Chatty & Cindy Hardin. 5 cass. (Running Time: 7 hrs.). Dramatization. 1979. 29.00 (C-10) Jimcin Record.
In Puritan New England, adultery was considered a crime against the state as well as a sin. Hester Prynne, convicted of this crime, is condemned to wear a scarlet "A" for the rest of her life. Her unknown lover finds his own form of punishment.

Scarlet Letter. unabr. ed. Nathaniel Hawthorne. Read by John Chatty & Cindy Hardin. 1 cass. (Running Time: 1 hr. 20 mins.). Dramatization. 1980. 7.95 (N-59) Jimcin Record.
Chapters 2, 3, 10 & 23 of the novel.

***Scarlet Letter.** unabr. ed. Nathaniel Hawthorne. 2010. audio compact disk 25.95 (978-1-58081-721-9(1)) L A Theatre.

Scarlet Letter. unabr. ed. Nathaniel Hawthorne. Perf. by Lesley Ann Warren. 4 cass. (Running Time: 6 hrs.). 2004. 25.00 (978-1-59007-134-2(4)) Pub: New Millenn Enter. Dist(s): PerseuPGW
An English scholar sends his young wife to Boston in the 17th century. He discovers his wife's illegitimate child, and banished from the city wearing a scarlet "A".

Scarlet Letter, unabr. ed. Nathaniel Hawthorne. Narrated by Flo Gibson. 6 cass. (Running Time: 9 hrs.). 1999. 51.00 (978-1-55690-459-2(2), 81270E7) Recorded Bks.
Hester Prynne wears the brand of adultery like a blazon in the strict society of 17th Century New England.

Scarlet Letter. unabr. ed. Nathaniel Hawthorne. Read by Dick Hill. (Running Time: 9 hrs.). 2004. 24.95 (978-1-59335-149-6(6), 1593351496) Soulmate Audio Bks.
The classic American story of Hester Prynne, accused of adultery, ostracized by her Puritan community & abandoned by both her lover & her husband Perhaps the first American novel to explore the ambiguities of morality, love & public judgement. The Scarlet Letter rightfully deserves its respected reputation.

Scarlet Letter. unabr. ed. Nathaniel Hawthorne. Read by Annie Wauters. 1 cd. (Running Time: 9 hrs 32 mins). (YA). 2002. audio compact disk 18.95 (978-1-58472-399-8(8), In Aud) Pub: Sound Room. Dist(s): Baker Taylor
MP3 format.

Scarlet Letter. unabr. ed. Nathaniel Hawthorne. Narrated by Shelly Frasier. (Running Time: 9 hrs. 0 mins. 0 sec.). (ENG.). 2008. 22.99 (978-1-4001-5855-3(9)); audio compact disk 32.99 (978-1-4001-0855-8(1)); audio compact disk 65.99 (978-1-4001-3855-5(8)) Pub: Tantor Media. Dist(s): IngramPubServ

Scarlet Letter. unabr. ed. Nathaniel Hawthorne. Read by Flo Gibson. (YA). 2006. 49.99 (978-1-59895-179-0(3)) Find a World.

Scarlet Letter. unabr. ed. Read by Annie Wauters. 8 CDs. (Running Time: 9 hrs. 30 mins.). 2002. audio compact disk 79.00 (978-1-58472-175-8(8), Commuters Library) Sound Room.
Classic novel of puritanism giving rise to twisted gender politics, hypocrisy, and strength of character in the face of public scorn.

Scarlet Letter. unabr. collector's ed. Nathaniel Hawthorne. Read by Donada Peters. 8 cass. (Running Time: 8 hrs.). (YA). 1991. 48.00 (978-0-7366-1910-3(0), 2736) Books on Tape.
Because Hester Prynne commits adultery & refuses to name her lover, she must wear a scarlet "A" on the breast of her gown for the rest of her life. In the course of the book, a complex interrelationship develops between Hester, her lover, her husband & the daughter of her adulterous union.

Scarlet Letter: Abridged. (ENG.). 2007. (978-1-60339-029-3(4)); cd-rom & audio compact disk (978-1-60339-030-9(8)) Listenr Digest.

Scarlet Letter: Classic Collection. unabr. ed. Nathaniel Hawthorne. Read by Kristen Underwood. (Running Time: 9 hrs. 30 mins.). 2008. 29.95 (978-0-7861-7271-9(1)) Blckstn Audio.

Scarlet Lion. Elizabeth Chadwick. 2007. 99.95 (978-1-84559-777-1(X)); audio compact disk 109.95 (978-1-84559-778-8(8)) Pub: Soundings Ltd GBR. Dist(s): Ulverscroft US

Scarlet Nights. abr. ed. Jude Deveraux. Read by Rick Holmes. (Running Time: 5 hrs. 30 mins. 0 sec.). (Edilean Ser.: Bk. 3). 2010. audio compact disk 29.99 (978-1-4423-0443-7(X)) Pub: S&S Audio. Dist(s): S and S Inc

***Scarlet Nights.** abr. ed. Jude Deveraux. Read by Rick Holmes. (Running Time: 5 hrs. 30 mins. 0 sec.). (ENG.). 2011. audio compact disk 14.99 (978-1-4423-4072-5(X)) Pub: S&S Audio. Dist(s): S and S Inc

Scarlet Pimpernel. Emmuska Orczy. Read by Flo Gibson. 6 cass. (Running Time: 9 hrs.). 1987. 24.95 (978-1-55685-110-0(3)) Audio Bk Con.
A British Lord's daring rescues of French nobility from the threat of the guillotine & the evil Chauvelin's efforts to track him down are part of the excitement of this swashbuckling tale.

***Scarlet Pimpernel.** Emmuska Orczy. Narrated by Flo Gibson. (ENG.). 2010. audio compact disk 29.95 (978-1-60646-168-6(0)) Audio Bk Con.

Scarlet Pimpernel. Emmuska Orczy. Narrated by Simon Williams. (Running Time: 2 hrs. 30 mins.). 2006. 14.95 (978-1-60083-032-7(3)) Iofy Corp.

Scarlet Pimpernel. Emmuska Orczy. Read by Derek Ronald Long & Kelsey Alexandra Johnson. Derek Ronald Long & Kelsey Alexandra Johnson. Prod. by Christopher Joseph O'Connell. Directed By Christopher Joseph O'Connell. Dramatization. 2006. 24.95 (978-0-9748741-1-1(6), Painted Rock Recs) Painted Rck Pubns.

Scarlet Pimpernel. abr. ed. Emmuska Orczy. Perf. by Christopher Cazenove. 4 cass. (Running Time: 6 hrs.). 2004. 25.00 (978-1-59007-136-6(0)) Pub: New Millenn Enter. Dist(s): PerseuPGW
Armed with only his wits and his cunning, one man recklessly defies the French revolutionaries and rescues scores of innocent men, women, and children from the deadly guillotine. His friends and foes know him only as the Scarlet Pimpernel. But the ruthless French agent Chauvelin is sworn to discover his identity and to hunt him down.

Scarlet Pimpernel. collector's ed. Emmuska Orczy. Read by Roe Kendall. 7 cass. (Running Time: 10 hrs. 30 min.). 1999. 56.00 (978-0-7366-4893-6(3)) Books on Tape.
A romantic adventure set during the French Revolution & the ensuing Reign of Terror. Inspired by a clandestine leader, a small band of titled Englishmen helps innocent victims escape. The hero, a man of many disguises, not only defies but taunts the French authorities: he leaves a blood red flower, a scarlet pimpernel, at the scene of each of his rescues.

Scarlet Pimpernel. unabr. ed. Emmuska Orczy. Read by Walter Zimmerman. (Running Time: 8 mins. 30 sec.). (J). 2007. 29.95 (978-0-7861-7901-5(5)); audio compact disk 63.00 (978-0-7861-7634-2(2)) Blckstn Audio.

Scarlet Pimpernel. unabr. ed. Emmuska Orczy. Read by Ralph Cosham. (Running Time: 30600 sec.). 2007. 54.95 (978-0-7861-2890-7(9)) Blckstn Audio.

Scarlet Pimpernel. unabr. ed. Emmuska Orczy. Read by Walter Zimmerman. 8 cass. (Running Time: 12 hrs.). (J). 1983. 56.00 (978-0-7366-3882-1(2), 9106) Books on Tape.
Set during the French Revolution & the ensuing Reign of Terror. Inspired by a clandestine leader, a small band of titled Englishmen helps innocent victims escape. The hero, a man of many disguises, not only defies but taunts the French authorities: he leaves a blood red flower, a scarlet pimpernel, at the scene of each of his rescues.

Scarlet Pimpernel. unabr. ed. Emmuska Orczy. Read by Michael Page. 6 cass. (Running Time: 8 hrs.). (Bookcassette Classic Collection). 1999. 57.25 (978-1-56740-678-8(5), 1567406785, Unabridge Lib Edns) Brilliance Audio.
Perhaps the most famous alias of all time, "The Scarlet Pimpernel" hides the identity of a British nobleman who, masked by various disguises, leads a band of young men to undermine the Reign of Terror after the French Revolution. The Scarlet Pimpernel makes daring raid after daring raid into the heart of France to save aristocrats condemned to the guillotine. At each rescue, he leaves his calling card: a small, blood-red flower - a pimpernel - mocking the power of Robespierre and his Committee of Public Safety. Having been told that his own wife was an informer who delivered an aristocrat into the hands of the Committee, the Scarlet Pimpernel must keep his identity and work a secret while he struggles against the love he feels for her. Until the day her own brother is taken prisoner.

Scarlet Pimpernel. unabr. ed. Emmuska Orczy. Read by Michael Page. (Running Time: 8 hrs.). 2005. 39.25 (978-1-59600-950-9(0), 9781596009509, BADLE); 24.95 (978-1-59600-949-3(7), 9781596009493, BAD); audio compact disk 39.25 (978-1-59600-948-6(9), 9781596009486, Brlnc Audio MP3 Lib); audio compact disk 24.95 (978-1-59600-947-9(0), 9781596009479, Brilliance MP3); audio compact disk 32.95 (978-1-59600-945-5(4), 9781596009455, Bril Audio CD Unabri) Brilliance Audio.

Scarlet Pimpernel. unabr. ed. Emmuska Orczy. Read by Ralph Cosham. (J). 2008. 54.99 (978-1-60514-918-9(7)) Find a World.

Scarlet Pimpernel. unabr. ed. Emmuska Orczy. Read by Walter Zimmerman. 8 cass. (Running Time: 10 hrs. 30 min.). 1984. 56.00 (C-106) Jimcin Record.
An elusive Englishman rescues Frenchmen from the guillotine during the "Reign of Terror".

Scarlet Pimpernel, unabr. ed. Emmuska Orczy. Narrated by Steven Crossley. 7 cass. (Running Time: 10 hrs.). (YA). 2000. 60.00 (95841X4) Recorded Bks.
As the French Revolution reaches its height, hundreds of aristocratic heads roll from the guillotine. One man, however, dares to move against the popular tide. Elusive & sly, the Scarlet Pimpernel is helping nobles & their families flee France.

Scarlet Pimpernel, unabr. ed. Emmuska Orczy. Read by Steven Crossley. 7 cass. (Running Time: 10 hrs.). (YA). 2000. pap. bk. & stu. ed. 73.20 (978-0-7887-3191-4(2), 40926X4) Recorded Bks.

Scarlet Pimpernel. unabr. ed. Emmuska Orczy. Narrated by Steven Crossley. 7 cass. (Running Time: 10 hrs.). (gr. 9 up). 2000. 60.00 (978-0-7887-3168-6(8), 95841E7) Recorded Bks.

Scarlet Pimpernel. unabr. ed. Emmuska Orczy. Narrated by Wanda McCaddon. (Running Time: 8 hrs. 30 mins. 0 sec.). (ENG.). 2009. audio compact disk 22.99 (978-1-4001-6276-5(9)); audio compact disk 65.99 (978-1-4001-4276-7(8)); audio compact disk 32.99 (978-1-4001-1276-0(1)) Pub: Tantor Media. Dist(s): IngramPubServ

Scarlet Pimpernel. unabr. ed. Emmuska Orczy. Read by Michael Page. (Running Time: 8 hrs.). (Classic Collection (Brilliance Audio) Ser.). 2005. audio compact disk 87.25 (978-1-59600-946-2(2), 9781596009462, BriAudCD Unabrid) Brilliance Audio.
Perhaps the most famous alias of all time, "The Scarlet Pimpernel" hides the identity of a British nobleman who, masked by various disguises, leads a band of young men to undermine the Reign of Terror after the French Revolution. The Scarlet Pimpernel makes daring raid after daring raid into the heart of France to save aristocrats condemned to the guillotine. At each rescue, he leaves his calling card: a small, blood-red flower - a pimpernel - mocking the power of Robespierre and his Committee of Public Safety. Having been told that his own wife was an informer who delivered an aristocrat into the hands of the Committee, the Scarlet Pimpernel must keep his identity and work a secret while he struggles against the love he feels for her. Until the day her own brother is taken prisoner.

Scarlet Pimpernel, Class Set. unabr. ed. Emmuska Orczy. Read by Steven Crossley. 7 cass. (Running Time: 10 hrs.). (YA). 1999. 130.30 (978-0-7887-3237-9(4), 46893) Recorded Bks.
As the French Revolution reaches its height, hundreds of aristocratic heads roll from the guillotine. One man, however, dares to move against the popular tide. Elusive & sly, the Scarlet Pimpernel is helping nobles & their families flee France.

Scarlet Ruse. unabr. collector's ed. John D. MacDonald. Read by Michael Prichard. 6 cass. (Running Time: 9 hrs.). (Travis McGee Ser.: Vol. 14). 1985. 48.00 (978-0-7366-0707-0(2), 1670) Books on Tape.
McGee was too busy with his beloved houseboat, the Busted Flush, to pay attention to the little old man with his missing postage stamps. Except they weren't ordinary stamps. They were rare stamps, $400,000 worth.

Scarlet Stain. (Paws & Tales Ser.: Vol. 24). (J). 2002. 3.99 (978-1-57972-432-0(9)); audio compact disk 5.99 (978-1-57972-433-7(7)) Insight Living.

Scarlet Thread. abr. ed. Francine Rivers. 2004. 11.99 (978-1-58926-721-3(4), 6721) Oasis Audio.

Scarlet Thread. abr. ed. Francine Rivers. Narrated by Aimee Lilly. (ENG.). 2004. 10.49 (978-1-60814-374-0(0)); audio compact disk 14.99 (978-1-58926-722-0(2), 6722) Oasis Audio.

Scarlett Pt. A: The Sequel to Margaret Mitchell's Gone with the Wind. unabr. ed. Alexandra Ripley. Read by Donada Peters. 11 cass. (Running Time: 16 hrs. 30 min. hrs.). 1992. 88.00 (978-0-7366-2308-7(6), 3091A) Books on Tape.
The story of Scarlett's & Rhett's love affair, begun in Gone With the Wind, continues in this long-awaited sequel.

Scarlett Pt. B: The Sequel to Margaret Mitchell's Gone with the Wind. Alexandra Ripley. Read by Donada Peters. 1992. 80.00 (978-0-7366-2309-4(4)) Books on Tape.

Scarlett Pt. B: The Sequel to Margaret Mitchell's Gone with the Wind. unabr. ed. Alexandra Ripley. Read by Donada Peters. 10 cass. (Running Time: 15 hrs.). 1992. 80.00 (3091B) Books on Tape.
The story of Scarlett's and Rhett's love affair, begun in Gone With the Wind, continues in this long-awaited sequel.

***Scarlett & Other Dance Solos & Duets.** Perf. by R. A. Zuckerman. Composed by R. A. Zuckerman. (ENG.). 2010. 12.95 (978-1-891083-23-5(6)) ConcertHall.

Scarlett Cord: Joshua 2. Ed Young. 1985. 4.95 (978-0-7417-1448-0(5), 448) Win Walk.

***Scarlett Fever.** unabr. ed. Maureen Johnson. Read by Jeannie Stith. (Running Time: 9 hrs.). 2010. 24.99 (978-1-4418-8339-1(8), 9781441883391, BAD); 39.99 (978-1-4418-8340-7(1), 9781441883407, BADLE) Brilliance Audio.

***Scarlett Fever.** unabr. ed. Maureen Johnson. Read by Jeannie Stith. (Running Time: 9 hrs.). (YA). 2010. 24.99 (978-1-4418-8337-7(1), 9781441883377, Brilliance MP3); 39.97 (978-1-4418-8338-4(X), 9781441883384, Brlnc Audio MP3 Lib); audio compact disk 29.99 (978-1-4418-8335-3(5), 9781441883353, Bril Audio CD Unabri); audio compact disk 71.97 (978-1-4418-8336-0(3), 9781441883360, BriAudCD Unabrid) Brilliance Audio.

Scarlett Letter: An A+ Audio Study Guide. unabr. ed. Nathaniel Hawthorne. (ENG.). 2006. 5.98 (978-1-59483-730-2(9)) Pub: Hachet Audio. Dist(s): HachBkGrp

Scarpetta. abr. ed. Patricia Cornwell. Read by Kate Reading. (Running Time: 6 hrs.). No. 16. (ENG.). (gr. 8). 2008. audio compact disk 29.95 (978-0-14-314365-9(4), PengAudBks) Penguin Grp USA.

Scarpetta. unabr. ed. Patricia Cornwell. Read by Kate Reading. 12 CDs. (Running Time: 15 hrs.). No. 16. (ENG.). (gr. 8). 2008. audio compact disk 39.95 (978-0-14-314364-2(6), PengAudBks) Penguin Grp USA.

Scarpetta. unabr. ed. Patricia Cornwell. Read by Kate Reading. 12 CDs. (Kay Scarpetta Ser.: No. 16). 2008. audio compact disk 100.00 (978-1-4159-6032-5(1), BksonTape) Pub: Random Audio Pubg. Dist(s): Random
Leaving behind her private forensic pathology practice in Charleston, South Carolina, Kay Scarpetta takes up an assignment in New York City, where the NYPD has asked her to examine an injured patient on Bellevue Hospital's psychiatric prison ward. The handcuffed and chained patient, Oscar Bane, has specifically asked for her, and when she literally has her gloved hands on him, he begins to talk - and the story he has to tell turns out to be one of the most bizarre she has ever heard. The injuries, he says, were sustained in the course of a murder . . . that he did not commit. Is

Bane a criminally insane stalker who has fixed on Scarpetta? Or is his paranoid tale true, and it is he who is being spied on, followed and stalked by the actual killer? The one thing Scarpetta knows for certain is that a woman has been tortured and murdered - and more violent deaths will follow. Gradually, an inexplicable and horrifying truth emerges: Whoever is committing the crimes knows where his prey is at all times. Is it a person, a government? And what is the connection among the victims? In the days that follow, Scarpetta, her forensic psychologist husband, Benton Wesley, and her niece Lucy, who has recently formed her own forensic computer investigation firm in New York, will undertake a harrowing chase through cyberspace and the all-too-real streets of the city - an odyssey that will take them at once to places they never knew but also much, much too close to home.

Scarpetta Factor. abr. ed. Patricia Cornwell. (Running Time: 8 hrs.). (Kay Scarpetta Ser.: No. 17). (ENG.). (gr. 12 up). 2009. audio compact disk 29.95 (978-0-14-314548-6(7), PengAudBks) Penguin Grp USA.

Scarpetta Factor. unabr. ed. Patricia Cornwell. Read by Kate Reading. 13 CDs. (Running Time: 16 hrs.). (Kay Scarpetta Ser.: No. 17). (ENG.). (gr. 12 up). 2009. audio compact disk 39.95 (978-0-14-314547-9(9), PengAudBks) Penguin Grp USA.

***Scarpetta Factor.** unabr. ed. Patricia Cornwell. Read by Kate Reading. 12 CDs. (Kay Scarpetta Ser.: No. 17). 2009. audio compact disk 100.00 (978-1-4159-6034-9(8), BksonTape) Pub: Random Audio Pubg. Dist(s): Random

Scarred by Struggle, Transformed by Hope. Speeches. Based on a book by Joan Chittister. 1. (Running Time: 60 mins). 2004. 7.00 (978-1-890890-36-0(7)) Benetvision.

Scarred Girl see James Dickey Reads His Poetry & Prose

Scars Remain. Contrib. by Disciple. Prod. by Travis Wyrick. 2007. audio compact disk 17.98 (978-5-557-63546-2(7)) INO Rec.

Scarves of Many Colors: Muslim Women & the Veil. 2000. pap. bk. 15.00 (978-1-878554-15-4(8)) Teaching Chng.

Scary Day. unabr. ed. Doreen Rappaport. 1 cass. (Running Time: 5 min.). (Happy Endings! Ser.). (J). (ps-1). 1988. pap. bk. 9.95 (978-0-87386-052-9(7)) Jan Prods.

Moving to a new house is very exciting, but it can also be very scary - especially when you also have to change schools! Children will empathize with Maggie's concerns about entering a new school in April, when friendships have already formed.

Scary Poems. Poems. 1 cass. (Running Time: 29 min.). 1991. 10.00 (102387) New Letters.

Various authors & readers celebrating Halloween through poetry.

Scary Snake Mystery. unabr. ed. David A. Adler. Narrated by Christina Moore. 1 cass. (Running Time: 30 min.). (Cam Jansen Ser.: No. 17). (J). 2003. 10.00 (978-1-4025-5551-0(2)) Recorded Bks.

Cam Jansen's trip into the big city promises to be exciting, and Cam's mother has brought along a video camera to record the action. When a scary snake frightens a man on the steps of the library, Cam's mother accidently tapes the funny scene. But later, a man in a red sweatshirt steals the video camera. Cam thinks there might be a connection between the two events and she's going to use her photographic memory to prove it!.

Scary Snake Mystery. unabr. ed. David A. Adler. Narrated by Christina Moore. 1 cass. (Running Time: 15 min.). (Cam Jansen Ser.: No. 17). 2003. 9.95 (978-1-4025-5552-7(0)) Recorded Bks.

Scary Sounds of Halloween. Audioscope. 1995. 5.00 (978-1-57375-075-2(1)); audio compact disk 8.00 CD. (978-1-57375-076-9(X)) Audioscope.

Scary Stories. unabr. ed. Alvin Schwartz. Perf. by George Irving. 3 CDs. (Running Time: 3 hrs. 30 min.). 2001. audio compact disk 22.00 (HarperChildAud) HarperCollins Pubs.

Scary Stories. unabr. ed. Alvin Schwartz. Perf. by George Irving. 3 cass. (Running Time: 3 hrs. 30 min.). 2001. 20.00 (HarperChildAud) HarperCollins Pubs.

Is it possible to die - and not know it? What if a person is buried too soon? What happens to a thief foolish enough to rob a corpse, or to a murderer whose victim returns from the grave? Read about these terrifying predicaments as well as what happens when practical jokes produce gruesome consequences and initiations go awry.

Scary Stories. unabr. ed. Alvin Schwartz. Read by George S. Irving. 3 cass. (Running Time: 3 hrs. 30 mins.). (J). (gr. 4-7). 2001. 20.00 (978-0-694-52615-4(0)) HarperCollins Pubs.

Scary Stories. unabr. ed. Alvin Schwartz & Alvin Schwartz. Read by George Irving. 3 CDs. (Running Time: 3 hrs. 30 mins.). (J). (gr. 4-7). 2001. audio compact disk 22.00 (978-0-694-52612-3(6)) HarperCollins Pubs.

Scary Stories. unabr. abr. ed. Alvin Schwartz. Perf. by George S. Irving. 1 cass. (Running Time: 42 min.). (J). (gr. 3-5). 1987. 12.00 (978-0-89845-758-2(0), CPN 1794, Harper Audio) HarperCollins Pubs.

Scary Stories for All Ages. unabr. ed. Roberta Simpson Brown. Read by Roberta Simpson Brown. 1 cass. (Running Time: 50 min.). (American Storytelling Ser.). 1993. 12.00 (978-0-87483-302-7(7)) Pub: August Hse. Dist(s): Natl Bk Netwk

Scat. unabr. ed. Carl Hiaasen. Narrated by Edward Asner. 8 CDs. (Running Time: 9 hrs. 18 mins.). (YA). (gr. 5-8). 2009. audio compact disk 60.00 (978-0-7393-7130-5(4), Listening Lib) Pub: Random Audio Pubg. Dist(s): Random

Scat. unabr. ed. Carl Hiaasen. Read by Edward Asner. (ENG.). (J). (gr. 5). 2009. audio compact disk 40.00 (978-0-7393-7128-2(2), Listening Lib) Pub: Random Audio Pubg. Dist(s): Random

Scat Like That: A Musical Word Odyssey. 1 CD. (Running Time: 42 mins.). 2005. audio compact disk 14.98 (978-1-57940-128-3(7)) Rounder Records.

Scattered Suns. abr. ed. Kevin J. Anderson. Read by David Colacci. (Running Time: 32400 sec.). (Saga of Seven Suns Ser.: Bk. 4). 2006. audio compact disk 19.99 (978-1-59737-210-7(2), 9781597372107, BCD Value Price) Brilliance Audio.

Please enter a Synopsis.

Scattered Suns. unabr. ed. Kevin J. Anderson. Read by David Colacci. (Running Time: 20 hrs.). (Saga of Seven Suns Ser.). 2005. 29.95 (978-1-59737-213-8(7), 9781597372138, BAD) Brilliance Audio.

Scattered Suns. unabr. ed. Kevin J. Anderson. Read by David Colacci. (Running Time: 20 hrs.). (Saga of Seven Suns Ser.: Bk. 4). 2005. 44.25 (978-1-59737-214-5(5), 9781597372145, BADLE); 112.25 (978-1-59737-206-0(4), 9781597372060, BrilAudUnabridg); 42.95 (978-1-59737-205-3(6), 9781597372053, BAU); audio compact disk 44.25 (978-1-59737-212-1(9), 9781597372121, Brinc Audio MP3 Lib); audio compact disk 29.95 (978-1-59737-211-4(0), 9781597372114, Brilliance MP3); audio compact disk 127.25 (978-1-59737-208-4(0), 9781597372084, BriAudCD Unabrid); audio compact disk 42.95 (978-1-59737-207-7(2), 9781597372077, Bril Audio CD Unabri) Brilliance Audio.

As the war escalates, the various civilizations across the Spiral Arm crack from the strain. Focused intently on the outside alien foe, leaders across the galaxy are failing to hold their nations together. Amid the mounting tensions, empires begin to crumble. In despair at his powerlessness to keep his human race alive, Chairman Basil Wenceslas grows increasingly irrational and tyrannical. Unable to effectively defend against the alien enemy, he blames the unruly colonies and independent human nations around the galaxy and punishes them with violence. Meanwhile, the leader of the Ildirans, Jora'h, flounders under a massive rebellion. For the first time in memory, Ildiran has taken up arms against Ildiran, and feeling every death through their psychic network, Jora'h suffers at the slaughter of his people. Every planet and colony across the spiral arm, human or alien, feels the devastation. No one is safe.

Scattering of Daisies. unabr. ed. Susan Sallis. Read by Jacqueline King. 11 cass. (Running Time: 15 hrs.). (Sound Ser.). 2001. 89.95 (978-1-85496-854-8(8)) Pub: UlverLrgPrint GBR. Dist(s): Ulverscroft US

Will Rising had dragged himself from humble beginnings to his own small tailoring business in Gloucester, and on the way he'd fallen violently in love with the refined and delicate Florence, who wanted something better for her children. March was the eldest girl, the least loved, the plain, unattractive one. However, March Rising was determined to find wealth, love and happiness.

Scavenger. abr. ed. David Morrell. Read by Patrick G. Lawlor. (Running Time: 14400 sec.). 2008. audio compact disk 14.99 (978-1-4233-2994-7(5), 9781423329947, BCD Value Price) Brilliance Audio.

Scavenger. unabr. ed. David Morrell. Read by Patrick G. Lawlor. (Running Time: 8 hrs.). 2007. 39.25 (978-1-4233-2990-9(2), 9781423329909, Brinc Audio MP3 Lib); 24.95 (978-1-4233-2989-3(9), 9781423329893, Brilliance MP3); 39.25 (978-1-4233-2992-3(9), 9781423329923, BADLE); 24.95 (978-1-4233-2991-6(0), 9781423329916, BAD); 74.25 (978-1-4233-2986-2(4), 9781423329862, BrilAudUnabridg); audio compact disk 87.25 (978-1-4233-2988-6(0), 9781423329886, BriAudCD Unabrid); audio compact disk 34.95 (978-1-4233-2987-9(2), 9781423329879, Bril Audio CD Unabri) Brilliance Audio.

Scavenger. unabr. ed. Tom Savage. Narrated by Richard Ferrone. 7 cass. (Running Time: 10 hrs. 15 mins.). 2000. 65.00 (978-0-7887-4389-4(9), 96242E7) Recorded Bks.

A hunt for a vicious serial killer intent on winning a deadly game where the rules are constantly changing. When a novel attracts the attention of someone who knows too much about a series of murders ten years ago, the novelist finds himself in the middle of a deadly scavenger hunt that could lead him to the identity of a killer long thought dead, if he can survive long enough to finish.

Scavenger Hunt. Janet Lorimer. 1 cass. (Running Time: 3775 sec.). (Pageturners Ser.). (J). 2002. 10.95 (978-1-56254-493-5(4), SP4934) Saddleback Edu.

Scavenger Reef. unabr. ed. Laurence Shames. Narrated by Richard Ferrone. 8 CDs. (Running Time: 9 hrs. 30 mins.). 1999. audio compact disk 73.00 (978-0-7887-3443-4(1), C1049E7) Recorded Bks.

Augie Silver's friends are ostensibly grief-stricken when he drowns in a shipwreck off Scavenger Reef, but most of them are nervous because his body wasn't found. Alive, his art isn't worth much, but dead, the price of his art is skyrocketing. If Augie isn't dead, he soon will be, if his "friends" get their way.

Scavenger Reef, unabr. ed. Laurence Shames. Narrated by Richard Ferrone. 7 cass. (Running Time: 9 hrs. 30 mins.). 1998. 60.00 (978-0-7887-1982-0(3), 95369E7) Recorded Bks.

Scavenger Reef. unabr. collector's ed. Laurence Shames. Read by Rob McQuay. 6 cass. (Running Time: 9 hrs.). 1998. 48.00 (978-0-7366-4080-0(0), 4589) Books on Tape.

Is he alive or dead? That's what everyone's wondering in this tale of an artist's disappearance in Key West.

Scene Behind the Screen: The Business Realities of the TV Industry. 8 cass. Incl. Alan Landsburg: President, Alan Landsburg Productions. 1978.; Don Ohlmeyer: Executive Producer, NBC Sports. 1978.; Joe Barbera, President, Hanna Barbera Productions, & Margaret Loesch, Director, Children's Programming, NBC-TV. 1978.; Lawrence Fraiberg, President, Metromedia TV, & Dennis Swanson, News Director, KABC-TV. 1978.; Norman Horowitz: President, Columbia Pictures Distribution. 1978.; Paul Klein: Executive Vice President Programming, NBC TV. 1978.; Richard C. Wald: Senior Vice President, News, ABC-TV. 1978.; Rowland Perkins: Talent Agent. 1978.; (Network Ser.). 1978. 15.00 ea.; 89.50 Set. (S117) J Norton Pubs.

Ten top professionals in the industry provide an in-depth examination of the programming process for network series, specials, children's TV, news, & sports; independent production; local & group station management; syndication, & more.

Scenes & Themes. Stanley Thornes. 1 cass. (C). 1985. 85.00 (978-0-7175-1324-6(6)) St Mut.

Scenes de la Vie Francaise. Read by Jean-Philippe Gaussens. 1 cass. (FRE.). 11.95 incl. text. (SAC 47-4) Spoken Arts.

These 13 dialogues are between a French father, mother & their young son & daughter.

Scenes from Childhood. Donia Blumenfeld Clenman. Read by Donia Blumenfeld Clenman. Perf. by Martin Clenman. 1 cass. (Running Time: 44 mins.). 8.95 Flo & Little CAN.

13 poems inspired by the piano music of Robert Schumann.

Scenes from My Life: An Autobiography. abr. ed. Andrea Bocelli. 2 cass. (Running Time: 3 hrs.). 2000. 18.98 (978-1-57042-967-5(7)) Hachet Audio.

Andrea Bocelli recounts the incredible story of how he overcame his blindness to become an international singing superstar. Singing in piano bars, Bocelli was discovered by the Italian pop star Zucchero & later Pavarotti. His career quickly skyrocketed when PBS aired a 1997 Bocelli concert. He has since become an international phenomenon who appeals to all ages.

Scenes from Shakespeare. Read by Paul Rogers. 10.95 (978-0-8045-0723-3(6), SAC 723) Spoken Arts.

Scenes of Clerical Life. unabr. ed. George Eliot. Narrated by Flo Gibson. 10 cass. (Running Time: 15 hrs.). 2003. 44.95 (978-1-55685-740-9(3)) Audio Bk Con.

"The Sad Fortunes of the Reverend Amos Barton", "Mr. Grifil's Love Story", and "Janet's Repentance" are full of rollicking laughter and hear-rending tears.

Scenes of Clerical Life. unabr. ed. George Eliot. Read by Nadia May. 10 cass. (Running Time: 14 hrs. 30 mins.). 1999. 69.95 (978-0-7861-1592-1(0), 2421) Blckstn Audio.

Eliot produced a form of fiction that ran counter to the debates regarding religion in her day. She had parted ways with Christian faith over a decade before writing it in 1857, becoming one of many Victorian era "Honest Doubters." Yet her mature views, never simple ones, shine through in this work. Under the surface orthodoxy are signs of her search for a "religion of Humanity," & her desire for conciliation with whatever was best in Christianity.

Scenes of Clerical Life. unabr. ed. George Eliot. (Running Time: 50400 sec.). 2007. audio compact disk 29.95 (978-0-7861-5916-1(2)); audio compact disk 99.00 (978-0-7861-5915-4(4)) Blckstn Audio.

Scent of Heather. abr. ed. Stella March. Read by Margaret Holt. 4 cass. (Running Time: 6 hrs.). (Sound Ser.). 2004. 44.95 (978-1-85496-434-2(8), 64348) Pub: UlverLrgPrint GBR. Dist(s): Ulverscroft US

***Scent of Rain & Lightning.** unabr. ed. Nancy Pickard. Read by Tavia Gilbert. (Running Time: 10 hrs.). 2010. 29.95 (978-1-4417-4775-4(3)); 65.95 (978-1-4417-4771-6(0)); audio compact disk 29.95 (978-1-4417-4774-7(5)); audio compact disk 90.00 (978-1-4417-4772-3(9)) Blckstn Audio.

Scent of Scandal. Carole Matthews. Read by Jennifer Van Dyck. 6 cass. 54.95 (978-0-7927-3397-3(5), CSL 726); audio compact disk 79.95 (978-0-7927-3398-0(3), SLD 726) AudioGO.

Scent of the Missing: Love & Partnership with a Search-and-Rescue Dog. unabr. ed. Susannah Charleson. (Running Time: 10 hrs. 0 mins.). 2010. 29.95 (978-1-4417-2962-0(3)); audio compact disk 29.95 (978-1-4417-2961-3(5)) Blckstn Audio.

***Scent of the Missing: Love & Partnership with a Search-and-Rescue Dog.** unabr. ed. Susannah Charleson. (Running Time: 10 hrs. 0 mins.). 2010. 59.95 (978-1-4417-2958-3(5)); audio compact disk 90.00 (978-1-4417-2959-0(3)) Blckstn Audio.

***Scent of Water: Discovering What Remains.** Naomi Zacharias. (ENG.). 2011. 16.99 (978-0-310-59045-3(0)) Zondervan.

Scent of Your Breath. unabr. ed. Melissa P. Read by Edwina Wren. (Running Time: 10200 sec.). 2007. audio compact disk 54.95 (978-1-921334-14-6(2), 9781921334146) Pub: Bolinda Pubng AUS. Dist(s): Bolinda Pub Inc

Schartz-Metterklume Method see Selected European Short Stories

Scheduling Time (Principle #11: Practice Kaizen) Psalm 90:10-12. Ed Young. 1997. 4.95 (978-0-7417-2132-7(5), 1132) Win Walk.

Scheherazade. unabr. ed. Anthony O'Neill. Narrated by Michael Carman. 12 cass. (Running Time: 18 hrs. 50 mins.). 2004. 96.00 (978-1-74030-580-8(9)) Pub: Bolinda Pubng AUS. Dist(s): Lndmrk Audiobks

***Scheherazade's Typewriter.** unabr. ed. Joe Hill. (ENG.). 2007. (978-0-06-155235-9(6)) HarperCollins Pubs.

Scherezade: Rimsky-Korsakov. 1994. 17.00 (978-0-7692-5005-2(X), Warner Bro) Alfred Pub.

Schindler's List. Thomas Keneally. 2004. 12.95 (978-0-7435-4804-5(3)) Pub: S&S Audio. Dist(s): S and S Inc

Schindler's List. unabr. ed. Thomas Keneally. Read by Walter Zimmerman. 12 cass. (Running Time: 18 hrs.). 1990. 96.00 (978-0-7366-1837-3(6), 2671) Books on Tape.

The true story of Oskar Schindler, German Catholic, industrialist & prison camp director - a man who saved more Jews from extermination than any other person during WW II. From the actual testimony of Schindlerjuden, (Schindler's Jews), a picture of this remarkable man emerges. Not only did he put his life at risk protecting Jews, but he spent his entire fortune in the effort. As the war drew to a close & as the Nazi administration pushed its extermination policies with incredible rigor, Schindler was able to safeguard more than a thousand otherwise doomed people.

Schindler's List, unabr. ed. Thomas Keneally. Narrated by Gordon Dulieu. 12 cass. (Running Time: 16 hrs. 45 min.). 1997. 97.00 (978-1-55690-460-8(6), 90066) Recorded Bks.

The utterly riveting story of a rather ordinary man who risked everything in the face of death for his fellow man.

Schirmer Inheritance. unabr. collector's ed. Eric Ambler. Read by Richard Brown. 6 cass. (Running Time: 9 hrs.). 1989. 48.00 (978-0-7366-1516-7(4), 2387) Books on Tape.

A wonderfully ingenious tangle of slow dissolving mystification which has the persuasive nag of truth.

Schizoaffective Disorder: Program from the Award Winning Public Radio Serie. Interview. Hosted by Fred Goodwin. Comment by John Hockenberry. 1 CD. (Running Time: 1 hr.). 2004. audio compact disk 21.95 (978-1-932479-90-4(2), LCM 315) Lichtenstein Creat.

Hundreds of thousands of Americans have schizoaffective disorder, an overlap of schizophrenia and manic depression. The illness can cause them to have both mood swings and cognitive symptoms including mania, depression and visual or aural hallucinations, and can be at grave risk of suicide.This week on The Infinite Mind, we explore schizoaffective disorder, what it's like to have the illness, how people have persevered in spite of it, and why it leaves so many doctors confused.Dr. Fred Goodwin's guests include Dr. Nassir Ghaemi, assistant professor of psychiatry at Harvard Medical School, Dr. Eden Evins, of the Massachusetts General Hospital Schizophrenia Program, and Dr. Corinne Cather, a cognitive behavioral therapist and clinical fellow at Massachusetts General Hospital.We'll also hear a gripping account of what it's like to live with schizoaffective disorder and hear a musical performance of Philippe Gaubert's "Nocturne et Allegro Scherzando" from Tracy Harris, a professional flutist living with the disorder, and a remarkable recreation of what it's like to hear aural hallucinations as recreated by a leading Broadway sound designer, based on the descriptions of a young woman who is living with the illness. John and Katie Cadigan discuss their new documentary film, "People Say I'm Crazy," which chronicles John's diagnosis with schizoaffective disorder. And John Hockenberry looks at the steep rise in the number of suicides on military bases, and what the resulting government response can teach the rest of us about the need for access to mental health care.

Schizophrenia. Prod. by Michelle Trudeau. 1 cass. (Running Time: 35 min.). 10.95 (I0180B090, HarperThor) HarpC GBR.

Schizophrenia: Program from the Award Winning Public Radio Series. Hosted by Fred Goodwin. Comment by John Hockenberry. Contrib. by Fred Frese et al. 1 cass. (Running Time: 1 hr.). (Infinite Mind Ser.). 1998. audio compact disk 15.00 (978-1-888064-43-8(9), LCM 12) Lichtenstein Creat.

What is schizophrenia? What's it like to experience its symptoms? Dr. Goodwin and several top researchers and advocates discuss the most recent developments in our understanding of schizophrenia and how to treat it. Psychologist Fred Frese, who himself has schizophrenia, explains that for the schizophrenic, life can be dreamlike. The ability to determine what is true, to control one's actions, to distinguish between internal and external aspects of one's experience - all can be altered. The ability to communicate with people who do not have schizophrenia may be lost.

Schizophrenia: Second Chances. Interview. Hosted by Fred Goodwin. 1 CD. (Running Time: 1 hr.). 2001. audio compact disk 21.95 (978-1-932479-91-1(0), LCM 162) Lichtenstein Creat.

Dramatic advances in schizophrenia research are providing new hope for people suffering from the disease. In this show, we'll explore recent genetic discoveries, as well as new developments in medical and therapeutic treatment. Guests include Dr. Linda Brzustowicz, Associate Professor of Genetics at Rutgers, the State University of New Jersey; Edith Shuttleworth, member of Fountain House; Dr. Nancy Andreasen, the Andrew H. Woods Chair of Psychiatry at The University of Iowa College of Medicine; Dr. Herbert Meltzer, Professor in the Departments of Psychology and Pharmacology at Vanderbilt Medical Center; and Dr. Xavier Amador, the

Director of Psychology at the New York State Psychiatric Institute and a Professor of Psychology in the Department of Psychiatry at Columbia University College of Physicians & Surgeons.

Schizophrenia: Survival World Normals. P.e.r. 1942. 115.00 (978-0-8002-4383-8(8), Pysch Press) Pub: Tay Francis Ltd GBR. Dist(s): Taylor and Fran

Schizophrenia: Voices of an Illness. Lichtenstein Creative Media, Inc. Staff. Read by Jason Robards. 1 cass. (Running Time: 1 hr.). 1994. 29.00 incl. script Lib. & inst. Lichtenstein Creat.
This Peabody-Award winning program is the first major radio documentary to feature people with the thought disorder telling their own stories in their own words. Eleven people - including a doctor, a writer & a teacher - provide intimate, first-person accounts of the onset, living with, & recovering from this most misunderstood illness. Presents leading clinicians, medical researchers & mental health advocates explaining this disease that affects one in 100 people & how a growing number of people are able to significantly improve thanks to new "second-generation" medications. Includes transcript & educational material written in conjunction with the National Institute of Mental Health.

Schizophrenia: Voices of an Illness. Lichtenstein Creative Media, Inc. Staff. Read by Jason Robards. 1 cd. (Running Time: 1 hr.). 1994. 25.00 incl. script. (978-1-888064-02-5(1)) Lichtenstein Creat.

Schizophrenia & the Double Bind. unabr. ed. Gregory Bateson. 1 cass. (Running Time: 1 hr. 30 min.). (Informal Esalen Lectures). 1976. 11.00 (02805) Big Sur Tapes.

Schizophrenia-Family & Society. R. D. Laing. 3 cass. 24.00 (OC63) Sound Horizons AV.

Schmidt Delivered. unabr. ed. Louis Begley. Narrated by George Guidall. 7 CDs. (Running Time: 8 hrs. 15 mins.). 2001. audio compact disk 78.00 (978-1-4025-0494-5(2), C1550) Recorded Bks.
Recently widowed, pushed into retirement by his law firm, at odds with his family, Albert Schmidt captivated readers with his cautious courage. Now he is facing ever mounting challenges of life, love, and age. Schmidt is happy living with his affectionate young girlfriend, Carrie. His grumpy daughter, on the other hand, seems to want only money from him. What really disturbs Schmidt, however, is the growing attention of his neighbor, the exotic Michael Mansour. Wealthy and persistent, Mansour seems determined to draw Schmidt into his lavish personal and financial affairs.

Schmidt Delivered. unabr. ed. Louis Begley. Narrated by George Guidall. 6 cass. (Running Time: 8 hrs. 15 mins.). 2001. 57.00 (978-0-7887-5512-5(9), 96505x7) Recorded Bks.
Recently widowed, pushed into retirement, at odds with his family, Albert Schmidt captivated readers with his cautious courage. Now he is facing greater challenges of life, love & age. The author's aim is perfect as he targets the emotional & financial pitfalls facing the resourceful ex-lawyer.

***Schmucks!** abr. ed. Jackie Mason & Raoul Felder. Read by Jackie Mason. (ENG.). 2007. (978-0-06-123031-8(6), Harper Audio); (978-0-06-123030-1(8), Harper Audio) HarperCollins Pubs.

Schmucks! Fakes, Frauds, Idiots, Liars, Good Guys Gone Bad, & the Armed & Dangerous. abr. ed. Jackie Mason & Raoul Felder. Read by Jackie Mason. 2007. audio compact disk 14.95 (978-0-06-114264-2(6)) HarperCollins Pubs.

Schneewittchen. Jacob W. Grimm & Wilhelm K. Grimm. 1 cass. (Running Time: 60 min.). (Bruder Grimm Kinder & Hausmarchen Ser.). (GER.). 1996. pap. bk. 19.50 (978-1-58085-220-3(3), GR-15) Interlingua VA.
Includes German transcription. Includes title story & Das Burle. The combination of written text & clarity & pace of diction will open the door for intermediate & advanced students to genuine comprehension & the use of literary texts for advancement in rapid understanding of written & oral language materials. The audio text plus written text concept makes foreign languages accessible to a much wider range of students than books alone.

Scholar Gypsy see Treasury of Matthew Arnold

School-Age Pregnancy, Pts. 1 & 2. 1 cass. (Running Time: 1 hr.). 10.95 (D024AB090, HarperThor) HarpC GBR.

School-Age Pregnancy, Pts. 3 & 4. 1 cass. (Running Time: 1 hr.). 10.95 (D024BB090, HarperThor) HarpC GBR.

School-Age Pregnancy, Pts. 5 & 6. 1 cass. (Running Time: 1 hr.). 10.95 (D024CB090, HarperThor) HarpC GBR.

School at Thrush Green. unabr. ed. Miss Read. Read by Gwen Watford. 4 cass. (Running Time: 6 hrs. 20 mins.). 2001. 24.95 (978-1-57270-186-1(2), M41186u, Audio Editions) Pub: Audio Partners. Dist(s): PerseuPGW
Dorothy Watson & Agnes Fogerty have been teachers forever, but now they're talking about retirement. The village is worried who can fill their shoes? In other, equally pressing matters, the Lovelock sisters may fire their domestic help & everyone's abuzz about that mysterious architectural student.

School at Thrush Green. unabr. ed. Miss Read & Gwen Watford. 6 cass. (Running Time: 6 hrs. 20 min.). (Thrush Green Chronicles Ser.). 1989. 54.95 (978-0-7451-6222-5(3), CAB 363) AudioGO.

School-Centered Applications of Empirically Based Assessment. Stephanie H. McConaughy. 1 cass. (Running Time: 45 mins.). 1999. 26.50 (9-23169) Riverside Pub Co.

School Choice: Making Your Decision & Making It Work. abr. ed. Dennis Rainey & Barbara Rainey. Ed. by Keith Lynch. 6 cass. (Running Time: 6 hrs.). 1995. 19.95 (978-1-57229-028-0(5)) FamilyLife.

School Days. 1 CD. (Running Time: 27 min.). (J). 2005. audio compact disk 14.95 (978-0-9765887-4-0(9)) S Edu Res LLC.

School Days. Perf. by Cedarmont Kids. 1 cass. (J). 1999. 3.99 (978-0-00-512412-3(3)); audio compact disk 5.99 (978-0-00-512418-5(2)) Provident Music.

School Days. Robert B. Parker. 5 CD. (Running Time: 6 Hrs.). (Spenser Ser.). 2005. audio compact disk 38.25 (978-1-4159-2440-2(6)) Pub: Books on Tape. Dist(s): NetLibrary CO

School Days. unabr. ed. Robert B. Parker. 4 cass. (Running Time: 6 hrs.). (Spenser Ser.). 2005. 36.00 (978-1-4159-2439-6(2)) Books on Tape.

School Days. unabr. ed. Robert B. Parker. Read by Joe Mantegna. (Running Time: 21600 sec.). (Spenser Ser.). (ENG.). 2008. audio compact disk 14.99 (978-0-7393-5825-2(1), Random AudioBks) Pub: Random Audio Pubg. Dist(s): Random

***School Days According to Humphrey.** Betty G. Birney. Contrib. by William Dufris. (Running Time: 4 hrs.). (ENG.). (J). 2011. audio compact disk 19.95 (978-0-14-242915-0(5), PengAudBks) Penguin Grp USA.

School Daze. Janet Gardner. Prod. by Alan Billingsley. 1 cass. (Running Time: 1 hr. 30 mins.). (ENG.). 1998. audio compact disk 16.95 (978-0-7390-0947-5(8), 16986) Alfred Pub.

School Daze - Sound Trax. Janet Gardner. Prod. by Alan Billingsley. 1 CD. (Running Time: 1 hr. 30 mins.). (ENG.). 1998. audio compact disk 59.95 (978-0-7390-0945-1(1), 16984) Alfred Pub.

School for Dark Thoughts. Charles Simic. Read by Charles Simic. 1 cass. (Running Time: 45 min.). (Watershed Tapes of Contemporary Poetry). 1978. 10.95 (23636) J Norton Pubs.
Combined live reading of this imaginative poet's work.

School for Managers: Six Hour Audio Cassette Series & Reference Guide. Andrew E. Schwartz. 1 cass. pap. bk. 94.95 (978-1-928950-52-3(3)); 89.95 (978-1-928950-50-9(7)) A E Schwartz.
Includes leadership, communication, goal setting, coaching motivation, time (self) management, delegation, problem solving & decision making.

School for Scandal see Theatre Highlights

School for Scandal see Sound of Classical Drama

School for Scandal, unabr. ed. Richard Brinsley Sheridan. Narrated by Flo Gibson. 3 cass. (Running Time: 3 hrs. 30 min.). 2003. 16.95 (978-1-55685-615-0(6)) Audio Bk Con.
A superb comedy of manners tossing daggers at the pretentiousness and affectation of aristocratic Londoners in the late 1700s. Such aptly named characters as Lady Sneerwell, Mrs. Candour, Sir Benjamin Backbite and Sir Joseph Surface take their turns at thrusts.

School for Scandal. unabr. ed. Richard Brinsley Sheridan. Perf. by Swan Theatre Players of Dublin. 3 cass. Dramatization. 10.95 ea. (SAC 7142/43/44) Spoken Arts.

School for the Blind. unabr. ed. Dennis McFarland. Read by William Schallert. 6 cass. (Running Time: 9 hrs.). 1995. 29.95 Set. (978-1-879371-84-2(7), 70030) Pub Mills.
Francis Brimm, a celebrated news photographer, has spent his peripatetic life as a professional voyeur, peering out with his camera at the lives of others but avoiding any gazes inward. Now retired, he returns to his childhood home on the Gulf Coast of Florida & reacquaints himself with his older sister, Muriel, whose circumscribed life has been the opposite of his own. Both brother & sister are haunted by images from the past, & when Francis stumbles upon evidence of a gruesome local murder, it shakes them profoundly. Gripped by a creeping vine of memory, they gradually confront their blindness to the hidden truths about their lives.

School for Wives. Molière. Tr. by Richard Wilbur. Contrib. by William Brown & Chicago's Court Theatre Cast. (Playaway Young Adult Ser.). (ENG.). 2009. 39.99 (978-1-60775-744-3(3)) Find a World.

School for Wives. abr. ed. Molière. Read by William Brown. Perf. by Cast of the Court Theatre Staff. 1 cass. (Running Time: 1 hr. 39 min.). 1999. 22.95 (978-1-58081-154-5(X), CTA69) L A Theatre.
In this biting comedy of Arnolph's errors,t he hapless man is done in by his own double dealing & double standards.

School House Bullies: Preventive Strategies for Professional Educators DVD & Facilitator's Guide. Judy M. Brunner & Dennis K. Lewis. 2005. 99.95 (978-1-4129-2625-6(4)) Pub: Corwin Pr. Dist(s): SAGE

***School Law: A California Perspective - Cd.** 4th rev. ed. Townley/Schmieder-Ramirez. (ENG.). 2010. audio compact disk 89.33 (978-0-7575-7678-2(8)) Kendall-Hunt.

School Libraries Technology Update. 2 cass. 1990. 16.00 set. Recorded Res.

School Mural/Diego Rivera. Steck-Vaughn Staff. (J). 1997. (978-0-8172-7383-5(2)) SteckVau.

School of Beauty & Charm. unabr. ed. Melanie Sumner. Narrated by Julia Gibson. 7 cass. (Running Time: 10 hrs. 15 mins.). 2001. 69.75 (978-1-4193-2076-7(9), SV022MC); audio compact disk 99.75 (978-1-4193-2078-1(5), CV024MC) Recorded Bks.

School of Country Guitar: Adv. Rhythm, Steel Bends & Hot Licks. Joe Carr. 2008. pap. bk. 14.95 (978-0-7866-7784-9(8)) Mel Bay.

School of Country Guitar: Chords, Accompaniment, Styles & Basic Leads. Joe Carr. (ENG.). 2009. pap. bk. 14.99 (978-0-7866-7775-7(9)) Mel Bay.

School of English Murder. unabr. ed. Ruth Dudley Edwards. Read by Bill Wallis. 6 CDs. (Running Time: 9 hrs.). 2002. audio compact disk 64.95 (978-0-7540-5454-2(3), CCD 145) AudioGO.

School of Essential Ingredients. unabr. ed. Erica Bauermeister. (Running Time: 6 hrs.). (ENG.). (gr. 12 up). 2009. audio compact disk 29.95 (978-0-14-314436-6(7), PengAudBks) Penguin Grp USA.

School of Essential Ingredients. unabr. ed. Erica Bauermeister. Read by Cassandra Campbell. 5 CDs. (Running Time: 6 hrs.). 2009. audio compact disk 80.00 (978-1-4159-6260-2(X), BksonTape) Pub: Random Audio Pubg. Dist(s): Random

***School of Fear.** Gitty Daneshvari. Read by Emma Walton Hamilton. (ENG.). (J). 2009. 49.99 (978-1-60788-395-1(3)) Find a World.

School of Fear. unabr. ed. Gitty Daneshvari. Read by Emma Walton Hamilton. (Running Time: 6 hrs.). (ENG.). 2009. 14.98 (978-1-60024-794-1(6)) Pub: Hachet Audio. Dist(s): HachBkGrp

School of Fear. unabr. ed. Gitty Daneshvari. Read by Emma Walton Hamilton. 5 CDs. (Running Time: 6 hrs.). (ENG.). (gr. 4-7). 2009. audio compact disk 19.98 (978-1-60024-793-4(8)) Pub: Hachet Audio. Dist(s): HachBkGrp

School of Life. Swami Amar Jyoti. 1 cass. 1988. 9.95 (A-42) Truth Consciousness.
What is mundane, what is spiritual? - one of the most difficult questions to solve in life.

School of Mandolin: Basic Chords & Soloing. Joe Carr. (ENG.). 2008. pap. bk. 14.95 (978-0-7866-7946-1(8)) Mel Bay.

School of Mandolin: Irish Mandolin. Joe Carr & Michael Gregory. 2009. pap. bk. 14.99 (978-0-7866-7778-8(3)) Mel Bay.

School of Mandolin - Blues. Joe Carr. (ENG.). 2009. pap. bk. 14.99 (978-0-7866-8159-4(4)) Mel Bay.

School of Obedience. unabr. ed. Andrew Murray. 2 CDs. (Running Time: 1 hr. 30 mins. 0 sec.). (ENG.). 2004. audio compact disk 15.98 (978-1-59644-045-6(7), Hovel Audio) christianaud.
With great gentleness, sensitivity and support, Andrew Murray describes the necessity of obedience, its enabling means, and its benefits. The School of Obedience is a pastoral encouragement that exudes tender humility, warmth and a magnanimous spirit.

***School of Obedience.** unabr. ed. Andrew Murray. Narrated by Paul Eggington. (ENG.). 2004. 9.98 (978-1-59644-046-3(5), Hovel Audio) christianaud.

School of Prayer. unabr. ed. Warren W. Wiersbe. Read by Warren W. Wiersbe. 1 cass. (Running Time: 45 min.). 1989. 4.95 (978-0-8474-2334-7(4)) Back to Bible.
Messages that take you through four levels in your understanding of prayer.

School of Prayer 2008. Lynne Hammond. 2008. audio compact disk 60.00 (978-1-57399-401-9(4)) Mac Hammond.

School of Prayer 2009. Lynne Hammond. 2009. audio compact disk 60.00 (978-1-57399-424-8(3)) Mac Hammond.

School of the Holy Spirit: Studies in Rosicrucian Mysteries. Instructed by Manly P. Hall. 8.95 (978-0-89314-244-5(1), C571103) Philos Res.

School on Heart's Content Road. unabr. ed. Carolyn Chute. Read by Susan Ericksen. (Running Time: 18 hrs.). 2008. 44.25 (978-1-4233-7459-6(2), 9781423374596, Brlnc Audio MP3 Lib); 44.25 (978-1-4233-7461-9(4), 9781423374619, BADLE); 29.95 (978-1-4233-7458-9(4), 9781423374589, Brilliance MP3); 29.95 (978-1-4233-7460-2(6), 9781423374602, BAD); audio compact disk 107.25 (978-1-4233-7457-2(6), 9781423374572, BriAudCD Unabrid); audio compact disk 39.99 (978-1-4233-7456-5(8), 9781423374565, Bril Audio CD Unabri) Brilliance Audio.

School Operations Program. James S. Benko. Read by James S. Benko. 6 cass. 1986. 89.00 ITA Inst.
A program for those who want to learn how to effectively & profitably operate a Dojang (school).

***School Participation Checklist: Companion CD.** Kandis Lighthall. (ENG.). 2008. audio compact disk 10.00 (978-0-9761517-8-4(2)) ABTA Pubns.

School Spirit; Scaredy Kat. unabr. ed. Elizabeth Cody Kimmel. (Suddenly Supernatural Ser.: Bks. 1-2). (ENG.). (J). (gr. 3). 2009. audio compact disk 44.00 (978-0-7393-7962-2(3), Listening Lib) Pub: Random Audio Pubg. Dist(s): Random

School Story. unabr. ed. Andrew Clements. 2 cass. (Running Time: 3 hrs. 17 mins.). (J). (gr. 3-7). 2004. 23.00 (978-0-8072-0676-8(8), Listening Lib) Random Audio Pubg.
Twelve-year-old Natalie has written a fabulous book and is determined to get it published. Luckily, she has connections to the publishing world - her mother is an assistant editor at a major publisher. However, Natalie doesn't want any favors and doesn't want her mom to know that she wrote a novel. So she and her best friend Zoe devise a plan. Natalie uses a pseudonym, Zoe pretends to be an agent, and with a little help from an English teacher, the girls succeed. Not only does Natalie's mom publish the novel, but it exceeds everyone's expectations and becomes a bestseller!.

School Story. unabr. ed. Andrew Clements. Read by Spencer Kayden. 2 vols. (Running Time: 3 hrs. 17 mins.). (Middle Grade Cassette Librariestm Ser.). (J). (gr. 3-7). 2004. pap. bk. 29.00 (978-0-8072-1000-0(5), S YA 352 SP, Listening Lib) Random Audio Pubg.

School Survival Skills: Student Syllabus. Kathleen L. McDonough. (J). 1985. 36.25 (978-0-89420-245-2(6), 340000) Natl Book.

School Terms. Harris Winitz. Illus. by Sydney M. Baker. (All about Language Ser.). (YA). (gr. 7 up). 1987. pap. bk. 32.00 (978-0-939990-49-8(0)) Intl Linguistics.

School Trip Estimation: Early Explorers Early Set B Audio CD. Clare O'Brien. Adapted by Benchmark Education Staff. (J). 2007. audio compact disk 10.00 (978-1-4108-8239-4(X)) Benchmark Educ.

School Trouble for Andy Russell. David A. Adler. Illus. by Will Hillenbrand. Narrated by Oliver Wyman. 2 cass. (Running Time: 2 hrs. 28 mins.). (J). (gr. 2-4). 2008. pap. bk. 24.95 (978-1-4301-0483-4(X)); 18.95 (978-1-4301-0481-0(3)) Live Oak Media.

School Trouble for Andy Russell. David A. Adler. Read by Oliver Wyman. Illus. by Will Hillenbrand. 2 CDs. (Running Time: 2 hrs. 28 mins.). (Andy Russell Ser.). (J). (gr. 2-5). 2008. pap. bk. 28.95 (978-1-4301-0484-1(8)) Live Oak Media.

School Trouble for Andy Russell. David A. Adler. Read by Oliver Wyman. Illus. by Will Hillenbrand. 2 CDs. (Running Time: 2 hrs. 28 mins.). (Andy Russell Ser.). (J). (gr. 2-4). 2008. audio compact disk 22.95 (978-1-4301-0482-7(1)) Live Oak Media.

Schoolboy see Brian Patten Reading His Poetry

Schooled. Gordon Korman. Read by Andy Paris. 4 cass. (Running Time: 5 hrs.). (YA). (gr. 9). 2007. 56.75 (978-1-4281-7186-2(X)) Recorded Bks.

Schooled. unabr. ed. Gordon Korman. Read by Andy Paris. 4 CDs. (Running Time: 5 hrs.). (YA). (gr. 6-9). 2007. audio compact disk 77.75 (978-1-4281-7191-6(6)) Recorded Bks.

Schoolhouse Rock. 4 cass. (Running Time: 6 hrs.). 2002. 31.92 (978-1-56826-985-6(4), 75573) Rhino Enter.
All four of the original series from ABC's Schoolhouse Rock(America Rock, Grammar Rock, Multiplication Rock, and Science Rock) are now available. Get to know the best teaching aid since chalk.

Schoolhouse Rock: Grammar Rock. 1 cass. (Running Time: 1 hr. 30 mins.). 2002. 7.98 (978-1-56826-825-5(4), 72612) Rhino Enter.
Includes "Lolly, Lolly, Lolly, Get YOur Adverbs Here" and "Conjunction Junction".

Schoolhouse Rock: Multiplication Rock. 1 cass. (Running Time: 1 hr. 30 mins.). 2002. 7.98 (978-1-56826-824-8(6), 72610) Rhino Enter.
Includes "Three Is A Magic Number," "My Hero, Zero," and "Little Twelvetoes".

Schoolhouse Rock: Schoolhouse Rocks the Vote. (J). 2002. 16.98 (978-1-56826-965-8(X), 75511) Rhino Enter.
Schoolhouse Rock teams up with some of the hottest names in music to take it to the street to out and vote.

Schoolhouse Rock: Science Rock. (J). 2002. 7.98 (978-1-56826-827-9(0), 72616) Rhino Enter.
Includes "The Body Machine," "Electricity, Electricity," and "Interplanet Janet".

Schoolhouse Rock: The Boxed Set. 4 CDs. (Running Time: 6 hrs.). 2002. audio compact disk 49.98 (978-1-56826-239-0(6), 72455) Rhino Enter.
New versions of "Electricity, Electricity" by Goodness and "My Hero, Zero" by the Lemonheads are included as bonus tracks as well as rare cuts from Scooter Computer and Mr. Chips and Money Rock.

Schoolhouse Rocks the Vote: A Benefit Album for Rock the Vote. 1 cass. 1998. 16.98 (978-1-56826-964-1(1)) Rhino Enter.

Schoolmaster's Daughter, unabr. ed. Dorothy Eden. Read by Diana Bishop. 7 cass. (Running Time: 7 hrs.). 1999. 61.95 (67177) Pub: Soundings Ltd GBR. Dist(s): Ulverscroft US

Schoolmaster's Daughter. unabr. ed. Dorothy Eden. Read by Diana Bishop. 7 cass. (Sound Ser.). 2004. 61.95 (978-1-85496-717-6(7)) Pub: UlverLrgPrint GBR. Dist(s): Ulverscroft US

Schoolproof. unabr. ed. Mary Pride. Read by Johanna Ward. 4 cass. (Running Time: 5 hrs. 30 mins.). 1992. 32.95 (978-0-7861-0285-3(3), 1250) Blckstn Audio.
Much more than a how-to book. You'll understand why different educational philosophies work - or don't work - & where we should go from here.

School's Out. unabr. ed. Wanda E. Brunstetter. Read by Ellen Grafton. (Running Time: 3 hrs.). (Rachel Yoder Ser.). 2009. 14.99 (978-1-4418-0678-9(4), 9781441806789, Brilliance MP3); 39.97 (978-1-4418-0679-6(2), 9781441806796, Brlnc Audio MP3 Lib); 14.99 (978-1-4418-0680-2(6), 9781441806802, BAD); 39.97 (978-1-4418-0681-9(4), 9781441806819, BADLE); audio compact disk 14.99 (978-1-4418-0676-5(8), 9781441806765, Bril Audio CD Unabri); audio compact disk 44.97 (978-1-4418-0677-2(6), 9781441806772, BriAudCD Unabrid) Brilliance Audio.

School's Out - Forever. abr. ed. James Patterson. Read by Valentina de Angelis. (Running Time: 5 hrs.). (Maximum Ride Ser.: No. 2). (ENG.). (J). (gr. 5-17). 2006. 9.98 (978-1-59483-517-9(9)) Pub: Hachet Audio. Dist(s): HachBkGrp

School's Out - Forever. abr. ed. James Patterson. Read by Valentina de Angelis. (Running Time: 5 hrs.). No. 2. (ENG.). 2008. audio compact disk 9.98 (978-1-60024-262-5(6)) Pub: Hachet Audio. Dist(s): HachBkGrp

School's Out - Forever. abr. ed. James Patterson. Read by Valentina de Angelis. (Running Time: 5 hrs.). (Maximum Ride Ser.: Bk. 2). (ENG.). 2009. 34.98 (978-1-60788-152-0(7)) Pub: Hachet Audio. Dist(s): HachBkGrp

School's Out - Forever. unabr. ed. James Patterson. Read by Nancy Wu & James R. Jenner. 9 CDs. (Running Time: 10 hrs. 30 mins.). (Maximum Ride Ser.: No. 2). (YA). 2006. audio compact disk 94.75 (978-1-4193-9420-1(7), C3728); 75.75 (978-1-4193-9415-7(0)) Recorded Bks.
Patterson ratchets-up the suspense and intensity in this thrilling sequel. The bird-girl Max is back and so is her flock of flying friends, heading south on a journey to reunite with their families. But they remain in danger; they carry the secret documents of the scientific experiments that made them what they are.

School's over Now What?(r): Get Hired! David Bowman. 2008. audio compact disk 19.95 (978-0-615-26480-6(8)) TTG Consultants.

Schools Then & Now Audio CD. Adapted by Benchmark Education Company Staff. Based on a work by Cynthia Swain. (Early Explorers Set C Ser.). (J). (gr. k). 2008. audio compact disk 10.00 (978-1-60437-512-1(4)) Benchmark Educ.

Schools We Need: And Why We Don't Have Them. unabr. ed. E. D. Hirsch, Jr. Read by Anna Fields. 9 cass. (Running Time: 13 hrs.). 1997. 62.95 (978-0-7861-1239-5(5), 1986) Blckstn Audio.
Research has shown that if children are taught in ways that empasize hard work & rigorous testing, their enthusiasm will grow & test scores will rise.

Schools We Need: And Why We Don't Have Them. unabr. ed. E. D. Hirsch, Jr. Read by Anna Fields. (Running Time: 45000 sec.). 2007. audio compact disk 90.00 (978-0-7861-5907-9(3)); audio compact disk 29.95 (978-0-7861-5908-6(1)) Blckstn Audio.

Schoonerman. unabr. collector's ed. Richard England. Read by Stuart Courtney. 9 cass. (Running Time: 13 hrs. 30 mins.). 1986. 72.00 (978-0-7366-0840-4(0), 1791) Books on Tape.
"Schoonerman" is a tribute to those tough individualists, the masters & crews, who spent their lives under sail. It is also a first-hand account of the schoonerman's life by one of their last survivors. Captain England who went to sea as a ship's boy in the 1920's when the schooners were enjoying their last sail describes the working of these vessels from the Master's viewpoint.

Schopenhauer in 90 Minutes. Paul Strathern. Read by Robert Whitfield. (Running Time: 1 hr. 30 mins.). 2004. 15.95 (978-0-7861-2784-9(8), 3317); audio compact disk 17.00 (978-0-7861-8529-0(5), 3317) Blckstn Audio.

Schopenhauer in 90 Minutes. unabr. ed. Paul Strathern. Read by Robert Whitfield. (Running Time: 1 hr. 30 mins.). (Philosophers in 90 Minutes Ser.). 2004. reel tape 14.95 (978-0-7861-2789-4(9)); audio compact disk 14.95 (978-0-7861-8528-3(7)) Blckstn Audio.

Schrodinger's Kitten. Short Stories. 1 CD. (Running Time: 76 mins). (Great Science Fiction Stories Ser.). 2004. audio compact disk 11.99 (978-1-884612-38-1(5)) AudioText.

Schrodinger's Kitten. unabr. ed. George Alec Effinger. 1 cass. (Running Time: 1 hr. 20 min.). 1998. 11.99 (978-1-884612-26-8(1)) AudioText.
In this Hugo & Nebula Award-winning tale, an Arab woman confronts the uncertainty principle in both practice & theory as she stands accused of killing a man who might do her harm in the future.

Schubert. Jeremy Siepmann. 4 CDs. audio compact disk 35.99 (978-1-84379-065-5(3), 8.558135-38) NaxMulti GBR.

Schubert: An Introduction to Piano Quintet in A Major "Trout" Jeremy Siepmann. (Classics Explained Ser.). 2003. pap. bk. (978-1-84379-018-1(1)) NaxMulti GBR.

Schubert: New Piano Transcriptions of Famous Masterworks. Composed by Franz Schubert. 2000. pap. bk. 15.95 (978-0-634-02606-5(2), 00296163) H Leonard.

Schubert: Songwriter & Symphonist. Narrated by Denis Matthews. 1 cass. 10.95 (ECN 198) J Norton Pubs.
Demonstrates that Schubert's gift for strong melodic lines was not confined to his songs alone but can be traced through the whole range of his music.

Schubert: The Domestic War. 1 cass. 11.95 (C11226) J Norton Pubs.
Franz Schubert's comic opera Der Hausliche Krieg.

Schubert German Lieder, Vol. I. John Wustman. 2003. pap. bk. 34.98 (978-1-59615-492-6(6), 586-050) Pub: Music Minus. Dist(s): Bookworld

***Schulz & Peanuts.** abr. ed. David Michaelis. Read by Holter Graham. (ENG.). 2007. (978-0-06-155467-4(7)); (978-0-06-155468-1(5)) HarperCollins Pubs.

Schulz & Peanuts: A Biography. abr. ed. David Michaelis. Read by Holter Graham. 2007. audio compact disk 39.95 (978-0-06-136707-6(9), Harper Audio) HarperCollins Pubs.

Schumann Frequency. unabr. ed. Christopher Ride. Read by Sean Mangan. (Running Time: 16 hrs. 45 mins.). 2008. audio compact disk 123.95 (978-1-921334-66-5(5), 9781921334665, Bolinda AudioAUS) Pub: Bolinda Pubng AUS. Dist(s): Bolinda Pub Inc

Schumann/Album for the Young. Perf. by Kim O'Reilly. 1 CD. (Alfred Masterwork Edition Ser.). (ENG.). 2000. audio compact disk 15.95 (978-0-7390-0806-5(4), 16796) Alfred Pub.

Schwa Was Here. unabr. ed. Neal Shusterman. Read by Neal Shusterman. 5 CDs. (Running Time: 6 hrs. 1 min.). (YA). (gr. 6-9). 2008. audio compact disk 50.00 (978-0-7393-7237-1(8), Listening Lib) Pub: Random Audio Pubg. Dist(s): Random

Schwedisch Ohne Muhe, Vol. 1. 1 cass. (Running Time: 1 hr. 30 min.).Tr. of Swedish with Ease. (GER & SWE.). 2000. bk. 75.00 (978-2-7005-1011-9(9)) Pub: Assimil FRA. Dist(s): Distribks Inc

Schwedisch Ohne Muhe, Vol. 2. 1 cass. (Running Time: 1 hr. 30 min.).Tr. of Swedish with Ease. (GER & SWE.). 2000. bk. 75.00 (978-2-7005-1012-6(7)) Pub: Assimil FRA. Dist(s): Distribks Inc

Schweitzer Mountain Poetry: A Collection of Poems with Schweitzer Mountain & Northwest Themes. 2006. 29.95 (978-1-59649-643-9(6)); audio compact disk 24.95 (978-1-59649-642-2(8)) Whsprng Pine.

Schweitzer Mountain Reflections. 2005. 29.95 (978-1-59649-059-8(4)); audio compact disk 24.95 (978-1-59649-058-1(6)) Whsprng Pine.

Sci-Fi Channel Presents Vol. 1: Seeing Ear Theatre. Perf. by Mark Hamill et al. 2 cass. (Running Time: 3 hr.). 1999. 17.98 (4416) Radio Spirits.

Sci-Fi Channel Presents Vol. 2: Seeing Ear Theatre. Featuring Peter Jurasik. 2 cass. (Running Time: 3 hrs.). 1999. 17.98 (4417) Radio Spirits.

Sci-Fi Channel Presents Vol. 2: Seeing Ear Theatre. Perf. by Peter Jurasik & Andreas Katsulas. 2 cass. (Running Time: 3 hr.). 1999. 17.98 (4417) Radio Spirits.

Sci-Fi Channel Presents - Seeing Ear Theatre Vol. 3: The Untold Story Behind the War of the Worlds, Featuring Orson Welles. 2 cass. (Running Time: 3 hr.). 1999. 17.98 (4419) Radio Spirits.

Sci-Fi Private Eye. unabr. ed. Fred Saberhagen. Ed. by Isaac Asimov et al. 4 cass. (Running Time: 6 hrs.). (Science Fiction Library). 1997. pap. bk. 21.95 (978-1-55656-273-0(X)) Pub: Dercum Audio. Dist(s): APG
Includes "The Adventure of the Metal Murderer," & "Mouthepiece".

Sci-Fi Shorts, Vol. II. Perf. by Steve Ziplow's Dandy Productions Staff. 1 cass. (Running Time: 1 hr. 10 mins.). 2001. 14.95 (HHIR006) Lodestone Catalog.
Funny stuff from: Return With Your Space Suit or On It & Story of the Century & Don't Go Out in Your Holy Underwear.

Sci-Fi Trilogy. Daniel Cline. 1 cass. (Running Time: 1 hr.). 2001. 12.95 (HHIR004) Lodestone Catalog.
Three stories by the author: General Emergency, The Lost Planeteers & Twin Engines. A wacky, over-the-top satire of bureaucracy & incompetence in a futuristic setting.

Sci Fiction Radio. 2004. 29.95 (978-1-57019-725-3(3)) Radio Spirits.

Sci-Five Live. Prod. by Jerry Stearns & Brian Price. 1 CD. audio compact disk 15.95 (JSBP006) Lodestone Catalog.

Science see Poetry of Robinson Jeffers

Science+ A Sampler. Holt, Rinehart and Winston Staff. (ENG & SPA.). 1997. 14.73 (978-0-03-050619-2(0)) Holt McDoug.

***Science: Grade 1.** Created by Harcourt School Publishers. 2005. audio compact disk 43.98 (978-0-15-342962-0(3)) Harcourt Schl Pubs.

Science & Discovery. Narrated by Edwin Newman. 15 cass. (Running Time: 22 hrs. 30 mins.). (Audio Classics Ser.). 1993. (978-1-56823-006-1(0)) Knowledge Prod.
Science & Discovery recreates one of history's most successful journeys - four thousand years of efforts to better understand & control the physical world. Science has often challenged & upset conventional wisdom or accepted practices; this is a story of vested interests & independent thinkers, experiments & theories, change & progress. Includes 15 different presentations covering the ideas of history's greatest scientists.

Science & Discovery: All you Want to Know. abr. ed. Edwin Newman. Read by Edwin Newman. 6 cass. (Running Time: 9 hrs.). 1999. 24.35 (978-0-671-03342-2(5)) S and S Inc.
Gives an accessible overview of the ideas and events which have shaped our world.

Science & Engineering of Novel Superconductors V. Ed. by P. Vincenzini & A. Fiorani. (Advances in Science & Technology Ser.: Vol. 47). audio compact disk 182.00 (978-3-908158-03-5(6)) Trans T Pub CHE.

Science & Engineering Sourcebook. Cass R. Lewart. 1982. 8.95 (978-0-686-98227-2(4)) Micro Text Pubns.

Science & Health with Key to the Scriptures. Mary Baker Eddy. 30 cass. (Running Time: 29 hrs. 31 min.). 1991. bk. 99.00 (978-0-87952-035-9(3), BPP25141); audio compact disk 140.00 (978-0-87952-036-6(1), BPP25380) Writings of Mary Baker.
This is a book for thinkers. When it was first published in 1875, Mary Baker Eddy's remarkable investigation of health, well-being, & the power of prayer challenged 19th-century mainstream beliefs about the nature of human existence & the phenomenon of healing. Today, Eddy's pathbreaking work continues to be one of the most effective & enduring books on spirituality & healing.

Science & Medicine. Sophia Millenotte. 1 cass. (Running Time: 90 min.). 10.00 (978-1-882834-74-7(7)) Seventh Ray.
A channeled work on healing.

Science & Religion. Instructed by Lawrence Principe. 6 cass. (Running Time: 6 hrs). 2006. 89.95 (978-1-59803-129-4(5)); audio compact disk 39.95 (978-1-59803-131-7(7)) Teaching Co.

Science & Secret of Prana. Swami Amar Jyoti. 1 dolby cass. 1986. 9.95 (O-29) Truth Consciousness.
Lord Indra, controller of prana, reveals its secrets for all humankind. Vedanta from the point of view of application.

Science & the Bible. Mac Hammond. 1 cass. (Running Time: 1 hour). 2005. 5.00 (978-1-57399-204-6(6)) Mac Hammond.

Science & the Bible: Are They Really Irrefutably Incompatible? Mac Hammond. 2 cass. 2001. 10.00 (978-1-57399-130-8(9)); audio compact disk 10.00 (978-1-57399-131-5(7)) Mac Hammond.
It's long been held that science and the Bible are diametrically opposed to one another. But are they? Mac Hammond refutes this contention saying the results of both actually corroborate one another!.

Science Audio CD Set: English Explorers Set A. Adapted by Benchmark Education Staff. (J). 2007. audio compact disk 450.00 (978-1-4108-9544-8(0)) Benchmark Educ.

Science Audio CD Set: English Explorers Set B. Adapted by Benchmark Education Staff. (J). 2007. audio compact disk 450.00 (978-1-4108-9538-7(6)) Benchmark Educ.

Science During the Renaissance. Compiled by Benchmark Education Staff. 2006. audio compact disk 10.00 (978-1-4108-6656-1(4)) Benchmark Educ.

Science E-Books: English Explorers Set B (Set Of 24) Compiled by Benchmark Education Staff. (J). 2007. audio compact disk 325.00 (978-1-4108-8577-7(1)) Benchmark Educ.

Science Early Explorers Take Home Book: CD Rom. Compiled by Benchmark Education Staff. (J). 2007. audio compact disk 10.00 (978-1-4108-9485-4(1)) Benchmark Educ.

Science Experiments. (gr. 10 up). 2004. DVD & audio compact disk 19.95 (978-0-7403-0735-5(5)) Alpha OmeGa Pub.

Science Experiments. (gr. 4 up). 2004. DVD & audio compact disk 19.95 (978-0-7403-0729-4(0)) Alpha OmeGa Pub.

Science Experiments. (gr. 6 up). 2004. DVD & audio compact disk 19.95 (978-0-7403-0731-7(2)) Alpha OmeGa Pub.

Science Experiments. (gr. 7 up). 2004. DVD & audio compact disk 19.95 (978-0-7403-0732-4(0)) Alpha OmeGa Pub.

Science Experiments. (gr. 8 up). 2004. DVD & audio compact disk 19.95 (978-0-7403-0733-1(9)) Alpha OmeGa Pub.

Science Experiments. (gr. 9 up). 2004. DVD & audio compact disk 19.95 (978-0-7403-0734-8(7)) Alpha OmeGa Pub.

Science Experiments on File, Vol. 1. Pam Walker & Elaine Wood. (gr. 6-12). 2005. audio compact disk 149.95 (978-0-8160-6257-7(9)) Facts On File.

Science Explorer: Section Summaries. Michael J. Padilla et al. (J). (gr. 6-8). audio compact disk 59.47 (978-0-13-115461-2(3)); audio compact disk 59.47 (978-0-13-115462-9(1)); audio compact disk 59.47 (978-0-13-115463-6(X)) PH School.

Science Explorer: Animals. Michael J. Padilla et al. (J). (gr. 6-8). stu. ed. 19.97 (978-0-13-181180-5(0)) PH School.

Science Explorer: Astronomy. Michael J. Padilla et al. (J). (gr. 6-8). stu. ed. 19.97 (978-0-13-181189-8(4)) PH School.

Science Explorer: Cells & Heredity. Michael J. Padilla et al. (J). (gr. 6-8). stu. ed. 19.97 (978-0-13-181182-9(7)) PH School.

Science Explorer: Chemical Building Blocks. Michael J. Padilla et al. (J). (gr. 6-8). stu. ed. 19.97 (978-0-13-181190-4(8)) PH School.

Science Explorer: Chemical Interactions. Michael J. Padilla et al. (J). (gr. 6-8). stu. ed. 19.97 (978-0-13-181191-1(6)) PH School.

Science Explorer Earth Science. Michael J. Padilla et al. (J). (gr. 6-8). audio compact disk 89.97 (978-0-13-181296-3(3)) PH School.

Science Explorer: Earth's Changing Surface. Michael J. Padilla et al. (J). (gr. 6-8). stu. ed. 19.97 (978-0-13-181186-7(4)) PH School.

Science Explorer: Earth's Waters. Michael J. Padilla et al. (J). (gr. 6-8). stu. ed. 19.97 (978-0-13-181187-4(8)) PH School.

Science Explorer: Electricity & Magnetism. Michael J. Padilla et al. (J). (gr. 6-8). stu. ed. 19.97 (978-0-13-181237-6(8)) PH School.

Science Explorer: Environmental Science. Michael J. Padilla et al. (J). (gr. 6-8). stu. ed. 19.97 (978-0-13-181184-3(3)) PH School.

Science Explorer: From Bacteria to Plants. Michael J. Padilla et al. (J). (gr. 6-8). stu. ed. 19.97 (978-0-13-181178-2(9)) PH School.

Science Explorer: Human Biology & Health. Michael J. Padilla et al. (J). (gr. 6-8). stu. ed. 19.97 (978-0-13-181183-6(5)) PH School.

Science Explorer: Inside Earth. Michael J. Padilla et al. (J). (gr. 6-8). stu. ed. 19.97 (978-0-13-181185-0(1)) PH School.

Science Explorer Life Science. Michael J. Padilla et al. (J). (gr. 6-8). stu. ed. 89.97 (978-0-13-181309-0(9)) PH School.

Science Explorer: Motion, Forces, & Energy. Michael J. Padilla et al. (J). (gr. 6-8). stu. ed. 19.97 (978-0-13-181192-8(4)) PH School.

Science Explorer Physical Science. Michael J. Padilla et al. (J). (gr. 6-8). audio compact disk 89.97 (978-0-13-181323-6(4)) PH School.

Science Explorer: Sound & Light. Michael J. Padilla et al. (J). (gr. 6-8). stu. ed. 19.97 (978-0-13-181236-9(X)) PH School.

Science Explorer: The Nature of Science & Technology. Michael J. Padilla et al. (J). (gr. 6-8). stu. ed. 19.97 (978-0-13-181193-5(2)) PH School.

Science Explorer: Weather & Climate. Michael J. Padilla et al. (J). (gr. 6-8). stu. ed. 19.97 (978-0-13-181188-1(6)) PH School.

Science Fair: A Story of Mystery, Danger, International Suspense & a Very Nervous Frog. Dave Barry & Ridley Pearson. Read by Phil Gigante. (Playaway Children Ser.). (J). 2008. 69.99 (978-1-60640-604-5(3)) Find a World.

Science Fair: A Story of Mystery, Danger, International Suspense & a Very Nervous Frog. unabr. ed. Dave Barry & Ridley Pearson. Read by Phil Gigante. 1 MP3-CD. (Running Time: 9 hrs.). 2008. 39.25 (978-1-4233-4775-0(7), 9781423347750, Brinc Audio MP3 Lib); 39.25 (978-1-4233-4777-4(3), 9781423347774, BADLE); 24.95 (978-1-4233-4774-3(9), 9781423347743, Brilliance MP3); 24.95 (978-1-4233-4776-7(5), 9781423347767, BAD); audio compact disk 97.25 (978-1-4233-4773-6(0), 9781423347736, BriAudCD Unabrid); audio compact disk 29.99 (978-1-4233-4772-9(2), 9781423347729, Bril Audio CD Unabri) Brilliance Audio.

Science Fairs: Integrating Science & Halacha. Shulamis Goldberg. 1 cass. (Running Time: 90 mins.). 1999. 6.00 (V60FO) Torah Umesorah.

Science Fair/Think Like a Scientist. Steck-Vaughn Staff. 1 cass. (Running Time: 90 mins.). (J). 1999. (978-0-7398-0922-8(9)) SteckVau.

Science Fiction: Best of Year 2006. (Running Time: 13 mins.). 2009. audio compact disk 36.95 (978-1-897304-62-4(5)) Dorch Pub Co.

***Science Fiction: Best of Year 2006.** (Running Time: 13 mins.). 2009. 19.95 (978-1-897331-16-3(9), AudioRealms) Dorch Pub Co.

Science Fiction: It's Future. Read by Isaac Asimov & Jack William. (Running Time: 30 min.). 14.95 (30428) MMI Corp.
Discuss man's literary response to social change in the genre of science fiction.

Science Fiction: It's Future. Isaac Asimov & Jack Williamson. 1 cass. (Running Time: 30 min.). 14.95 (30428) MMI Corp.

Science Fiction: The Best of the Year 2006. Rich Horton. Read by Brian Holsopple et al. (Running Time: 46800 sec.). 2006. audio compact disk 49.95 (978-0-8095-6270-1(7)) Pub: Wildside. Dist(s): Diamond Book Dists

Science Fiction: The Best of 2002. unabr. ed. Ed. by Robert A. Silverberg & Karen Haber. 6 cass. (Running Time: 10 hrs.). 2002. 32.00 (978-1-59040-553-6(6)) Audio Lit.
This audiobook presents the best short science fiction of the year as selected from magazines, anthologies, and journals. Featuring great authors, wonderful stories, and brilliant performances, it's a preview of what everyone will be talking about in months to come.

Science Fiction: The Literature of the Technological Imagination. Instructed by Eric Rabkin. 4 cass. (Running Time: 6 hrs.). 1994. 39.95 (978-1-56585-064-4(5)) Teaching Co.

Science Fiction Collection. unabr. ed. 4 cass. HarperCollins Pubs.

Science Fiction Favorites of Isaac Asimov. unabr. ed. Isaac Asimov. Read by Isaac Asimov. 6 cass. (Running Time: 6 hrs.). 1999. 44.98 (LL0018) AudioGO.

Science Fiction Favorites of Isaac Asimov. unabr. ed. Isaac Asimov. Read by Isaac Asimov. 6 cass. (Running Time: 5 hrs. 7 min.). Incl. Feeling of Power. 1975. (CXL 505CX); I Just Make Them up, See? 1975. (CXL 505CX); Immortal Bard. 1975. (CXL 505CX); Jokester. 1975. (CXL 505CX); Last Question. 1975. (CXL 505CX); Living Space. 1975. (CXL 505CX); Satisfaction Guaranteed. 1975. (CXL 505CX); Someday. 1975. (CXL 505CX); Spell My Name with an 'S' 1975. (CXL 505CX); Ugly Little Boy. (J). 1975. (CXL 505CX); 1975. 44.98 (978-0-8072-2928-6(8), CXL 505CX, Listening Lib) Random Audio Pubg.
A selection of some of Asimov's most enduring & unforgettable stories, these vintage tales encompass the full range of Asimov's versatility, while displaying his puckish sense of humor.

Science Fiction Favorites of Isaac Asimov. unabr. ed. Isaac Asimov. Read by Isaac Asimov. 6 cass. (Running Time: 5 hrs. 4 min.). (YA). 1999. 44.98 (Listening Lib) Random Audio Pubg.
Includes "I Just Make Them up, See?," "The Last Question," "The Immortal Bard," "Spell My Name with an 'S'," "The Ugly Little Boy," & more.

Science Fiction No. 1. 1 cass. (Running Time: 60 min.). Incl. Dimension X: Mars Is Heaven. (SF-9072); X Minus One: Tunnel under the World. (SF-9072); 7.95 (SF-9072) Natl Recrd Co.
In "Dimension X" the year is 1987 & the first space ship lands on Mars with 17 men aboard. Will they be welcomed or viewed as invaders? "X Minus One" takes you to the world of "could-be".

Science Fiction No. 2. 1 cass. (Running Time: 1 hr.). Incl. X Minus One: No Contact. (SF9074); X Minus One: The Vital Factor. (SF9074); 7.95 (SF9074) Natl Recrd Co.

Science Fiction No. 3. 1 cass. (Running Time: 1 hr.). Incl. Dimension X: Marionettes, Inc. (SF9076); X Minus One: The Lifeboat Mutiny. (SF9076); 7.95 (SF9076) Natl Recrd Co.

***Science Fiction Radio: Atom Age Adventures.** Perf. by Broadcasts Original Radio. 2009. audio compact disk 39.98 (978-1-57019-911-0(6)) Radio Spirits.

Science Fiction Stories, Vol. 1. unabr. ed. Narrated by Lawrence Kaiser. 2 cass. (Running Time: 3 hrs.). 1997. 17.00 Set. SEED Publishers Inc.
Includes six markedly different stories.

Science Fiction, the Early Days. Read by Heywood Hale Broun. 1 cass. (Running Time: 56 min.). (Broun Radio Ser.). 11.95 (40001) J Norton Pubs.
With Isaac Asimov & Frederick Pohl.

Science in a Nutshell. 2 cass. (Running Time: 2 hrs.). (J). (ps-3). 2001. 18.95 (KIM 1006C); lp 20.95 (KIM 1006) Kimbo Educ.
Fun songs about dinosaurs, electricity, hygiene, the senses & more. Expose youngsters to science concept at an early age, when they are so curious about eh world around them. Respiration, Your Senses Add Up to Five, Distant Star, Vegetable Soup, I'm Going to Plant a Garden, Electricity & more.

Science in Antiquity. unabr. ed. Jon Mandaville. Read by Edwin Newman. (Running Time: 10800 sec.). (Audio Classics: Science & Discovery Ser.). 2006. audio compact disk 25.95 (978-0-7861-6439-4(5)) Pub: Blckstn Audio. Dist(s): NetLibrary CO

Science in Antiquity. unabr. ed. Jon Mandaville. Read by Edwin Newman. Ed. by Jack Sommer & Mike Hassell. 2 cass. (Running Time: 2 hrs. 45 min.). Dramatization. (Science & Discovery Ser.). (YA). (gr. 11 up). 1992. 17.95 (978-0-938935-66-7(6), 10401) Knowledge Prod.
The scientific impulse can be said to have existed forever. But only with the written word did there emerge a record of speculations about how & why things happen. Middle Eastern civilizations developed ways to measure & describe (e.g. math & the alphabet); Greek philosophers classified natural objects & studied cause & effect. This is the story of ancient science, from China to the Mediterranean Basin.

Science in the 20th Century: A Social-Intellectual Survey, I-III. Instructed by Steven Goldman. 18 cass. (Running Time: 18 hrs.). 2004. bk. 79.95 (978-1-56585-889-3(1), 1220); bk. 99.95 (978-1-56585-891-6(3), 1220) Teaching Co.

Science Looks at Speech. D. B. Fry. 1 cass. (Running Time: 51 min.). 1973. 11.95 (33028) J Norton Pubs.
The remarkable ability of brain, tongue & ear that we take for granted in the use of speech is discussed.

Science Made Simple. Swami Amar Jyoti. 2 cass. 1978. 12.95 (O-10) Truth Consciousness.
The endless orbit of circular motion on the relative plane. Psychological paradox vs. spiritual Perfection. The spell of Maya. From untruth to Truth.

Science of Animal Agriculture. (C). 2006. audio compact disk 69.95 (978-1-4180-1974-7(7)) Pub: Delmar. Dist(s): CENGAGE Learn

Science of Being Great: The Practical Guide to a Life of Power. unabr. ed. Wallace D. Wattles. Read by Eliza Foss. (Running Time: 3 hrs.). (ENG.). (gr. 8). 2007. audio compact disk 19.95 (978-0-14-314284-3(4), PengAudBks) Penguin Grp USA.

Science of Being Great: The Secret to Real Power & Personal Achievement. unabr. ed. Wallace D. Wattles. Read by Erik Synnestvedt. (Running Time: 2 hrs. 30 mins.). (ENG.). 2008. 12.98 (978-1-59659-224-7(9), GildAudio) Pub: Gildan Media. Dist(s): HachBkGrp

Science of Being Well. unabr. ed. Wallace D. Wattles. Read by Sean Pratt. (Running Time: 2 hrs. 30 mins.). (ENG.). 2009. 14.98 (978-1-59659-327-5(X), GildAudio) Pub: Gildan Media. Dist(s): HachBkGrp

Science of Biofeedback: Breakthrough Techniques on Managing Stress & Relaxation. Thought Technology, Ltd. Staff. 8 cass. (Running Time: 8 hrs.). 1996. wbk. ed. 129.00 (13420AY) Nightingale-Conant.
This program reveals how to take control of your life through mental imagery, relaxation exercises & time management techniques.

Science of Conceptions. Swami Amar Jyoti. 1 cass. 1982. 9.95 (O-22) Truth Consciousness.
Creation, maintenance & results of conceptions. The problem of identification with them. Understading the nature of relativity. Courage to forsake identification.

Science of Enlightenment. Shinzen Young. 14 CDs. 2005. audio compact disk 99.00 (978-1-59179-232-1(0), AF00879D) Sounds True.
A leading meditation teacher and scientist invites us to test the enlightenment teachings of the world for ourselves, through direct experience.

Science of Ethics & the Ethics of Science. Manly P. Hall. 1 cass. 8.95 (978-0-89314-246-9(8), C890326) Philos Res.

Science of Fear: Why We Fear the Things We Should not- & Put Ourselves in Great Danger. unabr. ed. Daniel Gardner. Read by Scott Peterson. (Running Time: 12 hrs.). (ENG.). 2009. 29.98 (978-1-59659-432-6(2), GildAudio) Pub: Gildan Media. Dist(s): HachBkGrp

Science of Generic Design: Managing Complexity Through Systems Design. 3rd ed. John N. Warfield. 2003. pap. bk. (978-0-9716962-3-5(3)) Ajar Pubng.

Science of Getting Rich. Read by Patricia J. Crane & Rick Nichols. 4 CDs, 1 CD-ROM. 2004. audio compact disk 36.95 (978-1-893705-17-3(X), Cranes Nest) Hlth Horiz.

Science of Getting Rich. abr. ed. Wallace D. Wattles. Read by Charlie T. Jones. (Laws of Leadership Ser.). (ENG.). 2008. audio compact disk 19.95 (978-1-933715-61-2(8)) Executive Bks.

Science of Getting Rich. unabr. ed. Wallace D. Wattles. (ENG.). 2005. 3.98 (978-1-59659-051-9(3), GildAudio) Pub: Gildan Media. Dist(s): HachBkGrp

Science of Getting Rich. unabr. ed. Wallace D. Wattles. (Running Time: 1 hr. 30 mins.). (ENG.). 2007. audio compact disk 14.98 (978-1-59659-144-8(7), GildAudio) Pub: Gildan Media. Dist(s): HachBkGrp

Science of Getting Rich. unabr. ed. Wallace D. Wattles. Read by James Boles. Ed. by Ruth L. Miller. (Running Time: 2 hrs. 30 mins. 0 sec.). (ENG.). 2008. audio compact disk 14.95 (978-0-7435-7218-7(1)) Pub: S&S Audio. Dist(s): S and S Inc

Science of Getting Rich: The Proven Mental Program to a Life of Wealth. unabr. ed. Wallace D. Wattles. Read by Eliza Foss. 3 CDs. (Running Time: 3 hrs.). (ENG.). (gr. 8). 2007. audio compact disk 19.95 (978-0-14-314269-0(0), PengAudBks) Penguin Grp USA.

Science of Getting Rich: With MusiVation Mind Technology. Wallace D. Wattles. Read by M A Blood. (Science of Getting Rich Ser.). 2007. audio compact disk 29.95 (978-1-890679-28-6(3)) Micheles.

Science of Getting Rich or Financial Success Through Creative Thought, the [MP3 AUDIO] [UNABRIDGED]. Wallace D. Wattles. 2007. audio compact disk 19.99 (978-956-291-270-9(1)) Edit Benei CHL.

Science of Goal Achieving. Jack Boland. 4 cass. 1979. 34.95 (978-0-88152-003-3(9)) Master Mind.
Step into the magical world of goal achieving & watch your dreams come true. Let the mind's goal-seeking mechanism convert frustration into fun & failure into fulfillment.

Science of Inner Reality. unabr. ed. John Lilly. Narrated by Richard Phillips Feynman. 1 cass. (Running Time: 1 hr. 32 min.). 1977. 11.00 (03908) Big Sur Tapes.
A fascinating talk, introduced by Richard Feynman, on Lilly's decades of research with isolation tanks, sensory deprivation & solitude.

Science of Jurassic Park & the Lost World: Or, How to Build a Dinosaur, unabr. ed. Rob DeSalle & David Lindley. Narrated by Nelson Runger. 6 cass. (Running Time: 7 hrs. 30 mins.). 1997. 51.00 (978-0-7887-1762-8(6), 95240E7) Recorded Bks.
Examines how close we really are to making the dinosaurs from "Jurassic Park" & "The Lost World" a reality. Takes you to the outer edge of what is possible, where the science fiction of today approaches the hard science of tomorrow.

***Science of Liberty: Democracy, Reason, & the Laws of Nature.** unabr. ed. Timothy Ferris. (Running Time: 18 hrs.). 2011. audio compact disk 29.99 (978-1-4418-9242-3(7), 9781441892423, Bril Audio CD Unabri) Brilliance Audio.

Science of Medical Intuition: Self-Diagnosis & Healing with Your Body's Energy Systems. Caroline Myss & Norman Shealy. 12 CDs. (Running Time: 19 hrs.). 2002. wbk. ed. 199.00 (978-1-59179-006-8(9), AF00640D) Sounds True.
This book is designed to help listeners take control of their total health, through intuitive self-diagnosis and healing techniques. Complete on 12 enriching session, over 18 hours of learning, and enhanced by a large format workbook developed exclusively for this course.

Science of Medicine. unabr. ed. Paul Heidger. Read by Edwin Newman. Ed. by Jack Sommer & Mike Hassell. 2 cass. (Running Time: 2 hrs. 45 min.). Dramatization. (Science & Discovery Ser.). (YA). (gr. 11 up). 1993. 17.95 (978-0-938935-71-1(2), 10406) Knowledge Prod.
Though medical science began with the ancient Greek physician Hippocrates, dissection & the study of the human body was prohibited for religious reasons until the Renaissance. Only in 1628 did William Harvey theorize that blood circulates in the body; germs weren't discovered until the 19th century. Since then, surgery & drugs have greatly reduced deaths & pain from accident & disease. Genetic research & biotechnology hold the promise of even greater advances in the 21st century.

Science of Personal Achievement: Follow in the Footsteps of the Giants of Success. unabr. ed. Napoleon Hill. Read by Napoleon Hill. (Running Time: 7 hrs. 0 mins. 0 sec.). (ENG.). 2008. audio compact disk 29.95 (978-0-7435-7873-8(2)) Pub: S&S Audio. Dist(s): S and S Inc

Science of Personal Achievement: Management Secrets from John Wooden's Pyramid of Success. abr. ed. Napoleon Hill. 2004. 12.95 (978-0-7435-4808-3(6)) Pub: S&S Audio. Dist(s): S and S Inc

Science of Personal Achievement: The 17 Universal Principles of Success. unabr. ed. Napoleon Hill. 6 cass. (Running Time: 6 hrs.). 1992. wbk. ed. 59.95 (978-1-55525-009-6(2), 843A) Nightingale-Conant.
Napoleon Hill is credited with creating the first study ever, on the philosophies & commonalties of the worlds most successful people. He interviewed many of the leading successes of early.

Science of Recovery: Applying Neuroscience & Neuropsychology to Your Practice. Cardwell C. Nuckols. Perf. by Cardwell C. Nuckols. Executive Producer Dennis S. Miller. Photos by Charles Hodge. Charles Hodge. (ENG.). 2009. audio compact disk 50.00 (978-1-55982-016-5(0)) Grt Lks Training.

Science of Recovery: Applying Neuroscience & Neuropsycholorgy to Your Practice. Cardwell C. Nuckols. Ed. by Dennis S. Miller. Prod. by Charles Hodge. (ENG.). 2009. audio compact disk 45.00 (978-1-55982-017-2(9)) Grt Lks Training.

Science of Religion & Religion of Science. Instructed by Manly P. Hall. 8.95 (978-0-89314-247-6(6), C800143) Philos Res.

Science of Self-Confidence. Brian S. Tracy. Read by Brian S. Tracy. 6 cass. 1991. 39.95 incl. self assessment test. (857A) Nightingale-Conant.
All successful people have one shared trait - self confidence. The kind of unshakable self-confidence you'll find in this dynamic program. Brian Tracy shows you how through personal commitment, you can effect a real, positive & lasting change in your attitude & outlook. Learn powerful strategies to make failing virtually impossible! Includes self-assessment test.

Science of Self Discipline. Kerry L. Johnson. Read by Kerry L. Johnson. 6 cass. 59.95 incl. Progress Guide. (741AD) Nightingale-Conant.
Why do you persist in bad habits? Why do you procrastinate? Why do you avoid activities that are good for you? "The Science of Self-Discipline" is the first program to give you all the answers - everything that is now known by behavioral science on these crucial issues. You'll discover why you deliberately sabotage yourself...why pushing & punishing yourself can't work...why self-discipline has to be easy & automatic to be permanent.

Science of Sound. Duane Shinn. 1 cass. 19.95 (MU-6) Duane Shinn.
Discusses vibrations, pitch, fundamental tones, harmonies & ultrasonics.

Science of Sound: Bell Telephone Laboratories. 1 cass. 1990. (0-9307-45038-4-3) Smithsonian Folkways.
Recordings describe & demonstrate the phenomena of sound & explore how we hear.

Science of Star Wars: An Astrophysicist's Independent Examination of Space Travel, Aliens, Planets & Robots as Portrayed in the Star Wars Films & Books. unabr. ed. Jeanne Cavelos. Read by Doug Ordunio. 7 cass. (Running Time: 10 hrs. 30 min.). 1999. 29.95 (978-0-7366-4519-5(5), 4946) Books on Tape.
Former NASA scientist explores the questions & scientific possibilities raised by the films 7 books. Answers questions to the basic scientific principles underlying the technology of America's most popular science fiction series.

Science of Star Wars: An Astrophysicist's Independent Examination of Space Travel, Aliens, Planets & Robots as Portrayed in the Star Wars Films & Books. unabr. collector's ed. Jeanne Cavelos. Read by Doug Ordunio. 7 cass. (Running Time: 10 hrs. 30 min.). 1999. 56.00 (978-0-7366-4515-7(2), 4946) Books on Tape.
Former NASA scientist & "Star Wars" fan, the explores the scientific possibilities & questions raised by the "Star Wars" films & books. The author leaves no stone unturned in her attempt to question the basic scientific principles underlying the technology of America's most popular science fiction series. This is science at its best. Here you'll learn: the principles of quantum physics as exemplified by the "Millennium Falcon" & how close we are to creating our own R2-D2 & C-3PO like robots. Filled with mind-blowing facts.

Science of Staying Young. John Morley. 2009. audio compact disk 28.00 (978-1-933309-81-1(4)) Pub: A Media Intl. Dist(s): Natl Bk Netwk

Science of Success: How Market-Based Management Built the World's Largest Private Company. unabr. ed. Charles G. Koch. Read by Erik Synnestvedt. 3 CDs. (Running Time: 3 hrs. 30 mins.). (ENG.). 2008. audio compact disk 19.98 (978-1-59659-146-2(3), GildAudio) Pub: Gildan Media. Dist(s): HachBkGrp

Science of Success Individual Study Course. Napoleon Hill. 14 cass. (Running Time: 7 hrs.). 1996. pap. bk. 495.00 Incl. 6 wbks. (978-1-880369-10-4(9)) N Hill Found.
Home study course.

Science of Survival Lectures. L. Ron Hubbard. 4 cass. (Running Time: 6 hrs.). 2002. 40.00 (978-1-57318-231-7(1)) Bridge Pubns Inc.

Science of Vocal Pedagogy Tape 1: Soprano & Mezzo-Soprano. D. Ralph Appleman & D. Ralph Appelman. 1 cass. (Running Time: 60 min.). 1967. 7.95 (978-0-253-35112-8(X)) Ind U Pr.
Provides an acoustic model for use with the book of the same name.

Science of Vocal Pedagogy Tape 2: Tenor & Bass. D. Ralph Appleman & D. Ralph Appelman. 1 cass. (Running Time: 60 min.). 1967. 7.95 (978-0-253-35113-5(8)) Ind U Pr.

Science of Vocal Pedagogy Vol. 3: Two Songs. D. Ralph Appleman. 1 cass. (Running Time: 60 min.). 1986. 7.95 Ind U Pr.

Science of Vocal Pedagogyael. 3 cass. 17.95 Ind U Pr.

Science of Winning. Interview. Hosted by Peter Kramer. 1 CDs. (Running Time: 59 mins). (Infinite Mind Ser.: 444). 2006. 21.95 (978-1-933644-35-6(4)) Lichtenstein Creat.
"Whoever said 'It?s not whether you win or lose that counts,' probably lost." So says tennis star Martina Navratilova...it's the ethos of most top competitors at anything they do. But concept of "winning and losing" goes well beyond sports...today on The Infinite Mind, we look at the Science of Winning. We?ll listen in on a conversation with evolutionary biologists Howard Bloom and Dr. Neil Greenberg about biological consequences of winning and losing.Psychologist and conference-champion coach Dr. John Tauer will tell us how he explores internal and external motivation to help kids excel in his basketball camp, even when they don?t want to.Plus tennis superstar Martina Navratilova joins us from the road to talk about the role of competition in her life, and her future.And ZoneCoach Jim Fannin tells us how he keeps superstars in sports, business and everyday life, focused on what it takes to be a "true champion".Finally commentator John Hockenberry weighs in on the arenas of real tough-guy competition...where it's crush or be crushed...like chess and high school debate.

Science Plus 2002, Level Blue. 2nd ed. Holt, Rinehart and Winston Staff. 2001. audio compact disk 41.20 (978-0-03-064542-6(5)) Holt McDoug.

Science Plus 2002, Level Red. 2nd ed. Holt, Rinehart and Winston Staff. 2001. audio compact disk 41.20 (978-0-03-064537-2(9)) Holt McDoug.

Science Plus 2002 Level Green. Holt, Rinehart and Winston Staff. 2001. audio compact disk 41.20 (978-0-03-064532-7(8)) Holt McDoug.

Science, Politics & Gnosticism, unabr. ed. Eric Voegelin. Read by Robin Lawson. 2 cass. (Running Time: 2 hrs. 30 mins.). 1991. 17.95 (978-0-7861-0207-5(1), 1182) Blckstn Audio.
One of today's leading political theorists contends that certain modern movements, including Positivism, Hegelianism, Marxism & the "God is Dead" movement, are variants of the Gnostic tradition of antiquity. He attempts to resolve the intellectual confusion that has resulted from the dominance of gnostic thought by clarifying the distinction between political gnosticism & the philosophy of politics.

Science Projects for All Students. Ed. by Marty Berda & Mary Jean Blaisdell. (J). (gr. 4-9). 2000. audio compact disk 149.95 (978-0-8160-4203-6(9)) Facts On File.

Science Rock. Rhino Records Staff. 1 cass., 1 CD. (Schoolhouse Rock Ser.). 1998. 7.89 (978-1-56826-775-3(4)); 11.89 CD. (978-1-56826-776-0(2)) Rhino Enter.

***Science Rocks! Set 2 CD.** (Science Rocks! Set 2 CD Ser.). 2010. cd-rom 162.42 (978-1-60270-962-1(9)) ABDO Pub Co.

***Science Rocks! Set 2 Site CD.** (Science Rocks! Set 2 Site CD Ser.). 2010. cd-rom 342.42 (978-1-60270-976-8(9)) ABDO Pub Co.

Science Smarts by Dancing Beetle. Eugene Ely et al. 1 cass. (Running Time: 77 min.). (J). 1995. 10.00 Erthviibz.
Scientific facts, theories & nature sounds come together when Ms. Fire Toad & the spunky humans read & sing with Dancing Beetle.

Science Spectacular, Set. Holt, Rinehart and Winston Staff. 2004. audio compact disk 598.33 (978-0-03-038091-4(X)) Holt McDoug.

Science Spectacular, Set. 4th ed. Holman. 2004. audio compact disk 598.33 (978-0-03-038074-7(X)) Holt McDoug.

Science Spectrum: Guided Reading. Holt, Rinehart and Winston Staff. 2000. audio compact disk 247.13 (978-0-03-055524-4(8)) Holt McDoug.

Science Spectrum: Physics: Guide to Reading. 4th ed. Holt, Rinehart and Winston Staff. 2003. audio compact disk 235.66 (978-0-03-067093-0(4)) Holt McDoug.

Science Spectrum: Physics: Guided Reading Program. Holt, Rinehart and Winston Staff. 2000. audio compact disk 247.13 (978-0-03-055588-6(4)) Holt McDoug.

Science Spectrum: Physics: Guided Reading Program. 4th ed. Holt, Rinehart and Winston Staff. (SPA.). 2004. audio compact disk 228.80 (978-0-03-068334-3(3)) Holt McDoug.

Science Survey. William Schockley et al. 1 cass. 1990. 12.95 (TSE005) J Norton Pubs.
Twelve scientists discuss their work.

Science Take Home Book CD-ROM: Early. Benchmark Education Staff. (J). 2006. audio compact disk 10.00 (978-1-4108-7385-9(4)) Benchmark Educ.

Science Take Home Book CD-ROM: Emergent. Benchmark Education Staff. (J). 2006. audio compact disk 10.00 (978-1-4108-7382-8(X)) Benchmark Educ.

Science Take Home Book CD-ROM: Fluent. Benchmark Education Staff. (J). 2006. audio compact disk 10.00 (978-1-4108-7388-0(9)) Benchmark Educ.

Science vs. Fiction I. SERCON Panel. 1 cass. 9.00 (A0119-87) Sound Photosyn.
At the Science Fiction writers convention with Alan Bostick, Pohl, Bear, Murphy, & Rudy Rucker.

Science vs. Fiction II. SERCON Panel. 1 cass. 9.00 (A0127-87) Sound Photosyn.
At the SF writers convention featuring Paul Preuss, Knowles, Blumlein, Benfor & Whitmore.

Science Wars: What Scientists Know & How They Know It. Instructed by Steven L. Goldman. 12 cass. (Running Time: 12 hrs.). 2006. 129.95 (978-1-59803-204-8(6)); audio compact disk 69.95 (978-1-59803-206-2(2)) Teaching Co.

Science with Max Axiom, Super Scientist Part 2. Created by Playaway. (Playaway Children Ser.). (ENG.). (J). 2009. 39.99 (978-1-60775-755-9(9)) Find a World.

Science 1 Listening Cassette. 2nd rev. ed. 1988. 7.00 (978-1-57924-135-3(2)) BJUPr.

SciencePlus: Technology & Society Audiocassette. Holt, Rinehart and Winston Staff. (SPA & ENG.). 1997. 39.20 (978-0-03-095671-3(4)); 39.20 (978-0-03-095686-7(2)); 39.20 (978-0-03-095701-7(X)) Holt McDoug.

Scientific Color Measurement & Control. unabr. ed. Read by Eugene Allen. 5 cass. (Running Time: 6 hrs. 30 min.). 625.00 Incl. 251p. manual & color chip kit. (A4) Am Chemical.

Scientific Dilemmas: "What's Lurking Out There in Space?" Manly P. Hall. 8.95 (978-0-89314-248-3(4), C871101) Philos Res.
Explains philosophy & religion.

Scientific Discovery: Case Studies. Ed. by Thomas Nickles. (Boston Studies in the Philosophy of Science: No. 60). 1980. 155.00 (978-90-277-1092-5(9)) Spri.

Scientific Evidence. Irving Younger. Read by Irving Younger. 3 cass. (Running Time: 3 hrs.). 1985. pap. bk. 70.00 (978-0-943380-42-1(1)) PEG MN.

Scientific Evidence. Perf. by Irving Younger. Created by Irving Younger. 2 CDs. (Running Time: 3 hours). 2004. pap. bk. 199.00 (978-1-932831-05-4(3)) PEG MN.

Scientific Foundation Behind the Nervotron. 2nd rev. ed. Marco A. V. Bitetto. 1 cass. 1989. 37.00 (978-1-893375-97-0(8)) Tompkins Pr.
Explains the properties of natural neural systems & an innovative breakthrough in artificial intelligence based machines. This is done in easy to understand english.

Scientific Russian: The Key to Understanding a Vast World of Technical & Non-Technical Literature. Instructed by Lorraine T. Kapitanoff. 6 cass. (Running Time: 6 hrs.). 455.00 incl. 312pp. manual. (73) Am Chemical.
Introductory Russian language book for scientists & other professionals.

Scientific View of Meditation. Robert Ornstein. 1 cass. 1999. 11.00 (JN013) Big Sur Tapes.
1973 London.

Scientist: Researcher or World Citizen? Read by Linus Pauling. 1 cass. (Running Time: 26 min.). 10.95 J Norton Pubs.

Scientist As Evangelist. John Robbins. 1 cass. (Christianity & Science Ser.: No. 3). 5.00 Trinity Found.

Scientist in the City, unabr. ed. James S. Trefil. Narrated by Ed Blake. 7 cass. (Running Time: 10 hrs. 15 mins.). 1995. 60.00 (978-0-7887-0224-2(6), 94449E7) Recorded Bks.
A fascinating field trip into the modern city that will open your eyes to the hidden wonders of the man-made world around you. Trefil teaches some surprising truths about the forces that shape our world, as well as some unusual possibilities for the cities of tomorrow.

Scientists & Responsibility CD. Linus Pauling. 1 CD. (Running Time: 26 mins.). 2006. audio compact disk 12.95 (978-1-57970-409-4(3), C33032D, Audio-For) J Norton Pubs.

Scientology: A New Slant on Life. L. Ron Hubbard. (Running Time: 4 hrs. 55 mins. 0 sec.). (SPA.). 2007. audio compact disk 20.00 (978-1-4031-5643-3(3)) Bridge Pubns Inc.

***Scientology: A New Slant on Life.** L. Ron Hubbard. 2007. audio compact disk 20.00 (978-1-4031-5631-0(X)); audio compact disk 20.00 (978-1-4031-5644-0(1)); audio compact disk 20.00 (978-1-4031-5633-4(6)); audio compact disk 20.00 (978-1-4031-5695-2(6)); audio compact disk 20.00 (978-1-4031-5634-1(4)); audio compact disk 20.00 (978-1-4031-5632-7(8)); audio compact disk 20.00 (978-1-4031-5640-2(9)); audio compact disk 20.00 (978-1-4031-5639-6(5)); audio compact disk 20.00 (978-1-4031-5638-9(7)); audio compact disk 20.00 (978-1-4031-5637-2(9)); audio compact disk 20.00 (978-1-4031-5630-3(1)); audio compact disk 20.00 (978-1-4031-5641-9(7)); audio compact disk 20.00 (978-1-4031-5635-8(2)); audio compact disk 20.00 (978-1-4031-5642-6(5)); audio compact disk 20.00 (978-1-4031-5636-5(0)) Bridge Pubns Inc.

***Scientology: A New Slant on Life.** L. Ron Hubbard. (GER.). 2008. 14.00 (978-1-4031-5857-4(6)); 14.00 (978-1-4031-5858-1(4)); 14.00 (978-1-4031-5859-8(2)); 14.00 (978-1-4031-5856-7(8)); 14.00 (978-1-4031-5854-3(1)); 14.00 (978-1-4031-5855-0(X)) Bridge Pubns Inc.

***Scientology: A New Slant on Life.** L. Ron Hubbard. (GER.). 2010. audio compact disk 20.00 (978-1-4031-6921-1(7)); audio compact disk 20.00 (978-1-4031-6924-2(1)); audio compact disk 20.00 (978-1-4031-6868-9(7)); audio compact disk 20.00 (978-1-4031-6923-5(3)); audio compact disk 20.00 (978-1-4031-6929-7(2)); audio compact disk 20.00 (978-1-4031-6922-8(5)); audio compact disk 20.00 (978-1-4031-6928-0(4)); audio compact disk 20.00 (978-1-4031-6932-7(2)); audio compact disk 20.00 (978-1-4031-6925-9(X)); audio compact disk 20.00 (978-1-4031-6918-1(7)); audio compact disk 35.00 (978-1-4031-6926-6(8)); audio compact disk 20.00 (978-1-4031-6919-8(5)); audio compact disk 20.00 (978-1-4031-6927-3(6)); audio compact disk 20.00 (978-1-4031-6930-3(6)); audio compact disk 20.00 (978-1-4031-6920-4(9)); audio compact disk 20.00 (978-1-4031-6931-0(4)) Bridge Pubns Inc.

Scientology: A New Slant on Life. abr. ed. L. Ron Hubbard. Read by Harry Chase. (Running Time: 3 hrs. 58 mins. 0 sec.). (ENG.). 2007. audio compact disk 20.00 (978-1-4031-5541-2(0)) Bridge Pubns Inc.

***Scientology: Effective Knowledge.** L. Ron Hubbard. (ENG.). 2002. audio compact disk 15.00 (978-1-4031-1482-2(X)) Bridge Pubns Inc.

Scientology: Los Fundamentos del Pensamiento. L. Ron Hubbard. (Running Time: 3 hrs. 18 mins. 0 sec.). (SPA.). 2007. audio compact disk 20.00 (978-1-4031-5558-0(5)) Bridge Pubns Inc.

***Scientology: The Fundamentals of Thought.** L. Ron Hubbard. 2007. audio compact disk 20.00 (978-1-4031-5557-3(7)); audio compact disk 20.00 (978-1-4031-5550-4(X)); audio compact disk 20.00 (978-1-4031-5552-8(6)); audio compact disk 20.00 (978-1-4031-5555-9(0)); audio compact disk 20.00 (978-1-4031-5546-7(1)); audio compact disk 20.00 (978-1-4031-5547-4(X)); audio compact disk 20.00 (978-1-4031-5553-5(4)); audio compact disk 20.00 (978-1-4031-5629-7(8)); audio compact disk 20.00 (978-1-4031-5549-8(6)); audio compact disk 20.00 (978-1-4031-5693-8(X)); audio compact disk 20.00 (978-1-4031-5554-2(2)); audio compact disk 20.00 (978-1-4031-5545-0(3)); audio compact disk 20.00 (978-1-4031-5551-1(8)); audio compact disk 20.00 (978-1-4031-5556-6(9)); audio compact disk 20.00 (978-1-4031-5548-1(8)) Bridge Pubns Inc.

***Scientology: The Fundamentals of Thought.** L. Ron Hubbard. 2008. 14.00 (978-1-4031-5849-9(5)); 14.00 (978-1-4031-5852-9(5)); 14.00 (978-1-4031-5853-6(3)); 14.00 (978-1-4031-5851-2(7)); 14.00 (978-1-4031-5848-2(7)); 14.00 (978-1-4031-5850-5(9)) Bridge Pubns Inc.

***Scientology: The Fundamentals of Thought.** L. Ron Hubbard. 2010. audio compact disk 20.00 (978-1-4031-6945-7(4)); audio compact disk 20.00 (978-1-4031-6940-2(3)); audio compact disk 20.00 (978-1-4031-6947-1(0)); audio compact disk 20.00 (978-1-4031-6937-2(3)); audio compact disk 35.00 (978-1-4031-6943-3(8)); audio compact disk 20.00 (978-1-4031-6869-6(5)); audio compact disk 20.00 (978-1-4031-6933-4(0)); audio compact disk 20.00 (978-1-4031-6946-4(2)); audio compact disk 20.00 (978-1-4031-6936-5(5)); audio compact disk 20.00 (978-1-4031-6938-9(1)); audio compact disk 20.00 (978-1-4031-6944-0(6)); audio compact disk 20.00 (978-1-4031-6942-6(X)); audio compact disk 20.00 (978-1-4031-6934-1(9)); audio compact disk 20.00 (978-1-4031-6935-8(7)); audio compact disk 20.00 (978-1-4031-6941-9(1)); audio compact disk 20.00 (978-1-4031-6939-6(X)) Bridge Pubns Inc.

Scientology: The Fundamentals of Thought. abr. ed. L. Ron Hubbard. Read by Harry Chase. (Running Time: 2 hrs. 53 mins. 0 sec.). (ENG.). 2007. audio compact disk 20.00 (978-1-4031-5540-5(2)) Bridge Pubns Inc.

***Scientology & Ability.** L. Ron Hubbard. (ENG.). 2002. audio compact disk 15.00 (978-1-4031-1278-1(9)) Bridge Pubns Inc.

***Scientology & Ability.** L. Ron Hubbard. (NOR.). 2010. audio compact disk 15.00 (978-1-4031-7669-1(8)); audio compact disk 15.00 (978-1-4031-7672-1(8)); audio compact disk 15.00 (978-1-4031-7660-8(4)); audio compact disk 15.00 (978-1-4031-7675-2(2)); audio compact disk 15.00 (978-1-4031-7665-3(5)); audio compact disk 15.00 (978-1-4031-7674-5(4)); audio compact disk 15.00 (978-1-4031-7664-6(7)); audio compact disk 15.00 (978-1-4031-7671-4(X)); audio compact disk 15.00 (978-1-4031-7667-7(1)); audio compact disk 15.00 (978-1-4031-7666-0(3)); audio compact disk 15.00 (978-1-4031-7668-4(X)); audio compact disk 15.00 (978-1-4031-7663-9(9)); audio compact disk 15.00 (978-1-4031-7673-8(6)); audio compact disk 15.00 (978-1-4031-7661-5(2)); audio compact disk 15.00 (978-1-4031-7670-7(1)); audio compact disk 15.00 (978-1-4031-7662-2(0)) Bridge Pubns Inc.

Scientology & Effective Knowledge. L. Ron Hubbard. 1 cass. (Running Time: 1 hr.). 2002. 20.00 (978-0-88404-528-1(5)) Bridge Pubns Inc.

Scientology & Effective Knowledge. unabr. ed. L. Ron Hubbard. 1 cass. (Running Time: 1 hr.). 2001. 20.00 Bridge Pubns Inc.

***Scientology & Tradition.** L. Ron Hubbard. (ENG.). 2002. audio compact disk 15.00 (978-1-4031-1060-2(3)) Bridge Pubns Inc.

***Scientology, Its General Background.** L. Ron Hubbard. (ENG.). 2002. audio compact disk 15.00 (978-1-4031-1107-4(3)) Bridge Pubns Inc.

***Scientology, Its General Background.** L. Ron Hubbard. (SWE.). 2010. audio compact disk 15.00 (978-1-4031-7658-5(2)); audio compact disk 15.00 (978-1-4031-7649-3(3)); audio compact disk 15.00 (978-1-4031-7645-5(0)); audio compact disk 15.00 (978-1-4031-7654-7(X)); audio compact disk 15.00 (978-1-4031-7657-8(4)); audio compact disk 15.00 (978-1-4031-7659-2(0)); audio compact disk 15.00 (978-1-4031-7644-8(2)); audio compact disk 15.00 (978-1-4031-7647-9(7)); audio compact disk 15.00 (978-1-4031-7651-6(5)); audio compact disk 15.00 (978-1-4031-7646-2(9)); audio compact disk 15.00 (978-1-4031-7648-6(5)); audio compact disk 15.00 (978-1-4031-7656-1(6)); audio compact disk 15.00 (978-1-4031-7655-4(8)); audio compact disk 15.00 (978-1-4031-7653-0(1)); audio compact disk 15.00 (978-1-4031-7652-3(3)); audio compact disk 15.00 (978-1-4031-7650-9(7)) Bridge Pubns Inc.

***Scientology Zero.** L. Ron Hubbard. (ENG.). 2002. audio compact disk 15.00 (978-1-4031-1168-5(5)) Bridge Pubns Inc.

SCIFI Zone. Marco A. V. Bitetto. 1 cass. 2000. (978-1-58578-017-4(0)) Inst of Cybernetics.

Scimitar SL-2. Patrick Robinson. Read by Erik Steele. 10 cass. 84.95 (978-0-7927-3310-2(X), CSL 690); audio compact disk 110.95 (978-0-7927-3311-9(8), SLD 690); audio compact disk 49.95 (978-0-7927-3312-6(6), CMP 690) AudioGO.

***Scimitar SL-2.** abr. ed. Patrick Robinson. Read by David Mccallum. (ENG.). 2004. (978-0-06-081850-6(6), Harper Audio); (978-0-06-081851-7(4), Harper Audio) HarperCollins Pubs.

Scipio. Ross Leckie. Narrated by Paul Matthews. 12 cass. (Running Time: 16 hrs. 15 mins.). 102.00 (978-1-84197-375-3(0)) Recorded Bks.

***Scission.** Tim Winton. (Running Time: 4 hrs. 50 mins.). 2010. 59.99 (978-1-74214-618-8(X), 9781742146188) Pub: Bolinda Pubng AUS. Dist(s): Bolinda Pub Inc

***Scission.** unabr. ed. Tim Winton. Read by Samuel Johnson. (Running Time: 4 hrs. 50 mins.). 2009. audio compact disk 57.95 (978-1-74214-433-7(0), 9781742144337) Pub: Bolinda Pubng AUS. Dist(s): Bolinda Pub Inc

Scleroderma: Touching Deep With Music. Howard Richman. 1 cass. (Running Time: 24 min.). (Entrainment Music Ser.). 1995. 15.95 (978-1-882060-65-8(2), 98016-4) Sound Feelings.
Piano composition which helps to release the stress & frustration associated with this disease.

Scold's Bridle. unabr. ed. Minette Walters. Read by Sharon Williams. (Running Time: 11 hrs.). 2009. 39.97 (978-1-4233-7172-4(0), 9781423371724, Brlnc Audio MP3 Lib); 39.97 (978-1-4233-7174-8(7), 9781423371748, BADLE); 24.99 (978-1-4233-7171-7(2), 9781423371717, Brilliance MP3); 24.99 (978-1-4233-7173-1(9), 9781423371731, BAD) Brilliance Audio.

Scooby-Doo & the Alien Invaders. 1 cass. (Running Time: 1 hr. 30 mins.). (J). 2000. 9.98 (Rr 79869); audio compact disk 13.98 (R2 79870) Rhino Enter.

Scooby-Doo & the Alien Invaders. 2002. 9.98 (978-0-7379-0142-9(X), 79869); audio compact disk 13.98 (978-0-7379-0143-6(8), 79870) Rhino Enter.
Songs from the animated feature, plus other great alien songs, such as "The Purple People Eater," "Blast Off," and "The Martian Hop" performed by Scooby, Shaggy,a and the gang.

Scooby-Doo & the Witch's Ghost. 2002. 9.98 (978-0-7379-0038-5(5), 75708) Rhino Enter.
Scooby-Doo is back with music from the direct to video animated feature. Includes six original songs by The Hex Girls and two bonus songs from the Scooby-Doo On Zombie Island video.

Scooby-Doo & the Witch's Ghost. Perf. by Hex Girls, The. 2002. audio compact disk 13.98 (978-0-7379-0039-2(3), 75709) Rhino Enter.

Scooby-Doo! And the Witch's Ghost: Songs from the Animated Feature & More. 1 cass. (Running Time: 1 hr. 30 mins.). (J). 2001. 9.98 (R4 75708); audio compact disk 13.98 (R2 75709) Rhino Enter.

Scooby-Doo's Snack Tracks: The Ultimate Collection. 1 cass. (Running Time: 1 hr. 30 mins.). (Scooby-Doo Ser.). (J). (ps-3). 1998. 10.98 (978-1-56826-920-7(X), R475504); audio compact disk 16.98 (978-1-56826-921-4(8), R2 76505) Rhino Enter.

Scoop. abr. ed. Fern Michaels. Read by Natalie Ross. (Running Time: 5 hrs.). (Godmothers Ser.: Bk. 1). 2009. audio compact disk 14.99 (978-1-4233-4537-4(1), 9781423345374) Brilliance Audio.

Scoop. abr. ed. Fern Michaels. Read by Natalie Ross. (Running Time: 5 hrs.). (Godmothers Ser.: Bk. 1). 2010. audio compact disk 9.99 (978-1-4233-4538-1(X), 9781423345381, BCD Value Price) Brilliance Audio.

Scoop. unabr. ed. Fern Michaels. Read by Natalie Ross. (Running Time: 9 hrs.). (Godmothers Ser.: Bk. 1). 2009. 24.99 (978-1-4233-4533-6(9), 9781423345336, Brilliance MP3); 39.97 (978-1-4233-4534-3(7), 9781423345343, Brlnc Audio MP3 Lib); 24.99 (978-1-4233-4535-0(5), 9781423345350, BAD); 39.97 (978-1-4233-4536-7(3), 9781423345367, BADLE); audio compact disk 34.99 (978-1-4233-4531-2(2), 9781423345312); audio compact disk 97.97 (978-1-4233-4532-9(0), 9781423345329, BriAudCD Unabrid) Brilliance Audio.

Scoop: A Novel about Journalists. Evelyn Waugh. Read by Simon Cadell. 6 cass. (Running Time: 8 hrs.). 44.95 (CC/023) C to C Cassettes.
Boot was undoubtably one of the best writers around. Who better to send as Foreign Correspondent to cover the civil war in Ishmaelia? But due to a case of mistaken identity the wrong Boot ends up on the right foot.

Scoop: A Novel about Journalists. unabr. collector's ed. Evelyn Waugh. Read by David Case. 8 cass. (Running Time: 8 hrs.). 1991. 48.00 (978-0-7366-2080-2(X), 2885) Books on Tape.
In Scoop, surreptitiously dubbed a "newspaper adventure," Waugh flays Fleet Street & the social pastimes of its war correspondents. He tells how William Boot became the star of British super-journalism & how, leaving part of his shirt in the claws of the lovely Katchen, he returned from Ishmaeilia to London as the Daily Beast's most accoladed overseas reporter.

***Scorch Trials.** unabr. ed. James Dashner. Narrated by Mark Deakins. 9 CDs. (YA). (gr. 7-12). 2010. audio compact disk 44.00 (978-0-307-70661-4(3), Listening Lib) Pub: Random Audio Pubg. Dist(s): Random

***Scorch Trials.** unabr. ed. James Dashner. Read by Mark Deakins. (Running Time: 10 hrs. 23 mins.). (Maze Runner Ser.: Bk. 2). (ENG.). (J). 2010. audio compact disk 44.00 (978-0-307-70659-1(1), Listening Lib) Pub: Random Audio Pubg. Dist(s): Random

Scorched Earth. David L. Robbins. Narrated by Tom Stechschulte. 9 cass. (Running Time: 13 hrs. 15 mins.). 83.00 (978-1-4025-1862-1(5)) Recorded Bks.

Scorcher. unabr. ed. John Lutz. Read by Multivoice Production Staff. (Running Time: 7 hrs.). 2008. 39.25 (978-1-4233-5962-3(3), 9781423359623, BAD); 24.95 (978-1-4233-5959-3(3), 9781423359593, Brilliance MP3); 39.25 (978-1-4233-5960-9(7), 9781423359609, Brlnc Audio MP3 Lib); 24.95 (978-1-4233-5961-6(5), 9781423359616, BAD) Brilliance Audio.

Score. collector's ed. Richard Stark, pseud. Read by Michael Kramer. 4 cass. (Running Time: 6 hrs.). 1999. 32.00 (978-0-7366-4618-5(3), 5004) Books on Tape.
It was an impossible crime: knock off a huge plant payroll, all the banks & all the stores of one entire city in one night. But there was one thief good enough to try. That was Parker. All Parker needed was the right men, the right plan & the right kind of help from Lady Luck. He got the men & the plan. Lady Luck was another story. She turned out to be a good-looking blonde with a taste for booze & eyes for Parker. AndPparker knew this chilling caper would either be the perfect crime... or a set up that would put him in jail.

Score Takes Care of Itself: My Philosophy of Leadership. unabr. ed. Bill Walsh et al. (Running Time: 11 hrs. 0 mins. 0 sec.). (ENG.). 2009. 24.99 (978-1-4001-6331-1(5)); audio compact disk 69.99 (978-1-4001-4331-3(4)); audio compact disk 34.99 (978-1-4001-1331-6(8)) Pub: Tantor Media. Dist(s): IngramPubServ

Scorebusters. unabr. ed. Arleen W. Goldman. 2 cass. 13.95 (51596) Books on Tape.
Help teenagers bone up on vocabularies for the SAT. In this program, they'll never forget new words, because they're tied to music, rhyme & humor.

Scorebusters. unabr. ed. Arleen W. Goldman. 2 cass. (Running Time: 2 hrs.). (YA). 1992. bk. 29.95; 15.95 set incl. 300-word vocabulary list. (978-0-9628830-0-2(X)) Scorebusters.
Designed to quickly & easily boost verbal SAT scores. Done with humor, rhyme, mnemonic techniques in context of school, dating, driving, parental pressures. Easy-reference booklet included.

Scoring High on Bar Exam Essays: The CD Companion to the Highly-Acclaimed Book. Read by Mary Campbell Gallagher. 4. (Running Time: 3 hours). 2006. audio compact disk 43.95 (978-0-9706088-2-6(9)) M C Gallagher.

Scorn Not the Sonnet, Pt. A. Gilbert Highet. 1 cass. (Running Time: 30 min.). (Gilbert Highet Ser.). 11.95 (23322) J Norton Pubs.
Because the form of the sonnet is so tight, it has compelled many poets to produce fine poems as small & brightly polished as diamonds & the Japanese write some poems in a small neat form called haiku.

Scorpia. unabr. ed. Anthony Horowitz. Narrated by Simon Prebble. 7 CDs. (Running Time: 8 hrs. 15 mins.). (Alex Rider Ser.: Bk. 5). (YA). 2005. audio compact disk 69.75 (978-1-4193-5594-3(5), C3412); 54.75 (978-1-4193-4598-2(2), 98079) Recorded Bks.
Best-selling author Anthony Horowitz's Alex Rider adventure novels are a worldwide sensation. In Scorpia Alex must confront the legacy of the father he never knew. It turns out his father may have worked for Scorpia, a deadly terrorist organization. Now that Scorpia wants Alex on their team, the teenaged hero must face the hardest decision of his life.

Scorpio. Narrated by Patricia G. Finlayson. Music by Mike Cantwell. Contrib. by Marie De Seta & TMY Communications Staff. 1 cass. (Running Time: 30 min.). (Astrologer's Guide to the Personality Ser.: Vol. 8). 1994. 7.99 (978-1-878535-19-1(6)) De Seta-Finlayson.
Astrological description of the sign of Scorpio; individually customized, covering love, money, career, relationships & more.

Scorpio: October Twenty-Three - November Twenty-One. Barrie Konicov. 1 cass. (Hypno-Astrology Ser.). 11.98 (978-0-87082-098-4(2), 114) Potentials.
The author, Barrie Konicov, explains how each sign of the Zodiac has its positive & negative aspects, & that as individuals, in order to master our own destiny, we must enhance our positive traits.

Scorpio: Unleash the Power of Your True Self. 1 cass. (Running Time: 1 hr.). 1999. 9.99 (978-1-928996-07-1(8)) MonAge.

Scorpio: Your Relationship with the Energy of the Universe. Loy Young. 1993. 9.95 (978-1-882888-20-7(0)) Aquarius Hse.

Scorpio Connection: Astrological Perspective of Mafia I. Roger Mock. 1 cass. 8.95 (234) Am Fed Astrologers.
Charts of Godfathers, hitmen, events.

Scorpio Connection: Astrological Perspective of Mafia II. Roger Mock. 1 cass. 8.95 (235) Am Fed Astrologers.
Charts of Godfathers, hitmen, events.

Scorpio Illusion. unabr. ed. Robert Ludlum. Read by Michael Prichard. 13 cass. (Running Time: 19 hrs. 30 min.). 1993. 104.00 (978-0-7366-2485-5(6), 3247) Books on Tape.
Retired naval intelligence officer, now a Caribbean charter skipper, is the only one who can stop a woman assassin.

Scorpion. abr. ed. Louis Tridico. Abr. by Louis Tridico. Read by Carol Eason. 2 cass. (Running Time: 180 mins.). (Delta Code Ser.: No. 4). 2004. 18.00 (978-1-58807-372-3(6)) Am Pubng Inc.
As the Second Gulf War ends, Saddam Hussein knows he is defeated. He launches one last, vicious strike against the victorious Americans, a mission in preparation since the First Gulf War. To hearten resistance to the allied forces and terrorize his enemy, he sends a commando team with Weapons of Mass Destruction to attack and destroy a highly-visible military target in the continental United States. Former Delta Force officer Doug Malone and his corporate security specialists at High Ground, Inc., have been hired by the Department of Homeland Security to investigate an import-export company with suspected Cuban connections. With the help of a novice FBI agent, they uncover connections that extend quite a bit east of Cuba - like the Middle East. Can Malone and his team find out what is going down, before it is too late?.

Scorpion. abr. ed. Louis Tridico. Abr. by Louis Tridico. Read by Charlie O'Dowd. 3 CDs. (Running Time: 3 hrs.). (Delta Code Ser.: No. 4). 2004. audio compact disk 25.00 (978-1-58807-323-5(8)) Am Pubng Inc.

Scorpion: Delta Code #4. abr. ed. Louis Tridico. Abr. by Louis Tridico. Read by Carol Eason. 2 cass. (Running Time: 180 mins.). No. 4. 2004. (978-1-58807-640-3(7)) Am Pubng Inc.

Scorpion & the Frog: High Times & High Crimes. unabr. ed. Salvatore Lauria. Read by Scott Brick. As told by David S. Barry. 3 cass. (Running

Time: 5 hrs.). 2002. 34.95 (978-1-59007-226-4(X), N Millennium Audio) Pub: New Millenn Enter. Dist(s): PerseuPGW

Scorpion Down. unabr. ed. Ed Offley. Read by Richard Ferrone. (YA). 2007. 44.99 (978-1-60252-657-0(5)) Find a World.

Scorpion Down: Sunk by the Soviets, Buried by the Pentagon: The Untold Story of the USS Scorpion. unabr. ed. Edward Offley & Ed Offley. Read by Richard Ferrone. 12 CDs. (Running Time: 15 hrs.). (ENG.). 2007. audio compact disk 39.95 (978-1-59887-093-0(9), 1598870939) Pub: HighBridge. Dist(s): Workman Pub

Scorpion on a Stone. unabr. ed. Gwyn Griffin. Read by Wolfram Kandinsky. 8 cass. (Running Time: 8 hrs.). 1982. 48.00 (978-0-7366-0620-2(3), 1582) Books on Tape.

A collection of stories by Gwyn Griffin.

Scorpion Reef. unabr. collector's ed. Charles Williams. Read by Michael Russotto. 7 cass. (Running Time: 7 hrs.). 1993. 42.00 (978-0-7366-2402-2(3), 3171) Books on Tape.

Off Yucatan's coast lies a treasure in diamonds just waiting for someone who can take it & return.

Scorpion Signal. unabr. collector's ed. Adam Hall. Read by Robert Mundy. 8 cass. (Running Time: 8 hrs.). (Quiller Ser.). 1982. 48.00 (978-0-7366-0603-5(3), 1569) Books on Tape.

Quiller is older now, embittered, cynical & running on empty. A sorely needed vacation is rudely interrupted with an urgent mission to Moscow. A reliable British agent, Schrenk, an old partner of Quiller's, has been captured by the Russians & subjected to torture in the Lubyanka Prison. Schrenk has managed to escape, but he has disappeared & has made no contact with control in London. Quiller is entrusted with the task of finding him.

Scorpion Strike. unabr. ed. John J. Nance. Read by Brian Emerson. 8 cass. (Running Time: 11 hrs. 30 mins.). 1999. 56.95 (978-0-7861-1483-2(5), 2335) Blckstn Audio.

In the wake of operation Desert Storm, a defecting Iraqi scientist has revealed Saddam Hussein's horrifying plans for a devastating counter strike against his enemies...& the world. American forces must remobilize to locate & neutralize the underground laboratory where a lethal super-virus is ready to be unleashed.

Scorpion Strike. unabr. ed. John J. Nance. (Running Time: 39600 sec.). 2007. audio compact disk 29.95 (978-0-7861-5970-3(7)); audio compact disk 81.00 (978-0-7861-5969-7(3)) Blckstn Audio.

***Scorpions.** unabr. ed. Walter Dean Myers. Read by Peter Francis James. (ENG.). 2009. (978-0-06-180513-4(0)) HarperCollins Pubs.

Scorpions. unabr. ed. Walter Dean Myers. Narrated by Peter Francis James. 4 pieces. (Running Time: 5 hrs. 30 mins.). (gr. 6 up). 1997. 35.00 (978-0-7887-1815-1(0), 95285E7) Recorded Bks.

Twelve-year-old Jamal is having trouble at home, at school & on the street. Now he's expected to take over the leadership of the Scorpions, a Harlem street gang. Portrays the fear, frustration & despair of inner city life & peer pressure.

Scorpions, Class Set. unabr. ed. Walter Dean Myers. Read by Peter Francis James. 4 cass., 10 bks. (Running Time: 5 hrs. 30 min.). (J). 1997. bk. 105.30 (978-0-7887-2585-2(8), 46431) Recorded Bks.

Scorpions, Homework Set. unabr. ed. Walter Dean Myers. Read by Peter Francis James. 4 cass. (Running Time: 5 hrs. 30 min.). (J). 1997. bk. 48.20 (978-0-7887-1599-0(2), 40630) Recorded Bks.

***Scorpions: The Battles & Triumphs of FDR's Great Supreme Court Justices.** unabr. ed. Noah Feldman. (Running Time: 11 hrs.). (ENG.). 2010. 29.98 (978-1-60788-717-1(7)) Pub: Hachet Audio. Dist(s): HachBkGrp

***Scorpion's Bite.** unabr. ed. Aileen G. Baron. (Running Time: 8 hrs. 30 mins.). 2010. 19.95 (978-1-4417-5443-1(1)); 24.95 (978-1-4417-5439-4(3)); audio compact disk 49.00 (978-1-4417-5440-0(7)) Blckstn Audio.

Scorpion's Gate. unabr. ed. Richard A. Clarke. Read by Robertson Dean. 6 cass. (Running Time: 9 hrs.). 2005. 81.00 (978-1-4159-2385-6(X)); audio compact disk 99.00 (978-1-4159-2386-3(8)) Books on Tape.

***Scorpions Unabridged.** unabr. ed. Walter Dean Myers. Read by Peter Francis James. (ENG.). 2009. (978-0-06-178211-4(4)) HarperCollins Pubs.

Scott & Amundsen: Their Race to the South Pole. abr. ed. Roland Huntford. Narrated by Tim Pigott-Smith. 6 CDs. (Running Time: 7 hrs. 30 mins. 0 sec.). (ENG.). 2009. audio compact disk 31.95 (978-1-934997-33-8(1)) Pub: CSAWord. Dist(s): PerseuPGW

Scott Berg. A. Scott Berg. 1 cass. (Author Speaks Ser.). 1991. 14.95 J Norton Pubs.

Archival recordings of 20th-century authors.

Scott Blackwell: In the Beginning. Perf. by Scott Blackwell. 1 cass. 1999. 10.98 (KMGC8691); audio compact disk 16.98 (KMGD8691) Provident Mus Dist.

Scott Blackwell: Walk on the Wildside - Once upon a Time. Perf. by Scott Blackwell. 2 CDs. 1999. audio compact disk 12.99 (KMGD8674) Provident Mus Dist.

Scott Fitzgerald. unabr. ed. Jeffrey Meyers. Read by David Hilder. 11 cass. (Running Time: 16 hrs.). 1995. 76.95 (978-0-7861-0670-7(0), 1572) Blckstn Audio.

A romantic & tragic figure who embodied the decades between the two world wars, was a writer who took his material almost entirely from his life. This book is the first to analyze frankly the meaning as well as the events of Fitzgerald's life & to illuminate the recurrent patterns that reveal his inner self.

Scott Foresman-Addison Wesley Mathematics: Pre-K Mathematics. (Scott Foresman Addison Wesley Math Ser.). (ps up). 2004. audio compact disk (978-0-328-09169-0(3), Scott Frsmn) Addson-Wesley Educ.

Scott Foresman English. 2nd ed. J E Perpura et al. 3 cass. 2002. 50.10 (978-0-201-66412-6(7)); audio compact disk 50.10 (978-0-201-66418-8(6)) Longman.

Scott Foresman English, Bk. 1. 2nd ed. B. R. Denman. 2002. audio compact disk 50.10 (978-0-201-66404-1(6)) AddisonWesley.

Scott Foresman English 2e:In Contact 1, Bk. 1. 2nd ed. B. R. Denman. 3 cass. 2002. 47.70 (978-0-201-66402-7(X)) AddisonWesley.

Scott Foresman Literature & Integrated Studies. 1 cass. (Running Time: 1 hr.). (YA). (gr. 10). 1997. 96.67 (978-0-673-29477-7(3)) AddisonWesley.

Scott Foresman Literature & Integrated Studies. 1 cass. (Running Time: 1 hr.). (YA). (gr. 11). 1997. 96.97 (978-0-673-29478-4(1)) AddisonWesley.

Scott Foresman Literature & Integrated Studies. 1 cass. (Running Time: 1 hr.). (YA). (gr. 12). 1997. 96.97 (978-0-673-29479-1(X)) AddisonWesley.

Scott Foresman Literature & Integrated Studies. 1 cass. (Running Time: 1 hr.). (YA). (gr. 7). 1997. 96.97 (978-0-673-29474-6(9)) AddisonWesley.

Scott Foresman Literature & Integrated Studies. 1 cass. (Running Time: 1 hr.). (YA). (gr. 8). 1997. 96.97 (978-0-673-29475-3(7)) AddisonWesley.

Scott Foresman Literature & Integrated Studies. 1 cass. (Running Time: 1 hr.). (YA). (gr. 9). 1997. 96.97 (978-0-673-29476-0(5)) AddisonWesley.

Scott, Foresman Reading 2000. 1 cass. (Running Time: 1 hr.). (Scott Foresman Reading Ser.). (J). (gr. 2). 2001. 43.74 (978-0-673-62127-6(8), S-Foresman) AddWesSchl.

Readings of every Pupil Edition selection are presented at a pace that children can follow as they read along. One-minute reteach lessons reinforce the target comprehension skill of the week.

Scott, Foresman Reading 2000. 1 cass. (Running Time: 1 hr.). (Scott Foresman Reading Ser.). (J). (gr. 3). 2001. stu. ed. 67.95 (978-0-673-62128-3(6), S-Foresman); stu. ed. 98.52 (978-0-673-62304-1(1), S-Foresman) AddWesSchl.

Scott, Foresman Reading 2000. 1 cass. (Running Time: 1 hr.). (Scott Foresman Reading Ser.). (J). (gr. 4). 2001. stu. ed. 67.95 (978-0-673-62129-0(4), S-Foresman); stu. ed. 98.52 (978-0-673-62305-8(X), S-Foresman) AddWesSchl.

Scott, Foresman Reading 2000. 1 cass. (Running Time: 1 hr.). (Scott Foresman Reading Ser.). (J). (gr. 5). 2001. stu. ed. 67.95 (978-0-673-62130-6(8), S-Foresman); stu. ed. 98.52 (978-0-673-62306-5(8), S-Foresman) AddWesSchl.

Scott, Foresman Reading 2000. 1 cass. (Running Time: 1 hr.). (Scott Foresman Reading Ser.). (J). (gr. 6). 2001. stu. ed. 67.95 (978-0-673-62131-3(6), S-Foresman); stu. ed. 98.52 (978-0-673-62307-2(6), S-Foresman) AddWesSchl.

Scott, Foresman Reading 2000: Big Book Grade Level Package. 1 cass. (Running Time: 1 hr.). (Scott Foresman Reading Ser.). (J). 2001. 43.74 (978-0-673-62125-2(1), S-Foresman); audio compact disk 79.50 (978-0-673-62301-0(7), S-Foresman) AddWesSchl.

Scott Foresman Social Studies: Technology. (SPA.). (gr. k-2). 2003. audio compact disk (978-0-328-04338-5(9), Scott Frsmn) Addson-Wesley Educ.

Scott Foresman Social Studies: Technology. (gr. 1 up). 2003. audio compact disk (978-0-328-04805-2(4), Scott Frsmn) Addson-Wesley Educ.

Scott Foresman Social Studies: Technology. (gr. 2 up). 2003. audio compact disk (978-0-328-04806-9(2), Scott Frsmn) Addson-Wesley Educ.

Scott Foresman Social Studies: Technology. (SPA.). (gr. 3-5). 2003. audio compact disk (978-0-328-04339-2(7), Scott Frsmn) Addson-Wesley Educ.

Scott Foresman Social Studies: Technology. (gr. 3 up). 2003. audio compact disk (978-0-328-04807-6(0), Scott Frsmn) Addson-Wesley Educ.

Scott Foresman Social Studies: Technology. (gr. 4 up). 2003. audio compact disk (978-0-328-04808-3(9), Scott Frsmn) Addson-Wesley Educ.

Scott Foresman Social Studies: Technology. (gr. 5 up). 2003. audio compact disk (978-0-328-04809-0(7), Scott Frsmn) Addson-Wesley Educ.

Easy-to-follow recordings of all lessons in the Pupil Edition enable all students to access the content. Dramatic readings of You Are There features and biographies make social studies content come alive.

Scott Foresman Social Studies: Technology. (gr. 6 up). 2003. audio compact disk (978-0-328-04810-6(0), Scott Frsmn) Addson-Wesley Educ.

Scott Joplin & Age of Ragtime. Timothy Frew. (CD Ser.). 2001. bk. 16.98 (978-1-56799-305-9(2), Friedman-Fairfax) M Friedman Pub Grp Inc.

Scott Meek's Wildlife Art, Stephen Longfellow Fiske's "Earth Anthem" & The Monterey Bay Marine Sanctuary. Hosted by Nancy Pearlman. 1 cass. (Running Time: 29 min.). 10.00 (1113) Educ Comm CA.

Scott of the Antarctic. unabr. ed. Michael De-La-Noy. Read by Martyn Read. 2 cass. (Isis Ser.). (J). 2004. 24.95 (978-0-7531-0500-9(4), 981115) Pub: ISIS Lrg Prnt GBR. Dist(s): Ulverscroft US

The life of Captain Scott - Scott of the Antarctic - & the courage which he exemplified have marked him out as a hero to generations, despite his failure to be the first to reach the South Pole. This book describes his short life & the explorations which he & his team made. His journey across unforgiving, frozen wastes is vividly recreated.

Scott of the Antarctic. unabr. collector's ed. Elspeth Huxley. Read by Walter Zimmerman. 12 cass. (Running Time: 18 hrs.). 1990. 96.00 (978-0-7366-1723-9(X), 2564) Books on Tape.

"What qualities does a man need in order to become a national hero? He must be a man of action; he must be brave; he must be bold; & it is a great advantage, if not a necessity, that he should die in the attempt to reach his goal." Robert Falcon Scott was such a man. He led the British Antarctic Expedition in 1911, failed by one month to be the first to plant his country's flag at the South Pole, & died on the return trip from the Pole, just 11 miles from food & shelter. In this biography, Huxley takes the view that far from being a glamorous explorer, Scott was a reluctant hero, a complex, obstinate & reticent man. "His," says Huxley, "was the conquest of self, a feat perhaps more admirable than the conquest of the Pole".

Scott Turow: Interview with Scott Turow & Kay Bonetti. unabr. ed. 1 cass. 1989. 13.95 (978-1-55644-338-1(2), 9062) Am Audio Prose.

Scott Turow Omnibus: Presumed Innocent; The Burden of Proof; Pleading Guilty; The Laws of Our Fathers; One L, Set. abr. ed. Scott Turow et al. 14 cass. (Running Time: 200 min.). 1999. 49.95 (978-0-671-75840-0(3), Audioworks) S&S Audio.

Scottforesman English 2e:On Target 1, Bk. 1. 2nd ed. J E Perpura & D Pinkley. (Scott Foresman English Ser.). 2002. audio compact disk 50.10 (978-0-201-66414-0(3)) Longman.

Scottforesman English 2e:On Target 2. 2nd ed. J E Perpura & D Pinkley. 3 cass. (Scott Foresman English Ser.). 2002. 50.10 (978-0-201-66416-4(X)) Longman.

Scottish see Acting with an Accent

Scottish Airs & Ballads for Appalachian Dulcimer: Intermediate Level. Mark Nelson. 1997. spiral bd. 22.95 (978-0-7866-2321-1(7), 96022BCD) Mel Bay.

Scottish Airs & Ballads for Autoharp. Alex Usher. 2003. pap. bk. 14.95 (978-0-7866-0731-0(9), 99065BCD) Mel Bay.

Scottish Bride. abr. ed. Catherine Coulter. Read by Anne Flosnik. (Running Time: 21600 sec.). (Bride Ser.). 2007. audio compact disk 14.99 (978-1-59737-838-3(0), 9781597378383, BCD Value Price) Brilliance Audio.

Scottish Bride. unabr. ed. Catherine Coulter. Read by Josephine Bailey. 8 cass. (Running Time: 12 hrs.). 2001. 64.00 (978-0-7366-6196-6(4)) Books on Tape.

The lives of a dour vicar & his children are enlivened when he inherits a barony in Scotland & rescues a local lass.

Scottish Bride. unabr. ed. Catherine Coulter. Read by Josephine Bailey. 8 cass. (Running Time: 11 hrs.). 2002. 34.95 (978-0-7366-6750-0(4)) Books on Tape.

Tysen Sherbrooke is a dour vicor, a widower with three children who arrives in Scotland after inheriting a barony & a castle. When Tyson visits his new holdings, he steps into a beehive of complications - facing down dreadful people who would as willingly slit his English throat as look at him. Then the local bastard, a remarkable young woman blessed with a courageous spirit, comes unexpectedly into his life, in desperate need of his protection.

Scottish Bride. unabr. ed. Catherine Coulter. Read by Anne Flosnik. (Running Time: 11 hrs.). (Bride Ser.). 2006. 39.25 (978-1-59737-836-9(4), 9781597378369, BADLE); 24.95 (978-1-59737-835-2(6), 9781597378352, BAD); 39.25 (978-1-59737-834-5(8), 9781597378345, Brinc Audio MP3 Lib); 87.25 (978-1-59737-830-7(5), 9781597378307, BrilAudUnabridg); audio compact disk 97.25 (978-1-59737-832-1(1), 9781597378321, BriAudCD Unabrid); audio compact disk 36.95 (978-1-59737-831-4(3), 9781597378314, Bril Audio CD Unabri); audio compact disk 24.95 (978-1-59737-833-8(X), 9781597378338, Brilliance MP3) Brilliance Audio.

Dear Reader, All the Sherbrooke clan are alive, well and in rip-roaring spirits in August of 1815. Two months after Napoleon's defeat at Waterloo, Tysen Sherbrooke, the youngest of the three brothers, now thirty-one years old, a vicar, a widower, and the father of three children, has just been told by the earl that he's become the new Baron Barthwick of Kildrummy Castle in Scotland. Tysen feels it is his duty to visit his new holdings. His ten-year-old daughter, Meggie, insists she should accompany him. Tysen refuses, but Meggie is blessed with a full measure of Sherbrooke resolve, and a wily plan of action. Devout, thoughtful, honorable to his soul, Tysen's narrow, sober world explodes when he steps into a bee-hive of complications - facing down dreadful people who would as willingly slit his English throat as look at him. Then the Local Bastard, Mary Rose Fordyce, a remarkable young woman blessed with a soft, steady heart and a courageous spirit, comes unexpectedly into his life, in desperate need of his protection. This is the fourth and final book in the Bride series, and I like it the best of all. Tell me what you think. Catherine Coulter Write me at P.O. Box 17, Mill Valley, CA 94942 or e-mail me at ReadMoi@aol.com.

***Scottish Ceilidh Collection for Fiddlers - Volumes 1 And 2.** Christine Martin & Anne Hughes. (ENG.). 2005. pap. bk. 28.95 (978-1-871193-11-4(7), 1871193117) Pub: Music Sales. Dist(s): H Leonard

Scottish Christmas for Hammered Dulcimer: Intermediate Level. Maggie Sansone. 1997. pap. bk. 24.95 (978-0-7866-3010-3(8), 96515CDP); pap. bk. 19.95 (978-0-7866-3009-7(4), 96515P) Mel Bay.

Scottish Collection for Guitar. 1 CD. (Running Time: 90 mins.). 2004. audio compact disk 19.95 (978-1-871931-27-3(4)) Pub: Taigh Teud GBR. Dist(s): Music Sales

Scottish Fiddle Tunes: 60 Traditional Pieces for Violin. Iain Fraser. (ENG.). 2005. pap. bk. 24.95 (978-1-902455-58-7(4), 1902455584) Pub: Schott Music Corp. Dist(s): H Leonard

Scottish Highlands. unabr. ed. Ronald Hutton. Read by Ronald Hutton. Ed. by Craig Mayes. 2 cass. (Running Time: 2 hrs.). (Personal Courier Ser.). 1991. 19.95 Set. (978-1-878877-07-9(0)) Educ Excursions.

The tragic history of the Scottish Highlanders - with tales of Bonnie Prince Charlie, Stirling Castle, Bannockburn, Rob Roy & Robert the Bruce (& more). Ideal for travelers & armchair listeners alike.

Scottish Lute. Ronn McFarlane. Transcribed by Jamey Bellizzi. 1998. pap. bk. 29.95 (978-0-7866-2919-0(3), 96693CDP) Mel Bay.

Scottish Seas. Douglas M. Jones. Narrated by John Currie. 3 cass. (YA). 1998. 20.00 (978-1-59128-547-2(X)) Canon Pr ID.

Scottish Seas AudioBook. Douglas M. Jones. Read by John Currie. 3 cass. (ENG.). (YA). 1998. audio compact disk 20.00 (978-1-59128-546-5(1)) Canon Pr ID.

Scott's Last Expedition. Robert Falcon Scott. Narrated by William Sutherland. (Running Time: 19 hrs.). 1999. 50.95 (978-1-59912-586-2(2)) Iofy Corp.

Scott's Last Expedition: The Journals. unabr. ed. Robert Falcon Scott. Read by William Sutherland. 13 cass. (Running Time: 19 hrs.). 2000. 85.95 (978-0-7861-1749-9(4), 2553) Blckstn Audio.

In November 1910, the vessel Terra Nova left New Zealand carrying an international team of explorers led by Robert Falcon Scott, an Englishman determined to be the first man to reach the South Pole. Scott kept a detailed journal of his adventures until March 29, 1012, when he & the few remaining members of his team met their ends in a brutal blizzard.

Scottsboro Boys. 10.00 Esstee Audios.

The infamous trial of nine accused of rape.

Scottsboro, Too, Is Worth Its Song see Poetry of Countee Cullen

Scottsdale, AZ Technology Happens! unabr. ed. Innovation Groups Staff. 1 cass. (Running Time: 1 hrs. 15 min.). (Transforming Local Government Ser.: Vol. 9). 1999. 10.00 (978-1-882403-65-3(7), IG9909) Alliance Innov.

Scotty's Dream: Book & CD. Short Stories. Donna Fant. Ed. by Elizabeth C. Axford. Illus. by David McKeown. 1 CD. (Running Time: 5 mins.). (ENG.). (J). 2004. audio compact disk 14.99 (978-1-931844-17-8(8), PP1034) Pub: Piano Pr. Dist(s): BkWhole

Scoundrel Time. unabr. ed. Lillian Hellman. 3 cass. (Running Time: 4 hrs. 30 min.). 2003. 28.00 (978-0-7366-9466-7(8)) Books on Tape.

Scourby Bible-KJV-Dramatized. Narrated by Alexander Scourby. 2005. audio compact disk 99.95 (978-1-56563-825-9(5)) Hendrickson MA.

Scourby Compl Bible Aud. Ed. by Alexand Scourby. 2007. reel tape 79.99 (978-0-89957-760-9(1)) AMG Pubs.

Scourby Complete Bible-KJV. Narrated by Alexander Scourby. (Running Time: 252000 sec.). 2007. audio compact disk 79.99 (978-0-89957-593-3(5)) AMG Pubs.

Scourby KJV Audio New Testament, CD. Narrated by Alexander Scourby. 2005. audio compact disk 39.95 (978-1-56563-842-6(5)) Hendrickson MA.

Scourby KJV Audio New Testament, CD Dramatized. Narrated by Alexander Scourby. 2005. audio compact disk 39.95 (978-1-56563-885-3(9)) Hendrickson MA.

Scourge. unabr. ed. Jonathan B. Tucker. Read by Patrick Cullen. 8 CDs. (Running Time: 10 hrs.). 2002. audio compact disk 64.00 (978-0-7861-9495-7(2), 2965); 49.95 (978-0-7861-2241-7(2), 2965); audio compact disk 24.95 (978-0-7861-9205-2(4), 2965) Blckstn Audio.

Starting in the sixteenth century, the smallpox virus afflicted rich and poor, royalty and commoners, and repeatedly altered the course of human history. No safe way of preventing smallpox existed until 1796, when an English country doctor named Edward Jenner developed a vaccine against it. During the ensuing 170 years, vaccination banished smallpox from the industrialized countries, but it remained a major cause of death in the developing world, killing almost two million people per year. Finally, in 1967, the World Health Organization launched an intensified global campaign to eradicate smallpox. By early 1978, the disease had been eliminated worldwide.

Scourge. unabr. ed. Jonathan B. Tucker. Read by Patrick Cullen. 7 pieces. 2004. reel tape 35.95 (978-0-7861-2337-7(0)) Blckstn Audio.

Scourge of God. unabr. ed. S. M. Stirling. Narrated by Todd McLaren. (Running Time: 19 hrs. 0 mins. 0 sec.). (Change Ser.: No. 2). (ENG.). 2008. audio compact disk 49.99 (978-1-4001-0682-0(6)); audio compact disk 99.99 (978-1-4001-3682-7(2)); audio compact disk 34.99 (978-1-4001-5682-5(3)) Pub: Tantor Media. Dist(s): IngramPubServ

Scourge of the Swastika. unabr. ed. Lord Russell of Liverpool. Read by Richard Brown. 7 cass. (Running Time: 10 hrs. 30 min.). 1990. 56.00 (978-0-7366-1871-7(6), 2702) Books on Tape.

No sooner had WW II ended than the Allies began their search for the culprits. With great care & precision the mills of justice began to grind. Allied prosecutors sifted through millions of documents, as Allied tribunals heard the pleas. One distinguished participant, the author of this book, devoted most of his subsequent career to putting in readable form the enduring history of these events. The recital is not pleasant, but it is healthy. It gives vivid meaning to the phrase, "crimes against humanity." It reminds other would-be tyrants (& their accomplices) of our legal system's long memory & of its inexorable reach.

***Scouting the Divine: My Search for God in Wine, Wool, & Wild Honey.** Margaret Feinberg. (Running Time: 4 hrs. 56 mins. 0 sec.). (ENG.). 2009. 16.99 (978-0-310-77339-9(3)) Zondervan.

Scrambled Eggs Super! see Dr. Seuss Audio Collection

Scrambled Eggs Super! Dr. Seuss. (J). 1982. bk. 34.64 (978-0-676-31122-8(9)) SRA McGraw.

Scrambled Home Evening, abr. ed. Joni Hilton. 2 cass. (Running Time: 3 hrs.). 13.95 (978-1-57734-466-7(9), 07002068) Covenant Comms.

Scrambled States of America. 2004. bk. 24.95 (978-1-55592-056-2(X)); pap. bk. 18.95 (978-1-55592-462-1(X)); pap. bk. 18.95 (978-1-55592-464-5(6)); pap. bk. 38.75 (978-1-55592-463-8(8)); pap. bk. 32.75 (978-1-55592-306-8(2)); pap. bk. 32.75 (978-1-55592-465-2(4)); pap. bk. 14.95 (978-1-55592-091-3(8)); 8.95 (978-1-55592-996-1(6)); audio compact disk 12.95 (978-1-55592-922-0(2)) Weston Woods.

Scrambled States of America. Laurie Keller. Narrated by Jon Carroll & Chevy Chase. 1 cass. (Running Time: 15 min.). (J). (gr. 1-4). 2000. bk. 24.95 (QHRA392) Weston Woods.
Disenchanted in their fixed places on the map, the states decide to swap in hopes that each can get to see a different part of the country & do something different for a change.

***Scrambled States of America Talent Show.** Laurie Keller. Narrated by John Carroll. 1 CD. (Running Time: 16 mins.). (J). (gr. k-4). 2009. bk. 29.95 (978-0-545-19702-1(3)) Weston Woods.

***Scrambled States of America Talent Show.** unabr. ed. Laurie Keller. Narrated by John Carroll. 1 CD. (Running Time: 16 mins.). (J). (gr. k-4). 2009. audio compact disk 12.95 (978-0-545-19690-1(6)) Weston Woods.

Scrambled Yeggs. unabr. ed. Richard S. Prather. Read by Maynard Villers. 6 cass. (Running Time: 6 hrs. 36 min.). (Shell Scott Ser.: Bk. 5). 2001. 39.95 (978-1-55686-904-4(5)) Books in Motion.
A rash of hit and run deaths has the press in an uproar. When Shell Scott investigates, he finds a blackmail conspiracy, and his own death planned. But Shell Scott doesn't die easily.

***Scranimals.** abr. ed. Jack Prelutsky. Read by Jack Prelutsky. (ENG.). 2006. (978-0-06-135101-3(6), GreenwillowBks) HarperCollins Pubs.

***Scranimals.** unabr. ed. Jack Prelutsky. Read by Jack Prelutsky. (ENG.). 2007. (978-0-06-153697-7(0), GreenwillowBks) HarperCollins Pubs.

Scrapbooking Digitally: The Ultimate Guide to Saving Your Memories Digitally. Kerry Arquette et al. (ENG., 2008. 19.95 (978-1-56158-972-2(1), Taunt) Pub: Taunton. Dist(s): IngramPubServ

Scrapbooks of My Mind. Rick Jason. 2000. audio compact disk 14.99 (978-0-9701624-1-0(3)) Strange New Wrlds.

***Scratch a Woman.** unabr. ed. Laura Lippman. Read by Linda Emond & Francois Battiste. (ENG.). 2008. (978-0-06-176323-6(3), Harper Audio); (978-0-06-176318-2(7), Harper Audio) HarperCollins Pubs.

Scratch of a Pen: 1763 & the Transformation of North America. unabr. ed. Colin Calloway. Narrated by Simon Vance. 6 CDs. (Running Time: 7 hrs. 30 mins. 0 sec.). (ENG.). 2006. audio compact disk 29.99 (978-1-4001-0233-4(2)) Pub: Tantor Media. Dist(s): IngramPubServ
Most Americans know the significance of the Declaration of Independence or the Emancipation Proclamation, but not the Treaty of Paris. Yet 1763 was a year that shaped our history just as decisively as 1776 or 1862. This captivating book shows why.

Scratch of a Pen: 1763 & the Transformation of North America. unabr. ed. Colin Calloway. Narrated by Simon Vance. (Running Time: 7 hrs. 30 mins. 0 sec.). (ENG.). 2006. audio compact disk 19.99 (978-1-4001-5233-9(X)) Pub: Tantor Media. Dist(s): IngramPubServ

Scratch of a Pen: 1763 & the Transformation of North America. unabr. ed. Colin G. Calloway. Narrated by Simon Vance. 6 CDs. (Running Time: 7 hrs. 30 mins. 0 sec.). (ENG.). 2006. audio compact disk 59.99 (978-1-4001-3233-1(9)) Pub: Tantor Media. Dist(s): IngramPubServ

Scratch-Out! unabr. ed. Harley L. Sachs. 9 cass. (Running Time: 9 hrs.). 2001. 40.00 (978-0-9705390-4-5(5)) I D E V C O.

Scream for Me. unabr. ed. Karen Rose. (Running Time: 14 hrs. 50 mins.). 2008. 85.95 (978-1-4332-4711-8(9)) Blckstn Audio.

Scream for Me. unabr. ed. Karen Rose. Read by Tavia Gilbert. (Running Time: 59400 sec.). 2008. audio compact disk 29.95 (978-1-4332-4714-9(3)); audio compact disk & audio compact disk 29.95 (978-1-4332-4713-2(5)); audio compact disk & audio compact disk 110.00 (978-1-4332-4712-5(7)) Blckstn Audio.

Scream in the Night: Mothers & Babies. David Attenborough. 1 cass. (Running Time: 54 min.). (Animal Language Ser.). 10.95 J Norton Pubs.

Scream Museum. Paul Zindel. Narrated by Jeff Woodman. 3 CDs. (Running Time: 3 hrs. 30 mins.). (P. C. Hawke Mysteries Ser.: Vol. 1). (gr. 5 up). audio compact disk 29.00 (978-1-4025-3299-3(7)) Recorded Bks.

Scream Museum. Paul Zindel. Narrated by Jeff Woodman. 3 pieces. (Running Time: 3 hrs. 30 mins.). (P. C. Hawke Mysteries Ser.). (gr. 5 up). 2002. 28.00 (978-1-4025-1811-9(0)) Recorded Bks.
P.C. Hawke and his partner are on their toughest case yet. Their friend Tom has been accused of murdering a biologist at the Museum of Natural History. They uncover a strange artifact and a huge arachnid at the heart of the mystery.

Scream of the Haunted Mask. R. L. Stine. Read by Kate Simses. (Goosebumps HorrorLand Ser.: No. 4). (J). 2008. 34.99 (978-1-60640-845-2(3)) Find a World.

Scream of the Haunted Mask. R. L. Stine. (Goosebumps HorrorLand Ser.: No. 4). (ENG.). (J). (gr. 4-7). 2008. audio compact disk 29.95 (978-0-545-11328-1(8)) Scholastic Inc.

Scream of the Haunted Mask. R. L. Stine. Narrated by Kate Simses. (Goosebumps HorrorLand Ser.: No. 4). (J). (gr. 4-7). 2008. audio compact disk 9.95 (978-0-545-11153-9(6)) Scholastic Inc.

***Scream Street: Fang of the Vampire (Book #1) Fang of the Vampire (Book #1)** unabr. ed. Tommy Donbavand. (Running Time: 2 hrs.). 2010. 39.97 (978-1-4418-9035-1(1), 9781441890351, Candlewick Bril); 14.99 (978-1-4418-9034-4(3), 9781441890344, Candlewick Bril); audio compact disk 14.99 (978-1-4418-9032-0(7), 9781441890320, Candlewick Bril); audio compact disk 14.99 (978-1-4418-9030-6(0), 9781441890306, Candlewick Bril); audio compact disk 39.97 (978-1-4418-9033-7(5), 9781441890337, Candlewick Bril) Brilliance Audio.

***Scream Street: Fang of the Vampire (Book #1) Fang of the Vampire (Book #1)** unabr. ed. Tommy Donbavand. Read by MacLeod Andrews. (Running Time: 2 hrs.). (Scream Street Ser.). 2010. audio compact disk 39.97 (978-1-4418-9031-3(9), 9781441890313, Candlewick Bril) Brilliance Audio.

Screamfree Marriage: Turning Common Conflicts into a Deeper, Lifelong Connection. unabr. ed. Hal Edward Runkel & Jenny Runkel. Read by Hal Edward Runkel & Jenny Runkel. (ENG.). 2011. audio compact disk 30.00 (978-0-307-71258-5(3), Random AudioBks) Pub: Random Audio Pubg. Dist(s): Random

Screamfree Parenting: The Revolutionary Approach to Raising Your Kids by Keeping Your Cool. abr. unabr. ed. Hal Edward Runkel. Read by Hal Edward Runkel. (Running Time: 18000 sec.). (ENG.). 2007. audio compact disk 22.00 (978-0-7393-5720-0(4), Random AudioBks) Pub: Random Audio Pubg. Dist(s): Random

Screamin' Halloween Sounds. (J). 1997. 6.00 (978-1-57375-544-3(3)) Audioscope.

Screaming Eagles, unabr. ed. Peg Kehret. Narrated by Carine Montbertrand. 2 pieces. (Running Time: 3 hrs.). (Frightmares Ser.: No. 6). (gr. 5 up). 1997. 19.00 (978-0-7887-0830-5(9), 94975E7) Recorded Bks.
Rosie & Kayo are on a weekend trip in the North Cascades National Park, where they can't resist hiking a trail that takes them high into the rocks. When they see the eagle's nest, they are thrilled, until the poacher stalking the magnificent birds spots them. Now Rosie & Kayo are on the run.

Screaming Quietly. Short Stories. Hadassah Bat Haim. Read by Hadassah Bat Haim. 4 CDs. (Running Time: 250 mins.). 2002. audio compact disk 29.95 (978-1-889409-14-6(6)) Pub: LadybugPr CA. Dist(s): Baker Taylor
A humorous look at living with migraine while searching for a cure. Read by the author.

Screaming Skull. abr. ed. 1 cass. (Running Time: 1 hr.). (CBC Radio Ser.). 1997. 4.95 Tangled Web CAN.

Screaming with the Cannibals. Lee Maynard. Prod. by Ross Ballard. Music by Pops Walker. (ENG.). 2009. audio compact disk 28.95 (978-0-9795156-3-7(7)) Mtn Whispers Pubng.

Screech Owl at Midnight Hollow. C. Drew Lamm. Narrated by Alexi Komisar. Illus. by Joel Snyder. 1 cass. (Smithsonian's Backyard Ser.). (J). (ps-2). 1996. 5.00 (978-1-56899-269-3(6), C5010) Soundprints.
Something mysterious is happening in the backyard of the yellow house at Midnight Hollow! Bugs, grasshoppers, & mice are all disappearing. They are all easy food for Mother & Father Screech Owl & their five growing owlets. But as Father Screech Owl hunts in the yard, his awkward nestlings themselves become easy prey for other predators of the night!.

Screeches, Clanks & Howls. Audioscope. 1995. 5.00 (978-1-57375-079-0(4)); 8.00 (978-1-57375-080-6(8)) Audioscope.

Screen Director's Playhouse. 6 cass. 24.98 Moonbeam Pubns.

***Screen Directors Playhouse.** Perf. by Bette Davis et al. 2010. audio compact disk 39.98 (978-1-57019-951-6(5)) Radio Spirits.

***Screen Directors' Playhouse.** RadioArchives.com. (Running Time: 600). (ENG.). 2008. audio compact disk 29.98 (978-1-61081-128-6(3)) Radio Arch.

Screen Director's Playhouse. collector's ed. Perf. by Rosalind Russell et al. 6 cass. (Running Time: 9 hrs.). 2000. bk. 34.98 (978-1-57019-195-4(6), 4192) Radio Spirits.
Adaptations of famous movies. After each show, the director and stars gathered around the microphones to reminisce about the actual making of the film.18 episodes. Includes: "Hired Wife," "Magnificent Obsession," "The Prisoner of Zenda," "The Sky's the Limit," "Hold Back the Dawn," "Her Husband's Affair," "The Killers," "The Big Clock," "Appointment for Love," "Pitfall," "Love Letters," "Remember the Night," "Body and Soul," "All My Sons," "Tomorrow Is Forever" and more.

Screen Director's Playhouse: A Foreign Affair. Perf. by Lucille Ball & John Lund. 1 cass. (Running Time: 1 hr.). 2001. 6.98 (1937) Radio Spirits.

Screen Director's Playhouse: A Kiss in the Dark & It Happens Every Spring. Perf. by Ray Milland. 1 cass. (Running Time: 1 hr.). 2001. 6.98 (1700) Radio Spirits.

Screen Director's Playhouse: Bachelor Mother. Perf. by Bob Cummings & Lucille Ball. 1 cass. (Running Time: 1 hr.). 2001. 6.98 (2526) Radio Spirits.

Screen Director's Playhouse: Call Northside & The Affairs of Susan. 1 cass. (Running Time: 1 hr.). 2001. 6.98 (2045) Radio Spirits.

Screen Director's Playhouse: Champion & Chicago Deadline. 1 cass. (Running Time: 1 hr.). 2001. 6.98 (1918) Radio Spirits.

Screen Director's Playhouse: Humoresque. Perf. by Tallulah Bankhead & Steve Cochran. 1 cass. (Running Time: 1 hr.). 2001. 6.98 (2627) Radio Spirits.

Screen Director's Playhouse: It Had to Be You & The Sea Wolf. Perf. by Joan Fontaine & Edward G. Robinson. 1 cass. (Running Time: 1 hr.). 2001. 6.98 (2287) Radio Spirits.

Screen Director's Playhouse: It's in the Bag & The Paleface. Perf. by Fred Allen & Bob Hope. 1 cass. (Running Time: 1 hr.). 2001. 6.98 (1529) Radio Spirits.

Screen Director's Playhouse: Ivy. Perf. by Joan Fontaine & Charles Drake. 1 cass. (Running Time: 1 hr.). 2001. 6.98 (2503) Radio Spirits.

Screen Director's Playhouse: Let's Live a Little & The Exile. Perf. by Douglas Fairbanks, Jr. 1 cass. (Running Time: 1 hr.). 2001. 6.98 (1527) Radio Spirits.

Screen Director's Playhouse: Lifeboat. Perf. by Tallulah Bankhead & Jeff Chandler. 1 cass. (Running Time: 1 hr.). 2001. 6.98 (1702) Radio Spirits.

Screen Director's Playhouse: Lucky Jordan. Perf. by Alan Ladd & Sheldon Leonard. 1 cass. (Running Time: 1 hr.). 2001. 6.98 (1703) Radio Spirits.

Screen Director's Playhouse: Mr. & Mrs. Smith & Suddenly It's Spring. Perf. by Fred MacMurray. 1 cass. (Running Time: 1 hr.). 2001. 6.98 (1699) Radio Spirits.

Screen Director's Playhouse: Mrs. Mike. Perf. by Joseph Cotten. 1 cass. (Running Time: 1 hr.). 2001. 6.98 (1528) Radio Spirits.

Screen Director's Playhouse: Night Has a Thousand Eyes & Best Years of Our Lives. 1 cass. (Running Time: 1 hr.). 2001. 6.98 (1966) Radio Spirits.

Screen Director's Playhouse: One Way Passage & Magic Town. Perf. by James Stewart. 1 cass. (Running Time: 1 hr.). 2001. 6.98 (1896) Radio Spirits.

Screen Director's Playhouse: Prince of Foxes. Perf. by Raymond Burr & Douglas Fairbanks, Jr. 1 cass. (Running Time: 1 hr.). 2001. 6.98 (2486) Radio Spirits.

Screen Director's Playhouse: She Wouldn't Say Yes & The Ghost Breakers with Bob Hope. Perf. by Bob Hope. 1 cass. (Running Time: 1 hr.). 2001. 6.98 (1701) Radio Spirits.

Screen Director's Playhouse: The Big Lift. Perf. by Edmond O'Brien & Paul Douglas. 1 cass. (Running Time: 1 hr.). 2001. 6.98 (2546) Radio Spirits.

Screen Director's Playhouse: The Fighting O'Flynn & The Dark Mirror. 1 cass. (Running Time: 1 hr.). 2001. 6.98 (1858) Radio Spirits.

Screen Director's Playhouse: The Lady Gambles. Perf. by Barbara Stanwyck & Steven McNally. 1 cass. (Running Time: 1 hr.). 2001. 6.98 (2468) Radio Spirits.

Screen Director's Playhouse: You Were Meant for Me & The Perfect Marriage. 1 cass. (Running Time: 1 hr.). 2001. 6.98 (1566) Radio Spirits.

Screen Guild Players: Twelve O'Clock High. 1 hr. (Running Time: 1 cass.). 2001. 6.98 (2167) Radio Spirits.

Screen Guild Theater. Perf. by James Cagney et al. 3 CDs. (Running Time: 3 hrs.). 2002. audio compact disk 19.98 (27642); 17.98 Radio Spirits.
The Guild was able to draw more top Hollywood stars to its sound stage than any other program of the era. Undoubtedly that's because the stars were working for charity, their fees were donated to the Motion Picture Relief Fund, which provided housing for aging and indigent film stars. For this collection, the best of the best from the Golden Age of Cinema has been selected such as Yankee Doodle Dandy. Enjoy performances from the biggest stars of the 1940s in some of the greatest films of the day.

Screen Savers. Quintin Jardine. Read by Joe Dunlop. 8 cass. (Soundings Ser.). (J). 2005. 69.95 (978-1-84283-483-1(5)) Pub: ISIS Lrg Prnt GBR. Dist(s): Ulverscroft US

Screen Savers. Quintin Jardine. 8 CDs. (Running Time: 10 hrs.). (Soundings (CDs) Ser.). (J). 2005. audio compact disk 79.95 (978-1-84559-154-0(2)) Pub: ISIS Lrg Prnt GBR. Dist(s): Ulverscroft US

Screening & Early Detection of Gynecologic Malignancies. Contrib. by Ira R. Horowitz et al. 1 cass. (American Co[illegible] of Obstetrics & Gynecologists UPDATE: Vol. 23, No. 1). 1998. 20.00 [illegible] of Obstetric.

Screening Party. abr. ed. Dennis Hensley. [illegible]Ds. (Running Time: 4 hrs.). 2002. audio compact disk 24.95 (978-0-9702152-4-6(X)) Fluid Wds.
Fresh and funny look at some of our favorite movies from Dennis Hensley, has been getting together for years with a group of friends to watch and crack wise about films that for reasons both good and bad have made an impression on film and society.

Screenwriter Julius Epstein see I'm Too Busy to Talk Now

Screenwriting: How to Move Your Tale. abr. ed. Richard Walter. Read by Richard Walter. 1 cass. (Running Time: 90 mins.). 1990. 12.95 (978-1-880717-10-3(7),) Writers AudioShop.
How important is the story? Crucial, says the acclaimed head of UCLA's Department of Film & Television, in this edited workshop.

Screenwriting for Hollywood. Michael Hauge. Read by Michael Hauge. 2 cass. (Running Time: 3 hrs.). 1989. 17.95 (978-1-880717-39-4(5)) Writers AudioShop.
Details how to write & sell the Great American Screenplay. Covers structure, characters, selling your work & more. Includes ground-breaking information on "feminine-mode" movies.

Screenwriting for Hollywood. Michael Hauge. Perf. by Michael Hauge. 3 CDs. (ENG.). 2003. audio compact disk 29.95 (978-1-880717-60-8(3), 829-033) Writers AudioShop.

Screenwriting Tricks of the Trade: The Workshop. abr. ed. William Froug. Read by William Froug. 1 cass. (Running Time: 90 mins.). 1993. 12.95 (978-1-880717-30-1(1)) Writers AudioShop.
Write-from-the-gut advice that resounds with experience & integrity from the founder of UCLA's acclaimed film & television writing program. Edited from 1 1/2-day workshop sponsored by Austin Writers' League. Recorded live.

***Screw It, Let's Do It: Lessons in Life & Business.** unabr. ed. Read by Adrian Mulraney. Selected by Richard Branson. (Running Time: 6 hrs. 34 mins.). 2010. 43.95 (978-1-921334-17-7(7), 9781921334177); audio compact disk 77.95 (978-1-74214-744-4(5), 9781742147444) Pub: Bolinda Pubng AUS. Dist(s): Bolinda Pub Inc

Screwed: The Undeclared War Against the Middle Class - & What We Can Do about It. unabr. ed. Thom Hartmann. Read by Anthony Heald. (Running Time: 25200 sec.). 2008. 44.95 (978-1-4332-1513-1(6)); audio compact disk & audio compact disk 29.95 (978-1-4332-1517-9(9)); audio compact disk & audio compact disk 55.00 (978-1-4332-1514-8(4)) Blckstn Audio.

Screwtape Letters. C. S. Lewis. 2006. 24.95 (978-0-7861-4436-5(X)); audio compact disk 27.00 (978-0-7861-7349-5(1)) Blckstn Audio.

Screwtape Letters. abr. ed. C. S. Lewis. Read by John Cleese. 2 cass. (Running Time: 3 hrs.). (J). 1995. 16.95 (978-0-944993-15-6(X), 395018) Audio Lit.
Series of letters from a senior devil to a junior agent in the field, instructing him in the arts of temptation. A mix of brilliant humor with unsurpassed spiritual insight.

Screwtape Letters. abr. ed. C. S. Lewis. Read by John Cleese. 2 cass. (Running Time: 3 hrs.). (J). 1998. 16.85 (978-0-00-107177-3(7)) Ulvrscrft Audio.
Spiritual warfare and the invisible realities, which are part of our religious experience.

Screwtape Letters. abr. unabr. ed. Read by Ralph Cosham. 3 cass. (Running Time: 12600 sec.). 2006. 17.95 (978-0-7861-4475-4(0)); audio compact disk 17.95 (978-0-7861-7279-5(7)) Blckstn Audio.

Screwtape Letters, anniv. unabr. ed. C. S. Lewis. Read by John Cleese. 3 cass. (Running Time: 4 hrs. 30 mins.). (J). 1999. 21.95 (978-1-57453-261-6(8)) Audio Lit.
Speaks to seekers of all traditions, bringing the spiritual search into relation to life as it is actually lived in today's world.

Screwtape Letters. unabr. ed. C. S. Lewis. Read by Joss Ackland. 5 CDs. (Running Time: 6 hrs. 0 mins. 0 sec.). 2002. audio compact disk 29.99 (978-0-06-009366-2(8)) HarperCollins Pubs.

Screwtape Letters: First Ever Full-Cast Dramatization of the Diabolical Classic. adpt. ed. Prod. by Focus on the Family Staff. C. S. Lewis. Adapted by Paul McCusker. Created by Dave Arnold. 4 CDs. (Running Time: 4 hrs.). (Radio Theatre Ser.). (ENG.). 2009. audio compact disk 39.99 (978-1-58997-324-4(0), Tyndale Ent) Tyndale Hse.

Scribbleboy. Philip Ridley. Read by Russell Boulter. (Running Time: 14640 sec.). (J). (gr. 3-6). 2007. audio compact disk 34.95 (978-1-4056-5673-3(5), ChiversChildren) AudioGO GBR.

Scribbler of Dreams. unabr. ed. Mary E. Pearson. Read by Kate Rudd. (Running Time: 6 hrs.). 2010. audio compact disk 24.99 (978-1-4418-0516-4(8), 9781441805164, Bril Audio CD Unabri) Brilliance Audio.

***Scribbler of Dreams.** unabr. ed. Mary E. Pearson. Read by Kate Rudd. (Running Time: 6 hrs.). 2010. 24.99 (978-1-4418-0518-8(4), 9781441805188, Brilliance MP3); 39.97 (978-1-4418-0519-5(2), 9781441805195, Brinc Audio MP3 Lib); 24.99 (978-1-4418-0520-1(6), 9781441805201, BAD); 39.97 (978-1-4418-0521-8(4), 9781441805218, BADLE); audio compact disk 54.97 (978-1-4418-0517-1(6), 9781441805171, BriAudCD Unabrid) Brilliance Audio.

Scribbling the Cat: Travels with an African Soldier. unabr. ed. Alexandra Fuller. Read by Lisette Lecat. 7 cass. (Running Time: 9 hrs. 30 mins.). 2004. 69.75 (978-1-4025-8277-6(3)); audio compact disk 89.75 (978-1-4025-8279-0(X)) Recorded Bks.
Scribbling the Cat chronicles Fuller?s journey through Africa?s war-torn history with a battle-scarred veteran of the Rhodesian war. What emerges is a gripping portrait of men who struggle every day with the sins they cannot forget.

Scribbling the Cat: Travels with an African Soldier. unabr. ed. Alexandra Fuller. Narrated by Lisette Lecat. 6 cass. (Running Time: 9 hrs. 30 mins.). 2004. 24.99 (978-1-4025-7589-1(0), 04034) Recorded Bks.
The true story of her journey back through Africa's war-torn history with a battle-scarred veteran of the Rhodesian war. The man known as K is a banana farmer and born-again Christian. He is also touched by a deep sadness and haunted by the bloodshed of his past. Fuller and K travel from Zambia to Zimbabwe (formerly Rhodesia) to Mozambique, visiting scenes of unthinkable violence and meeting other war veterans with terrible stories to

share. What emerges is a gripping portrait of men who struggle every day to cope with the sins they can never forget.

Scribe. unabr. ed. Francine Rivers. Narrated by Chris Fabry. (Sons of Encouragement Ser.: Vol. 5). (ENG.). 2007. 13.99 (978-1-60814-375-7(9)); audio compact disk 19.99 (978-1-59859-250-4(5)) Oasis Audio.

Scribes from Alexandria. Caroline Lawrence. (Running Time: 3 hrs. 30 mins. 0 sec.). (Roman Mysteries Ser.). (ENG.). (J). (gr. 7-9). 2008. audio compact disk 24.99 (978-0-7528-9768-4(3)) Pub: OrnChdrns Bks GBR. Dist(s): IPG Chicago

Scripts for Winning Jobs: Trudoustrojstvo i Prodvizheniye po Sluzhbe. Natasha Cooper. (Power English Ser.: 5). (ENG & RUS.). 2007. per. 79.99 (978-1-932521-47-4(X)) Cooper Learn Syst.

Scriptural & Historical Foundations. Rick Joyner. 1 cass. (Running Time: 90 mins.). (Foundation Ser.: Vol. 2). 2000. 5.00 (RJ04-002) Morning NC.
Firmly establishing basic Christian principles, these messages also illuminate some of the primary enemies of truth, such as legalism & the control spirit.

Scriptural Basis for Gifts. Vincent M. Walsh. 1 cass. 1986. 4.00 Key of David.
Personal stories & examples told to promote a full understanding of the basic powers of the Renewal.

Scriptural Guidelines for Prayer. Kenneth E. Hagin. 6 cass. 24.00 (64H) Faith Lib Pubns.

Scriptural Response to the Five Points of Calvinism. Chris Jakway. 1 cass. 3.00 (CJ1) Evang Outreach.

Scriptural Rosary. Perf. by Catholic University of America, Drama Department. 2 cass. (Running Time: 1 hr. 28 min.). Dramatization. 1979. 17.95 Christianica.
Mysteries of Rosary dramatized by Drama Department of Catholic University.

Scriptural Sources of Ministry & Mission. Rea McDonnell. 3 cass. (Running Time: 3 hrs.). 1983. 24.95 Incl. shelf-case. (TAH103) Alba Hse Comns.
Presents definitons of ministry. Includes: Talk 1:God's Initiative, Our Response, Talk 2: Jesus, Missioned & Ministering, Talk 3 & 4: New Testament Witness to Mission & Ministry, Talk 5: Mid-Life for the Minister, Talk 6: the Future of Ministry.

Scripture & the Early Fathers of the Church. Joseph F. Girzone. Read by Joseph F. Girzone. 1 cass. (Running Time: 60 min.). 1992. 7.95 (978-0-911519-17-4(3)) Richelieu Court.
Girzone's public talk on these topics.

Scripture in Everyday Life: Comfort for the Suffering. David Powlison et al. (ENG.). 2006. audio compact disk 29.95 (978-1-934885-67-3(3)) New Growth Pr.

Scripture in Everyday Life: Comfort for the Suffering. unabr. ed. David Powlison et al. 3 CDs. (Running Time: 3 hrs.). 2003. audio compact disk 29.95 (978-1-930921-29-0(2)) Resources.

Scripture in Everyday Life: Comfort for the Suffering. unabr. ed. David Powlison et al. 3 cass. (Running Time: 3 hrs.). 2003. 29.95 (978-1-930921-04-7(7)) Resources.

Scripture Memory Songs. Prod. by Twin Sisters Productions Staff. 1 CD. (Running Time: 47 mins). (J). 2005. audio compact disk 6.99 (978-1-57583-814-4(1)) Twin Sisters.
Children will quickly and easily memorize God's Word with new, original Scripture memory songs! Impress God's Word upon tender hearts with contemporary, easy-to-sing, uplifting, and worshipful original music! Celebrate God's creation and amazing love. Worship with Psalms of praise and thanksgiving. Learn the Books of the Bible, the Fruit of the Spirit, the Golden Rule, and the Lord's Prayer. Sung by kids for kids, these Scripture memory songs are ideal for use at home, church, and school. BONUS! The ENHANCED CD includes 108 pages of sheet music that can be printed from your own computer!.

Scripture Memory Songs: Verses about Behaving. Max Lucado. (Max Lucado's Hermie & Friends Ser.). (J). (ps-2). 2007. audio compact disk 6.99 (978-1-4003-0914-6(X)) Nelson.

Scripture Memory Songs: Verses about Being Brave. unabr. ed. Created by Max Lucado. (Running Time: 3600 sec.). (Max Lucado's Hermie & Friends Ser.). (J). (ps-2). 2006. audio compact disk 6.99 (978-1-4003-0791-3(0)) Nelson.
Join Webster and all the garden friends as they teach Scripture to kids through this new CD series that will provide kids with a fun learning experience. Each CD will be comprised of 10-15 Scripture songs (in stereo) sung by kids and taken directly from Scriptures using ICB, KJV, NKJV, NAS and NCV. Each CD will feature a "missing word" version. As the song repeats, key words will be missing from the vocal in order to help reinforce Scripture memory. For parents who are looking for a tool to help kids learn God's Word, these Scripture Memory Songs will help kids of all ages learn with ease and fun as only Hermie and his garden friends can! Verses included on this volume: Psalm 4:8, 1 Peter 5:7, Heb 13:5b-6, Psalm 23, Psalm 18:1-3 and 2 Tim 1:7 as well as others.

Scripture Memory Songs: Verses about Being Special. unabr. ed. Created by Max Lucado. (Running Time: 1 hr.). (Hermie & Friends Ser.). (J). 2006. audio compact disk 6.99 (978-1-4003-0789-0(9)) Nelson.

Scripture Memory Songs: Verses about Being Truthful. unabr. ed. Created by Max Lucado. (Running Time: 3600 sec.). (J). (ps-2). 2006. audio compact disk 6.99 (978-1-4003-0790-6(2)) Nelson.
A fun, creative new way to teach children the Word of God, these sing-a-long scripture memory CDs are based upon the Hermie & Friends videos and the ICB text. Each CD is thematically based upon the correlating Hermie & Friends dvd/video. The songs are performed by children with Max, Hermie and their garden friends joining in on each scripture's lesson or truth. Each volume contains both track versions and bonus versions that omit words and phrases for the kids to sing along with, filling in the blanks for learning the scripture. Each project contains 12-15 songs on 4 CDs that go along with the existing Hermie and Friends dvd/videos.

Scripture Memory Songs: Verses about Praying. unabr. ed. Max Lucado. (Max Lucado's Hermie & Friends Ser.). (J). (ps-2). 2007. audio compact disk 6.99 (978-1-4003-0872-9(0)) Nelson.

Scripture Memory Songs: Verses about Sharing. unabr. ed. Created by Max Lucado. (Running Time: 3600 sec.). (Max Lucado's Hermie & Friends Ser.). (J). (ps-2). 2006. audio compact disk 6.99 (978-1-4003-0777-7(5)) Nelson.

Scripture Memory Songs: Verses & Songs about Christmas. unabr. ed. Created by Tommy Nelson. (Running Time: 3600 sec.). (Max Lucado's Hermie & Friends Ser.). (J). (ps-2). 2006. audio compact disk 6.99 (978-1-4003-0871-2(2)) Nelson.

Scripture Memory Songs - Buzby: Verses about Following the Rules. unabr. ed. Created by Max Lucado. (Running Time: 1 hr.). (Max Lucado's Hermie & Friends Ser.). (J). 2006. audio compact disk 6.99 (978-1-4003-0792-0(9)) Nelson.
Join Buzby and all the garden friends as they teach Scripture to kids through this new CD series that will provide kids with a fun learning experience. Each CD will be comprised of 10-15 Scripture songs (in stereo) sung by kids and taken directly from Scriptures using ICB, KJV, NKJV, NAS and NCV. Each CD will feature a "missing word" version. As the song repeats, key words will be missing from the vocal in order to help reinforce Scripture memory. For parents who are looking for a tool to help kids learn God's Word, these Scripture Memory Songs will help kids of all ages to learn God's Word with ease and fun as only Hermie and his garden friends can! Verses included on this volume: Deut 27:10, Prov 3:56, Psalm 119:5, Joshua 1:8, Matt 22:37-39, and Psalm 119:34-35 as well as others.

Scripture Memory Songs - Stanley: Verses about Being a Friend. unabr. ed. Created by Max Lucado. (Running Time: 1 hr.). (Max Lucado's Hermie & Friends Ser.). (J). 2006. audio compact disk 6.99 (978-1-4003-0793-7(7)) Nelson.
Join Stanley and his garden friends as they teach Scripture through this new CD series that will provide kids with a fun learning experience. Each CD will be comprised of 10-15 Scripture songs (in stereo) sung by kids and taken directly from Scriptures using ICB, KJV, NKJV, NAS and NCV. Each CD will feature a "missing word" version. As the song repeats, key words will be missing from the vocal in order to help reinforce Scripture memory. For parents who are looking for a tool to help kids learn God's Word, these Scripture Memory Songs will help kids of all ages to learn God's Word with ease and fun as only Hermie & Friends TM can! Verses included on this volume: 2 Cor 9:7, 1 John 4:7-8, 1 John 4:9-11, Col 3:12, Prov 17:17, and Eph 4:32 as well as others.

Scripture Rock. 1 cass. 1997. 7.99 (978-0-7601-1262-5(2), C80005); audio compact disk 11.99 (978-0-7601-1263-2(0), CD80005) Pub: Brentwood Music. Dist(s): Provident Mus Dist
A "Fun Upbeat Rockin' Way" for kids to memorize scriptures. Direct scriptures sung to all styles of "Rock n Roll" music. This is for the kids who are ready to learn in a fashion that has flair.

Scripture Songs. 1 CD. (Running Time: 1 hr. 34 mins.). 2002. audio compact disk 6.99 (978-1-57583-547-1(9), 3009CD) Twin Sisters.
It's amazing how quickly children learn Scripture verses that are set to music! Through catchy melodies and easy-to-sing songs, children will memorize verses that teach them about who God is and about His wonderful love for us. Adults and children alike will enjoy learning about the fruit of Spirit, the books of the Bible, and many life-changing Scripture verses through song.

Scripture Time: Blessing Your Family with Scripture Study. Jack Christianson. 2004. 9.95 (978-1-59156-383-9(6)); audio compact disk 11.95 (978-1-59156-384-6(4)) Covenant Comms.

Scriptures: Sleeping Aid or Power Source. Scott Simmons. 1 cass. 1998. 9.95 (978-1-57008-354-9(1), Bkcraft Inc) Deseret Bk.

Scrolls of Attikis & Ithaca. Kenneth R. Roberts & H. F. Noyes. Ed. by Kenneth R. Roberts. 2000. audio compact disk 20.00 (978-0-9703132-0-1(9)) ZZAPP.

SCSI-2 Common Access Method (CAM) 1 cass. 1990. 8.50 Recorded Res.

Scuba Dancing. unabr. abr. ed. Nicola Slade. Read by Hilary Neville. 6 cass. (Running Time: 28800 sec.). (Soundings Ser.). 2007. 54.95 (978-1-84559-380-3(4)) Pub: ISIS Lrg Prnt GBR. Dist(s): Ulverscroft US

Scudder Oration on Trauma: The Accident Hospital. 1 cass. (Named Lectures: C85-NL3). 1985. 7.50 (8533) Am Coll Surgeons.

Sculptor's Funeral see Women in Literature, the Short Story: A Collection

Sculptor's Funeral see Troll Garden

Sculptor's Funeral. unabr. ed. Willa Cather. Read by Walter Zimmerman. 1 cass. (Running Time: 82 min.). Dramatization. 1977. 7.95 (N-14) Jimcin Record.
The tragedy of sensitive people in a callous world.

Sculptress. abr. ed. Minette Walters. Read by Sandra Burr. 2 cass. (Running Time: 3 hrs.). 2000. 7.95 (978-1-57815-023-6(X), 1007, Media Bks Audio) Media Bks NJ.
A woman accepts commission to write a book about a mysterious & elusive convicted female murderer.

Sculptress. unabr. ed. Minette Walters. Read by Sandra Burr. (Running Time: 10 hrs.). 2009. 39.97 (978-1-4233-8346-8(X), 9781423383468, Brlnc Audio MP3 Lib); 39.97 (978-1-4233-8348-2(6), 9781423383482, BADLE); 24.99 (978-1-4233-8345-1(1), 9781423383451, Brilliance MP3); 24.99 (978-1-4233-8347-5(8), 9781423383475, BAD) Brilliance Audio.

***Scumble.** Ingrid Law. (ENG.). 2010. audio compact disk 29.95 (978-0-14-242814-6(0), PengAudBks) Penguin Grp USA.

***Scumbuster.** Tim Winton. Read by Stig Wemyss. (Running Time: 3 hrs.). (Lockie Leonard Ser.). (YA). 2009. 39.99 (978-1-74214-358-3(X), 9781742143583) Pub: Bolinda Pubng AUS. Dist(s): Bolinda Pub Inc

Scurvy: How a Surgeon, a Mariner, & a Gentleman Solved the Greatest Medical Mystery of the Age of Sail. unabr. ed. Stephen R. Bown. Read by Dan Cashman. 6 cass. (Running Time: 9 hrs.). 2004. 29.95 (978-1-59007-555-5(2)); audio compact disk 45.00 (978-1-59007-556-2(0)) Pub: New Millenn Enter. Dist(s): PerseuPGW

Se Deshabituer. unabr. ed. Robert A. Monroe. Read by Roland Simon. 1 cass. (Running Time: 30 min.). (Human Plus Ser.). (FRE.). 1993. 14.95 (978-1-56102-061-4(3)) Inter Indus.
Diminish & release detrimental physical, mental & emotional patterns or habits.

Se Escucha la LLuvia. Voice by Vino Nuevo Grupo alabanza. Prod. by Vino Nuevo. (SPA.). 2002. 7.99 (978-1-885630-68-1(9)) Jayah Producc.

Se Escucha la Lluvia. Voice by Vino Nuevo Grupo de Alabanza. (SPA.). 2002. audio compact disk 12.99 (978-1-885630-69-8(7)) Jayah Producc.

Se Oirá Otra Vez. unabr. ed. Musica Mesianica. 2002. audio compact disk 9.99 (978-0-8297-3362-4(0)) Zondervan.

Se Oirá Otra Vez. unabr. ed. Mesianic Musica. (SPA.). 2002. 9.99 (978-0-8297-3364-8(7)) Pub: Vida Pubs. Dist(s): Zondervan

Se Revigorer. unabr. ed. Robert A. Monroe. Read by Roland Simon. 1 cass. (Running Time: 30 min.). (Human Plus Ser.). (FRE.). 1993. 14.95 (978-1-56102-073-7(7)) Inter Indus.
Immediately restore high energy levels.

Se Transformer. unabr. ed. Robert A. Monroe. Read by Roland Simon. 1 cass. (Running Time: 30 min.). (Human Plus Ser.). (FRE.). 1993. 14.95 (978-1-56102-070-6(2)) Inter Indus.
Plan or change your personal reality.

Se Venden Gorras. Esphyr Slobodkina. Illus. by Esphyr Slobodkina. 11 vols. (Running Time: 10 mins.). 1999. bk. 28.95 (978-1-59519-195-3(X)); pap. bk. 39.95 (978-1-59519-194-6(1)); 9.95 (978-0-87499-515-2(9)); audio compact disk 12.95 (978-1-59519-192-2(5)) Live Oak Media.

Se Venden Gorras. Esphyr Slobodkina. Illus. by Esphyr Slobodkina. 11 vols. (Running Time: 10 mins.). (SPA.). (J). 1999. pap. bk. 18.95 (978-1-59519-193-9(3)) Pub: Live Oak Media. Dist(s): AudioGO

Se Venden Gorras. unabr. ed. Read by Esphyr Slobodkina & Angel Pineda. Tr. by Teresa Mlawer from ENG. Illus. by Esphyr Slobodkina. 11 vols. (Running Time: 10 mins.). (SPA., (J). (gr. k-3). 1999. bk. 25.95 (978-0-87499-513-8(2)); pap. bk. 16.95 (978-0-87499-512-1(4), LK3259) Pub: Live Oak Media. Dist(s): AudioGO
Cap salesman awakens from a nap to find his wares have disappeared.

Se Venden Gorras. unabr. ed. Read by Esphyr Slobodkina & Angel Pineda. Tr. by Teresa Mlawer. 14 vols. (Running Time: 10 mins.). (SPA., (J). (gr. k-3). 1999. pap. bk. & tchr. ed. 37.95 Reading Chest. (978-0-87499-514-5(0)) Live Oak Media.

Sea. unabr. ed. John Banville. Read by John Lee. 6 CDs. (Running Time: 21600 sec.). (ENG.). 2006. audio compact disk 29.95 (978-0-7393-3377-8(1), Random AudioBks) Pub: Random Audio Pubg. Dist(s): Random

Sea: A Timeless Procession of Ocean Waves. 1 cass. (Running Time: 1 hr.). 1992. 9.95 (978-1-55961-164-0(2)) Relaxtn Co.

Sea & Islands. unabr. ed. Hammond Innes. Read by Larry McKeever. 8 cass. (Running Time: 12 hrs.). 1987. 64.00 (978-0-7366-1231-9(9), 2149) Books on Tape.
A record of the travels of Innes & his wife on their yacht, to Scandinavia, Greece, Turkey, & the Indian Ocean.

Sea & Sardinia. unabr. collector's ed. D. H. Lawrence. Read by Richard Brown. 7 cass. (Running Time: 10 hrs. 30 mins.). 1989. 56.00 (978-0-7366-1601-0(2), 2462) Books on Tape.
D. H. Lawrence's importance to 20th-century literature extends beyond his achievement as a novelist: his uncompromising moral vision, his fierce puritanism, his vigorous devotion to the natural man defined a character in many ways more intense than those he created in fiction. In Sea & Sardinia, this character stands revealed against the stoney background of Sardinia. The island's hard & independent people, its little inns, the unique costumes & character of each village, come to sharp & vivid life through Lawrence's prose.

Sea & the Jungle. unabr. ed. H. M. Tomlinson. Read by Frederick Davidson. 8 cass. (Running Time: 11 hrs. 30 mins.). 1996. 56.95 (978-0-7861-0964-7(5), 1741) Blckstn Audio.
One rainy morning in the winter of 1909 a man with an altogether average look about him up & quit his job at the "London Morning Leader," kissed his wife & children goodbye & took a train to Swansea in Wales, where he talked his way aboard a freighter bound for somewhere in the upper reaches of the Amazon. Three years later Tomlinson published a book about his adventures. And the book made him famous.

Sea & the Jungle. unabr. ed. H. M. Tomlinson. Read by Frederick Davidson. (Running Time: 10 hrs. 5 mins.). 2009. 29.95 (978-1-4332-7042-0(0)); audio compact disk 90.00 (978-1-4332-7039-0(0)) Blckstn Audio.

Sea & the Jungle. unabr. ed. H. M. Tomlinson. Narrated by Ron Keith. 9 cass. (Running Time: 12 hrs. 30 mins.). 1991. 78.00 (978-1-55690-461-5(4), 91228E7) Recorded Bks.
An account of the author's journey to & into the Amazon Jungle in 1909.

Sea Break. unabr. ed. Antony Trew. Read by Peter Wickham. 8 cass. (Soundings Ser.). 2007. 69.95 (978-1-84559-391-9(X)) Pub: ISIS Lrg Prnt GBR. Dist(s): Ulverscroft US

Sea Burial from the Cruiser Reve see Richard Eberhart Reading His Poetry

Sea Change. unabr. ed. Robert Goddard. Read by Paul Shelley. 10 CDs. (Running Time: 15 hrs.). 2002. audio compact disk 94.95 (978-0-7540-5442-9(X), CCD 133) AudioGO.
The novel concerns the pursuit of a mysterious ledger whose contents could destroy the powerful and very likely overturn a monarchy.

Sea Change. unabr. ed. Robert Goddard. Read by Paul Shelley. 10 cass. (Running Time: 12 hrs.). 2001. 84.95 (978-0-7540-0680-0(8), CAB 2102) Pub: Chivers Audio Bks GBR. Dist(s): AudioGO
It's January, 1921. London is reeling from the effects of the greatest financial scandal of the age, the collapse of the South Sea Bubble. William Spandrel, a penniless mapmaker, is offered a discharge of his debts by his principal creditor, Sir Theodore Janssen, a director of the South Sea Company, on one condition: he must secretly convey an important package to Janssen's friend. The package safely delivered, spandrel barely survives an attempt on his life, only to be blamed for a murder...,.

Sea Change. unabr. ed. Robert B. Parker. 4 cass. (Running Time: 6 hrs.). (Jesse Stone Ser.: No. 5). 2006. 36.00 (978-1-4159-2751-9(0)); audio compact disk 45.00 (978-1-4159-2752-6(9)) Books on Tape.

***Sea Change: A Novel.** unabr. ed. Jeremy Page. (Running Time: 9.5 hrs. NaN mins.). (ENG.). 2010. 29.95 (978-1-4417-7371-5(1)); 59.95 (978-1-4417-7368-5(1)); audio compact disk 29.95 (978-1-4417-7370-8(3)); audio compact disk 90.00 (978-1-4417-7369-2(X)) Blckstn Audio.

Sea Change: Alone Across the Atlantic in a Wooden Boat. collector's ed. Peter Nichols. Read by Barrett Whitener. 6 cass. (Running Time: 9 hrs.). 1999. 29.95 (978-0-7366-4436-5(9)) Books on Tape.
A solo transatlantic passage that becomes a poignant personal voyage of sea & the self.

Sea Change Pt. 1: Alone Across the Atlantic in a Wooden Boat. unabr. collector's ed. Peter Nichols. Read by Barrett Whitener. 6 cass. (Running Time: 9 hrs.). 1998. 48.00 (978-0-7366-4102-9(5), 4607) Books on Tape.

Sea Coming Indoors see Poetry & Voice of Marilyn Hacker

Sea Drift see Twentieth-Century Poetry in English, No. 17, Walt Whitman Speaks for Himself

Sea el Factor de Cambio En Su Trabajo. Carlos Cuauhtemoc Sanchez. audio compact disk 15.95 (978-968-7277-58-5(0)) Pub: EdSelect MEX. Dist(s): Giron Bks

***Sea Escape: A Novel.** unabr. ed. Lynne Griffin. (Running Time: 9 hrs. 0 mins.). 2010. 15.99 (978-1-4001-8798-0(2)) Tantor Media.

***Sea Escape: A Novel.** unabr. ed. Lynne Griffin. Narrated by Tavia Gilbert. (Running Time: 8 hrs. 30 mins. 0 sec.). (ENG.). 2010. 24.99 (978-1-4001-6798-2(1)); audio compact disk 34.99 (978-1-4001-1798-7(4)); audio compact disk 83.99 (978-1-4001-4798-4(0)) Pub: Tantor Media. Dist(s): IngramPubServ

Sea Fairies, unabr. ed. L. Frank Baum. Read by Flo Gibson. 3 cass. (Running Time: 4 hrs.). (J). (gr. 2-4). 1997. 16.95 (978-1-55685-554-2(0)) Audio Bk Con.
Cap'n Bill & Trot join the mermaids under the sea where they meet many strange creatures & have exciting adventures.

***Sea Fangs.** L. Ron Hubbard. Read by Gino Montesinos et al. Narrated by R. F. Daley. 2 CDs. (Running Time: 1 hr. 20 mins.). (Stories from the Golden Age Ser.). (YA). 2010. audio compact disk 9.95 (978-1-59212-223-3(X)) Gala Pr LLC.

Sea Fever. Antony Trew. 2009. 61.95 (978-1-4079-0467-2(1)); audio compact disk 71.95 (978-1-4079-0468-9(X)) Pub: Soundings Ltd GBR. Dist(s): Ulverscroft US

Sea Fury. unabr. ed. James Pattinson. 5 cass. (Soundings Ser.). (J). 2006. 49.95 (978-1-84559-118-2(6)) Pub: ISIS Lrg Prnt GBR. Dist(s): Ulverscroft US

Sea Fury. unabr. ed. James Pattinson. Read by Peter Wickham. 6 CDs. (Running Time: 21600 sec.). (Soundings (CDs) Ser.). 2006. audio compact disk 64.95 (978-1-84559-144-1(5)) Pub: ISIS Lrg Prnt GBR. Dist(s): Ulverscroft US

Sea Garden. unabr. ed. Sam Llewellyn. Read by Gareth Armstrong. 10 cass. (Running Time: 13 hrs. 14 min.). (Isis Ser.). (J). 2001. 84.95 (978-0-7531-0832-1(1)) Pub: ISIS Lrg Prnt GBR. Dist(s): Ulverscroft US

When Victoria and Guy Jones inherit the tiny Cornish island of Trelise, they look on the restoration of the island's famous garden as a wonderful challenge. But as restoration begins, a skeleton is uncovered. Determined to find out whom the bones really belong to, Victoria begins to unravel a tormented family history that reaches back through five generations and discovers a secret that could do much more than shatter the island's idyllic charm.

Sea Garden. unabr. ed. Sam Llewellyn. Read by Gareth Armstrong. 4 CDs. (Running Time: 13 hrs. 14 min.). (Isis Ser.). (J). 2001. audio compact disk 51.95 (978-0-7531-1323-3(6)) Pub: ISIS Lrg Prnt GBR. Dist(s): Ulverscroft US

Sea Garden. unabr. ed. Sam Llewellyn. Read by Daniel Philpott & Gareth Armstrong. 12 CDs. (Isis Ser.). (J). 2001. audio compact disk 99.95 (978-0-7531-1321-9(X)) Pub: ISIS Lrg Prnt GBR. Dist(s): Ulverscroft US

Sea Glass. abr. ed. Anita Shreve. Read by Kyra Sedgwick. (ENG.). 2005. 14.98 (978-1-59483-262-8(5)) Pub: Hachet Audio. Dist(s): HachBkGrp

Sea Glass. unabr. ed. Anita Shreve. Read by Judith Ann Gantly. (ENG.). 2005. 16.98 (978-1-59483-390-8(7)) Pub: Hachet Audio. Dist(s): HachBkGrp

Sea Glass. unabr. ed. Anita Shreve. Read by Judith Ann Gantly. (Running Time: 9 hrs.). (ENG.). 2009. 49.98 (978-1-60788-091-2(1)) Pub: Hachet Audio. Dist(s): HachBkGrp

Sea Grieves see Poetry & Voice of Ted Hughes

Sea Gull. Anton Chekhov. Narrated by Flo Gibson. 2 cass. (Running Time: 2 hrs. 30 min.). 2001. 20.95 Audio Bk Con.

Konstantin Treplov's literary ambitions and his love for a young aspiring actress evade him. When Nina runs off with his mother's lover, the successful author Trigirin, he attempts suicide and compares himself to a dead seagull destroyed by a man's whim.

Sea Gull. unabr. ed. Anton Chekhov. Narrated by Flo Gibson. 2 cass. (Running Time: 2 hrs. 10 mins.). (gr. 10 up). 2002. 14.95 (978-1-55685-684-6(9),) Audio Bk Con.

Konstantin Treplov's literary ambitions & his love for a young aspiring actress evade him. When Nina runs off with his mother's lover, he attempts suicide & compares himself to a dead sea gull destroyed by a man's whim.

Sea Gulls: Music for Rest & Relaxation. Perf. by Hap Palmer. 1 cass. (J). 11.95 (EA 584C); lp 11.95 (EA 584) Kimbo Educ.

Savannah - Misty Canyon - Summer Rain & more.

Sea-Hawk see Richard Eberhart Reading His Poetry

Sea-Hawk. Rafael Sabatini. Read by John Bolen. (Running Time: 11 hrs. 30 mins.). 2002. 29.95 (978-1-60083-607-7(0), Audiofy Corp) Iofy Corp.

Sea-Hawk. Rafael Sabatini. Read by John Bolen. (ENG.). 2005. audio compact disk 96.00 (978-1-4001-3036-8(0)) Pub: Tantor Media. Dist(s): IngramPubServ

Sea-Hawk. unabr. ed. Rafael Sabatini. Narrated by John Bolen. 10 CDs. (Running Time: 11 hrs. 27 mins.). (ENG.). 2002. audio compact disk 48.00 (978-1-4001-0036-1(4)); audio compact disk 23.00 (978-1-4001-5036-6(1)) Pub: Tantor Media. Dist(s): IngramPubServ

Sea-Hawk. unabr. ed. Rafael Sabatini. Narrated by John Bolen. (Running Time: 11 hrs. 30 mins. 0 sec.). (ENG.). 2009. audio compact disk 22.99 (978-1-4001-6087-7(1)); audio compact disk 65.99 (978-1-4001-4087-9(0)) Pub: Tantor Media. Dist(s): IngramPubServ

Sea-Hawk. unabr. ed. Rafael Sabatini. Read by John Bolen. Narrated by John Bolen. (Running Time: 11 hrs. 30 mins. 0 sec.). (ENG.). 2009. audio compact disk 32.99 (978-1-4001-1087-2(4)) Pub: Tantor Media. Dist(s): IngramPubServ

Sea Hunters: True Adventures with Famous Shipwrecks, unabr. ed. Clive Cussler & Craig Dirgo. Read by Michael Prichard. 9 cass. (Running Time: 13 hrs. 30 min.). 1997. 72.00 (978-0-913369-58-6(6), 4282) Books on Tape.

Cussler tells of his lifelong love for the sea & ships & his dedication to the discovery & preservation of historic shipwrecks. After opening each story with a creative dramatization of a shipwreck, he then brings the story into the present by describing the immense research so often necessary to find a long lost ship.

Sea Hunters II: More True Adventures with Famous Shipwrecks. Clive Cussler & Craig Dirgo. 2002. 88.00 (978-0-7366-8933-5(8)); audio compact disk 104.00 (978-0-7366-8934-2(6)) Books on Tape.

Sea Lion Roars. C. Drew Lamm. 1 cass. (Running Time: 35 min.). (J). (ps-2). 2001. bk. 19.95 (SP 4013C) Kimbo Educ.

On his 1st birthday, Sea Lion departs from his rookery for San Francisco. Includes book.

Sea Lion Roars. C. Drew Lamm. Read by Peter Thomas. Illus. by Joel Snyder. Narrated by Peter Thomas. 1 cass. (Running Time: 13 min.). (Smithsonian Oceanic Collection). (J). (ps-2). 1997. 5.00 (978-1-56899-402-4(8), C4013) Soundprints.

Sea Lion leaves his rookery for San Francisco. All is well until he becomes entangled in a fishing net. Rescue is certain, but his future is not!.

Sea Monsters & other Delicacies: An Awfully Beastly Business Book Two. unabr. ed. David Sinden et al. Read by Gerard Doyle. (Running Time: 2 hrs. 30 mins. 0 sec.). (Awfully Beastly Business Ser.). (ENG.). (J). 2009. audio compact disk 19.99 (978-0-7435-8378-7(7)) Pub: S&S Audio. Dist(s): S and S Inc

Sea Music. unabr. ed. Sara MacDonald. 10 cass. (Running Time: 14 hrs. 38 mins.). (Isis Cassettes Ser.). (J). 2004. 84.95 (978-0-7531-1856-6(4)) Pub: ISIS Lrg Prnt GBR. Dist(s): Ulverscroft US

The house opposite the church, overlooking the Cornish coast, is home to three generations of Tremains. Fred Tremain came to this corner of England with his wife, Martha and their children, Anna, a successful lawyer and Barnaby, a clergyman to the parish. Also there is Kate, their beloved granddaughter, whose discoveries of hidden family papers unearths the first of the long-buried wartime secrets.

Sea Music. unabr. ed. Sara MacDonald. Read by Jilly Bond. 13 CDs. (Running Time: 14 hrs. 38 mins.). (Isis (CDs) Ser.). (J). 2006. audio compact disk 99.95 (978-0-7531-2501-4(3)) Pub: ISIS Lrg Prnt GBR. Dist(s): Ulverscroft US

Sea of Dreams. Susan Sallis. Read by Judith Porter. 10 CDs. (Running Time: 10 hrs.). 2001. audio compact disk (978-1-84283-119-9(4)) Soundings Ltd GBR.

Holly and Mark Jepson have always spent Christmas helping Uncle Reg with the guests in his holiday chalets on the Somerset coast. But this year Reg has to go into hospital, leaving Holly and Mark to welcome the motley assortment of guests - three elderly ladies, a clutch of children, an eccentric artist and his handsome daughter (but is she really his daughter?), a young married couple expecting their first baby (to the secret envy of childless Holly), and a wife escaping from a violent past. Each of them will play a part in the unexpected and at times shattering events which take place before the new millennium dawns. This is a magical story from this greatly-loved bestselling author, who is now firmly established as one of the most successful writers of contemporary family novels.

Sea of Dreams. unabr. ed. Susan Sallis. Read by Judith Porter. 10 cass. (Running Time: 10 hrs. 23 mins.). (Sound Ser.). (J). 2002. 84.95 (978-1-84283-047-5(3)) Pub: ISIS Lrg Prnt GBR. Dist(s): Ulverscroft US

Sea of Glory. abr. ed. Ken Wales & David Poling. Read by David Poling. 6 cass. (Running Time: 8 hrs.). 2001. 30.00 (978-1-58807-073-9(5)) Am Pubng Inc.

In the early morning hours of February 3, 1943, the American troop ship Dorchester is torpedoed by a German submarine en route to a top-secret radar installation in Greenland. The four Army chaplains on board could scarcely be more different from each other: Methodist pastor and WWI veteran George Fox; intellectual and athletic Rabbi Alex Goode; scholar, poet, and Dutch Reformed minister Clark Poling; baseball fan and "regular guy" Father John Washington. Yet in the terror and confusion following the attack by a deadly U-boat wolfpack, the chaplains unite in a final, triumphant sacrifice that transforms the life of every survivor who sees it - and inspires Sergeant Wesley Adams to exchange the bitterness of the past for the promise of the future.

Sea of Glory. unabr. ed. David Poling & Ken Wales. 6 vols. 2001. (978-1-58807-583-3(4)) Am Pubng Inc.

Sea of Glory: America's Voyage of Discovery, the U. S. Exploring Expedition, 1838-1842. abr. ed. Nathaniel Philbrick. Read by Dennis Boutsikaris. (Running Time: 6 hrs.). (ENG.). (gr. 12 up). 2006. audio compact disk 14.95 (978-0-14-305883-0(5), PengAudBks) Penguin Grp USA.

Sea of Glory: America's Voyage of Discovery, The U.S. Exploring Expedition, 1838-1842. unabr. ed. Nathaniel Philbrick. Read by Scott Brick. 10 CDs. (Running Time: 13 hrs. 12 min.). 2003. audio compact disk 79.20 (978-0-7366-9604-3(0)) Books on Tape.

An 1842 expedition charts the waters of the Pacific. Just as Lewis and Clark explored the American West, the 1842 expedition led by controversial lieutenant Charles Wilkes charted the waters of the Pacific Ocean. Comprised of six sailing vessels and 346 men, the Ex Ex represented the largest voyage of discovery in the history of the world.

Sea of Glory: America's Voyage of Discovery, The U.S. Exploring Expedition, 1838-1842. unabr. ed. Nathaniel Philbrick. Read by Scott Brick. 9 cass. (Running Time: 13 hrs. 30 min.). 2003. 64.80 (978-0-7366-9603-6(2)) Books on Tape.

Sea of Grass, unabr. ed. Conrad Richter. Narrated by Norman Dietz. 3 cass. (Running Time: 3 hrs. 45 mins.). (gr. 8 up). 1997. 27.00 (978-1-55690-615-2(3), 92308E7) Recorded Bks.

A vibrant tale of a great cattle ranch, a beautiful woman & a man determined to preserve the wild frontier. An authentic historical portrait of how the American West was transformed in the 1800s.

Sea of Monsters. unabr. ed. Rick Riordan. Read by Jesse Berns. 7 CDs. (Running Time: 7 hrs. 56 mins.). (Percy Jackson & the Olympians Ser.: Bk. 2). (J). (gr. 4-7). 2006. audio compact disk 46.75 (978-0-7393-3587-1(1), Listening Lib); 40.00 (978-0-7393-3586-4(3), Listening Lib) Pub: Random Audio Pubg. Dist(s): Random

Percy Jackson's seventh-grade year has been surprisingly quiet. Not a single monster has set foot on his New York prepschool campus. But when an innocent game of dodgeball among Percy and his classmates turns into a death match against an ugly gang of cannibal giants, things get - well, ugly. And the unexpected arrival of Percy's friend Annabeth brings more bad news: the magical borders that protect Camp Half-Blood have been poisoned by a mysterious enemy, and unless a cure is found, the only safe haven for demigods will be destroyed.

Sea of Monsters. unabr. ed. Rick Riordan. Read by Jesse Berns. 7 CDs. (Running Time: 28560 sec.). (Percy Jackson & the Olympians Ser.: Bk. 2). (ENG.). (J). (gr. 5-9). 2006. audio compact disk 37.00 (978-0-7393-3119-4(1), Listening Lib) Pub: Random Audio Pubg. Dist(s): Random

Sea of Poppies. unabr. ed. Amitav Ghosh. Read by Phil Gigante. (Running Time: 18 hrs.). (Ibis Ser.). 2008. 44.25 (978-1-4233-7379-7(0), 9781423373797, BADLE); 29.95 (978-1-4233-7378-0(2), 9781423373780, BAD); 44.25 (978-1-4233-7377-3(4), 9781423373773, Brinc Audio MP3 Lib); 29.95 (978-1-4233-7376-6(6), 9781423373766, Brilliance MP3); audio compact disk 122.97 (978-1-4233-7375-9(8), 9781423373759, BriAudCD Unabrid); audio compact disk 42.99 (978-1-4233-7374-2(X), 9781423373742, Bril Audio CD Unabri) Brilliance Audio.

Sea of Poppies Book Three. unabr. ed. Amitav Ghosh. (Running Time: 12 hrs.). (Ibis Ser.). 2012. 24.99 (978-1-4233-7390-2(1), 9781423373902, Brilliance MP3); 24.99 (978-1-4233-7392-6(8), 9781423373926, BAD); 39.97 (978-1-4233-7391-9(X), 9781423373919, Brinc Audio MP3 Lib); 39.97 (978-1-4233-7393-3(6), 9781423373933, BADLE); audio compact disk 38.25 (978-1-4233-7388-9(X), 9781423373889, Bril Audio CD Unabri); audio compact disk 92.97 (978-1-4233-7389-6(8), 9781423373896, BriAudCD Unabrid) Brilliance Audio.

Sea of Poppies Book Two. unabr. ed. Amitav Ghosh. (Running Time: 12 hrs.). (Ibis Ser.). 2010. 24.99 (978-1-4233-7383-4(9), 9781423373834, Brilliance MP3); 24.99 (978-1-4233-7385-8(5), 9781423373858, BAD); 39.97 (978-1-4233-7384-1(7), 9781423373841, Brinc Audio MP3 Lib); 39.97 (978-1-4233-7386-5(3), 9781423373865, BADLE); audio compact disk 38.99 (978-1-4233-7381-0(2), 9781423373810, Bril Audio CD Unabri); audio compact disk 92.97 (978-1-4233-7382-7(0), 9781423373827, BriAudCD Unabrid) Brilliance Audio.

Sea of Thunder: Four Commanders & the Last Great Naval Campaign 1941-1945. Evan Thomas. Read by George K. Wilson. (Running Time: 56700 sec.). 2006. audio compact disk 39.99 (978-1-4281-1183-7(2)) Recorded Bks.

Sea of Trolls. Nancy Farmer. Narrated by Gerard Doyle. 10 cass. (Running Time: 14 hrs.). (Sea of Trolls Trilogy: No. 1). (J). 2004. 88.75 (978-1-4193-0820-8(3)); audio compact disk 97.75 (978-1-4193-2090-3(4)) Recorded Bks.

Sea of Trolls. unabr. ed. Nancy Farmer. 11 CDs. (Running Time: 12 hrs.). (Sea of Trolls Trilogy: No. 1). 2004. audio compact disk 29.99 (978-1-4025-9344-4(9), 01742) Recorded Bks.

One of the most acclaimed children's authors in the world, Nancy Farmer won the National Book Award for The House of the Scorpion and has also earned several Newbery Honors. In The Sea of Trolls, this master storyteller crafts the tale of Jack, an apprentice bard, and his little sister, who are captured by Viking chief Olaf One-Brow and taken to the court of Ivar the Boneless. From there, they are sent on a perilous journey deep into the magical kingdom of the trolls!.

Sea Road West. Sally Rena. 5 cass. (Running Time: 6 hrs.). (Soundings Ser.). (J). 2005. 49.95 (978-1-84283-812-9(1)) Pub: ISIS Lrg Prnt GBR. Dist(s): Ulverscroft US

Sea Runners. unabr. collector's ed. Ivan Doig. Read by Paul Shay. 8 cass. (Running Time: 8 hrs.). 1987. 48.00 (978-0-7366-1227-2(0), 2145) Books on Tape.

Adventure story, set in the 19th century, of four serfs who escape from the Czar's Russia by canoe.

Sea Serpent Chantey see Poetry of Vachel Lindsay

Sea Serpent's Birthday Present. Steve J. Gall. Illus. by Pepper Hume. (J). 2002. pap. bk. 10.00 (978-1-931457-14-9(X)) Stargate Electronic.

Sea Star: Orphan of Chincoteague, unabr. ed. Marguerite Henry. Narrated by John McDonough. 3 pieces. (Running Time: 3 hrs. 45 mins.). (gr. 3 up). 2000. 30.00 (978-0-7887-3819-7(4), 95803E7) Recorded Bks.

Near Chincoteague, Paul & Maureen rescue a drowning newborn foal. They are delighted when their frisky pony appears in a popular children's book. But now movie makers want to buy her & take her away! This beguiling tale is based on real Maryland people & animals.

Sea Star: Orphan of Chincoteague, unabr. ed. Marguerite Henry. Read by John McDonough. 3 cass. (Running Time: 3 hrs. 45 mins.). (J). 2000. pap. bk. & stu. ed. 42.75 (978-0-7887-3853-1(4), 41051X4) Recorded Bks.

Sea Star: Orphan of Chincoteague, Class Set. unabr. ed. Marguerite Henry. Read by John McDonough. 3 cass. (Running Time: 3 hrs. 45 mins.). (YA). (gr. 3). 1999. 95.80 (978-0-7887-3879-1(8), 47045) Recorded Bks.

Sea Swept. Nora Roberts. Read by David Stuart. (Chesapeake Bay Ser.: Bk. 1). 2008. 69.99 (978-1-60640-807-0(0)) Find a World.

Sea Swept. abr. ed. Nora Roberts. Read by David Stuart. (Running Time: 3 hrs.). (Chesapeake Bay Ser.: Bk. 1). 2005. audio compact disk 62.25 (978-1-59600-088-9(0), 9781596000889, BACDLib Ed) Brilliance Audio.

A champion boat racer, Cameron Quinn traveled the world spending his winnings on champagne and women. But when his dying father calls him home to care for Seth, a troubled young boy not unlike Cameron once was, his life changes overnight. . . After years of independence, Cameron has to learn to live with his brothers again, while he struggles with cooking, cleaning, and caring for a difficult boy. Old rivalries and new resentments flare between Cameron and his brothers, but they try to put aside their differences for Seth's sake. In the end, a social worker, as tough as she is beautiful, will decide Seth's fate. She has the power to bring the Quinns together - or tear them apart. . .

Sea Swept. abr. rev. ed. Nora Roberts. Read by David Stuart. (Running Time: 3 hrs.). (Chesapeake Bay Ser.: Bk. 1). 2005. audio compact disk 14.99 (978-1-59600-087-2(2), 9781596000872) Brilliance Audio.

Sea Swept. unabr. ed. Nora Roberts. Read by David Stuart. 8 cass. (Running Time: 10 hrs.). (Chesapeake Bay Ser.: Bk. 1). 1998. 73.25 (978-1-56740-557-6(6), 1567405576, Unabridge Lib Edns) Brilliance Audio.

Sea Swept. unabr. ed. Nora Roberts. Read by David Stuart. (Running Time: 10 hrs.). (Chesapeake Bay Ser.: Bk. 1). 2005. 24.95 (978-1-59335-792-4(3), 9781593357924, Brilliance MP3); 39.25 (978-1-59710-672-6(0), 9781597106726, BADLE); 24.95 (978-1-59710-673-3(9), 9781597106733, BAD); 29.95 (978-1-59600-086-5(4), 9781596000865, BAU); 39.25 (978-1-59335-926-3(8), 9781593359263, Brinc Audio MP3 Lib) Brilliance Audio.

Sea Swept. unabr. ed. Nora Roberts. Read by David Stuart. (Running Time: 11 hrs.). (Chesapeake Bay Ser.: Bk. 1). 2008. audio compact disk 97.25 (978-1-4233-5646-2(2), 9781423356462, BriAudCD Unabrid); audio compact disk 36.95 (978-1-4233-5645-5(4), 9781423356455, Bril Audio CD Unabri) Brilliance Audio.

Sea Turtle Journey. 1 cass. (Running Time: 35 min.). (J). (gr. k-4). 2001. 19.95 (SP 4007C) Kimbo Educ.

Sea Turtle Journey: The Story of a Loggerhead Turtle. Lorraine A. Jay. Read by Peter Thomas. Illus. by Katie Lee. 1 cass. (Running Time: 1 hr.). (Smithsonian Oceanic Collection). (J). (ps-2). 1995. bk. 5.00 (978-1-56899-194-8(0), C4007) Soundprints.

Dozens of tiny loggerhead turtles thrash their way to the surface of a Florida beach. To escape the raccoons & ghost crabs, Loggerhead rushes to the ocean's edge to begin her journey far out to sea. She grows bigger & stronger after many years in the ocean. But her large body is no match for an abandoned fishing line that tangles her flippers. Such perils & adventures are captured in this exciting story of a loggerhead's mysterious ocean journey, only to return to the beach where she was born.

Sea Turtles. 1 cass. (Running Time: 35 min.). (J). (ps-4). 2001. bk. 15.95 (VX-583C) Kimbo Educ.

A variety of sea turtles are shown & their similarities & differences highlighted. Humans are presented as predators & protectors. Includes book.

Sea Turtles. 9.95 (978-1-59112-178-7(7)) Live Oak Media.

Sea Turtles. Gail Gibbons. Illus. by Gail Gibbons. 11 vols. (Running Time: 18 mins.). 1999. bk. 28.95 (978-1-59519-078-9(3)); pap. bk. 39.95 (978-1-59519-077-2(5)) Live Oak Media.

Sea Turtles. Gail Gibbons. Illus. by Gail Gibbons. 11 vols. (Running Time: 18 mins.). (J). 1999. pap. bk. 18.95 (978-1-59519-076-5(7)) Pub: Live Oak Media. Dist(s): AudioGO

Sea Turtles. Gail Gibbons. Illus. by Gail Gibbons. (Running Time: 18 mins.). (J). (gr. k-3). 1999. 9.95 (978-0-87499-582-4(5)); audio compact disk 12.95 (978-1-59519-075-8(9)) Live Oak Media.

Sea Turtles. unabr. ed. Gail Gibbons. Illus. by Gail Gibbons. Read by Paula Parker. 11 vols. (Running Time: 18 mins.). (Gail Gibbons' Creatures Great & Small Ser.). (J). (gr. 1-6). 1999. pap. bk. 16.95 (978-0-87499-583-1(3)) AudioGO.

Introduces sea turtles in an understandable manner suitable for young readers. Shows a variety of sea turtle species & their similarities & differences are highlighted. Humans are presented both as predators gathering turtle eggs & protectors standing watch over egg-hatching beaches.

Sea Turtles. unabr. ed. Gail Gibbons. Illus. by Gail Gibbons. Read by Paula Parker. 11 vols. (Running Time: 18 mins.). (Gail Gibbons' Creatures Great & Small Ser.). (J). (gr. 1-6). 1999. bk. 25.95 (978-0-87499-584-8(1)); pap. bk. & tchr. ed. 37.95 Reading Chest. (978-0-87499-581-7(7)) Live Oak Media.

Sea Was Our Village. unabr. ed. Miles Smeeton. Read by Bill Kelsey. 6 cass. (Running Time: 9 hrs.). 1991. 48.00 (978-0-7366-1936-3(4), 2758) Books on Tape.

Miles Smeeton is a byword among yachtsmen the world over. Born in 1906, educated at Wellington College, he joined the British Army & later transferred to the Indian Cavalry. In 1930 he married Beryl Boxer & together they attempted Tirich Mir in the Himalayas, where Beryl reached a height greater than any other woman had climbed at that time. So how was it that this soldier & his mountain-climbing wife took to the sea? This is their story, the story of a family with a great appetite for discovery. Their adventures, beautifully narrated, earned them the reputation of "first family of the sea".

Sea Wolf. Jack London. Narrated by Cindy Hardin. (Running Time: 10 hrs.). 2006. 19.95 (978-1-59912-377-6(0)) Iofy Corp.

Sea-Wolf, Jack London. Read by Arthur Addison. 8 cass. (Running Time: 11 hrs. 30 min.). 1995. 26.95 (978-1-55685-375-3(0)) Audio Bk Con.

At the center of this exciting sea adventure lies the epic battle between Humphrey Van Weyden, "Civilised man," & Wolf Larsen, London's blend of Milton's Lucifer, Melville's Ahab & Nietzsche's Superman. It is a Darwinian battle to determine who is fittest to survive; a battle for life, love & one man's soul.

Sea-Wolf. Jack London. Read by Brian Emerson. 7 cass. (Running Time: 10 hrs.30 mins.). 2000. 49.95 (978-0-7861-1833-5(4), 2632) Blckstn Audio.
Wolf Larsen, captain of the seal hunting Ghost, tormented by his convictions, was both fascinating & repellent to his reluctant crewman Humphrey Van Weyden. Throughout their long & perilous voyage together, the captain's ruthless belief in the survival of the fittest is pitted against Van Weyden's "civilization" a test between two opposing views of life.

Sea-Wolf. Jack London. Read by Garrick Hagon. 3 cass. (Running Time: 3 hrs. 30 mins.). 2002. 17.98 (978-962-634-751-5(1), NA325114); audio compact disk 22.98 (978-962-634-251-0(X), NA325112) Naxos.
Humphrey van Weyeden led a privileged existence during his early life, but suddenly finds himself cast into the sea, fighting for survival. Pitted against ruthless but educated captain Wolf Larsen, van Weyden's courage and determination allows him to fight adversity and learn valuable lessons along the way, in this American classic originally published in 1904.

Sea-Wolf. abr. ed. Jack London. Read by Stuart Whitman. 2 cass. (Running Time: 2 hrs. 53 min.). 2000. 15.95 (978-0-945353-47-8(2), F20000) Pub: Audio Partners. Dist(s): PerseuPGW
An American classic with a masterful performance that evokes the dramatic clash of safe, genteel comfort & a difficult set of circumstances.

Sea-Wolf. abr. ed. Jack London. Read by Stan Winiarski. Ed. by Marilyn Kay. 3 cass. (Running Time: 4 hrs. 30 min.). 1996. 15.95 (978-1-882071-08-1(5), 010) B-B Audio.
An epic of action-filled excitement. Rescued from drowning, a pampered gentleman awakens in a special kind of hell. Hes aboard the Ghost, a sailing schooner outbound for months of hunting. Wolf Larson, the devilish captain, a fiendish crew, the cruel.

Sea-Wolf. abr. ed. Jack London. Read by Will Patton. 4 cass. (Running Time: 6 hrs.). 2004. 25.00 (978-1-59007-137-3(9)) Pub: New Millenn Enter. Dist(s): PerseuPGW

Sea Wolf. abr. adpt. ed. Jack London. (Bring the Classics to Life: Level 3 Ser.). (ENG.). 2008. audio compact disk 12.95 (978-1-55576-477-7(0)) EDCON Pubng.

Sea Wolf. unabr. ed. Jack London. Read by Brian Emerson. (Running Time: 10 hrs.). 2000. 24.95 (978-0-7861-9362-2(X)) Blckstn Audio.

Sea Wolf. unabr. ed. Jack London. Read by Dick Hill. (Running Time: 10 hrs.). 2006. 39.25 (978-1-4233-1163-8(9), 9781423311638, BADLE); 24.95 (978-1-4233-1162-1(0), 9781423311621, BAD); audio compact disk 39.25 (978-1-4233-1161-4(2), 9781423311614, Brinc Audio MP3 Lib); audio compact disk 24.95 (978-1-4233-1160-7(4), 9781423311607, Brilliance MP3) Brilliance Audio.
"The danger lay in the heavy fog which blanketed the bay, and of which, as a landsman, I had little apprehension." This is the first line that the listener hears in this tale of a man uprooted and thrust into the unfamiliar and dangerous world of the sealing sailor. Humphrey Van Weyden, a San Francisco sophisticate and an intellectual finds himself the captive voyager aboard the Ghost, captained by the brutal and barbaric Wolf Larsen. The desperate character of Van Weyden's voyage is defined by the fact that he is out of his element, in unimaginable peril, and the slave of this cynical and wild soul, Larsen. The rights of man vanish as the coast of California vanishes over the horizon. Almost immediately, the slave plots his freedom - and must confront the weakness in his soul, mind and body. Generations have been spellbound by this harrowing story of danger on the sea, psychological confrontation, and the dual nature of humankind.

Sea Wolf. unabr. ed. Jack London. Narrated by Frank Muller. 6 cass. (Running Time: 9 hrs.). 1999. 51.00 (978-1-55690-462-2(2), 88230E7) Recorded Bks.
Wolf Larsen, captain of "The Ghost," seemed to have no other interest but life itself. And yet there was a magical attraction about this brutal man, some magnetism that hypnotized even as it repelled.

Sea-Wolf. unabr. ed. Jack London. Read by Brian Emerson. 9 CDs. (Running Time: 13 hrs. 30 min.). (J). (gr. 9-12). 2000. audio compact disk 72.00 (978-0-7861-9833-7(8), z2632) Blckstn Audio.
Capable of abandoning two sailors in an open boat, Wolf Larsen, captain of the seal hunting Ghost, was tormented by his own convictions, that made his enigma both fascinating & repellent to his reluctant crewman, Humphrey Van Weyden. Throughout their long & perilous voyage together, the captain's ruthless belief in the survival of the fittest is pitted against Van Weyden's "civilization" which was a test between two opposing views of life.

Sea-Wolf. unabr. ed. Jack London. Read by Patrick Treadway. 8 cass. (Running Time: 11 hrs.). 1989. 49.95 (978-1-55686-304-2(7), 304) Books in Motion.
A sea going soldier of fortune, Larsen is a strong independent anti-hero out to make a dollar any way he can.

Sea-Wolf. unabr. ed. Jack London. Read by John Chatty & Cindy Hardin. 7 cass. (Running Time: 10 hrs. 30 mins.). 1999. 56.00 (978-0-7366-3848-7(2), 9022) Books on Tape.
The struggle between two contrasting types, Wolf Larson & Humphrey Van Weyden. When Van Weyden's ship sinks in San Francisco Harbor, he is rescued by Larson, & is forced to serve as cook's scullion. Larson heads for the Bering Sea, where Van Weyden finds human cruelty is matched only by nature.

Sea-Wolf. unabr. ed. Jack London. Read by John Chatty & Cindy Hardin. 7 cass. (Running Time: 10 hrs.). 2001. 29.95 (978-0-7366-6775-3(X)) Books on Tape.
Brutality & magnificence on an ocean voyage to the Bering Sea.

Sea-Wolf. unabr. ed. Jack London. Read by Dick Hill. 9 CDS Library ed. (Running Time: 10 hrs.). (Classic Collection). 2001. audio compact disk 96.25 (978-1-58788-613-3(8), 1587886138, CD Unabrid Lib Ed); audio compact disk 37.95 (978-1-58788-612-6(X), 158788612X, CD Unabridged) Brilliance Audio.
"The danger lay in the heavy fog which blanketed the bay, and of which, as a landsman, I had little apprehension." This is the first line that the listener hears in this tale of a man uprooted and thrust into the unfamiliar and dangerous world of the sealing sailor. Humphrey Van Weyden, a San Francisco sophisticate and an intellectual finds himself the captive voyager aboard the Ghost, captained by the brutal and barbaric Wolf Larsen. The desperate character of Van Weyden's voyage is defined by the fact that he is out of his element, in unimaginable peril, and the slave of this cynical and wild soul, Larsen. The rights of man vanish as the coast of California vanishes over the horizon. Almost immediately, the slave plots his freedom - and must confront the weakness in his soul, mind and body. Generations have been spellbound by this harrowing story of danger on the sea, psychological confrontation, and the dual nature of humankind.

Sea-Wolf. unabr. ed. Jack London. Read by John Chatty & Cindy Hardin. 7 cass. (Running Time: 9 hrs. 30 min.). Dramatization. 1980. 39.00 (C-22) Jimcin Record.
The incredible saga of Wolf Larsen.

***Sea Wolf: Bring the Classics to Life.** adpt. ed. Jack London. (Bring the Classics to Life Ser.). 2008. pap. bk. 21.95 (978-1-55576-507-1(6)) EDCON Pubng.

Sea-Wolf & Other Selected Stories. collector's ed. Jack London. Read by John Edwardson. 10 cass. (Running Time: 15 hrs.). (J). 1999. 80.00 (978-0-7366-4817-2(8)) Books on Tape.
The struggle between two contrasting types, Wolf Larson & Humphrey Van Weyden. When Van Weyden's ship sinks in San Francisco Harbor, he is rescued by Larson & is forced to serve as cook's scullion. Larson heads for the Bering Sea, where Van Weyden finds human cruelty is matched only by nature.

Sea-Wolf & the Scarlet Plague. Jack London. 1 cass. (Running Time: 1 hr.). (Radiobook Ser.). 1987. 4.98 (978-0-929541-33-4(2)) Radiola Co.
Two complete stories.

SeaBabies... Clap-a-Long, Sing-a-Long. David G. Payton. Perf. by Kaleidascope Theatre Group. 1 cass. (Running Time: 20 min.). (J). (gr. k-6). 1997. 6.95 (978-0-9649745-5-5(X)); audio compact disk 11.95 CD. (978-0-9649745-6-2(8)) Cake & Candle.
Features 10 original songs which help to teach every land person the virtues of teamwork, responsibility, problem solving, caring, hard work & initiative, as well as the importance of keeping the oceans clean.

Seabiscuit. abr. ed. Laura Hillenbrand. Read by Campbell Scott. (YA). 2007. 39.99 (978-0-7393-7555-6(5)) Find a World.

Seabiscuit: An American Legend. abr. ed. Laura Hillenbrand. Read by Campbell Scott. (ENG.). 2010. audio compact disk 14.99 (978-0-7393-7083-4(9), Random AudioBks) Pub: Random Audio Pubg. Dist(s): Random

Seabiscuit: An American Legend. unabr. ed. Laura Hillenbrand. Narrated by Richard M. Davidson. 12 CDs. (Running Time: 13 hrs. 45 mins.). 2001. audio compact disk 116.00 (978-1-4025-0486-0(1), C1542) Recorded Bks.
Seabiscuit was a crooked little horse, built like a cinderblock, but there was something special about his attitude. In 1936, when a wealthy businessman, an aging trainer, and a destitute jockey focused their attention on Seabiscuit, they were astonished at the results. Despite heavy handicaps, Seabiscuit broke one track record after another. And despite the Great Depression, fans traveled hundreds of miles to see him.

Seabiscuit: An American Legend. unabr. ed. Laura Hillenbrand. Narrated by Richard M. Davidson. 10 cass. (Running Time: 13 hrs. 45 mins.). 2001. 94.00 (978-0-7887-9642-5(9), RF431) Recorded Bks.

Seabrooks' Gold. unabr. ed. G. M. Farley. Read by Jack Sondericker. 6 cass. (Running Time: 6 hrs. 15 min.). Dramatization. 1992. 39.95 (978-1-55686-450-6(7), 450) Books in Motion.
While sneaking along a creekbed in the middle of Ute Indian country, Charley Seabrook & his partner discovered gold. They hid the gold under a waterfall & drew a map before they were killed by the Indians. Later, a rancher & his sons have the map; they hope to get the gold before others do.

Seachran Si. Contrib. by Eamon O. Donnchadha. (ENG.). 1998. 13.95 (978-0-8023-7135-5(3)); audio compact disk 20.95 (978-0-8023-8135-4(9)) Pub: Clo Iar-Chonnachta IRL. Dist(s): Dufour

Seafarer see Caedmon Treasury of Modern Poets Reading Their Own Poetry

Seafaring I, Comb & Glass see Twentieth-Century Poetry in English, No. 26, Recordings of Poets Reading Their Own Poetry

Seafire. abr. ed. John E. Gardner. Read by Christopher Cazenove. 2 cass. (Running Time: 3 hrs.). 2001. 18.00 (978-1-59040-164-4(6), Phoenix Audio) Pub: Amer Intl Pub. Dist(s): PerseuPGW

Seafood Processing Equipment in India: A Strategic Reference 2007. Compiled by Icon Group International, Inc. Staff. 2007. ring bd. 195.00 (978-0-497-36022-1(5)) Icon Grp.

Seagull. Anton Chekhov. Narrated by Flo Gibson. (ENG.). 2007. audio compact disk 22.95 (978-1-55685-975-5(9)); audio compact disk 16.95 (978-1-55685-979-3(1)) Audio Bk Con.

Seagull. unabr. ed. Anton Chekhov. Narrated by Flo Gibson. 2 cass. (Running Time: 2 hrs. 30 mins.). (YA). 2003. 20.95 Audio Bk Con.
Konstantin Treplov's literary ambitions and his love for a young aspiring actress evade him. When Nina runs off with his mother's lover, the successful author Trigirin, he attempts suicide and compares himself to a dead seagull destroyed by a man's whim.

Seal Hunt - Alive or Dead. Hosted by Nancy Pearlman. 1 cass. (Running Time: 28 min.). 10.00 (227) Educ Comm CA.

Seal Killers. Susannah Brin. Narrated by Larry A. McKeever. (Adventure Ser.). (J). 2000. audio compact disk 14.95 (978-1-58659-283-7(1)) Artesian.

Seal Killers. unabr. ed. Susannah Brin. Narrated by Larry A. McKeever. 1 cass. (Running Time: 40 min.). (Take Ten Ser.). (J). (gr. 3-12). 2000. 10.95 (978-1-58659-019-2(7), 54109) Artesian.

Seal Maiden: A Celtic Musical. Narrated by Karan Casey. 1 cass. (Running Time: 52 min.). (YA). (gr. 4 up). 2000. 9.98 (978-1-56628-241-3(1)); audio compact disk 15.98 (978-1-56628-240-6(3)) MFLP CA.
Tells the story of Solanna the Elder whose daughter, Solanna the younger, becomes a silkie when she loses her sealskin after venturing too close to the shore.

Seal Maiden: A Celtic Musical. Perf. by Karan Casey. 1 cass. (Running Time: 90 mins.). (J). 2000. 9.98; audio compact disk 15.98 MFLP CA.
A musical inspired by the traditional tale of the selkie, a seal that is transformed into a girl.

***Seal Mo Chuarta.** Caitlin Ni Dhomhnaill. (ENG.). 1992. 11.95 (978-0-8023-7070-9(5)) Pub: Clo Iar-Chonnachta IRL. Dist(s): Dufour

Seal of Approval. Kenneth G. Mills. 1 cass. 1979. pap. bk. 10.95 Incl. trancription bklet. (978-0-919842-03-8(8), KGOM9) Ken Mills Found.
What must be the gift of God to His Son? asks the author in this New Year's Eve spontaneous lecture in Toronto. The reply is a timeless acknowledgement: "This is my beloved Son in whom I am well pleased.

Seal of Higher Destiny: Healing Beyond Health Series. Joseph Michael Levry. 2006. Rental 19.00 (978-1-885562-17-3(9)) Root Light.

Seal Pup Grows Up: The Story of a Harbor Seal. Kathleen Weidner Zoehfeld. 1 cass. (Running Time: 35 min.). (J). 2001. bk. 19.95 (SP 4002C) Kimbo Educ.
The story of a young seal pup's survival to adulthood along the coast of Maine. Includes book.

Seal Pup Grows Up: The Story of a Harbor Seal. unabr. ed. Kathleen Weidner Zoehfeld. Read by Peter Thomas, Jr. Illus. by Lisa Bonforte. Narrated by Peter Thomas, Jr. 1 cass. (Running Time: 9 min.). Dramatization. (Smithsonian Oceanic Collection). (J). (ps-2). 1994. 5.00 (978-1-56899-037-8(5)) Soundprints.
Cassette is a dramatized readalong of the storybook, with authentic sound effects added. It consists of two sides - one with & one without page turning signals.

Seal Pup Grows Up: The Story of a Harbor Seal, Set. Kathleen Weidner Zoehfeld. Illus. by Lisa Bonforte. 1 cass. (Smithsonian Oceanic Collection). (J). (ps-2). 1994. bk. 29.95 INCL. TOY. (978-1-56899-038-5(3)) Soundprints.

Seal Warrior: Death in the Dark - Vietnam, 1968-1972. unabr. ed. Thomas H. Keith & J. Terry Riebling. Narrated by Michael Prichard. 9 CDs. (Running Time: 11 hrs. 0 mins. 0 sec.). (ENG.). 2009. audio compact disk 34.99 (978-1-4001-1153-4(6)) Pub: Tantor Media. Dist(s): IngramPubServ

Seal Warrior - Vietnam: Three Tours of Duty, 1968-1972. unabr. ed. Thomas H. Keith & J. Terry Riebling. Narrated by Michael Prichard. 1 MP3-CD. (Running Time: 11 hrs. 0 mins. 0 sec.). (ENG.). 2009. 24.99 (978-1-4001-6153-9(3)); audio compact disk 69.99 (978-1-4001-4153-1(2)) Pub: Tantor Media. Dist(s): IngramPubServ

Seal Wife. unabr. ed. Kathryn Harrison. Read by Fred Stella. (Running Time: 5 hrs.). 2004. 39.25 (978-1-59335-404-6(5), 1593354045, Brinc Audio MP3 Lib) Brilliance Audio.

Seal Wife. unabr. ed. Kathryn Harrison. Read by Fred Stella. (Running Time: 5 hrs.). 2004. 39.25 (978-1-59710-674-0(7), 1597106747, BADLE); 24.95 (978-1-59710-675-7(5), 1597106755, BAD) Brilliance Audio.

Seal Wife. unabr. ed. Kathryn Harrison. Read by Fred Stella. (Running Time: 5 hrs.). 2004. 24.95 (978-1-59335-150-2(X), 159335150X) Soulmate Audio Bks.
A stunning and hypnotic novel by "a writer of extraordinary gifts" [Tobias Wolff], The Seal Wife tells the story of a young scientist and his consuming love for a woman known as Aleut. In 1915, Bigelow is sent to establish a weather observatory in Anchorage, Alaska, and finds that nothing has prepared him for the loneliness of a railroad town of over two thousand men and only a handful of women, of winter nights twenty hours long. And nothing can protect him from obsession-both with a woman, who seems in her silence and mystery to possess the power to destroy his life forever, and with the weather kite he designs to fly higher than any kite has ever flown before, a kite with which Bigelow plans to penetrate and know not just the sky but the heavens. A novel of passions both dangerous and generative, The Seal Wife explores the nature of desire and its ability to propel an individual beyond himself and outside conventions. Harrison brilliantly re-creates the Alaskan frontier during the period of the first World War and in lyrical prose explores the interior landscape of the psyche and human emotions - a landscape eerily continuous with the splendor and terror of the frozen frontier, the storms that blow over the earth and its face.

Sealed Book. 6 cass. (Running Time: 6 hrs.). 24.98 Moonbeam Pubns.

Sealed with a Kiss. abr. ed. Carly Phillips. Read by Marie Caliendo. (Running Time: 3 hrs.). 2008. audio compact disk 14.99 (978-1-4233-2768-4(3), 9781423327684, BCD Value Price) Brilliance Audio.

Sealed with a Kiss. unabr. ed. Carly Phillips. Read by Marie Caliendo. (Running Time: 8 hrs.). 2007. 39.25 (978-1-59737-204-6(8), 9781597372046, BADLE); 24.95 (978-1-59737-203-9(X), 9781597372039, BAD); audio compact disk 29.95 (978-1-59737-199-5(8), 9781597371995, Bril Audio CD Unabri); 74.25 (978-1-59737-198-8(X), 9781597371988, BrilAudUnabridg); audio compact disk 92.25 (978-1-59737-200-8(5), 9781597372008, BriAudCD Unabrid); audio compact disk 39.25 (978-1-59737-202-2(1), 9781597372022, Brinc Audio MP3 Lib); audio compact disk 24.95 (978-1-59737-201-5(3), 9781597372015, Brilliance MP3) Brilliance Audio.
Please enter a Synopsis.

Seals & Skins. Hosted by Nancy Pearlman. 1 cass. (Running Time: 28 min.). 10.00 (105) Educ Comm CA.

Seals in Penobscot Bay see Twentieth-Century Poetry in English, No. 28, Recordings of Poets Reading Their Own Poetry

Seals, Terns, Time see Richard Eberhart Reading His Poetry

Seamless Garment of Life. Megan McKenna. 1 cass. (Running Time: 1 hr. 35 min.). 1993. 8.95 (AA2593) Credence Commun.
These are stories about our position in the universe - the womb of God. The effect is to enrich the context & meaning of scripture & add a dimension to the other story.

Seamos Amigos: Easy-to-learn Children's Songs in Spanish. Lyrics by Alain Le Lait. Music by Alain Le Lait. Illus. by Christy Pitts. 1CD & 1 bk. (Running Time: 30 minutes). (SPA.). (J). 1999. pap. bk. 15.95 (978-0-9747122-2-2(1), SPCD100) Yadeeda.
Original songs by Alain Le Lait, performed in Spanish by Michelle Lobato.

Seamstress. unabr. ed. Frances De Pontes Peebles. Narrated by Justine Eyre. 21 CDs. (Running Time: 26 hrs.). 2008. audio compact disk 129.00 (978-1-4159-5789-9(4), BksonTape) Pub: Random Audio Pubg. Dist(s): Random
Taquaritinga do Norte, Brazil, 1928. As seamstresses, the young sisters Emília and Luzia dos Santos know how to cut, mend, and conceal. These are useful skills in the backcountry of Brazil, where ruthless land barons feud with bands of outlaw cangaceiros. While Emília dreams of falling in love with a gentleman and escaping to a big city, Luzia, scarred by a childhood accident that left her with a deformed arm, finds her escape in sewing and in secret prayers to the saints she believes once saved her life. But when Luzia is abducted by a group of cangaceiros led by the infamous Hawk, the sisters' quiet lives diverge in ways they never imagined. Emília stumbles into marriage with Degas Coelho, the son of a doctor whose wealth is rivaled only by his political power, and moves to the sprawling seaside city of Recife. Luzia, forced to trek through scrubland and endure a nomadic existence, proves her determination to survive and begins to see the cangaceiros as comrades, not criminals.

Seamus & Manus McGuire: The Humours of Lissadell. 1 cass. 9.98 (C-78) Folk-Legacy.
Superb Irish fiddling, some as duets.

Sean-Nos Cois Locha: Rogha Sean-Nos Milwaukee 2003-2005. (ENG.). 2006. audio compact disk 23.95 (978-0-8023-8162-0(6)) Pub: Clo Iar-Chonnachta IRL. Dist(s): Dufour

Sean O'Casey Reading I Knock at the Door & Other Works. abr. ed. Sean O'Casey. Perf. by Sean O'Casey. 1 cass. Incl. I Knock at the Door: Life Is More Than Meat. (SWC 1198); Rose & Crown: Ship in Full Sail. (SWC 1198); Sunset & Evening Star: Outside an Irish Window. (SWC 1198); Wearin' of the Green. (SWC 1198); 1984. 12.95 (978-0-694-50149-6(2), SWC 1198) HarperCollins Pubs.

Sean O'Casey Reading Juno & the Paycock & Other Works. Sean O'Casey. 1 cass. Incl. Inishfallen, Fare Thee Well: The Death of Mrs. Casside. (SWC 1012); Juno & the Paycock: Scenes from Acts One & Three. (SWC 1012); Pictures in the Hallway: Cat in Cage. (SWC 1012); 1984. 12.95 (978-0-694-50008-6(9), SWC 1012) HarperCollins Pubs.

Seance see Isaac Bashevis Singer Reader

Seaport Equipment in Indonesia: A Strategic Reference 2006. Compiled by Icon Group International, Inc. Staff. 2007. ring bd. 195.00 (978-0-497-36033-7(0)) Icon Grp.

Search. Gordon Korman. Read by Andrew Rannells & Christie Moreau. (Running Time: 2 hrs. 42 mins.). (Kidnapped Ser.: No. 2). (YA). (gr. 7). 2009. 39.99 (978-1-60775-998-0(5)) Find a World.

Search. Gordon Korman. Narrated by Andrew Rannells & Christie Moreau. 3 CDs. (Running Time: 2 hrs. 42 mins.). (Kidnapped Ser.: Bk. 2). (ENG.). (J). (gr. 4-7). 2009. audio compact disk 39.95 (978-0-545-03323-7(3)) Scholastic Inc.

***Search.** abr. ed. Nora Roberts. Read by Tanya Eby. (Running Time: 7 hrs.). 2010. 14.99 (978-1-4418-7478-8(X), 9781441874788, BAD); audio compact disk 26.99 (978-1-4418-0498-3(6), 9781441804983, BACD) Brilliance Audio.

Search. unabr. ed. Iris Johansen. Narrated by Barbara Rosenblat. 8 cass. (Running Time: 8 hrs. 45 mins.). 2000. 67.00 (978-0-7887-4852-3(1), 96344E7) Recorded Bks.
Sarah Patrick & her golden retriever, Monty, are a dedicated team.They are sent into the many difficult disaster areas on the roughest rescue missions. Through her work, Sarah has perfected a careful balance of tough courage & gentle compassion but when she discovers that she has been lured into a deadly conspiracy disguised as a search, she is furious. Who is behind it & how many victims will there be. Sarah is pulled deeper into the mission & she must draw on all her resources to protect her life & keep her emotions in check. Includes an Interview with the Author.

Search. unabr. ed. Iris Johansen. Narrated by Barbara Rosenblat. 9 CDs. (Running Time: 8 hrs. 45 mins.). 2001. audio compact disk 89.00 (978-0-7887-6174-4(9), C1398) Recorded Bks.
A harrowing journey into the life of a search-and-rescue expert. Sarah Patrick & her golden retriever, Monty, are a dedicated team. They are sent into the most difficult disaster areas on the roughest rescue missions. Through her work, Sarah has perfected a careful balance of tough courage & gentle compassion. But when she discovers that she has been lured into a deadly conspiracy disguised as a search, she is furious. Who is behind it, & how many victims will there be? As Sarah is pulled deeper into the mission, she must draw on all her resources to protect her life & keep her emotions in check. The Search offers fascinating scenes from the highly-trained world of professional rescue teams.

***Search.** unabr. ed. Nora Roberts. Read by Tanya Eby. (Running Time: 15 hrs.). 2010. 24.99 (978-1-4418-0496-9(X), 9781441804969, BAD); 24.99 (978-1-4233-9999-5(4), 9781423399995, Brilliance MP3); 39.97 (978-1-4418-0497-6(8), 9781441804976, BADLE); 39.97 (978-1-4418-0495-2(1), 9781441804952, Brinc Audio MP3 Lib); 39.99 (978-1-4418-7375-0(9)); audio compact disk 39.99 (978-1-4233-9997-1(8), 9781423399971, Bril Audio CD Unabri); audio compact disk 97.97 (978-1-4233-9998-8(6), 9781423399988, BriAudCD Unabrid) Brilliance Audio.

Search. unabr. ed. C. P. Snow. Read by Rupert Keenlyside. 7 cass. (Running Time: 10 hrs. 30 min.). (Strangers & Brothers Ser.). 1985. 56.00 (978-0-7366-0448-2(0), 1422) Books on Tape.
A brilliant young research scientist leaves his specialty to analyze the human muddle.

***Search: A Novel.** unabr. ed. Suzanne Woods Fisher. Narrated by Cassandra Campbell. (Running Time: 9 hrs. 0 mins. 0 sec.). (Lancaster County Secrets Ser.). (ENG.). 2011. audio compact disk 29.99 (978-1-59859-864-3(3)) Oasis Audio.

Search & Rescue. Susannah Brin. Narrated by Larry A. McKeever. (Thrillers Ser.). (J). 2004. audio compact disk 14.95 (978-1-58659-327-8(7)) Artesian.

Search & Rescue. unabr. ed. Susannah Brin. Narrated by Larry A. McKeever. 1 cass. (Running Time: 40 min.). (Take Ten Ser.). (J). 2004. 10.95 (978-1-58659-048-2(0), 54123) Artesian.

Search & Seizure Law in Missouri. unabr. ed. Morley Swingle. Read by Morley Swingle. 15 cass. (Running Time: 22 hrs.). 1998. 125.00 (978-0-9669429-0-3(6)) Missouri Law.
Treatise includes both search warrant law & law of warrantless search.

Search Engines in France: A Strategic Reference 2006. Compiled by Icon Group International, Inc. Staff. 2007. ring bd. 195.00 (978-0-497-35959-1(6)) Icon Grp.

Search for a Meaningful Past, Parts I-II, Vol. 1. Instructed by Darren Staloff. 8 cass. (Running Time: 12 hrs.). 1994. 129.95 (978-1-56585-097-2(1)) Teaching Co.

Search for a Meaningful Past Vol. 2: Philosophies, Theories & Interpretations of Human History. Instructed by Darren Staloff. 4 cass. (Running Time: 6 hrs.). 1994. 129.95 (978-1-56585-098-9(X)) Teaching Co.

Search for a Soul: Taylor Caldwell's Psychic Lives. unabr. collector's ed. Jess Stearn. Read by Roses Prichard. 8 cass. (Running Time: 12 hrs.). 1984. 64.00 (978-0-7366-0459-8(6), 1431) Books on Tape.
Jess Stearn takes us on an exploration of psychic phenomena with Taylor Caldwell. Under hypnosis, Caldwell relates her previous existences, all supported by remarkable details.

Search For Authority: Judges 21:25. Ed Young. 1987. 4.95 (978-0-7417-1604-0(6), 604) Win Walk.

Search for Belle Prater. unabr. collector's ed. Ruth White. Read by Alison Elliot. 3 cass. (Running Time: 3 hrs. 45 mins.). (J). (gr. 4-7). 2005. 30.00 (978-0-307-20631-2(9), BksonTape); audio compact disk 30.00 (978-0-307-20678-7(5), BksonTape) Random Audio Pubg.
Belle Prater is missing. Since she inexplicably disappeared about a year ago, her son, Woodrow, has been living with his grandparents, next door to his cousin Gypsy. The two are best friends, joined by their adventurous sprits and shared love of stories and magic. One night they receive a puzzling phone call, which provides a clue that sends Gypsy and Woodrow on a mission to find Belle. Joining them is Cassie Caulborne, the new girl in school, who, like Woodrow and Gypsy, has experienced the loss of a parent. She is also endowed with a valuable gift - she knows things, things that happened in the past and reveal themselves to her in dreams. Their quest leads them out of their sheltered life in Coal Station, Virginia, and eventually back to Woodrow's home in Crooked Ridge. On the road they meet new people with their own stories to tell. One is Joseph, who has to sit at the back of the buss because he is black. The young people join him in the rear and learn that he, too, is on a search - for his father. They help one another to find what they're looking for and gain friendship along the way.

Search for Delicious. Natalie Babbitt. Perf. by Natalie Babbitt. Perf. by Words Take Wing Repertory Company Staff. 2 cass. (Running Time: 2 hrs. 19 mins.). (J). 2000. 18.00 (978-0-7366-9172-7(3)) Books on Tape.

Search for Delicious. unabr. ed. Natalie Babbitt. Read by Natalie Babbitt. Read by WTW Repertory Company. 2 vols. (Running Time: 2 hrs. 41 mins.). Dramatization. (Words Take Wingtm Ser.). (J). (gr. 3-7). 1995. pap. bk. 29.00 (978-0-8072-7597-9(2), YA889SP, Listening Lib); 23.00 (978-0-8072-7596-2(4), YA889CX, Listening Lib) Random Audio Pubg.
What is the definition of delicious? A teasing fantasy-adventure that has the country on the brink of civil war.

Search for Emily: Sammy's Story. Short Stories. Dennis J. Deitz. Narrated by John Kessler. 2 cass. (Running Time: 1 hr. 25 mins.). 1999. 2.95 (978-0-938985-24-2(8)) Pub: Quarrier Pr. Dist(s): WV Book Co
Adaptation of the novel "The Search for Emily.".

Search for Enlightenment. Swami Amar Jyoti. 1 cass. 1991. 9.95 (M-83) Truth Consciousness.
All of us are searching; following the good rather than our likes & dislikes. Finding the way to the Light.

Search for Excellence: Ephesians 5:21-6:9. Ed Young. 1987. 4.95 (978-0-7417-1599-9(6), 599) Win Walk.

Search for Intelligent Life in Space. 6 cass. (Running Time: 6 hrs.). 1999. 89.95 (978-1-56585-005-7(X)) Teaching Co.

Search for Jesse Bram. Harley L. Sachs. 9 cass. (Running Time: 9 hrs.). 2001. 40.00 (978-0-9705390-6-9(1)) I D E V C O.
The young hero of this metaphysical science fiction adventure is unaware of his Urthling Jewish roots. An Eldre of mixed breed, he is marooned on the post-apocalyptic shunned variously view, Jesse as a bring of cargo for the half-breed Prefect Hrod, as the reborn Savior by Crypto-Christians & as a link to the past by a remnant of Jews. The Galactic Federation suspects him of treason & he is pursued by an enigmatic Trinian policeman.

Search for Jesus: Modern Scholarship Looks at the Gospels. Marcus J. Borg et al. Read by Marcus J. Borg et al. Moderated by Hershel Shanks. 4 cass. (Running Time: 5 hrs.). 32.95 Set. (978-1-880317-15-0(X), 7H44) Biblical Arch Soc.
Based on the 1993 BAS/Smithsonian Institution symposium, with leading New Testament scholars. Brings together drastic new evidence of historical Jesus studies.

Search for Justice: A Defense Attorney's Brief on the O. J. Simpson Case. abr. ed. Robert L. Shapiro. (ENG.). 2006. 14.98 (978-1-59483-825-5(9)) Pub: Hachet Audio. Dist(s): HachBkGrp

Search for Last Chance. unabr. ed. A. L. McWilliams. Read by Maynard Villers. 6 cass. (Running Time: 6 hrs. 36 min.). 1996. 39.95 (978-1-55686-711-8(5)) Books in Motion.
Two outlaws don't believe the eerie stories told by those who searched for the Last Chance Treasure & head for New Mexico's Sangre de Cristo Mountains & possibly, death.

***Search for Love.** unabr. ed. Nora Roberts. Read by Gayle Hendrix. (Running Time: 7 hrs.). 2011. audio compact disk 24.99 (978-1-4418-5728-6(1), 9781441857286, Bril Audio CD Unabri) Brilliance Audio.

Search for Maggie Ward. unabr. ed. Andrew M. Greeley. Read by Multivoice Production Staff. (Running Time: 15 hrs.). 2008. 24.95 (978-1-4233-5431-4(1), 9781423354314, Brilliance MP3); 24.95 (978-1-4233-5433-8(8), 9781423354338, BAD); 39.25 (978-1-4233-5432-1(X), 9781423354321, Brinc Audio MP3 Lib); 39.25 (978-1-4233-5434-5(6), 9781423354345, BADLE) Brilliance Audio.

Search for Modern China, Pt. 1. unabr. ed. Jonathan D. Spence. Read by Frederick Davidson. 14 cass. (Running Time: 38 hrs.). 1981. 89.95 (978-0-7861-0221-1(7), 1195A,B) Blckstn Audio.
The history of China is as rich & strange as that of any country on earth. With his command of character & event - the product of thirty years of research & reflection in the field - Spence dispels those myths in a powerful narrative.

Search for Modern China, Pt. 2. unabr. ed. Jonathan D. Spence. Read by Frederick Davidson. 12 cass. (Running Time: 38 hrs.). 1981. 83.95 (978-0-7861-0222-8(5), 1195A,B) Blckstn Audio.

Search for Nina Fletcher. unabr. ed. Stephen H. Martin. Read by Laurie Klein. 6 cass. (Running Time: 7 hrs. 24 min.). 1994. 39.95 (978-1-55686-540-4(6)) Books in Motion.
Rebecca Fletcher begins a search for the mother she never knew, the mother no one talked about. The search leads her into a Corsican feud & a nightmare of underworld intrigue.

Search for Sacredness. Keith J. Egan. 1 cass. (Running Time: 58 min.). 1986. 7.95 (TAH155) Alba Hse Comns.
Utilizes Sts. Thomas Aquinas, Teresa of Avila & John of the Cross in discovering the sacred.

Search for the Essential Meaning of Life. Manly P. Hall. 1 cass. 8.95 (978-0-89314-249-0(2)) Philos Res.

Search for the Real Mt. Sinai. 1 CD. (Running Time: 1 hr.). (YA). 2002. audio compact disk 9.95 (978-0-9675010-4-8(0)) Reel Prodns.
The Incredible Creatures That Defy Evolution series enters the fascinating world of animals to reveal sophisticated and complex designs that shake the traditional foundations of evolutionary theory. Incredible Creatures That Defy Evolution presents powerful evidence which proves that animal designs can only be attributed to a creator. They cannot possibly be explained by evolution. This program will inspire you to look more closely at the world around you.

Search for the Red Dragon. James A. Owen. Read by James Langton. (Chronicles of the Imaginarium Geographica (Playaway) Ser.). (YA). (gr. 7-12). 2008. 59.99 (978-1-60640-962-6(X)) Find a World.

Search for the Red Dragon. unabr. ed. James A. Owen. Read by James Langton. (Running Time: 9 hrs. 30 mins. 0 sec.). (Chronicles of the Imaginarium Geographica Ser.). (ENG.). (YA). 2008. audio compact disk 34.95 (978-0-7435-6913-2(X)) Pub: S&S Audio. Dist(s): S and S Inc

Search for the Self. Swami Amar Jyoti. 1 cass. 1989. 9.95 (M-78) Truth Consciousness.
In the Ocean of Consciousness, residing into True Being. Dharma, the foundation, leads to Awakening.

Search for Truth. unabr. ed. Kaza Kingsley. Kaza Kingsley. Read by Simon Jones. (Running Time: 13 hrs. 0 mins. 0 sec.). (Erec Rex Ser.). (ENG.). (J). 2009. audio compact disk 39.99 (978-0-7435-8386-2(8)) Pub: S&S Audio. Dist(s): S and S Inc

Search for Value - Toot Your Own Horn! Vol. 1: Demonstrating the Only Things Customers Care about. unabr. ed. Karl Walinskas. Perf. by Ted Ritsick & Beth Bloom-Wright. 1 cass. (Running Time: 50 min.). 1998. bk. 12.95 (978-0-9667084-4-8(X)) Speaking Connect.
Learn the only three things prospects care about, then position your product to do all three. Discover how to demonstrate your added value in black & white.

***Search for Well-Being.** unabr. ed. Martin Seligman. (Running Time: 10 hrs. 30 mins. 0 sec.). (ENG.). 2011. audio compact disk 39.99 (978-1-4423-3905-7(5)) Pub: S&S Audio. Dist(s): S and S Inc

Search for Whit, Vol. 27. AIO Team Staff. Prod. by Focus on the Family Staff. 4 CDs. (Running Time: 6 hrs.). (Adventures in Odyssey Ser.: Vol. 27). (ENG.). (J). (gr. 3-7). 1997. audio compact disk 24.99 (978-1-56179-528-4(3)) Pub: Focus Family. Dist(s): Tyndale Hse

Search for Wholeness. Thomas Merton. 1 cass. 8.95 (AA2370) Credence Commun.

***Search for WondLa.** unabr. ed. Tony DiTerlizzi. Read by Teri Hatcher. (Running Time: 10 hrs. 30 mins. 0 sec.). (ENG.). (J). 2010. audio compact disk 34.99 (978-1-4423-3428-1(2)) Pub: S&S Audio. Dist(s): S and S Inc

Search the Dark, unabr. ed. Charles Todd. Narrated by Samuel Gillies. 9 cass. (Running Time: 11 hrs. 45 mins.). (Inspector Ian Rutledge Mystery Ser.: Bk. 3). 1999. 79.00 (978-1-84197-039-4(5), H1039E7) Recorded Bks.
Dorset is the latest setting for the talents of Inspector Ian Rutledge, a veteran of the First World War still haunted - literally- by his actions. Indeed his personal ghost only serves to complicate things as his inner doubts blend into the trauma of the case. The disappearance of two children, the murder of a woman supposed to be their mother & an unstable suspect who may or may not be guilty form the bones of this thriller.

Search the Dark. unabr. ed. Charles Todd. Narrated by Samuel Gillies. 10 CDs. (Running Time: 11 hrs. 45 mins.). (Inspector Ian Rutledge Mystery Ser.: Bk. 3). 2001. audio compact disk 94.00 (978-1-84197-099-8(9), C1144E7) Recorded Bks.
The disappearance of two children, the murder of a woman supposed to be her mother & an unstable suspect who may or may not be guilty.

Searchers. unabr. ed. Will C. Knott. Read by Maynard Villers. 4 cass. (Running Time: 4 hrs. 24 min.). (Golden Hawk Ser.: Bk. 9). 1996. 26.95 (978-1-55686-705-7(0)) Books in Motion.
Hawk is in a race against time to head off a foul fur trader named Bannister who captured a beautiful Quaker woman to sell in the white slave market.

Searcher's Path: A Composer's Ways. Roger Reynolds. 1 cass. (I.S.A.M. Monographs). 1988. pap. bk. 12.00 (978-0-914678-28-1(0)) Inst Am Music.

Searching for Ancestors see Winter Count

Searching for Bobby Fischer. unabr. ed. Fred Waitzkin. Read by Lloyd James. 6 cass. (Running Time: 8 hrs. 30 mins.). 2001. 44.95 (978-0-7861-1972-1(1), 2742); audio compact disk 64.00 (978-0-7861-9753-8(6), 2742) Blckstn Audio.
From the moment Fred Waitzkin & his son Josh first sit down at a chessboard until he competes for the national championship, they are drawn into the insular, international network of chess. They must also navigate the difficult waters of their own relationship. All the while, Waitzkin searches for the elusive Bobby Fischer, whose myth still dominates the chess world & profoundly affects Waitzkin's dreams for his son.

Searching for Courtship Set: The Smart Woman's Guide to Finding a Good Husband. Winnifred B. Cutler. Read by Glynis Gould. 5 cass. (Running Time: 4 hrs. 30 mins.). (YA). 2000. bk. 35.00 (978-0-9651753-3-3(2)) Athena Inst.
Ten readings.

Searching for Dragons. unabr. ed. Patricia C. Wrede. 4 vols. (Running Time: 5 hrs. 55 mins.). (Enchanted Forest Chronicles: Bk. 2). (J). (gr. 5 up). 2004. pap. bk. 38.00 (978-0-8072-0670-6(9), Listening Lib); 32.00 (978-0-8072-0633-1(4), Listening Lib) Random Audio Pubg.
Those wicked wizards are at it again! This time they are draining power from the Enchanted Forest. And that does not sit well with Mendanbar the King. On the advice of the witch Morwen, Mendanbar decides to consult with Kazul, the King of the Dragons. When he arrives at Kazul's cave, he meets Princess Cimorene and learns that Kazul has been captured by those horrible wizards. Mendanbar and Cimorene will have to search for her, traveling over mountains and past man-eating giants, terrifying rock snakes and an assortment of magic-wielders.

Searching for God in America. Contrib. by Hugh Hewitt. 1 cass. 1996. 23.00 (978-0-8499-6233-2(1)) Nelson.

***Searching for God Knows What.** unabr. ed. Donald Miller. Narrated by Scott Brick. (ENG.). 2007. 14.98 (978-1-59644-546-8(7), Hovel Audio) christianaud.

Searching for God Knows What. unabr. ed. Donald Miller. Read by Scott Brick. (Running Time: 7 hrs. 15 mins. 0 sec.). (ENG.). 2007. audio compact disk 24.98 (978-1-59644-545-1(9), Hovel Audio) christianaud.

Searching for Paradise in Parker, PA. Kris Radish. Narrated by Barbara McCulloh. (Running Time: 41400 sec.). 2008. audio compact disk 34.99 (978-1-4281-7780-2(9)) Recorded Bks.

Searching for Schindler. Thomas Keneally. Read by Humphrey Bower. (Running Time: 9 hrs. 5 mins.). 2009. 79.99 (978-1-74214-252-4(4), 9781742142524) Pub: Bolinda Pubng AUS. Dist(s): Bolinda Pub Inc

Searching for Schindler. unabr. ed. Thomas Keneally. Read by Humprey Bower. (Running Time: 32700 sec.). 2008. audio compact disk 87.95 (978-1-921415-12-8(6), 9781921415128) Pub: Bolinda Pubng AUS. Dist(s): Bolinda Pub Inc

Searching for Schindler. unabr. ed. Thomas Keneally. Read by Humphrey Bower. (Running Time: 9 hrs. 5 mins.). 2009. 43.95 (978-1-74214-129-9(3), 9781742141299) Pub: Bolinda Pubng AUS. Dist(s): Bolinda Pub Inc

Searching for the Sound: My Life in the Grateful Dead. abr. ed. Phil Lesh. 2005. 17.95 (978-0-7435-5149-6(4)) Pub: S&S Audio. Dist(s): S and S Inc

Searching for the Star of Bethlehem, Michael Ballam. 2 cass. (Running Time: 3 hrs.). 2004. 14.98 (978-1-55503-432-0(2), 1100440) Covenant Comms.
Ballam guides you toward the star through music & symbols.

Searching for Tilly. Susan Sallis. 2008. 89.95 (978-1-4079-0022-3(6)); audio compact disk 99.95 (978-1-4079-0023-0(4)) Pub: Soundings Ltd GBR. Dist(s): Ulverscroft US

Searching Heart. unabr. ed. Janette Oke. Read by Marguerite Gavin. 5 cass. (Running Time: 7 hrs.). (Prairie Legacy Ser.: Bk. 2). 2001. 39.95 (978-0-7861-2099-4(1), 2861); audio compact disk 48.00 (978-0-7861-9675-3(0), 2861) Blckstn Audio.
Virginia Simpson managed to struggle through adolescence and was looking forward to stepping into adulthood. Now her graduation day arrives, and she walks to the podium as the class valedictorian to the proud grins of her grandparents, Marty and Clark Davis. College beckons, and life seems to be well in hand.

Searching Question: Mal. 3:8. Ed Young. 1991. 4.95 (978-0-7417-1846-4(4), 846) Win Walk.

Searching the Scriptures: Family Scripture Study. Gene R. Cook. 2005. audio compact disk 14.95 (978-1-59038-504-3(7)) Deseret Bk.

Searching the Scriptures: Personal Scripture Study. Gene R. Cook. 2005. audio compact disk 19.95 (978-1-59038-503-6(9)) Deseret Bk.

Sears, Roebock & Co 1902 Catalogue. Ed. by Tom Johnson. 2 CDs. (Running Time: 3 hrs.). 2002. audio compact disk 19.99 (978-0-9721709-0-1(1)) Princeton Imaging.
"This vast 1200 page catalog provides a unique historical perspective of life 100 years ago. This CD was created from high resolution scans of the original 1902 catalog and compressed using Lizard tech's advanced Djvu imaging technology. Runs on all MS windows versions from 95 and up, MACOS9 and OSX, Linux, various Unix versions.".

Seascape see Caedmon Treasury of Modern Poets Reading Their Own Poetry

Seascapes. 1 cass. (Solitudes Ser.). 9.95 (C11209) J Norton Pubs.
This tape tunes in the sounds & experiences of the natural environment.

Seashore. Dorling Kindersley Publishing Staff. (Eyewitness Videos Ser.). (ENG.). (J). 2010. 12.99 (978-0-7566-6296-7(6)) DK Pub Inc.

Seaside Images-Music. 2007. audio compact disk 16.95 (978-1-56136-400-8(2)) Master Your Mind.

Seaside Practice. Tom Smith. 2009. 54.95 (978-1-4079-0178-7(8)); audio compact disk 64.95 (978-1-4079-0179-4(6)) Pub: Soundings Ltd GBR. Dist(s): Ulverscroft US

Seaside Reflections-Music. 2007. audio compact disk 19.95 (978-1-56136-404-6(5)) Master Your Mind.

Seaside/Then Comes Marriage. unabr. ed. Terri Blackstock. 1 cass. (Running Time: 1 hr.). 2001. 19.99 (978-0-310-23464-7(6)) Zondervan.

Season. Charlotte Bingham. Read by Judy Bennett. 10 cass. (Running Time: 15 hrs.). 2002. 84.95 (978-0-7540-0722-7(7), CAB 2144) AudioGO.

Season. unabr. ed. Charlotte Bingham. Read by Judy Bennett. 2002. audio compact disk 110.95 (978-0-7540-5462-7(4), CCD 153) AudioGO.
Portia and Emily meet to launch their daughters on an unsuspecting Society for the London Season of 1913. Both are determined that their offspring, Phyllis and Edith, will catch the eye of their friend May's son, a future duke. If that wee all, the Season would be a relatively simple affair, but since Portia is recently widowed and Emily is away from her husband, life is bound to get more interesting.

Season & the Story. Rich Smith. 1 cass. 1.77 (10001190); audio compact disk 2.37 (2800845) Covenant Comms.
Capture the feelings of Christmas.

Season Deluxe. Robert Laughlin. Read by Robert Laughlin. 2 cass. (Running Time: 2 hrs.). 1994. pap. bk. 39.00 (978-0-929983-22-6(X)) New Schl Am Music.
Book explains chord method for 18 Christmas carols. Tapes demonstrate accompaniment styles for the first 10 songs in the book.

Season for Justice. abr. ed. Morris Dees & Steven Fiffer. Read by Morris Dees. 2 cass. (Running Time: 3 hrs.). 1991. 15.95 (978-1-879371-07-1(3)) Pub Mills.
This is the true story of Morris Dees, the grandson of a Ku Klux Klan member who became a crusader for civil rights & founder of the Southern Poverty Law Center.

Season for Murder. unabr. ed. Ann Granger & Alan Titchmarsh. Narrated by Judith Boyd & Alan Titchmarsh. 7 CDs. (Running Time: 7 hrs. 45 mins.). (Mitchell & Markby Mystery Ser.). 2000. audio compact disk 73.00 (978-1-84197-140-7(5), C1249E7) Recorded Bks.
Meredith Mitchell is none too happy to be back in Britain. Life as the British Consul of Yugoslavia was far more fun. Still, she's got the delightful opportunity to live in Oxfordshire, instead of London & what's more, she's in the vicinity of Chief Inspector Alan Markby.

Season for Murder: A Mitchell & Markby Mystery. unabr. ed. Ann Granger. Narrated by Judith Boyd. 8 cass. (Running Time: 10 hrs. 30 mins.). (Mitchell & Markby Mystery Ser.). 2000. 72.00 (978-1-84197-101-8(4), H1089E7) Recorded Bks.

Season in Hell. Interview with Percy Knauth. 1 cass. (Running Time: 1 hr.). 10.95 (OP-76-06-16, HarperThor) HarpC GBR.

Season in Purgatory. unabr. ed. Dominick Dunne. Read by Michael Kramer. 9 cass. (Running Time: 13 hrs. 30 min.). 1993. 72.00 (978-0-7366-2500-5(3), 3258) Books on Tape.
Cover-up of 20-year-old murder haunts rising politician's school chum.

Season in the Sun. unabr. collector's ed. Roger Kahn. Read by Michael Russotto. 6 cass. (Running Time: 6 hrs.). 1990. 36.00 (978-0-7366-1747-5(7), 2586) Books on Tape.
Baseball needs no defense, but it does occasionally need an interpreter, particularly because it is our national sport...& pastime. Most definitely the latter. Roger Kahn decided to spend some serious time with practitioners of his favorite sport. At any rate, he invested an entire season - from spring training through the Series - with baseball players of every stripe & competence. The result is this book. In it Kahn reports on a young New England ball club, a failing major league franchise, a small-town college team on a winning streak & a host of colorful past & present heroes of the sport. Along the way we rediscover the magic that baseball & America are all about.

Season of Angels. abr. ed. Debbie Macomber. Read by Kathy Garver. (Running Time: 6 hrs.). (Angels Everywhere Ser.: Bk. 1). 2008. 39.25 (978-1-4233-5880-0(5), 9781423358800, Brinc Audio MP3 Lib); 49.97 (978-1-4233-5882-4(1), 9781423358824, BADLE); 24.95 (978-1-4233-5881-7(3), 9781423358817, BAD); 24.95 (978-1-4233-5879-4(1), 9781423358794, Brilliance MP3) Brilliance Audio.

Season of Angels. abr. ed. Debbie Macomber. Read by Kathy Garver. (Running Time: 6 hrs.). (Angels Everywhere Ser.: Bk. 1). 2008. audio compact disk 14.99 (978-1-4233-5230-3(0), 9781423352303, BCD Value Price) Brilliance Audio.

Season of Angels - The Trouble with Angels - Touched by Angels. abr. ed. Debbie Macomber. Read by Kathy Garver. (Running Time: 18 hrs.). (Angel Ser.). 2007. audio compact disk 34.95 (978-1-4233-4904-4(0), 9781423349044, BACD) Brilliance Audio.

***Season of Divorce.** abr. ed. John Cheever. Read by Meryl Streep et al. (ENG.). 2009. (978-0-06-125303-4(0), Caedmon) HarperCollins Pubs.

***Season of Divorce.** unabr. ed. John Cheever. Read by Meryl Streep et al. (ENG.). 2009. (978-0-06-196868-6(4), Caedmon) HarperCollins Pubs.

Season of Dreams: Advent & Christmas Parables. Edward Hays. 3 cass. (Running Time: 3 hrs.). vinyl bd. 22.95 (For Peace Pubng) Ave Maria Pr.
No other time of the year is so rich in dreams as the Season of Advent & Christmas. Dreaming is seeded into the song of this season, songs like "O Come, O come, Emmanuel," & "I'm Dreaming of a White Christmas." "Season of Dreams" is a collection of original parables that will stir awake the "true meaning of Christmas" within you. From Isaiah & John the Baptizer's dream of a level road for the coming of Emmanuel, these six parables echo the Advent call to "stay awake," to remain faithful to the vision-dream of Jesus.

***Season of Gifts.** unabr. ed. Richard Peck. Read by Ron McLarty. 3 CDs. (Running Time: 3 hrs. 50 mins.). (J). (gr. 4-7). 2009. audio compact disk 30.00 (978-0-7393-8548-7(8), BksonTape) Pub: Random Audio Pubg. Dist(s): Random

Season of Gifts. unabr. ed. Richard Peck. (J). (gr. 5). 2009. audio compact disk 25.00 (978-0-7393-8546-3(1), Listening Lib) Pub: Random Audio Pubg. Dist(s): Random

Season of Hope. 2005. audio compact disk 4.95 (978-0-687-49306-7(4)) Abingdon.

Season of Hope: Rediscovering Our Advent Heritage. Contrib. by Brotherhood Of Hope Staff. (Running Time: 35 min.). 2004. audio compact disk 15.95 (978-5-559-53763-4(2)) Pub: Pt of Grace Ent. Dist(s): STL Dist NA

Season of Joy. bk. 4.95 (978-0-687-36343-8(8)) Abingdon.

Season of Joy, Pack. 2001. (978-1-931713-09-2(X)) Calvar ChalPub.

Season of Knives. unabr. ed. P. F. Chisholm. Read by Stephen Thome. 8 cass. (Running Time: 9 hrs. 30 min.). 2001. 69.95 (978-0-7531-0036-3(3), 970607) Pub: ISIS Audio GBR. Dist(s): Ulverscroft US
In Elizabethan England, Sir Robert Carey must battle with Sir Richard Lowther, his dishonest rival for the deputy warden's post, as well as raiders from the Debatable Land between Scotland & England, who plot to make off with Carey's married & virtuous love, Elizabeth Widdrington.

Season of Leaves. Catherine Law. 2009. 84.95 (978-0-7531-4076-5(4)); audio compact disk 99.95 (978-0-7531-4077-2(2)) Pub: Isis Pubng Ltd GBR. Dist(s): Ulverscroft US

Season of Light BookNote. John Beilenson. (BookNotes with CDs Ser.). 2001. bk. 14.99 (978-0-88088-415-0(0)) Peter Pauper.

Season of Lillian Dawes. Katherine Mosby. Narrated by Jeff Woodman. 6 cass. (Running Time: 7 hrs. 45 mins.). 54.00 (978-1-4025-1817-1(X)); audio compact disk 69.00 (978-1-4025-2108-9(1)) Recorded Bks.

Season of Lillian Dawes: A Novel. unabr. ed. Katherine Mosby. Read by Jeff Woodman. 6 cass. (Running Time: 9 hrs.). 2002. 34.95 (978-0-06-008297-0(6)) HarperCollins Pubs.

Season of Miracles: By Steve Brock. 2003. audio compact disk (978-1-59024-163-9(0)) B Hinn Min.

Season of Song Holiday Collection. Walt Disney Productions Staff. 1 cass., 1 CD. (J). 1996. audio compact disk 8.98 CD. (978-0-7634-0187-0(0)) W Disney Records.

Season of Song Holiday Collection. Walt Disney Productions Staff. 1 cass., 1 CD. (J). (ps-3). 1996. 5.98 (978-0-7634-0186-3(2)) W Disney Records.

Season of Souls. Perf. by Tulku. 1 cass., 1 CD. 8.78 (TRI 558007); audio compact disk 13.58 CD Jewel box. (TRI 558007) NewSound.
Featuring voices from Persia, India, Egypt, Turkey, Australian Aboriginal, Mayan & Native American. Featured artists include Krishna Das, Tim Reynolds, Daoud Al Jerrahi, Mayan Shaman Don Alejandro, Primeaux & more.

Season of the Machete. unabr. ed. James Patterson. Read by Lou Diamond Phillips. 5 CDs. (Running Time: 6 hrs.). (ENG.). 2006. audio compact disk 19.98 (978-1-59483-482-0(2)) Pub: GrandCentral. Dist(s): HachBkGrp

Season of the Machete. unabr. ed. James Patterson. Read by Lou Diamond Phillips. (Running Time: 6 hrs.). (ENG.). 2006. 14.98 (978-1-59483-511-7(X)) Pub: Hachet Audio. Dist(s): HachBkGrp

Season of the Machete. unabr. ed. James Patterson. Read by Lou Diamond Phillips. (Running Time: 6 hrs.). (ENG.). 2009. 29.98 (978-1-60788-120-9(9)) Pub: Hachet Audio. Dist(s): HachBkGrp

Season of the Snake. Claire Davis. Read by Hillary Huber. (Running Time: 39600 sec.). 2005. audio compact disk 81.00 (978-0-7861-8248-0(2)) Blckstn Audio.

Season of the Snake. unabr. ed. Claire Davis. 20 cass. (Running Time: 10 hrs.). 2005. reel tape 29.95 (978-0-7861-2899-0(2), E3393); audio compact disk 29.95 (978-0-7861-8318-0(7), ZM3393) Blckstn Audio.

Season of the Snake. unabr. ed. Claire Davis. Read by Hillary Huber. 8 CDs. (Running Time: 39600 sec.). 2005. audio compact disk 29.95 (978-0-7861-8249-7(0), ZE3393) Blckstn Audio.

Season of the Snake -Lib. (Running Time: 11 hrs. 0 mins.). 2005. 65.95 (978-0-7861-2900-3(X)) Blckstn Audio.

Season of the Swan, unabr. ed. Evan Maxwell. Narrated by Richard Poe. 6 cass. (Running Time: 7 hrs. 45 mins.). 1998. 51.00 (978-0-7887-2005-5(8), 95392E7) Recorded Bks.
A violinist is not sure what direction she wants her career to take after meeting a violin maker in rural Washington.

Season on the Mat: Dan Gable & the Pursuit of Perfection. Nolan Zavoral. Narrated by Robert O'Keefe. 8 CDs. (Running Time: 9 hrs. 15 mins.). audio compact disk 78.00 (978-1-4025-1565-1(0)) Recorded Bks.

Season on the Mat: Dan Gable & the Pursuit of Perfection. Nolan Zavoral. Narrated by Robert O'Keefe. 7 cass. (Running Time: 9 hrs. 15 mins.). 1998. 65.00 (978-1-4025-0912-4(X), 96719) Recorded Bks.
The greatest amateur wrestler and wrestling coach America has ever known. Through high school and college, Gable amassed 181 straight victories. He claimed Olympic gold without giving up a single point. He then turned the Iowa Hawkeyes into a wrestling behemoth, winning the Big Ten title every year he coached and capturing 15 NCAA championships.

Season on the Reservation. Kareem Abdul-Jabbar. Read by Carl Lumbly. 2004. 15.95 (978-0-7435-4087-2(5)) Pub: S&S Audio. Dist(s): S and S Inc

Season-4 CD audio Book. Thomas Henry Kelly. 2004. audio compact disk 35.00 (978-1-56142-183-1(9)) T Kelly Inc.

Seasons. 2004. 8.95 (978-0-7882-0078-6(X)); cass. & flmstrp 30.00 (978-0-89719-581-2(7)) Weston Woods.

Seasons: A Family Christmas Celebration. Perf. by Fred Penner. 1 cass. (J). (ps-5). 10.98 (978-0-945267-48-5(7), YM082-CN); audio compact disk 13.98 (978-0-945267-49-2(5), YM082-CD) Youngheart Mus.
Christmas songs include: "The Season"; "Children Go"; "Christmas Magic"; "Mao Tzur"; "Cantate Domino"; "O Tannenbaum"; "Leise Rieselt der Schnee"; "Vo Vyfleyemi"; "A 'Soalin"; "Riu Chiu"; "D'ou Viens Tu Bergere"; "Virgin Mary Had a Baby Boy" & more.

Seasons & Days: A Hunting Life. abr. ed. Thomas McIntyre. Narrated by Alan Sklar. (Running Time: 16200 sec.). 2005. audio compact disk 28.00 (978-1-932378-77-1(4)) Pub: A Media Intl. Dist(s): Natl Bk Netwk

Seasons & Holidays Clip Art. (Timesaving Software Tools for Teachers Ser.). 2004. audio compact disk 19.99 (978-1-57690-694-1(9)) Tchr Create Ma.

Seasons Change. 1 CD. (Running Time: 90 mins.). (Best of Contemporary Christian Ser.). 1999. audio compact disk 16.95 (978-1-56015-729-8(1)) Penton Overseas.
Contemporary Christian music including "Like I Love You," Marie Evans; "Radically Saved," Joseph Forrester; "Seasons Change," Shirley Church; "Butterfly Kisses," Carl W. Wright.

Seasons for Singing. 1995. 7.95 (1095); audio compact disk 14.95 CD. Revels Recs.
This collection celebrates spring, summer & autumn with love songs, carols, heart & soul songs.

Seasons for Singing. Ella Jenkins. 1 CD. (Running Time: 1 hr.). (J). 2001. audio compact disk 15.00 (FC 45031CD) Kimbo Educ.

Seasons for Singing. Perf. by Ella Jenkins. 1 cass. (J). (gr. 1-6). 1990. (0-9307-45031-4-0) Smithsonian Folkways.
A call & response session recorded live at a music workshop. Features original & traditional songs from around the world, such as "This Train," "On a Holiday" & "You Look So Sweet".

Seasons for Singing. Ella Jenkins. 1 cass. (Running Time: 33 min.). (J). 2000. 8.50 (SFW45031); audio compact disk 14.00 Smithsonian Folkways.
Notes include song texts.

Season's Greetings Accompaniment Cassette. Greg Skipper. 1999. 40.00 (978-0-7673-9748-3(7)) LifeWay Christian.

Seasons Greetings Cassette Kit. Greg Skipper. 1999. 54.95 (978-0-7673-9663-9(4)) LifeWay Christian.

Seasons Greetings Cassette Promo Pak. Greg Skipper. 1999. 8.00 (978-0-7673-9644-8(8)) LifeWay Christian.

Seasons Greetings Cd Kit. Greg Skipper. 1999. audio compact disk 59.95 (978-0-633-00298-5(4)) LifeWay Christian.

Seasons Greetings Cd Promo Pak. Greg Skipper. 1999. audio compact disk 12.00 (978-0-7673-9654-7(5)) LifeWay Christian.

Seasons Greetings Choral Cassette. Greg Skipper. 1999. 11.98 (978-0-7673-9712-4(6)) LifeWay Christian.

Seasons Greetings Stereo/Split Acc Cd. Greg Skipper. 1999. audio compact disk 50.00 (978-0-7673-9695-0(2)) LifeWay Christian.

Season's Greetings (You Can!0 Choral Cd. Greg Skipper. 1999. audio compact disk 16.98 (978-0-7673-9703-2(7)) LifeWay Christian.

Seasons in Cancer. abr. ed. George S. J. Anderson. Read by Alan Zimmerman. 2 cass. (Running Time: 180 min.). 2000. 18.00 (978-1-58807-039-5(5)) Am Pubng Inc.
Season in Cancer is an extraordinary chronicle of human conflict and resolution which generated five short stories over a seven year period.

Seasons of a Fisherman. abr. ed. Roderick L. Haig-Brown. (Running Time: 16200 sec.). 2008. audio compact disk 28.00 (978-1-933309-31-6(8)) Pub: A Media Intl. Dist(s): Natl Bk Netwk

Seasons of Beento Blackbird. unabr. ed. Akosua Busia. Read by Akosua Busia. (Running Time: 15 hrs.). 2008. 39.25 (978-1-4233-5356-0(0), 9781423353560, Brinc Audio MP3 Lib); 39.25 (978-1-4233-5358-4(7), 9781423353584, BADLE); 24.95 (978-1-4233-5355-3(2), 9781423353553, Brilliance MP3); 24.95 (978-1-4233-5357-7(9), 9781423353577, BAD) Brilliance Audio.

Seasons of Life: Ecc. 3:1-11. Ed Young. 1993. 4.95 (978-0-7417-1980-5(0), 980) Win Walk.

Seasons of Life: Reflections in Song. Sarah Barchas. Des. by Elizabeth Gething. Photos by Joseph A. Robbins. Prod. by King Roger. 1 CD. (Running Time: 50 mins). 2002. audio compact disk 16.98 (978-1-889686-17-2(4), HHM-111D) High Haven Mus.
Seasons of Life is an inspirational CD with lyrics booklet of 17 original songs in folk-acoustic style. The songs have themes of hope and healing, choices and chances, survival and loss, striving through adversity, and the fragility and complexity of life and relationships across passages of experience and time.

Seasons of Love. unabr. ed. Anna Jacobs. Read by Patience Tomlinson. 8 cass. (Soundings Ser.). (J). 2006. 69.95 (978-1-84559-338-4(3)); audio compact disk 84.95 (978-1-84559-363-6(4)) Pub: ISIS Lrg Prnt GBR. Dist(s): Ulverscroft US

Seasons of My Life, Hannah Hauxwell. Read by Hannah Hauxwell. 4 cass. (Running Time: 6 hrs.). 1999. 44.95 (63716) Pub: Soundings Ltd GBR. Dist(s): Ulverscroft US

Seasons of Revival. Stephen Mansfield. 1 cass. (Running Time: 90 mins.). (Studies in Church History Ser.: Vol. 5). 2000. 5.00 (SM02-005) Morning NC.
An in-depth look at different philosophies that have influenced church history, this series provides excellent keys for understanding how to effectively confront the important issues of our times.

Seasons of the Soul: Weather & Climate & the Psyche. Dennis Merritt. Read by Dennis Merritt. 1 cass. (Running Time: 1 hrs.). 1995. 9.95 (978-0-7822-0519-0(4), 587) C G Jung IL.
The upper midwest provides an ideal environment to symbolically explore the complete range of effects that weather has on humans. Dr. Merritt uses the many weather metaphors in the I Ching to delve into the deeper teachings offered by weather & climate.

Seasons under Heaven. Beverly LaHaye & Terri Blackstock. Narrated by Ruth Ann Phimister. 9 CDs. (Running Time: 10 hrs. 30 mins.). (Cedar Circle Ser.). audio compact disk 89.00 (978-0-7887-9887-0(1)) Recorded Bks.

***Seasons under Heaven.** Beverly LaHaye & Terri Blackstock. (Running Time: 9 hrs. 35 mins. 0 sec.). (Seasons Ser.). (ENG.). 2008. 14.99 (978-0-310-30510-1(1)) Zondervan.

Seasons under Heaven. unabr. ed. Beverly LaHaye & Terri Blackstock. Narrated by Ruth Ann Phimister. 8 cass. (Running Time: 10 hrs. 30 mins.). (Cedar Circle Ser.). 1999. 68.00 (978-0-7887-4960-5(9), K0012L8) Recorded Bks.
Cedar Circle is a typical cul-de-sac with typical families. Sylvia feels useless as she faces empty-nest syndrome. Tory can't start her writing career while raising two pre-schoolers. Cathy struggles to control her belligerent teenagers. And Brenda quietly tries to re-instill in her husband a love for Christ. But when one of Brenda's children becomes seriously ill, the families of Cedar Circle pull together to discover the incredible strength of accepting God's will for them.

Seasons Will Pass. unabr. ed. Audrey Howard. Read by Carole Boyd. 12 cass. (Running Time: 18 hrs.). 2002. 96.95 (978-0-7540-0752-4(9), CAB 2174) AudioGO.
Clare Hanrahan has nothing left to lose the day she stumbles into Lew Earnshaw's arms. Her family is gone, victims of the Irish potato famine; her own life hangs by a thread. By the time Lew and his kindly neighbors have nursed clare back to health, he is hopelessly in love with the frail Irish girl. But though she will always care for Lew, another man comes between them.

Seasons with Henry & Mudge. Cynthia Rylant. Illus. by Suçie Stevenson. 44 vols. (Running Time: 46 mins.). (Henry & Mudge Ser.). 2000. pap. bk. 68.95 (978-1-59112-855-7(2)) Live Oak Media.

Seasons with Henry & Mudge. Cynthia Rylant. Read by Suzanne Toren. Illus. by Suçie Stevenson. 44 vols. (Running Time: 46 mins.). (Henry & Mudge Ser.). (J). (gr. k-3). 2000. pap. bk. 61.95 (978-0-87499-573-2(6)) Live Oak Media.
Includes: "Henry & Mudge in the Green Time," "Henry & Mudge in Puddle Trouble," "Henry & Mudge in the Sparkle Days" & "Henry & Mudge under the Yellow Moon.".

Seat of Mercy. Chuck Missler & Bob Comuke. 1 CD and 1 CD-ROM. (Running Time: 2 hours). (Briefing Packages by Chuck Missler). 2001. audio compact disk 19.95 (978-1-57821-160-9(3)) Koinonia Hse.
What is the mystery that surrounds the Ark of the Covenant?Where is the Ark of God? And what is its ultimate destiny?The Ark of the Covenant, a prominent fixture in the narratives of the Old Testament, certainly seems to have disappeared from view after the Babylonian captivity, which began in 606 B.C. There are many theories as to what happened to the Ark of the Covenant. In the popularized and well-attended fantasy movie, Raiders of the Lost Ark, the mystery surrounding the Ark was dramatized. In this provocative study, Chuck and Bob discuss the mystery surrounding the Ark, new evidence of its possible location and the future role it may play in the end times.

Seat of the Soul. Swami Amar Jyoti. 1 cass. 1979. 9.95 (O-15) Truth Consciousness.
Finding the seat of the soul, the Cosmic Energy within. Renewal of energy, body & vitality. The religion of realism.

Seat of the Soul. unabr. ed. Gary Zukav. Read by William David Griffith. 5 cass. (Running Time: 7 hrs. 30 min.). 1999. 40.00 (978-0-7366-4483-9(0), 4923) Books on Tape.
Takes us on a penetrating exploration of the new phase of evolution we have now entered. Explains that we are evolving from a species that pursues power based upon the perception of the five senses & shows how the pursuit of external power has produced our survival-of-the-finest understanding of evolution & generated conflict between lovers, communities, & even superpowers. He believes that humans are immortal souls first, physical beings second, & that once we align our personalities with our soul - we will stimulate our spiritual growth & become better people in the process.

Seat of the Soul. unabr. ed. Gary Zukav. Read by Gary Zukav. 2006. 17.95 (978-0-7435-6454-0(5)); audio compact disk 29.95 (978-0-7435-5008-6(0)) Pub: S&S Audio. Dist(s): S and S Inc

Seattle. unabr. ed. Hank Mitchum. Read by Charlie O'Dowd. 4 vols. No. 7. 2003. 25.00 (978-1-58807-190-3(1)); (978-1-58807-591-8(5)) Am Pubng Inc.

Seattle & Its People. Pace International Research, Inc. Staff. 1984. 3.25 (978-0-89209-079-2(0)) Pace Grp Intl.

Seattle Interview on the Believer's Security. Dan Comer. 1 cass. 4.00 (SE) Evang Outreach.

Seatworks. 1 cass. (Running Time: 1 hr.). (J). 2001. pap. bk. 10.95 (KIM 9100C) Kimbo Educ.
Seated exercises concentrate on simple body movements. There are shoulder shrugs, toe walks, karate movements, arm stretches & strokes. Includes manual.

Seaview see Toby Olson

Seawitch. unabr. ed. Alistair MacLean. Read by Peter Wickham. 6 cass. (Running Time: 6 hrs.). 1996. 54.95 (978-0-7451-6680-3(6), CAB 1296) AudioGO.
"Seawitch," the massive oil-rig, is the hub of a huge empire owned by Lord Worth, who has clawed his way to great wealth. His only cares are for the "Seawitch" & his two daughters. One man knows this: John Cronkite, trouble-shooter for the world's top oilmen & Worth's ex-victim. Cronkite is spoiling for revenge & in one terrifying week, Worth's world explodes.

Seaworthy: A Swordboat Captain Returns to the Sea. unabr. ed. Linda Greenlaw. Read by Linda Greenlaw. 1 MP3-CD. (Running Time: 7 hrs.). 2010. 24.99 (978-1-4233-9006-0(7), 9781423390060, Brilliance MP3); 39.97 (978-1-4233-9007-7(5), 9781423390077, Brinc Audio MP3 Lib); 24.99 (978-1-4233-9008-4(3), 9781423390084, BAD); 39.97 (978-1-4233-9009-1(1), 9781423390091, BADLE); audio compact disk 24.99 (978-1-4233-9004-6(0), 9781423390046, Bril Audio CD Unabri); audio compact disk 82.97 (978-1-4233-9005-3(9), 9781423390053, BriAudCD Unabrid) Brilliance Audio.

Seazoo. Perf. by Jill Williamson. Composed by Lynne Cox. 1 cass. (Running Time: 10 min.). (J). 1997. 6.00 (978-1-891258-05-3(2), LCP05-2) L Cox Pubns.
Ten songs teaching the young child facts about sea creatures. The lyrics are in riddle format. Music styles range from a Latin-American beet (lobster) to chromaticism (Eel), etc.

Sebastian the Crab. Bob Marley et al. Perf. by Third World staff. 1 cass. (J). (ps up). 9.98 (2259); 21.98 Incl. toy crab. (5039); audio compact disk 17.98 (D2259) MFLP CA.
The beloved character from Disney's "Little Mermaid" does a great solo act with this collection of Caribbean tunes from Jamaica, the tropical land where it was recorded.

Sebby, Stee, the Garbos & Me. unabr. ed. Jane Godwin. Read by Stig Wemyss. (Aussie Bites Ser.). (J). 2002. audio compact disk 39.95 (978-1-74030-842-7(5)) Pub: Bolinda Pubng AUS. Dist(s): Bolinda Pub Inc

Sebby, Stee, the garbos & me, plus three More. unabr. ed. Margaret Clark et al. Read by Stig Wemyss. 2 cass. (Running Time: 3 hrs. 35 mins.). (Aussie Bites Ser.). (J). 2000. lib. bdg. 24.00 (978-1-74030-146-6(3), 500533) Pub: Bolinda Pubng AUS. Dist(s): Bolinda Pub Inc

SEC Section 16 Rules. 4 cass. (Running Time: 6 hrs.). 1991. 125.00 (T7-9343) PLI.

SECD Microprocessor: A Verification Case Study. Brian T. Graham. (International Series in Engineering & Computer Science Ser.). (C). 1992. audio compact disk 164.00 (978-0-7923-9245-3(0)) Spri.

Sechse Kommen Durch die Ganze Welt. Jacob W. Grimm & Wilhelm K. Grimm. 1 cass. (Running Time: 60 min.). (Bruder Grimm Kinder & Hausmarchen Ser.). (GER.). 1996. pap. bk. 19.50 (978-1-58085-209-8(2), GR-04) Interlingua VA.
Includes German transcription. Includes title story, Der Wolf und der Mensch, Der Wolf und der Fuchs, Der Fuchs und die Frau Gevatterin, Der Fuchs und die Katze, Die Nelke, Das kluge Gretel, Des Herrn und des Teufels Getier, Der Hahnenbalken. The combination of written text & clarity & pace of diction will open the door for intermediate & advanced students to genuine comprehension & the use of literary texts for advancement in rapid understanding of written & oral language materials. The audio text plus written text concept makes foreign languages accessible to a much wider range of students than books alone.

Second Angel. collector's ed. Philip Kerr. Read by Geoffrey Howard. 8 cass. (Running Time: 12 hrs.). 1999. 64.00 (978-0-7366-4649-9(3), 5030) Books on Tape.
It is July, 2069 & the new millennium is not working out well. Plagues have destroyed our major food supplies, climatic changes have brought constant winter to the once industrialized West & a new & virulent virus P (2) has infected the Earth's population. P (2) is curable but only with an infusion of clean, uninfected blood, available only in a lunar blood bank. The struggle for control of this vital cache powers this novel.

Second Annual Conference & Exhibition on High Definition Television. 33 cass. 1990. 195.00 Recorded Res.

Second Annual Current Issues for Child Advocates. 1998. bk. 99.00 (ACS-2025) PA Bar Inst.
The PBA Children's Rights Committee & PBI presented the second annual child advocate's training in April 1998. Now you have the opportunity to receive their practical advice in the manual. You will learn the methods of confronting the unique challenges faced by the child advocate in the areas of child custody, abuse, health benefits & dependency. This also takes a close look at the difficult ethical dilemmas faced by attorneys who are appointed guardians ad litem.

Second Annual Family Law Update. 1998. bk. 99.00 (ACS-2108) PA Bar Inst.
This is exclusively designed to provide matrimonial lawyers with an in-depth analysis of every major family law decision over the past year. It offers a review of practical implications & other significant cases in seven key areas. Rule & statutory changes are also addressed, including the recent changes to the Support Guidelines.

Second Best of Car Talk: More Used Calls from Click & Clack. Tom Magliozzi & Ray Magliozzi. 1 cass., 1 CD. 1998. 11.95 (978-1-55935-246-8(9)); audio compact disk 14.95 CD. (978-1-55935-221-5(3)) Soundelux.
More from the call-in radio show, in which Mr. Goodwrench meets the Marx Brothers.

Second Birthday. (Greetings Ser.: Vol. 2). (gr. 2-3). 10.00 (978-0-7635-5867-3(2)) Rigby Educ.

Second Book of the Tao. Stephen Mitchell. Read by Stephen Mitchell. (Running Time: 3 hrs.). (ENG.). (gr. 12 up). 2009. audio compact disk 25.95 (978-0-14-314437-3(5), PengAudBks) Penguin Grp USA.

***Second Chair.** John Lescroart. (Dismas Hardy Ser.). 2010. audio compact disk 9.99 (978-1-4418-5701-9(X)) Brilliance Audio.

Second Chair. abr. ed. John Lescroart. Read by David Colacci. (Running Time: 6 hrs.). (Dismas Hardy Ser.: No. 10). 2006. audio compact disk 16.99 (978-1-4233-1949-8(4), 9781423319498, BCD Value Price) Brilliance Audio.
Dismas Hardy is finally on top: As a managing partner at his thriving, newly reorganized law firm, he's a rainmaker and fix-it guy for clients leery of taking their chances in a courtroom. Now Hardy's up-and-coming associate, Amy Wu, brings him a high-profile case: Andrew Bartlett, the seventeen-year-old son of a prominent San Francisco family, has been arrested for the double slaying of his girlfriend and his English teacher. The D.A. wants to try him as an adult. Determined to get the case into juvenile court, and overwhelmed by the mounting evidence against her client, Wu asks Hardy to sit second chair for her in Bartlett's defense. As the Bartlett case moves swiftly to trial, another series of murders grips the city. An unseen killer seems to be shooting citizens wantonly, and as fear and anxiety build around the Executioner (as he is quickly dubbed in the ensuing media frenzy), Abe Glitsky, the newly promoted deputy chief of the Investigations Bureau, leads the desperate hunt to stop him. With the city on the verge of panic, Hardy and Glitsky are locked in a race against time - to save a client and to catch a murderer. But nothing is what it seems, and as both men's cases twist and turn to their shocking conclusions, the very foundations of San Francisco's legal system will be shaken to the core.

Second Chair. unabr. ed. John Lescroart. Read by David Colacci. 9 cass. (Running Time: 14 hrs.). (Dismas Hardy Ser.: No. 10). 2004. 97.25 (978-1-59086-376-3(3), 1590863763, BrilAudUnabridg); 34.95 (978-1-59086-375-6(5), 1590863755, BAU); audio compact disk 40.95 (978-1-59086-378-7(X), 159086378X, Bril Audio CD Unabri); audio compact disk 112.25 (978-1-59086-379-4(8), 1590863798, BriAudCD Unabrid) Brilliance Audio.
Dismas Hardy is finally on top: As a managing partner at his thriving, newly reorganized law firm, he's a rainmaker and fix-it guy for clients leery of taking their chances in a courtroom. Now Hardy's up-and-coming associate, Amy Wu, brings him a high-profile case: Andrew Bartlett, the seventeen-year-old son of a prominent San Francisco family, has been arrested for the double slaying of his girlfriend and his English teacher. The D.A. wants to try him as an adult. Determined to get the case into juvenile court, and overwhelmed by the mounting evidence against her client, Wu asks Hardy to sit second chair for her in Bartlett's defense. As the Bartlett case moves swiftly to trial, another series of murders grips the city. An unseen killer seems to be shooting citizens wantonly, and as fear and anxiety build around the Executioner (as he is quickly dubbed in the ensuing media frenzy), Abe Glitsky, the newly promoted deputy chief of the Investigations Bureau, leads the desperate hunt to stop him. With the city on the verge of panic, Hardy and Glitsky are locked in a race against time - to save a client and to catch a murderer. But nothing is what it seems, and as both men's cases twist and turn to their shocking conclusions, the very foundations of San Francisco's legal system will be shaken to the core.

Second Chair. unabr. ed. John Lescroart. Read by David Colacci. (Running Time: 14 hrs.). (Dismas Hardy Ser.: No. 10). 2004. 24.95 (978-1-59335-267-7(0), 1593352670, Brilliance MP3); 39.25 (978-1-59335-488-6(6), 1593354886, Brinc Audio MP3 Lib) Brilliance Audio.

Second Chair. unabr. ed. John Lescroart. Read by David Colacci. (Running Time: 14 hrs.). (Dismas Hardy Ser.: No. 10). 2004. 39.25 (978-1-59710-677-1(1), 1597106771, BADLE); 24.95 (978-1-59710-676-4(3), 1597106763, BAD) Brilliance Audio.

***Second Chair: A Stan Turner Mystery.** William Manchee. 2010. 15.00 (978-1-935722-52-6(2), TOP USA); audio compact disk 29.00 (978-1-935722-53-3(0), TOP USA) Top Pubns.

Second Chakra: Key to Flexibility, Contentment & Getting into the Flow. 1 cass. (Running Time: 90 min.). (Chakras Ser.). 9.95 (83T) Crystal Clarity.
Topics include: The water element in human consciousness, releasing the need for control & learning how to flow with life; living in the upper chakras as a route of joy.

Second Chance. Jane Green. Read by Rosalyn Landor. (Running Time: 12 hrs.). (ENG.). (gr. 12 up). 2007. audio compact disk 39.95 (978-0-14-314217-1(8), PengAudBks) Penguin Grp USA.

Second Chance. rev. ed. Sydney Banks. Read by Sydney Banks. 2001. (978-1-55105-297-7(0)) Lone Pine Publ CAN.

Second Chance. unabr. ed. Danielle Steel. 4 cass. (Running Time: 6 hrs.). 2004. 36.00 (978-1-4159-0086-4(8)); audio compact disk 38.25 (978-1-4159-0113-7(9)) Pub: Books on Tape. Dist(s): NetLibrary CO
A free-spirited fashion editor meets her match in this captivating tale of new hope and second chances.

Second Chance. unabr. ed. Elizabeth Waite. Read by Annie Aldington. 10 cass. (Running Time: 12 hrs. 30 min.). (Sound Ser.). 2001. 84.95 (978-1-86042-625-4(5)) Pub: UlverLrgPrint GBR. Dist(s): Ulverscroft US

Second Chance, Vol. 1. rev. ed. Sydney Banks. Read by Sydney Banks. (J). (gr. 4). 2001. audio compact disk 24.95 (978-1-55105-292-2(X)) Lone Pine.

Second Chance: Four Kids Face Earth's Last Days Together. Jerry B. Jenkins & Tim LaHaye. Narrated by Jeff Woodman. 2 pieces. (Running Time: 3 hrs.). (Left Behind Ser.: Bk. 2). (gr. 4 up). 22.00 (978-0-7887-5369-5(X)); audio compact disk 29.00 (978-1-4025-1971-0(0)) Recorded Bks.

Second Chance: The Story of Ajamila's Near-death Experience. 10 cass. 39.00 Set, incl. 1 vinyl album. Bhaktivedanta.
Adapted from Srila. Prabhupada's extensive lectures on this topic.

Second Chance: Three Presidents & the Crisis of American Superpower. unabr. ed. Zbigniew Brzezinski. Read by Dick Hill. (Running Time: 5 hrs. 30 mins. 0 sec.). (ENG.). 2007. audio compact disk 29.99 (978-1-4001-0459-8(9)); audio compact disk 19.99 (978-1-4001-5459-3(6)); audio compact disk 59.99 (978-1-4001-3459-5(5)) Pub: Tantor Media. Dist(s): IngramPubServ

Second Chance Christmas: A Symphonic Story. Scripts. Ric Reitz. Based on a poem by Ric Reitz. 1 CD. (Running Time: 58:00). Dramatization. (J). 2004. audio compact disk 14.95 (978-0-9670160-1-6(0), Sir Fir Bks) Sir Fir Ent.
On a cold Christmas Eve, in a town without joy,A law against music haunts each girl and boy.When a terrible storm strands touring musicians,Hope will return to break long-held traditions.(Full cast production features symphonic music by the Atlanta Symphony Youth Orchestra & Chorus, Jere Flint, Conductor.).

Second Chicken Soup for the Woman's Soul: 101 More Stories to Open the Hearts & Rekindle the Spirits of Women. abr. ed. Jack L. Canfield et al. 1 cass. (Running Time: 90 min.). (Chicken Soup for the Soul Ser.). 1998. 9.95 (978-1-55874-623-7(4)) Health Comm.
Selections of the best from the latest in the series.

Second Coming see Poetry of William Butler Yeats

Second Coming, George W. Pace. 2 cass. 11.98 (978-1-55503-028-5(9), 07002862) Covenant Comms.
Details prophecies to be fulfilled & warnings to heed.

Second Coming, unabr. ed. Walker Percy. Read by David Hilder. 9 cass. (Running Time: 13 hrs.). 1994. 62.95 (978-0-7861-0470-3(8), 1422) Blckstn Audio.
This is the story of Will Barrett of Linwood, North Carolina, a widower, & how he finds his way out of death-in-life with the help of Allison, the girl in the greenhouse. Allie, having just engineered her own escape from a mental institution, is working hard to make a new life for herself & install a big, black iron Grand Crown stove in the run-down greenhouse when Will, in a most unusual manner, crosses her path. Her marvelous, slightly crazy speech patterns & Will's peculiar tendency from his "petty mall" spells to fall down in strange places - golf courses, greenhouses, buses - astonishingly enough cement their relationship.

Second Coming: Great or Dreadful? Curtis Jacobs. 1 cass. 2004. 9.95 (978-1-57734-575-6(4), 06006167) Covenant Comms.
Two talks for our days.

Second Coming: The Great or Dreadful? Curtis Jacobs. 2004. audio compact disk 10.95 (978-1-57734-629-6(7)) Covenant Comms.

Second Coming of Christ: Being Prepared. Randall Bird. 1 cass. 2004. 7.98 (978-1-55503-952-3(9), 06005276) Covenant Comms.
Important doctrines of the Second Coming.

Second Coming of Christ Series. 4 cass. 32.00 incl. vinyl storage album. Crystal Clarity.
Examines: Who & What was Christ?; Christs Mission; The True Meaning of Christianity; Christ's Last Days.

Second Coming of the Santa Claus Spirit. Manly P. Hall. 8.95 (978-0-89314-250-6(6), C871221) Philos Res.
Inspirational & mystical beliefs - includes fiction, myths, & poetry.

Second Confession. unabr. ed. Rex Stout. Read by Michael Prichard. 6 cass. (Running Time: 8 hrs.). (Nero Wolfe Ser.). 2000. 29.95 (978-1-57270-132-8(3), N61132u) Pub: Audio Partners. Dist(s): PerseuPGW
When a millionaire businessman hires Nero Wolfe to uncover the background of his daughter's boyfriend, Wolfe isn't sure he wants to be involved. Then a mob boss counsels him to drop the matter, machine-gun fire rips apart his orchid room, & the boyfriend turns up dead. Wolfe must solve the murder to prevent his own.

Second Confession. unabr. ed. Rex Stout. Read by Michael Prichard. (Running Time: 28800 sec.). (Nero Wolfe Ser.). (ENG.). 2006. audio compact disk 29.95 (978-1-57270-501-2(9)) Pub: AudioGO. Dist(s): Perseus Dist
When a millionaire businessman hires Nero Wolfe to investigate his daughter's boyfriend, hoping to find that he's a member of the Communist Party, Wolfe suspects it's nothing more than an overprotective father. But after a powerful gangland boss "advises" him to drop the matter - and machine-gun fire rips into his beloved orchids - Wolfe realizes it's much more than a father's overactive imagination. And when the boyfriend turns up dead, leaving Archie Goodwin as the prime suspect, Wolfe realizes he must act fast to prevent another murder - his own.

Second Confession. unabr. collector's ed. Rex Stout. Read by Michael Prichard. 8 cass. (Running Time: 8 hrs.). (Nero Wolfe Ser.). 1995. 64.00 (978-0-7366-3070-2(8), 3752) Books on Tape.
Nero Wolfe cooperates with his mortal enemy in a case that squeezes the real culprit to confess. Sleuthing as a science.

***Second Contact.** unabr. ed. Harry Turtledove. Narrated by Patrick G. Lawlor. (Running Time: 28 hrs. 0 mins. 0 sec.). (Colonization Ser.). (ENG.). 2010. audio compact disk 109.99 (978-1-4001-4398-6(5)) Pub: Tantor Media. Dist(s): IngramPubServ

Second Corinthians. (LifeLight Bible Studies: Course 21). 13.95 Set. (20-2557) Concordia.

Second Day - Ewell's Attack. 1 cass. Dramatization. (Voices of Gettysburg Ser.). 1991. 12.95 Heritage.
Dramatized reconstructions of Civil War-era voices.

Second Day - Longstreet's Attack. 1 cass. Dramatization. (Voices of Gettysburg Ser.). 1991. 12.95 Heritage.

Second Death of Goodluck Tinubu: A Detective Kubu Mystery. unabr. ed. Michael Stanley. Narrated by Simon Prebble. (Running Time: 14 hrs. 0 mins. 0 sec.). (Detective Kubu Ser.). (ENG.). 2009. 29.99 (978-1-4001-6348-9(X)); audio compact disk 79.99 (978-1-4001-4348-1(9)); audio compact disk 39.99 (978-1-4001-1348-4(2)) Pub: Tantor Media. Dist(s): IngramPubServ

Second Decade of Love. abr. ed. Greg Johnson & Mike Yorkey. Narrated by Mike Trout. 2 cass. 1994. 14.99 Set. (978-0-8423-7434-7(5)) Tyndale Hse.
Most couples entering their second decade of marriage are met by challenges different from those faced during the first 10 years. This book targets such couples, giving reassurance for surviving - & thriving - over the following 10 years.

Second Decade 1993-2003. Contrib. by Michael W. Smith. 2003. audio compact disk 13.99 (978-5-550-26408-9(0)) Pt of Grace Ent.

Second Declaration. unabr. ed. Xiaoping Wang. Read by Marguerite Gavin. (Running Time: 14 hrs.). (ENG.). 2008. 39.98 (978-1-59659-295-7(8), GildAudio) Pub: Gildan Media. Dist(s): HachBkGrp

Second Dune. unabr. ed. Shelby Hearon. Narrated by Carol Monda. 4 cass. (Running Time: 5 hrs.). (Tcu Press Texas Tradition Ser.). 1973. 39.75 (978-1-4193-1229-8(4), S1075MC); audio compact disk 49.75 (978-1-4193-1231-1(6), CS025MC) Recorded Bks.

***Second Fiddle.** unabr. ed. Rosanne Parry. (ENG.). (J). 2011. audio compact disk 39.00 (978-0-307-74760-0(3), Listening Lib) Pub: Random Audio Pubg. Dist(s): Random

Second Fiddle. unabr. ed. Mary Wesley. Read by Anna Massey. 6 cass. (Running Time: 6 hrs.). (Audio Bks.). 1991. 54.95 set. (978-0-7451-6351-2(3)) AudioGO.
Laura Thornby manages her life with exquisite control. Her affairs are brief but delightful & her career is fulfilling. But when she meets Claude Bannister, struggling to be a writer, she is swept by an irresistible desire to manipulate & experiment with him. What she does not foresee, however, are the possibilities that he might one day be a good writer - & that she might fall in love.

Second Foundation. Isaac Asimov. Read by Scott Brick. 2002. 64.00 (978-0-7366-8958-8(3)); audio compact disk 72.00 (978-0-7366-9239-7(8)) Books on Tape.

Second Foundation. unabr. ed. Isaac Asimov. Read by Dan Lazar. 8 cass. (Running Time: 8 hrs.). 1979. 48.00 (978-0-7366-0196-2(1), 1196) Books on Tape.
Addresses the phenomenon of genetic mutation & its potential danger to a civilization. Tells of an overwhelmingly powerful mutant human being, born with the ability to mold men's minds & emotions. He has brought down the First Foundation; only the Second Foundation remains.

Second Generation. unabr. ed. Howard Fast. Read by Multivoice Production Staff. (Running Time: 15 hrs.). 2008. 39.25 (978-1-4233-7218-9(2), 9781423372189, BADLE); 39.25 (978-1-4233-7216-5(6), 9781423372165, Brinc Audio MP3 Lib); 24.95 (978-1-4233-7215-8(8), 9781423372158, Brilliance MP3); 24.95 (978-1-4233-7217-2(4), 9781423372172, BAD) Brilliance Audio.

Second Glance. 2004. DVD & audio compact disk 9.99 (978-0-01-222990-3(3)) D Christiano Films.

Second Glance. Jodi Picoult. 10 cass. (Running Time: 17 hrs.). 2004. 34.99 (978-1-4025-5647-0(0), 03244) Recorded Bks.

Second Grade Rules, Amber Brown. Paula Danziger. Read by Dana Lubotsky. Illus. by Tony Ross. 1 cass. (Running Time: 16 mins.). (J). (gr.

k-3). 2007. bk. 25.95 (978-1-4301-0071-3(0)); pap. bk. 18.95 (978-1-4301-0073-7(7)); pap. bk. 16.95 (978-1-4301-0070-6(2)) Live Oak Media.

Second Grade Rules, Amber Brown. Paula Danziger. Illus. by Tony Ross. Narrated by Dana Lubotsky. (J). (gr. k-3). 2007. audio compact disk 12.95 (978-1-4301-0069-0(9)) Live Oak Media.

Second Grade Rules, Amber Brown. unabr. ed. Paula Danziger. Read by Dana Lubotsky. Illus. by Tony Ross. 1 CD. (Running Time: 16 mins.). (J). (gr. k-3). 2007. bk. 28.95 (978-1-4301-0074-4(5)) Live Oak Media.

Second Grade Rules, Amber Brown, Set. Paula Danziger. Read by Dana Lubotsky. Illus. by Tony Ross. 1 CD. (Running Time: 16 mins.). (J). (gr. k-3). 2007. pap. bk. 31.95 (978-1-4301-0075-1(3)); pap. bk. 29.95 (978-1-4301-0072-0(9)) Live Oak Media.

Second Half of Life. Angeles Arrien. 1998. audio compact disk 69.95 (978-1-59179-536-0(2)) Sounds True.

Second Half of Life. Angeles Arrien. 2 CDs. 2005. audio compact disk 19.95 (978-1-59179-296-3(7), AW00936D) Sounds True.

Second Half of Marriage: Facing the Eight Challenges of Every Long-Term Marriage. abr. ed. Dave Arp & Claudia Arp. (Running Time: 2 hrs. 0 mins. 0 sec.). (ENG.). 2003. 9.99 (978-0-310-26096-7(5)) Zondervan.

Second Heaven. unabr. ed. Judith Guest. Interview with Judith Guest. 1 cass. (Running Time: 29 min.). 1984. 10.00 New Letters.
Guest talks about her writing & reads an excerpt from "Second Heaven." Short pieces of her "Ordinary People" which was made into the Academy Award-winning film are read by actors.

Second Heaven. unabr. ed. Judith Guest. Narrated by Sheri Blair. 7 cass. (Running Time: 9 hrs. 30 mins.). 1983. 60.00 (978-1-55690-463-9(0), 83049E7) Recorded Bks.
Cat Holzman opens her door & her heart to a teenage runaway. But the simple act of compassion becomes a call-to-arms to save this boy & herself from the mindless rush of convention, the law & her own shattered image.

Second Honeymoon. Vivien Young. Read by Elizabeth Henry. 3 cass. (Running Time: 3 hrs.). 1999. 34.95 (65646) Pub: Soundings Ltd GBR. Dist(s): Ulverscroft US

Second Horseman. abr. ed. Kyle Mills. 2006. 14.95 (978-1-59397-915-7(0)) Pub: Macmill Audio. Dist(s): Macmillan

Second John McPhee Reader, Pt. 1. unabr. ed. John McPhee. Narrated by Nelson Runger. 6 cass. (Running Time: 7 hrs. 45 mins.). 51.00 (978-0-7887-0654-7(3), 94831E7) Recorded Bks.
The writings gathered here show off a writer who not only is in absolute command of his craft, but also reveals the hidden fragility of the world around us. A must-listen for anyone interested in nature, or the state of the human condition. Available to libraries only.

Second John McPhee Reader, Pt. 2. unabr. ed. John McPhee. Narrated by Nelson Runger. 6 cass. (Running Time: 9 hrs.). 1999. 51.00 (978-0-7887-0670-7(5), 94847E7) Recorded Bks.

Second Journey: The Road Back to Yourself. unabr. ed. Joan Anderson. (Running Time: 5 hrs. NaN mins.). 2008. 19.95 (978-1-4332-1438-7(5)) Blckstn Audio.

Second Journey: The Road Back to Yourself. unabr. ed. Joan Anderson. Read by Pam Ward. (Running Time: 18000 sec.). 2008. audio compact disk 19.95 (978-1-4332-1440-0(7)); audio compact disk & audio compact disk 19.95 (978-1-4332-1439-4(3)) Blckstn Audio.

Second Journey: The Road Back to Yourself. unabr. ed. Anderson Joan. Read by Pam Ward. (Running Time: 18000 sec.). 2008. 34.95 (978-1-4332-1436-3(9)); audio compact disk & audio compact disk 40.00 (978-1-4332-1437-0(7)) Blckstn Audio.

Second Jungle Book. unabr. ed. Rudyard Kipling. Read by Flo Gibson. 5 cass. (Running Time: 7 hrs. 30 min.). (J). 1984. 20.95 (978-1-55685-057-8(3)) Audio Bk Con.
More of Mowgli's adventures with his jungle friends.

Second Jungle Book. unabr. ed. Rudyard Kipling. Read by Cindy Hardin & Walter Zimmerman. 5 cass. (Running Time: 7 hrs.). 1986. 39.95 (978-0-7861-0557-1(7), 2050) Blckstn Audio.
A continuation of "The Jungle Book," these adventures of Mowgli & his companions of the jungle are sure to delight listeners, young & old.

Second Jungle Book. unabr. ed. Rudyard Kipling. Read by Cindy Hardin & Walter Zimmerman. 8 cass. (Running Time: 1 hr. per cass.). Dramatization. (J). 1984. 42.00 (C-128) Jimcin Record.
More adventures of Mowgli, the jungle boy, & his friends.

Second Large Print Song Book. 2nd l.t. ed. Ulverscroft Staff. 1987. bk. 9.99 (978-0-7089-1670-0(3)) Pub: UlverLrgPrint GBR. Dist(s): Ulverscroft US

Second Large Print Song Book - Music Edition (Red) 2nd l.t. rev. ed. Ulverscroft Staff. 1987. bk. 18.99 (978-0-7089-1736-7(4)) Pub: UlverLrgPrint GBR. Dist(s): Ulverscroft US

Second Legacy. Joanna Trollope. Narrated by Virginia Leishman & Emily Gray. 11 cass. (Running Time: 15 hrs. 30 mins.). 98.00 (978-0-7887-9401-8(9)) Recorded Bks.

Second Life of Samuel Tyne. unabr. ed. Esi Edugyan. Narrated by Peter Jay Fernandez. 8 cass. (Running Time: 11 hrs.). 2004. 79.75 (978-1-4193-0556-6(5), F0193MC, Griot Aud) Recorded Bks.

Second Lives. unabr. ed. Tim Guest. (Running Time: 9 hrs. 0 mins.). 2008. audio compact disk 29.95 (978-1-4332-1020-4(7)) Blckstn Audio.

Second Lives: A Journey Through Virtual Worlds. unabr. ed. Tim Guest. Read by Paul Michael Garcia. (Running Time: 37800 sec.). 2008. 29.95 (978-1-4332-1019-8(3)); 65.95 (978-1-4332-1017-4(7)); audio compact disk 29.95 (978-1-4332-1021-1(5)); audio compact disk & audio compact disk 90.00 (978-1-4332-1018-1(5)) Blckstn Audio.

Second Look at the Genesis Myth - The Serpent As a Guide to Human Evolution. Bruce Hawkins. 1 cass. 9.00 (A0035-87) Sound Photosyn.

Second Look at the Law of Karma. Instructed by Manly P. Hall. 8.95 (978-0-89314-251-3(4), C861102) Philos Res.

Second Man: 1 Cor. 15:35-49. Ed Young. 1986. 4.95 (978-0-7417-1521-0(X), 521) Win Walk.

Second Manassas Expedition Guide: The Complete Guide to the Second Manassas Battlefield. Narrated by Chris Bryce. 2001. cd-rom & audio compact disk 24.95 (978-0-9705809-6-2(7), 949 951-3223) TravelBrains.

Second Mile Vol. 644: Matthew 5:41. Ed Young. 1988. 4.95 (978-0-7417-1644-6(5), 644) Win Walk.

Second Mouse. unabr. ed. Archer Mayor. Narrated by Christopher Graybill. 7 CDs. (Running Time: 28560 sec.). (Joe Gunther Ser.). 2006. audio compact disk 74.95 (978-0-7927-4524-2(8), SLD 1054); audio compact disk 44.95 (978-0-7927-4564-8(7), CMP 1054) AudioGO.

Second Mrs. Tanqueray. unabr. ed. Arthur Wing Pinero. Read by Flo Gibson. 2 cass. (Running Time: 3 hrs). 1998. bk. 14.95 (978-1-55685-538-2(9)) Audio Bk Con.
When the past revisits Paula Tanqueray there are dire consequences.

Second Nature. Alice Hoffman. 2004. 10.95 (978-0-7435-4594-5(X)) Pub: S&S Audio. Dist(s): S and S Inc

***Second Nature.** unabr. ed. Nora Roberts. Read by Allison Fraser. (Running Time: 6 hrs.). (Celebrity Magazine Ser.). 2011. 39.97 (978-1-4418-5737-8(0), 9781441857378, BADLE); 24.99 (978-1-4418-5735-4(4), 9781441857354, Brilliance MP3); 39.97 (978-1-4418-5736-1(2), 9781441857361, Brlnc Audio MP3 Lib); audio compact disk 24.99 (978-1-4418-5733-0(8), 9781441857330, Bril Audio CD Unabri); audio compact disk 69.97 (978-1-4418-5734-7(6), 9781441857347, BriAudCD Unabrid) Brilliance Audio.

Second Nature: A Gardener's Education. unabr. ed. Michael Pollan. Read by Michael Pollan. 8 CDs. (Running Time: 9 hrs.). 2010. audio compact disk 29.99 (978-1-4418-3455-3(9), 9781441834553, Bril Audio CD Unabri) Brilliance Audio.

***Second Nature: A Gardener's Education.** unabr. ed. Michael Pollan. Read by Michael Pollan. (Running Time: 9 hrs.). 2010. 24.99 (978-1-4418-3457-7(5), 9781441834577, Brilliance MP3); 24.99 (978-1-4418-3459-1(1), 9781441834591, BAD); 39.97 (978-1-4418-3458-4(3), 9781441834584, Brlnc Audio MP3 Lib); 39.97 (978-1-4418-3460-7(5), 9781441834607, BADLE); audio compact disk 92.97 (978-1-4418-3456-0(7), 9781441834560, BriAudCD Unabrid) Brilliance Audio.

***Second Nature: L-Book.** Jae. (ENG.). 2009. 30.95 (978-1-934889-45-9(8)) Lbook Pub.

Second Objective. unabr. ed. Mark Frost. Narrated by Erik Steele. (Running Time: 38160 sec.). (ENG.). 2007. audio compact disk 39.95 (978-1-60283-035-6(5)) Pub: AudioGO. Dist(s): Perseus Dist

Second Oldest Profession: Spice & Spying in the 20th Century. unabr. ed. Phillip Knightley. Narrated by Nelson Runger. 15 cass. (Running Time: 20 hrs. 45 mins.). 1988. 120.00 (978-1-55690-464-6(9), 88992E7) Recorded Bks.
An overview of the history of espionage in the 20th Century.

Second Opinion. abr. ed. Michael Palmer. Read by Franette Liebow. (Running Time: 6 hrs.). 2009. audio compact disk 14.99 (978-1-4233-0671-9(6), 9781423306719, BCD Value Price) Brilliance Audio.

Second Opinion. unabr. ed. Michael Palmer. Read by Franette Liebow. 1 MP3-CD. (Running Time: 10 hrs.). 2007. 39.97 (978-1-59737-077-6(0), 9781597370776, Brlnc Audio MP3 Lib); audio compact disk 107.97 (978-1-59737-075-2(4), 9781597370752, BriAudCD Unabrid) Brilliance Audio.
Please enter a Synopsis.

Second Opinion. unabr. ed. Michael Palmer. Read by Franette Liebow. (Running Time: 9 hrs.). 2009. 39.97 (978-1-59737-079-0(7), 9781597370790, BADLE); 24.99 (978-1-59737-078-3(9), 9781597370783, BAD); 24.99 (978-1-59737-076-9(2), 9781597370769, Brilliance MP3); audio compact disk 38.99 (978-1-59737-074-5(6), 9781597370745, Bril Audio CD Unabri) Brilliance Audio.

***Second Saladin.** abr. ed. Stephen Hunter. Read by Dick Hill. (Running Time: 6 hrs.). 2010. 9.99 (978-1-4418-9396-3(2), 9781441893963, BAD); audio compact disk 14.99 (978-1-4418-6156-6(4), 9781441861566, BACD) Brilliance Audio.

***Second Saladin.** unabr. ed. Stephen Hunter. Read by Dick Hill. (Running Time: 14 hrs.). 2010. 24.99 (978-1-4418-6154-2(8), 9781441861542, BAD); 39.97 (978-1-4418-6155-9(6), 9781441861559, BADLE); 24.99 (978-1-4418-6152-8(1), 9781441861528, Brilliance MP3); 39.97 (978-1-4418-6153-5(X), 9781441861535, Brlnc Audio MP3 Lib); audio compact disk 29.99 (978-1-4418-6150-4(5), 9781441861504, Bril Audio CD Unabri); audio compact disk 92.97 (978-1-4418-6151-1(3), 9781441861511, BriAudCD Unabrid) Brilliance Audio.

Second Sampler. (Running Time: 46 min.). (J). 1986. 9.95 (978-0-939065-18-9(5), GW 1018) Gentle Wind.
Nine more selections of songs & stories for all ages.

Second Sex. Simone de Beauvoir. 2 cass. (Running Time: 2 hrs. 40 min.).Tr. of Deuxième Sexe. 1995. 17.95 Set. (978-1-879557-25-3(8)) Audio Scholar.
Simone de Beauvoir wrote her controversial work of self-discovery to confront the question, "what is a woman?" To readers in the 1950's, her uninhibited critique of sexism was revolutionary.

***Second Siege.** unabr. ed. Henry H. Neff. Narrated by Jeff Woodman. 1 Playaway. (Running Time: 15 hrs.). (Tapestry Ser.: Bk. 2). (YA). (gr. 6-9). 2009. 64.75 (978-1-4407-2912-6(3)); 102.75 (978-1-4361-8653-7(6)); audio compact disk 108.75 (978-1-4361-8657-5(9)) Recorded Bks.

***Second Siege.** unabr. collector's ed. Henry H. Neff. Narrated by Jeff Woodman. 13 CDs. (Running Time: 15 hrs.). (Tapestry Ser.: Bk. 2). (YA). (gr. 6-9). 2009. audio compact disk 61.95 (978-1-4361-8661-2(7)) Recorded Bks.

Second Sight see Twentieth-Century Poetry in English, No. 4, Recordings of Poets Reading Their Own Poetry

Second Sight. abr. ed. Amanda Quick, pseud. Read by Anne Flosnik. (Running Time: 4 hrs.). (Arcane Society Ser.). 2007. audio compact disk 14.99 (978-1-4233-1483-7(2), 9781423314837, BCD Value Price) Brilliance Audio.

Second Sight. unabr. ed. Amanda Quick, pseud. Read by Anne Flosnik. (Running Time: 32400 sec.). (Arcane Society Ser.). 2006. audio compact disk 92.25 (978-1-4233-1477-6(8), 9781423314776, BriAudCD Unabrid) Brilliance Audio.
Financially straitened and on the path to spinsterhood, Venetia Milton thought her stay at the remote, ramshackle Arcane House would be a once-in-a-lifetime opportunity to engineer her own ravishment. She was there to photograph the artifacts collected by a highly secretive organization, founded two centuries earlier by an alchemist. And the alchemist's descendant - her employer, Gabriel Jones - had the eyes of a sorcerer... But despite her intent to seduce the man and move on, she is shattered to return home and, just a week later, read of his violent demise in the press. She uses the sizable fee Mr. Jones paid and establishes a new life, opening a gallery in London. Of course, posing as a respectable widow makes it easier to do business, so - in a private tribute to her lost, only lover - she takes on the identity of "Mrs. Jones." But her romantic whim will cause unexpected trouble. For one thing, Mr. Jones is about to stride, living and breathing, back into her life. And the two share more than a memory of passion - indeed, they are bonded by a highly unusual sort of vision, one that goes far beyond Venetia's abilities as a photographer. They also have in common a terrible threat - for someone has stolen a centuries-old notebook from Arcane House, containing a formula believed to enhance psychic powers of the kind Gabriel and Venetia possess. And the thief wants to know more - even if he must kill the keeper of the Arcane Society's treasures, or photographer who catalogued them, to obtain such knowledge.

Second Sight. unabr. ed. Amanda Quick, pseud. Read by Anne Flosnik. (Running Time: 9 hrs.). (Arcane Society Ser.). 2006. 39.25 (978-1-4233-1481-3(6), 9781423314813, BADLE); 24.95 (978-1-4233-1480-6(8), 9781423314806, BAD); 74.25 (978-1-4233-1475-2(1), 9781423314752, BriAudUnabridg); 29.95 (978-1-4233-1474-5(3), 9781423314745); audio compact disk 39.25 (978-1-4233-1479-0(4), 9781423314790, Brlnc Audio MP3 Lib); audio compact disk 24.95 (978-1-4233-1478-3(6), 9781423314783, Brilliance MP3); audio compact disk 34.95 (978-1-4233-1476-9(X), 9781423314769) Brilliance Audio.

Second Sight: An Intuitive Psychiatrist Tells Her Extraordinary Story & Shows You How to Tap Your Own Inner Wisdom. abr. ed. Judith Orloff. Read by Judith Orloff. 2 cass. (Running Time: 3 hrs.). 1997. 17.95 (978-1-57453-135-0(2)) Audio Lit.

Second Silence. unabr. ed. Eileen Goudge. Read by Sandra Burr. (Running Time: 13 hrs.). 2007. 39.25 (978-1-4233-3594-8(5), 9781423335948, BADLE); 24.95 (978-1-4233-3593-1(7), 9781423335931, BAD) Brilliance Audio.

Second Silence. unabr. ed. Eileen Goudge. Read by Sandra Burr. (Running Time: 13 hrs.). 2007. 39.25 (978-1-4233-3592-4(9), 9781423335924, Brlnc Audio MP3 Lib); 24.95 (978-1-4233-3591-7(0), 9781423335917, Brilliance MP3) Brilliance Audio.

***Second Sitting.** Stella Whitelaw. 2010. 76.95 (978-1-4079-0779-6(4)); audio compact disk 89.95 (978-1-4079-0780-2(8)) Pub: Soundings Ltd GBR. Dist(s): Ulverscroft US

Second Skin. Paul J. McAuley. Narrated by Jared Doreck. (Great Science Fiction Stories Ser.). 2007. audio compact disk 10.99 (978-1-884612-55-8(5)) AudioText.

Second Skin. abr. ed. Eric Lustbader. Read by Robert Forster. 4 cass. (Running Time: 6 hrs.). 2001. 25.00 (978-1-59040-101-9(8), Phoenix Audio) Pub: Amer Intl Pub. Dist(s): PerseuPGW

Second Spring. Connie Monk & Rachel Bavidge. 2009. 69.95 (978-1-84652-317-5(6)); audio compact disk 84.95 (978-1-84652-318-2(4)) Pub: Magna Story GBR. Dist(s): Ulverscroft US

Second Stain see Return of Sherlock Holmes

Second Stain: A Sherlock Holmes Adventure. Arthur Conan Doyle. (ENG.). 2007. 5.99 (978-1-60339-175-7(4)); audio compact disk 5.99 (978-1-60339-176-4(2)) Listenr Digest.

Second Step: A Cry for Help: Mark 9:14-24; Psalm 18:1-3. Ed Young. 1998. 4.95 (978-0-7417-2198-3(8), 1198) Win Walk.

Second Summer of the Sisterhood. abr. ed. Ann Brashares. Read by Angela Goethals. 2 CDs. (Running Time: 2 hrs. 29 mins.). (Sisterhood of the Traveling Pants Ser.: Bk. 2). (ENG.). (J). (gr. 7 up). 2003. audio compact disk 18.00 (978-0-8072-0967-7(8), ImaginStudio) Pub: Random Audio Pubg. Dist(s): Random

Second Summer of the Sisterhood. unabr. ed. Ann Brashares. Read by Amy Povich. 6 cass. (Running Time: 9 hrs. 2 mins.). (Sisterhood of the Traveling Pants Ser.: Bk. 2). (YA). (gr. 7 up). 2004. 40.00 (978-0-8072-0968-4(6), S YA 439 CX, Listening Lib); audio compact disk 51.00 (978-0-8072-1615-6(1), S YA 439 CD, Listening Lib) Pub: Random Audio Pubg. Dist(s): NetLibrary CO

Second Summer of the Sisterhood. unabr. ed. Ann Brashares. Read by Amy Povich. 7 CDs. (Running Time: 31500 sec.). (Sisterhood of the Traveling Pants Ser.: Bk. 2). (ENG.). (J). (gr. 7-12). 2007. audio compact disk 19.99 (978-0-7393-3922-0(2), Listening Lib) Pub: Random Audio Pubg. Dist(s): Random

Second Sun. Chris Stewart. (Great & Terrible Ser.: Vol. 3). 2005. audio compact disk 29.95 (978-1-59038-513-5(6)) Deseret Bk.

Second Thoughts. Mort Crim. 1999. Health Comm.

Second Thoughts of an Idle Fellow. unabr. ed. Jerome K. Jerome. 6 cass. 2005. 54.95 (978-1-86015-479-9(4)) Pub: Mgna Lrg Print GBR. Dist(s): Ulverscroft US

Second Time Around. Perf. by Emile Pandolfi. 1 cass., 1 CD. 7.98 (MMC 189); audio compact disk 12.78 CD Jewel box. (MMC 189) NewSound.

Second Time Around. abr. ed. Mary Higgins Clark. Read by Jan Maxwell. 2004. 15.95 (978-0-7435-4517-4(6)) Pub: S&S Audio. Dist(s): S and S Inc

Second Time Around. abr. ed. Mary Higgins Clark. Read by Jan Maxwell. (Running Time: 43 hrs. 0 mins. 0 sec.). (ENG.). 2010. audio compact disk 14.99 (978-1-4423-0009-5(4)) Pub: S&S Audio. Dist(s): S and S Inc

Second Time Around. unabr. ed. Julie Ellis. Read by Liza Ross. 8 vols. (Running Time: 11 hrs.). 1999. bk. 69.95 (978-0-7927-2288-5(4), CSL 177, Chivers Sound Lib) AudioGO.
After 17 years of marriage, Janet Ransome finds her husband in bed with a nubile 20-year-old. When Tim announces he is leaving, she moves to New York with her reluctant children to earn a living as a writer. Then fellow writer Dan Tempest moves into her apartment complex & Jan's attraction to him is instantaneous. But Tim shows up on the scene & she must make some serious choices.

Second to None. unabr. ed. Alexander Kent, pseud. Read by Michael Jayston. 10 cass. (Running Time: 15 hrs.). (Richard Bolitho Ser.: Bk. 24). 2000. 84.95 (978-0-7540-0526-1(7), CAB 1949) Pub: Chivers Audio Bks GBR. Dist(s): AudioGO
On the eve of Waterloo, a sense of finality & cautious hope pervade a nation wearied by decades of war. But peace will present its own challenges to Adam Bolitho, captain of His Majesty's Ship unrivaled, as many of his contemporaries face the prospect of discharge.

Second Touch. unabr. ed. Bodie Thoene & Brock Thoene. Narrated by Sean Barrett. (Running Time: 14 hrs. 35 mins. 4 sec.). (A. D. Chronicles Ser.). (ENG.). 2008. audio compact disk 49.99 (978-1-59859-501-7(6)) Oasis Audio.

Second Wife. unabr. ed. Denise Robertson. Read by Marlene Sidaway. 8 cass. (Running Time: 8 hrs.). 1999. 69.95 (978-0-7531-0420-0(2), 990313) Pub: ISIS Audio GBR. Dist(s): Ulverscroft US
Two things stand between Ellie & happiness. She is obsessed with thoughts of Julia, Richard's beautiful first wife who died young, & another spectre - this time from her own past. She slips away to her native north-east, hoping to recover the truth about her childhood. Richard, frantic to find Ellie & bring her home, enlists the help of her friend Terri, a spirited journalist & herself a second wife.

Second Wind. Dick Francis. Read by Michael Page. (Playaway Adult Fiction Ser.). (ENG.). 2009. 65.00 (978-1-60775-521-0(1)) Find a World.

Second Wind. unabr. ed. Dick Francis. Read by Michael Page. (Running Time: 8 hrs.). 2008. 39.25 (978-1-4233-3829-1(4), 9781423338291, BADLE); 24.95 (978-1-4233-3828-4(6), 9781423338284, BAD); audio compact disk 92.25 (978-1-4233-3825-3(1), 9781423338253, BriAudCD Unabrid); audio compact disk 39.25 (978-1-4233-3827-7(8), 9781423338277, Brlnc Audio MP3 Lib); audio compact disk 24.95 (978-1-4233-3826-0(X), 9781423338260, Brilliance MP3); audio compact disk 34.95 (978-1-4233-3824-6(3), 9781423338246, Bril Audio CD Unabri) Brilliance Audio.

Second Wind. unabr. ed. Dick Francis. Read by Michael Page. 6 cass. (Running Time: 6 hrs.). 1999. 57.25 (FS9-51032) Highsmith.

Second Wind for the Second Half: Twenty Ideas to Help You Reinvent Yourself for the Rest of the Journey. abr. ed. Patrick Morley. (Running Time: 2 hrs. 0 mins. 0 sec.). (ENG.). 2003. 9.99 (978-0-310-26097-4(3)) Zondervan.

Second World War. unabr. ed. Martin Gilbert. Read by David Case. 14 cass. (Running Time: 21 hrs.). 1996. 112.00 (4008-B) Books on Tape.

Audio MP3 Lib); audio compact disk 24.95 (978-1-4233-4900-6(8), 9781423349006, Brilliance MP3) Brilliance Audio.

Secret Cardinal: A Novel of Suspense. unabr. ed. Tom Grace. Read by Phil Gigante. (Running Time: 39600 sec.). (Nolan Kilkenny Ser.). 2007. audio compact disk 102.25 (978-1-4233-4899-3(0), 9781423348993, BriAudCD Unabrid); audio compact disk 36.95 (978-1-4233-4898-6(2), 9781423348986, Bril Audio CD Unabri) Brilliance Audio.

Secret Ceremonies, abr. ed. Deborah Laake. Read by Meredith MacRae. 2 cass. (Running Time: 3 hrs.). 2000. 7.95 (978-1-57815-138-7(4), 1097, Media Bks Audio) Media Bks NJ.

A frank yet compassionate depiction of the culture of the Mormon Church & also the mysteries of church's rituals & the beauty & rigor of its theology & traditions.

Secret Church. Louise Vernon. Narrated by Fern Ebersole. (ENG.). (J). 2008. audio compact disk 15.95 (978-0-9801244-5-3(X)) IG Publish.

***Secret Code of Success.** unabr. ed. Noah St. John. Read by Noah St. John. Read by Jack Canfield. (ENG.). 2010. (978-0-06-198630-7(5), Harper Audio) HarperCollins Pubs.

***Secret Code of Success: 7 Hidden Steps to More Wealth & Happiness.** unabr. ed. Noah St. John. Read by Noah St. John. Read by Jack Canfield. (ENG.). 2010. (978-0-06-197916-3(3), Harper Audio) HarperCollins Pubs.

Secret Combination for True Prosperity. Creflo A. Dollar. 2006. 20.00 (978-1-59944-069-9(5)); audio compact disk 28.00 (978-1-59944-070-5(9)) Creflo Dollar.

Secret Commonwealth see Spirits & Spooks for Halloween

Secret Confessions of the Applewood PTA. abr. ed. Ellen Meister. Read by Lisa Kudrow. (Running Time: 21600 sec.). 2007. audio compact disk 14.99 (978-1-4233-1217-8(1), 9781423312178, BCD Value Price) Brilliance Audio.

Secret Confessions of the Applewood PTA. unabr. ed. Ellen Meister. Read by Lisa Kudrow. (Running Time: 10 hrs.). 2006. 39.25 (978-1-4233-1215-4(5), 9781423312154, BADLE); 24.95 (978-1-4233-1214-7(7), 9781423312147, BAD); 82.25 (978-1-4233-1218-5(X), 9781423312185, BrilAudUnabridg); audio compact disk 97.25 (978-1-4233-1211-6(2), 9781423312116, BriAudCD Unabrid); audio compact disk 39.25 (978-1-4233-1213-0(9), 9781423312130, Brinc Audio MP3 Lib); audio compact disk 24.95 (978-1-4233-1212-3(0), 9781423312123, Brilliance MP3); audio compact disk 36.95 (978-1-4233-1210-9(4), 9781423312109, Bril Audio CD Unabri) Brilliance Audio.

Secret Confessions of the Applewood PTA is a novel about three women who come together when Hollywood announces plans to shoot a movie in their children's schoolyard. Maddie Schein is an emotionally-needy ex-lawyer whose marriage is on the rocks. Brash Ruth Moss has it all except for one thing: her husband was left brain-damaged and sexually uninhibited from a stroke. Timid Lisa Slotnick wants nothing more than to fade into the scenery, but is thrust before the spotlight by her alcoholic mother, a singer whose career has failed.

Secret Council of the Godhead. Derek Prince. 1 cass. (A-4094) Derek Prince.

Secret Creator Within: 23 Ways to Awaken Your Creative Genius. Victor K. Pryles. 2002. audio compact disk 29.95 (978-0-9786162-1-2(9)) V Pryles MA.

Secret De Louise. Di Bernardo. audio compact disk 12.95 (978-0-8219-3767-9(7)) EMC-Paradigm.

Secret de Shambhala. James Redfield. (FRE.). pap. bk. 18.95 (978-2-89558-095-9(2)) Pub: Coffragants CAN. Dist(s): Penton Overseas

Secret Diary of Adrian Mole Aged 13 3/4. unabr. ed. Sue Townsend. Read by Nicholas Barnes. 4 cass. (Running Time: 6 hrs.). 2000. 34.95 (978-0-7451-4333-0(4), CAB 1016) Pub: Chivers Audio Bks GBR. Dist(s): AudioGO

Discover the early teenage years of Adrian Mole, with references from his secret diary! Join Adrian as he gets acne, plays his records, reads intellectual books, and begins to fall in love with Pandora! So begins the life of the teenage Adrian Mole: misunderstood seer, thwarted lover and cult hero.

Secret Doctrine. abr. ed. Helena P. Blavatsky. Read by Ellen Burstyn. 2 cass. (Running Time: 3 hrs.). 1996. 17.95 (978-1-57453-067-4(4)) Audio Lit.

Examines the nature of the human being with testimony drawn from sacred scripture, traditions and legends.

Secret Empire. Philip Taubman. Read by Michael Prichard. (Running Time: 15 hrs. 45 mins.). 2003. 34.95 (978-1-60083-655-8(0), Audiofy Corp) Iofy Corp.

Secret Empire. unabr. ed. Philip Taubman. Narrated by Michael Prichard. (Running Time: 15 hrs. 43 mins. 48 sec.). (ENG.). 2003. audio compact disk 44.99 (978-1-4001-0089-7(5)) Pub: Tantor Media. Dist(s): IngramPubServ

Takes readers behind the closed doors of the Eisenhower administration to tell about the small group of Cold Warriors whose technological innovations-including the U2 spy plane and Corona, the country's first spy satellite-revolutionized espionage and intelligence gathering.

Secret Empire: Eisenhower, the CIA, & the Hidden Story of America's Space Espionage. unabr. ed. Philip Taubman. Narrated by Michael Prichard. (Running Time: 15 hrs. 43 mins. 48 sec.). (ENG.). 2003. audio compact disk 25.99 (978-1-4001-5089-2(2)) Pub: Tantor Media. Dist(s): IngramPubServ

Secret Empire: Eisenhower, the CIA, & the Hidden Story of America's Space Espionage. unabr. ed. Philip Taubman. Read by Michael Prichard. (Running Time: 15 hrs. 43 mins. 48 sec.). (ENG.). 2003. audio compact disk 89.99 (978-1-4001-3089-4(1)) Pub: Tantor Media. Dist(s): IngramPubServ

Secret Energy: The Soul at Rest in Christ. abr. ed. Bob Bew. Ed. by Rhett Ellis. Illus. by Dayton Cook. 3 vols. 2001. 19.95 (978-0-9670631-2-6(4)) Sparkling Bay.

Secret Esoteric Teachings in Star Wars. Robert A. Wilson & E. J. Gold. 2 cass. (Running Time: 2 hrs.). 1980. 18.98 (TP51) Union Label.

Robert Anton Wilson & E.J. Gold discuss the myth of transformation as represented in the characters & plot of "Star Wars" & demonstrate that the first stage of the space-age myth contains a hidden Tibetan teaching. This two hour discussion was held at the Cosmicon Convention in San Francisco.

Secret for a Nightingale. unabr. collector's ed. Victoria Holt. Read by Donada Peters. 9 cass. (Running Time: 13 hrs. 30 min.). 1993. 72.00 (978-0-7366-2486-2(4), 3248) Books on Tape.

Victorian Englishwoman is haunted by sinister physician responsible for tragedy in her marriage.

Secret Formulas of the Wizard of Ads. Roy H. Williams. 6 CDs. (Running Time: 4 hrs. 45 mins). 2000. audio compact disk 29.95 (978-0-9714769-2-9(6)) Wizard Academy.

Book two of the Wizard of Ads Trilogy on CD. In 100 chapters full of wit, wisdom and uncommon good sense, Secret Formulas conjures up more of the Wizard's provocative observations on advertising, business, and life that won The Wizard of Ads last year's Business Book of the Year Award?only this time, the book has nuts, bolt, and even more bite! The Wizard's secret formulas will show you: How to find a champion to sell your ideas; Why targeting your market can be a big mistake; How to get customers to remember you; Why bankers think backwards; How to write miraculous ads; Why the brain contains 100,000 new worlds; Why being 'out of style' can be profitable; How to hire wisely and fire compassionately; How Success can send you to the poor house; How to remember what's really important in life. Includes: 6 Audio CDs. Total running time: 4hours 45minutes.

***Secret Friend.** Chris Mooney. 2010. 61.95 (978-0-7531-3359-0(8)); audio compact disk 79.95 (978-0-7531-3360-6(1)) Pub: Isis Pubng Ltd GBR. Dist(s): Ulverscroft US

Secret Garden. Frances Hodgson Burnett. Narrated by Anne Flosnik. Prod. by Ralph LaBarge. (ENG.). (J). 2007. 12.95 (978-0-9798626-1-8(2)) Alpha DVD.

Secret Garden. Frances Hodgson Burnett. Narrated by Flo Gibson. (ENG.). (J). 2007. audio compact disk 29.95 (978-1-55685-913-7(9)) Audio Bk Con.

Secret Garden. Frances Hodgson Burnett. Narrated by Juliet Stevenson. (Running Time: 2 hrs.). 2006. 14.95 (978-1-59912-955-6(8)) Iofy Corp.

Secret Garden. Frances Hodgson Burnett. 2005. audio compact disk 29.95 (978-1-4193-5990-3(8)) Recorded Bks.

Secret Garden. Frances Hodgson Burnett. Narrated by Vanessa Maroney. (Running Time: 31200 sec.). (Unabridged Classics in MP3 Ser.). (ENG.). (J). 2008. audio compact disk 24.00 (978-1-58472-540-4(0), In Aud) Sound Room.

Secret Garden. Frances Hodgson Burnett. Narrated by Josephine Bailey. (ENG.). 2003. audio compact disk 78.00 (978-1-4001-3072-6(7)) Pub: Tantor Media. Dist(s): IngramPubServ

Secret Garden. Adapted by Dalmatian Press Staff. 2 cass. (Read-along Ser.). bk. 34.95 Set, incl. learner's guide & exercises. (S23948) J Norton Pubs.

Secret Garden. Perf. by Monterey SoundWorks. 2 cass. (Running Time: 2 hrs.). 2001. 16.95 (MOSW0007) Lodestone Catalog.

Secret Garden. abr. adpt. ed. Frances Hodgson Burnett. Adapted by Philip Glassborow & Paul McCusker. (Running Time: 240 hrs. 0 mins.). (Radio Theatre Ser.). (ENG.). (J). (gr. 3). 2007. audio compact disk 14.97 (978-1-58997-506-4(5), Tyndale Ent) Tyndale Hse.

Secret Garden, unabr. ed. Frances Hodgson Burnett. Read by Flo Gibson. 6 cass. (Running Time: 8 hrs.). (J). (gr. 4-8). 1987. 35.95 (978-1-55685-076-9(X)) Audio Bk Con.

An unhappy little orphan discovers a hidden garden & with it a special magic which spreads its wonders to the invalid Colin.

Secret Garden. unabr. ed. Frances Hodgson Burnett. Narrated by Wanda McCaddon. (Running Time: 27900 sec.). (ENG.). (J). (gr. 5). 2006. audio compact disk 29.95 (978-1-57270-522-7(1)) Pub: AudioGO. Dist(s): Perseus Dist

Secret Garden. unabr. ed. Frances Hodgson Burnett. Read by Vanessa Maroney. (J). 2006. 64.99 (978-1-59895-180-6(7)) Find a World.

***Secret Garden.** unabr. ed. Frances Hodgson Burnett. (ENG.). (J). 2010. audio compact disk 25.00 (978-0-307-74610-8(0), Listening Lib) Pub: Random Audio Pubg. Dist(s): Random

Secret Garden. unabr. ed. Frances Hodgson Burnett. Narrated by Josephine Bailey. (Running Time: 8 hrs. 0 mins. 0 sec.). (Tantor Unabridged Classics Ser.). (ENG.). (J). (gr. 3-7). 2008. audio compact disk 27.99 (978-1-4001-0844-2(6)); audio compact disk 19.99 (978-1-4001-5844-7(3)) Pub: Tantor Media. Dist(s): IngramPubServ

Secret Garden. unabr. ed. Frances Hodgson Burnett. Narrated by Josephine Bailey. (Running Time: 8 hrs. 0 mins. 0 sec.). (ENG.). (J). (gr. 4-7). 2008. audio compact disk 55.99 (978-1-4001-3844-9(2)) Pub: Tantor Media. Dist(s): IngramPubServ

Secret Garden. unabr. ed. Frances Hodgson Burnett & Johanna Ward. (Running Time: 8.5 hrs. NaN mins.). 2008. 29.95 (978-1-4332-5430-7(1)); audio compact disk 70.00 (978-1-4332-5429-1(8)) Blckstn Audio.

Secret Garden: A Young Reader's Edition of the Classic Story. Frances Hodgson Burnett. 2 CDs. (Running Time: 2 hrs. 15 min.). (Focus on the Family Radio Theatre Ser.). (J). 2000. audio compact disk 18.97 Bethany Hse.

Colin, the boy who thinks he's going to die, Dickon, who has a wondrous way with animals & gardens & Mary Lennox, the orphaned girl who uncovers the secrets of Misselthwaite Manor but unlike some television & movie adaptations, in this production the "magic" that makes flowers grow & brings healing to hurting people turns out to be God himself.

Secret Garden: A Young Reader's Edition of the Classic Story. Frances Hodgson Burnett. Read by Vanessa Maroney. (Running Time: 8 hrs. 45 mins.). 2002. 24.95 (978-1-59912-114-7(X), Audiofy Corp) Iofy Corp.

Secret Garden: A Young Reader's Edition of the Classic Story. Frances Hodgson Burnett. Read by Josephine Bailey. (Running Time: 8 hrs.). 2003. 27.95 (978-1-60083-640-4(2), Audiofy Corp) Iofy Corp.

Secret Garden: A Young Reader's Edition of the Classic Story. Frances Hodgson Burnett. Read by Jenny Agutter. 2 CDs. (Running Time: 3 hrs.). 2001. audio compact disk 15.98 (Naxos AudioBooks) Naxos.

Secret Garden: A Young Reader's Edition of the Classic Story. Frances Hodgson Burnett. Read by Jenny Agutter. 2 cass. (Running Time: 2 hrs. 30 min.). (Junior Classics Ser.). (YA). 2001. 13.98 (978-962-634-735-5(X), NA223514, Naxos AudioBooks) Naxos.

Secret Garden: A Young Reader's Edition of the Classic Story. Frances Hodgson Burnett. Read by Jenny Agutter. 2 CDs. (Running Time: 2 hrs. 30 min.). (Junior Classics Ser.). (J). (gr. 3-5). 2001. audio compact disk 17.98 (978-962-634-235-0(8), NA223512) Naxos.

Secret Garden: A Young Reader's Edition of the Classic Story. Frances Hodgson Burnett. Read by Susan Fitzgerald. 6 cass. (Running Time: 7 hrs. 55 min.). (J). 1987. 55.00 (978-0-8045-0071-5(1), PCC 71) Spoken Arts.

Mary Returns to Her Uncle's Estate in England from India. Orphaned by a Massacre, She Is a Cowed, Sickly Child. Her Discovery of the Secret Garden Leads to New Health & a New Vision of Wide Possibility.

Secret Garden: A Young Reader's Edition of the Classic Story, abr. ed. Frances Hodgson Burnett. Read by Elizabeth Rude. Ed. by Beth Baxter. 2 cass. (Running Time: 3 hrs.). (J). (gr. 3-7). 2000. 16.95 (978-1-882071-05-0(0), 006) B-B Audio.

Meet a spoiled, self-centered orphan girl who discovers the tragic secret of a once-beautiful garden that has been walled and locked for ten years. Share the magic as child and garden nurture each other. A tale of wonder for ages six to adult.

Secret Garden: A Young Reader's Edition of the Classic Story. abr. ed. Frances Hodgson Burnett. Read by Claire Bloom. 1 cass. Incl. Across the Moor. (J). (CPN 1463); Ben Weatherstaff. (J). (CPN 1463); Cry in the Coridor. (J). (CPN 1463); Dickon. (J). (CPN 1463); I Am Colin. (J). (CPN 1463); I Shall Live Forever. (J). (CPN 1463); In the Garden. Linda Tarr. (J). (CPN 1463); It Has Come! (J). (CPN 1463); Key of the Garden. (J). (CPN 1463); Magic. (J). (CPN 1463); Martha. (J). (CPN 1463); Mistress Mary Quite Contrary. (J). (CPN 1463); Nest of the Missel Thrush. (J). (CPN 1463); Robin Who Showed the Way. (J). (CPN 1463); Strangest House. (J). (CPN 1463); Tha' Munnot Waste No Time. (J). (CPN 1463); There's No One Left. (J). (CPN 1463); Where the Sun Went Down. (J). (CPN 1463); Young Rajah. (J). (CPN 1463); (J). 1984. 9.95 (978-0-89845-813-8(7), CPN 1463) HarperCollins Pubs.

Secret Garden: A Young Reader's Edition of the Classic Story. abr. ed. Frances Hodgson Burnett. Read by Claire Bloom. Illus. by Tasha Tudor. 1 cass. (Running Time: 1 hr. 04 min.). (J). (gr. 4-6). 1992. 12.00 (978-1-55994-650-6(4), HarperChildAud) HarperCollins Pubs.

Secret Garden: A Young Reader's Edition of the Classic Story, abr. ed. Frances Hodgson Burnett. Perf. by St. Charles Players. 2 cass. Dramatization. 1999. 16.95 (FS9-42730) Highsmith.

Secret Garden: A Young Reader's Edition of the Classic Story. abr. ed. Frances Hodgson Burnett. Read by Claire Bloom. 1 cass. (Running Time: 60 min.). (J). (gr. k up). 10.98 (383) MFLP CA.

Classic story about the healing power of nature & good thoughts in the metamorphosis of two "incurably disagreeable" children.

Secret Garden: A Young Reader's Edition of the Classic Story, abr. ed. Frances Hodgson Burnett. Perf. by St. Charles Players. 2 cass. (Running Time: 1 hr. 42 mins.). Dramatization. (Story Theatre for Young Readers Ser.). (J). (gr. 4-8). 1998. 16.95 (978-1-56994-510-0(1), 338634, Monterey SoundWorks) Monterey Media Inc.

The beloved children's classic of a young girl who comes to live with her moody, unhappy uncle in his run-down Victorian estate, where she discovers a secret gate leading to an abandoned garden. Enchanted by this place, she embarks on the adventure of bringing the garden & those around her back to life.

Secret Garden: A Young Reader's Edition of the Classic Story. abr. ed. Frances Hodgson Burnett. Read by Julie Christie. 4 cass. (Running Time: 6 hrs.). 2004. 25.00 (978-1-59007-138-0(7)) Pub: New Millenn Enter. Dist(s): PerseuPGW

Secret Garden: A Young Reader's Edition of the Classic Story. unabr. ed. Frances Hodgson Burnett. Read by Wanda McCaddon. 6 cass. (Running Time: 8 hrs.). (J). (gr. 4-7). 2004. 24.95 (978-1-57270-040-6(8), H61040u) Pub: Audio Partners. Dist(s): PerseuPGW

This children's classic opens the door to the innermost places of the heart. A bestseller since its original publication in 1911; the reader provides a truly special listening experience.

Secret Garden: A Young Reader's Edition of the Classic Story, unabr. ed. Frances Hodgson Burnett. Read by Johanna Ward. 6 cass. (Running Time: 8 hrs. 30 mins.). (gr. 3-5). 1992. 44.95 (978-0-7861-0374-4(4), 1329) Blckstn Audio.

Mary Lennox, a spoilt, ill tempered, & unhealthy child, comes to live with her reclusive uncle in Misselthwaite Manor after the death of her parents. There she meets a hearty housekeeper & her spirited brother, a dour gardener, a cheerful robin, & her willful, hysterical & sickly cousin, Master Colin. With the help of the robin, Mary finds the door to the secret garden, & from there the story takes the listener on a charming journey into the places of the heart where faith restores health, where flowers refresh the spirit, & where the magic of the garden coming to life after years of neglect brings to Colin health, & to Mary happiness.

Secret Garden: A Young Reader's Edition of the Classic Story. unabr. ed. Frances Hodgson Burnett. Read by Laurie Klein. 6 cass. (Running Time: 8 hrs.). Dramatization. (J). 1991. 39.95 (978-1-55686-362-2(4), 362) Books in Motion.

Orphaned, spoiled, & self-centered Mary Lennox is sent to her uncle's estate. Depressed & bewildered she discovers a magical secret garden that brings her happiness.

Secret Garden: A Young Reader's Edition of the Classic Story. unabr. ed. Frances Hodgson Burnett. Read by Carole Boyd. 6 cass. (Running Time: 9 hrs.). 2001. 54.95 (93061) Pub: ISIS Audio GBR. Dist(s): Ulverscroft US

Secret Garden: A Young Reader's Edition of the Classic Story. unabr. ed. Frances Hodgson Burnett. Read by Carole Boyd. 6 cass. (Running Time: 7 hrs. 15 min.). (Isis Ser.). (J). (gr. 4 up). 1994. 54.95 (978-1-85695-579-9(6), 93061) Pub: ISIS Audio GBR. Dist(s): Ulverscroft US

Secret Garden: A Young Reader's Edition of the Classic Story. unabr. ed. Frances Hodgson Burnett. 8 CDs. (Isis Ser.). (J). 2003. audio compact disk 79.95 (978-0-7531-1644-9(8)) Pub: ISIS Lrg Prnt GBR. Dist(s): Ulverscroft US

Secret Garden: A Young Reader's Edition of the Classic Story. unabr. ed. Frances Hodgson Burnett. (J). (gr. 3-5). 1990. pap. bk. 17.00 (978-0-8072-1124-3(9), Listening Lib) Random Audio Pubg.

Secret Garden: A Young Reader's Edition of the Classic Story, unabr. ed. Frances Hodgson Burnett. Narrated by Flo Gibson. 5 pieces. (Running Time: 7 hrs. 15 mins.). (gr. 6 up). 1987. 44.00 (978-1-55690-465-3(7), 87390E7) Recorded Bks.

Mary Lennox finds a locked garden in her new home in Yorkshire.

Secret Garden: A Young Reader's Edition of the Classic Story, unabr. ed. Frances Hodgson Burnett. Read by Vanessa Maroney. 6 cass. (Running Time: 9 hrs.). (Timeless Treasures Collection). (J). 1999. 56.50 (978-1-883049-77-5(6), Commuters Library) Sound Room.

The magical story of Mary & her friends & a garden which had been locked away for ten years.

Secret Garden: A Young Reader's Edition of the Classic Story. unabr. ed. Frances Hodgson Burnett. Read by Vanessa Maroney. 8 cds. (Running Time: 8 hrs 33 mins). (J). 2002. audio compact disk 39.95 (978-1-58472-320-2(3), 024, In Aud) Pub: Sound Room. Dist(s): Baker Taylor

The story of Mary Lennox and her friends and a garden which had been locked away for ten years.

Secret Garden: A Young Reader's Edition of the Classic Story. unabr. ed. Frances Hodgson Burnett. 8 CDs. (Running Time: 8 hrs. 40 mins.). (YA). (gr. 5-8). 2002. audio compact disk 79.00 (978-1-58472-111-6(1), Commuters Library) Sound Room.

Secret Garden: A Young Reader's Edition of the Classic Story. unabr. ed. Frances Hodgson Burnett. Read by Vanessa Maroney. 1 cd. (Running Time: 8 hrs 33 mins). (J). 2002. audio compact disk 18.95 (978-1-58472-400-1(5), In Aud) Pub: Sound Room. Dist(s): Baker Taylor

MP3 format.

Secret Garden: A Young Reader's Edition of the Classic Story. unabr. collector's ed. Frances Hodgson Burnett. Read by Penelope Dellaporta. 6 cass. (Running Time: 9 hrs.). (J). (gr. 4-7). 1983. 48.00 (978-0-7366-0688-2(2), 1648) Books on Tape.

"The Secret Garden" is the story of the awakening of friendship in two children who have been deprived of love & attention.

Secret Garden: BBC. unabr. ed. Frances Hodgson Burnett. 2 cass. (Running Time: 2 hrs. 40 min.). Dramatization. 1996. 16.99 (Random AudioBks) Random Audio Pubg.

Secret Garden Travelpak: The Secret Garden & Anne of Green Gables. abr. ed. Frances Hodgson Burnett. Read by Elizabeth Rude. 2 cass. (Running Time: 6 hrs.). (J). 1999. 34.95 (978-0-929071-54-1(9)) B-B Audio.

Plug-n-Play Travelpaks contain everything your customers will need for many hours of audiobook listening. 2 Fantastic Audiobooks with 1 Portable Cassette Player plus 1 Comfortable Headset plus 2 Batteries.

Secret Gift: How an Act of Kindness Revealed Hidden Lives of the Great Depression. unabr. ed. Ted Gup. Read by Mark Deakins. (ENG.). 2010. audio compact disk 35.00 (978-0-307-57803-7(8), Random AudioBks) Pub: Random Audio Pubg. Dist(s): Random

Secret Grotto & Mysterious World. (J). (gr. 3 up). 1997. bk. 6.98 W Disney Records.
Read-along titles feature characters from the re-released animated film The Little Mermaid.

Secret Handshake: Mastering the Politics of the Business Inner Circle. Kathleen Kelley Reardon. Narrated by Ruth Ann Phimister. 6 cass. (Running Time: 8 hrs. 15 mins.). 59.00 (978-0-7887-9003-4(X)); audio compact disk 69.00 (978-1-4025-3479-9(5)) Recorded Bks.

Secret Heart. David Almond. 3 cass. (Running Time: 3 hrs. 32 mins.). (J). (gr. 4-7). 2004. 30.00 (978-0-8072-0946-2(5), Listening Lib) Random Audio Pubg.
A tattered circus comes to town and Joey's world will never be the same again.

Secret History. unabr. ed. Donna Tartt. 1 cass. (Running Time: 1 hr. 30 mins.). 2002. 39.95 (978-0-06-051804-2(9)) HarperCollins Pubs.

***Secret History.** unabr. ed. Donna Tartt. Read by Donna Tartt. (ENG.). 2004. (978-0-06-078647-2(7), Harper Audio) HarperCollins Pubs.

***Secret History.** unabr. ed. Donna Tartt. Read by Donna Tartt. (ENG.). 2004. (978-0-06-081420-5(9), Harper Audio) HarperCollins Pubs.

Secret History of the War on Cancer. unabr. ed. Devra Davis. (Running Time: 19 hrs. 0 mins.). 2009. 44.95 (978-1-4332-5314-0(3)); 99.95 (978-1-4332-5311-9(9)); audio compact disk 123.00 (978-1-4332-5312-6(7)) Blckstn Audio.

Secret History of the World: As Laid down by the Secret Societies. Mark Booth. Read by John Lee. (ENG.). 2009. 69.99 (978-1-60775-791-7(5)) Find a World.

Secret History of the World: As Laid down by the Secret Societies. unabr. ed. Mark Booth. (Running Time: 17 hrs. 0 mins. 0 sec.). (ENG.). 2008. audio compact disk 79.99 (978-1-4001-3622-3(9)) Pub: Tantor Media. Dist(s): IngramPubServ

Secret History of the World: As Laid down by the Secret Societies. unabr. ed. Mark Booth. Read by John Lee. (Running Time: 17 hrs. 0 mins. 0 sec.). (ENG.). 2008. audio compact disk 39.99 (978-1-4001-0622-6(2)); audio compact disk 29.99 (978-1-4001-5622-1(X)) Pub: Tantor Media. Dist(s): IngramPubServ

***Secret History of Tom Trueheart.** unabr. ed. Ian Beck. Read by John Curless. (ENG.). 2007. (978-0-06-137604-7(3), GreenwillowBks); (978-0-06-137606-1(X), GreenwillowBks) HarperCollins Pubs.

Secret History of Tom Trueheart. unabr. ed. Ian Beck. Read by John Curless. 5 CDs. (Running Time: 19800 sec.). (J). (gr. 3-7). 2007. audio compact disk 25.95 (978-0-06-121498-1(1), HarperChildAud) HarperCollins Pubs.

Secret History of Tom Trueheart, Boy Adventurer. unabr. ed. Ian Beck. Read by Clive Mantle. 6 CDs. (Running Time: 5 hrs. 38 mins.). (J). (gr. 4-7). 2008. audio compact disk 59.95 (978-1-4056-5761-7(8), Chivers Child Audio) AudioGO.

Secret Holocaust Diaries. unabr. ed. Nonna Bannister et al. Narrated by Rebecca Gallagher. (ENG.). 2009. 19.59 (978-1-60814-471-6(2)) Oasis Audio.

Secret Holocaust Diaries: The Untold Story of Nonna Bannister. unabr. ed. Nonna Bannister et al. Narrated by Rebecca Gallagher. 7 CDs. (Running Time: 7 hrs. 35 mins. 16 sec.). (ENG.). 2009. audio compact disk 27.99 (978-1-59859-532-1(6)) Oasis Audio.

Secret Honor. W. E. B. Griffin. Read by Scott Brick. (Honor Bound Ser.: No. 3). 2000. audio compact disk 128.00 (978-0-7366-7129-3(3)) Books on Tape.

Secret Honor. unabr. ed. W. E. B. Griffin. Read by Scott Brick. 13 cass. (Running Time: 19 hrs. 30 mins.). (Honor Bound Ser.: Vol. 3). 2000. 104.00 (978-0-7366-4833-2(X), 5179) Books on Tape.
A story about espionage during World War II. A German general, realizing that his country is losing the war, tries to end it by assassinating Hitler. His son, an officer stationed in Buenos Aires, is suspected by the SS after a Nazi operation goes awry. An OSS agent accused of disobeying orders is nearly committed to a mental hospital. With detailed descriptions of the war's battles, its leaders, its aircraft and ships, the plot moves briskly.

Secret Honor. unabr. ed. W. E. B. Griffin. Read by Scott Brick. 13 cass. (Running Time: 19 hrs. 30 min.). (Honor Bound Ser.: No. 3). 2000. 104.00 (5179) Books on Tape.
Military espionage & thrills as World War II hastens to an end.

Secret Hour. abr. ed. Luanne Rice. Read by Linda Emond. 2004. 15.95 (978-0-7435-4873-1(6)) Pub: S&S Audio. Dist(s): S and S Inc

Secret House of Death. unabr. ed. Ruth Rendell. Read by Simon Russell Beale. 6 cass. (Running Time: 9 hrs.). 2000. 49.95 (978-0-7451-6733-6(0), CAB 1349) Pub: Chivers Audio Bks GBR. Dist(s): AudioGO
It was his third visit to the house on Orchard Drive, and each time Louise North greeted him at the door. Susan Townsend was the only resident who had no interest in their affair. But it was Susan who found the bodies of the lovers, locked not in passion, but in death. And her own life would be imperiled by a monstrous crime far beyond the imaginings of the vilest tongues.

Secret Hunter. Susanne Saville. Narrated by Anthony Richardson. Prod. by MediaMusicNow UK. (ENG.). 2008. audio compact disk 39.99 (978-0-9671399-1-3(0)) Cliocopia Pr.

Secret Hunters. Ranulph Fiennes. Narrated by Christopher Kay. 12 cass. (Running Time: 15 hrs. 45 mins.). 102.00 (978-1-84197-367-8(X)) Recorded Bks.

Secret Hunters. Ranulph Fiennes. Narrated by Christopher Kay. 13 CDs. (Running Time: 15 hrs. 45 mins.). 2001. audio compact disk 138.00 (978-1-4025-4045-5(0)) Recorded Bks.

Secret Identity. unabr. ed. Wendelin Van Draanen. Illus. by Brian Briggs. 2 cass. (Running Time: 1 hr. 50 mins.). (Shredderman Ser.: Bk. 1). (YA). (gr. 7-11). 2006. 18.95 (978-1-59519-760-3(5)) Live Oak Media.
Tired of the abuse that he's suffered because of bully Bubba Bixby, fifth-grader Nolan Byrd allows his inner super hero to emerge, inspired by a class project. Shredderman is born, and Nolan springs into action, armed with a computer, a cleverly concealed digital camera, and his own top-secret Web page, Shredderman.com. This clever story kicks off a series of fun-filled first chapter books.

Secret Identity. unabr. ed. Wendelin Van Draanen. 2 CDs. (Running Time: 6600 sec.). (Shredderman Ser.: Bk. 1). (J). (gr. 3-6). 2006. audio compact disk 22.95 (978-1-59519-761-0(3)) Live Oak Media.

Secret Ingredients: The New Yorker Book of Food & Drink. unabr. ed. Ed. by David Remnick. 20 CDs. (Running Time: 25 hrs.). 2007. audio compact disk 120.00 (978-1-4159-4281-9(1), BksonTape) Pub: Random Audio Pubg. Dist(s): Random
Since its earliest days, The New Yorker has been a tastemaker - literally. As the home of A. J. Liebling, Joseph Wechsberg, and M. F. K. Fisher, who practically invented American food writing, the magazine established a tradition that is carried forward today by irrepressible literary gastronomes including Calvin Trillin, Bill Buford, Adam Gopnik, Jane Kramer, and Anthony Bourdain. Now, in this indispensable collection, The New Yorker dishes up a feast of delicious writing on food and drink, from every age of its fabled eighty-year history. There are memoirs, short stories, tell-alls, and poems - ranging in tone from sweet to sour and in subject from soup to nuts. M. F. K. Fisher pays homage to "cookery witches," those mysterious cooks who possess "an uncanny power over food," while John McPhee valiantly trails an inveterate forager and is rewarded with stewed persimmons and white-pine-needle tea. There is Roald Dahl's famous story "Taste," in which a wine snob's palate comes in for some unwelcome scrutiny, and Julian Barnes's ingenious tale of a lifelong gourmand who goes on a very peculiar diet for still more peculiar reasons. Adam Gopnik asks if French cuisine is done for, and Calvin Trillin investigates whether people can actually taste the difference between red wine and white. We journey with Susan Orlean as she distills the essence of Cuba in the story of a single restaurant, and with Judith Thurman as she investigates the arcane practices of Japan's tofu masters. Closer to home, Joseph Mitchell celebrates the old New York tradition of the beefsteak dinner, and Mark Singer shadows the city's foremost fisherman-chef. Selected from the magazine's plentiful larder, SECRET INGREDIENTS celebrates all forms of gustatory delight.

Secret Inheritance. Elizabeth Lord. 2008. 69.95 (978-0-7531-3049-0(1)) Pub: ISIS Audio GBR. Dist(s): Ulverscroft US

Secret Inheritance. Elizabeth Lord. Read by Patricia Gallimore. (Running Time: 35100 sec.). 2008. audio compact disk 84.95 (978-0-7531-3050-6(5)) Ulverscroft US.

Secret Isaac. Jerome Charyn. Read by Jerome Charyn. 1 cass. (Running Time: 30 min). 13.95 (978-1-55644-003-8(0), 1021) Am Audio Prose.
Part of a sequence of novels centering on Isaac Sidel, Manhattan police inspector who is also a lover of James Joyce.

Secret Justice. unabr. ed. James W. Huston. Read by Christopher Lane. 10 CDs. (Running Time: 13 hrs.). 2003. audio compact disk 80.00 (978-0-7861-9184-0(8), 3141) Blckstn Audio.

Secret Justice. unabr. ed. James W. Huston. Read by Christopher Lane. 9 cass. (Running Time: 13 hrs.). 2003. 62.95 (978-0-7861-2508-1(X), 3141) Blckstn Audio.

Secret Justice. unabr. ed. James W. Huston. Read by Christopher Lane. (Running Time: 12 hrs. 30 mins.). 2009. audio compact disk 32.95 (978-1-4417-1181-6(3)) Blckstn Audio.

***Secret Kept.** unabr. ed. Tatiana de Rosnay. Read by Kate Reading & Simon Vance. 8 CDs. (Running Time: 9 hrs. 30 mins. 0 sec.). (ENG., 2010. audio compact disk 34.99 (978-1-4272-1095-1(0)) Pub: Macmill Audio. Dist(s): Macmillan

***Secret Kingdom - Audio.** Jenny Nimmo. (Chronicles of the Red King Ser.). (ENG.). 2011. audio compact disk 34.99 (978-0-545-32143-3(3)) Scholastic Inc.

***Secret Kingdom - Audio Library Edition.** Jenny Nimmo. (Chronicles of the Red King Ser.). (ENG.). 2011. audio compact disk 64.99 (978-0-545-32145-7(X)) Scholastic Inc.

Secret Language. unabr. ed. Frances Hodgson Burnett. 1 cass. (Running Time: 22 min.). (Middle Grade Cliffhangers Ser.). (J). (gr. 7). 1995. pap. bk. 15.98 (978-0-8072-1060-4(9), SWR7SP, Listening Lib) Random Audio Pubg.
The "Secret Language" lends itself well to discussions of feeling & emotions in general, especially those that change over the course of time. As an exercise in self-expression, students may wish to act out the first half of a chapter & make up their own endings.

Secret Language of Dolphins. Patricia St John. Read by Bernadette Dunne. (Running Time: 30600 sec.). 2005. audio compact disk 29.95 (978-0-7861-8209-1(1)) Blckstn Audio.

Secret Language of Dolphins -Lib. (Running Time: 9 hrs. 0 mins.). 2005. 59.95 (978-0-7861-3020-7(2)); audio compact disk 72.00 (978-0-7861-8087-5(0)) Blckstn Audio.

Secret Language of Girls. Frances O'Roark Dowell. 4 CDs. (Running Time: 4 hrs.). (J). (gr. 3-7). 2004. audio compact disk 35.00 (978-1-4000-8985-7(9), Listening Lib) Random Audio Pubg.

Secret Language of Girls. unabr. ed. Frances O'Roark Dowell. 3 cass. (Running Time: 4 hrs.). (J). (gr. 3-7). 2004. 30.00 (978-1-4000-8505-7(5), Listening Lib) Random Audio Pubg.
Kate and Marylin have always been the kind of best friends who don't need words to talk to one another; they always just knew what the other was thinking. But lately it's starting to feel as though they don't know each other at all anymore. Marylin decides Kate (who still chases fireflies!) still acts like a baby, while Kate doesn't understand Marylin's new obsession with painting her toenails or wanting to be a cheerleader (and becoming on eof those people who only thinks about her hair!). And even though, secretly, they both wish things could be the way they were, neither one of them know how to get back there.

Secret Language of Knitters. Mary Beth Temple. Narrated by Mary Beth Temple. (ENG.). 2009. audio compact disk 14.95 (978-0-9796073-9-4(6)) Knitting Out.

Secret Language of Persian Poets. Manly P. Hall. 1 cass. 8.95 (978-0-89314-252-0(2)) Philos Res.

Secret Laundry Monster Files. unabr. ed. John R. Erickson. 2 cass. (Running Time: 3 hrs.). (Hank the Cowdog Ser.: No. 39). (J). 2002. 24.00 (978-0-7366-8636-5(3)) Books on Tape.
Hank the Cowdog must come to grips with one of a dog's worst enemies: the dreaded laundry monster.

Secret Laundry Monster Files. unabr. ed. John R. Erickson. Read by John R. Erickson. 2 cass. (Running Time: 3 hrs.). (Hank the Cowdog Ser.: No. 39). (J). 2002. 17.99 (978-1-59188-339-5(3)) Maverick Bks.
Before he knows it, Hank finds himself caught up with his old friend Eddy the Rac and face-to-face with one of a dog's greatest enemies: the dreaded laundry monster.

Secret Laundry Monster Files. unabr. ed. John R. Erickson. Read by John R. Erickson. 3 CDs. (Hank the Cowdog Ser.: No. 39). (J). 2002. audio compact disk 19.99 (978-1-59188-639-6(2)) Maverick Bks.
When Hank the Cowdog hears suspicious sounds coming from near Sally May?s clothesline, it leads to a midnight investigation of the ranch. Before he knows it, Hank finds himself caught up with his old friend Eddy the Rac?and face-to-face with one of a dog?s greatest enemies: the dreaded Laundry Monster! Could this mean the end of everyone?s favorite Head of Ranch Security? Or is it just Eddy the Rac up to his old tricks? One thing?s for sure, Hank will keep readers laughing out loud in this latest hilarious adventure.Hear a rooster crow up the sun in ?Thus Spake J.T. Cluck? and Hank sings, ?Trudy, Trudy, What a Beauty!? to a visiting cocker spaniel.

Secret Laundry Monster Files, No. 39. unabr. ed. John R. Erickson. 3 CDs. (Running Time: 3 hrs.). (Hank the Cowdog Ser.: No. 39). (J). 2002. audio compact disk 28.00 (978-0-7366-8689-1(4)) Books on Tape.
Hank the Cowdog must come to grips with one of a dog's worst enemies: the dreaded laundry monster.

Secret Law of Attraction. 5th unabr. ed. Napoleon Hill. (ENG.). 2008. audio compact disk 29.95 (978-1-932429-38-1(7)) Pub: Highroads Media. Dist(s): Macmillan

Secret Life of Bees see Vida Secreta de las Abejas

Secret Life of Bees. Sue Monk Kidd. Read by Karen White. 10 cds. 2005. audio compact disk 80.00 (978-0-7366-9951-8(1)) Books on Tape.

Secret Life of Bees. Sue Monk Kidd. Contrib. by Jenna Lamia. (Running Time: 10 hrs.). (ENG.). (gr. 12 up). 2010. audio compact disk 34.95 (978-0-14-314555-4(X), PengAudBks) Penguin Grp USA.

Secret Life of Bees. movie tie-in unabr. ed. Sue Monk Kidd. Read by Jenna Lamia. 2008. audio compact disk 34.95 (978-1-59887-829-5(8)) Pub: HighBridge. Dist(s): Workman Pub

Secret Life of Bees. unabr. ed. Perf. by Sue Monk Kidd. 9 cass. (Running Time: 13 hrs. 30 mins.). 2002. 72.00 (978-0-7366-8555-9(3)) Books on Tape.

Secret Life of Bees. unabr. ed. Sue Monk Kidd. Read by Jenna Lamia. (YA). 2006. 44.99 (978-1-59895-648-1(5)) Find a World.

Secret Life of Houdini: The Making of America's First Superhero. abr. ed. William Kalush & Larry Sloman. Read by Adam Grupper. 2006. 17.95 (978-0-7435-6193-8(7)) Pub: S&S Audio. Dist(s): S and S Inc

Secret Life of Josephine: Napoleon's Bird of Paradise. unabr. ed. Carolly Erickson. Read by Margot Dionne. (YA). 2008. 79.99 (978-1-60514-502-0(5)) Find a World.

Secret Life of Laszlo, Count Dracula. abr. ed. Roderick Anscombe. 2 cass. (Running Time: 3 hrs.). 1999. (978-0-694-51469-4(1), 391531) HarperCollins Pubs.

Secret Life of Marilyn Monroe. abr. ed. J. Randy Taraborrelli. Read by Robert Petkoff. (Running Time: 8 hrs.). (ENG.). 2009. 14.98 (978-1-60024-652-4(4)) Pub: Hachet Audio. Dist(s): HachBkGrp

Secret Life of Marilyn Monroe. abr. ed. J. Randy Taraborrelli. Read by Robert Petkoff. (Running Time: 8 hrs.). (ENG., 2010. audio compact disk 14.98 (978-1-60788-255-8(8)) Pub: Hachet Audio. Dist(s): HachBkGrp

Secret Life of Prince Charming. unabr. ed. Deb Caletti. Read by Jeannie Stith. 1 MP3-CD. (Running Time: 10 hrs.). 2009. 24.99 (978-1-4233-9372-6(4), 9781423393726, Brilliance MP3); 39.97 (978-1-4233-9373-3(2), 9781423393733, Brlnc Audio MP3 Lib); 24.99 (978-1-4233-9374-0(0), 9781423393740, BAD); 39.97 (978-1-4233-9375-7(9), 9781423393757, BADLE); audio compact disk 29.99 (978-1-4233-9370-2(8), 9781423393702, Bril Audio CD Unabri); audio compact disk 97.97 (978-1-4233-9371-9(6), 9781423393719, BriAudCD Unabrid) Brilliance Audio.

Secret Life of the Soul. abr. ed. J. Keith Miller. Read by J. Keith Miller. 2 cass. (Running Time: 3 hrs.). 1997. 15.99 (978-0-8054-2817-9(8)) BH Pubng Grp.
A touchingly personal exploration of that place inside our lives, where we seldom take other people, where there is a secret life of the soul.

Secret Life of the Underwear Champ. Betty Miles. (J). 1989. 21.33 (978-0-07-540654-9(3)) SRA McGraw.

Secret Life of Walter Mitty see My World & Welcome to It

Secret Life of Walter Mitty. James Thurber. 1 cass. (Running Time: 22 min. per cass.). 1977. 10.00 (LSS1116) Esstee Audios.
Mitty, the henpecked husband, daydreams often on a grandiose scale to relieve himself from the tedium of his daily existence. His wife, the essential American Kvetch, is overdrawn, exaggerated, creating along with her spouse the archetypal naggers of the short story form.

Secret Life of Walter Mitty & You Could Look It up. James Thurber. 1 cass. (Running Time: 1 hr.). (Radiobook Ser.). 1987. 4.98 (978-0-929541-05-1(7)) Radiola Co.
Two complete stories.

Secret Lives of the Kudzu Debutantes: A Novel. unabr. ed. Cathy Holton. Read by Marguerite Gavin. (Running Time: 11 hrs. 0 mins.). (ENG.). 2009. 29.95 (978-1-4332-3466-8(1)); 65.95 (978-1-4332-3462-0(9)); audio compact disk 100.00 (978-1-4332-3463-7(7)) Blckstn Audio.

Secret Love. Stephanie Laurens. Narrated by Simon Prebble. 10 cass. (Running Time: 13 hrs. 45 mins.). (Cynster Family Ser.: Bk. 5). 54.00 (978-0-7887-9641-8(0)) Recorded Bks.

Secret Love. Stephanie Laurens. Narrated by Simon Prebble. 12 CDs. (Running Time: 13 hrs. 45 mins.). (Cynster Family Ser.: Bk. 5). 2000. audio compact disk 116.00 (978-1-4025-3816-2(2)) Recorded Bks.

Secret Lovers. unabr. ed. Charles McCarry. Read by Stefan Rudnicki. (Running Time: 39600 sec.). (Paul Christopher Novels Ser.). 2006. 29.95 (978-0-7861-4719-9(9)); audio compact disk 32.95 (978-0-7861-6577-3(4)); audio compact disk 29.95 (978-0-7861-7320-4(3)) Blckstn Audio.

Secret Lovers: A Paul Christopher Novel. unabr. ed. Charles McCarry. Read by Stefan Rudnicki. (Running Time: 39600 sec.). 2006. 65.95 (978-0-7861-4834-9(9)); audio compact disk 81.00 (978-0-7861-6136-2(1)) Blckstn Audio.

Secret Man: The Story of Watergate's Deep Throat. unabr. ed. Bob Woodward. 4 cass. (Running Time: 6 hrs.). 2005. 39.95 (978-1-4193-6292-7(5)); audio compact disk 49.75 (978-1-4193-6294-1(1)) Recorded Bks.

Secret Man: The Story of Watergate's Deep Throat. unabr. ed. Bob Woodward. Read by Boyd Gaines. 2005. 17.95 (978-0-7435-5226-4(1)) Pub: S&S Audio. Dist(s): S and S Inc

Secret Meeting. Jean Ure. 3 CDs. 2006. audio compact disk 29.95 (978-0-7540-6727-6(0), Chivers Child Audio) AudioGO.

***Secret Message of Jesus: Uncovering the Truth that Could Change Everything.** unabr. ed. Brian McLaren. Narrated by Paul Michael. (ENG.). 2006. 14.98 (978-1-59644-365-5(0), Hovel Audio) christianaud.

Secret Message of Jesus: Uncovering the Truth that Could Change Everything. unabr. ed. Brian D. McLaren. Narrated by Paul Michael. 1 MP3CD. (Running Time: 7 hrs. 18 mins. 0 sec.). (ENG.). 2006. lp 19.98 (978-1-59644-366-2(9), Hovel Audio) christianaud.
Pastor and bestselling author McLaren ("A New Kind of Christian") explores Jesus's teaching in this book, placing it in its Jewish context, analyzing its tenets and expression, and trying to work out how it should be lived today. McLaren starts with the assumption that the church may not have accurately understood Jesus's "secret message" (hidden "as a treasure one must seek in order to find"). He revisits the gospel material from a fresh -and at times radical -perspective. The church has focused on salvation as a means to "heaven after you die" for too long, according to McLaren; we should take Jesus at his word when he says "the kingdom of God is here now," and work to assist that kingdom by being peacemakers and loving others. McLaren admits to not exploring every topic here in depth, in an effort to keep the book brief, but he does an excellent job of capturing Jesus's quiet, revolutionary style -the prophet who spoke in parables, who didn't want people to talk about his miracles, who challenged established Jewish thought, and paradoxically found ultimate fulfillment and victory through death. Conservative evangelicals will be critical of some points (and there are weaknesses here), but this book will appeal to a broad spectrum of people who want to understand Jesus.

Secret Message of Jesus: Uncovering the Truth That Could Change Everything. unabr. ed. Brian D. McLaren. 6 CDs. (Running Time: 7 hrs. 18 mins. 0 sec.). (ENG.). 2006. audio compact disk 24.98 (978-1-59644-364-8(2)) christianaud.

Secret Nature Within You: Practical & Spiritual Tools & Insights for Your Journey of Self-Discovery. abr. ed. Christian Fisher. 2 cass. (Running Time: 2 hrs. 10 mins.). 1999. 16.95 (978-0-9677487-1-9(2)) Journey of Life.
This program will help you fill the gaps in your life where you feel less fulfilled. You'll learn how to bring to life, in natural ways, your own potential.

Secret of America's Strength. Spiro T. Agnew. 1 cass. (Running Time: 27 min.). 10.95 (150) J Norton Pubs.

Secret of an Untroubled Heart. Warren W. Wiersbe. Read by Warren W. Wiersbe. 2 cass. (Running Time: 2 hrs.). 1985. 9.95 (978-0-8474-2252-4(6)) Back to Bible.
Assurances that lead to an untroubled heart are discussed in these messages from John 14 - hope of heaven, knowledge of God as Father, privilege of prayer & the Father's love & peace.

Secret of Annexe 3. unabr. ed. Colin Dexter. Read by Michael Pennington. 6 cass. (Running Time: 6 hrs. 45 mins.). (Inspector Morse Mystery Ser.). 2000. 29.95 (978-1-57270-155-7(2), N61155u) Pub: Audio Partners. Dist(s): PerseuPGW
All the guests at the Hawthorne Hotel (with one exception) wake up late New Year's Day following a party the night before. The guest in Annexe 3, however, is found murdered - lying in a blood-soaked bed & still wearing his costume. To make matters worse, the victim's female companion & other guests have vanished. Inspector Morse's inquiries uncover a series of confusing identities that make this mystery a stretch even for Morse.

Secret of Annexe 3. unabr. ed. Colin Dexter. Read by Michael Pennington. 6 cass. (Running Time: 6 hrs.). (Inspector Morse Mystery Ser.). 1994. 54.95 (978-0-7451-4321-7(0), CAB 1004) AudioGO.
The guests of Haworth Hotel rose late, after New Year's Eve. But there was one exception, the guest in Annexe 3 missed New Year's Eve completely. He was still in his room, lying dead on the blood-soaked bed. Inspector Morse began investigating each of the guests. Was Mrs. Palmer really a faithful wife? Just who exactly were the Ballards? And, how had the hotel's booking confirmation been delivered to a nonexistent address?.

Secret of Annexe 3. unabr. ed. Colin Dexter. Read by Michael Pennington. 6 cass. (Running Time: 9 hrs.). (Inspector Morse Mystery Ser.: Bk. 7). 2000. 49.95 (CAB 1004) Pub: Chivers Audio Bks GBR. Dist(s): AudioGO
All of the guests of Haworth Hotel rose late on New Year's Day, except the guest in Annexe 3, who was still in his room, lying dead on the blood-soaked bed. Inspector Morse began investigating each of the guests. Was Mrs. Palmer really a faithful wife? Just who exactly were Mr. and Mrs. Ballard? And, how had the hotel's booking confirmation been delivered to an address that didn't exist?.

Secret of Being Unstoppable. Guy Finley. (ENG.). 2006. 7.49 (978-1-929320-61-5(2)) Life of Learn.

Secret of Castle Cant. unabr. ed. K. P. Bath. Narrated by Kerin McCue. 8 cass. (Running Time: 9 hrs. 45 mins.). 2005. 54.75 (978-1-4193-6689-5(0), 98239) Recorded Bks.
The widely-acclaimed stories of author K.P. Bath have been published in numerous literary journals. This spellbinding and grand adventure tale is populated by a cast of eccentric characters who spring to vibrant life with Kerin McCue's dazzling narration.

***Secret of Chanel No. 5: The Intimate History of the World's Most Famous Perfume.** unabr. ed. Tilar J. Mazzeo. (ENG.). 2010. (978-0-06-200714-8(9), Harper Audio) HarperCollins Pubs.

Secret of Chimneys. unabr. ed. Agatha Christie. Read by Flo Gibson. 6 cass. (Running Time: 7 hrs. 49 min.). (YA). (gr. 9 up). 2001. vinyl bd. 41.95 (978-1-55685-665-5(2)) Audio Bk Con.
International intrigue, stolen jewels, blackmail, murder & romance in a stately home in England.

Secret of Chimneys. unabr. ed. Agatha Christie. Read by Hugh Fraser. 6 cass. (Running Time: 8 hrs.). 2004. 29.95 (978-1-57270-386-5(5)) Pub: Audio Partners. Dist(s): PerseuPGW
Little did Anthony Cade suspect that a simple errand to deliver a manuscript on behalf of a friend would drop him right in the middle of an international conspiracy. Why were Count Stylptich's memoirs so important? And what was "King Victor" really after?.

Secret of Chimneys. unabr. ed. Agatha Christie. Read by Hugh Fraser. 7 CDs. (Mystery Masters Ser.). (ENG.). 2004. audio compact disk 29.95 (978-1-57270-387-2(3)) Pub: AudioGO. Dist(s): Perseus Dist

Secret of Concentration. Swami Amar Jyoti. 1 cass. 1988. 9.95 (P-63) Truth Consciousness.
Life as a Yoga. Patience & purification. Unity of within & without. The benevolent lessons of Mother Nature.

Secret of Crickley Hall. James Herbert. (Isis Cassettes Ser.). 2007. 104.95 (978-0-7531-3596-9(5)) Pub: ISIS Lrg Prnt GBR. Dist(s): Ulverscroft US

Secret of Crickley Hall. James Herbert. Read by Sean Barrett. (Running Time: 67800 sec.). (Isis (CDs) Ser.). 2007. audio compact disk 109.95 (978-0-7531-2665-3(6)) Pub: ISIS Lrg Prnt GBR. Dist(s): Ulverscroft US

Secret of Dominion. Susan Bayer & Richard Teneau. 4 cass. (Running Time: 5 hrs.). 19.95 Set. (978-1-882467-06-8(X), Wldstone Audio) Wildstone Media.
Full-cast sci-fi drama with music & sound effects.

Secret of Effective Leadership: Exodus 18. Ed Young. 1985. 4.95 (978-0-7417-1426-8(4), 426) Win Walk.

Secret of Elena's Tomb. Carl von Cosel. Read by Jack Hans Pedersen. 5 CDs. (Running Time: 5 hrs. 7 min.). Dramatization. 2003. audio compact disk 19.95 (978-0-9740883-0-3(7)) Howard Olsen.
These are the memoirs of Car Tanzler von Cosel, who fell in love with a beautiful tuberculosis patient named Elena Hoyos, in 1930's Key West. After her death he moved her body from the cemetery to his secret laboratory. There, for nearly eight years, he attempted to resurrect Elena with his inventions and experiments. He kept her body in a condition eerily close to that which it was in life, and when he was found out in 1938, this macabre story of love's transcendence of death began to unfold on a national stage.

***Secret of Excalibur: A Novel.** unabr. ed. Andy McDermott. Narrated by Gildart Jackson. (Running Time: 15 hrs. 0 mins.). (Nina Wilde/Eddie Chase Ser.). 2011. 20.99 (978-1-4526-7018-8(8)); 29.99 (978-1-4526-5018-0(7)); audio compact disk 39.99 (978-1-4526-0018-5(X)) Pub: Tantor Media. Dist(s): IngramPubServ

***Secret of Excalibur (Library Edition) A Novel.** unabr. ed. Andy McDermott. Narrated by Gildart Jackson. (Running Time: 15 hrs. 0 mins.). (Nina Wilde/Eddie Chase Ser.). 2011. 39.99 (978-1-4526-2018-3(0)); audio compact disk 95.99 (978-1-4526-3018-2(6)) Pub: Tantor Media. Dist(s): IngramPubServ

Secret of Father Brown. unabr. ed. G. K. Chesterton. Read by Geoffrey Matthews. 6 cass. (Running Time: 6 hrs. 40 mins.). (Father Brown Mystery Ser.). 2000. 29.95 (978-1-57270-175-5(7), N61176u, Audio Edits Mystry) Audio Partners.
One of fiction's best-loved amateur sleuths is its "high priest," Father Brown. This anthology includes eight delightfully clever mysteries that offer elegance, wit, wisdom & great entertainment.

Secret of Father Brown. unabr. ed. G. K. Chesterton. Read by Matthew Davis. 5 cass. (Running Time: 7 hrs.). (Father Brown Mystery Ser.). 1999. 39.95 (978-0-7861-0016-3(8), 1016) Blckstn Audio.
Detective fans of all races & creeds, of all tastes & fancies, will delight in the exploits of this wise & whimsical padre. Father Brown's powers of detection allow him to sit beside the immortal Holmes but he is also, a fascinating human being.

Secret of Father Brown. unabr. ed. G. K. Chesterton. Read by Geoffrey Matthews. 6 cass. (Running Time: 9 hrs.). (Father Brown Mystery Ser.). 2000. 49.95 (978-0-7451-5829-7(3), CAB 428) Pub: Chivers Audio Bks GBR. Dist(s): AudioGO
Flying fish, a man with two beards and the worst crime in the world - these are just some of the problems for Father Brown to solve. In his imitable way, the gentle, eccentric, extraordinary cleric-cum-detective sets about unraveling the threads of a colorful skein of mysteries. In the course of his investigations, Father Brown travels all over the world and through all walks of life.

Secret of Father Brown. unabr. collector's ed. G. K. Chesterton. Read by David Case. 7 cass. (Running Time: 7 hrs.). (Father Brown Mystery Ser.). 1994. 42.00 (978-0-7366-2755-9(3), 3478) Books on Tape.
Nine mystery stories featuring the priest-detective Father Brown.

Secret of Fearless Living: Going to God: 2007 CCEF Annual Conference. Featuring Tim Lane. 2007. audio compact disk 11.99 (978-1-934885-19-2(3)) New Growth Pr.

Secret of Freedom. Swami Jyotirmayananda. Read by Swami Jyotirmayananda. 1 cass. (Running Time: 45 min.). 10.00 (810) Yoga Res Foun.

Secret of Genius. 1 cass. (Opening Up to Superconsciousness Ser.). 9.95 (84TH) Crystal Clarity.
Topics include: What is genius?; energy as a form of faith; how to know what is "right"; the human nervous system - a vehicle for expressing spiritual realities; learning to relax into superconsciousness.

Secret of Greatness. 1978. 4.95 (978-0-7417-1012-3(9)) Win Walk.

Secret of Growth: Joshua 16:14-18. Ed Young. (J). 1985. 4.95 (978-0-7417-1457-2(4), 457) Win Walk.

Secret of Growth: 11 Peter 3:18. Ed Young. 1983. 4.95 (978-0-7417-1312-4(8), 312) Win Walk.

Secret of Gumbo Grove. Eleanora E. Tate. Narrated by Kim Staunton. 5 CDs. (Running Time: 5 hrs. 45 mins.). (gr. 5 up). audio compact disk 48.00 (978-1-4025-2336-6(X)) Recorded Bks.

Secret of Gumbo Grove, unabr. ed. Eleanora E. Tate. Narrated by Kim Staunton. 4 pieces. (Running Time: 5 hrs. 45 mins.). (gr. 5 up). 1997. 35.00 (978-0-7887-1771-0(5), 95249E7) Recorded Bks.
When 11-year-old Raisin helps to clean up the church cemetery, she discovers a real-life mystery that no one wants to talk about. Listeners of any age or race will identify with this spirited African-American girl who values truth & stands up for her beliefs.

Secret of Imagining. Neville Goddard. 1 cass. (Running Time: 62 min.). 1970. 8.00 (88) J & L Pubns.
Neville taught Imagination Creates Reality. He was a powerfully influential teacher of God as Consciousness.

Secret of Letting Go. Guy Finley. Read by Guy Finley. 6 cass. (Running Time: 6 hrs.). 1991. 59.95 (863A) Nightingale-Conant.
Everybody has two "selves" - one that seeks answers & one that knows them. Learn to get in touch with your intuitive side to make pleasure & happiness your true nature.

Secret of Longing. Swami Amar Jyoti. 1 cass. 1980. 9.95 (C-21) Truth Consciousness.
Where there is longing, the way is shown. Reaching the silent cave in the brain, our link with the cosmos.

Secret of Lost Things. Sheridan Hay. Read by Vanessa Benjamin. (Running Time: 41400 sec.). 2007. 72.95 (978-0-7861-4990-2(6)); audio compact disk 90.00 (978-0-7861-5755-6(0)) Blckstn Audio.

Secret of Lost Things. unabr. ed. Sheridan Hay. Read by Vanessa Benjamin. (Running Time: 41400 sec.). 2007. 29.95 (978-0-7861-4867-7(5)); audio compact disk 29.95 (978-0-7861-6079-2(9)); audio compact disk 29.95 (978-0-7861-7157-6(X)) Blckstn Audio.

Secret of Loving. Swami Amar Jyoti. 1 cass. 1980. 9.95 (A-16) Truth Consciousness.
What does it mean to be really loving? Love as a state of consciousness. Learning in this school of earth.

Secret of Macarger's Gulch see Eyes of the Panther & Other Stories

Secret of Magical Evocation. Featuring Donald Michael Kraig. 1988. 9.95 (978-1-59157-024-0(7)) Assn for Cons.

Secret of Mary. abr. ed. Louis de Montfort. Read by Jim Duffy. Adapted by Eddie Doherty. 1. (Running Time: 1 hr.). 2000. 9.95 (978-0-921440-62-8(6)) Madonna Hse CAN.

Secret of Old Mexico. Jerry Stemach. (Nick Ford Mysteries Ser.). 2000. audio compact disk 18.95 (978-1-4105-0142-4(6)) D Johnston Inc.

Secret of Old Mexico, Vol. 4. Jerry Stemach. Ed. by Jerry Stemach. Ed. by Gail Portnuff Venable & Dorothy Tyack. Illus. by Jeff Ham. Contrib. by Ed Smaron et al. (Start-to-Finish Books). (J). (gr. 2-3). 2000. 35.00 (978-1-58702-462-7(4)) D Johnston Inc.

Secret of Old Mexico, Vol. 4. Jerry Stemach. Ed. by Jerry Stemach. Ed. by Gail Portnuff Venable & Dorothy Tyack. Illus. by Jeff Ham. Contrib. by Ed Smaron et al. (Start-to-Finish Books). (J). (gr. 2-3). 2002. 100.00 (978-1-58702-984-4(7)) D Johnston Inc.

Secret of Old Mexico, Vol. 4. unabr. ed. Jerry Stemach. Ed. by Jerry Stemach. Ed. by Gail Portnuff Venable & Dorothy Tyack. Illus. by Jeff Ham. Contrib. by Ed Smaron et al. 1 cass. (Running Time: 1 hr.). (Start-to-Finish Books). (J). (gr. 2-3). 2000. (978-1-893376-54-0(0), F15K2) D Johnston Inc.
In this story, Jeff and Ken are invited to the Yucatan jungle to help on the archaeological dig of a Mayan temple. Someone on the dig team wants to steal valuable artifacts and smuggle them to the United States to sell on the black market. Kris and Mandy join the boys in Mexico while Nick goes to San Francisco to help open a new Museum of Latin Culture. In their attempt to stop the crime, they encounter poisoned artifacts, poisonous snakes and gold.

Secret of Personal Prayer. George King. 2007. audio compact disk (978-0-937249-45-1(9)) Aetherius Soc.

Secret of Personal Success. Sanford G. Kulkin. 8 cass. (Running Time: 4 hrs.). 1992. bk. & ring bd. 95.00 (978-1-58034-010-6(5)) IML Pubns.
Motivational messages focusing on the power of goal setting from the timeless perspective of the Bible.

Secret of Playing More Notes Without Reading More Notes: How to Play Piano from Chord Symbols. Duane Shinn. 1 cass. bk. 59.95 incl. fakebk. (CP-16) Duane Shinn.
Discusses how to make oneself into a pop pianist (or jazz, or rock, or whatever) by playing through the book, arranging each song from chord symbols.

Secret of Power Negotiating: Accelerated Learning Techniques Version. Roger Dawson & Colin Rose. 8 cass. (Running Time: 8 hrs.). 1996. wbk. ed. 79.95 (13780A) Nightingale-Conant.

Secret of Quarry House. unabr. ed. Claire Lorrimer. Read by Judith Boyd. 5 cass. (Running Time: 7 hrs. 30 min.). (Sound Ser.). 1993. 49.95 (978-1-85496-842-5(4), 68424) Pub: UlverLrgPrint GBR. Dist(s): Ulverscroft US
When Kate becomes mistress of Quarry House, it means a life of plots & ghosts from the past. There is her husband's brooding nature, rumors concerning the fates of the previous two Mrs. Rivers, & Kate's fears for his 3 young daughters.

Secret of Relaxation. Swami Amar Jyoti. 2 cass. 1988. 12.95 (K-107) Truth Consciousness.
What would happen if we relaxed? Why don't we? Reliance upon God.

Secret of Renunciation. Swami Jyotirmayananda. 1 cass. (Running Time: 45 min.). 1990. 10.00 Yoga Res Foun.

Secret of Ricena's Pond. Perf. by Riki Lipe. Composed by David Smith. Narrated by Reta Spears-Stewart. Contrib. by Ron Butler. 1 cass. (J). (ps-12). 1993. 9.95 (978-0-9659381-4-3(X)) Hoot N Cackle.

Secret of Robber's Cave. unabr. ed. Kristiana Gregory. (Cabin Creek Mysteries Ser.). (ENG.). 2008. 10.49 (978-1-60814-103-6(9), SpringWater) Oasis Audio.

Secret of Robber's Cave. unabr. ed. Kristiana Gregory. Read by Various Artists. (Running Time: 1 hr. 49 mins. 10 sec.). (Cabin Creek Mysteries Ser.). (ENG.). 2008. audio compact disk 14.99 (978-1-59859-344-0(7)) Oasis Audio.

Secret of Room 333. unabr. ed. Allan Zullo. Read by John Ratzenberger. 2008. 1.37 (978-1-4233-8069-6(X), 9781423380696, BAD) Brilliance Audio.

Secret of Sadhana. Swami Jyotirmayananda. 1 cass. (Running Time: 1 hr.). 1990. 12.99 Yoga Res Foun.

Secret of Santa Vittoria. unabr. ed. Robert Crichton. Read by Christopher Hurt. 10 cass. (Running Time: 14 hrs. 30 mins.). 1997. 69.95 (978-0-7861-1203-6(4), 1967) Blckstn Audio.
Santa Vittoria is a fictional town, still remote from the rest of war-torn Italy, where the citizens, led by their wine-loving mayor Bombolini, scheme & plot to prevent the Germans from locating & looting the town's only treasure - its fabulous wine cellars.

***Secret of Santa Vittoria: A Novel.** unabr. ed. Robert Crichton. Read by Christopher Hurt. (Running Time: 13 hrs. 30 mins.). 2010. 29.95 (978-1-4417-0337-8(3)); audio compact disk 109.00 (978-1-4417-0334-7(9)) Blckstn Audio.

Secret of Self-Restraint. Swami Jyotirmayananda. Read by Swami Jyotirmayananda. 1 cass. (Running Time: 45 min.). 10.00 (801) Yoga Res Foun.

Secret of Shakespeare. C. B. Purdom. 1 cass. (Running Time: 30 min.). 10.95 (23107) J Norton Pubs.
The analysis of nine Shakespearean plays serves to illustrate the essential nature of drama & to reveal the distinction between great drama & mere entertainment.

Secret of Shambhala: In Search of the Eleventh Insight? abr. ed. James Redfield & Salle Merrill Redfield. (ENG.). 2006. 9.98 (978-1-59483-686-2(8)) Pub: Hachet Audio. Dist(s): HachBkGrp

Secret of Shambhala: In Search of the Eleventh Insight. collector's ed. James Redfield. Read by LeVar Burton. 6 cass. (Running Time: 9 hrs.). 1999. 26.95 (978-0-7366-4778-6(3)) Books on Tape.
James Edfield takes readers to the mountains of Tibet in search of the mythical place called Shambhala. It is a paradise & spiritual utopia just as the book is part an adeventure travel story & part a metaphysical journey. Rather than preach his spiritual beliefs, he portrays himself as a pilgrim pondering the possibilities of living in a culture that is entirely focused on the life process.

Secret of Shambhala: In Search of the Eleventh Insight. unabr. ed. James Redfield. (ENG.). 2005. 14.98 (978-1-59483-676-3(0)) Pub: Hachet Audio. Dist(s): HachBkGrp

Secret of Shelter Island: Money & What Matters. unabr. ed. Alexander Green. Read by Erik Synnestvedt. (Running Time: 7 hrs. 30 mins.). (ENG.). 2009. 27.98 (978-1-59659-475-3(6), GildAudio) Pub: Gildan Media. Dist(s): HachBkGrp

Secret of St. John Bosco. Henri Gheon. 6 cass. 24.95 (753) Ignatius Pr.
Life of St. John Bosco by the great French author.

Secret of Successful Relationships. Earnie Larsen. 1 cass. (Running Time: 1 hr.). 1989. 10.95 (978-1-56047-007-6(0), A111) E Larsen Enterprises.
Explains why relationships work & how to make the work.

Secret of the Ages. Robert Collier. Read by Ned Neltner. Prod. by Mardig Sheridan. Music by Scott Cossu. 3 cass. (Running Time: 4 hrs.). 1997. 19.95 (978-0-912576-19-0(7)) R Collier.
Offers us the opportunity to become masters of our own lives. Stresses the unlimited power of the subconscious mind within us. Plots for us the course that is necessary to follow in order to reach that success which we all desire. Develop a positive mental attitude.

Secret of the Ages. abr. ed. Robert Collier. (Running Time: 7 hrs.). (ENG.). (gr. 8). 2008. audio compact disk 29.95 (978-0-14-314340-6(9), PengAudBks) Penguin Grp USA.

Secret of the Alchemist. unabr. ed. John Ward. Read by Colin Moody. 8 CDs. (Running Time: 7 hrs. 30 mins.). (Fate of the Stone Ser.). 2005. audio compact disk 87.95 (978-1-74093-565-4(9)) Pub: Bolinda Pubng AUS. Dist(s): Bolinda Pub Inc

Secret of the Caves. Franklin W. Dixon. (Hardy Boys Ser.: No. 7). (J). 2003. 23.00 (978-0-8072-1680-4(1), Listening Lib) Pub: Random Audio Pubg. Dist(s): Random

Secret of the Cure of Ars. Henri Gheon. 6 cass. 24.95 (705) Ignatius Pr.
Life of the Cure of Ars, remarkable confessor, miracle-worker, patron of all parish priests.

Secret of the Fox Hunter. abr. ed. Nathaniel Hawthorne. 2 pieces. (Running Time: 2 hrs.). 1991. 21.95 (978-1-55656-021-7(4)) Pub: Dercum Audio. Dist(s): APG

Secret of the Foxhunter see Classic Detective Stories, Vol. III, A Collection

***Secret of the Growing Gold.** Bram Stoker. 2009. (978-1-60136-490-6(3)) Audio Holding.

Secret of the Indian. unabr. ed. Lynne Reid Banks. Read by Lynne Reid Banks. 2 vols. (Running Time: 3 hrs. 22 mins.). (Indian in the Cupboard Ser.:

No. 3). (J). (gr. 3-7). 1991. pap. bk. 29.00 (978-0-8072-7327-2(9), YA829SP, Listening Lib) Random Audio Pubg.
In this sequel to "The Indian in the Cupboard" & "The Return of the Indian," a terrible battle leaves many of Little Bear's warriors wounded. Omri must find medical help while protecting the secret of the magic cupboard.

Secret of the Indian. unabr. ed. Lynne Reid Banks. Read by Lynne Reid Banks. 3 cass. (Running Time: 3 hrs. 22 min.). (Indian in the Cupboard Ser.: No. 3). (J). (gr. 4-7). 1991. 15.95 set. (YA 829 CXR, Listening Lib); 20.98 (YA 829 SP, Listening Lib) Random Audio Pubg.

Secret of the Junkyard Shadow. unabr. ed. Kristiana Gregory. (Running Time: 1 hr. 16 mins. 26 sec.). (Cabin Creek Mysteries Ser.). (ENG.). (J). 2009. 10.49 (978-1-60814-527-0(1), SpringWater); audio compact disk 14.99 (978-1-59859-587-1(3), SpringWater) Oasis Audio.

Secret of the Mansion: Trixie Belden. Julie Campbell. 3 vols. (Running Time: 4 hrs.). (J). (gr. 3-7). 2004. pap. bk. 29.00 (978-1-4000-9000-6(8), Listening Lib); 23.00 (978-1-4000-8980-2(8), Listening Lib) Random Audio Pubg.

Secret of the Night. Gaston Leroux. Read by John Bolen. (Running Time: 10 hrs.). 2001. 29.95 (978-1-60083-598-8(8), Audiofy Corp) Iofy Corp.

Secret of the Night. Gaston Leroux. Read by John Bolen. (ENG.). 2001. audio compact disk 90.00 (978-1-4001-3026-9(3)) Pub: Tantor Media. Dist(s): IngramPubServ

Secret of the Night. unabr. ed. Gaston Leroux. Read by John Bolen. 9 CDs. (Running Time: 10 hrs. 8 mins.). (ENG.). 2001. audio compact disk 45.00 (978-1-4001-0026-2(7)); audio compact disk 23.00 (978-1-4001-5026-7(4)) Pub: Tantor Media. Dist(s): IngramPubServ

Secret of the Night. unabr. ed. Gaston Leroux. Narrated by John Bolen. (Running Time: 10 hrs. 0 mins. 0 sec.). (ENG.). 2009. audio compact disk 22.99 (978-1-4001-6100-3(2)); audio compact disk 65.99 (978-1-4001-4100-5(1)) Pub: Tantor Media. Dist(s): IngramPubServ

Secret of the Night. unabr. ed. Gaston Leroux. Narrated by John Bolen. (Running Time: 10 hrs. 0 mins. 0 sec.). (ENG.). 2009. audio compact disk 32.99 (978-1-4001-1100-8(5)) Pub: Tantor Media. Dist(s): IngramPubServ

Secret of the Old Clock. unabr. ed. Carolyn Keene. Read by Laura Linney. 2 cass. (Running Time: 3 hrs. 14 mins.). (Nancy Drew Mystery Stories: Vol. 1). (J). (gr. 4-7). 2004. 23.00 (978-0-8072-0755-0(1), Listening Lib) Random Audio Pubg.
Nancy Drew's keen mind is tested when she searches for a missing will.

Secret of the Old Clock. unabr. ed. Carolyn Keene. Read by Laura Linney. (Running Time: 11640 sec.). (Nancy Drew Ser.). (ENG.). (J). (gr. 3-7). 2007. audio compact disk 14.95 (978-0-7393-4913-7(9), Listening Lib) Pub: Random Audio Pubg. Dist(s): Random

Secret of the Old Mill. unabr. ed. Franklin W. Dixon. Narrated by Flo Gibson. 3 cass. (Running Time: 4 hrs. 30 mins.). (J). 2003. 16.95 (978-1-55685-697-6(0)) Audio Bk Con.

Secret of the Old Mill Vol. 3. unabr. ed. Prod. by Listening Library Staff. 2 cass. (Running Time: 3 hrs. 25 mins.). (Hardy Boys Ser.). (J). (gr. 4-7). 2004. 23.00 (978-0-8072-0773-4(X), Listening Lib) Pub: Random Audio Pubg. Dist(s): Random

Secret of the Rosary. St. Louis De Montfort. 4 CDs. (Running Time: 4 hrs.). 2003. audio compact disk 26.95 (978-1-57058-588-3(1), rc17-cd) St Joseph Communs.
I wish to give you a rose-a crimson one, because the Precious Blood of Our Lord has fallen upon it. With these words St. Louis de Montfort invites you to discover a spiritual treasury of mental and vocal prayer blessed with the divine approval of heaven and the generous indulgence of the Church. Your life can change forever when you discover The Secret of the Rosary. Apostle of the Rosary A champion of prayer before the Blessed Sacrament, the author of True Devotion to Mary and the originator of total consecration to Mary, St. Louis de Montfort (1673-1716) remains one of the greatest apostles of Marian Devotion the world has ever known. Now, read by EWTN Radio personality Matthew Arnold on four CD?s, this all-new digital recording of de Montfort's timeless inspirational classic, The Secret of the Rosary, reveals to you dramatic evidence of the awesome spiritual power of this most Catholic of devotions-and how to experience it for yourself. The Rosary and You In 53 brief chapters that he calls "roses" St. Louis covers virtually every aspect of this amazing gift from heaven. You'll discover the origin of this great devotion, marvels and miracles of the Rosary, the meaning of the prayers, the testimony of other great saints, clergy and spiritual writers, and more. But this presentation is not merely a fascinating exploration of a devotion of inestimable value by a canonized master of Catholic spirituality, but also an intimate journey into the heart of Our Lord and Our Lady and an effective tool that will inspire and empower you to recite the Rosary with tremendous spiritual benefits to you and your loved ones. Spiritual Secrets Revealed A miracle of a book that has been changing lives for hundreds of years, millions of copies of The Secret of the Rosary have been sold in the twentieth century alone. Now, with the release of the SJC Audiobook version, this soul-transforming spiritual classic is more accessible than ever before. The Secret of the Rosary was written by a great saint to introduce you directly to the powerful intercession of the Mother of God. Order now, your rose is waiting for you. LEARN:How the Rosary is a "school of Christian life" Why you must know the difference between divine faith, human faith, and pious faith How the Rosary can be the means of your perfection Why the Rosary can be considered even more valuable than the Psalms of David How to offer each decade after the method of St. Louis de Montfort How the Angelic Salutation (the Hail Mary) was foretold by David What St. Jerome, St. Augustine, Tertullian and other Fathers of the Church teach about the Our Father How to identify the satanic trap that heretics of the past and over- critical Catholics of today often fall into without realizing it.

Secret of the Rosary. Saint Louis Grignon de Montfort. 5 cass. 22.95 (903) Ignatius Pr.
The spiritual classic on the Rosary by the great Marian Saint.

***Secret of the Rosary.** St. Louis de Montfort. Read by Karen Savage. (ELX.). 2009. audio compact disk 16.95 (978-1-936231-14-0(X)) Cath Audio.

Secret of the Secret: Unlocking the Mysteries of the Runaway Bestseller. unabr. ed. Karen Kelly. Read by Kathleen McInerney. 5 CDs. (Running Time: 6 hrs. 0 mins. 0 sec.). (ENG.). 2007. audio compact disk 29.95 (978-1-4272-0258-1(3)) Pub: Macmill Audio. Dist(s): Macmillan

Secret of the Snows. Katrina Wright. 1992. pap. bk. 34.95 (978-1-85496-624-7(3)) Pub: UlverLrgPrint GBR. Dist(s): Ulverscroft US

Secret of the Sperm. Neville Goddard. 1 cass. (Running Time: 62 min.). 1965. 8.00 (45) J & L Pubns.
Neville taught Imagination Creates Reality. He was a powerfully influential teacher of God as Consciousness.

Secret of the Universe: A Story of Love, Loss, & the Discovery of an Eternal Truth. (Running Time: 21 hrs., 47 min). (ENG.). 2008. 26.95 (978-0-9793880-1-9(5)) Truth Driven.

Secret of the Villa Mimosa, abr. ed. Elizabeth A. Adler. Read by Monica Buckley. 2 cass. (Running Time: 3 hrs.). 2000. 7.95 (978-1-57815-145-5(7), 1104, Media Bks Audio) Media Bks NJ.
Detective Franco Mahoney was looking for a killer, without a whisper of a clue. He needed Dr. Phyl Forster to unlock the victim's mind. But he wasn't prepared for the passion Dr. Phyl inspired or the passion ensued.

***Secret of the Villa Mimosa.** unabr. ed. Elizabeth A. Adler. Read by Monica Buckley. (Running Time: 11 hrs.). 2010. 24.99 (978-1-4418-4165-0(2), 9781441841650, Brilliance MP3); 39.97 (978-1-4418-4166-7(0), 9781441841667, Brlnc Audio MP3 Lib) Brilliance Audio.

Secret of Those Empowered by the Spirit. Read by Basilea Schlink. 1 cass. (Running Time: 30 min.). 1985. (0203) Evang Sisterhood Mary.
Discusses fundamentals of spiritual authority & mastering the future.

Secret of Yoga. Swami Jyotirmayananda. 1 cass. (Running Time: 1 hr.). 1990. 12.99 Yoga Res Foun.

Secret on the Wall. 2002. (978-0-7398-5155-5(1)) SteckVau.

Secret on the Wall Level 3. (J). 2002. audio compact disk (978-0-7398-5338-2(4)) SteckVau.

***Secret Order of the Gumm Street Girls.** abr. ed. Elise Primavera. Read by Colleen Delany. (ENG.). 2006. (978-0-06-123010-3(3)); (978-0-06-123011-0(1)) HarperCollins Pubs.

Secret Order of the Gumm Street Girls. unabr. ed. Elise Primavera. Read by Colleen Delany. (J). 2008. 54.99 (978-1-60514-503-7(3)) Find a World.

Secret Path. abr. ed. Paul Brunton. Read by Christopher Reeve. 1 cass. (Running Time: 1 hr. 15 mins.). 1995. 10.95 (978-0-944993-06-4(0)) Audio Lit.
Paul Brunton (1898-1981) is recognized as one of the pioneers who introduced yoga and meditation to the West. Written with the passion of an authentic pioneer and the thoughtfulness of a seasoned practitioner, his work is a beacon for all contemporary seekers.

Secret Path to Contract Programming Riches: An Expert Consultant's Step-by-Step Guide That Takes You from Having Little or No Computer Programming Experience, Virtually, Directly into High-Paid Contract Programming. Michael Nigohosian. 3 CDs. (Running Time: 3hrs. 16mins.). 2004. audio compact disk 47.97 (978-0-9712806-1-8(4)) Pub: McGil Wilcx Web. Dist(s): Baker Taylor
Now in audio CD format - the bestselling contract programming book, by veteran computer consultant, Michael Nigohosian! Written for the computer student, computer hobbyist and career-changer, this bestseller shows that you don't have to be a seasoned computer professional before you can consider creating a career as an expert programmer-consultant. - Mastery - Master the important, real-world fundamentals of quickly creating a rewarding, independent, computer programming career starting with learning how to learn computer science using Rapid Mastery Technology(tm). Discover how to concurrently get high-powered, real-world experience with your training and use it to increase your salary and position on your first job. Add to this, insider secrets on career control and longevity-and you can't do without this computer career success guide. - Uniqueness - What sets this bestseller apart from any other book on programming or consulting is that it is the only book that shows the computer hobbyist not only WHAT TO DO to become a high-paid contract programmer, but HOW TO DO IT! Some books explain what being a computer consultant is like from a day-to-day point of view and others teach you how to program in a specific language. But, no book provides a step-by-step system on how to become an absolute expert computer programmer and then take that knowledge to go virtually, directly into high-paid contract programming. - Timeliness - This powerful book comes at the right time and with the right information. Using the same technology developed and used by the author, the reader will be able to accelerate and concentrate the acquisition of specific industry experience. There's little corner-cutting here. Nigohosian stresses excellence, focus and determination throughout the book. By the time the reader is through with the program he or she will be ready to accept a high-paid contract programming position, by-passing many of the typical steps and years of experience needed.

Secret Pilgrim, unabr. ed. John le Carré. Read by Frederick Davidson. 9 cass. (Running Time: 13 hrs.). (George Smiley Ser.). 1992. 62.95 (978-0-7861-0325-6(6), 1286) Blckstn Audio.
Nothing is as it was. Old enemies embrace. The dark staging grounds of the Cold War - whose shadows barely obscured the endless games of espionage - are flooded with light; the rules are rewritten, the stakes changed, the future unfathomable. John le Carre has seized this momentous turning point in history to give us the most disturbing experience we have yet had of the frail & brutal world of spydom.

***Secret Pilgrim.** unabr. ed. John le Carré. (Running Time: 13 hrs.). 2010. audio compact disk 29.95 (978-1-4417-3554-6(2)) Blckstn Audio.

***Secret Pilgrim.** unabr. ed. John le Carré. Read by Frederick Davidson. (Running Time: 13 hrs.). 2010. 29.95 (978-1-4417-3555-3(0)); audio compact disk 109.00 (978-1-4417-3552-2(6)) Blckstn Audio.

Secret Pilgrim. unabr. ed. John le Carré. Read by Michael Jayston. 10 cass. (Running Time: 15 hrs.). (George Smiley Ser.: Bk. 8). 2000. 69.95 (978-0-7451-6467-0(6), CAB 1084) Pub: Chivers Audio Bks GBR. Dist(s): AudioGO
The Berlin Wall has fallen. Ned is the Secret Pilgrim, a loyal soldier of the British Intelligence. Approaching the end of his career, he is forced to revisit his early years in the British Intelligence as George Smiley gives back to Ned the dangerous edge of memory that cuts through his self-delusion and empowers him to finally frame the questions that have haunted him for thirty years.

Secret Pilgrim. unabr. ed. John le Carré. Narrated by John Franklyn-Robbins. 10 cass. (Running Time: 14 hrs.). (George Smiley Novels Ser.). 1992. 85.00 (978-1-55690-748-7(6), 92114E7) Recorded Bks.
George Smiley, master spy, delves into his past to recount incidents from his early days with the service.

Secret Pilgrim. unabr. collector's ed. John le Carré. Read by David Case. 9 cass. (Running Time: 13 hrs. 30 min.). (George Smiley Novels Ser.). 1992. 72.00 (978-0-7366-2119-9(9), 2922) Books on Tape.
Three decades in the Circus by the world's greatest spymaster.

***Secret Pilgrim: A BBC Full-Cast Radio Drama.** John le Carré. Narrated by Simon Russell Beale. (Running Time: 2 hrs. 0 mins. 0 sec.). (BBC Radio Ser.). (ENG.). 2010. audio compact disk 19.95 (978-1-60283-865-9(8)) Pub: AudioGO. Dist(s): Perseus Dist

Secret Place. Mac Hammond. 1 cass. (Running Time: 1 hr). 2005. 5.00 (978-1-57399-208-4(9)); audio compact disk 5.00 (978-1-57399-262-6(3)) Mac Hammond.

Secret Place. Mac Hammond. 2008. audio compact disk 6.00 (978-1-57399-383-8(2)) Mac Hammond.

Secret Pleasures of Menopause, Set. Christiane Northrup. 3 CDs. 2008. audio compact disk 19.95 (978-1-4019-2238-2(4)) Hay House.

Secret Plot to Make Ted Kennedy President: Inside the Real Watergate Conspiracy. unabr. ed. Geoff Shepard. Read by Jim Bond. (Running Time: 9 hrs.). 2008. 39.25 (978-1-4233-6069-8(9), 9781423360698, BADLE); 39.25 (978-1-4233-6067-4(2), 9781423360674, Brlnc Audio MP3 Lib); 24.95 (978-1-4233-6066-7(4), 9781423360667, Brilliance MP3); 24.95 (978-1-4233-6068-1(0), 9781423360681, BAD); audio compact disk 92.25 (978-1-4233-6065-0(6), 9781423360650, BriAudCD Unabrid); audio compact disk 34.95 (978-1-4233-6064-3(8), 9781423360643, Bril Audio CD Unabri) Brilliance Audio.

Secret Power of Personal Journals. Michael M. Kiefer. Read by Michael Monroe Kiefer. 1 cass. (Running Time: 40 min.). (Powermind Library). 1995. 14.00 (978-0-9645934-2-8(4)) Kiefer Enterprises.
Step-by-step instruction in self-discovery through journaling. Covers: journal selection, uses, review methods & applications.

Secret Power of Serendipity. Jack Boland. 2 cass. 1980. 19.95 (978-0-88152-005-7(5)) Master Mind.
Discover how you can create your own personal destiny.

Secret Prey, unabr. ed. John Sandford, pseud. Narrated by Richard Ferrone. 9 cass. (Running Time: 12 hrs. 30 mins.). (Prey Ser.). 1998. 80.00 (978-0-7887-2161-8(5), 95457E7) Recorded Bks.
The shooting death of the company chairman seems like an unfortunate accident - until Lucas Davenport investigates the members of the hunting party.

Secret Rider. Marta Randall. Dramatizati[illegible]35. 9.95 Audio Saga.
A science fiction tale of time travel in a[illegible]mpt to cheat death.

Secret River. unabr. ed. Kate Grenville. Read by Simon Vance. (Running Time: 43200 sec.). 2006. 72.95 (978-0-7861-4645-1(1)); audio compact disk 90.00 (978-0-7861-6792-0(0)); audio compact disk 29.95 (978-0-7861-7423-2(4)) Blckstn Audio.

Secret Roots of Alchemy. unabr. ed. Stephan Hoeller. 1 cass. (Running Time: 1 hr. 32 min.). 1985. 11.00 (40015) Big Sur Tapes.
Details C. G. Jung's explorations & elaborates on methods alchemists & Gnostics use to bring about psychological & spiritual transformation.

Secret Sanction. abr. ed. Brian Haig. Read by John Rubinstein. (ENG.). 2005. 14.98 (978-1-59483-411-0(3)) Pub: Hachet Audio. Dist(s): HachBkGrp

Secret Sanction. abr. ed. Brian Haig. Read by John Rubinstein. (Running Time: 6 hrs.). (ENG.). 2009. 44.98 (978-1-60788-092-9(X)) Pub: Hachet Audio. Dist(s): HachBkGrp

Secret Sanction. unabr. ed. Brian Haig. Read by Scott Brick. 10 cass. (Running Time: 15 hrs.). 2002. 80.00 (978-0-7366-8615-0(0)) Books on Tape.
Sean Drummond is a U.S. Army lawyer who is chosen to head an investigation with global implications. Thirty-five Central European victims have been executed, and the world media blames a team of Green Berets assigned to the area. The Green Berets protest their innocence, but Drummond can't take their word for it. A damaging leak to the White House, a reporter digging up dirt from Drummond's past, and a brutal murder at Drummond's doorstep all hinder him in his search. He must uneasily team up with Captain Lisa Morrow, the Army's best defense lawyer, only to discover that there is a vast conspiracy of frightening proportion at the bottom of these killings. Drummond must make his way through minefields of deception to find the truth.

Secret School. Avi. Narrated by Johanna Parker. 3 CDs. (Running Time: 3 hrs.). (J). 2001. audio compact disk 29.75 (978-1-4025-8064-2(9)) Recorded Bks.

Secret School. unabr. ed. Avi. Narrated by Johanna Parker. 2 pieces. (Running Time: 3 hrs.). 2001. 19.00 (978-1-4025-2205-5(3)) Recorded Bks.
In 1925 Colorado, 14-year-old Ida Bidson dreams of becoming a teacher, but she knows it won?t be easy. When the school board closes the town?s one-room school, threatening to keep Ida from finishing eighth grade and moving on to high school, it looks like her dream will never come true. Then she and her classmates come up with a plan for a secret school?with Ida as their teacher!.

***Secret Scooter.** Christianne C. Jones. Illus. by Mary Sullivan. (My First Graphic Novel Ser.). (ENG.). 2010. audio compact disk 14.60 (978-1-4342-2584-9(4)) CapstoneDig.

Secret Scripture. unabr. ed. Sebastian Barry. (Running Time: 9.5 hrs. NaN mins.). 2008. 59.95 (978-1-4332-6147-3(2)) Blckstn Audio.

Secret Scripture. unabr. ed. Sebastian Barry. Read by Wanda McCaddon. 1 MP3-CD. (Running Time: 9 hrs. 20 mins.). 2008. 29.95 (978-1-4332-6151-0(0)); audio compact disk 80.00 (978-1-4332-6148-0(0)); audio compact disk 19.95 (978-1-4332-6150-3(2)) Blckstn Audio.

Secret Servant. unabr. ed. Daniel Silva. Read by Phil Gigante. 11 CDs. (Running Time: 12 hrs.). (Gabriel Allon Ser.: No. 7). 2007. audio compact disk 38.95 (978-1-59600-035-3(X), 9781596000353, Bril Audio CD Unabri) Brilliance Audio.

Secret Seven Adventure, unabr. ed. Enid Blyton. Read by Sarah Greene. 2 cass. (Running Time: 3 hrs.). (Secret Seven Mystery Ser.). (J). (gr. 1-8). 1999. 18.95 (CCFA 3477, Chivers Child Audio) AudioGO.

Secret Sharer see Heart of Darkness & Other Stories

Secret Sharer. (1698) Books on Tape.

Secret Sharer. unabr. ed. Joseph Conrad. Read by Brian Parry. 1 cass. (Running Time: 1 hr. 30 min.). 1992. 7.95 (978-1-882071-09-8(3), 011) B-B Audio.
What strange power does a murder hold over a ships captain? Why would this captain risk the first vessel under his command for the sake of a mysterious sailor that he has never seen before, will never see again, and who is the self-confessed killer of on.

Secret Sharer & Other Stories. unabr. ed. Robert A. Silverberg. Read by Robertson Dean. 5 CDs. (Running Time: 5 hrs. 30 mins.). 2002. audio compact disk 40.00 (978-0-7861-9384-4(0), 3027); 32.95 (978-0-7861-2368-1(0), 3027) Blckstn Audio.
Includes The Secret Sharer, Good News from the Vatican, and the novella We Are for the Dark.

Secret Sharer & the Brute. unabr. ed. Joseph Conrad. Narrated by Flo Gibson. 2 cass. (Running Time: 3 hrs.). 2003. 14.95 (978-1-55685-708-9(X)) Audio Bk Con.
After pulling a fugitive from a murder that was accidental, on board the Captain hides him from his crew until he solves his dilemma. The second tale is about a brute of a ship that takes its toll.

Secret, Silent Screams. unabr. ed. Joan Lowery Nixon. Narrated by Alexandra O'Karma. 4 pieces. (Running Time: 5 hrs.). (gr. 7 up). 2001. 39.00 (978-0-7887-4568-3(9), 96337E7) Recorded Bks.
The coroner has ruled Barry Logan's death as the latest in a string of teen-age suicides. Marti Lewis, Barry's best friend, knows that he was murdered. She just can't get anyone to believe her.

Secret, Silent Screams. unabr. ed. Joan Lowery Nixon. Narrated by Christina Moore & Alexandra O'Karma. 5 CDs. (Running Time: 5 hrs.). (gr. 7 up).

2001. audio compact disk 48.00 (978-0-7887-5221-6(9), C1369E7) Recorded Bks.
The coroner has ruled Barry Logan's death as the latest string of teenage suicides. Marti Lewis, Barry's best friend, knows that he was murdered. She just can't get anyone to believe her.

Secret, Silent Screams. unabr. ed. Joan Lowery Nixon. Narrated by Alexandra O'Karma. 4 cass. (Running Time: 5 hrs.). (YA). 2001. pap. bk. & stu. ed. 53.24 Recorded Bks.
The coroner has ruled Barry Logan's death as the latest in a string of teen-age suicides. Marti Lewis, Barry's best friend, knows that he was murdered. She just can't get anyone to believe her.

***Secret Sins.** Kate Charles. 2010. 89.95 (978-1-4079-0268-5(7)); audio compact disk 99.95 (978-1-4079-0269-2(5)) Pub: Soundings Ltd GBR. Dist(s): Ulverscroft US

Secret Sins. Jeannie Johnson. 2009. 76.95 (978-1-4079-0392-7(6)); audio compact disk 84.95 (978-1-4079-0393-4(4)) Pub: Soundings Ltd GBR. Dist(s): Ulverscroft US

Secret Sits see Robert Frost in Recital

Secret Smile. abr. ed. Nicci French. Read by Anne Flosnik. (Running Time: 6 hrs.). 2004. audio compact disk 74.25 (978-1-59355-943-4(7), 1593559437) Brilliance Audio.
Miranda's sister, Kerri, has a new boyfriend. He's a raven-haired, handsome charmer who seems to dote on Kerri. But Brendan isn't the man he says he is. Miranda should know, because she broke off her own affair with him just a few weeks ago when she found him reading her diary. Now Brendan claims that it was he who ended their short-lived relationship - and everyone believes him. When he and Kerri announce their engagement, Miranda's parents are thrilled for their shyer, less confident daughter. Then Kerri and Brendan beg Miranda to let them live in her apartment until their new home is ready. Against her better judgment, Miranda agrees. Like a virus, Brendan starts spreading destruction throughout her life. He invades her privacy and disrupts her relationships with her family and friends. And then the real nightmare begins... Like the obscenities he whispers into her ear, his onslaughts are as undetectable as they are devastating. Those closest to her begin to doubt her mental stability and accuse her of the very thing she believes drives Brendan: obsession. When Miranda decides to take off the gloves, fight back, and discover what is behind her enemy's bemused, secret smile, the consequences will be terrifying.

Secret Smile. unabr. ed. Nicci French. Read by Anne Flosnik. (Running Time: 10 hrs.). 2004. 24.95 (978-1-59335-676-7(5), 1593356765, Brilliance MP3); 39.25 (978-1-59335-810-5(5), 1593358105, Brinc Audio MP3 Lib); 82.25 (978-1-59086-189-9(2), 1590861892, BrilAudUnabridg); 32.95 (978-1-59086-188-2(4), 1590861884, BAU) Brilliance Audio.

Secret Smile. unabr. ed. Nicci French. Read by Anne Flosnik. (Running Time: 10 hrs.). 2004. 49.97 (978-1-59710-679-5(8), 1597106798, BADLE); 24.95 (978-1-59710-678-8(X), 159710678X, BAD) Brilliance Audio.

***Secret Smile.** unabr. ed. Nicci French. Read by Anne Flosnik. (Running Time: 10 hrs.). 2010. audio compact disk 29.99 (978-1-4418-4111-7(3), 9781441841117, Bril Audio CD Unabri); audio compact disk 89.97 (978-1-4418-4112-4(1), 9781441841124, BriAudCD Unabrid) Brilliance Audio.

Secret Societies... & How They Affect Our Lives Today see Sociedades Secretas: Y como afectan nuestras vidas en la Actualidad

Secret Societies at Work in the Modern World. Instructed by Manly P. Hall. 8.95 (978-0-89314-253-7(0), C800126) Philos Res.

Secret Society. unabr. ed. Miasha. Read by Claudia Aleck. (Running Time: 7 hrs. 30 mins.). 2010. 29.95 (978-1-4417-2486-1(9)); 54.95 (978-1-4417-2482-3(6)); audio compact disk 69.00 (978-1-4417-2483-0(4)) Blckstn Audio.

Secret Society of Demolition Writers. unabr. ed. Ed. by Marc Parent. (Running Time: 7 hrs. 30 mins. 0 sec.). (ENG.). 2005. audio compact disk 29.99 (978-1-4001-0178-8(6)) Pub: Tantor Media. Dist(s): IngramPubServ

Secret Society of Demolition Writers. unabr. ed. Marc Parent et al. Narrated by Ellen Archer & Alan Sklar. (Running Time: 7 hrs. 30 mins. 0 sec.). (ENG.). 2005. audio compact disk 19.99 (978-1-4001-5178-3(3)); audio compact disk 59.99 (978-1-4001-3178-5(2)) Pub: Tantor Media. Dist(s): IngramPubServ

***Secret Soldier.** Alex Berenson. Read by George Guidall. (John Wells Novel Ser.). (ENG.). 2011. audio compact disk 39.95 (978-0-14-242892-4(2), PengAudBks) Penguin Grp USA.

***Secret Song of Garden Birds.** The British Library. (ENG.). 2010. audio compact disk 15.00 (978-0-7123-5104-1(3)) Pub: Britis Library GBR. Dist(s): Chicago Distribution Ctr

Secret Speech. unabr. ed. Tom Rob Smith. Ed. by Tom Rob Smith. Read by Dennis Boutsikaris. (Running Time: 11 hrs.). (ENG.). 2009. 19.98 (978-1-60024-578-7(1)) Pub: Hachet Audio. Dist(s): HachBkGrp

Secret Speech. unabr. ed. Tom Rob Smith. Ed. by Tom Rob Smith. Read by Dennis Boutsikaris. (Running Time: 11 hrs.). (ENG.). 2010. audio compact disk 19.98 (978-1-60788-385-2(6)) Pub: Hachet Audio. Dist(s): HachBkGrp

Secret Story of Hunchback of Notre Dame. Allen Holmquist. 1996. 7.98 (978-1-885505-14-9(0)) CMH Records.

Secret Streets. Ronnie Cone. 2007. audio compact disk 17.99 (978-1-60247-394-2(3)) Tate Pubng.

Secret Supper: A Novel. abr. ed. Javier Sierra. Read by Simon Jones. 2006. 17.95 (978-0-7435-5413-8(2)) Pub: S&S Audio. Dist(s): S and S Inc

Secret Supper: A Novel. unabr. ed. Javier Sierra. Read by Simon Jones. 2006. 23.95 (978-0-7435-6519-6(3)) Pub: S&S Audio. Dist(s): S and S Inc

***Secret Survivors: Real-Life Stories to Give You Hope for Healing.** Zondervan Publishing Staff et al. (Running Time: 2 hrs. 40 mins. 37 sec.). (ENG.). (YA). 2010. 14.99 (978-0-310-86999-3(4)) Zondervan.

Secret Teachings of All Ages: Atlantis & the Gods of Antiquity. Instructed by Manly P. Hall. 8.95 (978-0-89314-254-4(9), C800106) Philos Res.

Secret Teachings of All Ages: Initiation of the Pyramid. Instructed by Manly P. Hall. 8.95 (978-0-89314-255-1(7), C820627) Philos Res.

Secret Teachings of the Masters. Sai Maa Lakshmi Devi. 2004. audio compact disk 16.00 (978-1-933488-12-7(3)) HIU Pr.
Sai Maa's passionate commitment to uplift humanity is the inspiration for this transformative CD. Sai Maa boldly takes responsibility of offering the secret teachings of how to access the power and love of Almighty Victory, Hercules, the Elohims, the Realms of Angels, Ascended Masters, and the Karmic Board. Now is the time to return to our original light, drop all dark seeds of karma and move together into Global Enlightenment. Recorded May 2003, in Indianapolis, Indiana.

Secret Teachings of the Sacred Testaments: The Stairway to Heaven. Guy Finley. 2003. 24.95 (978-1-929320-09-7(4)) Life of Learn.

Secret Teachings of the Sacred Testaments: The Stairway to Heaven, Set. Guy Finley. 3 cass. (Running Time: 4 hrs.). 2001. 24.95 (978-1-929320-08-0(6)) Life of Learn.

Secret Things of God: Unlocking the Treasures Reserved for You. unabr. ed. Henry Cloud. Read by Henry Cloud. (Running Time: 5 hrs. 0 mins. 0 sec.). (ENG.). 2007. audio compact disk 29.95 (978-0-7435-7129-6(0)) Pub: S&S Audio. Dist(s): S and S Inc

Secret to Attracting Love. Kelly Howell. (Running Time: 3600 sec.). 2008. audio compact disk 14.95 (978-1-881451-02-0(X)) Brain Sync.

Secret to Attracting Money. abr. ed. Joe Vitale. Read by Joe Vitale. 2 CDs. (Running Time: 2 hrs. 0 mins. 0 sec.). (ENG.). 2010. audio compact disk 19.99 (978-1-4423-0063-7(9), Nightgale) Pub: S&S Audio. Dist(s): S and S Inc

Secret to Attracting Wealth. Kelly Howell. (Running Time: 3600 sec.). 2008. audio compact disk 14.95 (978-1-881451-07-5(0)) Brain Sync.

Secret to Believing Prayer, Elbert Willis. 4 cass. (Running Time: 4 hrs.). 13.00 Fill the Gap.

Secret to Enjoying Life: Ecc. 9:1-10. Ed Young. 1994. 4.95 (978-0-7417-1998-0(3), 998) Win Walk.

Secret to Life Transformation: How to Claim Your Destiny Now. Julie Chrystyn. (ENG.). 2009. audio compact disk 29.95 (978-1-59777-300-3(X)) IngramPubServ.

Secret to Loving Yourself. Diane Bills. 1 cass. (YA). 6.98 (978-1-55503-383-5(0), 06004393) Covenant Comms.
Teaches youth to survive in a put-down society.

Secret to Loving Yourself. Diane Bills. 1 cass. 2004. 3.95 (978-1-57734-376-9(X), 34441158) Covenant Comms.

Secret to Making Your Invention a Reality. David A. Fussell. 1 cass. 1993. 49.95 (978-0-9639336-0-7(4)) VenturSource.
Invention, new product development, licensing.

Secret to Manifesting: Audio Meditation Techniques. 2006. audio compact disk 8.95 (978-1-928843-32-0(8)) Ad Lib Res.

Secret to Manifesting: How to Get What You Really Want. 2005. audio compact disk 12.95 (978-1-928843-29-0(8)) Ad Lib Res.

***Secret to Teen Power.** unabr. ed. Paul Harrington. Read by Cassidy Lehrman et al. (Running Time: 4 hrs. 0 mins. 0 sec.). (ENG.). (YA). 2010. audio compact disk 29.99 (978-1-4423-0363-8(8)) Pub: S&S Audio. Dist(s): S and S Inc

Secret to True Happiness: Enjoy Today, Embrace Tomorrow. abr. ed. Joyce Meyer. Read by Sandra McCollom. (Running Time: 6 hrs.). (ENG.). 2008. 14.98 (978-1-60024-152-9(2)) Pub: Hachet Audio. Dist(s): HachBkGrp

Secret to True Happiness: Enjoy Today, Embrace Tomorrow. abr. ed. Joyce Meyer. Read by Sandra McCollom. (Running Time: 6 hrs.). (ENG.). 2009. audio compact disk 14.98 (978-1-60024-859-7(4)) Pub: Hachet Audio. Dist(s): HachBkGrp

Secret to Why Prayers Aren't Answered. Voice by Glenn Curtis Frazier, Sr. 1 CD. (Running Time: 77 mins. 05 Seconds). 2002. audio compact disk 8.00 (978-0-9721130-3-8(7)) Palace Pr Pubs.
Audio Book: Secret To Why Prayers Aren't Answered.

Secret Traditions in Arthurian Legend. Gareth Knight. 4 cass. 36.00 (OC133) Sound Horizons AV.

Secret Universal Mind Meditation. unabr. ed. Kelly Howell. Read by Kelly Howell. 1 CD. (Running Time: 1 hr.). 2006. audio compact disk 14.95 (978-1-881451-56-3(9)) Brain Sync.

Secret Universal Mind Meditation II. unabr. ed. Kelly Howell. Read by Kelly Howell. 1 CD. (Running Time: 1 hr.). 2008. audio compact disk 14.95 (978-1-881451-33-4(X)) Brain Sync.

Secret Vampire. unabr. ed. L. J. Smith. (Running Time: 6 hrs.). (Night World Ser.: Vol. 1). 2009. 39.97 (978-1-4418-0438-9(2), 9781441804389, Brinc Audio MP3 Lib); 19.99 (978-1-4418-0439-6(0), 9781441804396, BAD) Brilliance Audio.

Secret Vampire. unabr. ed. L. J. Smith. Read by Ellen Grafton. (Running Time: 6 hrs.). (Night World Ser.: Vol. 1). 2009. 19.99 (978-1-4418-0437-2(4), 9781441804372, Brilliance MP3); 39.97 (978-1-4418-0440-2(4), 9781441804402, BADLE); audio compact disk 19.99 (978-1-4418-0435-8(8), 9781441804358, Bril Audio CD Unabri); audio compact disk 59.97 (978-1-4418-0436-5(6), 9781441804365, BriAudCD Unabrid) Brilliance Audio.

Secret War Against Hitler, unabr. ed. William Casey. Read by Peter Kjenaas. 6 cass. (Running Time: 8 hrs. 30 mins.). 1988. 44.95 (978-0-7861-0013-2(3), 1012) Blckstn Audio.
Presents the author's account of his WWII service with the OSS, the Office of Strategic Services - which later evolved into the CIA. He recounts how the Allies gathered critical intelligence, thwarted Germany's atomic bomb development, & convinced German intelligence that the Normandy D-Day landings were to be a diversionary move while the main landing was to take place at Calais.

***Secret War against Hitler.** unabr. ed. William Casey. Read by Peter Kjenaas. (Running Time: 8 hrs. 30 mins.). 2010. 29.95 (978-1-4417-4597-2(1)); audio compact disk 76.00 (978-1-4417-4594-1(7)) Blckstn Audio.

Secret War with Iran: The 30-Year Clandestine Struggle Against the World's Most Dangerous Terrorist Power. Ronen Bergman. Read by Dick Hill. (Playaway Adult Nonfiction Ser.). (ENG.). 2009. 69.99 (978-1-60812-557-9(2)) Find a World.

Secret War with Iran: The 30-Year Clandestine Struggle Against the World's Most Dangerous Terrorist Power. unabr. ed. Ronen Bergman. Narrated by Dick Hill. (Running Time: 17 hrs. 0 mins. 0 sec.). (ENG.). 2008. audio compact disk 79.99 (978-1-4001-3982-8(1)); audio compact disk 29.99 (978-1-4001-5982-6(2)); audio compact disk 39.99 (978-1-4001-0982-1(5)) Pub: Tantor Media. Dist(s): IngramPubServ

Secret Warriors: A Men at War Novel, abr. ed. W. E. B. Griffin. Read by Edward Hermann. 4 cass. (Men at War Ser.: No. 2). (J). 1999. 24.95 (FS9-43230) Highsmith.

Secret Warriors: A Men at War Novel, unabr. ed. W. E. B. Griffin. 9 cass. (Running Time: 13 hrs. 30 mins.). (Men at War Ser.: No. 2). 1999. 72.00 (978-0-7366-4394-8(X), 4856) Books on Tape.
It is 1942, in Washington, D.C. the OSS under FDR & "Wild Bill" Donovan, escalates its tactical war & plunges into worldwide covert operations. In London, a difficult & exiled de Gaulle disrupts invasion plans & it is up to the OSS to force the General's hand. In the Belgian Congo, a desperate air maneuver drops OSS agents into Africa, with the aim of smuggling out uranium are essential to the arms race. And in Morrocco, OSS men plan a rendezvous with anti-Nazi Germans in an attempt to obtain critical weapons secrets.

Secret Wars of the CIA. Prod. by Other Americas Radio Network Staff. 1 cass. (Running Time: 2 hrs.). 16.95 (B0240B090, HarperThor) HarpC GBR.

Secret Watch: America's Secret Spy Planes. Ed. by Marco A. V. Bitetto. 1 cass. 2000. (978-1-58578-294-9(7)) Inst of Cybernetics.

Secret Weapon. Contrib. by MXPX. Prod. by Aaron Sprinkle. 2007. audio compact disk 17.99 (978-5-557-67465-2(9)) Tooth & Nail.

Secret Woman. unabr. ed. Victoria Holt. Read by Eva Haddon. 10 cass. (Running Time: 10 hrs.). 1997. 84.95 Set. (978-0-7451-6677-3(6), CAB 1293) AudioGO.
Anna Brett was a quiet woman whose only ambition was to carry on her aunt's profitable antiques business. So she did, until the memory of a cherished moment with a blue-eyed stranger returned to haunt her. It was then that Anna discovered the secret woman within: a daring & passionate creature willing to risk everything on a trip to a faraway island in the South Seas.

Secret Woman. unabr. collector's ed. Victoria Holt. Read by Donada Peters. 9 cass. (Running Time: 13 hrs. 30 mins.). 1994. 72.00 (978-0-7366-2891-4(6), 113269) Books on Tape.
To all appearances, Anna Brett has only one ambition: to carry on the antique business left to her by a spinster aunt. Then the memory of a cherished moment with a blue-eyed stranger suddenly returns with savage intensity & Anna risks everything to follow an impossible dream.

Secret World of Animals - Below & above the Ground. Canadian Museum of Nature Staff. 1992. 9.95 (978-0-660-13062-0(9)) Pub: U Ch Pr. Dist(s): Chicago Distribution Ctr

Secret World of Animals - In the Air. Canadian Museum of Nature Staff. 1992. 9.95 (978-0-660-13059-0(9)) Pub: U Ch Pr. Dist(s): Chicago Distribution Ctr

Secret World of Animals - On the Earth. Canadian Museum of Nature Staff. 1992. 9.95 (978-0-660-13061-3(0)) Pub: U Ch Pr. Dist(s): Chicago Distribution Ctr

Secret World of Og. Pierre Berton. Contrib. by Beverley Cooper. 1 CD. (Running Time: 3600 sec.). Dramatization. (J). (gr. k-4). 2006. audio compact disk 15.95 (978-0-660-19577-3(1), CBC Audio) Canadian Broadcasting CAN.

***Secret Zoo.** unabr. ed. Bryan Chick. Read by Patrick Lawlor. (ENG.). 2010. (978-0-06-199769-3(2), GreenwillowBks); (978-0-06-199526-2(6), GreenwillowBks) HarperCollins Pubs.

Secretarial Practice: Syllabus. 2nd ed. Carl W. Salser & Charlotte A. Butsch. (J). 1977. 101.00 (978-0-89420-183-7(2), 186700) Natl Book.

Secretarial Seminar. unabr. ed. 6 cass. (Running Time: 6 hrs.). (Seminars on Tape Ser.). 1980. pap. bk. 49.95 Prof Train TX.
Explains how to increase self-confidence, developing a role as a professional secretary, working smarter, controlling time wasters, taking a team approach to time management, overcoming communications barriers, polishing the key to verbal skills all together.

Secretarial Skills. Fred Pryor. 6 cass. (Running Time: 6 hrs.). (Fred Pryor Seminars Ser.). 1995. wbk. ed. 59.95 (11360AM) Nightingale-Conant.
Ideal for use as a training or reference tool.

Secretariat. Scripts. Text by Norman Corwin. Directed By Norman Corwin. 1 CD. (Running Time: 58 mins). Dramatization. 2005. audio compact disk 15.95 (978-1-59938-005-6(6)) Lode Cat.

Secretariat. Norman Corwin. Perf. by Hume Cronyn et al. Prod. by Mary Beth Kirchner. 1 cass. (Running Time: 90 min.). 12.95 (978-1-57677-080-1(X), CORW018) Lodestone Catalog.
A wonder-filled look at man's relationship with God in this inspiring banquet of food for thought. Production Script available.

Secretariat. Norman Corwin. 1 CD. (Running Time: 1 hr.). 2001. audio compact disk 15.95 (CORW025) Lodestone Catalog.

Secreto. unabr. ed. Rhonda Byrne. Read by Rebeca Sanchez Manriquez. (Running Time: 4 hrs. 30 mins. 0 sec.). (SPA.). 2007. audio compact disk 29.95 (978-0-7435-7178-4(9)) Pub: S&S Audio. Dist(s): S and S Inc

Secreto De Romina. Quiles. audio compact disk 12.95 (978-0-8219-3814-0(2)) EMC-Paradigm.

Secreto Mas Raro. Diana Nightingale & Earl Nightingale. Read by Multilinguel Communications Corp. Staff. 1 cass. (Running Time: 60 min.).Tr. of Strangest Secret. (SPA.). 1997. (978-0-9655760-5-5(1)) Keys Pbg FL.

Secreto Mas Raro. Earl Nightingale & Diana Nightingale. Read by Multilinguel Communications Corp. Staff. Tr. by Fred De Rosset. 1 cass. (Running Time: 60 min.). (Earl Nightingale's Library of Little Gems).Tr. of Strangest Secret. (ENG & SPA.). 1997. pap. bk. (978-0-9655760-6-2(X)) Keys Pbg FL.

Secreto Meditacion de la Menta Universal: Haga que la Ley de la Atracción Trabaje para Usted. Kelly Howell. (SPA.). 2006. audio compact disk 14.95 (978-1-881451-08-2(9)) Brain Sync.

***Secretos de los Triunfadores.** Ruben Gonzalez. Taller Del Exito Inc. 2009. audio compact disk 24.95 (978-1-60738-007-8(2)) Taller del Exito.

Secretos para la Buena Suerte. Carlos González. Read by Carlos González. Ed. by Dina Gonzalez. 1 cass. (Running Time: 32 min.). (SPA.). 2001. 10.00 (978-1-56491-022-6(9)) Imagine Pubs.
In Spanish. Mental drills to become a positive thinker and have a better attitud in life.

Secrets. abr. ed. Jude Deveraux. Read by Natalie Moore. (Running Time: 6 hrs. 0 mins. 0 sec.). 2009. audio compact disk 14.99 (978-0-7435-9972-6(1)) Pub: S&S Audio. Dist(s): S and S Inc

Secrets. unabr. ed. Jude Deveraux. Read by Barbara McCulloh. (Running Time: 11 hrs.). 2009. 56.75 (978-1-4407-0003-3(6)); 82.75 (978-1-4361-5129-0(5)); audio compact disk 123.75 (978-1-4361-5131-3(7)) Recorded Bks.

Secrets. unabr. ed. Kristen Heitzmann. Narrated by Katherine Kellgren. 16 CDs. (Running Time: 18 hrs. 30 mins.). 2005. audio compact disk 119.75 (978-1-4193-1877-1(2), CK125); 109.75 (978-1-4193-1875-7(6), K1130) Recorded Bks.
Adored for her sweeping Rocky Mountain Legacy series, Kristen Heitzmann inspires countless fans with her tales of Christian faith and romance. The search for a family secret drives Lance Michelli to the old villa once owned by his grandparents. But its present owner, Rese Barrett, is independent enough, and beautiful enough, to derail his efforts, distract his heart and stir his faith.

Secrets. unabr. collector's ed. Jude Deveraux. Read by Barbara McCulloh. 10 CDs. (Running Time: 11 hrs.). 2009. audio compact disk 51.95 (978-1-4361-5132-0(5)) Recorded Bks.

Secrets: A Memoir of Vietnam & the Pentagon Papers (Abridged) Daniel Ellsberg. (ENG.). 2007. 30.00 (978-1-4223-6419-2(4)) DIANE Pub.

Secrets about Life Every Woman Should Know. abr. ed. Barbara De Angelis. 3 CDs. (Running Time: 3 hrs. 0 mins. 0 sec.). (ENG.). 2005. audio compact disk 19.95 (978-1-59397-587-6(2)) Pub: Macmill Audio. Dist(s): Macmillan

Secrets & Mysteries of the World. abr. ed. Sylvia Browne. 2 CDs. 2005. audio compact disk 18.95 (978-1-4019-0091-5(7), 0917) Hay House.

Secrets for Good Luck see Los secretos de la buena Suerte

Secrets for Success & Happiness, unabr. ed. Og Mandino. Narrated by Nelson Runger. 8 cass. (Running Time: 11 hrs. 15 mins.). 1997. 70.00 (978-0-7887-1459-7(7), 95181E7) Recorded Bks.
Author encourages millions with his inspirational self-help books. First written as his personal journal, this glowing record of his heartwarming experiences & painful challenges shares his optimistic approach for life.

Secrets for Turning Your Great Product Idea into a Million Dollar Payday! Harvey Reese Tells You How It's Done. Speeches. Harvey Reese. 1 CD. (Running Time: 1 hr 10 mins). 2002. audio compact disk 14.95 (978-0-9745046-1-2(0)) H R Assocs PA.
Noted author and inventor Harvey Reese tells you his secrets for developing and licensing new product ideas.

***Secrets from Beyond the Grave.** unabr. ed. Perry Stone. Narrated by Tim Lundeen. (Running Time: 9 hrs. 20 mins. 20 sec.). (ENG.). 2010. 19.59 (978-1-60814-748-9(7)); audio compact disk 27.99 (978-1-59859-803-2(1)) Oasis Audio.

Secrets in the Heather. Gwen Kirkwood. 2009. 69.95 (978-1-4079-0764-2(6)); audio compact disk 84.95 (978-1-4079-0765-9(4)) Pub: Soundings Ltd GBR. Dist(s): Ulverscroft US

Secrets Leader Kit: Transforming Your Life & Marriage. Kerry Clarensau. 2009. pap. bk. 49.99 (978-0-88243-812-2(3)) Gospel Pub.

Secrets of a Civil War Submarine: Solving the Mysteries of the H. L. Hunley. unabr. ed. Sally M. Walker. Read by J. R. Horne. 3 CDs. (Running Time: 2 hrs. 34 mins.). (J). (gr. 4-7). 2007. audio compact disk 30.00 (978-0-7393-4871-0(X), Listening Lib) Pub: Random Audio Pubg. Dist(s): Random

Secrets of a Leadership Coach: The Coaching & Leadership Techniques of Marshall Goldsmith, Illustrated with Video, Teaching Executive Coaching, Behavioral Change, & Teamwork & Teambuilding, for Every Manager & Employee. Daniel Farb et al. 2004. audio compact disk 199.95 (978-0-9743674-0-8(0)) Pub: UnivofHealth. Dist(s): AtlasBooks

Secrets of a Modern Day Bounty Hunter. Richard James, Sr.. Based on a book by Richard James, Sr. Elaine Lanmon. 2008. 34.95 (978-0-9815294-3-1(7), Secrets Series) Our Gang Pubng.

Secrets of a Passionate Marriage. David Schnarch. 2003. audio compact disk 24.95 (978-1-59179-079-2(4)) Sounds True.

***Secrets of a Proper Lady.** unabr. ed. Victoria Alexander. Read by Charlotte Parry. (ENG.). 2007. (978-0-06-157760-4(X)); (978-0-06-157761-1(8)) HarperCollins Pubs.

Secrets of a Proper Lady. unabr. ed. Victoria Alexander. Read by Charlotte Parry. 8 CDs. (Running Time: 9 hrs. 30 mins.). 2007. audio compact disk 19.95 (978-0-06-143244-6(X), Harper Audio) HarperCollins Pubs.

Secrets of a Shoe Addict. unabr. ed. Beth Harbison. Read by Orlagh Cassidy. 7 CDs. (Running Time: 9 hrs. 0 mins. 0 sec.). (ENG.). 2008. audio compact disk 29.95 (978-1-4272-0423-3(3)) Pub: Macmill Audio. Dist(s): Macmillan

***Secrets of a Summer Night.** unabr. ed. Lisa Kleypas. Read by Rosalyn Landor. (Running Time: 11 hrs.). (Wallflower Ser.: Bk. 1). 2010. 24.99 (978-1-4418-5178-9(X), 9781441851789, Brilliance MP3); 39.97 (978-1-4418-5179-6(8), 9781441851796, Brlnc Audio MP3 Lib); 39.97 (978-1-4418-5182-6(8), 9781441851826, BADLE); audio compact disk 29.99 (978-1-4418-5177-2(1), 9781441851772, Bril Audio CD Unabri); audio compact disk 79.97 (978-1-4418-5180-2(1), 9781441851802, BriAudCD Unabrid) Brilliance Audio.

Secrets of a Truly Fulfilled Life: Enjoy Each Day - Stop Knocking Yourself. Shmuel Irons. 2 cass. (Running Time: 3 hrs.). 19.95 Set. (978-1-889648-02-6(7)) Jwish Her Fdtn.
Rabbi Irons applies the timeless truths found in the Bible & Talmud to gain knowledge, peace of mind, & the practical tools to live a happier & fulfilled life. Two lectures.

Secrets of a Truly Fulfilled Life: How to Raise Children You Can Be Proud of - How to Really Appreciate Your "Self" unabr. ed. Shmuel Irons. Read by Shmuel Irons. 2 cass. (Running Time: 3 hrs.). 19.95 (978-1-889648-10-1(8)) Jwish Her Fdtn.
Applies the timeless truths found in the Bible & Talmud to gain knowledge, peace of mind, & the practical tools to live a happier life.

Secrets of a Truly Fulfilled Life Vol. 2: How to Create Meaningful & Lasting Friendships - Secrets of Communication. unabr. ed. Shmuel Irons. Read by Shmuel Irons. 2 cass. (Running Time: 3 hrs.). 19.99 Set. (978-1-889648-11-8(6)) Jwish Her Fdtn.

Secrets of an Inspirational (In-Spirit) Life: Your Ultimate Calling. Wayne W. Dyer. Read by Wayne W. Dyer. 6 CDs. 2006. audio compact disk 45.00 (978-1-4019-0726-6(1)) Hay House.

Secrets of Anxiety & Stress Management. Joyce Alexander. Prod. by Joyce Alexander Productions. Music by Robin Miller. Photos by Steve Janowski. Steve Janowski. Photos by Russell Black. (ENG., (C). 2009. 24.97 (978-0-9709025-3-5(0)) Alex Prodns.

Secrets of Attracting Love, Money & Success Revealed! Paul Kyriazi. Ed. by Sid Campbell. Illus. by Sid Campbell. 3 cass. (Running Time: 3 hrs.). 1989. 29.95 (978-0-682-87176-1(1)) Gong Prods.
Explains the psychology, concepts, formulas, tried-&-true techniques that have made successful, happy & wealthy people what they are & how they have used their time, imagination & ambition to get what they have achieved.

Secrets of Being Unstoppable. Guy Finley. (ENG.). 2006. 79.95 (978-1-929320-44-8(2)); 95.00 (978-1-929320-30-1(2)); audio compact disk 95.00 (978-1-929320-27-1(2)) Life of Learn.
A collection of 16 empowering talks by best-selling self-realization author Guy Finley that reveal how to transform our limitless inborn potential into the reality of a truly limitless life. Includes Three Pillars of Spiritual Power, 5 Simple Steps to Make Yourself Fearless, The Power to Let Go and Live in the Now, Awaken the Greatness Within, Attract the Happiness Your Heart Longs For, 5 Words to Make You the Master of Your Life, and more!.

Secrets of Bredon Hill. unabr. ed. Fred Archer. Read by Brian Hewlett. 4 cass. (Running Time: 6 hrs.). 2001. 44.95 (978-0-7531-1232-8(9)) Pub: ISIS Audio GBR. Dist(s): Ulverscroft US

Secrets of Brideship. unabr. ed. R. Edward Miller. Read by R. Edward Miller. 3 cass. (Running Time: 3 hrs. 30 min.). 1997. 18.00 (978-0-945818-15-1(7)) Peniel Pubns.
Bridal relationship with Jesus Christ.

Secrets of Candlesticks, Volume I, English. 2004. audio compact disk 50.00 (978-0-9779729-1-3(7)) Win Wall Street.

Secrets of Candlesticks, Volume I, English. Marc Mandel. 2004. audio compact disk 100.00 (978-0-9779729-0-6(9)) Win Wall Street.

Secrets of Cleansing your Heart, Mind & Soul. Guy Finley. 3 cass. (Running Time: 2 hrs.). 1999. 24.95 (978-1-929320-06-6(X)) Life of Learn.
Reveals how to find the solid higher ground of self understanding & how to pull the punishing power out of negative states.

Secrets of Closing the Sale. Zig Ziglar. Read by Zig Ziglar. 12 cass. 1984. 119.95 (978-1-56207-228-5(5)) Zig Ziglar Corp.
Zig teaches you dozens of practical techniques you can use to improve your sales effectiveness.

Secrets of Closing the Sale. abr. ed. Zig Ziglar. Read by Zig Ziglar. 1 cass. (Running Time: 58 mins.). 1992. 13.00 (978-1-55994-470-0(6), CPN 5004) HarperCollins Pubs.

Secrets of Closing the Sale. abr. ed. Zig Ziglar. Read by Zig Ziglar. 4 CDs. (Running Time: 40 hrs. 0 mins. 0 sec.). (ENG.). 2004. audio compact disk 29.95 (978-0-7435-3725-4(4), Sound Ideas) Pub: S&S Audio. Dist(s): S and S Inc

Secrets of Closing the Sale. abr. ed. Zig Ziglar. 2004. 17.95 (978-0-7435-3915-9(X)) Pub: S&S Audio. Dist(s): S and S Inc

Secrets of Closing the Sale. unabr. ed. Zig Ziglar. Read by Zig Ziglar. 6 cass. (Running Time: 4 hrs.). 1988. 59.95 set. (978-0-671-63974-7(9)) S&S Audio.

Secrets of Communication & Expression. Gil Boyne. Read by Gil Boyne. 1 cass. (Running Time: 45 min.). (Hypnosis Motivation Cassettes Ser.). 1977. 9.95 (106) Westwood Pub Co.
How to present your ideas in a way that ensures acceptance. You can speak with absolute confidence & perfect poise, to an audience of hundreds, a small group, or a single person.

Secrets of Consulting. unabr. collector's ed. Gerald M. Weinberg. Read by Paul Shay. 8 cass. (Running Time: 8 hrs.). 1987. 48.00 (978-0-7366-1246-3(7), 2161) Books on Tape.
Guidance on pricing & marketing services, dealing with clients, etc.

Secrets of D-Day. unabr. ed. Larry Collins. 2004. 24.95 (978-1-59007-640-8(0), New Millenn Pr); audio compact disk 29.95 (978-1-59007-641-5(9), New Millenn Pr) New Millenn Enter.

Secrets of Deep Mind Mast. Gary F. Hutchison. 6 cass. (Running Time: 9 hrs.). 1994. 13.95 (978-1-885631-00-8(6)) G F Hutchison.
A self-help program to build self-esteem, happiness & a sense of personal integrity.

Secrets of Deliverance Audio. T. D. Jakes. 2004. 25.00 (978-1-57855-488-1(8)) T D Jakes.

Secrets of Droon Vol. 1: The Hidden Stairs & the Magic Carpet; Journey to the Volcano Palace; The Mysterious Island. unabr. ed. Tony Abbott. Read by Oliver Wyman. 3 CDs. (Running Time: 3 hrs. 16 mins.). (Secrets of Droon Ser.: Nos. 1-3). (ENG.). (J). (gr. 1). 2004. audio compact disk 25.00 (978-0-307-20692-3(0), ImaginStudio) Pub: Random Audio Pubg. Dist(s): Random

***Secrets of Eden.** unabr. ed. Chris Bohjalian. Narrated by Mark Bramhall et al. 9 CDs. (Running Time: 11 hrs. 15 mins.). 2010. audio compact disk 100.00 (978-0-307-70505-1(6), BksonTape) Pub: Random Audio Pubg. Dist(s): Random

Secrets of Eden. unabr. ed. Chris Bohjalian. Read by Mark Bramhall et al. (ENG.). 2010. audio compact disk 35.00 (978-0-307-70503-7(X), Random AudioBks) Pub: Random Audio Pubg. Dist(s): Random

Secrets of Enlightenment. Deepak Chopra. 2009. 14.98 (978-0-7662-4234-0(X)) Gaiam Intl.

Secrets of Getting What You Want. Jonathan Robinson. Read by Jonathan Robinson. 3 cass. (Running Time: 4 hrs.). 1991. pap. bk. 29.95 (978-1-57328-804-0(7)) Focal Pt Calif.
This series is designed to assist you in knowing exactly what you most desire, & formulating a guarantee plan to achieve it. Powerful techniques are revealed for helping you know what you really want, overcome fear & procrastination, & stay consistently motivated to achieve your goals. This program can help you achieve anything you desire, from financial abundance to peace of mind. It comes with an 8 page workbook to help guide you successfully towards the fulfillment of your personal dreams.

Secrets of Great Communicators. Jeff Myers. 2006. pap. bk. 49.99 (978-0-8054-6882-3(X)) BH Pubng Grp.

Secrets of Great Sex: From Personal Growth Programs. 6 cass. (Running Time: 6 hrs.). 59.95 (11040AM) Nightingale-Conant.
Awaken your ability to create sensual, erotic & exciting lovemaking that nurtures powerful feelings of attraction. Secrets of Great Sex shows you & your partner how to fulfill your deepest desires. Discover how to turn lovemaking into a lifelong adventure, understand your partner's attitudes about sex & communicate openly about your fantasies. Unlock the Secrets of Great Sex & forge a bond with your partner that will last forever.

Secrets of Great Sex: From Personal Growth Programs, John Gray. Read by John Gray. 2 cass. (Running Time: 2 hrs. 45 min.). (Secrets of Successful Relationships Ser.). 1994. 17.95 (978-1-886095-05-2(1)) Genesis Media Grp.
A seminar series helping people understand the opposite sex.

Secrets of Higher, Happier Human Relationships. Guy Finley. (ENG.). 2006. 7.49 (978-1-929320-62-2(0)) Life of Learn.

Secrets of Holographic Visualization. unabr. ed. Tag Powell. Read by Tag Powell. Ed. by Judith L. Powell. 2 cass. (Running Time: 80 min.). (Powell Life Improvement Programs Ser.). 1990. pap. bk. 19.95 (978-0-914295-57-0(8)) Top Mtn Pub.
Tape 1, Side A: Step-by-step procedure to improve visualization skills. Tape 1, Side B: Visualization/meditation experience designed to heighten mental senses. Tape 2, Side A: A seminar explaining the concepts & multi-usages of the technique of Holographic Visualization, a process to improve creativity & imagination using Neuro-Linguistic Programming. Tape 2, Side B: a guided Holographic Visualization practice session.

Secrets of How to Motivate Your People to Produce. Dave Johnson. (Dave Johnson Educational Library). 95.00 D Johnson.
Discusses various motivating ideas & concepts designed to bring out the potential of employees.

Secrets of Intercession - La: Joining Forces with the God of Love. Phillip Halverson & Fern Halverson. 2 CDs. 2007. audio compact disk 10.00 (978-1-57399-363-0(8)) Mac Hammond.

Secrets of Intercession - Minneapolis: Wrestling in the Heavenlies. Phillip Halverson. 1 cass. (Running Time: 1 hr.). 2005. 5.00 (978-1-57399-242-8(9)) Mac Hammond.
In prayer, some things are better "caught" than "taught". You're certain to "catch" a powerful impartation of Spirit-led prayer from this tape. Learn about warfare in the heavenlies, the "eyes" of your spirit, and the creative power of words prayed under the anointing.

Secrets of Intercession, Los Angeles: Joining Forces with the God of Love. Phillip Halverson & Fern Halverson. 1 cass. 1997. 12.00 (978-1-57399-036-3(1)) Mac Hammond.
Teaching on prayer.

***Secrets of Judas.** unabr. ed. James M. Robinson. Read by Eric Conger. (ENG.). 2006. (978-0-06-123385-2(4), Harper Audio); (978-0-06-123386-9(2), Harper Audio) HarperCollins Pubs.

Secrets of Love. J. Donald Walters. 2003. audio compact disk 15.95 (978-1-56589-771-7(4)) Pub: Crystal Clarity. Dist(s): Natl Bk Netwk

Secrets of Millionaire Moms: Learn How They Turned Great Ideas into Booming Businesses & How You Can Too! Tamara Monosoff. 2009. audio compact disk 28.00 (978-1-933309-72-9(5)) Pub: A Media Intl. Dist(s): Natl Bk Netwk

Secrets of Motivation. unabr. ed. Read by Bob Richards. 1 cass. (Running Time: 30 min.). 15.00 B R Motivational.
A recorded live speech by Bob Richards on the philosophy & attitude towards life that makes some people more successful than others - the "secrets" of a motivated person.

Secrets of Motivation. unabr. ed. Bob Richards. Read by Bob Richards. 12 cass. (Running Time: 6 hrs. 25 min.). 1992. 165.00 (CH-40) B R Motivational.
This is a complete set of all 12 taped speeches by Bob Richards, Olympic Champion. Includes the 11 listed for Chatham Films & the 12th is the re-issue of "How to Change Your Weakness to Power" (1968) - all in one 12-Cassette Album.

Secrets of Natural Hormone Therapy: Keys to Preventing Women's Most Serious Health Problems. Perf. by John R. Lee. Contrib. by David Zava. 2 cass. (Running Time: 2 hrs.). (Wellness Audio Ser.). 1999. 16.95 (978-1-56889-017-3(6), AW5720); 33.90 Set, incl. public performance rights for schools & libraries. Lghtwrks Aud & Vid.
Dr. Lee, author of "What Your Doctor May Not Tell You about Menopause & Hormone Balancing," presents empowering, life-changing natural alternatives to synthetic pharmacology that offer genuine options for wresting control of women's bodies back from the big drug companies & the doctors who prescribe for them.

Secrets of Network Marketing Success: Volume 1 4- CD Set. Randy Gage. (ENG.). 2009. audio compact disk 47.00 (978-0-9673164-3-7(X)) Prime Concepts Grp.

Secrets of Passion, John Gray. Read by John Gray. 2 cass. (Running Time: 3 hrs.). (Secrets of Successful Relationships Ser.). 1994. 17.95 (978-1-886095-02-1(7)) Genesis Media Grp.
A seminar series helping people understand the opposite sex.

Secrets of Persuasion. Maura Schreier-Fleming. (ENG.). 2005. 19.95i (978-0-9771483-0-1(0)) Best@Selling.

Secrets of Power Negotiating. Roger Dawson. Read by Roger Dawson. (Running Time: 7 hrs.). (C). 2005. 36.95 (978-1-59912-151-2(4)) Iofy Corp.

Secrets of Power Negotiating. Roger Dawson. Read by Roger Dawson. 6 cass. cass. & video 59.95 (474A) Nightingale-Conant.
Learn the caveats, hues, tactics, & techniques employed by master negotiator Roger Dawson. He discusses five key facts & three stages of all negotiations, plus more than 20 gambits you can use to get the best deal in every situation. Includes flashcards & workbook.

Secrets of Power Negotiating: How to Gain the Upper Hand in Any Negotiation. unabr. ed. Roger Dawson. Read by Roger Dawson. 7 CDs. (Running Time: 7 hrs.). (ENG.). 2005. audio compact disk 19.98 (978-1-59659-002-1(5), GildAudio) Pub: Gildan Media. Dist(s): HachBkGrp

Secrets of Power Persuasion. Roger Dawson. Read by Roger Dawson. 6 cass. (Running Time: 6 hrs.). 59.95 (711AD) Nightingale-Conant.
You'll discover why credibility & consistency are the cornerstones of persuasion. You'll learn the verbal skills that defuse resistence & empower you to prove your points, & you'll find out how you can use humor to strengthen your position. You'll develop the charisma that draws people to you & to your opinion, & that wins you lasting respect.

Secrets of Prayer. unabr. ed. R. Edward Miller. Read by R. Edward Miller. 4 cass. (Running Time: 5 hrs. 15 min.). 1997. 20.00 (978-0-945818-11-3(4)) Peniel Pubns.
How to pray effectively based on the biblical account of Nehemiah.

Secrets of Print-on-Demand: Print Your Book in a Week Without Filling Your Garage with Boxes. Featuring Don DeHart. Interview with Morgan Rebecca. 2000. 25.00 (978-1-930039-03-2(4)) Morgan Seminar.

Secrets of Prosperity: A Spiritual Boot Camp. Excerpts. Jaime J. Harris. Narrated by Mary Beth Murawski. Audio Download. (Running Time: 2 hours). 2002. 19.95 (978-0-9718387-3-4(9)) IngraFocus Mng.
Full dramatization of Secrets of Prosperity-A Spiritual Boot Camp read by the Authors.

Secrets of Raising Serious Money for Your Business Part 1: The Unlimited Potential of Limited Partnerships. unabr. ed. Linda Cline Chandler. 6 cass. (Running Time: 4 hrs. 30 min.). (Entrepreneurship Ser.). 1994. 149.95 (978-0-9639400-1-8(5)) Lrning Two-Thousand.
Takes listener through the Limited Partnership process. Describes one of the best ways to raise money for a new business concept or a growing business.

Secrets of Raising Serious Money for Your Business Part 2: Advanced Capital Formation Strategies for Fast Growth Companies. unabr. ed. Linda Cline Chandler. 6 cass. (Running Time: 6 hrs.). (Entrepreneurship Ser.). 1995. 149.95 Set. (978-0-9639400-3-2(1), L2A2) Lrning Two-Thousand.
Advanced audio course on capital formation. A must for all serious entrepreneurs & senior managers. Inspirational, full of practical knowledge & strategies that work.

Secrets of Savvy Networking: How to Make the Best Connections for Business & Personal Success. abr. ed. Susan RoAne. Read by Susan RoAne. 2 CDs. (Running Time: 5400 sec.). (ENG.). 2005. audio compact disk 14.95 (978-1-59397-859-4(6)) Pub: Macmill Audio. Dist(s): Macmillan

Secrets of Self-Confidence. Gil Boyne. Read by Gil Boyne. 1 cass. (Running Time: 45 min.). (Hypnosis Motivation Cassettes Ser.). 1977. 9.95 (101) Westwood Pub Co.
Explores how to radiate dynamic self-confidence. Improve your self-image. Overcome the fear of criticism, the fear of rejection, fear of failure. Feel more lovable & appreciate yourself more.

Secrets of Self-Management: Step-By-Step Exercises. Mike George. 3 cass. (Running Time: 4 hrs. 30 min.). bk., pap. bk., wbk. ed. (978-1-886872-15-8(5)) Brahma Kumaris.
Includes workbook & poster.

Secrets of Selling on eBay for Big Profits: Discover how to build a successful business on EBay. abr. ed. Sydney Johnston. Read by Robert Imbriale. (ENG.). 2006. audio compact disk (978-0-9785426-0-3(6)) Ultimate Wealth.

Secrets of Skull & Bones Revealed. 2005. audio compact disk 12.00 (978-1-892062-80-2(1)) Inner Light.

Secrets of Sonship. unabr. ed. R. Edward Miller. Read by R. Edward Miller. 3 cass. (Running Time: 3 hrs.). 1997. 18.00 Set. (978-0-945818-14-4(9)) Peniel Pubns.
How God brings forth new creatures into His own image, called "Sons of God".

Secrets of Spiritual Healing. Kriyananda, pseud. 1 cass. 9.95 (ST-77) Crystal Clarity.
Explores the nature of disease; how the "New Age" is affecting modern medicine; how to overcome physical suffering when it comes; why the spiritual is the key to all health.

Secrets of Stepparenting. 2004. audio compact disk 13.95 (978-1-930429-68-0(1)) Love Logic.

Secrets of Success. (Running Time: 7 hrs. 15 mins.). (C). 2005. 36.95 (978-1-59912-168-0(9)) Iofy Corp.

Secrets of Success. LaVell Edwards. 1 cass. 2004. 3.95 (978-1-57734-381-3(6), 34441204) Covenant Comms.

Secrets of Success. Swami Jyotirmayananda. Read by Swami Jyotirmayananda. 1 cass. (Running Time: 45 min.). 10.00 (816) Yoga Res Foun.

Secrets of Success: Eight Self-Help Classics That Have Changed the Lives of Millions. unabr. ed. James Allen. 8 CDs. (Running Time: 8 hrs.). (ENG., 2005. audio compact disk 29.98 (978-1-59659-037-3(8)) Pub: Gildan Media. Dist(s): HachBkGrp

Secrets of Success: Psalms. Read by Robert A. Cook. 4 cass. (Dr. Robert A. Cook's Teaching Ser.). 9.98 ea. (RC20) Chrstn Dup Intl.

Secrets of Success: Psalms. Robert A. Cook. Read by Robert A. Cook. 4 cass. (Running Time: 6 hrs.). 2000. 9.99 (978-7-902031-48-6(8)) Chrstn Dup Intl.

Secrets of Success Attitudes. Gil Boyne. Read by Gil Boyne. 1 cass. (Running Time: 45 min.). (Hypnosis Motivation Cassettes Ser.). 1977. 9.95 (104) Westwood Pub Co.
Discusses how to overcome your subconscious "will to fail" & move rapidly toward your career & financial goals. Develop a subconscious mental expectancy for success & riches.

Secrets of Success in Football, Family, & Friends. LaVell Edwards. 1 cass. 5.98 (978-1-55503-079-7(3), 06003516) Covenant Comms.

Secrets of Successful Blogging System: 101+ Tips for Blogging More Efficiently, Effectively, & Profitably. Ted Demopoulos. 2007. audio compact disk 97.00 (978-0-9788060-1-9(8)) Demopoulos.

Secrets of Successful Change Set: Putting the Laws of Change to Work for You. David Grudermeyer & Rebecca Grudermeyer. 2 cass. 18.95 INCL. HANDOUTS. (T-33) Willingness Wrks.

Secrets of Successful Self-Employment: Moving from Paycheck Thinking to Profit Thinking. Paul Edwards & Sarah Edwards. 6 cass. (Running Time: 6 hrs.). 1995. wbk. ed. 59.95 (13380AX) Nightingale-Conant.
You will master the 6 important steps to developing a marketing mindset & promoting yourself, what to say when people ask questions about your business & identify the 7 principles for building momentum with less effort.

Secrets of Successful Students. unabr. ed. James L. Warner. Read by James L. Warner. 1 cass. (Running Time: 51 min.). 1991. bk. 17.95 (978-0-9630611-0-2(0)) Stud Success.
A discussion of why it is important & how to succeed in school with descriptions of successful student behavior & methods.

Secrets of Successful Study. unabr. ed. Marianne L. McManus. 3 cass. 29.95 incl. album. (978-0-88432-181-1(9), S17050) J Norton Pubs.

***Secrets of Successful Time Management.** PUEI. 2009. audio compact disk 199.00 (978-1-935041-82-5(7), CareerTrack) P Univ E Inc.

Secrets of Successful Writers. Elizabeth R. Bills. 6 cass. (Running Time: 4 hrs. 37 mins.). 49.50 (978-0-88432-174-3(6), S23350) J Norton Pubs.
Learn the techniques & secrets of some of the most famous authors of world literature, profiting by their mistakes & becoming inspired by their words. Topics include getting started as a writer, making dialog sparkle, plotting a short story, beginning a story, bringing characters to life & writing a magazine article.

Secrets of Successful Writers. Elizabeth R. Bills. 6 CDs. (Running Time: 6 hrs.). 2005. audio compact disk 49.50 (978-1-57970-205-2(8), S23350D) J Norton Pubs.

Secrets of the Argentine Revival. unabr. ed. R. Edward Miller. Read by R. Edward Miller. 5 cass. (Running Time: 4 hrs. 30 min.). 1997. 22.50 (978-0-945818-16-8(5)) Peniel Pubns.

Secrets of the Baby Whisperer: How to Calm, Connect, & Communicate with Your Baby. abr. ed. Tracy Hogg. Read by Tracy Hogg. Told to Melinda Blau. 2 CDs. (Running Time: 2 hrs. 30 mins.). (ENG.). 2000. audio compact disk 24.95 (978-1-56511-458-6(2), 1565114582) Pub: HighBridge. Dist(s): Workman Pub

Secrets of the Cave. Phillipa Bowers & Colleen Prendergast. 2009. 76.95 (978-1-84652-350-2(8)); audio compact disk 89.95 (978-1-84652-335-9(4)) Pub: Magna Story GBR. Dist(s): Ulverscroft US

Secrets of the Dragon Sanctuary. Brandon Mull. (Fablehaven Ser.: Bk. 4). 2010. audio compact disk 39.95 (978-1-60641-064-6(4), Shadow Mount) Deseret Bk.

Secrets of the Everyday Leaders. Jeff Myers. 2006. DVD & audio compact disk 49.99 (978-0-8054-6888-5(9)) BH Pubng Grp.

Secrets of the Federal Reserve. Interview with Steven Jacobson. 1 cass. (Running Time: 60 min.). 9.95 (AT5777) Lghtwrks Aud & Vid.
Interview with Steven Jacboson about the untold story of the Federal Reserve System's economic stranglehold on the average American citizen.

Secrets of the Grand Canyon. 1 cass. (Running Time: 30 min.). (J). 1986. 12.95 incl. bk. minipack. (978-0-930399-05-4(6)); 9.95 incl. minipack. BackPax Int.
Here is a view deep into the heart of the canyon, where legends of prospectors & their prospects, archaeological mysteries & clues to worlds of nature still remain.

Secrets of the Great Rainmakers: The Keys to Success & Wealth. unabr. ed. Jeffrey J. Fox. Read by Jeffrey J. Fox. 2 CDs. (Running Time: 2 hrs. 30 mins. 0 sec.). (ENG.). 2006. audio compact disk 19.95 (978-1-59397-627-9(5)) Pub: Macmill Audio. Dist(s): Macmillan

Secrets of the Heart, Set. JoAnn Jolley. 2 cass. 1999. 12.95 (978-1-57734-332-5(8), 07001940) Covenant Comms.
A story of love, loss & healing.

Secrets of the Holy Spirit. unabr. ed. R. Edward Miller. Read by R. Edward Miller. 6 cass. (Running Time: 9 hrs.). 1998. 25.00 (978-0-945818-17-5(3)) Peniel Pubns.

Secrets of The Illuminati. Robert A. Wilson & E. J. Gold. 2 cass. 1980. 18.98 (TP53) Union Label.
Robert Anton Wilson & E.J. Gold explore the fascinating subject of the world-wide secret society of illumined individuals & cover a variety of perspectives on the illuminati. Given at the Cosmicon Convention in San Francisco, 1980.

Secrets of the Immortal: Advanced Teachings from a Course in Miracles. Gary Renard. (Running Time: 26100 sec.). 2006. audio compact disk 69.95 (978-1-59179-444-8(7)) Sounds True.

Secrets of the Immortal Nephilim: To Kill A Goddess. 2nd rev. ed. Rebecca Ellen Kurtz. (ENG.). 2010. 24.95 (978-0-9823135-1-0(9)) Ephesus Bks.

Secrets of the Jungle: Lessons on Survival & Success in Today's Organizations. Shirley Peddg. 1996. pap. bk. 29.95 (978-0-9651376-2-1(7)) Bullion Bks.

Secrets of the Kingdom: The Inside Story of the Secret Saudi-U. S. Connection. unabr. ed. Gerald L. Posner. Narrated by Alan Sklar. (Running Time: 9 hrs. 0 mins. 0 sec.). (ENG.). 2005. audio compact disk 69.99 (978-1-4001-3171-6(5)); audio compact disk 34.99 (978-1-4001-0171-9(9)); audio compact disk 22.99 (978-1-4001-5171-4(6)) Pub: Tantor Media. Dist(s): IngramPubServ

***Secrets of the Mental Game of Tennis.** David Ranney. 2009. 97.00 (978-1-61623-201-6(3)) Indep Pub IL.

***Secrets of the Millionaire Mind: Mastering the Inner Game of Wealth.** abr. ed. T. Harv Eker. Read by T. Harv Eker. (ENG.). 2005. (978-0-06-083893-5(0), Harper Audio); (978-0-06-083892-8(2), Harper Audio) HarperCollins Pubs.

Secrets of the Millionaire Mind: Mastering the Inner Game of Wealth. unabr. abr. ed. T. Harv Eker & T. H. Eker. Read by T. Harv Eker. 3 CDs. (Running Time: 3 hrs. 30 mins.). 2005. audio compact disk 22.95 (978-0-06-077657-2(9)) HarperCollins Pubs.

Secrets of the Monarch: What the Dead Can Teach Us about Living a Better Life. unabr. ed. Allison DuBois. Read by Renée Raudman. (Running Time: 5 hrs. 30 mins. 0 sec.). (ENG.). 2007. audio compact disk 24.99 (978-1-4001-0580-9(3)); audio compact disk 19.99 (978-1-4001-5580-4(0)); audio compact disk 49.99 (978-1-4001-3580-6(X)) Pub: Tantor Media. Dist(s): IngramPubServ

***Secrets of the Moneylab: How Behavioral Economics Can Improve Your Business.** unabr. ed. Kay-Yut Chen & Marina Krakovsky. Read by Don Hagen. (Running Time: 9 hrs.). (ENG.). 2010. audio compact disk 29.98 (978-1-59659-534-7(5), GildAudio) Pub: Gildan Media. Dist(s): HachBkGrp

Secrets of the Morning. V. C. Andrews. Read by Laurel Lefkow. 10 CDs. (Running Time: 12 hrs. 6 mins.). (Isis (CDs) Ser.). (J). 2004. audio compact disk 89.95 (978-0-7531-2276-1(6)) Pub: ISIS Lrg Prnt GBR. Dist(s): Ulverscroft US

Secrets of the Morning. unabr. ed. V. C. Andrews. Read by Donada Peters. 8 cass. (Running Time: 12 hrs.). (Cutler Ser.). 1993. 64.00 (978-0-7366-2356-8(6), 3131) Books on Tape.
Dawn hopes for a bright new life in the arts but events soon leave her victim of her grandmother's schemes.

Secrets of the Morning. unabr. ed. V. C. Andrews. Read by Laurel Lefkow. 10 cass. (Running Time: 12 hrs. 6 min.). (Isis Ser.). (J). 2003. 84.95 (978-0-7531-1773-6(8)) Pub: ISIS Lrg Prnt GBR. Dist(s): Ulverscroft US
Now a student at one of New York City's best music schools, Dawn's wish to become a singer can finally come true. But Dawn still dreams about Jimmy, her strong, intense boyfriend, and the love and anguished secrets they share. Then Michael Sutton arrives, a new teacher at the school, a singing star and the most wonderful-looking man Dawn has ever seen. In his embrace, Dawn awakens to disturbing, unfamiliar desires and his promises offer vision of music and romance forever...until he disappears.

Secrets of the Night. unabr. ed. Una-Mary Parker. Read by Anita Wright. 8 cass. (Running Time: 8 hrs.). 1999. 69.95 (978-0-7531-0467-5(9), 990402) Pub: ISIS Audio GBR. Dist(s): Ulverscroft US
To celebrate twenty-five years of marriage, Douglas & Julia Rutherford hold a glittering party on the grounds of their Hanmpshire manor house. With Julia's help, Douglas has become one of the country's leading restaurateurs. But once the party's in full swing, & the whole family is gathered together, an uninvited guest arrives with an unpleasant surprise for them all.

Secrets of the Past. unabr. ed. Rose Boucheron. Read by Sue Douglas. 8 cass. (Running Time: 10 hrs. 35 min.). 1999. 83.95 (978-1-85903-258-9(3)) Pub: Magna Story GBR. Dist(s): Ulverscroft US
After growing up in an orphanage, Lizzie Bartholomew goes into service. As a maid in a select academy for young ladies, she meets the wilful Sarah Chamberlain. When Sarah leaves in disgrace, Lizzie does not expect to hear from her again, until she receives a letter asking her to be Sarah's personal maid. Life is much better in the great house at Hyde Park Square. Both Lizzie's parents were in service in the same area but when she asks if anyone remembers them, she gets more than she bargained for.

Secrets of the Power of Intention. Wayne W. Dyer. 6 CDs. 2004. audio compact disk 59.95 (978-1-4019-0310-7(X), 310X) Hay House.

Secrets of the Power of Intention. unabr. ed. Wayne W. Dyer. 6 cass. (Running Time: 9 hrs.). (ENG.). 2004. reel tape 59.95 (978-1-4019-0311-4(8)) Hay House.

Secrets of the Sea. unabr. ed. Jessica Blair. Read by Maggie Mash. 12 cass. (Story Sound Ser.). (J). 2006. 94.95 (978-1-85903-855-0(7)) Pub: Mgna Lrg Print GBR. Dist(s): Ulverscroft US

Secrets of the Sea. unabr. ed. Jessica Blair & Maggie Mash. Read by Maggie Mash. 14 CDs. (Running Time: 16 hrs.). (Story Sound CD Ser.). (J). 2006. audio compact disk 104.95 (978-1-85903-944-1(8)) Pub: Mgna Lrg Print GBR. Dist(s): Ulverscroft US

Secrets of the Tai Chi Circle: Journey to Enlightenment. unabr. ed. Luke Chan. Read by Robert Allen. 4 cass. (Running Time: 5 hrs. 20 min.). 1994. 24.95 (978-0-9637341-1-2(3)) Benefactor.
A novel of a young student's spiritual jounrey which reveals the basic tenents of Taoism & Tai Chi in a manner that illustrates their applications in life.

Secrets of the Universe. abr. ed. Wayne W. Dyer & Dyer. Read by Wayne W. Dyer. 2 CDs. (Running Time: 2 hrs. 0 mins. 0 sec.). (ENG.). 2006. audio compact disk 19.95 (978-0-7435-5197-7(4), Nightgale) Pub: S&S Audio. Dist(s): S and S Inc

Secrets of the Vine. Global Vision Staff. 2002. 19.99 (978-1-932131-06-2(X)) Pub: Glob Vision. Dist(s): STL Dist NA

Secrets of the Vine Audio Cass. Global Vision Staff. 2002. 19.99 (978-1-932131-05-5(1)) Pub: Glob Vision. Dist(s): STL Dist NA

Secrets of the Widow's Son. David A Shugarts. 2005. audio compact disk 29.99 (978-1-4193-5753-4(0)) Recorded Bks.

***Secrets of the Yellow Jaguar.** unabr. ed. Jon Voelkel & Pamela Voelkel. Read by Scott Brick. (ENG.). (J). 2010. audio compact disk 44.00 (978-0-307-71202-8(8), Listening Lib) Pub: Random Audio Pubg. Dist(s): Random

Secrets of the Young & Successful Audio Program: How to Get Everything You Want Without Waiting a Lifetime. Jennifer Kushell & Scott Kaufman. 4 CDs. (Running Time: 5 hours). 2005. audio compact disk 30.00 (978-0-9748240-3-1(8)) Yng Succ Med.

Secrets of Vesuvius, Vol. 2. Caroline Lawrence. As told by Michael Praed. (Running Time: 3 hrs. 0 mins. 0 sec.). (Roman Mysteries Ser.). (ENG.). (J). (gr. 7-9). 2004. audio compact disk 24.99 (978-0-7528-6695-6(8)) Pub: OrnChdrns Bks GBR. Dist(s): IPG Chicago

Secrets of Weight Loss. Michael Klaper. Perf. by Sun. 1 cass. (Running Time: 30 min.). (Help Yourself to Health Ser.). 7.00 (978-0-929274-01-0(6)) Gentle World.
Improve your health & lose weight with pure vegetarian nutrition.

Secrets of Winning Tennis. Gil Boyne. Read by Gil Boyne. 1 cass. 9.95 (110) Westwood Pub Co.

Secrets of World Changers. Jeff Myers. 2006. DVD & audio compact disk 39.99 (978-0-8054-6885-4(4)) BH Pubng Grp.

Secrets of Your Own Healing Power. Wayne W. Dyer. Read by Wayne W. Dyer. 2 cass. (Running Time: 3 hrs.). 2000. 17.95 (978-1-56170-806-2(2), 4081) Hay House.

Secrets of Your Own Healing Power. abr. ed. Wayne W. Dyer. Read by Wayne W. Dyer. (YA). 2007. 34.99 (978-1-60252-792-8(X)) Find a World.

Secrets of Your Own Healing Power. abr. ed. Wayne W. Dyer. 2 CDs. 2005. audio compact disk 18.95 (978-1-4019-0426-5(2)) Hay House.

Secrets, Plots & Hidden Agendas: What You Don't Know about Conspiracy Theories. unabr. ed. Paul T. Coughlin. Read by Paul T. Coughlin. 6 cass. (Running Time: 8 hrs. 30 mins.). 1999. 44.95 (978-0-7861-1522-8(X), 2372) Blckstn Audio.
News of conspiracies has spread broadly. The theories are confirmed by some of the government's own declassified reports & by interpretations of Bible prophecy & alleged Bible codes that predict such events. But what is the truth?.

Secrets, Plots & Hidden Agendas: What You Don't Know about Conspiracy Theories. unabr. ed. Paul T. Coughlin. Read by Paul T. Coughlin. 5 cass. (Running Time: 7 hrs.). 1999. 27.95 (978-0-7861-1697-3(8)) Pub: Blckstn Audio. Dist(s): Penton Overseas
Summarizes the main ideas conspiracy theorists have about a one-world government as well as the role of the media, end-times teachings & the Jewish community.

Secrets, Plots & Hidden Agendas: What You Don't Know about Conspiracy Theories. unabr. ed. Paul T. Coughlin. Read by Paul T. Coughlin. 7 CDs. (Running Time: 8 hrs. 30 mins.). 2000. audio compact disk 56.00 (978-0-7861-9857-3(5), 2372) Blckstn Audio.
News of conspiracies has spread broadly by the Internet, radio talk shows & thriving publishing efforts. The theories are confirmed by some of the government's own declassified reports, by prominent leaders who publicly favor global government & by interpretations of Bible prophecy & alleged Bible codes that predict such events.

Secrets Revealed. Charlie Harding. 1 cass. (Running Time: 1 hr. 30 min.). 2000. 17.57 (978-0-9746197-1-2(X)) Seattle Parr Mar.
Includes information on Parrot Mental Stimulation Toys, chewable Toys, Puzzle Toys, Physical Activity Toys, Perma-Toys, Physiological and Psychological Effects of Bathing, including Skin Hygiene and Hydration. It goes on the explain Sleep Habits/Sleep Deprivation, Avian Diet, including recommended food for parrots. Further, it covers Environmental Stimulation including Humidity, Full Spectrum Lighting, and Timers. Additionally, Cigarette Smoking, Allocation of Time in and Out of the Cage, Picking the Right Cage, Playpens and Climbing Trees, Wing Clipping Techniques and the Step-Up Command, Come and Stay Command, To Shoulder or Not To Shoulder Command, Dealing with the One Person Bird are covered. There are also Chapters on Bird Health including the signs of illness, possible causes and solutions. And, common Household Hazards and Poisons.

Secret's Shadow. unabr. ed. Alex Matthews. Read by Lynda Evans. 8 cass. (Running Time: 9 hrs. 42 min.). (Cassidy McCabe Mystery Ser.). 1998. 49.95 (978-1-55686-745-3(X)) Books in Motion.
When a therapist is blamed for a patient's death, she decides to investigate.

Secrets to a Happier Life: Secrets to a Happier Marriage - the Secret of True Happiness. unabr. ed. Shmuel Irons. 2 cass. (Running Time: 3 hrs.). 19.95 Set. (978-1-889648-00-2(0)) Jwish Her Fdtn.
Rabbi Irons applies the timeless truths found in the Bible & Talmud to gain knowledge, peace of mind, & the practical tools to live a happier life.

Secrets to a Slimmer You. Dave E. David. 2 cass. 1997. 17.95 Set. (978-0-9655892-1-5(8)) Dr Davids.
Little known tips & techniques to help you slim down & keep body fat off forever.

Secrets to Creating Wealth: Learn How to Create Outrageous Wealth with Only 2 Pennies to Rub Together! Interview. Stephen A. Pierce & Pierce Litman. Moderated by Mike Litman. 2 CDs. 2006. audio compact disk 97.00 (978-1-933596-02-0(3)) Pub: Morgan James Pubng. Dist(s): IngramPubServ
Learn how to Create Outrageous Wealth With Only 2 Pennies to Rub Together! Discover the 7 Secrets to Creating Wealth Unabridged 2 Disc Audio Set and you will learn... The thrilling ?eternal? plan developed for anyone to become wealthy beyond their wildest dreams once they understand its power and purpose. This is one of the real MASTER-KEYS to becoming wealthy, and you will learn how to use it! Neutralize bad habits and heat-up powerful habits that can disintegrate poverty, lack and debt. This one INSIGHT alone could send shockwaves of confidence throughout your life! If you freak out when the unexpected happens, then here?s how to KNOCKOUT any surprise and survive any challenge you are facing. Experience relief in SECONDS with this proven stress reliever! People with this ?LIFESTYLE-CHANGE? almost always ooze with wealth and success. This is a sure path of transforming your dreams into reality! This age old lesson is worth a FORTUNE to those who tap into its relentless and unstoppable force. There?s nothing you can do to stop this force, so you better understand this one immediately! And many more proven practical and profitable strategies on the SECRETS TO CREATING WEALTH! ?Wealth is your birthright! And Stephen Pierce shows you exactly what it takes to claim the personal and financial success that should be rightfully yours. Stephen's story will inspire and motivate you. His wealth building strategies have made him rich and they can work for you too.? Will BonnerDirector, Agora Learning Institute ?Stephen Pierce is a perfect example of someone who doesn't just learn what everyone else learns, he applies what everyone else doesn't. His Wealth CD's will show anyone who is serious about really making it financially, how to do it. If you are one of those people who is looking to make it big by winning the lottery, this is NOT for you. However, if you are prepared to listen and follow the wisdom of a man who has risen from the depths of despair to multimillionaire, get these CD's now!? John AssarafNew York Times and Wall Street Journal Best-Selling Author?NOTHING teaches better than experience and example... and Stephen Pierce gives you BOTH! His Wealth CD's give you practical examples, steps, and tools that make a difference in your life - FAST! Within the first 5 minutes, Stephen gives you specific strategies you can use to change your DESTINY and they come straight from the depths of his own experiences.. the same experiences he used to transform his life into one of unlimited abundance. His genuine desire to help you succeed and find your own path to greatness shines through in every minute of this power-packed program! Do yourself and your family a favor, get this program NOW!? Jim EdwardsAuthor, ?5 Steps To Getting Anything You Want? ?Stephen Pierce's enthusiasm, zest and message is positively magnetic. With absolutely no advantages and everything against him Stephen shows you how anybody can rise above any obstacle to become successful, wealthy and happy. How? Just follow Stephen's message.? Yanik SilverInternet Marketing Expert, Author of Public Domain Riches ?Stephen Pierce's incredibly powerful strategies and techniques have helped us bring in an additional $173,317 dollars in revenue in the last 5 months. Stephen Pierce is in the top 1% of marketers and entrepreneurs in the world today. Eat every word he says up and immense profits will be your dessert.? Mike Litman#1 Best-Selling Author of Conversations with Millionaires.

Secrets to Getting over It. Patrick Wanis. As told by Patrick Wanis. (ENG.). 2008. 29.95 (978-0-9779192-6-0(9)) WOW Prods.

Secrets to Losing Weight, Being Thin, & Loving Your Body. Patrick Wanis. As told by Patrick Wanis. (ENG.). 2008. 147.95 (978-0-9779192-7-7(7)) WOW Prods.

Secrets to Manifesting Your Destiny. abr. ed. Wayne W. Dyer. 2 CDs. (Running Time: 22 hrs. 0 mins. 0 sec.). (ENG.). 2002. audio compact disk 19.95 (978-0-7435-2079-9(3), Nightgale) Pub: S&S Audio. Dist(s): S and S Inc

Teaches you how to: Understand that what you desire also desires you, realize that solutions to problems lie within, and feel worthy to receive your desires.

Secrets to Manifesting Your Destiny. unabr. ed. Wayne W. Dyer. 6 cass. (Running Time: 6 hrs.). 1996. suppl. ed. 59.95 mini poster. (978-1-55525-007-2(6), 14590); audio compact disk 69.95 (978-1-55525-008-9(4), 14590cd) Nightingale-Conant.

There's an amazing, ancient 20-minute technique that will enable you to create anything you want in life, whether it's love, money, improved health, a better job, or anything else you want or need.

Secrets to Normal Blood Sugars for Type 1 Diabetes by Dr. Richard K. Bernstein: An Education Program & Guide to Achieving Normal Blood Sugars. Directed By Diabetes In Control. 5 CDs. (Running Time: 6 hrs.). 2005. audio compact disk 149.95 (978-0-9772548-1-1(X)) Dia in Control.

For Type 1 diabetes, Secrets To Normal Blood Sugars is the entire education program taught by Dr. Richard K. Bernstein to his patients. A compilation of his two best selling books, Diabetes Solution, and The Diabetes Diet, the Secrets To Normal Blood Sugars contains new, more up-to-date information, and is being made available on 5 Audio CD's, categorized by subject, and containing 6 hours of education that can be listened to anywhere, making this beyond question, the easiest way to educate yourself and your patients, on how to better manage diabetes, and stop forever the complications of chronic high blood sugars.Never before has their been such a complete, easy to use, Diabetes Education Program available for both Type 1 or Type 2 diabetes. From the Dr. who is responsible for saving millions of peoples lives, and is credited as the founder of tight control, this complete education program is the perfect solution for anyone who suffers from Diabetes.As an added plus, Dr. Bernstein created a Bonus CD which contains information on the complications of diabetes and actual videos of him showing you how to give a painless injection, a muscle injection, and how to fill a syringe without bubbles. Included also on the bonus cd are sample meal plans and recipes you can print out.Available for Type 1 or Type 2 Diabetes.

Secrets to Normal Blood Sugars for Type 2 Diabetes: An Education Program & Guide to Achieving Normal Blood Sugars. Instructed by Richard K. Bernstein. 5 CDs. (Running Time: 6 hrs.). 2005. audio compact disk 149.95 (978-0-9772548-0-4(1)) Dia in Control.

For Type 2 diabetes, Secrets To Normal Blood Sugars is the entire education program taught by Dr. Richard K. Bernstein to his patients. A compilation of his two best selling books, Diabetes Solution, and The Diabetes Diet, the Secrets To Normal Blood Sugars contains new, more up-to-date information, and is being made available on 5 Audio CD's, categorized by subject, and containing 6 hours of education that can be listened to anywhere, making this beyond question, the easiest way to educate yourself and your patients, on how to better manage diabetes, and stop forever the complications of chronic high blood sugars.Never before has their been such a complete, easy to use, Diabetes Education Program available for both Type 1 or Type 2 diabetes. From the Dr. who is responsible for saving millions of peoples lives, and is credited as the founder of tight control, this complete education program is the perfect solution for anyone who suffers from Diabetes.As an added plus, Dr. Bernstein created a Bonus CD which contains information on the complications of diabetes and actual videos of him showing you how to give a painless injection, a muscle injection, and how to fill a syringe without bubbles. Included also on the bonus cd are sample meal plans and recipes you can print out.Available for Type 1 or Type 2 Diabetes.

Secrets to Scheduling the Executive Level Sales Call: How to Win over the Million-Dollar Decision Maker, abr. ed. Interview with Shelly Carlson. 2 cass. (Running Time: 2 hrs. 8 min.). 1998. 60.00 (978-0-9658697-2-0(5)) Lead Edge.

How to gain access to previously closed doors of the executive suite. For both experienced sales professionals & those who are new to sales.

***Secrets to the Grave.** unabr. ed. Tami Hoag. Read by Kirsten Potter. (ENG.). 2010. audio compact disk 40.00 (978-0-7393-6583-0(5), Random AudioBks) Pub: Random Audio Pubg. Dist(s): Random

Section 1983 Civil Rights Litigation & Attorneys' Fees: Current Developments. 8 cass. (Running Time: 10 hrs. 30 min.). bk. 95.00 incl. 1320-page course handbook. (T6-9140) PLI.

Section 608 Certification Exam Preparatory. ESCO Institute Staff. 1. 2003. audio compact disk 12.95 (978-1-930044-18-0(6), 608CD) ESCO PR.

Contains all the information necessary to pass the Section 608 Universal Certification.

Section 8. unabr. ed. K'Wan Foye. Read by Napiera Groves. (Running Time: 12 hrs. 30 mins.). (Hood Rat Novel Ser.). 2009. 29.95 (978-1-4417-2590-5(3)); 72.95 (978-1-4417-2586-8(5)); audio compact disk 105.00 (978-1-4417-2587-5(3)) Blckstn Audio.

Section 8. unabr. ed. K'Wan Foye. Read by Napiera Groves. (Running Time: 9 hrs. 30 mins.). 2009. audio compact disk 32.95 (978-1-4417-2589-9(X)) Blckstn Audio.

Sections & the Civil War 1826-1877. unabr. ed. Clarence B. Carson. (Running Time: 34200 sec.). (Basic History of the United States Ser.). 2007. audio compact disk 29.95 (978-0-7861-7302-0(5)); audio compact disk 72.00 (978-0-7861-6229-1(5)) Blckstn Audio.

Sector Trading Strategies: Turning Steady Profits Even in Stubborn Markets. Instructed by Deron Wagner. 1 cassette. (Running Time: 90 mins). (Trade Secrets Audio Ser.). 2002. 19.95 (978-1-931611-70-1(X)) Marketplace Bks.

Secular Franciscans. Curt Johnson. Read by Curt Johnson. 1 CD. (Running Time: 30 min.). 2003. audio compact disk 14.95 (978-1-881586-11-1(1)) Canticle Cass.

Historical and contemporary reflection on secular Franciscan movement.

Secular Humanism. Interview with Mother Angelica et al. 1 cass. (Running Time: 60 min.). (Mother Angelica Live Ser.). 1988. 10.00 (978-1-55794-104-6(1), T55) Eternal Wrd TV.

Secular Humanism: A Satire. 1 cass. (Running Time: 9 min.). 9.95 (F0550B090, HarperThor) HarpC GBR.

Secular Jihad in America (2006) Trinity Fest. 10. 2006. 28.00 (978-1-59128-485-7(6)); 35.00 (978-1-59128-487-1(2)) Canon Pr ID.

Secular Sabotage: How Liberals Are Destroying Religion & Culture in America. unabr. ed. William A. Donohue. Read by William A. Donohue. (Running Time: 8 hrs.). (ENG.). 2009. 18.98 (978-1-60024-938-9(8)); audio compact disk 26.98 (978-1-60024-937-2(X)) Pub: Hachet Audio. Dist(s): HachBkGrp

***Secularism & the Illusion of Neutrality.** Featuring Ravi Zacharias. 2005. audio compact disk 9.00 (978-1-61256-063-2(6)) Ravi Zach.

***Secularization.** Featuring Ravi Zacharias. 2003. audio compact disk 9.00 (978-1-61256-028-1(8)) Ravi Zach.

Secure in God's Choice, Pt. 1. Derek Prince. 1 cass. (I-136) Derek Prince.

Secure in God's Choice, Pt. 2. Derek Prince. 1 cass. (I-137) Derek Prince.

Secured Financing & Equipment Leasing. 9 cass. (Running Time: 13 hrs.). 1995. 360.00 Set; incl. study guide 592p. (M192) Am Law Inst.

Advanced course highlights recent significant developments in cross-border & domestic lease financing of transportation equipment, & the effects of regulatory requirements & of potential bankruptcy & workout issues in such deals. Other major areas of tax-advantaged financings are considered as well.

Secured Transactions. rev. ed. Douglass Boshkoff. 2 cass. (Running Time: 3 hrs.). (Outstanding Professors Ser.). 1995. 44.00 (978-0-940366-66-4(5), 28426) Pub: Sum & Substance. Dist(s): West Pub

Lecture given by a prominent American law school professor.

Secured Transactions under the Uniform Commercial Code. Contrib. by William A. Dreier et al. (Running Time: 4 hrs.). 1985. 90.00 incl. program handbook. NJ Inst CLE.

Includes filing, security agreements, financing statements, perfection, priority controversies, automatic stays, use of cash collateral, valuations, cramdown.

Secured Transactions, 2005 ed. (Law School Legends Audio Series) 2005th rev. ed. Michael I. Spak. (Law School Legends Audio Ser.). 2005. 52.00 (978-0-314-16116-1(3), gilbert); 47.95 (978-0-314-16115-4(5), gilbert) West.

Securing Your Financial Future: How to Maximize Your 401(k) Betty Meredith. Read by Susan Blauvelt. 6 cass. (Running Time: 6 hrs.). 1995. pap. bk. 59.95 (978-0-9702220-2-2(5)) Discover Learn.

You will create a personalized action plan by setting a retirement saving target, determining how much to save now & making an informed choice of investment options.

Securities Arbitration 1990. 4 cass. (Running Time: 5 hrs.). 1990. bk. 70.00 Set incl. course handbook. (T6-9149) PLI.

Securities Enforcement & Disclosure. 1997. bk. 99.00 (ACS-1234) PA Bar Inst.

The Private Securities Reform Act of 1995 made sweeping changes in how securities actions are litigated. This year, the "Fields Bill" was enacted, resulting in the first major overhaul of securities law in the last six years. The courts have not been silent during this period of rapid change, handing down important decisions on many issues, including use of the "misappropriaton theory" to prosecute insider trading cases.

Securities Filings, 1989: Review & Update. unabr. ed. Contrib. by Alan K. Austin. 8 cass. (Running Time: 10 hrs.). 1990. 50.00 course handbk. (T7-9243) PLI.

In this recording of PLI's December 1989 program, an experienced faculty examines the SEC's integrated disclosure rules, concentrating on: review procedures in the Department of Corporation Finance, disclosure problems, periodic reports under the Securities Exchange Act of 1934, proxy statements & annual reports to stockholders, filings under the Securities Act of 1933, ethics & securities practice, EDGAR, small & exempt offerings, resales of restricted securities, short-swing trading & forms required by the Williams Act.

Securities Law for Nonsecurities Lawyers. 9 cass. (Running Time: 12 hrs.). 1999. 295.00 Set; incl. study guide 347p. (MD57) Am Law Inst.

Designed to familiarize lawyers who do not regularly practice securities law with the basic structure of the federal securities laws, & where & how those laws may be relevant in a general or specialized business law practice.

Securities Law for the Non-Specialist. unabr. ed. Contrib. by Jeff Hoffman & Larry D. Soderquist. 8 cass. (Running Time: 11 hrs.). 1989. 50.00 course handbk. (T7-9228) PLI.

This recording of PLI's September 1989 program explains how a non-specialist should approach securities law questions & solve practical problems. Major topics include: how to approach securities law, business context of Securities Act registration, regulatory framework of Securities Act registration, Securities Act registration process, what is a security, Securities Act registration exemptions, resales of securities, liability for Securities Act violations, registration & reporting under the Exchange Act, regulation of proxy solicitation, regulation of tender offers, Rule 10b-5, short-swing trading & regulation of the securities business.

Securities Law Implications of Common Business Transactions. Read by Joan D. Maher. 1 cass. 1991. 20.00 (AL-108) PA Bar Inst.

Securities Litigation: Planning & Strategies. 6 cass. (Running Time: 9 hrs.). 1997. 137.50 Incl. course materials. (MB93) Am Law Inst.

Designed for outside & in-house counsel, members of the accounting profession, compliance officers within the securities & commodities industries,& members of government agencies. In addition to the examination confronted by the trial practitioner, attention is also directed to strategies used to avoid litigation & to litigation management techniques.

Securities Litigation, 1989. unabr. ed. Contrib. by Bruce G. Vanyo & Edward J. Yodowitz. 8 cass. (Running Time: 10 hrs.). 1989. 50.00 course handbk. (T7-9226) PLI.

In this recording of the September 1989 PLI program, all facets of securities litigation are covered. Fundamental issues such as scienter & materiality, plaintiff, defendant & prosecutor strategies are analyzed. In addition, the distinguished faculty of plaintiff & defense counsel, federal district judges & representatives from the SEC's Division of Enforcement discuss different types of securities litigation & the contrasting perspectives of the diverse parties to such litigation.

Securities Regulation. 3rd rev. ed. James D. Cox. (Sum & Substance Ser.). 2007. 74.00 (978-0-314-18821-2(5), West Lglwrks) West.

Security Analysis. 5th ed. Sidney Cottle et al. Read by Roger F. Murray. 1 cass. (Running Time: 60 min.). 1990. pap. bk. 9.95 (978-0-07-013238-2(0)) McGraw.

Explains the famous Graham-Dodd method & how to use it. It offers practical insights into investment decision making, the bond investment environment, & much more.

Security Analysis: The 1934 Original Edition. abr. ed. Benjamin Graham. (Running Time: 4 hrs. 30 min.). 2003. 24.00 (978-1-932378-06-1(5)); audio compact disk 28.00 (978-1-932378-07-8(3)) Pub: A Media Intl. Dist(s): Natl Bk Netwk

Security Design Pack: Microsoft Windows 2000. Richard A. McMahon, Sr. (Netability Ser.). 2005. tchr. ed. 69.95 (978-0-7638-1951-4(4)) EMC-Paradigm.

Security for Airport & Aerospace, Maritime & Port, & High-Threat Targets in Belgium: A Strategic Reference, 200609. Compiled by Icon Group International, Inc. Staff. 2007. ring bd. 195.00 (978-0-497-35828-0(X)) Icon Grp.

Security in the Spirit. 12 cass. 35.95 (20118, HarperThor) HarpC GBR.

Security of Salvation. 4 cass. 15.95 incl. study guide. (2036, HarperThor) HarpC GBR.

Security of the Believer. Michael Pearl. 3 CDs. 2003. audio compact disk (978-1-892112-46-0(9)) No Greater Joy.

Sedona Red Rock Country Tour. 2004. audio compact disk (978-0-9755800-2-8(7)) Waypoint Tours.

***Seduce Me.** abr. ed. Dahlia Schweitzer. Read by Kate Mcintyre. (ENG.). 2006. (978-0-06-123012-7(X), Harper Audio); (978-0-06-121511-7(2), Harper Audio) HarperCollins Pubs.

Seduce Me at Sunrise. abr. ed. Lisa Kleypas. Read by Rosalyn Landor. (Running Time: 5 hrs.). (Hathaways Ser.: No. 2). 2009. audio compact disk 24.99 (978-1-4418-0721-2(7), 9781441807212, BACD) Brilliance Audio.

Seduce Me at Sunrise. unabr. ed. Lisa Kleypas. Read by Rosalyn Landor. (Running Time: 10 hrs.). (Hathaways Ser.: No. 2). 2009. 24.99 (978-1-4233-8994-1(8), 9781423389941, Brilliance MP3); 39.97 (978-1-4233-8995-8(6), 9781423389958, Brlnc Audio MP3 Lib); 39.97 (978-1-4233-8997-2(2), 9781423389972, BADLE); audio compact disk 29.99 (978-1-4233-8992-7(1), 9781423389927, Bril Audio CD Unabri); audio compact disk 92.97 (978-1-4233-8993-4(X), 9781423389934, BriAudCD Unabrid) Brilliance Audio.

Seduce Me at Sunrise. unabr. ed. Lisa Kleypas. Read by Rosalyn Landor. (Running Time: 10 hrs.). (Hathaways Ser.: No. 2). 2009. 24.99 (978-1-4233-8996-5(4), 9781423389965, BAD) Brilliance Audio.

Seduced. unabr. collector's ed. Catherine Lanigan. Read by Anna Fields. 8 cass. (Running Time: 12 hrs.). 1996. 64.00 (978-0-7366-3525-7(4), 4162) Books on Tape.

The stranger flirting with Valentine St. James at the costume ball has guts. Sure, he wears a disguise, but his moves are especially conspicuous because partygoers expect an announcement on this night of Valentine's engagement to another man.

***Seduced by a Highlander: Children of the Mist series, Book 2.** unabr. ed. Paula Quinn. Read by Carrington MacDuffie. (Running Time: 13 hrs. NaN mins.). (Children of the Mist Ser.). 2010. 29.95 (978-1-4417-7553-5(6)); 59.95 (978-1-4417-7550-4(1)); audio compact disk 90.00 (978-1-4417-7551-1(X)) Blckstn Audio.

Seduced by Moonlight. abr. ed. Laurell K. Hamilton. Read by Laural Merlington. (Running Time: 6 hrs.). (Meredith Gentry Ser.: No. 3). 2008. audio compact disk 14.99 (978-1-4233-6236-4(5), 9781423362364, BCD Value Price) Brilliance Audio.

Seduced by Moonlight. unabr. ed. Laurell K. Hamilton. Read by Laural Merlington. (Running Time: 15 hrs.). (Meredith Gentry Ser.: No. 3). 2004. 34.95 (978-1-59355-418-7(4), 1593554184, BAU); 97.25 (978-1-59355-419-4(2), 1593554192, BrilAudUnabridg); audio compact disk 38.95 (978-1-59355-420-0(6), 1593554206, Bril Audio CD Unabri); audio compact disk 112.25 (978-1-59355-421-7(4), 1593554214, BriAudCD Unabrid) Brilliance Audio.

I am Meredith Gentry, P.I. and Princess Merry, heir to the throne of Faerie. Now there are those among us who whisper I am more. And who can blame them? I've awakened the dazzling magic that's slumbered in them for thousands of years. But the thing is, I can't figure out why. My aunt, Queen of Air and Darkness, is no longer distracted by her sadistic hobbies. Her obsession has turned unwaveringly to me. The mission to get me pregnant and beat my cousin Prince Cel to the crown is taking longer than expected. Even though I spend each night with the Queen's Ravens, my immortal guards, no child has come of our decadent pleasures. But something else is happening. My magic courses through me uncontrollably. And as I lock my half-mortal body with their full-Sidhe-blooded ones, the power surges like never before. It all began with a chalice. I dreamed of it, and it appeared, cool and hard, beside me when I awoke. My guards know the ancient relic well - its disappearance ages ago stripped them of all of their vital powers. But it is here with us now. My touch resonates with its force, and they're consumed with it, their Sidhe essences lit up by it. But even as they cherish me for this unexpected gift, there are those who loathe me for it. Me, a mongrel, only half fey and part mortal. The Unseelie court has suffered for so long, and there are some who would not have it weakened further by an impure queen. My enemies grow in number every day. But they do not know what I am capable of. Nor, for that matter, do I.

Seduced by Moonlight. unabr. ed. Laurell K. Hamilton. Read by Laural Merlington. (Running Time: 15 hrs.). (Meredith Gentry Ser.: No. 3). 2004. 39.25 (978-1-59335-548-7(3), 1593355483, Brlnc Audio MP3 Lib); 24.95 (978-1-59335-271-4(9), 1593352719, Brilliance MP3) Brilliance Audio.

Seduced by Moonlight. unabr. ed. Laurell K. Hamilton. Read by Laural Merlington. (Running Time: 15 hrs.). (Meredith Gentry Ser.: No. 3). 2004. 39.25 (978-1-59710-680-1(1), 1597106801, BADLE); 24.95 (978-1-59710-681-8(X), 159710681X, BAD) Brilliance Audio.

***Seduced by Shadows: A Novel of the Marked Souls.** unabr. ed. Jessa Slade & Jessa Slade. (Running Time: 13 hrs. 30 mins.). 2010. 79.95 (978-1-4417-3449-5(X)); audio compact disk 109.00 (978-1-4417-3450-1(3)) Blckstn Audio.

***Seduced by Shadows: A Novel of the Marked Souls.** unabr. ed. Jessa Slade. (Running Time: 13 hrs. 30 mins.). 2010. 29.95 (978-1-4417-3453-2(8)); audio compact disk 34.95 (978-1-4417-3452-5(X)) Blckstn Audio.

Seducing an Angel. unabr. ed. Mary Balogh. Read by Anne Flosnik. 1 MP3-CD. (Running Time: 11 hrs.). (Huxtable Quintet: Bk. 4). 2009. 39.97 (978-1-4233-8909-5(3), 9781423389095, Brlnc Audio MP3 Lib); 39.97 (978-1-4233-8911-8(5), 9781423389118, BADLE); 24.99 (978-1-4233-8908-8(5), 9781423389088, Brilliance MP3); 24.99 (978-1-4233-8910-1(7), 9781423389101, BAD); audio compact disk 97.97 (978-1-4233-8907-1(7), 9781423389071, BriAudCD Unabrid); audio compact disk 28.99 (978-1-4233-8906-4(9), 9781423389064, Bril Audio CD Unabri) Brilliance Audio.

Seducing the Spirits. unabr. ed. Louise Young. (Running Time: 11 hrs. 0 mins.). (ENG.). 2009. 29.95 (978-1-4332-6300-2(9)); 65.95 (978-1-4332-6296-8(7)); audio compact disk 100.00 (978-1-4332-6297-5(5)) Blckstn Audio.

Seduction. Composed by Ranjit Barot. 1 cass. 1996. (M96012); audio compact disk (CD M96012) Multi-Cultural Bks.

Midnight Flute, The Magic of the Mind, Rainswept (The Well of Longing), Sensuality, The Bridge of Sighs, The Garden of Maya, The Winds of Change, Seduction, The Dreams of Desire.

Seduction. unabr. ed. Amanda Quick, pseud. Read by Anne Flosnik. (Running Time: 12 hrs.). 2009. 39.97 (978-1-4233-8726-8(0), 9781423387268, Brlnc Audio MP3 Lib); 24.99 (978-1-4233-8725-1(2), 9781423387251, Brilliance MP3); 39.97 (978-1-4233-8728-2(7), 9781423387282, BADLE); 24.99 (978-1-4233-8727-5(9), 9781423387275, BAD); audio compact disk 82.97 (978-1-4233-8724-4(4), 9781423387244, BriAudCD Unabrid); audio compact disk 29.99 (978-1-4233-8723-7(6), 9781423387237) Brilliance Audio.

Seduction by Design. Erin St. Claire, pseud. Narrated by Jenna Stern. 5 CDs. (Running Time: 5 hrs. 30 mins.). audio compact disk 48.00 (978-1-4025-1528-6(6)) Recorded Bks.

Seduction by Design. Erin St. Claire, pseud. Read by Jenna Stern. (Running Time: 53 hrs. 0 mins. 0 sec.). 2004. audio compact disk 14.95 (978-0-7435-3785-8(8), S&S Encore) Pub: S&S Audio. Dist(s): S and S Inc *SANDRA BROWN'S BLOCKBUSTER BESTSELLER AT A NEW LOW PRICE! Seduction By Design Read by Jenna Stern Hailey Ashton projects an image that she's on top of everything, but no one realizes that she lives a life of quiet emptiness - not ready to have a relationship, not willing to give herself body and soul to a man. Never able to compete with her younger sister, the thoughtless beauty of the family, Hailey opted to be the "good girl." But when she meets Tyler Scott - her rich, attractive new boss - she longs to be anything but good.*

Seduction by Design. unabr. ed. Erin St. Claire, pseud. Narrated by Jenna Stern. 4 cass. (Running Time: 5 hrs. 30 mins.). 2001. 45.00 (978-0-7887-8856-7(6)) Recorded Bks.
Hailey Ashton has an exciting position as director of guest relations at a successful theme park. Instead of seeking a social life, the energetic readhead throws herself into her job responsibilities. But when Hailey meets Tyler Scott, the handsome owner of the park, her professionalism begins to melt under his direct, sexy gaze. Tyler's goal is to seduce Hailey. But as their passion grows, both start to wonder how much more their relationship could be.

Seduction in Death. abr. ed. J. D. Robb, pseud. Read by Susan Ericksen. (Running Time: 6 hrs.). (In Death Ser.). 2007. audio compact disk 14.99 (978-1-4233-1744-9(0), 9781423317449, BCD Value Price) Brilliance Audio.

Seduction in Death. unabr. ed. J. D. Robb, pseud. Read by Susan Ericksen. 7 cass. (Running Time: 10 hrs.). (In Death Ser.). 2001. 30.95 (978-1-58788-681-2(2), 1587886812, BAU) Brilliance Audio.

Seduction in Death. unabr. ed. J. D. Robb, pseud. Read by Susan Ericksen. 7 cass. (Running Time: 10 hrs.). (In Death Ser.:). 2001. 78.25 (978-1-58788-682-9(0), 1587886820, Unabridge Lib Edns) Brilliance Audio.

Seduction in Death. unabr. ed. J. D. Robb, pseud. Read by Susan Ericksen. (Running Time: 10 hrs.). (In Death Ser.). 2004. 39.25 (978-1-59335-395-7(2), 1593353952, Brinc Audio MP3 Lib) Brilliance Audio.
Dante had been courting his victim in cyberspace for weeks before meeting her in person. A few sips of wine and a few hours later, she was dead. The murder weapon: a rare, usually undetectable date-rape drug with a street value of a quarter million dollars. Detective Eve Dallas is playing and replaying the clues in her mind. The candlelight, the music, the rose petals strewn across the bed - a seduction meant for his benefit, not hers. He hadn't intended to kill her. But now that he has, he is left with only two choices: to either hole up in fear and guilt or start hunting again. .

Seduction in Death. unabr. ed. J. D. Robb, pseud. Read by Susan Ericksen. (Running Time: 10 hrs.). (In Death Ser.). 2004. 39.25 (978-1-59710-683-2(6), 1597106836, BADLE); 24.95 (978-1-59710-682-5(8), 1597106828, BAD) Brilliance Audio.

Seduction in Death. unabr. ed. J. D. Robb, pseud. Read by Susan Ericksen. (Running Time: 10 hrs.). (In Death Ser.). 2007. audio compact disk 36.95 (978-1-4233-1741-8(6), 9781423317418, Bril Audio CD Unabri); audio compact disk 97.25 (978-1-4233-1742-5(4), 9781423317425, BriAudCD Unabrid) Brilliance Audio.

Seduction in Death. unabr. ed. J. D. Robb, pseud. Read by Susan Ericksen. (Running Time: 10 hrs.). (In Death Ser.). 2004. 24.95 (978-1-59335-151-9(8), 1593351518) Soulmate Audio Bks.

***Seduction of a Proper Gentleman.** unabr. ed. Victoria Alexander. Read by Maxwell Caulfield & Rosalyn Landor. (ENG.). 2008. (978-0-06-169170-6(4)); (978-0-06-170607-3(8)) HarperCollins Pubs.

Seduction of Hillary Rodham. abr. ed. David Brock. 2 cass. (Running Time: 3 hrs.). 15.95 (57055) Books on Tape.
The First Lady's Struggle to maintain her integrity in the face of powerfully seductive forces: temptatations that unencumbered political power brings the appeal of Bill Clinton, who may have been both the best & the worst thing that ever happened to Hillary. As for Hillary, is she her husband's greatest asset or greatest liability.

Seduction of the Crimson Rose. unabr. ed. Lauren Willig. Read by Kate Reading. (Running Time: 14 hrs.). Bk. 4. (ENG.). (gr. 8 up). 2008. audio compact disk 39.95 (978-0-14-314295-9(X), PengAudBks) Penguin Grp USA.

Seduction of the Crimson Rose. unabr. ed. Lauren Willig. Narrated by Kate Reading. 11 CDs. (Running Time: 14 hrs.). (Pink Carnation Ser.: Bk. 4). 2008. audio compact disk 110.00 (978-1-4159-4808-8(9), BksonTape) Pub: Random Audio Pubg. Dist(s): Random
Lauren Willig continues the exciting, bestselling Pink Carnation series with her fourth novel, THE SEDUCTION OF THE CRIMSON ROSE, featuring Lord Vaughn, the delightfully devilish spy from The Masque of the Black Tulip, and Mary Alsworthy, the raven-haired beauty whose sister accidentally stole her suitor in The Deception of the Emerald Ring. Determined to secure another London Season without assistance from her new brother-in-law, Mary accepts a secret assignment from Lord Vaughn on behalf of the Pink Carnation: to infiltrate the ranks of the dreaded French spy, the Black Tulip, before he and his master can stage their planned invasion of England. Every spy has a weakness, and for the Black Tulip that weakness is black-haired women - his "petals" of the Tulip. A natural at the art of seduction, Mary easily catches the attention of the French spy, but Lord Vaughn never anticipates that his own heart will be caught as well. Fighting their growing attraction, impediments from their past, and, of course, the French, Mary and Vaughn find themselves lost in the shadows of a treacherous garden of lies. As our modern-day heroine, Eloise Kelly, digs deeper into England's Napoleonic-era espionage, she becomes even more entwined with Colin Selwick, the descendant of her spy subjects.

Seductions. Richard Kostelanetz. 1 cass. (Running Time: 56 min.). 1983. bk. 10.00 (978-0-932360-46-5(7)) Archae Edns.
Two formally experimental erotic narratives, respectively from "More Short Fictions" & "Autobiographies".

Seductive Image, unabr. ed. K. L. Billingsley. Read by Frederick Davidson. 6 cass. (Running Time: 8 hrs. 30 mins.). 1994. 44.95 (978-0-7861-0688-2(3), 1473) Blckstn Audio.
Billingsley takes us inside the Hollywood mindset that produces today's popular films & TV programs. He shows that a small group of people virtually controls their content. Far more liberal than the general public, these media managers promote an outlook critical of the United States, religion, morality & traditional values. Billingsley asserts that modern film has had a devastating impact on the human imagination & on society as a whole. He offers guidelines we can use to critique what we see & hear & thus be able to interact creatively with these powerful media.

Seductive Offer. Kathryn Smith. Narrated by Jill Tanner. 10 cass. (Running Time: 14 hrs.). 88.00 (978-1-4025-2152-2(9)) Recorded Bks.

See. 1998. 10.00 (978-1-58602-019-4(6)) E L Long.

See amid the Winter's Snow. Contrib. by Richard Kingsmore. (ENG.). 2008. audio compact disk 24.99 (978-5-557-43537-6(9)) Lillenas.

See & Say see Mira Y Habla

See & Say. 2004. 8.95 (978-1-56008-324-5(7)); cass. & flmstrp 30.00 (978-1-56008-760-1(9)) Weston Woods.

See-Be. Robert A. Monroe. Read by Robert A. Monroe. (Running Time: 30 min.). (Human Plus Ser.). 1989. 14.95 (978-1-56102-031-7(1)) Inter Indus.
Increase the efficiency of mental motor skills.

See Charlie Run. Brian Freemantle. Read by Hayward Morse. 10 CDs. (Running Time: 13 hrs. 30 min.). (Sound Ser.). (J). 2003. audio compact disk 89.95 (978-1-84283-583-8(1)) Pub: ISIS Lrg Prnt GBR. Dist(s): Ulverscroft US

See Charlie Run. unabr. ed. Brian Freemantle. Read by Hayward Morse. 9 cass. (Running Time: 13 hrs. 30 min.). (Sound Ser.). (J). 2003. 76.95 (978-1-84283-323-0(5)) Pub: ISIS Lrg Prnt GBR. Dist(s): Ulverscroft US

See Delphi & Die. Lindsey Davis. Narrated by Christian Rodska. 9 cass. (Running Time: 40740 sec.). (Marcus Didius Falco Ser.). 2006. 79.95 (978-0-7927-4258-6(3), CSL 972); audio compact disk 49.95 (978-0-7927-4259-3(1), CMP 972) AudioGO.

See Delphi & Die. unabr. ed. Lindsey Davis. Narrated by Christian Rodska. 9 CDs. (Running Time: 40740 sec.). (Marcus Didius Falco Ser.). 2006. audio compact disk 99.95 (978-0-7927-4065-0(3), SLD 972) AudioGO.

See, Hear, Touch, Taste, Smell. Sundance/Newbridge, LLC Staff. (Early Science Ser.). (gr. k-3). 2007. audio compact disk 12.00 (978-1-4007-6201-9(4)); audio compact disk 12.00 (978-1-4007-6200-2(6)); audio compact disk 12.00 (978-1-4007-6199-9(9)) Sund Newbrdge.

See How He Runs. Perf. by Jim Backus. 1 cass. (Running Time: 38 min.). (Suspense Radio Ser.). 10.95 (497) J Norton Pubs.
Jim Bacus plays the part of Poppy in "See How He Runs," the story of a blind small-time criminal with a guilty conscience & a lot of hidden money. Next Vincent Price stars as a southern plantation owner who is sentenced to death for sabotage during the Civil War. But he escapes the noose - or does he.

See how he runs/occurrence at owl creek Bridge. (ENG.). 1952. audio compact disk 12.95 (978-1-57970-511-4(1), Audio-For) J Norton Pubs.

See i told you So. Rush H. Limbaugh, III. 2004. 10.95 (978-0-7435-4595-2(8)) Pub: S&S Audio. Dist(s): S and S Inc

See, I Told You So. abr. ed. Rush H. Limbaugh, III. 2 cass. 12.95 (87222) Books on Tape.
Conservatism's most outspoken champion defends the fundamental values that have shaped the American character.

See It My Way. unabr. ed. Peter White. Read by Peter White. 8 cass. (Running Time: 12 hrs.). 2000. 69.95 (978-0-7540-0401-1(5), CAB1824) Pub: Chivers Audio Bks GBR. Dist(s): AudioGO

See Jane Lead: 99 Ways for Women to Take Charge at Work & in Life. abr. ed. Lois P. Frankel. (Running Time: 3 hrs. 30 mins.). (ENG.). 2007. 14.98 (978-1-59483-887-3(9)) Pub: Hachet Audio. Dist(s): HachBkGrp

See-More's Surprise. unabr. ed. Sandra Robbins. Perf. by Joe Rizzo et al. 1 cass. (Running Time: 32 min.). Dramatization. (See-More Ser.). (J). (ps-2). 1991. 7.95 (978-1-882601-02-8(5)) See-Mores Wrkshop.
Created for children based on Shadow Box Theatre's Production. Soundtrack of show.

See No Evil. abr. ed. Robert Baer. (Running Time: 18900 sec.). (ENG.). 2005. audio compact disk 14.99 (978-0-7393-2413-4(6), Random AudioBks) Pub: Random Audio Pubg. Dist(s): Random

See No Weevil see Thurber Country

See Rock City: A Story Journey Through Appalachia. Donald Davis. 1 cass. (Running Time: 54 mins.). (American Storytelling Ser.). (gr. 6 up). 1995. 12.00 (978-0-87483-452-9(X)) Pub: August Hse. Dist(s): Natl Bk Netwk
Now Donald Davis returns to Sulpher Springs through the wide eyes of an innocent, forthright narrator: "Years later I came to realize that when you come from a long-dammed-up Scots-Irish gene pool, it is an OK thing to wish for something, but it is not an OK thing to get it." So it is in the narrator's family. It was OK to want a new house. But once the family got the new house, nothing was to be OK for some time. The long-reliable Plymouth gave way. Then, on the first Sunday in the new house, they almost burned it down. With Mother warning, "Trouble always comes in threes!" the family embarked upon an ill-conceived Florida vacation. With two young boys in the back seat & two adults from the long-dammed-up Scots-Irish gene pool in the front - the trip was doomed. The title story's surprise ending resonates with Davis's trademark tsunami of good feelings.

See Rock City: A Story Journey Through Appalachia. abr. ed. Donald Davis. Read by Donald Davis. (Running Time: 3360 sec.). 1995. audio compact disk 14.95 (978-0-87483-771-1(5)) Pub: August Hse. Dist(s): Natl Bk Netwk

See the Lamb. Composed by Dennis Jernigan. Contrib. by Don Marsh. (ENG.). 2007. audio compact disk 24.98 (978-5-557-53090-3(8), Word Music) Word Enter.

See the Light. Perf. by True Vibe. 2002. audio compact disk Provident Mus Dist.

See the Morning. Contrib. by Chris Tomlin. 2007. 14.99 (978-5-557-57023-7(3)) Pt of Grace Ent.

See Them Die. unabr. ed. Ed McBain, pseud. Read by Jonathan Marosz. 6 cass. (Running Time: 6 hrs.). (87th Precinct Ser.: Bk. 13). 1996. 36.00 (978-0-7366-3359-8(6), 4009) Books on Tape.
Lt. Pete Byrnes & the cops of the 87th Precinct are at the end of their rope. Pepe Miranda - crook, murderer, hero of the street gangs - is hiding out & making fools of them, to the cheers of every street punk in the neighborhood. Then an anonymous tip comes in. Is it a trap? If Pepe hangs on, it's an open invitation to others like him to join in the fun. But bringing him in...well, that won't happen without a deadly showdown.

See You at the Top. Zig Ziglar. Read by Zig Ziglar. 6 cass. Orig. Title: Biscuits, Fleas, & Pump Handles. 59.95 Set. (172A) Nightingale-Conant.
A winner leads the way.

See You at the Top. 25th abr. anniv. ed. Zig Ziglar. Read by Zig Ziglar. (Running Time: 2 hrs. 30 mins. 0 sec.). Orig. Title: Biscuits, Fleas, & Pump Handles. (ENG.). 2009. audio compact disk 19.99 (978-0-7435-9678-7(1), Nightgale) Pub: S&S Audio. Dist(s): S and S Inc

See You at the Top. 25th anniv. ed. Narrated by Zig Ziglar. Orig. Title: Biscuits, Fleas, & Pump Handles. (ENG.). 2000. 59.95 (978-1-56554-857-2(4)) Pelican.

See You at the Top. 25th anniv. rev. ed. Narrated by Zig Ziglar & Kevin Hogan. (Running Time: 633 hrs. NaN mins.). Orig. Title: Biscuits, Fleas, & Pump Handles. (ENG.). 2009. audio compact disk 59.95 (978-1-58980-707-5(3)) Pelican.

See You in Second Grade! unabr. ed. Miriam Cohen. 1 cass. (Running Time: 9 min.). (Miriam Cohen Ser.). (J). (gr. k-3). 1990. bk. 15.95 (978-0-8045-6588-2(0), 6588) Spoken Arts.

See You in Spring: Early Explorers Early Set A Audio CD. Benchmark Education Staff. (J). 2006. audio compact disk 10.00 (978-1-4108-7616-4(0)) Benchmark Educ.

See You Later, Alligator. unabr. ed. William F. Buckley, Jr. Read by Jeff Cummings. (Running Time: 10 hrs. 50 mins.). (Blackford Oakes Mystery Ser.). 2009. 29.95 (978-1-4332-1625-1(6)); 65.95 (978-1-4332-1621-3(3)); audio compact disk 90.00 (978-1-4332-1622-0(1)) Blckstn Audio.

See You Later, Alligator. unabr. collector's ed. William F. Buckley, Jr. Read by Paul Shay. 8 cass. (Running Time: 12 hrs.). (Blackford Oakes Mystery Ser.). 1985. 64.00 (978-0-7366-0489-5(8), 1464) Books on Tape.
President Kennedy listens to the secret proposal & approves Operation Alligator. Can anyone tread the deadly waters between Cuba & the U.S. better than Blackford Oakes? Oakes is sent to negotiate a trade & noninvasion agreement initiated by Che Guevara. The story takes off when everyone - the Cuban leaders, the Russians, everyone, that is, except Oakes, discovers that our hero is being used as a pawn in an attempt by the Russians to deploy the missiles in Cuba.

See You on the Radio. Charles Osgood. Read by Charles Osgood. (Playaway Adult Nonfiction Ser.). 2008. 54.99 (978-1-60640-525-3(X)) Find a World.

See You on the Radio. abr. ed. Charles Osgood. Read by Charles Osgood. 2 cass. (Running Time: 3 hrs.). 1999. 17.95 Soundelux.
Commentaries from one of broadcasting's funniest writers & newsmen.

See You on the Radio, abr. ed. Charles Osgood. Read by Charles Osgood. 2 cass. (Running Time: 3 hrs.). 1999. 17.95 (978-1-55935-319-9(8)) Soundelux.
The best of Osgood's work from the last eight years as a news writer & broadcaster for CBS.

See You on the Radio. unabr. ed. Charles Osgood. Read by Charles Osgood. (Running Time: 13500 sec.). (ENG.). 2008. audio compact disk 18.95 (978-1-59887-591-1(4), 1598875914) Pub: HighBridge. Dist(s): Workman Pub

See Yourself Well: Visualizations for Whole Body Healing. Anne Fogelsanger. 1 cass. (Running Time: 60 min.). 1994. 10.95 (978-1-881025-31-3(4)) Pub: Equinox Pr. Dist(s): Natl Bk Netwk

See Yourself Well for People with AIDS-HIV Positive: Guided Visualizations & Relaxation Techniques. Anne Fogelsanger. 1 cass. (Running Time: 60 min.). 1994. 10.95 (978-1-881025-29-0(2)) Pub: Equinox Pr. Dist(s): Natl Bk Netwk

See Yourself Well for People with Cancer: Guided Visualizations & Relaxation Techniques. Anne Fogelsanger. 1 cass. (Running Time: 60 min.). 1994. 10.95 (978-1-881025-30-6(6)) Pub: Equinox Pr. Dist(s): Natl Bk Netwk

Seed Is the Word. Speeches. Joel Osteen. 1 Cass. (Running Time: 30 Mins.). 2000. 6.00 (978-1-59349-077-5(1)) J Osteen.

Seed Leaves see Richard Wilbur Readings

Seed Needs Help: Early Explorers Emergent Set A Audio CD. Benchmark Education Staff. (J). 2006. audio compact disk 10.00 (978-1-4108-7591-4(1)) Benchmark Educ.

Seed of Creation. Swami Amar Jyoti. 1 cass. 1988. 9.95 (O-35) Truth Consciousness.
How does variety arise? God is the main switch of all the circuits. Yogis & scientist. Samadhi, the Great Silence, where time & space are transcended.

Seed of Your Destiny. Candace Long. Composed by Candace Long. 2006. audio compact disk 8.95 (978-0-9788322-4-7(8)) auDEO Media.

Seed Principle: Sowing & Reaping Your Way to Prosperity. Mac Hammond. 6 Cass. (Running Time: 5 hrs.). (LAWS That Govern Prosperity Ser.: 2). 2005. 30.00 (978-1-57399-228-2(3)) Mac Hammond.
In this series, Mac Hammond explores the familiar concept of sowing and reaping with startling clarity and insight. You'll find keys to living a life that prospers on every level of existence.

Seed Principle: Sowing & Reaping Your Way to Prosperity. Mac Hammond. 1 cass. (LAWS That Govern Prosperity Ser.: Vol. 2). 1996. 36.00 (978-1-57399-018-9(3)) Mac Hammond.

Seed Will Meet Any Need. unabr. ed. Keith A. Butler. 6 cass. (Running Time: 9 hrs.). 2001. 30.00 (A119) Word Faith Pubng.

Seed Within. David Dorton. Read by Jack Labbe. 2 cass. (Running Time: 2 hrs. 12 min.). 1994. 16.95 (978-1-55686-511-4(2)) Books in Motion.
Colonel David Ryne last remembers attacking a 'bogey' & now finds himself in a strange world where time is only related to thought processes & age is no longer a factor.

Seedfolks. abr. ed. Paul Fleischman. 1 cass. (Running Time: 1 hr. 45 min.). (YA). (gr. 5 up). 2003. 18.95 (978-1-883332-89-1(3)); audio compact disk 24.95 (978-1-883332-95-2(8)) Audio Bkshelf.

Seedfolks. unabr. ed. Paul Fleischman. (J). 2008. 34.99 (978-1-60514-919-6(5)) Find a World.

Seeding for the Billion Flow. Featuring Bill Winston. 1 cass. 2006. 5.00 (978-1-59544-190-4(5)); audio compact disk 8.00 (978-1-59544-191-1(3)) Pub: B Winston Min. Dist(s): Anchor Distributors

Seeds & Crystals, No. 2. 1 cass. 10.00 (978-1-58429-004-9(8)) Rational Isl.
For poets & poetry lovers involved in re-evaluation counseling.

Seeds & Crystals, No. 3. 1 cass. 10.00 (978-1-58429-005-6(6)) Rational Isl.
For poets & poetry-lovers involved in re-evaluation counseling.

Seeds & Crystals, No. 4. 1 cass. 10.00 (978-1-58429-006-3(4)) Rational Isl.

Seeds Family Worship, Volume 1: Courage. Contrib. by Seeds Family Worship. (J). (ps-3). 2004. audio compact disk 12.99 (978-5-559-75543-4(5)) Pt of Grace Ent.

Seeds Get Around. Sundance/Newbridge, LLC Staff. (Early Science Ser.). (gr. k-3). 2007. audio compact disk 12.00 (978-1-4007-6345-0(2)); audio compact disk 12.00 (978-1-4007-6343-6(6)); audio compact disk 12.00 (978-1-4007-6344-3(4)) Sund Newbrdge.

Seeds of Change: Five Plants That Transformed Mankind. unabr. ed. Henry Hobhouse. Narrated by Nelson Runger. 7 cass. (Running Time: 10 hrs. 30 mins.). 1988. 60.00 (978-1-55690-466-0(5), 87880E7) Recorded Bks.
A history of our civilizations through the discovery & use of various plants & medicines. Examples written are about how did quinine, tea, cotton, sugar & the potato change the face of world history? Five fascinating tales in which the unwitting heroes are plants & spices.

Seeds of Contemplation. Thomas Merton. 5 cass. 22.95 (918) Ignatius Pr.
Thoughts & meditations on a wide range of topics concerning the spiritual life.

***Seeds of Enlightenment.** Featuring Mukti. (ENG.). 2010. audio compact disk 40.00 (978-1-933986-78-4(6)) Open Gate Pub.

Seeds of Greatness. Denis Waitley. Read by Denis Waitley. 6 cass. 49.95 Set. (700A) Nightingale-Conant.

Seeds of Greatness. Denis E. Waitley. Intro. by A. E. Whyte. 1 cass. (Running Time: 66 min.). (Listen & Learn USA! Ser.). 8.95 (978-0-88684-063-1(5)) Listen USA.
Contains revealing truths about traits of highly successful people.

Seeds of Greatness: Inspirational Excerpts for Success. abr. ed. Patricia W. Carson. Read by Patricia W. Carson. 1 cass. (Running Time: 60 min.). 1999. 10.00 (978-1-928652-01-4(8)) Motivational OH.

Seeds of Light. 2000. 15.99 (978-0-7435-0570-3(0), Audioworks) S&S Audio.

Seeds of Praise. Contrib. by Seeds Music. Prod. by Jason Houser. Contrib. by Michael Hagerty et al. (J). (gr. 4-7). 2005. audio compact disk 9.99 (978-5-558-80673-1(7)) Pt of Grace Ent.

Seeds of Purpose. Contrib. by Seeds Music. (J). (gr. 4-7). 2005. audio compact disk 9.99 (978-5-558-80672-4(9)) Pt of Grace Ent.

***Seeds of Summer.** unabr. ed. Deborah Vogts. (Running Time: 8 hrs. 40 mins. 47 sec.). (Seasons of the Tallgrass Ser.). (ENG.). 2010. 10.99 (978-0-310-77352-8(0)) Zondervan.

Seeds of Terror: How Heroin Is Bankrolling the Taliban & Al Qaeda. Gretchen Peters. Read by Laural Merlington. (Playaway Top Adult Picks C Ser.). (ENG.). 2009. 59.99 (978-1-61574-554-8(8)) Find a World.

Seeds of Terror: How Heroin Is Bankrolling the Taliban & Al Qaeda. unabr. ed. Gretchen Peters. Read by Laural Merlington. 1 MP3-CD. (Running Time: 8 hrs. 0 mins. 0 sec.). (ENG.). 2009. 19.99 (978-1-4001-6293-2(9)); audio compact disk 59.99 (978-1-4001-4293-4(8)); audio compact disk 29.99 (978-1-4001-1293-7(1)) Pub: Tantor Media. Dist(s): IngramPubServ

Seeds of Transformation: Inspirational Messages on Personal & Planetary Healing. Paul Ferrini. 2005. audio compact disk 48.00 (978-1-879159-63-1(5)) Heartways Pr.

Seeds of Yesterday. unabr. ed. V. C. Andrews. Read by Donada Peters. 11 cass. (Running Time: 16 hrs. 30 mins.). 1989. 88.00 (978-0-7366-1602-7(0), 2463) Books on Tape.
Flowers in the Attic is the tale of four innocent children locked away from the world by a cruel mother. It continues with Petals on the Wind & If There be Thorns. Now V. C. Andrews has created the final dark chapter in this story of incest. Each episode has captivated millions.

Seeds That Grew to Be a Hundred & The Day the Little Children Came. Donald Busboom. 1 cass. (J). (ps-3). 1998. pap. bk. 13.00 (978-0-570-06836-5(3), 59KM2133) Concordia.

Seedtime & Harvest. Bill Winston. 4 cass. (Running Time: 3hr.02min.). (C). 1995. 20.00 (978-1-931289-19-1(0)) Pub: B Winston Min. Dist(s): Anchor Distributors

Seeing. unabr. ed. J. Krishnamurti & Eugene Schallert. Read by J. Krishnamurti & Eugene Schallert. Ed. by Krishnamurti Foundation of America Staff. 1 cass. (Running Time: 60 min.). 1992. 8.50 (ARES721) Krishnamurti.
J. Krishnamurti & Rev. Eugene Schallert discuss seeing. This dialogue was recorded February 17, 1972 at KPBS-TV in San Diego. This is the 1st of a two part dialogue.

Seeing. unabr. ed. Bill Myers. (Running Time: 8 hrs. 0 mins. 0 sec.). (Soul Tracker Ser.). (ENG.). 2007. 12.99 (978-0-310-27355-4(2)) Zondervan.

Seeing a Large Cat. Elizabeth Peters, pseud. Narrated by Barbara Rosenblat. 12 CDs. (Running Time: 14 hrs. 45 mins.). (Amelia Peabody Ser.: No. 9). audio compact disk 118.00 (978-0-7887-9853-5(7)) Recorded Bks.

Seeing a Large Cat. unabr. ed. Elizabeth Peters, pseud. Narrated by Barbara Rosenblat. 10 cass. (Running Time: 14 hrs. 45 mins.). (Amelia Peabody Ser.: No. 9). 1997. 90.00 (978-0-7887-1297-5(7), 95131E7) Recorded Bks.
Receiving an anonymous message warning her away from a tomb in the awesome Valley of the Kings, Amelia won't rest until she finds the forbidden burial site. But when she excavates an unusual mummy, she suddenly must outsmart a demented killer, a bogus spiritualist & a predatory debutante.

Seeing As God Sees. John Bytheway. 2009. audio compact disk 14.95 (978-1-60641-133-9(0)) Deseret Bk.

Seeing Clearly, As It Is. Swami Amar Jyoti. 1 cass. 1984. 9.95 (L-11) Truth Consciousness.
Karma at different levels of consciousness. In clear seeing, without projections, beautiful wisdom unfolds. Applying this to relationships, seeing them as they really are.

Seeing Ear. 7 cass. 60.00 (978-0-614-25227-9(X)) Pub: UWA Pub AUS. Dist(s): Intl Spec Bk

Seeing Eye to Eye. 2002. (978-0-7398-5161-6(6)) SteckVau.

Seeing Eye to Eye. Steck-Vaughn Staff. 2002. pap. bk. 41.60 (978-0-7398-6974-1(4)) SteckVau.

Seeing Eye to Eye Level 3. (J). 2002. audio compact disk (978-0-7398-5345-0(7)) SteckVau.

Seeing Glass: A Memoir, abr. ed. Jacqueline Gorman. Read by Susan Clark. 2 cass. (Running Time: 3 hrs.). 1997. 17.95 (978-1-57453-185-5(9)) Audio Lit.
A sudden, unexplained loss of vision forces Gorman to see her life through the inner eye of memory. She returns to the world of light with a new gratitude for the gift of sight & a renewed understanding of the power of love.

***Seeing God: Twelve Reliable Signs of True Spirituality.** unabr. ed. Gerald McDermott. Narrated by Michael Kramer. (ENG.). 2005. 16.98 (978-1-59644-141-5(0), Hovel Audio) christianaud.

Seeing God: Twelve Reliable Signs of True Spirituality. unabr. ed. Gerald R. McDermott. Narrated by Michael Kramer. 7 CDs. (Running Time: 7 hrs. 30 mins. 0 sec.). (ENG.). 2005. audio compact disk 26.98 (978-1-59644-140-8(2), Hovel Audio); lp 19.98 (978-1-59644-139-2(9), Hovel Audio) christianaud.
TV evangelist scandals. More varieties of Christianity that Baskin-Robbins has flavors. These are times of pluralism and disenchantment with organized religion. How do Christians today know which leaders and companions in faith to trust? For help, Gerald McDermott returns to the work of Jonathon Edwards, the eighteenth century preacher and college president widely regarded as the greatest American theologian ever. Edwards wrestled expertly with similar questions arising from frontier revivalism. Now McDermott, not only a leading Edwards scholar but also a master teacher, makes Edwarda??s insights accessible and practical for todaya??s Christians. Seeing God offers a clarifying glimpse at the signs of genuine Christianity- yesterday, today and for the ages.

Seeing in the Dark: How Backyard Stargazers Are Probing Deep Space & Guarding Earth from Interplanetary Peril. unabr. ed. Timothy Ferris. Read by Timothy Ferris. 8 cass. (Running Time: 6 hrs.). 2004. 34.95 (978-1-59007-275-2(8)); audio compact disk 49.95 (978-1-59007-276-9(6)) Pub: New Millenn Enter. Dist(s): PerseuPGW
A poetic love letter to science and to the skies, Ferris invites us all to become stargazers. He recounts his own experiences as an enthralled lifelong amateur astronomer, and reports from around the glove, from England and Italy to the Florida Keys and the Chilean Andes, on the revolution that's putting millions in touch with the night sky. In addition, Ferris offers an authoritative and engaging report on what's out there to be seen, what Saturn, the Ring nebula, the Silver Coin galaxy and the Virgo supercluster really are, and how to find them.

***Seeing in the Dark: Myths & Stories to Reclaim the Buried, Knowing Woman.** Clarissa Pinkola Estes. (Running Time: 2:00:00). 2010. 19.95 (978-1-59179-969-6(4)) Sounds True.

Seeing Is Believing. unabr. ed. E. X. Ferrars. Read by Diana Bishop. 4 cass. (Running Time: 5 hrs. 15 min.). 1995. 44.95 (978-1-85695-754-0(3), 950605) Pub: ISIS Audio GBR. Dist(s): Ulverscroft US
The retired headmaster Malcolm Chance, lives quietly with his wife. However, his well-deserved & long awaited peace is rudely shattered when their next door neighbor, Peter Loxley, is shot to death in his own home while his wife Avril is in London. At first, suspicion centers on Fred Dyer, the local handyman, who was not only seen entering the Loxley house. Then it is discovered that Avril's marriage was floundering. It begins to look as though those with a motive for murder are almost as numerous as the passions that have been seething under the surface of an outwardly calm village life.

Seeing Life As It Is. unabr. ed. Perf. by Eknath Easwaran. 1 cass. (Running Time: 1 hr.). 1983. 7.95 (978-1-58638-604-7(2)) Nilgiri Pr.

Seeing Redd. Frank Beddor. Narrated by Gerard Doyle. 7 CDs. (Running Time: 32580 sec.). (Looking Glass Wars Trilogy: Bk. 2). (ENG.). (YA). (gr. 7-12). 2007. audio compact disk 34.95 (978-0-545-02387-0(4)) Scholastic Inc.

Seeing Redd. unabr. ed. Frank Beddor. Read by Gerard Doyle. (Looking Glass Wars Trilogy: Bk. 2). (YA). 2007. 54.99 (978-1-60252-793-5(8)) Find a World.

Seeing Redd. unabr. ed. Frank Beddor. Read by Gerard Doyle. (Running Time: 32580 sec.). (Looking Glass Wars Trilogy: Bk. 2). (ENG.). (YA). (gr. 7-12). 2007. audio compact disk 74.95 (978-0-545-02388-7(2)) Scholastic Inc.

Seeing Self-Interest As the Root of Fear. J. Krishnamurti. 1 cass. (Running Time: 75 min.). (Saanen, Switzerland Talks - 1985 Ser.: No. 3). 8.50 (AST853) Krishnamurti.
Why have we such deep rooted self-interest? Is self-interest a fence of self-protection to ward off any hurt?.

Seeing Stone. unabr. ed. Kevin Crossley-Holland. Read by Michael Maloney. 6 vols. (Running Time: 7 hrs. 53 mins.). (Young Adult Cassette Librariestm Ser.). (J). (gr. 6 up). 2004. pap. bk. 48.00 (978-0-8072-0999-8(6), S YA 327 SP, Listening Lib); 40.00 (978-0-8072-0546-4(X), Listening Lib) Random Audio Pubg.
It is 1199 and young Arthur de Caldicot is waiting impatiently to grow up and become a knight. One day his father's friend, Merlin, gives him a shining piece of obsidian and his life becomes entwined with that of his namesake, the Arthur whose story he sees unfold in the stone.

Seeing the Father's Heart. Steve Thompson. 1 cass. (Running Time: 90 mins.). (He Still Heals Ser.: Vol. 7). 2000. 5.00 (SAO1-007) Morning NC.
Learn about the healing power of God that is available to believers today.

Seeing the Franklin D. Roosevelt Home & Museum with Julian Padowicz, Julian Padowicz. Read by Julian Padowicz. 5 cass. (Running Time: 6 hrs. 10 mins.). 2000. 24.95 (978-1-881288-26-8(9)) BusnFilm Intl.
The story of Franklin & Eleanor Roosevelt,the world they lived in & the history they made, told through the exhibits.

Seeing the Multitudes. Francis Frangipane. 8 cass. (Running Time: 12 hrs.). 2000. 40.00 (FF07-000) Morning NC.
From the beatitudes, Francis draws applications for ministry to those who need Jesus.

Seeing Things. unabr. ed. Robin Klein. Read by Marcella Russo. 6 cass. (Running Time: 6 hrs.). 2002. (978-1-74030-042-1(4), 591114) Bolinda Pubng AUS.
It was strange how staring at things could alter their appearance, Miranda thought. It was weird how she could transmute quite ordinary things into images. Trouble is, it soon gets out of hand & it's about time they all discovered what is really going on.

Seeing Things: An Autobiography. Oliver Postgate. (ENG., 2001. (978-0-333-90727-6(2)) Macmillan UK GBR.

Seeing Things As They Are. Swami Amar Jyoti. 1 cass. 1979. 9.95 (P-25) Truth Consciousness.
A fresh approach without rejecting anything. The spiritual, initiated way of looking at the reality of things. Going by the "empty way".

***Seeing Through Death.** Barry Long. 2006. 17.95 (978-1-899324-22-4(4)) Pub: B Long Bks. Dist(s): AtlasBooks

Seeing Through Death: Facing the Fact Without Fear. Barry Long. 1 cass. (Running Time: 1 hr. 29 min.). (ENG.). 1996. audio compact disk 13.95 (978-1-899324-04-0(6)) Pub: B Long Bks. Dist(s): AtlasBooks
Helps you discover the reality of death & prepares you for the moment when death comes.

Seeing Through Native Eyes: Understanding the Language of Nature. Jon Young. Read by Jon Young. 6 cass. (Running Time: 9 hrs.). 1996. 49.95 Set. (978-1-57994-000-3(5), A1107) Owlink.
Weaves natural science & native philosophy & lore. Tracking, the language of birds, survival skills & trees, medicinal & edible plants, ecology, hazards of the wilderness & more.

Seeing Through Native Eyes - CD Collection: Understanding the Language of Nature. Jon Young. 2004. audio compact disk 67.95 (978-1-57994-017-1(X)) Owlink.

Seeing Through the Eyes of God. David Cooper. 2007. audio compact disk 69.95 (978-1-59179-592-6(3)) Sounds True.

Seeing Through the Game. 1 cass. (Running Time: 29 min.). 12.00 (L350) MEA A Watts Cass.

Seeing Tomorrow Today: Daniel 2:31-49. Ed Young. 1995. 4.95 (978-0-7417-2068-9(X), 1068) Win Walk.

Seeing What's Next: Using the Theories of Innovation to Predict Industry Change. unabr. ed. Clayton M. Christensen et al. Narrated by Joel Leffert. 8 cass. (Running Time: 11 hrs. 30 mins.). 2004. 89.75 (978-1-4193-1270-0(7), 97895MC) Recorded Bks.

Seeing with an Eye of Faith. Grant Von Harrison. Read by Ted Gibbons. 2 cass. (Personal Enrichment Ser.). 10.95 Jackman Pubng.
An essay on faith.

Seeing Without Glasses. 4 cass. (Running Time: 4 hrs.). 39.95 (978-0-941831-44-4(2)) Beyond Words Pub.

Seeing You Have a Woman see Twentieth-Century Poetry in English, No. 27, Recordings of Poets Reading Their Own Poetry

Seek. Paul Fleischman. 2 cass. (Running Time: 2 hrs. 42 mins.). (YA). (gr. 7 up). 2004. 23.00 (978-0-8072-0821-2(3), Listening Lib) Random Audio Pubg.
Told in a collage of voices describes Rob Radkovitz's search for his father, a search pursued not through San Francisco's streets, but through the labyrinth of the airwaves. Psychic readers, baseball announcers, pirate DJs, friends, and teachers join a rich, ringing aural autobiography that's as joyfully comic as it is compelling.

Seek. Paul Fleischman. Read by Paul Fleischman. 2 vols. (Running Time: 2 hrs. 42 mins.). (J). (gr. 7 up). 2004. pap. bk. 29.00 (978-0-8072-2285-0(2), Listening Lib) Random Audio Pubg.

Seek a New Dawn. E. V. Thompson. 11 CDs. (Running Time: 13 hrs.). (Soundings (CDs) Ser.). (J). 2005. audio compact disk 99.95 (978-1-84559-145-8(3)) Pub: ISIS Lrg Prnt GBR. Dist(s): Ulverscroft US

Seek a New Dawn. unabr. ed. E. V. Thompson. Read by Anne Dover. 12 cass. (Running Time: 13 hrs. 30 mins.). (Sound Ser.). 2002. 94.95 (978-1-84283-168-7(2)) Pub: UlverLrgPrint GBR. Dist(s): Ulverscroft US
When the Cornish copper mines close down at the end of the 1870s, Sam Hooper, like many men, sets sail for Austrailia in order to seek his fortune. But his hopes of taking his love, Emily, with him, are dashed by her father. Emily is not to be thwarted, however, and when her father dies, she decides to go to Australia and hung down Sam. On arriving at Kadina, however, Emily hears that Sam is married.

Seek after These Things. 2004. audio compact disk 14.95 (978-1-59156-327-3(5)) Covenant Comms.

Seek First the Kingdom. Paul Ferrini. Read by Paul Ferrini. 1 cass. (Running Time: 1 hrs. 30 mins.). (Christ Mind Talks & Workshops Ser.). 1997. audio compact disk 10.00 (978-1-879159-30-3(9)) Heartways Pr.
A talk given at Agape International Center of Truth in May 1997.

***Seek Me with All Your Heart.** unabr. ed. Beth Wiseman. (Running Time: 8 hrs. 45 mins. 0 sec.). (ENG.). 2010. audio compact disk 24.98 (978-1-59644-995-4(0)) christianaud.

Seek My Face. John Updike. Read by Kathryn Walker. 2002. audio compact disk 64.00 (978-0-7366-8846-8(3)) Books on Tape.

Seek My Face. unabr. ed. John Updike. 7 cass. (Running Time: 10 hrs. 30 mins.). 2002. 48.00 (978-0-7366-8845-1(5)) Books on Tape.

Seek That Which Is Above. unabr. ed. Joseph Ratzinger. Read by Al Covaia. 2 cass. 9.95 (940) Ignatius Pr.
A collection of meditations for the liturgical seasons & feasts, many for Eastertide.

Seek the Things That Are above. Read by Basilea Schlink. 1 cass. (Running Time: 30 min.). 1985. (0270) Evang Sisterhood Mary.
The Ascension of our Lord Jesus, as a challenge to His disciples to live for the heavenly goal; the joy of following Jesus.

Seeker. abr. ed. William Nicholson. Read by Michael Page. (Running Time: 4 hrs.). (Noble Warriors Trilogy: Bk. 1). 2007. audio compact disk 14.99 (978-1-4233-1838-5(2), 9781423318385, BCD Value Price) Brilliance Audio.

Seeker. unabr. ed. William Nicholson. Read by Michael Page. (Running Time: 36000 sec.). (Noble Warriors Trilogy: Bk. 1). (YA). (gr. 7-12). 2006. 82.25 (978-1-4233-1839-2(0), 9781423318392, BriAudUnabridg); audio compact disk 97.25 (978-1-4233-1840-8(4), 9781423318408, BriAudCD Unabrid) Brilliance Audio.
On the rocky island of Anacrea, in a garden within the great castle-monastery called the Nom, lives the All and Only, the god who made all things. He is protected by an elite band of fighter monks. These are the Nomana, the Noble Warriors. Seeker, who lives on the island, is now sixteen, at last old enough to follow his brother into the ranks of the Nomana. Far away, Morning Star, also just sixteen, is leaving home to achieve her lifelong wish to join the Nomana. And when a beautiful, violent river bandit know as the Wildman finds himself helpless before two Nomana, he, too, is determined to become a Noble Warrior. But these are dangerous times. Secret enemies have swom to destroy Anacrea, and in the imperial city of Radiance, where human sacrifices are thrown to their deaths every evening, elaborate plans to attack the Nom are in place. Soon, in a shocking turn of events, Seeker, Morning Star, and the Wildman are caught up in a bloody and harrowing race to save the Nomana - and themselves - from destruction.

Seeker. unabr. ed. William Nicholson. Read by Michael Page. (Running Time: 36000 sec.). (Noble Warriors Trilogy: Bk. 1). (YA). (gr. 7-12). 2006. audio compact disk 39.25 (978-1-4233-1841-5(2), 9781423318415, Brlnc Audio MP3 Lib); audio compact disk 24.95 (978-1-4233-1836-1(6), 9781423318361, Brilliance MP3) Brilliance Audio.

***Seeker: A Novel.** unabr. ed. Ann H. Gabhart. Narrated by Renee Ertl. (Running Time: 11 hrs. 49 mins. 40 sec.). (ENG.). 2010. 25.89 (978-1-60814-676-5(6)); audio compact disk 36.99 (978-1-59859-725-7(6)) Oasis Audio.

Seeker: Book One of the Noble Warriors. unabr. ed. William Nicholson. Read by Michael Page. (Running Time: 36000 sec.). (Noble Warriors Trilogy: Bk. 1). (YA). (gr. 7-12). 2006. audio compact disk 29.95 (978-1-4233-1835-4(8), 9781423318354) Brilliance Audio.

Seeker: Book One of the Noble Warriors. unabr. ed. William Nicholson. Read by Michael Page. (Running Time: 10 hrs.). (Noble Warriors Ser.). 2006. 39.25 (978-1-4233-1843-9(9), 9781423318439, BADLE); 24.95 (978-1-4233-1842-2(0), 9781423318422, BAD) Brilliance Audio.

Seeker & Social Values. Swami Amar Jyoti. 1 cass. 1989. 9.95 (M-99) Truth Consciousness.
The right way to deal with social valuations. "The true victory is over the self, not over others".

***Seeker Small Groups: Engaging Spiritual Seekers in Life-Changing Discussions.** Garry Poole. (Running Time: 11 hrs. 2 mins. 0 sec.). (ENG.). 2009. 21.99 (978-0-310-30515-6(2)) Zondervan.

Seekers. David Freudberg. Perf. by Howard Thurman et al. 6 cass. (Running Time: 6 hrs.). (Kindred Spirits Ser.: Vol. 2). 1983. 24.95 Set. (978-0-9640914-5-0(3)) Human Media.
A listening library of spiritual wisdom from the world's great traditions. Contains such wisdom from Rev. Howard Thurman; Robert Muller, Asst. Secretary General of the U.N.; M.R. Bawa Muhaiyaddeen, the luminous Sufi; Rev. Fred Rogers (Mr. Rogers), & others.

Seekers. abr. ed. Paul A. Hawkins. Read by Ben Hall. 4 cass. (Running Time: 6 hrs.). 2000. 24.95 (978-1-890990-50-3(7), 99050) Otis Audio.

Seekers. abr. ed. John Jakes. Read by Bruce Watson. 4 cass. (Running Time: 6 hrs.). (Kent Family Chronicles: No. 3). 2000. 12.99 (978-1-57815-162-2(7), 4411, Media Bks Audio) Media Bks NJ.

Seekers. unabr. collector's ed. John Jakes. Read by Michael Kramer. 13 cass. (Running Time: 19 hrs. 30 min.). (Kent Family Chronicles: No. 3). 1993. 104.00 (978-0-7366-2403-9(1), 3172) Books on Tape.
End of the colonies' fight for independence ushers in a new era for the Kent family.

Seekers: The Story of Man's Continuing Quest to Understand His World. abr. ed. Daniel J. Boorstin. Read by Denis DeBoisblanc. 4 cass. (Running Time: 4 hrs.). 1998. 22.95 (978-1-55935-284-0(1)) Soundelux.
A history of the greatest western heritage of ideas, told through the lives of those who still speak to us from Moses, Aristotle, & Plato, through Thucydydes, Thomas More, Machiavelli, & Voltaire, to Karl Marx, Carlyle, Emerson, & Einstein - to mention a few.

Seekers: The Story of Man's Continuing Quest to Understand His World. unabr. ed. Daniel J. Boorstin. Read by Michael Prichard. 10 cass. (Running Time: 15 hrs.). 1999. 80.00 (978-0-7366-4307-8(9), 4798) Books on Tape.
Describes people searching for an understanding of human existence. "Man is the asking animal," notes the author. It begins with the prophets of the Holy Land, the philosophers of ancient Greece, continues through the Renaissance & concludes with the modern era of the social sciences.

Seekers: The Story of Man's Continuing Quest to Understand His World. unabr. ed. Daniel J. Boorstin. Read by Donald Monat. 10 cass. (Running Time: 15 hrs.). 1998. 39.95 (978-1-57511-049-3(0)) Pub Mills.
Comprehensive overview of man's search for the meaning of life through the disciplines of philosophy & religion.

Seeker's Commitment. Swami Amar Jyoti. 1 cass. 1987. 9.95 (M-71) Truth Consciousness.
The life of the seeker, a different dimension. Dealing with the subconscious mind: the return journey . Education for life's purpose. Renunciation & strength. Looking to higher guidance.

***Seekers of the Supernatural Conversations with Ed & Lorraine Warren: Seekers of the Supernatural.** Seekers of the Supernatural LLC. (ENG.). 2010. 19.99 (978-0-9819624-6-7(7)) OmniMedia.

***Seekers #1: The Quest Begins.** unabr. ed. Erin Hunter. Read by Julia Fletcher. (ENG.). 2008. (978-0-06-157550-1(X)); (978-0-06-163057-6(8)) HarperCollins Pubs.

***Seekers #2: Great Bear Lake.** unabr. ed. Erin Hunter. Read by Julia Fletcher. (ENG.). 2009. (978-0-06-171507-5(7)); (978-0-06-172981-2(7)) HarperCollins Pubs.

***Seekers #3: Smoke Mountain.** unabr. ed. Erin Hunter. Read by Julia Fletcher. (ENG.). 2009. (978-0-06-184551-2(5)); (978-0-06-190181-2(4)) HarperCollins Pubs.

***Seekers #4: the Last Wilderness.** unabr. ed. Erin Hunter. Read by Julia Fletcher. (ENG.). 2010. (978-0-06-193824-5(6)); (978-0-06-196926-3(5)) HarperCollins Pubs.

***Seekers #5: Fire in the Sky.** unabr. ed. Erin Hunter. (ENG.). 2011. (978-0-06-206737-1(0)) HarperCollins Pubs.

***Seekers #6: Spirits in the Stars.** unabr. ed. Erin Hunter. (ENG.). 2011. (978-0-06-206733-3(8)) HarperCollins Pubs.

Seeking & Finding God (Audiobook CD) In Search of the True Faith. Dave Hunt. (Running Time: 4 hrs.). (ENG.). 2005. audio compact disk 16.99 (978-1-928660-40-8(1)) Pub: Berean Call. Dist(s): STL Dist NA

Seeking Beyond the Good Life. Swami Amar Jyoti. 1 dolby cass. 1983. 9.95 (A-27) Truth Consciousness.
The good life is not the supreme stage of being. A higher outlook. Full manhood on this earth.

Seeking God. Edd Anthony. 1 CD. (Running Time: 1 hr. 9 min.). 2003. audio compact disk 16.95 (978-1-881586-08-1(1)) Canticle Cass.

Seeking Him: Songs for Worship. Created by Life Action Ministries. (ENG.). 2004. audio compact disk 16.99 (978-0-940110-55-7(5)) Life Action Publishing.

Seeking Peace. Speeches. 6. (Running Time: 6 hrs). 2004. (978-0-9725627-7-5(X)); audio compact disk (978-0-9725627-8-2(8)) Medio Media Pubng.

Seeking Peace: Chronicles of the Worst Buddhist in the World. unabr. ed. Mary Pipher. Read by Kymberly Dakin. 1 MP3-CD. (Running Time: 8 hrs.). 2009. 39.97 (978-1-4233-8287-4(0), 9781423382874, Brlnc Audio MP3 Lib); 39.97 (978-1-4233-8289-8(7), 9781423382898, BADLE); 24.99 (978-1-4233-8286-7(2), 9781423382867, Brilliance MP3); 24.99 (978-1-4233-8288-1(9), 9781423382881, BAD); audio compact disk 82.97 (978-1-4233-8285-0(4), 9781423382850, BriAudCD Unabrid); audio compact disk 29.99 (978-1-4233-8284-3(6), 9781423382843, Bril Audio CD Unabri) Brilliance Audio.

Seeking Personal Guidance. unabr. ed. Robert A. Monroe. Read by Robert A. Monroe. (Running Time: 45 min.). (Explorer Ser.). 1987. 12.95 (978-1-56113-031-3(1), 32) Monroe Institute.
Explorer speaks about getting in touch with inner guidance.

Seeking the Ancestor: The Spiritual Search for Our Indigenous Root. Fred Gustafson. 2 cass. (Running Time: 3 hrs.). 1995. 18.95 set. (978-0-7822-0483-4(X), 559) C G Jung IL.
There is much interest today in indigenous cultures & particularly, on our soil, in Native Americans. Why this is so raises the issue of projection & what the American consciousness is now seeking. This seminar explores how we got to where we are. It looks at the projections that are both barriers to & opportunities for self discovery & at what the indigenous life really means. The seminar also includes a special sharing of the cosmology & ceremonial life of the Lakota (Sioux) & a discussion of how these interface with a Judeo-Christian western view.

Seeking the Gifts of Faith, Healing, Miracles, & Helps & Governments. unabr. ed. Duane S. Crowther. Read by Duane S. Crowther. 1 cass. (Running Time: 90 min.). 1998. 13.98 (978-0-88290-530-3(9), 1835) Horizon Utah.
Faith, faith to heal others, faith to be healed, miracles, & helps & governments are five important gifts specifically promised to the saints in the scriptures. Shows the scripturally based keys for acquiring them. True experiences cited.

Seeking the Gifts of Testimony, Knowledge, & Wisdom. unabr. ed. Duane S. Crowther. Read by Duane S. Crowther. 1 cass. (Running Time: 90 min.). 1998. 13.98 (978-0-88290-529-7(5), 1832) Horizon Utah.
Strengthens every listener's testimony of the Savior & his atonement & of spiritual gifts by presenting insights in four main areas including witnesses of personal knowledge that Jesus Christ is the Son of God & testimonies of his latter-day appearance.

Seeking the Inner Light. Swami Amar Jyoti. 1 cass. 1980. 9.95 (I-12) Truth Consciousness.
Everyone is seeking, consciously or unconsciously. Meditating on That alone. 'Thou art that Light & that Light is everywhere'.

Seeking the Truth. Swami Amar Jyoti. 1 cass. 1976. 9.95 (M-56) Truth Consciousness.
Truth is always available to everyone who is open to it. Truth seekers in humblest form, like children returning to the Father's house.

Seeking to Awaken. Swami Amar Jyoti. 1 cass. 1988. 9.95 (M-94) Truth Consciousness.
Direct & indirect knowledge; the role of questions. Putting energy into our awakening. Focus on the Highest. Finding our minus points & correcting them.

Seeking Wealth. Blaine Yorgason & Brenton Yorgason. Read by Marvin Payne. 1 cass. (Gospel Power Ser.). 6.95 (978-0-929985-49-7(4)) Jackman Pubng.
A father's letter to his son regarding using wealth under God's direction.

Seeking What We Already Are. Swami Amar Jyoti. 1 dolby cass. 1985. 9.95 (R-64) Truth Consciousness.
Discovering our inherent perfection. What is "want" & what is "renunciation"? Understanding is relaxing, coming in tune, direct communication.

Seems, the - the Glitch in Sleep. unabr. ed. John Hulme & Michael Wexler. Read by Oliver Wyman. (J). 2007. 49.99 (978-1-60252-932-8(9)) Find a World.

Seen It All & Done the Rest. unabr. ed. Pearl Cleage. Read by Robin Miles. (YA). 2008. 74.99 (978-1-60514-960-8(8)) Find a World.

Seen It All & Done the Rest: A Novel. unabr. ed. Pearl Cleage. Narrated by Robin Miles. 9 CDs. (Running Time: 10 hrs.). 2008. audio compact disk 89.95 (978-0-7927-5221-9(X)) AudioGO.
The toast of Europe, Josephine Evans had spent thirty years abroad establishing her reputation as one of the finest actresses of her generation. In Amsterdam, she redefined who and what an African American diva could be, and her legions of loyal fans loved her for it. But when a war she didn't even understand suddenly makes her the target of angry anti-American protests, Josephine is forced to return to America to see if she can find a new definition of home. Camping out with her granddaughter in Atlanta's West End, Josephine tries to reclaim her old life even as she scrambles to shape her new one. An unexpected reunion with an old friend, Abbie Allen Browning, soon offers her a chance to set things right. Rallying with Abbie against an unscrupulous land developer who threatens to tear the community apart, Josephine finds herself playing the most important role of her life, as she shows her neighbors what courage really is and learns the real meaning of coming home.

Seen It All & Done the Rest Uab. unabr. ed. Pearl Cleage. Narrated by Robin Miles. (ENG.). 2008. audio compact disk 29.95 (978-1-60283-341-8(9)) Pub: AudioGO. Dist(s): Perseus Dist

Seer of Shadows. unabr. ed. Avi. Narrated by Steven Boyer. 5 cass. (Running Time: 5 hrs. 45 mins.). (J). (gr. 5-7). 2008. 33.75 (978-1-4361-3725-6(X)); audio compact disk 46.75 (978-1-4361-3730-0(6)) Recorded Bks.

Sees Behind Trees. Michael Dorris. 2 cass. (J). 2000. 13.58 (398422) NewSound.
Set in sixteenth century America, Walnut, a Native American boy cannot see as well with his eyes as the others. He uses his senses to meet challenges. This earns him respect of others, as well as his adult name.

Sees Behind Trees, unabr. ed. Michael Dorris. Read by Joseph Bruchac. 2 cass. (Running Time: 2 hrs.). (J). (gr. 1-8). 1999. 23.00 (LL 0115, Chivers Child Audio) AudioGO.

Sees Behind Trees. unabr. ed. Michael Dorris. Read by Joseph Bruchac. 2 cass. (Running Time: 2 hrs.). (YA). 1999. 16.98 (FS9-34632) Highsmith.

Sees Behind Trees. unabr. ed. Michael Dorris. Read by Joseph Bruchac. 2 cass. (Running Time: 2 hrs. 29 mins.). (J). (gr. 4-6). 1998. pap. bk. 28.00 (978-0-8072-7957-1(9), YA949SP, Listening Lib) Random Audio Pubg.
A young Indian learns how to gain the respect of his people.

Sees Behind Trees. unabr. ed. Michael Dorris. Read by Joseph Bruchac. 2 cass. (Running Time: 2 hrs. 29 mins.). (J). (gr. 4-7). 1998. 23.00 (978-0-8072-7956-4(0), YA949CX, Listening Lib) Random Audio Pubg.

Sefiras Haomer - The Inner Count. Shira Smiles. 1 cass. (Running Time: 90 mins.). 1999. 6.00 (R60FB) Torah Umesorah.

Segregated Scholars: Black Social Scientists & the Creation of Black Labor Studies, 1890-1950. Francille Rusan Wilson. (Carter G. Woodson Institute Ser.). (ENG.). 2008. 22.50 (978-0-8139-2788-6(9)) U Pr of Va.

segundo Cumpleanos. (Saludos Ser.: Vol. 2). (SPA.). (gr. 2-3). 10.00 (978-0-7635-5879-6(6)) Rigby Educ.

Segundo Curso, Selected Readings with Program Notes. Holt, Rinehart and Winston Staff. (SPA.). 1997. 34.20 (978-0-03-095170-1(4)) Holt McDoug.

Segundo Dunes. Contrib. by Nancy Pearlman. 1 cass. (Running Time: 29 min.). 10.00 (102) Educ Comm CA.

***Seismic Shifts: The Little Changes That Make a Big Difference in Your Life.** Kevin G. Harney. (Running Time: 10 hrs. 40 mins. 0 sec.). (ENG.). 2009. 16.99 (978-0-310-30516-3(0)) Zondervan.

***Seize the Fire.** abr. ed. Adam Nicolson. Read by Adam Nicolson. (ENG.). 2005. (978-0-06-087935-8(1), Harper Audio); (978-0-06-087934-1(3), Harper Audio) HarperCollins Pubs.

Seize the Fire: Heroism, Duty, & the Battle of Trafalgar. abr. ed. Adam Nicolson. Read by Adam Nicolson. 2005. audio compact disk 29.95 (978-0-06-082484-6(0)) HarperCollins Pubs.

Seize the Night. unabr. ed. Dean Koontz. Read by Keith Szarabajka. 11 CDs. (Running Time: 14 hrs.). 2007. audio compact disk 96.00 (978-1-4159-3606-1(4)) Books on Tape.

Seize the Night, unabr. ed. Dean Koontz. Read by Keith Szarabajka. 10 cass. (Running Time: 10 hrs.). 1999. 39.95 (FS9-43278) Highsmith.

Seize the Night. unabr. ed. Dean Koontz. Read by Keith Szarabajka. (Dean Koontz Ser.). (ENG.). 2007. audio compact disk 29.95 (978-0-7393-4137-7(5), Random AudioBks) Pub: Random Audio Pubg. Dist(s): Random

Seizing the Enigma: The Race to Break the German U-Boat Codes, 1939-1943. unabr. ed. David Kahn. Read by Bernard Mayes. 10 cass. (Running Time: 14 hrs. 30 mins.). 1995. 69.95 (978-0-7861-0653-0(0), 1556) Blckstn Audio.
Provides the definitive account of how British & American codebreakers fought a war of wits against Nazi naval communications - & helped lead the Allies to victory in the crucial Battle of the Atlantic.

Seizure. unabr. ed. Robin Cook. 11 cass. Library ed. (Running Time: 15 hrs.). 2003. 98.00 (978-1-4025-2845-3(0)) Recorded Bks.

Seizure. unabr. collector's ed. Robin Cook. Narrated by George Guidall. 10 cass. (Running Time: 15 hrs.). 2003. 44.95 (978-1-4025-2846-0(9)) Recorded Bks.
Senator Ashley Butler is a notorious political icon of the South. His fervid support of America¿s traditional family values includes a kill-on-contact policy toward all pro-biotechnology legislation. When a subcommittee is created to introduce new legislation outlawing the rising swell of cloning technology, the senator knows that, by serving as chairman, he¿s found the key to continued political power.

Seizure. unabr. collector's ed. Robin Cook. Narrated by George Guidall. 12 CDs. (Running Time: 15 hrs.). 2004. audio compact disk 49.95 (978-1-4025-7719-2(2), CC016) Recorded Bks.

Seldom Disappointed: A Memoir. Tony Hillerman. Narrated by Tony Hillerman. 11 CDs. (Running Time: 12 hrs. 30 mins.). audio compact disk 111.00 (978-1-4025-2074-7(3)) Recorded Bks.

Seldom Disappointed: A Memoir. Tony Hillerman. Narrated by Tony Hillerman. 9 cass. (Running Time: 12 hrs. 30 mins.). 2001. 81.00 (978-1-4025-1175-2(2), 96709) Recorded Bks.
In the pages of his memoir, his fans will find the answer to the question he is most often asked: how does he know so much about Native American culture? But they will also hear about the rich life that extends far beyond the world of his novel.

Seleccion. 1 cass. (Running Time: 1 hr.). (SPA.). (gr. k up). 2000. 48.99 (978-0-673-64880-8(X)) Addson-Wesley Educ.
Readings of every Pupil Edition selection are presented at a pace that children can follow as they read along.

Select Readings. Jean Bernard & Linda Lee. 2006. audio compact disk 24.50 (978-0-19-439128-3(0)) OUP.

Select Readings. Linda Lee & Erik Gundersen. 2006. audio compact disk 24.50 (978-0-19-439127-6(2)) OUP.

Select Readings. Linda Lee et al. 2004. audio compact disk 24.50 (978-0-19-439126-9(4)) OUP.

Select Your Ideal Future. Bruce Goldberg. (ENG.). 2005. audio compact disk 17.00 (978-1-57968-090-9(9)) Pub: B Goldberg. Dist(s): Baker Taylor

Select Your Ideal Future. Bruce Goldberg. Read by Bruce Goldberg. 1 cass. (Running Time: 25 min.). (ENG.). 2007. 13.00 (978-1-885577-31-3(1)) Pub: B Goldberg. Dist(s): Baker Taylor
Through hypnotic age regression, Dr. Goldberg guides the listener into five future paths to choose the ideal future. Switch tracks to this ideal path.

***Selected American Short Stories.** Washington Irving et al. Narrated by John MacDonald et al. (ENG.). 2010. audio compact disk 16.95 (978-1-60646-136-5(2)) Audio Bk Con.

Selected American Short Stories, unabr. ed. Mark Twain et al. Read by Grover Gardner et al. 2 cass. (Running Time: 3 hrs.). Incl. Black Cat. Edgar Allan Poe. Read by Flo Gibson.; Chickamauga. Ambrose Bierce.; Mission of Jane. Edith Wharton.; Specter Bridegroom. Washington Irving.; Stolen White Elephant. Mark Twain.; 1999. 14.95 (978-1-55685-030-1(1)) Audio Bk Con.
Exciting adventure & humor with Irving's "The Specter Bridegroom", Twain's "The Stolen White Elephant", Bierce's "Chickamauga", Wharton's "The Mission of Jane" & Poe's "The Black Cat".

Selected Bosh. Edward Lear. Read by Alan Bennett. 1 cass. (Running Time: 40 min.). (J). (gr. 1 up). 9.00 (CC/043) C to C Cassettes.
A collection fo limericks & nonsense songs from the true master of bosh, that will appeal to both children & their parents.

Selected Canterbury Tales. Geoffrey Chaucer. Narrated by David Cutler. (Running Time: 32880 sec.). (Unabridged Classics in MP3 Ser.). (ENG.). 2008. audio compact disk 26.00 (978-1-58472-507-7(9), In Aud) Sound Room.

Selected Cases of Sherlock Holmes. Arthur Conan Doyle. Narrated by Grover Gardner. (ENG.). 2009. audio compact disk 16.95 (978-1-60646-101-3(X)) Audio Bk Con.

Selected Cases of Sherlock Holmes, unabr. ed. Arthur Conan Doyle. Read by Grover Gardner. 2 cass. (Running Time: 3 hrs. 30 min.). Incl. Adventure of the Greek Philosopher; Adventure of the Six Napoleons. Arthur Conan Doyle.; Adventure of the Speckled Band. Arthur Conan Doyle.; Selected Cases of Sherlock Holmes. Arthur Conan Doyle. Read by Grover Gardner.; Selected Cases of Sherlock Holmes. Arthur Conan Doyle. Read by Grover Gardner.; 1984. 14.95 (978-1-55685-031-8(X)) Audio Bk Con.
"The Adventure of the Speckled Band", "The Adventure of the Greek Philosopher" & "The Adventure of the six Napoleons".

Selected European Short Stories. Guy de Maupassant et al. Narrated by Flo Gibson et al. 2008. audio compact disk 16.95 (978-1-60646-064-1(1)) Audio Bk Con.

Selected European Short Stories, unabr. ed. Guy de Maupassant et al. Read by Grover Gardner et al. 2 cass. (Running Time: 2 hrs.). Incl. Duel. Guy de Maupassant.; Open Window. Saki. Read by Flo Gibson.; Scandal Monger. Anton Chekhov.; Schartz-Metterklume Method. Saki. Read by Flo Gibson.; Story-Teller. Saki. Read by Flo Gibson.; Umbrella. Guy de Maupassant.; Wardrobe. Thomas Mann.; 1984. 14.95 (978-1-55685-032-5(8)) Audio Bk Con.
Classic favorites, including "The Duel", "The Umbrella", The Schartz-Metterklume Method", The Open Window", The Story Teller", The Scandal monger", "Verochka" & "The Wardrobe".

Selected Issues in Criminal Trial Evidence. Read by Joseph Carson et al. (Running Time: 2 hrs. 30 min.). 1991. 70.00 Incl. 56p. tape materials. (CR-54189) Cont Ed Bar-CA.

Selected Issues in Employment Law Practice (91-92) Read by Cliff Palefsky et al. (Running Time: 2 hrs. 45 min.). 1991. 89.00 Incl. tape materials. (BU-55210) Cont Ed Bar-CA.
Experienced panelists, representing both employers & employees, bring you the latest developments while focusing more closely on landmark cases & hot issues in the field. Covers employment discrimination; workplace safety & health issues; Americans with Disabilities Act; wrongful termination; & related issues. New statutory requirements (IIPPs, Corporate Criminal Liability Act, ADA); arbitration (Gilmer); prohibition against sex-specific fetal protection policies (UAW v Johnson Controls); drug testing & privacy; sexual harassment; & wrongful termination.

Selected Issues in Search & Seizure Practice. Read by William Ridgeway et al. (Running Time: 2 hrs. 30 min.). 1991. 89.00 (CR-55291) Cont Ed Bar-CA.

Selected Just So Stories. Rudyard Kipling. (Running Time: 0 hr. 54 mins. 0 sec.). (PlainTales Classics Ser.). (ENG.). (J). (gr. k-2). 2009. audio compact disk 12.95 (978-0-9819032-6-2(6)) Pub: PlainTales. Dist(s): IPG Chicago

Selected Poems. Emily Dickinson. 1 cass. 1996. bk. & pap. bk. 5.95 (29118-9) Dover.

Selected Poems. Josephine Jacobsen. Read by Josephine Jacobsen. 1 cass. (Running Time: 28 min.). (Watershed Tapes of Contemporary Poetry). 1977. 10.95 (23626) J Norton Pubs.
Reading by the most recent woman Consultant in Poetry to the Library of congress.

Selected Poems. Carolyn Kizer. Read by Carolyn Kizer. 1 cass. (Running Time: 1 hr. 3 min.). (Watershed Tapes of Contemporary Poetry Ser.). 1977. 10.95 (23628) J Norton Pubs.
Compilation of two public readings.

Selected Poems. Pablo Neruda. Read by Pablo Neruda. 1 cass. (SPA.). 11.95 (978-0-8045-1114-8(4), SAC 1114) Spoken Arts.
Contains selections from "Residencia en la Tierra I," "Residencia en la Tierra II," & "Alturas de Macchu Picchu".

***Selected Poems.** Nuala Ni Dhomhniall. (ENG.). 1988. 11.95 (978-0-8023-0021-8(9)) Pub: Clo Iar-Chonnachta IRL. Dist(s): Dufour

Selected Poems of Dante. unabr. ed. Read by Jay Livernois. 2 cass. (Running Time: 3 hrs.). 1992. reel tape 17.95 (978-1-879816-09-1(1)) Pub: Spring Audio. Dist(s): Daimon Verlag
Jay Livernois reads from his translation, of selected cantos from Dante's epic, 'The Divine Comedy'. Listen to this tape for the rhythms of divine agony and desire!.

Selected Poems of Freddy the Pig. (J). (CP 1698) HarperCollins Pubs.

Selected Poems of Stephen Spender. unabr. ed. Stephen Spender. Read by Stephen Spender. 1 cass. 10.95 (SAC 7136) Spoken Arts.

Selected Poetry of Algernon Charles Swinburne. unabr. ed. Poems. Algernon Charles Swinburne. Perf. by James Mason. 1 cass. 1984. 12.95 (978-0-694-50301-8(0), SWC 1560) HarperCollins Pubs.

***Selected Poetry of Noel Coward.** abr. ed. Noel Coward. Read by Simon Jones. (ENG.). 2006. (978-0-06-125292-1(1), Harper Audio) HarperCollins Pubs.

Selected Poetry of William Wordsworth. unabr. ed. Poems. William Wordsworth. Perf. by Cedric Hardwicke. 1 cass. Incl. Composed upon Westminster Bridge, September 3, 1802. (SWC 1026); I Travelled among Unknown Men. (SWC 1026); It Is a Beauteous Evening, Calm & Free. (SWC 1026); My Heart Leaps up When I Behold. (SWC 1026); Nuns Fret Not at Their Convent's Narrow Room. (SWC 1026); Ode: Intimations of Immortality from Recollections of Early Childhood. (SWC 1026); Prelude, or, Growth of a Poet's Mind: Book Fifth: While I Was Seated in a Rocky Cave. (SWC 1026); Prelude, or, Growth of a Poet's Mind: Book First: Oh, Many a

Time Have I, a Five-Year's Child. (SWC 1026); Solitary Reaper. (SWC 1026); Strange Fits of Passions Have I Known. (SWC 1026); Tintern Abbey. (SWC 1026); World Is Too Much with Us. (SWC 1026); 1984. 12.95 (978-0-89845-243-3(0), SWC 1026) HarperCollins Pubs.

Selected Psalms & Parables. Narrated by George Vafiadis. (Running Time: 8640 sec.). (Unabridged Classics in MP3 Ser.). (ENG.). 2008. audio compact disk 24.00 (978-1-58472-651-7(2), In Aud) Sound Room.

Selected Psalms & Parables: 46 Psalms & 28 Parables Directly from the Holy Bible. Read by George Vafiadis. (Playaway Adult Nonfiction Ser.). 2008. 39.99 (978-1-60640-831-5(3)) Find a World.

Selected Readings. Holt, Rinehart and Winston Staff. (African American Literature Ser.). 1998. 58.26 (978-0-03-051099-1(6)) Holt McDoug.

Selected Readings from the Portable Dorothy Parker. Read by Lorna Raver. Ed. by Marion Meade. (Running Time: 48000 sec.). 2007. 79.95 (978-0-7861-4814-1(4)); audio compact disk 99.00 (978-0-7861-6188-1(4)) Blckstn Audio.

Selected Readings from the Portable Dorothy Parker. unabr. abr. ed. Dorothy Parker. Read by Lorna Raver. (Running Time: 48600 sec.). 2007. 25.95 (978-0-7861-4813-4(6)); audio compact disk 25.95 (978-0-7861-6187-4(6)); audio compact disk 29.95 (978-0-7861-7171-2(5)) Blckstn Audio.

Selected Readings in Chinese Communist Literature. rev. ed. Compiled by Tien-Yi Li. 8 cass. 1954. 8.95 ea. incl. suppl. materials. (978-0-88710-081-9(3)) Yale Far Eastern Pubns.

Selected Short Stories. unabr. ed. Short Stories. Thomas Hardy. Read by Richard Morant. 5 cass. (Running Time: 1 hrs. per cass.). 30.00 Set. (9903); Rental 12.50 Set. (9903) Books on Tape.

Selected Short Stories by Edith Wharton, unabr. ed. Edith Wharton. Read by Flo Gibson. 4 cass. (Running Time: 6 hrs.). Incl. Afterward. Edith Wharton. Read by Flo Gibson.; Angel at the Grave. Edith Wharton. Read by Flo Gibson.; Sanctuary. Edith Wharton. Read by Flo Gibson.; Souls Belated. Edith Wharton. Read by Flo Gibson.; 1985. 19.95 (978-1-55685-035-6(2)) Audio Bk Con.
"Sanctuary", "Afterward", "The Angel at the Grave", & "Souls Belated".

Selected Short Stories of Edgar Allan Poe. Short Stories. Edgar Allan Poe. Narrated by David Thorn. 6 Cds. (Running Time: 6 hrs.). Dramatization. 2005. audio compact disk 29.95 (978-0-9746806-3-7(X)) Alcazar AudioWorks.
A collection of the best horrorific Short Stories that Poe has to offer. Includes:The Tell Tale Heart,The Facts in the Case of M. ValdemarHop FrogMurder in the Rue MorgueThe Masque of the Red DeathThe Pit and the PendulumThe Fall of the House of UsherThe Black CatThe Cask of AmontilladoA production of Alcazar AudioWorks.

Selected Shorts, Vol. 1. unabr. ed. Richard Ford et al. Read by William Hurt et al. 2 cass. (Running Time: 2 hrs. 30 min.). 1989. 16.95 Symphony Space.
Classic & contemporary short fiction read by distinguished actors; recorded at Symphony Space in New York City before a live audience. The stories included consist of listeners' favorites from the popular show heard weekly on National Public Radio.

Selected Shorts, Vol. 2. unabr. ed. 2 cass. (Running Time: 2 hrs. 29 min.). (Live from Symphony Space Ser.). 1990. 15.98 set. (978-0-8072-3478-5(8), CB 125 CX, Listening Lib) Random Audio Pubg.
Recorded live at Symphony Space.

Selected Shorts, Vol. 2. unabr. ed. Thomas Meehan et al. Read by Christine Baranski et al. 2 cass. (Running Time: 2 hrs. 30 min.). 1989. 16.95 Symphony Space.
Classic & contemporary short fiction read by distinguished actors; recorded at Symphony Space in New York City before a live audience. The stories included consist of listeners' favorites from the popular show heard weekly on National Public Radio.

Selected Shorts, Vol. 3. unabr. ed. Michael Cunningham et al. Read by James Naughton et al. 2 cass. (Running Time: 2 hrs. 30 min.). 1990. 16.95 Symphony Space.

Selected Shorts, Vol. 6. unabr. ed. Laura Cunningham et al. Read by Linda Lavin et al. 2 cass. (Running Time: 2 hrs. 30 min.). 1992. 16.95 Symphony Space.

Selected Shorts: A Celebration of the Short Story. 6 cass. (Running Time: 9 hrs.). 1993. 37.98 (978-0-8072-3200-2(9), Listening Lib) Random Audio Pubg.

Selected Shorts: A Celebration of the Short Story. James Thurber et al. 3 CDs. (Running Time: 11700 sec.). (Selected Shorts Ser.). (ENG.). 2006. audio compact disk 28.00 (978-0-9719218-3-2(0)) Pub: Symphony Space. Dist(s): IPG Chicago

Selected Shorts: A Celebration of the Short Story, Vol. 7. unabr. ed. Davida Adedjouma et al. Read by Hattie Winston et al. 2 cass. (Running Time: 2 hrs. 30 min.). 1993. 16.95 Symphony Space.
Classic & contemporary short fiction read by distinguished film & theatre actors including Jane Curtin & Jack Davidson; recorded at Symphony Space in New York before a live audience. The stories on the cassette consist of listener's favorites from the popular show heard on National Public Radio.

Selected Shorts: American Classics. Ed. by Symphony Space Staff. 3 CDs. (Running Time: 3 hrs. 0 mins. 0 sec.). (Selected Shorts: A Celebration of the Short Story Ser.). (ENG.). 2010. audio compact disk 28.00 (978-1-934033-12-8(X)) Pub: Symphony Space. Dist(s): IPG Chicago

Selected Shorts: For Better & for Worse. unabr. ed. Symphony Space et al. 3 CDs. (Running Time: 3 hrs. 0 mins. 0 sec.). (Selected Shorts: A Celebration of the Short Story Ser.). (ENG.). 2008. audio compact disk 28.00 (978-1-934033-09-8(X)) Pub: Symphony Space. Dist(s): IPG Chicago

Selected Shorts Vol. 1: Listener Favorites Old & New: Fictions for Our Times. unabr. ed. Richard Ford et al. Read by William Hurt & Anne Pitoniak. 2 cass. (Running Time: 2 hrs. 27 min.). 1989. 15.98 (978-0-8072-3475-4(3), CB 124CX, Listening Lib) Random Audio Pubg.

Selected Shorts Vol. 3: Best Loved Stories. unabr. ed. 2 cass. (Running Time: 2 hrs. 56 min.). (Live from Symphony Space Ser.). 1991. 15.98 (978-0-8072-3482-2(6), CB 126CX, Listening Lib) Random Audio Pubg.

Selected Shorts Vol. 4: Celebrates Baseball. unabr. ed. 2 cass. (Running Time: 2 hrs.). 1991. 15.98 (978-0-8072-3485-3(0), CB 127 CX, Listening Lib) Random Audio Pubg.
Short stories recorded live at Symphony Space.

Selected Shorts Vol. 5: Selected Shorts Comedy Tonight! unabr. ed. Garrison Keillor et al. Read by Joe Grifasi et al. 2 cass. (Running Time: 2 hrs. 30 min.). 1991. 16.95 Symphony Space.
Classic & contemporary short fiction read by distinguished actors; recorded at Symphony Space in New York City before a live audience. The stories included consist of listeners' favorites from the popular show heard weekly on National Public Radio.

Selected Shorts Vol. 8: Food Fictions. 1 cass. 16.95 (CVIII) Symphony Space.
Includes: M. F. K. Fisher's "I Was Really Very Hungry" read by Tovah Feldshuh - A fantasy meal in a French country inn; Nora Ephron's "Heartburn" excerpt read by the author - Food, love & career in one casserole...with a dish of biting wit; Roald Dahl's "Taste" read by Geraldine Fitzgerald - A betting game in which a daughter is wagered on the vintage of a bottle of wine; & Angela Carter's "The Kitchen Child" read by Isaiah Sheffer - This Yorkshire kitchen legend is the sexiest souffle story in the history of English cuisine. Also Ogden Nash's Poems from "Food" read by Isaiah Sheffer; & Roy Blount, Jr.'s Poems from "SoupSongs" read by the author.

Selected Shorts Vol. 9: Best Loved Stories. 1 cass. 1995. 16.95 (CIX) Symphony Space.
Includes: Amy Bloom's "Silver Water" read by Linda Lavin; Max Steele's "The Hat of My Mother" read by Paul Hecht; Daniel Menaker's "The Treatment" read by Isaiah Sheffer; Terry McMillan's "Ma'Dear" read by Hattie Winston; & Charles Johnson's "Menagerie, a Child's Fable" read by Gloria Foster.

Selected Shorts Vol. 10: Best Loved Stories. Short Stories. 2 cass. Symphony Space.
Five selections by classic & contemporary authors.

Selected Shorts Vol. 11: Best Loved Stories. Short Stories. 2 cass. Symphony Space.

Selected Shorts Vol. 12: Best Loved Stories. Short Stories. 2 cass. Symphony Space.

Selected Shorts Celebrates Baseball, Vol. 4. unabr. ed. Short Stories. Roger Angell et al. Read by Roger Angell & A. Bartlett Giamatti. 2 cass. (Running Time: 2 hrs. 30 min.). 1991. 16.95 Symphony Space.
Classic & contemporary short fiction read by distinguished actors; recorded at Symphony Space in New York City before a live audience. The stories included on the cassettes consist of listeners' favorites from the popular show heard weekly on National Public Radio. Readers also include Stephen Lang, Jack Davidson, John Rubinstein, Jonathan Hadary, Arthur French & Fritz Weaver.

Selected Shorts Celebrates Baseball, Vol. 4. unabr. ed. Roger Angell et al. Read by Stephen Lang et al. 2 cass. (Running Time: 2 hrs. 30 min.). 1991. 16.95 set. Symphony Space.
Classic & contemporary short fiction read by distinguished actors; recorded at Symphony Space in New York City before a live audience. The stories included consist of listeners' favorites from the popular show heard weekly on National Public Radio.

Selected Shorts Comedy Tonight!, Vol. 5. unabr. ed. Short Stories. Garrison Keillor et al. Read by Joe Grifasi & Phyllis Newman. 2 cass. (Running Time: 2 hrs. 30 min.). (Selected Shorts on Audiocassette Ser.). 1991. 16.95 Symphony Space.
Classic & contemporary short fiction read by distinguished actors; recorded at Symphony Space in New York City before a live audience. The stories included on the cassettes consist of listeners' favorites from the popular show heard weekly on National Public Radio. Readers also include Malachy McCourt, Stockard Channing, Isaiah Sheffer, James Naughton, Charles Keating & David Margulies.

***Selected Shorts: Even More Laughs.** Symphony Space. (Running Time: 3 hrs. 0 mins. 0 sec.). (Selected Shorts: A Celebration of the Short Story Ser.). (ENG.). 2010. audio compact disk 28.00 (978-1-934033-14-2(6)) Pub: Symphony Space. Dist(s): IPG Chicago

Selected Songs for Cynical Scientists. Perf. by Ron Laskey. 2003. audio compact disk 18.00 (978-0-87969-685-6(0)) Cold Spring Harbor.

Selected Sonnets & Soliloques of Shakespeare. 10.95 (7005) Spoken Arts.

Selected Sonnets of Shakespeare. 1 cass. 10.95 (SAC 836) Spoken Arts.
Includes soliloquies from Hamlet, Othello & King Lear.

Selected Stories by O. Henry, O. Henry. Narrated by Grover Gardner. 2 cass. (Running Time: 3 hrs.). 1987. 14.95 (978-1-55685-090-5(5)) Audio Bk Con.
"A Madison Square Arabian Night", "The Lost Blend", "The Buyer from Cactus City", "Georgia's Ruling", "Blind Man's Holiday", "The Ransom of Red Chief", "Calloway's Code", & "The Last Leaf.".

Selected Stories from the Jungle Books. unabr. ed. Rudyard Kipling. Read by Ralph Cosham. 2 CDs. (Running Time: 2 hrs.). 2000. audio compact disk 19.95 (Commuters Library) Sound Room.

Selected Stories of Philip K. Dick: Volume 2. unabr. ed. Philip K. Dick. (Running Time: 8.5 hrs. NaN mins.). (ENG.). 2008. 29.95 (978-1-4332-2833-9(5)); 59.95 (978-1-4332-2829-2(7)); audio compact disk 70.00 (978-1-4332-2830-8(0)) Blckstn Audio.

Selected Stories of Philip K. Dick, Vol. 1. unabr. ed. Philip K. Dick. (Running Time: 14 hrs. NaN mins.). (ENG.). 2008. 29.95 (978-1-4332-2825-4(4)); 79.95 (978-1-4332-2821-6(1)); audio compact disk 99.00 (978-1-4332-2822-3(X)) Blckstn Audio.

Selected Studies from Proverbs. Charles R. Swindoll. 6 cass. (Running Time: 9 hrs.). 1998. 30.95 (978-1-57972-320-0(9)) Insight Living.

Selected Studies from Proverbs, Charles R. Swindoll. 6 cass. (Running Time: 6 hrs.). 1998. 30.95 (978-1-57972-145-9(1)) Insight Living.

Selected Tales by Edgar Allan Poe. unabr. ed. Edgar Allan Poe. Read by Grover Gardner. 2 cass. (Running Time: 3 hrs.). (gr. 8 up). 1989. 14.95 (978-1-55685-144-5(8)) Audio Bk Con.
Includes" "The Facts in the Case of M. Valdemar," "William Wilson," "Berenice," "The Oblong Box," & "The Fall of the House of Usher".

Selected Tales by Edgar Allen Poe. Edgar Allan Poe. Narrated by Grover Gardner. (ENG.). 2007. audio compact disk 16.95 (978-1-55685-984-7(8)) Audio Bk Con.

Selected Tax Issues in Estate Planning. Read by Richard Kinyon et al. (Running Time: 3 hrs.). 1992. 89.00 Incl. tape materials. (ES-55264) Cont Ed Bar-CA.
Experts cover selected complex issues of estate planning; tax & practical problems in allocating assets (including retirement funds) to fund marital deduction credit shelter & generation-skipping trusts (Richard Kinyon); examining valuation concepts & analyzing the effect of Chapter 14 on the transfer of business interests (Scott Beiser); & drafting buy-sell agreements with estate planning implications (Stuart Tobisman).

Selected Topics Set: Intermediate Listening Comprehension. Ellen Kisslinger. (Lecture Ser.). 1994. 66.00 (978-0-8013-0968-7(9)) Longman.

Selected Topics in Objectivist Esthetics. unabr. ed. Gary Hull. 4 cass. (Running Time: 4 hrs.). 1996. 39.95 Set. (978-1-56114-343-6(X), CH47D) Second Renaissance.
How one's artistic enjoyment is enhanced by an understanding of key principles.

Selected Topics in the Philosophy of Science. Harry Binswanger. 2 cass. (Running Time: 3 hrs.). 1991. 29.95 Set. (978-1-56114-122-7(4), CB04D) Second Renaissance.

Selected Works of Jean Genet. abr. ed. Jean Genet. Tr. by Bernard Frechtman. 1 cass. 1984. 12.95 (978-0-694-50099-4(2), SWC 1134) HarperCollins Pubs.
Cast of performers in the dramas includes: Max Adrian, Alan Webb, Brenda Bruce, Nigel Davenport, Sheila Burrell, Barbara Assoon, Olivier Cole, Jacqueline Le Maitre, Booker Bradshaw, John Thomas, Roy Stewart, Tarn Bassett, Pauline Jamieson, & Wendy Craige.

Selected Works of T. S. Spivet. unabr. ed. Reif Larsen. (Running Time: 14 hrs.). (gr. 12). 2009. audio compact disk 49.95 (978-0-14-314465-6(0), PengAudBks) Penguin Grp USA.

Selecting a Ghost see Tales of the Supernatural

Selecting & Influencing Your Jury. Speeches. Susan Jones. 6 cass. (Running Time: 6 hrs.). 2000. 185.00 (978-0-943380-70-4(7)) PEG MN.

Selecting Ideal Times. Carolyn Dodson. 1 cass. (Running Time: 90 min.). 1988. 8.95 (652) Am Fed Astrologers.

Selecting Individual Stocks for Your Portfolio. Carol S. Mull. 1 cass. 8.95 (247) Am Fed Astrologers.
What in a chart indicates a winning stock.

Selecting Mass Storage Peripherals. 2 cass. 1990. 17.00 set. Recorded Res.

Selecting Software for Your Personal Computer, Vol. 52. Michael Lodato. 1 cass. (Running Time: 45 min.). (Personal Computing Ser.). 1986. 7.95 B & H Comm.
Starting with a basic explanation of how programming works, reduces the anxiety the first time user may feel in respect to applying the PC to a particular task.

Selecting Your Divorce Lawyer: The Consumer Guide for Harris County, Texas. Peter Sperling. 2003. audio compact disk 24.95 (978-0-9726881-1-6(0)) Legal Guide.

Selection. (Scott Foresman Lectura Ser.). (SPA.). (gr. k up). 2000. audio compact disk 89.04 (978-0-673-64873-0(7)) Addson-Wesley Educ.

Selection. (Scott Foresman Lectura Ser.). (SPA.). (gr. 1 up). 2000. audio compact disk 89.04 (978-0-673-64874-7(5)) Addson-Wesley Educ.

Selection. (Scott Foresman Lectura Ser.). (SPA.). (gr. 2 up). 2000. audio compact disk 89.04 (978-0-673-64875-4(3)) Addson-Wesley Educ.

Selection. (Scott Foresman Lectura Ser.). (SPA.). (gr. 3 up). 2000. audio compact disk 110.34 (978-0-673-64876-1(1)) Addson-Wesley Educ.

Selection. 5 CDs. (High Point Ser.). (gr. 6-12). audio compact disk 69.15 (978-0-7362-0912-0(3)); audio compact disk 69.15 (978-0-7362-0944-1(1)) Hampton-Brown.

Selection, Set. 5 CDs. (High Point Ser.). (gr. 6-12). audio compact disk 69.15 (978-0-7362-0976-2(X)) Hampton-Brown.

Selection Chart. Carolyn Dodson. 1 cass. (Running Time: 90 min.). 1990. 8.95 (863) Am Fed Astrologers.

Selection Tape. (High Point Ser.). (gr. 6-12). reel tape 54.10 (978-0-7362-0938-0(7)); reel tape 54.10 (978-0-7362-0970-0(0)) Hampton-Brown.

Selection Tapes. (High Point Ser.). (gr. 6-12). reel tape 54.10 (978-0-7362-0906-9(9)) Hampton-Brown.

Selections from Catullus & Horace. unabr. ed. Gaius Valerius Catullus & Horace. Read by Robert P. Sonkowsky. Ed. by Stephen G. Daitz. 2 cass. (Running Time: 2 hrs.). (Living Voice of Greek & Latin Ser.). 1988. pap. bk. 39.95 (978-0-88432-262-7(9), S23800) J Norton Pubs.

Selections from Cicero. Robert P. Sonkowsky. 2 cass. J Norton Pubs.

Selections from Cicero. Read by Robert P. Sonkowsky. 2 cass. (Running Time: 2 hrs.). (Living Voice of Greek & Latin Ser.). 1985. pap. bk. 39.95 (978-0-88432-126-2(6), S23680) J Norton Pubs.

Selections from Dear Bill, Remember Me, & Other Stories. unabr. ed. Norma Fox Mazer. 2 cass. (Running Time: 3 hrs.). (J). 1987. 15.98 (978-0-8072-3436-5(2), Listening Lib) Random Audio Pubg.

Selections from Dreamsongs: Fan Fiction & Sci-Fi from Martin's Early Years, Vol. 1. abr. ed. George R. R. Martin. Read by George R. R. Martin. (Running Time: 15 hrs.). (ENG.). 2007. audio compact disk 34.95 (978-0-7393-5712-5(3), Random AudioBks) Pub: Random Audio Pubg. Dist(s): Random

Selections from Dreamsongs Vol. 1: Fan Fiction & SciFi from Martin's Early Years. unabr. ed. George R. R. Martin. 12 CDs. (Running Time: 15 hrs.). 2007. audio compact disk 129.00 (978-1-4159-4278-9(1)) Random.

Selections from Dreamsongs Vol. 2: Stories of Fantasy, Horror/Sci-Fi, & a Man Called Tuf. abr. ed. George R. R. Martin. Read by Mark Bramhall et al. 14 CDs. (Running Time: 61200 sec.). (ENG.). 2007. audio compact disk 34.95 (978-0-7393-5714-9(X), Random AudioBks) Pub: Random Audio Pubg. Dist(s): Random

Selections from Dreamsongs Vol. 2: Stories of Fantasy, Horror/Sci-Fi, & a Man Called Tuf. unabr. ed. George R. R. Martin. 14 CDs. (Running Time: 17 hrs.). 2007. audio compact disk 129.00 (978-1-4159-4290-1(0)) Random.

Selections from Dreamsongs Vol. 3: Selections from Wild Cards & More Stories from Martin's Later Years. unabr. abr. ed. George R. R. Martin. Read by Erik Davies et al. (Running Time: 72000 sec.). (ENG.). 2007. audio compact disk 34.95 (978-0-7393-5716-3(6), Random AudioBks) Pub: Random Audio Pubg. Dist(s): Random

Selections from Dreamsongs Vol. 3: Wild Cards & More Stories from Martin's Later Years. unabr. ed. George R. R. Martin. 17 CDs. (Running Time: 20 hrs.). 2008. audio compact disk 129.00 (978-1-4159-4299-4(4)) Random.

Selections from Greek Orators. Stephen G. Daitz. 2 cass. (Running Time: 2 hrs. 44 min.). 1989. 39.95 J Norton Pubs.

Selections from "Journey of the Rose" Gloria J. Burgess. 1998. audio compact disk 16.00 (978-1-892864-02-4(9)) Jazz Inc.

Selections from Ovid. Read by Robert P. Sonkowsky. Ed. by Stephen G. Daitz. 2 cass. (Running Time: 2 hrs.). (Living Voice of Greek & Latin Ser.). 2001. pap. bk. 39.95 (S23835) J Norton Pubs.

Selections from Saki, unabr. ed. Saki. Read by Flo Gibson. 2 cass. (Running Time: 3 hrs.). 1984. 14.95 (978-1-55685-034-9(4)) Audio Bk Con.
Short stories including "The Lumber Room", "The Interlopers", "Laura", "Mrs. Packletide's Tiger" & many more.

Selections from Samuel Pepys Diaries. Samuel Pepys. 4 CDs. (Running Time: 4 hrs.). (YA). 2003. audio compact disk 28.98 (978-962-634-288-6(9), NA428812, Naxos AudioBooks) Naxos.

Selections from Shui-hu Chuan. Ed. by James I. Crump, Jr. 1 cass. 1947. 7.95 incl. suppl. materials. (978-0-88710-086-4(4)) Yale Far Eastern Pubns.

Selections from the Adventures of Sherlock Holmes. Arthur Conan Doyle. Read by Ed Simone. 3 cass. (Running Time: 3 hrs.). Incl. Adventure of the Blue Carbuncle. Arthur Conan Doyle. 1987.; Case of the Five Orange Pips. Arthur Conan Doyle. 1987.; Red-Headed League. Arthur Conan Doyle. 1987.; Scandal in Bohemia. 1987.; (Chatham Audio Classics Ser.). 1987. Set bk. 15.95 Incl. case. Random Hse Value.

Selections from the Autobiography of Calvin Coolidge. Calvin Coolidge. Read by Jim Cooke. 1 cass. (Running Time: 1 hr. 30 min.). 1992. 10.00 (978-0-9650509-0-6(4)) I Do Not Choose.

Selections from the Decameron. Giovanni Boccaccio. Read by Stephen Thorne et al. Tr. by Richard Aldington. 4 cass. (Running Time: 4 hrs. 45 mins.). (YA). 2000. 22.98 (978-962-634-709-6(0), NA420914, Naxos AudioBooks); audio compact disk 26.98 (978-962-634-209-1(9), NA420912, Naxos AudioBooks) Naxos.
To escape an outbreak of the plague that ravished Europe in the 1340s, a group of ten friends enclosed themselves in a castle outside Florence.

Selections from the Faerie Queene. abr. ed. Edmund Spenser. Read by John Moffatt. 3 CDs. (Running Time: 14335 sec.). 2006. audio compact disk 22.98 (978-962-634-377-7(X), Naxos AudioBooks) Naxos.

Selections from the Greek Orators. Read by Stephen G. Daitz. Ed. by Stephen G. Daitz. 2 cass. (Running Time: 2 hrs.). (Living Voice of Greek & Latin Ser.). (GRE.). pap. bk. 39.95 (S23690) J Norton Pubs.
Includes Gorgias, Perikles, Lysias, Isokrates & Demosthenes.

Selections from the Mother Goose Treasury. 2004. 8.95 (978-1-56008-974-2(1)); cass. & flmstrp 30.00 (978-1-56008-720-5(X)) Weston Woods.

Selections from the Mother Goose Treasury; Twelve Days of Christmas, the; London Bridge Is Falling down!; Little Drummer Boy. 2004. (978-0-89719-828-8(X)); cass. & flmstrp (978-0-89719-736-6(4)) Weston Woods.

Selections from the New Testament. John W. Chu. 3 cass. 1966. 7.95 Incl. supp. materials. (978-0-88710-084-0(8)) Yale Far Eastern Pubns.

Selections from Tragedy & Comedy see Greek Poetry, A Recital of Ancient

Selections from Vergil. Read by Robert P. Sonkowsky. Ed. by Stephen G. Daitz. 2 cass. (Living Voice of Greek & Latin Ser.). (LAT.). 1985. pap. bk. 39.95 (978-0-88432-139-2(8), S23685) J Norton Pubs.

Selections of Greek Poetry. 4 cass. (GRE.). 42.50 (SGR401) J Norton Pubs.
Includes Solomos, Palamas, Karyotakis, Kazantzakis, & others.

(Selections of) the Old Testament. King James. (Running Time: 8 hrs.). 2000. 38.95 (978-1-60083-860-6(X)) Iofy Corp.

***Selections 2. 0.** Chris Funkhouser. 2007. audio compact disk 12.00 (978-983-41909-2-7(1)) Pub: We Pr. Dist(s): SPD-Small Pr Dist

Selena: Como la Flor. abr. ed. Joe Nick Patoski. 2 cass. (Running Time: 3 hrs.). 1997. 16.95 Set. (978-1-882071-75-3(1), 634018) B-B Audio.
The murder of Selena, the twenty-year-old Mexican-American singer, shocked Latino Americaand seized the attention of an Anglo audience that was largely unfamiliar with Tejano, the vibrant Tex-Mex musical fusion that Selena had popularized. Selena: Como.

Self: Center of the Psyche. Kenneth James. Read by Kenneth James. 2 cass. (Running Time: 1 hr. 45 min.). 1993. 16.95 (978-0-7822-0417-9(1), 504) C G Jung IL.

Self: Center of the Psyche. Read by Diane Martin. 2 cass. (Running Time: 2 hrs.). 1986. 16.95 (978-0-7822-0154-3(7), 206) C G Jung IL.

Self: Mirror of God. Vilma Seelaus. 1 cass. (Running Time: 48 min.). 1991. 7.95 (TAH254) Alba Hse Comns.
Spirituality.

Self- Esteem Children's. Scripts. Marjorie Baker Price. Illus. by David Price & Beth Price. 1 cassette. (Running Time: 60 minutes). (J). 1992. spiral bd. 12.95 (978-0-9713013-4-4(4)) Centering Pubns.
Cassette includes 15 minutes of dialogue on each side and 15 minutes of original music.

Self-Acceptance. 2 cass. (Running Time: 2 hrs.). (Personal Growth Ser.). 14.95 (ST-21) Crystal Clarity.
The importance of accepting things as they really are; the difference between accepting & affirming a fault; techniques for overcoming faults; why we have to fail before we succeed.

Self-Acceptance: Cultivate Appreciation & Acceptance of Yourself. Mark Bancroft. Read by Mark Bancroft. 1 cass., bklet. (Running Time: 1 hr.). (General Self-Development/Improvement Ser.). 1999. 12.95 (978-1-58522-008-3(6), 902, EnSpire Aud) EnSpire Pr.
Two complete sessions plus printed instruction manual/guidebook. With healing music soundtrack.

Self-Acceptance: Cultivate Appreciation & Acceptance of Yourself. Mark Bancroft. Read by Mark Bancroft. 1 CD, bklet. (Running Time: 1 hr.). (General Self-Development/Improvement Ser.). 2006. audio compact disk Rental 20.00 (978-1-58522-048-9(5)) EnSpire Pr.
Two complete sessions plus printed instructionmanual/guidebook. With healing music soundtrack.

Self-Accused: Freedom from Guilt. Kenneth Wapnick. 2008. 12.00 (978-1-59142-358-4(9)); audio compact disk 16.00 (978-1-59142-357-7(0)) Foun Miracles.

Self Actualization. 1 cass. (Running Time: 60 min.). 10.95 (041) Psych Res Inst.
Realize potential by making dreams & goals happen.

Self-Actualization. Michael Broder. 6 cass. (Running Time: 6 hrs.). 1993. 44.95 set. (686A) Nightingale-Conant.

Self-Actualization. unabr. ed. Abraham H. Maslow. 1 cass. (Running Time: 58 min.). 1966. 11.00 (04104) Big Sur Tapes.
Discusses how the author moved from the study of illness to the study of wellness in psychology.

***Self Analysis.** L. Ron Hubbard. (Running Time: 5 hrs. 4 mins. 0 sec.). (ENG.). 2010. audio compact disk 25.00 (978-1-4031-8853-3(X)); audio compact disk 25.00 (978-1-4031-9604-0(4)); audio compact disk 25.00 (978-1-4031-9611-8(7)); audio compact disk 25.00 (978-1-4031-9596-8(X)); audio compact disk 25.00 (978-1-4031-9601-9(X)); audio compact disk 25.00 (978-1-4031-9598-2(6)); audio compact disk 25.00 (978-1-4031-9600-2(1)); audio compact disk 25.00 (978-1-4031-9603-3(6)); audio compact disk 25.00 (978-1-4031-9606-4(0)); audio compact disk 25.00 (978-1-4031-9599-9(4)); audio compact disk 25.00 (978-1-4031-9602-6(8)); audio compact disk 25.00 (978-1-4031-9597-5(8)); audio compact disk 25.00 (978-1-4031-9608-8(7)); audio compact disk 25.00 (978-1-4031-9607-1(9)); audio compact disk 25.00 (978-1-4031-9610-1(9)); audio compact disk 25.00 (978-1-4031-9605-7(2)) Bridge Pubns Inc.

***Self Analysis.** L. Ron Hubbard. 2010. 17.50 (978-1-4031-8604-1(9)); 17.50 (978-1-4031-8605-8(7)); 17.50 (978-1-4031-8603-4(0)); 17.50 (978-1-4031-8606-5(5)) Bridge Pubns Inc.

Self & Sacredness: Twenty-First Century. David Spangler et al. 6 cass. 54.00 (OC309-67) Sound Horizons AV.

Self & Symbols of the Self. Read by Judith Hubback. 1 cass. (Running Time: 90 min.). 1979. 10.95 (978-0-7822-0094-2(X), 055) C G Jung IL.

Self & the Mulberry Tree. Marvin Bell. Read by Marvin Bell. 1 cass. (Running Time: 44 min.). (Watershed Tapes of Contemporary Poetry). 1976. 10.95 (23613) J Norton Pubs.
Selected poems.

Self Assured. Nicholas Rhea & Graham Padden. 2007. 54.95 (978-1-84652-105-8(X)); audio compact disk 71.95 (978-1-84652-106-5(8)) Pub: Magna Story GBR. Dist(s): Ulverscroft US

Self-Awakening Yoga: The Expansion of Consciousness Through the Body's Own Wisdom. Donna Heckman Stapleton. (Running Time: 60 mins.). 2004. bk. 24.95 (978-0-89281-183-0(8), Heal Arts VT) Inner Tradit.

Self Belief: Guided Meditations. Richard Latham. Created by Meditainment. (Running Time: 2700 sec.). (ENG.). 2007. audio compact disk 17.95 (978-0-9550584-5-5(7)) Meditainment Ltd GBR.

***Self Comes to Mind: Constructing the Conscious Brain.** unabr. ed. Antonio Damasio. (Running Time: 10 hrs.). 2010. 24.99 (978-1-4418-8046-8(1), 9781441880468, BAD); 39.97 (978-1-4418-8045-1(3), 9781441880451, Brinc Audio MP3 Lib); 39.97 (978-1-4418-8047-5(X), 9781441880475, BADLE); 24.99 (978-1-4418-8044-4(5), 9781441880444, Brilliance MP3) Brilliance Audio.

***Self Comes to Mind: Constructing the Conscious Brain.** unabr. ed. Antonio Damasio. Read by Fred Stella. (Running Time: 12 hrs.). 2010. audio compact disk 79.97 (978-1-4418-8043-7(7), 9781441880437, BriAudCD Unabrid); audio compact disk 29.99 (978-1-4418-8042-0(9), 9781441880420, Bril Audio CD Unabri) Brilliance Audio.

***Self-Compassion Diet: A Step-by-Step Program to Lose Weight with Loving-Kindness.** Jean Fain. (Running Time: 2:00:00). 2010. audio compact disk 19.95 (978-1-60407-077-4(3)) Sounds True.

Self Confidence. 2001. audio compact disk 19.95 (978-0-86580-008-3(1)) Success World.

Self Confidence. Rick Brown. Read by Rick Brown. Ed. by John Quatro. 1 cass. (Running Time: 30 min.). (Subliminal - New Age Ser.). 1993. 10.95 (978-1-57100-063-7(1), N136); 10.95 (978-1-57100-087-3(9), S136); 10.95 (978-1-57100-111-5(5), W136); 10.95 (978-1-57100-135-1(2), H136) Sublime Sftware.
Self confidence builds self esteem & character.

Self-Confidence. Robert E. Griswold. 1 cass. (Running Time: 55 min.). (Love Tapes Ser.). 1988. 10.95 (978-1-55848-040-7(4)) EffectiveMN.
Rid yourself of fear, feel happier, & perform better at whatever you choose to do.

Self-Confidence. Richard Jafolla & Mary-Alice Jafolla. Read by Richard Jafolla & Mary-Alice Jafolla. (Self-Improvement Ser.). 1986. 12.95 (200) Stppng Stones.
Motivational tapes that work on the subconscious mind (subliminal) & conscious mind to bring about self-improvement.

Self-Confidence. Barrie Konicov. 1 cass. (YA). 11.98 (978-0-87082-438-8(4), 115) Potentials.
Acquire the self-assurance to feel relaxed & at ease when you meet people & develop the confidence to say "no" without feeling guilty. Through this program start on the road to a more confident you.

Self-Confidence, Barrie Konicov. 1 cass., 1 video. (Video-Audio System Ser.). cass. & video 24.98 (978-0-87082-451-7(1), SYS115) Potentials.

Self-Confidence, Barrie Konicov. 2 cass. (YA). 16.98 (978-1-56001-302-0(8), SCII 115) Potentials.

Self-Confidence. Barrie Konicov. 1 CD. 2003. audio compact disk 19.98 (978-0-87082-955-0(6)) Potentials.
One of the greatest gifts you can bestow upon yourself is the gift of self-confidence. Acquire self-assured, relaxed feelings when you meet people. The road to a more confident you begins with this vital program. You will find the self-hypnosis on track 1 and the subliminal on track 2. The easy-listening music of the subliminal, together with the self-hypnosis, is the original format which most people love and with which they are most familiar.

Self-Confidence. Barrie Konicov. 2 CDs. 2003. audio compact disk 27.98 (978-1-56001-988-6(3)) Potentials.

Self-Confidence. Barry Tesar. 1 cass. (Running Time: 1 hr.). (Subliminal Inspiration Ser.). 1992. 9.98 (978-1-56470-015-5(1)) Success Cass.
Subliminal program.

Self-Confidence. abr. ed. Roger W. Bretemitz. 1 cass. (Running Time: 45 min.). 1985. pap. bk. 9.95 (978-1-893417-18-2(2)) Vector Studios.
Hypnosis: Instills a belief system that one can achieve all goals, make ideas become reality, & get what one wants out of life.

Self Confidence, No. E136. Rick Brown. Read by Rick Brown. Ed. by John Quatro. 1 cass. (Running Time: 30 min.). (Subliminal - Easy Listening Ser.). 1993. 10.95 (978-1-57100-015-6(1)) Sublime Sftware.
"Self Confidence builds self esteem & character.

Self Confidence, No. J136. Rick Brown. Read by Rick Brown. Ed. by John Quatro. 1 cass. (Running Time: 30 min.). (Subliminal - Jazz Ser.). 1993. 10.95 (978-1-57100-039-2(9)) Sublime Sftware.
"Self Confidence" builds self esteem & character.

Self Confidence: A Meditation to Help You Improve Self-Confidence & Reach Peak Performance. Belleruth Naparstek. Composed by Steven Mark Kohn. 1 cass. (Running Time: 1 hr.). (Health Journeys Ser.). 2000. 12.98 (978-1-881405-26-9(5)) Hlth Jrnys.
Designed to increase feelings of self-esteem & confidence; improve mastery & performance; reduce anxiety & fear of failure; heighten creativity, endurance & ability to focus within.

Self-Confidence: Confianza en Si Mismo. Barrie Konicov. 1 cass. (Running Time: 1 hr. 30 min.). (Spanish-Language Audios Ser.). (SPA.). (YA). 1995. 11.98 (978-0-87082-803-4(7), 115) Potentials.
Develop the confidence to say "no" without feeling guilty. Acquire the self-assurance to feel relaxed & at ease when meeting new people & situations. Bestow the greatest gift of all, self-confidence, upon yourself.

Self Confidence - Self Esteem. 1 cass. (Running Time: 60 min.). 10.95 (036) Psych Res Inst.
Positive reinforcement of self worth & confidence.

Self Confidence - Self Esteem. Pat Carroll. Read by Pat Carroll. Ed. by Tony Carroll. 1 cass. (Running Time: 30 min.). 10.00 Inner-Mind Concepts.
Demonstrates how to be in total control. Be confident at all times & success will naturally follow.

Self Confidence - Stage Fright. Bruce Goldberg. (ENG.). 2005. audio compact disk 17.00 (978-1-57968-097-8(6)) Pub: B Goldberg. Dist(s): Baker Taylor

Self Confidence - Stage Fright. Bruce Goldberg. Read by Bruce Goldberg. 1 cass. (Running Time: 25 min.). (ENG.). 2006. 13.00 (978-1-885577-61-0(3)) Pub: B Goldberg. Dist(s): Baker Taylor
Through self-hypnosis build up self-image, & eliminate fears of meeting & communicating with people.

Self-Confidence (Overcome Shyness) 1 cass. 10.00 (978-1-58506-029-0(1), 61) New Life Inst OR.
This program helps you feel calm & confident in any situation.

Self Control. Eldon Taylor. Interview with XProgress Aware Staff & Progress Aware Staff. 1 cass. (Running Time: 62 min.). (Inner Talk Ser.). 16.95 Incl. script. (978-1-55978-515-0(2), 53792F) Progress Aware Res.
Soundtrack - Babbling Brook with underlying subliminal affirmations.

Self Control: Leisure Listening. Eldon Taylor. 1 cass. 16.95 (978-0-940699-19-9(2), 53792B) Progress Aware Res.

Self-Control Anger. 1 cass. (Running Time: 45 min.). (Relationship Ser.). 9.98 (978-1-55909-057-5(X), 52S); 12.98 (52) Randolph Tapes.
No longer do you find yourself getting angry easily. Gone are those feelings of frustration. This tape works!.

Self-Control Anger. 1 cass. (Running Time: 45 min.). (Relationship Ser.). 1989. 15.98 90 min. extended length stereo music. (978-1-55909-058-2(8), 52X) Randolph Tapes.
Learn to be patient, work things out, & have self-control. Subliminal messages are heard 3-5 minutes before becoming ocean sounds or music.

Self-Control Sugar. 1 cass. (Running Time: 45 min.). (Health Ser.). 9.98 (978-1-55909-055-1(3), 51S); 9.98 90 min. extended length stereo music. (978-1-55909-056-8(1), 51X) Randolph Tapes.
Messages designed to use self-power in saying 'No' to sugar. Subliminal messages are heard 3-5 minutes before becoming ocean sounds or music.

Self-Deception: 11 Cor. 13:5-14. Ed Young. 1990. 4.95 (978-0-7417-1801-3(4), 801) Win Walk.

Self-Defense. unabr. ed. Jonathan Kellerman. Read by Alexander Adams. 8 cass. (Running Time: 12 hrs.). (Alex Delaware Ser.: No. 9). 1995. 64.00 (978-0-7366-2958-4(0), 3651) Books on Tape.
Psychologist Alex Delaware tries to find out if the meaning behind his patient's spooky dreams of a murder in progress will produce deadly, real-life consequences.

Self-Defense. unabr. ed. Jonathan Kellerman. Read by Alexander Adams. 10 CDs. (Running Time: 12 hrs.). (Alex Delaware Ser.: No. 9). 2004. audio compact disk 90.00 (978-1-4159-1622-3(5)) Books on Tape.
New patient - 24-year-old Lucy Lowell - has come to the semi-retired psychologist Alex Delaware, straight from the jury of a serial killer's grisly trial. The trial was harrowing enough, but now it's triggered a recurring and haunting dream in which Lucy - as a little girl - watches a gang of men bury a young woman's body in the woods. Dr. Delaware knows he may find the creepy dream's origin through hypnosis. He hopes to bring to the surface what seems to be Lucy's buried childhood memory. When Lucy becomes adamant that her life is in grave danger, it's up to Dr. Delaware to find out if her fears are imagined or if a desperate killer wants to eliminate a witness to a 20-year-old murder.

Self-Defense for Wimps (Yuppie Survival Guide of the 1990's) Sid Campbell. 3 cass. (Running Time: 4 hrs. 30 mins.). 1989. bk. 29.95 (978-0-682-87113-6(3)) Gong Prods.
Conveys practical ways in which the non-violent (aka Wimp or Wimpette) can defend themselves in potentially lethal or dangerous situations in modern society.

Self-Denial: Romans 15:1-13. Ed Young. 1984. 4.95 (978-0-7417-1403-9(5), 403) Win Walk.

Self-Determination for the American Indian: Development of Their Lands. Henry W. Hough. 1 cass. (Running Time: 50 min.). 10.95 (19008) J Norton Pubs.
Hough traces the history of reservations & discusses the present development of resources on Indian reservations.

Self-Directed Sales Success. 1 cass. (Running Time: 24 min.). 1999. 9.95 (C030) A Ellis Institute.

Self-Directed Sales Success. 1 cass. (Running Time: 24 min.). 14.95 (C030) Inst Rational-Emotive.
Teaches the techniques which research has demonstrated to be the key factors in sales success. Shows you how to identify behaviors & attitudes which prevents sales success, & demonstrates techniques for dramatically improving your sales behavior.

Self-Directed Work Teams. Fred Pryor. 6 cass. (Running Time: 6 hrs.). (Fred Pryor Seminars Ser.). 1995. wbk. ed. 59.95 (12340AM) Nightingale-Conant.
Ideal for use as a training or reference tool.

Self-Directed Work Teams: Proven & Practical Methods to Enhance Productivity, Reduce Costs, & Motivate Workers. 6 cass. wbk. ed. 59.95 (12340AS) Pryor Resources.
Learn why the self-directed team is a model for the high-performance organization.

Self-Discipline. 1 cass. 12.98 (978-0-87554-507-3(6), 1105) Valley Sun.
You are encouraged to be self-disciplined & to accomplish your personal & professional goals. Also: Direct your time & energy to manifest your desires. You do what you need to do to accomplish your goals. You control your thoughts & thus your actions. You are assertive & feel good about yourself. You commit to your goals. You do a job one step at a time until it's done. And many more suggestions.

Self-Discipline. Swami Jyotirmayananda. 1 cass. (Running Time: 1 hr.). 1990. 12.99 Yoga Res Foun.

Self Discipline. Short Stories. Joel Osteen. 1 Cass. (Running Time: 30 Mins). 2001. 6.00 (978-1-59349-088-1(7), JA0088) J Osteen.

Self-Discipline & Emotional Control. PUEI. 1994. audio compact disk 89.95 (978-1-933328-02-7(9), CareerTrack) P Univ E Inc.

Self-Discipline & Emotional Control: How to Change Your Negative Behaviors So You'll Stay Calm & Productive under Pressure. Tom Miller. 6 cass. (Running Time: 6 hrs. 20 min.). wbk. ed. 79.95 (V10171) CareerTrack Pubns.
This program will help you change your negative behaviors permanently. This powerful system is based on rational-emotive behavior therapy, which uses some of the most effective tools in modern psychology.

Self-Discipline & Emotional Control: How to Stay Calm & Productive under Pressure. abr. ed. Tom Miller. 2 cass. (Running Time: 3 hrs.). 2000. 17.95 (978-1-55977-340-9(5)) CareerTrack Pubns.

Self-Discipline & Moderation. Linda Eyre & Richard Eyre. 2 cass. (Running Time: 3 hrs.). (Teaching Your Children Values Ser.). (J). (ps-7). 2000. pap. bk. 16.95 (978-1-56015-790-8(9)) Penton Overseas.
Tape 1: a coaching, "how-to" program for parents; Tape 2: "Alexander's Amazing Adventures" program featuring stories, songs, sound effects & background music, that helps children ages 4-12 to develop social skills, communication skills & life skills. Includes activity cards.

Self Disciplined & Determined. Eldon Taylor. 1 cass. (Running Time: 62 min.). (Inner Talk Ser.). 16.95 incl. script. (978-1-55978-542-6(X), 5420F) Progress Aware Res.
Soundtrack - Brook with underlying subliminal affirmations.

Self Disciplined & Determined: Classics. Eldon Taylor. 1 cass. 16.95 (978-1-55978-641-6(8), 5420L) Progress Aware Res.

Self Discovery, 129. 1997. 24.95 (978-1-58557-005-8(2)) Dynamic Growth.

Self Effort & Divine Grace, No. 1. Swami Jyotirmayananda. 1 cass. (Running Time: 1 hr.). 1990. 12.99 Yoga Res Foun.

Self Effort & Divine Grace, No. 2. Swami Jyotirmayananda. 1 cass. (Running Time: 1 hr.). 1990. 12.99 Yoga Res Foun.

Self-Effort vs. Grace. 1 cass. (Yoga & Christianity Ser.). 9.95 (ST-50) Crystal Clarity.
Explores Christian theology as the product of materialistic (kali yuga) thinking; the role of grace in Eastern & Western religious traditions; the meaning of "salvation" how self-effort & grace become one.

Self-Employed. David Ignatow. Read by David Ignatow. 1 cass. (Running Time: 45 min.). (Watershed Tapes of Contemporary Poetry). 1977. 10.95 (23625) J Norton Pubs.
Poems of the 30's through the 70's.

Self-Empowerment. Jeff Salzman. 6 cass. (Running Time: 6 hrs.). 89.95 (C10102) CareerTrack Pubns.
Self-Empowerment is based on timeless philosophical principles. This program brings these principles alive, so you can apply them, & begin to use their power in your life.

Self-Empowerment: How to Take Charge of Your Work Life. 3 cass. (Running Time: 3 hrs.). pap. bk. & wbk. ed. 139.00 Incl. 2 multiple choice tests. (978-0-7612-0924-9(7), 80182) AMACOM.
You'll learn how to: Distinguish between "power" & "self-empowerment;" Differentiate between "being empowered by someone" & "being self-empowered;" Analyze the elements of self-empowerment as they apply to your work situation; Recognize organizational & personal obstacles to self-empowerment; Create a self-empowerment plan.

Self-Empowerment Affirmations. Liah Kraft-Kristaine. Read by Liah Kraft-Kristaine. 1 cass. (Running Time: 62 min.). 1988. 9.95 (978-1-878095-00-8(5)) LMI Prodns.
Increases self confidence, energy, & effectiveness.

Self Empowerment Men (Hypnosis), Vol. 15. Jayne Helle. 1 cass. (Running Time: 27 min.). 1997. 15.00 (978-1-891826-14-6(X)) Introspect.
It's time men own their inner power & be the happy self-fulfilled man they deserve to be, coming from personal respect & divine acceptance.

***Self Empowerment Through Self-Hypnosis CD Companion.** PhD, Joe H Slate & Carl Llewellyn Weschcke. (ENG.). 2011. audio compact disk 16.95 (978-0-7387-2672-4(9)) Llewellyn Pubns.

Self-Esteem. Nathaniel Branden. 2 cass. (Running Time: 1 hr. 28 min.). 19.95 (808-809); 11.95 (567) J Norton Pubs.
Why self-esteem is man's deepest psychological need - The consequences of the failure to achieve self-esteem.

Self-Esteem. Focus on the Family Staff. 3 cass. (Running Time: 3 hrs.). (Adventures in Odyssey Ser.). (J). (gr. 1-7). 2001. 9.99 (978-1-58997-022-9(5)) Pub: Focus Family. Dist(s): Tommy Nelson

Self-Esteem. Jennifer James. Read by Jennifer James. 1 cass. (Running Time: 43 min.). 1986. 9.95 (978-0-915423-11-8(1)) Jennifer J.
Self-esteem is developed by fate, family, experience & perception. Understand the development of your self-esteem & learn the steps to increase your self-worth.

Self Esteem. Liah Kraft-Kristaine. Read by Liah Kraft-Kristaine. 6 cass. (Running Time: 6 hrs.). 1992. 39.95 (978-1-878095-23-7(4)) LMI Prodns.
Method of healing the secret self.

Self Esteem. Gael Lindenfield. 1 cass. (Running Time: 1 hr.). (978-0-00-220065-3(1), HarperThor) HarpC GBR.

Self-Esteem. Betty L. Randolph. Read by Betty L. Randolph. Read by Leonard Baron. Ed. by Success Education Institute International Staff & Success Education Institute International. (Running Time: 45 min.). (Success Ser.). 1989. bk. 9.98 Adults. (978-1-55909-118-3(5), 95S) Randolph Tapes.

Self-Esteem. Betty L. Randolph. Read by Betty L. Randolph. Read by Leonard Baron. Ed. by Success Education Institute International Staff. (Running Time: 45 min.). (Success Ser.). 1989. bk. 9.98 Children. (978-1-55909-113-8(4), 93X); bk. 9.98; bk. 9.98 Teens. (978-1-55909-115-2(0), 94S); bk. 9.98 Teens. (978-1-55909-116-9(9), 94X); bk. 14.98 (978-1-55909-249-4(1), 370P) Randolph Tapes.
60,000 messages left-right brain. Male-female voice tracks with Megafonic Subliminals. Ocean (P) & Music (PM).

Self Esteem. Read by Mary Richards. (Subliminal Impact Ser.). 12.95 Master Your Mind.
Explains how to believe in oneself.

Self-Esteem. James Rosen. 4 cass. (Running Time: 4 hrs.). 1987. 29.95 (978-0-9620038-0-6(8)) Ouachita Psychol Servs.
Presents a program designed to build self-assertiveness & self-esteem.

Self Esteem. Standard Publishing Staff. 2006. cd-rom 24.99 (978-0-7847-1886-5(5)) Standard Pub.

Self Esteem. Eldon Taylor. Read by Eldon Taylor. Interview with Progress Aware Staff. Music by Steven Halpern. 1 cass. (Running Time: 62 min.). (EchoTech Ser.). 16.95 incl. script. (978-1-55978-338-5(9), 9902) Progress Aware Res.
Gentle coaching & soundtrack with underlying subliminal affirmations with tones & frequencies to alter brain wave activity.

Self-Esteem. Barry Tesar. 1 cass. (Running Time: 1 hr.). (Subliminal Inspiration Ser.). 1992. 9.98 (978-1-56470-009-4(7)) Success Cass.
Subliminal program.

Self-Esteem: Building a Positive Attitude in the Workplace. 1999. pap. bk. & wbk. ed. 30.00 (80225CHDG) AMACOM.

Self Esteem: Everybody's Special! Perf. by Janice Buckner. 1 cass. (Running Time: 1 hr.). (Learn along Song Ser.). (J). 2001. 10.00; audio compact disk 15.00 Moonlight Rose.
Includes full song lyrics and features a karaoke-style Sing-It-Yourself instrumental version of each tune. The feature is designed for classrooms, children's choirs and budding performers.

Self-Esteem: The Difference in Life. Charles B. Beckert. 1 cass. 2004. 7.98 (978-1-55503-186-2(2), 06003931) Covenant Comms.
Building esteem in ourselves & our families.

Self-Esteem: The Key to Success. unabr. ed. Clark Redwoods. Read by Johnny Rockit. 1 cass. (Running Time: 1 hr. 05 min.). (Mind Power Ser.). 1997. 12.99 (978-1-892654-06-9(7), BET070) FutureLife.
Practical advice, guidance, & motivation for building a positive mental self-image.

Self-Esteem: Your Fundamental Power. Caroline Myss. Read by Caroline Myss. (Playaway Adult Nonfiction Ser.). (ENG.). 2009. 59.99 (978-1-60812-780-1(X)) Find a World.

Self-Esteem: Your Fundamental Power. Caroline Myss. 3 cass. (Running Time: 3 hrs.). (Adventures in Odyssey). (J). (gr. k-4). 2001. 12.99 Pub: Focus Family. Dist(s): Tommy Nelson
Adventures in Odyssey stories packaged by theme.

Self-Esteem: Your Fundamental Power. unabr. ed. Caroline Myss. 4 CDs. (Running Time: 4 hrs. 45 mins.). 2006. audio compact disk 34.95 (978-1-59179-034-1(4), W687D) Sounds True.
Casts a new light on this often misunderstood subject, redefining self-esteem as an actual core power that is essential to our evolutionary progress. In fact, Myss teaches, your potential for success in life is determined by how greatly you esteem or value who you truly are.

Self-Esteem Set: Building a Positive Attitude in the Workplace. 4 cass. 1999. pap. bk. & wbk. ed. 129.00 incl. multiple choice tests. (80224CHDG) AMACOM.
The Institute for Certification, a department of Professional Secretaries International, will grant points toward CPS recertification to qualified individuals who successfully complete this course. 1 CEU.

Self-Esteem Affirmations: Motivational Affirmations for Achieving & Maintaining Optimum Health. Louise L. Hay. Read by Louise L. Hay. Music by Jerry Florence. Contrib. by Jeffrey Thompson. 1 cass. (Running Time: 60 min.). (Subliminal Mastery Ser.). 1990. 10.95 (978-0-937611-75-3(1), 706); audio compact disk 10.95 (978-1-56170-532-0(2), 441) Hay House.

Self-Esteem & Peak Performance. Jack L. Canfield. 6 cass. (Running Time: 6 hrs. 51 min.). 79.95 Set. (Q10073) CareerTrack Pubns.
Program highlights: How to get what you want in life by letting go of fear; When to learn from criticism & when - & how - to ignore it; How to muster the courage to stand up for what you know is true; How to hold onto your self-esteem after a big failure.

Self-Esteem & Peak Performance. Jack L. Canfield. 2 cass. (Running Time: 3 hrs.). 1995. 15.95 (978-1-55977-029-3(5)) CareerTrack Pubns.

Self-Esteem & Peak Performance. PUEI. 1995. audio compact disk 89.95 (978-1-933328-01-0(0), CareerTrack) P Univ E Inc.

Self-Esteem & Personal Evolution. Nathaniel Branden. 20 cass. (Running Time: 26 hrs.). 188.95 (621-640) J Norton Pubs.

Self-Esteem & the Christian. Dan Corner. 1 cass. 3.00 (81) Evang Outreach.

Self-Esteem & the Working Woman. Nathaniel Branden. 1 cass. (Running Time: 52 min.). 10.95 (846) J Norton Pubs.
A discussion about the need for women to learn new forms of self-assertiveness, because there is still a great deal of anxiety & belligerence rather than comfort with the working role.

Self-Esteem & Vulnerability/Being Authentic. Marianne Williamson. Read by Marianne Williamson. 1 cass. (Running Time: 90 mins.). (Lectures on a Course in Miracles). 1999. 10.00 (978-1-56170-263-3(3), M766) Hay House.

Self-Esteem (Child) 1 cass. (Young People Ser.). (J). 12.98 (93) Randolph Tapes.
Let your unique little person begin at an early age to develop a strong sense of self-worth.

Self-Esteem Facilitator's Kit. unabr. ed. Lilburn S. Barksdale. 8 Cass. (Running Time: 5 hrs. 43 min.). 1978. pap. bk. & stu. ed. 105.00 incl. 3 paperbacks, transparency, wall chart & daily companion. (978-0-918588-14-2(6), 200) NCADD.
This is a complete recording of the Barksdale Self-Esteem Workshop presentation, including exercises & provocative discussion questions for understanding the causes of self-rejection & the realities of human behavior. Steps for raising one's self-esteem complete the program.

Self-Esteem for Children. Shad Helmstetter. 1 cass. (Self-Talk Cassettes Ser.). 10.95 (978-0-937065-33-4(1)) Grindle Pr.

Self-Esteem for Women. PUEI. 2006. audio compact disk 89.95 (978-1-933328-63-8(0), Fred Pryor) P Univ E Inc.

Self-Esteem for Women: How to Increase Your Self-Worth & Satisfaction in Life. Instructed by Julie White. 6 cass. (Running Time: 4 hrs. 43 min.). pap. bk. & wbk. ed. 59.95 (Q10140) CareerTrack Pubns.
Program highlights: How to minimize the negativity of your inner critic; Why attacking yourself is often less painful than exposing yourself to attack from others; How to open your mind to new possibilities; The importance of "confiding relationships"; How to recognize your own growth & success; The telltale signs to self-defeating thinking; Why eliminating negative self-talk is even more powerful than increasing positive self-talk.

Self-Esteem Revolutions in Children: Understanding & Managing the Critical Transitions in Your Child's Life. unabr. ed. Thomas W. Phelan. 4 cass. (Running Time: 4 hrs.). (ENG.). 2003. 24.95 (978-1-889140-07-0(4)) Pub: ParentMagic. Dist(s): IPG Chicago
Self-Esteem Revolutions in Children describes the sweeping changes that youngsters experience as they grow up. Dr. Phelan explains why gimmicks & good intentions must be replaced by the hard work of both parents & children.

Self-Esteem Supercharger. Paul R. Scheele. 1 cass. (Paraliminal Tapes Ser.). 1988. 14.95 (978-0-925480-04-0(5)) Learn Strategies.
Face life's challenges with a positive belief in yourself. You may be surprised at how good you will feel after just one listening.

Self-Esteem (Teen) 1 cass. (Young People Ser.). (J). 12.98 (94) Randolph Tapes.
The teen years can be filled with good experiences & learning - or be just the opposite! Having this tape helps!.

Self-Esteem 2-CD Set. Nathaniel Branden. 2 CDs. (Running Time: 88 mins.). 2005. audio compact disk 19.95 (978-1-57970-254-0(6), AFNB06D, Audio-For) J Norton Pubs.
Reviewed are the many aspects of self-esteem: how it is reflected in one's dreams and fantasies, the correlation of self-esteem and one's level of creativity, as related to independence, and the various characteristics of low self-esteem.

***Self-Esteem, 3rd Ed. Low Price.** abr. ed. Matthew Mckay & Fanning Patrick. Read by Rob Shapiro. (ENG.). 2008. (978-0-06-157898-4(3)); (978-0-06-174414-3(X)) HarperCollins Pubs.

Self-Examination & Understanding of Breast Cancer. G. E. Caraker & H. E. Ulrich. 1 cass. (Running Time: 45 min.). 10.95 (495) J Norton Pubs.
This offers a discussion of cancer in general & breast cancer in particular, with a medically approved method of self-examination, accompanied by a chart.

Self-Healing. 1 cass. (Health Ser.). 12.98 (27) Randolph Tapes.
Everyone can benefit from these healing messages with Dr. Coue's powerful auto-suggestion. Amazing results! Also, good to use before & after surgery.

Self Healing. 1 cass. (Running Time: 60 min.). 10.95 (045) Psych Res Inst.
Designed to provide freedom from disease processes by inducing positive choices of health through mental imaging of natural healing powers & transference to the physical body.

Self Healing. Louise L. Hay. 1 CD. 2004. audio compact disk 10.95 (978-1-4019-0412-8(2)) Hay House.

Self-Healing. Barrie Konicov. 1 CD. 2003. audio compact disk 19.98 (978-0-87082-957-4(2)) Potentials.
If you have a mental, physical, or emotional area of your life that needs healing, Barrie's suggestions may help it to happen. First, choose programs that deal directly with your issue, then add this program which acts as a catalyst, to reinforce suggestions for change on the other programs. You will find the self-hypnosis on track 1 and the subliminal on track 2. The easy-listening music of the subliminal, together with the self-hypnosis, is the original format which most people love and with which they are most familiar.

Self-Healing. Barrie Konicov. 2 CDs. 2003. audio compact disk 27.98 (978-1-56001-989-3(1)) Potentials.

Self-Healing. Kriyananda, pseud. 1 cass. (Running Time: 80 min.). 9.95 (ST-46) Crystal Clarity.
Discusses the importance of seeing the body as energy flows; the patient's role in the healing process; why joy is the best healer; how to make God your healing partner.

Self Healing. Betty L. Randolph. Read by Betty L. Randolph. Read by Leonard Baron. Ed. by Success Education Institute International. 1 cass. (Running Time: 60 min.). (Health Ser.). 1989. bk. 9.98 (978-1-55909-188-6(6), 27B) Randolph Tapes.
Healing messages with auto-suggestion, also for use before & after surgery. Subliminal messages are heard 3-5 minutes before becoming ocean sounds or music.

Self Healing. Barry Tesar. 1 cass. (Running Time: 1 hr.). (Subliminal Inspiration Ser.). 1992. 9.98 (978-1-56470-010-0(0)) Success Cass.
Subliminal program.

Self-Healing. unabr. ed. Barrie Konicov. 1 cass. 11.98 (978-0-87082-361-9(2), 117) Potentials.
Professional hypnotist & author Barrie Konicov discusses types of mental, physical, or emotional areas of ones life that need to be healed & how to make it happen.

Self-Healing: Auto Curacion. Barrie Konicov. 1 cass. (Running Time: 1 hr. 30 min.). (Spanish-Language Audios Ser.). (SPA.). (YA). 1995. 11.98 (978-0-87082-809-6(6), 117) Potentials.
The suggestions found on this tape can help heal any type of mental, physical or emotional area of your life, acting as a catalyst & reinforcing the desire for change & healing.

Self-Healing: Hypnotic & Subliminal Learning. David Illig. 1985. 14.99i (978-0-86580-009-0(X)) Success World.

Self Healing is Natural. Eldon Taylor. 1 cass. (Running Time: 62 min.). (Inner Talk Ser.). 16.95 (978-1-55978-055-1(X), 5308A) Progress Aware Res.
Soundtrack - Tropical Lagoon with underlying subliminal affirmations.

Self-Healing Is Natural. Eldon Taylor. Read by Eldon Taylor. Ed. by Leslie Brice. 1 cass. (Running Time: 1 hr.). 1992. 16.95 (978-1-56705-200-8(2)) Gateways Inst.
Self improvement.

Self Healing is Natural: Babbling Brook. Eldon Taylor. 1 cass. 16.95 (978-1-55978-429-0(6), 5308F) Progress Aware Res.

Self Healing is Natural: Music Theme. Eldon Taylor. 1 cass. 16.95 (978-1-55978-057-5(6), 5308C) Progress Aware Res.

Self-Healing Strategies. Andrew Weil. 4 CDs. (Running Time: 4 hrs. 30 mins.). 2002. audio compact disk 34.95 (978-1-59179-004-4(2), AW00638D) Sounds True.
Dr. Weil introduces us to the specific arts of self-healing. These six practical one-on-one sessions cover: Keeping Your Immune System Strong, Preventing Chronic Disease, Living Longer and Aging Gracefully, Exploring Alternative Therapies and Living Well in the 21st Century.

Self-Healing with Energy Medicine. Andrew Weil MD & Ann Marie Chiasson MD. (Running Time: 2:28:12). 2009. audio compact disk 19.95 (978-1-59179-716-6(0)) Sounds True.

Self-Healing with Guided Imagery. Andrew Weil & Martin Rossman. 2 CDs. (Running Time: 2 hrs. 45 mins.). 2006. audio compact disk 19.95 (978-1-59179-132-4(4), W767D) Sounds True.

Self-Healing with Sound & Music. Andrew Weil & Kimba Arem. 2 CDs. (Running Time: 2 hrs. 15 mins.). 2006. audio compact disk 19.95 (978-1-59179-198-0(7), W842D) Sounds True.

Self-Help. Daniel Goleman. 1998. 39.95 Macmill Audio.

Self Help Groups & Pastoral Care. 1 cass. (Care Cassettes Ser.: Vol. 10, No. 1). 1983. 10.80 Assn Prof Chaplains.

Self Help Groups & Pastoral Care. Leonard Borman & Ronald Buch. 1986. 10.80 (0908) Assn Prof Chaplains.

Self-Help Pak: Love Tactics & How to Make Anyone Fall in Love with You. abr. ed. Thomas W. McKnight & Robert H. Phillips. Read by Franette Liebow & Leil Lowndes. 2 cass. (Running Time: 6 hrs.). 2001. 34.95 (978-0-929071-28-2(X)) B-B Audio.
Plugn Play Travelpaks contain everything your customers will need for many hours of audiobook listening. 2 Fantastic Audiobooks with1 Portable Cassette Player plus1 Comfortable Headset plus 2 Batteriers SELF-HELP PAK: 6 HoursLOVE TACTICS By Thoma.

Self Help Skills: Adaptive Behavior. Carol Michaelis. 2 cass. (Running Time: 2 hrs.). (J). 2001. pap. bk. 18.95 (KIM 8055C) Kimbo Educ.
Melodies offer lyrics that sing the task analysis of each skill. Hygiene, manners & more. Wipe My Nose, Wash My Hands, Comb Hair, Bathe, Clean Clothes, Time to Eat, Eat with Mouth Closed, Brush Teeth & more. IEP suggestions & charts to record behavior. Includes manual.

Self-Honesty & the Flow of Grace. 1 cass. (Running Time: 1 hr. 30 mins.). (Devotion Ser.). 9.95 (SS-87) Crystal Clarity.
Accepting things as they are; the inevitablity of divine law; the importance of not dwelling on mistakes; The importance of flowing with life's currents; tuning into how God wants to express Himself through us.

Self-Hypnosis. 1 cass. (Running Time: 45 min.). (Educational Ser.). 9.98 (978-1-55909-025-4(1), 33S) Randolph Tapes.
Used as an adjunct, to be more receptive to self-hypnosis training. Subliminal messages are heard 3-5 minutes before becoming ocean sounds or music.

Self Hypnosis. 1 cass. 12.95 (978-1-884305-62-7(8)) Changeworks.
For a relaxing time out. This tape takes you to a magical place that can be anything you want it to be. For stress reduction, goal setting, enhancing inner resource states, & getting fresh perspectives.

Self-Hypnosis. William Golden. 1 cass. (Running Time: 76 min.). 9.95 (C022) A Ellis Institute.
Demonstrates hypnotic & REBT techniques for helping control smoking, overeating, depression, shyness, & anxiety.

Self-Hypnosis. William Golden. 1 cass. (Running Time: 76 min.). 9.95 (C022) Inst Rational-Emotive.

Self-Hypnosis. Barrie Konicov. 1 cass. 11.98 (978-0-87082-302-2(7), 118) Potentials.
This self-hypnosis tape contains complete instructions for giving yourself suggestions, along with detailed procedures for entering into a state of self-hypnosis. After you have entered a quiet space where you can enter suggestions into your mind, you are gently guided back to awakening consciousness. Repeated use of this tape will help you develop into a good self-hypnosis subject.

Self-Hypnosis. Barrie Konicov. 1 CD. 2003. audio compact disk 19.98 (978-0-87082-980-2(7)) Potentials.
Learn to hypnotize yourself,to enter your own suggestions,and to guide yourself to awakening consciousness - renewed and refreshed.You will find the self-hypnosis on track 1 and the subliminal on track 2. The easy-listening music of the subliminal, together with the self-hypnosis, is the original format which most people love and with which they are most familiar.

Self-Hypnosis. Barrie Konicov. 2 CDs. 2003. audio compact disk 27.98 (978-1-56001-990-9(5)) Potentials.
Learn to hypnotize yourself, to enter your own suggestions, and to guide yourself to awakening consciousness - renewed and refreshed. This 2-CD program from our Super Consciousness series is our newest, most powerful format. On the self-hypnosis CD, SC programs have the Subliminal Persuasion soundtrack added under Barrie?s voice. And the 17th Century Baroque music on the Subliminal CD has the same beat as your body's natural rhythm, thereby allowing the suggestions to enter deeply and effortlessly.

An Asterisk (*) at the beginning of an entry indicates that the title is appearing for the first time.

Self Hypnosis. Read by Mary Richards. 12.95 (208) Master Your Mind.
Explains how to use the power of the mind to give oneself suggestions that increase one's confidence & self esteem.

Self Hypnosis. Created by Anne H. Spencer-Beacham. 1. 2003. audio compact disk (978-1-932163-68-1(9)) Infinity Inst.

Self-Hypnosis. abr. rev. unabr. ed. Edgar Cayce & Mark Thurston. Read by Stanley Ralph Ross. 1 CD. (Running Time: 1 hr. 0 mins. 0 sec.). (ENG.). 2002. audio compact disk 14.00 (978-1-55927-698-6(3)) Pub: Macmill Audio. Dist(s): Macmillan

Self-Hypnosis: Autohipnotismo. Barrie Konicov. 1 cass. (Running Time: 1 hr. 12 min.). (Spanish-Language Audios Ser.). (SPA.). 1995. 11.98 (978-0-87082-808-9(8), 118) Potentials.
Be guided into a state of hypnosis with key phrases & statements so you can utilize this level of mind any time you choose; detailed procedures are included for entering a state of self-hypnosis, as well as space for you to enter your own suggestions.

Self-Hypnosis: Hypnotic & Subliminal Learning. David Illig. 1985. 14.99 (978-0-86580-039-7(1)) Success World.

Self-Hypnosis - Self-Directed Inner-Mind Power. Norman J. Caldwell. Read by Norman J. Caldwell. Ed. by Achieve Now Institute Staff. 1 cass. (Running Time: 20 min.). (Self-Directed Improvement Ser.). 1988. 9.97 (978-1-56273-060-4(6)) My Mothers Pub.
Inner power & relaxation.

Self-Hypnosis & Meditation for Hair Growth: Whole-Body Approach to Restore Hair from Peach Fuzz to Full Crown of Glory. Created by Riquette Hofstein. Riquette International. 2008. audio compact disk 24.95 (978-0-9715088-1-1(X)) Riquette Intl.

Self-Hypnosis & Personal Development. Emmett E. Miller. 4 cass. 36.00 (OC7W) Sound Horizons AV.

Self Hypnosis Diet: Use the Power of Your Mind to Reach Your Perfect Weight. Steven Gurgevich. Read by Steven Gurgevich. (Playaway Adult Nonfiction Ser.). (ENG.). 2009. 59.99 (978-1-60812-781-8(8)) Find a World.

Self-Hypnosis Exercise. Bruce Goldberg. (ENG.). 2005. audio compact disk 17.00 (978-1-57968-029-9(1)) Pub: B Goldberg. Dist(s): Baker Taylor

Self-Hypnosis Exercise. Bruce Goldberg. Read by Bruce Goldberg. 1 cass. (Running Time: 25 min.). (ENG.). 2006. 13.00 (978-1-885577-79-5(6)) Pub: B Goldberg. Dist(s): Baker Taylor
A basic induction and deepening technique to guide the listener into a relaxed state.

Self-Hypnosis for a New Life. 1 cass. 10.00 (978-1-58506-000-9(3), 01) New Life Inst OR.
Acquire the skill of self-hypnosis easily & automatically.

Self-Hypnosis for Better Golf. Chuck Hogan. 2 cass. (Running Time: 1 hr. 30 mins.). 1995. 19.95 (978-0-9624504-3-3(X)) Sports Enhance.

Self Hypnosis for Mature Adults. Ormond McGill. 2000. (978-1-933332-19-2(0)) Hypnotherapy Train.

Self-Hypnosis for the Reiki Practitioner. Elisa J. Davenport. Read by Elisa J. Davenport. 1 cass. (Running Time: 1 hr. 12 min.). 1998. (978-0-9666343-1-0(4)); audio compact disk 17.00 CD. (978-0-9666343-0-3(6)) Ascension Quest.
Introduction plus short & long hypnosis sessions.

Self-Hypnosis for Women. Annellen M. Simpkins & C. Alexander Simpkins. 1 cass. (Running Time: 70 minutes). 2004. per. 29.95 (978-0-9679113-9-7(7)) Radiant Dolphin Pr.
The CD guides listeners into trance and shows how to use self- suggestion and self-hypnosis. The CD is an excellent suppliment to the material in the book. The authors lead listeners step-by-step to help them deepen their experience.

Self-Hypnosis Kit. Cherith Powell & Greg Forde. 1 cass. (Running Time: 60 min.). 1999. bk. 22.95 (20413) Courage-to-Change.
Provides all you need to practice self-hypnosis safely & effectively.

Self Hypnosis Made Easy. 1 CD. (Running Time: 40 min). 2002. audio compact disk (978-0-9726482-2-6(4)) Energy Way.

Self-Hypnosis or Self-Regulation. Read by Jack Schwarz. 3 cass. 35.00 (#200) Aletheia Psycho.

Self-Hypnosis Training. Betty L. Randolph. 1 stereo cass. (Running Time: 45 min.). (Self-Hypnosis Ser.). 9.98 (978-1-55909-162-6(2), 104) Randolph Tapes.
A program that trains in the use of self-hypnosis. Music background & spoken word.

Self Image. Created by Jerome Beacham. 1. 2003. audio compact disk (978-1-932163-58-2(1)) Infinity Inst.

Self Image. Pat Carroll. Read by Pat Carroll. Ed. by Tony Carroll. 1 cass. (Running Time: 30 min.). 10.00 Inner-Mind Concepts.
Intructs one how to overcome insecurities-.

Self-Image: How Come & How To. William Miller. 1986. 10.80 (0512) Assn Prof Chaplains.

Self-Image Builder Series. Created by Laura Boynton King. 6 cass. (Running Time: 6 hrs.). 2002. audio compact disk 109.95 (978-0-9748885-0-7(8)) Summit Dynamics.
A 6-volume series of Self-Hypnosis CD's designed to provide the tools needed to build self-confidence.

Self-Image II see Improve Your Self-Image

Self Improvement: Dream Recall - Creative Dream Interpretation. Diana Keck. Read by Diana Keck. 1 cass. 1985. 9.95 (978-0-929653-15-0(7), TAPE 602) Mntn Spirit Tapes.

Self Improvement: New Beginnings - Freedom from Guilt. Diana Keck. 1 cass. 1985. 9.95 (978-0-929653-13-6(0), TAPE 600) Mntn Spirit Tapes.

Self Improvement: On Becoming a Whole Person - Creative Problem Solving. Diana Keck. Read by Diana Keck. 1 cass. 1985. 9.95 (978-0-929653-14-3(9), TAPE 601) Mntn Spirit Tapes.

Self Improvement: Preparing to Study - Passing the Test. Diana Keck. 1 cass. 1985. 9.95 (978-0-929653-16-7(5), TAPE 603) Mntn Spirit Tapes.

***Self Improvement of Salvadore Ross.** 2010. audio compact disk (978-1-59171-222-0(X)) Falcon Picture.

Self-Improvement Speech Course: Advanced Course. Speechphone Staff. 3 cass. 39.50 (S23709); J Norton Pubs.
For the American & foreign students who wish to acquire the finer nuances of the language.

Self-Improvement Speech Course: Elementary Course. Speechphone Staff. 3 cass. 39.50 (S23701); J Norton Pubs.
Designed for foreign-born students who read & understand simple material but are unable to make themselves readily understood, or for Americans with limited vocabulary.

Self-Improvement Speech Course: Intermediate Course. Speechphone Staff. 3 cass. 39.50 (S23705); J Norton Pubs.
For the American student who wishes to eliminate a local accent, as well as for the advanced foreign student.

Self-Improvement Speech Course: Word List. Speechphone Staff. 3 cass. 39.50 (S23713); J Norton Pubs.
Up-to-date pronounciation of more than 3,000 words.

Self-Improvement Through Public Speaking. Orison Swett Marden. Read by Charlie Tremendous Jones. (Laws of Leadership Ser.). (ENG.). 2007. audio compact disk 19.95 (978-1-933715-42-1(1)) Executive Bks.

Self in Infancy & Childhood. Read by Mara Sidoli. 1 cass. (Running Time: 1 hr. 30 mins.). 1990. 10.95 (978-0-7822-0254-0(3), 409) C G Jung IL.

Self in Relationship Conference. 7 cass. (Running Time: 10 hrs.). 1988. 64.95 (978-0-7822-0005-8(2), SIR) C G Jung IL.

Self-Inquiry into Shining Reality. Swami Amar Jyoti. 1 dolby cass. 1986. 9.95 (R-80) Truth Consciousness.
Preparation for Vedantic meditation & Realization. The diamond-like spiritual wealth of the Upanishads. Maya, Divine Mother, in Vedanta.

Self Is God. Speeches. As told by Swami Prabhavananda. 1. (Running Time: 50). 2003. 9.95 (978-0-87481-354-8(9)) Vedanta Pr.
A lecture on one of the prime doctrine of vedanta: The concept of onesness with God.

Self Learning Schools Appraised. Mimsy Sadofsky. 1 cass. (Running Time: 1 hr.). 1996. 10.00 (978-1-888947-57-1(8)) Sudbury Valley.
Public radio interview about Sudbury Valley School, January 3, 1996.

Self Love. 2004. audio compact disk (978-0-9755937-6-9(5)) TheraScapes.

Self Love. Pat Carroll. Read by Pat Carroll. Ed. by Tony Carroll. 1 cass. (Running Time: 30 min.). 10.00 Inner-Mind Concepts.
Discusses how to initiate unrecognized feelings & activate positive self love.

Self-Made Woman. Wendy Robertson. Read by Diana Bishop. 8 cass. (Sound Ser.). (J). 2002. 69.95 (978-1-84283-206-6(9)) Pub: ISIS Lrg Prnt GBR. Dist(s): Ulverscroft US

Self Matters: Creating Your Life from the Inside Out. abr. ed. Phil McGraw. Read by Phil McGraw. 5 CDs. (Running Time: 60 hrs. 0 mins. 0 sec.). (ENG.). 2001. audio compact disk 32.00 (978-0-7435-0967-1(6), Sound Ideas) Pub: S&S Audio. Dist(s): S and S Inc

Self Matters: Creating Your Life from the Inside Out. abr. ed. Phil McGraw. 2005. 15.95 (978-0-7435-5528-9(7)) Pub: S&S Audio. Dist(s): S and S Inc

Self, Mind & Memory. Swami Amar Jyoti. 1 cass. 1982. 9.95 (J-43) Truth Consciousness.
Separation of mind from Self, the first fall from heaven. The Self, without memory, knows everything unto eternity. Nirvikalpa & Savikalpa Samadhi.

Self-Modification of Anxiety. Read by Marvin R. Godfried. 1 cass. 12.50 incl., 24p. self-instructional manual. (C29353) J Norton Pubs.
In language you can readily understand, Marvin R. Goldfried's clear instructions will help you to relax & restructure your cognitive skills. You can then apply this knowledge to daily anxiety-related situations.

Self-Motivation for Winners. 1978. audio compact disk (978-0-89811-288-7(5)) Meyer Res Grp.

Self-Motivation for Winners. Paul J. Meyer. 1 cass. (Running Time: 36 min.). 11.00 (978-0-89811-100-2(5), 7151) Meyer Res Grp.
Self-talk is a powerful influence on behavior & personal success - or lack of it. Learn to use affirmation. See yourself as you can be - successful, respected, & filled with honest self-appreciation.

Self-Motivation for Winners. Paul J. Meyer. 1 cass. 10.00 (SP100029) SMI Intl.
What you say & think about yourself may be more important than you ever imagined. Self-talk is a powerful influence on behavior & personal success - or lack of it. Learn to use affirmations. See yourself as you can be - successful, respected, & filled with honest self-appreciation.

Self-motivator. unabr. ed. Paul Hanna. Read by Paul Hanna. 2009. 43.95 (978-1-74214-485-6(3), 9781742144856) Pub: Bolinda Pubng AUS. Dist(s): Bolinda Pub Inc

Self-Nurture: Learning to Care for Yourself As Effectively As You Care for Everyone Else. Alice D. Domar & Henry Dreher. Read by Juliette Parker. 8 cass. (Running Time: 11 hrs.). 2000. 29.95 (978-0-7366-4940-7(9)) Books on Tape.
Domar believes that learning to nurture themselves is essential for women whose lives often feel overwhelming. Most women have to juggle the roles of caregiver, breadwinner and nurturer - and have been taught to put everyone else's needs ahead of their own. The result is a near epidemic of physical, emotional and spiritual fatigue. She doesn't believe you have to give up your life to enrich it. Here she shows you how to restructure your life in a way that lets you breathe. Here are inspiring stories, easy-to-follow exercises and meditations that will shift your focus from self-sacrifice to self-care. Domar draws on her many years of clinical experience and research to offer women practical ways to nurture body, mind and spirit.

Self-Nurture: Learning to Care for Yourself As Effectively As You Care for Everyone Else. collector's ed. Alice D. Domar. Read by Juliette Parker. 8 cass. (Running Time: 12 hrs.). 2000. 64.00 (978-0-7366-5006-9(7)) Books on Tape.
Inspiring stories, easy-to-follow exercises, & meditations that will shift your focus from self-sacrifice to self-care.

Self Peace. Eldon Taylor. Read by Eldon Taylor. Interview with Progress Aware Staff. 1 cass. (Running Time: 62 min.). 16.95 incl. script. (978-1-55978-292-0(7), 020106) Progress Aware Res.
Verbal coaching soundtrack with underlying subliminal affirmations & sound matrix frequencies for brain entrainment.

***Self-Power: Answers to Life's Greatest Challenges.** unabr. ed. Deepak Chopra. (ENG.). 2012. audio compact disk 35.00 (978-0-307-87771-0(X), Random AudioBks) Pub: Random Audio Pubg. Dist(s): Random

Self Programming: Self Hypnosis. Pat Carroll. Read by Pat Carroll. Ed. by Tony Carroll. 1 cass. (Running Time: 30 min.). 10.00 Inner-Mind Concepts.
A quiet space is allowed in the center for suggestions. Then one is guided through a positive visual affirmation of one's goal as a fact.

Self Promotion Basics Audio MP3. Ilise Benun. 2006. 12.95 (978-0-9791245-9-4(X)) Marktg Mentor.

Self-Publishing for the Clueless(r). Created by Mike Rounds. Narrated by Mike Rounds. 1 CD. (Running Time: 53 mins., 07 seconds). (ENG.). 2007. audio compact disk 24.95 (978-1-891440-36-6(5)) CPM Systems.

Self-Publishing in Audio & Making Money from the Start. unabr. ed. Julian Padowicz. Read by Julian Padowicz. 1 cass. (Running Time: 1 hr. 18 mins.). 1997. 12.95 (978-1-881288-15-2(3), BFI AudioBooks) BusnFilm Intl.
A discussion by author-publisher, Julian Padowicz, of his experiences developing a profitable self-publishing business. Also advice on how listener can do the same.

Self-Purification Toward the Goal. unabr. ed. Swami Amar Jyoti. 1 cass. (Running Time: 1 hr.). (Satsangs of Swami Amar Jyoti Ser.). 1999. 9.95 (978-0-933572-60-7(3), M-113) Truth Consciousness.
Paying the price for our karmas. Seeking Go'd help versus doing it ourselves. Focus on the Goal.

Self-Realization: The Inner & the Outer Path. Paramhansa Yogananda. 11.50 (978-0-87612-433-8(3)) Self Realization.

Self-Realization: The Inner & the Outer Path. Paramhansa Yogananda. (Running Time: 53 mins.). 2007. audio compact disk 14.00 (978-0-87612-440-6(6)) Self Realization.

Self-Realization - Looking Within. unabr. ed. Lilburn S. Barksdale. Read by William Wolff & June Wolff. 1 cass. (Running Time: 36 min.). 1978. 9.95 (978-0-918588-38-8(3), 121) NCADD.
Two exercises are given to confirm the truth about yourself & your relationship to a beneficent universe. This inspiring tape puts you in touch with your inner being, affirms your innate worth & importance, & reflects on the meaning & purpose of life.

Self-Relaxation: A Chinese Qigong Meditation. Jwing-Ming Yang. Read by Kathleen Iacobacci. 1 cass. (Running Time: 53 min.). 1996. bk. 12.95 (978-1-886969-38-4(8), A001) Pub: YMAA Pubn. Dist(s): Natl Bk Netwk
Background theoretical information about Chinese Qigong & guided Qigong meditation.

Self-Reliance see Great American Essays: A Collection

Self-Reliance. unabr. ed. Ralph Waldo Emerson. Read by Jim Killavey. 1 cass. (Running Time: 1 hr. 12 mins.). Dramatization. 1980. 7.95 (N-48) Jimcin Record.
Essays on independent thinking.

Self-Reliance & Potential. Linda Eyre & Richard Eyre. 2 cass. (Running Time: 3 hrs.). (Teaching Your Children Values Ser.). (J). (ps-7). 2000. bk. 16.95 (978-1-56015-789-2(5)) Penton Overseas.
Tape 1: a coaching, "how-to" program for parents; Tape 2: "Alexander's Amazing Adventures" program featuring stories, songs, sound effects & background music, that helps children ages 4-12 to develop social skills, communication skills & life skills. Includes activity cards.

Self-Sabotage. 5th ed. Alyce P. Cornyn-Selby. 1 cass. 1987. 9.95 (978-0-941383-10-3(5)) Beynch Pr.
Explores fascinating human behavior of self-sabotage: when we say we want something & then go about making sure it doesn't happen. Writer's block, overweight, procrastination - self-sabotage as a creative act.

Self Syndicate: Your Way to Success. Larry White. 1 cass. (Running Time: 1 hr. 30 mins.). 1990. 8.95 (723) Am Fed Astrologers.

Self-Talk for Exercising. Shad Helmstetter. 1 cass. (Self-Talk Ser.). 10.95 (978-0-937065-48-8(X)) Grindle Pr.
Companion Self-Talk Cassettes as mentioned in the book, "What To Say When You Talk To Your Self".

Self-Talk for Managing. Shad Helmstetter. 1 cass. (Self-Talk Ser.). 10.95 (978-0-937065-52-5(8)) Grindle Pr.

Self-Talk for Weight-Loss. Shad Helmstetter. 4 cass. 29.95 incls. Self-Talk Pocket Card Packs, Weekly Progress Guides & Daily Plan Bklet. (978-0-937065-98-3(6)) Grindle Pr.
This program works with your attitudes about how you eat & how much-the cravings, temptations, frustrations, & rationalizations that surround weight gain. Self-Talk for Weight-Loss gives you the daily support & determination you need to get started & stay with any good diet or exercise plan.

Self-Transcendence: The Motivational Theory of Logotherapy. Viktor E. Frankl. 1 cass. (Running Time: 40 min.). 10.95 (25004) J Norton Pubs.
Issue is taken with the motivational theories based on the Homeostasis principle (fulfillment for its own sake) as the final goal of human life.

Self-Transformation Through the New Hypnosis. Daniel L. Aaroz. 4 cass. wbk. ed. 50.00 (S1835) J Norton Pubs.
This program of eight mind exercises trains you to generate mental images & helps you discover your true feelings about persons, events, & memories. Through the use of non-traditional hypnotherapy, where no trances or deepening instructions are used, you can discover your own realistic agenda for self-improvement & be able to pursue whatever goals you set.

Self under Siege: Philosophy in the Twentieth Century. Instructed by Rick Roderick. 4 cass. (Running Time: 6 hrs.). 1993. 39.95 (978-1-56585-095-8(5)) Teaching Co.

Self Worth: The Power of Self Appreciation. Carol Rios. 2007. audio compact disk 18.95 (978-1-4276-2337-9(6)) AardGP.

Selfish Giant see Favorite Children's Stories: A Collection

Selfish Giant see Happy Prince & Other Stories

Selfish Giant. 2004. 8.95 (978-1-56008-325-2(5)); cass. & flmstrp 30.00 (978-1-56008-761-8(7)) Weston Woods.

Selfish Giant. unabr. ed. Oscar Wilde. 1 cass. (Running Time: 56 min.). Dramatization. (J). 1978. 7.95 (G-3); 9.95 incl. follow along script. Jimcin Record.
A giant learns to love & a classic myth re-told for children.

Selfishness: The Root to All Evil. Speeches. Creflo A. Dollar. 4 cass. (Running Time: 5 hrs.). 2004. 20.00 (978-1-59089-896-3(6)); audio compact disk Rental 28.00 (978-1-59089-897-0(4)) Creflo Dollar.

Selfless Love: Healing & Pathology in Devotion, Cherishing & Adoration, Nos. 22, 23 & 24. Carl Faber. 3 cass. (Running Time: 3 hrs. 45 min.). 1984. 28.50 (978-0-918026-50-7(4), SR 60-011) Perseus Pr.

Selfless Service, No. 1. Swami Jyotirmayananda. Read by Swami Jyotirmayananda. 1 cass. (Running Time: 1 hr.). 12.99 (735) Yoga Res Foun.

Selfless Service, No. 2. Swami Jyotirmayananda. 1 cass. (Running Time: 1 hr.). 1990. 12.99 Yoga Res Foun.

Selfless Service, No. 3. Swami Jyotirmayananda. 1 cass. (Running Time: 1 hr.). 1990. 12.99 Yoga Res Foun.

Selichos Service. 10.00 (RJ130) Esstee Audios.

Selkie: Irish Traditional Fiddle Music. Contrib. by Mick Conneely. (ENG.). 2001. audio compact disk 22.95 (978-0-8023-8148-4(0)) Pub: Clo Iar-Chonnachta IRL. Dist(s): Dufour

Selkie Girl. 2004. bk. 24.95 (978-0-7882-0590-3(0)); pap. bk. 14.95 (978-0-7882-0664-1(8)); 8.95 (978-1-56008-440-2(5)); cass. & flmstrp 30.00 (978-0-89719-578-2(7)) Weston Woods.

Sell Benefits. (Running Time: 38 min.). 12.95 (205) Salenger.
Features advice on selling.

Sell in the USA. (ENG.). 2009. 19.99 (978-0-9713031-1-9(8)) Flow Pubng.

Sell It by Owner & Save: The Complete Guide to Selling Your Home Without a Real Estate Agent. Excerpts. Michael M. Kloian. 2 CDs. (Running Time: 150 mins). 2003. audio compact disk 14.95 (978-0-9707346-3-1(8)) H-Two Pr.
Power packed information on 2 CDs, Abridged.

Sell It with the Million Dollar Attitude. Joel Weldon. Read by Joel Weldon. 6 cass. 54.95 Set. (120A) Nightingale-Conant.

***SELL LIKE A PRO Unabridged.** abr. ed. Dale Carnegie Training (Firm) Staff. (Running Time: 6 hrs. 30 mins. 0 sec.). (ENG.). 2010. audio compact disk 29.99 (978-1-4423-0384-3(0), Nightgale) Pub: S&S Audio. Dist(s): S and S Inc

Sell Like the Pros: Selling with Service, Integrity & Added Value. Orvel R. Wilson. 1 cass. (Running Time: 4 hrs. 23 min.). 59.95 Set. (V10074) CareerTrack Pubns.
In this high-content, no-hype program, you'll gain valuable insights to help you become more "in tune" with your customers. You'll not only make easier sales, you'll develop the bonds that lead to long-term loyalty.

Sell Your Way to the Top. Zig Ziglar. Read by Zig Ziglar. 6 cass. (Running Time: 6 hrs.). 59.95 (1941AD) Nightingale-Conant.
With Zig, you'll learn not just one or two, but 44 proven ways to close any sale, plus the five basic reasons why prospects don't buy & how to overcome them. And there's more: Zig alerts you to the 24 negative words that can kill any sale & how to communicate such irresistible enthusiasm that your prospects will literally sell themselves. You'll learn the crucial importance of correct phrasing, effective voice inflections, & appropriate body language, & you'll find out how to become "selectively deaf" when objections are raised.

Sell Your Way to the Top. abr. ed. Zig Ziglar. 2 CDs. (Running Time: 20 hrs. 0 mins. 0 sec.). (ENG., 2002. audio compact disk 20.00 (978-0-7435-0920-6(X), Nightgale) Pub: S&S Audio. Dist(s): S and S Inc
Success can be yours with Zig Ziglar's Sell Your Way To The Top! Learn from America's sales mentor Drawing on his own proven selling strategies that build successful sales careers, mega-bestselling author Zig Ziglar (Goals, How To Get What You Want) tells you how to turn every no into a yes and improve your prospecting, overcome price objections, and close more deals with finesse and style. Combining vivid scenarios and crystal clear instructions, Ziglar will motivate you to reach your peak as a sales star. You'll learn how to add the personal touch to client relations making you more effective than ever at demonstrating the need for your product or service. With these important skills, you'll become a word merchant who paints verbal pictures that capture your client's full attention. More than a guide to closing one single sale, Sell Your Way To The Top will help you open the door to a profitable sales career - because no one can teach you how to make your sales percentages skyrocket like Zig Ziglar can.

Sellevision: A Novel. unabr. ed. Augusten Burroughs. Read by Robin Miles. 6 CDs. (Running Time: 7 hrs. 0 mins. 0 sec.). (ENG.). 2006. audio compact disk 29.95 (978-1-59397-852-5(9)) Pub: Macmill Audio. Dist(s): Macmillan

Selling. J. Douglas Edwards. Read by J. Douglas Edwards. 2 cass. (Running Time: 2 hrs.). 1993. 35.00 Set. (978-0-938636-31-1(6), 5015) T Hopkins Intl.
Selling strategies of the 60's.

Selling. 2nd rev. ed. Tom Hopkins. Read by Brett Barry. (Running Time: 12600 sec.). (For Dummies Ser.). 2006. audio compact disk 14.95 (978-0-06-115324-2(9)) HarperCollins Pubs.

Selling: The Proud Profession. Zig Ziglar. Read by Zig Ziglar. 1 cass. (Zig Ziglar Presents Ser.). 1990. 9.95 (978-1-56207-009-0(6)) Zig Ziglar Corp.
A sales career can be the foundation for success & the cornerstone of satisfaction. Zig will renew your confidence, recharge your enthusiasm & increase your sales.

Selling: 12.5 Principles of Sales Greatness. unabr. ed. Jeffrey H. Gitomer. Read by Jeffrey H. Gitomer. (Running Time: 4 hrs. 30 mins. 0 sec.). (ENG.). 2008. audio compact disk 29.95 (978-0-7435-7254-5(8)) Pub: S&S Audio. Dist(s): S and S Inc

Selling above the Crowd: 365 Strategies for Sales Excellence. unabr. ed. Dave Anderson. Read by Dave Anderson. 1 cass. 1999. 29.95 (978-0-9700018-0-1(0)) D Anderson Corp.

Selling Across the Gender Divide. Pat Heim. 1 cass. (Running Time: 37 mins.). 2000. 12.95 (978-1-891531-05-7(0)) Heim Gp.
Uncovers the secrets of targeting your sales strategy to be equally successful with men & women.

Selling Advantage. 12 cass. 1991. 149.95 (232A) Nightingale-Conant.
Learn the techniques & inspirational abilities of over 40 grand masters of sales.

Selling & Serving. Emmet L. Robinson. Read by Emmet L. Robinson. 1 cass. (Running Time: 1 hr. 10 min.). 1994. 14.95 King Street.
How a new sales philosophy can increase your closing ratio.

Selling at Mach 1: Motivational Acceleration. unabr. ed. Steve Sullivan. Read by Steve Sullivan. 4 cass. (Running Time: 2 hrs. 56 min.). 1995. 19.95 (978-0-9641053-6-2(5)) Motivat Resources.
Redefines the nature of successful selling & gives the listener the eight components necessary for accelerated sales success.

Selling At the Top Vols. 1 & 2: Winning in the Hypercompetitive 90's; How to Focus Your Business-to-Business Sales Strategy. Jim Pancero. 12 cass. (Running Time: 9 hrs. 30 min.). 1992. pap. bk. 121.50 Incl. action guides. (2018) Dartnell Corp.
Outfits sales staffs with the advanced selling skill powers you need to succeed in any selling situation - even complicated, lengthy sales cycles that last six months or more.

Selling Ben Cheever: Back to Square One in a Service Economy. Benjamin Cheever. Narrated by Benjamin Cheever. 7 cass. (Running Time: 10 hrs. 15 mins.). 65.00 (978-1-4025-1239-1(2)); audio compact disk 89.00 (978-1-4025-1559-0(6)) Recorded Bks.

Selling Edge. unabr. ed. Michael Levokove. Read by Noah Waterman. 4 cass. (Running Time: 5 hrs. 30 mins.). 1996. 32.95 (978-0-7861-0976-0(9), 1753) Blckstn Audio.
Explores the changing business environment of today's marketplace & identifies the tools & techniques to make you more efficient, more responsive, & as a result, more successful in this highly competitive sales environment. It focuses on business-to-business selling & takes a comprehensive look at the top performing salespeople.

Selling Edge. unabr. ed. Michael Levokove. Read by Noah Waterman. 4 cass. (Running Time: 6 hrs.). 1996. 32.95 (1753) Blckstn Audio.

***Selling for Dummies.** abr. ed. Tom Hopkins. Read by Brett Barry. (ENG.). 2006. (978-0-06-123028-8(6), Harper Audio); (978-0-06-123029-5(4), Harper Audio) HarperCollins Pubs.

Selling from Strength. 6 CDs. (Running Time: 5 hrs, 28 mins). 2003. pap. bk. 299.95 (978-0-9722587-2-2(8)) Caskey Ach Strat.
This is a 6 CD set that includes an operations manual.

Selling from Strength Preview. Bill Caskey. 1 CD. (Running Time: 1 hr.). 2004. audio compact disk 24.95 (978-0-9758510-8-1(X)) Caskey Ach Strat.
Your journey toward the goal of ?Selling From Strength? is a path is full of obstacles, excitement, and thoughts. For you to accomplish this goal it will require some amount of study and contemplation. This CD is a preview to our package Selling From Strength, to give a chance to learn some new strategies and begin implementing them in your marketplace immediately. The optimum way to use this is to listen to the CDonce, then listen to it again, and again, and again. There are exercises for you to complete that aredesigned to help you get better in touch with your value and learn how to sell from strength.One CautionBecause this methodology is applied in our local training practice to hundreds of differentindustries, we believe that these principles and thoughts will apply to almost anyone.However, we also understand the words of your profession may be a little bit different.As you listen you may have to slightly alter the words. I just won?t say the right thing or I won?t say the words in the way that you would say them.That is totally okay. Not only are you free to make those changes, but you should modify what doesn?t work for you?adapt it to your world. And try to have fun while you?re doing it.I have yet to find an industry in B2B selling that parts or all of this program doesn?t apply to. But I fully recognize that I won?t be with you one-on-one. There will be things that don?t fit. I wish you luck on this journey to operating in the business marketplace in a position of strength. It will bring you more satisfaction, more happiness, and more money. I applaud you for taking the first step to tapping into the abundance that?s in each and every market and that is yours for the asking.

Selling Heart. Jack Kinder, Jr. & Garry Kinder. 1 cass. 10.00 (SP100067) SMI Intl.
Selling is an art & the great salespeople are great artists. But like the artist who paints, you must learn the techniques first before you can really express yourself in the art. This tape is about sales techniques & strategy. It is intended to help you get started & keep going successfully & professionally in a sales career.

Selling Heart. Jack Kinder & Garry D. Kinder. 1 cass. 11.00 (978-0-89811-260-3(5), 9452) Meyer Res Grp.
Tape is about sales techniques & strategy. Helps you get started & keep going successfully & professionally in a sales career.

Selling in the Nineties. Larry Wilson. Read by Larry Wilson. 2 cass. 95.00 (586VD) Nightingale-Conant.
You'll learn how to "change the game" on your competition so that even if you find yourself seeing fewer prospects, you'll be twice as productive.

Selling in Tough Times: Secrets to Selling When No One Is Buying. unabr. ed. Tom Hopkins. Read by Tom Hopkins. (Running Time: 7 hrs.). (ENG.). 2010. 16.98 (978-1-60024-927-3(2)); audio compact disk 24.98 (978-1-60024-925-9(6)) Pub: Hachet Audio. Dist(s): HachBkGrp

Selling Made Simple. Steve Sullivan. 1999. 11.95 (978-1-890522-07-0(4)) Pub: Motivat Resources. Dist(s): HRD Press

Selling More... No Matter What. John Graham. Read by John Graham. Read by Christen P. Heide et al. 6 cass. (Running Time: 5 hrs.). 1991. pap. bk. 49.95 (2009) Dartnell Corp.
Practical solutions to boosting sales in the face of tough competition, a sluggish economy, & a struggling sales force.

***Selling of the American Economy: How Foreign Companies Are Remaking the American Dream.** unabr. ed. Micheline Maynard. Read by Marguerite Gavin. (Running Time: 6 hrs. 30 mins.). (ENG.). 2009. 27.98 (978-1-59659-493-7(4), GildAudio) Pub: Gildan Media. Dist(s): HachBkGrp

Selling Out America's Children. David Walsh. 1 cass. (Running Time: 1 hr. 30 mins.). 9.95 (978-1-890423-01-8(7)) Natl Inst Media.
How Americans put profit before values & what parents can do.

Selling Power, Vol. 1. unabr. collector's ed. 12 cass. (Running Time: 12 hrs.). 2001. 7.95 Personal Selling.
Practical selling tips and ideas that are guaranteed to boost your sales and profits. If your business depends on sales, you need Selling Power Live!.

Selling Power, Vol. 11. unabr. collector's ed. 12 cass. (Running Time: 12 hrs.). 2001. 79.95 Personal Selling.

Selling Power, Vol. 111. unabr. collector's ed. 12 cass. (Running Time: 12 hrs.). 2001. 79.00 Personal Selling.
A year's worth of selling skills and success motivation in one handsome album.

Selling Power Live! Laura Day et al. Read by Laura Day et al. 1998. Personal Selling.

Selling Safety in the Nineties. Art Fettig. 6 cass. (Running Time: 6 hrs.). Dramatization. 1990. 59.95 (SSA) Growth Unltd.
A six tape program that will help you sell yourself & all you come in contact with on the importance of safety.

Selling Solutions: The Key to Unlocking Your Hidden Value & Increasing Your Margins, Vol. 1. unabr. ed. Karl Walinskas. Perf. by Ted Ritsick & Beth Bloom-Wright. Narrated by Jim Rising. 6 cass. (Running Time: 5 hrs. 30 min.). 1998. bk. 59.95 Set. (978-0-9667084-0-0(7)) Speaking Connect.
Learn to sell as a consulting partner, not a vendor, & close more sales at higher margins.

Selling Strategies for Internet Marketers: How to Immediately Transform Your Results by Adding Powerful Sales Strategies to Your Marketing Efforts. abr. ed. Eric Lofholm & Robert Imbriale. 2006. audio compact disk (978-0-9785426-1-0(4)) Ultimate Wealth.

Selling Success: Using Hypnosis to Sell. Narrated by Dean A. Montalbano. (Hypnotic Sensory Response Audio Ser.). 2000. 250.00 (978-0-9708772-1-5(8)) L Lizards Pub Co.

Selling Success Again: An HSR Edutainment Tape. Speeches. Dean A. Montalbano. 12 cass. (Running Time: 12 hrs). (Hypnotic Sensory Response Audio Ser.). (C). 2002. (978-1-932086-07-2(2)) L Lizards Pub Co.
Learn to use hypnotic language and NLP techniques to sell. This new, expanded edition includes two new recordings complete with Exercises to help you LEARN!.

Selling the Invisible: Modern Marketing. Harry Beckwith. Narrated by George Wilson. 5 cass. (Running Time: 6 hrs. 15 mins.). 52.00 (978-0-7887-5343-5(6)); audio compact disk 48.00 (978-1-4025-3828-5(6)) Recorded Bks.

Selling the Invisible: Modern Marketing. abr. ed. Harry Beckwith. (ENG.). 2006. 9.98 (978-1-59483-715-9(5)) Pub: Hachet Audio. Dist(s): HachBkGrp

Selling the Invisible: Modern Marketing. abr. ed. Harry Beckwith. Read by Jeffrey Jones. (Running Time: 3 hrs.). (ENG.). 2008. audio compact disk 16.98 (978-1-60024-101-7(8)) Pub: Hachet Audio. Dist(s): HachBkGrp

Selling to the Japanese Market. unabr. ed. David K. Luhman. Read by David K. Luhman. 1 cass. (Running Time: 55 min.). (Doing Busines in Japan Ser.: Vol. 3). 1994. 10.00 (978-1-889297-02-6(X)) Numen Lumen.
Distribution systems, product localization, returned goods, retailers vs. manufacturers, Large Store Law, consignment sales, direct marketing, payment methods, telemarketing, price fixing, advertising.

Selling Toy & Game Ideas. John Landers. 1 cass. (Running Time: 55 min.). 10.95 (946) J Norton Pubs.

Selling Women: Proven Techniques from the Top. Dottie Walters & Laura Larman. 2 cass. (Running Time: 2 hrs.). 1999. 55.00 (978-0-934344-49-4(3)) Royal Pub.
How to sell more to the people who buy the most. Sell to women; sell as a woman.

Selling You: A Practical Guide to Achieving the Most by Becoming Your Best. abr. unabr. ed. Napoleon Hill. Read by Napoleon Hill. Read by Joe Slattery. 2 CDs. (Running Time: 2 hrs. 0 mins. 0 sec.). (ENG.). 2000. audio compact disk 22.95 (978-1-55927-617-7(7)) Pub: Highroads Media. Dist(s): Macmillan

Selling You! A Practical Guide to Achieving the Most by Becoming Your Best. unabr. ed. Napoleon Hill. Read by Napoleon Hill. Read by Michael McConnohie & Joe Slattery. Contrib. by Julien Cook. Prod. by Bill Hartley. 8 CDs. (Running Time: 8 hrs. 0 mins. 0 sec.). (ENG.). 2006. audio compact disk 39.95 (978-1-932429-29-9(8)) Pub: Highroads Media. Dist(s): Macmillan

Selling Your Book's Subsidiary Rights. Jeff Davidson. 1 CD. (Running Time: 59 min.). 2006. audio compact disk 23.95 (978-0-9771296-2-1(4)); audio compact disk (978-1-60729-567-9(9)) Breath Space Inst.

Selling Your Book's Subsidiary Rights. Jeff Davidson. 2006. 13.95 (978-1-60729-341-5(2)) Breath Space Inst.

Selling Your Home. Heather Kibbey & John F. Scott. 1 cass. (Running Time: 1 hr.). 1987. 8.95 incl. worksheet. (978-0-9615067-4-2(1)) Panoply Pr.
Professionals share trade secrets for a quick, profitable transaction.

Selling Your Personal Experiences to Magazines. Read by Lois Duncan. 1 cass. 10.95 (AF1963) J Norton Pubs.
Popular professional writer Lois Duncan shares her secrets for lucrative freelancing by telling you how to write a query letter, use your own experience as subject matter, outline & write an article & slant a subject to appeal to more than one magazine.

Selling Yourself. Jeff Davidson. 6 cass. (Running Time: 6 hrs.). 1995. 59.95 Set. (12590A) Nightingale-Conant.

Selling Yourself: Strategies for Successful Self-Promotion. Jeff Davidson. 6 cass. 59.95 Set. (12590AM) Nightingale-Conant.
This powerful program will give you the tools you need to advance your career & build a reputation for excellence. Why leave recognition & its rewards to chance, when you can put the odds in your favor & gain the recognition & rewards you deserve? Unlock the sure way to business success with this program.

Sellout. 2 CD. (Running Time: 2 hr. 30 mins.). Dramatization. 2000. audio compact disk 19.95 (978-0-9706323-1-9(2)) Kookalook.
The award-winning audio book "Sellout" is a rare treat - 14 performers, an original score, and countless sound effects makes this an entirely new listening/reading experience!.

Sellout. Contrib. by Matthew West. 2006. audio compact disk 11.99 (978-5-558-40877-5(4)) Pt of Grace Ent.

Selma & Eva: Audio Book of Selma Metzger Winkler: Her Experience in Nazi Concentration Camp. Read by [illegible] Feder. Based on a book by Martin A. Winkler. 2006. audio compac[illegible] 6.99 (978-0-9788925-2-4(6)) M Winkler.

Selu: Seeking the Corn-Mother's Wisdom. abr. ed. Marilou Awiakta. 2 cass. (Running Time: 3 hrs.). 1995. 16.95 (978-0-944993-95-8(8)) Audio Lit.
In this collection of essays, poems & stories, the living Cherokee Corn-Mother spirit, called Selu, shows us how to find unity & balance in our selves & in our world.

Selu & Kana'Ti: Cherokee Corn Mother & Lucky Hunter. As told by Red Earth. 1 cass. (Running Time: 30 mins.). (Folktales Ser.). (J). (ps-4). 1999. 7.95 (978-1-57255-656-0(0)) Mondo Pubng.
Meet Selu, Kana'ti & their children & find out how farming & hunting came to the people.

Selznick: The Man Who Produced "Gone with the Wind" abr. ed. Bob Thomas. Read by Carl Reiner. Frwd. by Peter Bart. 4 cass. (Running Time: 6 hrs.). (Hollywood Classics Ser.: Vol. 3). 2004. 25.00 (978-1-931056-20-5(X), N Millennium Audio) New Millenn Enter.
David Selznick (1902-1965) belonged to a select group of Hollywood producers as well-known as the actors they employed. Neurotic, a perfectionist & an acknowledged genius, Selznick was in many ways his own creation. He also collaborated on some of Alfred Hitchcock's most successful pictures.

Semana Santa 2009. Charles R. Swindoll.Tr. of 2009 Easter Messages. 2009. audio compact disk 10.00 (978-1-57972-852-6(9)) Insight Living.

***Semana Santa 2010.** Charles R. Swindoll.Tr. of Easter 2010 Messages. 2010. audio compact disk 12.00 (978-1-57972-884-7(7)) Insight Living.

Semantics in Business Systems: The Savvy Manager's Guide. Dave McComb. 8. (Running Time: 8). 2004. audio compact disk 44.95 (978-0-9754368-1-3(3)) First Princpls.

Semantics in Business Systems: The Savvy Manager's Guide. abr. ed. Dave McComb. 2 CDs. (Running Time: 2 hours). 2004. audio compact disk 19.95i (978-0-9754368-0-6(5)) First Princpls.

Semi-Attached Couple, unabr. ed. Emily Eden. Read by Flo Gibson. 6 cass. (Running Time: 8 hrs.). (gr. 9-12). 1987. 24.95 (978-1-55685-100-1(6)) Audio Bk Con.
The adjustments of a marriage in aristocratic society in England in the early 1800's.

Semi-Detached Couple, unabr. ed. Emily Eden. Read by Peter Joyce. 6 cass. 1999. 54.95 T T Beeler.

Semi-Detached House, unabr. ed. Emily Eden. Read by Flo Gibson. 4 cass. (Running Time: 5 hrs. 30 min.). (gr. 9-12). 1987. 19.95 (978-1-55685-101-8(4)) Audio Bk Con.
The affectation of an avaricious nouveau riche pair are contrasted with the kindness & consideration of landed gentry & neighboring villagers.

Semi-Detached House. unabr. ed. Emily Eden. Read by Peter Joyce. 4 cass. (Running Time: 4 hrs.). 1998. 44.95 (978-1-86015-459-1(X)) Pub: UlverLrgPrint GBR. Dist(s): Ulverscroft US
When Blanch's husband is away she decides to let a house with her sister & soon learns that her new neighbors are already acquainted with her husband.

Semi for a Sleign. 2005. audio compact disk 15.95 (978-1-59433-020-9(4)) Publ Consult.

Semiautomatic: A Novel. Robert Reuland. Read by Jason Collins. 8 vols. 2004. bk. 39.95 (978-0-7927-3261-7(8), SLD 671, Chivers Sound Lib) AudioGO.

Semiconductor Production Equipment in Taiwan: A Strategic Reference 2007. Compiled by Icon Group International, Inc. Staff. 2007. ring bd. 195.00 (978-0-497-82434-1(5)) Icon Grp.

Semilla de Mostaza. unabr. ed. (SPA.). 2001. 9.99 (978-0-8297-3414-0(7)) Pub: Vida Pubs. Dist(s): Zondervan

Semilla de Mostaza. unabr. ed. 2001. audio compact disk 14.99 (978-0-8297-3412-6(0)) Zondervan.

semilla necesita ayuda Audio CD: Emergent Set A. Benchmark Education Staff. Ed. by Katherine Scraper. (Early Explorers Ser.). (J). 2008. audio compact disk 10.00 (978-1-60437-240-3(0)) Benchmark Educ.

Seminar for Executive Secretaries. unabr. ed. 6 cass. (Running Time: 6 hrs.). (Seminars on Tape Ser.). 1980. pap. bk. 49.95 Prof Train TX.
Explains how to manage professional growth, getting control of the day & more.

Seminar for Supervisors. unabr. ed. Read by George Varchola. 6 cass. (Running Time: 6 hrs.). (Seminars on Tape Ser.). 1981. pap. bk. 49.95 Prof Train TX.
Designed to help strengthen motivational skills, communicate more clearly, solve employee performance problems & manage time more effectively.

Seminar on Consumer Finance. Larry Burkett. 1990. 20.00 (978-1-56427-110-5(2)) Crown Fin Min Inc.

Seminar on the Three Yanas of Tibetan Buddhism. T'ai Situ. 4 cass. 1982. 36.00 Vajradhatu.

Seminar Tidbits of the Fifties & Sixties. Clara Darr. 1 cass. 8.95 (076) Am Fed Astrologers.
Information from astrologers at early AFA conventions.

Seminole. Donald Clayton Porter. Read by Lloyd James. 4 vols. No. 12. 2004. (978-1-58807-759-2(4)); audio compact disk 30.00 (978-1-58807-412-6(9)) Am Pubng Inc.

Seminole. Dana Fuller Ross, pseud. Read by Lloyd James. 5 vols. No. 12. 2004. audio compact disk (978-1-58807-876-6(0)) Am Pubng Inc.

Seminole. abr. ed. Donald Clayton Porter. Read by Lloyd James. 4 vols. (Running Time: 6 hrs.). 2004. 25.00 (978-1-58807-228-3(2)) Am Pubng Inc.

Semper Fi. unabr. collector's ed. W. E. B. Griffin. Read by Michael Russotto. 9 cass. (Running Time: 13 hrs. 30 mins.). (Corps Ser.: No. 1). 1992. 72.00 (978-0-7366-2196-0(2), 2991) Books on Tape.
In Semper Fi meet the old corps as it existed between the world wars & witness the relentless approach of Pearl Harbor.

Sempster's Tale. Margaret Frazer. 2008. 84.95 (978-1-4079-0188-6(5)); audio compact disk 89.95 (978-1-4079-0189-3(3)) Pub: Soundings Ltd GBR. Dist(s): Ulverscroft US

Senate Amendment Procedure (CD) Featuring Walter Oleszek. Prod. by TheCapitol.Net. 2006. 107.00 (978-1-58733-041-4(5)) TheCapitol.

Senate Scheduling & Floor Procedures. Ed. by TheCapitol.Net. 2005. audio compact disk 107.00 (978-1-58733-023-0(7)) TheCapitol.

Senator Charles Percy: G. O. P. Foreign Policy see Buckley's Firing Line

Senator Edward Long: Electronic Bugging see Buckley's Firing Line

Senator Gaylord Nelson Speaks Out on Wilderness; Reports about Texas Parks' Trail Building by Boy Scouts; Eagle Release & Caddo Lake Tourism. Hosted by Nancy Pearlman. 1 cass. (Running Time: 28 min.). 10.00 (1208) Educ Comm CA.

Senator Mark Hatfield: Goldwater Candidacy see Buckley's Firing Line

Senator Sam Ervin, Last of the Founding Fathers. Karl Campbell. (ENG.). 2007. 34.95 (978-0-8078-8504-8(5)); audio compact disk 39.95 (978-0-8078-8506-2(1)) U of NC Pr.

Senator Thomas Dodd: Misconduct Charges see Buckley's Firing Line

Senator was Indiscreet. Perf. by William Powell. 1949. (CC-5060) Natl Recrd Co.

Senatorial Privilege: The Chappaquiddick Cover-Up, unabr. ed. Leo Damore. Read by Joe Vincent. 10 cass. (Running Time: 14 hrs. 30 mins.). 1988. 69.95 (978-0-7861-0026-2(5), 1025) Blckstn Audio.
Argues that Senator Kennedy exercised privilege associated with his family name, wealth, office & political power to cover-up numerous facts & implications. With on-the-record statements by leading participants, including Kennedy's cousin Joseph A. Gargan, as well as exclusive first-time-ever interviews, he reveals how Senator Kenndy exercised privilege to emerge unscathed, legally, morally & to a great extent, politically. He weaves the facts into a captivating narrative, illustrating the Kennedy mystique & revealing some explosive quotes.

Senatorial Privilege: The Chappaquiddick Cover-Up. unabr. collector's ed. Leo Damore. Read by Dick Estell. 12 cass. (Running Time: 18 hrs.). 1989. 96.00 (978-0-7366-2502-9(X), 3260) Books on Tape.
Two decades have passed since a car driven by Senator Edward Kennedy plunged off Dike Bridge on Chappaquiddick Island killing former staffer Mary Jo Kopechne. Kennedy has seen the specter of that mishap haunt, frustrate & finally end his presidential ambitions. Not even the Kennedy's political weight has suppressed the questions left unresolved by the accident investigations. Why was Kennedy with Kopechne in a remote part of the island? Why did he flee - how could he flee - an accident scene while she drowned? And why didn't he report the accident until the following morning? Chappaquiddick came to symbolize cover-up, incompetence, raw power &, in the end, a cruel travesty of justice. In seeking the answers to the many questions remaining, Leo Damore conducted over 200 interviews with people close to the case - including Joe Gargan, Kennedy's cousin, co-host of the Chappaquiddick party - accessed the DA's files & the investigator's personal notes.

Senator's Daughter. abr. ed. Victoria Gotti. Read by Mia Sara. 4 cass. (Running Time: 6 hrs.). 1997. 23.00 (978-1-56876-065-0(5)) Soundlines Ent.
Taylor Brooke is defending Tommy Washington, a young kid accused of killing union strong man Joe Sessio. The case becomes personally complicated when Senator Frank Morgan, the father who abandoned her, surfaces in her life.

Senator's Wife. unabr. ed. Sue Miller. Narrated by Blair Brown. 9 CDs. (Running Time: 10 hrs. 15 mins.). 2008. audio compact disk 100.00 (978-1-4159-4583-4(7)) Random.

Senator's Wife. unabr. ed. Sue Miller. Read by Blair Brown. (Running Time: 37800 sec.). (ENG.). 2008. audio compact disk 34.95 (978-0-7393-5851-1(0), Random AudioBks) Pub: Random Audio Pubg. Dist(s): Random

Senator's Wife, unabr. ed. Karen Robards. Read by Paula Parker. 10 vols. (Running Time: 10 hrs.). 1999. bk. 84.95 (978-0-7927-2297-7(3), CSL 186, Chivers Sound Lib) AudioGO.
Ronnie Honneker is the senator's second wife. The Honorable Lewis Honneker, a man twice her age, is wealthy, successful, & revered by voters in his home state of Mississippi. What the public doesn't know is that this pillar of the community is quite unfaithful. Now he's up for re-election, & he hires Tom Quinlan, a political strategist, to head his campaign. The attraction between Tom & Ronnie is instantaneous. When the senator mysteriously dies, scandal breaks & Tom & Ronnie must now risk everything for each other.

Send: The Essential Guide to Email for Office & Home. abr. ed. David Shipley & Will Schwalbe. Read by David Shipley & Will Schwalbe. (Running Time: 7200 sec.). (ENG.). 2007. audio compact disk 19.95 (978-0-7393-4435-4(8), Random AudioBks) Pub: Random Audio Pubg. Dist(s): Random

Send for Paul Temple. unabr. ed. Francis Durbridge. Read by Alistair McGowan. 5 cass. (Running Time: 6 hrs. 15 min.). 2001. 49.95 (978-1-85695-797-7(7), 940208) Pub: ISIS Audio GBR. Dist(s): Ulverscroft US
For years the exclusive Knave of Diamonds has eluded capture in South Africa where he had carried out a series of baffling jewel robberies & murders. Suddenly, this pattern of crimes makes its appearance in London. Scotland Yard is baffled & they cannot think which way to turn. Paul Temple - aided by the beautiful & intrepid Miss Steve Trent, reporter for the Evening Post - is soon on the trail of the mastermind & his dangerous gang of criminals.

Send for Paul Temple Again! Francis Durbridge. 2008. 61.95 (978-0-7531-3796-3(8)); audio compact disk 79.95 (978-0-7531-2777-3(6)) Pub: ISIS Audio GBR. Dist(s): Ulverscroft US

Send in the Clowns: II Cor. 4:10. Ed Young. 1990. 4.95 (978-0-7417-1793-1(X), 793) Win Walk.

Send Me. Contrib. by Graeme Press. 2007. audio compact disk 24.99 (978-5-557-54321-7(X)) Allegis.

Send Me an Angel. Perf. by Heather Miler. 1 CD. (Running Time: 1 hr.). 1999. audio compact disk (978-0-7601-3494-8(4), SO401061) Brentwood Music.
Songs include: "Angel," "We Will See Him," "In Your Arms," "Life to Me" & more.

Send No Flowers, abr. ed. Sandra Brown. Read by Alison Frasier. 2 cass. 1999. 18.00 (FS9-43330) Highsmith.

Send No Flowers. abr. ed. Sandra Brown. Read by Alison Fraser. 3 CDs. (Running Time: 10800 sec.). (ENG.). 2006. audio compact disk 14.99 (978-0-7393-2495-0(0), Random AudioBks) Pub: Random Audio Pubg. Dist(s): Random

Send Your Rain. Perf. by Donnie Harper & New Jersey Mass Choir. 1 cass. 1995. 6.98 (978-1-57908-114-0(2), 9244); audio compact disk 8.98 CD. (978-1-57908-113-3(4)) Platinm Enter.
Sunday morning choir singing is an important part of the American cultural landscape, & since its inception, The New Jersey Mass Choir has made its mark within this culture on the ever-demanding gospel circuit. Since being featured on Foreigner's international, Grammy-nominated hit, "I Want to Know What Love Is," this choir has garnered a huge following & reputation as one of America's most spiritual & creative vocal ensembles. Throughout their successful career, the choir has been led by their founder Donnie Harper who, as director, composer, arranger & performer, adds an original flair to their fresh-sounding compositions.

Sendero. unabr. ed. Stephen D. Stainkamp. Read by Rusty Nelson. 12 cass. (Running Time: 13 hrs. 30 min.). 2001. 64.95 (978-1-55686-988-4(6)) Books in Motion.
Bodyguard and Texas rancher Clint Travis finds his job to protect the Chief Operating Officer for a computer firm more difficult than he had imagined, when the firm's Chief Executive Officer is slain.

Sendero del Mago. Deepak Chopra. 2 cass. (Running Time: 2 hrs.).Tr. of Way of the Wizard. (SPA.). 2002. (978-968-5163-07-1(3)) Taller del Exito.
Twenty spiritual lessons for creating the life you want.

Seneca. Tim Nelson. Read by Tim Nelson. 4 cass. (Running Time: 6 hrs.). (White Indian Ser.: No. 9). 2004. (978-1-58807-940-4(6)) Am Pubng Inc.
Fierce warrior of the Seneca, Ghonkaba, grandson of Renno the White Indian, feels his blood run hot as the American colonists revolt against the British. But the Seneca refuse to break their traditional alliance with England to join the colonists' fight. His noble heart burning, Ghonkaba realizes the only chance for freedom for the Seneca is to become a traitor to his heritage and family to follow the patriots' star-spangled banner into a long and dangerous war. Only his superb scouting skills can lead the fledgling American army to safety in a series of narrow escapes from the Redcoats. Then the Manitou, sacred spirits of the Seneca, guide Ghonkaba as he guides General Washington's troops in a daring midwinter attack across the Delaware River that will stun the world with a victory for a nation struggling to be born.

Seneca. abr. ed. Donald Clayton Porter. Read by Lloyd James. Abr. by Edward McClure. 5 vols. (Running Time: 6 hrs.). No. 9. 2004. audio compact disk 30.00 (978-1-58807-409-6(9)); audio compact disk (978-1-58807-848-3(5)) Am Pubng Inc.

Seneca. abr. ed. Donald Clayton Porter. Read by Tim Nelson. Abr. by Ted McClure. 4 cass. (Running Time: 6 hrs.). (White Indian Ser.: No. 9). 2004. 25.00 (978-1-58807-225-2(8)) Am Pubng Inc.

Seneca Warrior. Donald Clayton Porter. Read by Lloyd James. 4 vols. No. 17. 2004. 25.00 (978-1-58807-233-7(9)); (978-1-58807-764-6(0)) Am Pubng Inc.

Senior Bacclaureate Service. Ed Young. 1995. 4.95 (978-0-7417-2059-7(0), 1059) Win Walk.

Senior Fitnessize. Mike Cinquanto. 1 cass. 19.95 Incl. exercise manual.; 59.95 Incl. Audio cass., video & manual. Image Media.
Aims at promoting senior adult fitness through a safe, scientifically sound exercise program designed by professionals.

Senior Musician Accompaniment. 2002. 25.00 (978-0-633-06479-2(3)) LifeWay Christian.

Senior Musician Accompaniment. 2003. 3.25 (978-0-633-07783-9(6)) LifeWay Christian.

Senior Musician Accompaniment. 2004. 3.25 (978-0-633-08155-3(8)) LifeWay Christian.

Senior Musician Accompaniment. 2004. 3.25 (978-0-633-08407-3(7)) LifeWay Christian.

Senior Musician Accompaniment. 2004. 3.25 (978-0-633-08657-2(6)) LifeWay Christian.

Senior Musician Accompaniment. 2004. 3.25 (978-0-633-17459-0(9)) LifeWay Christian.

Senior Musician Accompaniment. 2005. 3.25 (978-0-633-17654-9(0)) LifeWay Christian.

Senior Musician Accompaniment. 2005. 25.00 (978-0-633-17795-9(4)) LifeWay Christian.

Senior Musician Accompaniment CD. 2003. 25.00 (978-0-633-07715-0(1)) LifeWay Christian.

Senior Musician Accompaniment CD. 2004. 25.00 (978-0-633-08087-7(X)) LifeWay Christian.

Senior Musician Accompaniment CD. 2004. 25.00 (978-0-633-08339-7(9)) LifeWay Christian.

Senior Musician Accompaniment CD. 2004. 25.00 (978-0-633-08589-6(8)) LifeWay Christian.

Senior Musician Accompaniment CD. 2004. 25.00 (978-0-633-17403-3(3)) LifeWay Christian.

Senior Musician Accompaniment CD. 2005. 25.00 (978-0-633-17597-9(8)) LifeWay Christian.

Senior Musician Accompaniment CD. 2005. 3.25 (978-0-633-17852-9(7)) LifeWay Christian.

Senor Blues. Perf. by Taj Mahal. 1 cass., 1 CD. 8.78 (PM 82151); audio compact disk 13.58 CD. (PM 82151) NewSound.
Featuring a melange of well known Blues, Jazz & R&B. Includes: "Mr. Pitiful," & others.

Senor de Este Siglo. 2001. 7.99 (978-0-8297-3444-7(9)) Pub: Vida Pubs. Dist(s): Zondervan

señor de la Familia. P. Juan Rivas. (SPA.). 2005. audio compact disk 18.95 (978-1-935405-72-6(1)) Hombre Nuevo.

Senorita Runfio. 2004. pap. bk. 32.75 (978-1-55592-344-0(5)) Weston Woods.

Senorita Runfio. Barbara Cooney. Narrated by Claire Danes. Music by John Jennings. 1 cass., 5 bks. (Running Time: 18 min.).Tr. of Miss Rumphius. (J). pap. bk. 32.75 Weston Woods.
As a young girl, Alice dreams of traveling to faraway places & finding a home by the sea. "There is a third thing you must do," says her grandfather, "You must do something to make the world more beautiful." After many years, Alice finds the answer to her lifelong search in a simple handful of seeds.

Senorita Runfio. Barbara Cooney. Narrated by Claire Danes. Music by John Jennings. 1 cass. (Running Time: 18 min.).Tr. of Miss Rumphius. (J). (gr. k-5). bk. 24.95 Weston Woods.

Senorita Runfio. Barbara Cooney. Narrated by Claire Danes. Music by John Jennings. Prod. by Sarah Kerruish. 1 cass. (Running Time: 18 min.).Tr. of Miss Rumphius. (J). (gr. k-5). 2000. pap. bk. 12.95 (QPRA396) Weston Woods.

Senorita Runfio. Barbara Cooney.Tr. of Miss Rumphius. (J). (gr. 2-3). 2004. 8.95 (978-1-55592-988-6(5)) Weston Woods.

Senorita Runfio. Barbara Cooney. 1 cass. (Running Time: 18 min.).Tr. of Miss Rumphius. (SPA.). (J). (gr. 2-4). 2004. 8.95 (978-1-55592-979-4(6), WW30965) Weston Woods.
After many years, Alice finds her lifelong search to make the world more beautiful in a handful of seeds.

Sens. Contrib. by Evan Anthem. Prod. by Mark Lee Townsend. 2005. audio compact disk 13.98 (978-5-558-96639-8(4)) Mono Vs Ster.

Sensation, Perception, & the Aging Process. Instructed by Francis B. Colavita. 12 cass. (Running Time: 12 hrs.). 2006. 129.95 (978-1-59803-227-7(5)); audio compact disk 69.95 (978-1-59803-228-4(3)) Teaching Co.

Sensational Sex. Dick Sutphen. 1 cass. (Running Time: 1 hr.). (RX17 Ser.). 14.98 (978-0-87554-388-8(X), RX152) Valley Sun.

Sensations (Readings From) Poems. Barbara Rosenthal. Read by Barbara Rosenthal. (Running Time: 30 MINS.). 2005. audio compact disk 25.00 (978-0-9760793-5-4(6)) eMedialoft.
Digitized from the author's live performance of text with slides at The Poetry Project, NYC, this reading contains 25 very brief prose-poetry short stories and fables, often of unstable characters negotiating a highly unstable landscape.

Sense & Nonsense. 1 cass. 10.95 (C23327) J Norton Pubs.
A look at the differences between sense, meta-sense, & nonsense.

Sense & Nonsense, Pt. I. Gilbert Highet. 1 cass. (Running Time: 30 min.). (Gilbert Highet Ser.). 11.95 (23326) J Norton Pubs.
What is the difference between sense, almost sense, & nonsense & what does it matter?.

***Sense & Nonsense about Heaven & Hell.** Zondervan. (Running Time: 5 hrs. 51 mins. 43 sec.). (Sense & Nonsense Ser.). (ENG.). 2010. 9.99 (978-0-310-86934-4(X)) Zondervan.

Sense & Nonsense & Well-Adjusted. 1 cass. (Recovery Is Forever Ser.). 1981. 8.95 (1534G) Hazelden.

Sense & Sensibility. Jane Austen. Narrated by Anne Flosnik. (ENG.). 2008. 12.95 (978-0-9801087-9-8(9)) Alpha DVD.

***Sense & Sensibility.** Jane Austen. Narrated by Flo Gibson. 2010. audio compact disk 34.95 (978-1-60646-137-2(0)) Audio Bk Con.

Sense & Sensibility. Jane Austen. Narrated by Annette Crosbie. 2004. audio compact disk 39.95 (978-0-563-52483-0(9)) AudioGO.

Sense & Sensibility. Jane Austen. 10 Cds. (Running Time: 12 hrs.). 2002. audio compact disk 68.00 (978-0-7366-8691-4(6)) Pub: Books on Tape. Dist(s): NetLibrary CO
Two sisters try to find enduring love in a world marked by class and social differences.

Sense & Sensibility. Jane Austen. Read by Sarah Badel. 9 cass. (Running Time: 10 hrs. 30 min.). 75.00 (CC/033) C to C Cassettes.
Elinor & Marianne Dashwood appear to be images of sense & sensibility, as they confront the straitened circumstances they find themselves in due to their selfish stepbrother.

Sense & Sensibility. Jane Austen. Read by Susannah Harker. 10 cass. (Running Time: 15 hrs.). 2001. 69.95 (SAB 133) Pub: Chivers Audio Bks GBR. Dist(s): AudioGO
Two sisters, Elinor and Marianne, each quite different in appearance and temperament. Elinor's good sense contrasts with Marianne's impulsive candor. Yet in the face of a highly competitive marriage market their experience of love causes both to readjust.

Sense & Sensibility. Jane Austen. Narrated by Nadia May. (Running Time: 12 hrs.). (C). 2000. 34.95 (978-1-59912-588-6(9)) Iofy Corp.

Sense & Sensibility. Jane Austen. Abr. by Laurie Knox. (ENG.). 2007. 5.99 (978-1-60339-159-7(2)); audio compact disk 5.99 (978-1-60339-160-3(6)) Listenr Digest.

Sense & Sensibility. Jane Austen. Read by Allison Green. 8 cass. (Running Time: 11 hrs.). 1993. 50.60 (978-1-56544-001-2(3), 350006); Rental 9.50 30 day rental Set. (350006) Literate Ear.
Nineteenth century British society is the setting of this romantic story of sisters Elinor & Marianne Dashwood, as each overcomes her limits in her quest for virtue & true love.

Sense & Sensibility. Jane Austen. Read by Juliet Stevenson. 3 cass. (Running Time: 3 hrs. 45 mins.). (Works of Jane Austen). 1996. 17.98 (978-962-634-593-1(4), NA309314, Naxos AudioBooks) Naxos.

Sense & Sensibility. Jane Austen. Contrib. by Julie Christie. (Classic, Audio Ser.). (ENG., (gr. 12 up). 2003. 16.95 (978-0-14-086105-1(X), PenGlobal) Penguin Grp USA.

Sense & Sensibility. Jane Austen. Narrated by Flo Gibson. 7 cas. (Running Time: 11 hrs.). 19.95 (978-1-4025-3324-2(1)) Recorded Bks.

Sense & Sensibility. abr. ed. Jane Austen. Read by Glenda Jackson. (Running Time: 23400 sec.). 2007. audio compact disk 19.95 (978-1-4332-0703-7(6)); audio compact disk & audio compact disk 45.00 (978-1-4332-1351-9(6)) Blckstn Audio.

Sense & Sensibility. abr. ed. Jane Austen. 2001. 7.95 (978-1-57815-242-1(9), Media Bks Audio) Media Bks NJ.

Sense & Sensibility. abr. ed. Jane Austen. Read by Juliet Stevenson. 3 CDs. (Running Time: 3 hrs. 45 mins.). (Works of Jane Austen). 1996. audio compact disk 22.98 (978-962-634-093-6(2), NA309312, Naxos AudioBooks) Naxos.

Sense & Sensibility. abr. ed. Jane Austen. Perf. by Glenda Jackson. 4 cass. (Running Time: 6 hrs.). 2004. 25.00 (978-1-59007-139-7(5)) Pub: New Millenn Enter. Dist(s): PerseuPGW
Timeless novel from 1811 has won over a new generation of readers (and movie-goers). Intricate plot follows the loves and losses of the recently impoverished Dashwood sisters, straitlaced Elinor and lively Marianne.

Sense & Sensibility. abr. ed. Jane Austen & Julie Christie. (Running Time: 6 hrs.). (ENG.). (gr. 12 up). 2005. audio compact disk 16.95 (978-0-14-305808-3(8), PengAudBks) Penguin Grp USA.

Sense & Sensibility. abr. unabr. ed. Jane Austen. Narrated by Annette Crosbie. (Running Time: 12600 sec.). (BBC Radio Classics Ser.). (ENG.). 2007. audio compact disk 19.95 (978-1-60283-314-2(1)) Pub: AudioGO. Dist(s): Perseus Dist

Sense & Sensibility. unabr. ed. Jane Austen. Read by Flo Gibson. 8 cass. (Running Time: 11 hrs. 30 min.). (YA). (gr. 9 up). 1990. 26.95 (978-1-55685-184-1(7)) Audio Bk Con.
The discreet Elinor (sense) & the romantic & reckless Marianne (sensibility) find the course of true love full of brambles & disillusionment. Their neighborhood & London are peopled with characters in the special Austenian mold.

Sense & Sensibility. unabr. ed. Jane Austen. Read by Sarah Badel. 8 cass. (Running Time: 10 hrs. 30 min.). (Studies in Austrian Literature, Culture, & Thought). (gr. 9-12). 2004. 34.95 (978-1-57270-070-3(X), F81070u) Pub: Audio Partners. Dist(s): PerseuPGW
The story revolves around the Dashwood sisters, Elinor & Marianne. Whereas the former is a sensible, rational creature, her younger sister is wildly romantic - a characteristic that offers Austen plenty of scope for both satire & compassion. Commenting on Edward Ferrars, a potential suitor for Elinor's hand, Marianne admits that while she "loves him tenderly", she finds him disappointing as a possible lover for her sister.

Sense & Sensibility. unabr. ed. Jane Austen. Read by Susannah Harker. 10 CDs. (Running Time: 15 hrs.). 2002. audio compact disk 94.95 (978-0-7540-5495-5(0), CCD186) AudioGO.

Sense & Sensibility. unabr. ed. Jane Austen. Read by Sarah Badel. (Running Time: 37800 sec.). (ENG.). 2006. audio compact disk 37.95 (978-1-57270-552-4(3)) Pub: AudioGO. Dist(s): Perseus Dist

Sense & Sensibility. unabr. ed. Jane Austen. Read by Nadia May. 9 cass. (Running Time: 13 hrs.). 2000. 62.95 (978-0-7861-1822-9(9), 2621); audio compact disk 80.00 (978-0-7861-9849-8(4), 2621) Blckstn Audio.

Sense & Sensibility. unabr. ed. Jane Austen. 8 cass. (Running Time: 12 hrs.). 2002. 64.00 (978-0-7366-8624-2(X)) Books on Tape.
Two sisters try to find enduring love in a world marked by class and social differences.

Sense & Sensibility. unabr. ed. Jane Austen. Read by Nadia May. (YA). 2006. 64.99 (978-1-59895-349-7(4)) Find a World.

Sense & Sensibility. unabr. ed. Jane Austen. Read by Jill Masters. 10 cass. (Running Time: 10 hrs.). 1999. 69.95 (FS9-34248) Highsmith.

Sense & Sensibility. unabr. ed. Jane Austen. Read by Jill Masters. 9 cass. (Running Time: 12 hrs. 30 min.). 1982. 52.00 (C-71) Jimcin Record.
The two main characters Elinor & Marianne Dashwood, are of contrasting characters - one practical, the other emotional. The struggle for each to see the other's point of view provides the conflict in this novel.

Sense & Sensibility. unabr. ed. Jane Austen. Read by Juliet Stevenson. 11 CDs. (Running Time: 45805 sec.). 2005. bk. 67.98 (978-962-634-361-6(3)) Naxos UK GBR.

Sense & Sensibility. unabr. ed. Jane Austen. Narrated by Flo Gibson. 8 cass. (Running Time: 11 hrs.). 1981. 70.00 (978-1-55690-468-4(1), 81110E7) Recorded Bks.
Elinor & Marianne Dashwood pursue love & happiness in polite English society.

Sense & Sensibility. unabr. ed. Jane Austen. Narrated by Wanda McCaddon. 9 CDs. (Running Time: 11 hrs. 30 mins. 0 sec.). (ENG.). 2008. audio compact disk 34.99 (978-1-4001-0689-9(3)) Pub: Tantor Media. Dist(s): IngramPubServ

Sense & Sensibility. unabr. ed. Jane Austen. Read by Wanda McCaddon. Narrated by Wanda McCaddon. 1 MP3-CD. (Running Time: 11 hrs. 30 mins. 0 sec.). (ENG.). 2008. 24.99 (978-1-4001-5689-4(0)); audio compact disk 69.99 (978-1-4001-3689-6(X)) Pub: Tantor Media. Dist(s): IngramPubServ

Sense & Sensibility. unabr. collector's ed. Jane Austen. Read by Jill Masters. 10 cass. (Running Time: 15 hrs.). (J). 1982. 80.00 (978-0-7366-3864-7(4), 9071) Books on Tape.
Elinor & Marianne Dashwood have contrasting qualities of character, one practical & conventional, the other emotional & sentimental. The outcome turns on these young women mastering their primary Characteristics & finding true happiness when in the one - sense gives way to sensibility & in the other sensibility to sense.

***Sense & Sensibility: (Unabridged Audiobook)** Wendy Mullen. 2010. audio compact disk 24.95 (978-1-4276-4634-7(1)) AardGP.

Sense & Sensibility & Sea Monsters. unabr. ed. Jane Austen & Ben H. Winters. Read by Katherine Kellgren. (Running Time: 11 hrs.). (Quirk Classic Ser.). 2009. 24.99 (978-1-4418-2436-3(7), 9781441824363, Brilliance MP3); 39.97 (978-1-4418-2437-0(5), 9781441824370, Brlnc Audio MP3 Lib); 39.97 (978-1-4418-2438-7(3), 9781441824387, BADLE); audio compact disk 29.99 (978-1-4418-2434-9(0), 9781441824349, Bril Audio CD Unabri); audio compact disk 97.97 (978-1-4418-2435-6(9), 9781441824356, BriAudCD Unabrid) Brilliance Audio.

***Sense & Sensuality: Jesus Talks with Oscar Wilde on the Pursuit of Pleasure.** unabr. ed. Ravi Zacharias. Narrated by Simon Vance. (ENG.). 2005. 9.98 (978-1-59644-237-5(9), Hovel Audio) christianaud.

Sense & Sensuality: Jesus Talks with Oscar Wilde on the Pursuit of Pleasure. unabr. ed. Ravi Zacharias. Narrated by Simon Vance. 2 CDs. (Running Time: 2 hrs. 0 mins. 0 sec.). (ENG.). 2005. audio compact disk 15.98 (978-1-59644-236-8(0), Hovel Audio) christianaud.

Sense of Beauty. unabr. ed. George Santayana. Read by Robert L. Halvorson. 6 cass. (Running Time: 6 hrs.). 42.95 (78) Halvorson Assocs.

Sense of Belonging. unabr. ed. Margaret T. Davis. Narrated by Jean Simmons. 12 cass. (Running Time: 16 hrs. 30 mins.). 1999. 101.00 (978-1-84197-036-3(0), H1039E7) Recorded Bks.
Sequel to "A Woman of Property." Elizabeth's world is wrecked when she finds Christina Monkton, model of sophistication & success, is not her mother. To find her true origins is her only hope to balance the constant misery she feels in love & life. The goal of her search, Annalie Gordon, has her own problems. As a dancer, she stars with the fiery Tony Carlino, whose interest is more personal than professional. Her rejection of his uncontained passion is catastrophic, as tempers rage & emotions intensify, Annalie is alone again, but fate has a surprise in store.

Sense of Evil. unabr. ed. Kay Hooper. Narrated by Alyssa Bresnahan. 10 CDs. (Running Time: 10 hrs. 45 min.). 2003. audio compact disk 69.00 (978-1-4025-5751-4(5), C2289) Recorded Bks.
Beautiful, successful, blonde women are being murdered in a small, peaceful town where such horrible atrocities are not supposed to happen. Police Chief Rafe Sullivan knows he has to find the killer fast, but he doesn?t know where to begin. Enter FBI profiler Isabel Adams. She?s tough, fearless, and determined. Not to mention psychic, and blonde.

Sense of Evil. unabr. ed. Kay Hooper. Read by Alyssa Bresnahan. 7 cass. (Running Time: 11 hrs. 45 mins.). 2004. 29.99 (978-1-4025-5772-9(8), 03274) Recorded Bks.
In a small southern town, blondes are becoming an endangered species, led to their bloody deaths by an attacker that none of them seems to have resisted.

Sense of Music. Stephen Brown. 6 cass. (J). (ps). 1988. 22.00 (978-0-15-579639-3(9)) Harcourt CAN CAN.

Sense of Nonsense. 1 cass. (Running Time: 23 min.). 12.00 (L440) MEA A Watts Cass.

Sense of Place. Wallace Stegner. Read by Wallace Stegner. 2 cass. (Running Time: 3 hrs.). 1994. 16.95 (978-0-939643-19-6(7), 3526, NrthWrd Bks) TandN Child.
Pulitzer Prize-winning author includes eight essays, reflects his bond with his surroundings from the Saskatchewan prairie, to Utah & Montana & finally, to his home in California.

Sense of Precious: Human Nature's Missing Ingredient. Gary F. Hutchison. 1 cass. (Running Time: 1 hr. 30 mins.). 1994. pap. bk. 7.50 (978-1-885631-08-4(1)) G F Hutchison.
A discussion of the concept of helping children acquire a sense that all human beings are precious & therefore to be protected & nurtured.

Sense of Reality. Graham Greene & Richard Woodman. Read by Derek Jacobi. 6 cass. (Isis Cassettes Ser.). 1992. 69.95 (978-1-85695-587-4(7)) Pub: ISIS Lrg Prnt GBR. Dist(s): Ulverscroft US

Sense of Reality. unabr. ed. Graham Greene. Read by Derek Jacobi. 6 cass. (Running Time: 7 hrs. 17 min.). (Cassette Library). 1991. 44.98 (978-0-8072-3169-2(X), CXL549CX, Listening Lib) Random Audio Pubg.
A collection that captures a wealth of the writer's diverse themes.

Sense of Smell: Program from the Award Winning Public Radio Serie. Interview. Hosted by Fred Goodwin. 1 CD. (Running Time: 1 hr). 2001. audio compact disk 21.95 (978-1-932479-92-8(9), LCM 188) Lichtenstein Creat.
You're visiting a friend for dinner. How does the simple act of sniffing the air tell you if you'll be having curry for dinner... or lasagna? This show explores the sophisticated chemical sensing system we know as sense of smell. Dr. Stuart Firestein, Professor of Biology at Columbia University, describes new breakthroughs in our understanding of how we recognize smells. Dr. Sophia Grojsman, of International Flavors and Fragrances, talks about the blend of artistry and chemistry that she brings to her work as a perfume creator. Aromatherapist Trigve Harris, owner of New York's essential oils store Enfleurage, recommends essential oils to comfort the grief-stricken and soothe the frazzled. Joseph "Jofish" Kaye, of the Media Lab at the Massachusetts Institute of Technology, explores new uses of scent to convey abstract information. Dr. Sarah Rachel Herz, Assistant Professor of Psychology at Brown University, shares her findings on the emotionaly link between sense of smell and memory. And anthropologist Dr. David Howes, of Montreal's Concordia University, offers insight into olfactory codes the world over.

Sense of the Past. unabr. ed. Henry James. Narrated by Flo Gibson. 5 cass. (Running Time: 7 hrs. 30 mins.). 2003. 20.95 (978-1-55685-732-4(2)) Audio Bk Con.
Delves into the life of a young American who returns to the land of his forefathers where he falls in love with his cousin. Recommended for true Jamesian enthusiasts who are used to convolution.

Sense of Touch: Program from the Award Winning Public Radio Series. Featuring Susan Lederman. (Infinite Mind Ser.). 2002. audio compact disk 21.95 (978-1-888064-58-2(7), LCM 241) Lichtenstein Creat.
This week on The Infinite Mind: Sense of Touch. Guests include Dr. Tiffany Field, director of the Touch Research Institute, University of Miami Medical School; Dr. Susan Lederman, director of the Touch Laboratory Queen's University in Ontario; Dr. Shelby Taylor, adjunct professor of psychology at the California State University, Fullerton; Ann Cunningham, a tactile artist and teacher at The Colorado Center for the Blind; Greg Wong, a student of Ann Cunningham's; and Julie Deden, director of The Colorado Center for the Blind. Also featured is a report by Devorah Klahr on an infant massage class that Stoney Brook University Hospital offers free to parents of premature infants. Plus, John Hockenberry on what he's learned about sense of touch by living with a spinal cord injury that's led to the loss of sensation through much of his body.

Sense of Urgency. John P. Kotter. Read by Bill Weideman. (Playaway Adult Nonfiction Ser.). (ENG.). 2009. 49.99 (978-1-60775-860-0(1)) Find a World.

Sense of Urgency. unabr. ed. John P. Kotter. Read by Bill Weideman. (Running Time: 5 hrs.). 2008. 39.25 (978-1-4233-6940-0(8), 9781423369400, BADLE); 24.95 (978-1-4233-6937-0(8), 9781423369370, Brilliance MP3); 39.25 (978-1-4233-6938-7(6), 9781423369387, Brlnc Audio MP3 Lib); 24.95 (978-1-4233-6939-4(4), 9781423369394, BAD); audio compact disk 69.25 (978-1-4233-6936-3(X), 9781423369363, BriAudCD Unabrid); audio compact disk 24.95 (978-1-4233-6935-6(1), 9781423369356, Bril Audio CD Unabri) Brilliance Audio.

Sense of Where You Are & The Headmaster. unabr. ed. John McPhee. Read by Walter Zimmerman. 7 cass. (Running Time: 7 hrs.). 1989. 42.00 (978-0-7366-1526-6(1), 2397) Books on Tape.
Stories of basketball legend & Senator, Bill Bradley & headmaster, Frank Boyden.

Sense of Wonder. unabr. ed. Rachel Carson. (Running Time: 1800 sec.). 2007. 15.95 (978-1-4332-0721-1(4)); audio compact disk 19.95 (978-1-4332-0723-5(0)); audio compact disk 17.00 (978-1-4332-0722-8(2)) Blckstn Audio.

Sensible Life. unabr. ed. Mary Wesley. Read by Eleanor Bron. 10 cass. (Running Time: 10 hrs. 50 min.). (Isis Ser.). (J). 1990. 84.95 (978-1-85089-610-4(0), 90114) Pub: ISIS Lrg Prnt GBR. Dist(s): Ulverscroft US

Sensible Weight Loss, No. I. 1 cass. (Running Time: 1 hr.). 12.95 (978-1-884305-67-2(9)) Changeworks.
Tape I is Motivation & Preparation. It will help you identify any hidden causes of overeating & evaluate any healthy lifestyle changes that may be necessary. Tape II is Acting & Maintaining. It will help you begin to lose weight & naturally include the new changes into your daily life & future.

Sensible Weight Loss, No. II. 1 cass. (Running Time: 1 hr.). 12.95 Tape II. (978-1-884305-68-9(7)) Changeworks.

Sensible Weight Loss, Nos. I & II. 2 cass. (Running Time: 2 hrs.). (978-1-884305-69-6(5)) Changeworks.

Sensibly Thin Motivational Weight Loss Program. 1 cass. 1994. 14.95 (978-0-9636350-2-0(6)) Sensibly Thin.

Sensing the Right Time for Ministry. 1 cass. (Care Cassettes Ser.: Vol. 13, No. 3). 1986. 10.80 Assn Prof Chaplains.

Sensitive New Age Spy. unabr. ed. Geoff McGeachin. Read by Peter Hosking. (Running Time: 21600 sec.). 2008. audio compact disk 63.95 (978-1-921415-15-9(0), 9781921415159) Pub: Bolinda Pubng AUS. Dist(s): Bolinda Pub Inc

Sensitive Nodal Degrees. Jan Snodgrass. 1 cass. 8.95 (714) Am Fed Astrologers.
An AFA Convention workshop tape.

Sensitive Points, Vol. 1. Clara Darr. 1 cass. (Running Time: 1 hr. 30 mins.). 1988. 8.95 (647) Am Fed Astrologers.

Sensitive Points, Vol. 2. Clara Darr. 1 cass. (Running Time: 1 hr. 30 mins.). 1988. 8.95 (648) Am Fed Astrologers.

Sensitivity of Heart. Kenneth Copeland. 2 cass. 1985. 10.00 (978-0-88114-765-0(6)) K Copeland Pubns.
Biblical teaching on knowing God.

Senso. Camillo Boito. Read by Cecile Brune. 1 cass. 1996. 16.95 (1861-LV) Olivia & Hill.
In her diary, Countess Livia, recounts her love for the handsome lieutenant, Remigio, some 20 years before.

Sensor Sweep. Don Pendleton. (Stony Man Ser.: No. 84). 2006. audio compact disk (978-1-59950-141-3(4)) GraphicAudio.

Sensory: Hearing. abr. ed. Robert A. Monroe. Read by Robert A. Monroe. (Running Time: 30 min.). (Human Plus Ser.). 1989. 14.95 (978-1-56102-032-4(X)) Inter Indus.
Amplify or decrease your sense of hearing.

Sensory: Seeing. abr. ed. Robert A. Monroe. Read by Robert A. Monroe. (Running Time: 30 min.). (Human Plus Ser.). 1989. 14.95 (978-1-56102-033-1(8)) Inter Indus.
Improve & fine-tune sense of sight.

Sensory: Smell. Robert A. Monroe. Read by Robert A. Monroe. (Human Plus Ser.). 1989. 14.95 (978-1-56102-034-8(6)) Inter Indus.
Amplify of decrease your sense of smell.

Sensory: Taste. Robert A. Monroe. Read by Robert A. Monroe. (Running Time: 30 min.). (Human Plus Ser.). 1989. 14.95 (978-1-56102-035-5(4)) Inter Indus.
Develop discriminating taste buds.

Sensory: Touch. abr. ed. Robert A. Monroe. Read by Robert A. Monroe. (Running Time: 30 min.). (Human Plus Ser.). 1989. 14.95 (978-1-56102-036-2(2)) Inter Indus.
Increase or decrease your sense of touch at will.

Sensory Development Self-Study Course. 2nd ed. David Longmire. 2 cass. (CIL Publications & Audiobooks). 1997. bk. 22.00 (978-1-890786-00-7(4)) Visions-Srvs.
Teaches skills to visually impaired people.

Sensual Enhancement: Hypnosis for Couples. Created by Randall Maynard. 1 CD. (Running Time: 40 min). 2002. audio compact disk (978-0-9633737-9-3(X)) Nordique.

Sensual Lovemaking. Read by Mary Richards. (Subliminal - Self Hypnosis Ser.). 12.95 (812) Master Your Mind.

Sensual Sensual. Perf. by B-Tribe Staff. 1 cass., 1 CD. 8.78 (ATL 83080); audio compact disk 13.58 CD Jewel box. (ATL 83080) NewSound.

Sensuous, Loving Woman. Read by Mary Richards. 1 cass. (Running Time: 83 min.). (Series Two Thousand). 2007. audio compact disk 19.95 (978-1-56136-106-9(2)) Master Your Mind.

Sensuous Woman. unabr. collector's ed. Read by Violet Cielo. 4 cass. (Running Time: 4 hrs.). 1979. 24.00 (978-0-7366-0214-3(3), 1212) Books on Tape.
The first how-to manual of sexual practice & manipulation.

***Sent.** unabr. ed. Margaret Peterson Haddix. Narrated by Chris Sorensen. 1 Playaway. (Running Time: 7 hrs. 45 mins.). (Missing Ser.: Bk. 2). (YA). (gr. 5-9). 2009. 59.75 (978-1-4407-2677-4(9)); 51.75 (978-1-4407-2668-2(X)); audio compact disk 77.75 (978-1-4407-2672-9(8)) Recorded Bks.

***Sent.** unabr. collector's ed. Margaret Peterson Haddix. Narrated by Chris Sorensen. 7 CDs. (Running Time: 7 hrs. 45 mins.). (Missing Ser.: Bk. 2). (YA). (gr. 5-9). 2009. audio compact disk 44.95 (978-1-4407-2676-7(0)) Recorded Bks.

Sent By the Father. Perf. by Point of Grace Staff. 1 cass. 1999. Provident Music.

Sent for You Yesterday. John Edgar Wideman. Read by John Edgar Wideman. Interview with Kay Bonetti. 1 cass. (Running Time: 1hr. 30 mins.). 1985. 13.95 (978-1-55644-136-3(3), 5081) Am Audio Prose.
Wideman reads excerpts from two of his works.

Sentence Patterns of Indonesian. Soenjono Dardjowidjojo. (PALI Language Text Ser.). 1994. bk. 502.00 (978-0-8248-1624-7(2)) UH Pr.

Sentence Sense, Vol. 1. Edith Chevat. 4 cass. (YA). 59.00 Incl. activity bks., guide. (978-0-89525-173-2(6), AKC 334) Ed Activities.
Activity centers around subject-verb agreement & the building of sentences using structured, linguistic approach. The concept of first, second, or third person & present, past, or future tense is explained.

sentido de la Vida. P. Juan Rivas. (SPA.). (YA). 2005. audio compact disk 18.95 (978-1-935405-71-9(3)) Hombre Nuevo.

Sentimental. Perf. by Kayleen Anderson & Gary Romer. 1 cass. 1995. 8.00 (978-1-890672-14-0(9)) Phil Don.
Western.

Sentimental Christmas. Perf. by Kathy Troccoli et al. 1 cass. 1999. (978-0-7601-2926-5(6)); audio compact disk (978-0-7601-2925-8(8)) Brentwood Music.
The classic sound of the big band combined with Kathy's rich, warm vocals. Includes: "White Christmas"; "It's the Most Wonderful Time of the Year"; "O Little Town of Bethlehem/Away in a Manger"; "Walking in a Winter Wonderland"; "What Child Is This?"; "Let It Snow"; "I'll Be Home for Christmas"; "Christmas Song"; "Sleigh Ride"; "Silent Night"; "Have Yourself a Merry Little Christmas" & the all-new "Only Always.".

Sentimental Education: The Story of a Young Man. unabr. ed. Gustave Flaubert. Read by Michael Maloney. 12 cass. (Running Time: 18 hrs.). 2003. 96.95 (978-0-7540-0867-5(3), CAB 2289) AudioGO.

Sentimental Journey. Perf. by Doris Day. 1 cass. (Running Time: 34 min.). 1953. 7.98; audio compact disk 10.98 Lifedance.
Includes "Be Anything (But Be Mine)," "Blue Skies," "Don't Worry 'Bout Me," "I Can't Give You Anything but Love," "I Got It Bad (& That Ain't Good)," "I'm a Big Girl Now," "I've Gotta Sing Away These Blues," "Love to Be with You," "My Blue Heaven," "Sentimental Journey," "Sweet Evening Breeze," "You Oughta Be in Pictures," & more. Demo CD or cassette available.

Sentimental Journey, abr. ed. Laurence Sterne. Read by Robert L. Halvorson. 4 cass. (Running Time: 4 hrs.). 28.95 (90) Halvorson Assocs.

Sentimental Journey: Songs of the World War II Era. Friedman-Fairfax and Sony Music Group. 1 cass. (CD Ser.). 1995. pap. bk. 15.98 (978-1-56799-127-7(0), Friedman-Fairfax) M Friedman Pub Grp Inc.

Sentimental Journey Through France & Italy. unabr. ed. Laurence Sterne. Read by Walter Covell. 3 cass. (Running Time: 3 hrs. 10 min.). 1991. 21.00 set. (C-206) Jimcin Record.
In his unique style, Sterne relates a humorous account of his travels.

Sentimental Safari. unabr. collector's ed. Kermit Roosevelt. Read by Bob Erickson. 7 cass. (Running Time: 10 hrs. 30 mins.). 1984. 56.00 (978-0-7366-0847-3(8), 1798) Books on Tape.
Kermit Roosevelt, son of Kermit & grandson of Theodore Roosevelt, has always had an urge to retrace the trails of the great African hunt which his grandfather & his father had engaged in during 10 eventful months.

Sentimental Tommy, J. M. Barrie. Read by Flo Gibson. 7 cass. (Running Time: 10 hrs. 30 min.). 1995. 25.95 (978-1-55685-380-7(7)) Audio Bk Con.
Imaginative, kind & mischievous Tommy walks right into our hearts as he takes care of his little sister, after their mother's death, & shares adventures with Grizel, the daughter of a madwoman.

Sentinel. Arthur C. Clarke. 1 cass. 10.95 (SAC 1159) Spoken Arts.

Sentinel. abr. ed. Barry Sadler. Read by Charlton Griffin. 2 vols. (Casca Ser.: No. 9). 2003. (978-1-58807-535-2(4)) Am Pubng Inc.

Sentinel. abr. ed. Barry Sadler. Read by Charlton Griffin. 2 vols. (Running Time: 3 hrs.). (Casca Ser.: No. 9). 2003. 18.00 (978-1-58807-109-5(X)) Am Pubng Inc.
Casca Longinus: Cursed by Christ on Golgotha. Condemned to outlive the ages and wander the globe as a constant soldier. Forever fighting, surviving, waiting for Him to return. Awakened from frozen slumber by the touch of a beautiful young woman, the mighty Casca journeys from the northern wasteland to legendary Constantinople and the war-ravaged shores of North Africa. Casca must struggle with the agony of an eternal curse and triumph over the razor-sharp fanaticism of the bloody Brotherhood.

Sentinel. abr. ed. Barry Sadler. Read by Charlton Griffin. 2 vols. (Casca Ser.: No. 9). 2004. audio compact disk 25.00 (978-1-58807-283-2(5)); audio compact disk (978-1-58807-714-1(4)) Am Pubng Inc.

***Sentry.** abr. ed. Robert Crais. (Running Time: 6 hrs.). (Elvis Cole/Joe Pike Novels Ser.). 2011. 9.99 (978-1-4418-9403-8(9), 9781441894038, BAD) Brilliance Audio.

Sentry. abr. ed. Robert Crais. Read by Luke Daniels. (Running Time: 5 hrs.). (Elvis Cole/Joe Pike Novels Ser.). 2011. audio compact disk 24.99 (978-1-4233-7562-3(9), 9781423375623, BACD) Brilliance Audio.

Sentry. abr. ed. Robert Crais. (Running Time: 6 hrs.). 2011. audio compact disk 14.99 (978-1-4233-7563-0(7), 9781423375630, BCD Value Price) Brilliance Audio.

Sentry. unabr. ed. Robert Crais. (Running Time: 8 hrs.). (Elvis Cole/Joe Pike Novels Ser.). 2011. 24.99 (978-1-4233-7560-9(2), 9781423375609, BAD); 39.97 (978-1-4233-7561-6(0), 9781423375616, BADLE) Brilliance Audio.

Sentry. unabr. ed. Robert Crais. Read by Luke Daniels. (Running Time: 8 hrs.). (Elvis Cole/Joe Pike Novels Ser.). 2011. 24.99 (978-1-4233-7558-6(0), 9781423375586, Brilliance MP3); 39.97 (978-1-4233-7559-3(9), 9781423375593, Brlnc Audio MP3 Lib); audio compact disk 34.99 (978-1-4233-7556-2(4), 9781423375562, Bril Audio CD Unabri); audio compact disk 87.97 (978-1-4233-7557-9(2), 9781423375579, BriAudCD Unabrid) Brilliance Audio.

***Seoda Chonamara: Connemara Favourites.** Artists Chonamara. (ENG.). 11.95 (978-0-8023-7019-8(5)) Pub: Clo Iar-Chonnachta IRL. Dist(s): Dufour

Seoda Sean-Nois as Tir Chonaill. Contrib. by Aine Ui Laoi. (ENG.). 1996. 13.95 (978-0-8023-7118-8(3)); audio compact disk 20.95 (978-0-8023-8118-7(9)) Pub: Clo Iar-Chonnachta IRL. Dist(s): Dufour

Seoul, Korea. Compiled by Benchmark Education Staff. 2006. audio compact disk 10.00 (978-1-4108-6613-4(0)) Benchmark Educ.

Separate Beds. unabr. ed. LaVyrle Spencer. Read by Liz Dykhouse. 9 cass. (Running Time: 13 hrs.). 2003. 32.95 (978-1-59355-164-3(9), 1593551649, BAU); 92.25 (978-1-59355-165-0(7), 1593551657, BrilAudUnabridg) Brilliance Audio.
Readers have long flocked to the works of LaVyrle Spencer, one of America's most cherished storytellers. From The Fulfillment to Morning Glory to Then Came Heaven, her touching, emotionally charged novels have examined love in all its forms. In Separate Beds, two attractive, headstrong people meet - and fireworks ensue. Catherine Anderson and Clay Forrester come from two completely different worlds, but one blind date leaves them forever linked. Clay, a handsome law student, and Catherine, a serious, bookish undergrad, experience an evening they will never forget. Fortified by the beauty of the night, as well as a bottle of wine, they share a night together. A few short months later, Catherine discovers she's pregnant. They agree to a marriage of convenience, an arrangement that suits them both - until they begin to fall in love. Moving and deeply affecting, Separate Beds is a celebration of the healing power of love.

Separate Beds. unabr. ed. LaVyrle Spencer. Read by Liz Dykhouse. (Running Time: 13 hrs.). 2004. 39.25 (978-1-59335-499-2(1), 1593354991, Brlnc Audio MP3 Lib) Brilliance Audio.

Separate Beds. unabr. ed. LaVyrle Spencer. Read by Liz Dykhouse. (Running Time: 13 hrs.). 2004. 39.25 (978-1-59710-684-9(4), 1597106844, BADLE) Brilliance Audio.

Separate Beds. unabr. ed. LaVyrle Spencer. Read by Liz Dykhouse. (Running Time: 13 hrs.). 2004. 24.95 (978-1-59335-225-7(5), 1593352255) Soulmate Audio Bks.

Separate Beds. unabr. ed. LaVyrle Spencer. Read by Liz Dykhouse. (Running Time: 13 hrs.). 2004. 24.95 (978-1-59710-685-6(2), 1597106852, BAD) Brilliance Audio.

***Separate Beds: A Novel.** Elizabeth Buchan. (Running Time: 13 hrs.). (ENG.). 2011. audio compact disk 39.95 (978-0-14-242885-6(X), PengAudBks) Penguin Grp USA.

***Separate Country.** Robert Hicks. Read by Kevin T. Collins et al. (Playaway Adult Fiction Ser.). (ENG.). 2009. 89.99 (978-1-60788-393-7(7)) Find a World.

Separate Country. unabr. ed. Robert Hicks. Read by Kevin T. Collins et al. (Running Time: 17 hrs.). (ENG.). 2009. 26.98 (978-1-60024-763-7(6)); audio compact disk 39.98 (978-1-60024-762-0(8)) Pub: Hachet Audio. Dist(s): HachBkGrp

***Separate Country.** unabr. ed. Robert Hicks. Read by Sherman Howard et al. (Running Time: 17 hrs.). (ENG.). 2011. audio compact disk 19.98 (978-1-60788-642-6(1)) Pub: Hachet Audio. Dist(s): HachBkGrp

Separate Flights. unabr. collector's ed. Andre Dubus. Read by Dan Lazar. 8 cass. (Running Time: 8 hrs.). 1981. 48.00 (978-0-7366-0463-5(4), 1435) Books on Tape.
This Dubus sampler includes a novella & seven short stories. Themes range from violence & confrontation to tenderness & affection.

Separate Peace. John Knowles. Read by Matthew Modine. 2 cass. (Running Time: 2 hrs. 15 mins.). 2000. 18.00 (978-0-7366-9039-3(5)) Books on Tape.
Classic story of two best friends at a New England boarding school during World War II. The friendship of these young men is a starkly moving parable of lost innocence & tortured adolescence in a generation coming of age during the dark years of war.

Separate Peace. John Knowles. Narrated by Spike McClure. 6 CDs. (Running Time: 6 hrs. 30 mins.). 2000. audio compact disk 58.00 (978-0-7887-4665-9(0), C1224E7) Recorded Bks.
Story of friendship between boys at summer school while outside the world is ravaged by war.

Separate Peace. John Knowles. Narrated by Spike McClure. (Running Time: 23400 sec.). (YA). (gr. 7). 2006. audio compact disk 19.99 (978-1-4281-2438-7(1)) Recorded Bks.

Separate Peace. Tom Stoppard. Perf. by Christopher Cazenove & Anghared Rees. 1 cass. 10.95 (ECN 168) J Norton Pubs.
The doctor in charge of a private nursing home is persuaded to admit a mysterious patient who does not appear to be ill but has a suitcase full of money.

Separate Peace. unabr. ed. John Knowles. Narrated by Scott Snively. 4 cass. (Running Time: 6 hrs.). 2002. 34.95 (978-1-883332-49-5(4), 2-02); audio compact disk 54.00 (978-1-883332-76-1(1), CD2-02) Audio Bkshelf.
Now a modern classic, this story of two boys' friendship at an exclusive New Hampshire prep school as it parallels the inescapable and escalating atmosphere of World War II, is intense and engaging to the last word.

Separate Peace, unabr. ed. John Knowles. Narrated by Spike McClure. 5 cass. (Running Time: 6 hrs. 30 mins.). 1999. 46.00 (978-1-55690-469-1(X), 91111E7) Recorded Bks.
Story of friendship between boys at summer school while outside the world is ravaged by war.

Separate Peace. unabr. ed. John Knowles. Read by Scott Snively. (YA). 2008. 64.99 (978-1-60514-797-0(4)) Find a World.

Separate Reality: Further Conversations with Don Juan. abr. ed. Carlos Casteneda. Read by Peter Coyote. 2 cass. (Running Time: 3 hrs.). 1995. 16.95 (978-0-944993-33-0(8)) Audio Lit.
Casteneda's teacher demonstrates the seriousness & danger of the sorcerer's way.

Separated & Divorced: A Guide to the Tasks of Healing. Kathleen Kircher. 4 cass. (Running Time: 4 hrs.). 2001. vinyl bd. 34.95 (A5950) St Anthony Mess Pr.
Discusses the psychosocial and relisious dimensions of separation, divorce and remarriage.

Separated from the Light A training Series for Professionals: Professional CD. William Tollefson. (ENG.). 2009. 79.00 (978-0-9760554-1-9(4)) W Tollefson.

Separated from the Light Training for Survivors: Healing Intrusive Memory CD. William Tollefson. (ENG.). 2009. 39.00 (978-0-9760554-2-6(2)) W Tollefson.

Separation. Henry W. Wright. (ENG.). 2008. audio compact disk 17.95 (978-1-934680-31-5(1)) Be in Hlth.

Separation & Forgiveness: The Four Splits & Their Undoing. Kenneth Wapnick. 9 CDs. 2006. audio compact disk 56.00 (978-1-59142-294-5(9), CD57) Foun Miracles.

Separation & Forgiveness: The Four Splits & Their Undoing. Kenneth Wapnick. 1 CD. (Running Time: 10 hrs. 22 mins. 51 secs.). 2007. 50.00 (978-1-59142-295-2(7), 3m57) Foun Miracles.

Separation of Power. Vince Flynn. (Running Time: 50 hrs. 0 mins. 0 sec.). No. 3. (ENG.). 2004. audio compact disk 14.95 (978-0-7435-3797-1(1), S&S Encore) Pub: S&S Audio. Dist(s): S and S Inc

Separation of Power. abr. ed. Vince Flynn. (Mitch Rapp Ser.: No. 3). 2004. 15.95 (978-0-7435-4874-8(4)) Pub: S&S Audio. Dist(s): S and S Inc

Sept approches a un Corpus: Analyses du francais Parle. Ed. by Hanne L. Andersen & Christa Thomsen. Directed By Alain Berrendonner et al. (Sciences Pour la Communication Ser.: Vol. 71). (FRE.). 2004. bk. 54.95 (978-3-906770-89-5(3)) Pub: P Lang CHE. Dist(s): P Lang Pubng

Sept Contes, Michel Tournier. Read by Michel Tournier. 2 cass. (Running Time: 2 hrs.). (FRE.). 1991. bk. 35.95 (1GA060) Olivia & Hill.
Modern adaptation of traditional tales & characters, as well as his original stories.

Sept. 2001 Lessons Learned: Resilience (the Infinite Mind Vol. 445) Interview. Hosted by Fred Goodwin. 1 CDs. (Running Time: 59 mins). 2006. 21.95 (978-1-933644-36-3(2)) Lichtenstein Creat.
How is it that adversity can defeat some people, and bring out the best in others? Since the terrorists attacks on the United States five years ago, many Americans have risen to new challenges with courage and grace. This show explores what lets some people not only "bounce back" from disaster, but even gain in strength through adversity. The show includes interviews with psychologist Dr. Al Siebert, author of The Survivor Personality; and Dr. Karen Reivich, Co-Director of the Penn Resiliency Project at the University of Pennsylvania. One of the world's best known neuro-biologists, Dr. Robert Sapolsky, discusses how stress harms us . . . and helps us. And storyteller Laura Simms shares an Arabic story that reveals how even in grief we are not alone. Plus, John Hockenberry contributes a moving, insightful commentary on volcanos, SCUD missiles, terrorism, and resiliency.

September. unabr. ed. Rosamunde Pilcher. Read by Eve Karpf. 16 cass. (Running Time: 21 hrs. 15 min.). 1992. 124.95 (978-0-7451-6197-6(9), CAB 625) AudioGO.
It is May in Scotland, & invitations are being written for a party in September, a moment which will be the turning point in the lives of a small group of people. Among them are Virginia Aird & her husband, facing the unanswered questions behind their apparently happy marriage; Alexa, discovering love for the first time; & Lottie whose meddling is seen as malicious.

September. unabr. ed. Rosamunde Pilcher. Read by Penelope Dellaporta. 15 cass. (Running Time: 22 hrs. 30 min.). 1990. 120.00 (978-0-7366-1777-2(9), 2616) Books on Tape.
September is an extraordinary month in Scotland, when a brief but glorious summer is ending & the long, gray winter has yet to begin. It is a time of parties, house guests & hospitality. It is a month of excess, when marriage is proposed & marriages break up, when people drink too much & dance too late, when promises are made, hearts broken & family secrets come to light. September begins in May as invitations are sent for a 21st birthday party. May becomes June, summer begins, & the tug of an inexorable fate propels Pilcher's characters to their inevitable - & often surprising - destinies.

September in the Park **see Twentieth-Century Poetry in English, No. 27, Recordings of Poets Reading Their Own Poetry**

September Morning. unabr. ed. Rowena Summers. Read by Julia Franklin & Marie McCarthy. 9 cass. (Storysound Ser.). (J). 2001. 76.95 (978-1-85903-380-7(6)) Pub: Mgna Lrg Print GBR. Dist(s): Ulverscroft US

September, September, unabr. ed. Shelby Foote. 9 cass. (Running Time: 12 hrs. 15 mins.). 1994. 78.00 (978-0-7887-0103-0(7), 94344E7) Recorded Bks.
In the Memphis of 1957, three scam artists attempt to take advantage of current tension between the races by kidnapping for ransom the son of a wealthy black businessman.Their story, by turns ribald, thought-provoking & chilling, is a compelling portrait of the racial tensions in the South of the late 50s.

September Starlings. unabr. ed. Ruth Hamilton. Read by Marlene Sidaway. 18 cass. (Running Time: 27 hrs.). 2001. 109.95 (990613) Pub: ISIS Audio GBR. Dist(s): Ulverscroft US

September Starlings. unabr. ed. Ruth Hamilton. Read by Marlene Sidaway. 18 cass. (Running Time: 24 hrs.). 1999. 109.95 (978-0-7531-0515-3(2), 990613) Pub: UlverLrgPrint GBR. Dist(s): Ulverscroft US
Laura, now wealthy & successful, has survived a bitter past. She fled from a tyrannical mother into the clutches of a sadistic man, enduring poverty & fear. Then along came Ben Starling, older, wiser, smoothing her path & giving her love & security but now Ben has become stranger who has slipped beyond her reach. As her stability threatens to disintegrate once more, a waif-like girl from Liverpool who is to prove a link to her past thrusts her way into Laura's life, but no one can help Laura make her decision she must forge her own future.

September 1, 1939 **see Dylan Thomas Reads the Poetry of W. B. Yeats & Others**

September 11 & the New Global Jihad. unabr. ed. Quintan Wiktorowicz. 2 cds. 2002. audio compact disk 24.95 (978-1-58472-268-7(1), In Aud) Pub: Sound Room. Dist(s): Baker Taylor

Septenaries. Manly P. Hall. 5 cass. (Running Time: 150 min.). 1999. 40.00 Set. (978-0-89314-256-8(5)) Philos Res.
Includes: "The Seven Creative Powers of the Godhead;" "The Seven Great Ages of the Earth;" "The Seven Races of Mankind;" "The Seven Laws of Governing Human Life;" & "The Seven Schools of Mystery Religions".

Septimouse, Supermouse; Septimouse, Big Cheese! unabr. ed. Ann Jungman. Read by Nigel Lambert. 2 cass. (Running Time: 2 hrs.). (J). 1997. 18.95 (CCA 3359, Chivers Child Audio) AudioGO.

***Septimus Heap, Book Four: Queste.** unabr. ed. Angie Sage. Read by Gerald Doyle. (ENG.). 2008. (978-0-06-157551-8(8)); (978-0-06-163241-9(4)) HarperCollins Pubs.

***Septimus Heap, Book One: Magyk.** unabr. ed. Angie Sage. Read by Allan Corduner. (ENG.). 2005. (978-0-06-084049-5(8), KTegenBooks); (978-0-06-084048-8(X), KTegenBooks) HarperCollins Pubs.

***Septimus Heap, Book Three: Physik.** unabr. ed. Angie Sage. Read by Gerald Doyle. (ENG.). 2007. (978-0-06-143827-1(8), KTegenBooks); (978-0-06-137688-7(4), KTegenBooks) HarperCollins Pubs.

***Septimus Heap, Book Two: Flyte.** unabr. ed. Angie Sage. Read by Gerald Doyle. (ENG.). 2007. (978-0-06-114980-1(2), KTegenBooks); (978-0-06-116143-8(8), KTegenBooks) HarperCollins Pubs.

Sepulchre. James Herbert & Jonathan Firth. 3 CDs. (Running Time: 3 hrs. 0 mins. 0 sec.). (ENG.). 2008. audio compact disk 27.95 (978-0-230-70444-2(1)) Pub: Macmillan UK GBR. Dist(s): IPG Chicago

Sepulchre. unabr. ed. James Herbert. Read by Sean Barrett. 10 cass. (Running Time: 11 hr. 45 min.). 1998. 84.95 (978-0-7531-0441-5(5), 980902) Pub: ISIS Audio GBR. Dist(s): Ulverscroft US
There is a house, hidden away in a small valley, that holds a dark & dreadful secret. There is a psychic that lives in this house who is part of its secret. There is a guardian of the house & of the psychic & of that secret, known as the Keeper. Together they serve a force that threatens mankind itself. An outsider named Halloran is thrust upon the scene & will discover the horrific & awesome secret of the Sepulchre.

Sepulchre. unabr. ed. James Herbert. Read by Sean Barrett. 10 CDs. (Running Time: 11 hrs. 45 mins.). 1999. audio compact disk 89.95 (978-0-7531-0712-6(0), 107120) Pub: ISIS Audio GBR. Dist(s): Ulverscroft US

Sequential Simplex Optimization. Instructed by Stanley N. Deming. Prod. by American Chemical Society Staff. 5 cass. (Running Time: 4 hrs. 30 min.). 39.00 manual. Am Chemical.
Course explains how to use sequential sequence optimization, a highly efficient experimental design strategy, to improve system response. Sequential sequence optimization is an alternate evolutionary operation technique that is not based on traditional factorial designs. This technique can be used to optimize several factors - not just two or three - in a single study. Course lessons are designed to improvid a sound understanding of the use of sequential simples designs in research & development. The course will help improve processes & methods, decrease project development time, & provide optimized processes for statistical process control.

Sequimos United 2. Contrib. by Uncion Tropical. (SPA.). (gr. 13). 2007. audio compact disk 14.99 (978-0-8297-5251-9(X)) Zondervan.

Ser Excelente. Miguel Angel Cornejo. 1 cass. (Running Time: 1 hr. 30 mins.).Tr. of How to Be Excllent. (SPA.). 2001. Astran.

Ser Excelente. Miguel Angel Cornejo. 2 cass. (Running Time: 2 hrs.).Tr. of On Being Excellent. (SPA.). 2002. (978-968-6210-03-3(2)) Taller del Exito.
Presents the attitudes and qualities characteristic of those who succeed in life.

Ser Superior. Deepak Chopra. 1 cass. (Running Time: 1 hr. 30 mins.).Tr. of Higher Self. (SPA.). 2001. Astran.

Ser Superior. Deepak Chopra. 6 cass. (Running Time: 5 hrs. 30 mins.).Tr. of Higher Self. (SPA.). 2002. (978-1-931059-22-0(5)) Taller del Exito.
Demonstrates how combining western medicine with ancient eastern philosophies can lead to a healthier, more fulfilled life.

Ser y Dociau Newydd. Dafydd Huws & Cyfres y. Dolffin. 2005. 5.90 (978-0-00-077009-7(4)) Zondervan.

Ser 24 Audio Hotsheets 16E. Ed. by Kaplan Publishing Staff. 2005. 29.00 (978-1-4195-1327-5(3)) Dearborn Financial.

Ser 24 Audio Hotsheets 17E. Ed. by Kaplan Publishing Staff. 2006. 29.00 (978-1-4195-1526-2(8)) Dearborn Financial.

Ser 26 Audio Hotsheets 16E. Ed. by Kaplan Publishing Staff. 2005. 29.00 (978-1-4195-1209-4(9)) Dearborn Financial.

Ser 26 Audio Hotsheets 17E. Ed. by Kaplan Publishing Staff. 2005. 29.00 (978-1-4195-1472-2(5)) Dearborn Financial.

Ser 26 Audio Hotsheets 18E. Ed. by Kaplan Publishing Staff. 2006. 29.00 (978-1-4195-1571-2(3)) Dearborn Financial.

Ser 6 Audio Hotsheets 25E. Ed. by Kaplan Publishing Staff. 2005. 29.00 (978-1-4195-1368-8(0)) Dearborn Financial.

Ser 6 Audio Hotsheets 26E. Ed. by Kaplan Publishing Staff. 2006. 29.00 (978-1-4195-1607-8(8)) Dearborn Financial.

Ser 63 Audio Hotsheets 21E. Ed. by Kaplan Publishing Staff. 2005. 29.00 (978-1-4195-1366-4(4)) Dearborn Financial.

Ser 63 Audio Hotsheets 22E. Ed. by Kaplan Publishing Staff. 2005. 29.00 (978-1-4195-1499-9(7)) Dearborn Financial.

Ser 65 Audio Hotsheets 13E. Ed. by Kaplan Publishing Staff. 2005. 29.00 (978-1-4195-1437-1(7)) Dearborn Financial.

Ser 65 Audio Hotsheets 14E. Ed. by Kaplan Publishing Staff. 2006. 29.00 (978-1-4195-1597-2(7)) Dearborn Financial.

Ser 66 Audio Hotsheets 12E. Ed. by Kaplan Publishing Staff. 2005. 29.00 (978-1-4195-1199-8(8)) Dearborn Financial.

Ser 66 Audio Hotsheets 13E. Ed. by Kaplan Publishing Staff. 2005. 29.00 (978-1-4195-1466-1(0)) Dearborn Financial.

Ser 66 Audio Hotsheets 14E. Ed. by Kaplan Publishing Staff. 2006. 29.00 (978-1-4195-1567-5(5)) Dearborn Financial.

Ser 7 Audio Hotsheets 17E. Ed. by Kaplan Publishing Staff. 2005. 29.00 (978-1-4195-1381-7(8)) Dearborn Financial.

Ser 7 Audio Hotsheets 18E. Ed. by Kaplan Publishing Staff. 2006. 29.00 (978-1-4195-1585-9(3)) Dearborn Financial.

***Seraph Seal.** unabr. ed. Leonard Sweet & Lori Wagner. 2011. audio compact disk 24.99 (978-1-4003-1710-3(X)) Nelson.

Serbo-Croate sans Peine. 1 cass. (Running Time: 1 hr. 30 min.). (FRE & SBC.). 2000. bk. 75.00 (978-2-7005-1342-4(8)) Pub: Assimil FRA. Dist(s): Distribks Inc

Serbo-Croatian. 2 cass. (Running Time: 80 min.). (Language - Thirty Library). bk. 16.95 vinyl binding. Moonbeam Pubns.
Using the proven method based on the famous U.S. Military accelerated language learning program, Language/30 courses stress conversationally useful words & phrases.

Serbo-Croatian. Ed. by Charles Berlitz. 2 cass. (Running Time: 1 hr. 30 mins.). (Language/30 Brief Course Ser.). pap. bk. 21.95 (AF1039) J Norton Pubs.
Quick, highly condensed introduction to the words & phrases you'll need to communicate effectively in the country you're visiting. Cassettes & phrase guide book are in a vinyl album.

Serbo-Croatian, Vol. 1. Foreign Service Institute Staff. 12 cass. (Running Time: 12 hrs. 30 mins.). 2001. pap. bk. 225.00 (AFY601) J Norton Pubs.
Basic sentences & conversation drills in the text are given in both Roman & Cyrillic alphabets. The course also uses a "standard" form of Serbo-Croatian understood throughout the Balkans, with accepted regional variations in vocabulary & pronunciation.

Serbo-Croatian, Vol. 2. Foreign Service Institute Staff. 24 cass. (Running Time: 32 hrs.). 2001. pap. bk. 295.00 (AFY650) J Norton Pubs.

Serbo-Croatian: Language/30. unabr. ed. Educational Services Corporation Staff. Intro. by Charles Berlitz. 2 cass. (CRO & SER.). 1975. pap. bk. 21.95 (978-0-910542-17-3(1)) Educ Svcs DC.
Serbo-Croation self-teaching language course.

Serbo Croatian Basic Course Levels 1 & 2. Hodge et al. (Multilingual Books Intensive Cassette Foreign Language Ser.). 1965. spiral bd. 395.00 (978-1-58214-167-1(3)) Language Assocs.

Serbo-Croatian (FSI), Vol. 1. 22 CDs. (Running Time: 12 hrs. 30 mins.). (Foreign Service Institute Basic Course Ser.). (SBC.). 2005. audio compact disk 245.00 (978-1-57970-206-9(6), AFY601D) J Norton Pubs.

Serbo-Croatian (FSI), Vol. 2. 21 CDs. (Running Time: 32 hrs.). (Foreign Service Institute Basic Course Ser.). (SBC.). 2005. audio compact disk 295.00 (978-1-57970-207-6(4), AFY650D) J Norton Pubs.

Serena. unabr. ed. Ron Rash. Read by Phil Gigante. (Running Time: 11 hrs.). 2008. 24.95 (978-1-4233-7367-4(7), 9781423373674, Brilliance MP3); 39.25 (978-1-4233-7370-4(7), 9781423373704, BADLE); 39.25 (978-1-4233-7368-1(5), 9781423373681, Brinc Audio MP3 Lib); 24.95 (978-1-4233-7369-8(3), 9781423373698, BAD); audio compact disk 97.25 (978-1-4233-7366-7(9), 9781423373667, BriAudCD Unabrid); audio compact disk 34.99 (978-1-4233-7365-0(0), 9781423373650, Bril Audio CD Unabri) Brilliance Audio.

Serena & the Sea Serpent. unabr. ed. Garth Nix. Read by Stig Wemyss. (Aussie Bites Ser.). (J). (gr. 1-7). 2006. audio compact disk 39.95 (978-1-74093-343-8(5)) Pub: Bolinda Pubng AUS. Dist(s): Bolinda Pub Inc

Serenade. Bro Halff. 1989. 5.00 (978-1-885238-07-8(X)) Simpler Gifts.

Serenata Espiritual. unabr. ed. 2001. audio compact disk 11.99 (978-0-8297-3502-4(X)) Zondervan.

Serenity. 1 cass. (Subliminal Affirmations for Twelve Step Living Ser.). 1988. 9.95 (978-0-89486-522-0(6), 5615G) Hazelden.

Serenity. (713) Yoga Res Foun.

Serenity. S. Eckels. 1 cass. (Running Time: 40 min.). 11.95 (978-0-938586-88-3(2), S) Whole Person.
Guaranteed to alter your state of consciousness. Classical guitarist Steven Zdenek Eckels draws on Gregorian chant, Native American melodies, the rhythms of Lake Superior, & the spirit of the North Woods for inspiration to compose his musical prayers for healing. Summer or winter, he prepares his creative spirit by hiking along the rocky wind-swept shore, then returns to his cozy studio to compose in front of the picture window or fireplace, accompanied by the aromas of cedar, sage, pine, or angelica. Music composed in this peaceful environment is certain to bring you peace of mind.

Serenity. Swami Jyotirmayananda. 1 cass. (Running Time: 1 hr.). 1990. 12.99 Yoga Res Foun.

Serenity. Eldon Taylor. 1 cass. (Running Time: 62 min.). (Inner Talk Ser.). 16.95 incl. script. (978-1-55978-771-0(6), 53878F) Progress Aware Res.
Soundtrack - Babbling Brook with underlying subliminal affirmations.

Serenity. Eldon Taylor. Read by Eldon Taylor. Interview with Progress Aware Staff. 2 cass. (Running Time: 62 min. per cass.). (Omniphonics Ser.). 29.95 incl. script Set. (978-1-55978-802-1(X), 4003) Progress Aware Res.
3-D soundtrack with underlying subliminal affirmations, night & day versions.

Serenity. Eldon Taylor. 1 CD. (Running Time: 52 min.). (Whole Brain Innertalk Ser.). 1998. audio compact disk (978-1-55978-775-8(9)) Progress Aware Res.

Serenity. Eldon Taylor. 1 CD. (Running Time: 52 min.). (Whole Brain Innertalk Ser.). 1999. audio compact disk (978-1-55978-923-3(9)) Progress Aware Res.

Serenity: Inspirational Scriptures for Living: Faith & Deliverance. Voice by Elizabeth Morgan. Music by Spencer Lackey. Des. by Crawford Designs And Promotions. 2006. audio compact disk 10.00 (978-1-4276-0640-2(4)) AardGP.

Serenity Prayer. 1 CD. 1981. audio compact disk 16.95 (978-1-55841-128-9(3)) Emmett E Miller.
Dr. Miller finds this prayer the most concise and profound guide to wise, health and successful living. Experience this message more clearly than ever. Affirmations, music, poetry and ageless wisdom guide your thoughts while you work or play.

Serenity Prayer. Emmett E. Miller. Read by Emmett E. Miller. 1 cass. (Running Time: 1 hr.). 1996. 10.00 (978-1-56170-369-2(9), 394) Hay House.
Dedicate yourself to the creation of a future inspired by the wisdom of the Serenity Prayer.

Serenity Prayer: Affirmations & Meditations for Recovery. 1 cassette. 1981. 12.95 (978-1-55841-060-2(0)) Emmett E Miller.
Dr. Miller calls the Serenity Prayer the most concise and profound guide to wise, healthy and successful living. Experience this message more clearly than ever, in an entertaining and inspiring way. Affirmations, music, poetry and ageless wisdom guide your thoughts while you work or play.

Serenity (zen heart Serenity) Orig. Title: Zen heart of Serenity. 2005. audio compact disk (978-1-59250-616-3(X)) Gaiam Intl.

Sergeant Lamb of the Ninth. unabr. collector's ed. Robert Graves. Read by Bill Kelsey. 9 cass. (Running Time: 13 hrs. 30 mins.). 1990. 72.00 (978-0-7366-1724-6(8), 2565) Books on Tape.
Robert Graves first came across the name of Roger Lamb in 1914, when Graves was an English officer instructing his platoon in regimental history. Lamb was a British soldier, a sergeant, who had served his King during the American Revolution & whose claim to a footnote in history is that he managed to escape twice from American prison camp.

Sergeant Lamb's America. unabr. ed. Robert Graves. Narrated by Ron Keith. 10 cass. (Running Time: 14 hrs. 30 mins.). 1990. 85.00 (978-1-55690-470-7(3), 90104E7) Recorded Bks.
A meticulous recreation of the American Revolution from a British soldier's point of view.

Sergeant Preston of the Yukon. Perf. by Paul Sutton & Dewey Cole. 2009. audio compact disk 24.95 (978-1-57019-897-7(7)) Radio Spirits.

Sergeant Preston of the Yukon, Vol. 1. collector's ed. 6 cass. (Running Time: 9 hrs.). 1998. bk. 34.98 (4047) Radio Spirits.
The sergeant & his wonder dog Yukon King meet the challenge of the Yukon in 18 action-packed adventures.

Sergeant Preston of the Yukon, Vol. 2. collector's ed. Perf. by Jay Michael. 6 cass. (Running Time: 9 hrs.). 2000. bk. 34.98 (4545) Radio Spirits.
In this series, a.k.a. "The Challenge of the Yukon," a Northwest Mounted policeman, along with his trusted lead dog, King, fought for law and order in the tumultuous Yukon. 36 episodes.

Sergeant Preston of the Yukon: A Freind in Need & The Telltale Knife. Perf. by Paul Sutton. 1 cass. (Running Time: 1 hr.). (J). 2001. 6.98 (2628) Radio Spirits.

Sergeant Preston of the Yukon: Blind Man's Bluff & Jailbreak. Perf. by Paul Sutton. 1 cass. (Running Time: 1 hr.). (J). 2001. 6.98 (2527) Radio Spirits.

Sergeant Preston of the Yukon: Casper Mott's Adventure & Circumstantial Evidence. Perf. by Paul Sutton. 1 cass. (Running Time: 1 hr.). (J). 2001. 6.98 (2504) Radio Spirits.

Sergeant Preston of the Yukon: Contention & Whistling in the Dark. Perf. by Paul Sutton. 1 cass. (Running Time: 1 hr.). 2001. 6.98 (2610) Radio Spirits.

Sergeant Preston of the Yukon: Design Murder, Duke Bows, Outlaw's Nemesis & The Idol. Perf. by Paul Sutton. 1 cass. (Running Time: 1 hr.). (J). 2001. 6.98 (1530) Radio Spirits.

***Sergeant Preston of the Yukon: Klondike Gold.** Perf. by Paul Sutton & Dewey Cole. 2010. audio compact disk 24.95 (978-1-57019-927-1(2)) Radio Spirits.

Sergeant Preston of the Yukon: Meeting, Proven Dead, Swindler & Footprint. Perf. by Paul Sutton. 1 cass. (Running Time: 1 hr.). (J). 2001. 6.98 (1704) Radio Spirits.

Sergeant Preston of the Yukon: Silvertip & The Debt. Perf. by Paul Sutton. 1 cass. (Running Time: 1 hr.). (J). 2001. 6.98 (2046) Radio Spirits.

Sergeant Preston of the Yukon: The Claim Jumpers & A Large Sum of Money on a Wrecked Ship. Perf. by Paul Sutton. 1 cass. (Running Time: 1 hr.). (J). 2001. 6.98 (2024) Radio Spirits.

Sergeant Preston of the Yukon: The Clue of the Silver Pup & Passport to Death. Perf. by Paul Sutton. 1 cass. (Running Time: 1 hr.). 2001. 6.98 (2588) Radio Spirits.

Sergeant Preston of the Yukon: The Dawson Fire & Preston Turns the Tables. Perf. by Paul Sutton. 1 cass. (Running Time: 1 hr.). (J). 2001. 6.98 (1709) Radio Spirits.

Sergeant Preston of the Yukon: The Last Cabin & The Fraud. Perf. by Paul Sutton. 1 cass. (Running Time: 1 hr.). (J). 2001. 6.98 (1706) Radio Spirits.

Sergeant Preston of the Yukon: The Runaway Heir & Flaming Valley. Perf. by Paul Sutton. 1 cass. (Running Time: 1 hr.). (J). 2001. 6.98 (2547) Radio Spirits.

Sergeant Preston of the Yukon: The Second Chance & Manhunt. Perf. by Paul Sutton. 1 cass. (Running Time: 1 hr.). (J). 2001. 6.98 (2565) Radio Spirits.

Sergeant Preston of the Yukon: The Showdown & The Emerald in the Nugget. Perf. by Paul Sutton. 1 cass. (Running Time: 1 hr.). (J). 2001. 6.98 (1708) Radio Spirits.

Sergeant Preston of the Yukon: The White Hawk & Underground Ambush. Perf. by Paul Sutton. 1 cass. (Running Time: 1 hr.). (J). 2001. 6.98 (1710) Radio Spirits.

Sergeant Preston of the Yukon: Trader Muldoon & Old Moby's Cairn. Perf. by Paul Sutton. 1 cass. (Running Time: 1 hr.). (J). 2001. 6.98 (1707) Radio Spirits.

Sergeant Preston of the Yukon: 11th Hr., ABCs, Self Defense & Revenge. Perf. by Paul Sutton. 1 cass. (Running Time: 1 hr.). (J). 2001. 6.98 (1580) Radio Spirits.

Sergeant Preston of the Yukon & Nick Carter Master Detective. unabr. ed. 1 cass. (Running Time: 60 min.). Dramatization. 7.95 Norelco box. (MM-6764) Natl Recrd Co.
Sergeant Preston of the Northwest Mounted Police & his Wonder Dog, Yukon King, take us back to the days of the Gold Rush...a stampede to the Klondike. A young couple inherit a gold mine & then their problems begin! Presented by Quaker Puffed Wheat & Quaker Puffed Rice ("the delicious cereals shot from guns"). Nick Carter: Death in the Pines: Or, Nick Carter & the mystery of the murdered river. "Yes, it's another case for that most famous of all man-hunters, the detective whose ability at solving crime is unequalled in the history of detective fiction!" This caper involves a "protective agency" forced on a trucking company. Broadcast March 4, 1944.

Sergeant Simpson's Sacrifice. unabr. ed. Nicholas Rhea. Contrib. by Gareth Armstrong. 7 cass. (Story Sound Ser.). (J). 2006. 61.95 (978-1-85903-917-5(0)) Pub: Mgna Lrg Print GBR. Dist(s): Ulverscroft US

Sergeant Simpson's Sacrifice. unabr. ed. Nicholas Rhea & Gareth Armstrong. Contrib. by Gareth Armstrong. 8 vols. (Story Sound CD Ser.). (J). 2006. audio compact disk 79.95 (978-1-85903-951-9(0)) Pub: Mgna Lrg Print GBR. Dist(s): Ulverscroft US

Sergeants' Tale. Bernice Rubens. 6 CDs. (Running Time: 6 hrs. 55 mins.). (Isis (CDs) Ser.). (J). 2005. audio compact disk 64.95 (978-0-7531-2424-6(6)) Pub: ISIS Lrg Prnt GBR. Dist(s): Ulverscroft US

Sergeants' Tale. unabr. ed. Bernice Rubens. Read by Stephen Greif. 6 cass. (Running Time: 6 hrs. 55 mins.). (Isis Cassettes Ser.). (J). 2004. 54.95 (978-0-7531-1879-5(3)) Pub: ISIS Lrg Prnt GBR. Dist(s): Ulverscroft US

Sergio Ramirez. unabr. ed. Sergio Ramírez. Read by Sergio Ramírez. Read by Tim Richards. Prod. by Rebekah Presson. 1 cass. (Running Time: 29 min.). 1991. 10.00 (042691) New Letters.
Considered by many to be Nicaragua's premier prose writer, Ramirez was also Vice President of the country until last year. Ramirez, who was recorded in Managua by Tim Richards, talks about the influences of German cinema, popular music, history & politics on his work.

Serial Killers & Mass Murderers. Roger Mock. 2 cass. 1992. 8.95 ea. Am Fed Astrologers.

Serial Killers Club. unabr. ed. Jeff Povey. Read by Holter Graham. (Running Time: 7 hrs. 30 mins.). (ENG.). 2006. 14.98 (978-1-59483-639-8(6)) Pub: Hachet Audio. Dist(s): HachBkGrp

Serial Killers Club. unabr. ed. Jeff Povey. Read by Holter Graham. (Running Time: 7 hrs. 30 mins.). (ENG.). 2009. 19.98 (978-1-60788-160-5(8)) Pub: Hachet Audio. Dist(s): HachBkGrp

Serial Sneak Thief. E. W. Hildick. Illus. by E. W. Hildick. 2000. 9.95 (978-0-87499-643-2(0)); 9.95 (978-0-87499-644-9(9)); 9.95 (978-0-87499-645-6(7)) Live Oak Media.

Serial Sneak Thief. unabr. ed. E. W. Hildick. Read by Carol Jordan Stewart. 3 cass. (Running Time: 4 hrs.). (Felicity Snell Mystery Ser.: No. 2). (J). (gr. 4-7). 2000. 23.95 (978-0-87499-646-3(5), OAK005) Pub: Live Oak Media. Dist(s): AudioGO

Serial Sneak Thief: A Felicity Snell Mystery. unabr. ed. E. W. Hildick. Read by Carol Jordan Stewart. 3 vols. (Running Time: 4 hrs.). (J). (gr. 4-7). 2000. bk. 38.95 (978-0-87499-648-7(1)) Live Oak Media.
This new story features intrepid children's librarian & former private investigator Felicity Snell. "Not since John Bellairs introduced us to Miss Eells have children's librarians gotten such an image boost! Both books will make great read-alouds & the Great One-Day Cluefinders Contest has potential as a real library program".

Serialist. unabr. ed. David Gordon. (Running Time: 8 hrs. 30 mins.). 2010. 29.95 (978-1-4417-2788-6(4)); 54.95 (978-1-4417-2784-8(1)); audio compact disk 76.00 (978-1-4417-2785-5(X)) Blckstn Audio.

Serie Clásicos. unabr. ed. Dante Gebel. Read by Dante Gebel. (SPA.). 2009. audio compact disk 19.99 (978-0-8297-5634-0(5)) Pub: Vida Pubs. Dist(s): Zondervan

Serie Inspiración. Dante Gebel. Read by Dante Gebel. (SPA.). 2009. audio compact disk 19.99 (978-0-8297-5635-7(3)) Pub: Vida Pubs. Dist(s): Zondervan

Serie Integridad: Pack 1. unabr. ed. Dante Gebel. (SPA.). 2006. audio compact disk 19.99 (978-0-8297-4758-4(3)) Pub: Vida Pubs. Dist(s): Zondervan

Serie los Nuevos. unabr. ed. Dante Gebel. Read by Dante Gebel. (SPA.). 2009. audio compact disk 19.99 (978-0-8297-5636-4(1)) Pub: Vida Pubs. Dist(s): Zondervan

Serie Sobre Cuidados para la Afliccion. Doug Manning. Frank Johnson. 2 CDS. (Running Time: 2 hrs, 30 mins). (SPA.). 2006. audio compact disk 15.95 (978-1-892785-54-1(4)) In-Sight Bks Inc.

Serie Vida Cristiana: Pack 2. unabr. ed. Dante Gebel. (SPA.). 2006. audio compact disk 19.99 (978-0-8297-4757-7(5)) Pub: Vida Pubs. Dist(s): Zondervan

Series of Murders. unabr. ed. Simon Brett. Read by Simon Brett. 4 cass. (Running Time: 4 hrs.). 1993. 39.95 (978-0-7451-5801-3(3), CAB 427) AudioGO.

Series of Murders. unabr. ed. Simon Brett. Narrated by Simon Prebble. 4 cass. (Running Time: 5 hrs. 30 mins.). (Charles Paris Mystery Ser.: Vol. 13). 1989. 39.75 (978-1-4193-2606-6(6), 97950MC) Recorded Bks.

***Series of Unfortunate Events #1 Multi-Voice, A: the Bad Beginning.** abr. ed. Lemony Snicket, pseud. Read by Tim Curry. (ENG.). 2004. (978-0-06-081790-9(9)); (978-0-06-081791-6(7)) HarperCollins Pubs.

***Series of Unfortunate Events #10: the Slippery Slope.** abr. ed. Lemony Snicket, pseud. Read by Tim Curry & Stephin Merritt. (ENG.). 2004. (978-0-06-079350-0(3)); (978-0-06-081445-8(4)) HarperCollins Pubs.

***Series of Unfortunate Events #11: the Grim Grotto.** abr. ed. Lemony Snicket, pseud. Read by Tim Curry. (ENG.). 2004. (978-0-06-079349-4(X)) HarperCollins Pubs.

***Series of Unfortunate Events #11:the Grim Grotto.** abr. ed. Lemony Snicket, pseud. Read by Tim Curry. (ENG.). 2004. (978-0-06-081446-5(2)) HarperCollins Pubs.

***Series of Unfortunate Events #12.** abr. ed. Lemony Snicket, pseud. Read by Tim Curry. (ENG.). 2005. (978-0-06-079685-3(5)); (978-0-06-089757-4(0)) HarperCollins Pubs.

***Series of Unfortunate Events #13: the End.** abr. ed. Lemony Snicket, pseud. Read by Tim Curry. (ENG.). 2006. (978-0-06-123027-1(8)); (978-0-06-123026-4(X)) HarperCollins Pubs.

***Series of Unfortunate Events #3: the Wide Window.** abr. ed. Lemony Snicket, pseud. Read by Lemony Snicket, pseud. (ENG.). 2004. (978-0-06-079345-6(7)); (978-0-06-081447-2(0)) HarperCollins Pubs.

***Series of Unfortunate Events #4: the Miserable Mill.** abr. ed. Lemony Snicket, pseud. Read by Lemony Snicket, pseud. (ENG.). 2004. (978-0-06-079344-9(9)); (978-0-06-081448-9(9)) HarperCollins Pubs.

***Series of Unfortunate Events #5: the Austere Academy.** abr. ed. Lemony Snicket, pseud. Read by Lemony Snicket, pseud. (ENG.). 2004. (978-0-06-081450-2(0)); (978-0-06-079343-2(0)) HarperCollins Pubs.

***Series of Unfortunate Events #6: the Ersatz Elevator.** abr. ed. Lemony Snicket, pseud. Read by Tim Curry. (ENG.). 2004. (978-0-06-081451-9(9)); (978-0-06-079342-5(2)) HarperCollins Pubs.

***Series of Unfortunate Events #7: the Vile Village.** abr. ed. Lemony Snicket, pseud. Read by Tim Curry. (ENG.). 2004. (978-0-06-079341-8(4)) HarperCollins Pubs.

***Series of Unfortunate Events #7: the Vile Village.** abr. ed. Lemony Snicket, pseud. Read by Lemony Snicket, pseud. (ENG.). 2004. (978-0-06-081452-6(7)) HarperCollins Pubs.

***Series of Unfortunate Events #8: the Hostile Hospital.** abr. ed. Lemony Snicket, pseud. Read by Tim Curry. (ENG.). 2004. (978-0-06-079340-1(6)) HarperCollins Pubs.

***Series of Unfortunate Events #8: the Hostile Hospital.** abr. ed. Lemony Snicket, pseud. Read by Lemony Snicket, pseud. (ENG.). 2004. (978-0-06-081453-3(5)) HarperCollins Pubs.

***Series of Unfortunate Events #9: the Carnivorous Carnival.** abr. ed. Lemony Snicket, pseud. Read by Tim Curry. (ENG.). 2004. (978-0-06-081454-0(3)); (978-0-06-079339-5(2)) HarperCollins Pubs.

Serious. 2005. audio compact disk (978-5-559-15983-6(2)) Pt of Grace Ent.

Serious Business of Small Talk. Carol Fleming. 4 cass. (Running Time: 4 hrs.). 1996. 34.95 incl. script. (978-1-878542-59-5(1), 11-0403) SkillPath Pubns.
Human communications foibles that leap out when least expected.

Serious Call to a Devout & Holy Life. William Law. (Pure Gold Classics Ser.). (ENG., 2008. pap. bk. 14.99 (978-0-88270-453-1(2)) Bridge-Logos.

Serious Christian Living. Dan Corner. 1 cass. 3.00 (82) Evang Outreach.

Serious Intent. unabr. ed. Margaret Yorke. Read by Christian Rodska. 8 cass. (Running Time: 12 hrs.). 2000. 59.95 (978-0-7451-6626-1(1), CAB 1242) Pub: Chivers Audio Bks GBR. Dist(s): AudioGO
Richard Gardner struggles with his moody wife, Verity, and her two rebellious sons. Meanwhile, a new neighbor is drawn into their troubled lives and discovers criminal undercurrents in the village of Haverscot. She is unaware that her purchase of the property will upset the plans of a convicted killer: his quest to reclaim the hidden murder weapon and determination to finish a job begun years ago.

Serious Kitchen Play. 2001. audio compact disk 9.95 (978-1-930805-21-7(7)) XC Pubng.

Serious Talk see Nobody Said Anything

***Serious Times: Making Your Life Matter.** unabr. ed. James Emery White. Narrated by Lloyd James. (ENG.). 2005. 12.98 (978-1-59644-145-3(3), Hovel Audio) christianaud.

Serious Times: Making Your Life Matter in an Urgent Day. unabr. ed. James Emery White. Narrated by Lloyd James. 4 CDs. (Running Time: 5 hrs. 0 mins. 0 sec.). (ENG.). 2005. audio compact disk 21.98 (978-1-59644-144-6(5), Hovel Audio) christianaud.
How can we make our lives matter? John Adams and Thomas Jefferson lived in serious times. And because they chose to live serious lives, they turned the course of history. Serious times met with serious lives. This is the

means by which the kingdom of God is advanced and the life of a Christ follower is measured. As the modern era transitions into postmodern turbulence, we too find ourselves in serious times. There is a great movement of God that has been set loose in the world. In this book, James Emery White explores what it means to be in the front lines of what God is doing. Ita??s about action. But more than that, ita??s about character and our connectedness with God. Come and discover a life of significance.

Seriousness Rut. Swami Amar Jyoti. 1 cass. 1980. 9.95 (J-38) Truth Consciousness.
What is the genesis of seriousness? Concentration & seriousness are two different things. How to get out of the rut.

Sermon from the Underground see Berrigan Raps

Sermon on the Monitor. Saint Silicon. 2 cass. (Running Time: 2 hrs.). 18.00 (A0175-87) Sound Photosyn.
More hacker hilarity from the software patrons' saint.

Sermon on the Mount. 2004. (978-1-931713-98-6(7)) Word For Today.

Sermon on the Mount. Richard Rohr. 7 cass. (Running Time: 7 hrs.). 2001. vinyl bd. 59.95 (A6120) St Anthony Mess Pr.
Explains the challenge of Jesus to let go of the conventional wisdom that comes with contemporary American culture and travel in a path of life which unfolds into freedom.

Sermon on the Mount. unabr. ed. Jack Boland. Read by Jack Boland. 4 cass. (Running Time: 4 hrs.). 34.95 (978-0-88152-056-9(X), BA22) Master Mind.

Sermon on the Mount, Vol. 1. 2004. audio compact disk (978-1-931713-96-2(0)) Word For Today.

Sermon on the Mount, Vol. 2. 2004. audio compact disk (978-1-931713-97-9(9)) Word For Today.

Sermon on the Mount: A Biblical Interpretation. Concept by Ermance Rejebian. (ENG.). 2007. 5.99 (978-1-60339-149-8(5)); audio compact disk 5.99 (978-1-60339-150-4(9)) Listenr Digest.

Sermon on the Mount: Vol 1. Read by Douglas Wilson. 12. 1994. 32.00 (978-1-59128-515-1(1)); 40.00 (978-1-59128-517-5(8)) Canon Pr ID.

Sermon on the Mount - Special Number 1. C. S. Lovett. 6 cass. 1986. 29.95 (9206) Prsnl Christianity.

Sermon on the Mount - Special Number 2. C. S. Lovett. 6 cass. 1986. 29.95 (9215) Prsnl Christianity.

Sermon on the Mount - Special Number 3. C. S. Lovett. 6 cass. 1986. 29.95 (9216) Prsnl Christianity.

Sermon on the Mount According to Vedanta. Ed. by Swami Prabhavananda. 2000. bk. 50.00 (978-0-87481-398-2(0)) Vedanta Pr.

Sermon on the Mount According to Vedanta MP3 - CD. Speeches. Swami Prabhavananda. 1 cd. (Running Time: 10 hrs). 2007. 29.95 (978-0-87481-977-9(6)) Vedanta Pr.

Sermon on the Mount Introductory. C. S. Lovett. 1 cass. 4.95 (7000) Prsnl Christianity.

***Sermon on Themount - Parables & Miracles of Jesus, Pt. 1.** unabr. ed. Zondervan. (Running Time: 0 hr. 18 mins. 41 sec.). (Best-Loved Stories of the Bible, NIrV Ser.). (ENG.). (J). 2010. 1.99 (978-0-310-86529-2(8)) Pub: Zondkidz. Dist(s): Zondervan

Sermon Studies, Vols. 1-10. Northwest Publishing Staff. 2000. audio compact disk 179.00 (978-0-8100-0993-6(5)) Northwest Pub.

Sermons: Biblical Wisdom for Daily Living. abr. ed. Peter J. Gomes. Read by Peter J. Gomes. 2 cass. (Running Time: 2 hrs.). 1998. 17.95 (978-1-55935-280-2(9)) Soundelux.
Offers tools needed to understand the Bible & the joy & inspiration it can bring to everyday life.

Sermons by Marshall Keeble. Marshall Keeble. 2 CDs. (Running Time: 3 hrs.). audio compact disk 19.99 (978-0-89098-258-7(9)) Twent Cent Christ.
Marshall Keeble was indeed a legend in his own time. He personally baptized more than 40,000 people. This CD collection of four outstanding sermons is a tribute to the man and his vital Christian service to all men.

Sermons from the Heart: A Collection of Divinely Inspired Devotional Sermons: A Special Tribute. Berlinda A. Love. (Running Time: 12300 sec.). 2008. audio compact disk 19.99 (978-1-60247-195-5(9)) Tate Pubng.

Sermons to Dispel Anxiety: Self-Help Series. unabr. ed. Charles Kingsley et al. Narrated by Don Randall & Dick Fisher. 2 CDs. (Running Time: 2 hrs. 20 mins.). 2006. audio compact disk 25.95 (978-0-9790364-1-5(0)) A Audiobooks.
An effective alternative to vapid "flavor-of-the-day" pop psychology, these sermons offer deeply-founded and time-proven relief for the troubles of the soul. These works provide inspiration for all, religious or not, and are highly entertaining!Included in this audiobook: "The Distracted Mind", "Terror by Night" and "The Torment of Fear" by Charles Kingsley; "Parting Words" by James Martineau; "Christ and the Fear of Death" by George H. Morrison; "Self-Reliance" by Ralph Waldo Emerson; "Fearing and Trusting" by Charles H. Spurgeon; and "Love and Fear" by Alexander Maclaren.

Serpent. Clive Cussler & Paul Kemprecos. 12 cass. (Running Time: 18 hrs.). (NUMA Files Ser.: No. 1). 2001. 96.00 (978-0-7366-6192-8(1)) Books on Tape.
Cussler introduces a hero for the new millennium. When Kurt Austin, leader of a courageous National Underwater & Marine Agency exploration team, rescues beautiful marine archaeologist Nina Kirov off the coast of Morocco, he becomes the next target of Texas industrialist, Don Halcon.

Serpent. Clive Cussler & Paul Kemprecos. Read by Michael Prichard. (NUMA Files Ser.: No. 1). 2001. audio compact disk 120.00 (978-0-7366-8527-6(8)) Books on Tape.

Serpent, abr. ed. Clive Cussler & Paul Kemprecos. Read by David Purdham. 4 cass. (Running Time: 4 hrs.). (NUMA Files Ser.: No. 1). 1999. 24.00 (FS9-50946) Highsmith.

Serpent: Chinese Feng Shui Music. Hsiao-ping Wu. Perf. by Shanghai Chinese Traditional Orchestra. Conducted by Xia Fei-yun. 1 CD. (Running Time: 1 hr.). audio compact disk (978-1-57606-052-0(7)) Wind Recs.
Serpent, god of the center, is associated with the element of earth & with kung of the five Chinese tones. Its music reflects the terrestrial characteristics of earth & is believed to have therapeutic functions for people lacking earth energy. Play Serpent if you live in a tall building, or if your home faces southwest or northeast. Detailed liner notes.

Serpent Gate. Michael McGarrity. (Kevin Kerney Ser.: Bk. 3). 2000. 15.99 (978-0-7435-0557-4(3), Audioworks) S&S Audio.

Serpent Gate. Michael McGarrity. (Kevin Kerney Ser.: Bk. 3). 2004. 15.95 (978-0-7435-4875-5(2)) Pub: S&S Audio. Dist(s): S and S Inc

Serpent Gate. unabr. ed. Michael McGarrity. Narrated by George Guidall. 6 cass. (Running Time: 8 hrs. 30 mins.). (Kevin Kerney Ser.: Bk. 3). 1998. 53.00 (978-0-7887-2598-2(X), 95497E7) Recorded Bks.
As a former Santa Fe policeman returns to duty, he must confront powerful state politicians & a deadly enemy from the past.

***Serpent on the Crown.** abr. ed. Elizabeth Peters. Read by Barbara Rosenblat. (ENG.). 2005. (978-0-06-084071-6(4), Harper Audio); (978-0-06-084069-3(2), Harper Audio) HarperCollins Pubs.

***Serpent on the Crown.** unabr. ed. Elizabeth Peters. Read by Barbara Rosenblat. (ENG.). 2005. (978-0-06-084073-0(0), Harper Audio); (978-0-06-084072-3(2), Harper Audio) HarperCollins Pubs.

Serpent on the Crown. unabr. ed. Elizabeth Peters, pseud. Read by Barbara Rosenblat. (Amelia Peabody Ser.: No. 17). 2005. audio compact disk 39.95 (978-0-06-076013-7(3)) HarperCollins Pubs.

Serpent on the Crown. unabr. ed. Elizabeth Peters, pseud. Narrated by Barbara Rosenblat. 11 CDs. (Running Time: 12 hrs. 15 mins.). (Amelia Peabody Ser.: No. 17). 2005. audio compact disk 119.75 (978-1-4193-2278-5(8), C2989); 89.75 (978-1-4193-2276-1(1), 97948) Recorded Bks.
It's 1922, and The Great War is over. With the world at peace, Amelia and her family return to the Valley of the Kings to explore its storied sands. But they are quickly troubled by treacherous secrets and murder. A woman presents them with a priceless but dangerous artifact - a golden king said to bring death to all who possess it. The woman's husband has already fallen, and now she needs help to return the relic to its tomb.

Serpent on the Crown. unabr. abr. ed. Elizabeth Peters, pseud. Read by Barbara Rosenblat. (Amelia Peabody Ser.: No. 17). 2005. audio compact disk 29.95 (978-0-06-076012-0(5)) HarperCollins Pubs.

serpent Scenario. A. J. Butcher. Read by Sean Mangan. (Running Time: 6 hrs. 45 mins.). (Spy High Ser.). (YA). 2009. 69.99 (978-1-74214-303-3(2), 9781742143033) Pub: Bolinda Pubng AUS. Dist(s): Bolinda Pub Inc

Serpent Scenario. unabr. ed. Read by Sean Mangan. (Running Time: 24300 sec.). (Spy High Ser.). (J). (ps-7). 2008. audio compact disk 77.95 (978-1-74093-800-6(3)) Pub: Bolinda Pubng AUS. Dist(s): Bolinda Pub Inc

Serpent's Bride see Black Fairy Tales

Serpent's Children, unabr. ed. Laurence Yep. Narrated by Alyssa Bresnahan. 5 pieces. (Running Time: 6 hrs. 45 mins.). (Golden Mountain Chronicles). (gr. 7 up). 1997. 44.00 (978-0-7887-1334-7(5), 95183E7) Recorded Bks.
In this tale of early 19th century China, a teenaged girl describes how she kept her family together through years of violence, famine & drought. Shortly after eight-year-old Cassia's father marches off to fight the demons in the Opium War, Mother dies. The villagers insist on separating her & her younger brother, but Cassia knows Mother would expect her to take over. Sequel to "Dragon's Gate".

Serpent's Children. unabr. ed. Laurence Yep. Read by Alyssa Bresnahan. 5 cass. (Running Time: 6 hrs. 45 min.). (Golden Mountain Chronicles). (J). (gr. 2). 1997. Rental 13.50 Recorded Bks.

Serpent's Children, unabr. ed. Laurence Yep. Read by Alyssa Bresnahan. 5 cass. (Running Time: 6 hrs. 45 min.). (Golden Mountain Chronicles). (YA). (gr. 7). 1997. pap. bk. 58.20 (978-0-7887-1714-7(6), 40582) Recorded Bks.

Serpent's Tale. unabr. ed. Ariana Franklin, pseud. Read by Kate Reading. 10 CDs. (Running Time: 13 hrs.). (ENG.). (gr. 8). 2008. audio compact disk 39.95 (978-0-14-314287-4(9), PengAudBks) Penguin Grp USA.

Serpent's Tooth. Faye Kellerman. (Peter Decker & Rina Lazarus Novel Ser.). 2004. 15.95 (978-0-7435-4876-2(0)) Pub: S&S Audio. Dist(s): S and S Inc

Serpent's Tooth. unabr. ed. Faye Kellerman. Read by Bernadette Dunne. 9 cass. (Running Time: 13 hrs. 30 min.). (Peter Decker & Rina Lazarus Novel Ser.). 1997. 72.00 (978-0-7366-4049-7(5), 4548) Books on Tape.
The author's latest thriller pits Lieutenant Peter Decker & his wife, Rina Lazarus, against an adversary who is pure evil. A lone gunman walks into a trendy L.A. restaurant & when the shooting stops, he lies among the dead. Enough of the triggerman's face remains to identify him as a former bartender & would-be actor. The papers paint him psycho, but Decker thinks it's all too pat. Pursuing the crime, he delves into the moneyed enclaves f Southern California. When he enters a world where everything's for sale, Decker & his reputation come under fire. As the attacks heat up, he finds unexpected allies in mysterious but welcome places.

Serpent's Tooth. unabr. ed. Michelle Paver. Read by Bentinck. 9 cass. (Running Time: 12 hrs. 35 mins.). (Isis Cassettes Ser.). (J). 2005. 76.95 (978-0-7531-1613-5(8)); audio compact disk 99.95 (978-0-7531-2477-2(7)) Pub: ISIS Lrg Prnt GBR. Dist(s): Ulverscroft US

Serpents Trail. unabr. ed. Sue Henry. Read by Lee Adams. 6 cass. (Running Time: 9 hrs.). (Maxie & Stretch Mystery Ser.). 2004. 72.00 (978-1-4159-9982-0(1)) Books on Tape.
An on-the go Alaskan RVing retiree discovers there's murder at every rest stop.

Serrano Legacy (Book 3) Winning Colors (Part 1) Based on a book by Eliz Moon. 2008. 12.99 (978-1-59950-546-6(0)) GraphicAudio.

Serrano Legacy (Book 4) Once a Hero (Part 1) 2008. 12.99 (978-1-59950-548-0(7)) GraphicAudio.

Serrano Legacy (Book 5) Rules of Engagement (Part 1) Based on a book by Elizabeth mo. 2009. 12.99 (978-1-59950-550-3(9)) GraphicAudio.

***Servant Heart.** 2010. audio compact disk (978-0-9769068-7-2(2)) Mid A Bks & Tapes.

Servant of the Bones. unabr. ed. Anne Rice. Read by Michael Prichard. 11 cass. (Running Time: 16 hrs. 30 min.). 1996. 88.00 (978-0-7366-3430-4(4), 4074) Books on Tape.
Marshaling his strength & wit to defeat them, Azriel embarks on a perilous journey through time, to Manhattan in the 1990s. There he sees a young girl murdered & challenges her father, a powerful televangilist who embodies all that Azriel has fought against. Azriel uses his own powers to forestall a conspiracy that threatens the world. But can he finally redeem his immortal soul?.

Servant of the Bones, unabr. ed. Anne Rice. Read by Michael Prichard. 12 cass. (Running Time: 12 hrs.). 1999. 44.95 (FS9-34629) Highsmith.

Servanthood. Derek Prince. 1 cass. (Running Time: 60 min.). 5.95 (B-4238) Derek Prince.

Servanthood: The Pathway to Greatness. 2 cass. (Running Time: 2 hrs.). (Passing the Test Ser.: 4). 2002. 10.00 (978-1-57399-153-7(8)) Mac Hammond.
In this installment of the Passing the Test series, Mac Hammond reveals the Bible's secret for finding success that lasts. Jesus described that secret this way: to be the greatest of all, you must be the servant of all. If you've been unable to find your road to success, discover the Bible's route to servanthood in this two-part message.

Servanthood: The Pathway to Greatness. Mac Hammond. 2 cass. (Running Time: 2 hr.). (Passing the Test Ser.: 4). 2005. 10.00 (978-1-57399-230-5(5)) Mac Hammond.

Servant's Heart. Chuck Smith. 6 cass. (Running Time: 5 hrs. 15 mins.). (Leadership Ser.). 2001. (978-0-936728-94-0(9)) Word For Today.
A collection of seven messages designed for those pursuing ministry.

Servant's Heart Vol. 1: Leadership Series, Pack. 2003. audio compact disk (978-1-931713-88-7(X)) Word For Today.

Servants of the Queen. (J). 1980. (N-66) Jimcin Record.

Servants of the Shadow. unabr. ed. Stephan Hoeller. 1 cass. (Running Time: 1 hr. 30 min.). 1982. 11.00 (40005) Big Sur Tapes.
Through history many individuals & groups have been taken over by the shadow of their own nature, or by the universal shadow. Hoeller explains the inevitable aspect of human nature that attempts to rid itself of the dark, the inacceptable & evil side of itself by projecting that shadow in someone else.

Servants of Truth: A Weekend Inquiry with Adyashanti recorded September 16-17 2006. Featuring Adyashanti. 7 CDs. (Running Time: 8 hours). 2006. audio compact disk 65.00 (978-1-933986-12-8(3)) Open Gate Pub.

Servants of Twilight. unabr. ed. Leigh Nichols, pseud. Read by Kyle Prue. 9 cass. (Running Time: 13 hrs. 30 min.). 1993. 72.00 (978-0-7366-2543-2(7), 3294) Books on Tape.
Religious fanatics target a six-year-old boy. They think he's the Antichrist.

Servants or Friends? Another Look at God. Graham Maxwell. Illus. by Susan Kelley. 1992. 15.95 (978-1-56652-002-7(9)) Pine Knoll Pubns.

Servant's Tale see Widow's Children

Serve One Another: Teach Kids 6-12 to Serve. Created by Standard Publishing. (God Rocks! Bibletoons Ser.). (J). (gr. 1-7). 2007. DVD & audio compact disk 39.99 (978-0-7847-1981-7(0)) Standard Pub.

Serve Self. Perf. by Left Out. 1 CD. audio compact disk 15.98 CD. (978-1-57908-331-1(5), 1393) Platinm Enter.

Serve the Lord with Your Heart. Grant Von Harrison. Read by Ted Gibbons. 1 cass. (Missionary Success Ser.). 6.95 (978-0-929985-34-3(6)) Jackman Pubng.
Explores the idea of being called to serve the Lord.

Serve with Gladness. Greg Skipper. 1997. 40.00 (978-0-7673-3024-4(2)) LifeWay Christian.

Serve with Gladness Senior Adult. Greg Skipper. 1997. 11.98 (978-0-7673-3022-0(6)) LifeWay Christian.

Server Down. unabr. ed. J. M. Hayes. (Running Time: 7 hrs. 0 mins.). (ENG.). 2009. 29.95 (978-1-4332-8995-8(4)); 54.95 (978-1-4332-8991-0(1)); audio compact disk 60.00 (978-1-4332-8992-7(X)) Blckstn Audio.

Service: Finding Something of Your Own to Give. Tara Singh. Read by Tara Singh. 2 cass. (Running Time: 1 hr. 40 min.). 1992. 14.95 (978-1-55531-261-9(6)) Life Action Pr.
Service is the watchword of the decade. Many of us are questioning our meaningless routines & know there must be something more to life. In These two tapes Tara Singh explores in-depth what service really is & how we can discover what we have to give to others.

Service Dress Blues: A Rep & Melissa Pennyworth Mystery. unabr. ed. Michael Bowen. (Running Time: 8 hrs. 0 mins.). (ENG.). 2009. 29.95 (978-1-4332-9454-9(0)); 54.95 (978-1-4332-9450-1(8)); audio compact disk 76.00 (978-1-4332-9451-8(6)) Blckstn Audio.

Service Excellence Audible. Price Pritchett. (ENG.). 2007. 9.95 (978-0-944002-40-7(4)) Pritchett.

Service Music & Music from Taize. bk. 10.00 (978-0-687-04916-5(4)) Abingdon.

Service of All the Dead. unabr. ed. Colin Dexter. Read by Terrence Hardiman. 6 cass. (Running Time: 9 hrs.). (Inspector Morse Mystery Ser.: Bk. 4). 2000. 49.95 (978-0-7451-6497-7(8), CAB 1113) Pub: Chivers Audio Bks GBR. Dist(s): AudioGO
"Churchwarden murdered during Service," the headline read. After the second death, the apparent suicide of the murderer, the case was closed. But Chief Inspector Morse had already found discrepancies in the case. Then a chance meeting among the tombstones reveals a startling conspiracy. Morse realized there was much more to the case, two more bodies, in fact.

Service of Clouds. Delia Falconer. Read by Jenny Seedsman. 6 cass. (Running Time: 10 hrs.). 2000. 44.95 (978-0-7861-1742-0(7), 2547) Blckstn Audio.
It is 1907 & the Blue Mountains are filled with the grand dreams of elsewhere. Eureka Jones, a young pharmacist's assistant with historical eyes, falls in love with Harry Kitchings, a man who takes pictures of clouds & succumbs to the "madness of photography." Set in a vast landscape haunted by sadness, romance, illness & the secret desires men & women bring to the mountains.

Service of Love see Favorite Stories by O. Henry

Service, the Life of the Believer. Chuck Smith. (ENG.). 2001. audio compact disk 22.99 (978-1-932941-15-9(0)) Word For Today.

Service with a Smile. Read by Nigel Lambert. 6 vols. (Running Time: 23580 sec.). 2003. audio compact disk 64.95 (978-0-7540-8755-7(7)) Pub: Chivers Audio Bks GBR. Dist(s): AudioGO

***Service with a Smile.** P. G. Wodehouse. Read by Martin Jarvis. (Running Time: 5 hrs. 0 mins. 0 sec.). (Blandings Castle Saga Ser.). (ENG.). 2010. audio compact disk 26.95 (978-1-934997-64-2(1)) Pub: CSAWord. Dist(s): PerseuPGW

Service with a Smile, unabr. ed. P. G. Wodehouse. Read by Frederick Davidson. 5 cass. (Running Time: 7 hrs.). 1990. 39.95 (978-0-7861-0210-5(1), 1185) Blckstn Audio.
This is a priceless tale filled with a wonderfully batty assemblage of characters: the pompous duke, the doddering earl, the haughty secretary, the plebeian swineherder. At Lord Emsworth's invitation Uncle Fred intervenes at Blanding Castle & thwarts another plot of the mad Duke of Dunstable to eliminate the prize pig.

Service with a Smile. unabr. ed. P. G. Wodehouse. Read by Nigel Lambert. 6 cass. (Running Time: 12 hrs.). (Blandings Castle Comedies Ser.). 1998. 49.95 (978-0-7540-0220-8(9), CAB 1643) Pub: Chivers Audio Bks GBR. Dist(s): AudioGO
Lord Emsworth needs an ally at his side to remove unwanted & troublesome guests from his home, so he can tend to his beloved pig, Empress of Blandings.

***Servicio al cliente conexion al Exito.** Javier Madera Camacho.Tr. of Customer Service. (SPA.). 2008. audio compact disk 39.95 (978-0-9827086-1-3(0)) JMC Prof Semin.

Servidumbre Humana. abr. ed. Somerset Maugham. Read by Fabio Camero. 3 CDs.Tr. of Of Human Bondage. (SPA.). 2002. audio compact disk 17.00 (978-958-8161-25-9(8)) YoYoMusic.

Servile State, unabr. ed. Hilaire Belloc. Read by Robin Lawson. 3 cass. (Running Time: 4 hrs.). 1991. 23.95 (978-0-7861-0078-1(8), 1072) Blckstn Audio.
Hilaire Belloc defines the servile state as "that arrangement of society in which so considerable a number of families & individuals are constrained by positive law to labor for the advantage of other families & individuals as to stamp the whole community with the mark of such labor.".

Serving in Silence. unabr. ed. Margarethe Cammermeyer & Chris Fisher. Narrated by Barbara Caruso. 8 cass. (Running Time: 11 hrs. 45 mins.). 1995. 70.00 (978-0-7887-0196-2(7), 94420E7) Recorded Bks.
Autobiography of a Vietnam nurse, mother of four & the highest-ranking officer to challenge the military's anti-gay policy.

***Servolution: Starting a Church Revolution through Serving.** unabr. ed. Dino Rizzo. (Running Time: 5 hrs. 49 mins. 0 sec.). (Leadership Network Innovation Ser.). (ENG.). 2009. 16.99 (978-0-310-78900-0(1)) Zondervan.

Ses Amis. Mary Alice Fontenot. Narrated by Julie Landry. (Clovis Crawfish Ser.). (FRE.). (J). 1996. 9.95 (978-1-56554-729-2(2)) Pelican.

Sesame & Lilies. unabr. ed. John Ruskin. Read by Robert L. Halvorson. 4 cass. (Running Time: 4 hrs.). 28.95 (74) Halvorson Assocs.

Sesame Road. 1 cass. (J). 1995. 9.98 (Sony Wonder); audio compact disk 13.98 CD. Sony Music Ent.
Includes two new tracks, & features The Sesame Street Beetles & friends singing popular tunes such as "I Want to Hold Your Ear," "A Little Yelp from My Friends" & "Rebel L".

Sesame Street Christmas. 1 cass. (J). 1995. 9.98 (Sony Wonder) Sony Music Ent.
Features the "Sesame Street" characters singing re-recorded & re-mixed versions of their favorite holiday tunes. Included is a lyric book so you can sing with Bert, Ernie, Elmo, Herry Monster, Prairie Dawn & The Count on "Deck the Halls;" join Hoots the Owl, Bob, Elmo & company on "True Blue Miracle;" & sing along with 12 favorite "Sesame Street" characters including Cookie Monster, Elmo, Oscar the Grouch, Bert, Ernie & Big Bird on "The Twelve Days of Christmas".

Sesame Street Christmas. 1 cass. (J). 2000. audio compact disk 10.98 Sony Music Ent.

Sesame Street Country. Perf. by Glen Campbell et al. 1 cass. (Running Time: 42 min.). (J). 1993. 11.99 compact disc. (5685, Gold Bks) RH Chldrns.
Includes Kin Folk, Sesame Jamboree, Keep on Smilin', The Last Cookie Roundup, Count Von Count's Continuous Country Cookin' Downhome Diner, Songs, Count on Me, Takin' Turns, Roll Over.

Sesame Street in Harmony, Vol. I. 1 cass. (J). 7.98 (978-1-880528-93-8(2), M5 3481) Warner Bros.
Various children's songs.

Sesame Street Music Collection. 4 cass. (J). (ps-3). 19.95 Set. (282) MFLP CA.
The ultimate Sesame Street collection, featuring 72 of the best songs from the television series with performances by Big Bird, Bert, Ernie, Cookie Monster & all the gang.

Sesame Street Platinum: All Time Favorites. 1 cass. (Sesame Street Ser.). (J). 1995. bk. 9.98 (Sony Wonder); audio compact disk 13.98 CD. Sony Music Ent.
Features many of the classic songs that helped make "Sesame Street" number one with kids around the world. Also included is a lyric book with words to such hits as the "Sesame Street Theme," "C Is for Cookie," "Sing," & "Bein' Green".

Sesame Street Splish Splash: Bath Time Fun. 1 cass. (Sesame Street Ser.). (J). 1995. 9.98 (Sony Wonder); audio compact disk 13.98 CD. Sony Music Ent.
Little Richard is sure to have kids yelling for their favorite bath toys with his upbeat version of "Rubber Duckie", & they'll continue to rock while they wash to songs such as "Splish Splash", "Everybody Wash" & "Comb Your Face".

Sespe Creek of Ventura County, California - A Proposed National Wild & Scenic River. Hosted by Nancy Pearlman. 1 cass. (Running Time: 28 min.). 10.00 (1019) Educ Comm CA.

Set A: 1 Audiocassette (6 Titles) (gr. k-3). 10.00 (978-0-7635-5031-8(0)) Rigby Educ.

Set B: 1 Audiocassette (6 Titles) (gr. k-3). 10.00 (978-0-7635-5032-5(9)) Rigby Educ.

Set C: 3 Audiocassettes (6 Titles) 3 cass. (gr. k-3). 30.00 (978-0-7635-4337-2(3)) Rigby Educ.

Set D: 3 Audiocassettes (7 Titles) 3 cass. (gr. k-3). 30.00 (978-0-7635-4338-9(1)) Rigby Educ.

Set for Life. 1 cass. (Running Time: 3 hrs.). (Wiley Audio Ser.). 2000. 18.95 Penton Overseas.

Set for Life: Financial Peace for People over 50. Bambi Holzer. 2 cass. (Running Time: 3 hrs.). 2000. 18.95 Penton Overseas.

Set Free Indeed. Perf. by Rose Leibundguth. 3 cass. (Running Time: 3 hrs). 2002. 10.00 (978-1-931262-09-5(8)) Rose Leibund.
Testimony of Rose Leibundgut (Formerly Rose Warnke from Warnke Ministries).

***Set in Stone.** Kay Stephens. Read by Julia Franklin. 2010. 64.95 (978-1-84652-818-7(6)); audio compact disk 71.95 (978-1-84652-819-4(4)) Pub: Magna Story GBR. Dist(s): Ulverscroft US

Set in Stone. unabr. ed. Robert Goddard. Read by Michael Kitchen. 10 cass. (Running Time: 10 hrs.). 2000. 84.95 (978-0-7540-0483-7(X), CAB1906) AudioGO.
Recovering from the recent tragedy of his wife's death in a cliff fall, Tony Sheridan goes to stay with his sister-in-law Lucy & her husband at their new home "Otherways," a strange circular, moated house. Sheridan is troubled by weird & vivid dreams, as well as his growing attraction to Lucy. As he & Lucy begin a secret & passionate affair, he begins uncovering the truth about "Otherways".

Set in Stone. unabr. ed. Robert Goddard. Read by Michael Kitchen. 10 CDs. (Running Time: 10 hrs.). 2000. audio compact disk 94.95 (978-0-7540-5378-1(4), CCD069) AudioGO.
Recovering from his wife's recent death, Tony Sheridan goes to stay with his sister-in-law, Lucy & her husband at their strange, circular moated house, Otherways. Disturbed by memories of his wife & a growing attraction to Lucy. Sheridan is also troubled by weird & vivid dreams. As he & Lucy embark on a secret & passionate affair, Sheridan begins uncovering the truth about, Otherways.

Set Me Free. Contrib. by Myron Butler & Ken Pennell. 2005. audio compact disk 17.99 (978-5-558-77433-7(9)) Pt of Grace Ent.

Set Me Free. Contrib. by Casting Crowns. (Sound Performance Soundtracks Ser.). 2006. audio compact disk 5.98 (978-5-558-43568-9(2)) Pt of Grace Ent.

Set of the Sail Vol. 620: James 1:9-18. Ed Young. 1987. 4.95 (978-0-7417-1620-0(8), 620) Win Walk.

***Set of 12 Bilingual Quest for Success.** ed. Carl Sommer. (Quest for Success Bilingual Ser.). (ENG & SPA.). (YA). 2009. bk. 299.40 (978-1-57537-247-1(9)) Advance Pub.

***Set of 12 Quest for Success.** Carl Sommer. (Quest for Success Ser.). (ENG.). (YA). 2009. bk. 239.40 (978-1-57537-323-2(8)) Advance Pub.

Set of 2 CDs for Young Bret Rabbit, Vol. 2. Music by H. S. A. Calkin-Clough. audio compact disk 12.95 (978-0-88045-163-5(7)) Stemmer Hse.

***Set of 6 English Paperbacks, Plus CD: Gus the Hedgehod.** (Read-It! Readers: Gus the Hedgehog Ser.). (ENG.). 2007. audio compact disk 23.70 (978-1-4048-4143-7(1)) CapstoneDig.

Set on Stone. Perf. by Kifenora Fiddle Ceili Band. 1 cass., 1 CD. 8.78 (GH 10041); audio compact disk 12.78 CD Jewel box. (GH 10041) NewSound.

Set the World on Fire. Contrib. by Britt Nicole. (Mastertrax Ser.). 2007. audio compact disk 9.98 (978-5-557-51419-4(8)) Pt of Grace Ent.

Set This House on Fire, Pt. 1. unabr. collector's ed. William Styron. Read by Wolfram Kandinsky. 9 cass. (Running Time: 13 hrs. 30 min.). 1986. 72.00 (978-0-7366-0557-1(6), 1530-A) Books on Tape.
The narrator, Peter Leverett, a government employee returning to the U.S., stops in the Italian village of Sambuco to see his old schoolmate Mason Flagg. The next morning Flagg is found dead at the base of a cliff, a peasant girl has been beaten to death, & Cass Kinsolving, a drunken American painter, is gone. The case is written off as a murder & a suicide, but Leverett doesn't believe it & searches for the truth.

Set This House on Fire, Pt. 2. collector's ed. William Styron. Read by Wolfram Kandinsky. 9 cass. (Running Time: 13 hrs. 30 min.). 1986. 72.00 (978-0-7366-0558-8(4), 1530-B) Books on Tape.

Set Up. unabr. ed. Claire McNab. 4 cass. (Running Time: 5 hrs. 37 mins.). 2004. 32.00 (978-1-74030-532-7(9)) Pub: Bolinda Pubng AUS. Dist(s): Lndmrk Audiobks

Set up for Success. Arynne Simon. 1 cass. 1995. 14.95 (978-1-882389-20-9(4)) Wilarvi Communs.
How reality concepts can help dreams come true. It's possible to remain vulnerable & kind in one's heart, while getting more out of life.

Set Your Soul Free! Tape 2: How to Play Soul Gospel. Robert L. Jefferson. 1992. 9.95 (978-1-880549-03-2(4)) Pensacola Pubns.

Set Yourself Free: Releasing Fears & Concerns of Pregnancy, Childbirth & Motherhood. Lea Blumberg. 1CD. 2005. audio compact disk 19.95 (978-0-9747487-4-0(9)) L Blumberg.

Set Yourself Free & Enjoy Your Life. Bill Ferguson. Read by Bill Ferguson. 8 cass. (Running Time: 8 hrs.). 1990. 64.95 (978-1-878410-01-6(6)) Return Heart.
This series of eight audio cassettes will show you how to have every aspect of your life be effortless & supportive. You will discover how to set yourself free inside & restore your natural aliveness & effectiveness. You will discover why areas of your life don't work & what you can do to resolve them. You will discover something about yourself that will permanently alter the way you live your life. This series contains each of the following eight audio tapes.

Setbacks. Ann Seagrave & Faison Covington. Read by Ann Seagrave & Faison Covington. (Anxiety Treatment Ser.). 15.50 CHAANGE.
Presents a talk between Ann, the therapist, & Elizabeth & Don, who are both recovered from agoraphobia through the CHAANGE process. They describe what a setback is (& isn't) & how to deal appropriately with those times.

***Seth Baumgartner's Love Manifesto.** unabr. ed. Eric Luper. Read by Nick Podehl. (Running Time: 7 hrs.). 2010. 24.99 (978-1-4418-5965-5(9), 9781441859655, Brilliance MP3); 39.97 (978-1-4418-5966-2(7), 9781441859662, Brinc Audio MP3 Lib); 24.99 (978-1-4418-5967-9(5), 9781441859679, BAD); 39.97 (978-1-4418-5968-6(3), 9781441859686, BADLE); audio compact disk 69.97 (978-1-4418-5964-8(0), 9781441859648, BriAudCD Unabrid) Brilliance Audio.

***Seth Baumgartner's Love Manifesto.** unabr. ed. Eric Luper. Read by Nick Podehl. (Running Time: 7 hrs.). (YA). 2010. audio compact disk 24.99 (978-1-4418-5963-1(2), 9781441859631, Bril Audio CD Unabri) Brilliance Audio.

SETH: Electronic Swept Frequencies 1 & 2: From Ancient Egyptian, Mayan & Druid Temples. John McAuliffe & Dotti McAuliffe. 1 cass. (Running Time: 46 min.). 1990. 12.00 (978-1-878976-00-0(1)) D McAuliffe.
Meditation, self-help tape, consisting of frequencies recorded in ancient temples.

SETH: Electronic Swept Frequencies 3 & 4: From Ancient Egyptian, Mayan & Druid Temples. John McAuliffe & Dotti McAuliffe. 1 cass. (Running Time: 46 min.). 1990. 12.00 (978-1-878976-01-7(X)) D McAuliffe.

SETH: Electronic Swept Frequencies 5 & 6: From Ancient Egyptian, Mayan & Druid Temples. John McAuliffe & Dotti McAuliffe. 1 cass. (Running Time: 46 min.). 1990. 12.00 (978-1-878976-02-4(8)) D McAuliffe.
Meditation, self-help tape, consisting of electronic frequencies recorded in ancient temples.

SETH: Electronic Swept Frequencies 7 & 8: From Ancient Egyptian, Mayan & Druid Temples. John McAuliffe & Dotti McAuliffe. 1 cass. (Running Time: 46 min.). 1990. 12.00 (978-1-878976-04-8(4)) D McAuliffe.

SETH: Electronic Swept Frequencies 9 & 10: From Ancient Egyptian, Mayan & Druid Temples. John McAuliffe & Dotti McAuliffe. 1 cass. (Running Time: 46 min.). 1990. 12.00 (978-1-878976-05-5(2)) D McAuliffe.

Setons. unabr. ed. O. Douglas. Read by Gordon Reid. 6 cass. (Running Time: 8 hrs.). (Isis Ser.). (J). 2000. 54.95 (978-0-7531-0624-2(8), 991114) Pub: ISIS Lrg Prnt GBR. Dist(s): Ulverscroft US
This gentle classic, set in Glasgow in 1913, follows the lives of a Scottish minister, his exuberant family & parishioners. His vivacious daughter, Elizabeth, whose outspokenness in turn charms & exasperates; Buff, her spirited younger brother whose innocent mumbled remarks always hit on some inappropriate truth; & the widowed minister himself, who drinks too much tea for his own good. O. Douglas has a sharp eye for snobbery & an ability to mingle believable characters & social satire whilst recognizing the importance of everyday events & World Wars in the lives of ordinary people.

Setting & Achieving Goals. 1 cass. 10.00 (978-1-58506-036-8(4), 68) New Life Inst OR.
This program helps you set your goals & help you accomplish them.

Setting & Achieving Goals (Subliminal & Hypnosis), Vol. 29. Jayne Helle. 1 cass. (Running Time: 28 min.). 1996. 15.00 (978-1-891826-28-3(X)) Introspect.
Goal setting is more than a road map of life. It is the energy generator to help one over the rough spots.

Setting & Attaining Realistic Goals. Norman J. Caldwell. Read by Norman J. Caldwell. Ed. by Achieve Now Institute Staff. 1 cass. (Running Time: 20 min.). (Success Now Ser.). 1988. 9.97 My Mothers Pub.
Attaining realistic goals.

Setting & Reaching Goals. Shad Helmstetter. 1 cass. (Self-Talk Cassettes). 10.95 (978-0-937065-02-0(1)) Grindle Pr.

***Setting Boundaries with Difficult People: A Survival Guide for People Pleasers.** unabr. ed. David J. Lieberman. Read by Sean Pratt. (Running Time: 34 mins.). (ENG.). 2010. 6.98 (978-1-59659-603-0(1), GildAudio) Pub: Gildan Media. Dist(s): HachBkGrp

Setting Business Strategy. Brian S. Tracy. Read by Brian S. Tracy. 2 cass. (Running Time: 2 hrs.). (Effective Manager Seminar Ser.: No. 5). cass. & video 95.00 (744VD) Nightingale-Conant.
This program teaches you how.

Setting Free. Contrib. by Tola Custy. (ENG.). 1994. 13.95 (978-0-8023-7098-3(5)); audio compact disk 21.95 (978-0-8023-8098-2(0)) Pub: Clo Iar-Chonnachta IRL. Dist(s): Dufour

Setting Free the Bears. unabr. collector's ed. John Irving. Read by Dan Lazar. 8 cass. (Running Time: 12 hrs.). 1981. 64.00 (978-0-7366-0381-2(6), 1358) Books on Tape.
This novel juxtaposes selected events in World War II with the rebellion of youth in the late 1960's. One spring day in Vienna, Graff, an earnest young Austrian student who has just failed his exams, meets Siggy, a wildly eccentric motorcycle mechanic & philosopher. Together they roam the countryside astride a 700cc Royal Enfield racer. Lovely long-limbed Gallen soon joins them. The drama climaxes in "the great zoo bust" as all forms of beast, including human, break free.

Setting Goals: Children's. (Running Time: 45 min.). (Educational Ser.). (J). 12.98 (978-1-55909-111-4(8), 91S) Randolph Tapes.

Setting Goals in Marriage: Gal. 5:22, 727. Ed Young. 1989. 4.95 (978-0-7417-1727-6(1), 727) Win Walk.

Setting Goals to Improve Your Life & Happiness. Edwin Locke. 1 cass. (Running Time: 90 min.). 1985. 12.95 (978-1-56114-035-0(X), IL02C) Second Renaissance.
How can one plan & organize the activities of one's life to achieve success? This valuable "how-to" talk explains why setting well-defined goals is vital & offers advice on how to make difficult goals achievable.

Setting Limits in the Classroom. Robert J. Mackenzie. 1 cass. (Running Time: 1 hr. 28 min.). 1998. bk. 20.00 (978-1-58111-067-8(7)) Contemporary Medical.
Discusses providing guidance for children, temperament of limit setting, ways to communicate with children & approaches for teachers.

Setting of the Sunshine: Judges 14:1-3. Ed Young. (J). 1980. 4.95 (978-0-7417-1143-4(5), A0143) Win Walk.

Setting Priorities & Managing Time. Shad Helmstetter. 1 cass. (Self-Talk Cassettes Ser.). 10.95 (978-0-937065-03-7(X)) Grindle Pr.

Setting the East Ablaze. unabr. collector's ed. Peter Hopkirk. Read by Richard Brown. 6 cass. (Running Time: 9 hrs.). 1987. 48.00 (978-0-7366-1143-5(6), 2068) Books on Tape.
Shortly after seizing power in Russia, the Bolsheviks tried to "set the East ablaze" with the heady new gospel of Marxism. It is a tale of intrigue & treachery, barbarism & civil war & sometimes pure farce.

Setting the Stage for Fatima: The World Situation in 1917. Robert I. Bradley. 1 cass. 1989. 2.50 (978-1-56036-068-1(2)) AMI Pr.

***Setting the Table.** abr. ed. Danny Meyer. Read by Danny Meyer. (ENG.). 2006. (978-0-06-125269-3(7), Harper Audio); (978-0-06-125268-6(9), Harper Audio) HarperCollins Pubs.

Setting the Table: The Transforming Power of Hospitality in Business. abr. ed. Danny Meyer. Read by Danny Meyer. (Running Time: 21600 sec.). 2007. audio compact disk 14.95 (978-0-06-137415-9(6), Harper Audio) HarperCollins Pubs.

Setting up a Small Business. Interview. Contrib. by Audiotopics. 2 CDs. (Running Time: 9000 sec.). (AudioTopics Ser.). 2006. audio compact disk 14.95 (978-0-9647401-6-7(8)) Western Media.
AUDIOTOPICS is a series of radio talk-show style audio CD programs on current practical topics of interest to a wide audience. The guest experts offer consultation in subject areas that affect all of us: finance, business, home, family, health, safety, etc. The target audience is the commuter who spends hours a week in the car. And anyone who likes listening to information.

Setting Your Church Free. Neil T. Anderson & Charles Mylander. Read by Neil T. Anderson & Charles Mylander. Ed. by Wycliff Media Staff & Summer Institute of Linguistics Staff. 8 cass. (Running Time: 8 hrs.). 1994. pap. bk. 34.99 (978-1-884284-32-8(9)); 34.99 set. (978-1-884284-29-8(9)) Freedom in Christ.
Eight one hour messages on releasing the power of God through your Church by dealing directly with corporate sins. This is for pastors, elders, & concerned laymen.

Setting Youth Free. Read by Dave Parks. Perf. by James Long. Contrib. by Frank Allnutt. 1 cass. (Running Time: 1 hr. 42 min.). (ICEL Three Ser.). 1996. cass. & video 6.00 (978-1-57838-060-2(X)) CrossLife Express.
Christian living.

Settle down Sounds. Scripts. Voice by Georgette Baker. 1CD. (Running Time: 30 mins).Tr. of Sonidos Serenos. (J). 2005. audio compact disk 9.95 (978-1-892306-08-1(5)) Cantemos-bilingual.
10 three minute relaxation exercises to help children settle down after lunch, recess, before test taking or any time. One for each day of the school week, two weeks total.

Settlements & Annuities. 1 cass. 15.00 (AL-87) PA Bar Inst.

Seven: The Number for Happiness, Love, & Success. unabr. ed. Jacqueline Leo. (Running Time: 8 hrs.). 2009. audio compact disk 29.95 (978-1-4417-1197-7(X)) Blckstn Audio.

Seven: The Number for Happiness, Love, & Success. unabr. ed. Jacqueline Leo. Read by Pam Ward. (Running Time: 8 hrs. 0 mins.). 2009. 29.95 (978-1-4417-1198-4(8)); 54.95 (978-1-4417-1194-6(5)); audio compact disk 76.00 (978-1-4417-1195-3(3)) Blckstn Audio.

Seven Ages: An Anthology of Poetry with Music. Read by Ian McKellen. 2 cass. (Running Time: 2 hrs. 33 mins.). 2000. 13.98 (978-962-634-689-1(2), NA218914); audio compact disk 17.98 (978-962-634-189-6(0), NA218912) Naxos.
This exceptional anthology, based on Lord David Owen's book, Seven-Ages-Poetry for a Lifetime, features many of Britain's leading actors, reading over 100 poems.

***Seven Ages of Man: The Ego in Action.** Kenneth Wapnick. 2010. 20.00 (978-1-59142-493-2(3)); audio compact disk 25.00 (978-1-59142-492-5(5)) Foun Miracles.

Seven Bible Truths Violated by Christian Dating. As told by S. M. Davis. 1 CD. (Running Time: 1 hr. 14 mins.). 2003. audio compact disk 10.00 (978-1-929241-92-7(5)) Vsn Forum.

Seven Blind Mice. Ed Young. Read by B. D. Wong. (Running Time: 8 hrs.). 2007. 8.95 (978-0-439-02779-3(9)); audio compact disk 12.95 (978-0-439-02778-6(0)) Scholastic Inc.

Seven Blind Mice. Ed Young. Illus. by Ed Young. Read by B. D. Wong. (Running Time: 8 hrs.). 2007. pap. bk. 18.95 (978-0-439-02785-4(3)) Scholastic Inc.

Seven Blind Mice. Ed Young. Illus. by Ed Young. Read by B. D. Wong. (Running Time: 8 hrs.). 2007. pap. bk. 14.95 (978-0-439-02784-7(5)) Scholastic Inc.

Seven Blind Mice. Ed Young. Illus. by Ed Young. Read by B. D. Wong. 1 cass. (Running Time: 7 mins.). (J). (gr. k-3). 2007. bk. 24.95 (978-0-439-02782-3(9)) Scholastic Inc.

Seven by Gershwin (Contemporary Settings of Seven Classic Songs by George Gershwin & Ira Gershwin for Solo Voice & Piano) Medium High Voice. Composed by George Gershwin & Ira Gershwin. (ENG.). 2007. audio compact disk 13.95 (978-0-7390-4710-1(8)) Alfred Pub.

Seven by Gershwin (Contemporary Settings of Seven Classic Songs by George Gershwin & Ira Gershwin for Solo Voice & Piano) Medium Low Voice. Composed by George Gershwin & Ira Gershwin. (ENG.). 2007. audio compact disk 13.95 (978-0-7390-4711-8(6)) Alfred Pub.

Seven by Mercer: Contemporary Settings of Seven Classic Songs by Johnny Mercer (High Voice) Alfred Publishing Staff. (ENG.). 2009. audio compact disk 13.95 (978-0-7390-6139-8(9)) Alfred Pub.

Seven by Mercer: Contemporary Settings of Seven Classic Songs by Johnny Mercer (Low Voice) Alfred Publishing Staff. (ENG.). 2009. audio compact disk 13.95 (978-0-7390-6142-8(9)) Alfred Pub.

Seven by Porter: Contemporary Settings of Seven Classic Songs by Cole Porter. Contrib. by Mark Hayes. (ENG.). 2008. audio compact disk 13.95 (978-0-7390-5262-4(4)) Alfred Pub.

Seven by Porter: Contemporary Settings of Seven Classic Songs by Cole Porter (Medium Low Voice) Composed by Cole Porter & Mark Hayes. (ENG.). 2008. audio compact disk 13.95 (978-0-7390-5265-5(9)) Alfred Pub.

Seven Candles for Kwanzaa. 2004. pap. bk. 18.95 (978-1-55592-746-2(7)); pap. bk. 38.75 (978-1-55592-753-0(X)); pap. bk. 32.75 (978-1-55592-307-5(0)); pap. bk. 14.95 (978-1-55592-046-3(2)); audio compact disk 12.95 (978-1-55592-733-2(5)) Weston Woods.

Seven Candles for Kwanzaa. Andrea Davis Pinkney. Illus. by Brian Pinkney. Narrated by Alfre Woodard. 1 cass., 5 bks. (Running Time: 9 min.). (J). pap. bk. 32.75 Weston Woods.
African-American holiday commemorates the strength of family ties, respect for ancestors, commitment to growth of community & gratitude of life's bounties.

Seven Candles for Kwanzaa. Andrea Davis Pinkney. Illus. by Brian Pinkney. Narrated by Alfre Woodard. 1 cass. (Running Time: 9 min.). (J). (ps-4). pap. bk. 12.95 Weston Woods.

Seven Candles for Kwanzaa. Created by Andrea Davis Pinkney. Contrib. by Brian Pinkney. Music by Crystal Taliefero. Narrated by Alfre Woodard. 1 cass. (Running Time: 9 mins.). (Story Hour Collection). (J). (ps-4). 1998. pap. bk. 24.95 (JHRA371) Weston Woods.
African-American holiday commemorating the strength of family ties, respect for ancestors, commitment to the growth of community, & gratitude for life's bounties. For each day of Kwanzaa, a new candle is lit & children & adults share their thoughts, songs, stories from the past, dreams about the future, & a delicious feast on the last day.

Seven Candles for Kwanzaa. unabr. ed. Andrea Davis Pinkney. Music by Crystal Taliefero. Narrated by Alfre Woodard. 1 cass. (Running Time: 9 mins.). (J). (ps-4). 1997. 8.95 (978-1-56008-819-6(2), RAC371) Weston Woods.
African-American holiday commemorates the strength of family ties, respect for ancestors, commitment to growth of community & gratitude of life's bounties.

Seven Candles for Kwanzaa. unabr. ed. Andrea Davis Pinkney. Music by Crystal Taliefero. Narrated by Alfre Woodard. 1 cass. (Running Time: 9 mins.). (J). (ps-4). 1997. bk. 24.95 (978-0-7882-0671-9(0), HRA371) Weston Woods.

Seven Cats & the Art of Living. abr. ed. Jo Coudert. Read by Sandra Burr. (Running Time: 3 hrs.). 2008. 39.25 (978-1-4233-5270-9(X), 9781423352709, BADLE); 24.95 (978-1-4233-5269-3(6), 9781423352693, BAD); audio compact disk 39.25 (978-1-4233-5268-6(8), 9781423352686, Brlnc Audio MP3 Lib); audio compact disk 24.95 (978-1-4233-5267-9(X), 9781423352679, Brilliance MP3) Brilliance Audio.

Seven Characteristics of Higher Consciousness. Guy Finley. 3 cass. (Running Time: 2 hrs. 30 mins.). 1998. 24.95 (978-1-929320-05-9(1)) Life of Learn.
Reveals how to realize a whole new you beyond self defeating thoughts & feelings.

Seven Choices: Taking the Steps to New Life after Losing Someone You Love. abr. ed. Elizabeth H. Neeld. Read by Elizabeth H. Neeld. 2 cass. 1998. 18.95 Set. (978-0-937897-50-8(7)) Centerpoint Pr.

Seven Classic Plays. (Running Time: 13 hrs.). (C). 2002. 35.95 (978-1-59912-589-3(7)) Iofy Corp.

Seven Classic Plays, Vol. 1. unabr. ed. Perf. by F. Murray Abraham et al. Prod. by Yuri Rosavsky. 7 cass. (Running Time: 10 hrs.). 2002. 49.95 (978-0-7861-2291-2(9), 3016); audio compact disk 80.00 (978-0-7861-9394-3(8), 3016) Blckstn Audio.
Illustrates the development of European drama from ancient times to the threshold of the modern theater. Includes Euripides - Medea, Shakespeare - The Tempest, Moliere - The Imaginary Invalid, Dumas - Camille, Ibsen - An Enemy of the People, Shaw - Arms and the Man, and Chekhov - Uncle Vanya.

Seven Classic Plays, Vol. 1. unabr. ed. Prod. by Yuri Rosavsky. 2002. audio compact disk 19.95 (978-0-7861-9150-5(3), PZM3016) Brilliance Audio.

Seven Classic Plays: Medea; the Tempest; the Imaginary Invalid; Camille; an Enemy of the People; Arms & the Man; Uncle Vanya. unabr. ed. Euripides et al. Read by Full Cast Production Staff. (YA). 2008. 64.99 (978-1-60514-751-2(6)) Find a World.

Seven Council Fires of Sweet Medicine. David Seals. Read by David Seals. Ed. by Motseyoef & Wakanoiayas. 16 cass. (Running Time: 24 hrs.). (National Epic of Native America Ser.). (C). 1996. 129.00 (978-1-887786-34-8(1)) Sky & Sage Bks.
An integrated learning series. The most popular linguistic & mythic drama among Canadian & American Natives themselves. With extensive scholarly introductions in anthropology & mythology, it follows the spiritual life & death of the historical Cheyenne culture hero Sweet Medicine, told in modern allegorical idiom. From the acclaimed 1979 novel "The Powwow Highway" through the controversial 1995 screenplay on the spiritual life of "Crazy Horse," this is appropriate for high school & college Indian Studies & Literature instruction.

Seven Daughters of Eve. unabr. ed. Bryan Sykes. Narrated by Bryan Sykes. 7 cass. (Running Time: 10 hrs.). 2002. 64.00 (978-1-84197-422-4(6)) Recorded Bks.
An account of scientific inquiries into the origins of humans.

Seven Days in May. Kristin Sergel. Perf. by Edward Asner & Fred Thompson. Based on a book by Charles Bailey, II & Fletcher Knebel. 2 CDs. (Running Time: 2 hrs. 1 min.). 2002. audio compact disk 25.95 (978-1-58081-243-6(0), CDWTA14) Pub: L A Theatre. Dist(s): NetLibrary CO
During the height of the Cold War, an American President negotiates a highly unpopular disarmament treaty with the Soviet Union. Is a Presidential coup possible? A cautionary tale for anyone who assumes that American democracy is immune to palace revolution.

Seven Days in May. Kristin Sergel. Perf. by Edward Asner et al. Based on a book by Charles Bailey, II et al. 2 cass. (Running Time: 2 hrs. 1 min.). 2002. 22.95 (978-1-58081-236-8(8), WTA14) L A Theatre.

Seven Days in May. unabr. ed. Fletcher Knebel & Charles W. Bailey, II. Read by Wolfram Kandinsky. 8 cass. (Running Time: 12 hrs.). 1978. 64.00 (978-0-7366-0161-0(9), 1163) Books on Tape.
Cast in Washington & centered around the Pentagon, the action begins on a quiet Sunday morning as Colonel Martin J. "Jiggs" Casey, Director of Research for the Joint Chiefs of Staff, assumes his once-monthly stint as officer of the day. The President's popularity is at an all-time low, due principally to his engineering a controversial disarmament treaty with Russia. By Tuesday, Colonel Casey accidently uncovers a fantastic plot to overthrow the President.

Seven Days in May. unabr. ed. Kristen Sergel et al. Read by Edward Asner. (YA). 2008. 34.99 (978-1-60514-986-8(1)) Find a World.

Seven Days to a Killing. unabr. ed. Clive Egleton. Narrated by Simon Prebble. 5 cass. (Running Time: 7 hrs.). 44.00 (978-0-7887-0362-1(5), 94554E7) Recorded Bks.
Major John Tarrant works for British Military Intelligence, handling information filtered in from Russia & the Warsaw Pact countries. His life is peaceful until a Russian agent known as Drabble kidnaps his son & demands a ransom of 500,000 pounds in uncut diamonds. Tarrant has seven days to come up with the ransom & less time to realize that his greatest enemy is not Drabble; it is a traitor of the highest rank in the British military. Available to libraries only.

Seven Days to Petrograd. unabr. ed. Tom Hyman. Narrated by Sam Gray. 11 cass. (Running Time: 15 hrs. 45 mins.). 1992. 91.00 (978-1-55690-691-6(9), 92347E7) Recorded Bks.
A "sealed" train has left for Petrograd carrying a dangerous passenger: Vladimir Lenin. Only a rogue American ex-ballplayer named Henry Bauer can stop the "internationalist" from changing the course of war.

Seven Deadly Sins. Read by Douglas Wilson. 2000. 17.00 (978-1-59128-350-8(7)); 21.00 (978-1-59128-352-2(3)) Canon Pr ID.

Seven Deadly Wonders. Matthew Reilly. Read by William Dufris. (Jack West Junior Ser.: No. 1). 2006. audio compact disk 29.95 (978-0-7927-3958-6(2), CMP 892) AudioGO.

Seven Deadly Wonders. Matthew Reilly. Read by William Dufris. 7 cass. (Running Time: 46500 sec.). (Jack West Junior Ser.: No. 1). 2006. 59.95 (978-0-7927-3874-9(8), CSL 892); audio compact disk 94.95 (978-0-7927-3875-6(6), SLD 892) AudioGO.

Seven Decisions: With Andy Andrews. As told by Andy Andrews. 2005. audio compact disk 19.99 (978-0-9776246-2-1(5)) Lightning Crown Pub.

***Seven Desires of Every Heart.** Mark Laaser & Debra Laaser. (Running Time: 5 hrs. 53 mins. 0 sec.). (ENG.). 2008. 19.99 (978-0-310-30271-1(4)) Zondervan.

Seven Dials. unabr. ed. Anne Perry. Read by Michael Page. 8 cass. (Running Time: 11 hrs.). (Thomas Pitt Ser.). 2003. 34.95 (978-1-59086-497-5(2), 1590864972); 87.25 (978-1-59086-498-2(0), 1590864980); audio compact disk 40.95 (978-1-59086-500-2(6), 1590865006, CD); audio compact disk 102.25 (978-1-59086-501-9(4), 1590865014) Brilliance Audio.
In the first gray of a mid-September morning, Thomas Pitt, mainstay of Her Majesty's Special Branch, is summoned to Connaught Square mansion where the body of a junior diplomat lies huddled in a wheelbarrow. Nearby stands the tenant of the house, the beautiful and notorious Egyptian woman Ayesha Zakhari, who falls under the shadow of suspicion. Pitt's orders, emanating from Prime Minister Gladstone himself, are to protect-at all costs-the good name of the third person in the garden: senior cabinet minister Saville Ryerson. This distinguished public servant, whispered to be Ayesha's lover, insists that she is as innocent as he is himself. Could it be true? In the dead man's less-than-stellar reputation, Pitt finds hope. But in ancient Alexandria, where the victim was once an army officer, hope grows dim. For there, Pitt receives intimations of deadly entanglements stretching from Egyptian cotton fields to Manchester cotton mills, from the noxious London slum known as Seven Dials to the madhouse called Bedlam. Meanwhile, in a packed courtroom at the Old Bailey, time is ticking away for Ayesha and Saville. With Pitt and his clients racing against the hangman, the trial reaches its pulse-pumping climax.

Seven Dials. unabr. ed. Anne Perry. Read by Michael Page. (Running Time: 11 hrs.). (Thomas Pitt Ser.). 2004. 39.25 (978-1-59335-600-2(5), 1593356005, Brlnc Audio MP3 Lib) Brilliance Audio.

Seven Dials. unabr. ed. Anne Perry. Read by Michael Page. (Running Time: 11 hrs.). (Thomas & Charlotte Pitt Ser.). 2004. 39.25 (978-1-59710-686-3(0), 1597106860, BADLE); 24.95 (978-1-59710-687-0(9), 1597106879, BAD) Brilliance Audio.

Seven Dials. unabr. ed. Anne Perry. Read by Michael Page. (Running Time: 11 hrs.). (Thomas Pitt Ser.). 2004. 24.95 (978-1-59335-152-6(6), 1593351526) Soulmate Audio Bks.

Seven Dials Mystery. unabr. ed. Agatha Christie. Read by Emilia Fox. 5 cass. (Running Time: 7 hrs. 30 min.). 2005. 27.95 (978-1-57270-450-3(0)) Pub: Audio Partners. Dist(s): PerseuPGW

Seven Dials Mystery. unabr. ed. Agatha Christie. Read by Emilia Fox. 7 Cds. (Running Time: 7 Hrs. 50 Mins). (Mystery Masters Ser.). (ENG.). 2005. audio compact disk 31.95 (978-1-57270-451-0(9)) Pub: AudioGO. Dist(s): Perseus Dist
At the home of Lord Caterham and his daughter, Lady Eileen Brent (aka Bundle), Sir Oswald and Lady Maria Coote throw a party for some weekend guests. But the young guests play a practical joke on someone who turns up murdered the following morning. It's up to Bundle and her friends to solve the case, which only gets worse with the appearance of a second corpse. The trail of bodies leads to the mysterious Seven Dials Club. Actress Emilia Fox's exciting reading brings Christie's vivid mystery, first published in 1929, to scintillating life. Read by Emilia Fox.

Seven Dimensions of Creation. George King. 2007. audio compact disk (978-0-937249-35-2(1)) Aetherius Soc.

Seven Dimensions of Spirituality. 1 cass. (Care Cassettes Ser.: Vol. 11, No. 7). 1984. 10.80 Assn Prof Chaplains.

Seven Directions Movement Meditation CD: Understanding the Cycles of Truth. Narrated by White Feather Curtiss. 1 CD. (Running Time: 46 mins.). 2000. audio compact disk 14.95 (978-0-9792830-2-4(7)) White Pine NY.

***Seven Dirty Words: The Life & Crimes of George Carlin.** unabr. ed. James Sullivan. (Running Time: 12 hrs. 0 mins.). 2010. 17.99 (978-1-4001-8469-9(X)) Tantor Media.

***Seven Dirty Words: The Life & Crimes of George Carlin.** unabr. ed. James Sullivan. Narrated by Alan Sklar. (Running Time: 10 hrs. 30 mins. 0 sec.). 2010. 19.99 (978-1-4001-6469-1(9)); audio compact disk 59.99 (978-1-4001-4469-3(8)); audio compact disk 29.99 (978-1-4001-1469-6(1)) Pub: Tantor Media. Dist(s): IngramPubServ

Seven Dudley Sins. Greg Nelson. Prod. by Greg Nelson. 4 CDs. (Running Time: 3 hrs. 30 mins.). 2005. audio compact disk 29.95 (978-0-660-19222-2(5)) Pub: Canadian Broadcasting CAN. Dist(s): Georgetown Term

Seven Dumbest Relationship Mistakes Smart People Make. unabr. ed. Carolyn N. Bushong. Read by Carolyn N. Bushong. 4 cass. (Running Time: 6 hrs.). 1997. 24.95 Set. (978-1-57511-028-8(8)) Pub Mills.
Bushong applies her twenty years of experience as a relationship counselor & extensive media experience to detailing & solving the seven most common relationship mistakes everyone makes & gives practical advice on how to repair damage or avoid it altogether.

***Seven Events That Made America America: And Proved That the Founding Fathers Were Right All Along.** unabr. ed. Larry Schweikart. (Running Time: 10 hrs. 30 mins.). 2010. 34.99 (978-1-4001-9725-5(2)); 16.99 (978-1-4001-8725-6(7)) Tantor Media.

***Seven Events That Made America America: And Proved That the Founding Fathers Were Right All Along.** unabr. ed. Larry Schweikart. Narrated by Peter Berkrot. 1 MP3-CD. (Running Time: 10 hrs. 0 mins. 0 sec.). 2010. 24.99 (978-1-4001-6725-8(6)); audio compact disk 83.99 (978-1-4001-4725-0(5)); audio compact disk 34.99 (978-1-4001-1725-3(9)) Pub: Tantor Media. Dist(s): IngramPubServ

Seven Facets of the Anointing. Creflo A. Dollar. 45.00 (978-1-59089-002-8(7)) Pub: Creflo Dollar. Dist(s): STL Dist NA

Seven Factors of Enlightenment. Scott Morrison. 1 cass. (Running Time: 1 hr.). 1999. 7.50 (978-1-882496-51-8(5)) Twnty Frst Cntry Ren.
The nuts-&-bolts "how to" of spiritual awakening & self-realization.

***Seven Faith Tribes: Who They Are, What They Believe, & Why They Matter.** unabr. ed. George Barna. (ENG.). 2009. 14.98 (978-1-59644-734-9(6), christianSeed) christianaud.

Seven Faith Tribes: Who They Are, What They Believe, & Why They Matter. unabr. ed. George Barna. Read by George Barna. (Running Time: 7 hrs. 30 mins. 0 sec.). (ENG.). 2009. audio compact disk 24.98 (978-1-59644-733-2(8), Hovel Audio) christianaud.

Seven for a Secret. Judy Astley. (Isis (CDs) Ser.). (J). 2005. audio compact disk 84.95 (978-0-7531-2400-0(9)) Pub: ISIS Lrg Prnt GBR. Dist(s): Ulverscroft US

Seven for a Secret. unabr. ed. Judy Astley. Read by Patricia Gallimore. 8 cass. (Running Time: 12 hrs.). 2001. 69.95 (978-0-7531-0843-7(7), 001211) Pub: ISIS Audio GBR. Dist(s): ISIS Pub
It is Heather's silver wedding anniversary. But this milestone does not mark her marriage to Tom, her often-absent airline pilot husband & father of their children. It is for her first marriage - a wildly romantic secret affair: when she was sixteen, she & Iain - twelve years older than her & the heir to a Scottish baronetcy - eloped after school speech day. The marriage had not lasted, but secrets have a habit of coming out & Heather is horrified to find her ex-husband amongst a visiting film crew. Many secrets are revealed & the peaceful Oxfordshire village community buzzes with scandal.

Seven for a Secret. unabr. ed. Mary Reed & Eric Mayer. Read by James Adams. (Running Time: 32400 sec.). (John the Eunuch Mystery Ser.). 2008. 65.95 (978-1-4332-1163-8(7)); audio compact disk 29.95 (978-1-4332-1165-2(3)); audio compact disk & audio compact disk 90.00 (978-1-4332-1164-5(5)) Blckstn Audio.

Seven for a Secret. unabr. collector's ed. Victoria Holt. Read by Donada Peters. 8 cass. (Running Time: 12 hrs.). 1993. 64.00 (978-0-7366-2442-8(2), 3195) Books on Tape.
Young women's world crumbles under weight of hidden truths, but love & fidelity triumph at last.

Seven Gothic Tales. unabr. collector's ed. Isak Dinesen. Read by Donada Peters. 11 cass. (Running Time: 16 hrs. 30 mins.). 1989. 88.00 (978-0-7366-1603-4(9), 2464) Books on Tape.
Features a collection of seven short stories. Includes "The Deluge at Norderney," "The Old Chevalier," "The Monkey" & "The Roads Round Pisa." Rounding out the collection are "The Supper at Elsinore," "The Dreamers" & "The Poet".

Seven Habits of Highly Effective People see 7 Habitudes des Gens Efficaces

Seven Habits of Highly Effective People see Siete Habitos de las Personas Altamente Eficaces

Seven Habits of Highly Effective People see 7 Habitos de la Gente Altamente Efectiva

Seven Hidden Secrets of Motivation: Unlocking the Genius Within. unabr. ed. Todd Beeler. Read by Todd Beeler. 6 CDs. (Running Time: 6 hrs.). (ENG.). 2006. audio compact disk 19.98 (978-1-59659-030-4(0)) Pub: Gildan Media. Dist(s): HachBkGrp

Seven Hundred Fifty Plus Sure Fire Interview Questions see Matchmaker

Seven Hundred Forty Eight Lifetime Secrets of Positive Paul. Paul Stanyard. 1 cass. 12.50 Alpha Tape.

Seven Keys of Great Teaching. Created by Oliver DeMille. (YA). 2008. audio compact disk 15.00 (978-0-9840990-0-9(X)) Institute for Ex.

Seven Keys to a Happy Marriage see Siete Claves para Tener un Matrimonio Feliz

Seven Keys to Anointing. 2 cass. 1993. 12.00 (978-1-881256-09-0(X)) Wrld Outreach Church.

Seven Keys to Baldpate. abr. ed. Earl Derr Biggers. Narrated by Marvin Miller. 2 cass. (Running Time: 3 hrs. 4 min.). 12.95 (978-0-89926-157-7(4), 845) Audio Bk.

Seven Keys to Baldpate. unabr. ed. Earl Derr Biggers. Read by Jim Killavey. 6 cass. (Running Time: 9 hrs.). (J). (gr. 6-12). 1993. vinyl bd. 29.00 Jimcin Record.
A summer resort in the dead of winter ought to be secluded & quiet, but Baldpate is the scene for mystery, romance & murder.

Seven Keys to Changing: Your Life, Health & Wealth. abr. ed. Linda L. McNeil. Read by Linda L. McNeil. 1 cass. 1998. 14.95 (978-1-891446-09-2(6)) Open Mind.
Linda McNeil has lost 1/3 of her body weight & kept it off for 18 years; gone from poor health & the brink of bankruptcy to health & wealth. Learn the 7 keys to transform your own life through changing your thinking.

Seven Keys to Prosperity & Fullfillment - How to Get What You Want. Robert E. Griswold. Read by Robert E. Griswold. 1 cass. (Super Strength Ser.). 1995. 10.95 (978-1-55848-318-7(7)) EffectiveMN.
Two complete non-subliminal programs to help easily eliminate the roadblocks to prosperity & gain many other valuable benefits.

Seven Keys to Victory. Steve Hill. 2007. audio compact disk 10.00 (978-1-892853-79-0(5)) Togthr Hrvest.

Seven Kinds of Death. unabr. ed. Kate Wilhelm. (Running Time: 7 hrs. NaN mins.). 2008. 29.95 (978-1-4332-3065-3(8)); 54.95 (978-1-4332-3061-5(5)); audio compact disk 60.00 (978-1-4332-3062-2(3)) Blckstn Audio.

Seven Last Words: Lenten Reflections for Today's Believers. abr. ed. Alice Camille. Perf. by Alice Camille. Score by Sheldon Cohen. 1 cass. (Running Time: 1 hr. 19 mins.). 1998. 9.95 (978-0-87946-192-8(6), 341) ACTA Pubns.
Meditations on the last words of Christ from the cross.

Seven Last Words from the Cross. Benedict J. Groeschel. 1 cass. (Running Time: 1 hr. 29 min.). 1991. 7.95 (TAH241) Alba Hse Comns.
A powerful Good Friday meditation takes its starting point from Christ's Seven Last Words & goes on to provide a searching examination of the hard aspects of the Christian life.

Seven Last Words of Jesus. Jack Deere. 1 cass. (Running Time: 1 hr. 30 mins.). (Cross Ser.: Vol. 1). 2000. 5.00 (JD01-001) Morning NC.
These are outstanding messages on the work & power of the most important truths of our faith.

Seven Laws of the Learner Audio Album. Instructed by Bruce Wilkinson. 1991. 29.95 (978-1-885447-27-2(2)) Walk Thru the Bible.
Helps teachers uncover student's real learning needs. Reveals how to motivate low achievers and problem students.Helps teachers create the best environment for learning. Guides instructors in cooperating with the Holy Spirit.

Seven Laws of the Teacher Audio Album. Instructed by Howard Hendricks. 1994. 29.95 (978-1-885447-36-4(1)) Walk Thru the Bible.
Taught by Dr. Howard Hendricks.Full of vivid graphics and realistic classroom dramas.Helps teachers stay motivated in the face of great challenges.Unlocks the principles of teaching found in the Bible.Helps teachers prevent burnout and stay excited about their work.

Seven Lessons for Leading in Crisis. unabr. ed. Bill George. (Running Time: 3 hrs.). (ENG.). 2009. 19.98 (978-1-59659-466-1(7), GildAudio) Pub: Gildan Media. Dist(s): HachBkGrp

Seven Lessons for Leading in Crisis. unabr. ed. Bill George. (Running Time: 3 hrs.). (ENG.). 2010. audio compact disk 19.98 (978-1-59659-447-0(0), GildAudio) Pub: Gildan Media. Dist(s): HachBkGrp

Seven Levels of Intimacy: The Art of Loving & the Joy of Being Loved. abr. ed. Matthew Kelly. Read by Matthew Kelly. 2005. 17.95 (978-0-7435-5222-6(9)); audio compact disk 29.95 (978-0-7435-5190-8(7), Sound Ideas) Pub: S&S Audio. Dist(s): S and S Inc

Seven Little Australians. unabr. ed. Ethel Turner. Ed. by Candyce Kanuchok. Illus. by Hatem Aly. Narrated by Drew de Carvalho. Prod. by Antland Productions Staff. Executive Producer Hannah Kanuchok. (ENG.). 2009. 75.00 (978-0-9819988-0-0(1)) Kalliope.

Seven Lost Secrets of Success: Million Dollar Ideas of Bruce Barton, America's Forgotten Genius. unabr. ed. Joe Vitale, Jr. (Running Time: 3 hrs. 30 mins.). (ENG.). 2007. 14.98 (978-1-59659-175-2(7), GildAudio) Pub: Gildan Media. Dist(s): HachBkGrp

Seven Magic Steps to Speed Sight Reading. Duane Shinn. 1 cass. (Running Time: 1 hr. 30 mins.). bk. 39.95 (MR-2) Duane Shinn.
Reveals secrets of sight-reading music instantly such as: how to increase your eye span; how to look at an entire measure & identify it as only one chord; how to instantly recognize inversions, intervals, & arpeggios; & much more.

Seven Marriages of Your Marriage: How Couples Can Make Love Last by Understanding & Managing the Many Marriages & Divorces in Every Committed Relationship. unabr. collector's ed. Mel Krantzler & Patricia B. Krantzler. Read by Mary Peiffer. 8 cass. (Running Time: 8 hrs.). 1995. 48.00 (978-0-7366-2997-3(1), 3686) Books on Tape.
Veteran marriage counselors say a marriage is actually seven "mini marriages" that reflect a couple's changing needs. Empowerment to make love last.

Seven Mistakes Artists Make - & How You Can Avoid Them All. Kathy Gulrich. Prod. by Nicole Kang. 1 CD. (Running Time: 30 mins.). 2005. audio compact disk 17.00 (978-0-9746533-1-0(4)) Center City.
This is a unique instructional CD created specifically for artists just beginning their professional art careers. New York artist and art coach Kathy Gulrich gives artists practical suggestions and action steps that will enable them to turn the most common artist mistakes into a personal checklist for success. Gulrich is the author of '187 Tips for Artists: How to Create a Successful Art Career - and Have Fun in the Process!' and is a frequent contributor to leading artist magazines.

Seven Mysteries of Enlightenment. unabr. ed. Stan Kendz. Read by Stan Kendz. 1 cass. (Running Time: 60 min.). 1995. 10.00 (978-1-57582-011-8(0)) HAPPE Progs.
Discussion of the 7 stages of enlightenment.

Seven Nazis & a Hunter. Dana Holiday. 1 cass. 8.95 (163) Am Fed Astrologers.
Charts of seven Nazi leaders and Simon Wiesenthal.

Seven of Hearts see Extraordinary Adventures of Arsene Lupin

Seven (or Mabye Ten) Habits of Pretty Good Writers: A Writer's Primer. Featuring Ken Rand. 2005. (978-1-933846-02-6(X)) Med Man.

Seven Paths to Understanding: A Practical Guide to Symbolic Exploration. Caroline Myss. (Seven Paths to Understanding). 2000. 55.00 (978-1-893869-61-5(X)) Celbrtng Life.

Seven-Per-Cent Solution. unabr. collector's ed. Nicholas Meyer. Read by David Case. 7 cass. (Running Time: 7 hrs.). 1994. 42.00 (978-0-7366-2794-8(4), 3509) Books on Tape.
The unique collaboration of Sherlock Holmes & the equally great detective of the human psyche, Sigmund Freud.

Seven Pictures of God's People. Derek Prince. 4 cass. (Running Time: 4 hrs.). 19.95 (I-SP1); 11.90 Set. (051-052) Derek Prince.
God's Word, our mirror, reveals all that He intends us to become as His redeemed people.

Seven Pillars of Health: The Natural Way to Better Health for Life. unabr. ed. Don Colbert. Narrated by Jon Gauger. (ENG.). 2008. 27.99 (978-1-60814-376-4(7)); audio compact disk 39.99 (978-1-59859-353-2(6)) Oasis Audio.

Seven Pillars of Wisdom. T. E. Lawrence. Read by Jim Norton. 3 cass. (Running Time: 3 hrs. 51 mins.). 1994. 17.98 (978-962-634-510-8(1), NA301014, Naxos AudioBooks) Naxos.
Lawrence of Arabia's role in leading the Arab Revolt against the Turks during the first World War. A reluctant leader, wracked by guilt at the duplicity of the British, he threw himself into this role, suffering the blistering desert conditions and masterminding triumphant military campaigns.

Seven Pillars of Wisdom. abr. ed. T. E. Lawrence. Read by James Wilby. Abr. by Gordon House. 6 CDs. (Running Time: 7 hrs. 0 mins. 0 sec.). (ENG.). 2009. audio compact disk 31.95 (978-1-934997-20-8(X)) Pub: CSAWord. Dist(s): PerseuPGW

Seven Pillars of Wisdom. abr. ed. T. E. Lawrence. Read by Jim Norton. 3 CDs. (Running Time: 3 hrs. 45 mins.). 1994. audio compact disk 22.98 (978-962-634-010-3(X), NA301012, Naxos AudioBooks) Naxos.

Seven Pillars of Wisdom. abr. ed. T. E. Lawrence. Read by James Wilby. (Playaway Adult Nonfiction Ser.). 2008. 64.99 (978-1-60640-929-9(8)) Find a World.

Seven Pillars of Wisdom, Pt. 1. unabr. ed. T. E. Lawrence. Read by Rupert Keenlyside. 19 cass. (Running Time: 13 hrs. 30 min.). 1984. 72.00 (978-0-7366-0641-7(6), 1600-A) Books on Tape.
This is Lawrence's vivid & stirring account of the Arabian campaigns. Scouting, battles, military strategy & politics are interspread with unforgettable descriptions of the country, self-criticism & philosophy.

Seven Pillars of Wisdom, Pt. 2. T. E. Lawrence. Read by Rupert Keenlyside. 10 cass. (Running Time: 15 hrs.). 80.00 (1600-B) Books on Tape.

Seven Plays from American Literature. rev. ed. Adapted by George P. McCallum. (J). (gr. 9-12). 1977. 39.50 (978-0-87789-126-0(5), 1205) ELS Educ Servs.

Seven Powerful Scriptures for Solving Life's Problems. Rand H. Packer. 1 cass. 1998. 9.95 (978-1-57008-426-3(2), Bkcraft Inc) Deseret Bk.

Seven Powers: Building Bridges to Your Higher Possibilities. Guy Finley. (ENG.). 2007. 24.95 (978-1-929320-37-0(X)); audio compact disk 34.95 (978-1-929320-33-2(7)) Life of Learn.

Seven Principles for Teaching Christian Morality. Richard C. Sparks. 1 cass. (Running Time: 1 hr.). 2001. 8.95 (A6701) St Anthony Mess Pr.
By reflecting on guilt-ridden confessions by basically good people and noting the eloquence of Joseph Cardinal Bernardin's life and witness, Sparks offers principles for teaching Catholic Christian morality.

Seven Problems That Are Plaguing the World. Manly P. Hall. 8.95 (978-0-89314-257-5(3), C871206) Philos Res.
Deals with psychology & self-help.

Seven Rays. unabr. ed. Jessica Bendinger. Read by Angela Dawe. (Running Time: 8 hrs.). 2009. 24.99 (978-1-4418-2683-1(1), 9781441826831, BAD); 39.97 (978-1-4418-2682-4(3), 9781441826824, Brlnc Audio MP3 Lib); 39.97 (978-1-4418-2684-8(X), 9781441826848, BADLE); 24.99 (978-1-4418-2681-7(5), 9781441826817, Brilliance MP3); audio compact disk 69.97 (978-1-4418-2680-0(7), 9781441826800, BriAudCD Unabrid); audio compact disk 29.99 (978-1-4418-2679-4(3), 9781441826794) Brilliance Audio.

Seven Rays Workshop, No. 1. Mae R. Wilson-Ludlam. 1 cass. 8.95 (445) Am Fed Astrologers.

Seven Rays Workshop, No. 2. Mae R. Wilson-Ludlam. 1 cass. 8.95 (446) Am Fed Astrologers.

Seven Rays Workshop, No. 3. Mae R. Wilson-Ludlam. 1 cass. 8.95 (447) Am Fed Astrologers.

Seven Rays Workshop, No. 4. Mae R. Wilson-Ludlam. 1 cass. 8.95 (448) Am Fed Astrologers.

Seven Responsibilities of the New Age. Kryon. Read by Lee Carroll. 1 cass. (Running Time: 53 min.). 1996. 10.00 (978-1-888053-02-9(X)) Kryon Writings.
Recording of live event. Channeling of spiritual information.

Seven Rewards of a Renewed Soul. As told by Frank Damazio. 8 Cass. 1998. 40.00 (978-1-886849-53-2(6)) CityChristian.

Seven Sacred Truths. Denis Waitley. Read by Denis Waitley. (Running Time: 6 hrs.). (C). 2005. 36.95 (978-1-59912-155-0(7)) Iofy Corp.

Seven Sacred Truths: A Lifetime of Wisdom While You're Young Enough to Enjoy It! unabr. ed. Denis Waitley. Read by Denis Waitley. 6 CDs. (Running Time: 6 hrs.). (ENG.). 2005. audio compact disk 19.98 (978-1-59659-007-6(6), GildAudio) Pub: Gildan Media. Dist(s): HachBkGrp

***Seven Seasons of the Man in the Mirror: Guidance for Each Major Phase of Your Life.** Zondervan. (Running Time: 11 hrs. 27 mins. 22 sec.). (ENG.). 2010. 9.99 (978-0-310-86920-7(X)) Zondervan.

Seven Secrets: Success & the Self-Fulfilling Prophecy. 1 cass. 1996. 10.00 (978-1-879630-03-1(6)) Black Hawk Pub.
How to be more successful in every aspect of life.

Seven Secrets: Uncovering Genuine Greatness. abr. ed. John Hagee. 3 cass. (Running Time: 4 hrs.). 2004. 49.25 (978-1-59355-551-1(2), 1593555512); audio compact disk 69.25 (978-1-59355-553-5(9), 1593555539) Brilliance Audio.
Everyone longs to be successful but very few have a clue of what true success really means. Pastor John Hagee explores seven areas of life that help listeners recognize and define genuine greatness in their lives. Listeners will learn how to press in closer to their potential, overcome their frustration in current situations and achieve great things by using godly principles to resolve difficult issues. Here are a few topics that Pastor Hagee discusses in this motivational message: Entering the School of Success (A Personal Story) False Definitions of Success The Real Picture of Success The Secrets of Attitude, Perseverance, Self-Esteem, Self-Mastery, Communication, Prosperity and Prayer The Challenge Those looking for suggestions about improving personal effectiveness and personal growth will both enjoy and benefit from The Seven Secrets.

Seven Secrets: Uncovering Genuine Greatness. abr. ed. John Hagee. Read by J. Charles. 3 cass. (Running Time: 4 hrs.). 2004. 19.95 (978-1-59355-550-4(4), 1593555504); audio compact disk 21.95 (978-1-59355-552-8(0), 1593555520) Brilliance Audio.

Seven Secrets: Uncovering Genuine Greatness. abr. ed. John Hagee. Read by J. Charles. (Running Time: 4 hrs.). 2006. 39.25 (978-1-4233-0318-3(0), 9781423303183, Brlnc Audio MP3 Lib); 24.95 (978-1-4233-0317-6(2), 9781423303176, Brilliance MP3); 39.25 (978-1-4233-0320-6(2), 9781423303206, BADLE); 24.95 (978-1-4233-0319-0(9), 9781423303190, BAD) Brilliance Audio.

Seven Secrets of Influence. Elaine Zuker. 1 cass. 1991. 9.95 (978-0-07-073084-7(9)) Pub: McGraw-Hill Trade. Dist(s): McGraw
With organizations being reshaped & hierarchies shaken, managers need new skills to gain support across departmental lines. Here Zuker instructs listeners on how to analyze their own styles of influence & that of others to sharpen the competitive edge.

Seven Secrets of the Corporate Mystic. unabr. ed. Gay Hendricks. 4 CDs. (Running Time: 5 hrs.). 2002. audio compact disk 34.95 (978-1-56455-930-2(0), AW00570D) Sounds True.
Includes: How modern mystics are initiated into the mysteries of corporate life, while pursuing their visions with passion and compassion. The enduring qualities that set visionary leaders apart, and how to cultivate them. How meditation, creativity, and intuition are helping to solve problems in our cathedrals of enterprise, and much more.

Seven Secrets to Becomming a Multi-Millionare. Bill Staton. Read by Bill Staton. (Running Time: 6 hrs.). (C). 2005. 36.95 (978-1-59912-160-4(3)) Iofy Corp.

Seven Secrets to Greater Happiness. Jonathan Robinson. Read by Jonathan Robinson. 1 cass. (Running Time: 60 min.). 1990. 9.95 (978-1-57328-783-8(0)) Focal Pt Calif.
People who are particularly happy are not any smarter, better looking, richer, or luckier than other people. Yet, almost all highly fulfilled people do use seven key behaviors or attitudes that make a tremendous difference in their lives. This tape presents these seven secrets to greater happiness, & instructs you in how to apply them in your life. With humorous stories & practical techniques, you'll be guided towards a deeper experience of personal fulfillment.

Seven Signs. Steven C. Warner. 1 cass. 1999. 11.00 (978-0-937690-72-7(4), 7236) Wrld Lib Pubns.
Catholic music.

Seven Signs. Steven C. Warner. 1 cass. (Running Time: 1 hr. 4 mins.). 1999. audio compact disk 17.00 CD. (978-0-937690-71-0(6), 7238) Wrld Lib Pubns.

***Seven Simons.** Anonymous. 2009. (978-1-60136-605-4(1)) Audio Holding.

Seven Sins: The Tyrant Ascending. unabr. ed. Jon Land. Read by Alan Sklar. Narrated by Alan Sklar & Patrick G. Lawlor. (Running Time: 12 hrs. 30 mins. 0 sec.). (ENG.). 2008. audio compact disk 24.99 (978-1-4001-5774-7(9)); audio compact disk 75.99 (978-1-4001-3774-9(8)) Pub: Tantor Media. Dist(s): IngramPubServ

Seven Sins: The Tyrant Ascending. unabr. ed. Jon Land. Read by Alan Sklar. Narrated by Alan Sklar & Patrick G. Lawlor. (Running Time: 12 hrs. 30 mins. 0 sec.). (ENG.). 2008. audio compact disk 37.99 (978-1-4001-0774-2(1)) Pub: Tantor Media. Dist(s): IngramPubServ

Seven Sisters. Margaret Drabble. (Isis (CDs) Ser.). (J). 2006. audio compact disk 89.95 (978-0-7531-2563-2(3)) Pub: ISIS Lrg Prnt GBR. Dist(s): Ulverscroft US

Seven Sisters. unabr. ed. Margaret Drabble. 8 cass. (Isis Cassettes Ser.). (J). 2005. 69.95 (978-0-7531-1590-9(5)) Pub: ISIS Lrg Prnt GBR. Dist(s): Ulverscroft US

Seven Sisters. unabr. ed. Anthony Sampson. Read by Paul Shay. 10 cass. (Running Time: 15 hrs.). 1987. 88.00 (978-0-7366-1142-8(8), 2067) Books on Tape.
The Seven Sisters: Exxon, Gulf, Texaco, Mobil, Socal, British Petroleum & Shell. How did they get to run your life.

Seven Sleepers. unabr. ed. Elizabeth Ferrars. Read by Garard Green. 6 cass. (Running Time: 7 hrs. 30 min.). 1998. 54.95 (978-0-7531-0241-1(2), 971114) Pub: ISIS Audio GBR. Dist(s): Ulverscroft US
The late professor Garvie-Brown of Edinburgh University departed this life full of honors, professional esteem, & leaving a considerable estate. Many years later, evidence has emerged of seven wives, four bigamous, & all murdered. Young Luke Latimer, along with a devious private detective are dragged into the ambit of a family, the professors' descendants, who are desperate - even murderously - determined to prevent public scandal.

Seven Songs of Merlin. T. A. Barron. 6 cass. (Running Time: 9 hrs. 59 mins.). (Lost Years of Merlin Ser.: Bk. 2). (J). (gr. 5-9). 2004. 38.25 (978-0-8072-0959-2(7), Listening Lib) Pub: Random Audio Pubg. Dist(s): NetLibrary CO
Young Merlin must master the Seven Songs of Wisdom in order to save his ailing mother.

Seven Songs of Merlin. T. A. Barron. Intro. by T. A. Barron. Read by Kevin Isola. 6 vols. (Running Time: 9 hrs. 59 mins.). (Lost Years of Merlin Ser.: Bk. 2). (J). (gr. 5-9). 2004. pap. bk. 48.00 (978-0-8072-2099-3(X), Listening Lib) Random Audio Pubg.

Seven Spiritual Laws for Parents: Guiding Your Children to Success & Fulfillment. abr. ed. Deepak Chopra. Read by Deepak Chopra. 1 cass. (Running Time: 1 hr. 30 mins.). 1997. 14.00 (Random AudioBks) Random Audio Pubg.

Seven Spiritual Laws for Parents: Guiding Your Children to Success & Fulfillment. abr. ed. Deepak Chopra. Read by Deepak Chopra. 2 CDs. (Running Time: 5400 sec.). (Deepak Chopra Ser.). (ENG.). 2006. audio compact disk 14.99 (978-0-7393-1953-6(1)) Pub: Random Audio Pubg. Dist(s): Random

Seven Spiritual Laws of Success see Siete Leyes Espirituales del Exito

Seven Spiritual Laws of Success: A Practical Guide to the Fulfillment of Your Dreams. Deepak Chopra. 1 cass. (Running Time: 1 hr. 30 mins.). 11.95 (AN5726) Lghtwrks Aud & Vid.
Based on natural laws which govern all of creation, this presentation shatters the myth that success is the result of hard work, exacting plans or driving ambition. Deepak Chopra, M.D. distills the essence of his spiritual teachings into seven simple yet powerful principles that can easily be applied to create success in all areas of your life.

Seven Spiritual Laws of Success: A Practical Guide to the Fulfillment of Your Dreams. abr. ed. Deepak Chopra. 1 cass. 1996. 9.95 (87842) Books on Tape.
The New Age physician says minding key spiritual principles guarantees success & happiness.

Seven Spiritual Laws of Success: A Practical Guide to the Fulfillment of Your Dreams. unabr. ed. Deepak Chopra. Read by Deepak Chopra. 2 CDs. (Running Time: 1 hr. 30 mins.). (Chopra, Deepak Ser.). (ENG.). 2002. audio compact disk 17.95 (978-1-878424-75-4(0)) Amber-Allen Pub.
Deepak Chopra distills the essence of his teachings into seven simple, yet powerful principles that can easily be applied to create success in all areas of your life. Based on natural laws that govern all of creation, this audio shatters the myth that success is the result of hard work, exacting plans, or driving ambition. Filled with timeless wisdom and practical steps you can apply right away, this is an audio you will want to listen to again and again.

Seven Spiritual Laws of Success: A Practical Guide to the Fulfillment of Your Dreams. unabr. ed. Deepak Chopra. 2 CDs. (Running Time: 41 mins.). 2002. audio compact disk 17.95 (978-1-878424-14-3(9)) Amber-Allen Pub.
Distills the essence of his teachings into seven simple yet powerful principles that can easily be applied to create success in all areas of your life.

Seven Spritual Laws of Success. abr. ed. Deepak Chopra. 1 cass. 9.95 (87842) Books on Tape.
The New Age physician says minding key spiritual principles guarantees success & happiness.

Seven Stars. unabr. ed. Anthea Fraser. Read by Gordon Griffin. 6 cass. (Running Time: 6 hrs. 30 min.). 2001. (978-1-84283-095-6(3)) Soundings Ltd GBR.
British detective David Webb's latest assignment finds him tracking a country house burglar who also dabbled in murder.Bad weather forces Helen Campbell to cut her road trip short and spend the night in the Seven Star Guest House, where she innocently picks up the local rag to read her horoscope. Little does she suspect that the stars hold much more information than just the day's outlook.

Seven States of Consciousness. unabr. ed. Stan Kendz. Read by Stan Kendz. 1 cass. (Running Time: 50 min.). 1995. 10.00 (978-1-57582-002-6(1)) HAPPE Progs.
Tape discusses waking, sleeping, dreaming, transcendent, cosmic, divine, & universal states of consciousness.

Seven Steps for Creating a New You. Jane E. Hart. (ENG.). 2008. audio compact disk 10.00 (978-0-9753047-5-4(5)) J E Hart.

Seven Steps for Successful Life Transitions. Jane E. Hart. (ENG.). 2008. audio compact disk 15.00 (978-0-9753047-4-7(7)) J E Hart.

Seven Steps to a Turn Around. 1 cass. 1997. 20.00 (978-1-57855-007-4(6)) T D Jakes.

Seven Steps to Christian Love. Derek Prince. 1 cass. (I-4054) Derek Prince.

Seven Steps to Healthy Eating. Annemarie Colbin. 1 cass. (Running Time: 1 hr.). 1993. 9.95 (978-1-57124-012-5(8)) Creat Seminars.
Better health through better eating.

Seven Steps to Heaven. Perf. by Ray Brown. 1 cass., 1 CD. 7.98 (TA 33384); audio compact disk 12.78 CD Jewel box. (TA 83384) NewSound.

Seven Steps to Move a Mountain. 1999. 59.95 (978-1-893027-33-6(3)) Path of Light.

Seven Steps to Oneness: Journey to a Whole New Life. Guy Finley. (ENG.). 2006. 24.95 (978-1-929320-47-9(7)); 34.95 (978-1-929320-25-7(6)); audio compact disk 34.95 (978-1-929320-26-4(4)) Life of Learn.
This groundbreaking audio program, recorded live by best-selling self-realization author Guy Finley, teaches listeners to discover and work with timeless principles that empower the evolution of the soul. Includes ways to realize the greatest gifts heaven and earth have to offer, including unshakable confidence, perfect peace, timeless beauty, incorruptible love, sensitive strength, total freedom, and conscious compassion.

Seven Steps to Prayer That Bring Results. Kenneth Copeland. 4 cass. (Running Time: 4 hrs.). 1982. stu. ed. 20.00 (978-0-938458-59-3(0)) K Copeland Pubns.
Biblical teaching on prayer.

Seven Steps to Revival. Derek Prince. 4 cass. (Running Time: 4 hrs.). 19.95 (SS1); 14.95 Set. (SS2) Derek Prince.
"If My people will humble themselves" is the first step in praying for revival. The Lord allows His people to reach a place of utter helplessness & total reliance. But, when our prayer is based on this realization, the Lord's compassion prevails.

Seven Steps to Successful FHA Marketing. Chip Cummings. (ENG.). 2008. audio compact disk 97.00 (978-0-9746975-4-3(0)) Northwind Financial.

Seven Storey Mountain. abr. ed. Thomas Merton. Read by Sidney Lanier. 2 cass. (Running Time: 3 hrs.). 1995. 16.95 (978-0-944993-38-5(9)) Audio Lit.

Seven Storey Mountain. unabr. ed. Thomas Merton. Read by Wolfram Kandinsky. 13 cass. (Running Time: 19 hrs. 30 min.). 1984. 104.00 (978-0-7366-0903-6(2), 1846) Books on Tape.
This is Thomas Merton's account of his conversion to Catholicism. Already enjoying recognition as a poet, Merton's spiritual restiveness leads to his pilgrimage to a Trappist monastery in Kentucky.

Seven Stories. Short Stories. James Kelman. Read by James Kelman. 1 CD. (Running Time: 1 hr.). (AK Press Audio Ser.). (ENG.). 2000. audio compact disk 13.98 (978-1-873176-34-4(1)) Pub: AK Pr GBR. Dist(s): Consort Bk Sales

Seven Strange & Ghostly Tales, unabr. ed. Short Stories. Brian Jacques. Read by Brian Jacques. 3 cass. (Running Time: 3 hrs.). (YA). 1999. 23.98 (FS9-26774) Highsmith.

Seven Strange & Ghostly Tales. unabr. ed. Short Stories. Read by Brian Jacques. Ed. by Brian Jacques. 3 vols. (Running Time: 4 hrs. 4 mins.). (J). (gr. 4-7). 1996. pap. bk. 36.00 (978-0-8072-7613-6(8), YA899SP, Listening Lib) Random Audio Pubg.
Seven genuinely scary stories with touches of humor.

Seven Strange & Ghostly Tales. unabr. ed. Brian Jacques. Read by Brian Jacques. 3 cass. (Running Time: 4 hrs. 4 mins.). (J). (gr. 4-7). 1996. 30.00 (978-0-8072-7612-9(X), YA899CX, Listening Lib) Random Audio Pubg.
Presents seven creepy stories of ghosts, vampires & spooky things that creep around in the dark.

Seven Summits. Dick Bass & Frank Wells. 9 cass. (Running Time: 13 hrs. 30 mins.). 2001. 72.00 (978-0-7366-6182-9(4)) Books on Tape.
Frank Wells & Dick Bass had a dream. It was as straightforward as it was difficult: climb the highest mountain on each of the world's seven continents; a feat that had eluded the world's best mountaineers. What made it all the more extraordinary was that Frank & Dick were businessmen, not mountaineers.

Seven Test of Obedience: 1 Kings 18:41-46. Ed Young. 1987. 4.95 (978-0-7417-1597-5(X), 597) Win Walk.

Seven Things God Hates. Warren W. Wiersbe. Read by Warren W. Wiersbe. 2 cass. (Running Time: 3 hrs.). 1987. 9.95 (978-0-8474-2305-7(0)) Back to Bible.
Features messages dealing with seven specific sins listed in Proverbs 6:16-19.

Seven Things God Hates: Proverbs 6:16-19. Ed Young. 1991. 4.95 (978-0-7417-1894-5(4), 894) Win Walk.

Seven Things I Hate about Satan. unabr. ed. Doug Giles. Read by Doug Giles. 1 cass. (Running Time: 40 mins.). 2000. 14.95 (978-0-9667501-1-9(X)) Clash Ministries.
A modernization of Thomas Brook's Puritan classic, "Precious Remedies Against Satan's Devices".

Seven Things That Steal Your Joy: Overcoming the Obstacles to Your Happiness. unabr. ed. Joyce Meyer. Read by Joyce Meyer. 5 CDs. (Running Time: 6 hrs.). (ENG.). 2004. audio compact disk 29.98 (978-1-58621-641-2(4)) Pub: Hachet Audio. Dist(s): HachBkGrp

Seven Things That Steal Your Joy: Overcoming the Obstacles to Your Happiness. unabr. ed. Joyce Meyer. (ENG.). 2005. 14.98 (978-1-59483-313-7(3)) Pub: Hachet Audio. Dist(s): HachBkGrp

Seven Things That Steal Your Joy: Overcoming the Obstacles to Your Happiness. unabr. ed. Joyce Meyer. (Running Time: 6 hrs.). (ENG.). 2009. 44.98 (978-1-60024-586-2(2)) Pub: Hachet Audio. Dist(s): HachBkGrp

Seven Things You Should Know about Divine Healing. Kenneth E. Hagin. 6 cass. (Running Time: 6 hrs.). 1993. 24.00 (69H) Faith Lib Pubns.

Seven Universal Rays. Mae R. Wilson-Ludlam. 1 cass. (Running Time: 90 min.). 1990. 8.95 (836) Am Fed Astrologers.

Seven Up. Janet Evanovich. Read by Lorelei King. (Stephanie Plum Ser.: No. 7). 2005. 20.95 (978-1-59397-795-5(6)) Pub: Macmill Audio. Dist(s): Macmillan

Seven Up. abr. ed. Janet Evanovich. Read by Lorelei King. (Stephanie Plum Ser.: No. 7). 2005. 11.95 (978-1-59397-794-8(8)); audio compact disk 19.95 (978-1-59397-774-0(3)) Pub: Macmill Audio. Dist(s): Macmillan

Seven Up. unabr. abr. ed. Janet Evanovich. Read by Lorelei King. 7 CDs. (Running Time: 8 hrs. 30 mins. 0 sec.). (Stephanie Plum Ser.: No. 7). (ENG.). 2005. audio compact disk 34.95 (978-1-59397-775-7(1)) Pub: Macmill Audio. Dist(s): Macmillan

Seven Upper Halls: Meditation. Warren Kenton. 2 cass. 18.00 (OC136) Sound Horizons AV.

Seven Upper Halls: Workshop. 5 cass. 40.00 (OC135) Sound Horizons AV.

Seven Ways to Make TV Work for Your Family. Joseph B. Walker. 1 cass. 7.95 (Bkcraft Inc) Deseret Bk.

Seven Weeks to Better Sex. abr. ed. Domeena Renshaw. 2 cass. (Running Time: 2 hrs.). 1996. 18.00 (978-0-694-51623-0(6), CPN 2533) HarperCollins Pubs.
This recording is designed for couples willing to overcome sexual roadblocks or simply enrich their sexual relationship. A new chapter serves each week, building confidence, communication, enjoyment, fulfillment & fun.

Seven Wheels of Light. Joel Andrews. 1 cass. (Running Time: 1 hr.). 1996. 9.95 (978-1-55961-351-4(3)); audio compact disk 14.95 (978-1-55961-350-7(5)) Relaxtn Co.

Seven Wonders of Grace. Charles H. Spurgeon. Read by J. Gerald Harris. 2008. audio compact disk 21.95 (978-0-615-21809-0(1)) Sapphire Dig.

Seven Wonders of Sassafras Springs. unabr. ed. Betty G. Birney. Read by Joseph Buttler. 3 CDs. (Running Time: 3 hrs. 37 mins.). (J). (gr. 4-7). 2006. audio compact disk 30.00 (978-0-7393-3633-5(9), Listening Lib); 30.00 (978-0-7393-3634-2(7), Listening Lib) Pub: Random Audio Pubg. Dist(s): Random
When Eben McAllister reads about the Seven Wonders of the World, he longs to escape the small farming community of Sassafras Springs and do some exploring of his own. No one else ever seems to want to leave Sassafras, however - not even his best pal, Jeb - and so, for now, Eben figures he's stuck on the farm with Pa and Aunt Pretty until he grows up.All that changes when his pa, tired of Eben's moping, challenges him to find Seven Wonders in Sassafras Springs that can stand up to the real Seven Wonders of the World. And if he does? Then Eben will get the adventure he's been craving for - a trip out West. Eben doesn't reckon he'll have any luck - he can't think of even one thing that could be called "interesting," let alone wondrous, in Sassafras, but he figures he'll give it a try.

Seven Wonders of Sassafras Springs. unabr. ed. Betty G. Birney. Read by Joseph Buttler. (Running Time: 13020 sec.). (ENG.). (J). (gr. 7-7). 2006. audio compact disk 27.00 (978-0-7393-3641-0(X), Listening Lib) Pub: Random Audio Pubg. Dist(s): Random

Seven Wonders of the Universe. 1 cass. (Running Time: 21 min.). 14.95 (8371) MMI Corp.
Relating celestial phenomena to the Universe: Constellations, globular clusters, a star that died 900 years ago, a place where night would be brighter than day.

Seven Wonders of the World, Ancient & Modern. Instructed by Manly P. Hall. 8.95 (978-0-89314-258-2(1), C580504) Philos Res.

Seven Words for Three Hours. Edmund Newell. bk. 31.00 (978-0-232-52645-5(1)) D Longman & Todd GBR.

Seven Worst Things Parents Do. abr. ed. John C. Friel & Linda D. Friel. Read by John C. Friel & Linda D. Friel. Read by Jeffrey Hedquist. 1 cass. (Running Time: 1 hr. 30 mins.). 1999. 9.95 (978-1-55874-737-1(0)) Health Comm.
Parents can learn to recognize their inefficient parenting techniques & make appropriate changes to become better parents. Parenting is a great challenge & many parents unknowingly create unhealthy behavior in their children by making mistakes in their parenting. The tape ends with the authors offering words of encouragement to all parents.

***Seven Year Switch.** unabr. ed. Claire Cook. Narrated by Coleen Marlo. (Running Time: 7 hrs. 30 mins.). 2010. 14.99 (978-1-4001-8777-5(X)); 19.99 (978-1-4001-6777-7(9)); audio compact disk 29.99 (978-1-4001-1777-2(1)); audio compact disk 71.99 (978-1-4001-4777-9(8)) Pub: Tantor Media. Dist(s): IngramPubServ

Seven-Year Zig Zag, Richard Green. 2 cass. (Running Time: 2 hrs. 20 mins.). 19.95 (NSME001) Lodestone Catalog.

Seven-Year Zig Zag. Richard Green. 2 CDs. (Running Time: 2 hrs.). 2001. audio compact disk 24.95 (NSME002) Lodestone Catalog.

Seven Years in Tibet. unabr. ed. Heinrich Harrer. Read by David Case. 9 CDs. (Running Time: 13 hrs. 30 mins.). 2000. audio compact disk 72.00 (978-0-7366-6048-8(8)) Books on Tape.
This is the memoir of a young Austrian who escaped from an internment camp in India & made his way to the side of the Dalai Lama.

Seven Years in Tibet. unabr. collector's ed. Heinrich Harrer. Read by David Case. 7 cass. (Running Time: 10 hrs. 30 mins.). 1987. 56.00 (978-0-7366-1122-0(3), 2045) Books on Tape.
In 1943, Heinrich Harrer made a successful escape from an internment camp in India through the rugged Himalayan passes to the Forbidden City of Lhasa in Tibet. From destitute vagabond, he rose to the position of tutor & confidant to the fourteen-year-old Dalai Lama until their parting in 1950, when the Chinese Communists overran the country. His work of travel, adventure & brilliant observation has been updated to include post-1950 events.

Seven Years to Seven Figures: The Fast-Track Plan to Becoming a Millionaire. unabr. ed. Michael Masterson. Read by Norman Dietz. (Running Time: 10 hrs. 0 mins. 0 sec.). (ENG.). 2001. audio compact disk 59.99 (978-1-4001-3342-0(4)); audio compact disk 19.99 (978-1-4001-5342-8(5)) Pub: Tantor Media. Dist(s): IngramPubServ

Seven Years to Seven Figures: The Fast-Track Plan to Becoming a Millionaire. unabr. ed. Michael Masterson. Read by Norman Dietz. 8 CDs. (Running Time: 10 hrs. 0 mins. 0 sec.). (ENG.). 2007. audio compact disk 29.99 (978-1-4001-0342-3(8)) Pub: Tantor Media. Dist(s): IngramPubServ

Sevenfold Mystery of Love. Instructed by Manly P. Hall. 8.95 (978-0-89314-259-9(X), C860511) Philos Res.

Seventeen, unabr. ed. Booth Tarkington. Read by Flo Gibson. 5 cass. (Running Time: 7 hrs.). 1992. 20.95 (978-1-55685-251-0(7)) Audio Bk Con.
The awful, but amusing circumstances of William Sylvanus Baxter's first love when he is smitten by the charms of Lola Pratt, a visitor in town, who talks baby talk to her dog & many admirers, is told with relish. If certain racial insensitivities offend you, let us rejoice over the distance we have come!.

Seventeen Evidences of the True Church. Floyd Weston. 2004. audio compact disk 10.95 (978-1-57734-655-5(6)); 9.95 (978-1-55503-302-6(4), 06004288) Covenant Comms.
A classic & incredible talk by a great modern missionary.

Seventeen Months see Carl Sandburg's Poems for Children

***Seventeen Second Miracle.** unabr. ed. Jason F. Wright. (Running Time: 7 hrs.). (ENG.). 2010. audio compact disk 29.95 (978-0-14-242854-2(X), PengAudBks) Penguin Grp USA.

Seventeen Seconds to Anywhere. Perf. by Liz Story. 1 cass., 1 CD. 8.78 (WH 11291); audio compact disk 13.58 CD Jewel box. (WH 11291) NewSound.

Seventeen Seventy-Six: Year of Illusions. Thomas J. Fleming & Roland Van Zandt. 1 cass. (Running Time: 56 min.). 10.95 (40213) J Norton Pubs.
Author Fleming & historian Van Zandt recreate with Heywood Hale Broun our year of independence, not as a year of high purpose & unity, but a year of self-interest, stupidity & even greed. The founding fathers, they remind us, were as human as ourselves, & living through a time of extraordinary events.

Seventeen Success Principles. unabr. ed. Jack Boland. Read by Jack Boland. 6 cass. (Running Time: 6 hrs.). 49.95 (978-0-88152-058-3(6), BA23) Master Mind.

Seventeen Syllables, Pt. B. (23322) J Norton Pubs.

Seventh. Richard Stark, pseud. 3 cass. (Running Time: 4.5 hrs.). 2001. 28.00 (978-0-7366-6358-8(4)) Books on Tape.

Seventh Annual Criminal Law Symposium. 1990. 95.00 (AC-566) PA Bar Inst.

Seventh Commandment. Lawrence Sanders. 2004. 10.95 (978-0-7435-4597-6(4)) Pub: S&S Audio. Dist(s): S and S Inc

Seventh Commandment. unabr. ed. Sarah Shears. Read by Tanya Myers. 5 cass. (Running Time: 6 hrs. 35 min.). 1999. 63.95 (978-1-85903-245-9(1)) Pub: Magna Story GBR. Dist(s): Ulverscroft US
The third volume of the author's autobiography. A love affair that lasted for sixteen years & which isolated her from family, friends & the normal satisfaction of middle age.

Seventh Day. Fran Avni. Read by Fran Avni. 1 cass. (J). 1992. 9.98 (978-1-877737-88-6(7), MLP 268) MFLP CA.
A joyous & creative celebration of Shabbat.

Seventh Day. unabr. ed. Bodie Thoene & Brock Thoene. Narrated by Sean Barrett. (Running Time: 8 hrs. 15 mins. 0 sec.). (A. D. Chronicles Ser.). (ENG.). 2009. audio compact disk 29.99 (978-1-59859-541-3(5)) Oasis Audio.

Seventh Heaven. Catherine Anderson. Narrated by Julia Gibson. 10 cass. (Running Time: 14 hrs. 45 mins.). 88.00 (978-0-7887-9964-8(9)) Recorded Bks.

Seventh Heaven. Alice Hoffman. Read by Roberta Germaine. 7 CDs. 2004. audio compact disk 74.95 (978-0-7927-3151-1(4), SLD 231, Chivers Sound Lib) AudioGO.

Seventh Heaven. unabr. ed. Alice Hoffman. Read by Roberta Germaine. 6 vols. (Running Time: 9 hrs.). 2000. bk. 54.95 (978-0-7927-2266-3(3), CSL 155, Chivers Sound Lib) AudioGO.
It is 1959. Nora Silk is extraordinary: she's strong, passionate, mysterious and determined to raise her two children without a husband. She's a woman whose liberated spirit foreshadows the 1960's. At first, the residents view Nora and her children as outcasts. But slowly, everyone in town is drawn to her, and in the mirror of her magnetism, people begin to see themselves as never before.

Seventh Man see Classic Ghost Stories, Vol. 3, A Collection

Seventh Man, unabr. ed. Max Brand. Read by Ian Esmo. 6 cass. (Running Time: 9 hrs.). 1999. 44.95 (978-0-7861-1526-6(2), 2376) Blckstn Audio.
His name is Dan Barry, & they call him "the Manslayer." His best friend is a savage wolf dog no other man can touch. They say his gun is faster than summer lightning & has never missed its mark. His lifeblood is danger.

Seventh Man, unabr. ed. Max Brand. Read by Ian Esmo. 6 cass. (Running Time: 6 hrs.). 1999. 44.95 (FS9-50927) Highsmith.

Seventh Man. unabr. collector's ed. Max Brand. Read by Jonathan Marosz. 7 cass. (Running Time: 7 hrs.). 1995. 42.00 (978-0-7366-2959-1(9), 3652) Books on Tape.
Whistling Dan Barry stands up against the law for six-time killer Vic Gregg, but a seventh murder finally convinces Barry he's wrong.

Seventh Scroll. unabr. ed. Wilbur Smith. Read by Stephen Thorne. 16 cass. (Running Time: 16 hrs.). 1996. 124.95 (978-0-7451-6640-7(7), CAB 1256) AudioGO.
Duraid Al Simmu & his wife Royan, were the first to discover the tomb of Queen Lostris. And with it, they found the scrolls that recorded the burial of Pharoah Mamose & his vast treasure. But as they search in Ethiopia, Duraid is murdered, the scrolls are stolen & Royan flees to England.

Seventh Scroll. 4th abr. ed. Wilbur Smith. Read by James Fox. 2 cass. (Running Time: 3 hrs.). (Egyptian Ser.). (ENG., 2001. 16.99 (978-0-333-66113-0(3)) Pub: Macmillan UK GBR. Dist(s): IPG Chicago

Seventh Scroll, Pt. 1. unabr. ed. Wilbur Smith. Read by David Case. 8 cass. (Running Time: 12 hrs.). (Courtney Novels). 1995. 64.00 (978-0-7366-3152-5(6), 3826 A) Books on Tape.

Seventh Scroll, Pt. 2. unabr. ed. Wilbur Smith. Read by David Case. 8 cass. (Running Time: 12 hrs.). (Courtney Novels). 1995. 64.00 (3826-B) Books on Tape.

Seventh Seal. Jessica Draper & Richard Draper. 7 CDs. 2004. audio compact disk 19.95 (978-1-59156-192-7(2)) Covenant Comms.

Seventh Sense: A Different Way to See. M. Therese Crowley. Perf. by M. Therese Crowley. 3 CDs. (Running Time: 2 hrs. 57 mins., 06 sec.). 2006. audio compact disk 25.00 (978-0-9788359-0-3(5)) MTCSeven.
Tune in, lose your worry and shake loose your thinking about time & energy, what's possible, creative and true. An effervescent adventure written for audio by Therese the visionary former WCBS anchorwoman-turned coach/energy healer. Light, deep, humorous, and eternally hopeful. Original Method to tune into the body and "the voice inside that knows", your own special power and purpose. Original music illustrates the marriage of the mystic and the scientific, the creative process and telepathy and her beautiful visions preceding 9-11. Perfect for people with a sixth sense, those in recovery, career change, artists, entrepreneurs, athletes and the young vanguard. Played as a science experiment in life: We are guided by the theorem that no matter what happens, we are held safe within the mind of God.

Seventh Sinner, unabr. ed. Elizabeth Peters, pseud. Read by Grace Conlin. 4 cass. (Running Time: 5 hrs. 30 mins.). 1998. 32.95 (978-0-7861-1324-8(3), 2249) Blckstn Audio.
For vibrant, lovely Jean Suttman, the fellowship to study in Rome is the culmination of all of her dreams, until she undertakes an innocent expedition to the ancient subterranean Temple of Mithra. Someone is stalking Jean, someone ruthless & determined. Before long she can see no chance of rescue from the ever-present terror, no hope of escape, nothing but death.

Seventh Sinner. unabr. ed. Elizabeth Peters, pseud. Read by Grace Conlin. 5 CDs. (Running Time: 5 hrs. 30 mins.). 2000. audio compact disk 40.00 (978-0-7861-9942-6(3), 2249) Blckstn Audio.
Jean Suttman, on a fellowship to study in Rome undertakes an expedition to the ancient subterranean Temple of Mithra. She discovers the corpse of one of her fellow students. Then one small accident after another occurs, that come dreadfully close to killing her.

Seventh Sinner. unabr. ed. Elizabeth Peters, pseud. Read by Grace Conlin. (Running Time: 5 hrs. 30 mins.). (Jaqueline Kirby Ser.: Vol. 1). 2000. 24.95 (978-0-7861-9670-8(X), 2249) Blckstn Audio.

Seventh Sinner. unabr. ed. Elizabeth Peters, pseud. Read by Grace Conlin. 1 CD. (Running Time: 12 hrs.). 2001. audio compact disk 19.95 (zm2249) Blckstn Audio.
For vibrant, lovely Jean Suttman, the fellowship to study in Rome is the culmination of all of her dreams, until she undertakes an innocent expedition to the ancient subterranean Temple of Mithra. Someone is stalking Jean, someone ruthless & determined. Before long she can see no chance of rescue from the ever-present terror, no hope of escape, nothing but death.

Seventh Son. Orson Scott Card. Read by Scott Brick et al. (Running Time: 32400 sec.). (Tales of Alvin Maker Ser.). 2007. 59.95 (978-1-4332-0094-6(5)); audio compact disk 72.00 (978-1-4332-0095-3(3)); audio compact disk 29.95 (978-1-4332-0096-0(1)) Blckstn Audio.

Seventh Son. Orson Scott Card. Read by Orson Scott Card. 5 cass. (Running Time: 7 hrs. 30 min.). (Tales of Alvin Maker Ser.: No. 1). 1993. 47.00

(978-1-56544-018-0(8), 550003); Rental 7.80 30 day rental Set. (550003) Literate Ear.
In an alternative frontier America, where settlers & natives alike exchange the mysteries of folk magic, an enchanted child is born.

Seventh Son. unabr. ed. Reay Tannahill. Read by Stephen Thorne. 10 cass. (Running Time: 15 hrs.). 2002. 84.95 (978-0-7540-0846-0(0), CAB 2268) Pub: Chivers Pr GBR. Dist(s): AudioGO

Seventh Wave. Emma Sinclair. Read by Nicolette McKenzie. 20 cass. (Sound Ser.). (J). 2003. 109.95 (978-1-84283-337-7(5)) Pub: ISIS Lrg Prnt GBR. Dist(s): Ulverscroft US

Seventh Wave. Emma Sinclair. Read by Nicolette McKenzie. 19 CDs. (Running Time: 22 hrs. 40 mins.). (Soundings (CDs) Ser.). (J). 2004. audio compact disk 124.95 (978-1-84283-782-5(6)) Pub: ISIS Lrg Prnt GBR. Dist(s): Ulverscroft US

Seventies' Disco Ball. 1 cass. 1998. 31.98 (978-1-56826-871-2(8)) Rhino Enter.

Seventies' Disco Ball with Other, 2 cass. (Running Time: 2 hrs.). 1998. 24.98 (978-1-56826-938-2(2)) Rhino Enter.

Seventy Basic Phonograms: Hearing How & Why. abr. ed. Wanda Sanseri. Read by Wanda Sanseri. 1 cass. (Running Time: 1 hr. 32 min.). 1991. 5.95 (978-1-880045-02-2(8)) Back Home Indust.
Tape made in live training class. Wanda Sanseri explains how to write & says the 70 Basic Phonograms used in English spelling & speech.

Seventy-Ninth Prince. Patricia White. Perf. by High Sierra Players Staff. Narrated by Frank Riley. Score by David Fabrizio. Directed By David Fabrizio. 2 CDs. (Running Time: 1 hr. 30 mins.). Dramatization. (ENG.). 2004. audio compact disk 16.95 (978-1-58124-729-9(X)) Pub: Fiction Works. Dist(s): Brodart

Seventy's Walking One: (Beginner) Bruce Blackmon. 1 cass. (Running Time: 1 hr. 2 min.). 1991. 12.95 (978-1-56481-006-9(2)) Sports Music.
A one hour beginner level fitness walking program featuring well known songs from the 1970's.

Seventy's Walking Three: (Advanced) Bruce Blackmon. 1 cass. (Running Time: 1 hr. 2 min.). 1991. 12.95 (978-1-56481-008-3(9)) Sports Music.
A one hour advanced level fitness walking program featuring well known songs from the 1970's.

Seventy's Walking Two: (Intermediate) Bruce Blackmon. 1 cass. (Running Time: 1 hr. 2 min.). 1991. 12.95 (978-1-56481-007-6(0)) Sports Music.
A one hour fitness walking program (intermediate level) featuring well known songs from the 1970's.

***Severance: A Novel.** unabr. ed. Elliott Sawyer. Read by Kirby Heyborne. (Running Time: 9.5 hrs. NaN mins.). (ENG.). 2010. 29.95 (978-1-4417-7829-1(2)); 44.95 (978-1-4417-7826-0(8)); audio compact disk 24.95 (978-1-4417-7828-4(4)); audio compact disk 55.00 (978-1-4417-7827-7(6)) Blckstn Audio.

Severance Park & Those "Revolting" Americans. unabr. ed. Gerald J. Morse. Read by Brooks Baldwin. 1 cass. (Running Time: 75 min.). 9.95 (978-0-939969-04-3(1)); Talk-a-Walk.
A Talk-A-Walk guide thru Independence National Historic Park in Philadelphia providing a history of people, places, events & architecture; packaged with a detailed map to guide you through the 45-acre site.

Severe Mercy. unabr. ed. Sheldon Vanauken. Read by Peter Kjenaas. 6 cass. (Running Time: 9 hrs.). 1989. 44.95 (978-0-7861-0017-0(6), 1017) Blckstn Audio.
This is a poetic autobiography tracing Sheldon & Jean (Davy) Vanauken's love & their intense search for Christian faith. At Oxford they met C. S. Lewis & through his influence, became Christians. Then Jean contracted a mysterious illness.

Seville Communion. abr. ed. Arturo Pérez-Reverte. Read by Christopher Cazenove. 4 cass. (Running Time: 6 hrs.). 2002. 25.00 (978-1-59040-038-8(0), Phoenix Audio) Pub: Amer Intl Pub. Dist(s): PerseuPGW
A magnificant old church in Spain faces demolition until a handful of supporters rally to save the landmark. But soon the church's defenders begin to die. Accidents or murder? The task of unraveling the mystery falls to the Vatican's handsome and sophisticated Father Lorenzo Quart. But first he must track down the identity of a savvy computer hacker known only as Vespers, and find a way to resist the considerable charms of a stunning Spanish beauty bent on seduction.

Sewage Sludge/"Biosolids" Prod. by Perelandra Staff. 2004. 14.95 (978-0-927978-54-5(7)) Perelandra Ltd.

Sewing Together: A Birthday Quilt. Jocelyn Riley. 1 cass. (Running Time: 15 min.). (YA). 1996. 12.00 (978-1-877933-67-7(8), 19003) Her Own Words.

Sex. Vajracarya. 1 cass. 1970. 9.00 Vajradhatu.
A seminar by the scholar & meditation master trained in the philosophical & meditative traditions of Buddhism in Tibet.

Sex: An Oral History. abr. ed. Harry Maurer. 2 cass. (Running Time: 3 hrs.). 1996. 16.95 Set. (978-1-886238-08-4(1)) Passion Press.
A revealing first person narrative by a diverse group of people who speak about their sexual needs & how they try to fulfill them. Gentle sex, rough sex...gay, straight, & bi...their voices will captivate you with their frankness, their humor, their guilt & their pathos.

Sex: An American Obsession: Romans 1:25. Ed Young. 1995. 4.95 (978-0-7417-2045-0(0), 1042) Win Walk.

Sex & Dating for Teens. Taffi L. Dollar & Eric Harris. (ENG.). 2000. 25.00 (978-1-59089-084-4(1)) Pub: Creflo Dollar. Dist(s): STL Dist NA

Sex & Ethics. Milton Diamond. 1 cass. (Running Time: 1 hr.). (Human Sexuality Ser.). 11.95 (34029) J Norton Pubs.

Sex & Other Changes. unabr. ed. David Nobbs. Read by Glen McCready. 8 cass. (Running Time: 11 hrs.). (Isis Cassettes Ser.). (J). 2005. 69.95 (978-0-7531-3459-7(4)); audio compact disk 89.95 (978-0-7531-2492-5(0)) Pub: ISIS Lrg Prnt GBR. Dist(s): Ulverscroft US

Sex & Other Touchy Subjects. Shelley L. Stockwell. Perf. by Frank Unzueta & Betsy Moreland. 1 cass. (Running Time: 49 min.). 1990. 10.00 Creativity Unltd Pr.
Shelley Stockwell's song & spoken word is guaranteed to make you roar, make you sing & celebrate the rites of spring. Features: Static Grid on My CB, Dating Game Reject, Yes, I'm Positive & Frustration is the "F" Word. An unusual book on tape from her best seller of the same title.

Sex & Shopping: The Confessions of a Nice Jewish Girl. abr. ed. Judith Krantz. Read by Judith Krantz. 4 cass. (Running Time: 6 hrs.). 2001. 25.00 (978-1-59040-076-0(3), Phoenix Audio) Pub: Amer Intl Pub. Dist(s): PerseuPGW
Judith Krantz openly and humorously discusses her transformation from virginal Welesley graduate Judy Tarcher to sophisticated world-travelled Judith Krantz.

Sex & Spirit. abr. ed. John Gray & John Selby. 2004. 11.95 (978-0-7435-3925-8(7)) Pub: S&S Audio. Dist(s): S and S Inc

Sex & the Arts. Milton Diamond. 1 cass. (Running Time: 55 min.). (Human Sexuality Ser.). 1975. 11.95 (34028) J Norton Pubs.
A discussion about art as an expression of sexuality & how it helps the artist make his statement.

Sex & the City. Candace Bushnell. 2002. 24.98 (978-1-58621-121-9(8)) Hachet Audio.

Sex & the City. abr. ed. Candace Bushnell. Read by Cynthia Nixon. (YA). 2007. 54.99 (978-1-60252-794-2(6)) Find a World.

Sex & the City. abr. ed. Candace Bushnell. Read by Cynthia Nixon. (ENG.). 2005. 14.98 (978-1-59483-452-3(0)) Pub: Hachet Audio. Dist(s): HachBkGrp

Sex & the City. abr. ed. Candace Bushnell. Read by Cynthia Nixon. 5 CDs. (Running Time: 6 hrs.). (ENG.). 2008. audio compact disk 16.98 (978-1-60024-283-0(9)) Pub: Hachet Audio. Dist(s): HachBkGrp

Sex & the City. abr. ed. Candace Bushnell. Read by Cynthia Nixon. (Running Time: 6 hrs.). (ENG.). 2009. 24.98 (978-1-60788-138-4(1)) Pub: Hachet Audio. Dist(s): HachBkGrp

Sex & the Law. Milton Diamond. 1 cass. (Running Time: 1 hr.). (Human Sexuality Ser.). 11.95 (34027) J Norton Pubs.

Sex & the Married Girl: From Clicking to Climaxing... the Complete Truth about Modern Marriage. unabr. ed. Mandi Norwood. Read by Mandi Norwood. 8 cass. (Running Time: 13 hrs.). 2004. 34.95 (978-1-59007-402-2(5)); audio compact disk 55.00 (978-1-59007-403-9(3)) Pub: New Millenn Enter. Dist(s): PerseuPGW

Sex & the Sacred City: Meditations on the Theology of the Body. Speeches. Voice by Steve Kellmeyer. 1 CD. (Running Time: 1 hr). 2005. audio compact disk 11.95 (978-0-9767368-1-3(0)) Bridegroom.

Sex & the Seasoned Woman: Pursuing the Passionate Life. abr. ed. Gail Sheehy. Read by Gail Sheehy. (Running Time: 18000 sec.). (ENG.). 2006. audio compact disk 27.95 (978-0-7393-2204-8(4), Random AudioBks) Pub: Random Audio Pubg. Dist(s): Random

Sex & the Single: Gen. 39:1-12. Ed Young. 1988. 4.95 (978-0-7417-1679-8(8), 679) Win Walk.

***Sex & the Soul of a Woman: The Reality of Love & Romance in an Age of Casual Sex.** Paula Rinehart. (Running Time: 4 hrs. 45 mins. 0 sec.). (ENG.). 2009. 14.99 (978-0-310-30517-0(9)) Zondervan.

Sex Attraction - Sex Appeal. 1 cass. (Running Time: 60 min.). 10.95 (027) Psych Res Inst.
Arouse an awakening of natural attractiveness to the opposite sex by programming desirability subconsciously.

***Sex Crime Scenario Cd.** rev. ed. Tolbert. (ENG.). 2010. audio compact disk 50.99 (978-0-7575-3156-9(3)) Kendall-Hunt.

Sex, Death & Genius. Arthur Schopenhauer. 2 cass. (Running Time: 2 hrs. 25 min.). 1995. 17.95 (978-1-879557-24-6(X)) Audio Scholar.
Arthur Schopenhauer was one of the most influential philosophers of the nineteenth century. He drew upon the teachings of Eastern religions to give ultimate meaning to life & existence. Schopenhauer here applies his famous philosophy of the Will to a variety of human concerns.

Sex, Deception & Jealousy. R. D. Laing. 3 cass. 24.00 (OC64) Sound Horizons AV.

***Sex Detox.** unabr. ed. Ian Kerner. Read by Ian Kerner. (ENG.). 2008. (978-0-06-125744-5(3), Harper Audio); (978-0-06-125745-2(1), Harper Audio) HarperCollins Pubs.

Sex Detox: Recharge Desire. Revitalize Intimacy. Rejuvenate Your Love Life. Ian Kerner. 2007. audio compact disk 39.95 (978-0-06-123075-2(8)) HarperCollins Pubs.

Sex Differences: Myths & Realities. Carole Offir. 1 cass. 10.95 (29300) J Norton Pubs.
Talks about the contributions of biology & culture to sexual development, & hypothesizes that male social dominance has an economic base.

Sex Drive. Robert A. Monroe. Read by Robert A. Monroe. (Running Time: 30 min.). (Human Plus Ser.). 1989. 14.95 (978-1-56102-037-9(0)) Inter Indus.
For complete control of sex drive.

Sex, Drugs, & Cocoa Puffs: A Low Culture Manifesto. abr. ed. Chuck Klosterman. Read by Chuck Klosterman. 2006. 17.95 (978-0-7435-6430-4(8), Audioworks); audio compact disk 29.95 (978-0-7435-5488-6(4), Audioworks) Pub: S&S Audio. Dist(s): S and S Inc

Sex Education. Milton Diamond. 1 cass. (Running Time: 1 hr.). (Human Sexuality Ser.). 11.95 (34023) J Norton Pubs.

Sex Education: Syllabus. Lester A. Kirkendall & Ruth F. Osborne. (J). 1971. 82.60 (978-0-89420-184-4(0), 180800) Natl Book.

Sex God: Exploring the Endless Connections Between Sexuality & Spirituality. Rob Bell. Read by Rob Bell. (Running Time: 4 hrs. 24 mins. 0 sec.). (ENG.). 2007. audio compact disk 19.99 (978-0-310-27290-8(4)) Zondervan.

Sex God: Exploring the Endless Connections Between Sexuality & Spirituality. Zondervan Publishing Staff & Rob Bell. (Running Time: 4 hrs. 24 mins. 0 sec.). (ENG.). 2007. 14.99 (978-0-310-27292-2(0)) Zondervan.

Sex in Marriage - Part 11 (God's Word to the Wife) 1 Cor. 7:15-20. Ed Young. (C). 1995. 4.95 (978-0-7417-2047-4(7), 1047) Win Walk.

Sex in Marriage Is Not OK. unabr. ed. Phyllis Hill & Glenn Hill. 2005. audio compact disk 22.69 (978-1-933803-09-8(6), SBKCD1) Child Sens Comm.

Sex in the Bible Audio Book. Zondervan Publishing Staff. 2007. audio compact disk 14.99 (978-0-8297-4959-5(4)) Pub: Vida Pubs. Dist(s): Zondervan

Sex in the Christian Marriage. Creflo A. Dollar. (ENG.). 2000. 18.00 (978-1-59089-092-9(2)) Pub: Creflo Dollar. Dist(s): STL Dist NA

Sex Is Important: Ephesians 5:21-28. Ed Young. (J). 1981. 4.95 (978-0-7417-1168-7(0), A0168) Win Walk.

Sex Is the Most Stressful Thing in the History of the Universe (an Essay from Things I've Learned from Women Who've Dumped Me) abr. ed. Dan Vebber. Read by Dan Vebber. Ed. by Ben Karlin. (Running Time: 15 mins.). (ENG.). 2008. 1.98 (978-1-60024-329-5(0)) Pub: Hachet Audio. Dist(s): HachBkGrp

Sex, Laughter & God Realization. Ruchira Avatar Adi Da Samraj. 1 cass. 1975. 11.95 (978-1-57097-048-1(3), AT-SCG) Dawn Horse Pr.

Sex Lies & Superspeedways. Henry Smokey Yunick. Read by John DeLorean. 2 cass. (Running Time: 6 hrs). 2002. (978-0-9711469-5-2(0)) Carb Pr.

Sex Lies & Superspeedways. Excerpts. Henry Smokey Yunick. Read by John DeLorean. 6 cds. (Running Time: 6 hrs. 40 min.). 2002. audio compact disk 29.95 (978-0-9724378-0-6(0), Carbon Pr) Carb Pr.

Sex Lives of Cannibals: Adrift in the Equatorial Pacific. unabr. ed. J. Maarten Troost. Read by Simon Vance. (Running Time: 21600 sec.). 2007. 19.95 (978-1-4332-0174-5(7)); audio compact disk 19.95 (978-1-4332-0175-2(5)) Blckstn Audio.

Sex Lives of Cannibals: Adrift in the Equatorial Pacific. unabr. ed. J. Maarten Troost. Read by Simon Vance. (Running Time: 30600 sec.). 2007. 54.95 (978-1-4332-0286-5(7)); audio compact disk 29.95 (978-1-4332-0176-9(3)); audio compact disk 63.00 (978-1-4332-0287-2(5)) Blckstn Audio.

***Sex, Love, & Money: Revenge & Ruin in the World of High-Stakes Divorce.** unabr. ed. Gerald Nissenbaum & John Sedgwick. Narrated by Patrick G. Lawlor. (Running Time: 10 hrs. 0 mins.). 2010. 16.99 (978-1-4001-8641-9(2)); 24.99 (978-1-4001-6641-1(1)); audio compact disk 69.99 (978-1-4001-4641-3(0)); audio compact disk 34.99 (978-1-4001-1641-6(4)) Pub: Tantor Media. Dist(s): IngramPubServ

Sex Magic. Michael P. Marshall. Read by Michael P. Marshall. Ed. by Jonathan C. Renaud. Music by Ted Crook. 1 cass. (Running Time: 52 min.). 1995. 9.00 (978-0-912403-07-6(1)) Prod Renaud.
Sexuality is a tremendous power, recognized & hence regulated & directed by every society & every major world religion. This session focuses on wise, loving, magical harnessing of that power.

***Sex, Mom, & God: A Religiously Obsessed Sexual Memoir (or a Sexually Obsessed Religious Memoir)** unabr. ed. Frank Schaeffer. Read by Author. (Running Time: 7 hrs.). (ENG.). 2011. 27.00 (978-1-59659-644-3(9), GildAudio); audio compact disk 29.98 (978-1-59659-633-7(3), GildAudio) Pub: Gildan Media. Dist(s): HachBkGrp

Sex Money KISS. ltd. unabr. ed. Scripts. Gene Simmons. Read by Gene Simmons. 4 cass. (Running Time: 6 hrs.). 2003. 39.95 (978-1-59007-315-5(0), N Millennium Audio) Pub: New Millenn Enter. Dist(s): PerseuPGW

Sex Money KISS. ltd. unabr. ed. Scripts. Gene Simmons. Read by Gene Simmons. 5 CDs. (Running Time: 6 hrs.). 2004. 49.95 (978-1-59007-316-2(9)) Pub: New Millenn Enter. Dist(s): PerseuPGW

Sex Money KISS. unabr. ed. Gene Simmons. 4 cass. 2004. 25.00 (978-1-59007-417-6(3)); audio compact disk 37.95 (978-1-59007-418-3(1)) New Millenn Enter.

Sex on the Brain: 12 Lessons to Enhance Your Love Life. Daniel G. Amen. Read by Patrick G. Lawlor. (Playaway Adult Nonfiction Ser.). 2008. 64.99 (978-1-60640-697-7(3)) Find a World.

Sex on the Brain: 12 Lessons to Enhance Your Love Life. unabr. ed. Daniel G. Amen. Read by Patrick G. Lawlor. (Running Time: 8 hrs. 30 mins. 0 sec.). (ENG.). 2007. audio compact disk 34.99 (978-1-4001-0402-4(5)); audio compact disk 24.99 (978-1-4001-5402-9(2)); audio compact disk 69.99 (978-1-4001-3402-1(1)) Pub: Tantor Media. Dist(s): IngramPubServ

***Sex on the Moon: The Amazing Story Behind the Most Audacious Heist in History.** unabr. ed. Ben Mezrich. (ENG.). 2011. audio compact disk 35.00 (978-0-307-75076-1(0), Random AudioBks) Pub: Random Audio Pubg. Dist(s): Random

Sex, Power & Pericles, unabr. ed. Reid Buckley. Read by Reid Buckley. 6 cass. (Running Time: 8 hrs. 30 mins.). 1998. 44.95 (978-0-7861-1255-5(7), 2164) Blckstn Audio.
A timely & joyous reminder that rhetoric is the domain of thoroughbreds who are unthreatened by tension & understand its uses. Aided by his vast erudition & his knack of marshaling the fragmentary reflections of his well-traveled life, Buckley has written an expert how-to manual on podium performance that is also a wise & witty cultural essay demonstrating that the art of speaking & the art of living are one.

Sex-Restraint. (705) Yoga Res Foun.

Sex-Restraint. Swami Jyotirmayananda. 1 cass. (Running Time: 1 hr.). 1990. 12.99 Yoga Res Foun.

Sex, Should We Wait? J. C. Willke & Willke. 2 cass. (Running Time: 60 min.). 1969. 13.95 (978-0-910728-18-6(6)) Hayes.
Discuss aspects of premarital sex & its complications.

Sex Slaves of the Dragon Tong. F. Paul Wilson. (Dark Voices Ser.). 2007. audio compact disk 25.00 (978-1-880325-90-2(X)) Pub: Borderlnds NH. Dist(s): Diamond Book Dists

Sex-Spirituality & Relationships. D. Charlotte Kasl. 2 cass. (Running Time: 2 hrs.). 1992. 18.00 (OC291-64) Sound Horizons AV.

Sex Talk: Program from the Award-Winning Public Radio Series, 431. Interview. Hosted by Peter Kramer. 1 CD. (Running Time: 59 minutes). 2006. audio compact disk 21.95 (978-1-933644-31-8(1)) Lichtenstein Creat.
On TV and radio, people are "exposing themselves"...why would anyone air their most private thoughts in the most public of media? On-air sex talk is entertaining to be sure, and there's more of it now than ever. But is it helpful medicine? Viagra aside, is it medicine at all? Join us we speak with three of the leading "sexperts" on the phenomena.We start with a report from The Infinite Mind's Mary Carmichael on just how helpful or harmful these shows can be. She speaks with Dr. Spencer Eth, chair of the American Psychiatric Association's ethics committee, Dr. Joy Davidson; clinical psychologist, bestselling author and certified sex therapist, and media theorist Mimi White.Next we turn to the grandmother of all the sex experts...literally, in this case...Dr. Ruth Westheimer, who speaks candidly about her role on her radio show vs. her private therapy practice.Dr. Drew Pinsky...well-known and well-loved as co-host of MTV's "LoveLine"...shares his thoughts on how little real therapy goes on during his show, but that he feels it's still an important tool for reaching America's youth.Perhaps known best for his frank, graphic advice in the column Savage Love, Dan Savage takes on every sex-related question you can imagine (and some you probably can't). He shares his unique point of view with The Infinite Mind.Finally, commentator Sharon Lerner talks about contrast of sex education in our schools with the sex education they get from TV and radio.

Sex Technique & Sex Problems in Marriage. Ed Wheat. 2 cass. 19.95 Set. (978-0-00-497832-1(3)) Script Coun.

Sex, Truth & Real Life: 1 Thes. 4:3-8. Ed Young. 1991. 4.95 (978-0-7417-1886-0(3), 886) Win Walk.

Sexaholics Anonymous. 5 cass. (Running Time: 5 hrs.). 1997. 30.00 (978-0-9622887-4-6(8)) SA Literature.
A program of recovery for those who want to stop their sexually self-destructive thinking & behavior.

Sexual Abuse: The Dark Side of Childhood. 1 cass. (Running Time: 30 min.). 9.95 (D0150B090, HarperThor) HarpC GBR.

Sexual Abuse of Children: A Comprehensive Guide to Current Knowledge & Intervention Strategies. Jeffrey J. Haugaard & N. Dickon Reppucci. (Social & Behavioral Science Ser.). 1988. bk. 53.50 (978-1-55542-077-2(X), Jossey-Bass) Wiley US.

Sexual Addiction. 2007. audio compact disk 19.95 (978-1-56136-092-5(9)) Master Your Mind.

Sexual Addiction: New Life Clinic, Stephen Arterburn et al. 2 cass. (Running Time: 3 hrs.). (Minirth Meier New Life Clinic Ser.). 1997. 12.99 (978-1-886463-03-5(4)) Oasis Audio.
Would life be better without that sexual addiction? Helps the listener identify the problem, the cause, the prognosis & the first step to recovery.

Sexual Aliveness. Dick Sutphen. 1 cass. (Running Time: 1 hr.). (Probe Seven Ser.). 14.98 (978-0-87554-368-0(5), P104) Valley Sun.
"Sex gets better & better. Yes, it does. You accept this. Enjoy. Do it. Yes, Fun sex...".

An Asterisk (*) at the beginning of an entry indicates that the title is appearing for the first time.

Sexual Attraction: Program from the Award Winning Public Radio Serie. Interview. Hosted by Fred Goodwin. Comment by John Hockenberry. 1 CD. (Running Time: 1 hr.). 2000. audio compact disk 21.95 (978-1-932479-93-5(7), LCM 97) Lichtenstein Creat.
Sexual attraction is the key to the perpetuation of the human species. It pervades our everyday lives in numerous ways, including how we behave, how we interact with each other, even the advertisements we see. In this hour of The Infinite Mind, we take a look at sexual attraction from the point of view of evolution, anthropology, biology - and cabaret. With David Buss, a professor of psychology at the University of Texas and the author of "The Evolution of Desire" and "The Dangerous Passion", and Helen Fisher, an anthropologist at Rutgers University and the author of "Anatomy of Love" and "The First Sex: The Natural Talents of Women and How they are Changing the World," cabaret performer Sidney Meyer, Dr. Charles Wysocki, a neuroscientist at the Monell Chemical Senses Center in Philadelphia, and Dr. George Preti, a chemist at the Monell Center, and an adjunct professor in the Department of Dermatology at the University of Pennsylvania, Simon LeVay, whose 1990 report that he found differences between the size of the hypothalmus in gay and straight men sparked controversy. With commentary by John Hockenberry.

Sexual Bliss for Men. Bruce Goldberg. (ENG.). 2005. audio compact disk 17.00 (978-1-57968-049-7(6)) Pub: B Goldberg. Dist(s): Baker Taylor

Sexual Bliss for Men. Bruce Goldberg. Read by Bruce Goldberg. 1 cass. (Running Time: 25 min.). (ENG.). 2006. 13.00 (978-1-885577-40-5(0)) Pub: B Goldberg. Dist(s): Baker Taylor
Share with one's partner the most enjoyable and fulfilling sex one is capable of reaching with this self-hypnosis technique.

Sexual Bliss for Women. Bruce Goldberg. (ENG.). 2005. audio compact disk 17.00 (978-1-57968-048-0(8)) Pub: B Goldberg. Dist(s): Baker Taylor

Sexual Bliss for Women. Bruce Goldberg. Read by Bruce Goldberg. 1 cass. (Running Time: 25 min.). (ENG.). 2006. 13.00 (978-1-885577-39-9(7)) Pub: B Goldberg. Dist(s): Baker Taylor
Experience the ultimate in sexual joy and attain complete fulfillment on many levels through self-hypnosis.

Sexual Chaos: Romans 1:21-32. Ed Young. 1995. 4.95 (978-0-7417-2054-2(X), 1054) Win Walk.

Sexual Commerce. Milton Diamond. 1 cass. (Running Time: 1 hr.). (Human Sexuality Ser.). 11.95 (34019) J Norton Pubs.

Sexual Development. Milton Diamond. 1 cass. (Running Time: 1 hr.). (Human Sexuality Ser.). 11.95 (34005) J Norton Pubs.

Sexual Enrichment for Men. Gil Boyne. Read by Gil Boyne. 1 cass. (Running Time: 45 min.). (Hypnosis Motivation Cassettes Ser.). 1977. 9.95 (115) Westwood Pub Co.
Experience the joy of total sexual fulfillment.

Sexual Enrichment for Women. Gil Boyne. Read by Gil Boyne. 1 cass. (Running Time: 45 min.). (Hypnosis Motivation Cassettes Ser.). 1977. 9.95 (116) Westwood Pub Co.
A Major breakthrough in realizing your true sexual potential. Experience the joy of total sexual fulfillment. Learn to be all that you can be!.

Sexual Ethics & Morality. Jack Deere. 1 cass. (Running Time: 90 mins.). (Proverbs Ser.: Vol. 3). 2000. 5.00 (JD08-003) Morning NC.
Practical wisdom for everyday living is brought to life in Jack's thorough exposition of this important book of the Bible.

Sexual Ethics in Ministry. 1 cass. (Care Cassettes Ser.: Vol. 19, No. 1). 1993. 10.80 Assn Prof Chaplains.

Sexual Fringes. Milton Diamond. 1 cass. (Running Time: 1 hr.). (Human Sexuality Ser.). 11.95 (34018) J Norton Pubs.

Sexual Fulfillment. Richard Jafolla & Mary-Alice Jafolla. Read by Richard Jafolla & Mary-Alice Jafolla. (Relationships). 1986. 12.95 (360) Stppng Stones.
Motivational tapes that work on the subconscious mind (subliminal) & conscious mind to bring about self-improvement.

Sexual Fulfillment Experience Cassette Album, Bruce Goldberg. Read by Bruce Goldberg. 6 cass. (Running Time: 3 hrs.). (ENG.). 2005. 65.00 (978-1-885577-78-8(8)) Pub: B Goldberg. Dist(s): Baker Taylor
Learn to overcome any sexual difficulty and then experience the maximum in sexual fulfillment through self-hypnosis techniques.

Sexual Fulfillment Experience CD Album. Bruce Goldberg. (ENG.). 2005. audio compact disk 75.00 (978-1-57968-054-1(2)) Pub: B Goldberg. Dist(s): Baker Taylor

Sexual Game. Dorothy Santangelo. 1 cass. 8.95 (303) Am Fed Astrologers.
Each sign has own attitudes & energies playing "mating game".

Sexual Harassment: Litigating, Preventing & Resolving Claims. S. Beville May. 1 cass. 1994. 35.00 bk. (4923) Natl Prac Inst.

Sexual Harassment in the Workplace. S. Beville May. 1994. 135.00 Natl Prac Inst.

Sexual Harassment Update. 2 cass. (Running Time: 2 hrs.). 1998. 25.00 Incl. study outline. (M213) Am Law Inst.
Includes discussion of the U.S. Supreme Court decision in "Burlington Industries, Inc. v. Ellerth" & its practical effect on the workplace.

Sexual Harassment Update. 1998. 99.00 (ACS-2185) PA Bar Inst.
In this past term, the U.S. Supreme Court made sweeping pronouncements in the law of sexual harassment, clarifying many areas that the lower courts have been grappling with for years. The Court analyzed the issues of employer liability for harassing acts of supervisory employees, whether an employee must suffer job-related harm as a result of the harassemnt, same-sex harassment & school district liability for teachers' sexual harassment of students.

Sexual Healing. Excerpts. Peter A. Levine. 2 CDs. (Running Time: 2.5 hours). 2003. audio compact disk 24.95 (978-1-59179-039-6(5)) Sounds True.
On "Sexual Healing," Peter Levine - a pioneer in the healing of emotional trauma - offers crucial new information and self-guided exercises for those seeking help.

***Sexual Healing: A Meditation CD.** David Elliott. (ENG.). 2005. 15.00 (978-0-9753910-4-4(6)) Hawk Pr CA.

Sexual Healing: Q & A Logos 2/27/00. Ben Young. 2000. 4.95 (978-0-7417-6171-2(8), B0171) Win Walk.

Sexual Healing & Spiritual Awakening: What about Sex? abr. ed. Scott Morrison. 1 cass. (Running Time: 1 hr.). 1998. 7.50 (978-1-882496-28-0(0)) Twnty Frst Cntry Ren.
Wisdom, honesty, & compassion in matters of lovemaking & celibacy; sex vs. the idea of sex.

Sexual Honesty. 2005. audio compact disk 7.95 (978-1-932927-70-2(0)) Ascensn Pr.

Sexual Identity. Milton Diamond. 1 cass. (Running Time: 1 hr.). (Human Sexuality Ser.). 11.95 (34015) J Norton Pubs.

Sexual Intimacy. 1 cassette. 1986. 12.95 (978-1-55841-052-7(X)) Emmett E Miller.
Lovely music and imagery support the voices of Dr. Miller and Sandra Miller, providing gentle, sensitive, compassionate guidance for opening your heart and body to the beauty of loving. Use side 1 alone and side 2 with a partner.

Sexual Intimacy. 1 CD. 1986. audio compact disk 16.95 (978-1-55841-125-8(9)) Emmett E Miller.

Sexual Love in Marriage: Heb. 13:4, 728. Ed Young. 1989. 4.95 (978-0-7417-1728-3(X)) Win Walk.

Sexual Processes. Milton Diamond. 1 cass. (Running Time: 1 hr.). (Human Sexuality Ser.). 11.95 (34004) J Norton Pubs.

Sexual Purity & Marital Fidelity. unabr. ed. Jack Deere. 2 cass. (Running Time: 3 hrs.). 2000. 10.00 (JD07-000) Morning NC.
"God is the Judge" & "the Glory of Sexual Purity." Marriages are under attack, but God has ordained spiritual principles that will enable us to stand strong.

Sexual Satisfaction. 1 cass. (Running Time: 60 min.). 10.95 (018) Psych Res Inst.
Enhances sexual desire in lovemaking situations.

Sexual Satisfaction (Subliminal & Hypnosis), Vol. 34. Jayne Helle. 1 cass. (Running Time: 28 min.). 1998. 15.00 (978-1-891826-33-7(6)) Introspect.
Let go of old fears, guilts & doubts, in order to enjoy the physical relationship one desires.

Sexual Wars Nos. 1, 2, & 3: A Weary Male Talks. Carl Faber. 3 cass. (Running Time: 3 hrs. 45 min.). 1982. 28.50 (978-0-918026-51-4(2)) Perseus Pr.

Sexual Wars Nos. 19, 20 & 21: What Men Need for Themselves & from Other Men. Carl Faber. 3 cass. (Running Time: 3 hrs. 45 min.). 1983. 28.50 (978-0-918026-55-2(5), SR 51-861) Perseus Pr.

Sexual Wars Nos. 37, 38 & 39: Pornography, Rage, & the Abuse of Women. Carl Faber. 3 cass. (Running Time: 3 hrs. 45 min.). 1985. 28.50 (978-0-918026-53-8(9), SR 64-276) Perseus Pr.

Sexual Wars Nos. 47, 48 & 49: Celibacy & Isolation. Carl Faber. 3 cass. (Running Time: 3 hrs. 45 min.). 1986. 28.50 (978-0-918026-52-1(0), SR 73-806) Perseus Pr.

Sexual Wars Nos. 58, 59 & 60: Surrender, Passion & Romance. Carl Faber. 3 cass. (Running Time: 3 hrs. 45 min.). 1987. 28.50 (978-0-918026-54-5(7), SR 85-967) Perseus Pr.

Sexualidad. unabr. ed. Carlos González. 1 cass. (Running Time: 32 min.). (SPA.). 1995. 12.00 incl. Norelco box. (978-1-56491-063-9(6)) Imagine Pubs.
Self improvement - improve the idea of sex in modern society.

Sexuality: Celibate, Chastity & the Life Cycle. Sean Sammon. 3 cass. 1988. 25.95 (TAH203) Alba Hse Comns.
This series gives insight to the hurting, hope for the desperate, & reassurance for those who delight in their God-given vocations. The series is wholistic & outlines the steps to be taken in reaching the goal of integrity & the achievement of a healthy identity that every celibate needs.

Sexuality & Celibacy. Sivananda Radha. 1 cass. 1989. 7.95 (978-0-931454-51-6(4)) Timeless Bks.
A frank discussion of the idea of sexuality & celibacy on the spiritual path.

Sexuality & the Nursing Home Resident. unabr. ed. Charlotte Eliopoulos. Read by Charlotte Eliopoulos. 1 cass. (Running Time: 20 min.). 1991. 15.00 (978-1-882515-08-0(0)) Hlth Educ Netwk.
Describes age-related changes to sexual function & measures nursing home staff can use to promote sexuality in residents.

Sexuality As Identity. Read by Ann Belford Ulanov & Barry Ulanov. 1 cass. (Running Time: 90 min.). 1987. 10.95 (978-0-7822-0309-7(4), 241) C G Jung IL.

Sexuality As Identity (Workshop) Read by Ann Belford Ulanov & Barry Ulanov. 1 cass. (Running Time: 2 hrs.). 1987. 12.95 (978-0-7822-0310-3(8), 247) C G Jung IL.

Sexuality Factor. Keith Clark. 3 cass. (Running Time: 2 hrs. 23 min.). 1994. 27.95 Set. (TAH318) Alba Hse Comns.
Fr. Clark, in these three one hour talks, shows you the difference between romantic pursuit & response; & how to understand & practically apply the dynamics of response to your life.

Sexuality (Female) 1 stereo cass. (Running Time: 45 min.). (Self-Hypnosis Ser.). 9.98 (978-1-55909-150-3(9), 810) Randolph Tapes.
Ocean & music to put you in the mood & increase responses. Music background & spoken word.

Sexuality, Human Series. Milton Diamond. 30 cass. (Running Time: 30 hrs.). 285.00 (978-0-88432-227-6(0), S34001) J Norton Pubs.

Sexuality in Illness & Health. Earl Hackett & Myrna Hackett. 1986. 10.80 (0608) Assn Prof Chaplains.

Sexuality in Marriage: Genesis 2:23. Ed Young. 1986. 4.95 (978-0-7417-1534-0(1), 534) Win Walk.

Sexuality (Male) Betty L. Randolph. 1 stereo cass. (Running Time: 45 min.). (Self-Hypnosis Ser.). 9.98 (978-1-55909-149-7(5), 809) Randolph Tapes.
Helps to program desires, releases & hang-ups. Music background & spoken word.

Sexuality of Intimacy: Lovemaking with - Without Sex, David Grudermeyer & Rebecca Grudermeyer. 2 cass. (Running Time: 2 hrs.). 18.95 Incl. handouts. (T-59) Willingness Wrks.

Sexually Confident Wife: Connect with Your Husband in Mind, Heart, Body, Spirit. unabr. ed. Shannon Ethridge. Narrated by Shannon Ethridge. (Running Time: 6 hrs. 58 mins. 16 sec.). (ENG.). 2008. audio compact disk 25.99 (978-1-59859-427-0(3)) Oasis Audio.

Sexually Confident Wife: Connect with Your Husband in Mind, Heart, Body, Spirit. unabr. ed. Shannon Ethridge. Narrated by Shannon Ethridge. (Running Time: 6 hrs. 58 mins. 16 sec.). (ENG.). 2008. 18.19 (978-1-60814-377-1(5), SpringWater) Oasis Audio.

Sexually Fulfilled Man. Read by Mary Richards. (Subliminal Impact Ser.). 12.95 (628) Master Your Mind.
Having freed one's mind from the negative teachings of the past, & having gained new heights in sexual self esteem, one can give & receive pleasure & joy.

Sexually Fulfilled Woman. Read by Mary Richards. (Subliminal Impact Ser.). 12.95 (627) Master Your Mind.
Discusses ways to take responsibility for your sexuality.

Sexually Transmitted Disease: Nineteen Eighty-Five. Moderated by King K. Holmes. Contrib. by Willard Cates, Jr. et al. 1 cass. (Running Time: 90 min.). 1985. 12.00 (A8502) Amer Coll Phys.
This topic is discussed by a moderator & experts who offer differing opinions.

Sexually Transmitted Diseases - Changing Concepts. 2 cass. (General Sessions Ser.: C84-GO7). 1984. 15.00 (8438) Am Coll Surgeons.

Sexy Years: Discover the Hormone Connection - The Secret to Fabulous Sex, Great Health, & Vitality, for Women & Men. unabr. ed. Suzanne Somers. 7 cass. (Running Time: 10 hrs. 30 min.). 2004. 63.00 (978-0-7366-9751-4(9)) Books on Tape.
Middle age doesn't have to be about hot flashes, irritable tempers, and no sex drive. Rigorously researched and engagingly written, Suzanne Somers' THE SEXY YEARS is women's indispensable guide to life after 50. Making the case that the key to happiness lies in the replacement of lost hormones, Somers shares some of the benefits she had first-handedly experienced as a result: increased energy levels, improved sex drive, better weight management, and much more. Included are interviews with several doctors and such vital information as why natural hormones are better than synthetic, the difference between male and female menopause, and how a woman can reinvent herself after 50.

Seymour Bernstein - A Retrospective, Set. Contrib. by Seymour Bernstein. 2003. audio compact disk 19.95 (978-0-634-07770-8(8), 00220097) H Leonard.

Seymour Bernstein Performs His Own Compositions. Composed by Seymour Bernstein. 2005. pap. bk. 19.95 (978-0-634-09850-5(0), 00220146) H Leonard.

Seymour Krim. Interview. Interview with Seymour Krim & Kay Bonetti. 1 cass. (Running Time: 1 hr.). 13.95 (978-1-55644-112-7(6), 4112) Am Audio Prose.
Interview, including discussion of Krim's concept of art as action, his contribution to New Journalism & what he thinks now about his earlier stand on the subject.

Seymour Melman: Disarmament **see Buckley's Firing Line**

SF Soundbook. unabr. ed. Sbc104 Cae. 4 cass. Incl. Foundation: The Psychohistorians. (SBC 104); Gentlemen, Be Seated. (SBC 104); Green Hills of Earth. Robert A. Heinlein. (SBC 104); Martian Chronicles. Ray Bradbury. (SBC 104); Mimsy Were the Borogoves. Swc1509 Cae. 1976. 12.95 (978-0-694-50282-0(0), SWC 1509); 1977. 29.95 (978-0-89845-036-1(5), SBC 104) HarperCollins Pubs.

Sgt. Preston of the Yukon. Contrib. by Jay Michael. (Running Time: 10800 sec.). 2004. 9.98 (978-1-57019-584-6(6)); audio compact disk 9.98 (978-1-57019-585-3(4)) Radio Spirits.

Shabanu: Daughter of the Wind, unabr. ed. Suzanne Fisher Staples. Narrated by Christina Moore. 5 pieces. (Running Time: 6 hrs. 45 mins.). (gr. 8 up). 1995. 44.00 (978-0-7887-0189-4(4), 94414E7) Recorded Bks.
A vibrant young girl of the Pakistani desert finds her future in jeopardy when her father must offer her in marriage to a rich old man.

Shabbat Anthology. Created by Hal Leonard Corporation Staff. 2003. pap. bk. 34.95 (978-0-8074-0877-3(8), 993207) Pub: URJ Pr. Dist(s): H Leonard

Shabbat Anthology, Vol. 2. Mark Dunn & Joel Eglash. 2004. pap. bk. 34.95 (978-0-8074-0920-6(0), 993248) Pub: URJ Pr. Dist(s): H Leonard

Shabbat Anthology, Vol. 3. Ed. by Joel N. Eglash & Jonathan B. Hall. 2005. pap. bk. 34.95 (978-0-8074-0939-8(1), 993280) Pub: URJ Pr. Dist(s): H Leonard

Shabbat Anthology, Vol. 4. 2007. pap. bk. 34.95 (978-0-8074-0992-3(8), 993293) URJ Pr.

Shabbat Sing-Along for Kids. 1 cass. (C5192N) Brentwood Music.
Great for the home & Synagogue, features the beautiful, exciting songs that are an important part of the Sabbath. A blend of Hebrew & English songs that it's educational as well as a lot of fun for everyone.

Shabbath. Leah Novick. 2 cass. 18.00 set. (A0698-89) Sound Photosyn.
The first woman Rabbi shares the feeling & tradition. Powerful & fun.

Shabbatt Seder: The Sabbath Seder. Ron Wolfson. Illus. by Torah Auro Production Staff. (Art of Jewish Living Ser.). 1985. 4.00 (978-0-935665-02-4(1)) Fed Jewish Mens Clubs.

Shack. William Paul Young. Read by Roger Mueller. (Playaway Adult Nonfiction Ser.). 2008. 59.99 (978-1-60640-653-3(1)) Find a World.

Shack. unabr. ed. William Paul Young. Read by Roger Mueller. (Running Time: 8 hrs. 30 mins.). 2009. 59.99 (978-1-60640-151-4(3)) Find a World.

Shack: Where Tragedy Confronts Eternity. unabr. ed. William Paul Young. Narrated by Roger Mueller. (Running Time: 8 hrs. 30 mins. 50 sec.). (ENG.). 2008. 19.59 (978-1-60814-378-8(3)); audio compact disk 27.99 (978-1-59859-419-5(2)) Oasis Audio.

Shackles. Contrib. by Don Moen. Created by Integrity Music. Prod. by Israel Houghton et al. (Shout Praises! Kids Ser.). (J). (ps-3). 2006. audio compact disk 9.99 (978-5-558-16557-9(X)) Integrity Music.

Shackleton's Way. Margot Morrell & Stephanie Capparell. Read by Tim Pigott-Smith. (Running Time: 2 hrs. 30 mins.). 2006. 25.95 (978-1-59912-969-3(8)) Iofy Corp.

Shackleton's Way: Leadership Lessons from the Great Antarctic Explorer. Margot Morrell & Stephanie Capparell. 5 cass. (Running Time: 7 hrs. 30 mins.). 2001. 40.00 (978-0-7366-6214-7(6)) Books on Tape.
From 1914 to 1916, Ernest Shackleton & his men survived the wreck of their ship Endurance, crushed in the Antarctic ice, stranded twelve hundred miles from civilization with no means of communication & no hope for rescue.

Shackleton's Way: Leadership Lessons from the Great Antarctic Explorer. Margot Morrell & Stephanie Capparell. Read by Richard Matthews. 2001. audio compact disk 48.00 (978-0-7366-7510-9(8)) Books on Tape.

Shackleton's Way: Leadership Lessons from the Great Antarctic Explorer. unabr. ed. Margot Morrell & Stephanie Capparell. Read by Richard Matthews. 5 cass. (Running Time: 8 hrs.). 2002. 24.95 (978-0-7366-6748-7(2)) Books on Tape.
Shipwrecked in the Antarctic from 1914 to 1916, Sir Ernest Shackleton & his men survived due to his incredible leadership.

Shaddai. Contrib. by Paul Wilbur et al. 2005. audio compact disk 14.98 (978-5-559-07874-8(3)) Hosanna NM.

Shaddai: The God Who Is More than Enough, Vol. 1. Speeches. Creflo A. Dollar. 3 cass. (Running Time: 4 hrs.). 2000. 15.00 (978-1-59089-169-8(4)) Creflo Dollar.

Shaddai - Winans Phase II. 1 cass. 1999. 7.98 (978-0-7601-2884-8(7)) Provident Music.

Shade. unabr. ed. Neil Jordan. Read by Terry Donnelly. (YA). 2007. 49.99 (978-1-60252-715-7(6)) Find a World.

***Shade.** unabr. ed. Jeri Smith-Ready. Read by Khristine Hvam. (Running Time: 9 hrs.). 2010. 24.99 (978-1-4418-5895-5(4), 9781441858955, Brilliance MP3); 39.97 (978-1-4418-5896-2(2), 9781441858962, Brlnc Audio MP3 Lib); 39.97 (978-1-4418-5897-9(0), 9781441858979, BADLE); audio compact disk 24.99 (978-1-4418-5893-1(8), 9781441858931, Bril Audio CD Unabri); audio compact disk 69.97 (978-1-4418-5894-8(6), 9781441858948, BriAudCD Unabrid) Brilliance Audio.

***Shades of Blue.** Karen Kingsbury. (Running Time: 11 hrs. 10 mins. 0 sec.). (ENG.). 2009. 14.99 (978-0-310-77282-8(6)) Zondervan.

Shades of Blue. unabr. ed. Karen Kingsbury. (Running Time: 11 hrs. 10 mins. 0 sec.). (ENG.). 2009. audio compact disk 19.99 (978-0-310-32419-5(X)) Zondervan.

Shades of Blue. unabr. ed. Bill Moody. Read by Grover Gardner. (Running Time: 30600 sec.). (Evan Horne Ser.). 2008. 54.95 (978-1-4332-1151-5(3));

audio compact disk & audio compact disk 29.95 (978-1-4332-1153-9(X)); audio compact disk & audio compact disk 70.00 (978-1-4332-1152-2(1)) Blckstn Audio.

Shades of Blue & Gray. unabr. ed. Herman Hattaway. Read by Lloyd James. 8 cass. (Running Time: 11 hrs. 30 mins.). 1998. 56.95 (978-0-7861-1299-9(9), 2201) Blckstn Audio.
An introductory military history of the American Civil War, places the 1861-1865 conflict within the broad context of evolving warfare. The evolution of professionalism in the American military serves as an important connective theme throughout.

Shades of Blue & Gray: An Introductory Military History of the Civil War. unabr. ed. Herman Hattaway. (Running Time: 41400 sec.). 2007. audio compact disk 81.00 (978-0-7861-5955-0(3)); audio compact disk 29.95 (978-0-7861-5956-7(1)) Blckstn Audio.

Shades of Blue & Gray: An Introductory Military History of the Civil War. unabr. ed. Herman Hattaway. Narrated by Richard M. Davidson. 8 cass. (Running Time: 11 hrs. 45 mins.). 2000. 70.00 (978-0-7887-1781-9(2), 95255E7) Recorded Bks.
An account of the conflict that split the nation. With careful scholarship & colorful anecdotes, illustrates the technology, tactics, & leadership involved in the major campaigns.

Shades of Fortune. unabr. ed. Stephen Birmingham. Read by Roger Ellis. (Running Time: 17 hrs.). 2009. 24.99 (978-1-4418-0793-9(4), 9781441807939, Brilliance MP3); 24.99 (978-1-4418-0795-3(0), 9781441807953, BAD); 39.97 (978-1-4418-0794-6(2), 9781441807946, Brlnc Audio MP3 Lib); 39.97 (978-1-4418-0796-0(9), 9781441807960, BADLE) Brilliance Audio.

Shades of Gray. unabr. ed. Carolyn Reeder. Narrated by John McDonough. 4 pieces. (Running Time: 5 hrs. 15 mins.). (gr. 5 up). 35.00 (978-0-7887-1793-2(6), 95265E7) Recorded Bks.
Now that the Civil War left him an orphan, 12-year-old Will Page has to live with relatives in Virginia. But his uncle refused to fight - how can Will stay with a coward? Available to libraries only.

Shades of Grey: The Road to High Saffron. unabr. ed. Jasper Fforde. Contrib. by John Lee. (Running Time: 14 hrs.). (ENG.). (gr. 12). 2009. audio compact disk 39.95 (978-0-14-314326-0(3), PengAudBks) Penguin Grp USA.

***Shades of Grey: The Road to High Saffron.** unabr. ed. Jasper Fforde. Narrated by John Lee. 11 CDs. (Running Time: 11 hrs. 30 mins.). 2010. audio compact disk 100.00 (978-1-4159-5528-4(X), BksonTape) Pub: Random Audio Pubg. Dist(s): Random

***Shades of Midnight.** unabr. ed. Lara Adrian. Narrated by Hillary Huber. (Running Time: 10 hrs. 30 mins.). (Midnight Breed Ser.). 2011. 16.99 (978-1-4001-8463-7(0)); 24.99 (978-1-4001-6463-9(X)); audio compact disk 34.99 (978-1-4001-1463-4(2)) Pub: Tantor Media. Dist(s): IngramPubServ

***Shades of Midnight (Library Edition)** unabr. ed. Lara Adrian. Narrated by Hillary Huber. (Running Time: 10 hrs. 30 mins.). (Midnight Breed Ser.). 2011. 34.99 (978-1-4001-9463-6(6)); audio compact disk 83.99 (978-1-4001-4463-1(9)) Pub: Tantor Media. Dist(s): IngramPubServ

Shades of Red. unabr. ed. Doris Mortman. 9 cass. (Running Time: 13 hrs. 30 min.). 2005. 99.00 (978-1-4159-1683-4(7)) Books on Tape.

Shades of Shadow. Perf. by Paul Speer. 1 cass. 9.98 (MPC3001); audio compact disk 14.98 CD. Miramar Images.
The debut from melody maker Quintana with the trademark guitar & production of Paul Speer. This album brings new light to the music of the 90's.

Shades of Twilight. abr. ed. Linda Howard. Read by Natalie Ross. (Running Time: 5 hrs.). 2009. audio compact disk 24.99 (978-1-4418-0714-4(4), 9781441807144, BACD) Brilliance Audio.

Shades of Twilight. abr. ed. Linda Howard. Read by Natalie Ross. (Running Time: 5 hrs.). 2010. audio compact disk 14.99 (978-1-4418-1703-7(4), 9781441817037, BCD Value Price) Brilliance Audio.

Shades of Twilight. unabr. ed. Linda Howard. Read by Natalie Ross. (Running Time: 14 hrs.). 2009. 39.97 (978-1-4233-6327-9(2), 9781423363279, Brlnc Audio MP3 Lib); 24.99 (978-1-4233-6326-2(4), 9781423363262, Brilliance MP3); 24.99 (978-1-4233-6328-6(0), 9781423363286, BAD); audio compact disk 92.97 (978-1-4233-6325-5(6), 9781423363255, BriAudCD Unabrid); audio compact disk 29.99 (978-1-4233-6324-8(8), 9781423363248, Bril Audio CD Unabri) Brilliance Audio.

Shades of Twilight. unabr. ed. Linda Howard. Read by Natalie Ross. (Running Time: 14 hrs.). 2009. 39.97 (978-1-4418-5030-0(9), 9781441850300, BADLE) Brilliance Audio.

Shadow see Tales of Terror & the Supernatural: A Collection

Shadow. 1 cass. (Running Time: 1 hr. 30 mins.). Incl. Shadow: Stake Out. Perf. by Orson Welles & Agnes Moorehead. (MM-5540); Shadow: The Moment of Darkness. Perf. by Peter Lorre. (MM-5540); 7.95 (MM-5540) Natl Recrd Co.
In "Stake Out," Lamont Cranston & lovely Margo Lane get involved in a couple of murders with Silky & Duke. In "The Moment of Darkness," action takes place on a crack express train between Paris & the French Riviera, also in Monte Carlo. George Revel, who is about to be exposed as a fake, conducts a seance & warns of danger.

Shadow. 3 cass. (Running Time: 3 hrs.). (3-Hour Collectors' Editions Ser.). audio compact disk 19.98 (978-1-57019-515-0(3), 27592) Radio Spirits.

Shadow. 3 CDs. (Running Time: 3 hrs.). 2002. audio compact disk 19.98 (27592); 17.98 (27594) Radio Spirits.
"Who knows what evil lurks in the hearts of men? The Shadow knows!" JOin Lamont Cranston, the lovely Margot Lane and, of course, Cranston's alter ego, The Shadow, as they protect the innocent and punish the guilty in six exciting, never-before-released episodes.

Shadow. 2004. cass. & flmstrp 30.00 (978-0-89719-519-5(1)) Weston Woods.

Shadow. Radio Spirits Staff. Read by Orson Welles. 12 CDs. (Running Time: 12 hrs.). 2005. audio compact disk 39.98 (978-1-57019-539-6(0), 4334) Radio Spirits.

Shadow. Radio Spirits Staff. 2007. audio compact disk 39.98 (978-1-57019-798-7(9)) Pub: Radio Spirits. Dist(s): AudioGO

Shadow, Perf. by Orson Welles & Agnes Moorehead. 6 cass. (Running Time: 9 hrs.). 34.98 (Q106) Blckstn Audio.
Includes "The Tomb of Terror," "The Oracle of Death," "The Shadow Challenged," "Murder Incorporated," "Death on the Bridge," & "White God.".

Shadow. Perf. by Orson Welles & Agnes Moorehead. 1 cass. (Running Time: 60 min.). Incl. Bones of the Dragon. (MM-7070); Silent Avenger. (MM-7070); 7.95 (MM-7070) Natl Recrd Co.
In "The Silent Avenger," a condemned criminal has his shell-shocked, sharp-shooting, sniper brother carry out a vendetta against those that sentenced him to death. In "The Bones of the Dragon," Chinatown is beginning its New Year celebration & the Dragon parades through the streets. Gifts of money are offered & The Shadow & lovely Margo Lane accompany their friend Johnnie Lee to collect these gifts. By evening the money box holds a fortune...& murder.

Shadow. Perf. by Orson Welles & Bret Morrison. 1 cass. (Running Time: 60 min.). (Old Time Radio Classic Singles Ser.). 4.95 (978-1-57816-120-1(7), SD117) Audio File.
Includes: 1) "Silent Avenger" (3/13/38). 2) "Bones of the Dragon". Blue Coal (1/11/48).

Shadow. abr. ed. Nina Mattikow. Perf. by Orson Welles. 4 cass. (Running Time: 4 hrs.). Dramatization. (Four Cassette Crates Ser.). 1992. 16.95 Set. (978-1-55569-152-3(8), 577008) Great Am Audio.
Who knows what evil lurks in the hearts of men?.

Shadow. abr. ed. Nina Mattikow. 8 cass. (Running Time: 8 hrs.). Dramatization. (Eight Cassette Collector Packs Ser.). 1992. 29.95 Set. (978-1-55569-577-4(9), 48003) Great Am Audio.
Sixteen original broadcasts from radio's golden age.

Shadow, collector's ed. Perf. by Orson Welles & Margot Stevenson. 6 cass. (Running Time: 9 hrs.). 1998. bk. 34.98 (4049) Radio Spirits.
Eighteen original shows; "The Tomb of Terror," "The Oracle of Death," "The Ghost on the Stair," "The Leopard Strikes," "The Ghost Building," "The shadow Challenged," "The Cat that Killed," "Murder in the Death House," "The Precipice Called Death," "Doom & the Limping Man," "The Comic Strip Killer," "Stake Out," "Murder Incorporated," "Death on the Bridge," "Death Speaks Twice," "The Ghost Wore a Silver Slipper," "The Unburied Dead," "White God".

Shadow. unabr. ed. 2 CDs. (Running Time: 2 Hrs.). bk. 15.95 (978-1-57816-159-1(2), DSD908); 10.95 (978-1-57816-073-0(1), SD2401) Audio File.
Four mystery/adventure shows from the radio Program.

Shadow. unabr. ed. 8 cass. (Running Time: 12 hrs.). 2003. 39.98 (978-1-57019-540-2(4), 40014) Radio Spirits.

Shadow, 1998th ed. 8 cass. (Running Time: 8 hrs.). 1998. bk. 29.98 (4058) Radio Spirits.

Shadow, Vol. 1. Perf. by Orson Welles. 4 cass. (Running Time: 4 hrs.). 1998. bk. 13.98 (4059); bk. 32.98 (4060) Radio Spirits.

Shadow, Vol. 2. Short Stories. 2 Cassette. (Running Time: 2hrs). Dramatization. 2004. 10.95 (978-1-57816-166-9(5)); audio compact disk 12.95 (978-1-57816-170-6(3)) Audio File.

Shadow, Vol. 2. 4 cass. (Running Time: 4 hrs.). 1998. bk. 13.98 (4061) Radio Spirits.

Shadow, Vol. 3. 4 cass. (Running Time: 4 hrs.). 1998. bk. 13.98 (4062) Radio Spirits.

Shadow: Death in a Black Fedora & The House That Death Built. 1 cass. (Running Time: 1 hr.). 2001. 6.98 (2127) Radio Spirits.

Shadow: Death Rides a Broomstick & Murder from the Grave. 1 cass. (Running Time: 1 hr.). 2001. 6.98 (1878) Radio Spirits.

Shadow: Death Stalks the Shadow & Prelude to Terror. 1 cass. (Running Time: 1 hr.). 2001. 6.98 (2406) Radio Spirits.

Shadow: Murder Underground & The Walking Corpse. 1 cass. (Running Time: 1 hr.). 2001. 6.98 (2089) Radio Spirits.

Shadow: Our Holy Grit. unabr. ed. Jacquelyn Small. 2 cass. (Running Time: 3 hrs.). 1994. bk. 16.00 (978-0-939344-10-9(6)) Eupsychian.
According to Carl Jung, at the very core of our being is a duality - the shadow & the true self. This teaches us how to relate to our shadow, those aspects of ourselves we try to deny, repress, & leave behind.

Shadow: Poison Death & Murder on Approval. 1 cass. (Running Time: 1 hr.). 2001. 6.98 (2487) Radio Spirits.

***Shadow: Radio Treasures.** Perf. by Bill Johnstone & Bret Morrison. 2010. audio compact disk 35.95 (978-1-57019-945-5(0)) Radio Spirits.

Shadow: Rare Radio Gems. 4 cass. (Running Time: 4 hrs.). 2002. 29.95 (978-0-7413-0171-0(7)) Radio Spirits.

Shadow: Rare Radio Gems. collector's ed. Perf. by Orson Welles et al. 4 cass. (Running Time: 4 hrs.). 2001. bk. 19.95 (4698); bk. 29.95 (4699) Radio Spirits.
"Caverns of Death," "Death Under the Chapel," "The Sandhog Murders," "The Case of the Three Frightened Policemen," "The Ring of Light," "The Return of Anatol Chevanic," "Death Speaks Twice," "Death Gives an Encore," "Dead Men Tell".

Shadow: Stake Out see Shadow

Shadow: Strange Puzzles. Perf. by Orson Welles et al. 2009. audio compact disk Rental 35.95 (978-1-57019-902-8(7)) Radio Spirits.

Shadow: The Lost Shows. collector's ed. Perf. by Orson Welles. 5 hrs. (Running Time: 5 CDs). 2001. bk. & pap. bk. 39.95 (4064) Radio Spirits.
Ten original radio broadcasts, including book with rare photos and historical anecdotes. Includes "The Death House Rescue," "Death Keeps a Deadline," "The Hoodoo Ship," "The Altar of Death," "Out of This World," "The Brief Fame of John Cooper," "Seance with Death," "Death Is a Colored Dream," "The 'Nursery Rhyme Murders," "The Man Who Was Death".

Shadow: The Lost Shows, collector's ed. Perf. by Orson Welles. 5 cass. (Running Time: 5 hrs.). 1999. bk. & pap. bk. 29.95 (4063) Radio Spirits.

Shadow: The Moment of Darkness see Shadow

Shadow: The Night Side of the Ego. Read by Boris Matthews. 1 cass. (Running Time: 2 hrs.). 1986. 12.95 (978-0-7822-0164-2(4), 223) C G Jung IL.

Shadow: The Nursery Rhyme Murders. Perf. by Orson Welles & Agnes Moorehead. 1 cass. (Running Time: 60 min.). 7.95 (MM-0602) Natl Recrd Co.
In "The Nursery Rhyme Murders," Lamont Cranston & lovely Margo Lane get involved in a private nursing home mystery. In the story "The Bakery," Simon Templar visits a bakery to buy a loaf of bread. When some unsavory characters enter the store, Peggy, the clerk, hurriedly gives the Saint a cake & sends him away.

Shadow: The Tenor with the Broken Voice. Perf. by Orson Welles & Agnes Morehead. 1930. (MM8425) Natl Recrd Co.

Shadow: The Terror at Wolf's Head Knoll & The Nursery Rhyme Murders. 1 cass. (Running Time: 1 hr.). 2001. 6.98 (2168) Radio Spirits.

Shadow: Unearthly Specters. Perf. by Orson Welles et al. 2009. audio compact disk 35.95 (978-1-57019-887-8(X)) Radio Spirits.

***Shadow: Weird Adventure.** Perf. by Orson Welles & Bill Johnstone. 2010. audio compact disk 35.95 (978-1-57019-922-6(1)) Radio Spirits.

Shadow No. 2: "When the Grave Is Open" & "House of Fun" unabr. ed. 1 cass. (Running Time: 60 min.). Dramatization. 7.95 Norelco box. (MM-8787) Natl Recrd Co.
When the Grave Is Open: Two grave robbers try to deliver the wrong body to their clients, & force him into a partnership. The Shadow believes there is something sinister to these thefts. Starring Bret Morrison as Lamont Cranston with Grace Matthews as the lovely Margo Lane. Blue Coal, 1947. House of Fun: A prosperous businessman is kidnapped in the Fun House at a carnival. It involves a racket by gangsters. Starring Bill Johnstone as Lamont Cranston with Agnes Moorehead as the lovely Margo Lane. Mutual Network, 1939.

Shadow No. 3: "Terror at Wolf's Head Knoll" & "The Ghost Building" unabr. ed. 1 cass. (Running Time: 60 min.). Dramatization. 7.95 Norelco box. (MM8788) Natl Recrd Co.
Terror at Wolf's Head Knoll: Margo & Cranston seek shelter in a mysterious mansion after a minor accident. A strange "doctor" treats Margo's sprained ankle. Starring Bret Morrison as Lamont Cranston, with Grace Matthews as the lovely Margo Lane. Blue Coal, 1948. The Ghost Building: Mysterious deaths occur while constructing the largest building in the world. The Shadow breaks into suspect's office & discovers another death. Starring Bill Johnstone as Lamont Cranston with Marjorie Anderson as the lovely Margo Lane. Blue Coal, 1941.

Shadow Account. Stephen Frey. Read by Ken Kliban. 8 vols. 2004. bk. 69.95 (978-0-7927-3191-7(3), CSL 645, Chivers Sound Lib); bk. 94.95 (978-0-7927-3192-4(1), SLD 645, Chivers Sound Lib); bk. 29.95 (978-0-7927-3193-1(X), CMP 645, Chivers Sound Lib) AudioGO.

Shadow & Fairy Tales. unabr. ed. John Boe. 1 cass. (Running Time: 55 min.). 1986. 11.00 (13401) Big Sur Tapes.
Boe, an award-winning writer & teacher, as well as a witty & charming storyteller, taps the underside of fairy tales, weaving stories & trickster myths from many dimensions with insightful commentary from a Jungian perspective.

Shadow & Light. unabr. ed. Jonathan Rabb. Narrated by Simon Prebble. (Running Time: 12 hrs. 30 mins. 0 sec.). (ENG.). 2009. audio compact disk 24.99 (978-1-4001-6217-8(3)); audio compact disk 69.99 (978-1-4001-4217-0(2)); audio compact disk 34.99 (978-1-4001-1217-3(6)) Pub: Tantor Media. Dist(s): IngramPubServ

Shadow & Persona. Read by Boris Matthews. 1 cass. (Running Time: 2 hrs.). 1986. 12.95 (978-0-7822-0163-5(6), 201) C G Jung IL.

Shadow Baby. unabr. ed. Margaret Forster. Read by Phyllida Law. 12 cass. (Running Time: 12 hrs.). 1999. 96.95 (978-0-7540-0283-3(7), CAB1706) AudioGO.

Shadow Baby. unabr. ed. Alison McGhee. Narrated by Christina Moore. 5 cass. (Running Time: 6 hrs. 45 mins.). 2001. 45.00 (978-0-7887-5209-4(X), 96537E7) Recorded Bks.
Tales shimmering with shrewd truth & wild imaginings. From a missing father, sister & grandfather & a mother who won't explain.

Shadow Behind Somoza see Sombras Nada Mas

Shadow Boxing: The Dynamic 2-5-14 Strategy to Defeat the Darkness Within. Henry Malone. Read by Carol Cavazos. Frwd. by Jack Taylor. (Running Time: 18000 sec.). (ENG.). 2006. audio compact disk 29.95 (978-0-9717065-3-8(0)) Pub: Vis life. Dist(s): STL Dist NA

Shadow-Boxing: 1 Cor. 9:19-27. Ed Young. 1986. 4.95 (978-0-7417-1501-2(5), 501) Win Walk.

Shadow Catcher. unabr. ed. Michelle Pav... Read by Anna Bentick. 13 CDs. (Isis Ser.). (J). 2003. audio compact di... 95 (978-0-7531-1729-3(0)) Pub: ISIS Lrg Prnt GBR. Dist(s): Ulverscroft US

Shadow Catcher. unabr. ed. Marianne Wiggins. Read by Bernadette Dunne. 8 CDs. 2007. audio compact disk 79.95 (978-0-7927-4893-9(X)) AudioGO.

Shadow Catcher: A Spellbinding Novel about Families, Secrets & Dreams. unabr. ed. Michelle Paver. 12 cass. (Isis Ser.). (J). 2003. 94.95 (978-0-7531-1610-4(3)) Pub: ISIS Lrg Prnt GBR. Dist(s): Ulverscroft US

***Shadow Chaser.** unabr. ed. Alexey Pehov. (Running Time: 16 hrs.). (Chronicles of Siala Ser.). 2011. audio compact disk 34.99 (978-1-4418-1443-2(4), 9781441814432, Bril Audio CD Unabri) Brilliance Audio.

Shadow Chronicles. collector's ltd. ed. Featuring Bill Johnstone. 5 vols. (Running Time: 5 hrs.). (Limited Edition Chronical Ser.). 1999. bk. 39.95 (978-1-55569-823-2(9), OTR49500) Pub: Great Am Audio. Dist(s): AudioGO

Shadow Chronicles. collector's ltd. ed. Perf. by Orson Welles et al. Intro. by Gertrude Chandler Warner. 5 vols. (Running Time: 5 hrs.). (Limited Edition Chronical Ser.). 2002. bk. 39.95 (978-1-55569-822-5(0), OTR43500) Radio Spirits.
Radio's most popular mystery man made his debut on September 26, 1937 and thrilled and chilled listeners until December 26, 1954. In addition to eight original radio broadcasts, this collection also includes a fascinating 60-minute Shadow audio documentary featuring more than 60 rare clips of the actors, writers and directors from the series.

Shadow Command. abr. ed. Dale Brown. Read by Phil Gigante. (Running Time: 6 hrs.). 2009. audio compact disk 14.99 (978-1-4233-2443-0(9), 9781423324430, BCD Value Price) Brilliance Audio.

Shadow Command. unabr. ed. Dale Brown. Read by Phil Gigante. (Running Time: 13 hrs.). 2008. 39.25 (978-1-4233-2441-6(2), 9781423324416, BADLE); 24.95 (978-1-4233-2440-9(4), 9781423324409, BAD) Brilliance Audio.

Shadow Command. unabr. ed. Dale Brown & Dale Brown. Read by Phil Gigante. 9 CDs. (Running Time: 46800 sec.). 2008. audio compact disk 36.95 (978-1-4233-2436-2(6), 9781423324362, Bril Audio CD Unabri); audio compact disk 24.95 (978-1-4233-2438-6(2), 9781423324386, Brilliance MP3); audio compact disk 39.25 (978-1-4233-2439-3(0), 9781423324393, Brlnc Audio MP3 Lib); audio compact disk 97.25 (978-1-4233-2437-9(4), 9781423324379, BriAudCD Unabrid) Brilliance Audio.

Shadow Country: A New Rendering of the Watson Legend. unabr. ed. Peter Matthiessen. Read by Anthony Heald. (Running Time: 38 hrs. 50 mins.). (ENG.). 2009. 59.95 (978-1-4332-7897-6(9)) Blckstn Audio.

Shadow Country: A New Rendering of the Watson Legend, Pt. A. unabr. ed. Peter Matthiessen. Read by Anthony Heald. (Running Time: 38 hrs. 50 mins.). (ENG.). 2009. 105.95 (978-1-4332-7893-8(6)); audio compact disk 125.00 (978-1-4332-7894-5(4)) Blckstn Audio.

Shadow Country: A New Rendering of the Watson Legend, Pt. B. unabr. ed. Peter Matthiessen. Read by Anthony Heald. (Running Time: 38 hrs. 50 mins.). (ENG.). 2009. 89.95 (978-1-4332-8765-7(X)); audio compact disk 120.00 (978-1-4332-8766-4(8)) Blckstn Audio.

Shadow Dance. Julie Garwood. Read by Joyce Bean. (Playaway Adult Fiction Ser.). (ENG.). 2009. 64.99 (978-1-60775-688-0(9)) Find a World.

Shadow Dance. abr. ed. Julie Garwood. Read by Joyce Bean. (Running Time: 21600 sec.). 2007. audio compact disk 14.99 (978-1-4233-0644-3(9), 9781423306443, BCD Value Price) Brilliance Audio.

Shadow Dance. unabr. ed. Julie Garwood. Read by Joyce Bean. (Running Time: 9 hrs.). 2006. 39.25 (978-1-59710-879-9(0), 9781597108799, BADLE); 24.95 (978-1-59710-878-2(2), 9781597108782, BAD); audio compact disk 36.95 (978-1-59086-260-5(0), 9781590862605, Bril Audio CD Unabri); 74.25 (978-1-59086-258-2(9), 9781590862582, BrilAudUnabridg); audio compact disk 92.25 (978-1-59086-261-2(9), 9781590862612, BriAudCD Unabrid); audio compact disk 39.25 (978-1-59335-819-8(9), 9781593358198, Brlnc Audio MP3 Lib); audio compact disk 24.95 (978-1-59335-685-9(4), 9781593356859, Brilliance MP3) Brilliance Audio.
Please enter a Synopsis.

Shadow Dance: Understanding Repetitive Patterns in Relationships. Rebeca E. Eigen. 1 cass. (Running Time: 1 hr.). 2000. (978-0-9709258-2-4(4)) Libra Press.
Cassette of a video presentation on the shadow, a concept of C.G. Jung's, an unconscious aspect of everyone.

Shadow Dance Vol. 1: Understanding Repetitive Patterns in Relationships. Rebeca E. Eigen. 1 cass. (Running Time: 1 hr.). 1998. (978-0-9709258-0-0(8)) Libra Press.
Live presentation based on C.G. Jung's theories of the shadow, an unconscious aspect of everyone.

Shadow Divers: The True Adventure of Two Americans Who Risked Everything to Solve One of the Last Mysteries of World War II. abr. ed. Robert Kurson. Read by Campbell Scott. 5 CDs. (Running Time: 6 hrs.). (ENG.). 2005. audio compact disk 14.99 (978-0-7393-2083-9(1)) Pub: Random Audio Pubg. Dist(s): Random

Shadow Dragons. unabr. ed. James A. Owen. Read by James Langton. (Running Time: 11 hrs. 0 mins. 0 sec.). (Chronicles of the Imaginarium Geographica Ser.). (ENG.). (YA). 2009. audio compact disk 34.99 (978-0-7435-8374-9(4)) Pub: S&S Audio. Dist(s): S and S Inc

***Shadow Effect: Illuminating the Hidden Power of Your True Self.** unabr. ed. Deepak Chopra et al. Read by Deepak Chopra & Marianne Williamson. 2010. (978-0-06-199308-4(5), Harper Audio); (978-0-06-199307-7(7), Harper Audio) HarperCollins Pubs.

Shadow Effect: Illuminating the Hidden Power of Your True Self. unabr. ed. Deepak Chopra et al. Read by Deepak Chopra & Marianne Williamson. 2010. audio compact disk 29.99 (978-0-06-198850-9(2), Harper Audio) HarperCollins Pubs.

Shadow Falls. unabr. ed. Claire Lorrimer. Read by Judith Boyd. 6 cass. (Running Time: 9 hrs.). 1996. 54.95 (978-1-86042-125-9(3), 21253) Pub: Soundings Ltd GBR. Dist(s): Ulverscroft US
After Samantha & Greg's wedding celebration, he is seen in the company of a mysterious woman. A stranger is lurking around, & Samantha begins to fear for her new marriage & for herself.

Shadow Game. Michael Underwood. Read by Gordon Griffin. 6 cass. (Running Time: 6 hrs.). 1999. 54.95 (68564) Pub: Soundings Ltd GBR. Dist(s): Ulverscroft US

Shadow Hunter. unabr. ed. Geoffrey Archer. Read by Bill Wallis. 10 cass. (Running Time: 15 hrs.). 2000. 84.95 (978-0-7540-0532-2(1), CAB 1955) Pub: Chivers Audio Bks GBR. Dist(s): AudioGO
HMS Truculent is a nuclear-powered, hunter-killer submarine & one of the most deadly weapon systems in the world. Phil Hitchems is a distinguished British commander, who has broken away from a NATO exercise & embarked on his own darkly vengeful & deadly mission.

***Shadow Hunter.** unabr. ed. Pat Murphy. (Running Time: 9 hrs. 0 mins.). 2010. 29.95 (978-1-4332-2001-2(6)); 59.95 (978-1-4332-1997-9(2)); audio compact disk 90.00 (978-1-4332-1998-6(0)) Blckstn Audio.

Shadow in Renegade Basin. Les Savage. (Running Time: 1 hr. 24 mins.). 1999. 10.95 (978-1-60083-488-2(4)) Iofy Corp.

***Shadow in Renegade Basin.** Les Savage, Jr. 2009. (978-1-60136-412-8(1)) Audio Holding.

Shadow in the North. Philip Pullman. Read by Anton Lesser. (Playaway Children Ser.). (J). 2008. 59.99 (978-1-60640-680-9(9)) Find a World.

Shadow in the North. Philip Pullman. Read by Anton Lesser. 6 cass. (Sally Lockhart Ser.: Bk. 2). 2004. 40.00 (978-1-4000-8971-0(9), Listening Lib) Random Audio Pubg.

Shadow in the North. unabr. ed. Philip Pullman. Read by Anton Lesser. (Sally Lockhart Ser.: Bk. 2). (ENG.). (J). (gr. 7). 2008. audio compact disk 50.00 (978-0-7393-7152-7(5), Listening Lib) Pub: Random Audio Pubg. Dist(s): Random

Shadow in the Sands. Sam Llewellyn. Read by Richard Heffer. 8 CDs. (Running Time: 9 hrs. 39 mins.). (Isis (CDs) Ser.). (J). 2004. audio compact disk 79.95 (978-0-7531-2277-8(4)) Pub: ISIS Lrg Prnt GBR. Dist(s): Ulverscroft US

Shadow in the Sands. unabr. ed. Sam Llewellyn. Read by Richard Heffer. 10 cass. (Running Time: 15 hrs.). (Isis Ser.). (J). 2001. 84.95 (978-0-7531-0907-6(7), 001212) Pub: ISIS Lrg Prnt GBR. Dist(s): Ulverscroft US

Shadow Issues in the Daughter's Father Complex. Julia Jewett. Read by Julia Jewett. 2 cass. (Running Time: 2 hrs. 15 min.). 1991. 18.95 (978-0-7822-0381-3(7), 469) C G Jung IL.
This workshop explores the shadowy dynamics in the relationship between father & daughter, using fairy tale & art therapy techniques as ways to imaginally enter this often mysterious bond.

Shadow Killer. unabr. ed. Matthew Scott Hansen. Read by William Dufris. 14 CDs. (Running Time: 15 hrs. 0 mins. 0 sec.). (ENG.). 2007. audio compact disk 39.99 (978-1-4001-0325-6(8)); audio compact disk 29.99 (978-1-4001-5325-1(5)); audio compact disk 79.99 (978-1-4001-3325-3(4)) Pub: Tantor Media. Dist(s): IngramPubServ

Shadow Kingdoms. Robert E. Howard. (Running Time: 6 mins.). 2009. audio compact disk 29.95 (978-1-897304-12-9(9)) Dorch Pub Co.

Shadow Kingdoms. Robert E. Howard. (Running Time: 19800 sec.). (Weird Works of Robert E. Howard). 2007. audio compact disk 19.95 (978-0-8095-6227-5(8)) Pub: Wildside. Dist(s): Diamond Book Dists

Shadow Kingdoms, Vol. 1. unabr. ed. Robert E. Howard. Read by Brian Holsopple et al. Prod. by Fred Godsmark. 5 CDs. (Running Time: 19800 sec.). (Weird Works of Robert E. Howard). 2007. audio compact disk 29.95 (978-0-8095-6228-2(6)) Pub: Wildside. Dist(s): Diamond Book Dists

Shadow Knight of Darkness. Perf. by Orson Welles et al. (ENG.). 2008. audio compact disk 35.95 (978-1-57019-872-4(1)) Radio Spirits.

Shadow Leader. unabr. ed. Tara K. Harper. Read by Karen White Eyes. 10 cass. (Running Time: 15 hrs.). 2001. 80.00 (978-0-7366-8095-0(0)) Books on Tape.
Dion, her wolf Gray Hishn, and their friends have just escaped from slavers, and are trying to return home so that they can warn their people about the likelihood of impending war. Dion and her wolf share a telepathic bond. Together, they are superior scouts of terrain, and her wolf amplifies Dion's healing abilities so that together, they can heal people wholly. Nonetheless, they face many battles as they make their way. There is much gritty fighting that needs doing, many frozen mountains that need to be traversed, and enemy agents scour the countryside for the group that includes them. Now, Dion's abilities may make her stand out and bring harm to her friends.

Shadow-Line. Joseph Conrad. Narrated by Fred Williams. (Running Time: 5 hrs. 30 mins.). 2004. 24.95 (978-1-59912-714-9(8)) Iofy Corp.

Shadow-Line. Joseph Conrad & Fred Williams. 2002. 23.95 (978-0-7861-2716-0(3)) Blckstn Audio.

Shadow-Line. unabr. ed. Joseph Conrad. Read by Fred Williams. (Running Time: 5 hrs. 30 mins.). 2004. 24.95 (978-0-7861-8574-0(0)); audio compact disk 32.00 (978-0-7861-8638-9(0)) Blckstn Audio.

Shadow-Line. unabr. ed. Joseph Conrad. Read by Fred Williams. (YA). 2008. 39.99 (978-1-60514-920-2(9)) Find a World.

***Shadow Lines.** unabr. ed. Amitav Ghosh. (Running Time: 11 hrs.). 2010. 24.99 (978-1-4418-3510-9(5), 9781441835109, BAD); 39.97 (978-1-4418-3511-6(3), 9781441835116, BADLE) Brilliance Audio.

***Shadow Lines.** unabr. ed. Amitav Ghosh. Read by Raj Varma. (Running Time: 10 hrs.). 2010. 24.99 (978-1-4418-3508-6(3), 9781441835086, Brilliance MP3); 39.97 (978-1-4418-3509-3(1), 9781441835093, Brinc Audio MP3 Lib); audio compact disk 29.99 (978-1-4418-3506-2(7), 9781441835062, Bril Audio CD Unabri); audio compact disk 89.97 (978-1-4418-3507-9(5), 9781441835079, BriAudCD Unabrid) Brilliance Audio.

Shadow Lost Shows. ltd. ed. 5 vols. (Running Time: 5 hrs.). (Limited Edition Chronical Ser.). 2003. bk. 39.95 (978-1-55569-952-9(9), OTR49503) Pub: Great Am Audio. Dist(s): AudioGO

Shadow Lost Shows. ltd. ed. Read by The Shadow Staff. 5 vols. (Running Time: 5 hrs.). (Limited Edition Chronical Ser.). 2002. bk. (978-1-55569-950-5(2), OTR43503) Radio Spirits.
The Lost Shows features 10 original radio programs available for the first time in more than 50 years. This special collector's set includes the long-lost premier broadcast of The ShadowTM, which first introduced radio listeners to the characters of Lamont Cranston and Margot Lane and gave the young Orson Welles his first starring role in a radio series.

Shadow Man. John Katzenbach. Read by Stacy Keach. 2004. 10.95 (978-0-7435-4598-3(2)) Pub: S&S Audio. Dist(s): S and S Inc

***Shadow Market: How a Group of Wealthy Nations & Powerful Investors Secretly Dominate the World.** unabr. ed. Eric Weiner. (Running Time: 9 hrs. 0 mins. 0 sec.). 2010. 24.99 (978-1-4001-6893-4(7)); 15.99 (978-1-4001-8893-2(8)); audio compact disk 34.99 (978-1-4001-1893-9(X)) Pub: Tantor Media. Dist(s): IngramPubServ

***Shadow Market (Library Edition) How a Group of Wealthy Nations & Powerful Investors Secretly Dominate the World.** unabr. ed. Eric J. Weiner. (Running Time: 9 hrs. 0 mins. 0 sec.). (ENG.). 2010. audio compact disk 83.99 (978-1-4001-4893-6(6)) Pub: Tantor Media. Dist(s): IngramPubServ

Shadow Men. unabr. ed. Jonathon King. Read by David Colacci. (Running Time: 7 hrs.). (Max Freeman Ser.: No. 3). 2004. 29.95 (978-1-59355-306-7(4), 1593553064, BAU); 69.25 (978-1-59355-307-4(2), 1593553072, BrilAudUnabridg); audio compact disk 29.95 (978-1-59355-308-1(0), 1593553080, Bril Audio CD Unabri); audio compact disk 87.25 (978-1-59355-309-8(9), 1593553099, BriAudCD Unabrid) Brilliance Audio.
It begins with an 80-year-old mystery. Three men - a father and his two sons - vanished while working as laborers on a dangerous project to build the first road through the Florida Everglades. Now, years later, a series of letters are unexpectedly discovered by a descendent of these men. Driven by the need to know what happened to these lost members of the family, he starts asking questions - and is quickly stonewalled. With nowhere else to turn, he enlists the help of former Philadelphia police officer Max Freeman. Living in his isolated shack in the Glades, Max starts his longshot investigation into the fate of the men. A newly minted private investigator working with his friend and attorney, Billy Manchester, Max is surprised to meet resistance immediately at every turn. The search for the truth quickly turns violent - and Max finds he has more to worry about than just 80-year-old ghosts. For there are powerful interests that want to make sure that the shadows of the past remain undisturbed - including some who will kill to make sure they do.

Shadow Men. unabr. ed. Jonathon King. Read by David Colacci. (Running Time: 7 hrs.). (Max Freeman Ser.: No. 3). 2004. 39.25 (978-1-59335-545-6(9), 1593355459, Brinc Audio MP3 Lib); 24.95 (978-1-59335-289-9(1), 1593352891, Brilliance MP3) Brilliance Audio.

Shadow Men. unabr. ed. Jonathon King. Read by David Colacci. (Running Time: 7 hrs.). (Max Freeman Ser.). 2004. 39.25 (978-1-59710-690-0(9), 1597106909, BADLE); 24.95 (978-1-59710-691-7(7), 1597106917, BAD) Brilliance Audio.

Shadow Music. abr. ed. Julie Garwood. Read by Davina Porter. (ENG.). 2008. audio compact disk 14.99 (978-0-7393-8235-6(7)) Pub: Random Audio Pubg. Dist(s): Random

Shadow Music. unabr. ed. Julie Garwood. Read by Rosalyn Landor. (Running Time: 41400 sec.). (ENG.). 2007. audio compact disk 44.95 (978-0-7393-5758-3(1), Random AudioBks); audio compact disk 100.00 (978-1-4159-4338-0(9), BksonTape) Pub: Random Audio Pubg. Dist(s): Random
For Princess Gabrielle of St. Biel, Scotland is a land of stunning vistas, wild chieftains, treacherous glens, and steep shadows - skulduggery, betrayal, and now murder. Prized for her exquisite beauty, the daughter of one of England's most influential barons, Gabrielle is also a perfect bargaining chip for a king who needs peace in the Highlands: King John has arranged Gabrielle's marriage to a good and gentle laird. But this marriage will never take place. For Gabrielle, everything changes in one last burst of freedom - when she and her guards come upon a scene of unimaginable cruelty. With one shot from her bow and arrow, Gabrielle takes a life, saves a life, and begins a war. Within days, the Highlands are aflame with passions as a battle royal flares between enemies old and new. Having come to Scotland to be married, Gabrielle is instead entangled in Highland intrigue. For two sadistic noblemen, underestimating Gabrielle's bravery and prowess may prove fatal. But thanks to a secret Gabrielle possesses, Colm MacHugh, the most feared man in Scotland, finds a new cause for courage. Under his penetrating gaze, neither Gabrielle's body nor heart is safe.

Shadow of a Bull. Maia Wojciechowska. Read by Francisco Rivela. 2 cass. (J). 13.58 Blisterpack. (BYA 934) NewSound.
Manolo Olivar, son of the greatest bullfighter in Spain, looks just like his father, & is expected to repeat his success. But he knows he does not have the courage a bullfighter needs. Caught up in the plans to prepare him for the bullring, Manolo struggles to retain his pride, self-respect & independence - struggles that boys everywhere must face.

Shadow of a Bull. unabr. ed. Maia Wojciechowska. Read by Francisco Rivela. 2 cass. (Running Time: 2 hrs.). (J). 1997. 23.00 (LL0097) AudioGO.

Shadow of a Bull. unabr. ed. Maia Wojciechowska. Read by Rita Moreno. 2 cass. (J). 1986. 15.95 (978-0-89845-544-1(8), A 2094) HarperCollins Pubs.

Shadow of a Bull, unabr. ed. Maia Wojciechowska. Read by Francisco Rivela. 2 cass. (Running Time: 2 hrs.). (YA). 1999. 16.98 (FS9-31555) Highsmith.

Shadow of a Bull. unabr. ed. Maia Wojciechowska. Read by Francisco Rivela. 2 vols. (Running Time: 3 hrs. 34 mins.). (J). (gr. 4-7). 1997. pap. bk. 29.00 (978-0-8072-7851-2(3), YA934SP, Listening Lib); 23.00 (978-0-8072-7850-5(5), YA934CX, Listening Lib) Random Audio Pubg.
Manolo Olivar is the son of the greatest bullfighter in Spain. He does not have the urge to fight that a bullfighter needs. Manolo struggles to maintain his pride & independence.

Shadow of a Doubt. Perf. by Joseph Cotton & Jeff Chandler. 1946. (DD-8405) Natl Recrd Co.

Shadow of a Noose. Ralph Compton. 4 cass. (Running Time: 6 hrs.). 2001. 24.95 (978-1-890990-71-8(X)) Otis Audio.
One year after their sister rode off to avenge their father's death, Tim & Jed Strange are on the brink of losing the family farm. They head west hoping to find their sister, but find trouble instead. Accused of a murder they didn't commit, they're on the run & seeking the true killers.

Shadow of Clorinda. abr. ed. Katrina Wright. Read by Vivian Younger. 2 cass. (Running Time: 3 hrs.). 1994. 24.95 (978-1-85496-213-3(2), 62132) Pub: UlverLrgPrint GBR. Dist(s): Ulverscroft US

Shadow of Death. Alison Joseph & Julia Franklin. 2008. 61.95 (978-1-84652-113-3(0)); audio compact disk 79.95 (978-1-84652-114-0(9)) Pub: Magna Story GBR. Dist(s): Ulverscroft US

Shadow of Death, unabr. collector's ed. William X. Kienzle. Read by Edward Holland. 7 cass. (Running Time: 10 hrs. 30 min.). (Father Koesler Mystery Ser.: No. 5). 1999. 56.00 (978-0-7366-4330-6(3), 4824) Books on Tape.
A cardinal is murdered in his own church. Another is slain in the Vatican. A clue - the black imprint of a clenched fist - is left at the scene of each crime. Who's behind these sinister attacks? And is the ultimate target the Holy Office of the Pope himself? On a detective's trail from Detroit to Dublin to Rome, Father Koesler, the ferreting father, plunges back into his own haunted past - & becomes a candidate for assassination.

Shadow of Doubt. Terri Blackstock. Narrated by John McDonough. 9 cass. (Running Time: 12 hrs. 30 mins.). (Newpointe 911 Ser.: Vol. 1). 82.00 (978-0-7887-9904-4(5)) Recorded Bks.

***Shadow of Doubt.** Terri Blackstock. (Running Time: 11 hrs. 12 mins. 0 sec.). (Newpointe 911 Ser.). (ENG.). 2009. 14.99 (978-0-310-30491-3(1)) Zondervan.

Shadow of Doubt. Amy Maida Wadsworth. 3 cass. 2004. 14.95 (978-1-59156-221-4(X)) Covenant Comms.

Shadow of Doubt. unabr. ed. Terri Blackstock. Read by Juanita Parker. 10 CDs. (Running Time: 11 hrs.). 2001. audio compact disk 65.00 (978-1-58116-116-8(6)) Books in Motion.
Defense attorney Jill Clark's client, accused of the arsenic poisoning of her husband, harbors a guilty past. Clark can't quite decide if her client's Christian faith is a sham, or if evidence points to a game of deadly frame-up.

Shadow of Doubt. unabr. ed. Terri Blackstock. Read by Juanita Parker. 8 cass. (Running Time: 11 hrs.). (Newpointe 911 Ser.: Bk. 2). 2001. 49.95 (978-1-58116-077-2(1)) Books in Motion.

***Shadow of Fu Manchu.** RadioArchives.com. (Running Time: 675). (ENG.). 2010. audio compact disk 29.98 (978-1-61081-008-1(2)) Radio Arch.

Shadow of Heaven: Hebrews 8:1-6. 1992. 4.95 (978-0-7417-1902-7(9), 901) Win Walk.

Shadow of His Wings. unabr. ed. Gilbert Morris. Read by Maynard Villers. 8 cass. (Running Time: 9 hrs. 30 min.). (Appomattox Ser.: Bk. 6). 1998. 49.95 (978-1-55686-840-5(5)) Books in Motion.
Lowell Rocklin, who has lost his leg in battle, finds the inspiration to continue.

***Shadow of Power.** unabr. ed. Steve Martini. Read by George Guidall. (ENG.). 2008. (978-0-06-163237-2(6)); (978-0-06-163238-9(4)) HarperCollins Pubs.

Shadow of Power. unabr. ed. Steve Martini. Read by George Guidall. (Running Time: 48600 sec.). (Paul Madriani Ser.: No. 9). 2008. audio compact disk 44.95 (978-0-06-145306-9(4), Harper Audio) HarperCollins Pubs.

Shadow of Saganami. unabr. ed. David Weber. Read by Jay Snyder. (Running Time: 31 hrs.). (Honorverse Ser.). 2009. 44.97 (978-1-4233-9541-6(7), 9781423395416, Brinc Audio MP3 Lib); 29.99 (978-1-4233-9540-9(9), 9781423395409, Brilliance MP3); 44.97 (978-1-4233-9542-3(5), 9781423395423, BADLE); audio compact disk 49.99 (978-1-4233-9538-6(7), 9781423395386, Bril Audio CD Unabri); audio compact disk 99.97 (978-1-4233-9539-3(5), 9781423395393, BriAudCD Unabrid) Brilliance Audio.

Shadow of Silver Tip. unabr. ed. Max Brand. Read by Buck Schirner. (Running Time: 28800 sec.). 2007. audio compact disk 24.95 (978-1-4233-3499-6(X), 9781423334996, Brilliance MP3) Brilliance Audio.

Shadow of Silver Tip. unabr. ed. Max Brand. Read by Buck Schirner. (Running Time: 8 hrs.). 2007. 39.25 (978-1-4233-3502-3(3), 9781423335023, BADLE); 24.95 (978-1-4233-3501-6(5), 9781423335016, BAD); audio compact disk 39.25 (978-1-4233-3500-9(7), 9781423335009, Brinc Audio MP3 Lib) Brilliance Audio.

Shadow of Silver Tip. unabr. ed. Max Brand. Read by Buck Schirner. (Running Time: 9 hrs.). 2009. audio compact disk 19.99 (978-1-4418-0479-2(X), 9781441804792, Bril Audio CD Unabri); audio compact disk 59.97 (978-1-4418-0480-8(3), 9781441804808, BriAudCD Unabrid) Brilliance Audio.

Shadow of the Almighty. Elisabeth Elliot. Read by Elisabeth Elliot. 5 cass. (Running Time: 5 hrs.). 1989. 22.95 (978-0-8474-2005-6(1)) Back to Bible.
Discusses the story of the authors life with missionary Jim Elliot in the jungles of the Amazon.

Shadow of the Almighty. unabr. ed. Elisabeth Elliot. Read by Elisabeth Elliot. 8 cass. (Running Time: 11 hrs. 30 mins.). 2003. 56.95 (978-0-7861-0750-6(2), 1600) Blckstn Audio.
Jim Elliot & four other young men sat together on a strip of white sand on the Curaray River, deep in Ecuador's rain forest, waiting for the arrival of a group of men whom they loved, but had never met - savage Stone Age killers, men now known to all the world as Aucas. The circumstances of the death of these men are by now known throughout the world in one of the great missionary adventure stories of modern times. But this is the first account of the whole life of one of them - a tremendous biography of an adventurous & inspirational life.

***Shadow of the Almighty: The Life & Testament of Jim Elliot.** unabr. ed. Elisabeth Elliot. Read by Elisabeth Elliot. (Running Time: 11 hrs. 5 mins.). (ENG.). 2011. 29.95 (978-1-4417-8419-3(5)); audio compact disk 100.00 (978-1-4417-8417-9(9)) Blckstn Audio.

Shadow of the Bull. Maia Waiciechowska. Read by Francisco Rivela. 2 cass. (Running Time: 3 hrs. 30 mins.). (J). 2000. 18.00 (978-0-7366-9163-5(4)) Books on Tape.
Manolo Olivar, son of the greatest bullfighter in Spain, who struggles to retain his pride, self-respect & independence.

Shadow of the Eagle. unabr. ed. Richard Woodman. Read by Stephen Thorne. 8 cass. (Running Time: 12 hrs.). (Nathaniel Drinkwater Ser.: Bk. 13). 2000. 59.95 (978-0-7540-0108-9(3), CAB 1531) Pub: Chivers Audio Bks GBR. Dist(s): AudioGO
It is 1814 and Napoleon has abdicated as Emperor of France. Although King Louis XVII returns from exile, discontented Bonapartists plot to restore the eagle whose shadow still lies across Europe. At the service of the king, Captain Nathaniel Drinkwater receives news of an imminent threat to the peace. Seizing the opportunity, Drinkwater steps out of retirement to risk his life for his country.

Shadow of the Giant. abr. ed. Orson Scott Card. 4 cass. (Running Time: 6 hrs.). (Shadow Ser.). 2002. 25.00 (978-1-57453-493-1(9)) Audio Lit.
Describes the relentlessly brutal education of Andrew "Ender" Wiggin, a preadolescent military genius believed to be humankind's last, best hope against the anticipated invasion of an insectile race of aliens called the Formics. As the novel opens, the Formics, popularly known as "the Buggers", have already made two unsuccessful attempts to conquer and colonize Earth, and xenophobia now runs rampant, temporarily uniting a wide range of political and ideological factions. Ender, together with a handpicked group of gifted, if slightly less brilliant children, is conscripted and sent to a remote space station called the Battle School, where he participates in a series of war games that prepare him, by the age of 9, for the responsibilities of military command. Eventually, the games turn real, and Ender leads his youthful forces to a bitter and ironic "victory" over the Buggers.

Shadow of the Giant. unabr. ed. Orson Scott Card. Read by Scott Brick & Gabrielle De Cuir. 2 pieces. (Shadow Ser.). 2005. 49.95 (978-0-7927-3709-4(1), CMP 827); 79.95 (978-0-7927-3707-0(5), CSL 827); audio compact disk 112.95 (978-0-7927-3708-7(3), SLD 827) AudioGO.

Shadow of the Giant, No. 4. unabr. rev. ed. Orson Scott Card. Read by David Birney et al. Ed. by Beth Meacham. 9 CDs. (Running Time: 12 hrs. 0 mins. 0 sec.). (Ender's Shadow Ser.). (ENG.). 2005. audio compact disk 39.95 (978-1-59397-496-1(5)) Pub: Macmill Audio. Dist(s): Macmillan

Shadow of the Giant: Ender's shadow. unabr. ed. Geraldine Brooks. Read by Richard Easton. 9 CDs. 2005. audio compact disk 89.95 (978-0-7927-3488-8(2), SLD 760) AudioGO.

Shadow of the Grizzly. unabr. ed. Larry Jay Martin. Read by Maynard Villers. 6 cass. (Running Time: 6 hrs. 48 min.). 2001. 39.95 (978-1-55686-965-5(7)) Books in Motion.
For Clint Ryan, his San Joaquin Valley ranch is a land of hope and promise. But the isolated spread seems like easy pickings to the vicious Stokes boys. And stalking Clint's land is an even greater threat - a massive and elusive grizzly called Twotoes.

Shadow of the Hegemon. unabr. ed. Orson Scott Card. Read by David Birney et al. 11 CDs. (Running Time: 13 hrs. 0 mins. 0 sec.). (Shadow Ser.). (ENG.). 2006. audio compact disk 44.95 (978-1-59397-480-0(9)) Pub: Macmill Audio. Dist(s): Macmillan

Shadow of the Lynx. unabr. ed. Victoria Holt. Read by Lin Sagovsky. 10 cass. (Running Time: 10 hrs.). 1998. 84.95 Set. (978-0-7540-0103-4(2), CAB1526) AudioGO.
Arriving in Australia, Nora Tamasin found herself under the guardianship of Charles Herrick, known as the Lynx. The search for gold has obsessed everyone, including the Lynx, because it was necessary for his plan of revenge. Nora is overwhelmed & fascinated by the Lynx, finding herself involved in his evil schemes.

Shadow of the Lynx, unabr. ed. Victoria Holt. Narrated by Virginia Leishman. 10 cass. (Running Time: 14 hrs. 30 mins.). 1997. 85.00 (978-0-7887-0852-7(X), 94998E7) Recorded Bks.
Recently orphaned, beautiful young Nora Tamasin leaves her home in Victorian England & sails to Australia to live with her guardian, the Lynx, a man who can safeguard her finances, but cannot control her heart.

Shadow of the Lynx. unabr. collector's ed. Victoria Holt. Read by Donada Peters. 9 cass. (Running Time: 13 hrs. 30 min.). 1994. 72.00 (978-0-7366-2892-1(4), 3592) Books on Tape.
Spirited Nora Tamasin can't help being seduced by the power of a strange man called Lynx...or falling in love with his son.

Shadow of the Moon, Pt. 1. unabr. collector's ed. M. M. Kaye. Read by Kate Reading. 12 cass. (Running Time: 18 hrs.). 1998. 96.00 (978-0-7366-4127-2(0), 4631-A) Books on Tape.
A beautiful heiress returns to the British Raj where she falls in love with her handsome protector.

Shadow of the Moon, Pt. 2. unabr. collector's ed. M. M. Kaye. Read by Kate Reading. 10 cass. (Running Time: 15 hrs.). 1998. 80.00 (978-0-7366-4128-9(9), 4631-B) Books on Tape.

Shadow of the Mountains: Cheney Duvall. unabr. ed. Lynn Morris & Gilbert Morris. Narrated by Kate Forbes. 9 cass. (Running Time: 12 hrs.). 2000. 81.00 (978-0-7887-4319-1(8), 96007E7) Recorded Bks.
Dr. Cheney Duvall takes her medical skills to the Ozark Mountains of Arkansas, where a pregnant friend needs medical care. But when Cheney extends her help to the mountain people, superstition & family fueding become constant obstacles & Cheney's own well-being is quickly threatened.

Shadow of the Other: A Critical Look at the New Age. unabr. ed. Richard Grossinger. 2 cass. 1987. 18.00 Set. (978-1-56964-770-7(4), A0305-87) Sound Photosyn.

Shadow of the Past. Judith Cutler. 2009. 61.95 (978-0-7531-3948-6(0)); audio compact disk 84.95 (978-0-7531-3949-3(9)) Pub: Isis Pubng Ltd GBR. Dist(s): Ulverscroft US

Shadow of the Pomegranate. unabr. ed. Jean Plaidy & Anne Flosnik. (Running Time: 12 hrs. 5 mins.). 2008. 29.95 (978-1-4332-5344-7(5)); 72.95 (978-1-4332-5341-6(0)); audio compact disk 90.00 (978-1-4332-5342-3(9)) Blckstn Audio.

Shadow of the Protector. Elizabeth Lord. 5 cass. (Running Time: 6 hrs. 35 mins.). (Story Sound Ser.). (J). 2005. 49.95 (978-1-85903-837-6(9)) Pub: Mgna Lrg Print GBR. Dist(s): Ulverscroft US

Shadow of the Raven. Concept by Joseph Vargo. Composed by Joseph Vargo. Composed by William Piotrowski. Engineer William Piotrowski. Nox Arcana. 2007. audio compact disk 13.99 (978-0-9788857-3-1(2)) Monolith.

Shadow of the Silk Road. Colin Thubron. Read by Jonathan Keeble. (Running Time: 47100 sec.). 2007. 84.95 (978-0-7531-3702-4(X)); audio compact disk 99.95 (978-0-7531-2716-2(4)) Pub: ISIS Audio GBR. Dist(s): Ulverscroft US

Shadow of the Sun, unabr. ed. A. S. Byatt. Read by Frances Jeater. 10 cass. (Running Time: 12 hrs. 30 min.). (Isis Ser.). (J). 2001. 84.95 (978-1-85695-858-5(2), 941110) Pub: ISIS Lrg Prnt GBR. Dist(s): Ulverscroft US

Shadow of Your Cross. Contrib. by Joel Engle. (Praise Hymn Soundtracks Ser.). 2006. audio compact disk 8.98 (978-5-558-47746-7(6)) Pt of Grace Ent.

Shadow of Your Smile. abr. ed. Mary Higgins Clark. Read by Jan Maxwell. 5 CDs. (Running Time: 5 hrs.). 2010. audio compact disk 29.99 (978-1-4423-0023-1(X)) Pub: S&S Audio. Dist(s): S and S Inc

***Shadow of Your Smile.** unabr. ed. Mary Higgins Clark. Narrated by Jan Maxwell. 8 cass. (Running Time: 9 hrs.). 2010. 67.75 (978-1-4407-9347-9(6)); audio compact disk 92.75 (978-1-4407-9348-6(4)) Recorded Bks.

***Shadow of Your Smile.** unabr. ed. Mary Higgins Clark. Narrated by Jan Maxwell. 1 Playaway. (Running Time: 9 hrs.). 2010. 59.75 (978-1-4407-9350-9(6)) Recorded Bks.

Shadow of Your Smile. unabr. ed. Mary Higgins Clark. Read by Jan Maxwell. 8 CDs. (Running Time: 9 hrs. 0 mins. 0 sec.). 2010. audio compact disk 39.99 (978-1-4423-0025-5(6)) Pub: S&S Audio. Dist(s): S and S Inc

***Shadow of Your Smile.** unabr. collector's ed. Mary Higgins Clark. Narrated by Jan Maxwell. 8 CDs. (Running Time: 9 hrs.). 2010. audio compact disk 44.95 (978-1-4407-9349-3(2)) Recorded Bks.

***shadow on the Glass.** unabr. ed. Ian Irvine. Read by Grant Cartwright. (Running Time: 21 hrs. 36 mins.). (View from the Mirror Ser.). 2010. audio compact disk 123.95 (978-1-74214-718-5(6), 9781742147185) Pub: Bolinda Pubng AUS. Dist(s): Bolinda Pub Inc

***shadow on the Glass.** unabr. ed. Ian Irvine. Read by Grant Cartwright. (Running Time: 21 hrs. 36 mins.). (view from the Mirror Ser.). 2010. 54.95 (978-1-74214-767-3(4), 9781742147673) Pub: Bolinda Pubng AUS. Dist(s): Bolinda Pub Inc

Shadow on the Snow. Anne Schraff. Narrated by Larry A. McKeever. (Standing Tall 2 Mystery Ser.). (J). 2000. audio compact disk 14.95 (978-1-58659-272-1(6)) Artesian.

Shadow on the Snow. unabr. ed. Anne Schraff. Narrated by Larry A. McKeever. 1 cass. (Running Time: 40 min.). (Standing Tall 2 Mystery Ser.). (J). 2000. 10.95 (978-1-58659-098-7(7), 54138) Artesian.

Shadow over Babylon. unabr. ed. David Mason. Read by Steven Pacey. 14 cass. (Running Time: 21 hrs.). 2000. 89.95 (978-0-7451-4244-9(3), CAB 927) Pub: Chivers Audio Bks GBR. Dist(s): AudioGO
In early 1992, nine men entered Saudi Arabia illegally. Almost three weeks later, they secretly crossed the border into Iraq. Their mission was to assassinate President Sadam Hussei. Did they succeed? Did they survive? And did it really happen?.

Shadow over Innsmouth. unabr. ed. Adapted by Gregory Nicoll. Featuring Berl Boykin et al. 1 cass. (Running Time: 90 min.). Dramatization. 2002. 12.95 (978-0-929483-33-7(2)) Centauri Express Co.
There is something wrong in the decayed seacoast town of Innsmouth. Something wrong in the crumbling buildings. Something wrong in the cold deep waters.

Shadow over Second. unabr. ed. Matt Christopher. Narrated by Kerin McCue. 1 cass. (Running Time: 1 hr.). (Peach Street Mudders Ser.). (gr. 2 up). 1998. 10.00 (978-0-7887-1115-2(6), 95109E7) Recorded Bks.
Nicky Chong is very superstitious when it comes to playing baseball. To make matters worse, someone has locked him in the shed for the second to last game of the season. He puts together all the clues left behind & the reasons why.

***Shadow Pass: A Novel of Suspense.** unabr. ed. Sam Eastland. (ENG.). 2011. audio compact disk 35.00 (978-0-307-87666-9(7), Random AudioBks) Pub: Random Audio Pubg. Dist(s): Random

***Shadow People: An Audio Exclusive Adventure.** Scott Handcock. Narrated by Elisabeth Sladen. (Running Time: 1 hr. 0 mins. 0 sec.). (ENG.). 2011. audio compact disk 24.95 (978-1-4084-2669-2(2)) Pub: AudioGO. Dist(s): Perseus Dist

Shadow, Persona & the Contrasexual. Read by James Wyly. 1 cass. (Running Time: 2 hrs.). 1987. 12.95 (978-0-7822-0334-9(5), 263) C G Jung IL.

***Shadow Play.** (ENG.). 2010. audio compact disk (978-1-59171-267-1(X)) Falcon Picture.

Shadow Play. unabr. ed. Frances Fyfield. Read by Rula Lenska. 8 cass. (Running Time: 8 hrs.). (Prosecutor Helen West Mysteries Ser.). 1994. 69.95 (978-0-7451-4232-6(X), CAB 915) AudioGO.
Time after time the sinister Mr. Logo eludes the accusations of numerous crimes with acquittals. Prosecuter Helen West has been trying to convict him for some time, but now overwhelmed by personal & professional problems, West takes a break from the case. Suddenly, she is pulled into a maze of violence & fear, where Logo & his grubby world somehow divide & rule.

Shadow Play. unabr. ed. Frances Fyfield. Read by Rula Lenska. 8 cass. (Running Time: 12 hrs.). (West & Bailey Mystery Ser.). 2000. 59.95 (CAB 915) Pub: Chivers Audio Bks GBR. Dist(s): AudioGO

***Shadow Prey.** abr. ed. John Sandford, pseud. Read by Ken Howard. 2006. (978-0-06-122894-0(X), Harper Audio) HarperCollins Pubs.

Shadow Prey. abr. ed. John Sandford, pseud. Read by Ken Howard. 2 cass. (Running Time: 3 hrs.). (Prey Ser.). 2000. 7.95 (978-1-57815-054-0(X), 1036, Media Bks Audio) Media Bks NJ.
Twin Cities Detective Lucas Davenport teams up with NYPD Lt. Lily Rothenberg to track down an elusive serial killer, known only as Shadow Love.

Shadow Prowler. unabr. ed. Alexey Pehov. Read by MacLeod Andrews. 1 MP3-CD. (Running Time: 15 hrs.). (Chronicles of Siala Ser.). 2010. 24.99 (978-1-4418-1439-5(6), 9781441814395, Brilliance MP3); 24.99 (978-1-4418-1441-8(8), 9781441814418, BAD); 39.97 (978-1-4418-1440-1(X), 9781441814401, Brlnc Audio MP3 Lib); 39.97 (978-1-4418-1442-5(6), 9781441814425, BADLE); audio compact disk 29.99 (978-1-4418-1437-1(X), 9781441814371, Bril Audio CD Unabri); audio compact disk 99.97 (978-1-4418-1438-8(8), 9781441814388, BriAudCD Unabrid) Brilliance Audio.

Shadow Puppets. unabr. ed. Orson Scott Card. Read by David Birney et al. 9 CDs. (Running Time: 11 hrs. 0 mins. 0 sec.). (Shadow Ser.). (ENG.). 2007. audio compact disk 39.95 (978-1-59397-482-4(5)) Pub: Macmill Audio. Dist(s): Macmillan

Shadow Riders. abr. ed. Terry C. Johnston. Read by Dick Wilkinson. 2002. 25.00 (978-1-59183-001-6(X)) Pub: Otis Audio. Dist(s): Lndmrk Audiobks

Shadow Rising. abr. ed. Robert Jordan. Read by Mark Rolston. 2 cass. (Running Time: 3 hrs.). (Wheel of Time Ser.: Bk. 4). 1992. 15.95 (978-1-879371-30-9(8), 40130) Pub Mills.
The Dark One sends evil to touch the Dragon Reborn. Must he die in the forbidden city of Rhuidean?.

Shadow Rising. unabr. rev. ed. Robert Jordan. Read by Kate Reading & Michael Kramer. 34 CDs. (Running Time: 43 hrs. 0 mins. 0 sec.). (Wheel of Time Ser.: Bk. 4). (ENG.). 2004. audio compact disk 89.95 (978-1-59397-535-7(X)) Pub: Macmill Audio. Dist(s): Macmillan

Shadow Rising, Pt. 1. unabr. ed. Robert Jordan. Read by Michael Kramer & Kate Reading. 14 cass. (Running Time: 21 hrs.). (Wheel of Time Ser.: Bk. 4). 1997. 112.00 (978-0-7366-3679-7(X), 4359-A) Books on Tape.
The seals of Shayol Ghul have weakened, & the Dark One reaches out. The shadow is rising to cover humankind. Can he be stopped.

Shadow Rising, Pt. 2. unabr. ed. Robert Jordan. Read by Michael Kramer & Kate Reading. 15 cass. (Running Time: 22 hrs. 30 min.). (Wheel of Time Ser.: Bk. 4). 1997. 120.00 (978-0-7366-3680-3(3), 4359-B) Books on Tape.

Shadow Ruler of Your Chart. Pat Strickland. 1 cass. 8.95 (465) Am Fed Astrologers.
An AFA Convention workshop tape.

Shadow Side of Every Day Life. Jeremiah Abrams. 2 cass. (Running Time: 2 hrs.). 1992. 18.00 (OC319-69) Sound Horizons AV.

Shadow Soldier. unabr. ed. C. K. Crigger. Read by Stephanie Brush. 8 cass. (Running Time: 11 hrs. 30 min.). (Time Travel Gunsmith Ser.: Bk. 2). 2001. 49.95 (978-1-58116-025-3(9)) Books in Motion.
Boothenay Irons possesses a mysterious power that allows her to go back in time and experience the history held with an antique gun. Boothenay must go back to 1918, where her fiancee Caleb is trapped on a WWI battlefield.

Shadow Song. Terry Kay. 2004. 10.95 (978-0-7435-4599-0(0)) Pub: S&S Audio. Dist(s): S and S Inc

Shadow Song, unabr. ed. Terry Kay. Narrated by George Guidall. 8 cass. (Running Time: 11 hrs. 30 mins.). 1999. 70.00 (978-0-7887-0299-0(8), 94492E7) Recorded Bks.
Fifty-five-year-old Madison Lee "Bobo" Murphy returns to the breath-taking beauty of the Catskill Mountains to settle the estate of a long-time friend. Bobo once again hears the dreams of his youth, a strange & beautiful music calling him from his marriage, his career & his home toward a love larger than himself.

Shadow Spinner, unabr. ed. Susan Fletcher. Narrated by Suzanne Toren. 5 pieces. (Running Time: 6 hrs. 30 mins.). (gr. 6 up). 1999. 46.00 (978-0-7887-2977-5(2), 95747E7) Recorded Bks.
As a serving girl helps the beautiful Shahrazad find new tales to tell the Sultan, a new chapter in the poor girl's life begins. Listeners of all ages will love this fresh view of the ancient collection of 1001 tales.

Shadow Spinner. unabr. ed. Susan Fletcher. Read by Suzanne Toren. 5 cass. (Running Time: 6 hrs. 30 mins.). (J). (gr. 5). 1999. pap. bk. & stu. ed. 59.24 (978-0-7887-3007-8(X), 40889) Recorded Bks.

Shadow Spinner. unabr. ed. Susan Fletcher. Narrated by Suzanne Toren. 1 CD. (J). 2000. audio compact disk 58.00 (C1200W5) Recorded Bks.

Shadow Spinner. unabr. ed. Susan Fletcher. Narrated by Suzanne Toren. 6 CDs. (Running Time: 6 hrs. 30 mins.). (gr. 6 up). 2001. audio compact disk 58.00 (978-0-7887-4649-9(9), C1200E7) Recorded Bks.

Shadow Spinner, Class Set. unabr. ed. Susan Fletcher. Read by Suzanne Toren. 5 cass. (Running Time: 6 hrs. 30 mins.). (J). 1999. 116.70 (978-0-7887-3037-5(1), 46854) Recorded Bks.

***Shadow Tag: A Novel.** unabr. ed. Louise Erdrich. Read by Coleen Marlo. (ENG.). 2010. (978-0-06-195363-7(6), Harper Audio); (978-0-06-196763-4(7), Harper Audio) HarperCollins Pubs.

Shadow Warriors: Inside the Special Forces. Tom Clancy et al. Read by Jonathan Marosz. 2002. 120.00 (978-0-7366-8875-8(7)) Books on Tape.

Shadow Warriors: Inside the Special Forces. unabr. ed. Tom Clancy. Read by Carl Stiner. 2002. 64.00 (978-0-7366-8591-7(X)) Books on Tape.

Shadow Warriors: Inside the Special Forces. unabr. ed. Tom Clancy & Carl Steiner. 14 cass. (Running Time: 22 hrs. 30 min.). 2002. 64.00 (978-0-7366-8438-5(7)) Books on Tape.
Teams of dedicated, highly specialized soldiers trained to a higher standard than regular forces; an armamentarium of advanced weapons and tactics; a variety of exotic, critical assignments for the good of the nation; in short, the U.S.

Shadow Warriors Pts. A & B: Inside the Special Forces. unabr. ed. Tom Clancy et al. Read by Jonathon Marosz. 18 CDs. (Running Time: 22 hrs. 30 mins.). 2002. audio compact disk 144.00 (978-0-7366-8619-8(3)) Books on Tape.

Shadow Watch, abr. ed. Read by J. K. Simmons. Created by Tom Clancy & Martin Greenberg. 2 cass. (Tom Clancy's Power Plays Ser.: No. 3). 1999. 18.00 (FS9-51095) Highsmith.

***Shadow Wolf.** Kathryn Lasky. (ENG.). 2010. audio compact disk 49.99 (978-0-545-25502-8(3)) Scholastic Inc.

***Shadow Wolf.** Kathryn Lasky. Narrated by Erik Davies. (ENG.). 2010. audio compact disk 29.99 (978-0-545-25501-1(5)) Scholastic Inc.

Shadow Woman. unabr. ed. Thomas Perry. Narrated by Joyce Bean. (Running Time: 14 hrs. 30 mins. 0 sec.). (Jane Whitefield Ser.). (ENG.). 2009. audio compact disk 79.99 (978-1-4001-4024-4(2)) Pub: Tantor Media. Dist(s): IngramPubServ

Shadow Woman. unabr. abr. ed. Thomas Perry. Narrated by Joyce Bean. (Running Time: 14 hrs. 30 mins. 0 sec.). (Jane Whitefield Ser.). (ENG.). 2009. audio compact disk 39.99 (978-1-4001-1024-7(6)); audio compact disk 29.99 (978-1-4001-6024-2(3)) Pub: Tantor Media. Dist(s): IngramPubServ

Shadow Women. Angela Elwell Hunt. 12 cass. (Running Time: 16 hrs. 45 mins.). 2002. 98.00 (978-1-4025-3607-6(0)) Recorded Bks.

***Shadow Zone.** abr. ed. Iris Johansen & Roy Johansen. (Running Time: 6 hrs.). 2010. 14.99 (978-1-4418-8423-7(8), 9781441884237, BAD) Brilliance Audio.

***Shadow Zone.** abr. ed. Iris Johansen & Roy Johansen. Read by Jennifer Van Dyck. 5 CDs. (Running Time: 6 hrs.). 2010. audio compact disk 24.99 (978-1-4418-8422-0(X), 9781441884220, BACD) Brilliance Audio.

***Shadow Zone.** unabr. ed. Iris Johansen & Roy Johansen. (Running Time: 11 hrs.). 2010. 24.99 (978-1-4418-8420-6(3), 9781441884206, BAD); 39.97 (978-1-4418-8421-3(1), 9781441884213, BADLE) Brilliance Audio.

***Shadow Zone.** unabr. ed. Iris Johansen & Roy Johansen. Read by Jennifer Van Dyck. 1 MP3-CD. (Running Time: 11 hrs.). 2010. 24.99 (978-1-4418-8418-3(1), 9781441884183, Brilliance MP3); 39.97 (978-1-4418-8419-0(X), 9781441884190, Brlnc Audio MP3 Lib); audio compact disk 36.99 (978-1-4418-8416-9(5), 9781441884169, Bril Audio CD Unabri); audio compact disk 97.97 (978-1-4418-8417-6(3), 9781441884176, BriAudCD Unabrid) Brilliance Audio.

Shadowcatchers: A Journey in Search of the Teachings of Native American Healers. abr. ed. Steve Wall. Read by Apesanahkwat et al. 2 cass. (Running Time: 3 hrs.). 1996. 17.95 (978-1-57453-006-3(2), 330062) Audio Lit.
Join "National Geographic" photographer Steve Wall as he seeks out Native American elders, tribal leaders, healers, high priests & sorcerers.

***Shadowfever.** unabr. ed. Karen Marie Moning. Read by Natalie Ross and Phil Gigante. (Running Time: 22 hrs.). (Fever Ser.). 2011. 29.99 (978-1-4233-4216-8(X), 9781423342168, Brilliance MP3); 44.97 (978-1-4233-4217-5(8), 9781423342175, Brlnc Audio MP3 Lib) Brilliance Audio.

***Shadowfever.** unabr. ed. Karen Marie Moning. Read by Natalie Ross & Phil Gigante. (Running Time: 22 hrs.). (Fever Ser.). 2011. audio compact disk 34.99 (978-1-4233-4214-4(3), 9781423342144) Brilliance Audio.

***Shadowfever.** unabr. ed. Karen Marie Moning. Read by Natalie Ross and Phil Gigante. (Running Time: 22 hrs.). (Fever Ser.). 2011. audio compact disk 92.97 (978-1-4233-4215-1(1), 9781423342151, BriAudCD Unabrid) Brilliance Audio.

Shadowfires. unabr. ed. Leigh Nichols, pseud. Read by Jonathan Marosz. 11 cass. (Running Time: 16 hrs. 30 min.). 1994. 88.00 (978-0-7366-2699-6(9), 3433) Books on Tape.
He died in a hideous accident. Or is he alive, watching her, stalking her, seeking revenge, at her very door?.

Shadowfires. unabr. ed. Leigh Nichols, pseud. Read by Sandra Burr. (Running Time: 18 hrs.). 2008. 29.95 (978-1-4233-5131-3(2), 9781423351313,

Brilliance MP3); 29.95 (978-1-4233-5133-7(9), 9781423351337, BAD); 44.25 (978-1-4233-5134-4(7), 9781423351344, BADLE); audio compact disk 122.25 (978-1-4233-5130-6(4), 9781423351306, BriAudCD Unabrid); audio compact disk 46.95 (978-1-4233-5129-0(0), 9781423351290, Bril Audio CD Unabri) Brilliance Audio.

Shadowfires. unabr. ed. Leigh Nichols, pseud & Dean Koontz. Read by Sandra Burr. (Running Time: 18 hrs.). 2008. 44.25 (978-1-4233-5132-0(0), 9781423351320, Brinc Audio MP3 Lib) Brilliance Audio.

***Shadowheart: Shadowmarch: Volume IV.** unabr. ed. Tad Williams. (Running Time: 25 hrs.). (Shadowmarch Ser.). 2010. 39.97 (978-1-4418-9125-9(0), 9781441891259, BADLE); 24.99 (978-1-4418-9124-2(2), 9781441891242, BAD) Brilliance Audio.

***Shadowheart: Shadowmarch: Volume IV.** unabr. ed. Tad Williams. Read by Dick Hill. (Running Time: 33 hrs.). (Shadowmarch Ser.). 2010. 27.99 (978-1-4418-9122-8(6), 9781441891228, Brilliance MP3); 39.97 (978-1-4418-9123-5(4), 9781441891235, Brinc Audio MP3 Lib); audio compact disk 99.97 (978-1-4418-9121-1(8), 9781441891211, BriAudCD Unabrid); audio compact disk 39.99 (978-1-4418-9120-4(X), 9781441891204, Bril Audio CD Unabri) Brilliance Audio.

Shadowland. unabr. ed. Jenny Carroll, pseud. Narrated by Johanna Parker. 5 cass. (Running Time: 6 hrs.). (Mediator Ser.: Bk. 1). (J). (gr. 3-7). 2005. bk. 68.99 (978-1-4193-4144-1(8), 42055); 52.75 (978-1-4193-4142-7(1), 98045) Recorded Bks.

Meg Cabot is the New York Times best-selling author of The Princess Diaries series. Susannah Simon is a teenager who can see ghosts. As a bridge between the living and the dead, she gets called on to help ghosts take care of unfinished business. After she and her mother move from New York City to sunny California, Suze meets the sexiest boy she's ever seen - too bad he's a ghost, too.

Shadowland. unabr. ed. Alyson Noël. Read by Katie Schorr. (Running Time: 9 hrs. 30 mins. 0 sec.). (Immortals Ser.: Bk. 3). (ENG., (YA). (gr. 7-12). 2009. audio compact disk 17.99 (978-1-4272-0884-2(0)) Pub: Macmill Audio. Dist(s): Macmillan

Shadowlands. William Nicholson. Perf. by Harriet Harris. 2 CDs. (Running Time: 1 hr. 44 mins.). (L. A. Theatre Works). 2002. audio compact disk 25.95 (978-1-58081-246-7(5), CDTPT159) Pub: L A Theatre. Dist(s): NetLibrary CO

Shadowlands. William Nicholson. Perf. by Harriet Harris & Martin Jarvis. 2 cass. (Running Time: 1 hr. 44 mins.). 2002. 23.95 (978-1-58081-241-2(4), TPT159) L A Theatre.

The story of shy Oxford don and children's author C.S. Lewis and American poet Joy Gresham. Shows the love, and the risk of loss, transformed this great man's relationships, even with God.

Shadowlands. abr. ed. Brian Sibley. Read by Joss Ackland. 2 cass. (Running Time: 3 hrs.). 1998. 16.85 Set. (978-0-00-104796-9(5)) Ulvrscrft Audio.

In the summer of 1952 C.S. Lewis met Hoy Gresham, a 37 year old Christian convert taking time out from an unfaithful husband; & so began one of the most unlikely & beautiful love stories of all times.

***Shadowmaker.** Roy Lewis & Martyn Waites. 2010. 64.95 (978-1-84652-928-3(X)); audio compact disk 71.95 (978-1-84652-929-0(8)) Pub: Magna Story GBR. Dist(s): Ulverscroft US

Shadowmaker. unabr. ed. Joan Lowery Nixon. Narrated by Stina Nielsen. 4 pieces. (Running Time: 5 hrs. 15 mins.). (gr. 10 up). 2001. 36.00 (978-0-7887-5185-1(9), 96360E7) Recorded Bks.

A tale of the evil that lurks in the shadows of a seemingly ordinary town.

Shadowmancer. G. P. Taylor. 4 cass. (Running Time: 7 hrs.). (J). (gr. 5 up). 2004. 36.00 (978-1-4000-8518-7(7), Listening Lib) Random Audio Pubg.

***Shadowmarch: Shadowmarch: Volume I.** unabr. ed. Tad Williams. (Running Time: 28 hrs.). (Shadowmarch Ser.). 2010. 24.99 (978-1-4418-9106-8(4), 9781441891068, BAD); 39.97 (978-1-4418-9107-5(2), 9781441891075, BADLE) Brilliance Audio.

***Shadowmarch: Shadowmarch: Volume I.** unabr. ed. Tad Williams. Read by Dick Hill. (Running Time: 29 hrs.). (Shadowmarch Ser.). 2010. 27.99 (978-1-4418-9104-4(8), 9781441891044, Brilliance MP3); 39.97 (978-1-4418-9105-1(6), 9781441891051, Brinc Audio MP3 Lib); audio compact disk 39.99 (978-1-4418-9102-0(1), 9781441891020, Bril Audio CD Unabri); audio compact disk 99.97 (978-1-4418-9103-7(X), 9781441891037, BriAudCD Unabrid) Brilliance Audio.

***Shadowplay: Shadowmarch: Volume II.** unabr. ed. Tad Williams. (Running Time: 29 hrs.). (Shadowmarch Ser.). 2010. 24.99 (978-1-4418-9112-9(9), 9781441891129, BAD); 39.97 (978-1-4418-9113-6(7), 9781441891136, BADLE); 27.99 (978-1-4418-9110-5(2), 9781441891105, Brilliance MP3) Brilliance Audio.

***Shadowplay: Shadowmarch: Volume II.** unabr. ed. Tad Williams. Read by Dick Hill. (Running Time: 30 hrs.). (Shadowmarch Ser.). 2010. 39.97 (978-1-4418-9111-2(0), 9781441891112, Brinc Audio MP3 Lib); audio compact disk 39.99 (978-1-4418-9108-2(0), 9781441891082, Bril Audio CD Unabri); audio compact disk 99.97 (978-1-4418-9109-9(9), 9781441891099, BriAudCD Unabrid) Brilliance Audio.

***Shadowrise: Shadowmarch: Volume III.** unabr. ed. Tad Williams. (Running Time: 25 hrs.). (Shadowmarch Ser.). 2010. 27.99 (978-1-4418-9116-7(1), 9781441891167, Brilliance MP3); 24.99 (978-1-4418-9118-1(8), 9781441891181, BAD); 39.97 (978-1-4418-9119-8(6), 9781441891198, BADLE) Brilliance Audio.

***Shadowrise: Shadowmarch: Volume III.** unabr. ed. Tad Williams. Read by Dick Hill. (Running Time: 25 hrs.). (Shadowmarch Ser.). 2010. 39.97 (978-1-4418-9117-4(X), 9781441891174, Brinc Audio MP3 Lib); audio compact disk 39.99 (978-1-4418-9114-3(5), 9781441891143, Bril Audio CD Unabri); audio compact disk 99.97 (978-1-4418-9115-0(3), 9781441891150, BriAudCD Unabrid) Brilliance Audio.

Shadows. unabr. ed. John Saul. Read by J. Charles. (Running Time: 12 hrs.). 2005. 39.25 (978-1-59737-605-1(1), 9781597376051, BADLE); 24.95 (978-1-59737-604-4(3), 9781597376044, BAD); audio compact disk 36.95 (978-1-59737-600-6(0), 9781597376006, Bril Audio CD Unabri); audio compact disk 24.95 (978-1-59737-602-0(7), 9781597376020, Brilliance MP3); audio compact disk 102.25 (978-1-59737-601-3(9), 9781597376013, BriAudCD Unabrid); audio compact disk 39.25 (978-1-59737-603-7(5), 9781597376037, Brinc Audio MP3 Lib) Brilliance Audio.

From the author of fifteen consecutive New York Times bestsellers, comes a tale of evil genius that illustrates the most horrifying powers of a dark mind. Housed in a clifftop mansion overlooking the Pacific coast, "The Academy" is a school for special children. Children gifted with extraordinary minds. Children soon to become influenced by and ultimately the victims of, a mind even more brilliant than their own. By all appearances, some of the most brilliant students at the Academy have committed suicide. But as wiz kid Josh McCallum begins to realize what is really happening to the children around him, he also realizes that no one will believe him. To save his friends from the shadows, he must pit his superior intellect against a mind so powerful and so evil, it seems that nothing may prevail against it.

Shadows. unabr. ed. Jacqueline West. (ENG.). 2010. audio compact disk 29.95 (978-0-14-314571-4(1), PengAudBks) Penguin Grp USA.

Shadows among Us: Discovering the path to spiritual liberation & Wholeness. Robin M. Bertram. 2008. audio compact disk 44.99 (978-1-60604-735-4(3)) Tate Pubng.

Shadows & Strongholds. Elizabeth Chadwick. 14 cass. (Soundings Ser.). (J). 2005. 99.95 (978-1-84283-981-2(0)); audio compact disk 109.95 (978-1-84559-002-4(3)) Pub: ISIS Lrg Prnt GBR. Dist(s): Ulverscroft US

Shadow's Edge. unabr. ed. Brent Weeks. Narrated by Paul Boehmer. (Running Time: 20 hrs. 30 mins. 0 sec.). (Night Angel Trilogy: Bk. 2). (ENG.). 2009. 34.99 (978-1-4001-6287-1(4)); audio compact disk 49.99 (978-1-4001-1287-6(7)); audio compact disk 99.99 (978-1-4001-4287-3(3)) Pub: Tantor Media. Dist(s): IngramPubServ

***Shadow's Edge, Pt. 1 of 2.** Brent Weeks. (Night Angel Trilogy: Bk. 2). 2010. audio compact disk 19.99 (978-1-59950-669-2(6)) GraphicAudio.

***Shadow's Edge, Pt. 2 of 2** Brent Weeks. (Night Angel Trilogy: Bk. 2). 2010. audio compact disk 19.99 (978-1-59950-677-7(7)) GraphicAudio.

Shadows in Bronze. Lindsey Davis. (Running Time: 3 hrs. 0 mins. 0 sec.). (ENG.). 2009. audio compact disk 29.95 (978-1-60283-752-2(X)) Pub: AudioGO. Dist(s): Perseus Dist

Shadows in Bronze. unabr. ed. Lindsey Davis. Narrated by Donal Donnelly. 12 cass. (Running Time: 18 hrs. 15 mins.). (Marcus Didius Falco Ser.). 1992. 97.00 (978-1-55690-728-9(1), 92223E7) Recorded Bks.

The setting is Rome, A.D. 70. Marcus Didius Falco, "gumshoe" in a toga, tries to unravel the complicates caused by the death of the traitor Pertinax.

Shadows in the Jungle: The Alamo Scouts Behind Japanese Lines in World War II. unabr. ed. Larry Alexander. Read by Norman Dietz. (Running Time: 11 hrs. 30 mins. 0 sec.). (ENG.). 2009. audio compact disk 34.99 (978-1-4001-1055-1(6)); audio compact disk 24.99 (978-1-4001-6055-6(3)); audio compact disk 69.99 (978-1-4001-4055-8(2)) Pub: Tantor Media. Dist(s): IngramPubServ

Shadows in the Twilight. Henning Mankell. Read by Francis Greenslade. (Running Time: 4 hrs. 55 mins.). (Joel Gustafson Stories). (J). 2009. 64.99 (978-1-74214-412-2(8), 9781742144122) Pub: Bolinda Pubng AUS. Dist(s): Bolinda Pub Inc

Shadows in the Twilight. unabr. ed. Henning Mankell. Read by Francis Greenslade. (Running Time: 4 hrs. 55 mins.). (Joel Gustafson Stories). (J). 2008. audio compact disk 63.95 (978-1-74214-002-5(5), 9781742140025) Pub: Bolinda Pubng AUS. Dist(s): Bolinda Pub Inc

Shadows in Their Blood. Marian Babson. Read by Diana Bishop. 2003. 54.95 (978-0-7540-8366-5(7)) Pub: Chivers Audio Bks GBR. Dist(s): AudioGO

Shadows of Glory. Owen Parry. Read by Paul Boehmer. 2001. 64.00 (978-0-7366-6031-0(3)) Books on Tape.

Shadows of Limitation. Kenneth Wapnick. 4 CDs. 2005. audio compact disk 25.00 (978-1-59142-179-5(9), CD107) Foun Miracles.

Shadows of Power. unabr. ed. Jennifer Bacia. Read by Melissa Eccleston. 6 cass. (Running Time: 11 hrs. 5 mins.). 2004. 48.00 (978-1-74030-162-6(5), 500848) Pub: Bolinda Pubng AUS. Dist(s): Lndmrk Audiobks

***Shadows of Power.** unabr. ed. James W. Huston. (Running Time: 15 hrs.). 2010. 29.95 (978-1-4417-5673-2(6)); 65.95 (978-1-4417-5669-5(8)); audio compact disk 29.95 (978-1-4417-5672-5(8)); audio compact disk 100.00 (978-1-4417-5670-1(1)) Blckstn Audio.

Shadows of Steel. unabr. ed. Dale Brown. Read by Edward Lewis. 9 cass. (Running Time: 13 hrs. 30 mins.). 2000. 72.00 (978-0-7366-5444-9(5), 5315) Books on Tape.

A new Gulf War is erupting. A newly powerful Iran is flexing its military muscle in the Middle East. The Iranians have declared the Persian Gulf their territorial waters, and an American ship has just been sunk to prove the point. With a military wracked by budget cuts and a public reluctant to fight, the president must end the crisis before it escalates. The solutions: Project Future Flight, a surgical stealth campaign to silence Iran's modern weapons. The personnel: Colonel Patrick McLanahan and the surviving crew of the Old Dog. The stakes: success or full-scale war.

Shadows of the Canyon. abr. ed. Tracie Peterson. Read by Sandra Burr. (Running Time: 10800 sec.). (Desert Roses Ser.: Vol. 1). 2002. audio compact disk 24.95 (978-1-4233-0413-5(6), 9781423304135, Brilliance MP3) Brilliance Audio.

Tracie Peterson will captivate her legion of readers with this romantic historical novel of loss and love, longing and fulfillment. Working as a Harvey Girl at the luxury resort El Tovar, located on the south rim of the Grand Canyon, Alexandra Keegan feels she is in a dream come true. But when her father's indiscretions come to light and her mother is suspected of murder, Alex finds herself the center of some unwelcome attention. Will she soon find herself alone in the world?.

Shadows of the Canyon. abr. ed. Tracie Peterson. Read by Sandra Burr. 2 cass. (Running Time: 3 hrs.). (Desert Roses Ser.: Vol. 1). 2002. 17.95 (978-1-59086-683-2(5), 1590866835); 44.25 (978-1-59086-684-9(3), 1590866843); audio compact disk 24.95 (978-1-59086-685-6(1), 1590866851); audio compact disk 62.25 (978-1-59086-686-3(X), 159086686X) Brilliance Audio.

Shadows of the Canyon. abr. ed. Tracie Peterson. Read by Sandra Burr. (Running Time: 3 hrs.). (Desert Roses Ser.: Vol. 1). 2006. 39.25 (978-1-4233-0416-6(0), 9781423304166, BADLE); 24.95 (978-1-4233-0415-9(2), 9781423304159, BAD); 39.25 (978-1-4233-0414-2(4), 9781423304142, Brinc Audio MP3 Lib) Brilliance Audio.

Shadows of the Female Self. Joan Chamberlain Engelsman. Read by Joan Chamberlain Engelsman. 1 cass. (Running Time: 90 min.). 1987. 10.95 (978-0-7822-0063-8(X), 242) C G Jung IL.

Shadows of the Voice. Earnest Robson & Larry Wendt. 12.00 Primary Pr.

Includes: a phonetic symphony "Voices in the Rivers", a phonetic dirge "Requiem for Lost Sperm", & five text sound compositions "It Takes All of A Kind", "Azure", "Elegy for F.T. Marinetti" & "Disco" & "OK Corral".

Shadows of the Workhouse. Jennifer Worth. 2009. 76.95 (978-1-4079-0274-6(1)); audio compact disk 84.95 (978-1-4079-0275-3(X)) Pub: Soundings Ltd GBR. Dist(s): Ulverscroft US

***Shadows of Yesterday.** Sandra Brown. 2010. audio compact disk 9.99 (978-1-4418-5702-6(8)) Brilliance Audio.

Shadows of Yesterday. unabr. ed. Sandra Brown. Read by Joyce Bean. (Running Time: 6 hrs.). 2005. 39.25 (978-1-59710-692-4(5), 9781597106924, BADLE); 24.95 (978-1-59710-693-1(3), 9781597106931, BAD); 24.95 (978-1-59355-908-3(9), 9781593559083, BAU); 24.95 (978-1-59335-767-2(5), 9781593357672, Brilliance MP3); 39.25 (978-1-59335-901-0(2), 9781593359010, Brinc Audio MP3 Lib); 62.25 (978-1-59355-909-0(7), 9781593559090, BriAudUnabridg); audio compact disk 74.25 (978-1-59355-911-3(9), 9781593559113, BriAudCD Unabrid) Brilliance Audio.

Leigh...She was terrifyingly alone on a Texas highway about to deliver her first child when a rugged stranger in a pickup truck stopped to help her. Leigh Bransom had lost her husband eight months before when he was tragically killed on the job. Now a fateful meeting on a lonesome highway brought a new man into her life - one with secrets and the power to make her lonely once again. Chad...A man who pursued a dangerous business, Chad Dillon kept his past a mystery. He was determined to make Leigh care for him, but there were no guarantees that his love could protect her from the very thing she feared most.

Shadows of Yesterday. unabr. ed. Sandra Brown. Read by Joyce Bean. (Running Time: 21600 sec.). 2007. audio compact disk 14.99 (978-1-4233-3357-9(8), 9781423333579, BCD Value Price) Brilliance Audio.

Shadows on the Coast of Maine: An Antique Print Mystery. unabr. ed. Lea Wait. Read by Celeste Lawson. 6 CDs. (Running Time: 10 hrs.). 2003. audio compact disk 48.00 (978-0-7861-9144-4(9), 3146); 44.95 (978-0-7861-2513-5(6), 3146) Blckstn Audio.

A spooky house, a gorgeous Maine setting, and some fascinating antique prints provide the perfect ingredients for a riveting new mystery in the series.

Shadows on the Ivy. Lea Wait. Ed. by Celeste Lawson. 6 cass. (Running Time: 8 hrs.). 2004. 44.95 (978-0-7861-2837-2(2), 3369); audio compact disk 56.00 (978-0-7861-8338-8(1), 3369) Blckstn Audio.

Shadows on the Ivy. Lea Wait. Narrated by Nadia May. (Running Time: 13 hrs.). (C). 2004. 32.95 (978-1-59912-590-9(0)) Iofy Corp.

Shadows on the Rock: Women, Violence, & the Church. Read by Joan Chamberlain Engelsman. 1 cass. (Running Time: 80 min.). 1991. 10.95 (978-0-7822-0368-4(X), 467) C G Jung IL.

This lecture utilizes the novel Shadows on the Rock by Willa Cather to help illustrate the shadow of Christianity, as reflected by the problems confronting women & the staggering statistics of family violence. Part of the conference set Gold in Dark Places: Shadow Work in the Struggle for Selfhood.

Shadows on the Sea. unabr. ed. 3 cass. (Running Time: 4 hrs. 30 min.). (J). 2004. 28.00 (978-1-4025-7015-5(5)) Recorded Bks.

Shadows on the Sun. Michael Jan Friedman. (Star Trek Ser.). 2004. 10.95 (978-0-7435-4674-4(1)) Pub: S&S Audio. Dist(s): S and S Inc

Shadows on the Sun. Kathryn Haig. 12 cass. (Soundings Ser.). (J). 2005. 94.95 (978-1-84283-906-5(3)) Pub: ISIS Lrg Prnt GBR. Dist(s): Ulverscroft US

Shadows on the Wall see Wind in the Rose Bush & Other Stories of the Supernatural

Shadows on the Wall. 1982. (S-45) Jimcin Record.

Shadows Over Stonewycke. unabr. ed. Michael R. Phillips & Judith Pella. Narrated by Davina Porter. 13 cass. (Running Time: 18 hrs. 15 mins.). (Stonewycke Legacy Ser.: No. 2). 2002. 98.00 (978-0-7887-5272-8(3), RG202) Recorded Bks.

With World War II looming on the horizon, Allison and Logan Macintyre's once-idyllic relationship has become a shadow of its former self. With Allison in London, and Logan working as a British spy in France, they are spending more and more time apart. Can their marriage survive with the world at war.

Shadows Still Remain. unabr. ed. Peter de Jonge. Read by Tina Benko. 2009. audio compact disk 29.99 (978-0-06-180496-0(7), Harper Audio) HarperCollins Pubs.

***Shadows Still Remain.** unabr. ed. Peter De Jonge. Read by Tina Benko. (ENG.). 2009. (978-0-06-189657-6(8), Harper Audio); (978-0-06-189656-9(X), Harper Audio) HarperCollins Pubs.

Shadrach's Crossing see Smugglers' Island

Shahid Parvez (Sitar), Vol. 1. Music by Shahid Parvez. 1 cass. (Music Today Presents Ser.). 1992. (A92022) Multi-Cultural Bks.

Shahid Parvez (Sitar), Vol. 2. Music by Shahid Parvez. 1 cass. (Music Today Presents Ser.). 1992. (A92023) Multi-Cultural Bks.

Shake a Leg. Norman Foote. 1 cass. (J). (ps-7). 10.98 (978-0-945267-35-5(5), YM042-CN); audio compact disk 13.98 (978-0-945267-36-2(3), YM042-CD) Youngheart Mus.

Songs include: "Shake a Leg"; "Oodles of Doodles"; "Wonderful Pals"; "Smelly Feet"; "Yard Sale"; "The Bear & the Mountain"; "Eye Spy"; "Bird Tales" "Brand New Shoes"; "Able the Table"; "My Neighbor's Dog" & "Take Us on the Rides.".

Shake & Learn Grammar & Usage. (YA). 2002. spiral bd. 119.95 (978-0-9746001-3-0(X)) Salt Prod Inc.

Shake & Learn Language Arts. 2000. spiral bd. 119.95 (978-0-9746001-0-9(5)) Salt Prod Inc.

Shake & Learn Mathematics. (YA). 2001. spiral bd. 119.95 (978-0-9746001-1-6(3)) Salt Prod Inc.

Shake & Learn Pre-K & K Early Literacy. (YA). 2003. 119.95 (978-0-9746001-4-7(8)) Salt Prod Inc.

Shake & Learn Pre-K & K Mathematics. (YA). 2003. 119.95 (978-0-9746001-5-4(6)) Salt Prod Inc.

Shake & Learn Science. (YA). 2001. spiral bd. 119.95 (978-0-9746001-2-3(1)) Salt Prod Inc.

Shake Hands Forever. unabr. ed. Ruth Rendell. Read by Nigel Anthony. 6 cass. (Running Time: 9 hrs.). (Inspector Wexford Mystery Ser.: Bk. 9). 2000. 49.95 (978-0-7540-0301-4(9), CAB 1724) Pub: Chivers Audio Bks GBR. Dist(s): AudioGO

Wexford could discover no motive, reason or suspect. He was probably reading meaning where there was none; and probably Angela Hathall really had picked up a stranger, and that stranger had killed her. By why such doubt? Was Wexford becoming cynical and untrusting, or was this simply one of the most ingenious crimes he had ever tackled?.

Shake It All About. Perf. by Little Richard. 1 cass. (Running Time: 37 min.). (J). 1992. 9.98 (978-1-55723-378-3(0)); audio compact disk (978-1-55723-380-6(2)) W Disney Records.

Kids will be compelled to dance, sing & clap along to such classics as a zydeco "She'll Be Comin' Around the Mountain" & a very funky rendition of "Zip-a-Dee-Doo-Dah." Parents will also be amused to hear this new twist in the career of another veteran musician who has turned his attention to tomorrow's adults. Featured on paino throughout, Richard brings an infectious humor to these doings. Selections like "Twinkle, Twinkle, Little Star" (to the tune of "Hand Jive") & "Here We Go Loopty-Loo" (with a Caribbean feel) indicate that this artist's strong sense of style may well influence yet another generation.

Shake It, Break It & Hang It on the Wall. abr. ed. Guys' All-Star Shoe Band Staff. Told to Garrison Keillor. 1 CD. (Running Time: 1 hr.). (ENG.). 1996. audio compact disk 16.95 (978-1-56511-263-6(6), 1565112636) Pub: HighBridge. Dist(s): Workman Pub

Shake It to the One That You Love the Best: Play Songs & Lullabies from Black Musical Traditions. Cheryl W. Mattox. 1 cass. (Running Time: 1 hr. 30 mins.). 1989. bk. 15.95 (978-0-9623381-3-7(3)) Warren-Mattox.

Shake It to the One You Love the Best. 1 cass. (J). 1991. 9.98 (978-1-877737-70-1(4), MLP 2211) MFLP CA.

Songs from African, African-American, Creole & Carribean cultures. Jazz, reggae, gospel, rhythm & blues performed by top artists.

Shake It to the One You Love the Best: Play Songs & Lullabies from Black Musical Traditions. (J). bk. 16.98 (661); 9.98 (2211) MFLP CA.

Songs from African, African-American, Creole & Caribbean cultures, in jazz, reggae, gospel, rhythm & blues & classical styles, performed by top artists including Taj Mahal.

Shake off the Dust. Myron Madden & Wilbur Schwartz. 1986. 10.00 (0210A) Assn Prof Chaplains.

Shake, Rattle & Roll - ShowTrax. Perf. by Bill Haley and the Comets Staff. Arranged by Kirby Shaw. 1 CD. (Running Time: 5 mins.). 2000. audio compact disk 19.95 (08201246) H Leonard.
Your guys will love to perform this anthem from rock's early era.

Shake Sugaree. Taj Mahal. 1 cass. (Running Time: 34 min.). (J). (ps up). 1988. 9.98 Norelco. (978-1-877737-01-5(1), MLP 272); audio compact disk 12.98 CD Norelco. (978-1-877737-45-9(3), MLP D 272) MFLP CA.
Music for children.

***Shaken.** unabr. ed. J. A. Konrath. (Running Time: 6 hrs.). (Jacqueline Jack Daniels Ser.). 2010. 9.99 (978-1-61106-329-5(9), 9781611063295, BAD) Brilliance Audio.

***Shaken.** unabr. ed. J. A. Konrath. (Running Time: 6 hrs.). (Jacqueline Jack Daniels Ser.). 2011. 39.97 (978-1-61106-330-1(2), 9781611063301, BADLE) Brilliance Audio.

***Shaken.** unabr. ed. J. A. Konrath. Read by Angela Hill. (Running Time: 6 hrs.). (Jacqueline Jack Daniels Ser.). 2011. 39.97 (978-1-61106-328-8(0), 9781611063288, Brinc Audio MP3 Lib) Brilliance Audio.

***Shaken.** unabr. ed. J. A. Konrath. Read by Dick Hill & Angela Dawe. (Running Time: 6 hrs.). (Jacqueline Jack Daniels Ser.). 2011. 19.99 (978-1-61106-232-8(2), 9781611062328, Brilliance MP3) Brilliance Audio.

***Shaken.** unabr. ed. J. A. Konrath. Read by Angela Dawe. (Running Time: 6 hrs.). (Jacqueline Jack Daniels Ser.). 2011. audio compact disk 69.97 (978-1-61106-231-1(4), 9781611062311, BriAudCD Unabrid) Brilliance Audio.

***Shaken.** unabr. ed. J. A. Konrath. Read by Dick Hill. (Running Time: 6 hrs.). (Jacqueline Jack Daniels Ser.). 2011. audio compact disk 19.99 (978-1-61106-230-4(6), 9781611062304, Bril Audio CD Unabri) Brilliance Audio.

***Shaken & Stirred.** Adapted by Siren Audio Studios. Prod. by Siren Audio Studios. Based on a novel by Lois Cutts Sullivan. (ENG.). 2010. audio compact disk (978-0-9844180-2-2(4)) Siiren Audio.

Shakers at Sabbathday Lake. 1 cass. (Running Time: 1 hr.). 9.00 (H0320B090, HarperThor) HarpC GBR.

Shakespeare see Treasury of Matthew Arnold

Shakespeare. abr. ed. William Shakespeare. 8 cass. Dramatization. Incl. King Lear. (A-424); Macbeth. William Shakespeare. (A-424); Romeo & Juliet. (A-424); Twelfth Night. (A-424); 47.60 (A-424); 9.95 rental. Audio Bk.
Eight of Shakespeare's finest works, in condensed form, are presented by some of England's finest actors.

Shakespeare. unabr. ed. Anthony Holden. Narrated by Paul Matthews. 11 cass. (Running Time: 14 hrs. 30 mins.). 2000. 98.00 (978-1-84197-234-3(7), H1185L8) Recorded Bks.
A racy, incident-packed account of Shakespeare as husband, father, actor, poet & Stratford lad who found subsequent immortality via the stage of Elizabethan London.

Shakespeare. unabr. ed. Anthony Holden. Narrated by Paul Matthews. 11 CDs. (Running Time: 14 hrs. 30 mins.). 2001. audio compact disk 124.00 (978-1-4025-1015-1(2), C1593) Recorded Bks.
Holden's portrayal is a racy, incident-packed account of Shakespeare as husband, father, actor, poet and Stratford lad who found subsequent immortality via the stage of Elizabethan London. There are also some controversial, but intriguing claims. Not only was Shakespeare a covert Catholic, who spent his so-called "lost years" as a budding actor in Catholic households in Lancashire under the name of "Shakeshafte," but he also suffered from sexually transmitted diseases, a nervous breakdown, fathered an illegitimate son via his middle-aged landlady, and sailed close to the political wind with what Holden sees as his residual Catholic and republican instincts.

Shakespeare: A Light & Enlightening Lecture, Featuring Elliot Engel. 2000. bk. 15.00 (978-1-890123-36-9(6)) Media Cnslts.

Shakespeare: Comedies, Histories, & Tragedies (Introduction) Instructed by Peter Saccio. 6 cass. (Running Time: 6 hrs.). 1999. 89.95 (978-1-56585-960-9(X)); audio compact disk 134.95 (978-1-56585-962-3(6)) Teaching Co.

Shakespeare: His Life & Work. unabr. abr. ed. Richard Hampton & David Weston. Read by Judi Dench & Timothy West. 2 cass. (Running Time: 2 hrs. 32 mins.). (gr. 9-12). 2000. 17.95 (978-1-57270-178-6(1), E21178a); audio compact disk 19.95 (978-1-57270-179-3(X), E21179a) Pub: Audio Partners. Dist(s): PerseuPGW
Welcome to Shakespeare's world! The authors, experienced actors & directors with the Royal Shakespeare Company, provide a fascinating look at Shakespeare's influences. Plus, two great Shakespearean actors perform excerpts from 22 plays including best-loved speeches & many other passages that are equally enticing.

Shakespeare: The Biography. unabr. ed. Peter Ackroyd. Read by Simon Vance. 11 CDs. (Running Time: 68400 sec.). (ENG.). 2005. audio compact disk 49.95 (978-0-7393-2376-2(8), Random AudioBks) Pub: Random Audio Pubg. Dist(s): Random

***Shakespeare: The Essential Tragedies.** unabr. ed. William Shakespeare. Narrated by Full Cast. 9 CDs. (Running Time: 10 hrs. 0 mins. 0 sec.). (ENG.). 2010. audio compact disk 49.95 (978-1-60998-006-1(9)) Pub: AudioGO. Dist(s): Perseus Dist

Shakespeare: The Last Plays. Instructed by Peter Saccio. 2 cass., 4 lectures. (Running Time: 3 hrs.). (SuperStar Teachers Ser.). 19.95 (978-1-56585-146-7(3)) Teaching Co.
Professor Saccio concentrates on words & actions as he discusses the providential romances Cymbeline, The Winter's Tale, The Tempest & the providentially-inflected history play, Henry VIII. A fantastically elaborated plot is the chief glory of Cymbeline. Converting human actions into lasting art is a central concern of The Winter's Tale. The Tempest entails actions that can be seen as imperialist or magical or Christian. In Henry VIII, Shakespeare develops a new mode of dramaturgy to depict history as a series of magnificent ceremonies.

***Shakespeare: The World as Stage.** unabr. ed. Bill Bryson. Read by Bill Bryson. (ENG.). 2007. (978-0-06-155533-6(9)); (978-0-06-155534-3(7)) HarperCollins Pubs.

Shakespeare: The World as Stage. unabr. ed. Bill Bryson. Read by Bill Bryson. 2008. audio compact disk 14.99 (978-0-06-167137-1(1), Harper Audio) HarperCollins Pubs.

Shakespeare Pts. I-II: The Word & the Action. Instructed by Peter Saccio. 16 CDs. (Running Time: 12 hrs.). 1995. bk. 69.95 (978-1-56585-307-2(5), 273) Teaching Co.

Shakespeare Vol. 1, Parts I-II: The Word & the Action. Instructed by Peter Saccio. 8 cass. (Running Time: 12 hrs.). 1995. 54.95 (978-1-56585-053-8(X), 273) Teaching Co.

Shakespeare Vol. 2: The Word & the Action. Instructed by Peter Saccio. 4 cass. (Running Time: 6 hrs.). 1995. 129.95 (978-1-56585-054-5(8)); audio compact disk 179.95 (978-1-56585-308-9(3)) Teaching Co.

Shakespeare Vol. 2: The Word & the Action, Course 273. Instructed by Peter Saccio. 8 cass. (Running Time: 12 hrs.). 2000. 129.95 (273) Teaching Co.
Experience Shakespeare's words as he meant them to be experienced. Shows the extraordinary ways in which he used language, action, & structure to create the dramatic impact & deep insight that forever set him apart. 16 lectures.

Shakespeare - Love to Madness: Contemporary Renderings of the Sonnets in Song, for Piano & Voice. William Shakespeare. Composed by Richard Caruso. 1 CD. (YA). (gr. 11-12). 1998. audio compact disk 15.00 (978-0-9665894-0-5(8)) R Caruso.

Shakespeare & Ecology by Dancing Beetle. Perf. by Eugene Ely. 1 cass. (Running Time: 1 hr. 27 mins.). (J). 1990. 10.00 Erthviibz.
Shakespeare, ecology, parody & nature sounds come together when Ms. Jellyfish & the spunky musical humans read & sing with Dancing Beetle.

Shakespeare & Money by Dancing Beetle. Perf. by Eugene Ely. 1 cass. (Running Time: 1 hr. 20 mins.). (J). 1993. 10.00 Erthviibz.
Shakespeare, money management, parody & nature sounds come together when Ms. Hyena & the spunky musical humans read & sing with Dancing Beetle.

Shakespeare & Mother Nature by Dancing Beetle. Perf. by Eugene Ely. 1 cass. (Running Time: 89 min.). (J). 1992. 10.00 Erthviibz.
Shakespeare's nature poetry & nature's sounds come together when Ms. Pelican & the spunky musical humans read & sing with Dancing Beetle.

Shakespeare & Passion by Dancing Beetle. Perf. by Eugene Ely. 1 cass. (Running Time: 1 hr. 15 mins.). (J). 1994. 10.00 Erthviibz.
Shakespeare, love & nature sounds come together when Ms. Walrus & the spunky musical humans read & sing with Dancing Beetle.

Shakespeare & the English Language. G. Wilson Knight. 1 cass. (Running Time: 30 min.). (Shakespeare's Critics Speak Ser.). 1965. 11.95 (23105) J Norton Pubs.
A talk on Shakespeare's use of the manifold resources, drawn from different tongues, of Elizabethan English; the variations to which he put these for different purposes; & how the multi-racial origins of his medium have helped to make him a dramatic poet of universal appeal.

Shakespeare & the English Language. G. Wilson Knight. 1 CD. (Running Time: 30 mins.). 2006. audio compact disk 12.95 (978-1-57970-362-2(3), C23105D, Audio-For) J Norton Pubs.
A talk on Shakespeare's use of manifold resources, drawn from different tongues, of Elizabethan English; the variations to which he put these for different purposes; and how the multiracial origins of his medium have helped make him a a dramatic poet of universal appeal.

Shakespeare & the Fundamental Law of Drama. C. B. Purdom. 1 cass. (Running Time: 28 min.). (Shakespeare's Critics Speak). 1965. 11.95 (23106) J Norton Pubs.
Attention is focused on the fundamental principals that govern drama in an attempt to answer the question, "What is the quality that makes Shakespeare the supreme dramatist?".

Shakespeare at Work. Gilbert Highet. Read by Gilbert Highet. 1 cass. (Running Time: 30 min.). 11.95 (23285-A) J Norton Pubs.

Shakespeare Audio Collection. unabr. abr. ed. William Shakespeare. Prod. by Shakespeare Recording Society. Intro. by Harold Bloom. Illus. by Maurice Sendak. 7 CDs. (Running Time: 8 hrs.). 1999. audio compact disk 50.00 (978-0-694-52270-5(8)) HarperCollins Pubs.

Shakespeare by Another Name: The Life of Edward de Vere, Earl of Oxford, the Man Who Was Shakespeare. abr. ed. Mark Anderson. Read by Simon Prebble. 8 CDs. (Running Time: 10 hrs.). (ENG.). 2005. audio compact disk 34.95 (978-1-56511-994-9(0), 1565119940) Pub: Penguin-HghBrdg. Dist(s): Penguin Grp USA

Shakespeare Christmas Carol. Prod. by Actors Scene Unseen. Based on a play by Kathy Feininger. Music by Alan Kaufman. (ENG.). 2008. audio compact disk 12.99 (978-0-9817573-1-5(6)) Scene Unseen.

Shakespeare Collection. Abr. by iSummaries Staff. (YA). 2007. audio compact disk 39.95 (978-1-934488-25-6(9)) L England.

Shakespeare Collection. William Shakespeare. 6 cass. (Running Time: 6 hrs.). 1997. 39.95 (978-1-880184-43-1(5)) Scarab Bk Ltd.
Presents summaries of 22 works by history's most celebrated playwright. Become versed in "The Merchant of Venice," "Hamlet," "King Lear," "Julius Caesar," "Othello," "The Taming of the Shrew" & 16 more of "the Bard's" best!.

Shakespeare for Children. Charles Lamb. Read by Josephine Bailey. (Running Time: 5 hrs.). 2005. 25.95 (978-1-60083-658-9(5), Audiofy Corp) Iofy Corp.

Shakespeare for Children. Charles Lamb & Mary Lamb. Read by Josephine Bailey & Simon Vance. (Running Time: 19800 sec.). (Unabridged Classics in Audio Ser.). (ENG.). (J). 2005. audio compact disk 19.99 (978-1-4001-5092-2(2)) Pub: Tantor Media. Dist(s): IngramPubServ

Shakespeare for Children. Charles Lamb & Mary Lamb. Read by Josephine Bailey & Simon Vance. (Running Time: 19800 sec.). (Unabridged Classics in Audio Ser.). (ENG.). (J). (ps-7). 2005. audio compact disk 49.99 (978-1-4001-3092-4(1)) Pub: Tantor Media. Dist(s): IngramPubServ

Shakespeare for Children. Short Stories. Based on a play by William Shakespeare. As told by Jim Weiss. 1 cass. (Running Time: 1 hr.). Dramatization. (Storyteller's Version Ser.). (YA). (gr. 2 up). 1999. 10.95 (978-1-882513-15-4(0), 1124-15); audio compact disk 14.95 (978-1-882513-40-6(1), 1124-015) Greathall Prods.
The glorious richness of two of Shakespeare's best loved plays on a level children can grasp. "A Midsummer Night's Dream" and "The Taming of the Shrew".

Shakespeare for Children. Read by Jim Weiss. 1 cass. (J). (gr. 3-12). 1999. 9.95 (978-1-882513-71-0(1), 1124-15) Greathall Prods.
The glorious richness of two of Shakespeare's best loved plays on a level children can grasp. "A Midsummer Night's Dream" & "The Taming of the Shrew".

Shakespeare for Children. Read by Jim Weiss. 1 cass., 1 CD. (Running Time: 1 hr.). (J). (GHP15) NewSound.

Shakespeare for Children. unabr. ed. Charles Lamb & Mary Lamb. Narrated by Josephine Bailey & Simon Vance. (Running Time: 5 hrs. 30 mins. 0 sec.). (ENG.). (J). (gr. 4-7). 2008. 19.99 (978-1-4001-5854-6(0)); audio compact disk 22.99 (978-1-4001-0854-1(3)); audio compact disk 45.99 (978-1-4001-3854-8(X)) Pub: Tantor Media. Dist(s): IngramPubServ

Shakespeare for Children. unabr. ed. Lamb et al. Read by Josephine Bailey & Simon Vance. (J). 2008. 44.99 (978-1-60514-675-1(7)) Find a World.

Shakespeare, His Life & Work. Richard Hampton & David Weston. Read by Judi Dench & Timothy West. (Running Time: 2 hrs.). 2003. 21.95 (978-1-59912-934-1(5)) Iofy Corp.

Shakespeare His Life & Work. William Shakespeare. 2 cass. (Running Time: 2 hrs.). 1999. 16.85 Set. (978-1-901768-28-2(7)) Pub: CSA Telltapes GBR. Dist(s): Ulverscroft US

Shakespeare: His Life & Work. William Shakespeare. Contrib. by Judi Dench & Timothy West. Narrated by Richard Hampton & David Weston. (Playaway Adult Nonfiction Ser.). 2008. 39.99 (978-1-60640-925-1(5)) Find a World.

Shakespeare Is Hip-Hop. unabr. ed. Flocabulary. Read by Flocabulary. (YA). 2008. 34.99 (978-1-60514-504-4(1)) Find a World.

Shakespeare Looks at Revolution. 10.00 (MC1001) Esstee Audios.

Shakespeare on Stage. Contrib. by Robert Speaight et al. 1 cass. 8.95 (ECN 113) J Norton Pubs.
An actor, a director, & a critic look at the way productions of Shakespeare have changed over the years & the ideas that have influenced these changes.

Shakespeare Sonnets. unabr. ed. William Shakespeare. Read by Ronald Colman. 3 cass. 17.85 (E-603) Audio Bk.
The complete selection, 154 of the sonnets.

Shakespeare Stealer. Gary L. Blackwood. Narrated by Ron Keith. 5 CDs. (Running Time: 5 hrs. 45 mins.). (gr. 5 up). audio compact disk 48.00 (978-1-4025-1970-3(2)) Recorded Bks.

Shakespeare Stealer. unabr. ed. Gary L. Blackwood. Narrated by Ron Keith. 4 cass. (Running Time: 5 hrs. 45 mins.). (YA). 2001. pap. bk. & stu. ed. 54.24 Recorded Bks.
Life has always been bleak for the orphan Widge. He is apprenticed to a cruel, unfeeling cutthroat, when he is ordered to steal a play called Hamlet.

Shakespeare Stealer. unabr. ed. Gary L. Blackwood. Narrated by Ron Keith. 4 pieces. (Running Time: 5 hrs. 45 mins.). (gr. 5 up). 2001. 39.00 (978-0-7887-4733-5(9), 96407E7) Recorded Bks.

***Shakespeare: the Essential Comedies, Volume One: Four BBC Full-Cast Radio Dramas.** William Shakespeare. Narrated by Full Cast. (Running Time: 9 hrs. 0 mins. 0 sec.). (ENG.). 2010. audio compact disk 49.95 (978-1-60998-007-8(7)) Pub: AudioGO. Dist(s): Perseus Dist

Shakespeare the Man. unabr. ed. A. L. Rowse. Read by Richard Green. 7 cass. (Running Time: 10 hrs. 30 mins.). 1978. 56.00 (978-0-7366-0080-4(9), 1090) Books on Tape.
A narrative of Shakespeare's life as he moved from his Stratford boyhood to fame & acclaim in the London of Queen Bess. There he encountered the "Dark Lady" & wooed her with his love & sonnets.

Shakespeare Without the Boring Bits. unabr. ed. Humphrey Carpenter. Read by Carole Boyd. 2 CDs. (Running Time: 7500 sec.). (J). 2002. audio compact disk 21.95 (978-0-7540-6505-0(7), CHCD 005, Chivers Child Audio) AudioGO.

Shakespeare Without the Boring Bits, Set. unabr. ed. Humphrey Carpenter. Read by Carole Boyd. 2 cass. (J). (gr. 1-8). 1999. 18.95 (CCA 3486, Chivers Child Audio) AudioGO.

Shakespearean Actor Prepares. abr. ed. Adriane Brine & Michael York. Perf. by Michael York. 4 cass. (Running Time: 6 hrs.). 2004. 25.00 (978-1-59007-036-9(4)) Pub: New Millenn Enter. Dist(s): PerseuPGW
Offers sound, practical advice for effective acting by its cogent explanations of the operations and functions of Shakespeare's language and techniques of characterization.

Shakespeare's Comedies. Thomas M. Parrott. 1 cass. (Running Time: 23 min.). (Shakespeare's Critics Speak Ser.). 1953. 11.95 (23096) J Norton Pubs.
"A Midsummer Night's Dream" & "The Merchant of Venice" are compared & contrasted.

Shakespeare's Comedies. Mark Van Doren. 1 cass. (Running Time: 59 min.). 1953. 11.95 (C23226) J Norton Pubs.

Shakespeare's Critics Speak. 15 cass. 160.00 Set. (S104) J Norton Pubs.

Shakespeare's Dreams & Dreamers. Gilbert Highet. Read by Gilbert Highet. 1 cass. (Running Time: 30 min.). 11.95 (23286-A) J Norton Pubs.

Shakespeare's Greatest Hits. unabr. ed. William Shakespeare. Read by Amy Irving & Peter Aylward. Adapted by Barbara Gaines. 1 CD. (Running Time: 1 hr. 15 mins.). 2009. audio compact disk 25.95 (978-1-58081-559-8(6)) L A Theatre.

Shakespeare's Greatest Hits: A Midsummer's Night Dream; Macbeth; Romeo & Juliet; Twelth Night. unabr. ed. Bruce Coville. Read by Full Cast Production Staff. (YA). 2007. 34.99 (978-1-59895-942-0(5)) Find a World.

Shakespeare's Henry V, William Shakespeare. 3 cass. (Running Time: 3 hrs.). 1994. 21.95 (978-0-88432-457-7(5), SCN089) J Norton Pubs.

Shakespeare's Lovers. Excerpts. William Shakespeare. Ed. by Estelle Kohler & Bill Homewood. 2 cass. (Running Time: 2 hrs 33 mins.). Dramatization. (Classic Literature with Classical Music Ser.). 1994. 13.98 (978-962-634-524-5(1), NA202414, Naxos AudioBooks) Naxos.
Many of the greatest lovers and the greatest love scenes from nearly 20 plays are performed. Includes "Romeo and Juliet," "As You Like It," "Hamlet," "Henry V," "Much Ado about Nothing," "Twelfth Night," "Macbeth" and many more.

Shakespeare's Lovers. unabr. ed. Excerpts. William Shakespeare. Perf. by Estelle Kohler & Bill Homewood. 2 CDs. (Running Time: 2 hrs. 33 mins.). Dramatization. (Classic Literature with Classical Music Ser.). 1994. audio compact disk 15.98 (978-962-634-024-0(X), NA202412, Naxos AudioBooks) Naxos.

Shakespeare's Plays in Story Form. unabr. ed. Charles Lamb & Mary Lamb. Read by Sean Pratt. 9 cds. (Running Time: 10 hrs 34 mins). (YA). 2002. pap. bk. (978-1-58472-358-5(0), In Aud) Sound Room.
A retelling of eighteen of Shakespeare's most loved plays. It includes Romeo and Juliet, The Winter's Tale, Measure for Measure, Taming of the Shrew, Hamlet, Macbeth, As You Like It, The Tempest, A Midsummer Night's Dream, King Lear, Much Ado About Nothing, All's Well That Ends Well, The Two Gentlemen of Verona, The Merchant of Venice, The Comedy of Errors, Twelth Night, Or What You Will, Timon of Athens, Othello.

Shakespeare's Plays in Story Form. unabr. ed. Short Stories. Charles Lamb & Mary Lamb. Read by Sean Pratt. 5 cds. (YA). 2002. audio compact disk 29.95 (978-1-58472-324-0(6), In Aud) Pub: Sound Room. Dist(s): Baker Taylor
Contains Romeo and Juliet, Hamlet, Macbeth, Othello, Merchant of Venice, As You Like It, Mid Summer's Night Dream, Taming of the Shrew, King Lear, The Tempest.

Shakespeare's Plays in Story Form. unabr. ed. Charles Lamb & Mary Lamb. Read by Sean Pratt. 1 cd. (Running Time: 10 hrs 34 mins). (YA). 2002. audio compact disk 18.95 (978-1-58472-401-8(3), In Aud) Pub: Sound Room. Dist(s): Baker Taylor
MP3 format.

Shakespeare's Rhetoric. G. Wilson Knight. 1 cass. (Running Time: 24 min.). (Shakespeare's Critics Speak Ser.). 11.95 (23109) J Norton Pubs.
A selection of readings of some of Shakespeare's long speeches, with comments on the various points of structure which the readings are intended to illustrate.

Shakespeare's Secret. unabr. ed. Elise Broach. Narrated by Jenny Ikeda. 5 CDs. (Running Time: 5 hrs. 45 mins.). 2005. audio compact disk 48.75

An Asterisk (*) at the beginning of an entry indicates that the title is appearing for the first time.

(978-1-4193-5582-0(1), C3409); 37.75 (978-1-4193-5067-2(6), 98114) Recorded Bks.
This Junior Library Guild selection by Elise Broach is sure to become a favorite of all young sleuths. Sixth-grader Hero is captivated by the stories about her new home, especially the mystery of the missing million-dollar diamond and a 500-year-old necklace. As she searches for clues to their whereabouts she stumbles upon another perplexing question: Who was the real William Shakespeare?.

Shakespeare's Sonnets. William Shakespeare. Read by David Butler. (Running Time: 2 hrs. 21 mins.). 2003. 17.95 (978-1-59912-116-1(6), Audiofy Corp) Iofy Corp.

Shakespeare's Sonnets. William Shakespeare. Read by Flo Gibson. 2 cass. (Running Time: 2 hrs. 30 min.). 1995. 14.95 (978-1-55685-397-5(1)) Audio Bk Con.
154 sonnets to a friend, about the woman he loves, & to his muse.

***Shakespeare's Sonnets.** William Shakespeare. Narrated by Flo Gibson. (ENG.). 2010. audio compact disk 16.95 (978-1-60646-202-7(4)) Audio Bk Con.

Shakespeare's Sonnets. William Shakespeare. Narrated by David Butler. (Running Time: 8460 sec.). (Unabridged Classics in MP3 Ser.). (ENG.). 2008. audio compact disk 24.00 (978-1-58472-648-7(2), In Aud) Sound Room.

Shakespeare's Sonnets. unabr. ed. William Shakespeare. Read by Simon Callow. (Running Time: 2 hrs.). (ENG.). 2005. audio compact disk 18.95 (978-1-59887-007-7(6), 1598870076) Pub: HighBridge. Dist(s): Workman Pub

Shakespeare's Sonnets. unabr. ed. William Shakespeare. 4 cass. (Running Time: 6 hrs.). 29.95 (978-1-85998-223-5(9), HoddrStoughton) Pub: Hodder General GBR. Dist(s): Trafalgar
This recording contains Keats's most famous works: "La Belle Dame Sans Merci," "The Eve of St. Agnes," "Ode to a Nightingale," "On a Grecian Urn," along with many lesser-known short poems such as "To Mrs. Reynolds' Cat" that exhibit the poet's more fanciful side. Reading all of Shakespeare's sonnets written between 1593 and 1601, actor Simon Callow conveys the dramatic potential.

Shakespeare's Sonnets. unabr. ed. Poems. William Shakespeare. Read by David Butler. 2 cds. (Running Time: 2 hrs 21 mins.). 2002. audio compact disk 18.95 (978-1-58472-322-6(X), 087, In Aud) Pub: Sound Room. Dist(s): Baker Taylor
All 154 of Shakespeare's rich sonnets.

Shakespeare's Sonnets & Tales from Shakespeare. unabr. ed. Shakespeare. Read by David Butler & Sean Pratt. (YA). 2006. 44.99 (978-1-59895-181-3(5)) Find a World.

Shakespeare's Storybook. 2007. audio compact disk 19.99 (978-1-84148-414-3(8)) BarefootBksMA.

Shakespeare's Storybook: Folk Tales That Inspired the Bard. Patrick Ryan. Narrated by Patrick Ryan. 2 CDs. (Running Time: 4 mins. 7 sec.). (ENG., (J). (gr. 3-6). 2001. audio compact disk 19.99 (978-1-84148-415-0(6)) BarefootBksMA.
Traditional stories that are at the heart of seven of Shakespeare's masterpieces. Includes leaflet.

Shakespeare¿s Tragedies. Instructed by Clare R. Kinney. 12 cass. (Running Time: 12 hrs.). 54.95 (978-1-59803-306-9(9)) Teaching Co.

Shakespeare¿s Tragedies. Instructed by Clare R. Kinney. 12 CDs. (Running Time: 12 hrs.). 2007. audio compact disk 69.95 (978-1-59803-307-6(7)) Teaching Co.

Shakespeare's Tragedies. Mark Van Doren. 1 cass. (Running Time: 1 hr.). 1953. 11.95 (C23227) J Norton Pubs.

Shakespeare's Tragic Structure in King Lear. Derek Traversi. 1 cass. (Running Time: 40 min.). (Shakespeare's Critics Speak Ser.). 1965. 11.95 (23100) J Norton Pubs.
A study of King Lear as the most complex & universal of Shakespeare's tragic structures.

Shakespear's Sonnets. unabr. ed. Narrated by David Butler. 3 CDs. (Running Time: 2 hrs. 21 mins.). (YA). (gr. 9 up). 2002. audio compact disk 34.00 (978-1-58472-170-3(7), Commuters Library) Sound Room.
The simplicity and elegance of Shakespear's lyric poetry is apparent in this audio rendition. All 154 sonnets are read in order, each one identified by its number which corresponds with the CD track number, making it easy to locate a particular choice. This form of poetry is characterized by 14 lines of rhymed, iambic pentameter in a scheme of three quatrains followed by a couplet.

Shakin' a Tailfeather. Perf. by Taj Mahal. 1 cass.; 1 CD. 1998. 9.98 (978-1-56628-147-8(4), 72940); audio compact disk 15.98 CD. (978-1-56628-146-1(6), 72940D) MFLP CA.

Shakin' It. Perf. by Parachute Express Staff. 1 cass., 1 CD. (J). 7.98 (TLR 1001); audio compact disk 11.18 CD Jewel box. (TLR 1001) NewSound.

Shakin' It Up! Sally K. Albrecht & Jay Althouse. 1 CD. (Running Time: 1 hr.). (ENG.). 2000. audio compact disk 39.95 (978-0-7390-0847-8(1), 19807) Alfred Pub.

Shakin' Loose with Mother Goose, Vols. 1-4. Steve Allen & Jayne Meadows. Intro. by Kathleen Bullock. 2 read-along cass. (Running Time: 1 hr. 20 min.). (J). (ps-8). 1986. pap. bk. 14.95 (978-0-89411-009-2(8), KM006); 19.95 incl. four pap. bks. (978-0-89411-010-8(1)) Wisdom Ex.

Shakin' Loose with Mother Goose: Hey Diddle Rock. David B. Zaslow et al. Illus. by Kathleen Bullock. 1 read-along cass. (Running Time: 20 min.). (Shakin' Loose with Mother Goose Ser.: No. 3). (J). (ps-8). 1986. pap. bk. 7.95 (978-0-89411-006-1(3)) Wisdom Ex.

Shakin' Loose with Mother Goose: Hickory Dickory Rock. David B. Zaslow et al. Illus. by Kathleen Bullock. 1 read-along cass. (Running Time: 20 min.). (Shakin' Loose with Mother Goose Ser.: No. 1). (J). (ps-8). 1986. pap. bk. 7.95 (978-0-89411-004-7(7)) Wisdom Ex.

Shakin' Loose with Mother Goose: Humpty Dumpty Rock. David B. Zaslow et al. Illus. by Kathleen Bullock. 1 read-along cass. (Running Time: 20 min.). (Shakin' Loose with Mother Goose Ser.: No. 4). (J). (ps-8). 1986. pap. bk. 7.95 (978-0-89411-007-8(1)) Wisdom Ex.

Shakin' Loose with Mother Goose: Rock-a-Doodle-Doo. David B. Zaslow et al. Illus. by Kathleen Bullock. 1 read-a-long cass. (Running Time: 20 min.). (Shakin' Loose with Mother Goose Ser.: No. 2). (J). (ps-8). 1986. pap. bk. 7.95 (978-0-89411-005-4(5)) Wisdom Ex.

Shaking: The Original Path to Ecstasy & Healing. abr. ed. Bradford P. Keeney. (Running Time: 22500 sec.). 2008. audio compact disk 69.95 (978-1-59179-895-8(7)) Sounds True.

Shakira: Woman Full of Grace. Ximena Diego. Narrated by Monica Steuer. 3 cass. (Running Time: 4 hrs. 30 mins.). 42.00 (978-1-4025-0381-8(4)) Recorded Bks.

Shaklee Files: Marketing Your Business. Randy Gage. 6 cass. (Running Time: 6 hrs.). 99.00 (978-1-884667-04-6(X)) Prime Concepts Grp.
Business training.

Shakti, Vol. 1. Music by Bhimsen Joshi & Shruti Sadolikar. 1 cass. (Bhaktimala Ser.). 1992. (D92005); audio compact disk (CD D92005) Multi-Cultural Bks.

Shakti, Vol. 2. Music by Pandit Jasraj & Ashwini Bhide. 1 cass. (Bhaktimala Ser.). 1992. (D92006); audio compact disk (CD D92006) Multi-Cultural Bks.

Shakti Rhythms. Shiva Rea. 1 CD. (Running Time: 1 hr. 16 mins.). 2006. audio compact disk 16.98 (978-1-59179-185-0(5), M820D) Sounds True.
At the cutting edge of today?s growing flow yoga phenomenon, Shiva Rea is renowned for creating original music compilations to accompany her popular Southern California classes and sold-out international workshops. Shakti Rhythms ? music drawn from her new Yoga Shakti DVD ? is designed to bring listeners into the flow of this dynamic practice.Perfect for yoga and creative movement of all kinds, Shakti Rhythms melts the boundaries between ancient and modern music ? with a unique mix of ecstatic chant, underground, ambient, and driving rhythms.Features Cheb I Sabbah, Jai Uttal, Dum Dum Project, Laylo and Bushwacka, Swami Ramananda, Tumbara, DJ Pathaan, and more.

Shakuhachi Meditation Music: Traditional Japanese Flute for Zen Contemplation. unabr. ed. Perf. by Stan Richardson. 2 CDs. (Running Time: 2 hrs. 22 mins.). 1999. audio compact disk 18.98 (978-1-56455-420-8(1), MM00301D) Sounds True.
The virtuoso offers authentic bamboo flute selections in the traditional Zen style, each one a soothing contemplation meant to still the mind & awaken attention.

Shal Pyaler Bane. A. Mohit. Voice by Sheema Mohit. 1 cd. 1999. audio compact disk 10.00 (978-0-9647672-7-0(9)) Beacon Hse IN.

Shalimar the Clown. unabr. ed. Salman Rushdie. Narrated by Aasif Mandvi. 15 CDs. (Running Time: 18 hrs.). 2005. audio compact disk 119.75 (978-1-4193-4000-0(X), C3295); 109.75 (978-1-4025-7661-4(7), 97670) Recorded Bks.
In Shalimar the Clown, Rushdie effortlessly weaves a series of interconnected narratives to form a sweeping and ambitious tale - at once timeless and startlingly modern - that reaches back through the years and across the continents.

Shalimar the Clown. unabr. ed. Salman Rushdie. Narrated by Aasif Mandvi. 15 CDs. (Running Time: 65700 sec.). 2005. audio compact disk 39.99 (978-1-4193-3999-8(0)) Recorded Bks.

Shall I Compare Thee (A Poem from the Poets' Corner) The One-and-Only Poetry Book for the Whole Family. unabr. ed. William Shakespeare & John Lithgow. Read by John Lithgow. (Running Time: 10 mins.). (ENG.). 2008. 0.99 (978-1-60024-327-1(4)) Pub: Hachet Audio. Dist(s): HachBkGrp

Shall I Compare Thee to a Summer's Day: Sonnet 18 see Palgrave's Golden Treasury of English Poetry

Shall Not God? Luke 18:7. Ed Young. (J). 1979. 4.95 (978-0-7417-1051-2(X), A0052) Win Walk.

Shall We Gather. Jerry Galipeau. 1 cass., 1 CD. (Running Time: 40 min.). (Piano Portrait Ser.). 1996. 9.95 (978-0-87946-142-3(X), 319); audio compact disk 14.95 CD. (978-0-87946-144-7(6), 403) ACTA Pubns.
Includes "Ave Maria," "Amazing Grace," "Tantum Ergo," "Were You There?," "Veni Creator Spirtus," "Jesus Christ is Risen Today," "Attende Domine," "Let All Mortal Flesh Keep Silence," "Shall We Gather," & six more selections ranging from ancient chant tones to contemporary American hymns.

Shall We Tell the President? abr. ed. Jeffrey Archer. Read by Tim Pigott-Smith. 2000. 16.95 (978-0-00-105019-8(2)) Pub: HarpC GBR. Dist(s): Trafalgar

Shall We Tell the President? abr. rev. ed. Jeffrey Archer. Narrated by Lorelei King. 3 CDs. (Running Time: 3 hrs. 30 mins. 0 sec.). (ENG.). 2009. audio compact disk 14.95 (978-1-59397-529-6(5)) Pub: Macmill Audio. Dist(s): Macmillan

Shall We Tell the President? unabr. ed. Jeffrey Archer. Read by E. C. Kelly. 6 cass. (Running Time: 9 hrs.). 2001. 49.95 (978-0-7451-6807-4(8), CAB 319) Pub: Chivers Audio Bks GBR. Dist(s): AudioGO
It is the not-to-distant future, and Florentyna Kane is the first woman president of the United States. Threats on her life abound. At 7:30 one evening, the FBI learns of a plot to kill Florentyna. An hour later, five people know the details. By 9:30, four of these people are dead. Only FBI agent Mark Andrews remains, and only he knows why and when the killer will strike. But where and how?.

Shallow Grave. unabr. ed. Cynthia Harrod-Eagles. Read by Terry Wale. 10 cass. (Running Time: 13 hrs. 30 min.). (Bill Slider Mystery Ser.: No. 7). 1999. 84.95 (978-1-86042-521-9(6), 25216) Pub: UlverLrgPrint GBR. Dist(s): Ulverscroft US

Shallowness of a Life Without Passion. J. Krishnamurti. 1 cass. (Running Time: 75 min.). (Madras, India Talks 1985 Ser.: No. 3). 1999. 8.50 (AMT853) Krishnamurti.
Krishnamurti addresses the timeless questions which mankind has always asked & he invites each one of us to suspend our beliefs & theories, to observe together, to walk together with the speakers as we inquire into the human condition.

Shallows. unabr. ed. Tim Winton. Read by Tracey Callander. 7 cass. (Running Time: 9 hrs. 15 mins.). 2004. 56.00 (978-1-876584-71-9(8), 591105); audio compact disk 87.95 (978-1-74093-101-4(7)) Pub: Bolinda Pubng AUS. Dist(s): Bolinda Pub Inc

***Shallows: What the Internet Is Doing to Our Brains.** unabr. ed. Nicholas Carr. Read by William Hughes. (Running Time: 8 hrs. 30 mins.). 2010. 29.95 (978-1-4417-5000-6(2)); 54.95 (978-1-4417-4996-3(9)); audio compact disk 29.95 (978-1-4417-4999-4(3)); audio compact disk 76.00 (978-1-4417-4997-0(7)) Blckstn Audio.

Shaman, Jhankri & Nele: Music Healers of Indigenous Cultures. Ellipsis Arts Staff. 1997. bk. & pap. bk. 29.95 (978-1-55961-456-6(0), Ellipsis Arts) Relaxtn Co.

Shaman Journey. Tara Sutphen. Read by Tara Sutphen. 1 cass. (Running Time: 60 min.). 1991. 11.98 (978-0-87554-481-6(9), TS202) Valley Sun.
A beautiful guided meditation to explore your joys, burdens, goals & new directions.

Shamaneya. Perf. by Shelley Snow. 1 cass., 1 CD. 7.98 (SHAM 1110); audio compact disk 12.78 CD Jewel box. (SHAM 1110) NewSound.

Shamanic Approaches to the UFO. Terence McKenna. 1 cass. (AA & A Symposium Ser.). 9.00 (A0256-87) Sound Photosyn.

Shamanic Call to Acca-demia: My Studies with Ellen Marit Gaup-Dunfield, the Shaman of Samiland. Gloria Orenstein. 1 cass. 9.00 (A0378-88) Sound Photosyn.
Good story! A comedic romp through a deep & important personal adventure. From the 1988 ICSS with Berney & Saklani.

Shamanic Dreaming. Stanley Krippner. 1 cass. 9.00 (OC154) Sound Horizons AV.

Shamanic Drum: A Guide to Sacred Drumming. Michael Drake. 1 cass. (Running Time: 60 min.).Tr. of Samanske Bubny. 1993. 10.00 (978-0-9629002-1-1(4)) Talking Drum.
Shamanism.

Shamanic Drumming. Perf. by Alexander Alich. Prod. by Alexander Alich. Kati Meden. 1 CD. (Running Time: 50 mins.). Orig. Title: Here & Here. 2003. audio compact disk 17.00 (978-0-9710275-1-0(X), FoxTales) FoxFire Institute.
Shamanic Drumming for Journeys, Ritual and Ceremony.

Shamanic Experience: A Practical Guide to Psychic Powers. Kenneth Meadows. (Running Time: 47 mins.). 2003. bk. 20.00 (978-1-59143-002-5(X)) Bear & Co.

Shamanic Film Festival. Bruce Hawkins. 1 cass. 9.00 (A0038-88) Sound Photosyn.

Shamanic Journey. Felicitas Goodman. 1 cass. 9.00 (A0207-87) Sound Photosyn.
Experiential session at ICSS '87.

Shamanic Journeying & Active Imagination. Nancy Dougherty. 1 cass. (Running Time: 1 hrs. 20 min.). 1997. 10.95 (598) C G Jung IL.
Shamanic journeying is an ancient process which may be considered the ground for what Jung describes as active imagination. The shaman travels into the upper or lower world to interact with whom or what is found there. In active imagination, we face & take an active stance toward our inner world, interacting with the images & respecting the psychic reality from which they emerge.

Shamanic Meditations: Guided Journeys for Insight, Vision, & Healing. Sandra Ingerman. (Running Time: 2:24:00). 2010. audio compact disk 19.95 (978-1-59179-757-9(8)) Sounds True.

Shamanic Navigation. John Perkins. 2002. audio compact disk 24.95 (978-1-56455-904-3(1)) Sounds True.

Shamanic Overview. Ruth-Inge Heinze. 1 cass. 7.00 (A0039-85) Sound Photosyn.
Ruth-Inge Heinze founded & continues the annual International Conference for the Study of Shamanism, along with many other ground breaking scholastic & public events. She is included in "Shape Shifters," a book about Bay Area shamans.

Shamanic Technologies in Contemporary Society. Thomas Pinkson. 1 cass. 9.00 (A0323-88) Sound Photosyn.
A concentrated & personal ritual for healing.

Shamanism. Terence McKenna. 4 cass. (Running Time: 4 hrs.). 1993. 36.00 (OC347-73) Sound Horizons AV.

Shamanism: Before & Beyond History. Terence McKenna & Ralph Metzner. 7 cass. (Running Time: 7 hrs.). 63.00 (A0332-88) Sound Photosyn.
The entire workshop on the hilltop at Ojai. Among many stories, Metzner tells the ancient story of Gilgamesh & Inkidu, & his aspirations in the Gaia arena while dialoguing with shamanologicaly wired McKenna.

Shamanism: Before & Beyond History: A Weekend at Ojai. Ralph Metzner & Terence McKenna. 7 cass. (Running Time: 7 hrs.). 56.00 (A0332-88) Sound Photosyn.
The two excellent philosopher/storytellers with plenty of space atop the California hills to expand their points of view.

Shamanism: If This Is a Quest, Who's the Psychopomp? Read by John Van Eenwyk. 1 cass. (Running Time: 90 min.). (Patterns of Divinity Ser.: No. 7). 1988. 10.95 (978-0-7822-0316-5(7), 307) C G Jung IL.

Shamanism & Analytical Psychology. Donald Sander. 1 cass. 9.00 (A0222-87) Sound Photosyn.
From the 1987 ICSS Shamanism, with Oliver Ocskay on tape.

Shamanism & Contemporary Visual Arts. Mark Levy. 1 cass. 9.00 (A0216-87) Sound Photosyn.
A humorous survey from ICSS '87.

Shamanism & Deep Hypnosis. Etzel Cardena. 1 cass. 9.00 (A0225-87) Sound Photosyn.
From the 1987 ICSS, with William Leikem on the tape.

Shamanism & Gaia Consciousness. Ralph Metzner. 2 cass. (Running Time: 2 hrs.). 18.00 (A0614-90) Sound Photosyn.
Ralph quite polished with an elegant collection of slides - a sincere & consciousness expanding talk.

Shamanism & Healing. 1 cass. (Running Time: 1 hr.). 1990. 8.95 (978-0-8356-1901-1(X)) Theos Pub Hse.
Native American & Hawaiian healers.

Shamanism & Homosexuality. An Painter. 1 cass. 9.00 (A0224-87) Sound Photosyn.
Renato Berger is featured on this tape from the 1987 ICSS.

Shamanism & the Archetypes. Oliver Ocskay. 1 cass. 9.00 (A0221-87) Sound Photosyn.
From ICSS '87 with Donald Sander.

Shamanism, Mysticism, Pantheism, & the Holographic Paradigm. Beverly Rubik. 1 cass. 9.00 (A0349-88) Sound Photosyn.
ICSS '88 with Heinze & Walsh.

Shamanism, Symbiosis & the Psychedelic Experience. Terence McKenna. 2 cass. (Running Time: 2 hrs.). 18.00 set. (A0325-89) Sound Photosyn.
A two hour wowie zowie workshop to transport you to McKenna land.

Shamanistic Family Therapy. Paul M. Brala. 1 cass. 9.00 (A0351-88) Sound Photosyn.
ICSS '88 with Siegel, Waller, & Palmer on tape.

Shamanistic Use of Sacred Places in Health & Healing. Jim Swan. 1 cass. 9.00 (A0138-86) Sound Photosyn.
ICSS '86.

Shamanology. unabr. ed. Terence McKenna. 3 cass. (Running Time: 3 hrs.). 1984. 27.00 (978-1-56964-008-1(4), A0083-84) Sound Photosyn.
An intimate gathering with much intelligent interchange, this is a very relaxed & articulate examination of the topic.

Shamanology of the Amazon. Nicole Maxwell & Terence McKenna. 7 cass. (Running Time: 7 hrs.). 63.00 (A0478-78) Sound Photosyn.
Nicole the explorer & storyteller swaps tales with mercury minded Terence.

Shaman's Body. Carolyn Marks. 1 cass. 9.00 (A0393-88) Sound Photosyn.
From ICSS '88.

Shaman's Power: A North American Indian Perspective. Royal E. Allsup. 1 cass. 9.00 (A0389-88) Sound Photosyn.
ICSS '88 with Norton & Carroll.

Shambhala Warrior Training. Cynthia Kneen. 2007. audio compact disk 69.95 (978-1-59179-433-2(1)) Sounds True.

Shambleau. abr. ed. C. L. Moore. Perf. by C. L. Moore. 1 cass. 1984. 8.98 (CP 1667) HarperCollins Pubs.

Shame see Richard Wilbur Readings

Shame. Pia Mellody. Read by Pia Mellody. 2 cass. 18.00 Set. (A5) Featuka Enter Inc.
Discusses the emotion shame & its relationship to the disease of codependence & recovery.

Shame: The Social Emotion. Lois F. Timmins. 1 cass. (Running Time: 55 min.). 1986. 12.95 (978-0-931814-10-5(3)) Comn Studies.
Although shame is one of the most uncomfortable feelings and the most difficult to cope with, it makes one aware of & responsive to the opinions & feelings of others; it highlights deficiencies & deviant behavior. Coping with shame helps define identity & achieve intimacy & mutual love.

Understanding shame give insight into dependancy on others & encourages self-reform.

Shame & Grace. Lewis B. Smedes. 2 cass. (Running Time: 1 hr.). 1992. 14.99 (978-0-310-59898-5(2)) Zondervan.
This audio edition provides listeners with practical insight into the differences between good or creative shame & bad or destructive shame.

Shame & the Paralysis of Feminine Initiative. Laura McGrew. Read by Laura McGrew. 1 cass. (Running Time: 90 min.). 1991. 10.95 (978-0-7822-0362-2(0), 461) C G Jung IL.
Described by analyst Laura McGrew, the Athene-Persephone woman is seen by the world as responsible, articulate, intelligent, & successful, yet experiences internally an unexplained sense of emptiness & sadness. This lecture utilizes material based on the analyses of twenty women extending over nine years to examine the concept of shame in the Athene-Persephone woman - shame as an archetypal affect of the Self & as the source of wounding & key to healing.

Shame-Based Family. John E. Bradshaw. (Running Time: 7200 sec.). 2008. audio compact disk 70.00 (978-1-57388-159-3(7)) J B Media.

Shame the Devil. unabr. ed. George P. Pelecanos. Read by Richard J. Brewer. 6 cass. (Running Time: 9 hrs.). 2001. 29.95 (978-1-57511-077-6(6)) Pub Mills.
Crime tale follows the lives of the relatives of the victims of a robbery turned massacre. As they deal with their grief, the killers itch to escape their low-profile "under the radar" existence, forcing a nasty showdown.

***Shameless.** unabr. ed. Karen Robards. (Running Time: 13 hrs.). (Banning Sisters Ser.). 2010. 24.99 (978-1-4418-6425-3(3), 9781441864253, BAD); 39.97 (978-1-4418-6426-0(1), 9781441864260, BADLE) Brilliance Audio.

***Shameless.** unabr. ed. Karen Robards. Read by Rosalyn Landor. (Running Time: 13 hrs.). (Banning Sisters Ser.). 2010. 24.99 (978-1-4418-6423-9(7), 9781441864239, Brilliance MP3); 39.97 (978-1-4418-6424-6(5), 9781441864246, Brlnc Audio MP3 Lib); audio compact disk 36.99 (978-1-4418-6421-5(0), 9781441864215, Bril Audio CD Unabri); audio compact disk 92.97 (978-1-4418-6422-2(9), 9781441864222, BriAudCD Unabrid) Brilliance Audio.

Shan Newspaper Reader. Irving Glick & Sao T. Moeng. 1 cass. (Running Time: 1 hr. 30 min. per cass.). (SHN.). 1996. 12.00 (3127) Dunwoody Pr.
Intended for students who have learned the basic elements of the language & want to improve their proficiency & gain experience in reading natural language. Twenty-four articles, taken from the newspaper "Independence," published in the years 1991-1994.

Shan Phonological Drills, Eileen M. Scott & Sao T. Moeng. 3 cass. (Running Time: 4 hrs. 30 mins.). (SHN.). 1987. 24.00 (3072) Dunwoody Pr.
Intended for advanced students & designed to provide practice in producing the sounds of Shan.

Shan Phonological Drills with Workbook. Contrib. by Sao T. Moeng. 1987. pap. bk. 24.00 (978-0-931745-45-4(4)) Dunwoody Pr.

Shanah Tovah: A Good Year, Songs for Jewish Holidays. 1 cass., 1 CD. (Running Time: 33 min.). (J). (ps-6). 1996. 9.95 (978-1-890161-25-5(X)); audio compact disk 15.95 CD. (978-1-890161-26-2(8)) Sounds Write.
A delightful collection of 13 upbeat Jewish holiday songs.

Shandilya Upasana. (715) Yoga Res Foun.

Shandilya Upasana. Swami Jyotirmayananda. 1 cass. (Running Time: 1 hr.). 1990. 12.99 Yoga Res Foun.

Shane. unabr. ed. Jack Schaefer. Read by Walter Zimmerman. 6 cass. (Running Time: 6 hrs.). 1988. 36.00 (2205) Books on Tape.
Quiet, but dangerous, Shane takes the settlers side in a fatal duel with ranchers.

***Shane.** unabr. ed. Jack Schaefer. Read by Grover Gardner. (Running Time: 4 hrs. 0 mins.). 2010. 19.95 (978-1-4417-3267-5(5)); 24.95 (978-1-4417-3263-7(2)); audio compact disk 49.00 (978-1-4417-3264-4(0)) Blckstn Audio.

***Shane.** unabr. ed. Jack Schaefer. Read by Grover Gardner. (Running Time: 4 hrs.). 2010. audio compact disk 19.95 (978-1-4417-3266-8(7)) Blckstn Audio.

Shane. unabr. collector's ed. Jack Shaefer. Read by Walter Zimmerman. 6 cass. (Running Time: 6 hrs.). (J). 1988. 36.00 (978-0-7366-1298-2(X), 2205) Books on Tape.
Shane is a drifter who rides into a small Wyoming valley in the summer of 1889. He settles in with the Starretts, a family of homesteaders. Shane soon finds himself a reluctant part of the feud between rangers & those like the Starretts who are proving their land claims.

Shanghai Common Expressions. 1989. 39.00 (978-0-931745-53-9(5)) Dunwoody Pr.

Shanghai Common Expressions. Ed. by Jim Mathias. 6 cass. (Running Time: 9 hrs.). (CHI.). 1988. 39.00 (3073) Dunwoody Pr.
Represents 600 colloquial sentences from a variety of social situations that will enable English speakers to learn basic phrases necessary when visiting Shanghai (Romanizations are included).

Shanghai Dialect: An Introduction to Speaking the Contemporary Language. (C). 1994. 12.00 (978-1-881265-15-3(3)) Dunwoody Pr.

Shanghai Dialect: An Introduction to Speaking the Contemporary Language. Lance Eccles. 1 cass. (Running Time: 1 hr. 30 min. per cass.). (CHI.). 1993. 12.00 (3092) Dunwoody Pr.
Twenty-nine units intended chiefly for those who already have some knowledge of Putonghua.

Shanghai Girls. unabr. ed. Lisa See. Read by Janet Song. (ENG.). 2009. audio compact disk 39.95 (978-0-7393-5933-4(9), Random AudioBks) Pub: Random Audio Pubg. Dist(s): Random

Shanghai Moon. unabr. ed. S. J. Rozan. Narrated by Samantha Quan. 1 Playaway. (Running Time: 13 hrs. 30 mins.). 2009. 74.95 (978-0-7927-6184-6(7)); 59.95 (978-0-7927-6183-9(9)) AudioGO.

Shanghai Moon. unabr. ed. S. J. Rozan. Narrated by Samantha Quan. 11 CDs. (Running Time: 13 hrs. 30 mins.). 2009. audio compact disk 99.95 (978-0-7927-6030-6(1)) AudioGO.

***Shanghai Tango.** Jin Xing. Read by Keith Brockett. (Running Time: 7 hrs. 5 mins.). 2009. 49.99 (978-1-74214-185-5(4), 9781742141855) Pub: Bolinda Pubng AUS. Dist(s): Bolinda Pub Inc

Shanghai Tango. unabr. ed. Jin Xing. Read by Keith Brockett. (Running Time: 7 hrs. 5 mins.). 2008. audio compact disk 77.95 (978-1-921415-75-3(4), 9781921415753) Pub: Bolinda Pubng AUS. Dist(s): Bolinda Pub Inc

Shangri-La. unabr. collector's ed. Eleanor Cooney & Daniel Altieri. Read by Kate Reading. 7 cass. (Running Time: 10 hrs. 30 mins.). 1996. 56.00 (978-0-7366-3526-4(2), 4163) Books on Tape.
Hugh Conway returns to Shangri-La, the utopian city hidden in the Himalayas, to repel a destructive enemy. It's 1966 & China's Cultural Revolution has reached Tibet. A Chinese general zeroes in on Shangri-La for his ultimate plunder.

Shangri-la Diet. Seth Roberts. Read by Alan Sklar. (Playaway Adult Nonfiction Ser.). (ENG.). 2008. 39.99 (978-1-60640-862-9(3)) Find a World.

Shangri-la Diet: The No Hunger Eat Anything Weight-Loss Plan. unabr. ed. Seth Roberts. Narrated by Alan Sklar. (Running Time: 3 hrs. 30 mins. 0 sec.). (ENG.). 2006. audio compact disk 39.99 (978-1-4001-3257-7(6)); audio compact disk 19.99 (978-1-4001-5257-5(7)); audio compact disk 19.99 (978-1-4001-0257-0(X)) Pub: Tantor Media. Dist(s): IngramPubServ
With the publication of this unique and groundbreaking book, Seth Roberts's program will be available to anyone who wants to lose weight-a little or a lot-and keep it off. The Shangri-La Diet includes specific instructions for tailoring the program for individual needs and goals, as well as expert tips, variations, success stories, and an illuminating explanation of how Roberts devised the diet and why it works so well. A diet program simple enough for anyone to try, The Shangri-La Diet has the potential to radically change the way we think about weight loss - -and deliver remarkably easy, sustainable results.

Shanji. unabr. ed. James C. Glass. Read by Maynard Villers. 12 cass. (Running Time: 13 hrs. 42 min.). 1996. 64.95 (978-1-55686-677-7(1)) Books in Motion.
A feudal empire exists on the star Shanji, but a neighboring star desires to establish a progressive society. A leader is trained to rule Shanji but it leads to war between the two stars.

Shank. unabr. collector's ed. Roderick Anscombe. Read by Barrett Whitener. 8 cass. (Running Time: 12 hrs.). 1997. 64.00 (978-0-7366-3577-6(7), 4229) Books on Tape.
Dan Cody adores his wife, so he killed her. She was HIV-positive & she begged him to do it - or so he says.

Shankari Blue Pearl Meditation. Perf. by Shankari the Alchemist. Shankari the Alchemist. Tr. by Tomomi Tanizaki. Prod. by Cainan Ashton. Engineer Cainan Ashton. (JPN.). 2007. audio compact disk 15.00 (978-1-921370-00-7(9)) Red Truck AUS.

Shannon: A Novel. unabr. ed. Frank Delaney. Read by Frank Delaney. (ENG.). 2009. audio compact disk 44.95 (978-0-7393-3372-3(0), Random AudioBks) Pub: Random Audio Pubg. Dist(s): Random

Shannon to Sligo. 1 cass. (Running Time: 1 hr 30 min.). 12.95 (978-1-55606-022-9(X), CCI-455) Comp Comms Inc.
Features the lakes of Fergus, Cliffs of Moher, & the town of Limerick.

Shantaram. unabr. ed. Gregory David Roberts. Read by Bower Humphrey. (Running Time: 15600 sec.). 2006. audio compact disk 35.95 (978-0-7861-7465-2(X)) Blckstn Audio.

Shantaram. unabr. ed. Gregory David Roberts. Read by Humphrey Bower. 35 CDs. (Running Time: 154800 sec.). 2006. audio compact disk 44.95 (978-0-7861-6876-7(5)) Blckstn Audio.

Shantaram. unabr. ed. Gregory David Roberts. Read by Humphrey Bower. (YA). 2008. 184.99 (978-1-60514-921-9(7)) Find a World.

Shantaram, Pt. 1. Gregory David Roberts. Read by Bower Humphrey. (Running Time: 77400 sec.). 2006. 90.95 (978-0-7861-4612-3(5)) Blckstn Audio.

Shantaram, Pt. 1. Gregory David Roberts. Read by Humphrey Bower. (Running Time: 82800 sec.). 2006. audio compact disk 99.00 (978-0-7861-6882-8(X)) Blckstn Audio.

Shantaram, Pt. 2. Gregory David Roberts. Read by Humphrey Bower. (Running Time: 75900 sec.). 2006. 90.95 (978-0-7861-4613-0(3)) Blckstn Audio.

Shantaram, Pt. 2. Gregory David Roberts. Read by Bower Humphrey. (Running Time: 72000 sec.). 2006. audio compact disk 99.00 (978-0-7861-6881-1(1)) Blckstn Audio.

Shanti Mandir. Brahmacharini Mirabai. 1984. 7.00 (2304) Self Realization.
Ten selections from Paramahansa Yogananda's "Cosmic Chants" sung in Hindi by Brahmacharini Mirabai.

Shantih: Music for Peace & Relaxation. unabr. ed. Yogi Hari. 1998. audio compact disk 14.95 (978-1-57777-036-7(6), 407-010) Pub: Nada Prodns. Dist(s): Bookworld

Shape: Find & Fulfill Your Unique Purpose in Life. Zondervan Publishing Staff & Erik Rees. (Running Time: 7 hrs. 30 mins. 0 sec.). (ENG.). 2007. 14.29 (978-0-310-27350-9(1)) Zondervan.

Shape of Dread. unabr. ed. Marcia Muller. Read by Bernadette Dunne. 6 cass. (Running Time: 9 hrs.). (Sharon McCone Mystery Ser.: No. 9). 1999. 48.00 (978-0-7366-4455-6(5), 4900) Books on Tape.
Bobby Foster, car-hop at the chic Cafe Comedie, is going to the gas chamber since he's already confessed to the murder of Tracy Kostakos, the club's rising star. The final appeal sends San Francisco's #1 P.I. Sharon McCone, into the fractured world of Tracy's privileged family & the mind of a young comedienne who was not the good little girl they thought they knew.

Shape of Flesh & Bond, from Act Five see Twentieth-Century Poetry in English: Recordings of Poets Reading Their Own Poetry

Shape of Mercy. unabr. ed. Susan Meissner. (Running Time: 9 hrs. 0 mins. 0 sec.). (ENG.). 2008. audio compact disk 24.98 (978-1-59644-658-8(7)) christianaud.

***Shape of Mercy: A Novel.** unabr. ed. Susan Meissner. Narrated by Tavia Gilbert. (ENG.). 2008. 14.98 (978-1-59644-659-5(5), christaudio) christianaud.

Shape of Snakes. Minette Walters. Read by Frances Barber. 10 CDs. (Running Time: 15 hrs.). 2001. audio compact disk 94.95 (978-0-7540-5429-0(2), CCD 120) Pub: Chivers Audio Bks GBR. Dist(s): AudioGO
November 1978, the winter of discontent. Britain is on strike. The dead lie unburied, rubbish piles in the streets, and somewhere in West London a black woman dies in a gutter. She was known as "Mad Annie" and was despised by her neighbors. Her passing would have gone unnoticed and unmourned but for the young woman who finds her and believes apparently against reason, that she was murdered.

Shape of Snakes. unabr. ed. Minette Walters. Read by Frances Barber. 10 cass. (Running Time: 15 hrs.). 2001. 84.95 (978-0-7540-0657-2(3), CAB 2079) Pub: Chivers Audio Bks GBR. Dist(s): AudioGO

Shape of Snakes. 2nd abr. ed. Minette Walters. 4 CDs. (Running Time: 5 hrs.). (ENG., 2001. audio compact disk (978-0-333-90721-4(3)) Macmillan UK GBR.

Shape of Specialized Ministries in the United States. 1 cass. (Care Cassettes Ser.: Vol. 9, No. 12). 1982. 10.80 Assn Prof Chaplains.

Shape of Water. unabr. ed. Andrea Camilleri. Read by Grover Gardner. (Running Time: 14400 sec.). (Inspector Montalbano Mystery Ser.). 2006. 24.95 (978-0-7861-4670-3(2)); audio compact disk 36.00 (978-0-7861-6736-4(X)); audio compact disk 19.95 (978-0-7861-7401-0(3)) Blckstn Audio.

Shape Shifter. unabr. ed. Tony Hillerman. Read by George Guidall. (Running Time: 25200 sec.). (Joe Leaphorn & Jim Chee Novel Ser.). 2006. audio compact disk 29.95 (978-0-06-057899-2(8)) HarperCollins Pubs.

Shape up with Vitamins. Earl Mindell. 1 cass. 8.95 Listen USA.
Explains how vitamins affect your health & how to choose the right vitamin program for your needs.

Shapely Sleepy Sheep. Rory Zuckerman. Illus. by Maryn Roos. 1 CD. (Running Time: 18 mins.). (Sleepy Sheep Ser.). (J). (ps). 2007. bds. 7.95 (978-0-9796393-4-0(4)) Little Lion Pr.

Shapes. (Metro Math Readers Red Ser.). (J). (gr. 12). 2000. 5.58 (978-1-58120-559-6(7)) Metro Teaching.

Shapes & Patterns Theme Audio CD. ed. (J). 2004. audio compact disk (978-1-4108-1833-1(0)) Benchmark Educ.

Shapes & Solids: Early Explorers Early Set B Audio CD. Michelle Schaub. Adapted by Benchmark Education Staff. (J). 2007. audio compact disk 10.00 (978-1-4108-8243-1(8)) Benchmark Educ.

Shapes & Solids Outdoors: Early Explorers Fluent Set B Audio CD. Sophie Caribacas. Adapted by Benchmark Education Staff. (J). 2007. audio compact disk 10.00 (978-1-4108-8255-4(1)) Benchmark Educ.

Shapes at My House: Early Explorers Early Set B Audio CD. Anna Lee. Adapted by Benchmark Education Staff. (J). 2007. audio compact disk 10.00 (978-1-4108-8242-4(X)) Benchmark Educ.

Shapes in Action. 1 cass. (Running Time: 1 hr.). (J). 2001. pap. bk. 10.95 (KIM 7031C) Kimbo Educ.
Fun activities with triangles, circles & squares to catchy original tunes. Action-packed games & rhythmic activities teach the basic shapes. Includes manual.

Shapes of Animal Life. David Nichols. 1 cass. 1990. 12.95 (ECN023) J Norton Pubs.
Amoeba to man.

Shapeshifter. 2000. audio compact disk 9.95 (978-1-930805-08-8(X)) XC Pubng.

Shapes/Together & Apart. Created by Steck-Vaughn Staff. (Running Time: 566 sec.). (Shutterbug Bks.). 2002. (978-0-7398-5909-4(9)) SteckVau.

Shaping of a Christian Family. 1 cass. 1992. 9.99 (978-0-8474-2053-7(1)) Loizeaux.
Christian Life.

Shaping of a Soul. Interview with Mother Angelica & Adrian Kaam. 1 cass. (Running Time: 60 min.). (Mother Angelica Live Ser.). 10.00 (978-1-55794-065-0(7), T16) Eternal Wrd TV.

Shaping Self-Concept. 2004. audio compact disk (978-1-930429-51-2(7)) Love Logic.

Shaping Self-Concept: Encouraging Kids to Take Risks & Learn. unabr. ed. Jim Fay. Interview with Bert G. Mizke. 2 cass. (Running Time: 3 hrs.). 1999. 17.95 (978-0-944634-94-3(X)) Pub: Love Logic. Dist(s): Penton Overseas
Gives adults techniques & skills to help children become more self-confident & to see themselves as winners.

Shaping Self-Concept: Encouraging Kids to Take Risks & Learn. unabr. ed. Jim Fay. Read by Jim Fay. 2 cass. (Running Time: 3 hrs.). 2000. 17.95 Penton Overseas.

Shaping the Game: The New Leader's Guide to Effective Negotiating. unabr. ed. Lyndon Baines Johnson Library & Michael Watkins. Read by Grover Gardner. (Running Time: 5 hrs.). (ENG.). 2007. audio compact disk 29.98 (978-1-59659-092-2(0), GildAudio) Pub: Gildan Media. Dist(s): HachBkGrp

Shaping Your Destiny: By Receiving from the Fivefold Ministry. Speeches. 5 cass. (Running Time: 5 hrs.). (Annointing Ser.: 6). 2002. 25.00 (978-1-57399-100-1(7)) Mac Hammond.
Mac and Lynne Hammond team up to explain why knowing how to recive from each of the fivefold ministry gifts is essential to maturing as a believer and vital to knowing God's specific plans and purposes for your life.

Shaping Your Sound (SYS) Learning Kit. 1 cass. (YA). (gr. 9 up). 29.95 (978-1-56552-010-3(6), 301) First Light.
This learning kit contains supplementary materials to help you practice microphone & signal processing techniques.

Shardik, Vol. 2. collector's ed. Richard Adams. Read by Dan Lazar. 7 cass. (Running Time: 10 hrs. 30 min.). 1986. 56.00 (978-0-7366-0416-1(2)) Books on Tape.
A fantasy epic centered in the long-awaited reincarnation of the gigantic, ferocious & unpredictable bear, Lord Shardik, the Power of God.

Shards of Honor. unabr. ed. Lois McMaster Bujold. Read by Grover Gardner. (Running Time: 8 hrs. 0 mins.). (ENG.). 2009. 29.95 (978-1-4332-3193-3(X)); 54.95 (978-1-4332-3189-6(1)); audio compact disk 70.00 (978-1-4332-3190-2(5)) Blckstn Audio.

Shards of Honor. unabr. ed. Lois McMaster Bujold. 1 CD (MP3). (Running Time: 8 hrs. 24 min.). (Vorkosigan Ser.). 1999. audio compact disk 24.95 (978-1-885585-16-5(0)) Readers Chair.
Commander Cordelia Naismith of Beta Colony & Captain Aral Vorkosigan of Barrayar suddenly find themselves at war with each other, abandoned by their respective forces on an uncharted planet & dependent on each other for their very survival. Trapped in an endless war without victory or glory & only one thing worth fighting for..."Shards of Honor".

Shards of Honor. unabr. ed. Lois McMaster Bujold. Perf. by Carol Cowan & Michael Hanson. 7 cass. (Running Time: 8 hrs. 24 min.). (Vorkosigan Ser.). 1996. 42.00 Set. (978-1-885585-00-4(4)) Readers Chair.

Share in Death. Deborah Crombie. Read by Michael Deehy. 6 CDs. (Duncan Kincaid/Gemma James Novel Ser.). 2004. audio compact disk 32.95 (978-0-7927-3265-5(0), SLD 673, Chivers Sound Lib) AudioGO.

Share It. Rosenshontz. Perf. by Gary Rosen & Bill Shontz. 1 cass. (Rosenshontz Ser.). (J). (ps-6). 1992. 8.98 (978-1-879496-56-9(9)); audio compact disk 13.98 CD. (978-1-56896-040-1(9)) Lightyear Entrtnmnt.
A two-man group singing delightful children's songs.

Share It. Rosenshontz. Perf. by Gary Rosen & Bill Shontz. 1 cass. (Running Time: 1 hr.). (Rosenshontz Ser.). (J). (ps-6). 1993. pap. bk. 8.98 Incl. long box. (978-1-879496-57-6(7)) Lightyear Entrtnmnt.

Share Jesus Without Fear. William Fay. (ENG.). 2005. audio compact disk 3.99 (978-0-8054-2873-5(9)) BH Pubng Grp.

Share the Laughter. Perf. by Vickie Winans. 1 CD. (Running Time: 36 mins.). audio compact disk 16.98 (978-1-57908-469-1(9), 5339) Platinm Enter.

Share the Laughter, unabr. ed. Perf. by Vickie Winans. 1 cass. (Running Time: 36 mins.). 10.98 (978-1-57908-470-7(2), 5339) Platinm Enter.

Share This World. Read by Jim Rule. Perf. by Jim Rule. Prod. by Patrick Woodland. 1 cass. (Running Time: 36 min.). 1994. 10.00 (978-1-886037-02-1(7), PN02701); audio compact disk 15.00 PNO Tuna.
A collection of 12 original songs intended for children & parents.

Share Your Song. Perf. by Skip West. 1 CD. (Running Time: 30 mins.). (J). 2002. audio compact disk 12.98 (978-1-893967-16-8(6)) Emphasis Ent.

Shared Care for Prostatic Diseases. Roger S. Kirby et al. Frwd. by Louis J. Denis & E. Darracott Vaughan, Jr. 1995. 29.95 (978-1-899066-19-3(5), Informa Health) Pub: Tay Francis Ltd GBR. Dist(s): Taylor and Fran

Shared Experience. Neville Goddard. 1 cass. (Running Time: 62 min.). 1965. 8.00 (70) J & L Pubns.
Neville taught Imagination Creates Reality. He was a powerfully influential teacher of God as Consciousness.

An Asterisk (*) at the beginning of an entry indicates that the title is appearing for the first time.

Shared Heart Cassette Tape: The Relationship of Love. Barry Vissell & Joyce Vissell. 1 cass. (Running Time: 45 min.). 1985. 9.95 Ramira Pub.
Introduces visualizations & practices for individuals & couples written & narrated by the authors of the book, The Shared Heart.

Shared Responsibilities: NACADA Webinar Series 11. Featuring Jennifer Joslin & Casey Self. 2008. audio compact disk 140.00 (978-1-935140-53-5(1)) Nat Acad Adv.

Shared Visions for the Future. Stephen Gaskin. 2 cass. 18.00 set. (A0723-90) Sound Photosyn.
The Tao is going up for '60's stock, & Steven has kept it viable. Hear how.

Shared Visions in World Religions. Nicholson & Theosophical Society America Staff. 2 cass. (Running Time: 2 hrs.). 1989. 10.95 (978-0-8356-2090-1(5), Quest) Pub: Theos Pub Hse. Dist(s): Natl Bk Netwk
Surveys the major world religions, drawing similarities.

Shari Lewis Tells Her One Minute Bedtime Stories. Shari Lewis. (J). 1987. 29.95 (HarperChildAud) HarperCollins Pubs.

Sharing a Song. Perf. by Bob Schneider. 3 cass. (Running Time: 7 hrs. 30 min.). (J). (ps-6). 1990. 13.32 ea. AddisonWesley.
Multicultural songs for whole language classroom experiences.

Sharing Adoption with Children: When, Where & How. Hosted by Mardie Caldwell. (ENG.). 2008. audio compact disk 19.95 (978-1-935176-05-3(6)) Pub: Am Carrage Hse Pubng. Dist(s): STL Dist NA

Sharing God's Vision. Derek Prince. 1 cass. (I-4149) Derek Prince.

Sharing Good Times. unabr. ed. Jimmy Carter. Read by Jimmy Carter. 3 cass. (Running Time: 4 hrs. 30 mins.). 2005. 29.75 (978-1-4193-3003-2(9), 97980) Recorded Bks.
Former president and Nobel Laureate Jimmy Carter has crafted his most intimate self-portrait to date. Carter reflects on some of the more pleasant moments he has shared with his family and friends. He stresses that true pleasure and understanding come from having these shared experiences. He also discusses how his relationship with his wife matured over time and how he came to depend on her as an equal partner in their marriage.

Sharing Good Times. unabr. ed. Jimmy Carter. Read by Jimmy Carter. 2006. 17.95 (978-0-7435-6165-5(1)) Pub: S&S Audio. Dist(s): S and S Inc

Sharing Knife. unabr. ed. Lois McMaster Bujold. (Running Time: 46800 sec.). (Legacy Ser.). 2007. 72.95 (978-1-4332-0778-5(8)); audio compact disk 29.95 (978-1-4332-0780-8(X)); audio compact disk 90.00 (978-1-4332-0779-2(6)) Blckstn Audio.

Sharing Knife, Vol. 3: Passage. unabr. ed. Lois McMaster Bujold. Read by Bernadette Dunne. (Running Time: 14 hrs. 0 mins.). 2008. 79.95 (978-1-4332-3490-3(4)) Blckstn Audio.

Sharing Knife, Vol. 4: Horizon. unabr. ed. Lois McMaster Bujold. Read by Bernadette Dunne. (Running Time: 16 hrs. 0 mins.). (ENG.). 2009. 29.95 (978-1-4332-3596-2(X)); 89.95 (978-1-4332-3592-4(7)); audio compact disk 118.00 (978-1-4332-3593-1(5)) Blckstn Audio.

Sharing Nature Walk. Joseph Cornell. 1 cass. (Running Time: 1 hr. 15 mins.). 1996. 9.95 (978-1-56589-003-9(5), ES-18) Dawn CA.
"Come for a walk in the forest," & along the way meet a number of interesting people! Draw a mystery animal, call in & identify birds, sing delightful nature songs. Side 2 contains adult teaching resources.

Sharing Our Stories: Early Explorers Fluent Set A Audio CD. Benchmark Education Staff. (J). 2006. audio compact disk 10.00 (978-1-4108-7638-6(1)) Benchmark Educ.

Sharing the Gospel in the 21st Century: Introduction to Eternity. Marc Estes. 2 cass. (Running Time: 3 hrs.). 2000. (978-1-886849-20-4(X)) CityChristian.

Sharing Through Primary Songs: Sharing Time Lessons That Combine Music & Gospel Principles; I'll Follow Him in Faith. Alison Palmer. 2006. pap. bk. 17.99 (978-0-88290-814-4(6)) CFI Dist.

Sharing Through Song: My Eternal Family. Alison Palmer. 2008. audio compact disk 12.99 (978-0-88290-954-7(1), HorPubs) CFI Dist.

Sharing Your Faith Naturally: 2007 CCEF Annual Conference. Featuring John Leonard. (ENG.). 2007. audio compact disk 11.99 (978-1-934885-14-7(2)) New Growth Pr.

Shariyat-Ki-Sugmad. unabr. ed. Paul Twitchell. Read by Barbara Kooyman. 6 cass. (Running Time: 10 hrs. 29 mins.). 2004. 28.00 (978-1-57043-175-3(2)) Pub: Eckankar. Dist(s): Hushion Hse

Shariyat-Ki-Sugmad, Vol. 2. unabr. ed. Paul Twitchell. Read by Susan Miller. 6 cass. (Running Time: 10 hrs. 54 mins.). 2004. 28.00 (978-1-57043-189-0(2)) Pub: Eckankar. Dist(s): Hushion Hse

Shark: The Biography of Greg Norman. unabr. ed. Lauren St. John. Read by Ian Esmo. 8 cass. (Running Time: 11 hrs. 30 mins.). 1999. 56.95 (978-0-7861-1641-6(2), 2469) Blckstn Audio.
Norman is golf's most complex & controversial celebrity & perhaps its most gifted & charismatic player. Winner of more than 70 tournaments, including the 1986 & 1993 British Opens, he has reigned as the world's number-one-ranked golfer for most of a decade & began 1998 as the PGA Tour's career-earnings leader with almost $12 million.

Shark! The Truth Behind the Terror. Mike Strong. (High Five Reading - Red Ser.). (ENG.). (gr. 2-3). 2007. audio compact disk 5.95 (978-1-4296-1416-0(1)) CapstoneDig.

Shark & the Goldfish: Positive Ways to Thrive During Waves of Change. unabr. ed. Jon Gordon. (Running Time: 40 hrs.). (ENG.). 2009. 9.98 (978-1-59659-470-8(5), GildAudio) Pub: Gildan Media. Dist(s): HachBkGrp

Shark Bait. unabr. ed. Graham Salisbury. Narrated by Graham Salisbury. 3 pieces. (Running Time: 3 hrs. 15 mins.). (gr. 6 up). 1998. 27.00 (978-0-7887-1808-3(8), 95280E7) Recorded Bks.
Twelve-year-old Mokes is torn between obeying his father, the police chief in a small Hawaiian town & hanging out with his trouble-seeking friends.

Shark Bait. unabr. ed. Graham Salisbury. Read by Graham Salisbury. 3 cass. (Running Time: 3 hr. 15 min.). (J). (gr. 6). 1998. 39.75 Hmwk set. (978-0-7887-1957-8(2), 40658) Recorded Bks.
Twelve-year-old Mokes is torn between obeying his father, a police chief in a small Hawaiian town, & being with his trouble-seeking friends.

Shark Beneath the Reef. unabr. ed. Jean Craighead George. Narrated by Jeff Woodman. 4 pieces. (Running Time: 5 hrs. 15 mins.). (gr. 6 up). 1993. 35.00 (978-1-55690-858-3(X), 93226E7) Recorded Bks.
Fourteen-year old Tomas, who lives in Mexico on the Sea of Cortez, must choose between his hopes of becoming a marine biologist & helping his poor family by quitting school to become a fisherman.

Shark in the Park. Created by Rigby Staff. (Rigby Literacy Ser.). (J). 2000. 9.70 (978-0-7635-7200-6(4), Rigby PEA) Pearson EdAUS AUS.

Shark Mutiny. Patrick Robinson. Narrated by George Guidall. 13 cass. (Running Time: 15 hrs. 30 mins.). 124.00 (978-1-4025-1529-3(4)) Recorded Bks.

Shark Mutiny. Patrick Robinson. Narrated by George Guidall. 11 cass. (Running Time: 15 hrs. 30 mins.). 2001. 97.00 (978-0-7887-5349-7(5), 96571) Recorded Bks.
When China and Iran seize the world's oil supply, four United States carrier battlegroups are dispatched to break up the partnership with a bold display of force. But will the U.S. forces become entrapped by an elaborate diversion.

Shark Mutiny. abr. ed. Patrick Robinson. Read by David McCallum. 4 cass. (Running Time: 6 hrs.). 2001. 25.95 (978-0-694-52554-6(5)) HarperCollins Pubs.

***Shark Mutiny.** abr. ed. Patrick Robinson. Read by David Mccallum. (ENG.). 2004. (978-0-06-081826-5(3), Harper Audio); (978-0-06-081825-8(5), Harper Audio) HarperCollins Pubs.

Shark Net: Memories & Murder. unabr. ed. Robert Drewe. Read by Michael Carman. 7 cass. (Running Time: 8 hrs. 30 mins.). 2001. 56.00 (978-1-74030-440-5(3)) Pub: Bolinda Pubng AUS. Dist(s): Bolinda Pub Inc

Shark Net: Memories & Murder. unabr. ed. Robert Drewe. Read by Michael Carman. 7 CDs. (Running Time: 8 hrs. 30 mins.). 2003. audio compact disk 83.95 (978-1-74093-091-8(6)) Pub: Bolinda Pubng AUS. Dist(s): Bolinda Pub Inc

Shark Net: Memories & Murder. unabr. ed. Robert Drewe. Read by Michael Carmen. (Running Time: 8 hrs. 30 mins.). (YA). 2008. 43.95 (978-1-921415-91-3(6), 9781921415913) Pub: Bolinda Pubng AUS. Dist(s): Bolinda Pub Inc

Shark River. Randy Wayne White. Narrated by Ron McLarty. 9 CDs. (Running Time: 10 hrs. 15 mins.). (Doc Ford Ser.: No. 8). audio compact disk 89.00 (978-1-4025-1526-2(X)) Recorded Bks.

Shark River. Randy Wayne White. Narrated by Ron McLarty. 7 cass. (Running Time: 10 hrs. 15 mins.). (Doc Ford Ser.: No. 8). 2001. 67.00 (978-0-7887-8857-4(4)) Recorded Bks.
Marine biologist Doc Ford is spending two weeks on luxurious Guava Key in a cushy, temporary job. But when two young women at the resort are attacked, Doc is pulled into a plan of revenge that becomes more deadly with each passing hour.

Shark! the Truth behind the Terror. Mike Strong. (High Five Reading Ser.). (ENG.). (gr. 4 up). 2002. audio compact disk 5.95 (978-0-7368-9558-3(2)) CapstoneDig.

Shark Trouble: True Stories & Lessons about the Sea. unabr. ed. Peter Benchley. 4 cass. (Running Time: 6 hrs.). 2002. 32.00 (978-0-7366-8710-2(6)) Books on Tape.
Three decades of experience with the ocean to share stories and information about sharks and other marine animals, and to help the reader approach the ocean and its creatures with understanding and respect. Benchley distinguishes between dangerous and benign sharks, discusses what to tell children about the sea, and tells how to swim safely in the ocean, how to read tides and currents, and how to survive when danger suddenly strikes.

Shark Trouble: True Stories & Lessons about the Sea. unabr. ed. Peter Benchley. 5 CDs. (Running Time: 6 hrs.). 2002. audio compact disk 40.00 (978-0-7366-8711-9(4)) Books on Tape.

Sharkman Six. abr. ed. Owen West. 2004. 15.95 (978-0-7435-4877-9(9)) Pub: S&S Audio. Dist(s): S and S Inc

***Sharkproof.** abr. ed. Harvey Mackay. Read by Harvey Mackay. (ENG.). 2007. (978-0-06-155442-1(1)); (978-0-06-155443-8(X)) HarperCollins Pubs.

Sharkproof. unabr. ed. Harvey Mackay. Read by Harvey Mackay. (Running Time: 7 hrs.). 2009. 39.97 (978-1-4233-9049-7(0), 9781423390497, BADLE) Brilliance Audio.

Sharkproof. unabr. ed. Harvey B. Mackay. Read by Harvey B. Mackay. (Running Time: 7 hrs.). 2009. 39.97 (978-1-4233-9047-3(4), 9781423390473, Brinc Audio MP3 Lib) Brilliance Audio.

Sharkproof. unabr. ed. Harvey B. Mackay. Read by Harvey B. Mackay. (Running Time: 7 hrs.). 2009. 24.99 (978-1-4233-9048-0(2), 9781423390480, BAD) Brilliance Audio.

Sharkproof. unabr. ed. Harvey Mackay & Harvey B. Mackay. Read by Harvey Mackay & Harvey B. Mackay. (Running Time: 7 hrs.). 2009. 24.99 (978-1-4233-9046-6(6), 9781423390466, Brilliance MP3) Brilliance Audio.

Sharks. 1 cass. (Running Time: 35 min.). (J). (gr. k-4). 2001. pap. bk. 15.95 (VX-58C) Kimbo Educ.
World of sharks, from the tiny dwarf to the gigantic whale shark. Includes read along book.

Sharks. 9.95 (978-1-59112-174-9(4)) Live Oak Media.

Sharks. 1 cass. (Running Time: 1 hr.). Dramatization. (J). pap. bk. 6.95 (978-0-86545-105-6(2)) Spizzirri.
Covers sharks from some of the smallest to the large whale shark.

Sharks. California Academy of Sciences Staff & Kay Productions Staff. 1 cass. (Running Time: 25 min.). (Science in Action Learning Ser.). (J). 1988. bk. 11.45 Kay Productions.

Sharks. Gail Gibbons. Illus. by Gail Gibbons. 11 vols. (Running Time: 14 mins.). 1992. bk. 28.95 (978-1-59519-082-6(1)); pap. bk. 39.95 (978-1-59519-081-9(3)) Live Oak Media.

Sharks. Gail Gibbons. Illus. by Gail Gibbons. 11 vols. (Running Time: 14 mins.). (J). 1992. pap. bk. 18.95 (978-1-59519-080-2(5)) Pub: Live Oak Media. Dist(s): AudioGO

Sharks. Gail Gibbons. Illus. by Gail Gibbons. (Running Time: 14 mins.). (J). (gr. k-3). 1992. 9.95 (978-1-59112-117-6(5)); 12.95 (978-1-59519-079-6(1)) Live Oak Media.

Sharks. unabr. ed. Gail Gibbons. Illus. by Gail Gibbons. Read by Peter Fernandez. 11 vols. (Running Time: 14 mins.). (Creatures Great & Small Ser.). (J). (gr. 1-6). 1992. pap. bk. 16.95 (978-0-87499-275-5(3)) AudioGO.
From the tiny dwarf shark to the gigantic whale shark, Gail Gibbons' clear text and illustrations acquaint readers with these ever-fascinating creatures.

Sharks. unabr. ed. Gail Gibbons. Illus. by Gail Gibbons. Read by Peter Fernandez. 11 vols. (Running Time: 14 mins.). (Gail Gibbons' Creatures Great & Small Ser.). (J). (gr. 1-6). 1992. bk. 25.95 (978-0-87499-276-2(1)); pap. bk. & tchr. ed. 37.95 Reading Chest. (978-0-87499-277-9(X)) Live Oak Media.
A fact-filled look at sharks & their environment.

Sharks. unabr. ed. Gail Gibbons. 1 cass. (Running Time: 14 min.). (J). (gr. 2-5). 1993. 9.95 Live Oak Media.

Sharks Don't Get Cancer: How Shark Cartilage Could Save Your Life. abr. ed. I. William Lane & Linda Comac. Read by Tim Kenney & Bert Gurule. Ed. by Bert Gurule & Doug Brand. 2 cass. (Running Time: 2 hrs. 54 min.). 1996. 17.95 (978-0-944634-30-1(3)) Love Logic.
Offers alternative therapy for cancer through use of shark cartilage. Shark cartilage inhibits the growth of blood vessels that nourish cancerous tumors, ultimately destroying them.

Sharks Never Sleep. unabr. ed. William F. Nolan. Read by Barrett Whitener. 6 cass. (Running Time: 8 hrs. 30 mins.). 1999. 44.95 (978-0-7861-1629-4(3), 2457) Blckstn Audio.
In a another vivid re-creation of Hollywood's Golden Age, Erle Stanley Gardner is accused of murder & becomes a hunted fugitive, staying just one step ahead of the law in a desperate attempt to find the real killer.

Sharks Never Sleep. unabr. ed. William F. Nolan. Read by Barrett Whitener. (Running Time: 30600 sec.). 2007. audio compact disk 29.95 (978-0-7861-5818-8(2)) Blckstn Audio.

Sharks Never Sleep: A Black Mask Mystery Featuring Erle Stanley Gardner. unabr. ed. William F. Nolan. Read by Barrett Whitener. (Running Time: 30600 sec.). 2007. audio compact disk 63.00 (978-0-7861-5817-1(4)) Blckstn Audio.

Sharks Still Don't Get Cancer. abr. ed. I. William Lane & Linda Comac. Read by Tim Kenney & Bert Gurule. Ed. by Bert Gurule & Doug Brand. 2 cass. (Running Time: 3 hrs.). 1996. 17.95 (978-0-944634-98-1(2)) Love Logic.
An update of research sighted in Dr. Lane's first audio, "Sharks Don't Get Cancer." Explains alternative therapy for cancer through use of shark cartilage. It also updates the listener on types of shark cartilage to purchase, where to find it & doctors using this therapy.

Sharon Mountain Harmony. 1 cass. 9.98 (C-86) Folk-Legacy.
A splendid collection of traditional gospel songs with harmonies.

Sharon Olds. unabr. ed. Read by Sharon Olds & Rebekah Presson. Ed. by James McKinley. 1 cass. (Running Time: 29 min.). (New Letters on the Air Ser.). 1992. 10.00 (122592); 18.00 2-sided cass. New Letters.
Olds reads from Father & talks to Rebekah Presson about writing "personal" poems that reveal the details of her life.

Sharon Osbourne Extreme: My Autobiography. abr. ed. Sharon Osbourne. (Running Time: 3 hrs. 30 mins.). (ENG.). 2006. 14.98 (978-1-59483-799-9(6)) Pub: Hachet Audio. Dist(s): HachBkGrp

Sharon Osbourne Extreme: My Autobiography. abr. ed. Sharon Osbourne. (Running Time: 3 hrs. 30 mins.). (ENG.). 2009. 34.98 (978-1-60788-274-9(4)) Pub: Hachet Audio. Dist(s): HachBkGrp

Sharp Edges. Jayne Ann Krentz. 2004. 10.95 (978-0-7435-4601-0(6)) Pub: S&S Audio. Dist(s): S and S Inc

Sharp Edges. unabr. ed. Jayne Ann Krentz. Read by Stephanie Diaz. 8 vols. (Running Time: 12 hrs.). 2001. bk. 69.95 (978-0-7927-2424-7(0), CSL 313, Chivers Sound Lib); audio compact disk 94.95 (978-0-7927-9905-4(4), SLD 056, Chivers Sound Lib) AudioGO.
Eugenia Swift, a young woman of singular sensibilities & director of the Leabrook Glass Museum, has been asked to travel to Frog Cove Island to catalog an important collection of art glass. But unsavory rumors surround the collector's death, so the museum insists she take along a private investigator. She fears her secret mission will be discovered, while he hopes she will be a mask for his own hidden agenda.

Sharp Focus on Our Lives. Swami Amar Jyoti. 1 cass. 1982. 9.95 (A-13) Truth Consciousness.
Exploring the facts of our lives with thorough honesty. The secret of our living. When we go to God, everyone benefits.

Sharp Through the Hawthorn. unabr. ed. Sybil Marshall. Read by Norma West. 16 cass. (Running Time: 24 hrs. 21 mins.). (Sound Ser.). 2002. 104.95 (978-1-84283-025-3(2)) Pub: UlverLrgPrint GBR. Dist(s): Ulverscroft US

Sharpen Your Brain Power. Eldon Taylor. Read by Eldon Taylor. Ed. by Leslie Brice. 6 cass. (Running Time: 6 hrs.). 1992. 69.95 (978-1-56705-371-5(8)) Gateways Inst.
Self improvement.

Sharpening Your Legal Negotiating Skills: How to Improve Settlement Results. Read by Charles B. Craver. 4 cass. (Running Time: 4 hrs. 45 min.). 1989. 125.00 Incl. 95p. tape materials. (CP-52247) Cont Ed Bar-CA.
Nationally acclaimed author & lecturer Charles B. Craver covers preparation; when & what to disclose, blocking techniques, inducing first offer; power bargaining; weakening opponent's position; interpreting nonverbal signals; understanding different cultures & sex role expectations; dealing with "strategic misrepresentation;" & ethical considerations.

Sharper Thinking. 1 cass. (Running Time: 60 min.). 10.95 (050) Psych Res Inst.
Fine tuning of the mind to think & react quickly, accurately & automatically.

Sharpe's Battle: Richard Sharpe & the Battle of Fuentes de Oñoro, May 1811. Bernard Cornwell. Narrated by Frederick Davidson. (Running Time: 11 hrs.). (Richard Sharpe Adventure Ser.: No. 12). 1999. 34.95 (978-1-59912-591-6(9)) Iofy Corp.

Sharpe's Battle: Richard Sharpe & the Battle of Fuentes de Oñoro, May 1811. unabr. ed. Bernard Cornwell. Read by William Gaminara. 10 cass. (Running Time: 10 hrs.). (Richard Sharpe Adventure Ser.: No. 12). 1996. 84.95 (978-0-7451-6642-1(3), CAB 1258) AudioGO.
The Spring of 1811 brings one of the worst battles of the Peninsular War on which all British hopes of victory in Spain will depend. Sharpe is given a poorly trained battalion & while comered in a crumbling fort, they are attacked by the French! With thousands of French troops massing nearby, Sharpe must lead his men to glory.

Sharpe's Battle: Richard Sharpe & the Battle of Fuentes de Oñoro, May 1811. unabr. ed. Bernard Cornwell. Read by Frederick Davidson. 8 cass. (Running Time: 11 hrs. 30 mins.). (Richard Sharpe Adventure Ser.: No. 12). 2000. 56.95 (978-0-7861-1689-8(7), 2512) Blckstn Audio.
As Napoleon threatens to crush Britain in Battle, Lt. Col. Richard Sharpe leads a ragtag army to exact a personal revenge. A skilled leader & proven hero, Sharpe takes charge of an Irish battalion from the king of Spain's household guard. But ill-equipped & untrained, they are easily ambushed by an elite French unit commanded by Sharpe's deadly enemy, Brigadier General Guy Loup.

Sharpe's Battle: Richard Sharpe & the Battle of Fuentes de Oñoro, May 1811. unabr. ed. Bernard Cornwell. Read by Frederick Davidson. (Running Time: 11 hrs. 50 mins.). (Richard Sharpe Adventure Ser.: No. 12). 2009. audio compact disk 24.95 (978-1-4332-6946-2(5)) Blckstn Audio.

Sharpe's Battle: Richard Sharpe & the Battle of Fuentes de Oñoro, May 1811. unabr. ed. Bernard Cornwell. Read by Frederick Davidson. (Running Time: 11 hrs. 0 mins.). (Richard Sharpe Adventure Ser.: No. 12). 2009. 29.95 (978-0-7861-7972-5(4)); audio compact disk 100.00 (978-0-7861-7748-6(9)) Blckstn Audio.

Sharpe's Battle: Richard Sharpe & the Battle of Fuentes de Oñoro, May 1811. unabr. ed. Bernard Cornwell. Read by William Gaminara. 10 cass. (Running Time: 15 hrs.). (Richard Sharpe Adventure Ser.: No. 12). 2000. 69.95 (CAB 1258) Pub: Chivers Audio Bks GBR. Dist(s): AudioGO
The Spring of 1811 brings one of the worst battles of the Peninsular War on which all British hopes of victory in Spain will depend. Sharpe is given a poorly trained battalion & while cornered in a crumbling fort, they are attacked by the French! With thousands of French troops massing nearby, Sharpe must lead his men to glory.

Sharpe's Company: Richard Sharpe & the Siege of Badajoz, January to April 1812. Bernard Cornwell. Read by David Case. (Richard Sharpe Adventure Ser.: No. 13). 2000. 56.00 (978-0-7366-5914-7(5)) Books on Tape.

Sharpe's Company: Richard Sharpe & the Siege of Badajoz, January to April 1812. unabr. ed. Bernard Cornwell. Read by William Gaminara. 8 cass. (Running Time: 8 hrs.). (Richard Sharpe Adventure Ser.: No. 13). 1994. 69.95 (978-0-7451-4336-1(9), CAB 1019) AudioGO.
Richard Sharpe had lost his command to a wealthy man who literally bought the promotion Sharpe coveted, & his oldest enemy, the ruthless Hakeswill, appeared on the scene determined to ruin Sharpe. But Sharpe was ready to

change his luck by leading an attack on the fortress of Badajoz, a road to almost certain death or unimaginable glory.

Sharpe's Company: Richard Sharpe & the Siege of Badajoz, January to April 1812, unabr. ed. Bernard Cornwell. Read by Frederick Davidson. 7 cass. (Running Time: 10 hrs.). (Richard Sharpe Adventure Ser.: No. 13). 1995. 49.95 (978-0-7861-0770-4(7), 1619) Blckstn Audio.
The British must mount a bloody attack that no man could survive - no man except Captain Richard Sharpe. Looming on the border of Portugal & Spain is the fortress of Badajoz. To lead an assault on its thick, sheer walls & battlements is suicide, yet Richard Sharpe must lead one. Inside the walls are his wife & daughter, & only he can save them. Outside is the misshapen, vengeance-crazed Sergeant Obadiah Hakeswill, a man determined to kill Sharpe. Sharpe knows that in the heat of battle only the cold steel of his battered sword & the ruthless bloodlust of a soldier at war will protect him from the danger of both sides.

Sharpe's Company: Richard Sharpe & the Siege of Badajoz, January to April 1812. unabr. ed. Bernard Cornwell. Read by Frederick Davidson. (Running Time: 10 hrs. 0 mins.). (Richard Sharpe Adventure Ser.: No. 13). 2009. audio compact disk 24.95 (978-1-4332-6140-4(5)) Blckstn Audio.

Sharpe's Company: Richard Sharpe & the Siege of Badajoz, January to April 1812. unabr. ed. Bernard Cornwell. Read by Frederick Davidson. (Running Time: 9.5 hrs. 0 mins.). (Richard Sharpe Adventure Ser.: No. 13). 2009. 29.95 (978-1-4332-9421-1(4)); audio compact disk & audio compact disk 90.00 (978-1-4332-9420-4(6)) Blckstn Audio.

Sharpe's Company: Richard Sharpe & the Siege of Badajoz, January to April 1812. unabr. ed. Bernard Cornwell. Read by David Case. 7 cass. (Running Time: 10 hrs. 30 min.). (Richard Sharpe Adventure Ser.: No. 13). 2000. 56.00 Books on Tape.
Sharpe must lead a suicide assault against the impregnable Fortress of Badajoz in order to save his wife & daughter.

Sharpe's Devil: Richard Sharpe & the Emperor, 1820-1821. Bernard Cornwell. Narrated by Frederick Davidson. (Running Time: 10 hrs.). (Richard Sharpe Adventure Ser.: No. 21). 1998. 30.95 (978-1-59912-592-3(7)) Iofy Corp.

Sharpe's Devil: Richard Sharpe & the Emperor, 1820-1821. unabr. ed. Bernard Cornwell. Read by William Gaminara. 8 cass. (Running Time: 8 hrs.). (Richard Sharpe Adventure Ser.: No. 21). 1994. 69.95 (978-0-7451-4252-4(4), CAB 935) AudioGO.
Five years after Waterloo & Sharpe's retirement is interrupted by a plea for help. An old friend, Don Blas Vivar, is missing in Chile. Vivar's wife convinces Sharpe to find her husband. Sharpe & his companion, Patrick Harper, are certain that they are only on a mission to collect a corpse, but neither can imagine the dangers in Chile.

Sharpe's Devil: Richard Sharpe & the Emperor, 1820-1821. unabr. ed. Bernard Cornwell. Read by Frederick Davidson. 7 cass. (Running Time: 10 hrs.). (Richard Sharpe Adventure Ser.: No. 21). 1999. 49.95 (978-0-7861-1667-6(6), 2495) Blckstn Audio.
A honored veteran of the Napoleonic Wars, Lt. Col. Richard Sharpe is drawn into a deadly battle, both on land & on the high seas. In 1820, Richard Sharpe has become a peaceful farmer following Waterloo, but comes out of retirement to undertake a perilous mission. He must find Don Blas Vivar, Captain-General of the Spanish colony of Chile & an old friend, who vanished without a trace half a world away.

Sharpe's Devil: Richard Sharpe & the Emperor, 1820-1821. unabr. ed. Bernard Cornwell. Read by Frederick Davidson. (Running Time: 10 hrs. 0 mins.). (Richard Sharpe Adventure Ser.: No. 21). 2009. audio compact disk 24.95 (978-1-4332-6958-5(9)) Blckstn Audio.

Sharpe's Devil: Richard Sharpe & the Emperor, 1820-1821. unabr. ed. Bernard Cornwell. Read by Frederick Davidson. (Running Time: 10 hrs. 0 mins.). (Richard Sharpe Adventure Ser.: No. 21). 2009. audio compact disk 29.95 (978-1-4332-6959-2(7)); audio compact disk 90.00 (978-1-4332-6956-1(2)) Blckstn Audio.

Sharpe's Devil: Richard Sharpe & the Emperor, 1820-1821. unabr. ed. Bernard Cornwell. Read by William Gaminara. 8 cass. (Running Time: 12 hrs.). (Richard Sharpe Adventure Ser.: No. 21). 2000. 59.95 (CAB 935) Pub: Chivers Audio Bks GBR. Dist(s): AudioGO
Five years after Waterloo, Sharpe's retirement is interrupted by a plea for help. An old friend, Don Blas Vivar, is missing in Chile. Vivar's wife pleads with Sharpe to find her husband. Sharpe is soon convinced that they are only on a journey to collect a corpse, but neither can imagine the dangers ahead!.

Sharpe's Eagle: Richard Sharpe & the Talavera Campaign, July 1809. Bernard Cornwell. Read by David Case. (Richard Sharpe Adventure Ser.: No. 8). 2000. 56.00 (978-0-7366-4825-7(9)) Books on Tape.

Sharpe's Eagle: Richard Sharpe & the Talavera Campaign, July 1809. unabr. ed. Bernard Cornwell. Read by William Gaminara. 8 cass. (Running Time: 8 hrs.). (Richard Sharpe Adventure Ser.: No. 8). 1993. bk. 69.95 (978-0-7451-5879-2(X), CAB 429) AudioGO.

Sharpe's Eagle: Richard Sharpe & the Talavera Campaign, July 1809, unabr. ed. Bernard Cornwell. Read by Frederick Davidson. 7 cass. (Running Time: 10 hrs.). (Richard Sharpe Adventure Ser.: No. 8). 1995. 49.95 (978-0-7861-0662-2(X), 1564) Blckstn Audio.
At Talavera in July of 1809, Captain Richard Sharpe, bold, professional, & ruthless, prepares to lead his men against the armies of Napoleon into what will be the bloodiest battle of the war. Sharpe has earned his captaincy, but there are others, such as the foppish Lieutenant Gibbons & his uncle, Colonel Henry Simmerson, who have bought their commissions despite their incompetence. After their cowardly loss of the regiment's colors, their resentment toward the upstart Sharpe turns to treachery, & Sharpe must battle his way through sword fights & bloody warfare to redeem the honor of his regiment.

Sharpe's Eagle: Richard Sharpe & the Talavera Campaign, July 1809. unabr. ed. Bernard Cornwell. Read by Frederick Davidson. 8 CDs. (Running Time: 10 hrs.). (Richard Sharpe Adventure Ser.: No. 8). 2001. audio compact disk 64.00 (978-0-7861-9744-6(7), 1564) Blckstn Audio.

Sharpe's Eagle: Richard Sharpe & the Talavera Campaign, July 1809. unabr. ed. Bernard Cornwell. 7 cass. (Running Time: 34200 sec.). (Richard Sharpe Adventure Ser.: No. 8). 2005. 29.95 (978-0-7861-3664-3(2), E1564); audio compact disk 29.95 (978-0-7861-7737-0(3), ZE1564) Blckstn Audio.

Sharpe's Eagle: Richard Sharpe & the Talavera Campaign, July 1809. unabr. ed. Bernard Cornwell. Read by Frederick Davidson. 13 vols. (Running Time: 10 hrs.). (Richard Sharpe Adventure Ser.: No. 8). 2005. audio compact disk 24.95 (978-0-7861-8660-0(7), ZM1564) Blckstn Audio.

Sharpe's Eagle: Richard Sharpe & the Talavera Campaign, July 1809. unabr. ed. Bernard Cornwell. Read by Frederick Davidson. (Running Time: 10 hrs. 0 mins.). (Richard Sharpe Adventure Ser.: No. 8). 2009. audio compact disk 24.95 (978-1-4332-6497-9(8)) Blckstn Audio.

Sharpe's Eagle: Richard Sharpe & the Talavera Campaign, July 1809. unabr. ed. Bernard Cornwell. Read by David Case. 7 cass. (Running Time: 10 hrs. 30 mins.). (Richard Sharpe Adventure Ser.: No. 8). 2000. 42.00 (5171) Books on Tape.
Captain Richard Sharpe boldly leads his men against Napoleon's armies in a bloody battle to capture a Gold Eagle.

Sharpe's Enemy: Richard Sharpe & the Defense of Portugal, Christmas 1812. Bernard Cornwell. Read by David Case. (Richard Sharpe Adventure Ser.: No. 15). 2000. 64.00 (978-0-7366-6026-6(7)) Books on Tape.

Sharpe's Enemy: Richard Sharpe & the Defense of Portugal, Christmas 1812. unabr. ed. Bernard Cornwell. Read by William Gaminara. 10 cass. (Running Time: 10 hrs.). (Richard Sharpe Adventure Ser.: No. 15). 1995. 84.95 (978-0-7451-6569-1(9), CAB 1185) AudioGO.
Newly promoted Major Richard Sharpe leads his regiment into the mountains. His task is to rescue some women being held hostage by deserters. But one of the renegades is Sergeant Hakeswill, Sharpe's biggest enemy! Once again, with his back against the wall, Sharpe must fight for the regiment & his own personal honor.

Sharpe's Enemy: Richard Sharpe & the Defense of Portugal, Christmas 1812. unabr. ed. Bernard Cornwell. Read by Frederick Davidson. 8 cass. (Running Time: 11 hrs. 30 mins.). (Richard Sharpe Adventure Ser.: No. 15). 1996. 56.95 (978-0-7861-0923-4(8), 1717) Blckstn Audio.
A band of renegades led by Sharpe's vicious mortal enemy, Obadiah Hakeswill, holds a group of British & French women hostage in a strategic mountain pass. On the other side of the pass, Napoleon's Grande Armee seeks to smash through & crush the British army in Portugal. Outnumbered & attacked from two sides, Sharpe must hold his ground or die in the attempt. "The charm of the Sharpe novels is that of meticulously researched stories, books with a passionate correctness as to the details of military organization...& an old-fashioned devotion to heroic conduct".

Sharpe's Enemy: Richard Sharpe & the Defense of Portugal, Christmas 1812. unabr. ed. Bernard Cornwell. Read by Frederick Davidson. (Running Time: 11 hrs. 0 mins.). (Richard Sharpe Adventure Ser.: No. 15). 2008. audio compact disk 90.00 (978-1-4332-4990-7(1)) Blckstn Audio.

Sharpe's Enemy: Richard Sharpe & the Defense of Portugal, Christmas 1812. unabr. ed. Bernard Cornwell. Read by Frederick Davidson. (Running Time: 11 hrs. 0 mins.). (Richard Sharpe Adventure Ser.: No. 15). 2009. audio compact disk 24.95 (978-1-4332-6142-8(1)) Blckstn Audio.

Sharpe's Enemy: Richard Sharpe & the Defense of Portugal, Christmas 1812. unabr. ed. Bernard Cornwell. Read by William Gaminara. 10 cass. (Running Time: 15 hrs.). (Richard Sharpe Adventure Ser.: No. 15). 2000. 69.95 (CAB 118) Pub: Chivers Audio Bks GBR. Dist(s): AudioGO
Newly promoted Major Richard Sharpe leads his regiment into the mountains to rescue some women being held hostage by deserters. But one of the renegades is Sergeant Hakeswill, Sharpe's biggest enemy! With his back against the wall, Sharpe must fight for the regiment and his own personal honor.

***Sharpe's Escape.** unabr. ed. Bernard Cornwell. Read by Patrick Tull. (ENG.). 2005. (978-0-06-083888-1(4), Harper Audio); (978-0-06-078452-2(0), Harper Audio) HarperCollins Pubs.

Sharpe's Escape: Richard Sharpe & the Bussaco Campaign 1810. unabr. ed. Bernard Cornwell. Read by Patrick Tull. (Richard Sharpe Adventure Ser.: No. 10). 2004. 39.95 (978-0-06-059172-4(2)) HarperCollins Pubs.

Sharpe's Fortress: Richard Sharpe & the Siege of Gawilghur, December 1803. Bernard Cornwell. Read by Paul McGann. 2 cass. (Running Time: 3 hrs.). (Richard Sharpe Adventure Ser.: No. 3). 1999. 16.85 (978-0-00-105562-9(3)) Ulvrscrft Audio.
Sharpe, just promoted to an officer, faces his toughest battle, Sergeant Hakeswill wants Sharpe dead, & Hakeswill has powerful friends while Sharpe has only an orphaned Arab boy as his ally. Who rules in Gawilghur, it is said, rules India, & Dodd knows that the fortress is impregnable. There, behind its double walls, in the towering twin forts, Sharpe must face his enemies in what will prove to be Wellesley's last battle on Indian soil.

Sharpe's Fortress: Richard Sharpe & the Siege of Gawilghur, December 1803. unabr. ed. Bernard Cornwell. Read by William Gaminara. 10 cass. (Running Time: 11 hrs.). (Richard Sharpe Adventure Ser.: No. 3). 1999. 84.95 (978-0-7540-0391-5(4), CAB1814) Pub: Chivers Audio Bks GBR. Dist(s): AudioGO
Sharpe is now an officer in Sir Arthur Wellesley's army that is seeking to end the Mahratta War. Having just risen from the ranks, he discovers that his fellow officers are not welcoming. Unsure of his authority, Sharpe's failure seems assured when he discovers that Hakeswell, his oldest enemy, is plotting treason.

Sharpe's Fortress: Richard Sharpe & the Siege of Gawilghur, December 1803. unabr. ed. Bernard Cornwell. Read by William Gaminara. 10 CDs. (Running Time: 15 hrs.). (Richard Sharpe Adventure Ser.: No. 3). 2000. audio compact disk 99.95 (978-0-7540-5319-4(9), CCD 010) Pub: Chivers Audio Bks GBR. Dist(s): AudioGO

***Sharpe's Fury.** abr. ed. Bernard Cornwell. Read by Paul Mcgann. (ENG.). 2006. (978-0-06-124009-6(5), Harper Audio); (978-0-06-124008-9(7), Harper Audio) HarperCollins Pubs.

Sharpe's Fury: Richard Sharpe & the Battle of Barrosa, March 1811. abr. ed. Bernard Cornwell. Read by Paul McGann. (Running Time: 21600 sec.). (Richard Sharpe Adventure Ser.: No. 11). 2007. audio compact disk 14.95 (978-0-06-137416-6(4), Harper Audio) HarperCollins Pubs.

Sharpe's Fury: Richard Sharpe & the Battle of Barrosa, March 1811. unabr. ed. Bernard Cornwell. Read by Steven Crossley. 10 CDs. (Running Time: 12 hrs.). (Richard Sharpe Adventure Ser.: No. 11). 2006. audio compact disk 123.75 (978-1-4281-1563-7(3)) Recorded Bks.

Sharpe's Gold: Richard Sharpe & the Destruction of Almeida, August 1810. unabr. ed. Bernard Cornwell. Read by William Gaminara. 8 cass. (Running Time: 8 hrs.). (Richard Sharpe Adventure Ser.: No. 9). bk. 69.95 (978-0-7451-5874-7(9), CAB 510) AudioGO.

Sharpe's Gold: Richard Sharpe & the Destruction of Almeida, August 1810. unabr. ed. Bernard Cornwell. Read by Frederick Davidson. 6 cass. (Running Time: 8 hrs. 30 mins.). (Richard Sharpe Adventure Ser.: No. 9). 1995. 44.95 (978-0-7861-0716-2(2), 1594) Blckstn Audio.
Only a year after its stunning victory at Talavera in July of 1809, Wellington's Peninsular army - vastly outnumbered, its coffers empty - was on the brink of collapse. The Spanish government had fallen, the last Spanish armies had been crushed by the French, & all that was left were the peasants fighting the guerrillas, the "little war." But Wellington had one hope left. He knew that in the dangerous Portugese hills lay a fortune in gold, enough gold perhaps to turn the Peninsular War around. And he knew of one fighting man capable of stealing it: Captain Richard Sharpe of the South Essex Regiment.

Sharpe's Gold: Richard Sharpe & the Destruction of Almeida, August 1810. unabr. ed. Bernard Cornwell. Read by Frederick Davidson. 8 CDs. (Running Time: 8 hrs. 30 mins.). (Richard Sharpe Adventure Ser.: No. 9). 2001. audio compact disk 64.00 (978-0-7861-9745-3(5), 1594) Blckstn Audio.

Sharpe's Gold: Richard Sharpe & the Destruction of Almeida, August 1810. unabr. ed. Bernard Cornwell. Read by Frederick Davidson. (Running Time: 9 hrs. 0 mins.). (Richard Sharpe Adventure Ser.: No. 9). 2009. audio compact disk 24.95 (978-1-4332-6139-8(1)) Blckstn Audio.

Sharpe's Gold: Richard Sharpe & the Destruction of Almeida, August 1810. unabr. ed. Bernard Cornwell. Read by David Case. 6 cass. (Running Time: 9 hrs.). (Richard Sharpe Adventure Ser.: No. 9). 2000. 48.00 (978-0-7366-4901-8(8), 5206) Books on Tape.
A year after the victory at Talavera, Wellington's army outnumbered and out of money, is on the verge of collapse. Its only hope lies in a cache of gold hidden in the Portuguese mountains and the only man capable of stealing it is Captain Richard Sharpe.

Sharpe's Gold: Richard Sharpe & the Destruction of Almeida, August 1810. unabr. ed. Bernard Cornwell. Read by William Gaminara. 8 cass. (Running Time: 12 hrs.). (Richard Sharpe Adventure Ser.: No. 9). 2000. 59.95 (CAB 510) Pub: Chivers Audio Bks GBR. Dist(s): AudioGO

Sharpe's Havoc: Richard Sharpe & the Campaign in Northern Portugal, Spring 1809. unabr. ed. Bernard Cornwell. 9 cass. (Running Time: 12 hrs. 30 min.). (Richard Sharpe Adventure Ser.: No. 7). 2003. 89.00 (978-1-4025-4373-9(5)) Recorded Bks.
In 1809 Lieutenant Sharpe and his riflemen are in Portugal, preparing for Napoleon's next strike. The smaller English force will probably pull out before it's too late, but not Sharpe. His orders are to find the missing daughter of an English wine shipper. Just as Sharpe and his men begin their mission, the French launch their punishing assault.

Sharpe's Honor: Richard Sharpe & the Vitoria Campaign, February to June, 1813. unabr. ed. Bernard Cornwell. Read by Frederick Davidson. (Running Time: 37800 sec.). (Richard Sharpe Adventure Ser.: No. 16). 2008. audio compact disk 29.95 (978-1-4332-4502-2(7)); audio compact disk & audio compact disk 90.00 (978-1-4332-4501-5(9)) Blckstn Audio.

Sharpe's Honour: Richard Sharpe & the Vitoria Campaign, February to June, 1813. unabr. ed. Bernard Cornwell. Read by William Gaminara. 8 cass. (Running Time: 8 hrs.). (Richard Sharpe Adventure Ser.: No. 16). 1995. 69.95 (978-0-7451-6475-5(7), CAB 1091) AudioGO.
Major Richard Sharpe awaits the opening shots of the army's campaign with grim expectancy. For victory depends on the increasingly fragile alliance between Britain & Spain, an alliance that must be kept at any cost. Pierre Ducos, a French Intelligence Officer, sees a chance to destroy both the alliance & to achieve personal revenge on Sharpe. Soon Sharpe finds himself a fugitive from ally & enemy alike.

Sharpe's Honour: Richard Sharpe & the Vitoria Campaign, February to June, 1813, unabr. ed. Bernard Cornwell. Read by Frederick Davidson. 8 cass. (Running Time: 11 hrs. 30 mins.). (Richard Sharpe Adventure Ser.: No. 16). 1996. 56.95 (978-0-7861-0943-2(2), 1693) Blckstn Audio.
An unfinished duel, a midnight murder, & the treachery of a beautiful prostitute lead to the imprisonment of Sharpe. Condemned to die as an assassin, he is the pawn in a plot conceived by his archenemy, Pierre Ducos. Caught in a web of political intrigue for which his military experience has left him fatally unprepared, Sharpe becomes a fugitive - a man hunted by both ally & enemy alike.

Sharpe's Honour: Richard Sharpe & the Vitoria Campaign, February to June, 1813. unabr. ed. Bernard Cornwell. Read by Frederick Davidson. (Running Time: 10 hrs. 50 mins.). (Richard Sharpe Adventure Ser.: No. 16). 2009. audio compact disk 24.95 (978-1-4332-6143-5(X)) Blckstn Audio.

Sharpe's Honour: Richard Sharpe & the Vitoria Campaign, February to June, 1813. unabr. ed. Bernard Cornwell. 8 cass. (Running Time: 12 hrs.). (Richard Sharpe Adventure Ser.: No. 16). 2001. 64.00 (978-0-7366-6348-9(7)) Books on Tape.
An unfinished duel, a midnight murder, and the treachery of a beautiful prostitute lead to Sharpe's imprisonment. Caught in a web of political intrigue for which his military experience has left him fatally unprepared, Sharpe becomes a fugitive - a man hunted by both ally and enemy alike.

Sharpe's Honour: Richard Sharpe & the Vitoria Campaign, February to June, 1813. unabr. ed. Bernard Cornwell. Read by William Gaminara. 8 cass. (Running Time: 12 hrs.). (Richard Sharpe Adventure Ser.: No. 16). 2000. 59.95 (CAB 1091) Pub: Chivers Audio Bks GBR. Dist(s): AudioGO
Major Richard Sharpe awaits the opening shots of the army's campaign with grim expectancy. For victory depends on the increasingly fragile alliance between Britain & Spain, an alliance that must be kept at any cost. Pierre Ducos, a French Intelligence Officer, sees a chance to destroy both the alliance & to achieve personal revenge on Sharpe. Soon Sharpe finds himself a fugitive from ally & enemy alike.

Sharpe's Prey: Richard Sharpe & the Expedition to Copenhagen 1807. unabr. ed. Bernard Cornwell. Narrated by Patrick Tull. 9 cass. (Running Time: 12 hrs. 30 mins.). (Richard Sharpe Adventure Ser.: No. 5). 2002. 84.00 (978-1-4025-1864-5(1)) Recorded Bks.

Sharpe's Prey: Richard Sharpe & the Expedition to Copenhagen 1807. unabr. ed. Bernard Cornwell. Narrated by Patrick Tull. 9 cass. (Running Time: 12 hrs. 30 mins.). (Richard Sharpe Adventure Ser.: No. 5). 2002. 42.95 (978-1-4025-1865-2(X), RF930) Recorded Bks.

Sharpe's Regiment: Richard Sharpe & the Invasion of France, June to November 1913. Bernard Cornwell. Read by David Case. (Richard Sharpe Adventure Ser.: No. 17). 2001. 64.00 (978-0-7366-6830-9(6)) Books on Tape.

Sharpe's Regiment: Richard Sharpe & the Invasion of France, June to November 1913. unabr. ed. Bernard Cornwell. Read by Frederick Davidson. 8 cass. (Running Time: 11 hrs. 30 mins.). (Richard Sharpe Adventure Ser.: No. 17). 1996. 56.95 (978-0-7861-0966-1(1), 1743) Blckstn Audio.
A corrupt political enemy is determined to disband the South Essex Regiment & destroy the life of Major Richard Sharpe. Sharpe returns to England & discovers an illegal recruiting ring that sells soldiers like cattle to other division. The ringleaders know Sharpe is on their trail, & they try to kill him at every turn.

Sharpe's Regiment: Richard Sharpe & the Invasion of France, June to November 1913. unabr. ed. Bernard Cornwell. Read by Frederick Davidson. (Running Time: 11 hrs. 50 mins.). (Richard Sharpe Adventure Ser.: No. 17). 2009. audio compact disk 24.95 (978-1-4332-6144-2(8)) Blckstn Audio.

Sharpe's Regiment: Richard Sharpe & the Invasion of France, June to November 1913. unabr. ed. Bernard Cornwell. Read by Frederick Davidson. (Running Time: 11 hrs. 0 mins.). (Richard Sharpe Adventure Ser.: No. 17). 2009. 29.95 (978-1-4332-9417-4(6)); audio compact disk & audio compact disk 100.00 (978-1-4332-9416-7(8)) Blckstn Audio.

Sharpe's Regiment: Richard Sharpe & the Invasion of France, June to November 1913. unabr. ed. Bernard Cornwell. Read by William Gaminara. 10 cass. (Running Time: 15 hrs.). (Richard Sharpe Adventure Ser.: No. 17). 2000. 69.95 (CAB 770) Pub: Chivers Audio Bks GBR. Dist(s): AudioGO
Major Richard Sharpe's men are in danger, not from the French, but from the bureaucrats of Whitehall! Unless reinforcements can be delivered, the

regiment will be disbanded. Refusing to let his men die, Sharpe returns to England and uncovers a nest of high-ranking traitors.

Sharpe's Revenge: Richard Sharpe & the Peace of 1814. unabr. ed. Bernard Cornwell. Read by Frederick Davidson. 8 cass. (Running Time: 11 hrs. 30 mins.). (Richard Sharpe Adventure Ser.: No. 19). 1996. 56.95 (978-0-7861-1013-1(9), 1791) Blckstn Audio.
It is 1814 & the defeat of Napoleon seems imminent - if the well-protected city of Toulouse can be conquered. For Richard Sharpe, the battle turns out to be one of the bloodiest of the Peninsula Wars, & he must draw on his last reserves of strength to lead his troops to victory. But before Sharpe can lay down his sword, he must fight a different sort of battle. Accused of stealing Napoleon's personal treasure, Sharpe escapes from a British military court & embarks on the battle of his life - armed only with the unflinching resolve to protect his honor.

Sharpe's Revenge: Richard Sharpe & the Peace of 1814. unabr. ed. Bernard Cornwell. Read by Frederick Davidson. (Running Time: 11 hrs. 0 mins.). (Richard Sharpe Adventure Ser.: No. 19). 2008. 29.95 (978-1-4332-5046-0(2)); audio compact disk 90.00 (978-1-4332-5045-3(4)) Blckstn Audio.

Sharpe's Revenge: Richard Sharpe & the Peace of 1814. unabr. ed. Bernard Cornwell. Read by Frederick Davidson. (Running Time: 11 hrs. 0 mins.). (Richard Sharpe Adventure Ser.: No. 19). 2009. audio compact disk 24.95 (978-1-4332-6146-6(4)) Blckstn Audio.

Sharpe's Revenge: Richard Sharpe & the Peace of 1814. unabr. ed. Bernard Cornwell. Read by William Gaminara. 10 cass. (Running Time: 15 hrs.). (Richard Sharpe Adventure Ser.: No. 19). 2000. 69.95 (CAB 642) Pub: Chivers Audio Bks GBR. Dist(s): AudioGO
It is 1814, and after an exhausting series of battles, the British and Spanish armies are pushing into south-western France. Major Richard Sharpe is accused of stealing Napoleon's treasure en route to Elba, and he must now be on the lookout for his captors and track down the unknown enemy who has tried to frame him. Accompanied by Captain Frederickson, the two men set out to resolve an ingenious and devastating revenge.

Sharpe's Revenge: Richard Sharpe & the Peace of 1814. unabr. ed. Bernard Cornwell. Read by William Gaminara. 10 cass. (Running Time: 12 hrs. 15 min.). (Richard Sharpe Adventure Ser.: No. 19). 1992. 84.95 (978-0-7451-5875-4(7), CAB 642) Pub: Chivers Audio Bks GBR. Dist(s): AudioGO
It is 1814. After a long & exhausting series of battles, the British & Spanish armies are pushing into southwestern France from Spain. But before the French are finally defeated & Sharpe can lay down his sword, one of the bloodiest conflicts of the war must be fought: the battle for the city of Toulouse.

Sharpe's Rifles: Richard Sharpe & the French Invasion of Galicia, January 1809. Bernard Cornwell. Read by David Case. (Richard Sharpe Adventure Ser.: No. 6). 2000. 64.00 (978-0-7366-4979-7(4)) Books on Tape.

Sharpe's Rifles: Richard Sharpe & the French Invasion of Galicia, January 1809. unabr. ed. Bernard Cornwell. Read by William Gaminara. 8 cass. (Running Time: 9 hrs. 43 min.). (Richard Sharpe Adventure Ser.: No. 6). 1990. 69.95 (978-0-7451-5876-1(5), CAB 352) AudioGO.
In the bitter winter of 1809, the French are winning the war in Spain. The British are quickly retreating - but the troop of young Richard Sharpe is cut off & surrounded. Worse, Sharpe is mistrusted by his men, & can rely on only three things: a Spanish cavalryman, a young woman attempting to return home to England, & his own savage determination.

Sharpe's Rifles: Richard Sharpe & the French Invasion of Galicia, January 1809. unabr. ed. Bernard Cornwell. 1 CD. (Running Time: 10 hrs. 30 mins.). (Richard Sharpe Adventure Ser.: No. 6). 2001. audio compact disk 19.95 (zm1650) Blckstn Audio.
It's 1809 & the powerful French juggernaut is sweeping across Spain. Lieutenant Sharpe is newly in command of the demoralized, distrustful men of the 95th Rifles. He must lead them to safety & the only means of escape is a treacherous trek through the enemy-infested mountains of Spain.

Sharpe's Rifles: Richard Sharpe & the French Invasion of Galicia, January 1809, unabr. ed. Bernard Cornwell. Read by Frederick Davidson. 8 cass. (Running Time: 11 hrs. 30 mins.). (Richard Sharpe Adventure Ser.: No. 6). 1995. 56.95 (978-0-7861-0852-7(5), 1650) Blckstn Audio.

Sharpe's Rifles: Richard Sharpe & the French Invasion of Galicia, January 1809. unabr. ed. Bernard Cornwell. Read by Frederick Davidson. 9 CDs. (Running Time: 11 hrs. 30 mins.). (Richard Sharpe Adventure Ser.: No. 6). 2000. audio compact disk 72.00 (978-0-7861-9856-6(7), 1650) Blckstn Audio.

Sharpe's Rifles: Richard Sharpe & the French Invasion of Galicia, January 1809. unabr. ed. Bernard Cornwell. 8 cass. (Running Time: 041400 sec.). (Richard Sharpe Adventure Ser.: No. 6). 2005. 29.95 (978-0-7861-3443-4(7)) Blckstn Audio.

Sharpe's Rifles: Richard Sharpe & the French Invasion of Galicia, January 1809. unabr. ed. Bernard Cornwell. Read by Frederick Davidson. 13 vols. (Running Time: 11 hrs. 30 mins.). (Richard Sharpe Adventure Ser.: No. 6). 2005. audio compact disk 24.95 (978-0-7861-9601-2(7), 1650) Blckstn Audio.

Sharpe's Rifles: Richard Sharpe & the French Invasion of Galicia, January 1809. unabr. ed. Bernard Cornwell. Read by Frederick Davidson. (Running Time: 11 hrs. 50 mins.). (Richard Sharpe Adventure Ser.: No. 6). 2009. audio compact disk 24.95 (978-1-4332-6138-1(3)) Blckstn Audio.

Sharpe's Rifles: Richard Sharpe & the French Invasion of Galicia, January 1809. unabr. ed. Bernard Cornwell. Read by William Gaminara. 8 cass. (Running Time: 12 hrs.). (Richard Sharpe Adventure Ser.: No. 6). 2000. 59.95 (CAB 352) Pub: Chivers Audio Bks GBR. Dist(s): AudioGO
In the bitter winter of 1809, the French are winning the war in Spain. Britain's forces, hotly pursued by Napoleon's troops, are retreating, and Lieutenant Richard Sharpe's regiment has been cut off. Surrounded by the enemy, and distrusted by his men, it is up to Sharpe and his unlikely ally, Blas Vivar, a Spanish calvary officer, to win back the trust of the regiment and stop the advancement of the French.

Sharpe's Siege: Richard Sharpe & the Winter Campaign 1814. Bernard Cornwell. Illus. by Bernard Cornwell. Read by David Case. (Richard Sharpe Adventure Ser.: No. 18). 2001. 64.00 (978-0-7366-7155-2(2)) Books on Tape.

Sharpe's Siege: Richard Sharpe & the Winter Campaign 1814. Bernard Cornwell. Narrated by Frederick Davidson. (Running Time: 12 hrs.). (Richard Sharpe Adventure Ser.: No. 18). 1995. 34.95 (978-1-59912-593-0(5)) Iofy Corp.

Sharpe's Siege: Richard Sharpe & the Winter Campaign 1814. unabr. ed. Bernard Cornwell. Read by William Gaminara. 10 cass. (Running Time: 11 hrs. 10 min.). (Richard Sharpe Adventure Ser.: No. 18). 1991. 84.95 (978-0-7451-5877-8(3), CAB 573) AudioGO.
The invasion of France is underway, & the British Navy has called upon the services of Major Richard Sharpe. He & a small force of riflemen are to capture a fortress & secure a landing on the French coast. It is to be one of the most dangerous missions of his career.

Sharpe's Siege: Richard Sharpe & the Winter Campaign 1814. unabr. ed. Bernard Cornwell. Read by Frederick Davidson. 8 cass. (Running Time: 11 hrs. 30 mins.). (Richard Sharpe Adventure Ser.: No. 18). 1996. 56.95 (978-0-7861-0993-7(9), 1770) Blckstn Audio.
Sharpe's mission had seemed simple: capture a small unguarded French coastal fort, cripple Napoleon's supply lines, & retreat across the sea. But behind the lines, Sharpe's old enemy, Pierre Ducos, awaits Sharpe's arrival with a battalion of French soldiers & a vicious commanding general who keeps the scalps of his dead enemies as trophies. Outmaneuvered by Ducos's treachery & abandoned by his own navy, Sharpe has only two choices: To escape with the aid of the charming, unscrupulous American mercenary, Cornelius Killick, or die.

Sharpe's Siege: Richard Sharpe & the Winter Campaign 1814, unabr. ed. Bernard Cornwell. Read by Frederick Davidson. 8 cass. (Running Time: 12 hrs.). (Richard Sharpe Adventure Ser.: No. 18). 1996. 56.95 (1770) Blckstn Audio.

Sharpe's Siege: Richard Sharpe & the Winter Campaign 1814. unabr. ed. Bernard Cornwell. Read by Frederick Davidson. (Running Time: 11 hrs. 50 mins.). (Richard Sharpe Adventure Ser.: No. 18). 2009. audio compact disk 24.95 (978-1-4332-6145-9(6)) Blckstn Audio.

Sharpe's Siege: Richard Sharpe & the Winter Campaign 1814. unabr. ed. Bernard Cornwell. Read by Frederick Davidson. (Running Time: 10 hrs. 50 mins.). (Richard Sharpe Adventure Ser.: No. 18). 2009. 29.95 (978-1-4332-9423-5(0)); audio compact disk & audio compact disk 100.00 (978-1-4332-9422-8(2)) Blckstn Audio.

Sharpe's Siege: Richard Sharpe & the Winter Campaign 1814. unabr. ed. Bernard Cornwell. Read by William Gaminara. 10 cass. (Running Time: 15 hrs.). (Richard Sharpe Adventure Ser.: No. 18). 2000. 69.95 (CAB 573) Pub: Chivers Audio Bks GBR. Dist(s): AudioGO
The invasion of France is underway, and the British Navy has called upon the services of Major Richard Sharpe. He and a small force of Riflemen are to capture a fortress and secure a landing on the French coast. Through the incompetence of a reckless naval commander and the machinations of his enemy, French spy-master Pierre Ducos, Sharp finds himself abandoned in the heart of enemy territory, facing overwhelming forces and the very real prospect of defeat.

Sharpe's Siege: Richard Sharpe & the Winter Campaign 1814. unabr. collector's ed. Bernard Cornwell. Read by David Case. 8 cass. (Running Time: 12 hrs.). (Richard Sharpe Adventure Ser.: No. 18). 2001. 64.00 Books on Tape.
Sharpe, ordered to take a French coastal fort, has his back to the sea until he adopts a cunning strategy to defeat the French.

Sharpe's Sword: Richard Sharpe & the Salamanca Campaign, June & July 1812. Bernard Cornwell. 8 cass. (Running Time: 12 hrs.). (Richard Sharpe Adventure Ser.: No. 14). 2001. 64.00 (978-0-7366-6190-4(5)) Books on Tape.
Colonel Leroux, France's most ruthless assassin, is killing Britain's most valuable spies & it's up to Richard Sharpe to stop him. Thrust into the unfamiliar world of political & military intrigue, Sharp must tangle with LaMarquesa, a beguiling, extraordinarily beautiful woman whose embrace is as calculating as it is passionate.

Sharpe's Sword: Richard Sharpe & the Salamanca Campaign, June & July 1812. unabr. ed. Bernard Cornwell. Read by William Gaminara. 8 cass. (Running Time: 8 hrs.). (Richard Sharpe Adventure Ser.: No. 14). 1997. 69.95 (978-0-7451-6785-5(3), CAB 1401) AudioGO.
The Salamanca Campaign, 1812. Richard Sharpe is once again at war. But this time his enemy is the ruthless & sadistic Colonel Leroux. Sharpe's mission is to safeguard El Mirador, the spy whose network of agents is vital for a British victory. In this new world of political & military intrigue in the unfamiliar aristocratic Spanish society, Sharpe's only guide is the beautiful Marquesa, a woman with her own secrets to conceal.

Sharpe's Sword: Richard Sharpe & the Salamanca Campaign, June & July 1812, unabr. ed. Bernard Cornwell. Read by Frederick Davidson. 8 cass. (Running Time: 11 hrs. 30 mins.). (Richard Sharpe Adventure Ser.: No. 14). 1995. 56.95 (978-0-7861-0898-5(3), 1670) Blckstn Audio.
Colonel Leroux is killing Britain's most valuable spies, & it's up to Richard Sharpe to stop him. Thrust into the unfamiliar world of political & military intrigue, Sharpe must tangle with La Marquesa, a beguiling, extraordinarily beautiful woman whose embrace is as calculating as it is passionate. As she leads him through a maze of secrecy, cunning, & deception, Sharpe relentlessly pursues Leroux, determined to exact his revenge with the cold steel of his sword.

Sharpe's Sword: Richard Sharpe & the Salamanca Campaign, June & July 1812. unabr. ed. Bernard Cornwell. Read by Frederick Davidson. (Running Time: 11 hrs. 50 mins.). (Richard Sharpe Adventure Ser.: No. 14). 2009. audio compact disk 24.95 (978-1-4332-6141-1(3)) Blckstn Audio.

Sharpe's Sword: Richard Sharpe & the Salamanca Campaign, June & July 1812. unabr. ed. Bernard Cornwell. Read by Frederick Davidson. (Running Time: 10 hrs. 0 mins.). (Richard Sharpe Adventure Ser.: No. 14). 2009. 29.95 (978-1-4332-9419-8(2)); audio compact disk & audio compact disk 100.00 (978-1-4332-9418-1(4)) Blckstn Audio.

Sharpe's Sword: Richard Sharpe & the Salamanca Campaign, June & July 1812. unabr. ed. Bernard Cornwell. Read by William Gaminara. 8 cass. (Running Time: 12 hrs.). (Richard Sharpe Adventure Ser.: No. 14). 2000. 59.95 (CAB 1401) Pub: Chivers Audio Bks GBR. Dist(s): AudioGO
The Salamanca Campaign, 1812, Richard Sharpe is once again at war. But this time his enemy is the ruthless and sadistic Colonel Leroux. Sharpe's mission is to safeguard El Mirador, the spy whose network of agents is vital to the British victory. In this new world of political and military intrigue in the unfamiliar aristocratic Spanish society, Sharpe's only guide is the beautiful Marquesa, a woman with her own secrets to conceal.

Sharpe's Sword: Richard Sharpe & the Salamanca Campaign, June & July 1812. unabr. ed. Bernard Cornwell. Read by William Gaminara. 8 CDs. (Running Time: 9 hrs. 30 mins.). (Richard Sharpe Adventure Ser.: No. 14). 2000. audio compact disk 79.95 (978-0-7540-5346-0(6), CCD 037) Pub: Chivers Audio Bks GBR. Dist(s): AudioGO
Sharpe's mission is to safeguard El Mirador, the spy whose network is vital to the British victory. In this Spanish society of political & military intrigue, Sharpe's only guide is Marquesa, a woman with her own secrets to conceal.

Sharpe's Tiger: Richard Sharpe & the Siege of Seringapatam 1799. Bernard Cornwell. 11 CDs. (Running Time: 16 hrs. 30 mins.). (Richard Sharpe Adventure Ser.: No. 1). 2000. audio compact disk 88.00 (ZP2536) Blckstn Audio.
It is 1799: as the British Army fights its way through India toward a diabolical trap, the young & illiterate private Richard Sharpe must battle both man & beast behind enemy lines, in an attempt to push the ruthless Tippoo of Mysore from his throne & drive his French allies out of India.

Sharpe's Tiger: Richard Sharpe & the Siege of Seringapatam 1799. Bernard Cornwell. Read by Frederick Davidson. 11 CDs. (Running Time: 13 hrs.). (Richard Sharpe Adventure Ser.: No. 1). 2003. audio compact disk 88.00 (978-0-7861-9842-9(7), 2536) Blckstn Audio.

Sharpe's Tiger: Richard Sharpe & the Siege of Seringapatam 1799. unabr. ed. Bernard Cornwell. Read by William Gaminara. 12 CDs. (Running Time: 18 hrs.). (Richard Sharpe Adventure Ser.: No. 1). 2002. audio compact disk 110.95 (978-0-7540-5481-8(0), CCD 172) AudioGO.
Sharpe and the rest of his battalion are about to embark upon the siege of Seringapatam, island citadel of the Tippoo of Mysore. The British must move this potentate from his tiger throne, but he has gone to extraordinary lengths to defend his city from attack. AS always he is surrounded by tigers, both living and ornamental.

Sharpe's Tiger: Richard Sharpe & the Siege of Seringapatam 1799. unabr. ed. Bernard Cornwell. Read by Frederick Davidson. 9 cass. (Running Time: 13 hrs.). (Richard Sharpe Adventure Ser.: No. 1). 2003. 62.95 (978-0-7861-1731-4(1), 2536) Blckstn Audio.
It is1799: as the British Army fights its way through India toward a diabolical trap, the young & illiterate private Richard Sharpe must battle both man & beast behind enemy lines, in an attempt to push the ruthless Tippoo of Mysore from his throne & drive his French allies out of India.

Sharpe's Tiger: Richard Sharpe & the Siege of Seringapatam 1799. unabr. ed. Bernard Cornwell. Read by Frederick Davidson. 9 pieces. (Richard Sharpe Adventure Ser.: No. 1). 2004. reel tape 39.95 (978-0-7861-2557-9(8)) Blckstn Audio.

Sharpe's Tiger: Richard Sharpe & the Siege of Seringapatam 1799. unabr. ed. Bernard Cornwell. Read by Frederick Davidson. (Running Time: 13 hrs. 0 mins.). (Richard Sharpe Adventure Ser.: No. 1). 2009. audio compact disk 24.95 (978-1-4332-6937-0(6)) Blckstn Audio.

Sharpe's Tiger: Richard Sharpe & the Siege of Seringapatam 1799. unabr. ed. Bernard Cornwell. Read by William Gaminara. 10 cass. (Running Time: 12 hrs. 9 mins.). (Richard Sharpe Adventure Ser.: No. 1). 1998. 69.95 (978-0-7540-0135-5(0), CAB1558) Pub: Chivers Audio Bks GBR. Dist(s): AudioGO
Richard Sharpe & the rest of his battalion are about to embark upon the siege of Seringapatam, the island citadel of the Tippoo of Mysore. The British must remove this fierce tiger from power, but he has gone to extraordinary lengths to defend his city from attack.

Sharpe's Trafalgar: Richard Sharpe & the Battle of Trafalgar, October 21, 1805. unabr. ed. Bernard Cornwell. Read by William Gaminara. 10 cass. (Running Time: 15 hrs.). (Richard Sharpe Adventure Ser.: No. 4). 2001. 84.95 (978-0-7540-0564-3(X), CAB1987) Pub: Chivers Audio Bks GBR. Dist(s): AudioGO
It's 1805 & Ensign Richard Sharpe is on his way home from India. However, his ship is riven with treachery & threatened by a French warship, the Revenant, which is terrorizing British shipping. As the French warship races home, carring a treaty that could ignite India into a new war against the British & the hunt turns into a stern chase.

Sharpe's Trafalgar: Richard Sharpe & the Battle of Trafalgar, October 21, 1805. unabr. ed. Bernard Cornwell. Read by William Gaminara. 10 CDs. (Running Time: 15 hrs.). (Richard Sharpe Adventure Ser.: No. 4). 2001. audio compact disk 94.95 (978-0-7540-5400-9(4), CCD091) Pub: Chivers Audio Bks GBR. Dist(s): AudioGO

Sharpe's Trafalgar: Richard Sharpe & the Battle of Trafalgar, October 21, 1805. unabr. ed. Bernard Cornwell. Narrated by Patrick Tull. 9 cass. (Running Time: 13 hrs. 15 mins.). (Richard Sharpe Adventure Ser.: No. 4). 2001. 84.00 (978-0-7887-7242-9(2)) Recorded Bks.
Richard Sharpe is returning from his latest campaign against Napoleon. Anticipating an uneventful voyage, he finds himself in the middle of the Battle of Trafalgar.

Sharpe's Traflagar. unabr. ed. 2001. 29.99 (978-0-7887-8952-6(X)) Recorded Bks.

Sharpe's Triumph: Richard Sharpe & the Battle of Assaye, September 1803. Bernard Cornwell. Read by Frederick Davidson. 8 cass. (Running Time: 11 hrs. 30 mins.). (Richard Sharpe Adventure Ser.: No. 2). 2001. 56.95 (978-0-7861-1908-0(X), 2701) Blckstn Audio.
In the four years since he earned his sergeant's stripes, young Richard Sharpe has led a peaceful existence. But this relatively easy life meets with a brutal end when he is the sole survivor of a murderous attack at the hands of Major William Dodd.

Sharpe's Triumph: Richard Sharpe & the Battle of Assaye, September 1803. unabr. ed. Bernard Cornwell. Read by William Gaminara. 8 cass. (Running Time: 8 hrs.). (Richard Sharpe Adventure Ser.: No. 2). 1999. 69.95 (978-0-7540-0268-0(3), CAB1691) AudioGO.
India, 1803. Sergeant Richard Sharpe has discovered the easiest billet in the British army. But when he witnesses a murderous act of treachery by an English officer who has defected from the East India Company, he is ordered to hunt for the renegade deep in enemy territory.

Sharpe's Triumph: Richard Sharpe & the Battle of Assaye, September 1803. unabr. ed. Bernard Cornwell. Read by William Gaminara. 10 CDs. (Running Time: 15 hrs.). (Richard Sharpe Adventure Ser.: No. 2). 2002. audio compact disk 94.95 (978-0-7540-5474-0(8), CCD 165) AudioGO.
It is four years since Richard Sharpe earned his sergeant's stripes, and four years in which Sharpe seems to have discovered the easiest billet in the British army. But that comfort is rudely shattered when he witnesses a murderous act of treachery by an English officer who has defected from the East India company. Sharpe is ordered to join the hunt for the renegade Englishman, and it is a hunt that will take him deep into the enemy's territory.

Sharpe's Triumph: Richard Sharpe & the Battle of Assaye, September 1803. unabr. ed. Bernard Cornwell. Read by Frederick Davidson. (Running Time: 11 hrs. 30 mins.). (Richard Sharpe Adventure Ser.: No. 2). 2000. audio compact disk 24.95 (978-0-7861-9468-1(5), 2701) Blckstn Audio.

Sharpe's Triumph: Richard Sharpe & the Battle of Assaye, September 1803. unabr. ed. Bernard Cornwell. Read by Frederick Davidson. 10 CDs. (Running Time: 11 hrs. 30 mins.). (Richard Sharpe Adventure Ser.: No. 2). 2000. audio compact disk 80.00 (978-0-7861-9787-3(0), 2701) Blckstn Audio.
In the four years since he earned his sergeant's stripes, young Richard Sharpe has led a peaceful existence. But this relatively easy life meets with a brutal end when he is the sole survivor of a murderous attack at the hands of Major William Dodd.

Sharpe's Triumph: Richard Sharpe & the Battle of Assaye, September 1803. unabr. ed. Bernard Cornwell. Narrated by Frederick Davidson. 8 pieces. (Running Time: 11 hrs. 30 mins.). (Richard Sharpe Adventure Ser.: No. 2). 2004. reel tape 39.95 (978-0-7861-2571-5(3), 100379); audio compact disk 49.95 (978-0-7861-9082-9(5), 110320) Blckstn Audio.

Sharpe's Triumph: Richard Sharpe & the Battle of Assaye, September 1803. unabr. ed. Bernard Cornwell. Read by Frederick Davidson. (Running Time: 11 hrs. 50 mins.). (Richard Sharpe Adventure Ser.: No. 2). 2009. audio compact disk 24.95 (978-1-4332-6941-7(4)) Blckstn Audio.

Sharpe's Waterloo: Richard Sharpe & the Waterloo Campaign, 15 June to 18 June 1815. abr. ed. Bernard Cornwell. Read by William Gaminara. 10 cass. (Running Time: 11 hrs. 50 min.). (Richard Sharpe Adventure Ser.: No. 20). 1992. 84.95 (978-0-7451-5878-5(1), CAB 671) AudioGO.
As Europe heads towards one of the most decisive battles in history, the British & their allies are preparing for a grand society ball in Brussels. Among the names on the glittering guest list is one very reluctant, newly promoted Lieutenant-Colonel Sharpe. Sharpe's scouting reports of the huge French army marching towards Brussels go unheeded by a young & inexperienced commander, the Prince of Orange, who is infinitely more concerned with the flair of his dancing steps than apparent impending doom.

Sharpe's Waterloo: Richard Sharpe & the Waterloo Campaign, 15 June to 18 June 1815. unabr. ed. Bernard Cornwell. Read by Frederick Davidson. (Running Time: 13 hrs. 0 mins.). (Richard Sharpe Adventure Ser.: No. 20). 2009. audio compact disk 24.95 (978-1-4332-6951-6(1)) Blckstn Audio.

Sharpe's Waterloo: Richard Sharpe & the Waterloo Campaign, 15 June to 18 June 1815. unabr. ed. Bernard Cornwell. Read by William Gaminara. 10 cass. (Running Time: 15 hrs.). (Richard Sharpe Adventure Ser.: No. 20). 2000. 69.95 (CAB 671) Pub: Chivers Audio Bks GBR. Dist(s): AudioGO
It is June of 1815, and as Europe heads toward one of the most decisive battle in history, Lieutenant-Colonel Richard Sharpe finds himself under the command of the Prince of Orange, who is in charge of a large proportion of the Allied Forces. However, the Prince refuses to listen to Sharpe's scouting reports of an enormous French army marching towards Brussels with the recently returned Emperor Napoleon at its head.

Sharpshooter Craps. unabr. ed. Frank Scoblete. 1 cass. (Running Time: 1 hr.). 1997. audio compact disk 16.95 CD. (978-1-882173-06-8(6)) Paone Pr.
For advanced craps players. Explains the five count, the captain's supersystems, "Dark-Sider" attack methods & setting & controling the dice.

***Shattered.** Karen Robards. Contrib. by Susan Ericksen. (Playaway Adult Fiction Ser.). (ENG.). 2010. 69.99 (978-1-4418-5617-3(X)) Find a World.

Shattered. abr. ed. Karen Robards. Read by Susan Ericksen. 5 CDs. (Running Time: 6 hrs.). 2010. audio compact disk 19.99 (978-1-4233-6844-1(4), 9781423368441, BACD) Brilliance Audio.

Shattered. abr. ed. Karen Robards. (Running Time: 6 hrs.). 2011. audio compact disk 9.99 (978-1-4233-6849-6(5), 9781423368496, BCD Value Price) Brilliance Audio.

Shattered. unabr. ed. Dick Francis. Read by Fiacre Douglas. 5 cass. (Running Time: 7 hrs.). 2000. 29.95 (978-1-58788-063-6(6), 1587880636, BAU); 57.25 (978-1-58788-064-3(4), 1587880644, Unabridge Lib Edns) Brilliance Audio.
When jockey Martin Stukely dies after a fall at Cheltenham, he accidentally embroils his friend Gerard Logan in a perilous search for a stolen videotape. Logan is a glassblower on the verge of widespread acclaim. Long accustomed to the frightful dangers inherent in molten glass and in maintaining a glassmaking furnace at never less than 1800 degrees Fahrenheit, Logan is suddenly faced with terrifying threats to his business, his courage, and his life. Believing that the missing video holds the key to a priceless treasure, and wrongly convinced that Logan knows where to find it, criminal forces set out to press him for information he doesn't have. To survive, he realizes that he himself must sort out the truth. The final race to the tape throws more hazards in Logan's way than his dead jockey friend could ever have imagined. Glass shatters. Logan doesn't. . . but it's a close-run thing.

Shattered. unabr. ed. Dick Francis. Read by Fiacre Douglas. (Running Time: 7 hrs.). 2004. 39.25 (978-1-59600-498-6(3), 1596004983, BADLE); 24.95 (978-1-59600-497-9(5), 1596004975, BAD); 39.25 (978-1-59600-496-2(7), 1596004967, Brlnc Audio MP3 Lib); 24.95 (978-1-59600-495-5(9), 1596004959, Brilliance MP3) Brilliance Audio.

Shattered. unabr. ed. Dick Francis. Read by Fiacre Douglas. (Running Time: 25200 sec.). 2007. audio compact disk 82.25 (978-1-4233-3368-5(3), 9781423333685, BriAudCD Unabrid); audio compact disk 29.95 (978-1-4233-3367-8(5), 9781423333678, Bril Audio CD Unabri) Brilliance Audio.

Shattered. unabr. ed. Gabrielle Lord. Read by Caroline Lee. (Running Time: 14 hrs. 15 mins.). 2008. audio compact disk 108.95 (978-1-921415-31-9(2), 9781921415319) Pub: Bolinda Pubng AUS. Dist(s): Bolinda Pub Inc

Shattered. unabr. ed. Karen Robards. Read by Susan Ericksen. 1 MP3-CD. (Running Time: 13 hrs.). 2010. 39.97 (978-1-4233-6848-9(7), 9781423368489, Brlnc Audio MP3 Lib); audio compact disk 32.99 (978-1-4233-6843-4(6), 9781423368434, Bril Audio CD Unabri) Brilliance Audio.

***Shattered.** unabr. ed. Karen Robards. Read by Susan Ericksen. 1 MP3-CD. (Running Time: 13 hrs.). 2010. 24.99 (978-1-4233-6845-8(2)); audio compact disk 92.97 (978-1-4233-6847-2(9), 9781423368472, BriAudCD Unabrid) Brilliance Audio.

***Shattered: Struck down, but Not Destroyed.** unabr. ed. Frank Pastore & Ellen Vaughn. Narrated by Frank Pastore. (Running Time: 6 hrs. 17 mins. 39 sec.). (ENG.). 2010. 18.19 (978-1-60814-744-1(4)); audio compact disk 25.99 (978-1-59859-842-1(2)) Oasis Audio.

Shattered Air: A True Account of Catastrophe & Courage on Yosemite's Half Dome. unabr. ed. Bob Madgic. Read by Anthony Heald. (Running Time: 28800 sec.). 2007. 59.95 (978-1-4332-1111-9(4)); audio compact disk 29.95 (978-1-4332-1113-3(0)) Blckstn Audio.

Shattered Air: A True Account of Catastrophe & Courage on Yosemite's Half Dome. unabr. ed. Bob Madgic & Adrian Esteban. (Running Time: 8 mins. 30 sec.). 2007. audio compact disk 63.00 (978-1-4332-1112-6(2)) Blckstn Audio.

Shattered Dreams: My Life as a Polygamist's Wife. unabr. ed. Irene Spencer. Read by Laural Merlington. (Running Time: 14 hrs. 0 mins. 0 sec.). (ENG.). 2007. audio compact disk 39.99 (978-1-4001-0594-6(3)); audio compact disk 29.99 (978-1-4001-5594-1(0)); audio compact disk 79.99 (978-1-4001-3594-3(X)) Pub: Tantor Media. Dist(s): IngramPubServ

***Shattered Vows: Hope & Healing for Women Who Have Been Sexually Betrayed.** unabr. ed. Debra Laaser. (Running Time: 7 hrs. 27 mins. 0 sec.). (ENG.). 2009. 12.99 (978-0-310-77196-8(X)) Zondervan.

Shattering. unabr. ed. Kathryn Lasky. (Running Time: 4.5 hrs. NaN mins.). (Guardians of Ga'Hoole Ser.: Bk. 5). 2008. 34.95 (978-1-4332-2605-2(7)); audio compact disk 40.00 (978-1-4332-2606-9(5)) Blckstn Audio.

Shattering. unabr. ed. Kathryn Lasky. Read by Pamela Garelick. (Running Time: 4 hrs. 30 mins.). (Guardians of Ga'Hoole Ser.: Bk. 5). 2010. 19.95 (978-1-4332-2609-0(X)) Blckstn Audio.

***Shattering.** unabr. ed. Kathryn Lasky. Read by Pamela Garelick. (Running Time: 4 hrs 30 mins.). (Guardians of Ga'Hoole Ser.: Bk. 5). 2010. audio compact disk 19.95 (978-1-4332-2608-3(1)) Blckstn Audio.

Shattering Glass. Gail Giles. 3 cass. (Running Time: 5 hrs. 34 mins.). (J). (gr. 7 up). 2004. 30.00 (978-0-8072-1640-8(2), Listening Lib) Random Audio Pubg.

Shattering Glass. Gail Giles. Read by Scott Brick. 3 vols. (Running Time: 5 hrs. 34 mins.). (J). (gr. 7 up). 2004. pap. bk. 37.00 (978-1-4000-9013-6(X), Listening Lib) Random Audio Pubg.

Shaw-Terry Letters. abr. ed. George Bernard Shaw et al. Perf. by Peggy Ashcroft & Cyril Cusack. 1 cass. (J). 1984. 12.95 (978-0-694-50083-3(6), SWC 1108) HarperCollins Pubs.

Shawl. unabr. ed. Cynthia Ozick. Read by Cynthia Ozick. Read by Yelena Shmulenson. 2 CDs. (Running Time: 1 hrs. 30 mins.). (ENG., 2008. audio compact disk 18.95 (978-1-59887-684-0(8), 1598876848) Pub: HighBridge. Dist(s): Workman Pub

Shawn McLemore: Wait on Him. 1997. 10.98; audio compact disk 16.98 Pub: Brentwood Music. Dist(s): Provident Mus Dist
Includes "Holy Hand," "Wait on Him," "Your Love," "Christ Did It All," & more.

Shawn Michaels. unabr. ed. Donald V. Allen. Read by Shawn Michaels. 1 cass. (Running Time: 30 min.). Dramatization. (Official Audio Biography Series of the World Wrestling Federation). 5.99 (978-1-56703-045-7(9)) High-Top Sports.

Shawnee Trail. abr. ed. Ralph Compton. Read by Jim Gough. 4 cass. (Running Time: 6 hrs.). (Trail Drive Ser.: Bk. 6). 1998. Rental 24.95 (978-1-890990-05-3(1)) Otis Audio.
Driving two thousand cattle north from Texas, Cajun cowboy Long John Coons must brave stampedes, cattle rustlers, renegade Indians & the love of a beautiful woman with a sordid past to get his longhorns to the Kansas railroad.

Shawshank Redemption. Stephen King. Read by Frank Muller. (Running Time: 4 hrs.). (ENG.). (gr. 12 up). 2009. audio compact disk 19.95 (978-0-14-314395-6(6), PengAudBks) Penguin Grp USA.

***Shawshank Redemption.** unabr. ed. Stephen King. (Running Time: 4 hrs.). (ENG.). 2010. audio compact disk 14.95 (978-0-14-242802-3(7), PengAudBks) Penguin Grp USA.

Shayla's Double Brown Baby Blues. unabr. ed. Lori Aurelia Williams. Read by Heather Alicia Simms. 7 cass. (Running Time: 10 hrs. 30 mins.). (J). (gr. 7 up). 2004. 46.00 (978-0-8072-0581-5(8), Listening Lib) Random Audio Pubg.

She see Richard Wilbur Readings

She. unabr. ed. H. Rider Haggard. Read by Richard Brown. 9 cass. (Running Time: 12 hrs. 30 min.). (gr. 8 up). 1990. 28.95 (978-1-55685-185-8(5)) Audio Bk Con.
She, or Ayesha, is a beautiful & powerful African sorceress who appears to be immortal. Young Leo Vincey sets out on a dangerous journey to avenge her murder of his ancestor, an ancient priest of Isis.

She, unabr. ed. H. Rider Haggard. Read by Fred Williams. 9 cass. (Running Time: 13 hrs. 30 min.). 1996. 62.95 (978-0-7861-0947-0(5), 1696) Blckstn Audio.
A dangerous quest in underground tombs, ancient Egyptian relics, a beautiful, ruthless Queen who possesses magical powers, & a narrow escape by the narrator from her clutches - have become prototypes for today's adventure books & films, from "Raiders of the Lost Ark" to "Jurassic Park." More than just great escape fiction, "She" is great literature. It contains the embodiment of one of the most formidable & ambivalent characters of Western mythology: a female who is both monstrous & beautiful.

She: Safe, Healthy, & Empowered. unabr. ed. Rebecca St. James & Linda Bjorkland. (ENG.). 2004. 19.59 (978-1-60814-368-9(6)) Oasis Audio.

She & He: Adventures in Mythology. Short Stories. As told by Jim Weiss. 1 CD. (Running Time: 1 hr.). Dramatization. (Storyteller's Version Ser.). (J). (gr. k up). 1999. audio compact disk 14.95 (978-1-882513-34-5(7), 1124-0009) Greathall Prods.
Collection of myths addresses the equality of the sexes and the value of love and honor. Includes: "Psyche and Cupid," "Pygmalion and Galatea," "Echo and Narcissus," "Atlanta and the Golden Apples" and "Baucis and Philemon".

She & He: Adventures in Mythology. Short Stories. As told by Jim Weiss. 1 cass. (Running Time: 1 hr.). Dramatization. (Storyteller's Version Ser.). (J). (gr. k up). 1991. 10.95 (978-1-882513-09-3(6), 1124-09) Greathall Prods.

She & He: Adventures in Mythology. Read by Jim Weiss. 1 cass. (Running Time: 1 hr.). (J). (GHP9) NewSound.

She Baby. Prod. by Jordan Davis. 1 CD. (Running Time: 40 mins.). audio compact disk 15.00 (VCEE302) Lodestone Catalog.

She Came Back, unabr. ed. Patricia Wentworth. Read by Nadia May. 5 cass. (Running Time: 7 hrs.). 1993. 39.95 (978-0-7861-0319-5(1), 1280) Blckstn Audio.
It takes two murders, an attempted third, the whispered arrogant command that tags the culprit & the unobtrusively ubiquitous Miss Silver to prove Sir Philip's theory regarding his young wife's return from the dead.

***She Comes First: The Grammer of Oral Sex.** abr. ed. Ian Kerner. Read by Ian Kerner. (ENG.). 2005. (978-0-06-083526-2(5), Harper Audio); (978-0-06-083525-5(7), Harper Audio) HarperCollins Pubs.

***She Comes First: Introduction: The Grammer of Oral Sex.** abr. ed. Ian Kerner. Read by Ian Kerner. (ENG.). 2006. (978-0-06-201483-2(8), Harper Audio); (978-0-06-134113-7(4), Harper Audio) HarperCollins Pubs.

She Dwelt among the Untrodden Ways see Treasury of William Wordsworth

She Goes to War. unabr. ed. Edith Pargeter. Read by Carol Boyd. 8 cass. (Running Time: 10 hrs.). (Isis Ser.). (J). 1995. 69.95 (978-1-85695-893-6(0), 950504) Pub: ISIS Lrg Prnt GBR. Dist(s): Ulverscroft US

She Got up off the Couch: And Other Heroic Acts from Mooreland, Indiana. Haven Kimmel. Read by Haven Kimmel. (Playaway Adult Nonfiction Ser.). 2008. 54.99 (978-1-60640-631-1(0)) Find a World.

She Got up off the Couch: And Other Heroic Acts from Mooreland, Indiana. unabr. ed. Haven Kimmel. Read by Haven Kimmel. 8 CDs. (Running Time: 11 hrs.). (ENG.). 2006. audio compact disk 34.95 (978-1-59887-011-4(4), 1598870114) Pub: Penguin-HghBrdg. Dist(s): Penguin Grp USA

She Is Me. unabr. ed. Cathleen Schine. Read by Patricia Kalember. (ENG.). 2005. 14.98 (978-1-59483-342-7(7)) Pub: Hachet Audio. Dist(s): HachBkGrp

She May Not Leave. Fay Weldon. Narrated by Rula Lenska. (Running Time: 28440 sec.). (Sound Library). 2006. audio compact disk 74.95 (978-0-7927-4071-1(8)) AudioGo GBR.

She Said - He Said: Gender Differences in the Business Setting. Pat Heim. 1 cass. (Running Time: 1 hr.). 1995. 12.95 (978-1-891531-01-9(8)) Heim Gp.
Explores the divergent rules men & women learned about "appropriate" adult behavior & how they cause us problems at work & at home.

She Said Yes Set: The Unlikely Martyrdom of Cassie Bernall. unabr. ed. Misty Bernall. 2 cass. 1999. 34.25 (FS9-51044) Highsmith.

She Set Out to Seek Her Fortune. Ruth Halpern. 1 cass. (Running Time: 1 hr.). (J). (gr. 1-8). 1997. 10.00 (978-0-9661114-0-8(0)) Word for Word.
Folktales & original stories about heroines from many cultures.

She Stoops to Conquer see Sound of Classical Drama

She Stoops to Conquer. Oliver Goldsmith. 2 cass. Dramatization. 10.95 ea. (SAC 8047/8048) Spoken Arts.

She Stoops to Conquer. unabr. ed. Oliver Goldsmith. Narrated by Flo Gibson. (Running Time: 2 hrs. 43 mins.). 1999. 14.95 (978-1-55685-722-5(5)) Audio Bk Con.

She Walks in Beauty see Poetry of Byron

***She Walks in Beauty.** Caroline Kennedy. 2011. audio compact disk 24.99 (978-1-4013-2600-5(5)) Hyperion.

She Walks These Hills. abr. ed. Sharyn McCrumb. Read by Buck Schirner. 2 cass. (Running Time: 3 hrs.). (Ballad Ser.: No. 3). 2000. 7.95 (978-1-57815-025-0(6), 1027, Media Bks Audio) Media Bks NJ.
An aging folkhero escaped from prison, a pioneer woman's ghost & an Appalachian hiker cross paths.

She Walks These Hills, unabr. ed. Sharyn McCrumb. Narrated by Sally Darling. 9 cass. (Running Time: 12 hrs. 45 mins.). (Ballad Ser.: No. 3). 1999. 78.00 (978-0-7887-0229-7(7), 94454E7) Recorded Bks.
A tale of journeys from the historic journey of Katie Wyler, kidnapped by the Shawnee in 1789, to the pilgrimage of Hiram Sorley, an escapee from Mountain City's prison.

She Wasn't the One (an Essay from Things I've Learned from Women Who've Dumped Me) abr. ed. Bruce Jay Friedman. Read by Bruce Jay Friedman. Ed. by Ben Karlin. (Running Time: 15 mins.). (ENG.). 2008. 1.98 (978-1-60024-353-0(3)) Pub: Hachet Audio. Dist(s): HachBkGrp

***She Who Laughs, Lasts! Laugh-Out-Loud Stories from Today's Best-Known Women of Faith.** Compiled by Ann Spangler. (Running Time: 5 hrs. 41 mins. 0 sec.). (ENG.). 2008. 14.99 (978-0-310-30518-7(7)) Zondervan.

She Who Remembers. unabr. collector's ed. Linda L. Shuler. Read by Donada Peters. 11 cass. (Running Time: 16 hrs. 30 min.). 1992. 88.00 (978-0-7366-2310-0(8), 3092) Books on Tape.
Kwani. A beautiful woman born in the American southwest long before Columbus...whose blue eyes marked her as a witch & set her apart from the Indian tribe that raised her.

Shearwater. unabr. ed. Andrea Mayes. Read by Marie-Louise Walker. (Running Time: 8 hrs. 30 mins.). 2008. audio compact disk 87.95 (978-1-921415-32-6(0), 9781921415326) Pub: Bolinda Pubng AUS. Dist(s): Bolinda Pub Inc

Shed Stress. Eldon Taylor. Read by Eldon Taylor. Interview with XProgress Aware Staff. Music by Steven Halpern. Interview with XProgress Aware. 1 cass. (Running Time: 62 min.). (EchoTech Ser.). 16.95 incl. script. (978-1-55978-341-5(9), 9905) Progress Aware Res.
Gentle coaching & soundtrack with underlying subliminal affirmations with tones & frequencies to alter brain wave activity.

Shedding Light on Our Dark Side Series, Charles R. Swindoll. 6 cass. (Running Time: 11 hrs.). 1994. 30.95 (978-1-57972-029-2(3)) Insight Living.
Bible study discussing sin's serious effects & how to recover from them.

Sheen on the Silk. unabr. ed. Anne Perry. Read by Angela Dawe. 16 CDs. (Running Time: 19 hrs.). 2010. audio compact disk 32.99 (978-1-4418-2488-2(X), 9781441824882, Bril Audio CD Unabri) Brilliance Audio.

***Sheen on the Silk.** unabr. ed. Anne Perry. Read by Angela Dawe. 2 MP3-CDs. (Running Time: 19 hrs.). 2010. 24.99 (978-1-4418-2490-5(1), 9781441824905, Brilliance MP3); 39.97 (978-1-4418-2491-2(X), 9781441824912, Brlnc Audio MP3 Lib); 39.97 (978-1-4418-2493-6(6), 9781441824936, BADLE); 24.99 (978-1-4418-2492-9(8), 9781441824929, BAD); audio compact disk 89.97 (978-1-4418-2489-9(8), 9781441824899, BriAudCD Unabrid) Brilliance Audio.

Sheep see Poetry & Voice of Ted Hughes

Sheep Country. unabr. ed. M. Lehman. Read by Gene Engene. 4 cass. (Running Time: 4 hrs. 42 min.). 1994. 26.95 (978-1-55686-500-8(7)) Books in Motion.
Unaware of the range war brewing over her uncle's sheep ranch located in cattle country, Kim Demming leaves Seattle, Washington to live on her uncle's ranch in Wyoming.

Sheep in a Jeep. Nancy E. Shaw. Illus. by Margot Apple. (Carry-Along Book & Cassette Favorites Ser.). (ENG.). (J). (gr. k-3). 1999. pap. bk. 10.99 (978-0-395-95990-9(X)) HM Harcourt.

Sheep in a Jeep. Nancy E. Shaw. Illus. by Margot Apple. (J). (ps-k). 2005. audio compact disk 6.00 (978-0-618-70898-7(7)) HM Harcourt.

Sheep in Wolves' Clothing. unabr. ed. Satoshi Kitamura. Narrated by John McDonough. 1 cass. (Running Time: 15 mins.). (ps up). 1997. 10.00 (978-0-7887-0905-0(4), 95043E7) Recorded Bks.
Three playful sheep go to the beach the last day of summer. While they swim, four helpful wolves watch their wooly coats. But when the sheep get out of the water, their coats are gone & so are the wolves! Portrays the dangers of being too trusting.

Sheep-Pig. Dick King-Smith. Read by Stephen Thorne. 2 cass. (Running Time: 1 hr. 50 min.). (J). (gr. 1-5). 12.95 (CC/030) C to C Cassettes.
Farmer Hogget wins a piglet at the fair. His sheepdog Fly adopts the motherless orphan & is delighted to find he learns all that she has to teach him.

***Sheep Thief: How Anyone, Anywhere, Can Make a Positive Change in Life.** Al Walker. Read by Al Walker. Frwd. by Bob Johnson. (ENG.). 2010. pap. bk. 24.95 (978-1-936354-00-9(4), TremLifeBks) Executive Bks.

***Sheepfarmer's Daughter.** unabr. ed. Elizabeth Moon. (Running Time: 18 hrs.). (Deed of Paksenarrion Ser.). 2010. 44.97 (978-1-4418-5121-5(6), 9781441851215, BADLE) Brilliance Audio.

***Sheepfarmer's Daughter.** unabr. ed. Elizabeth Moon. Read by Jennifer Van Dyck. (Running Time: 16 hrs.). (Deed of Paksenarrion Ser.). 2010. 29.99 (978-1-4418-5119-2(4), 9781441851192, Brilliance MP3); 44.97 (978-1-4418-5120-8(8), 9781441851208, Brlnc Audio MP3 Lib); audio compact disk 99.97 (978-1-4418-5118-5(6), 9781441851185, BriAudCD Unabrid); audio compact disk 29.99 (978-1-4418-5117-8(8), 9781441851178, Bril Audio CD Unabri) Brilliance Audio.

Sheepfold. Derek Prince. 1 cass. (B-122) Derek Prince.

Sheepwrecked. Jackie Moffat & Patricia Gallimore. 2007. 69.95 (978-1-84652-151-5(3)); audio compact disk 84.95 (978-1-84652-152-2(1)) Pub: Magna Story GBR. Dist(s): Ulverscroft US

Sheer Mischief. Jill Mansell. 2009. 89.95 (978-0-7531-3225-8(7)); audio compact disk 99.95 (978-0-7531-3226-5(5)) Pub: Isis Pubng Ltd GBR. Dist(s): Ulverscroft US

***Sheila Butt - Seasons of Service.** Arranged by Polishing the Pulpit. 2010. audio compact disk 25.00 (978-1-60644-117-6(5)) Heart Heart.

Sheila O'Connor. unabr. ed. Sheila O'Connor. Read by Sheila O'Connor. Interview with Rebekah Presson. 1 cass. (Running Time: 29 min.). 1990. 10.00 (122890) New Letters.
O'Connor's first novel, "Tokens of Grace", is told in brief vignettes that have been compared to prose poems. She reads from this work & talks about combining memory with imagination in writing.

An Asterisk (*) at the beginning of an entry indicates that the title is appearing for the first time.

Sheila Rae, the Brave. Kevin Henkes. 14 vols. (Running Time: 8 mins.). (J). 2002. pap. bk. & tchr.'s planning gde. ed. 33.95 (978-0-87499-954-9(5)) Live Oak Media.
The challenge of facing fears head on is humorously conveyed when Sheila Rae, a fearless and boastful mouse, decides to take a new route home from school. and wanders into unfamiliar territory.

Sheila Rae, the Brave. Kevin Henkes. 11 vols. (Running Time: 8 mins.). (J). (ps-3). 2002. bk. 25.95 (978-0-87499-953-2(7)) Live Oak Media.

Sheila Rae, the Brave. Kevin Henkes. Illus. by Kevin Henkes. (Running Time: 8 mins.). 2002. audio compact disk 12.95 (978-1-59112-325-5(9)) Live Oak Media.

Sheila Rae, the Brave. Kevin Henkes. Illus. by Kevin Henkes. 14 vols. (Running Time: 8 mins.). 2002. pap. bk. 35.95 (978-1-59112-549-5(9)) Live Oak Media.

Sheila Rae, the Brave. Kevin Henkes. Illus. by Kevin Henkes. (Running Time: 8 mins.). (J). (ps-2). 2002. 9.95 (978-0-87499-951-8(0)) Live Oak Media.

Shelby's Secret Treasure-Search for Ephesians. (J). 2002. 9.95 (978-1-56623-101-5(9)) Pub: Imprenta. Dist(s): STL Dist NA

She'll Be Comin' round the Mountain. 2004. 8.95 (978-1-56008-326-9(3)); cass. & flmstrp 30.00 (978-1-56008-762-5(5)) Weston Woods.

Shell Beach. unabr. ed. Nancy Thayer. Narrated by Renée Raudman. (Running Time: 9 hrs. 30 mins. 0 sec.). (ENG.). 2008. audio compact disk 69.99 (978-1-4001-3775-6(6)) Pub: Tantor Media. Dist(s): IngramPubServ

Shell Game. James Swallow. 2009. audio compact disk 15.95 (978-1-84435-346-0(X)) Pub: Big Finish GBR. Dist(s): Natl Bk Netwk

Shell Game, unabr. ed. Carol O'Connell. Read by Roberta Germaine. 12 vols. (Running Time: 17 hrs.). (Chivers Sound Library American Collections). 1999. bk. 96.95 (978-0-7927-2347-9(3), CSL 236, Chivers Sound Lib) AudioGO.
On live television the re-creation of a legendary magic trick goes horribly awry, a terrible accident everyone agrees. But two people know it is not.

Shell Game, Pt. 1. unabr. ed. Douglas Terman. Read by Michael Prichard. 7 cass. (Running Time: 10 hrs. 30 min.). Incl. Pt. II. Shell Game. 7 cass. (Running Time: 10 hrs. 30 min.). Douglas Terman. Read by Michael Prichard. 1985. 56.00 (1274-B); 1985. 56.00 (978-0-7366-0284-6(4), 1274-A) Books on Tape.
A thriller set in Cuba during the missile crisis, "Shell Game" combines political espionage & dramatic adventure. As a tale of two brothers divided by love & war, it exposes what may be in reality the most deadly deception of the nuclear age. What if the Soviets removed only the missile casings & not the missiles themselves?.

Shell Seekers. Rosamunde Pilcher. Read by Penelope Dellaporta. 1990. 72.00 (978-0-7366-1697-3(7)) Books on Tape.

Shell Seekers, unabr. ed. Rosamunde Pilcher. Narrated by Barbara Rosenblat. 16 cass. (Running Time: 23 hrs.). 1990. 128.00 (978-1-55690-471-4(1), 90008E7) Recorded Bks.
A warm family saga of three generations of heroines: Penelope, her daughter Olivia & a young girl named Antonia, whom Olivia & Penelope have adopted as surrogate child. Confronted with her own mortality, Penelope returns to the Cornwall coast to come to terms with her son Noel, with Antonia's haunted young boyfriend Danus & with the memory of Richard, the soldier who never returned.

Shell Seekers, Pt. A. unabr. ed. Rosamunde Pilcher. Read by Penelope Dellaporta. 10 cass. (Running Time: 15 hrs.). 1990. 72.00 (978-0-7366-1696-6(9), 2542-A) Books on Tape.
Set in London & Cornwall from WWII to the present. The story of the Keeling family & of the passions & heartbreak that have held them together for three generations. The family centers around Penelope & it is her love & courage that determine the course of all their lives. One of Penelope's treasured possessions is the Shell Seekers, a painting her father left her as a rememberance & a legacy. It is this painting that symbolizes to Penelope the ties between the generations. It is the link between the past, the present & the future. But it is also this painting that just may tear the family apart.

Shell Seekers, Pt. B. unabr. ed. Rosamunde Pilcher. Read by Penelope Dellaporta. 9 cass. (Running Time: 13 hrs. 30 min.). 1990. 72.00 (2542-B) Books on Tape.
A magical painting holds a family together for three generations.

***Shelter.** 2010. audio compact disk (978-1-59171-294-7(7)) Falcon Picture.

Shelter. Perf. by Gary Chapman & Amy Grant. Prod. by Michael Omartian. 1 cass. 1996. audio compact disk Brentwood Music.
The 1996 Dove Award Male Vocalist of the Year brings you Shelter, including the No. 1 song, One of Two, featuring his wife, Amy Grant. Features: Man After Your Own Heart.

Shelter from the Storm. unabr. ed. Rowena Summers. Read by Julie Maisie. 7 cass. (Running Time: 9 hrs. 15 mins.). (Story Sound Ser.). 2007. 61.95 (978-1-84652-008-2(8)); audio compact disk 79.95 (978-1-84652-009-9(6)) Pub: Mgna Lrg Print GBR. Dist(s): Ulverscroft US

Shelter in the Time of Storm. Patti Drennan. 2008. pap. bk. 29.95 (978-1-59235-215-9(4), Glory Snd) Pub: Shawnee Pr. Dist(s): H Leonard

***Shelter of God's Promises.** unabr. ed. Sheila Walsh. (Running Time: 6 hrs. 0 mins. 0 sec.). (ENG.). 2011. audio compact disk 24.98 (978-1-61045-038-6(8)) christianaud.

Sheltering Stones. Perf. by Richard Searles. 1 cass. 9.98; audio compact disk 16.98 Lifedance.
Gently cheerful music, culled from Searles' vast library, has a sweet medieval flavor that both comforts & delights. Demo CD or cassette available.

Sheltering Tree. unabr. ed. Iris Bromige. Read by Carol Marsh. 6 cass. (Running Time: 6 hrs. 45 min.). 2001. 54.95 (978-1-85089-633-3(X), 30591) Pub: ISIS Audio GBR. Dist(s): Ulverscroft US
A car crash robs Jennifer Barbury of two close friends, & puts an end to her musical career. In her search for a new purpose in life Jennifer takes a job as housekeeper to the autocratic Joel Vurney.

***Shelters of Stone.** unabr. ed. Jean M. Auel. Read by Sandra Burr. (Running Time: 33 hrs.). (Earth's Children Ser.). 2011. 19.99 (978-1-61106-461-2(9), 9781611064612, Brilliance MP3); audio compact disk 29.99 (978-1-61106-459-9(7), 9781611064599); audio compact disk 99.97 (978-1-61106-460-5(0), 9781611064605, BriAudCD Unabrid) Brilliance Audio.

Shelters of Stone: Earth's Children. Jean M. Auel. Read by Sandra Burr. (Playaway Adult Fiction Ser.). (ENG.). 2009. 149.99 (978-1-60775-702-3(8)) Find a World.

Shelters of Stone: Earth's Children. unabr. ed. Jean M. Auel. Read by Sandra Burr. 20 cass. (Running Time: 33 hrs.). (Earth's Children Ser.: Bk. 5). 2002. 189.25 (978-1-58788-990-5(0), 1587889900, Unabridge Lib Edns) Brilliance Audio.

Shelters of Stone: Earth's Children. unabr. ed. Jean M. Auel. Read by Sandra Burr. 28 CDs. (Running Time: 33 hrs.). (Earth's Children Ser.: Vol. 5). 2002. audio compact disk 209.25 (978-1-58788-992-9(7), 1587889927, CD Unabrid Lib Ed); 59.95 (978-1-58788-989-9(7), 1587889897, BAU); audio compact disk 79.95 (978-1-58788-991-2(9), 1587889919, CD Unabridged) Brilliance Audio.
After their epic journey across Europe, Ayla and Jondalar have reached his home, the Ninth Cave of the Zelandonii, the old stone age settlement in the region known today as southwest France. Jondalar's family greet him warmly, but they are initially wary of the beautiful young woman he has brought back, with her strange accent and her tame wolf and horses. Ayla has much to learn from the Zelandonii and much to teach them. She is intrigued by their clothes, their crafts, and their home, and wants to learn their customs and the ways that they live, so that she will fit in. She is delighted when she meets Zelandoni, the spiritual leader of her people, a fellow healer with whom she can share medicinal skills and knowledge. The Zelandonii are surprised to learn she was found and raised by the Clan, the ones that they call flatheads and think of as animals, and are skeptical when she tells them they are people. After the rigors and dangers that have characterized her extraordinary life so far, Ayla yearns for peace and tranquility, to be Jondalar's mate and to have children. But her unique spiritual gifts cannot be ignored, and even as she gives birth to her eagerly-awaited child, she is coming to accept that she has a greater role to play in the destiny of the Zelandonii.

Shelters of Stone: Earth's Children. unabr. ed. Jean M. Auel. Read by Sandra Burr. (Running Time: 118800 sec.). (Earth's Children Ser.). 2004. audio compact disk 44.25 (978-1-59335-588-3(2), 1593355882, Brlnc Audio MP3 Lib) Brilliance Audio.

Shelters of Stone: Earth's Children. unabr. ed. Jean M. Auel. Read by Sandra Burr. (Running Time: 33 hrs.). (Earth's Children Ser.). 2004. 44.25 (978-1-59710-694-8(1), 1597106941, BADLE); 24.99 (978-1-59710-695-5(X), 159710695X, BAD) Brilliance Audio.

Shelters of Stone: Earth's Children. unabr. ed. Jean M. Auel. Read by Sandra Burr. (Running Time: 33 hrs.). (Earth's Children Ser.: Vol. 5). 2004. 29.95 (978-1-59335-106-9(2), 1593351062) Soulmate Audio Bks.

Shem Creek. abr. ed. Dorothea Benton Frank. Read by Sandra Burr & Dick Hill. (Running Time: 6 hrs.). (Lowcountry Tales Ser.: No. 4). 2004. audio compact disk 74.25 (978-1-59355-974-8(7), 1593559747, BACDLib Ed) Brilliance Audio.
Meet Linda Breland, single parent of two teenage daughters. The oldest, Lindsey, who always held her younger sister in check, is leaving for college. And Gracie, her Tasmanian devil, is giving her nightmares. Linda's personal life? Well, between the married men, the cold New Jersey winters, her pinched wallet and her ex-husband who marries a beautiful, successful woman ten years younger than she is - let's just say, Linda has seen enough to fill a thousand pages. As the story opens, she is barreling down Interstate 95, bound for Mount Pleasant, South Carolina, the land of her ancestors. Welcomed by the generous heart of her advice-dispensing sister, Mimi, Linda and her daughters slowly begin to find their way and discover a sweeter rhythm of life. And then there's Brad Jackson, a former investment banker of Atlanta, Georgia who hires her to run his restaurant on Shem Creek. Like everyone else, Brad's got a story of his own - namely an almost ex-wife, Loretta who is the kind of gal who gives women a bad name. The real protagonist of this story is the Lowcountry itself. The magical waters of Shem Creek, the abundant wildlife and the astounding power of nature give this tiny corner of the planet its infallible reputation as a place for introspection, contemplation and healing. As in all her previous work, you'll find Shem Creek to be compulsively readable, irreverent but warm and blazingly authentic - and you'll dread reaching the last page. It is her vivid writing, colorful characters and rich narrative that have made Dorothea Benton Frank one of our nation's greatest storytellers. Shem Creek is a triumphant novel that proves we are all entitled to a second chance. The challenge is to learn how to recognize it when it comes and to know which chance to take.

Shem Creek. abr. ed. Dorothea Benton Frank. Read by Sandra Burr et al. (Running Time: 6 hrs.). (Lowcountry Tales Ser.: No. 4). 2005. audio compact disk 16.99 (978-1-59600-410-8(X), 9781596004108, BCD Value Price) Brilliance Audio.

Shem Creek. unabr. ed. Dorothea Benton Frank. Read by Sandra Burr & Dick Hill. (Running Time: 11 hrs.). (Lowcountry Tales Ser.: No. 4). 2004. 24.95 (978-1-59335-777-1(X), 159335777X, Brilliance MP3); 39.25 (978-1-59335-911-9(X), 159335911X, Brlnc Audio MP3 Lib); 32.95 (978-1-59355-970-0(4), 1593559704, BAU); 87.25 (978-1-59355-971-7(2), 1593559712, BrilAudUnabridg) Brilliance Audio.

Shem Creek. unabr. ed. Dorothea Benton Frank. Read by Sandra Burr et al. (Running Time: 11 hrs.). (Lowcountry Tales Ser.: No. 4). 2004. 39.25 (978-1-59710-697-9(6), 1597106976, BADLE); 24.95 (978-1-59710-696-2(8), 1597106968, BAD) Brilliance Audio.

***Shem Creek.** unabr. ed. Dorothea Benton Frank. Read by Sandra Burr et al. (Running Time: 11 hrs.). 2010. audio compact disk 29.99 (978-1-4418-3992-3(5), 9781441839923, Bril Audio CD Unabri); audio compact disk 89.97 (978-1-4418-3993-0(3), 9781441839930, BriAudCD Unabrid) Brilliance Audio.

Shem Creek-Abr. abr. ed. Dorothea Benton Frank. (Running Time: 6 hrs.). 2010. audio compact disk 9.99 (978-1-4418-4191-9(1), 9781441841919) Brilliance Audio.

Shen: Five Parts of the Soul: Five Parts of the Soul. Scripts. Bruce Goldberg. Read by Bruce Goldberg. 1 cass. (Running Time: 25 min.). (ENG.). 2006. 13.00 (978-1-57968-007-7(0)) Pub: B Goldberg. Dist(s): Baker Taylor
Through self-hypnosis be guided to connect to the five parts of the soul.

Shenandoah. James Reasoner. Read by Lloyd James. (Running Time: 11 mins. 30 sec.). (Civil War Battle Ser.: Bk. 8). 2005. 65.95 (978-0-7861-3692-6(8)); audio compact disk 81.00 (978-0-7861-7679-3(2)) Blckstn Audio.

Shenandoah. unabr. ed. James Reasoner. Read by Lloyd James. (Running Time: 11 mins. 30 sec.). (Civil War Battle Ser.: Bk. 8). 2005. 29.95 (978-0-7861-7917-6(1)) Blckstn Audio.

Shepherd: Coping Strategies for the Modern Era. Foundation of Human Understanding. (Running Time: 300 minutes). (ENG.). (YA). 2009. audio compact disk 15.00 (978-0-9824951-2-4(9)) Foun Human Under.

Shepherd & Other Christmas Favourites. Frederick Forsyth. Read by Alan Maitland. 2005. audio compact disk 15.95 (978-0-660-19282-6(9)) Canadian Broadcasting CAN.

Shepherd God: The 23rd Psalm for Today. Paul Nagano. Ed. by Rennie Mau. 1989. pap. bk. (978-0-318-66305-0(8)) Media Bridge.

***Shepherd Looks at Psalm 23.** W. Phillip Keller. (Running Time: 3 hrs. 44 mins. 0 sec.). (ENG.). 2008. 14.99 (978-0-310-30519-4(5)) Zondervan.

Shepherd Looks at Psalm 23. abr. ed. W. Phillip Keller. 1 cass. (Running Time: 60 min.). 1988. 12.99 (978-0-310-26798-0(6), 6780T) Zondervan.

Shepherd Looks at Psalm 23. abr. ed. W. Phillip Phillip Keller. (Running Time: 1 hr. 0 mins. 0 sec.). (ENG.). 2003. 7.99 (978-0-310-26098-1(1)) Zondervan.

Shepherd of the Hills. unabr. ed. Harold Bell Wright. Read by Jack Sondericker. 6 cass. (Running Time: 7 hrs. 30 min.). Dramatization. 1990. 39.95 (978-1-55686-356-1(X), 752382) Books in Motion.
Strangers aren't well received in the Mutton Hollow neighborhood of the Ozarks. But there was something different about this old gentleman. He carried himself with the unconscious air of one long used to power & influence. No one knew his past, or why he came to the hollow. But his presence was soon to be felt by every family.

Shepherd of the Second Spring. Jude Mead. 11 cass. 43.95 (757) Ignatius Pr.
The life of Passionist Father, Blessed Dominic Barberi.

Shepherd Song. 1988. audio compact disk 16.00 (978-1-58459-109-2(9)) Wrld Lib Pubns.

Shepherd Song. Music by Michael John Poirier. 1988. 11.00 (978-1-58459-108-5(0)) Wrld Lib Pubns.

Shepherd Song: Christmas Carols for Contemporary Christians. Perf. by New Horizon Singers et al. Contrib. by Sheldon Cohen. 1 cass., 1 CD. (Running Time: 40 min.). 1997. 9.95 (978-0-87946-171-3(3), 340); audio compact disk 14.95 CD. (978-0-87946-172-0(1), 405) ACTA Pubns.
Traditional songs include: "Rise up Shepherd & Follow," "Go Tell it on a Mountain," "The March of the Kings," "Away in a Manager," "Pat-a-Pan," "O Come O Come Emmanuel," "Dona Nobis Pacem," "Coventry Carol," "O Little Town of Bethlehem," "Lo How a Rose E're Blooming" & "Sleep Well Little Child".

Shepherding a Child's Heart. 2006. audio compact disk 26.00 (978-0-9723046-5-8(7)) Shepherd Pr PA.

Shepherding a Child's Heart. unabr. ed. Tedd Tripp. Photos by Tedd Tripp. 1 cass. (Running Time: 1 hr. 30 mins.). 2001. 20.00 (978-0-9663786-5-8(2), Shepherd Press) Calvary Press.
Reading of Shepherding a Child's Heart by the author.

Shepherding Young People. 6 cass. 1990. 18.00 (978-1-59128-205-1(5)) Canon Pr ID.

Shepherding Young People. Douglas Wilson. 6 CDs. (ENG.). 1990. audio compact disk 18.00 (978-1-59128-204-4(7)) Canon Pr ID.

Shepherds Abiding; Esther's Gift; The Mitford Snowmen. unabr. ed. Jan Karon. 6 CDs. (Running Time: 7 hrs.). Bk. 8. (ENG.). (gr. 12 up). 2005. audio compact disk 12.95 (978-0-14-305821-2(5), PengAudBks) Penguin Grp USA.

Shepherd's Heart. Rick Joyner. 1 cass. (Running Time: 90 mins.). (Ministry of The Pastor Ser.: Vol. 2). 2000. 5.00 (RJ08-002) Morning NC.
"The Mandates of the Pastoral Ministry" & "The Shepherd's Heart." This brief series gives a revolutionary understanding of this most misunderstood ministry.

Shepherds Song. Dennis Allen. 1998. 8.00 (978-0-7673-9247-1(7)); 75.00 (978-0-7673-9244-0(2)); audio compact disk 85.00 (978-0-7673-9248-8(5)); audio compact disk 12.00 (978-0-7673-9245-7(0)) LifeWay Christian.

Shepherd's Song. Dennis Allen. 1998. audio compact disk 16.98 (978-0-7673-9243-3(4)) LifeWay Christian.

Shepherd's Song. Dennis Allen. 1998. 11.98 (978-0-7673-9242-6(6)) LifeWay Christian.

Shepherd's Story. Hal H. Hopson. Contrib. by Carol McClure. (gr. 2-5). bk. 40.00 (978-0-687-05018-5(9)) Abingdon.

Shepherd's Tale: Accompaniment/Performance. Composed by Dave Perry & Jean Perry. (ENG.). 2003. audio compact disk 45.00 (978-0-7390-3078-3(7)) Alfred Pub.

Shepherd's Tale: Preview Pack. Composed by Dave Perry & Jean Perry. (ENG.). 2003. audio compact disk 12.95 (978-0-7390-3077-6(9)) Alfred Pub.

Shepherds, Wiseman, Etc: Luke 2:1-10. Ed Young. 1993. 4.95 (978-0-7417-1992-8(4), 992) Win Walk.

Sheppard Murder Case: Dr. Sam Sheppard Interview Tapes. Illus. by William Levy. Contrib. by Sam Sheppard. 4 CDs. (Running Time: 4 hrs.). 2001. audio compact disk 24.95 (978-0-9716934-0-1(4)) B Levy Pro.
Interview with Dr. Sam Sheppard done in 1965 and 1966 during his retrial for the murder of his wife Marilyn. The interview were used by William Levy to ghost write "Endure and Conquer", Dr. Sam Sheppards autobiography.

***Sherbrooke Bride.** Catherine Coulter. (Bride Ser.). 2010. audio compact disk 9.99 (978-1-4418-5700-2(1)) Brilliance Audio.

Sherbrooke Bride. abr. ed. Catherine Coulter. Read by Anne Flosnik. (Running Time: 6 hrs.). (Bride Ser.). 2006. audio compact disk 16.99 (978-1-59737-788-1(0), 9781597377881, BCD Value Price) Brilliance Audio.
Dear Reader, Douglas Sherbrooke, Earl of Northcliffe, is a man besieged. He must have an heir. Thus he must first provide himself with the requisite bride. Alexandra Chambers, youngest daughter of the Duke of Beresford, has loved Douglas Sherbrooke since she was fifteen. Unfortunately, it is her sister, the incomparable Melissande, he wishes to wed. But life never ladles out what one expects, and Douglas finds himself wed to the wrong sister. If having an unwanted wife isn't enough, he is also plagued by The Virgin Bride, a ghost that is reputedly seen in the countess's bedchamber. Does the willowy phantom really appear to Douglas? Does she speak to him? I hope you enjoy reading about the exploits of Alexandra and Douglas as much as I enjoyed writing them. You will see them again in The Hellion Bride. Please write me at P.O. Box 17, Mill Valley, CA 94942 or email me at ReadMoi@aol.com. Catherine Coulter.

Sherbrooke Bride. abr. ed. Catherine Coulter. Read by Juliet Mills. 2 cass. (Running Time: 3 hrs.). (Bride Trilogy: Bk. 1). 1992. 15.95 Set. (978-1-879371-17-0(0), 40070) Pub Mills.
The first in the Bride Trilogy, this book is about a man beseiged. His name is Lord Douglas Sherbrooke, the Earl of Northcliffe. He must marry & produce an heir. He has underhandedly been fooled by his cousin into marrying his beautiful bride to be's less desirable sister.

Sherbrooke Bride. unabr. ed. Catherine Coulter. Read by Anne Flosnik. (Running Time: 11 hrs.). (Bride Ser.). 2005. 39.25 (978-1-59737-786-7(4), 9781597377867, BADLE); 24.95 (978-1-59737-785-0(6), 9781597377850, BAD); 32.95 (978-1-59737-779-9(1), 9781597377799, BAU); 87.25 (978-1-59737-780-5(5), 9781597377805, BrilAudUnabridg); audio compact disk 24.95 (978-1-59737-783-6(X), 9781597377836, Brilliance MP3); audio compact disk 36.95 (978-1-59737-781-2(3), 9781597377812, Bril Audio CD Unabri); audio compact disk 97.25 (978-1-59737-782-9(1), 9781597377829, BriAudCD Unabrid); audio compact disk 39.25 (978-1-59737-784-3(8), 9781597377843, Brlnc Audio MP3 Lib) Brilliance Audio.
Dear Reader, Douglas Sherbrooke, Earl of Northcliffe, is a man besieged. He must have an heir. Thus he must first provide himself with the requisite bride. Alexandra Chambers, youngest daughter of the Duke of Beresford, has loved Douglas Sherbrooke since she was fifteen. Unfortunately, it is her sister, the incomparable Melissande, he wishes to wed. But life never ladles out what one expects, and Douglas finds himself wed to the wrong sister. If having an unwanted wife isn't enough, he is also plagued by The Virgin Bride, a ghost that is reputedly seen in the countess's bedchamber. Does the willowy phantom really appear to Douglas? Does she speak to him? I hope you enjoy reading about the exploits of Alexandra and Douglas as much as I enjoyed writing them. You will see them again in The Hellion

Bride. Please write me at P.O. Box 17, Mill Valley, CA 94942 or email me at ReadMoi@aol.com. Catherine Coulter.

Sherbrooke Twins. abr. ed. Catherine Coulter. Read by Anne Flosnik. (Running Time: 6 hrs.). (Bride Ser.). 2008. audio compact disk 14.99 (978-1-4233-6228-9(4), 9781423362289, BCD Value Price) Brilliance Audio.

Sherbrooke Twins. unabr. ed. Catherine Coulter. Read by Anne Flosnik. 5 CDs. (Running Time: 10 hrs.). (Bride Ser.). 2004. audio compact disk 97.25 (978-1-59086-909-3(5), 1590869095, BACDLib Ed) Brilliance Audio.
Dear Reader: The Sherbrooke family saga continues with James and Jason Sherbrooke, identical male twins who look exactly like their beautiful Aunt Melissande, and not at all like their father, the earl, which riles him no end. James, twenty-eight minutes older than his brother, is the heir. He is solid, is James. He's a student of astronomy, rides like a centaur, and, unlike his brother, Jason, enjoys learning the ropes of managing his father's estates. He no longer sows excessive wild oats, as his neighbor, Corrie Tybourne Barrett, a brat he's known since she was three-years-old, looks forward to doing since she turned eighteen. When she nearly shoves him off a cliff, sneering all the while, James hauls off and spanks her. A promising start. Then, unfortunately, the earl, Douglas Sherbrooke, is shot at. This leads to Georges Cadoudal, a Frenchman in the employ of the English war ministry with whom Douglas had dealings with some years before. But Cadoudal died in 1815, fifteen years before. Were there children who might want revenge against Douglas? But the question is why: Georges and Douglas parted friends, at least Douglas believed that they had. Adventures compound; Corrie hurls herself into the thick of things. As for Jason, not quite a half an hour younger, he loves horses, wants to start a stud farm, still sows more oats than a man should be allowed, but finally meets a girl who stops him in his tracks. And then what happens? You will have to listen to the book to find out. I hope you enjoy yourself. The characters are rich, colorful, and a hoot to boot. The mystery will confound you. Do let me know what you think. Write me at P.O. Box 17, Mill Valley, CA., 94942 or email me at readmoi@aol.com. Keep an eye on my web site at www.CatherineCoulter.com. Catherine Coulter [signature].

Sherbrooke Twins. unabr. ed. Catherine Coulter. Read by Anne Flosnik. (Running Time: 10 hrs.). (Bride Ser.). 2004. 39.25 (978-1-59710-698-6(4), 1597106984, BADLE); 24.95 (978-1-59710-699-3(2), 1597106992, BAD) Brilliance Audio.

Sheri Dew COLL. Sheri Dew. 2009. audio compact disk 49.95 (978-1-60641-171-1(3)) Deseret Bk.

Sherida. unabr. ed. Judy Turner. 4 cass. (Running Time: 4 hrs.). 1998. 57.95 (978-1-85903-004-2(1)) Pub: Magna Story GBR. Dist(s): Ulverscroft US

Sheridan: The Life & Wars of General Phil Sheridan. unabr. ed. Roy Morris, Jr. Read by Jonathan Reese. 11 cass. (Running Time: 16 hrs. 30 min.). 1993. 88.00 (978-0-7366-2357-5(4), 3132) Books on Tape.
General Phil Sheridan was the Civil War's most famous Union cavalry commander who went West to lead operations against the Indians.

Sheriff & the Branding Iron Murders. abr. ed. Doris R. Meredith. Read by Bernard Bridges. Ed. by Stephen Holland. 4 cass. 1994. 24.95 set. (978-1-883268-12-1(5)) Spellbinders.
When cowboy artist Willie Russell is murdered, Sheriff Charles Matthews is called upon to find the killer & solve the mystery of the missing Santiago Crucifix.

Sheriff & the Panhandle Murders. abr. ed. Doris R. Meredith. Read by Jay Maxwell. Ed. by Stephen Holland. 4 cass. 1994. 24.95 Set. (978-1-883268-08-4(7)) Spellbinders.
Sheriff Charles Matthews solves the mystery of who hated good ol' boy Billy Joe Williams & beautiful Maria Martinez enough to kill them.

Sheriff & the Pheasant Hunt Murders. abr. ed. Doris R. Meredith. Read by Ronald Wilcox. Ed. by Stephen Holland. 4 cass. 1994. 24.95 set. (978-1-883268-07-7(9)) Spellbinders.
The story of a ruthless banker killed on the opening day of the annual Panhandle pheasant hunt.

Sheriff Daisy & Deputy Bud: Join Us in the Old West as Daisy & Bud Stop Robbers, Rustlers, & Buffalo Poachers. (Running Time: 3300 sec.). (J). (gr. k-6). 2006. audio compact disk 12.95 (978-1-933781-01-3(7)) TallTales Aud.

Sheriff of Yrnameer. unabr. ed. Michael Rubens. Narrated by William Dufris. (Running Time: 9 hrs. 30 mins. 0 sec.). (ENG.). 2009. audio compact disk 69.99 (978-1-4001-4325-2(X)) Pub: Tantor Media. Dist(s): IngramPubServ

Sheriff of Yrnameer: A Novel. unabr. ed. Michael Rubens. Narrated by William Dufris. (Running Time: 9 hrs. 30 mins. 0 sec.). (ENG.). 2009. 24.99 (978-1-4001-6325-0(0)); audio compact disk 34.99 (978-1-4001-1325-5(3)) Pub: Tantor Media. Dist(s): IngramPubServ

Sheriff Star's Skits. 1 cass. (Running Time: 1 hr.). (J). 9.95 Let Us Tch Kids.

***Sherlock Dance Fantasy.** Perf. by R. A. Zuckerman. Composed by R. A. Zuckerman. (ENG.). 2010. 12.95 (978-1-891083-24-2(4)) ConcertHall.

Sherlock Holmes. 2003. bk. 15.99 (978-1-57815-574-3(6), Media Bks Audio) Media Bks NJ.

Sherlock Holmes. (Nostalgia Classics Ser.). 19.98 Moonbeam Pubns.
Includes "The Blackmailer;" "Scandal in Bohemia;" "The Red Headed League;" "A Case of Identity;" "The Traitor;" "Rare Disease;" "The Norwood Builder;" "The Speckled Band;" "The Final Problem;" "The Empty House;" "The Second Stain;" "The Solitary Cyclist".

Sherlock Holmes. Radio Spirits Staff. Read by John Stanley. 2005. audio compact disk 39.98 (978-1-57019-624-9(9)) Radio Spirits.

Sherlock Holmes. Perf. by Basil Rathbone & Nigel Bruce. 1 cass. (Running Time: 60 min.). (Old Time Radio Classic Singles Ser.). 4.95 (978-1-57816-121-8(5), SH118) Audio File.
Two adventures. 1) "Scandal in Bohemia" (12/10/45). 2) "Great Gondolfo" (10/22/45) Petri Wines.

Sherlock Holmes, Vol. 1. abr. ed. Nina Mattikow. 8 cass. (Running Time: 8 hrs.). Dramatization. (Eight Cassette Collector Packs Ser.). 1992. 29.95 (978-1-55569-542-2(6), 48001) Great Am Audio.
Sixteen complete original radio broadcasts of the world's most famous detective.

Sherlock Holmes, Vol. 1. unabr. ed. 2 cass. (Running Time: 2 hrs.). (Double Value Pack Ser.). 1990. 9.95 (978-1-55569-369-5(5), 7102) Great Am Audio.
Classic adventures of "The Red-Headed League," "Six Napoleons," "The Blue Carbuncle" & "The Speckled Band".

Sherlock Holmes, Vol. 2. abr. ed. Nina Mattikow. 8 cass. (Running Time: 8 hrs.). Dramatization. (Eight Cassette Collector Packs Ser.). 1992. 29.95 Set. (978-1-55569-543-9(4), 48002) Great Am Audio.
Sixteen complete original radio broadcasts of the world's most famous detective.

Sherlock Holmes, Vol. 2. unabr. ed. 2 cass. (Running Time: 2 hrs.). (Double Value Pack Ser.). 1990. 9.95 (978-1-55569-370-1(9), 7103) Great Am Audio.
"The Traitor," "The Blackmailer," "A Case of Identity" & "The Yastley Case". Four classic adventures.

Sherlock Holmes, Vol. 3. unabr. ed. 2 cass. (Running Time: 2 hrs.). (Double Value Pack Ser.). 1990. 9.95 (978-1-55569-371-8(7), 7104) Great Am Audio.
"Rare Disease," "The Solitary Bicyclist," "The Empty House" & "The Mystery of the Second Stain". Four complete adventures.

Sherlock Holmes: A Baker's Street Dozen. unabr. ed. Arthur Conan Doyle. Perf. by John Gielgud et al. 6 cass. (Running Time: 6 hrs.). Dramatization. 1998. 26.95 (978-1-55935-200-0(0)) Soundelux.
Includes "The Blue Carbuncle," "The Yoxley Case," "The Norwood Builder," "Solitary Bicyclist," "The Final Problem," "A Case of Identity," "Six Napoleons," "The Mystery of the Second Stain," "Rare Disease," "The Speckled Bank," "The Blackmailer" & "A Scandal in Bohemia".

Sherlock Holmes: A Case of Identity. Arthur Conan Doyle. Narrated by Edward Raleigh. (Running Time: 1 hr. 30 mins.). 2006. 11.95 (978-1-60083-010-5(2)) Iofy Corp.

***Sherlock Holmes: A Case of Identity, the Adventure of the Empty House, & the Adventure of the Golden Pince-Nez.** Arthur Conan Doyle. 2009. (978-1-60136-563-7(2)) Audio Holding.

Sherlock Holmes: A Scandal in Bohemia. Arthur Conan Doyle. Narrated by Edward Raleigh. (Running Time: 2 hrs. 30 mins.). 2006. 14.95 (978-1-59912-995-2(7)) Iofy Corp.

Sherlock Holmes: A Study in Scarlet. unabr. ed. Arthur Conan Doyle. 2 vols. (Running Time: 4 hrs.). 2003. audio compact disk 29.95 (978-0-563-49682-3(7), BBCD 031) BBC Worldwide.
An unmarked corpse, a wedding ring and a mysterious message scrawled in blood are the intrepid pair's only clues as they follow the trail of a man driven to fulfil a terrible oath, which he swore more than twenty years before.

Sherlock Holmes: A Study in Scarlet & The Sign of the Four. abr. ed. Arthur Conan Doyle. Read by John Whitaker. 5 vols. (Great Mystery Ser.). 2001. audio compact disk 14.99 (978-1-57815-532-3(0), Media Bks Audio) Media Bks NJ.

Sherlock Holmes: Adventure of Illustrious Client. Arthur Conan Doyle. Narrated by Edward Raleigh. (Running Time: 1 hr.). 2006. 11.95 (978-1-60083-014-3(5)) Iofy Corp.

Sherlock Holmes: Adventure of Sussex Vampire. Arthur Conan Doyle. Narrated by Edward Raleigh. (Running Time: 1 hr.). 2006. 11.95 (978-1-60083-016-7(1)) Iofy Corp.

Sherlock Holmes: Adventure of the Blanched Soldier. Arthur Conan Doyle. Narrated by Edward Raleigh. (Running Time: 1 hr.). 2006. 11.95 (978-1-60083-012-9(9)) Iofy Corp.

Sherlock Holmes: Adventure of the Bruce Partington Plans. Arthur Conan Doyle. Narrated by Edward Raleigh. (Running Time: 1 hr.). 2006. 11.95 (978-1-60083-011-2(0)) Iofy Corp.

Sherlock Holmes: Adventure of the Creeping Man. Arthur Conan Doyle. Narrated by Edward Raleigh. (Running Time: 1 hr. 30 mins.). 2006. 11.95 (978-1-60083-017-4(X)) Iofy Corp.

Sherlock Holmes: Adventure of the Lion's Mane. Arthur Conan Doyle. Narrated by Edward Raleigh. (Running Time: 1 hr.). 2006. 11.95 (978-1-60083-013-6(7)) Iofy Corp.

Sherlock Holmes: Adventure of Wisteria Lodge. Arthur Conan Doyle. Narrated by Edward Raleigh. (Running Time: 1 hr.). 2006. 11.95 (978-1-60083-018-1(8)) Iofy Corp.

Sherlock Holmes: Casebook. unabr. ed. Arthur Conan Doyle. Read by John Barnes. 2 cass. (Running Time: 2 hrs.). 1997. 12.95 B-B Audio.
In "The Man with the Twisted Lip," Holmes & Dr. Watson comb the London waterfront looking for Neville St. Claire, son of the 7th Duke of Holdernesse.

Sherlock Holmes: Classic Mysteries. unabr. ed. Arthur Conan Doyle. Read by Ralph Cosham. 2 cass. (Running Time: 3 hrs.). 1996. bk. 16.95 (978-1-883049-67-6(9), Commuters Library) Sound Room.
These are the best of the early stories which excited the imagination of readers the world over. A man comes to Holmes & Watson perplexed by his dealings with "The Red-Headed League" which requires its members to have brilliant red hair. A young man must be cleared of the murder of his father in "The Boscombe Valley Mystery." A whistle in the night prior to the mysterious death of a young woman begins "The Adventure of the Speckled Band." "The Five Orange Pips" has an American connection to the accidental deaths of these successive generations.

Sherlock Holmes: Selected Stories. abr. ed. Arthur Conan Doyle. 4 cass. (Running Time: 4 hrs.). HarperCollins Pubs.

Sherlock Holmes: Selected Stories. abr. ed. Arthur Conan Doyle. 4 cass. Incl. Adventures of the Speckled Band. (SBC 107); Redheaded League. (SBC 107); Scandal in Bohemia. Arthur Conan Doyle. (SBC 107); Silver Blaze. (SBC 107); 1985. 29.95 (978-0-89845-032-3(2), SBC 107) HarperCollins Pubs.

Sherlock Holmes: Selected Stories. unabr. ed. Arthur Conan Doyle. Read by William Barker. 2 cass. (Running Time: 3 hrs. 10 min.). Incl. Case of Identity. 1986.; Musgrave Ritual. 1986.; Red-Headed League. Arthur Conan Doyle. 1986.; Scandal in Bohemia. Arthur Conan Doyle. 1986.; 1986. 16.95 library case. (978-1-55656-003-3(6)) Dercum Audio.

Sherlock Holmes: Selected Stories. unabr. ed. Arthur Conan Doyle. 4 cass. (Running Time: 4 hrs.). 1986. 17.95 (978-1-55569-116-5(1), 5770-06) Great Am Audio.
Four complete adventures of the world's most famous detective including "The Red Headed League," "A Case of Identity," "The Man with the Twisted Lip" & "The Musgrave Ritual".

Sherlock Holmes: Selected Stories, Vol. 3. Arthur Conan Doyle. 2 cass. (Running Time: 2 hrs.). Dramatization. 1991. 14.95 Minds Eye.
Dramatizations with Carleton Hobbs & Norman Shelley.

***Sherlock Holmes: The Adventure of Black Peter & the Red-headed League.** Arthur Conan Doyle. 2009. (978-1-60136-567-5(5)) Audio Holding.

***Sherlock Holmes: The Adventure of Charles Augustus Milverton & the Adventure of the Illustrious Client.** Arthur Conan Doyle. 2009. (978-1-60136-559-0(4)) Audio Holding.

***Sherlock Holmes: The Adventure of the Blanched Soldier & the Boscombe Valley Mystery.** Arthur Conan Doyle. 2009. (978-1-60136-565-1(9)) Audio Holding.

***Sherlock Holmes: The Adventure of the Blue Carbuncle & the Adventure of the Dancing Men.** Arthur Conan Doyle. 2009. (978-1-60136-568-2(3)) Audio Holding.

***Sherlock Holmes: The Adventure of the Creeping Man & the Adventue of the Abbey Grange.** Arthur Conan Doyle. 2009. (978-1-60136-569-9(1)) Audio Holding.

***Sherlock Holmes: The Adventure of the Engineer's Thumb & A Scandal in Bohemia.** Arthur Conan Doyle. 2009. (978-1-60136-566-8(7)) Audio Holding.

***Sherlock Holmes: The Adventure of the Lion's Mane & the Adventure of the Speckled Band.** Arthur Conan Doyle. 2009. (978-1-60136-560-6(8)) Audio Holding.

***Sherlock Holmes: The Adventure of the Mazarin Stone, & the Adventure of the Bruce-Partington Plans.** Arthur Conan Doyle. 2009. (978-1-60136-555-2(1)) Audio Holding.

***Sherlock Holmes: The Adventure of the Missing Three-Quarter & the Adventure of the Six Napoleons.** Arthur Conan Doyle. 2009. (978-1-60136-571-2(3)) Audio Holding.

***Sherlock Holmes: The Adventure of the Noble Bachelor & the Adventure of the Beryl Coronet.** Arthur Conan Doyle. 2009. (978-1-60136-570-5(5)) Audio Holding.

***Sherlock Holmes: The Adventure of the Solitary Cyclist & the Adventure of the Copper Beeches.** Arthur Conan Doyle. 2009. (978-1-60136-564-4(0)) Audio Holding.

***Sherlock Holmes: The Adventure of the Sussex Vampire & the Adventure of the Second Stain.** Arthur Conan Doyle. 2009. (978-1-60136-557-6(8)) Audio Holding.

***Sherlock Holmes: The Adventure of the Three Garridebs & the Adventure of the Priory School.** Arthur Conan Doyle. 2009. (978-1-60136-556-9(X)) Audio Holding.

***Sherlock Holmes: The Adventure of the Three Students & the Naval Treaty.** Arthur Conan Doyle. 2009. (978-1-60136-558-3(6)) Audio Holding.

***Sherlock Holmes: The Adventure of the Veiled Lodger & the Adventure of Wisteria Lodge.** Arthur Conan Doyle. 2009. (978-1-60136-554-5(3)) Audio Holding.

Sherlock Holmes: The Black Peter & The Missing Three Quarter. 1 cass. (Running Time: 1 hr.). 2001. 6.98 (1711) Radio Spirits.

Sherlock Holmes: The Classics, unabr. ed. Arthur Conan Doyle. Perf. by John Gielgud et al. 2 cass. (Running Time: 2 hrs.). Dramatization. 1997. 17.95 (978-1-55935-272-7(8)) Soundelux.
Includes "The Empty House," "The Red-Headed League," "The Traitor - Sherlock Holmes" & "Silver Blaze.".

***Sherlock Holmes: The Five Orange Pips & the Adventure of the Norwood Builder.** Arthur Conan Doyle. 2009. (978-1-60136-561-3(6)) Audio Holding.

Sherlock Holmes: The Hound of the Baskervilles. abr. ed. Arthur Conan Doyle. Read by Michael J. Bennett. 5 cass. (Running Time: 7 hrs. 30 min.). (Great Mystery Ser.). 2001. audio compact disk 14.99 (978-1-57815-531-6(2), Media Bks Audio) Media Bks NJ.

Sherlock Holmes: The Hound of the Baskervilles. abr. ed. Arthur Conan Doyle. 2 cass. (Running Time: 120 min.). 2004. reel tape 18.99 (978-1-894003-26-1(8)) Pub: Scenario Prods CAN. Dist(s): PerseuPGW

Sherlock Holmes: The Hound of the Baskervilles. unabr. ed. Arthur Conan Doyle. Read by Ralph Cosham. 5 cds. (Running Time: 5 hrs 26 mins). (YA). 2002. audio compact disk 29.95 (978-1-58472-328-8(9), 018, In Aud) Pub: Sound Room. Dist(s): Baker Taylor
Sherlock Holmes must tackle the mystery of the demonic hound and the curse of the House of the Baskervilles.

Sherlock Holmes: The Man with the Twisted Lip. Arthur Conan Doyle. Narrated by Edward Raleigh. (Running Time: 2 hrs. 30 mins.). 2006. 14.95 (978-1-60083-065-5(X)) Iofy Corp.

***Sherlock Holmes: The Musgrave Ritual & Man with the Twisted Lip.** Arthur Conan Doyle. 2009. (978-1-60136-562-0(4)) Audio Holding.

Sherlock Holmes: The Musgrave Ritual & The Final Problem. unabr. ed. Arthur Conan Doyle. Read by Ralph Cosham. 2 CDs. (Running Time: 2 hrs.). 2000. audio compact disk 19.95 (Commuters Library) Sound Room.

Sherlock Holmes: The Naval Treaty. Arthur Conan Doyle. Narrated by Edward Raleigh. (Running Time: 1 hr.). 2006. 11.95 (978-1-60083-023-5(4)) Iofy Corp.

Sherlock Holmes: The Red-Headed Le... & The Adventures of the Speckled Band. unabr. ed. Arthur Cona... Doyle. Read by Ralph Cosham. 2 CDs. (Running Time: 2 hrs.). 2000. audio compact disk 19.95 (Commuters Library) Sound Room.

Sherlock Holmes: Three Tales of Avarice. unabr. ed. Arthur Conan Doyle. Read by Edward Hardwicke. 3 CDs. (Running Time: 2 hrs. 30 mins. 0 sec.). (ENG.). 2009. audio compact disk 9.95 (978-1-60283-715-7(5)) Pub: AudioGO. Dist(s): Perseus Dist

Sherlock Holmes: Three Tales of Intrigue. unabr. ed. Arthur Conan Doyle. Read by Edward Hardwicke. 3 CDs. (Running Time: 2 hrs. 30 mins. 0 sec.). (ENG.). 2009. audio compact disk 9.95 (978-1-60283-659-4(0)) Pub: AudioGO. Dist(s): Perseus Dist

Sherlock Holmes: 3 Tales of Avarice. unabr. ed. Arthur Conan Doyle. Read by Edward Hardwicke. 2 cass. (Running Time: 3 hrs.). 2000. 17.95 (978-1-57270-173-1(0), N21173u) Pub: Audio Partners. Dist(s): PerseuPGW
Three complete stories: "Red-Headed League", Holmes catches one of London's most daring criminals while investigating the strange business of the redheaded league, "The Adventure of the Priory School", Motivated by greed & jealousy, a wicked scheme to kidnap a young lord results in a far greater tragedy, "The Adventure of the Blue Caruncle", An unusual sequence of events leads Holmes to discover the precious blue carbuncle of the Countess of Morcar.

Sherlock Holmes: 3 Tales of Avarice. unabr. ed. Arthur Conan Doyle. Read by Edward Hardwicke. 3 CDs. (Running Time: 3 hrs.). 2000. audio compact disk 24.95 (978-1-57270-176-2(5), N21176u, Audio Edits Mystry) Pub: Audio Partners. Dist(s): PerseuPGW
Three complete stories: "Adventure of the Priory School," "Red-Headed League" & " Adventure of the Blue Carbuncle".

Sherlock Holmes: 3 Tales of Betrayal. unabr. ed. Arthur Conan Doyle. Read by Edward Hardwicke. 2 cass. (Running Time: 3 hrs.). 2000. 17.95 (978-1-57270-142-7(0), N21142u) Pub: Audio Partners. Dist(s): PerseuPGW
"A Scandal in Bohemia," a story of love, intrigue & scandal as Holmes first encounters New Jersey born opera singer Irene Adler, "Silver Blaze," A trusted horse trainer is murdered. Holmes & Watson are on the case, but a strange knife & a missing horse confuse the investigation, "The Adventure of the Copper Beeches," Copper beeches in the front of a mysterious house expose betrayal.

Sherlock Holmes: 3 Tales of Intrigue. unabr. ed. Arthur Conan Doyle. Read by Edward Hardwicke. 2 cass. (Running Time: 2 hrs. 30 min.). 2001. 17.95 (978-1-57270-192-2(7), N21192u, Audio Edits Mystry) Pub: Audio Partners. Dist(s): PerseuPGW

Sherlock Holmes: 3 Tales of Intrigue. unabr. ed. Arthur Conan Doyle. Read by Edward Hardwicke. 3 CDs. (Running Time: 2 hrs. 30 min.). 2001. audio compact disk 24.95 (978-1-57270-193-9(5), N35193u, Audio Edits Mystry) Pub: Audio Partners. Dist(s): PerseuPGW

Sherlock Holmes - Tales from Baker Street. Radio Yesteryear Staff. 4 cass. 1993. 16.95 Set. (978-0-929541-71-6(5)) Radiola Co.

***Sherlock Holmes - the Complete Novels: A Study in Scarlet , the Sign of Four , the Hound of the Baskervilles & the Valley of Fear.** Arthur Conan Doyle. Narrated by Flo Gibson & Grover Gardner. (ENG.). 2010. audio compact disk 48.95 (978-1-60646-194-5(X)) Audio Bk Con.

Sherlock Holmes - the Hound of the Baskervilles. unabr. ed. Arthur Conan Doyle. Read by Ralph Cosham. (YA). 2006. 39.99 (978-1-59895-182-0(3)) Find a World.

Sherlock Holmes - Volume 1. Arthur Conan Doyle. Read by Edward Hardwicke. 2008. audio compact disk 39.35 (978-1-906147-32-7(9)) CSA Telltapes GBR.

Sherlock Holmes: A Baker Street Dozen. unabr. ed. Arthur Conan Doyle. Read by John Gielgud & Orson Welles. Contrib. by John Gielgud et al. (ENG.). 2009. audio compact disk 24.95 (978-1-59887-916-2(2), 1598879162) Pub: HighBridge. Dist(s): Workman Pub

Sherlock Holmes & Selecting a Ghost. Arthur Conan Doyle. 2 CDs. (Running Time: 2 hrs. 30 mins.). (J). 2003. audio compact disk 17.99 (978-1-58926-184-6(4), C05M-0020, Oasis Kids) Oasis Audio.

Sherlock Holmes & The Falcon: The Missing Submarine Plans & Murder Is a Family Affair. unabr. ed. Perf. by Basil Rathbone & Nigel Bruce. 1 cass. (Running Time: 60 min.). Dramatization. 7.95 Norelco box. (MM3344) Natl Recrd Co.
Sherlock Holmes: Holmes is visited by his brother, a government official, who asks Sherlock to solve the mystery of a government employee that is found dead in the subway. British Security is involved...top secret papers are missing from the dead man's pockets. The Falcon: Ray Sinclair kills his wife's lover & is sentenced to die. He asks Michael Waring, The Falcon, to look after his kid brother Danny. Danny decides to try his hand at murder & this keeps the story moving along at a fast pace. Presented by Gem Blades..."avoid the five o'clock shadow".

***Sherlock Holmes & the Ghosts of Bly: And Other New Adventures of the Great Detective.** Donald Thomas. (Running Time: 10 hrs. 0 mins. 0 sec.). (ENG.). 2011. audio compact disk 29.95 (978-1-60998-173-0(1)) Pub: AudioGO. Dist(s): Perseus Dist

Sherlock Holmes & the Hapsburg Tiara. unabr. ed. Alan Vanneman. Read by Robert Whitfield. 7 cass. (Running Time: 10 hrs.). 2004. 49.95 (978-0-7861-2671-2(X), 3229); audio compact disk 72.00 (978-0-7861-8748-5(4), 3229) Blckstn Audio.
A fabulous diamond, a vanishing duke, and a murdered servant boy launch an original, new, and ingeniously contrived Holmesian adventure.

Sherlock Holmes & the Hound of the Baskervilles. 2 CDs. (Running Time: 2 hrs. 30 mins.). 2004. audio compact disk 24.99 (978-1-894003-39-1(X)) Pub: Scenario Prods CAN. Dist(s): PerseuPGW

Sherlock Holmes & the Mark of the Beast. unabr. ed. Ronald C. Weyman. Read by Ronald C. Weyman. 5 cass. (Running Time: 5 hrs. 20 min.). Dramatization. 1995. vinyl bd. 28.95 (978-1-888728-01-9(9)) Clssic Spclties.
During Mr. Holmes' hiatus after the incident at Reichenbach Falls, he travels to Canada to undertake adventures critical to The Crown & to the very survival of The Empire!.

"Sherlock Holmes" Approach to the Detection of Bleeding Disorders. Read by Richard J. Cohen. 1 cass. (Running Time: 90 min.). 1985. 12.00 (C8548) Amer Coll Phys.

Sherlock Holmes Arrives Too Late see Extraordinary Adventures of Arsene Lupin

Sherlock Holme's Classic Mysteries. unabr. ed. Arthur Conan Doyle. Read by Ralph Cosham. 3 cds. (Running Time: 3 hrs 3 mins). (YA). 2002. audio compact disk 22.95 (978-1-58472-326-4(2), In Aud) Pub: Sound Room. Dist(s): Baker Taylor
Contains The Adventure of the Speckled Band, The Red-Headed League, The Musgrave Ritual, and The Final Problem.

Sherlock Holme's Classic Mysteries: 4 Great Musteries. Arthur Conan Doyle. Narrated by Ralph Cosham. (Running Time: 10800 sec.). (Unabridged Classics in MP3 Ser.). (ENG.). 2008. audio compact disk 24.00 (978-1-58472-660-9(1), In Aud) Sound Room.

Sherlock Holmes Collection. Arthur Conan Doyle. Narrated by Ralph Cosham. (Running Time: 29700 sec.). (Unabridged Classics in MP3 Ser.). (ENG.). 2008. audio compact disk 24.00 (978-1-58472-545-9(1), In Aud) Sound Room.

Sherlock Holmes Collection: Study in Scarlet & the Sign of the Four. Arthur Conan Doyle. 3 cass. (Running Time: 3 hrs.). 1999. 17.95 (Bkcassette) Brilliance Audio.

***Sherlock Holmes Essentials: The Favorite Stories of Conan Doyle, Volume One.** Arthur Conan Doyle. Narrated by Clive Merrison et al. (Running Time: 5 hrs. 0 mins. 0 sec.). (BBC Radio Ser.). (ENG.). 2010. audio compact disk 16.95 (978-1-60998-060-3(3)) Pub: AudioGO. Dist(s): Perseus Dist

Sherlock Holmes for Children. Short Stories. Based on a book by Arthur Conan Doyle. As told by Jim Weiss. 1 cass. (Running Time: 1 hr.). Dramatization. (Storyteller's Version Ser.). (J). (gr. 2 up). 1991. 10.95 (978-1-882513-10-9(X), 1124-10); audio compact disk 14.95 (978-1-882513-35-2(5), 1124-010) Greathall Prods.
Brings the world of Sherlock Holmes and Doctor Watson to life for children. Includes "The Mazarin Stone," "The Adventure of the Speckled Band," "The Musgrave Ritual" and "The Adventure of the Blue Carbuncle".

Sherlock Holmes for Children. Read by Jim Weiss. 1 cass. (Running Time: 1 hr.). (J). (gr. 3-12). 1999. 9.95 (1124-10); audio compact disk 14.95 (1124-010) Greathall Prods.

Sherlock Holmes for Children. Read by Jim Weiss. 1 cass., 1 CD. (Running Time: 1 hr.). (J). (GHP10) NewSound.

Sherlock Holmes No. 2. Perf. by Basil Rathbone & Nigel Bruce. 1 cass. (Running Time: 60 min.). Incl. Adventure of the Speckled Band. Arthur Conan Doyle. (MM-8450); Murder by Moonlight. (MM-8450); 7.95 (MM-8450) Natl Recrd Co.
In "The Adventure of the Speckled Band," it was early in April, 1883, that Holmes was awakened by Helen Stoner, a terrified young lady, who feels certain it is just a matter of time before she will be murdered by her brutal stepfather. Her twin sister had died suddenly & strangely, two years previously. Her sisters last words were "speckled band." In "Murder by Moonlight," the entire adventure takes place aboard a small steamer sailing in the stormy seas of the Indian Ocean. A woman asks for Holmes' help, as she fears someone aboard ship will kill her.

Sherlock Holmes on American Radio. Compiled by Lawrence Nepodahl. 2000. 12.95 (978-1-888728-14-9(0)) Clssic Spclties.

Sherlock Holmes Stories, Vol. 2. unabr. ed. Arthur Conan Doyle. Read by Tim Behrens. 6 cass. (Running Time: 6 hrs. 30 min.). 1989. 39.95 (978-1-55686-310-3(1), 310) Books in Motion.
The six short stories included in this album are: "The Adventure of the Speckled Band", "The Adventure of the Copper Beeches", "The Adventure of the Silver Blaze", "The Adventure of the Yellow Face", "The Adventure of the MusgraVe Ritual", "The Adventure of the Crooked Man".

Sherlock Holmes Stories, Vol. 3. unabr. ed. Arthur Conan Doyle. Read by Tim Behrens. 6 cass. (Running Time: 6 hrs. 30 min.). 1989. 39.95 (978-1-55686-311-0(X), 311) Books in Motion.
The six short stories included are: "The Adventure of the Greek Interpreter", "The Adventure of the Naval Treaty", "The Adventure of the Final Problem", "The Adventure of the Empty House", "The Adventure of the Norwood Builder", "The Adventure of the Solitary Cyclist".

Sherlock Holmes Stories, Vol. 4. unabr. ed. Arthur Conan Doyle. Read by Tim Behrens. 6 cass. (Running Time: 6 hrs. 30 min.). 1989. 39.95 (978-1-55686-312-7(8), 312) Books in Motion.
The six stories included are: "The Adventure of the Priory School", "The Adventure of the Six Napoleons", "The Adventure of the Three Students", "The Adventure of the Golden Pince-Nez", "The Adventure of the Abbey Grange", "The Adventure of the Second Stain".

Sherlock Holmes Tales of Mystery: The Adventure of the Empty House; The Adventure of the Devil's Foot; The Adventure of the Abbey Grange. Arthur Conan Doyle. 2 cass. (Sherlock Holmes Ser.). 1998. 16.95 (978-1-896552-24-8(2)) Pub: Tangled Web CAN. Dist(s): Lndmrk Audiobks

***Sherlock Holmes: the Rediscovered Railway & Other Stories.** John Taylor. Narrated by Benedict Cumberbatch. (Running Time: 2 hrs. 0 mins. 0 sec.). (ENG.). 2011. audio compact disk 24.95 (978-1-4084-2625-8(0)) Pub: AudioGO. Dist(s): Perseus Dist

Sherlock Holmes Theatre. Arthur Conan Doyle & Yuri Rasovsky. Read by Arthur Conan Doyle & Yuri Rasovsky. 4 CDs. (Running Time: 4 hrs. 30 mins.). 2005. audio compact disk 34.95 (978-0-7861-3010-8(5), 3420) Blckstn Audio.

Sherlock Holmes Theatre. Arthur Conan Doyle & Yuri Rasovsky. 5 CDs. (Running Time: 4 hrs. 30 mins.). 2005. audio compact disk 45.00 (978-0-7861-8092-9(7), 3420) Blckstn Audio.

Sherlock Holmes Theatre. unabr. ed. Arthur Conan Doyle. Read by Full Cast Production Staff. 4 CDs. (Running Time: 16200 sec.). 2005. audio compact disk 24.95 (978-0-7861-7991-6(0)) Blckstn Audio.

Sherlock Holmes Theatre. unabr. ed. Arthur Conan Doyle & Yuri Rasovsky. 4 cass. (Running Time: 7 hrs.). 2005. 19.95 (978-0-7861-3441-0(0)); audio compact disk 29.95 (978-0-7861-8215-2(6), 3420) Blckstn Audio.

***Sherlock Holmes: Three Tales of Betrayal.** Arthur Conan Doyle. Narrated by Edward Hardwicke. (Running Time: 3 hrs. 0 mins. 0 sec.). (ENG.). 2011. audio compact disk 9.95 (978-1-60998-161-7(8)) Pub: AudioGO. Dist(s): Perseus Dist

Sherlock Holmes Through the Magnifying Glass: A Female Perspective. unabr. ed. David Stuart Davies. Read by Vanessa Maroney. Intro. by Catherine Cooke. 1 cass. (Running Time: 1 hr. 2 min.). Dramatization. 1995. 9.95 (978-1-888728-00-2(0)) Clssic Spclties.
Ms. Maroney begins with an insightful reading of Catherine Cooke's erudite analysis of the relationships between Mr. Holmes & all of the major canonical women; she then continues by dramatizing the identities of Irene Adler; Mrs. Watson "the unknown lady" & Carrie Trevor.

Sherlock Holmes Was Wrong: Reopening the Case of the Hound of the Baskervilles. unabr. ed. Pierre Bayard. Narrated by John Lee. (Running Time: 4 hrs. 0 mins. 0 sec.). (ENG.). 2008. audio compact disk 19.99 (978-1-4001-5983-3(0)); audio compact disk 49.99 (978-1-4001-3983-5(X)); audio compact disk 24.99 (978-1-4001-0983-8(3)) Pub: Tantor Media. Dist(s): IngramPubServ

Sherlock Holmes's Mysteries. unabr. ed. Short Stories. Arthur Conan Doyle. Read by Ralph Cosham. 1 cd. (Running Time: 8 hrs 29 mins). (YA). 2002. audio compact disk 18.95 (978-1-58472-402-5(1), In Aud) Pub: Sound Room. Dist(s): Baker Taylor
MP3 format. Includes Hound of the Baskervilles, The Musgrave Ritual, The Final Problem, The Adventure of the Speckled Band, and the Red-Headed League.

***Sherlockian.** unabr. ed. Graham Moore. Read by Steven Crossly. (Running Time: 9 hrs.). (ENG.). 2010. 24.98 (978-1-60788-723-2(1)) Pub: Hachet Audio. Dist(s): HachBkGrp

Sherlock's Secret Life: Volume 1&2. unabr. ed. Ed Lange. 2 cass. (Running Time: 003296 sec.). Dramatization. (Family Classic Audio Bks.). (gr. 9 up). 1998. 16.95 (978-1-892613-03-5(4), SL1998) NYS Theatre Inst.
An original mystery-comedy about young Sherlock Holmes & his familiar cohorts, Dr. Watson & Professor Moriarty on an early case that brought the detective to the brink of lovelorn heartbreak.WINNER OF 2000 AUDIE AWARD.CHOSEN BY ALA as a Selected Audiobook for Young Adults.

Sherman. unabr. ed. Steven E. Woodworth. (Running Time: 7 hrs. NaN mins.). 2009. 29.95 (978-1-4332-4690-6(2)); audio compact disk 24.95 (978-1-4332-4689-0(9)) Blckstn Audio.

Sherman: Great Generals Series. unabr. ed. Steven E. Woodworth. (Running Time: 7 hrs. NaN mins.). 2009. audio compact disk 60.00 (978-1-4332-4688-3(0)); audio compact disk 44.95 (978-1-4332-4687-6(2)) Blckstn Audio.

Sherman: Soldier, Realist, American. unabr. collector's ed. Basil H. Liddell-Hart. Read by Bill Kelsey. 12 cass. (Running Time: 18 hrs.). 1988. 96.00 (978-0-7366-1338-5(2), 2241) Books on Tape.
Focuses on the life of the Civil War general. His great campaign of destruction through the South was 100 years ahead of its time & foreshadowed both the totality & nobility of W. W. II. His mind was imaginative & uncompromising & no matter our profession, we can study its working with profit.

Sherman Brothers: Walt Disney's Supercalifragilistic Songwriting Team. Robert Sherman & Richard Sherman. Perf. by Maurice Chevalier et al. Contrib. by Walter Elias Disney. 1 cass. (Running Time: 69 min.). 1992. 8.95 (978-1-55723-314-1(4)); audio compact disk (978-1-55723-315-8(2)) W Disney Records.
This compilation of 26 remastered songs by the award-winning composers introduces many classics to a new generation while providing older listeners with a trip down memory lane. The songs - "It's a Small World" & "A Spoonful of Sugar" - have as much appeal today as when they were written. The album's final cut, a session with the Shermans & Disney himself, is a fitting tribute to the man who started it all.

Sherman McClellan: The McClellan Oscillator & Summation Index. Read by Sherman McClellan. 1 cass. (Running Time: 1 hr.). 30.00 Dow Jones Telerate.
Focus on techniques for interpreting both indices for market timing, showing techniques for overlaying similar Summation Index chart patterns. This technique helped properly forecast the explosive market rally that occurred in December, 1991. Overlays of Oscillator patterns forecast the May, 1970 bottom within one day in real time. Sherman discusses how bull market tops & bear market bottoms develop, & how the Oscillator & Summation indices give advance warning & real-time confirmation of these events & insight into the meaning of extreme Summation Index readings.

Sherman's March. unabr. ed. Richard Wheeler. Read by Jeff Riggenbach. 5 cass. (Running Time: 7 hrs.). 1995. 39.95 (978-0-7861-0763-6(4), 1612) Blckstn Audio.
Offers a new view of Sherman as a man of compassion as well as conviction & as a military leader who was ahead of his time in understanding that the destruction of supplies & property, the means to wage war, was as important as meeting & destroying enemy armies. An historically accurate narrative created by carefully selecting extracts from letters, diaries, memoirs & first-person reports from the period & then linking them.. A fresh & detailed account of this important campaign which, though highly destructive, doubtlessly shortened the Civil War appreciably, saving thousands of lives.

Sherman's March. unabr. collector's ed. Burke Davis. Read by Dick Estell. 9 cass. (Running Time: 13 hrs. 30 min.). 1988. 72.00 (978-0-7366-1364-4(1), 2263) Books on Tape.
In the final days of the Civil War, Sherman cut a swath through Georgia "from Atlanta to the sea." It sounded the Confederacy's death knell.

Sherman's March: An Eyewitness History of the Cruel Campaign that Helped End a Crueler War. unabr. ed. Richard Wheeler. Read by Jeff Riggenbach. (Running Time: 7 hrs. NaN mins.). 2008. 29.95 (978-1-4332-5834-3(X)); audio compact disk 60.00 (978-1-4332-5831-2(5)) Blckstn Audio.

Sherod Santos. unabr. ed. Ed. by Jim McKinley. Prod. by Rebekah Presson. 1 cass. (Running Time: 29 min.). (New Letters on the Air Ser.). 1994. 10.00 (103093) New Letters.
Santos' Third Book of Poems, "City of Women" is "A Sustained meditation on the nature & origins of erotic love." One critic says of the poems, "Their achievement is to canvass the dark side of the erotic argument - where power is mistaken for authority - with all the lyric gifts of powerless regret & real feeling".

She's All That. abr. ed. Kristin Billerbeck. Read by Kristin Billerbeck. 4 CDs. (Running Time: 18000 sec.). (Spa Girls Ser.). 2005. audio compact disk 25.99 (978-1-59859-038-8(3)) Oasis Audio.

She's All That. abr. ed. Kristin Billerbeck. Narrated by Brooke Sanford. (ENG.). 2005. 18.19 (978-1-60814-379-5(1)) Oasis Audio.

She's Come Undone. Read by Kathy Najimy. 2004. 15.95 (978-0-7435-1941-0(8)) Pub: S&S Audio. Dist(s): S and S Inc

She's Come Undone. abr. ed. Wally Lamb. 2 cass. (Running Time: 4 hrs.). 1997. 17.60 (978-0-671-57736-0(0), 908768, Audioworks) S&S Audio.

She's Come Undone. abr. ed. Wally Lamb. Read by Kathy Najimy. (Running Time: 5 hrs. 30 mins. 0 sec.). (ENG.). 2008. audio compact disk 14.99 (978-0-7435-7957-5(7)) Pub: S&S Audio. Dist(s): S and S Inc

She's Come Undone. unabr. ed. Wally Lamb. Narrated by Linda Stephens. 12 cass. (Running Time: 18 hrs. 15 mins.). 1999. 102.00 (978-0-7887-1763-5(4), 95241K8) Recorded Bks.
When teenage Dolores Price satisfies her cravings for love & happiness with potato chips, wisecracks & sitcoms, the results are both heartbreaking & comical.

She's Leaving Home. unabr. ed. Edwina Currie. Read by Judy Bennett. 16 cass. (Running Time: 16 hrs.). 1998. 124.95 (978-0-7540-0136-2(9), CAB1559) AudioGO.
Helen Majinsky is 16, Jewish & obsessed with the Beatles. After school, she & her friend Colette escape to the Cavern Club & dance to the fresh, exciting sounds of 1963. Helen dreams of going to college & escaping Liverpool. And as the prospect of a place at Oxbridge shimmers into view, Helen knows that the world is now at her feet.

She's Pregnant: A Guy's View to Adoption. Hosted by Mardie Caldwell. (ENG.). 2008. audio compact disk 12.95 (978-1-935176-02-2(1)) Pub: Am Carrage Hse Pubng. Dist(s): STL Dist NA

She's So Dead to Us. unabr. ed. Kieran Scott. Read by Keith Nobbs & Rebecca Soler. (Running Time: 8 hrs. 0 mins. 0 sec.). (ENG.). (YA). 2010. audio compact disk 17.95 (978-1-4423-0463-5(4)) Pub: S&S Audio. Dist(s): S and S Inc

She's the One. Sandra Kitt. Narrated by Patricia Floyd. 8 cass. (Running Time: 11 hrs. 30 mins.). 74.00 (978-1-4025-1592-7(8)) Recorded Bks.

Shest Rasskazov. Anton Chekhov. 1 cass. (Running Time: 1 hrs.). (RUS.). 1997. pap. bk. 19.50 (978-1-58085-562-4(8)) Interlingua VA.

Shh! We're Writing the Constitution. 2004. bk. 24.95 (978-1-56008-220-0(8)); bk. 24.95 (978-1-55592-680-9(0)); pap. bk. 18.95 (978-1-55592-681-6(9)); pap. bk. 32.75 (978-1-55592-353-2(4)); pap. bk. 14.95 (978-1-55592-679-3(7)); 8.95 (978-0-7882-0079-3(8)); 8.95 (978-1-55592-677-9(0)); 8.95 (978-0-7882-0080-9(1)); cass. & flmstrp 30.00 (978-0-89719-590-4(6)); audio compact disk 12.95 (978-1-55592-678-6(9)) Weston Woods.

Shh! We're Writing the Constitution. Jean Fritz. Illus. by Tomie dePaola. 1 cass., 5 bks. (Running Time: 1 hr.). 2001. pap. bk. 32.75 Weston Woods.

Shh! We're Writing the Constitution. Jean Fritz. Illus. by Tomie dePaola. 1 cass. (Running Time: 1 hr.). (J). 2001. bk. 24.95 Weston Woods.

Shh! We're Writing the Constitution. Jean Fritz. Illus. by Tomie dePaola. 1 cass. (Running Time: 1 hr.). (J). 2004. pap. bk. 14.95 (978-1-56008-226-2(7)) Weston Woods.

Shhh... Activities for Quiet Times & Rainy Days. Read by Pamela Ott. 1 cass. (Running Time: 1 hr. 02 min.). (Music & Movement Ser.). 14.95 (978-1-886655-06-5(5), 85078) Corwin Pr.
A collection of beautifully arranged instrumental songs suitable for play while reading, relaxing, cuddling or falling asleep.

Shhh... Activities for Quiet Times & Rainy Days. Pamela Ott. 1 CD. (Teaching Tunes Ser.). 2000. audio compact disk 14.95 (978-0-8039-6873-8(6), 85077) Corwin Pr.

Shhh! It's Special Ed. Your School District's Best Kept Secret. Peter M. Geil M.Ed. 2007. audio compact disk 27.99 (978-1-60247-480-2(X)) Tate Pubng.

Shibumi. Trevanian. (Running Time: 61200 sec.). 2005. 89.95 (978-0-7861-3483-0(6)) Blckstn Audio.

Shibumi. Trevanian. (Running Time: 61200 sec.). 2005. audio compact disk 108.00 (978-0-7861-7937-4(6)) Blckstn Audio.

Shibumi. unabr. ed. Trevanian. Read by Christopher Lane. 13 vols. (Running Time: 15 hrs.). 2005. 29.95 (978-0-7861-8111-7(7)) Blckstn Audio.

Shibumi. unabr. ed. Trevanian. Read by Joe Barrett. 10 cass. (Running Time: 61200 sec.). 2005. 32.95 (978-0-7861-3446-5(1)) Blckstn Audio.

Shibumi. unabr. ed. Trevanian & Trevanian. Read by Joe Barrett. 12 CDs. (Running Time: 61200 sec.). 2005. audio compact disk 34.95 (978-0-7861-7978-7(3)) Blckstn Audio.

Shield: Ephesians 6:16. Ed Young. 1988. 4.95 (978-0-7417-3647-5(0), AV0647) Win Walk.

Shield: Ephesians 6:16, Vol. 647. Ed Young. 1988. 4.95 (978-0-7417-1647-7(X), 647) Win Walk.

Shield & the Sword. unabr. collector's ed. Ernle Bradford. Read by Walter Zimmerman. 6 cass. (Running Time: 9 hrs.). 1986. 48.00 (978-0-7366-0775-9(7), 1729) Books on Tape.
The Knights of St. John trace their origin to Jerusalem where they began in charity & penance. But when they embraced the church militant, they made themselves pre-eminent in the Mediterranean. They threatened Turkish expansion & the Turks set out to destroy them, a task to which they brought great numerical superiority.

Shield Out Hostility: Healthy Protection against Emotional Assault. Scripts. Richard Driscoll. 1 CD. (Running Time: 31 mins.). 2005. pap. bk. 19.50 (978-0-9634126-7-6(1)) Westside Pubng.
Book and Training CD.

Shield's Lady. unabr. ed. Amanda Glass, pseud & Jayne Ann Krentz. Read by Natalie Ross. (Running Time: 12 hrs.). (Lost Colony Ser.). 2009. 39.97 (978-1-4233-8714-5(7), 9781423387145, Brlnc Audio MP3 Lib); 24.99 (978-1-4233-8713-8(9), 9781423387138, Brilliance MP3); 39.97 (978-1-4233-8716-9(3), 9781423387169, BADLE); 24.99 (978-1-4233-8715-2(5), 9781423387152, BAD); audio compact disk 82.97 (978-1-4233-8712-1(0), 9781423387121, BriAudCD Unabrid); audio compact disk 29.99 (978-1-4233-8711-4(2), 9781423387114, Bril Audio CD Unabri) Brilliance Audio.

Shields of Achilles. (23298-A) J Norton Pubs.

Shiendele. unabr. ed. Rami Danon & Amnon Levi. Perf. by Theo Bikel et al. 1 cass. (Running Time: 1 hrs. 35 min.). 1998. 19.95 (978-1-58081-116-3(7)) L A Theatre.

The searing love story takes us into a world rarely glimpsed by outsiders - the Mea Shearim quarter in Jerusalem, home to the ultra-orthodox Hassidic community. The community's powerful rabbis want Yoelish to divorce the childless Sheindele. When Sheindele rebels, her passion ignites a struggle that threatens to separate husband & wife forever.

Shift. movie tie-in ed. Wayne W. Dyer. Ethan Lipton & Christopher Ferreira. (ENG.). 2009. audio compact disk 15.00 (978-1-4019-2635-9(5), 1190) Hay House.

***Shift, Pt. 1.** unabr. ed. Tim Kring & Dale Peck. Read by Robert Forster. (ENG.). 2010. audio compact disk 45.00 (978-0-307-75034-1(5), Random AudioBks) Pub: Random Audio Pubg. Dist(s): Random

Shifting Fog. unabr. ed. Kate Morton. Read by Caroline Lee. (Running Time: 69300 sec.). 2006. audio compact disk 123.95 (978-1-74093-837-2(2)) Pub: Bolinda Pubng AUS. Dist(s): Bolinda Pub Inc

Shifting Ground. 2002. (978-0-7398-5159-3(4)) SteckVau.

Shifting Ground Level 3. (J). 2002. audio compact disk (978-0-7398-5342-9(2)) SteckVau.

Shifting Through Neutral. unabr. ed. Bridgett M. Davis. Narrated by Susan Spain. 8 cass. (Running Time: 11 hrs.). 2004. 79.75 (978-1-4193-1035-5(6), F0196MC, Griot Aud) Recorded Bks.

Shifting Tide. unabr. ed. Anne Perry. Read by David Colacci. (Running Time: 12 hrs.). (William Monk Novel Ser.). 2004. 34.95 (978-1-59355-779-9(5), 1593557795, BAU); 92.25 (978-1-59355-780-5(9), 1593557809, BrilAudUnabridg); audio compact disk 38.95 (978-1-59355-782-9(5), 1593557825, Bril Audio CD Unabri); audio compact disk 107.25 (978-1-59355-783-6(3), 1593557833, BriAudCD Unabrid) Brilliance Audio.

William Monk knows London's streets like the back of his hand; after all, they are where he earns his living. But the river Thames and its teeming docks - where towering schooners and clipper ships unload their fabulous cargoes and wharf rats and night plunderers ply their trades - is unknown territory. Only dire need persuades him to accept an assignment from shipping magnate Clement Louvain to investigate the theft of a cargo of African ivory from Louvain's recently docked schooner, the Maude Idris. Monk is desperate for work, not only to feed himself and his wife, Hester, but to keep open the doors of her clinic, a last resort for sick and starving street women. But he wonders: Why didn't Louvain report the ivory theft directly to the River Police? Why did he warn Monk not to investigate the murder of one of the Maude Idris crew? Even more mysterious, why has Louvain brought to Hester's clinic a desperately ill woman who, he claims, is the discarded mistress of an old friend? Neither Hester nor Monk anticipates the nightmare answers to these questions . . . nor the trap that soon so fatefully ensnares them.

Shifting Tide. unabr. ed. Anne Perry. Read by David Colacci. 8 CDs. (Running Time: 12 hrs.). (William Monk Novel Ser.). 2004. 39.25 (978-1-59335-531-9(9), 1593355319, Brlnc Audio MP3 Lib); 24.95 (978-1-59335-298-1(0), 1593352980, Brilliance MP3) Brilliance Audio.

Shifting Tide. unabr. ed. Anne Perry. Read by David Colacci. (Running Time: 12 hrs.). (William Monk Ser.). 2004. 39.25 (978-1-59710-701-3(8), 1597107018, BADLE); 24.95 (978-1-59710-700-6(X), 159710700X, BAD) Brilliance Audio.

Shiite/Sunni: The Two Houses of Islam. Avi Lipkin. 2 CD's. 2007. audio compact disk 19.95 (978-1-57821-393-1(2)) Koinonia Hse.

Shiksa Goddess: Or, How I Spent My Forties. abr. ed. Wendy Wasserstein. Perf. by Wendy Wasserstein. 4 cass. (Running Time: 6 hrs.). 2004. 25.00 (978-1-59007-015-4(1)); audio compact disk 34.95 (978-1-59007-016-1(X)) Pub: New Millenn Enter. Dist(s): PerseuPGW

When the Pulitzer Prize-winning playwright turned 40, she made a To Do list, most of which repeated the items she had listed when she turned 30: lose weight, become a better citizen, move, fall in love, & - at the very end - decide about a baby. In this book of essays, the author takes on these & other midlife quests & obsessions with her famous, appealing humor. She writes about diets & cooking, the theater, attending the Golden Globes, Chekhov & George Abbott, hiring a personal trainer & the surprising truth about her denominational heritage.

Shiksa Syndrome. unabr. ed. Laurie Graff. (Running Time: 9 hrs. NaN mins.). 2008. 59.95 (978-1-4332-4699-9(6)); audio compact disk 29.95 (978-1-4332-4701-9(1)) Blckstn Audio.

Shiksa Syndrome. unabr. ed. Laurie Graff. Read by Hillary Huber. 1 MP3-CD. (Running Time: 9 hrs. 30 mins.). 2008. 29.95 (978-1-4332-4702-6(X)); audio compact disk 80.00 (978-1-4332-4700-2(3)) Blckstn Audio.

Shilling for Candles. unabr. ed. Josephine Tey. Read by Stephen Thorne. 6 cass. (Running Time: 7 hrs.). 2001. 29.95 (978-1-57270-166-3(8), N6166u) Pub: Audio Partners. Dist(s): PerseuPGW

When the body of famous screen actress Christine Clay isfound on a beach on the southern coast of England, Inspector Alan Grant is faced with too many clues & too many motives. It seems the world is full of people who wanted Christine Clay dead.

Shilling for Candles, unabr. ed. Josephine Tey. Read by Nadia May. 5 cass. (Running Time: 7 hrs.). 1991. 39.95 (978-0-7861-0224-2(1), 1197) Blckstn Audio.

The plot concerns a naive young man who is suspected of murdering a famous film star. The novel was the basis for Alfred Hitchcock's film "Young & Innocent".

Shiloh. Phyllis Reynolds Naylor. Read by Peter MacNicol. 2 cass. (Running Time: 3 hrs.). (Shiloh Ser.). (J). 2000. 64.00 (978-0-7366-9046-1(8)) Books on Tape.

Eleven-year-old Marty Preston happens upon a beagle puppy that has been abused. The animal follows the boy home & in a test of courage & integrity, Marty learns difficult lessons of morality & kindness.

Shiloh. James Reasoner. Read by Lloyd James. (Running Time: 10 hrs. 30 mins.). (Civil War Battle Ser.: Bk. 2). (J). 2003. 34.95 (978-1-59912-594-7(3)) Iofy Corp.

Shiloh. unabr. ed. Phyllis Reynolds Naylor. Read by Peter MacNicol. (Running Time: 2 hrs. 39 mins.). (ENG.). (J). (gr. 5). 2004. audio compact disk 14.99 (978-1-4000-8500-2(4), Listening Lib) Pub: Random Audio Pubg. Dist(s): Random

Shiloh. unabr. ed. Phyllis Reynolds Naylor. Read by Peter MacNicol. 3 CDs. (Running Time: 2 hrs. 39 mins.). (Middle Grade Cassette Librariestm Ser.). (J). (gr. 3-7). 2004. audio compact disk 25.50 (978-0-8072-1159-5(1), S YA 164 CD, Listening Lib); 23.00 (978-0-8072-8328-8(2), LL0176, Listening Lib) Random Audio Pubg.

Shiloh. unabr. ed. Phyllis Reynolds Naylor. Narrated by Peter MacNicol. 2 cass. (Running Time: 2 hrs.). (J). pap. bk. 23.00 (LL0137AC) Weston Woods.

Shiloh. unabr. ed. James Reasoner. Read by Lloyd James. 8 CDs. (Running Time: 11 hrs. 30 mins.). (Civil War Battle Ser.: Bk. 2). 2003. audio compact disk 72.00 (978-0-7861-9136-9(8), 3154); 56.95 (978-0-7861-2521-0(7), 3154) Blckstn Audio.

As the Civil War sweeps across the country, it finds the most wayfaring member of the Brannon family of Culpeper County, Virginia, working as a wharf rat at the Mississippi River port of New Madrid, Missouri.

Shiloh, Bk. 1. abr. ed. Dalton Walker. Read by Dick Wilkinson. 2 cass. (Running Time: 3 hrs.). (Shiloh: Vol. 1). 1999. Rental 16.95 (978-1-890990-23-7(X)) Otis Audio.

Shiloh, No. 1. unabr. ed. Phyllis Reynolds Naylor. Read by Peter MacNicol. 2 vols. (Running Time: 2 hrs. 39 mins.). (J). (gr. 3-7). 2004. pap. bk. 29.00 (978-0-8072-8329-5(0), YA164SP, Listening Lib) Random Audio Pubg.

Eleven-year-old Marty Preston happens upon a beagle puppy that has been abused. The animal follows the boy home & in a test of courage & integrity, Marty learns difficult lessons of morality & kindness.

Shiloh: A Novel. unabr. ed. Shelby Foote. Narrated by Shelby Foote. 4 cass. (Running Time: 5 hrs. 30 mins.). 1992. 35.00 (978-1-55690-653-4(6), 92341E7) Recorded Bks.

The story of the Civil War battle of Shiloh, April 1862, as told through the eyes of several fictional participants, both Northern & Southern.

Shiloh: A Novel. unabr. ed. Shelby Foote. Read by Shelby Foote. 5 CDs. (Running Time: 5 hrs. 30 mins.). 2000. audio compact disk 42.00 (978-0-7887-3963-7(8), C1118E7) Recorded Bks.

Fictional history that recreates two days of intense battle in the Civil War, as seen through the eyes of the officers & foot soldiers in a single squad.

Shiloh Renewal. unabr. ed. Joan Leslie Woodruff. (Running Time: 16200 sec.). (J). (gr. 4-7). 2007. audio compact disk 19.95 (978-1-4332-0591-0(2)) Blckstn Audio.

Shiloh Renewal. unabr. ed. Joan Leslie Woodruff. Read by Rebecca Rogers. (Running Time: 16200 sec.). (J). (gr. 4-7). 2007. 34.95 (978-1-4332-0589-7(0)); audio compact disk 36.00 (978-1-4332-0590-3(4)) Blckstn Audio.

Shiloh Season. Phyllis Reynolds Naylor. Read by Michael Moriarty. 2 cass. (Running Time: 3 hrs.). (Shiloh Ser.: No. 2). (J). (gr. 4-7). 2000. 18.00 (978-0-7366-9047-8(6)) Books on Tape.

This dramatic tale furthers the adventures of a young country boy, Marty Preston & the dog he rescued from neighbor Judd Travers, a hard-drinking miscreant who attempts to hunt on the Preston's land.

Shiloh Season. unabr. ed. Phyllis Reynolds Naylor. Read by Michael Moriarty. 2 vols. (Running Time: 2 hrs. 37 mins.). (Shiloh Ser.: No. 2). (J). (gr. 3-7). 2004. pap. bk. 29.00 (978-0-8072-8707-1(5), YA242SP, Listening Lib); 23.00 (978-0-8072-8706-4(7), YA242CX, Listening Lib) Random Audio Pubg.

Eleven-year-old Marty Preston happens upon a beagle puppy that has been abused. The animal follows the boy home & in a test of courage & integrity, Marty learns difficult lessons of morality & kindness.

Shiloh Season. unabr. ed. Phyllis Reynolds Naylor. Read by Michael Moriarty. (ENG.). (J). (gr. 3). 2009. audio compact disk 19.99 (978-0-7393-8104-5(0), Listening Lib) Pub: Random Audio Pubg. Dist(s): Random

Shiloh! the Soldiers Story. Short Stories. Gary C. Martin. Narrated by Luke Behan. 4CDs. (Running Time: 4 hours). 2003. audio compact disk 14.95 (978-0-9721444-6-9(3)) Audio History.

The true story of the Battle at Shiloh TN April 6,7 1862 as told by the participants. From the Official Records of the War of the Rebellion & letters from the soldiers who fought there. Over 30 narrations with sound effects & original music background.

Shimmer. unabr. ed. David Morrell. Read by Phil Gigante. (Running Time: 11 hrs.). 2009. 24.99 (978-1-4233-9721-2(5), 9781423397212, Brilliance MP3); 24.99 (978-1-4233-9723-6(1), 9781423397236, BAD); 39.97 (978-1-4233-9722-9(3), 9781423397229, Brlnc Audio MP3 Lib); 39.97 (978-1-4233-9724-3(X), 9781423397243, BADLE); audio compact disk 29.99 (978-1-4233-9719-9(3), 9781423397199, Bril Audio CD Unabri); audio compact disk 87.97 (978-1-4233-9720-5(7), 9781423397205, BriAudCD Unabrid) Brilliance Audio.

***Shimmer.** unabr. ed. Alyson Noël. (ENG.). (J). 2011. audio compact disk 19.99 (978-1-4272-1250-4(3)) Pub: Macmill Audio. Dist(s): Macmillan

Shine. Contrib. by Salvador. Prod. by Nic Gonzales & Chris Bevins. (Studio Ser.). 2006. audio compact disk 9.98 (978-5-558-10891-0(6), Word Records) Word Enter.

Shine: Selected Songs for Grown-Ups. Rachel Coleman. (J). 2006. audio compact disk 9.99 (978-1-933543-34-5(5)) Tw Li Ha Pr LLC.

Shine! Sing & Praise Worship for Kids. Directed By Brian Shumate. Contrib. by Thom Schultz. Created by Group Publishing. Prod. by Brenda Kraft. 2007. 19.99 (978-5-557-54493-1(3)) Group Pub.

Shine - a Prayer for Children Everywhere. (J). audio compact disk 19.00 (978-0-9666199-7-3(8)) DreamDog Press.

Shine, Perishing Republic see Poetry of Robinson Jeffers

***Shine Your Light!** Composed by Greg Gilpin. (Running Time: 3 mins.). (ENG.). 2010. audio compact disk 26.99 (978-1-4234-8808-8(3), 1423488083) Pub: Shawnee Pr. Dist(s): H Leonard

Shiniest Star (Nativity) Sara Ridgeley. (Class Act Productions Ser.). (ENG., 2005. audio compact disk 11.95 (978-1-85909-656-7(5), Warner Bro) Alfred Pub.

Shining. unabr. ed. Stephen King. Read by Campbell Scott. 2005. 29.95 (978-0-7435-5165-6(6)); audio compact disk 49.95 (978-0-7435-3700-1(9)) Pub: S&S Audio. Dist(s): S and S Inc

Shining Company. unabr. ed. Rosemary Sutcliff. Read by Johanna Ward. 6 cass. (Running Time: 8 hrs. 30 mins.). 2001. 44.95 (978-0-7861-2003-1(7), 2773); audio compact disk 56.00 (978-0-7861-9726-2(9), 2773) Blckstn Audio.

A white stag and a dagger transform the life of Prosper, a Welsh chieftain's son. With Conn, his bondservant, he leaves his isolated valley and joins the war band of King Mynyddog the Golden as a shieldbearer. For the Saxons have returned to threaten the northern tribes of Britain and the Shining Company'a brotherhood of three hundred chosen warriors' must make a desperate attempt to repel the invaders.

Shining Company, unabr. ed. Rosemary Sutcliff. Narrated by Ron Keith. 7 pieces. (Running Time: 9 hrs. 30 mins.). (gr. 7 up). 1994. 60.00 (978-0-7887-0133-7(9), 94358E7) Recorded Bks.

Around A.D. 600, a young boy joins the 300 warriors sent by the Celtic King Mynyddog to fight the invading Saxons & becomes one of the few survivors of the ill-fated raid.

Shining Like the Sun: The Chants of Transfiguration. Contrib. by Gloriae Dei Schola. 2005. audio compact disk 16.95 (978-1-55725-364-4(1), GDCD035) Paraclete MA.

Shining Star. Contrib. by Jump5. Prod. by Mark Hammond. 2005. audio compact disk 11.99 (978-5-558-69883-1(7)) Pt of Grace Ent.

Shining Star: Audio Program. Created by Pearson-Longman. 4 CDs. 2003. audio compact disk 220.66 (978-0-13-049951-6(X)) Longman.

Shining Threads. unabr. ed. Audrey Howard. Read by Carole Boyd. 14 cass. (Running Time: 14 hrs.). 1998. 110.95 (978-0-7540-0228-4(4), CAB 1651) AudioGO.

Young Tessa Harrison & her twin cousins are unprepared for running a cotton mill, but first she must deal with the attraction she feels for her foreman.

Shinrai: Building Trusting Relationships with Japanese Colleagues. Dianne Saphiere & Yuko Kipnis. (Running Time: approximately 1 hour). 2002. audio compact disk 39.95 (978-0-9708463-2-7(0)) Nipp Assocs.

A combination of cultural information and key Japanese phrases to enable non-Japanese to build trusting and productive relationships with Japanese colleagues.

Shinsokan Meditation. Prod. by Seicho-No-Ie. Voice by Bruce Mallery. (ENG.). 2009. audio compact disk 15.00 (978-0-9825725-0-4(6)) Seicho-No.

Shinto & Japanese New Religions. unabr. ed. Byron Earhart. Read by Ben Kingsley. (Running Time: 10800 sec.). (Religion, Scriptures, & Spirituality Ser.). 2006. audio compact disk 25.95 (978-0-7861-6478-3(6)) Pub: Blckstn Audio. Dist(s): NetLibrary CO

Shinto & Japanese New Religions. unabr. ed. Byron Earhart. Read by Ben Kingsley. Ed. by Walter Harrelson & Mike Hassell. 2 cass. (Running Time: 3 hrs.). Dramatization. (Religion, Scriptures & Spirituality Ser.). 1994. 17.95 (978-1-56823-014-6(1), 10457) Knowledge Prod.

The traditional religion known as Shinto was present in Japan from prehistoric times, long before Buddhism & other traditions arrived from the Asian continent. One of its forms, shrine Shinto, is centered around local shrines & seasonal festivals; it has greatly influenced Japanese culture. Sect Shinto is characterized by more highly organized institutions, which attract many members; folk Shinto consists of beliefs & practices apart from these institutions, especially in the home. This presentation also discusses the dynamic new Japanese religions formed during the last century & a half.

Shiny Dinah: Sing, Dance & Read with Me, Read-Along with Big Book. Susan James. 1 CD. (Running Time: 1 hr). (J). (ps-3). 2000. pap. bk. 29.95 (978-1-931127-50-9(6), 986-009) Kindermusik Intl.

Choo-Choo! Shiny Dinah shines her way through tunnels, around the bands, all day long & into the night, clickety-clacking down the track.

Shiny Red Sled. Barbara Davoll & Dennis Hockerman. Illus. by Dennis Hockerman. 1 cass. (Christopher Churchmouse Ser.). (J). (ps-2). 1989. bk. 11.99 (978-0-89693-031-5(9), 3-1203) David C Cook.

Shinyel. Nikolai Gogol. Read by Eugene Shago. 2 cass. (Running Time: 2 hrs.).Tr. of Overcoat. (RUS.). 1995. pap. bk. 29.50 (978-1-58085-556-3(3)) Interlingua VA.

Includes text & English vocabulary, intermediate level. The combination of written text & clarity & pace of diction will open the door for intermediate & advanced students to genuine comprehension & the use of literary texts for advancement in rapid understanding of written & oral language materials. The audio text plus written text concept makes foreign languages accessible to a much wider range of students than books alone.

Ship. unabr. collector's ed. C. S. Forester. Read by Thomas Whitworth. 7 cass. (Running Time: 7 hrs.). 1985. 42.00 (978-0-7366-2200-4(4), 2995) Books on Tape.

The ship is the British light cruiser "Artemis." Half-way through W.W.II in the Mediterranean, en route to Malta, an uneventful afternoon turns into a lethal night action when a major strike force of the Italian fleet moves in to attack.

***Ship Breaker.** unabr. ed. Paolo Bacigalupi. Read by Joshua Swanson. (Running Time: 9 hrs.). (YA). 2010. 19.99 (978-1-4418-8348-3(7), 9781441883483, Brilliance MP3); 39.97 (978-1-4418-8349-0(5), 9781441883490, Brlnc Audio MP3 Lib); 39.97 (978-1-4418-8350-6(9), 9781441883506, BADLE); audio compact disk 19.99 (978-1-4418-8346-9(0), 9781441883469, Bril Audio CD Unabri); audio compact disk 49.97 (978-1-4418-8347-6(9), 9781441883476, BriAudCD Unabrid) Brilliance Audio.

Ship Is Dying. unabr. ed. Brian Callison. Read by Dan Lazar. 7 cass. (Running Time: 7 hrs.). 1980. 42.00 (978-0-7366-0253-2(4), 1248) Books on Tape.

Three minutes before the collision, the second mate caught a glimpse of a foam-shrouded shape lurking half a mile ahead. Seventeen minutes afterward, the ship plunged beneath the icy waters of the North Sea. Into this brief space of time is paced a lifetime of turbulence & tragedy; moments of pathos, moments of humor; even, incredibly, moments of boredom & of exultation. Heroes, cowards, suicides, plain fools & a possible murderer emerge from rather ordinary men.

Ship Must Die. unabr. ed. Douglas Reeman. Read by David Rintoul. 8 cass. (Running Time: 12 hrs.). 2000. 59.95 (978-0-7451-4192-3(7), CAB 875) Pub: Chivers Audio Bks GBR. Dist(s): AudioGO

In January 1944, British ships on the Indian Ocean are being destroyed by German raiders. The HMS Andromeda, lead by Captain Richard Blake, prepares to engage in a bloody combat against the Nazi's. And in this conflict, one ship must die!.

Ship of Death see Dylan Thomas Reading

***Ship of Destiny.** unabr. ed. Robin Hobb. Narrated by Anne Flosnik. (Running Time: 33 hrs. 30 mins. 0 sec.). (Liveship Traders Ser.). (ENG.). 2010. 44.99 (978-1-4001-6439-4(7)); 30.99 (978-1-4001-8439-2(8)); 64.99 (978-1-4001-9439-1(3)); audio compact disk 129.99 (978-1-4001-4439-6(6)); audio compact disk 64.99 (978-1-4001-1439-9(X)) Pub: Tantor Media. Dist(s): IngramPubServ

Ship of Fools. unabr. ed. Katherine Anne Porter. Read by Grace Conlin. 16 cass. (Running Time: 23 hrs. 30 mins.). 1995. 99.95 (978-0-7861-0864-0(9), 1662) Blckstn Audio.

***Ship of Fools.** unabr. ed. Katherine Anne Porter. Read by Grace Conlin. (Running Time: 22 hrs.). 2010. 44.95 (978-1-4417-6644-1(8)); audio compact disk 140.00 (978-1-4417-6642-7(1)) Blckstn Audio.

Ship of Ghosts: The Story of the USS Houston, FDR's Legendary Lost Cruiser, & the Epic Saga of Her Survivors. abr. ed. James D. Hornfischer. Read by Robertson Dean. (Running Time: 21600 sec.). (ENG.). 2006. audio compact disk 29.95 (978-0-7393-1143-1(3)) Pub: Random Audio Pubg. Dist(s): Random

Ship of Ghosts: The Story of the USS Houston, FDR's Legendary Lost Cruiser, & the Epic Saga of Her Survivors. unabr. ed. James D. Hornfischer. Read by Marc Cashman. 14 CDs. 2006. audio compact disk 102.00 (978-1-4159-3133-2(X)) Pub: Books on Tape. Dist(s): NetLibrary CO

Ship of Line. Diane Carey. (Star Trek). 2004. 10.95 (978-0-7435-4633-1(4)) Pub: S&S Audio. Dist(s): S and S Inc

***Ship of Magic.** unabr. ed. Robin Hobb. Narrated by Anne Flosnik. (Running Time: 35 hrs. 30 mins. 0 sec.). (Liveship Traders Ser.). (ENG.). 2010. 44.99 (978-1-4001-6437-0(0)); 34.99 (978-1-4001-8437-8(1)); audio compact disk

129.99 (978-1-4001-4437-2(X)); audio compact disk 64.99 (978-1-4001-1437-5(3)) Pub: Tantor Media. Dist(s): IngramPubServ

Ship of State see Treasury of Henry Wadsworth Longfellow

Ship of the Line. abr. ed. Diane Carey. Read by Kevin Conway. 2 cass. (Running Time: 3 hrs.). (Star Trek). 1997. 18.00 S&S Audio.

Ship Possessed. unabr. ed. Alton L. Gansky. Narrated by Jack Garrett. 8 cass. (Running Time: 11 hrs.). 2001. 68.00 (978-0-7887-5474-6(2), K0061E7) Recorded Bks.
Fifty years after it was lost at sea, a World War II submarine, the USS Triggerfish, washes up on the California shore. When retired Navy Captain J. D. Stanton is called into duty to investigate, he begins to see disturbing evidence that someone, or something, is aboard the ship. The supernatural secrets lurking below Triggerfish's deck will stretch the limits of Stanton's courage & his beliefs.

Ship Shapes. 1 cass. (Running Time: 90 mins.). (Pooh Learning Ser.). (J). (ps-3). 2000. pap. bk. 6.98 (978-0-7634-0471-0(3)) W Disney Records.

Ship That Died of Shame see Monsarrat at Sea

Ship That Died of Shame. unabr. collector's ed. Nicholas Monsarrat. Read by Victor Rumbellow. 8 cass. (Running Time: 8 hrs.). Incl. Dinner Party. 1984. (1217); I Was There. 1984. (1217); Licensed to Kill. 1984. (1217); List. 1984. (1217); Man Who Wanted a Mark IX. 1984. (1217); Oh to Be in England. 1984. (1217); Postscript. 1984. (1217); Postscript. 1984. (1217); Reconciliation. 1984. (1217); Thousand Islands Snatch. 1984. (1217); Up the Garden Path. 1984. (1217); 1980. 48.00 (978-0-7366-0219-8(4), 1217) Books on Tape.
The title story takes us on board a small motor gunboat with a distinguished World War II record; the boat's shame is that it is being used as a smuggler.

Ship to Remember see Monsarrat at Sea

Shipbuilding in China: A Strategic Reference 2006. Compiled by Icon Group International, Inc. Staff. 2007. ring bd. 195.00 (978-0-497-35893-8(X)) Icon Grp.

Shipment of Mute Fate see Escape

Shipping News. Annie Proulx. Read by Annie Proulx. 2004. 15.95 (978-0-7435-4057-5(3)) Pub: S&S Audio. Dist(s): S and S Inc

Shipping News. Annie Proulx. Adapted by Annie Proulx. 2000. 15.99 (978-0-7435-0552-9(2), Audioworks) S&S Audio.

Shipping News. unabr. ed. Annie Proulx. Adapted by Annie Proulx. Read by Kimberly Schraf. 9 cass. (Running Time: 13 hrs. 30 min.). 1993. 72.00 (978-0-7366-3141-9(0), 113380) Books on Tape.
After his two-timing wife dies, Quoyle, a hack reporter, moves with his two daughters & an aged aunt to their ancestral home in a remote Newfoundland village. In this starkly beautiful country of coast & cove, the lumpish Quoyle, who hides a gentle heart within his bulk, cobbles up a new life for himself. He's sheltered in the tiny community; his talents come alive & he breaks the link between love & misery. Pulitzer Prize winner.

Shipping News. unabr. ed. Annie Proulx. Adapted by Annie Proulx. Narrated by Paul Hecht. 9 cass. (Running Time: 13 hrs.). 78.00 (978-0-7887-0343-0(9), 94535E7) Recorded Bks.
Quoyle, a timid New York newspaper reporter, retreats to his ancestral home on the starkly beautiful coast of Newfoundland. He finds a job reporting the shipping news & meets a colorful collection of local characters - including drowned Herald & cane-twirling Beety - who teach him that love isn't always painful. Available to libraries only.

Shipping News. unabr. ed. Annie Proulx. Adapted by Annie Proulx. Narrated by Paul Hecht. 11 CDs. (Running Time: 13 hrs.). 1999. audio compact disk 100.00 (978-0-7887-3708-4(2), C1064E5) Recorded Bks.

Ships. unabr. ed. Ed. by Linda Spizzirri. 1 cass. (Running Time: 15 min.). Dramatization. (Educational Coloring Book & Cassette Package Ser.). (J). (gr. k-8). 1989. 6.95 (978-0-86545-156-8(7)) Spizzirri.
Discusses ships from the Egyptian Sahure to the English Tanker.

Ships & Boats in China: A Strategic Reference 2006. Compiled by Icon Group International, Inc. Staff. 2007. ring bd. 195.00 (978-0-497-35894-5(8)) Icon Grp.

Ships in the Sky. unabr. collector's ed. John Toland. Read by John MacDonald. 10 cass. (Running Time: 15 hrs.). 1989. 80.00 (978-0-7366-1488-7(5), 2364) Books on Tape.
They cruised serenely above the earth's surface, carried tons of cargo, crossed oceans & continents, & were felt by many to be the logical next step in transportation.

Ships of Earth: Homecoming: Volume 3. unabr. ed. Orson Card Scott & Stefan Rudnicki. (Running Time: 13 hrs. NaN mins.). 2008. 29.95 (978-1-4332-1889-7(5)); 72.95 (978-1-4332-1885-9(2)); audio compact disk 90.00 (978-1-4332-1886-6(0)) Blckstn Audio.

***Ships of Song: A Parable of Ascension.** (ENG.). 2010. 13.95 (978-0-9823691-6-6(6)) Awakening Pubns Inc.

Shipwreck. unabr. ed. Gordon Korman. Read by Holter Graham. (J). 2007. 34.99 (978-1-60252-840-6(3)) Find a World.

Shipwreck. unabr. ed. Gordon Korman. Read by Holter Graham. 2 CDs. (Running Time: 8940 sec.). (Island Ser.: Bk. 1). (ENG.). (J). (gr. 4-7). 2007. audio compact disk 29.95 (978-0-439-02331-3(9)) Scholastic Inc.

Shipwreck at the Bottom of the World: The Extraordinary True Story of Shackleton & the Endurance. unabr. ed. Jennifer Armstrong. Read by Taylor Mali. 4 CDs. (Running Time: 4 hrs.). (YA). 2000. audio compact disk 39.95 (978-1-883332-54-9(0)) Audio Bkshelf.
When their ship, "Endurance," became icebound in Antarctica & sank in 1914, Sir Ernest Shackleton & his 27 crewmen were 100 miles from land. Unbelievably, they all survived. At first, the men played on the ice to kill time, but after the ship sank, they took to their life boats & spent a year & a half traveling over ice, water & mountains to reach safety. Includes 2 maps.

Shipwreck at the Bottom of the World: The Extraordinary True Story of Shackleton & the Endurance. unabr. ed. Jennifer Armstrong. Read by Taylor Mali. 4 cass. (Running Time: 4 hrs.). (YA). (gr. 5 up). 2000. 24.95 (978-1-883332-39-6(7)) Audio Bkshelf.

Shipwreck That Saved Jamestown: The Sea Venture Castaways & the Fate of America. unabr. ed. Lorri Glover & Daniel Smith. Narrated by Michael Prichard. (Running Time: 10 hrs. 0 mins. 0 sec.). (ENG.). 2008. audio compact disk 24.99 (978-1-4001-5947-5(4)); audio compact disk 69.99 (978-1-4001-3947-7(3)) Pub: Tantor Media. Dist(s): IngramPubServ

Shipwreck that Saved Jamestown: The Sea Venture Castaways & the Fate of America. unabr. ed. Lorri Glover & Daniel Smith. Narrated by Michael Prichard. (Running Time: 10 hrs. 0 mins. 0 sec.). (ENG.). 2008. audio compact disk 34.99 (978-1-4001-0947-0(7)) Pub: Tantor Media. Dist(s): IngramPubServ

Shiralee. unabr. ed. D'Arcy Niland. Read by James Condon. 6 cass. (Running Time: 8 hrs.). 1998. 48.00 (978-1-86340-626-0(3), 560107) Pub: Bolinda Pubng AUS. Dist(s): Lndmrk Audiobks
An Austrailian classic. Macauley, a rough, tough & proud street fighter & "Swaggie," is forced to walk the roads in the vast & beautiful outback in search of work during the Great Depression. He returns home unexpectedly to find his wife in bed with another man. Judging her unfit to raise their four-year-old daughter, Buster, he takes the child on the road with him. She becomes his "Shiralee," his burden.

Shiralee. unabr. ed. D'Arcy Niland. Read by James Condon. (Running Time: 8 hrs.). 2009. audio compact disk 87.95 (978-1-74214-510-5(8), 9781742145105) Pub: Bolinda Pubng AUS. Dist(s): Bolinda Pub Inc

Shirim al Galgalim: Songs on Wheels. Debbie Friedman. Ed. by Randee Friedman. Tr. by Randee Friedman. 1 cass. (Running Time: 30 min.). 1994. 9.95 (978-1-890161-19-4(5)) Sounds Write.
Twelve original children's songs that teach about Jewish holidays & daily experiences.

Shirim al Galgalim: Songs on Wheels. Debbie Friedman. Ed. by Randee Friedman. Tr. by Randee Friedman. 1 CD. (Running Time: 30 min.). 1995. audio compact disk 15.95 (978-1-890161-20-0(9)) Sounds Write.

Shirley. Charlotte Brontë. 2007. 117.25 (978-0-7531-3732-1(1)); audio compact disk 139.95 (978-0-7531-2698-1(2)) Pub: ISIS Audio GBR. Dist(s): Ulverscroft US

Shirley, unabr. ed. Charlotte Brontë. Read by Flo Gibson. 15 cass. (Running Time: 22 hrs.). 1992. 43.95 (978-1-55685-246-6(0)) Audio Bk Con.
The heroine, Shirley Keeldar, is the authoress' tribute to her sister Emily. Two Belgian brothers fall in love with two young ladies of Yorkshire during a period that encompasses the Napoleonic Wars, Luddite riots, economic hardships due to poor harvests & the oppression of women.

Shirley: Your Favorites & Mine. Perf. by Shirley Keller. 1 cass. (Running Time: 60 min.). (J). (gr. 3 up). 10.00 (978-1-879846-07-4(1)) Cloudstone NY.
19 traditional & contemporary folksongs on guitar, banjo, autoharp, dolcimer, featuring "Library Song".

Shirley Ann Grau: Interview with Shirley Ann Grau & Kay Bonetti. Shirley Ann Grau. 1 cass. 1989. 13.95 (978-1-55644-326-8(9), 9022) Am Audio Prose.

Shirley Caesar: The Definitive Gospel Collection. Contrib. by Shirley Caesar. (Definitive Gospel Collection). 2008. audio compact disk 7.99 (978-5-557-49744-2(7), Word Records) Word Enter.

Shirley MacLaine Gift Set: The Camino, Going Within, Out on a Limb. Shirley MacLaine. 1 CD. 2001. audio compact disk 49.95 (978-0-7435-0447-8(X), Audioworks) S&S Audio.

Shiva, Vol. 1. Music by Rajan Mishra et al. 1 cass. (Running Time: 60 mins.). (Bhaktimala Ser.). 1992. (D92003); audio compact disk (CD D92003) Multi-Cultural Bks.

Shiva, Vol. 2. Music by Veena Sahasrabuddhe et al. 1 cass. (Running Time: 60 mins.). (Bhaktimala Ser.). 1992. (D92004); audio compact disk (CD D92004) Multi-Cultural Bks.

Shiva in Steel. unabr. ed. Fred Saberhagen. Read by Edward Lewis. 7 cass. (Running Time: 10 hrs.). (Berserker Ser.). 2001. 49.95 (978-0-7861-1938-7(1), 2709); audio compact disk 64.00 (978-0-7861-9781-1(1), 2709) Blckstn Audio.
In a sector of the Galaxy occupied by Earth descended people, one berserk computer has suddenly & mysteriously developed a tactical strategy unlike anything the human opposition has been before.

Shiva-Shakti, Vol. 2. Music by Pandit Jasraj & Shruti Sadolikar. 1 cass. (Running Time: 60 mins.). (Bhaktimala Ser.). 1992. (D92016); audio compact disk (CD D92016) Multi-Cultural Bks.

Shiva's Fire. unabr. ed. Suzanne Fisher Staples. Narrated by Johnny Heller. 6 cass. (Running Time: 7 hrs. 20 mins.). (YA). (gr. 7). 2001. 56.00 (96338E7) Recorded Bks.
Born in the south of India during a storm that destroys her village, Parvati is immediately recognized as a child with mystical abilities. Then one day she meets a young man with magical abilities of his own.

Shiva's Fire. unabr. ed. Suzanne Fisher Staples. Narrated by Johnny Heller. 6 cass. (Running Time: 7 hrs. 30 mins.). (YA). 2001. pap. bk. & stu. ed. 82.00 Recorded Bks.

Shiva's Fire. unabr. ed. Suzanne Fisher Staples. Narrated by Johnny Heller & Christina Moore. 6 CDs. (Running Time: 7 hrs. 15 mins.). (gr. 7 up). 2001. audio compact disk 58.00 (978-0-7887-5222-3(7), C1370E7) Recorded Bks.

Shiver. Read by Jenna Lamia & David LeDoux. Ed. by Maggie Stiefvater. (ENG.). (J). 2009. 69.99 (978-1-61574-571-5(8)) Find a World.

Shiver. Maggie Stiefvater. Narrated by Jenna Lamia & David LeDoux. (J). (gr. 8). 2009. audio compact disk 39.95 (978-0-545-16506-8(7)) Scholastic Inc.

Shiver. abr. ed. Lisa Jackson. Read by Joyce Bean. (Running Time: 6 hrs.). (New Orleans Ser.: Bk. 3). 2007. audio compact disk 14.99 (978-1-4233-1512-4(X), 9781423315124, BCD Value Price) Brilliance Audio.

Shiver. abr. ed. Lisa Jackson. Read by Joyce Bean. (Running Time: 6 hrs.). (New Orleans Ser.: Bk. 3). 2009. audio compact disk 9.99 (978-1-4418-0827-1(2), 9781441808271, BCD Value Price) Brilliance Audio.

Shiver. unabr. ed. Lisa Jackson. Read by Joyce Bean. (Running Time: 16 hrs.). (New Orleans Ser.: Bk. 3). 2006. 39.25 (978-1-4233-1510-0(3), 9781423315100, BADLE); 24.95 (978-1-4233-1509-4(X), 9781423315094, BAD); 87.25 (978-1-4233-1504-9(9), 9781423315049, BrilAudUnabridg); 34.95 (978-1-4233-1503-2(0), 9781423315032); audio compact disk 39.25 (978-1-4233-1508-7(1), 9781423315087, Brinc Audio MP3 Lib); audio compact disk 102.25 (978-1-4233-1506-3(5), 9781423315063, BriAudCD Unabrid); audio compact disk 24.95 (978-1-4233-1507-0(3), 9781423315070, Brilliance MP3); audio compact disk 38.95 (978-1-4233-1505-6(7), 9781423315056) Brilliance Audio.
Detective Reuben "Diego" Montoya is back in New Orleans. Thanks to years of working with the dark side of society, his youthful swagger is gone, replaced by a determined, take-no-prisoners stride. He'll need every bit of it, because a serial killer is turning the Big Easy into his personal playground. The victims are killed in pairs - no connection, no apparent motive, no real clues. Somebody's playing a sick game, and Montoya intends to beat him to it. As more bodies are found, Montoya's in a desperate race to find a killer whose crimes are getting more terrifying and closer all the time. Plunging deep into a nightmare investigation will uncover a shocking revelation. For the past is never completely gone. Its sins must be avenged, its wrongs righted. And this time, Detective Reuben Montoya may pay the price.

Shiver. unabr. ed. Maggie Stiefvater. Narrated by David LeDoux & Jenna Lamia. 9 CDs. (Running Time: 10 hrs. 43 mins.). (ENG.). (YA). (gr. 8 up). 2009. audio compact disk 79.95 (978-0-545-16508-2(3)) Scholastic Inc.

Shiveree. unabr. ed. Sophie Dunbar. Read by Lynda Evans. 8 cass. (Running Time: 10 hrs. 30 min.). (Claire & Dan Claiborne Eclaire Mystery Ser.). 2001. 49.95 (978-1-55686-929-7(0)) Books in Motion.
Claire and Dan Claiborne are faced with the elements of murder when they attend their friends' wedding. It seems that a New Orleans high society event, and missing jewels do not mix well.

Shivering Sands. unabr. ed. Victoria Holt. 8 cass. (Running Time: 39600 sec.). 1997. 69.95 (978-0-7451-6731-2(4), CAB 1347) AudioGO.
Caroline Verlaine, a young widow, comes to the legendary Stacy estate to investigate the disappearance of her sister, Roma. As Caroline falls under the strange spell of the Stacy family & its haunting past, she discovers a deadly secret amid the nearby ruins, a secret that had cost Roma her life & now threatens Caroline.

Shivering Sands. unabr. collector's ed. Victoria Holt. Read by Jonathan Marosz. 8 cass. (Running Time: 12 hrs.). 1995. 64.00 (978-0-7366-2921-8(1), 3619) Books on Tape.
Caroline Verlaine arrives at the legendary Stacy estate, seeking answers about the disappearance of her sister, Roma. As Caroline falls under the strange spell of the Stacy family, she begins to believe Roma had discovered a deadly secret, one that now threatens Caroline.

Shlomo Vinner. unabr. ed. Shlomo Vinner. 1 cass. (Running Time: 29 min.). (New Letters on the Air Ser.). 1992. 10.00 (060791) New Letters.
The Israeli poet talks about his disillusionment with his hometown & reads poems from his translated collection, "Jerusalem As She Is.".

Sh'ma Yisrael: Hear O Israel. Perf. by Barry Segal & Batya Segal. Prod. by Martin Smith. 1 CD. (Running Time: 60 mins.). 1999. audio compact disk (978-0-7601-3140-4(6)) Brentwood Music.
Blends rhythmic praise & ethnic overtones with passionate worship towards the "Holy One of Israel.".

Sh'Ma Yisrael: Hear O Israel. Perf. by Barry Segal & Batya Segal. Prod. by Martin Smith. 1 cass. (Running Time: 60 mins.). 1999. (978-0-7601-3141-1(4)) Brentwood Music.

Shobies' Story. Short Stories. Ursula K. Le Guin. Narrated by Amy Bruce. 1 CD. (Running Time: 68 mins.). (Great Science Fiction Stories Ser.). 2004. audio compact disk 10.99 (978-1-884612-37-4(7)) AudioText.

Shobies' Story. unabr. ed. Ursula K. Le Guin. Read by Amy Bruce. Ed. by Allan Kaster. 1 cass. (Running Time: 1 hr. 08 min.). (Great Science Fiction Stories Ser.). 1996. 10.99 (978-1-884612-09-1(1), 2091) AudioText.

Shock. Robin Cook. Narrated by C. J. Critt. 11 CDs. (Running Time: 13 hrs.). audio compact disk 111.00 (978-1-4025-1525-5(1)) Recorded Bks.

Shock. unabr. ed. Robin Cook. Narrated by C. J. Critt. 9 cass. (Running Time: 13 hrs.). 2001. 83.00 (978-0-7887-4923-0(4), 96387) Recorded Bks.
Two egg donors discover that a fertility clinic is engaged in cloning experiments that defy all ethical boundaries. Resonating with sharp scientific details and nonstop action, it's a disturbing vision of the future.

Shock - Burns & Smoke Inhalation. Robert Luten & John Templeton. 1 cass. (Running Time: 90 mins.). (Pediatric Emergencies: The National Conference for Practioners Ser.). 1986. 9.00 (978-0-932491-67-1(7)) Res Appl Inc.

Shock Doctrine: The Rise of Disaster Capitalism. abr. ed. Naomi Klein. Read by Jennifer Wiltsie. (Running Time: 9 hrs. 0 mins. 0 sec.). (ENG.). 2007. audio compact disk 29.95 (978-1-4272-0088-4(2)) Pub: Macmill Audio. Dist(s): Macmillan

Shock Rock. abr. ed. 4 CDs. (Running Time: 6 hrs.). 2001. audio compact disk 35.00 (978-1-57511-067-7(9)) Mills Pub KS.

Shock Rock, abr. ed. Read by Joan Jett et al. Ed. by Jeff Gelb. 4 cass. (Running Time: 4 hrs.). 1998. 24.95 (978-1-57511-008-0(3)) Pub Mills.
Put on your headphones & rock to this horrific compilation where martyred musical superlegends return from the dead & where other worldly specters pirate human souls not records. Experience the dark side of rock-n-roll where the party stops & the terror begins. A collection of short stories featuring the living legends & rising stars in horror writing. An all-access pass into the otherworldly terror & rafter rousing noise of rock-n-horror. A superstar jam for those who are not faint of heart.

Shock to the System. unabr. ed. Simon Brett. 8 cass. (Running Time: 9 hrs. 30 min.). (Mystery Library). 1997. pap. bk. Set. Dercum Audio.
Details one man's highly unique method of career planning. Graham Marshall had all the elements of success. He cultivated the right people, had a pretty wife, had moved quickly up the rungs of the giant conglomerate where he worked. Everything was going according to plan. Then the unthinkable happened & his plans for further upward mobility would have to be shelved, unless... Unless certain inconvenient people were to die.

Shock to the System. unabr. ed. Simon Brett. Read by Simon Brett. 7 cass. (Running Time: 8 hrs.). (Isis Ser.). (J). 2004. 61.95 (978-1-85695-498-3(6), 90062) Pub: ISIS Lrg Prnt GBR. Dist(s): Ulverscroft US

Shock Value. Contrib. by Twelve Gauge. Prod. by Fred Archambault. 2006. audio compact disk 16.99 (978-5-558-21026-2(5)) Solid State MO.

Shock Wave. unabr. ed. Clive Cussler. Read by Michael Prichard. 13 cass. (Running Time: 19 hrs. 30 min.). (Dirk Pitt Ser.). 1996. 104.00 (978-0-7366-3341-3(3), 3990) Books on Tape.
How would it feel to have the weight of a million lives on your shoulders? It's just part of the job for Dirk Pitt, eco-warrior for a national marine agency, on a case in the year 2000. Pitt's after a diamond tycoon who mines the Pacific with high-frequency, undersea sound waves. The sound's incredible energy kills everything in range, setting off a marine holocaust that threatens to reach Honolulu.

Shockaholic. abr. ed. Carrie Fisher. Read by Carrie Fisher. (Running Time: 60 hrs. 0 mins. 0 sec.). (ENG.). 2011. audio compact disk 29.99 (978-0-7435-5026-0(9), Audioworks) Pub: S&S Audio. Dist(s): S and S Inc

Shocker on Shock Street. R. L. Stine. 1 cass. (Running Time: 60 min.). (Goosebumps Ser.: No. 35). (J). (gr. 3-7). 1996. 6.98 (978-0-7634-0084-2(X)) W Disney Records.

Shocking Facts That Will Save Anyone. 2005. audio compact disk 11.95 (978-0-911203-96-7(6)) New Life.

Shocking Truth about the Pope & the Bible. 2005. audio compact disk 27.95 (978-1-888992-73-1(5)) Catholic Answers.

Shocking World of Electricity with Max Axiom, Super Scientist. Liam O'Donnell & Charles Barnett III. Illus. by Richard Dominguez. (Graphic Science Ser.). (ENG.). (gr. 3-4). 2007. audio compact disk 6.95 (978-1-4296-1127-5(8)) CapstoneDig.

Shockwave. unabr. ed. Colin Forbes. Read by Peter Wickham. 14 cass. (Running Time: 18 hrs. 5 min.). 2001. (978-0-7531-0944-1(1)) ISIS Audio GBR.
Tweed, victim of a ruthless frame-up, has to flee into snowbound Europe. Paula Grey insists on accompanying him on his journey into the unknown. But Europe?s top security chiefs, once his friends, are warned to track him down. His unknown enemy hires a top assassin. His mission: kill Tweed.

Shoe Addicts Anonymous. unabr. ed. Beth Harbison. Read by Orlagh Cassidy. 7 CDs. (Running Time: 9 hrs. 0 mins. 0 sec.). (ENG.). 2007. audio compact disk 29.95 (978-1-4272-0102-7(1)) Pub: Macmill Audio. Dist(s): Macmillan

Shoe Bird. Samuel Jones. Contrib. by Jim Dale & Eudora Welty. (ENG.). (J). 2009. 34.99 (978-1-60775-668-2(4)) Find a World.

Shoe Bird: A Musical Fable. unabr. ed. Samuel Jones. Read by Jim Dale. Based on a book by Eudora Welty. 1 MP3-CD. (Running Time: 1 hr.). 2008. 14.95 (978-1-4233-7740-5(0), 9781423377405, Brilliance MP3); audio compact disk 24.95 (978-1-4233-7739-9(7), 9781423377399, BriAudCD Unabrid); audio compact disk 14.95 (978-1-4233-7738-2(9), 9781423377382, Bril Audio CD Unabri) Brilliance Audio.

Shoe Bird: A Musical Fable. unabr. ed. Eudora Welty & Samuel Jones. Read by Jim Dale. (Running Time: 1 hr.). 2008. 24.97 (978-1-4233-7743-6(5), 9781423377436, BADLE); 24.95 (978-1-4233-7741-2(9), 9781423377412, Brlnc Audio MP3 Lib); 14.95 (978-1-4233-7742-9(7), 9781423377429, BAD) Brilliance Audio.

Shoe Bird (Jewel Case Edition) A Musical Fable by Samuel Jones. Based on a Story by Eudora Welty. unabr. ed. Samuel Jones. Read by Jim Dale. (Running Time: 1 hr.). 2008. audio compact disk 14.95 (978-1-4233-8052-8(5), 9781423380528, Bril Audio CD Unabri) Brilliance Audio.

Shoeless Joe. unabr. ed. W. P. Kinsella. Read by Grover Gardner. 6 cass. (Running Time: 8 hrs. 30 mins.). 1991. 44.95 (978-0-7861-0258-7(6), 1226) Blckstn Audio.
Soul-stirring novel on which the movie "Field of Dreams" is based. It is more than just another baseball story. Kinsella captures the spiritual dimension that baseball represents for its most determined devotees. It is about the love & the power of dreams to make people come alive.

Shoeless Joe. unabr. ed. W. P. Kinsella. Read by Grover Gardner. (Running Time: 8 hrs. 0 mins.). 2008. 29.95 (978-1-4332-4994-5(4)); audio compact disk 70.00 (978-1-4332-4993-8(6)) Blckstn Audio.

Shoemaker & the Elves. unabr. ed. Naomi Fox. Illus. by Neal Fox. Music by Neal Fox. Narrated by Robert Guillaume. 1 cass. (Running Time: 15 min.). Dramatization. (J). (ps-1). 1993. pap. bk. 9.95 (978-1-882179-15-2(3)) Confetti Ent.
The Confetti Company, a cast of multi-ethnic children, reenact the classic fairytale told in a modern, upbeat tempo.

Shoes. Elizabeth Winthrop. Read by Peter Fernandez. (Live Oak Readalong Ser.). pap. bk. 18.95 (978-1-59519-349-0(9)) Pub: Live Oak Media. Dist(s): AudioGO

Shoes. Elizabeth Winthrop. Illus. by William Joyce. Narrated by Peter Fernandez. (J). 1988. audio compact disk 12.95 (978-1-59519-348-3(0)) Live Oak Media.

Shoes. Elizabeth Winthrop. Illus. by William Joyce. (Running Time: 4 mins.). 1988. 9.95 (978-1-59112-118-3(3)) Live Oak Media.

Shoes. Elizabeth Winthrop. Read by Peter Fernandez. Illus. by William Joyce. 14 vols. (Running Time: 4 mins.). (J). (gr. k-3). 1988. pap. bk. & tchr. ed. 33.95 (978-0-87499-114-7(5)) Live Oak Media.

Shoes. abr. ed. Elizabeth Winthrop. Read by Peter Lerangis. Illus. by William Joyce. Contrib. by Peter Lerangis. 1 cass. (Running Time: 35 min.). (Tell Me a Story Bks.). (J). (ps-3). 1996. 8.95 (978-0-694-70037-0(1)) HarperCollins Pubs.

Shoes. unabr. ed. Elizabeth Winthrop. Illus. by William Joyce. 1 cass. (Running Time: 4 min.). (J). (gr. k-2). 1988. 9.95 Live Oak Media.
A tribute in rhyme to something usually taken for granted - shoes.

Shoes. unabr. ed. Elizabeth Winthrop. Read by Peter Fernandez. Illus. by William Joyce. 11 vols. (Running Time: 4 mins.). (J). (gr. k-3). 1988. pap. bk. 16.95 (978-0-87499-112-3(9)) Live Oak Media.

Shoes for Industry. Perf. by Firesign Theatre Firesign Theatre Staff. 2001. audio compact disk 24.95 Lodestone Catalog.
The best of the Firesign Theatre! Favorite cuts from beloved early albums including Dwarf, Bozos, Dear Friends, Electrician, more.

Shoes for Industry. Perf. by Firesign Theatre Firesign Theatre Staff. 2 CDs. (Running Time: 2 hrs.). audio compact disk 24.95 (SONY004) Sony Corp.

Shoes of the Fisherman. unabr. ed. Morris West. Narrated by Paul Hecht. 8 cass. (Running Time: 10 hrs. 45 mins.). (Vatican Trilogy). 2000. 72.00 (978-0-7887-4322-1(8), 96228E7) Recorded Bks.
Tells a timeless story of a newly elected Pope & his struggles with faith & his church's role in a changing world.

Shoes of the Fisherman. unabr. ed. Morris West. Narrated by Paul Hecht. 10 CDs. (Running Time: 10 hrs. 45 mins.). (Vatican Trilogy). 2001. audio compact disk 97.00 (978-0-7887-5197-4(2), C1354E7) Recorded Bks.
A timeless story of a newly elected Pope & his struggles with faith & his church's role in a changing world.

Shoes of Wandering see Poetry & Voice of Galway Kinnell

Shoes Were for Sunday. unabr. ed. Molly Weir. Read by Molly Weir. 4 cass. (Running Time: 4 hrs.). 23.80 (D-129) Audio Bk.
In spite of what may seem a grim background, there was fun & laughter & Weir brings lively observation & warm affection to her pictures of a Glasgow upbringing.

***Shoeshine Man's Regrets.** unabr. ed. Laura Lippman. Read by Linda Emond & Francois Battiste. (ENG.). 2008. (978-0-06-176319-5(5), Harper Audio); (978-0-06-176320-5(9), Harper Audio) HarperCollins Pubs.

Shoestring Murders. 1 cass. (Running Time: 1 hr. 30 mins.). (SmartReader Ser.). (J). 1999. pap. bk. & tchr. ed. 19.95 (978-0-7887-0115-3(0), 79303T3) Recorded Bks.
Sargent Ellison knows how the two murders were committed: both victims were found with a shoe lace from the Green Sox uniform wrapped around their necks. But he doesn't know who the killer is. Should he question the entire team, or can a few clues help him narrow the list of suspects?.

Shofar. James T. Barbarossa. 3 cass. (Running Time: 30 mins. per cass.). 1998. 15.00 (978-0-9676380-5-8(4)) Step By Step Min.
Barbarossa teaches about the Shofar.

Shogun, Pt. 1. unabr. collector's ed. James Clavell. Read by David Case. 11 cass. (Running Time: 16 hrs. 30 mins.). 1999. 88.00 (978-0-7366-4858-5(5), 5170-A) Books on Tape.
A beautiful woman is torn between two ways of life when she must choose between a bold English adventurer & an invincible Japanese warlord. They are all brought together in a mighty saga of a time & place aflame with conflict, passion, ambition, lust & the struggle for power.

Shogun, Pt. 2 unabr. collector's ed. James Clavell. Read by David Case. 12 cass. (Running Time: 18 hrs.). 1999. 96.00 (978-0-7366-4896-7(8), 5170-B&C) Books on Tape.

Shogun, Pt. 3. collector's ed. James Clavell. Read by David Case. 12 cass. (Running Time: 18 hrs.). 1999. 96.00 (978-0-7366-4897-4(6)) Books on Tape.

Shona. Foreign Service Institute Staff. 10 cass. (Running Time: 8 hrs.). (SHO.). (YA). (gr. 10-12). 1970. pap. bk. 255.00 (978-0-88432-290-0(4), AFSH10) J Norton Pubs.
Although English is the official language of Zimbabwe (formerly Rhodesia). Shona is the most important language among the black nationals, with close to six million speakers.

Shona Basic Course, FSI CDs & Text. ed. Ed. by Earl W. Stevick. 10 CDs. (Running Time: 8 hrs.). (Foreign Service Institute Basic Course Ser.). (SHO.). 2005. audio compact disk 255.00 (978-1-57970-335-6(6), AFSH10D, Audio-For) J Norton Pubs.

Shoofly, Vol. 1, No. 1. Ed. by Arlene Furman & Jack Nestor. (J). 2006. 12.95 (978-1-887066-21-1(7)); audio compact disk 12.95 (978-1-887066-20-4(9)) Shoofly.

Shoofly, Vol. 1, No. 2. Ed. by Arlene Furman & Jack Nestor. (J). 2006. 12.95 (978-1-887066-23-5(3)); audio compact disk 12.95 (978-1-887066-22-8(5)) Shoofly.

Shoofly, Vol. 1, No. 3. Ed. by Arlene Furman & Jack Nestor. (J). 2006. 12.95 (978-1-887066-25-9(X)) Shoofly.

Shoofly, Vol. 1, No. 3. Ed. by Nestor Furman & Jack Nestor. (J). 2006. audio compact disk 12.95 (978-1-887066-24-2(1)) Shoofly.

Shoofly, Vol. 1, No. 4. Ed. by Arlene Furman & Jack Nestor. (J). 2006. 12.95 (978-1-887066-27-3(6)); audio compact disk 12.95 (978-1-887066-26-6(8)) Shoofly.

Shoofly, Vol. 2, No. 1. Ed. by Arlene Furman & Jack Nestor. (J). 2006. 12.95 (978-1-887066-29-7(2)); audio compact disk 12.95 (978-1-887066-28-0(4)) Shoofly.

Shoofly, Vol. 2, No. 2. Ed. by Arlene Furman & Jack Nestor. (J). 2006. 12.95 (978-1-887066-31-0(4)); audio compact disk 12.95 (978-1-887066-30-3(6)) Shoofly.

Shoofly, Vol. 2, No. 3. Ed. by Arlene Furman & Jack Nestor. (J). 2006. 12.95 (978-1-887066-33-4(0)); audio compact disk 12.95 (978-1-887066-32-7(2)) Shoofly.

Shoofly, Vol. 2, No. 4. Ed. by Arlene Furman & Jack Nestor. (J). 2006. 12.95 (978-1-887066-35-8(7)); audio compact disk 12.95 (978-1-887066-34-1(9)) Shoofly.

Shoofly, Vol. 3, No. 1. Ed. by Arlene Furman & Jack Nestor. (J). 2006. 12.95 (978-1-887066-37-2(3)); audio compact disk 12.95 (978-1-887066-36-5(5)) Shoofly.

Shoofly, Vol. 3, No. 2. Ed. by Arlene Furman & Jack Nestor. (J). 2006. 12.95 (978-1-887066-39-6(X)); audio compact disk 12.95 (978-1-887066-38-9(1)) Shoofly.

Shoofly, Vol. 3, No. 3. Ed. by Arlene Furman & Jack Nestor. (J). 2006. audio compact disk 12.95 (978-1-887066-40-2(3)) Shoofly.

Shoofly: An Audiomagazine for Children, Vol. 3, No. 3. Ed. by Arlene Furman & Jack Nestor. (J). 2006. 12.95 (978-1-887066-41-9(1)) Shoofly.

Shoofly: An Audiomagazine for Children, Vol. 3, No. 4. Ed. by Arlene Furman & Jack Nestor. (J). 2006. 12.95 (978-1-887066-43-3(8)); audio compact disk 12.95 (978-1-887066-42-6(X)) Shoofly.

Shoofly: An Audiomagazine for Children, Vol. 4, No. 1. Ed. by Nestor Furman & Jack Nestor. (J). 2006. audio compact disk 12.95 (978-1-887066-44-0(6)) Shoofly.

Shoofly: An Audiomagazine for Children, Vol. 4, No. 2. Ed. by Arlene Furman & Jack Nestor. (J). 2006. 12.95 (978-1-887066-47-1(0)); audio compact disk 12.95 (978-1-887066-46-4(2)) Shoofly.

Shoofly: An Audiomagazine for Children, Vol. 4, No. 3. Ed. by Arlene Furman & Jack Nestor. (J). 2006. 12.95 (978-1-887066-49-5(7)); audio compact disk 12.95 (978-1-887066-48-8(9)) Shoofly.

Shoofly: An Audiomagazine for Children, Vol. 4, No. 4. Ed. by Arlene Furman & Jack Nestor. (J). 2006. 12.95 (978-1-887066-51-8(9)) Shoofly.

Shoofly: An Audiomagazine for Children, Vol. 4, No. 4. Ed. by Jack Nestor & Arlene Furman. (J). 2006. audio compact disk 12.95 (978-1-887066-50-1(0)) Shoofly.

Shoofly: An Audiomagazine for Children, Vol. 5, No. 1. Ed. by Arlene Furman & Jack Nestor. (J). 2006. 12.95 (978-1-887066-53-2(5)); audio compact disk 12.95 (978-1-887066-52-5(7)) Shoofly.

Shoofly: An Audiomagazine for Children, Vol. 5, No. 2. Ed. by Arlene Furman & Jack Nestor. (J). 2006. 12.95 (978-1-887066-55-6(1)) Shoofly.

Shoofly: An Audiomagazine for Children, Vol. 5, No. 3. Ed. by Jack Nestor & Arlene Furman. (J). 2008. 8.00 (978-1-887066-57-0(8)); audio compact disk 12.95 (978-1-887066-56-3(X)) Pub: Shoofly. Dist(s): Baker Taylor

Shoofly: An Audiomagazine for Children, Vol. 41. Ed. by Arlene Furman & Jack Nestor. (J). 2006. 12.95 (978-1-887066-45-7(4)) Shoofly.

Shoofly Vol. 2, No. 1: An Audiomagazine for Children. Poems. Ed. by Arlene Furman & Jack Nestor. 1 cass. (Running Time: 61 min.). Dramatization. (J). (ps-2). 1995. 9.95 (978-1-877066-04-7(4)) Shoofly.
Literature, children's poetry. Featuring blues guitarist Lightnin' Wells.

Shoofly: An Audiomagazine for Children, Vol. 5, No. 2. Ed. by Arlene Furman & Jack Nestor. (J). 2006. audio compact disk 12.95 (978-1-887066-54-9(3)) Shoofly.

Shoot. unabr. collector's ed. Elleston Trevor. Read by Grover Gardner. 5 cass. (Running Time: 7 hrs. 30 min.). 1987. 40.00 (978-0-7366-1212-8(2), 2130) Books on Tape.
Thriller set on a Pacific island, where a scientific team is working on a new space probe.

Shoot Don't Shoot. unabr. ed. J. A. Jance. Read by Ellen Travolta. 8 cass. (Running Time: 10 hrs.). (Joanna Brady Mystery Ser.). 1996. 49.95 (978-1-55686-656-2(9)) Books in Motion.
A vigilante killer is depositing his partially clad victims in the cool desert, terrifying even the most intrepid Arizona women.

***Shoot Don't Shoot.** unabr. ed. J. A. Jance. Read by Hillary Huber. (ENG.). 2009. (978-0-06-195391-0(1), Harper Audio); (978-0-06-196765-8(3), Harper Audio) HarperCollins Pubs.

Shoot Don't Shoot. unabr. ed. J. A. Jance. Narrated by C. J. Critt. 8 cass. (Running Time: 11 hrs.). (Joanna Brady Mystery Ser.). 1996. 70.00 (978-0-7887-0477-2(X), 94670E7) Recorded Bks.
A tale of kidnapping, murder & psychological drama set against the holiday season in the American Southwest.

Shoot Him If He Runs. unabr. ed. Stuart Woods. (Running Time: 8 hrs.). No. 14. (ENG.). (gr. 8). 2008. audio compact disk 14.95 (978-0-14-314382-6(4), PengAudBks) Penguin Grp USA.

Shoot, Minnie, Shoot! Happy Jack Feder. (Running Time: 6 hrs. 18 mins.). 2005. 44.95 (978-0-7861-3491-5(7)); audio compact disk 55.00 (978-0-7861-7889-6(2)) Blckstn Audio.

Shoot, Minnie, Shoot! The Story of the 1904 Fort Shaw Indian Girls. Happy Jack Feder. Read by Anna Fields. (Running Time: 23400 sec.). 2005. audio compact disk 29.95 (978-0-7861-8072-1(2)) Blckstn Audio.

***Shoot-Out.** unabr. ed. Mike Lupica. Contrib. by Keith Nobbs. (Running Time: 3 hrs.). (Comeback Kids Ser.). (ENG.). (J). 2010. audio compact disk 19.95 (978-0-14-314572-1(X), PengAudBks) Penguin Grp USA.

Shoot Out: Surviving the Fame & (Mis)Fortune of Hollywood. unabr. ed. Peter Bart & Peter Gruber. Read by Peter Bart & Peter Gruber. 6 cass. (Running Time: 9 hrs.). 2004. 29.95 (978-1-59007-230-1(8)) Pub: New Millenn Enter. Dist(s): PerseuPGW
Two of Hollywood's major players come together to share their insights and anecdotes about the art and business of filmmaking in the twenty-first century. Inspired by the graduate course that they have taught at the UCLA School of Theater, Film, and Television, Shoot Out is animated by observations from more than three decades in Hollywood.

Shoot the Lawyer Twice: Rep & Melissa Pennyworth Mystery. unabr. ed. Michael Bowen. (Running Time: 8 hrs. NaN mins.). 2008. 29.95 (978-1-4332-5206-8(6)); 54.95 (978-1-4332-5204-4(X)); audio compact disk 70.00 (978-1-4332-5205-1(8)) Blckstn Audio.

Shoot the Moon. abr. ed. Billie Letts. Read by Lou Diamond Phillips. (ENG.). 2005. 14.98 (978-1-59483-157-7(2)) Pub: Hachet Audio. Dist(s): HachBkGrp

Shoot the Moon. abr. ed. Billie Letts. Read by Lou Diamond Phillips. (Running Time: 6 hrs.). (ENG.). 2009. 44.98 (978-1-60788-053-0(9)) Pub: Hachet Audio. Dist(s): HachBkGrp

Shoot the Singer! Marie Korpe. 2004. (978-1-84277-506-6(5)) Zed Books GBR.

Shoot to Thrill. unabr. ed. P. J. Tracy. Read by Buck Schirner. (Running Time: 9 hrs.). (Monkeewrench Ser.). 2010. 24.99 (978-1-4233-3680-8(1), 9781423336808, Brilliance MP3); 39.97 (978-1-4233-3681-5(X), 9781423336815, Brinc Audio MP3 Lib); 39.97 (978-1-4233-3683-9(6), 9781423336839, BADLE); audio compact disk 29.99 (978-1-4233-3678-5(X), 9781423336785, Bril Audio CD Unabri); audio compact disk 87.97 (978-1-4233-3679-2(8), 9781423336792, BriAudCD Unabrid) Brilliance Audio.

Shooter. abr. ed. Paul A. Hawkins. Narrated by Ben Hall. 4 cass. (Running Time: 6 hrs.). 2000. 24.95 (978-1-890990-48-0(5), 99048) Otis Audio.

Shooter. unabr. ed. 3 cass. (Running Time: 3 hrs. 45 min.). 2004. audio compact disk 45.75 (978-1-4025-8492-3(X)) Recorded Bks.

***Shooter.** unabr. ed. Walter Dean Myers. Read by Chad Coleman et al. (ENG.). 2005. (978-0-06-083919-2(8)); (978-0-06-083918-5(X)) HarperCollins Pubs.

Shooter: The Autobiography of the Top-Ranked Marine Sniper. Jack Coughlin et al. Read by Dick Hill. (Running Time: 9 mins.). 2005. 59.95 (978-0-7861-3754-1(1)) Blckstn Audio.

Shooter: The Autobiography of the Top-Ranked Marine Sniper. unabr. ed. Jack Coughlin et al. Read by Dick Hill. 7 cass. (Running Time: 9 hrs.). 2005. 29.95 (978-0-7861-3755-8(X), E3551) Blckstn Audio.
With more than sixty confirmed kills, Gunnery Sgt. Jack Coughlin is the Marine Corps' top-ranked sniper. Shooter is his harrowing first-person account of a sniper's life on and off the modern battlefield. At the age of nineteen, Coughlin joined the Marines and spent the next twenty years behind the scope of a long-range precision rifle as a sniper. In that time, he accumulated one of the most successful sniper records in the Corps. Now Coughlin has written a highly personal story about his deadly craft, taking readers deep inside an invisible society that is off-limits to outsiders. This is not a heroic battlefield memoir but the careful study of an exceptional man who must keep his sanity while carrying forward one of the deadliest legacies in the U.S. military today.

Shooter: The Autobiography of the Top-Ranked Marine Sniper. unabr. ed. Jack Coughlin et al. Told to Donald A. Davis. 1 MP3. (Running Time: 32400 sec.). 2005. audio compact disk 29.95 (978-0-7861-7907-7(4), ZM3551) Blckstn Audio.

Shooter: The Autobiography of the Top-Ranked Marine Sniper. unabr. ed. Jack Coughlin et al. Read by Dick Hill. 8 CDs. (Running Time: 32400 sec.). 2005. DVD, audio compact disk, audio compact disk 72.00 (978-0-7861-7641-0(5)) Blckstn Audio.

Shooter: The Autobiography of the Top-Ranked Marine Sniper. unabr. ed. Jack Coughlin et al. Read by Dick Hill. Told to Donald A. Davis. 7 CDs. (Running Time: 32400 sec.). 2005. audio compact disk 29.95 (978-0-7861-7640-3(7), ZE3551) Blckstn Audio.

Shooters. abr. ed. Terrill Lankford. Perf. by Eric Roberts. 2 cass. (Running Time: 3 hrs.). 1997. 17.00 (978-1-56876-068-1(X)) Soundlines Ent.
Nick Gardner, a superstar fashion photographer gets caught up in murder & finds his secret past comes back to haunt him.

Shooters. unabr. ed. W. E. B. Griffin. Read by Dick Hill. 15 CDs. (Running Time: 18 hrs.). No. 4. (ENG.). (gr. 8). 2008. audio compact disk 49.95 (978-0-14-314245-4(3), PengAudBks) Penguin Grp USA.

Shooters. unabr. ed. W. E. B. Griffin. Read by Dick Hill. 15 cass. (Running Time: 18 hrs. 75 mins.). (Presidential Agent Ser.: Bk. 4). 2007. 113.75 (978-1-4281-9813-5(X)); audio compact disk 123.75 (978-1-4281-9815-9(6)) Recorded Bks.

Shooter's Point: A Martha Chainey Mystery. Gary Phillips. Narrated by Patricia Floyd. 6 cass. (Running Time: 8 hrs.). 2001. 56.00 (978-1-4025-3613-7(5)) Recorded Bks.

Shooting at Loons. unabr. ed. Margaret Maron. Narrated by C. J. Critt. 5 cass. (Running Time: 7 hrs. 15 mins.). (Deborah Knott Mystery Ser.: No. 3). 2000. 44.00 (978-0-7887-0665-3(9), 94842E7) Recorded Bks.
Judge Deborah Knott is enjoying the first day of vacation on the idyllic tip of the Outer Banks. Her relaxation is quickly replaced by horror, however, when she finds the drowned body of a local fisherman floating by a sandbar. Turning him over, she sees a bullet hole in his chest. Suddenly Judge Knott finds herself caught in a battle between the traditional fisher folks and aggressive developers.

***Shooting Balibo.** Tony Maniaty. Read by Humphrey Bower. (Running Time: 13 hrs. 40 mins.). 2010. 99.99 (978-1-74214-619-5(8), 9781742146195) Pub: Bolinda Pubng AUS. Dist(s): Bolinda Pub Inc

Shooting Balibo. unabr. ed. Tony Maniaty. Read by Humphrey Bower. (Running Time: 13 hrs. 40 mins.). 2009. audio compact disk 103.95 (978-1-74214-565-5(5), 9781742145655) Pub: Bolinda Pubng AUS. Dist(s): Bolinda Pub Inc

Shooting Elvis. Stuart Pawson. Contrib. by Andrew Wincott. 7. 2007. 61.95 (978-1-84652-068-6(1)) Pub: ISIS Audio GBR. Dist(s): Ulverscroft US

Shooting Elvis. Stuart Pawson. Read by Andrew Wincott. 8. 2007. audio compact disk 79.95 (978-1-84652-069-3(X)) Pub: ISIS Audio GBR. Dist(s): Ulverscroft US

Shooting History: A Personal Journey. abr. ed. Jon Snow. Read by Jon Snow. 5 CDs. (Running Time: 0 hr. 60 mins. 0 sec.). (ENG.). 2004. audio compact disk 25.00 (978-0-00-719254-0(1)) Pub: HarpC GBR. Dist(s): IPG Chicago

Shooting in the Dark. John Baker. Read by Cornelius Garrett. 9 CDs. (Running Time: 10 hrs. 45 mins.). (Isis (CDs) Ser.). (J). 2004. audio compact disk 84.95 (978-0-7531-2327-0(4)) Pub: ISIS Lrg Prnt GBR. Dist(s): Ulverscroft US

Shooting in the Dark. unabr. ed. John Baker. Read by Cornelius Garrett. 10 cass. (Running Time: 11 hrs.). (Isis Ser.). (J). 2002. 84.95 (978-0-7531-1370-7(8)) Pub: ISIS Lrg Prnt GBR. Dist(s): Ulverscroft US
Angeles Falco seemed like something straight from a fifties detective movie when she walked into Sam Turner's office. Beautiful, dark and enigmatic - but made strangely vulnerable by her damaged eyesight. All she would say is that she and her sister were being followed. But by whom or for what purpose she didn't know - and she feared for their lives.

Shooting Monarchs. unabr. ed. 3 cass. (Running Time: 3 hrs. 30 min.). 2003. 28.00 (978-1-4025-5899-3(6)) Recorded Bks.
Takes an unflinching look at the way even tiny events can echo through lives, with both tragic and uplifting consequences. Loners Macy and Danny are each following paths that will lead them to an explosive and unforgettable encounter. And at the intersection of those paths is beautiful Leah, the girl Danny has loved since the first time he saw her.

Shooting of Dan McGrew see Poetry of Robert W. Service

Shooting Script. unabr. ed. Laurence Klavan. Read by Nick Sullivan. 2005. 29.95 (978-0-7927-3536-6(6), CMP 769); 49.95 (978-0-7927-3508-3(0), CSL 769); audio compact disk 64.95 (978-0-7927-3509-0(9), SLD 769) AudioGO.

***Shooting Star.** unabr. ed. Wallace Stegner. Read by Bernadette Dunne. (Running Time: 17 hrs. 30 mins.). 2010. 44.95 (978-1-4417-3634-5(4)); 95.95 (978-1-4417-3630-7(1)); audio compact disk 123.00

(978-1-4417-3631-4(X)); audio compact disk 34.95 (978-1-4417-3633-8(6)) Blckstn Audio.

Shooting Star. unabr. ed. Peter Temple. Read by David Tredinnick. 5 cass. (Running Time: 7 hrs.). 2001. 40.00 (978-1-74030-359-0(8)) Pub: Bolinda Pubng AUS. Dist(s): Bolinda Pub Inc

Shooting Star. unabr. ed. Peter Temple. Read by David Tredinnick. (Running Time: 24360 sec.). 2007. audio compact disk 77.95 (978-1-74093-968-3(9), 9781740939683) Pub: Bolinda Pubng AUS. Dist(s): Bolinda Pub Inc

Shooting Star; Happy Birthday. Sal Fiorilla. Perf. by Jerry Pitts. 1 cass. (Running Time: 10 min.). (Flower for Iggey Ser.: No. 1). (J). (gr. k-4). 1993. 1.95 (978-1-885527-12-7(8)) Feather Fables.
Two songs based on the book "A Flower for Iggey".

Shooting Stars. Mary Blakely. 1 cass. (Running Time: 60 mins.). (Starbrights Ser.). (978-1-882995-02-8(3)) Azuray Learn.
Self-empowerment educational songs - ages 6-12.

Shooting Stars. LeBron James & Buzz Bissinger. Contrib. by Moe Irvin. (Running Time: 7 hrs.). (ENG.). (gr. 12 up). 2009. audio compact disk 29.95 (978-0-14-314502-8(9), PengAudBks) Penguin Grp USA.

Shooting the Monkey. Colin Turner. Read by Colin Turner. 2 cass. (Running Time: 2 hrs.). 1999. (978-1-84032-131-9(8), HoddrStoughton) Hodder General GBR.
Best-selling business author shares how you can be the master of the fast-changing new business world & not its slave.

Shooting the Moon. unabr. ed. Frances O'Roark Dowell. Narrated by Jessica Almasy. 3 cass. (Running Time: 3 hrs. 15 mins.). (YA). (gr. 5-8). 2008. 30.75 (978-1-4361-4861-0(8)); audio compact disk 30.75 (978-1-4361-4866-5(9)) Recorded Bks.

Shooting to Thrill. unabr. ed. P. J. Tracy. Read by Buck Schirner. (Running Time: 9 hrs.). (Monkeewrench Ser.). 2010. 24.99 (978-1-4233-3682-2(8), 9781423336822, BAD) Brilliance Audio.

Shoovy Jed. unabr. ed. Maureen Stewart. Read by Stig Wemyss. 2 cass. (Running Time: 2 hrs.). 2002. (978-1-74030-348-4(2)) Bolinda Pubng AUS.

Shop Class As Soulcraft: An Inquiry into the Value of Work. Matthew B. Crawford. Read by Max Bloomquist. (Playaway Adult Nonfiction Ser.). 2009. 59.99 (978-1-4418-1097-7(8)) Find a World.

Shop Class As Soulcraft: An Inquiry into the Value of Work. unabr. ed. Matthew B. Crawford. Read by Max Bloomquist. (Running Time: 7 hrs.). 2009. 39.97 (978-1-4418-0011-4(5), 9781441800114, Brinc Audio MP3 Lib); 39.97 (978-1-4418-0031-2(X), 9781441800312, BADLE); 24.99 (978-1-4418-0030-5(1), 9781441800305, BAD); 24.99 (978-1-4418-0010-7(7), 9781441800107, Brilliance MP3); audio compact disk 82.97 (978-1-4418-0009-1(3), 9781441800091, BriAudCD Unabrid); audio compact disk 29.99 (978-1-4418-0008-4(5), 9781441800084, Bril Audio CD Unabri) Brilliance Audio.

***Shop on Blossom Street.** abr. ed. Debbie Macomber. Read by Linda Edmond. (ENG.). 2004. (978-0-06-081822-7(0), Harper Audio); (978-0-06-081821-0(2), Harper Audio) HarperCollins Pubs.

Shop on Blossom Street. abr. ed. Debbie Macomber. Read by Linda Emond. (Blossom Street Ser.: No. 1). 2005. audio compact disk 14.95 (978-0-06-082098-5(5)) HarperCollins Pubs.

Shopaholic Abroad see Shopaholic Takes Manhattan

Shopaholic & Baby. abr. ed. Sophie Kinsella, pseud. Read by Katherine Kellgren. (Running Time: 21600 sec.). (Shopaholic Ser.: Bk. 5). (ENG.). 2007. audio compact disk 14.99 (978-0-7393-6574-8(6), Random AudioBks) Pub: Random Audio Pubg. Dist(s): Random

Shopaholic & Sister. abr. ed. Sophie Kinsella, pseud. Read by Katherine Kellgren. 5 CDs. (Running Time: 21600 sec.). (Shopaholic Ser.: Bk. 4). (ENG.). 2005. audio compact disk 14.99 (978-0-7393-2148-5(X), RH Aud Price) Pub: Random Audio Pubg. Dist(s): Random

Shopaholic & Sister. unabr. ed. Sophie Kinsella, pseud. (Shopaholic Ser.: Bk. 4). 2004. audio compact disk 76.50 (978-1-4159-0334-6(4)) Pub: Books on Tape. Dist(s): NetLibrary CO

Shopaholic & Sister. unabr. ed. Sophie Kinsella, pseud. (Shopaholic Ser.: Bk. 4). 2004. 72.00 (978-1-4159-0333-9(6)) Books on Tape.

Shopaholic Takes Manhattan. Sophie Kinsella, pseud. Narrated by Emily Gray. 9 cass. (Running Time: 12 hrs. 45 mins.). (Shopaholic Ser.: Bk. 2). Orig. Title: Shopaholic Abroad. 2002. 86.00 (978-1-4025-3882-7(0)) Recorded Bks.

Shopaholic Takes Manhattan. Sophie Kinsella, pseud. 7 cass. (Running Time: 13 hrs.). (Shopaholic Ser.: Bk. 2). Orig. Title: Shopaholic Abroad. 2004. 29.99 (978-1-4025-3624-3(0), 02534) Recorded Bks.

Shopaholic Ties the Knot. Sophie Kinsella, pseud. 9 cass. (Running Time: 14 hrs. 45 mins.). (Shopaholic Ser.: Bk. 3). 2004. 29.99 (978-1-4025-3625-0(9), 02544) Recorded Bks.

Shopgirl. movie tie-in unabr. ed. Steve Martin. Read by Steve Martin. 4 CDs. (Running Time: 40 hrs. 0 mins. 0 sec.). (ENG.). 2005. audio compact disk 14.95 (978-0-7435-5090-1(0)) Pub: S&S Audio. Dist(s): S and S Inc

Shopgirl. unabr. ed. Steve Martin. Read by Steve Martin. 3 vols. (Running Time: 4 hrs. 30 mins.). 2000. bk. 29.95 (978-0-7927-2449-0(6), CSL 338, Chivers Sound Lib) AudioGO.
Marabelle works behind the glove counter at Neiman Marcus "selling things that nobody buys anymore" Marabelle captures the attention of a wealthy businessman almost twice her age. The both struggle to decipher the language of love with consequences that are both comic & heartbreaking.

Shopgirl. unabr. ed. Steve Martin. Read by Steve Martin. 4 CDs. (Running Time: 6 hrs.). 2001. audio compact disk 49.95 (978-0-7927-9906-1(2), SLD 057, Chivers Sound Lib) AudioGO.
Marabelle works behind the glove counter at Neiman Marcus "selling things that nobody buys anymore". Marabelle captures the attention of a wealthy businessman almost twice her age. The both struggle to decipher the language of love with consequences that are both comic & heartbreaking.

Shopgirl. unabr. ed. Steve Martin. Read by Steve Martin. 2006. 17.95 (978-0-7435-6378-9(6), Audioworks) Pub: S&S Audio. Dist(s): S and S Inc

Shopping for Meat in Winter see Twentieth-Century Poetry in English, No. 26, Recordings of Poets Reading Their Own Poetry

Shopping with the Nicholas Family: Early Explorers Early Set A Audio CD. Benchmark Education Staff. (J). 2006. audio compact disk 10.00 (978-1-4108-7628-7(4)) Benchmark Educ.

***Shopportunity!** unabr. ed. Kate Newlin. Read by Kimberly Schraf. (ENG.). 2006. (978-0-06-113462-3(7), Harper Audio); (978-0-06-113461-6(9), Harper Audio) HarperCollins Pubs.

***Short & Easy Method of Prayer.** unabr. ed. Madame Guyon. Narrated by Marguerite Gavin. (ENG.). 2005. 9.98 (978-1-59644-309-9(X), Hovel Audio) christianaud.

Short & Easy Method of Prayer. unabr. ed. Madame Guyon. Narrated by Marguerite Gavin. 2 CDs. (Running Time: 2 hrs. 0 mins. 0 sec.). (ENG.). 2005. audio compact disk 15.98 (978-1-59644-308-2(1), Hovel Audio) christianaud.

Short & Easy Method of Prayer by Madame Guyon: Unabridged audio e-book CD in MP3 Format. Narrated by Stephanie Sandberg. (ENG.). 2007. 15.00 (978-1-931848-09-1(2)) Christ Class Ethereal.

Short & Shivery: Thirty Chilling Tales. unabr. ed. Short Stories. Retold by Robert D. San Souci. Narrated by Mark Hammer. 4 pieces. (Running Time: 5 hrs.). (gr. 5 up). 1995. 35.00 (978-0-7887-0178-8(9), 94403E7) Recorded Bks.
This multicultural collection of hair-raising tales introduces listeners to a Japanese skeleton, a Russian vampire, a Norwegian ghost & many other spooky creatures from around the world.

Short & Tall Tales: Moose County Legends Collected by James Mackintosh Qwilleran. abr. ed. James MacKintosh & Lilian Jackson Braun. Narrated by George Guidall. 3 cass. (Running Time: 4 hrs. 15 mins.). 2002. 26.95 (RG191) Recorded Bks.
Whimsical mystery featuring the popular Jim Qwilleran and his two Siamese cats, Koko and Yum Yum. In her latest book, Qwill is writing a history of Moose County and delights in telling audiences of its legends and mysteries.

Short & Tall Tales: Moose County Legends Collected by James MacKintosh Qwilleran. unabr. ed. Lilian Jackson Braun. Narrated by George Guidall. 2 cass. (Running Time: 1 hr. 30 mins.). 2002. 34.00 (978-1-4025-3036-4(6)) Recorded Bks.

Short-Chain Acyl-Coenzyme A Dehydrogenase Deficiency - A Bibliography & Dictionary for Physicians, Patients, & Genome Researchers. Compiled by Icon Group International, Inc. Staff. 2007. ring bd. 28.95 (978-0-497-11291-2(4)) Icon Grp.

Short Change. unabr. ed. Patricia Smiley. Read by Allyson Ryan. 9 CDs. (Running Time: 10 hrs. 30 mins.). (Tucker Sinclair Ser.: Bk. 3). 2007. audio compact disk 90.00 (978-1-4159-4161-4(0)) Books on Tape.

Short Course in Spoken English. Ronald Mackin. (J). (gr. 9-12). 1975. 55.00 (978-0-87789-140-6(0), 1173) ELS Educ Servs.

Short Course in Statistics. George Noonan. 1 cass. 8.95 (572) Am Fed Astrologers.

***Short Drink from a Certain Fountain.** 2010. audio compact disk (978-1-59171-163-6(0)) Falcon Picture.

Short Fix. abr. ed. Robert A. Monroe. Read by Robert A. Monroe. 2 cass. (Running Time: 3 hrs.). (Human Plus Ser.). 1989. 14.95 (978-1-56102-038-6(9)) Inter Indus.
Provide temporary relief of pain in any part of body.

Short Friday see Isaac Bashevis Singer Reader

Short Girls. unabr. ed. Bich Minh Nguyen. (Running Time: 9 hrs.). 2009. 39.97 (978-1-4233-9107-4(1), 9781423391074, BADLE) Brilliance Audio.

Short Girls. unabr. ed. Bich Minh Nguyen. Read by Alice H. Kennedy. (Running Time: 9 hrs.). 2009. 24.99 (978-1-4233-9104-3(7), 9781423391043, Brilliance MP3); 39.97 (978-1-4233-9105-0(5), 9781423391050, Brinc Audio MP3 Lib); 24.99 (978-1-4233-9106-7(3), 9781423391067, BAD); audio compact disk 28.99 (978-1-4233-9102-9(0), 9781423391029, Bril Audio CD Unabri); audio compact disk 92.97 (978-1-4233-9103-6(9), 9781423391036, BriAudCD Unabrid) Brilliance Audio.

Short Grass. unabr. collector's ed. Thomas W. Blackburn. Read by Christopher Lane. 6 cass. (Running Time: 6 hrs.). 1994. 36.00 (978-0-7366-2893-8(2), 3593) Books on Tape.
An indifferent law lets a gang of ruthless ranchers make the rules - until Steve Lewellyn decides to stand up to them.

Short Happy Life of Francis Macomber see Hemingway Short Stories

Short Happy Life of Francis Macomber see Stories of Ernest Hemingway

Short Happy Life of Francis Macomber. Ernest Hemingway. 1 cass. (Running Time: 90 mins.). 10.00 (LSS1119) Esstee Audios.

Short Hindi-Urdu Stories on Tape: Step 1. unabr. ed. Read by Harinder J. Dhillon. 1 cass. (Running Time: 1 hr. 30 min.). (URD.). 1992. 10.00 H J Dhillon.
This tape is for listening comprehension. Beginning stories with English translation. Not based on a book.

Short History of Africa. unabr. ed. Roland Oliver & J. D. Fage. Read by Geoffrey Howard. 7 cass. (Running Time: 10 hrs.). 1996. 49.95 (978-0-7861-0987-6(4), 1764) Blckstn Audio.
The dramatic alterations in political power have corrected the vision of a European-centered world. While the centers of European culture flourished, decayed & sprouted in turn, empires in Africa rose, ruled, resisted & succumbed. Much of Africa's past has now been excavated from ignorance & error, revealing a rich & previously little-known human heritage. In this classic work, the authors have drawn on the whole range of literature about Africa & on the evidence provided by archaeology, oral traditions, language relationships & social institutions.

Short History of Africa. unabr. ed. Roland Oliver & J. D. Fage. Read by Geoffrey Howard. (Running Time: 9.5 hrs. 0 mins.). (ENG.). 2009. 29.95 (978-1-4417-0313-2(6)); audio compact disk 90.00 (978-1-4417-0310-1(1)) Blckstn Audio.

Short History of Byzantium. unabr. ed. John Julius Norwich. Narrated by John McDonough. 16 cass. (Running Time: 23 hrs. 30 mins.). 1997. 130.00 (978-0-7887-3105-1(X), 95816E7) Recorded Bks.
Guides you through the Byzantine Empire's dramatic history, from its foundation by Constantine the Great in AD 330 to the agonizing days of its final defeat by the Turks in 1453.

Short History of Myth. unabr. ed. Karen Armstrong. Read by Sandra Burr. (Running Time: 3 hrs.). (Myths Ser.). 2005. 39.25 (978-1-4233-0774-7(7), 9781423307747, BADLE); 24.95 (978-1-4233-0773-0(9), 9781423307730, BAD); 44.25 (978-1-4233-0768-6(2), 9781423307686, BrilAudUnabridg); 19.95 (978-1-4233-0767-9(4), 9781423307679, BAU); audio compact disk 39.25 (978-1-4233-0772-3(0), 9781423307723, Brinc Audio MP3 Lib); audio compact disk 62.25 (978-1-4233-0770-9(4), 9781423307709, BriAudCD Unabrid); audio compact disk 19.95 (978-1-4233-0769-3(0), 9781423307693, Bril Audio CD Unabri); audio compact disk 24.95 (978-1-4233-0771-6(2), 9781423307716, Brilliance MP3) Brilliance Audio.
What are myths? How have they evolved? And why do we still so desperately need them? The history of myth is the history of humanity; our stories and beliefs, our curiosity and attempts to understand the world, link us to our ancestors and each other. Myths help us make sense of the universe. Armstrong takes us from the Palaeolithic period and the myths of the hunters right up to the "Great Western Transformation" of the last five hundred years and the discrediting of myth by science. Heralding a major series of retellings of international myths by authors from around the world, Armstrong's characteristically insightful and eloquent book serves as a brilliant and thought-provoking introduction to myth in the broadest sense - and why we dismiss it only at our peril. "Witty, informative and contemplative: Ms. Armstrong can simplify complex ideas, but she is never simplistic." - New York Times Book Review "Armstrong writes with sensitivity and wisdom. She employs a breadth of learning that reflects the scintillating, shifting light and shade of human experience." - The Times.

Short History of Nearly Everything. Bill Bryson. 2006. cd-rom 34.99 (978-1-59895-482-1(2)) Find a World.

Short History of Nearly Everything. abr. ed. Bill Bryson. Read by Bill Bryson. (YA). 2006. 44.99 (978-0-7393-7557-0(1)) Find a World.

Short History of Nearly Everything. abr. ed. Bill Bryson. Read by Bill Bryson. 5 CDs. (Running Time: 6 hrs.). (ENG.). 2003. audio compact disk 29.95 (978-0-7393-0294-1(9)) Pub: Random Audio Pubg. Dist(s): Random

Short History of Nearly Everything. unabr. ed. Bill Bryson. 15 CDs. (Running Time: 15 hrs.). 2003. audio compact disk 68.00 (978-0-7366-9320-2(3)) Pub: Books on Tape. Dist(s): NetLibrary CO

Short History of Progress: The 2004 CBC Massey Lectures. Ronald Wright. 2005. audio compact disk 39.95 (978-0-660-19330-4(2)) Canadian Broadcasting CAN.

Short History of the American Nation. 7th ed. John A. Garraty. (C). 1998. (978-0-321-04375-7(8)) Addson-Wesley Educ.

Short History of the Civil War: From the American Heritage Short History. unabr. ed. Bruce Catton. Narrated by Alan Bergreen. 5 cass. (Running Time: 7 hrs.). 1985. 44.00 (978-1-55690-105-8(4), 85440E7) Recorded Bks.
A general history of the American Civil War.

Short History of the Gospel in England, Scotland, & America (1999) 1999. 22.00 (978-1-59128-329-4(9)) Canon Pr ID.

Short History of the Korean War. unabr. ed. James L. Stokesbury. Narrated by Richard Poe. 7 cass. (Running Time: 10 hrs. 15 mins.). 1994. 60.00 (978-1-55690-729-6(X), 92224E7) Recorded Bks.
For a long time this war, fought over the course of 3 1/2 years, & costing the United Nations Command thousands of casualties, was not considered a war at all, but rather a "bandit incursion," a "police action." In this third volume in a series, we find out the whys & wherefores of America's most bewildering war. Highlights include: the intervention of China; the amphibious landing at Inchon; the dismissal of General MacArthur; the endless negotiations for cease-fire; the propaganda war; the embarrassing difficulties with South Korea's president, Syngman Rhee; & America's changing attitudes toward the war.

Short History of the United States. abr. ed. Robert V. Remini. Read by Oliver Wyman. 2008. audio compact disk 39.95 (978-0-06-166923-1(7), Harper Audio) HarperCollins Pubs.

***Short History of the United States.** abr. ed. Robert V. Remini. Read by Oliver Wyman. (ENG.). 2008. (978-0-06-171013-1(X)); (978-0-06-171014-8(8)) HarperCollins Pubs.

Short History of the United States. abr. ed. Robert Vincent Remini. Read by Oliver Wyman. (Playaway Adult Nonfiction Ser.). (ENG.). 2009. 64.99 (978-1-60812-714-6(1)) Find a World.

Short History of Tractors in Ukranian. unabr. ed. Marina Lewycka. 8 CDs. (Running Time: 31680 sec.). 2006. audio compact disk 79.95 (978-0-7927-4528-0(0), SLD 1058) AudioGO.

***Short History of Women.** unabr. ed. Kate Walbert. Read by Eliza Foss et al. (ENG.). 2010. audio compact disk 29.95 (978-1-61573-096-4(6), 1615730966) Pub: HighBridge. Dist(s): Workman Pub

Short History of World War I. unabr. ed. James L. Stokesbury. Narrated by Nelson Runger. 11 cass. (Running Time: 15 hrs. 30 mins.). 1991. 91.00 (978-1-55690-472-1(X), 91316E7) Recorded Bks.
A history of World War I, its causes & consequences.

Short History of World War II. unabr. ed. James L. Stokesbury. Narrated by Nelson Runger. 12 cass. (Running Time: 18 hrs.). 1991. 97.00 (978-1-55690-473-8(8), 91204E7) Recorded Bks.
A comprehensive short history of the conflict with ideas on its genesis & effects.

***Short Life of Jonathan Edwards.** unabr. ed. George M. Marsden. Narrated by Grover Gardner. (ENG.). 2008. 12.98 (978-1-59644-661-8(7), Hovel Audio) christianaud.

Short Life of Jonathan Edwards. unabr. ed. George M. Marsden. Narrated by Grover Gardner. 4 CDs. (Running Time: 5 hrs. 0 mins. 0 sec.). (ENG.). 2008. audio compact disk 21.98 (978-1-59644-660-1(9)) christianaud.

Short Manifesto see Winter Count

Short Month see Great American Essays: A Collection

Short Ode see Poetry of Benet

Short Panjabi Stories on Tape: Step 1. unabr. ed. Read by Harinder J. Dhillon. 1 cass. (Running Time: 1 hr. 30 min.). (ENG & PAN.). 1992. 10.00 H J Dhillon.
This tape is for listening comprehension. Beginning Panjabi stories with English translation. Not based on a book.

Short Reading. Ursula K. Le Guin. 1 cass. 9.00 (A0061-87) Sound Photosyn.
A warm, humorous, poignant reading giving the anima a moment in the limelight. Also featured on this cassette is Albert Alveros Rios.

Short Reference Grammar of Moroccan Arabic. 1 cass. (ARA.). 19.95 264p. text. (AFA996) J Norton Pubs.

Short Reference Grammar of Moroccan Arabic. 1 cass. (Running Time: 20 mins.). (ARA.). (YA). (gr. 10-12). pap. bk. 34.95 (978-0-88432-244-3(0), AFA460) J Norton Pubs.
Description of principal grammar facts of the language in the text & examples of phonology on the cassette.

***Short Second Life of Bree Tanner.** unabr. ed. Stephenie Meyer. (Twilight Saga Ser.). (ENG.). (J). 2010. audio compact disk 28.00 (978-0-307-74681-8(X), Listening Lib) Pub: Random Audio Pubg. Dist(s): Random

***Short Squeeze.** Chris Knopf. Narrated by Deanna Hurst. (Running Time: 9 hrs. 20 mins. 0 sec.). (ENG.). 2011. audio compact disk 29.95 (978-1-60998-158-7(8)) Pub: AudioGO. Dist(s): Perseus Dist

Short Stories: The Nostalgia Collection. (ENG.). 2008. audio compact disk 40.32 (978-1-906147-36-5(1), CSAW) CSA Telltapes GBR.

***Short Stories: The Vintage Collection.** unabr. ed. P. G. Wodehouse & Jerome K. Jerome. Read by Hugh Laurie et al. Ed. by CSA Word Editors. 6 CDs. (Running Time: 7 hrs.). 2010. audio compact disk 31.95 (978-1-934997-62-8(5)) Pub: CSAWord. Dist(s): PerseusPGW

Short Stories & Poetry. A. J. Spencer, 1st. (ENG.). 2008. audio compact disk 7.99 (978-0-9755851-1-5(8)) A Eanes.

Short Stories Audio CD: For Creative Language Classrooms. Joanne Collie & Stephen Slater. (Running Time: 1 hr. 19 mins.). (ENG.). 2009. audio compact disk 24.00 (978-0-521-12329-7(1)) Cambridge U Pr.

Short Stories by American Ladies of Literature. unabr. ed. Kate Chopin et al. Narrated by Flo Gibson. 3 cass. (Running Time: 4 hr. 30 mins.). (gr. 10 up). 1999. 16.95 (978-1-55685-626-6(1)) Audio Bk Con.
The erotic "The Storm", the grim "Life in the Iron Mills", the tender "A Humble Romance" & four other tales of comprise this collection .

***Short Stories by Anton Chekhov Vol. 1: A Tragic Actor & Other Stories, Bk. 1.** unabr. ed. Anton Chekhov. Read by Max Bollinger. Tr. by Constance Garnett. 1 CD. (Running Time: 1 hr. 4 mins.). (ENG.). 2009. cd-rom 25.00 (978-0-9561165-4-3(X), Sovereig) Max Bollinger GBR.

***Short Stories by Anton Chekhov Vol. 2: Talent & Other Stories, Bk. 2.** unabr. ed. Anton Chekhov. Tr. by Constance Garnett. Music by Pyotr Tchaikovsky. Narrated by Max Bollinger. 1 CD. (Running Time: 1 hr. 4 mins.). 2010. audio compact disk 25.00 (978-0-9561165-5-0(8), Sovereig) Max Bollinger GBR.

Short Stories by Saki. Saki. Narrated by Frederick Davidson & Nadia May. (Running Time: 11 hrs. 30 mins.). 1996. 34.95 (978-1-59912-595-4(1)) Iofy Corp.

Short Stories by Saki. unabr. ed. Saki. Read by Frederick Davidson & Nadia May. 8 cass. (Running Time: 13 hrs.). 1997. 56.95 (978-0-7861-1212-8(3), 1993) Blckstn Audio.
His eccentric characters, humorous dialogue & engaging situations all reveal a penetrating insight into human nature.

Short Stories Gift Edition. Ernest Hemingway. Read by Stacy Keach. 2006. 35.95 (978-0-7435-6377-2(8), Audioworks) Pub: S&S Audio. Dist(s): S and S Inc

Short Stories of Ambrose Bierce, Vol. 1. unabr. ed. Ambrose Bierce. 3 cass. (Running Time: 3 hrs. 9 min.). 2000. 24.00 (978-1-929718-05-4(5), 1601-4) Audio Conn.

Short Stories of Anton Chekhov, Vol. 1. unabr. ed. Anton Chekhov. 3 cass. (Running Time: 3 hrs. 57 min.). 2000. 24.00 (978-1-929718-04-7(7)) Audio Conn.

Short Stories of Bernard Malamud. unabr. ed. Read by Eli Wallach & Anne Jackson. 6 cass. (Running Time: 7 hrs. 23 min.). 1988. 44.98 (978-0-8072-3054-1(5), CXL 531 CX, Listening Lib) Random Audio Pubg.
Collection of the Pulitzer Prize-winning author's most celebrated works.

Short Stories of E. M. Forster. unabr. ed. Read by Charles Kay. 6 cass. (Running Time: 9 hrs.). 1999. 44.98 (LL 0024) AudioGO.

Short Stories of E. M. Forster. unabr. ed. Read by Charles Kay. 6 cass. (Running Time: 7 hrs. 20 min.). 1988. 44.98 (978-0-8072-3106-7(1), CXL 542 CX, Listening Lib) Random Audio Pubg.
Explore such subjects as freedom, alienation, enlightenment, & progress & rely on fantasy & myth.

Short Stories of Ernest Hemingway. unabr. gif. ed. Ernest Hemingway. Read by Stacy Keach. 15 CDs. (ENG.). 2003. audio compact disk 59.95 (978-0-7435-3525-0(1), Audioworks) Pub: S&S Audio. Dist(s): S and S Inc
ALL THREE VOLUMES OF HEMINGWAY'S SHORT STORIES TOGETHER IN ONE DELUXE EDITION Before he gained wide fame as a novelist, Ernest Hemingway established his literary reputation with his short stories. Set in the varied landscapes of Spain, Africa, and the American Midwest, this definitive audio collection traces the development and maturation of Hemingway's distinct and revolutionary storytelling style - from the plain bald language of his first story to his mastery of seamless prose that contained a spare, eloquent pathos, as well as a sense of expansive solitude. These stories showcase the singular talent of a master, the most important American writer of the twentieth century. The Short Stories Gift Edition features Stacy Keach reading such favorites as: The Short Happy Life of Francis Macomber; The Snows of Kilimanjaro; The Doctor and the Doctor's Wife; The End of Something; My Old Man; Hills Like White Elephants; The Killers; Ten Indians; Now I Lay Me; A Clean, Well-lighted Place; A Way You'll Never Be; The Gambler; and Fathers and Sons.

Short Stories of Ernest Hemingway, Vol. 1. abr. ed. Ernest Hemingway. Read by Stacy Keach. 5 CDs. (Running Time: 50 hrs. 0 mins. 0 sec.). (ENG.). (gr. 9-12). 2002. audio compact disk 30.00 (978-0-7435-2632-6(5)) Pub: S&S Audio. Dist(s): S and S Inc
Before he gained wide fame as a novelist, Ernest Hemingway established his literary reputation with his short stories. Set in the varied landscapes of Spain, Africa, and the American Midwest, this definitive audio collection traces the development and maturation of Hemingway's distinct and revolutionary storytelling style - from the plain bald language of his first story to his mastery of seamless prose that contained a spare, eloquent pathos, as well as a sense of expansive solitude. These stories showcase the singular talent of a master, the most important American writer of the twentieth century. The Short Stories Volume I features Stacy Keach reading such favorites as: The Short Happy Life of Francis Macomben The Capital of the Work- The Snows of Kilimanjaro; Old Man at the Briage; Up in Michigan; On the Quai at Smyma; Indian Camp; The Doctor and the Doctor's Wife, The End of Something; The Three-Day Blow, The Battler; A Very Short Story, Soldier's Home, The Revolutionist; Mr. and Mrs. Elliot, Cat in the Rain; Out of Season; and Cross-Country Snow.

Short Stories of Ernest Hemingway, Vol. 1. unabr. ed. Ernest Hemingway. Read by Stacy Keach. 2006. 17.95 (978-0-7435-6374-1(3), Audioworks) Pub: S&S Audio. Dist(s): S and S Inc

Short Stories of Ernest Hemingway, Vol. 2. unabr. ed. Ernest Hemingway. Read by Stacy Keach. 5 CDs. (Running Time: 50 hrs. 0 mins. 0 sec.). (ENG.). 2002. audio compact disk 30.00 (978-0-7435-2718-7(6), Audioworks) Pub: S&S Audio. Dist(s): S and S Inc
ERNEST HEMINGWAY The Short Stories VOLUME II Before he gained wide fame as a novelist, Ernest Hemingway established his literary reputation with his short stories. Set in the varied landscapes of Spain, Africa, and the American Midwest, this definitive audio collection traces the development and maturation of Hemingway's distinct and revolutionary storytelling style - from the plain bold language of his first story to his mastery of seamless prose that contained a spare, eloquent pathos, as well as a sense of expansive solitude. These stories showcase the singular talent of a master, the most important American writer of the twentieth century. The Short Stories Volume II features Stacy Keach reading such favorites as: My Old Man; Big Two-Hearted River: Part I and Part II; The Undefeated; In Another Country; Hills Like White Elephants; The Killers; Che Ti Dice La Patria?; Fifty Grand; A Simple Enquiry; Ten Indians; and A Canary for One.

Short Stories of Ernest Hemingway, Vol. 2. unabr. ed. Ernest Hemingway. Read by Stacy Keach. 2006. 17.95 (978-0-7435-6375-8(1), Audioworks) Pub: S&S Audio. Dist(s): S and S Inc

Short Stories of Ernest Hemingway, Vol. 3. unabr. ed. Ernest Hemingway. Read by Stacy Keach. (Running Time: 50 hrs. 0 mins. 0 sec.). (ENG.). 2003. audio compact disk 30.00 (978-0-7435-2729-3(1), Audioworks) Pub: S&S Audio. Dist(s): S and S Inc
Before he gained wide fame as a novelist, Ernest Hemingway established his literary reputation with his short stories. Set in the varied landscapes of Spain, Africa, and the American Midwest, this definitive audio collection traces the development and maturation of Hemingway's distinct and revolutionary storytelling style - from the plain bald language of his first story to his mastery of seamless prose that contained a spare, eloquent pathos, as well as a sense of expansive solitude. These stories showcase the singular talent of a master, the most important American writer of the twentieth century. The Short Stories Volume I features Stacy Keach reading such favorites as: The Short Happy Life of Francis Macomben The Capital of the Work- The Snows of Kilimanjaro; Old Man at the Briage; Up in Michigan; On the Quai at Smyma; Indian Camp; The Doctor and the Doctor's Wife, The End of Something; The Three-Day Blow, The Battler; A Very Short Story, Soldier's Home, The Revolutionist; Mr. and Mrs. Elliot, Cat in the Rain; Out of Season; and Cross-Country Snow.

Short Stories of Ernest Hemingway, Vol. 3. unabr. ed. Ernest Hemingway. Read by Stacy Keach. 2006. 17.95 (978-0-7435-6376-5(X), Audioworks) Pub: S&S Audio. Dist(s): S and S Inc

Short Stories of Guy De Maupassant. abr. ed. Short Stories. Guy de Maupassant. Read by Anthony Quayle. 2 cass. (Running Time: 3 hrs.). 2000. 7.95 (978-1-57815-125-7(2), 1087, Media Bks Audio) Media Bks NJ.

Short Stories of Guy De Maupassant, Vol. 1. unabr. ed. Guy de Maupassant. 2 cass. (Running Time: 2 hrs. 51 min.). 2000. 16.00 (978-1-929718-01-6(2), 1201-4) Audio Conn.
Five selections in volume one.

Short Stories of Isaac Bashevis Singer. unabr. ed. Isaac Bashevis Singer. Read by Eli Wallach. 1 cass. (Running Time: 63 min.). 10.95 (SAC 1153) Spoken Arts.
The famous short story writer shares his view of life in two works: "The Seance" & "The Lecture.".

Short Stories of Sherlock Holmes. abr. ed. Edgar Rice Burroughs. (YA). 2001. 17.95 (978-1-882071-03-6(4)) B-B Audio.

Short Stories of Sherlock Holmes, Vol. 1. unabr. ed. Arthur Conan Doyle. Read by Tim Behrens. 6 cass. (Running Time: 7 hrs.). 1989. 39.95 (978-1-55686-301-1(2), 301) Books in Motion.
Stories included are: "A Scandal in Bohemia", "The Red-Headed League", "A Case of Identity", "The Five Orange Pips", "The Man with the Twisted Lip", "The Adventure of the Blue Carbuncle".

Short Stories of Thomas Mann. Short Stories. Thomas Mann. 1 cass. (Running Time: 1 hr.). 12.95 (SGE515) J Norton Pubs.
Four short stories written between 1903 and 1930 are discussed in English by two professors of German.

Short Stories of William Somerset Maugham, Vol. 1. unabr. ed. W. Somerset Maugham. 3 cass. (Running Time: 3 hrs. 42 min.). 2000. 24.00 (978-1-929718-00-9(4)) Audio Conn.
5 selections in Volume 1. Some of the most unforgettable literary characters of the 20th century.

Short Stories of William Somerset Maugham, Vol. 2. unabr. ed. 3 cass. (Running Time: 4 hrs. 30 mins.). 2002. 24.00 (978-1-929718-11-5(X), 1102-4) Audio Conn.
Includes An Official Position, The Verger, Home, Mayhew, The Alien Corn, and others.

Short Stories Theme: Reader's Theater Classics Set A Read Aloud Think Aloud CD Rom. Compiled by Benchmark Education Staff. 2007. audio compact disk 10.00 (978-1-4108-8555-5(0)) Benchmark Educ.

Short Story Collection: Adventures in Far-Off Places, unabr. ed. Short Stories. Jack London et al. Narrated by Frank Muller et al. 3 cass. (Running Time: 2 hrs. 30 mins.). 1998. 26.00 (978-0-7887-0663-9(2), 95217E7) Recorded Bks.
Includes: "To Build a Fire," "Isle of Voices" & "Rikki-Tikki-Tavi".

Short Story Collection: Spooky, Mysterious Tales. unabr. ed. Short Stories. Arthur Conan Doyle et al. Narrated by Recorded Books Staff. 3 cass. (Running Time: 3 hrs. 15 mins.). 2001. 26.00 (978-0-7887-0798-8(1), 95218E7) Recorded Bks.
A collection filled with thrills & dark suspense, by the masters of mystery & horror.

***Short Straw.** Stuart Woods. (Running Time: 7 hrs.). (ENG.). 2010. audio compact disk 14.95 (978-0-14-242865-8(5), PengAudBks) Penguin Grp USA.

Short Straw. unabr. ed. Stuart Woods. Read by Michael Kramer. 6 cass. (Running Time: 9 hrs.). (Ed Eagle Ser.). 2006. 54.00 (978-1-4159-3456-2(8)); audio compact disk 72.00 (978-1-4159-3457-9(6)) Books on Tape.

Short Tales of Joseph Conrad. unabr. collector's ed. Short Stories. Joseph Conrad. Read by Wolfram Kandinsky. 9 cass. (Running Time: 13 hrs. 30 min.). 1993. 72.00 (978-0-7366-2544-9(5), 3295) Books on Tape.
Eight short stories from a master at shining a light in those dark recesses of human character that make us squirm.

Short, Tall, Big or Small? Sundance/Newbridge, LLC Staff. (Early Math Ser.). (gr. k-1). 2000. 12.00 (978-1-58273-311-1(2)) Sund Newbrdge.

Short-Term Solutions to the Energy Crisis. Armen A. Alchian et al. 1 cass. (Running Time: 1 hr. 50 min.). 12.50 (221) J Norton Pubs.
This concentrates on the role of wage-price controls in causing & prolonging the energy crisis, & the need for their repeal.

Short Victorious War. unabr. ed. David Weber. Read by Allyson Johnson. (Running Time: 12 hrs.). (Honor Harrington Ser.: Bk. 3). 2009. 24.99 (978-1-4233-9525-6(5), 9781423395256, Brilliance MP3); 39.97 (978-1-4233-9526-3(3), 9781423395263, Brlnc Audio MP3 Lib); 39.97 (978-1-4233-9527-0(1), 9781423395270, BADLE); audio compact disk 99.97 (978-1-4233-9524-9(7), 9781423395249, BriAudCD Unabrid); audio compact disk 29.99 (978-1-4233-9523-2(9), 9781423395232, Bril Audio CD Unabri) Brilliance Audio.

Short Vowel Sounds, Level 2. (Laubach Way to Reading Ser.). 1993. 12.00 (978-0-88336-915-9(X)) New Readers.

Short Vowels. Steven Traugh & Susan Traugh. Ed. by Rozanne Lanczak Williams. Illus. by Diane Valko. (Fun Phonics Ser.: Vol. 8026). 1999. pap. bk. & tchr. ed. 13.99 (978-1-57471-640-5(9), 8026) Creat Teach Pr.

Short Vowels Set: Level B. (Sing-along Songs Ser.). (ps-2). bk. 48.46 (978-0-7362-0420-0(2)) Hampton-Brown.

Short Walk from Harrods. unabr. ed. Dirk Bogarde. Read by Dirk Bogarde. 8 cass. (Running Time: 8 hrs.). (Autobiography Ser.: Vol. 3). 1994. 69.95 (978-0-7451-4294-4(X), CAB 977) AudioGO.
Dirk Bogarde, renowned actor & author, continues with the third volume in his autobiography series. Bogarde covers the latter years of his life, his lifelong relatioinship with E.L.L. Forwood & his time spent in Southern France. Bogarde has starred in over sixty films & written more than ten novels.

Short Walk from Harrods. unabr. ed. Dirk Bogarde. Read by Dirk Bogarde. 8 CDs. 2000. audio compact disk 79.95 (978-0-7540-5340-8(7), CCD 031) Pub: Chivers Audio Bks GBR. Dist(s): AudioGO
Covers the latter years of Dirk Bogarde's life, describing his lifelong relationship with E.L.L. Forwood & his time spent in Southern France. Bogarde has starred in over sixty films & written more than ten novels.

Short Walk in the Hindu Kush. unabr. ed. Eric Newby. Read by Richard Mitchley. 6 cass. (Running Time: 9 hrs.). 1988. 49.00 (978-1-55690-474-5(6), 88850) Recorded Bks.
An account of the author's trek into the Nuristan Mountains of Afghanistan.

Short Walk in the Hindu Kush. unabr. collector's ed. Eric Newby. Read by Donald Monat. 6 cass. (Running Time: 9 hrs.). 1992. 48.00 (978-0-7366-2265-3(9), 3053) Books on Tape.
No mountaineer, Newby set out with a friend to explore the formidable peaks of the Nuristan Mountains in northeast Afghanistan. His witty, unorthodox report is packed with incidents both ghastly & ecstatic as he takes us where few Western feet have trod.

Short Works of Louisa May Alcott. unabr. ed. Short Stories. Louisa May Alcott. Read by Laurie Klein. 2 cass. (Running Time: 2 hrs. 30 min.). Dramatization. (J). 1992. 16.95 (978-1-55686-396-7(9), 396) Books in Motion.
Here are a few of Alcott's most powerful & mature writings. The stories included are: Onawandah, Patty's Place, Cupid Chow Chow, & Roses.

Shortcut to French. Colette Dulac. (J). (gr. 9 up). 1977. 25.00 (978-0-685-79306-0(0), 58442) Prentice ESL.

Shortcut to Santa Fe. unabr. ed. Medora Sale. Read by Lynda Evans. 8 cass. (Running Time: 9 hrs. 30 min.). (Inspector John Sanders Mystery Ser.). 2001. 49.95 (978-1-55686-922-8(3)) Books in Motion.
While taking a New Mexico vacation, Inspector John Sanders is thrust into a scene terror when bus passengers are trapped, far from civilization. And a killer is stalking the victims nightly.

***Shortcuts.** Tarrin Webb. Read by Marguerite Gavin. (Running Time: 55). (ENG.). 2009. 2.99 (978-1-61114-012-5(9)); audio compact disk 2.99 (978-0-9825278-3-2(7)) Mind Wings Aud.

Shortcuts on Wine: Everything the Wine Lover Needs to Know. Edmond Masciana. 2 cass. 1998. 19.95 Set. (978-0-9663996-0-8(9)) Crtve Audio.

***shorter history of Australia.** unabr. ed. Geoffrey Blainey. Read by Humphrey Bower. (Running Time: 11 hrs. 3 mins.). 2010. audio compact disk 93.95 (978-1-74214-660-7(0), 9781742146607) Pub: Bolinda Pubng AUS. Dist(s): Bolinda Pub Inc

Shortest Day: Murder at the Revels. unabr. collector's ed. Jane Langton. Read by Kate Reading. 7 cass. (Running Time: 7 hrs.). (Homer Kelly Mystery Ser.). 1996. 42.00 (978-0-7366-3331-4(6), 3982) Books on Tape.
Every year Homer Kelly, a Harvard professor, endures the rehearsals for the Christmas Revels, for which his wife sings in the chorus. It's a ho-hum affair for him. But this production is different - more interesting.

Shortest Journey. unabr. ed. Hazel Holt. 5 CDs. (Sheila Malory Mystery Ser.: No. 3). 2006. audio compact disk 59.95 (978-1-84559-531-9(9)) Pub: ISIS Lrg Prnt GBR. Dist(s): Ulverscroft US

Shortest Journey. unabr. ed. Hazel Holt & Hazel Holt. Read by Patricia Gallimore. 5 cass. (Running Time: 19800 sec.). (Sheila Malory Mystery Ser.: No. 3). 2006. 49.95 (978-1-84559-489-3(4)) Pub: ISIS Lrg Prnt GBR. Dist(s): Ulverscroft US

Shortest Way to Hades. unabr. ed. Sarah Caudwell. Read by Eva Haddon. 7 CDs. (Running Time: 6 hrs. 50 min.). (Isis Ser.). (J). 2003. audio compact disk 71.95 (978-0-7531-2223-5(5)) Pub: ISIS Lrg Prnt GBR. Dist(s): Ulverscroft US
It seemed the perfect way to avoid three million in taxes on a five-million-pound estate: change the Trust arrangement. Everyone in the family agreed to support the heiress, Camilla Galloway, in her court petition - except dreary cousin Deirdre, who suddenly demanded a small fortune for her signature. Then Dreary Deirdre has a terrible accident which is the moment when the London barristers handling the trust - Cantrip, Selena, Ragwort and Julia - decide to summon their Oxford mentor Professor Hilary Tamar to Lincoln's Inn.And when deadly accidents in the family escalate, Hilary is dispatched on the most perilous quest of all: to find the truth and unmask the killer . .

Shortest Way to Hades. unabr. ed. Sarah L. Caudwell. Read by Eva Haddon. 6 cass. (Running Time: 24600 sec.). (Isis Ser.). 2003. 54.95 (978-0-7531-1688-3(X)) Pub: ISIS Lrg Prnt GBR. Dist(s): Ulverscroft US
It seemed the perfect way to avoid three million in taxes on a five-million-pound estate, change the Trust arrangement. Everyone in the family agreed to support the heiress, Camilla Galloway, in her court petition except dreary cousin Deirdre. Then Dreary Deirdre has a terrible accident which is the moment when the London barristers handling the Trust decide to summon their Oxford mentor Professor Hilary Tamar to find the truth and unmask the killer.

Shorthand Speed Development Audio Program. Donald J. Macksoud. Ed. by Elizabeth Gray. 10 cass. 1995. 142.00 incl. transcript. (978-0-937901-09-0(1)) Reinforcement Lrn.
Twenty shorthand speed building lessons designed to rapidly build speed for any shorthand program up to 60 WPM.

Shorthand Speed Test Tapes Audio Program. rev. ed. Donald J. Macksoud. Ed. by Elizabeth Gray. 10 cass. 1995. 142.00 incl. transcript. (978-0-937901-10-6(5)) Reinforcement Lrn.
Twenty shorthand test sessions designed to both test & build speed to 60 WPM.

Shot see Great French & Russian Stories, Vol. 1, A Collection

Shot. Philip Kerr. Narrated by George Guidall. 12 CDs. (Running Time: 13 hrs. 30 mins.). audio compact disk 116.00 (978-0-7887-9854-2(5)) Recorded Bks.

Shot. Jamie Murphy. 1 cass. (Running Time: 5 min.). (YA). (gr. 7-12). 1999. 4.98 (978-0-9630373-1-2(5)) Earth Healing.
"The Shot" is a song that tells the story of what a parent & their child go through during vaccination. It is a powerful & moving social commentary about the dangers of vaccines.

Shot. Jamie Murphy. Ed. by Carol White. 1 cass. (Running Time: 5 min.). (YA). (gr. 7-12). 1996. pap. bk. 18.95 (978-0-9630373-2-9(3)) Earth Healing.

***Shot.** Jenny Siler. Read by Humphrey Bower. (Running Time: 8 hrs. 20 mins.). 2009. 79.99 (978-1-74214-286-9(9), 9781742142869) Pub: Bolinda Pubng AUS. Dist(s): Bolinda Pub Inc

Shot. unabr. ed. Philip Kerr. Narrated by George Guidall. 10 cass. (Running Time: 13 hrs. 30 mins.). 2001. 94.00 (978-0-7887-5006-9(2), 96511E7) Recorded Bks.
Covers the mythology surrounding the assassination of John F. Kennedy. Hitman Tom Jefferson accepts a Mafia contract to slay Fidel Castro, but uncovers stunning information about Kennedy & changes his agenda.

Shot. unabr. ed. Alexander Pushkin. Read by Walter Zimmerman. 1 cass. (Running Time: 84 min.). Dramatization. 1979. 8.95 (N-31) Jimcin Record.
Two tragic duels & their aftermaths.

Shot. unabr. ed. Jenny Siler. Read by Humphrey Bower. (Running Time: 8 hrs. 20 mins.). 2006. audio compact disk 87.95 (978-1-74093-776-4(7)) Pub: Bolinda Pubng AUS. Dist(s): Bolinda Pub Inc

Shot Rolling Ship. unabr. ed. David Donachie. Read by Peter Wickham. 10 cass. (Soundings Ser.). 2007. 84.95 (978-1-84559-478-7(9)) Pub: ISIS Lrg Prnt GBR. Dist(s): Ulverscroft US

Shotgun. unabr. ed. Ed McBain, pseud. Read by Jonathan Marosz. 5 cass. (Running Time: 5 hrs.). (87th Precinct Ser.: Bk. 23). 1997. 30.00 (978-0-7366-3578-3(5), 4230) Books on Tape.
The men of the 87th Precinct know exactly who fired a shotgun point blank into the faces of a young couple: he's a psycho named Walter Damascus, also a third-rate actor. Damascus is on the loose, but the cops know he'll surface. They'll be waiting - for the biggest shock of their careers.

Shotgun Alley. Andrew Klavan. Read by Andrew Klavan. 6 cass. 54.95 (978-0-7927-3328-7(2), CSL 697); audio compact disk 79.95

(978-0-7927-3329-4(0), SLD 697); audio compact disk 29.95 (978-0-7927-3330-0(4), CMP 697) AudioGO.

Shotgun Tantra. Christopher S. Hyatt. Interview with Linda Miller & Nick Tharcher. (ENG.). 2008. audio compact disk 31.00 (978-1-935150-02-2(2)) Orig Falcon.

Shots on Goal, unabr. ed. Rich Wallace. Narrated by Johnny Heller. 3 pieces. (Running Time: 4 hrs.). (gr. 9 up). 1998. 27.00 (978-0-7887-1919-6(X), 95340E7) Recorded Bks.
Follows two high school soccer players on their path to adulthood in a small Pennsylvania town, as they discover unexpected lessons about the darker sides of friendship & loyalty.

Shots on Goal, unabr. ed. Rich Wallace. Read by Johnny Heller. 3 casss. . (Running Time: 4 hrs.). (YA). (gr. 5). 1998. 40.24 homework pack/realong pack . (978-0-7887-1947-9(5), 40654) Recorded Bks.
This story follows a high school soccer player on his path to adulthood in a small Pennsylvania town.

Should I Learn Astrology. Sue Lovett. 1 cass. 8.95 (556) Am Fed Astrologers.
Yes! Change your life for the better.

Should Lanterns Shine see Dylan Thomas Reading: And Death Shall Have No Dominion and Other Poems

Should Lanterns Shine see Dylan Thomas Reading His Poetry

Should Religious Organizations Be Involved in Partisan Politics? Instructed by Manly P. Hall. 1 cass. (Running Time: 90 mins.). 8.95 (978-0-89314-260-5(3), C800727) Philos Res.

Should We Change the World, or Change Worlds? Huston Smith. 1 cass. 9.00 (A0135-87) Sound Photosyn.
An elegant philosophical exploration with detailed cross-referencing of multicultural systems of understanding.

***Should We Fire God? Finding Hope in God When We Don't Understand.** unabr. ed. Jim Pace. Narrated by Jim Pace. (Running Time: 5 hrs. 58 mins. 39 sec.). (ENG.). 2010. 18.19 (978-1-60814-674-1(X)); audio compact disk 25.99 (978-1-59859-723-3(X)) Oasis Audio.

Should You Have a Say in Decisions Affecting Your Life? Hosted by Leonard Peikoff. 1 cass. (Philosophy: Who Needs It? Ser.). 1998. 12.95 (LPXXC67) Second Renaissance.

Should You Keep an Open Mind? I. Hosted by Leonard Peikoff. 1 cass. (Philosophy: Who Needs It? Ser.). 1998. 12.95 (LPXXC65) Second Renaissance.

Shoulda, Coulda, Woulda: Release Regret, Find Your Future. abr. ed. Les Parrott, III. (Running Time: 3 hrs. 0 mins. 0 sec.). (ENG.). 2003. 14.99 (978-0-310-26099-8(X)) Zondervan.

Shoulda, Coulda, Woulda: Release Regret, Find Your Future. abr. unabr. ed. Les Parrott, III. 2 CDs. (Running Time: 3 hrs. 0 mins. 0 sec.). (ENG.). 2004. audio compact disk 24.99 (978-0-310-25188-0(5)) Zondervan.

Shoulda, Coulda, Woulda: Release Regret, Find Your Future. abr. unabr. ed. Les Parrott, III. 2004. 19.99 (978-0-310-24088-4(3)) Zondervan.

Shoulder Dystocia. Contrib. by Thomas J. Benedetti et al. 1 cass. (Running Time: 90 mins.). (American College of Obstetrics & Gynecologists UPDATE: Vol. 21, No. 1). 1998. 20.00 Am Coll Obstetric.

Shoulder the Sky. Anne Perry. Read by Michael Page. (Playaway Adult Fiction Ser.). (ENG.). 2009. 74.99 (978-1-60775-695-8(1)) Find a World.

Shoulder the Sky. unabr. ed. Anne Perry. Read by Michael Page. (Running Time: 12 hrs.). (World War One Ser.). 2004. 39.25 (978-1-59710-704-4(2), 1597107042, BADLE); 24.95 (978-1-59710-705-1(0), 1597107050, BAD); 32.95 (978-1-59355-051-6(0), 1593550510, BAU); 87.25 (978-1-59355-052-3(9), 1593550529, BrilAudUnabridg); audio compact disk 36.95 (978-1-59355-054-7(5), 1593550545, Bril Audio CD Unabri); 24.95 (978-1-59335-704-7(4), 1593357044, Brilliance MP3); 39.25 (978-1-59335-838-9(5), 1593358385, Brlnc Audio MP3 Lib); audio compact disk 102.25 (978-1-59355-055-4(3), 1593550553, BriAudCD Unabrid) Brilliance Audio.
By April 1915, as chaplain Joseph Reavley tends to the soldiers in his care, the nightmare of trench warfare is impartially cutting down England's youth. On one of his rescue forays into no-man's-land, Joseph finds the body of an arrogant war correspondent, Eldon Prentice. A nephew of the respected General Owen Cullingford, Prentice was despised for his prying attempts to elicit facts that would turn public opinion against the war. Most troublesome to Joseph, Prentice has been killed not by German fire but, apparently, by one of his own compatriots. What Englishman hated Prentice enough to kill him? Joseph is afraid he may know, and his sister, Judith, who is General Cullingford's driver and translator, harbors her own fearful suspicions. Meanwhile, Joseph and Judith's brother, Matthew, an intelligence officer in London, continues his quiet search for the sinister figure they call the Peacemaker, who, like Eldon Prentice, is trying to undermine the public support for the struggle - and, as the Reavley family has good reason to believe, is in fact at the heart of a fantastic plot to reshape the entire world. An intimate of kings, the Peacemaker kills with impunity, and his dark shadow stretches from the peaceful country lanes of Cambridgeshire to the twin hells of Ypres and Gallipoli.

Shoulder to Shoulder. Terry Franklin & Barbi Franklin. (Running Time: 30 min.). 2002. 9.95 (978-7-901440-63-0(5)); audio compact disk 14.95 (978-7-901440-70-8(8)) Pub: Tylis Music. Dist(s): STL Dist NA

Shoulder to Shoulder: The Journey from Isolation to Brotherhood. Rodney L. Cooper. Read by Rodney L. Cooper. 2 cass. (Running Time: 2 hrs.). 1997. 14.99 (978-0-310-21192-1(1)) Zondervan.
Powerful, practical help for men to break down barriers of isolation & experience dynamic, life-giving relationships with other men.

Shout! The Beatles in Their Generation. unabr. collector's ed. Philip Norman. Read by Edward Lewis. 12 cass. (Running Time: 18 hrs.). 1997. 96.00 (978-0-7366-3623-0(4), 4283) Books on Tape.
The Beatles came to America in the early sixties & have been an integral part of our culture ever since. Philip Norman, a journalist who began covering the Fab Four in 1968, tells the fascinating story of four unknowns from Liverpool & how they became world-famous.

Shout at the Devil. unabr. ed. Wilbur Smith. Read by Nigel Davenport. 10 cass. (Running Time: 12 hrs. 39 min.). 1989. 84.95 (978-0-7451-6299-7(1), CAB 386) AudioGO.
On the eve of world war I in German-occupied East Africa, Flynn is engaged in the risky - but profitable - occupation of ivory poaching. Playing a dangerous game of hide-and-seek with the local German commissioner, he enjoys remarkable success. Then War Breaks out, and what was impetuous sport becomes a desperate fight to stay alive.

Shout at the Devil. unabr. collector's ed. Wilbur Smith. Read by Richard Brown. 10 cass. (Running Time: 15 hrs.). (Courtney Novels). 1990. 80.00 (978-0-7366-1698-0(5), 2543) Books on Tape.
"This scheme has flair!" roars Flynn Patrick O'Flynn. The year is 1912. The place: East Africa. The action: ivory poaching deep in the German-occupied delta of the Rufiji River. But Flynn, elephant hunter, likes to enjoy the spoils of his sport without much effort. The arrival of rich young Sebastian Oldsmith is a windfall he can't resist. Sebastian is plunged into an ivory hunt...& a murderous game of hide & seek with Flynn's outraged enemy, the German Commissioner. When war is declared Flynn sets out with his daughter & Sebastian to find the German warship, Blucher. They learn that death & violence are no longer a grotesque joke - but a savage reality.

Shout On No. 3: The Leadbelly Legacy. 1 CD. audio compact disk Smithsonian Folkways.

Shout Praises Kids Hymns: the Solid Rock. Created by Provident-Integrity Distribution. Prod. by Jeff Sandstrom. Contrib. by Don Moen & Craig Dunnagan. (Shout Praises! Kids Ser.). (J). (ps-3). 2005. audio compact disk 10.99 (978-5-558-80688-5(5)) Integrity Music.

***Shout Praises Kids 3 - CD.** unabr. ed. Integrity Music. 2003. audio compact disk 10.98 (978-7-472-02707-0(3)) Nelson.

Shout to the Lord. 1 cass. (Max Lucado's Opening Windows Ser.). 1998. 8.98 Mastertrax. (978-1-58229-051-5(2)) Brentwood Music.

Shout to the Lord. Perf. by Aaron Benward. 1 cass. 1999. 7.98 (978-0-7601-2937-1(1)) Provident Music.
Hi Lo Track.

Shout to the Lord. Contrib. by Hillsong & Michael Coleman. 2008. audio compact disk 19.98 (978-5-557-39780-3(9)) Integrity Music.

Shout to the Lord. Perf. by Max Lucado. 1 cass. 1999. 8.99 (Howard Bks) S and S.
Songs of praise & words of inspiration by Max Lucado.

Shout to the Lord. Contrib. by Don Moen. Prod. by Jeff Sandstrom. (Shout Praises! Kids Ser.). (J). (ps-3). 2006. audio compact disk 9.99 (978-5-558-16711-5(4)) Integrity Music.

***Shout to the Lord Kids! For Kids of All Ages.** unabr. ed. Thomas Nelson. 2001. audio compact disk 15.00 (978-7-472-01821-4(X)) Nelson.

***Shout to the Lord 2.** unabr. ed. Integrity Music. 2001. 6.98 (978-7-472-02083-5(4)); audio compact disk 10.98 (978-7-472-02082-8(6)) Nelson.

Shout with Joy. Camp Kirkland. 1998. 30.00 (978-0-7673-9952-4(8)) LifeWay Christian.

Show: The Inside Story of the Spectacular Los Angeles Lakers in the Words of Those Who Lived It. abr. ed. Roland Lazenby. Read by Chris Ryan. (Running Time: 16200 sec.). 2006. audio compact disk 28.00 (978-1-933309-02-6(4)) Pub: A Media Intl. Dist(s): Natl Bk Netwk

Show a Little Love. Janeen Brady. Illus. by Nina Grover. 1 cass. (J). (ps-6). 1981. 9.95 (978-0-944803-28-8(8)) Brite Music.

Show & Tell. Nelson George. Narrated by Dion Graham. 4 cass. (Running Time: 5 hrs. 30 mins.). 38.00 (978-1-4025-1594-1(4)) Recorded Bks.

Show & Tell. Nelson George. Narrated by Dion Graham. 5 CDs. (Running Time: 5 hrs. 30 mins.). 2001. audio compact disk 48.00 (978-1-4025-3823-0(5)) Recorded Bks.

Show & Tell. abr. ed. David Spangler & Marc Elliot. Read by Molly McKloskey & Joey Lawrence. 1 cass. 1986. 8.98 (978-0-89845-439-0(5)) HarperCollins Pubs.

Show Boat. abr. ed. Edna Ferber. 1 cass. 1984. 12.95 (978-0-694-50362-9(2), SWC 1719) HarperCollins Pubs.

Show Boat. unabr. ed. Edna Ferber. Narrated by Flo Gibson. (Running Time: 11 hrs. 10 mins.). 1999. 26.95 (978-1-55685-699-0(7)) Audio Bk Con.

Show Business Kills. unabr. ed. Iris Rainer Dart. Read by Gayle Humphrey. 10 vols. (Running Time: 15 hrs.). 2000. bk. 84.95 (978-0-7927-2203-8(5), CSL 092, Chivers Sound Lib) AudioGO.
A hard-driving movie executive, a beloved soap opera diva, a screenwriter nominated for an Oscar, and a well-known actress married to TV's King of Late Night. Four friends who have led charmed Hollywood lives facing middle age. They have always shared a "Girl's Night Out", but suddenly it becomes a painful vigil as three of the women watch their friend fight for her life in an intensive care unit. She has been attacked by a stalker who is obsessed with all four women. Will the bonds of friendship that have linked them together for years enable them to survive this chilling night?.

Show Me the Buffet. Perf. by John Pinette. 2000. audio compact disk 16.98 (978-1-929243-18-1(9)) Uproar Ent.

Show Me Your Faith. John MacArthur, Jr. 2 cass. (Running Time: 1 hr.). pap. bk. 8.25 (HarperThor) HarpC GBR.

Show Me Your Glory. Speeches. Creflo A. Dollar. 5 cass. (Running Time: 6 hrs.). 2003. 25.00 (978-1-59089-788-1(9)); audio compact disk 34.00 (978-1-59089-789-8(7)) Creflo Dollar.

Show Me Your Way. Perf. by Glen Campbell. 1 CD. (Running Time: 90 mins.). audio compact disk 15.99 (D2011) Diamante Music Grp.

Show No Fear. abr. ed. Perri O'Shaughnessy. Read by Dagmara Dominczyk. (Running Time: 6 hrs. 0 mins. 0 sec.). (ENG.). 2008. audio compact disk 29.99 (978-0-7435-7193-7(2)) Pub: S&S Audio. Dist(s): S and S Inc

Show No Fear. unabr. ed. Perri O'Shaughnessy. Narrated by Johanna Parker. 10 CDs. (Running Time: 11 hrs. 45 mins.). 2009. audio compact disk 123.75 (978-1-4361-7835-8(5)) Recorded Bks.

Show No Fear. unabr. collector's ed. Perri O'Shaughnessy. Narrated by Johanna Parker. 10 CDs. (Running Time: 11 hrs. 45 mins.). 2009. audio compact disk 49.95 (978-1-4361-7836-5(3)) Recorded Bks.

***Show No Fear: A Nina Reilly Novel.** abr. ed. Perri O'Shaughnessy. Read by Dagmara Dominczyk. (Running Time: 6 hrs. 0 mins. 0 sec.). (ENG.). 2011. audio compact disk 14.99 (978-1-4423-4070-1(3)) Pub: S&S Audio. Dist(s): S and S Inc

Show That Never Aired. Eddie Cantor. 1 cass. 1993. (978-1-887958-03-5(7)) B Gari.
Old time radio.

Show Your Appreciation. Emmet L. Robinson. Read by Emmet L. Robinson. 1 cass. (Running Time: 18 min.). 1994. 7.95 King Street.
How to make effective & profitable use of positive re-inforcement.

Showboat. 1 cass., 1 CD. 8.78 (RCA 61182); audio compact disk 14.38 CD Jewel box. (RCA 61182) NewSound.

Showdown. abr. ed. Tilly Bagshawe. Read by Sonya Walger. (Running Time: 6 hrs.). (ENG.). 2006. 14.98 (978-1-59483-520-9(9)) Pub: Hachet Audio. Dist(s): HachBkGrp

Showdown. abr. ed. Tilly Bagshawe. Read by Sonya Walger. (Running Time: 6 hrs.). (ENG.). 2009. 44.98 (978-1-60788-159-9(4)) Pub: Hachet Audio. Dist(s): HachBkGrp

Showdown. unabr. ed. Tilly Bagshawe. Read by Gillian Doyle. 12 cass. (Running Time: 19 hrs.). 2006. 99.00 (978-1-4159-3366-4(9)); audio compact disk 104.00 (978-1-4159-3367-1(7)) Books on Tape.
Bobby Cameron is a cowboy through and through. After inheriting Highwood, his father's magnificent but debt-ridden ranch in California's Santa Ynez Valley, Bobby travels wherever he's wanted, breaking horses for their wealthy owners and raising the cash he needs to protect his land. That's all he cares about - until he meets a young English girl named Milly Lockwood Groves. Forbidden to race because of a childhood accident and her mother's notions about unladylike behavior, the seventeen-year-old daughter of a millionaire Newmarket breeder is still secretly determined to follow her dreams. Then Bobby Cameron strides into her life, and nothing is ever the same. She accepts his offer to work for a year at Highwood, desperate to make a name for herself in racing...and for Bobby to see her as a woman. Caught up in a world where unscrupulous horse owners and billionaire media moguls rub shoulders - and more - with oversexed racing widows and fiercely ambitious jockeys, Milly must discover if she has what it takes to be a winner - on the track, in the bedroom, and, ultimately, in the game of love.

Showdown. unabr. ed. Ted Dekker. Narrated by Kevin King. (Running Time: 12 hrs. 47 mins. 30 sec.). (Books of History Chronicles: Bk. 1). (ENG.). 2005. 24.49 (978-1-60814-380-1(5)); audio compact disk 34.99 (978-1-59859-105-7(3)) Oasis Audio.

***Showdown at Anchor.** Peter Dawson. 2009. (978-1-60136-403-6(2)) Audio Holding.

Showdown at Anchor. Peter Dawson. (Running Time: 1 hr. 30 mins.). 1998. 10.95 (978-1-60083-467-7(1)) Iofy Corp.

Showdown at Dry Gulch: Leader Accompanist Edition. Henry Hinnant. 1 cass. (Running Time: 40 mins.). (gr. 3-8). 2004. bk. 12.00 (978-0-687-09133-1(0)) Abingdon.
Nonseasonal musical uses the story of Elijah to teach about obedience to God and steadfast faith. For grades 3-8. 35-40 minutes in length.

Showdown at Dry Gulch: Leader Accompanist Edition. unabr. ed. Henry Hinnant. 10 cass. (Running Time: 40 mins.). (gr. 3-8). 2004. bk. 40.00 (978-0-687-09134-8(9)) Abingdon.

Showdown at Lonesome Pellet. unabr. ed. Paul Ra'tz de Tagyos. 1 cass. (Running Time: 8 min.). (J). (gr. k-4). 1994. bk. 25.90 (978-0-8045-6831-9(6), 6831) Spoken Arts.

Showdown at Snakegrass Junction. unabr. ed. Gary McCarthy. Read by Gene Engene. 6 cass. (Running Time: 6 hrs. 24 min.). (Derby Man Ser.: Bk. 2). 1994. 39.95 (978-1-55686-550-3(3)) Books in Motion.
Darby Buckingham takes over as sheriff for the town of Running Springs, Wyoming. Gun-slick honchos of neighboring Snakegrass Junction seem determined to destroy Running Springs.

Showdown at Two Bit Creek: Gunfighter Series. unabr. abr. ed. Ralph Compton Novel. (Running Time: 5 hrs.). (ENG.). 2003. audio compact disk 22.95 (978-1-56511-806-5(5), 1565118065) Pub: HighBridge. Dist(s): Workman Pub

Showdown in Texas. abr. ed. Jake Logan. Read by Michelle de Long & Dick Wilkinson. 2 cass. (Running Time: 3 hrs.). (Jake Logan Ser.: No. 263). 2001. 16.95 (978-1-890990-67-1(1)) Otis Audio.
A trio of lowlife gunslingers is terrorizing Austin & the sheriff is powerless to stop them. It's up to Slocum to let them know that three's a crowd.

Showdown on Mt Carmel: 1 Kings 18:1-40. Ed Young. 1987. 4.95 (978-0-7417-1595-1(3), 595) Win Walk.

Showdown on the Hogback. Louis L'Amour. Narrated by Grover Gardner. (Running Time: 5 hrs.). 1995. 24.95 (978-1-59912-596-1(X)) Iofy Corp.

Showdown on the Hogback. unabr. ed. Louis L'Amour. Read by Lloyd James. 30 cass. (Running Time: 5 hrs. 30 mins.). 2005. reel tape 19.95 (978-0-7861-2887-7(9), E3387); audio compact disk 19.95 (978-0-7861-8289-3(X), ZE3387); audio compact disk 29.95 (978-0-7861-8351-7(9), ZM3387) Blckstn Audio.

Showdown on the Hogback -Lib. (Running Time: 5.3 hrs. 0 mins.). 2005. 34.95 (978-0-7861-2888-4(7)); audio compact disk 45.00 (978-0-7861-8288-6(1)) Blckstn Audio.

***Showdown with Rance Mcgrew.** 2010. audio compact disk (978-1-59171-217-6(3)) Falcon Picture.

Showers in Season. Beverly LaHaye & Terri Blackstock. Narrated by Ruth Ann Phimister. 9 cass. (Running Time: 13 hrs.). (Cedar Circle Ser.). 84.00 (978-0-7887-9902-0(9)) Recorded Bks.

***Showers in Season.** Zondervan Publishing Staff. (Running Time: 11 hrs. 24 mins. 7 sec.). 2010. 9.99 (978-0-310-86952-8(8)) Zondervan.

Showers of Blessings. Evelyn Murray. Read by Evelyn Murray. 8 cass. (Running Time: 8 hrs.). 1997. 28.00 Set. Evelyn Murray.
A tale of faith & courage, a woman building a home with scant resources for her family, the neighbors ostracized them, they persisted. They built a town & caused others to follow.

Showing God's Kindness & Mercy. Short Stories. Joel Osteen. 1 Cass. (Running Time: 30 Mins.). 2002. 6.00 (978-1-59349-152-9(2), Ja0152) J Osteen.

Showing My Color Set: Impolite Essays on Race in America. abr. ed. Clarence Page. Read by Clarence Page. 2 cass. (Running Time: 3 hrs.). 1996. 18.00 (978-0-694-51647-6(3), 393557) HarperCollins Pubs.
This gritty series of all-original essays concerns itself with many of the central questions of color, race, gender & ethnic identity that have emerged since the great civil rights reforms of the mid-60s, certain to knock down the walls of political correctness while fearlessly tackling some of the most difficult subjects of our times.

***Showing up for Life: Thoughts on the Gifts of a Lifetime.** unabr. ed. Bill Gates, Sr. & Mary Ann Mackin. Narrated by Patrick Egan. 3 CDs. (Running Time: 3 hrs. 30 mins.). 2009. audio compact disk 40.00 (978-1-4159-6214-5(6), BksonTape) Pub: Random Audio Pubg. Dist(s): Random

Showing up for Life: Thoughts on the Gifts of a Lifetime. unabr. ed. Bill Gates, Sr. & Mary Ann Mackin. Read by Bill Gates, Sr. & Patrick Egan. Frwd. by Bill Gates. (ENG.). 2009. audio compact disk 25.00 (978-0-7393-7071-1(5)) Pub: Random Audio Pubg. Dist(s): Random

Showtime for the Sheep? The Passion of the Christ. T. A. McMahon. Read by T. A. McMahon. (Running Time: 4 hrs.). (ENG.). 2005. audio compact disk 25.99 (978-1-928660-41-5(X)) Pub: Berean Call. Dist(s): STL Dist NA

Shrapnel Academy. unabr. ed. Fay Weldon. Narrated by Davina Porter. 5 cass. (Running Time: 6 hrs. 30 mins.). 1988. 44.00 (978-1-55690-475-2(4), 88370) Recorded Bks.
A satire of class warfare. Cut off by a blizzard, the Shrapnel Academy's "Upstairs" guests find themselves besieged by a revolution "Downstairs".

Shred Jam Trax for Guitar. Ralph Agresta. 1997. pap. bk. 49.95 (978-0-8256-1414-9(7), AM91475) Beekman Bks.

Shrek! William Steig. (J). (ps-3). 2001. pap. bk. 15.95 (VX-454C) Kimbo Educ.
A horrid little ogre encounters a nasty witch, a knight in armor, a dragon & true love with a princess who's even uglier than he is. Includes read along book.

Shrek! William Steig. Read by Bob Severa. 14 vols. (Running Time: 3 mins.). 1998. pap. bk. & tchr. ed. 33.95 Reading Chest. (978-0-87499-456-8(X)) Live Oak Media.
When a horrid little ogre ventures out into the world, he encounters a nasty witch, a knight in armor, a dragon &... true love with a princess who's even uglier than he is.

Shrek! William Steig. Illus. by William Steig. (Running Time: 3 mins.). 1998. 9.95 (978-0-87499-457-5(8)); audio compact disk 12.95 (978-1-59112-327-9(5)) Live Oak Media.

Shrek! William Steig. Illus. by William Steig. 11 vols. (Running Time: 3 mins.). (J). 2005. pap. bk. 18.95 (978-1-59112-328-6(3)) Pub: Live Oak Media. Dist(s): AudioGO

Shrek! unabr. ed. William Steig. Read by Bob Sevra. 11 vols. (Running Time: 3 mins.). (J). (gr. k-3). 1998. pap. bk. 16.95 (978-0-87499-454-4(3)) Pub: Live Oak Media. Dist(s): AudioGO

Shrike & the Chipmunks see World of James Thurber

Shrimp. unabr. ed. Rachel Cohn. Narrated by Carine Montbertrand. 9 CDs. (Running Time: 10 hrs.). (YA). (gr. 9 up). 2005. audio compact disk 89.79 (978-1-4193-6793-9(5), C3511); 61.75 (978-1-4193-5250-8(4), 98129) Recorded Bks.
Rachel Cohn delivers an irresistible sequel to her extremely popular debut novel, Gingerbread (RB# 98125). Cyd Charisse has returned to San Francisco from her summer in New York City to begin her senior year of high school. Cyd has changed in many ways but one thing remains the same - her feelings for Shrimp. But, how does he feel about her? After all, he has changed too.

Shrine. James Herbert. 12 CDs. (Running Time: 15 hrs. 14 mins.). (Isis (CDs) Ser.). (J). 2005. audio compact disk 99.95 (978-0-7531-2416-1(5)) Pub: ISIS Lrg Prnt GBR. Dist(s): Ulverscroft US

Shrine. unabr. ed. James Herbert. 11 cass. (Running Time: 15 hrs. 14 mins.). (Isis Cassettes Ser.). (J). 2005. 89.95 (978-0-7531-2144-3(1)) Pub: ISIS Lrg Prnt GBR. Dist(s): Ulverscroft US

Shrine of Temptation. (SWC 1593) HarperCollins Pubs.

Shringar, Vol. 1. Music by Girija Devi. 1 cass. 1993. (B93005) Multi-Cultural Bks.

Shringar, Vol. 2. Music by Shobha Gurtu. 1 cass. 1993. (B93006) Multi-Cultural Bks.

Shringar, Vol. 3. Music by Lakshmi Shankar. 1 cass. 1993. (B93007) Multi-Cultural Bks.

Shringar, Vol. 4. Music by Ajoy Chakraborty. 1 cass. 1993. (B93008) Multi-Cultural Bks.

Shrink Rap. unabr. ed. Robert Parker-Munn. Narrated by Deborah Raffin. 5 cass. (Running Time: 5 hrs. 45 mins.). 2002. 44.95 (2C369) Recorded Bks.
Boston P.I. Sunny Randall is working as a bodyguard for popular romance writer Melanie Hall, who is being stalked by her psychiatrist ex-husband. To find out what the shrink is up to, Sunny goes undercover as his new patient. But his therapy soon threatens both her sanity and her life.

Shrink Rap. unabr. ed. Robert B. Parker. Read by Deborah Raffin. 5 cass. (Running Time: 9 hrs.). (Sunny Randall Ser.: No. 3). 2004. 29.95 (978-1-59007-271-4(5)); audio compact disk 34.95 (978-1-59007-272-1(3)) Pub: New Millenn Enter. Dist(s): PerseuPGW
Sunny Randall, the beautiful blond P.I. with a yen for dogs, painting, and her ex-husband, Richie, has won over even the most hardcore of Robert B. Parker's fans.

Shrink Rap. unabr. ed. Robert B. Parker. Narrated by Deborah Raffin. 5 cass. (Running Time: 6 hrs.). (Sunny Randall Ser.: No. 3). 2002. 45.00 (978-1-4025-2858-3(2)) Recorded Bks.
Sunny Randall, the beautiful private investigator, is hired by famous author, Melanie Joan, to protect her from her stalking ex-husband while she's on a book tour. When Sunny learns that the ex is a psychotherapist and therefore not the average stalker, she decides the only way to stop him is from inside his world. Entering therapy herself, she soon discovers her own personal demons, which puts her very existence on the line.

Shrink Rap. unabr. ed. Robert B. Parker. Narrated by Deborah Raffin. 5 CDs. (Running Time: 6 hrs.). (Sunny Randall Ser.: No. 3). 2003. audio compact disk 58.00 (978-1-4025-4230-5(5)) Recorded Bks.

Shrink Rap. unabr. ed. Robert B. Parker. Narrated by Deborah Raffin. 5 cass. (Running Time: 6 hrs.). (Sunny Randall Ser.: No. 3). 2003. 32.95 (978-1-4025-2859-0(0)) Recorded Bks.

Shrink Survey 1995. 1 cass. (America's Supermarket Showcase '96 Ser.). 1996. 11.00 (NGA96-013) Sound Images.

Shrinkboard's Psychiatry Board Review: Psychiatric Diagnostic Criteria. Created by FDL Psychiatry Staff. 2009. (978-0-9840972-4-1(4)) Term Un Pub.

Shrinkboard's Psychiatry Board Review: Psychopharmacology. Created by FDL Psychiatry. (ENG.). 2009. 49.00 (978-0-9840972-0-3(1)) Term Un Pub.

Shrinkboard's Psychiatry Board Review: Q & A: Adult Psychopathology. Created by FDL Psychiatry. (ENG.). 2009. 24.00 (978-0-9840972-1-0(X)) Term Un Pub.

Shrinkboard's Psychiatry Board Review: Q & A: Neurology. Created by FDL Psychiatry. 2009. 49.00 (978-0-9840972-5-8(2)) Term Un Pub.

Shrinking of Treehorn. unabr. ed. Florence Parry Heide. 1 cass. (Running Time: 23 min.). (J). (gr. 1-3). 1994. pap. bk. 15.98 (978-0-8072-0215-9(0), Listening Lib) Random Audio Pubg.
Uplifting for any child who's been feeling "small.".

Shrinking Violet. 2004. bk. 24.95 (978-1-55592-174-3(4)); 8.95 (978-1-55592-831-5(5)); audio compact disk 12.95 (978-1-55592-887-2(0)) Weston Woods.

Shrot-Term Missions Language Program: Spanish. Scripts. 1 CD. (Running Time: 60 mins). 2003. pap. bk. 19.95 (978-0-9746182-0-3(9)) Short Term Mis.
Program comes with one audio CD and one pocket-size booklet.

Shroud. Robert K. Wilcox. Read by Paul T. Brandon. Engineer Hope Harbor Records Staff. 6 CDs. 2000. audio compact disk 64.95 (978-1-58444-058-1(9)) DiscUs Bks.

Shroud for a Nightingale. unabr. ed. P. D. James. Read by Penelope Dellaporta. 9 cass. (Running Time: 13 hrs. 30 min.). (Adam Dalgliesh Mystery Ser.). 1993. 72.00 (978-0-7366-2443-5(0), 3208) Books on Tape.
Adam Dalgliesh investigates murder at a hospital nursing school, uncovering its secret world of sex & ambition.

Shroud for a Nightingale. unabr. ed. P. D. James. Read by Michael Jayston. 8 cass. (Running Time: 12 hrs.). (Adam Dalgliesh Mystery Ser.). 2000. 59.95 (978-0-7451-6069-6(7), CAB 388) Pub: Chivers Audio Bks GBR. Dist(s): AudioGO
When Nurse Peace died grotesquely within the precincts of Nightingale House, a nurse training school, murder was strongly suspected. Superintendent Adam Dalgliesh arrived to investigate, and he rapidly found himself caught in a deadly web of intrigue and corruption. Then another nurse is found dead.

Shroud of Silence. Nancy Buckingham. 1992. pap. bk. 44.95 (978-1-85496-598-1(0)) Pub: UlverLrgPrint GBR. Dist(s): Ulverscroft US

Shroud of Silence. unabr. ed. Nancy Buckingham. Read by Jacqueline King. 4 cass. (Running Time: 6 hrs.). 1999. 44.95 (65980) Pub: Soundings Ltd GBR. Dist(s): Ulverscroft US

Shroud of Turin: The Controversy & the Truth. August Accetta. 5 cass. (Running Time: 5 hrs.). 2000. 29.95 (20228) Cath Treas.
Is this the burial cloth that covered Jesus in the tomb nearly 2000 years ago? Or is it a fraud & a hoax that has fooled millions of experts & scientists for centuries? Explore the scientific investigations currently ongoing into what Pope John Paul II has called, "the greatest relic of all Christendom." Dr. Accetta gives a riveting overview & history of the Shroud. He concludes this electrifying series with what he calls "The Liturgy of the Shroud." He shows how the Last Supper, the Eucharist, the Passover & the Passover Lamb are all tied together & wrapped up in this miraculous cloth.

Shrouded Destiny. Richard W. Bates. 2002. audio compact disk 5.95 (978-1-59201-001-1(6)) Bks Unbound Pubng Co.

Shrouds of Glory. unabr. collector's ed. Winston Groom. Read by Barrett Whitener. 9 cass. (Running Time: 13 hrs. 30 min.). 1996. 72.00 (978-0-7366-3233-1(6), 3894) Books on Tape.
In the late afternoon of its war of secession, the Confederacy pinned its hopes on a young general, John Bell Hood, head of the 20,000-man army of Tennessee. His mission: to head northwest from the ashes of Atlanta & regain Nashville. Can this desperate offensive turn the tide? It's November 30, 1864. Bands playing Dixie on one side, Battle Hymn of the Republic on the other, set the stage for what will become the bloodiest encounter of the entire Civil War: the battle for Franklin. It could alter the course of history.

Shrugg la Bugg Cassette. Stephen Cosgrove. 2004. 5.00 (978-1-58804-361-0(4)) PCI Educ.

Shruti Sadolikar (Vocal), Vol. 1. Music by Shruti Sadolikar. 1 cass. (Music Today Presents Ser.). 1992. (A92026) Multi-Cultural Bks.

Shruti Sadolikar (Vocal), Vol. 2. Music by Shruti Sadolikar. 1 cass. (Music Today Presents Ser.). 1992. (A92027) Multi-Cultural Bks.

***Sh*t My Dad Says.** unabr. ed. Justin Halpern. Read by Sean Schemmel. (ENG.). 2010. (978-0-06-201619-5(9), Harper Audio); (978-0-06-201236-4(3), Harper Audio) HarperCollins Pubs.

***Sh*t My Dad Says Low Price.** unabr. ed. Justin Halpern. Read by Sean Schemmel. 2010. audio compact disk 9.99 (978-0-06-207340-2(0), Harper Audio) HarperCollins Pubs.

Shtopalschik (The Clothsmender) Nikolai Leskov. Read by Leonid Schulman. 1 cass. (Running Time: 1 hrs.). (RUS.). 1997. pap. bk. 19.50 Interlingua VA.

Shuffle up & Deal: The Ultimate No Limit Texas Hold 'Em Guide. Mike Sexton. 1 CD-ROM. 2005. audio compact disk 19.95 (978-0-06-076251-3(9)) HarperCollins Pubs.

Shug. unabr. ed. Jenny Han. Read by Liz Morton. 5 CDs. (Running Time: 6 hrs.). (J). 2006. audio compact disk 49.75 (978-1-4193-8248-2(9), C3642); 39.75 (978-1-4193-8243-7(8), 98306) Recorded Bks.
Meet 12-year-old Annemarie "Shug" Wilcox. What's not to like about her? She's smart, she's tall, and she has lots of freckles. She lives in a small Georgia town with her popular, gorgeous older sister and intellectual mother. Shug is excited about starting the seventh-grade, but she's not prepared for all the vicious teasing that comes with the new school year.

Shunamite Woman. John Kilpatrick. 1 cass. 1996. 7.00 (978-0-7684-0022-9(8)) Destiny Image Pubs.

Shunning. unabr. ed. Beverly Lewis. Read by Marguerite Gavin. (Running Time: 7 hrs.). (Heritage of Lancaster County Ser.). 2003. audio compact disk 48.00 (978-0-7861-8995-3(9)) Blckstn Audio.

Shunning. unabr. ed. Beverly Lewis. Read by Marguerite Gavin. (Running Time: 7 hrs.). (Heritage of Lancaster County Ser.: No. 1). 2003. 24.95 (978-0-7861-8817-8(0)); 39.95 (978-0-7861-2577-7(2)) Blckstn Audio.

Shunning. unabr. ed. Beverly Lewis. Narrated by Barbara Caruso. 6 cass. (Running Time: 8 hrs. 45 mins.). (Heritage of Lancaster County Ser.: No. 1). 1998. 51.00 (978-0-7887-2192-2(5), 95488E7) Recorded Bks.
In a quiet Amish community in Pennsylvania, beautiful Katie prepares for her wedding. She discovers a satin infant gown hidden in a musty trunk. From that moment, she is determined to learn the truth, even if it destroys the only life she has known.

Shunyata. Read by Chogyam Trungpa. 1 cass. 1972. 12.50 (A004) Vajradhatu.
Four talks. The Shunyata principle is the emptiness of phenomena, which can only be perceived by non-conceptual mind. In this space, compassion & wisdom manifest.

Shurangama Mantra Recitation. 5.00 (978-0-88139-717-8(2)) Buddhist Text.

Shurangama Mantra Recitation for Beginners. 5.00 (978-0-88139-609-6(5)) Buddhist Text.

Shut Out That Moon see Poetry of Thomas Hardy

Shut Your Mouth & Open Your Mind: The Rise & Reckless Fall of Lenny Bruce. Keith Rodway & Chrome Dreams Staff. (Enlightenment Ser.). (ENG.). 2000. audio compact disk 15.95 (978-1-84240-085-2(1)) Pub: Chrome Dreams GBR. Dist(s): IPG Chicago

Shutochka, Skripka Rotshilda, Posle Teatra. Anton Chekhov. 1 cass. (Running Time: 1 hrs.). (RUS.). 1996. pap. bk. 19.50 (978-1-58085-571-6(7)) Interlingua VA.

Shutter Island. Dennis Lehane. Read by David Strathairn. 1975. 14.95 (978-0-06-074353-6(0)); 9.99 (978-0-06-074360-4(3)) HarperCollins Pubs.

***Shutter Island.** abr. ed. Dennis Lehane. Read by David Strathairn. (ENG.). 2008. (978-0-06-180506-6(8), Harper Audio); (978-0-06-180512-7(2), Harper Audio) HarperCollins Pubs.

***Shutter Island.** unabr. ed. Dennis Lehane. Read by Tom Stechschulte. (ENG.). 2008. (978-0-06-180509-7(2), Harper Audio); (978-0-06-180508-0(4), Harper Audio) HarperCollins Pubs.

Shutter Island. unabr. movie tie-in ed. Dennis Lehane. Read by David Strathairn & Tom Stechschulte. 2009. audio compact disk 19.99 (978-0-06-190628-2(X), Harper Audio) HarperCollins Pubs.

Shutterbug A-D. Steck-Vaughn Staff. (Benchmark Bks.). 2002. 10.00 (978-0-7398-6122-6(0)); 10.00 (978-0-7398-6594-1(3)) SteckVau.

Shutterbug E-I. Steck-Vaughn Staff. (Benchmark Bks.). 2002. 10.00 (978-0-7398-6123-3(9)); 10.00 (978-0-7398-6124-0(7)); 10.00 (978-0-7398-6595-8(1)) SteckVau.

Shutterbug A-D A-D. Steck-Vaughn Staff. (Benchmark Bks.). 2002. 10.00 (978-0-7398-6121-9(2)) SteckVau.

Shutterbug Early Emergent. Raintree Steck-Vaughn Staff. (J). 2002. (978-0-7398-5916-2(1)) SteckVau.

Shutterbug Emergent Stage. Steck-Vaughn Staff. (J). 2002. (978-0-7398-6000-7(3)) SteckVau.

Shuttle. 1 cass. (Read-along Ser.). bk. 34.95 Set, incl. learner's guide & exercises. (S23914) J Norton Pubs.

Shuttle Down. abr. ed. Mack Maloney. Read by Charlie O'Dowd. 2 vols. No. 3. 2003. (978-1-58807-572-7(9)) Am Pubng Inc.

Shuttle Down. abr. ed. Mack Maloney. Read by Charlie O'Dowd. 4 cass. (Running Time: 6 hrs.). (Chopper Ops Ser.: No. 3). 2003. 25.00 (978-1-58807-097-5(2)) Am Pubng Inc.
Under strict secrecy, the Pentagon launches a shuttle intended to capture a classified space camera and bring it back to Earth. But the shuttle disappears upon reentry. When satellite reconnaissance spots the craft in western China, the U.S. government wants it recovered immediately. They provide Chopper Ops with the ultimate in high-tech copters equipped to retrieve the shuttleor destroy it before another country can get ahold of its top secret cargo.But the trip to China is only the start of something far more complicated and dangerous. The final stage of their mission will take the team to the Bershewr region of Pakistan, a place so barren and isolated it makes the moon look like an oasis. And as national security hangs in the balance, theyll have to finish the jobbefore it finishes them.

Shy Boy Set: The Horse That Came in from the Wild. unabr. ed. Monty Roberts. Read by Monty Roberts. 3 cass. 1999. 24.00 (FS9-50902) Highsmith.

Shy Guy. unabr. ed. David R. Addleman. Read by Cameron Beierle. 8 cass. (Running Time: 8 hrs. 18 min.). (David R. Addleman Mystery Ser.). 2001. 49.95 (978-1-58116-151-9(4)) Books in Motion.
Ex-Navy Seal James Gearing hires on with Hadley & Emerson Detective Agency. When the attempted robbery of a client's bank is put down by James' quick action, the mob's retribution results, and no-one is safe from hit-men who come to kill, and are hired by competing factions.

Shy Person's Guide to Successful Dating. Eric Weber. Narrated by Alan Ishack. 1 cass. (Running Time: 1 hr.). 1983. 20.95 (978-0-914094-53-1(X)) Symphony Pr.
Interpersonal relationships.

Shylock. George B. Harrison. 1 cass. (Running Time: 35 min.). (Shakespeare's Critics Speak Ser.). 11.95 (23104) J Norton Pubs.
A presentation of the various interpretations of the character Shylock with some reading of the principle relevant speeches.

Shyness. Philip G. Zimbardo. 1 cass. (Running Time: 1 hr.). 10.95 (29354) J Norton Pubs.
Shyness can be a crippling problem, whether it affects one in a range of situations or in a single context. This shows how to socialize freely in a number of everyday situations & gives clear examples of how to pinpoint & treat specific problem areas.

Shyness: Program from the Award Winning Public Radio Series. Interview. Hosted by Fred Goodwin. 1CD. (Running Time: 1 hr). (Infinite Mind Ser.). 2001. audio compact disk 21.95 (978-1-888064-95-7(1), LCM 157) Lichtenstein Creat.
Everyone feels shy sometimes. Have you ever wondered what's going on in our minds and bodies when we experience shyness? This week, we look into both the social aspects and the biology of shyness. Guests include singer-songwriter Suzanne Vega, who talks about being a shy performer; Dr. Bernardo Carducci, the Director of the Shyness Research Institute at Indiana University Southeast; and two preeminent developmental psychologists, Dr. Jerome Kagan and Dr. Nathan Fox, who discuss whether shyness is an inborn trait. We also visit a support a support group for shy people.

Si quiere caminar sobre las aguas tiene que salir de la barca, audio Libro. Read by John Ortberg. (SPA.). 2009. audio compact disk 19.99 (978-0-8297-5354-7(0)) Pub: Vida Pubs. Dist(s): Zondervan

¡Sí! Salud Integral CD Profesional: Vida Integral y Abundante. 2nd ed. John B. Youngberg et al. Tr. by Carmen Collins.Tr. of WIN! Wellness Professional CD. (SPA., 2008. audio compact disk 149.95 (978-0-9815123-2-7(1)) WIN Wellness.

¡Sí Se Puede! Aprender Inglés Fácil en la industria de Construcción y Jardinería. Elizabeth Budner. Text by Norma Valles. Voice by Norma Valles. Engineer Kelley Aaron. (SPA.). 2006. audio compact disk (978-0-9786863-0-7(6)) ITRON.

¡Sí Se Puede! Aprender Inglés Fácil en la industria de Restaurante y Hotelería. Elizabeth Budner. Voice by Norma Valles. Moderated by Norma Valles. Engineer Kelley Aaron. (SPA.). 2006. audio compact disk (978-0-9786863-1-4(4)) ITRON.

Si Se Puede Tener 'Exito. Charles Gonzalez. (SPA.). 1999. bk. 17.95 (978-0-7931-3339-0(4)) Kaplan Pubng.

Si Tu No Estás. unabr. ed. Gloria Santamaría & Luis Santiago. (SPA.). 1998. 9.99 (978-0-8297-2709-8(4)) Pub: Vida Pubs. Dist(s): Zondervan

Siamese Twin Mystery. unabr. ed. Ellery Queen. Read by Scott Harrison. 7 cass. (Running Time: 10 hrs.). 1998. 49.95 (978-0-7861-1266-1(2), 2203) Blckstn Audio.
At the mountain lodge, trouble came in twos. Two corpses, two clues. Two strange youths turned into one. Pitted against this double-trouble were two sleuths-Ellery Queen & Inspector Queen-who knew that every time they didn't succeed, someone was going to die.

Siamese Twin Mystery. unabr. collector's ed. Ellery Queen. Read by Michael Prichard. 8 cass. (Running Time: 8 hrs.). 1978. 48.00 (978-0-7366-0136-8(8), 1140) Books on Tape.
This finds Ellery Queen & his father, the irascible Inspector Queen, trapped in a mountain retreat by a raging forest fire. The members of the household are a strange lot indeed & the mysterious murder of the retreat's host indicates to our hero that not only is he isolated with an odd assortment of characters, but a dangerous killer as well.

***Siar Ar Bhoithrin Na Smaointe.** Maire Begley O. Seaghdha. (ENG.). 1990. 11.95 (978-0-8023-7030-3(6)) Pub: Clo Iar-Chonnachta IRL. Dist(s): Dufour

Sibelius: Educational Edition. 2001. audio compact disk 319.95 (978-0-634-04495-3(8), 00631207) H Leonard.

Sibelius: Educational 5-User Lab Pack. 2001. audio compact disk 899.95 (978-0-634-04496-0(6), 00631208) H Leonard.

Sibelius: Educational 5-User Lab Pack & Photoscore Bundle. 2001. audio compact disk 999.95 (978-0-634-04505-9(9), 00631217) H Leonard.

Sibelius: Professional Edition & Photoscore Bundle. 2001. audio compact disk 699.95 (978-0-634-04507-3(5), 00631219) H Leonard.

Siberian Alterna. abr. ed. Axel Kilgore. Read by Charlton Griffin. 2 vols. (Running Time: 3 hrs.). No. 14. 2004. 18.00 (978-1-58807-170-5(7)) Am Pubng Inc.

Siberian Alternative. Axel Kilgore. Read by Carol Eason. 2 vols. No. 14. 2004. (978-1-58807-661-8(X)) Am Pubng Inc.

Sibling. unabr. collector's ed. Adam Hall. Read by Rupert Keenlyside. 6 cass. (Running Time: 9 hrs.). 1983. 48.00 (978-0-7366-0731-5(5), 1688) Books on Tape.
A brother & sister whose wickedness & cruelty led to their separation in childhood meet years later. They find a strange fascination in each other's company as old bitterness is submerged. But the madness of childhood suddenly surfaces.

Sibling Relationships: Program from the Award Winning Public Radio Series. Featuring Laurie Kramer. (Infinite Mind Ser.). 2002. audio compact disk 21.95 (978-1-888064-57-5(9), LCM 240) Lichtenstein Creat.
In this hour, we explore Sibling Relationships. Four out of five Americans have a brother or sister. Best friend? Worst enemy? One thing's for sure - nobody can push your buttons like a sibling. How do the bonds between brothers and sisters change over time? Are birth order and spacing between siblings less important than we thought? We'll have the latest research. Guests include: psychologists Dr. Judy Dunn, Dr. Laurie Kramer, and Dr. Peter Goldenthal; brothers Matt Lee and Ted Lee, who share a byline in The New York Times; and the brother and sister who lead the musical group the Cowboy Junkies.

Sibling Revelry: The Best of the Smothers Brothers. Smothers Brothers. 1 CD. (Running Time: 1 hr. 30 mins.). 2001. audio compact disk 16.98 (R2 75235) Rhino Enter.

An Asterisk (*) at the beginning of an entry indicates that the title is appearing for the first time.

Sibling Rivalry. 3 cass. (Running Time: 3 hrs.). (Adventures in Odyssey). (J). (gr. k-4). 2001. 12.99 Pub: Focus Family. Dist(s): Tommy Nelson
Adventures in Odyssey stories packaged by theme.

Sibling Rivalry. Focus on the Family Staff. 3 cass. (Running Time: 3 hrs.). (Adventures in Odyssey Ser.). (J). (gr. 1-7). 2001. 9.99 (978-1-58997-021-2(7)) Pub: Focus Family. Dist(s): Tommy Nelson

Sibling Rivalry: A Parent Guide to Managing Sibling Conflicts. Robert H. Meyer. 1 cass. 1989. 10.95 (978-0-9622490-0-6(9)) Parent Tapes.
Designed to help parents achieve a better understanding of sibling rivalry & provide parents with methods for dealing with common sibling problems in the home.

Sibling Rivalry: Strategies for Teaching Your Kids How to Get Along. Charles Fay. Illus. by Jackie Dussiau-Beilke. 2008. audio compact disk 21.95 (978-1-930429-93-2(2)) Love Logic.

Sibyl. Par Lagerkvist. Read by Lorna Raver et al. Tr. by Naomi Walford. 4 CDs. (Running Time: 4 hrs. 30 mins.). 2004. audio compact disk 36.00 (978-0-7861-8280-0(6)) Blckstn Audio.

Sibyl. Pär Lagerkvist. Narrated by Yuri Rasovsky. (Running Time: 4 hrs. 30 mins.). 2004. 22.95 (978-1-59912-715-6(6)) Iofy Corp.

Sibyl. unabr. ed. Par Lagerkvist. Read by Lorna Raver et al. 30 cass. (Running Time: 5 hrs. 30 mins.). 2005. reel tape 19.95 (978-0-7861-2895-2(X), E3391); audio compact disk 19.95 (978-0-7861-8281-7(4), ZE3391); audio compact disk 24.95 (978-0-7861-8356-2(X), ZM3391) Blckstn Audio.

Sibyl. unabr. ed. Par Lagerkvist. Read by and Kristoffer Tabori, Lorna Raver Yuri Rasovsky. (Running Time: 5 hrs. 30 mins.). 2004. 34.95 (978-0-7861-2896-9(8)) Blckstn Audio.

Sibyl in Her Grave. unabr. ed. Sarah Caudwell. Read by Eva Haddon. 8 cass. (Running Time: 9 hrs. 51 mins.). (Isis Cassettes Ser.). (J). 2004. 69.95 (978-0-7531-1689-0(8)) Pub: ISIS Lrg Prnt GBR. Dist(s): Ulverscroft US

Sibyl in Her Grave. unabr. ed. Sarah Caudwell. 8 CDs. (Running Time: 9 hrs. 51 mins.). (Isis (CDs) Ser.). (J). 2004. audio compact disk 79.95 (978-0-7531-2356-0(8)) Pub: ISIS Lrg Prnt GBR. Dist(s): Ulverscroft US

Sic a Wife As Willie Had see Poetry of Robert Burns & Border Ballads

Sichtwechsel NEU: Text- und Arbeitsbuch, Level 1. S. Bachmann et al. (GER.). (C). 1995. 34.25 (978-3-12-675023-3(0)) Pub: Klett Ernst Verlag DEU. Dist(s): Intl Bk Import

Sicilian. unabr. ed. Mario Puzo. Read by multivoice. (Running Time: 11 hrs.). 2009. 24.99 (978-1-4233-9689-5(8), 9781423396895, Brilliance MP3); 24.99 (978-1-4233-9691-8(X), 9781423396918, BAD); 39.97 (978-1-4233-9690-1(1), 9781423396901, Brinc Audio MP3 Lib); 39.97 (978-1-4233-9692-5(8), 9781423396925, BADLE) Brilliance Audio.

Sicilian. unabr. ed. Mario Puzo. Read by multivoice. (Running Time: 12 hrs.). 2010. audio compact disk 29.99 (978-1-4418-3574-1(1), 9781441835741, Bril Audio CD Unabri); audio compact disk 89.97 (978-1-4418-3575-8(X), 9781441835758, BriAudCD Unabrid) Brilliance Audio.

Sicilian. unabr. ed. Mario Puzo. Narrated by Richard Ferrone. 11 cass. (Running Time: 16 hrs. 30 mins.). 1992. 91.00 (978-1-55690-730-2(3), 92230E7) Recorded Bks.
In this sequel to "The Godfather," Michael Corleone is at the end of his two-year exile in Sicily. He is charged with bringing back to America the man known as Turi Guiliano, a self-styled bandit who fights for his countrymen against the corruption of Rome. But Turi & now Michael, encounters opposition from an unanticipated quarter: Don Croce Malo, the Capo di Capi of the Sicilian Mafia.

Sicilian Romance. Ann Radcliffe. Read by Anais 9000. 2009. 27.95 (978-1-60112-216-2(0)) Babblebooks.

Sick as a Parrot. unabr. ed. Liz Evans. Read by Catherine Thompson. 8 CDs. (Running Time: 33900 sec.). (Isis (CDs) Ser.). 2006. audio compact disk 79.95 (978-0-7531-2503-8(X)) Pub: ISIS Lrg Prnt GBR. Dist(s): Ulverscroft US

Sick As a Parrot. unabr. ed. Liz Evans. Read by Catherine Thompson. 8 cass. (Running Time: 37200 sec.). (Isis Cassettes Ser.). 2006. 69.95 (978-0-7531-2153-5(0)) Pub: ISIS Lrg Prnt GBR. Dist(s): Ulverscroft US

Sick Bay. Sharon Olexa Crandall. Illus. by Sue Kemp. (J). 2001. pap. bk. 14.95 (978-0-9662378-5-6(4)) Astoria Prodns.

Sick Heart River. unabr. ed. John Buchan. Read by Alistair Maydon. 10 cass. (Running Time: 9 hrs. 15 min.). 2001. 69.95 (978-1-85695-580-5(X), 93016) Pub: ISIS Audio GBR. Dist(s): Ulverscroft US
Terminally ill, Sir Edward Leithan, barrister & adventurer, decides not to wait passively for death. Instead he sets off to search for Francis Galliard, an explorer who disappeared in the Canadian Arctic. His search exposes him to physical hardship but also leads to an awareness of a greater world of the spirit which allows him to come to terms with his situation.

Sick of Being Sick? Miss Dee. 1 cass. 8.95 (749) Am Fed Astrologers.

Sick Puppy. unabr. ed. Carl Hiaasen. Read by Nick Sullivan. 8 vols. (Running Time: 12 hrs.). 2000. bk. 69.95 (978-0-7927-2361-5(9), CSL 250, Chivers Sound Lib) AudioGO.
Twilly Spree, a man dedicated to saving Florida's wilderness, has vengeance on his mind. After watching Palmer Stoat dump a trail of fast-food out the window of his car, Twilly decides to teach him a lesson. And when Twilly discovers that Stoat is one of Florida's cockiest political fixers, whose latest project is the "malling" of a pristine Gulf Coast island, the real fun begins.

Sicken & So Die. unabr. ed. Simon Brett. Read by Geoffrey Howard. 4 cass. (Running Time: 5 hrs. 30 mins.). (Charles Paris Mystery Ser.). 1997. 32.95 (978-0-7861-1108-4(9), 1874) Blckstn Audio.
Charles Paris is forced to deal with a wild young director whose idea of Shakespeare the bard himself would hate.

Sicken & So Die. unabr. ed. Simon Brett. Read by Geoffrey Howard. 5 CDs. (Running Time: 5 hrs. 30 mins.). (Charles Paris Mystery Ser.). 2000. audio compact disk 40.00 (978-0-7861-9896-2(6), 1874) Blckstn Audio.

Sicken & So Die. unabr. ed. Simon Brett. Read by Geoffrey Howard. 1 CD. (Running Time: 5 hrs. 30 mins.). 2001. audio compact disk 19.95 (zm1874) Blckstn Audio.
Paris, the often out-of-work actor, has a good part for a change playing Sir Toby Belch in a summer festival production of "Twelfth Night." But when the director takes ill it's not long until the bodies start to turn up.

Sicken & So Die. unabr. ed. Simon Brett. Read by Simon Brett. 6 cass. (Running Time: 9 hrs.). (Charles Paris Mystery Ser.: Bk. 16). 2000. 49.95 (CAB 1314) Pub: Chivers Audio Bks GBR. Dist(s): AudioGO
Things are going suspiciously well for Charles Paris: he's moved in with his ex-wife and he's got a leading role in the production of Twelfth Night! But the director of the play is taken ill, and now it's only a matter of time before Charles is out on a limb! On the first night of the play, someone tries to kill him.

Sickle Cell Anemia - A Bibliography & Dictionary for Physicians, Patients, & Genome Researchers. Compiled by Icon Group International, Inc. Staff. 2007. ring bd. 28.95 (978-0-497-11292-9(2)) Icon Grp.

***Sickness & Healing.** Kenneth Wapnick. 2010. 54.00 (978-1-59142-496-3(8)); audio compact disk 61.00 (978-1-59142-495-6(X)) Foun Miracles.

***Sid & Sam.** unabr. ed. Nola Buck. (ENG.). 2008. (978-0-06-179921-1(1)); (978-0-06-169485-1(1)) HarperCollins Pubs.

***Sid Guy: The Case of the Mysterious Woman & the Case of the Missing Boxer.** Prod. by Siren Audio Studios. Created by L. N. Nolan & W. W. Marciano. (ENG.). 2010. audio compact disk 25.99 (978-0-9844180-0-8(8)) Siiren Audio.

Siddhartha. Hermann Hesse. Narrated by Harish Bhimani. (ENG.). 2008. 12.95 (978-0-9801087-8-1(0)) Alpha DVD.

Siddhartha. Hermann Hesse. Tr. by Joachim Neugroschel. Narrated by Firdous Bamji. (Running Time: 19800 sec.). 2006. audio compact disk 19.99 (978-1-4193-7793-8(0)) Recorded Bks.

Siddhartha. abr. ed. Hermann Hesse. Read by Derek Jacobi. 2 cass. (Running Time: 3 hrs.). (Mondo Folktales Ser.). 2004. 17.95 (978-1-57270-048-2(3), M21048) Pub: Audio Partners. Dist(s): PerseuPGW
A compelling tale of spiritual quest, this fictionalized story of Buddha was inspired by Hesse's travels in India.

Siddhartha. unabr. ed. Hermann Hesse. Read by Christian Baron. (YA). 2008. 54.99 (978-1-60514-857-1(1)) Find a World.

Siddhartha. unabr. ed. Hermann Hesse. Narrated by Michael Thompson. 3 cass. (Running Time: 4 hrs. 15 mins.). 1999. 26.00 (978-1-55690-476-9(2), 89640E7) Recorded Bks.
A young man sets out from his opulent home in search of truth.

***Siddhartha.** unabr. ed. Hermann Hesse. Narrated by James Langton. (Running Time: 4 hrs. 30 mins.). 2009. 12.99 (978-1-4001-8547-4(5)) Tantor Media.

***Siddhartha.** unabr. ed. Hesse, Hermann. Narrated by Langton, James. (Running Time: 4 hrs. 30 mins. 0 sec.). (ENG.). 2009. 19.99 (978-1-4001-6547-6(4)); audio compact disk 19.99 (978-1-4001-1547-1(7)); audio compact disk 39.99 (978-1-4001-4547-8(3)) Pub: Tantor Media. Dist(s): IngramPubServ

Siddhartha: A New Translation. unabr. ed. Hermann Hesse. Read by Baron Christian. Tr. by Sherab Chodzin Kohn. (Running Time: 18000 sec.). (ENG.). 2008. audio compact disk 24.95 (978-1-59030-551-5(5)) Pub: Shambhala Pubns. Dist(s): Random

Side by Side. Jane Voss & Hoyle Osborne. Perf. by Jane Voss & Hoyle Osborne. 1 cass. (Running Time: 44 min.). (J). (gr. k-3). 1985. 9.95 (978-0-939065-29-5(0), GW1033) Gentle Wind.
Songs & oldtime ragtime music for children.

Side by Side. Perf. by Jane Voss & Hoyle Osborne. 1985. audio compact disk 14.95 (978-1-58467-001-8(0)) Gentle Wind.

Side by Side, Bk. 1. 3rd ed. Steven J. Molinsky. 2 cass. (C). 2000. wbk. ed. & act. bk. ed. 46.00 (978-0-13-026746-7(5)) Longman.

Side by Side, Bk. 1. 3rd ed. Steven J. Molinsky & Bill Bliss. 7 CDs. (C). 2000. bk. & stu. ed. 135.00 (978-0-13-026748-1(1)) Longman.

Side by Side Leadership: Achieving Outstanding Results Together. Dennis A. Romig. Read by Dennis A. Romig. (ENG.). 2006. audio compact disk 19.95 (978-0-9672350-2-8(2)) Perf Res Pr.

Side Effect. Sandra S. Feder. 5 cassettes. (Running Time: 6 hrs. 45 mins.). 2001. 32.95 (978-1-930541-10-8(4)) Thornwood Pub Co.
Complete, unabridged text of the novel, Side Effect, read by the author, Sandra Feder.

Side Effects. abr. ed. Michael Palmer. Read by Heather McLennan. 4 cass. Library ed. (Running Time: 6 hrs.). 2003. 62.25 (978-1-59086-854-6(4), 1590868544, BAudLibEd); audio compact disk 74.25 (978-1-59086-856-0(0), 1590868560, BACDLib Ed) Brilliance Audio.
Kate Bennet. A bright hospital pathologist with a loving husband and a solid future. Until one day her world turns dark. A strange, puzzling illness has killed two women. Now it endangers Kate's closest friend. Soon it will threaten Kate's marriage. Her sanity. Her life. Kate has uncovered a horrifying secret. Important people will stop at nothing to protect it. It is a terrifying medical discovery. And its roots lie in one of the greatest evils in the history of humankind.

Side Effects. abr. ed. Michael Palmer. Read by Heather McLennan. (Running Time: 6 hrs.). 2005. audio compact disk 16.99 (978-1-59600-401-6(0), 9781596004016, BCD Value Price) Brilliance Audio.

Side Effects. abr. ed. Michael Palmer. Read by Heather McLennan. (Running Time: 6 hrs.). 2006. 24.95 (978-1-4233-0203-2(6), 9781423302032, BAD); 39.25 (978-1-4233-0202-5(8), 9781423302025, Brlnc Audio MP3 Lib); audio compact disk 24.95 (978-1-4233-0201-8(X), 9781423302018, Brilliance MP3) Brilliance Audio.
Kate Bennett. A bright hospital pathologist with a loving husband and a solid future. Until one day her world turns dark. A strange, puzzling illness has killed two women. Now it endangers Kate's closest friend. Soon it will threaten Kate's marriage. Her sanity. Her life. Kate has uncovered a horrifying secret. Important people will stop at nothing to protect it. It is a terrifying medical discovery. And its roots lie in one of the greatest evils in the history of humankind.

Side Effects. abr. ed. Michael Palmer. Read by Heather McLennan. (Running Time: 6 hrs.). 2009. audio compact disk 9.99 (978-1-4418-0831-8(0), 9781441808318, BCD Value Price) Brilliance Audio.

Side Effects. unabr. ed. Michael Palmer. Read by Angela Dawe. (Running Time: 11 hrs.). 2009. 39.97 (978-1-4418-0122-7(7), 9781441801227, Brlnc Audio MP3 Lib); 39.97 (978-1-4418-0124-1(3), 9781441801241, BADLE); 24.99 (978-1-4418-0123-4(5), 9781441801234, BAD); 24.99 (978-1-4418-0121-0(9), 9781441801210, Brilliance MP3); audio compact disk 87.97 (978-1-4418-0120-3(0), 9781441801203, BriAudCD Unabrid); audio compact disk 29.99 (978-1-4418-0119-7(7), 9781441801197, Bril Audio CD Unabri) Brilliance Audio.

***Side Jobs.** Jim Butcher. (Running Time: 11 hrs.). (Dresden Files Ser.). (ENG.). 2010. audio compact disk 39.95 (978-0-14-242826-9(4), PengAudBks) Penguin Grp USA.

Sidetracked. unabr. ed. Henning Mankell. Read by Dick Hill. (Running Time: 52200 sec.). (Kurt Wallander Ser.). 2007. 79.95 (978-1-4332-0278-0(6)); audio compact disk 99.00 (978-1-4332-0279-7(4)); audio compact disk 29.95 (978-1-4332-0280-3(8)) Blckstn Audio.

Sidetracked. unabr. ed. Henning Mankell. Read by Dick Hill. (Running Time: 14 hrs. 50 mins.). (Kurt Wallander Ser.). 2009. audio compact disk 29.95 (978-1-4332-7079-6(X)) Blckstn Audio.

Sidetracked Home Executives(TM) From Pigpen to Paradise. unabr. ed. Pam Young & Peggy Jones. Read by Anna Stone & Gabra Zackman. (Running Time: 3 hrs.). (ENG.). 2010. 14.98 (978-1-60024-886-3(1)) Pub: Hachet Audio. Dist(s): HachBkGrp

Sidewalk Counseling: Still a Constitutional Right. Walter Weber. 1 cass. 4.00 (95A) IRL Chicago.
How recent laws & Supreme Court decisions affect peaceful pro-life activities. January 1995 talk.

Sideways. Rex Pickett. (Running Time: 10 hrs. 0 mins.). 2005. 65.95 (978-0-7861-3477-9(1)) Blckstn Audio.

Sideways. Rex Pickett. Read by Scott Brick. (Running Time: 11 hrs.). 2004. 34.95 (978-1-59912-597-8(8)) Iofy Corp.

Sideways: The Ultimate Road Trip. Rex Pickett. Read by Scott Brick. 8 cass. (Running Time: 7 hrs.). 2005. 29.95 (978-0-7861-3476-2(3)); audio compact disk 29.95 (978-0-7861-8107-0(9)) Blckstn Audio.

Sideways: The Ultimate Road Trip. unabr. ed. Rex Pickett. Read by Scott Brick. 9 CDs. (Running Time: 11 hrs.). 2005. audio compact disk 29.95 (978-0-7861-7929-9(5)) Blckstn Audio.

Sideways: The Ultimate Road Trip / the Last Hurrah. Rex Pickett. Read by Scott Brick. (Running Time: 39600 sec.). 2005. audio compact disk 81.00 (978-0-7861-7930-5(9)) Blckstn Audio.

Sideways Stories from Wayside School. Louis Sachar. Read by Lionel Wilson. 2 cass. (Running Time: 3 hrs.). (J). 2000. 18.00 (978-0-7366-9105-5(7)) Books on Tape.
All thirty classrooms at Wayside School are on top of each other, instead of side by side. Maybe that's why there are wacky goings on especially on the thirteenth floor!.

Sideways Stories from Wayside School. unabr. ed. Louis Sachar. Read by Lionel Wilson. 2 vols. (Running Time: 2 hrs. 48 mins.). (J). (gr. 3-7). 1993. pap. bk. 29.00 (978-0-8072-7401-9(1), YA851SP, Listening Lib); 23.00 (978-0-8072-7400-2(3), YA851CX, Listening Lib) Random Audio Pubg.

Sidewinder, abr. ed. Dalton Walker. Read by Dick Wilkinson. 2 cass. (Running Time: 3 hrs.). (Shiloh Ser.: Vol. 6). 1999. 16.95 (978-1-890990-33-6(7), 99033) Otis Audio.
A crooked, cold-blooded killer & gambler leaves a trail of blood & bodies across the mining country of California. Shiloh the bounty hunter is hot on his trail & won't stop until the killer is swinging from the gallows.

Sidewinders 1. William W. Johnstone & J. A. Johnstone. (Sidewinders Ser.: No. 1). 2009. audio compact disk 19.99 (978-1-59950-564-0(9)) GraphicAudio.

Sidewinders 2: Massacre at Whiskey Flats. William W. Johnstone & J. A. Johnstone. (Sidewinders Ser.: No. 2). 2009. audio compact disk 19.99 (978-1-59950-583-1(5)) GraphicAudio.

Sidewinders 3: Cutthroat Canyon. Based on a novel by William W. Johnstone & J. A. Johnstone. (Sidewinders Ser.: No. 3). 2009. audio compact disk 19.99 (978-1-59950-609-8(2)) GraphicAudio.

***Sidewinders 4: Mankiller Colorado.** William W. Johnstone. 2011. audio compact disk 19.99 (978-1-59950-726-2(9)) GraphicAudio.

Sidney: Test Title. Conde Sidney. 1992. 26.00 (978-0-312-55555-9(5)) Pub: St Martin. Dist(s): Macmillan

Sidney & Norman: A Tale of Two Pigs. unabr. ed. Phil Vischer. Narrated by Phil Vischer. (ENG.). (J). 2007. 6.29 (978-1-60814-381-8(3)) Oasis Audio.

Sidney Sheldon see Movie Makers Speak: Writers

Sidney Sheldon's Mistress of the Game. unabr. ed. Sidney Sheldon & Tilly Bagshawe. (Running Time: 11 hrs. 0 mins.). 2009. 29.95 (978-1-4332-9391-7(9)); 65.95 (978-1-4332-9387-0(0)) Blckstn Audio.

Sidney Sheldon's Mistress of the Game. unabr. ed. Sidney Sheldon & Tilly Bagshawe. Read by Karen Ziemba. 9 CDs. (Running Time: 12 hrs.). 2009. audio compact disk 100.00 (978-1-4332-9388-7(9)) Blckstn Audio.

Sidney Sheldon's Mistress of the Game. unabr. ed. Sidney Sheldon & Tilly Bagshawe. Read by Karen Ziemba. 2009. audio compact disk 39.99 (978-0-06-184194-1(3), Harper Audio) HarperCollins Pubs.

***Sidney Sheldon's Mistress of the Game.** unabr. ed. Sidney Sheldon & Tilly Bagshawe. Read by Karen Ziemba. (ENG.). 2009. (978-0-06-190262-8(4), Harper Audio); (978-0-06-190261-1(6), Harper Audio) HarperCollins Pubs.

Sido ma mere, Lettres de Sido a Colette. Excerpts. Sidonie-Gabrielle Colette. Read by Sidonie-Gabrielle Colette. Read by Edwige Feuillere. 1 cass. (FRE.). 1991. 24.95 (1035-EF) Olivia & Hill.
Colette reads excerpts from her novel "Sido," based on memories of her mother.

Sidrah Stories: A Torah Companion Vol 1: Stories Inspired by the Book of Genesis. Steven M. Rosman. Read by Steven M. Rosman. Perf. by Yael Leiman et al. Contrib. by David Kumin. 1 cass. (J). 9.95 (571600) URJ Pr.
The author reads six selections, relating to the Book of Genesis, that appear in his popular book. With his friendly, sensitive voice, Rabbi Rosman makes these tales truly come to life. Enhanced by an original music score.

SIDS - Near Drowning. Susan Wooley & Robert Felter. (Pediatric Emergencies: The National Conference for Practioners Ser.). 1986. 9.00 (978-0-932491-73-2(1)) Res Appl Inc.

Siege. Seymour Krim. Read by Seymour Krim. 1 cass. (Running Time: 1 hr.). 13.95 (978-1-55644-111-0(8), 4111) Am Audio Prose.
One of the fathers of New Journalism or "creative non-fiction" reads from his long prose-poem jazz meditation on the state of American culture, which has been in progress for 10 years.

Siege. abr. ed. Stephen White. Read by Dick Hill. (Running Time: 6 hrs.). (Dr. Alan Gregory Ser.). 2009. audio compact disk 26.99 (978-1-4418-0720-5(9), 9781441807205, BACD) Brilliance Audio.

Siege. abr. ed. Stephen White. Read by Dick Hill. (Running Time: 6 hrs.). (Dr. Alan Gregory Ser.). 2010. audio compact disk 14.99 (978-1-4418-2612-1(2), 9781441826121, BCD Value Price) Brilliance Audio.

Siege. unabr. ed. Helen Dunmore. Read by Jilly Bond. 8 cass. (Running Time: 10 hrs. 38 mins.). (Isis Ser.). (J). 2002. 69.95 (978-0-7531-1260-1(4)); audio compact disk 89.95 (978-0-7531-1492-6(5)) Pub: ISIS Lrg Prnt GBR. Dist(s): Ulverscroft US
Leningrad, September 1941, German forces surround the city, imprisoning those who live there. The besieged people of Leningrad face shells, starvation and the Russian winter. What is it like to be so hungry you simmer your leather manicure case to make soup, so cold you burn first your furniture and then your books? The Siege is a brilliantly imagined novel about war and the wounds it inflicts on ordinary people's lives. It is also a profoundly moving celebration of love, life and survival.

Siege. unabr. ed. Kathryn Lasky. Read by Pamela Garelick. (Running Time: 18000 sec.). (Guardians of Ga'Hoole Ser.: Bk. 4). (J). (gr. 4-7). 2007. 34.95 (978-1-4332-0571-2(8)); audio compact disk 36.00 (978-1-4332-0572-9(6)) Blckstn Audio.

***Siege.** unabr. ed. Kathryn Lasky. Read by Pamela Garelick. (Running Time: 5 hrs.). (Guardians of Ga'Hoole Ser.: Bk. 4). 2010. audio compact disk 19.95 (978-1-4417-5538-4(1)) Blckstn Audio.

Siege. unabr. ed. Kathryn Lasky. Read by Pamela Garelick. (Running Time: 5 hrs.). (Guardians of Ga'Hoole Ser.: Bk. 4). (gr. 4-7). 2010. audio compact disk 19.95 (978-1-4332-0573-6(4)) Blckstn Audio.

Siege. unabr. ed. Stephen White. Read by Dick Hill. (Running Time: 12 hrs.). (Dr. Alan Gregory Ser.). 2009. 24.99 (978-1-4233-9036-7(9), 9781423390367, Brilliance MP3); 24.99 (978-1-4233-9038-1(5), 9781423390381, BAD); 39.97 (978-1-4233-9037-4(7), 9781423390374, Brlnc Audio MP3 Lib); 39.97 (978-1-4233-9039-8(3), 9781423390398, BADLE); audio compact disk 38.99 (978-1-4233-9034-3(2), 9781423390343, Bril Audio CD Unabri); audio compact disk 99.97 (978-1-4233-9035-0(0), 9781423390350, BriAudCD Unabrid) Brilliance Audio.

Siege: Malta 1940-1943. unabr. collector's ed. Ernle Bradford. Read by Walter Zimmerman. 8 cass. (Running Time: 12 hrs.). 1988. 64.00 (978-0-7366-1460-3(5), 2340) Books on Tape.
The siege of Malta began in June 1940 & lasted until the end of 1942, making it the longest in the history of warfare. Day & night the tiny island of Malta (21 miles long, 12 miles wide) was the most heavily bombed place on earth.

Siege & Fall of Troy. unabr. ed. Robert Graves. Read by David Case. 6 cass. (Running Time: 1 hr. per cass.). 1992. 36.00 set. (3026); Rental 14.50 set. (3026) Books on Tape.
Helen's beauty, Odysseus' cunning, Achilles' vulnerable heel are all proverbial. As well known as the incidents & characters are, however, Robert Graves' new telling brings fresh life to this story of the Trojan War.

Siege & Fall of Troy & Greek Gods & Heroes. unabr. collector's ed. Robert Graves. Read by David Case. 6 cass. (Running Time: 6 hrs.). (J). 1992. 36.00 (978-0-7366-2236-3(5), 3026) Books on Tape.
In "The Siege & Fall of Troy," Robert Graves' new telling brings fresh life to the story of the Trojan War. "Greek Gods & Heroes" recounts the days when gods dwelt on Mount Olympus.

Siege at Peking. unabr. collector's ed. Peter Fleming. Read by David Case. 7 cass. (Running Time: 10 hrs. 30 min.). 1988. 56.00 (978-0-7366-1299-9(8), 2206) Books on Tape.
On June 20, 1900 the foreign legations at Peking were attacked by Boxers & Imperial Chinese troops, with the equivocal support of the Empress Dowager, Tz'u Hsi. The ensuing siege was to last for 55 days, & the news of it shook the world.

Siege of Krishnapur. abr. ed. J. G. Farrell. Narrated by Tim Pigott-Smith. (Running Time: 5 hrs. 0 mins. 0 sec.). (ENG.). 2009. audio compact disk 26.95 (978-1-934997-48-2(X)) Pub: CSAWord. Dist(s): PerseuPGW

Siege of London. Read by Jonathan Epstein. Prod. by Jason Brown. Berkshire Visual Enterprises. (ENG.). 2007. audio compact disk 24.50 (978-0-9663401-9-8(1)) BMA Studios.

Siege of Mecca: The Forgotten Uprising in Islam's Holiest Shrine & the Birth of Al-Qaeda. unabr. ed. Yaroslav Trofimov. Narrated by Todd McLaren. (Running Time: 8 hrs. 30 mins. 0 sec.). (ENG.). 2007. audio compact disk 34.99 (978-1-4001-0534-2(X)) Pub: Tantor Media. Dist(s): IngramPubServ

Siege of Mecca: The Forgotten Uprising in Islam's Holiest Shrine & the Birth of Al-Qaeda. unabr. ed. Yaroslav Trofimov. Narrated by Todd McLaren. (Running Time: 8 hrs. 30 mins. 0 sec.). 2007. audio compact disk 24.99 (978-1-4001-5534-7(7)); audio compact disk 69.99 (978-1-4001-3534-9(6)) Pub: Tantor Media. Dist(s): IngramPubServ

Siege of Mecca: The Forgotten Uprising in Islam's Holiest Shrine & the Birth of Al Qaeda. unabr. ed. Yaroslav Trofimov. Read by Todd McLaren. (YA). 2008. 59.99 (978-1-60514-676-8(5)) Find a World.

Siege of the Villa Lipp. unabr. collector's ed. Eric Ambler. Read by Richard Brown. 9 cass. (Running Time: 13 hrs. 30 min.). 1989. 72.00 (978-0-7366-1622-5(5), 2482) Books on Tape.
In the shadowy areas of international law, able criminals work hard at figuring loopholes. One such wheeler-dealer is Paul Firman. He pursues his own ends in a quiet, unobtrusive way. Why would anyone want to bother about him? But he is unaware that an obsessive academician, Professor Krom, has stumbled on Firman's activities & is determined to expose him. Two of Krom's colleagues are on hand as witnesses as Krom prepares to confront Firman. But none have bargained with a third party threatening to put a permanent stop to the encounter. The booby-trapped grounds of the Mediterranean Villa Lipp, a hovering motor cruiser, a sudden attack - Krom is prepared for none of these. But Firman, always cool & self-possessed, responds with force & decision, & in the end pulls Krom's chestnuts out of the fire.

Siege of Vicksburg. unabr. collector's ed. Richard Wheeler. Read by Dick Estell. 7 cass. (Running Time: 10 hrs. 30 min.). 1995. 56.00 (978-0-7366-3033-7(3), 3715) Books on Tape.
When the Union Army took Vicksburg after a seven-month siege, it doomed the Confederacy.

Siegfried: The Hero As an Adult Child. Jean S. Bolen. Read by Jean Shinoda Bolen. 1 cass. (Running Time: 50 min.). 1993. 9.95 (978-0-7822-0422-3(8), 506-3) C G Jung IL.
Part three of the set The Ring of Power: A Jungian Understanding of Wagner's Ring Cycle.

Siegfried von Gegesack: Tanja. 2 cass. (GER.). 24.95 Set. (SGE350) J Norton Pubs.

Siempre Adelante: A Brief Course for Intermediate Spanish. Jorge H. Cubillos. 2 cass. (Running Time: 3 hrs.l). 2001. 24.50 (978-0-8384-0558-1(4)) Heinle.
A one-semester Intermediate Spanish program that will benefit both students preparing for upper-level work and students who are completing their study in Spanish.

Siena Summer, Set. unabr. ed. Teresa Crane. Read by Jan Francis. 8 cass. 1999. 69.95 (978-0-7540-0361-8(2), CAB1784) AudioGO.
While Kit Enever recuperates from a leg wound as world War I draws to a close, Isobel Brookes captivates & ensnares him. A decade later, Isobel invites her sister Poppy to come to Siena. When Poppy arrives, she finds a disturbing undercurrent in Isobel & Kit's relationship & an equally disturbing third party on the scene.

Sierra Triumph. Scripts. Dana Fuller Ross, pseud. 5 CDs. (Running Time: 6 hrs.). (Holts, an American Dynasty Ser.: Vol. 6). 2005. 30.00 (978-1-58943-025-9(5)) Am Pubng Inc.
Frank Blake, seventeen with a wanderlust, finds himself in the California oil fields as a labor strike threatens. Tim Holt, falls for a suffragist bent on securing the right to vote for women. The nation is changing, in ferment, and it will take people willing to seize the future to preserve its ideals - people like the Holts.

***Sierra's Homecoming.** unabr. ed. Linda Lael Miller. Read by Nellie Chalfant. (Running Time: 7 hrs.). (McKettrick Ser.). 2010. 19.99 (978-1-4418-7109-1(8), 9781441871091, Brilliance MP3); 39.97 (978-1-4418-7111-4(X), 9781441871114, BADLE); 39.97 (978-1-4418-7110-7(1), 9781441871107, Brinc Audio MP3 Lib); audio compact disk 19.99 (978-1-4418-7107-7(1), 9781441871077, Bril Audio CD Unabri); audio compact disk 69.97 (978-1-4418-7108-4(X), 9781441871084, BriAudCD Unabrid) Brilliance Audio.

Sieste Assassinee. l.t. ed. Philippe Delerm. (French Ser.). 2001. bk. 30.99 (978-2-84011-411-6(9)) Pub: UlverLrgPrint GBR. Dist(s): Ulverscroft US

Siete Ahorcados. abr. ed. Leonidas Nikolaievich Andreiev. Tr. by G. Portnof from RUS. (SPA.). 2007. audio compact disk 17.00 (978-958-8218-95-3(0)) YoYoMusic.

Siete Claves para Tener un Matrimonio Feliz. Rafael Ayala. 2 cass. (Running Time: 2 hrs.).Tr. of Seven Keys to a Happy Marriage. (SPA.). 2003. 20.00 (978-1-931059-13-8(6)) Taller del Exito.
Allows you to see your marriage from a new perspective. By listening and practicing these important tips, your married life will improve in the following areas: education of your children, family goals, sexuality, relationship with God, finances, health and affective relationships with your spouse.

Siete Habitos de las Familias Altamente Efectivas. Stephen R. Covey. 4 cass. (Running Time: 4 hrs.). (SPA.). 2002. bk. 20.95 (978-970-05-1016-3(6)) Taller del Exito.
Shows how to balance individual and family needs.

Siete Habitos de las Personas Altamente Eficaces. abr. ed. Stephen R. Covey. 1 CD. (Running Time: 13 hrs. 0 mins. 0 sec.).Tr. of Seven Habits of Highly Effective People. (SPA & ENG.). 2004. audio compact disk 19.95 (978-0-7435-3852-7(8), Sound Ideas) Pub: S&S Audio. Dist(s): S and S Inc

Siete Leyes Espirituales del Exito. Deepak Chopra. 1 cass. (Running Time: 1 hr. 30 mins.).Tr. of Seven Spiritual Laws of Success. (SPA.). 2001. Astran.

Siete Leyes Espirituales del Exito. Deepak Chopra. 2 cass. (Running Time: 2 hrs.).Tr. of Seven Spiritual Laws of Success. (SPA.). 2002. (978-968-5163-05-7(7)) Taller del Exito.
Shatters the myth that success is the result of hard work, exacting plans, or driving ambition.

Sift & Splash: Sand & Water Play. 1 cass. (Running Time: 1 hr.). (J). 2001. 10.95 (KUB 9000C); audio compact disk 14.95 (KUB 9000CD) Kimbo Educ.
Add a musical blast to one of kids' favorite pastimes. Sift, Shape, Pour & Scoop, Measure, Mix & more! 14 songs include Finger Fish, Float or Sink, Sandbox & more. Abundant learning opportunities.

Sigan la Bandera. Contrib. by Donna Pena. 2006. audio compact disk 17.00 (978-5-557-94936-1(4)) OR Catholic.

Sight for Sore Eyes. Ruth Rendell. Read by Donada Peters. 9 cass. (Running Time: 13 hrs.). 2000. 34.95 (978-0-7366-4591-1(8)) Books on Tape.
When the lives of a fragile girl, an aging beauty and a sociopathic killer converge, the effect is surprising, harrowing and unforgettable.

Sight for Sore Eyes. collector's unabr. ed. Ruth Rendell. Read by Donada Peters. 10 CDs. (Running Time: 10 hrs.). 2000. audio compact disk 80.00 (978-0-7366-5174-5(8)) Books on Tape.
Francine, a child, has been scolded & sent to her room. Peeking downstairs she witnesses the brutal killing of her mother. The experience has left her mute; it will be nine months until Francine can speak & she will be unable to identify the killer. Harriet, an aging beauty, scans the local newspapers for handymen to perform odd jobs around the house, including services in the bedroom. A boy, Teddy, born to barely socialized parents, grows into a physically beautiful but sociopathic young man who discovers that killing is an easy way to get what he wants. When these three lives converge, the effect is surprising, harrowing & unforgettable.

Sight for Sore Eyes. unabr. ed. Ruth Rendell. Narrated by Jenny Sterlin. 11 cass. (Running Time: 15 hrs. 45 mins.). 1999. 91.00 (978-0-7887-2505-0(X), 95577E7) Recorded Bks.
A tale of murder & redemption. This probes the depths of the human psyche to the relationship between two psychologically damaged, but physically beautiful young people.

Sight for Sore Eyes. unabr. collector's ed. Ruth Rendell. Read by Donada Peters. 9 cass. (Running Time: 13 hrs. 30 min.). 1999. 72.00 (978-0-7366-4504-1(7), 4939) Books on Tape.
Francine, just a child, witnesses the brutal murder of her mother. The experience has left her mute. It will be nine months until Francine can speak & she will be unable to identify the killer. Harriet, an aging beauty married to an older man, scans the local newspapers for handymen to perform services around the house & in her bedroom. A boy, Teddy, born to barely socialized parents, grows into a physically beautifully but sociopathic young man who discovers killing is an easy way to get what he wants.

Sight for Sore Eyes, Set. abr. ed. Ruth Rendell. Read by Tim Pigott-Smith. 2 cass. 1999. 18.00 (FS9-43377) Highsmith.

Sight of the Stars. unabr. ed. Belva Plain. 7 cass. (Running Time: 10 hrs. 30 min.). 2003. 81.00 (978-0-7366-9694-4(6)) Books on Tape.

Sight Singing Made Simple. David Bauguess. (Classroom Methods Ser.). 1995. audio compact disk 14.95 (978-0-7935-9973-8(3), HL47819111) H Leonard.

Sight Unseen. unabr. ed. Donald Margulies. 2 CDs. (Running Time: 1 hr. 52 mins.). 2005. audio compact disk 25.95 (978-1-58081-274-0(0), CDTPT185) Pub: L A Theatre. Dist(s): NetLibrary CO
The milieu is the art world, and Pulitzer Prize-winning playwright Donald Margulies takes us on a rocky backward and forward journey through the career, values, and loves of a now-famous painter. It's about the art scene, the loss of love, and the price of assimilation-both ethnic and intellectual-in an America where authenticity often has little to do with an artist's, or anyone's rise to the top.

Sights & Sounds Creation. Contrib. by J. Daniel Smith. (Running Time: 3300 sec.). (ENG.). 2008. audio compact disk 16.99 (978-5-557-48308-7(X), Brentwood-Benson Music) Brentwood Music.

Sights & Sounds Creation: Alto. Contrib. by J. Daniel Smith. 2008. audio compact disk 5.00 (978-5-557-48303-2(9), Brentwood-Benson Music) Brentwood Music.

Sights & Sounds Creation: Bass. Contrib. by J. Daniel Smith. 2008. audio compact disk 5.00 (978-5-557-48301-8(2), Brentwood-Benson Music) Brentwood Music.

Sights & Sounds Creation: Soprano. Contrib. by J. Daniel Smith. 2008. audio compact disk 5.00 (978-5-557-48304-9(7), Brentwood-Benson Music) Brentwood Music.

Sights & Sounds Creation: Tenor. Contrib. by J. Daniel Smith. 2008. audio compact disk 5.00 (978-5-557-48302-5(0), Brentwood-Benson Music) Brentwood Music.

Sights & Sounds Creation: Your Visual Choir Experience. Contrib. by Johnathan Crumpton et al. Prod. by J. Daniel Smith. (ENG.). 2008. audio compact disk 90.00 (978-5-557-48307-0(1), Brentwood-Benson Music) Brentwood Music.

Sights Unseen. Kaye Gibbons. 2004. 10.95 (978-0-7435-4603-4(2)) Pub: S&S Audio. Dist(s): S and S Inc

Sights Unseen. unabr. ed. Kaye Gibbons. Read by Kate Fleming. 4 vols. (Running Time: 6 Hrs.). 2000. bk. 39.95 (978-0-7927-2412-4(7), CSL 301, Chivers Sound Lib) AudioGO.
An unforgettable tale of unconditional love & of a Southern family's desperate search for normalcy in the midst of madness.

Sights Unseen. unabr. ed. Kaye Gibbons. Read by Kate Fleming. 6 CDs. (Running Time: 9 hrs.). 2001. audio compact disk 64.95 (978-0-7927-9955-9(0), SLD 006, Chivers Sound Lib) AudioGO.
Sights Unseen is an unforgettable tale of unconditional love & of a Southern family's desperate search for normalcy in the midst of madness.

Sigma Protocol. Robert Ludlum. Read by Jeff Harding. 16 cass. (Sound Ser.). (J). 2002. 104.95 (978-1-84283-204-2(2)) Pub: ISIS Lrg Prnt GBR. Dist(s): Ulverscroft US

Sigma Protocol. Robert Ludlum. Narrated by Paul Michael. 17 CDs. (Running Time: 19 hrs. 45 mins.). audio compact disk 160.00 (978-1-4025-2076-1(X)) Recorded Bks.

Sigma Protocol. Robert Ludlum. Narrated by Paul Michael. 14 cass. (Running Time: 19 hrs. 45 mins.). 2001. 144.00 (978-1-4025-0784-7(4), 96915) Recorded Bks.
A chance encounter with an old friend plunges a wealthy businessman into a terrifying maze of murder, deception and secret CIA codes.

Sigma Protocol. abr. ed. Robert Ludlum. Read by Paul Michael. 6 CDs. (Running Time: 6 hrs. 0 mins. 0 sec.). (ENG.). 2008. audio compact disk 14.95 (978-1-4272-0486-8(1)) Pub: Macmill Audio. Dist(s): Macmillan

Sigma Protocol, Pt. 1. Robert Ludlum. Read by Michael Prichard. 8 cass. (Running Time: 12 hrs.). 2001. 64.00 (978-0-7366-8076-9(4)) Books on Tape.
Ben Hartman, scion of a financial empire, encounters a childhood friend on what should be a relaxing vacation in Switzerland. Astonishingly, the friend tries to shoot him, and ends up killing himself and everyone except Ben. At the same time, DOJ Field Agent Anna Navarro has commenced her investigation on a suspicious series of worldwide killings of elderly men, linked only by an old OSS file codenamed Sigma. Ben and Anna's paths intersect, and they realize that behind Sigma lies a series of earth-shattering truths about themselves, their families, and world history. They must fight to save not only their own lives, but also the future of the world.

Sigma Protocol, Pt. 2. unabr. ed. Robert Ludlum. Read by Michael Prichard. 8 cass. (Running Time: 12 hrs.). 2001. 64.00 (978-0-7366-8375-3(5)) Books on Tape.

Sigmund Freud. 1 cass. (Running Time: 1 hr. 11 min.). (History Maker Ser.). 10.95 (41013) J Norton Pubs.
The outline of Sigmund Freuds' life & work are traced, showing how the man's personality & experiences affected the course of his research.

Sigmund Freud: A Concise Biography. unabr. ed. Stephen Wilson. Read by Martyn Read. 2 cass. (Running Time: 2 hrs. 15 min.). (Pocket Biography Ser.). 1998. 24.95 (978-0-7531-0332-6(X), 980517) Pub: ISIS Audio GBR. Dist(s): Ulverscroft US
The founder of psychoanalysis whose name has become a landmark in cultural history. His theories concerning sexuality, memory, dreams, self-deception & the unconscious mind created a furore when first advanced & have never ceased to invite controversy. In recent times, both the man & the discipline he invented - psychoanalysis - have come under reevaluation (& attack) on both sides of the Atlantic. This depicts his life & ideas, from birth above a blacksmith's forge to his death in 1939 in London.

Sigmund Freud: Psychoanalytic Theory. Robert Stone. 1 cass. 1983. 10.00 (978-0-938137-06-1(9)) Listen & Learn.
Analyzes the structure of personality: the Id, Ego & Superego, personality development, anxiety, instinct, the unconscious mind, the psychosexual stages of development, the mechanisms of defense, psychic energy, dream interpretation.

Sign. Raymond Khoury. (Running Time: 17 hrs.). (ENG.). (gr. 12 up). 2009. audio compact disk 39.95 (978-0-14-314421-2(9), PengAudBks) Penguin Grp USA.

Sign Here, John Hancock. 2004. pap. bk. 32.75 (978-1-55592-360-0(7)) Weston Woods.

Sign Language Studies 1972-1993, Vol. 1-81. Ed. by William C. Stokoe. 2004. audio compact disk 39.95 (978-1-56368-301-5(6)) Gallaudet Univ Pr.

Sign of Chaos. Roger Zelazny. Read by Roger Zelazny. 2 vols. (Chronicles of Amber: Bk. 8). 2003. (978-1-58807-530-7(3)) Am Pubng Inc.

Sign of Chaos. Roger Zelazny. Read by Roger Zelazny. 2 vols. (Chronicles of Amber: Bk. 8). 2004. audio compact disk 25.00 (978-1-58807-260-3(6)); audio compact disk (978-1-58807-691-5(1)) Am Pubng Inc.

Sign of Chaos. abr. ed. Roger Zelazny. 2 cass. (Running Time: 3 hrs.). (Chronicles of Amber: Bk. 8). 2003. 18.00 (978-1-58807-133-0(2)) Am Pubng Inc.
The epic story of the royal family of Amber enters an exciting new chapter as Merlin, son of Prince Corwin, pursues his noble destiny against a shifting panorama of shadow worlds and deadly intrigue, powerful computers, and magic gone out of control. A violent vendetta, renegade sorcery, and whirlwind adventure lead Merlin to a monumental confrontation at the Keep of the Four Worlds, where astonishing secrets and mysterious identities will at last be revealed.

Sign of Christmas Is a Star. Kenneth Wapnick. 1 CD. (Running Time: 2 hrs. 9 mins. 36 secs.). 2007. 10.00 (978-1-59142-320-1(1), 3m46); audio compact disk 13.00 (978-1-59142-319-5(8), CD46) Foun Miracles.

***Sign of Four.** Arthur Conan Doyle. Narrated by Flo Gibson. (ENG.). 2010. audio compact disk 19.95 (978-1-60646-140-2(0)) Audio Bk Con.

Sign of Four. Arthur Conan Doyle. Narrated by Walter Covell. (Running Time: 4 hrs.). 1979. 22.95 (978-1-59912-873-3(X)) Iofy Corp.

Sign of Four. Arthur Conan Doyle. Read by David Timson. 2003. pap. bk. 22.98 (978-962-634-796-6(1)); pap. bk. 28.98 (978-962-634-296-1(X), Naxos AudioBooks) Naxos.
Mary Morstan comes to Holmes in the hope that he will be able to solve a mystery. Ten years earlier her father, Captain Arthur Morstan, had returned to London on leave from his regiment in India where it is said that he and one Thadeus Sholto, "came into possession of a considerable treasure." By the time his daughter arrived at his hotel, he had vanished without a trace.

Sign of Four. unabr. ed. Arthur Conan Doyle. Narrated by Flo Gibson. 3 cass. (Running Time: 4 hrs. 30 mins.). 2003. 16.95 (978-1-55685-738-6(1)) Audio Bk Con.
Master sleuth Sherlock Holmes and Dr. Watson pursue a murderer and search for missing treasure in the Far East.

Sign of Four. unabr. ed. Arthur Conan Doyle. Read by Walter Covell. 5 cass. (Running Time: 5 hrs.). 2001. 24.95 (978-0-7366-6805-7(5)) Books on Tape.
With his customary skill & by close observations, Holmes solves the mystery of the Indian treasure.

***Sign of Four.** unabr. ed. Arthur Conan Doyle. (Running Time: 5 hrs.). 2010. 14.99 (978-1-4418-3944-2(5), 9781441839442, BAD); 49.97 (978-1-4418-3945-9(3), 9781441839459, BADLE) Brilliance Audio.

Sign of Four. unabr. ed. Arthur Conan Doyle. Read by Michael Page. (Running Time: 4 hrs.). 2010. audio compact disk 14.99 (978-1-4418-3920-6(8), 9781441839206, Bril Audio CD Unabri) Brilliance Audio.

***Sign of Four.** unabr. ed. Arthur Conan Doyle. Read by Michael Page. (Running Time: 4 hrs.). 2010. 49.97 (978-1-4418-3943-5(7), 9781441839435, Brinc Audio MP3 Lib); 14.99 (978-1-4418-3942-8(9), 9781441839428, Brilliance MP3); audio compact disk 49.97 (978-1-4418-3941-1(0), 9781441839411, BriAudCD Unabrid) Brilliance Audio.

Sign of Four. unabr. ed. Arthur Conan Doyle. Read by Walter Covell. 3 cass. (Running Time: 4 hrs.). Dramatization. 1980. 18.00 (C-21) Jimcin Record.
In "The Sign of the Four," Sherlock Holmes solves the mystery of the Indian treasure for Miss Mary Marston.

Sign of Four. unabr. ed. Arthur Conan Doyle. Narrated by Patrick Tull. 3 cass. (Running Time: 4 hrs. 30 mins.). (Sherlock Holmes Mystery Ser.). 1986. 26.00 (978-1-55690-477-6(0), 86240E7) Recorded Bks.
Sherlock Holmes & Dr. Watson stalk mysterious killers from the East.

Sign of Four. unabr. ed. Arthur Conan Doyle. Narrated by Simon Prebble. (Running Time: 5 hrs. 0 mins. 0 sec.). (ENG.). 2009. 19.99 (978-1-4001-6514-8(8)); 13.99 (978-1-4001-8514-6(9)); audio compact disk 17.99 (978-1-4001-1514-3(0)); audio compact disk 45.99 (978-1-4001-4514-0(7)) Pub: Tantor Media. Dist(s): IngramPubServ

Sign of Four. unabr. collector's ed. Arthur Conan Doyle. Read by Walter Covell. 5 cass. (Running Time: 5 hrs.). (J). 1983. 30.00 (978-0-7366-3966-8(7), 9508) Books on Tape.
Published in 1889, Holmes solves the mystery of the Indian treasure & strengthens his hold on our imagination.

Sign of Four, Set. unabr. ed. Arthur Conan Doyle. Read by Walter Covell. 3 cass. 1999. 23.95 (FS9-34235) Highsmith.

Sign of Seven CD Collection: Blood Brothers; The Hollow; The Pagan Stone. abr. ed. Nora Roberts. (Running Time: 18 hrs.). (Sign of Seven Trilogy: Bks. 1-3). 2009. audio compact disk 34.99 (978-1-4233-9730-4(4), 9781423397304, BACD) Brilliance Audio.

Sign of the Beaver. Elizabeth George Speare. Read by Greg Schaffert. 2 cass. (Running Time: 3 hrs.). (J). 2000. 18.00 (978-0-7366-9107-9(3)) Books on Tape.
Alone in the Maine wilderness, 12-year-old Matt must decide if he should wait for his father's return or start a new life with the Beaver tribe.

Sign of the Beaver. Elizabeth George Speare. 2 cass. (J). 13.58 Set, blisterpack. (BYA 950) NewSound.
Until the day his father returns to their cabin in the Maine wilderness, 12-year-old Matt must try to survive on his own.

Sign of the Beaver. unabr. ed. Elizabeth George Speare. Read by Greg Schaffert. 2 cass. (Running Time: 3 hrs.). (J). (gr. 1-8). 1999. 23.00 (LL 0112, Chivers Child Audio) AudioGO.

Sign of the Beaver. unabr. ed. Elizabeth George Speare. Read by Greg Schaffert. 2 vols. (Running Time: 3 hrs. 9 mins.). (J). (gr. 4-7). 1998. pap. bk. 29.00 (978-0-8072-7960-1(9), YA950 SP, Listening Lib); 23.00 (978-0-8072-7959-5(5), JD91R, Listening Lib) Random Audio Pubg.
The friendship between two boys in the Maine wilderness.

Sign of the Beaver. unabr. ed. Elizabeth George Speare. Read by Greg Schaffert. (Running Time: 3 hrs. 9 mins.). (ENG.). (J). (gr. 5). 2004. audio compact disk 14.99 (978-1-4000-8497-5(0), Listening Lib) Pub: Random Audio Pubg. Dist(s): Random

Sign of the Beaver, Set. unabr. ed. Elizabeth George Speare. Read by Greg Schaffert. 2 cass. (YA). 1999. 16.98 (FS9-34542) Highsmith.

Sign of the Book. unabr. ed. John Dunning. Read by George Guidall. 9 CDs. (Running Time: 10 hrs.). (Cliff Janeway Novel Ser.). 2005. audio compact disk 99.75 (978-1-4193-4076-5(X)); 69.75 (978-1-4193-4074-1(3)) Recorded Bks.
Dunning's fourth Cliff Janeway novel finds the Denver antiquarian book dealer acting as investigator for criminal defense attorney Erin D'Angelo, his lover. Erin's former boyfriend, Bobby Marshall, has been murdered in the small town of Paradise, CO, and his wife, Laura, once Erin's best friend, has been charged. Laura's having stolen Bobby from Erin is only one of several complications. In addition, Jerry, the Marshall's adopted son, who has never spoken, may have witnessed the killing, while the local deputy sheriff does everything he can to impede Cliff's investigation, Cliff's expertise comes into play when he discovers Bobby's hugh collection of books signed by celebrities.

Sign of the Book. unabr. ed. John Dunning. (Cliff Janeway Novel Ser.). 2005. audio compact disk 39.99 (978-1-4193-3857-1(9)) Recorded Bks.

Sign of the Cross. unabr. ed. Chris Kuzneski. Read by Dick Hill. 1 MP3-CD. (Running Time: 16 hrs.). (Payne & Jones Ser.: Bk. 2). 2009. 24.99 (978-1-4233-8659-9(0), 9781423386599, Brilliance MP3); 39.97 (978-1-4233-8660-5(4), 9781423386605, Brinc Audio MP3 Lib); 39.97 (978-1-4233-8662-9(0), 9781423386629, BADLE); 24.99 (978-1-4233-8661-2(2), 9781423386612, BAD); audio compact disk 92.97 (978-1-4233-8658-2(2), 9781423386582, BriAudCD Unabrid); audio compact disk 29.99 (978-1-4233-8657-5(4), 9781423386575) Brilliance Audio.

***Sign of the Four.** unabr. ed. Arthur Conan Doyle. Read by Ralph Cosham. (Running Time: 5 hrs. 30 mins.). 2010. 29.95 (978-1-4417-3905-6(X)); 34.95 (978-1-4417-3901-8(7)); audio compact disk 55.00 (978-1-4417-3902-5(5)) Blckstn Audio.

Sign of the Salamander. Eugenia Miller. Read by Talmadge Ragan. Engineer Worth Keeter. Naz Arandi. (ENG.). (J). 2007. (978-0-9725297-0-9(5)) Blue Kiss.

Sign of the Unicorn. Roger Zelazny. Read by Roger Zelazny. 2 vols. (Chronicles of Amber: Bk. 3). 2002. (978-1-58807-510-9(9)) Am Pubng Inc.

Sign of the Unicorn. Roger Zelazny. Read by Roger Zelazny. 2 vols. (Chronicles of Amber: Bk. 3). 2003. audio compact disk 25.00 (978-1-58807-255-9(X)); audio compact disk (978-1-58807-686-1(5)) Am Pubng Inc.

Sign of the Unicorn. abr. ed. Roger Zelazny. Read by Roger Zelazny. 2 vols. (Running Time: 3 hrs.). (Chronicles of Amber: Bk. 3). 2002. 18.00 (978-1-58807-128-6(6)) Am Pubng Inc.
Amber is the one real world, of which all others - including our own Earth - are but Shadows. A traitor has revealed the royal family's greatest secret: the ability to manipulate Shadow and travel through all possible worlds, enabling a plot towards Amber's destruction. Corwin, Prince of the Blood, must risk everything in a deadly assault on evil's stronghold. Now, beset by demonic powers beyond imagination and betrayed by a bizarre conspiracy among his own kin, Corwin walks a perilous path toward ultimate knowledge and terrifying discovery.

Sign, Symbol & Code. Umberto Eco. 2 cass. (Running Time: 2 hrs. 30 min.). 1996. 17.95 (978-1-879557-37-6(1)) Audio Scholar.
Theoretical writings offer the listener a survey and analysis of semiotic theories from Aristotle to Lacan, threading its way through the Scriptures, Kabbalistic literature, Romanticism, Jungian symbolism, the genetic code and more.

Signal see De Maupassant Short Stories

Signal - Close Action! unabr. ed. Alexander Kent, pseud. Read by Michael Jayston. 8 cass. (Richard Bolitho Ser.: Bk. 12). 2005. 69.95 (978-0-7927-3502-1(1), CSL 766); audio compact disk 94.95 (978-0-7927-3503-8(X), SLD 766) AudioGO.

Signal Zero. unabr. ed. George L. Kirkham. Read by Dan Lazar. 7 cass. (Running Time: 7 hrs.). 1977. 42.00 (978-0-7366-0089-7(2), 1097) Books on Tape.
This gives a new comprehension of police problems.

Signale, Systeme und Klangsynthese: Grundlagen der Computermusik. Martin Neukom. 2 vols. (Zurcher Musikstudien. Forschung und Entwicklung an der Hmt Zurich Ser.). (GER.). 2003. bk. 96.95 (978-3-03910-125-2(0)) Pub: P Lang CHE. Dist(s): P Lang Pubng

Signalman see Classic Ghost Stories, Vol. 1, A Collection

Signalman. unabr. ed. Charles Dickens. Read by Walter Covell. 1 cass. (Running Time: 58 min.). Dramatization. 1980. 7.95 (N-39) Jimcin Record.
Restless spirits haunt the world of men.

Signature. Contrib. by Moya Brennan. 2007. audio compact disk 13.99 (978-5-557-59355-7(1)) Pt of Grace Ent.

Signature of God. Grant R. Jeffrey. 2 cass. 1997. 15.99 Set. (978-0-921714-29-3(7)) Pub: Fon3tier Res CAN. Dist(s): Spring Arbor Dist
Bible, Prophecies.

***Signature of God: Conclusive Proof That Every Teaching, Every Command, Every Promise in the Bible Is True.** unabr. ed. Grant R. Jeffrey. Narrated by Grant R. Jeffrey. (Running Time: 11 hrs. 41 mins. 26 sec.). (ENG.). 2010. 20.99 (978-1-60814-679-6(0)); audio compact disk 29.99 (978-1-59859-728-8(0)) Oasis Audio.

Signature Series, Vol. 1. Music by Ali Akbar Khan. 1 cass. 1997. (L97001); audio compact disk (CD L97001) Multi-Cultural Bks.

Signature Series, Vol. 2. Music by Ali Akbar Khan. 1 cass. 1997. (L97002); audio compact disk (CD L97002) Multi-Cultural Bks.

Signature Series, Vol. 3. Music by Ali Akbar Khan. 1 cass. 1997. (L97003); audio compact disk (CD L97003) Multi-Cultural Bks.

Signature Series, Vol. 4. Music by Ali Akbar Khan. 1 cass. 1997. (L97004); audio compact disk (CD L97004) Multi-Cultural Bks.

Signature Songs: Glad the Band. Perf. by Glad the Band. 1 CD. (Running Time: 60 mins.). 2000. audio compact disk 9.99 (978-0-7601-3472-6(3), SO33210) Pub: Brentwood Music. Dist(s): Provident Mus Dist
Songs include: "Be Ye Glad," "Good News," "Faith Makes," "Color Outside the Lines," "Holy Fire" & more.

Signature Songs: Michael O'Brien. Perf. by Michael O'Brien. 1 CD. (Running Time: 60 mins.). 2000. audio compact disk 9.99 (978-0-7601-3476-4(6), SO33210) Pub: Brentwood Music. Dist(s): Provident Mus Dist
Songs include: "Somebody Cares," "If Ever I Forget," "Higher & Higher," "Let There Be Light," "Christ in Me" & more.

Signature Songs: Twila Paris. Perf. by Twila Paris. 1 CD. (Running Time: 60 mins.). 2000. audio compact disk 9.99 (978-0-7601-3474-0(X), SO33210) Pub: Brentwood Music. Dist(s): Provident Mus Dist
Songs include: "The Warrior Is a Child," "We Bow Down," "We Will Glorify," "Do I Trust You," "Clearer Vision" & more.

Signed, Sealed, & Committed, Vol. 29. AIO Team Staff. Prod. by Focus on the Family Staff. 4 CDs. (Running Time: 6 hrs.). Dramatization. (Adventures in Odyssey Ser.). (ENG.). (J). (gr. 3-7). 1998. audio compact disk 24.99 (978-1-56179-623-6(9)) Pub: Focus Family. Dist(s): Tyndale Hse

Signed, Sealed, Delivered, I'm Yours - ShowTrax. Arranged by Alan Billingsley. 1 CD. (Running Time: 5 mins.). 2000. audio compact disk 19.95 (08201224) H Leonard.
The 1970 pop hit by Stevie Wonder in a full-blown show choir setting. Sensational!.

Significance - Death of a Longed for Child, Vol. 1. Doug Manning. 1 cass. (Running Time: 20 min.). 1991. 9.95 (978-1-892785-14-5(5)) In-Sight Bks Inc.
A miscarriage or still birth is a lonely type of grief. Author uses his insight & warmth to help the family begin to heal after such a loss.

Significance of Cultural-Ethical Issues in Moral Decision Making. 1 cass. (Care Cassettes Ser.: Vol. 21, No. 4). 1994. 10.80 Assn Prof Chaplains.

Significance of Kriya Yoga for the Modern Age. Kriyananda, pseud. 1 cass. (Running Time: 75 min.). 9.95 (ST-14) Crystal Clarity.
Topics include: how the practice of Kriya Yoga will usher in an age that will see major changes in the arts, politics, business & how people live; yoga teachings in the Bible.

Significance of Tat Twam Asi. (206) Yoga Res Foun.

Significance of Tat Twam Asi. Swami Jyotirmayananda. 1 cass. (Running Time: 1 hr.). 1990. 12.99 Yoga Res Foun.

Significance of the Goldwater Campaign. Ayn Rand. 1 cass. (Running Time: 50 min.). 1993. 12.95 (978-1-56114-337-5(5), AR50C) Second Renaissance.

Significance of the Synod of Bishops for Rebirth of Religious Life. John J. O'Connor. 1 cass. (National Meeting of the Institute, 1995 Ser.). 4.00 (95N1) IRL Chicago.

Significant Conversations: NACADA Webinar Series 19: the Art & Science of Communication in Transformational Advising. Featuring Jose Rodriguez. (ENG.). 2008. audio compact disk 140.00 (978-1-935140-61-0(2)) Nat Acad Adv.

Significant Experience. unabr. ed. Gwyn Griffin. Read by Wolfram Kandinsky. 3 cass. (Running Time: 3 hrs.). 1983. 18.00 (978-0-7366-0619-6(X), 1581) Books on Tape.
An ingenious young cadet at a British regimental training facility in Egypt becomes the victim of a brutal disciplinary action inflicted by officers of the old school.

***Significant Others.** abr. ed. Armistead Maupin. Read by Armistead Maupin. (ENG.). 2009. (978-0-06-197739-8(X), Harper Audio); (978-0-06-197738-1(1), Harper Audio) HarperCollins Pubs.

Significant Past. A Challenging Future: Hope Beyond the Hurt. 2004. audio compact disk 7.00 (978-1-57972-589-1(9)) Insight Living.

***Significant Seven.** unabr. ed. John McEvoy. (Running Time: 13 hrs. 0 mins.). (Jack Doyle Mysteries Ser.). 2010. 29.95 (978-1-4417-3227-9(6)); 54.95 (978-1-4417-3223-1(3)); audio compact disk 76.00 (978-1-4417-3224-8(1)) Blckstn Audio.

Signing Time! Songs Series Two Volumes 1-7. Prod. by Two Little Hands Productions. (J). 2007. audio compact disk 13.99 (978-1-933543-52-9(3)) Tw Li Ha Pr LLC.

Signing Time! Songs Series Two Volumes 8-13. Prod. by Two Little Hands Productions. (J). 2007. audio compact disk 13.99 (978-1-933543-53-6(1)) Tw Li Ha Pr LLC.

Signing Time! Songs Volumes 1-3. Rachel Coleman. (ENG.). (J). 2002. audio compact disk 13.99 (978-1-933543-30-7(2)) Tw Li Ha Pr LLC.

Signing Time! Songs Volumes 10-12. Rachel Coleman. (J). 2006. audio compact disk 13.99 (978-1-933543-33-8(7)) Tw Li Ha Pr LLC.

Signing Time! Songs Volumes 4-6. Rachel Coleman. (J). 2002. audio compact disk 13.99 (978-1-933543-31-4(0)) Tw Li Ha Pr LLC.

Signing Time! Songs Volumes 7-9. Rachel Coleman. (J). 2005. audio compact disk 13.99 (978-1-933543-32-1(9)) Tw Li Ha Pr LLC.

Signora da Vinci: A Novel. unabr. ed. Robin Maxwell. (Running Time: 16 hrs. 0 mins.). (ENG.). 2009. 29.95 (978-1-4332-9494-5(X)); 89.95 (978-1-4332-9490-7(7)); audio compact disk 118.00 (978-1-4332-9491-4(5)) Blckstn Audio.

Signposts along Life's Journey. Charles R. Swindoll. 3 cass. 1998. 16.95 (978-1-57972-100-8(1)) Insight Living.

Signposts of Purification. Swami Amar Jyoti. 1 cass. 1980. 9.95 (P-38) Truth Consciousness.
The stages in letting go of ego; what all the hard work is for. "Purify your hearts, you shall know.".

Signposts on the Road to Success. unabr. ed. E. W. Kenyon. Read by Stephen Sobozenski. 1 cass. (Running Time: 1 hr. 10 min.). 2000. 8.50 (978-1-57770-026-5(0)) Kenyons Gospel.
Every young person should read this book; it will stir ambition in the hearts of young men and women.

Signs & Wonders. Gloria Copeland & Billye Brim. 3 Cass. (BVOV Ser.). 2006. 15.00 (978-1-57562-889-9(9)); audio compact disk 15.00 (978-1-57562-890-5(2)) K Copeland Pubns.

Signs & Wondes Now: Living the Book of Acts. Phillip Halverson. 1 cass. (Running Time: 1 hr). 2005. 5.00 (978-1-57399-243-5(7)) Mac Hammond.
Signs and wonders will increase as we near the coming of the Lord. Learn how you can move with the Spirit of God as He manifests His glory in the earth.

Signs in the Heavens. Chuck Missler. 2 CD's. (Running Time: 120 mins.). (Briefing Packages by Chuck Missler). 1994. audio compact disk 19.95 (978-1-57821-295-8(2)) Koinonia Hse.
Is there a message hidden behind the 'Signs of the Zodiac'? Are there secrets hidden in the original names of the constellations?What we know as the "Signs of the Zodiac" is known in Hebrew as "the Mazzeroth." This briefing pack explores the possibility that the Mazzeroth, the pre-Babylonian original, anticipated God's total plan for mankind.The Long Day of JoshuaThe recent insights from celestial mechanics, including orbital resonance, may shed new light on the famous Biblical Battle of Beth-Horon (Joshua Chapter 10) and suggest the possibility that the Planet Mars may have been a fearsome participant.Implications on ancient calendars and other events are also addressed.

Signs in the Heavens. Chuck Missler. 2 cass. (Running Time: 2.5 hours +). (Briefing Packages by Chuck Missler). 1991. vinyl bd. 14.95 Incls. notes. (978-1-880532-74-4(3)) Koinonia Hse.
What Sign are You?What we know as the "Signs of the Zodiac" is known in Hebrew as "the Mazzeroth." The possibility that the original Mazzeroth (which was pre-Babylonian) anticipated God's total plan for mankind is explored.The Long Day of JoshuaThe recent insights from celestial mechanics, including orbital resonance, may shed new light on the famous Biblical Battle of Beth-Horon (Joshua Chapter 10) and suggest the possibility that the Planet Mars may have been a fearsome participant.Implications on ancient calendars and other events are also addressed.

Signs-Making Money. Kathleen B. Johnson. 1 cass. 8.95 (678) Am Fed Astrologers.
An AFA Convention workshop tape.

Signs of a Believer. Mike Craig & Kim Craig. 1 cass. (Running Time: 90 mins.). (He Still Heals Ser.: Vol. 6). 2000. 5.00 (SAO1-006) Morning NC.
Learn about the healing power of God that is available to believers today.

Signs of Christmas. Created by Pam Andrews. 2004. audio compact disk 10.00 (978-5-559-53188-5(X)) Lillenas.

Signs of Christ's Return, Vol. I. 7 cass. 21.95 (20144, HarperThor) HarpC GBR.

Signs of Christ's Return, Vol. 2. John MacArthur, Jr. 8 cass. 24.95 (20149, HarperThor) HarpC GBR.

Signs of His Coming 2002 Prophecy Update Tape Pack. 2002. (978-1-931713-13-9(8)) Word For Today.

Signs of Pastoral Care: Language of Symbols: Communication of Sacraments. Edward Mahnke. 1986. 10.80 (0311) Assn Prof Chaplains.

Signs of Progress. unabr. ed. Perf. by Eknath Easwaran. 1 cass. (Running Time: 1 hr.). 1987. 7.95 (978-1-58638-605-4(0)) Nilgiri Pr.

Signs of Separation. Lynne Hammond. 1 CD. 2005. audio compact disk 5.00 (978-1-57399-286-2(0)) Mac Hammond.

Signs of Spiritual Progress & Finding a True Teaching. 9.95 (SS-89, ST-133) Crystal Clarity.
Topics Includes: Spiritual progress as all we take with us at death; guideposts of spritual growth; the importance of knowing that you need God; why the spiritual search begins in suffering; a 3-point test for evaluating a spiritual teaching.

Signs of the End. Neville Goddard. 1 cass. (Running Time: 62 min.). 1968. 8.00 (44) J & L Pubns.
Neville taught Imagination Creates Reality. He was a powerfully influential teacher of God as Consciousness.

Signs of the Times. 1998. 6.00 (978-1-58602-054-5(4)) E L Long.

Signs of the Times. Narrated by Gary Frazier. (ENG.). 2006. audio compact disk 19.99 (978-1-930034-71-6(7)) Casscomm.

Signs of the Times: A Bible Prophecy Multimedia Study Kit. Perf. by Dave Reagan et al. 1998. tchr. ed. 45.00 (978-0-945593-04-1(X)) Lamb Lion Minstrs.

Signs of the Times, Are We Ready? Don J. Black. 1 cass. 7.98 (978-1-55503-670-6(8), 06004873) Covenant Comms.
Triumphing over adversity.

Signs of the Zodiac: The Elena Duran Collection 2, Volume 2. Ed. by Elena Duranm. Composed by Charles Matthews. 2007. pap. bk. 24.95 (978-1-902455-36-5(3), 1902455363) Pub: Schott Music Corp. Dist(s): H Leonard

Signs/Wonders, Have Tongues/Prophecy Ceased? Logos 01/17/99. Ben Young. 1999. 4.95 (978-0-7417-6115-6(7), B0115) Win Walk.

Siguiendo la Fe de Abraham. Kenneth Copeland. Tr. by Kenneth Copeland Publications Staff from ENG. 6 cass. (SPA.). 1986. 30.00 Set. (978-0-88114-495-6(9)) K Copeland Pubns.
Indepth study of Abraham's faith.

Siguiendo la Fe de Abraham, Vol. 1. Kenneth Copeland. Tr. by Kenneth Copeland Publications Staff from ENG. 1 cass. (SPA.). 1986. 5.00 (978-0-88114-496-3(7)) K Copeland Pubns.

Siguiendo la Fe de Abraham, Vol. 2. Kenneth Copeland. Tr. by Kenneth Copeland Publications Staff from ENG. 1 cass. (SPA.). 1986. 5.00 (978-0-88114-497-0(5)) K Copeland Pubns.

Siguiendo la Fe de Abraham, Vol. 3. Kenneth Copeland. Tr. by Kenneth Copeland Publications Staff from ENG. 1 cass. (SPA.). 1986. 5.00 (978-0-88114-498-7(3)) K Copeland Pubns.

Siguiendo la Fe de Abraham, Vol. 4. Kenneth Copeland. Tr. by Kenneth Copeland Publications Staff from ENG. 1 cass. (SPA.). 1986. 5.00 (978-0-88114-499-4(1)) K Copeland Pubns.

Siguiendo la Fe de Abraham, Vol. 5. Kenneth Copeland. Tr. by Kenneth Copeland Publications Staff from ENG. 1 cass. (SPA.). 1986. 5.00 (978-0-88114-500-7(9)) K Copeland Pubns.

Siguiendo la Fe de Abraham, Vol. 6. Kenneth Copeland. Tr. by Kenneth Copeland Publications Staff from ENG. 1 cass. (SPA.). 1986. 5.00 (978-0-88114-501-4(7)) K Copeland Pubns.

Siguiendo la Nube. Created by C. C. Vino Nuevo. 2007. audio compact disk 12.99 (978-1-933172-38-5(X)) Jayah Producc.

Silage: Vegas Car Chasers. Perf. by Silage. 1 cass., 1 CD. 1998. (978-0-7601-2595-3(3)); audio compact disk (978-0-7601-2596-0(1)) Provident Mus Dist.
Issues of materialism & wordly trappings, & their effect on Christians in our own personal lives.

Silage Watusi. 1997. 10.98 (978-0-7601-1382-0(3), CSUB70020); audio compact disk 15.98 (978-0-7601-1383-7(1), CDSUB70020) Pub: Brentwood Music. Dist(s): Provident Mus Dist
Combines the Ska sound with horns, punk & rap. Ministry oriented band features blatantly Christian lyrics.

Silas Marner. George Eliot. Narrated by Flo Gibson. 2009. audio compact disk 27.95 (978-1-60646-098-6(6)) Audio Bk Con.

Silas Marner. George Eliot. Read by Nadia May. (Playaway Young Adult Ser.). (ENG.). (YA). 2008. 49.99 (978-1-60514-786-4(9)) Find a World.

Silas Marner. George Eliot. Narrated by Hannah Gordon. 2 cass. (Running Time: 3 hrs. 0 mins. 0 sec.). (HarperCollinsAudioBooks Ser.). (ENG., 1996. 16.99 (978-0-00-105243-7(8)) Pub: HarpC GBR. Dist(s): IPG Chicago
Marner becomes a compendium of virtues whose lot is to care for a small golden-haired girl whose mother freezes to death in the snow outside his cottage.

Silas Marner. George Eliot. Narrated by Donna Barkman. (Running Time: 7 hrs. 30 mins.). 2006. 24.95 (978-1-59912-812-2(8)) Iofy Corp.

Silas Marner. George Eliot. Read by Alec McCowen. Adapted by Eileen Capel. 5 cass. 25.95 (SCN 210) J Norton Pubs.
The traditional order prevails but as the story progresses it becomes clear social relationships are changing & the old is giving way to the new.

Silas Marner. George Eliot. Read by Donna Barkman. 6 cass. (Running Time: 7 hrs.). 1989. 36.00 incl. album. (C-85) Jimcin Record.
Poignant story of a weaver.

Silas Marner. abr. ed. George Eliot. Perf. by Basil Rathbone & Cathleen Nesbitt. 2 cass. Dramatization. 1984. 19.95 (SWC 2024) HarperCollins Pubs.
Cast includes: George Rose, Eileen Atkins, & Dawn Brookes.

Silas Marner. abr. adpt. ed. George Eliot. (Bring the Classics to Life: Level 2 Ser.). 2008. audio compact disk 12.95 (978-1-55576-463-0(0)) EDCON Pubng.

Silas Marner, unabr. ed. George Eliot. Narrated by Flo Gibson. 5 cass. (Running Time: 7 hrs. 30 min.). 1984. 20.95 (978-1-55685-036-3(0)) Audio Bk Con.
Embittered by a false accusation Silas Marner retreats to his loom & to hoard his gold. When his treasure is stolen his spirit is restored by the arrival of a foundling child.

Silas Marner. unabr. ed. George Eliot. Read by Andrew Sachs. 6 cass. (Running Time: 6 hrs. 44 mins.). 2003. 29.95 (978-1-57270-338-4(5)) Pub: Audio Partners. Dist(s): PerseuPGW
A moral allegory about the redemptive power of love. The weaver, Silas Marner, is embittered by a false accusation, disappointed in friendship and love and has retreated into a life alone with his loom and his gold. Silas hoards a treasure that kills his spirit until fate steals it from him and replaces it with a golden-haired foundling child.

Silas Marner. unabr. ed. George Eliot. Read by Andrew Sachs. 6 CDs. (Running Time: 6 hrs. 44 mins.). (Audio Editions Ser.). (ENG.). 2003. audio compact disk 29.95 (978-1-57270-339-1(3)) Pub: AudioGO. Dist(s): Perseus Dist

Silas Marner. unabr. ed. George Eliot. Read by Nadia May. 5 cass. (Running Time: 7 hrs.). 1989. 39.95 (978-0-7861-0040-8(0), 1039) Blckstn Audio.
Silas Marner is a gentle linen weaver who is wrongly accused of a heinous theft committed by his best friend. After going into seclusion, he finds redemption & spiritual rebirth issuing from his unselfish love of an abandoned child who mysteriously appears one day in his cottage. George Eliot shows how character is rewarded in this ageless, heartwarming novel.

Silas Marner. unabr. ed. George Eliot. Read by Nadia May. (Running Time: 25200 sec.). (Classic Collection (Blackstone Audio) Ser.). 2008. 19.95 (978-1-4332-1252-9(8)); audio compact disk 19.95 (978-1-4332-1253-6(6)) Blckstn Audio.

Silas Marner. unabr. ed. George Eliot. Read by Donada Peters. 5 cass. (Running Time: 7 hrs. 30 min.). 1994. 35.00 (3383) Books on Tape.
Silas Marner is a compendium of virtues whose lot is to care for a small golden-haired girl whose mother freezes to death in the snow outside his cottage.

Silas Marner. unabr. ed. George Eliot. Read by John Peakes. 6 cass. (Running Time: 7 hrs.). (Bookcassette Classic Collection). 1993. 57.25 (978-1-56100-165-1(1), 1561001651, Unabridge Lib Edns) Brilliance Audio.
The story of Silas Marner's redemption and restoration, which is interwoven with the live of Eppie, Dolly Winthrop, Dunstan and Godfrey, is part beautifully realized portraiture of rural England and part fairy tale. "Silas Marner" has long been the most beloved and widely read book by George Eliot, the pen name for the 19th century English woman writer Marian Evans. "Silas Marner" is an amazing presentation of Eliot's power to combine symbolic and realistic narrative. In the story of an isolated, misanthropic old weaver - whose life is forever changed by the appearance of a little girl (Eppie) in his cottage - Eliot created a compact, tightly structured, pleasingly patterned novel. The tale is one that endorses the common goodness of rural people, yet remains agnostic as to the ultimate cause of good and evil.

Silas Marner. unabr. ed. George Eliot. Read by John Peakes. (Running Time: 7 hrs.). 2006. 39.25 (978-1-4233-1075-4(6), 9781423310754, BADLE); 24.95 (978-1-4233-1074-7(8), 9781423310747, BAD); audio compact disk 82.25 (978-1-4233-1071-6(3), 9781423310716, BriAudCD Unabrid); audio compact disk 39.25 (978-1-4233-1073-0(X), 9781423310730, Brlnc Audio MP3 Lib); audio compact disk 29.95 (978-1-4233-1070-9(5), 9781423310709, Bril Audio CD Unabri); audio compact disk 24.95 (978-1-4233-1072-3(1), 9781423310723, Brilliance MP3) Brilliance Audio.
The story of Silas Marner's redemption and restoration, which is interwoven with the lives of Eppie, Dolly Winthrop, Dunstan and Godfrey, is part beautifully realized portraiture of rural England and part fairy tale. Silas Marner has long been the most beloved and widely read book by George Eliot, the pen name for the 19th century English woman writer Marian Evans. Silas Marner is an amazing presentation of Eliot's power to combine symbolic and realistic narrative. In the story of an isolated, misanthropic old weaver - whose life is forever changed by the appearance of a little girl (Eppie) in his cottage - Eliot created a compact, tightly structured, pleasingly patterned novel. The tale is one that endorses the common goodness of rural people, yet remains agnostic as to the ultimate cause of good and evil.

Silas Marner. unabr. ed. George Eliot. Read by Stephanie Beacham. 4 cass. (Running Time: 6 hrs.). 2004. 25.00 (978-1-59007-140-3(9)) Pub: New Millenn Enter. Dist(s): PerseuPGW
Silas Marner, a weaver who has no friends and cares only for the gold he has saved, is robbed. But shortly thereafter, he finds an abandoned baby girl, whom he raises as his own child. His love for her redeems his character.

Silas Marner, unabr. ed. George Eliot. Narrated by Margaret Hilton. 5 cass. (Running Time: 7 hrs. 15 mins.). 1988. 44.00 (978-1-55690-478-3(9), 88270E7) Recorded Bks.
A reclusive weaver finds comfort in his love for an orphan.

***Silas Marner.** unabr. ed. George Eliot. Narrated by Rosalyn Landor. (Running Time: 8 hrs. 0 mins.). 2010. 15.99 (978-1-4001-8608-2(0)) Tantor Media.

***Silas Marner.** unabr. ed. George Eliot. Narrated by Rosalyn Landor. (Running Time: 7 hrs. 30 mins. 0 sec.). (ENG.). 2010. 19.99 (978-1-4001-6608-4(X)); audio compact disk 27.99 (978-1-4001-1608-9(2)); audio compact disk 55.99 (978-1-4001-4608-6(9)) Pub: Tantor Media. Dist(s): IngramPubServ

Silas Marner. unabr. collector's ed. George Eliot. Read by Donada Peters. 5 cass. (Running Time: 7 hrs. 30 min.). 1994. 40.00 (978-0-7366-2646-0(8), 9058) Books on Tape.
Silas Marner is a compendium of virtues whose lot is to care for a small golden-haired girl whose mother freezes to death in the snow outside his cottage.

Silas Marner, Set. unabr. ed. George Eliot. Read by Andrew Sachs. 6 cass. (Running Time: 9 hrs.). 1999. 54.95 (978-0-7540-0393-9(0), CAB 1816) AudioGO.
Exiled by superstition & betrayal & cut off from human love, for fifteen years the solitary & simple-hearted weaver Silas Marner has plied his loom in Raveloe & devoted himself to amassing a hoard of golden guineas. His chance of redemption, thought, is intimately connected with the fate of Godfrey Cass, son of the village Squire.

Silas Marner, Set. unabr. ed. George Eliot. Read by Andrew Sachs. 6 CDs. 2000. audio compact disk 69.95 (978-0-7540-5320-0(2), CCD 011) Pub: Chivers Audio Bks GBR. Dist(s): AudioGO

Silas Marner: Abridged. (ENG.). 2007. (978-1-60339-019-4(7)); cd-rom & audio compact disk (978-1-60339-020-0(0)) Listenr Digest.

***Silas Marner: Bring the Classics to Life.** adpt. ed. George Eliot. (Bring the Classics to Life Ser.). 2008. pap. bk. 21.95 (978-1-55576-500-2(9)) EDCON Pubng.

Silas Marner: Classic Collection. unabr. ed. George Eliot. Read by Nadia May. (Running Time: 7 hrs. 0 mins.). 2008. 29.95 (978-1-4332-1254-3(4)) Blckstn Audio.

Silas Marner: The Weaver of Raveloe. adpt. ed. Created by Focus on the Family Radio Theatre. (Running Time: 240 hrs. 0 mins.). (Radio Theatre Ser.). (ENG.). (J). (gr. 3). 2007. audio compact disk 14.97 (978-1-58997-516-3(2)) Pub: Focus Family. Dist(s): Tyndale Hse

Silbale a Guillermito. Tr. of Whistle for Willie. (SPA.). 2004. 8.95 (978-0-7882-0274-2(X)) Weston Woods.

***Silence.** 2010. audio compact disk (978-1-59171-239-8(4)) Falcon Picture.

Silence. Read by Thomas Merton. 1 cass. (Running Time: 60 min.). (Thomas Merton Ser.). 8.95 (AA2133) Credence Commun.

***Silence.** unabr. ed. Shusaku Endo. Narrated by David Holt. (Running Time: 7 hrs. 40 mins. 41 sec.). (ENG.). 2010. audio compact disk 29.99 (978-1-59859-741-7(8), SpringWater) Oasis Audio.

Silence. unabr. ed. Thomas Perry. Read by Michael Kramer. (YA). 2008. 64.99 (978-1-60514-505-1(X)) Find a World.

Silence. unabr. ed. Thomas Perry. (Running Time: 13 hrs. 0 mins. 0 sec.). (ENG.). 2007. audio compact disk 29.99 (978-1-4001-5447-0(2)) Pub: Tantor Media. Dist(s): IngramPubServ

Silence. unabr. ed. Thomas Perry. Read by Michael Kramer. 11 CDs. (Running Time: 13 hrs. 0 mins. 0 sec.). (ENG.). 2007. audio compact disk 39.99 (978-1-4001-0447-5(5)); audio compact disk 79.99 (978-1-4001-3447-2(1)) Pub: Tantor Media. Dist(s): IngramPubServ

Silence: The Universal Solvent. unabr. ed. Gangaji Foundation Staff. Read by Gangaji Foundation Staff. 3 cass. (Running Time: 4 hrs. 50 min.). 1994. 24.00 set. (978-0-9632194-6-6(4)) The Gangaji Fnd.
Gangaji reveals the secret for direct self-realization & ending egoic suffering.

Silence & Awareness: A Retreat Experience in Christian-Buddhist Meditation. Daniel Chowning et al. Read by Daniel Chowning et al. 12 cass. (Running Time: 16 hrs.). 1992. 84.95 Set. (978-7-900781-31-4(5), AA2515) Credence Commun.
How to pray using discipline, structure, techniques & practice.

Silence As the Ground of the Eternal. J. Krishnamurti. 1 cass. (Running Time: 75 min.). (Saanen, Switzerland Talks - 1985 Ser.: No. 5). 8.50 Krishnamurti.
Desire is the result of sensation given shape & image by thought. Is love put together by thought? If there is no time, is there death?.

Silence de la Mer. Vercors. Read by Philippe De Boissy. 1 cass. (FRE.). 1991. 21.95 (1294-VSL) Olivia & Hill.
This short novel published clandestinely in 1942 has become a classic of wartime resistance literature. When a refined German officer is billeted in the country house of a French writer & his niece, their decision not to speak to the enemy becomes increasingly difficult to maintain.

Silence de la Mer. Vercors. pap. bk. 24.95 (978-88-7754-162-8(8)) Pub: Cideb ITA. Dist(s): Distribks Inc

Silence in Hanover Close. unabr. ed. Anne Perry. Narrated by Davina Porter. 9 cass. (Running Time: 12 hrs. 45 mins.). (Thomas Pitt Ser.). 2005. 89.75 (978-1-4193-3947-9(8)) Recorded Bks.
In this latest Charlotte and Thomas Pitt novel, Perry is at her best. Thomas has been ordered to look into a three-year-old murder and use the utmost discretion when dealing with the family of the deceased. However, the closer he gets to solving this case, the more uneasy his supervisor becomes. When Thomas himself is accused of murdering a witness and is jailed, his wife, Charlotte, and her sister Elizabeth, quickly realize that Thomas's life is dependent upon their resolution of these murders. The author keeps the listener's attention as danger lurks around every corner and even those in high society find murder in their midst.

Silence Is Golden. unabr. ed. Jeanne M. Dams. 5 cass. (Running Time: 7 hrs. 30 mins.). (Hilda Johansson Mystery Ser.: Bk. 4). 2002. 40.00 (978-0-7366-8708-9(4)); audio compact disk 48.00 (978-0-7366-8709-6(2)) Books on Tape.
Her woman on the spot, Hilda Johansson, a maid in the Studebaker household in South Bend, sees what's going on among the rich, suffers what's going on among the less fortunate...and has no trouble telling it like it is. In the fourth in this series, Hilda's situation is still fragile. She's still crammed into a small house with her family of seven, and her happiness at being reunited with them is bittersweet. Worst of all, her 12-year-old brother, Eric, can't hold a job. When a friend of Eric's runs away to join the circus and is found beaten, perhaps worse, events take a desperate turn.

Silence Kills: Speaking Out & Saving Lives. Ed. by Lee Gutkind. 2008. 25.95 (978-0-87074-523-2(9)) SMU Press.

Silence of Adam. abr. ed. Larry Crabb et al. (Running Time: 2 hrs. 0 mins. 0 sec.). (ENG.). 2003. 9.99 (978-0-310-26110-0(4)) Zondervan.

Silence of Adam Audio: Finding the Courage to Be a Man in a World of Chaos. Larry Crabb et al. 2 cass. (Running Time: 2 hrs.). 1995. 14.99 set. (978-0-310-24658-9(X)) Zondervan.
God calls men to move into situations where there are no clear guidelines for success, but men are paralyzed. Crabb challenges men to own their own cowardice in the face of terror & to follow their true calling.

Silence of God: Job 23:3. 1983. 44.95 (978-0-7417-1321-6(7), 321) Win Walk.

Silence of God: Romans 1:24. Ed Young. 1990. 4.95 (978-0-7417-1825-9(1), 825) Win Walk.

Silence of the Lambs. Thomas Harris. Narrated by Frank Muller. 9 CDs. (Running Time: 10 hrs. 45 mins.).Tr. of Chen mo de gao yang. audio compact disk 89.00 (978-1-4025-3496-6(5)) Recorded Bks.

Silence of the Lambs. abr. ed. Thomas Harris.Tr. of Chen mo de gao yang. 2004. 10.95 (978-0-7435-4604-1(0)) Pub: S&S Audio. Dist(s): S and S Inc

Silence of the Lambs, unabr. ed. Thomas Harris. Narrated by Frank Muller. 8 cass. (Running Time: 10 hrs. 45 mins.).Tr. of Chen mo de gao yang. 70.00 (978-1-55690-830-9(X), 93142E7) Recorded Bks.
The FBI, working desperately to locate a serial killer poised to strike again, sends a young trainee to interview an imprisoned psychopathic genius in the hope he will assist their investigation. Available to libraries only.

Silence, on Dort. Kidzup Productions Staff. 1 cass. (Running Time: 90 mins.). (Kidzup Foreign Language Ser.). (FRE.). (J). 1999. 8.99 (978-1-894281-39-3(X)); audio compact disk 12.99 (978-1-894281-40-9(3)) Pub: Kidzup CAN. Dist(s): Penton Overseas
A classic collection of all time favorites. Guaranteed to soothe your baby to sleep.

Silence to Sainthood (James The Less) Matthew 10:3. Ed Young. 1985. 4.95 (978-0-7417-1475-6(2), 475) Win Walk.

Silencer. unabr. ed. Campbell Armstrong. Narrated by Richard Ferrone. 8 cass. (Running Time: 11 hrs. 30 mins.). 1997. 79.75 (978-1-4193-1303-5(7), H1766MC, Clipper Audio) Recorded Bks.

***Silencer.** unabr. ed. James W. Hall. Narrated by Ed Sala. (Running Time: 9 hrs. 30 mins.). (Thorn Mysteries Ser.). 2010. 16.99 (978-1-4001-8557-3(2)) Tantor Media.

***Silencer.** unabr. ed. James W. Hall. Narrated by Ed Sala. (Running Time: 9 hrs. 30 mins. 0 sec.). (Thorn Mysteries Ser.). (ENG.). 2010. 24.99 (978-1-4001-6557-5(1)); audio compact disk 69.99 (978-1-4001-4557-7(0)); audio compact disk 34.99 (978-1-4001-1557-0(4)) Pub: Tantor Media. Dist(s): IngramPubServ

***Silencing of God: The Dismantling of America's Christian Heritage.** Dave Miller. Prod. by World Video Bible School , World Video Bible School. (ENG.). 2007. 24.00 (978-1-60063-003-3(0)) Pub: Apologetic Pr. Dist(s): STL Dist NA

***Silencing Sam: A Novel.** unabr. ed. Julie Kramer. Narrated by Renée Raudman. (Running Time: 9 hrs. 30 mins.). 2010. 16.99 (978-1-4001-8787-4(7)); 24.99 (978-1-4001-6787-6(6)); audio compact disk 34.99 (978-1-4001-1787-1(9)); audio compact disk 83.99 (978-1-4001-4787-8(5)) Pub: Tantor Media. Dist(s): IngramPubServ

Silencing the Clutter of the Mind. Swami Amar Jyoti. 1 cass. 1977. 9.95 (J-8) Truth Consciousness.
The bell is always ringing; we hear it only when we are quiet. How to silence?.

***Silent Alarm.** John Blumberg. 2005. 14.95 (978-0-9765266-4-3(6)) Rosedale Pr IL.

Silent Angel see Poetry & Voice of James Wright

Silent Avenger see Shadow

Silent Boy. unabr. ed. Lois Lowry. Read by Karen Allen. 3 cass. (Running Time: 3 hrs. 57 mins.). (J). (gr. 5 up). 2004. 30.00 (978-0-8072-1692-7(5), Listening Lib); audio compact disk 35.00 (978-0-8072-1766-5(2), Listening Lib) Random Audio Pubg.

Silent Boy. unabr. ed. Lois Lowry. Read by Karen Allen. (ENG.). (J). (gr. 5). 2009. audio compact disk 30.00 (978-0-7393-8233-2(0), Listening Lib) Pub: Random Audio Pubg. Dist(s): Random

Silent Bride. abr. ed. Leslie Glass. Read by M. J. Wilde. Abr. by Mary Bevoni. 4 cass. (Running Time: 6 hrs.). 2003. 27.00 (978-1-58807-098-2(0), 691064) Am Pubng Inc.

Silent Bride. abr. ed. Leslie Glass. Read [illegible] J. Wilde. Abr. by Mary Bevoni. 4 vols. No. 7. 2003. (978-1-58807-735[illegible] Am Pubng Inc.

***silent Country.** unabr. ed. Di Morrissey. Read by Kate Hood & Humphrey Bower. (Running Time: 15 hrs. 41 mins.). 2010. audio compact disk 113.95 (978-1-74214-505-1(1), 9781742145051) Pub: Bolinda Pubng AUS. Dist(s): Bolinda Pub Inc

Silent Cradle. Margaret Cathbert. 2004. 10.95 (978-0-7435-4605-8(9)) Pub: S&S Audio. Dist(s): S and S Inc

Silent Cradle. abr. ed. Margaret Cuthbert. Read by Tonya Pinkins. 2 cass. (Running Time: 3 hrs.). 1999. 16.85 (978-0-671-01116-1(2)) S and S Inc.
A riveting thriller about a female obstetrician's attempt to unravel the mystery surrounding a string of childbirth fatalities.

Silent Eloquence of Truth. Swami Amar Jyoti. 1 dolby cass. 1984. 9.95 (K-66) Truth Consciousness.
Truth shatters false ego structures as sunshine scatters darkness. Renunciation of falsehood, seeing the Truth & living what we believe in.

***Silent Gift.** abr. ed. Michael Landon Jr. & Cindy Kelley. Narrated by Tavia Gilbert. (ENG.). 2009. 14.98 (978-1-59644-776-9(1), christaudio) christianaud.

Silent Gift. abr. ed. Michael Landon, Jr. & Cindy Kelley. (Running Time: 7 hrs. 15 mins. 0 sec.). (ENG.). 2009. audio compact disk 24.98 (978-1-59644-775-2(3), christaudio) christianaud.

Silent Gun. unabr. ed. Douglas Hirt. Read by Rusty Nelson. 6 cass. (Running Time: 6 hrs. 6 min.). 2001. 39.95 (978-1-58116-067-3(4)) Books in Motion.

Silent Holy Night: Children's Music for the Christmas Season. Mark Friedman & Janet Vogt. Read by Mark Friedman & Janet Vogt. 1 cass. (J). (gr. k-12). 1994. 11.95 (9924); audio compact disk 19.95 (10905) OR Catholic.
Readings, songs and stories for use at worship in the classroom or as a children's Christmas program.

Silent Hour. unabr. ed. Michael Koryta. (Running Time: 10 hrs. 50 mins.). (Lincoln Perry Ser.: Vol. 4). 2009. 29.95 (978-1-4332-9241-5(6)); 65.95 (978-1-4332-9237-8(8)); audio compact disk 100.00 (978-1-4332-9238-5(6)) Blckstn Audio.

Silent House. Ed Greenwood. Narrated by Simon Vance. (Running Time: 16 hrs.). 2004. 44.95 (978-1-59912-716-3(4)) Iofy Corp.

Silent House. unabr. ed. Ed Greenwood. Read by Simon Vance. 11 cass. (Running Time: 16 hrs.). 2004. 76.95 (978-0-7861-2792-4(9)); audio compact disk 24.95 (978-0-7861-8467-5(1)); audio compact disk 104.00 (978-0-7861-8484-2(1)) Blckstn Audio.

***Silent Joe.** abr. ed. T. Jefferson Parker. Read by James Daniels. (Running Time: 5 hrs.). 2010. audio compact disk 9.99 (978-1-4418-6708-7(2), 9781441867087, BCD Value Price) Brilliance Audio.

An Asterisk (*) at the beginning of an entry indicates that the title is appearing for the first time.

Silent Joe. unabr. ed. T. Jefferson Parker. Read by James Daniels. 8 cass. (Running Time: 11 hrs.). 2001. 32.95 (978-1-58788-428-3(3), 1587884283, BAU); 78.25 (978-1-58788-429-0(1), 1587884291, Unabridge Lib Edns) Brilliance Audio.
With the horrible remnants of a childhood tragedy forever visible across his otherwise handsome face, Joe Trona is scarred in more ways than one. Rescued from an orphanage by Will Trona, a charismatic Orange County politician who sensed his dark potential, Joe is swept into the maelstrom of power and intimidation that surrounds his adoptive father's illustrious career. Serving as Will's right hand man, Joe is trained to protect and defend his father's territory - but he can't save the powerful man from his enemies. Will Trona is murdered, and Joe will stop at nothing to find out who did it. Looking for clues as he sifts through the remains of his father's life - his girlfriends, acquaintances, deals, and enemies - Joe comes to realize how many secrets Will Trona possessed, and how many people he had the power to harm. But two leads keep rising to the surface: a little girl who was kidnapped by her mentally disturbed brother, and two rival gangs who seem to have joined forces. As Joe deepens his investigation - and as he is forced to confront painful events of his troubled childhood - these two seemingly disconnected threads will intersect. Just how and why form the crux of this intricate, intelligent mystery that satisfies the mind as well as the heart - and reveals yet again the impeccable detail, vivid characterization, and emotional complexity that make a T. Jefferson Parker novel impossible to resist.

Silent Joe. unabr. ed. T. Jefferson Parker. Read by James Daniels. (Running Time: 11 hrs.). 2004. 39.25 (978-1-59335-396-4(0), 1593353960, Brlnc Audio MP3 Lib) Brilliance Audio.

Silent Joe. unabr. ed. T. Jefferson Parker. Read by James Daniels. (Running Time: 11 hrs.). 2004. 39.25 (978-1-59710-706-8(9), 1597107069, BADLE); 24.95 (978-1-59710-707-5(7), 1597107077, BAD) Brilliance Audio.

***Silent Joe.** unabr. ed. T. Jefferson Parker. Read by James Daniels. (Running Time: 10 hrs.). 2010. audio compact disk 29.99 (978-1-4418-4117-9(2), 9781441841179, Bril Audio CD Unabri); audio compact disk 89.97 (978-1-4418-4118-6(0), 9781441841186, BriAudCD Unabrid) Brilliance Audio.

Silent Joe. unabr. ed. T. Jefferson Parker. Read by James Daniels. (Running Time: 11 hrs.). 2004. 24.95 (978-1-59335-156-4(9), 1593351569) Soulmate Audio Bks.

Silent Justice. unabr. ed. William Bernhardt. Read by Jonathan Marosz. 10 cass. (Running Time: 15 hrs.). (Ben Kincaid Ser.: No. 9). 2000. 80.00; 80.00 (978-0-7366-5001-4(6), 5259) Books on Tape.
Ben Kincaid believes that the class action suit he has just taken on is a suicide mission but he can't forget the innocent children whose untimely deaths cry out for justice. The Blaylock Corporation is charged with dumping toxic chemicals into the community's drinking water. As Ben prepares for legal battle, a group of Blaylock employees are fighting for their lives against a sadistic killer. With each gruesome murder, a terrifying connection is drawn between Ben's quest for justice and another man's relentless hunt for the spoiled of his own private, and very dirty, war.

Silent Lady. Catherine Cookson. Read by Anne Dover. 10 CDs. (Running Time: 11 hrs. 27 min.). (Sound Ser.). (J). 2003. audio compact disk 89.95 (978-1-84283-117-5(8)) Pub: ISIS Lrg Prnt GBR. Dist(s): Ulverscroft US

Silent Lady. unabr. ed. Catherine Cookson. Read by Anne Dover. 12 cass. (Running Time: 18 hrs.). 2001. 94.95 (978-1-86042-986-6(6), 2-986-6) Pub: Soundings Ltd GBR. Dist(s): Ulverscroft US
The silent lady who presented herself at the firm of London solicitors was clearly a vagrant. But when Alexander Armstrong, the firm's senior partner, learned her name everyone was amazed at his reaction. For Irene Baindor had a past & her emergence is to signal the unravelling of a mystery that had baffled Armstrong for years. What Irene had been doing emerged over the following weeks as Armstrong met the unlikely benefactors who had helped her to build a satisfying life in a sheltered environment. Now she is able to confront her violent past & find happiness with the help of old friends & some newer ones.

***Silent Land: A Novel.** unabr. ed. Graham Joyce. (Running Time: 8 hrs. NaN mins.). (ENG.). 2011. 29.95 (978-1-4417-8033-1(5)); audio compact disk 29.95 (978-1-4417-8032-4(7)) Blckstn Audio.

***Silent Land: A Novel.** unabr. ed. Graham Joyce. Read by To be Announced. (Running Time: 8 hrs. NaN mins.). (ENG.). 2011. 54.95 (978-1-4417-8030-0(0)); audio compact disk 76.00 (978-1-4417-8031-7(9)) Blckstn Audio.

Silent Man. unabr. ed. Alex Berenson. Read by George Guidall. 10 CDs. (Running Time: 12 hrs.). (ENG.). (gr. 12 up). 2009. audio compact disk 39.95 (978-0-14-314413-7(8), PengAudBks) Penguin Grp USA.

Silent Man. unabr. ed. Alex Berenson. Narrated by George Guidall. 11 CDs. (Running Time: 12 hrs. 30 mins.). 2009. audio compact disk 123.75 (978-1-4361-7502-9(X)) Pub: Recorded Bks. Dist(s): NetLibrary CO

***Silent Mercy.** Linda Fairstein. (ENG.). 2011. audio compact disk 39.95 (978-0-14-242875-7(2), PengAudBks) Penguin Grp USA.

Silent Night see Christmas Stories

Silent Night. 1 cass., 1 CD. audio compact disk 10.98 CD. (978-1-57908-381-6(1), 1545) Platinm Enter.

Silent Night. 1 cass. 1999. 5.99 (978-7-5126-7916-0(5), PHC8014); audio compact disk 7.99 (978-7-5126-7917-7(3), PHD8014) Provident Mus Dist.
A Christmas collection of 16 songs including 6 original arrangements.

Silent Night. abr. ed. Mary Higgins Clark. Read by Jennifer Beals. (Running Time: 20 hrs. 0 mins. 0 sec.). (ENG.). 2009. audio compact disk 9.99 (978-0-7435-8351-0(5)) Pub: S&S Audio. Dist(s): S and S Inc

Silent Night: A Christmas Suspense Story. unabr. ed. Mary Higgins Clark. Read by William Dufris. 4 vols. (Running Time: 6 hrs.). 2000. bk. 39.95 (978-0-7927-2422-3(4), CSL 311, Chivers Sound Lib) AudioGO.
When Catherine Dorman's husband is diagnosed with leukemia, she & their two young sons travel with him to New York for a lifesaving operation. On Christmas Eve, Catherine takes them to see Rockefeller Center's famous Christmas tree, where seven year old Brian notices a woman taking his mother's wallet. Brian follows the thief into the subway & the most adventure of his life begins.

Silent Night: A Christmas Suspense Story. unabr. ed. Mary Higgins Clark. Read by William Dufris. 4 CDs. (Running Time: 6 hrs.). 2001. audio compact disk 49.95 (978-0-7927-9929-0(1), SLD 080, Chivers Sound Lib) AudioGO.
When Catherine Dorman's husband is diagnosed with leukemia, she and their children travel with him to New York for a lifesaving operation. On Christmas Eve, Catherine takes them to see Rockefeller Center's famous Christmas Tree, where seven-year-old Brian notices a woman taking his mother's wallet. Brian follows the thief into the subway, and the most dangerous adventure of his young life begins.

Silent Night: A Mouse Tale. Betsy Hernandez & Donny Monk. Illus. by Joe Boddy. 1 cass. (J). 1993. bk. 17.95 (978-0-917143-11-3(6)) Sparrow TN.

Silent Night: All Through the Night. Mary Higgins Clark. Read by Jennifer Beals & Carol Higgins Clark. (Running Time: 5 hrs. 0 mins. 0 sec.). (ENG.). 2006. audio compact disk 19.95 (978-0-7435-6433-5(2)) Pub: S&S Audio. Dist(s): S and S Inc

Silent Night: Luke 2:1-20. Ed Young. 1999. 4.95 (978-0-7417-2241-6(0), 1241) Win Walk.

Silent Night: The Remarkable 1914 Christmas Truce. unabr. ed. Stanley Weintraub. Read by Edward Holland. 4 cass. (Running Time: 6 hrs.). 2001. 32.00 (978-0-7366-8322-7(4)) Books on Tape.
In the beginning months of World War I, a very strange thing happened. After the fierce trench warfare of November and December, on Christmas Eve, 1914, the fighting spontaneously stopped. Men on both sides laid down their arms and came to celebrate Christmas with each other. They shared food parcels across the lines, sang carols together, and erected Christmas trees with candles. They buried the dead, exchanged presents, and even played soccer together.

Silent Option. Jamie Fredric. 2000. audio compact disk 14.99 (978-1-930252-06-6(4), Bks OnScreen) PageFree Pubg.

Silent Outcry. Marcel Marceau. 1 cass. (Running Time: 45 min.). 1968. 11.95 (11015) J Norton Pubs.
Morgan Upton interviews Marcel Marceau on the development of art, & its place in the current world of social protest.

Silent Partner. abr. ed. Jonathan Kellerman. Read by John Rubinstein. (Running Time: 3 hrs.). (Alex Delaware Ser.: No. 4). (ENG.). 2003. audio compact disk 14.99 (978-0-7393-0376-4(7), Random AudioBks) Pub: Random Audio Pubg. Dist(s): Random

Silent Partner. unabr. ed. Jonathan Kellerman. Read by Alexander Adams. 11 cass. (Running Time: 16 hrs. 30 min.). (Alex Delaware Ser.: No. 4). 1992. 88.00 (978-0-7366-2266-0(7), 3054) Books on Tape.
Alex Delaware, a professional psychologist & occasional detective, has never quite put his affair with Sharon to rest. So years later, when he meets her again, it brings back the bittersweet of their love & its breakup. The next day she's found dead, apparently by suicide. Alex vows to find the truth of her death as he attempts to make peace with her memory.

Silent Passage, Set. unabr. ed. Gail Sheehy. Read by Gail Sheehy. 2 cass. (Running Time: 3 hrs. 30 min.). 1992. 17.00 (978-1-55994-787-9(X), 391575) HarperCollins Pubs.
Gail Sheehy's groundbreaking examination of America's last taboo: menopause. Examines both the social & psychological aspects of the menopausal years & presents the most current medical information to help women assess their options & calculate their risks.

Silent Places. unabr. ed. Stewart Edward White. Read by David Sharp. 6 cass. (Running Time: 6 hrs. 12 min.). 1995. 39.95 (978-1-55686-595-4(3)) Books in Motion.
Two woodsmen are hired by the Hudson Bay Company to venture into the silent, frozen north, track down an Indian who reneged on his charge account, & bring him back alive.

Silent Pool. Patricia Wentworth. 2009. 61.95 (978-0-7531-3138-1(2)); audio compact disk 79.95 (978-0-7531-3139-8(0)) Pub: Isis Pubng Ltd GBR. Dist(s): Ulverscroft US

Silent Power. Stuart Wilde. One CD. 2005. audio compact disk 10.95 (978-1-4019-0658-0(3)) Hay House.

Silent Predator. unabr. ed. Tony Park. Read by Mark Davis. (Running Time: 15 hrs. 25 mins.). 2009. audio compact disk 113.95 (978-1-74214-135-0(8), 9781742141350) Pub: Bolinda Pubng AUS. Dist(s): Bolinda Pub Inc

Silent Prey. John Sandford, pseud. Narrated by Richard Ferrone. 10 CDs. (Running Time: 11 hrs. 15 mins.). (Prey Ser.). 2000. audio compact disk 97.00 (978-0-7887-4907-0(2), C1282E7) Recorded Bks.
In this sequel to "Eyes of Prey," a psychotic murderer escapes from jail, prompting Lucas Davenport, the Minneapolis cop who put him away, to come out of retirement.

***Silent Prey.** abr. ed. John Sandford, pseud. Read by Ken Howard. (ENG.). 2006. (978-0-06-122893-3(1), Harper Audio); (978-0-06-122895-7(8), Harper Audio) HarperCollins Pubs.

Silent Prey. unabr. ed. John Sandford, pseud. Narrated by Richard Ferrone. 8 cass. (Running Time: 11 hrs. 15 mins.). (Prey Ser.). 1993. 70.00 (978-1-55690-918-4(7), 93414K8) Recorded Bks.

Silent Running. unabr. ed. James F. Calvert. Read by Kevin Patrick. 7 cass. (Running Time: 10 hrs.). 1997. 49.95 Set. (978-0-7861-1149-7(6), 1916) Blckstn Audio.
An American hero relives the perils & triumphs of eight harrowing patrols aboard one of America's most successful World War II submarines.

***Silent Scream.** Carl Sommer. (Quest for Success Ser.). (ENG.). (YA). 2009. bk. 19.95 (978-1-57537-336-2(X)); pap. bk. 11.95 (978-1-57537-385-0(8)) Advance Pub.

***Silent Scream.** unabr. ed. Karen Rose. (Running Time: 20 hrs. 30 mins.). 2010. 44.95 (978-1-4417-6983-1(8)); 105.95 (978-1-4417-6980-0(3)); audio compact disk 34.95 (978-1-4417-6982-4(X)); audio compact disk 123.00 (978-1-4417-6981-7(1)) Blckstn Audio.

***Silent Scream: An Anna Travis Mystery.** Lynda La Plante. Narrated by K. I. m. Hicks. (Running Time: 12 hrs. 42 mins. 0 sec.). (ENG.). 2011. audio compact disk 29.95 (978-1-60998-138-9(3)) Pub: AudioGO. Dist(s): Perseus Dist

***Silent Scream / el Grito Silencioso.** ed. Carl Sommer. (Quest for Success Bilingual Ser.). (ENG & SPA.). (YA). 2009. bk. 21.95 (978-1-57537-435-2(8)) Advance Pub.

Silent Sea. abr. ed. Clive Cussler & Jack Du Brul. Contrib. by Jason Culp. (Running Time: 6 hrs.). (ENG.). (gr. 12 up). 2010. audio compact disk 29.95 (978-0-14-314541-7(X), PengAudBks) Penguin Grp USA.

Silent Sea. unabr. ed. Clive Cussler & Jack Du Brul. Contrib. by Scott Brick. 9 CDs. (Running Time: 11 hrs.). (ENG.). (gr. 12 up). 2010. audio compact disk 39.95 (978-0-14-314540-0(1), PengAudBks) Penguin Grp USA.

***Silent Sea.** unabr. ed. Clive Cussler & Jack Du Brul. Read by Scott Brick. 9 CDs. (Running Time: 11 hrs. 15 mins.). 2010. audio compact disk 100.00 (978-0-307-71413-8(6), BksonTape) Pub: Random Audio Pubg. Dist(s): Random

Silent Sleep of the Dying. Keith Mccarthy. 2007. 76.95 (978-0-7531-3771-0(2)); audio compact disk 99.95 (978-0-7531-2740-7(7)) Pub: ISIS Audio GBR. Dist(s): Ulverscroft US

Silent Snow, unabr. ed. Steve Thayer. Narrated by George Guidall. 7 cass. (Running Time: 10 hrs.). 1999. 66.00 (978-0-7887-3767-1(8), 95984E7) Recorded Bks.
Investigative reporter Rick Beanblossum, "the man without a face," is about to spend the most harrowing week of his life. Someone has snatched his infant son in a crime ominously similar to the Lindbergh kidnapping 60 years ago. In a race against time, Rick must solve the the infamous case, even though it may already be too late to save his son.

Silent Speaker. abr. ed. Rex Stout. Read by Michael Prichard. 6 cass. (Running Time: 9 hrs.). (Nero Wolfe Ser.). 2002. 29.95 (978-1-57270-270-7(2)) Pub: Audio Partners. Dist(s): PerseuPGW
When a powerful government official turns up dead, the great Nero Wolfe takes notice. On the edge of financial ruin, the orchid-loving detective grudgingly accepts the case. Soon another victim is found, a stenographer tape disappears, and the dead man speaks, after a fashion. As the business world clamors for a solution, Wolfe patiently lays a trap.

Silent Speaker. unabr. ed. Rex Stout. Read by Michael Prichard. (ENG.). 2009. audio compact disk 29.95 (978-1-60283-564-1(0)) Pub: AudioGO. Dist(s): AudioGo

Silent Speaker. unabr. collector's ed. Rex Stout. Read by Michael Prichard. 6 cass. (Running Time: 9 hrs.). (Nero Wolfe Ser.). 1994. 48.00 (978-0-7366-2837-2(1), 3545) Books on Tape.
Murder tops the menu at a Waldorf dinner party when the guest speaker never makes it to the podium. Nero Wolfe finds out why.

Silent Spillbills. unabr. ed. Tor Seidler. Narrated by Christina Moore. 3 pieces. (Running Time: 4 hrs.). (gr. 5 up). 2000. 29.00 (978-0-7887-4028-2(8), 95862E7) Recorded Bks.
At school, Katya is embarrassed about her stuttering problem; she never speaks to anyone. Only when she's out bird-watching with her father, does Katya feel happy. But when her favorite birds, the spillbills, are threatened by extinction, Katya must overcome her self-consciousness to save them.

Silent Spillbills. unabr. ed. Tor Seidler. Read by Christina Moore. 3 cass. (Running Time: 4 hrs.). (J). (gr. 5). 2000. pap. bk. & stu. ed. 50.95 (978-0-7887-4153-1(5), 41116) Recorded Bks.

Silent Spillbills, Class Set. unabr. ed. Tor Seidler. Read by Christina Moore. 3 cass. (Running Time: 4 hrs.). (J). 2000. 186.80 (978-0-7887-4154-8(3), 47109) Recorded Bks.

***Silent Superstitions.** unabr. ed. Catherine Marshall. Adapted by C. Archer. Narrated by Jaimee Draper. (Catherine Marshall's Christy Ser.). (ENG.). 2010. 7.00 (978-1-60814-701-4(0), SpringWater) Oasis Audio.

Silent Temples, Songful Hearts: Traditional Music of Cambodia. 1 cass. (Running Time: 45 mins.). 1991. pap. bk. 29.95 (978-0-88432-980-0(1), S11345) J Norton Pubs.
Ranges from children's etiquette songs to stories told through song & narration. English translations & historical background are given.

Silent Temples, Songful Hearts: Traditional Music of Cambodia. Sam-Ang Sam & Patricia S. Campbell. Ed. by Judith C. Tucker. Pref. by Terry Miller. Frwd. by Chinry Ung. (YA). (gr. 7). 1991. pap. bk. 24.95 (978-0-937203-74-3(2)) World Music Pr.

Silent Temples, Songful Hearts: Traditional Music of Cambodia. unabr. ed. 1 cass., bklet. (Running Time: 45 mins.). pap. bk. 18.95 (S11345) J Norton Pubs.

Silent Temples, Songful Hearts: Traditional Music of Cambodia. unabr. ed. Sam-Ang Sam & Patricia S. Campbell. Perf. by Sam, Sam-Ang, Ensemble of Cambodian Musicians. Ed. by Judith C. Tucker. Pref. by Terry Miller. Frwd. by Chinry Ung. 1 cass. (Running Time: 40 min.). 1991. pap. bk. 20.95 (978-0-937203-36-1(X)) World Music Pr.
The first introduction in English to the tradition music & culture of Cambodia, including children's songs, instrumental, vocal & dance music, percussion pieces & stories. History, culture & musical analysis are included with study guides for classroom/community use. Grades 2 - adult. Illustrated with photos, drawings, map, & transcriptions.

Silent Thunder. Iris Johansen. Read by Jennifer Van Dyck. (Playaway Adult Fiction Ser.). (ENG.). 2009. 70.00 (978-1-60775-529-6(7)) Find a World.

Silent Thunder. abr. ed. Iris Johansen & Roy Johansen. Read by Jennifer Van Dyck. 5 CDs. (Running Time: 6 hrs.). 2008. audio compact disk 26.95 (978-1-4233-2957-2(0), 9781423329572, BACD) Brilliance Audio.

Silent Thunder. abr. ed. Iris Johansen & Roy Johansen. Read by Jennifer Van Dyck. (Running Time: 6 hrs.). 2009. audio compact disk 14.99 (978-1-4233-2958-9(9), 9781423329589, BCD Value Price) Brilliance Audio.

Silent Thunder. unabr. ed. Iris Johansen & Roy Johansen. Read by Jennifer Van Dyck. 1 MP3-CD. (Running Time: 10 hrs.). 2008. 24.95 (978-1-4233-2953-4(8), 9781423329534, Brilliance MP3); 39.25 (978-1-4233-2956-5(2), 9781423329565, BADLE); 39.25 (978-1-4233-2954-1(6), 9781423329541, Brlnc Audio MP3 Lib); 24.95 (978-1-4233-2955-8(4), 9781423329558, BAD); audio compact disk 36.95 (978-1-4233-2951-0(1), 9781423329510, Bril Audio CD Unabri); audio compact disk 97.25 (978-1-4233-2952-7(X), 9781423329527, BriAudCD Unabrid) Brilliance Audio.

Silent Thunder: A Civil War Story. Andrea Davis Pinkney. Narrated by Peter Jay Fernandez & Andrea Johnson. 5 CDs. (Running Time: 5 hrs. 30 mins.). (gr. 4 up). audio compact disk 48.00 (978-0-7887-6160-7(9)) Recorded Bks.

Silent Thunder: A Civil War Story. unabr. ed. Andrea Davis Pinkney. Narrated by Peter Jay Fernandez & Andrea J. Johnson. 5 pieces. (Running Time: 5 hrs. 30 mins.). (gr. 4 up). 2001. 48.00 (978-0-7887-4721-2(5), 96395E7) Recorded Bks.
Both Summer & her older brother Roscoe have a roaring through their souls. She longs to read, Roscoe wants to join the Union army. They were told by other slaves to keep their feelings private & also they face difficult decisions that will change their lives forever.

Silent Thunder: A Civil War Story. unabr. ed. Andrea Davis Pinkney. Narrated by Peter Jay Fernandez & Andrea J. Johnson. 5 cass. (Running Time: 5 hrs. 30 mins.). (J). 2001. pap. bk. & stu. ed. 70.99 Read-along pack. Recorded Bks.

Silent Thunder: A Civil War Story. unabr. ed. Andrea Davis Pinkney. Narrated by Peter Jay Fernandez & A. Johnson. 5 CDs. (Running Time: 5 hrs. 30 min.). (J). (gr. 10-13). 2001. audio compact disk 48.00 (C1384) Recorded Bks.
Both 11-year-old Summer & her older brother Roscoe have a "silent thunder" roaring through their souls. Summer yearns to learn letters, so she can read. Roscoe wants to join the Union forces & fight in the Civil War. But they are slaves in Virginia & their wishes are forbidden. Their friend Thea says that silent thunder is something slaves have to keep private, but Summer & Roscoe can?t resist their feelings. Before 1862 comes to a close, they both find unexpected allies who help them act on their desires. Now they must make difficult, painful decisions that will forever change their lives.

Silent to the Bone. unabr. ed. E. L. Konigsburg. Read by Howard McGillin. 4 vols. (Running Time: 5 hrs. 19 mins.). (Middle Grade Cassette Librariestm Ser.). (J). (gr. 5-9). 2004. pap. bk. 38.00 (978-0-8072-8741-5(5), S YA 253 SP, Listening Lib); 32.00 (978-0-8072-8740-8(7), YA253CX, Listening Lib) Random Audio Pubg.
On Wednesday, November 25, Branwell Zamborska is struck dumb. Nikki, his baby half sister, has slipped into a coma. Branwell dials 911, but when the emergency operator answers, he cannot speak. He cannot utter a sound. The au pair from England, takes over. She tells the emergency medical team that Branwell dropped Nikki & shook her. As Branwell's best friend, Connor investigates the events leading up to the silence, he slowly discovers what his problems really are & what it takes to help Branwell reveal what happened that Wednesday afternoon.

Silent Treatment. Michael Palmer. Narrated by George Guidall. 13 CDs. (Running Time: 14 hrs. 45 mins.). audio compact disk 124.00 (978-0-7887-7178-1(7)) Recorded Bks.

Silent Treatment. unabr. ed. Michael Palmer. Narrated by George Guidall. 10 cass. (Running Time: 14 hrs. 45 mins.). 85.00 (978-0-7887-0268-6(8), 94477E7) Recorded Bks.
When his wife mysteriously dies the night before she is scheduled for surgery, Dr. Harry Corbett realizes a killer is moving through the wards of Good Samaritan Hospital, a killer so sophisticated & silent that he can only be a doctor. Available to libraries only.

Silent Treatment. unabr. ed. Michael Palmer. Narrated by George Guidall. 10 CDs. (Running Time: 14 hrs. 45 min.). 2001. audio compact disk 124.00 (C1428) Recorded Bks.

Silent Valley. unabr. ed. Carey Cleaver. 8 cass. 1998. 83.95 Set. (978-1-85903-154-4(4)) Pub: Magna Story GBR. Dist(s): Ulverscroft US

Silent Victim. 1997. bk. 99.00 (ACS-1438) PA Bar Inst.
Retained to prosecute a winning personal injury case, victory could be jeopardized by unfamiliarity with technical requirements. Be aware of the important procedural steps & substantive issues involved in securing authority to act & protect case where the victim is a minor, is incapacitated, or dies. The authors provide practical guidance in identifying & handling the issues which arise at each stage of the representation & litigation.

Silent War. Ben Bova. Read by Amanda Karr & Christian Noble. (Asteroid Wars Ser.: Bk. III). 2005. 26.95 (978-1-59397-653-8(4)) Pub: Macmill Audio. Dist(s): Macmillan

Silent War. unabr. ed. Amanda Karr & Ben Bova. Read by Christian Noble. 11 CDs. (Running Time: 13 hrs. 0 mins. 0 sec.). (Grand Tour; also Asteroid Wars Ser.: Bk. 3). (ENG.). 2005. audio compact disk 44.95 (978-1-59397-504-3(X)) Pub: Macmill Audio. Dist(s): Macmillan

Silent Wing. unabr. ed. Jose Raul Bernardo. Read by Adams Morgan. 6 cass. (Running Time: 8 hrs. 30 mins.). 1999. 44.95 (978-0-7861-1554-9(8), 2384) Blckstn Audio.
A Cuban poet is exiled from his homeland for demonstrating in favor of his country's independence from the tyrannical hold of Spain.

Silent Witness. unabr. ed. Nigel McCrery. Read by Paddy Glynn. 6 cass. (Running Time: 12 hrs.). (Isis Cassettes Ser.). 2000. 54.95 (978-0-7531-0598-6(5), 991205) Pub: ISIS Audio GBR. Dist(s): Ulverscroft US
Tramping around a graveyard in the dark is not how Dr. Sam Ryan, forensic pathologist, planned to spend her day off. But then she finds herself fascinated. The evidence seems to point to a ritualistic killing linked to the black arts. The murder bears an uncanny resemblance to a local crime committed many years ago. Then another death is discovered. Sam is under pressure to come up with evidence the police desperately need. By now, though, the killer has decided that Sam is a threat that had far better be removed.

Silent Witness. unabr. ed. Nigel Mccrery. Ed. by Paddy Glynn. 8 CDs. (Isis Ser.). (J). 2003. audio compact disk 79.95 (978-0-7531-1726-2(6)) Pub: ISIS Lrg Prnt GBR. Dist(s): Ulverscroft US

Silent Witness. unabr. ed. Michael Norman. Read by William Dufris. (Running Time: 30600 sec.). 2008. 72.95 (978-1-4332-3511-5(0)); audio compact disk 29.95 (978-1-4332-3515-3(3)); audio compact disk & audio compact disk 90.00 (978-1-4332-3512-2(9)) Blckstn Audio.

Silent Witness. unabr. ed. Richard North Patterson. Read by T. J. Edwards. 13 cass. (Running Time: 19 hrs. 30 min.). 1997. 104.00 (978-0-913369-44-9(6), 4231) Books on Tape.
It's 1967 & Tony Lord, Lake City's star high school athlete, seems destined for greatness outside his small town. But when someone murders his girlfriend, his life turns upside down.

***Silent Witness: A Forensic Investigation of Terri Schiav.** unabr. ed. Mark Fuhrman. Read by John Hinch. (ENG.). 2005. (978-0-06-087605-0(0), Harper Audio); (978-0-06-087604-3(2), Harper Audio) HarperCollins Pubs.

Silent World of Nicholas Quinn. Colin Dexter. 2 cass. (Running Time: 3 hrs.). (ENG., 2001. (978-0-333-90440-4(0)) Macmillan UK GBR.

Silent World of Nicholas Quinn. unabr. ed. Colin Dexter. Read by Terrence Hardiman. 6 cass. (Running Time: 9 hrs.). (Inspector Morse Mystery Ser.: Bk. 3). 2000. 49.95 (978-0-7451-6607-0(5), CAB 1223) Pub: Chivers Audio Bks GBR. Dist(s): AudioGO
The Foreign Examinations Syndicate at Oxford is a small unit that supervises the examinations of people in Third World countries. Complete integrity from its small staff is essential. And when a member of the staff is murdered, Inspector Morse spots a clue telling him the integrity has been breached. And he's soon convinced that one of the five executives is the murderer, but which one?.

Silhouette in Scarlet. unabr. ed. Elizabeth Peters, pseud. Narrated by Barbara Rosenblat. 5 cass. (Running Time: 6 hrs. 45 mins.). (Vicky Bliss Mystery Ser.). 44.00 (978-0-7887-0160-3(6), 94385E7) Recorded Bks.
A single crimson rose and a plane ticket to Stockholm neatly mailed in a mysterious package sound like the formula for a romantic weekend. And a note in the bottom of the box fuels Vicky's already insatiable curiosity. It is written in a archaic language even the capable Dr. Bliss cannot decipher. Is she embarking on a journey of romance or something else? Available to libraries only.

Silicon Gold Rush: The Next Generation of High-Tech Stars Rewrite the Rules of Business. unabr. ed. Karen Southwick. Read by Sneha Mathan. 6 cass. (Running Time: 5 hrs. 30 mins.). 2000. 44.95 (978-0-7861-1824-3(5), 2623) Blckstn Audio.
A hotbed of activity for farsighted thinkers & determined doers, the high technology industry has given rise to a pioneering group of entrepreneurs & executives that is not only behind today's most innovative technological advances, but at the forefront of a dynamic new movement in business. Armed with groundbreaking management approaches, the members of this visionary group are changing the way companies are modeled & offering new ideas on how companies should be run. They offer invaluable lessons for executives & managers in all industries.

Silicon Gold Rush: The Next Generation of High-Tech Stars Rewrite the Rules of Business. unabr. ed. Karen Southwick. Read by Sneha Mathan. 6 cass. (Running Time: 9 hrs.). 2001. (978-0-7861-1917-2(9)) Blckstn Audio.
The high-technology industry has given rise to a pioneering group of entrepreneurs and executives that is not only behind today's most innovative technological advances, but at the forefront of a dynamic new movement in business.

***Silicon Gold Rush: The Next Generation of High-Tech Stars Rewrites the Rules of Business.** unabr. ed. Karen Southwick. Read by Sneha Mathan. (Running Time: 8.5 hrs. NaN mins.). (ENG.). 2011. 29.95 (978-1-4417-8513-8(2)); audio compact disk 76.00 (978-1-4417-8511-4(6)) Blckstn Audio.

Silk. Nicola Thorne. Read by Joanna David. (Chivers Audio Bks.). 2003. 96.95 (978-0-7540-8421-1(3)) Pub: Chivers Audio Bks GBR. Dist(s): AudioGO

Silk & Steel. Catherine King & Maggie Mash. 2009. 84.95 (978-1-84652-303-8(6)); audio compact disk 99.95 (978-1-84652-304-5(4)) Pub: Magna Story GBR. Dist(s): Ulverscroft US

Silk Road. Sichou Zhi Lu. 2 CDs. (Light on China Ser.). audio compact disk 14.95 (978-7-88581-113-6(1), VCDTR-42) China Bks.

Silk Stockings see Women in Literature, the Short Story: A Collection

Silks. unabr. ed. Dick Francis & Felix Francis. Narrated by Martin Jarvis. 9 CDs. (Running Time: 11 hrs.). (ENG.). (gr. 12 up). 2008. audio compact disk 34.95 (978-0-14-314385-7(9), PengAudBks) Penguin Grp USA.

Silks. unabr. ed. Dick Francis & Felix Francis. Read by Martin Jarvis. 6 cass. (Running Time: 10 hrs. 30 mins.). 2008. 100.00 (978-1-4159-5969-5(2), BksonTape); audio compact disk 100.00 (978-1-4159-5962-6(5), BksonTape) Pub: Random Audio Pubg. Dist(s): Random

Silksinger. unabr. ed. Laini Taylor. Read by Cassandra Campbell. (Running Time: 10 hrs.). (Faeries of Dreamdark Ser.: No. 2). 2009. 39.97 (978-1-4418-0233-0(9), 9781441802330, Brlnc Audio MP3 Lib); 24.99 (978-1-4418-0232-3(0), 9781441802323, Brilliance MP3); 24.99 (978-1-4418-0234-7(7), 9781441802347, BAD); 39.97 (978-1-4418-0235-4(5), 9781441802354, BADLE); audio compact disk 29.99 (978-1-4418-0230-9(4), 9781441802309, Bril Audio CD Unabri) Brilliance Audio.

Silksinger. unabr. ed. Laini Taylor. Read by Cassandra Campbell. 11 CDs. (Running Time: 13 hrs.). (Faeries of Dreamdark Ser.: No. 2). (gr. 5-9). 2009. audio compact disk 79.97 (978-1-4418-0231-6(2), 9781441802316, BriAudCD Unabrid) Brilliance Audio.

Silla de Pedro. Tr. of Peter's Chair. (SPA.). 2004. 8.95 (978-0-7882-0281-0(2)) Weston Woods.

Sillon para Mi Mama. Contrib. by Vera B. Williams. 9.95 (978-1-59112-161-9(2)) Live Oak Media.

Sillon para Mi Mama. Vera B. Williams. Illus. by Vera B. Williams. 14 vols. (Running Time: 11 mins.). 1994. pap. bk. 39.95 (978-1-59519-198-4(4)); 9.95 (978-1-59112-119-0(1)) Live Oak Media.

Sillon para Mi Mama. Vera B. Williams. Illus. by Vera B. Williams. (Running Time: 11 mins.). (J). 1994. audio compact disk 12.95 (978-1-59519-196-0(8)) Live Oak Media.

Sillon para Mi Mama. Vera B. Williams. Illus. by Vera B. Williams. 11 vols. (Running Time: 11 mins.). (SPA.). (J). (gr. k-4). 1994. pap. bk. 18.95 (978-1-59519-197-7(6)) Live Oak Media.

Sillon para Mi Mama. unabr. ed. Vera B. Williams. Illus. by Vera B. Williams. Read by Susan Rybin. 11 vols. (Running Time: 11 mins.). (SPA.). (J). (gr. k-2). 2004. pap. bk. 16.95 (978-0-87499-335-6(0), LK6260) Pub: Live Oak Media. Dist(s): AudioGO
Daughter, mother, and grandmother all dream of saving enough coins to buy a new chair to replace the one that was destroyed in the fire that ravaged their apartment.

Sillon para Mi Mama, Grades 1-6. unabr. ed. Vera B. Williams. Illus. by Vera B. Williams. Read by Susan Rybin. 14 vols. (Running Time: 11 mins.).Tr. of Chair for My Mother. (SPA.). (J). 1994. pap. bk. & tchr. ed. 37.95 Reading Chest. (978-0-87499-337-0(7)) Live Oak Media.
Daughter, mother, & grandmother all share the dream of saving enough coins to buy a new easy chair to replace the one that was destroyed in the fire that ravaged their apartment. The story is told by the young girl who helps her mother & grandmother in their quest.

Silly Billy see Pony Engine & Other Stories for Children

Silly Chicken. Idries Shah. Illus. by Jeff Jackson. (J). (ps-3). 2006. pap. bk. 18.95 (978-1-883536-80-0(4), Hoopoe Books) ISHK.

Silly Chicken/el Pollo Bobo. Idries Shah. Tr. by Rita Wirkala. Illus. by Jeff Jackson. (J). (ps-3). 2006. pap. bk. 18.95 (978-1-883536-82-4(0), Hoopoe Books) ISHK.

Silly Favorites. 1 cass.; 1 CD. 1998. 7.98 (978-1-56628-169-0(5), 75503); audio compact disk 11.98 CD. (978-1-56628-193-5(8), 75503D) MFLP CA.

***Silly Mammo: An Ethiopian Tale.** Read by Gebregeorgis Yohannes. (Running Time: 20).Tr. of Kilu Mammo. (ENG & AMH.). (J). 2010. 10.00 (978-1-883701-03-1(1)) Sololia.

Silly N Spooky Tales of Kids in Hawaii. Jeff Gere. 2006. audio compact disk 16.95 (978-0-9762190-4-0(2)) Pub: J Gere. Dist(s): Islander Grp

Silly Old Bear Songs. 1 cass. (My First Sing-Alongs Ser.). (J). bk. 7.99 (978-0-7634-0368-3(7)) W Disney Records.

Silly Sing-Alongs. abr. ed. Nina Mattikow. Perf. by Purple Balloon Players. 1 cass. (Running Time: 60 min.). (Cassettes for Kids Ser.). (J). 1992. 5.95 (978-1-55569-528-6(0), 20004) Great Am Audio.
Sing-along with: "I'm a Little Teapot," "Jack & Jill," & many more.

Silly Songbook. Esther Nelson & Bruce Haack. 1 cass. (Running Time: 60 min.). (J). (ps-5). 1987. 9.95 (978-0-945110-00-2(6), D211) Dragonhawk Pub.
Instructs children to follow directions given to misic, with the goal of intensifying the listeners imagination & creativity through body movement.

Silly Songs. (Silly-Wacky-Goofy-Flaky Ser.). (J). 1997. 7.00 (978-1-57375-372-2(6)) Audioscope.

Silly Songs. 1 cass. (J). 9.98 (Sony Wonder); audio compact disk 13.98 CD. Sony Music Ent.
A zany fun time sing-along featuring the Muppets singing "Sesame Street" favorites such as "The Transylvania Polka".

Silly Songs. 1 cass. (Classic Collections). (J). 7.99 (978-1-55723-211-3(3)); 7.99 Norelco. (978-1-55723-212-0(1)); audio compact disk 13.99 CD. (978-1-55723-213-7(X)); audio compact disk 13.99 (978-1-55723-515-2(5)) W Disney Records.

Silly Songs. Perf. by Cedarmont Kids. 1 cass. 1999. 5.99 (978-0-00-507231-8(X)); 3.99 (978-0-00-546333-8(5)) Provident Music.

Silly Songs. Ed. by Publications International Staff. (J). 2007. audio compact disk 3.98 (978-1-4127-3791-3(5)) Pubns Intl Ltd.

Silly Songs, Set. 1 cass. (Let's Sing & Learn Ser.). (J). 1997. pap. bk. 7.95 (978-0-8092-3052-5(6), 305260, Contemporary) McGraw-Hill Trade.

***Silly Tilly & the Easter Bunny.** unabr. ed. Lillian Hoban. (ENG.). 2008. (978-0-06-169486-8(X)); (978-0-06-171322-4(8)) HarperCollins Pubs.

***Silly Tilly's Valentine.** unabr. ed. Lillian Hoban. (ENG.). 2008. (978-0-06-169487-5(8)); (978-0-06-171325-5(2)) HarperCollins Pubs.

Silly Tunes. Penton Overseas, Inc. Staff. 1 cass. (Running Time: 60 mins.). (Ready-Set-Sing Collection). (ENG.). (J). 2003. 4.49 (978-1-56015-975-9(8)) Penton Overseas.
Includes: "Yankee Doodle," "Pat-A-Cake," "London Bridge" and more.

Silly Willy Discovers Fitness & Phonics: Long Vowels Movement Songs, Vol. 1. 1 cass. (Running Time: 30 min.). (Silly Willy Ser.). (J). (gr. k-3). 1997. audio compact disk 14.95 CD. Ed Activities.
Helps children hear the vowel sounds as they move to catchy rhythms & imaginative stories.

Silly Willy Discovers Fitness & Phonics: Long Vowels Movement Songs, Vol. 2. 1 cass. (Running Time: 30 min.). (Willy Willy Ser.). (J). (gr. k-3). audio compact disk 14.95 CD. Ed Activities.

Silly Willy Discovers Fitness & Phonics Vol. 1: Long Vowels Movement Songs. 1 cass. (Running Time: 30 min.). (Silly Willy Ser.). (J). (gr. k-3). 1997. 11.95 (978-0-7925-4163-9(4), AC557) Ed Activities.

Silly Willy Discovers Fitness & Phonics Vol. 2: Long Vowels Movement Songs. 1 cass. (Running Time: 30 min.). (Willy Willy Ser.). (J). (gr. k-3). 11.95 (978-0-7925-4159-2(6), AC558) Ed Activities.

Silly Willy Moves Through the ABC's. 1 cass. (Running Time: 30 min.). (Silly Willy Ser.). (J). (gr. k-3). 1996. 11.95 (978-0-7925-4091-5(3), AC550); audio compact disk 14.95 CD. Ed Activities.
Each letter of the alphabet is introduced, then followed by original songs that will capture a child's imagination while developing fitness & locomotor skills.

Silly Willy Will. unabr. ed. Poems. John Schmidt. Read by John Schmidt. Music by Cornplanter Staff. 2 cass. (Running Time: 3 hrs.). (C). 2000. 12.99 (978-0-9639132-8-9(X)) Path Pubng.
Silly Willy is Everyman in the 21st century; will he begin his rise to perfection & become a fourth-dimentional being, master of space & time, before Earth ends, or forever be silly? This is the question posed in Silly Willy Will, a 3-hour poetry collection.

Silly Willy Workout. 1 cass.; 1 CD. (Running Time: 30 min.). (Silly Willy Ser.). (J). (gr. k-3). 1995. 12.95 (978-0-8113-3500-3(3), AC548) Ed Activities.
Upbeat contemporary music & activities to allow children to receive a high energy "state of the art" workout including warm up, cool down & stretches. Contains a talk-through section that lets teacher help students with the movements.

Sillytime Magic. Joanie Bartels. 1 cass. (Running Time: 50 min.). (J). (gr. k up). 1989. 9.95 Discov Music.

Sillytime Magic. Read by Joanie Bartels. 1 cass. (Running Time: 35 min.). (Magic Ser.). (J). 1989. pap. bk. 8.95 incl. lyric bk. (978-1-881225-05-8(4)) Discov Music.
New packaging includes full length audio cassette & complete full color lyric book with words to "Sillytime songs" & photos of Joanie & kids.

Sillytime Magic. Read by Joanie Bartels. 1 cass. (J). (ps). 9.98 (2228) MFLP CA.
Collection of silly songs sung by Joanie Bartels. Includes "The Name Game," "The Witch Doctor," "Mairzy Doats," "This Old Man" & more.

Silmarillion. J. R. R. Tolkien. 10 cass. (Running Time: 14 hrs.). 1998. 65.55 (978-0-00-105534-6(8)) Ulvrscrft Audio.
Ancient history of Middle-earth, the foundations of the world & it's peoples.

Silmarillion. abr. ed. J. R. R. Tolkien. Perf. by Christopher Tolkien. 1 cass. 1984. 12.95 (978-0-694-50305-6(3), SWC 1564) HarperCollins Pubs.

Silmarillion. unabr. ed. J. R. R. Tolkien. Read by Martin Shaw. 12 cass. (Running Time: 15 hrs.). (Middle Earth Chronicles). (J). (gr. 7 up). 2004. pap. bk. 75.00 (978-0-8072-8295-3(2), LL0188, Listening Lib) Random Audio Pubg.
Tells of the Elder Days, of the First Age of Tolkien's World, when Morgoth, the first Dark Lord, dwelt in Middle Earth & the High Elves made war upon them for the recovery of the Silmarils, the jewels containing the pure light of Valinor. It is to this ancient drama that the characters in "The Lord of the Rings" so often look back.

Silmarillion (Boxed Set), Set. unabr. ed. J. R. R. Tolkien. Read by Martin Shaw. 13 CDs . (Running Time: 15 hrs.). (J. R. R. Tolkien Ser.). (ENG.). 1998. audio compact disk 65.00 (978-0-553-45606-6(7)) Pub: Random Audio Pubg. Dist(s): Random

Silos, Politics, & Turf Wars: A Leadership Fable about Destroying the Barriers That Turn Colleagues into Competitors. Patrick Lencioni. 2006. 13.95 (978-1-59397-861-7(8)) Pub: Macmill Audio. Dist(s): Macmillan

Silos, Politics, & Turf Wars: A Leadership Fable about Destroying the Barriers That Turn Colleagues into Competitors. unabr. ed. Patrick Lencioni. Read by Eric Conger. 4 CDs. (Running Time: 5 hrs. 0 mins. 0 sec.). (ENG.). 2006. audio compact disk 22.95 (978-1-59397-860-0(X)) Pub: Macmill Audio. Dist(s): Macmillan

Silva - Athletic Success. unabr. ed. José Silva & Tag Powell. Read by Tag Powell. 1 cass. (Running Time: 40 min.). (Silva Master Keys to Success Ser.). 1987. pap. bk. 12.95 (978-0-914295-11-2(X)) Top Mtn Pub.
Side A presents a Mental Training Exercise designed to remove mental limitations & blockages, & to improve reaction time, increase speed, & sharpen skills under pressure, to experience peak sports performance. Side B presents subliminal athletic-building suggestions hidden in ocean-type sound.

Silva - Become a Non-Smoker. unabr. ed. José Silva & Tag Powell. Read by Tag Powell. 1 cass. (Running Time: 40 min.). (Silva Master Keys to Success Ser.). 1987. pap. bk. 12.95 (978-0-914295-16-7(0)) Top Mtn Pub.
Side A presents an exercise designed to re-program old, limiting beliefs & habits, & build control & success over the smoking habit. Side B presents subliminal non-smoking suggestions hidden in ocean-type sound.

Silva - Dissolve Anger. unabr. ed. José Silva & Tag Powell. Read by Tag Powell. 1 cass. (Running Time: 40 min.). (Silva Master Keys to Success Ser.). 1987. pap. bk. 12.95 (978-0-914295-08-2(X)) Top Mtn Pub.
Side A presents a Mental Training Exercise designed to free one's self from anger by controlling negative emotions & gaining clamness, confidence, & tolerance. Side B presents anger-easing suggestions hidden in ocean-type sound.

Silva - Dissolve Fear. unabr. ed. José Silva & Tag Powell. Read by Tag Powell. 1 cass. (Running Time: 40 min.). (Silva Master Keys to Success Ser.). 1987. pap. bk. 12.95 (978-0-914295-10-5(1)) Top Mtn Pub.
Side A presents a Mental Training Exercise designed to remove negative expectations of the future & build a positive, confident outlook, free of fear. Side B presents subminal confidence-building & fear-eliminating suggestions hidden in ocean-type sound.

Silva - Enjoy Exercise. unabr. ed. José Silva & Tag Powell. Read by Tag Powell. 1 cass. (Running Time: 40 min.). (Silva Master Keys to Success Ser.). 1987. pap. bk. 12.95 (978-0-914295-14-3(4)) Top Mtn Pub.
Side A presents exercises designed to mentally condition the body & enjoy better love relationships, job success & personal self-confidence. Side B presents subliminal exercise-motivating suggestions hidden in ocean-type sounds.

Silva - Enjoy Life More. unabr. ed. José Silva & Tag Powell. Read by Tag Powell. 1 cass. (Running Time: 40 min.). (Silva Master Keys to Success Ser.). 1987. pap. bk. 12.95 (978-0-914295-13-6(6)) Top Mtn Pub.
Side A presents Mental Training Exercise designed to rid one's self of boredom at work & in family lives. Side B presents subliminal suggestions hidden in ocean-type sound.

Silva - Goal Setting. unabr. ed. José Silva & Tag Powell. Read by Tag Powell. 1 cass. (Running Time: 40 min.). (Silva Master Keys to Success Ser.). 1987. pap. bk. 12.95 (978-0-914295-15-0(2)) Top Mtn Pub.
Side A presents exercises designed to develop the habits & confidence to plan immediate & long-range future. Side B presents subliminal goal-reaching suggestions hidden in ocean-type sound.

Silva - Improve Creativity. unabr. ed. José Silva & Tag Powell. Read by Tag Powell. 1 cass. (Running Time: 40 min.). (Silva Master Keys to Success Ser.). 1987. pap. bk. 12.95 (978-0-914295-17-4(9)) Top Mtn Pub.
Side A presents Mental Training exercises designed to produce & release untapped creativity & to induce creative answers to problems & decisions by brain-storming. Side B presents subliminal creativity-enhancement suggestions hidden in ocean-type sound.

Silva - Increase Concentration. unabr. ed. José Silva & Tag Powell. Read by Tag Powell. 1 cass. (Running Time: 40 min.). (Silva Master Keys to Success Ser.). 1987. pap. bk. 12.95 (978-0-914295-19-8(5)) Top Mtn Pub.
Side A presents exercises designed to increase powers of visualization, ability to focus thoughts, & to improve problem-solving talents. Side B presents subliminal concentration-building suggestions hidden in ocean-type sounds.

Silva - Increase Motivation & Decrease Procrastination. unabr. ed. José Silva & Tag Powell. Read by Tag Powell. 1 cass. (Running Time: 40 min.). (Silva Master Keys to Success Ser.). 1987. pap. bk. 12.95 (978-0-914295-21-1(7)) Top Mtn Pub.
Side A presents exercises designed to teach the mind how to make decisions, gain confidence, & take action by dispelling fears of failure & rejection. Side B presents subliminal action-orientating suggestions hidden in ocean-type sound.

Silva - Increase Sales. unabr. ed. José Silva & Tag Powell. Read by Tag Powell. 1 cass. (Running Time: 40 min.). (Silva Master Keys to Success Ser.). 1987. pap. bk. 12.95 (978-0-914295-22-8(5)) Top Mtn Pub.
Side A presents Mental Training Excerises designed to help attract clients & customers by removing inner mental blocks against success. Side B presents subliminal sales-communication skills suggestions hidden in ocean-type sound.

Silva - Increase Self-Confidence. unabr. ed. José Silva & Tag Powell. Read by Tag Powell. 1 cass. (Running Time: 40 min.). (Silva Master Keys to Success Ser.). 1987. pap. bk. 12.95 (978-0-914295-20-4(9)) Top Mtn Pub.
Side A presents exercises designed to develop self-confidence through the rejection of old, negative images, & by concentrating on positive, out-going, open & friendly feelings & images. Side B presents subliminal confidence-boosting suggestions hidden in ocean-type sound.

Silva - Memory Improvement. unabr. ed. José Silva & Tag Powell. Read by Tag Powell. 1 cass. (Running Time: 40 min.). (Silva Master Keys to Success Ser.). 1987. pap. bk. 12.95 (978-0-914295-07-5(1)) Top Mtn Pub.
Side A presents a Mental Training Excerise designed to develop & enhance memory skills. Side B presents subliminal memory-improvement suggestions hidden in ocean-type sounds.

Silva - Pain Control. Tag Powell & José Silva. Read by Tag Powell. 1 cass. (Running Time: 40 min.). (Silva Master Keys to Success Ser.). 12.95 (12-8) Top Mtn Pub.
Pain can be controlled with the use of your mind: sore muscles, nagging pain, etc. Side A: relaxation exercise; Side B: subliminals in ocean.

Silva - Pain Control. unabr. ed. José Silva & Tag Powell. Read by Tag Powell. 1 cass. (Running Time: 40 min.). (Silva Master Keys to Success Ser.). 1987. pap. bk. 12.95 (978-0-914295-12-9(8)) Top Mtn Pub.
Side A presents Mental Training Exercise designed to decrease & dissolve emotional, mental & physical pain. Side B presents subliminal pain-controlling suggestions hidden in ocean-type sound.

Silva - Time Management. unabr. ed. José Silva & Tag Powell. Read by Tag Powell. 1 cass. (Running Time: 40 min.). (Silva Master Keys to Success Ser.). 1987. pap. bk. 12.95 (978-0-914295-18-1(7)) Top Mtn Pub.
Side A presents excercises designed to help one accomplish more by mentally stretching the clock through organizing the mind to prioritize tasks, & get rid of extraneous thoughts. Side B presents subliminal time management suggestions hidden in ocean-type sound.

Silva - Weight Control. unabr. ed. José Silva & Tag Powell. Read by Tag Powell. 1 cass. (Running Time: 40 min.). (Silva Master Keys to Success Ser.). 1987. pap. bk. 12.95 (978-0-914295-09-9(8)) Top Mtn Pub.
Side A presents exercises designed to program the mind to take off weight effortlessly & permanently. Side B presents subliminal weight-control suggestions hidden in ocean type sound.

Silva Long Relaxation Exercise. Narrated by Tag Powell. 1 cass. 1988. 12.95 (978-1-56087-122-4(9)) Top Mtn Pub.
Side A: The classic "Silva Mental Training Exercise" with health improvement statements for self-controlled awareness. Side B: Silva Alpha-Centering sound only. Use it to help you maintain an Alpha level while at a relaxed state, & to make your own tapes for your personal use. Includes instructions, Alphamatic card in book-size box.

Silva Master Keys to Success Series. unabr. ed. José Silva & Tag Powell. Read by Tag Powell. 8 cass. (Running Time: 5 hrs. 20 min.). 1987. pap. bk. 79.95 Set. (978-0-914295-54-9(3)) Top Mtn Pub.
Mental Training Exercises designed to program your mind for success in all sixteen basic areas of life.

Silva Method. Robert Stone. Read by Robert Stone. Read by Laura Silva & José Silva. 6 cass. 1991. 59.95 set. (521A) Nightingale-Conant.
Unlock the amazing powers of your mind, this experiential step by step program will help you use & access the under-utilized right side of your brain.

Silva Method: Tapping the Secrets of the Mind for Total Self Mastery. Robert Stone. 6 cass. (Running Time: 6 hrs.). 1991. wbk. ed. (978-1-55525-084-3(X), 521A) Nightingale-Conant.
Discover the most popular relaxation method.

Silva Method in Action. Laura Silva. 1 cass. cass. & video 39.95 (1048VM) Nightingale-Conant.
Learn to use & enhance the power of your mind. Access your Alpha-level brain waves via The Silva Method to improve memory, creativity, problem solving, stress management & more.

Silva Mind Control Method of Mental Dynamics. Jose Silva. Read by Burt Goldman. 2004. 7.95 (978-0-7435-4224-1(X)) Pub: S&S Audio. Dist(s): S and S Inc

Silva Mind Mastery Seminar Audiocassette Album. Tag Powell & Judith L. Powell. Read by Tag Powell. 8 cass. (Running Time: 8 hrs.). 1988. 79.95 set in vinyl library album. (978-1-56087-026-5(5)) Top Mtn Pub.
At Last! The World Famous Seminar in your own home, at your own schedule, & at your own pace. You can enjoy the benefits of this event now...with this all-encompassing package. You will gain an increase & hone skills in: instant attitude adjustment, goal setting, better communication skills, study of trigger mechanisms, the holographic brain, subjective programming, stress & relaxation techniques, alphatime management, remembering names & faces, Silva long relaxation exercise...to name a few.

Silva Ultramind ESP System. 2000. 99.95 (978-1-55525-099-7(8)); audio compact disk 109.95 (978-1-55525-100-0(5)) Nightingale-Conant.

Silver. Contrib. by Starflyer 59. 2005. audio compact disk 13.98 (978-5-558-97844-5(9)) Tooth & Nail.

Silver: The Super Investment of the Coming Decade. Charles Stahl. 1 cass. (Running Time: 34 min.). 10.95 (1105) J Norton Pubs.
In this tape Stahl gives statistics on visible silver stocks & the amount remaining in India in one form or another; discusses new potential demands in industry & for energy conservation; predicts real shortages in the 80's.

Silver Anniversary Guitar Case Chord Book. Peter Pickow. 1 CD. (Running Time: 1 hr.). 2004. audio compact disk 9.95 (978-0-8256-1728-7(6)) Music Sales.

Silver Bears. unabr. collector's ed. Paul E. Erdman. Read by Dan Lazar. 8 cass. (Running Time: 8 hrs.). 1980. 48.00 (978-0-7366-0301-0(8), 1289) Books on Tape.
This story involves a bank founded by the Mafia in Switzerland, an ancient silver mine rediscovered in Iran, the bullion smugglers of Dubai on the Persian Gulf, & a billionaire American speculator living in England.

***Silver Bells.** Debbie Macomber. 2010. audio compact disk 9.99 (978-1-4418-6131-3(9)) Brilliance Audio.

Silver Bells. unabr. ed. Debbie Macomber. Read by Tanya Eby. (Running Time: 2 hrs.). 2009. 39.97 (978-1-4418-0757-1(8), 9781441807571, Brlnc Audio MP3 Lib); 24.99 (978-1-4418-0756-4(X), 9781441807564, Brilliance MP3); 24.99 (978-1-4418-0758-8(6), 9781441807588, BAD); 39.97 (978-1-4418-0759-5(4), 9781441807595, BADLE); audio compact disk 26.99 (978-1-4418-0754-0(3), 9781441807540, Bril Audio CD Unabri); audio compact disk 69.97 (978-1-4418-0755-7(1), 9781441807557, BriAudCD Unabrid) Brilliance Audio.

***Silver Birches: A Novel.** unabr. ed. Adrian Plass. (Running Time: 6 hrs. 17 mins. 0 sec.). (ENG.). 2009. 12.99 (978-0-310-77342-9(3)) Zondervan.

Silver Blaze see Sherlock Holmes: Selected Stories

Silver Blaze. Retold by John Bergez. Arthur Conan Doyle. (Sherlock Holmes Mysteries Ser.). 2000. audio compact disk 18.95 (978-1-4105-0156-1(6)) D Johnston Inc.

Silver Blaze. Arthur Conan Doyle. Ed. by Jerry Stemach. Retold by John Bergez. Narrated by Nick Sandys. 2000. audio compact disk 200.00 (978-1-58702-491-7(8)) D Johnston Inc.

Silver Blaze, Vol. 1. Arthur Conan Doyle. Ed. by Jerry Stemach et al. Retold by John Bergez. Illus. by Michael Letwenko & Edward Letwenko. Narrated by Nick Sandys. Contrib. by Ted S. Hasselbring. 1 cass. (Running Time: 1 hr.). (Start-to-Finish Books). (J). (gr. 2-3). 2000. (978-1-58702-327-9(X), F28K2) D Johnston Inc.
A champion racehorse named Silver Blaze has been kidnapped from his stable, just one week before a famous race called the Wessex Cup. The horses trainer, John Straker, has been brutally murdered. Sherlock Holmes, Englands greatest detective, and Dr. Watson, his learned sidekick, head for the open moors of Wessex to investigate. The police have already arrested a young man named Fitzroy Simpson for the murder of John Straker. But Holmes is unconvinced of his crime.

Silver Blaze, Vol. 1. Arthur Conan Doyle. Ed. by Jerry Stemach et al. Retold by John Bergez. Illus. by Michael Letwenko & Edward Letwenko. Narrated by Nick Sandys. Contrib. by Ted S. Hasselbring. (Start-to-Finish Books). (J). (gr. 2-3). 2000. 35.00 (978-1-58702-492-4(6)) D Johnston Inc.

Silver Blaze: A Sherlock Holmes Adventure. (ENG.). 2007. (978-1-60339-067-5(7)); cd-rom & audio compact disk (978-1-60339-068-2(5)) Listenr Digest.

Silver Boxes: The Gift of Encouragement. Florence Littauer. 1 cass. 1989. 10.99 (978-0-8499-1259-7(8)) Nelson.
Urges Christians to "impart grace" by their words.

Silver Branch. unabr. ed. Rosemary Sutcliff. Read by Johanna Ward. 7 CDs. (Running Time: 7 hrs.). 2002. audio compact disk 56.00 (978-0-7861-9749-1(8), 2747) Blckstn Audio.
Justin & Flavius are accidentally caught up in the struggle for power after they discover a plot to overthrow the Emperior Carausius. They are forced to play a lone hand when a series of adventures carries them across England to the Wall & down again to the South where they become secret agents in the service of Rome.

Silver Branch. unabr. ed. Rosemary Sutcliff. Read by Johanna Ward. 5 cass. (Running Time: 7 hrs.). 2001. 39.95 (978-0-7861-1977-6(2), 2747) Blckstn Audio.

Silver brumbies of the South. Elyne Mitchell. Read by Caroline Lee. (Running Time: 6 hrs. 45 mins.). (Silver Brumby Ser.). (YA). 2009. 69.99 (978-1-74214-342-2(3), 9781742143422) Pub: Bolinda Pubng AUS. Dist(s): Bolinda Pub Inc

Silver Brumbies of the South. unabr. ed. Elyne Mitchell. 5 cass. (Running Time: 7 hrs.). 2002. (978-1-74030-373-6(3)) Bolinda Pubng AUS.

Silver Brumbies of the South. unabr. ed. Elyne Mitchell. Read by Caroline Lee. (Running Time: 24300 sec.). (Silver Brumby Ser.). (J). (gr. 4-7). 2006. audio compact disk 77.95 (978-1-74093-893-8(3)) Pub: Bolinda Pubng AUS. Dist(s): Bolinda Pub Inc

silver Brumby. Elyne Mitchell. Read by Caroline Lee. (Running Time: 6 hrs.). (Silver Brumby Ser.). (YA). 2009. 69.99 (978-1-74214-343-9(1), 9781742143439) Pub: Bolinda Pubng AUS. Dist(s): Bolinda Pub Inc

Silver Brumby. unabr. ed. Elyne Mitchell. Read by Caroline Lee. 6 CDs. (Running Time: 6 hrs.). (Silver Brumby: Ser.). (YA). 2004. audio compact disk 77.95 (978-1-74093-456-5(3)) Pub: Bolinda Pubng AUS. Dist(s): Bolinda Pub Inc

Silver Brumby. unabr. ed. Elyne Mitchell. Read by Caroline Lee. 4 cass. (Running Time: 6 hrs.). (Silver Brumby: Ser.). (YA). 2004. 32.00 (978-1-74030-050-6(5), 591115) Pub: Bolinda Pubng AUS. Dist(s): Bolinda Pub Inc
Thowra, the magnificent silver stallion, is king of mustangs. But he must defend his herd from the mighty horse, The Brolga, in the most savage of struggles.

Silver Brumby Kingdom. unabr. ed. Elyne Mitchell. 4 cass. (Running Time: 5 hrs. 45 mins.). 2002. (978-1-74030-539-6(6)) Bolinda Pubng AUS.

Silver Brumby Whirlwind. unabr. ed. Elyne Mitchell. Read by Caroline Lee. 3 cass. (Running Time: 4 hrs.). 2002. (978-1-74030-596-9(5)) Bolinda Pubng AUS.

***silver brumby's Daughter.** Elyne Mitchell. Read by Caroline Lee. (Running Time: 6 hrs. 55 mins.). (Silver Brumby Ser.). (YA). 2009. 49.99 (978-1-74214-344-6(X), 9781742143446) Pub: Bolinda Pubng AUS. Dist(s): Bolinda Pub Inc

Silver Brumby's Daughter. unabr. ed. Elyne Mitchell. Read by Caroline Lee. 5 cass. (Running Time: 6 hrs. 55 mins.). 2002. (978-1-74030-102-2(1), 500222) Bolinda Pubng AUS.

Silver Brumby's Daughter. unabr. ed. Elyne Mitchell. Read by Caroline Lee. 6 CDs. (Running Time: 25200 sec.). (Silver Brumby: Ser.). (J). (gr. 3-8). 2005. audio compact disk 77.95 (978-1-74093-688-0(4)) Pub: Bolinda Pubng AUS. Dist(s): Bolinda Pub Inc

Silver Bullet Audio MCAT Science Review MP3. Brett Ferdinand. (ENG., 2004. 59.99 (978-0-9780941-1-9(5)) RuveneCo CAN.

Silver Cascades. 1 cass. (Running Time: 60 min.). 1994. audio compact disk 15.95 CD. (2612, Creativ Pub) Quayside.
Melodious sounds of a clear mountain creek blended with original contemporary piano & guitar-based music by Chuck Lange.

Silver Cascades. 1 cass. (Running Time: 60 min.). 1994. 9.95 (2611, NrthWrd Bks) TandN Child.

Silver Chair see Chronicles of Narnia

Silver Chair see Chronicles of Narnia Super-Soundbook

Silver Chair. C. S. Lewis. 2 cass. (Chronicles of Narnia Ser.: Bk.4). (J). (gr. 4-8). 16.99 (BMDD018, Random AudioBks) Random Audio Pubg.

Silver Chair. adpt. ed. C. S. Lewis. (Running Time: 240 hrs. 0 mins.). (Radio Theatre: Chronicles of Narnia Ser.). (ENG.). (J). (gr. 3). 2007. audio compact disk 14.97 (978-1-58997-517-0(0)) Pub: Focus Family. Dist(s): Tyndale Hse

Silver Chair. unabr. ed. C. S. Lewis. 2 cass. (Running Time: 3 hrs.). (Chronicles of Narnia Ser.). (J). (gr. 4-8). 18.00 (D103) Blckstn Audio.
The perilous quest to find Prince Caspian before his father dies.

***Silver Chair.** unabr. ed. C. S. Lewis. Read by Jeremy Northam. 2005. (978-0-06-085440-9(5)); (978-0-06-085439-3(1)) HarperCollins Pubs.

Silver Chair. unabr. ed. C. S. Lewis. Read by Jeremy Northam. 6 cds. (Running Time: 021600 sec.). 2005. audio compact disk 29.95 (978-0-06-079336-4(8)) HarperCollins Pubs.

Silver Chair. unabr. abr. ed. C. S. Lewis. Read by Jeremy Northam. 4 cass. (Running Time: 6 hrs.). (Chronicles of Narnia Ser.). (J). 2004. audio compact disk 27.50 (978-0-06-058257-9(X)) HarperCollins Pubs.

Silver Chalice, Pt. 1. unabr. collector's ed. Thomas B. Costain. Read by David Case. 9 cass. (Running Time: 13 hrs. 30 min.). 1993. 72.00 (978-0-7366-2487-9(2), 3249A) Books on Tape.
SKay Scarpetta, Virginia's chief medical examiner, investigates an arson-murder & discovers evidence that sheds light on a series of unsolved crimes.

Silver Chalice, Pt. 2. collector's ed. Thomas B. Costain. Read by David Case. 8 cass. (Running Time: 12 hrs.). 1993. 64.00 (978-0-7366-2488-6(0), 3249-B) Books on Tape.
Kay Scarpetta, Virginia's chief medical examiner, investigates an arson-murder & discovers evidence that sheds light on a series of unsolved crimes.

Silver Cord/In Memoriam. adpt. ed. Focus on the Family Staff. Prod. by Dave Arnold. Adapted by Paul McCusker. (Running Time: 240 hrs. 0 mins.). (Radio Theatre Ser.). (ENG.). (J). (gr. 3). 2007. audio compact disk 14.97 (978-1-58997-511-8(1), Tyndale Ent) Tyndale Hse.

Silver Cow. 2004. bk. 24.95 (978-0-7882-0584-2(6)); pap. bk. 14.95 (978-0-7882-0652-8(4)); 8.95 (978-0-89719-956-8(1)); cass. & flmstrp 30.00 (978-0-89719-568-3(X)) Weston Woods.

Silver Crown. unabr. ed. 6 cass. (Running Time: 7 hrs. 45 min.). 2003. 54.00 (978-1-4025-6625-7(5)) Recorded Bks.

silver Donkey. Sonya Hartnett. Read by Richard Aspel. (Running Time: 4 hrs. 15 mins.). (J). 2009. 59.99 (978-1-74214-394-1(6), 9781742143941) Pub: Bolinda Pubng AUS. Dist(s): Bolinda Pub Inc

Silver Donkey. unabr. ed. Sonya Hartnett. Read by Richard Aspel. 4 CDs. (Running Time: 15300 sec.). (J). (gr. 3-8). 2005. audio compact disk 57.95 (978-1-74093-586-9(1)) Pub: Bolinda Pubng AUS. Dist(s): Bolinda Pub Inc

Silver Ghost. Charlotte MacLeod. Read by Mary Peiffer. 2001. 40.00 (978-0-7366-7175-0(7)) Books on Tape.

Silver Ghost. unabr. collector's ed. Charlotte MacLeod. Read by Mary Peiffer. 5 cass. (Running Time: 7 hrs. 30 min.). (Kelling/Bittersohn Ser.: Bk. 8). 2001. 40.00 Books on Tape.
Sarah and Max must untangle a series of events including robbery, murder and the disappearance of Aunt Bodicea Kelling.

***Silver Girl.** unabr. ed. Elin Hilderbrand. (Running Time: 12 hrs.). (ENG.). 2011. 26.98 (978-1-60941-294-4(X)); audio compact disk & audio compact disk 34.98 (978-1-60941-288-3(5)) Pub: Hachet Audio. Dist(s): HachBkGrp

Silver Hand. unabr. ed. Stephen R. Lawhead. Read by Stuart Langston. 9 cass. (Running Time: 13 hrs. 30 min.). (Song of Albion Ser.: Bk. 2). 2002. 62.95 (978-0-7861-2363-6(X)); audio compact disk 80.00 (978-0-7861-9429-2(4)) Blckstn Audio.
Illustrates the development of European drama from ancient times to the threshold of the modern theater. Includes Euripides - Medea, Shakespeare - The Tempest, Moliere - The Imaginary Invalid, Dumas - Camille, Ibsen - An Enemy of the People, Shaw - Arms and the Man, and Chekhov - Uncle Vanya.

Silver Hand. unabr. ed. Stephen R. Lawhead. Read by Stuart Langston. 1 MP3. (Running Time: 13 hrs.). (Song of Albion Ser.: Bk. 2). 2002. audio compact disk 24.95 (978-0-7861-9120-8(1)) Blckstn Audio.

***Silver Hand: The Song of Albion Trilogy, Book 2.** unabr. ed. Stephen R. Lawhead. Read by Stuart Langton. (Running Time: 13 hrs.). (Song of Albion Ser.). 2010. audio compact disk 29.95 (978-1-4417-5204-8(8)) Blckstn Audio.

Silver Harvest. Kay Stephens. (Story Sound Ser.). (J). 2005. 54.95 (978-1-85903-731-7(3)) Pub: Mgna Lrg Print GBR. Dist(s): Ulverscroft US

Silver Hatchet see Tales of the Supernatural

Silver Horde. unabr. ed. Rex Ellingwood Beach. Read by David Sharp. 8 cass. (Running Time: 11 hrs.). 1994. 49.95 (978-1-55686-557-2(0)) Books in Motion.
After failing at gold mining, Boyd Emerson stakes his future on the salmon canning industry in Alaska. But in those early days of the industry, fortunes were won or lost as fast as mining.

Silver Lining. unabr. ed. Catrin Collier. Read by Helen Griffin. 10 cass. (Running Time: 15 cass.). 2000. 84.95 (978-0-7540-0434-9(1), CAB 1857) Pub: Chivers Audio Bks GBR. Dist(s): AudioGO
Alma Moore is betrayed by the man she loves, left alone to face the whisperings of an uptight society. Bethan Powell returns to her home town without her husband, carrying a child whose arrival has irrevocably shattered a marriage. Two women, ostracized & forced to confront society. One man, haunted by his past, is prepared to stretch out a helping hand to both.

Silver Lining. unabr. ed. Read by Kirk Douglas et al. 2 cass. (Running Time: 49 min.). 1996. 19.95 Set. (978-1-888453-00-3(1), BMP Audio) BMP Music.
Twenty-three of the world's most distinguished actors read their favorite poems. Includes: "The Stolen Child" by W. B. Yeats; "Pity This Busy Monster, Manunkind" by E. E. Cummings; "Snake" by D. H. Lawrence; "Hope Is the Thing with Feathers" & more.

Silver Linings. unabr. ed. Matthew Quick. (Running Time: 9.5 hrs. NaN mins.). (J). 2008. 29.95 (978-1-4332-5369-0(0)) Blckstn Audio.

Silver Linings. unabr. ed. Matthew Quick. (Running Time: 9.5 hrs. NaN mins.). 2008. 59.95 (978-1-4332-5367-6(4)) Blckstn Audio.

Silver Linings. unabr. ed. Matthew Quick. Read by Ray Porter. 6 CDs. (Running Time: 7 hrs. 30 mins.). 2008. audio compact disk 80.00 (978-1-4332-5368-3(2)) Blckstn Audio.

Silver Linings. unabr. collector's ed. Jayne Ann Krentz. Read by Mary Peiffer. 7 cass. (Running Time: 10 hrs. 30 min.). 1996. 56.00 (978-0-7366-3262-1(X), 3919) Books on Tape.
When you get rejected in love, you naturally build walls. Mattie Sharpe, a shy but successful art dealer, lays bricks sky-high after Hugh Abbott, an adventurer, breaks her heart. She vows that she'll only meet Hugh again over her - better his - dead body.

Silver Master. abr. ed. Jayne Castle, pseud. Read by Joyce Bean. (Running Time: 6 hrs.). (Harmony Ser.: No. 5). 2008. audio compact disk 14.99 (978-1-4233-3347-0(0), 9781423333470, BCD Value Price) Brilliance Audio.

Silver Master. unabr. ed. Jayne Castle, pseud. Read by Joyce Bean. (Running Time: 9 hrs.). (Harmony Ser.: No. 5). 2007. 39.25 (978-1-4233-3345-6(4),

9781423333456, BADLE); 24.95 (978-1-4233-3344-9(6), 9781423333449, BAD); 74.25 (978-1-4233-3339-5(X), 9781423333395, BrilAudUnabridg); audio compact disk 24.95 (978-1-4233-3342-5(X), 9781423333425, Brilliance MP3); audio compact disk 34.95 (978-1-4233-3340-1(3), 9781423333401, Bril Audio CD Unabri); audio compact disk 39.25 (978-1-4233-3343-2(8), 9781423333432, Brlnc Audio MP3 Lib); audio compact disk 92.25 (978-1-4233-3341-8(1), 9781423333418, BriAudCD Unabrid) Brilliance Audio.

Silver Meadow. unabr. ed. Robert C. Reade. Read by Maynard Villers. 6 cass. (Running Time: 7 hrs. 12 min.). 2001. 39.95 (978-1-55686-989-1(4)) Books in Motion.
The plans of young Matt Reynolds to settle down and marry in Belmont, Nevada are thrown into crisis, when the son of a wealthy mine owner forces Matt to defend himself, resulting in the young man's death. For power and position can twist justice in this mining town.

Silver Moons, Black Steel. Tara K. Harper. Read by Karen White. 2002. 112.00 (978-0-7366-8787-4(4)) Books on Tape.

Silver on the Tree. unabr. ed. Susan Cooper. 6 cass. (Running Time: 9 hrs. 27 mins.). (Dark Is Rising Sequence Ser.). (J). (gr. 4-7). 2004. 40.00 (978-0-8072-0679-9(2), Listening Lib) Random Audio Pubg.

Silver on the Tree. unabr. ed. Susan Cooper. Read by Alex Jennings. 6 vols. (Running Time: 9 hrs. 27 mins.). (Dark Is Rising Sequence Ser.). (J). (gr. 4-7). 2004. 46.00 (978-0-8072-0795-6(0), S YA 353 SP, Listening Lib) Random Audio Pubg.
"The Dark is rising in its last and greatest bid to control the world. Will Stanton must join forces with his ageless master Merriman and Bran, the Welsh boy whose destiny ties him to the Light as well as the three Drew children. These six fight fear and death, in a quest through time and space that touches the most ancient myths of the British Isles and that brings Susan Cooper's masterful sequence of novels to a satisfying close.".

Silver Pigs. Lindsey Davis. Read by Christian Rodska. 6 cass. (Marcus Didius Falco Ser.). 54.95 (978-0-7927-3814-5(4), CSL 873); audio compact disk 29.95 (978-0-7927-3851-0(9), CMP 873) AudioGO.

Silver Pigs. Lindsey Davis. Read by Christian Rodska. 8 CDs. (Running Time: 33060 sec.). (Marcus Didius Falco Ser.). 2005. audio compact disk 79.95 (978-0-7927-3815-2(2), SLD 873) AudioGO.

Silver Pigs. unabr. ed. Lindsey Davis. Narrated by Donal Donnelly. 8 cass. (Running Time: 11 hrs. 45 mins.). (Marcus Didius Falco Ser.). 1992. 70.00 (978-1-55690-635-0(8), 92103E7) Recorded Bks.
Marcus Didius Falco is a private informer in Rome, 50 A.D. His assignment - to break an illegal traffic in precious metal.

Silver Pigs: A BBC Full-Cast Radio Drama. unabr. ed. Lindsey Davis. Narrated by Full Cast. (Running Time: 2 hrs. 0 mins. 0 sec.). (ENG.). 2010. audio compact disk 24.95 (978-1-60283-851-2(8)) Pub: AudioGO. Dist(s): Perseus Dist

Silver Shoes: Shoes Through the Ages. Steck-Vaughn Staff. (J). 1999. (978-0-7398-0931-0(8)) SteckVau.

Silver Shot. unabr. ed. Gary McCarthy. Read by Gene Engene. 6 cass. (Running Time: 6 hrs. 12 min.). (Derby Man Ser.: Bk. 5). 1994. 39.95 (978-1-55686-552-7(X)) Books in Motion.
Darby Buckingham sets out to expose a spellbinding stock manipulator. But his opponent has the disposition of a rattlesnake & gets even by sabotaging a mine shaft into a pit of death.

Silver Spitfire. Roger Harvey. Read by Gordon Griffin. 3 cass. (Running Time: 30 min.). 1988. 34.95 (978-1-85496-114-3(4), 61144) Pub: Soundings Ltd GBR. Dist(s): Ulverscroft US

Silver Spoon. John Galsworthy. Read by David Case. (Running Time: 34200 sec.). 2007. audio compact disk 72.00 (978-0-7861-5829-4(8)) Blckstn Audio.

Silver Spoon. unabr. ed. John Galsworthy. Read by David Case. (Running Time: 34200 sec.). (Forsyte Chronicles Ser.). 2007. 65.95 (978-0-7861-4967-4(1)); audio compact disk 29.95 (978-0-7861-6970-2(2)) Blckstn Audio.

Silver Spoon & Passers By. unabr. collector's ed. John Galsworthy. Read by David Case. 7 cass. (Running Time: 10 hrs. 30 min.). (Forsyte Saga Ser.). 1999. 56.00 (978-0-7366-4385-6(0), 4846) Books on Tape.
Detailed picture of the British propertied class, from the wealth & security of the mid-Victorian era through Edwardian high-noon to a post-WW I world of change, strikes & social malaise. By showing the Forsytes in all their strengths & weaknesses against a detailed background of English life - Parliament, the Courts, the City, sports, philanthropy, art, wars - Galsworthy has made THE WHITE MONKEY & the other volumes in THE FORSYTE SAGA valuable social history as well as great fiction.

Silver Spoon of Solomon Snow. unabr. ed. Kaye Umansky. Read by Jenny Sterlin. 5 CDs. (Running Time: 5 hrs. 15 mins.). (J). (gr. 4-7). 2006. audio compact disk 49.75 (978-1-4193-7113-4(4), C3546); 39.75 (978-1-4193-7108-0(8), 98271) Recorded Bks.
Nottinghamshire Book Award winner Kaye Umansky combines humor and a Dickensian atmosphere to bring young readers into the unlikely world of Solomon Snow. Solly's life stinks. He lives with Ma and Pa Scubbins in a rundown cottage outside of the village of Boring working as a delivery boy for their laundry service. But his luck soon changes when Ma lets slip a little secret - Solly was left on their doorstep as an infant with a silver spoon in his mouth. Solly sets out to find his spoon with the help of some ragamuffin friends he picks up along the way. But will Solly ever find his spoon and his real parents?.

Silver Street. Elizabeth Gill & Trudy Harris. 2009. 54.95 (978-1-84652-453-0(9)); audio compact disk 71.95 (978-1-84652-454-7(7)) Pub: Magna Story GBR. Dist(s): Ulverscroft US

Silver Swan. unabr. ed. Benjamin Black. Narrated by Timothy Dalton. 1 MP3-CD. (Running Time: 8 hrs. 46 mins.). 2008. 44.95 (978-0-7927-5302-5(X)); audio compact disk 74.95 (978-0-7927-5246-2(5)) AudioGO.
Two years have passed since the events of the bestselling Christine Falls, and much has changed for Quirke, the irascible, formerly hard-drinking Dublin pathologist.With much to regret from his last inquisitive foray, Quirke ought to know better than to let his curiosity get the best of him. Yet when an almost-forgotten acquaintance comes to him about his beautiful young wife's apparent suicide, Quirke's "old itch to cut into the quick of things, to delve into the dark of what was hidden" is roused again. As he begins to probe further into the shadowy circumstances of Deirdre Hunt's death, he discovers many things that might better have remained hidden, as well as grave danger to those he loves.

Silver Swan. unabr. ed. Benjamin Black & John Banville. Read by Timothy Dalton. 7 CDs. (Running Time: 9 hrs. 0 mins. 0 sec.). (ENG.). 2008. audio compact disk 34.95 (978-1-4272-0289-5(3)) Pub: Macmill Audio. Dist(s): Macmillan

Silver Sword. Ian Serraillier. Read by Michael Maloney. 1 cass. (Running Time: 3 hrs. 0 mins. 0 sec.). (ENG., 2001. (978-0-14-180254-1(5), PengAudBks) Penguin Grp USA.
Although the silver sword was only a paper knife, it became the symbol of hope and courage which kept the four children alive through the years of Nazi occupation when they had to fend for themselves. And afterwards, it inspired them to keep going on the exhausting and dangerous journey from war-torn Poland to Switzerland, where they hoped to find their parents.

Silver Sword, Set. unabr. ed. Ian Serraillier. Read by Sean Barrett. 3 cass. (Running Time: 3 hrs.). (J). 1995. 24.95 (978-1-85549-051-2(X), CTC 050) AudioGO.

Silver Touch. Rosalind Laker, pseud. 12 CDs. (Running Time: 13 hrs. 30 mins.). (Soundings (CDs) Ser.). (J). 2004. audio compact disk 99.95 (978-1-84283-860-0(1)) Pub: ISIS Lrg Prnt GBR. Dist(s): Ulverscroft US

Silver Touch. Rosalind Laker, pseud. Read by Annie Aldington. 11 cass. (Running Time: 13 hrs. 30 mins.). (Soundings Ser.). (J). 2004. 89.95 (978-1-84283-706-1(0)) Pub: ISIS Lrg Prnt GBR. Dist(s): Ulverscroft US

Silver Tower. abr. ed. Dale Brown. Read by Richard Allen. 4 cass. (Running Time: 6 hrs.). 2003. 62.25 (978-1-59086-809-6(9), 1590868099, CD Lib Edit); audio compact disk 74.25 (978-1-59086-816-4(1), 1590868161, CD Lib Edit) Brilliance Audio.
Iran has been invaded. And America responds in a grueling counterattack by air, by sea - and by a brave new technology that will redefine war. The most sophisticated laser defense system ever. It is called Silver Tower. And it will change the balance of world power forever.

Silver Tower. abr. ed. Dale Brown. Read by Richard Allen. (Running Time: 21600 sec.). 2005. audio compact disk 16.99 (978-1-59600-438-2(X), 9781596004382, BCD Value Price) Brilliance Audio.

Silver Tower. abr. ed. Dale Brown. Read by Richard Allen. (Running Time: 6 hrs.). 2006. 39.25 (978-1-4233-0206-3(0), 9781423302063, Brlnc Audio MP3 Lib); 24.95 (978-1-4233-0205-6(2), 9781423302056, Brilliance MP3); 39.25 (978-1-4233-0208-7(7), 9781423302087, BADLE) Brilliance Audio.

Silver Tower. abr. ed. Dale Brown. Read by Richard Allen. (Running Time: 6 hrs.). 2006. 24.95 (978-1-4233-0207-0(9), 9781423302070, BAD) Brilliance Audio.

Silver Tower. abr. ed. Dale Brown. Read by Richard Allen. (Running Time: 6 hrs.). 2009. audio compact disk 9.99 (978-1-4418-0812-7(4), 9781441808127, BCD Value Price) Brilliance Audio.

Silver Wattle. Belinda Alexandra. Read by Caroline Lee. (Running Time: 16 hrs. 15 mins.). 2009. 109.99 (978-1-74214-190-9(0), 9781742141909) Pub: Bolinda Pubng AUS. Dist(s): Bolinda Pub Inc

Silver Wattle. unabr. ed. Belinda Alexandra. Read by Caroline Lee. (Running Time: 59100 sec.). 2008. audio compact disk 118.95 (978-1-921334-63-4(0), 9781921334634) Pub: Bolinda Pubng AUS. Dist(s): Bolinda Pub Inc

Silver Wedding. unabr. ed. Maeve Binchy. Read by Kate Binchy. 8 cass. (Running Time: 12 hrs.). 2000. 59.95 (CAB 384) Pub: Chivers Audio Bks GBR. Dist(s): AudioGO
A unique family occasion is looming for the O'Hagans. Desmond and Deirdre will have been married 25 years in October. Naturally there will be a celebration, but who will arrange it? And will the right people come? It's unthinkable to not have a party, but do they really want one? The past secrets and present fears of the family and their close friends are gradually unveiled in this collection of stories.

Silver Winds. unabr. ed. Gary McCarthy. Read by Stephanie Brush. 12 cass. (Running Time: 14 hrs. 30 min.). 1997. 64.95 (978-1-55686-732-3(8)) Books in Motion.
Six people, enroute to the richest silver strike in history - the Comstock Lode -, meet in a Sierra blizzard. Who among them will survive the failures, successes & dangers that lay ahead.

Silverado Squatters. abr. ed. Excerpts. Robert Louis Stevenson. Narrated by Francis Balfour. Photos by Craig Duddles. Prod. by Craig Duddles. Abr. by David Duddles. Epil. by David Duddles. 2 CDs. (Running Time: 2 hrs. 30 mins.). 2005. audio compact disk 27.90 (978-0-9765765-0-1(3)) Blue Pylon.
Like the wine makers he visited, Robert Louis Stevenson bottled the flavors of the Napa Valley in the summer of 1880.He had just married Fanny Osbourne and set up camp in a bunkhouse near an abandoned silver mine. The unique characters and serene beauty of the valley gave the young author much to write about. Beautifully written, this travelogue is classic Stevenson. Francis Balfour, the Scottish narrator, provides authenticity and entertainment. The CD case is beautifully enhanced with photos from site of the story.

SilverFin. unabr. ed. Charlie Higson. Read by Nathaniel Parker. 5 cass. (Running Time: 8 hrs. 29 mins.). (Young Bond Ser.). (J). (gr. 4-7). 2006. 40.00 (978-0-307-28574-4(X), Listening Lib); audio compact disk 55.00 (978-0-307-28575-1(8), Listening Lib) Pub: Random Audio Pubg. Dist(s): Random

SilverFin. unabr. ed. Charlie Higson. Read by Nathaniel Parker. 7 CDs. (Running Time: 30600 sec.). (Young Bond Ser.). (ENG.). (J). (gr. 5). 2006. audio compact disk 37.00 (978-0-307-28437-2(9), Listening Lib) Pub: Random Audio Pubg. Dist(s): Random

***Silverlicious.** unabr. ed. Victoria Kann. (ENG.). 2011. (978-0-06-200767-4(X)) HarperCollins Pubs.

Silvertongue. Charlie Fletcher. Narrated by Jim Dale. (Stoneheart Trilogy: Bk. 3). (J). (gr. 4-7). 2009. audio compact disk 39.95 (978-0-545-02747-2(0)) Scholastic Inc.

Silvertongue. unabr. ed. Charlie Fletcher. Narrated by Jim Dale. 9 CDs. (Running Time: 10 hrs. 45 mins.). (Stoneheart Trilogy: Bk. 3). (ENG.). (J). (gr. 4-7). 2009. audio compact disk 84.95 (978-0-545-03321-3(7)) Scholastic Inc.

Silverwing. unabr. ed. Kenneth Oppel. Narrated by John McDonough. 6 pieces. (Running Time: 7 hrs. 30 mins.). (Silverwing Saga: Bk. 1). (gr. 4 up). 1997. 54.00 (978-1-4025-0752-6(6), 96898) Recorded Bks.
Shade, a young silverwing bat, is the runt of his colony. Determined to show how brave he is, Shade breaks one of the ancient rules that governs the bats. As punishment, owls burn the bats' roost, forcing them to migrate earlier than normal. While on the trip south to the Hibernaculum, Shade becomes separated from his flock during a rain storm. His destination is millions of wing beats away. Now he must find a way to make the journey on his own. Along the way, he'll meet up with bats of different species - some friendly, some not. Shade will have to learn quickly which ones to trust if he's ever going to see his family again.

Silvestre Y la Piedrecita. 2004. pap. bk. 32.75 (978-1-55592-345-7(3)) Weston Woods.

Silvestre y la Piedrecita Magica. William Steig. Illus. by William Steig. 11 vols. (Running Time: 20 mins.). 1992. bk. 28.95 (978-1-59519-202-8(6)); pap. bk. 45.95 (978-1-59519-201-1(8)); 9.95 (978-1-59112-120-6(5)); audio compact disk 12.95 (978-1-59519-199-1(2)) Live Oak Media.

Silvestre y la Piedrecita Magica. William Steig. Illus. by William Steig. 11 vols. (Running Time: 20 mins.). (SPA.). (J). 1992. pap. bk. 18.95 (978-1-59519-200-4(X)) Pub: Live Oak Media. Dist(s): AudioGO

Silvestre y la Piedrecita Magica. William Steig. 1 cass. (Running Time: 10 min.). (SPA.). (J). pap. bk. 12.95; pap. bk. 32.75 Weston Woods.
The Duncan family is beside itself when son Sylvester turns himself into a rock to escape the jaws of a hungry lion.

Silvestre y la Piedrecita Magica. William Steig. (SPA.). (J). 2004. 8.95 (978-0-7882-0127-1(1)) Weston Woods.

Silvestre y la Piedrecita Magica. unabr. ed. William Steig. Illus. by William Steig. Read by Angel Pineda. 14 vols. (Running Time: 20 mins.). (SPA.). (J). 1992. pap. bk. & tchr. ed. 41.95 Reading Chest. (978-0-87499-273-1(7)) Live Oak Media.
Readalong of Spanish translation of Silvester & the Magic Pebble.

Silvestre y la Piedrecita Magica. unabr. ed. William Steig. Illus. by William Steig. Read by Angel Pineda. 11 vols. (Running Time: 20 mins.). (SPA.). (J). (gr. 1-6). 1992. bk. 25.95 (978-0-87499-272-4(9)); pap. bk. 16.95 (978-0-87499-271-7(0)) Pub: Live Oak Media. Dist(s): AudioGO

Silvestre y la Piedrecita Magica. unabr. ed. William Steig. 1 cass. (Running Time: 20 min.). (SPA.). (J). 1992. 9.95 Live Oak Media.

Simandl - Complete Etudes: 4-CD Double Bass Play-along. Composed by Franz Simandl. 2006. pap. bk. 39.98 (978-1-59615-636-4(8), 1596156368) Pub: Music Minus. Dist(s): H Leonard

Simba's Favorites. Prod. by Walt Disney Records Staff. 1 cass . (J). 1998. 12.98 (978-0-7634-0480-2(2)); audio compact disk 22.50 (978-0-7634-0481-9(0)) W Disney Records.

Simba's Pride Read-Along. Prod. by Walt Disney Records Staff. 1 cass. (J). (ps-3). 1998. pap. bk. 6.98 (978-0-7634-0439-0(X)) W Disney Records.

Simbolo Perdido. unabr. ed. Dan Brown. Read by Gustavo Rex. (ENG & SPA.). 2009. audio compact disk 50.00 (978-0-307-73692-5(X), Random AudioBks) Pub: Random Audio Pubg. Dist(s): Random

Simeon Stylites see Twentieth-Century Poetry in English, No. 29, Recordings of Poets Reading Their Own Poetry

Simeon's Bride. unabr. ed. Alison Taylor. Read by Steve Hodson. 10 cass. (Running Time: 15 hrs.). 2002. 84.95 (978-0-7540-0756-2(1), CAB 2178) AudioGO.
A woman, little more than a skeleton, is found hanging in dense woodland outside Bangor, hands bound behind her back. Detective Chief Inspector Michael McKenna and his colleagues, seeking her identity and her killer, become enmeshed in deceit and half-truths as they chase shadows in an area of spectacular beauty.

Simisola. unabr. ed. Ruth Rendell. Read by Donada Peter. 8 cass. (Running Time: 12 hrs.). (Inspector Wexford Mystery Ser.: Bk. 16). 1996. 64.00 (978-0-7366-3263-8(8), 3920) Books on Tape.
A doctor's daughter disappears. One woman turns up dead, then another - neither one the daughter. A third woman, beaten & unconscious, may hold the key to the mystery.

Simisola. unabr. ed. Ruth Rendell. Read by Christopher Ravenscroft. 10 cass. (Running Time: 15 hrs.). (Inspector Wexford Mystery Ser.: Bk. 16). 2000. 69.95 (978-0-7451-6515-8(X), CAB 1131) Pub: Chivers Audio Bks GBR. Dist(s): AudioGO
When Melanie Akande, daughter of Inspector Wexford's Nigerian-born GP, goes missing, the family prepares for the worst. And when the body of a young black girl is found buried in the countryside, the whiff of deceit lingers around key witnesses. Inspector Wexford finds that he must battle through the prejudices of color, age and social class to discover the shocking truth.

S'Immuniser. unabr. ed. Robert A. Monroe. Read by Roland Simon. 1 cass. (Running Time: 30 min.). (Human Plus Ser.). (FRE.). 1993. 14.95 (978-1-56102-068-3(0)) Inter Indus.
Alert immune system to seek out & destroy disease producing organisms.

Simon Bloom, the Gravity Keeper. unabr. ed. Michael Reisman. Read by Nicholas Hormann. 6 CDs. (Running Time: 7 hrs. 22 mins.). (YA). (gr. 5-9). 2008. audio compact disk 50.00 (978-0-7393-6218-1(6), Listening Lib) Pub: Random Audio Pubg. Dist(s): Random
Ordinary sixth-grader Simon Bloom has just made the biggest discovery since gravity - and it literally fell into his lap. Or onto his head, anyway. You see, Simon has found the Teacher's Edition of Physics, a magical reference book containing the very formulas that control the laws that govern the universe! By reciting the formulas out loud, he's able to do the impossible - like reverse the force of gravity to float weightlessly, and reduce friction to zoom across any surface! But a book that powerful isn't safe with Simon for long. Before he knows it, he is being pursued by evil forces bent on gaining control of the formulas. And they'll do anything to retrieve them. Now, Simon and his friends must use their wits and the magic of science in a galactic battle for the book, and the future of the universe, in this funny, fast-paced science fiction adventure from first-time author Michael Reisman.

Simon Bloom, the Gravity Keeper. unabr. ed. Michael Reisman. Read by Nicholas Hormann. (Running Time: 26520 sec.). (ENG.). (J). (gr. 4-7). 2008. audio compact disk 34.00 (978-0-7393-6353-9(0), Listening Lib) Pub: Random Audio Pubg. Dist(s): Random

Simon Bloom, the Octopus Effect. unabr. ed. Michael Reisman. (ENG.). (J). (gr. 4). 2009. audio compact disk 40.00 (978-0-7393-8238-7(1), Listening Lib) Pub: Random Audio Pubg. Dist(s): Random

Simon Fehfer's Junkland Jam. Prod. by Greg Clayman. 1 cass. 1997. 19.95 (978-1-57304-914-6(X)) Hachet Audio.

Simon Legree: A Negro Sermon see Poetry of Vachel Lindsay

Simon the Coldheart. Georgette Heyer. Read by Ben Elliot. 7 cass. (Running Time: 10 hrs.). (Isis Cassettes Ser.). (J). 2005. 61.95 (978-0-7531-3405-4(5)) Pub: ISIS Lrg Prnt GBR. Dist(s): Ulverscroft US

Simon the Coldheart. unabr. ed. Georgette Heyer. Read by Ben Elliot. 9 CDs. (Running Time: 35400 sec.). (Isis (CDs) Ser.). 2005. audio compact disk 84.95 (978-0-7531-2458-1(0)) Pub: ISIS Lrg Prnt GBR. Dist(s): Ulverscroft US

Simon the Cyrenian Speaks see Poetry of Countee Cullen

Simone de Beauvoir: Knowledge Products Production. unabr. ed. LaDelle McWhorter. Read by Lynn Redgrave. (Running Time: 3 mins.). (J). 2006. audio compact disk 25.95 (978-0-7861-6385-4(2)) Pub: Blckstn Audio. Dist(s): NetLibrary CO

Simone Weil. Francine Du Plessix Gray. 2001. 40.00 (978-0-7366-7035-7(1)) Books on Tape.
A thoughtful and compelling biography of an enigmatic figure and early feminist.

Simone Weil. unabr. ed. Francine Du Plessix Gray. 4 cass. (Running Time: 6 hrs.). 2001. 24.95 (978-0-7366-6812-5(8)) Books on Tape.
In this thoughtful & compelling biography, du Plessix Gray illuminates an enigmatic figure & early feminist whose passion & pathos will fascinate a wide audience of readers.

Simon's Pond. Perf. by Monroe Alfrey. 1 cass. (J). (ps-3). 9.95 (1-888-FUN-SONG); audio compact disk 12.95 CD. (NG) Five Speed Prods.
A collection of ten lively songs for children aged 2-8. A plumber by trade, Alfrey harbored a hobby for musical composition for years. His now 19-month-old son loved the song Dad created just for him, "Simon's Pond." When friends overheard Alfrey singing his other original tunes for Simon,

including "The Monkey & the Lion" & "Daddy's Tools," they convinced him to share them with other children. Selected "Outstanding" by Parent's Councel Limited.

Simple. 2004. audio compact disk 16.99 (978-7-5124-0295-9(3)) Destiny Image Pubs.

Simple. Jack Deere. 1 cass. (Running Time: 90 mins.). (Proverbs Ser.: Vol. 7). 2000. 5.00 (JD08-007) Morning NC.
Practical wisdom for everyday living is brought to life in Jack's thorough exposition of this important book of the Bible.

Simple Abundance see Abondance Dans la Simplicitee

Simple Abundance: Living by Your Own Lights. abr. ed. Sarah Ban Breathnach. Read by Sarah Ban Breathnach. 3 CDs. (Running Time: 3 hrs.). (ENG.). 2002. audio compact disk 24.98 (978-1-58621-407-4(1)) Pub: Hachet Audio. Dist(s): HachBkGrp

Simple Abundance: Living by Your Own Lights. abr. ed. Sarah Ban Breathnach. (ENG.). 2005. 14.98 (978-1-59483-354-0(0)) Pub: Hachet Audio. Dist(s): HachBkGrp

Simple Act of Faith. Swami Amar Jyoti. 1 cass. 1976. 9.95 (D-13) Truth Consciousness.
We see Light in direct proportion to our degree of faith. Personal choice, self-interest & the will of God.

Simple & Easy: The little things you can do that will have a BIG impact on your performance, success, & Happiness. Ned Parks. (ENG.). 2007. audio compact disk 19.95 (978-0-9798623-0-4(2)) New Dir.

Simple Answers from the Cosmos. Swami Amar Jyoti. 1 cass. 1992. 9.95 (P-60) Truth Consciousness.
The cosmos always provides answers depending upon our level of understanding; the higher you go, the simpler it is.

Simple Approach to Horoscope Interpretation. Sue Lovett. 1 cass. 8.95 (217) Am Fed Astrologers.
Qualities & elements are key to simplified interpretation.

Simple Chinese for Adoptive Families. Amy Kendall. 2007. spiral bd. 30.00 (978-0-9796813-1-8(6)) Simple Language.

Simple Choices, Powerful Changes. Read by Dean Ornish. 2 cass. (Running Time: 2 hrs. 10 min.). (Love & Survival Ser.). 1999. 17.95 Set. (83-0054) Explorations.
Illustrates how simple choices in diet & lifestyle can cause powerful changes in our health & well-being, & offers important lifestyle changes we can make to live healthier, better lives.

Simple Christianity. unabr. ed. John MacArthur. Narrated by Scott Grunden. (Running Time: 5 hrs. 36 mins. 0 sec.). (ENG.). 2009. audio compact disk 21.98 (978-1-59644-671-7(4), christianSeed) christianaud.

***Simple Christianity: Rediscover the Principle Foundations of Faith.** unabr. ed. John MacArthur. Narrated by Scott Grunden. (ENG.). 2009. 12.98 (978-1-59644-672-4(2), christianSeed) christianaud.

Simple Christmas. Contrib. by John M. DeVries. 1997. 7.98 (978-0-7601-1749-1(7), 75602106); 55.00 (978-0-7601-1750-7(0), 75606322) Pub: Brentwood Music. Dist(s): H Leonard

Simple Christmas: Twelve Stories That Celebrate the True Holiday Spirit. unabr. ed. Mike Huckabee. Read by Mike Huckabee. (Running Time: 6 hrs.). (ENG.). (gr. 12 up). 2009. audio compact disk 29.95 (978-0-14-314549-3(5), PengAudBks) Penguin Grp USA.

Simple Christmas Pageant. Composed by Cindy Sterling & Sheldon Curry. (ENG.). 2009. audio compact disk 16.95 (978-0-7390-6296-8(4)); audio compact disk 59.95 (978-0-7390-6295-1(6)) Alfred Pub.

***Simple Christmas Pageant: Preview Pack, Choral Score & CD.** Composed by Cindy Sterling & Sheldon Curry. (ENG.). 2009. audio compact disk 12.95 (978-0-7390-6298-2(0)) Alfred Pub.

Simple Christmas Pageant: 10 CDs. Composed by Cindy Sterling & Sheldon Curry. (ENG.). 2009. audio compact disk 89.95 (978-0-7390-6297-5(2)) Alfred Pub.

***Simple Church: Returning to God's Process for Making Disciples.** unabr. ed. Sam Rainer & Eric Geiger. Narrated by Grover Gardner. (ENG.). 2008. 14.98 (978-1-59644-568-0(8), Hovel Audio) christianaud.

Simple Church: Returning to God's Process for Making Disciples. unabr. ed. Thom S. Rainer & Eric Geiger. Read by Grover Gardner. (Running Time: 6 hrs. 36 mins. 0 sec.). (ENG.). 2008. audio compact disk 24.98 (978-1-59644-567-3(X)) christianaud.

***Simple Compassion: Devotions to Make a Difference in Your Neighborhood & Your World.** Keri Wyatt Kent. (Running Time: 8 hrs. 47 mins. 0 sec.). (ENG.). 2009. 9.99 (978-0-310-77335-1(0)) Zondervan.

Simple Concepts in Estate Planning: Successful Strategies for Distribution-Oriented Planning. Instructed by Robert E. Hales. (Running Time: 120 mins.). 2004. audio compact disk 19.95 (978-1-59280-126-8(9)) Marketplace Bks.
Sometimes the most important lessons are learned by going back to the basics. Now, business planning expert Robert E. Hales revisits the essential elements of estate planning - but offers a significant new twist: He shows how slightly tweaking standard estate planning strategies can lead to more optimal effectiveness. With his appealing mix of humor and professional insight, Hale clearly underscores the need for integrating both the 'bean counter" and "visionary" approach into the estate planning process.Hale's 90-minute workshop outlines the fundamentals of distribution-oriented estate planning in clear, acronym-free English, and furnishes fresh new approaches to common concepts, including: ?Tax reduction vs. distribution - the goal of an estate plan?Benefits of Q-Tip trusts?Advantages of generation-skipping trusts?Use and shortcomings of buy-sell agreements?Using life insurance to pay estate taxes, second-to-die polices, and more.Plus, many estate planners focus on minimizing - or eliminating taxes - as the primary goal of estate planning, Hale feels ?distribution? should be the primary focus of an estate plan. After all, he argues, if estate assets do not go to whom they are supposed to, an estate plan is a failed document - regardless of how much tax savings it may generate. Even experienced practitioners will discover new ways to increase your estate planning acumen - with this entertaining new presentation from an industry veteran.

Simple Email Marketing to Skyrocket Sales-Even without a Website. Kris Solie-Johnson. 2007. 49.95 (978-0-939069-09-5(1)) Amer Inst Small Bus.

Simple Faith. 2002. audio compact disk 43.00 (978-1-57972-450-4(7)) Insight Living.

Simple Faith. 2002. 34.95 (978-1-57972-443-6(4)) Insight Living.

Simple Faith. Perf. by Craig Duncan & Mountain View Players Staff. 1996. 9.98; audio compact disk 14.98 Pub: Brentwood Music. Dist(s): Provident Mus Dist
Celebrates hope & belief with a collection of favorite hymns performed with simple, authentic acoustic mountain instruments. Includes "Softly & Tenderly," "The Old Rugged Cross," "Power in the Blood," "Oh, How I Love Jesus," & many more.

Simple Faith. Rick Joyner. 1 cass. (Running Time: 90 mins.). (Growing in Faith Ser.: Vol. 4). 2000. 5.00 (RJ14-004) Morning NC.
With fresh & practical messages centering on faith, this tape series will enable you to better understand essential principles of the Christian walk.

Simple Faith, Charles R. Swindoll. 7 cass. (Running Time: 12 hrs.). 1991. 34.95 (978-1-57972-028-5(5)) Insight Living.
Bible study based Jesus' Sermon on the Mount & how it can inspire us to simplify our lives.

Simple Faith of Mister Rogers: Spiritual Insights from the Worl's Most Beloved Neighbor. unabr. ed. Amy Hollingsworth. Narrated by Amy Hollingsworth. (ENG.). 2005. 18.19 (978-1-60814-382-5(1)) Oasis Audio.

Simple Faith of Mr. Rogers. abr. ed. Amy Hollingsworth. 2005. 23.99 (978-1-58926-840-1(7), 6840); audio compact disk 25.99 (978-1-58926-841-8(5), 6841) Pub: Oasis Audio. Dist(s): TNT Media Grp

Simple Folk Dances. 1 cass. (J). (ps). 2001. pap. bk. 10.95 (KIM 07042C); pap. bk. 11.95 (KIM 07042) Kimbo Educ.
Involves children in gross motor activities with easy folk dances. Slow tempos ideal for preschool. Danish Dance of Greeting, Chimes of Dunkirk, Shoemakers Dance & more. Includes manual.

Simple Genius. abr. ed. David Baldacci. Read by Ron McLarty. (Running Time: 6 hrs.). (Sean King & Michelle Maxwell Ser.: No. 3). (ENG.). 2007. 14.98 (978-1-59483-902-3(6)) Pub: Hachet Audio. Dist(s): HachBkGrp

Simple Genius. abr. ed. David Baldacci. Read by Ron McLarty. (Running Time: 6 hrs.). (Sean King & Michelle Maxwell Ser.: No. 3). (ENG.). 2008. audio compact disk 14.98 (978-1-60024-474-2(2)) Pub: Hachet Audio. Dist(s): HachBkGrp

Simple Genius. unabr. ed. David Baldacci. Read by Scott Brick. (Running Time: 12 hrs.). (Sean King & Michelle Maxwell Ser.: No. 3). (ENG.). 2007. 16.98 (978-1-59483-905-4(0)) Pub: Hachet Audio. Dist(s): HachBkGrp

***Simple Gifts.** Lori Copeland. (Running Time: 9 hrs. 17 mins. 0 sec.). (ENG.). 2009. 14.99 (978-0-310-30522-4(5)) Zondervan.

Simple Gifts. Perf. by Aaron Copland. 1 cass. (J). 9.98 (2129); audio compact disk 17.98 (D2129) MFLP CA.
Shaker melodies are emotional & inspiring. Aaron Copland takes the listener full circle through a selection of Shaker hymns, songs & dances.

Simple Gifts. Christopher Leonard. 1 cass. 1995. 9.95 (978-1-887756-03-7(5)) Richmond Hill.
Musical recording.

Simple Gifts. Lightwood Duo Staff. 1 cass. 9.95 (1001387); audio compact disk 14.95 (28001044) Covenant Comms.
A beautiful mixture of guitar & clarinet perform Sunday favorites.

Simple Gifts. Chris Raschka. Perf. by Elza Muller-Roemer. 1 cass. (Running Time: 90 mins.). (Music Makers Ser.). (J). (ps up). 2000. bk. 24.95 (978-0-87499-641-8(4)) Live Oak Media.
A traditional Shaker hymn receives a new interpretation by Raschka, (that) turns out right. One by one, a cat, a bluebird, a squirrel, a turtle & a rabbit enter a forest made up of swirling shapes that evoke the Shakers' passion for "turning," that is, dancing in circles, a brilliantly original interpretation of traditional material but also, in its harmony of image & text & its dynamic movement from page to page, an unforgettable picture book that adults will appreciate as much as children.

Simple Gifts. Chris Raschka. Illus. by Chris Raschka. (Running Time: 5 mins.). 2000. 9.95 (978-0-87499-639-5(2)); audio compact disk 12.95 (978-1-59112-413-9(1)) Live Oak Media.

Simple Gifts. Chris Raschka. Perf. by Elza Muller-Roemer. 11 vols. (Running Time: 5 mins.). (Live Oak Readalong Ser.). (J). 2003. pap. bk. 16.95 (978-0-87499-640-1(6)) Pub: Live Oak Media. Dist(s): AudioGO

Simple Gifts. Chris Raschka. Illus. by Chris Raschka. 14 vols. (Running Time: 5 mins.). 2003. pap. bk. 41.95 (978-0-87499-642-5(2)); pap. bk. 43.95 (978-1-59112-604-1(5)) Live Oak Media.

Simple Gifts: Making the Most of Life's KI Moments. Contrib. by Judy Ringer. (ENG.). 2009. audio compact disk 15.00 (978-0-9776149-2-9(1)) OnePoint.

Simple Gifts of Christmas, Accompaniment. Steve Kupferschmid & Jean Anne Shafferman. 1 cass. (Running Time: 1 hr.). (ENG.). 1993. 59.95 (978-0-7390-1882-8(5), 4669) Alfred Pub.

***Simple Government: Twelve Things We Really Need from Washington (And a Trillion That We Don't!)** Mike Huckabee. Read by Mike Huckabee. (Running Time: 8 hrs.). (ENG.). 2011. audio compact disk 29.95 (978-0-14-242879-5(5), PengAudBks) Penguin Grp USA.

Simple Guide to Yoga. Frances Kean & Susan Voorhees. 2005. bk. 14.99 (978-0-88088-416-7(9)) Peter Pauper.

Simple Guides for Daily Growth, Problem Solving & Purposeful Relaxation, Set. Russell E. Mason. Read by Russell E. Mason. 3 cass. (Running Time: 2 hrs. 57 min.). 1975. pap. bk. 23.00 (978-0-89533-001-7(6), 50.GT-GP) F I Comm.
Practice for relaxation methods including a brief one of 17 minutes. Also techniques for bodily feeling awareness & for desired substitutions of feeling & actions & reactions.

Simple Habana Melody: (From When the World Was Good) unabr. ed. Oscar Hijuelos. Read by Jimmy Smits. 6 cass. (Running Time: 9 hrs.). 2002. 34.95 (978-0-06-009480-5(X)) HarperCollins Pubs.

Simple Haitian Creole for Adoptive Families. Amy Kendall. 2007. spiral bd. 30.00 (978-0-9796813-0-1(8)) Simple Language.

Simple Kabbalah: A Simple Wisdom Book, unabr. ed. Kim Zetter. Read by Theodore Bikel. 4 cass. (Running Time: 5 hrs.). 2000. 25.00 (978-1-57453-377-4(0)) Audio Lit.

Simple Kyriale. J. Michael Thompson. 1 cass. 16.00 (978-1-58459-014-9(9)) Wrld Lib Pubns.
Mass in English & Latin.

Simple Life. Eknath Easwaran. Read by Eknath Easwaran. 1 cass. (Running Time: 1 hr.). 1988. 7.95 (978-1-58638-606-1(9)) Nilgiri Pr.

Simple Life. unabr. ed. Rosie Thomas. Read by Clare Higgins. 10 cass. (Running Time: 15 hrs.). 1996. 69.95 (978-0-7451-6636-0(9), CAB 1252) Pub: Chivers Audio Bks GBR. Dist(s): AudioGO
Dinah Steward has everything she could hope for: a loving husband, two well-adjusted sons & a beautiful house in Franklin, Massachusetts. But Dinah has a secret that she & her husband never mention & knowing it could rock their comfortable existence. Then a chance meeting stirs up Dinah's past & she can no longer deny the events that happened 15 years ago. But in returning to England to face it, she risks destroying her family life forever.

Simple Living & High Thinking. 1 cass. (Running Time: 1 hr.). 12.99 (186); (196) Yoga Res Foun.

Simple Living & High Thinking, No. 2. Swami Jyotirmayananda. 1 cass. (Running Time: 1 hr.). 1990. 12.99 Yoga Res Foun.

Simple Machines. Sundance/Newbridge, LLC Staff. (Early Science Ser.). (gr. k-3). 2007. audio compact disk 12.00 (978-1-4007-6615-4(X)); audio compact disk 12.00 (978-1-4007-6616-1(8)); audio compact disk 12.00 (978-1-4007-6614-7(1)) Sund Newbrdge.

Simple Massage Deck & Disc. 2002. pap. bk. 14.95 (978-1-931918-04-6(X)) Compass Labs.

simple Plan. Scott Smith. Read by Griffin Dunne. 2004. 10.95 (978-0-7435-4612-6(1)) Pub: S&S Audio. Dist(s): S and S Inc

Simple Plan. abr. ed. Scott Smith. Read by Griffin Dunne. (Running Time: 3 hrs. 0 mins. 0 sec.). (ENG.). 2006. audio compact disk 9.95 (978-0-7435-6503-5(7)) Pub: S&S Audio. Dist(s): S and S Inc

Simple Plan. unabr. ed. Scott B. Smith. Read by Alexander Adams. 8 cass. (Running Time: 12 hrs.). 1994. 64.00 (978-0-7366-2757-3(X), 3480) Books on Tape.
Hank Mitchell, steady, solid, devoted husband, proud new father, finds an immense cache of money with two other men. The three agree to a simple plan that will allow them to hide, keep & eventually share the fortune. But when suspicion, blackmail, betrayal & murder come on the scene, Hank's orderly universe begins to crumble.

Simple Prayers. abr. ed. Michael Golding. (ENG.). 2006. 14.98 (978-1-59483-717-3(1)) Pub: Hachet Audio. Dist(s): HachBkGrp

Simple Sacred Songs for Children: 6 Delightfully Easy Songs for Unison or 2-Part with Reproducible Song Sheets. Composed by Jean Anne Shafferman & Tim Hayden. (ENG.). 2007. audio compact disk 29.95 (978-0-7390-4800-9(7)) Alfred Pub.

Simple Scripts for New Managers. PUEI. 2007. audio compact disk 19.95 (978-1-934147-49-8(4), CareerTrack) P Univ E Inc.

Simple Scripts for Problems at Work. PUEI. 2006. audio compact disk 19.95 (978-1-933328-96-6(7), Fred Pryor) P Univ E Inc.

***Simple Scripts for Problems at Work.** PUEI. 2009. audio compact disk 199.00 (978-1-935041-69-6(X), CareerTrack) P Univ E Inc.

Simple Scripts for Team Conflict. PUEI. audio compact disk 19.95 (978-1-934147-69-6(9), Fred Pryor) P Univ E Inc.

Simple Scripts to Say No Without Feeling Guilty. PUEI. 2007. audio compact disk 19.95 (978-1-934147-29-0(X), CareerTrack) P Univ E Inc.

Simple Simon. Ryne Douglas Pearson. 2004. 10.95 (978-0-7435-4957-8(0)) Pub: S&S Audio. Dist(s): S and S Inc

Simple Simon, unabr. ed. Ryne Douglas Pearson. Narrated by George Guidall. 6 cass. (Running Time: 8 hrs.). 1997. 51.00 (978-0-7887-0814-5(7), 94964E7) Recorded Bks.
When a autistic teenager innocently cracks a government code, shadowy powers from around the globe target him. An FBI agent comes to his aid, but soon he is also in danger.

Simple Social Graces: The Lost Art of Gracious Victorian Living. unabr. ed. Linda S. Lichter. Read by Nadia May. 8 cass. (Running Time: 11 hrs. 30 mins.). 1999. 56.95 (978-0-7861-1528-0(9), 2378) Blckstn Audio.
Shattering myths revealing the provocative truths of our forbears' lives, laced with intriguing anecdotes, offers us an abundance of practical inspirations. Retrieves the lost arts & forgotten rituals of a sensibility that still resonates in every aspect of our lives today.

Simple Solutions to Getting the Cash You Need for Your International or Domestic Business. Donald M. Gartrell. 1 cass. (Running Time: 30 min.). 1998. bk. 12.38 (978-1-893461-01-7(7)) Gartrell.
Discusses: how to select a banker & bank, what documentation the bank requires to establish a credit line, how working capital credit lines are established for the mature company & start up, the criteria of asset-based lending, bankers acceptance financing & various other options on how to get money for a business.

Simple Soul & Other Stories. unabr. ed. Catherine Cookson. Read by Susan Jameson. 6 cass. (Running Time: 9 hrs.). 2002. 54.95 (978-0-7540-0810-1(X), CAB 2232) AudioGO.

Simple Soul & Other Stories. unabr. ed. Catherine Cookson. Read by Susan Jameson. 6 CDs. (Running Time: 21720 sec.). 2003. audio compact disk 64.95 (978-0-7540-5503-7(5), CCD 194) Pub: Chivers Pr GBR. Dist(s): AudioGO

Simple Spanish for Adoptive Families. Amy Kendall. 2007. spiral bd. 30.00 (978-0-9796813-2-5(4)) Simple Language.

Simple Steps. Lisa Lelas et al. Read by Lisa Lelas & Celeste Lawson. (Running Time: 7 hrs.). 2004. 27.95 (978-1-59912-598-5(6)) Iofy Corp.

Simple Steps: 10 Weeks to Getting Control of Your Life. unabr. ed. Lisa Lelas et al. Read by Lisa Lelas & Celeste Lawson. 5 cass. (Running Time: 7 hrs.). 2004. 39.95 (978-0-7861-2768-9(6), 3251); reel tape 29.95 (978-0-7861-2646-0(9)); audio compact disk 29.95 (978-0-7861-8729-4(8)); audio compact disk 24.95 (978-0-7861-8557-3(0), 3251); audio compact disk 48.00 (978-0-7861-8625-9(9), 3251) Blckstn Audio.

Simple Steps to Impossible Dreams: The 15 Power Secrets of the World's Most Successful Women & Men. Steven K. Scott. 8 cass. (Running Time: 8 hrs.). 1999. wbk. ed. (978-1-55525-062-1(9), 19940a) Nightingale-Conant.
Take 15 steps to realize your dreams.

Simple Story. Elizabeth Inchbald. 7 cass. (Running Time: 10 hrs.). 2000. 47.95 Audio Bk Con.
Miss Milner rebels after she marries her stern moral husband. Her daughter suffers the consequences, but love prevails.

***Simple Stress Relief Through Thanksgiving & Praise.** Kenneth Copeland & Gloria Copeland. (ENG.). 2010. audio compact disk 5.00 (978-1-57562-808-0(2)) K Copeland Pubns.

Simple Thinking. unabr. ed. Gregory Bateson. 1 cass. (Running Time: 1 hr. 13 min.). (Informal Esalen Lectures). 1980. 11.00 (02811) Big Sur Tapes.

***Simple Times: Crafts for Poor People.** unabr. ed. Amy Sedaris. Read by Amy Sedaris. (Running Time: 2 hrs. 30 mins.). (ENG.). 2010. 19.98 (978-1-60024-729-3(6)) Pub: Hachet Audio. Dist(s): HachBkGrp

***Simple Times: Crafts for Poor People.** unabr. ed. Amy Sedaris. Read by Amy Sedaris. 3 CDs. (Running Time: 2 hrs. 30 mins.). (ENG., 2010. audio compact disk 24.98 (978-1-60024-728-6(8)) Pub: Hachet Audio. Dist(s): HachBkGrp

Simple Trust & Love: Eleven Vietnamese Catholic Songs. Huy Phung.Tr. of Mot Chut Tin Yeu. (ENG & VIE., 2009. audio compact disk 7.00 (978-0-9662708-3-9(5)) Nghia Sinh.

Simple Truth. David Baldacci. Read by Tony Roberts. 4 cass. (Running Time: 6 hrs.). 1999. 24.35 (978-0-671-03345-3(X)) S and S Inc.
As a young conscripted soldier, Rufus Harms was jailed for the brutal killing of a schoolgirl. A stray letter from the US Army reveals new facts about the night of the murder.

Simple Truth. Swami Amar Jyoti. 1 dolby cass. 1984. 9.95 (K-62) Truth Consciousness.
Our complex minds are attracted to the freedom of simplicity. Then "what's the hitch?" A radical analysis. Women as seekers. The only valid question.

Simple Truth. abr. ed. David Baldacci. (Running Time: 4 hrs.). (ENG.). 2006. 14.98 (978-1-59483-771-5(6)) Pub: Hachet Audio. Dist(s): HachBkGrp

Simple Truth, abr. ed. David Baldacci. Read by Tony Roberts. 4 cass. 1999. 24.98 (FS9-43314) Highsmith.

Simple Truth. unabr. ed. David Baldacci. Read by Jonathan Marosz. 9 cass. (Running Time: 13 hrs. 30 mins.). 1998. 72.00 (978-0-7366-4251-4(X), 4750) Books on Tape.
Rufus Harm has spent the last twenty-five years in prison for a murder he's sure he committed, then he realizes he is not guilty.

Simple Truth. unabr. ed. David Baldacci. Read by Jonathan Marosz. 11 CDs. (Running Time: 16 hrs. 30 mins.). 2001. audio compact disk 88.00 Books on Tape.
Rufus Harm has spent the last twenty-five years in prison for a murder he's sure he committed. However, when he receives a letter from the army, Rufus' memory is jogged. As the events play out in his mind, Rufus comes to a realization: he's not guilty. From his prison cell Rufus secretly files an appeal with the Supreme Court. When the Supreme Court clerk, who is the first to see Rufus' appeal and Harm's own lawyer are murdered, Harm knows the real killers are on to him. Rufus also knows he's quickly running out of time. Sprung from prison with the help of his brother, Rufus must elude capture long enough to expose a cover-up and save his own life.

Simple Truth. unabr. ed. David Baldacci. Read by Jonathan Marosz. 2001. 24.98 (978-1-57042-774-9(7)) Hachet Audio.
A look behind the scenes of the U.S. Supreme Court to witness a battleground of egos, intellects, and power.

Simple Ways to Minimize Stress & Conflict While Bringing Out the Best in Yourself & Others. Richard Carlson. Read by Richard Carlson. 2 cass. (Running Time: 2 hrs.). 1999. 16.85 Set. (978-1-84032-163-0(6)) Ulvrscrft Audio.
How to interact more peaceably & joyfully with colleagues, clients & bosses.

Simplenomics. abr. unabr. ed. Joel Greenblatt. (Running Time: 8 hrs. 0 mins. 0 sec.). (ENG.). 2011. audio compact disk 29.99 (978-0-7435-6258-4(5)) Pub: S&S Audio. Dist(s): S and S Inc

Simpleology: The Simple Science of Getting What You Want. unabr. ed. Mark Joyner. Read by Mark Joyner. (Running Time: 6 hrs.). (ENG.). 2007. audio compact disk 29.98 (978-1-59659-089-2(0), GildAudio) Pub: Gildan Media. Dist(s): HachBkGrp

Simpler Way. abr. ed. Margaret J. Wheatley & Myron Kellner-Rogers. Read by Margaret J. Wheatley & Myron Kellner-Rogers. 2 cass. (Running Time: 3 hrs.). 1996. 17.95 (978-1-57453-053-7(4)) Audio Lit.

Simplest Thing in the World. Ayn Rand. Read by Ayn Rand. 1 cass. (Running Time: 30 min.). 1963. 12.95 (978-1-56114-064-0(3), AR01C) Second Renaissance.
A short story, written & narrated by Ayn Rand, about the functioning of an artist's creative process.

SimpleTalk! Spanish for Contractors Pocket Guide. Created by Roger G. Thomas. (SPA & ENG.). 2004. audio compact disk 6.95 (978-0-9754727-1-2(2)) SimpleTalk.

SimpleTalk! Spanish for Contractors Pocket Guide. Created by Roger G. Thomas. Voice by Lauren Thomas. 1 CD. (Running Time: 30 mins). (SPA & ENG.). 2004. audio compact disk 19.95 (978-0-9754727-0-5(4)) SimpleTalk.
Spanish learning CD for Contracting/Building Industry to accompany included pocket guide.

Simpleton Peter see Dick Whittington & His Cat & Other English Fairy Tales

Simplexity: Why Simple Things Become Complex. unabr. ed. Jeffrey Kluger. Read by Holter Graham. (Running Time: 30600 sec.). 2008. audio compact disk 34.95 (978-1-4013-9024-2(2)) Pub: Hyperion. Dist(s): HarperCollins Pubs

Simplicity: How to Focus on the Vital Few Rather than the Trivial Many. Jeff Davidson. 1999. audio compact disk 59.95 (978-1-60729-125-1(8)) Breath Space Inst.

Simplicity: How to Focus on the Vital Few Rather than the Trivial Many. Jeff Davidson. 1999. 54.95 (978-1-60729-359-0(5)) Breath Space Inst.

Simplicity: How to Focus on the Vital Few Rather Than the Trivial Many, unabr. ed. Jeff Davidson & Tony Allesandra. Read by Jeff Davidson & Tony Allesandra. 6 cass. (Running Time: 6 hrs.). 1997. 59.95 (978-1-57294-138-0(3), 11-0616) SkillPath Pubns.
Learn to take charge of your life without sacrificing what's really important to you. Set your own ground rules, stomp out false expectations, & reclaim your sanity.

Simplicity & the Art of Living. Read by Tara Singh. 2 cass. (Running Time: 2 hrs.). 1995. 15.95 (978-1-55531-276-3(4)) Life Action Pr.
Simplicity is the answer to busy & yet unfulfilled & exhausted life. It frees us from the pressure of uncertain economy & introduces us to our natural goodness.

Simplicity & the Practice of Lineage. Read by Chogyam Trungpa. 4 cass. 1979. 38.50 (A125) Vajradhatu.
Six talks. Simplicity is the only way to bring about enlightened mind. It has been experienced & taught by Kagyu lineage teachers up to the present day, through the practice of meditation.

Simplicity & The Practice of Lineage, RMDC. Vajracarya. 4 cass. 1979. 38.50 Vajradhatu.
Teaches that simplicity is the only way to bring about enlightened mind; It has been experienced & taught by each of the Kagyu lineage teachers, down to the present, by the practice of meditation.

Simplicity Christ; Visualization & Transenergization. Jonathan Murro & Ann Ree Colton. 1 cass. 7.95 A R Colton Fnd.
Discusses the goal of God-Realization.

Simplicity for the Soul. John Williamsen. Perf. by John Williamsen. Dannye Williamsen. 2007. audio compact disk 15.95 (978-0-9726058-4-7(3)) Williamsen Pubns.

Simplicity, Loyalty, Unity. unabr. ed. Perf. by Eknath Easwaran. 1 cass. (Running Time: 1 hr.). 1987. 7.95 (978-1-58638-607-8(7)) Nilgiri Pr.

Simplicity Meditation: Cultivate Inner & Outer Simplicity. Mark Bancroft. Read by Mark Bancroft. 1 cass., bklet. (Running Time: 1 hr.). (Spirituality & Consciousness Ser.). 1999. 12.95 (978-1-58522-012-0(4), 708, EnSpire Aud) EnSpire Pr.
Two complete sessions plus printed instruction manual/guidebook. With healing music soundtrack.

Simplicity Meditation: Cultivate Inner & Outer Simplicity. Mark Bancroft. Read by Mark Bancroft. 1 CD, 1 bklet. (Running Time: 1 hr.). (Spirituality & Consciousness Ser.). 2006. audio compact disk 20.00 (978-1-58522-064-9(7)) EnSpire Pr.
Two complete sessions plus printed instructionmanual/guidebook. With healing music soundtrack.

Simplicity of Salvation. Kenneth Wapnick. 11 CDs. 2006. audio compact disk 64.00 (978-1-59142-226-6(4), CD1) Foun Miracles.

Simplicity of Salvation. Kenneth Wapnick. 1 CD. (Running Time: 11 hrs. 55 mins. 49 secs.). 2006. 57.00 (978-1-59142-247-1(7), 3m1) Foun Miracles.

Simplicity of Spiritual Practice. Jack Kornfield. 1 cass. (Running Time: 1 hr. 30 min.). 1982. 11.00 (03602) Big Sur Tapes.

Simplified Behavior & Feeling State Change & Goal Accomplishments, Russell E. Mason. Read by Russell E. Mason. 6 cass. (Running Time: 5 hrs. 54 min.). (Train-Ascendance Ser.). 1975. pap. bk. 45.00 (978-0-89533-002-4(4), 51.GT-BF) F I Comm.
Guides for purposeful relaxation, awareness of positive feelings & of values for goal accomplishments.

Simplified Extended, Deep & or Meditative Relaxation, Set-R. Russell E. Mason. Read by Russell E. Mason. 3 cass. (Running Time: 2 hrs. 57 min.). (Train-Ascendance Ser.). 1975. pap. bk. 23.00 (978-0-89533-004-8(0), 53.GT-RM) F I Comm.
Orientation for practice & applications of varied relaxation techniques.

Simplified Folk Songs. Perf. by Hap Palmer. 1 cass. (J). 11.95 (EA 518C); lp 11.95 (EA 518) Kimbo Educ.
He's Got the Whole World in His Hands - Michael Row the Boat Ashore - The Paw Paw Patch & more.

Simplified Horary Astrology. Gilbert Navarro. 1 cass. (Running Time: 90 min.). 1990. 8.95 (883) Am Fed Astrologers.

Simplified Insight into Solar Returns. unabr. ed. Nance McCullough. Read by Nance McCullough. 1 cass. (Running Time: 1 hr. 22 mins.). 1991. 6.20 (978-0-936916-50-7(8)) NAMAC.
Astrology: Based on yearly solar return charts & what each one predicts.

Simplified Purposeful Relaxation for Comfort or Effectiveness, Set-PR. Russell E. Mason. 3 cass. (Running Time: 2 hrs. 57 min.). (Train-Ascendance Cassettes Ser.). 1975. pap. bk. 23.00 (978-0-89533-003-1(2), 52.GT-RP) F I Comm.
Orientation & practice for purposefulness, values, & types of relaxation.

Simplified Relaxation, Problem Solutions & Substitutions & Value Considerations, Set-S. Russell E. Mason. Read by Russell E. Mason. 9 cass. (Running Time: 8 hrs. 51 min.). (Train-Ascendance Ser.). 1975. pap. bk. 65.00 (978-0-89533-020-8(2), 65.GT-SV) F I Comm.
Includes growth, awareness, problem solving, value considerations, & details concerning each positive & negative feeling state as applicable to understanding personality & behavior changes.

Simplified Rhythm Stick Activities. 1 LP . (Running Time: 1 hr.). (J). 2001. pap. bk. 11.95 (KIM 2015); pap. bk. 14.95 (KIM2015CD) Kimbo Educ.
Children perform basic rhythm stick activities. Develops motor skills & coordination. Sesame Street, The Wizard of Oz, It's a Small, Small World, Mickey Mouse March & more. Includes instructional manual.

Simplified Rhythm Stick Activities. 1 cass. (Running Time: 1 hr.). (J). (ps-3). 2001. pap. bk. 10.95 (KIM 2015C) Kimbo Educ.

Simplifiez-vous la Vie. unabr. ed. Werner Tiki Kustenmacher & Lothar J. Seiwert. Read by Pierre Forest. (YA). 2007. 79.99 (978-2-35569-011-2(1)) Find a World.

Simplify Your Life. Jennifer Crow. 2 cass. (Running Time: 2 hrs.). 2001. (978-1-931537-01-8(1)) Vision Comm Creat.

Simplify Your Life, 2nd ed. Linda M. Buell. Read by Linda M. Buell. 1 cass. (Running Time: 50 min.). 1997. pap. bk. & wbk. ed. 49.95 (978-1-928607-03-8(9), 9901) Simplify Life.
A detailed approach to creating the life you will love to live in the audiotape supported by a workbook of activities that help you uncover, define, simplify & start creating the life you really want.

Simplify Your Life: Seven Simple Strategies for Doing What You Love to Do. Linda M. Buell. 1 cass. (Running Time: 50 min.). (C). 1997. 10.00 (978-1-928607-02-1(0), 97-01) Simplify Life.
A detailed approach to creating the life you will love to live. Based on personal experiences, Linda Manassee Buell uses proven strategies for success with basic rules of the game & true stories to illustrate how you can reclaim your life.

Simplify Your Life with Kids. Elaine St. James. Read by Elaine St. James. 2 cass. 1997. 17.95 Set. (978-1-55935-256-7(6)) Soundelux.
Simple step-by-step guide for simplifying our desire to create a happy, healthy family life for ourselves & our children.

Simplifying Tax Legislation: Strategies for Maximizing Plan Distributions. Instructed by Frank Rainaldi. 2 CDs. (Running Time: 180 mins.). 2004. audio compact disk 19.95 (978-1-59280-106-0(4)) Marketplace Bks.
Despite new tax "simplification" legislation, financial professionals know that grappling with tax laws regulating the nation's retirement plans is anything but simple. Now, get welcome relief with a new workshop outlining an array of simple strategies for customizing retirement plan payouts to meet each client's unique situation.From individuals seeking income to support early retirement, to those looking to convert qualified-plan assets into inheritance vehicles, this presentation addresses the full spectrum of client needs and circumstances. In every instance, retirement specialist Frank Rainaldi explains how advisors can maximize a client's investments while also minimizing client taxes and penalties - a combination that can dramatically enhance advisor revenues, as well.Rainaldi highlights critical guidelines and a variety of key strategies for optimizing and customizing distributions from qualified retirement plans including ??Taking advantage of systematic lifetime withdrawals?Establishing a stretch-out Qualified Plan distribution?IRA Rollover vs. tax-deferred annuity: Pros & Cons?Incorporating Q-Tip Trusts and insurance policies into Qualified Plan asset planning?The basics of defined benefit payout options ?Bequeathing an IRA to a charity - and so much more.Whether you're calculating the required minimum distribution amount, or clarifying the rules regarding Qualified Plan beginning distribution dates or designated beneficiaries - you'll find all the "need-to-know" details in this comprehensive tutorial.

Simplifying the Budgeting Process. Dora C. Fowler. 2 cass. (Running Time: 2 hrs.). 1992. pap. bk. 19.95 (978-1-57323-014-8(6)) Natl Inst Child Mgmt.

Simply Al Denson. Contrib. by Al Denson. (Simply (Provident) Ser.). 2005. audio compact disk 6.97 (978-5-559-01294-0(7)) Pt of Grace Ent.

Simply Barbara Bush, Set. unabr. ed. Donnie Radcliffe. Read by Flo Gibson. 4 cass. (Running Time: 6 hrs.). (gr. 8 up). 1991. 19.95 (978-1-55685-228-2(2)) Audio Bk Con.
Our former first lady is exposed as the warm, witty, wonderful person she truly is.

Simply Carolyn Arends. Contrib. by Carolyn Arends. (Simply (Provident) Ser.). 2005. audio compact disk 6.97 (978-5-559-01293-3(9)) Pt of Grace Ent.

***Simply Christian.** unabr. ed. N. T. Wright. Read by Simon Prebble. (ENG.). 2008. (978-0-06-167371-9(4)) HarperCollins Pubs.

***Simply Christian: Why Christianity Makes Sense.** unabr. ed. N. T. Wright. Read by Simon Prebble. (ENG.). 2008. (978-0-06-164953-0(8)) HarperCollins Pubs.

Simply Clay Crosse. Contrib. by Clay Crosse. (Simply (Provident) Ser.). 2005. audio compact disk 6.97 (978-5-559-01382-4(X)) Pt of Grace Ent.

Simply Coaching, Vol. 1. Lynn M. Coffey. 1 cass. (Running Time: 2 hrs.). 1997. 29.95 (978-0-9660342-0-2(1)) Busn Coaching.
Description of how & why personal & professional coaching began.

Simply Dino. Contrib. by Dino. (Simply (Provident) Ser.). 2005. audio compact disk 6.97 (978-5-559-01291-9(2)) Pt of Grace Ent.

Simply Divine. unabr. ed. Wendy Holden. Narrated by Jenny Sterlin. 12 CDs. (Running Time: 13 hrs. 45 mins.). 2001. audio compact disk 116.00 (978-0-7887-7169-9(8), C1422) Recorded Bks.
Despite jobs at magazines like Gorgeous & Fabulous, Jane feels anything but. Her relationship with the man in her life is at a dead-end, & the body she sees each morning in the mirror simply refuses to cooperate. But Jane's life is about to receive some divine intervention: shes been chosen to ghost-write the racy doings of celebrity socialite Champagne D'Vyne, the grand diva of self-promotion. As Jane follows Champagne's antics from one rich boyfriend & glamorous hotel to the next, Holden observes the London social scene with a wit as sharp as a stiletto heel.

Simply Divine. unabr. ed. Wendy Holden. Narrated by Jenny Sterlin. 10 cass. (Running Time: 13 hrs. 45 mins.). 2000. 88.00 (978-0-7887-4858-5(0), 96427E7) Recorded Bks.
Takes readers on a fun-filled romp through the viciously glamorous world of glossy magazines & London single life. Despite jobs at Gorgeous & Fabulous, Jane feels anything but. Her relationship with the man in her life is at a dead-end & the body she sees each morning in the mirror simply refuses to cooperate but Jane's life is about to receive some divine intervention. She's been chosen to ghost-write the racy doings of celebrity socialite Champagne D'Vyne.

Simply... Femme M'amie. Perf. by Femme M'amie. 1 cass. (Running Time: 43 mins.). 2000. (978-0-9655068-2-3(7)) Femme Mamie.
A live recording of Femme M'amie, an extraordinary blend of seven women's voices. Rich harmonies & musical passion filll this recording of original, contempory & classic selections with a touch of seasonal good will.

Simply Glad. Contrib. by Glad. (Simply (Provident) Ser.). 2005. audio compact disk 6.97 (978-5-559-01292-6(0)) Pt of Grace Ent.

Simply God, Encouragement for the Soul. Cathy Jodeit. 2007. audio compact disk 24.99 (978-1-60462-009-2(9)) Tate Pubng.

Simply Kim Hill. Contrib. by Kim Hill. (Simply (Provident) Ser.). 2005. audio compact disk 6.97 (978-5-559-01296-4(3)) Pt of Grace Ent.

Simply Love. unabr. ed. Mary Balogh. Read by Rosalyn Landor. 9 CDs. (Running Time: 11 hrs.). (Simply Quartet). 2006. audio compact disk 99.00 (978-1-4159-2553-9(4)) Books on Tape.
At the center of this spellbinding novel is Anne Jewell, a teacher haunted by a scandalous past - until she meets a man who teaches her the most important lesson of all: nothing is simple when it comes to love. She spies him in the deepening dusk of a Wales evening - a lone figure of breathtaking strength and masculinity, his handsome face branded by a secret pain. For single mother and teacher Anne Jewell, newly arrived with her son at a sprawling estate in Wales on the invitation of an influential friend, Sydnam Butler is a man whose sorrows - and passions - run deeper than she could have ever imagined. As steward of a remote seaside manor, Sydnam lives a reclusive existence far from the pity and disdain of others. Yet almost from the moment Anne first appears on the cliffs, he senses in this lovely stranger a kindred soul, and between these two wary hearts, desire stirs. Unable to resist the passion that has rescued them both from loneliness, Anne and Sydnam share an afternoon of exquisite lovemaking. Now the unwed single mother and war-scarred veteran must make a decision that could forever alter their lives. For Sydnam, it is a chance to heal the pain of the past. For Anne, it is the glorious promise of a future with the man who will dare her to reveal her deepest secrets - before she can give him all her heart.

Simply Magic, Vol. 1. Read by Joanie Bartels. 1 cass. (Running Time: 1 hr.). (J). 1993. 14.98 (978-1-881225-16-4(X)) Discov Music.
Joanie takes songs from her award-winning "Magic Series" & turns them into a video spectacular wrapped within a fun-filled storyline.

Simply Plumb. Contrib. by Plumb. (Simply (Provident) Ser.). 2005. audio compact disk 6.97 (978-5-559-01295-7(5)) Pt of Grace Ent.

Simply Quit Drinking: An Inspirational Journey from near Death. 2008. 24.95 (978-0-9816134-1-3(1), R P Pub); 13.95 (978-0-9816134-2-0(X), R P Pub) Reach Peak.

Simply Rich Mullins. Contrib. by Rich Mullins. (Simply (Provident) Ser.). 2005. audio compact disk 6.97 (978-5-559-01297-1(1)) Pt of Grace Ent.

Simply Romantic. Perf. by Joe Burke. 1 cass. 9.98; audio compact disk 15.98 Lifedance.
Some of the great love songs of the 40's, including "Always on My Mind," "At Last," "Beautiful in My Eyes," "By Myself," "Funny How Time Slips Away," "Here's That Rainy Day," "I Could Write a Book," "I'll Be Seeing You," "I'm Beginning to See the Light," "Let's Get Away," "The Way You Look Tonight" & "Where is Love." Demo CD or cassette available.

Simply Romantic. abr. ed. Dennis Rainey & Barbara Rainey. Ed. by Keith Lynch. 1 cass. (Running Time: 45 min.). 1996. 24.95 (978-1-57229-050-1(1)) FamilyLife.
A 12 month collection of fun, creative ideas you can use to enhance the romance in your marriage.

***Simply Sacred.** Gary Thomas. (ENG.). 2010. 22.99 (978-0-310-58674-6(7)) Zondervan.

Simply... the Best Easter, Volume 3: Satb. Contrib. by Robert Sterling et al. (Simply... the Best Ser.). 2007. audio compact disk 34.98 (978-5-557-53115-3(7), Word Music) Word Enter.

Simply Unforgettable. unabr. ed. Mary Balogh. Read by Rosalyn Landor. 11 CDs. (Running Time: 11 hrs. 30 mins.). (Simply Quartet). 2005. audio compact disk 99.00 (978-1-4159-1643-8(8)); 81.00 (978-1-4159-1642-1(X)) Books on Tape.
They meet in a ferocious snowstorm. She is a young teacher with a secret past. He is the cool, black-caped stranger who unexpectedly comes to her rescue. Between these two unlikely strangers, desire is instantaneous - and utterly impossible to resist. Stranded together in a rustic country inn, Lucius Marshall, who is the Viscount Sinclair, and Frances Allard share a night of glorious, unforgettable passion. But Frances knows her place - and it is far from the privileged world of the sensual aristocrat. Due to begin her teaching position at Miss Martin's School in Bath, Frances must try to forget that one extraordinary night - and the man who touched her with such exquisite tenderness and abandon. But Frances cannot hide forever. And when fate once again throws them together, Lucius refuses to take no for an answer. If Frances will not be his wife, he will make her his mistress. So begins an odyssey fraught with intrigue, one that defies propriety and shocks the straitlaced ton. For Lucius's passionate, single-minded pursuit is about to force Frances to give up all her secrets - except one - to win the heart of the man she already loves.

***Simply Wisdom Audiobook.** Read by Tiffanydenise. 2010. 14.99 (978-0-9675432-2-2(3)) Nia Bks.

Simpsons: An Uncensored, Unauthorized History. unabr. ed. John Ortved. Narrated by John Allen Nelson & Justine Eyre. 1 MP3-CD. (Running Time: 11 hrs. 30 mins. 0 sec.). 2009. 24.99 (978-1-4001-6448-6(6)) Pub: Tantor Media. Dist(s): IngramPubServ

Simpsons: An Uncensored, Unauthorized History. unabr. ed. John Ortved. Narrated by Justine Eyre & John Allen Nelson. (Running Time: 11 hrs. 30 mins. 0 sec.). (ENG.). 2009. audio compact disk 34.99

(978-1-4001-1448-1(9)); audio compact disk 69.99 (978-1-4001-4448-8(5)) Pub: Tantor Media. Dist(s): IngramPubServ

***Simpsons: An Uncensored, Unauthorized History.** unabr. ed. John Ortved. Narrated by John Allen Nelson & Justine Eyre. (Running Time: 11 hrs. 30 mins.). 2009. 17.99 (978-1-4001-8448-4(7)) Tantor Media.

Simpsons: Go Simpsonic with the Simpsons. Perf. by Sonic Youth et al. 1 cass. (Running Time: 1 hr.). (J). 2002. 10.98 (978-1-56826-975-7(7), 75480); audio compact disk 17.98 (978-0-7379-0099-6(7), 75480) Rhino Enter.
The much anticipated follow up to Songs in the Key of Springfield. Includes performances from some of the show's guest stars plus four never before heard tracks that never made it to broadcast.

Simpsons: Judges 14:1-3. Ed Young. 1991. 4.95 (978-0-7417-1851-8(0), 851) Win Walk.

Simpsons: Songs in the Key of Springfield: Original Music from the Television Series. Created by Matt Groening. 1 cass. (Running Time: 1 hr.). 1998. 10.98 (978-1-56826-814-9(9)); audio compact disk 15.98 (978-1-56826-815-6(7)) Rhino Enter.

Simpsons: Songs in the Key of Springfield Original Music from the TV Series. Score by Alf Clausen. 1 CD. (Running Time: 1 hr.). (J). 2002. audio compact disk 17.98 (978-1-56826-765-4(7), 72723) Rhino Enter.
Hilarious cuts from the first seven years of The Simpsons animated series. Features original score and a slew of different versions of the closing theme.

Simsalabim. unabr. ed. Ursula Hirschfeld & Kerstin Reinke. 1 cass. (Running Time: 1 hr. 25 mins.). (GER.). 2005. 16.50 (978-3-468-90541-4(6)) Langenscheidt.

Simultaneous Translation. Terrance Cox. (ENG.). 2005. audio compact disk 12.95 (978-0-937821-60-2(8)) Pub: Sig2nature Eds CAN. Dist(s): U Toronto Pr

Sin. unabr. ed. Wendy MacLeod. Perf. by Steve Carell et al. 1 cass. (Running Time: 1 hr. 55 min.). 1995. 19.95 (978-1-58081-103-3(5)) L A Theatre.
"Sin" subtitled "a contemporary morality play," features Avery Bly on High, the helicopter traffic reporter for a San Francisco radio station. She's trying to keep herself above life's messiness, but finding that most people, unlike herself above life's messiness, are less than perfect. Her soon to be ex husband is guilty of sloth; her roommate is a glutton; she's envied by her co worker; & her blind date wallows in greed. It takes her dying brother to make her see that pride is the deadliest of sins, & it just might take an Act of God to bring her back down to earth.

Sin: Overcoming the Ultimate Deadly Addiction. Keith Miller. Read by J. Keith Miller. 1 cass. (Running Time: 60 min.). 1988. bk. 8.95 (978-0-06-065715-4(4)) HarperCollins Pubs.
The author presents an inspiring account of his struggle with anxiety, frustration, & compulsive behavior. Addressing himself directly to the people in the pews who are searching for healing & growth, he offers practical steps for recovery.

Sin - "The Fooler"; Christian "I" Trouble. C. S. Lovett. 1 cass. 6.95 (7020) Prsnl Christianity.
Expands on teaching of the book, "Dynamic Truths".

Sin & a Shame. unabr. ed. (Running Time: 16 hrs.). (J). 2006. 29.95 (978-0-7861-7101-9(4)) Blckstn Audio.

Sin & a Shame. unabr. ed. Victoria Christopher Murray. Read by Monalisa Wilson. 7 cass. (Running Time: 36000 sec.). 2006. 59.95 (978-0-7861-4901-8(9)); audio compact disk 72.00 (978-0-7861-5979-6(0)) Blckstn Audio.

***Sin Boldly: A Field Guide for Grace.** unabr. ed. Cathleen Falsani. (Running Time: 5 hrs. 15 mins. 0 sec.). (ENG.). 2008. 19.99 (978-0-310-30273-5(0)) Zondervan.

Sin by Any Other Name: Luke 15:13-20. Ed Young. 1992. 4.95 (978-0-7417-1944-7(4), 944) Win Walk.

Sin Eater. Gary D. Schmidt. Narrated by Johnny Heller. 5 CDs. (Running Time: 5 hrs. 45 mins.). (YA). 1996. audio compact disk 48.75 (978-1-4025-8082-6(7)) Recorded Bks.

Sin Eater. unabr. ed. Gary D. Schmidt. Narrated by Johnny Heller. 4 cass. (Running Time: 5 hrs. 45 mins.). (gr. 6 up). 1997. 35.00 (978-0-7887-1349-1(3), 95199E7) Recorded Bks.
After his mother dies, Cole & his father return to the ancient family farm in New Hampshire to live with Grandma & Grandpa Emerson. There, as his father becomes more & more withdrawn, Cole listens to stories of his ancestors & a mysterious healer called the Sin Eater. Through these tales, Cole will learn forgiveness & find the strength to survive another tragedy.

Sin God Will Not Permit: Daniel 4:1-37. Ed Young. 1995. 4.95 (978-0-7417-2071-9(X), 1071) Win Walk.

Sin in the Second City: Madams, Ministers, Playboys, & the Battle for America's Soul. unabr. ed. Karen Abbott. Read by Joyce Bean. (Running Time: 11 hrs. 30 mins. 0 sec.). (ENG.). 2007. audio compact disk 34.99 (978-1-4001-0466-6(1)); audio compact disk 69.99 (978-1-4001-3466-3(8)); audio compact disk 24.99 (978-1-4001-5466-1(9)) Pub: Tantor Media. Dist(s): IngramPubServ

Sin Killer. Larry McMurtry. Narrated by Henry Strozier. 6 cass. (Running Time: 8 hrs.). (Berrybender Narratives Ser.: Bk. 1). 64.00 (978-1-4025-2391-5(2)) Recorded Bks.

Sin Killer. unabr. ed. Larry McMurtry. Narrated by Henry Strozier. 6 cass. (Running Time: 8 hrs.). (Berrybender Narratives Ser.: Bk. 1). 2002. 34.95 (978-1-4025-2392-2(0), RG086) Recorded Bks.
Set in the 1830s, Sin Killer traces the perilous voyage of the Berrybenders, a family of English aristocrats, as they make their way across the wild American continent. Listeners from all walks of life are sure to relish this masterpiece of the old West filled with a cast of unique characters.

Sin Killer. unabr. ed. Larry McMurtry. 8 CD. (Running Time: 80 hrs. 0 mins. 0 sec.). Bk. 1. (ENG.). 2002. audio compact disk 39.95 (978-0-7435-2511-4(6), Audioworks) Pub: S&S Audio. Dist(s): S and S Inc

Sin No More. Michael Pearl. 9 CDs. (ENG.). 2006. audio compact disk 28.00 (978-1-892112-25-5(6)) Pub: No Greater Joy. Dist(s): STL Dist NA

Sin No More. unabr. ed. Kimberla Lawson Roby. Narrated by Tracey Leigh. 7 CDs. (Running Time: 8 hrs.). (Reverend Curtis Black Ser.: Bk. 5). 2008. audio compact disk 74.95 (978-0-7927-5269-1(4)) AudioGO.

Sin No More. unabr. ed. Kimberla Lawson Roby. Narrated by Tracey Leigh. 7 CDs. (Running Time: 8 hrs.). (Reverend Curtis Black Ser.: Bk. 5). (ENG.). 2008. audio compact disk 29.95 (978-1-60283-359-3(1)) Pub: AudioGO. Dist(s): Perseus Dist

Sin No More. unabr. ed. Kimberla Lawson Roby. Read by Tracey Leigh. (Reverend Curtis Black Ser.: Bk. 5). (YA). 2008. 64.99 (978-1-60514-922-6(5)) Find a World.

Sin Novedad en el Frente. abr. ed. Erich-Maria Remarque. 3 CDs.Tr. of All Quiet in the Western Front. (SPA.). 2002. audio compact disk 17.00 (978-958-43-0191-8(8)) YoYoMusic.

***Sin Temor: Imagina tu vida sin Preocupacion.** unabr. ed. Max Lucado. Narrated by David Rojas. (Running Time: 4 hrs. 35 mins. 13 sec.). (SPA.). 2010. 13.99 (978-1-60814-756-4(8)); audio compact disk 19.99 (978-1-59859-835-3(X)) Oasis Audio.

***Sin Undone.** unabr. ed. Larissa Ione. Read by Cinnamon Dizon & A. C. Edwards. (Running Time: 12 hrs.). (Demonica Ser.). (ENG.). 2010. 24.98 (978-1-60788-638-9(3)) Pub: Hachet Audio. Dist(s): HachBkGrp

Sin unto Death. Kenneth E. Hagin. 1 cass. 4.95 (SH20) Faith Lib Pubns.

Sinatra: The Life. unabr. collector's ed. Anthony Summers & Robbyn Swan. Read by Scott Brick. 18 CDs. (Running Time: 19 hrs.). 2005. audio compact disk 144.00 (978-1-4159-2244-6(6)); 120.00 (978-1-4159-2243-9(8)) Books on Tape.
From the best-selling author of Goddess: The Secret Lives of Marilyn Monroe, the first fully documented, comprehensively researched, birth-to-death biography - the definitive life -of Frank Sinatra. Sinatra is the story of an American icon who held the imagination of millions for more than fifty years and whose influence in popular music was unsurpassed in the twentieth century. As a child, he said, he had heard "symphonies from the universe" in his head. No one could have imagined where those sounds would lead him. Tracing the arc of this incredible life, from the humble beginnings in Hoboken to the twilight years as a living legend in Malibu, Sinatra follows a career built on raw talent, sheer willpower - and criminal connections. Drawing on a treasure trove of documents and interviews, Anthony Summers and Robbyn Swan reveal stunning new information about Sinatra's links to such Mafia figures as Sam Giancana and Lucky Luciano. And we see for the first time where the Mafia connection began, how and why it lasted, and how it impinged on others, not least President John F. Kennedy. Here, too, is the core of the private Sinatra - alternately caustic and sympathetic - that the singer - so long - concealed. The heartbreaking truth about his passion for Ava Gardner emerges from never-before-published conversations with Gardner herself. In exclusive, intimate interviews, the women who loved Sinatra - some of them unknown to the public until now - share memories of the joy and pain of their relationships with him. And we learn what it was like to be the friend of a man who was generous and loyal to a fault, yet - as some of his fellow Rat Packers discovered - who could turn abruptly into a vindictive brute.

Sinatra Solution (Second Edition) Metabolic Cardiology. unabr. ed. M.D., F.A.C.C., Stephen T Sinatra. Read by Brian Emerson. (Running Time: 8.5 hrs. 0 mins.). (ENG.). 2009. 29.95 (978-1-4332-2233-7(7)); 54.95 (978-1-4332-2229-0(9)); audio compact disk 76.00 (978-1-4332-2230-6(2)) Blckstn Audio.

Since I Fell for You. Perf. by Lori Wilke. 1 cass. (Running Time: 6 min.). 1988. 9.98 Sound track. (978-1-891916-15-1(7)) Spirit To Spirit.

Since I Love You So Much: A New Look at the Ten Commandments. Dick Duerksen. 10 cass. (Running Time: 10 hrs.). bk. 30.00 (8063) Family Mtrs.
Bible stories to help you listen again to the Ten Commandments.

Since Yesterday: The 1930s in America, unabr. ed. Frederick Lewis Allen. Read by Christopher Lane. 8 cass. (Running Time: 11 hrs. 30 mins.). 1994. 56.95 (978-0-7861-0825-1(8), 1545) Blckstn Audio.
In this panorama of the thirties, Allen combines an eye for the significant trivia of everyday existence with a facility for neatly dissecting the political monoliths of the era.

Since You Went Away. Dean Hughes. Read by Dean Hughes. (Children of the Promise Ser.: Vol. 2). 2003. 19.95 (978-1-57345-293-9(9)) Deseret Bk.
Continues with Wally Thomas's struggle to survive as a prisoner of war on the Bataan Peninsula while his family begin to disperse due to the war.

Sincerity. Swami Amar Jyoti. 1 cass. 1977. 9.95 (K-12) Truth Consciousness.
What leads us beyond all the angles & pairs of opposites? The positive role of suffering. Short-cut to finish desires.

Sincerity & Honesty for the Goal. Swami Amar Jyoti. 1 cass. 1977. 9.95 (M-2) Truth Consciousness.
Why don't we see God? The role of thoroughly honest sincere will. Removing the separating tendency.

Sincerity in Spiritual Practices. Swami Amar Jyoti. 1 cass. 1991. 9.95 (P-56) Truth Consciousness.
Regular, sustained practices, truthful dealing with our mind, purify us, lead us to ascending aspiration for Enlightenment. Conscious destiny.

Sinclair Lewis: The Roaring Twenties. Joseph Schiffman. 1 cass. (Running Time: 25 min.). (Six American Authors Ser.). 1969. 11.95 (23055) J Norton Pubs.
The life, thought, art & relevance of Sinclair Lewis.

Sinews of Peace: Post War Speeches. Read by Winston L. S. Churchill. 1 cass. 10.95 (SAC 917) Spoken Arts.
The historic speech delivered by the late Prime Minister at Westminster College, Fulton, Missouri, in March 1946.

Sinful Nature. Michael Paerl. 4 CDs. 2003. audio compact disk (978-1-892112-42-2(6)) No Greater Joy.

Sing! - ShowTrax, Pt. 2. Arranged by Larry Farrow. 1 CD. (Running Time: 5 mins.). 2000. audio compact disk 19.95 (08742399) H Leonard.
This unique scat-style contemporary original will reach out & grab your audience. Fun, fun, fun!.

Sing a Jewish Song. Perf. by Jackie Silberg. 1 cass. (J). 1988. 10.95 (978-0-939514-26-7(5)) Miss Jackie.
Miss Jackie performed this live concert for parents & their preschool children.

Sing a Little Gay Song. Silvia Silk. 1984. (978-0-938861-08-9(5)) Jasmine Texts.

Sing-a-Long Bus. 1 cass. 1995. pap. bk. 11.95 (978-1-55569-698-6(8)) Great Am Audio.

Sing-a-Long Soup. Michael A. Farber. 1 cass. (Running Time: 28 min.). (J). (ps-5). 1996. 9.95 (978-0-9646094-2-6(8), R2996) KF Classix.
A collection of ten songs for children ages 3 & up about values. Each song is about a different value, from honesty & responsibility to keeping our environment clean & leading a healthy lifestyle. Each of the songs is also written in a different style of music. Designed for use by parents & educators as a fun & multicultural educational tool.

Sing-a-Long Train. 4 cass. (Running Time: 4 hrs.). (Wood Cassette Toys Ser.). (J). 1991. 19.95 (978-1-55569-487-6(X), 8330) Great Am Audio.
Tape-1, Traveling along songs, Tape-2, Animal Kingdom, Tape-4, Musical Stories, Tape-3, Silly Songs.

Sing a Song. 1 cass. (Running Time: 15 min.). (ITA.). (J). Incl. bklet. with lyrics & music. (978-88-85148-39-0(5)) Midwest European Pubns.
Songs include: "Yankee Doodle," "Jingle Bells," "Twinkle, Twinkle Little Star," "On My Farm," "Brother Peter," "This is the Way," & "Head & Shoulders".

Sing a Song of Death. unabr. ed. Catherine Dain. Read by Stephanie Brush. 6 cass. (Running Time: 6 hrs. 12 min.). (Freddie O'Neal Mystery Ser.: Bk. 2). 2001. 39.95 (978-1-58116-108-3(5)); audio compact disk 39.00 (978-1-58116-204-2(9)) Books in Motion.
On the Tahoe stage set, Vince Marino had a few enemies off-stage. And, when he shows up dead, everything points to his ex-wife as the killer. But Freddie believes otherwise.

Sing a Song of Joy. Jack Miffleton. 1 cass. (Running Time: 1 hr.). (J). (gr. k-6). pap. bk. 16.00 (978-0-937690-93-2(7), 6107); audio compact disk 24.00 CD. (978-0-937690-92-5(9), 6109) Wrld Lib Pubns.
Religious text & music.

Sing a Song of Science. 1 CD. (Running Time: 24 min.). (J). (ps). 1999. audio compact disk 15.95 Frnds St Music.
This toe-tapping collection of songs can be used to introduce a topic, as an activity break in the lesson or to reinforce a unit. Hand-clapping, dancing & singing along are great ways to gain the children's attention & aid retention.

Sing a Song of Science. 1 cass. (Running Time: 24 min.). (J). (ps-1). 1999. 9.95 (978-1-885430-17-5(5)) Frnds St Music.

Sing a Song of Scripture. Compiled by Ken Bible. 1 cass. (Running Time: 1 hr.). (J). (gr. 3-7). 1986. 12.99 (TA-9074C) Lillenas.
One hundred Scripture songs in a variety of styles. Includes traditional & contemporary favorites, along with new songs, providing a wealth of fun & meaningful music for both general & seasonal uses. Arranged with melody line, easy keyboard accompaniment & chord symbols, this volume is ideal for many situations: Sunday School, children's church, Vacation Bible School, children's choirs or home use. Alphabetical, topical & Scripture reference indexes included. All 100 songs are attractively recorded on two double-length stereo cassettes.

Sing a Song of Scripture. Contrib. by Ken Bible. 1 cass. (Running Time: 1 hr.). (J). (gr. 3-7). 1986. 12.99 (TA-9075C) Lillenas.
One hundred Scripture songs in a variety of styles. Includes traditional & contemporary favorites, along with new songs, providing a wealth of fun & meaningful music for both general & seasonal uses. Arranged with melody line, easy keyboard accompaniment & chord symbols, this volume is ideal for many situations: Sunday School, children's church, Vacation Bible School, children's choirs & home use. Alphabetical, topical & Scripture reference indexes included. All 100 songs are attractively recorded on two double-length stereo cassettes.

Sing a Song of Scripture, Vol. 1. Ken Bible. 1 cass. (Running Time: 1 hr.). (J). (gr. 3-7). 1986. 12.99 (MU-9074C) Lillenas.
One hundred Scripture songs in a variety of styles, especially suited for children 8 to 12. Includes traditional & contemporary favorites, along with new songs, providing a wealth of fun & meaningful music for both general & seasonal uses. Arranged with melody line, easy keyboard accompaniment & chord symbols, this volume is ideal for many situations: Sunday School, children's church, Vacation Bible School, children's choirs & home use. Alphabetical, topical & Scripture reference indexes included. All 100 songs are attractively recorded on two double-length stereo cassettes. Complete accompaniment tapes are provided in a split-channel format, with voices on one channel & instruments on the other for easy learning.

Sing a Song of Scripture, Vol. 2. Ken Bible. 1 cass. (Running Time: 1 hr.). (J). 1986. 12.99 (MU-9075C) Lillenas.

Sing a Song of Scripture, Vols. 1 & 2. Compiled by Ken Bible. 2 cass. (Running Time: 2 hrs.). (J). (gr. 3-7). 1986. 90.00 (MU-9075CB) Lillenas.
Demo cassette, Music only, no voices.

Sing a Song of Scripture Vols. 1 & 2: 100 Scripture Songs for Kids. Arranged by Joseph Linn. 2 cass. (Running Time: 2 hrs.). (J). (gr. 3-7). 1986. 19.99 (TA-9075B) Lillenas.
One hundred Scripture songs in a variety of styles. Includes traditional & contemporary favorites, along with new songs, providing a wealth of fun & meaningful music for both general & seasonal uses. Arranged with melody line, easy keyboard accompaniment & chord symbols, this volume is ideal for many situations: Sunday School, children's church, Vacation Bible School, children's choirs & home use. Alphabetical, topical & Scripture reference indexes included. All 100 songs are attractively recorded on two double-length stereo cassettes.

Sing a Song of Seasons. Rachel Buchman. 1 cass. (Running Time: 51 min.). (J). 1997. 9.98 (978-1-886767-98-0(X)); audio compact disk 14.98 (978-1-886767-97-3(1)) Rounder Records.
Twenty-two songs, activities, and poems that symbolize each of the four seasons. This recording is as valuable a storytime resource as Buchman's wonderful toddler recording, "Hello Everybody".

Sing a Song of Seasons. Mary Thienes-Schunemann. Illus. by Lura Schwarz Smith. Intro. by Cynthia Aldinger. (J). 2000. bk. 21.95 (978-0-9708397-0-1(7)) Pub: Naturally You. Dist(s): SteinerBooks Inc

Sing a Song of Six-Packs. Jerry Kent. 1998. bk. 11.95 (978-0-9620314-4-1(5)) WNY Wares.

Sing a Song of Sixpence, the King's Special Pie Audio CD. Adapted by Benchmark Education Company Staff. Based on a work by Jeffrey B. Fuerst. (Reader's Theater Nursery Rhymes & Songs Ser.). (J). (gr. k-1). 2008. audio compact disk 10.00 (978-1-60634-003-5(4)) Benchmark Educ.

Sing a Song of Tuna Fish: Hard-to-Swallow Stories from the Fifth Grade. unabr. ed. Prod. by Listening Library Staff. 2 cass. (Running Time: 2 hrs. 30 mins.). 2005. 23.00 (978-1-4000-9903-0(X), Listening Lib); audio compact disk 20.40 (978-0-307-20681-7(5), Listening Lib) Pub: Random Audio Pubg. Dist(s): NetLibrary CO

Sing a Song, Sing Along. Perf. by Faith Petric. 1 cass. (Running Time: 30 min.). (J). (gr. 1-7). 1982. 9.95 (978-0-939065-15-8(0), GW 1015) Gentle Wind.
Features songs as "Oh, He!, on Helen,I love you" & HIFI Stereo, Color TV.

Sing a Song with Baby. Mary Thienes-Schunemann. Illus. by Lurs Schwarz Smith. Intro. by Rena Osmer. (J). 2003. bk. 21.95 (978-0-9708397-5-6(8)) Pub: Naturally You. Dist(s): SteinerBooks Inc

***Sing a Spring Song: Incorporating Mendelssohn's Spring Song.** Composed by Jill Gallina & Felix Mendelssohn. (Running Time: 2 mins.). (ENG.). 2010. audio compact disk 26.99 (978-1-4234-8614-5(5), 1423486145) Pub: Shawnee Pr. Dist(s): H Leonard

Sing a Sum or a Remainder. Alan Stern. (J). 1997. 11.95 Ed Activities.

Sing A to Z. Perf. by Sharon, Lois and Bram Staff. 1 cass. (J). (ps-2). 9.98 (254); audio compact disk 17.98 (D254) MFLP CA.
Listeners go on a witty romp through the alphabet, matching 26 tunes with letters as they proceed.

Sing about Me. Janet Gari. 1 cass. (Running Time: 1 hr.). (J). 1995. pap. bk. (978-1-887958-06-6(1)) B Gari.
Children's songs.

Sing! Accompaniment CD. 2005. audio compact disk 16.95 (978-1-934477-20-5(6)) DictionSing.

Sing Again with Sydney. Christine Wyrtzen & Paula Bussard. 1 cass. (50-Day Spiritual Adventure Ser.). (J). (gr. k-2). 1994. 8.99 (978-1-879050-69-3(2)) Chapel of Air.
Sing along for the 1995 50-Day Spiritual Adventure.

Sing Alleluia. Perf. by City on a Hill. 2002. audio compact disk 17.98 Essential Recs.

Sing along & Read along with Dr. Jean All-in-One Pack (with Lap Books) Voice by Jean Feldman. 2009. pap. bk. 58.86 (978-1-60689-163-6(4)) Pub: Youngheart Mus. Dist(s): Creat Teach Pr

An Asterisk (*) at the beginning of an entry indicates that the title is appearing for the first time.

Sing Me a Song: Low Voice. Ed. by Sally K. Albrecht. (ENG.). 2008. audio compact disk 13.95 (978-0-7390-5085-9(0)) Alfred Pub.

Sing Me a Song Vol. One: Songs to Share Series. 1997. (978-0-9715448-1-9(6)) Walden Green.

Sing Me a Story. (J). 1986. audio compact disk 14.95 (978-0-939065-63-9(0)) Gentle Wind.

Sing Me a Story. Heather Forest. Read by Heather Forest. 1 cass. (Running Time: 50 min.). (J). (ps-1). 1986. 9.95 (978-0-939065-33-2(9), GW1037) Gentle Wind.

Stories such as, "The Little Red Hen," "Three Billy Goats Gruff," "Stone Soup" & others are presented with a weave of song & story.

Sing Me a Story. Heather Forest. 1 cass. (J). (GW1037) NewSound.

Sing Me a Story, Read Me a Song. Kathryn L. Cloonan. Read by Kathryn L. Cloonan. 1 cass. pap. bk. 25.95 (978-1-879813-25-0(4), PER-ST01); 10.95 (PER-C001) Child Like.

How to make old favorite kids songs into fun, clever big books & mini books. Includes: "Bingo," "Hickory, Dickory, Dock," "Ten in the Bed," "Happy birthday," "Baa Baa Black Sheep," "Twinkle, Twinkle Little Star," "Wheels on the Bus" & more.

***Sing Me to Sleep - Indie Lullabies.** Perf. by Jenny Owen Youngs et al. Prod. by American Laundromat R. American Laundromat Records. Stars et al. 2010. audio compact disk 25.00 (978-0-9807823-0-1(9)) GestaltP AUS.

Sing Me to Sleep, Daddy. (J). 1997. 9.99 (C80002); audio compact disk 12.99 (CD80002) Pub: Brentwood Music. Dist(s): Provident Mus Dist

Christian music's best known fathers express their love for their creator & their children through words & music. Includes "Safe in Your Daddy's Arms," "I Will Be There," "Oh Little One," & more.

Sing Me to Sleep, Daddy. 1 cass., 1 CD. (J). 7.99; audio compact disk 11.99 CD. Provident Mus Dist.

Sing Me to Sleep, Daddy. Perf. by Michael James et al. 1 cass., 1 CD. (J). 8.78 (BD 80002); audio compact disk 12.78 CD Jewel box. (BD 80002) NewSound.

Endearing moments between father & child can now be shared in these songs of love. Includes: "Safe in Your Daddy's Arms," "You Steal My Heart Away," "You Were His Idea" & more.

Sing Me to Sleep, Mommy: A Collection of Original Ballads & Lullabies. 1 CD. 1998. audio compact disk 16.98 (978-0-7601-2708-7(5)) Provident Music.

Tender ballads & peaceful lullabies.

Sing Me to Sleep, Mommy: A Collection of Original Ballads & Lullabies. Perf. by Brentwood Kids Staff. 1 cass. 1998. 10.98 (978-0-7601-2707-0(7)) Provident Music.

Sing More Songs. 1 cass. (Running Time: 25 min.). (ITA.). (J). Incl. bklet. with lyrics, music, teaching suggestions. (978-88-85148-99-4(9)) Midwest European Pubns.

Songs include: "10 Little Indians," "Good Morning," "Santa Claus," "I Hear Thunder," "One, Two, Three, Four, Five," "I Like to Jump," "The Muffin Man," "If You're Happy," "What Time Is It?," "Pop Goes the Weasel," "We Wish You a Merry Christmas," "The Wheels of the Bus," "Tipperary," "Baa, Baa, Black Sheep," "Sing, Sing, Sing," & "Row, Row, Row Your Boat".

Sing, Move, Learn. Jenny Clark Brack. Perf. by Mark Cosgrove. Arranged by Mark Thies. (ENG.). (J). 2009. audio compact disk 19.95 (978-1-934575-41-3(0)) Autism Aspgr.

Sing 'n Learn Chinese: Introduce Chinese with Favorite Children's Songs. Trio Jan Jeng & Selina Yoon. 1 CD. (Running Time: 46 min.). (Sing 'n Learn Ser.). (CHI & ENG., (J). (ps-6). 1997. pap. bk. 17.95 (978-1-888194-17-3(0)); pap. bk. 14.95 (978-1-888194-06-7(5)) Master Commn.

Introduces Chinese through familiar melodies. Children will enjoy the learning basic vocabulary through popular themes such as numbers, family animals weather, colors & more.

Sing 'n Learn Japanese One Vol. 1: Introduce Japanese with Favorite Children's Songs. Tazuko Inui & Selina Yoon. 1 cass. (Running Time: 1 hr.). (Sing 'n Learn Ser.). (ENG & JPN., (J). (ps-6). 1998. pap. bk. 14.95 (978-1-888194-21-0(9)); pap. bk. 17.95 (978-1-888194-22-7(7)) Master Commn.

Basic vocabulary is taught through popular themes such as numbers, greetings, animals, colors, & more.

Sing 'n Learn Japanese Two: More Japanese Through Favorite Songs, Vol. 2. Tazuko Inui & Selina Yoon. 1 cass. (Running Time: 1 hr.). (Sing 'n Learn Ser.). (ENG & JPN., (J). (ps-6). 1998. pap. bk. 14.95 (978-1-888194-23-4(5)) Master Commn.

Learn Japanese language & culture through favorite songs. Themes include festivals, holidays, seasons, games, food & more.

Sing 'n Learn Japanese Two Vol. 2: More Japanese Through Favorite Songs. Tazuko Inui & Selina Yoon. 1 CD. (Running Time: 30 mins.). (Sing 'n Learn Ser.). (ENG & JPN., (J). (ps-6). 1998. pap. bk. 17.95 (978-1-888194-24-1(3)) Master Commn.

Sing 'n Learn Korean: Introduce Korean with Favorite Children's Songs. Bo-Kyung Kim & Selina Yoon. 1 CD. (Running Time: 46 min.). (Sing 'n Learn Ser.). (ENG & KOR., (J). (ps-6). 1997. pap. bk. 17.95 (978-1-888194-18-0(9)); pap. bk. 14.95 (978-1-888194-08-1(1)) Master Commn.

Multicultural Education Council Award-1998. Introduces Korean with many familiar melodies. Children will enjoy learning basic vocabulary through popular themes such as greetings, numbers, family, weather, colors & more.

Sing 'n Learn Vietnamese: Introduce Vietnamese with Favorite Children's Songs. Hop Thi Nguyen & Selina Yoon. Interview with Dong Nguyen. 1 cass. (Running Time: 1 hr.). (Sing 'n Learn Ser.). (ENG & VIE., (J). (ps-6). 1998. pap. bk. 14.95 (978-1-888194-16-6(2)); pap. bk. 17.95 (978-1-888194-19-7(7)) Master Commn.

Introduces Vietnamese language & culture with favorite children's songs, with traditional & familiar melodies, children will enjoy learning basic vocabulary through popular themes such as numbers, family, animals, colors, & more.

Sing 'n Sign for Fun. Perf. by Gaia. 1 cass.; 1 CD. 1998. 10.95; audio compact disk 14.95 CD. Hrtsong Comm.

Features the alphabet plus songs & signs for greetings & feelings. Offers upbeat, unforgettable songs that encourage positive values, self-confidence & acceptance of others.

Sing 'n Sign for Fun. Perf. by Gaia. Illus. by Diana Bonadurer-Sullivan. Prod. by Ed Tossing. 1 cass. (Running Time: 66 min.). 1995. 9.95 Hrtsong Comm.

Side A, the "Sing" side, features seven original, fun & empowering songs to sing & dance along with including "I Can Do Anything," "I'll Be Friends with You," "Open Your Heart America," "People Havin' Fun," "The Unicorn Song," "Global Thread (the Ribbon Dance Song)" & "Oh Tree". Side B is the "Sign" side where Gaia teaches signing the manual alphabet, greetings & feelings, a rap song called "I Sign Like This," & the signs for three songs from Side A to create a blend of music, fun & education in the language skill of American Sign Language.

Sing 'n Sign for Fun - Gaia! Gaia. 1 cass. (Running Time: 1 hr.). (J). 2001. 10.95 (KHS 1003C) Kimbo Educ.

Gaia's songs touch on self-esteem & caring for one another, involving children in activities with sign language, signing & dancing. Includes a "sing" & a "sign" side. People Have'n Fun, I Can Do Anything, Greeting Signs, Feeling Signs, The Manual Alphabet & more. Guide includes lyrics & signs.

Sing 'n Sign for Fun - Gaia. Gaia. 1 CD. (Running Time: 1 hr.). (J). 2001. audio compact disk 14.95 (KHS 1005CD) Kimbo Educ.

Sing 'n Sign Holiday Time: Songs for Christmas, Kwanzaa & Hannukah by Gaia! Gaia. 1 cass. (Running Time: 40 min.). (J). (ps-6). 2001. pap. bk. & tchr. ed. 10.95 (KIM9163C); pap. bk. & tchr. ed. 14.95 (KIM9163CD) Kimbo Educ.

Traditional and original songs, including "Up on the Housetop," "Everyday a Holiday," "Hanukkah, Oh Hanukkah," "It's Kwanzaa Time," "The Twelve Days of Christmas" and more. Includes drawings of basic signs (ASL).

Sing No Sad Songs. unabr. ed. Christian Thompson. Read by Jonathan Keeble. 5 cass. (Running Time: 6 hrs. 35 mins.). (Story Sound Ser.). (J). 2005. 49.95 (978-1-85903-859-8(X)) Pub: Mgna Lrg Print GBR. Dist(s): Ulverscroft US

Sing No Sad Songs, Set. Lys Holland. 4 cass. (Running Time: 6 hrs.). 1990. 44.95 (978-1-85496-344-4(9)) Pub: UlverLrgPrint GBR. Dist(s): Ulverscroft US

Aubrey Mainwaring was a rich young Victorian musician who lived as a virtual hermit - until he heard a voice he couldn't live without. From that moment on, his life was to revolve around three very unusual women.

Sing Noel with Gloriae Dei Cantores. Gloriae Dei Cantores. 1 CD. 1999. audio compact disk 16.95 (978-1-55725-229-6(7), GDCD105) Paraclete MA.

Sing of My Redeemer. Greg Skipper. 1996. 40.00 (978-0-7673-0712-3(7)); 11.98 (978-0-7673-0677-5(5)) LifeWay Christian.

Sing of My Redeemer Cassette Kit. Greg Skipper. 1996. 54.95 (978-0-7673-0152-7(8)) LifeWay Christian.

Sing Praise &Thanksgiving. Composed by Michael Joncas. 1 CD. 1989. audio compact disk 16.00 (978-0-937690-77-2(5)) Wrld Lib Pubns.

Sing praises to our God: A selection of Orthodox liturgical Hymns. St Tikhon's Seminary Choir. 2008. audio compact disk 17.00 (978-1-878997-78-4(5)) St Tikhons Pr.

Sing science Intermediate Science Songs Collection #1: [Re-issued for Grades 3 - 8]. (ENG.). (J). 2008. audio compact disk 25.00 (978-0-9791493-2-0(0)) SingScience.

Sing Science Primary Science Songs Collection #1: For K, 1st, & 2nd Grade. 1 CD. (J). 2006. audio compact disk 15.00 (978-0-9791493-0-6(4)) SingScience.

Sing-Song of Old Man Kangaroo. Rudyard Kipling. 1 cass. (World of Words Ser.). (J). 15.00 (SAC 6503D); Spoken Arts.

Sing the Faith (Cd Accompaniment) New Hymns for Presbyterians. 2004. audio compact disk 349.99 (978-0-664-50276-8(8)) Westminster John Knox.

Sing the Glory Down. (Family of God Ser.). 1997. 4.98; audio compact disk 7.98 Pub: Brentwood Music. Dist(s): Provident Mus Dist

Original versions of classic songs including "I Bowed on My Knees & Cried Holy" by the Gaither Vocal Band, "Jesus Is Coming Soon" by the Oak Ridge Boys, & many more.

Sing the God of Ultimate Justice: Music for the End Time. Perf. by Schola Cantorum of St. Peter's in the Loop Church. Contrib. by J. Michael Thompson. 1 CD. (Running Time: 1 hr.). 2005. audio compact disk 16.95 CD. (978-0-8146-7925-8(0)) Liturgical Pr.

Featuring a broad spectrum of music from Gregorian chant to the composers of the twentieth century. Selections convey the thoughts of the Church concerning the Four Last Things with beauty and insight. Far from being "music for a funeral," this recording puts Christ's gospel of justice into its eternal and cosmic context.

Sing the Hits. Contrib. by Luke Gambill et al. (Running Time: 3300 sec.). (ChartSong Ser.). (ENG.). 2008. audio compact disk 16.99 (978-5-557-48298-1(9), Brentwood-Benson Music) Brentwood Music.

Sing the Hits. Contrib. by Luke Gambill. Prod. by Luke Gambill et al. (ChartSong Ser.). (ENG.). 2008. audio compact disk 90.00 (978-5-557-48297-4(0), Brentwood-Benson Music) Brentwood Music.

Sing the Hits: Alto. Contrib. by Luke Gambill et al. (ChartSong Ser.). 2008. audio compact disk 5.00 (978-5-557-48294-3(6), Brentwood-Benson Music) Brentwood Music.

Sing the Hits: Bass. Contrib. by Luke Gambill et al. (ChartSong Ser.). 2008. audio compact disk 5.00 (978-5-557-48293-6(8), Brentwood-Benson Music) Brentwood Music.

Sing the Hits: Soprano. Contrib. by Luke Gambill et al. (ChartSong Ser.). 2008. audio compact disk 5.00 (978-5-557-48295-0(4), Brentwood-Benson Music) Brentwood Music.

Sing Them Home. Stephanie Kallos. Read by Tavia Gilbert. (Running Time: 70200 sec.). 2008. 65.95 (978-1-4332-0335-0(9)); audio compact disk 90.00 (978-1-4332-0336-7(7)) Blckstn Audio.

Sing Them Home. unabr. ed. Stephanie Kallos. (Running Time: 11 hrs. 50 mins.). 2008. 29.95 (978-1-4332-0339-8(1)) Blckstn Audio.

Sing Them Home. unabr. ed. Stephanie Kallos. Read by Tavia Gilbert. 9 CDs. (Running Time: 11 hrs. 50 mins.). 2008. audio compact disk 29.95 (978-1-4332-0338-1(3)) Blckstn Audio.

Sing Them Home. unabr. ed. Stephanie Kallos. (Running Time: 11 hrs. 30 mins.). 2009. 29.95 (978-1-4332-0337-4(5)) Blckstn Audio.

***Sing to the Lord: for All Seasons, Volume 1.** Prod. by Steve Bowersox. (ENG.). 1998. audio compact disk 39.99 (978-0-00-523185-2(X)) Lillenas.

***Sing to the Lord, Praise & Worship, Volume 1: MIDI Hymn Trax.** Prod. by Steve Bowersox. (ENG.). 1998. audio compact disk 39.99 (978-0-00-523179-1(5)) Lillenas.

***Sing to Your Baby: Love Songs & Sing-Plays for New Families.** Community Music, Incorporated Staff & Marcy Marxer. Illus. by James Nocito. 2010. bk. 19.95 (978-0-9651036-5-7(X)) Cmmnty Music.

Sing Together with Ladybug. 1 cass. (J). (ps-1). 2002. 10.95 (978-0-8126-0080-3(0)) Pub: Cricket Bks. Dist(s): PerseuPGW

Sing with Eleni - Fun Songs for Children. Perf. by Elaine J. Konugres. 1 cass. (Running Time: 40 min.). (J). 1997. (978-0-9660591-2-0(3)); CD. (978-0-9660591-1-3(5)) Eleni Prodns.

Includes twenty sing-along songs.

Sing with Me: Bible ABCs. Created by C. D. Dudley. Illus. by C. Neal. (ENG.). (J). 2008. pap. bk. 19.95 (978-0-615-22370-4(2)) Exc Way.

Sing with Me ABC. Bente Martinsen & Solveig Pedersen. (J). 2001. pap. bk., tchr. ed., wbk. ed. 16.95 (978-1-928595-03-8(0)) Citron Bay.

Sing Your Heart Out. Arthur Samuel Joseph. 3 CDs. (Running Time: 2 hrs 45 mins). 2005. audio compact disk 24.95 (978-1-59179-315-1(7), AW00341D) Sounds True.

If you?ve ever been told you can?t even carry a tune ? think again. On Sing Your Heart Out, vocal coach and master teacher Arthur Joseph shows you how to discover your authentic singing voice through self-discovery exercises that are simple to practice and profoundly effective. For over 35 years, Joseph?s methods have helped thousands of students find their natural vocal talents ? quickly and naturally. From the sound stages of Hollywood to everyday neighborhoods, from the halls of Yale to corporate boardrooms, his methods have transformed voices yearning to be heard into living instruments rich with life, love, and power. On Sing Your Heart Out, you will learn Joseph?s groundbreaking system, which integrates spiritual principles for self-awareness with his secrets for using your mind and body to sing powerfully and easily. While you learn along with original exercises and delightful songs, Joseph offers gentle guidance with the ease of an expert who has helped ordinary people develop extraordinary confidence in their vocal gifts.

Sing Your Own Song. (J). 2001. audio compact disk 14.95 (978-1-55942-187-4(8)) Marsh Media.

Sing Your Praise. Daughters of St Paul. 2001. audio compact disk 16.95 (978-0-8198-7055-1(2), 332-353) Pauline Bks.

Sing your way To 2252. bk. 28.00 (978-2-7005-3020-9(9)) Pub: Assimil FRA. Dist(s): Distribks Inc

Singable Nursery Rhymes. 1 cass. (Running Time: 1 hr.). (J). (ps). 2001. pap. bk. 10.95 (KIM 8035C) Kimbo Educ.

Here they are, nursery rhymes for today's child! All our favorite characters are here in these upbeat arrangements that your child will love. The complete collection of songs include Humpty Dumpty, Jack & Jill, Little Miss Muffet, Sing a Song of Sixpence, Mary Had a Little Lamb & more. Includes guide.

Singable Songs. Perf. by Raffi. 1 cass.; 1 CD. 1998. 10.98 (32100); audio compact disk 16.98 CD. (32100D) MFLP CA.

Singable Songs Collection. Perf. by Raffi. 3 cass. (Running Time: 1 hr. 25 mins.). (J). 1999. (978-1-886767-83-6(1)); audio compact disk (978-1-886767-82-9(3)) Rounder Records.

Over 50 musical delights! An irresistible blend of traditional & original favorites for the young & the young at heart.

Singable Songs Collection. gif. ed. Perf. by Raffi. 3 cass. (Running Time: 3 hrs.). (J). 15.98 (RDR 8077) NewSound.

***Singable Songs for Letter & Sounds.** Created by Heidi Butkus. Lyrics by Heidi Butkus. Arranged by Mike Cravens. (ENG.). (J). 2008. audio compact disk 15.00 (978-0-9845641-8-7(7)) HeidiSongs.

Singable Songs for the Very Young. Perf. by Raffi. 1 cass. (J). (ps). 10.98 (2100); audio compact disk 17.98 (D2100) MFLP CA.

Raffi sings his favorite toddler songs in a style that delights the young. Includes: The More We Get Together, Aiken Drum, Down by the Bay, Brush Your Teeth, My Dreidel, Five Little Frogs, Must Be Santa & 15 more singable tunes.

Singable Songs for the Very Young. Perf. by Raffi. 1 cass., 1 CD. (J). 7.98 (RDR 8051); audio compact disk 12.78 CD Jewel box. (RDR 8051) NewSound.

Singable Songs for the Very Young. Perf. by Raffi. (J). (978-1-886767-57-7(2)) Rounder Records.

Raffi's first & best selling allbum. A children's classic: favorites & originals, rhyming fun, counting songs - irrestible!.

Singable Songs for the Very Young. Perf. by Raffi. (J). 1999. (978-1-886767-31-7(9)); audio compact disk (978-1-886767-30-0(0)); audio compact disk (978-1-886767-56-0(4)) Rounder Records.

Raffi's first & best selling album. A children's classic: favorites & originals, rhyming fun, counting songs - irresistible!.

Singable Songs for the Very Young. Perf. by Raffi & Ken Whiteley. 1 cass. (Running Time: 1 hr.). (J). 2001. 10.95 (KSR 8102C); lp 10.95 (KSR 8102); audio compact disk 16.95 (KSR 8102CD) Kimbo Educ.

The More We Get Together - Down by the Bay - Brush Your Teeth - Willoughby Wallaby Woo & more.

Singable Songs Gift Collection. Perf. by Raffi. 3 cass., 3 CD. (J). audio compact disk 23.93 CD Jewel box, Gift pack. (RDR 8077) NewSound.

Singalong Live at Sanders Theatre, 1980. Perf. by Pete Seeger. 1 cass. 1992. (0-9307-400270-9307-40027-2-8); audio compact disk (0-9307-40027-2-8) Smithsonian Folkways.

Addresses salient social issues. Includes "If I Had a Hammer," "Greensleeves" & "We Shall Not Be Moved." Recorded live.

Singe en Hiver. Antoine Blondin. 4 cass. (Running Time: 4 hrs.). (FRE.). 1992. 34.95 (1525-VSL) Olivia & Hill.

Set in a small village in Normandy, an old innkeeper combats the humiliation of the German Occupation by drinking. After the war he reforms, but is tempted by a visiting stranger into one last drinking binge. Read by a cast of actors.

Singenpoo Shoots Through. unabr. ed. Paul Jennings. Read by Stig Wemyss. 1 cass. (Running Time: 38 mins.). 2002. (978-1-74030-474-0(8)) Bolinda Pubng AUS.

Singenpoo Strikes Again. unabr. ed. Paul Jennings. Read by Stig Wemyss. 1 cass. (Running Time: 36 mins.). 2002. (978-1-74030-473-3(X)) Bolinda Pubng AUS.

Singenpoo's Secret Weapon. unabr. ed. Paul Jennings. 1 cass. (Running Time: 27 mins.). 2002. (978-1-74030-475-7(6)) Bolinda Pubng AUS.

Singer. 11.00 (978-1-59166-059-0(9)) BJUPr.

Singer of All Songs: The Chanters of Tremaris Trilogy. Kate Constable. 5 cass. (Running Time: 9 hrs.). (J). (gr. 5 up). 2004. 36.00 (978-1-4000-8515-6(2), Listening Lib) Random Audio Pubg.

Singer Trilogy: A Classic Retelling of Cosmic Conflict. unabr. ed. Calvin Miller. Narrated by Adam Verner. (Running Time: 5 hrs. 12 mins. 54 sec.). (ENG.). 2009. 13.99 (978-1-60814-538-6(7)); audio compact disk 19.99 (978-1-59859-598-7(9)) Oasis Audio.

Singer's Gilbert & Sullivan: Men's Edition. 1 CD. (Running Time: 90 mins.). (Orchestra Accompaniment Ser.). 2000. pap. bk. 19.95 (00740056) H Leonard.

Contains two versions of each selection: one with singer & one with orchestra accompaniment only. Book contains historical & plot notes about each opera, operetta or show & piano/vocal reductions of the music. The singers are top professionals from Covent Garden, English National Opera & other main stages. Includes: The Gondoliers: "Take a Pair of Sparkling Eyes"; HMS Pinafore: "When I Was a Lad I Served a Term"; Iolanthe: "When You're Lying Awake with a Dismal Headache"; The Mikado: "A Wand'ring Minstrel I," "As Some Day It May Happen," "Willow, Tit-Willow" & more.

Singer's Gilbert & Sullivan: Women's Edition. 1 CD. (Running Time: 90 mins.). (Orchestra Accompaniment Ser.). 2000. bk. 19.95 (00740055) H Leonard.

Singer's Library of Arias: High Voice. Composed by Patrick M. Liebergen. (ENG.). 2008. audio compact disk 13.95 (978-0-7390-5138-2(5)) Alfred Pub.

Singer's Library of Arias: Low Voice. Composed by Patrick M. Liebergen. (ENG.). 2008. audio compact disk 13.95 (978-0-7390-5141-2(5)) Alfred Pub.

Singer's Library of Musical Theatre, Vol 1: Baritone/Bass Voice, 2 CDs. Alfred Publishing Staff. (Singer's Library of Musical Theatre Ser.). (ENG.). 2009. audio compact disk 22.95 (978-0-7390-6101-5(1)) Alfred Pub.

Singer's Library of Musical Theatre, Vol 1: Mezzo Soprano/Alto Voice, 2 CDs. Alfred Publishing Staff. (Singer's Library of Musical Theatre Ser.). (ENG.). 2009. audio compact disk 22.95 (978-0-7390-6097-1(X)) Alfred Pub.

Singer's Library of Musical Theatre, Vol 1: Soprano Voice, 2 CDs. Alfred Publishing Staff. (Singer's Library of Musical Theatre Ser.). (ENG.). 2009. audio compact disk 22.95 (978-0-7390-6095-7(3)) Alfred Pub.

Singer's Library of Musical Theatre, Vol 1: Tenor Voice, 2 CDs. Alfred Publishing Staff. (Singer's Library of Musical Theatre Ser.). (ENG.). 2009. audio compact disk 22.95 (978-0-7390-6099-5(6)) Alfred Pub.

Singer's Library of Musical Theatre, Vol 2: Baritone/Bass Voice. Alfred Publishing Staff. (Singer's Library of Musical Theatre Ser.). (ENG.). 2009. audio compact disk 22.95 (978-0-7390-6109-1(7)) Alfred Pub.

Singer's Library of Musical Theatre, Vol 2: Mezzo Soprano/Alto Voice. Alfred Publishing Staff. (Singer's Library of Musical Theatre Ser.). (ENG.). 2009. audio compact disk 22.95 (978-0-7390-6105-3(4)) Alfred Pub.

Singer's Library of Musical Theatre, Vol 2: Soprano Voice. Alfred Publishing Staff. (Singer's Library of Musical Theatre Ser.). (ENG.). 2009. audio compact disk 22.95 (978-0-7390-6103-9(8)) Alfred Pub.

Singer's Library of Musical Theatre, Vol 2: Tenor Voice. Alfred Publishing Staff. (Singer's Library of Musical Theatre Ser.). (ENG.). 2009. audio compact disk 22.95 (978-0-7390-6107-7(0)) Alfred Pub.

Singer's Library of Song: High Voice. Ed. by Patrick M. Liebergen. (ENG.). 2005. audio compact disk 19.95 (978-0-7390-3665-5(3)) Alfred Pub.

Singer's Library of Song: Low Voice. Ed. by Patrick M. Liebergen. (ENG.). 2005. audio compact disk 19.95 (978-0-7390-3666-2(1)) Alfred Pub.

Singer's Library of Song: Medium Voice. Ed. by Patrick M. Liebergen. (ENG.). 2005. audio compact disk 19.95 (978-0-7390-3667-9(X)) Alfred Pub.

Singer's Musical Theatre Anthology. Ed. by Richard Walters. Created by Hal Leonard Corporation Staff. 2005. pap. bk. 22.95 (978-0-634-06020-5(1), 0634060201) H Leonard.

Singer's Musical Theatre Anthology, Vol. 2. Created by Hal Leonard Corporation Staff. 2005. pap. bk. 22.95 (978-0-634-06186-8(0), 0634061860) H Leonard.

Singer's Musical Theatre Anthology, Vol. 2. Ed. by Richard Walters. Created by Hal Leonard Corporation Staff. 2005. pap. bk. 22.99 (978-0-634-06201-8(8), 0634062018) H Leonard.

Singer's Musical Theatre Anthology, Vol. 3. Created by Hal Leonard Corporation Staff. 2005. pap. bk. 22.95 (978-0-634-06014-4(7), 0634060147) H Leonard.

Singer's Musical Theatre Anthology: Duets Accompaniment. Ed. by Richard Walters. Created by Hal Leonard Corporation Staff. (Vocal Collections: Vol. 1). 2005. pap. bk. 22.95 (978-0-634-06018-2(X), 063406018X) H Leonard.

Singer's Musical Theatre Anthology: Soprano Accompaniment. Created by Hal Leonard Corporation Staff. (Vocal Collections). 2005. pap. bk. & pap. bk. 22.95 (978-0-634-06012-0(0), 0634060120) H Leonard.

Singer's Musical Theatre Anthology: Soprano Accompaniment. Created by Hal Leonard Corporation Staff. (Vocal Collections: Vol. 3). 2005. pap. bk. 22.95 (978-0-634-06013-7(9), 0634060139) H Leonard.

Singer's Musical Theatre Anthology: Soprano Accompaniment. 2nd ed. Created by Hal Leonard Corporation Staff. (Vocal Collections: Vol. 2). 2005. pap. bk. 22.95 (978-0-634-06011-3(2), 0634060112) H Leonard.

Singer's Musical Theatre Anthology: Tenor Accompaniment. Created by Hal Leonard Corporation Staff. (Vocal Collections: Vol. 3). 2005. pap. bk. 22.95 (978-0-634-06185-1(2), 0634061852) H Leonard.

Singer's Musical Theatre Anthology: Tenor Accompaniment. rev. ed. Ed. by Richard Walters. Created by Hal Leonard Corporation Staff. (Vocal Collections: Vol. 1). 2005. pap. bk. 22.95 (978-0-634-06183-7(6), 0634061836) H Leonard.

Singer's Musical Theatre Anthology: Tenor Accompaniment. rev. ed. Ed. by Richard Walters. Created by Hal Leonard Corporation Staff. (Vocal Collections: Vol. 2). 2005. pap. bk. 22.95 (978-0-634-06184-4(4), 0634061844) H Leonard.

Singer's Musical Theatre Anthology: Baritone/Base Volume 4. Ed. by Richard Walters. (Singer's Musical Theatre Anthology Accompaniment Tapes). 2005. pap. bk. 19.95 (978-1-4234-0026-4(7), 1423400267) H Leonard.

Singer's Musical Theatre Anthology: Baritone/Bass Volume 4, Vol. 4. Created by Hal Leonard Corporation Staff. (Singer's Musical Theatre Anthology Accompaniment Tapes). 2006. pap. bk. 22.95 (978-1-4234-0030-1(5), 1423400305) H Leonard.

Singer's Musical Theatre Anthology: Mezzo-Soprano/Belter Volume 4, Vol. 4. Created by Hal Leonard Corporation Staff. (Singer's Musical Theatre Anthology Accompaniment Tapes). 2006. pap. bk. 22.95 (978-1-4234-0028-8(3), 1423400283) H Leonard.

Singer's Musical Theatre Anthology: Soprano Volume 4, Vol. 4. Created by Hal Leonard Corporation Staff. (Singer's Musical Theatre Anthology Accompaniment Tapes). 2006. pap. bk. 22.95 (978-1-4234-0027-1(5), 1423400275) H Leonard.

Singer's Musical Theatre Anthology: Tenor Volume 4, Vol. 4. Created by Hal Leonard Corporation Staff. (Singer's Musical Theatre Anthology Accompaniment Tapes). 2006. pap. bk. 22.95 (978-1-4234-0029-5(1), 1423400291) H Leonard.

Singin' Collection: With Songbook. unabr. ed. 1 CD. (Running Time: 1 hr. 5 min.). (J). 2003. audio compact disk 16.95 (978-0-9723972-1-6(3)) Wiggle Tune.
This collection of 31 activity songs comes from Wiggles 'n Tunes, a music program designed to develop rhythmic and tonal music awareness in young children.

Singin' in the Bathrub. 1 cass. (Running Time: 40 min.). 1999. 9.98 (Sony Wonder); 13.98 CD. Sony Music Ent.

Singin' on a Star. Purly Gates & David Levine. 1 cass. (Running Time: 30 min.). (J). (ps-7). 1985. 9.95 (978-0-939065-30-1(4), GW 1034) Gentle Wind.
Features childrens songs such as swingin on a star, if you like tails, Dad's old mule & Others.

Singin' on a Star. David Levine. Afterword by Purly Gates. (J). 1985. audio compact disk 14.95 (978-0-939065-71-4(1)) Gentle Wind.

Singin' Sidesaddle. Perf. by Nancy Stewart & Mary L. Sunseri. 1 cass., 1 CD. (Running Time: 46 min.). (J). (gr. 5-10). 1997. 10.00 (978-1-885430-14-4(0)); audio compact disk 15.00 CD. (978-1-885430-15-1(9)) Frnds St Music.

Singin' Steve's Alphabet Town & More Alphabet Town. (J). 1997. 9.95 (978-1-882500-14-7(8)) SmartSong.

Singin' Steve's Learning Land & Rainbow Village. (J). 1997. 10.95 (978-1-882500-16-1(4)) SmartSong.

Singin' Steve's Learning Land & Rainbow Village. Stephen H. Lemberg. Illus. by Darrell Baker. 1 cass. (Running Time: 30 min.). (Singin' Steve's SmartSongs Ser.). (J). (ps-1). 1999. bk. 14.95 (978-1-882500-17-8(2)); 19.95 SmartSong.
Teaches preschoolers about color, lines & shapes in preparation for letter & numerical recognition.

Singin' Steve's More Numberville. Singin' Steve. 1 cass. (Running Time: 30 min.). (Singin' Steve's SmartSongs Ser.). (J). (ps-2). 1996. bk. 9.95 (978-1-882500-10-9(5)) SmartSong.
Teaches comparison concepts like big/little, more/less, heavy/light & double digit numerals in preparation for addition.

Singin' Steve's Numberville & More Numberville. (J). 1997. 10.95 (978-1-882500-15-4(6)); (978-1-882500-12-3(1)) SmartSong.

Sing'in the Word Kid's Scripture Songs, Vol. I. l.t. ed. Music by Cliff White & Lisa White. 1 CD. (Running Time: 28 min.). (YA). 2003. audio compact disk 14.99 (978-0-9716523-4-7(1)) Pub: Hope Harvest Pub. Dist(s): Baker Taylor
Singin The Word Kids Songs and the companion book gives your kids all the tools they need to learn Bible verses and to have God's Word permanently hidden in their heart. The lyrics are pure scripture and nothing else, with verse references on each song. This CD has become a favorite for kids of all ages and their parents!.

Singing Bell see Asimov's Mysteries

Singing Bible: The Fun & Easy Way to Learn Scripture. Prod. by Focus on the Family Staff. (Running Time: 2 hrs. 40 mins. 0 sec.). (ENG.). (J). (ps-2). 2007. audio compact disk 19.99 (978-1-58997-463-0(8), Tyndale Ent) Tyndale Hse.

Singing Bowl Chakra Meditation. Hans De Back. 1 cass. (Running Time: 1 hr.). 10.00 (978-1-57863-053-0(3), Red); audio compact disk 16.95 (978-1-57863-052-3(5), Red) Red Wheel Weiser.
Various Himalayan bowls, bells & gongs, finely in tune for a simple but awesome interplay, from the very deep reverberation of the gong to the high pitch of the temple bells.

Singing Bowl Meditation I: Music for Relaxation & Meditation. Perf. by Hans De Back. 1 cass. (Running Time: 65 min.). 10.00 (978-1-57863-059-2(2), Red) Red Wheel Weiser.
Beautiful improvisations on Tibetan singing bowls for healing, meditation, love-making or pure listening pleasure.

Singing Bowls of Tibet. Interview with Alain Presencer et al. 1 cass. 10.95 (ECN 177) J Norton Pubs.
From his collection of singing Tibetan bowls, Presencer demonstrates his ability to induce strange & hypnotic sounds.

Singing Bowls Package. Jansen De Beck. 1998. bk. 27.95 (978-90-74597-30-2(0)) Pub: Binkey Kok NLD. Dist(s): Red Wheel Weiser

Singing Cowboy Stars. Robert W. Phillips. 1995. bk. 25.95 (978-0-87905-593-6(6)) GibbsSmith Pub.

Singing Cure. Paul Newham. 6 cass. (Running Time: 9 hrs.). 1999. stu. ed. 59.95 (83-0060) Explorations.
Unique professional training course on therapeutic singing, utilizing simple exercises adapted from many healing traditions, including indigenous cultures, to investigate who you are & how you feel, to express yourself with confidence & clarity.

Singing Dead. unabr. ed. Ron Ellis. Read by Trevor Nichols. 6 cass. (Storysound Ser.). (J). 2003. 54.95 (978-1-85903-518-4(3)) Pub: Mgna Lrg Print GBR. Dist(s): Ulverscroft US

Singing Earth (Sacred Music) unabr. ed. Prem Das & Don Jose. 1 cass. (Running Time: 1 hr. 25 min.). 1980. 11.00 (00502) Big Sur Tapes.
Explains the function of the ancient Huichol songs & Don Jose, a Huichol shaman, sings them for us. The Huichols feel the songs are the earth singing to herself through the shaman, & the shaman uses them to guide the flow of visions during peyote ceremonies.

Singing English Irregular Verbs CD. Suzanne Medina. (ENG., 2004. audio compact disk (978-0-9700490-4-9(8)) Forefront Pubs.

Singing for Beginners. Ferdinand Banda. 1 CD. (Running Time: 1 hr. 30 mins.). 2000. audio compact disk (978-0-7390-0422-7(0), 19333) Alfred Pub.

Singing French Songs. Perf. by Petite Chanteurs de Paris. 1 cass. bk. 14.95 (SFR250) J Norton Pubs.
The National Boys Choir, sings traditional French songs. This group of 24 boys, ages 8-14, is trained in vocal & music techniques as well as the history of French music. Lyric sheet in French included. Side 2 provides solo piano accompaniment to the selections. Lyric sheet in French included.

Singing french Songs: Les petits chanteurs de Paris. Perf. by LES PETITS CHANTEURS DE PARIS. 1 CD. (FRE.). 2005. audio compact disk 14.95 (978-1-57970-230-4(9), SFR250D) J Norton Pubs.

Singing Games. 1 cass. (J). (ps-5). 10.98 (2138) MFLP CA.
Collection of singing games includes familiar songs with dance games - walking, running, sliding, galloping & skipping. Includes simple explanations & popular songs such as "Skip to My Lou," "Farmer in the Dell," "Hokey Pokey," "Garden Game," "German Clap Dance" & more.

Singing Games for Little People. 1 cass. (J). 10.95 incl. guide. (KIM 0880C) Kimbo Educ.
Thirteen all-time favorite singing games.

***Singing Grammar Audio CD: Teaching Grammar through Songs.** Mark Hancock. (Running Time: 1 hr. 17 mins.). (Cambridge Copy Collection). (ENG.). 2010. audio compact disk 41.00 (978-0-521-17467-1(8)) Cambridge U Pr.

Singing Guns. unabr. ed. Max Brand. Narrated by George Guidall. 6 cass. (Running Time: 8 hrs.). 1992. 51.00 (978-1-55690-797-5(4), 92425E7) Recorded Bks.
The story of the growing friendship & respect between two oddly matched men: a notorious fugitive & the sheriff whose job it is to bring him to justice.

Singing Heart: Ephesians 5:19. Ed Young. 1983. 4.95 (978-0-7417-1276-9(8), 276) Win Walk.

Singing in the African American Tradition. 6 cass. (Running Time: 6 hrs.). bk. 59.95 (S11150) J Norton Pubs.

Singing in the Comeback Choir. unabr. ed. Bebe Moore Campbell. Read by Rebecca Nicholas. 8 cass. (Running Time: 12 hrs.). 1998. 64.00 (978-0-7366-4208-8(0), 4705) Books on Tape.

Singing in the Presence of God. Perf. by Robert Kochis & Robin Kochis. 1 cass. (Running Time: 45 mins.). 1999. 9.95 (T9418); audio compact disk 14.95 (K7150) Liguori Pubns.
Songs include: "I Am the Bread of Life," "Be Not Afraid," "Gift of Life," "Hosea" & more.

Singing in the Rain: Psalm 3. Ed Young. 1989. 4.95 (978-0-7417-1749-8(2), 749) Win Walk.

***Singing in the Shrouds.** Ngaio Marsh. Read by Anton Lesser. (Running Time: 2 hrs. 56 mins.). (ENG.). 2010. audio compact disk 22.95 (978-1-4055-0800-1(0)) Pub: Little BrownUK GBR. Dist(s): IPG Chicago

Singing in the Shrouds. unabr. ed. Ngaio Marsh. Read by James Saxon. 6 cass. (Running Time: 9 hrs.). 2002. 49.95 (978-0-7540-0771-5(5), CAB 2193, Chivers Sound Lib) AudioGO.
The police found the third corpse on a wharf in the Pool of London, her body covered with flower petals and pearls. Once again, the killer walked away, singing. Within the hour, he was safe at sea, and among his fellow passengers were four more potential victims.

Singing Is Fun CD. 2003. cd-rom & audio compact disk (978-0-7428-0577-4(8)) CCLS Pubg Hse.
Singing is Fun! For children over 6Two CDs and a booklet with the lyrics to 77 songsChildren?s songs and old favorites for classroom usePlay them anytime, anywhere ? on a CD player, or play and record on a computer, karaoke styleThe upbeat way for kids to enjoy and practice English!.

Singing Lesson see Garden Party

Singing Lesson. (Running Time: 300 sec.). (J). (ps-3). 2007. audio compact disk 9.99 (978-1-60247-108-5(8)) Tate Pubng.

Singing, Moving & Fun. 1 cass. (Running Time: 1 hr.). (J). 2001. 10.95 (KUB 1000C) Kimbo Educ.
11 action tunes teach subjects such as, saying "No" to strangers, expressing feelings & self-help skills. Body Bop, What Color is This?, Angry, Happy, I Got a Mosquito & more.

Singing My Him Song. unabr. ed. Malachy McCourt. Read by Malachy McCourt. 6 vols. (Running Time: 9 hrs.). 2001. bk. 54.95 (978-0-7927-2455-1(0), CSL 344, Chivers Sound Lib); audio compact disk 94.95 (978-0-7927-9901-6(1), SLD 052, Chivers Sound Lib) AudioGO.
The author grew up amid death, squalor, poverty & abuse in the lanes of Limerick, Ireland. When he came to America as a young man, he brought a gargantuan appetite for what life had to offer & an equal drive to forget what had happened to him.

Singing News Top Ten 2002. 2002. audio compact disk Provident Mus Dist.

Singing of the Dead. Dana Stabenow. 6 cass. (Running Time: 9 hrs.). (Kate Shugak Ser.). 2001. 48.00 (978-0-7366-6853-8(5)) Books on Tape.

Singing of the Dead. unabr. ed. Dana Stabenow. Read by Marguerite Gavin. 5 cass. (Running Time: 7 hrs.). (Kate Shugak Ser.). 2001. 24.95 (978-0-7366-6747-0(4)) Books on Tape.
Aleutian PI Kate Shugak joins the staff of a political campaign to work security for a Native woman running for state senator. Kate is to become her shadow, but just as she's getting started the campaign is rocked by the murder of the staff researcher, who, Kate discovers, was in possession of damning information about the pasts of both candidates. To track the killer, Kate will have to delve into the grisly murder of a "good-time girl" during the Klondike Gold Rush in 1915. Little can she guess the impact a ninety-year-old unsolved case could have on a modern-day killer.

Singing People for Little People. 1 cass. (Running Time: 1 hr.). (J). 2001. pap. bk. 10.95 (KIM 0880C) Kimbo Educ.
13 all-time favorite singing games, such as Farmer in the Dell, London Bridge, A Tisket-a-Tasket, Hokey Pokey, Jump Josie, See Saw, Kitty White, Did You Ever See a Lassie?, Hansel & Gretel, The Snail & more. Includes guide.

Singing Rails. Wayne Erbsen. 2002. per. 27.95 (978-0-7866-6608-9(0), 96901BCD) Mel Bay.

Singing Rails: Fourteen Railroadin' Songs. unabr. ed. Wayne Erbsen. Perf. by Wayne Erbsen. 1 cass. (Running Time: 42 min.). 1997. pap. bk. 9.95 (978-1-883206-30-7(8), NGB-900) Native Ground.
Classic railroad songs performed on old-time instruments.

Singing Rails: Fourteen Railroadin' Songs. unabr. ed. Perf. by Wayne Erbsen. 1 cass. (Running Time: 42 min.). 1997. audio compact disk 14.95 CD. (978-1-883206-28-4(6), NG-CD-910) Native Ground.

Singing Rainbow. Composed by Lynne Cox. Contrib. by Jill Williamson. 1 cass. (J). 1996. 6.00 Incl. J card & shrink wrapped. (978-1-891258-02-2(8), LCP3); 15.95 Incl. box of crayons, gift package, coloring pages. (978-1-891258-00-8(1), LCP1) L Cox Pubns.
Five songs sung with accompaniment five minutes duration, same program each side.

Singing Rat see Ellery Queen

Singing Sands. unabr. ed. Josephine Tey. Read by Stephen Thorne. 6 cass. (Running Time: 9 hrs.). (Inspector Grant Mystery Ser.: Bk. 6). 2000. 49.95 (978-0-7451-6322-2(X), CAB 401) Pub: Chivers Audio Bks GBR. Dist(s): AudioGO
While on vacation in the Western Highlands, Inspector Grant comes across the sleeping-car attendant of the night train trying to rouse the passenger in B-Seven. But it's an impossible task, for the man is dead. Upon picking up a newspaper on the floor, Grant notices lines of poetry written on it. Who wrote it and why? Inspector Grant was going to find out.

Singing Science. 1 CD. (Running Time: 1 hr. 5 min.). (J). (gr. 4-7). 2001. audio compact disk 14.98 (978-0-945337-16-4(7)) Tickle Tune Typhoon.
Familiar folk songs and original tunes on all aspects of science are presented in a mixture of musical styles. Sing along to "Home on the Sea" which is sung to the tune of "Home on the Range," and "I Am an Insect" which is sung to "B-I-N-G-O." Also includes "The Blue Mammal Waltz," a takeoff on Strauss's "Blue Danube".

Singing Spears. unabr. ed. E. V. Thompson. Read by Jon Cartwright. 12 cass. (Running Time: 16 hrs. 58 min.). 1995. 94.95 (978-1-85089-728-6(X), 90036) Pub: ISIS Audio GBR. Dist(s): Ulverscroft US
Daniel grew to manhood during the years of flood tide in the chronicles of Africa. The son of John & Miriam, he settles with his wife & children on a homestead in a valley of Matabeleland. It is now the 1880s & the Matabele impis are advancing with their singing spears toward the death-dealing Maxim guns of the white man. Daniel's loyalties, plans & dreams are swept by destiny into the savage whirlpool of history.

Singing Steve's Alphabet Town & More Numbersville. Stephen H. Lemberg. Illus. by Darrell Baker. 1 CD. (Singin' Steve's SmartSongs Ser.). (J). 1999. audio compact disk 19.95 (978-1-882500-19-2(9)) SmartSong.
Teaches children 2-6 each letter's shape, name & letter sounds in preparation for reading.

Singing Steve's Alphabet Town & More Numbersville. Stephen H. Lemberg. Illus. by Darrell Baker. 1 cass. (Singin' Steve's SmartSongs Ser.). (J). (ps-1). 1999. 14.95 (978-1-882500-18-5(0)) SmartSong.
Teaches children 2-6 each letter's shape, name & letter sounds in preparation for reading.

Singing Stone. Ellika Linden. Music by Bert Karlsson & Danny Solomon. (Running Time: 1 hr.). (J). (ps up). 6.00 Story Stone.
A beautiful tale of a young girl and her search for truth to save her people's sacred mountain.

Singing Stones, unabr. ed. Phyllis A. Whitney. Read by Anna Fields. 6 cass. (Running Time: 9 hrs.). 1999. 44.95 (2416) Blckstn Audio.
Despite her misgivings, child psychologist Lynn McLeod can't ignore the plea to help ten-year-old Jilly, daughter of her ex-husband, Stephen. But immediately upon her return to Virginia's Blue Ridge Mountains, Lynn is drawn subtly into the lives of everyone in the secluded household. The

dangers that threaten Stephen & his daughter soon close tightly around Lynn. And all the while, the soft, hypnotic sound in the wind - the eerie yet beautiful music of the Singing Stones - lures Lynn into a realm of mystery, murder & dormant passion.

Singing Stones. unabr. ed. Phyllis A. Whitney. Read by Anna Fields. 6 cass. (Running Time: 8 hrs. 30 mins.). 2001. 44.95 (978-0-7861-1587-7(4), 2416) Blckstn Audio.

Singing Stones. unabr. ed. Phyllis A. Whitney. Read by Anna Fields. 6 cass. (Running Time: 6 hrs.). 1999. 44.95 (FS9-51039) Highsmith.

Singing Stories for Children, Raffles & Other. 1 cass. (J). bk. 19.95 (S11125) J Norton Pubs.

Singing the Daily Office. Perf. by The Society of Saint John The Evangelist. 2 CDs. (Running Time: 1 hr. 42 mins.). 1999. audio compact disk 14.95 (978-1-56101-154-4(1)) Cowley Pubns.

Singing the Psalms. Cynthia Bourgeault. 4 CDs. (Running Time: 4 Hrs 15 Mins). 2005. audio compact disk 29.95 (978-1-59179-385-4(8), AW00379D) Sounds True.

Fifteen hundred years ago, St. Benedict established a system of ora et labora - prayer and work - that monastics still follow today. Central to this prayerful integration of body and spirit is psalmody, or chanting the psalms. On Singing the Psalms, Episcopal priest Cynthia Bourgeault shows how the psalms - 150 exquisite paeans of praise and supplication to God - can awaken rich spiritual and psychological insights. This ancient path is accessible to you today, whatever your level of vocal skill or theological understanding. An ideal support for both solitary and group practice, Singing the Psalms includes a mini-psalter (psalm book) with instructions, musical notations, rhythmic and melodic suggestions, and more.Topics include: How psalmody can deepen contemplative prayer, Antiphons: the verses you use to "personalize" your psalmody, How to "bring your mind in harmony with your voice", Specific instructions for singing seven psalms and three other sacred songs, The three functions of psalmody in spiritual transformation, How to create your own musical settings, and much more.

Singing the Sacred: Musical Gifts from Native American Communities. Compiled by Alvin Deer. (ARP, OJI, CHO, CHR & NAV.). 2008. audio compact disk 12.95 (978-1-933663-24-1(3), GBGMusik) Pub: Gnl Brd Glbl Minis. Dist(s): Cokesbury

Singing the Sacred Yes. Valerie Joi. 1 CD. 2006. audio compact disk 16.98 (978-1-59179-516-2(8), MM001070D) Sounds True.

Singing Wind: Songs & Melodies from Ecuador. Elizabeth Villarreal Brennan. 1998. audio compact disk 14.95 (978-0-937203-91-0(2)) World Music Pr.

Singing with Young Children. Bonnie Phipps. Illus. by Hal Aqua. 1 cass. (Running Time: 1 hr.). 1991. pap. bk. 17.95 (978-0-88284-492-3(X), 3558) Alfred Pub.

Single Again. Howard B. Lyman. 6 cass. (Running Time: 2 hrs. 20 min.). 55.00 (35020-35026) J Norton Pubs.

Single & Single. John le Carré. 4 cass. (Running Time: 6 hrs.). 1999. (978-1-84032-196-8(2), HoddrStoughton) Hodder General GBR.

Single & Single. abr. ed. John le Carré. Read by John le Carré. 4 cass. (Running Time: 4 hrs.). 1999. 25.00 (FS9-43368) Highsmith.

Single & Single. abr. ed. John le Carré. 2006. 14.95 (978-0-7435-6143-3(0)) Pub: S&S Audio. Dist(s): S and S Inc

Single Audits of State & Local Governments. Lucinda V. Upton. 4 cass. 1995. bk. 199.00 set. (CPE0640) Bisk Educ.

An in-depth discussion of the auditor's responsibilities in a single audit for reporting on the financial stmts., the supplementary schedule of federal financial assistance, the internal control structure & compliance with laws & regulations.

Single Aussie Bites: Crackle! unabr. ed. Margaret Clark. (Aussie Bites Ser.). (YA). 2003. audio compact disk 39.95 (978-1-74030-959-2(6)) Pub: Bolinda Pubng AUS. Dist(s): Bolinda Pub Inc

Single Aussie Bites: Holly & the Dream Fixer. unabr. ed. Rosemary Hayes. (Aussie Bites Ser.). (YA). 2003. audio compact disk 39.95 (978-1-74030-957-8(X)) Pub: Bolinda Pubng AUS. Dist(s): Bolinda Pub Inc

Single Aussie Bites: No Place for Grubbs! unabr. ed. Max Dann. (Aussie Bites Ser.). (YA). 2003. audio compact disk 39.95 (978-1-74030-962-2(6)) Pub: Bolinda Pubng AUS. Dist(s): Bolinda Pub Inc

Single but Not Alone 2004 Conference. 10 CASS. Orig. Title: Singles Conference 2004. 2004. 50.00 (978-1-58602-195-5(8)) E L Long.

Single but Not Alone 2004 Conference: Singles Conference 2004. 10 CDS. 2004. audio compact disk 65.00 (978-1-58602-196-2(6)) E L Long.

Single by Choice: Matt. 19:11-12, 1 Cor 7:7-9. Ed Young. 1993. 4.95 (978-0-7417-1956-0(8), 956) Win Walk.

Single Global Currency - Common Cents for the World. Morrison Bonpasse. (ENG.). 2006. audio compact disk 38.00 (978-0-9778426-1-2(4)) Single Global.

Single-Handed. unabr. collector's ed. C. S. Forester. Read by David Case. 5 cass. (Running Time: 5 hrs.). 1993. 30.00 (978-0-7366-2595-1(X), 3340) Books on Tape.

Lives of British naval officer & his sailor son unknowingly intersect during WW I hunt for German cruiser.

Single Hero see Twentieth-Century Poetry in English, No. 1, Recordings of Poets Reading Their Own Poetry

Single Life: How to Make It Work for You. Michael Broder. 1 cass. 1996. 12.95 (C065) A Ellis Institute.

Addresses the issues of being single, & ways to achieve the feelings of freedom that happy singles almost universally point to as the most positive aspect of single life. Strategies are presented for dealing with loneliness, & keeping it from driving you into inappropriate involvements. Through interactive exercises, you will learn successful social strategies, as well as how to build a support system & how to enjoy your own solitude.

Single Life: How to Make It Work for You - with or Without a Relationship. Michael Broder. 1 cass. 14.95 (C065) Inst Rational-Emotive.

Learn to enjoy the freedom of being single & not let loneliness overwhelm you. Through interactive exercises, you will learn successful social strategies, as well as how to build a support system & enjoy your own solitude.

Single Life: 1 Cor. 7:7-8. Ed Young. 1989. 4.95 (978-0-7417-1736-8(0), 736) Win Walk.

Single Life Special. Ben Young. 1997. 4.95 (978-0-7417-6035-7(5), B0035) Win Walk.

Single-Man see Complete Ghost Stories

Single Man. unabr. ed. Christopher Isherwood. Read by Simon Prebble. 4 CDs. (Running Time: 4 hrs. 30 mins.). 2009. audio compact disk 24.95 (978-1-61573-058-2(3), 1615730583) Pub: HighBridge. Dist(s): Workman Pub

Single Minderness. Elbert Willis. 1 cass. (Spirit of a Finisher Ser.). 4.00 Fill the Gap.

***Single Sashimi.** Camy Tang. (Running Time: 9 hrs. 26 mins. 0 sec.). (Sushi Ser.). (ENG.). 2009. 14.99 (978-0-310-30276-6(5)) Zondervan.

Single Shard. unabr. ed. Linda Sue Park. Read by Graeme Malcolm. (Running Time: 3 hrs. 12 mins.). (ENG.). (J). (gr. 5). 2004. audio compact disk 14.99 (978-1-4000-8495-1(4), Listening Lib) Pub: Random Audio Pubg. Dist(s): Random

Single Shard. unabr. ed. Linda Sue Park. 3 cass. (Running Time: 3 hrs. 12 mins.). (J). (gr. 5-9). 2004. 30.00 (978-0-8072-0702-4(0), Listening Lib) Random Audio Pubg.

Single Shard. unabr. ed. Linda Sue Park. Read by Graeme Malcolm. 3 vols. (Running Time: 3 hrs. 12 mins.). (Middle Grade Cassette Librariestm Ser.). (J). (gr. 5-9). 2004. pap. bk. 36.00 (978-0-8072-1760-3(3), S YA 349 SP, Listening Lib); audio compact disk 30.00 (978-0-8072-1607-1(0), S YA 349 CD, Listening Lib) Random Audio Pubg.

Single Shot. unabr. ed. Ron Ellis. Read by Trevor Nichols. 6 cass. (Running Time: 8 hrs.). (Story Sound Ser.). (J). 2004. 54.95 (978-1-85903-679-2(1)) Pub: Mgna Lrg Print GBR. Dist(s): Ulverscroft US

Single Shot. unabr. ed. Matthew F. Jones. Read by Richard Choate. 6 cass. (Running Time: 9 hrs.). 1996. 48.00 (978-0-7366-3399-4(5), 4046) Books on Tape.

John Moon thinks he's hit rock bottom. He lives in a trailer, his wife left him & took their son. He makes ends meet doing odd jobs & poaching.

Single Spies: A BBC Radio Full-Cast Dramatization. Alan Bennett. (Running Time: 1 hr. 30 mins. 0 sec.). (ENG.). 2009. audio compact disk 24.95 (978-1-60283-738-6(4)) Pub: AudioGO. Dist(s): Perseus Dist

***Single Thread.** unabr. ed. Marie Bostwick. (Running Time: 9 hrs. 30 mins.). (Cobbled Court Ser.). 2010. 29.95 (978-1-4417-7046-2(1)); 59.95 (978-1-4417-7043-1(7)); audio compact disk 90.00 (978-1-4417-7044-8(5)) Blckstn Audio.

Single to Paris. Alexander Fullerton. 2009. audio compact disk 89.95 (978-1-4079-0483-2(3)) Pub: Soundings Ltd GBR. Dist(s): Ulverscroft US

Singled Out. Trisha Ashley. Read by Eva Haddon. 8 cass. (Running Time: 34800 sec.). (Isis Cassettes Ser.). 2005. 69.95 (978-0-7531-2103-0(4)) Pub: ISIS Lrg Prnt GBR. Dist(s): Ulverscroft US

Singled Out. unabr. ed. Trisha Ashley. Read by Eva Haddon. 9 CDs. (Running Time: 9 hrs. 42 mins.). (Isis (CDs) Ser.). (J). 2005. audio compact disk 84.95 (978-0-7531-2468-0(8)) Pub: ISIS Lrg Prnt GBR. Dist(s): Ulverscroft US

Singled Out. unabr. l.t. ed. Simon Brett. Read by Simon Brett. 5 cass. (Running Time: 7 hrs.). 2001. 49.95 (978-0-7531-0013-4(4), 960207) Pub: ISIS Audio GBR. Dist(s): Ulverscroft US

Laura sets out to have a baby as an assertion of her independence, a sign that she has overcome an upbringing of terrifying violence. Then she sees something in the newspaper about the father of her child that shocks her to the core.

Singleness: The Blueprint to Successful Relationships. Creflo A. Dollar & Taffi L. Dollar. (ENG.). 2006. 15.00 (978-1-59944-139-9(X)); audio compact disk 21.00 (978-1-59944-140-5(3)) Creflo Dollar.

Singles Conference 2004 see Single but Not Alone 2004 Conference

Singles Rap Up: Phil. 4:11-13. Ed Young. 1991. 4095.00 (978-0-7417-1888-4(X), 888) Win Walk.

Sings for Children. Lead Belly et al. 1 CD. (Running Time: 62 min.). (J). 1999. audio compact disk 14.00 Smithsonian Folkways.

Singsation. Jacquelin Thomas. Narrated by Susan Spain. 6 cass. (Running Time: 8 hrs. 30 mins.). 54.00 (978-1-4025-1607-8(X)) Recorded Bks.

Singsation. Jacquelin Thomas. Narrated by Susan Spain. 7 CDs. (Running Time: 8 hrs. 30 mins.). 2001. audio compact disk 69.00 (978-1-4025-3825-4(1)) Recorded Bks.

Singular's Illustrated Dictionary of Audiology. Lisa Lucks Mendel et al. 2000. audio compact disk 68.95 (978-0-7693-0067-2(7), Singular) Pub: Delmar. Dist(s): CENGAGE Learn

Sinhalese Basic Course, Vol. 1. ed. G. H. Fairbanks et al. 19 CDs. (Running Time: 16 hrs.). (SNH.). 2005. audio compact disk 275.00 (978-1-57970-336-3(4), AFSN10D, Audio-For) J Norton Pubs.

Volume 1 has 24 lessons, each containing a conversation, grammar section, and exercises. Romanization is used in the first 12 lessons; Sinhalese script is introduced in Lesson 5. Beginning with Lesson 13, all new material is in script.

Sinhalese Basic Course CDs & Text: Colloquial Sinhala, Vol. 2. ed. G. H. Fairbanks et al. 7 CDs. (Running Time: 11 hrs.). (SNH.). 2005. audio compact disk 225.00 (978-1-57970-337-0(2), AFSN20D, Audio-For) J Norton Pubs.

Sinhalese, Colloquial, Vol. II. 12 cass. (Running Time: 11 hrs.). pap. bk. 225.00 (978-0-88432-692-2(6), AFSN20) J Norton Pubs.

Has 12 lessons & contains an appendix of noun & verb forms & comprehensive Sinhalese-English & English-Sinhalese glossaries.

Sinister Pig. collector's unabr. ed. Tony Hillerman. Narrated by George Guidall. 4 cass. (Running Time: 5 hrs. 45 min.). (Joe Leaphorn & Jim Chee Novel Ser.). 2003. 29.95 (978-1-4025-5649-4(7)) Recorded Bks.

A wealthy Washington businessman will do anything to protect a covert operation that earns him millions of dollars. But when his activities attract the attention of reservation police, his power becomes as unstable as the desert wind.

Sinister Pig. unabr. ed. Tony Hillerman. Read by George Guidall. 5 CDs. (Running Time: 7 hrs.). (Joe Leaphorn & Jim Chee Novel Ser.). 2003. audio compact disk 29.95 (978-0-06-054448-5(1)) HarperCollins Pubs.

Sinister Pig. unabr. ed. Tony Hillerman. Narrated by George Guidall. 4 cass. Library Ed. (Running Time: 5 hrs. 45 min.). (Joe Leaphorn & Jim Chee Novel Ser.). 2003. 29.95 (978-1-4025-5648-7(9)); audio compact disk 48.00 (978-1-4025-5681-4(0)) Recorded Bks.

Sinister Substitute. unabr. ed. Wendelin Van Draanen. Read by Marc Cashman. (Gecko & Sticky Ser.: Bk. 4). (ENG.). (J). (gr. 3). 2010. audio compact disk 25.00 (978-0-7393-7926-4(7), Listening Lib) Pub: Random Audio Pubg. Dist(s): Random

Sinister Swindler. unabr. ed. Frank Roderus. Read by Kevin Foley. 4 cass. (Running Time: 5 hrs.). (Heller Ser.: Bk. 7). 1995. 26.95 (978-1-55686-642-5(9)) Books in Motion.

Carl Heller gets himself marked for death while investigating a seemingly simple case involving the swindle of a Ute Indian tribal fund.

Sink or Float? Sundance/Newbridge, LLC Staff. (Early Science Ser.). (gr. k-3). 2007. audio compact disk 12.00 (978-1-4007-6273-6(1)); audio compact disk 12.00 (978-1-4007-6271-2(5)); audio compact disk 12.00 (978-1-4007-6272-9(3)) Sund Newbrdge.

Sink or Swim. unabr. ed. Kate Cann. Read by Nicky Talacko. 6 CDs. (Running Time: 6 hrs. 10 mins.). (YA). (gr. 9 up). 2007. audio compact disk 77.95 (978-1-74093-895-2(X)) Pub: Bolinda Pubng AUS. Dist(s): Bolinda Pub Inc

Sink or Swim Money Program: A 6-Step Plan for Teaching Your Teens Financial Responsibility. John E. Whitcomb. Narrated by Robert O'Keefe. 5 CDs. 2000. audio compact disk 48.00 (978-1-4025-4399-9(9)) Recorded Bks.

Sink the Gizmo. unabr. ed. Paul Jennings. Narrated by Francis Greenslade. 1 cass. (Running Time: 30 mins.). 2002. (978-1-74030-368-2(7)) Bolinda Pubng AUS.

Sink the Gizmo. unabr. ed. Paul Jennings. Read by Francis Greenslade. 1 CD. (Running Time: 30 mins.). (Gizmo Ser.). 2002. audio compact disk 18.00 (978-1-74030-752-9(6)) Pub: Bolinda Pubng AUS. Dist(s): Bolinda Pub Inc

Sinkiang Executive. unabr. collector's ed. Adam Hall. Read by Rupert Keenlyside. 6 cass. (Running Time: 9 hrs.). (Quiller Ser.). 1985. 48.00 (978-0-7366-0605-9(X), 1571) Books on Tape.

Whirling silently through space, satellite cameras pick up a suspicious new Soviet missile complex which must be identified. Quiller gets the job using the latest & fastest MiG, which a defecting Soviet pilot has conveniently landed in the West.

Sinking of the Bismarck. unabr. collector's ed. William L. Shirer. Read by Larry McKeever. 4 cass. (Running Time: 4 hrs.). 1987. 24.00 (978-0-7366-1080-3(4), 2007) Books on Tape.

At 8:00 a.m. on May 21, 1941, a coded message arrived at the Admiralty in London. The Bismarck, the world's most powerful battleship, has been sighted heading for the North Atlantic. Swiftly, the British organize an armada of fighting ships to pursue. Before the Bismarck can get a chance to fire on any of the British convoys, she must be sunk.

Sinking the Bismark. Kenneth Bruce. 1 cass. (Running Time: 1 hr.). Dramatization. (Excursions in History Ser.). 12.50 Alpha Tape.

Sinking the Eight Ball: Ruby Joe. Perf. by Ruby Joe. 1 cass., 1 CD. 1997. 10.98 (978-0-7601-1806-1(X)); audio compact disk 15.98 CD. Provident Mus Dist.

***Sinner.** abr. ed. Tess Gerritsen. Read by Dennis Boutsikaris. (ENG.). 2011. audio compact disk 14.99 (978-0-307-93311-9(3), Random AudioBks) Pub: Random Audio Pubg. Dist(s): Random

Sinner. unabr. ed. Ted Dekker. Narrated by Adam Verner. (Running Time: 11 hrs. 4 mins. 34 sec.). (Books of History Chronicles: Bk. 3). (ENG.). 2008. 24.49 (978-1-60814-383-2(X)); audio compact disk 34.99 (978-1-59859-520-8(2)) Oasis Audio.

Sinners in the Hands of an Angry God. 1 CD. 2004. audio compact disk 9.95 (978-1-931047-40-1(5)) Fellow Perform Arts.

Sins. abr. ed. Judith Gould. Read by Juliet Mills. 2 cass. (Running Time: 3 hrs.). 2000. 7.95 (978-1-57815-061-8(2), 1045, Media Bks Audio) Media Bks NJ.

About ambition & desire & the daring women who ruled the world's most successful magazine empire.

Sins. abr. ed. Judith Gould. Read by Juliet Mills. 3 vols. (YA). 2001. audio compact disk 11.99 (978-1-57815-520-0(7), Media Bks Audio) Media Bks NJ.

Sins. abr. ed. Judith Gould. Read by Juliet Mills. 2 cass. (Running Time: 3 hrs.). 1994. 15.95 (978-1-879371-03-3(0), 40040) Pub Mills.

Nothing was too much for Helene Junot. She was the most successful woman in the fashion world. Women envied her, men desired her. With her beauty & brains she built the greatest magazine empire on Earth. But Helene never forgot the horrors of her childhood in France, her mother's brutal murder, the rape of her sister by Nazis, her nightmarish years as a penniless orphan.

Sins Against Poverty. Thomas Merton. 1 cass. (Running Time: 60 min.). (Poverty Ser.). 4.50 (AA2103) Credence Commun.

Discusses sins against poverty in our society & the demands of poverty in the monastery.

***Sins of Omission.** abr. ed. Fern Michaels. Read by Joyce Bean. (Running Time: 6 hrs.). 2010. 14.99 (978-1-4418-8446-6(7), 9781441884466, BAD); audio compact disk 14.99 (978-1-4418-8445-9(9), 9781441884459, BACD) Brilliance Audio.

***Sins of Omission.** unabr. ed. Fern Michaels. Read by Joyce Bean. (Running Time: 22 hrs.). 2010. 24.99 (978-1-4418-8441-1(6), 9781441884411, Brilliance MP3); 39.97 (978-1-4418-8442-8(4), 9781441884428, Brlnc Audio MP3 Lib); 24.99 (978-1-4418-8443-5(2), 9781441884435, BAD); 39.97 (978-1-4418-8444-2(0), 9781441884442, BADLE); audio compact disk 34.99 (978-1-4418-8439-8(4), 9781441884398, Bril Audio CD Unabri); audio compact disk 89.97 (978-1-4418-8440-4(8), 9781441884404, BriAudCD Unabrid) Brilliance Audio.

Sins of Omission: Hos. 4:1-19. Ed Young. 1988. 4.95 (978-0-7417-1654-5(2)) Win Walk.

Sins of the Assassin. unabr. ed. Robert Ferrigno. Read by L. J. Ganser. (YA). 2008. 94.99 (978-1-60514-954-7(3)) Find a World.

Sins of the Father: Joseph P. Kennedy & the Dynasty He Founded. Ronald Kessler. 1997. (978-1-57042-554-7(X)) Hachet Audio.

Sins of the Fathers. 2003. 29.95 (978-1-888992-35-9(2)) Catholic Answers.

***Sins of the Fathers.** James Scott Bell. (Running Time: 10 hrs. 7 mins. 0 sec.). (ENG.). 2009. 14.99 (978-0-310-30527-9(6)) Zondervan.

Sins of the Fathers. abr. ed. John Blackthorn, pseud. Read by Julio Perez. 2 cass. (Running Time: 3 hrs.). 1999. 17.95 (978-1-55935-292-5(2)) Soundelux.

An American scholar stumbles on a plot to blow up Castro & his ministers on the 40th anniversary of the Cuban revolution.

Sins of the Fathers. unabr. ed. Lawrence Block. Read by Alan Sklar. 4 vols. (Running Time: 6 hrs.). (Matthew Scudder Mystery Ser.: No. 1). 2000. bk. 39.95 (978-0-7927-2372-1(4), CSL 261, Chivers Sound Lib) AudioGO.

The hooker was young, pretty & dead, butchered in a Greenwich Village apartment. The prime suspect, a minister's son, was also dead, the victim of a jailhouse suicide. The case is closed, as far as the NYPD is concerned. Now the murdered prostitute's father wants it opened again & that's where Matthew Scudder comes in.

Sins of the Fathers. unabr. ed. Ruth Rendell. Read by Nigel Anthony. 6 CDs. (Running Time: 7 hrs.). (Inspector Wexford Mystery Ser.: Bk. 2). 2008. audio compact disk 69.95 (978-0-7927-5509-8(X), Chivers Sound Lib) AudioGO.

Sins of the Fathers, Pt. 1 of 2. unabr. ed. Susan Howatch. Read by Robert Whitfield. 11 cass. (Running Time: 24 hrs. 30 mins.). 2004. 76.95 (978-0-7861-2664-4(7), 3223A,B) Blckstn Audio.

Sins of the Fathers, Pt. 2 of 2. unabr. ed. Susan Howatch. Read by Robert Whitfield. 7 cass. (Running Time: 24 hrs. 30 mins.). 2004. 49.95 (978-0-7861-2667-5(1), 3223A,B) Blckstn Audio.

***Sins of the Flesh.** abr. ed. Fern Michaels. Read by Joyce Bean. (Running Time: 6 hrs.). 2010. 14.99 (978-1-4418-8466-4(1), 9781441884664, BAD); audio compact disk 14.99 (978-1-4418-8465-7(3), 9781441884657, BACD) Brilliance Audio.

***Sins of the Flesh.** unabr. ed. Fern Michaels. Read by Joyce Bean. (Running Time: 18 hrs.). 2010. 24.99 (978-1-4418-8461-9(0), 9781441884619, Brilliance MP3); 24.99 (978-1-4418-8463-3(7), 9781441884633, BAD); 39.97 (978-1-4418-8462-6(9), 9781441884626, Brlnc Audio MP3 Lib); 39.97 (978-1-4418-8464-0(5), 9781441884640, BADLE); audio compact disk 34.99 (978-1-4418-8459-6(9), 9781441884596, Bril Audio CD Unabri); audio compact disk 89.97 (978-1-4418-8460-2(2), 9781441884602, BriAudCD Unabrid) Brilliance Audio.

Sins of the Wolf. unabr. ed. Anne Perry. Narrated by Davina Porter. 11 cass. (Running Time: 16 hrs.). (William Monk Novel Ser.). 2000. 91.00 (978-0-7887-0272-3(6), 94481E7) Recorded Bks.
When her wealthy Scottish employer dies of an overdose of heart medication, Nurse Latterly is charged with murder & locked up in Newgate Prison. To save his friend from the gallows, Inspector Monk works feverishly to identify a cold-blooded killer in the victim's greatly admired - and coolly silent - family.

Sins Out of School. Jeanne M. Dams. Read by Kate Reading. (Dorothy Martin Mystery Ser.: Bk. 8). 2002. 56.00 (978-0-7366-8929-8(X)); audio compact disk 56.00 (978-0-7366-8930-4(3)) Books on Tape.

Sintesis: Curso Intermedio de Espanol. Mercedes Belchi Arevalo & Paul J. Carter. 1 cass. (Running Time: 1 hr. 30 mins.). (SPA & ENG.), (978-84-7861-999-3(2)) Coloquio Edit ESP.

Sioux Shaman. unabr. ed. Joseph Henderson. 1 cass. (Running Time: 1 hr. 19 min.). 1970. 11.00 (06602) Big Sur Tapes.
On Black Elk's vision & seven secret rites of the soul.

Sioux Songs, Traditional. 1 cass. (Running Time: 1 hr.). 12.95 (C11150) J Norton Pubs.

Sir Apropos of Nothing. abr. ed. Peter David. Read by Peter David. 4 cass. (Running Time: 6 hrs.). 2001. 24.95 (978-1-57511-092-9(X)) Pub Mills.
The result of the midnight rape of a tavern wench, Apropos is an unlikely hero: rogue, rascal, scoundrel, cheat, & those are his good points. Lame but cunning, he thinks that chivalry is not dead simply because he isn't finished with it.

Sir Bentley & Holbrook Court. unabr. ed. Chuck Black. Narrated by Andy Turvey et al. (Running Time: 4 hrs. 58 mins. 6 sec.). (Knights of Arrethtrae Ser.). (ENG.). 2009. 13.99 (978-1-60814-500-3(X)) Oasis Audio.

Sir Bentley & Holbrook Court. unabr. ed. Chuck Black. Narrated by Andy Turvey et al. (Running Time: 4 hrs. 58 mins. 6 sec.). (Knights of Arrethtrae Ser.). (ENG.). 2009. audio compact disk 19.99 (978-1-59859-516-1(4)) Oasis Audio.

Sir Billy Bear & Other Friends. unabr. ed. Rose Impey. Read by June Whitfield. 3 cass. (Running Time: 3 hrs.). (J). (gr. 1-8). 1999. 24.95 (CCA 3475, Chivers Child Audio) AudioGO.

Sir Charles: The Wit & Wisdom of Charles Barkley. abr. ed. Charles Barkley. (ENG.). 2006. 5.98 (978-1-59483-761-6(9)) Pub: Hachet Audio. Dist(s): HachBkGrp

Sir Dalton & the Shadow Heart. unabr. ed. Chuck Black. Narrated by Andy Turvey & Dawn Marshall. (Running Time: 5 hrs. 0 mins. 0 sec.). (Knights of Arrethtrae Ser.). (ENG.). 2010. 13.99 (978-1-60814-617-8(0)); audio compact disk 19.99 (978-1-59859-671-7(3)) Oasis Audio.

Sir Dominic Sarsfield see Tales of Terror & the Supernatural: A Collection

Sir Dominic Sarsfield. unabr. ed. J. Sheridan Le Fanu. Read by Jack Benson. 1 cass. (Running Time: 78 min.). Dramatization. 1980. 7.95 (N-40) Jimcin Record.
The devil gets his due & a foolish young man escapes his.

Sir Francis Drake. unabr. ed. John Sugden. Narrated by Ian Stuart. 14 cass. (Running Time: 19 hrs. 30 mins.). 1992. 112.00 (978-1-55690-680-0(3), 92332E7) Recorded Bks.
A biographical account of the English explorer Sir Francis Drake. A swashbuckling tale of adventure on the high seas.

Sir Gawain & the Green Knight. unabr. ed. Read by Bill Wallis. Tr. by Simon Armitage. (YA). 2008. 59.99 (978-1-60514-606-5(4)) Find a World.

Sir Gawain & the Green Knight: New Verse Translation. Read by Jasper Britton. Tr. by Benedict Flynn. (Running Time: 8056 sec.). (Classic Literature with Classical Music Ser.). 2008. audio compact disk 17.98 (978-962-634-865-9(8), Naxos AudioBooks) Naxos.

Sir Gawain & the Green Knight, Pearl, Sir Orfeo. unabr. ed. J. R. R. Tolkien. Read by Terry Jones. 2 cass. (Running Time: 3 hrs.). 1997. 17.99 (978-0-00-105373-1(6)) Pub: HarpC GBR. Dist(s): Trafalgar
This 14th-century poem tells of love and sex, honour and integrity, chivalry and magic, and above all right and wrong.

Sir Gawaine & the Green Knight see Twentieth-Century Poetry in English, No. 7, Recordings of Poets Reading Their Own Poetry

Sir Harry Hotspur of Humblethwaite. Anthony Trollope. Read by Tony Britton. (Running Time: 28200 sec.). 2003. audio compact disk 79.95 (978-0-7540-8764-9(6)) Pub: Chivers Audio Bks GBR. Dist(s): AudioGO

Sir Harry Hotspur of Humblethwaite. Anthony Trollope. Read by Peter Joyce. 2002. pap. bk. 54.95 (978-1-86015-472-0(7)) Ulverscroft US.

Sir Harry Hotspur of Humblethwaite, unabr. ed. Anthony Trollope. Read by Flo Gibson. 5 cass. (Running Time: 6 hrs. 30 min.). 1998. bk. 20.95 (978-1-55685-550-4(8)) Audio Bk Con.
Tells of a father's vacillation over his daughter's wish to marry his nephew, who will inherit the family title, but is a scamp & wastrel.

Sir Harry Hotspur of Humblethwaite. unabr. ed. Anthony Trollope. Read by Tony Britton. 8 cass. (Running Time: 12 hrs.). 2001. 69.95 (978-0-7540-0572-8(0), CAB1995) AudioGO.
Upon the death of his only son, the wealthy baronet Sir Harry Hotspur had determined to give his property to his daughter Emily, who is vigorous, beautiful & as strong-willed & high-principled as her father. She falls in love with George Hotspur, heir to the title & black sheep of the family Sir Harry must choose between losing family honor & happiness & losing his beloved daughter.

Sir John Betjeman Reading His Poetry. unabr. ed. John Betjeman. 1 cass. Incl. Anglo-Catholic Congresses. (SWC 1557); Barrow-on-the-Hill. (SWC 1557); Bay in Anglesey. (SWC 1557); Caprice. (SWC 1557); Five O'Clock Shadow. (SWC 1557); Good-bye. (SWC 1557); Great Central Railway. (SWC 1557); Greenaway. (SWC 1557); Harvest Hymn. (SWC 1557); Hon. Sec. (SWC 1557); Hunters Trials. (SWC 1557); Ireland's Own. (SWC 1557); Matlock Bath. (SWC 1557); Meditation on the A-Thirty. (SWC 1557); Reproof Deserved. (SWC 1557); Russell Flint. (SWC 1557); Subaltern's Love Song A. (SWC 1557); Sun & Fun. (SWC 1557); Tregardock. (SWC 1557); Youth & Age on Beaulieu River, Hants. (SWC 1557); Chap. 1 extracts from Chap. 2. Summoned by the Bells. (SWC 1557); 1984. 12.95 (978-0-694-50299-8(5), SWC 1557) HarperCollins Pubs.

Sir Kendrick & the Castle of Bel Lione. unabr. ed. Chuck Black. Narrated by Andy Turvey & Dawn Marshall. (Running Time: 5 hrs. 1 mins. 20 sec.). (Knights of Arrethtrae Ser.). (ENG.). 2009. 13.99 (978-1-60814-499-0(2)); audio compact disk 19.99 (978-1-59859-515-4(6)) Oasis Audio.

Sir Lancelot of the Lake. unabr. ed. 1 cass. (Running Time: 20 min.). Dramatization. (Magic Looking Glass Ser.). (J). (gr. 2-6). 1989. 9.95 (978-0-7810-0055-0(6), NIM-CW-131-6-C) NIMCO.
An English folk tale.

Sir Michael Tippett. Hosted by Colin Davis. Contrib. by Peter Pears et al. 1 cass. 10.95 (ECN 217) J Norton Pubs.
Extensive extracts from these operas & other compositions are used to illustrate this feature & there are contributions from musicians & artists who have been closely associated with Tippett's work.

Sir Nigel. Arthur Conan Doyle. Read by Anais 9000. 2008. 27.95 (978-1-60112-167-7(9)) Babblebooks.

Sir Nigel. Arthur Conan Doyle. 2009. 94.95 (978-0-7531-4157-1(4)); audio compact disk 104.95 (978-0-7531-4158-8(2)) Pub: Isis Pubng Ltd GBR. Dist(s): Ulverscroft US

Sir Oliver's Song. 1 cass. (J). 9.95 (ASOS) Brdgstn Multimed Grp.
Fun & lively musical lessons about the Ten Commandments.

Sir Oliver's Song. 1 cass. (Running Time: 1 hr.). (J). 2000. 6.99 HARK Ent.
Will fill your home with fun-filled praise of the Lord. Provides wholesome messages that are sure to last a lifetime.

Sir Olivers Song. Bridgestone Staff. 2004. audio compact disk 7.98 (978-1-56371-033-9(1)) Brdgstn Multimed Grp.

***Sir Quinlan & the Swords of Valor.** unabr. ed. Chuck Black. (Running Time: 5 hrs. 42 mins. 2 sec.). (Knights of Arrethtrae Ser.). (ENG.). 2010. 13.99 (978-1-60814-780-9(0)); audio compact disk 19.99 (978-1-59859-788-2(4)) Oasis Audio.

***Sir Rowan & the Camerian Conquest.** unabr. ed. Chuck Black. (Running Time: 5 hrs. 25 mins. 33 sec.). (Knights of Arrethtrae Ser.). (ENG.). 2010. 13.99 (978-1-60814-781-6(9)); audio compact disk 19.99 (978-1-59859-789-9(2)) Oasis Audio.

Sir Thursday. unabr. ed. Garth Nix. Read by Allan Corduner. 7 CDs. (Running Time: 7 hrs. 52 mins.). (Keys to the Kingdom Ser.: No. 4). (J). (gr. 4-7). 2006. audio compact disk 55.00 (978-0-307-28568-3(5), Listening Lib); 40.00 (978-0-8072-1736-8(0), Listening Lib) Pub: Random Audio Pubg. Dist(s): Random
It's Thursday. Following their adventure on the Border Sea, Arthur and Leaf are set on heading home. But only Leaf can make it through the Front Door. Arthur is blocked because someone - or something - has assumed his identity and it taking over his life. Before Arthur can take action, his is drafted by the strange Sir Thursday and forced to join the Glorious Army of the Architect. While Leaf tries to banish Arthur's double on earth, Arthur must survive his basic training, avoid getting posted to the Front, and work out how he can free Part Four of the Will. Is this a war that Arthur can win... or is his only hope to escape it?.

Sir Thursday. unabr. ed. Garth Nix. Read by Allan Corduner. 6 CDs. (Running Time: 28380 sec.). (Keys to the Kingdom Ser.: No. 4). (ENG.). (J). (gr. 4). 2010. audio compact disk 45.00 (978-0-8072-1735-1(2), Listening Lib) Pub: Random Audio Pubg. Dist(s): Random

Sir Walter's Lady. Judith Saxton. Read by Anna Bentinck. 6 cass. (Running Time: 6 hrs. 30 mins.). (Soundings Ser.). (J). 2004. 54.95 (978-1-84283-471-8(1)); audio compact disk 64.95 (978-1-84283-861-7(X)) Pub: ISIS Lrg Prnt GBR. Dist(s): Ulverscroft US

Sir William Walton: A Portrait. Narrated by William Walton. Contrib. by Sacheverell Sitwell et al. 1 cass. 10.95 (ECN 219) J Norton Pubs.
He talks about his personal life & the way it has influenced his music.

Sir Winston Churchill: His Finest Hour. unabr. ed. Winston L. S. Churchill. 1 CD. (Running Time: 1 hr. 30 mins.). 2001. audio compact disk 20.95 Books on Tape.

Sire de Maletroit's Door see Suicide Club & Other Stories

Sire de Maletroit's Door. unabr. ed. Robert Louis Stevenson. 1 cass. (Running Time: 52 min.). Dramatization. 1977. 7.95 (D-8) Jimcin Record.
Two stories of the macabre.

***Siren.** Tara Moss. Read by Edwina Wren. (Running Time: 11 hrs. 36 mins.). 2010. 94.99 (978-1-74214-613-3(9), 9781742146133) Pub: Bolinda Pubng AUS. Dist(s): Bolinda Pub Inc

Siren. unabr. ed. Tara Moss. Read by Edwina Wren. (Running Time: 11 hrs. 36 mins.). 2009. audio compact disk 98.95 (978-1-74214-518-1(3), 9781742145181) Pub: Bolinda Pubng AUS. Dist(s): Bolinda Pub Inc

***Siren.** unabr. ed. Tricia Rayburn. Read by Nicola Barber. (Running Time: 10 hrs.). 2010. 39.97 (978-1-4418-8859-4(4), 9781441888594, BADLE) Brilliance Audio.

***Siren.** unabr. ed. Tricia Rayburn. Read by Nicola Barber. (Running Time: 9 hrs.). (YA). 2010. 24.99 (978-1-4418-8857-0(8), 9781441888570, Brilliance MP3); 39.97 (978-1-4418-8858-7(6), 9781441888587, Brlnc Audio MP3 Lib); audio compact disk 24.99 (978-1-4418-8855-6(1), 9781441888556, Bril Audio CD Unabri); audio compact disk 54.97 (978-1-4418-8856-3(X), 9781441888563, BriAudCD Unabrid) Brilliance Audio.

Siren Land. unabr. collector's ed. Norman Douglas. Read by Richard Brown. 7 cass. (Running Time: 10 hrs. 30 mins.). 1988. 56.00 (978-0-7366-1339-2(0), 2242) Books on Tape.
The author was born in 1868, mid-Victorian, & received a classical education. To a lad of spirit & imagination, England was no place to stay. So he shipped to Italy & there remained, steeped in the land & tradition, 100 years ahead of his time. In books such as Siren Land, he wrote of the timeless things that come to us from antiquity. His books are erudite & humane, rather like a seminar with a favorite professor.

Siren Psalms: Poems in Her Own Voice. Siobhan Pitchford. Perf. by Siobhan Pitchford. Executive Producer David M. Pitchford. David M. Pitchford. 2006. audio compact disk 14.95 (978-1-933923-09-3(1), DaybrePr) Pitch-Black.

Siren Song. Perf. by Connemara. 1 cass. 10.98; audio compact disk 17.98 Lifedance.
Celtic harp, vocals, fiddle, & dulcimer. The tender voices of women echo with a sense of mystery, with harp or fiddle adding a simple accompaniment. The words are in Gaelic; occasional instrumental ballads offer a tender repose. Demo CD or cassette available.

Sirens & Sea Monsters, unabr. ed. Mary Pope Osborne. Illus. by James Simmons. 2 cass. (Running Time: 3 hrs.). (Tales from the Odyssey Ser.: Bk. 3). 2004. 18.00 (978-0-06-052434-0(0), HarperChildAud) HarperCollins Pubs.

Sirens of Baghdad. unabr. ed. Yasmina Khadra & Jason Collins. Tr. by John Cullen. (Running Time: 9 hrs. NaN mins.). 2008. 29.95 (978-1-4332-2937-4(4)); 59.95 (978-1-4332-2933-6(1)); audio compact disk 70.00 (978-1-4332-2934-3(X)) Blckstn Audio.

Sirens of Titan. unabr. collector's ed. Kurt Vonnegut. Read by Dan Lazar. 8 cass. (Running Time: 8 hrs.). 1978. 48.00 (978-0-7366-0113-9(9), 1120) Books on Tape.
We meet Malachi Constant, "the richest man in America," who feels a calling to probe the depths of space. He leaves a life of unequaled indulgence to voyage through the solar system. He participates in a Martian invasion of Earth, mates with the wife of an astronaut who is adrift in the tides of time, & from start to finish follows the irresistible lure of the "Sirens of Titan".

Sirens Sang of Murder. unabr. ed. Sarah Caudwell. Read by Eva Haddon. 7 CDs. (Running Time: 8 hrs. 2 mins.). (Isis (CDs) Ser.). (J). 2004. audio compact disk 71.95 (978-0-7531-2271-6(5)) Pub: ISIS Lrg Prnt GBR. Dist(s): Ulverscroft US

Sirens Sang of Murder. unabr. ed. Sarah L. Caudwell. Read by Eva Haddon. 6 cass. (Running Time: 28800 sec.). (Isis Cassettes Ser.). 2004. 54.95 (978-0-7531-1690-6(1)) Pub: ISIS Lrg Prnt GBR. Dist(s): Ulverscroft US

Sirius Crossing. John Creed. Read by Sean Barrett. 7 CDs. (Running Time: 8 hrs. 26 mins.). (Isis (CDs) Ser.). (J). 2004. audio compact disk 71.95 (978-0-7531-2321-8(5)) Pub: ISIS Lrg Prnt GBR. Dist(s): Ulverscroft US

Sirius Crossing. unabr. ed. John Creed. Read by Sean Barrett. 7 cass. (Running Time: 8 hrs. 26 mins.). (Isis Cassettes Ser.). (J). 2004. 61.95 (978-0-7531-1668-5(5)) Pub: ISIS Lrg Prnt GBR. Dist(s): Ulverscroft US

Siro, unabr. ed. David Ignatius. Narrated by George Guidall. 12 cass. (Running Time: 18 hrs.). 1991. 97.00 (978-1-55690-479-0(7), 91303E7) Recorded Bks.
An aging "prince" at the CIA stages a covert mission in South Russia to save the agency from itself.

Sirocco see Robert Penn Warren Reads Selected Poems

Sirocco at Deya see Robert Graves Reads from His Poetry & the White Goddess

SIRS Discoverer: Getting Started Manual Fall 2003. (J). 2003. cd-rom 630.00 (978-0-89777-528-1(7)) SIRS Pubng.

SIRS Renaissance: Getting Started Manual Fall 2003. (YA). 2003. cd-rom Rental 850.00 (978-0-89777-532-8(5)) SIRS Pubng.

Sister. unabr. ed. Poppy Adams. Read by Juliet Mills. 9 CDs. (Running Time: 11 hrs.). (ENG.). 2008. audio compact disk 39.95 (978-0-7393-6673-8(4), Random AudioBks) Pub: Random Audio Pubg. Dist(s): Random

Sister Aimee: The Life of Aimee Semple McPherson. unabr. collector's ed. Daniel Mark Epstein. Read by Frances Cassidy. 12 cass. (Running Time: 18 hrs.). 1995. 96.00 (978-0-7366-3001-6(5), 3689) Books on Tape.
After Aimee Semple McPherson realized her calling, she built a powerful, glittering ministry that captivated the public. Relics still survive.

Sister Bernetta Quinn & W. R. Moses. unabr. ed. Bernetta Quinn & W. R. Moses. Read by Bernetta Quinn & W. R. Moses. 1 cass. (Running Time: 29 min.). Incl. Dancing in Stillness; 1987. 10.00 New Letters.
A well known literary critic & an author read from their works.

Sister Bishop's Christmas Miracle. Janene W. Baadsgaard. 1 cass. 1998. 7.95 (978-1-57008-589-5(7), Bkcraft Inc) Deseret Bk.

Sister Carrie. Theodore Dreiser. Read by C. M. Hebert. 15 CDs. (Running Time: 17 mins.). 2005. audio compact disk 120.00 (978-0-7861-8130-8(3), 2522) Blckstn Audio.

Sister Carrie. Theodore Dreiser. Read by Rebecca Burns. (Playaway Adult Fiction Ser.). (ENG.). 2008. 89.99 (978-1-60640-875-9(5)) Find a World.

Sister Carrie. Theodore Dreiser. Narrated by Jim Killavey. (Running Time: 17 hrs.). 1988. 36.95 (978-1-59912-864-1(0)) Iofy Corp.

Sister Carrie. Theodore Dreiser. Read by Jim Killavey. 13 cass. (Running Time: 19 hrs. 10 min.). 1989. 59.00 incl. album. (C-203) Jimcin Record.
Realistic view of life at the turn of the century.

Sister Carrie. Theodore Dreiser. Read by Rebecca C. Burns. (Running Time: 66600 sec.). (Unabridged Classics in Audio Ser.). (ENG.). 2006. audio compact disk 34.99 (978-1-4001-5270-4(4)); audio compact disk 99.99 (978-1-4001-3270-6(3)); audio compact disk 49.99 (978-1-4001-0270-9(7)) Pub: Tantor Media. Dist(s): IngramPubServ

Sister Carrie, unabr. ed. Theodore Dreiser. Read by Flo Gibson. 10 cass. (Running Time: 15 hrs.). 1990. 44.95 (978-1-55685-186-5(3)) Audio Bk Con.
Suppressed as "immoral" when first published, this vigorous realistic story of a fallen woman, or the demoralization of an actress, is filled with brilliant insight into American culture. Carrie's spiritual innocence is brought into conflict with the reckless driving forces, material temptations & amoral ways of the big city & we witness the gradual ruination of her lover, Hurstwood.

Sister Carrie, unabr. ed. Theodore Dreiser. Read by C. M. Herbert. 12 cass. (Running Time: 17 hrs. 30 mins.). 2000. 83.95 (978-0-7861-1718-5(4), 2522) Blckstn Audio.
The story of Carrie Meeber, a Midwestern country girl who moves to Chicago. She meets a salesman, Charles Rouet & after a period of unemployment becomes his mistress. Soon, however, she becomes disillusioned with him & takes up with his friend George Hurstwood, a middle-aged, married restaurant manager. He embezzles money & elopes with Carrie to New York, where he opens a saloon which fails.

Sister Carrie. unabr. ed. Theodore Dreiser. Read by C. M. Herbert. (Running Time: 17 mins.). 2005. 44.95 (978-0-7861-7903-9(1)) Blckstn Audio.

Sister Carrie. unabr. ed. Theodore Dreiser. Read by Rebecca C. Burns. (Running Time: 18 hrs. 30 mins. 0 sec.). (Tantor Unabridged Classics Ser.). (ENG.). 2009. audio compact disk 79.99 (978-1-4001-3905-7(8)) Pub: Tantor Media. Dist(s): IngramPubServ

Sister Carrie. unabr. collector's ed. Theodore Dreiser. Read by Rebecca C. Burns. 13 cass. (Running Time: 19 hr. 30 min.). 1997. 104.00 (978-0-7366-3700-8(1), 4385-A) Books on Tape.
Theodore Dreiser's first & perhaps greatest novel, Sister Carrie appeared in 1900. It met with outraged disapproval & was immediately withdrawn as "too shocking & sordid for polite readers." But it is precisely in Dreiser's compassionate exploration of ordinary men & women, their frailty & humanity, that this stormy controversial novel remains supreme.

Sister Carrie, with EBook. unabr. ed. Theodore Dreiser. Narrated by Rebecca C. Burns. (Running Time: 18 hrs. 30 mins. 0 sec.). (ENG.). 2009. audio compact disk 29.99 (978-1-4001-5905-[illegible]; audio compact disk 39.99 (978-1-4001-0905-0(1)) Pub: Tantor M[illegible] Dist(s): IngramPubServ

Sister Images Audiotape. Mary Zimmer. [illegible]s. 1994. 4.00 (978-0-687-00815-5(8)) Abingdon.
A collection of twenty commentaries & guided imagery meditations on women in the Bible, which offers women a new look at biblical women & the truth of their stories which has been obscured by traditional scholarship.

Sister, Sister. Eric Jerome Dickey. 6 cass. (Running Time: 8 hrs. 30 mins.). 56.00 (978-1-4025-3027-2(7)); audio compact disk 89.00 (978-1-4025-3071-5(4)) Recorded Bks.

Sister, Sister. abr. ed. Eric Jerome Dickey. 4 cass. (Running Time: 6 hrs.). 2002. 24.95 (978-1-57511-105-6(5)) Pub Mills.
Focuses on two young, upwardly mobile African American sisters. Valerie is married to Walter, who just wants to sit in front of the TV. She's willing to fight for her marriage but there's a snag, Daniel. Ina has a different problem, his name is Raymond. He's got smooth moves and another woman on the side.

Sister Stew, Fiction & Poetry by Women. Poems. Ed. by Juliet S. Kono & Cathy Song. 1 cass. (Running Time: 1 hr.). (YA). 1991. pap. bk. 8.00 (978-0-910043-25-0(6)); pap. bk. Bamboo Ridge Pr.

Sister to Sister. 16.50 (978-0-8170-1455-1(1)) Judson.

Sister to Sister: Devotions for & from African American Women. Ed. by Suzan D. Johnson Cook. 1 cass. (Running Time: 1 hr. 52 mins.). 2003. 11.00 Judson.

Sister to Sister: Devotions for & from African American Women Audiocassette. Short Stories. Read by Suzan D. Johnson Cook. 1 cass. (Running Time: 1 hr. 52 mins.). 2003. 11.00 (978-0-8170-1454-4(3)) Judson.
This inspiring collection of original meditations is now available on audiotape. For years, the reflections in the 80,000-copy bestseller Sister to Sister: Devotions for and from African American Women have been a source of strength, renewal, healing, and celebration. The editor of the volume, best-selling author Rev. Dr. Suzan Johnson Cook, breathes the messages to life with her inspiring voice. Each section is prefaced by an

An Asterisk (*) at the beginning of an entry indicates that the title is appearing for the first time.

introduction from Cook. Select readings from the book focus on topics such as relationships, family, prayer, determination, faith, and worship.

Sister Water. unabr. ed. Nancy Willard. Narrated by George Guidall. 6 cass. (Running Time: 8 hrs.). 1993. 51.00 (978-1-55690-913-9(6), 93409E7) Recorded Bks.
The spirit world often makes its presence felt along the Huron river, where Jessie Woolman & her family struggle to make sense of their changing lives.

Sister Wit: Devotions for Women. abr. ed. Jacqueline Jakes. (ENG.). 2005. 14.98 (978-1-59483-369-4(9)) Pub: Hachet Audio. Dist(s): HachBkGrp

Sister Writes see Twentieth-Century Poetry in English, No. 24, Recordings of Poets Reading Their Own Poetry

Sisterchicks Do the Hula. Robin Jones Gunn. (Sisterchicks Ser.: Bk. 2). (ENG.). 2004. audio compact disk 15.99 (978-1-59052-132-8(3), Mult Fiction) Pub: Doubday Relig. Dist(s): Random

Sisterchicks in Sombreros. Robin Jones Gunn. (Sisterchicks Ser.: Bk. 3). (ENG.). 2004. audio compact disk 15.99 (978-1-59052-466-4(7), Mult Fiction) Pub: Doubday Relig. Dist(s): Random

Sisterchicks on the Loose! unabr. ed. Robin Jones Gunn. Narrated by C. J. Critt. 6 cass. (Running Time: 8 hrs. 30 mins.). (Sisterchicks Ser.: Bk. 1). 2004. 59.75 (978-1-4193-1027-0(5), K1124MC) Recorded Bks.

Sisterhood. abr. ed. Colin Forbes. Read by William Franklyn. 2 cass. (Running Time: 3 hrs.). (ENG., 2001. 16.99 (978-0-333-73221-2(9)) Pub: Macmillan UK GBR. Dist(s): Trafalgar
They're back again! England's top SIS agents Tweed, Paula Grey and international foreign correspondent Bob Newman, along with ace sniper Marler and heavies Butler and Nield are facing a dangerous threat. Europe is under attack as various high ranking politicians seriously concerned with the lack of leadership and military spending in Europe are being taken out one by one. Tweed is on the list. Paula is almost kidnapped by Arab fundamentalists in Vienna. In Slovakia, Arab leader Hassan has made his residence and is planning a major military strike. Tanks and mechanised infantry are massing in Iraq. Tweed and his crew head for Geneva and then Austria on the trail of Hassan and his professional female assassins, known as the Sisterhood.

Sisterhood. abr. ed. Michael Palmer. Read by J. Charles. 4 cass. Library ed. (Running Time: 6 hrs.). 2003. 62.25 (978-1-59086-842-3(0), 1590868420, BAudLibEd); audio compact disk 74.25 (978-1-59086-844-7(7), 1590868447, BACDLib Ed) Brilliance Audio.
Inside Boston Doctors Hospital, patients are dying. In the glare of the operating room, they survive the surgeon's knife. But in the dark, hollow silence of the night, they die. Suddenly, inexplicably, horribly. A tough, bright doctor will risk his very life for a dedicated young nurse who unknowingly holds the answers.

Sisterhood. abr. ed. Michael Palmer. Read by J. Charles. (Running Time: 6 hrs.). 2006. 39.25 (978-1-4233-0212-4(5), 9781423302124, BADLE); 24.95 (978-1-4233-0211-7(7), 9781423302117, BAD); 39.25 (978-1-4233-0210-0(9), 9781423302100, Brlnc Audio MP3 Lib); audio compact disk 24.95 (978-1-4233-0209-4(5), 9781423302094, Brilliance MP3) Brilliance Audio.

Sisterhood. abr. ed. Michael Palmer. Read by J. Charles. (Running Time: 6 hrs.). 2010. audio compact disk 9.99 (978-1-4418-0832-5(9), 9781441808325, BCD Value Price) Brilliance Audio.

Sisterhood. unabr. ed. Michael Palmer. Read by Renée Raudman. (Running Time: 11 hrs.). 2009. 39.97 (978-1-4418-0128-9(6), 9781441801289, Brlnc Audio MP3 Lib); 39.97 (978-1-4418-0130-2(8), 9781441801302, BADLE); 24.99 (978-1-4418-0129-6(4), 9781441801296, BAD); 24.99 (978-1-4418-0127-2(8), 9781441801272, Brilliance MP3); audio compact disk 87.97 (978-1-4418-0126-5(X), 9781441801265, BriAudCD Unabrid); audio compact disk 29.99 (978-1-4418-0125-8(1), 9781441801258, Bril Audio CD Unabri) Brilliance Audio.

***Sisterhood Everlasting: A Novel.** unabr. ed. Ann Brashares. (ENG.). 2011. audio compact disk 40.00 (978-0-307-91222-0(1), Random AudioBks) Pub: Random Audio Pubg. Dist(s): Random

Sisterhood of the Traveling Pants. Angela Goethals. 4 vols. (Running Time: 6 hrs. 35 mins.). (Sisterhood of the Traveling Pants Ser.: Bk. 1). (YA). (gr. 7 up). 2004. pap. bk. 40.00 (978-0-8072-2286-7(0), Listening Lib) Random Audio Pubg.

Sisterhood of the Traveling Pants. unabr. ed. Ann Brashares. 6 CDs. (Running Time: 6 hrs. 35 mins.). (Sisterhood of the Traveling Pants Ser.: Bk. 1). (YA). (gr. 7 up). 2004. audio compact disk 42.50 (978-0-8072-1161-8(3), S YA 326 CD, Listening Lib) Pub: Random Audio Pubg. Dist(s): NetLibrary CO
"Four best friends go their separate ways for the summer, but share their stories through one magical pair of jeans.".

Sisterhood of the Traveling Pants. unabr. ed. Ann Brashares. Read by Angela Goethals. 4 cass. (Running Time: 6 hrs. 35 mins.). (Sisterhood of the Traveling Pants Ser.: Bk. 1). (YA). (gr. 7 up). 2004. 32.00 (978-0-8072-0590-7(7), Listening Lib) Random Audio Pubg.
Carmen got the jeans at a thrift shop. They didn't look all that great; they were worn, dirty and speckled with bleach. On the night before she and her friends part for the summer, Carmen decides to toss them. But Tibby, Lena and Bridget think they're fabulous. Lena decides they should all try them on and whoever they fit best will get them. Nobody knows why, but the pants fit everyone perfectly. They decide to form a sisterhood and take the vow of "The Sisterhood of the Traveling Pants"... the next morning, they say good-bye. Now the journey of the pants - and the most memorable summer of their lives - begins.

Sisterhood of the Traveling Pants. unabr. ed. Ann Brashares. Read by Angela Goethals. (Running Time: 23700 sec.). (Sisterhood of the Traveling Pants Ser.: Bk. 1). (ENG.). (J). (gr. 7-12). 2007. audio compact disk 19.99 (978-0-7393-5681-4(X), Listening Lib) Pub: Random Audio Pubg. Dist(s): Random

Sisters. abr. ed. Danielle Steel. Read by Sam Freed. (Running Time: 21600 sec.). (ENG.). 2008. audio compact disk 14.99 (978-0-7393-5824-5(3), Random AudioBks) Pub: Random Audio Pubg. Dist(s): Random

Sisters. unabr. ed. James Joyce. Read by Richard Setlok. 2 cass. (Running Time: 2 hrs. 15 min.). 1993. lib. bdg. 18.95 set incl. vinyl case with notes, author's picture & biography. (978-1-883049-19-5(9)) Sound Room.
A collection of stories from "Dubliners." "The Sisters," "The Boarding House," "A Painful Case," "Eveline," "An Encounter," "A Mother," & "Two Gallants." "Audio Best of the Year" - Publishers Weekly.

Sisters. unabr. ed. Short Stories. James Joyce. Read by Richard Setlok. Ed. by Richard Setlok. 2 cass. (Running Time: 2 hrs. 15 mins.). 1993. pap. bk. 16.95 (978-1-883049-00-3(8), 390215, Commuters Library) Sound Room.
A collection of stories from "Dubliners," Includes: "The Sisters," the experiences of a boy whose best friend, an old priest, has died. Also included: "The Boarding House," "A Painful Case," "Eveline," "An Encounter," "A Mother" & "Two Gallants.".

Sisters. unabr. ed. Robert Littell. Read by Scott Brick. 7 cass. (Running Time: 10 hrs. 30 mins.). 2004. 32.95 (978-1-59007-413-8(0)); audio compact disk 55.00 (978-1-59007-414-5(9)) Pub: New Millenn Enter. Dist(s): PerseuPGW

Sisters. unabr. ed. Hilda McKenzie. 10 cass. (Running Time: 10 hrs.). 1998. 98.95 (978-1-85903-097-4(1)) Pub: Magna Story GBR. Dist(s): Ulverscroft US

Sisters. unabr. ed. Danielle Steel. Read by Sam Freed. 10 CDs. (Running Time: 38700 sec.). (Danielle Steel Ser.). (ENG.). 2007. audio compact disk 44.95 (978-0-7393-1360-2(6)) Pub: Random Audio Pubg. Dist(s): Random

Sisters, No. 1. 1 cass. 10.00 (978-1-58429-007-0(2)) Rational Isl.
Shared experiences of women & everyone interested in women's liberation & about women using re-evaluation counseling.

Sisters, No. 2. 1 cass. 10.00 (978-1-58429-008-7(0)) Rational Isl.

Sisters, No. 3. 3 cass. 10.00 ea. (978-1-58429-009-4(9)) Rational Isl.

Sisters, No. 4. 4 cass. 10.00 ea. (978-1-58429-010-0(2)) Rational Isl.

Sisters, No. 5. 6 cass. 10.00 ea. (978-1-58429-011-7(0)) Rational Isl.

Sisters, No. 6. 7 cass. 10.00 ea. (978-1-58429-012-4(9)) Rational Isl.

Sisters All... & One Troll. Short Stories. Retold by Mary Hamilton. 1 CD. (Running Time: 1 hr. 5 min. 18 sec.). Dramatization. (J). 2005. audio compact disk 15.00 (978-1-885556-08-0(X)) Hidden Sprng.
Mary Hamilton retells three tales of active heroines, "Kate Crackernuts," "Three Sisters and the Troll," and "Eleven Cinderellas." Mary's unique multicultural compilation and retelling of the Cinderella tale.

Sisters & Husbands. Amanda Brookfield. Narrated by Patricia Gallimore. 9 cass. (Running Time: 12 hrs. 15 mins.). 82.00 (978-1-84197-415-6(3)) Recorded Bks.

Sisters & Lovers. unabr. ed. Connie Briscoe. Narrated by Robin Miles & Myra Lucretia Taylor. 9 cass. (Running Time: 12 hrs. 30 mins.). 2001. 81.00 (978-0-7887-5117-2(4), F0020F7) Recorded Bks.
Three sisters wishing their lives were just a little different. Beverly, 29 & single, would love to be in love. Charmaine, with a beautiful child & irresponsible husband. And Evelyn, a successful psychologist with a lawyer husband, is finding out that paradise isn't exactly what it seems.

Sister's Choice. abr. ed. Judith Pella. Narrated by Brooke Sanford. (Patchwork Circle Ser.). (ENG.). 2008. 16.09 (978-1-60814-384-9(8)) Oasis Audio.

Sister's Choice. abr. ed. Judith Pella. Narrated by Brooke Sanford. (Running Time: 5 hrs. 31 mins. 29 sec.). (Patchwork Circle Ser.: Bk. 2). (ENG.). 2008. audio compact disk 22.99 (978-1-59859-340-2(4)) Oasis Audio.

***Sisters Club, the: Cloudy with a Chance of Boys: Cloudy with a Chance of Boys.** unabr. ed. Megan McDonald. (Running Time: 5 hrs.). (Sisters Club Ser.). 2011. 39.97 (978-1-4558-0362-0(6), 9781455803620, Candlewick Bril); 19.99 (978-1-4558-0361-3(8), 9781455803613, Candlewick Bril); 19.99 (978-1-4558-0358-3(8), 9781455803583, Candlewick Bril); 39.97 (978-1-4558-0359-0(6), 9781455803590, Candlewick Bril); audio compact disk 19.99 (978-1-4558-0356-9(1), 9781455803569, Candlewick Bril); audio compact disk 49.97 (978-1-4558-0357-6(X), 9781455803576, Candlewick Bril) Brilliance Audio.

***Sisters Club, the: Rule of Three: Rule of Three.** unabr. ed. Megan McDonald. (Running Time: 6 hrs.). (Sisters Club Ser.). 2011. 39.97 (978-1-4558-0355-2(3), 9781455803552, Candlewick Bril); 19.99 (978-1-4558-0354-5(5), 9781455803545, Candlewick Bril); 19.99 (978-1-4558-0351-4(0), 9781455803514, Candlewick Bril); 39.97 (978-1-4558-0352-1(9), 9781455803521, Candlewick Bril); audio compact disk 19.99 (978-1-4558-0349-1(9), 9781455803491, Candlewick Bril); audio compact disk 49.97 (978-1-4558-0350-7(2), 9781455803507, Candlewick Bril) Brilliance Audio.

***Sisters from Hardscrabble Bay.** unabr. ed. Beverly Jensen. Read by Bernadette Dunne. (Running Time: 11 hrs.). 2010. 29.95 (978-1-4417-4791-4(5)); 65.95 (978-1-4417-4787-7(7)); audio compact disk 32.95 (978-1-4417-4790-7(7)); audio compact disk 100.00 (978-1-4417-4788-4(5)) Blckstn Audio.

Sisters-Hermanas, unabr. ed. Gary Paulsen. Narrated by Alyssa Bresnahan & Graciela Lecube. 2 pieces. (Running Time: 2 hrs. 15 mins.). (ENG & SPA.). (gr. 8 up). 1995. 19.00 (978-0-7887-0188-7(6), 94413E7) Recorded Bks.
The stories of two Texas fourteen-year-old girls, one an illegal Mexican immigrant working as a prostitute, the other, a wealthy pampered teenager being groomed for marriage.

Sisters-in-Law. unabr. ed. Gertrude Franklin Horn Atherton. Read by Meb Bowden. 8 cass. (Running Time: 12 hrs.). (Timeless Bestsellers Ser.). 1996. 69.95 Set. (978-1-884428-08-1(8), 428088) Eye Ear.
Set in the early 1900's, Alexina, the young lady of the house has social status & "old money." She falls for a social climbing ne'er do well, & begins a relationship with her sister that spans twenty years, moving from San Francisco to France.

Sisters in Song Rejoice. Directed By Christopher Walker. 2005. audio compact disk 17.00 (978-5-559-48727-4(9)) OR Catholic.

Sisters, Ink. unabr. ed. Rebeca Seitz. Narrated by Brooke Sanford. (Scrapbooker's Ser.). (ENG.). 2008. 19.59 (978-1-60814-385-6(6)); audio compact disk 27.99 (978-1-59859-319-8(6)) Oasis Audio.

Sisters Mortland. abr. ed. Sally Beauman. 5 CDs. (Running Time: 6 hrs.). 2006. audio compact disk 29.98 (978-1-59483-105-8(X)) Hachet Audio.

Sisters O'Donnell. unabr. ed. Lyn Andrews. Read by Jacqueline King. 13 cass. (Running Time: 19 hrs.). 2000. 99.95 (978-1-85496-948-4(X), 6948X) Pub: Soundings Ltd GBR. Dist(s): ISIS Pub
The sisters O'Donnell all had the flaming red hair of the O'Donnell clan & tempers to match. When they came from County Tipperary to seek their fortunes in the Liverpool of the 1920s, they were full of ambition & hope. However, the city wasn't what they thought it would be & neither was their Aunt Maura, who turned out to be a miserable slattern. Work was impossible to find & their money was running out. The girls had a long way to go before they could realize their dreams.

Sisters of the Golden Circle see Favorite Stories by O. Henry

Sisters of the Yam (audio Edition) Black Women & Self-Recovery. bell hooks. Narrated by Ayo Sesheni. (ENG.). 2009. audio compact disk 25.00 (978-0-89608-789-7(1)) Pub: South End Pr. Dist(s): Consort Bk Sales

Sisters Red. unabr. ed. Jackson Pearce. Read by Michal Friedman et al. (Running Time: 10 hrs.). (ENG.). 2010. 19.98 (978-1-60788-302-9(3)); audio compact disk 22.98 (978-1-60788-301-2(5)) Pub: Hachet Audio. Dist(s): HachBkGrp

Sisters Rosensweig. unabr. ed. Wendy Wasserstein. Perf. by Caroline Aaron et al. 2 CDs. (Running Time: 2 hrs. 8 mins.). 2000. audio compact disk 25.95 (978-1-58081-179-8(5), CDTPT129) Pub: L A Theatre. Dist(s): NetLibrary CO

Sisters Rosensweig. unabr. ed. Wendy Wasserstein. Perf. by Jamie Lee Curtis et al. 2 cass. (Running Time: 2 hrs. 8 mins.). 2000. 23.95 (978-1-58081-135-4(3), TPT129) L A Theatre.
Chronicles three Jewish sisters from Brooklyn as they gather in London to celebrate a birthday.

Sisters Three. unabr. ed. Jessica Stirling. Read by Vivien Heilbron. 12 cass. (Running Time: 14 hrs.). 2002. 96.95 (978-0-7540-0774-6(X), CAB 2196) AudioGO.
In Prized Possessions, Jessica Stirling introduced the Conway women: indomitable Lizzie, who endures despite everything that life in Glasgow's notorious Gorbals slums can throw at her, and Lizzie's three daughters, each of whom combines her iron will with her own desires and ambitions. Set against the vibrant streets of 1930s Glasgow on the eve of war, this is a story of unfulfilled ambitions, desires, and passionate romance.

Sisters Three. unabr. ed. Jessica Stirling. Read by Vivien Heilbron. 12 CDs. (Running Time: 18 hrs.). 2002. audio compact disk 110.95 (978-0-7540-5485-6(3), CCD 176) AudioGO.

Sisters Who Would Be Queen: Mary, Katherine, & Lady Jane Grey - A Tudor Tragedy. unabr. ed. Leanda de Lisle. Narrated by Wanda McCaddon. (Running Time: 11 hrs. 0 mins. 0 sec.). (ENG.). 2009. 24.99 (978-1-4001-6366-3(8)); audio compact disk 69.99 (978-1-4001-4366-5(7)); audio compact disk 34.99 (978-1-4001-1366-8(0)) Pub: Tantor Media. Dist(s): IngramPubServ

***Sisters Who Would Be Queen: Mary, Katherine, & Lady Jane Grey - A Tudor Tragedy.** unabr. ed. Leanda de Lisle. Narrated by Wanda McCaddon. (Running Time: 11 hrs. 0 mins.). 2009. 17.99 (978-1-4001-8366-1(9)) Tantor Media.

Sit Down & Be Counted: Prov. 20:6; Gal. 5:23. Ed Young. 1993. 4.95 (978-0-7417-1969-0(X), 969) Win Walk.

Sit-in with jim Chapin. Jim Chapin. 1994. pap. bk. 34.98 (978-1-59615-119-2(6), 586-031) Pub: Music Minus. Dist(s): Bookworld

Sita, Speak! unabr. ed. Julian C. Hollick. 1 cass. (Running Time: 60 min.). (Passages to India Ser.). 1991. 15.00 (978-1-56709-017-8(6), 1017) Indep Broadcast.
Although women have been portrayed in Hindu mythology as creative & all-powerful, in practice, Indian women have often been submissive. An examination of how new legislation & women's self-assertions in today's India clash with centuries of tradition & immobilism.

Site Lic/Ug-Skillbuilding Made Easy with Web Reporting. (C). 2007. audio compact disk 1126.95 (978-0-538-72989-5(9)) Pub: South-West. Dist(s): CENGAGE Learn

Sitka, Alaska: From Russian Orthodox to American Paradox. Tim Hostiuck. Read by Tim Hostiuck. 1 cass. (Running Time: 40 min.). 1993. 12.00 (978-1-928952-03-9(8)) Misty Peaks.
This 1818 to 1884 transformation of Russian American capital New Archangel, to American frontier town Sitka, reveals how it's Golden era of Russian First Ladies degenerated to Dark Decades of American misrule.

Sittaford Mystery. Agatha Christie. 2004. audio compact disk 29.95 (978-0-563-52413-7(8)) AudioGO.

Sittaford Mystery. unabr. ed. Agatha Christie. Read by Nathaniel Parker. 4 cass. (Running Time: 6 hrs. 14 mins). 2003. 25.95 (978-1-57270-316-2(4)) Pub: Audio Partners. Dist(s): PerseuPGW
As amateur occultists play an innocent parlor game on a winter night, a prediction of doom appears. The house's owner, wealthy Captain Trevelyan, fulfills the prophecy by turning up dead. The intrepid Miss Emily Trefusis must delve deep into the spirit world to find the decidedly human murderer. She's convinced that someone planned Trevelyan's demise and planted the message of doom, but who.

Sittaford Mystery. unabr. ed. Agatha Christie. Narrated by Nathaniel Parker. 5 CDs. (Running Time: 6 hrs. 15 mins.). 2008. audio compact disk 59.95 (978-0-7927-5280-6(5)) AudioGO.
Holding a séance is an innocent diversion for Mrs. Willet's guests; after all, the supernatural is a fad - but when the spirit spells M-U-R-D-E-R, the spooked party turns the lights on fast. Within hours Captain Trevelyn is found dead, brutally killed by a blow to the head. Intrepid Emily Trefusis descends on the village to defend the police's #1 suspect - her fiancé, Jim. With the help of newshound Charles Enderby and retired Inspector Narracott, Emily tracks down the very human - and dangerous - haunt of Hazelmoor.

Sittercise. 1 cass . (Running Time: 1 hr.). (J). 2001. pap. bk. 10.95 (KIM 2045C); pap. bk. 11.95 (KIM 2045); audio compact disk 14.95 (KIM 2045CD) Kimbo Educ.
A runaway bestseller that gives your class an exercise break without getting out of their seats. Imaginative way for kids to get fit while they sit. Ideal for all ages & great with senior citizens, too. Rocky Too!, Harlem Smoke, The T-Bird & more. Includes guide.

Sittin' in the Front Pew. Parry Brown. 6 cass. (Running Time: 8 hrs. 30 mins.). 2002. 58.00 (978-1-4025-4606-8(8)) Recorded Bks.

***Sitting at the Feet of Rabbi Jesus: How the Jewishness of Jesus Can Transform Your Faith.** unabr. ed. Ann Spangler & Lois Tverberg. (Running Time: 7 hrs. 46 mins. 42 sec.). (ENG.). 2010. 21.99 (978-0-310-77310-8(5)) Zondervan.

Sitting Bull & His World. Albert Marrin. Narrated by Ed Sala. 6 pieces. (Running Time: 9 hrs.). (gr. 7 up). 2000. 52.00 (978-0-7887-5033-5(X), 96501E7); audio compact disk 78.00 (978-1-4025-1490-6(5), C1615) Recorded Bks.
Sitting Bull, the great Lakota chief, warrior, and holy an, is commonly remembered for leading his people during the Battle of Little Bighorn. His is a story of both extraordinary achievement and unthinkable hardship. Respected among Indians as no other chief in history, he was inhumanely despised by whites as an evil, violent savage.

Sitting by the Well. Marion Woodman. 2007. audio compact disk 69.95 (978-1-59179-596-4(6)) Sounds True.

Sitting down to Eat. Shad Helmstetter. 1 cass. (Self-Talk Cassettes Ser.). 10.95 (978-0-937065-43-3(9)) Grindle Pr.

Sitting Fit: Yoga Bits. Susan W. Ward. 1 cass. (Yoga for the Young at Heart Ser.: Vol. 1). 1996. 10.00 (978-0-9651409-1-1(1)) Yoga for the Yng.
Exercises that can be done in a chair - anytime, anywhere. Great for desk-bound, physically challenged & seniors.

***Sitting in the Light: Guided Meditations for Relaxation & Self-Balancing.** Angela Hryniuk. (ENG.). 2008. audio compact disk 14.99 (978-1-894692-21-2(7)) Pub: McGillig Bks CAN. Dist(s): U Toronto Pr

Sitting on My Hands. unabr. ed. Bill Harley. Read by Bill Harley. 1 cass. (Running Time: 52 min.). (C). 1995. 10.00 (978-1-878126-18-4(0), RRR402) Round Riv Prodns.
Short commentaries as aired on National Public Radios "All Things Considered". Combining humor with meaning Bill talks about parenting, education & "being a grownup". Also included on this track are: Full Moon Walk; Sledding; Pukey Butthead; Stuffed Duck; Nintendo; Releaming the Box Step; Trading Cards; That Hunger Within; Spring Peepers; & Learning to Be Stupid.

Sitting Pretty. Al Young. Read by Al Young. 1 cass. (Running Time: 33 min.). (J). 1981. 13.95 (978-1-55644-031-1(6), 1171) Am Audio Prose.
Performance voice of S. J. Prettyman, a 55-year-old Huck Finn seeking to win his family's love & respect, finding in the process that he already has it.

Sitting Well: A Practical Guide to Improve Your Sitting. Ann L. Rodiger. 1 cass. 1987. 9.95 Balance Arts.
Instructions on correct posture, breathing, & mental attitude for desk-workers.

Situacion Humana see Human Situation

Situation Tragedy. Simon Brett. Narrated by Simon Prebble. 5 cass. (Running Time: 6 hrs. 30 mins.). (Charles Paris Mystery Ser.: Vol. 7). 1981. 44.00 (978-0-7887-3491-5(1), 95898E7) Recorded Bks.
Charles Paris has landed a role as a bartender in West End Television's new smash comedy, but a rash of nasty "accidents" threatens the show's success.

Situation Tragedy. unabr. ed. Simon Brett. Read by Geoffrey Howard. 4 cass. (Running Time: 5 hrs. 30 mins.). 1996. 32.95 (978-0-7861-0965-4(3), 1742) Blckstn Audio.
"Is everything all right?" the producer kept asking, & for a while everything was. "The Strutters" was destined to be the situation comedy hit of the year, with just the right mix of stars & schmaltz - along with none other than hard-drinking Charles Paris in the role of (irony of ironies!) the barman. But before Charles could get used to being in a megahit, things began going wrong. First it was the aggressive production assistant, then the hotshot young director, soon fatal accidents were becoming contagious, & nobody was dying laughing. While "The Strutters" marched on, Charles Paris began prying - & found himself stepping into a backstage drama of blackmail, murder, & madness.

Situational Functional Japanese Vol. 1: Drills. 2nd ed. 1 cass. (Running Time: 1 hr. 30 mins.). (JPN.). 38.90 (978-4-89358-165-5(1)) Pub: Bonjinsha JPN. Dist(s): Cheng Tsui

Situational Functional Japanese Vol. 1: Notes. 1 cass. (Running Time: 1 hr. 30 mins.). 38.90 (978-4-89358-164-8(3)) Pub: Bonjinsha JPN. Dist(s): Cheng Tsui

Situational Functional Japanese Vol. 2: Drills. 2nd ed. 1 cass. (Running Time: 1 hr. 30 mins.). (JPN.). 38.90 (978-4-89358-284-3(4)) Pub: Bonjinsha JPN. Dist(s): Cheng Tsui

Situational Functional Japanese Vol. 2: Notes. 2nd ed. 1 cass. (Running Time: 1 hr. 30 mins.). (JPN.). 29.20 (978-4-89358-283-6(6)) Pub: Bonjinsha JPN. Dist(s): Cheng Tsui

Situational Functional Japanese Vol. 3: Drills. 1 cass. (Running Time: 1 hr. 30 mins.). 38.90 (978-4-89358-299-7(2)) Pub: Bonjinsha JPN. Dist(s): Cheng Tsui

Situational Functional Japanese Vol. 3: Notes. 1 cass. (Running Time: 1 hr. 30 mins.). 34.80 (978-4-89358-298-0(4)) Pub: Bonjinsha JPN. Dist(s): Cheng Tsui

Situations et Contextes. 2nd ed. Siskin. (FRE.). 1993. pap. bk. & tchr. ed. 32.95 (978-0-470-00268-1(9), JWiley) Wiley US.

Situations et Contextes. 2nd ed. H. Jay Siskin. 2002. wbk. ed. & lab manual ed. 87.95 (978-0-470-00610-8(2), JWiley) Wiley US.

Situations et Contextes: Instructor's Testing Program, with Testing Cassettes. 2nd ed. Siskin. 1994. pap. bk. & tchr. ed. 51.95 (978-0-470-00492-0(4), JWiley) Wiley US.

Situations et Contextes: Tapescript. 2nd ed. Siskin. 1993. pap. bk. 64.95 (978-0-470-00265-0(4), JWiley) Wiley US.

Situations et Contextes: Testing Cassettes. 2nd ed. Siskin. (FRE.). 1993. pap. bk. 28.95 (978-0-470-00284-1(0), JWiley) Wiley US.

Siva Siva. Sivananda Radha. 1 cass. (Running Time: 60 min.). 1994. 9.95 (978-0-931454-63-9(8)) Timeless Bks.
Swami Radha chants traditional ancient Mantra. Effective in keeping the mind centered while working, or for meditation.

Six A. M., Boston, Summer Sublet see Poetry & Voice of Margaret Atwood

Six Adventures of Tintin, Vol. 1. Hergé. Perf. by Leo McKern et al. 2 cass. (Running Time: 3 hrs.). (J). 2000. 18.00 (978-0-7366-9095-9(6)) Books on Tape.
Young reporter-sleuth Tintin & a hilarious cast of characters that include his faithful dog Snowy, Captain Haddock & the look-alike detectives Thompson & Thompson, romp through six adventures from the Sahara Desert to the moon. Includes: "The Island," "The Secret for the Unicorn," "Red Rackham's Treasure," "Destination Moon," "Explorers on the Moon," & "Tintin in Tibet.".

Six Adventures of Tintin, Vol. 1. unabr. ed. Hergé. Read by BBC Cast Staff. 2 cass. (Running Time: 2 hrs.). (J). (gr. 1-8). 1999. 23.00 (LL 0137, Chivers Child Audio) AudioGO.

Six Adventures of Tintin, Vol. 1. unabr. ed. Hergé. 2 cass. (Running Time: 2 hrs. 56 mins.). (J). (gr. 3-9). 1999. 23.00 (978-0-8072-8087-4(9), YA999CX, Listening Lib) Random Audio Pubg.
Young reporter-sleuth TinTin & a hilarious, nefarious cast of characters including faithful dog Snowy, Captain Haddock & the look-alike detectives Thompson & Thomson romp through six adventures from the Sahara Desert, to the high seas, to the surface of the moon.

Six American Authors. Joseph Schiffman. 6 cass. (Running Time: 2 hrs. 21 min.). 65.00 (S115) J Norton Pubs.
This series includes: Nathaniel Hawthorne; Ralph Waldo Emerson; Herman Melville; Henry David Thoreau; John Steinbeck; Sinclair Lewis.

Six Armies in Normandy. John Keegan. Narrated by Fred Williams. (Running Time: 18 hrs.). (C). 2000. 48.95 (978-1-59912-599-2(4)) Iofy Corp.

Six Armies in Normandy. unabr. ed. John Keegan. Read by Fred Williams. 12 cass. (Running Time: 17 hrs. 30 mins.). 2001. 83.95 (978-0-7861-2024-6(X), 2792); audio compact disk 120.00 (978-0-7861-9713-2(7), 2792) Blckstn Audio.
John Keegan tells the story of the Allies greatest military achievement as he chronicles the 1944 invasion of Normandy, from D-Day to the liberation of Paris.

Six Armies in Normandy. unabr. ed. John Keegan. 12 CDs. (Running Time: 15 hrs.). 2005. audio compact disk 34.95 (978-1-4193-5159-4(1)) Recorded Bks.
Historic author and military strategist, John Keegan, dramatically brings D-Day and the following stages of the Normandy invasion to life - on the beaches, in the air, and throughout the countryside. Including fascinating details and anecdotes, he expertly chronicles the individual successes and setbacks of six separate national armies - American, Canadian, English, German, Polish, and French - as they struggle for control. Keegan clearly depicts each nation¿s values and their approach to war with unique insight and intelligence. Using writings and eyewitness accounts, he vividly captures the feelings of military participants, from key leaders to the troops in the field. Robert Sevra¿s skillful narration takes the listener through the planning sessions onto the battlefield, portraying the fear and honor warriors universally share. Six Armies in Normandy is a memorable must-listen for anyone who enjoys human drama.

Six Armies in Normandy. unabr. collector's ed. John Keegan. Read by Christopher Hurt. 9 cass. (Running Time: 13 hrs. 30 min.). 1986. 72.00 (978-0-7366-0999-9(7), 1933) Books on Tape.
On D-Day, 1944, the armies of six nations converged on the beaches of France & began the final dramatic chapter of WW II. The analysis of this historic action is carried out on many levels.

Six Armies in Normandy: From D-Day to the Liberation of Paris. John Keegan. Read by Robert Sevra. 9 Cass. (Running Time: 15 Hours). 34.95 (978-1-4025-4530-6(4)) Recorded Bks.

Six Armies in Normandy: From D-Day to the Liberation of Paris. unabr. ed. John Keegan. Narrated by Robert Sevra. 10 cass. (Running Time: 15 hrs.). 1997. 85.00 (978-0-7887-0824-4(4), 94974E7) Recorded Bks.
Author & military historian, dramatically brings to life the D-Day invasion & following battles that liberated Paris. With details & anecdotes, he carefully chronicles the individual successes & setbacks of six separate national armies & universal fear & honor.

Six Armies in Normandy: From D-Day to the Liberation of Paris. unabr. ed. John Keegan. Narrated by Robert Sevra. 10 cass. (Running Time: 15 hrs.). 2002. 44.95 (978-0-7887-6437-0(3), RC989) Recorded Bks.

Six Bad Things. unabr. ed. Charlie Huston. Read by Christian Conn. 2005. 29.95 (978-0-7927-3688-2(5), CMP 821); 54.95 (978-0-7927-3686-8(9), CSL 821); audio compact disk 74.95 (978-0-7927-3687-5(7), SLD 821) AudioGO.

Six Battles Every Man Must Win: ... & the Ancient Secrets You'll Need to Succeed. Bill Perkins. (ENG.). 2009. audio compact disk 21.99 (978-1-934384-06-0(2)) Pub: Treasure Pub. Dist(s): STL Dist NA

***Six Characteristics of Highly Effective Change Leaders.** Brett Clay. (ENG.). 2010. 2.95 (978-0-9822952-8-1(6)) ARIVA Publg.

Six Characters in Search of an Author. unabr. ed. Luigi Pirandello. 2 cass. (Running Time: 3 hrs.). 2005. audio compact disk 15.95 (978-0-660-18528-6(8)) Pub: Canadian Broadcasting CAN. Dist(s): Georgetown Term

Six Crows. Leo Lionni. 1 cass. (Running Time: 1 hr.). (J). 1989. bk. 35.98 (978-0-676-87376-4(6)) SRA McGraw.

Six-Day Financial Makeover: Transform Your Financial Life in Less Than a Week! unabr. ed. Robert Pagliarini. Read by Robert Pagliarini. 8 cass. (Running Time: 34200 sec.). 2006. 27.95 (978-0-7861-4624-6(9)); 59.95 (978-0-7861-4847-9(0)); audio compact disk 27.95 (978-0-7861-6845-3(5)); audio compact disk 29.95 (978-0-7861-7463-8(3)); audio compact disk 72.00 (978-0-7861-6091-4(8)) Blckstn Audio.

Six Day War. 10.00 (RME116) Esstee Audios.
Analyzes the various events that made the 1967 war between Israel & the Arab nations inevitable & is a good summary of the reasons for its occurrence & outcome.

Six Days of War: June 1967 & the Making of the Modern Middle East. unabr. ed. Michael B. Oren. Read by Robert Whitfield. 2 CDs. (Running Time: 19 hrs.). 2003. audio compact disk 39.95 (978-0-7861-8971-7(1), 3090); 85.95 (978-0-7861-2455-8(5), 3090) Blckstn Audio.
The most comprehensive history of the six days of intense Arab-Israeli fighting in the summer of 1967 that transformed the world.

Six Days of War: June 1967 & the Making of the Modern Middle East. unabr. ed. Michael B. Oren. Read by Robert Whitfield. 13 pieces. 2004. reel tape 49.95 (978-0-7861-2566-1(7)) Blckstn Audio.

Six Days of War: June 1967 & the Making of the Modern Middle East. unabr. ed. Michael B. Oren. Read by Robert Whitfield. 15 CDs. (Running Time: 19 hrs.). 2006. audio compact disk 120.00 (978-0-7861-9232-8(1), 3090) Blckstn Audio.

Six Days of War: June 1967 & the Making of the Modern Middle East. unabr. ed. Michael B. Oren. Read by Robert Whitfield. 15 CDs. (Running Time: 64800 sec.). 2006. audio compact disk 34.95 (978-0-7861-7079-1(4)) Blckstn Audio.

Six Days That Shook the Walt. Tim Burns & Brian Moffatt. Perf. by Tim Burns & Brian Moffatt. Perf. by Kathy Laskey. 3 cass. (Running Time: 4 hrs. 30 mins.). 2005. audio compact disk 19.95 (978-0-660-18186-8(X)) Pub: Canadian Broadcasting CAN. Dist(s): Georgetown Term

Six Degrees of Separation. unabr. ed. John Guare. Perf. by Alan Alda et al. 2 CDs. (Running Time: 1 hr. 22 mins.). Dramatization. 2000. audio compact disk 25.95 (978-1-58081-173-6(6), CDTPT121); 20.95 (978-1-58081-141-5(8), TPT121) L A Theatre.
When a young man enters the Fifth Avenue home of Flanders & Ouisa Kittredge claiming to be a friend of their children & son of actor Sidney Poitier, the couple is charmed by his manners, wit & intelligence. When the Kittredges discover that "Paul" isn't all he claims to be, they find themselves stuck between embarrassment & fascination.

Six Disciplines Execution Revolution Audio. Gary Harpst. 2008. audio compact disk 19.95 (978-0-9816411-1-9(3)) Six Disc Pub.

Six Disciplines for Excellence Audio. Gary Harpst. 2008. audio compact disk 19.95 (978-0-9816411-2-6(1)) Six Disc Pub.

Six Events: The Restoration Model for Solving Life's Problems. Stephen R. Covey. 6 CDs. 2004. audio compact disk 21.95 (978-1-59038-365-0(6)) Deseret Bk.
How do you help a struggling teen, an overwhelmed mother, a teacher who feel inadequate, a divorced man struggling with feelings of self-worth? The Lord has shown theway. The pattern he used to restore the gospel in a world filled with darkness provides a perfect model for our own spiritual and social development. The most vital questions of life - Who are we? What is our relationship with God and Christ? What would they have us do? - can be answered more clearly each day with the simple but profound program for internalizing the gospel. In his first book in more than twenty years written specifically to an LDS audience, Dr. Stephen R. Covey explores six transcendent events of teh Restoration and demonstrates the significance of those events and their sequence in our lives today.

Six Figure Networking. abr. ed. Clyde C. Lewstuter & David P. Robertson. Intro. by Arnold N. Carter. 6 cass. (Running Time: 4 hrs. 30 min.). (In Search of the Perfect Job Ser.). 1994. pap. bk. 129.95 Set. (978-1-886025-00-4(2)) RL Communs.
Audio learning system teaches the listeners job-hunting strategies, particularly networking which accelerates their career search efforts.

Six Foolish Fishermen see Pony Engine & Other Stories for Children

Six Foundation Stones. Derek Prince. 2 cass. (Running Time: 2 hrs.). 11.90 (4350-4351) Derek Prince.
Six basic doctrines of the New Testament form the only secure foundation for Christian living. Are they part of your life?.

Six Frigates: The Epic History of the Founding of the U. S. Navy. abr. ed. Ian W. Toll. Read by Stephen Lang. 2006. 17.95 (978-0-7435-6529-5(0)); audio compact disk 29.95 (978-0-7435-3684-4(3)) Pub: S&S Audio. Dist(s): S and S Inc

Six Fundamentals of Success: The Rules for Getting It Right for Yourself & Your Organization. unabr. ed. Stuart Levine. Narrated by Alan Sklar. (Running Time: 2 hrs. 30 mins. 0 sec.). (ENG.). 2006. audio compact disk 39.99 (978-1-4001-3321-5(1)) Pub: Tantor Media. Dist(s): IngramPubServ

Six Fundamentals of Success: The Rules for Getting It Right for Yourself & Your Organization. unabr. ed. Stuart Levine. Read by Alan Sklar. (Running Time: 2 hrs. 30 mins. 0 sec.). (ENG.). 2006. audio compact disk 19.99 (978-1-4001-5321-3(2)) Pub: Tantor Media. Dist(s): IngramPubServ

Six Fundamentals of Success: The Rules for Getting It Right for Yourself & Your Organization. unabr. ed. Stuart R. Levine. Narrated by Alan Sklar. 3 CDs. (Running Time: 2 hrs. 30 mins. 0 sec.). (ENG.). 2006. audio compact disk 19.99 (978-1-4001-0321-8(5)) Pub: Tantor Media. Dist(s): IngramPubServ

Six Great Adventures of Sherlock Holmes. Arthur Conan Doyle. Read by Edward Hardwicke. 4 cass. (Running Time: 6 hrs.). bk. 19.95 (978-1-878427-47-2(4), XC600) Cimino Pub Grp.
This collection contains: "The Adventure of the Empty House," "The Adventure of the Devil's Foot," "The Adventure of the Abbey Grange," "The Adventure of the Cardboard Box," "The Man with the Twisted Lip," & "The Adventure of the Bruce Partington Plan".

Six Great Ideas, unabr. ed. Mortimer J. Adler. Read by Robin Lawson. 6 cass. (Running Time: 8 hrs. 30 mins.). 1991. 44.95 (978-0-7861-0237-2(3), 1207) Blckstn Audio.
Each summer, Mortimer J. Adler conducts a seminar at the Aspen Institute in Colorado. At the 1981 seminar, leaders from the worlds of business, literature, education & the arts joined him in an in-depth consideration of the six great ideas that are the subject of this book: Truth, Goodness & Beauty - the ideas we judge by; & Liberty, Equality & Justice - the ideas we act on.

Six Great Scientists. unabr. ed. J. G. Crowther. Read by Roe Kendall. 6 cass. (Running Time: 18 hrs. 30 mins.). 2001. 44.95 (978-0-7861-2095-6(9), 2857); audio compact disk 64.00 (978-0-7861-9678-4(5), 2857) Blckstn Audio.
All of the geniuses in Six Great Scientists had one thing in common: the determination to do scientific research whatever the obstacles. They all had the imagination to conceive great ideas and the force of will not to be defeated. Nicolaus and his modern scientific outlook, Galileo Galilei and the use of the telescope, Isaac Newton's comprehensive account of the entire physical universe, Charles Darwin's belief in evolution and living organisms, Marie Curie's discovery of radium and the disclosed secret of the atom and finally, Albert Einstein's theory of relativity and the equivalence of mass and energy.

***Six Great Scientists: Copernicus, Galileo, Newton, Darwin, Marie Curie, Einstein.** unabr. ed. J. G. Crowther. Read by Patrick Cullen. (Running Time: 9 hrs.). 2010. 29.95 (978-1-4417-6696-0(0)) Blckstn Audio.

Six Guided Meditations with the Twelve Archangels, Vol. I. unabr. ed. 1 cass. (Running Time: 2 hrs.). 2000. 39.95 (978-0-9655457-6-1(8)) Theo Press.
Remarkable guided meditations given to us by twelve Archangels Meditations for Manifestation Healing, Connecting with Angels & Spirit Guides Multidimensional Experiences, Soul Integration opening hear.

Six-Gun Atonement. unabr. ed. Lauran Paine. Read by William Dufris. 4 cass. (Running Time: 6 hrs.). (Sagebrush Western Ser.). (J). 2005. 44.95 (978-1-57490-314-0(4)) Pub: ISIS Lrg Prnt GBR. Dist(s): Ulverscroft US

Six-Gun Caballero. L. Ron Hubbard. Read by Jim Meskimen et al. Narrated by R. F. Daley. (Stories from the Golden Age Ser.). 2009. audio compact disk 9.95 (978-1-59212-340-7(6)) Gala Pr LLC.

Six-Gun Caballero. L. Ron Hubbard. 1996. 10.95 (978-1-57318-003-0(3)) Bridge Pubns Inc.

Six-Gun Caballero. abr. ed. L. Ron Hubbard. Read by Geoffrey Lewis. 1 cass. (Running Time: 1 hr. 30 min.). 10.95 (978-1-59212-017-8(2)) Gala Pr LLC.
One man, Michael Obanon, stands in the way of a lawless band of desperados ruthlessly bent on seizing United States territory that, until recently, had belonged to Mexico.

Six-Gun Cabellero. abr. ed. L. Ron Hubbard. 2 CDs. (Western Audiobooks Ser.). 2006. 14.95 (978-1-59212-227-1(2)) Gala Pr LLC.

Six-Gun Trail. unabr. ed. M. Lehman. Read by Gene Engene. 3 cass. (Running Time: 4 hrs. 12 min.). Dramatization. 1993. 21.95 (978-1-55686-455-1(8), 455) Books in Motion.
Tyler Justin finds his neighbor dead. Tyler is suspected & jailed for the murder. With a desire to clear his name, Tyler breaks out of jail & goes in pursuit of the real killers.

Six Keys to Enjoying Life, Pt. 2. Speeches. Joel Osteen. 1 Cass. (Running Time: 30 Mins.). 2001. Rental 6.00 (978-1-59349-110-9(7), JA0110) J Osteen.

Six Keys to Happiness, Contrib. by Tsering Everest. 2 cass. (Running Time: 2 hrs.). 1996. 12.00 (978-1-881847-20-5(9), PP-AVSKH) Padma Pub CA.
Our inability to find lasting happiness stems from our mistaken focus on self & our failure to recognize the true nature of mind Lama Tsering Everest addresses this situation from the perspective of six key issues: impermanence, compassion, karma, self-centeredness, the relative truth of ordinary reality & the perfection of absolute reality.

Six Lessons for Six Sons. unabr. ed. Massengale Joe & Clow David. (Running Time: 7 hrs. 30 mins.). (J). 2007. audio compact disk 29.95 (978-0-7861-7450-8(1)) Blckstn Audio.

Six Lessons for Six Sons: An Extraordinary Father, a Simple Formula for Success. unabr. ed. Joe Massengale & David Clow. Frwd. by George Foreman. (Running Time: 27000 sec.). 2006. audio compact disk 55.00 (978-0-7861-6834-7(X)) Blckstn Audio.

Six Lessons for Six Sons: An Extraordinary Father, a Simple Formula for Success. unabr. ed. Joe Massengale & David Clow. Read by Full Cast Production Staff. Frwd. by George Foreman. (Running Time: 27000 sec.). 2006. 44.95 (978-0-7861-4638-3(9)) Blckstn Audio.

Six Lessons for Six Sons: An Extraordinary Father, a Simple Formula for Success. unabr. ed. John Massengale & David Clow. Read by Full Cast Production Staff. (Running Time: 27000 sec.). 2007. 19.95 (978-0-7861-4808-0(X)) Blckstn Audio.

Six Lessons for Six Sons: An Extraordinary Father, a Simple Formula for Success. unabr. ed. John Massengale & David Clow. Read by Full Cast Production Staff. Frwd. by George Foreman. (Running Time: 27000 sec.). 2007. audio compact disk 19.95 (978-0-7861-6193-5(0)) Blckstn Audio.

Six Little Ducks. 1 cass. (Running Time: 1 hr.). (J). (ps-2). 1997. pap. bk. 10.95 (KIM-9147C); pap. bk. 14.95 (KIM-9147CD) Kimbo Educ.
Children will love all of the singable songs on this recording. In addition, each song connects with a creative extension activity & literature link in the guide. A must for every classroom & home! These classics include Mr. Sun, ABC Song, Take Me Out to the Ball Game & more. Includes guide with lyrics & activities.

Six Little Ducks. 1 cass., 1 CD. (J). 8.78 (KE 9147); audio compact disk 11.98 CD Jewel box. (KE 9147) NewSound.

Six Month Course in Theory & Harmony. 6 cass. (Running Time: 6 hrs.). wbk. ed. 295.00 (V-6) Duane Shinn.
Understanding music theory is really the key that unlocks a vast world of musical insight & pleasure. This course starts at square one & goes through advanced harmonic concepts. Provides a month to complete each workbook before a new workbook arrives at the start of each month. Learn about figured bass, voicing, part writing, transposition, non-harmonic tones of various sorts, cadences, motion, form, analysis, & writing compositions. Learn to write for vocal parts, as well as for transposing instruments such as trumpet, sax & violin.

Six of the Best. abr. ed. John Bird. 1 cass. 1998. 11.25 (978-1-897774-85-4(0)) LaughStockProd GBR.

Six One One. Created by Janet Kuypers. 2002. audio compact disk 6.22 (978-1-891470-52-3(3)) Scars Pubns.
Designed for a live performance June 11 2002, This CD is the performance Art show Janet Kuypers did in Chicago, covering poetry, journals and storytelling about a variety of topics.

Six Pixels of Separation: Everyone Is Connected. Connect Your Business to Everyone. unabr. ed. Mitch Joel. Read by Mitch Joel. (Running Time: 7 hrs. 30 mins.). (ENG.). 2009. 27.98 (978-1-59659-440-1(3), GildAudio) Pub: Gildan Media. Dist(s): HachBkGrp

Six Pixels of Separation: Everyone Is Connected. Connect Your Business to Everyone. unabr. ed. Mitch Joel. Read by Mitch Joel. (Running Time: 7 hrs. 30 mins.). (ENG.). 2009. audio compact disk 29.98 (978-1-59659-378-7(4), GildAudio) Pub: Gildan Media. Dist(s): HachBkGrp

Six Power Moves of Chess: A Breakthrough Approach which shows you how to use the simplest moves in the game to beat any Player! (ENG., 2009. DVD 16.95 (978-0-9822243-9-7(7)) Lingo Arts.

Six Powers of Poetry. Robert Bly. 1 cass. (Running Time: 1 hr. 30 min.). 1983. 11.00 Big Sur Tapes.
Examines American Poetry & discusses the properties that poets use to bring words alive. What qualities constitute great poetry?.

Six Realms of Being in the Bardo. Read by Chogyam Trungpa. 7 cass. 1971. 72.00 (A201) Vajradhatu.
Seven talks. The bardo refers to an intermediate state. At such times the realms of being emerge to form & colour our experience.

***Six Rules of Maybe.** unabr. ed. Deb Caletti. Read by Teri Clark Linden. (Running Time: 10 hrs.). 2010. 24.99 (978-1-4233-9669-7(3), 9781423396697, BAD); 39.97 (978-1-4233-9668-0(5), 9781423396680, Brlnc Audio MP3 Lib); 39.97 (978-1-4233-9670-3(7), 9781423396703, BADLE); 24.99 (978-1-4233-9667-3(7), 9781423396673, Brilliance MP3); audio compact disk 92.97 (978-1-4233-9666-6(9), 9781423396666, BriAudCD Unabrid) Brilliance Audio.

***Six Rules of Maybe.** unabr. ed. Deb Caletti & Young Adult. Read by Teri Clark Linden. (Running Time: 10 hrs.). 2010. audio compact disk 29.99 (978-1-4233-9665-9(0), 9781423396659) Brilliance Audio.

Six-Second Way to Control Stress. 1 cass. (Running Time: 44 min.). 9.95 (I0060B090, HarperThor) HarpC GBR.

Six Secrets of Change: What the Best Leaders Do to Help Their Organizations Survive & Thrive. unabr. ed. Michael Fullan. Read by Erik Synnestvedt. (Running Time: 4 hrs.). (ENG.). 2008. 24.98 (978-1-59659-248-3(6), GildAudio) Pub: Gildan Media. Dist(s): HachBkGrp

Six Secrets of Sales Magnets. 2005. audio compact disk 24.95 (978-1-59801-230-9(4)) Huge Arch.

Six Servants see Favorite Children's Stories: A Collection

Six Servants see Favorite Tales by the Brothers Grimm

Six Shooter. 6 cass. (Running Time: 6 hrs.). 24.98 Moonbeam Pubns.

Six Shooter. Read by James Stewart. (Running Time: 10 hrs.). 2004. 39.98 (978-1-57019-685-0(0)) Radio Spirits.

Six Shooter. Perf. by Jimmy Stewart. 2 cass. (Running Time: 2 hrs.). vinyl bd. 10.95 (978-1-57816-078-5(2), SS2401) Audio File.
Includes: "Jenny Garver" (9-30-53) First show in the series. Britt Ponset finds a wounded man & brings him to a cabin where a single woman lives by herself. "The New Sheriff" (9-29-53) There's a new look to the jail in the town of Dawson. "The Young Gunslinger" (3-21-54) A tough young gunfighter wants to pick a fight with Ponset. "The Wyoming Kid" (5-20-54) The townspeople & the sheriff give credit to the Six Shooter for bringing down a wanted desperado.

Six Shooter, collector's ed. Perf. by James Stewart. 6 cass. (Running Time: 9 hrs.). 1998. bk. 34.98 (4131) Radio Spirits.

Six Shooter: Hiram Garver's Strike & The Silver Buckle. Perf. by James Stewart. 1 cass. (Running Time: 1 hr.). 2001. 6.98 (2025) Radio Spirits.

Six Shooter: "The Swedish Mail-Order Bride" 1 cass. (Running Time: 60 min.). 1953. 7.95 (WW-8090) Natl Recrd Co.
In "The Six Shooter" episode an attractive young lady arrives from Sweden to be married, only to discover that her husband-to-be is in jail with a murder charge against him. "The Death Valley Days" episode concerns two old prospectors, Smitty & Ole, who meet up with a white burro that plays an important part in their lives.

Six Short Novels. unabr. ed. Herman Melville. Read by Dan Lazar. 8 cass. (Running Time: 8 hrs.). 1975. 48.00 (1008); Rental 15.50 Set. (1008) Books on Tape.
These six short novels show Melville to have been not just a brooding genius, but also a writer possessed of wit & humor. Includes "Billy Budd," "Bartleby the Scrivener," "The Apple Tree Table," & "The Piazza".

Six Sigma: The Breakthrough Management Strategy Revolutionizing the World's Top Corporations. abr. ed. Mikel J. Harry & Richard Schroeder. Read by James Lurie. 5 CDs. (Running Time: 5 hrs. 15 mins.). (ENG.). 1999. audio compact disk 29.95 (978-0-553-45669-1(5)) Pub: Random Audio Pubg. Dist(s): Random

***Six Sigma for Dummies.** abr. ed. Bruce Williams & Neil Decarlo. (ENG.). 2008. (978-0-06-176497-4(3), Harper Audio); (978-0-06-176496-7(5), Harper Audio) HarperCollins Pubs.

Six Sigma Leader: Putting the Power of Business Excellence into Everything You Do. Peter Pande. 2007. audio compact disk 28.00 (978-1-933309-36-1(9)) Pub: A Media Intl. Dist(s): Natl Bk Netwk

Six Sigma Simplified Money Belt Training: How to Save $250,000 & Add It to Your Bottom Line. Scripts. Jay Arthur. 4 cass. (Running Time: 4 hrs.). 2002. 49.95 (978-1-884180-19-4(1), 225) Pub: LifeStar. Dist(s): AtlasBooks
Proven, step-by-step system for implementing Six Sigma to achieve breakthrough improvements.

Six Sigma Start-Up: Six Sigma Awarness Training for Everyone in Your Organization. Created by Resource Engineering, Inc. Staff. (Personal Trainer Ser.). 2001. audio compact disk 495.00 (978-1-882307-30-2(5)) Res Engineering.

Six Sigma Way: How GE, Motorola, & Other Top Companies Are Honing Their Performance. abr. ed. Peter S. Pande et al. 3 cass. (Running Time: 4 hrs. 30 mins.). (McGraw Hill Audiobks.). 2003. 24.00 (978-0-9724462-7-3(3)) Pub: A Media Intl. Dist(s): Natl Bk Netwk
This is the first book to provide basic, non-technical information on understanding and implementing Six Segma.

Six Sigma Way: How GE, Motorola, & Other Top Companies Are Honong Their Performance. abr. ed. Peter S. Pande et al. 4 CDs. (Running Time: 4 hrs. 30 mins.). (McGraw Hill Audiobks.). 2003. audio compact disk 28.00 (978-0-9724889-5-2(2)) Pub: A Media Intl. Dist(s): Natl Bk Netwk
This is the first book to provide basic, non-technical information on understanding and implementing Six Sigma.

Six Signs of a Healthy Impacting Church. As told by Frank Damazio. 6 cass. 2002. 59.99 (978-1-886849-94-5(3)) CityChristian.

Six Sillies see Favorite Children's Stories: A Collection

Six Stages of the Masculine Journey. Featuring John Eldredge. (ENG.). 2009. audio compact disk 12.99 (978-1-933207-36-0(1)) Ransomed Heart.

Six States of the Bardo. Read by Chogyam Trungpa. 9 cass. 1971. 96.75 (A202) Vajradhatu.
Nine talks. The bardo teachings provide a guide to dealing with the groundlessness we experience, both in everyday life & at death.

Six Steps to Enjoying Life. Speeches. Joel Osteen. 6 audio cass. (J). 2001. 24.00 (978-1-931877-14-5(9), JAS010) J Osteen.

Six Steps to Enjoying Life. Speeches. Joel Osteen. 3 CDs. (J). 2002. audio compact disk 24.00 (978-1-931877-31-2(9), JCS010) J Osteen.

Six Steps to Enjoying Life, Pt. 1. Speeches. Joel Osteen. 1 Cass. (Running Time: 30 Mins.). 2001. 6.00 (978-1-59349-109-3(3), JA0109) J Osteen.

Six Steps to Enjoying Life: Lighten up & Learn to Laugh. Speeches. Told to Joel Osteen. 1 Cass. (Running Time: 30 Mins.). 2001. 6.00 (978-1-59349-111-6(5), JA0111) J Osteen.

Six Steps to Enjoying Life Pt. 4: Be Positive. Speeches. Told to Joel Osteen. 1 Cass. (Running Time: 30 Mins.). 2001. 6.00 (978-1-59349-112-3(3), JA0112) J Osteen.

Six Steps to Enjoying Life Pt. 5: Refuse to Worry. Speeches. Told to Joel Osteen. 1 Cass. (Running Time: 30 Mins.). 2001. 6.00 (978-1-59349-113-0(1), JA0113) J Osteen.

Six Steps to Enjoying Life Pt. 6: Live to Give. Speeches. Joel Osteen. 1 Cass. (Running Time: 30 Mins.). 2001. 6.00 (978-1-59349-114-7(X), JA0114) J Osteen.

Six Steps to Excellence in Ministry. Kenneth Copeland. 6 cass. (Running Time: 6 hrs.). 1983. bk. & stu. ed. 30.00 (978-0-938458-29-6(9)) K Copeland Pubns.
How to excell in ministry.

Six Steps to Excellence in Selling: The Step-by-Step Guide to Effective Selling. Warren M. Wechsler. 2 cass. (Running Time: 2 hrs.). 19.95 Set. (978-1-886656-05-5(3)) Better Books.

***Six Suspects.** Vikas Swarup. Narrated by Full Cast Production Staff. (Running Time: 2 hrs. 30 mins. 0 sec.). (ENG.). 2010. audio compact disk 24.95 (978-1-4084-2731-6(1)) Pub: AudioGO. Dist(s): Perseus Dist

***Six Suspects.** unabr. ed. Vikas Swarup. Narrated by Lyndam Gregory. 1 Playaway. (Running Time: 17 hrs. 30 mins.). 2010. 115.95 (978-0-7927-6989-7(9)); audio compact disk 115.95 (978-0-7927-6988-0(0)) AudioGO.

Six Vital Ingredients of Self-Esteem: How to Develop Them in Young People. Bettie B. Youngs. 1990. 49.95 (978-0-940221-07-9(1)) Lrng Tools.

Six Ways to Become All You Are Capable of Being. Speeches. Aaron Lumpkin. 1 cass. (Running Time: 55 mins). 2001. 11.95 (978-0-9711605-1-4(1)) Winning TN.

***Six Wise Neighbors.** Anonymous. 2009. (978-1-60136-614-6(0)) Audio Holding.

Six Wives of Henry VIII. Alison Weir. Narrated by Simon Prebble. 16 cass. (Running Time: 22 hrs. 30 mins.). 1991. 124.00 (978-1-4025-4020-2(5)) Recorded Bks.

Six Year Plan for Music Appreciation in the Elementary Schools. 2002. 12.99 (978-0-9744270-7-2(1)) Take Note.

Six Years in Hell. unabr. ed. Jay R. Jensen. Read by Jay R. Jensen. 3 cass. (Running Time: 4 hrs. 30 min.). 1989. bk. 26.00; pap. bk. 26.00 (978-1-877898-08-2(2)) Pubns Of Worth.

Six Young Men see Poetry & Voice of Ted Hughes

Sixes & Sevens, Vol. 1. unabr. ed. O. Henry. Read by Gene Engene. 6 cass. (Running Time: 8 hrs. 6 min.). 2001. 39.95 (978-1-58116-079-6(8)); audio compact disk 55.95 (978-1-58116-117-5(4)) Books in Motion.
To readers and listeners all over the world, O. Henry - one of the most famous pen names in history - means the very best in short story writing. Included are 19 stories with both East Coast and Southwest settings.

Sixes & Sevens, Vol. II. unabr. ed. O. Henry. Read by Gene Engene. 6 cass. (Running Time: 7 hrs. 30 min.). 2001. 39.95 (978-1-58116-094-9(1)); audio compact disk 55.95 (978-1-58116-118-2(2)) Books in Motion.
Short stories from the anthology published as Sixes and Sevens.

Sixguns & Double Eagles. abr. ed. Ralph Compton. Read by Jim Gough. 4 cass. (Running Time: 6 hrs.). (Gun Ser.). 2000. 24.95 (978-1-890990-57-2(4), 99057) Otis Audio.
Wes Stone was once a lawman, but that was before the ruthless Sandlin Gang gunned down his father-Nathan Stone, the Gunfighter. Now, having traded in his badge for his father's guns, he's sworn blood vengeance on every last member of the Gang. But little does he realize that the Sandlins are part of a much larger criminal organization, one whose influence stretches across the entire west & knows his every move!.

***Sixkill.** unabr. ed. Robert B. Parker. (ENG.). 2011. audio compact disk 32.00 (978-0-7393-8487-9(2), Random AudioBks) Pub: Random Audio Pubg. Dist(s): Random

Sixpence in Her Shoe. Frances McNeil et al. 2008. 84.95 (978-1-84652-191-1(2)); audio compact disk 99.95 (978-1-84652-192-8(0)) Pub: Magna Story GBR. Dist(s): Ulverscroft US

Sixteen Harry Christophers. Perf. by Sixteen Harry Christophers. Composed by Antonio Vivaldi et al. 1992. 10.95 (365); audio compact disk 15.95 (365) GIA Pubns.

Sixteen in Nome. unabr. ed. Max Brand. Read by Arthur Addison. 7 cass. (Running Time: 7 hrs.). 1996. 42.00 (978-0-7366-3624-7(2), 4284) Books on Tape.
"Sixteen in Nome" would be Joe May's epitaph if he didn't find work soon. The frail teen has eaten once in thirty-six hours. Hugh Massey has a job for Joe, but it involves a little travel. In fact, it's a dogsled trek across Alaska, miles of frozen sea, rough overland & the river of ice known as the Yukon.

Sixteen in Nome. unabr. ed. Max Brand. Read by David Stuart. (Running Time: 7 hrs.). 2007. 39.25 (978-1-4233-3542-9(2), 9781423335429, BADLE); 24.95 (978-1-4233-3541-2(4), 9781423335412, BAD) Brilliance Audio.

Sixteen in Nome. unabr. ed. Max Brand. Read by David Stuart. (Running Time: 25200 sec.). 2007. audio compact disk 24.95 (978-1-4233-3539-9(2), 9781423335399, Brilliance MP3); audio compact disk 39.25 (978-1-4233-3540-5(6), 9781423335405, Brlnc Audio MP3 Lib) Brilliance Audio.

Sixteen in Nome. unabr. ed. Max Brand. Read by David Stuart. (Running Time: 6 hrs.). 2009. audio compact disk 59.97 (978-1-4418-0474-7(9), 9781441804747, BriAudCD Unabrid); audio compact disk 19.99 (978-1-4418-0473-0(0), 9781441804730, Bril Audio CD Unabri) Brilliance Audio.

***Sixteen-Millimeter Shrine.** 2010. audio compact disk (978-1-59171-293-0(9)) Falcon Picture.

Sixteen Short Stories by Outstanding Writers for Young Adults. unabr. ed. Read by Barbara Caruso et al. Ed. by Donald R. Gallo. 6 cass. (Running Time: 5 hrs. 35 min.). (Cassette Library). (J). 1987. 44.98 (978-0-8072-3026-8(X), CXL527CX, Listening Lib) Random Audio Pubg.
Contains works by Joan Aiken, Judie Angell, Robin F. Brancato, Robert Cormier, Diane Duane, Bette Greene, Rosa Guy, M. E. Kerr, Robert Lipsyte, Kevin Major, Harry Mazer, Norma Fox Mazer, Richard Peck, Susan Beth Pfeffer, Ouida Sebestyen & Marjorie Sharmat.

Sixteen Wounded. Eliam Kraiem. Perf. by Annabelle Gurwitch et al. 2 CDs. (Running Time: 1 hr. 49 mins.). 2005. audio compact disk 25.95 (978-1-58081-306-8(2), LA 073) Pub: L A Theatre. Dist(s): NetLibrary CO

Sixteenth & Seventeenth Century. 1 cass. (Golden Treasury of Poetry & Prose Ser.). 1991. 16.95 (1058-SA) Olivia & Hill.

Sixth Annual Criminal Law Symposium. 1989. 95.00 (AC-495) PA Bar Inst.

Sixth Annual Municipal Law Forum. Contrib. by William L. Forester et al. (Running Time: 4 hrs.). 1985. 80.00 incl. program handbook. NJ Inst CLE.
Discusses resource recovery, the law governing municipal sewer & water utility authorities, cable TV, land use, the cost of such recent developments to the municipality.

Sixth Annual Tax Day for New Jersey Practitioners. Contrib. by Frank S. Berall et al. Moderated by Charles M. Costenbader. (Running Time: 7 hrs. 30 min.). 1985. 90.00 incl. program handbook. NJ Inst CLE.
Includes resolving current estate planning problems, time value of money, recent developments on subchapter C, criminal tax investigations.

Sixth Bowl of Chicken Soup for the Soul. abr. ed. Jack L. Canfield & Mark Victor Hansen. Read by Jack L. Canfield & Mark Victor Hansen. 1 CD. (Running Time: 1 hr. 30 mins.). (Chicken Soup for the Soul Ser.). 1999. 19.95 (978-1-55874-665-7(X)); audio compact disk 11.95 (978-1-55874-664-0(1)) Health Comm.
Filled with wisdom, love & inspiration.

Sixth Commandment. abr. ed. Lawrence Sanders. 2004. 10.95 (978-0-7435-4722-2(5)) Pub: S&S Audio. Dist(s): S and S Inc

Sixth Covenant. unabr. ed. Bodie Thoene & Brock Thoene. Narrated by Sean Barrett. (Running Time: 11 hrs. 0 mins. 0 sec.). (A. D. Chronicles Ser.). (ENG.). 2009. audio compact disk 34.99 (978-1-59859-540-6(7)) Oasis Audio.

Sixth House of Health. Harold Hason. 1 cass. 8.95 (416) Am Fed Astrologers.
Decanates & dwads help accurately diagnose.

***Sixth Man.** abr. ed. David Baldacci. (Running Time: 7 hrs.). (ENG.). 2011. 19.98 (978-1-60941-984-4(7)); audio compact disk & audio compact disk 29.98 (978-1-60788-581-8(6)) Pub: Hachet Audio. Dist(s): HachBkGrp

***Sixth Man.** unabr. ed. David Baldacci. (Running Time: 13 hrs.). (ENG.). 2011. 26.98 (978-1-60788-582-5(4)); audio compact disk & audio compact disk 39.98 (978-1-60788-580-1(8)) Pub: Hachet Audio. Dist(s): HachBkGrp

Sixth Seal. unabr. ed. Mary Wesley. Read by Carole Boyd. 5 cass. (Running Time: 6 hrs. 10 min.). 1993. 49.95 (978-1-85089-665-4(8), 91102) Pub: ISIS Audio GBR. Dist(s): Ulverscroft US
Unnatural incidents begin to occur, such as falls of brilliantly colored snow, until a deadly storm wipes the life out of everything it touches. Muriel, her son Paul, & his friend Henry are amongst the few who survive, having been safely underground when the storm hit. They bond together with others who have also escaped to make the most of their changed world.

Sixth Seal, unabr. ed. Mary Wesley. Read by Carole Boyd. 6 CDs. (Running Time: 6 hrs. 10 min.). (Isis Ser.). (J). (gr. 7-12). 2000. audio compact disk 64.95 (978-0-7531-0713-3(9), 107139) Pub: ISIS Lrg Prnt GBR. Dist(s): Ulverscroft US

Sixth Sense: RADIO DIVINITY. Concept by Apple Feng.Tr. of Case Samples in Chinese. 2008. audio compact disk 14.99 (978-0-9815053-0-5(9)) Assential.

Sixth Sense Calle Faith. Tsea. 2007. audio compact disk (978-0-9797500-3-8(2)) TSEA.

Sixth Sense... Faith. Speeches. Joel Osteen. 1 Cass. (Running Time: 30 Mins.). 2000. 6.00 (978-1-59349-080-5(1), JA0080) J Osteen.

Sixth Shooter. 1998th ed. Perf. by Jimmy Stewart. 6 cass. (Running Time: 9 hrs.). 1998. bk. 24.98 (4131) Radio Spirits.
An easy going frontier drifter, Britt Ponset is a friendly cowboy, & when he had to be a tough gunfighter he got his nickname, "The Six Shooter," from his trusty gray steel & rainbow mother-of-pear revolves.

Sixth Shotgun. Louis L'Amour. Read by Christopher Walker. (Running Time: 0 hr. 30 mins.). 1998. 10.95 (978-1-60083-452-3(3)) Iofy Corp.

Sixth Step: What You Own Is What You Get: Mark 5:1-18. Ed Young. 1998. 4.95 (978-0-7417-2202-7(X), 1202) Win Walk.

Sixties Rock Sessions for Guitar. Ed. by Ed Lazano. Contrib. by Louis Rochman & Peter Marunzak. 1 CD. (Running Time: 1 hr.). 1998. pap. bk. 12.95 (978-0-8256-1628-0(X), AM945186) Music Sales.

***Sixty-Eight Rooms.** unabr. ed. Marianne Malone. (ENG.). (J). 2011. audio compact disk 35.00 (978-0-307-91633-4(2), Listening Lib) Pub: Random Audio Pubg. Dist(s): Random

Sixty Feet, Six Inches: A Hall of Fame Pitcher & a Hall of Fame Hitter Talk about How the Game Is Played. abr. ed. Bob Gibson et al. Read by Dominic Hoffman & Mirron Willis. (ENG.). 2009. audio compact disk 30.00 (978-0-7393-8483-1(X), Random AudioBks) Pub: Random Audio Pubg. Dist(s): Random

Sixty-Minute Shakespeare: Romeo & Juliet. Cass Foster. 1 cass. (Running Time: 10 min.). 1992. 5.00 (978-1-877749-04-9(4)) Five Star AZ.
Sound effects tape.

Sixty-Minute Shakespeare: Romeo & Juliet. Ed. by Mary E. Hawkins. Abr. by Cass Foster. Based on a play by William Shakespeare. 1 cass. (Running Time: 10 min.). (J). (gr. 9 up). 1990. pap. bk. 5.00 (978-1-877749-00-1(1)) Five Star AZ.
Sound effects tape for The Sixty-Minute Shakespeare: Romeo & Juliet.

Sixty Minutes Towards Computer Literacy. 2nd unabr. ed. Julian Padowicz & Donna K. Carter. Read by Julian Padowicz. 1 cass. (Running Time: 80 min.). 1993. 12.95 (978-1-881288-06-0(4), BFI AudioBooks) BusnFilm Intl.
Explains basic computer terms & concepts through analogies to which all can relate.

Sixty Minutes Towards Computer Literacy & Internet Explained Short & Sweet. unabr. ed. Julian Padowicz & Donna K. Carter. Read by Julian Padowicz. 2 cass. (Running Time: 2 hrs. 27 min.). 1996. 21.95 (978-1-881288-11-4(0), BFI AudioBooks) BusnFilm Intl.
Explains basic concepts of computers & the Internet.

Sixty Silly Songs. Alan Billingsley & Daniel Fox. 1 cass. (Running Time: 1 hr.). 1998. pap. bk. 39.95 (978-0-88284-871-6(2), 16973) Alfred Pub.

Sixty-Six. unabr. ed. Barry Levinson. Narrated by Johnny Heller. 5 cass. (Running Time: 8 hrs. 15 mins.). 2004. 24.99 (978-1-4025-5988-4(7), 03614) Recorded Bks.
Academy Award(r)-winning filmmaker Barry Levinson, director of such classics as Diner and Rain Man, taps into his storytelling magic to craft a nostalgic look at a time when the innocence of an entire generation was shattered. Baltimore in 1966 is a quiet, blue-collar town. But all that will soon change for one group of young men about to confront the realities of growing up in a changing world. Featuring the razor-sharp dialogue Levinson's films are known for, Sixty-Six brilliantly captures America's most turbulent decade.

Sixty's Party Walking One: (Beginner) Bruce Blackmon. 1 cass. (Running Time: 1 hr. 2 min.). 1991. 12.95 (978-1-56481-003-8(8)) Sports Music.
A one hour beginner level fitness walking program featuring well known songs from the 1960's.

Sixty's Party Walking Three: (Advanced) Bruce Blackmon. 1 cass. (Running Time: 1 hr. 2 min.). 1991. 12.95 (978-1-56481-005-2(4)) Sports Music.
A one hour advanced level fitness walking program featuring well known songs from the 1960's.

Sixty's Party Walking Two: (Intermediate) Bruce Blackmon. 1 cass. (Running Time: 1 hr. 2 min.). 1991. 12.95 (978-1-56481-004-5(6)) Sports Music.
A one hour intermediate level fitness walking program featuring well known songs from the 1960's.

Siyahamba - ShowTrax. Arranged by Cheryl Lavender. 1 CD. 2000. audio compact disk 19.95 (09970206) H Leonard.
This popular South African freedom song is now available in a great 2-part arrangement.

Size Matters. unabr. ed. Judy Astley. 7 cass. (Running Time: 8 hrs. 3 mins.). (Isis Cassettes Ser.). (J). 2004. 61.95 (978-0-7531-2318-8(5)) Pub: ISIS Lrg Prnt GBR. Dist(s): Ulverscroft US

Size Matters. unabr. ed. Judy Astley. Read by Trudy Harris. 8 CDs. (Running Time: 29100 sec.). (Isis (CDs) Ser.). 2004. audio compact disk 79.95 (978-0-7531-2348-5(7)) Pub: ISIS Lrg Prnt GBR. Dist(s): Ulverscroft US

Size 14 Is Not Fat Either. Meg Cabot. (Heather Wells Mystery Ser.: No. 2). 2006. audio compact disk 29.95 (978-0-06-123084-4(7)) HarperCollins Pubs.

***Size 14 Is Not Fat Either.** unabr. ed. Meg Cabot. Read by Kristen Kairos. (ENG.). 2006. (978-0-06-134057-4(X), Harper Audio); (978-0-06-134056-7(1), Harper Audio) HarperCollins Pubs.

***Sizzle: A Novel.** unabr. ed. Julie Garwood. Read by Susan Denaker. 8 CDs. (Running Time: 9 hrs. 45 mins.). 2010. audio compact disk 100.00 (978-0-307-57784-9(8), BksonTape) Pub: Random Audio Pubg. Dist(s): Random

Sizzle: A Novel. unabr. ed. Julie Garwood. Read by Susan Denaker. (ENG.). 2009. audio compact disk 40.00 (978-0-7393-5766-8(2), Random AudioBks) Pub: Random Audio Pubg. Dist(s): Random

Sizzle & Burn. abr. ed. Jayne Ann Krentz. Read by Sandra Burr. 5 CDs. (Running Time: 21600 sec.). (Arcane Society Ser.). 2008. audio compact disk 26.95 (978-1-4233-2631-1(8), 9781423326311, BACD) Brilliance Audio.

Sizzle & Burn. abr. ed. Jayne Ann Krentz. Read by Sandra Burr. (Running Time: 6 hrs.). (Arcane Society Ser.). 2009. audio compact disk 14.99 (978-1-4233-2632-8(6), 9781423326328, BCD Value Price) Brilliance Audio.

Sizzle & Burn. unabr. ed. Jayne Ann Krentz. Read by Sandra Burr. 1 MP3-CD. (Running Time: 10 hrs.). (Arcane Society Ser.). 2008. 24.95 (978-1-4233-2627-4(X), 9781423326274, Brilliance MP3); 39.25 (978-1-4233-2630-4(X), 9781423326304, BADLE); 24.95 (978-1-4233-2629-8(6), 9781423326298, BAD); 87.25 (978-1-4233-2602-1(4), 9781423326021, BrilAudUnabridg); audio compact disk 36.95 (978-1-4233-2609-0(1), 9781423326090, Bril Audio CD Unabri); audio compact disk 92.25 (978-1-4233-2622-9(9), 9781423326229, BriAudCD Unabrid); audio compact disk 39.25 (978-1-4233-2628-1(8), 9781423326281, Brinc Audio MP3 Lib) Brilliance Audio.

***Sizzling.** unabr. ed. Susan Mallery. Read by Alyson Silverman. (Running Time: 8 hrs.). 2011. 19.99 (978-1-4418-7623-2(5), 9781441876232, Brilliance MP3); 39.97 (978-1-4418-7625-6(1), 9781441876256, BADLE); 39.97 (978-1-4418-7624-9(3), 9781441876249, Brlnc Audio MP3 Lib); audio compact disk 19.99 (978-1-4418-7621-8(9), 9781441876218, Bril Audio CD Unabri); audio compact disk 79.97 (978-1-4418-7622-5(7), 9781441876225, BriAudCD Unabrid) Brilliance Audio.

***Sizzling Sixteen.** abr. ed. Janet Evanovich. Read by Lorelei King. 3 CDs. (Running Time: 4 hrs.). Bk. 16. 2010. audio compact disk 19.99 (978-1-4272-0965-8(0)) Pub: Macmill Audio. Dist(s): Macmillan

***Sizzling Sixteen.** unabr. ed. Janet Evanovich. Narrated by Lorelei King. 1 Playaway. (Running Time: 7 hrs.). 2010. 79.95 (978-0-7927-7212-5(1)); 44.95 (978-0-7927-7211-8(3)); audio compact disk 74.95 (978-0-7927-7156-2(7)) AudioGO.

***Sizzling Sixteen.** unabr. ed. Janet Evanovich. Read by Lorelei King. 7 CDs. (Running Time: 7 hrs.). Bk. 16. (ENG.). 2010. audio compact disk 34.99 (978-1-4272-0967-2(7)) Pub: Macmill Audio. Dist(s): Macmillan

SK-0-The Krishna Consciousness. 1 cass. 3.95 Bhaktivedanta.
Includes the Hare Krsna mantra & purport.

SK-1-The Govinda Album. A. C. Bhaktivedanta Prabhupada. 1 cass. 3.95 Bhaktivedanta.
Prayers from the Brahma-Samhita chanted in original Sanskrit texts.

SK-2-Vande'ham Album. A. C. Bhaktivedanta Prabhupada. 1 cass. 3.95 Bhaktivedanta.

SK-3-The Krishna Meditation Album. 1 cass. 3.95 Bhaktivedanta.
Bhaktivedanta Swami chants bhajans with harmonium.

Ska La-La-La-La. Perf. by Bunch of Believers Staff. 1 cass. (J). 1999. 10.99 (KMGC8932); audio compact disk 16.99 (KMGD8932) Provident Mus Dist.
B.O.B. offer old favorites: "Joy to the World"; "O Come All Ye Faithful"; "Deck the Halls"; "Jingle Bells"; "O Come, O Come Emmanuel"; "God Rest Ye Merry Gentlemen." They also wrote some originals: "Snowball Fight"; "Putting on a Play"; "Light up the World"; "Jesus's Birthday Party"; "So Many Santas"; "Room in Your Heart.".

Skakuhachi Meditation Music. Perf. by Stan Richardson. 1 cass., 1 CD. 9.58 Double. (STA 301); audio compact disk 14.38 CD Jewel box, double. (STA 301) NewSound.
Thirteen authentic bamboo flute selections played in the traditional Len style.

Skalleluia Too! Perf. by Insyderz, The. 1 cass. 1998. (978-0-7601-3095-7(7)); audio compact disk (978-0-7601-3094-0(9)) Brentwood Music.

Skaneateles Model 5 Plans: Documentation Record & Notes of a Classic Double End Rowboat. John Wilson. 2005. audio compact disk 40.00 (978-0-9729947-3-6(4)) Home Shop.

***Skate Trick: A Robot & Rico Story.** Anastasia Suen. Illus. by Mike Laughead. (Robot & Rico Ser.). (ENG.). 2010. audio compact disk 14.60 (978-1-4342-2588-7(7)) CapstoneDig.

Skate Your Personal Best - Sound Advice for Controlling Nervousness, Mentally Preparing for Competitions & Getting to Sleep. abr. ed. Sandra Foster & Tracy Prussaek. 1 cass. (Running Time: 2 hrs.). 1998. 19.95 (978-0-945213-29-1(8)) Rudi Pub.
For skaters motivation, inspiration & relaxation.

Skateboard City Level 1. (J). 2002. (978-0-7398-5089-3(X)); audio compact disk (978-0-7398-5326-9(0)) SteckVau.

Skateboarding. Joanne Mattern. (Rourke Discovery Library (CD-ROM) Ser.). (J). 2008. audio compact disk 24.95 (978-1-60472-771-5(3)) Rourke FL.

Skeletal Structure of a Story. Elizabeth R. Bills. 1 cass. (Running Time: 30 min.). (Secrets of a Successful Writers Ser.). 1963. 11.95 (23022) J Norton Pubs.
Disciplined structure requires that the writer concern himself with the rules of traditional form & the three elements of craftmanship: unity, compression & dramatic design.

Skeleton. Dorling Kindersley Publishing Staff. (DK Eyewitness Bks.). (ENG.). (J). (gr. 1). 2006. 12.99 (978-0-7566-2833-8(4)) DK Pub Inc.

Skeleton Canyon, unabr. ed. J. A. Jance. Read by Stephanie Brush. 8 cass. (Running Time: 11 hrs.). (Joanna Brady Mystery Ser.). 1999. 49.95 (978-1-55686-883-2(9)) Books in Motion.
When teenager Brianna O'Brien is murdered the prime suspect is her misfit boyfriend. It doesn't take long for Sheriff Brady to suspect that this was more than an isolated crime of passion, & she is proved correct when another girl disappears. Soon, the investigation exposes a complete web of crime & deception that stretches from a desert canyon to a luxurious mansion.

***Skeleton Canyon.** unabr. ed. J. A. Jance. Read by C. J. Critt. (ENG.). 2010. (978-0-06-195392-7(X), Harper Audio); (978-0-06-196726-9(2), Harper Audio) HarperCollins Pubs.

Skeleton Coast. unabr. ed. Clive Cussler & Jack Du Brul. Read by Scott Brick. (Running Time: 55800 sec.). No. 4. (ENG.). (gr. 8). 2006. audio compact disk 39.95 (978-0-14-305935-6(1), PengAudBks) Penguin Grp USA.

Skeleton Crew: Selections. unabr. ed. Stephen King. Read by Stephen King. Read by Matthew Broderick et al. (ENG.). 2009. audio compact disk 29.95 (978-1-59887-844-8(1), 1598878441) Pub: Penguin-HghBrdg. Dist(s): Workman Pub

Skeleton Crew Readalong. Janet Lorimer. 1 cass. (Running Time: 1 hr.). (Ten-Minute Thrillers Ser.). (YA). (gr. 6-12). 1995. pap. bk. 12.95 (978-0-7854-1080-5(5), 40819) Am Guidance.

Skeleton Dance. unabr. ed. Aaron Elkins. Narrated by George Guidall. 6 cass. (Running Time: 8 hrs.). (Gideon Oliver Mystery Ser.). 2000. 57.00 (978-0-7887-4867-7(X), 96245E7) Recorded Bks.
Seattle professor Gideon Oliver travels to France to study bones found in a burial cave once explored by l'Institut de Prehistoire but his arrival sets off a chain of events that threatens to tear apart the dignified institute & destroy his own safety. A twisting trail of lies & bloodshed through this lively mystery.

Skeleton Dance. unabr. ed. Aaron Elkins. Narrated by George Guidall. 7 CDs. (Running Time: 8 hrs.). (Gideon Oliver Mystery Ser.). 2001. audio compact disk 69.00 (978-0-7887-6178-2(1), C1403) Recorded Bks.
When Seattle professor Gideon Oliver travels to France to apply his famed skill in forensic medicine, the bodies & puzzles pile up. A dog has uncovered some bones in an ancient burial cave that the prestigious l'Institut de Prehistoire explored years ago. Hoping to find some answers, French police inspector Joly calls up his old friend Gideon, the Skeleton Detective. But when Gideon arrives, he sets off a chain of events that threatens to tear apart the dignified institute & destroy his own safety.

Skeleton in Armor see Best Loved Poems of Longfellow

Skeleton in God's Closet. abr. ed. Paul L. Maier. Read by J. Charles. 2 cass. (Running Time: 3 hrs.). 2003. 17.95 (978-1-59355-259-6(9), 1593552599); 44.25 (978-1-59355-260-2(2), 1593552602); audio compact disk 19.95 (978-1-59355-261-9(0), 1593552610); audio compact disk 62.25 (978-1-59355-262-6(9), 1593552629) Brilliance Audio.
Dr. Jonathan Weber, Harvard professor and biblical scholar, is looking forward to his sabbatical year on an archaeological dig in Israel. But a spectacular find that seems to be an archaeologist's dream-come-true becomes a nightmare that could be the death rattle of Christianity. Meanwhile, Weber's strong interest in Shannon Jennings, daughter of the dig's director, is an exhilarating complication. Carefully researched and compellingly written, this fast-paced thriller takes you from the dust of an archaeological dig to the laboratories of dedicated scientists to the halls of political and religious power, where world reaction is instant, fierce, and shattering. Moreover, A Skeleton in God's Closet explores the tension between doubt and faith, science and religion, and one man's determination to find the truth - no matter what the cost.

Skeleton in God's Closet. abr. ed. Paul L. Maier. Read by J. Charles. (Running Time: 3 hrs.). 2006. 39.25 (978-1-4233-0344-2(X), 9781423303442, BADLE); 24.95 (978-1-4233-0343-5(1), 9781423303435, BAD); 39.25 (978-1-4233-0342-8(3), 9781423303428, Brlnc Audio MP3 Lib); audio compact disk 24.95 (978-1-4233-0341-1(5), 9781423303411, Brilliance MP3) Brilliance Audio.

Skeleton in Search of a Cupboard. unabr. ed. E. X. Ferrars. Read by Celia Gordon. 5 cass. (Running Time: 6 hrs. 15 min.). 2001. 49.95 (978-1-85695-610-9(5), 93075) Pub: ISIS Audio GBR. Dist(s): Ulverscroft US
On the night of Henrietta's 80th birthday her house burns down. It appears the fire was intentional & meant to cover up a theft of valuable paintings. But the fire reveals more than it hides, & Henrietta finds herself in the center of a murder hunt.

Skeleton in Search of a Cupboard, unabr. ed. E. X. Ferrars. Read by Celia Gordon. 6 CDs. (Running Time: 6 hrs. 15 min.). 2000. audio compact disk 64.95 (978-0-7531-0703-4(1), 107031) Pub: ISIS Audio GBR. Dist(s): Ulverscroft US

Skeleton in the Closet. M. C. Beaton, pseud. Read by Donada Peters. 2001. audio compact disk 40.00 (978-0-7366-8294-7(5)) Books on Tape.

Skeleton in the Closet. unabr. ed. M. C. Beaton, pseud. 4 cass. (Running Time: 6 hrs.). 2001. 32.00 (978-0-7366-6849-1(7)) Books on Tape.

Skeleton Key. unabr. ed. Prod. by Recorded Books Staff. 5 cass. (Running Time: 7 hrs.). 2003. 48.00 (978-1-4025-2476-9(5)) Recorded Bks.
Alex Rider of Point Blank (RB# 97134) is back in another hair raising adventure. Although the 14-year-old has escaped great dangers and has twice saved the world, he now faces his most perilous foe. A Russian man with a huge grudge against the free world has a nuclear weapon and is threatening to use it. It's up to Alex to stop him.

Skeleton Lode. abr. ed. Ralph Compton. 4 cass. (Running Time: 6 hrs.). (Sundown Riders Ser.). 2001. 24.95 (978-1-890990-64-0(7)) Otis Audio.
Arlo Wells & Dallas Holt are two ex-cowpunchers who've hit a patch of bad luck, until a dying friend tells them of a lost gold mine. They jump at the chance to get the fortune. But Arlo & Dallas aren't the only ones who know about the mine & their streak of bad luck is about to turn into a fight for survival.

Skeleton Man. unabr. ed. Joseph Bruchac. Read by Carine Montbertrand. 2 cass. (Running Time: 2 hrs. 35 mins.). (YA). 2004. 19.75 (978-1-4025-9398-7(8)) Recorded Bks.
Master storyteller and author Joseph Bruchac transforms an ancient Native American legend into a terrifying thriller with the novel Skeleton Man. One day Molly wakes up to discover her parents are missing. Soon the welfare services people bring her to live with a great-uncle she never knew she had. Facing uncertain circumstances, Molly struggles to stay brave with the help of her favorite school teacher.

Skeleton Man. unabr. ed. Tony Hillerman. 5 cass. (Running Time: 6 hrs. 30 mins.). (Joe Leaphorn & Jim Chee Novel Ser.). 2004. 49.75 (978-1-4193-1584-8(6), 97912MC) Recorded Bks.

Skeleton Man. unabr. ed. Tony Hillerman. 6 CDs. (Running Time: 6 hrs. 30 min.). (Joe Leaphorn & Jim Chee Novel Ser.). 2004. audio compact disk 34.95 (978-1-4193-1586-2(2)) Recorded Bks.

Skeleton on the Skateboard, unabr. ed. Tom B. Stone. Narrated by Jeff Woodman. 2 cass. (Running Time: 2 hrs. 30 mins.). (Graveyard School Ser.: No. 2). (gr. 3-7). 2001. 19.00 (978-0-7887-0706-3(X), 94881E7) Recorded Bks.
An adventure of spooky danger & grisly humor centers around a school so weird that its students are dying to go to class.

Skeleton Staff, unabr. ed. Elizabeth Ferrars. Read by Sheila Mitchell. 5 cass. (Running Time: 6 hrs. 30 min.). 1997. 49.95 (978-0-7531-0130-8(0), 970502) Pub: ISIS Audio GBR. Dist(s): Ulverscroft US
A mystery set in Madeira, where wealthy Roberta Ellison & her husband had settled after Roberta had been crippled in a car accident. When Roberta is left suddenly widowed, she finds that her staff problems have only just begun. Her young half-sister, Camilla, comes out to help find her a companion, but Camilla brings problems of her own with her, problems which at first seem trivial, but soon involve the sisters in violent & mystifying events that lead up to murder.

Skeletons. unabr. ed. Kate Wilhelm. Read by C. M. Herbert. 6 cass. (Running Time: 8 hrs. 30 mins.). 2002. 44.95 (978-0-7861-2293-6(5), 2982); audio compact disk 64.00 (978-0-7861-9477-3(4), 2982) Blckstn Audio.
Lee Donne has an eidetic memory that maintains a visual representation of everything she has ever seen. Without a job or prospects, Lee is relieved to be house-sitting at her grandfather's isolated Oregon home. But her stay soon becomes a nightmare when she is tormented by strange and menacing noises at night. Determined to track down the haunting sounds, Lee finds their source - a young man who is accidentally killed during the course of her investigation.

Skeletons at the Feast. unabr. ed. Chris Bohjalian. Narrated by Mark Bramhall. 10 CDs. (Running Time: 12 hrs.). 2008. audio compact disk 110.00 (978-1-4159-4889-7(5), BksonTape) Pub: Random Audio Pubg. Dist(s): Random

Skeletons at the Feast. unabr. ed. Chris Bohjalian. (Running Time: 12 hrs.). (ENG.). 2008. 22.50 (978-0-7393-6624-0(6)) Pub: Random Audio Pubg. Dist(s): Random

Skeletons at the Feast. unabr. ed. Chris Bohjalian. Read by Mark Bramhall. 10 CDs. (Running Time: 12 hrs.). (ENG.). 2008. audio compact disk 34.95 (978-0-7393-6623-3(8)) Pub: Random Audio Pubg. Dist(s): Random

Skellig. David Almond. Read by David Almond. 2 cass. (Running Time: 2 hrs. 13 mins.). (J). 2000. 18.00 (978-0-7366-9025-6(5)) Books on Tape.
Michael's family moves to a new house & everything starts to go wrong, his baby sister is ill, his parents are frantic & Dr. Death has come to call. One day in the crumbling garage, he discovers something beneath the spider webs & dead flies.

Skellig. abr. ed. David Almond. Read by David Almond. 2 cass. (Running Time: 3 hrs.). (J). 1999. 15.00 (978-1-84032-224-8(1)) Ulvrscrft Audio.
Michael steps into the crumbling garage & discovers something beneath the spider's webs & dead flies. Is it a human being, or a strange kind of beast never seen before?.

Skellig. unabr. ed. David Almond. (ENG.). (J). (gr. 5). 2009. audio compact disk 27.00 (978-0-7393-8585-2(2), Listening Lib) Pub: Random Audio Pubg. Dist(s): Random

Skepticism & Religious Relativism. unabr. ed. Nicholas Capaldi. Read by Ben Kingsley. (Running Time: 10800 sec.). (Religion, Scriptures, & Spirituality Ser.). 2006. audio compact disk 25.95 (978-0-7861-6492-9(1)) Pub: Blckstn Audio. Dist(s): NetLibrary CO

Skepticism & Religious Relativism. unabr. ed. Nicholas Capaldi. Read by Ben Kingsley. Ed. by Walter Harrelson & Mike Hassell. 2 cass. (Running Time: 3 hrs.). Dramatization. (Religion, Scriptures & Spirituality Ser.). 1994. 17.95 (978-1-56823-020-7(6), 10463) Knowledge Prod.
The longstanding ideas of humanism, agnosticism, & atheism have increasingly challenged traditional religious doctrines or practices. Yet reason alone often fails to secure the commitments & values of a healthy personal & communal life; spiritual & emotional life can diminish to the dangerous level of nihilism & despair. Meanwhile, some theologians have challenged the "truth" of any religion with the radical view that all beliefs are equally true. These tapes explore how religious commitment can be reconciled with life in a rational, skeptical world.

***Skeptics & Believers: Religious Debate in the Western Intellectual Tradition.** Instructed by Tyler Roberts. 2009. 199.95 (978-1-59803-609-1(2)); audio compact disk 269.95 (978-1-59803-610-7(6)) Teaching Co.

Skeptic's Despair: Ecc. 3:16-4:3. Ed Young. 1993. 4.95 (978-0-7417-1982-9(7), 982) Win Walk.

Sketch of Chinese History. 2 cass. (Running Time: 2 hrs.). 1985. 7.95 Incl. supp. materials) Set. (978-0-88710-093-2(7)) Yale Far Eastern Pubns.

Sketches by Boz. Charles Dickens. Read by Anais 9000. 2008. 33.95 (978-1-60112-192-9(X)) Babblebooks.

Sketches of Spain. Perf. by Miles Davis. 1 cass., 1 CD. 4.78 (CBS 65142); audio compact disk 9.58 CD Jewel box. (CBS 65142) NewSound.

Skies of Pern. unabr. ed. Anne McCaffrey. Read by Dick Hill. 10 cass. (Running Time: 14 hrs.). (Dragonriders of Pern Ser.). 2001. 34.95 (978-1-58788-065-0(2), 1587880652, BAU); 107.25 (978-1-58788-066-7(0), 1587880660, Unabridge Lib Edns) Brilliance Audio.
The magic of Anne McCaffrey's dragons and their riders lives on, in this exciting new adventure for all McCaffrey fans - and especially for lovers of her bestselling Dragonriders of Pern series. Now that Pern can look forward to a future without the threat of Threadfall, the people are free to leave their protective stone holds and spread across more of the planet, as well as improve their lives with the newly discovered ancient technology. Not everyone is happy, though. Some resist the change, and consider anything new to be an "abomination." And the dragonriders are uncertain: without Thread, what will their purpose be in Pernese society? Then a new danger - again from the skies - looms. Once again, the people must pull together . . . And turn to the only ones who can solve the crisis: the dragonriders of Pern!.

Skies of Pern. unabr. ed. Anne McCaffrey. Read by Dick Hill. (Running Time: 14 hrs.). (Dragonriders of Pern Ser.). 2004. 39.25 (978-1-59335-445-9(2), 1593354452, Brlnc Audio MP3 Lib) Brilliance Audio.

Skies of Pern. unabr. ed. Anne McCaffrey. Read by Dick Hill. (Running Time: 16 hrs.). (Dragonriders of Pern Ser.). 2004. 39.25 (978-1-59710-710-5(7), 1597107107, BADLE); 24.95 (978-1-59710-711-2(5), 1597107115, BAD) Brilliance Audio.

Skies of Pern. unabr. ed. Anne McCaffrey. Read by Dick Hill. (Running Time: 16 hrs.). (Dragonriders of Pern Ser.). 2007. audio compact disk 117.25 (978-1-4233-3396-8(9), 9781423333968, BriAudCD Unabrid); audio compact disk 38.95 (978-1-4233-3395-1(0), 9781423333951, Bril Audio CD Unabri) Brilliance Audio.

Skies of Pern. unabr. ed. Anne McCaffrey. Read by Dick Hill. (Running Time: 14 hrs.). (Pern Ser.). 2004. 24.95 (978-1-59335-165-6(8), 1593351658) Soulmate Audio Bks.

Skiing. 1 cass. (Running Time: 60 min.). 10.95 (SP7) Psych Res Inst.

Skiing Banff. unabr. ed. Gail Taylor. Read by Gail Taylor. Ed. by James B. Kirgan. 1 cass. (Running Time: 1 hr. 30 min.). (Essence of Nature Ser.: Vol. 3). (J). 1989. 12.99 stereo. (978-1-878362-03-2(8)) Emerald Ent.

On this tape Thumper, the adventure dog, skies across the Columbia Ice Fields & down into the Banff National Park in Canada. This tape includes the actual sounds of nature in this Canadian National Park.

Skiing with the Wind. Barrie Konicov. 1 cass. 11.98 (978-0-87082-424-1(4), 120) Potentials.

The author explains how to breathe, slowly exhale, move down the slopes & be at one with your skiis.

Skill-Building System Set: Teaching Students Strategies for Successful Living. Bertie Ryan Synowiec. (Successful Living Ser.). (YA). (gr. 7 up). 1997. pap. bk. 199.95 (978-1-885335-10-4(5)) Positive Support.

Skill Cd-Calc Earl Trans. 5th ed. (C). 2002. audio compact disk 16.95 (978-0-534-39326-7(8)) Pub: Brooks-Cole. Dist(s): CENGAGE Learn

***Skill Development Drills Timing Audio Files CD.** Pat Mantabe. 2010. 0.00 (978-0-9828538-9-4(0)) South Coast.

Skill Development Model to Help Others Change. Gary Applegate. 2 cass. 1986. 20.00 Berringer Pub.

Skill Development's founder, Dr. Gary Applegate, presents the unique Skill Development approach to successful change.

Skill Measure: Microsoft Access 2000. Presenting Solutions Staff. 2000. audio compact disk 12.95 (978-0-619-02116-0(0)) Course Tech.

Skillful Means & Wisdom Seminar. Read by Chogyam Trungpa. 4 cass., 3 pts. 1976. 25.00 Pt. 1. (A026); 43.00 Pt. 2. (A026); 34.00 Pt. 3. (A026) Vajradhatu.

Eighteen talks: An overview of the 3 yana path. Part One: Hinayana, 5 talks; Part Two: Mahayana, 7 talks; Part Three: Vajrayana, 6 talks. It is recommended that the Vajrayana material be studied only after the Hinayana & Mahayana talks.

Skillful Means & Wisdom Seminar Pt. I: Hinayana. 2 cass. 1976. 25.00 Vajradhatu.

Talks about impulse & deception, mind, true renunciation, expectations & answers & meditation in action.

Skillful Means & Wisdom Seminar Pt. II: Mahayana. 4 cass. 1976. 43.00 Vajradhatu.

Explores the expansive approach, heroism of Bodhicitta, the Paramitas, discipline & patience, exertion & meditation, Prajna & Vajra-like Samadhi.

Skillful Means & Wisdom Seminar Pt. III: Vajrayana. 3 cass. 1976. 34.00 Vajradhatu.

Discusses Vajradhatu & Dharmadhatu, theism & nontheism, The Vajra Master, Samaya, Deception & Discipline, skillfull means & wisdom.

Skillfull & Godly Wisdom for Today's Women. Terri Pearsons. 7 CDs. 2006. audio compact disk (978-1-57562-852-3(X)) K Copeland Pubns.

Skills & Strategies. 2nd ed. Deborah Phillips. 2002. 51.10 (978-0-201-84677-5(2)) Longman.

Skills for Management Effectiveness. Roger Burgraff. 6 cass. (Running Time: 6 hrs.). 1991. pap. bk. 79.50 bklt. (978-0-88432-437-9(0), S03050) J Norton Pubs.

Success at work can be improved via this practical approach to interpersonal effectiveness.

Skills for Managing Conflict: National Association of Evangelicals, 47th Annual Convention, Columbus, Ohio, March 7-9, 1989. Richard Blackburn. 1 cass. (Workshops Ser.: No. 14-Wednesd). 1989. 4.24 ea. 1-8 tapes.; 4.00 ea. 9 tapes or more. Nat Assn Evan.

Skills for Personal & Family Living: Teaching Package PowerZone Challenge Game. Frances Baynor Parnell. (gr. 8-12). 2004. audio compact disk 118.64 (978-1-59070-106-5(2)) Goodheart.

Skills for Personal & Family Living: Teaching Package Teacher's Resource (Windows) Frances Baynor Parnell. (gr. 8-12). tchr. ed. 200.00 (978-1-59070-105-8(4)) Goodheart.

Skills of Constructive Negotiating. Scott. 1990. audio compact disk 61.95 (978-0-566-02812-0(3)) Ashgate Pub Co.

Skimper-Scamper/My Wild Woolly. Created by Steck-Vaughn Staff. (Running Time: 446 sec.). (Primary Take-Me-Home Books Level A Ser.). 1998. 9.80 (978-0-8172-8659-0(4)) SteckVau.

Skin. Ted Dekker. Read by Adam Verner. (Playaway Adult Fiction Ser.). (ENG.). 2009. 60.00 (978-1-60775-597-5(1)) Find a World.

Skin. unabr. ed. Ted Dekker. Narrated by Adam Verner. (ENG.). 2007. 24.49 (978-1-60814-386-3(4)); audio compact disk 34.99 (978-1-59859-231-3(9)) Oasis Audio.

Skin & Blister. Victoria Blake & Trudy Harris. 2008. 76.95 (978-1-84652-209-3(9)); audio compact disk 89.95 (978-1-84652-210-9(2)) Pub: Magna Story GBR. Dist(s): Ulverscroft US

Skin & Its Disorders. Milady Publishing Company Staff. 1 cass. (Standard Ser.: Chapter 21). 1995. 9.95 (978-1-56253-293-2(6), Milady) Delmar.

***Skin Deep.** unabr. ed. Nora Roberts. Read by Marie Caliendo. (Running Time: 7 hrs.). (O'Hurleys Ser.). 2010. 14.99 (978-1-4418-5740-8(0), 9781441857408, Brilliance MP3); 39.97 (978-1-4418-5741-5(9), 9781441857415, Brinc Audio MP3 Lib); 39.97 (978-1-4418-5742-2(7), 9781441857422, BADLE); audio compact disk 14.99 (978-1-4418-5738-5(9), 9781441857385, Bril Audio CD Unabri); audio compact disk 79.97 (978-1-4418-5739-2(7), 9781441857392, BriAudCD Unabrid) Brilliance Audio.

Skin Deep: A Body of Evidence Thriller. unabr. ed. Christopher Golden. Narrated by Julie Dretzin. 5 pieces. (Running Time: 7 hrs.). (gr. 9 up). 2000. 45.00 (978-1-4025-0998-8(7), 96681) Recorded Bks.

Jenna Blake's second semester in college is off to a good start. She has a new boyfriend and a job she loves in the county medical examiner's office. Then an African-American couple on campus is brutally attacked. Racial tension suddenly floods her normally liberal campus. The African-American students don't think the police are doing all they can to find the killer. When a white student is killed, the campus erupts in a storm of protests, rallies and peace marches. As the violence escalates, Jenna finds herself defending her own interracial romance and frantically looking for clues to the killer's identity.

Skin Healing. Steven Gurgevich. (ENG.). 2004. audio compact disk 19.95 (978-1-932170-25-2(1), HWH) Tranceformation.

Skin Hunger. unabr. ed. Kathleen Duey. Narrated by Andy Paris. 9 CDs. (Running Time: 10 hrs.). (Resurrection of Magic Ser.: Bk. 1). (YA). (gr. 7 up). 2008. audio compact disk 97.75 (978-1-4361-1616-9(3)); 67.75 (978-1-4361-1611-4(2)) Recorded Bks.

Kathleen Duey launches a mesmerizing trilogy with a book that has been honored as a National Book Award Finalist. In Sadima's time, magic has been banned and she is forced to hide her ability to communicate with animals. But then a young nobleman bent on bringing magic back to the world sends his servant to find Sadima, and a new life opens before her. Centuries later, an academy of magic welcomes 10 applicants, but only one will graduate.

Skin I'm In. unabr. ed. 3 cass. (Running Time: 4 hrs.). 2004. 28.75 (978-1-4025-8472-5(5)) Recorded Bks.

Maleeka Madison is a dark-skinned African-American girl. She feels uncomfortable and wishes she had lighter skin. When her teacher, Miss Saunders, who suffers from a rare skin condition, shows that there is more to people than the color of their skin, Maleeka learns to appreciate and accept who she truly is. Sisi Aisha Johnson's gripping narration makes this story come.

***Skin Map.** unabr. ed. Stephen R. Lawhead. (Bright Empires Ser.). 2010. audio compact disk 29.99 (978-1-4003-1673-1(1)) Nelson.

Skin Problems. Bruce Goldberg. (ENG.). 2005. audio compact disk 17.00 (978-1-57968-045-9(3)) Pub: B Goldberg. Dist(s): Baker Taylor

Skin Problems. Bruce Goldberg. 1 cass. (Running Time: 20 min.). (ENG.). 2006. 13.00 (978-1-885577-12-2(5)) Pub: B Goldberg. Dist(s): Baker Taylor

This self hypnosis program trains the listener to build up their immune system to overcome skin problems.

Skin Tight. unabr. ed. Carl Hiaasen. Narrated by George Wilson. 10 cass. (Running Time: 14 hrs. 45 mins.). 1993. 85.00 (978-1-55690-846-0(6), 93213E7) Recorded Bks.

A famous plastic surgeon performs a fatal nose job & will stop at nothing - not even murder - to keep the world from discovering the truth.

Skin Trade. abr. ed. Laurell K. Hamilton. Read by Kimberly Alexis. (Running Time: 9 hrs.). (Anita Blake, Vampire Hunter Ser.: No. 17). (ENG.). (gr. 12 up). 2009. audio compact disk 29.95 (978-0-14-314518-9(5), PengAudBks) Penguin Grp USA.

Skin Trade. unabr. ed. Laurell K. Hamilton. Read by Kimberly Alexis. (Running Time: 19 hrs.). (Anita Blake, Vampire Hunter Ser.: No. 17). (ENG.). (gr. 12 up). 2009. audio compact disk 39.95 (978-0-14-314517-2(7)) Penguin Grp USA.

***Skin Trade.** unabr. ed. Laurell K. Hamilton. Read by Kimberly Alexis. 15 CDs. (Running Time: 18 hrs. 15 mins.). (Anita Blake, Vampire Hunter Ser.: No. 17). 2009. audio compact disk 100.00 (978-1-4159-6743-0(1), BksonTape) Pub: Random Audio Pubg. Dist(s): Random

Skin Walkers. Scott Handcock. 2009. audio compact disk 15.95 (978-1-84435-376-7(1)) Pub: Big Finish GBR. Dist(s): Natl Bk Netwk

Skinned. unabr. ed. Robin Wasserman. Read by Kate Reinders. 1 MP3-CD. (Running Time: 9 hrs.). 2008. 24.99 (978-1-4233-7470-1(3), 9781423374701, Brilliance MP3); 24.99 (978-1-4233-7472-5(X), 9781423374725, BAD); 39.97 (978-1-4233-7471-8(1), 9781423374718, Brinc Audio MP3 Lib); 39.97 (978-1-4233-7473-2(8), 9781423374732, BADLE); audio compact disk 29.99 (978-1-4233-7468-8(1), 9781423374688, Bril Audio CD Unabri); audio compact disk 72.97 (978-1-4233-7469-5(X), 9781423374695, BriAudCD Unabrid) Brilliance Audio.

Skinner's Ghost. unabr. ed. Quintin Jardine. Read by James Bryce. 10 cass. (Running Time: 15 hrs.). 2001. 84.95 (978-0-7531-1022-5(9), 001112) Pub: ISIS Audio GBR. Dist(s): ISIS Pub

Deputy Chief Constable Bob Skinner could be forgiven for thinking that someone is out to get him. With his marriage already on the rocks, he suddenly finds his private life plastered across the pages of a tabloid. And then a woman already linked to Skinner by tragedy is found dead, with her young son a kidnap victim. Skinner finds himself at the center of a deadly maze of conspiracy & unless he can clear his name he stands to lose everything.

Skinner's Ghost. unabr. ed. Quintin Jardine. Read by James Bryce. 10 CDs. (Running Time: 11 hrs. 15 min.). (Isis Ser.). (J). 2001. audio compact disk 89.95 (978-0-7531-1271-7(X)) Pub: ISIS Lrg Prnt GBR. Dist(s): Ulverscroft US

Skinner's Mission. unabr. ed. Quintin Jardine. Read by Robbie MacNab. 8 cass. (Running Time: 10 hrs. 35 mins.). 1999. 83.95 (978-1-85903-291-6(5)) Pub: Magna Story GBR. Dist(s): Ulverscroft US

When an Edinburgh car showroom is torched, leaving a badly charred body, Deputy Chief Constable Bob Skinner wonders if a life of crime has finally caught up with the owner, Jackie Charles. But the corpse turns out to be that of Jackie's wife, Carole. Skinner's number one priority, though, is a murder much closer to home. The question of how his first wife, Myra, really died has become an obsession. As he & his daughter, Alex, unlock the hidden secrets of Myra's past, they discover her bloody fate is linked inextricably across the years with the death of Carole Charles.

***Skinning of Black Coyote.** Henry W. Allen. 2009. (978-1-60136-475-3(X)) Audio Holding.

Skinning of Black Coyote. Will Henry. (Running Time: 0 hr. 42 mins.). 2000. 10.95 (978-1-60083-526-1(0)) Iofy Corp.

Skinny Bastard: A Kick-in-the-Ass for Real Men Who Want to Stop Being Fat & Start Getting Buff. unabr. ed. Rory Freedman & Kim Barnouin. Read by Hillary Huber. (Running Time: 4 hrs.). 2009. audio compact disk 24.95 (978-1-4332-7986-7(X)) Blckstn Audio.

Skinny Bastard: A Kick-in-the-Ass for Real Men Who Want to Stop Being Fat & Start Getting Buff. unabr. ed. Rory Freedman & Kim Barnouin. (Running Time: 4 hrs. 0 mins.). 2009. 29.95 (978-1-4332-7987-4(8)); 24.95 (978-1-4332-7983-6(5)); audio compact disk 40.00 (978-1-4332-7984-3(3)) Blckstn Audio.

Skinny Bitch: A No-Nonsense, Tough-Love Guide for Savvy Girls Who Want to Stop Eating Crap & Start Looking Fabulous! deluxe unabr. ed. Rory Freedman & Kim Barnouin. Read by Renée Raudman. 5 CDs. (Running Time: 4 hrs. 30 mins. 0 sec.). (ENG.). 2007. audio compact disk 34.99 (978-1-4001-0563-2(3)) Pub: Tantor Media. Dist(s): IngramPubServ

Skinny Bitch: A No-Nonsense, Tough-Love Guide for Savvy Girls Who Want to Stop Eating Crap & Start Looking Fabulous! unabr. ed. Rory Freedman & Kim Barnouin. Read by Renée Raudman. (YA). 2008. 44.99 (978-1-60514-607-2(2)) Find a World.

Skinny Bitch: A No-Nonsense, Tough-Love Guide for Savvy Girls Who Want to Stop Eating Crap & Start Looking Fabulous! unabr. ed. Rory Freedman & Kim Barnouin. Narrated by Renée Raudman. 4 CDs. (Running Time: 4 hrs. 0 mins. 0 sec.). (ENG.). 2007. audio compact disk 24.99 (978-1-4001-0562-5(5)) Pub: Tantor Media. Dist(s): IngramPubServ

Skinny Bitch: A No-Nonsense, Tough-Love Guide for Savvy Girls Who Want to Stop Eating Crap & Start Looking Fabulous! unabr. ed. Rory Freedman & Kim Barnouin. Read by Renée Raudman. 1 MP3-CD. (Running Time: 4 hrs. 0 mins. 0 sec.). (ENG.). 2007. 19.99 (978-1-4001-5562-0(2)); audio compact disk 49.99 (978-1-4001-3562-2(1)) Pub: Tantor Media. Dist(s): IngramPubServ

Skinny Bitch & Skinny Bitch in the Kitch. deluxe unabr. ed. Rory Freedman & Kim Barnouin. Read by Renée Raudman. 1 MP3-CD. (Running Time: 4 hrs. 30 mins. 0 sec.). (ENG.). 2007. audio compact disk 24.99 (978-1-4001-5563-7(0)) Pub: Tantor Media. Dist(s): IngramPubServ

Skinny Bitch & Skinny Bitch in the Kitch. unabr. deluxe ed. Rory Freedman & Kim Barnouin. Read by Renée Raudman. 5 CDs. (Running Time: 4 hrs. 30 mins. 0 sec.). (ENG.). 2007. audio compact disk 69.99 (978-1-4001-3563-9(X)) Pub: Tantor Media. Dist(s): IngramPubServ

***Skinny Bitch Deluxe Edition: Promotional.** unabr. ed. Rory Freedman & Kim Barnouin. Narrated by Renée Raudman. (Running Time: 4 hrs. 30 mins. 0 sec.). (ENG.). 2010. audio compact disk 14.95 (978-1-4001-2026-0(8)) Pub: Tantor Media. Dist(s): IngramPubServ

Skinny Dip. abr. ed. Carl Hiaasen. Read by Barry Bostwick. 4 CDs. (Running Time: 5 hrs.). (ENG.). 2005. audio compact disk 14.99 (978-0-7393-2087-7(4)) Pub: Random Audio Pubg. Dist(s): Random

Skinny Dip. unabr. ed. Carl Hiaasen. 4 cass. (Running Time: 6 hrs.). 2004. 81.00 (978-1-4159-0091-8(4)); audio compact disk 84.15 (978-1-4159-0204-2(6)) Pub: Books on Tape. Dist(s): NetLibrary CO

When Chaz Perron's wife discovers that he is posing as a marine biologist, he tries to kill her-but she 'comes back' to haunt him.

Skinny Man. unabr. ed. James Colbert. Narrated by Mark Hammer. 5 cass. (Running Time: 6 hrs. 30 mins.). 1993. 44.00 (978-1-55690-930-6(6), 93426E7) Recorded Bks.

A cop on suspension for questionable behavior investigates a deadly fire.

Skinny Melon & Me. Jean Ure. Read by Eve Karpf. 3 cass. (Running Time: 3 hrs. 40 min.). (J). 2001. 15.95 (978-0-7540-5214-2(1)) AudioGO.

Cherry's English teacher says that keeping a diary is a good way to unclog your head of all the bits & pieces that worry you or make you angry. So that's just what Cherry & Skinny Melon do.

Skinny Women Are Evil: Note of a Big Girl in a Small-Minded World. abr. ed. Mo'Nique. 2004. 11.95 (978-0-7435-4779-6(9)) Pub: S&S Audio. Dist(s): S and S Inc

Skinnygirl Rules: For Getting & Staying Naturally Thin. adpt. unabr. ed. Bethenny Frankel. Read by Bethenny Frankel. 3 CDs. (Running Time: 3 hrs. 0 mins. 0 sec.). 2009. audio compact disk 14.99 (978-1-4423-0050-7(7)) Pub: S&S Audio. Dist(s): S and S Inc

Skinwalkers. Tony Hillerman. Read by Tony Hillerman. 2 cass. (Running Time: 3 hrs.). 1990. 15.95 HarperCollins Pubs.

Skinwalkers. Tony Hillerman. Read by Walter Hawn. 4 cass. (Running Time: 6 hrs.). (Joe Leaphorn & Jim Chee Novel Ser.). 1993. 39.80 Set. (978-1-56544-007-4(2), 250032); Rental 7.30 30 day rental Set. (250032) Literate Ear.

For the first time, officer Jim Chee & Lieutenant Joe Leaphorn appear together to solve a crime in which, it seems, Jim Chee is somehow personally involved.

Skinwalkers. Tony Hillerman. Read by George Guidall. 4. (Running Time: 7 Hours). (Joe Leaphorn & Jim Chee Novel Ser.). 19.95 (978-1-4025-4531-3(2)); audio compact disk 2003.00 (978-1-4025-4532-0(0)) Recorded Bks.

Skinwalkers. abr. ed. Tony Hillerman. Read by Tony Hillerman. 2 cass. (Running Time: 4 hrs.). (Joe Leaphorn & Jim Chee Novel Ser.). 1991. 18.00 (978-1-55994-166-2(9), CPN 2152) HarperCollins Pubs.

Skinwalkers. unabr. ed. Tony Hillerman. Read by Jonathan Marosz. 6 cass. (Running Time: 6 hrs.). (Joe Leaphorn & Jim Chee Novel Ser.). 1994. 48.00 (978-0-7366-2795-5(2), 3510) Books on Tape.

Jim Chee & Lt. Joe Leaphorn enter a dark world of ritual witchcraft & blood - all tied to the elusive, evil "skinwalker".

Skinwalkers. unabr. ed. Tony Hillerman. Narrated by George Guidall. 5 cass. (Running Time: 7 hrs.). (Joe Leaphorn & Jim Chee Novel Ser.). 1990. 44.00 (978-1-55690-480-6(0), 90074E7) Recorded Bks.

Lieutenant Joe Leaphorn & his colleague, Sergeant Jim Chee, set out to solve a trail of murders.

Skip-a-Star: The Legend of the Christmas Snow. 2nd ed. Carolyn E. Graves. (Skip-a-Star Ser.: Bk. 1). (J). (gr. 2-4). 1993. 5.00 (978-1-882716-04-3(3)) PAVE.

Skip-Counting. Sundance/Newbridge, LLC Staff. (Early Math Ser.). (gr. k-1). 2000. 12.00 (978-1-58273-880-2(7)) Sund Newbrdge.

Skip Counting Songs. Narrated by Caryl Schlicher. Lyrics by Caryl Schlicher. A Bridge To Excellence. (ENG.). (J). 2009. audio compact disk 15.95 (978-0-9841942-1-6(5)) Bridg Excel.

Skip Gorman: New Englander's Choice. 1 cass. 9.98 (C-95) Folk-Legacy.

A wide variety of popular New England fiddle tunes.

Skip Gorman: Trail to Mexico. 1 cass. 9.98 (C-103) Folk-Legacy.

More excellent & unusual western songs & tunes.

Skip, Hop & Wobble - Dobro Edition. Transcribed by Stacy Phillips. 1997. pap. bk. 24.95 (978-0-7866-3098-1(1), 95765CDP) Mel Bay.

Skipper Ireson's Ride see **Barefoot Boy**

Skipping Christmas/Christmas with the Kranks: A Novel. unabr. ed. John Grisham. Read by Dennis Boutsikaris. 2001. 28.00 (978-0-7366-8856-7(0)); audio compact disk 32.00 (978-0-7366-8857-4(9)) Books on Tape.

Skippyjon Jones. Judy Schachner. Narrated by Robert Ramirez. (Running Time: 30 mins.). (Skippyjon Jones Ser.). (J). 2003. audio compact disk 12.75 (978-1-4193-1749-1(0)) Recorded Bks.

Skirmish see **Tom McGuane Reads Three Untitled Short Stories from Work in Progress**

Skirt. unabr. ed. Gary Soto. Narrated by Eileen Galindo. 1 cass. (Running Time: 1 hr. 30 mins.). (gr. 4 up). 1993. 10.00 (978-1-55690-875-0(X), 93317E7) Recorded Bks.

When Miata leaves her folkorico skirt on the school bus, she needs all her wits to get it back without her parent's finding out that she had lost something yet again. A captivating introduction to the culture & traditions of Mexico.

Skirt Man. unabr. ed. Shelly Reuben. Read by Anna Fields. (Running Time: 21600 sec.). 2006. 44.95 (978-0-7861-4874-5(8)); audio compact disk 45.00 (978-0-7861-6038-9(1)); audio compact disk 29.95 (978-0-7861-7122-4(7)) Blckstn Audio.

Skits in English. Mary E. Hines. (C). (gr. 9-12). 1987. bk. 105.00 (978-0-13-812421-2(3), 58855) Prentice ESL.

Skorzeny Project. unabr. ed. Clive Egleton. Read by Christopher Kay. 11 cass. (Running Time: 16 hrs. 30 mins.). 2001. 89.95 (978-1-86042-545-5(3), 25453) Pub: Soundings Ltd GBR. Dist(s): Ulverscroft US

Skulduggery. unabr. ed. Mark Shand. Read by Paul Shelley. 4 cass. (Running Time: 4 hrs.). (Mini-CAB Audio Bks.). 1994. 39.95 (978-0-7451-4345-3(8), CAB 1028) AudioGO.

Mark Shand takes a fascinating journey to New Guinea, into the heart of cannibal & orangutan country. So begins a vivid account by Shand through the wilds of New Guinea where his stops include: canoeing down untamed rivers, negotiating with a village of headhunters, & their eventual encounter with hundreds of orangutans.

***Skulduggery Pleasant.** unabr. ed. Derek Landy. Read by Rupert Degas. (ENG.). 2007. (978-0-06-144891-1(5)); (978-0-06-134106-9(1)) HarperCollins Pubs.

Skulduggery Pleasant. unabr. ed. Derek Landy. Read by Rupert Degas. 6 CDs. (Running Time: 7 hrs. 30 mins.). (Skulduggery Pleasant Ser.: Bk. 3).

(J). (gr. 3-7). 2007. audio compact disk 27.95 (978-0-06-134104-5(5), Harper Audio) HarperCollins Pubs.

*Skulduggery Pleasant: Playing with Fire. unabr. ed. Derek Landy. Read by Rupert Degas. (ENG.). 2008. (978-0-06-171450-4(X)); (978-0-06-171575-4(1)) HarperCollins Pubs.

*Skulduggery Pleasant: the Faceless Ones. unabr. ed. Derek Landy. Read by Rupert Degas. (ENG.). 2009. (978-0-06-180834-0(2)); (978-0-06-180832-6(6)) HarperCollins Pubs.

Skull & Rose. John Buckmann. 4 CDs. (Running Time: 6 hrs.). 2005. audio compact disk 24.95 (978-0-660-18917-8(8)) Pub: Canadian Broadcasting CAN. Dist(s): Georgetown Term

*Skull Beneath the Skin: A BBC Full-Cast Radio Drama. P. D. James. Narrated by Greta Scaachi. 3 CDs. (Running Time: 3 hrs. 0 mins. 0 sec.). (ENG.). 2010. audio compact disk 29.95 (978-0-563-52931-6(8)) Pub: AudioGO. Dist(s): Perseus Dist

Skull Beneath the Skin: A BBC Full-Cast Radio Drama. unabr. ed. P. D. James. Read by Penelope Dellaporta. 11 cass. (Running Time: 16 hrs. 30 min.). 1994. 88.00 (978-0-7366-2647-7(6), 3384) Books on Tape.
Clarissa Lisle, an actress famous for her beauty & intrigue, wins a starring role on the death-shrouded island of Courcy. It's Clarissa's last performance, & Cordelia Gray, searching for clues, finds everything turns to illusion...except her quest, where it's her life or the murderer's.

Skull Beneath the Skin: Radio Dramatization. abr. ed. P. D. James. 3 CDs. (Running Time: 4 hrs. 30 mins.). 2003. audio compact disk 39.95 (978-0-563-49608-3(8), BBCD 016) BBC Worldwide.

Skull of Truth. Bruce Coville. Read by Bruce Coville. 3 cass. (Running Time: 4 hrs. 30 mins.). (Magic Shop Bks.). (J). 2000. 24.00 (978-0-7366-9140-6(5)) Books on Tape.
The third Magic Shop book delivers an uproarious tale of truth & far-out consequences when Charlie Eggleston stumbles into Mr. Elives' strange store & departs with the "skull of truth".

Skull of Truth. unabr. ed. Bruce Coville. Read by Full Cast Production Staff. 2 cass. (Running Time: 2 hrs.). (Magic Shop Bks.). (J). 1997. 23.00 (LL 0100, Chivers Child Audio) AudioGO.

Skull of Truth, unabr. ed. Bruce Coville. 3 cass. (Running Time: 3 hrs.). (Magic Shop Bks.). (YA). 1999. 16.98 (FS9-34193) Highsmith.

Skull of Truth. unabr. ed. Bruce Coville. Read by Bruce Coville. Read by Words Take Wing Repertory Company Staff. 3 cass. (Running Time: 3 hrs. 50 min.). (Magic Shop Bks.). (J). (gr. 4-7). 1997. 30.00 (978-0-8072-7828-4(9), 496002, Listening Lib) Random Audio Pubg.
Charlie stumbles into Mr. Elives' strange store & departs with the skull of truth.

Skull of Truth. unabr. ed. Bruce Coville. Read by WTW Repertory Company. 3 cass. (Running Time: 3 hrs. 50 mins.). (Magic Shop Bks.). (J). (gr. 5-7). 1997. pap. bk. 35.00 (978-0-8072-7829-1(7), YA927SP, Listening Lib) Random Audio Pubg.

Skull Session. Daniel Hecht. Read by Christopher Lane. (Running Time: 17 hrs. 30 mins.). 2005. audio compact disk 120.00 (978-0-7861-7727-1(6)) Blckstn Audio.

Skull Session. Daniel Hecht. Read by Christopher Lane. (Running Time: 63000 sec.). 2005. 89.95 (978-0-7861-3667-4(7)); audio compact disk 44.95 (978-0-7861-7956-5(2)) Blckstn Audio.

Skull Session. Daniel Hecht. Narrated by Christopher Lane. (Running Time: 17 hrs. 30 mins.). 2005. 48.95 (978-1-59912-600-5(1)) Iofy Corp.

Skunk at Hemlock Circle. Victoria Sherrow. Illus. by Allen Davis. 1 cass. (Running Time: 1 hr.). (J). (ps-2). 1994. bk. 32.95 Incl. toy. (978-1-56899-046-0(4)) Soundprints.

Skunk at Hemlock Circle. unabr. ed. Victoria Sherrow. Read by Alexi Komisar. Illus. by Allen Davis. Narrated by Alexi Komisar. 1 cass. (Running Time: 7 min.). Dramatization. (Smithsonian's Backyard Ser.). (ENG.). (J). (ps-2). 1994. 19.95 (978-1-56899-047-7(2)); 5.00 cass. (978-1-56899-045-3(6)) Soundprints.
Cassette is a dramatized readalong of the storybook, with authentic sound effects added. It consists of two sides - one with & one without page turning signals.

Skunk Hour see Robert Lowell: A Reading

Skunk Hour from "Life Studies" see Twentieth-Century Poetry in English, No. 32-33, Recordings of Poets Reading Their Own Poetry

Skunk Works. unabr. collector's ed. Ben R. Rich & Leo Janos. Read by Arthur Addison. 9 cass. (Running Time: 13 hrs. 30 min.). 1995. 72.00 (978-0-7366-3108-2(9), 3784) Books on Tape.
Project boss Rich & co-author Janos chronicle the high-stakes drama, cold war confrontations & Gulf War air combat.

Skverniy Anekdot. Fyodor Dostoyevsky. Read by Igor Dmitriev. 1 cass. (Running Time: 1 hrs.). (RUS.). 1996. pap. bk. 19.50 (978-1-58085-553-2(9)) Interlingua VA.

Sky & the Forest. unabr. collector's ed. C. S. Forester. Read by David Case. 6 cass. (Running Time: 9 hrs.). 1992. 48.00 (978-0-7366-2120-5(2), 2923) Books on Tape.
A central African kingdom is invaded by European explorers. Helps us imagine the plight of primitive people.

Sky Bears: Winter Festival Music from Around the World. Perf. by Nancy Raven. 1 cass. (Running Time: 26 min.). (J). (ps-6). 1987. 10.00 (978-1-885292-07-0(4)) Lizards Rock.
Folk music for children, teachers.

Sky Can Still Remember. Contrib. by Sherri Youngward. 2006. audio compact disk 12.99 (978-5-558-15499-3(3)) BEC Recordings.

Sky Club. Scripts. Ian Feldman. 4 cass. (Running Time: 5 hrs. 50 mins). 2007. 29.95 (978-0-9743673-5-4(4), 0-9743673-5-4); audio compact disk 29.95 (978-0-9743673-4-7(6), 0-9743673-4-6) SSI.
A man on his final mission for Britain's MI5 unseals a secret document concealed for over fifty years revealing a shocking truth from the past:In 1939, one of the world's most renowned nuclear physicist's wrote the definitive formula for a thermonuclear bomb on a classroom chalkboard for all to see, at Cal-Tech near San Francisco.He proved that with a limited amount of Uranium-235 in a shell casing of liquid heavy hydrogen, the device would be be over five hundred times more powerful than the atomic bomb eventually dropped on Hiroshima.At the same time in 1939, a secret Nazi organization, unknown even to Churchill's MI5 and the Allies was formed in Germany using Aryan nuclear scientists and extorted American Jewish physicists to exploit that incredible formula in a diabolical conspiracy to create the world's first Hydrogen Bomb.Caught in an emotional struggle between his idealism for the Reich and exploding the Nazi's Super Bomb on innocent civilians as Germany nears it's disastrous end in 1945, the secret organization's leader Horst Deeke inevitably becomes the only Naziwith the ability to destroy it. . . .Crossing the globe, it's high-energy plot adroitly races between the forces of good and evil in a dark tale of fearless men, lavishly beautiful women and mysterious locales, beginning in the pre-war idealism of Germany's propaganda schemes.As Horst's future is viciously destroyed by his vindictive Nazi Kommandant, his transformation finally drives a fanatical revenge to destroy his own creation.But, after being stripped of his authority, he may be left powerless to stop Nazi Germany's diabolical leaders from exploding their disastrous horror somewhere in the Allied world. . .

Sky-Crasher. unabr. ed. L. Ron Hubbard. Read by Shannon Evans et al. Narrated by R. F. Daley. 2 CDs. (Running Time: 2 hrs.). (Stories from the Golden Age Ser.). 2009. audio compact disk 9.95 (978-1-59212-387-2(2)) Gala Pr LLC.

Sky Fisherman: A Novel. unabr. ed. Craig Lesley. Narrated by Ed Sala. 9 cass. (Running Time: 13 hrs.). 1997. 78.00 (978-0-7887-0722-3(1), 94899E7) Recorded Bks.
Laced with love of the great outdoors & infused with colorful local characters, this is the poignant story of a young man coming of age in a small Oregon town.

Sky Ghost. abr. ed. Mack Maloney. 2 cass. (Running Time: 3 hrs.). (Wingman Ser.: Vol. 14). 2002. 9.95 (978-1-931953-06-1(6)) Listen & Live.

Sky High/Hot Air Balloons. Steck-Vaughn Staff. 1997. (978-0-8172-7369-9(7)) SteckVau.

Sky in Gray see Bloodline

*Sky Is Everywhere. Jandy Nelson. Contrib. by Julia Whelan. (Playaway Young Adult Ser.). (ENG.). (J). 2010. 49.99 (978-1-4418-5587-9(4)) Find a World.

Sky Is Everywhere. unabr. ed. Jandy Nelson. Read by Julia Whelan. 6 CDs. (Running Time: 7 hrs.). 2010. audio compact disk 24.99 (978-1-4418-2013-6(2), 9781441820136, Bril Audio CD Unabri) Brilliance Audio.

*Sky Is Everywhere. unabr. ed. Jandy Nelson. Read by Julia Whelan. 1 MP3-CD. (Running Time: 7 hrs.). 2010. 24.99 (978-1-4418-2015-0(9), 9781441820150, Brilliance MP3); 39.97 (978-1-4418-2016-7(7), 9781441820167, Brinc Audio MP3 Lib); 24.99 (978-1-4418-2017-4(5), 9781441820174, BAD); 39.97 (978-1-4418-2018-1(3), 9781441820181, BADLE); audio compact disk 60.97 (978-1-4418-2014-3(0), 9781441820143, BriAudCD Unabrid) Brilliance Audio.

Sky Is Falling. Sidney Sheldon. Narrated by Kate Forbes. 8 CDs. (Running Time: 8 hrs. 45 mins.). 2001. audio compact disk 78.00 (978-0-7887-5152-3(2), C1315E7) Recorded Bks.
Television news anchor Dana Evans is beautiful, intelligent & fearless, having been a correspondent during the Bosnian War. But when she begins to investigate a string of murders that has wiped out one of America'a most prominent families, she is shocked.

Sky Is Falling. abr. ed. Sidney Sheldon. Read by Karen Allen. 3 CDs. (Running Time: 4 hrs.). 2004. audio compact disk 14.95 (978-0-06-059441-1(1)) HarperCollins Pubs.

*Sky Is Falling. abr. ed. Sidney Sheldon. Read by Karen Allen. (ENG.). 2004. (978-0-06-081456-4(X), Harper Audio); (978-0-06-078658-8(2), Harper Audio) HarperCollins Pubs.

Sky Is Falling. collector's unabr. ed. Sidney Sheldon. Narrated by Kate Forbes. 6 cass. (Running Time: 8 hrs. 45 mins.). 2001. 35.95 (978-0-7887-5133-2(6)) Recorded Bks.

*Sky Is Falling. unabr. ed. Sidney Sheldon. Read by Kate Forbes. (ENG.). 2004. (978-0-06-079238-1(8), Harper Audio); (978-0-06-081417-5(9), Harper Audio) HarperCollins Pubs.

Sky Is Falling. unabr. ed. Sidney Sheldon. Narrated by Kate Forbes. 6 cass. (Running Time: 8 hrs. 45 mins.). 2001. 59.00 (978-0-7887-4498-3(4), 96302E7) Recorded Bks.

Sky Is Low, the Clouds Are Mean see Poems & Letters of Emily Dickinson

Sky Island. unabr. ed. L. Frank Baum. Read by Flo Gibson. 4 cass. (Running Time: 5 hrs. 30 min.). (J). (gr. 2-4). 1989. 19.95 (978-1-55685-138-4(3)) Audio Bk Con.
A magic umbrella transports Trot, Buttonbright & Captain Bill to an island in the sky inhabited by the blues, the pinks & the evil Boolooroo.

Sky-Liners. unabr. ed. Louis L'Amour. Read by Jason Culp. (Running Time: 21600 sec.). (Sacketts Ser.: No. 13). (ENG.). 2008. audio compact disk 25.95 (978-0-7393-4222-0(3), Random AudioBks) Pub: Random Audio Pubg. Dist(s): Random

Sky of Stone. unabr. ed. Homer H. Hickam, Jr. Read by Dick Hill. (Running Time: 12 hrs.). 2004. 39.25 (978-1-59710-713-6(1), 1597107131, BADLE); 24.95 (978-1-59710-712-9(3), 1597107123, BAD) Brilliance Audio.

Sky of Stone: A Memoir. unabr. ed. Homer H. Hickam, Jr. Read by Dick Hill. 9 cass. (Running Time: 12 hrs.). 2001. 34.95 (978-1-58788-884-7(X), 158788884X, BAU); 96.25 (978-1-58788-885-4(8), 1587888858, Unabridge Lib Edns) Brilliance Audio.
In the summer of '61, Homer "Sonny" Hickam, a year of college behind him, is dreaming of sandy beaches and rocket ships. But before Sonny can reach the seaside fixer-upper where his mother is spending the summer, a telephone call sends him back to the place he thought he had escaped, the gritty coal-mining town of Coalwood, West Virginia. There, Sonny's father, the mine's superintendent, has been accused of negligence in a man's death. Sonny's mother, Elsie, has commanded her son to spend the summer in Coalwood to support his father. But within hours of his arrival, Sonny realizes two things: His father, always cold and distant with his second son, doesn't want him there... and his parents' marriage has begun to unravel. For Sonny, so begins a summer of discovery - a time when he will learn about love, loss, and a closely guarded secret that threatens to destroy his father and his town. As the days of summer grow shorter, Sonny finds himself changing in surprising ways, taking the first real steps toward adulthood. But it's a journey he can make only by unraveling the story of a man's death and a father's secret - the mysteries that lie at the heart of Coalwood.

Sky of Stone: A Memoir. unabr. ed. Homer H. Hickam, Jr. Read by Dick Hill. (Running Time: 12 hrs.). 2004. 39.25 (978-1-59335-529-6(7), 1593355297, Brinc Audio MP3 Lib) Brilliance Audio.

Sky of Stone: A Memoir. unabr. ed. Homer H. Hickam, Jr. Read by Dick Hill. (Running Time: 12 hrs.). 2004. 24.95 (978-1-59335-182-3(8), 1593351828) Soulmate Audio Bks.

Sky Over Taos: A. Invocation; B. Dusk; C. Morning Song see Twentieth-Century Poetry in English, No. 1, Recordings of Poets Reading Their Own Poetry

Sky Passage. 1 cass. (Running Time: 45 min.). 1994. audio compact disk 15.95 CD. (2824, Creativ Pub) Quayside.
Kurnow's flights of natural & musical fancy.

Sky Passage. 1 cass. (Running Time: 45 min.). 1994. 9.95 (2822, NrthWrd Bks) TandN Child.

Sky People. unabr. ed. S. M. Stirling. Read by Todd McLaren. (YA). 2008. 64.99 (978-1-60514-754-3(0)) Find a World.

Sky People. unabr. ed. S. M. Stirling. Narrated by Todd McLaren. (Running Time: 10 hrs. 30 mins. 0 sec.). (Lords of Creation Ser.). (ENG.). 2001. audio compact disk 29.99 (978-1-4001-5345-9(X)); audio compact disk 79.99 (978-1-4001-3345-1(9)) Pub: Tantor Media. Dist(s): IngramPubServ

Sky People. unabr. ed. S. M. Stirling. Narrated by Todd McLaren. 9 CDs. (Running Time: 10 hrs. 30 mins. 0 sec.). (Lords of Creation Ser.). (ENG.). 2007. audio compact disk 39.99 (978-1-4001-0345-4(2)) Pub: Tantor Media. Dist(s): IngramPubServ

Sky Rider. Nancy Springer. Narrated by Christina Moore. 3 CDs. (Running Time: 2 hrs. 45 mins.). (gr. 9 up). audio compact disk 32.00 (978-1-4025-1972-7(9)) Recorded Bks.

Sky Rider. Nancy Springer. Narrated by Christina Moore. 2 pieces. (Running Time: 2 hrs. 45 mins.). (gr. 9 up). 2001. 22.00 (978-0-7887-5313-8(4)) Recorded Bks.
Ever since Dusty's mom died, life has been rough. A car accident has permanently injured Dusty's back. Now, Dusty's crippled horse will be put down. But a curiously pale boy appears in the barn and rides away on Tazz.

Sky Suspended. Jim Bailey. Read by Graham Seed. 5 cass. (Running Time: 5 hrs. 55 mins.). (Isis Cassettes Ser.). (J). 2005. 49.95 (978-0-7531-3425-2(X)) Pub: ISIS Lrg Prnt GBR. Dist(s): Ulverscroft US

Sky Suspended. Jim Bailey. (Isis (CDs) Ser.). 2006. audio compact disk 64.95 (978-0-7531-2568-7(4)) Pub: ISIS Lrg Prnt GBR. Dist(s): Ulverscroft US

Sky Talk see Carl Sandburg's Poems for Children

Sky That Needed Mending. Chaitania Hein. Read by Chaitania Hein. Read by Bob Kechley. 1 cass. (Running Time: 60 min.). (Dance Impulse with Chaitania Ser.). (J). (ps-2). 1987. 9.99 (978-0-929676-01-2(7)) Alim Azim Prodns.
Storytelling with music & creative dance instruction.

Sky Took Him. unabr. ed. Donis Casey. (Running Time: 9 hrs. NaN mins.). 2009. 29.95 (978-1-4332-6004-9(2)); audio compact disk 59.95 (978-1-4332-6000-1(X)); audio compact disk 70.00 (978-1-4332-6001-8(8)) Blckstn Audio.

Sky Woman Falling. 2005. 79.95 (978-0-7861-4359-7(2)) Blckstn Audio.

Sky Woman Falling. Kirk Mitchell. Read by Dick Hill. (Running Time: 48600 sec.). 2005. audio compact disk 99.00 (978-0-7861-7498-0(6)) Blckstn Audio.

Sky Woman Falling. unabr. ed. Kirk Mitchell. Read by Dick Hill. 2005. 29.95 (978-0-7861-7813-1(2)) Blckstn Audio.

Skybreaker. unabr. ed. Kenneth Oppel. Read by David Kelly. (J). 2008. 54.99 (978-1-60514-608-9(0)) Find a World.

Skydancer. unabr. ed. Geoffrey Archer. Read by Bill Wallis. 8 cass. (Running Time: 8 hrs.). 2000. 69.95 (978-0-7540-0475-2(9), CAB1898) AudioGO.
Project Skydancer: the brainchild of the Ministry of Defense & terrifying in its simplicity. For Aldermaston scientist Peter Joyce, it was the pinnacle of his career. Until documents from the project turn up on Parliament Hill & he is left with two alternatives: write off a billion dollar project, or approve tests which could give Russia the power to wipe out the West at the touch of a button.

Skydive! unabr. ed. Gary Paulsen. Narrated by Jeff Woodman. 1 cass. (Running Time: 1 hr.). (Gary Paulsen's World of Adventure Ser.: Bk. 11). (gr. 4 up). 1997. 10.00 (978-0-7887-0796-4(5), 94946E7) Recorded Bks.
Jesse Rodriguez can't wait to turn 16 so he can make his first free-fall jump from a plane. But when he discovers a drug-smuggling scheme at the tiny airport he uses, he's forced to think about jumping sooner than he expected.

Skye O'Malley. abr. ed. Bertrice Small. Read by Deborah McLiam. 1 cass. (Running Time: 90 min.). 1994. 5.99 (978-1-57096-019-2(4), RAZ 920) Romance Alive Audio.
From her lush Irish homeland through the harem courts of Algiers to the stately homes of London, Skye O'Malley uses all her wit & wisdom in this classic historical romance to find love with her virile & dashing sea-captain.

Skyfire. abr. ed. Mack Maloney. 2 cass. (Running Time: 3 hrs.). (Wingman Ser.: Vol. 8). 2002. 9.95 (978-1-931953-00-9(7)) Listen & Live.

Skygods: The Fall of Pan Am. unabr. collector's ed. Robert Gandt. Read by Jonathan Reese. 9 cass. (Running Time: 13 hrs. 30 min.). 1996. 72.00 (978-0-7366-3527-1(0), 4164) Books on Tape.
In 1966, Pan Am reached the zenith of its wealth & experience. The airline rose from a Latin American mail carrier to preeminence in world commerce, making millions & commissioning the most modern fleet of planes.

Skyhook. John J. Nance. 2009. audio compact disk 9.99 (978-1-4418-2655-8(6)) Brilliance Audio.

Skyhook. abr. ed. John J. Nance. Read by John J. Nance. 5 CDs. (Running Time: 6 hrs.). 2003. audio compact disk 74.25 (978-1-59086-840-9(4), 1590868404, BACDLib Ed) Brilliance Audio.
The "boomerang box," a high-tech computer program designed to save a plane experiencing flight trouble, is Dr. Ben Cole's baby. After a test run over the Gulf of Alaska goes awry, he suspects someone has sabotaged the plane's computer systems. And mysteriously, and almost simultaneously, April Rosen is horrified to learn that her father's plane has narrowly escaped a mid-air collision over the same patch of sea. While Dr. Cole considers the uncomfortable notion that someone within his own company might wish him harm, Rosen begins her search for the cause of her father's hair-raising "near miss." But what both don't know is this: their fears have a common source. They are being watched by people in the Pentagon, who believe that the two might stumble upon the secret that will destroy them all before Skyhook has a chance to succeed. What is Skyhook's real purpose? Is it commercial or military? And will its early implementation compromise the safety of flyers everywhere?.

Skyhook. abr. ed. John J. Nance. Read by John J. Nance. 5 CDs. (Running Time: 21600 sec.). 2005. audio compact disk 16.99 (978-1-59600-408-5(8), 9781596004085, BCD Value Price) Brilliance Audio.

Skyhook. unabr. ed. John J. Nance. Read by John J. Nance. 9 cass. (Running Time: 13 hrs.). 2003. 34.95 (978-1-59086-588-0(X), 159086588X, BAU); 87.25 (978-1-59086-589-7(8), 1590865898, CD Unabrid Lib Ed) Brilliance Audio.

Skyhook. unabr. ed. John J. Nance. Read by John J. Nance. (Running Time: 13 hrs.). 2004. 39.25 (978-1-59335-429-9(0), 1593354290, Brinc Audio MP3 Lib) Brilliance Audio.

Skyhook. unabr. ed. John J. Nance. Read by John J. Nance. (Running Time: 13 hrs.). 2004. 39.25 (978-1-59710-714-3(X), 159710714X, BADLE) Brilliance Audio.

Skyhook. unabr. ed. John J. Nance. Read by John J. Nance. (Running Time: 13 hrs.). 2004. 24.95 (978-1-59335-204-2(2), 1593352042) Soulmate Audio Bks.

Skyhook. unabr. ed. John J. Nance. Read by John J. Nance. (Running Time: 13 hrs.). 2004. 24.95 (978-1-59710-715-0(8), 1597107158, BAD) Brilliance Audio.

*Skyjack: The Hunt for D. B. Cooper. unabr. ed. Geoffrey Gray. (ENG.). 2011. audio compact disk 35.00 (978-0-307-73579-9(6), Random AudioBks) Pub: Random Audio Pubg. Dist(s): Random

Skylab Mission. 1 cass. (Running Time: 27 min.). 14.95 (CBC1030) MMI Corp.
Techniques & technology of an ambitious program. Discusses two main objects, flood control & other practical applications. A 13 year-old girl converses with NASA engineers who explain the complex instrumentation.

Skylar. unabr. ed. Gregory Mcdonald. Read by Alexander Adams. 8 cass. (Running Time: 8 hrs.). (Skylar Ser.: No. 1). 1997. 48.00 (978-0-7366-3790-9(7), 4464) Books on Tape.
Everyone loves Skylar Whitfield. But it looks like Skylar's the only one who could have killed Mary Lou Simes.

Skylar. unabr. ed. Gregory Mcdonald. Read by Dick Hill. (Running Time: 8 hrs.). 2009. 39.97 (978-1-4233-7158-8(5), 9781423371588, BADLE); 39.97 (978-1-4233-7156-4(9), 9781423371564, Brinc Audio MP3 Lib); 24.99 (978-1-4233-7155-7(0), 9781423371557, Brilliance MP3); 24.99 (978-1-4233-7157-1(7), 9781423371571, BAD) Brilliance Audio.

Skylar in Yankeeland. unabr. ed. Gregory Mcdonald. Read by Alexander Adams. 6 cass. (Running Time: 6 hrs.). (Skylar Ser.: No. 2). 1998. 36.00 (978-0-7366-4007-7(X), 4505) Books on Tape.
Finds the southern playboy in Boston amid jewel heist & murder.

Skylark. unabr. ed. Jo Beverley. Narrated by Jill Tanner. 9 cass. (Running Time: 12 hrs. 45 mins.). 2004. 79.75 (978-1-4193-1197-0(2), L1133MC) Recorded Bks.

Skylark. unabr. ed. Patricia MacLachlan. Read by Glenn Close. (J). 2008. 39.99 (978-1-60514-609-6(9)) Find a World.

Skylark. unabr. ed. Patricia MacLachlan. 1 cass. (Running Time: 1 hr. 30 mins.). 2003. 7.99 (978-0-06-058461-0(0)) HarperCollins Pubs.

***Skylark.** unabr. ed. Patricia Maclachlan. Read by Glenn Close. (ENG.). 2008. (978-0-06-180014-6(7), KTegenBooks); (978-0-06-180015-3(5), KTegenBooks) HarperCollins Pubs.

Skylark. unabr. abr. ed. Patricia MacLachlan. Read by Glenn Close. 1 cass. (Running Time: 1 hr. 30 min.). (J). 2001. 12.00 (978-0-694-52595-9(2), HarperChildAud) HarperCollins Pubs.

Skylight Confessions. unabr. ed. Alice Hoffman. Read by Mare Winningham. (Running Time: 7 hrs. 30 mins.). (ENG.). 2007. 14.98 (978-1-59483-614-5(0)) Pub: Hachet Audio. Dist(s): HachBkGrp

Skylight Confessions. unabr. ed. Alice Hoffman. Read by Mare Winningham. (Running Time: 7 hrs. 30 mins.). (ENG.). 2009. 44.98 (978-1-60788-293-0(0)) Pub: Hachet Audio. Dist(s): HachBkGrp

Skylight Room see Favorite Stories by O. Henry

Sky's the Limit. Dave Arnold et al. Created by Focus on the Family Staff. (Running Time: 14400 sec.). (Adventures in Odyssey Ser.). (ENG.). (J). (gr. 4-7). 2008. audio compact disk 24.99 (978-1-58997-473-9(5), Tyndale Ent) Tyndale Hse.

Sky's the Limit. Perf. by Fred Astaire. (DD8835) Natl Recrd Co.

Sky's the Limit: Passion & Property in Manhattan. abr. ed. Steven Gaines. (ENG.). 2005. 14.98 (978-1-59483-242-0(0)) Pub: Hachet Audio. Dist(s): HachBkGrp

Sky's the Limit: Passion & Property in Manhattan. abr. ed. Steven Gaines. (Running Time: 6 hrs.). (ENG.). 2009. 44.98 (978-1-60788-048-6(2)) Pub: Hachet Audio. Dist(s): HachBkGrp

Skyway Arizona MP3. Mark Paul Sebar. 2001. 9.99 (978-1-930246-27-0(7), 1930246277) Sebar Pubng.

Skywriting: A Life Out of the Blue. unabr. ed. Jane Pauley. 2004. 25.95 (978-1-4159-0322-3(0)); audio compact disk 90.00 (978-1-4159-0001-7(9)) Books on Tape.

Slab Rat. Ted Heller. Narrated by Johnny Heller. 9 CDs. (Running Time: 11 hrs.). 2001. audio compact disk 89.00 (978-0-7887-5171-4(9), C1333E7) Recorded Bks.
Zach Post is an editor for It magazine with an impressive history: his father is a famous architect, his mother a socialite & he has attended Colgate, Berkley & Liverpool University. Or, at least that's what everyone thinks. When obnoxious new editor Mark Larkin is quickly promoted, Zach's secrets are threatened & his future no longer seems bright. But he knows what to do - Mark Larkin must be eliminated.

Slab Rat. unabr. ed. Ted Heller. Narrated by Johnny Heller. 9 cass. (Running Time: 11 hrs.). 2000. 74.00 (978-0-7887-4375-7(9), 96241E7) Recorded Bks.
The glossy magazine industry receives a scathing examination in this wicked tale about climbing the corporate ladder. Zach Post is an editor whose secret past is threatened when new company favorite Mark Larkin appears & is rapidly promoted. But Zach knows what to do with his obnoxious new co-worker. Mark Larkin must be eliminated.

Slake's Limbo. unabr. ed. Felice Holman. Read by Neil Patrick Harris. 2 vols. (Running Time: 2 hrs. 23 mins.). (J). (gr. 7 up). 2004. pap. bk. 29.00 (978-0-8072-8744-6(X), YA254SP, Listening Lib); 23.00 (978-0-8072-8743-9(1), YA254CX, Listening Lib) Random Audio Pubg.
Desperate, driven, harassed to the breaking point, Slake decides to go underground - into the sheltering depths of the New York City Subway where he ends up staying for one hundred & twenty-one days. This is the story about survival & about a 13-year-old misfit's attempts to find footing in a hostile & threatening world.

Slam. unabr. ed. Nick Hornby. Read by Nicholas Holt. 6 CDs. (Running Time: 7 hrs.). (ENG.). (J). (gr. 6-12). 2007. audio compact disk 29.95 (978-0-14-314283-6(6), PengAudBks) Penguin Grp USA.

Slam! unabr. ed. Walter Dean Myers. Narrated by Thomas Penny. 4 pieces. (Running Time: 5 hrs. 15 mins.). (gr. 9 up). 2001. 39.00 (978-0-7887-3245-4(5), 95849E7) Recorded Bks.
Greg "Slam" Harris can play basketball. But off the court, every day is a struggle to keep things together. The author reflects the hopes & desires shared by many budding stars as they chase their dreams on & off the basketball courts.

Slam! unabr. ed. Walter Dean Myers. Narrated by Thomas Penny. 4 cass. (Running Time: 5 hrs. 15 mins.). (YA). 2001. pap. bk. & stu. ed. 53.24 Recorded Bks.

Slammin' on the West Side. Perf. by Luther Johnson. 7.98 (TA 33389); audio compact disk 12.78 CD Jewel box. (TA 83389) NewSound.

Slamming Slime. Lavaille Lavette. Narrated by Cynthia Cooper. 1 cass. (Running Time: 840 sec.). (Adventures of Roopster Roux Ser.). (ENG.). (J). (gr. k-3). 1998. 5.95 (978-1-56554-401-7(3)) Pelican.
The evil Tegore is planning on taking over the town and the world with his stinky green slime. What can Roopster Roux do?.

Slan. A. E. Van Vogt. 2 cass. (Running Time: 1 hr. 10 mins.). 2001. 19.95 (ZIGG002) Lodestone Catalog.
In the 25th century mankind fought against the hated telepathic Slan race, resulting in the extermination of almost all Slans & the establishment of a worldwide police state. In the 30th century, Slan Johnny Cross has escaped extermination & is tracking down other Slans to solve the mystery of their strange existence.

Slan. A. E. Van Vogt. Adapted by Bob E. Flick. Engineer Bob E. Flick. Des. by Adam Mayefsky. 2 CDs. (Running Time: 2 hrs. 10 mins.). Dramatization. 1993. audio compact disk 19.00 (978-1-884214-16-5(9)) Ziggurat Prods.
A classic tale from one of the all-time great science-fiction authors! In the 25th Century, mankind fought the hated telepathic Slan race in the fierce "Slan Wars." The result was the extermination of almost all Slans, and the establishment of a world-wide police state. Now, in the 30th Century, Slan Jommy Cross has escaped extermination and is living in theworld of cruel humans. Amid grave danger, Jommy is determined to avoid detection, track down other surviving Slans, and with them solve the mystery of the Slans' strange existence and superiority.

Slan. abr. ed. A. E. Van Vogt. Prod. by Perry Jacob. Directed By Perry Jacob. Prod. by Bob Flick. Engineer Bob Flick. 2 cass. (Running Time: 2 hr. 30 min.). Dramatization. 1993. 12.95 (978-1-884214-00-4(2), 1-884214-00-2) Ziggurat Prods.
In time 25th-century, mankind fought the hated, telepathic Slan race in the fierce "Slan wars." Almost all Slans were exterminated. But now in the 30th-century, Johnny Cross has escaped.

Slanderer see Bet

Slangman Guide to Biz Speak 1: Slang, Idioms, & Jargon Used in Business English. Excerpts. 2 Cass. (Running Time: 2 hrs. 20mins.). (Slangman Guides to Biz Speak Ser.). Orig. Title: Biz Talk One. 2001. 25.00 (978-1-891888-36-6(6)) Slangman Pubng.

Slangman Guide to Biz Speak 1: Slang Idioms & Jargon Used in Business English. Excerpts. 2 CDs. (Running Time: 2 hrs. 20mins.). 2001. audio compact disk 35.00 (978-1-891888-35-9(8)) Slangman Pubng.

Slangman Guide to Biz Speak 2: Slang, Idioms, & Jargon Used in Business English. Excerpts. 2 Cass. (Running Time: 2 hrs. 20 mins.). (Slangman Guides to Biz Speak Ser.). Orig. Title: Biz Talk Two. 2002. 25.00 (978-1-891888-38-0(2)) Slangman Pubng.

Slangman Guide to Biz Speak 2: Slang Idioms & Jargon Used in Business English. Excerpts. 2 CDs. (Running Time: 2 hrs. 20 mins.). 2002. audio compact disk 35.00 (978-1-891888-37-3(4)) Slangman Pubng.

Slangman Guide to Street French 1: The Best of French Slang. David Burke. (Slangman Guide To Ser.). (ENG & FRE.). 2002. audio compact disk 35.00 (978-1-891888-67-0(6)) Slangman Pubng.

Slangman Guide to Street French 2: The Best of French Idioms. David Burke. (Slangman Guide To Ser.). (ENG & FRE.). 2002. audio compact disk 14.95 (978-1-891888-68-7(4)) Slangman Pubng.

Slangman Guide to Street French 3: The Best of Naughty French. David Burke. (Slangman Guide To Ser.). (ENG & FRE.). 2002. audio compact disk 35.00 (978-1-891888-69-4(2)) Slangman Pubng.

Slangman Guide to Street Spanish 1: The Best of Spanish Slang. David Burke. (ENG & SPA.). 2002. audio compact disk 35.00 (978-1-891888-70-0(6)) Slangman Pubng.

Slangman Guide to Street Spanish 2: The Best of Spanish Idioms. David Burke. (ENG & SPA.). 2002. audio compact disk 35.00 (978-1-891888-71-7(4)) Slangman Pubng.

Slangman Guide to Street Spanish 3: The Best of Naughty Spanish. David Burke. (Slangman Guides). (ENG & SPA.). 2002. audio compact disk 35.00 (978-1-891888-72-4(2)) Slangman Pubng.

Slangman Guide to Street Speak 1: The Complete Course in American Slang & Idioms. Excerpts. 2 Cass. (Running Time: 2 hrs. 20 mins.). (Slangman Guide To Ser.). Orig. Title: Street Talk One. 2000. 25.00 (978-1-891888-30-4(7)) Slangman Pubng.

Slangman Guide to Street Speak 1: The Complete Course in American Slang & Idioms. abr. ed. Excerpts. 2 CDs. (Running Time: 2 hrs. 20 mins.). (Slangman Guides). Orig. Title: Street Talk One. 2000. audio compact disk 35.00 (978-1-891888-29-8(3)) Slangman Pubng.

Slangman Guide to Street Speak 2: The Complete Course in American Slang & Idioms. Excerpts. 2 Cass. (Running Time: 2 hrs. 20 mins.). (Slangman Guide To Ser.). Orig. Title: Street Talk Two. 2000. 25.00 (978-1-891888-32-8(3)) Slangman Pubng.

Slangman Guide to Street Speak 2: The Complete Course in American Slang & Idioms. abr. ed. Excerpts. 2 CDs. (Running Time: 2 hrs. 20 mins.). (Slangman Guides). Orig. Title: Street Talk Two. 2000. audio compact disk Rental 35.00 (978-1-891888-31-1(5)) Slangman Pubng.

Slangman Guide to Street Speak 3: The Complete Course in American Slang & Idioms. Excerpts. 2 Cass. (Running Time: 2 hrs. 20mins.). (Slangman Guide To Ser.). Orig. Title: Street Talk Three. 2002. 25.00 (978-1-891888-34-2(X)); audio compact disk 35.00 (978-1-891888-33-5(1)) Slangman Pubng.

Slant of Sun. Beth Kephart. Read by Bernadette Dunne. 6 cass. (Running Time: 9 hrs.). 1999. 29.95 (978-0-7366-4589-8(6)) Books on Tape.
In the fall of 1991, Beth Kephart's son Jeremy was diagnosed with a broad spectrum of difficulties, including a behavioral disorder related to autism. There were no definitive medical answers & no guidebooks to Jeremy's inner world. Kephart shares the painful & inspiring experience of loving a child whose "special needs" bring tremendous frustration & incalculable rewards. With the help of passionate parental involvement & the kindness of a few open hearts, Jeremy slowly emerges from a world of obsessive play rituals, atypical language constructions & endless pacing & begins to engage others, describe his thoughts & build essential friendships. Ultimately this is a story of the shallowness of medical labels compared to a child's courage & a mother's love.

Slant of Sun: One Child's Courage. collector's ed. Beth Kephart. Read by Bernadette Dunne. 6 cass. (Running Time: 9 hrs.). 1999. 48.00 (978-0-7366-4556-0(X), 4951) Books on Tape.
In the fall of 1991, Beth Kephart's son Jeremy was diagnosed with a broad spectrum of difficulties, including a behavioral disorder related to autism. There were no definitive medical answers & no guidebooks to Jeremy's inner world. Kephart shares the painful & inspiring experience of loving a child whose "special needs" bring tremendous frustration & incalculable rewards. With the help of passionate parental involvement & the kindness of a few open hearts, Jeremy slowly emerges from a world of obsessive play rituals, atypical language constructions & endless pacing & begins to engage others, describe his thoughts & build essential friendships. Ultimately this is a story of the shallowness of medical labels compared to a child's courage & a mother's love.

***Slap.** Christos Tsiolkas. Read by Alex Dimitriades. (Running Time: 16 hrs.). 2010. 109.99 (978-1-74214-805-2(0), 9781742148052) Pub: Bolinda Pubng AUS. Dist(s): Bolinda Pub Inc

***Slap.** unabr. ed. Christos Tsiolkas. Read by Alex Dimitriades. (Running Time: 16 hrs.). 2010. 43.95 (978-1-74214-589-1(2), 9781742145891); audio compact disk 113.95 (978-1-74214-576-1(0), 9781742145761) Pub: Bolinda Pubng AUS. Dist(s): Bolinda Pub Inc

Slap Happy: How to Play World-Beat Rhythms with Just Your Body & a Buddy. Alan Dworsky & Betsy Sansby. (gr. 3-6). 2002. bk. 19.95 (978-0-9638801-7-8(9)) Pub: Dancing Hands. Dist(s): SCB Distributors

Slap Technique for Bass Guitar: From Beginner to Professional Level. Stephan Richter. 1 CD. (Progressive Ser.). 1997. pap. bk. 19.95 (978-0-947183-16-5(7), 256-162) Kolala Music SGP.

Slappin' A Complete Study of Slap Technique for Bass. Marc Ensign. 1 CD. (Running Time: 1 hr.). 1997. pap. bk. 19.95 (978-0-7866-2701-1(8), 96534BCD) Mel Bay.

SLAPPs - Strategic Lawsuits Against Public Participation in Government Set: Managing Litigation Against Citizen Political Action. 8 cass. (Running Time: 10 hrs. 30 min.). (ALI-ABA Course of Study Ser.). 1994. 310.00 incl. course materials. (M155) Am Law Inst.
This course of study will provide an in-depth review of current issues in litigation & legislation involving political activists, citizens, groups, & organizations. The course is designed for attorneys; government officials; academics; real estate developers; corporations; businesses; unions; federal-state-local government employees; national & local environmental organizations; citizen lobbies; good government groups; neighborhood & condominium associations; consumer groups; civil rights, women's, taxpayers', & other advocacy organizations; election-issue campaigns & their lawyers; & others involved in the government decision-making process.

Slapstick & Mother Night. collector's ed. Kurt Vonnegut. Read by Dan Lazar. 8 cass. (Running Time: 8 hrs.). (J). 1979. 48.00 (978-0-7366-3055-9(4), 3737) Books on Tape.
In which we discover "ice nine," a new invention from one of the fathers of the atomic bomb.

Slashback, abr. ed. Paul Levine. Read by Robert Lawrence. 2 cass. (Running Time: 3 hrs.). (Jake Lassiter Mystery Ser.: Bk. 5). 2000. 7.95 (978-1-57815-144-8(9), 1103, Media Bks Audio) Media Bks NJ.
The Dolphin linebacker, turned trial-lawyer has two things on his mind: somebody's stole 1.5 million from his favorite client, Sam Kazdoy & someone has murdered Berto Zaldivar, an old buddy who changed careers from being a lawyer to drug smuggling.

Slater Creed. unabr. ed. Larry D. Names. Read by Maynard Villers. 12 cass. (Running Time: 12 hrs 36 min.). (Creed Ser.: Bk. 1). 2001. 64.95 (978-1-55686-799-6(9)) Books in Motion.
Confederate Captain Clete Slater returns to Post-Civil War Texas to find everything changed, including ownership of his plantation. Slater is accused of post-war murder.

Slaughter in the Ashes. abr. ed. William W. Johnstone. Read by Michael Kramer. 2 cass. (Running Time: 3 hrs.). (Ashes Ser.: No. 23). 1998. 16.95 (978-1-882071-94-4(8)) B-B Audio.
America has been brought to its knees by nuclear apocalypse. Decent citizens have united and are praying for a leader who can protect them. Luckily, one of the survivors is Ben Raines.Rebel leader Ben Raines created the Tri-States, but no system is.

Slaughter Run. abr. ed. Axel Kilgore. Read by Charlton Griffin. 2 vols. No. 2. 2003. (978-1-58807-649-6(0)) Am Pubng Inc.

Slaughter Run. abr. ed. Axel Kilgore. 2 vols. (Running Time: 3 hrs.). (Mercenary Ser.: No. 2). 2003. 18.00 (978-1-58807-158-3(8)) Am Pubng Inc.
Assassination in the Swiss Alps...terrorism in the Central Americana jungle...treachery in Washington...and Hank Frost right in the middle! The wise-cracking mercenary captain is up to his eyepatch in brutal violence, torture, and betrayal. There's the presidential bodyguard force he'd be a fool to trust; the fighting right-wing general whose republic is aflame with revolt; his seductive wife who'll have Frost as her lover - or have Frost dead; and the Communist Terrorist Army that's out for a final bloodbath!.

Slaughter Run. abr. ed. Axel Kilgore. Read by Carol Eason. 3 CDs. (Running Time: 3 hrs.). (Mercenary Ser.: No. 2). 2004. audio compact disk 25.00 (978-1-58807-326-6(2)) Am Pubng Inc.
Assassination in the Swiss Alps...terrorism in the Central American jungle...treachery in Washington...and Hank Frost is right in the middle! The wise-cracking mercenary captain is up to his eyepatch in brutal violence, torture, and betrayal. There's the presidential bodyguard force he'd be a fool to trust; the fighting right-wing general whose republic is aflame with revolt; his seductive wife who'll have Frost as her lover - or have Frost dead; and the Communist Terrorist Army that's out for a final bloodbath!.

Slaughterer see Isaac Bashevis Singer Reader

***Slaughterhouse Five.** unabr. ed. Kurt Vonnegut. Read by Ethan Hawke. (ENG.). 2003. (978-0-06-073555-5(4), Harper Audio); (978-0-06-079916-8(1), Harper Audio) HarperCollins Pubs.

Slaughterhouse-Five: A Duty Dance with Death. unabr. ed. Kurt Vonnegut. Read by Ethan Hawke. 2003. 25.95 (978-0-06-056492-6(X)) HarperCollins Pubs.

Slaughterhouse-Five: Or, the Children's Crusade, A Duty Dance with Death. unabr. ed. Kurt Vonnegut. (Running Time: 9.5 hrs. NaN mins.). 2009. 29.95 (978-1-4332-6972-1(4)); audio compact disk 80.00 (978-1-4332-6969-1(4)); audio compact disk 59.95 (978-1-4332-6968-4(6)) Blckstn Audio.

Slaughterhouse-Five Vol. 5: Or the Children's Crusade - A Duty Dance with Death. unabr. ed. Kurt Vonnegut. Read by Ethan Hawke. 2003. audio compact disk 29.95 (978-0-06-057377-5(5)) HarperCollins Pubs.

Slave. unabr. ed. Isaac Bashevis Singer. 6 cass. (Running Time: 9 hrs.). 2001. 39.95 Jewish Contempry Classics.

Slave. unabr. ed. Isaac Bashevis Singer. Narrated by David Chandler & Tracy Sallows. Directed By Susan Dworkin. 8 CDs. (Running Time: 10 hrs). 2002. audio compact disk 69.95 (978-1-893079-12-0(0), JCCAUDIOBOOKS) Jewish Contempry Classics.
A novel of passion & love between Jew & gentile girl, set in Medieval Poland.

***Slave: How One Forgotten Word Can Restore Your True Christian Freedom.** unabr. ed. John MacArthur. 2011. audio compact disk 24.99 (978-1-4003-1677-9(4)) Nelson.

***Slave Across the Street: How an American Teen Survived the World of Human Trafficking.** unabr. ed. Theresa L. Flores. Read by Theresa L. Flores. 5 CDs. (Running Time: 5 hrs. 36 mins. 0 sec.). (ENG.). 2010. audio compact disk 21.98 (978-1-59644-876-6(8)) christianaud.

***Slave Across the Street: The True Story of How an American Teen Survived the World of Human Trafficking.** unabr. ed. Theresa Flores. Narrated by Renée Raudman. (ENG.). 2010. 12.98 (978-1-59644-877-3(6)) christianaud.

Slave Dancer. Paula Fox. Read by Peter MacNicol. 4 cass. (Running Time: 4 hrs. 10 mins.). (J). 2000. 30.00 (978-0-7366-9034-8(4)) Books on Tape.
In a tale at once fascinating & horrifying, young Jessie suffers capture & indenture on a slave ship. His job is to "dance" the slaves by playing his wife while they're forced to engage in daily movement.

Slave Dancer. unabr. ed. Paula Fox. Read by Peter MacNicol. 4 vols. (Running Time: 4 hrs. 10 mins.). (J). (gr. 5-9). 2004. pap. bk. 38.00 (978-0-8072-0458-0(7), Listening Lib); 32.00 (978-0-8072-0457-3(9), Listening Lib) Random Audio Pubg.

Slave Dancer, unabr. ed. Paula Fox. Narrated by George Guidall. 3 pieces. (Running Time: 4 hrs. 15 mins.). (gr. 6 up). 1993. 27.00 (978-1-55690-952-8(7), 93444E7) Recorded Bks.
Snatched from the docks of New Orleans, a 13-year-old white boy is thrown aboard a slave ship & forced to play music for the African prisoners & to become a witness to the horrors of slavery.

Slave-Girl from Jerusalem. Caroline Lawrence. (Running Time: 3 hrs. 30 mins. 0 sec.). (Roman Mysteries Ser.). (ENG., (J). (gr. 7-9). 2007. audio compact disk 24.99 (978-0-7528-9066-1(2)) Pub: OrnChdrns Bks GBR. Dist(s): IPG Chicago

Slave No More: Two Men Who Escaped to Freedom, Including Their Own Narratives of Emancipation. abr. ed. David W. Blight. Read by David W. Blight. Read by Richard Allen & Dion Graham. 5 CDs. (Running Time: 6 hrs.). (ENG.). 2007. audio compact disk 29.95 (978-0-7393-1951-2(5)) Pub: Random Audio Pubg. Dist(s): Random

Slave of Sarna. abr. ed. Jeffrey Lord. Read by Carol Eason. Abr. by Odin Westgaard. 3 CDs. (Running Time: 3 hrs.). (Richard Blade Adventure Ser.: No. 4). 2004. audio compact disk 25.00 (978-1-58807-495-9(1)) Am Pubng Inc.

Richard Blade's newest mission: Projection to Dimension X, to track down and kill the Russian agent posing as his double. In Sarna, land of weird customs and barbaric punishments, failure means live burial or being hurled into the flaming jaws of Bek-Tor. And always the lurking danger from the man who was his double - and who might prove to be his destruction.

Slave of Sarna. abr. ed. Jeffrey Lord. Read by Lloyd James. Abr. by Odin Westgaard. 2 vols. 2003. 18.00 (978-1-58807-359-4(9)) Am Pubng Inc.

Slave of Sarna. abr. ed. Jeffrey Lord. Read by Lloyd James. Abr. by Odin Westgaard. 2 vols. No. 4. 2003. (978-1-58807-777-6(2)) Am Pubng Inc.

Slave of the Warmonger. Carol Eason. Read by Carol Eason. 3 CDs. (Running Time: 3 hrs.). (Mercenary Ser.: No. 7). 2004. audio compact disk 25.00 (978-1-58807-331-0(9)) Am Pubng Inc.

Hank Frost, the one-eyed merc Captain, gets an offer he can't refuse. The exquisitely beautiful daughter of a New York Mafia capo has been kidnapped by white slavers in the Middle East and sold into the harem of a militant Arab oil sheik. The capo and his own crime syndicate soldiers are powerless to get her out. But rescuing the capo's daughter is just the beginning of Frost's troubles. The sheik and his neo-Nazi advisors are plotting to assassinate the President of Egypt, putting the blame on Jewish extremists and making the Middle East explode in all-out war!.

Slave of the Warmonger. Carol Eason. Read by Carol Eason. 3 CDs. (Running Time: 3 hrs.). (Mercenary Ser.: No. 7). 2004. audio compact disk (978-1-58807-897-1(3)) Am Pubng Inc.

Slave of the Warmonger. abr. ed. Axel Kilgore. Read by Carol Eason. Abr. by Mary Bevoni. 2 vols. No. 7. 2003. 18.00 (978-1-58807-163-7(4)); (978-1-58807-654-0(7)) Am Pubng Inc.

Slave or Master: Romans 6:15-23. Ed Young. 1984. 4.95 (978-0-7417-1372-8(1), 372) Win Walk.

Slave Ship: A Human History. Marcus Rediker. Read by David Drummond. (Playaway Adult Nonfiction Ser.). 2008. 69.99 (978-1-60640-712-7(0)) Find a World.

Slave Ship: A Human History. unabr. ed. Marcus Rediker. Read by David Drummond. 2 MP3-CDs. (Running Time: 13 hrs. 0 mins. 0 sec.). (ENG.). 2007. 29.99 (978-1-4001-5479-1(0)); audio compact disk 39.99 (978-1-4001-0479-6(3)); audio compact disk 79.99 (978-1-4001-3479-3(X)) Pub: Tantor Media. Dist(s): IngramPubServ

Slave Voices: Things Past Telling. 1 cass. (Running Time: 30 min.). 9.95 (HO-87-12-29, HarperThor) HarpC GBR.

Slavery: A Re-evaluation. Eugene D. Genovese. 1 cass. (Running Time: 55 min.). 10.95 (40093) J Norton Pubs.

In an interview with Heywood Hale Broun. Genovese has compiled a reassessment of the role of the slave in the Old South that breaks many myths about the slave-master relationship prior to the Civil War. James Shenton, an American History professor at Columbia, is the guest.

Slaves & Masters: Romans 6:15-23. Ben Young. 1996. 4.95 (978-0-7417-6004-3(5), B0004) Win Walk.

Slaves of Obsession. Anne Perry. Read by Terrence Hardiman. 10 cass. (Running Time: 15 hrs.). (William Monk Novel Ser.). 2002. 84.95 (978-0-7927-2775-0(4)) Pub: Chivers Audio Bks GBR. Dist(s): AudioGO

Slaves of Quentaris. unabr. ed. Paul Collins. Read by Richard Aspel. 3 CDs. (Running Time: 10800 sec.). (Quentaris Chronicles: Ser.). (J). (gr. 5-11). 2005. audio compact disk 54.95 (978-1-74093-319-3(2)) Pub: Bolinda Pubng AUS. Dist(s): Bolinda Pub Inc

Slaves of Sleep & the Masters of Sleep. abr. ed. L. Ron Hubbard. Read by Rene Auberjonois. 4 cass. (Running Time: 6 hrs.). 1993. 19.95 (978-0-88404-656-1(7)) Bridge Pubns Inc.

A vivid Arabian Nights fantasy depicting a man's life in "eternal wakefulness".

Slaves of Sleep & the Masters of Sleep. abr. ed. L. Ron Hubbard. (Running Time: 6 hrs.). audio compact disk 27.95 (978-1-59212-219-6(1)) Gala Pr LLC.

Slaves of Sleep & the Masters of Sleep. abr. ed. L. Ron Hubbard. Read by Rene Auberjonois. 2 cass. (Running Time: 21600 sec.). 1993. 24.95 (978-1-59212-018-5(0)) Gala Pr LLC.

Slaves' War: The Civil War in the Words of Former Slaves. Andrew Ward. Read by Richard Allen. (Playaway Adult Nonfiction Ser.). 2008. 64.99 (978-1-60640-563-5(2)) Find a World.

Slaves' War: The Civil War in the Words of Former Slaves. unabr. ed. Andrew Ward. Narrated by Richard Allen. 11 CDs. (Running Time: 14 hrs. 0 mins. 0 sec.). (ENG.). 2008. audio compact disk 39.99 (978-1-4001-0614-1(1)); audio compact disk 29.99 (978-1-4001-5614-6(9)) Pub: Tantor Media. Dist(s): IngramPubServ

Slaves' War: The Civil War in the Words of Former Slaves. unabr. ed. Andrew Ward. Read by Richard Allen. (Running Time: 14 hrs. 0 mins. 0 sec.). (ENG.). 2008. audio compact disk 79.99 (978-1-4001-3614-8(8)) Pub: Tantor Media. Dist(s): IngramPubServ

Slavs. abr. ed. Kushner. 1 cass. (Running Time: 90 min.). 2000. 15.00 (978-0-671-52160-8(8), Audioworks) S&S Audio.

Slay-Ride. unabr. ed. Dick Francis. Read by David Case. 7 cass. (Running Time: 7 hrs.). 1991. 56.00 (978-0-7366-2081-9(8), 2886) Books on Tape.

Robert Sherman is a champion jockey. He's sure to win the upcoming Norwegian National - that is, until he suddenly drops out of sight. Called in to investigate, David Cleveland sets out to find his man. What he uncovers instead is a series of deaths that, if he is not careful, will soon include his own!.

Slay Your Giant. 2006. audio compact disk 29.95 (978-0-9790578-0-9(9)) Rhino Nation.

Slayers: Best of TV & Radio. 1 CD. 2004. audio compact disk 14.98 (978-1-57813-433-5(1), CSL/003, ADV Music) A D Vision.

Slayers: Return. 2002. audio compact disk 14.98 (978-1-57813-432-8(3)) A D Vision.

Slayers: The Motion Picture. 1 disc. (JPN.). 2003. audio compact disk 14.98 (978-1-57813-431-1(5), CSL/001) A D Vision.

Slayground. unabr. ed. Richard Stark, pseud. Read by Michael Kramer. 4 cass. (Running Time: 6 hrs.). 2000. 32.00 (978-0-7366-6020-4(8)) Books on Tape.

Parker figured his number had finally come up. An armored car heist had gone sour. His partners were dead or dying. He had escaped with the loot, but holing up in a deserted amusement park with only one exit had turned into a fatal mistake.

Slaying the Dragon. Michael Johnson. 1 cass. 1977. 18.00 (978-0-694-51822-7(0), 685760) HarperCollins Pubs.

Slaying the Dragon. Putting Pornography to Death once & for All. 2006. audio compact disk (978-0-9786075-2-4(X)) Burn Bush Comm.

SLCG Adult Leadership Training Seminar: Adult Partnership in Student-Led-Cell Groups. Ted M. Stump. 1 cass. (Running Time: 1 hr. 30 mins.). (YA). 2000. 12.95 (978-1-891793-68-4(3)) High Impact.

Sleep. David Ison. (Running Time: 1:00:00). 2009. audio compact disk 9.99 (978-1-60297-021-2(1)) Sounds True.

Sleep. Dorothy J. Papin-Griffith. 2005. audio compact disk 14.95 (978-0-9765935-5-3(6)) Gry L Prodns Inc.

Sleep. Betty L. Randolph. 1 stereo cass. (Running Time: 45 min.). (Self-Hypnosis Ser.). 9.98 (978-1-55909-145-9(2), 804) Randolph Tapes.

Promotes restful sleep. Music background & spoken word.

Sleep. abr. ed. Robert A. Monroe. Read by Robert A. Monroe. (Running Time: 30 min.). (Human Plus Ser.). 14.95 (978-1-56102-039-3(7)) Inter Indus.

Use to establish optimum regulation of your sleep cycle.

Sleep: Program from the Award Winning Public Radio Serie. Interview. Hosted by Fred Goodwin. 1 CD. (Running Time: 1 hr.). 1997. audio compact disk 21.95 (978-1-932479-94-2(5), LCM 0) Lichtenstein Creat.

In the premiere program, Dr. Fred Goodwin takes a fascinating look at sleep and our lives - why we sleep, the role of dreams, why some people can't sleep, why some people can't not. We hear about a recent study that puts people in the dark for 12 hours a day and examined their nocturnal patterns, we hear from a man who, literally and involuntarily, acts out his dreams, a narcoleptic who can't stay awake, and from John Updike on insomnia. We also hear about the effects of not sleeping on clinical depression.

Sleep - Deep & Restful. Norman J. Caldwell. Read by Norman J. Caldwell. Ed. by Achieve Now Institute Staff. 1 cass. (Running Time: 20 min.). (Better Health Ser.). 1988. 9.97 (978-1-56273-046-8(0)) My Mothers Pub.

Falling into a deep, restful sleep is as easy as listening to this tape - sleeping soundly all night.

Sleep - Deep & Restful: Fall into A deep Restful Sleep. Interview. 1 CD. (Running Time: 50 Minutes). 1988. 14.95 (978-1-56273-001-7(0)) My Mothers Pub.

Sleep - The Ultimate Secret to Ageless Achievement. Fawn O'Connor. 2002. per. 29.95 (978-0-9725341-1-6(3)) Ronnoco Pub.

Sleep Aid for Children. Eldon Taylor. Read by Eldon Taylor. Ed. by Leslie Brice. 1 cass. (Running Time: 1 hr.). 1992. 24.95 (978-1-56705-264-0(9)) Gateways Inst.

Self improvement.

Sleep & awaken a better Golfer: The lazy persons way to golfing Sucess. Lee Carlin. 2006. audio compact disk 49.99 (978-1-4276-0708-9(7)) AardGP.

Sleep & awaken a better Sportsperson: The lazy persons way to sporting Sucess. Lee Carlin. 2006. audio compact disk 39.99 (978-1-4276-0706-5(0)) AardGP.

Sleep & awaken De-stressed: Relax & let Go. Carlin ee. 2006. audio compact disk 19.99 (978-1-4276-0709-6(5)) AardGP.

Sleep & awaken Slimmer: The secret of slimming Success. Lee Carlin. 2006. audio compact disk 19.99 (978-1-4276-0705-8(2)) AardGP.

Sleep & Dream Enhancement: Sailing the Cosmic Sea. unabr. ed. Kim Falcone & Steven Falcone. Read by Steven Falcone. 1 cass. (Running Time: 76 min.). 1994. 10.95 (978-1-887799-06-5(0), 1-906-456) Creat Aware.

This program helps to create healthy sleep patterns & to remember dreams.

Sleep Apnea & Sleep Problems. Contrib. by Gerald M. Loughlin et al. 1 cass. (American Academy of Pediatrics UPDATE: Vol. 17, No. 1). 1998. 20.00 Am Acad Pediat.

Sleep, Baby, Sleep. abr. ed. Jessica Auerbach. Read by Jean Reed Bahle. 2 cass. (Running Time: 3 hrs.). 2000. 7.95 (978-1-57815-027-4(2), 1032, Media Bks Audio) Media Bks NJ.

Tale of a mother in a desperate search for her stolen child.

Sleep Baby Sleep. abr. ed. Nina Mattikow. Perf. by Purple Balloon Players. 1 cass. (Running Time: 60 min.). (Cassettes for Kids Ser.). (J). 1992. 5.95 (978-1-55569-526-2(4), 20002) Great Am Audio.

Your baby will go to sleep easily & happily to the sounds of ocean waves & soft lullaby melodies.

Sleep, Baby, Sleep. unabr. ed. Jessica Auerbach. Read by Jean Reed-Bahle. (Running Time: 8 hrs.). 2008. 39.25 (978-1-4233-5298-3(X), 9781423352983, BADLE); 24.95 (978-1-4233-5297-6(1), 9781423352976, BAD); audio compact disk 39.25 (978-1-4233-5296-9(3), 9781423352969, Brlnc Audio MP3 Lib); audio compact disk 24.95 (978-1-4233-5295-2(5), 9781423352952, Brilliance MP3) Brilliance Audio.

Sleep Beautiful Sleep. Shelley L. Stockwell. 1 cass. (Running Time: 60 min.). (Self Hypnosis Ser.). 1986. 10.00 (978-0-912559-01-8(2)) Creativity Unltd Pr.

Proven stress reliever created by an expert on Jet Lag. Use self-hypnosis, guided imagery & the sound of the ocean, to sleep soundly throughout the night.

Sleep Better. Michael Reed Gach. (Running Time: 1 hr. 15 mins.). 2006. audio compact disk 15.95 (978-1-59179-084-6(0), W717D) Sounds True.

Sleep Better: Acupressure & Gentle Yoga. Michael Reed Gach. Read by Michael Reed Gach. (Playaway Adult Nonfiction Ser.). (ENG.). 2009. 39.99 (978-1-60812-777-1(X)) Find a World.

Sleep Blissful Sleep. R. M. Peluso. Perf. by R. M. Peluso. 2005. audio compact disk 19.95 (978-0-9794674-0-0(3)) R M Peluso.

Sleep Easy. abr. ed. Robert A. Monroe. Read by Robert A. Monroe. (Running Time: 30 min.). (Human Plus Ser.). 1989. 14.95 (978-1-56102-040-9(0)) Inter Indus.

Use to achieve normal sleep in non-routine or adverse circumstances.

Sleep Easy. unabr. ed. Ronald Soderquist & Lynn di Sarro. 1 CD. (Running Time: 1 hr.). 2001. audio compact disk 49.77 (978-0-9712609-1-7(5)) Westlke Hyp.

Sleep Ezee (Subliminal & Hypnosis), Vol. 37. Jayne Helle. 1 cass. (Running Time: 56 min. per cass.). 1998. 15.00 (978-1-891826-36-8(0)) Introspect.

Get that long awaited deep sleep, waking up feeling refreshed & wonderful.

Sleep Impression see Carl Sandburg's Poems for Children

Sleep in Heavenly Peace. unabr. ed. M. William Phelps. Read by J. Charles. (Running Time: 13 hrs.). 2008. 39.25 (978-1-4233-4956-3(3), 9781423349563, BADLE); 39.25 (978-1-4233-4954-9(7), 9781423349549, Brlnc Audio MP3 Lib); 24.95 (978-1-4233-4955-6(5), 9781423349556, BAD); 24.95 (978-1-4233-4953-2(9), 9781423349532, Brilliance MP3); audio compact disk 102.25 (978-1-4233-4952-5(0), 9781423349525, BriAudCD Unabrid); audio compact disk 29.99 (978-1-4233-4951-8(2), 9781423349518, Bril Audio CD Unabri) Brilliance Audio.

Sleep in the Woods. unabr. ed. Dorothy Eden. Read by Nicolette McKenzie. 10 CDs. (Running Time: 15 hrs.). (Isis Ser.). (J). 1999. audio compact disk 89.95 (978-0-7531-1177-2(2), 111772) Pub: ISIS Lrg Prnt GBR. Dist(s): Ulverscroft US

Sleep in the Woods. unabr. ed. Dorothy Eden. Read by Nicolette McKenzie. 8 cass. (Running Time: 9 hrs. 20 mins.). (Isis Ser.). (J). 2001. 69.95 (978-0-7531-0527-6(6), 990207) Pub: ISIS Lrg Prnt GBR. Dist(s): Ulverscroft US

New Zealand was a place where rigid class distinctions could be forgotten, where the most eligible bachelor in Wellington proposed to a servant girl because he admired the arrogant slimness of her body & the spirit that made her confident she would be a good wife to him, although she would not pretend she was in love. So it was that Briar went to live with Saul Whitmore in his beautiful house in the heart of Maori country.

Sleep Judea Fair. Perf. by Choir of Grace Cathedral & Christopher Putnam. Contrib. by John Fenstermaker. 1 cass. 1997. 11.95 (MoreHse Pubng) Church Pub Inc.

Live recording featuring favorites from the Men & Boys choir's annual Christmas concerts. Includes "The Holly & the Ivy," "What Child Is This?" "I Saw Three Ships" & "No Room at the Inn".

Sleep Judea Fair. Perf. by Christopher Putman & Choir of Grace Cathedral. Contrib. by John Fenstermaker. 1 cass. 1997. audio compact disk 16.95 CD. (MoreHse Pubng) Church Pub Inc.

Sleep Like a Baby. Dick Sutphen. 1 cass. (Running Time: 1 hr.). (RX17 Ser.). 1986. 14.98 (978-0-87554-303-1(0), RX112) Valley Sun.

You now sleep peacefully through the night. Shortly after lying down, you fall into a deep, natural sleep. Your relaxation technique puts you to sleep. After a full night's sleep, you awaken relaxed & refreshed. Peaceful sleep now becomes your reality.

Sleep Like a Baby. unabr. ed. Mercedes Leidlich. Read by Mercedes Leidlich. 1 cass. (Running Time: 1 hr.). 1992. 10.95 in Norelco box. (978-1-882174-07-2(0), MLL-008) UFD Pub.

A gentle, soothing tape to induce sleep. Side A of this tape teaches about sleep & the different brain waves involved in the process of relaxing into the sleep state. Side B contains breath work & progressive relaxation that calm the body & mind, & quietly induce tranquil sleep.

Sleep Little Baby. MTL Staff. Illus. by Kathleen Francour. (Flitterbyes Relaxation Ser.). (J). 2003. audio compact disk 20.95 (978-1-59125-411-9(6)) Penton Overseas.

Sleep My Sweet Baby: A Lullaby. Dolly Braida. Composed by Dolly Braida. Perf. by Martha D. Petersen. Ed. by Christine Vaughan. Illus. by Mark Byans. Contrib. by Edward Abarr & Christine Vaughan. 1 cass. (J). (ps-1). 1997. pap. bk. 7.95 (978-0-9658113-0-9(1)) Jo-Eric.

A beautiful illustrated book. Tape is vocal on one side & instrumental on the other. A comforting lullaby which can be sung or read to a child.

Sleep My Sweet Baby: A Lullaby. Read by Frances Roznowski & Martha D. Peterson. Composed by Dolly Braida. 1 cass. (Running Time: 1 hr.). (J). 1997. pap. bk. 10.95; 3.50 (978-0-9658113-1-6(X)) Jo-Eric.

A children's lullaby for adults to read or sing to them. One side includes words, the other is instrumentation only, so your child can hear the lullaby in your own voice.

Sleep No More. abr. ed. Greg Iles. Read by Dick Hill. (Running Time: 21600 sec.). 2007. audio compact disk 14.99 (978-1-4233-3184-1(2), 9781423331841, BCD Value Price) Brilliance Audio.

Sleep No More. unabr. ed. Greg Iles. Read by Dick Hill. 8 cass. (Running Time: 11 hrs.). 2002. 32.95 (978-1-59086-106-6(X), 159086106X, BAU); 82.25 (978-1-59086-107-3(8), 1590861078, Unabridge Lib Edns); audio compact disk 38.95 (978-1-59086-211-7(2), 1590862112, CD Unabridged); audio compact disk 92.25 (978-1-59086-212-4(0), 1590862120, CD Unabrid Lib Ed) Brilliance Audio.

In Sleep No More, Greg Iles returns to the territory of some of his best-loved works, the steamy and hypnotic small town Mississippi where Iles himself grew up. In this new novel, John Waters is a husband and father happy with his lot in life, though he has not always felt that way. Years earlier he escaped an obsessive love affair, which he feared might consume him. The woman in question disappeared after Waters married, and later he heard that she was killed in New Orleans. But now, Waters has an uneasy feeling that she has resurfaced to trouble him - and entice him - once again. A woman he meets casually stuns him with a smile and a secret only this former lover would know. But when this alluring stranger is suddenly murdered, Waters's quiet life is enveloped in a whirlwind of guilt and suspicion, revealing the shadowy sides of love and friendship, and the terror that can result when passion becomes obsession.

Sleep No More. unabr. ed. Greg Iles. Read by Dick Hill. (Running Time: 11 hrs.). 2004. 39.25 (978-1-59335-425-1(8), 1593354258, Brlnc Audio MP3 Lib) Brilliance Audio.

Sleep No More. unabr. ed. Greg Iles. Read by Dick Hill. (Running Time: 11 hrs.). 2004. 39.25 (978-1-59710-717-4(4), 1597107174, BADLE); 24.95 (978-1-59710-716-7(6), 1597107166, BAD) Brilliance Audio.

Sleep No More. unabr. ed. Greg Iles. Read by Dick Hill. (Running Time: 11 hrs.). 2004. 24.95 (978-1-59335-192-2(5), 1593351925) Soulmate Audio Bks.

Sleep of Reason. unabr. ed. C. P. Snow. Read by Jack Hrkach. 11 cass. (Running Time: 16 hrs. 30 min.). (Strangers & Brothers Ser.). 1985. 88.00 (978-0-7366-0445-1(6), 1419) Books on Tape.

Out of duty to his old friend, the lawyer George Passant, Lewis Eliot agrees to help in a murder trial. The case is shocking: two lesbians are charged with torturing & killing an 8-year old boy.

Sleep of the Dead. unabr. ed. Tom Bradby. Read by Steven Pacey. 10 cass. (Running Time: 15 hrs.). 2002. 84.95 (978-0-7540-0849-1(5), CAB 2271) Pub: Chivers Pr GBR. Dist(s): AudioGO

Sleep of the Innocent. unabr. ed. Medora Sale. Read by Lynda Evans. 8 cass. (Running Time: 9 hrs. 18 min.). (Inspector John Sanders Mystery Ser.). 1999. 49.95 (978-1-55686-906-8(1)) Books in Motion.

A wealthy businessman is found shot in a Toronto luxury hotel. The only witness is a young pop singer known as Stormi Knight, who was seen fleeing from the crime scene. Inspector John Sanders, with the aid of photographer Harriet Jeffries, must figure out what the businessman & Stormi have in common before the killer strikes again.

Sleep off Pounds. 1 cass. 12.98 (978-0-87554-504-2(1), 1102) Valley Sun.

Positive affirmations to support healthy, intelligent weight-loss also program you to lose weight now, stick to your decisions & your diet, eat only at meal time & to draw upon the regulating power of your mind to assist you in fulfilling your weightloss goals. Also: You take the necessary steps to support your weight loss goals. Eat healthy foods. Eat more fiber. Manage stress. And many more suggestions.

Sleep Problems: Settling, Night Awakening & Sleep Walking. unabr. ed. Robert B. Speigel. Read by Robert B. Speigel. 2 cass. (Running Time: 1 hr.). (Audio Suggestion Bedtime Story Tapes Ser.). (J). 1993. 16.95 Incl. coloring poster. (978-0-937977-01-9(2)) Speigel&Assoc.

Psychotherapist Robert B. Speigel tells a story from his own childhood & leads children through a series of relaxation & positive visualization exercises designed to help them gain confidence to overcome bad habits & negative thinking. A helpful "Parent Information" cassette is included that

provides positive daytime techniques & facts about each problem compiled from current research.

Sleep Reduction. Eldon Taylor. Read by Eldon Taylor. Interview with XProgress Aware Staff & Progress Aware Staff. 1 cass. (Running Time: 62 min.). (Inner Talk Ser.). 16.95 (978-1-55978-559-4(4), 5346L) Progress Aware Res.
Soundtrack - Classics with underlying subliminal affirmations.

Sleep Reduction: Babbling Brook. Eldon Taylor. 1 cass. 16.95 (978-1-55978-753-6(8), 5346F) Progress Aware Res.

Sleep Reduction: Music Theme. Eldon Taylor. 1 cass. 16.95 (978-0-940699-06-9(0), 5346C) Progress Aware Res.

Sleep Reduction: Ocean. Eldon Taylor. Read by Eldon Taylor. Ed. by Leslie Brice. 1 cass. (Running Time: 1 hr.). 1992. 16.95 (978-1-56705-349-4(1)) Gateways Inst.
Self improvement.

Sleep Solutions. Roberta Shapiro. 2009. audio compact disk 11.99 (978-1-4276-3834-2(9)) AardGP.

Sleep Sound in Jesus. Illus. by Michael Card. 1 cass. (Running Time: 1 hr.). (J). bk. 17.95 calendar . (978-0-917143-18-2(3)) Sparrow TN.

Sleep Soundly. Steven Halpern. 1 cass. (Soundwave Two Thousand, the Audio Active Subliminal Ser.). 1990. (2012) Inner Peace Mus.
Relaxing music with subliminal affirmations.

Sleep Soundly. Eldon Taylor. 1 cass. (Running Time: 62 min.). (Inner Talk Ser.). 16.95 incl. script. (978-1-55978-479-5(2), 5347F) Progress Aware Res.
Soundtrack - Babbling Brook with underlying subliminal affirmations.

Sleep Soundly: Classic. Eldon Taylor. Read by Eldon Taylor. Ed. by Leslie Brice. 1 cass. (Running Time: 1 hr.). 1992. 16.95 (978-1-56705-125-4(1)) Gateways Inst.
Self improvement.

Sleep Soundly: Easy. Eldon Taylor. Read by Eldon Taylor. Ed. by Leslie Brice. 1 cass. (Running Time: 1 hr.). 1992. 16.95 (978-1-56705-126-1(X)) Gateways Inst.

Sleep Soundly: Harmonies. Eldon Taylor. Read by Eldon Taylor. Ed. by Leslie Brice. 1 cass. (Running Time: 1 hr.). 1992. 16.95 (978-1-56705-127-8(8)) Gateways Inst.

Sleep Soundly: Ocean. Eldon Taylor. Read by Eldon Taylor. Ed. by Leslie Brice. 1 cass. (Running Time: 1 hr.). 1992. 16.95 (978-1-56705-128-5(6)) Gateways Inst.

Sleep Soundly: Pastoral Theme. Eldon Taylor. 1 cass. 16.95 (978-1-55978-433-7(4), 5347M) Progress Aware Res.

Sleep Soundly: Stream. Eldon Taylor. Read by Eldon Taylor. Ed. by Leslie Brice. 1 cass. (Running Time: 1 hr.). 1992. 16.95 (978-1-56705-129-2(4)) Gateways Inst.

Sleep, Sweet Baby. MTL Staff. Illus. by Kathleen Francour. (Flitterbyes Relaxation Ser.). (J). 2003. audio compact disk 6.95 (978-1-59125-412-6(4)) Penton Overseas.

Sleep Sweet Baby. Penton Overseas, Inc. Staff. 1 CD. (Running Time: 1 hr. 30 mins.). (Relaxation Ser.). (ENG.). (J). 2003. audio compact disk 7.95 (978-1-59125-332-7(2)) Penton Overseas.

Sleep Through Insomnia. unabr. ed. Krs Edstrom. Read by Krs Edstrom. 1 cass. (Running Time: 40 min.). (Inner Mastery Ser.). 1994. 9.95 Norelco size. (978-1-886198-11-1(X)); 12.95 (978-1-886198-03-6(9), IMS04) Soft Stone Pub.
Provides techniques that WORK, delivering not only immediate results, but also internalizes skills to draw on forever. You learn to dissolve the barriers that keep you from sleep. Guided meditation and relaxation skills with celestial music composed to help guide you to the "land of nod." A great tape to have on hand at all times for occasional or chronic sleep problems. Endorsed by hospitals, airlines and psychologists. Total running time: 40 minutes. One of six audios in the Inner Mastery Series.

Sleep Through Insomnia: Meditations to Quiet the Mind & Still the Body. unabr. ed. Krs Edstrom. 1 CD. (Running Time: 40 mins.). 2006. audio compact disk 16.95 (978-1-886198-18-0(7)) Soft Stone Pub.
A great audio to have on hand for occasional or chronic sleep problems - NO PILLS NEEDED! Take the pressure and "failure" out of insomnia as you learn how to break old patterns and develop a wonderful new relationship with sleep. Mindfulness meditation skills blended with celestial music guide you to the "land of nod." Provides not only immediate results, but also internalizes skills to draw on forever.

Sleep Tight: 12 Lullaby Favorites for Your Bee-Autiful Baby. Created by Word Records. 2008. audio compact disk 3.99 (978-5-557-47085-8(9), Word Records) Word Enter.

Sleep to Go. 2003. audio compact disk (978-1-59250-104-5(4)) Gaiam Intl.

Sleep Well. 1 cass. 10.00 (978-1-58506-011-5(9), 17) New Life Inst OR.
You can conquer insomnia & sleep soundly.

Sleeper. abr. ed. Gene Riehl. Read by David Colacci. (Running Time: 4 hrs.). (Puller Monk Ser.). 2005. audio compact disk 69.25 (978-1-59355-941-0(0), 9781593559410, BACDLib Ed) Brilliance Audio.
FBI agent Puller Monk is losing his mind. His father passed away six months ago and left him a predisposition for Alzheimer's disease. Add to that a lethal American spy raised by the North Koreans, and Monk's life just got a lot more complicated. Aware of his dark side and willingness to take chances no matter what the risk, Monk is asked by the NSA to go undercover. His mission: find the sleeper spy, infiltrate the contact she's been seducing, and stop her before she carries out her shadowy objective. A gambling man with a jones for adrenaline, Monk lives for this moment: It's time to go rogue, to work in the shadows, to follow his own "Quantico rules." But with his failing mind and his demons close at his heels, can he even trust himself? Riehl exploded on the scene with his hit debut, Quantico Rules, but in Sleeper he takes Puller Monk, the most fascinatingly flawed espionage figure in years, to the next level and listeners on a ride unlike any they've experienced before.

Sleeper. unabr. ed. Gene Riehl. Read by David Colacci. (Running Time: 11 hrs.). (Puller Monk Ser.). 2005. 39.25 (978-1-59710-718-1(2), 9781597107181, BADLE); 24.95 (978-1-59710-719-8(0), 9781597107198, BAD); 39.25 (978-1-59335-826-6(1), 9781593358266, Brlnc Audio MP3 Lib); 24.95 (978-1-59335-692-7(7), 9781593356927, Brilliance MP3); 32.95 (978-1-59086-938-3(9), 9781590869383, BAU); 87.25 (978-1-59086-939-0(7), 9781590869390, BAudLibEd) Brilliance Audio.

Sleeper. unabr. ed. Gillian White. Read by Tracey Lord. 8 cass. (Running Time: 12 hrs.). 2001. 69.95 (978-0-7531-0612-9(4), 991107) Pub: ISIS Audio GBR. Dist(s): Ulverscroft US

Sleepers see Treasury of Walt Whitman

Sleepiness: Milton Erman Interviewed by Stephen M. Stahl. Interview. Interview with Stephen M. Stahl. Featuring Milton Erman. 1 CD. 2005. audio compact disk (978-1-4225-0006-4(3)) NEI Pr.

Sleeping Arrangements. unabr. ed. Madeleine Wickham. Read by Annie Aldington. 6 cass. (Running Time: 8 hrs. 10 min.). (978-0-7531-1171-0(3)) ISIS Audio GBR.
Chloe needs a holiday. She?s sick of making wedding dresses and her partner Philip has trouble at work. Her wealthy friend Gerard has offered the loan of his luxury villa in Spain perfect. Hugh is not a happy man. His immaculate wife Amanda seems more interested in the granite for the new kitchen than in him, and he works so hard to pay for it all, he barely has time for his family. But his old school friend Gerard has lent them a luxury villa in Spain perfect. Both families arrive at the villa and get a shock: Gerard?s double-booked. An uneasy week of sharing begins, and tensions soon mount in the soaring heat. But there?s also a secret history between the families and as tempers fray, an old passion begins to resurface.

Sleeping Arrangements. unabr. ed. Madeleine Wickham. Read by Katherine Kellgren. 6 CDs. (Running Time: 8 hrs. 30 mins. 0 sec.). (ENG.). 2008. audio compact disk 29.95 (978-1-4272-0439-4(X)) Pub: Macmill Audio. Dist(s): Macmillan

Sleeping at the starlite motel & other adventures on the way back Home: And Other Adventures on the Way Back Home. Bailey White. 2004. 11.95 (978-0-7435-4780-2(2)) Pub: S&S Audio. Dist(s): S and S Inc

Sleeping Beastly: Lazy Jack; Sleeping Beastly; Iron John & the Little Drummer Boy; Piggy Wiggy; the Little Moose Who Couldn't Go to Sleep. unabr. ed. Willy Claflin. Read by Willy Claflin. (J). 2007. 34.99 (978-1-60252-514-6(5)) Find a World.

Sleeping Beauty see Stories Children Love to Hear

Sleeping Beauty see Sleeping Beauty & Other Stories

Sleeping Beauty see Bella Durmiente

Sleeping Beauty. (J). 1975. (D 5) Soundelux.

Sleeping Beauty. 1 cass. (Read-Along Ser.). (J). bk. 7.99 (978-1-55723-010-2(2)); 11.99 Norelco. (978-0-7634-0226-6(5)); audio compact disk 19.99 (978-1-55723-770-5(0)) W Disney Records.

Sleeping Beauty. 1 cass. (Classics Ser.). (J). 1997. 11.99 (978-0-7634-0225-9(7)); audio compact disk 19.99 CD. (978-1-55723-803-0(0)) W Disney Records.

Sleeping Beauty. Read by Charles Biddle, Jr. Illus. by Annabel Malak. 1 cass. (Running Time: 15 mins.). (Classic Stories Ser.). (J). (ps-2). 2000. audio compact disk 9.95 (978-2-921997-74-4(6)) Coffragants CAN.
Will enchant little princesses as well as future princes.

Sleeping Beauty. Read by Denise Bryer. 1 cass. (J). (ps-2). 3.98 (978-1-55886-037-7(1)); 3.98 (978-1-55886-029-2(0)) Smarty Pants.
A children's fairy tale about a beautiful princess.

Sleeping Beauty. Classics for Family staff. 1 cass., 2 CD. (J). 1996. bk. 39.98; 24.98 Consort Bk Sales.

Sleeping Beauty. Robert Guillaume. (J). 1992. 9.95 (978-1-882179-08-4(0)) Confetti Ent.

Sleeping Beauty. Judith Ivory. Narrated by Violet Primm. 8 cass. (Running Time: 11 hrs. 30 mins.). 74.00 (978-0-7887-5976-5(0)); audio compact disk 97.00 (978-1-4025-3079-1(X)) Recorded Bks.

Sleeping Beauty. Phillip Margolin. Read by Suzanne Houston. 8 vols. 2004. bk. 69.95 (978-0-7927-3229-7(4), CSL 659, Chivers Sound Lib); bk. 94.95 (978-0-7927-3230-3(8), SLD 659, Chivers Sound Lib); bk. 29.95 (978-0-7927-3231-0(6), CMP 659, Chivers Sound Lib) AudioGO.

***Sleeping Beauty.** abr. ed. Phillip Margolin. Read by Margaret Whitton. (ENG.). 2004. (978-0-06-079789-8(4), Harper Audio); (978-0-06-081423-6(3), Harper Audio) HarperCollins Pubs.

Sleeping Beauty. l.t. ed. Illus. by Graham Percy. 1 cass. (Running Time: 1 hr. 30 mins.). (J). (ps-3). 2001. bk. 8.99 (978-84-87650-26-0(0)) Pub: Peralt Mont ESP. Dist(s): imaJen

Sleeping Beauty. unabr. ed. 1 cass. (Running Time: 20 min.). Dramatization. (Magic Looking Glass Ser.). (J). (gr. 2-6). 1989. 9.95 (978-0-7810-0023-9(8), NIM-CW-127-2-C) NIMCO.
A folk tale of German descent.

Sleeping Beauty. unabr. ed. Naomi Fox. Illus. by Neal Fox. Narrated by Robert Guillaume. 1 cass. (Running Time: 15 min.). Dramatization. (Confetti Company Proudly Presents Ser.). (J). (ps-1). 1992. pap. bk. 9.95 (978-1-882179-13-8(7)) Confetti Ent.
The Confetti Company, a cast of children, reenact the classic fairy tale with a modern upbeat tempo.

Sleeping Beauty. unabr. ed. Judith Ivory. 2001. 71.00 (L1000L8) Recorded Bks.

Sleeping Beauty. unabr. ed. Elizabeth Lowell. Read by Tom Parker. 6 cass. (Running Time: 6 hrs.). 1999. 44.95 (FS9-43272) Highsmith.

Sleeping Beauty. unabr. ed. Ross MacDonald. Read by Tom Parker. (Running Time: 27000 sec.). (Lew Archer Mystery Ser.). 2008. audio compact disk & audio compact disk 60.00 (978-1-4332-3416-3(5)) Blckstn Audio.

Sleeping Beauty. unabr. ed. Ross MacDonald, pseud. Read by Harris Yulin et al. 6 cass. (Running Time: 6 hrs. 51 mins.). Dramatization. (Lew Archer Mystery Ser.). 2004. 29.95 (978-1-57270-049-9(1), N61049u) Pub: Audio Partners. Dist(s): PerseuPGW
An original music score, a 35-person cast & a plot that features Lew Archer dealing with a Southern California oil spill, a missing girl & two men dead creates a compelling audio gem.

Sleeping Beauty. unabr. ed. Ross MacDonald, pseud. Read by Tom Parker. 6 cass. (Running Time: 8 hrs. 30 mins.). (Lew Archer Mystery Ser.). 1998. 44.95 (978-0-7861-1320-0(0), 2245) Blckstn Audio.
"Sleeping Beauty" plunges detective Lew Archer into a fascinating & intricate case connected to a disastrous oil spill on the Southern California coast. He becomes involved with three generations of the imposing Lennox family whose offshore oil platform caused the spill & whose young heiress, glimpsed for a haunting moment on the beach, has disappeared.

Sleeping Beauty. unabr. ed. Ross MacDonald, pseud. 6 cass. (Running Time: 7 hrs.). (Lew Archer Mystery Ser.). 2001. 34.95 (AUPA001) Lodestone Catalog.

***Sleeping Beauty.** unabr. ed. Phillip Margolin. Read by Suzanne Houston. (ENG.). 2004. (978-0-06-075574-4(1), Harper Audio); (978-0-06-081344-4(X), Harper Audio) HarperCollins Pubs.

Sleeping Beauty. unabr. ed. Arthur Thomas Quiller-Couch. Read by Roe Kendall. 3 CDs. (Running Time: 2 hrs. 30 mins.). 2006. audio compact disk 27.00 (978-0-7861-8132-2(X), 2425) Blckstn Audio.

Sleeping Beauty: A Lew Archer Novel. unabr. ed. Ross MacDonald. Read by Tom Parker. (Running Time: 27000 sec.). (Lew Archer Mystery Ser.). 2008. audio compact disk & audio compact disk 29.95 (978-1-4332-3417-0(3)) Blckstn Audio.

Sleeping Beauty & Other Children's Favorites. (J). 2005. audio compact disk (978-1-933796-35-2(9)) PC Treasures.

Sleeping Beauty, & Other Fairy Tales. Arthur Thomas Quiller-Couch. Read by Roe Kendall. 2 cass. (Running Time: 2 hrs. 30 mins.). 1999. 17.95 (978-0-7861-1596-9(3), 2425) Blckstn Audio.

Sleeping Beauty & Other Stories. unabr. ed. Charles Perrault. Read by Caroline Noone. 2 cass. (Running Time: 1 hr. 45 min.). Incl. Donkey Skin. (J).; Hop O' My Thumb. (J).; Little Red Riding Hood. (J).; Puss in Boots. (J).; Ricky with the Tuft. (J).; Sleeping Beauty. (J).; (J). 16.95 Set, library case. (978-1-55656-044-6(3)) Dercum Audio.
Composed in the early 1700's, Charles Perrault's stories are distinguished by the simplicity of ideas & situations. They therefore remain the most timeless & entertaining of all the classic collections of fairy tales.

Sleeping Beauty & Other Stories. unabr. ed. Charles Perrault. 2 cass. (Running Time: 2 hrs.). (Classic Literature Ser.). 1997. pap. bk. 16.95 (978-1-55656-199-3(7)) Pub: Dercum Audio. Dist(s): APG
Includes "Cinderella," "Little Red Riding Hood" & "Puss in Boots" among others.

Sleeping Beauty & the Five Questions: A Parable about the Hearts of Fathers & Daughters. Douglas W. Phillips. 1 CD. (Running Time: 1 hr. 5 mins.). 2004. audio compact disk 10.00 (978-0-9744689-9-0(1)) Pub: Vision Forum. Dist(s): STL Dist NA

Sleeping Cruelty. Lynda La Plante. 2 cass. (Running Time: 3 hrs.). 2001. (978-0-333-78244-6(5)) Macmillan UK GBR.

Sleeping Cruelty. unabr. ed. Lynda La Plante. Read by Christian Rodska. 10 cass. (Running Time: 10 hrs.). 2001. 84.95 (978-0-7540-0638-1(7)) Pub: Chivers Audio Bks GBR. Dist(s): AudioGO
Sir William Benedict had it all: wealth, position, a career that knows no bounds & an island in the Caribbean. His world was a perfect place, until Andrew Maynard commits suicide, leaving Benedict's flawless reputation in shambles. Now the worm is ready to turn. His enemies are the people once closest to him & now he has all the money he needs to satisfying revenge.

Sleeping Dogs. unabr. ed. E. X. Ferrars. Read by Angela Down. 5 cass. (Running Time: 7 hrs. 30 min.). (Sound Ser.). 2004. 49.95 (978-1-85496-662-9(6), 66626) Pub: UlverLrgPrint GBR. Dist(s): Ulverscroft US
Elsbeth Marris' brother-in-law, Bernard, was to ghostwrite the story of Teresa Swale, who was acquitted of a murder charge. But when he comes down with pneumonia, Elsbeth finds herself enquiring after this oddly elusive woman with a sensational past & questionable morals. And Elsbeth learns that she is not the only one looking for Teresa, & that to be involved in an unsolved murder could be a dangerous, frightening thing.

Sleeping Dogs. unabr. ed. Sonya Hartnett. 3 cass. (Running Time: 4 hrs.). 2002. (978-1-74030-266-1(4)) Bolinda Pubng AUS.

Sleeping Dogs. unabr. ed. Sonya Hartnett. Read by Kate Hosking. (Running Time: 14400 sec.). (J). 2006. audio compact disk 57.95 (978-1-74093-129-8(7)) Pub: Bolinda Pubng AUS. Dist(s): Bolinda Pub Inc

Sleeping Dogs. unabr. ed. Thomas Perry. Narrated by Michael Kramer. (Running Time: 12 hrs. 30 mins. 0 sec.). (ENG.). 2009. audio compact disk 75.99 (978-1-4001-4028-2(5)); audio compact disk 37.99 (978-1-4001-1028-5(9)); audio compact disk 24.99 (978-1-4001-6028-0(6)) Pub: Tantor Media. Dist(s): IngramPubServ

Sleeping Doll. abr. ed. Jeffery Deaver. Read by Anne Twomey. (Running Time: 6 hrs. 0 mins. 0 sec.). No. 1. (ENG.). 2009. audio compact disk 14.99 (978-0-7435-8295-7(0)) Pub: S&S Audio. Dist(s): S and S Inc

Sleeping Doll. unabr. ed. Jeffery Deaver. Read by Anne Twomey. (Running Time: 16 hrs. 0 mins. 0 sec.). No. 1. (ENG.). 2007. audio compact disk 49.95 (978-0-7435-6612-4(2)) Pub: S&S Audio. Dist(s): S and S Inc

Sleeping Easily - Creative Dreaming. Nathaniel Branden. 1 cass. (Running Time: 20 min.). 10.95 (856) J Norton Pubs.
Learn to have a deeply satisfying night's sleep &, at the same time, to utilize dreams to solve problems.

Sleeping Freshmen Never Lie. unabr. ed. David Lubar. Read by Full Cast Production Staff. (YA). 2007. 44.99 (978-1-59895-943-7(3)) Find a World.

Sleeping Fury see Twentieth-Century Poetry in English, No. 2, Recordings of Poets Reading Their Own Poetry

Sleeping in America: The Secret War. Avi Lipkin. 2 CDs. (Running Time: 2 hrs). (Briefing Packages by Chuck Missler). 2003. audio compact disk 19.95 (978-1-57821-239-2(1)) Koinonia Hse.
Iraq and Afghanistan have drawn significant media attention and are obvious battlefields. However, while soldiers walk the streets of the Middle East, Muslim extremists both at home and abroad are working out the steps of an involved plot to convert the world to Islam by any means necessary, whether through violence or through propaganda. In this newest briefing, Avi talks about fanatical Islam's invasion techniques and how they are being put into effect in Canada, the EU and in the U.S.Each Audio Briefing Pack contains two high-quality cassette tapes, with extensive supporting study notes, all packaged in a sturdy clear-plastic case.

Sleeping Lady. unabr. ed. Sue Henry. Read by Mary Peiffer. 6 cass. (Running Time: 9 hrs.). (Jessie Arnold Mystery Ser.). 1999. 48.00 (978-0-7366-4458-7(X), 4903) Books on Tape.
Alaska State Trooper Alex Jensen is faced with solving the mystery of what became of pilot Norm Lewis, whose plane disappeared six months ago in the vast white wilderness. Even more puzzling is the discovery of the plane - with the frozen body of an unidentified woman strapped in the passenger seat. Norm is nowhere to be found, & his wife, Rochelle, has flown in demanding to be included in the search. Jensen & Rochelle begin their probe, an emotional trek through the forbidding Alaskan wilderness - a trail that turns even more ominous as they follow the fateful path of a man who has vanished without a trace.

Sleeping Lady. unabr. ed. Sue Henry. Read by Mary Peiffer. 6 cass. (Running Time: 9 hrs.). (Jessie Arnold Mystery Ser.). 2001. (978-0-7366-4961-2(1)) Books on Tape.

Sleeping Life. unabr. ed. Ruth Rendell. Read by Nigel Anthony. 6 cass. (Running Time: 9 hrs.). (Inspector Wexford Mystery Ser.: Bk. 10). 2000. 49.95 (978-0-7540-0036-5(2), CAB 1459) Pub: Chivers Audio Bks GBR. Dist(s): AudioGO
The body under the hedge was that of a middle-aged woman. The gray eyes were wide and staring, and in them Inspector Wexford thought he saw a sardonic gleam. But that must have been his imagination. the woman was a stranger. There was nothing to give him her address, name or occupation, let alone any clues that might lead to her killer.

Sleeping Murder. Agatha Christie. (Running Time: 26100 sec.). (Miss Marple Ser.: No. 15). (ENG.). 2007. audio compact disk 29.95 (978-1-57270-849-5(2)) Pub: AudioGO. Dist(s): Perseus Dist

***Sleeping Murder.** Agatha Christie. Narrated by June Whitfield & Full Cast Production Staff. (Running Time: 2 hrs. 0 mins. 0 sec.). (ENG.). 2010. audio compact disk 24.95 (978-1-84607-039-6(2)) Pub: AudioGO. Dist(s): Perseus Dist

Sleeping Murder. unabr. ed. Agatha Christie. Read by Rosemary Leach. 6 cass. (Running Time: 7 hrs. 18 min.). (Miss Marple Ser.: No. 15). 2002. 29.95 (978-1-57270-285-1(0), Audio Editions) Pub: Audio Partners. Dist(s): PerseuPGW

Sleeping Queen: The Child As Saviour. Read by John Giannini. 1 cass. (Running Time: 2 hrs.). (Fairytales Ser.: No. 8). 1987. 12.95 (978-0-7822-0069-0(9), 238) C G Jung IL.

Sleeping Reader: 4 CD Day/Night Audio Reading Program. Jason Allen Miller. Prod. by Sleeping Reader. (ENG.). (J). 2008. audio compact disk 39.95 (978-0-615-26615-2(0)) Learn Sleep.

Sleeping the Loaf. Poems. John M. Bennett. Read by John Bennett. Music by Dick Metcalf. 1 cass. (Running Time: 1 hr.). 1995. 5.00 (978-0-935350-57-9(8)) Luna Bisonte.
Avant-garde poetry with experimental music.

Sleeping Through Gethsemane: The Atonement & You. Diana Hoelscher. 2004. 9.95 (978-1-59156-228-3(7)); audio compact disk 11.95 (978-1-59156-229-0(5)) Covenant Comms.

Sleeping Through the Rain. Matthew Sigmon & Julie Anderson. 1 cass. (Running Time: 30 min.). (Meta Music Artist Ser.). 1991. 14.95 (978-1-56102-240-3(3)) Inter Indus.
Segues between the wakefulness theme & the sleep theme. Hemi-Sync patterns support the piece.

Sleeping Through the Rain. unabr. ed. Matthew Sigmon & Julie Anderson. Read by Matthew Sigmon & Julie Anderson. 1 cass. (Running Time: 30 min.). (TimeOut Ser.). 1991. 14.95 (978-1-56102-807-8(X)) Inter Indus.
Restful music.

Sleeping Tiger. unabr. ed. Rosamunde Pilcher. Read by Jan Carey. 6 cass. (Running Time: 6 hrs.). 1996. 54.95 (978-0-7451-6710-7(1), CAB1326) AudioGO.
Selina impulsively leaves her fiance behind to search for the father she never knew on the island of San Antonio. But what she finds is the unexpected truth about herself & a man who holds the key not only to her past, but to her heart.

Sleeping Tiger. unabr. ed. Rosamunde Pilcher. Read by Donada Peters. 5 cass. (Running Time: 5 hrs.). 1991. 40.00 (978-0-7366-2082-6(6), 2887) Books on Tape.
Engaged to a wealthy young lawyer, herself the proud owner of a chic London flat, Selina Bruce seems to have it all. But it's a facade. For Selina's an orphan. Her mother died giving her life, her father in the war. She never knew either of them, & she feels empty because of it. Then evidence turns up that Selina's dad may still be alive. Following the clue, she flies to San Antonio, a tiny island off the Spanish coast. She finds more there than the prospect of her father: she finds George Dyer, a man who holds the key to her past...also to her heart.

Sleeping with Fear. abr. ed. Kay Hooper. Read by Kathy Garver. (Running Time: 14400 sec.). (Fear Trilogy: Bk. 3). 2007. audio compact disk 14.99 (978-1-4233-0946-8(4), 9781423309468, BCD Value Price) Brilliance Audio.

Sleeping with Fear. unabr. ed. Kay Hooper. Read by Kathy Garver. (Running Time: 7 hrs.). (Fear Trilogy: Bk. 3). 2006. 39.25 (978-1-4233-0944-4(8), 9781423309444, BADLE); 24.95 (978-1-4233-0943-7(X), 9781423309437, BAD); 69.25 (978-1-4233-0938-3(3), 9781423309383, BrilAudUnabridg); audio compact disk 39.25 (978-1-4233-0942-0(1), 9781423309420, Brinc Audio MP3 Lib); audio compact disk 87.25 (978-1-4233-0940-6(5), 9781423309406, BriAudCD Unabrid); audio compact disk 24.95 (978-1-4233-0941-3(3), 9781423309413, Brilliance MP3); audio compact disk 32.95 (978-1-4233-0939-0(1), 9781423309390, Bril Audio CD Unabri) Brilliance Audio.
New York Times bestselling author Kay Hooper saves the best for last in the almost unbearably intense conclusion to her spellbinding Fear Trilogy, which already has over one million copies of the first two books in print. Agent Riley Crane of the FBI's Special Crimes Unit is used to dealing with bizarre situations and violent death, but when she wakes up alone, head pounding and covered in blood - human blood - she knows she's entered a new kind of nightmare. The trouble is, that's all she knows. With the last two weeks of her life wiped from her memory, Riley's in the middle of an undercover operation where friend and foe look terrifyingly alike, and where the murderer could be someone close to her. Perhaps someone she loves. Perhaps even...herself.

Sleeping with Schubert: A Novel of Genius, Passion, & Hair. unabr. ed. Bonnie Marson. 2004. 72.00 (978-1-4159-0085-7(X)); 90.00 (978-1-4159-0116-8(3)) Random Audio Pubg.

Sleeping with Strangers. Eric Jerome Dickey. Read by Dion Graham. (Playaway Adult Fiction Ser.). (ENG.). 2009. 65.00 (978-1-60775-530-2(0)) Find a World.

Sleeping with Strangers. abr. ed. Eric Jerome Dickey. Read by Dion Graham. (Running Time: 5 hrs.). (Gideon Ser.). 2008. audio compact disk 14.99 (978-1-4233-0665-8(1), 9781423306658, BCD Value Price) Brilliance Audio.

Sleeping with Strangers. unabr. ed. Eric Jerome Dickey. (Running Time: 9 hrs.). (Gideon Ser.). 2007. 24.95 (978-1-59335-751-1(6), 9781593357511, Brilliance MP3); 39.25 (978-1-59335-768-9(0), 9781593357689, Brinc Audio MP3 Lib); 74.25 (978-1-59600-011-7(2), 9781596000117, BrilAudUnabridg); audio compact disk 92.25 (978-1-59600-014-8(7), 9781596000148, BriAudCD Unabrid); audio compact disk 36.95 (978-1-59600-013-1(9), 9781596000131, Bril Audio CD Unabri) Brilliance Audio.
Please enter a Synopsis.

Sleeping with Strangers. unabr. ed. Eric Jerome Dickey. Read by Dion Graham. (Running Time: 9 hrs.). (Gideon Ser.). 2007. 39.25 (978-1-59710-871-3(5), 9781597108713, BADLE); 24.95 (978-1-59710-870-6(7), 9781597108706, BAD) Brilliance Audio.

Sleeping with the Devil. abr. ed. Suzanne Finstad. Read by Suzanne Finstad. 2 cass. (Running Time: 3 hrs.). 1991. 15.95 set. (978-1-879371-06-4(5), 20120) Pub Mills.
This is the true story of a young, beautiful & motivated girl whose goal is to become a doctor. While on a skiing vacation, she meets an older man, they fall in love & she moves to Houston to be with him, even enrolling in medical school there. She learns that he is not divorced, contrary to what he told her, but his wife soon files for divorce.

Sleeping with the Devil. unabr. ed. Suzanne Finstad. Read by Donada Peters. 9 cass. (Running Time: 13 hrs. 30 min.). 1991. 72.00 (978-0-7366-2083-3(4), 2888) Books on Tape.
Barbara Piotrowski & Richard Minns were something special - even in the world of the Texas rich. Barbara was a beauty queen & pre-med student, Richard a self-made millionaire & bodybuilder, 24 years Barbara's senior. They cut a real swath. Or so it appeared. But the reality was all wrong. Richard's world began to unravel. He blamed Barbara & not just a little. He hired a killer to do her in.

Sleeping with the Enemy. unabr. ed. Nancy Price. Read by Donada Peters. 7 cass. (Running Time: 10 hrs. 30 min.). 1987. 56.00 (978-0-7366-2025-3(7), 2840) Books on Tape.
Sara Burney is desperate. She's trapped in a violent marriage. She'll do anything to escape. When a storm blows up during a sail, Sara sees her chance. She disappears overboard. It's perfect cover for her getaway. Presumed dead, she goes for deep cover. But her husband finds one clue, then another. Finally convinced that she's hiding, he stalks her with a vengeance. He wants her back, literally dead or alive.

Sleeping with the Fishes. Perf. by Music Workshop for Kids. 1 cass. (Running Time: 50 min.). (J). 1997. 10.98 (3007-4); audio compact disk 15.98 (3007-2) Baby Music.
Featuring both original & traditional lullabies.

Sleepless. unabr. ed. Charlie Huston. (Running Time: 12 hrs. 30 mins.). 2010. 29.95 (978-1-4417-2636-0(5)); 72.95 (978-1-4417-2632-2(2)) Blckstn Audio.

Sleepless. unabr. ed. Charlie Huston. Read by Mark Bramhall & Ray Porter. 11 CDs. (Running Time: 12 hrs. 30 mins.). 2010. audio compact disk 105.00 (978-1-4417-2633-9(0)) Blckstn Audio.

Sleepover. 1 CD. (Running Time: 20 min.). (Good to Grow Ser.). (J). (ps-3). 2001. audio compact disk 8.95 (978-1-929962-03-7(7)) Write BIG.
When her older brother asks her to guard his invention only to have it demolished during her sleepover, Shelly Kelly comes face-to-face with a lesson in responsibility.

Sleepover Party. Perf. by Mary-Kate Olsen & Ashley Olsen. 1 cass. (Running Time: 1 hr.). (You're Invited To Mary-Kate & Ashley's Ser.). (J). 2002. 8.98 (978-1-56896-189-7(8), 54202-4); audio compact disk 15.98 (978-1-56896-188-0(X), 54202-2) Lightyear Entrtnmnt.
America has watched the Olsen twins grow up from their TV series "Full House" to their current series "So Little Time". The whole family can enjoy this series titles. Featuring Gimme Pizza, OUr Dog Has Eaten OUr HOmework, Stayin' Cool, I'd Rather Be Surfing.

***Sleepwalk with Me: And Other Painfully True Stories.** unabr. ed. Mike Birbiglia. (Running Time: 5 hrs. 30 mins.). 2010. 13.99 (978-1-4001-8919-9(5)) Tantor Media.

***Sleepwalk with Me (Library Edition) And Other Painfully True Stories.** unabr. ed. Mike Birbiglia. (Running Time: 5 hrs. 30 mins.). 2010. 24.99 (978-1-4001-9919-8(0)) Tantor Media.

***Sleepwalkers.** unabr. ed. Paul Grossman. 2010. audio compact disk 34.95 (978-1-61573-105-3(9), 1615731059) Pub: HighBridge. Dist(s): Workman Pub

Sleepy Angels: Beautiful TLC Music for Children. Perf. by Jim Oliver. 1 cass. (978-0-9627593-9-0(2)) Quiet Tymes.

Sleepy Child for Happy Dreams. Read by Mary Richards. 1 cass. (Running Time: 50 min.). (J). 2007. audio compact disk 19.95 (978-1-56136-172-4(0)) Master Your Mind.

Sleepy Hollow. Washington Irving. (YA). 2007. audio compact disk 15.00 (978-1-4276-2425-3(9)) AardGP.

Sleepy Locust. unabr. ed. Robert A. Monroe. Read by Robert A. Monroe. 1 cass. (Running Time: 30 min.). (TimeOut Ser.). 1990. 14.95 (978-1-56102-803-0(7)) Inter Indus.
A modern fable that lulls you into sleep.

Sleepy Lullabies Sing-a-Long. (Hello Kitty Babies Ser.). (J). 1997. 8.00 (978-1-57375-387-6(4)) Audioscope.

Sleepy Ocean & Rain. abr. ed. Jeffrey Thompson. (Running Time: 2:00:00). 2007. audio compact disk 19.98 (978-1-55961-854-0(X)) Sounds True.

Sleepy on Sunday. (Language of Mathematics Ser.). 1989. 7.92 (978-0-8123-6478-1(3)) Holt McDoug.

Sleepy Songs & Stories. Read by Carole Boyd & James Good. 1 cass. (Running Time: 1 hr. 20 min.). (J). 1998. 7.95 (978-1-84032-046-6(X), HoddrStoughton) Pub: Hodder General GBR. Dist(s): Trafalgar

Sleepy Time Hypnosis. Scripts. Steven Gurgevich. Prod. by Steven Gurgevich. 1 CD. (Running Time: 45 min). (ENG.). 2002. audio compact disk 19.95 (978-1-932170-05-4(7), HWH) Tranceformation.

Sleepy Time Lullabies. Perf. by Rachel Sumner. 1 cass; 1 CD. (Running Time: 41 min.). (ENG.). (J). 1995. audio compact disk 14.98 (978-1-886673-04-5(7), Songs by Rachel) Rachels Recs.

Sleepy Time Lullabies. Perf. by Rachel Sumner. 1 cass; 1 CD. (Running Time: 41 min.). (J). (ps). 1995. 9.98 (978-1-886673-03-8(9), Songs by Rachel) Rachels Recs.

Sleepy Time Rock-a-Byes. Kidzup Productions Staff. 1 cass. (Running Time: 90 mins.). (Kidzup Lullabies Ser.). (J). 1999. 8.99 (978-1-894281-07-2(1)); audio compact disk 12.99 (978-1-894281-08-9(X)) Pub: Kidzup CAN. Dist(s): Penton Overseas
A classic collection of all time favorites. Guaranteed to soothe your baby to sleep.

Sleepy Times: Classic Children's Bedtime Stories. Created by Radio Spirits. (Running Time: 10800 sec.). 2004. audio compact disk 9.98 (978-1-57019-801-4(2)) Radio Spirits.

Sleepytime Serenade. Linda Schrade. 1 cass. (Running Time: 39 min.). (J). (ps-6). 1988. 9.95 (978-0-939065-44-8(4), GW 1048) Gentle Wind.
Gentle lullabyes accompanied by guitar & flute.

Sleepytime Serenade. Perf. by Linda Schrade. (J). 1999. audio compact disk 14.95 (978-0-939065-76-9(2)) Gentle Wind.

Sleepytime Showers. Bernie Krause. 1 cass. (Running Time: 60 min.). (Nature's Lullabyes Ser.). 1994. 7.95 (2660, NrthWrd Bks) TandN Child.
Features the gentle voices of birds in a rainshower with the distant murmur of thunder.

Sleepytime Slumber Stories. 1 cass. (Barney Ser.). (J). bk. 6.38 Blisterpack. (LY 9577) NewSound.
Expressive voices, charming music, & a calm pace. A great collection of entertaining children's classics narrated by Barney.

Sleepytime Songs. Gobo Books Staff. (Baby Sing & Play Ser.). (J). (ps). 2007. bds. 12.95 (978-1-932915-42-6(7)) Sandvik Inn.

Sleigh Bells Are Ringing. Scripts. Dave Privett. Prod. by One Way Street Staff. (Running Time: 27 minutes). 2002. audio compact disk Rental 18.00 (978-1-58302-219-1(8)) One Way St.
Snowed in at Grandpa's house, two youngsters, Marie and Gilbert learn the secret of Santa's flying sleigh. they are delighted as Grandpa introduces them to Luiz, a singing penguin who used to be one of Santa's sleigh mechanics. This 20-minute secular Christmas musical gives us a whimsical look at christmas and points us to the power of the holiday which is, love!Song titles include: Let it Snow; Jingle Bells; Little Saint Nick; We Wish you a Merry Christmas.

Sleight of Hand. unabr. ed. (Running Time: 14 hrs.). (J). 2006. 29.95 (978-0-7861-7104-0(9)) Blckstn Audio.

Sleight of Hand. unabr. ed. Kate Wilhelm. Read by Anna Fields. (Running Time: 36000 sec.). 2006. 79.95 (978-0-7861-4897-4(7)); audio compact disk 99.00 (978-0-7861-5982-6(0)) Blckstn Audio.

***Sleights of Mind: What the Neuroscience of Magic Reveals about Our Everyday Deceptions.** unabr. ed. Stephen L. Macknik et al. Narrated by Lloyd James. (Running Time: 10 hrs. 30 mins. 0 sec.). 2010. 24.99 (978-1-4001-6990-0(9)); 16.99 (978-1-4001-8990-8(X)); audio compact disk 34.99 (978-1-4001-1990-5(1)) Pub: Tantor Media. Dist(s): IngramPubServ

***Sleights of Mind (Library Edition) What the Neuroscience of Magic Reveals about Our Everyday Deceptions.** unabr. ed. Stephen L. Macknik et al. Narrated by Lloyd James. (Running Time: 10 hrs. 30 mins.). 2010. 34.99 (978-1-4001-9990-7(5)); audio compact disk 83.99 (978-1-4001-4990-2(8)) Pub: Tantor Media. Dist(s): IngramPubServ

Slender & Gorgeous: Attain a total makeover the simple Way! Created by Christine Sherborne. (ENG.). 2007. audio compact disk 19.95 (978-0-9582712-5-7(9)) Pub: Colourstory AUS. Dist(s): APG

Slender Knowledge. unabr. ed. Stan Kendz. Read by Stan Kendz. 1 cass. (Running Time: 50 min.). 1994. 10.00 (978-1-57582-008-8(0)) HAPPE Progs.
Learn to balance your body naturally with food & daily routine & lose weight naturally without diets.

Slender Thread. unabr. ed. Tracie Peterson. Narrated by Ruth Ann Phimister. 10 cass. (Running Time: 12 hrs. 45 mins.). 2000. 93.00 (978-0-7887-4844-8(0), K0006E7) Recorded Bks.
Five sisters, abondoned by their mother, have been driven apart by pain & trials. But when they attend their mother's funeral, they begin to salvage their frayed relationships held together only by a slender thread. As new tragedies pass their way, they struggle to maintain the tenuous bonds of sisterhood.

Slender Thread: Rediscovering Hope at the Heart of Crisis. abr. ed. Diane Ackerman. Read by Lisa Rafel. 2 cass. (Running Time: 3 hrs.). 1998. 18.95 (978-1-57453-257-9(X)) Audio Lit.
The author mixes stories from her work at a crisis center with her observations of the natural world. Luminous in its insight into human nature.

***Slice of Heaven.** unabr. ed. Sherryl Woods. (Running Time: 11 hrs.). (Sweet Magnolias Ser.). 2010. 19.99 (978-1-4418-6460-4(1), 9781441864604, Brilliance MP3); 19.99 (978-1-4418-6462-8(8), 9781441864628, BAD); 39.97 (978-1-4418-6461-1(X), 9781441864611, Brinc Audio MP3 Lib); 39.97 (978-1-4418-6463-5(6), 9781441864635, BADLE) Brilliance Audio.

***Slice of Heaven.** unabr. ed. Sherryl Woods. Read by Janet Metzger. (Running Time: 11 hrs.). (Sweet Magnolias Ser.). 2010. audio compact disk 19.99 (978-1-4418-6458-1(X), 9781441864581, Bril Audio CD Unabri); audio compact disk 79.97 (978-1-4418-6459-8(8), 9781441864598, BriAudCD Unabrid) Brilliance Audio.

Slice of Life. Al Lucia & Brian Gareau. Narrated by Jim McCabe. 2008. audio compact disk 19.95 (978-1-60031-043-0(5)) Spoken Books.

Slicky Boys. abr. ed. Martin Limón. Read by Martin Limón. 4 cass. (Running Time: 6 hrs.). 1997. 23.00 (978-1-56876-067-4(1)) Soundlines Ent.
George Sueno & Ernie Bascom have found a home in the U. S. Army Criminal Division in Korea. When a soldier ends up dead the two are drawn into a plot with more than just murder.

Slide. unabr. ed. Victor Pemberton. Narrated by Full Cast. (Running Time: 3 hrs. 30 mins. 0 sec.). (ENG.). 2010. audio compact disk 29.95 (978-1-60283-818-5(6)) Pub: AudioGO. Dist(s): Perseus Dist

Slide Guitar. Rikky Rooksby. (Fast Forward Ser.). 2000. audio compact disk 15.95 (978-0-7119-8200-0(7), AM958903) Pub: Wise Publns GBR. Dist(s): Music Sales

Slide Guitar-Tindal, No. 1. Pete Tindal. 1 CD. (Running Time: 1 hr.). 1998. pap. bk. 17.95 (978-0-7866-0585-9(5), 95553BCD) Mel Bay.

Slide Rule: The Autobiography of an Engineer. Nevil Shute. 8 CDs. (Running Time: 9 hrs.). (Soundings (CDs) Ser.). (J). 2005. audio compact disk 79.95 (978-1-84559-150-2(X)) Pub: ISIS Lrg Prnt GBR. Dist(s): Ulverscroft US

Slide Rule: The Autobiography of an Engineer. unabr. ed. Nevil Shute. 7 cass. (Running Time: 9 hrs.). (Soundings Ser.). (J). 2005. 61.95 (978-1-84559-069-7(4)) Pub: ISIS Lrg Prnt GBR. Dist(s): Ulverscroft US

Slide Rule: The Autobiography of an Engineer. unabr. collector's ed. Nevil Shute. Read by Grover Gardner. 8 cass. (Running Time: 8 hrs.). 1986. 48.00 (978-0-7366-1045-2(6), 1975) Books on Tape.
Nevil Shute's autobiography discusses his life long love of airplanes.

Slider: The Leo Butterburger Story. Michael Shaw. Read by Michael Shaw. 2 CDs. (Running Time: 2 hrs. 10 mins.). (YA). 2004. audio compact disk 24.95 (978-0-9747666-3-8(1)) Amer Retro LLC.
Leo was born near Cincinnati, Ohio. He had a passion for sports but not much athletic ability. When it came to neighborhood ball games, he was the kid nobody ever wanted on their team. So, Leo created his own games that he played by himself in his basement on St. John's Street. Then one day he invented a game called Slider that touched millions of people across America and changed his life forever.

Slight Trick of the Mind. unabr. ed. Mitch Cullin. Read by Simon Jones. (YA). 2007. 54.99 (978-1-60252-628-0(1)) Find a World.

Slight Trick of the Mind. unabr. ed. Mitch Cullin. 6 CDs. (Running Time: 7 hrs.). (ENG.). 2005. audio compact disk 29.95 (978-1-56511-950-5(9), 1565119509) Pub: HighBridge. Dist(s): Workman Pub

Slightest Reminders of Your Being... Three Decades of Exile: 1974-2004. Bronislava Volkova. 2005. audio compact disk 15.00 (978-0-9719130-5-9(6)) Explorer Ed.

Slightly Bad Girls of the Bible: Flawed Women Loved by a Flawless God. unabr. ed. Liz Curtis Higgs. Narrated by Liz Curtis Higgs. (ENG.). 2007. 18.19 (978-1-60814-387-0(2)) Oasis Audio.

Slightly Scary Stories for Halloween: Space Case; What's under My Bed?; Georgie; Teeny-Tiny & the Witch Woman. unabr. ed. Edward Marshall et al. Read by Christopher Lloyd et al. (J). 2007. 44.99 (978-1-60252-701-0(6)) Find a World.

Slightly Scary Stories, Volume 2. Alison McGhee et al. Read by Elle Fanning et al. (Playaway Children Ser.). (ENG.). (J). 2009. 44.99 (978-1-60812-599-9(8)) Find a World.

Slightly Shady. unabr. ed. Amanda Quick, pseud. Narrated by Barbara Rosenblat. 9 CDs. (Running Time: 10 hrs.). 2001. audio compact disk 89.00 (978-1-4025-1004-5(7), C1583) Recorded Bks.
Besieged by gambling debts, a desperate gentleman purchases a diary as a tool for blackmail. But he does not live to carry out his plans. He is murdered, and the diary is stolen. Now Tobias March, discrete private investigator, has been hired to find the incriminating diary. Tobias is familiar with danger, but when his inquiries lead him to the beautiful entrepreneur Lavinia Lake, his emotions are sidetracked.

Slightly Shady. unabr. ed. Amanda Quick, pseud. Narrated by Barbara Rosenblat. 7 cass. (Running Time: 10 hrs.). 2001. 68.00 (978-0-7887-5315-2(0)) Recorded Bks.

Sligo to Cork. 1 cass. (Running Time: 1 hr. 30 min.). 12.95 (978-1-55606-023-6(8), CCI-456) Comp Comms Inc.
Features central & eastern Ireland including Dublin, Wexford, & Waterford.

SLII Audio Tape Training System. Ken Blanchard. 6 cass. (Running Time: 6 hrs.). 69.95 (SL0040) K Blanchard.
Learn about Situational Leadership, the four leadership styles, & the three skills of a Situational Leader: Flexibility, Diagnosis & Contracting for Leadership Style.

Slim Forever - for Men: Subliminal Self Help. abr. ed. Audio Activation Staff. 1 CD. (Running Time: 1 hr.). (ENG.). 2003. audio compact disk 9.99 (978-0-7393-0959-9(5)) Pub: Random Audio Pubg. Dist(s): Random

Slim Forever for Women: Subliminal Self-Help. abr. ed. Kelly Howell & Alyson Daniels. 1 CD. (Running Time: 1 hr.). (ENG.). 2003. audio compact disk 9.99 (978-0-7393-0893-6(9)) Pub: Random Audio Pubg. Dist(s): Random

Slim Goodbody: Inside Out. unabr. ed. Perf. by John Burstein. 1 cass. (J). 1984. 8.98 (978-0-89845-170-2(1), CP 1712) HarperCollins Pubs.

Slim Goodbody's Galactic Health Adventure. unabr. ed. Perf. by John Burstein et al. 1 cass. (J). 1984. 8.98 (978-0-89845-136-8(1), CP 1729) HarperCollins Pubs.
Slim's space adventure is designed to teach children healthy living through good nutrition.

Slim Image II: Weight Control. Read by Robert E. Griswold. 1 cass. 1991. 10.95 (978-1-55848-046-9(3)) EffectiveMN.
A new program that incorporates the more recently acquired knowledge & techniques of weight control.

Slim Image II Weight Control. 1 CD. (Running Time: 4140 sec.). (Love Tapes Ser.). 2005. audio compact disk 15.98 (978-1-55848-154-1(0), Love Tapes) EffectiveMN.
This highly-effective and enjoyable CD will help you look and feel exactly as you choose - quickly, easily, and permanently. This is one of the most popular self-improvement programs of all times and comes with a 100% satisfaction guarantee.This CD contains 3 programs. The first is a guided meditation with powerful imagery and techniques for achieving your ideal weight. It also includes two excellent subliminal programs, one with the sound of ocean waves and the other with relaxing original music.

Slim Naturally: Advanced Weight Loss System. Read by Kelly Howell. 1 cass. (Running Time: 60 min.). 1993. 11.95 (978-1-881451-10-5(0)) Brain Sync.
Scientists have now proved beyond doubt that the contents of our thoughts, feelings & emotions have a direct & immediate influence upon our physical being. By means of purely mental techniques such as positive self-suggestion & guided visualization, "Slim Naturally" actually helps regulate physiology. Effortlessly guided into a state of hyper-suggestibility, affirmative information has the most powerful & lasting impact. Both physical & emotional selves are able to "reshape" as thoughts & feelings about self are repatterned & reprogrammed.

Slim Naturally: Advanced Weight Loss System. Kelly Howell. 2000. audio compact disk 14.95 (978-1-881451-66-2(6)) Brain Sync.

Slime Lake, unabr. ed. Tom B. Stone. Narrated by Jeff Woodman. 2 cass. (Running Time: 2 hrs. 15 mins.). (Graveyard School Ser.: No. 7). (gr. 3-7). 2001. 19.00 (978-0-7887-0694-3(2), 94884E7) Recorded Bks.
An adventure of spooky danger & grisly humor centers around a school so weird that its students are dying to go to class.

Slimmer You. 1 cass. (Running Time: 55 min.). 9.95 (I0090B090, HarperThor) HarpC GBR.

Slim's Good-Bye. John R. Erickson. 1 cass. (Running Time: 2 hrs. 10 mins.). (Hank the Cowdog Ser.: No. 34). (J). (gr. 2-5). 2000. 16.95 (978-0-87719-375-3(4)) Lone Star Bks.

Slim's Good-Bye. unabr. ed. John R. Erickson. Read by John R. Erickson. 3 CDs. (Running Time: 3 hrs. 36 mins.). (Hank the Cowdog Ser.: No. 34). (J). (gr. 4-7). 2001. audio compact disk 14.95 Books on Tape.
When hard times hit the ranch, Slim hits the road in search of a new job, not knowing that Hank is in the back of the pickup.

Slim's Good-Bye. unabr. ed. John R. Erickson. Read by John R. Erickson. (Hank the Cowdog Ser.: No. 34). (J). (gr. 4-7). 2001. 24.00 (978-0-7366-6249-9(9)) Books on Tape.
Things are not looking good for the ranch. When Loper heads into town to negotiate with the banker, Slim hits the road in search of a new home. Meanwhile, Hank and his faithful sidekick, Drover, hitch a ride in the back of slim's pick-up. Before long, they come to a stop in an unfamiliar town. When Slim lands himself a new job, Hank finds that he's no longer the Head of Ranch Security,but the Head of Chicken House Security. Hank knows this new life is for the birds...but will he ever see the ranch again.

Slim's Good-Bye. unabr. ed. John R. Erickson. Read by John R. Erickson. 2 cass. (Running Time: 2 hrs.). (Hank the Cowdog Ser.: No. 34). (J). (gr. 4-7). 2001. 12.95 (978-0-7366-6923-8(X)) Books on Tape.
When hard times hit the ranch, Slim hits the road in search of a new job, not knowing that Hank is in the back of the pickup.

Slim's Good-Bye. unabr. ed. John R. Erickson. Read by John R. Erickson. 3 CDs. (Running Time: 1 hr. 12 mins.). (Hank the Cowdog Ser.: No. 34). (J). (gr. 4-7). 2001. audio compact disk 28.00 (978-0-7366-7556-7(6)) Books on Tape.
Things are not looking good for the ranch. When Loper heads into town to negotiate with the banker, Slim hits the road in search of a new home. Meanwhile, Hank and his faithful sidekick, Drover, hitch a ride in the back of slim's pick-up. Before long, they come to a stop in an unfamiliar town. When Slim lands himself a new job, Hank finds that he's no longer the Head of Ranch Security,but the Head of Chicken House Security. Hank knows this new life is for the birds...but will he ever see the ranch again.

Slim's Good-Bye. unabr. ed. John R. Erickson. Read by John R. Erickson. 2 cass. (Running Time: 3 hrs.). (Hank the Cowdog Ser.: No. 34). (J). 2002. 17.99 (978-1-59188-334-0(2)) Maverick Bks.
Things are not looking good for the ranch. So when Loper heads into town to negotiate with the banker, Slim hits the road in search of a new home.

Slim's Good-Bye. unabr. ed. John R. Erickson. Read by John R. Erickson. 3 CDs. (Running Time: Approx. 3 hours). (Hank the Cowdog Ser.: No. 34). (J). 2002. audio compact disk 19.99 (978-1-59188-634-1(1)) Maverick Bks.

Slim's Good-Bye, unabr. ed. John R. Erickson. Read by John R. Erickson. 2 cass. (Running Time: 2 hrs. 30 mins.). (Hank the Cowdog Ser.: No. 34). (J). (gr. 2-5). 2000. 18.00 (978-0-8072-8265-6(0), Listening Lib) Random Audio Pubg.

Slimy, Secret, & Scary: Day of the Field Trip Zombies/Ooze Slingers from Outer Space/Tiger Moth Insect Ninja. Aaron Reynolds et al. (Playaway Children Ser.). (ENG.). (J). 2009. 35.00 (978-1-60775-618-7(8)) Find a World.

Slingshot, unabr. ed. Jack D. Hunter. Read by Tom Parker. 9 cass. (Running Time: 13 hrs.). 1995. 62.95 (978-0-7861-0872-5(X), 1642) Blckstn Audio.
Against a future backdrop of growing American middle class discontent & rebellion, investigative reporter Matt Cooper single-mindedly probes the murder of his father, a successful novelist with mysterious ties to World War II Nazi Germany. His obsessive search takes Cooper halfway around the globe & to the very core of the international conspiracy that uses the incipient citizens' rebellion as a screen for its own efforts to usurp the faltering U.S. government.

Slingshot. unabr. ed. Jack D. Hunter. Read by Tom Parker. (Running Time: 45000 sec.). 2007. audio compact disk 90.00 (978-0-7861-6116-4(7)); audio compact disk 29.95 (978-0-7861-6117-1(5)) Blckstn Audio.

Slip of the Knife. unabr. ed. Denise Mina. Narrated by Jane MacFarlane. (Running Time: 10 hrs. 45 mins.). 2008. 54.95 (978-0-7927-5375-9(5)); audio compact disk 89.95 (978-0-7927-5335-3(6)) AudioGO.
Paddy Meehan is no stranger to murder - as a reporter she lives at crime scenes - but nothing has prepared her for this visit from the police. Her former boyfriend and fellow journalist Terry Patterson has been found hooded and shot through the head. Paddy knows she will be of little help - she had not seen Terry in more than six months. So she is bewildered to learn that in his will he has left her his house and several suitcases full of notes. Drawn into a maze of secrets and lies, Paddy begins making connections to Terry's murder that no one else has seen, and soon finds herself trapped in the most important - and dangerous - story of her career.

Slip, Sliding Away: Hebrews 2:1-4. Ed Young. 1991. 4.95 (978-0-7417-1876-1(6), 876) Win Walk.

Slipback. Eric Saward. (Running Time: 1 hr.). 2001. audio compact disk 15.99 (978-0-563-47794-5(6)) London Brdge.

Slipknot. unabr. ed. Linda Greenlaw. Read by Sandra Burr. (Running Time: 8 hrs.). (Jane Bunker Ser.). 2007. 39.25 (978-1-4233-3178-0(8), 9781423331780, BADLE); 24.95 (978-1-4233-3177-3(X), 9781423331773, BAD); 69.25 (978-1-4233-3172-8(9), 9781423331728, BrilAudUnabridg); audio compact disk 24.95 (978-1-4233-3175-9(3), 9781423331759, Brilliance MP3); audio compact disk 29.95 (978-1-4233-3173-5(7), 9781423331735, Bril Audio CD Unabri); audio compact disk 39.25 (978-1-4233-3176-6(1), 9781423331766, Brinc Audio MP3 Lib); audio compact disk 87.25 (978-1-4233-3174-2(5), 9781423331742, BriAudCD Unabrid) Brilliance Audio.

Slippery Slope. unabr. abr. ed. Lemony Snicket, pseud. Read by Tim Curry. 6 CDs. (Running Time: 6 hrs.). (Series of Unfortunate Events Ser.: Bk. 10). (gr. 3-8). 2003. audio compact disk 25.99 (978-0-06-056441-4(5)) HarperCollins Pubs.

Slipping-down Life. unabr. ed. Anne Tyler. Read by Mary Woods. 6 cass. (Running Time: 6 hrs.). 1987. 36.00 (978-0-7366-1105-3(3), 2031) Books on Tape.
Drum Casey surprised Evie like the discovery of an island surprises a drowning person...If it wasn't love between them, it was at least dry land.

Sliver. unabr. ed. Ira Levin. Read by Multivoice Production Staff. (Running Time: 5 hrs.). 2008. 39.25 (978-1-4233-5292-1(0), 9781423352921, Brinc Audio MP3 Lib) Brilliance Audio.

Sliver. unabr. ed. Ira Levin. Read by Multivoice Production Staff. (Running Time: 5 hrs.). 2008. 39.25 (978-1-4233-5294-5(7), 9781423352945, BADLE); 24.95 (978-1-4233-5293-8(9), 9781423352938, BAD); 24.95 (978-1-4233-5291-4(2), 9781423352914, Brilliance MP3) Brilliance Audio.

Sloan & Philamena see Hug Me & Other Stories

Slobberers. unabr. ed. Morris Gleitzman & Paul Jennings. Read by Kate Hosking & Stig Wemyss. (Running Time: 1 hr.). (Wicked! Ser.: Bk. 1). (J). audio compact disk 18.00 (978-1-74093-423-7(7)) Bolinda Pubng AUS.

Slobberers. unabr. ed. Morris Gleitzman & Paul Jennings. Read by Kate Hosking. (Running Time: 1 hr.). (Wicked! Ser.: Bk. 1). (J). 2001. 18.00 (978-1-74030-457-3(8)) Pub: Bolinda Pubng AUS. Dist(s): Bolinda Pub Inc

Slobbering Love Affair: The True (and Pathetic) Story of the Torrid Romance Between Barack Obama & the Mainstream Media. unabr. ed. Bernard Goldberg. Narrated by Alan Sklar. (Running Time: 4 hrs. 30 mins. 0 sec.). (ENG.). 2009. audio compact disk 24.99 (978-1-4001-1204-3(4)); audio compact disk 19.99 (978-1-4001-6204-8(1)) Pub: Tantor Media. Dist(s): IngramPubServ

Slobbering Love Affair: The True (And Pathetic) Story of the Torrid Romance Between Barack Obama & the Mainstream Media. unabr. ed. Bernard Goldberg. Narrated by Alan Sklar. 4 CDs. (Running Time: 4 hrs. 30 mins. 0 sec.). (ENG.). 2009. audio compact disk 49.99 (978-1-4001-4204-0(0)) Pub: Tantor Media. Dist(s): IngramPubServ

Slocum & the Ambush Trail. abr. ed. Jake Logan. Narrated by Michelle de Long & Dick Wilkinson. 2 cass. (Running Time: 3 hrs.). (Jake Logan Ser.: No. 262). 2001. 16.95 (978-1-890990-61-9(2)) Otis Audio.
Slocum escorts four brides-to-be on a wagon trip through rugged territory. But what's outside ain't as dangerous as what's inside: four fiery women hankering for their first-and last-taste of freedom.

Slocum & the Blue-Eyed Hostage. Jake Logan. 2 cass. (Running Time: 3 hrs.). (Jake Logan Ser.: No. 266). 2001. 16.95 (978-1-890990-72-5(8)) Otis Audio.
Slocum signs on to guard a wealthy Comanchero trader for some quick cash & gets a white squaw in the bargain. The only problem is that the brutal Comanche Chief Black Horn wants her back & promises slow death to any who would dare stop him.

Slocum & the Friendly Foe. abr. ed. Jake Logan. Read by Dick Wilkinson & Michelle DeLong. 2 cass. (Running Time: 3 hrs.). (Jake Logan Ser.: Vol. 271). 2002. 16.95 (978-1-890990-83-1(3), 99083) Otis Audio.
Adult western with sound effects.

Slocum & the Gambler's Woman. abr. ed. Jake Logan. Narrated by Michelle de Long & Dick Wilkinson. 2 cass. (Running Time: 3 hrs.). (Jake Logan Ser.: Vol. 51). 2000. 16.95 (978-1-890990-42-8(6), 99042) Otis Audio.
Since the alleged killing of Billy the Kid, things have been pretty peaceful on New Mexico's old Fort Sumner settlement. But a gambling cheat who beats his girlfriend is trying to spoil the mood. And there's nothing Slocum hates more than a cheater or loves more than a pretty woman in distress. Especially one who's happy to show her gratitude night after night.

Slocum & the Gila Rangers. abr. ed. Jake Logan. Narrated by Dick Wilkinson & Michelle de Long. 2 cass. (Running Time: 3 hrs.). (Jake Logan Ser.: No. 260). 2001. 16.95 (978-1-890990-59-6(0), 99059) Otis Audio.

Slocum & the Gunrunners. abr. ed. Jake Logan. Narrated by Michelle de Long & Dick Wilkinson. 2 cass. (Running Time: 3 hrs.). (Jake Logan Ser.: Vol. 52). 2000. 16.95 (978-1-890990-43-5(4), 99043) Otis Audio.
Apache uprisings are forcing local homesteaders to abandon their land. And a group of outlaws plans to sell them a lot more firepower. But Slocum's prepared to defuse the situation before the frontier explodes.

Slocum & the Hired Gun, No. 268. Jake Logan. 2 cass. (Running Time: 3 hrs.). 2001. 16.95 (978-1-890990-76-3(0)) Otis Audio.

Slocum & the Jersey Lily. abr. ed. Jake Logan. Read by Dick Wilkinson & Michelle DeLong. 2 cass. (Running Time: 3 hrs.). (Jake Logan Ser.: Vol. 50). 2000. 16.95 (978-1-890990-41-1(8), 99041) Otis Audio.
Western with sound effects & music, multi-voice.

Slocum & the Lakota Lady. Jake Logan. Read by Dick Wilkinson & Michelle DeLong. 2 cass. (Running Time: 3 hrs.). (Jake Logan Ser.: No. 264). 2001. 16.95 (978-1-890990-68-8(X), 99068) Otis Audio.
After Slocum risks his life to help a Lakota woman, she "heals" his injuries quite effectively. Soon, Slocum befriends her people & vows to help when the government starts pushing them around.

Slocum & the Mountain Spirit. abr. ed. Jake Logan. Narrated by Dick Wilkinson & Michelle de Long. 2 cass. (Running Time: 3 hrs.). (Jake Logan Ser.). 2000. 16.95 (978-1-890990-52-7(3), 99052) Otis Audio.

Slocum & the Nebraska Storm. abr. ed. Jake Logan. Narrated by Dick Wilkinson & Michelle de Long. 2 cass. (Running Time: 3 hrs.). (Jake Logan Ser.: Vol. 53). 2000. 16.95 (978-1-890990-44-2(2),) Otis Audio.
Slocum's under the weather during one of Nebraska's worst storms. A Sioux warrior has taken it upon himself to watch over Slocum while he heals & protect him from the notorious One-eyed Jacks & his liquor-guzzling, troublemaking crew.

Slocum & the Pomo Chief. abr. ed. Jake Logan. Narrated by Dick Wilkinson & Michelle de Long. 2 cass. (Running Time: 3 hrs.). (Jake Logan Ser.). 2000. 16.95 (978-1-890990-51-0(5), 99051) Otis Audio.
Needing cash, Slocum gets a lumberjacking job in the forests of Northern California. And though the superintendent's daughter is willing to take Slocum to heaven, some renegade Indians are ready to take him to hell.

Slocum & the Rich Man's Son, No. 265. Jake Logan. 2 cass. (Running Time: 3 hrs.). 2001. 16.95 (978-1-890990-70-1(1)) Otis Audio.
Slocum is on the hunt for Michael Porges, whose wealthy father wants him brought back home. Now, Slocum will learn more about the Porges family than he ever wanted to, if he lives long enough to find out the truth.

Slocum & the Senorita. abr. ed. Jake Logan. Narrated by Michelle de Long & Dick Wilkinson. 2 cass. (Running Time: 3 hrs.). (Jake Logan Ser.: No. 261). 2001. 16.95 (978-1-890990-60-2(4)) Otis Audio.
Pistoleros & bounty hunters are hot on Slocum's trail, after he rescues a pretty young Mexican girl from a brutal attack.

Slocum & the Undertaker. abr. ed. Jake Logan. Read by Michelle de Long & Dick Wilkinson. 2 cass. (Running Time: 3 hrs.). (Jake Logan Ser.: Vol. 55). 2000. 16.95 (978-1-890990-46-6(9), 99046) Otis Audio.
In the strange little town of Lost Soul, where the marshal doesn't carry a gun & the undertaker has taken over everything, Slocum finds that getting out is a lot tougher than getting in.

Slocum & Wild Bill's Lady. abr. ed. Jake Logan. Read by Michelle de Long & Dick Wilkinson. 2 cass. (Running Time: 3 hrs.). (Jake Logan Ser.: No. 259). 2000. 16.95 (978-1-890990-54-1(X), 99054) Otis Audio.
Slocum's always got a lovely lady on his arm. But when he gets involved with Wild Bill Hickok's favorite girl everyone in Abilene sees trouble brewing.

Slocum on Ghost Mesa. abr. ed. Jake Logan. Read by Dick Wilkinson & Michelle DeLong. 2 cass. (Running Time: 3 hrs.). (Jake Logan Ser.: Vol. 270). 2001. 16.95 (978-1-890990-80-0(9), 99080) Otis Audio.
Adult western with music and sound effects.

Slocum's Close Call. abr. ed. Jake Logan. Read by Michelle de Long & Dick Wilkinson. 2 cass. (Running Time: 3 hrs.). (Jake Logan Ser.: Vol. 54). 2000. 16.95 (978-1-890990-45-9(0), 99045) Otis Audio.
Slocum becomes a guardian angel when he helps out a rancher on the run from a wild bunch of rustlers. But keeping this man alive could put Slocum six feet under.

Slocum's Partner. abr. ed. Jake Logan. Read by Dick Wilkinson & Michelle DeLong. 2 cass. (Running Time: 3 hrs.). (Jake Logan Ser.). 2000. 16.95 (978-1-890990-53-4(1), 99053) Otis Audio.
Adult western with sound effects & music.

Slocum's Sidekick, No. 267. Jake Logan. 2 cass. (Running Time: 3 hrs.). 2001. 16.95 (978-1-890990-73-2(6)) Otis Audio.
The last three mail drivers who tried to make it to Prescott turned up dead. But that doesn't stop Slocum from trying. Until a young runaway with a big secret shows up by his side & greets Slocum with a real dangerous surprise.

***Sloppy Joe.** unabr. ed. Dave Keane. Read by Fred Berman. (ENG.). 2009. (978-0-06-179287-8(X)); (978-0-06-190246-8(2)) HarperCollins Pubs.

Slot Conquest. unabr. ed. Frank Scoblete. 1 cass. (Running Time: 1 hr.). 1997. audio compact disk 16.95 CD. (978-1-882173-05-1(8)) Paone Pr.
New strategies for today's one armed bandits including the placement of the loose & tight machines.

Slouching Towards Gomorrah: Modern Liberalism & American Decline, unabr. ed. Robert H. Bork. Read by Barrett Whitener. 10 cass. (Running Time: 14 hrs. 30 mins.). 1997. 69.95 (978-0-7861-1182-4(8), 1941) Blckstn Audio.
One of our nation's most distinguished conservative scholars offers a prophetic & unprecedented view of a culture in decline, a nation in such serious moral trouble that its very foundation is crumbling.

Slough of Despond from "Lord Weary's Castle" see Twentieth-Century Poetry in English, No. 32-33, Recordings of Poets Reading Their Own Poetry

Slovak, Beginning. Oscar E. Swan & Sylvia Galova-Lorinc. 8 cass. (Running Time: 8 hrs.). (SLO & ENG., (C). 1990. pap. bk. (978-0-89357-214-3(4), AFSL10) Slavica.
Foreign Language Instruction. Modern, Full-length course of Slovak.

Slovak Phrase Book. Sylvia Galova-Lorinc & Stephen R. Hoferka, Jr. Ed. by John M. Lorinc. 1991. 9.50 (978-0-9644998-1-2(9)) Lor-Hof Pub.

Slovak Songs in Latin, Slovak & English with 170 Music Score. Ed. by Ivan Reguli et al. Tr. by Bystrik Muransky. Contrib. by Viktor Stefanec. Music by Jan Eambal. Illus. by Joseph Cincik. 2007. audio compact disk 39.00 (978-0-86516-567-0(X)) Bolchazy-Carducci.

Slow Awakening. Catherine Cookson. Read by Anne Dover. 8 cass. (Running Time: 12 hrs.). 1999. 69.95 (65247) Pub: Soundings Ltd GBR. Dist(s): Ulverscroft US

Slow Awakening. unabr. ed. Catherine Cookson. Read by Anne Dover. 8 cass. (Running Time: 12 hrs.). 1991. 69.95 (978-1-85496-524-0(7), 65247) Pub: Soundings Ltd GBR. Dist(s): Ulverscroft US
In the mid-1850's orphan Kirsten was sold at 14 to a vicious traveling tinker. Rescued, she gave birth to a child, just as the mistress of the house was told that her newborn was dead. A secret bargain was struck which would change Kirsten's fortune.

Slow Birds. Short Stories. Ian Watson. Narrated by Jim Bond. 1CD. (Running Time: 72 mins.). (Great Science Fiction Stories Ser.). 2004. audio compact disk 10.99 (978-1-884612-34-3(2)) AudioText.

Slow Birds. unabr. ed. Ian Watson. Read by Jim Bond. Ed. by Allan Kaster. 1 cass. (Running Time: 1 hr. 12 min.). (Great Science Fiction Stories Ser.). 1996. 10.99 (978-1-884612-10-7(5)) AudioText.

Slow Boat to Mongolia. unabr. ed. Lydia Laube. Read by Deidre Rubenstein. 6 cass. (Running Time: 9 hrs.). 1998. (978-1-86442-290-0(4), 580745) Bolinda Pubng AUS.
Lydia tells of her travels by ship, train & bone-shaking bus through Indonesia & China on her way to fabled Outer Mongolia, where she stays in a ger in the snow, & rides a horse through waist-high silvery grass.

Slow Boats Home. unabr. ed. Gavin Young. 12 cass. (Isis Ser.). (J). 2004. 94.95 (978-1-85089-847-4(2)) Pub: ISIS Lrg Prnt GBR. Dist(s): Ulverscroft US

Slow Boats to China. unabr. collector's ed. Gavin Young. Read by Bill Kelsey. 13 cass. (Running Time: 19 hrs. 30 mins.). 1991. 104.00 (978-0-7366-1961-5(5), 2782) Books on Tape.
It was a simple idea, the kind all of us have had at one time or another. Take a series of ships of different sizes & kinds, go where they lead & see what happens. Inspired by great sea writers, like Jack London, Herman Melville & Joseph Conrad, Gavin Young decided he would port-hop to some far destination on the other side of the world. The end of the line would be China.

Slow Burn. abr. ed. Julie Garwood. Read by Laural Merlington. (Running Time: 21600 sec.). 2006. audio compact disk 16.99 (978-1-59600-834-2(2), 9781596008342, BCD Value Price) Brilliance Audio.

Slow Burn. abr. ed. Julie Garwood. Read by Laural Merlington. (Running Time: 6 hrs.). 2010. audio compact disk 9.99 (978-1-4418-0825-7(6), 9781441808257, BCD Value Price) Brilliance Audio.

Slow Burn. unabr. ed. Julie Garwood. Read by Joyce Bean. (Running Time: 9 hrs.). 2005. 39.25 (978-1-59710-876-8(6), 9781597108768, BADLE); 24.95 (978-1-59710-877-5(4), 9781597108775, BAD) Brilliance Audio.

Slow Burn. unabr. ed. Julie Garwood. Read by Laural Merlington & Joyce Bean. (Running Time: 9 hrs.). 2005. 39.25 (978-1-59335-818-1(0), 9781593358181, Brlnc Audio MP3 Lib) Brilliance Audio.
Living a successful life in Charleston, South Carolina, Kate MacKenna has always been able to turn her challenges into triumphs. But now the fates seem to be lining up against her . . . in a lethal fashion. While attending a reception at a friend's estate for a controversial artist, Kate is nearly killed by an explosion. Once home, Kate is hit with the news that the prosperous fragrance company she has nurtured from the ground up is in jeopardy: It turns out that her late mother used the business as collateral for a huge loan, and full payment is due in three weeks. Kate's still reeling from this devastating news when her younger sister's volatile ex-boyfriend shows up and threatens her. Then Kate receives a call from her best friend, Jordan Buchanan, who is hospitalized and scheduled for surgery in Boston. Though stretched to the limit, Kate immediately rushes to her side. Once she knows that Jordan is going to be fine, Kate abandons her calm façade and allows herself a major meltdown, doing something that is totally uncharacteristic: She has a one-night stand with Jordan's brother Dylan. Coming to her senses, Kate returns home determined to get back on track and save her business. But the mishaps keep coming. At Jordan's insistence, Dylan checks up on Kate. He's convinced that she's merely having a spell of bad luck - until he discovers how many people want Kate MacKenna dead.

Slow Burn. unabr. ed. Julie Garwood. Read by Joyce Bean. 6 cass. (Running Time: 32400 sec.). 2005. 32.95 (978-1-59086-251-3(1), 9781590862513, BAU); audio compact disk 36.95 (978-1-59086-254-4(6), 9781590862544, Bril Audio CD Unabri); audio compact disk 92.25 (978-1-59086-255-1(4), 9781590862551, BriAudCD Unabrid); audio compact disk 24.95 (978-1-59335-684-2(6), 9781593356842, Brilliance MP3) Brilliance Audio.

***Slow Burn: A Novel.** Mary E. DeMuth. (Running Time: 10 hrs. 4 mins. 0 sec.). (Defiance Texas Ser.). (ENG.). 2009. 14.99 (978-0-310-77295-8(8)) Zondervan.

Slow Burning. unabr. ed. Stanley Pottinger. Narrated by Richard Ferrone. 15 cass. (Running Time: 20 hrs. 30 mins.). 2000. 119.00 (978-0-7887-4305-4(8), 96200E7) Recorded Bks.
As a boy in Mississippi, Cush Walker watched the Klan lynch his father. Now a brain surgeon in New York, he is working on a procedure designed to eradicate that kind of hatred. But how far can he stretch his ethics & medical expertise? Includes an exclusive interview with the author.

Slow Dollar. unabr. ed. Margaret Maron. Narrated by C. J. Critt. 6 cass. (Running Time: 8 hrs. 45 mins.). (Deborah Knott Mystery Ser.: No. 9). 2002. 85.00 (978-1-4025-1821-8(8)) Recorded Bks.

Slow Down: Awaken to Your Own Spiritual Path. David Essel. (ENG.). 2007. audio compact disk 12.00 (978-1-893074-19-4(6)) D Essel Inc.

Slow Down: Shift Your Energy Through Meditation. David Essel. (ENG.). 2007. audio compact disk 12.00 (978-1-893074-20-0(X)) D Essel Inc.

Slow Down: The Fastest Way to Get Everything You Want. David Essel. (ENG.). 2007. audio compact disk 28.00 (978-1-893074-18-7(8)) D Essel Inc.

Slow Down: Transform Your Stress into Success. David Essel. (ENG.). 2007. audio compact disk 12.00 (978-1-893074-17-0(X)) D Essel Inc.

Slow down & Live. 1 cass. (Running Time: 1 hr.). 1982. 7.95 (978-1-58638-608-5(5)) Nilgiri Pr.
Install brakes on the mind.

Slow Heat in Heaven. abr. ed. Sandra Brown. Read by Dick Hill. (Running Time: 21600 sec.). 2007. audio compact disk 14.99 (978-1-4233-2472-0(2), 9781423324720, BCD Value Price) Brilliance Audio.

Slow Heat in Heaven. unabr. ed. Sandra Brown. Read by Dick Hill. (Running Time: 15 hrs.). 2006. 39.25 (978-1-4233-2470-6(6), 9781423324706, BADLE); 24.95 (978-1-4233-2469-0(2), 9781423324690, BAD); 97.25 (978-1-4233-2464-5(1), 9781423324645, BrilAudUnabridg); audio compact disk 117.25 (978-1-4233-2466-9(8), 9781423324669, BriAudCD Unabrid); audio compact disk 39.25 (978-1-4233-2468-3(4), 9781423324683, Brlnc Audio MP3 Lib); audio compact disk 38.95 (978-1-4233-2465-2(X), 9781423324652, Bril Audio CD Unabri); audio compact disk 24.95 (978-1-4233-2467-6(6), 9781423324676, Brilliance MP3) Brilliance Audio.
The adopted daughter of the most powerful man in town, Schyler Crandall had left Heaven, Louisiana, a broken-hearted girl. Now a crisis brings her home to a family in conflict, a logging empire on the brink of disaster, and secrets that make Heaven hotter than hell.

Slow Moon. unabr. ed. Elizabeth Cox. (Running Time: 28800 sec.). 2007. 54.95 (978-1-4332-0619-1(6)); audio compact disk 29.95 (978-1-4332-0621-4(8)); audio compact disk 63.00 (978-1-4332-0620-7(X)) Blckstn Audio.

Slow Motion Riot. unabr. ed. Peter Blauner & Malcolm Hillgartner. (Running Time: 15 hrs. 5 mins.). 2008. 29.95 (978-1-4332-5435-2(2)); 89.95 (978-1-4332-5433-8(6)); audio compact disk 110.00 (978-1-4332-5434-5(4)) Blckstn Audio.

***Slow Sex: The Art & Craft of the Female Orgasm.** unabr. ed. Nicole Daedone. (Running Time: 7 hrs. 30 mins.). (ENG.). 2011. 24.98 (978-1-60788-297-8(3)) Pub: Hachet Audio. Dist(s): HachBkGrp

***Slow Wave Sleep.** Kelly Howell. (ENG.). 2010. audio compact disk 14.95 (978-1-60568-065-1(6)) Brain Sync.

Slow World. Music by Liquid Mind. Composed by Chuck Wild. 1 CD. (Running Time: 59 mins.). 1996. audio compact disk 15.98 (978-0-9742661-1-4(6)) Chuck Wild Recs.

Slowing down the Aging Process. Bruce Goldberg. Read by Bruce Goldberg. 1 cass. (Running Time: 30 min.). (ENG.). 2007. 13.00 (978-1-885577-28-3(1)) Pub: B Goldberg. Dist(s): Baker Taylor
This self hypnosis program trains you to tap into your natural healing abilities and raise the immune system, thus slowing down the aging process.

Slowing down the Aging Process DVD. Bruce Goldberg. (ENG.). 2005. audio compact disk 17.00 (978-1-57968-042-8(9)) Pub: B Goldberg. Dist(s): Baker Taylor

Slowly down the Ganges. unabr. collector's ed. Eric Newby. Read by David Case. 9 cass. (Running Time: 13 hrs. 30 min.). 1995. 72.00 (978-0-7366-3109-9(7), 3785) Books on Tape.
The spirit is lively as they meet an inviting mix of characters. The spirit is tranquil as the dusty simplicity of India quiets & mystifies their souls. Throughout the pages, the Mother Ganges runs through, a sacred presence.

Slowness. unabr. collector's ed. Milan Kundera. Read by Barrett Whitener. 3 cass. (Running Time: 3 hrs.). 1997. 18.00 (978-0-7366-3579-0(3), 4232) Books on Tape.
Underlying this fanatasy is a profound meditation on contemporary life: about the bond between slowness & memory & about how our era has surrendered to the demon of speed.

Sluggers Collection. unabr. ed. Loren Long & Phil Bildner. Read by Josh Hamilton. (Running Time: 5 hrs. 0 mins. 0 sec.). (J). 2009. audio compact disk 19.99 (978-0-7435-7960-5(7)) Pub: S&S Audio. Dist(s): S and S Inc

Slugs at Sea. Perf. by Banana Slug String Band Staff. 1 cass. (Running Time: 31 min.). 1991. 9.98 (978-1-877737-71-8(2), MLP 2141) MFLP CA.
Scientifically accurate & entertaining music about ocean & wetland environments done in coordination with the Oceanic Society's Project OCEAN. Fun & lively!.

Slumber Mountain. unabr. ed. Max Brand. Read by Steve Pietrofesa. 5 cass. (Running Time: 7 hrs.). (Sagebrush Western Ser.). (J). 1998. 49.95 (978-1-57490-220-4(2)) Pub: ISIS Lrg Prnt GBR. Dist(s): Ulverscroft US

Slumber of Christianity: Awakening a Passion for Heaven on Earth. Ted Dekker. 2005. 19.99 (978-1-59859-033-3(2)); audio compact disk 27.99 (978-1-59859-032-6(4)) Oasis Audio.

Slumber of Christianity: Awakening a Passion for Heaven on Earth. abr. ed. Ted Dekker. (Running Time: 3 hrs. 30 mins.). 2005. audio compact disk 24.99 (978-0-7852-1240-9(X)) Nelson.

Slumber of Christianity: Awakening a Passion for Heaven on Earth. unabr. ed. Ted Dekker. Narrated by Kelly Ryan Dolan. (ENG.). 2005. 19.59 (978-1-60814-388-7(0)) Oasis Audio.

***Slumdog Millionaire.** unabr. ed. Vikas Swarup. Narrated by Christopher Simpson. 1 Playaway. (Running Time: 10 hrs. 45 mins.). 2009. 89.95 (978-0-7927-6601-8(6)); audio compact disk 89.95 (978-0-7927-6162-4(6)) AudioGO.

Slumdog Millionaire. unabr. ed. Vikas Swarup. Narrated by Christopher Simpson. 9 CDs. (Running Time: 10 hrs. 45 mins.). (ENG.). 2009. audio compact disk 29.95 (978-1-60283-466-8(0)) Pub: AudioGO. Dist(s): Perseus Dist

Slumgullion Stew: An Edward Abbey Reader. unabr. collector's ed. Edward Abbey. Read by Paul Shay. 10 cass. (Running Time: 15 hrs.). 1988. 80.00 (978-0-7366-1461-0(3), 2341) Books on Tape.
Besides excerpts from seven novels - including a work in process - there are offerings from the author's personal histories of travel, ideas, people, nature, places & adventures including Abbey's Road, Beyond the Wall & Down the River.

Slumming. unabr. ed. 4 cass. (Running Time: 4 hrs. 30 min.). (YA). 2003. 38.00 (978-1-4025-6475-8(9)) Recorded Bks.

Slummy Mummy. unabr. ed. Fiona Neill. Read by Katherine Kellgren. (YA). 2007. 44.99 (978-1-60252-861-1(6)) Find a World.

Slummy Mummy. unabr. ed. Fiona Neill. Read by Katherine Kellgren. 10 CDs. (Running Time: 43200 sec.). 2007. audio compact disk 29.95 (978-1-59316-101-9(8)) Listen & Live.

Sly Fox & the Chicks. Short Stories. Carl Sommer. Narrated by Carl Sommer. 1 cass. Dramatization. (Another Sommer-Time Story Ser.). (J). (gr. 1-4). 2003. bk. 16.95 (978-1-57537-553-3(2)) Advance Pub.

***Sly Fox & the Chicks / el Zorro Astutoso Y Los Pollit.** ed. Carl Sommer. Illus. by Kennon James. (Another Sommer-Time Story Bilingual Ser.). (ENG & SPA.). (J). 2009. bk. 26.95 (978-1-57537-191-7(X)) Advance Pub.

Sly Fox & the Chicks Read-along. Carl Sommer. Narrated by Carl Sommer. 1 cass. Dramatization. (Another Sommer-Time Story Ser.). (J). 2003. lib. bdg. 23.95 (978-1-57537-754-4(3)) Advance Pub.
Character Education story with a character song by Karacter Kidz.

***Sly Moves.** unabr. ed. Sylvester Stallone. Read by Robb Webb. (ENG.). 2005. (978-0-06-088526-7(2), Harper Audio); (978-0-06-088527-4(0), Harper Audio) HarperCollins Pubs.

Sly Moves: My Proven Program to Lose Weight, Build Strength, Gain Will Power, & Live Your Dream. unabr. ed. Sylvester Stallone. Read by Robb Webb. 2005. audio compact disk 22.95 (978-0-06-078773-8(2)) HarperCollins Pubs.

Sly Vengeance. unabr. ed. Dorothy R. Kliewer. Read by Denise S. Utter. 4 cass. (Running Time: 5 hrs. 24 min.). 1994. 26.95 (978-1-55686-541-1(4)) Books in Motion.
Kyla Kurtis, investigative reporter for the New-Times stumbles into a murder mystery surrounding the mysterious deaths of a former Belmont mayor & a private investigator.

Sm Trato Hecho: Spanish Real Life Cassette. 2nd ed. McMinn. (SPA.). (C). 2000. 42.67 (978-0-13-021666-3(6), Prentice Hall) P-H.

Smakebiter av Norsk og Norge: An 8-Lesson Norwegian Language Course for Adult Learners. 2000. audio compact disk 32.95 (978-0-9702065-0-3(X)) Kari Norsk.

***Small Adventure of Popeye & Elvis.** unabr. ed. Barbara O'Connor. Narrated by Scott Sowers. 1 Playaway. (Running Time: 2 hrs. 30 mins.). (J). (gr. 3-6). 2009. 54.75 (978-1-4407-5036-6(X)); 30.75 (978-1-4407-5026-7(2)); audio compact disk 30.75 (978-1-4407-5030-4(0)) Recorded Bks.

***Small Adventure of Popeye & Elvis.** unabr. collector's ed. Barbara O'Connor. Narrated by Scott Sowers. 2 CDs. (Running Time: 2 hrs. 30 mins.). (J). (gr. 3-6). 2009. audio compact disk 22.95 (978-1-4407-5031-1(9)) Recorded Bks.

Small Business. 2nd abr. ed. Eric Tyson & Jim Schell. Read by Brett Barry. (Running Time: 12600 sec.). 2007. audio compact disk 14.95 (978-0-06-117594-7(3)) HarperCollins Pubs.

Small Business Basics: How to Run a Business - From Opening Day to Tax Day! rev. ed. Richard Stim. (ENG.). 2008. audio compact disk & audio compact disk 34.99 (978-1-4133-0914-0(3)) Nolo.

Small Business Bible: Everything You Need to Know to Succeed in Your Small Business. unabr. rev. ed. Steven D. Strauss. (Running Time: 9 hrs.). (ENG.). 2006. audio compact disk 29.98 (978-1-59659-074-8(2), GildAudio) Pub: Gildan Media. Dist(s): HachBkGrp

Small Business Bible, 2E: Everything You Need to Know to Succeed in Your Small Business. unabr. ed. Steven D. Strauss. Read by Walter Dixon. (Running Time: 15 hrs. 30 mins.). (ENG.). 2009. 39.98 (978-1-59659-414-2(4), GildAudio) Pub: Gildan Media. Dist(s): HachBkGrp

***Small Business for Dummies 2nd Ed.** abr. ed. Eric Tyson & Jim Schell. Read by Brett Barry. (ENG.). 2006. (978-0-06-128730-5(X), Harper Audio); (978-0-06-128729-9(6), Harper Audio) HarperCollins Pubs.

Small Business Library. Ed. by Socrates Media Editors. 2005. audio compact disk 49.95 (978-1-59546-117-9(5)) Pub: Socrates Med LLC. Dist(s): Midpt Trade

Small Business Owner's Guide to a Good Night's Sleep. unabr. ed. Debra Koontz Traverso. Read by Anna Fields. 5 cass. (Running Time: 7 hrs.). 2002. 39.95 (978-0-7861-2179-3(3), 2930); audio compact disk 56.00 (978-0-7861-9542-8(8), 2930) Blckstn Audio.
Tells you how to prepare for the surprises most likely to throw small businesses off course. Helps you anticipate both predictable hurdles and devastating ordeals, so that no crisis will catch you off guard. You'll have a plan of response for everything.

Small Business Planning. Melvin B. Seiden & John C. Wisdom. 3 cass. bk. 159.00 set. (CPE4675) Bisk Educ.
Discusses issues involving business start-ups, choosing the best form of business entity, finding the necessary financing, & writing & using a business plan. Learn how to advise clients about their insurance needs, employee hiring practices, pricing strategies, valuation methods, buying & selling a business, & more.

Small Business Resource Guide. unabr. ed. Stasia Kelly & Dennis Baxter. Read by Stasia Kelly & Steve Woodburn. Ed. by Dennis Baxter & Ed Baker. 2 cass. (Running Time: 1 hr. 40 min.). (In Sight Ser.). 1992. pap. bk. 12.95 set. (978-1-882944-00-2(3)) Creat Sound.
General guideline for starting & maintaining a business.

Small Cabin see Poetry & Voice of Margaret Atwood

Small Day see Erskine Caldwell

Small Death in Lisbon. unabr. ed. Robert Wilson. Read by Sean Barrett. 15 CDs. (Running Time: 15 hrs. 45 mins.). (Isis Ser.). (J). 2002. audio compact disk 104.95 (978-0-7531-1473-5(9)) Pub: ISIS Lrg Prnt GBR. Dist(s): Ulverscroft US
As the start of the Second World War, a portuguese bank is founded on the back of Nazi wartime deals. Over half a century later a young girl is murdered in Lisbon. Inspector Ze Coelho is put in charge of the investigation, and soon finds that his search for the truth leads him to some shocking revelations.

Small Death in Lisbon. unabr. ed. Robert Wilson & Sean Barrett. 14 cass. (Running Time: 15 hrs. 45 mins.). (Isis Ser.). (J). 2002. 99.95 (978-0-7531-0985-4(9)) Pub: ISIS Lrg Prnt GBR. Dist(s): Ulverscroft US

Small Dragon see Brian Patten Reading His Poetry

***Small Faith, Great God.** unabr. ed. N. T. Wright. (Running Time: 4 hrs. 30 mins. 0 sec.). (ENG.). 2010. audio compact disk 18.98 (978-1-61045-074-4(4), Hovel Audio) christianaud.

Small Favor. unabr. ed. Jim Butcher. Read by James Marsters. 12 CDs. (Running Time: 11 hrs.). Bk. 10. (ENG.). (gr. 12 up). 2008. audio compact disk 44.95 (978-0-14-314339-0(5), PengAudBks) Penguin Grp USA.

Small Fires. unabr. ed. Interview with Christopher Cerf & Marina Albee. Prod. by Rebekah Presson. 1 cass. (Running Time: 29 min.). 1990. 10.00 (122190) New Letters.
Theme program featuring interviews with the editors of "Small Fires: Letters from the Soviet People to Obonyok Magazine, 1987-1990". Includes readings from the book.

Small Firm Logistics: Turning Your Practice into a Business. Edward Poll. 2008. audio compact disk 79.00 (978-0-9797610-0-3(X)) E Poll & Assocs.

***Small Furry Prayer: Dog Rescue & the Meaning of Life.** unabr. ed. Steven Kotler. Narrated by Kevin Foley. (Running Time: 9 hrs. 30 mins.). 2010. 16.99 (978-1-4001-8987-8(X)); 24.99 (978-1-4001-6987-0(9)); audio compact disk 34.99 (978-1-4001-1987-5(1)) Pub: Tantor Media. Dist(s): IngramPubServ

***Small Furry Prayer (Library Edition) Dog Rescue & the Meaning of Life.** unabr. ed. Steven Kotler. Narrated by Kevin Foley. (Running Time: 9 hrs. 30 mins.). 2010. 34.99 (978-1-4001-9987-7(5)); audio compact disk 83.99 (978-1-4001-4987-2(8)) Pub: Tantor Media. Dist(s): IngramPubServ

Small Gods. Terry Pratchett. Read by Tony Robinson. 2 cass. (Running Time: 3 hrs.). (Discworld Ser.). 2000. 16.99 (978-0-552-14416-2(9)) Pub: Transworld GBR. Dist(s): Trafalgar
Where there are gods galore, there are priests, high and low, and, there are novices. Brutha is a novice with little chance to become a priest - thinking does not come easily to him, although believing does. But it is to Brutha that the great god Om manifests, in the lowly form of a tortoise.

Small Gods. unabr. ed. Terry Pratchett. Read by Nigel Planer. 8 cass. (Running Time: 11 hr.). (Discworld Ser.). (J). 1997. 69.95 (978-0-7531-0141-4(6), 970201) Pub: ISIS Lrg Prnt GBR. Dist(s): Ulverscroft US
Brutha is the Chosen One. His god has spoken to him, admittedly while currently in the shape of a tortoise. Brutha is a simple lad. He can't read. He can't write. He's pretty good at growing melons. And his wants are few. He wants to overthrow a huge & corrupt church, he wants to prevent a horribly holy war, he wants peace & justice & brotherly love. But most of all, what he really wants, more than anything else, is for his god to Choose Someone Else.

Small Gods. unabr. ed. Terry Pratchett. Read by Stephen Briggs & Nigel Planer. 9 CDs. (Discworld Ser.). 2007. audio compact disk 84.95 (978-0-7531-1555-8(7)) Pub: ISIS Lrg Prnt GBR. Dist(s): Ulverscroft US

Small, Good Thing & Other Stories. unabr. ed. Raymond Carver. Read by Tim Behrens. 2 cass. (Running Time: 2 hrs. 24 min.). Dramatization. 1992. 16.95 (978-1-55686-459-9(0), 459) Books in Motion.
Three stories; A Small, Good Thing, Fever, & The Students Wife. A young boy is struck by an automobile driver & seriously injured. The parents are trying to cope with the difficulty when they begin to receive crank telephone calls from the baker for a birthday cake they didn't pick up.

Small Group Support for Advent. Clarence Thomson. Perf. by Karen Blomgren. 2 cass. (Running Time: 1 hr. 30 min.). 1995. Set. Credence Commun.
If you don't have a theologian & a musician in your group, this is the next best thing for Advent.

Small Harp. Alison Kinnaerd. 2004. audio compact disk 24.95 (978-0-9511204-2-2(5), TR00805) Pub: [illegible]mor GBR. Dist(s): Music Sales

Small Homes see Carl Sandburg's Poe[illegible] [illegible]r Children

Small House at Allington. Anthony Trollo[illegible] [illegible]ead by Simon Vance. (Running Time: 82800 sec.). 2007. 119.95 (978-1-4332-0607-8(2)) Blckstn Audio.

Small House at Allington. unabr. ed. Anthony Trollope. (Running Time: 82800 sec.). 2007. audio compact disk 140.00 (978-1-4332-0608-5(0)); audio compact disk 44.95 (978-1-4332-0609-2(9)) Blckstn Audio.

Small House at Allington. unabr. ed. Anthony Trollope. Read by David Case. 17 cass. (Running Time: 24 hrs.). (Barsetshire Chronicles Ser.). 1993. 136.00 (3209A\B) Books on Tape.
Trollope's most charming heroine, Lily Dale, is introduced onto the Barsetshire scene.

Small House at Allington. unabr. ed. Anthony Trollope & Simon Vance. 2007. audio compact disk 119.95 (978-1-4662-0607-6(1)) Blckstn Audio.

Small House at Allington, Pt. 1. unabr. collector's ed. Anthony Trollope. Read by David Case. 9 cass. (Running Time: 13 hrs. 30 mins.). 1993. 72.00 (978-0-7366-2444-2(9), 3209-A) Books on Tape.
Introducing Trollope's most charming heroine, Lily Dale, onto the Barsetshire scene. Lily is the niece of Squire Dale, an idiosyncratic bachelor entrenched in the Great House at Allington. Dale's sister-in-law lives at the adjacent Small House with her two daughters, one of whom is Lily. Relations between the two houses & the romantic entanglements of the girls drive the story.

Small House at Allington, Pt. 2. collector's ed. Anthony Trollope. Read by David Case. 8 cass. (Running Time: 12 hrs.). 1993. 64.00 (978-0-7366-2445-9(7), 3209-B) Books on Tape.

Small House at Allington, Set. unabr. ed. Anthony Trollope. Read by Flo Gibson. 16 cass. (Running Time: 23 hrs.). 1994. 46.95 (978-1-55685-345-6(9)) Audio Bk Con.
Touching love stories emerge from the romantic entanglements of the Dale sisters. Snobbery & pride in London are contrasted with gracious country living in rural Barsetshire.

Small Is the New Big. abr. ed. Seth Godin. Read by Seth Godin. (Running Time: 27000 sec.). (ENG.). 2006. audio compact disk 29.95 (978-1-59887-056-5(4), 1598870564) Pub: HighBridge. Dist(s): Workman Pub

Small Is the New Big: And Other Riffs, Rants, & Remarkable Business Ideas. abr. ed. Seth Godin. Read by Seth Godin. (YA). 2007. 54.99 (978-1-60252-709-6(1)) Find a World.

Small Miracles: Extraordinary Coincidences from Everyday Life. Yitta Halberstam. 2004. 7.95 (978-0-7435-4225-8(8)) Pub: S&S Audio. Dist(s): S and S Inc

Small miracles II: Bush, Clinton, & the Generals. Yitta Halberstam & Judith Leventhal. 2004. 7.95 (978-0-7435-4226-5(6)) Pub: S&S Audio. Dist(s): S and S Inc

Small One. 1 cass. (J). 1996. pap. bk. 6.99 (978-0-7634-0154-2(4)) W Disney Records.
Religious - Christian.

Small One. Alex Walsh. (J). 2005. pap. bk. 15.99 (978-0-7868-1350-6(4)) Pub: Hyprn Ppbks. Dist(s): HachBkGrp

***Small Pig.** unabr. ed. Arnold Lobel. Read by Mark Linn-baker. (ENG.). 2009. (978-0-06-196769-6(6)); (978-0-06-190161-4(X)) HarperCollins Pubs.

Small Sacrifices: A True Story of Passion & Murder. Ann Rule. 2004. 10.95 (978-0-7435-4611-9(3)) Pub: S&S Audio. Dist(s): S and S Inc

Small Steps. unabr. ed. Louis Sachar. Read by Curtis McClarin. 5 CDs. (Running Time: 5 hrs. 12 mins.). (YA). 2005. audio compact disk 38.25 (978-0-307-28226-2(0), Listening Lib) Pub: Random Audio Pubg. Dist(s): NetLibrary CO
Two years after being released from Camp Green Lake, Armpit is home in Austin, Texas, trying to turn his life around. But it¿s hard when you have a record, and everyone expects the worst from you. The only person who believes in him is Ginny, his 10-year old disabled neighbor. Together, they are learning to take small steps. And he seems to be on the right path, until X-Ray, a buddy from Camp Green Lake, comes up with a get-rich-quick scheme. This leads to a chance encounter with teen pop sensation, Kaira DeLeon, and suddenly his life spins out of control, with only one thing for certain. He¿ll never be the same again.

Small Steps. unabr. ed. Louis Sachar. Read by Curtis McClarin. 3 cass. (Running Time: 5 hrs. 12 mins.). (YA). 2006. 30.00 (978-0-307-28225-5(2), Listening Lib) Pub: Random Audio Pubg. Dist(s): Random

Small Steps. unabr. ed. Louis Sachar. Read by Curtis McClarin. 5 CDs. (Running Time: 18720 sec.). (ENG.). (J). (gr. 7-9). 2006. audio compact disk 30.00 (978-0-307-28223-1(6), Listening Lib) Pub: Random Audio Pubg. Dist(s): Random

Small Store Operations: Growth & Survival. 1 cass. (America's Supermarket Showcase '96 Ser.). 1996. 11.00 (NGA96-041) Sound Images.

Small Talk see Carl Sandburg's Poems for Children

Small Talk. Carolyn Graham. (Jazz Chants Ser.). 1992. 24.50 (978-0-19-434639-9(0)) OUP.

Small Talk. Carolyn Graham. (Jazz Chants Ser.). 2003. audio compact disk 24.50 (978-0-19-438608-1(2)); audio compact disk 24.50 (978-0-19-438609-8(0)) OUP.

Small Town see Twentieth-Century Poetry in English, No. 24, Recordings of Poets Reading Their Own Poetry

***Small Town.** abr. ed. Lawrence Block. Read by Lawrence Block. (ENG.). 2004. (978-0-06-078316-7(8), Harper Audio) HarperCollins Pubs.

***Small Town.** abr. ed. Lawrence Block. Read by Lawrence Block. (ENG.). 2004. (978-0-06-081398-7(9), Harper Audio) HarperCollins Pubs.

Small Town. unabr. ed. Lawrence Block. Narrated by George Guidall. 11 cass. (Running Time: 15 hrs. 15 mins.). 2003. 114.00 (978-1-4025-0619-2(8)) Recorded Bks.

Small Town. unabr. collector's ed. Sloan Wilson. Read by Ron Shoop. 11 cass. (Running Time: 16 hrs. 30 min.). 1987. 88.00 (978-0-7366-1181-7(9), 2101) Books on Tape.
A story of the passions that lie just below the surface of a deceptively placid upstate New York village.

Small Town: Accompaniment Cassette. Austin C. Lovelace. 2001. bk. 5.00 (978-0-687-07077-0(5)) Abingdon.

Small-Town Browny. unabr. ed. Simon Silva. Read by Simon Silva. Music by Pedro Rubalcava. 2 CDs. (Running Time: 3 hrs.). (J). 2000. audio compact disk 18.00 (978-0-9660773-8-4(5)) Pub: Calaca Pr. Dist(s): SPD-Small Pr Dist

Small Town Christmas. Michael Mish. 1 cass. 1999. (978-1-888311-02-0(9), MMM2011) Mish Mash Music.
Traditional Christmas music.

Small Town in Germany. unabr. ed. John le Carré. Read by Barry Phillips. 9 cass. (Running Time: 13 hrs. 30 min.). (George Smiley Novels Ser.). 1987. 72.00 (978-0-7366-1141-1(X), 2066) Books on Tape.
A British diplomat carrying confidential files stolen from the embassy in Bonn suddenly vanishes. A tough London investigator is assigned to the case. This is a relentless thriller that turns on a rusty key & leads to a secret on which England's survival, Germany's future & the fate of the whole world may depend.

Small Town in Germany. unabr. ed. John le Carré. Read by Michael Jayston. 10 cass. (Running Time: 15 hrs.). 1998. 69.95 (978-0-7540-0174-4(1), CAB 1597) Pub: Chivers Audio Bks GBR. Dist(s): AudioGO
The missing man: Harting, a Junior something in the British Embassy in Bonn. The missing files: 43 of them, all confidential. The timing: appalling & probably not accidental. London's security officer Alan Turner is sent to Bonn to find the missing man & files, as Germany's past, present & future threaten to collide in a nightmare of violence.

Small Town in Germany, unabr. ed. John le Carré. Narrated by Simon Prebble. 9 cass. (Running Time: 13 hrs. 15 mins.). (George Smiley Novels Ser.). 1991. 78.00 (978-1-55690-481-3(9), 91233E7) Recorded Bks.
A British diplomat & a confidential file go missing from the Embassy in Bonn, setting off a trail of suspicion & betrayal.

Small Towns Can Be Murder. unabr. ed. Connie Shelton. Read by Lynda Evans. 6 cass. (Running Time: 6 hrs. 48 min.). (Charlie Parker Mystery Ser.: No. 4). 2001. 39.95 (978-1-55686-749-1(2)) Books in Motion.
A bizarre incidence of miscarriages in a small New Mexico town finds Charlie investigating the health care industry with deadly consequences.

Small Vices. David Armstrong. 7 cass. (Soundings Ser.). (J). 2005. 61.95 (978-1-84283-883-9(0)) Pub: ISIS Lrg Prnt GBR. Dist(s): Ulverscroft US

Small Vices. Robert B. Parker. Contrib. by Burt Reynolds. (Spenser Ser.). 2008. 59.99 (978-1-60640-678-6(7)) Find a World.

Small Vices. unabr. ed. Robert B. Parker. Read by Burt Reynolds. 6 cass. (Running Time: 9 hrs.). (Spenser Ser.). 2004. 34.95 (978-1-59007-210-3(3)); audio compact disk 49.95 (978-1-59007-557-9(9)) Pub: New Millenn Enter. Dist(s): PerseuPGW

Small Victories: The Real World of a Teacher, Her Students & Their High School. Samuel G. Freedman. 2 cass. (Running Time: 90 min. per cass.). 1990. 15.95 HarperCollins Pubs.

Small Voice Within. abr. ed. Eileen Caddy. 2 CDs. (Running Time: 2 hrs.). (ENG.). 2005. audio compact disk 21.99 (978-1-84409-057-0(4)) Pub: Findhorn Pr GBR. Dist(s): IPG Chicago

***Small Wars.** unabr. ed. Sadie Jones. Narrated by Stephen Hoye. (Running Time: 10 hrs. 30 mins. 0 sec.). (ENG.). 2010. audio compact disk 69.99 (978-1-4001-4556-0(2)) Pub: Tantor Media. Dist(s): IngramPubServ

***Small Wars: A Novel.** unabr. ed. Sadie Jones. Narrated by Stephen Hoye. (Running Time: 10 hrs. 30 mins. 0 sec.). (ENG.). 2010. 24.99 (978-1-4001-6556-8(3)); 16.99 (978-1-4001-8556-6(4)); audio compact disk 34.99 (978-1-4001-1556-3(6)) Pub: Tantor Media. Dist(s): IngramPubServ

Small White Scar. unabr. ed. K. A. Nuzum. Read by Steven Boyer. 4 cass. (Running Time: 4 hrs.). (J). (gr. 5-7). 2006. 30.75 (978-1-4281-0453-2(4)); audio compact disk 46.75 (978-1-4281-0458-7(5)) Recorded Bks.

***Small Wolf.** unabr. ed. Nathaniel Benchley. (ENG.). 2008. (978-0-06-169488-2(6)); (978-0-06-172145-8(X)) HarperCollins Pubs.

***Small Wonder.** abr. ed. Barbara Kingsolver. Read by Barbara Kingsolver. (ENG.). 2005. (978-0-06-089459-7(8), Harper Audio); (978-0-06-089458-0(X), Harper Audio) HarperCollins Pubs.

Small Wonder. unabr. ed. Barbara Kingsolver. 6 cass. (Running Time: 9 hrs.). 2002. 45.00 (2C361) Recorded Bks.
In 23 wonderfully articulate essays, the author raises her voice in praise of nature, family, literature, and the joys of everyday life while examining the genesis of war, violence, poverty in our world and the anguish over September 11.

***Smallbiz America Talks: 12 Expert Interviews to Transform Your Business.** David Wolf. (ENG.). 2010. 4.99 (978-0-9827081-4-9(9)) AuthorsDig.

Smallbone Deceased. unabr. ed. Michael Gilbert. Read by Phil Garner. 5 cass. (Running Time: 6 hrs. 15 min.). (Isis Ser.). (J). 1998. 49.95 (978-1-85695-614-7(8), 931204) Pub: ISIS Lrg Prnt GBR. Dist(s): Ulverscroft US

Smallest Cow in the World. abr. ed. Katherine Paterson. Read by Cyd Quilling. Illus. by Jane C. Brown. Contrib. by Cyd Quilling. (Running Time: 25 min.). (I Can Read Bks.). (J). (ps-3). 1996. 8.99 (978-0-694-70036-3(3)) HarperCollins Pubs.

Smart & Simple Financial Strategies for Busy People. abr. ed. Jane Bryant Quinn. Read by Jane Bryant Quinn. 2006. 17.95 (978-0-7435-5567-8(8)) Pub: S&S Audio. Dist(s): S and S Inc

Smart Business - France: What to Expect...What to Do... When Doing Business with the French. Peregrine Media Group. 1 cass. 19.95 (978-1-881487-05-0(9)) Peregrine Media.

Smart Business - Mexico. Narrated by Francis M. Brunetto. 1 cass. (Smart Business Ser.). 1997. 19.95 Incl. bklet. (978-1-881487-02-9(4)) Peregrine Media.
Contains the essentials for success in a foreign business environment, covering subjects ranging from negotiating strategies & contracts to key points on legal & banking systems together with hints on thinking like a local & imaginative ways to deal with business differences.

Smart Business - Morocco. Narrated by Francis M. Brunetto. 1 cass. (Smart Business Ser.). 1997. 19.95 Incl. bklet. (978-1-881487-04-3(0)) Peregrine Media.

Smart Business Brazil: What to Expect... What to Do... When Doing Business with Brazilians. Frank Brunetto. 1 cass. 1998. 19.95 (978-1-881487-06-7(7)) Peregrine Media.

Smart Business China: What to Expect & What to Do When Doing Business with Chinese. Audio. 1 cass. (Running Time: 1 hr.). 1995. 19.95 (978-1-881487-03-6(2)) Peregrine Media.
The vital facts & solid fundamentals together with comments & insights from major market players on how to be most effective when doing business in The Peoples Republic of China.

Smart Business Germany: What to Do & What Not to Do When Doing Business with Germans. Francis M. Brunetto. 1 cass. 1992. 19.95 (978-1-881487-00-5(8)) Peregrine Media.
A unique "quick study" packed with vital information for executives operating in a 1990s German business environment.

Smart Business Japan: What to Do & What Not to Do When Doing Business with Japanese. Francis M. Brunetto. 1 cass. 1992. 19.95 (978-1-881487-01-2(6)) Peregrine Media.
A unique "quick study" packed with vital information for executives operating in 1990s Japanese business environment.

Smart Business Series. Francis M. Brunetto. (Running Time: 1 hr.). 1997. 12.95 Peregrine Media.

Smart Child for Happy Dreams. Read by Mary Richards. 1 cass. (Running Time: 45 min.). (J). 2007. audio compact disk 19.95 (978-1-56136-173-1(9)) Master Your Mind.
For bed time or quiet time. Voice of Mary Richards, music & waves. Going to wonderland just for the children, expanding the fun of learning: "I am 100 percent O.K. I learn something new every day." Both sides guided.

Smart Choices for a New Century. unabr. ed. Jane Anderson. Perf. by Arye Gross et al. 1 cass. (Running Time: 1 hr. 03 min.). 1994. 19.95 (978-1-58081-072-2(1)) L A Theatre.
One act plays explore the challenges of life in Los Angeles, from gun violence to earthquakes.

Smart Cookie Approach to Dieting: The Habitual Dieter's Best Friend. Judy Payne. Read by Judy Payne. 4 cass. (Running Time: 6 hrs.). 1987. 29.95 (978-0-9617452-0-2(7)) Long Term Success.
Six hours of diet motivation & wisdom. Unique, enjoyable, witty, sensible, loving help for the intelligent woman dieter who wants to take control of her life & her weight forever.

Smart Cookies' Guide to Making More Dough: How Five Young Women Got Smart, Formed a Money Group, & Took Control of Their Finances. The Smart Cookies. Read by Andrea Baxter. Told to Jennifer Barrett. Frwd. by Jean Chatzky. (Playaway Adult Nonfiction Ser.). (ENG.). 2009. 59.99 (978-1-60847-881-1(5)) Find a World.

Smart Cookies' Guide to Making More Dough: How Five Young Women Got Smart, Formed a Money Group, & Took Control of Their Finances. unabr. ed. Jennifer Barrett. (Running Time: 7 hrs. 0 mins. 0 sec.). (ENG.). 2008. audio compact disk 19.99 (978-1-4001-6015-0(4)); audio compact disk 59.99 (978-1-4001-4015-2(3)) Pub: Tantor Media. Dist(s): IngramPubServ

Smart Cookies' Guide to Making More Dough: How Five Young Women Got Smart, Formed a Money Group, & Took Control of Their Finances. unabr. ed. Smart Cookies Staff & Jennifer Barrett. Read by Andrea Baxter. (Running Time: 7 hrs. 0 mins. 0 sec.). (ENG.). 2008. audio compact disk 29.99 (978-1-4001-1015-5(7)) Pub: Tantor Media. Dist(s): IngramPubServ

Smart Couples Finish Rich: 9 Steps to Creating a Rich Future for You & Your Partner. abr. ed. David Bach. 3 CDs. (Running Time: 3 hrs. 0 mins. 0 sec.). (ENG.). 2005. audio compact disk 19.95 (978-1-59397-589-0(9)) Pub: Macmill Audio. Dist(s): Macmillan

Smart Guys Readalong. Prescott Hill. 1 cass. (Running Time: 1 hr.). (Ten-Minute Thrillers Ser.). (YA). (gr. 6-12). 1995. pap. bk. 12.95 (978-0-7854-1081-2(3), 40822) Am Guidance.

Smart Keno Play. Keith L. Hall & Ronald L. Dikmyhr. 2005. audio compact disk (978-1-888436-18-1(2)) Jackpot Pub.

Smart Kids Allowance System: Tool Kit. Kathleen Duey & Ron Berry. 1 cass. (Running Time: 1 hr.). (J). (gr. 1-6). 2000. pap. bk. 14.95 (978-1-891100-68-0(8)) Pub: Smart Kids Publ. Dist(s): Penton Overseas
The best program on the market today for teaching kids the value of money & family responsibility. Fun-to-use tools include: allowance chart, chore label sheet, point tokens sheet, chore list & the Smart Kids Contract, plus step-by-step Money Management Guidebook. Tape is a humorous look inside 3 different families' attempts to give allowances.

Smart Leadership. Michael A. Podolinsky. 2 cass. (Running Time: 1 hrs. 47 min.). (Smart Tapes Ser.). 1996. pap. bk. 19.99 (978-1-55678-063-9(X), 3275) Oasis Audio.
Smart Leadership is a simple, effective way to achieve cooperation, respect, & teamwork. These simple daily actions will help you inspire extraordinary performance from ordinary people.

Smart Love: The Compassionate Alternative to Discipline That Will Make You a Better Parent & Your Child a Better Person. unabr. ed. Martha Heineman Pieper. Narrated by Suzanne Toren & George Guidall. 9 CDs. (Running Time: 10 hrs.). 2000. audio compact disk 81.00 (978-0-7887-3984-2(0), C1147E7) Recorded Bks.
The smart love approach offers a way to steer through the extremes of tough love & unbridled permissiveness. The Piepers draw from decades of experience as parents & therapists. An inspiring message of love & compassion.

Smart Love: The Compassionate Alternative to Discipline That Will Make You a Better Parent & Your Child a Better Person. unabr. ed. Martha Heineman Pieper & William J. Pieper. Narrated by Suzanne Toren & George Guidall. 7 cass. (Running Time: 10 hrs.). 1999. 60.00 (978-0-7887-3749-7(X), 95894E7) Recorded Bks.

Smart Money: How the World's Best Sports Bettors Beat the Bookies Out of Millions. abr. ed. Michael Konik. Read by Michael Konik. 4 cass. (Running Time: 5 hrs.). (ENG.). 2006. 26.00 (978-0-7435-4994-3(5)) Pub: S&S Audio. Dist(s): S and S Inc

Smart Money: How the World's Best Sports Bettors Beat the Bookies Out of Millions. abr. ed. Michael Konik. Read by Michael Konik. 2006. 17.95 (978-0-7435-6432-8(4)) Pub: S&S Audio. Dist(s): S and S Inc

Smart Moves: Building Enrollment Through Parent Satisfaction. George B. Fowler. 4 cass. (Running Time: 6 hrs.). 1992. pap. bk. 59.00 (978-1-57323-015-5(4)) Natl Inst Child Mgmt.
Child care management training material.

Smart Moves 1: Tots thru Pre-K. Prod. by Angela Russ. (ENG.). (J). 2004. audio compact disk 14.99 (978-0-9747064-0-5(X), ABridge) Russ Invis.

Smart Moves 2: Preschool Thru 1st. Prod. by Angela Russ. (ENG.). (J). 2004. audio compact disk 14.99 (978-0-9747064-1-2(8), ABridge) Russ Invis.

Smart Music Cartime. 1 CD. (Running Time: 1 hr.). (J). (ps). 2001. audio compact disk 15.98 (BS-5CD) Kimbo Educ.
Enrich a baby's learning through exposure to classical music. Friendly melodies.

Smart Music Playtime. 1 CD. (Running Time: 1 hr.). (J). (ps). 2001. audio compact disk 15.98 (BS-4CD) Kimbo Educ.

Smart Music Sleepytime. 1 CD. (Running Time: 1 hr.). (J). (ps). 2001. audio compact disk 15.98 (BS-6CD) Kimbo Educ.

Smart Negotiating. James C. Freund. 2004. 7.95 (978-0-7435-4227-2(4)) Pub: S&S Audio. Dist(s): S and S Inc

Smart Parenting. Peter J. Favaro. 6 cass. (Running Time: 6 hrs.). 1994. wbk. ed. 59.95 (11220AB) Nightingale-Conant.
With Smart Parenting, you'll see how to step outside of a problem & analyze it while still empathizing with your child's concerns & discover how to combine your parental authority with sensitivity to affect a suitable solution. Parenting will become easier, more rewarding, less stressful - & more fun.

Smart Parenting: Thirty-Six Powerful Ways to Be a Better Parent. unabr. ed. Perry Buffington. Read by Perry Buffington. Ed. by Greg Womble. 4 cass. (Running Time: 3 hrs.). 1992. 29.95 (978-1-883233-00-6(3)) Vanguard Audio.
Effective & powerful parenting insights. Many child-rearing subjects covered.

Smart Reading. Learn Inc. Staff. 2 cass. (Running Time: 2 hrs. 22 min.). (Smart Tapes Ser.). 1999. pap. bk. 19.99 (978-1-55678-067-7(2), 3350) Oasis Audio.
Shows a proven way to double reading speed & comprehension.

Smart Reading. unabr. ed. Russell G. Stauffer & Marcia Reynolds. 2 CDs. (Smart Tapes Ser.). (ENG.). 2003. audio compact disk 19.99 (978-1-58926-074-0(0)) Oasis Audio.

Smart Reading. unabr. ed. Russell Stauffer & Marcia Reynolds. (Smart Tapes Ser.). (ENG.). 2003. 13.99 (978-1-60814-389-4(9)) Oasis Audio.

***Smart Solutions to Control Healthcare & Benefit Costs.** PUEI. 2009. audio compact disk 199.00 (978-1-935041-55-9(X), CareerTrack) P Univ E Inc.

Smart Songs for Kids 1. Prod. by Angela Russ. Composed by Bill Burchell. 1 CD. (Running Time: 34 mins.). (J). 2003. audio compact disk 14.99 (978-0-9720234-6-7(1), ABridge) Russ Invis.
It's the first CD of this VERBALLY INTERACTIVE series, and it takes children on a musical journey of learning and discovery. This fun-filled music CD introduces young children to topics such as planets in orbit, the characteristics of insects, long vowels, identifying shapes, personal safety, Spanish numbers, and many more. A variety of subjects and concepts from preschool and kindergarten curriculum are set to lyrics that encourage children to sing along, mimic a phrase, or shout a response. Guest singers are Tim Russ (Tuvok), and Robert Picardo (The Doctor) from the TV series, Star Trek:Voyager. Lyrics and teaching tips are available on-line.

Smart Songs for Kids 2. Prod. by Angela Russ. Composed by Bill Burchell. 1 CD. (Running Time: 34 mins.). (J). 2003. audio compact disk 14.99 (978-0-9720234-7-4(X), ABridge) Russ Invis.
It's the first CD of this VERBALLY INTERACTIVE series, and it takes children on a musical journey of learning and discovery. This fun-filled CD introduces young children to topics such as good manners, the library, 7 days a week, color identification, short vowels, counting patterns, Spanish animals, and many more. A variety of subjects and concepts from preschool and kindergarten curriculum are set to lyrics that encourage children to sing

along, mimic a phrase, or shout a response. Guest singers are Tim Russ (Tuvok), and Robert Picardo (The Doctor) from the TV series, Star Trek:Voyager. Lyrics and teaching tips are available on-line.

Smart Start. Perf. by London Symphony Orchestra. 2000. audio compact disk 14.98 (978-1-930800-11-3(8), Prop Voice) Iliad TN.

Smart Steps: 3rd Grade. (Smart Steps Ser.). (J). (gr. 3). 1999. audio compact disk 29.95 (978-0-7894-4538-4(7)) DK Pub Inc.

Smart Steps: 4th Grade. (Smart Steps Ser.). (J). (gr. 4). 1999. audio compact disk 29.95 (978-0-7894-4539-1(5)) DK Pub Inc.

Smart Steps: 5th Grade. (Smart Steps Ser.). (J). (gr. 5). 1999. audio compact disk 29.95 (978-0-7894-4540-7(9)) DK Pub Inc.

Smart Study. abr. ed. Roger W. Bretemitz. 1 cass. (Running Time: 45 min.). 1985. pap. bk. 9.95 (978-1-893417-20-5(4)) Vector Studios.
Hypnosis: Implants suggestions on strong study habits, memory retention, goal achievement, & absorbing new knowledge & concepts.

Smart Technology Demonstrators & Devices 2001. Manson. 2002. audio compact disk 219.95 (978-0-7503-0875-5(3), IP656) Taylor and Fran.

Smart Way to Buy a House. unabr. ed. Read by John Adams. Ed. by Dennis Baxter. 2 cass. (Running Time: 1 hr. 30 min.). (Insight Ser.). pap. bk. 12.95 set. (978-1-882944-02-6(X)) Creat Sound.
Step by step guideline to purchase real estate.

***Smartest Investment Book You'll Ever Read: The Simple, Stress-Free Way to Reach You.** unabr. ed. Dan Solin. Read by Craig Wollman. (ENG.). 2006. (978-0-06-128406-9(8), Harper Audio); (978-0-06-128407-6(6), Harper Audio) HarperCollins Pubs.

Smartest Investment Book You'll Ever Read: The Simple, Stress-Free Way to Reach Your Investment Goals. unabr. ed. Dan Solin. Read by Craig Wollman. (Running Time: 10800 sec.). 2006. audio compact disk 22.95 (978-0-06-124075-1(3)) HarperCollins Pubs.

Smartest 401 (k)* Book You'll Ever Read: Maximize Your Retirement Savings... the Smart Way! (*Smartest 403(b) & 457(b), Too!) unabr. ed. Daniel R. Solin. Read by Arthur Morey. (Running Time: 4 hrs. 0 mins.). (ENG.). 2009. 24.95 (978-1-4332-7097-0(8)); audio compact disk 40.00 (978-1-4332-7098-7(6)) Blckstn Audio.

Smartest 401(k)* Book You'll Ever Read: Maximize Your Retirement Savings... the Smart Way! (*Smartest 403(b) & 457(b), Too!) unabr. ed. Daniel R. Solin. (Running Time: 4 hrs. 0 mins.). 2009. 19.95 (978-1-4332-7101-4(X)); audio compact disk 19.95 (978-1-4332-7100-7(1)) Blckstn Audio.

SmartFrench Beginner. SmartFrench Staff. 2003. pap. bk. (978-0-9729474-1-1(8)) SmartPolyglot.

SmartFrench Intermediate/Advanced. SmartFrench Staff. 2003. pap. bk. (978-0-9729474-2-8(6)) SmartPolyglot.

SmartLink for MBAA: Advanced Commercial Real Estate Values & Investments. David Geltner & Norman Miller. 2003. audio compact disk 150.00 (978-0-324-20659-3(3)) Pub: South-West. Dist(s): CENGAGE Learn

SmartLink for MBAA: Intro to Commercial Real Estate. Geltner. 2003. audio compact disk 150.00 (978-0-324-20660-9(7)) Pub: South-West. Dist(s): CENGAGE Learn

SmartLink for MBAA: Real Estate Math. Betty J. Armbrust. (C). 2003. audio compact disk 150.00 (978-0-324-20301-1(2)) Pub: South-West. Dist(s): CENGAGE Learn

SmartSpanish Audio CDs Int/Adv: The Smart Way to Learn Spanish. C. Aubert. 2005. audio compact disk 34.95 (978-0-9729474-7-3(7)) SmartPolyglot.

SmartSpanish CDs Beginner: The Smart Way to Learn Spanish. C. Aubert. 2005. audio compact disk 34.95 (978-0-9729474-6-6(9)) SmartPolyglot.

Smarty Pants. J. Melser & J. Cowley. 1 read-along cass. (J). 1986. 5.95 incl. bk. (978-0-86867-050-8(2)) Wright Group.
Smarty Pants flies, plays, swims, skiis & swings, all in rhyme & repetition.

Smarty's New Friend. Joseph C. Dennie & Joseph Weathers. Ed. by Charlotte A. Bonnette. Illus. by Vanessa R. Williams & Mariama K. Washington. (J). (gr. 1-4). 1994. pap. bk. 7.95 (978-1-877971-11-2(1)) Mid Atl Reg Pr.

Smash. unabr. ed. David Caddy. Read by Peter Hardy. 2 cass. (Running Time: 2 hrs.). 2002. (978-1-74030-254-8(0)) Bolinda Pubng AUS.

Smash Cut. abr. ed. Sandra Brown. Read by Victor Slezak. (Running Time: 6 hrs. 0 mins. 0 sec.). (ENG.). 2008. audio compact disk 29.99 (978-0-7435-7229-3(7)) Pub: S&S Audio. Dist(s): S and S Inc

Smash Cut. unabr. ed. Sandra Brown. Read by Victor Slezak. 12 CDs. (Running Time: 13 hrs. 0 mins. 0 sec.). 2008. audio compact disk 49.99 (978-0-7435-7231-6(9)) Pub: S&S Audio. Dist(s): S and S Inc

***Smash Cut: A Novel.** abr. ed. Sandra Brown. Read by Victor Slezak. (Running Time: 6 hrs. 0 mins. 0 sec.). (ENG.). 2011. audio compact disk 14.99 (978-1-4423-4071-8(1)) Pub: S&S Audio. Dist(s): S and S Inc

Smashed: Story of a Drunken Girlhood. unabr. ed. Koren Zailickas & Koren Zailckas. Read by Ellen Archer. (Running Time: 10 hrs. 30 mins. 0 sec.). (ENG.). 2005. audio compact disk 69.99 (978-1-4001-3154-9(5)); audio compact disk 22.99 (978-1-4001-5154-7(6)) Pub: Tantor Media. Dist(s): IngramPubServ

Smashed: Story of a Drunken Girlhood. unabr. ed. Koren Zailckas. Read by Ellen Archer. (Running Time: 10 hrs. 30 mins. 0 sec.). (ENG.). 2005. audio compact disk 34.99 (978-1-4001-0154-2(9)) Pub: Tantor Media. Dist(s): IngramPubServ

Smasher: The Ugly Puppy. unabr. ed. Dick King-Smith. Read by Bernard Cribbins. 1 cass. (Running Time: 1 hr., 30 mins.). (J). (gr. 1-8). 1999. 9.95 (CTC 783, Chivers Child Audio) AudioGO.

Smashing Out of the Comfort Zone. abr. ed. Ken Ready. 2 cass. (Running Time: 1 hr. 39 min.). 1998. bk. 16.95 Set. (978-0-9670558-0-0(6)) Life Mgmt Org.
A powerful & dynamic success formula broken into simple steps & exercises.

Smashing Scroll. unabr. ed. Michael Dahl. 1 CD. (Zone Bks.). (J). (gr. 1-4). 2008. audio compact disk 14.60 (978-1-4342-0606-0(8)) CapstoneDig.
An ancient curse sends a stone silo crashing across the countryside. Houses, barns, and cars are crushed in its path. The silo contains a giant scroll, sent by the foul Spellbinder to imprison the entire earth within its vast, unrolling page. Even the mighty Librarian is overpowered by the Spellbinder's steamrolling magic. Can anyone stop the smashing scroll?.

Smell! see William Carlos Williams Reads His Poetry

Smell of the Night. unabr. ed. Andrea Camilleri. Read by Grover Gardner. 4 cass. (Running Time: 4 hrs.). (Inspector Montalbano Mystery Ser.). 2005. 34.95 (978-0-7861-3783-1(5)) Blckstn Audio.

Smell of the Night. unabr. ed. Andrea Camilleri. Read by Grover Gardner. 4 CDs. (Running Time: 18000 sec.). (Inspector Montalbano Mystery Ser.). 2005. audio compact disk 36.00 (978-0-7861-7542-0(7)) Blckstn Audio.

Smell of the Night. unabr. ed. Andrea Camilleri. Tr. by Stephen Sartarelli. 8 CDs. (Running Time: 18000 sec.). (Inspector Montalbano Mystery Ser.). 2005. audio compact disk 29.95 (978-0-7861-7742-4(X), ZE3522); audio compact disk 29.95 (978-0-7861-7968-8(6), ZM3522) Blckstn Audio.

Smell of the Night. unabr. ed. Andrea Camilleri. Tr. by Stephen Sartarelli. 7 cass. (Running Time: 18000 sec.). (Inspector Montalbano Mystery Ser.). 2005. 29.95 (978-0-7861-3653-7(7), E3522) Blckstn Audio.

Smickamookum Drinks Belly. S. A. Blackman. Illus. by Lillian Gubitosi. 1 cass. (Running Time: 90 min.). (J). (ps-k). 2003. bk. 16.95 (978-1-929409-02-0(8)) Blade Pubg.
About a mommy explaining to her 3-year-old why & how she breastfeeds the little girl's baby sister, Veronica. Pro-breastfeeding without condemning or judging bottle feeding.

Smiggy Weevil Cassette. Stephen Cosgrove. 2004. 5.00 (978-1-58804-424-2(6)) PCI Educ.

Smile see Fantastic Tales of Ray Bradbury

Smile. Contrib. by Kutless. (Premiere Performance Plus Ser.). 2006. audio compact disk 9.98 (978-5-558-01627-7(2)) BEC Recordings.

Smile! Geraldine McCaughrean. 2005. audio compact disk 9.95 (978-0-7540-6708-5(4), Chivers Child Audio) AudioGO.

Smile. Emmet L. Robinson. Read by Emmet L. Robinson. 1 cass. (Running Time: 33 min.). 1994. 12.95 King Street.
How the expression on your face can put money in your pocket.

Smile for All Seasons. unabr. ed. Pamela Evans. Read by Heather Williams. 10 cass. (Running Time: 44340 sec.). (Detrolt Ser.). 2000. 84.95 (978-0-7540-0480-6(5), CAB1903) AudioGO.
In 1963, Eve Peters has it all or so it seems. Young & beautiful, she has a gorgeous husband, Ken, with whom she's still madly in love. She has dreams of them owning a house in Ealing where they can start a family with Ken working so hard it shouldn't be long before these dreams come true. However, life is not always rosy & a horrific tragedy leaves Eve a widow at the age of twenty-six with Ken's baby on the way.

Smile for Auntie. 2004. bk. 24.95 (978-0-7882-0570-5(6)); pap. bk. 14.95 (978-0-7882-0634-4(6)); 8.95 (978-1-56008-328-3(X)); cass. & flmstrp 30.00 (978-1-56008-763-2(3)) Weston Woods.

Smile of a Ghost. Phil Rickman. 13 CDs. (Merrily Watkins Ser.). 2006. audio compact disk 99.95 (978-0-7531-2581-6(1)) Pub: ISIS Lrg Prnt GBR. Dist(s): Ulverscroft US

Smile of a Ghost. Phil Rickman. Read by Emma Powell. 11 cass. (Running Time: 14 hrs. 35 mins.). (Merrily Watkins Ser.). 2006. 89.95 (978-0-7531-3594-5(9)) Pub: ISIS Lrg Prnt GBR. Dist(s): Ulverscroft US

Smile of the Buddha. unabr. ed. Jack Kornfield. 1 cass. (Running Time: 1 hr. 15 min.). 1982. 11.00 (03601) Big Sur Tapes.

Smile on the Face of the Tiger. unabr. ed. Loren D. Estleman. Read by John Kenneth. 5 cass. (Running Time: 7 hrs.). (Amos Walker Ser.). 2000. 27.95 (978-1-56740-374-9(3), 1567403743, BAU); 57.25 (978-1-56740-741-9(2), 1567407412) Brilliance Audio.
"I never thought I'd see her again. But never is longer than forever." She is book editor, Louise Starr, a beautiful and scheming ghost from Amos Walker's past; and she wants the Detroit private eye to find Eugene Booth, a missing paperback writer from the 1950s and ask him why he turned down his first book contract in 40 years. Eugene Booth's trail leads to a rustic motel cabin, where the crusty old pro is hammering out his first novel in decades on a battered Smith Corona with a case of bourbon for inspiration. But when the writer winds up hanging from his own belt, Walker must discover the connection between the apparent suicide, the murder of Booth's wife 40 years before - and a deadly secret as old as World War II.

Smile on the Face of the Tiger. unabr. ed. Loren D. Estleman. Read by John Kenneth. (Running Time: 7 hrs.). (Amos Walker Ser.). 2005. 39.25 (978-1-59600-562-4(9), 9781596005624, BADLE); 24.95 (978-1-59600-561-7(0), 9781596005617, BAD); 39.25 (978-1-59600-560-0(2), 9781596005600, Brlnc Audio MP3 Lib); 24.95 (978-1-59600-559-4(9), 9781596005594, Brilliance MP3) Brilliance Audio.

Smile, Smile, Smile: Poems. Poems. Gurumayi Chidvilasananda. Read by Gurumayi Chidvilasananda. 2 cass. (Running Time: 2 hrs. 24 mins.). 1999. 19.95 (978-0-911307-79-5(6), 105464, Siddha Yoga Pubs) SYDA Found.
Throughout the ages, great spiritual mastershave offered their teachings in spontaneous outpourings of poetry.Demonstrates the mystical process of spiritual contemplation, offering an awareness of the perfection of the soul.

Smile, Smile, Smile: Poems. Gurumayi Chidvilasananda. Read by Gurumayi Chidvilasananda. 2 CDs. (Running Time: 2 hrs. 24 mins.). 2001. audio compact disk 22.95 (978-0-911307-80-1(X), 106464, Siddha Yoga Pubs) SYDA Found.
Throughout the ages, great spiritual masters have offered their teachings in spontaneous outpourings of poetry. In the tradition of the poet-saints of India, this collection of 30 poems nourishes the heart's need for the highest vision of humanity and the world. Each poem contains a teaching that gently merges into your being.

Smiles on Smoking. Virgil B. Smith. Read by Dell Smith. Perf. by Tom Drury et al. 1 cass. (Running Time: 12 min.). (J). (gr. 7 up). 1972. 5.95 (978-1-878507-02-0(8), 25C) Human Grwth Services.
Songs, narration, & skits poking fun at some ridiculous aspects of smoking, deglamorizing the use of tobacco; using the power of laughter as a social influence without any preaching or warning about effects of tobacco.

Smiles to Go. unabr. ed. Jerry Spinelli. Read by Conor Donovan. (J). 2008. 54.99 (978-1-60514-799-4(0)) Find a World.

***Smiles to Go.** unabr. ed. Jerry Spinelli. Read by Conor Donovan. (ENG.). 2008. (978-0-06-163235-8(X)); (978-0-06-163236-5(8)) HarperCollins Pubs.

Smiles to Go. unabr. ed. Jerry Spinelli. Read by Conor Donovan. (Running Time: 14400 sec.). (J). (gr. 5). 2008. audio compact disk 22.95 (978-0-06-155186-4(4), HarperChildAud) HarperCollins Pubs.

Smiley's People. John le Carré. 2 cass. (George Smiley Ser.). bk. 34.95 Set, incl. learner's guide & exercises. (S23912) J Norton Pubs.

Smiley's People, unabr. ed. John le Carré. Read by Frederick Davidson. 11 cass. (Running Time: 16 hrs.). (George Smiley Ser.). 1992. 76.95 (978-0-7861-0265-5(9), 1232) Blckstn Audio.
Spy chief George Smiley intends to retire. However, his brain does not. So when the Circus asks him to go just one more round, his response is predictable. Smiley's opponent in this conclusive match is Karla, his mortal enemy (& opposite) inside the Soviet Union.

***Smiley's People.** unabr. ed. John le Carré. (Running Time: 16 hrs. 30 mins.). 2010. audio compact disk 29.95 (978-1-4417-3548-5(8)) Blckstn Audio.

***Smiley's People.** unabr. ed. John le Carré. Read by Frederick Davidson. (Running Time: 13 hrs.). 2010. 29.95 (978-1-4417-3549-2(6)) Blckstn Audio.

Smiley's People. unabr. ed. John le Carré. Read by Rupert Keenlyside. 12 cass. (Running Time: 18 hr.). (George Smiley Novels Ser.). 1986. 96.00 (978-0-7366-0967-8(9), 1909) Books on Tape.
This is the final confrontation between George Smiley & Karla, his mortal enemy & opposite number inside the Soviet Union. Paris, London, Germany & Switzerland are backdrops for this finale.

Smiley's People. unabr. ed. John le Carré. Read by Michael Jayston. 12 cass. (Running Time: 18 hrs.). (George Smiley Ser.). 2000. 79.95 (978-0-7451-6679-7(2), CAB 1295) Pub: Chivers Audio Bks GBR. Dist(s): AudioGO
Two seemingly unrelated events summoned George Smiley from his retirement. The first was a woman in Paris promised the return of the daughter she'll never see, and second was a hand-over on a steamer in Hamburg. And when Smiley finds himself contemplating the corpse of an old acquaintance on Hampstead Heath, the events seem to take on a new and deadly importance in the Cold War.

Smiley's People. unabr. ed. John le Carré. Narrated by Frank Muller. 10 cass. (Running Time: 13 hrs. 45 mins.). (George Smiley Novels Ser.). 1999. 85.00 (978-1-55690-482-0(7), 90091E7) Recorded Bks.
This brings the conflict between George Smiley & his counterpart, the Russian spymaster Karla, to a final confrontation.

***Smiley's People.** unabr. ed. John le Carré. Read by Frederick Davidson. (Running Time: 13 hrs.). 2010. audio compact disk 118.00 (978-1-4417-3546-1(1)) Blckstn Audio.

***Smiley's People: A BBC Full-Cast Radio Drama.** John le Carré. Narrated by Simon Russell Beale. (Running Time: 3 hrs. 0 mins. 0 sec.). (BBC Radio Ser.). (ENG.). 2010. audio compact disk 19.95 (978-1-60283-864-2(X)) Pub: AudioGO. Dist(s): Perseus Dist

Smilin' Island of Song. Read by Cedella M. Booker & Taj Mahal. 1 cass. (Running Time: 55 min.). 1992. 9.98 (978-1-877737-10-7(0), MLP258/WB42521-4) MFLP CA.
Stories & music of Jamaica by the mother of the legendary Bob Marley, with her friends David Lindley & Taj Mahal.

Smiling at Death. unabr. ed. Betty Rowlands. Read by Phyllida Nash. 6 cass. (Running Time: 6 hrs.). 1998. 54.95 Set. (978-0-7540-0106-5(7), CAB1529) AudioGO.
After a third murder within three months, the residents of Thanebury village now live in fear. Despite her local reputation for solving mysteries, crime writer Melissa Craig has no intention of getting involved, until a fourth victim turns up in her own village of Upper Benbur. As Melissa hunts for clues, a fifth murder occurs, & it becomes clear that at least one very disturbed mind is at work.

Smiling Country. Elmer Kelton. Narrated by George Guidall. 7 CDs. (Running Time: 7 hrs. 45 mins.). (Hewey Calloway Ser.). audio compact disk 69.00 (978-1-4025-2091-4(3)) Recorded Bks.

Smiling Country. Elmer Kelton. Narrated by George Guidall. 6 cass. (Running Time: 7 hrs. 45 mins.). (Hewey Calloway Ser.). 1998. 57.00 (978-0-7887-9444-5(2), S1003) Recorded Bks.
Filled with pathos and humor, this endearing tale is set in the last days of the Old West. Hewey Calloway may be pushing 45, but he can still rope and outride most things on four legs. When he is critically injured by a wild horse, he finally admits that his world is passing away.

Smilla's Sense of Snow, unabr. ed. Peter Hoeg. Tr. by Tiina Nunnally. Narrated by Alyssa Bresnahan. 12 cass. (Running Time: 17 hrs. 45 mins.). 1994. 97.00 (978-0-7887-0023-1(5), 94222E7) Recorded Bks.
Isaiah, the son of one of Smilla Jasperson's neighbors, is found face-down in the snow outside her Copenhagen apartment building, leaving the usually stoical Smilla disturbed. She quickly rejects the official verdict of accidental death when she observes the footprints the boy left in the snow.

Smith. unabr. ed. Leon Garfield. Narrated by Ron Keith. 5 pieces. (Running Time: 6 hrs. 30 mins.). (gr. 6 up). 2001. 44.00 (978-0-7887-5370-1(3)) Recorded Bks.
Smith, a penniless and illiterate 12-year-old urchin, has so far survived the streets of 18th century London. But when he picks a piece of paper from an old man's pocket, Smith's life takes a direction he never could have predicted.

Smith & Jones. (1243) Books on Tape.

Smith-Lemli-Opitz Syndrome - A Bibliography & Dictionary for Physicians, Patients, & Genome Researchers. Compiled by Icon Group International, Inc. Staff. 2007. ring bd. 28.95 (978-0-497-11293-6(0)) Icon Grp.

Smith-Magenis Syndrome - A Bibliography & Dictionary for Physicians, Patients, & Genome Researchers. Compiled by Icon Group International, Inc. Staff. 2007. ring bd. 28.95 (978-0-497-11294-3(9)) Icon Grp.

Smithsonian Collection of Classic Jazz. rev. ed. Anno. by Martin Williams. Selected by Martin Williams. 6 CDs. (Running Time: 6 hrs.). 1990. audio compact disk 68.00 (978-0-393-99487-2(2)) Norton.

Smithsonian Dashiell Hammett. 2004. 34.98 (978-1-57019-719-2(9)) Radio Spirits.

Smithsonian Edgar Allan Poe. 2004. 34.98 (978-1-57019-721-5(0)) Radio Spirits.

Smithsonian Institution. abr. ed. Gore Vidal. 2 cass. 1998. 17.95 (978-1-55935-276-5(0), 896823) Soundelux.

Smithsonian Institution. unabr. ed. Gore Vidal. Read by Grover Gardner. 6 cass. (Running Time: 9 hrs.). (American Chronicles Ser.). 1998. 48.00 (978-0-7366-4156-2(4), 4659) Books on Tape.
Washington, D.C., Good Friday, 1939. A teenage math prodigy, known only as T, gets an unexpected summons to the Smithsonian. Deep in its cavernous basement, arcane projects proliferate. meanwhile, museum displays come alive after hours & an adventurous First Lady from the inaugural gowns exhibit interrupts T's scientific work to introduce him to the joys of sex. Combining inventive energy with historical themes, Vidal stages a glittering cast from the past, among them, Lincoln, Lindbergh, Albert Einstein & Adolf Hitler.

Smithsonian Legendary Performers. Edgar Allan Poe. 6 CDs. (Running Time: 6 hrs.). 2005. audio compact disk 34.98 (978-1-57019-720-8(2), OTR 50462) Pub: Radio Spirits. Dist(s): AudioGO

Smithsonian Legendary Performers: Dashiell Hammett. Dashiell Hammett. 6 CDs. (Running Time: 6 hrs.). 2005. audio compact disk 34.98 (978-1-57019-718-5(0), OTR 50452) Pub: Radio Spirits. Dist(s): AudioGO

***Smitten.** unabr. ed. Janet Evanovich. Read by C. J. Critt. (ENG.). 2006. (978-0-06-113479-1(1), Harper Audio); (978-0-06-113480-7(5), Harper Audio) HarperCollins Pubs.

Smitten. unabr. ed. Janet Evanovich. Read by C. J. Critt. (Running Time: 18000 sec.). 2006. audio compact disk 14.95 (978-0-06-073707-8(7)) HarperCollins Pubs.

Smoke. unabr. ed. John Ed Bradley. Read by Christopher Hurt. 10 cass. (Running Time: 14 hrs. 30 mins.). 1998. 69.95 (978-0-7861-1368-2(5), 2276) Blckstn Audio.
High comedy, high jinx, unrequited love, & small town eccentrics confronting big business come together in this engaging tale.

Smoke. unabr. ed. John Ed Bradley. Read by Christopher Hurt. (Running Time: 50400 sec.). 2008. audio compact disk 29.95 (978-0-7861-6221-5(X)) Blckstn Audio.

Smoke. unabr. ed. Ivan Turgenev. Read by Stewart Lankton. 5 cass. (Running Time: 7 hrs. 30 min.). 2000. 39.95 (978-0-7861-1733-8(8), 2538) Blckstn Audio.
Study of politics & society & an enduringly poignant love story. European setting, barbed wit & visionary call for Russia to look west, became the center of a famous philosophical breach between Turgenev & Dostoevsky.

Smoke. unabr. ed. Ivan Turgenev. Read by Stuart Langton. 5 cass. (Running Time: 23400 sec.). 2000. audio compact disk 48.00 (978-0-7861-9906-8(7), 2538) Blckstn Audio.

Smoke. unabr. ed. Ivan Turgenev. Read by Stuart Langton. (Running Time: 59400 sec.). 2007. audio compact disk 29.95 (978-0-7861-4997-1(3)) Blckstn Audio.

Smoke. unabr. collector's ed. Donald E. Westlake. Read by Michael Kramer. 9 cass. (Running Time: 13 hrs. 30 min.). (Dortmunder Ser.). 1996. 72.00 (978-0-7366-3332-1(4), 3983) Books on Tape.
Any thief knows he can't get fingered for a burglary if no one sees him. So you'd think Freddie Noon, smalltime crook, would jump for joy after he inadvertently breaks into a tobacco-industry research lab, swallows an experimental serum & becomes completely invisible. It's a thief's fantasy come true...or is it?.

Smoke, Set. unabr. ed. John Ed Bradley. Read by Christopher Hurt. 10 cass. 1999. 69.95 (FS9-51123) Highsmith.

Smoke & Whispers. Mick Herron. 2009. 69.95 (978-0-7531-4408-4(5)); audio compact disk 84.95 (978-0-7531-4409-1(3)) Pub: Isis Pubng Ltd GBR. Dist(s): Ulverscroft US

Smoke Bellew. unabr. ed. Jack London. Read by Gene Engene. 8 cass. (Running Time: 10 hrs.). Dramatization. 1990. 49.95 (978-1-55686-361-5(6), 361) Books in Motion.
Tenderfoot, journalist Kit Bellew, nicknamed "Smoke" accepts his grandfather's challenge to pack into the Klondike. Kit is faced with unexpected dangers.

Smoke Enders: A Self Hypnosis Tape Set. (Hypnotic Sensory Response Audio Ser.). 1999. 39.95 (978-0-9708772-4-6(2)) L Lizards Pub Co.

Smoke Free. 2004. audio compact disk (978-0-9755937-1-4(4)) TheraScapes.

Smoke Free. Created by Ellen Chernoff Simon. 3 CDs. (Running Time: 2 hrs.). 2004. audio compact disk 58.00 (978-0-9765587-1-2(8)) Imadulation.

Smoke-Free. Paul R. Scheele. 1 cass. (Running Time: 40 min.). (Paraliminal Tapes Ser.). 1989. 24.95 (978-0-925480-07-1(X)) Learn Strategies.
Designed for smokers who desire to quit smoking and who have tried in the past.

***Smoke Free Forever: Hypnosis to Help You Be Smoke Free.** Paul Dale Anderson. Perf. by Paul Dale Anderson. (ENG.). 2010. audio compact disk 21.00 (978-0-937491-13-3(6)) TwoAM Pubns.

Smoke-Free in 30 Days: The Pain-Free, Permanent Way to Quit. abr. unabr. ed. Daniel F. Seidman. Read by Daniel F. Seidman. (ENG.). 2009. audio compact disk 20.00 (978-0-307-71479-4(9), Random AudioBks) Pub: Random Audio Pubg. Dist(s): Random

Smoke-Free Life. Carla Czybora. Music by Jim Adams. 1 cass. 10.00 New Bgnnngs.
Features self hypnosis using affirmations for behavior modification of smoking tobacco.

Smoke Free Today. 2004. audio compact disk (978-0-9755937-3-8(0)) TheraScapes.

Smoke Free Tomorrow. 2004. audio compact disk (978-0-9755937-4-5(9)) TheraScapes.

Smoke Free Yesterday. 2004. audio compact disk (978-0-9755937-2-1(2)) TheraScapes.

Smoke in Mirrors. abr. ed. Jayne Ann Krentz. Narrated by James Daniels & Aasne Vigesaa. 5 CDs. (Running Time: 4 hrs.). 2002. audio compact disk 61.25 (978-1-58788-703-1(7), 1587887037, CD Lib Edit) Brilliance Audio.

Smoke in Mirrors. unabr. ed. Jayne Ann Krentz. Narrated by James Daniels & Aasne Vigesaa. 6 cass. (Running Time: 9 hrs.). 2002. 29.95 (978-1-58788-699-7(5), 1587886995, BAU); 69.25 (978-1-58788-700-0(2), 1587887002, Unabridge Lib Edns) Brilliance Audio.
A con artist and seductress, Meredith Spooner lived fast - and died young. Now it seems Meredith's last scam - embezzling more than a million dollars from a college endowment fund - is coming back to haunt Leonora Hutton. An email just arrived in which Meredith - in fear for her life - explains that the money is waiting for Leonora in an offshore account ... and a safe-deposit key is on the way. Leonora wants nothing to do with the tainted money. She's already been accused of being in on the theft by Thomas Walker - who, it seems, was a victim of Meredith's knack for both scams and seductions. Eager to prove him wrong, Leonora sets out to collect the cash and hand it over. But she discovers two other items in the safe-deposit box. One is a book about Mirror House - a mansion filled with antique mirrors, where Meredith engineered her final deception. The other is a set of newspaper stories about a thirty-year-old murder that occurred there - unsolved to this day. Now Leonora has an offer for Thomas Walker. She'll hand over the money - if he helps her figure out what's happening. Meredith had described Walker as "a man you can trust." But in a funhouse-mirror world of illusion and distortion, Leonora may be out of her league.

Smoke in Mirrors. unabr. ed. Jayne Ann Krentz. Read by James Daniels Aasne Vigesaa. (Running Time: 9 hrs.). 2004. 39.25 (978-1-59335-512-8(2), 1593355122, Brlnc Audio MP3 Lib) Brilliance Audio.

Smoke in Mirrors. unabr. ed. Jayne Ann Krentz. Read by James Daniels Aasne Vigesaa. (Running Time: 9 hrs.). 2004. 39.25 (978-1-59710-721-1(2), 1597107212, BADLE); 24.95 (978-1-59710-720-4(4), 1597107204, BAD) Brilliance Audio.

***Smoke in Mirrors.** unabr. ed. Jayne Ann Krentz. Read by James Daniels Aasne Vigesaa. (Running Time: 9 hrs.). 2010. audio compact disk 29.99 (978-1-4418-4073-8(7), 9781441840738, Bril Audio CD Unabri); audio compact disk 89.97 (978-1-4418-4074-5(5), 9781441840745, BriAudCD Unabrid) Brilliance Audio.

Smoke in Mirrors. unabr. ed. Jayne Ann Krentz. Read by James Daniels Aasne Vigesaa. (Running Time: 9 hrs.). 2004. 24.95 (978-1-59335-243-1(3), 1593352433) Soulmate Audio Bks.

Smoke Jensen: Blood of the Mountain Man: the Mountain Man 11. Based on a novel by William W. Johnstone. (Mountain Man Ser.: No. 11). 2010. audio compact disk 19.99 (978-1-59950-634-0(3)) GraphicAudio.

Smoke Jensen: Code of the Mountain Man: the Mountain Man 8. Based on a book by William W. Johnstone. (Mountain Man Ser.: No. 8). 2009. audio compact disk 19.99 (978-1-59950-602-9(5)) GraphicAudio.

Smoke Jensen: Courage of the Mountain Man: the Mountain Man 10. Based on a novel by William W. Johnstone. (Mountain Man Ser.: No. 10). 2010. audio compact disk 19.99 (978-1-59950-625-8(4)) GraphicAudio.

***Smoke Jensen: Cunning of the Mountain Man: the Mountain Man 14.** William W. Johnstone. (Mountain Man Ser.: No. 14). 2010. audio compact disk 19.99 (978-1-59950-660-9(2)) GraphicAudio.

Smoke Jensen: Fury of the Mountain Man: the Mountain Man 12. Based on a novel by William W. Johnstone. (Mountain Man Ser.: No. 12). 2010. audio compact disk 19.99 (978-1-59950-641-8(6)) GraphicAudio.

Smoke Jensen: Journey of the Mountain Man: the Mountain Man 5. William W. Johnstone. (Mountain Man Ser.: No. 6). 2009. audio compact disk 19.99 (978-1-59950-568-8(1)) GraphicAudio.

Smoke Jensen: Law of the Mountain Man: the Mountain Man 6. William W. Johnstone. (Mountain Man Ser.: No. 5). 2009. audio compact disk 19.99 (978-1-59950-574-9(6)) GraphicAudio.

***Smoke Jensen: Power of the Mountain Man: the Mountain Man 15.** William W. Johnstone. (Mountain Man Ser.: No. 15). 2010. audio compact disk 19.99 (978-1-59950-676-0(9)) GraphicAudio.

Smoke Jensen: Pursuit of the Mountain Man: the Mountain Man 9. Based on a novel by William W. Johnstone. (Mountain Man Ser.: No. 9). 2009. audio compact disk 19.99 (978-1-59950-611-1(4)) GraphicAudio.

***Smoke Jensen: Rage of the Mountain Man: the Mountain Man 13.** William W. Johnstone. (Mountain Man Ser.: No. 13). 2010. audio compact disk 19.99 (978-1-59950-652-4(1)) GraphicAudio.

Smoke Jensen: Return of the Mountain Man: the Mountain Man 2. William W. Johnstone. (Mountain Man Ser.: No. 2). 2009. audio compact disk 19.99 (978-1-59950-533-6(9)) GraphicAudio.

Smoke Jensen: Revenge of the Mountain Man: the Mountain Man 4. William W. Johnstone. (Mountain Man Ser.: No. 4). 2009. audio compact disk 19.99 (978-1-59950-560-2(6)) GraphicAudio.

Smoke Jensen: The Last Mountain Man: the Mountain Man 1. unabr. ed. William W. Johnstone. Read by Mort Shelby et al. 5 CDs. (Mountain Man Ser.: No. 1). 2009. audio compact disk 19.99 (978-1-59950-525-1(8)) GraphicAudio.

Smoke Jensen: Trail of the Mountain Man: the Mountain Man 3. William W. Johnstone. (Mountain Man Ser.: No. 3). 2009. audio compact disk 19.99 (978-1-59950-557-2(6)) GraphicAudio.

Smoke Jensen: War of the Mountain Man: the Mountain Man 7. William W. Johnstone. (Mountain Man Ser.: No. 7). 2009. audio compact disk 19.99 (978-1-59950-582-4(7)) GraphicAudio.

Smoke Jumper. abr. ed. Nicholas Evans. Read by Luke Perry. 5 CDs. (Running Time: 8 hrs. 35 mins.). (ENG.). 2001. audio compact disk 29.95 (978-0-553-71456-2(2)) Pub: Random Audio Pubg. Dist(s): Random

Smoke No More. 2 cassettes. 1985. 19.45 (978-1-55841-221-7(2)) Emmett E Miller.
Develop a clear, positive image of your goals; teach your mind to reject smoking and create a more healthy substitute behavior. Eliminate the desire to smoke and manage the stress of quitting or cutting down.

Smoke No More. 2 CDs. 1985. audio compact disk 25.50 (978-1-55841-136-4(4)) Emmett E Miller.
Develop a clear, positive image of your goals, teach your mind to reject smoking and create a more healthy substitute behavior. Elimate the desire to smoke and manage the stress of quitting or cutting down.

Smoke No More. 1. (Running Time: 20 nin). 2002. audio compact disk (978-0-9726482-1-9(6)) Energy Way.
Sellf help audio program to Stop Smoking.

Smoke No More. Mary Lee LaBay. 2007. audio compact disk 19.95 (978-1-934705-14-8(4)) Awareness Engin.

Smoke No More. Betty L. Randolph. Read by Betty L. Randolph. Read by Leonard Baron. Ed. by Success Education Institute International. 1 cass. (Running Time: 60 min.). (Health Ser.). 1989. bk. 14.98 Ocean Format. (978-1-55909-260-9(2), 500P); bk. 14.98 Music Format. (978-1-55909-261-6(0), 500PM) Randolph Tapes.
60,000 messages left-right brain. Male-females voice tracks with Megafonic Subliminals. Ocean (P) & Music (PM).

Smoke No More. Dick Sutphen. 1 cass. (Running Time: 1 hr.). (Probe Seven Ser.). 14.98 (978-0-87554-371-0(5), P107) Valley Sun.
"You have the self discipline to stop smoking. You do. You quit. You accept this. Yes...".

Smoke Ring. unabr. ed. Larry Niven. Read by Pat Bottino. 7 cass. (Running Time: 10 hrs.). 1996. 49.95 (978-0-7861-1012-4(0), 1790) Blckstn Audio.
In the free-fall environment of the Smoke Ring, the descendants of the crew of the "Discipline" no longer remembered their Earth roots - or the existence of Sharls Davis Kendy, the computer-program despot of the ship. Until Kendy initiated contact once more. Fourteen years later, only Jeffer, the Citizens Tree Scientist, knew that Kendy was still watching - & waiting. Then the Citizens Tree people rescued a family of loggers & learned for the first time of the Admiralty, a large society living in free fall amid the floating debris called the Clump. And it was likely that the Admiralty had maintained, intact, "Discipline's" original computer library. Exploration was a temptation neither Jeffer nor Kendy could resist, & neither Citizens Tree nor Sharls Davis Kendy would ever be the same again.

Smoke Ring. unabr. ed. Larry Niven. Read by Pat Bottino. (Running Time: 36000 sec.). 2007. audio compact disk 72.00 (978-0-7861-5808-9(5)); audio compact disk 29.95 (978-0-7861-5809-6(3)) Blckstn Audio.

Smoke Screen. abr. ed. Sandra Brown. Read by Victor Slezak. (Running Time: 6 hrs. 0 mins. 0 sec.). (ENG.). 2010. audio compact disk 14.99 (978-1-4423-0472-7(3)) Pub: S&S Audio. Dist(s): S and S Inc

Smoke Screen. unabr. ed. Sandra Brown. Narrated by Victor Slezak. 12 CDs. (Running Time: 14 hrs. 15 mins.). 2008. audio compact disk 123.75 (978-1-4361-2335-8(6)) Recorded Bks.

Smoke Screen. unabr. ed. Sandra Brown. Read by Victor Slezak. 12 cass. (Running Time: 14 hrs. 15 mins.). 2008. 98.75 (978-1-4361-2333-4(X)) Recorded Bks.

Smoke Screen. unabr. ed. Sandra Brown. Read by Victor Slezak. 12 CDs. (Running Time: 15 hrs. 0 mins. 0 sec.). (ENG.). 2008. audio compact disk 49.95 (978-0-7435-7227-9(0)) Pub: S&S Audio. Dist(s): S and S Inc

Smoke Screen. unabr. ed. Vincent Patrick. Narrated by Richard Ferrone. 10 cass. (Running Time: 13 hrs. 45 mins.). 1999. 85.00 (978-0-7887-3895-1(X), 95936E7) Recorded Bks.
Cuba has the ultimate biological weapon: a virus so deadly it can wipe out millions of lives in a few days. In America, an envoy from Castro will demonstrate its power. To stop him & keep the virus secret, the President's advisor invents a smoke screen. During a hotel robbery, Castro's messenger will be nabbed as one of the hostages. The stakes are high & so are the chances for something going wrong.

Smoke Without Fire. unabr. ed. E. X. Ferrars. Read by George Hagan. 6 cass. (Running Time: 7 hrs. 1 min.). 2001. 54.95 (978-1-85089-878-8(2), 92085) Pub: ISIS Audio GBR. Dist(s): Ulverscroft US
Andrew Basnett didn't like Christmas. He preferred to spend it with his friends in the peace of their country home. But peace & goodwill was not to be. The day before Christmas Eve their neighbor was blown up by a bomb. No one knew he was returning to Berkshire. Had the bomb been intended for someone else?.

Smokejumpers: Battling the Forest Flames. Diana Briscoe. (High Five Reading - Green Ser.). (ENG.). (gr. 3-4). 2007. audio compact disk 5.95 (978-1-4296-1423-8(4)) CapstoneDig.

Smoker: An Atticus Kodiak Novel. unabr. ed. Greg Rucka. Narrated by George Wilson. 8 cass. (Running Time: 11 hrs. 45 mins.). 2000. 71.00 (978-0-7887-4926-1(9), 95844E7) Recorded Bks.
Security expert Atticus Kodiak has been hired to make sure there are no weak points in a witness protection team. But meanwhile, one of the ten most dangerous contract killers in the world plans to destroy the operation. Studded with the latest technological tools of the security trade, zinging with split second decisions.

Smokescreen. Dick Francis. Read by Geoffrey Howard. 5 CDs. (Running Time: 5 mins. 30 sec.). 2005. audio compact disk 40.00 (978-0-7861-8780-5(8), 2364) Blckstn Audio.

Smokescreen. Dick Francis. 2 cass. (Running Time: 90 min. per cass.). 1990. 15.95 HarperCollins Pubs.

***Smokescreen.** Betty Rowlands. 2010. 61.95 (978-1-4079-0798-7(0)); audio compact disk 79.95 (978-1-4079-0799-4(9)) Pub: Soundings Ltd GBR. Dist(s): Ulverscroft US

Smokescreen. abr. ed. Dick Francis. Read by Edward Woodward. 2 cass. (Running Time: 3 hrs.). 2000. 7.95 (978-1-57815-049-6(3), 1046, Media Bks Audio) Media Bks NJ.
Link is there to save horses, but first he must save himself.

Smokescreen. unabr. ed. Dick Francis. Read by Tony Britton. 6 cass. (Running Time: 6 hrs.). 1995. 54.95 (978-0-7451-6832-6(9), CAB 486) AudioGO.
Big-time racing provides the background for this brilliant suspense novel. International superstar Edward Lincoln is acting as detective again, but this time there is no script & a poor performance could mean a bullet in the head.

Smokescreen. unabr. ed. Dick Francis. Read by Geoffrey Howard. 4 cass. (Running Time: 5 hrs. 30 mins.). 1999. 32.95 (978-0-7861-1514-3(9), 2364) Blckstn Audio.
Edward Lincoln is a worldwide celebrity who plays impossibly daring detectives on the big screen. But in reality he is an ordinary man currently stuck in an extraordinary spot. Nerissa, his ailing godmother, has pleaded with him to travel to South Africa to do some investigating - she's afraid someone is tampering with her racehorses. Feeling helpless, Lincoln nevertheless cannot refuse her request.

Smokescreen. unabr. ed. Dick Francis. Read by David Case. 7 cass. (Running Time: 7 hrs.). 1994. 56.00 (978-0-7366-2838-9(X), 3546) Books on Tape.
While investigating racehorse tampering, Edward Lincoln is confronted by sudden perils & even murder.

Smokescreen. unabr. ed. Dick Francis. Read by Tony Britton. 6 cass. (Running Time: 9 hrs.). 2000. 49.95 (CAB 486) Pub: Chivers Audio Bks GBR. Dist(s): AudioGO
International superstar Edward Lincoln is acting as detective again, but this time there is no script and a poor performance.

Smokescreen, unabr. ed. Dick Francis. Read by Geoffrey Howard. 4 cass. 1999. 32.95 (FS9-50914) Highsmith.

Smokescreen. unabr. ed. Dick Francis. Narrated by Simon Prebble. 5 cass. (Running Time: 7 hrs.). 2000. 44.00 (978-0-7887-0231-0(9), 94456E7) Recorded Bks.

Smokey Brandon Duo Pack. abr. ed. Noreen Ayres. Read by Jennifer Durand & John Durand. Prod. by Brad Fregger. 4 cass. (Running Time: 6 hrs.). (Smokey Brandon Mystery Ser.: Nos. 1 & 2). 1995. 24.00 Set. (978-1-886392-02-1(1), Parrot Bks) Walberg Pubng.
Kirkus reviews says "(She) is tough, hip, visceral & lusty enough to make both Wambaugh & Spillane sit up...a macho heroine".

Smokey Mountain Christmas for Guitar. Steve Kaufman. 1994. spiral bd. 18.95 (978-0-7866-1141-6(3), 95308P) Mel Bay.

Smokey Mountain Christmas for Guitar. Steve Kaufman. 1998. spiral bd. 24.95 (978-0-7866-4436-0(2), 95308CDP) Mel Bay.

Smokey Mountain Christmas for Guitar. Steve Kaufman. (ENG.). 2002. per. 24.95 (978-0-7866-6551-8(3)) Mel Bay.

Smokey Mountain Christmas for Mandolin. Steve Kaufman. 1994. pap. bk. 24.95 (978-0-7866-0691-7(6), 95474CDP) Mel Bay.

Smokey Mountain Christmas for Mandolin. Steve Kaufman. (ENG.). 2002. per. 24.95 (978-0-7866-6565-5(3)) Mel Bay.

***Smokin' Seventeen: A Stephanie Plum Novel.** unabr. ed. Janet Evanovich. (ENG.). 2011. audio compact disk 32.00 (978-0-307-93223-5(0), Random AudioBks) Pub: Random Audio Pubg. Dist(s): Random

Smoking. Bruce Goldberg. (ENG.). 2005. audio compact disk 17.00 (978-1-57968-083-1(6)) Pub: B Goldberg. Dist(s): Baker Taylor

Smoking. Bruce Goldberg. Read by Bruce Goldberg. 1 cass. (Running Time: 25 min.). (ENG.). 2006. 13.00 (978-1-885577-48-1(6)) Pub: B Goldberg. Dist(s): Baker Taylor
Through self-hypnosis eliminate this nasty habit without gaining weight by removing its cause.

Smoking Cessation. Bruce A. Baldwin. Read by Bruce A. Baldwin. (Running Time: 60 min.). 1983. 8.95 (978-0-933583-14-6(1), PDC833) Direction Dynamics.
Side A is a relaxation & reinforcement program to use when "Awake & Aware". Side B does the same in a hypnotic relaxation format.

Smoking Control, Relaxation For. Brian G. Danaher. 1 cass. (Running Time: 39 min.). 10.95 (29355) J Norton Pubs.
Teaches how to achieve a state of deep muscular relaxation quickly & to use this skill to aid in the control, & eventual, elimination of smoking habits.

Smoking in a Hot Bath see **J. B. Priestley**

Smoking, Stop: Quit for Good! Elin Rhoderick & Rhoderick Elin. 3 cass. 1990. pap. bk. 39.50 Set incl. 31 p. bklt. (978-0-88432-287-0(4), S01670) J Norton Pubs.
Uses stress management techniques to help you quit smoking for good.

Smoky Hill. unabr. ed. Don Coldsmith. Read by Maynard Villers. 8 cass. (Running Time: 9 hrs. 42 min.). (Rivers West Ser.: Bk. 2). 1996. 49.95 (978-1-55686-655-5(0)) Books in Motion.
The Smoky Hill River runs through the rolling grasslands of Kansas, a rich source of opportunity for those bold enough to risk the dream-killing territory.

Smoky Joe's Cafe. unabr. ed. Bryce Courtenay. Read by Humphrey Bower. 4 cass. (Running Time: 5 hrs. 15 mins.). 2005. 32.00 (978-1-74030-537-2(X)); audio compact disk 63.95 (978-1-74030-689-8(9)) Pub: Bolinda Pubng AUS. Dist(s): Bolinda Pub Inc

Smoky Mountain Hymns, Vol. 1. 7.99 (978-1-55897-350-3(8), C-5137N); audio compact disk 9.99 (978-1-55897-352-7(4), CD-5137J) Brentwood Music.

Smoky Mountain Kids. 1 cass. (J). bk. (978-1-55897-511-8(X), CSBK5202); (978-1-55897-208-7(0), V5225) Brentwood Music.
Action-filled recording featuring hand-crafted instruments & songs of simplicity. Features: Deep & Wide, Simple Gifts, This Little Light of Mine & others.

Smoky Mountains Audio Cassette Tour: The Newfound Gap Road. unabr. ed. Paul Sagan. Read by Ed Markmann. Ed. by Steve Kemp. 2 cass. (Running Time: 2 hrs.). 1992. 9.95 (978-0-937207-06-2(3), 03-008) GSMA.
An audio tour of the Newfound Gap Road in Great Smoky Mountains National Park, featuring explanations of landmarks, interviews with former residents & park rangers.

Smoky the Cowhorse. unabr. collector's ed. Will James. Read by Dan Lazar. 5 cass. (Running Time: 7 hrs. 30 mins.). (J). (gr. 4-7). 1981. 40.00 (978-0-7366-0401-7(4), 1378) Books on Tape.
If you'd like to meet a real cow puncher, you'll like Clint, the bronc peeler. He'll tell you all about his favorite pony, Smoky, who lived a full horse's life in cow country around the time of World War I.

Smooth - ShowTrax. Arranged by Mac Huff. 1 CD. (Running Time: 5 mins.). 2000. audio compact disk 19.95 (08201205) H Leonard.
This Grammy Award winner by Santana was #1 for weeks. Its great Latin groove will show your pop group at its best.

Smooth Jazz. Windham Hill Staff. 1 cass. 1998. 15.00 (978-1-56170-561-0(6)) Hay House.

Smooth Talking: A Curriculum for School-Age Children Who Stutter. 2nd ed. Nola T. Radford. 2009. spiral bd. 159.95 (978-1-59756-243-0(2)) Plural Pub Inc.

Smooth Talking Stranger. abr. ed. Lisa Kleypas. Read by Emily Durante. (Running Time: 5 hrs.). 2010. audio compact disk 14.99 (978-1-59737-878-9(X), 9781597378789, BCD Value Price) Brilliance Audio.

Smooth Talking Stranger. unabr. ed. Lisa Kleypas. Read by Emily Durante. 1 MP3-CD. (Running Time: 10 hrs.). 2009. 24.99 (978-1-59737-873-4(9), 9781597378734, Brilliance MP3); 39.97 (978-1-59737-876-5(3), 9781597378765, BADLE); 39.97 (978-1-59737-874-1(7), 9781597378741, Brinc Audio MP3 Lib); 24.99 (978-1-59737-875-8(5), 9781597378758, BAD); audio compact disk 36.99 (978-1-59737-871-0(2), 9781597378710, Bril Audio CD Unabri); audio compact disk 97.97 (978-1-59737-872-7(0), 9781597378727, BriAudCD Unabrid) Brilliance Audio.

Smooth Trippin' Martin Mlecko. 2006. pap. bk. 49.95 (978-3-937406-22-0(0)) Pub: edel CLASS DEU. Dist(s): Natl Bk Netwk

Smothers Brothers. Interview. Interview with Smothers Brothers. 1 cass. (Running Time: 30 min.). 9.95 (A0230B090, HarperThor) HarpC GBR.

Smugglers. unabr. ed. Iain Lawrence. Narrated by Ron Keith. 4 pieces. (Running Time: 5 hrs. 45 mins.). (gr. 7 up). 2000. 37.00 (978-0-7887-4242-2(6), 96056E7) Recorded Bks.
It's been two years since John Spencer & his father were shipwrecked & nearly murdered. Now 16-year-old John is making their new schooner's maiden voyage to London. Not long out to sea, John realizes that the captain & crew are smugglers, steering their own course & prepared to kill anyone who tries to stop them.

Smugglers. unabr. ed. Iain Lawrence. Read by Ron Keith. 4 cass. (Running Time: 5 hrs. 45 mins.). (YA). 2000. pap. bk. & stu. ed. 59.95 (978-0-7887-4348-1(1), 41142); 204.80 (978-0-7887-4448-8(8), 47139) Recorded Bks.

Smugglers. unabr. ed. Iain Lawrence. Narrated by Ron Keith. 5 CDs. (Running Time: 5 hrs. 45 mins.). (gr. 7 up). 2000. audio compact disk 48.00 (978-0-7887-4734-2(7), C1263E7) Recorded Bks.

Smugglers' Island, unabr. ed. Avi. Narrated by George Guidall. 3 pieces. (Running Time: 4 hrs.). Orig. Title: Shadrach's Crossing. (gr. 5 up). 1997. 27.00 (978-0-7887-0375-1(7), 94566E7) Recorded Bks.
Gain fascinating insights into the historical & political complications of Prohibition. Set in the 1930s, it is the story of an Irish-American boy who concocts a dangerous plan to bust the liquor smugglers who are terrorizing his island home.

Smuggler's Moon. Bruce Alexander. Read by John Lee. 2001. 56.00 (978-0-7366-8324-1(0)) Books on Tape.

Smuggler's Trail. unabr. collector's ed. Max Brand. Read by Wolfram Kandinsky. 6 cass. (Running Time: 9 hrs.). 1993. 48.00 (978-0-7366-2358-2(2), 3133) Books on Tape.
In jail for counterfeiting, Jack Ripley thinks his trail has ended. But U.S. Marshall Tom Dallas offers him his freedom - for a price. In a desperate try for justice, Dallas arranges Ripley's escape, hoping that Ripley can succeed where others have failed to capture the West's most murderous band of smugglers. For the first time in his life, Ripley's guns are shooting for the law, not at it!.

Snack Thief. unabr. ed. Andrea Camilleri. Read by Grover Gardner. (Running Time: 21600 sec.). (Inspector Montalbano Mystery Ser.). 2007. 44.95 (978-1-4332-0212-4(3)); audio compact disk 45.00 (978-1-4332-0213-1(1)); audio compact disk 29.95 (978-1-4332-0214-8(X)) Blckstn Audio.

Snafu: The Littlest Clown. Lillian B. Pennington. Illus. by Earle Gardner. (J). (gr. 1-6). 1972. pap. bk. 7.94 (978-0-87783-225-6(0)) Oddo.

Snaggle Doodles. unabr. ed. Patricia Reilly Giff. 1 cass. (Running Time: 1 hr.). (Follow the Reader Ser.). (J). (gr. 1-2). 1985. pap. bk. 17.00 incl. bk. & guide. (978-0-8072-0104-6(9), FTR107SP, Listening Lib) Random Audio Pubg.
Follow the kids in Ms. Rooney's second grade class as they learn & grow through an entire school year filled with fun & surprises. Corresponding Month - April.

Snail Boy & the Toilet Bots. Susan Gates. Read by Nigel Lambert. (Running Time: 18000 sec.). (J). 2001. audio compact disk 59.95 (978-0-7540-6743-6(2)) AudioGo GBR.

Snail Eggs & Samphire: Dispatches from the Food Front. Derek Cooper. Read by Stephen Thorne. 10 cass. (Running Time: 15 hrs.). 2002. 84.95 (978-0-7540-0691-6(3), CAB 2113) AudioGO.

Snail Mail No More. unabr. ed. Paula Danziger & Ann M. Martin. 3 vols. (Running Time: 4 hrs. 36 mins.). (J). (gr. 3-7). 2004. pap. bk. 36.00 (978-0-8072-8413-1(0), Listening Lib) Random Audio Pubg.

Snail Mail No More. unabr. ed. Paula Danziger & Ann M. Martin. Read by Paula Danziger & Ann M. Martin. 3 cass. (Running Time: 4 hrs. 36 mins.). (J). (gr. 3-7). 2004. 30.00 (978-0-8072-8412-4(2), YA194CX, Listening Lib) Random Audio Pubg.
Best friends Elizabeth & Tara Starr are still totally different. Tara Starr accessorizes with glitter & sequins & loves the spotlight. Elizabeth loves reading & writing poetry & hates to be the center of attention. Though the two live far from each other, they continue to correspond regularly now, via e-mail. But distance & life events out of their control, put the girls' friendship to the test.

Snake Charmer: A Life & Death in Pursuit of Knowledge. unabr. ed. Jamie James. Read by William Hughes. (Running Time: 12 hrs. 50 mins.). 2008. 29.95 (978-1-4332-1218-5(8)) Blckstn Audio.

Snake Charmer: A Life & Death in Pursuit of Knowledge. unabr. ed. Jamie James. Read by William Hughes. (Running Time: 30600 sec.). 2008. 29.95 (978-1-4332-1216-1(1)); 54.95 (978-1-4332-1214-7(5)); audio compact disk 29.95 (978-1-4332-1217-8(X)); audio compact disk 63.00 (978-1-4332-1215-4(3)) Blckstn Audio.

Snake Chief: A Story from Nelson Mandela's Favorite African Folktales. Read by Scarlett Johansson. Compiled by Nelson Mandela. Composed by Johnny Clegg. (Running Time: 7 mins.). (ENG.). 2009. 1.99 (978-1-60024-813-9(6)) Pub: Hachet Audio. Dist(s): HachBkGrp

Snake in the Heart: Poems & Music by Chicago Spoken Word Performers. Chicago Spoken Word Performers & Tia Chucha Press Staff. 1994. audio compact disk 15.00 (978-1-882688-06-7(6)) Pub: Tia Chucha Pr. Dist(s): Chicago Distribution Ctr

Snake Oil. (Paws & Tales Ser.: Vol. 13). (J). 2001. 3.99 (978-1-57972-410-8(8)); audio compact disk 5.99 (978-1-57972-411-5(6)) Insight Living.

Snake Oil & Other Preoccupations. unabr. ed. John Diamond. Read by Neil Pearson. 8 cass. (Running Time: 33540 sec.). 2003. 74.95 (978-0-7540-0823-1(1), CAB 2245) Chivers Pr GBR.

Snake River. unabr. ed. Winfred Blevins. Read by Michael Taylor. 8 cass. (Running Time: 11 hrs. 6 min.). (Rivers West Ser.: Bk. 7). 1998. 49.95 (978-1-55686-772-9(7)) Books in Motion.
A rugged mountain man faces a great challenge in the form of a strong-willed missionary woman.

Snake-Stone. unabr. ed. Berlie Doherty. Read by Dermot Crowley. 3 cass. (Running Time: 3 hrs.). (J). 1997. 24.95 (CCA 3361) AudioGO.

Snake Stone. unabr. ed. Jason Goodwin. Read by Stephen Hoye. (Running Time: 11 hrs. 0 mins. 0 sec.). (Yashim the Eunuch Mysteries Ser.). (ENG.). 2009. audio compact disk 69.99 (978-1-4001-4011-4(0)) Pub: Tantor Media. Dist(s): IngramPubServ

Snake Stone. unabr. ed. Jason Goodwin. Read by Stephen Hoye. Narrated by Stephen Hoye. (Running Time: 11 hrs. 0 mins. 0 sec.). (Yashim the Eunuch Mysteries Ser.). (ENG.). 2009. audio compact disk 24.99 (978-1-4001-6011-2(1)) Pub: Tantor Media. Dist(s): IngramPubServ

Snake Stone. unabr. ed. Jason Goodwin & Jason Goodwin. Read by Stephen Hoye. (Running Time: 11 hrs. 0 mins. 0 sec.). (Yashim the Eunuch Mysteries Ser.). (ENG.). 2009. audio compact disk 34.99 (978-1-4001-1011-7(4)) Pub: Tantor Media. Dist(s): IngramPubServ

Snake Tattoo. unabr. ed. Linda Barnes. Narrated by C. J. Critt. 5 cass. (Running Time: 7 hrs. 15 mins.). (Carlotta Carlyle Mystery Ser.). 1993. 44.00 (978-1-55690-923-8(3), 93419E7) Recorded Bks.
Boston private eye Carlotta Carlyle investigates the disappearance of a prostitue who was the witness to a crime.

Snake, the Crocodile & the Dog. unabr. ed. Elizabeth Peters, pseud. Narrated by Barbara Rosenblat. 11 cass. (Running Time: 15 hrs. 15 mins.). (Amelia Peabody Ser.: No. 7). 1992. 91.00 (978-1-55690-783-8(4), 92422E7) Recorded Bks.
In this lively romp, eminent Victorian Egyptologist Radcliffe Emerson disappears into the desert, & it is up to his intrepid wife, Amelia Peabody, to solve the mystery & rescue him.

Snakecharm. unabr. ed. Amelia Atwater-Rhodes. Narrated by Norm Lee. 4 cass. (Running Time: 5 hrs. 15 mins.). (Kiesha'ra Ser.: Bk. 2). (YA). 2005. 39.75 (978-1-4193-2660-8(0), 97959) Recorded Bks.
Amelia Atwater-Rhodes is a brilliant young author whose books have been ALA Quick Picks for Young Adults. Hawksong (RB# 97919) was a School Library Journal Best Book of the Year. In this sequel, the story is told from the point of view of Zane Cobriana, a snake shapeshifter. He and Danica, an avian shapeshifter, are now happily married and expecting a child that will represent the union of their two kingdoms. Trouble surfaces, though, when a powerful representative from another kingdom arrives and raises questions about how a child of mixed heritage will be received.

Snakecharm. unabr. ed. Amelia Atwater-Rhodes. Read by Norm Lee. 4 CDs. (Running Time: 5 hrs. 15 mins.). (Kiesha'ra Ser.: Bk. 2). (YA). 2005. audio compact disk 48.75 (978-1-4193-3868-7(4), C3282) Recorded Bks.

Snakehead. unabr. ed. Anthony Horowitz. Narrated by Simon Prebble. 8 cass. (Running Time: 9 hrs. 45 mins.). (Alex Rider Ser.: Bk. 7). (YA). 2007. 46.95 (978-1-4281-8273-8(X)) Recorded Bks.

Snakehead. unabr. ed. Anthony Horowitz. Narrated by Simon Prebble. 8 cass. (Running Time: 9 hrs. 45 mins.). (Alex Rider Ser.: Bk. 7). (YA). (gr. 5-10). 2007. 67.75 (978-1-4281-8272-1(1)); audio compact disk 97.75 (978-1-4281-8277-6(2)) Recorded Bks.

Snakehead. unabr. ed. Peter May. (Running Time: 12 hrs. 0 mins.). 2009. 29.95 (978-1-4332-6450-4(1)); audio compact disk 90.00 (978-1-4332-6447-4(1)); audio compact disk 72.95 (978-1-4332-6446-7(3)) Blckstn Audio.

Snakehead: An Epic Tale of the Chinatown Underworld & the American Dream. abr. ed. Patrick Radden Keefe. Read by Patrick Radden Keefe. (ENG.). 2009. audio compact disk 29.95 (978-0-7393-8291-2(8), Random AudioBks) Pub: Random Audio Pubg. Dist(s): Random

Snakes! Deadly Predators or Harmless Pets? Sarah Houghton. (High Five Reading - Purple Ser.). (ENG.). (gr. 4-5). 2007. audio compact disk 5.95 (978-1-4296-1428-3(5)) CapstoneDig.

Snakes & Ladders, Vol. 2. unabr. ed. Dirk Bogarde. Read by Andrew Sachs. 10 cass. (Running Time: 10 hrs.). 1998. 84.95 (978-0-7451-6704-6(7), CAB1320) AudioGO.
The acclaimed autobiography covers the years from World War II to the making of "Death in Venice." These are the spellbinding years in which he transformed himself from a celebrity matinee idol into one of the finest actors of our time.

Snakes & Ladders: Glimpses of Modern India, abr. ed. Gita Mehta. Read by Gita Mehta. 2 cass. (Running Time: 3 hrs.). 1997. 17.95 (978-1-57453-189-3(1)) Audio Lit.
Mehta looks at contemporary India in a series of engrossing sketches. Her evocative reports cover India from ancient cultures to her encounters with film directors & poets & the complicated machination of the world's largest democracy. In her engaging style, she provides unique insight into the Indian mind & heart.

Snakes Apes & Bees. Narrated by Sandra Crowe. 3 cass. (Running Time: 3 hrs.). 1997. 19.95 (978-0-9658131-0-5(X)) Pivotal Pt.
Provides concrete action steps you can use today when challenged with frustrating, difficult people interactions.

Snakes! Deadly Predators or Harmless Pets? (High Five Reading Ser.). (ENG.). (gr. 4 up). 2001. audio compact disk 5.95 (978-0-7368-9508-8(6)) CapstoneDig.

Snakes on a Plane. 2006. audio compact disk 19.99 (978-1-59950-166-6(X)) GraphicAudio.

***Snakewoman of Little Egypt.** unabr. ed. Robert Hellenga. Narrated by Coleen Marlo. (Running Time: 10 hrs. 30 mins. 0 sec.). 2010. audio compact disk 83.99 (978-1-4001-4791-5(3)) Pub: Tantor Media. Dist(s): IngramPubServ

***Snakewoman of Little Egypt: A Novel.** unabr. ed. Robert Hellenga. (Running Time: 12 hrs. 0 mins.). 2010. 17.99 (978-1-4001-8791-1(5)) Tantor Media.

***Snakewoman of Little Egypt: A Novel.** unabr. ed. Robert Hellenga. Narrated by Coleen Marlo. (Running Time: 10 hrs. 30 mins. 0 sec.). 2010. 24.99 (978-1-4001-6791-3(4)); audio compact disk 34.99 (978-1-4001-1791-8(7)) Pub: Tantor Media. Dist(s): IngramPubServ

Snap! unabr. ed. Margaret Clark. (Aussie Bites Ser.). (YA). 2003. audio compact disk 39.95 (978-1-74030-964-6(2)) Pub: Bolinda Pubng AUS. Dist(s): Bolinda Pub Inc

Snap Out of It! You've Only Been Hypnotized into Believing You're over the Hill. Based on a book by Mariann Aalda. 1 CD. (Running Time: 1 hr. 10 min). 2004. audio compact disk 18.95 (978-0-9711867-1-2(5)) PeopleLikeUs.
Wit, wisdom and wisecracks for women over forty...and those planning on living to be...a "how -to" for living "the good life" after midlife!.

Snap Training & Assessment: Text with CD & Snap Assessment. audio compact disk 37.90 (978-0-7638-2111-1(X)); audio compact disk 36.90 (978-0-7638-2108-1(X)); audio compact disk 36.90 (978-0-7638-2104-3(7)) Paradigm MN.

Snap Training & Assessment: Text with CD & Snap Training & Assessment. audio compact disk 39.90 (978-0-7638-2135-7(7)); audio compact disk 39.90 (978-0-7638-2132-6(2)); audio compact disk 39.90 (978-0-7638-2128-9(4)) Paradigm MN.

Snap Web-Based Training & Assessment: Text with CD & Snap Assessment. audio compact disk 65.90 (978-0-7638-2113-5(6)); audio compact disk 47.90 (978-0-7638-2125-8(X)); audio compact disk 64.90 (978-0-7638-2124-1(1)); audio compact disk 67.90 (978-0-7638-2119-7(5)); audio compact disk 64.90 (978-0-7638-2112-8(8)); audio compact disk 33.90 (978-0-7638-2110-4(1)); audio compact disk 27.90 (978-0-7638-2123-4(3)); audio compact disk 64.90 (978-0-7638-2109-8(8)); audio compact disk 33.90 (978-0-7638-2107-4(1)); audio compact disk 27.90 (978-0-7638-2121-0(7)); audio compact disk 64.90 (978-0-7638-2105-0(5)); audio compact disk 33.90 (978-0-7638-2103-6(9)); audio compact disk 27.90 (978-0-7638-2120-3(9)); audio compact disk 51.90 (978-0-7638-2106-7(3)); audio compact disk 27.95 (978-0-7638-2122-7(5)) Paradigm MN.

Snap Web-Based Training & Assessment: Text with CD & Snap Training & Assessment. audio compact disk 68.90 (978-0-7638-2137-1(3)); audio compact disk 49.90 (978-0-7638-2149-4(7)); audio compact disk 67.90 (978-0-7638-2148-7(9)); audio compact disk 70.90 (978-0-7638-2905-6(6)); audio compact disk 67.90 (978-0-7638-2136-4(5)); audio compact disk 36.90 (978-0-7638-2134-0(9)); audio compact disk 30.90 (978-0-7638-2147-0(0)); audio compact disk 36.90 (978-0-7638-2131-9(4)); audio compact disk 30.90 (978-0-7638-2145-6(4)); audio compact disk 67.90 (978-0-7638-2129-6(2)); audio compact disk 36.90 (978-0-7638-2127-2(6)); audio compact disk 30.90 (978-0-7638-2144-9(6)); audio compact disk 54.90 (978-0-7638-2130-2(6)); audio compact disk 30.95 (978-0-7638-2146-3(2)) Paradigm MN.

Snap Web-Based Training & Assessment: Text with Encore CD & Snap Assessment. audio compact disk 47.95 (978-0-7638-2254-5(X)); audio compact disk 55.95 (978-0-7638-2255-2(8)); audio compact disk 67.95 (978-0-7638-2256-9(6)) Paradigm MN.

Snapped: A Novel. unabr. ed. Tracy Brown. (Running Time: 15 hrs. 30 mins.). 2010. 29.95 (978-1-4417-2898-2(8)); 85.95 (978-1-4417-2894-4(5)); audio compact disk 34.95 (978-1-4417-2897-5(X)); audio compact disk 118.00 (978-1-4417-2895-1(3)) Blckstn Audio.

Snapped in Cornwall. Janie Bolitho. (Soundings Ser.). (J). 2006. 49.95 (978-1-84559-258-5(1)); audio compact disk 64.95 (978-1-84559-375-9(8)) Pub: ISIS Lrg Prnt GBR. Dist(s): Ulverscroft US

Snappy Answers!! Tim Sample. 1 cass. (Running Time: 48 min.). 1989. 8.95 (17) Bert and I Inc.
Tales of Hubert, Unc's Cow, Wilbur's Wife, Hutch Wins the Lottery.

Snappy Auction Photos: The online Auction Seller's Guide to Digital Photography. David Steiner. Ed. by Ina Steiner. 2002. 12.99 (978-0-9723764-0-2(2), AuctionBytes) Steiner Assoc.
A guide to digital photography for those who sell on eBay, Yahoo, Amazon, ePier, Bidfields, uBid and other online marketplaces. You will learn how to make your items appealing and obtain more bids and higher selling prices. This jam-packed book takes you through the complete process of adding images to your auctions.

Snapshot. unabr. ed. Linda Barnes. Narrated by C. J. Critt. 8 cass. (Running Time: 10 hrs. 45 mins.). (Carlotta Carlyle Mystery Ser.). 1994. 70.00 (978-1-55690-969-6(1), 94112E7) Recorded Bks.
Carlotta Carlyle, private investigator, looks into the death of a critically ill child in a Boston hosptial.

Snare Drum Duets. 2004. audio compact disk 14.95 (978-0-8258-4990-9(X)) Fischer Inc NY.

Snare of Serpents. unabr. ed. Victoria Holt. Read by Morag Hood. 10 cass. (Running Time: 10 hrs.). 1993. 84.95 (978-0-7451-4201-2(X), CAB 884) AudioGO.
After the death of her mother, Davina Glentyre's father seemed changed. He married Zillah Grey, an unlikely choice for a spouse. But during the first year of their marriage, Mr. Glentyre was murdered. Now Davina stands on trial for the murder of her father! How can she prove she is not the killer?.

Snare of Serpents. unabr. collector's ed. Victoria Holt. Read by Donada Peters. 8 cass. (Running Time: 12 hrs.). 1991. 64.00 (978-0-7366-1962-2(3), 2783) Books on Tape.
Davina Glentyre, a proper young woman of turn-of-the-century Scotland, sees her beloved governess unjustly dismissed so that her father can bring his mistress, Zillah, into the household. When her father marries Zillah & soon after dies under suspicious circumstances, Davina finds herself accused of murder.

Snare of the Hunter. unabr. collector's ed. Helen MacInnes. Read by Penelope Dellaporta. 9 cass. (Running Time: 13 hrs. 30 min.). 1981. 72.00 (978-0-7366-0396-6(4), 1373) Books on Tape.
As Irina Kusak flees across Czechoslovakia into Austria to seek her Nobel-laureate father, she finds herself drawn into a political intrigue with dimensions more terrifying than at first she realizes.

Snares to Avoid. Elbert Willis. 1 cass. (Learning Divine Healing Ser.). 4.00; 4.00 Fill the Gap.

Snark. David Denby. Read by William Dufris. (Playaway Adult Nonfiction Ser.). (ENG.). 2009. 39.99 (978-1-60847-870-5(X)) Find a World.

Snark: It's Mean, It's Personal, & It's Ruining Our Conversation. unabr. ed. David Denby. Read by William Dufris. (Running Time: 4 hrs. 0 mins. 0 sec.). (ENG.). 2009. audio compact disk 19.99 (978-1-4001-1160-2(9)); audio compact disk 39.99 (978-1-4001-4160-9(5)); audio compact disk 19.99 (978-1-4001-6160-7(6)) Pub: Tantor Media. Dist(s): IngramPubServ

Snarkout Boys & the Avocado of Death. Adapted by James Sie. Contrib. by Daniel M. Pinkwater et al. 1 cass. (Running Time: 1 hr. 40 min.). 1996. 18.95 (978-1-58081-106-4(X), CTA43) L A Theatre.
Welcome to Baconburg (a city that strongly resembles Chicago), where three oddballs join forces with the Chicken Man & the great detective Osgood Sigerson in search of a captive orangutan, a missing mad scientist, an earth-saving avocado & a diabolical archfiend. A mystery so wacky it could only have come from the mind of Daniel Pickwater.

Snatch. unabr. ed. Gerald Hammond. Contrib. by Cathleen McCarron. 4 cass. (Story Sound Ser.). 2006. 44.95 (978-1-85903-922-9(7)) Pub: Mgna Lrg Print GBR. Dist(s): Ulverscroft US

Snatch. unabr. ed. Gerald Hammond & Cathleen McCarron. Contrib. by Cathleen McCarron. 5 CDs. (Story Sound CD Ser.). 2006. audio compact

An Asterisk (*) at the beginning of an entry indicates that the title is appearing for the first time.

disk 59.95 (978-1-84652-039-6(8)) Pub: Mgna Lrg Print GBR. Dist(s): Ulverscroft US

Snatch of Sliphorn Jazz see Carl Sandburg's Poems for Children

Snatched! Graham Marks. Read by Toby Longworth. (Running Time: 19860 sec.). (J). (gr. 3-6). 2007. audio compact disk 59.95 (978-1-4056-5635-1(2), ChiversChildren) AudioGo GBR.

Sneaky People. unabr. collector's ed. Thomas Berger. Read by Christopher Hurt. 7 cass. (Running Time: 10 hrs. 30 mins.). 1988. 56.00 (978-0-7366-1462-7(1), 2342) Books on Tape.
Owner of a used-car lot & father of a 15-year-old son with a penchant for sex manuals, Buddy has decided to murder his wife & marry his mistress Laverne. Buddy's only problem is how to arrange the crime.

Sneaky Pete & the Wolf; The Carnival of the Animals. P. D. Q. Bach. 1 cass., 1 CD. (J). 7.98 (TA 30350); audio compact disk 12.78 CD. (TA 80350) NewSound.
A take on Tahaikovsky's classic "Peter & the Wolf," & Camille Saint-Saens' "The Carnival of the Animals.

Snickerdoodle! Stories & Songs for Little Guys Who Think Big! 2nd ed. Clare Ham Grosgebauer. Illus. by Clare Ham Grosgebauer. 1 CD. (Running Time: 43 mins.). (J). (ps-3). 2005. audio compact disk 8.00 (978-0-9741888-0-5(8)) Pub: Sm Wond. Dist(s): AtlasBooks
An audio CD of 3 humorous children's stories about "Snickerdoodle", a tiny tall-tale hero from American folklore. Narrated by Gary Lloyd, member of the National Storytelling Network. Includes 6 songs (American folk tune melodies) performed by Tom Stamp's bluegrass band and a "Rap".

Sniggles, Squirrels & Chicken Pox, Vol. 1. Perf. by Jackie Silberg. 1 cass. (J). (ps-3). 1988. 10.95 (978-0-939514-19-9(2)) Miss Jackie.
Features treasury of seasonal, holiday, & anytime ditties.

Sniggles, Squirrels of Chicken Pox, Vol. 2. Perf. by Jackie Silberg. 1 cass. (J). (ps-3). 1988. 10.95 (978-0-939514-21-2(4)) Miss Jackie.
Features 23 original songs from the book of the same name. The recording contains many musical styles including Dixieland, Rock & Roll, Calypso, Rousing Marches, Mexican Mariachi Band, Middle Eastern Music & a Gospel tribute to Dr. Martin Luther King.

Snip. Read by Jerry Lyden & Giz Coughlin. Engineer Todd Lewis. Prod. by Custom Recording at RFB&D. (ENG.). 2009. 28.00 (978-0-9785717-3-3(8)) Pub: Floating Word. Dist(s): Partners-West

Snobbery with Violence. Marion Chesney. Narrated by Davina Porter. 5 cass. (Running Time: 23880 sec.). (Edwardian Murder Mysteries Ser.). 2006. 49.95 (978-0-7927-4024-7(6), CSL 941); audio compact disk 64.95 (978-0-7927-4025-4(4), SLD 941) AudioGO.

Snobs. unabr. ed. Julian Fellowes & Richard Morant. 6 cass. 2005. 54.95 (978-0-7927-3454-3(8), CSL 750); audio compact disk 89.95 (978-0-7927-3455-0(6), SLD 750) AudioGO.

Snooze Music. unabr. ed. Rick Scott. 1 CD. (Running Time: 44 mins.). 2006. audio compact disk 10.00 (978-0-9733515-2-1(7)) JSTR CAN.

Snopp on the Sidewalk & Other Poems see Rolling Harvey down the Hill

Snort of Kings. Ron Ellis. 2008. 54.95 (978-1-4079-0287-6(3)); audio compact disk 64.95 (978-1-4079-0288-3(1)) Pub: Soundings Ltd GBR. Dist(s): Ulverscroft US

Snout for Chocolate. Denys Cazet. Illus. by Denys Cazet. Read by John Beach. 1 cass. (Running Time: 11 mins.). (Grandpa Spanielson's Chicken Pox Stories Ser.). (J). (ps-3). 2008. pap. bk. 16.95 (978-1-4301-0463-6(5)); pap. bk. 18.95 (978-1-4301-0466-7(X)) Live Oak Media.

Snout for Chocolate, Set. Denys Cazet. Illus. by Denys Cazet. Narrated by John Beach. 1 cass. (Running Time: 11 mins.). (J). (ps-2). 2008. pap. bk. 29.95 (978-1-4301-0465-0(1)); pap. bk. 31.95 (978-1-4301-0468-1(6)) Live Oak Media.

Snow. pap. bk. 18.95 (978-1-59112-353-8(4)) Pub: Live Oak Media. Dist(s): AudioGO

Snow. Contrib. by Go Fish. Prod. by Darren Rust & Jamie Statema. (J). (ps-3). 2006. audio compact disk 14.98 (978-5-558-15171-8(4), Word Records) Word Enter.

Snow. Uri Shulevitz. Read by George Guidall. Music by Chris Kubie. (Running Time: 6 mins.). (J). 2000. 9.95 (978-0-87499-625-8(2)) Live Oak Media.
The innocent, small boy with his dog, uncluttered by adult experience, can see clearly what is happening around him. Lovely background music imitates quiet snowfall.

Snow. Uri Shulevitz. Read by George Guidall. Music by Chris Kubie. 11 vols. (Running Time: 6 mins.). (J). (gr. k-3). 2000. bk. 25.95 (978-0-87499-627-2(9)) Live Oak Media.

Snow. Uri Shulevitz. Illus. by Uri Shulevitz. 11 vols. (Running Time: 6 mins.). 2000. bk. 28.95 (978-1-59112-354-5(2)); audio compact disk 12.95 (978-1-59112-352-1(6)) Live Oak Media.

Snow. unabr. ed. Orhan Pamuk. Read by John Lee. (Running Time: 66600 sec.). (ENG.). 2007. audio compact disk 34.95 (978-0-7393-5430-8(2), Random AudioBks) Pub: Random Audio Pubg. Dist(s): Random

Snow Angels. unabr. ed. Read by Malcolm Hillgartner. 5 cass. (Running Time: 23400 sec.). 2008. 44.95 (978-1-4332-1494-3(6)); audio compact disk 17.95 (978-1-4332-1593-3(4)); audio compact disk 45.00 (978-1-4332-1495-0(4)); audio compact disk 29.95 (978-1-4332-1512-4(8)) Blckstn Audio.

Snow Blind. abr. ed. P. J. Tracy. Read by Mel Foster. (Running Time: 5 hrs.). (Monkeewrench Ser.). 2007. audio compact disk 14.99 (978-1-59737-671-6(X), 9781597376716, BCD Value Price) Brilliance Audio.

Snow Blind. abr. unabr. ed. P. J. Tracy. Read by Mel Foster. (Running Time: 8 hrs.). (Monkeewrench Ser.). 2006. audio compact disk 87.25 (978-1-59600-135-0(6), 9781596001350, BACDLib Ed) Brilliance Audio.
Please enter a Synopsis.

Snow Blind. unabr. ed. Read by Mel Foster. (Running Time: 28800 sec.). (Monkeewrench Ser.). 2006. 74.25 (978-1-59600-133-6(X), 9781596001336, BrilAudUnabridg); audio compact disk 39.25 (978-1-59335-941-6(1), 9781593359416, Brinc Audio MP3 Lib); audio compact disk 24.95 (978-1-59335-940-9(3), 9781593359409, Brilliance MP3); audio compact disk 32.95 (978-1-4233-0176-9(5), 9781423301769, Bril Audio CD Unabri) Brilliance Audio.

Snow Blind. unabr. ed. P. J. Tracy. Read by Mel Foster. (Running Time: 8 hrs.). (Monkeewrench Ser.). 2006. 39.25 (978-1-59710-944-4(4), 9781597109444, BADLE); 24.95 (978-1-59710-945-1(2), 9781597109451, BAD) Brilliance Audio.

Snow-Bound see Barefoot Boy

Snow-Bound see Classic American Poetry

Snow Bound. unabr. ed. Harry Mazer. 1 cass. (Running Time: 1 hr. 26 min.). (Young Adult Cliffhangers Ser.). (YA). (gr. 7 up). 1985. 15.98 incl. bk. & guide. (978-0-8072-1824-2(3), JRH 112SP, Listening Lib) Random Audio Pubg.
Stranded during a severe snow storm, Tony & Cindy waste precious time fighting with each other while waiting to be rescued. Finally they realize their lives are in danger & they must cooperate to survive.

Snow Child. Freya Littledale. 1 cass. (Running Time: 16 min.). (J). (gr. k up). 1989. bk. 5.95 Scholastic Inc.

***Snow Day!** Lester L. Laminack. Read by Lester L. Laminack. Illus. by Adam Gustavson. (ENG.). (J). 2010. audio compact disk 6.95 (978-1-56145-556-0(3)) Peachtree Pubs.

***Snow Day: A Novel.** unabr. ed. Billy Coffey. Narrated by Tim Gregory. (Running Time: 5 hrs. 30 mins. 36 sec.). (ENG.). 2010. 16.09 (978-1-60814-776-2(2), SpringWater); audio compact disk 22.99 (978-1-59859-838-4(4)) Oasis Audio.

Snow Dreams. 1 cass. (Running Time: 60 min.). (Interludes Music Ser.). 1989. 9.95 (978-1-55569-281-0(8), MOD-3902) Great Am Audio.

Snow Falcon. abr. ed. Stuart Harrison. Read by Dick Hill. 2 cass. 1999. 17.95 (FS9-43329) Highsmith.

Snow Falling on Cedars. David Guterson. Read by Barrett Whitener. 1996. audio compact disk 88.00 (978-0-7366-6168-3(9)) Books on Tape.

Snow Falling on Cedars. David Guterson. Read by Tim Pigott-Smith. 2 cass. 1998. 16.85 Set. (978-0-00-105207-9(1)) Ulvrscrft Audio.
San Piedro Island in Puget Sound is a place so isolated that no one who lives there can afford to make enemies. But in 1954 a local fisherman is found suspiciously drowned.

Snow Falling on Cedars. unabr. ed. David Guterson. Read by Peter Marinker. 12 CDs. (Running Time: 18 hrs.). 2002. audio compact disk 110.95 (978-0-7540-5452-8(7), CCD 143) AudioGO.
On San Piedro, an island of rugged, spectacular beauty in Puget Sound, a Japanese-American fisherman stands trial for murder. Set in 1954 in the shadow of World War II, Snow Falling on Cedars is a beautifully crafted courtroom drama, love story, and war novel, illuminating the psychology of a community, the ambiguities of justice, the racism that persists even between neighbors, and the necessity of individual moral action despite the indifference of nature and circumstance.

Snow Falling on Cedars. unabr. ed. David Guterson. Read by Barrett Whitener. 10 cass. (Running Time: 15 hrs.). 1996. 80.00 (978-0-913369-19-7(5), 4165) Books on Tape.
It's 1954 & a young fisherman, Carl Heine, is found dead in the waters off of San Piedro, an island in Puget Sound. Police charge Kabuo Miyamoto, another fisherman, with murder. Around Miyamoto's trial, Guterson composes a fugue of memory, guilt & longing, whose themes include the childhood romance between a caucasian boy & a Japanese girl & a land dispute.

Snow Falling on Cedars. unabr. ed. David Guterson. Read by Barrett Whitener. 10 cass. (Running Time: 13 hrs.). 2001. 34.95 (978-0-7366-6753-1(9)) Books on Tape.
On San Piedro, an island of rugged spectacular beauty in Puget Sound, home to salmon fisherman & strawberry farmers, a Japanese-American fisherman stands trial, charged with cold-blooded murder. The year is 1954 & the shadow of World War II, with its brutality abroad & internment of Japanese-Americans at home, hangs over the courtroom. Ishmael Chambers, who lost an arm in the Pacific war & now runs the island newspaper inherited from his father, is among the journalists covering the trial - a trial that brings him close, once again, to Hatsue Miyomoto, the wife of the accused man & Ishmael's never-forgotten boyhood love.

Snow Falling on Cedars. unabr. ed. David Guterson. Read by Peter Marinker. 10 cass. (Running Time: 15 hrs.). 2000. 69.95 (SAB 118) Pub: Chivers Audio Bks GBR. Dist(s): AudioGO
On the island of San Pedro, a Japanese-American fisherman stands trial for murder. It is 1954, and the shadow of World War II's brutal internment of Japanese-Americans hangs over the courtroom. Ishmael Chambers, who fought in the war and now runs the island newspaper, is covering the trial that brings him close to Hatsue Miyamoto, the wife of the accused and Ishmael's first love. The island community is faced with the ambiguities of justice, racism, and the necessity of moral action.

Snow Falling on Cedars. unabr. ed. David Guterson. Narrated by George Guidall. 13 CDs. (Running Time: 15.75 hrs.). audio compact disk 49.95 (978-1-4025-2378-6(5)); 91.00 (978-0-7887-0585-4(7), 94738E7) Recorded Bks.
As a Japanese-American fisherman stands trial for murder on an island in Puget Sound, snow blankets the countryside. The whiteness covers the courthouse, but it cannot conceal the memories at work inside: the internment of Japanese Americans during World War II, an unrequited love & the ghosts of racism that still haunt the islanders. Available to libraries only.

Snow Falling on Cedars. unabr. ed. David Guterson. Read by George Guidall. 9 Cass. (Running Time: 15.75 Hrs). 39.95 (978-1-4025-2359-5(9)) Recorded Bks.

Snow Falling on Cedars, unabr. ed. David Guterson. Narrated by George Guidall. 13 CDs. (Running Time: 15 hrs. 45 mins.). 2000. audio compact disk 116.00 (978-0-7887-3718-3(X), C1075E7) Recorded Bks.

Snow Flower & the Secret Fan. abr. ed. Lisa See. Read by Jodi Long. (Running Time: 18000 sec.). (ENG.). 2006. audio compact disk 14.99 (978-0-7393-3467-6(0), Random AudioBks) Pub: Random Audio Pubg. Dist(s): Random

Snow Flower & the Secret Fan. unabr. ed. Lisa See. Read by Janet K. Song. 9 CDs. (Running Time: 12 hrs.). 2005. audio compact disk 53.55 (978-1-4159-2154-8(7)); 54.00 (978-1-4159-2014-5(1)) Books on Tape.
Lily is haunted by memories - of who she once was, and of a person, long gone, who defined her existence. She has nothing but time now, as she recounts the tale of Snow Flower, and asks the gods for forgiveness. In nineteenth-century China, when wives and daughters were foot-bound and lived in almost total seclusion, the women in one remote Hunan county developed their own secret code for communication: nu shu ("women's writing"). Some girls were paired with laotongs, "old sames," in emotional matches that lasted throughout their lives. They painted letters on fans, embroidered messages on handkerchiefs, and composed stories, thereby reaching out of their isolation to share their hopes, dreams, and accomplishments. With the arrival of a silk fan on which Snow Flower has composed for Lily a poem of introduction in nu shu, their friendship is sealed and they become "old sames" at the tender age of seven. As the years pass, through famine and rebellion, they reflect upon their arranged marriages, loneliness, and the joys and tragedies of motherhood. The two find solace, developing a bond that keeps their spirits alive. But when a misunderstanding arises, their lifelong friendship suddenly threatens to tear apart. Snow Flower and the Secret Fan is a brilliantly realistic journey back to an era of Chinese history that is as deeply moving as it is sorrowful. With the period detail and deep resonance of Memoirs of a Geisha, this lyrical and emotionally charged novel delves into one of the most mysterious of human relationships: female friendship.

Snow Garden. unabr. ed. Christopher Rice. Read by James Daniels. 9 cass. (Running Time: 13 hrs.). 2002. 34.95 (978-1-58788-731-4(2), 1587887312, BAU); 96.25 (978-1-58788-732-1(0), 1587887320, Unabridge Lib Edns) Brilliance Audio.
Atherton University, freshman year. Kathryn, Randall, and Jesse come from different worlds, but find themselves drawn together in unexpected ways. For each of them, college promises a bright future and a way to disconnect from a dark, haunted past. But as winter sets in, their secret histories threaten to disrupt the layers of deceit that protect their fragile new lives. One dark night a professor's wife is found drowned in an icy river, and rumors of murder threaten the safe haven of Atherton. Within days, Randall's illicit affair with the professor is about to be revealed in the local press. Then, an old mystery emerges from the shadows - the discovery of a co-ed's corpse in a frozen creek twenty years before makes these accidents of the past and the present look a little too closely connected. Gradually, the three friends find themselves snared in a web of lies, a web spun long before their days at Atherton. Snowbound on the university campus, they are unwitting captives of a malevolent force that drives them inexorably toward the "snow garden" of the title - a place of nightmares that is all too real, and all too near.

Snow Garden. unabr. ed. Christopher Rice. Read by James Daniels. (Running Time: 13 hrs.). 2004. 39.25 (978-1-59335-397-1(9), 1593353979, Brlnc Audio MP3 Lib) Brilliance Audio.

Snow Garden. unabr. ed. Christopher Rice. Read by James Daniels. (Running Time: 13 hrs.). 2004. 39.25 (978-1-59710-723-5(9), 1597107239, BADLE); 24.95 (978-1-59710-722-8(0), 1597107220, BAD) Brilliance Audio.

Snow Garden. unabr. ed. Christopher Rice. Read by James Daniels. (Running Time: 13 hrs.). 2004. 24.95 (978-1-59335-163-2(1), 1593351631) Soulmate Audio Bks.

Snow Geese. unabr. ed. William Fiennes. Read by Steve Hodson. 6 cass. (Running Time: 8 hrs.). (Isis Ser.). (J). 2002. 54.95 (978-0-7531-1526-8(3)); audio compact disk 79.95 (978-0-7531-1588-6(3)) Pub: ISIS Lrg Prnt GBR. Dist(s): Ulverscroft US
Snow geese spend their summers on the tundra of the Canadian Arctic. Each autumn they migrate south to Delaware, California and the Gulf of Mexico. In the spring they fly north again. William Fiennes decided to go with them. The book that resulted from his travels thrums with ideas, stories and anecdotes, with humankind as well as fowl, with the funny and acute insights of an assured and highly entertaining writer.

Snow in April. unabr. ed. Rosamunde Pilcher. Read by Hannah Gordon. 4 cass. (Running Time: 4 hrs.). 1997. 39.95 (978-0-7451-6561-5(3), CAB 1177) AudioGO.
Caroline Cliburn is to be married next week. She & her brother Jody have taken a drive to Scotland in search of their missing brother Angus. As the landscape grows stark & wintry with each mile, Caroline recognizes a coldness inside her. She never dreamed a sudden spring blizzard would leave them stranded, or that snow in April could give her one last chance to find the healing warmth of love.

Snow in April. unabr. ed. Rosamunde Pilcher. Read by Donada Peters. 5 cass. (Running Time: 5 hrs.). 1992. 40.00 (978-0-7366-2158-8(X), 2957) Books on Tape.
Stranded in a sudden snowstorm a young woman discovers true warmth in the arms of a stranger. Touching & romantic.

Snow in August. abr. ed. Pete Hamill. Read by Tom Merritt. 2 cass. 1998. 17.95 (978-1-55935-250-5(7)) Soundelux.
Evokes the exquisite joys, pains, & mysteries of youth.

Snow in August. unabr. collector's ed. Pete Hamill. Read by Michael Mitchell. 8 cass. (Running Time: 12 hrs.). 1997. 64.00 (978-0-7366-3755-8(9), 4430) Books on Tape.
Despite their age & cultural differences, a mutual love for major league baseball cements a friendship between an Irish Catholic boy & an immigrant rabbi.

Snow King. unabr. ed. Frank Roderus. Read by Kevin Foley. 4 cass. (Running Time: 4 hrs. 30 min.). (Heller Ser.: Bk. 8). 1996. 26.95 (978-1-55686-698-2(4)) Books in Motion.
Carl Heller goes undercover as a big time investor in the Snow King resort scam to help find a missing man & finds a desperate gunfight in the snow instead.

Snow Leopard. unabr. ed. Peter Matthiessen. Read by John MacDonald. 8 cass. (Running Time: 12 hrs.). 1989. 64.00 (978-0-7366-1604-1(7), 2465) Books on Tape.
Across the most awesome mountains on earth, the Himalayas, Peter Matthiessen went in search of the rare snow leopard. His dangerous trip became a pilgrimage, a luminous journey of the heart.

Snow Leopard & On the River Styx. Short Stories. Peter Matthiessen. Read by Peter Matthiessen. 1 cass. (Running Time: 79 min.). 1987. 13.95 (978-1-55644-183-7(5), 7041) Am Audio Prose.
One of our most distinguished & versatile authors reads generous selections from The Snow Leopard, winner of the 1978 National Book Award, & a short story.

Snow Man. unabr. ed. Carolyn Chute. Read by Julia Delfino. 4 cass. (Running Time: 6 hrs.). 1999. 32.00 Books on Tape.
A senator's wife & daughter shelter a member of a right-wing militia who is wanted for murder.

***Snow Melts in Spring.** Zondervan. (Running Time: 8 hrs. 19 mins. 23 sec.). (Seasons of the Tallgrass Ser.). (ENG.). 2010. 14.99 (978-0-310-87065-4(8)) Zondervan.

Snow Queen. Hans Christian Andersen. Illus. by Hans Christian Andersen. Perf. by NYS Theatre Institute. Adapted by Adrian Mitchell. Composed by Richard Peaslee. Directed By Patricia Birch. 2 CDs. (Running Time: 2 hours). Dramatization. (J). 2003. audio compact disk 16.95 (978-1-892613-09-7(3)) NYS Theatre Inst.
Hans Christian Andersen's classic tale of Gerda and Kai. The Snow Queen steals the boy, Kai, and carries him off to the land of endless cold and snow. Kai's friend Gerda risks everything to rescue her dear friend. An original musical that premiered at NYSTI and played for a month on London's West End.WINNER OF THE GOLDEN HEADPHONES AWARD.

Snow Queen. Hans Christian Andersen. Illus. by Hans Christian Andersen. (What's a Good Story? Ser.). (YA). 1993. pap. bk. & stu. ed. 99.00 (60797) Phoenix Films.
Follows the travails of Kay & Gerda, two children who are deftly moved from innocence to awareness.

Snow Queen. abr. ed. Susan Jeffers. Narrated by Sigourney Weaver. Based on a story by Hans Christian Andersen. 1 CD. (Running Time: 44 min.). (Stories to Remember Ser.). (J). (gr. 1-5). 1991. audio compact disk 13.98 CD. Lightyear Entrtnmnt.
Powerful tale of a young girl's quest to rescue her playmate from the icy palace of the Snow Queen. Based on the Hans Christian Andersen story.

Snow Queen. unabr. ed. Hans Christian Andersen. Illus. by Hans Christian Andersen. Narrated by Aurora Wetzel. 1 cass. (J). (ps up). 1994. 9.95 (978-1-887393-06-5(4)) Aurora Audio.
Little Gerda's search for Kay.

Snow Queen. unabr. ed. Adrian Mitchell & Richard Peaslee. Narrated by Jonathan Pryce. Based on a story by Hans Christian Andersen. 2 CDs. (Running Time: 2 hours). Dramatization. (Family Classic Audio Bks.). (J). 1997. 16.95 Set. (978-1-892613-02-8(6), SQ1997) NYS Theatre Inst.
Fully dramatized musical.

Snow Queen & Other Stories. unabr. ed. Hans Christian Andersen. 2 vols. (Running Time: 2 hrs.). (Classic Literature Ser.). 1997. pap. bk. 16.95 (978-1-55656-202-0(0)) Pub: Dercum Audio. Dist(s): APG
Includes "The Ugly Duckling," "The emperor's New Suit," "The Princess & the Pea," "The Little Mermaid" & "The Little Match-Seller," stories that charm & delight while dispensing thoughtful life lessons.

Snow Spider. unabr. ed. Jenny Nimmo. Read by John Keating. (J). 2007. 34.99 (978-1-60252-702-7(4)) Find a World.

Snow Spider. unabr. ed. Jenny Nimmo & Jenny Nimmo. Read by John Keating. 3 CDs. (Running Time: 3.5 hrs.). (Snow Spider Trilogy: Bk. 1). (ENG.). (J). (gr. 4-7). 2006. 24.95 (978-0-439-89553-8(7), Scholastic) Scholastic Inc.

Snow Storm see Poetry of Ralph Waldo Emerson

Snow-Storm see Ralph Waldo Emerson: Poems and Essays

Snow Treasure, unabr. ed. Marie McSwigan. Narrated by John McDonough. 3 pieces. (Running Time: 4 hrs.). (gr. 3 up). 2000. 28.00 (978-0-7887-2971-3(3), 95743E7) Recorded Bks.
For twelve-year-old Peter Lundstrom, the Norwegian winter of 1940 begins like any other. But when Nazis come, the town wants to hide the bank's gold bullion. Soon the men think of a daring plan that relies on Peter & his friends. Will the village children be able to fool the suspicious soldiers?.

Snow Treasure, unabr. ed. Marie McSwigan. Read by John McDonough. 3 cass. (Running Time: 4 hrs.). (J). 2000. pap. bk. & stu. ed. 40.24 (978-0-7887-3001-6(0), 40883X4) Recorded Bks.

Snow Treasure. unabr. ed. Marie McSwigan. Narrated by John McDonough. 4 CDs. (Running Time: 4 hrs.). (gr. 3 up). 2000. audio compact disk 31.00 (978-0-7887-3731-2(7), C1102E7) Recorded Bks.

Snow Treasure, Class Set. unabr. ed. Marie McSwigan. Read by John McDonough. 3 cass. (Running Time: 4 hrs.). (J). 1999. 88.70 (978-0-7887-3031-3(2), 46848) Recorded Bks.

Snow Walker. Margaret K. Wetterer & Charles Wetterer. Illus. by Mary O. Young. 9.95 (978-1-59112-292-0(9)) Live Oak Media.

Snow Walker. Margaret K. Wetterer & Charles Wetterer. Illus. by Mary O. Young. 14 vols. (Running Time: 22 mins.). 1997. pap. bk. 39.95 (978-1-59112-670-6(3)) Live Oak Media.

Snow Walker. Margaret K. Wetterer & Charles Wetterer. Illus. by Mary O. Young. (Running Time: 22 mins.). (J). (gr. k-4). 1997. 9.95 (978-1-59112-121-3(3)); audio compact disk 12.95 (978-1-59112-668-3(1)) Live Oak Media.

Snow Walker. Margaret K. Wetterer & Charles M. Wetterer. Read by Larry Robinson. 11 vols. (Running Time: 22 mins.). (On My Own History Ser.). (J). 2005. pap. bk. 18.95 (978-1-59112-669-0(X)) Pub: Live Oak Media. Dist(s): AudioGO

Snow Walker. unabr. ed. Farley Mowat. Read by Wolfram Kandinsky. 7 cass. (Running Time: 7 hrs.). 1994. 42.00 (978-0-7366-2849-5(5), 3557) Books on Tape.
Collection of stories dealing with Arctic survival.

Snow Walker. unabr. ed. Margaret K. Wetterer & Charles M. Wetterer. Read by Larry Robinson. Illus. by Mary O'Keefe Young. 1 cass. (Running Time: 22 mins.). (Historical Fiction Ser.). (J). (gr. 1-6). bk. 24.95 (978-0-87499-394-3(6)) Live Oak Media.
One morning in March 1888, twelve year-old Milton Daub awoke to find the world buried in snow. The Blizzard of 1888 set records in the Northeast that are still unbroken. Milton didn't let the snow stop him from helping neighbors in need.

Snow Walker. unabr. ed. Margaret K. Wetterer & Charles M. Wetterer. Read by Larry Robinson. Illus. by Mary O'Keefe Young. 11 vols. (Running Time: 22 mins.). (On My Own History Ser.). (J). (gr. 1-6). 2005. pap. bk. 16.95 (978-0-87499-393-6(8)) Pub: Live Oak Media. Dist(s): AudioGO

Snow Walker, Grades 1-6. Margaret K. Wetterer & Charles M. Wetterer. Read by Larry Robinson. Illus. by Mary O'Keefe Young. 14 vols. (Running Time: 22 mins.). (Historical Fiction Ser.). 1997. pap. bk. & tchr. ed. 37.95 Reading Chest. (978-0-87499-395-0(4)) Live Oak Media.

Snow Was Black. unabr. collector's ed. Georges Simenon. Read by Michael Prichard. 7 cass. (Running Time: 7 hrs.). 1982. 42.00 (978-0-7366-0531-1(2), 1505) Books on Tape.
The story of Frank Friedmaier, the only son of a brothel madam who grows up in a bordello in postwar Europe.

Snow Way Out! A Vacation in Winter's Wonderland: A Mini-Musical for Unison & 2-Part Voices. Composed by Sally K. Albrecht et al. (ENG.). 2009. audio compact disk 54.95 (978-0-7390-5834-3(7)) Alfred Pub.

Snow White. 1 cass. (Read-Along Ser.). (J). bk. 7.99 (978-1-55723-387-5(X)) W Disney Records.

Snow White. Read by Macha Grenon. Illus. by Andre Pijet. 1 cass. (Running Time: 15 mins.). (Classic Stories Ser.). (J). (ps-2). 2000. cass. & audio compact disk 9.95 (978-2-921997-87-4(8)) Coffragants CAN.
Rather than being an homage to frivolous beauty, Snow White teaches children the futility of jealousy & helps them appreciate the privilege of having friends who care about you.

Snow White. Jacob W. Grimm et al. (J). 1983. bk. 26.26 (978-0-676-30134-2(7)) RandomHse Pub.

Snow White. Read by Marjorie Westbury. 1 cass. (J). (ps-2). 3.98 (978-1-55886-019-3(3)) Smarty Pants.
A children's fairy tale of a princess & her Prince Charming.

Snow White & Other Children's Favorites. (J). 2005. audio compact disk (978-1-933796-28-4(6)) PC Treasures.

Snow White & Other Tales. unabr. ed. Gioia Timpanelli. 2 cass. 1983. 18.00 (978-1-56964-818-6(2), A0145-83) Sound Photosyn.

***Snow White & Red Rose.** Anonymous. 2009. (978-1-60136-585-9(3)) Audio Holding.

Snow White & Rose Red. unabr. ed. Ed McBain, pseud. Read by Michael Prichard. 8 cass. (Running Time: 8 hrs.). (Matthew Hope Mystery Ser.: No. 5). 1986. 48.00 (978-0-7366-1036-0(7), 1966) Books on Tape.
Shimmering blonde hair framing an exquisite pale face, deep green eyes, a generous mouth - Matthew Hope took one look & fell instantly in love. Sarah Whittaker has everything but her freedom. He probes Sarah's story of a mother driven by hate to confine her only child to a mental institution & decides she is telling the truth. He takes the case & is led into a hall of mirrors in which reality & delusion blur into murder, mutilation & the greatest danger he has ever known.

Snow White & the Seven Dwarfs see Stories Children Love to Hear

Snow White & the Seven Dwarfs see Blanche Neige et les Sept Nains

Snow White & the Seven Dwarfs. (Ladybird Bks.). (ARA., (J). (gr. 1-12). 1987. bk. 12.95 (978-0-86685-636-2(6)) Intl Bk Ctr.

Snow White & the Seven Dwarfs. Perf. by Edgar Bergen & Charlie McCarthy. 1 cass. (Running Time: 60 min.). (J). 1946. 7.95 (CC-5075) Natl Recrd Co.

Snow White & the Seven Dwarfs. Prod. by Walt Disney Productions Staff. 1 cass. (J). (ps-3). 1998. 19.95 (978-0-7634-0384-3(9)) W Disney Records.
Music - Popular.

Snow White & the Seven Dwarfs: Read Along. 1 CD. (Running Time: 1 hr. 30 mins.). (J). 2001. audio compact disk 9.99 (978-0-7634-1826-7(9)) W Disney Records.

Snow White & the Seven Dwarfs - The Golden Pears - Cinderella - The Ant & Thegrasshopper. EDCON Publishing Group Staff. (ENG.). 2008. audio compact disk 12.95 (978-0-8481-0417-7(X)) EDCON Pubng.

Snow White, Simbad the Sailor, Alice's Adventures in Wonderland & Many More Tales see Blanca Nieves y Muchos Cuentos Mas

Snow White Soundtrack. 1 cass. (J). 1993. 12.98 (978-1-55723-384-4(5)) W Disney Records.

Snow White Soundtrack. 1 cass. 1994. 19.98 (978-1-55723-386-8(1)) W Disney Records.

Snow White,Sinbad the Sailor, Alice's Adventures in Wonderland & Many More Tales. (Running Time: 1 hr.). 2001. 14.95 (978-1-60083-132-4(X), Audiofy Corp) Iofy Corp.

Snow Wolf. unabr. ed. Glenn Meade. Read by Rob McQuay. 13 cass. (Running Time: 19 hrs. 30 min.). 1997. 104.00 (978-0-913369-65-4(9), 4308) Books on Tape.
In the tradition of Frederick Forsyth & Robert Ludlum comes Glenn Meade's thriller of espionage during 1953, the iciest year of The Cold War.

Snowball: Warren Buffett & the Business of Life. abr. ed. Alice Schroeder. Read by Richard McGonagle. 8 CDs. (Running Time: 10 hrs.). (ENG.). 2008. audio compact disk 40.00 (978-0-7393-3406-5(9), Random AudioBks) Pub: Random Audio Pubg. Dist(s): Random

Snowball in Hell. Christopher Brookmyre. 2009. 89.95 (978-0-7531-3875-5(1)); audio compact disk 99.95 (978-0-7531-3876-2(X)) Pub: Isis Pubng Ltd GBR. Dist(s): Ulverscroft US

Snowball, the Lost Cat. Princess Martin. 1 cass. 1986. 12.95 (978-0-931814-16-7(2)) Comn Studies.
Snowball, the Lost Cat (Side 1): Account of Southwestern small-town family life as revealed through little lost Snowball. Side 2: West Texas rancher's wife discloses small town's judgemental attitudes toward the new minister's family.

Snowbears of Lake Louise. David Chesky. 1 cass. (J). 1998. 19.95 (978-0-9658787-4-6(0)) Chesky Recs.

Snowboarding to Nirvana. unabr. ed. Frederick Lenz. Read by Jonathan Marosz. 7 cass. (Running Time: 7 hrs.). 1997. 42.00 (978-0-7366-4053-4(3), 4564) Books on Tape.
A champion snowboarder searches for Buddhist enlightenment in the Himalayas.

Snowbound! Steck-Vaughn Staff. 2003. (978-0-7398-8436-2(0)) SteckVau.

Snowfall at Willow Lake. abr. ed. Susan Wiggs. Read by Joyce Bean. 5 CDs. (Running Time: 21600 sec.). (Lakeshore Chronicles: Bk. 4). 2008. audio compact disk 26.95 (978-1-4233-5183-2(5), 9781423351832, BACD) Brilliance Audio.

Snowfall at Willow Lake. abr. ed. Susan Wiggs. Read by Joyce Bean. (Running Time: 6 hrs.). (Lakeshore Chronicles: Bk. 4). 2009. audio compact disk 14.99 (978-1-4233-5184-9(3), 9781423351849, BCD Value Price) Brilliance Audio.

Snowfall at Willow Lake. unabr. ed. Susan Wiggs. Read by Joyce Bean. (Running Time: 12 hrs.). (Lakeshore Chronicles: Bk. 4). 2008. 39.25 (978-1-4233-5182-5(7), 9781423351825, BADLE); 24.95 (978-1-4233-5181-8(9), 9781423351818, BAD); 97.25 (978-1-4233-5176-4(2), 9781423351764, BrilAudUnabridg); audio compact disk 39.25 (978-1-4233-5180-1(0), 9781423351801, Brlnc Audio MP3 Lib); audio compact disk 102.25 (978-1-4233-5178-8(9), 9781423351788, BriAudCD Unabrid); audio compact disk 24.95 (978-1-4233-5179-5(7), 9781423351795, Brilliance MP3); audio compact disk 38.95 (978-1-4233-5177-1(0), 9781423351771, Bril Audio CD Unabri) Brilliance Audio.

Snowflake Bentley. 2004. bk. 24.95 (978-1-55592-622-9(3)); 8.95 (978-1-55592-618-2(5)); audio compact disk 12.95 (978-1-55592-620-5(7)) Weston Woods.

Snowflake Bentley. Jacqueline Briggs Martin. Narrated by Tom Stechschulte. (Running Time: 30 mins.). (J). 1998. 10.75 (978-1-4193-0813-0(0)) Recorded Bks.

***Snowing in Greenwich Village: A Selection from the John Updike Audio Collection.** unabr. ed. John Updike. Read by John Updike. (ENG.). 2009. (978-0-06-196253-0(8), Caedmon); (978-0-06-196254-7(6), Caedmon) HarperCollins Pubs.

Snowman. 1 cass. (Running Time: 30 min.). (J). 4.98 (443) MFLP CA.
Beautifully haunting song accompanies the friends as they fly through the air on their wintertime adventure.

Snowman. 2004. 8.95 (978-1-56008-329-0(8)); cass. & flmstrp 30.00 (978-1-56008-764-9(1)) Weston Woods.

***Snowman.** unabr. ed. Jo Nesbo. Tr. by Don Bartlett. (ENG.). 2011. audio compact disk 40.00 (978-0-307-91750-8(9), Random AudioBks) Pub: Random Audio Pubg. Dist(s): Random

Snowman, the; Miss Nelson Is Missing!; Most Wonderful Egg in the World, the; Goodnight Moon. 2004. (978-0-89719-857-8(3)); cass. & flmstrp (978-0-89719-757-1(7)) Weston Woods.

Snows of Kilimanjaro see Hemingway Short Stories

Snows of Kilimanjaro see Stories of Ernest Hemingway

Snows of Kilimanjaro. abr. ed. Ernest Hemingway. Read by Charlton Heston. 1 cass. (Running Time: 47 min.). (gr. 9-12). 1998. 12.00 (978-0-89845-955-5(9), CPN 1840) HarperCollins Pubs.

Snows of Kilimanjaro. abr. unabr. ed. Ernest Hemingway. Read by Charlton Heston. (Running Time: 3600 sec.). 2008. audio compact disk 14.95 (978-0-06-145784-5(1), Caedmon) HarperCollins Pubs.

Snows of Kilimanjaro; The Short Happy Life of Francis Macomber. Ernest Hemingway. Read by Alexander Adams. 2000. audio compact disk 24.00 (978-0-7366-6732-6(6)) Books on Tape.

Snows of Kilimanjaro; The Short Happy Life of Francis Macomber. collector's ed. Ernest Hemingway. Read by Alexander Adams. 2 cass. (Running Time: 3 hrs.). 2000. 24.00 (978-0-7366-5069-4(5)) Books on Tape.
The protagonist perishes of gangrene alone out in the bush, recognizing his failure as a writer, a writer who never had the nerve to write. He dies with stoic acceptance & a view of the famous summit unseen by any alive. Francis is too wimpy to face down a wounded lion, let alone satisfy his wife in bed.

Snows of Kilimanjaro; The Short Happy Life of Francis Macomber. unabr. ed. Ernest Hemingway. Read by Alexander Adams. 2 cass. (Running Time: 3 hrs.). 2000. 17.95 (978-0-7366-5026-7(1)) Books on Tape.
Two of Hemingway's greatest tales of great white hunters facing tests of courage, corruption and morality.

Snows of Kilimanjaro; The Short Happy Life of Francis Macomber. unabr. ed. Ernest Hemingway. Read by Alexander Adams. 3 CDs. (Running Time: 3 hrs.). 2001. audio compact disk 24.95 (978-0-7366-5702-0(9)) Books on Tape.
In "The Snows of Kilmanjaro," the protagonist perishes of gangerene alone in the bush, recognizing his failure as a writer who never had the nerve to write. "The Short Happy Life of Francis Macomber" deals with a character too wimpy to face down a wounded lion, let alone satisfy his wife in bed.

Snowstorm in January see Twentieth-Century Poetry in English, No. 10, Recordings of Poets Reading Their Own Poetry

Snowy Day see Dia de Nieve

Snowy Day. 9.95 (978-1-59112-162-6(0)) Live Oak Media.

Snowy Day. 2004. bk. 24.95 (978-0-89719-686-4(4)); pap. bk. 18.95 (978-1-55592-811-7(0)); pap. bk. 18.95 (978-1-55592-777-6(7)); pap. bk. 38.75 (978-1-55592-761-5(0)); pap. bk. 38.75 (978-1-55592-724-0(6)); pap. bk. 32.75 (978-1-55592-308-2(9)); pap. bk. 32.75 (978-1-55592-309-9(7)); pap. bk. 14.95 (978-1-56008-074-9(4)); pap. bk. 14.95 (978-0-7882-0509-5(9)); 8.95 (978-1-56008-330-6(1)); 8.95 (978-0-7882-0271-1(5)); cass. & flmstrp 30.00 (978-0-89719-619-2(8)); audio compact disk 12.95 (978-1-55592-868-1(4)) Weston Woods.

Snowy Day. Ezra Jack Keats. Read by Linda Terheyden. 1 cass. (J). 2000. pap. bk. 19.97 (978-0-7366-9215-1(0)) Books on Tape.
Sparkling with atmosphere, a small boy experiences the joys of a snowy day. Points out his new awareness.

Snowy Day. Ezra Jack Keats. 1 cass. (Running Time: 35 min.). (J). 2001. pap. bk. 15.95 (VX-11C) Kimbo Educ.
A small boy experiences the joys of a snowy day. An expression of environmental awareness. Includes book.

Snowy Day. Ezra Jack Keats. Illus. by Ezra Jack Keats. 14 vols. (Running Time: 5 mins.). 1982. pap. bk. 35.95 (978-1-59112-747-5(5)); 9.95 (978-1-59112-122-0(1)); audio compact disk 12.95 (978-1-59112-744-4(0)) Live Oak Media.

Snowy Day. Ezra Jack Keats. Illus. by Ezra Jack Keats. 11 vols. (Running Time: 5 mins.). (J). 1982. pap. bk. 18.95 (978-1-59112-745-1(9)) Pub: Live Oak Media. Dist(s): AudioGO

Snowy Day. Ezra Jack Keats. (J). 1985. bk. 18.66 (978-0-394-07685-0(0)) SRA McGraw.

Snowy Day. Ezra Jack Keats. 1 cass., 5 bks. (Running Time: 6 min.). (J). pap. bk. 32.75; 8.95 (RAC061) Weston Woods.
One side with page turn signals, one side without.

Snowy Day. Ezra Jack Keats. 1 cass. (Running Time: 6 min.). (J). (ps-1). bk. 24.95 Weston Woods.
A small boy's enchantment with a city's snowfall has him making snow angels & snowballs, sliding down snow mountains & looking forward to going outside again.

Snowy Day. Ezra Jack Keats. 1 read-along cass. (Running Time: 6 min.). (J). (ps-1). 2000. pap. bk. 12.95 (PRA061) Weston Woods.
One side with page turn signals, one side without.

Snowy Day. Ezra Jack Keats. (J). 2004. 8.95 (978-1-56008-427-3(8)) Weston Woods.

Snowy Day. unabr. ed. Ezra Jack Keats. 1 read-along cass. (Running Time: 5 min.). (J). 1974. 9.95 Live Oak Media.
A small boy experiences the joys of a snowy day.

Snowy Day. unabr. ed. Ezra Jack Keats. Read by Linda Terheyden. 11 vols. (Running Time: 5 mins.). (J). (gr. k-3). 1974. bk. 25.95 (978-0-670-65405-5(1)); pap. bk. 16.95 (978-0-670-65408-6(6)); pap. bk. & tchr. ed. 33.95 Reading Chest. (978-0-670-65402-4(7)) Live Oak Media.

Snowy Day & Other Stories by Ezra Jack Keats: The Snowy Day; Apt. #3; Goggles!; Whistle for Willie; Pet Show; Peter's Chair. unabr. ed. Ezra Jack Keats. Read by Charles Turner et al. (J). 2008. 44.99 (978-1-60514-923-3(3)) Find a World.

Snowy Day, the see Dia Nevado

Snowy Day, the; Cow Who Fell in the Canal, the; Happy Owls, the; Norman the Doorman. 2004. (978-0-89719-814-1(X)); cass. & flmstrp (978-0-89719-723-6(2)) Weston Woods.

Snowy Day; Un Dia de Nieve. unabr. ed. Ezra Jack Keats. Illus. by Ezra Jack Keats. 22 vols. (Running Time: 6 mins.). (ENG & SPA.). (J). (gr. k-3). 1999. pap. bk. 33.95 (978-0-87499-563-3(9)) Live Oak Media.

Snuff. 2004. 8.95 (978-1-56008-331-3(X)); cass. & flmstrp 30.00 (978-1-56008-765-6(X)) Weston Woods.

Snuff. unabr. ed. Chuck Palahniuk. Read by Todd McLaren. (YA). 2008. 44.99 (978-1-60514-967-7(5)) Find a World.

Snuff. unabr. ed. Chuck Palahniuk. Narrated by Todd McLaren. 5 CDs. (Running Time: 5 hrs. 30 mins. 0 sec.). (ENG.). 2008. audio compact disk 24.99 (978-1-4001-0733-9(4)); audio compact disk 19.99 (978-1-4001-5733-4(1)) Pub: Tantor Media. Dist(s): IngramPubServ

Snuff. unabr. ed. Chuck Palahniuk. Read by William Dufris. Narrated by Todd McLaren. 5 CDs. (Running Time: 5 hrs. 30 mins. 0 sec.). (ENG.). 2008. audio compact disk 49.99 (978-1-4001-3733-6(0)) Pub: Tantor Media. Dist(s): IngramPubServ

Snuff; Could Anything Be Worse?; Jack Jouett's Ride; Arrow to the Sun. 2004. (978-0-89719-839-4(5)); cass. & flmstrp (978-0-89719-747-2(X)) Weston Woods.

Snugg N Flitter Cassette. Stephen Cosgrove. 2004. 5.00 (978-1-58804-391-7(6)) PCI Educ.

Snuggle & Listen, Bible Stories, Vol. 1. Short Stories. Arranged by Rich Herman. 1 CD. (Running Time: approx. 30 mins). (J). 2005. audio compact disk 16.95 (978-0-9765630-8-2(8)) Family Bks N CDs.
Snuggle & Listen, Bible Stories Volume 1 - Includes an Adorable Teddy Bear and a Children's Audio Book. This gift set is great for traveling, birthday gifts, Christmas gifts, or any occasion. The audio book contains six fun and inspiring bible stories. Great music and voice talent make these stories come to life. Stories include: Daniel and the Lion's Den, How Moses Was Saved, In The Beginning, Jesus Calms the Storm, David and Goliath, and The King and the Bees.

Snuggle & Listen, Famous Americans, Vol. 1. Short Stories. Arranged by Rich Herman. 1 CD. (Running Time: Approx. 30 mins). (J). 2005. audio compact disk 16.95 (978-0-9765630-9-9(6)) Family Bks N CDs.
Snuggle & Listen, Famous Americans Volume 1 - Includes an Adorable Teddy Bear and a Children's Audio Book. This gift set is great for traveling, birthday gifts, Christmas gifts, or any occasion. The audio book contains six fun and exciting stories about Famous Americans. Great music and voice talent make these stories come to life. Stories include: A True Story About A Girl(Louisa Alcott), Ben Franklin and the Kite, Going to Sea(George Washington), Kit Carson and the Bears, Lincoln Saves the Birds, and Stories About Jefferson.

Snuggle & Listen, Story Classics, Vol. 1 Short Stories. Arranged by Rich Herman. 1 CD. (Running Time: approx. 30 mins). (J). 2005. audio compact disk 16.95 (978-0-9765630-7-5(X)) Family Bks N CDs.
Snuggle & Listen, Story Classics Volume 1 - Includes an Adorable Teddy Bear and a Children's Audio Book. This gift set is great for traveling, birthday gifts, Christmas gifts, or any occasion. The audio book contains six fun and exciting classical stories. Great music and voice talent make these stories come to life. Stories include: Little Red Riding Hood, Read and You Will Know, The Boy and the Robbers, The Gingerbread Man, The Little Half-Chick, and The Little Red Hen.

Snuggle down & Say Goodnight. unabr. ed. 1 CD. (Running Time: 42 mins.). (YA). 2006. audio compact disk 13.95 (978-0-615-13232-7(4)) Fine Feather.
Relaxation Instructions, an Engaging Bedtime Story, andOriginal Lullaby Music. Helps children go to sleep happily; Teaches children to calm themselves and relax their own bodies; Guides children to develop self-awareness and mental focus; Coaches children to remember good things that happened today; and to expect good things to happen tomorrow.

Snuggle Up: A Gift of Songs for Sweet Dreams. Ed. by J. Aaron Brown. Illus. by Cruise Lines Creative Agency Staff. 1 cass. (Running Time: 60 min.). (J). (ps). 1992. bk. 12.95 (978-0-927945-06-6(1)) Someday Baby.
Fully orchestrated, original songs on one side, with an instrumental version that allows for sing-along on side two. The well-designed die-cut box contains a full-color lyric booklet. The nine selections have titles like "Sweeet Dreams," "Sweet Lullaby" & "Dream Carousel".

Snuggle Up: A Gift of Songs for Sweet Dreams. Ed. by J. Aaron Brown. 1 cass. (Running Time: 60 min.). (J). (ps). 1995. bk. 15.95 CD. (978-0-927945-11-0(8)) Someday Baby.

Snuggle up Cozy. David S. Jack. 1 cass. (J). 8.78 (KE 201) NewSound.

Snuggle up Cozy. David S. Jack & Susan J. Cooper. Perf. by David S. Jack. 1 cass. (J). (ps-5). 1987. 9.98 (978-0-942181-00-5(X)) Ta-Dum Prodns.
Eleven (11) original lullabies contemporary in style.

So B. It. unabr. ed. Sarah Weeks. Read by Cherry Jones. (J). 2004. audio compact disk 25.95 (978-0-06-075481-5(8), HarperChildAud) HarperCollins Pubs.

***So B. It.** unabr. ed. Sarah Weeks. Read by Cherry Jones. (ENG.). 2005. (978-0-06-083491-3(9), Harper Audio); (978-0-06-083492-0(7), Harper Audio) HarperCollins Pubs.

So Beautiful: Divine Design for Life & the Church. unabr. ed. Len Sweet. (Running Time: 7 hrs. 0 mins. 0 sec.). (ENG.). 2009. audio compact disk 24.98 (978-1-59644-696-0(X), christianSeed) christianaud.

***So Beautiful: Divine Design for Life & the Church.** unabr. ed. Len Sweet. Narrated by Tom Weiner. (ENG.). 2009. 14.98 (978-1-59644-697-7(8), christianSeed) christianaud.

So Big. 1 CD. (Running Time: 1 hr.). (J). 2001. pap. bk. 14.95 (EA 678CD); 11.95 (EA 678C) Kimbo Educ.
Easy-to-learn activity songs! So Happy You're Here, I'm a Pretzel, Ten Wiggle Worms, Rock & Roll Freeze Dance & more. Includes guide.

So Big. Hap Palmer. 1 CD. (Running Time: 1 hr.). (J). 2001. audio compact disk 14.95 (HP 107 CD) Hap-Pal Music.
Easy to learn activity songs for pre-school & primary grade learners which tap children's natural desire to move, sing & make-believe. The whole child is engaged in developing movement skills, enriching language, experiencing basic math & science concepts & stimulating imaginative powers. Each song is repeated in an instrumental version. Complete guide with lyrics & activities included.

So Big. Perf. by Hap Palmer. 1 cass. (Running Time: 1 hr.). (J). 2001. 9.95 (HP 107) Hap-Pal Music.

So Big, unabr. ed. Edna Ferber. Read by Flo Gibson. 7 cass. (Running Time: 10 hrs. 30 min.). (Classic Books on Cassettes Coll.). 1998. 56.00 Audio Bk Con.
Selina Peake de Jong is a memorable literary heroine, strong, proud, devoted equally to her son Dirk & what she sees as "the pursuit of beauty." When fortune casts her as the wife of a young farmer in the midwestern plains, she tackles the role with customary zest. The plot turns on her relationship with Dirk & his failure to fulfill his early promise. In Selina, Ferber catches the hope & attention parents lavish on their children to help us understand why those we love are truly "hostages to fortune".

So Big. unabr. collector's ed. Edna Ferber. Read by Flo Gibson. 7 cass. (Running Time: 10 hrs. 30 mins.). 1983. 56.00 (978-0-7366-0664-6(5), 1626) Books on Tape.
Selina Peake Du Jong is proud, strong, devoted equally to her son Dirk & what she sees as "the pursuit of beauty." When fortune casts her as the wife of a young farmer in the vast mid-western plains, she tackles the role with customary zest. The plot turns on her relationship with Dirk & his failure to fulfill an early promise.

So Brave, Young & Handsome. unabr. ed. Leif Enger. Read by Dan Woren. 7 CDs. (Running Time: 8 hrs. 30 mins.). (ENG.). 2008. audio compact disk 34.95 (978-0-7393-6922-7(9), Random AudioBks) Pub: Random Audio Pubg. Dist(s): Random

***So Close the Hand of Death.** unabr. ed. J. T. Ellison. Read by Joyce Bean. (Running Time: 12 hrs.). (Taylor Jackson Ser.). 2011. 19.99 (978-1-61106-300-4(0), 9781611063004, BAD); 19.99 (978-1-61106-298-4(5), 9781611062984, Brilliance MP3); 39.97 (978-1-61106-299-1(3), 9781611062991, Brinc Audio MP3 Lib); 39.97 (978-1-61106-301-1(9), 9781611063011, BADLE); audio compact disk 19.99 (978-1-61106-296-0(9), 9781611062960, Bril Audio CD Unabri); audio compact disk 79.97 (978-1-61106-297-7(7), 9781611062977, BriAudCD Unabrid) Brilliance Audio.

So Cold the River. unabr. ed. Michael Koryta. Read by Robert Petkoff. (Running Time: 14 hrs.). (ENG.). 2010. 29.98 (978-1-60788-303-6(1)) Pub: Hachet Audio. Dist(s): HachBkGrp

So Disdained. unabr. ed. Nevil Shute. Read by Stephen Thorne. 8 cass. (Running Time: 12 hrs.). 2000. 69.95 (978-0-7540-0234-5(9), CAB 1657) Pub: Chivers Audio Bks GBR. Dist(s): AudioGO
On a rain-swept night on the Sussex Downs during the uneasy peace between wars, Peter Moran stops his car to give a man a ride. His unexpected passenger turns out to be an old wartime comrade, a pilot who has just crash-landed a high speed French bomber, Trapped between old loyalties and enmeshed in a sheet of treason, Moran is about to be swept into a desperate manhunt across Europe.

So Far. Kelsey Grammer. Read by Kelsey Grammer. 4 cass. (Running Time: 6 hrs.). 12.99 (978-1-57815-295-7(X), 4441, Media Bks Audio) Media Bks NJ.
Grammer's life from tragedy and heartbreak to triumph. From the murder of his father and sister, to his addiction to drugs and alcohol, to his award-winning sitcoms.

So Far. abr. ed. Kelsey Grammer. Read by Kelsey Grammer. 5 CDs. (Running Time: 6 hrs.). 2002. audio compact disk 14.99 (978-1-57815-552-1(5), Media Bks Audio) Media Bks NJ.

So Far from Heaven. unabr. collector's ed. Richard Bradford. Read by Dan Lazar. 8 cass. (Running Time: 8 hrs.). 1977. 48.00 (978-0-7366-0091-0(4), 1099) Books on Tape.
The story of the Tafoya clan, a Chicano family with a flair for misadventure. The Tafoyas include a physician-philosopher, a radical daughter with a degree from Bryn Mawr, a clumsily stupid son & a governor of New Mexico.

So Far from the Sea. unabr. ed. Eve Bunting. Narrated by Alyssa Bresnahan. 1 cass. (Running Time: 15 mins.). (J). (gr. 1). 1998. 12.00 (978-0-7887-2332-2(4), 95543E7) Recorded Bks.
Seven-year-old Laura & her parents are visiting grandfather's grave in the ruins of the Manzanar War Relocation Center, a camp built in California to confine people of Japanese ancestry during World War II. Laura begins to understand a dark chapter in American history & its impact on generations of Japanese-Americans.

So Far So Good. Perf. by Kim Hill. 1 cass. 1994. audio compact disk Brentwood Music.
Kim Hill's venture into the country music genre, features the fun two-steppin' tune, Is There Any Love Left, written by Amy Grant & Wayne Kirkpatrick.

So Far: the Acoustic Sessions. Contrib. by Bethany Dillon. Prod. by Ian Fitchuck & Justin Loucks. 2008. audio compact disk 9.99 (978-5-557-47118-3(9)) Pt of Grace Ent.

So Five Minutes Ago: A Novel. abr. ed. Hilary De Vries. Read by Laura Hamilton. 5 CDs. (Running Time: 6 hrs.). (What's New Ser.). 2004. audio compact disk 29.95 (978-1-59316-022-7(4), LL114) Listen & Live.
Alex Davidson is a thirtysomething celebrity publicist for a down-at-heels Los Angeles PR firm known for taking on clients whose careers have crashed and burned. A professional hand-holder and spinmeister, she?s one notch above a nanny on the Hollywood food chain.L.A. is already losing its luster in Alex?s eyes when her firm is bought out by the hottest agency in town. Will it mean massive layoffs or a chance at a big promotion? In between signing a new client (a once-hot-now-not actor just out of rehab) and wondering if one of the partners is putting the moves on her, Alex grows wary of her new boss, a sharklike exec who?s forcing out Alex?s old boss under suspicious circumstances. Is there anything she can do to save her and her boss?s jobs, and maybe right some wrongs against women in Hollywood along the way?Packed with razor-sharp humor and featuring a winning protagonist, So 5 Minutes Ago will satisfy even the most hard-to-pleaser celebriholics who long to find out what goes on after a star steps off the red carpet.

So Glad. Ed. by Phillip Feaster & Jeral Gray, Sr. Contrib. by Kevin Vassar & Ken Pennell. Prod. by Percy Gray. 2006. audio compact disk 17.99 (978-5-558-21027-9(3)) Pt of Grace Ent.

So Glad I'm Here. Perf. by Bessie Jones. 1 cass. (Running Time: 37 min.). (Family Ser.). (J). 1975. 9.98 (2015) Rounder Records.
The late Bessie Jones was the leading performer of traditional music from the Georgia Sea Islands. These islands were a rich source of African American oral history & culture, primarily because of their isolation from the mainland. These recordings feature Bessie's game songs learned from the islanders & from her grandfather who had been sold into slavery in the 1840s.

So Good It Hurts: The Pain. the Fight. the Love. Read by Na'Kisha Crawford & Sherri Anderson. Based on a book by Na'Kisha Crawford. (ENG.). 2008. audio compact disk 17.95 (978-0-9744769-2-6(7)) Pathway Pubng CA.

So Great a Salvation. 2000. 75.00 (978-0-633-00686-0(6)); 11.98 (978-0-633-00684-6(X)); audio compact disk 85.00 (978-0-633-00687-7(4)); audio compact disk 16.98 (978-0-633-00685-3(8)) LifeWay Christian.

So Great Salvation. Gloria Copeland. 6 cass. 1987. 30.00 Set incl. study guide. (978-0-88114-793-3(1)) K Copeland Pubns.
In-depth study of God's salvation.

So Great Salvation. Speeches. Taffi L. Dollar. 2 cass. (Running Time: 3 hrs.). 2003. 10.00 (978-1-59089-752-2(8)); audio compact disk 14.00 (978-1-59089-753-9(6)) Creflo Dollar.

So Help Me God. unabr. ed. Roy Moore. 2005. 25.99 (978-1-58926-852-4(0), 6852); audio compact disk 27.99 (978-1-58926-853-1(9), 6853) Pub: Oasis Audio. Dist(s): TNT Media Grp

So Help Me God: The Ten Commandments, Judicial Tyranny, & the Battle for Religious Freedom. unabr. ed. Roy S. Moore. Narrated by Roy S. Moore. (ENG.). 2005. 20.99 (978-1-60814-390-0(2)) Oasis Audio.

So Horrible a Place. unabr. ed. Margaret Duffy. Read by Jilly Bond. 7 cass. (Running Time: 9 hrs. 15 mins.). (Story Sound Ser.). (J). 2006. 61.95 (978-1-85903-898-7(0)) Pub: Mgna Lrg Print GBR. Dist(s): Ulverscroft US

So into You. Perf. by Rici. 1 cass. 1997. audio compact disk 15.99 CD. (D7085) Diamante Music Grp.
In spite of all the negative things out there for teenagers to get into, 16-year old Rici Bell wants youth around the globe to know that it's okay to be into God.

So Long, & Thanks for All the Fish. unabr. ed. Douglas Adams. Read by Douglas Adams. 5 CDs. (Running Time: 6 hrs.). 2004. audio compact disk 39.95 (978-1-59007-261-5(8)) Pub: New Millenn Enter. Dist(s): PerseuPGW

So Long, & Thanks for All the Fish. unabr. ed. Douglas Adams. Read by Martin Freeman. (Running Time: 16200 sec.). (ENG.). 2006. audio compact disk 29.95 (978-0-7393-3211-5(2), Random AudioBks) Pub: Random Audio Pubg. Dist(s): Random

So Long, & Thanks for All the Fish. unabr. abr. ed. Douglas Adams. Read by Douglas Adams. 4 cass. (Running Time: 6 hrs.). 2004. 25.00 (978-1-59007-260-8(X)) Pub: New Millenn Enter. Dist(s): PerseuPGW

So Long As You Both Shall Live. unabr. ed. Ed McBain, pseud. Read by Jonathan Marosz. 5 cass. (Running Time: 5 hrs.). (87th Precinct Ser.: Bk. 31). 1998. 40.00 (978-0-7366-3778-7(8), 4451) Books on Tape.
Augusta mysteriously disappears sometime between 11:20 & 11:25 p.m.

So Long, Insecurity: You've Been a Bad Friend to Us. unabr. ed. Beth Moore. (ENG.). 2010. audio compact disk 29.99 (978-1-4143-3474-5(5)) Tyndale Hse.

So Many Gifts. unabr. ed. Anne M. Pierce. Read by Julie Briskman Hall. Ed. by Tom Lindquist. 1 cass. (Running Time: 50 min.). (J). (gr. k-6). 1992. 7.50 (978-0-9623937-1-6(1)) Forword MN.
A story of how Santa chose his career & how helpers keep his dream alive.

So Many Gifts. unabr. ed. Anne M. Pierce. Read by Julie Briskman Hall. Ed. by Tom Lindquist. Illus. by Donna P. Campbell. 1 cass. (Running Time: 50 min.). (J). (gr. k-6). 1993. bk. 25.00 (978-0-9623937-0-9(3)) Forword MN.

So Much Blood. unabr. ed. Simon Brett. Narrated by Simon Prebble. 5 cass. (Running Time: 6 hrs. 15 mins.). (Charles Paris Mystery Ser.: Vol. 2). 1997. 44.00 (978-0-7887-0931-9(3), 95071E7) Recorded Bks.
Planning a restful break from the London theater, Charles takes a role in a Scottish drama festival. But his working vacation is tarnished after a cast member dies in a suspicious dress rehearsal accident.

***So Much for That.** Lionel Shriver. Contrib. by Dan John Miller. (Playaway Adult Fiction Ser.). (ENG.). 2010. 74.99 (978-1-4418-5588-6(2)) Find a World.

So Much for That. abr. ed. Lionel Shriver. (Running Time: 6 hrs.). 2011. audio compact disk 14.99 (978-1-4233-6106-0(7), 9781423361060, BCD Value Price) Brilliance Audio.

So Much for That. unabr. ed. Lionel Shriver. Read by Dan John Miller. (Running Time: 17 hrs.). 2010. 44.97 (978-1-4233-6102-2(4), 9781423361022, Brinc Audio MP3 Lib); 29.99 (978-1-4233-6101-5(6), 9781423361015, Brilliance MP3); 44.97 (978-1-4233-6104-6(0), 9781423361046, BADLE); 29.99 (978-1-4233-6103-9(2), 9781423361039, BAD); audio compact disk 36.99 (978-1-4233-6099-5(0), 9781423360995, Bril Audio CD Unabri); audio compact disk 97.97 (978-1-4233-6100-8(8), 9781423361008, BriAudCD Unabrid) Brilliance Audio.

***So Much for That.** unabr. ed. Lionel Shriver. Read by Michael Mcconnohie et al. (ENG.). 2010. (978-0-06-197751-0(9), Harper Audio) HarperCollins Pubs.

***So Much for That: A Novel.** unabr. ed. Lionel Shriver. Read by Michael Mcconnohie et al. (ENG.). 2010. (978-0-06-195372-9(5), Harper Audio) HarperCollins Pubs.

So Much of Life Ahead. Dean Hughes. 6 CDs. (Hearts of the Children Ser.: Vol. 5). 2005. audio compact disk 21.95 (978-1-59038-500-5(4)) Deseret Bk.

So Much to Tell You. unabr. ed. John Marsden. Narrated by Kate Hosking. 3 CDs. (Running Time: 3 hrs. 25 mins.). (YA). (gr. 7-9). 2006. audio compact disk 54.95 (978-1-74093-719-1(8)) Pub: Bolinda Pubng AUS. Dist(s): Bolinda Pub Inc

So Much to Tell You. unabr. ed. John Marsden. Read by Kate Hosking. (Running Time: 3 hrs. 25 mins.). (YA). 2009. 43.95 (978-1-74214-435-1(7), 9781742144351) Pub: Bolinda Pubng AUS. Dist(s): Bolinda Pub Inc

So My Soul Can Sing. Poems. Etheridge Knight. Read by Etheridge Knight. Intro. by Gwendolyn Brooks. 1 cass. (Running Time: 51 min.). 1986. 10.95 (23662) J Norton Pubs.
This popular Black poet writes poetry rooted in both rural Mississippi & the ghettoes of urban America.

So Shall We Stand. Elyse Larson. Narrated by Vanessa Benjamin. (Running Time: 15 hrs.). (C). 2005. 44.95 (978-1-59912-601-2(X)) Iofy Corp.

So Shall We Stand. Elyse Larson. (Running Time: 15 hrs. 0 mins.). 2005. 85.95 (978-0-7861-3489-2(5)); audio compact disk 99.00 (978-0-7861-7891-9(4)) Blckstn Audio.

So Shall We Stand. Elyse Larson & Vanessa Benjamin. (Running Time: 15 hrs. 0 mins.). 2005. 29.95 (978-0-7861-8074-5(9)) Blckstn Audio.

So Sure of Death. collector's ed. Dana Stabenow. Read by Marguerite Gavin. 7 cass. (Running Time: 10 hrs. 30 min.). (Liam Campbell Mystery Ser.: Bk. 2). 1999. 56.00 (978-0-7366-4795-3(3), 5143) Books on Tape.
When the bodies of a local family are found adrift at sea, horribly murdered, Alaska State Trooper Liam Campbell is drawn straight into the heart of a family scandal involving adultery, tribal taboos & forbidden romance. To find the killer, Liam will have to wade into the murky depths of Native-Alaskan politics, tribal mores & deeply held secret.

So the Loud Torrent, unabr. ed. R. C. House. Read by Rusty Nelson. 6 cass. (Running Time: 7 hrs.). 1999. 39.95 (978-1-55686-903-7(7)) Books in Motion.
Old Smith, big Rome Jordan & Gunsight Kirby are experienced mountainmen who have lived through the toughest challenges offered by nature. Abby Freeman asks the men to help her find her husband, who is said to be captured by Indians. Fearing for the woman's safety, the men refuse her offer, but are soon persuaded by her offer of a cash reward. The party sets out to find that more than just hostile Indians will block their progress.

So We're Not a New Creation after All? 1985. (0228) Evang Sisterhood Mary.

So What. (Choices & Decisions Ser.). (J). (gr. k-1). 1990. 7.92 (978-0-8123-6444-6(9)) Holt McDoug.

So What? unabr. ed. Miriam Cohen. 1 cass. (Running Time: 7 min.). (J). (gr. k-3). 1990. pap. bk. 13.90 (978-0-8045-6541-7(4), 6541-B) Spoken Arts.

So What Do I Do with My Left Hand? 1 cass. 19.95 Incl. left hand style sheet. (V-4) Duane Shinn.
Explains a dozen unique bass styles, including - swing bass, continuity bass; upward inversions, pyramids, string bass style, arps in 10ths, hand-over arps; boogie-bass; Western bass; elephant bass; break-it-up bass.

So What If You're Right?! Getting Your Power Back by Giving up "Looping", Set. David Grudermeyer & Rebecca Grudermeyer. 2 cass. 18.95 (T-53) Willingness Wrks.

So, What's Your Father Like: Logos 11/01/98. Ben Young. 1998. 4.95 (978-0-7417-6104-0(1)) Win Walk.

So Yesterday. unabr. ed. Scott Westerfeld. Read by Scott Brick. 4 cass. (Running Time: 6 hrs. 33 mins.). (YA). 2006. 35.00 (978-0-307-28457-0(3), Listening Lib); audio compact disk 42.50 (978-0-307-28458-7(1), Listening Lib) Pub: Random Audio Pubg. Dist(s): NetLibrary CO

So You Don't Want to Go to Church Anymore: An Unexpected Journey. unabr. ed. Jake Colsen. Narrated by Wayne Jacobsen. (Running Time: 5 hrs. 27 mins. 32 sec.). (ENG.). 2008. 16.09 (978-1-60814-391-7(0)); audio compact disk 22.99 (978-1-59859-521-5(0)) Oasis Audio.

So You Made a Mistake/Support in Healing. Marianne Williamson. Read by Marianne Williamson. 1 cass. (Running Time: 90 mins.). (Lectures on a Course in Miracles). 1999. 10.00 (978-1-56170-264-0(1), M767) Hay House.

So, You Think You're Done? Speeches. Kevin Aguanno. 1 CD. (Running Time: 63 mins). 2005. audio compact disk 14.87 (978-1-895186-59-8(5)) Multi-Media ON CAN.
Project closeout always presents challenges: getting final approvals, performing administrative and contract closure, capturing lessons learned, and others. In a world moving at the speed of e-business, efficient project closure is a must and may even give you a competitive edge. This presentation covers best practices for getting final signoffs and closing out IT projects.

So, You Want to Be a Networker? Kim Klaver. 1 cass. (Running Time: 50 min.). 1996. 7.95 (978-1-891493-00-3(0)) Max Out Prodns.
Humorous overview of what it takes to make it in a business of your own.

So You Want to Be a Wizard. Diane Duane. Narrated by Christina Moore. 7 CDs. (Running Time: 7 hrs. 30 mins.). (gr. 5 up). audio compact disk 69.00 (978-0-7887-4968-1(4)) Recorded Bks.

So You Want to Be a Wizard. Diane Duane. Narrated by Christina Moore. 7 CDs. (Running Time: 7 hrs. 30 min.). (J). (gr. 5 up). 2000. audio compact disk 69.00 (C1313E7) Recorded Bks.
When a 13-year-old hides in the library from a gang of bullying classmates, she finds the help she needs in a book of wizardry.

So You Want to Be a Wizard, unabr. ed. Diane Duane. Narrated by Christina Moore. 5 pieces. (Running Time: 7 hrs. 30 mins.). (gr. 5 up). 1998. 44.00 (978-0-7887-2079-6(1), 95432E7) Recorded Bks.

So You Want to Be an Author. 1 cass. 11.95 (978-1-57025-009-5(X)) Whole Person.

So You Want to Be an Interpreter? 6 cass. Dramatization. 49.95 Set. (978-0-9640367-5-8(4), A-T1) Sign Enhancers.
Too busy to read? Learn more about the profession while driving to your next assignment.

So You Want to Be an Interpreter? Study Guide. Janice H. Humphrey. audio compact disk 49.95 (978-0-9640367-9-6(7)) H & H Pub.

So, You Want to Be Like Christ? see Asi Que, Quiere Ser Como Cristo?

So, You Want to Be Like Christ? 2005. audio compact disk 34.00 (978-1-57972-684-3(4)) Insight Living.

So, You Want to Be Like Christ? Musical Companion. 2005. audio compact disk 17.00 (978-1-57972-622-5(4)) Insight Living.

So You Want to Be President? 2004. pap. bk. 38.75 (978-1-55592-642-7(8)); pap. bk. 32.75 (978-1-55592-363-1(1)); pap. bk. 14.95 (978-1-55592-167-5(1)) Weston Woods.

So You Want to Be President? Judith St. George. Illus. by David Small. 1 cass. (Running Time: 22 mins.). (J). (gr. 1-6). 2004. bk. 24.95 (978-1-55592-094-4(2)); 8.95 (978-1-55592-963-3(X)); audio compact disk 12.95 (978-1-55592-933-6(8)) Weston Woods.
Celebrates the public and private lives of 42 presidents.

So You Want to Be President? unabr. ed. Judith St. George. Narrated by Brian Keeler. 1 cass. (Running Time: 30 mins.). (gr. 1 up). 2002. 14.00 (978-1-4025-1020-5(9)) Recorded Bks.
A humorous and informative look at America's highest office.

So You Want to Be Published? A Guide to Getting into Print. Roisin Conroy. 1992. 65.00 (978-1-85549-056-7(0)) St Mut.

So, You Want to Get a Job Seminar Audio Series Set: Fishing for a Job from an Employer's Perspective, unabr. ed. Kenneth Guinup & Michael Lukens. Prod. by Joe Hardwick. 3 cass. (Running Time: 30 mins. per cass.). 2000. 17.95 (978-0-615-11578-8(0), 201) SoBooks.com.
Whether you are a beginner or an experienced job seeker this easy to understand step-by-step program will help you.

So You Want to Have a Christian Home Vol. 1: Eight Secrets to Transforming Your Family, Robert D. Wolgemuth. 4 cass. (Running Time: 45 min.). 29.99 Set. (978-1-892037-00-8(9)) RDW Inc.
Presentation filled with lots of humor & practical ideas for making any home a place that truly honors God.

So Your Teen Knows All the Answers..., Corrie Lynne Player. 2 cass. 13.95 (978-1-57734-533-6(9), 07002211) Covenant Comms.

So, You're Out of a Job? Barrie Konicov. 1 cass. 11.98 (978-0-87082-440-1(6), 121) Potentials.
A personal portrayal of being out of a job, living off unemployment & how to handle the situation.

So You've Got a Great Idea. unabr. collector's ed. Steve Fiffer. Read by Larry McKeever. 8 cass. (Running Time: 8 hrs.). 1987. 48.00 (978-0-7366-1232-6(7), 2150) Books on Tape.
Offers advice for developing & marketing innovative products & ideas.

So You've Got This Great Idea: Inventor's Roadmap. Edward N. Horton, II. Interview with Bob Beavers & Marvin Glaser. (Running Time: 3 hr.). 1999. 59.95 (978-0-9675959-0-0(8)) Inventions Unlimit.
A first-time inventors dream. A round-table discussion about what works, what doesn't, & how to make the invention process work for you.

***So You've Graduated, Now What Are You Going to Do? A new & simple twist to finding your true career Path.** Al Auger. (Running Time: 40 minutes divided in 7 tracks). (ENG.). (YA). 2010. audio compact disk 15.49 (978-0-615-36157-4(9)) Al Auger.

Soaking Presence. John Belt. (Sounds of Worship Ser.). 2002. audio compact disk 15.00 (978-0-9748236-0-7(0)) Pub: Live in His Presence. Dist(s): STL Dist NA

Soap! Soap! Don't Forget the Soap! An Appalachian Folktale. unabr. ed. Tom Birdseye. Narrated by Tom Stechschulte. 1 cass. (Running Time: 15 mins.). (gr. k up). 1997. 10.00 (978-0-7887-0745-2(0), 94922E7) Recorded Bks.
Forgetful young Plug Honeycutt can't quite remember what his mother sent him to the store to buy, but one thing leads to another & he eventually gets it right.

Soap Suds. abr. ed. Nina Mattikow. 1 cass. Dramatization. (At the Sound of the Beep Ser.). 1992. 6.95 (978-1-55569-573-6(6), 41506) Great Am Audio.
Let your favorite vamps, villains, heroines, hunks & heart throbs answer your calls...sixteen hilarious impersonations of soap stars & their fans will have your callers staying tuned for the beep!.

Soapbox. Contrib. by R-Swift & John K. Wells. 2008. audio compact disk 13.99 (978-5-557-39783-4(3)) C Mason Res.

Soapsuds. abr. ed. Finola Hughes & Digby Diehl. Read by Finola Hughes. (Running Time: 21600 sec.). 2005. audio compact disk 74.25 (978-1-59737-326-5(5), 9781597373265, BACDLib Ed) Brilliance Audio.
Having escaped to Hollywood after catching her boyfriend in bed with her best friend, London stage actress Kate McPhee is offered a gig on the popular daytime television series Live for Tomorrow. As Devon Merrick - police detective, car crash victim, and love interest for at least two men - she knows all the secrets and sins pulsating in fictional Hope Canyon. But the real drama is off the set, where the soap is indeed slippery. Enter Meredith Contini, the show's power-wielding diva. Meredith has two rules: Know your place and Stay in it. Kate broke both on day one, which is why she suddenly found her character switching sexual orientation. That brilliant solution came from Daphne del Valle, the show's barking-mad obsessive/compulsive producer, who drives herself and her actors to enthrall the audience. ("Sell the hurt. Sell the rage. Sell the hunger. Sell the loooooove.") As gay detective Devon Merrick, Kate is a smash. The show is a hit. But Kate's private life seems to be becoming something of a drama itself. Especially since everybody thinks she really is gay, which is a problem since she thinks the best cure for her real-life broken heart is to get a man into her bed. But who? Kirk, her sexy, tan, and talented leading man, is involved with Meredith. There's Matt, the magician who makes her tea, but will her fourteen-hour days keep them from the promise of tangled sheets? And there's Wyatt, her handsome new co-star, who Kate believes is the great love of her life. Except that he's married, and his wife, Christine, is Kate's new makeup artist and the one sane friend she has made in Los Angeles. As the line between television and reality blurs with increasing speed, tension tightens and passions surge. Does Wyatt want Kate as much as she wants him? Will Christine find out? Will Kate lose her new friend? Will Meredith finally have Kate fired? Will Kate ever get to "come out" as heterosexual on the set? Are her steamy kiss scenes fated to be only with beautiful women? Emmy Award-winning actress Finola Hughes whips up a frothy, scathingly funny novel worthy of any afternoon time slot in this delicious romp that takes listeners through the twists, turns, and dish that drive the madness that is daytime television.

Soapsuds. abr. ed. Finola Hughes & Digby Diehl. Read by Finola Hughes. (Running Time: 21600 sec.). 2006. audio compact disk 16.99 (978-1-59737-327-2(3), 9781597373272) Brilliance Audio.

Soapsuds. unabr. ed. Finola Hughes & Digby Diehl. Read by Anne Flosnik. (Running Time: 15 hrs.). 2005. 39.25 (978-1-59737-331-9(1), 9781597373319, BADLE); 24.95 (978-1-59737-330-2(3), 9781597373302, BAD); 39.25 (978-1-59737-329-6(X), 9781597373296, Brlnc Audio MP3 Lib); 34.95 (978-1-59737-323-4(0), 9781597373234, BAU); cass., cass., DVD 97.25 (978-1-59737-324-1(9), 9781597373241, BrilAudUnabridg); DVD & audio compact disk 24.95 (978-1-59737-328-9(1), 9781597373289, Brilliance MP3) Brilliance Audio.

Soar the Universe: To Connect to All That Is! (ENG., 2009. audio compact disk 19.95 (978-0-9766735-3-8(3)) R Seals.

Soar un Crimen. Rosana Acquaroni. (Coleccion Leer en Espanol: Nivel 1 Ser.). 2008. pap. bk. 13.99 (978-84-9713-058-5(8)) Santillana.

Soar Unafraid: Learning to Trust No Matter What. Jo Franz. 2007. audio compact disk 50.99 (978-1-60247-656-1(X)) Tate Pubng.

Soaring Self Confidence. Eldon Taylor. Read by Eldon Taylor. Interview with XProgress Aware Staff. 1 cass. (Running Time: 62 min.). 16.95 incl. script. (978-1-55978-289-0(7), 020103) Progress Aware Res.
Verbal coaching soundtrack with underlying subliminal affirmations & sound matrix frequencies for brain entrainment.

Soaring Self-Confidence: OZO. Eldon Taylor. Read by Eldon Taylor. Ed. by Leslie Brice. 1 cass. (Running Time: 1 hr.). 1992. 19.95 (978-1-56705-008-0(5)) Gateways Inst.
Self improvement.

Soaring Self Esteem. Eldon Taylor. 1 CD. (Running Time: 52 min.). (Whole Brain Innertalk Ser.). 1998. audio compact disk (978-1-55978-870-0(4)); audio compact disk (978-1-55978-947-9(6)) Progress Aware Res.

Soaring with the Eagles Series. Kenneth W. Hagin, Jr. 2 cass. 1996. 8.00 Set. (35J) Faith Lib Pubns.

Soaring with the Phoenix: Renewing the Vision, Reviving the Spirit, & Re-Creating the Success of Your Company. abr. ed. Scripts. James A. Belasco. Read by David Ackroyd. 4 cass. (Running Time: 6 hrs.). 2004. 25.00 (978-1-59007-166-3(2)) Pub: New Millenn Enter. Dist(s): PerseuPGW

Sober After Suboxone: When to Stop Buprenorphine Treatment? Created by Jeffrey T. Junig. 2009. 19.99 (978-0-9840972-3-4(6)) Term Un Pub.

Sober & Free-Subliminal. 2007. audio compact disk 19.95 (978-1-56136-123-6(2)) Master Your Mind.

Sobornost: Experiencing Unity of Mind, Heart & Soul. unabr. ed. Catherine Doherty. Read by Patrick McNulty. 4 cass. (Running Time: 4 hrs.). 24.95 (978-0-921440-57-4(X)) Madonna Hse CAN.
In Sobornost, the Russian word for "unity," Catherine Doherty leads her readers on the journey of a lifetime. She guides us along the pathway that takes us home to God's house, into the graced intimacy of eternal belonging. Here we rediscover the final unity that flows from Divine Persons, one in love-Father, Son, and Spirit. Here Catherine holds the lost key, the forgotten path, the secret to the most profound of all worlds-to a new civilization of love. Sobornost enters our hearts through the grace of the Trinity. This unity transcends our emotions, our ideas, our identities and opens immense horizons. It is a mystery to be understood more with the heart than with the mind. Catherine shares her own experience of it in a way that rings true and brings readers to the heart of the mystery. She writes in a simple, conversational tone, from a heart full of immense love for God and neighbour. Around the theme of spiritual unity Catherine weaves various threads of Christian spirituality: the primacy and meaning of Baptism, Eucharist, service to others in love, and contemplation. Attaining sobornost is vital in this technological age with its loneliness, alienation, and fragmentation.

Sobrenatural. 1 cass. 16.95 (CSP310) J Norton Pubs.
Six legends with multicultural significance, from ancient to modern times.

Sobrenatural. Marcos Witt. 2008. audio compact disk 15.99 (978-0-8297-5604-3(3)) Pub: Vida Pubs. Dist(s): Zondervan

Sobreviviendo: Guia Para el Bienestar. Gretchen Chandler. Read by Irene Keeser. Ed. by Neva Duyndam. 1 cass. (SPA.). 1989. 9.95 (978-1-878159-09-0(7)) Duvall Media.
Gives practical steps the author took toward recovery from manic depression.

Sobrevivir Entre Piranas. Joachim de Posada. 2008. audio compact disk 24.95 (978-1-933499-75-8(3)) Fonolibro Inc.

Soccer. Eldon Taylor. 1 cass. (Running Time: 62 min.). (Inner Talk Ser.). 16.95 incl. script. (978-1-55978-533-4(0), 53892F) Progress Aware Res.
Soundtrack - Babbling Brook with underlying subliminal affirmations.

Soccer: Music Theme. Eldon Taylor. 1 cass. 16.95 (978-0-940699-65-6(6), 53892C) Progress Aware Res.

Soccer: Rhythm. Eldon Taylor. Read by Eldon Taylor. Ed. by Leslie Brice. 1 cass. (Running Time: 1 hr.). 1992. 16.95 (978-1-56705-254-1(1)) Gateways Inst.
Self improvement.

Soccer: Stream. Eldon Taylor. Read by Eldon Taylor. Ed. by Leslie Brice. 1 cass. (Running Time: 1 hr.). 1992. 16.95 (978-1-56705-255-8(X)) Gateways Inst.

Soccer War. unabr. collector's ed. Ryszard Kapuscinski. Read by Geoffrey Howard. 5 cass. (Running Time: 7 hrs. 30 min.). 1997. 40.00 (978-0-7366-4031-2(2), 4530) Books on Tape.
This chronicle of small wars throughout the world is among the most respected works of contemporary journalism.

Social Action: Proceedings of the 45th Annual Convention National Association of Evangelicals Buffalo, New York. Read by O. Hatfield. 1 cass. (Running Time: 60 min.). 1987. 4.00 (345) Nat Assn Evan.

Social Action & Spiritual Life. unabr. ed. Ram Dass. 1 cass. (Running Time: 1 hr. 24 min.). 1982. 11.00 (00611) Big Sur Tapes.
If the universe is perfect, as the mystic contends, why is there so much suffering in the world? This ancient dilemna, & how to work with it, spurs the ever-eloquent Ram Dass into a moving talk on action & acceptance.

Social Action & the Compassionate Heart. Ram Dass. 1 cass. (Running Time: 56 min.). (How Then Shall We Live? Ser.). 1987. 9.95 Original Face.
Addresses the challenge of developing compassion in our individual lives & bringing it to bear on political decision making in our communities & the world.

Social Change. Harvey Jackins. 1 cass. 10.00 (978-1-58429-013-1(7)) Rational Isl.
A lecture about social change.

Social Confidence. unabr. ed. Judith L. Powell. Read by Judith L. Powell. 1 cass. (Running Time: 40 min.). (Successful Living Ser.). 1987. pap. bk. 12.95 (978-0-914295-29-7(2), 29-2) Top Mtn Pub.
Side A presents exercises designed to improve conversation skills, build security in encounters, overcome shyness & attracting friends. Side B presents subliminal sociable suggestions hidden in New Age Music.

Social Consciousness. David Freudberg. Perf. by Roger Fisher et al. 6 cass. (Running Time: 6 hrs.). (Kindred Spirits Ser.: Vol. 4). 1985. 24.95 Set. (978-0-9640914-7-4(X)) Human Media.
A listening library of spiritual wisdom from the world's great traditions. Covers subjects such as Helping Hands, The Quaker Conscience, Martin Luther King's Spiritual Journey, Business Ethics, & On Reaching Agreement.

Social Contract & Arts & Sciences, abr. ed. Jean-Jacques Rousseau. Read by Robert L. Halvorson. 6 cass. (Running Time: 6 hrs.). 1975. 28.95 Halvorson Assocs.
Rousseau's writings influenced the thinking of our founding fathers & U. S. Constitution.

Social Control in Europe. Herman Roodenburg. (History of Crime & Criminal Justice Ser.). 2004. audio compact disk 19.95 (978-0-8142-9048-4(5)) Pub: Ohio St U Pr. Dist(s): Chicago Distribution Ctr

Social Crimes. Jane Stanton Hitchcock. Read by Barbara Rosenblat. (Running Time: 12 hrs.). 2003. 36.95 (978-1-59912-602-9(8)) Iofy Corp.

Social Crimes. unabr. ed. Jane Stanton Hitchcock. Read by Barbara Rosenblat. 10 CDs. (Running Time: 13 hrs.). 2003. audio compact disk 80.00 (978-0-7861-9236-6(4), 3120); 62.95 (978-0-7861-2441-1(5), 3120) Blckstn Audio.
When husband Lucius dies under rather sordid and suspicious circumstances, prominent New York socialite Jo Slater is shocked to learn that he has left his sizable estate to a mysterious French countess. Exiled from the kingdom of money, power, and privilege, Jo struggles to rebuild her life only to find herself thwarted at every turn by the countess, sliding down the social ladder until she hits rock bottom, buying a pair of Hush Puppies (on sale) for her aching feet. Obsessed with recovering her fortune and place as queen of New York, Jo concocts an audacious scheme of revenge. Can she pull it off?.

Social Crimes. unabr. ed. Jane Stanton Hitchcock. Read by Barbara Rosenblat. 10 CDs. 2004. audio compact disk 49.95 (978-0-7861-9276-2(3)); reel tape 39.95 (978-0-7861-2469-5(5)) Blckstn Audio.

Social Crimes. unabr. ed. Jane Stanton Hitchcock. Read by Barbara Rosenblat. 1 MP3. (Running Time: 12 hrs.). 2005. 24.95 (978-0-7861-9000-3(0), ZM3120); 29.95 (978-0-7861-3756-5(8), E3120) Blckstn Audio.
Dark secrets lurk beneath the glamour and glitter of New York's high society life in this riveting tale of murder, obsession, and revenge. Jo Slater, one of the grandest of New York's grande dames is knocked off her pedestal when her husband of twenty years dies under strange circumstances and leaves his fortune to a mysterious French countess. When Jo discovers she has been the victim of a plot, she decides to set things straight. And nothing is going to get in her way.

Social Crimes. unabr. ed. Jane Stanton Hitchcock. Read by Barbara Rosenblat. 10 CDs. (Running Time: 43200 sec.). 2005. audio compact disk 29.95 (978-0-7861-7639-7(3), ZE3120) Blckstn Audio.

Social Dance Cha-Cha Music. Composed by Richard Gardzina. Contrib. by Judy P. Wright. 1 cass. (Running Time: 50 min.). (Steps to Success Activity Ser.). 1991. 9.95 Incl. text. (978-0-7360-2958-2(3), MGAR0194); 39.95 Set of 5, incl. text. (MGAR0191) HumanKinUSA.
Music to accompany the book of instruction, "Social Dance: Steps to Success," by Judy Patterson Wright.

Social Dance Fox-Trot Music. Composed by Richard Gardzina. Contrib. by Judy P. Wright. 1 cass. (Running Time: 50 min.). (Steps to Success Activity Ser.). 1991. 9.95 Incl. text. (978-0-7360-2959-9(1), MGAR0195); 39.95 Set of 5, incl. text. (MGAR0191) HumanKinUSA.

Social Dance Polka Music. Composed by Richard Gardzina. Contrib. by Judy P. Wright. 1 cass. (Running Time: 50 min.). (Steps to Success Activity Ser.). (AFA.). 1991. 9.95 Incl. text. (978-0-7360-2960-5(5), MGAR0196); 39.95 Set of 5, incl. text. (MGAR0191) HumanKinUSA.

Social Dance Swing Music. Composed by Richard Gardzina. Contrib. by Judy P. Wright. 1 cass. (Running Time: 50 min.). (Steps to Success Activity Ser.). 1991. 9.95 Incl. text. (978-0-7360-2956-8(7), MGAR0192); 39.95 Set of 5, incl. text. (MGAR0191) HumanKinUSA.

Social Dance Waltz Music. Composed by Richard Gardzina. Contrib. by Judy P. Wright. 1 cass. (Running Time: 50 min.). (Steps to Success Activity Ser.). 1991. 9.95 Incl. text. (978-0-7360-2957-5(5), MGAR0193); 39.95 Set of 5, incl. text. (MGAR0191) HumanKinUSA.

Social Groups in Action & Interaction. Charles Stangor. 2005. audio compact disk (978-1-84169-413-9(4), Pysch Press) Tay Francis Ltd GBR.

Social Intelligence: The New Science of Human Relationships. abr. ed. Daniel Goleman. Read by Daniel Goleman. 4 CDs. (Running Time: 21600 sec.). (ENG.). 2006. audio compact disk 24.95 (978-1-59397-984-3(3)) Pub: Macmill Audio. Dist(s): Macmillan

Social Intelligence: The New Science of Human Relationships. unabr. ed. Daniel Goleman. Narrated by Dennis Boutsikaris. 11 CDs. 2006. audio compact disk 99.95 (978-0-7927-4369-9(5), SLD 993) AudioGO.

Social Intelligence: The New Science of Human Relationships. unabr. ed. Daniel Goleman. Narrated by Dennis Boutsikaris. 2 CDs. (Running Time: 43440 sec.). 2006. audio compact disk 59.95 (978-0-7927-4556-3(6), CMP 993) AudioGO.

Social Intelligence: The New Science of Human Relationships. unabr. ed. Daniel Goleman. Read by Dennis Boutsikaris. (Running Time: 12 hrs. 0 mins. 0 sec.). (ENG.). 2006. audio compact disk 44.95 (978-1-59397-371-1(3), Rena Bks) Pub: St Martin. Dist(s): Macmillan

Social Life of the Newt see Best of Benchley

Social Lives of Dogs: The Grace of Canine Company, Set. abr. ed. Elizabeth Marshall Thomas. Read by Elizabeth Marshall Thomas. 2 cass. (Running Time: 3 hrs.). 2000. 18.00 (978-1-55935-342-7(2)) Soundelux.
The Thomas household has always been made up of dogs, cats, parrots & humans, in varying rations.

***Social Media 101: Tactics & Tips to Develop Your Business Online.** unabr. ed. Chris Brogan. (Running Time: 6 hrs. 30 mins.). (ENG.). 2010. 27.98 (978-1-59659-553-8(1), GildAudio) Pub: Gildan Media. Dist(s): HachBkGrp

Social Problems: Instructor's Resource CD. 2nd rev. ed. John J. Macionis. audio compact disk 18.97 (978-0-13-189191-3(X)) PH School.

Social Revolution. 10.00 (HT403) Esstee Audios.

Social Science: an Introduction to the Study of Society: Instructor's Resource CD-ROM. 11th rev. ed. Hunt & Colander. audio compact disk 18.97 (978-0-13-184990-7(5)) PH School.

Social Science Reprints. Ed. by Marco A. V. Bitetto. 1 cass. 2000. (978-1-58578-059-4(6)) Inst of Cybernetics.

Social Security. Peter Ferrara. 1 cass. (Running Time: 60 min.). 1986. 9.95 (978-0-945999-18-8(6)) Independent Inst.
In-Depth Expose of the Precarious Nature of Social Security, Making the Case for Privatization Through a System of IRAs.

Social Security Disability Claims. 1991. 40.00 (AC-613) PA Bar Inst.

Social Security Disability Practice - The Basics. 1996. bk. 99.00 (ACS-1107) PA Bar Inst.
For the uninformed, making sense of the Social Security Disability adjudication process can be the equivalent of wandering in a cleverly designed maze. This provides the essentials of disability practice necessary to navigate this process.

Social Security Disability Update. 1998. bk. 99.00 (ACS-2088); bk. 99.00 (ACS-2088) PA Bar Inst.
Wouldn't it be nice to walk into your next disability hearing with the latest developments at your fingertips & several new strategies to use when confronted with vocational & medical expert testimony? All of this & more has been packed into this book written by experienced Administrative Law Judges & authors.

Social Skills Training for Nonverbal Communication. Maria Antoniadis & Kathryn McCarthy. 1 cass. (Running Time: 1 hrs. 19 min.). 1997. bk. 15.00 (978-1-58111-013-5(8)) Contemporary Medical.
Discusses treatment models of social skills group; defines social competence; addresses non-verbal communication & specific socioemotional/adaptational difficulties of NLD.

Social Standards at School: Set Social & Behavioral Guidelines. Judi Kinney & Tom Kinney. (gr. 1-6). 2002. spiral bd. 39.00 (978-1-57861-155-3(5), IEP Res) Attainment.

Social Studies. (AMF-22) Am Audio Prose.

Social Studies: Music of the World. 3rd ed. Holt, Rinehart and Winston Staff. 2002. audio compact disk 47.20 (978-0-03-065441-1(6)) Holt McDoug.

Social Studies Unit 2: Text on Tape: Florida Edition. 2nd ed. Harcourt School Publishers Staff. (J). (gr. 3). 2002. 12.90 (978-0-15-320894-2(5)) Harcourt Schl Pubs.

Social Studies Unit 3: Text on Tape: Florida Edition. 2nd ed. Harcourt School Publishers Staff. (J). (gr. 3). 2002. 12.90 (978-0-15-320895-9(3)) Harcourt Schl Pubs.

Social Studies Unit 4: Text on Tape: Florida Edition. 2nd ed. Harcourt School Publishers Staff. (J). (gr. 3). 2002. 12.90 (978-0-15-320896-6(1)) Harcourt Schl Pubs.

Social Studies Unit 6: Text on Tape: Florida Edition. 2nd ed. Harcourt School Publishers Staff. (J). 2002. 12.90 (978-0-15-320897-3(X)) Harcourt Schl Pubs.

Social Studies Audio CD Set: English Explorers Set A. Adapted by Benchmark Education Staff. (J). 2007. audio compact disk 450.00 (978-1-4108-9545-5(9)) Benchmark Educ.

Social Studies Audio CD Set: English Explorers Set B. Adapted by Benchmark Education Staff. (J). 2007. audio compact disk 450.00 (978-1-4108-9539-4(4)) Benchmark Educ.

Social Studies Big Book Audiocassette Collection. Dahia Shabaka. (Living & Working Together Ser.). (J). (gr. k). 2000. 39.95 (978-1-58830-307-3(1)) Metro Teaching.

Social Studies E-Books: English Explorers Set B (Set Of 24) Compiled by Benchmark Education Staff. (J). 2007. audio compact disk 325.00 (978-1-4108-8578-4(X)) Benchmark Educ.

Social Studies Early Explorers Take Home Book: CD Rom. Compiled by Benchmark Education Staff. (J). 2007. audio compact disk 10.00 (978-1-4108-9486-1(X)) Benchmark Educ.

Social Studies Take Home Book-CD Rom: Early. Benchmark Education Staff. (J). 2006. audio compact disk 10.00 (978-1-4108-7386-6(2)) Benchmark Educ.

Social Studies Take Home Book-CD Rom: Emergent. Benchmark Education Staff. (J). 2006. audio compact disk 10.00 (978-1-4108-7383-5(8)) Benchmark Educ.

Social Studies Take Home Book-CD Rom: Fluent. Benchmark Education Staff. (J). 2006. audio compact disk 10.00 (978-1-4108-7389-7(7)) Benchmark Educ.

Socialism, Pt. 1. unabr. ed. Ludwig von Mises. Read by Bernard Mayes. 8 cass. (Running Time: 11 hrs. 30 mins.).Tr. of Gemeinwirtschaft. 1990. 56.95 (978-0-7861-0191-7(1), 1168-A,B) Blckstn Audio.
Published in 1922, it stunned the Socialist world. Mises has given us a profoundly important treaties which assaults Socialism in all its guises; a work which discusses every major aspect of Socialism & leaves no stone unturned.

Socialism, Pt. 2. unabr. ed. Ludwig von Mises. Read by Bernard Mayes. 10 cass. (Running Time: 11 hrs. 30 mins.).Tr. of Gemeinwirtschaft. 1990. 69.95 (978-0-7861-0192-4(X), 1168-A,B) Blckstn Audio.

Socialism & Liberalism: Anarchy in Medieval Iceland. David Friedman. 1 cass. (Running Time: 53 min.). 10.95 (989) J Norton Pubs.

Socialism vs. Capitalism (Debate) Harry Binswanger et al. 1 cass. (Running Time: 90 min.). 1989. 12.95 (978-1-56114-135-7(6), HB11C) Second Renaissance.

Socialism, Why Always Fails. Ludwig von Mises. 1 cass. (Running Time: 1 hr. 26 min.). 11.95 (155) J Norton Pubs.
Von Mises describes the nature of society based on the principle of socialism, & contrasts it with society under the principle of free market exchange. He exposes the inherent weaknesses of socialism, why many people unwisely advocate it, & outlines how the free market helps men achieve their goals.

Socialist Thought, the Anarchists, Ethics. Robert LeFevre. 1 cass. (Running Time: 1 hr. 52 min.). 12.50 (1011) J Norton Pubs.
Is the good determined by the group? U. S. & its socialist communes before Marx.

Socialization Skills: Adaptive Behavior. Carol Michaelis. 2 cass. (Running Time: 2 hrs.). (J). 2001. 18.95 (KIM 8056C) Kimbo Educ.
16 songs present lyrics that teach sharing, emotional awareness, social skills, manners & listening. Thank You, Please, Sorry, Excuse Me, Telephone, Your Turn, Sharing & more. IEP suggestions & aids to chart behavior. Includes manual.

Socially Intelligent Computing. Clay Shirky & Daniel Goleman. (ENG.). 2007. 10.95 (978-1-934441-02-2(3)) More Than Snd.

Sociedades Secretas: Y como afectan nuestras vidas en la Actualidad. Sylvia Browne. 2 CDs.Tr. of Secret Societies... & How They Affect Our Lives Today. 2007. audio compact disk 18.95 (978-1-4019-1677-0(5)) Hay House.

Society. abr. ed. Michael Palmer. Read by J. Charles. (Running Time: 21600 sec.). 2006. audio compact disk 16.99 (978-1-4233-1494-3(8), 9781423314943, BCD Value Price) Brilliance Audio.
At the headquarters of Boston's Eastern Quality Health, the wealthy and powerful CEO is brutally murdered. She's not the first to die - nor the last. A vicious serial killer is on the loose and the victims have one thing in common: they are all high-profile executives in the managed care industry. Dr. Will Grant is an overworked and highly dedicated surgeon. He has experienced firsthand the outrages of a system that cares more about the bottom line than about the life-and-death issues of patients. As a member of the Hippocrates Society, Will seeks to reclaim the profession of medicine from the hundreds of companies profiting wildly by controlling the decisions that affect the delivery of care. But the doctor's determination has attracted a dangerous zealot who will stop at nothing to make Will his ally. Soon Will is both a suspect and a victim, a pawn in a deadly endgame. Then, in one horrible moment, Will's professional and personal worlds are destroyed and his very life placed in peril. Rookie detective Patty Moriarity is in danger of being removed from her first big case - the managed care killings. To save her career, she has no choice but to risk trusting Will, knowing he may well be the killer she is hunting. Together they have little to go on except the knowledge that the assassin is vengeful, cunning, ruthless - and may not be working alone. That - and a cryptic message that grows longer with each murder: a message Grant and Moriarity must decipher if they don't want to be the next victims.

***Society.** abr. ed. Michael Palmer. Read by J. Charles. (Running Time: 6 hrs.). 2010. audio compact disk 9.99 (978-1-4418-5689-0(7), 9781441856890, BCD Value Price) Brilliance Audio.

Society. unabr. ed. Michael Palmer. 10. (Running Time: 13 hrs.). 2004. audio compact disk 107.25 (978-1-59355-710-2(8), 1593557108, BriAudCD Unabrid) Brilliance Audio.

Society. unabr. ed. Michael Palmer. Read by J. Charles. (Running Time: 13 hrs.). 2004. 24.95 (978-1-59335-750-4(8), 1593357508, Brilliance MP3); 39.25 (978-1-59335-884-6(9), 1593358849, Brlnc Audio MP3 Lib); 36.95 (978-1-59355-706-5(X), 159355706X, BAU); 92.25 (978-1-59355-707-2(8), 1593557078, BrilAudUnabridg); audio compact disk 39.95 (978-1-59355-709-6(4), 1593557094, Bril Audio CD Unabri) Brilliance Audio.

Society. unabr. ed. Michael Palmer. Read by J. Charles. (Running Time: 13 hrs.). 2004. 39.25 (978-1-59710-725-9(5), 1597107255, BADLE); 24.95 (978-1-59710-724-2(7), 1597107247, BAD) Brilliance Audio.

Society in the Golden Age. Swami Amar Jyoti. 1 cass. 1982. 9.95 (A-23) Truth Consciousness.
The unified gaze of full awakening. Burning the seeds of discord within us first. Being worthy members of society. Stages of life in a perfect civilization.

Society of Others. unabr. ed. William Nicholson. 2005. audio compact disk 34.99 (978-1-4193-2678-3(3)) Recorded Bks.

Society of S. unabr. ed. Susan Hubbard. (Running Time: 10 hrs. 0 mins. 0 sec.). (ENG.). 2007. audio compact disk 69.99 (978-1-4001-3426-7(9)) Pub: Tantor Media. Dist(s): IngramPubServ

Society of S. unabr. ed. Susan Hubbard. Read by Joyce Bean. (Running Time: 10 hrs. 0 mins. 0 sec.). (ENG.). 2007. audio compact disk 24.99 (978-1-4001-5426-5(X)) Pub: Tantor Media. Dist(s): IngramPubServ

Society of S. unabr. ed. Susan Hubbard. Read by Joyce Bean. 8 CDs. (Running Time: 10 hrs. 0 mins. 0 sec.). (ENG.). (YA). (gr. 9 up). 2007. audio compact disk 34.99 (978-1-4001-0426-0(2)) Pub: Tantor Media. Dist(s): IngramPubServ

Society of the Mind, Eric Harry. 2 cass. 1996. 18.00 (978-0-694-51642-1(2), 628136) HarperCollins Pubs.
Brimming with dangerous scientific possibility & the lunacies of an eccentric genius. The story of Laura Aldrich, a young Harvard psychology professor, offered 1 million dollars for a week's work at the island compound belonging to genius-eccentric Joseph Gray. This mesmerizing audio sheds uncertainty into areas of artificial intelligence which are no longer progressive - let alone safe.

Socio-Sexual Experience of Homosexuality. unabr. ed. Del Martin & Phyllis Lyon. 1 cass. (Running Time: 90 min.). 1973. 11.00 (09701) Big Sur Tapes.
Offer a distillation of their experiences as "other" women. They see lesbianism as a political statement as well as a sexual orientation. Even though they were part of the Gay Liberation Movement of the time, they discuss why their concerns are more closely allied with the women's movement.

Socioeconomic Aspects of Human Behavioral Ecology. Ed. by N. Dannhaeuser et al. (Research in Economic Anthropology Ser.). 2004. 150.95 (978-0-7623-1082-1(0)) Pub: E G Pubng GBR. Dist(s): TurpinDistUSA

Sociopath Next Door. unabr. ed. Martha Stout. Read by Shelly Frasier. (Running Time: 7 hrs. 30 mins. 0 sec.). (ENG.). 2005. audio compact disk 29.99 (978-1-4001-0156-6(5)); audio compact disk 19.99 (978-1-4001-5156-1(2)); audio compact disk 59.99 (978-1-4001-3156-3(1)) Pub: Tantor Media. Dist(s): IngramPubServ

Socios: Curso Basico de Espanol Orientado al Mundo del Trabajo: Cuaderno de Ejercicios & Transcript Cassette. M. González & F. Martin. 2 vols. (SPA., bk. 39.95 (978-84-89344-68-6(X), DIF468X) Pub: Difusion Centro Inv ESP. Dist(s): Continental Bk

Socios: Curso Basico de Espanol Orientado al Mundo del Trabajo: Libro del Alumno & Transcript. M. González & F. Martin. 2 vols. (Running Time: 1 hr.). (SPA., 2000. stu. ed. 39.95 (978-84-89344-67-9(1), DIF4671) Pub: Difusion Centro Inv ESP. Dist(s): Continental Bk
"Socios es el primer metodo de E/LE basado en el enfoque por tareas dirigido a personas que necesitan el espanol para desenvolverse en el mundo laboral. El metodo consta de dos niveles, inicial e intermedio, y abarca diferentes ambitos del mundo del trabajo. Socios capacita al alumno para llevar a cabo actividades como negociar, escribir cartas comerciales o pronunciar un discurso, e invita a la reflexion sobre aspectos socioculturales. Ademas, sus contenidos preparan al alumno para el ""Certificado Basico de Espanol de los Negocios""."

Sockdolager! Davy Crockett. Read by Davy Crockett. 1 cass. 1998. (978-0-912986-24-1(7)) Am Media.

Sockeye's Journey Home. 1 cass. (Running Time: 35 min.). (J). (gr. k-4). 2001. pap. bk. 19.95 (SP 4019C) Kimbo Educ.
Sockeye Salmon must swim from the Pacific Ocean, through Seattle's Puget Sound & Lake Washington & finally into the Cedar River where it will be time to spawn. Includes readalong book.

Sockeye's Journey Home. Barbara Gaines Winkelman. Illus. by Joanie Popeo. Narrated by Peter Thomas. (J). 2000. bk. (978-1-56899-837-4(6)) Soundprints.

***Socks.** abr. ed. Beverly Cleary. Read by Neil Patrick Harris. (ENG.). 2004. (978-0-06-079047-9(4)); (978-0-06-081402-1(0)) HarperCollins Pubs.

Socks. unabr. ed. Beverly Cleary. 1 read-along cass. (Running Time: 1 hr.). (Middle Grade Cliffhangers Ser.). (J). (gr. 3-4). 1985. 15.98 incl. bk. & guide. (978-0-8072-1134-2(6), SWR50SP, Listening Lib) Random Audio Pubg.
Socks the cat has always lead a charmed life with the Brickers. But everything changes when the new baby comes home, & Socks finds himself vying with the little newcomer for love & attention.

Socrates. Tom Brickhouse & Nicholas Smith. Read by Lynn Redgrave. 2 cass. (Running Time: 3 hrs.). Dramatization. (World of Philosophy Ser.: No. 1). 1995. 17.95 Set. (978-1-56823-036-8(2), 10551) Knowledge Prod.
Though he left no written works, Socrates was the first great philosopher of the West. His conversations & dramatic death in ancient Athens were recorded by a number of writers (including Plato); they show that Socrates was deeply interested in "self-knowledge" & "virtue." Socrates also believed in the "rule of law" even refusing to flee when he was condemned to death. His ceaseless questionings have set timeless standards for the relentless pursuit of truth.

Socrates: The Man & His Thought. unabr. ed. A. E. Taylor. Read by Frederick Davidson. 3 cass. (Running Time: 4 hrs.). 1993. 23.95 (978-0-7861-0400-0(7), 1352) Blckstn Audio.
Without question the finest short biography of the world's greatest philosopher. Provides us with an excellent introduction to Socratic thought. Although Socrates himself left no writings, Professor Taylor consolidates all that can be known about the life & death of Socrates through the Dialogues of Plato, Aristotle's treatises & Xenophon's discourses.

Socrates in 90 Minutes. unabr. ed. Paul Strathern. Read by Robert Whitfield. (Running Time: 2 hrs. NaN mins.). 2009. audio compact disk 22.95 (978-0-7861-3680-3(4)); audio compact disk 27.00 (978-1-4332-6792-5(6)) Blckstn Audio.

Sodbusters. unabr. ed. Gary McCarthy. Read by Gene Engene. 6 cass. (Running Time: 6 hrs. 6 min.). 1996. 39.95 (978-1-55686-697-5(6)) Books in Motion.
Two teen-aged farm children from Wyoming set out for Texas on foot. Ignorant of the geography & hostility of the prairie, they are faced with an incredible journey.

Sodom & Gomorrah: Cities of the Plain. Marcel Proust. Read by Neville Jason. Tr. by C. K. Scott Moncrieff from FRE. Adapted by Neville Jason. 3 cass. (Running Time: 4 hrs.). (Remembrance of Things Past Ser.: Vol. VII). 1998. 17.98 (978-962-634-661-7(2), NA316114, Naxos AudioBooks) Naxos.
Introduces the theme of homosexuality with sympathy for the pain and frustration it causes those whose sexual nature is condemned by society and who are obliged to live lives of secrecy and duplicity.

Sodom & Gomorrah: Cities of the Plain. abr. ed. Marcel Proust. Read by Neville Jason. Tr. by C. K. Scott Moncrieff. Adapted by Neville Jason. 3 CDs. (Running Time: 4 hrs.). (Remembrance of Things Past Ser.: Vol. VII). 1998. audio compact disk 22.98 (978-962-634-161-2(0), NA316112, Naxos AudioBooks) Naxos.

Sodom & Gomorrah Pt. 2: Cities of the Plain. Marcel Proust. Read by Neville Jason. Tr. by C. K. Scott Moncrieff. Adapted by Neville Jason. 3 cass. (Running Time: 4 hrs.). (Remembrance of Things Past Ser.: Vol. VIII). 1999. 17.98 (978-962-634-667-9(1), NA316714, Naxos AudioBooks) Naxos.
Marcel continues his voyage of discovery through the homosexual world, where the affairs of the aging Baron de Charlus lead to unexpected and hilarious adventures.

Sodom & Gomorrah Pt. 2: Cities of the Plain, Vol. 2. abr. ed. Marcel Proust. Read by Neville Jason. Tr. by C. K. Scott Moncrieff. Adapted by Neville Jason. 3 CDs. (Running Time: 4 hrs.). (Remembrance of Things Past Ser.: Vol. VIII). 1999. audio compact disk 22.98 (978-962-634-167-4(X), NA316712, Naxos AudioBooks) Naxos.

Sodom & Gomorrah & Houston: Genesis 17:1. Ed Young. (J). 1980. 4.95 (978-0-7417-1148-9(6), A0148) Win Walk.

Sodoma Y Gomorra. unabr. ed. Proust Marcel. Read by Santiago Munevar. (SPA.). 2007. audio compact disk 17.00 (978-958-8318-18-9(1)) Pub: Yoyo Music COL. Dist(s): YoYoMusic

Sody Saleratus & Other Tales. Retold by George Pilling. 1 CD. (Running Time: 1 hr. 3 mins.). (J). (gr. k-4). 2007. audio compact disk 16.95 (978-0-9665930-2-0(2)) Sound Stories.

Soeurs. l.t. ed. Cristina Comencini. (French Ser.). (FRE., 2000. bk. 30.99 (978-2-84011-353-9(8)) Pub: UlverLrgPrint GBR. Dist(s): Ulverscroft US

Sofia Petrovna. Short Stories. Lidiya Chukovskaya & Olga Kagan. Adapted by Mara Kashper. 3 CDs. (Running Time: 4 hrs. 30 min.). (Student Editions in Russian Ser.). (RUS.). (C). 2002. audio compact disk 34.95 (978-1-58510-015-6(3)) Focus Pub-R Pullins.

Soft & Hard: Early Explorers Emergent Set B Audio CD. Katherine Scraper. Adapted by Benchmark Education Staff. (J). 2007. audio compact disk 10.00 (978-1-4108-8209-7(8)) Benchmark Educ.

Soft & Still. abr. ed. Robert A. Monroe. Read by Robert A. Monroe. (Mind Food Ser.). 1983. 14.95 (978-1-56102-415-5(5)) Inter Indus.
Solitude of sea & coastal breezes.

***Soft Focus.** abr. ed. Jayne Ann Krentz. Read by Dick Hill & Susie Breck. (Running Time: 5 hrs.). 2010. audio compact disk 9.99 (978-1-4418-6705-6(8), 9781441867056, BCD Value Price) Brilliance Audio.

Soft Focus. unabr. ed. Jayne Ann Krentz. Read by Dick Hill & Breck Susie. (Running Time: 9 hrs.). 2004. 24.95 (978-1-59600-459-7(2), 1596004592, Brilliance MP3) Brilliance Audio.

Soft Focus. unabr. ed. Jayne Ann Krentz. Read by Dick Hill & Susie Breck. (Running Time: 9 hrs.). 2004. 49.97 (978-1-59600-462-7(2), 1596004622, BADLE); 24.95 (978-1-59600-461-0(4), 1596004614, BAD); 39.25 (978-1-59600-460-3(6), 1596004606, Brlnc Audio MP3 Lib) Brilliance Audio.
Elizabeth Cabot is all business. She knows how to maximize her investments and cut her losses - in both her career and her personal life. So when she discovers that Jack Fairfax has deceived her, she's determined to end their relationship. Putting a stop to their budding romance is easy, but breaking up their business deal will be more difficult. Despite all her efforts, she has no luck disentangling herself from Jack's client company, Excalibur. But the situation becomes even more strained when a lethal act of sabotage threatens to put both their companies out of business for good. Elizabeth is no fool. If she can help Jack save Excalibur, she'll recoup her substantial investment plus millions in profits. Putting her emotions aside, she insists on helping him search for the scientist who's disappeared with a valuable new crystal that could revolutionize their high-tech industry. She'll go in, solve the problem, and get out. The trail leads Elizabeth and Jack to a fringe film festival, but their goal is as elusive as the shadowy black-and-white images from the classic noir films. Life starts to imitate art, and double-dealing seems to be the name of the game. For these business adversaries turned reluctant partners, keeping an eye on each other - and the lid on their sizzling attraction - seems to be the only insurance against further treachery. But with millions at stake, trust can turn to betrayal in the blink of an eye.

***Soft Focus.** unabr. ed. Jayne Ann Krentz. Read by Dick Hill & Susie Breck. (Running Time: 9 hrs.). 2010. audio compact disk 29.99 (978-1-4418-4097-4(4), 9781441840974, Bril Audio CD Unabri); audio compact disk 89.97 (978-1-4418-4098-1(2), 9781441840981, BriAudCD Unabrid) Brilliance Audio.

Soft in the Middle: The Contemporary Softcore Feature in Its Contexts. David Andrews. 2006. audio compact disk 9.95 (978-0-8142-9106-1(6)) Pub: Ohio St U Pr. Dist(s): Chicago Distribution Ctr

Soft May Morn. Bonnie Rideout. 1997. pap. bk. 22.95 (978-0-7866-0663-4(0), 95571P); pap. bk. 27.95 (978-0-7866-0665-8(7), 95571CDP) Mel Bay.

Soft May Morn - Scottish Fiddle. Bonnie Rideout. 2002. bk. 27.95 (978-0-7866-6572-3(6), 95571BCD) Mel Bay.

Soft Metal. 1 CD. 2003. audio compact disk (978-1-932616-06-4(3)) Feng Shui Para.
If You are the Element SOFT METAL...In Feng Shui you are the personal Trigram TUI (pronounced "dewey") and you represent the youngest daughterWhen in balance, you are refined, organized, focused, analytical, and can create order out of chaos. You are creative and visionary, exude clarity, optimism, and charm, and are very social and spiritual in nature.When you are not in balance, you can be obsessive-compulsive, caught up in doing, defensive, withdrawn, and picky. You can be arrogant, emotionally unavailable, isolated and sorrowful.The above is just a brief excerpt from the SOFT METAL audio program. Discover the hidden mysteries of your life, recorded in China's ancient art, history and science. Learn about your lucky number and season, along with the kind of homes and offices that support you, and the types of locations that can deplete your

business, health and finances. You will learn specific power directions to help you negotiate a sale, communicate with your friends and family, increase your wealth, improve your health, along with optimum directions to capitalize on to enhance love and good fortune in your life. This and more is available, today, on Suzee's audio program... SOFT METAL.

Soft Metal. unabr. ed. Max Brand. Read by Lloyd James. 6 cass. (Sagebrush Western Ser.). (J). 2005. 49.95 (978-1-57490-312-6(8)) Pub: ISIS Lrg Prnt GBR. Dist(s): Ulverscroft US

Soft Sell, the New Art of Selling, Self-Empowerment & Persuasion. 3 CDs. (Running Time: 3 hrs.). 2003. audio compact disk 19.95 Penton Overseas.

Soft Selling in a Hard World: Plain Talk on the Art of Persuasion. 2nd rev. ed. 2001. audio compact disk (978-0-9629610-1-4(9)) Vass Co.

Soft Target. Stephen Leather. 13 CDs. (Running Time: 15 hrs. 40 mins.). (Isis (CDs) Ser.). (J). 2005. audio compact disk 99.95 (978-0-7531-2418-5(1)) Pub: ISIS Lrg Prnt GBR. Dist(s): Ulverscroft US

Soft Target. unabr. ed. Stephen Leather. 12 cass. (Running Time: 15 hrs. 40 mins.). (Isis Cassettes Ser.). (J). 2005. 94.95 (978-0-7531-2147-4(6)) Pub: ISIS Lrg Prnt GBR. Dist(s): Ulverscroft US

Soft-Tissue Sarcoma: Patterns of Care & Perspectives for Management: Cancer Symposium. Moderated by Walter Lawrence, Jr. 3 cass. (Spring Sessions Ser.: SP-10). 1986. 28.50 (8682) Am Coll Surgeons.

Soft Wood. 1 CD. 2003. audio compact disk (978-1-932616-07-1(1)) Feng Shui Para.
If You are the Element SOFT WOOD...In Feng Shui you are the personal Trigram SUN (pronounced "soon") and you represent the oldest daughterWhen in balance, you are patient, a clear thinker, open minded, capable of leadership, intelligent, able to thrive under pressure, a good organizer and pragmatic. You are hungry for knowledge and information and loyal to home, family and friends.When you are not in balance, you can be demanding, fault finding, arrogant, judgmental, opportunistic, impatient, always on the edge and addicted to doing, as well as prone to depression.The above is just a brief excerpt from the SOFT WOOD audio program. Discover the hidden mysteries of your life, recorded in China's ancient art, history and science. Learn about your lucky number and season, along with the kind of homes and offices that support you, and the types of locations that can deplete your business, health and finances. You will learn specific power directions to help you negotiate a sale, communicate with your friends and family, increase your wealth, improve your health, along with optimum directions to capitalize on to enhance love and good fortune in your life. This and more is available, today, on Suzee's audio program... SOFT WOOD.

Soft Words, Warm Nights: The Most Romantic Poems Ever Spoken. 1 cass. (Running Time: 45 min.). 1993. 9.95 (978-0-9644619-0-1(0), Word Music); audio compact disk 12.95 CD. (978-0-9644619-1-8(9)) Word Enter.
An anthology of classical & contemporary love/romance poetry.

Softly & Tenderly. Perf. by Bernhard Herms. 1 cass. 1999. 7.99 (978-0-7601-2107-8(9)); audio compact disk 10.99 (978-0-7601-2108-5(7)) Provident Music.

***Softly & Tenderly.** unabr. ed. Sara Evans et al. (Running Time: 9 hrs. 0 mins. 0 sec.). (Songbird Novel Ser.). (ENG.). 2011. audio compact disk 29.99 (978-1-59859-856-8(2)) Oasis Audio.

Softly We Sing. unabr. ed. Kim Mitzo Thompson. Perf. by Karen Mitzo Hilderbrand. 1 CD. (Running Time: 1 hr. 05 min.). (Growing Minds with Music Ser.). (J). 1999. audio compact disk 12.99 CD. (978-1-57583-168-8(6), 165CD) Twin Sisters.
The sweet-sounding voices of children will soothe parents & babies alike during quiet time or bedtime. Each song is played again as an instrumental sing-along.

Software Performance for Jukebox-Based Systems: Off-the-Shelf vs. Customized Software for Jukeboxes. 1 cass. 1990. 8.50 Recorded Res.

Software Protection, Contracts, Tax Reform Impact: An Analysis of Computer Law. 1987. bk. 90.00 incl. book.; 55.00 cass. only.; 35.00 book only. PA Bar Inst.

Software Tools in Pascal: Tape. Brian W. Kernighan & P. L. Plauger. 1976. bk. 99.95 (978-0-201-03668-8(1)) AddisonWesley.

Soham Upasana. Swami Jyotirmayananda. 1 cass. (Running Time: 1 hr.). 1990. 12.99 Yoga Res Foun.

Soho Square. unabr. ed. Claire Rayner. Read by Anne Cater. 10 cass. (Running Time: 14 hrs.). (Performers Ser.: Vol. 4). (J). 2003. 84.95 (978-1-84283-489-3(4)) Pub: ISIS Lrg Prnt GBR. Dist(s): Ulverscroft US

Soil Wetting Agents. 2005. audio compact disk 40.00 (978-0-89118-558-1(5)) Am Soc Agron.

Soir de Demi-Brume. 1 cass. (Running Time: 60 mins.). Dramatization. (Maitres du Mystere Ser.). (FRE.). 1996. 11.95 (1832-MA) Olivia & Hill.
Popular radio thriller, interpreted by France's best actors.

Sojourn. Daughters of St Paul. 2001. audio compact disk 16.95 (978-0-8198-7049-0(8), 332-351) Pauline Bks.

Sojourner & Mollie Sinclair (Floyd) Perf. by Patricia Neway & Norman Treigle. Conducted by Julius Rudel. 1 CD. audio compact disk 16.99 VAI Audio.
Comic one-act opera by the composer of Susannah, with the cast and conductor of the work's premiere.

***Sojourner Truth: From Slave to Activist for Freedom.** unabr. ed. Mary G. Butler. Read by Allyson Johnson. (Running Time: 2 hrs.). (J). 2011. audio compact disk 24.99 (978-1-4558-0182-4(8), 9781455801824, Bril Audio CD Unabri); audio compact disk 29.97 (978-1-61106-485-8(6), 9781611064858, BriAudCD Unabrid) Brilliance Audio.

Solace. Michael Hoppe. 1 CD. (Running Time: 1 hr. 21 min.). 2003. audio compact disk (978-1-891319-75-4(2)) Spring Hill CO.

Solace. Perf. by Mike Rowland. 1 cass. (Running Time: 37 min.). 10.95 Credence Commun.
A sequel to Fairy Ring, Rowland's beautiful piano is supported by lush strings to create an atmosphere of utter tranquility.

Solace (Adagio Music for Relaxation) (YA). 2005. audio compact disk (978-1-59250-619-4(4)) Gaiam Intl.

Solace of Open Spaces & Other Essays. Gretel Ehrlich. Read by Gretel Ehrlich. 2 cass. (Running Time: 2 hrs. 35 min.). 1988. 16.95 (978-0-939643-06-6(5), NrthWrd Bks) TandN Child.
A celebration of life in Wyoming ranch country.

Solace of Sin. unabr. ed. Catherine Cookson. Read by Susan Jameson. 8 cass. (Running Time: 8 hrs.). 1999. 69.95 (978-0-7540-0250-5(0), CAB1673) AudioGO.
With her marriage on the brink of collapse, Constance decides to sell her apartment & buy the house on the moors north of Hexham. To buy it, she has to negotiate with the mysterious Vincent O'Connor. When the house is hers, she discovers that mystery is a way of life with him.

Solace of Sin. unabr. ed. Catherine Cookson. Read by Susan Jameson. 8 CDs. (Running Time: 12 hrs.). 2002. audio compact disk 79.95 (978-0-7540-5523-5(X), CCD 214) Pub: Chivers Pr GBR. Dist(s): AudioGO

***Solace of the Road.** unabr. ed. Siobhan Dowd. Read by Sile Bermingham. 6 CDs. (Running Time: 7 hrs. 5 mins.). (YA). (gr. 8-11). 2009. audio compact disk 50.00 (978-0-7393-8591-3(7), BksonTape) Pub: Random Audio Pubg. Dist(s): Random

Solace of the Road. unabr. ed. Siobhan Dowd. Read by Sile Bermingham. (ENG.). (J). (gr. 9). 2009. audio compact disk 34.00 (978-0-7393-8589-0(5), Listening Lib) Pub: Random Audio Pubg. Dist(s): Random

Solanus Casey: One Man's Journey Toward Sanctity. Michael Crosby. 4 cass. (Running Time: 4 hrs.). 2001. 32.95 (A6670) St Anthony Mess Pr.
Solanus Casey was a Capuchin Franciscan who dies in 1957, after leading a remarkable life. These talks focus on his life story and the invitation that if we realized God's graces, as Solanus did, we would be saints the next day.

***Solar.** unabr. ed. Ian McEwan. Read by Roger Allam. 9 CDs. (Running Time: 11 hrs. 30 mins.). 2010. audio compact disk 34.99 (978-1-4498-1951-4(6)) Recorded Bks.

***Solar.** unabr. ed. Ian McEwan. Read by Roger Allam. 1 Playaway. (Running Time: 12 hrs.). 2010. 64.75 (978-1-4498-0679-8(1)); 82.75 (978-1-4498-0676-7(7)); audio compact disk 123.75 (978-1-4498-0677-4(5)) Recorded Bks.

Solar & Lunar Returns. M. O. Brown. 1 cass. 1992. 8.95 (1015) Am Fed Astrologers.

Solar & Other Returns. Nona G. Press. 1 cass. 1992. 8.95 (1087) Am Fed Astrologers.

Solar Arc Age Method of Predicting. Jan W. Allen. 1 cass. 1992. 8.95 (1003) Am Fed Astrologers.

Solar Conscience - Lunar Conscience. Murray Stein & Josip Pasic. Read by Murray Stein & Josip Pasic. 1 cass. (Running Time: 68 min.). 1994. 10.95 (978-0-7822-0445-2(7), 523) C G Jung IL.

Solar Cooking & Yosemite Restoration. Hosted by Nancy Pearlman. 1 cass. (Running Time: 28 min.). 10.00 (504) Educ Comm CA.

Solar Destiny vs. Lunar Fate. Howard S. Berg. 1 cass. (Running Time: 90 min.). 1988. 8.95 (637) Am Fed Astrologers.

Solar Eclipse. Lee Ferns. 1 cass. 8.95 (659) Am Fed Astrologers.
An AFA Convention workshop tape.

Solar Electric Car Races. Hosted by Nancy Pearlman. 1 cass. (Running Time: 30 min.). 10.00 (1106) Educ Comm CA.

Solar Energy in Germany: A Strategic Reference 2006. Compiled by Icon Group International, Inc. Staff. 2007. ring bd. 195.00 (978-0-497-35985-0(5)) Icon Grp.

Solar Flare. Larry Burkett. 2 cass. (Running Time: 3 hrs.). 1998. 14.99 Set. (978-1-881273-41-7(5)) Northfield Pub.

Solar Labyrinth. Short Stories. (4151) Am Audio Prose.

Solar Return from Beginning to End. Mary Shea. 8.95 (313) Am Fed Astrologers.
Intro & professional tips on interpretation.

Solar Returns. S. Hopkins. Read by S. Hopkins. 1 cass. (Running Time: 90 min.). 1994. 8.95 (1168) Am Fed Astrologers.

Solar Returns. Sophia Mason. Read by Sophia Mason. 1 cass. (Running Time: 90 min.). 1994. 8.95 (1107) Am Fed Astrologers.
Using solar return charts to forecast events.

Solar Returns in Your Life. M. O. Brown. 1 cass. 1992. 8.95 (1016) Am Fed Astrologers.

Solar Revolutions. Susan Horton. 1 cass. 8.95 (165) Am Fed Astrologers.
How to calculate and interpret this predictive tool.

Solar System. Read by Franklyn M. Branley. 1 cass. (Running Time: 26 min.). 14.95 (23560) MMI Corp.
Discusses the sun & its relatives, their satellites, asteroids, comets, meteors, etc.

Solar System: Includes Cassette. unabr. ed. Brad Caudle & Melissa Caudle. Read by Brad Caudle. Illus. by Anthony Guerra. 1 cass. (Running Time: 40 min.). (Rock 'N Learn Ser.). (J). (gr. 2 up). 1997. pap. bk. 12.99 (978-1-878489-60-9(7), RL960) Rock N Learn.
Songs teach the order of the planets & much more. Separate songs for each planet, the sun & the moon. Full-color lyrics book includes illustrations & highly detailed photos from NASA.

Solar System, the Audio CD Theme Set: Set of 6 Set B. Adapted by Benchmark Education Staff. (English Explorers Ser.). (J). (gr. 3-6). 2007. audio compact disk 60.00 (978-1-4108-9815-9(6)) Benchmark Educ.

Solaria: L-Book. Fran Heckrotte. (ENG.). 2008. 14.95 (978-1-934889-18-3(0)) Lbook Pub.

Solaris. unabr. ed. Stanislaw Lem. Narrated by Full Cast. (Running Time: 2 hrs. 0 mins. 0 sec.). (ENG.). 2010. audio compact disk 24.95 (978-1-60283-819-2(4)) Pub: AudioGO. Dist(s): Perseus Dist

***Solaris.** unabr. ed. Stanislaw Lem. Narrated by Michael Kramer. (Running Time: 7 hrs. 30 mins.). 2010. 14.99 (978-1-4001-8993-9(4)) Tantor Media.

***Solaris (Library Edition)** unabr. ed. Stanislaw Lem. Narrated by Michael Kramer. (Running Time: 7 hrs. 30 mins.). 2010. 29.99 (978-1-4001-9993-8(X)) Tantor Media.

Solas. Perf. by Ronan Hardiman. 1 cass. (Running Time: 1 hr.). 8.78 (PHI 539438); audio compact disk 13.58 CD Jewel box. (PHI 539438) NewSound.
Presents original compositions steeped in a rich to ancient Celtic musical heritage.

Solas Con Dios. unabr. ed. Claudio Freidzon. 1 cass. (Running Time: 90 min.). (SPA.). 2001. 7.99 (978-0-8297-3109-5(1)) Pub: Vida Pubs. Dist(s): Zondervan
Description: The songs are: . Hoy quiero Alabarte: 2. Sopla sobre Mi: 3. Nadie como Tu. 4. No hay Nadie como Tu.

Solas con Dios. unabr. ed. Claudio Freidzon. (SPA.). 2001. audio compact disk 11.99 (978-0-8297-3110-1(5)) Pub: Vida Pubs. Dist(s): Zondervan

Sold Out. Radical X Generation. (Running Time: 1 hr.). 2003. audio compact disk 16.98 (978-5-552-41383-6(0)) Pub: Pt of Grace Ent. Dist(s): STL Dist NA

Soldadito de Plomo. l.t. ed. Short Stories. Illus. by Graham Percy. 1 cass. (Running Time: 10 mins.). Dramatization.Tr. of Steadfast Tin Soldier. (SPA.). (J). (ps-3). 2001. 9.95 (978-84-86154-54-7(5)) Peralt Mont ESP.

Soldier see Robert Frost in Recital

Soldier see Twentieth-Century Poetry in English, No. 6, Recordings of Poets Reading Their Own Poetry

Soldier. John Whitman. 1999. (978-1-57042-722-0(4)) Hachet Audio.

Soldier: A Poet's Childhood. June Jordan. Narrated by Robin Miles. 4 cass. (Running Time: 5 hrs.). 38.00 (978-0-7887-8999-1(6)) Recorded Bks.

Soldier: The Life of Colin Powell. abr. ed. Karen DeYoung. Read by Roscoe Orman. (Running Time: 21600 sec.). (ENG.). 2006. audio compact disk 29.95 (978-0-7393-4008-0(5), Random AudioBks) Pub: Random Audio Pubg. Dist(s): Random

Soldier: The Life of Colin Powell. unabr. ed. Karen DeYoung. Read by Coleen Marlo. 18 CDs. (Running Time: 27 hrs.). 2006. audio compact disk 144.00 (978-1-4159-3342-8(1)) Books on Tape.

Soldier Blue. unabr. collector's ed. Theodore V. Olsen. Read by Christopher Lane. 7 cass. (Running Time: 7 hrs.). 1995. 42.00 (978-0-7366-3185-3(2), 3853) Books on Tape.
The Cheyenne chief won't rest until he recaptures the beautiful woman he took for a wife. Can the U.S. soldier protect his charge?.

Soldier in Buckskin. abr. ed. Ray Hogan. Read by Buck Schirner. (Running Time: 10800 sec.). (Five Star Westerns Ser.). 2007. audio compact disk 24.95 (978-1-4233-3579-5(1), 9781423335795, Brilliance MP3) Brilliance Audio.

Soldier in Buckskin. abr. ed. Ray Hogan. Read by Buck Schirner. (Running Time: 3 hrs.). (Five Star Westerns Ser.). 2008. 39.25 (978-1-4233-3582-5(1), 9781423335825, BADLE); 24.95 (978-1-4233-3581-8(3), 9781423335818, BAD) Brilliance Audio.

Soldier in Buckskin. abr. ed. Sunzi. Read by Buck Schirner. (Running Time: 10800 sec.). (Five Star Westerns Ser.). 2007. audio compact disk 39.25 (978-1-4233-3580-1(5), 9781423335801, Brinc Audio MP3 Lib) Brilliance Audio.

Soldier in Buckskin. unabr. ed. Ray Hogan. Read by Larry McKeever. 8 cass. (Running Time: 12 hrs.). 1997. 64.00 (978-0-7366-3815-9(6), 105783) Books on Tape.
Kit Carson, the famed frontiersman, fur trapper, Army scout, military officer & trusted friend to the Indian nations. Set before 1850, this focuses on Carson's relations with the Indians & his marriage to Singing Grass, an Arapaho.

Soldier in Paradise. unabr. ed. John Mort. Read by Jerry Sciarrio. 6 cass. (Running Time: 6 hrs. 30 min.). 2001. 39.95 (978-1-58116-135-9(2)); audio compact disk 39.00 (978-1-58116-136-6(0)) Books in Motion.
Jimmy Donnelly returns home after serving his country as part of the "Lonely Patrol" in Vietnam.

Soldier in the Wheatfield. unabr. ed. Philip Hook. Read by Simon Shepherd. 10 cass. 1999. 84.95 (978-0-7540-0296-3(9), CAB 1719) AudioGO.

Soldier in the Wheatfield, Set. unabr. ed. Philip Hook. Read by Simon Shepherd. 10 cass. 1999. 84.95 (CAB 1719) AudioGO.

Soldier of Fortune. abr. ed. Barry Sadler. Read by Charlton Griffin. 2 vols. (Casca Ser.: No. 8). 2003. (978-1-58807-531-4(1)) Am Pubng Inc.

Soldier of Fortune. abr. ed. Barry Sadler. Read by Charlton Griffin. 2 vols. (Running Time: 3 hrs.). (Casca Ser.: No. 8). 2003. 18.00 (978-1-58807-108-8(1)) Am Pubng Inc.
When Major Shan of Taiwanese military intelligence is contracted to rescue a merchant family from the jungles of Cambodia, he selects Casca aka Casey Romain to do the job. Always waiting for the next inevitable battle, Casey decides to take the offer even though this mission might be his last. In order to even the odds a little, Casey enlists the aid of three friends: a former South Viet soldier named Van, a mountain tribesman known as George, and Phang, a Kamserai bandit familiar with the deadly Cambodian jungles. Together, this rugged and determined band of soldiers race against time and the natural dangers of the jungle to find the family...while a small, but savage Cambodian army led by a ruthless general races after them.

Soldier of Fortune. abr. ed. Barry Sadler. Read by Charlton Griffin. 2 vols. (Casca Ser.: No. 8). 2004. audio compact disk 25.00 (978-1-58807-282-5(7)); audio compact disk (978-1-58807-713-4(6)) Am Pubng Inc.

Soldier of Gideon. Barry Sadler. Read by Charlton Griffin. 2 vols. (Casca Ser.: No. 20). 2004. 18.00 (978-1-58807-120-0(0)); (978-1-58807-560-4(5)) Am Pubng Inc.

Soldier of Peace. unabr. ed. Dan Kurzman. Read by Geoffrey Howard. 14 cass. (Running Time: 21 hrs.). 1999. 112.00 (5022) Books on Tape.
Rabin's evolution from desert warrior to pioneering peacemaker.

Soldier of the Great War. abr. unabr. ed. Mark Helprin. Narrated by David Colacci. (Running Time: 111600 sec.). (ENG.). 2007. audio compact disk 49.95 (978-1-60283-312-8(5)) Pub: AudioGO. Dist(s): Perseus Dist

Soldier of the Great War. unabr. ed. Mark Helprin. Read by David Colacci. (YA). 2008. 124.99 (978-1-60514-506-8(8)) Find a World.

Soldier of the Mist. Gene Wolfe. Read by Ray Verna. 7 cass. (Running Time: 10 hrs.). 1993. 53.60 (978-1-56544-016-6(1), 550015); Rental 9.10 30 day rental Set. (550015) Literate Ear.
Papyrus scrolls found in the basement of the British Museum, apparently unused, are bought by a Detroit dealer & collector. He discovers that the sticks on which the ancient paper was wound contain minute characters which yield the writings of "Latro" & his ancient fantastic world!.

Soldier of the Queen. Philip McCutchan. 8 cass. (Running Time: 9 hrs.). (James Ogilvie Ser.). (J). 2004. 69.95 (978-1-84283-757-3(5)); audio compact disk 79.95 (978-1-84283-874-7(1)) Pub: ISIS Lrg Prnt GBR. Dist(s): Ulverscroft US

Soldier of the Spirit. Michel Carrouges. Read by Wayne Jordan. 9 cass. (Running Time: 9 hrs.). 1987. 39.95 (746) Ignatius Pr.

Soldier Returns: A Long Tan Veteran Discovers the Other Side of Vietnam, unabr. ed. Terry Burstall. Read by Peter Hosking. 6 cass. (Running Time: 9 hrs.). 2001. (978-1-876584-41-2(6), 590895) Bolinda Pubng AUS.
The Vietnamese looked on Long Tan as a key victory for them & in the sequel to The Soldiers' Story. He makes a veteran's emotional journey back to the battlefield after twenty-five years.

Soldier, Sail North. James Pattinson. Read by Michael Tudor Barnes. 7 cass. (Soundings Ser.). (J). 2005. 61.95 (978-1-84283-610-1(2)) Pub: ISIS Lrg Prnt GBR. Dist(s): Ulverscroft US

Soldier Spies: A Men at War Novel. W. E. B. Griffin. Read by Scott Brick. 1999. audio compact disk 88.00 (978-0-7366-5194-3(2)) Books on Tape.

Soldier Spies: A Men at War Novel, abr. ed. W. E. B. Griffin. Read by Stephen Lang. 4 cass. (Men at War Ser.: No. 3). 1999. 24.95 (FS9-50936) Highsmith.

Soldier Spies: A Men at War Novel. unabr. ed. W. E. B. Griffin. Read by Scott Brick. 9 cass. (Running Time: 13 hrs. 30 mins.). 1999. 72.00 (978-0-7366-4646-8(9), 5027) Books on Tape.
November 1942. War is raging in Europe. The invasion of North Africa has begun. In Washington, OSS chief William J. Donovan finds himself fighting a rear-guard battle against rival intelligence chiefs back home. In Morocco, Second Lieutenant Eric Fulmar waits in the desert for a car containing two top-level defectors - or will it be full of SS men instead? And in England, Major Richard Canidy gets the mission of his life: to penetrate into the heart of Germany and bring out the man with the secret of the jet engine, before the Germans grab him first.

Soldier Spies: A Men at War Novel. unabr. ed. W. E. B. Griffin. Read by Scott Brick. 11 CDs. (Running Time: 16 hrs. 30 mins.). (Men at War Ser.: No. 3). 2001. audio compact disk 88.00 Books on Tape.

Soldier Spies: A Men at War Novel, unabr. ed. W. E. B. Griffin. Read by Scott Brick. 9 cass. (Running Time: 13 hrs. 30 mins.). (Men at War Ser.: No. 3). 2000. 72.00 (5027) Books on Tape.
Story about the O.S.S. agents during World War II.

Soldiers & Heroes: The Poems of Kipling & Macaulay. Poems. National Theatre Staff. 1 cass. 10.95 (ECN 208) J Norton Pubs.
Side 1 contains Kipling's "Barrack Room Ballads" depicting the lot of 'Tommy Atkins' - the soubriquet gives to the common British soldier. Side 2 offers an extract, "Horatius," from 'the Lays of Ancient Rome' based on the ballad tradition of Scotland & England.

Soldier's Heart. Gary Paulsen. Read by George Wendt. 2 cass. (Running Time: 2 hrs.). (J). 2000. 18.00 (978-0-7366-9011-9(5)) Books on Tape.
The nightmare of the Civil War, based on the real life experiences of a young enlistee.

Soldier's Heart. Gary Paulsen. Read by George Wendt. 2 vols. (Running Time: 1 hr. 39 mins.). (J). (gr. 7 up). 2004. pap. bk. 29.00 (978-0-8072-8301-1(0), Listening Lib) Random Audio Pubg.

Soldier's Heart. unabr. ed. Gary Paulsen. Read by George Wendt. 2 cass. (Running Time: 1 hr. 39 mins.). (J). (gr. 7 up). 2004. 23.00 (978-0-8072-8300-4(2), LL0185, Listening Lib) Random Audio Pubg.
Includes an exclusive author interview.

Soldiers of an Unfinished Revolution. Rick Joyner. 1 cass. (Running Time: 90 mins.). (Church History & the Coming Move of God Ser.: Vol. 6). 2000. 5.00 (RJ11-006) Morning NC.
Church history is brought to life with practical applications & insights into how the enemy uses the same strategy against every new move of God.

Soldiers of Faith: Crusaders & Moslems at War. unabr. ed. Ronald C. Finucane. Narrated by Peter Johnson. 6 cass. (Running Time: 8 hrs. 15 mins.). 1988. 51.00 (978-1-55690-483-7(5), 88280E7) Recorded Bks.
The great crusades of the middle ages swept men & women up in an irresistible current of events. Homes, farms & families were abandoned in pursuit of a cause greater than men had ever known - the rescue of the Holy Land from the unbeliever.

Soldiers of Fortune, unabr. ed. Richard Harding Davis. Read by Flo Gibson. 5 cass. (Running Time: 7 hrs.). 1997. 20.95 (978-1-55685-496-5(X), 496-X) Audio Bk Con.
Adventurers, engineers & miners from the U.S. become involved in a South American revolution. A beautiful love story is intertwined.

Soldiers of Halla. unabr. ed. D. J. MacHale. Read by William Dufris. (Running Time: 18 hrs.). (Pendragon Ser.: Bk. 10). 2009. 44.97 (978-1-59737-314-2(1), 9781597373142, BADLE); 29.99 (978-1-59737-313-5(3), 9781597373135, BAD); 39.97 (978-1-59737-312-8(5), 9781597373128, Brilnc Audio MP3 Lib); 24.99 (978-1-59737-311-1(7), 9781597373111, Brilliance MP3); audio compact disk 69.97 (978-1-59737-310-4(9), 9781597373104, BriAudCD Unabrid); audio compact disk 29.99 (978-1-59737-309-8(5), 9781597373098, Bril Audio CD Unabri) Brilliance Audio.
Please enter a Synopsis.

***Soldiers of the Cross.** Contrib. by Joseph Linn. (ENG.). 1994. audio compact disk 90.00 (978-0-00-503056-1(0)) Lillenas.

Soldiers' Pay. unabr. collector's ed. William Faulkner. Read by Wolfram Kandinsky. 9 cass. (Running Time: 13 hrs. 30 min.). 1994. 72.00 (978-0-7366-2839-6(8), 3547) Books on Tape.
Disillusion & fulfillment, sensuality & beauty, love & hate - all blended with humor, insight & pity in Faulkner's first novel.

Soldier's Promise: The Heroic True Story of an American Soldier & an Iraqi Boy. abr. ed. Daniel Hendrex. Read by Lee Sellars. Told to Wes Smith. 2006. 17.95 (978-0-7435-5577-7(5), Audioworks) Pub: S&S Audio. Dist(s): S and S Inc

Soldier's Return. Melvyn Bragg. Read by Mark McGann. 2003. audio compact disk 79.95 (978-0-7540-8774-8(3)) Pub: Chivers Audio Bks GBR. Dist(s): AudioGO

Soldier's Return. unabr. ed. Melvyn Bragg. Read by Mark McGann. 8 cass. 2000. 69.95 (978-0-7540-0419-6(8), CAB 1842) AudioGO.
In the Spring of 1946, ex-corporal Samuel Richardson returns home from World War II to his wife, Ellen. He finds a town in which little has changed. Sam, however, has changed: the war has left him with traumatic memories, while Ellen has gained a sense of independence. And there's six-year-old Joe, a baby when Sam volunteered, who can scarcely remember his father. As all three strive to adjust, the bonds of love & loyalty become stretched to a breaking point..

Soldier's Stand see Twentieth-Century Poetry in English, No. 24, Recordings of Poets Reading Their Own Poetry

Soldiers' Story: The Battle at Xa Long Tan Vietnam, August 18, 1966. unabr. ed. Terry Burstall. Read by Peter Hosking. 5 cass. (Running Time: 7 hrs. 30 mins.). 2001. (978-1-876584-40-5(8), 590791) Bolinda Pubng AUS.
The controversial Battle at Xa Long Tan was not only a critical episode in Australia's Vietnam involvement, it was also a textbook nightmare in the history of jungle warfare. Reconstructing this dramatic action from secret documents & the vivid recollections of many diggers who fought at Long Tan. This is a challenge of the official army version.

Soldiers' Story: Vietnam in their Own Words. unabr. ed. Ron Steinman. 10 cass. (Running Time: 15 hrs.). 2001. 80.00 (978-0-7366-6201-7(4)) Books on Tape.
This powerful book brings to life the triumphs and tragedies experienced by American soldiers in Vietnam.

Soldier's Testament see Classical Russian Poetry

Soldier's Wife. unabr. ed. Mary Sydney Burke. Read by Marlene Sidaway. 6 cass. (Running Time: 5 hrs. 45 mins.). (Isis Audio Reminiscence Ser.). (J). 2002. 54.95 (978-0-7531-1304-2(X)) Pub: ISIS Lrg Prnt GBR. Dist(s): Ulverscroft US
In this light-hearted true story, Mary Sydney Burke relates how she strove to bring up her children in wartime England on a meager army allowance while her husband was on active service with the Grenadier Guards. After being reunited for a spell of post-war duty in Singapore, the family returned to England before finally migrating to Austrailia in a spirit of adventure and hope. She writes frankly of the later problems caused by her husband's failing health, during which she struggled to keep the family from falling apart. Her indomitable spirit and deep faith shine out in a story by turns amusing, moving and perceptive.

Soldier's Wife. unabr. ed. Rachel Moore. Read by Tanya Myers. 9 cass. (Running Time: 12 hrs.). (Story Sound Ser.). (J). 2005. 76.95 (978-1-85903-853-6(0)) Pub: Mgna Lrg Print GBR. Dist(s): Ulverscroft US

***Soldiers without Borders.** unabr. ed. Ian McPhedran. Read by Peter Byrne. (Running Time: 12 hrs. 17 mins.). 2010. 43.95 (978-1-74214-761-1(5), 9781742147611) Pub: Bolinda Pubng AUS. Dist(s): Bolinda Pub Inc

***Soldiers Without Borders: Beyond the SAS - A Global Network of Brothers-in-Arms.** unabr. ed. Ian McPhedran. Read by Peter Byrne. (Running Time: 12 hrs. 17 mins.). 2010. audio compact disk 103.95 (978-1-74214-704-8(6), 9781742147048) Pub: Bolinda Pubng AUS. Dist(s): Bolinda Pub Inc

Sole Survivor. Ruthanne Lum McCumm. Read by Johanna Ward. (Running Time: 7 hrs.). 2002. 27.95 (978-1-59912-603-6(6)) Iofy Corp.

Sole Survivor, abr. ed. Derek Hansen. Read by Christopher Cazenove. 4 cass. 1999. 25.00 (FS9-43395) Highsmith.

Sole Survivor. unabr. ed. Derek Hansen. Read by Peter Wickham. 12 cass. (Running Time: 18 hrs.). 2001. (500738) Bolinda Pubng AUS.

Sole Survivor. unabr. ed. Dean Koontz. Read by David Birney. (Running Time: 12 hrs. 30 mins.). (Dean Koontz Ser.). (ENG.). 2006. audio compact disk 29.95 (978-0-7393-3423-2(9), Random AudioBks) Pub: Random Audio Pubg. Dist(s): Random

Sole Survivor: A Story of Record Endurance at Sea. unabr. ed. Ruthanne Lum McCunn. Read by Johanna Ward. 5 cass. (Running Time: 7 hrs.). 2002. 39.95 (978-0-7861-2312-4(5), 2998); audio compact disk 48.00 (978-0-7861-9436-0(7), 2998) Blckstn Audio.
On November 23, 1942, German U-Boats torpedoed the British ship Benlomond, and it sank in the Atlantic in two minutes. The sole survivor was a second steward named Poon Lim, who, with no knowledge of the sea, managed to stay alive for 133 days on a small wooden raft. Sole Survivor, based on three years of interviews with Poon, reconstructs his remarkable ordeal.

Soli Deo Gloria Beneath the Tree of Life: A Communion Service for All the Churches. Marty Haugen. 1 cass. 1999. 10.95 (CS-463); audio compact disk 15.95 (CD-463) GIA Pubns.

Solicitation of Clients under the New Rules of Professional Conduct. Read by Frank J. Benasutti. 1 cass. 1989. 20.00 (AL-64) PA Bar Inst.

Soliciting the Major Gift. Julian Padowicz. Read by Julian Padowicz. 1 cass. (Running Time: 40 min.). 1996. bk. 14.95 (978-1-881288-13-8(7), BFI AudioBooks) BusnFilm Intl.
How-to for fund raising solicitors - instructions in face-to-face solicitation.

Solid & Medical Waste Treatment Services in China: A Strategic Reference 2006. Compiled by Icon Group International, Inc. Staff. 2007. ring bd. 195.00 (978-0-497-35895-2(6)) Icon Grp.

Solid As a Rock. Dennis Allen & Nan Allen. 1 cass. (Running Time: 55 min.). (YA). 1992. 80.00 (MU-9147C); audio compact disk 80.00 (MU-9147T) Lillenas.
Youth will be enthusiastic to perform the contemporary songs made popular by their favorite Christian artists, like Petra, Al Denson, Michael English, First Call & 4Him. Use as a choral collection for 2 & 3-part choir; in small thematic packages as a complete musical. Complete accompaniment attractively recorded on stereo cassette. Side A, split-channel; Side B, stereo trax.

Solid As the Rock. Contrib. by Nan Allen. Arranged by Dennis Allen. 1 cass. (Running Time: 55 min.). (YA). 1992. 12.99 (TA-9147C) Lillenas.

Solid Foundation for Growth. Swami Amar Jyoti. 1 cass. 1987. 9.95 (M-69) Truth Consciousness.
The hard work of foundation building. On temptation & fair means. Fear, a major cause of illness. Our zero point, the bottom line, starting point on the path.

Solid Gold Marketing Tactics: Tips & Strategies to Increase Your Response. Sheryl L. Roush. (ENG.). 2000. audio compact disk 19.95 (978-1-880878-05-7(4)) Sparkle Present.

Solid Gold Newsletter Design: 253 Treasures, Tips, Tools & Techniques for Turning Your Newsletter into a "Gold Mine" Sheryl L. Roush. 1 cass. (Running Time: 90 mins.). (YA). (gr. 7-12). 2000. 19.95; audio compact disk 19.95 Sparkle Present.
Discover how to: promote your organization, communicate your message & market your product, service, business or ideas.

Solid Gold Newsletter Design: 253 Treasures, Tips, Tools & Techniques for Turning Your Newsletter into a "Gold Mine" Sheryl L. Roush. 1 CD. (Running Time: 90 mins.). (YA). (gr. 7-12). 2000. per. 39.95; per. 39.95 Sparkle Present.

Solid Gold Soul: 1966. 1 cass. 1999. 9.99 (TYA9Z6); audio compact disk 9.99 (TZA920) Time-Life.

Solid Shapes! Sundance/Newbridge, LLC Staff. (Early Math Ser.). (gr. k-1). 2000. 12.00 (978-1-58273-885-7(8)) Sund Newbrdge.

Solid Tax Planning Tips for Self-Employed Clients. Joseph R. Oliver. 1 cass. (Running Time: 8 hrs.). 1995. 119.00 incl. wkbk. (752380EZ) Am Inst CPA.
The best interests of your self-employed clients are pointed out in this comprehensive course. You'll find a wealth of innovative tips & techniques that will save taxes & protect self-employed clients from embarrassing & costly tax traps.

Solid Truth about States of Matter with Max Axiom, Super Scientist. Agnieszka Biskup. (Graphic Science Ser.). (ENG.). (gr. 3-4). 2009. audio compact disk 6.95 (978-1-4296-4222-4(X)) CapstoneDig.

Solid Waste Equipment & Services in Mexico: A Strategic Reference 2007. Compiled by Icon Group International, Inc. Staff. 2007. ring bd. 195.00 (978-0-497-82360-3(8)) Icon Grp.

Soliloquies see Poetry of Geoffrey

Soliloquy of the Spanish Cloister see Browning's Last Duchess

Solitaire Mystery. unabr. ed. Jostein Gaarder. Read by Barrett Whitener. 6 cass. (Running Time: 9 hrs.). 1997. 48.00 (978-0-7366-3668-1(4), 4343) Books on Tape.
Memoir of a sailor shipwrecked in 1842 on a strange island where a deck of cards has come to life.

***Solitary.** unabr. ed. Alexander Gordon Smith. Read by Alex Kalajzic. (Running Time: 7 hrs.). (Escape from Furnace Ser.). (YA). 2010. 24.99 (978-1-4418-4286-2(1), 9781441842862, Brilliance MP3); 39.97 (978-1-4418-4287-9(X), 9781441842879, Brlnc Audio MP3 Lib); 24.99 (978-1-4418-4288-6(8), 9781441842886, BAD); 39.97 (978-1-4418-4289-3(6), 9781441842893, BADLE); audio compact disk 24.99 (978-1-4418-4284-8(5), 9781441842848, Bril Audio CD Unabri); audio compact disk 60.97 (978-1-4418-4285-5(3), 9781441842855, BriAudCD Unabrid) Brilliance Audio.

***Solitary: A Novel.** unabr. ed. Travis Thrasher. (Running Time: 10 hrs. 0 mins. 0 sec.). (Solitary Tales Ser.). (ENG.). 2011. audio compact disk 29.99 (978-1-59859-878-0(3)) Oasis Audio.

Solitary Blue, unabr. ed. Cynthia Voigt. Narrated by Jeff Woodman. 6 pieces. (Running Time: 8 hrs. 30 mins.). (Tillerman Cycle Ser.: Bk. 3). (gr. 7 up). 1998. 51.00 (978-0-7887-1910-3(6), 95331E7) Recorded Bks.
Moving tale of a youngster discovering genuine family love. If Jeff is perfect, maybe his father won't leave like his mother. A teenaged boy's struggles to accept himself before he can really know others.

Solitary Blue, unabr. ed. Cynthia Voigt. Read by Jeff Woodman. 6 cass. (Running Time: 8 hrs. 30 mins.). (Tillerman Cycle Ser.: Bk. 3). (YA). (gr. 6). 1998. 75.00 (978-0-7887-1938-7(6), 40645) Recorded Bks.
A teenage boy's poignant struggle to accept himself before he can really know others.

Solitary Cyclist see Return of Sherlock Holmes

Solitary Daffodil see Twentieth-Century Poetry in English, No. 26, Recordings of Poets Reading Their Own Poetry

Solitary Freedom: Meditations for Piano. Contrib. by Peter B. Allen. (Running Time: 1 hr 5 min.). 2004. audio compact disk 15.95 (978-5-559-78856-2(2)) Pub: Pt of Grace Ent. Dist(s): STL Dist NA

Solitary Freedom Piano. Peter B. Allen. 2004. pap. bk. 24.95 (978-5-559-78365-9(X)) Pub: Pt of Grace Ent. Dist(s): STL Dist NA

***Solitary Man.** Stephen Leather. 2010. 99.95 (978-0-7531-4130-4(2)); audio compact disk 104.95 (978-0-7531-4131-1(0)) Pub: Isis Pubng Ltd GBR. Dist(s): Ulverscroft US

Solitary Man. unabr. ed. Stephen Leather. Read by Steven Pacey. 14 cass. (Running Time: 14 hrs.). 1998. 110.95 (978-0-7540-0113-3(X), CAB1536) AudioGO.
Chris Hutchinson is on the run. Imprisoned for a crime he didn't commit, Hutch escapes from a maximum security prison & begins a new life in Hong Kong. But when a face from the past catches up with him, Hutch is forced to help a former terrorist break out of Bangkok Prison. Journalist Jennifer Leigh is convinced there is more to Hutch's story than meets the eye & he could be her ticket to the front page.

Solitary Reaper see Treasury of William Wordsworth

Solitary Reaper see Selected Poetry of William Wordsworth

Solitary Shores. Doug Wood. 2005. audio compact disk 14.95 (978-0-9719971-5-8(2)) Pub: Wind In The Pines. Dist(s): Adventure Pubns

Solitary Thyroid Nodule - Diagnosis & Treatment. 2 cass. (Otorhinolaryngology Ser.: C85-OT4). 1985. 15.00 (8576) Am Coll Surgeons.

Solitude see Children

Solitude: Breaking the Heart. Read by Thomas Merton. 1 cass. (Running Time: 60 min.). (Thomas Merton Ser.). 8.95 Credence Commun.

Solitude & Resurrection. Thomas Merton. 1 cass. (Running Time: 60 min.). (Solitude Ser.). 8.95 (AA2100) Credence Commun.
Merton speaks on the attitudes which led him to live a hermits life for a time.

Solitude & Sacred Places in Shamanic Training. Jack Norton. 1 cass. 9.00 (A0386-88) Sound Photosyn.
From ICSS '88 with Sarah Dubin-Vaughn.

Solitude of Latin America, Program 1. Read by Gabriel García Márquez. (F007AB090) Natl Public Radio.

Solitude of Prime Numbers. unabr. ed. Paolo Giordano. Read by Luke Daniels. 6 CDs. (Running Time: 7 hrs.).Tr. of Solitudine Dei Numeri Primi. 2010. audio compact disk 29.99 (978-1-4418-3671-7(3), 9781441836717, Bril Audio CD Unabri) Brilliance Audio.

***Solitude of Prime Numbers.** unabr. ed. Paolo Giordano. Read by Luke Daniels. (Running Time: 8 hrs.).Tr. of Solitudine Dei Numeri Primi. 2010. 24.99 (978-1-4418-3675-5(6), 9781441836755, BAD); 39.97 (978-1-4418-3674-8(8), 9781441836748, Brlnc Audio MP3 Lib); 39.97 (978-1-4418-3676-2(4), 9781441836762, BADLE); 24.99 (978-1-4418-3673-1(X), 9781441836731, Brilliance MP3); audio compact disk 89.97 (978-1-4418-3672-4(1), 9781441836724, BriAudCD Unabrid) Brilliance Audio.

Solitude of Thomas Cave. unabr. ed. Georgina Harding. Read by John Lee. (Running Time: 19800 sec.). 2007. 44.95 (978-1-4332-0760-0(5)); audio compact disk 29.95 (978-1-4332-0762-4(1)) Blckstn Audio.

Solitude of Thomas Cave. unabr. ed. Georgina Harding & John Lee. (Running Time: 19800 sec.). 2007. audio compact disk 45.00 (978-1-4332-0761-7(3)) Blckstn Audio.

Solitudine Dei Numeri Primi see Solitude of Prime Numbers

Solo. Jill Mansell. Read by Penelope Freeman. 13 CDs. (Running Time: 14 hrs. 48 mins.). (Isis (CDs) Ser.). (J). 2005. audio compact disk 99.95 (978-0-7531-2437-6(8)) Pub: ISIS Lrg Prnt GBR. Dist(s): Ulverscroft US

Solo. unabr. ed. Jill Mansell. 12 cass. (Running Time: 14 hrs. 48 mins.). (Isis Cassettes Ser.). (J). 2005. 94.95 (978-0-7531-1657-9(X)) Pub: ISIS Lrg Prnt GBR. Dist(s): Ulverscroft US

Solo Alabanza, Volume 2. Created by Canzion. (SPA.). 2008. audio compact disk 11.99 (978-0-8297-5436-0(9)) Pub: CanZion. Dist(s): Zondervan

Solo en Una Cancion (Gustavo Velázquez) 1. 1998. 5.00 (978-1-59305-044-3(5)); audio compact disk 5.00 (978-1-59305-043-6(7)) Good News Prod Intl.

Solo Guitar Playing, Vol. 1. Frederick Noad. (ENG.). 1996. audio compact disk 12.95 (978-0-7210-0566-9(7), 0721005667) H Leonard.

Solo Impressions: For Timpani & Piano. Vic Firth. 2004. audio compact disk 19.95 (978-0-8258-4557-4(2)) Fischer Inc NY.

Solo Jazz Piano: The Linear Approach. Composed by Neil Olmstead. 2003. audio compact disk 39.95 (978-0-634-00761-3(0), 50449444, Berklee Pr) H Leonard.

Solo la Muerte see Pablo Neruda Reading His Poetry

Solo Plus: My First Recital for Alto Saxophone with Piano Accompaniment. David Pearl. (Solo Plus Ser.). 2004. audio compact disk 12.95 (978-0-8256-1682-2(4), AM947452) Pub: Music Sales. Dist(s): H Leonard

Solo Plus: My First Recital for Clarinet with Piano Accompaniment. David Pearl. (Solo Plus Ser.). 2004. audio compact disk 12.95 (978-0-8256-1680-8(8), AM947430) Pub: Music Sales. Dist(s): H Leonard

Solo Plus: My First Recital for Trumpet with Piano Accompaniment. David Pearl. (Solo Plus Ser.). 2004. audio compact disk 12.95 (978-0-8256-1683-9(2), AM947463) Pub: Music Sales. Dist(s): H Leonard

Solo Plus: My First Recital for Violin with Piano Accompaniment. David Pearl. (Solo Plus Ser.). 2004. audio compact disk 12.95 (978-0-8256-1656-3(5), AM945714) Pub: Music Sales. Dist(s): H Leonard

Solo Plus: Trumpet with Piano Accompaniment. David Pearl. 1 CD. (Running Time: 1 hr.). (Solo Plus Ser.). 1998. audio compact disk 12.95 (978-0-8256-1651-8(4), AM945660) Pub: Music Sales. Dist(s): H Leonard

Solo Plus Clarinet: Standards & Jazz with Piano Accompaniment. (Solo Plus Ser.). 1998. audio compact disk 12.95 (978-0-8256-1665-5(4), AM947474) Pub: Music Sales. Dist(s): H Leonard

Solo Solutions 4 Guitar: 3 Steps to Successful Lead Guitar Playing. Chris Korblein. 1999. pap. bk. 19.95 (978-0-7866-5260-0(8)) Voggenreiter Pubs DEU.

Soloist. unabr. ed. Steve Lopez. Read by William Hughes. (Running Time: 23400 sec.). 2008. 19.95 (978-1-4332-1521-6(7)); 44.95 (978-1-4332-1519-3(5)); audio compact disk 29.95 (978-1-4332-1523-0(3)); audio compact disk & audio compact disk 60.00 (978-1-4332-1520-9(9)) Blckstn Audio.

Soloist. unabr. ed. Steve Lopez. Read by William Hughes. (Running Time: 23400 sec.). 2009. audio compact disk 19.95 (978-1-4332-1522-3(5)) Blckstn Audio.

Solomon see Salomon

Solomon. 1998. 20.95 (978-1-57972-301-9(2)) Insight Living.

Solomon. Charles R. Swindoll. 2008. audio compact disk 34.00 (978-1-57972-832-8(4)) Insight Living.

Solomon & the Witch see Dylan Thomas Reads the Poetry of W. B. Yeats & Others

Solomon Gursky Was Here. Mordecai Richler. (Running Time: 30 min.). 1990. 8.95 (AMF-230) Am Audio Prose.
Richler talks about Canada, history, bootleggers, judaism, & cultural snobbery.

Solomon: The First Recordings, 1942-43. Solomon. (Running Time: 1 hr. 18 mins.). lp Audio Bks Ltd GBR.

Solomon vs. Lord. 2005. 72.95 (978-0-7861-4358-0(4)) Blckstn Audio.

Solomon vs. Lord. Paul Levine. Read by Christopher Lane. (Running Time: 43200 sec.). 2005. audio compact disk 90.00 (978-0-7861-7497-3(8)) Blckstn Audio.

Solomon vs. Lord. unabr. ed. Paul Levine. Read by Christopher Lane. 2005. 29.95 (978-0-7861-7812-4(4)) Blckstn Audio.

Solomon's Angels. Doreen Virtue. 2008. audio compact disk 23.95 (978-1-4019-2324-2(0)) Hay House.

Solomon's Fine Featherless Friends. Esther Hicks & Jerry Hicks. Read by Jerry Hicks. (Sara Ser.: Bk. 2). 2008. audio compact disk 19.95 (978-1-4019-2026-5(8)) Hay House.

Solomon's Mines see Poetry of Geoffrey

***Solomon's Oak: A Novel.** unabr. ed. Jo-Ann Mapson. (Running Time: 11 hrs. 0 mins. 0 sec.). (ENG.). 2010. 24.99 (978-1-4001-6899-6(6)); 17.99 (978-1-4001-8899-4(7)); audio compact disk 34.99 (978-1-4001-1899-1(9)) Pub: Tantor Media. Dist(s): IngramPubServ

***Solomon's Oak (Library Edition) A Novel.** unabr. ed. Jo-Ann Mapson. (Running Time: 11 hrs. 0 mins. 0 sec.). (ENG.). 2010. audio compact disk 83.99 (978-1-4001-4899-8(5)) Pub: Tantor Media. Dist(s): IngramPubServ

Solomons Seal. unabr. collector's ed. Hammond Innes. Read by Dan Lazar. 8 cass. (Running Time: 12 hrs.). 1986. 64.00 (978-0-7366-0862-6(1), 1813) Books on Tape.
A beautiful young heiress, Perenna Holland, falls on hard times & enlists Roy Slingsby, estate agent to sell the family manse. He uncovers an album of stamps with a singular story to tell. Tracing its origin, he joins a ship where the cargo is contraband, sails to an island seething with rebellion & finds the stamps are rooted to a dark secret in Perenna's family. How will she take this information?.

Solomon's Song. Bryce Courtenay. Read by Humphrey Bower. (Running Time: 19 hrs. 25 mins.). 2009. 114.99 (978-1-74214-206-7(0), 9781742142067) Pub: Bolinda Pubng AUS. Dist(s): Bolinda Pub Inc

Solomon's Song. unabr. ed. Bryce Courtenay. Narrated by Humphrey Bower. 13 cass. (Running Time: 19 hrs. 25 mins.). 2000. 104.00 (978-1-74030-142-8(0)) Pub: Bolinda Pubng AUS. Dist(s): Bolinda Pub Inc

Solomon's Song. unabr. ed. Bryce Courtenay. Read by Humphrey Bower. 17 CDs. (Running Time: 19 hrs. 25 mins.). 2001. audio compact disk 123.95 (978-1-74030-394-1(6)) Pub: Bolinda Pubng AUS. Dist(s): Bolinda Pub Inc

Solomon's Song. unabr. ed. Bryce Courtenay. Read by Humphrey Bower. (Running Time: 19 hrs. 25 mins.). 2009. 54.95 (978-1-74214-478-8(0), 9781742144788) Pub: Bolinda Pubng AUS. Dist(s): Bolinda Pub Inc

Solos for Young Cellists, Vol. 2. Ed. by Carey Cheney. Compiled by Carey Cheney. 1 CD. (Running Time: 1 hr. 30 min.). (ENG.). 2003. audio compact disk 13.95 (978-1-58951-217-7(0)) Alfred Pub.

Solos for Young Cellists: Selections from the Cello Repertoire. Carey Cheney. (ENG.). 2006. audio compact disk 13.95 (978-0-7390-3880-2(X)) Alfred Pub.

Solos for Young Cellists: Selections from the Cello Repertoire. Contrib. by Carey Cheney & David Dunford. (Solos for Young Cellists Ser.). (ENG.). 2006. audio compact disk 14.95 (978-0-7390-3881-9(8)) Alfred Pub.

Solos for Young Cellists: Selections from the Cello Repertoire. Contrib. by Carey Cheney & David Dunford. (Solos for Young Cellists Ser.). (ENG.). 2007. audio compact disk 13.95 (978-0-7390-4676-0(4)); audio compact disk 13.95 (978-0-7390-4678-4(0)) Alfred Pub.

Solos for Young Cellists, Vol 1: Selections from the Cello Repertoire. Carey Cheney. (ENG.). 2003. audio compact disk 13.95 (978-1-58951-216-0(2)) Alfred Pub.

Solos for Young Cellists, Vol 3: Selections from the Cello Repertoire. Carey Cheney. (ENG.). 2005. audio compact disk 13.95 (978-1-58951-218-4(9)) Alfred Pub.

Solos for Young Cellists, Vol 4: Selections from the Cello Repertoire. Carey Cheney. (ENG.). 2005. audio compact disk 13.95 (978-1-58951-219-1(7)) Alfred Pub.

Solos for Young Violinists: Selections from the Student Repertoire. Contrib. by Barbara Barber & Trudi Post. (ENG.). 1995. audio compact disk 13.95 (978-0-7579-2438-5(7)); audio compact disk 13.95 (978-0-7579-2440-8(9)); audio compact disk 13.95 (978-0-7579-2439-2(5)); audio compact disk 13.95 (978-0-7579-2437-8(9)) Alfred Pub.

Solos for Young Violinists: Selections from the Student Repertoire. Contrib. by Barbara Barber & Trudi Post. (ENG.). 1995. audio compact disk 13.95 (978-0-7579-2436-1(0)) Alfred Pub.

Solos for Young Violists, Vol 1: Selections from the Viola Repertoire. Barbara Barber. (ENG.). 2003. audio compact disk 13.95 (978-1-58951-189-7(1)) Alfred Pub.

Solos for Young Violists, Vol 2: Selections from the Viola Repertoire. Barbara Barber. (ENG.). 2003. audio compact disk 13.95 (978-1-58951-190-3(5)) Alfred Pub.

Solos for Young Violists, Vol 3: Selections from the Viola Repertoire. Barbara Barber. (ENG.). 2003. audio compact disk 13.95 (978-1-58951-191-0(3)) Alfred Pub.

Solos for Young Violists, Vol 4: Selections from the Viola Repertoire. Barbara Barber. (ENG.). 2004. audio compact disk 13.95 (978-1-58951-192-7(1)) Alfred Pub.

Solos for Young Violists, Vol 5: Selections from the Viola Repertoire. Barbara Barber. (ENG.). 2004. audio compact disk 13.95 (978-1-58951-193-4(X)) Alfred Pub.

Solos Plus Classical Flute: With Piano Accompaniment. David Pearl. 1 CD. (Running Time: 1 hr.). (Solo Plus Ser.). 1998. audio compact disk 12.95 (978-0-8256-1649-5(2), AM 945648) Pub: Music Sales. Dist(s): H Leonard

Solos Young Violinists V-2/Cd, Vol. 2. Barbara Barber. (ENG.). 1995. audio compact disk 13.95 (978-0-7692-5259-9(1), Warner Bro) Alfred Pub.

Solstice. Short Stories. James Patrick Kelly. Narrated by Pat Bottino. 2 CDs. (Running Time: 1 hr. 31 min.). (Great Science Fiction Stories Ser.). 2005. audio compact disk 14.99 (978-1-884612-41-1(5)) AudioText.

Solstice. Joyce Carol Oates. Read by Joyce Carol Oates. 1 cass. (Running Time: 30 min.). 8.95 (AMF-25) Am Audio Prose.
The author reads from her novel & talks about seasonal mood changes & artistic vampirism.

Solstice. unabr. ed. James Patrick Kelly. 1 cass. (Running Time: 1 hr. 30 min.). 1998. 11.99 (978-1-884612-28-2(8)) AudioText.
A famous drug artist wants a woman who would be uniquely his. All it took was some of his genetically sculptured cells & lots of money. The result was not his daughter nor was it exactly his clone.

Solstice Points. Bobbye Bratcher-Hill. 1 cass. 8.95 (036) Am Fed Astrologers.
Importance of solstice points in all chart work.

Soluciones. Carlos Gonzalez. 1 cass. (Running Time: 40 mins). (SPA.). 2004. audio compact disk 15.00 (978-1-56491-108-7(X)) Imagine Pubs.

Solution. unabr. ed. Joe Vitale. Read by Joe Vitale. (Running Time: 1 hr.). (ENG.). 2009. 10.98 (978-1-59659-392-3(X), GildAudio) Pub: Gildan Media. Dist(s): HachBkGrp

Solution Kit 1: Launching Your Solution. Laurel Mellin. Ed. by Kristen Shepos-Salvatore. Illus. by Teka Luttrell. 2003. bk. 99.95 (978-1-893265-51-6(X)) Sweetest Fruit Pr.

Solution to Problems. Swami Amar Jyoti. 1 cass. 1979. 9.95 (J-22) Truth Consciousness.
Problems are complexities, solution is always simple. When spirituality guides each fiber of our existence, problems are over.

Solutions for LDS Families. Paula Fellingham. 5 cass. 2004. 19.95 (978-1-59156-290-0(2)); audio compact disk 19.95 (978-1-59156-291-7(0)) Covenant Comms.

Solutions Manual for Air Quality. 4th ed. Thad Godish. (C). 2003. audio compact disk (978-1-56670-677-3(7)) CRC Pr.

Solutions, Relaxation or Understanding of Tense, Anxious, Depressive, Hostile (Irritable) & Disgust States & Problems, Russell E. Mason. Read by Russell E. Mason. 6 cass. (Running Time: 5 hrs. 54 min.). 1976. pap. bk. 45.00 (978-0-89533-010-9(5), 59.GT-DH) F I Comm.
Guides for purposeful relaxation & desired positive substitution for each of seven negative, bodily feeling states, along with focus on associated attitudes & behavior.

Solve a Mystery, Bk. 1. unabr. ed. Marian L. Clish. Illus. by Stephen Crombie. 1 cass. (Running Time: 20 min.). (J). (gr. k-5). 1999. pap. bk. 8.95 (978-1-928632-02-3(5)) Writers Mrktpl.
Match wits with the famous detective. Includes 14 mini-mysteries with answers in code in the back of the book.

Solve a Mystery, Bk. 1. unabr. ed. Marian Lee. Illus. by Stephen Crombie. 1 CD. (J). (gr. k-5). 1999. pap. bk. 12.95 (978-1-928632-03-0(3)) Writers Mrktpl.
Match wits with the famous detective. Includes 14 mini-mysteries to solve with answers in code at the back of the book.

Solve a Mystery, Bk. 2. unabr. ed. Marian Lee. Illus. by Stephen Crombie. 1 cass. (Running Time: 20 min.). (J). (gr. k-5). 1999. pap. bk. 8.95 (978-1-928632-10-8(6)); pap. bk. 12.95 (978-1-928632-11-5(4)) Writers Mrktpl.
Match wits with the famous detective by helping to solve these mysteries.

Solve It! Sundance/Newbridge, LLC Staff. (Early Math Ser.). (gr. k-1). 2000. 12.00 (978-1-58273-313-5(9)) Sund Newbrdge.

Solving Driver Licensing Problems II. 1998. bk. 99.00 (ACS-2104) PA Bar Inst.
Geared towards the general practitioner, this offers an overview which helps you handle your client's driver licensing problems. Without the proper knowledge of how to handle these cases, you can actually create more problems for your client. The experienced authors make you aware of the pitfalls you should avoid & steps you must take to save your clients time & frustration.

Solving Emotional Problems. Albert Ellis. 1 cass. (Running Time: 46 min.). 9.95 (C023) A Ellis Institute.
Clearly summarizes the REBT system of problem-solving & ABC's of emotional disturbance.

Solving Emotional Problems. Albert Ellis. 1 cass. (Running Time: 46 min.). 9.95 (C023) Inst Rational-Emotive.
Clearly summarizes the REBT system of problem-solving & ABC's of emotional disturbance. A fine example of the incomparable Ellis style & wit.

Solving IRS Problems. Ed. by Socrates Media Editors. 2005. audio compact disk 29.95 (978-1-59546-089-9(6)) Pub: Socrates Med LLC. Dist(s): Midpt Trade

Solving Our Confusion. Swami Amar Jyoti. 1 cass. 1976. 9.95 (K-74) Truth Consciousness.
If we were not confused 'it would happen'. Basis of confusion. Humility on the spiritual path. Righteousness balances our vibrations.

Solving Our Problems. Swami Amar Jyoti. 1 cass. 1983. 9.95 (A-20) Truth Consciousness.
The genesis of all our problems. How we usually handle problems & the only abiding solution.

Solving Real Estate Title Problems. 1993. bk. 99.00 (ACS-826) PA Bar Inst.
A tool that enables you to recognize real estate title problems & offer effective solutions.

Solving Real Estate Title Problems. 1989. 45.00 (AC-484) PA Bar Inst.

Solving the Marriage Maze. Charles Beckert. 1 cass. 3.95 (978-1-57734-373-8(5), 34441115) Covenant Comms.

Solving the Marriage Maze. Charles B. Beckert. 1 cass. 5.98 (978-1-55503-265-4(6), 06004008) Covenant Comms.
Discusses codependency & other marital patterns.

Solving the Population Crisis. Hosted by Nancy Pearlman. 1 cass. (Running Time: 29 min.). 10.00 (218) Educ Comm CA.

Solving the Problem of Evil. unabr. ed. Perf. by Eknath Easwaran. 1 cass. (Running Time: 1 hr.). 1992. 7.95 (978-1-58638-609-2(3)) Nilgiri Pr.

Solving Your Child's Sleeping Problems: A Guide for Tired Parents. Tim Jordan. Read by Tim Jordan. 1 cass. (Running Time: 40 mins.). 1996. 10.00 (978-0-9705335-0-0(0)); audio compact disk 10.00 (978-0-9705335-5-5(1)) Child & Families.
Teaches parents about sleep patterns & physiology of sleep & how to get babies & toddlers to sleep through the night.

Solzhenitsyn Reads. Aleksandr Solzhenitsyn. Read by Aleksandr Solzhenitsyn. 3 cass. (Running Time: 4 hrs.). 29.50 (SRU101) J Norton Pubs.
Solzhenitsyn reads, in Russian, One Day in the Life of Ivan Denisovich.

Solzhenitsyn Reads in Russian. Aleksandr Solzhenitsyn. Read by Aleksandr Solzhenitsyn. 3 cass. (Running Time: 4 hrs.). 2001. 39.95 (SRU101) J Norton Pubs.
The author reads "One Day in the Life of Ivan Denisovich".

Solzhenitsyn's America (Hosea) Hos. 1;1-11. Ed Young. 1988. 4.95 (978-0-7417-1650-7(X), 650) Win Walk.

Soma: An Experience in Psychoacoustic Healing. Tom Kenyon. 1 cass. (Running Time: 1 hr.). 9.95 (978-1-55961-505-1(2)) Relaxtn Co.

Soma: An Experience in Psychoacoustic Healing. Tom Kenyon. 1 CD. (Running Time: 1 hr.). 1998. pap. bk. 14.95 (978-1-55961-502-0(8)) Relaxtn Co.

Somali Handbook. 1993. 19.00 (978-0-931745-95-9(0)) Dunwoody Pr.

Somali Handbook (a Phrasebook with Indexes) Madina Osman & R. David Zorc. 2 cass. (Running Time: 1 hr. 30 min. per cass.). (SOM.). 1992. 19.00 (3048) Dunwoody Pr.
Designed for emergency & relief workers in Somalia. General, military, medical, relief & time expressions are covered.

Somali Newspaper Reader. 1984. 20.00 (978-0-931745-13-3(6)) Dunwoody Pr.

Somali Newspaper Reader, Abdullahi A. Issa & John D. Murphy. 4 cass. (Running Time: 6 hrs.). (SOM.). 1984. 29.00 (3053) Dunwoody Pr.
Fifty-one articles.

Sombra de Galdos: Libra De Lectura, Repaso y Conversacion. Benito Pérez Galdós. Ed. by Rudolph Cardona. (C). 1964. (978-0-393-99114-7(8)) Norton.

Sombra de Mi Alma see Poesia y Drama de Garcia Lorca

Sombra de un Pajaro. Rodolfo Walsh. 1 cass. (Running Time: 90 mins.). (SPA., 16.95 (CSP305) J Norton Pubs.
Psychological insight & the shadow of a bird unravel the mysterious death of the beautiful Mariana.

Sombra Muchacha Flor. unabr. ed. Marcel Proust. Read by Daniel Quintero. (SPA.). 2007. audio compact disk 17.00 (978-958-8318-16-5(5)) Pub: Yoyo Music COL. Dist(s): YoYoMusic

Sombras Nada Mas. unabr. ed. Sergio Ramirez. Read by Francisco Rivela. 9 cass. (Running Time: 12 hrs.).Tr. of Shadow Behind Somoza. (SPA.). 2004. 42.95 (978-1-4025-6675-2(1)) Recorded Bks.
Sombras Nada Mas is placed alongside La Fiesta Del Chivo as one of the best novels portraying political and social events of Latin America in the last decades of the 20th century. Accused of participating in criminal actions of the Somoza regime, Alirio Martinica is tried and judged by Sandinistas and is forced to defend his case. Meticulously researched this audiobook is an art masterpiece.

Sombrero de Luis Lucero. Cecilia O. Avalos. 1 cass. (Running Time: 60 mins.). (SPA.). 2003. 5.95 (978-1-56801-044-1(3), SW4021) Sund Newbrdge.

Sombrero de Tres Picos. abr. ed. Pedro Antonio de Alarcón. 3 CDs.Tr. of Three Cornered Hat. (SPA.). 2001. audio compact disk 17.00 (978-958-9494-18-9(8)) YoYoMusic.

Sombrero of Luis Lucero. Cecilia O. Avalos. (SPA.). 2001. (978-1-56801-043-4(5)) Sund Newbrdge.

Some Americans Aboard. unabr. ed. Richard Nelson. Perf. by Ken Baltin et al. 1 cass. (Running Time: 1 hr. 29 min.). 1993. 19.95 (978-1-58081-090-6(X)) L A Theatre.
A witty comedy in which a group of American academics with a gaggle of students in tow are in England to refresh themselves at the fountain of English culture. They expose their charges to English theatre at the rate of a play a night. From the head of the department to temporary lecturer, they have all brought with them their personal & professional problems.

Some Americans Abroad. Richard Nelson. Perf. by Julie Harris et al. 1 cass. (Running Time: 1 hr. 29 min.). 15.95 (NTN6) L A Theatre.
A witty comedy about a group of American academics & students in London struggling to refresh themselves at the fountain of English culture.

Some Assembly Required. Excerpts. Ed. by Leslie Morris. 1. (Running Time: 90 Mins). 2006. audio compact disk 19.95 (978-0-9760095-1-1(X)) NewYearPubng.

Some Assured. unabr. ed. Nicholas Rhea. Read by Graham Padden. 6 cass. (Running Time: 8 hrs.). (Story Sound Ser.). (J). 2005. 54.95 (978-1-85903-876-5(X)) Pub: Mgna Lrg Print GBR. Dist(s): Ulverscroft US

Some Assured. unabr. ed. Nicholas Rhea & Graham Padden. Read by Graham Padden. 7 CDs. (Running Time: 8 hrs.). (Story Sound CD Ser.). (J). 2005. audio compact disk 71.95 (978-1-85903-912-0(X)) Pub: Mgna Lrg Print GBR. Dist(s): Ulverscroft US

Some Awesome Stuff. 2 cass. (Running Time: 2 hrs.). 4.99 (978-0-529-06995-5(4), WBC-31) Nelson.
Original tunes that use the first 9 chapters of Proverbs.

Some Awesome Stuff. 2 CD. 1999. audio compact disk (978-0-529-07005-0(7), CD) Nelson.

Some Buried Caesar. unabr. ed. Rex Stout. Read by Michael Prichard. 6 cass. (Running Time: 8 hrs.). (Nero Wolfe Ser.). 2004. 29.95 (978-1-57270-054-3(8), N61154u) Pub: Audio Partners. Dist(s): PerseuPGW
Will the $45,000 championship bull become barbecue, or be preserved for its lineage? Before this family feud is resolved, two people are murdered & the bull mysteriously dies. It is all told from Archie's viewpoint with his usual wry humor.

Some Buried Caesar. unabr. ed. Rex Stout. (Running Time: 27720 sec.). (Nero Wolfe Ser.). (ENG.). 2007. audio compact disk 29.95 (978-1-57270-734-4(8)) Pub: AudioGO. Dist(s): Perseus Dist

Some Buried Caesar. unabr. collector's ed. Rex Stout. Read by Michael Prichard. 6 cass. (Running Time: 9 hrs.). (Nero Wolfe Ser.). 1994. 48.00 (978-0-7366-2746-7(4), 3471) Books on Tape.
A family feud over a prize bull worth 45,000 dollars. It gets ugly. Then it draws in Nero Wolfe.

***Some by Fire.** Stuart Pawson & Andrew Wincott. 2010. 61.95 (978-1-84652-381-6(8)); audio compact disk 79.95 (978-1-84652-382-3(6)) Pub: Magna Story GBR. Dist(s): Ulverscroft US

Some Can Whistle. unabr. collector's ed. Larry McMurtry & Michael Prichard. 7 cass. (Running Time: 10 hrs. 30 min.). 1990. 56.00 (978-0-7366-1803-8(1), 2640) Books on Tape.
No novelist recycles characters & locales to better effect than Larry McMurtry. Here, he resurrects Danny Deck, the protagonist of his 1972 novel All My Friends Are Going to Be Strangers, & sets him down in the East Texas of The Last Picture Show & Texasville.

Some Cats Know (The Songs of Peggy Lee) Perf. by Jeanie Bryson. 7.98 (TA 33391); audio compact disk 12.78 CD Jewel box. (TA 83391) NewSound.

Some Champions. unabr. collector's ed. Ring Lardner. Read by Daniel Grace. 7 cass. (Running Time: 7 hrs.). 1976. 42.00 (978-0-7366-0024-8(8), 1035) Books on Tape.
Ring Lardner has been resurrected as an authentic American humorist. Wit & style flash from this fresh collection of Lardner imporbables. Listening to the stories & these current Larnder themes of innocence, of worldliness & its miscues, one realizes the people & times of which Lardner writes, while an authentic part of our recent past, are now dead as the dodo. A bracing illustration of the change in our national character, if any is needed.

Some Day You'll Thank Me for This: The Official Southern Ladies' Guide to Being a Perfect Mother. Gayden Metcalfe & Charlotte Hays. Read by Marguerite Gavin. (Playaway Adult Nonfiction Ser.). (ENG.). 2009. 49.99 (978-1-60847-872-9(6)) Find a World.

Some Day You'll Thank Me for This: Th[illegible]cial Southern Ladies Guide to Being a Perfect Mother. unabr. ed. G[illegible] Metcalfe & Charlotte Hays. Read by Marguerite Gavin. (Running Tim[illegible] 4 hrs. 30 mins. 0 sec.). (ENG.). 2009. audio compact disk 49.99 (978-1-4001-4044-2(7)); audio compact disk 19.99 (978-1-4001-6044-0(8)); audio compact disk 24.99 (978-1-4001-1044-5(0)) Pub: Tantor Media. Dist(s): IngramPubServ

Some Days You Gotta Dance - ShowTrax. Perf. by Dixie Chicks. Arranged by Mac Huff. 1 CD. (Running Time - 5 mins.). 2000. audio compact disk 19.95 (08201136) H Leonard.
Audiences can't resist this lively toe-tapping 1999 hit by the Dixie Chicks. Excellent show choir number!.

Some Dog & Other Kentucky Wonders. Short Stories. Retold by Mary Hamilton. 1 CD. (Running Time: 71 Minutes). 2001. audio compact disk 15.00 (978-1-885556-07-3(1)) Hidden Sprng.
Kentucky Tales told by Mary Hamilton, a native Kentuckian. Stories include folktales - "Lazy Jack" "Stormwalker" "The Farmer's Daughter" "Some Dog" a Hamilton family anecdote - "Jeff Rides the Rides" and a personal narrative - "Jump Rope Kingdom".

Some Dog & Other Kentucky Wonders. Short Stories. Retold by Mary Hamilton. 1 cass. (Running Time: 60 min.). (J). (gr. 1 up). 1992. 10.00 (978-1-885556-01-1(2)) Hidden Sprng.
Kentucky tales told by a native Kentuckian. Includes "Lazy Jack," "The Farmer's Smart Daughter," "Stormwalker" & "Some Dog".

***Some Enchanted Evening.** abr. ed. Christina Dodd. Read by Elizabeth Sastre. (ENG.). 2005. (978-0-06-085433-1(2), Harper Audio); (978-0-06-085434-8(0), Harper Audio) HarperCollins Pubs.

***Some Experiences of an Irish R. M.** Edith Somerville & Martin Ross. Read by Alfred von Lecteur. 2009. 27.95 (978-1-60112-973-4(4)) Babblebooks.

***Some Girls: My Life in a Harem.** unabr. ed. Jillian Lauren. Narrated by Tavia Gilbert. (Running Time: 8 hrs. 30 mins.). 2010. 29.99 (978-1-4001-9878-8(X)); 15.99 (978-1-4001-8878-9(4)) Tantor Media.

***Some Girls: My Life in a Harem.** unabr. ed. Jillian Lauren. Narrated by Tavia Gilbert. 1 MP3-CD. (Running Time: 8 hrs. 30 mins. 0 sec.). 2010. 19.99 (978-1-4001-6878-1(3)); audio compact disk 29.99 (978-1-4001-1878-6(6)); audio compact disk 71.99 (978-1-4001-4878-3(2)) Pub: Tantor Media. Dist(s): IngramPubServ

***Some Girls Bite.** unabr. ed. Chloe Neill. Narrated by Cynthia Holloway. (Running Time: 12 hrs. 0 mins.). (Chicagoland Vampires Ser.). 2010. 17.99 (978-1-4001-8936-6(5)); 24.99 (978-1-4001-6936-8(4)); audio compact disk 34.99 (978-1-4001-1936-3(7)) Pub: Tantor Media. Dist(s): IngramPubServ

***Some Girls Bite (Library Edition)** unabr. ed. Chloe Neill. Narrated by Cynthia Holloway. (Running Time: 12 hrs. 0 mins.). (Chicagoland Vampires Ser.). 2010. 34.99 (978-1-4001-9936-5(0)); audio compact disk 83.99 (978-1-4001-4936-0(3)) Pub: Tantor Media. Dist(s): IngramPubServ

***Some Golden Harbor.** David Drake. Narrated by David Drake. Narrated by Victor Bevine. (Playaway Adult Fiction Ser.). 2009. 69.99 (978-1-61587-807-9(6)) Find a World.

Some Haunted Houses see Classic Ghost Stories, Vol. 3, A Collection

Some Hope. unabr. ed. Edward St. Auben. Narrated by Edward Hibbert. 11 cass. (Running Time: 15 hrs. 15 mins.). 2003. 99.75 (978-1-4025-7587-7(4), H1592MC, Griot Aud) Recorded Bks.

Some Horary Basics. John Somoza. Read by John Somoza. 1 cass. (Running Time: 90 min.). 1994. 8.95 (1132) Am Fed Astrologers.
Horary astrology - basic guidelines.

Some Irish Songs for My Nana. Marylee Sunseri. 1 cass. 1995. 9.95 (978-1-887795-02-9(2)) Piper Grove Mus.
Traditional & original Irish songs & stories.

***Some Job.** James Pattinson. 2010. 44.95 (978-1-4079-0855-7(3)); audio compact disk 51.95 (978-1-4079-0856-4(1)) Pub: Soundings Ltd GBR. Dist(s): Ulverscroft US

Some Key-Points of Hindi Grammar. Harinder J. Dhillon. Read by Harinder J. Dhillon. 1 cass. (Running Time: 1 hr. 30 min.). 1990. pap. bk. 10.00 H J Dhillon.
Based on the book with the same title.

Some Key-Points of Panjabi Grammar (Gurmukhi or Persian Script) Harinder J. Dhillon. Read by Harinder J. Dhillon. 1 cass. (Running Time: 1 hr. 30 min.). 1990. pap. bk. 10.00 H J Dhillon.

Some Key-Points of Urdu Grammar. Harinder J. Dhillon. Read by Harinder J. Dhillon. 1 cass. (Running Time: 1 hr. 30 min.). pap. bk. 10.00 H J Dhillon.

***Some Kind of Wonderful.** unabr. ed. Debbie Macomber. Read by Teri Clark Linden. (Running Time: 5 hrs.). (Legendary Lovers Ser.: Bk. 2). 2010. 14.99 (978-1-4418-5354-7(5), 9781441853547, Brilliance MP3); 14.99 (978-1-4418-5355-4(3), 9781441853554, BAD); audio compact disk 14.99 (978-1-4418-5353-0(7), 9781441853530, Bril Audio CD Unabri) Brilliance Audio.

Some Lie & Some Die. unabr. ed. Ruth Rendell. Read by Nigel Anthony. 6 cass. (Running Time: 6 hrs.). (Inspector Wexford Mystery Ser.: Bk. 8). 1998. 54.95 (978-0-7540-0216-1(0), CAB 1639) AudioGO.
Inspector Wexford investigates a gruesome body found in a nearby quarry.

Some Lie & Some Die. unabr. ed. Ruth Rendell. Read by Nigel Anthony. 6 cass. (Running Time: 9 hrs.). (Inspector Wexford Mystery Ser.: Bk. 8). 2000. 54.95 (CAB 1639) Pub: Chivers Audio Bks GBR. Dist(s): AudioGO
For a while, the rock festival at Sundays went well. The sun would shine as the bands played, and everyone, except a few angry neighbors, seemed to enjoy themselves. Then the weather changed. And in a nearby quarry, a body is found that made even Inspector Wexford's stomach lurch.

Some Like It Haute. Julie K. L. Dam. (Running Time: 32400 sec.). 2006. 65.95 (978-0-7861-4450-1(5)) Blckstn Audio.

Some Like It Haute. Julie K. L. Dam. Read by Carrington MacDuffie. (Running Time: 32400 sec.). 2006. audio compact disk 81.00 (978-0-7861-7333-4(5)) Blckstn Audio.

Some Like It Haute. unabr. ed. Julie K. L. Dam. Read by Carrington MacDuffie. 7 cass. (Running Time: 32400 sec.). 2006. 29.95 (978-0-7861-4393-1(2)); audio compact disk 29.95 (978-0-7861-7445-4(5)); audio compact disk 29.95 (978-0-7861-7801-8(9)) Blckstn Audio.

Some Miracles Take Time. Art E. Berg. 1 cass. 1991. (978-1-883437-01-5(6)) Invictus Comm.
Are all miracles instantaneous? Through Art's humor style, he relates his own experiences with miracles.

Some Mispalced Ideas on Democracy CD. Albert Szent-Gyorgyi. 1 CD. (Running Time: 25 mins.). (Sound Seminars Ser.). 2006. audio compact disk 12.95 (978-1-57970-368-4(2), C27022D, Audio-For) J Norton Pubs.
Szent-Gyorgyi discusses creativity and its importance in the future of humankind, and notes that the development of creative people is hindered by a misplaced idea about democracy: the idea that all people are created equal. He says that nature is not democratic in this sense, and that this idea leads to the tendency to replace quality with quantity. Originally broadcast by Pacifica Radio station WBAI in 1961.

Some Misplaced Ideas on Democracy. Albert Szent-Gyorgyi. 1 cass. (Running Time: 25 min.). 10.95 (27022) J Norton Pubs.
Discusses creativity & its importance to the future of mankind. The author notes that development of creative people is hindered by the misplaced idea that all men are created equal; Nature is not democratic in that sense, & so we tend to replace quality with quantity.

Some Must Watch While Some Must Sleep: Exploring the World of Sleep. unabr. collector's ed. William C. Dement. Read by Michael Prichard. 6 cass. (Running Time: 6 hrs.). 1984. 36.00 (978-0-7366-0973-9(3), 1915) Books on Tape.
A study of the nature of sleep & what happens when you sleep & dream.

Some Notes about Tomorrow. Leonard Peikoff. 1 cass. (Running Time: 90 min.). 1992. 14.95 (978-1-56114-159-3(3), LP27C) Second Renaissance.

Some Observations on Naturalism. James T. Farrell. Read by James T. Farrell. 1 cass. (Running Time: 26 min.). 1954. 11.95 (23009) J Norton Pubs.
Zola's theory of naturalism provides the basis for this noted author's lecture on the topic.

Some of My Best Friends Are...the Piano Players. Perf. by Ray Brown. 1 cass., 1 CD. 7.98 (TA 33373); audio compact disk 12.78 CD Jewel box. (TA 83373) NewSound.

Some of My Best Friends Are...the Tenor Saxists: The Tenor Saxists. Perf. by Ray Brown. 1 cass. 7.98 (TA 33388); audio compact disk 12.78 CD Jewel box. (TA 83388) NewSound.

Some of the Most Important Truths Ever Taught. Dan Comer. 1 cass. 3.00 (83) Evang Outreach.

Some of Us Are Brave: Strategies for Surviving As a Pioneer Chaplain. 1 cass. (Care Cassettes Ser.: Vol. 12, No. 1). 1985. 10.80 Assn Prof Chaplains.

Some Perspectives on How We Create Our Own Reality. Jon Klimo. 2 cass. 18.00 (A0471-89) Sound Photosyn.
Double speak that makes perfect sense if you have the two ears for it.

Some Reflections on the Subject of Earthquakes. Instructed by Manly P. Hall. 8.95 (978-0-89314-261-2(1), C821010) Philos Res.

***Some Sing, Some Cry.** unabr. ed. Ntozake Shange & Ifa Bayeza. Read by Robin Miles. (Running Time: 26 hrs.). 2010. 44.97 (978-1-4418-8006-2(2), 9781441880062, Brinc Audio MP3 Lib); 44.97 (978-1-4418-8007-9(0), 9781441880079, BADLE); 29.99 (978-1-4418-8005-5(4), 9781441880055, Brilliance MP3); audio compact disk 29.99 (978-1-4418-8003-1(8), 9781441880031, Bril Audio CD Unabri) Brilliance Audio.

***Some Sing, Some Cry.** unabr. ed. Ntozake Shange & Ifa Bayeza Shange. Read by Robin R. Mileham & Robin Miles. (Running Time: 27 hrs.). 2010. audio compact disk 79.97 (978-1-4418-8004-8(6), 9781441880048, BriAudCD Unabrid) Brilliance Audio.

Some Sunday. Margaret Johnson-Hodge. Narrated by Robin Miles. 9 cass. (Running Time: 12 hrs.). 82.00 (978-1-4025-1779-2(3)) Recorded Bks.

Some Sweet Day, Jennie L. Hansen. 2 cass. 1997. 11.98 (978-1-57734-105-5(8), 07001495) Covenant Comms.

Some Tame Gazelle, unabr. ed. Barbara Pym. Narrated by Flo Gibson. 6 cass. (Running Time: 9 hrs.). 1984. 24.95 (978-1-55685-037-0(9)) Audio Bk Con.
Days in the lives of spinster sisters peopled & enhanced by the local curates & villagers.

Some Things You Just Have to Live With: Musings on Middle Age. Barbara Cawthorne Crafton. 2003. audio compact disk 30.00 (978-0-8192-1978-7(9), MoreHse Pubng) Church Pub Inc.

Some Time with Thurber. James Thurber. Read by Joe Knight. 1 cass. (Running Time: 38 min. per cass.). 1981. 10.00 (LSS1201) Esstee Audios.
Three Thurber stories - "The MacBeth Murder Mystery," "Sex ex Machina," & "University Days".

***Some We Love, Some We Hate, Some We Eat: Why It's So Hard to Think Straight about Animals.** unabr. ed. Hal Herzog. (Running Time: 9 hrs. 30 mins.). 2010. 16.99 (978-1-4001-8921-2(7)); 24.99 (978-1-4001-6921-4(6)); audio compact disk 34.99 (978-1-4001-1921-9(9)); audio compact disk 83.99 (978-1-4001-4921-6(5)) Pub: Tantor Media. Dist(s): IngramPubServ

***Some We Love, Some We Hate, Some We Eat (Library Edition) Why It's So Hard to Think Straight about Animals.** unabr. ed. Hal Herzog. (Running Time: 9 hrs. 30 mins.). 2010. 34.99 (978-1-4001-9921-1(2)) Tantor Media.

Some Wildflower in My Heart. Jamie Langston Turner. Narrated by Cynthia Darlow. 10 cass. (Running Time: 14 hrs. 15 mins.). 94.00 (978-0-7887-9614-2(3)) Recorded Bks.

Somebody: The Reckless Life & Remarkable Career of Marlon Brando. unabr. ed. Stefan Kanfer. 1 MP3-CD. (Running Time: 15 hrs.). 2008. 29.95 (978-1-4332-5118-4(3)); 85.95 (978-1-4332-5115-3(9)); audio compact disk 32.95 (978-1-4332-5117-7(5)); audio compact disk 110.00 (978-1-4332-5116-0(7)) Blckstn Audio.

Somebody Bit the Moon. Perf. by Sherban Cira. 1 CD. audio compact disk 14.00 Amused Prodns.

Somebody Else's Daughter. unabr. ed. Elizabeth Brundage. Contrib. by Mark Bramhall & Bernadette Dunne. 11 CDs. (Running Time: 13 hrs.). (ENG.). (gr. 12 up). 2008. audio compact disk 39.95 (978-0-14-314346-8(8), PengAudBks) Penguin Grp USA.

Somebody Else's Daughter. unabr. ed. Elizabeth Brundage. Read by Bernadette Dunne. 11 CDs. (Running Time: 13 hrs.). 2008. audio compact disk 90.00 (978-1-4159-5492-8(5), BksonTape) Pub: Random Audio Pubg. Dist(s): Random
Two young drifters, Nate and Cat - bottomed out on drugs and living on the margins of San Francisco - are forced by stress and circumstance to give up their infant daughter. Seventeen years later, Nate comes to the idyllic setting of the Berkshires to teach at the elite private Pioneer School - as his daughter's teacher. Willa Golding, ensconced in a magnificent country home with her parents, has never worried much about being adopted. But when the world she's always trusted becomes a foreign place, she learns that her adoptive parents have not been totally honest with her - nor with others in their privileged circle. Claire Squire is a visual artist struggling on the outskirts of her profession. It is a lucky break to get her troubled son, Teddy, a backdoor acceptance to Pioneer. But Teddy soon finds it's a precarious place well disguised by preppy ties, plaid skirts, and activities designed to look good on college applications. SOMEBODY ELSE'S DAUGHTER is a collision of two very different fathers - biological and adoptive; a woman whose independence and talent have led her to dead ends in life and love; and a villain whose intentions slowly unfold with the help, witting and unwitting, of all those around him. An electric, suspenseful tale of conflicted characters and the fractured landscape of the American psyche, it scratches the surface of the Berkshire dream.

Somebody Loves You. Lucile Johnson. 2004. 7.95 (978-1-57734-659-3(9)) Covenant Comms.

Somebody Owes Me Money. unabr. ed. Donald E. Westlake. Narrated by Stephen Thorne. (Running Time: 6 hrs. 30 mins.). 2008. 49.95 (978-0-7927-5565-4(0)); audio compact disk 79.95 (978-0-7927-5453-4(0)) AudioGO.
Cab driver Chet Conway was hoping for a good tip from his latest fare, the sort he could spend. But what he got was a tip on a horse race. Which might have turned out okay, except that when he went to collect his winnings, Chet found his bookie lying dead on the living room floor. Chet knows he had nothing to do with it-but just try explaining that to the cops, to the two rival criminal gangs who each think Chet's working for the other, and to the dead man's beautiful sister, who has flown in from Las Vegas to avenge her brother's murder.

***Somebody Pick up My Pieces.** unabr. ed. J. D. Mason. (Running Time: 10 hrs. 5 mins.). (ENG.). 2011. 29.95 (978-1-4417-7427-9(0)); 65.95 (978-1-4417-7424-8(6)); audio compact disk 29.95 (978-1-4417-7426-2(2)); audio compact disk 100.00 (978-1-4417-7425-5(4)) Blckstn Audio.

Somebody Somewhere. abr. ed. Donna Williams. Read by Debra Winger. 2 cass. (Running Time: 3 hrs.). 1995. 16.95 (978-0-944993-86-6(9)) Audio Lit.
A continuation of the author's battle with autism begun in "Nobody Nowhere".

Somebody to Love? A Rock-and-Roll Memoir. unabr. ed. Grace Slick & Andrea Cagan. (ENG.). 2006. 14.98 (978-1-59483-719-7(8)) Pub: Hachet Audio. Dist(s): HachBkGrp

Somebody's Darling: A Novel. unabr. collector's ed. Larry McMurtry. Read by Wolfram Kadinsky. 8 cass. (Running Time: 12 hrs.). 1986. 64.00 (978-0-7366-0791-9(9), 1743) Books on Tape.
Jill Peel is the first woman to make Hollywood's bigtime as a director. She has other interests as well - Joe Percy, a veteran screenwriter & Owens Oarson, an oportunist. All three travel in a world of easy sex & available drugs, of astronomical salaries & artistic compromise.

Somebody's Gotta Say It. abr. ed. Neal Boortz. Read by Neal Boortz. (Running Time: 21600 sec.). 2007. audio compact disk 29.95 (978-0-06-089790-1(2)) HarperCollins Pubs.

***Somebody's Gotta Say It.** abr. ed. Neal Boortz. Read by Neal Boortz. (ENG.). 2007. (978-0-06-113502-6(X), Harper Audio); (978-0-06-113503-3(8), Harper Audio) HarperCollins Pubs.

Somebody's Son see Your Own World

Someday see Science Fiction Favorites of Isaac Asimov

Someday see Isaac Asimov Library

Someday. Karen Kingsbury. Read by Sandra Burr. (Baxter Family Drama: Sunrise Ser.). (ENG.). 2009. 69.99 (978-1-60775-879-2(2)) Find a World.

Someday. Jackie French Koller. Narrated by Julia Gibson. 2003. 45.00 (978-1-4025-4791-1(9)) Recorded Bks.

***Someday.** Alison McGhee. Illus. by Peter H. Reynolds. Narrated by Janine Turner. 1 cass. (Running Time: 7 mins.). (J). (ps-2). 2008. bk. 27.95 (978-0-8045-6975-0(4)); bk. 29.95 (978-0-8045-4200-5(7)) Spoken Arts.

Someday. abr. ed. Karen Kingsbury. Read by Sandra Burr. 5 CDs. (Running Time: 6 hrs.). (Sunrise Ser.: No. 3). 2008. audio compact disk 26.95 (978-1-59600-219-7(0), 9781596002197, BACD) Brilliance Audio.
Please enter a Synopsis.

***Someday.** abr. ed. Karen Kingsbury. Read by Sandra Burr. (Running Time: 6 hrs.). (Sunrise Ser.). 2010. audio compact disk 9.99 (978-1-4418-7838-0(6), 9781441878380, BCD Value Price) Brilliance Audio.

Someday. unabr. ed. Karen Kingsbury. Read by Sandra Burr. (Running Time: 10 hrs.). (Sunrise Ser.: No. 3). 2008. 39.25 (978-1-59737-984-7(0), 9781597379847, BADLE); 24.95 (978-1-59737-983-0(2), 9781597379830, BAD); audio compact disk 24.95 (978-1-59737-981-6(6), 9781597379816, Brilliance MP3); audio compact disk 39.25 (978-1-59737-982-3(4), 9781597379823, Brinc Audio MP3 Lib); audio compact disk 97.25 (978-1-4233-4400-1(6), 9781423344001, BriAudCD Unabrid); audio compact disk 36.95 (978-1-4233-4399-8(9), 9781423343998, Bril Audio CD Unabri) Brilliance Audio.

Someday, Somewhere. unabr. ed. Eileen Ramsay. Read by Pamela Donald. 10 cass. (Running Time: 13 hrs. 15 mins.). (Story Sound Ser.). (J). 2004. 84.95 (978-1-85903-667-9(8)); audio compact disk 99.95 (978-1-85903-737-9(2)) Pub: Mgna Lrg Print GBR. Dist(s): Ulverscroft US

Someday the Rabbi Will Leave. unabr. ed. Harry Kemelman. Narrated by George Guidall. 5 cass. (Running Time: 6 hrs. 45 mins.). (Rabbi Small Mystery Ser.). 1985. 46.00 (978-0-7887-3110-5(6), 95821E7) Recorded Bks.
Rabbi David Small must face two problems that threatens to destroy his career. The new president of the temple is determined to get rid of him, & a young man in the congregation has been arrested for murder. Can he maintain his position in the temple while helping the young man?.

Someday This Pain Will Be Useful to You. unabr. ed. Peter Cameron. Read by Lincoln Hoppe. 6 CDs. (Running Time: 7 hrs. 7 mins.). (YA). (gr. 10 up). 2008. audio compact disk 50.00 (978-0-7393-7253-1(X), Listening Lib) Pub: Random Audio Pubg. Dist(s): Random

Someday This Pain Will Be Useful to You. unabr. ed. Peter Cameron. Read by Lincoln Hoppe. (ENG.). (J). (gr. 7). 2008. audio compact disk 39.00 (978-0-7393-7289-0(0), Listening Lib) Pub: Random Audio Pubg. Dist(s): Random

Someone Else's Dream. E. Jean Beres. Read by Marc Cashman & Gale Van Cott. 2009. audio compact disk 5.49 (978-0-9821192-4-2(0)) Mind Wings Aud.

***Someone Else's Dream.** E. Jean Beres. Read by Marc Cashman & Gale Van Cott. (Running Time: 60). (ENG.). 2009. 2.99 (978-1-61114-004-0(8)) Mind Wings Aud.

Someone in the House, unabr. ed. Barbara Michaels, pseud. Narrated by Barbara Rosenblat. 6 cass. (Running Time: 9 hrs.). 1993. 51.00 (978-1-55690-838-5(5), 93206E7) Recorded Bks.
A young writer & her collaborator encounter ghostly mischief while spending the summer working on a book at an old manor house.

Someone Knows My Name. unabr. ed. Read by Adenrele Ojo. Ed. by Lawrence Hill. 14 CDs. (Running Time: 18 hrs.). 2007. audio compact disk 129.00 (978-1-4159-4590-2(X), BksonTape) Pub: Random Audio Pubg. Dist(s): Random
Aminata Diallo ("an amazing literary creation," Literary Review of Canada) is the beguil-ing heroine of Lawrence Hill's SOMEONE KNOWS MY NAME. In it, Hill exquisitely imagines the tale of an eighteenth-century woman's life, spanning six decades and three continents. The fascinating story that Hill tells is a work of the soul and the imagination. Aminata is a character who will stir listeners, from her kid-napping from Africa through her journeys back and forth across the ocean. Enslaved on a South Carolina plantation, Aminata works in the indigo fields and as a mid-wife. When she is bought by an entrepreneur from Charleston, she is torn from friends and family. The chaos of the Revolutionary War allows her to escape. In British-held Manhattan, she helps pen the Book of Negroes, a list of blacks rewarded for wartime service to the King with safe passage to Nova Scotia. During her travels in Canada, Sierra Leone, and England, Aminata strives for her free-dom and that of her people - even when it comes at a price.

Someone Like You. unabr. ed. Sarah Dessen. Read by Katherine Powell. 4 cass. (Running Time: 6 hrs. 48 mins.). (J). (gr. 7 up). 2004. 29.75 (978-0-8072-1565-4(1), S YA 422 CX, Listening Lib) Pub: Random Audio Pubg. Dist(s): NetLibrary CO

Someone Like You: A Novel. unabr. ed. Cathy Kelly. Read by Brett O'Brien. 18 cass. (Running Time: 21 hrs. 45 min.). 2001. (978-0-7531-1289-2(2)) ISIS Audio GBR.
Emma, Leonie and Hannah all want just one thing in life and then they'll be truly happy. For just-married Emma, happiness means escaping the control of her domineering father and conceiving a much longed-for child with her beloved husband. For Leonie, divorced mother of three teenagers, it means finding the true love that was missing from her ten-year marriage. And for Hannah, striking out alone after the man she loved abandoned her, happiness means independence and security - something she doesn't think any man can provide.

Someone Not Really. Sarah Challis. Read by Myra Platt. 3 cass. 29.95 (978-0-7927-3345-4(2), CSL 704) AudioGO.

Someone Not Really Her Mother. unabr. ed. Harriet Scott Chessman. 4 CDs. (Running Time: 4 hrs. 30 mins.). 2004. audio compact disk 49.95 (978-0-7927-3346-1(0), Chivers Sound Lib) AudioGO.

Someone Said No. Excerpts. Based on a work by Robert Briggs. 1 CD. (Running Time: 1 hr. 12 min.). Dramatization. 2003. audio compact disk 14.95 (978-0-931191-19-0(X)) Rob Briggs.
This CD examines the disturbing uncertainty of the today's war on terrorism by tracing it back to the 1950s. Through the breakdown of a friend, Harmon Crow, Briggs tells the tale of a troubled Beat who survives the collapse by believing there is "more to life than living.".

Someone, Somewhere, Some Other Time. Alex R. Teixeira. 2007. audio compact disk 12.95 (978-1-60031-022-5(2)) Infinity PubPA.

Someone Special - You! Janeen Brady. Illus. by Clarkson & Evan Twede. (J). (gr. k-9). 1991. 12.95 (978-0-944803-74-5(1)) Brite Music.

Someone Talking to Himself see Richard Wilbur Readings

***Someone to Blame.** unabr. ed. Susanne Lakin & C. S. Lakin. (Running Time: 10 hrs. 11 mins. 10 sec.). (ENG.). 2010. 13.99 (978-0-310-57750-8(0)) Zondervan.

Someone to Hold. Anita Stansfield. 3 cass. 2004. 14.95 (978-1-57734-992-1(X)) Covenant Comms.

Someone to Love. abr. ed. Jude Deveraux. Read by Dagmara Dominczyk. (Running Time: 6 hrs. 0 mins. 0 sec.). (ENG.). 2009. audio compact disk 14.99 (978-0-7435-8042-7(7)) Pub: S&S Audio. Dist(s): S and S Inc

Someone to Love, unabr. ed. Francess L. Lantz. Narrated by Kate Forbes. 5 pieces. (Running Time: 7 hrs. 15 mins.). (gr. 9 up). 1998. 46.00 (978-0-7887-2710-8(9), 95454E7) Recorded Bks.
Fifteen-year-old Sarah is surprised when her parents tell her they are going to adopt a baby. Meeting Iris, the teenaged birth mother, she envies her life of freedom. As Sarah writes series of letters to the unborn baby, she chronicles her path from anger & rebellion to what genuine love requires.

Someone Was Watching, unabr. ed. David Patneaude. Narrated by Jeff Woodman. 4 pieces. (Running Time: 5 hrs. 30 mins.). (gr. 7 up). 1997. 35.00 (978-0-7887-1282-1(9), 95169E7) Recorded Bks.
It's been three long months since Chris' little sister, Molly, has disappeared from the riverbank. Refusing to accept a drowning verdict, he & his best friend embark upon a desperate journey to prove an impossible hunch.

Someone Was Watching. unabr. ed. David Patneaude. Read by Jeff Woodman. 4 cass. (Running Time: 5 hrs. 30 min.). (YA). (gr. 2). 1997. Rental 11.50 Recorded Bks.

Someone Was Watching, unabr. ed. David Patneaude. Read by Jeff Woodman. 4 cass. (Running Time: 5 hrs. 30 min.). (YA). (gr. 7). 1997. pap. bk. 38.95 (978-0-7887-1252-4(7), 40498) Recorded Bks.

Someone Who Dared! 1985. (0252) Evang Sisterhood Mary.

Something. unabr. ed. Natalie Babbitt. 1 read-along cass. (Running Time: 6 min.). (Follow the Reader Ser.). (J). (gr. k-2). 1982. 15.98 incl. bk. & guide. (978-0-8072-0024-7(7), FTR 67 SP, Listening Lib) Random Audio Pubg.
Mylo is afraid of the dark because "the Something" might come, something he can't explain. But when he makes a statue of "the Something" with modelling clay, he can face his unnamed fear.

Something about a Soldier, unabr. ed. Mark Harris. Narrated by George Guidall. 5 cass. (Running Time: 6 hrs. 15 mins.). 1991. 44.00 (978-1-55690-485-1(1), 91220E7) Recorded Bks.
A young man undergoes the trials of enlistment & basic training, learning much about growing up thereby.

Something about Poetry. W. H. Auden. 1 cass. (Running Time: 22 min.). 1969. 10.95 (23154) J Norton Pubs.
Describes the verbal world of poetry & the use of words for two purposes: as a code of communication & to share experiences.

Something about That Name: Matthew 6:9. Ed Young. (J). 1979. 4.95 (978-0-7417-1075-8(7), A0075) Win Walk.

Something Beautiful. unabr. ed. Sharon Dennis Wyeth. Narrated by Lynne Thigpen. 1 cass. (Running Time: 15 mins.). (gr. 1 up). 1999. 10.00 (978-0-7887-2960-7(8), 95734E7) Recorded Bks.
Saddened by the trash & graffiti around her apartment, a little girl walks through her neighborhood looking for something beautiful. One by one, as her friends show her their beautiful things, the girl finds the power to look beyond her bleak surroundings.

Something Beautiful. unabr. ed. Sharon Dennis Wyeth. Read by Lynne Thigpen. 1 cass. (Running Time: 15 mins.). (YA). (ps up). 1999. pap. bk. & stu. ed. 33.95 (978-0-7887-2990-4(X), 40872) Recorded Bks.

Something Beautiful, Class Set. unabr. ed. Sharon Dennis Wyeth. Read by Lynne Thigpen. 1 cass. (Running Time: 15 mins.). (J). 1999. 187.80 (978-0-7887-3020-7(7), 46837) Recorded Bks.

Something Beautiful: 1 Peter 3:3-5, Vol. 704. Ed Young. 1989. 4.95 (978-0-7417-1703-0(4), 704) Win Walk.

Something Beautiful for God. Malcolm Muggeridge. 4 cass. 18.95 (309) Ignatius Pr.
A tribute to Mother Teresa of Calcutta by a world-renowned Christian journalist & commenatator.

Something Beautiful for God, unabr. ed. Malcolm Muggeridge. Read by Leonard Muggeridge & Nadia May. 3 cass. (Running Time: 4 hrs.). 1993. 23.95 (978-0-7861-0452-9(X), 1404) Blckstn Audio.
First published in 1977, this is the work that introduced Mother Teresa of Calcutta to the Western world. Malcolm Muggeridge paints a profound & moving portrait of a lady whose love for Christ & the needy has deeply impacted many a life - including the author's.

Something Beautiful for God. unabr. ed. Malcolm Muggeridge. 1998. audio compact disk 90.00 (978-0-7861-0122-1(9)) Blckstn Audio.

Something Big Has Been Here. Jack Prelutsky. (J). 1991. (978-0-8072-0208-1(8), Listening Lib) Random Audio Pubg.

***Something Big Has Been Here.** unabr. ed. Jack Prelutsky. Read by Jack Prelutsky. (ENG.). 2007. (978-0-06-144892-8(3), GreenwillowBks); (978-0-06-144893-5(1), GreenwillowBks) HarperCollins Pubs.

Something Big Has Been Here. unabr. abr. ed. Jack Prelutsky. Read by Jack Prelutsky. (Running Time: 3600 sec.). (J). (ps-3). 2007. 14.95 (978-0-06-135942-2(4), HarperChildAud) HarperCollins Pubs.

Something Big Has Been Here & the New Kid on the Block. unabr. ed. Jack Prelutsky. Read by Jack Prelutsky. 1 cass. (Running Time: 47 mins.). (J). (gr. 4-7). 1991. 11.00 (978-0-8072-0202-9(9), FTR147CX, Listening Lib) Random Audio Pubg.
poems.

Something Blue. abr. ed. Emily Giffin. Read by Jennifer Wiltsie. 4 CDs. (Running Time: 5 hrs. 0 mins. 0 sec.). (ENG.). 2005. audio compact disk 24.95 (978-1-59397-745-0(X)) Pub: Macmill Audio. Dist(s): Macmillan

***Something Blue.** abr. ed. Emily Giffin. Read by Jennifer Wiltsie. (Running Time: 5 hrs. 0 mins. 0 sec.). (ENG.). 2010. audio compact disk 14.99 (978-1-4272-1027-2(6)) Pub: Macmill Audio. Dist(s): Macmillan

Something Blue. unabr. ed. Emily Giffin. 7 cass. (Running Time: 40020 sec.). 2005. cass., cass., DVD 59.95 (978-0-7927-3633-2(8), CSL 800); audio compact disk 89.95 (978-0-7927-3634-9(6), SLD 800) AudioGO.

***Something Borrowed.** abr. ed. Emily Giffin. Read by Jennifer Wiltsie. (Running Time: 5 hrs. 0 mins. 0 sec.). (ENG.). 2011. audio compact disk 14.99 (978-1-4272-1194-1(9)) Pub: Macmill Audio. Dist(s): Macmillan

Something Borrowed. abr. ed. Emily Giffin. Read by Jennifer Wiltsie. 4 CDs. (Running Time: 5 hrs. 0 mins. 0 sec.). (ENG.). 2009. audio compact disk 24.95 (978-1-4272-0698-5(8), Rena Bks) Pub: St Martin. Dist(s): Macmillan

Something Dangerous. abr. ed. Patrick Redmond. 2 cass. (Running Time: 2 hrs.). 1999. 17.95 (978-1-55935-325-0(2)) Soundelux.
Kirkston Abbey is no place for weak or sensitive boys. So Jonathan Palmer can't believe his good fortune when Richard Rokeby seeks out his friendship.

Something Familiar. Pamela Reid. 3 cass. 2004. 14.95 (978-1-59156-162-0(0)) Covenant Comms.

Something for Nothing: The All-Consuming Desire That Turns the American Dream into A Social Nightmare. unabr. ed. Brian Tracy. Narrated by Brian Tracy. (ENG.). 2005. 18.19 (978-1-60814-392-4(9)); audio compact disk 25.99 (978-1-59859-109-5(6)) Oasis Audio.

Something-for-Nothing Syndrome. Leonard E. Read. 1 cass. (Ludwig von Mises Lecture Ser.). 10.95 (M 20) J Norton Pubs.

Something Fresh. unabr. ed. P. G. Wodehouse. Read by Frederick Davidson. 6 cass. (Running Time: 8 hrs. 30 mins.). 1995. 44.95 (978-0-7861-0897-8(5), 1671) Blckstn Audio.
The one thing that could be expected to militate against the peace of life at Blandings is the constant incursion of impostors. Blandings has impostors like other houses have mice. On this particular occasion there are two of them - both intent on a dangerous enterprise. Lord Emsworth's secretary, the Efficient Baxter, is on the alert & determined to discover what is afoot - despite the distractions caused by the Hon. Freddie Threepwood's hapless affair of the heart.

Something Happened. unabr. collector's ed. Joseph Heller. Read by Dan Lazar. 11 cass. (Running Time: 16 hrs. 30 mins.). 1981. 88.00 (978-0-7366-0472-7(3), 1447) Books on Tape.
This explores the wartime generation's new predicament...as husband, progenitor, provider & survivalist. What happened to all the youthful dreams & those who people them? Gone to ruin.

Something Higher Than Ideas. 2002. audio compact disk 11.95 (978-0-911203-54-7(0)) New Life.

Something in Disguise. unabr. ed. Elizabeth Jane Howard. Read by Eleanor Bron. 8 cass. (Running Time: 12 hrs.). 2000. 59.95 (978-0-7540-0212-3(8), CAB 1635) Pub: Chivers Audio Bks GBR. Dist(s): AudioGO
Mary's second marriage to Colonel Herbert Brown-Lacey is turning out to be a terrible mistake. her children find the Colonel's presence oppressive and leave home: Oliver drifts from one affair to another, and Elizabeth goes to London in search of love and security. Even Herbert's own daughter tries to escape his sinister behavior.

Something in the Blood. J. G. Goodhind. 2008. 61.95 (978-1-4079-0304-0(7)); audio compact disk 79.95 (978-1-4079-0305-7(5)) Pub: Soundings Ltd GBR. Dist(s): Ulverscroft US

Something Is Rotten. J. M. Gregson. 2009. 61.95 (978-1-4079-0337-8(3)); audio compact disk 71.95 (978-1-4079-0338-5(1)) Pub: Soundings Ltd GBR. Dist(s): Ulverscroft US

Something I've Been Meaning to Tell You: Thirteen Stories. unabr. collector's ed. Alice Munro. Read by Jeanne Hopson. 6 cass. (Running Time: 9 hrs.). 1984. 48.00 (978-0-7366-0512-0(6), 1486) Books on Tape.
This is a collection of 13 varied stories addressing the questions, fears, doubts & observations of childhood & adolescence.

***Something Like Fate.** unabr. ed. Susane Colasanti. Read by Jeannie Stith. (Running Time: 6 hrs.). 2010. 19.99 (978-1-4418-5882-5(2), 9781441858825, Brilliance MP3); 19.99 (978-1-4418-5884-9(9), 9781441858849, BAD); 39.97 (978-1-4418-5883-2(0), 9781441858832, Brlnc Audio MP3 Lib); 39.97 (978-1-4418-5885-6(7), 9781441858856, BADLE); audio compact disk 19.99 (978-1-4418-5880-1(6), 9781441858801, Bril Audio CD Unabri); audio compact disk 54.97 (978-1-4418-5881-8(4), 9781441858818, BriAudCD Unabrid) Brilliance Audio.

Something, Maybe. unabr. ed. Elizabeth Scott. Read by Ellen Grafton. (Running Time: 5 hrs.). 2009. 39.97 (978-1-4233-9759-5(2), 9781423397595, Brlnc Audio MP3 Lib); 24.99 (978-1-4233-9758-8(4), 9781423397588, Brilliance MP3); 39.97 (978-1-4233-9761-8(4), 9781423397618, BADLE); 24.99 (978-1-4233-9760-1(6), 9781423397601, BAD); audio compact disk 26.99 (978-1-4233-9756-4(8), 9781423397564, Bril Audio CD Unabri) Brilliance Audio.

Something, Maybe. unabr. ed. Elizabeth Scott. Read by Ellen Grafton. 5 CDs. (Running Time: 5 hrs.). (YA). (gr. 9 up). 2009. audio compact disk 54.97 (978-1-4233-9757-1(6), 9781423397571, BriAudCD Unabrid) Brilliance Audio.

Something More. Contrib. by Ginny Owens & Don Donahue. Prod. by Monroe Jones. 2004. audio compact disk 16.98 (978-5-559-72891-9(8)) Rocket.

Something More. unabr. ed. Janet Dailey. Read by Renée Raudman. (YA). 2008. 59.99 (978-1-60514-507-5(6)) Find a World.

Something More. unabr. ed. Janet Dailey. Read by Renée Raudman. (Running Time: 11 hrs. 0 mins. 0 sec.). (ENG.). 2007. audio compact disk 34.99 (978-1-4001-0511-3(0)); audio compact disk 69.99 (978-1-4001-3511-0(7)); audio compact disk 24.99 (978-1-4001-5511-8(8)) Pub: Tantor Media. Dist(s): IngramPubServ

Something More: Excavating Your Authentic Self. abr. ed. Sarah Ban Breathnach. (ENG.). 2006. 14.98 (978-1-59483-721-0(X)) Pub: Hachet Audio. Dist(s): HachBkGrp

Something Nasty in the Woodshed. Kyril Bonfiglioli. Read by Simon Prebble. (Running Time: 21600 sec.). (Charlie Mortdecai Mysteries Ser.). 2006. 44.95 (978-0-7861-4582-9(X)); audio compact disk 45.00 (978-0-7861-7032-6(8)) Blckstn Audio.

Something Nasty in the Woodshed. unabr. ed. Kyril Bonfiglioli. Read by Simon Prebble. 5 cass. (Running Time: 27000 sec.). (Charlie Mortdecai Mysteries Ser.). 2006. 24.95 (978-0-7861-4394-8(0)); audio compact disk 25.95 (978-0-7861-7444-7(7)) Blckstn Audio.

Something Nasty in the Woodshed. unabr. ed. Kyril Bonfiglioli. Read by Simon Prebble. (Running Time: 21600 sec.). (Charlie Mortdecai Mysteries Ser.). 2006. audio compact disk 29.95 (978-0-7861-7800-1(0)) Blckstn Audio.

Something New. Contrib. by Jimmy Fitzgerald. (ENG.). 1995. 13.95 (978-0-8023-7109-6(4)); audio compact disk 21.95 (978-0-8023-8109-5(X)) Pub: Clo Iar-Chonnachta IRL. Dist(s): Dufour

Something New. P. G. Wodehouse. Read by Anais 9000. 2009. 27.95 (978-1-60112-209-4(8)) Babblebooks.

Something of an Achievement. unabr. ed. Gwyn Griffin. Read by Wolfram Kandinsky. 6 cass. (Running Time: 9 hrs.). 1983. 48.00 (978-0-7366-0618-9(1), 1580) Books on Tape.
This is the story of Cecil Spurgeon, a middle-aged Chief of Rural Police in a British East Africa colony & his quest to fill the soon-to-be vacant post of Deputy Commissioner of Police.

Something Old, Something New. Connie Monk. Read by Margaret Sircom. 8 cass. (Storysound Ser.). (J). 2003. 69.95 (978-1-85903-491-0(8)) Pub: Mgna Lrg Print GBR. Dist(s): Ulverscroft US

Something Old, Something New. unabr. ed. O. Henry et al. 6 cass. (Running Time: 6 hrs.). (AudioDrama 101 Ser.: Vol. 8). 2001. 14.95 (978-1-892077-08-0(6)) Lend-A-Hand Soc.
This volume contains stories such as The Caliph & the Cad, The Baby Party, The Old Man in the Sea, The Emperor's New Clothes, Demons on the Wall.

Something Old, Something New: 1 John 2:1-11. Ed Young. 1984. 4.95 (978-0-7417-1366-7(7), 366) Win Walk.

Something Queer Is Going On. unabr. ed. Elizabeth Levy. Illus. by Mordicai Gerstein. 1 read-along cass. (Running Time: 19 min.). (Something Queer Ser.). (J). (gr. 2-5). 1983. pap. bk. 15.98 incl. bk. & guide. (978-0-8072-0046-9(8), FTR 78 SP, Listening Lib) Random Audio Pubg.
When Jill's dog Fletcher disappears, she & pal, Gwen, know something is queer - Fletcher never even moves. They dog his trail until Fletcher is recovered, with wonderful consequences for all.

Something Rotten. abr. ed. Engle & Barnes. Read by Full Cast Production Staff. (Running Time: 7200 sec.). (Strange Matter Ser.). (J). (gr. 4-7). 2006. audio compact disk 9.95 (978-1-4233-0842-3(5), 9781423308423, BACD) Brilliance Audio.

Something Rotten. abr. ed. Engle & Barnes. (Running Time: 2 hrs.). (Strange Matter Ser.). 2006. 9.95 (978-1-4233-0844-7(1), 9781423308447, BAD) Brilliance Audio.

Something Rotten. abr. ed. Engle & Julian Barnes. Read by Multivoice Production Staff. (Running Time: 2 hrs.). (Strange Matter Ser.). 2006. 25.25 (978-1-4233-0845-4(X), 9781423308454, BADLE) Brilliance Audio.

Something Rotten. abr. ed. Marion Engle & Johnny Ray Barnes, Jr. Read by Multivoice Production Staff. (Running Time: 7200 sec.). (Strange Matter Ser.). (J). (gr. 4-7). 2006. audio compact disk 25.25 (978-1-4233-0843-0(3), 9781423308430, BACDLib Ed) Brilliance Audio.

Something Rotten. unabr. ed. Jasper Fforde. 10 CDs. (Running Time: 12 hrs. 30 mins.). (Thursday Next Ser.: No. 4). 2004. audio compact disk 34.99 (978-1-4025-9430-4(5), 01812) Recorded Bks.
Literary time traveller Thursday has returned to England-with Hamlet and a pair of dodos-only to find a man aspiring to be dictator so he can invade the Welsh Socialist Republic.

Something Rotten. unabr. ed. Alan Gratz. Read by Erik Davies. 5 CDs. (Running Time: 5 hrs. 42 mins.). (YA). (gr. 7 up). 2007. audio compact disk 50.00 (978-0-7393-6150-4(3), Listening Lib) Pub: Random Audio Pubg. Dist(s): Random
Denmark, Tennessee, stinks. Bad. The smell hits Horatio Wilkes the moment he pulls into town to visit his best friend, Hamilton Prince. And it's not just the paper plant and the polluted Copenhagen River that's stinking up Denmark: Hamilton's father has been poisoned and the killer is still at large. Why? Because nobody believes Rex Prince was murdered. Nobody except Horatio and Hamilton. Now they need to find the killer before someone else dies, but it won't be easy. It seems like everyone's a suspect. But who has committed murder most foul? If high school junior Horatio Wilkes can just get past the smell, he might get to the bottom of all this. A cool and clever twist on the tale of Hamlet, where one-liners crackle and mystery abounds. Think you already know the story? Think again.

Something Rotten in the Village. Steck-Vaughn Staff. 2002. pap. bk. 41.60 (978-0-7398-6975-8(2)) SteckVau.

Something Rotten in the Village Market: Level 4. 2002. (978-0-7398-5346-7(5)) SteckVau.

Something Rotten Village. 2002. (978-0-7398-5190-6(X)) SteckVau.

***Something Special for Me.** unabr. ed. Vera B. Williams. Read by Martha Plimpton. (ENG.). 2009. (978-0-06-176310-6(1), GreenwillowBks); (978-0-06-180607-0(2), GreenwillowBks) HarperCollins Pubs.

Something That Can't Be Borrowed: Matthew 2:31-46. Ed Young. 1993. 4.95 (978-0-7417-1967-6(3), 967) Win Walk.

Something to Hide. unabr. collector's ed. Nicholas Monsarrat. Read by Stuart Courtney. 6 cass. (Running Time: 9 hrs.). 1983. 48.00 (978-0-7366-0249-5(6), 1243) Books on Tape.
Something is the story of a teenage pregnancy. Two embassy officials defect to the enemy.

Something to Say. Arranged by Good News Productions Int'l. (YA). 2009. audio compact disk 6.00 (978-1-59305-170-9(0)) Good News Prod Intl.

Something to Say. Contrib. by Matthew West. Prod. by Brown Bannister et al. 2008. audio compact disk 13.99 (978-5-557-50594-9(6)) Pt of Grace Ent.

Something Upstairs, unabr. ed. Avi. Narrated by George Guidall. 3 pieces. (Running Time: 3 hrs. 15 mins.). (gr. 6 up). 1992. 27.00 (978-1-55690-613-8(7), 92306E7) Recorded Bks.
Kenny Huldorf's family moves to Providence, Rhode Island & Kenny finds his room already inhabited. He meets the ghost of a 100-year-old slave & plunges into a terrifying plot of murder & time travel.

Something Wicked. David Roberts. 2009. 69.95 (978-1-4079-0559-4(7)); audio compact disk 79.95 (978-1-4079-0560-0(0)) Pub: Soundings Ltd GBR. Dist(s): Ulverscroft US

Something Wicked. unabr. ed. Carolyn G. Hart. Read by Kate Reading. 6 cass. (Running Time: 9 hrs.). (Death on Demand Mystery Ser.: No. 3). 2000. 48.00 (978-0-7366-5463-0(1)) Books on Tape.
Annie must find who drew final curtain in a summer stock production or she'll be the star in the next death scene.

Something Wicked, unabr. ed. Jennifer Rowe. Read by Tracey Callander. 8 cass. (Running Time: 10 hrs. 30 mins.). 1999. (978-1-86442-386-0(2), 590377) Bolinda Pubng AUS.
When burnt-out pop star Adam Quinn is found grotesquely dead on a secluded mountain property called Haven, it looks like a case of suicide. But is it? Bliss, Skye & Astral Brydie, the three sisters found at Haven with Quinn's body are vague about what happened the night he died & their mother is nowhere to be found. The girls seem terrified, as if they are holding something back. As Senior Detective Tessa Vance & her partner Steve Hayden work to penetrate the web of fear, suspicion & deceit that shrouds Haven, as the dark secrets of the place are slowly exposed, Tessa must fight to stay clear-headed & to come to terms with the truth.

Something Wicked This Way Comes. Ray Bradbury. Narrated by Paul Hecht. 7 CDs. (Running Time: 8 hrs.). audio compact disk 69.00 (978-0-7887-4637-6(5)) Recorded Bks.

Something Wicked This Way Comes. unabr. ed. Ray Bradbury. Read by Stefan Rudnicki. 1 MP3. (Running Time: 10 hrs. 30 mins.). 2005. 29.95 (978-0-7861-7872-8(8), ZM3559) Blckstn Audio.

Something Wicked This Way Comes. unabr. ed. Ray Bradbury. Told to Jerry Robbins & Colonial Radio Players. (Running Time: 7200 sec.). 2007. 22.95 (978-1-4332-1078-5(9)); audio compact disk 24.00 (978-1-4332-1079-2(7)); audio compact disk 19.95 (978-1-4332-1080-8(0)) Blckstn Audio.

Something Wicked This Way Comes. unabr. ed. Ray Bradbury. Read by Paul Hecht. 5 Cass. (Running Time: 8 Hours). 1999. 24.95 (978-1-4025-2492-9(7)) Recorded Bks.

Something Wicked This Way Comes. unabr. ed. Ray Bradbury. Narrated by Paul Hecht. 6 cass. (Running Time: 8 hrs.). 1999. 51.00 (978-0-7887-3494-6(6), 95691E7) Recorded Bks.
The legendary storyteller weaves dreams & nightmares, childhood memories & fantasies for a darkly poetic, magical tale of two boys encountering evil secrets.

Something Wicked This Way Comes. unabr. ed. Ray Bradbury. Narrated by Paul Hecht. 7 CDs. (Running Time: 8 hrs.). 2000. audio compact disk 69.00 (C1212E7) Recorded Bks.
Legendary storyteller weaves dreams & nightmares, childhood memories & fantasies for a darkly poetic, magical tale of two boys encountering evil secrets.

***Something Wicked This Way Comes.** unabr. ed. Ray Bradbury. Narrated by Kevin Foley. (Running Time: 8 hrs. 30 mins. 0 sec.). (ENG.). 2010. 19.99 (978-1-4001-6825-5(2)); 15.99 (978-1-4001-8825-3(3)); audio compact disk 29.99 (978-1-4001-1825-0(5)); audio compact disk 71.99 (978-1-4001-4825-7(1)) Pub: Tantor Media. Dist(s): IngramPubServ

Something Wicked This Way Comes; A Sound of Thunder. Ray Bradbury. (Running Time: 34200 sec.). 2005. 59.95 (978-0-7861-4353-5(3)); audio compact disk 72.00 (978-0-7861-7535-2(4)) Blckstn Audio.

Something Wicked This Way Comes; A Sound of Thunder. unabr. ed. Ray Bradbury. Read by Stefan Rudnicki. 9 CDs. (Running Time: 34200 sec.). 2005. audio compact disk 29.95 (978-0-7861-7626-7(1), ZE3559); 29.95 (978-0-7861-3766-4(5), ZE3559) Blckstn Audio.
Something Wicked This Way Comes - One Autumn midnight, on the crest of the wind, something evil arrives in a small Midwestern town. A "dark carnival" with frightening attractions and supernatural characters sets up stakes. And two thirteen-year-old boys, James Nightshade and William Halloway, must figure out a way to save the souls of the town in this unforgettable modern Gothic masterpiece. A Sound of Thunder - A small safari company promises to transport adventurers back in time for a chance to hunt any animal that ever existed. The animals are specially selected according to their natural time of death. Nothing else may be altered because it just might change the whole course of the future. But when one foolish hunter comes face to face with a tyrannosaurus rex, the carefully constructed safari goes awry and the future is up for grabs.

Something Wonderful. abr. ed. Judith McNaught. Read by Noel Taylor. 1 cass. (Running Time: 90 min.). 1993. 5.99 (978-1-57096-001-7(1), RAZ 902) Romance Alive Audio.
When innocent Alexandra Lawrence enters into marriage with the arrogant Duke of Hawthorne, Jordan Townsende, she never dreams that an enforced separation will eventually reveal to them both that their love for each other is something wonderful.

Something's Fishy at Camp Wiganishie. Al Simmons. 1 cass. (J). 1994. 10.98 Consort Bk Sales.

Something's Fishy at Camp Wiganishie. Perf. by Al Simmons. 1 cass. (J). (ps-7). 10.98 (978-0-945267-37-9(1), YM047-CN); audio compact disk 13.98 (978-0-945267-38-6(X), YM047-CD) Youngheart Mus.
Songs include: "Camp Wiganishie"; "The Woodpecker Song"; "I Want a Pancake"; "I Got My Axe"; "Bling Blang"; "Lego House"; "I Got a Horse"; "Something in My Shoe"; "Counting Feathers"; "I Collect Rocks"; "The Stew Song"; "It's Raining, It's Pouring" & more.

Something's Gone Wrong with the Harvest: Galatians 6:7-8. Ed Young. 1985. 4.95 (978-0-7417-1455-8(8), 455) Win Walk.

Something's Happening! Zsuzsanna E. Budapest. 1 cass. (Roy Tuckman Interview Ser.). 9.00 (A0434-89) Sound Photosyn.

Something's Happening! Bob Nelson. 1 cass. (Roy Tuckman Interview Ser.). 9.00 (A0689-90) Sound Photosyn.

Something's Happening! Daniel Sheehan. 1 cass. (Roy Tuckman Interview Ser.). 9.00 (A0474-89) Sound Photosyn.
The Chief Council & vanguard force of the intrepid integrity mongers, the Cristic Institute, clarifies some questions.

Something's Happening! unabr. ed. Terence McKenna. 2 cass. (Roy Tuckman Interview Ser.). 1987. 18.00 Set. (978-1-56964-047-0(5), A0085-87) Sound Photosyn.

***Sometimes I Feel Like a Nut: Essays & Observations.** unabr. ed. Jill Kargman. (ENG.). 2011. (978-0-06-206260-4(3), Harper Audio) HarperCollins Pubs.

Somewhere Behind the Morning. unabr. ed. Frances McNeil. Read by Margaret Sircom. 10 cass. (Story Sound Ser.). (J). 2006. 84.95 (978-1-85903-919-9(7)) Pub: Mgna Lrg Print GBR. Dist(s): Ulverscroft US

Somewhere Behind the Morning. unabr. ed. Frances McNeil & Margaret Sircom. Read by Margaret Sircom. 11 CDs. (Running Time: 13 hrs. 15 mins.). (Story Sound CD Ser.). (J). 2006. audio compact disk 99.95 (978-1-85903-968-7(5)) Pub: Mgna Lrg Print GBR. Dist(s): Ulverscroft US

***Somewhere I'll Find You.** unabr. ed. Lisa Kleypas. Read by Rosalyn Landor. (Running Time: 10 hrs.). 2011. 24.99 (978-1-4418-5215-1(8), 9781441852151, Brilliance MP3); 39.97 (978-1-4418-5216-8(6), 9781441852168, Brlnc Audio MP3 Lib); audio compact disk 29.99 (978-1-4418-5213-7(1), 9781441852137, Bril Audio CD Unabri); audio compact disk 79.97 (978-1-4418-5214-4(X), 9781441852144, BriAudCD Unabrid) Brilliance Audio.

Somewhere in a Turret see Poetry & Voice of Marilyn Hacker

Somewhere in Heaven: The Remarkable Love Story of Dana & Christopher Reeve. unabr. ed. Christopher Andersen. Narrated by Edward Herrmann. (Running Time: 6 hrs.). 2008. 56.75 (978-1-4361-6498-6(2)); audio compact disk 44.95 (978-1-4361-3888-8(4)) Recorded Bks.
Christopher Andersen, senior editor for People and acclaimed author of numerous books, spotlights Dana and Christopher Reeve - examining their unique partnership and the romance, faith, and fortitude that defined it. This bittersweet saga shows the couple bearing the painful hand of providence with unbelievable grace, courage, and humor.

Somewhere in Southern Indiana: Poems of Midwestern Origins. Norbert Krapf. 1993. 12.95 (978-1-877770-91-3(4)) Time Being Bks.

Somewhere in the Crowd. Scott Houghton. 1999. audio compact disk 14.99 (978-1-878046-54-3(3)) Hart Res Ctr.

***Somewhere in Time.** unabr. ed. Richard Matheson. Read by Scott Brick. (Running Time: 10 hrs. 30 mins.). 2010. 29.95 (978-1-4417-2221-8(1)); 65.95 (978-1-4417-2217-1(3)); audio compact disk 29.95 (978-1-4417-2220-1(3)); audio compact disk 100.00 (978-1-4417-2218-8(1)) Blckstn Audio.

Somewhere in Time. unabr. collector's ed. Richard Matheson. Read by Christopher Hurt. 7 cass. (Running Time: 10 hrs. 30 min.). 1989. 56.00 (978-0-7366-1517-4(2), 2388) Books on Tape.
Somewhere in Time is a haunting blend of great romance & mesmerizing mystery.

Somewhere in Time: The Songs & Spirit of WW II. Perf. by Bob Hope & Dolores Reade Hope. 2 cass. Dramatization. (This Is Bob "On the Air" Hope Ser.). 1994. pap. bk. Hope Enterprise.
Dolores Reade Hope sings songs of WW II. Excerpts from Bob Hope Radio Shows of WW II.

***Somewhere Inside.** unabr. ed. Laura Ling & Lisa Ling. Read by Laura Ling & Lisa Ling. (ENG.). 2010. (978-0-06-201620-1(2), Harper Audio) HarperCollins Pubs.

***Somewhere Inside: One Sister's Captivity in North Korea & the Other's Fight to Bring Her Home.** unabr. ed. Laura Ling & Lisa Ling. Read by Laura Ling & Lisa Ling. (ENG.). 2010. (978-0-06-201241-8(X), Harper Audio) HarperCollins Pubs.

***Somewhere More Holy: Stories from a Bewildered Father, Stumbling Husband, Reluctant Handyman, & Prodigal Son.** Zondervan Publishing Staff & Tony Woodlief. (Running Time: 4 hrs. 46 mins. 51 sec.). (ENG.). 2010. 12.99 (978-0-310-41256-4(0)) Zondervan.

Somewhere off the Coast of Maine. collector's ed. Ann Hood. Read by Kimberly Schraf. 5 cass. (Running Time: 7 hrs. 30 min.). 2000. 40.00 (978-0-7366-5447-0(X)) Books on Tape.
It is 1969, Suzanne, a poet, lives in a Maine beach house awaiting the birth of her love child, who she will name Sparrow. Claudia, who weds a farmer during college, is planning to raise three strong sons. Elizabeth & Howard get married, organize protest marches & try to raise their two children with their own earthy, hippie values. By 1985, things have changed, Suzanne, now with an MBA, has taken to calling Sparrow Susan. After personal tragedy, Claudia spirals backward into her sixties world & madness & Elizabeth, fatally ill, watches despairingly as her children yearn for a split level house & a gleaming station wagon. Looking into their pasts, each woman attempts to reconcile her youthful life with what she had become.

Somewhere Out There. 1987. audio compact disk 22.95 (978-0-634-09202-2(2)) H Leonard.

Somewhere, Someday. Josephine Cox. Read by Carole Boyd. 8 cass. (Running Time: 12 hrs.). 2000. 69.95 (978-0-7540-0522-3(4), CAB 1945) Pub: Chivers Audio Bks GBR. Dist(s): AudioGO

Somewhere, Someday. unabr. ed. Josephine Cox. Read by Carole Boyd. 8 CDs. (Running Time: 12 hrs.). 2000. audio compact disk 79.95 (978-0-7540-5387-3(3), CCD 078) Pub: Chivers Audio Bks GBR. Dist(s): AudioGO
Kelly had always known Barney would leave, but she could never have envisioned how his leaving would turn her whole world upside down. But now he was gone & she wondered if she would ever see him again. Being alone with her past, she recalls the mother that had disowned her & the time when the family was torn apart. Now, after years of regret, she knows that she must return to her past & lay to rest the ghosts that haunted her.

Somewhere South of Here. William Kowalski. Narrated by Tom Stechschulte. 7 cass. (Running Time: 9 hrs.). 65.00 (978-1-4025-0232-3(X)) Recorded Bks.

Somewhere to Belong. abr. ed. Judith Miller. Narrated by Rebecca Gallagher. (Running Time: 7 hrs. 53 mins. 4 sec.). (Daughters of Amana Ser.: Bk. 1). 2010. 19.59 (978-1-60814-623-9(5)); audio compact disk 27.99 (978-1-59859-677-9(2)) Oasis Audio.

Somme & Back to Ypres: July 1916 - July 1917. Max Arthur. 2 cass. (Running Time: 3 hrs. 0 mins. 0 sec.). (Forgotten Voices Ser.). (ENG., 2003. 17.50 (978-1-85686-687-3(4), Audiobks) Pub: Random GBR. Dist(s): IPG Chicago

Sommeil Profond. unabr. ed. Robert A. Monroe. Read by Roland Simon. 1 cass. (Running Time: 30 min.). (Mind Food Ser.). 1992. 14.95 (978-1-56102-430-8(9)) Inter Indus.
Get a good night's sleep with the Hemi-Sync signal.

***Sommer-Time Stories, Set.** Carl Sommer. (Another Sommer-Time Story Ser.). (J). 2009. bk. 406.80 (978-1-57537-548-9(6)) Advance Pub.

Somos los Ninos de Zoo-Phonics. Charlene Wrighton et al. 1 cass. (Running Time: 1 hr. 30 mins.). (J). 1994. bk. 16.95 (978-1-886441-15-6(4)) Zoo-phonics.
Teaches the sounds of the Spanish alphabet through songs & stories. Includes lyrics booklet.

Son Años. unabr. ed. Fuerte Torre & Heriberto Hermosillo. (SPA.). 1999. 4.99 (978-0-8297-2821-7(X)) Pub: Vida Pubs. Dist(s): Zondervan

Son, I Loved You at Your Darkest. Contrib. by As Cities Burn. Prod. by Matt Goldman & Josh Scogin. 2005. audio compact disk 13.98 (978-5-558-97849-0(X)) Solid State MO.

Son of a Wanted Man. abr. ed. Louis L'Amour. Read by Dramatization Staff. (Running Time: 3 hrs.). (Louis L'Amour Ser.). (ENG.). 2005. audio compact disk 14.99 (978-0-7393-1730-3(X)) Pub: Random Audio Pubg. Dist(s): Random

***Son of a Witch.** unabr. ed. Gregory Maguire. Read by Gregory Maguire. (ENG.). 2005. (978-0-06-112488-4(5), Harper Audio); (978-0-06-112489-1(3), Harper Audio) HarperCollins Pubs.

Son of a Witch. unabr. ed. Gregory Maguire. Read by Gregory Maguire. (Wicked Years Ser.: No. 2). 2009. audio compact disk 19.99 (978-0-06-190621-3(2), Harper Audio) HarperCollins Pubs.

Son of David. Contrib. by Various Artists & Yochanan Ben Yehuda. Prod. by Yochanan Ben Yehuda & Jerry Marcellino. 2008. audio compact disk 17.98 (978-5-557-43329-7(5)) Pt of Grace Ent.

Son of God. Contrib. by Starfield. (Praise Hymn Soundtracks Ser.). 2006. audio compact disk 8.98 (978-5-558-20108-6(8)) Pt of Grace Ent.

Son of God Manifested. Kenneth E. Hagin. (Spiritual Life & Scriptual Healing Ser.). 24.00 Faith Lib Pubns.

Son of Hamas: A Gripping Account of Terror, Betrayal, Political Intrigue, & Unthinkable Choices. unabr. ed. Mosab Hassan Yousef. Told to Ron Brackin. (ENG.). 2010. audio compact disk 29.99 (978-1-4143-3309-0(9), Tyndale Audio) Tyndale Hse.

Son of Light Vol. 1. unabr. ed. Christian Jacq. Narrated by George Guidall. 8 cass. (Running Time: 11 hrs. 15 mins.). 1998. 70.00 (978-0-7887-1893-9(2), 95315E7) Recorded Bks.
Historical novel of court intrique, treason & romance. A rare look at the Egypt of 3,000 years ago.

Son of Satan Audio Series. Speeches. James A. Scudder. 6. (Running Time: 90). 2002. audio compact disk 30.00 (978-0-9719262-0-2(4)) Victin Grace Min.

Son of Tarzan. 2003. 16.95 (978-0-929071-84-8(0)) B-B Audio.
Follows the adventures of Tarzan's son, Jack. Despite all the civilizing efforts of his parents, Jack feels the call of the wild and sets off for Africa. The Son of Tarzan escapes from the drawing rooms of London as a teenager with Akut, the great ape, and learns to live in the jungle.

Son of Tarzan. Edgar Rice Burroughs. Read by Shelly Frasier. (Running Time: 9 hrs. 45 mins.). 2002. 27.95 (978-1-60083-625-1(9), Audiofy Corp) Iofy Corp.

Son of Tarzan. Edgar Rice Burroughs. Read by Shelly Frasier. (Tarzan Ser.). (ENG.). 2005. audio compact disk 84.00 (978-1-4001-3056-6(5)) Pub: Tantor Media. Dist(s): IngramPubServ

Son of Tarzan. unabr. ed. Edgar Rice Burroughs. Narrated by Edgar Rice Burroughs. (Running Time: 9 hrs. 43 mins.). (Tarzan Ser.). (ENG.). 2002. audio compact disk 20.00 (978-1-4001-5056-4(6)) Pub: Tantor Media. Dist(s): IngramPubServ
Unabridged Audiobook. 1 MP3 CD - 9 hours, 43 minutes. Narrated by Shelly Frasier.Paulvitch seeks revenge against Tarzan once again, this time by luring Lord Greystoke's rebellious son away from London. The great ape Akut foils the plot of revenge as he helps the boy escape the wrath of Paulvitch. Akut and the son flee to the savage African jungle where Tarzan was reared.In his quest to survive, the young civilized boy reckons with life and death as he encounters the same dangers that his father once faced and ultimately matures into the mighty warrior, ?Korak the Killer?. In one of his many adventures, Korak rescues a young beauty, Meriem from an Arabian band of raiders. Like Tarzan, Korak discovers that the perils of the jungle are nothing compared to the evils of men. Tarzan Series #4.

Son of Tarzan. unabr. ed. Edgar Rice Burroughs. Narrated by Shelly Frasier. (Running Time: 9 hrs. 30 mins. 0 sec.). (Tarzan Ser.). (ENG.). 2009. 22.99 (978-1-4001-5924-6(5)); lab manual ed. 65.99 (978-1-4001-3924-8(4)); audio compact disk 32.99 (978-1-4001-0924-1(8)) Pub: Tantor Media. Dist(s): IngramPubServ

Son of Tarzan, Bk. 4. unabr. ed. Edgar Rice Burroughs. Read by David Sharp. 8 cass. (Running Time: 9 hrs. 24 min.). Dramatization. 1993. 49.95 (978-1-55686-481-0(7), 481) Books in Motion.
Reared in England, Tarzan's son Jack inherited the wild, jungle countenance of his father. Jack leads us away from the sheltered shores of 19th century England, back to the primitive jungle. Young Lord Greystoke quickly asserts his natural authority in the jungle.

Son of the Circus. unabr. ed. John Irving. Read by David Colacci. (Running Time: 93600 sec.). 2007. audio compact disk 29.95 (978-1-4233-3599-3(6), 9781423335993, Brilliance MP3) Brilliance Audio.

Son of the Circus. unabr. ed. John Irving. Read by David Colacci. (Running Time: 26 hrs.). 2007. 44.25 (978-1-4233-3602-0(X), 9781423336020, BADLE); 29.95 (978-1-4233-3601-3(1), 9781423336013, BAD); audio compact disk 44.25 (978-1-4233-3600-6(3), 9781423336006, Brlnc Audio MP3 Lib) Brilliance Audio.

***Son of the Long One.** Anonymous. 2009. (978-1-60136-597-2(7)) Audio Holding.

Son of the Middle Border. Hamlin Garland. (Running Time: 48600 sec.). 2005. 79.95 (978-0-7861-3778-7(9)) Blckstn Audio.

Son of the Middle Border. Hamlin Garland. Read by Grover Gardner. (Running Time: 48600 sec.). 2005. audio compact disk 99.00 (978-0-7861-7588-8(5)) Blckstn Audio.

Son of the Middle Border. unabr. ed. Hamlin Garland. Read by Grover Gardner. (Running Time: 48600 sec.). 2005. audio compact disk 29.95 (978-0-7861-7863-6(9)) Blckstn Audio.

Son of the Mob. unabr. ed. Gordon Korman. 3 cass. (Running Time: 4 hrs. 36 mins.). (J). (gr. 7 up). 2004. 30.00 (978-0-8072-0971-4(6), S YA 412 CX, Listening Lib) Random Audio Pubg.

Son of the Morning. abr. ed. Linda Howard. Read by Natalie Ross. (Running Time: 6 hrs.). 2009. audio compact disk 19.99 (978-1-4418-0716-8(0), 9781441807168, BACD) Brilliance Audio.

Son of the Morning. abr. ed. Linda Howard. Read by Natalie Ross. (Running Time: 6 hrs.). 2010. audio compact disk 9.99 (978-1-4418-1674-0(7), 9781441816740, BCD Value Price) Brilliance Audio.

Son of the Morning. unabr. ed. Linda Howard. Read by Natalie Ross. (Running Time: 14 hrs.). 2009. 39.97 (978-1-4233-6332-3(9), 9781423363323, Brlnc Audio MP3 Lib); 24.99 (978-1-4233-6331-6(0), 9781423363316, Brilliance MP3); 24.99 (978-1-4233-6333-0(7), 9781423363330, BAD); 39.97 (978-1-4418-5031-7(7), 9781441850317, BADLE); audio compact disk 92.97 (978-1-4233-6330-9(2), 9781423363309, BriAudCD Unabrid); audio compact disk 29.99 (978-1-4233-6329-3(9), 9781423363293, Bril Audio CD Unabri) Brilliance Audio.

Son of the Morning Star: Custer & the Little Bighorn, abr. ed. Evan S. Connell. Read by Joseph Campanella. 2 cass. (Running Time: 3 hrs.). 1991. 15.95 (978-1-879371-05-7(7), 391614) Pub Mills.
This is the bestselling book which provided a keen & anecdotal analysis of the military career & personal life of General George Armstrong Custer & how the two led to his demise at the Little Bighorn. It was named one of the ten best non-fiction books of the 80's by Time Magazine.

Son of the Morning Star: Custer & the Little Bighorn. unabr. ed. Evan S. Connell. Narrated by Adrian Cronauer. 14 cass. (Running Time: 21 hrs.). 1985. 112.00 (978-1-55690-486-8(X), 85420E7) Recorded Bks.
An expansive account of the Battle of Little Big Horn & the events leading up to it.

Son of the Morning Star Pt. 1: Custer & the Little Bighorn, unabr. collector's ed. Evan S. Connell. Read by Christopher Hurt. 7 cass. (Running Time: 10 hrs. 30 min.). 1986. 56.00 (978-0-7366-1052-0(9), 1980-A) Books on Tape.
George Armstrong Custer was a hero to some, a disaster to others. When he first saw the line of Indian camps opposing him, a line more than four miles long, he whooped, "Hurrah, boys, we've got them." Disregarding a Cheyenne warning, Custer rode to his death & led to death every man of the Seventh Cavalry who followed. This is part biography of Custer & part history of the Plains Indian Wars.

Son of the Morning Star Pt. 2: Custer & the Little Bighorn, collector's ed. Evan S. Connell. Read by Christopher Hurt. 7 cass. (Running Time: 10 hrs. 30 min.). 1986. 56.00 (978-0-7366-1053-7(7), 1980-B) Books on Tape.

Son of the Sun see Captain David Grief

Son of the Sun. unabr. ed. Jack London. Read by Patrick Treadway. 4 cass. (Running Time: 5 hrs. 15 min.). Dramatization. 1992. 26.95 (978-1-55686-431-5(0), 431) Books in Motion.
In the world of the South Pacific Islands, Captain Grief was always ready for the unexpected. With a quick eye for the promise of danger, Grief was not afraid to resort to raw fists & guns to obtain the treasures & power for which he searched.

Son of the Whirlwind. unabr. ed. Elyne Mitchell. Read by Caroline Lee. 4 cass. (Running Time: 4 hrs. 15 mins.). 2002. (978-1-74030-151-0(X), 500638) Bolinda Pubng AUS.

Son of the Wilderness: The Life of John Muir, unabr. ed. Linnie M. Wolfe. Read by James Armstrong. 10 cass. (Running Time: 15 hrs.). 1996. 69.95 (978-0-7861-1222-7(0), 2161) Blckstn Audio.
Creates a full portrait of the subject, not only as America's firebrand conservationist & founder of the national park system, but also as husband, father, & friend.

Son of the Wolf. unabr. ed. Jack London. Read by John Chatty & Jim Roberts. 4 cass. (Running Time: 6 hrs.). Incl. In a Far Country. 1984. (C-104); Men of Forty Mile. 1984. (C-104); Odyssey of the North. 1984. (C-104); Priestly Prerogative. 1984. (C-104); To the Man on Trail. 1984. (C-104); White Silence. 1984. (C-104); Wife of a King. 1984. (C-104); Wisdom of the Trail. 1984. (C-104); 1984. 28.00 (C-104) Jimcin Record.

Son of the Wolf. unabr. collector's ed. Jack London. Read by John Chatty & Jim Roberts. 6 cass. (Running Time: 6 hrs.). (J). 1983. 36.00 (978-0-7366-3881-4(4), 9105) Books on Tape.
Tales of the Yukon, including "The White Silence," "The Son of the Wolf," "The Men of Forty Mile," "In a Far Country," "To the Man on Trail," "The Priestly Prerogative," "The Wisdom of the Trail," "The Wife of a King" & "An Odyssey of the North".

Son of Thunder (John) Luke 9:54-56. Ed Young. 1985. 4.95 (978-0-7417-1468-8(X), 468) Win Walk.

Son of War. unabr. ed. Melvyn Bragg. Read by Mark McGann. 10 cass. (Running Time: 15 hrs.). 2002. 84.95 (978-0-7540-0795-1(2), CAB 2217) AudioGO.

Son Revealed. Neville Goddard. 1 cass. (Running Time: 62 min.). 1969. 8.00 (79) J & L Pubns.
Neville taught Imagination Creates Reality. He was a powerfully influential teacher of God as Consciousness.

Sonando Tambores (Dreaming Drums) Shakti for Children Staff et al. Perf. by Prem Dass & Muruga. 1 cass. 10.00 (A0729-90) Sound Photosyn.
Cultures around the world use dream time to gain information. Shamanic dream time, upon which this album is based, & Nada Yoga, the ancient science of sound, blend to produce a transcendent state.

***Sonata A Kreutzer.** abr. ed. Leon Tolstoi. Read by Daniel Quintero. (SPA.). 2008. audio compact disk 17.00 (978-958-8318-32-5(7)) Pub: Yoyo Music COL. Dist(s): YoYoMusic

Sonatas of Praise. Don Wyrtzen. 1996. audio compact disk 16.98 (978-0-8054-9554-6(1)) BH Pubng Grp.

Sonatas of Praise. Don Wyrtzen. 1994. 11.98 (978-0-7673-0653-9(8)) LifeWay Christian.

Sonatas of Praise Ii. Don Wyrtzen. 1996. 11.98 (978-0-8054-9516-4(9)) BH Pubng Grp.

Sonatina Album. Kim Newman & Lucille Schreibman. (Alfred Masterwork Edition Ser.). (ENG.). 1994. audio compact disk 14.95 (978-0-7390-1657-2(1), 3997) Alfred Pub.

Sonatina Album, Volume 1: Schirmer Performance Editions Series. Created by Hal Leonard Corporation Staff. 2006. pap. bk. 12.95 (978-1-4234-0509-2(9), 1423405099, G Schirmer) H Leonard.

Sonderberg Case. unabr. ed. Elie Wiesel. Read by Mark Bramhall. Tr. by Catherine Temerson. 2010. audio compact disk 30.00 (978-0-307-73463-1(3), Random AudioBks) Pub: Random Audio Pubg. Dist(s): Random

Sonderling: The Franz Jaegerstatter Story. unabr. ed. James F. Sinnott. Read by Adams Morgan. 11 cass. (Running Time: 16 hrs.). 1999. 76.95 (978-0-7861-1589-1(0), 2418) Blckstn Audio.
Follows the life of young Franz who, as a child, sees his father go off to fight in The Great War & as a young man about to marry, finds himself under the shadow of Hitler's Nazi Germany. The dilemmas created by Hitler's oppression of Catholics & the Vatican's fear of the same enemy Hitler has declared - Soviet atheistic communism - takes Franz, his childhood friends & the Catholic priests who have helped in his upbringing through an odyssey of intrigue, resistance & survival during the dark years of WWII.

Sonetti (The Sonnets) Original 78 Sonnets Read in Italian with Text & the J. A. Symonds Verse Translation. Michelangelo Buonarroti. Read by Elsa Proverbio. 2 cass. (Running Time: 2 hrs.). (ITA.). 1997. pap. bk. 29.50 (978-1-58085-452-8(4)) Interlingua VA.

Song see Poetry & Voice of Muriel Rukeyser

Song see Evening with Dylan Thomas

Song: Go & Catch a Falling Star see Love Poems of John Donne

Song: Sweetest Love, I Do Not Go see Love Poems of John Donne

Song - Sweet Beast, I Have Gone Prowling see Twentieth-Century Poetry in English, No. 29, Recordings of Poets Reading Their Own Poetry

Song - The Heart of Christmas. Perf. by Kenneth G. Mills & Star-Scape Singers. 1 cass. (Running Time: 1 hr. 2 min.). 1990. 9.98 (KGOC28); audio compact disk 14.98 CD. (KGOD28) Ken Mills Found.
Kenneth G. Mills conducts The Star-Scape Singers. Christmas carols old & new 16 carols.

Song (A Poem from the Poets' Corner) The One-and-Only Poetry Book for the Whole Family. unabr. ed. John Donne & John Lithgow. Read by John Lithgow. (Running Time: 10 mins.). (ENG.). 2008. 0.99 (978-1-60024-315-8(0)) Pub: Hachet Audio. Dist(s): HachBkGrp

Song about Myself see Poetry of Keats

Song & Dance Man. Karen Ackerman. (J). 1989. 18.66 SRA McGraw.
Grandpa a vaudeville entertainer demonstrates for his grandchildren some of the songs, dances and jokes he performed.

Song & Play Time. Perf. by Pete Seeger. 1 cass. (J). (ps-6). 1990. (0-9307-45023-4-1) Smithsonian Folkways.
Focuses on memory skills & variations of a theme using time-honored songs "Go In & Out the Window," "She'll Be Comin' Round the Mountain," "Little Sally Walker" & others.

Song & the Silence: Songs of Meditation & Healing. Marty Haugen. 1 cass. 1998. 10.95 (CS-449); audio compact disk 15.95 (CD-449) GIA Pubns.

Song at Twilight. unabr. ed. Lilian Harry. 12 CDs. (Soundings (CDs) Ser.). 2007. audio compact disk 99.95 (978-1-84559-527-2(0)) Pub: ISIS Lrg Prnt GBR. Dist(s): Ulverscroft US

Song at Twilight. unabr. ed. Lilian Harry. Read by Anne Dover. 12 cass. (Soundings Ser.). 2007. 94.95 (978-1-84559-332-2(4)) Pub: ISIS Lrg Prnt GBR. Dist(s): Ulverscroft US

Song Box Sets & Resources:Save the Tree for Me Cass. McGraw-Hill Staff. (Song Box Ser.). (gr. 1-2). bk. 8.50 (978-0-7802-2265-6(2)) Wright Group.

Song Flung up to Heaven. unabr. ed. Maya Angelou. Read by Maya Angelou. 3 cass. (Running Time: 4 hrs. 30 mins.). 2002. 28.00 (978-0-7366-8556-6(1)); audio compact disk 32.00 (978-0-7366-8606-8(1)) Books on Tape.
opens in 1964 as she returns from Africa to the United States to work with Malcolm X. No sooner does she arrive there than she learns that Malcolm X has been assassinated. Devastated, she tries to put her life back together, working on the stage in local theaters and even conducting a door-to-door survey in Watts until it erupts in riot. When Martin Luther King is assassinated, Angelou completely withdraws from the world, unable to deal with this horrible event. Finally, James Baldwin forces her out of isolation and insists that she accompany him to a dinner party - where the idea for writing this book was born.

Song for a Dark Girl see Poetry of Langston Hughes

Song for Billie Holliday see Poetry of Langston Hughes

Song for Koko: An Introduction to the Language of Jazz for the Native American Flute. John Vames. 2008. pap. bk. 29.95 (978-0-9740486-1-1(5)) Molly Moon.

Song for Mary: An Irish-American Memory. Dennis Smith. 2000. (978-1-57042-885-2(9)) Hachet Audio.

Song for Mary: An Irish-American Memory, abr. ed. Dennis Smith. Read by Dennis Smith. 2 cass. 1999. 17.98 (FS9-43332) Highsmith.

Song for Mary: An Irish American Memory. abr. ed. Dennis Smith. (ENG.). 2006. 14.98 (978-1-59483-849-1(6)) Pub: Hachet Audio. Dist(s): HachBkGrp

Song for Saint Cecilia's Day see Treasury of John Dryden

Song for St. Cecilia's Day see Palgrave's Golden Treasury of English Poetry

Song for Successful Parenting. Created by Barbara Lynn Taylor. 2001. 11.95 (978-1-880283-53-0(0)) Active Parenting.

Song for the Asking, unabr. ed. Steve Gannon. Narrated by George Guidall. 9 cass. (Running Time: 12 hrs. 15 mins.). 1997. 83.00 (978-0-7887-0919-7(4), 95059E7) Recorded Bks.
During the summer-long vacation at the family's California beach house, a tyrannical father attempts to mold his four children into strong-willed copies of himself. Soon his misguided love brings rebellion, brutality & despair.

Song in a Strange Land. 2006. 65.95 (978-0-7861-4437-2(8)); audio compact disk 90.00 (978-0-7861-7348-8(3)) Blckstn Audio.

Song in a Strange Land. unabr. ed. Gilbert Morris. Read by Robert Whitfield. 2006. 29.95 (978-0-7861-7723-3(3)) Blckstn Audio.

***Song in the Air.** Anne Douglas. 2010. 69.95 (978-1-4079-0891-5(X)); audio compact disk 84.95 (978-1-4079-0892-2(8)) Pub: Soundings Ltd GBR. Dist(s): Ulverscroft US

Song in the Wood see Gathering of Great Poetry for Children

Song Lee & the "I Hate You" Notes. unabr. ed. Suzy Kline. Narrated by Johnny Heller. 1 cass. (Running Time: 30 mins.). (gr. 2 up). 2000. 10.00 (978-0-7887-3811-1(9), 96025E7) Recorded Bks.
Everyone in Mrs. Mackle's class knows that Horrible Harry likes to do horrible things. But when someone sends Song Lee two "I hate you" notes, no one thinks of Harry. He wouldn't send mean notes to the nicest person in the class.

Song Lee & the "I Hate You" Notes. unabr. ed. Suzy Kline. Read by Johnny Heller. 1 cass. (Running Time: 30 mins.). (J). 2000. pap. bk. & stu. ed. 30.99 (978-0-7887-3854-8(2), 41052X4) Recorded Bks.

Song Lee & the "I Hate You" Notes, Class Set. unabr. ed. Suzy Kline. Read by Johnny Heller. 1 cass. (Running Time: 30 mins.). (YA). (gr. 2 up). 1999. 158.20 (978-0-7887-3880-7(1), 47046) Recorded Bks.

Song Lee & the Leech Man. Suzy Kline. Narrated by Johnny Heller. 1 cass. (Running Time: 30 mins.). (gr. 2 up). 2001. 10.00 (978-0-7887-5522-4(6)) Recorded Bks.
Song Lee is excited about the class field trip to a pond. Before the students get on the bus, Sydney has made Horrible Harry angry. Harry wants revenge. Suddenly, his plan backfires, and Harry is covered in trouble. Can Song Lee save him?.

Song Lee in Room 2B. unabr. ed. Suzy Kline. Narrated by Johnny Heller. 1 cass. (Running Time: 45 mins.). (gr. 2 up). 1998. 10.00 (978-0-7887-1902-8(5), 95323E7) Recorded Bks.
Everyone knows that Song Lee is shy, but Horrible Harry & his classmates soon find that he is also full of surprises. Join the students in Room 2B in four adventures starring Song Lee.

Song Lee in Room 2B. unabr. ed. Suzy Kline. Read by Johnny Heller. 1 cass. (Running Time: 45 min.). (J). (gr. 2). 1998. 22.24 Hmwk Set. (978-0-7887-1930-1(0), 40637) Recorded Bks.
Everyone in room 2B knows that Song Lee is shy, but Horrible Harry & his classmates soon find that quiet Song Lee is also full of surprises.

Song of a Dark Angel: A Medieval Mystery Featuring Hugh Corbett. unabr. ed. Paul C. Doherty. 6 cass. 1998. 69.95 Set. (978-1-85903-104-9(8)) Pub: Magna Story GBR. Dist(s): Ulverscroft US

song of an innocent Bystander. Ian Bone. Read by Caroline Lee. (Running Time: 10 hrs.). (YA). 2009. 84.99 (978-1-74214-299-9(0), 9781742142999) Pub: Bolinda Pubng AUS. Dist(s): Bolinda Pub Inc

Song of an Innocent Bystander. unabr. ed. Ian Bone. Read by Caroline Lee. 7 cass. (Running Time: 10 hrs.). 2003. 56.00 (978-1-74093-046-8(0)) Pub: Bolinda Pubng AUS. Dist(s): Bolinda Pub Inc
Hostage. Nine-year-old Freda trapped in a restaurant with a fanatic and his gun. Survivor. No parents to protect her, two men dead. Ten years later. Live by the rules: keep yourself small, don't let them ask you questions. A dead man's words ... 'Are you living a good life, Freda?' The answer lies in hunting down the ghosts of the past. Gripping and moving, The Song of an Innocent Bystander is a novel you won't easily forget. As reviewed in the American May 2004 issue of Kliatt.

Song of an Innocent Bystander. unabr. ed. Ian Bone. Read by Caroline Lee. 9 CDs. (Running Time: 36000 sec.). (YA). (gr. 8-12). 2006. audio compact disk 93.95 (978-1-74093-793-1(7)) Pub: Bolinda Pubng AUS. Dist(s): Bolinda Pub Inc

Song of Angels: Experiencing the Atmosphere of Heaven. gif. ed. Freddy Hayler. 2001. bk. 17.99 (978-0-88368-664-5(3), 776643) Pub: Whitaker Hse. Dist(s): Anchor Distributors

Song of Bernadette, unabr. ed. Franz Werfel. Read by Johanna Ward. 13 cass. (Running Time: 19 hrs. 30 min.). 1997. 85.95 (1889) Blckstn Audio.
In June 1940, Franz Werfel & his wife were on a desperate flight across France, seeking to escape death at the hands of the Nazis. Franz had written many articles & given radio speeches denouncing their tyranny. They found temporary refuge in the small town of Lourdes, home of the famous shrine where the virtuous Bernadette received visions of the Virgin Mary. Werfel became fascinated with Bernadette's story & he swore that, should he & his wife be granted escape, he would write the story of Bernadette for all the world to savor.

Song of Bernadette. unabr. ed. Franz Werfel. Read by Johanna Ward. (Running Time: 18 hrs. 30 mins.). 1998. 85.95 (978-0-7861-1124-4(0)) Blckstn Audio.

Song of Creation. Medicine Story. 1 cass. (Running Time: 1 hr.). 6.00 Story Stone.
Creation tales of the Wampanoag people.

Song of Devotion. Read by Osel Tendzin. 4 cass. 1979. 45.00 (A117) Vajradhatu.
Four talks. "Devotion is the point of view of the student & devotion is the state of mind of the guru".

Song of Guinevere: A Defense of Arthur's Wife in Verse, Vol. 1. unabr. ed. Alicia Snow. Read by Alicia Snow. 8 cass. (Running Time: 16 hrs.). 1999. 49.95 Set. (978-0-9660643-5-3(6)) Belgrave Hse.
Epic poem/historical fiction of Arthurian court and Guinevere.

Song of Hiawatha: Hiawatha's Childhood see Best Loved Poems of Longfellow

Song of Hiawatha & More. Henry Wadsworth Longfellow. Read by Flo Gibson. 3 cass. 1996. Rental 23.50 Audio Bk Con.

Song of Hiawatha & More Poems, Henry Wadsworth Longfellow. Read by Flo Gibson. 3 cass. (Running Time: 4 hrs.). 1996. 16.95 (978-1-55685-420-0(X)) Audio Bk Con.
The title poem, "The Wreck of the Hesperus," "April Day," "Autumn," "Woods in Winter," "The Village Blacksmith," "Endymion," & "The Day Is Done" comprise a large part of this familiar collection.

***Song of Hiawatha & Other Poems.** Henry Wadsworth Longfellow. Narrated by Flo Gibson. 2009. audio compact disk 19.95 (978-1-60646-106-8(0)) Audio Bk Con.

Song of Hope, Marilyn Arnold. 2 cass. 1999. 13.95 (978-1-57734-430-8(8), 07002033) Covenant Comms.
Sequel to "Desert Song.".

Song of La Selva. 1 cass. (Running Time: 35 min.). (J). (gr. k-4). 2001. pap. bk. 19.95 (SP 7009C) Kimbo Educ.
An adventurous story of the Costa Rican Rain Forest.

Song of Love: Spiritual Canticle. Keith J. Egan. 4 cass. 1988. 32.95 (TAH207) Alba Hse Comns.
This workshop explores The Spiritual Canticle, poem & commentary, as an interpretation of God's word for us, as a way of understanding God's will for us, & as an invitation to persevere in our journey to God.

Song of Love: The Spiritual Canticle of John of the Cross. Keith J. Egan. Read by Keith J. Egan. 4 cass. (Running Time: 4 hrs. 30 min.). 32.95 set. (TAH207) Alba Hse Comns.

Song of Mark. Marty Haugen. 1995. 10.95 (356); audio compact disk 15.95 (356) GIA Pubns.

Song of Myself see Twentieth-Century Poetry in English, No. 16, Walt Whitman Speaks for Himself

Song of Prayer: Workshop on the Pamphlet. Kenneth Wapnick. 13 CDs. 2004. audio compact disk 75.00 (978-1-59142-136-8(5), CD18) Foun Miracles.
This workshop presents a line-by-line commentary on the companion pamphlet to the Course, scribed by Helen Schucman from Jesus; looks at the role of prayer as a reflection of the process of our acceptance of the true meaning of Jesus' presence in our lives; presents Jesus' relationship with Helen as the model for understanding the nature of prayer.

Song of Redemption. unabr. ed. Lynn Austin. Read by Suzanne Toren. 12 CDs. (Running Time: 14 hrs.). (Chronicles of the Kings: Bk. 2). 2005. audio compact disk 119.75 (978-1-4193-4829-7(9), CK160); 94.75 (978-1-4193-4827-3(2), K1169) Recorded Bks.
The second book in her Chronicles of the Kings series, Song of Redemption is a retelling of the life of Hezekiah, King of Judah from 716 to 687 BC After years of idolatry, Judah's temple has been cleansed and Hezekiah has brought God's law back to his people. But when he incurs the wrath of the barbaric Assyrians, he will need help from a surprising source.

Song of Rhanna. unabr. ed. Christine M. Fraser. Read by Vivien Heilbron. 10 cass. (Running Time: 10 hrs.). 1994. 84.95 (978-0-7451-4271-5(0), CAB 954) AudioGO.
Ruth now feels complete in her marriage to Lorn. Her oldest friend, Rachel, is planning a visit to Rhanna & to Ruth's surprise, Lorn is strangely disinterested. Yet, Rachel's arrival would bring Ruth more heartache than she could imagine & drive her away from the island she loved.

Song of Roland. 2 cass. (Running Time: 3 hrs.). 2001. 19.95 (BLKS001) Lodestone Catalog.
This 12th-century French legend was based on the famous "Oxford Roland" which was about Charlemagne battling the Saracens for control of Europe in the year 778.

Song of Roland. Narrated by Flo Gibson. 2008. 19.95 (978-1-55685-981-6(3)) Audio Bk Con.

Song of Roland. unabr. ed. Poems. Read by D.D.R. Owen. Tr. by D.D.R. Owen. 2 cass. (Running Time: 2 hrs. 30 mins.). 1998. 17.95 Set. (978-0-7861-1364-4(2), 2133) Blckstn Audio.
One of the great medieval "chansons de geste" (songs of great deeds), a composite of several hero legends interlaced with Christian moral sentiments. Centered on battles, heroic feats, & knightly ideals, it may have its roots in the Basque ambush of AD 778 on the rear guard of Charlemagne's army during a retreat through the Pyrenees. Presents psychological, emotional & sociological realities that transcend factual data to reach a new plateau of reality that reflects the spirit of the times rather than its substance.

Song of Solomon. Kelley Varner. 4 cass. 1992. 25.00 Set. (978-0-938612-78-0(6)) Destiny Image Pubs.

Song of Solomon. unabr. ed. Toni Morrison. Narrated by Lynne Thigpen. 9 cass. (Running Time: 13 hrs. 30 mins.). 1999. 83.00 (978-0-7887-3467-0(9), 95887E7) Recorded Bks.
This new version creates a magical world out of four generations of black life in America. A powerful, sensual, & poetic exploration of a family mistakenly named Dead. We discover a century's worth of secrets, ghosts & troubles.

Song of Solomon: A Study of Love, Sex, Marriage & Romance. unabr. ed. Tommy Nelson. 6 cass. (Running Time: 6 hrs.). 1995. bk. 34.95 (978-1-928828-01-3(9)) Hudson Prods.
Biblical & practical teaching of the Old Testament book.

Song of Solomon Vol. 2: From the King James Version, Read by Eric Martin. 1 cass. (Running Time: 27 min.). 1997. 5.25 (978-1-891320-01-9(7)) Jodacom Intl.

Song of Solomon Classic CD: A Study of Love, Marriage & Sex. Perf. by Tommy Nelson. (ENG.). 2009. audio compact disk 59.95 (978-1-928828-11-2(6)) Hudson Prods.

Song of Songs. Lorenza Ponce & Ben Zebelman. 1 CD. (Running Time: 29 min.). 2002. audio compact disk (978-1-891319-73-0(6)) Spring Hill CO.

Song of Songs: A New Translation. abr. ed. Read by Jill Eikenberry & Michael Tucker. Tr. by Ariel Bloch & Chana Bloch from HEB. 2 cass. (Running Time: 3 hrs.). 1998. 18.95 (978-1-57453-280-7(4)) Audio Lit.
The Song of Songs, often referred to as the Song of Solomon, is one of the great love poems of all time. For over 2,000 years its passionate depiction of love as a cosmic force has been a source of inspiration for poets & lovers. In this lyrical new translation, an eminent scholar of ancient Semitic languages & a distinguished poet & translator restore the sensuousness of the original with scrupulous faithfulness to the Hebrew text & a new sense of the beauty & spirit of the poem.

Song of Songs & the Letters of Heloise & Abelard. abr. ed. Perf. by Claire Bloom et al. 1 cass. 1984. 12.95 (978-0-694-50067-3(4), SWC 1085) HarperCollins Pubs.

Song of Songs & the Spiritual Canticle. Roland E. Murphy. 1 cass. (Running Time: 60 min.). 1988. 7.95 (TAH211) Alba Hse Comns.
In a lively & entertaining manner, Roland Murphy, OCARm presents the meaning & background of the Song of Songs on the level of historical criticism. He discusses the relationship of the Song of Songs of John of the

Cross' Spiritual Canticle, & concludes by drawing out the significance of the Song for contemporary spirituality.

Song of Survival. unabr. ed. Helen Colijn. Read by Nadia May. 5 cass. (Running Time: 8 hrs. 30 mins.). 1998. 39.95 (978-0-7861-1261-6(1), 2183) Blckstn Audio.
Account of the author's wartime experiences is a window into a largely overlooked dimension of World War II-the imprisonment of women & children in Southeast Asia by the Japanese & how these prisoners of war responded to their dire circumstances. Their courage, faith, resiliency, ingenuity, & camaraderie provide us with enduring lessons on living.

Song of Survival: Women Interned. unabr. ed. Helen Colijn. (Running Time: 25200 sec.). 2007. audio compact disk 55.00 (978-0-7861-5937-6(5)); audio compact disk 29.95 (978-0-7861-7063-0(8)) Blckstn Audio.

Song of Susannah. unabr. ed. Stephen King. Narrated by George Guidall. (Dark Tower Ser.: Bk. 6). 2004. audio compact disk 49.95 (978-1-4025-9392-5(9)) Recorded Bks.
Roland and his gunslingers have to save the endangered Rose-the beautifully understated manifestation of the Dark Tower in our world, which grows in a vacant lot in New York City. But thugs and a pregnant female demon named Mia, who has possessed wheel-chair bound Susannah, have been dispatched by the Crimson King to wreak havoc and prevent the gunslingers' noble quest from its fulfillment.

Song of Susannah. unabr. ed. Stephen King. Read by George Guidall. 12 CDs. (Running Time: 140 hrs. 0 mins. 0 sec.). Bk. 6. (ENG.). 2004. audio compact disk 59.95 (978-0-7435-3670-7(3)) Pub: S&S Audio. Dist(s): S and S Inc

Song of Susannah. unabr. ed. Stephen King. Read by George Guidall. (Dark Tower Ser.: Bk. 6). 2006. 35.95 (978-0-7435-6170-9(8)) Pub: S&S Audio. Dist(s): S and S Inc

Song of the Broad-Axe see Twentieth-Century Poetry in English, No. 17, Walt Whitman Speaks for Himself

Song of the Cheyenne. unabr. ed. Jory Sherman. Read by Kevin Foley. 4 cass. (Running Time: 5 hrs. 30 min.). 1996. 26.95 (978-1-55686-657-9(7)) Books in Motion.
He was called Sun Runner. As a boy he carried the medicine arrows into battle for the first time & saw his first victory. They knew then he was a Cheyenne warrior destined for greatness.

Song of the Divine Lovers. unabr. ed. Rama Berch. 1 CD. (Chants of Awakening Ser.: Vol. 4). 1999. audio compact disk (978-1-930559-16-5(X)) STC Inc.

Song of the Dodo Pt. 1: Island Biogeography in an Age of Extinctions, unabr. collector's ed. David Quammen. Read by Larry McKeever. 10 cass. (Running Time: 15 hrs.). 1997. 80.00 (978-0-7366-3705-3(2), 4391-A) Books on Tape.
An adventure in the great outdoors, also a wake-up call to the age of extinctions.

Song of the Dodo Pt. 2: Island Biogeography in an Age of Extinctions, unabr. collector's ed. David Quammen. Read by Larry McKeever. 10 cass. (Running Time: 15 hrs.). 1997. 80.00 (978-0-7366-3706-0(0), 4391-B) Books on Tape.

***Song of the Dragon: The Annals of Drakis: Book One.** unabr. ed. Tracy Hickman. (Running Time: 15 hrs.). (Annals of Drakis Ser.). 2010. 24.99 (978-1-4418-7053-7(9), 9781441870537, Brilliance MP3); 39.97 (978-1-4418-7054-4(7), 9781441870544, Brinc Audio MP3 Lib); audio compact disk 34.99 (978-1-4418-7051-3(2), 9781441870513, Bril Audio CD Unabri) Brilliance Audio.

***Song of the Dragon: The Annals of Drakis: Book One.** unabr. ed. Tracy Hickman. Read by Phil Gigante. (Running Time: 15 hrs.). (Annals of Drakis Ser.). 2010. 24.99 (978-1-4418-7055-1(5), 9781441870551, BAD); 39.97 (978-1-4418-7056-8(3), 9781441870568, BADLE); audio compact disk 89.97 (978-1-4418-7052-0(0), 9781441870520, BriAudCD Unabrid) Brilliance Audio.

Song of the Exile. unabr. ed. David Ambrose & Kiana Davenport. Narrated by Cristine McMurdo-Wallis. 12 cass. (Running Time: 16 hrs.). 1999. 93.00 (978-0-7887-3772-5(4), 95989E7) Recorded Bks.
This haunting novel bares the soul of a Hawaiin-American family during WWII. As you share in the Meahuna family's misfortunes & triumphs, a sense of intense intimacy evolves.

Song of the Exposition see Twentieth-Century Poetry in English, No. 16, Walt Whitman Speaks for Himself

Song of the Gargoyle, unabr. ed. Zilpha Keatley Snyder. Narrated by Richard Ferrone. 6 cass. (Running Time: 7 hrs. 45 mins.). (gr. 6 up). 1992. 51.00 (978-1-55690-601-5(3), 92206E7) Recorded Bks.
When Komus, the court jester in the magical kingdom of Austerneve, is kidnapped, his 13-year-old son joins an enchanted gargoyle on a mission to rescue him.

Song of the Heart. unabr. ed. Helene Wiggin. Read by Cathleen McCarron. 7 cass. (Running Time: 9 hrs. 15 mins.). (Story Sound Ser.). (J). 2006. 61.95 (978-1-85903-897-0(2)) Pub: Mgna Lrg Print GBR. Dist(s): Ulverscroft US

Song of the Lark, unabr. ed. Willa Cather. Read by Flo Gibson. 9 cass. (Running Time: 13 hrs. 30 min.). 1991. 28.95 (978-1-55685-190-2(1)) Audio Bk Con.
Thea Kronborg, gifted & passionate, struggles to leave the confines & constraints of a small Colorado town in order to achieve an operatic career.

Song of the Lark, unabr. ed. Willa Cather. Narrated by Barbara Caruso. 11 cass. (Running Time: 15 hrs. 30 mins.). 2001. 91.00 (978-0-7887-0657-8(8), 94834E7) Recorded Bks.
Thea Kronberg has a voice that can call down angels & the soul of a Colorado pioneer girl. But as she develops her talents & devotes herself to the life of an artist, she must consider the cost of the creative path she follows.

***Song of the Lark.** unabr. ed. Willa Cather. Narrated by Pam Ward. (Running Time: 16 hrs. 30 mins. 0 sec.). 2010. 27.99 (978-1-4001-6978-8(X)); 21.99 (978-1-4001-8978-6(0)); audio compact disk 35.99 (978-1-4001-1978-3(2)) Pub: Tantor Media. Dist(s): IngramPubServ

***Song of the Lark (Library Edition)** unabr. ed. Willa Cather. Narrated by Pam Ward. (Running Time: 16 hrs. 30 mins.). 2010. 35.99 (978-1-4001-9978-5(6)); audio compact disk 85.99 (978-1-4001-4978-0(9)) Pub: Tantor Media. Dist(s): IngramPubServ

Song of the Ocean. 1 cass. (Running Time: 60 min.). 1994. audio compact disk 15.95 CD. (2746, Creativ Pub) Quayside.
Blending original piano music with the power of ocean surf. Acoustic grand piano orchestrations of Steven C.

Song of the Ocean. 1 cass. (Running Time: 60 min.). 1994. 9.95 (2745, NrthWrd Bks) TandN Child.

Song of the Old Mother see Caedmon Treasury of Modern Poets Reading Their Own Poetry

Song of the Road. Dorothy Garlock. Read by Isabel Keating. 11 vols. 2004. bk. 44.95 (978-0-7927-3241-9(3), SLD 663, Chivers Sound Lib) AudioGO.

Song of the Slasher. 1945. (MM-5795) Natl Recrd Co.

Song of the Soul: Guided Meditation for Healing & Relaxation. Lynne Newman. Narrated by Lynne Newman. Music by Steven Mark Kohn. 1 CD. (Running Time: 60 min.). (Health Journeys Ser.: 2601). 2004. audio compact disk 17.98 (978-1-881405-74-0(5)) Hlth Jmys.
Track One is a civinely inspired, lyrical, utterly original, 30 minute guided meditation of extraordinary beauty and power. Its heartfelt richness and integrity will take you deeper into yourself and illuminate your own, unique inner journey. Track Two allows you to listen to Steven Mark Kohn's exquisite music by itself, giving your imagination permission and space to work on its own.

Song of the Sun. Andrew Harvey. 5 CDs. (Running Time: 6 Hrs). 2006. audio compact disk 34.95 (978-1-59179-493-6(5), AW00427D) Sounds True.
Sifting through the many legends associated with the Persian poet Rumi's life, Andrew Harvey emerges with a rare and inspiring portrait of what a human being in love with and empowered by God can become. Features some of Rumi's most inspired love poetry.

Song of the Teeny-Tiny Mosquito. Alma Flor Ada. Illus. by Viví Escrivá. (Stories for the Telling Ser.). (J). (gr. k-3). 4.95 (978-1-58105-323-4(1)) Santillana.

Song of the Wanderer. Bruce Coville. Read by Bruce Coville. (Running Time: 6 hrs.). (Unicorn Chronicles: Bk. 2). 2002. 32.95 (978-1-60083-343-4(8)) Iofy Corp.

Song of the Wanderer. unabr. ed. Bruce Coville. Read by Full Cast Production Staff. (J). 2007. 44.99 (978-1-60252-543-6(9)) Find a World.

Song of the Whip. unabr. collector's ed. Max Brand. Read by Jonathan Marosz. 7 cass. (Running Time: 7 hrs.). 1998. 42.00 (978-0-7366-4029-9(0), 4528) Books on Tape.
A young American has crossed back into Mexico, lured by a cruel tune. It's the song of the whip, & his mission is to free the peasants who live under the lash. He is El Keed, an outcast among his own people, an outlaw with a price on his head. Joining an army of ruthless bandits, he challenges the powerful Lerraza family & their hired guns, singing them a new song straight from hell.

Song of Wandering Aengus see Gathering of Great Poetry for Children

Song of Wandering Aengus see Poetry of William Butler Yeats

Song or Two for You. Nick Seeger. (J). (ps-7). 9.95 (GW1002) Gentle Wind.
The tape of silly songs, sing-along songs & just plain pretty songs will delight you & your children.

Song or Two for You. Perf. by Nick Seeger. (J). 1981. 9.95 (978-0-939065-02-8(9)); audio compact disk 14.95 (978-0-939065-95-0(9)) Gentle Wind.

Song Train: 56 Great 2-Chord Songs Anyone Can Play. Harvey Reid & Joyce Andersen. 2007. bk. 49.95 (978-0-9759219-1-3(6)) Woodpecker Rec.

Song yet Sung. unabr. ed. James McBride. Read by Leslie Uggams. (Running Time: 11 hrs.). (ENG.). 2008. audio compact disk 39.95 (978-0-14-314291-1(7), PengAudBks) Penguin Grp USA.

Songames for Sensory Integration, Aubrey Lande & Bob Wiz. 2 CDs. (Running Time: 1 hr. 27 mins.). (Sensory Processing Ser.). (J). (gr. k-3). 1999. bk. 21.00 (978-1-893601-07-9(2), BCRI-8CD) Sensory Res.
25 therapist created musical activities designed to improve gross motor skills, muscle strength & rhythm among children with sensory integration dysfunction.

Songames for Sensory Integration: Therapeutic Play along Activities, Level 1. Aubrey Lange et al. 1 cass. (Running Time: 1 hr.). (Belle Curve Clinical Ser.). (J). (ps-2). 1999. 20.00 (978-1-893601-00-0(5), BCRI-8) Sensory Res.
Activity based song games designed to promote motor, sensory, cognitive & visual integrative development.

Songbird. Perf. by Eva Cassidy. 1 cass. 1998. 10.98; audio compact disk 18.98 Lifedance.
Includes: "Wade in the Water," "Over the Rainbow," "I Know You by Heart," "People Get Ready," "Wayfaring Stranger," "Songbird," "Fields of Gold," "Time is a Healer," "Autumn Leaves," & more.

Songbird Sunrise & Thunderstorm. abr. ed. Jeffrey Thompson. (Running Time: 2 hrs. 0 mins. 0 sec.). 2007. audio compact disk 19.98 (978-1-55961-797-0(7)) Pub: Relaxtn Co. Dist(s): S and S Inc

Songbird Symphony. 1 cass. (Running Time: 60 min.). 1994. audio compact disk 15.95 CD. (2994, Creativ Pub) Quayside.
Songbirds. Blended with classical music by the Masters.

Songbird Symphony. 1 cass. (Running Time: 60 min.). 1994. 9.95 (2292, NrthWrd Bks) TandN Child.

Songbook for Orchestra. Perf. by Erich Kunzel et al. 1 cass., 1 CD. 7.98 (TA 30375) NewSound.

Songbook of Arrurruz see Poetry of Geoffrey

Songbook of Micah. Contrib. by Micah Stampley et al. 2007. audio compact disk 17.99 (978-5-557-67284-9(2)) Pt of Grace Ent.

Songcatcher. unabr. ed. Sharyn McCrumb. Narrated by James Daniels & Aasne Vigesa. 7 cass. (Running Time: 10 hrs.). (Ballad Ser.: No. 6). 2001. 32.95 (978-1-58788-130-5(6), 1587881306, BAU) Brilliance Audio.
Folksinger Lark McCourry is haunted by the memory of a song. As a child she heard it from her relatives in the North Carolina mountains, and she knows that the song has been in her family since 1759, when her ancestor, nine-year-old Malcolm MacQuarry, kidnapped from the Scottish island of Islay, learned it aboard an English ship. The song accompanied young Malcolm when he made his way to Morristown, New Jersey, where he apprenticed with an attorney, became a lawyer himself, and fought in the American Revolution. The song came with Malcolm in 1790, when he left his family and traveled the Wilderness Road to homestead in western North Carolina, where he remarried and raised a second family. The song, passed down through the generations, carries Malcolm's descendants through the settling of the frontier, the Civil War, the coming of the railroads, and into modern times, providing both solace in the present and a link to the past. Over the years, though, the memory of the old song has dimmed and Lark McCourry's only hope of preserving her family legacy lies in mountain wise-woman Nora Bonesteel, who talks to both the living and the dead.

Songcatcher. unabr. ed. Sharyn McCrumb. Read by James Daniels & Aasne Vigesaa. (Running Time: 36000 sec.). (Ballad Ser.: No. 6). 2004. audio compact disk 39.25 (978-1-59335-393-3(6), 1593353936, Brinc Audio MP3 Lib) Brilliance Audio.

Songcatcher. unabr. ed. Sharyn McCrumb. Read by James Daniels Aasne Vigesaa. (Running Time: 10 hrs.). (Ballad Ser.). 2004. 39.25 (978-1-59710-727-3(1), 1597107271, BADLE) Brilliance Audio.

Songcatcher. unabr. ed. Sharyn McCrumb. Read by James Daniels Aasne Vigesaa. (Running Time: 10 hrs.). (Ballad Ser.: No. 6). 2004. 24.95 (978-1-59335-164-9(X), 159335164X) Soulmate Audio Bks.

Songcatcher. unabr. ed. Sharyn McCrumb. Read by James Daniels Aasne Vigesaa. (Running Time: 10 hrs.). (Ballad Ser.). 2004. 24.95 (978-1-59710-726-6(3), 1597107263, BAD) Brilliance Audio.

Songmaster. unabr. ed. Orson Scott Card. Read by Stefan Rudnicki. (Running Time: 45000 sec.). 2006. 72.95 (978-0-7861-3509-7(3)); audio compact disk 90.00 (978-0-7861-7842-1(6)); audio compact disk 29.95 (978-0-7861-8057-8(9)) Blckstn Audio.

Songmaster. unabr. ed. Di Morrissey. 11 cass. (Running Time: 14 hrs. 30 mins.). 2004. 88.00 (978-1-74030-482-5(9)) Pub: Bolinda Pubng AUS. Dist(s): Lndmrk Audiobks

Songprints: The Musical Experience of Five Shoshone Women. Judith Vander. (Music in American Life Ser.). 1988. 10.95 (978-0-252-01531-1(2)) Pub: U of Ill Pr. Dist(s): Chicago Distribution Ctr

Songs. Voice by Lucy Hyman. (ENG & SPA.). 1980. 6.95 (978-0-89265-496-3(1)) Randall Hse.

Songs. Perf. by Rich Mullins. 1 cass. 1999. 10.98 (978-7-01-011652-5(0)); audio compact disk 16.98 (978-7-01-011672-3(5)) Provident Music.

Songs: Rich Mullins. Perf. by Rich Mullins. 1 cass. (Running Time: 1 hr.). 1998. 10.98; audio compact disk 16.98 CD. Provident Mus Dist.

Songs about Insects, Bugs & Squiggly Things. Jane Murphy. 1 cass. (Running Time: 1 hr.). (J). (ps-4). 2001. pap. bk. 10.95 (KIM 9127C); lp 11.95 (KIM 9127); audio compact disk 14.95 (KIM 9127CD) Kimbo Educ.
Whole language at it's best! Here are all the facts children want & need to know about insects, toads, snakes, butterflies, spiders & more! They'll love it. Science comes alive in Patty's Pet Python, Bees in the Hive, Instinct, Ants On Parade, Praying Mantis, Spunky Spider, Make a Snake, The Bee Bop, Hi, Hi Firefly, Grasshoppers & more. Includes song guide.

Songs about Me. Perf. by William Janiak. 1 cass. (Running Time: 1 hr.). (J). 2001. pap. bk. 10.95 (KIM 70223C); pap. bk. 11.95 (KIM 70223) Kimbo Educ.
Stand up, Sit Down, Count My Fingers, I'm Swaying My Body, There Are Seven Days in the Week, Do You Like Foods?, The Slow Fast, Soft Loud Clap Song, Point to My Clothes, Why Me? Includes guide.

Songs about Me. unabr. ed. Cake and Candle Cassettes, Inc. Staff. Read by Ron Trigilio. 1 cass. (Running Time: 18 min.). (J). (gr. k-6). 1989. 7.95 (978-0-9649745-2-4(5)) Cake & Candle.
Mentions a child's first name eleven times. Three original songs help a child to care, share, feel good & develop a healthy self image.

Songs about Me & My World Vol. 2: Every Child Needs to Feel Special, Douglas J. Albert & Ron Trigilio. Perf. by Ron Trigilio & Mary Giles Edes. 1 CD. (Running Time: 40 Min.). (J). (gr. k-6). 1999. audio compact disk 12.95 Incl. slide tray. (978-0-9649745-7-9(6), Sammy-1) Cake & Candle.
A compilation of 2 previous cassette titles, "Songs About Me & My World" is a 40 min. CD that encourages young listerers to have confident and positive thinking. It's theme extends to caring for and appreciating nature.

Songs about Native Americans. 1 CD. (Running Time: 1 hr.). (J). (ps-3). 2001. pap. bk. 14.95 (KIM 9132CD) Kimbo Educ.
A unique introduction to the rich cultural heritage of Native Americans. Descriptive lyrics & contemporary music depict the environments that shaped lifestyles & traditions. Includes The Circle of Life, Sun & Rain. Activity book & lyrics included.

Songs about Native Americans. 1 cass. (Running Time: 1 hr.). (J). (ps-5). 2001. pap. bk. 10.95 (KIM 9132C); pap. bk. 11.95 (KIM 9132) Kimbo Educ.

Songs & Activities. 1 cass. (Running Time: 1 hr.). (Scott Foresman Ciencias Ser.). (SPA.). (gr. k up). 2000. 37.49 (978-0-673-59428-0(9)); audio compact disk 50.09 (978-0-673-62639-4(3)) Addson-Wesley Educ.
Entertaining and educational lyrics from Children's Television Workshop let students begin every chapter with a science sing-along. We've set science to music in engaging songs students can take home and share with their families. A great way to reinforce learning! Includes content in English and Spanish.

Songs & Activities. 1 cass. (Running Time: 1 hr.). (Scott Foresman Ciencias Ser.). (SPA.). (gr. 1 up). 2000. 37.49 (978-0-673-59429-7(7)); audio compact disk 50.09 (978-0-673-62640-0(7)) Addson-Wesley Educ.

Songs & Activities. 1 cass. (Running Time: 1 hr.). (Scott Foresman Ciencias Ser.). (SPA.). (gr. 2 up). 2000. 37.49 (978-0-673-59430-3(0)); audio compact disk 50.09 (978-0-673-62641-7(5)) Addson-Wesley Educ.

Songs & Activities. 1 cass. (Running Time: 1 hr.). (Scott Foresman Science Ser.). (SPA.). (gr. 3 up). 2000. 37.49 (978-0-673-65139-6(8)); audio compact disk 50.09 (978-0-673-65117-4(7)) Addson-Wesley Educ.

Songs & Activities for Early Learners. Sara Jordan. Illus. by Hector Obando. 1 cass. (Running Time: 45 min. 16 secs.). (J). (ps-2). 1993. pap. bk. 14.95 (978-1-895523-38-6(9), JMP105K) Jordan Music.
Kids learn about the alphabet, farm animals, counting, family members, parts of the body, days of the week, colors, fruit, opposites and shapes through these lively action-packed songs. A bonus complement of music accompaniment tracks on the CD allows for kids to become performers! Great for school performances!.

Songs & Activities for Early Learners. abr. ed. Sara Jordan. Prod. by Sara Jordan. 1 CD. (Running Time: 30 min.). (Songs that Teach Early Learning Ser.). (ENG., (J). (gr. 4-7). 1993. audio compact disk 13.95 (978-1-894262-29-3(8), JMP 105CD) Pub: S Jordan Publ. Dist(s): CrabtreePubCo

Songs & Dances of the Middle Ages: Recorder/Flute Edition. John Holenko & Hazel Ketchum. 2002. bk. 25.95 (978-0-7866-6606-5(4), 96861BCD) Mel Bay.

Songs & Dances of the Middle Ages - Guitar Edition. John Holenko & Hazel Ketchum. 1998. pap. bk. 25.95 (978-0-7866-4307-3(2), 96712CDP) Mel Bay.

Songs & Dances of the Middle Ages - Recorder/Flute. John Holenko & Hazel Ketchum. 1998. pap. bk. 25.95 (978-0-7866-4306-6(4), 96861CDP) Mel Bay.

Songs & Games from Around the World. Perf. by Rachel Buchman. 1 cass. (Running Time: 39 hrs. 10 min.). (Family Ser.). (J). (ps-5). 1988. 9.98 (8006) Rounder Records.
Presents material in English, Spanish, Italian & Chinese & finds the award-winning performer where she is most at home - singing with a group of young children.

Songs & More Songs by Tom Lehrer. Tom Lehrer. 1 CD. (Running Time: 1 hr. 30 mins.). 1996. audio compact disk 16.98 (R2 72776) Rhino Enter.

Songs & Readings from Poetry with a Porpoise. unabr. ed. Rick Peoples. 1 cass. (Running Time: 28 min.). (J). 1998. 5.95 incl. script. (978-0-9668328-1-5(7)) Appenzell Pr.
Includes 8 songs & 10 readings.

Songs & Scenes: A Visual Choir Collection. Contrib. by Johnathan Crumpton. Created by Johnathan Crumpton. Created by Luke Gambill. Prod. by Luke Gambill. (ENG.). 2008. 149.99 (978-5-557-38251-9(8), Brentwood-Benson Music); audio compact disk 59.99 (978-5-557-38252-6(6), Brentwood-Benson Music) Brentwood Music.

Songs & Scenes: A Visual Choir Collection. Created by Johnathan Crumpton & Luke Gambill. (ENG.). 2008. audio compact disk 12.99 (978-5-557-38253-3(4), Brentwood-Benson Music); audio compact disk 10.00 (978-5-557-38250-2(X), Brentwood-Benson Music) Brentwood Music.

Songs & Sonnets. Larry Beckett. bk. 35.00 (978-1-879082-14-4(4)) Rainy Day CA.

Songs & Sounds of the Humpback Whale. 1 cass. (Running Time: 45 min.). 1994. audio compact disk 15.95 CD. (0266, Creativ Pub) Quayside.
The songs of the male can last up to 30 minutes each. Side One was recorded off the coast of Maui, Hawaii. Side Two features over 1,000 porpoise chattering & playing off the Baja Peninsula. A fantastic underwater adventure.

Songs & Sounds of the Humpback Whale. 1 cass. (Running Time: 45 min.). 1994. 9.95 (0242, NrthWrd Bks) TandN Child.

Songs & Stories for Christmas. 6 cass. 15.98 (3444317) Covenant Comms.

Songs & Stories for Happy Kids. Ed. by Publications International Staff. (J). 2007. audio compact disk 15.98 (978-1-4127-8180-0(9)) Pubns Intl Ltd.

Songs & Stories from Uganda. W. Moses Serwadda. Ed. by Hewitt Pantaleoni. Illus. by Leo Dillon. 1 cass. (Running Time: 64 min.). (J). (gr. k up). 1987. pap. bk. 17.95 (978-0-937203-17-0(3)) World Music Pr.
Story songs, lullabies & work songs narrated by Moriah Vecchia, songs performed by Moses Serwadda & daughter. Two-color woodcuts throughout book by Leo & Diane Dillon.

Songs & Stories of Africa. Gcina Mhlophe. audio compact disk (978-1-86914-084-7(2)) KwazuluNatal ZAF.

Songs Are Free. adpt. ed. Perf. by Bernice Johnson Reagon. Interview with Bernice Johnson Reagon. Interview with Bill Moyers. 1 cass. (Running Time: 58 min.). 1994. 10.95 (978-1-56176-902-5(9)) Mystic Fire.
Moyers joins Reagon for a celebration of the power of song - the music & singing that continue to preserve & transmit the spiritual strength of African-American culture.

Songs Children Love to Sing. Ella Jenkins. 1 cass. (Running Time: 1 hr.). (J). 2001. 10.95 (FC 45042C); audio compact disk 15.00 (FC 45042CD) Kimbo Educ.
Fortieth Anniversary Collection! 17 songs that are especially popular with children. This a Way, Miss Mary Mack, Muffin Man, Many Pretty Trees, Toom Bah Ee Lero & much more.

Songs Children Love to Sing. Perf. by Ella Jenkins. 1 cass. (Running Time: 41 min.). (J). (ps-4). 1996. (0-9307-450420-9307-45042-2-4); audio compact disk (0-9307-45042-2-4) Smithsonian Folkways.
Anthology of 17 songs, selected by Jenkins, celebrating 40 years of recordings.

Songs for a Family Seder. Perf. by Robert S. Friedman. 1 cass. (Running Time: 40 mins.). (J). (ps-6). 1987. 7.95 (978-0-929371-02-3(X), Kar-Ben) Lerner Pub.
Features thirty traditional blessings & songs from the Passover seder including several children's songs.

Songs for a Gentle World. Light. Read by Sun. 1 cass. (Running Time: 32 min.). 1989. 7.00 (978-0-929274-15-7(6)) Gentle World.
Features uplifting songs.

Songs for a Purpose Driven Life. 2002. audio compact disk Maranatha Music.

Songs for a Purpose Driven Life. Maranatha Music. 2003. audio compact disk 17.98 (978-0-310-64473-6(9)) Zondervan.

Songs for All Seasons see Cantos para Nuestros Tiempos

Songs for All Seasons. 1 cass. (Running Time: 1 hr. 30 mins.). 2000. 16.95 (978-1-57972-359-0(4)) Insight Living.

Songs for All Seasons: Choral Selections to Highlight Special Days. Compiled by Ken Bible & Marty Parks. 2007. audio compact disk 16.99 (978-5-557-54404-7(6)) Lillenas.

Songs for All Seasons: Choral Selections to Highlight Special Days. Created by Ken Bible & Marty Parks. 2007. audio compact disk 12.00 (978-5-557-54405-4(4)) Lillenas.

Songs for All Seasons: Choral Selections to Highlight Special Days. Contrib. by Marty Parks & Ken Bible. 2007. audio compact disk 90.00 (978-5-557-54402-3(X)); audio compact disk 90.00 (978-5-557-54401-6(1)) Lillenas.

Songs for Cats & the People Who Love Them. Ellen Bernfeld & Anne Bryant. Interview with Tony Iatrois. 1 cass. (Running Time: 30 mins.). 1997. pap. bk. 11.95 (978-0-9648762-6-2(4)); pap. bk. 15.95 (978-0-9648762-5-5(6)) Gloryvision.
A dramatic musical fantasy about cats in the music business.

Songs for Children of All Ages. Perf. by Robin Williamson. 1 cass. (J). 1999. Rounder Records.
Robin Williamson is something of a modern day Scottish bard. Multi-instrumentalist, poet & prolific writer of songs & stories, he is perhaps best remembered for his decade-long stint as part of beloved cult folk group, the Incredible String Band. Williamson's first album for children ("of all ages") was issued in 1987 & contains his arrangements of traditional children's songs from Scotland,I Ireland, France, Canada & America (including such chestnuts as "The Raggle Taggle Gypsies" & "Froggy Would a-Wooing Go") & several originals, including updated versions of the ISB classics, "Witch's Hat" & "The Water Song". Robin accompanies himself on harp guitar, cittern, mandolin, fiddle, small-pipes, whistle, Jew's harp, mouth organ, kazoo, washboard & hand drums. Joining him are vocalist Krysia Krystianne, hammered dulcimer player Judy Gameral & hurdy-gurdy man Bryan Tolley.

Songs for Communion. Contrib. by Hillsong. 2006. audio compact disk 19.95 (978-5-558-16263-9(5)) Hillsong Pubng AUS.

Songs for Easy Piano: Famous Scottish Songs. 1 cass. bk. 16.95 (S11255) J Norton Pubs.

Songs for Easy Piano: One Hundred Irish Ballads. 1 cass. bk. 16.95 (S11245) J Norton Pubs.

Songs for Easy Piano: One Hundred Irish Ballads. (YA). 1981. bk. 16.95 (978-0-7119-1868-9(6), S11245) J Norton Pubs.

Songs for Easy Piano: One Hundred Scottish Songs. 1 cass. bk. 16.95 (S11250) J Norton Pubs.

Songs for Easy Piano: Popular Irish Songs. 1 cass. bk. 16.95 (S11260) J Norton Pubs.

Songs for Easy Piano: Popular Irish Songs. (YA). 1989. bk. 16.95 (978-0-7119-1866-5(X), S11260) J Norton Pubs.

***Songs for Every Season.** Perf. by Shari Tallon & Jerry Tallon. 1 CD. (Running Time: 28 mins.). (J). (gr. k-3). 2009. audio compact disk (978-0-9739996-8-6(3)) Narroway ProCN CAN.

Songs for God's Little Ones. Arranged by Joseph Linn. 1 cass. (Running Time: 1 hr.). (J). (ps). 2001. pap. bk. 12.99 (TA-9194C) Lillenas.
These 32 songs were arranged specifically for use with nursery-age children. Side A of the cassette contains songs for use in Sunday School or anytime young children use music; side B is useful for worship & quiet times. The companion songbook features words & simple piano accompaniment for all the songs on side A.

Songs for Growin. Kol B'seder. (gr. k-3). pap. bk. 22.95 (978-0-8074-0878-0(6), 993167) URJ Pr.

Songs for I Love You Rituals. Becky Bailey. 1 cass. (J). 10.95 (978-1-889609-07-2(2), AT-112); audio compact disk 13.95 CD. (978-1-889609-08-9(0), AT-113) Loving Guidnce.
Twenty-nine selections by which combining touch & music in an atmosphere of love, optimal brain development is supported.

***Songs for I Love You Rituals Vol II.** 2nd ed. Becky A. Bailey. Mar Harman. (ENG.). (J). 2010. audio compact disk 15.00 (978-1-889609-21-8(8)) Loving Guidnce.

Songs for LDS Children. D's. 1 cass. (J). 5.98 (1900560) Covenant Comms.
The D's sing for LDS children (and mommies & daddies).

Songs for Learning. Kim Mitzo Thompson & Karen Mitzo Hilderbrand. Arranged by Hal Wright. (J). 2001. audio compact disk 12.99 (978-1-57583-379-8(4), Twin 173CD) Twin Sisters.

Songs for Learning. unabr. ed. Twin Sisters Productions. Read by Twin Sisters. (J). 2008. 59.99 (978-1-60514-605-8(6)) Find a World.

Songs for Life, Vol. 1. 1 CD. (Running Time: 1 hr. 30 min.). 12.95 (978-1-56212-626-1(1), 100030); 12.95 (978-1-56212-628-5(8), 100030) FaithAliveChr.

Songs for Life, Vol. 2. 1 cass. (Running Time: 1 hr. 30 min.). (Children's Music Ser.). 12.95 (978-1-56212-629-2(6), 100040); audio compact disk 12.95 (978-1-56212-627-8(X), 100045) FaithAliveChr.

Songs for Little People. 1 CD. (Running Time: 27 min.). (J). (ps-3). 2001. audio compact disk 14.99 Mission Grp.
Ten songs.

Songs for Mom & Me: Songs to Sing, Things to Do, for Mom & Me & Teacher Too. Tonja Evetts Weimer. (J). (ps-3). 1997. 9.95 (978-0-936823-16-4(X)) Pearce Evetts.

Songs for Motivation: Motivation for the Nation. Michele Blood & Bob Proctor. 2007. audio compact disk 14.95 (978-1-890679-26-2(7)) Micheles.

Songs for Music Time. (J). (gr. k-3). 2003. audio compact disk 14.95 (978-0-633-09162-0(6)) LifeWay Christian.

Songs for Music Time, Vol. 7. (J). (gr. k-3). 2004. audio compact disk 14.95 (978-0-633-19512-0(X)) LifeWay Christian.

Songs for Play Time. Kim Mitzo Thompson & Karen Mitzo Hilderbrand. Arranged by Hal Wright. (J). 2001. audio compact disk 12.99 (978-1-57583-387-3(5), Twin 175CD) Twin Sisters.

Songs for Rest Time. Kim Mitzo Thompson & Karen Mitzo Hilderbrand. Arranged by Hal Wright. (Running Time: 1 hr. 12 mins.). (J). 2001. audio compact disk 12.99 (978-1-57583-417-7(0), Twin 170CD) Twin Sisters.

Songs for Silly Time. Kim Mitzo Thompson & Karen Mitzo Hilderbrand. Arranged by Hal Wright. (J). 2001. audio compact disk 12.99 (978-1-57583-421-4(9), Twin 171CD) Twin Sisters.

Songs for Silly Time. unabr. ed. Twin Sisters Productions. Read by Twin Sisters. (J). 2008. 59.99 (978-1-60252-907-6(8)) Find a World.

Songs for Singing Children. 1 cass. (J). (ps-3). 1996. 7.95 (CA 8586); audio compact disk 14.95 (CD 8586) Revels Recs.

Songs for Singing Children. Perf. by John Langstaff. 1 cass., 1 CD. (J). 1996. 7.95 (8586); audio compact disk 14.95 CD. Revels Recs.
A collection of folk songs, singing games, rounds & story songs, sung by a lively group of children.

Songs for Successful Parenting. Barbara Lynn Taylor & Kim Ratz. 1 CD. (Running Time: 90 min.). 2004. audio compact disk 16.95 (978-1-880283-52-3(2)) Pub: Active Parenting. Dist(s): Natl Bk Netwk

Songs for Sunday. 1997. audio compact disk 19.99 (978-0-8066-3401-2(4), 14-3401) Augsburg Fortress.

Songs for the Brave. Read by Joe Gebhardt. Ed. by Ann J. Davidson. 2001. 20.00 (978-0-9688765-1-0(X)) SCW1 CAN.

Songs for the Brave. l.t. ed. Read by Joe Gebhardt. Ed. by Ann J. Davidson. Date not set. per. 20.00 (978-0-9688765-3-4(6)) SCW1 CAN.

Songs for the Earth - Environmental Music Videos. Hosted by Nancy Pearlman. 1 cass. (Running Time: 29 min.). 10.00 (808) Educ Comm CA.

Songs for the High Holidays. Contrib. by Frances Goldman. 1 cass. (Running Time: 30 mins.). (J). 1990. 7.95 (978-0-929371-22-1(4), Kar-Ben) Lerner Pub.

Songs for the High Holidays. Francis T. Goldman. Prod. by Mason Stevens. (Running Time: 30 mins.). (J). audio compact disk 15.95 (978-1-58013-177-3(8), Kar-Ben) Lerner Pub.

Songs for the Inner Child. Contrib. by Shaina Noll. 1992. audio compact disk 15.99 (978-5-552-14437-2(6)) Azerneor AZE.

Songs for the Inner Child. Shaina Noll. (Running Time: 42 min.). 1992. audio compact disk 15.99 (978-5-559-68408-6(2)) Pub: Pt of Grace Ent. Dist(s): STL Dist NA

Songs for the Journey. Contrib. by Sandi Patty. Prod. by David Hamilton. 2008. audio compact disk 13.99 (978-5-557-43333-4(3)) INO Rec.

Songs for the Missing. unabr. ed. Stewart O'Nan. Narrated by Emily Janice Card. (Running Time: 10 hrs.). 2008. 39.95 (978-1-4406-5674-3(6), PengAudBks) Penguin Grp USA.

Songs for the Soul, Vol. 2. Perf. by Daryl Coley et al. 2002. audio compact disk Provident Mus Dist.

Songs for the World CD: Hymns by Charles Wesley. Executive Producer S. T. Kimbrough, Jr. (ENG.). 2001. audio compact disk 12.95 (978-1-890569-43-3(7), GBGMusik) Pub: Gnl Brd Glbl Minis. Dist(s): Cokesbury

Songs for Traveling. Kim Mitzo Thompson & Karen Mitzo Hilderbrand. Arranged by Hal Wright. (J). 2001. audio compact disk 12.99 (978-1-57583-375-0(1), Twin 172CD) Twin Sisters.

Songs for You & Me: Learn about Feelings & Emotions. Perf. by Jane Murphy. 1 LP. (Running Time: 1 hr.). (J). 2001. pap. bk. 11.95 (KIM 8085); 10.95 (KIM 8085C) Kimbo Educ.
Youngsters learn about various emotions & explore acceptable & unacceptable ways of expressing them. Feelings include jealousy, anger, fear, honesty & more. Babies Are People, Pass the Pickles, Monsters Are Only Make Believe, Can We Be Friends? & others. Includes guide.

Songs from a Long Undressing. James Broughton. 1 cass. 1986. 9.95 SPD-Small Pr Dist.

Songs from a Parent to a Child. Art Garfunkel. 1997. 13.98 CD. (Sony Wonder) Sony Music Ent.
Sentiments of joy & wonder pervade this eclectic, fine crafted assemblage of tunes that celebrate day-to-day parent-child quality time.

Songs from an Appalachian Childhood. 2000. audio compact disk 12.99 (978-0-9706527-0-6(4)) Montville Pr.

Songs from Around the World see Chansons Autour du Monde pour les Grandes

Songs from Around the World. 1 cass. 1998. 10.98 (978-1-56826-942-9(0)); audio compact disk 16.98 (978-1-56826-943-6(9)) Rhino Enter.

Songs from Faithweaver: Fall 1999. 1 CD. (Faithweaver Children's Church Ser.). audio compact disk 14.99 Group Pub.

Songs from Faithweaver: Winter. 1 CD. (Faithweaver Children's Church Ser.). 1999. audio compact disk 14.99 CD. Group Pub.

Songs from Grandma's Piano Bench: Fifty Years of Children's Music. abr. ed. Read by Connie K. Anderson. Perf. by Connie K. Anderson. Perf. by Andrew Witchger. 1 cass. (Running Time: 40 min.). (J). (ps-2). 1996. 9.95 (978-0-9649986-1-2(0)); audio compact disk 12.95 CD. (978-0-9649986-2-9(9)) Iguana Prodns.
Valuable old songs about animals, places, people, & nature that expand a child's listening, language, & musical knowledge; to be used in any setting. Two introductory songs are 1995 originals by the author.

Songs from Grandma's Piano Bench: Fifty Years of Children's Music. unabr. ed. Connie K. Anderson. Perf. by Connie K. Anderson. Perf. by Andrew J. Witchger & Jessica Witchger. 1 cass. (Running Time: 43 min.). (J). (ps-2). 1995. audio compact disk 15.95 CD. Iguana Prodns.
17 valuable old songs about animals, places, people, & nature that expand a child's listening, language, & musical knowledge; to be used in any setting. Introductory song is a 1995 original by the author. The music is accompanied by a coloring book with lyrics so that children can choose to listen, read, or color.

Songs from Grandma's Piano Bench: Fifty Years of Children's Music. unabr. ed. Perf. by Connie K. Anderson et al. 1 cass. (Running Time: 43 min.). (J). (ps-2). 1995. bk. 11.95 (978-0-9649986-0-5(2)) Iguana Prodns.

Songs from My Childhood. L. Stanford. 1 cass. (Running Time: 1 hr.). cass. & lp 15.00 (BOD8401C); lp 15.00 (BOD8401); lp & audio compact disk 18.00 (BOD8401CD) Kimbo Educ.
An entire ballet class performed to children's song & nursery rhymes. Barre & center for all levels of dance instruction.

Songs from Sorrow, Songs from Joy: Contemporary Songs from Grief to Healing. Robert Ellis Krout. Composed by Robert Ellis Krout. 1999. per. 19.95 (978-1-58106-011-9(4), ST556) MMB Music.

Songs from the Beginners Bible. Illus. by Jodi Benson. 1 cass. (J). 10.98 (978-0-917143-19-9(1)) Sparrow TN.

Songs from the Cozy Cottage. Read by Clair LeBear. Perf. by Clair LeBear. 1 CD. (Running Time: 1 hr.). (Clair's Cozy Cottage Music Ser.). 2000. audio compact disk 14.95 (978-0-9706321-2-8(6), CC001) Cozy Cottage.
Childrens songs.

Songs from the Garden of Eden: Jewish Lullabies & Nursery Rhymes. Nathalie Soussana. Illus. by Beatrice Alemagna. 1 CD. (Running Time: 52 mins.). (J). (gr. 3). 2009. bk. 16.95 (978-2-923163-46-8(X)) Pub: MontagnSecrete CAN. Dist(s): Natl Bk Netwk

Songs from the Heart. Perf. by Yolanda Adams. 1 cass. 1999. (978-0-7601-2546-5(5)); audio compact disk (978-0-7601-2547-2(3)) Brentwood Music.

Songs from the Iroquois Longhouse. ed. William N. Fenton. Compiled by William N. Fenton. 1 CD. (Running Time: 47 min.). (IRO.). 2005. audio compact disk 16.95 (978-1-57970-339-4(9), S11156D, Audio-For) J Norton Pubs.
Tribal members of the original Iroquois Confederacy-MOhawk, Oneida, Onondaga, Cauyga, and Seneca-lived in a communal household called the longhouse. Iroquois songs of the longhouse are among the earliest annotated music from the Americas. Father Gabriel Sagard recognized as early as 1623 that a charactistic of Iroquois songs was the preponderance of nonsense (or burden) syllables recurring in regular meter not to dissimilar from the song idiom of "tra-la-la." Included in the song collection are The Creator's Songs, songs of medicine societies, of war and peace, and social dances.

Songs from the Iroquois Longhouse. Interview with William N. Fenton. 1 cass. (Running Time: 47 min.). 1999. pap. bk. 16.95 (978-1-57970-043-0(8), S11156) J Norton Pubs.
Collection of Iroquois confederation songs, including the creator's songs, songs of medicine societies, of war & peace, & social dances.

Songs from the Land Before Time. 1 cass. (Running Time: 1 hr.). (J). 5.58 (UNI 56001); audio compact disk 7.98 CD Jewel box. (UNI 56002) NewSound.

Songs from the Land Before Time. 1 cass. (Running Time: 1 hr.). 1997. 6.98 (978-0-7832-2540-1(7), 56001); audio compact disk 9.98 (978-0-7832-2541-8(5), 56002) U Studios Home Vid.
Collection of ten original songs.

Songs from the Loft. Perf. by Amy Grant et al. 1 cass. 1993. Brentwood Music.
These songs were birthed out of the youth outreach held weekly in Amy & Gary's barn. This Dove Award winning album & near gold selling release features the songs, We Believe in God, Hope Set High & Where Do I Go.

Songs from the New Mormon Hymnbook. 1 cass. 7.98 (1000462) Covenant Comms.
An introduction to new hymns by contemporary composers.

Songs from the Other Side. Speeches. LaMar Boschman. 4 CD's. (Running Time: 45 min). 2006. audio compact disk 29.99 (978-0-9759165-3-7(X)) WorshipInstitute.

Songs from the Street: 35 Years of Music. 3 CDs. (Running Time: 30 min). 2004. audio compact disk 44.98 (978-0-7389-2277-5(3)) Sony Music Ent.

Songs from Wildwood. 2004. 8.00 (978-1-57972-601-0(1)); audio compact disk 12.00 (978-1-57972-600-3(3)) Insight Living.

Songs II. Perf. by Rich Mullins. 1 cass. 1999. (978-0-7601-2936-4(3)); audio compact disk (978-0-7601-2935-7(5)) Brentwood Music.
Goes deeper into the writing & theology of Rich's songs & brings out the treasures that truly show how great of a writer & performer Rich was. Songs include: "Step by Step"; "Where You Are"; "I Will Sing/Hope to Carry on"; "I See You"; "The Just Shall Live"; "Somewhere"; "Growing Young"; "Brother's Keeper"; "Home"; "Here in America"; "Bound to Come Some Trouble/The Love of God"; "Ready for the Storm"; "Peace"; "Be With You."

Songs in Ordinary Time. unabr. ed. Mary McGarry Morris. Read by Frances Cassidy. 10 cass. (Running Time: 15 hrs.). 1997. 80.00 (978-0-7366-3743-5(5), 4418-B) Books on Tape.
Epic of everyday life takes us to Vermont in the early sixties and into the turbulent Fermoyle family.

Songs in Ordinary Time. unabr. ed. Mary McGarry Morris. Read by Frances Cassidy. 20 cass. (Running Time: 30 hrs.). 2000. 80.00 (978-0-7366-3742-8(7)) Books on Tape.
Takes us to Vermont in the early sixties & into the turbulent Fermoyle family.

Songs in Ordinary Time. unabr. ed. Mary McGarry Morris. Read by Sandra Burr. (Running Time: 30 hrs.). 2008. 44.25 (978-1-4233-5300-3(5), 9781423353003, Brinc Audio MP3 Lib); 44.25 (978-1-4233-5302-7(1), 9781423353027, BADLE); 29.95 (978-1-4233-5301-0(3), 9781423353010, BAD); 29.95 (978-1-4233-5299-0(8), 9781423352990, Brilliance MP3) Brilliance Audio.

Songs in Ordinary Time. unabr. ed. Mary McGarry Morris. Read by Kate Burton. 4 cass. (Running Time: 6 hrs.). 1997. 24.95 (PengAudBks) Penguin Grp USA.

Songs in Ordinary Time, Pt. 1. unabr. ed. Mary McGarry Morris. Read by Frances Cassidy. 10 cass. (Running Time: 15 hrs.). 1997. 80.00 (4418-A) Books on Tape.

An Asterisk (*) at the beginning of an entry indicates that the title is appearing for the first time.

Songs in Ordinary Time, Pt. 2. unabr. ed. Mary McGarry Morris. Read by Frances Cassidy. 10 cass. (Running Time: 15 hrs.). 1997. 80.00 (4418-B) Books on Tape.

Songs Kids Love. Alexa S. Lambert. 1 cass. (Running Time: 30 min.). (J). (ps-5). 1988. 6.99 (978-0-9639375-0-6(2)) ASL Music.
A collection of old gospel & folk songs, but including one original song of Lambert's simply accompanied by Lambert on guitar.

Songs of America: 18 Classic Songs from Childhood. Prod. by Sue Martin Gay. Directed By Sue Martin Gay & Mike Gay. (C). audio compact disk 5.99 Provident Mus Dist.

Songs of Blue & Gold. Deborah Lawrenson. 2009. 76.95 (978-0-7531-4271-4(6)); audio compact disk 99.95 (978-0-7531-4272-1(4)) Pub: Isis Pubng Ltd GBR. Dist(s): Ulverscroft US

Songs of Christmas. unabr. ed. Warren W. Wiersbe. Read by Warren W. Wiersbe. 2 cass. (Running Time: 2 hrs. 30 min.). 1989. 9.95 (978-0-8474-2360-6(3)) Back to Bible.
This series examines the songs & testimonies of Mary, the angels & others at Christ's birth.

Songs of Earth & Sky. Perf. by Bill Douglas & Ars Nova Singers. 1 cass. 9.98; audio compact disk 17.98 Lifedance.
Various wind instruments share the melodies while vocals, piano, electronic instruments & some percussion provide a delicate balance. Demo CD or cassette available.

Songs of England. Jerry Silverman. 1991. 9.98 (978-1-56222-110-2(8), 94408C) Mel Bay.

Songs of Enlightenment. Poems. Ilchi Lee. 1 CD. (Running Time: 50mins.). 2002. audio compact disk 18.00 (978-0-9720282-2-6(6)) Healing Society.
This CD contains selected poems of enlightenment, given form and voice through the personal experiences of Ilchi Lee. Ilchi Lee!?s beautiful words are both inspirational in their power to stir the soul, as well as straight forward in their message of truth. His poems provide us a place to rest, a soothing touch upon our hearts, and a guiding hand for our souls, giving us the courage and determination to transform ourselves.Let the inspired reading of Ilchi Lee!?s enlightenment poems, accompanied by powerful and stirring music, transport you to a place deep within where you will experience an awakening communion with your soul.

Songs of Experience see Poetry of William Blake

Songs of Faith. Mormon Tabernacle Choir. 1 cass. 4.98 (1500589); audio compact disk 8.98 (1400444) Covenant Comms.
Includes "How Firm a Foundation" & "A Mighty Fortress".

Songs of Faith: Sing-Along for 25 Hymns & Gospel Songs. Prod. by Dawn Wooderson & Kurt Kaiser. 2000. 10.00; audio compact disk 15.00 WoodSong Pub.

***Songs of Garden Birds: The Definitive Audio Guide to British Garden Birds.** British Library Staff & Vrej Nersessian. (Running Time: 1 hr. 12 mins.). (ENG.). 2010. audio compact disk 15.00 (978-0-7123-0519-8(X)) Pub: Britis Library GBR. Dist(s): Chicago Distribution Ctr

Songs of Good Cheer. Donald Walters. 2002. audio compact disk 15.95 (978-1-56589-778-6(1)) Pub: Crystal Clarity. Dist(s): Natl Bk Netwk

Songs of Hispanic America. Ruth DeCesare. (SPA.). 1997. audio compact disk 11.95 (978-0-7390-1325-0(4), 16416) Alfred Pub.

Songs of Hispanic Americans. 1 cass. (Running Time: 90 mins.). (SPA.). pap. bk. 21.95 (SSP290) J Norton Pubs.
A varied collection of folk songs in Spanish & English from the Mexican-American border, the American Southwest & Puerto Rico. Manual includes music & lyrics, a guide to Spanish pronunciation, selected references & a reading list.

Songs of Innocence see Poetry of William Blake

Songs of Inspiration. 1 cass. 1999. 9.99 (P7AAF2); audio compact disk 9.99 (P8AAFI) Time-Life.

Songs of Ireland. Jerry Silverman. 1991. 9.98 (978-1-56222-114-0(0), 94395C) Mel Bay.

Songs of Jabez. George Bloomer. audio compact disk Whitaker Hse.

Songs of Jabez. Perf. by George Bloomer. 1 CD. (Running Time: 90 mins.). 2001. audio compact disk 13.99 (978-0-88368-681-2(3), 776813) Pub: Whitaker Hse. Dist(s): Anchor Distributors

Songs of Joy. 1 cass. 1995. 4.95 (978-1-55569-724-2(0)) Great Am Audio.

Songs of Jubilation. James Chepponis. 1995. 10.95 (368) GIA Pubns.

Songs of Jubilation: Ritual Music of James Chepponis. James Chepponis. 1995. audio compact disk 15.95 (368) GIA Pubns.

Songs of Love. 1 cass. 1995. 4.95 (978-1-55569-726-6(7)) Great Am Audio.

***Songs of Love & Marriage.** Terry Franklin & Barbi Franklin. (ENG.). 2006. audio compact disk 14.95 (978-0-9778908-1-1(3)) Pub: Tylis Pubng. Dist(s): STL Dist NA

Songs of Love & Politics: The Folkway Years 1955-1992. Anno. by Charles Seeger et al. 1 cass. 1992. (0-9307-400480-9307-40048-2-1); audio compact disk (0-9307-40048-2-1) Smithsonian Folkways.
Includes "Freight Train," "First Time Ever I Saw Your Face" & "Gonna Be an Engineer".

Songs of Milarepa. Vajracarya. 9 cass. 1976. 85.50 Vajradhatu.

Songs of My Heart. Paramhansa Yogananda. 1984. 7.00 (2004) Self Realization.
This recording, made in the last years of Yogananda's life, includes the following selections of chants & prayers: "Prayer at Noon"; "The Hound of Heaven" (excerpt from Francis Thompson's poem); "Cloud-Colored Christ"; "I Will Be Thine Always" (English); "I Will Be Thine Always" (Hindi); "Do Not Dry the Ocean of My Love"; "Prayer at Night".

Songs of My Heart: Chants, Poems, & Prayers. Contrib. by Paramhansa Yogananda. (Running Time: 1 hr. 9 mins.). 2005. audio compact disk 14.00 (978-0-87612-502-1(X)) Self Realization.

Songs of Parting see Twentieth-Century Poetry in English, No. 17, Walt Whitman Speaks for Himself

Songs of Polish Heritage. Perf. by Spiewane Prezez Choir. 1 cass. (Running Time: 1 hr.). 14.95 (C11350) J Norton Pubs.
A choir of 80 voices sings traditional songs, polkas & songs of friendship & festival celebrations, accompanied by a string orchestra.

Songs of Power. unabr. ed. Hilari Bell. Narrated by Ruth Ann Phimister. 4 cass. (Running Time: 5 hrs. 30 mins.). (YA). 2001. pap. bk. & stu. ed. 60.99 Recorded Bks.
Imina lives in a scientific community on the ocean floor where no one believes she can perform magic. But when accidents begin to happen, Imina must use her own power to prevent a disaster to the air.

Songs of Power. unabr. ed. Hilari Bell. Narrated by Ruth Ann Phimister. 4 pieces. (Running Time: 5 hrs. 30 mins.). (gr. 5 up). 2001. 37.00 (978-0-7887-4645-1(6), 96375E7) Recorded Bks.

Songs of Praise. 1 cass. 1995. 4.95 (978-1-55569-725-9(9)) Great Am Audio.

Songs of Praise. Perf. by Cedarmont Kids. 1 cass. 1999. 3.99 (978-0-00-546330-7(0)); audio compact disk 5.99 (978-0-00-507232-5(8)) Provident Music.

Songs of Praise. Prod. by Twin Sisters Productions Staff. 1 CD. (J). 2005. audio compact disk 6.99 (978-1-57583-808-3(7)) Twin Sisters.
No one is ever too young to praise the Lord! Kids will worship Him with songs that celebrate His love and greatness. And together with their friends and family, kids will sing to God, "I love and thank YOU!" This new collection of traditional praise songs and choruses arranged for today's kids is perfect for leading young children in worship at home, church, or school. BONUS! The ENHANCED CD includes 68 pages of sheet music that can be printed from your own computer!.

Songs of Saints & Scholars: A Celtic Pilgrimage with the University of Notre Dame Folk Choir. Directed By Steven C. Warner & Karen Schneider Kirner. Contrib. by University of Notre Dame Folk Choir. (ENG.). 2009. audio compact disk 17.00 (978-1-58459-426-0(8)) Wrld Lib Pubns.

Songs of Sioux. 1 cass. (Running Time: 1 hr.). 12.95 (C11149) J Norton Pubs.

Songs of Strength, Michael Ballam. 2 cass. 14.95 (978-1-57734-324-0(7), 1100807) Covenant Comms.
Music has dramatic power to help us through difficult times. A charming mixture of words & music.

***Songs of Taize: O LORD, HEAR MY PRAYER & MY SOUL IS at REST.** (ENG.). 2006. audio compact disk 17.99 (978-92-822-2102-0(4)) Pub: Kingsway Pubns GBR. Dist(s): STL Dist NA

Songs of the Aberdeen: Stories of Great Scottish Terriers from the Pages of Great Scots Magazine. Joseph Harvill. Read by Joseph Harvill. 2 cass. (Running Time: 1 hrs. 20 mins.). 2000. 18.00 (978-0-9703701-1-2(3)) Tartan Scottie.

Songs of the Apache. Willard Rhodes. 1 cass. 1999. pap. bk. 14.95 (978-1-57970-041-6(1), 511157) J Norton Pubs.
Includes three love songs & recorded in 1954.

Songs of the Apache audio CD & Booklet. 1 CD. (Running Time: 35 mins.). (APA.). 2005. audio compact disk 14.95 (978-1-57970-233-5(3), S111157D) J Norton Pubs.

Songs of the Bible. Kidzup Productions Staff. 1 cass. (Running Time: 90 mins.). (Kidzup Ser.). (J). 2000. 8.99 (978-1-894281-53-9(5)); audio compact disk 12.99 (978-1-894281-52-2(7)) Pub: Kidzup CAN. Dist(s): Penton Overseas

Songs of the Cat. abr. unabr. ed. Intro. by Garrison Keillor. Told to Frederica Von Stade. 1 CD. (Running Time: 1 hr.). (ENG.). 1991. audio compact disk 13.95 (978-0-942110-55-5(2), 0942110552) Pub: HighBridge. Dist(s): Workman Pub

Songs of the Century: Southern Gospel's Top 20, Vol. 2. 2002. audio compact disk Provident Mus Dist.

Songs of the Civil War. 1 cass. (Running Time: 1 hr.). 7.98 (CMH 8028); audio compact disk 11.18 CD Jewel box. (CMH 8028) NewSound.

Songs of the Covenant: 100 Songs for Children Learning Covenantal Catechism. Voice by Erin Rice. Contrib. by Emily VanDyken. (J). 2002. audio compact disk 12.98 (978-0-9705251-7-8(6)) Line of Promise Pr.
Three recordings are to teach children the songs assigned in books 1-4 of the Covenantal Catechism Curriculum. Mot of the songs are from the Psalms.

Songs of the CSA, No. 1. 1 cass. (Running Time: 60 min.). 11.95 (CCWS310) Comp Comms Inc.
Features everybody's Dixie, God Save the South, Maryland My Maryland, Rose of Alabama, All Quiet Alon the Potomac Tonight.

Songs of the CSA, No. 2. 1 cass. (Running Time: 60 min.). 11.95 (CCWS311) Comp Comms Inc.
Features Wait For the Wagon, Virginia Marseillaise, Jine the Calvalry, You Are Going to the Wars Willie Boy, Evelina.

Songs of the CSA, No. 3. 1 cass. (Running Time: 1 hr.). 11.95 (CCWS312) Comp Comms Inc.
Features Old Abners Shoes, Cheer Boys Cheer, God Save The Southern Land, Root Hog or Die, Somebody's Darling & Others.

Songs of the CSA, No. 4. (Running Time: 60 min.). 1990. 11.95 (CC314) Comp Comms Inc.
Everybody's Dixie, Maryland My Maryland, Rose of Alabama, All Quiet Along the Potomac Tonight, Stonewall Jacksons Way, The Homespun Dress, Battle Cry of Freedom, Yellow Rose of Texas, The Rebel Soldier, Bonnie Blue Flag, Riding a Raid, Lorena, Twas at the Siege of Vicksburg, Home Sweet Home, Oh I'm a Good Old Rebel, Long Ago, Dixie.

Songs of the Differently Abled: Physical Challenges. Perf. by Janice Buckner. 1 CD. (Running Time: 1 hr. 20 min.). (Learn along Song Ser.). (J). 2001. audio compact disk 15.00 Moonlight Rose.
Celebrates the courage & unique abilities of the physically challenged.

Songs of the Differently Abled: Physical Challenges. Perf. by Janice Buckner. 1 cass. (Running Time: 1 hr. 20 min.). (Learn along Song Ser.: Vol. 4). (J). 1992. 9.98 (978-1-56479-105-4(X), MR105-4) Moonlight Rose.

Songs of the Doomed. Thompson. 2004. 10.95 (978-0-7435-4609-6(1)) Pub: S&S Audio. Dist(s): S and S Inc

Songs of the Doomed: More Notes on the Death of the American Dream. abr. ed. Hunter S. Thompson. Read by Hunter S. Thompson. 2 cass. (Running Time: 3 hrs.). (Gonzo Papers: Vol. 3). 15.95 Set. S&S Audio.

***Songs of the Dying Earth: Stories in Honor of Jack Vance.** Dan Simmons. Ed. by George R. R. Martin & Gardner Dozois. Contrib. by Arthur Morey et al. (Playaway Adult Nonfiction Ser.). (ENG.). 2009. 69.99 (978-1-4418-2711-1(0)) Find a World.

Songs of the Dying Earth: Stories in Honor of Jack Vance. unabr. ed. George R. R. Martin. Read by Arthur Morey. (Running Time: 29 hrs.). 2009. 29.99 (978-1-4418-0702-1(0), 9781441807021, Brilliance MP3) Brilliance Audio.

Songs of the Dying Earth: Stories in Honor of Jack Vance. unabr. ed. Read by Arthur Morey. Ed. by George R. R. Martin & Gardner Dozois. (Running Time: 29 hrs.). 2009. 44.97 (978-1-4418-0703-8(9), 9781441807038, Brinc Audio MP3 Lib); 29.99 (978-1-4418-0704-5(7), 9781441807045, BAD) Brilliance Audio.

Songs of the Dying Earth: Stories in Honor of Jack Vance. unabr. ed. Read by Arthur Morey. Ed. by George R. R. Martin. (Running Time: 26 hrs.). 2009. 44.97 (978-1-4418-0705-2(5), 9781441807052, BADLE) Brilliance Audio.

Songs of the Dying Earth: Stories in Honor of Jack Vance. unabr. ed. Read by Arthur Morey. Ed. by George R. R. Martin & Gardner Dozois. (Running Time: 29 hrs.). 2009. audio compact disk 99.97 (978-1-4418-0701-4(2), 9781441807014, BriAudCD Unabrid); audio compact disk 34.99 (978-1-4418-0700-7(4), 9781441807007, Bril Audio CD Unabri) Brilliance Audio.

***Songs of the Humpback Whale.** unabr. ed. Jodi Picoult. Narrated by Jim Colby et al. 1 Playaway. (Running Time: 15 hrs. 15 mins.). 2009. 64.75 (978-1-4407-1336-1(7)); 92.75 (978-1-4407-1333-0(2)); audio compact disk 123.75 (978-1-4407-1334-7(0)) Recorded Bks.

***Songs of the Humpback Whale.** unabr. collector's ed. Jodi Picoult. Narrated by Jim Colby et al. 12 CDs. (Running Time: 15 hrs. 15 mins.). 2009. audio compact disk 56.95 (978-1-4407-1335-4(9)) Recorded Bks.

Songs of the Kings. Barry Unsworth. Read by Andrew Sachs. 8 vols. (Running Time: 12 hrs.). 2003. 69.95 (978-0-7540-8374-0(8)) Pub: Chivers Audio Bks GBR. Dist(s): AudioGO

Songs of the Kiowa. Willard Rhodes. 1 cass. (Running Time: 37 mins.). 1999. pap. bk. 14.95 (978-1-57970-045-4(4), S511154) J Norton Pubs.
Song collection including songs typical of Plains indians, such as sun dance, war dance, & ghost dance songs as well as songs of legend, Christian prayer, & peyote.

Songs of the Kiowa CD & Booklet. ed. Ed. by Willard Rhodes. Compiled by Willard Rhodes. Frwd. by David P. MacAllester & Douglas McKay. 1 CD. (Running Time: 37 mins.). (MIS.). 2005. audio compact disk 14.95 (978-1-57970-340-0(2), S11154D, Audio-For) J Norton Pubs.
Unlike Sioux music, Kiowa songs are distinguished by narrowness of melodic range and lack of drums, whistles, or accompaniment. This song collection includes those typical of Plains Indians, such as Sun Dance, War Dance, and Ghost Dance songs, as well as songs of legend, Christian prayer, and peyote.

Songs of the Navajo. Willard Rhodes. 1 cass. (Running Time: 36 min.). 1999. pap. bk. 14.95 (978-1-57970-042-3(X), S11153) J Norton Pubs.
Collection of Navajo songs, including blessingway.

Songs of the Navajo CD & Booklet: From the Library of Congress Archive of Folk Culture. ed. Ed. by Willard Rhodes. Compiled by Willard Rhodes. Frwd. by David McKay & David P. McAllester. 1 CD. (Running Time: 36 mins.). (NAV.). 2005. audio compact disk 14.95 (978-1-57970-341-7(0), S11153D, Audio-For) J Norton Pubs.
Includes selections such as "Yeibichai" or "Night Chant"; chant fromt he "Blessingway," described as the backbone of the Navajo religion; corn-grinding songs; mocassin game songs; social dance song; peyote song; circle dance songs; and an interesting Song Commemorating Flag Raising at Iwo Jina, composed by Teddy Draper.

Songs of the Peyote Road. Perf. by Joe Shields, III et al. 1 cass. 7.98 (CANR 6311) NewSound.
Performers sing 24 peyote songs in Lakota; accompanied by a rattle & special waterdrum.

Songs of the Santa Fe Trail & the Far West. Perf. by Mark L. Gardner. 1 cass. (Running Time: 33 min.). 1996. 9.95 (NG003); audio compact disk 14.95 CD. (NG-CD-003) Native Ground.
Documented songs & instrumentals of the 19th Century American West performed with period instruments.

Songs of the Season. Contrib. by Randy Travis & Tim Marshall. Prod. by Kyle Lehning. 2007. audio compact disk 18.99 (978-5-557-58829-4(9), Word Records) Word Enter.

Songs of the Seasons, Vol. 1. Music by Girija Devi. 1 cass. 1994. (B94001) Multi-Cultural Bks.

Songs of the Seasons, Vol. 2. Music by Shobha Gurtu. 1 cass. 1994. (B94002) Multi-Cultural Bks.

Songs of the Seasons, Vol. 3. Music by Lakshmi Shankar. 1 cass. 1994. (B94003) Multi-Cultural Bks.

Songs of the Seasons, Vol. 4. Music by Shubha Mudgal. 1 cass. 1994. (B94004) Multi-Cultural Bks.

Songs of the Sioux. Willard Rhodes & Frances Densmore. Interview with Frances Densmore. 2 cass. (Running Time: 1 hr. 15 min.). 1999. pap. bk. 29.50 (978-1-57970-044-7(6), S11158) J Norton Pubs.
Collection of Sioux songs, including ghost dance, sun dance, war dance, lullaby & Hunka.

Songs of the Sioux CDs & Booklets: From the Library of Congress Archive of Folk Song. ed. Ed. by Frances Densmore & Willard Rhodes. Compiled by Frances Densmore & Willard Rhodes. Pref. by Duncan Emrich. Frwd. by Douglas McKay & David P. McAllester. 2 CDs. (Running Time: 75 mins.). (SIO.). 2005. audio compact disk 29.50 (978-1-57970-342-4(9), S11158D, Audio-For) J Norton Pubs.
Sioux music has several distinguishing features: singing is pitched high and sung with tensed vocal cords, producing a sharp, clear, penetrating sound; melodies spread over an octave or more, and then descend in a series of terraced phrases. The style is also influenced by the genre of the song, such as Ghost Dance, Sun Dance, War Dance, Lullaby, and Adoption, all among the songs included in this collection.

Songs of the Spiritual Masters. 1 cass. (Running Time: 1 hr.). 4.95 (CD-3); audio compact disk 14.95 Bhaktivedanta.

Songs of the Union Army, Vol. 2. (Running Time: 60 min.). 1990. 11.95 (CC315) Comp Comms Inc.
Battle Hymn of the Republic, The Girl I left Behind me, Johnny is my Darling, Aura Lea, Clear the Tracks, Lincoln & Liberty, The Army Bean, Brother Green, The Invalid Corps, The Flag of Columbia, Whats the Matter, Garyowen, Just Before the Battle Mother, Corporal Schnapps, We are marching on to Richmond, Virginias Bloody Soil, When Johnny Comes Marching Home.

Songs of the Voyageurs. Theodore C. Blegen. Perf. by Universite de Moneton Choir Canada. 1 cass. (Running Time: 25 min.). (MHS Minnesota Musical Traditio Ser.). (FRE., 1998. cass. & audio compact disk 16.95 (978-0-87351-361-6(4), 361-4) Pub: Minn Hist. Dist(s): Chicago Distribution Ctr
Selection of traditional voyageur songs celebrates the French-Canadian canoe men of the North American fur trade who sang as they paddled over rivers & lakes during the 17th, 18th & early 19th centuries. The book contains the song texts in French and a description of voyageur life.

Songs of the Whimple Wood, Vol. 1. Louisa Branscomb. 1 cass. (Running Time: 30 min.). (J). (ps-2). 1995. 6.95 Chinky-Po Tree.
A strange combination of beautiful bluegrass & folk music mixed with overly-cute lyrics. The recording centers around the imaginary world of Whimple World. The residents include the Whango-Whee who lives in the Chinky-Po Tree, the Wapiti-Hoo, & the Flapper-Jack-Whacker, all who intrude throughout several songs.

Songs of the Winds: Tree top winds-Mountain Winds-Waterfall Winds-Blue Heron Flies-Path to the Cave of the Bear. Alice Damon. 1999. audio compact disk 10.00 (978-1-4276-1111-6(4)) AardGP.

Songs of the Woodcutter: Zen Poems of Wang Wei & Taigu Ryokan. Wang Wei. 2003. audio compact disk 15.00 (978-0-933087-80-4(2)) Pub: Bottom Dog Pr. Dist(s): SPD-Small Pr Dist

Songs of Victory (Cassette) Compiled by Sunday School Publishing Board. (J). 2004. 3.99 (978-1-932972-03-0(X)) Townsnd-Pr.

Songs of Victory (CD) Compiled by Sunday School Publishing Board. (J). 2004. audio compact disk Rental 5.99 (978-1-932972-04-7(8)) Townsnd-Pr.

Songs of Vietnam. Thich Nhat Hanh. Perf. by Chan Khong. 1 cass. 10.00 (99018) Parallax Pr.
Nine Vietnamese poems set to music. Each story explained in English.

Songs of Warm Fuzzy. 1 cass. (J). 12.95 (JP9003-C) Jalmar Pr.

Soon I Will Be Invincible. unabr. ed. Austin Grossman. Read by J. Paul Boehmer & Coleen Marlo. (YA). 2007. 59.99 (978-1-60252-716-4(4)) Find a World.

Soon to Be a Major Motion Picture: A Novel. Warren Dunford. Read by Mitchell Anderson. 4 cass. (Running Time: 6 hrs. 30 mins.). 2001. 24.95 (978-0-9702152-1-5(5)) Fluid Wds.
Mitchell Draper, a gay Toronto office temp & would-be screenwriter, is chronicling his misadventures as they develop. His big break comes when Carmen Denver offers him a chance to script her top-secret blockbuster. When all his friends experience a turn of good fortune & everyone is happy, the complications begin.

***Sooner or Later.** abr. ed. Debbie Macomber. Read by Natalie Ross. (Running Time: 5 hrs.). 2010. audio compact disk 14.99 (978-1-4418-1982-6(7), 9781441819826) Brilliance Audio.

Sooner or Later. unabr. ed. Debbie Macomber. Read by Natalie Ross. (Running Time: 9 hrs.). 2010. audio compact disk 29.99 (978-1-4418-1976-5(2), 9781441819765, Bril Audio CD Unabri) Brilliance Audio.

***Sooner or Later.** unabr. ed. Debbie Macomber. Read by Natalie Ross. (Running Time: 9 hrs.). 2010. 24.99 (978-1-4418-1978-9(9), 9781441819789, Brilliance MP3); 39.97 (978-1-4418-1979-6(7), 9781441819796, Brinc Audio MP3 Lib); 39.97 (978-1-4418-1981-9(9), 9781441819819, BADLE); 24.99 (978-1-4418-1980-2(0), 9781441819802, BAD); audio compact disk 87.97 (978-1-4418-1977-2(0), 9781441819772, BriAudCD Unabrid) Brilliance Audio.

***Sooner the Better.** abr. ed. Debbie Macomber. Read by Renée Raudman. (Running Time: 5 hrs.). 2010. audio compact disk 14.99 (978-1-4418-1927-7(4), 9781441819277, BACD) Brilliance Audio.

***Sooner the Better.** abr. ed. Debbie Macomber & Renée Raudman. (Running Time: 5 hrs.). 2010. 14.99 (978-1-4418-9238-6(9), 9781441892386, BAD) Brilliance Audio.

***Sooner the Better.** unabr. ed. Debbie Macomber. (Running Time: 8 hrs.). 2010. 24.99 (978-1-4418-1923-9(1), 9781441819239, Brilliance MP3) Brilliance Audio.

Sooner the Better. unabr. ed. Debbie Macomber. Read by Renée Raudman. (Running Time: 9 hrs.). 2010. audio compact disk 29.99 (978-1-4418-1921-5(5), 9781441819215, Bril Audio CD Unabri) Brilliance Audio.

***Sooner the Better.** unabr. ed. Debbie Macomber. Read by Renée Raudman. (Running Time: 8 hrs.). 2010. 24.99 (978-1-4418-1925-3(8), 9781441819253, BAD); 39.97 (978-1-4418-1926-0(6), 9781441819260, BADLE); 39.97 (978-1-4418-1924-6(X), 9781441819246, Brinc Audio MP3 Lib); audio compact disk 92.97 (978-1-4418-1922-2(3), 9781441819222, BriAudCD Unabrid) Brilliance Audio.

Soong Dynasty. unabr. ed. Sterling Seagrave. Read by Alexander Adams. 13 cass. (Running Time: 19 hrs. 30 min.). 1995. 104.00 (978-0-7366-3110-5(0), 3786) Books on Tape.
The Soongs had their fingers in every pot, shaping American policy through a U.S. lobbyist & helping shift control to Chiang Kai-shek at home.

Soothing Classics. Gordon Jeffries. 4 cass., 4 CDs. 1999. 23.95 Set. (45732); audio compact disk 34.95 CD Set. (45734) Courage-to-Change.
Beautiful & soothing musical masterpieces including classics from Mozart, Beethoven, Bach, Vivaldi, & more.

Soothing Classics: Satie/Bach, Debussy/Vivaldi, Mozart/Beethoven. 4 cass. (Running Time: 3 hrs.). 23.95 (978-1-55961-122-0(7)) Relaxtn Co.

Soothing Classics: Satie/Bach, Debussy/Vivaldi, Mozart/Beethoven. Gordon Jeffries. 3 CDs. (Running Time: 2 hrs. 36 min.). 1991. audio compact disk 19.95 (978-1-55961-092-6(1)) Relaxtn Co.
Jeffries augments the musical splendor of Satie, Bach, Vivaldi, Dubussy, Mozart, & Beethoven by combining them with the soothing, relaxing sounds of the oceans, streams, meadows, & gentle rainfall. Thus he has created an exquisite feast for the listener's ears.

Soothing Classics Satie-Bach. Perf. by Gordon Jeffries. 1 cass. (Running Time: 60 min.). 1991. 9.95 (978-1-55961-135-0(9)); 9.95 (978-1-55961-091-9(3)) Relaxtn Co.
The pensive richness of Satie is combined with the irrepressible delights of Bach to create a program of wonderfully refreshing music. Gordon Jeffries calls on his extensive background in both jazz & classical music to make these ageless compositions new.

Soothing Classics/Vivaldi/Debussy. Gordon Jeffries. 1 cass. (Running Time: 48 min.). (Soothing Classics Ser.). 1991. bk. (978-1-55961-108-4(1)) Relaxtn Co.

Soothing Sounds. Executive Producer Twin Sisters Productions Staff. 1 CD. (Running Time: 73 mins). (Growing Minds with Music Ser.). (J). 2004. audio compact disk 12.99 (978-1-57583-733-8(1)) Twin Sisters.
Household noises to keep baby-and others-sleeping through the night. Features authentic recordings of Window Fan Hum, Clothes Dryer Drone, Pitter-Patter Bathwater, Vacuum Cleaner Rumble, White Noise, and A Ride In The Car.

Sop Doll & Other Tales of Mystery & Mayhem. Milbre Burch. Perf. by Milbre Burch. (ENG.). 2002. audio compact disk 15.00 (978-0-9795271-2-8(0)) Kind Crone.

Sopa de Piedras. 1 cass. (Running Time: 1 hr.).Tr. of Stone Soup. (SPA.). (J). 2001. 15.95 (VXS-40C) Kimbo Educ.

Sopa de Piedras. Tr. of Stone Soup. 9.95 (978-1-59112-163-3(9)) Live Oak Media.

Sopa de Piedras. Tr. of Stone Soup. (SPA.). 2004. 8.95 (978-0-7882-0256-8(1)) Weston Woods.

Sopa de Piedras. Marcia Brown. Illus. by Marcia Brown. (Running Time: 16 mins.).Tr. of Stone Soup. 1992. 9.95 (978-1-59112-123-7(X)); audio compact disk 12.95 (978-1-59519-203-5(4)) Live Oak Media.

Sopa de Piedras. Marcia Brown. Illus. by Marcia Brown. 11 vols. (Running Time: 16 mins.).Tr. of Stone Soup. (SPA.). (J). 1992. pap. bk. 18.95 (978-1-59519-204-2(2)) Pub: Live Oak Media. Dist(s): AudioGO

Sopa de Piedras. Marcia Brown. Illus. by Marcia Brown. 11 vols. (Running Time: 16 mins.).Tr. of Stone Soup. 1992. bk. 28.95 (978-1-59519-206-6(9)); pap. bk. 43.95 (978-1-59519-205-9(0)) Live Oak Media.

Sopa de Piedras. Marcia Brown. 1 cass. (Running Time: 10 min.).Tr. of Stone Soup. (SPA.). (J). bk. 24.95; pap. bk. 15.95 Weston Woods.
Three clever soldiers devise a plan to get food & lodging from the selfish inhabitants of a French village during the time of Napoleon.

Sopa de Piedras. unabr. ed. Marcia Brown. Illus. by Marcia Brown. Read by Angel Pineda. 11 vols. (Running Time: 16 mins.).Tr. of Stone Soup. (SPA.). (J). (gr. k-3). 1992. pap. bk. 16.95 (978-0-87499-278-6(8), LK4670) Pub: Live Oak Media. Dist(s): AudioGO
Three hungry soldiers outwit greedy villagers into providing them with a feast, in this classic based on an old French tale.

Sopa de Piedras. unabr. ed. Marcia Brown. Illus. by Marcia Brown. Read by Angel Pineda. 11 vols. (Running Time: 16 mins.).Tr. of Stone Soup. (SPA.). (J). (gr. 1-3). 1992. bk. 25.95 (978-0-87499-279-3(6)); pap. bk. & tchr. ed. 41.95 Reading Chest. (978-0-87499-280-9(X)) Live Oak Media.
Readalong of Spanish translation of Stone Soup.

Sophia: The Fall, Redemption, Sin & Ascension, Set. Stephan Hoeller. 4 cass. 1999. 36.00 (40034) Big Sur Tapes.
1990 Los Angeles.

Sophia Loren. unabr. ed. Warren G. Harris. Read by Nadia May. 12 cass. (Running Time: 17 hrs. 30 mins.). 1998. 83.95 (978-0-7861-1267-8(0), 2202) Blckstn Audio.
An in-depth portrait, with many new facts about Loren's personal life. Born Sofia Scicolone, an illegitimate child in Fascist Italy, Sophia Loren grew up a sickly & undernourished girl who blossomed into one of the world's great beauties. After her screen debut as a teenager, she made several movies in Italy that left directors impressed with her stunning looks & range of emotion.

***Sophie & the Rising Sun (DN) (UAB)** unabr. ed. Augusta Trobaugh. (Running Time: 4 hrs.). (ENG.). 2001. 12.95 (978-0-553-75510-7(2), Random AudioBks) Pub: Random Audio Pubg. Dist(s): Random

Sophie's Choice. William Styron. Read by William Hope. 2003. 145.95 (978-0-7540-8436-5(1)) Pub: Chivers Audio Bks GBR. Dist(s): AudioGO

Sophie's Choice. abr. ed. William Styron. Read by Norman Snow. (Running Time: 10800 sec.). (ENG.). 2007. audio compact disk 14.99 (978-0-7393-5445-2(0), Random AudioBks) Pub: Random Audio Pubg. Dist(s): Random

Sophie's Choice, Pt. 1. unabr. collector's ed. William Styron. Read by Wolfram Kandinsky. 9 cass. (Running Time: 13 hrs. 30 min.). 1984. 72.00 (978-0-7366-0934-0(2), 1878A) Books on Tape.

Sophie's Choice, Pt. 2. collector's ed. William Styron. Read by Wolfram Kandinsky. 10 cass. (Running Time: 15 hrs.). 1984. 80.00 (978-0-7366-0935-7(0), 1878-B) Books on Tape.
Three stories are told: a young Southerner wants to become a writer, a turbulent love-hate affair between a brilliant Jew & a beautiful Polish woman; & an awful wound in that woman's past, one that impels both Sophie & Nathan toward destruction.

Sophie's Dilemma. abr. ed. Lauraine Snelling. Narrated by Renee Ertl. (Running Time: 8 hrs. 30 mins. 14 sec.). (Daughters of Blessing Ser.). (ENG.). 2008. 19.59 (978-1-60814-393-1(7)); audio compact disk 27.99 (978-1-59859-443-0(5)) Oasis Audio.

Sophie's Misfortune see Malheurs de Sophie

Sophie's World. unabr. ed. Jostein Gaarder. Read by Donada Peters. 12 cass. (Running Time: 18 hrs.). 1996. 96.00 (978-0-7366-3431-1(2), 4075) Books on Tape.
Mysterious notes about the purpose of life send a young girl on a philosophical jorney.

Sophie's World. unabr. ed. Jostein Gaarder. Read by Simon Vance. Tr. by Paulette Moller. (Running Time: 18 hrs. 0 mins. 0 sec.). (ENG.). 2007. audio compact disk 59.95 (978-1-4272-0087-7(4)) Pub: Macmill Audio. Dist(s): Macmillan

Sophisticated Estate Planning. 5 cass. (Running Time: 5 hrs.). 1986. pap. bk. 99.95 (543-0077-01); 69.95 (543-0076-01) Amer Bar Assn.
Informs lawyers about provisions from the Tax Reform Act of 1986 that affect the way they counsel clients on their estates. Includes discussions of planning without deductions, new taxes on trusts & estates, the use of subchapter S corporations & personal holding companies, & the new generation-skipping transfer tax.

Sophisticated Estate Planning Techniques. 9 cass. (Running Time: 13 hrs.). 1998. 345.00 Set; incl. study guide 697p. (MD17) Am Law Inst.
Examines cutting-edge techniques in the bread-&-butter areas of estate planning generation skipping, marital deduction, qualified plans, charitable giving, closely held family businesses, trusts, & ethical considerations that affect all of these areas.

Sophisticated Estate Planning Techniques. 1 cass. (Running Time: 13 hrs.). 1999. 345.00 Incl. study guide. (AE09) Am Law Inst.

Sophocles' Electra. Perf. by Jane Lapotaire & Michael Pennington. Tr. by Derek Coltman. 2 cass. (Running Time: 1 hr. 28 mins.). 17.95 (SCN 171) J Norton Pubs.
The return of Orestes to Argos to avenge the death of his father is one of the best-known stories in the Troy cycle. With the help of his sister Electra, Orestes kills his mother & her lover, but is destined to be pursued & tormented by the Furies.

***Sophomore Switch.** unabr. ed. Abby McDonald. (Running Time: 7 hrs.). 2010. 39.97 (978-1-4418-8975-1(2), 9781441889751, Candlewick Bril); 14.99 (978-1-4418-8974-4(4), 9781441889744, Candlewick Bril) Brilliance Audio.

***Sophomore Switch.** unabr. ed. Abby McDonald. Read by Katherine Kellgren. (Running Time: 7 hrs.). 2010. audio compact disk 19.99 (978-1-4418-8970-6(1), 9781441889706, Candlewick Bril); audio compact disk 14.99 (978-1-4418-8972-0(8), 9781441889720, Candlewick Bril); audio compact disk 39.97 (978-1-4418-8973-7(6), 9781441889737, Candlewick Bril); audio compact disk 54.97 (978-1-4418-8971-3(X), 9781441889713, Candlewick Bril) Brilliance Audio.

Sopla en Mi. unabr. ed. Claudio Freidzon. (SPA.). 1999. 7.99 (978-0-8297-2713-5(2)) Pub: Vida Pubs. Dist(s): Zondervan

Soprano Solos. Ed. by Joan Frey Boytim. Created by Hal Leonard Corporation Staff. (ENG.). 1997. audio compact disk 18.99 (978-0-7935-8647-9(X), 079358647X, G Schirmer) H Leonard.

Sor - Classic Guitar Duos: 2-CD Set. Composed by Fernando Sor. 2006. pap. bk. 34.98 (978-1-59615-390-5(3), 1596153903) Pub: Music Minus. Dist(s): H Leonard

Sorcerer, Bks. 4-6. unabr. ed. Tony Abbott. Read by Oliver Wyman. 2 cass. (Running Time: 3 hrs. 16 mins.). (Secrets of Droon Ser.: No. 4). (J). (ps-3). 2005. 23.00 (978-0-307-24604-2(3)) Books on Tape.

Sorcerer's Apprentice. unabr. ed. Composed by Paul Dukas. Contrib. by London Philharmonic Orchestra. Narrated by Yadu. Conducted by Stephen Simon. 1 CD. (Running Time: 41 mins.). (Stories in Music Ser.). (J). (ps-3). 2002. audio compact disk 16.98 (978-1-932684-07-0(7)) Simon Simon.

Sorcerer's Apprentice. unabr. ed. Emily Rodda. Read by Rebecca Macauley. 3 CDs. (Running Time: 3 hrs.). (Raven Hill Mysteries Ser.: Bk. 2). (YA). 2006. audio compact disk 54.95 (978-1-74093-698-9(1)) Pub: Bolinda Pubng AUS. Dist(s): Bolinda Pub Inc

Sorcerer's Apprentice, Pt. 1. unabr. collector's ed. Elspeth Huxley. Read by Donada Peters. 7 cass. (Running Time: 10 hrs. 30 min.). 1988. 56.00 (978-0-7366-1432-0(X), 2316-A) Books on Tape.
Presents visits to Kenya, Tanganyika, Zanzibar & Uganda.

Sorcerer's Apprentice, Pt. 2. unabr. collector's ed. Elspeth Huxley. Read by Donada Peters. 6 cass. (Running Time: 9 hrs.). 1988. 48.00 (978-0-7366-1433-7(8), 2316-B) Books on Tape.

Sorcerer's Apprentice: Stories in Music - A Learn to Listen CD. (J). 2006. audio compact disk 16.98 (978-1-932684-06-3(9)) Simon Simon.

Sorceress see Poetry of Vachel Lindsay

Sorceress. unabr. ed. Michael Scott. Read by Paul Boehmer. (Secrets of the Immortal Nicholas Flamel Ser.: Bk. 3). (ENG.). (J). (gr. 7). 2009. audio compact disk 50.00 (978-0-7393-8055-0(9), Listening Lib) Pub: Random Audio Pubg. Dist(s): Random

***Sorceress: The Secrets of the Immortal Nicholas Flamel.** unabr. ed. Michael Scott. Read by Paul Boehmer. 11 CDs. (Running Time: 14 hrs.). (YA). (gr. 6-9). 2009. audio compact disk 60.00 (978-0-7393-8057-4(5), Listening Lib) Pub: Random Audio Pubg. Dist(s): Random

Soren Kierkegaard: Denmark (1813-1855) abr. ed. Narrated by Charlton Heston. (Running Time: 7579 sec.). (Audio Classics: the Giants of Philosophy Ser.). 2006. audio compact disk 25.95 (978-0-7861-6934-4(6)) Pub: Blckstn Audio. Dist(s): NetLibrary CO

Soren Kierkegaard: Denmark (1813-1855) unabr. ed. George Connell. Read by Charlton Heston. Ed. by George H. Smith & Wendy McElroy. 2 cass. (Running Time: 3 hrs.). (Giants of Philosophy Ser.). 1991. 17.95 Set. (978-0-938935-26-1(7), 10310) Knowledge Prod.
Kierkegaard believed that truth emerges only from our subjective, private lives; but neither the selfish search for pleasure nor a responsible social life can fully satisfy us. A deeply religious thinker, he believed God's existence cannot be proved, but that only a religious leap of faith can make our own finitude bearable & endow life with meaning.

Soren Kierkegaard: Denmark (1813-1855), Set. unabr. ed. Read by Charlton Heston. 2 cass. (Giants of Philosophy Ser.). 17.95 (K126) Blckstn Audio.
See how one of the world's most important philosophers created a complete system of thought, including his views on ethics, metaphysics, politics & aesthetics. Learn about his epistemology - how we know what we know.

Sorpresa de Mama Coneja. Alma Flor Ada. (Cuentos Para Todo el Ano Ser.). (SPA.). (J). (gr. k-3). 4.95 (978-1-58105-246-6(4)) Santillana.

Sorrow. Short Stories. (5121) Am Audio Prose.

Sorrow-Acre see Winter's Tales

Sorrowful Mysteries / Misterios Dolorosos: The Holy Rosary Audio CD / el Santo Rosario Audio CD, Vol. 3. Kenneth L. Davison, Jr. & Shana Buck. Kenneth L. Davison, Jr. Prod. by Brian Shields. Music by William Straub. (ENG & SPA.). (J). 2008. audio compact disk 15.00 (978-0-9801121-2-2(5)) Holy Heroes.

Sorrowful Mysteries of the Rosary. unabr. ed. Perf. by Benedictine Sisters of Erie Staff. 1 cass. (Running Time: 30 min.). 1998. 7.00 (978-1-890890-32-2(4)) Benetvision.
Contemporary & creative presentation of the rosary includes meditations & musical accompaniments.

Sorrows & Smiles. unabr. ed. Dee Williams. Read by Kim Hicks. 8 cass. (Running Time: 12 hrs.). 2001. 69.95 (978-0-7540-0573-5(9), CAB1996) Pub: Chivers Audio Bks GBR. Dist(s): AudioGO
Young Pam King cannot believe her ears when her grandmother, Ivy, forbids her to see Robbie Bennetti. Pam & her mother live with Ivy in Rotherhithe & Pam has always gotten along well with her grandmother. But she won't say why she's so against Robbie, except to announce that the Bennettis are a bad lot. But anyone can see the Robbie's a lovely lad & not half as dangerous as cheeky Lu Cappa, who's always giving Pam the eye.

***Sorrow's Anthem.** unabr. ed. Michael Koryta. Read by Scott Brick. (Running Time: 12 hrs.). (Lincoln Perry Ser.: Vol. 2). 2010. 29.95 (978-1-4417-5841-5(0)); 72.95 (978-1-4417-5837-8(2)); audio compact disk 105.00 (978-1-4417-5838-5(0)); audio compact disk 32.95 (978-1-4417-5840-8(2)) Blckstn Audio.

Sorrows of Empire: Militarism, Secrecy, & the End of the Republic. unabr. ed. Chalmers Johnson. Read by Tom Weiner. (Running Time: 39600 sec.). 2007. 72.95 (978-1-4332-0480-7(0)); audio compact disk 29.95 (978-1-4332-0484-5(3)) Blckstn Audio.

Sorrows of Empire: Militarism, Secrecy, & the End of the Republic. unabr. ed. Chalmers Johnson. Read by Tom Weiner. (Running Time: 41400 sec.). 2007. 24.95 (978-1-4332-0482-1(7)); audio compact disk 24.95 (978-1-4332-0483-8(5)) Blckstn Audio.

Sorrows of Empire: Militarism, Secrecy, & the End of the Republic. unabr. ed. Chalmers Johnson & Tom Weiner. (Running Time: 39600 sec.). 2007. audio compact disk 90.00 (978-1-4332-0481-4(9)) Blckstn Audio.

***Sorrows of Gin.** abr. ed. John Cheever. Read by Meryl Streep et al. (ENG.). 2009. (978-0-06-125305-8(7), Caedmon) HarperCollins Pubs.

***Sorrows of Gin.** unabr. ed. John Cheever. Read by Meryl Streep et al. (ENG.). 2009. (978-0-06-196869-3(2), Caedmon) HarperCollins Pubs.

Sorrows of Young Werther. unabr. ed. Johann Wolfgang von Goethe. Read by Tom Beyer. 6 cass. (Running Time: 5 hrs. 15 min.). Dramatization. 1991. 36.95 set. (978-1-55686-387-5(X), 387) Books in Motion.
A young man's passion for a woman he can't possess progresses from the rapture of love, to painful obsession, to suicidal delirium.

***Sorrows of Young Werther.** unabr. ed. Johann Wolfgang von Goethe. Read by Don Hagen. (Running Time: 5 hrs.). (ENG.). 2010. 9.98 (978-1-59659-517-0(5), GildAudio) Pub: Gildan Media. Dist(s): HachBkGrp

Sorry: Wrong Number. 10.00 (MC1004) Esstee Audios.

Sorry, Right Number: And Other Stories. unabr. ed. Stephen King. Read by Stephen King. Read by Joe Mantegna et al. (Running Time: 3 hrs. 30 mins. 0 sec.). (ENG.). 2009. audio compact disk 14.99 (978-0-7435-9825-5(3)) Pub: S&S Audio. Dist(s): S and S Inc

Sorry, Wrong Number. Perf. by Agnes Moorehead. 1946. (DD-8430) Natl Recrd Co.

Sorry You've Been Troubled. unabr. ed. Peter Cheyney. Read by Terry Wale. 7 cass. (Running Time: 10 hrs. 30 min.). (Sound Ser.). 2004. 61.95 (978-1-85496-790-9(8), 67908) Pub: UlverLrgPrint GBR. Dist(s): Ulverscroft US
Slim Callaghan - dead bodies - beautiful women - fast cars. A story that will keep you guessing, banish your blues & put back the twinkle in your eye.

Sort It Out. Sundance/Newbridge, LLC Staff. (Early Math Ser.). (gr. k-1). 2000. 12.00 (978-1-58273-310-4(4)) Sund Newbrdge.

Sort of Life. unabr. ed. Graham Greene. Read by Ian Whitcomb. 7 cass. (Running Time: 7 hrs.). 42.00 (978-0-7366-0629-5(7), 1590) Books on Tape.
Story of the author's childhood & youth is the first installment of his autobiography.

Sorta Like a Rock Star. unabr. ed. Matthew Quick. Read by Cynthia Holloway. (J). 2010. audio compact disk 34.00 (978-0-307-73811-0(6), Listening Lib) Pub: Random Audio Pubg. Dist(s): Random

Sorting at the Nature Center: Early Explorers Emergent Set A Audio CD. Benchmark Education Staff. (J). 2006. audio compact disk 10.00 (978-1-4108-7604-1(7)) Benchmark Educ.

Sorting at the Park: Early Explorers Emergent Set A Audio CD. Benchmark Education Staff. (J). 2006. audio compact disk 10.00 (978-1-4108-7601-0(2)) Benchmark Educ.

Sorting Out This Marriage Thing... Our Relationships Affect Our Health. Henry W. Wright. (ENG.). 2008. audio compact disk 17.95 (978-1-934680-29-2(X)) Be in Hlth.

SOS Help! My Flesh Needs Discipline. Creflo A. Dollar. 30.00 (978-1-59089-088-2(4)) Pub: Creflo Dollar. Dist(s): STL Dist NA

Sotheby's: Bidding for Class. unabr. ed. Robert Lacey. Narrated by Simon Prebble. 7 cass. (Running Time: 9 hrs. 45 mins.). 1999. 62.00 (978-1-84197-013-4(1), H1013E7) Recorded Bks.
In this splendid account of the world's oldest & richest auction house, Lacey brings to life the personalities, ambition & shrewd business dealings behind the glamour & the glitz. From its beginnings in eighteenth-century London as a modest book dealer, Sotheby's owes its rise to a succession of clever & colourful entrepreneurs who knew how to read the winds of economic change & sniff out buyers & sellers of the moment.

Sotheby's Set: Bidding for Class. unabr. ed. Robert Lacey. Narrated by Simon Prebble. 7 cass. 1999. 62.00 (H1013K4, Clipper Audio) Recorded Bks.

Sotho Newspaper Reader, Grammar Sketch & Lexicon. R. David Zorc & Paul Mokabe. 1 cass. (Running Time: 1 hr. 30 min.). (MIS.). 1998. 12.00 (3140) Dunwoody Pr.
Twenty-eight selections representing both the South African & Lesotho press. The orthography of both the grammar & lexicon is that of South Africa since most grammatical studies to date are in the Lesotho version.

Sotos Syndrome - A Bibliography & Dictionary for Physicians, Patients, & Genome Researchers. Compiled by Icon Group International, Inc. Staff. 2007. ring bd. 28.95 (978-0-497-11382-7(1)) Icon Grp.

Sotto Voce. unabr. ed. Dave Kenney & Tena Hess. Perf. by Tena Hess. Ed. by Charles Beres & Randy Beres. 1 cass. (Running Time: 38 min.). 1995. 9.95 (978-1-883152-06-2(2)); audio compact disk 15.95 CD. (978-1-883152-07-9(0)) Amirra Pr.
Light classical favorites performed on flute, hammered dulcimer & cello.

Soul. Erikka Haa. (Musicbooks Ser.). 1997. bk. 13.50 (978-1-56799-544-2(6), Friedman-Fairfax) M Friedman Pub Grp Inc.

***Soul: Good or Evil?** L. Ron Hubbard. (ENG.). 2002. audio compact disk 15.00 (978-1-4031-0627-8(4)) Bridge Pubns Inc.

***Soul: Good or Evil?** L. Ron Hubbard. 2010. audio compact disk 15.00 (978-1-4031-7689-9(2)); audio compact disk 15.00 (978-1-4031-7687-5(6)); audio compact disk 15.00 (978-1-4031-7678-3(7)); audio compact disk 15.00 (978-1-4031-7688-2(4)); audio compact disk 15.00 (978-1-4031-7680-6(9)); audio compact disk 15.00 (978-1-4031-7677-6(9)); audio compact disk 15.00 (978-1-4031-7679-0(5)); audio compact disk 15.00 (978-1-4031-7676-9(0)); audio compact disk 15.00 (978-1-4031-7690-5(6)); audio compact disk 15.00 (978-1-4031-7682-0(5)); audio compact disk 15.00 (978-1-4031-7684-4(1)); audio compact disk 15.00 (978-1-4031-7683-7(3)); audio compact disk 15.00 (978-1-4031-7686-8(8)); audio compact disk 15.00 (978-1-4031-7681-3(7)); audio compact disk 15.00 (978-1-4031-7691-2(4)); audio compact disk 15.00 (978-1-4031-7685-1(X)) Bridge Pubns Inc.

Soul: How to Make Godly Decisions by Controlling Your Mind, Will, & Emotions. 8. (Running Time: 8 hrs.). (Soul Control Ser.: 2). 2002. 40.00 (978-1-57399-108-7(2)); audio compact disk 40.00 (978-1-57399-158-2(9)) Mac Hammond.
In this series, Mac teaches how we can train and discipline our soul to make decisions for life and blessing every time. Make sure your eternal destiny is one you can live with. Take control of your soul and start making decisions for life and blessing today!.

Soul Aerobics: Soul-Utions to Experience Success Beyond Your Wildest Dreams. Jesse Weeks. 1 cass. 1996. 9.95 Sovrgnty Pubng.
Part I: Introduction to the qualities of the soul & how they promote success. Part II: Exercises to develop soul qualities (joy, love, peace, etc.) & atrophy fear & limitation.

Soul & Belonging: The Power & Presence of Poetry. David Whyte. 1 cass. (Running Time: 1 hr. 23 min.). 1995. 10.95 (978-0-7822-0500-8(3), 575) C G Jung IL.
Poetry is not only a doorway to profound experience but a celebration of experience itself. As we attempt to bring more sense of soul to our work, our relationships, & our society. Poetry can be of immense use in taking real steps toward the life we desire for ourselves. This tape explores these ideas in this moving presentation of poetry & talk.

Soul & Everyday Life. Thomas Moore. 2 cass. (Running Time: 3 hrs.). 1995. pap. bk. 19.95 set. (978-1-879323-16-2(8)) Sound Horizons AV.
On these two tapes Moore takes the listener through an actual lecture & workshop weekend on the soul conducted at The Open Center in New York, where he discusses his ideas on work, money, futility, creativity & answers questions from the audience.

***Soul & Its Mechanism: Mp3.** Alice A. Bailey. (ENG.). 2009. audio compact disk 13.00 (978-0-85330-215-5(4)) Lucis Pr GBR.

Soul & Psyche: A Child Psychiatrist's View of the World see Soul & Psyche: The Crossing Point

Soul & Psyche: On the Spiritual Instinct: A Jungian Point of View see Soul & Psyche: The Crossing Point

Soul & Psyche: Panel Discussion see Soul & Psyche: The Crossing Point

Soul & Psyche: Psychology & Religion Intertwined: Their Place in Spiritual Development see Soul & Psyche: The Crossing Point

Soul & Psyche: Quaker Experience of Prayer & the Inward Work of Christ see Soul & Psyche: The Crossing Point

Soul & Psyche: Religion & Psychology: Hits & Misses in Institutional Christianity see Soul & Psyche: The Crossing Point

Soul & Psyche: Religious Experience & Psychotic Experience see Soul & Psyche: The Crossing Point

Soul & Psyche: The Crossing Point. 10 cass. Incl. Soul & Psyche: A Child Psychiatrist's View of the World. Elinor E. Weeks. 1982.; Soul & Psyche: On the Spiritual Instinct: A Jungian Point of View. Stephen A. Martin. 1982.; Soul & Psyche: Panel Discussion. 1982.; Soul & Psyche: Psychology & Religion Intertwined: Their Place in Spiritual Development. Dorothy Reichardt. 1982.; Soul & Psyche: Quaker Experience of Prayer & the Inward Work of Christ. William Taber. 1982.; Soul & Psyche: Religion & Psychology: Hits & Misses in Institutional Christianity. Albert Neilson. 1982.; Soul & Psyche: Religious Experience & Psychotic Experience. Roberto J. Serruya. 1982.; Soul & Psyche: The Dimensions of Transpersonal Psychology & Mysticism. Zalman Schachter-Shalomi. 1982.; Soul & Psyche: The Journey Inward: The Personal Perspective & Struggle. Virginia H. Davis. 1982.; Soul & Psyche: Women's Perspectives in Religion & Psychology. Damaris Wehr. 1982.; 1982. 30.00 Set.; 4.50 ea. Pendle Hill.

Soul & Psyche: The Dimensions of Transpersonal Psychology & Mysticism see Soul & Psyche: The Crossing Point

Soul & Psyche: The Journey Inward: The Personal Perspective & Struggle see Soul & Psyche: The Crossing Point

Soul & Psyche: Women's Perspectives in Religion & Psychology see Soul & Psyche: The Crossing Point

Soul & Psyche (Readings From) Excerpts. Barbara Rosenthal. Read by Barbara Rosenthal. (Running Time: 30 mins). 2003. audio compact disk 25.00 (978-0-9728260-6-8(8), Soul & Psyche CD) eMedialoft.
Originally presented on WNYE-FM Radio, Media Poet/Writer/Photographer/Conceptual Artist Barbara Rosenthal reads the first page from each of the six years in "Soul & Psyche," her book of Surreal Photography and Journal-Poetry, which has been described by Buzz Spector as "a kind of shorthand which lets all sorts of interesting other meanings enter into its narrative of days." Highly inventive experimental condensed language-form abbreviates English to only those letters and symbols absolutely necessary for comprehension. This artist shares startling personal revelations about her attempts to face the outside world of imposed stress, and she provides deep insights into the nature of High Art, with passages negotiated through her "Lumpy Potato theory of the Universe" and socio-political commentary, to bring the listener into a mysterious tiny distorted universe, as Rosenthal continues her uphill struggle to find a place in it. One Surreal Photograph on front cover; author portrait and signature on back.

Soul & Spirit in the World. Robert Sordello & Thomas Moore. 3 cass. 1993. 27.00 set. (OC338-72) Sound Horizons AV.

Soul & the City: Art, Literature, & Urban Life. 4 cass. (Running Time: 6 hrs.). 1991. 39.95 (978-1-56585-136-8(6)) Teaching Co.

Soul Catcher. unabr. ed. Michael White. 13 CDs. (Running Time: 16 hrs. 0 mins. 0 sec.). (ENG.). 2007. audio compact disk 39.99 (978-1-4001-0521-2(8)) Pub: Tantor Media. Dist(s): IngramPubServ

Soul Catcher. unabr. ed. Michael White. Read by William Dufris. (Running Time: 16 hrs. 0 mins. 0 sec.). (ENG.). 2007. audio compact disk 29.99 (978-1-4001-5521-7(5)) Pub: Tantor Media. Dist(s): IngramPubServ

Soul Catcher. unabr. ed. Michael C. White. Read by William Dufris. (YA). 2007. 64.99 (978-1-60252-814-7(4)) Find a World.

Soul Catcher. unabr. ed. Michael C. White. Read by William Dufris. (Running Time: 16 hrs. 0 mins. 0 sec.). (ENG.). 2007. audio compact disk 79.99 (978-1-4001-3521-9(4)) Pub: Tantor Media. Dist(s): IngramPubServ

Soul Circus. unabr. ed. George P. Pelecanos. Read by Richard Allen. (Running Time: 9 hrs.). (Derek Strange/Terry Quinn Ser.). 2004. 24.95 (978-1-59710-729-7(8), 1597107298, BAD) Brilliance Audio.

Soul City. unabr. ed. Toure. Narrated by Kevin R. Free. 5 cass. (Running Time: 5 hrs.). 2004. 49.75 (978-1-4193-1250-2(2), F0198MC, Griot Aud) Recorded Bks.

Soul Communication: Opening Your Spiritual Channels for Success & Fulfillment. unabr. ed. Zhi Gang Sha. Read by Marilyn Smith. (Running Time: 14 hrs. 0 mins. 0 sec.). (ENG.). 2008. audio compact disk 49.99 (978-0-7435-7678-9(0)) Pub: S&S Audio. Dist(s): S and S Inc

***Soul Custody: Choosing to Care for the one & Only You.** unabr. ed. Stephen Smith. (ENG.). 2010. 12.98 (978-1-59644-905-3(5)); audio compact disk 21.98 (978-1-59644-904-6(7)) christianaud.

Soul Cutz, Vol. 1. 1 CD. (Running Time: 1 hrs. 30 mins.). audio compact disk 16.98 (978-5-559-36289-2(1)) Pub: Pt of Grace Ent. Dist(s): STL Dist NA

Soul Eater. unabr. ed. Michelle Paver. Read by Ian McKellen. 6 cass. (Running Time: 6 hrs. 45 mins.). (Chronicles of Ancient Darkness: Bk. 3). (YA). (gr. 5 up). 2007. 51.75 (978-1-4281-4604-4(0)); audio compact disk 66.75 (978-1-4281-4609-9(1)) Recorded Bks.

Soul Eclipsed: Greed, Violence, & the Loss of Wonder. John Van Eenwyk. 1 cass. (Running Time: 1 hr. 14 min.). 1995. 10.95 (978-0-7822-0502-2(X), 577) C G Jung IL.
Trying to define the soul is an exercise in futility. This provocative presentation says that to achieve that understanding we must first look at ourselves.

Soul Enchilada. unabr. ed. David Macinnis Gill. Read by Michelle Carmen Gomez. 1 MP3-CD. (Running Time: 9 hrs.). 2009. 24.99 (978-1-4233-8226-3(9), 9781423382263, Brilliance MP3); 39.97 (978-1-4233-8227-0(7), 9781423382270, Brlnc Audio MP3 Lib) Brilliance Audio.

Soul Enchilada. unabr. ed. David Macinnis Gill. Read by Michelle Carmen. (Running Time: 9 hrs.). 2009. 39.97 (978-1-4233-8229-4(3), 9781423382294, BADLE) Brilliance Audio.

Soul Enchilada. unabr. ed. David Macinnis Gill. Read by Michelle Carmen Gomez. (Running Time: 9 hrs.). 2009. 24.99 (978-1-4233-8228-7(5), 9781423382287, BAD); audio compact disk 87.97 (978-1-4233-8225-6(0), 9781423382256, BriAudCD Unabrid); audio compact disk 29.99 (978-1-4233-8224-9(2), 9781423382249, Bril Audio CD Unabri) Brilliance Audio.

Soul Escape. Roger Neal. (Running Time: 42 hrs. 26 mins.). 2005. audio compact disk 14.98 (978-5-558-98206-0(3)) Freed Recs.

Soul Food: Satisfying Your Spiritual Hunger. G. P. Holt. 6 cass. (Running Time: 9 hrs.). 24.99 (978-0-89098-250-1(3)) Twent Cent Christ.

Soul Friend: Meditations for Healing. unabr. ed. Karen Ander Francis. 1 cass. (Running Time: 30 mins.). 2001. 6.95 Innerwork.
Each side has a guided meditation to heal the soul of the spiritual wounds associated with childhood abuse. Accompanies the book, "The Soul Friend," Model of spiritual direction with adults abused as children. Can be used separately.

Soul Harvest: An Experience in Sound & Drama. unabr. ed. Tim LaHaye & Jerry B. Jenkins. Read by Jack Sondericker. 10 CDs. (Running Time: 11 hrs. 12 min.). (Left Behind Ser.: Bk. 4). 2001. audio compact disk 65.00 (978-1-58116-128-1(X)) Books in Motion.
Tribulation Force members Rayford Steele and Buck Williams have survived, and are separately looking for loved ones, as the world is forced to take sides.

Soul Harvest: The World Takes Sides. Tim LaHaye & Jerry B. Jenkins. Narrated by Richard Ferrone. 9 CDs. (Running Time: 11 hrs. 15 mins.). (Left Behind Ser.: Bk. 4). 2000. audio compact disk 89.00 (978-0-7887-4902-5(1), C1277E7) Recorded Bks.
A global earthquake caused widespread destruction. Although the evil world leader, Carpathia, shrugs at this evidence of the wrath of the Lamb, believers see it as the beginning of the great harvest of faithful souls.

Soul Harvest: The World Takes Sides. unabr. ed. Tim LaHaye & Jerry B. Jenkins. Read by Jack Sondericker. 8 cass. (Running Time: 11 hrs. 12 min.). (Left Behind Ser.: Bk. 4). 2001. 49.95 (978-1-55686-917-4(7)) Books in Motion.
Tribulation Force members Rayford Steele and Buck Williams have survived, and are separately looking for loved ones, as the world is forced to take sides.

Soul Harvest: The World Takes Sides. unabr. ed. Tim LaHaye & Jerry B. Jenkins. Narrated by Richard Ferrone. 8 cass. (Running Time: 11 hrs. 15 mins.). (Left Behind Ser.: Bk. 4). 1999. 70.00 (978-0-7887-3896-8(8), 95693E7) Recorded Bks.
A global earthquake caused widespread destruction. Although the evil world leader, Carpathia, shrugs at this evidence of the wrath of the Lamb, believers see it as the beginning of the great harvest of faithful souls.

Soul Harvest: The World Takes Sides. unabr. ed. Tim LaHaye & Jerry B. Jenkins. Read by Richard Ferrone. 7 cass. (Running Time: 11 hrs. 15 mins.). (Left Behind Ser.: Bk. 4). 2004. 29.95 (978-0-7887-5126-4(3), 00064) Recorded Bks.

Soul Harvest: The World Takes Sides, unabr. ed. Tim LaHaye & Jerry B. Jenkins. Read by Richard Ferrone. 9 CDs. (Running Time: 11 hrs. 15 mins.). (Left Behind Ser.: Bk. 4). 2004. audio compact disk 39.95 (978-0-7887-5135-6(2), 00062) Recorded Bks.

Soul in Exile. Read by Marion Woodman. 1 cass. (Running Time: 90 min.). 1987. 10.95 (978-0-7822-0332-5(9), 239) C G Jung IL.

Soul in Nature, unabr. ed. Hans C. Oerstad. Read by Robert L. Halvorson. 2 cass. (Running Time: 3 hrs.). 14.95 (59) Halvorson Assocs.

Soul in Torment & other Stories. adpt. ed. Read by Adrian Plass et al. Prod. by Dave Arnold. Adapted by Paul McCusker. (Running Time: 240 hrs. 0 mins.). (Radio Theatre Ser.). (ENG.). (J). (gr. 3). 2007. audio compact disk 14.97 (978-1-58997-501-9(4), Tyndale Ent) Tyndale Hse.

Soul Interpretations. Perf. by Excelsior. audio compact disk 16.98 Provident Mus Dist.

Soul Kiss. unabr. ed. Shay Youngblood. Narrated by Patricia R. Floyd. 5 cass. (Running Time: 7 hrs. 15 mins.). 1997. 45.00 (978-0-7887-5331-2(2), F0011L8) Recorded Bks.
Mariah is abandoned at seven by her mother & raised by maiden aunts in Georgia. Over the next decade she will begin a journey that takes her to California to meet her father & back to Georgia in her quest to find the meaning of love. Along the way, she will find that the most satisfying love comes with self-acceptance.

Soul Life Set: How to Nourish & Deepen Your Everyday Life, Thomas Moore. 6 cass. 1994. 59.95 (10060PAX) Nightingale-Conant.
Your soul is an inner universe: vast, mysterious, powerful. It embraces every aspect of your life - all moods, all experiences & all emotions. And it is a part of life's defining mystery, reaching to the infinite depths within you. Best-selling author Thomas Moore takes you on a journey full of discovery to the farthest reaches of this complex realm. He presents a compelling approach to everyday life that takes place not on a scientific-mechanical level, but on the deepest human plane. Includes: Tape 1: Introduction to Soul Life; Tape 2: Soul & the Family; Tape 3: Work & Soul; Tape 4: Art & Soul; Tape 5: Soul & Place; Tape 6: Religion & Soul.

Soul Mates. Christopher Love. Read by Christopher Love. 1 cass. (Running Time: 30 min.). 1997. 10.95 (978-1-891820-21-2(4)) World Sangha Pubg.
Self-hypnosis meditation for healing, self-improvement & realizing our full & powerful potential as spiritual beings.

***Soul Mates.** abr. ed. Thomas Moore. Read by Thomas Moore. (ENG.). 2005. (978-0-06-089366-8(4), Harper Audio); (978-0-06-089365-1(6), Harper Audio) HarperCollins Pubs.

Soul Mates: Honoring the Mysteries of Love & Relationship, unabr. ed. Thomas Moore. Narrated by Nelson Runger. 8 cass. (Running Time: 10 hrs. 45 mins.). 70.00 (978-0-7887-0253-2(X), 94462E7) Recorded Bks.
The companion volume to "Care of the Soul" explores how relationships of all kinds, even with all their difficulties, deepen our lives & help fulfill the needs of the soul. Teaches that sometimes the slightest shift of imagination can have more impact on a relationship than most major efforts at change, bringing both partners a deeper sense of person satisfaction. Available to libraries only.

Soul Mates- Reflections on Love's Mysteries. abr. ed. Thomas Moore & Thomas Moore. Read by Thomas Moore. 2 cass. (Running Time: 3 hrs.). 1994. 18.00 (978-1-55994-941-5(4), CPN 2419, Harper Audio) HarperCollins Pubs.

Soul Mates & Family. Terrie Brill. Read by Terrie Brill. 1 cass. (Running Time: 90 min.). 1994. 8.95 (1166) Am Fed Astrologers.

Soul Mates & Twin Flames: The Spiritual Dimension of Love & Relationships. unabr. ed. Elizabeth Clare Prophet. 1 cass. (Running Time: 1 hr. 30 mins.). 2002. 10.95 (978-0-922729-75-3(1), 942-061) Pub: Summit Univ. Dist(s): Natl Bk Netwk

Soul Mates Dissipate. Mary B. Morrison. Narrated by Indigo Brown. 5 cass. (Running Time: 7 hrs. 15 mins.). 45.00 (978-1-4025-3953-4(3)) Recorded Bks.

Soul Mountain. Xingjian Gao. Read by Brian Keeler. 11 Cass. (Running Time: 19 Hrs.). 39.95 (978-1-4025-4533-7(9)) Recorded Bks.

Soul Mountain. unabr. ed. Xingjian Gao. Tr. by Mabel Lee. Narrated by Brian Keeler. 13 cass. (Running Time: 19 hrs.). 2002. 99.00 (978-0-7887-8871-0(X)) Recorded Bks.

Soul Music. Terry Pratchett. Read by Tony Robinson. 2 cass. (Running Time: 3 hrs.). (Discworld Ser.). (ENG.). 1996. 16.99 (978-0-552-14424-7(X)) Pub: Transworld GBR. Dist(s): IPG Chicago
Susan Sto Helit is rather bored at her boarding school in the city of Ankh-Morpork, which is just as well, since it seems that her family business - she is the granddaughter of Death, suddenly needs a new caretaker.

Soul Music. Perf. by Woody Rock. audio compact disk 17.98 Provident Music.

Soul Music. unabr. ed. Terry Pratchett. Read by Nigel Planer. 8 cass. (Running Time: 9 hr. 30 min.). (Discworld Ser.). (J). 2001. 69.95 (978-0-7531-0120-9(3), 961204) Pub: ISIS Lrg Prnt GBR. Dist(s): Ulverscroft US
It's hard to grow up normally when Grandfather rides a white horse & wields a scythe-especially when you have to take over the family business & everyone mistakes you for the Tooth Fairy. And Especially when you have to face the new & addictive music that has entered the Discworld. It's lawless. It changes people. It's called "Music With Rocks In". It's got a beat & you can dance to it, but ... it's alive. And it won't fade away.

Soul Music. unabr. ed. Terry Pratchett. Read by Nigel Planer. 9 CDs. (Running Time: 37500 sec.). (Discworld Ser.). 2007. audio compact disk 84.95 (978-0-7531-2216-7(2)) Pub: ISIS Lrg Prnt GBR. Dist(s): Ulverscroft US

Soul of a New Machine. unabr. ed. Tracy Kidder. Read by Grover Gardner. 7 cass. (Running Time: 10 hrs. 30 min.). 1987. 56.00 (978-0-7366-1247-0(5), 2162) Books on Tape.
Everything actually happened. No names have been changed. Nothing controversial has been left out. In 1979 Tracy Kidder went underground into the closely guarded research basement of Data General to observe a crack team of computer wizards about to embark on a crash program to design & build a fast new computer. "The Soul of a New Machine" is the Pulitzer Prize-winning result.

Soul of an Age. abr. ed. William Shakespeare. Perf. by Ralph Richardson & Michael Redgrave. 1 cass. 1984. 12.95 (SWC 1170) HarperCollins Pubs.

***Soul of an Age.** abr. ed. William Shakespeare. (ENG.). 2006. (978-0-06-112633-8(0), Caedmon); (978-0-06-112634-5(9), Caedmon) HarperCollins Pubs.

Soul of Elizabeth Seton. unabr. ed. Joseph I. Dirvin. Read by Maureen O'Leary. 6 cass. 24.95 Set. (769) Ignatius Pr.
This moving biography & inspiring record of St. Elizabeth Seton's interior journey gives us a profound spiritual portrait of a multi-faceted saint who is a particularly important model for our times. Mother Seton embodies the truth that sainthood & modernity can mix.

Soul of Leadership: Unlocking Your Potential for Greatness. abr. unabr. ed. Deepak Chopra. Read by Deepak Chopra. (ENG.). 2010. audio compact disk 30.00 (978-0-7393-8524-1(0), Random AudioBks) Pub: Random Audio Pubg. Dist(s): Random

Soul of Lion. unabr. ed. Gene Veith. 2005. 25.99 (978-1-58926-873-9(3), 6873) Pub: Oasis Audio. Dist(s): TNT Media Grp

***Soul of Sex.** abr. ed. Thomas Moore. Read by Thomas Moore. (ENG.). 2005. (978-0-06-089386-6(9), Harper Audio); (978-0-06-089385-9(0), Harper Audio) HarperCollins Pubs.

Soul of the Apostolate. Dom Chautard. 8 cass. 32.95 (920) Ignatius Pr.
The classic on the spiritual life. A favorite of St. Pius X.

Soul of the Fire. unabr. ed. Terry Goodkind. Read by Buck Schirner. 13 cass. (Running Time: 24 hrs.). (Sword of Truth Ser.: Bk. 5). 1999. 137.25 (978-1-56740-632-0(7), 1567406327, Unabridge Lib Edns) Brilliance Audio.
Terry Goodkind returns to the epic Sword of Truth saga in a tale of sweeping fantasy adventure bound to enthrall his growing legion of fans. In Temple of the Winds, the New York Times bestselling fourth novel in the series, the Seeker of Truth Richard Rahl and Mother Confessor Kahlan Amnell risked their lives and souls to free the land of D'Hara from the scourge of a magical plague. But in doing so they accidentally unleashed the Chimes, a magic whose threat will reach far beyond D'Hara. Now it has become terrifyingly clear that the Chimes have the potential to bring down all that Richard and Kahlan have worked to protect, and even the power of the Sword of Truth may not be enough to stem the tide of their unleashed magical force. But if the Chimes cannot be stopped, first they will ravage Richard and Kahlan, then all of D'Hara, and then the entire world .

Soul of the Fire. unabr. ed. Terry Goodkind. Read by Buck Schirner. 16 cass. (Running Time: 24 hrs.). (Sword of Truth Ser.: Bk. 5). 2002. 39.95 (978-1-59086-297-1(X), 159086297X, BAU) Brilliance Audio.

Soul of the Fire. unabr. ed. Terry Goodkind. Read by Buck Schirner. (Running Time: 24 hrs.). (Sword of Truth Ser.: Bk. 5). 2004. 44.25 (978-1-59335-432-9(0), 1593354320, Brlnc Audio MP3 Lib) Brilliance Audio.

Soul of the Fire. unabr. ed. Terry Goodkind. Read by Buck Schirner. (Running Time: 24 hrs.). (Sword of Truth Ser.). 2004. 44.25 (978-1-59710-730-3(1), 1597107301, BADLE); 29.95 (978-1-59710-731-0(X), 159710731X, BAD) Brilliance Audio.

Soul of the Fire. unabr. ed. Terry Goodkind. Read by Buck Schirner. (Running Time: 24 hrs.). (Sword of Truth Ser.: Bk. 5). 2007. audio compact disk 150.25 (978-1-4233-1398-4(4), 9781423313984, BriAudCD Unabrid); audio compact disk 38.95 (978-1-4233-1397-7(6), 9781423313977, Bril Audio CD Unabri) Brilliance Audio.

Soul of the Fire. unabr. ed. Terry Goodkind. Read by Buck Schirner. (Running Time: 24 hrs.). (Sword of Truth Ser.: Bk. 5). 2004. 29.95 (978-1-59335-118-2(6), 1593351186) Soulmate Audio Bks.

Soul of the Indian. Charles A. Eastman. Narrated by Jim Killavey. (Running Time: 2 hrs.). 2006. 16.95 (978-1-59912-817-7(9)) Iofy Corp.

Soul of the Indian. Charles Alexander Eastman. Read by Scott Peterson. (Running Time: 2 hrs. 30 mins.). 2002. 17.95 (978-1-59912-717-0(2)) Iofy Corp.

Soul of the Indian. unabr. ed. Charles Alexander Eastman. Read by Scott Peterson. 2 CDs. (Running Time: 2 hrs. 30 mins.). 2003. audio compact disk 16.00 (978-0-7861-9340-0(9), 3048); 17.95 (978-0-7861-2346-9(X), 3048) Blckstn Audio.
Charles Alexander Eastman (1858-1939), an educated and well-known Sioux, saw both sides of the great divide between Indians and whites. Part history, part reminiscence, and coupled with folk tales, this book treats the listener to the ethics and morality of a culture that few people know about.

Soul of the Koto. 1 cass. 11.95 (7218) J Norton Pubs.

Soul of the Lion Witch, & the Wardrobe. unabr. ed. Gene Veith. (Running Time: 21600 sec.). 2005. audio compact disk 27.99 (978-1-58926-872-2(5), 6872) Oasis Audio.

Soul of the Lion,the Witch, & the Wardrobe. unabr. ed. Gene Veith. Narrated by Stasi Eldredge. (ENG.). 2005. 19.59 (978-1-60814-394-8(5)) Oasis Audio.

Soul Plane Ascension. Bruce Goldberg. (ENG.). 2005. audio compact disk 17.00 (978-1-57968-035-0(6)) Pub: B Goldberg. Dist(s): Baker Taylor

Soul Plane Ascension. Bruce Goldberg. 1 cass. (Hypnotic Time Travel Ser.). (ENG.). 2006. 13.00 (978-1-885577-07-8(9)) Pub: B Goldberg. Dist(s): Baker Taylor
Self hypnosis program that takes you to the soul plane & allows you to receive information from the higher plane.

Soul Prints: Your Path to Fulfillment. Marc Gafni. Read by Marc Gafni. 2004. 15.95 (978-0-7435-1942-7(6)) Pub: S&S Audio. Dist(s): S and S Inc

Soul Prints: Your Path to Fulfillment. unabr. ed. Marc Gafni. Read by Philip Goodwin. 8 vols. (Running Time: 12 hrs.). 2001. bk. 69.95 (978-0-7927-2493-3(3), CSL 382, Chivers Sound Lib); audio compact disk 94.95 (978-0-7927-9920-7(8), SLD 071, Chivers Sound Lib) AudioGO.
Addressing our age-old desire to feel connected, the author uses spiritual stories to teach us how to live fuller, happier lives. The secret is to "live your story" & we do this by identifying our true, unique selves, what he calls our "soul prints." Only then can we connect on a far deeper level with the world & with those sharing it alongside us. While based on the realm of spirituality & philosophy, this book speaks to all readers, regardless of religious beliefs or practices, or lack thereof.

Soul Proprietor: 101 Lessons from a Lifestyle Entrepreneur. unabr. ed. Perf. by Eileen Lawless. 4 CDs. (Running Time: 4 hrs.). 2003. audio compact disk 39.95 (978-0-9746225-0-7(8)) J Pollak.
A primer on the daily lessons that business ownership teaches, this book explores how to maintain a balanced and joyful life while striking out on an entrepreneurial mission. Ultimately, Pollak's story illustrates that structuring a business to reflect personal values is the true key to success.

Soul Purpose: Discovering & Fulfilling Your Purpose. Mark Thurston. Read by Mark Thurston. 1 cass. (Running Time: 60 min.). 1990. 9.95 HarperCollins Pubs.

Soul Quest. 1 cass. (Ultra-Depth Hypnosis Ser.). 14.98 (978-0-87554-589-9(0), UDC802); audio compact disk 19.98 CD. (978-0-87554-588-2(2), UD102) Valley Sun.

Soul Reflections: A Personal Odyssey in Poetry. Miriam Arman. 2003. audio compact disk 15.95 (978-0-9674181-3-1(5)) Music Visions.

Soul Retrieval. Christopher Love. Read by Christopher Love. 1 cass. (Running Time: 30 min.). 1997. 10.95 (978-1-891820-08-3(7)) World Sangha Pubg.
Self-hypnosis meditation for healing, self-improvement & realizing our full & powerful potential as spiritual beings.

Soul Retrieval Journey. Sandra Ingerman. 3 CDs. (Running Time: 6 Hrs). 2006. audio compact disk 24.95 (978-1-59179-484-4(6), AW00342D) Sounds True.
Over 40,000 years ago the first shamans ventured into the spirit realms in search of wisdomand healing. What they found was a secret world of teachers, animal spirits, and the soul fragments of those suffering in the ordinary world. On The Soul Retrieval Journey, you will joinSandra Ingerman (director of the Foundation for Shamanic Studies) as she shares the rituals of the shaman and explains how these powerful tools for selfhealing and insight are available to anyone. Ingerman offers the shamanic perspective on illness, explaining how parts of the soulcan be lost through personal tragedy, physical injury, or the negative emotions of others.Through the ages, she teaches, shamans have used a powerful process called ?soul retrieval? toretum people to their original wholeness and health. In step-by-step detail, she explains this technique, including exercises that use singing, dancing, praying, sacred spaces, and talismans to welcome the soul home. Here is a fascinating introduction to shamanic healing, as taught by one of the West?s preeminent authorities and modern-day practitioners.

Soul Revision: A Hawaii Story, Death in the Belly of a Pelagic Shark. abr. ed. Richard M. Esterle. 1 CD. (Running Time: 1 hr. 16 mins.). 2002. audio compact disk (978-0-9721807-0-2(2)) R Esterle.
A true story about a man's revelations while swimming to his death and how the experience transforms his life.

***Soul School: Enrolling in a Soulful Lifestyle for Youth Ministry.** unabr. ed. Jeanne Stevens. (Running Time: 5 hrs. 21 mins. 0 sec.). (Soul Shaper Ser.). (ENG.). 2009. 15.99 (978-0-310-77202-6(8)) Zondervan.

Soul Search. Tyler Higgins. Narrated by David Bindewald, Jr. 2009. (978-1-936204-03-8(7)) Ineffable.

Soul Search: A Scientist Explores the Afterlife. abr. ed. David Darling. Read by Michael Toms. 2 cass. (Running Time: 3 hrs.). 1996. 17.95 (978-1-57453-004-9(6), 330065) Audio Lit.
Is there a spirit that exists independently from the brain and can this spirit survive death? Scientist David Darling examines the merger between science, religion and mysticism to examine the great mystery of life after death.

Soul Searchers: Finding Peace of Mind. Ben Saltzman. 4 CDs and 40 pg. wor. (Running Time: 3 hrs, 30 min.). 2002. audio compact disk 69.95 (978-0-9671010-2-6(6)) Lifestrides Pubg.
You are not at the mercy of the people and events in your life. Stress and anxiety are symptoms, not a way of life. This seminar teaches you to be the calm eye in the hurricane.

Soul Seekers. Contrib. by Soul Seekers et al. 2005. audio compact disk 17.98 (978-5-559-23190-7(8)) Pt of Grace Ent.

Soul Selects Her Own Society see Poems & Letters of Emily Dickinson

Soul Sex Audio: A Sexual Adventure through the Chakras with Erotic Escapades in Exotic Lands. As told by Pavitra. Based on a book by Pavitra. Music by Trevor Coleman. 5 CDs. (Running Time: 5 hrs. 15 mins.). 2004. audio compact disk 34.95 (978-0-9684928-5-7(1)) ShellDen.
An erotic fantasy fiction adventure story about a woman who travels the world in search of the ultimate experience of all, Soul Sex. Read word for word from the book Soul Sex, by Pavitra.

Soul Space. Ronald D. Bissell. Read by Ronald D. Bissell. 1 cass. (Running Time: 1 hr. 40 min.). 1992. 12.95 (978-0-9639446-1-0(4)) Inn Voice Prods.
Guided meditations set to music to allow the listener to experience their "Soul Space" & obtain its wisdom to aid them in their daily lives.

***soul Stealer.** A. J. Butcher. Read by Sean Mangan. (Running Time: 6 hrs. 45 mins.). (Spy High Ser.). (YA). 2009. 49.99 (978-1-74214-305-7(9), 9781742143057) Pub: Bolinda Pubng AUS. Dist(s): Bolinda Pub Inc

Soul Stealer. unabr. ed. A. J. Butcher. Read by Sean Mangan. 6 CDs. (Running Time: 6 hrs. 45 mins.). (Spy High Ser.: Vol. 6). (YA). (gr. 7 up). 2008. audio compact disk 77.95 (978-1-74093-970-6(0), 9781740939706) Pub: Bolinda Pubng AUS. Dist(s): Bolinda Pub Inc

Soul Stories. unabr. ed. Gary Zukav. Read by Gary Zukav. 4 cass. (Running Time: 53 hrs. 0 mins. 0 sec.). (ENG.). 2000. 25.00 (978-0-7435-0662-5(6), Sound Ideas) Pub: S&S Audio. Dist(s): S and S Inc
Story of the author's own personal evolution. He writes openly & intimately about periods of his life when he felt jealousy, competitiveness, fear, anger, & about how his understanding of these emotions changed with his awakening consciousness & recognition of a Universe that is alive & compassionate.

Soul Survivor: The Reincarnation of a World War II Fighter Pilot. unabr. ed. Bruce Leininger et al. Narrated by Paul Boehmer. (Running Time: 9 hrs. 0 mins. 0 sec.). (ENG.). 2009. 19.99 (978-1-4001-6387-8(0)); audio compact disk 59.99 (978-1-4001-4387-0(X)); audio compact disk 29.99 (978-1-4001-1387-3(3)) Pub: Tantor Media. Dist(s): IngramPubServ

Soul Symphony of Yin Yang: For Healing & Rejuvenation. unabr. ed. Master Zhi Gang Sha & Chun Yen Chiang. (Running Time: 0 hr. 36 mins. 0 sec.). (ENG.). 2009. audio compact disk 17.99 (978-1-4423-0467-3(7)) Pub: S&S Audio. Dist(s): S and S Inc

Soul Talk. 2005. audio compact disk 15.00 (978-0-9762037-3-5(1)) Ctr Soulful.

Soul, the Garment of Glory. Manly P. Hall. 1 cass. 8.95 (978-0-89314-262-9(X), C890604) Philos Res.

Soul Thief. Charles Baxter. Narrated by Jefferson Mays. (Running Time: 22500 sec.). 2008. audio compact disk 29.99 (978-1-4281-7797-0(3)) Recorded Bks.

Soul Thief. unabr. ed. Charles Baxter. Narrated by Jefferson Mays. 5 cass. (Running Time: 6 hrs. 15 mins.). 2007. 36.95 (978-1-4281-7799-4(X)); 41.75 (978-1-4281-7798-7(1)); audio compact disk 56.75 (978-1-4281-7800-7(7)) Recorded Bks.

Soul to Soul: Communications from the Heart. unabr. ed. Gary Zukav. Read by Gary Zukav. 6. (Running Time: 6 hrs. 0 mins. 0 sec.). (ENG.). 2007. audio compact disk 29.95 (978-0-7435-6983-5(0)) Pub: S&S Audio. Dist(s): S and S Inc

Soul Tracker. abr. ed. Bill Myers. (Running Time: 9 hrs. 27 mins. 0 sec.). (Soul Tracker Ser.). (ENG.). 2005. 10.99 (978-0-310-26965-6(2)) Zondervan.

Soul Trance. Joseph Michael Levry. 2002. 19.00 (978-1-885562-05-0(5)) Root Light.

Soul Truth Set: A Remarkable Dialogue with Twelve Archangels. 6 cass. (Running Time: 6 hrs. 42 mins.). 2000. 69.95 (978-0-9655457-2-3(5)) Theo Press.
Guiding us through he most profound shift in consciousness & spiritual awakening ever before witnessed on our planet are the twelve Archangels collectively known as "Theo". Following a near death experience in 1969, world renowned spiritual medium Sheila Gillette became the channel for these angelic messengers from God who are now exalting humanity into a new way of thinking & being.

Soul Truth Vol. I: A Remarkable Dialogue with Twelve Archangels. 3 cass. 1999. 34.95 (978-0-9655457-3-0(3)) Theo Press.
Guiding us through the most profound shift in consciousness & spiritual awakening ever before witnessed on our planet are the twelve archangels collectively know as "Theo". Following a near death experience in 1969, world renowned spiritual medium Sheila Giuetti became the channel for these angelic messengers from God who are now exalting humanity into a new way of thinking & being.

Soul Truth Vol. II: A Remarkable Dialogue with Twelve Archangels. 3 cass. 1999. 34.95 (978-0-9655457-4-7(1)) Theo Press.
Guiding us through the most profound shift in consciousness & spiritual awakening ever before witnessed on our planet are the twelve Archangels collectively known as "Theo". Following a near death experience in 1969, world renowned spiritual medium Sheila Gillette became the channel for these angelic messengers from God who are now exalting humanity into a new way of thinking & being.

Soul Walk: Tarot & Expression of Your Soul. Poems. Text by Twainhart Hill. 1 CD. (Running Time: 46 minutes). 2005. audio compact disk 18.00 (978-0-9765803-0-0(6)) Twain H.
Written and narrated by Twainhart Hill. Learn about the 22 Major tarot cards. Each card symbolizes the behaviors, attitudes, and beliefs we experience when we recognize and acknowledge that spirit is a part of our life. This CD uses the voices of narration and poetry, and the poetic language of music to interpret these meanings. No prior study of the tarot is necessary, and there is something here all all tarot enthusiasts.

Soul Winning. Dan Corner. 1 cass. 3.00 (117) Evang Outreach.

Soul-Winning. C. S. Lovett. 1 cass. (Running Time: 35 min.). cass. & flmstrp 8.95 filmstrip & cass. (204) Prsnl Christianity.
Motivational color filmstrip & cassette to get church involved.

Soul Winning Demo. C. S. Lovett. Read by C. S. Lovett. 1 cass. (Running Time: 15 min.). 4.95 (203) Prsnl Christianity.
Demonstrates the soul-winning interview with prospect. You hear every step of the soul-winning dialogue. Side 2 demonstrates how to use the rejection technique when a prospect says No to Jesus.

Soul Wisdom: Practical Soul Treasures to Transform Your Life. unabr. ed. Zhi Gang Sha. Read by Marilyn Smith. (Running Time: 16 hrs. 0 mins. 0 sec.). (ENG.). 2008. audio compact disk 49.95 (978-0-7435-7676-5(4)) Pub: S&S Audio. Dist(s): S and S Inc

Soulagement. unabr. ed. Robert A. Monroe. Read by Roland Simon. 1 cass. (Running Time: 30 min.). (Human Plus Ser.). (FRE.). 1993. 14.95 (978-1-56102-074-4(5)) Inter Indus.
Provide temporary relief of pain in any part of the body.

Soulforge. abr. ed. Margaret Weis & Tracy Hickman. Read by Carol Stewart. 2 cass. (Running Time: 3 hrs.). (DragonLance: Vol. 1). 1998. 17.95 (978-1-55935-251-2(5), 395621) Soundelux.
Raistlin Majere is six when he is introduced to the archmage who enrolls him in a school for the study of magic. There the gifted & talented but tormented boy comes to see magic as his salvation. As Raistlin draws near his goal of becoming a wizard, he must take the dreaded Test in the Tower of High Sorcery. It will change his life forever, if he survives.

Soulful Christmas Carol. unabr. ed. Wendy Woods Jackson. 1 cass. (Running Time: 1 hr.). 2002. 14.95 (978-1-890222-05-5(4)) Envoi Pubg.
This book writes the spirit of Ebenezer Scrooge with Afrocentric aesthetics and revealsits main character Teleda Monet Washington in a winning combination of drama, intelligence, retrospect and humor.

Soulful Mass of St. Alphonsus. Danny DuMaine & Maurice Nutt. 1 cass. (Running Time: 54 mins.). 1999. 9.95 (978-0-89243-892-1(4), T9480) Liguori Pubns.
Songs include: "Call To Worship," "Be Thy Strength," "Lord Have Mercy," "Gloria" & more.

Soulful Soak. abr. ed. Relaxation Company Staff. 1 CD. (Running Time: 1 hr. 0 mins. 0 sec.). (ENG.). 2007. audio compact disk 19.98 (978-1-55961-847-2(7)) Pub: Relaxtn Co. Dist(s): S and S Inc

Soulless CD: The Right-Wing Church of Hate. Susan Estrich. 2007. audio compact disk 29.95 (978-0-06-125647-9(1), Harper Audio) HarperCollins Pubs.

Soulmate. unabr. ed. L. J. Smith. (Running Time: 6 hrs.). (Night World Ser.: Vol. 6). 2010. 19.99 (978-1-4418-2059-4(0), 9781441820594, BAD) Brilliance Audio.

Soulmate. unabr. ed. L. J. Smith. Read by Kate Rudd. (Running Time: 6 hrs.). (Night World Ser.: Vol. 6). 2010. 19.99 (978-1-4418-2057-0(4), 9781441820570, Brilliance MP3); 39.97 (978-1-4418-2058-7(2), 9781441820587, Brlnc Audio MP3 Lib); 39.97 (978-1-4418-2060-0(4), 9781441820600, BADLE); audio compact disk 59.97 (978-1-4418-2056-3(6), 9781441820563, BriAudCD Unabrid); audio compact disk 19.99 (978-1-4418-2055-6(8), 9781441820556, Bril Audio CD Unabri) Brilliance Audio.

Soulmate, Vol. 6, set. Jonathan Parker. Read by Jonathan Parker. 2 CDs. (Running Time: 2 hrs.). (Guided Meditation Ser.: Vol. 6). 1999. audio compact disk (978-1-58400-061-7(9)) QuantumQuests Intl.

***Soulmate Secret.** unabr. ed. Arielle Ford. Read by Arielle Ford. (ENG.). 2008. (978-0-06-177136-1(8), Harper Audio); (978-0-06-177134-7(1), Harper Audio) HarperCollins Pubs.

Soulmate Secret: Manifest the Love of Your Life with the Law of Attraction. unabr. ed. Arielle Ford. Read by Arielle Ford. 2009. audio compact disk 23.99 (978-0-06-176906-1(1), Harper Audio) HarperCollins Pubs.

***Soulprint: Discovering your Divine Destiny.** unabr. ed. Mark Batterson. (Running Time: 5 hrs. 30 mins. 0 sec.). (ENG.). 2011. audio compact disk 21.98 (978-1-61045-051-5(5)) christianaud.

Souls Belated see Selected Short Stories by Edith Wharton

Souls, God's Heartbeat. Gary V. Whetstone. (Theology Ser.: Vol. TH 205). 1994. 80.00 (978-1-58866-129-6(6)) Gary Whet Pub.

Souls, God's Heartbeat. Gary V. Whetstone. (Theology Ser.: Vol. TH 205). (C). 1994. 160.00 (978-1-58866-128-9(8)) Gary Whet Pub.

Souls Illuminated by Light: Guided Meditations for All Seasons. ldr.'s ed. Debra Donnelly-Barton. 2001. bk. 19.95 (978-0-8192-0002-0(6), MoreHse Pubng) Church Pub Inc.

Soul's Journey Into Human Form - At the Crossroads of the Heart. Ralph Metzner. 1 cass. 10.50 (A0036-87) Sound Photosyn.
A guided meditation with helpful sounds of shamanic instruments.

Souls of Black Folk. W. E. B. Du Bois. Read by Anais 9000. 2009. 27.95 (978-1-60112-219-3(5)) Babblebooks.

Souls of Black Folk. W. E. B. Du Bois. Read by Richard Allen. (Playaway Adult Nonfiction Ser.). (ENG.). 2009. 59.99 (978-1-60812-540-1(8)) Find a World.

Souls of Black Folk. W. E. B. Du Bois. Narrated by Walter Covell. (Running Time: 8 hrs.). 1993. 32.95 (978-1-59912-874-0(8)) Iofy Corp.

Souls of Black Folk, unabr. ed. W. E. B. Du Bois. Read by Walter Covell. 6 cass. (Running Time: 8 hrs. 30 mins.). 1994. 44.95 (978-0-7861-0745-2(6), 2126) Blckstn Audio.
One of the most prophetic works in all of American literature. In this collection of fifteen essays, first published in 1903, Du Bois dared to describe the racism which prevailed at that time in America. And he demanded an end to it. Du Bois draws on his early experiences, from teaching in the hills of Tennessee to the death of his infant son & his historic break with the conciliatory position of Booker T. Washington. After receiving a Ph.D. from Harvard in 1895, Du Bois became a professor of economics & history at Atlanta University. His dynamic leadership in the cause of social reform on behalf of his fellow blacks anticipated & inspired much of the black activism of the 1960s.

Souls of Black Folk. unabr. ed. W. E. B. Du Bois. Read by Walter Covell. 6 cass. (Running Time: 8 hrs.). 1992. vinyl bd. 42.00 (C-244) Jimcin Record.
Considered one of the most prophetic & influential works in American literature.

Souls of Black Folk. unabr. ed. W. E. B. Du Bois. 2003. 44.99 (978-0-9742088-0-0(9)) MasterBuy Audio Bks.

Souls of Black Folk. unabr. ed. W. E. B. Du Bois. Read by Theodore Eagans. 2001. audio compact disk 29.95 (978-0-9708860-0-2(4)) Phoenix Pubng Corp.
The 1903 Classic is a social study of the life of African Americans from emancipation through the beginning of the 20th century. The book explores the role of government, economics and the then current African American leadership in the development of post-slavery Black society.

Souls of Black Folk. unabr. ed. W. E. B. Du Bois. Narrated by Richard Allen. (Running Time: 9 hrs. 0 mins. 0 sec.). (Tantor Unabridged Classics Ser.). (ENG.). 2008. audio compact disk 59.99 (978-1-4001-3995-8(3)); audio compact disk 19.99 (978-1-4001-5995-6(4)) Pub: Tantor Media. Dist(s): IngramPubServ

Souls of Black Folk. unabr. ed. W. E. B. Du Bois. Read by Richard Allen. (Running Time: 9 hrs. 0 mins. 0 sec.). (Tantor Unabridged Classics Ser.). (ENG.). 2008. audio compact disk 29.99 (978-1-4001-0995-1(7)) Pub: Tantor Media. Dist(s): IngramPubServ

***Souls of Black Folk.** unabr. ed. W. e. b. Du Bois. Read by Walter Covell. (Running Time: 8 hrs. 30 mins.). 2010. 29.95 (978-1-4417-4387-9(1)) Blckstn Audio.

***Souls of Black Folk.** unabr. ed. W. e. b. Du Bois. Read by Mirron Willis. (Running Time: 8 hrs. NaN mins.). (ENG.). 2010. 29.95 (978-1-4417-8111-6(0)); 54.95 (978-1-4417-8108-6(0)) Blckstn Audio.

***Souls of Black Folk.** unabr. ed. W. e. b. Du Bois. Read by Walter Covell. (Running Time: 8 hrs. 30 mins.). 2010. audio compact disk 76.00 (978-1-4417-4384-8(7)) Blckstn Audio.

***Souls of Black Folk.** unabr. ed. W. e. b. Du Bois. Read by Mirron Willis. (Running Time: 8 hrs. NaN mins.). (ENG.). 2010. audio compact disk 76.00 (978-1-4417-8109-3(9)) Blckstn Audio.

Souls of the Slain see Poetry of Thomas Hardy

***Soul's Religion.** abr. ed. Thomas Moore. Read by Thomas Moore. (ENG.). 2005. (978-0-06-089372-9(9), Harper Audio); (978-0-06-089371-2(0), Harper Audio) HarperCollins Pubs.

Soul's Religion: Cultivating a Profoundly Spiritual Way of Life. unabr. ed. Thomas Moore. Narrated by Nelson Runger. 9 cass. (Running Time: 12 hrs. 15 mins.). 2002. 85.00 (978-1-4025-0617-8(1)) Recorded Bks.

Souls United in Love. Swami Amar Jyoti. 1 cass. 1983. 9.95 (R-52) Truth Consciousness.
Love springs from the soul; it makes union possible. Matured feelings, catching the subtle vibrations. Love is something higher - what it is & is not.

Soulsalsa. unabr. ed. Dr. Leonard Sweet. 2000. 17.99 (978-0-310-23482-1(4)) Zondervan.

Soulsalsa: 17 Surprising Steps for Godly Living in the 21st Century. abr. ed. Zondervan Publishing Staff. (Running Time: 2 hrs. 0 mins. 0 sec.). (ENG.). 2003. 10.99 (978-0-310-26101-8(5)) Zondervan.

Soulspeak: The Outward Journey of the Soul. Poems. Justin Spring. Frwd. by Stephen Larsen. 1 CD. (Running Time: 71 mins.). Dramatization. 2002. per. 34.95 (978-0-9717374-0-2(1)) Sara Poet Thetre.

Soultsunami: Sink or Swim in New Millennium Culture. abr. ed. Leonard Sweet. (Running Time: 3 hrs. 0 mins. 0 sec.). (ENG.). 2003. 14.99 (978-0-310-26102-5(3)) Zondervan.

Sound. Sundance/Newbridge, LLC Staff. (Early Science Ser.). (gr. k-3). 2007. audio compact disk 12.00 (978-1-4007-6397-9(5)); audio compact disk 12.00 (978-1-4007-6398-6(3)); audio compact disk 12.00 (978-1-4007-6399-3(1)) Sund Newbrdge.

Sound Advantage Set: A Pronunciation Book. Stacy A. Hagen & Patricia E. Grogan. 2001. 86.85 (978-0-13-816349-5(9)) Longman.

Sound Adventures. 1 cass. 1997. Incl. bklet. (04-64652) Amer Assn Teach German.

Sound Advice. Stacy A. Hagen. 1 cass. 1988. 83.50 (978-0-13-823170-5(2)) P-H.

Sound Advice Set: A Basis for Listening. 2nd ed. Stacy A. Hagen. 2002. 52.45 (978-0-13-081363-3(X)) Longman.

Sound Advice on Selling Your Car. Jack Burke. Read by Jack Burke. Read by David Banks et al. 1 cass. (Running Time: 50 min.). 9.95 (SMRTL 101) Sound Mktg.

Sound & Fury see Favorite Stories by O. Henry

Sound & Fury: Two Powerful Lives, One Fateful Friendship. Dave Kindred. Read by Dick Hill. (Running Time: 52200 sec.). 2006. 72.95 (978-0-7861-4534-8(X)); audio compact disk 99.00 (978-0-7861-7145-3(6)) Blckstn Audio.

Sound & Fury: Two Powerful Lives, One Fateful Friendship. abr. unabr. ed. Dave Kindred. Read by Dick Hill. 9 cass. (Running Time: 52200 sec.). 2006. 29.95 (978-0-7861-4461-7(0)); audio compact disk 29.95 (978-0-7861-7291-7(6)) Blckstn Audio.

Sound & Fury: Two Powerful Lives, One Fateful Friendship. abr. unabr. ed. Dave Kindred. Read by Dick Hill. (Running Time: 52200 sec.). 2006. audio compact disk 29.95 (978-0-7861-7713-4(6)) Blckstn Audio.

Sound & Healing. unabr. ed. Jill Purce & Elizabeth Gips. 1 cass. (Running Time: 90 min.). 1998. 11.00 (32004) Big Sur Tapes.

Sound & Restful Sleep. 1998. 24.95 (978-1-58557-012-6(5)) Dynamic Growth.

Sound & Sense in Poetry. George B. Harrison. Read by C. B. Harrison. 1 cass. (Running Time: 57 min.). 1963. 10.95 (23153) J Norton Pubs.
The great importance of sound in understanding poetry is illustrated by the reading of some well-known poems by Sidney, Shakespeare, Donne, Milton, Marvel, Browning, & others. Commentary is given on each poet.

Sound & Style of American English. 2nd unabr. ed. David A. Stern. Read by David A. Stern. 3 cass. (Running Time: 4 hrs. 42 min.). 1992. 29.95 Set. Dialect Accent.
Course in accent reduction for all speakers of English as a second language.

Sound & the Fury. William Faulkner. Read by Grover Gardner. 2002. 72.00 (978-0-7366-8956-4(7)); audio compact disk 88.00 (978-0-7366-9124-6(3)) Books on Tape.

Sound & the Fury. unabr. ed. William Faulkner. Read by Wolfram Kandinsky. 9 cass. (Running Time: 13 hrs. 30 mins.). 1995. 72.00 (978-0-7366-2922-5(X), 113262) Books on Tape.
The author creates the tragic Caddy Compson & projects her through the eyes of her three brothers: the idiot Benjy, the neurotic Quentin & the monstrous Jason.

Sound & the Fury. unabr. ed. William Faulkner. Read by Grover Gardner. (Running Time: 8 hrs.). (ENG.). 2005. audio compact disk 19.95 (978-0-7393-2535-3(3), Random AudioBks) Pub: Random Audio Pubg. Dist(s): Random
First published in 1929, Faulkner created his "heart's darling," the beautiful and tragic Caddy Compson, whose story Faulkner told through separate monologues by her three brothers - the idiot Benjy, the neurotic suicidal Quentin and the monstrous Jason. From the Trade Paperback edition.

Sound Beginnings: Develop Your Baby's Natural Gift for Languages, Just by Listening! unabr. ed. Beth Huddleston et al. 3 cass. (Running Time: 4 hrs. 30 mins.). (Sound Beginnings Ser.). (FRE, GER, SPA, RUS & JPN.). (J). 2004. pap. bk. 19.95 (978-1-885278-00-5(4)) Pub: Snd Beginnings. Dist(s): Penton Overseas
Features nursery rhymes, lullabies, words, phrases and traditional music of six foreign languages. Designed for ages birth to preschool-The Critical "Listening" Period. Simply by listening, neural pathways are activated and sound recognition skills are increased, making it easier to acquire languages later in life. Sound Beginnings cassette set includes: 3 90-minute cassettes, 16-page translation guide Spanish, French, German, Russian, Japanese, Hebrew Double Compact Disc Set Spanish, French, German, Russian, Hebrew, Japanese, and English.

Sound Beginnings Set: Languages & Music of the World. 3 cass. (Running Time: 90 mins.). (SPA.). (J). 1993. Snd Beginnings.
Children can hear language & music segments in Spanish, French, German, Russian, Hebrew, Japanese & English.

Sound Choices for the Future. Timothy Leary. 1 cass. 9.00 (A0628-90) Sound Photosyn.
Faustin & Brian take a visit to the home of the wizard to hear what he has to say about music, computers, & the state of the union.

Sound Drama before Marconi. Narrated by W. M. S. Russell. 1 cass. 10.95 (ECN 137) J Norton Pubs.
Dr. Russell explains, in an entertaining & witty way, why he considers Seneca's plays such good candidates for model 'sound dramas'.

Sound Effects for Church Productions, Vol. 3: Over 85 General Sounds, Voiceovers, Musical Underscores & Musical Themes. Created by Lillenas Drama. (ENG.). 2008. audio compact disk 39.99 (978-5-557-40951-3(3)) Lillenas.

Sound Effects Library. unabr. ed. 60 CDs. 2006. audio compact disk 895.00 (978-0-7927-3565-6(X), BBCD080) AudioGO.

Sound Guide to the Grasshoppers & Crickets of Western Europe. David R. Ragge & W.J. Reynolds. 1998. 50.00 (978-0-946589-50-0(X)) Pub: Apollo Books DNK. Dist(s): Intl Spec Bk

Sound Healers; Four Pioneers Explore the Healing Power of Music. 4 CDs. 1997. 34.95 (978-1-55961-416-0(1)) Relaxtn Co.

Sound Healing. Perf. by Dean Evenson. 1 cass. (Running Time: 1 hr.). 7.98 (SOP 7174); audio compact disk 11.98 CD Jewel box. (SOP 7174) NewSound.

Sound Healing: Balance mind & Body. Kelly Howell. 1 CD. (Running Time: 60 mins.). 2006. audio compact disk 14.95 (978-1-881451-16-7(X)) Pub: Brain Sync. Dist(s): Music Design Inc
Support physical healing with Brain Wave Therapy. Within minutes, soothing music and Delta waves induce peaceful states of reverie. These are mind-body states that are proven to enhance immune function, reduce pain and activate your body's natural healing abilities. Recovery is often swifter: blood loss is reduced, less pain is perceived, and fewer analgesics are needed. Moreover, the immune system seems to respond better, and hospital stays can be shortened. If you are preparing for surgery or if you need to heal on any level, Sound Healing will help.

Sound Healing: Balance Mind & Body. unabr. ed. Kelly Howell. 1 cass. (Running Time: 60 mins.). 1992. 11.95 (978-1-881451-15-0(1)) Brain Sync.
You experience a delightful floating sensation as you literally "lighten up" in mind, body & spirit. An experience that will create a vibrant state of health & well being.

***Sound Healing Collection: Sessions from Six Sound Healing Pioneers.** Dr. Jeffrey Thompson et al. (Running Time: 6:00:00). 2011. audio compact disk 39.98 (978-1-60297-073-1(4)) Sounds True.

Sound Hearing or Hearing What You Miss. S. Harold Collins. Prod. by Cal Scott. 1 cass. (Running Time: 30 min.). 1988. pap. bk. 9.95 (978-0-931993-26-8(1), GP-026) Garlic Pr.
Provides listening samples to illustrate sound, hearing and hearing loss. Listeners will hear as impaired people might.

***Sound Innovations for Concert Band: Combined Percussion, Book 1: A Revolutionary Method for Beginning Musicians.** Composed by Robert Sheldon et al. (Sound Innovations Ser.). (ENG., 2010. pap. bk. (978-0-7390-6740-6(0)) Alfred Pub.

***Sound Innovations for Concert Band: Tuba, Book 1: A Revolutionary Method for Beginning Musicians.** Composed by Robert Sheldon et al. (Sound Innovations Ser.). (ENG., 2010. pap. bk. (978-0-7390-6736-9(2)) Alfred Pub.

Sound Is Energy. Compiled by Benchmark Education Staff. 2006. audio compact disk 10.00 (978-1-4108-6678-3(5)) Benchmark Educ.

Sound of Classical Drama. abr. ed. Anton Chekhov et al. Perf. by Michael Redgrave & Swan Theatre Players. 6 cass. (Running Time: 4 hrs. 30 min.). Dramatization. Incl. Anton Chekhov - Selected Readings. Anton Chekhov. 1986. (PCC 21); School for Scandal. Richard Brinsley Sheridan. 1986. (PCC 21); She Stoops to Conquer. Oliver Goldsmith. Perf. by Swan Theatre Players of Dublin. 1986. (PCC 21); 1986. 55.00 (978-0-8045-0021-0(5), PCC 21) Spoken Arts.

Sound of Gospel: Bb Clarinet. Stephen Bulla. 2007. pap. bk. 14.95 (978-90-431-2444-7(3), 9043124443) H Leonard.

Sound of Gospel: Bb Trumpet/Bb Euphonium TC. Stephen Bulla. 2007. pap. bk. 14.95 (978-90-431-2424-9(9), 9043124249) H Leonard.

Sound of Gospel: BC Instruments (Bassoon, Euphonium, Tromone & Others) Stephen Bulla. 2007. pap. bk. 14.95 (978-90-431-2427-0(3), 9043124273) H Leonard.

Sound of Gospel: C Instruments (Flute, Oboe & Others) Stephen Bulla. 2007. pap. bk. 14.95 (978-90-431-2423-2(0), 9043124230) H Leonard.

Sound of Gospel: F/Eb Horn. Stephen Bulla. 2007. pap. bk. 14.95 (978-90-431-2426-3(5), 9043124265) H Leonard.

Sound of Honor. unabr. ed. Jim Stovall. Narrated by Bill Myers. (Running Time: 4 hrs. 57 mins. 45 sec.). (ENG.). 2009. 16.09 (978-1-60814-603-1(0)); audio compact disk 22.99 (978-1-59859-655-7(1)) Oasis Audio.

Sound of Many Voices. 1979. 4.95 (978-0-7417-1001-7(3)) Win Walk.

Sound of Melodies. Contrib. by Leeland. 2006. audio compact disk 11.99 (978-5-558-26040-3(8)) Essential Recs.

Sound of Modern Drama: The Crucible. abr. ed. John Van Druten et al. 6 cass. (Running Time: 4 hrs. 46 min.). Incl. Death of a Salesman. Arthur Miller. Illus. by Arthur Miller. 1986. (PCC 22); Druid Circle. John Van Druten. 1986. (PCC 22); I Am a Camera. John Van Druten. 1986. (PCC 22); I've Got Sixpence. John Van Druten. 1986. (PCC 22); Krapp's Last Tape. Samuel Beckett. 1986. (PCC 22); Lady in the Dark. Moss Hart. 1986. (PCC 22); Man Who Came to Dinner. Moss Hart. 1986. (PCC 22); Plays & Memories. W. B. Yeats. 1986. (PCC 22); Voice of the Turtle. John Van Druten. 1986. (PCC 22); Zoo Story. Edward Albee. 1986. (PCC 22); Sound of Modern Drama: The Crucible. Arthur Miller. 1986. (PCC 22); 1986. 55.00 (978-0-8045-0022-7(3), PCC 22) Spoken Arts.
Modern playwrights read & discuss their work.

Sound of Music. Erich Kunzel. Perf. by Rogers and Hammerstein & Cincinnati Pops Orchestra. 1 cass., 1 CD. 7.98 (TA 30162); audio compact disk 12.78 CD Jewel box. (TA 80162) NewSound.

***Sound of Music: Vocal Selections with CD.** Composed by Richard Rodgers & Oscar Hammerstein II. (ENG.). 2010. pap. bk. 22.99 (978-1-4234-9800-1(3), 1423498003) H Leonard.

Sound of No Hands Clapping: A Memoir. Toby Young. Read by Simon Vance. (Playaway Adult Nonfiction Ser.). (ENG.). 2008. 64.99 (978-1-60640-863-6(1)) Find a World.

Sound of No Hands Clapping: A Memoir. unabr. ed. Toby Young. Narrated by Simon Vance. (Running Time: 8 hrs. 0 mins. 0 sec.). (ENG.). 2006. audio compact disk 69.99 (978-1-4001-3249-2(5)); audio compact disk 24.99 (978-1-4001-5249-0(6)); audio compact disk 34.99 (978-1-4001-0249-5(9)) Pub: Tantor Media. Dist(s): IngramPubServ
Now Tinseltown beckons. After receiving a once-in-a-lifetime opportunity from a big Hollywood producer, Toby sets his sights anew on a high-flying career, this time on the West Coast. But it doesn't take long for Toby's fabled "brown thumb" and self-sabotaging instincts to reassert themselves. On the home front, though, things seem to be looking up: Toby manages to persuade his girlfriend to marry him and move to Los Angeles - -but then she decides to abandon her promising legal career in order to become a fulltime homemaker . . . and mother. Toby's increasingly hapless attempts to pursue a glamorous showbiz career while buried in diapers will strike a chord with all modern fathers struggling to find the right work/life balance . . . and with their utterly exasperated wives. Failure - -and fatherhood - -have never been funnier.

Sound of One Voice Marching: A Spoken Word Project. Detrick Oliver Hughes. Intro. by Janette Hughes. Text by Wole Sabande. Photos by Gregory Prescott. 1 cass. 1999. 11.99 (978-0-9648980-6-6(3)) Poet D H.

Sound of Shear, No. 45. Read by Carl Faber. 1 cass. (Running Time: 45 min.). 1985. 9.50 (978-0-918026-56-9(3), SR 64-517) Perseus Pr.

Sound of Spanish. Carmen P. Clough & James Saddler. 4 cass. (Running Time: 4 hrs.). (Spanish in the Field Ser.). 36.00; 59.95 Incl. pocket dictionary. Ag Access.
Accompanies Spanish in the Field, practical Spanish as spoken on the ranches & farms of the Southwest.

Sound of the Dove: Singing in Appalachian Primitive Baptist Churches. Beverly B. Patterson. 1 cass. (Music in American Life Ser.). 1995. 11.00 (978-0-252-02173-2(8)) Pub: U of Ill Pr. Dist(s): Chicago Distribution Ctr

Sound of the Trumpet. Perf. by Lori Wilke. 1 cass. 1988. 9.98 (978-1-891916-17-5(3)) Spirit To Spirit.

Sound of Thunder see Fantastic Tales of Ray Bradbury

Sound of Thunder. unabr. ed. Wilbur Smith. Read by Steven Crossley. 14 cass. (Running Time: 22 hrs.). (Sean Courtney Adventure Ser.). 1998. 89.95 (978-0-7540-0189-8(X), CAB 1612) Pub: Chivers Audio Bks GBR. Dist(s): AudioGO
Sean Courtney, the impulsive adventurer of "When the Lion Feeds," returns from the wilderness a rich man. Until he is robbed by the Boers of his wagons, his gold & the woman he loves. A grim homecoming finds his country in the cruel grip of war. But in the bloody days ahead, conflicts within his family will prove far worse.

Sound of Thunder. unabr. collector's ed. Wilbur Smith. Read by Richard Brown. 12 cass. (Running Time: 18 hrs.). (Courtney Novels). 1989. 96.00 (978-0-7366-1474-0(5), 2352) Books on Tape.
An epic of the Boer War & the unstable peace that followed.

Sound of Wind Driven Rain. Perf. by William Ackerman. 1 cass., 1 CD. 8.78 (WH 11250); audio compact disk 13.58 CD Jewel box. (WH 11250) NewSound.

Sound of Wine: A Wine Audio Digest. abr. ed. Read by Eric Brotman. Compiled by Eric Brotman. 1 cass. (Running Time: 1 hr. 30 mins.). 1995. 10.95 (978-0-944993-54-5(0)) Audio Lit.
Vignettes from the vineyard. Includes interviews with Julia Child & Robert Mondavi, plus fascinating facts & lore about the virtues of wine.

Sound of Writing. 1989. (HarperThor) HarpC GBR.

Sound of Writing. Ed. by Alan Cheuse & Caroline Marshall. 6 cass. (Running Time: 9 hrs.). 1993. 43.60 (978-1-56544-031-9(5), 450007); Rental 8.50 30 day rental Set. (450007) Literate Ear.
A compilation of 38 of the best short stories from the pens of established masters & brand-new talents, written especially for & aired on National Public Radio.

Sound of Your Voice. Carol Fleming. 6 cass. (Running Time: 6 hrs.). 59.95 (635AX) Nightingale-Conant.
Interpersonal Communication expert Carol Fleming reveals the 24 dimensions of verbal behavior - including modifying regional accents. She teaches you how to add depth, strength, vitality & resonance to your voice. And she shows you how to take control of your voice & make it a real asset in everyday conversations, speeches & presentations. Includes listener's guide.

Sound of Your Voice. abr. ed. Carol Fleming. Read by Carol Fleming. 1 cass. (Running Time: 1 hr.). 2004. 10.95 (978-0-88690-234-6(7), L58051a) Pub: Audio Partners. Dist(s): PerseuPGW
Shows you how to analyze your own voice & develop the "voice image" that fits your life today. Learn how to develop stronger speech style, eliminate annoying mannerisms & more.

Sound of Your Voice. abr. ed. Carol Fleming. 2004. 17.95 (978-0-7435-4946-2(5)) Pub: S&S Audio. Dist(s): S and S Inc

Sound of Your Voice. abr. ed. Carol Fleming. Read by Carol Fleming. 4 CDs. (Running Time: 40 hrs. 0 mins. 0 sec.). (ENG.). 2006. audio compact disk 29.95 (978-0-7435-5179-3(6), Sound Ideas) Pub: S&S Audio. Dist(s): S and S Inc

Sound of Your Voice. unabr. ed. Carol Fleming. Read by Carol Fleming. 6 cass. (Running Time: 5 hrs.). 1988. instr.'s gde. ed. 59.95 (978-0-671-67695-7(4)) S&S Audio.
How to speak with ease, confidence & clarity. Make your voice a powerful tool & a super asset.

Sound Photosynthesis Asks Ed. Ed Rosenthal. 1 cass. 9.00 (A0562-89) Sound Photosyn.
The first of a series of interviews with Ed, arranged to shed light on the confusing political, social, & spiritual ramifications of the new regime's approach to marijuana & personal freedoms.

Sound Self-Esteem & the Joy of Loving: Talking to Myself on Self-Esteem. unabr. ed. Lilburn S. Barksdale. Read by Lilburn S. Barksdale. 1 cass. (Running Time: 20 min.). 1977. 9.95 (978-0-918588-36-4(7), 110) NCADD.
Talks by L.S. Barksdale, about who we are & how we actually function, clearly & logically reveal the realities of human behavior & the priceless benefits of sound self-esteem.

***Sound Shapes, Rhythms & More! Activities for the Music Classroom.** Composed by Tom Anderson. (ENG.). 2007. pap. bk. 29.95 (978-1-4234-2605-9(3), 1423426053) H Leonard.

Sound-Sight Skills, Vol. 1. Howard Schivera. 6 cass. (J). (gr. 1-4). 89.00 set, incl. 10 activity bks. & guide. (978-0-89525-022-3(5), AC 14) Ed Activities.
Challenges students to listen, reason & follow directions while completing a variety of puzzle, game & skill tasks, which develop hand-eye-ear coordination. Objectives include: developing listening skills; following directions; working in logical sequential order; working with basic maps & charts; reinforcing mathematics skills; using alphabetical & numerical order.

Sound-Sight Skills, Vol. 2. Howard Schivera. 6 cass. (J). (gr. 4-6). 89.00 set, incl. 10 activity bks. & guide. (978-0-914296-47-8(7), AC 119) Ed Activities.
Challenges students to listen, reason, & follow directions while completing a variety of puzzle, game, & skill tasks which develop hand-eye-ear coordination. Objectives include developing listening skills, following directions, working in logical sequential order, working with basic maps & charts, reinforcing mathematics skills, using alphabetical & numerical order.

Sound Sleep. Richard Jafolla & Mary-Alice Jafolla. Read by Richard Jafolla & Mary-Alice Jafolla. (Health & Healing Ser.). 1986. 12.95 (260) Stppng Stones.
Motivational tapes that work on the subconscious mind (subliminal) & conscious mind to bring about self-improvement.

Sound Sleep: Relax for Deep Sleep. unabr. ed. Kelly Howell. 1 cass. (Running Time: 60 mins.). 1991. 11.95 (978-1-881451-05-1(4)) Brain Sync.

Sound Sleep: Relax for Deep Sleep. unabr. ed. Kelly Howell. 1 CD. (Running Time: 1 hr.). 2000. audio compact disk 14.95 (978-1-881451-63-1(1)) Brain Sync.

Sound Sleeper. abr. ed. Robert A. Monroe. Read by Robert A. Monroe. 2 cass. (Mind Food Ser.). 1986. 14.95 (978-1-56102-416-2(3)) Inter Indus.
Get a good night's sleep with the Hemi-Sync signal.

Sound Sleeper. unabr. ed. Robert A. Monroe. Read by Robert A. Monroe. 1 cass. (Running Time: 30 min.). (TimeOut Ser.). 1992. 14.95 (978-1-56102-802-3(9)) Inter Indus.
Guides you into a deep, refreshing, full night's sleep.

Sound the Trumpet. unabr. ed. Gilbert Morris. Narrated by Robert Whitfield. 7 cass. (Running Time: 10 hrs.). 2002. 49.95 (978-0-7861-2188-5(2), 2949); audio compact disk 64.00 (978-0-7861-9579-4(7), 2949) Blckstn Audio.
Daniel Bradford, a poor young Britisher, is separated from his sister, Lyna, and left infamous Dartmoor Prison. His only hope for escape is when he agrees to a seven-year indenture in America. But he discovers he had traded one imprisonment for another under a cruel and exacting master, Sir Leo Rochester. But eventually, Daniel marries a young woman, Holly Blanchard, and they settle near Mount Vernon, Virginia. Daniel meets George Washington and experiences the taste of freedom sweeping the land. Then tragedy strikes and Daniel moves his family to Boston, where he meets Sam Adams, the patriot for independence. Bound by his loyalty to England, he struggles as he sees two of his sons caught up with the Sons of Liberty.

Sound Track. unabr. ed. John Timpson. Read by John Timpson. 8 cass. (Running Time: 10 hrs. 52 min.). 1994. 69.95 (978-1-85695-685-7(7), 93055) Pub: ISIS Audio GBR. Dist(s): Ulverscroft US
While working for a provincial newspaper, Charles spots an ad for a job & makes the pilgrimage back to the city. But in the end the provincial newspaper & Rebecca begin to look more attractive.

Sound Voyage. 1 cass. 9.98 (KGOC25) Ken Mills Found.
Kenneth G. Mills conducts The Star-Scape Singers in a tonal journey of new compositions & spirituals.

Sound/el Sonido: Loud, Soft, High, & Low/Fuerte, Suave, Alto y Bajo. abr. ed. Natalie M. Rosinsky. Tr. by Sol Robledo. Illus. by Matthew John. (Amazing Science Ser.). (SPA.). (gr. k). 2008. audio compact disk 14.60 (978-1-4048-4473-5(2)) CapstoneDig.

Sounder. William H. Armstrong. (J). 1970. 20.00 (978-0-394-66795-9(6)) SRA McGraw.

Sounder. unabr. ed. William H. Armstrong. Read by Avery Brooks. (J). 2008. 34.99 (978-1-60514-974-5(8)) Find a World.

***Sounder.** unabr. ed. William H. Armstrong. Read by Avery Brooks. (ENG.). 2006. (978-0-06-114650-3(1)); (978-0-06-114651-0(X)) HarperCollins Pubs.

Sounder. unabr. ed. William H. Armstrong. Narrated by Avery Brooks. 2 cass. (Running Time: 3 hrs.). (J). (gr. 6). 1997. 21.00 (21622) Recorded Bks.
A true American classic - the bittersweet story of a man & his faithful dog.

Sounder. 4th rev. unabr. ed. William Howard Armstrong. Read by Avery Brooks. (Running Time: 9000 sec.). (J). (gr. 4-7). 2006. audio compact disk 17.95 (978-0-06-085270-2(4), HarperChildAud) HarperCollins Pubs.

***Sounding Forth the Trumpet Audio Book.** Peter J. Marshall. 2001. audio compact disk 25.00 (978-0-9827444-0-6(4)) Pet Mars Mini.

Sounding the Trumpet. Jim Bakker et al. 6 cass., 5 videos. 30.00 Set. (NY01-000) Morning NC.
Developed from a New Year's Eve weekend meetings & contains relevant words for the days that we are now approaching.

Soundings. unabr. ed. Perf. by Noirin Ni Riain. 1 CD. (Running Time: 49 mins.). 1995. audio compact disk 16.98 (978-1-56455-343-0(4), MM00272D) Sounds True.
Fourteen spiritual classics from many world traditions: The Shakers, Irish laments, Hildegard of Bingen & more.

Soundings: A Cape Cod Notebook. Robert Finch. Read by Robert Finch. 2 cass. (Running Time: 3 hrs.). 1994. 16.95 (978-0-939643-21-9(9), 3580, NrthWrd Bks) TandN Child.
An exploration of the Cape Cod coast. The author reflects his belief that, in the modern age, it is essential to know deeply and personally the place one calls home.

Soundings: Spaxter & Spaxterback - Plague & the Tuning, Bk. 1. Jeff Green. 2 cass. (Running Time: 3 hrs.). 1996. 16.95 (978-1-57677-056-6(7)) Lodestone Catalog.
Superb writing, sensual special effects, & great electronic music will evoke every emotion from laughter to horror. "Spaxter" & Spaxterback" will appeal to anyone who likes a good detective/future story - except it's not your average future, & he's not your average detective. "Plague" is a terrifying story about a deadly virus, but has a final message of hope. "The Turning" is about a world where the whole human race is totally immersed in a global interactive network.

Soundings: The Jeff Green Collection. Jeff Green. 6 cass. (Running Time: 10 hrs.). 2001. 39.95 (MAXM126); audio compact disk 69.95 (MAXM030) Lodestone Catalog.
Outstanding science fiction, horror, comedy, satire & mystery in this collection. Powerful gripping stories include Spaxter, Spaxterback, Plague, Epiphanies, Christmas is Coming to the District of Drudge, Flash, Psychotherapy, Vigilante & She Dreams of Atlantis.

Soundless. unabr. ed. Lysa Williams. Read by Christopher Lane. 7 CDs. (Running Time: 10 hrs.). 2003. audio compact disk 56.00 (978-0-7861-9325-7(5), 3057); 49.95 (978-0-7861-2380-3(X), 3057) Blckstn Audio.
Nick Raze is a famous violinist who successfully hides his dark past until friendship is offered in the form of a trusting young woman and her daughter, and his facade begins to crack.

Sounds. 1 cass. (First Steps in Science Ser.). (J). 12.00 (6352-0, Natl Textbk Co) M-H Contemporary.
Helps children in grades 1-4 discover the process of scientific investigation. Part of the First Steps in Science Program.

Sounds a Little Fishy to Me. Donna Amorosia & Lori Weidermann. 1992. audio compact disk 35.00 (978-0-7935-2892-9(5)) H Leonard.

Sounds All Around Us. 1 cass. (Running Time: 30 min.). (J). (ps-3). 1987. 12.20 incl. 32pg. book. Sound World Record.

Sounds & Lettersb Set: Level A. (Sing-along Songs Ser.). (ps-2). audio compact disk 66.18 (978-0-7362-0419-4(9)) Hampton-Brown.

***Sounds & Silences.** 2010. audio compact disk (978-1-59171-207-7(6)) Falcon Picture.

Sounds & Sweet Airs: Songs from Shakespeare. William Shakespeare. 1 cass. 10.95 (SAC 7011) Spoken Arts.

Sounds Easy! Sharron Bassano. Illus. by Craig Cornell. (Sounds Easy Ser.). 1980. 10.95 (978-0-88084-041-5(2)) Alemany Pr.

Sounds for Healing. Selected by Rainer Tillman. (Running Time: 1 hr. 13 mins.). 2000. audio compact disk 16.95 (978-1-57863-068-4(1), Red) Red Wheel Weiser.

Sounds for Healing I. Selected by Rainer Tillman. 1 cass. (Running Time: 74 min.). 2000. 10.00 (978-1-57863-069-1(X), Red) Red Wheel Weiser.
Contains a unique combination of ancient Tibetan singing bowls & contemporary crystal singing bowls. Rainer Tillman begins performing solely on singing bowls; in the second part, he adds other instruments, such as cymbals & chimes. Tibetan singing bowls have transparent, clear overtones, whereas the crystal bowls have a softer sound, with unexpected, crisp overtones.

Sounds Like Business: Improving English Pronunciation Skills. Sheri Miller & Berry Garber. 1 cass. (C). 1994. (978-0-9640809-0-4(7)) S Miller.

Sounds of a Revolution. 2004. audio compact disk 15.00 (978-0-9792335-0-0(X)) Faith Christn.

Sounds of American Speech Vol. 1: A Practice Regimen for the Neurological Patient. unabr. ed. Harold Stearns. Illus. by Jaime Servine. 4 cass. (Running Time: 4 hrs.). 1998. spiral bd. 89.50 (978-0-924799-27-3(7)) Am Articulat.
A training & practice program for neurologically affect speech patients.

Sounds of American Speech Vol. 2: A Practice Regimen for the Neurological Patient. unabr. ed. Harold Stearns. Illus. by Jaime Servine. 4 cass. (Running Time: 4 hrs.). 1998. spiral bd. 89.50 (978-0-924799-28-0(5)) Am Articulat.
A training & practice program for neurologically affect speech patients.

Sounds of Big Sur. David Schiffman. 1 cass. (Running Time: 1 hr. 30 min.). 9.98 (978-0-89334-122-0(3)) Humanics Pub Grp.

Sounds of Celebration. 2000. audio compact disk 12.95 (978-0-634-01941-8(4)) H Leonard.

Sounds of Celebration Vol. 2: Solos with Ensemble Arrangements for Two or More Players. 2002. audio compact disk 19.95 (978-0-634-04693-3(4)) H Leonard.

Sounds of Creation: Genesis in Song. Prod. by Randee Friedman. 1 cass. (Running Time: 38 mins.). (HEB.). 1988. 9.95 (978-1-890161-00-2(4)) Sounds Write.
A contemporary Hebrew or English song to accompany each weekly portion of Exodus.

Sounds of Creation, Sounds of Freedom. Tr. by Randee Friedman. 1 CD. (Running Time: 74 min.). 1992. audio compact disk 15.95 CD. (978-1-890161-02-6(0)) Sounds Write.
A combined compact disc of Genesis & Exodus in song.

Sounds of Freedom: Exodus in Song. Prod. by Randee Friedman. 1 cass. (Running Time: 36 mins.). (HEB.). 1991. 9.95 (978-1-890161-01-9(2)) Sounds Write.
An upbeat Hebrew or English contemporary song to accompany each weekly portion of Genesis.

Sounds of Heaven. Perf. by Kathy Troccoli. 1 cass. 1995. audio compact disk Brentwood Music.
One of the best selling releases of 1996, contains 5 No. 1 songs, including Go Light Your World, Sounds of Heaven, I Will Choose Christ, Fill My Heart & That's How Much I Love You.

Sounds of Holiness: Leviticus in Song. Prod. by Randee Friedman. (Running Time: 42 mins.). (HEB.). 2000. 9.95 (978-1-890161-40-8(3)) Sounds Write.

Sounds of Holiness, Sounds of Sinai, Sounds of Promise: A Contemporary Anthology Featuring a Song for Every Torah Portion in the Books of Leviticus, Numbers, & Deuteronomy. Prod. by Randee Friedman. 2 CDs. (Running Time: 112 mins.). (HEB.). 2000. audio compact disk 24.95 (978-1-890161-43-9(8)) Sounds Write.

Sounds of Korean: A Pronunciation Guide. Miho Choo & William O'Grady. (Running Time: 2000 mins.). (ENG & KOR., 2003. bk. 24.00 (978-0-8248-2601-7(9)) UH Pr.

Sounds of Music & Voice. 1 cass. (Running Time: 35 min.). 10.95 (SM-81-10-10, HarperThor) HarpC GBR.

Sounds of Neotropical Rainforest Mammals: An Audio Field Guide. Louise H. Emmons et al. 1998. audio compact disk 24.95 (978-0-938027-40-9(9)) Pub: Crows Nest Bird. Dist(s): Chicago Distribution Ctr

Sounds of Our World. Perf. by Barry Weiss. 1 cass. (Running Time: 50 min.). 1998. (978-1-892450-27-2(5), 126) Promo Music.
Relaxation music.

Sounds of Peace. unabr. ed. Nawang Khechog. Read by Nawang Khechog. 1 CD. (Running Time: 49 min.). 1996. audio compact disk 16.98 (978-1-56455-413-0(9), MM00296D) Sounds True.
A blissful, deeply-felt prayer for the ears & spirit. With long, soothing phrases, he invites us to experience the profound interior calm that allows for cultivation of a loving spirit. Each phrase & note invokes an extraordinary tranquility (one hospital has used it hundreds of times to soothe women in childbirth), & is regarded as a valuable meditation tool itself. Through this spare, haunting work we become the wind, the clouds, the mountains, the rivers - we become peace.

Sounds of Planets: Meditations with the Planet Sounds of Tibetan Singing Bowls, Vol. 1. Rainer Tillman. 1 CD. (Running Time: 1 hr. 13 mins.). 1998. audio compact disk 16.95 (978-1-57863-063-9(0), Red) Red Wheel Weiser.

Sounds of Planets No. 2: Meditations with the Planet Sounds of Tibetan Singing Bowls. Rainer Tillman. 2000. audio compact disk 16.95 (978-1-57863-065-3(7), Red); audio compact disk 10.00 (978-1-57863-066-0(5), Red) Red Wheel Weiser.
Rainer Tillman plays on various singing bowls, bells & cymbals, Thailand soundplates & some handmade chimes. No gongs are used.

Sounds of Planets Vol. 1: Meditations with the Planet Sounds of Tibetan Singing Bowls. Rainer Tillman. 1 cass. (Running Time: 73 min.). 1998. 10.00 (978-1-57863-064-6(9), Red) Red Wheel Weiser.
According to the law of resonance, chaotic sounds create chaos & harmonic sounds create harmony. This recording contains pure, meditative sounds, which correlate with the planetary ratio harmonies & can connect the harmonies or our solar system with the harmonies of our own inner being.

Sounds of Promise: Deuteronomy in Song. Prod. by Randee Friedman. (Running Time: 45 mins.). (HEB.). 2000. 9.95 (978-1-890161-42-2(X)) Sounds Write.

Sounds of Serenity: Musical Meditations & Nature's Chorus. K. R. S. Edstrom. 1 CD. (Running Time: 40 mins.). 2009. audio compact disk 16.95 (978-1-886198-20-3(9)) Pub: Soft Stone Pub. Dist(s): Ingram Bk Co

Sounds of Silence: Chants to the Divine. Miller Richard. (ENG.). 2009. 15.00 (978-1-893099-10-4(5)) Pub: Anahata Pr. Dist(s): Ctr of Timeless

Sounds of Sinai: Numbers in Song. Prod. by Randee Friedman. (Running Time: 44 mins.). (HEB.). 2000. 9.95 (978-1-890161-41-5(1)) Sounds Write.

Sounds of Spanish: Examples. Excerpts. Robert M. Hammond. 1 CD. (Running Time: 67 mins.). 2002. audio compact disk 10.00 (978-1-57473-218-4(8)) Cascadilla Pr.
This standard audio CD contains recordings of hundreds of examples from The Sounds of Spanish: Analysis and Application, showing how pronunciation rules are applied.

Sounds of Texas Birds, Vol. 2. Robert Benson & Karen Benson. 1 cass. (Louise Lindsey Merrick Natural Environment Ser.: No. 18). (J). (gr. 7-12). 1994. 10.95 (978-0-89096-570-2(6)) Tex AM Univ Pr.
Nature education/appreciation.

Sounds of the Alaskan Arctic Ocean. Cornell Laboratory of Ornithology Staff. 1 cass. 9.95 (978-0-938027-05-8(0)) Crows Nest Bird.
Recordings to introduce the sounds of marine mammals & ice from the Alaskan Arctic Ocean.

Sounds of the Chakras. Harish Johari. (Running Time: 60 mins.). 2004. audio compact disk 12.95 (978-1-59477-001-2(8)) Inner Tradit.

Sounds of the Colorado Rockies. 2001. audio compact disk 19.95 (978-0-9713164-1-6(4)) Television Schl.

***Sounds of the Deep: An Exploration of Life in Our Seas.** British Library Sound Archive Staff & Vrej Nersessian. (ENG.). 2010. audio compact disk 15.00 (978-0-7123-0526-6(2)) Pub: Britis Library GBR. Dist(s): Chicago Distribution Ctr

Sounds of the Eternal CD: Meditative Chants & Prayers. J. Philip Newell. Music by Suzanne Adam. Composed by Linda Larkin. (ENG.). 2008. audio compact disk 22.00 (978-0-9798958-1-4(2), NewBeg) Mat Media.

Sounds of the Ether: Healing Beyond Medicine Series. Joseph Michael Levry. 2005. 19.00 (978-1-885562-12-8(8)) Root Light.

***Sounds of the Heart: Energize Your Heart in 4 Dimensions.** Susanna Bair. (ENG.). 2009. audio compact disk 15.95 (978-0-9795269-2-3(2)) Lvng Hrt Med.

Sounds of the Phoenix. Voice by Patricia Strawser. 1 Cd. (Running Time: 48 mins). 2005. audio compact disk (978-0-9755695-5-9(4)) My Lvng Solutions.
The Phoenix Sounds is a collection of six tracks harmoniously composed to relax the mind while soothing the soul. Its inspirational messages and beautifully crafted melodies are perfect for meditation and relaxation. We offer this CD to introduce the concept of "The Phoenix People." Through spiritual transformation, these mortals have learned to emerge triumphant from adversity, challenges, failures, and successes. They use these experiences to enhance their devotion to God and to forge practical tools for loving service to others.

Sounds of the San Diego Beach. 2001. audio compact disk 19.95 (978-0-9713164-2-3(2)) Television Schl.

Sounds of the Season, Vol. 1. Maggie Sansone. audio compact disk 15.98 (978-1-56222-867-5(6), 95021CD) Mel Bay.

Sounds of the Season, Vol. 2. Maggie Sansone. 1996. bk. 22.95 (978-0-7866-2598-7(8), 95566CDP); bk. 17.95 (978-0-7866-2599-4(6), 95566P) Mel Bay.

Sounds of the Season, Vol. 2. Maggie Sansone. 2002. bk. 22.95 (978-0-7866-6571-6(8), 95566BCD) Mel Bay.

Sounds of the Texas Plains. (Sounds of the Texas Plains). 2001. audio compact disk 19.95 (978-0-9713164-3-0(0)) Television Schl.

Sounds of the '70s. 1 cass. (Running Time: 1 hr. 10 min.). 1999. 9.99 (PBXTY8); audio compact disk 9.99 (PCXUE2) Time-Life.

Sounds of the '80s: 1986. 1 cass. (Running Time: 1 hr. 30 min.). 1999. 9.99 (SEDEK4); audio compact disk 9.99 (SFDEM9) Time-Life.
Ever tried to find the best songs of the '80s? Well, look no further. Time-Life Music has collected all the great hits of the decade into the most definitive, year-by-year '80s collection ever.

Sounds of United States English. Hal Kornell. Read by Hal Kornell. 1 cass. (Running Time: 47 min.). (J). (gr. 4 up). 1994. 19.95 incl. script. Snds US English.
A scale of U.S. speech sounds to measure pronunciation accuracy, with exercises to increase proficiency & consistency in vocal communication. Special ESL benefits.

Sounds that Haunt Your House. Audioscope. 1 cass. (Running Time: 30 mins.). 1995. 5.00 (978-1-57375-077-6(8)); 8.00 CD. (978-1-57375-078-3(6)) Audioscope.

Sounds True Anthology of Sacred World Music. unabr. ed. Perf. by Nawang Khechog et al. 1 CD. (Running Time: 64 mins.). 1998. audio compact disk 8.98 (978-1-56455-580-9(1), MM00005D) Sounds True.
From the African coast to the Himalayas, this music sampler takes listeners on a trip around the globe & into the ecstatic world of sacred sound.

Soundscape: South California. Arranged by Ric Flauding. 1 CD . 1999. audio compact disk 14.98 (978-1-57919-127-6(4)) Randolf Prod.

Soundscape: South California. Ric Flauding. 1 cass. 1999. 10.98 Randolf Prod.

Soundscapes: Musical Landscapes Inspired by Nature. Andrew Stewart. 1 cass. (Running Time: 1 hr.). (Art of Relaxation Ser.). 9.95 (978-1-55961-111-4(1)) Relaxtn Co.

Soundscapes Recordings: Exploring Music in a Changing World. Kay Kaufman Shelemay. (C). 2001. cass. & cd-rom (978-0-393-10422-6(2)) Norton.

SoundsRomantic Sugar Series: Pillow Talk. 2006. audio compact disk 15.95 (978-0-9777105-4-6(8)) Sounds Pubng Inc.

Soundtrack to Nothing. 2000th ed. Ed. by Rhiannon Kubicka. Photos by Christy Bush. Christy Bush. Music by Sam Fogarino & Dagan James. Mark Ohe. Des. by Lara Topping. 2006. bk. 40.00 (978-0-9785013-0-3(6)) Bespoke Gall.

Soundview Career Building Blocks Collection #1. (Running Time: 4 hrs.). 2006. 49.50 (978-1-59912-189-5(1), Audiofy Corp) Iofy Corp.

Soundview Career Building Blocks Collection #2. (Running Time: 3 hrs. 30 mins.). 2006. 49.50 (978-1-59912-190-1(5), Audiofy Corp) Iofy Corp.

Soundview Career Building Blocks Collection #3. (Running Time: 3 hrs. 30 mins.). 2006. 49.50 (978-1-59912-191-8(3), Audiofy Corp) Iofy Corp.

Soundview Career Building Blocks Collection #4. (Running Time: 3 hrs. 30 mins.). 2006. 49.50 (978-1-59912-192-5(1), Audiofy Corp) Iofy Corp.

Soundview Career Building Blocks Collection #5. (Running Time: 3 hrs. 30 mins.). 2006. 49.50 (978-1-59912-193-2(X), Audiofy Corp) Iofy Corp.

Soundview Career Building Blocks Collection #6. (Running Time: 3 hrs. 30 mins.). 2006. 49.50 (978-1-59912-194-9(8), Audiofy Corp) Iofy Corp.

Soundview Complete Business Library. (Running Time: 84 hrs.). 2006. 399.95 (978-1-59912-188-8(3), Audiofy Corp) Iofy Corp.

Soundview Executive Book Summary Leadership Collection 2006. (Running Time: 5 hrs. 30 mins.). 2006. 99.95 (978-1-60083-381-6(0), Audiofy Corp) Iofy Corp.

Soundview 2001 Yearly Summary Collection. (Running Time: 14 hrs.). 2002. 149.95 (978-1-59912-184-0(0), Audiofy Corp) Iofy Corp.

Soundview 2002 Yearly Summary Collection. (Running Time: 14 hrs.). 2003. 149.95 (978-1-59912-185-7(9), Audiofy Corp) Iofy Corp.

Soundview 2003 Yearly Summary Collection. (Running Time: 14 hrs.). 2004. 149.95 (978-1-59912-186-4(7), Audiofy Corp) Iofy Corp.

Soundview 2004 Yearly Summary Collection. (Running Time: 14 hrs.). 2005. 149.95 (978-1-59912-001-0(1), Audiofy Corp) Iofy Corp.

Soundview 2005 Yearly Summary Collection. (Running Time: 14 hrs.). 2006. 149.95 (978-1-59912-187-1(5), Audiofy Corp) Iofy Corp.

Soundz of Praize. Perf. by Joyful Noize. 2002. audio compact disk Provident Mus Dist.

Sountrack for the Law of Attraction: The Law of Attraction. Prod. by Nikkos Zorbas. (ENG.). 2008. audio compact disk (978-0-9820802-0-7(4)) Nikko.

Soup. unabr. ed. Robert Newton Peck. Read by Amon Purinton. 2 CDs. (Running Time: 1 hr. 30 min.). (YA). 1995. audio compact disk 24.95 (978-1-883332-68-6(0)) Audio Bkshelf.
With over a dozen books now in the Soup series, Robert Newton Peck started it all with this hilarious account of nonstop mischief & timeless friendship.

Soup. unabr. ed. Robert Newton Peck. Read by Amon Purinton. 2 cass. (Running Time: 1 hr. 30 min.). (YA). (gr. 2 up). 1995. 14.95 (978-1-883332-14-3(1)) Audio Bkshelf.

Soup, unabr. ed. Robert Newton Peck. Narrated by Norman Dietz. 2 pieces. (Running Time: 2 hrs.). (gr. 4 up). 1994. 19.00 (978-0-7887-0140-5(1), 94365E7) Recorded Bks.
Two best friends, growing up in a small Vermont town, create continual adventures & excitement in the world around them.

Soup Ahoy, unabr. ed. Robert Newton Peck. Narrated by Norman Dietz. 3 cass. (Running Time: 3 hrs. 45 mins.). (gr. 4 up). 1994. 27.00 (978-0-7887-0081-1(2), 94314E7) Recorded Bks.
Mayhem ensues when Soup & Rob's favorite radio personality, Sinker O. Sailor, pays a visit to the town.

Soup & Me, unabr. ed. Robert Newton Peck. Narrated by Norman Dietz. 3 cass. (Running Time: 3 hrs. 15 mins.). (gr. 4 up). 1994. 27.00 (978-0-7887-0174-0(6), 94399E7) Recorded Bks.
The misadventures of two mischievous boys in a small Vermont town in the early twentieth century. Their escapades include skinny-dipping in Putt's Pond, chasing runaway pumpkins through the Baptist church & giving a lonely old schoolteacher a Christmas she'll never forget.

Soup Has Many Eyes: From Shtetl to Chicago - A Memoir of One Family's Journey Through History. unabr. ed. Joann Rose Leonard. Narrated by Suzanne Toren. 4 cass. (Running Time: 5 hrs.). 2001. 38.00 (978-0-7887-8919-9(8)) Recorded Bks.
Story of the author's Jewish ancestry. Using soup as a metaphor, Leonard adds stories from her past to the pot, creating a nourishing "meal" that will enrich the lives of all who share.

Soup in Love, unabr. ed. Robert Newton Peck. Narrated by Norman Dietz. 2 cass. (Running Time: 2 hrs. 45 mins.). (gr. 4 up). 1992. 19.00 (978-1-55690-599-5(8), 92204E7) Recorded Bks.
When Jovial Joe Spazzatura, owner of Joe's Diner, lends them a refrigerator crate, Soup & Rob concoct a plan to build the biggest Valentine in the world.

Soupy Saturdays with the Pain & the Great One. unabr. ed. Judy Blume. Read by Judy Blume. Read by Fred Berman & Kathleen McInerney. (Running Time: 4380 sec.). (ENG.). (J). (gr. 1-3). 2007. audio compact disk 14.95 (978-0-7393-5624-1(0), Listening Lib) Pub: Random Audio Pubg. Dist(s): Random

Soupy Saturdays with the Pain & the Great One. unabr. ed. Judy Blume. Read by Fred Berman & Kathleen McInerny. 1 CD. (Running Time: 1 hr. 13 mins.). (J). (ps-3). 2007. audio compact disk 20.00 (978-0-7393-6105-4(8), Listening Lib) Pub: Random Audio Pubg. Dist(s): Random

Sour Lemon Score. Richard Stark, pseud. Read by Michael Kramer. 3 cass. (Running Time: 4 hrs. 30 mins.). 2001. 28.00 (978-0-7366-8070-7(5)) Books on Tape.
Anti-hero Parker in this story of a heist that, paradoxically, goes right. It's just the aftermath that explodes. Parker is in on the job with three other men: Weiss, Andrews, and Uhl. Disappointed with the meager amount they've gotten, the men are about to split up when Uhl blows away Weiss and Andrews. Parker gets away out a window, and that's Uhl's mistake. Now he's got all the money, but he's got Parker on his trail, and Parker is not pleased. Parker tracks Uhl up and down the Eastern seaboard, but as they play cat and mouse, others become interested in the money.

Sour Puss. Rita Mae Brown & Sneaky Pie Brown. Narrated by Kate Forbes. (Running Time: 27000 sec.). (Mrs. Murphy Mystery Ser.). 2006. audio compact disk 29.99 (978-1-4193-7167-7(3)) Recorded Bks.

Sour Puss. unabr. ed. Rita Mae Brown & Sneaky Pie Brown. Read by Kate Forbes. 6 cass. (Running Time: 7 hrs. 30 mins.). (Mrs. Murphy Mystery Ser.). 2006. 59.75 (978-1-4193-6170-8(8), 98189); audio compact disk 74.75 (978-1-4193-6172-2(4), C3436) Recorded Bks.
Sour Puss has all the red herrings and surprising plot twists fans adore. When world-renowned grape and fungus expert Professor Vincent Forland is decapitated in Crozet, Virginia, it looks like a political killing. Forland had recently lectured on how distilled fungus plays a critical role in chemical warfare. But then another headless body turns up, and the residents of Crozet wonder who will be next.

Source. Swami Amar Jyoti. 2 cass. 1978. 12.95 (N-8) Truth Consciousness.
Relaxing into the Source within; the vital sheath; on forgiveness, fasting, celibacy, austerity & more.

Source. unabr. ed. James A. Michener. Read by Larry A. McKeever. 12 cass. (Running Time: 18 hrs.). 1993. 104.00 (978-0-7366-2490-9(2), 2350-B) Books on Tape.
Archeological dig in Makor, an ancient city in Gaillee, backdrops this story of the Jewish people.

Source. unabr. ed. James A. Michener. Read by Larry McKeever. 13 cass/. (Running Time: 19 hrs. 30 mins.). 1993. 104.00 (978-0-7366-2491-6(0), 3250-C) Books on Tape.

Source, Pt. 1. unabr. ed. James A. Michener. Read by Larry McKeever. 13 cass. (Running Time: 19 hrs. 30 min.). 1993. 104.00 (978-0-7366-2489-3(9), 3250A) Books on Tape.
Archaeological dig in the ancient city of Makor in Galilee is the backdrop for story of the Jewish people.

Source for Stuttering & Cluttering. David A. Daly. 1 cass. (Running Time: 60 mins.). 1996. spiral bd. 41.95 (978-0-7606-0108-2(9), 6-0108-9) LinguiSystems.
Helps clients reflect on their feeling about stuttering while working toward fluent speech. Includes a section on cluttering remediation techniques plus an audiotape to model speech patterns.

Source Meditation. 1 CD. 1987. audio compact disk 16.95 (978-1-55841-122-7(4)) Emmett E Miller.
Training in two effective meditation techniques - active and receptive - for opening to inner peace and energy. After a brief period of guidance, you meditate on your own to a soothing background of ocean surf and positive "threshold affirmations" which gently carress the edge of your consciousness.

Source Meditation: Opening Gates to Universal Energy. 1 cassette. 1987. 12.95 (978-1-55841-042-8(2)) Emmett E Miller.
Training in two effective meditation techniques - active and receptive - for opening to inner peace and energy. After a brief period of guidance, you meditate on your own to a soothing backgground of oceansurf and positive "threshold affirmations" which gently carress the edge of your consiousness.

Source of All Love. Read by Mother Basilea Schlink. 1 cass. (Running Time: 30 min.). 1985. (0254) Evang Sisterhood Mary.
Topics are: A Father's Love; Together with Jesus; Have You Prayed for It?; Unremovable Traces; A Gift Beyond Compare.

Source of Light see Long & Happy Life

Source of Miracles: 7 Steps to Transforming Your Life Through the Lord's Prayer. unabr. ed. Kathleen McGowan, pseud. Read by Kathleen McGowan, pseud. (Running Time: 6 hrs. 0 mins. 0 sec.). (ENG.). 2009. audio compact disk 29.99 (978-0-7435-9732-6(X)) Pub: S&S Audio. Dist(s): S and S Inc

Source of Peace/Our Work in the World. Marianne Williamson. Read by Marianne Williamson. 1 cass. (Running Time: 90 mins.). (Lectures on a Course in Miracles). 1999. 10.00 (978-1-56170-619-8(1), M858) Hay House.

Source of Pleasure. Swami Amar Jyoti. 1 cass. 1980. 9.95 (B-9) Truth Consciousness.
Attachment to pleasure creates forgetfulness & pain follows. The hard work of going beyond it to that Bliss of which pleasure is a small ray.

Source of the Anointing. Kenneth Copeland. Perf. by Kenneth Copeland. 1 cass. (Anointed & His Anointing Ser.: Tape 2). 1995. cass. & video 5.00 (978-1-57562-029-9(4)) K Copeland Pubns.

Sourcery. unabr. ed. Terry Pratchett. Read by Nigel Planer. 6 cass. (Running Time: 8 hrs. 30 min.). (Discworld Ser.). (J). 2001. 54.95 (978-1-85695-862-2(0), 950701) Pub: ISIS Lrg Prnt GBR. Dist(s): Ulverscroft US

Sourcery. unabr. ed. Terry Pratchett. 7 CDs. (Discworld Ser.). 2006. audio compact disk 71.95 (978-0-7531-1833-7(5)) Pub: ISIS Lrg Prnt GBR. Dist(s): Ulverscroft US

Sources of Creation Spirituality: A Jungian Commentary. Read by John Giannini. 2 cass. (Running Time: 2 hrs.). 1990. 16.95 (978-0-7822-0077-5(X), 425) C G Jung IL.

Sources of Information. Milton Diamond. 1 cass. (Running Time: 1 hr.). (Human Sexuality Ser.). 11.95 (34002) J Norton Pubs.

Sources of Passion. unabr. ed. Jennifer James. Read by Jennifer James. 1 cass. (Running Time: 1 hr.). 9.95 (978-0-915423-24-8(3)) Jennifer J.

***Sourland.** unabr. ed. Joyce Carol Oates. Read by Coleen Marlo. 2010. (978-0-06-200699-8(1), Harper Audio); (978-0-06-204192-0(4), Harper Audio) HarperCollins Pubs.

South see Poetry & Reflections

South. Edward Shackleton. Read by Sean Barrett. 8 cass. (Running Time: 12 hrs.). 2001. 69.95 (8910X) Pub: ISIS Audio GBR. Dist(s): Ulverscroft US

South. unabr. ed. Ernest Shackleton. Read by Geoffrey Howard. (Running Time: 13 hrs.). 2003. audio compact disk 24.95 (978-0-7861-9567-1(3), 2523) Blckstn Audio.

South. unabr. ed. Ernest Shackleton. Read by Geoffrey Howard. 9 pieces. 2004. reel tape 39.95 (978-0-7861-2216-5(1)) Blckstn Audio.

South: A Memoir of the Endurance Voyage. unabr. ed. Ernest Shackleton. Read by Geoffrey Howard. (Running Time: 12 hrs. 0 mins.). 2009. audio compact disk 34.95 (978-0-7861-7434-8(X)) Blckstn Audio.

South: A Memoir of the Endurance Voyage. unabr. ed. Ernest Henry Shackleton. Read by Geoffrey Howard. 1 CD. (Running Time: 12 hrs. 30 mins.). 2001. audio compact disk 19.95 (zm2523) Blckstn Audio.
His destination Antarctica, his expectations high, veteran explorer Sir Ernest Shackleton set out, on the eve of the First World War, in pursuit of his goal to lead the first expedition across the last unknown continent. Instead, his ship, the "Endurance," became locked in sea ice & for nine months Shackleton fought a losing battle with the elements before the drifting ship was crushed & his crew marooned.

South: The Story of Shackleton's Last Expedition, 1914-1917. unabr. ed. Ernest Henry Shackleton. Read by Geoffrey Howard. 9 cass. (Running Time: 13 hrs.). 2003. 62.95 (978-0-7861-1719-2(2), 2523) Blckstn Audio.

South: The Story of Shackleton's Last Expedition, 1914-1917. unabr. ed. Ernest Henry Shackleton. Read by Geoffrey Howard. 11 CDs. (Running Time: 13 hrs.). 2000. audio compact disk 88.00 (978-0-7861-9910-5(5), 2523) Blckstn Audio.

South: The Story of Shackleton's Last Expedition, 1914-1917. unabr. ed. Ernest Henry Shackleton. Read by Sean Barrett. 8 cass. (Running Time: 10 hrs.). (Isis Ser.). 1994. 69.95 Set. (978-1-85089-735-4(2), 8910X) Eye Ear.
Sir Ernest Shackleton was determined to lead the first expedition to cross Antarctica via the South Pole. Setting off in 1914, the expedition failed in its grand design - but in failure, they recorded one of the great stories of human endurance.

South: A Memoir of the Endurance Voyage: A Memoir of the Endurance Voyage. Ernest Shackleton. Read by Geoffrey Howard. (Running Time: 12 hrs. 30 mins.). 1999. 36.95 (978-1-59912-605-0(2)) Iofy Corp.

South Africa. unabr. ed. Joeseph Stromberg. Read by Harry Reasoner. (Running Time: 10800 sec.). (World's Political Hot Spots Ser.). 2006. audio compact disk 25.00 (978-0-7861-6231-4(7)) Blckstn Audio.

South Africa. unabr. ed. Joseph Stromberg. Read by Harry Reasoner et al. 2 cass. (Running Time: 3 hrs.). (World's Political Hot Spots Ser.). 1991. 17.95 Set. (978-0-938935-87-2(9), 10352) Knowledge Prod.
South Africa has become the world's symbol of racism. From the moment the Dutch colonists set foot on the Cape in 1652, this nation has steered a straight course toward apartheid; civil unrest has resulted.

South Africa: A World Leader in Conservation. Hosted by Nancy Pearlman. 1 cass. (Running Time: 29 min.). 10.00 (1029) Educ Comm CA.

South Africa: The Struggle Against Apartheid. 1 cass. (Running Time: 30 min.). 9.95 (H0290B090, HarperThor) HarpC GBR.

South African Gold Investment. John McFalls. 1 cass. (Running Time: 1 hr. 6 min.). 11.95 (414) J Norton Pubs.

***South Beach Diet.** abr. ed. Arthur S. Agatston. Read by Arthur S. Agatston. (ENG.). 2004. (978-0-06-078330-3(3), Harper Audio) HarperCollins Pubs.

***South Beach Diet.** abr. ed. Arthur S. Agatston. Read by Arthur S. Agatston. (ENG.). 2004. (978-0-06-081431-1(4), Harper Audio) HarperCollins Pubs.

South Beach Diet: The Delicious, Doctor-Designed, Foolproof Plan for Fast & Healthy Weight Loss. abr. ed. Arthur Agatston. Read by Arthur Agatston. (Running Time: 10800 sec.). 2006. audio compact disk 14.95 (978-0-06-087726-2(X)) HarperCollins Pubs.

South Beach Diet Supercharged: Faster Weight Loss & Better Health for Life. unabr. ed. Arthur Agatston. Narrated by Arthur Agatston. Narrated by L. J. Ganser & Elisabeth S. Rogers. Told to Joseph Signorile. (Running Time: 40500 sec.). (South Beach Diet: Ser.). (ENG.). 2008. audio compact disk 24.95 (978-1-60283-385-2(0)) Pub: AudioGO. Dist(s): Perseus Dist

South Beach Diet Supercharged: Faster Weight Loss & Better Health for Life. unabr. ed. Arthur Agatston & Joseph Signorile. 1 MP3-CD. (Running Time: 11 hrs. 6 mins.). 2008. 54.95 (978-0-7927-5513-5(8)); audio compact disk 84.95 (978-0-7927-5450-3(6)) AudioGO.
The Latest on This Revolutionary Diet, Plus a Metabolism-Revving Exercise Plan for Faster Weight Loss and Better Overall Health! In the all-new The South Beach Diet Supercharged, Dr. Arthur Agatston shows you how to rev up your metabolism and lose weight faster while following the proven healthy eating principles of the original diet: choose good carbs, good fats, lean protein, and low-fat dairy. Collaborating with Dr. Joseph Signorile, a professor of exercise physiology at the University of Miami, Dr. Agatston presents a cutting-edge, three-phase workout that perfectly complements the three phases of the diet itself. Based on the latest exercise science, this ease-into-it fitness program combines low- and high-intensity interval exercise (with a focus on walking) and functional core body-toning exercises. The result: You'll feel better and you'll burn more fat and calories all day long. " The audio program includes an enhanced CD with PDF versions of all charts, photos, meal plans, and recipes from the book.

South Beach Shakedown: The Diary of Gideon Pike. unabr. ed. Don Bruns. Read by Paul Michael Garcia. (Running Time: 30600 sec.). 2006. 54.95 (978-0-7861-4905-6(1)); audio compact disk 63.00 (978-0-7861-5975-8(8)); audio compact disk 29.95 (978-0-7861-7072-2(7)) Blckstn Audio.

South Dakota: A Journey Through Time. 4th ed. John E. Miller. Narrated by Bertram Getzug. (YA). (gr. 3 up). 2001. (978-1-57579-132-6(3)) Pine Hill Pr.

South Florida (I-95) Barnabas B. Hicks & Robert W. Magee. Read by Grover Gardner et al. 2 cass. (Running Time: 2 hrs. 15 min.). (Ride with Me Ser.). 1996. 17.95 (978-0-942649-36-9(2)) RWM Assocs.
Narrative on history & development of South Florida between Daytona Beach & Miami keyed to highway milepost markers. Original work.

South of Broad. unabr. ed. Pat Conroy. Read by Mark Deakins. (ENG.). 2009. audio compact disk 45.00 (978-0-7393-8293-6(4), Random AudioBks) Pub: Random Audio Pubg. Dist(s): Random

***South of Broad.** unabr. ed. Pat Conroy. Read by Mark Deakins. 16 CDs. 2009. audio compact disk 100.00 (978-1-4159-6539-9(0), BksonTape) Pub: Random Audio Pubg. Dist(s): Random

South of Cape Horn. unabr. collector's ed. Armstrong Sperry. Read by Paul Shay. 5 cass. (Running Time: 5 hrs.). (YA). 1988. 30.00 (978-0-7366-1463-4(X), 2343) Books on Tape.
Tells the story of a boy who became a seaman at 14 & master of a ship sailing in unknown waters.

South of Deadwood; Too Tough to Brand; Showdown Trail. unabr. ed. Louis L'Amour. Read by Dramatization Staff. (ENG.). 2008. audio compact disk 14.99 (978-0-7393-5887-0(1), Random AudioBks) Pub: Random Audio Pubg. Dist(s): Random

South of the Border. abr. ed. Jake Logan. Read by Dick Wilkinson & Michelle DeLong. 2 cass. (Running Time: 3 hrs.). 2002. 16.95 (978-1-890990-84-8(1), 99084) Otis Audio.
Adult western with sound effects.

South of Truth. unabr. ed. Sandra Heiss. Read by Sandra Heiss. 2 cass. (Running Time: 3 hrs. 20 min.). 1996. 13.95 Set. (978-1-890038-00-7(8)) HmeGrown Pubng.
"Coming of Age" novel of young girl in the 60s rural South.

***South Phoenix Rules: A David Mapstone Mystery.** unabr. ed. Jon Talton. (Running Time: 8 hrs. 30 mins.). (David Mapstone Mysteries Ser.). 2010. 29.95 (978-1-4417-6502-4(6)); 59.95 (978-1-4417-6499-7(2)); audio compact disk 76.00 (978-1-4417-6500-0(X)) Blckstn Audio.

South Sea Tales. Jack London. Narrated by Lloyd James. (Running Time: 7 hrs.). 2002. 27.95 (978-1-59912-606-7(0)) Iofy Corp.

South Sea Tales. unabr. ed. Jack London. Read by Lloyd James. 1 MP3. (Running Time: 7 hrs. 30 min.). 2002. audio compact disk 19.95 (978-0-7861-9113-0(9)); 39.95 (978-0-7861-2369-8(9)) Blckstn Audio.
Presents the people who lived on these exotic islands as individuals who had to deal with the white man's intrusions, the racism, foreign diseases, biased legal systems, and brutality.

South Sea Tales. unabr. ed. Jack London. Read by Lloyd James. 5 CDs. (Running Time: 7 hrs. 30 min.). 2002. audio compact disk 40.00 (978-0-7861-9481-0(2)) Blckstn Audio.

South Shore Smugglers. Sandy Laurence. 1 cass. (Running Time: 20 min.). (J). (gr. 4-8). 1983. bk. 16.99 (978-0-934898-54-6(5)) Jan Prods.
Suspense & danger abound when two young Nova Scotians, Andrew MacLean & his twin sister Glenda, accidentally learn of the arrival of a large drug shipment on the South Shore of the province.

South Shore Smugglers. Sandy Laurence. Illus. by Alyssa Walker. 1 cass. (Running Time: 20 min.). (J). (gr. 4-8). 1983. bk. 9.95 (978-0-934898-22-5(7)) Jan Prods.

South Sotho Language/30 CDs & Booklet. 2 CDs. (Running Time: 1 hr. 30 mins.). (SOT.). 2005. audio compact disk 26.95 (978-1-57970-140-6(X), AF1051D) J Norton Pubs.

South Street to Maiden Lane to Louise Nevelson Plaza to Firefighters Museum to St. Pauls Chapel to World Trade Center, No. 3. (Running Time: 90 min.). (New York - Lower Manhattan Ser.). 1990. 12.95 (CC218) Comp Comms Inc.
A detailed look at New Amsterdam & Old New York. Each street is an outdoor museum with its treasures carefully selected & defined.

South to Java, unabr. ed. William P. Mack & William P. Mack, Jr. Narrated by Nelson Runger. 10 cass. (Running Time: 14 hrs. 30 mins.). 1989. 85.00 (978-1-55690-488-2(6), 89650E7) Recorded Bks.
The USS O'Leary, a rusting four-stack destroyer, heads for a showdown in the South Pacific in 1941.

South Was Right! abr. ed. Narrated by James Ronald Kennedy & Walter Donald Kennedy. 10 cass. (Running Time: 15 hrs.). (ENG.). 2002. 25.00 (978-1-58980-040-3(0)) Pelican.

*South Wind Through the Kitchen: The Best of Elizabeth David.** Elizabeth David. Narrated by Melissa Hughes. 2010. 19.95 (978-0-9825470-1-4(3)) Knitting Out.

Southampton Row. Anne Perry. Read by Michael Page. (Playaway Adult Fiction Ser.). 2009. 49.99 (978-1-60775-861-7(X)) Find a World.

Southampton Row. abr. ed. Anne Perry. Read by Michael Page. 5 CDs. (Running Time: 6 hrs.). (Thomas Pitt Ser.). 2002. audio compact disk 69.25 (978-1-58788-917-2(X), 158788917X, CD Lib Edit) Brilliance Audio.

***Southampton Row.** abr. ed. Anne Perry. Read by Michael Page. (Running Time: 6 hrs.). (Thomas & Charlotte Pitt Ser.). 2010. audio compact disk 9.99 (978-1-4418-6692-9(2), 9781441866929, BCD Value Price) Brilliance Audio.

Southampton Row. unabr. ed. Anne Perry. Read by Michael Page. (Running Time: 11 hrs.). (Thomas Pitt Ser.). 2004. 39.25 (978-1-59335-602-6(1), 1593356021, Brinc Audio MP3 Lib) Brilliance Audio.

Southampton Row. unabr. ed. Anne Perry. Read by Michael Page. (Running Time: 11 hrs.). (Thomas & Charlotte Pitt Ser.). 2004. 49.97 (978-1-59710-732-7(8), 1597107328, BADLE); 24.95 (978-1-59710-733-4(6), 1597107336, BAD) Brilliance Audio.

Southampton Row. unabr. ed. Anne Perry. Read by Michael Page. (Running Time: 11 hrs.). (Thomas Pitt Ser.). 2004. 24.95 (978-1-59335-166-3(6), 1593351666) Soulmate Audio Bks.
A riveting new Thomas and Charlotte Pitt novel, in which Anne Perry again proves her mastery of the people, the mores, and the politics of the Victorian era she has made her own. A general election is approaching and Thomas is called to monitor the bitter struggle for one crucial London seat. The Tory candidate is Charles Voisey, ruthless Number One of the Inner Circle and old enemy of Pitt. His Liberal opponent is Aubrey Serracold, whose wife, Rose, is passionately committed to a socialist agenda and a liability to Serracold as she is immersed in spiritualism. Rose is one of the three participants in a late-night seance held by clairvoyant Maude Lamont, which becomes notorious when Madame Lamont's brutally murdered body is found the next morning. To Pitt's heavy burdens is now added the investigation of this baffling crime.

***Southampton Row.** unabr. ed. Anne Perry. Read by Michael Page. (Running Time: 12 hrs.). (Thomas & Charlotte Pitt Ser.). 2010. audio compact disk 29.99 (978-1-4418-4039-4(7), 9781441840394, Bril Audio CD Unabri); audio compact disk 89.97 (978-1-4418-4040-0(0), 9781441840400, BriAudCD Unabrid) Brilliance Audio.

Southeast Indians. unabr. ed. Peter M. Spizzirri. Read by Charles Fuller. Ed. by Linda Spizzirri. 1 cass. (Running Time: 15 min. per cassette). Dramatization. (Educational Coloring Book & Cassette Ser.). (J). (gr. 1-8). pap. bk. 6.95 (978-0-86545-092-9(7)) Spizzirri.
The Creek, Cherokee, Choctaw & the Semiole of the Everglades are a few of the Indian cultures you will learn about in this book.

Southeast Region. Compiled by Benchmark Education Staff. 2006. audio compact disk 10.00 (978-1-4108-6624-0(6)) Benchmark Educ.

Southeastern Washington Heritage Corridor: Richland to Clarkston. Text by Jens Lund. (ENG., 1999. spiral bd. 12.00 (978-1-891466-01-4(1)) NW Heritage.

Southern Bells. unabr. ed. Donald Davis. Read by Donald Davis. 1 cass. (Running Time: 55 min.). (American Storytelling Ser.). (gr. 5 up). 1997. 12.00 (978-0-87483-390-4(6)) Pub: August Hse. Dist(s): Natl Bk Netwk

Southern Classics, Volume II. Contrib. by Gaither Vocal Band. (Gaither Gospel Ser.). 1996. audio compact disk 13.98 (978-7-474-00066-8(0)) Sprg Hill Music Group.

Southern Cross. Patricia Cornwell. Read by Kate Reading. (Andy Brazil Ser.: No. 2). 1999. audio compact disk 80.00 (978-0-7366-5162-2(4)) Books on Tape.

Southern Cross. Patricia Cornwell. Narrated by Cristine McMurdo-Wallis. 11 CDs. (Running Time: 12 hrs. 30 mins.). (Andy Brazil Ser.: No. 2). 2001. audio compact disk 99.00 (978-0-7887-3721-3(X), C1078E7) Recorded Bks.
In Richmond, the lives of a gullible redneck, a harried police chief & a skinny kid named Weed are on a collision course. When they meet, surprises spring from all directions.

Southern Cross, abr. ed. Patricia Cornwell. Read by Roberta Maxwell. 4 cass. (Running Time: 4 hrs.). (Andy Brazil Ser.: No. 2). 1999. 24.95 (FS9-43334) Highsmith.

Southern Cross. abr. ed. Patricia Cornwell. 2 cass. (Running Time: 3 hrs.). (Andy Brazil Ser.: No. 2). 1999. 16.85 (978-1-85686-611-8(4)) Ulvrscrft Audio.

Southern Cross. unabr. ed. Patricia Cornwell. Read by Kate Reading. 8 cass. (Running Time: 12 hrs.). (Andy Brazil Ser.: No. 2). 1999. 64.00 (978-0-7366-4447-1(4), 4892) Books on Tape.
Chief Judy Hammer, Deputy Virginia West & rookie cop Andy Brazil are dispatched to Richmond, VA by an NIJ grant, to quell the growing gang problem & modernize the beleaguered Richmond PD. Unfortunately the trio could not have been prepared for the resentment they would confront or for the bizarre cast of characters they would find upon their arrival. In the face of overwhelming public scrutiny, the trio must find the link between the desecration of Confederate president Jefferson Davis' statue & the brutal murder of an elderly woman.

Southern Cross. unabr. ed. Patricia Cornwell. Read by Kate Reading. 10 CDs. (Running Time: 15 hrs.). (Andy Brazil Ser.: No. 2). 2001. audio compact disk 80.00 Books on Tape.
Chief Judy Hammer, Deputy Virginia West & rookie cop Andy Brazil are dispatched to Richmond, Virginia by an NIJ grant to quell the growing gang problem & modernize the beleaguered Richmond PD. Unfortunately the trio could not have been prepared for the resentment they would confront or for the bizarre cast of characters they would find upon their arrival. In the face of overwhelming public scrutiny, the trio must find the link between the desecration of Confederate president Jefferson Davis' statue & the brutal murder of an elderly woman.

Southern Cross. unabr. ed. Patricia Cornwell. Read by Cristine McMurdo-Wallis. 8 cass. (Running Time: 8 hrs.). (Andy Brazil Ser.: No. 2). 1999. 39.95 (FS9-43348) Highsmith.

Southern Cross. unabr. ed. Patricia Cornwell. Narrated by Cristine McMurdo-Wallis. 9 cass. (Running Time: 12 hrs. 30 mins.). (Andy Brazil Ser.: No. 2). 1999. 83.00 (978-0-7887-2591-3(2), 95612E7) Recorded Bks.
The author laces broad strands of humor into a story of deception & danger. In Richmond, the lives of a gullible redneck, a harried police chief & a skinny kid named Weed are on a collision course. When they meet, surprises spring from all directions.

Southern Cross to Pole Star. unabr. collector's ed. A. F. Tschiffely. Read by John MacDonald. 9 cass. (Running Time: 13 hrs. 30 mins.). 1989. 72.00 (978-0-7366-1652-2(7), 2503) Books on Tape.
Southern Cross to Pole Star is an enduring adventure story of one of history's greatest rides. Aime Felix Tschiffely, a young Swiss living in Argentina in the early 1900s, took two aging Creole horses on a 10,000-mile, 30-month journey over the Andes, through the wilds of Bolivia, across the Isthmus of Panama & on to Washington, D. C. Undeterred by tropical fever, quicksand & bandits.

Southern Cultures: The Fifteenth Anniversary Reader, 1993-2008. Ed. by Harry L. Watson & Larry J. Griffin. (ENG., 2008. 26.95 (978-0-8078-8649-6(1)); audio compact disk 26.95 (978-0-8078-8651-9(3)) U of NC Pr.

Southern Discomfort. unabr. ed. Margaret Maron. Narrated by C. J. Critt. 6 cass. (Running Time: 7 hrs. 45 mins.). (Deborah Knott Mystery Ser.: No. 2). 1994. 51.00 (978-0-7887-0032-3(4), 94231E7) Recorded Bks.
Newly created the only female judge in Colleton County, North Carolina, Deborah Knott finds herself investigating her young cousin's assault.

Southern Exposure. Lynn Foster. (ENG.). 2009. 3.75 (978-0-615-28741-6(7)) Coral Sands.

Southern Fried Divorce: A Woman Unleashes Her Hound & His Dog in the Big Easy. Judy Conner. 2004. audio compact disk 29.99 (978-1-4193-2757-5(7)) Recorded Bks.

Southern Fried Rock. Friedman-Fairfax and Sony Music Staff. 1 CD. (CD Ser.). 1995. pap. bk. 16.98 (978-1-56799-232-8(3), Friedman-Fairfax) M Friedman Pub Grp Inc.

Southern Gates of Arabia. unabr. collector's ed. Freya Stark. Read by Donada Peters. 6 cass. (Running Time: 9 hrs.). 1990. 48.00 (978-0-7366-1748-2(5), 2587) Books on Tape.
In 1935, Freya Stark landed on the coast of South Arabia, intent on being the first woman to venture alone into the country's interior by way of its ancient Incense Road. She traveled close to the country...by donkey, car & foot. She stayed in villages beset by poverty, & made her way through hostile tribes. She spoke the local dialects, adopted the customs, mixed with people along the way - she even let soldiers use her face cream to shine their daggers & learned the rites of hookah.

Southern Ghost. unabr. ed. Carolyn G. Hart. Read by Kate Reading. 7 cass. (Running Time: 10 hrs. 30 mins.). (Death on Demand Mystery Ser.: No. 8). 1996. 56.00 (978-0-7366-3501-1(7), 4141) Books on Tape.
Annie Darling can hardly believe it. The police say her husband, Max, sits behind bars. They speak of him with a beautiful blonde. The baffling mystery leads to the home of a venerable Southern family with a violent history. A killer wants to hide the family's secrets & it's up to Annie to stop him.

Southern Gospel: Great 80's. 1 cass. 1999. 8.98 (978-5-552-82021-4(5)); audio compact disk 13.98 (978-5-552-81960-7(8)) Provident Music.

Southern Gospel Favorites: Unison/2-Part. Created by Luke Gambill. (Running Time: 3300 sec.). (Simple Ser.). 2007. audio compact disk 16.98 (978-5-557-53246-4(3), Brentwood-Benson Music); audio compact disk 10.00 (978-5-557-53244-0(7), Brentwood-Benson Music) Brentwood Music.

Southern Gospel Favorites: Unison/2-Part. Created by Luke Gambill. (Running Time: 3300 sec.). (Simple Ser.). 2007. audio compact disk 90.00 (978-5-557-53245-7(5), Brentwood-Benson Music) Brentwood Music.

Southern Gospel's Top Twenty All Time Favorites, Vol. 2. Perf. by Cathedral Quartet et al. 1 cass. (Running Time: 1 hr.). 1997. audio compact disk 15.99 (D2038) Diamante Music Grp.
Also including: Kingsmen, McKameys, Spencers, Inspirations, Perrys, Hoppers, Speers, Singing Echoes, Kingsboys & Marksmen.

Southern Gospel's 15 All-Time Favorites. 2007. audio compact disk 16.99 (978-5-558-16551-7(0)) Pt of Grace Ent.

Southern Joy: Featuring Southern Gospel's Top Twenty Artists & Songs. Perf. by Jeff Easter et al. 1 cass. audio compact disk 15.99 (D2024) Diamante Music Grp.
Also includes the Will Perry Sisters & others.

Southern Landmarks by Blacks. Rex A. Barnett. (Running Time: 15 min.). (YA). 1990. 16.99 (978-0-924198-10-6(9)) Hist Video.
Black achievements throughout the south by landmark, are reviewed.

Southern Lights. abr. ed. Danielle Steel. Read by Nick Podehl. 5 CDs. (Running Time: 6 hrs.). 2009. audio compact disk 26.99 (978-1-4233-2076-0(X), 9781423320760, BACD) Brilliance Audio.

Southern Lights. abr. ed. Danielle Steel. Read by Nick Podehl. (Running Time: 6 hrs.). 2010. audio compact disk 14.99 (978-1-4233-2077-7(8), 9781423320777, BCD Value Price) Brilliance Audio.

Southern Lights. unabr. ed. Danielle Steel. Read by Nick Podehl. 1 MP3-CD. (Running Time: 9 hrs.). 2009. 24.99 (978-1-4233-2072-2(7), 9781423320722, Brilliance MP3); 39.97 (978-1-4233-2073-9(5), 9781423320739, Brinc Audio MP3 Lib); 24.99 (978-1-4233-2074-6(3), 9781423320746, BAD); 39.97 (978-1-4233-2075-3(1), 9781423320753, BADLE); audio compact disk 38.99 (978-1-4233-2070-8(0), 9781423320708, Bril Audio CD Unabri); audio compact disk 99.97 (978-1-4233-2071-5(9), 9781423320715, BriAudCD Unabrid) Brilliance Audio.

Southern Mammy Sings see Poetry of Langston Hughes

Southern Mammy Sings see Poetry & Reflections

Southern Mountain Banjo. Wayne Erbsen. 1995. pap. bk. 24.95 Book cassette pack . (978-0-7866-0890-4(0), 95275P) Mel Bay.

Southern Mountain Classics: Sixteen Old-Time Instrumentals. Perf. by Wayne Erbsen. 1 cass. (Running Time: 48 min.). 1991. 9.95 (978-0-9629327-5-5(2), NG002); audio compact disk 14.95 (978-0-9629327-6-2(0), NG-CD-100) Native Ground.
A rollicking collection of classic 19th century American tunes popular not only on rural front porches, but also with early pioneers heading west.

Southern Mountain Classics: 16 Old-Time Instrumentals. Wayne Erbsen. (Running Time: 2880 sec.). 2007. audio compact disk 15.98 (978-0-7866-0819-5(6)) Native Ground.

Southern Mountain Dulcimer. Wayne Erbsen. 1995. pap. bk. 22.95 (978-0-7866-0892-8(7), 95274P); spiral bd. 27.95 (978-0-7866-0891-1(9), 95274CDP) Mel Bay.

Southern Mountain Fiddle. Wayne Erbsen. 1995. spiral bd. 21.95 (978-0-7866-0884-3(6), 95278P); spiral bd. 26.95 (978-0-7866-0883-6(8), 95278CDP) Mel Bay.

Southern Mountain Guitar. Wayne Erbsen. 1995. spiral bd. 21.95 (978-0-7866-0888-1(9), 95276P) Mel Bay.

Southern Mountain Mandolin. Wayne Erbsen. 1995. pap. bk. 21.95 (978-0-7866-0886-7(2), 95277P); spiral bd. 25.95 (978-0-7866-0885-0(4), 95277CDP) Mel Bay.

Southern Pacific see Carl Sandburg Reading Cool Tombs & Other Poems

Southern Sky. 1 cass. (Running Time: 29 min.). 14.95 (23572) MMI Corp.
Astronomers talk about Alpha Centauri, Southern Cross, other configurations in the S. Hemisphere.

Southern Soldier Boy: Sixteen Authentic Tunes of the Civil War. Perf. by Wayne Erbsen. 1 cass. (Running Time: 45 min.). 1992. 9.95 (978-0-9629327-7-9(9), NG005); audio compact disk 14.95 (978-1-883206-19-2(7), NG-CD-005) Native Ground.
A popular collection of music as was played by common soldiers. Includes spirited rallying songs, mournful laments, popular pieces of the day, & a lively buckdance tune.

Southern Sotho. Ed. by Charles Berlitz. 2 cass. (Running Time: 1 hr. 30 mins.). (Language/30 Brief Course Ser.). 1980. pap. bk. 24.95 (978-0-88432-407-2(9), AF1051) J Norton Pubs.
Quick, highly condensed introduction to the words & phrases you'll need to communicate effectively in the country you're visiting. Cassettes & phrase guide book are in a vinyl album.

Southern Stories. Muyiwa. (ENG.). 2008. bk. (978-0-9814970-0-6(4)) Two Zero Nine.

***Southern Storm.** Terri Blackstock. (Running Time: 10 hrs. 41 mins. 0 sec.). (Cape Refuge Ser.). (ENG.). 2008. 14.99 (978-0-310-30433-3(4)) Zondervan.

***Southern Storm: Sherman's March to the Sea.** abr. ed. Noah Andre Trudeau. Read by Eric Conger. (ENG.). 2008. (978-0-06-166149-5(X)); (978-0-06-166150-1(3)) HarperCollins Pubs.

Southern Strings. Music by V. Doreswamy Iyenger et al. 1 CD. (Running Time: 1 hr.). 1994. audio compact disk (CD C94011) Multi-Cultural Bks.

Southern U. S. see Acting with an Accent

Southern Woman: New & Selected Fiction. unabr. ed. Elizabeth Spencer. (Running Time: 15 hrs. 50 mins.). (ENG.). 2009. 29.95 (978-1-4332-2417-1(8)); 85.95 (978-1-4332-2413-3(5)); audio compact disk 118.00 (978-1-4332-2414-0(3)) Blckstn Audio.

Southpaw, unabr. ed. Mark Harris. Narrated by John Randolph Jones. 9 cass. (Running Time: 12 hrs. 45 mins.). 1991. 78.00 (978-1-55690-489-9(4), 91222E7) Recorded Bks.
When things were going just right, the crowd would recede into the background like a dull hum & he could hear his boys, his team, reaching out to him in their own individual ways, telling him they were behind him, like a real ball club, 100%. And it would come over him like wave, that this was where he would always want to be, digging his toe with authority into the resin dust on top of the mound, winding up for the pitch of his life.

Southpaw. unabr. ed. Eric Simonson. Perf. by Edward Asner et al. 1 cass. (Running Time: 1 hr. 31 min.). 1997. 19.95 (978-1-58081-098-2(5)) L A Theatre.
Coming of age in America by way of the baseball diamond, left hander Henry Wiggen grows to manhood in a right handed world. From his small town beginnings to the top of the game, Henry finds out how hard it is to please his coach, his girl, the sports page & himself, all at once. The first installment of a series which includes "Bang the Drum Slowly, The Southpaw" is a comic & poignant look at Henry Wiggen's first season in the majors.

Southpaw. unabr. collector's ed. Mark Harris. Read by Christopher Hurt. 8 cass. (Running Time: 12 hrs.). 1989. 64.00 (978-0-7366-1532-7(6), 2402) Books on Tape.
This is a story about coming of age in America by Way of the Baseball diamond.

Southwest Airlines Way: Using the Power of Relationships to Achieve High Performance. Jody Hoffer Gittell. Read by Jody Hoffer Gittell. 2 cass. (Running Time: 3 hrs.). 2004. 24.00 (978-1-932378-18-4(9)); audio compact disk 28.00 (978-1-932378-19-1(7)) Pub: A Media Intl. Dist(s): Natl Bk Netwk
Learn from this rich story and adapt the lessons. - -Thomas A. Kochan.

Southwest Chamber see Wind in the Rose Bush & Other Stories of the Supernatural

Southwest Folk Tales. unabr. ed. Ed McCurdy. (Running Time: 50 min.). 10.95 (978-0-8045-0722-6(8), SAC 7041) Spoken Arts.

Southwest Indians. unabr. ed. Peter M. Spizzirri. Read by Charles Fuller. Ed. by Linda Spizzirri. 1 cass. (Running Time: 15 min.). Dramatization. (Educational Coloring Book & Cassette Ser.). (J). (gr. 1-8). pap. bk. 6.95 (978-0-86545-093-6(5)) Spizzirri.
If you would like to know how the Hopi, Apache, Mohave lived years ago, you will enjoy this book.

Southwest Region. Compiled by Benchmark Education Staff. 2006. audio compact disk 10.00 (978-1-4108-6625-7(4)) Benchmark Educ.

Southwestern Prehistoric American Indian Civilizations & Archaeology. Hosted by Nancy Pearlman. 1 cass. (Running Time: 29 min.). 10.00 (1027) Educ Comm CA.

Souvenir. unabr. ed. Patricia Carlon. Read by Joy Mitchell. 5 cass. (Running Time: 5 hrs.). 2001. (978-1-86340-663-5(8), 561016) Bolinda Pubng AUS.
An early morning murder in the park of a quiet country town. Two hitch hiking girls, one of them innocent - one of them a liar. Four years on, Marion still has to know who killed her brother. She needs to call on Jefferson Shields - she's been told that he solves puzzles.

Souvenir: A Daughter Discovers Her Father's War. Louise Steinman. Narrated by Suzanne Toren. 6 cass. (Running Time: 6 hrs. 30 mins.). 54.00 (978-1-4025-0531-7(0)) Recorded Bks.

Souvenir: A Daughter Discovers Her Father's War. unabr. ed. Louise Steinman. Narrated by Suzanne Toren. 6 cass. (Running Time: 6 hrs. 30 mins.). 2002. 34.95 (978-1-4025-0533-1(7), RF564) Recorded Bks.
Louise Steinman never understood the private hell that tormented her father. Years later, among her late parents' belongings, she discovers a metal ammo box. In it are almost 500 letters written by her father to her mother during World War II. It also contains a silk Japanese flag inscribed to Yoshio Shimizu. When she reads the letters, Steinman begins to see what her father experienced in the endless days of combat. She also embarks on a decade-long search to find out who Shimizu was-a search which culminates in a trip to Japan to return his flag. The result is a powerful story of discovery, connection, and reconciliation. Weaving together her father's letters, historical details and the political propaganda of both sides, Steinman creates a narrative that is a unique examination of the personal and universal costs of war.

Souvenirs of Solitude. unabr. ed. Brennan Manning. (Running Time: 4 hrs. 0 mins. 0 sec.). (ENG.). 2009. audio compact disk 24.98 (978-1-59644-803-2(2), Hovel Audio) christianaud.

***Souvenirs of Solitude: Finding Rest in Abba's Embrace.** unabr. ed. Brennan Manning. Narrated by Arthur Morey. (ENG.). 2009. 14.98 (978-1-59644-804-9(0), Hovel Audio) christianaud.

Sovay. unabr. ed. Celia Rees. Narrated by Bianca Amato. (Running Time: 12 hrs. 15 mins.). (YA). (gr. 9 up). 2008. 61.75 (978-1-4361-9894-3(1)); 97.75 (978-1-4361-5978-4(4)); audio compact disk 108.75 (978-1-4361-5983-8(0)) Recorded Bks.

Sovay. unabr. collector's ed. Celia Rees. Narrated by Bianca Amato. 11 CDs. (Running Time: 12 hrs. 15 mins.). (YA). (gr. 9 up). 2008. audio compact disk 49.95 (978-1-4361-5987-6(3)) Recorded Bks.

Sovereign for a Song. Annie Wilkinson. Read by Trudy Harris. 8 cass. (Running Time: 10 hrs. 35 mins.). 2005. 69.95 (978-1-85903-797-3(6)); audio compact disk 84.95 (978-1-85903-883-3(2)) Pub: UlverLrgPrint GBR. Dist(s): Ulverscroft US

Sovereign Governmental & Official Immunity. Read by Andrew H. Cline. 1 cass. 1990. 20.00 (AL-99) PA Bar Inst.

Sovereignty of God. Arthur W. Pink. (Pure Gold Classics Ser.). (ENG., 2007. pap. bk. 14.99 (978-0-88270-424-1(9)) Bridge-Logos.

Sovereignty of God. unabr. ed. Arthur W. Pink. Read by Robert Whitfield. 5 CDs. (Running Time: 5 hrs. 30 mins.). 2000. audio compact disk 40.00 (978-0-7861-9900-6(8), 2555) Blckstn Audio.
"Present day conditions," writes Pink, "call loudly for a new examination & new presentation of God's omnipotence, God's sufficiency, God's sovereignty. From every pulpit in the land it needs to be thundered forth that God still lives, that God still observes, that God still reigns.".

Sovereignty of God, unabr. ed. Arthur W. Pink. Read by Robert Whitfield. 4 cass. (Running Time: 5 hrs. 30 mins.). 2000. 32.95 (978-0-7861-1751-2(6), 2555) Blckstn Audio.

Sovereignty of God: Daniel 2:1-30. Ed Young. 1995. 4.95 (978-0-7417-2067-2(1), 1067) Win Walk.

Sovereignty of God: Matt. 6:23. Ed Young. (J). 1990. 4.95 (978-0-7417-1832-7(4), 832) Win Walk.

Sovereignty of Man. Chuck Missler. 2 cass. (Running Time: 3 hrs.). (Briefing Packages by Chuck Missler). 1996. vinyl bd. 14.95 (978-1-880532-41-6(7)) Koinonia Hse.
From the beginning of time, thinkers have puzzled over the paradox of fate vs. Free will. In theological terms, this leads to the struggle between Calvinism and Arminianism. As we explore this paradox we find that examining the fruit of each position reveals that the River of Life seems to flow between these two extremes, and that again, truth involves a careful balance.We hear a lot about the "Sovereignty of God"; and the prerogatives of our Creator are pretty obvious.As the children's riddle goes, "Where does the gorilla sleep in the forest?""Anywhere he wants to."And, as most of you have discovered, He has also given us one of His greatest treasures - His Word. Jealous as He is of His Name, Psalm 138:2 highlights: "...for thou hast magnified thy word above thy name."And indeed, God has declared in detail the responsibilities He desires of His people. The Bible lays out just how He desires to be worshipped, etc.Beyond the mysteries associated with the "sovereignty of God" - and the libraries are full of studies on that subject - there emerges what is, to many of us, an even more troubling mystery: The Sovereignty of Man!Internationally recognized Biblical authority, Chuck Missler, explores the fundamental paradox underlying our ultimate destiny.

Sovereignty of Man. Chuck Missler. 2 CD's. (Running Time: 120 mins.). (Briefing Packages by Chuck Missler). 1995. audio compact disk 19.95 (978-1-57821-301-6(0)) Koinonia Hse.

Sovereingty of God: Logos Sept. 7, 1997. Ben Young. 1997. 4.95 (978-0-7417-6046-3(0), B0046) Win Walk.

Soviet Army. unabr. ed. Basil H. Liddell-Hart. Read by Bill Kelsey. 12 cass. (Running Time: 18 hrs.). 1987. 96.00 (2056) Books on Tape.
Traces the evolution of Russia'a Army during the first half of the twentieth century. It was written by men who knew their subject: officers who had fought with or against the Russians. It is crammed with gripping, vital information.

Soviet Army. unabr. collector's ed. Basil H. Liddell-Hart. Read by Bill Kelsey. 12 cass. (Running Time: 18 hrs.). 1987. 96.00 (978-0-7366-1133-6(9), 2056) Books on Tape.
A historical perspective on Russia's great weapon.

Soviet Economy: The Brezhnev Era. R. A. Lewis. 1 cass. 1986. 11.95 (R7879) J Norton Pubs.
Examines the economic history of the Soviet Union since Krushchev's fall in 1964. Analyzes the economy & agriculture, Soviet industry & its development under Brezhnev, & the emergence of new technologies.

Sow What? Matthew 13:3-12. Ed Young. (J). 1981. 4.95 (978-0-7417-1189-2(3), A0189) Win Walk.

Sower. Neville Goddard. 1 cass. (Running Time: 62 min.). 1965. 8.00 (54) J & L Pubns.
Neville taught Imagination Creates Reality. He was a powerfully influential teacher of God as Consciousness.

Sower Sows the Word. Kenneth Copeland. 4 cass. (Running Time: 4 hrs.). 1983. bk. & stu. ed. 20.00 (978-0-938458-46-3(9)) K Copeland Pubns.
How to reap the word in your life.

Sowers. unabr. ed. H.S. Merriman. 8 cass. 2005. 69.95 (978-1-86015-480-5(8)) Ulverscroft US.

Sowieso. H. Funk & Neuner. (Sowieso Ser.). (GER.). 1998. audio compact disk 15.50 (978-3-468-47669-3(8)) Langenscheidt.

Sowieso. Hermann Funk et al. 2 cass. (Sowieso Ser.). (GER.). (YA). (gr. 9-12). 1994. 22.50 (978-3-468-47653-2(1)) Langenscheidt.
A revolutionary German Course that teaches High School students how to learn.

Sowieso, Level 1. H. Funk et al. (Sowieso Ser.). (GER.). 2005. audio compact disk 22.50 (978-3-468-47668-6(X)) Langenscheidt.

Sowieso 2, Level II, 2B. unabr. ed. H. Funk et al. 1 cass., 1 CD. (Sowieso Ser.). (GER.). (YA). 2005. wbk. ed. 9.95 (978-3-468-47674-7(4)); audio compact disk 9.95 (978-3-468-47688-4(4)) Langenscheidt.

Sowieso 2, Level 2A. unabr. ed. H. Funk et al. 2 cass. (Sowieso Ser.). (GER.). (YA). 2005. 36.50 (978-3-468-47673-0(6)); audio compact disk 36.50 (978-3-468-47687-7(6)) Langenscheidt.

Sowieso 3, Level 3A. unabr. ed. Funk et al. 2 CDs. (Running Time: 1 hr.). (Sowieso Ser.). (GER.). (YA). 2005. audio compact disk 36.50 (978-3-468-47700-3(7)) Langenscheidt.

Sowieso 3, Level 3A, Set. unabr. ed. Funk et al. 2 cass. (Sowieso Ser.). (GER.). (YA). 2005. 36.50 (978-3-468-47693-8(0)) Langenscheidt.

Sowieso 3, Level 3B. unabr. ed. Funk et al. 1 cass. (Sowieso Ser.). (GER.). (YA). 2005. 11.50 (978-3-468-47694-5(9)); audio compact disk 11.50 (978-3-468-47701-0(5)) Langenscheidt.

Sowing & Reaping, Set. Read by Tim Greenwood. 2 cass. (Running Time: 2 hrs.). 1999. 10.00 (978-0-9666689-2-6(8)) TGMinist.

Sowing to the Wind: Hos. 8:1-14. Ed Young. 1988. 4.95 (978-0-7417-1658-3(5), 658) Win Walk.

Sow's Ears & Silk Purses. unabr. ed. Ann Drysdale. Read by Ann Drysdale. 4 cass. (Running Time: 5 hrs. 20 min.). (Isis Audio Reminiscence Ser.). (J). 2001. 44.95 (978-0-7531-1041-6(5)) Pub: ISIS Lrg Prnt GBR. Dist(s): Ulverscroft US
Author tells of her further efforts on a small independent hill farm in the North York Moors. These tales of a Londoner coming to terms with country life are written with warmth and affection for her family of children and animals. Working hard to turn her "sow's ear", Hagg House Farm, into a "silk purse" of a home and small business.

Soy de dos lugares: Poesia Juvenil. (Saludos Ser.: Vol. 2). (SPA.). (gr. 3-5). 10.00 (978-0-7635-1768-7(2)) Rigby Educ.

Soy Mi Propia Autoridad: Elimine la Auto-condena y el Sentimiento de Culpa. unabr. ed. Lilburn S. Barksdale. Read by Juan Francisco Estrada & Elizabeth Trabanino. Tr. by George Teague. 1 cass. (Running Time: 37 min.). (SPA.). 1994. 9.95 (978-0-918588-43-2(X), 123S) NCADD.
Side one helps you take conscious charge of your life. Side two explains why guilt is irrational despite the fact that each of us is inescapably responsible for everything we think, say & do.

Soy una Pizza. Perf. by Charlotte Diamond. 1 cass., 1 CD. (SPA.). (CD323) NewSound.
Includes: "Cuatro Abrazos Al Dia" (Four Hugs a Day), "Di Dinosaurio" (Dicky Dinosaur), & "La Bamba," & "De Colores".

Soybean Capital of the World. Mark Costello. Read by Mark Costello. Contrib. by AAPL Staff. 1 cass. (Running Time: 46 min.). 13.95 (978-1-55644-040-3(5), 2041) Am Audio Prose.
Reads excerpts & short stories.

Soyons Amis: Easy to Learn French Songs for Children. Perf. by Alain Le Lait. Music by Alain Le Lait. Des. by Christy Pitts. 1 CD and 1 Book. (Running Time: 35 minutes). (FRE., (J). 1999. pap. bk. 15.95 (978-0-9747122-1-5(3), FRCD100) Yadeeda.
12 original songs in French along with two traditional recordings.

***Spa: Favorite Recipes from Celebrated Spas, Soothing Classical Piano Music.** Sharon O'Connor. 1998. pap. bk. 24.95 (978-1-883914-37-0(X)) Menus & Music.

***Spa Deadly: An Allie Armington Mystery.** Louise Gaylord. Narrated by Mara Purl. (Running Time: 326). (YA). 2010. 8.99 (978-0-9827081-6-3(5)) AuthorsDig.

Spa Decameron. unabr. ed. Fay Weldon. Narrated by Rula Lenska. 11 CDs. (Running Time: 12 hrs. 45 mins.). 2009. audio compact disk 99.95 (978-0-7927-5791-7(2)) AudioGO.

Spa: Dreaming. Jordan Peters. (Running Time: 60 mins.). 2002. audio compact disk 15.99 (978-1-904451-97-6(7)) Global Jrny GBR GBR.

***Spa Healing in a Box: Rest-Rebalance-Heal.** unabr. ed. Made for Success. Read by Crystal Dwyer. (Made for Success Ser.). 2010. audio compact disk 19.95 (978-1-4417-6777-6(0)) Blckstn Audio.

***Spa Healing in a Box (Library Edition) Rest-Rebalance-Heal.** unabr. ed. Made for Success. Read by Crystal Dwyer. (Running Time: 1 hr. 30 mins.). (Made for Success Ser.). 2010. audio compact disk 30.00 (978-1-4417-6776-9(2)) Blckstn Audio.

Space. Composed by Zakir Hussain. 1 cass. (Elements Ser.: Vol. 5). 1995. (M95011); (CD M95011) Multi-Cultural Bks.
Shwas-Uchhashwas, Deep Space, The Zen of Space, Brahmand: The Final Frontier.

Space, Pt. 1. unabr. ed. James A. Michener. Read by Larry McKeever. 14 cass. (Running Time: 21 hrs.). 1994. 112.00 (978-0-7366-2607-1(7), 3350A) Books on Tape.
It stretches billions of miles beyond the Earth. It's the focus of dreams & daring. It's the last great frontier in our human drama. It's Space. Michener's Space gives life to those who seek the stars, from engineers & scientists to politicians & astronauts. They live the quest; reporters rush their stories to a breathless world.

Space, Pt. 2. unabr. ed. James A. Michener. Read by Larry McKeever. 14 cass. (Running Time: 21 hrs.). 1993. 112.00 (3350B) Books on Tape.

Space: Isaac Asimov on "Moon Colonies" Isaac Asimov. Read by Isaac Asimov. 1 cass. (Running Time: 30 min.). 14.95 (CBC197) MMI Corp.
Suggests why man should go ahead & colonize the moon.

Space: The Infinite Frontier. unabr. ed. Roadrunner Audio Staff. Ed. by Lee Matthew. Intro. by Harrison Schmitt. 1 cass. (Running Time: 1 hr.). (Audio Science Tour Ser.). 1989. 13.95 (978-0-944857-06-9(X)) Matthew Media.
Introduces a story of the courageous first explorers of space - and the revolutionary thinkers back on Earth who extended the frontiers of knowledge.

Space Vol. 120: Get Kids Excited About Space! unabr. ed. Ken Thompson & Karen Mitzo Hilderbrand. 1 CD. (Running Time: 40 min.). (Get Kids Excited about Ser.). (J). (ps-4). 1999. audio compact disk 12.99 (978-1-57583-200-5(3)) Twin Sisters.
Through 12 sing-along songs, children will learn about weightlessness, the history of space travel, and the possibility of living in space someday!.

Space - Communication with Alien Beings. Read by Everett Hafner. 1 cass. (Running Time: 30 min.). 14.95 (CBC198) MMI Corp.
Talks about theories of communication with beings in outer space.

Space Activity Book Set. 2004. audio compact disk 13.99 (978-1-57583-356-9(5)) Twin Sisters.

Space Adventure. Nancy Shaw. Illus. by Kelly McMahon. (Two Can Read Ser.). 2002. reel tape Rental 2.99 (978-1-56472-660-5(6)) Edupress Inc.

Space Adventure, No. 2. (Adventure Ser.). 35.00 (978-1-56997-094-2(7)) Knowldge Adv.

Space Age As Creative Challenge. unabr. ed. Ray Bradbury. 1 cass. (Running Time: 1 hr. 27 min.). 1970. 11.00 (11301) Big Sur Tapes.
An entertaining talk about the space age, about how technology has changed the world, & how each of us can change the world through dedicating ourselves to the work we love.

***Space Between: New & Selected Poems, 1984-1992.** Gabriel Fitzmaurice. (ENG.). 1993. 11.95 (978-0-8023-0014-0(6)) Pub: Clo Iar-Chonnachta IRL. Dist(s): Dufour

Space Between the Stars: My Journey to an Open Heart. abr. ed. Louis L'Amour & Deborah Santana. Read by Deborah Santana. 4 cass. (Running Time: 5 hrs.). (ENG.). 2004. 14.95 (978-0-7393-1682-5(6), Random AudioBks) Pub: Random Audio Pubg. Dist(s): Random

Space Between the Stars: My Journey to an Open Heart. unabr. ed. Deborah Santana. 11 CDs. (Running Time: 9 hrs. 30 mins.). 2005. audio compact disk 99.00 (978-1-4159-1672-8(1)); 81.00 (978-1-4159-1587-5(3)) Books on Tape.
Space Between the Stars is a moving account of self-discovery, rendered in raw, beautiful prose, by a woman whose heart has remained pure even in times of despair. As Deborah Santana talks frankly about her lifelong fight against racial injustice and her deep-seated loyalty to her family, ultimately it is the struggle to remain a spiritual and artistic force in her own right, in the shadow of one of the world¿s most revered musicians, that shines through as her most indomitable pursuit.

Space Boy. Orson Scott Card. Read by Stefan Rudnicki. (Running Time: 7200 sec.). (J). 2007. audio compact disk 24.00 (978-1-4332-0764-8(8)); audio compact disk 19.95 (978-1-4332-0765-5(6)) Blckstn Audio.

Space Boy. Orson Scott Card. Read by Stefan Rudnicki. (Running Time: 7200 sec.). (J). (gr. 5). 2007. 22.95 (978-1-4332-0763-1(X)) Blckstn Audio.

Space Cadet Training: 11 Cor. 4:13-18. Ed Young. 1990. 4.95 (978-0-7417-1782-5(4), 782) Win Walk.

Space Camp: 12 Bible Sessions/Grades 1-6. Tracy Carpenter. (J). 2007. audio compact disk 59.99 (978-0-7847-1979-4(9)) Standard Pub.

Space Case. 2004. pap. bk. 18.95 (978-1-55592-114-9(0)); pap. bk. 38.75 (978-1-55592-643-4(6)); pap. bk. 32.75 (978-1-55592-310-5(0)); pap. bk. 14.95 (978-1-55592-063-0(2)); 8.95 (978-1-55592-989-3(3)); audio compact disk 12.95 (978-1-55592-944-2(3)) Weston Woods.

Space Case. Edward Marshall. Illus. by James Marshall. Narrated by Christopher Lloyd. Music by Scotty Huff & Robert Reynolds. Animated by Virginia Wilkos. 1 cass. (Running Time: 13 min.). (J). (ps-4). 2000. pap. bk. 12.95 (QPRA397) Weston Woods.
Funny things happen when a creature from outer space visits Earth on Halloween. This zany story of a small space traveler & the young boy he befriends is vividly brought to life through lively animation & an upbeat musical score.

Space Case. unabr. ed. Edward Marshall. 1 cass. (Running Time: 6 min.). (J). (gr. k-4). 1992. pap. bk. 15.90 (978-0-8045-6597-4(X), 6597) Spoken Arts.

Space Command Novella. Marco A. V. Bitetto. 1 cass. 2000. (978-1-58578-124-9(X)) Inst of Cybernetics.

Space Craft. 1 cass. Dramatization. (J). pap. bk. 6.95 (978-0-86545-110-0(9)) Spizzirri.
Covers space crafts, including the space shuttle "Columbia", that were developed to put man in space.

Space Craft. Ed. by Linda Spizzirri. Illus. by Peter M. Spizzirri. 1 cass. Dramatization. (J). (gr. 1-8). pap. bk. 4.98 incl. educational coloring bk. (978-0-86545-036-3(6)) Spizzirri.

Space Enterprise. Ed. by Marco A. V. Bitetto. 1 cass. 1999. (978-1-58578-310-6(2)) Inst of Cybernetics.

Space Enterprise. Ed. by Marco A. V. Bitetto. 1 cass. 2000. (978-1-58578-077-8(4)) Inst of Cybernetics.

Space Explorers. Peter M. Spizzirri. 1 cass. Dramatization. (J). pap. bk. 6.95 (978-0-86545-111-7(7)) Spizzirri.
Interesting facts about the first U.S. rockets to the unmanned satellites visiting planets throughout our galaxy.

Space for God in Words & Music. Don Postema. 1 CD. (Running Time: 1 hr. 30 mins.). (What the Bible Teaches Ser.). audio compact disk 12.95 (978-5-550-36047-7(0), 150985) Pub: Nairi ARM. Dist(s): FaithAliveChr

Space for God in Words & Music. Don Postema. 1 cass. (Running Time: 1 hr. 30 mins.). (What the Bible Teaches Ser.). 1998. 12.95 (978-5-550-35987-7(1), 150980) Pub: Nairi ARM. Dist(s): FaithAliveChr

Space Ghost: Brak Presents The Brak Album. Perf. by Freddie Prinze, Jr. et al. 2002. audio compact disk 17.98 (978-0-7379-0105-4(5), 79772) Rhino Enter.
Space Ghost's Brak now takes center stage with his very own album.

Space Ghost: Brak Presents The Brak Album. Perf. by Freddie Prinze, Jr. et al. (Running Time: 40 mins.). 2002. 10.98 (978-0-7379-0106-1(3), 79772) Rhino Enter.

Space Ghost's Musical Bar-B-Que. 1 CD. (Running Time: 40 mins.). (J). 2001. audio compact disk 17.98 (R2 72876) Rhino Enter.
Forty minutes of pure insanity featuring 25 hickory-smoked harmonies and laid-back one-liners from Cartoon Planet's Space Ghost, Zorak and Brak.

Space Ghost's Surf & Turf. 1 CD. (Running Time: 1 hr. 30 mins.). (J). 2001. audio compact disk 17.98 (R2 75487) Rhino Enter.
Here comes the luau to end all luaus! You'll have a blast with 22 tiki-torched tunes, along with loads of side-splitting dialogue from your favorite Space Ghost characters.

Space Ghost's Surf & Turf. 1 cass. 1998. 16.98 (978-1-56826-913-9(7)) Rhino Enter.

Space of Contemplation. Swami Amar Jyoti. 1 cass. 1987. 9.95 (K-89) Truth Consciousness.
Space, the secret of existence. Blending inner & outer life; activity in peace & joy, without tension. Perversions of the iron age.

Space Pirates. Doctor Who. 2 CDs. (Running Time: 3 hrs.). 2003. audio compact disk 19.99 (978-0-563-53505-8(9)) BBC Worldwide.

Space Play, Level 4. 2002. (978-0-7398-5192-0(6)) SteckVau.

Space Play Level 4. (J). 2002. audio compact disk (978-0-7398-5348-1(1)) SteckVau.

Space Play Single. Steck-Vaughn Staff. 2002. pap. bk. 41.60 (978-0-7398-6977-2(9)) SteckVau.

Space Ship One: Making History in Outerspace. Tom Sibila. (High Five Reading Ser.). (ENG., (gr. 4-5). 2005. audio compact disk 5.95 (978-0-7368-5754-3(0)) CapstoneDig.

Space Shuttle Mystery. George Khoury. 1 cass. (Running Time: 20 min.). (Adventures Abounds Ser.). (J). (gr. 3-6). 1984. bk. 16.99 (978-0-934898-64-5(2)); pap. bk. 9.95 (978-0-934898-77-5(4)) Jan Prods.
Excitement comes into the life of a boy living on a faraway space colony when a vital space shuttle is reported missing. How he & his computer sidekick, Harold, try to track down the mysterious shuttle makes high adventure reading.

Space Songs for Children. Tonja Evetts Weimer. 1 cass. (Running Time: 25 min.). (J). (ps-3). 1993. 9.98 (978-0-936823-12-6(7)) Pearce Evetts.
Multiple award winning book & cassette. Fun songs & activities about outer space. Activity book provides parents & teachers additional ideas & activities to do with their children.

Space Songs for Children. Tonja Evetts Weimer. Illus. by Manuela Bernardez. 1 cass. (Running Time: 25 min.). (J). (ps-3). 1993. pap. bk. 14.95 (978-0-936823-11-9(9)) Pearce Evetts.

***Space Station Rat.** Michael J. Daley. Read by Daniel Bostick. (ENG.). (J). 2010. audio compact disk 34.00 (978-1-936223-05-3(8)) Full Cast Audio.

Space Station 7th Grade, unabr. ed. Jerry Spinelli. Narrated by Johnny Heller. 5 pieces. (Running Time: 7 hrs.). (gr. 6 up). 1998. 44.00 (978-0-7887-1917-2(3), 95338E7) Recorded Bks.
Jason recounts how his boggled mind tries to keep pace with his changing body, friends, family & school.

Space Station 7th Grade, unabr. ed. Jerry Spinelli. Read by Johnny Heller. 5 cass. (Running Time: 6 hr. 45 min.). (YA). (gr. 6). 1998. 58.20 Hmwk . (978-0-7887-1945-5(9), 40652); 124.30 Class set. (978-0-7887-3802-9(X), 46462) Recorded Bks.
Jason recounts his seventh-grade year from his first big crush to popping his first pimple as his boggle mind tries to keep pace with this friends, family & school.

Space, Time & Energy. Read by Osel Tendzin. 3 cass. 1983. 31.50 (A071) Vajradhatu.
Three talks: 1) Space as ground from which everything arises; 2) Time as either struggle, or activity of compassion; 3) Energy as chaotic force or brilliant display of magic.

Space, Void & Cosmos. Read by H. Bondi. 1 cass. (Running Time: 30 min.). 14.95 (CBC151) MMI Corp.
Talks about theories of the Universe, in particular, the "big bang" theory.

Space, Void & Cosmos. Read by Thomas Gold. 1 cass. (Running Time: 30 min.). 14.95 (CBC174) MMI Corp.
Discusses quasars, the most powerful & largest objects in the universe.

Space, Void & Cosmos. Read by Edward Grant. 1 cass. (Running Time: 30 min.). 14.95 (CBC152) MMI Corp.
Talks about the West's earliest organized notions about the nature of space & medieval concepts of space.

Space Voyage: Hitching A Ride Through the Solar System. John Bergez. (World Around Us Ser.). 2003. pap. bk. 69.00 (978-1-4105-0020-5(9)); audio compact disk 18.95 (978-1-4105-0199-8(X)) D Johnston Inc.

Space War Novella. Read by Marco A. V. Bitetto. 1 cass. 2000. (978-1-58578-120-1(7)) Inst of Cybernetics.

Space Warfare: Fact Is Stranger Than Fiction. Ed. by Marco A. V. Bitetto. 1 cass. 1999. (978-1-58578-326-7(9)) Inst of Cybernetics.

Space 1999 Resurrection. William Latham. Read by Barry Morse. 6 CDs. 2004. audio compact disk 40.00 (978-0-9677280-6-3(1)) Powys.

Spaceship Earth. unabr. ed. Tom Schwartz. Narrated by Tom Schwartz. (Running Time: 3 hrs. 30 mins.). (ENG.). (J). 2009. audio compact disk 19.95 (978-1-57545-358-3(4), RP Audio Pubng) Pub: Reagent Press. Dist(s): OverDrive Inc

SpaceShipOne: Making Dreams Come True. (High Five Reading - Blue Ser.). (ENG.). (gr. 1-2). 2007. audio compact disk 5.95 (978-1-4296-1431-3(5)) CapstoneDig.

Spade Skin. Honoré de Balzac. Read by Laura Garcia. (Running Time: 3 hrs.). 2002. 16.95 (978-1-60083-260-4(1), Audiofy Corp) Iofy Corp.

Spaghetti for the Soul. Kathy Troccoli & Ellie Lofaro. Read by Laural Merlington. (ENG.). 2009. 59.99 (978-1-60775-676-7(5)) Find a World.

Spaghetti for the Soul: A Feast of Faith, Hope, & Love. unabr. ed. Kathy Troccoli & Ellie Lofaro. Read by Laural Merlington. 1 MP3-CD. (Running Time: 7 hrs.). 2008. 39.25 (978-1-4233-6922-6(X), 9781423369226, Brinc Audio MP3 Lib); 24.95 (978-1-4233-6921-9(1), 9781423369219, Brilliance MP3); 39.25 (978-1-4233-6924-0(6), 9781423369240, BADLE); 24.95 (978-1-4233-6923-3(8), 9781423369233, BAD); audio compact disk 82.25 (978-1-4233-6920-2(3), 9781423369202, BriAudCD Unabrid); audio compact disk 29.95 (978-1-4233-6919-6(X), 9781423369196, Bril Audio CD Unabri) Brilliance Audio.

***Spailpin Fanach.** 'ac Dhonncha, Sean. (ENG.). 1988. 11.95 (978-0-8023-7006-8(3)) Pub: Clo Iar-Chonnachta IRL. Dist(s): Dufour

Spain. Robert S. Kane. 1 cass. (Running Time: 1 hr.). (Passport's Travel Paks Ser.). bk. & pap. bk. 29.95 (978-0-8442-9201-4(X), Passport Bks) McGraw-Hill Trade.
An introduction to the country's culture & customs, plus brief language orientation of common words, phrases & expressions.

Spain Explores the Americas. Compiled by Benchmark Education Staff. 2005. audio compact disk 10.00 (978-1-4108-5474-2(4)) Benchmark Educ.

Span-Bktrax-Disc-Divine Revelation of Hell. Mary K. Baxter. 2 CDs. 2005. audio compact disk 14.99 (978-0-88368-888-5(3)) Whitaker Hse.

Span-Bktrax-Disc-Divine Revelation of Hell. abr. ed. Mary K. Baxter. 2005. audio compact disk 9.99 (978-0-88368-887-8(5)) Whitaker Hse.

Span-Disc-Rvr 1960 Complete Bible-Nylon Zip. 62 CDs. (SPA.). 2004. audio compact disk 89.98 (978-0-88368-821-2(2)) Whitaker Hse.

Spandau Pt. 1: The Secret Diaries. unabr. collector's ed. Albert Speer. Read by Michael Prichard. 8 cass. (Running Time: 12 hrs.). 1983. 64.00 (978-0-7366-0323-2(9), 1310-A) Books on Tape.
This account, together with his "Inside the Third Reich," comprises the most exhaustive & reliable memoir of any of the leaders of Nazi Germany. In flashbacks he recalls events & conversations in detail & brings insight to the complex personalities of Hitler & those around him.

Spandau Pt. 2: The Secret Diaries. collector's ed. Albert Speer. Read by Michael Prichard. 7 cass. (Running Time: 10 hrs. 30 min.). 1983. 64.00 (978-0-7366-0324-9(7), 1310-B) Books on Tape.

Spandau Phoenix. abr. ed. Greg Iles. Narrated by Dick Hill. 4 cass. Library ed. (Running Time: 6 hrs.). 2002. 62.25 (978-1-59086-125-7(6), 1590861256, Lib Edit) Brilliance Audio.
The Spandau Diary - what was in it? Why did the secret intelligence agencies of every major power want it? Why was a brave and beautiful woman kidnapped to get it? Why did a chain of deception and violent death lash out across the globe, from survivors of the Nazi past to warriors in this new conflict about to explode? Why did the world's entire history of World War II have to be rewritten as the future hung over a nightmare abyss?.

Spandau Phoenix. abr. ed. Greg Iles. Read by Dick Hill. (Running Time: 6 hrs.). 2006. 24.95 (978-1-4233-0215-5(X), 9781423302155, BAD) Brilliance Audio.

Spandau Phoenix. abr. ed. Greg Iles. Read by Dick Hill. 5. (Running Time: 21600 sec.). 2007. audio compact disk 14.99 (978-1-4233-3181-0(8), 9781423331810, BCD Value Price) Brilliance Audio.

Spandau Phoenix. unabr. ed. Greg Iles. Read by Dick Hill. (Running Time: 27 hrs.). 2010. 24.99 (978-1-4418-1154-7(0), 9781441811547, Brilliance MP3); 24.99 (978-1-4418-1156-1(7), 9781441811561, BAD); 39.97 (978-1-4418-1155-4(9), 9781441811554, Brinc Audio MP3 Lib); 39.97 (978-1-4418-1157-8(5), 9781441811578, BADLE); audio compact disk 39.99 (978-1-4418-1152-3(4), 9781441811523, Bril Audio CD Unabri); audio compact disk 99.97 (978-1-4418-1153-0(2), 9781441811530, BriAudCD Unabrid) Brilliance Audio.

Spanglish: Un Curso de Communicacion Celebrando Similaridad (A Course of Communication Celebrating Similarity) 1 cass. (Running Time: 1 hr.). (SPA & ENG.). 1999. pap. bk. (978-0-9674526-2-3(7)); pap. bk. (978-0-9674526-1-6(9)) Spanglish NC.

Spaniard's Daughter. Melanie Gifford & Maggie Mash. 2008. 84.95 (978-1-84652-139-3(4)); audio compact disk 99.95 (978-1-84652-140-9(8)) Pub: Magna Story GBR. Dist(s): Ulverscroft US

Spanisch in der Praxis. 1 cass. (Running Time: 1 hr. 30 min.).Tr. of Using Spanish. (GER & SPA.). 2000. bk. 75.00 (978-2-7005-1018-8(6)) Pub: Assimil FRA. Dist(s): Distribks Inc

Spanisch Ohne Muhe Heute. 1 cass. (Running Time: 1 hr. 30 min.).Tr. of Spanish with Ease. (GER & SPA., 1997. pap. bk. 75.00 (978-2-7005-1002-7(X)) Pub: Assimil FRA. Dist(s): Distribks Inc

Spanish see Acting with an Accent

Spanish. Untza Otaola Alday. (Colloquial Ser.). (ENG & SPA., 1995. bk. 21.95 (978-0-415-12681-6(9)) Pub: Routledge. Dist(s): Taylor and Fran

Spanish. Ed. by Charles Berlitz. 2 cass. (Running Time: 1 hr. 30 mins.). (Language/30 Brief Course Ser.). pap. bk. 21.95 (AF1030) J Norton Pubs.
Quick, highly condensed introduction to the words & phrases you'll need to communicate effectively in the country you're visiting. Cassettes & phrase guide book are in a vinyl album.

Spanish. Ed. by Berlitz Publishing. (In 60 MINUTES Ser.). 2008. audio compact disk 9.95 (978-981-268-396-0(8)) Pub: APA Pubns Serv SGP. Dist(s): Langenscheidt

Spanish. Ed. by Berlitz Publishing Staff. (Running Time: 1 hr.). (Berlitz Rush Hour Express Ser.). (ESP, SPA & ENG.). 2004. audio compact disk 9.95 (978-981-246-598-6(7), 465987); audio compact disk 9.95 (978-981-246-617-4(7), 466177) Pub: APA Pubns Serv SGP. Dist(s): IngramPubServ

Spanish. Created by Berlitz Publishing Staff. (Berlitz Guaranteed Ser.). (ENG., 2007. audio compact disk 19.95 (978-981-268-234-5(1)) Pub: APA Pubns Serv SGP. Dist(s): IngramPubServ

Spanish. Contrib. by Berlitz Publishing Staff. (NOVA PREMIER Ser.). (ENG.). 2008. audio compact disk 49.95 (978-0-8416-0044-7(9)) Pub: APA Pubns Serv SGP. Dist(s): IngramPubServ

Spanish. Ed. by Berlitz Publishing Staff. (Berlitz iPhrase Ser.). (ENG.). 2008. audio compact disk 12.95 (978-981-268-488-2(3)) Pub: APA Pubns Serv SGP. Dist(s): IngramPubServ

Spanish. Ed. by Berlitz Publishing Staff. 3 CDs. (ADVANCED Ser.). 2008. audio compact disk 34.95 (978-981-268-322-9(4)) Pub: Berlitz Pubng. Dist(s): Langenscheidt

Spanish. Carmen Garcia del Rio & Collins UK Staff. Contrib. by Rosi McNab. (Running Time: 3 hrs. 0 mins. 0 sec.). (Collins Easy Learning Audio Course Ser.). (ENG.). 2009. audio compact disk 13.95 (978-0-00-727175-7(1)) Pub: HarpC GBR. Dist(s): IPG Chicago

Spanish. Juan Kattán-Ibarra. 1 cass. (Running Time: 60 min.). (Language Complete Course Packs Ser.). 1993. 17.95 (Passport Bks) McGraw-Hill Trade.

Spanish. Living Language Staff. 2 cass. (Running Time: 1 hr. 20 mins.). (Language - Thirty Library). bk. 16.95 vinyl album. Moonbeam Pubns.
Using the proven method based on the famous U.S. Military accelerated language learning program, Language/30 courses stress conversationally useful words & phrases.

Spanish. Living Language Staff. 1 cass. (Running Time: 1 hr.). (Listen & Learn a Language Ser.). (SPA.). (J). bk. (TWIN 409) NewSound.

Spanish. Living Language Staff. (Vocabulearn-CE Ser.). 1996. audio compact disk 39.95 (978-1-56015-890-5(5)) Penton Overseas.

Spanish. Living Language Staff. (Vocabulearn-CE Ser.). 1996. audio compact disk 39.95 (978-1-56015-840-0(9)) Penton Overseas.

Spanish. Harold Stearns. 4 cass. (Running Time: 6 hrs.). (Accent English Ser.). (SPA & ENG.). 1991. bk. 89.50 set, incl. visual aids cards. J Norton Pubs.
English as a second language instructional program.

Spanish. Kim Mitzo Thompson & Karen Mitzo Hilderbrand. 1 cass. (Running Time: 1 hr. 40 min.). (Listen & Learn a Language Ser.). (J). (ps-6). 1994. pap. bk. 9.98 (978-1-882331-25-3(7), TWIN 409) Twin Sisters.
This unique bilingual teaching series entertains children as they begin to learn a foreign language. Words & phrases are taught using simple rhythms & then a cheerful melody incorporates the learned words in a wonderfully captivating song. Children will enjoy listening to the varied musical styles & authentic sound effects while learning becomes automatic. Over 100 words are learned.

Spanish. rev. ed. Berlitz Editors. (Running Time: 1 hr. 30 min.). (Cassette Packs Ser.). (SPA., 1998. pap. bk. 18.95 (978-2-8315-6335-0(6)) Berlitz Intl Inc.
For travelers.

Spanish. rev. ed. Berlitz Publishing Staff. 1 CD. (Running Time: 1 hr.). (Berlitz Kids Language Pack Ser.). (SPA & ENG., 2003. audio compact disk 26.95 (978-981-246-369-2(0), 463690) Pub: Berlitz Pubng. Dist(s): Langenscheidt

Spanish. rev. ed. Living Language Staff. 2 cass. (Running Time: 3 hrs.). (Basic Courses Ser.). 1993. bk. 30.00 (LivingLang) Random Info Grp.

Spanish. unabr. ed. Behind the Wheel Staff. 8 CDs. (Running Time: 8 hrs. 0 mins. 0 sec.). (ENG & SPA.). 2009. audio compact disk 49.95 (978-1-4272-0631-2(7)) Pub: Macmill Audio. Dist(s): Macmillan

Spanish. unabr. ed. Linguistics Staff. Narrated by Linguistics Staff. Created by Oasis Audio Staff. (Running Time: 2 hrs. 17 mins. 31 sec.). (Complete Idiot's Guide Ser.). (ENG.). 2005. audio compact disk 19.99 (978-1-59859-054-8(5)) Oasis Audio.

Spanish. unabr. ed. Linguistics Staff. Narrated by Linguistics Staff. Created by Oasis Audio Staff. 2 cass. (Running Time: 3 hrs.). (Complete Idiot's Guide to Languages Ser.). (ENG & SPA.). 2005. audio compact disk 9.99 (978-1-59859-117-0(7)) Oasis Audio.

Spanish. unabr. ed. Oasis Audio Staff & Linguistics Staff. Narrated by Linguistics Staff. (Complete Idiot's Guides). (ENG.). 2005. audio compact disk 39.99 (978-1-59859-060-9(X)) Oasis Audio.

Spanish. 2nd ed. Carmén del Rio et al. Contrib. by Rosi McNab. (Running Time: 3 hrs. 0 mins. 0 sec.). (Collins Easy Learning Audio Course Ser.). (SPA & ENG.). 2009. audio compact disk 17.95 (978-0-00-728754-3(2)) Pub: HarpC GBR. Dist(s): IPG Chicago

Spanish. 2nd rev. ed. Created by Berlitz Guides. (Berlitz Deluxe Language Pack Ser.). (SPA & ENG., 2008. audio compact disk 79.95 (978-981-268-406-6(9)) Pub: Berlitz Pubng. Dist(s): Langenscheidt

Spanish. 3rd rev. ed. Created by Berlitz Publishing Staff. 6 CDs. (Berlitz Basic Ser.). (SPA & ENG., 2007. audio compact disk 29.95 (978-981-268-229-1(5)) Pub: APA Pubns Serv SGP. Dist(s): Langenscheidt

Spanish. 3rd rev. abr. ed. Howard Beckerman. Created by Berlitz Publishing Staff. (Berlitz Rush Hour Ser.). 2008. audio compact disk 19.95 (978-981-268-425-7(5)) Pub: Berlitz Pubng. Dist(s): Langenscheidt

Spanish, Pack. deluxe ed. Created by Berlitz Guides Staff. 12. (Berlitz Deluxe Language Ser.). (ENG & SPA., 2005. audio compact disk 79.95 (978-981-246-707-2(6), 467076) Pub: Berlitz Pubng. Dist(s): Langenscheidt

Spanish, Set. 2004. bk. 13.99 (978-1-57583-299-9(2)) Twin Sisters.

***Spanish, Set.** Carmen García del Rio & Ronan Fitzsimons. Contrib. by Rosi McNab. (Running Time: 6 hrs. 50 mins.). (Collins Easy Learning Audio Course Ser.). (SPA & ENG.). 2010. audio compact disk 24.95 (978-0-00-734778-0(2)) Pub: HarpC GBR. Dist(s): IPG Chicago

Spanish, Vol. I. unabr. ed. Brad Caudle & Richard Caudle. Perf. by Brad Caudle et al. Perf. by Jean July et al. Illus. by Bart Harlan. 1 cass. (Running Time: 55 min.). (Rock 'N Learn Ser.). (J). (gr. 1-12). 1993. pap. bk. 12.99 (978-1-878489-19-7(4), RL919) Rock N Learn.
Original, pop/rock music with a Spanish twist & educational lyrics teach beginning Spanish. Covers counting, colors, parts of the body, travel phrases, & more. Includes illustrated book. Also can be used to teach English as a second language to native Spanish-speakers.

Spanish: Advanced III, 4 cass. (Learn While You Drive Ser.). (SPA.). 1995. bk. 47.95 (5057-AMR) Olivia & Hill.
Language course designed specifically for use in your car. The sentence in the foreign language is always followed by an English translation. Assumes a basic knowledge of the language. Complex sentence structure & grammar are taught within the context of practical everyday situations: conversations, newspapers, the day's events, medical problems, shopping, politics, schools, social occasions, etc.

Spanish: Advanced IV, 4 cass. (Running Time: 4 hrs.). (Learn While You Drive Ser.). (SPA.). 1995. bk. 44.95 (5058-AMR) Olivia & Hill.

Spanish: All the Spanish You Need to Get Started in a Simple Auido-Only Program. unabr. l.t. ed. Living Language Staff. (Starting Out In... Ser.). (ENG.). 2008. audio compact disk 15.95 (978-1-4000-2462-9(5), LivingLang) Pub: Random Info Grp. Dist(s): Random

Spanish: Basic II, 4 cass. (Running Time: 4 hrs.). (Learn While You Drive Ser.). (SPA.). 1995. bk. 47.95 (5056-AMR) Olivia & Hill.
Language course designed specifically for use in your car. The sentence in the foreign language is always followed by an English translation. Subjects covered: travel, shopping, ordering meals, placing telephone calls, telling time, counting money, using postal system, sightseeing, theater, arranging & attending business meetings & above all, making friends. Recorded with voices from various Latin American countries.

Spanish: Basic 1, 4 cass. (Running Time: 4 hrs.). (Learn While You Drive Ser.). (SPA.). 1995. bk. 44.95 (5055-AMR) Olivia & Hill.

Spanish: Language/30. Educational Services Corporation Staff. (SPA.). 2004. pap. bk. 21.95 (978-1-931850-09-4(7)) Educ Svcs DC.

Spanish: Learn to Speak & Understand Latin American Spanish with Pimsleur Language Programs. 2nd unabr. ed. Pimsleur Staff. Created by Simon and Schuster Staff. 5 CDs. (Running Time: 50 hrs. 0 mins. 0 sec.). (Basic Ser.). (SPA & ENG.). 2005. audio compact disk 24.95 (978-0-7435-5070-3(6), Pimsleur) Pub: S&S Audio. Dist(s): S and S Inc

Spanish: Learn to Speak & Understand Spanish with Pimsleur Language Programs. Pimsleur Staff. (Running Time: 11 hrs. 50 mins. 0 sec.). (Express Ser.). (ENG.). 2003. audio compact disk 11.95 (978-0-7435-3393-5(3), Pimsleur) Pub: S&S Audio. Dist(s): S and S Inc

Spanish: Speak & Read the Pimsleur Way. Pimsleur Staff. (Running Time: 7 hrs. 30 mins. 0 sec.). (Go Ser.). (ENG.). 2009. audio compact disk 29.99 (978-0-7435-9655-8(2)) Pub: S&S Audio. Dist(s): S and S Inc

Spanish: Start Speaking Today. rev. ed. Educational Services Corporation Staff. Intro. by Charles Berlitz. 2 cass. (SPA.). 1992. pap. bk. 21.95 (978-0-910542-62-3(7)) Educ Svcs DC.
Spanish self-teaching language course.

Spanish Vol. II: Includes Cassette. unabr. ed. Melissa Caudle & Trey Herbert. Perf. by Trey Herbert et al. Illus. by Anthony Guerra. 1 cass. (Running Time: 55 min.). (Rock 'N Learn Ser.). (ENG & SPA.). (J). (gr. 1-12). 1995. pap. bk. 12.99 Includes illustrated bk. (978-1-878489-34-0(8), RL934) Rock N Learn.
Fun pop/rock music with a Spanish twist teaches subject pronouns, telling time to the hour, days of the week, months of the year, "question words," phrases to use while traveling, & much more. Picks up where Rock n Learn Spanish, Vol. I leaves off. Also great for E. S. L.

Spanish - Chinese, Level 1. Vocabulearn. 2 cass. (Running Time: 90 min. ea.). (VocabuLearn Ser.). (SPA & CHI.). 1995. pap. bk. 15.95 (978-957-9330-83-1(2)) Penton Overseas.

Spanish Alive!, Level 1. Lonnie Dai Zovi. (Spanish Alive! Spanish for Young Children Ser.). (SPA., (J). (ps-3). 1990. pap. bk. 13.95 (978-0-935301-72-4(0)) Vibrante Pr.

Spanish Alive! for Children. (J). 1986. 18.95 tchr's. manual. Vibrante Pr.
A Spanish program appropriate for young children, Encompassing a variety of methods such as Total Physical Response (TPR), The Natural Method, & many others all combined to produce a fun & lasting learning experience. The lessons revolve around 10 original & classic stories & 15 jazzy & vibrant songs, all interwoven with related activities. This is an aural-oral approach, no reading is introduced.

Spanish-American War & World War I, Part 1: Knowledge Products. unabr. ed. Stromberg Joseph & Raico Ralph. Read by George C. Scott. 2006. audio compact disk 25.95 (978-0-7861-6691-6(6)) Pub: Blckstn Audio. Dist(s): NetLibrary CO

Spanish American War & World War One, Pt. 1, set. unabr. ed. Joseph Stromberg & Ralph Raico. Ed. by Wendy McElroy. Narrated by George C. Scott. 4 cass. (Running Time: 6 hrs.). Dramatization. (United States at War Ser.). (YA). (gr. 9 up). 1989. 17.95 (978-0-938935-57-5(7), 692311) Knowledge Prod.
By the turn of the twentieth century, the United States was an international power. From the Spanish-American War, America acquired colonies in both the Atlantic & Pacific; she also acquired a taste for international politics. Then the first world war erupted. The U. S. had a deep tradition of avoiding foreign wars, but the Spanish-American War had challenged this tradition. World War I would shatter it.

Spanish & English Sing & Learn by Ms Blanca. Blanca Castro. (ENG & SPA.). (J). 2006. audio compact disk 12.99 (978-0-9793633-0-6(6)) Little Xavier.

Spanish Basic Course (FSI) Advanced Level A. 18 CDs. (Running Time: 13 hrs.). (SPA.). 2005. audio compact disk 225.00 (978-1-57970-151-2(5), AFS153D) J Norton Pubs.

Spanish Basic Course (FSI) Advanced Level Part B. 18 CDs. (Running Time: 12 hrs. 30 mins.). (SPA.). 2005. audio compact disk 225.00 (978-1-57970-152-9(3), AFS170D) J Norton Pubs.

Spanish Bible. Narrated by Samuel Montoya. 48 cass. (Running Time: 72 hrs.). (SPA.). 1999. 99.98 (978-7-902031-21-9(6)) Chrstn Dup Intl.

Spanish Bible. Narrated by Samuel Montoya. 61 CDs. (Running Time: 92 hrs.). (SPA.). 1999. audio compact disk 199.98 (978-7-902031-84-4(4)) Chrstn Dup Intl.

Spanish Bible: RVR 2000. Read by Juan Ovalle. 15 CDs. (SPA.). 2005. audio compact disk 29.98 (978-0-88368-822-9(0)) Whitaker Hse.

Spanish Bible - Complete (Spoken Word) 1960 Reina-Valera Revision. Read by Samuel Montoya. 48 cass. (Running Time: 72 hrs.). (SPA.). 1994. 99.97 Set. (978-1-58968-035-7(9), 2025A) Chrstn Dup Intl.
Includes the Old & New Testaments.

Spanish Bible - New Testament (Spoken Word) 1909 Antigua Reina-Valera Revision. Read by Samuel Montoya. 12 cass. 1994. 39.97 (978-1-58968-041-8(3), 2002A) Chrstn Dup Intl.

Spanish Bible - New Testament (Spoken Word) 1960 Reina-Valera Revision. Read by Samuel Montoya. 12 cass. 1994. 29.97 (978-1-58968-034-0(0), 2006A) Chrstn Dup Intl.

Spanish Bible - Old Testament (Spoken Word) 1909 Antigua Reina-Valera Revision. Read by Samuel Montoya. 36 cass. 1994. 99.97 (978-1-58968-040-1(5), 2001A) Chrstn Dup Intl.

Spanish Bible - Old Testament (Spoken Word) 1960 Reina-Valera Revision. Read by Samuel Montoya. 36 cass. 1994. 79.97 (978-1-58968-033-3(2), 2005A) Chrstn Dup Intl.

Spanish Book of Mormon, Set. Narrated by Omar Canals. 17 cass. (SPA.). 2004. 29.95 (978-1-55503-571-6(X), 520012) Covenant Comms.

Spanish Cape Mystery. unabr. ed. Ellery Queen. Read by Scott Harrison. 7 cass. (Running Time: 10 hrs. 30 mins.). 1999. 49.95 (978-0-7861-1326-2(X), 2219) Blckstn Audio.
Rosa Godfrey & her uncle, David Kummer, were kidnapped by a grotesque, one-eyed giant; & John Marco, Rosa's handsome gigolo, was found dead on the terrace. The only clue: an opera cape wrapped around Marco's dead, naked body.

Spanish Cape Mystery. unabr. collector's ed. Ellery Queen. Read by Michael Prichard. 8 cass. (Running Time: 8 hrs.). 1978. 48.00 (978-0-7366-0103-0(1), 1111) Books on Tape.
The story is a study in jealousy, revenge, & mistaken identity. The setting is a brooding headland called the Spanish Cape. The cast contains the monstrous Captain Kidd, the ill-fated David Cumer & his beautiful niece Rosa, Rosa's suitors, including the woeful Earl Court & glib John Marco. Into this scene drives Ellery Queen, intent on a holiday. Instead he must solve a baffling kidnap-murder.

***Spanish Chat for Business CD: 180 useful business phrases & 15 conversational role plays pronounced by Native Speakers.** Julie Pospishil & Bradley Pospishil. Prod. by Spanish Chat Company. (ENG & SPA.). 2010. 14.95 (978-0-9824625-1-5(4)) Spanish Chat.

Spanish Complete Set. unabr. ed. University of Iowa, CEEDE Staff. 1 cass. (You & Others Ser.). (SPA.). 1989. 17.00 Incl. tchr's. guide & student text. (978-0-7836-0732-0(6), 8928) Triumph Learn.
Spanish readings of fictional episodes which address common situations. An awareness program for interpersonal relationships & situations.

***Spanish Crossing.** Alan LeMay. 2009. (978-1-60136-461-6(X)) Audio Holding.

Spanish Crossing. Alan LeMay. (Running Time: 0 hr. 6 mins.). 2000. 10.95 (978-1-60083-550-6(3)) Iofy Corp.

Spanish Culture Capsules. 1 cass. (Running Time: 1 hr.). 12.95 (978-0-88432-509-3(1), CCSP01) J Norton Pubs.
The brief culture capsules recorded in English at the end of each lesson unit of the introductory courses are available as separate cassettes. An indispensable aid for the vacationer or business traveler. Includes getting around in Spain, cuisine, doing business, festival, fiestas & bullfights & much more.

Spanish Doctrine & Covenants & Pearl of Great Price, Set. Narrated by Oscar Underwood. 12 cass. (SPA.). 22.95 (978-1-55503-572-3(8), 520020) Covenant Comms.

Spanish Early Explorers Audio CD Set. Based on a work by 04. (Early Explorers Ser.). (J). (gr. k-2). 2008. audio compact disk 225.00 (978-1-60437-674-6(0)) Benchmark Educ.

Spanish Early Explorers Emergent Take Home Books: Set A CD-ROM. Compiled by Benchmark Education Staff. (J). 2007. audio compact disk 10.00 (978-1-4108-9048-1(1)) Benchmark Educ.

Spanish Early Math Take Home Book: CD-ROM. Compiled by Benchmark Education Staff. (J). 2007. audio compact disk 10.00 (978-1-4108-8967-6(X)) Benchmark Educ.

Spanish Early Science Take Home Book: CD-ROM. Compiled by Benchmark Education Staff. (J). 2007. audio compact disk 10.00 (978-1-4108-8965-2(3)) Benchmark Educ.

Spanish Early Social Studies Take Home Book: CD-ROM. Compiled by Benchmark Education Staff. (J). 2007. audio compact disk 10.00 (978-1-4108-8966-9(1)) Benchmark Educ.

Spanish Early/Fluent Extension Take Home Books: CD Rom. Compiled by Benchmark Education Staff. (J). 2007. audio compact disk 10.00 (978-1-4108-9263-8(8)) Benchmark Educ.

Spanish Emergent Extension Take Home Books: CD Rom. Compiled by Benchmark Education Staff. (J). 2007. audio compact disk 10.00 (978-1-4108-9262-1(X)) Benchmark Educ.

Spanish Emergent Math Take Home Book: CD-ROM. Compiled by Benchmark Education Staff. (J). 2007. audio compact disk 10.00 (978-1-4108-8964-5(5)) Benchmark Educ.

Spanish Emergent Science Take Home Book: CD-ROM. Compiled by Benchmark Education Staff. (J). 2007. audio compact disk 10.00 (978-1-4108-8962-1(9)) Benchmark Educ.

Spanish Emergent Social Studies Take Home Book: CD-ROM. Compiled by Benchmark Education Staff. (J). 2007. audio compact disk 10.00 (978-1-4108-8963-8(7)) Benchmark Educ.

Spanish (Espanol) Contrib. by Twin Sisters Productions Staff. 1 CD. (SPA.). 1997. bk. 19.95 (978-1-57583-032-2(9)) Twin Sisters.

SPANISH Especially for You, Favorites. Scripts. Created by Sharon Mentkowski. Tey Lin. (Running Time: 30 mins.). (ENG & SPA.). (J). 2005. audio compact disk 12.99 (978-0-9774742-0-2(8)) LGE Espc For You.
SPANISH Especially For You, Favorites CD, is a fun Spanish-learning CD for young children. The CD helps children learn the Spanish terms related to colors, numbers, farm animals, school, weather, and feelings & needs. Each Spanish term is introduced contextually and with a sound effect, and each term is repeated 5 times within the CD.

SPANISH Especially for You, Personalized CD. Created by Sharon Mentkowski. Tey Lin. (Running Time: 30 mins.). (ENG & SPA.). (J). 2005. audio compact disk 15.99 (978-0-9774742-1-9(6)) LGE Espc For You.
SPANISH Especially For You, Personalized CD, is a personalized, customized, fun Spanish-learning CD for young children. The CD is personalized with a child's name on the cover and within the audio of the CD, and the customer can select six categories of child-friendly terms to be included in the CD. Each Spanish term is introduced contextually and with a sound effect, and each term is repeated 5 times within the CD.

SPANISH Especially for You, Personalized Extra-Long CD. Scripts. Created by Sharon Mentkowski. Tey Lin. (Running Time: 60 mins.). (ENG & SPA.). (J). 2005. audio compact disk 24.99 (978-0-9774742-2-6(4)) LGE Espc For You.
SPANISH Especially For You, Personalized Extra-Long CD, is a personalized, customized, fun Spanish-learning CD for young children. The CD is personalized with a child's name on the cover and within the audio of the CD, and the customer can select twelve categories of child-friendly terms to be included in the CD. Each Spanish term is introduced contextually and with a sound effect, and each term is repeated 5 times within the CD.

Spanish Fluency Kit Audio CD: Levels F-M (9-28) Benchmark Education Staff. (J). 2006. audio compact disk 10.00 (978-1-4108-7697-3(7)) Benchmark Educ.

Spanish Fluency Kit Audio CD: Levels N-U (30-50) Benchmark Education Staff. (J). 2006. audio compact disk 10.00 (978-1-4108-7698-0(5)) Benchmark Educ.

Spanish Fluent Math Take Home Book: CD-ROM. Compiled by Benchmark Education Staff. (J). 2007. audio compact disk 10.00 (978-1-4108-8970-6(X)) Benchmark Educ.

Spanish Fluent Science Take Home: CD-ROM. Compiled by Benchmark Education Staff. (J). 2007. audio compact disk 10.00 (978-1-4108-8968-3(8)) Benchmark Educ.

Spanish Fluent Social Studies Take Home Book: CD-ROM. Compiled by Benchmark Education Staff. (J). 2007. audio compact disk 10.00 (978-1-4108-8969-0(6)) Benchmark Educ.

Spanish for Banking. abr. ed. Stacey Kammerman. (Running Time: 3600 sec.). (Spanish on the Job Ser.). (ENG.). 2006. audio compact disk 15.95 (978-1-934842-34-8(6)) Pub: KAMMS Consult. Dist(s): Natl Bk Netwk

Spanish for Banking, Set. Stacey Kammerman. 2006. audio compact disk 19.95 (978-0-9788099-3-5(9)) Pub: KAMMS Consult. Dist(s): Natl Bk Netwk

Spanish for Banking (Digital) Stacey Kammerman. 2006. audio compact disk 15.95 (978-1-934842-07-2(9)) KAMMS Consult.

Spanish for Beginners. Contrib. by Angela Wilkes. 1 cass. (Passport's Languages for Beginners Ser.). (SPA.). (J). 1999. bk. 12.95 (978-0-8442-1607-2(0), 16070, Passport Bks) McGraw-Hill Trade.
Foreign language study.

Spanish for Bus-Finance. 3rd ed. Ana C. Jarvis et al. (ENG & SPA.). (C). 1988. 31.16 (978-0-669-12248-0(3)) HM Harcourt.

Spanish for Business. Albert C. Eyde & Beatriz P. Zeller. 6 cass. (Running Time: 6 hrs.). (SPA.). 1984. pap. bk. 185.00 (978-0-88432-129-3(0), S24300) J Norton Pubs.
For anyone who has already acquired a basic knowledge of Spanish & now wants to communicate effectively with the language in business situations. Provides dialogs, exercises & specialized vocabulary used in a wide range of business situations, such as the business meeting, bank & credit & import/export procedures. This course is self-testing: you may monitor your progress using the self-evaluations that follow each unit.

***Spanish for Business Cds & Book.** Albert C. Eyde & Beatriz Presedo Zeller. (ENG & SPA.). 2005. pap. bk. 185.00 (978-1-57970-338-7(0), Audio-For) J Norton Pubs.

Spanish for Children. AMR Staff. 1 cass. (AMR Language Ser.). (J). (gr. 3-9). 1988. 13.95 (978-1-55536-473-1(X)) Oasis Audio.
This AMR product is designed to teach children simple Spanish words & phrases in a playful setting. Songs & games by the main character "Senor Toto" are introduced.

Spanish for Child Care Facilities. Ed. by Sam L. Slick & Maryjane Dunn. 4 cass. (Running Time: 2 hrs. 15 min.). (C). 1999. ring bd. 34.95 (978-1-888467-19-2(3)) Command Spanish.

Spanish for Communication. 3rd ed. Ana C. Jarvis et al. (ENG & SPA.). (C). 1988. 31.16 (978-0-669-12246-6(7)) HM Harcourt.

Spanish for Construction. abr. ed. Stacey Kammerman. (Running Time: 3600 sec.). (Spanish on the Job Ser.). (ENG.). 2006. audio compact disk 15.95 (978-1-934842-32-4(X)) Pub: KAMMS Consult. Dist(s): Natl Bk Netwk

Spanish for Construction, Set. Stacey Kammerman. 2006. audio compact disk 19.95 (978-0-9762750-6-0(6)) Pub: KAMMS Consult. Dist(s): Natl Bk Netwk

Spanish for Construction (Amazon) Stacey Kammerman. 2006. audio compact disk 15.95 (978-0-9788099-9-7(8)) KAMMS Consult.

Spanish for Construction (Digital) Stacey Kammerman. 2006. audio compact disk 15.95 (978-1-934842-08-9(7)) KAMMS Consult.

Spanish for Construction Site Supervisors. Sam Slick. (ENG.). 2009. 14.95 (978-1-888467-74-1(6)) Command Spanish.

Spanish for Dental Hygienists - Audio CD. Sam Slick. (ENG.). 2009. 14.95 (978-1-888467-82-6(7)) Command Spanish.

Spanish for Dental Staff. Sam L. Slick. (SPA.). 1997. ring bd. 34.95 (978-1-888467-12-3(6)) Command Spanish.

Spanish for Dentists - Audio CD. Sam Slick. (ENG.). 2009. 14.95 (978-1-888467-81-9(9)) Command Spanish.

Spanish for Dummies. unabr. ed. Jessica Langemeier. Read by Becky Wilmes & Angel Banda. (YA). 2008. 34.99 (978-1-60514-508-2(4)) Find a World.

Spanish for Dummies Audio Set. Jessica Langemeier. (For Dummies Ser.). (SPA & ENG.). 2007. audio compact disk 19.99 (978-0-470-09585-0(7), For Dummies) Wiley US.

Spanish for Educators. 1 CD. (Running Time: 1 hr). 2003. audio compact disk 19.95 (978-0-9762750-0-8(7)) KAMMS Consult.
The CD is designed for educators, counselors, administrators and other school officials who interact with Hispanic students. Educators will benefit from this Audio CD by learning words and phrases that will help them to communicate more efficiently with Spanish-speaking students and their parents. This improved communication will result in better understanding and performance of the Spanish-speaking students and enhanced parent/teacher relationships. It contains over 350 Spanish words and phrases that relate to classroom instruction and parent conferences.

Spanish for Educators. abr. ed. Stacey Kammerman. (Running Time: 3600 sec.). (Spanish on the Job Ser.). (ENG.). 2005. audio compact disk 15.95 (978-1-934842-27-0(3)) Pub: KAMMS Consult. Dist(s): Natl Bk Netwk

Spanish for Educators, Set. Stacey Kammerman. 2 CDs. (Running Time: 2 hrs). 2006. audio compact disk 19.95 (978-0-9762750-9-1(0)) Pub: KAMMS Consult. Dist(s): Natl Bk Netwk

Spanish for Educators (Digital) Stacey Kammerman. 2005. audio compact disk 15.95 (978-1-934842-09-6(5)) KAMMS Consult.

Spanish for Emergency Medical Services - Audio CD. Sam Slick. (ENG.). 2009. 14.95 (978-1-888467-86-4(X)) Command Spanish.

Spanish for Financial Institutions - Audio CD. Sam Slick. (ENG.). 2009. 14.95 (978-1-888467-70-3(3)) Command Spanish.

Spanish for Health. Melston et al. 2000. reel tape 16.75 (978-0-8384-0783-7(8)) Heinle.

Spanish for Health Care. Stacey Kammerman. 2 CDs. (Running Time: 2 hrs). 2006. audio compact disk 19.95 (978-0-9762750-3-9(1)) Pub: KAMMS Consult. Dist(s): Natl Bk Netwk

Spanish for Health Care: Student Audio CDs. Patricia Rush. 3 CDs. audio compact disk 19.97 (978-0-13-096905-7(2)) PH School.

Spanish for Health Care Workers: A Cassette Study Course for Beginning to Intermediate Spanish Speakers. unabr. ed. Sarah Ison. Read by Translation Services International Staff. 2 cass. (Running Time: 1 hr. 40 min.). 1997. pap. bk. & wbk. ed. 44.95 (978-0-9655168-4-6(9)) Around Wrld Pub.
Spanish instruction for medical personnel. Covers adult & pediatric exams, OB/GYN, emergency care & public health topics.

Spanish for Healthcare. abr. ed. Stacey Kammerman. (Running Time: 3600 sec.). (Spanish on the Job Ser.). (ENG.). 2006. audio compact disk 15.95 (978-1-934842-26-3(5)) Pub: KAMMS Consult. Dist(s): Natl Bk Netwk

Spanish for Healthcare (Digital) Stacey Kammerman. 2006. audio compact disk 15.95 (978-1-934842-10-2(9)) KAMMS Consult.

Spanish for Home Managers. unabr. ed. Joseph N. Granados & Mary P. Granados. 2 cass. (Running Time: 2 hrs.). 1984. pap. bk. 29.50 (978-1-879090-12-5(0), S107) Granados Schl.
Spanish language instruction in conversation used to communicate with household employees.

Spanish for Hospital Nurses - Audio CD. Sam Slick. (ENG.). 2008. 14.95 (978-1-888467-73-4(8)) Command Spanish.

Spanish for Hospitality. 1 CD. (Running Time: 75 mins). 2005. audio compact disk 15.95 (978-0-9762750-1-5(5)) KAMMS Consult.

Spanish for Housekeeping. abr. ed. Stacey Kammerman. (Running Time: 3600 sec.). (Spanish on the Job Ser.). (ENG.). 2006. audio compact disk 15.95 (978-1-934842-30-0(3)) Pub: KAMMS Consult. Dist(s): Natl Bk Netwk

Spanish for Housekeeping, Set. Stacey Kammerman. 2006. audio compact disk 19.95 (978-0-9788099-2-8(0)) Pub: KAMMS Consult. Dist(s): Natl Bk Netwk

Spanish for Housekeeping (Digital) Stacey Kammerman. 2006. audio compact disk 15.95 (978-1-934842-11-9(7)) KAMMS Consult.

Spanish for Human Resources. abr. ed. Stacey Kammerman. (Running Time: 3600 sec.). (Spanish on the Job Ser.). (ENG.). 2006. audio compact disk 15.95 (978-1-934842-24-9(9)) Pub: KAMMS Consult. Dist(s): Natl Bk Netwk

Spanish for Human Resources, Set. Stacey Kammerman. 2006. audio compact disk 19.95 (978-0-9762750-7-7(4)) Pub: KAMMS Consult. Dist(s): Natl Bk Netwk

Spanish for Human Resources (Digital) Stacey Kammerman. 2006. audio compact disk 15.95 (978-1-934842-12-6(5)) KAMMS Consult.

Spanish for Kids: And the Whole Family. unabr. ed. Pamela Rand. Perf. by Erika Luckett & Jackie Rago. Illus. by Sara Mordecai. Intro. by Ivan Barzakov. 2 cass. (Running Time: 1 hr.). (J). (ps-6). 1990. pap. bk. 19.95 Incl. activity wkbk., parental guide. (978-1-878245-01-4(5)) OptimaLearning.
Original songs & lively conversations by native speakers. Based on renown OptimaLearning method. Course is highly motivational for children & whole family.

Spanish for Landscaping. abr. ed. Stacey Kammerman. (Running Time: 3600 sec.). (Spanish on the Job Ser.). (ENG.). 2006. audio compact disk 15.95 (978-1-934842-29-4(X)) Pub: KAMMS Consult. Dist(s): Natl Bk Netwk

Spanish for Landscaping, Set. Stacey Kammerman. 2006. audio compact disk 19.95 (978-0-9788099-1-1(2)) Pub: KAMMS Consult. Dist(s): Natl Bk Netwk

Spanish for Landscaping (Digital) Stacey Kammerman. 2006. audio compact disk 15.95 (978-1-934842-13-3(3)) KAMMS Consult.

***Spanish for Latter Day Saints - Level 1: Getting to Know Your Neighbors.** Adrian R. Escalante. (ENG.). 2010. pap. bk. 149.00 (978-0-9768797-0-1(0)) Daily Dose.

***Spanish for Latter Day Saints - Level 2: Sharing the Gospel in Spanish.** Adrian R. Escalante. (ENG.). 2010. pap. bk. 149.00 (978-0-9768797-2-5(7)) Daily Dose.

***Spanish for Latter Day Saints - Levels 1 And 2: Prepare to Serve.** Adrian R. Escalante. (ENG.). 2010. pap. bk. 249.00 (978-0-9768797-4-9(3)) Daily Dose.

Spanish for Law Enforcement. AMR Staff. 4 cass. (Running Time: 6 hr.). (AMR Language Ser.). (SPA.). 1998. pap. bk. 49.95 (978-1-886463-40-0(9)) Oasis Audio.
Spanish language learning for law enforcement & fire fighters.

Spanish for Law Enforcement. Kate Brown & James W. Moore. 2001. reel tape 16.75 (978-0-8384-0792-9(7)) Heinle.

Spanish for Law Enforcement. Patricia Rush & Patricia Houston. 3 CDs. stu. ed. 19.97 (978-0-13-193150-3(4)) PH School.

Spanish for Law Enforcement. abr. ed. Stacey Kammerman. (Running Time: 3600 sec.). (Spanish on the Job Ser.). (ENG.). 2006. audio compact disk 15.95 (978-1-934842-28-7(1)) Pub: KAMMS Consult. Dist(s): Natl Bk Netwk

Spanish for Law Enforcement. 3rd ed. Ana C. Jarvis et al. (ENG & SPA.). (C). 1988. 31.16 (978-0-669-12253-4(X)) HM Harcourt.

Spanish for Law Enforcement, Set. Stacey Kammerman. 2 CDs. (Running Time: 2 hrs). 2006. audio compact disk 19.95 (978-0-9762750-2-2(3)) Pub: KAMMS Consult. Dist(s): Natl Bk Netwk

Spanish for Law Enforcement (Digital) Stacey Kammerman. 2006. audio compact disk 15.95 (978-1-934842-14-0(1)) KAMMS Consult.

Spanish for Law Enforcement Officers. Sam Slick. (ENG.). 2008. 14.95 (978-1-888467-69-7(X)) Command Spanish.

Spanish for Library Personnel - Audio CD. Sam Slick. (ENG.). 2008. 14.95 (978-1-888467-75-8(4)) Command Spanish.

Spanish for Med-Personnel. 3rd ed. Ana C. Jarvis et al. (ENG & SPA.). (C). 1988. 31.16 (978-0-669-12250-3(5)) HM Harcourt.

Spanish for Medical Office Nurses - Audio CD. Sam Slick. (ENG.). 2008. 14.95 (978-1-888467-72-7(X)) Command Spanish.

Spanish for Medical Personnel. Created by Donna Lynn Smith. (ENG.). 2007. audio compact disk 19.95 (978-0-9793655-0-8(3)) R Language.

Spanish for Medical Receptionist. abr. ed. Stacey Kammerman. (Running Time: 3600 sec.). (Spanish on the Job Ser.). (ENG.). 2006. audio compact disk 15.95 (978-1-934842-33-1(8)) Pub: KAMMS Consult. Dist(s): Natl Bk Netwk

Spanish for Medical Receptionist (Digital) Stacey Kammerman. 2006. audio compact disk 15.95 (978-1-934842-15-7(X)) KAMMS Consult.

Spanish for Medical Receptionists. Stacey Kammerman. 2006. audio compact disk 19.95 (978-0-9762750-4-6(X)) Pub: KAMMS Consult. Dist(s): Natl Bk Netwk

Spanish for Nursing. Sam L. Slick. 5 cass. (Running Time: 3 hrs. 45 min.). 1998. ring bd. 34.95 (978-1-888467-13-0(4)) Command Spanish.
Spanish for nursing professionals.

Spanish for OB/GYN Clinics - Digital Multimedia Course Vol. 8: 2 books, 4 Audio CDs & 2 DVDs (120 mins. Ea.) 7th ed. Scripts. Maria Susana Peluffo. Created by Julio Aramburu. 4 Cds, 2 Dvds, 2 Boo. (Running Time: 240 mins.). Dramatization. (SPA & ENG.). 2004. DVD & audio compact disk 299.00 (978-0-9758550-3-4(4)) Spanish Audio.
CONTENTS:GUIDE TO PRONUNCIATION-GREETINGS AND COMMON PHRASES-GENERAL VOCABULARY-THE HUMAN BODY-GETTING ACQUAINTED WITH THE HOSPITAL-GIVING DIRECTIONS-SOCIAL AND FINANCIAL INFORMATION-ADMISSION , SIGNATURES AND PERMISSIONS-ADMISSION OF PATIENT TO THE ROOM-VISITING HOURS-NURSING CARE AND HYGIENE-DISCHARGE-PREGNANCY AND DELIVERY-PRESENT PREGNANCY-MONTHLY EXAMINATIONS-LABOR AND DELIVERY-INFORMATION FOR CERTIFICATE OF LIVE BIRTH-FAMILY PLANNING-BIRTH CONTROL PILL-DIAPHRAGM-CONDOMS, FOAM AND VAGINAL TABLETS-IUD-RHYTHM METHOD-INFANT CARE: IMMUNIZATION -PREVENTIVE CARE-CLEANLINESS / AIR-PRECAUTIONS-LACTATION AND NUTRITION-REPRODUCTIVE SYSTEM-PHYSICAL EXAMINATION-VAGINAL DISCHARGE-PELVIC INFLAMMATION-SEXUAL FUNCTION-BREAST EXAM-STERILIZATION-MENOPAUSE-INFERTILITY MAN-INFERTILITY WOMAN-COMMON PEDIATRIC PROBLEMS:VOMITING AND FEVER-CHILD WITH ASTHMA-DIARRHEA AND CONSTIPATION-CHILDHOOD ILLNESSES:DIPHTERIA-WOOPING COUGH-MEASLES / SCARLET FEVER-CHICKEN POX / MUMPS-CARE OF THE PATIENT BEFORE SURGERY-CARE OF THE PATIENT AFTER THE OPERATION-DICTIONARY OF TERMS-ANATOMICAL TERMS-PREGNANCY, CHILDBIRTH AND POSTNATAL CARE.

Spanish for Pharmacy Personnel - Audio CD. Sam Slick. (ENG.). 2008. 14.95 (978-1-888467-76-5(2)) Command Spanish.

Spanish for Physical Therapy - Audio CD. Sam Slick. (ENG.). 2009. 14.95 (978-1-888467-84-0(3)) Command Spanish.

Spanish for Physicians - Audio CD. Sam Slick. (ENG.). 2008. 14.95 (978-1-888467-77-2(0)) Command Spanish.

Spanish for Police & Firefighters, Jose Cerrudo. 5 cass. (Running Time: 4 hrs.). (SPA.). 1994. pap. bk. 75.00 (978-0-88432-826-1(0), SSP450) J Norton Pubs.
Designed to teach both basic & specialized expressions, phrases & terminology needed to communicate with Spanish-speaking people in a variety of human services situations.

Spanish for Police & Firefighters. José Cerrudo. 5 CDs. (Running Time: 4 hrs.). Orig. Title: Practical Spanish for Policemen & Firemen. (SPA.). 2005.

audio compact disk 75.00 (978-1-57970-268-7(6), SSP450D, Audio-For) J Norton Pubs.
This practical audio/book course is designed to teach both basic and specialized expressions, phrases, and terminology needed to communicate with Spanish-speaking people in a variety of human-services situations.

Spanish for Professionals Medical Vocabulary. unabr. ed. Maria L. Oliveira. Read by Maria Oliveira & Glen Cordon. 1 cass. (Running Time: 1 hr.). 1997. 15.95 (978-1-888165-30-2(8)) M Oliveira.
Provides the necessary Spanish vocabulary to facilitate communication between Spanish speaking patients & health care providers.

Spanish for Real Estate. abr. ed. Stacey Kammerman. (Running Time: 3600 sec.). (Spanish on the Job Ser.). (ENG.). 2006. audio compact disk 15.95 (978-1-934842-31-7(1)) Pub: KAMMS Consult. Dist(s): Natl Bk Netwk

Spanish for Real Estate, Set. Stacey Kammerman. 2006. audio compact disk 19.95 (978-0-9762750-5-3(8)) Pub: KAMMS Consult. Dist(s): Natl Bk Netwk

Spanish for Real Estate (Digital) Stacey Kammerman. 2006. audio compact disk 15.95 (978-1-934842-16-4(8)) KAMMS Consult.

Spanish for Real Estate Sales - Audio CD. Sam Slick. (ENG.). 2008. 14.95 (978-1-888467-78-9(9)) Command Spanish.

Spanish for Respiratory Therapists - Audio CD. Sam Slick. (ENG.). 2009. 14.95 (978-1-888467-83-3(5)) Command Spanish.

Spanish for Restaurant Staff. Ed. by Sam L. Slick. 4 cass. (Running Time: 2 hrs. 45 min.). (C). 2000. ring bd. 34.95 (978-1-888467-24-6(X)) Command Spanish.

Spanish for Restaurants. abr. ed. Stacey Kammerman. (Running Time: 3600 sec.). (Spanish on the Job Ser.). (ENG.). 2006. audio compact disk 15.95 (978-1-934842-25-6(7)) Pub: KAMMS Consult. Dist(s): Natl Bk Netwk

Spanish for Restaurants, Set. Stacey Kammerman. 2006. audio compact disk 19.95 (978-0-9762750-8-4(2)) Pub: KAMMS Consult. Dist(s): Natl Bk Netwk

Spanish for Restaurants (Digital) Stacey Kammerman. 2006. audio compact disk 15.95 (978-1-934842-17-1(6)) KAMMS Consult.

Spanish for Retail - Audio CD. Sam Slick. (ENG.). 2009. 14.95 (978-1-888467-85-7(1)) Command Spanish.

Spanish for Retail Business. abr. ed. Stacey Kammerman. (Running Time: 3600 sec.). (Spanish on the Job Ser.). (ENG.). 2006. audio compact disk 15.95 (978-1-934842-35-5(4)) Pub: KAMMS Consult. Dist(s): Natl Bk Netwk

Spanish for Retail Business, Set. Stacey Kammerman. 2006. audio compact disk 19.95 (978-0-9788099-0-4(4)) Pub: KAMMS Consult. Dist(s): Natl Bk Netwk

Spanish for Retail Business (Digital) Stacey Kammerman. 2006. audio compact disk 15.95 (978-1-934842-18-8(4)) KAMMS Consult.

Spanish for Retail Sales. 2000. spiral bd. (978-1-888467-22-2(3)) Command Spanish.

Spanish for School Personnel. Patricia Rush & Patricia Houston. 3 CDs. stu. ed. 19.97 (978-0-13-140982-8(4)) PH School.

Spanish for School Teachers - Audio CD. Sam Slick. (ENG.). 2009. 14.95 (978-1-888467-80-2(0)) Command Spanish.

Spanish for Social Services. 3rd ed. Ana C. Jarvis et al. (ENG & SPA.). (C). 1988. 31.16 (978-0-669-12255-8(6)) HM Harcourt.

Spanish for the Business Traveler. Terri Morrison & Wayne A. Conaway. 1 cass. (ENG & SPA.). 1996. bk. 21.95 (978-0-8120-8399-6(7)) Barron.

Spanish for the Community - Audio CD. Sam Slick. (ENG.). 2008. 14.95 (978-1-888467-71-0(1)) Command Spanish.

Spanish for the Health Professional. 4 CDs. (Running Time: 3 hrs.). (SPA.). 2005. audio compact disk 65.00 (978-1-57970-143-7(4), SSP300D) J Norton Pubs.

Spanish for the Health Professional, Jose Cerrudo. 4 cass. (Running Time: 3 hrs.). (SPA.). 1994. pap. bk. 65.00 (978-0-88432-650-2(0), SSP300) J Norton Pubs.
Designed for admission personnel, nurses, volunteer hospital aides, medical technicians & paramedics who need to communicate with Spanish-speaking patients.

Spanish for the Physician's Office. Ed. by Sam L. Slick. 4 cass. (Running Time: 2 hrs.). (C). 1999. ring bd. 34.95 (978-1-888467-14-7(2)) Command Spanish.

Spanish for the Workforce - Audio CD. Sam Slick. (ENG.). 2009. 14.95 (978-1-888467-79-6(7)) Command Spanish.

Spanish for Travel - Audio CD. Sam Slick. (ENG.). 2009. 14.95 (978-1-888467-87-1(8)) Command Spanish.

Spanish for Your Trip. Berlitz Publishing Staff. (Berlitz for Your Trip Ser.). 2007. audio compact disk 9.95 (978-981-268-047-1(0)) Pub: Berlitz Pubng. Dist(s): Langenscheidt

Spanish Gambit see Tapestry of Spies

Spanish Game. unabr. ed. Charles Cumming. Narrated by Simon Vance. (Running Time: 11 hrs. 0 mins. 0 sec.). (ENG.). 2008. lab manual ed. 69.99 (978-1-4001-4042-8(0)); audio compact disk 24.99 (978-1-4001-6042-6(1)); audio compact disk 34.99 (978-1-4001-1042-1(4)) Pub: Tantor Media. Dist(s): IngramPubServ

Spanish Genesis. Narrated by Samuel Montoya. 4 cass. (Running Time: 6 hrs.). (SPA.). 1997. 9.98 (978-7-902032-24-7(7)) Chrstn Dup Intl.

Spanish Genesis 1960. Narrated by Samuel Montoya. 4 cass. 9.98 (2007A) Chrstn Dup Intl.

Spanish Grammar Songs. unabr. ed. Gale Mackey. 1 cass. (Running Time: 15 Min.). (SPA.). (J). 1997. 11.95 (978-0-929724-41-6(0)) Command Performance.
Simple, catchy songs for learning irregular Spanish verb forms.

Spanish Grammar with Pronunciation. 1 cass. (Running Time: 80 min.). Orig. Title: Spanish Grammar with Pronunciation Tape. (SPA.). (YA). (gr. 10-12). 1992. bk. 24.95 (978-0-88432-455-3(9), SSP350) J Norton Pubs.
Practical & concise presentation of the essentials of Spanish grammar.

Spanish Grammar with Pronunciation. 1 CD. (Running Time: 80 mins.). Orig. Title: Spanish Grammar with Pronunciation Tape. (SPA.). 2005. audio compact disk 24.95 (978-1-57970-269-4(4), SSP350D, Audio-For) J Norton Pubs.
This practical and concise presentation of the essentials of Spanish grammar was designed to supplement and aid self-study. Explanations have been made as brief as possible. Spanish translations of the end-of-unit exercises are given in the extensive appendix.

Spanish Grammar with Pronunciation Tape see Spanish Grammar with Pronunciation

Spanish Hablemos en Espanol. Mariano Garcia. 1 cass. 175.00 10 cass. (978-0-8325-9659-9(0), Natl Textbk Co); 175.00 10 cass. (978-0-8325-9654-4(X), Natl Textbk Co) M-H Contemporary.
Using immediate classroom situations, plus real-life experiences, students quickly learn to converse & acquire the cultural awareness needed to interact with confidence in casual, social & work situations.

Spanish Hawk. James Pattinson & James Pattinson. (Soundings (CDs) Ser.). 2007. audio compact disk 59.95 (978-1-84559-443-5(6)) Pub: ISIS Lrg Prnt GBR. Dist(s): Ulverscroft US

Spanish Hawk. unabr. ed. James Pattinson & James Pattinson. Read by Peter Wickham. 5 cass. (Soundings Ser.). 2007. 49.95 (978-1-84559-325-4(1)) Pub: ISIS Lrg Prnt GBR. Dist(s): Ulverscroft US

Spanish I, 1996th ed. Paul Pimsleur. 16 cass. (Running Time: 16 hrs.). (Pimsleur Language Learning Ser.). 1996. pap. bk. & stu. ed. 345.00 SyberVision.

Spanish I: Learn to Speak & Understand Latin American Spanish with Pimsleur Language Programs. 2nd unabr. ed. Pimsleur Staff. 16 CDs. (Running Time: 160 hrs. 0 mins. 0 sec.). (Comprehensive Ser.). (SPA & ENG.). 2002. audio compact disk 345.00 (978-0-7435-2357-8(1), Pimsleur) Pub: S&S Audio. Dist(s): S and S Inc

Spanish I: Learn to Speak & Understand Spanish with Pimsleur Language Programs. 2nd rev. ed. Pimsleur Staff & Pimsleur. 8 CDs. (Running Time: 400 hrs. 0 mins. NaN sec.). (Quick & Simple Ser.). (SPA & ENG.). 2002. audio compact disk 19.95 (978-0-7435-2355-4(5), Pimsleur) Pub: S&S Audio. Dist(s): S and S Inc

Spanish I Basic. Paul Pimsleur. 8 lessons on 4 cass. (Pimsleur Language Learning Ser.). 1995. 29.95 (52161-1) SyberVision.

Spanish (Iberian) unabr. ed. Pimsleur Staff. 30 lessons on 16 ca. (SPA.). 295.00 Set. (978-0-671-57948-7(7), Pimsleur) S&S Audio.

Spanish II, Set. 1996th ed. Paul Pimsleur. 16 cass. (Pimsleur Language Learning Ser.). 1996. pap. bk. & stu. ed. 345.00 (0671-57071-4) SyberVision.

Spanish II: Learn to Speak & Understand Latin American Spanish. 3rd ed. Pimsleur Staff. (Running Time: 160 hrs. 0 mins. 0 sec.). (Comprehensive Ser.). (ENG.). 2003. audio compact disk 345.00 (978-0-7435-2893-1(X), Pimsleur) Pub: S&S Audio. Dist(s): S and S Inc

Spanish III, 1994th ed. Paul Pimsleur. 16 cass. (Running Time: 16 hrs.). (Pimsleur Language Learning Ser.). 1994. pap. bk. & stu. ed. 345.00 SyberVision.

Spanish III: Learn to Speak & Understand Latin American Spanish with Pimsleur Language Programs. 2nd ed. Pimsleur Staff. (Running Time: 160 hrs. 0 mins. 0 sec.). (Comprehensive Ser.). (ENG.). 2004. audio compact disk 345.00 (978-0-7435-2895-5(6), Pimsleur) Pub: S&S Audio. Dist(s): S and S Inc

Spanish in a Minute. 1 cass. (Language in a Minute Cassette Ser.). 5.95 (978-0-943351-15-5(4), XC1002) Cimino Pub Grp.
Feel at home in any foreign country with these 101 esssential words & phrases. Hear each word introduced in English, hear them pronounced by a Voice of America instructor. Practice at your own pace, you can check yourself with the wallet sized dictionary included.

Spanish in Health Care. unabr. ed. Jane Westberg. Read by Jane Westberg. Read by Wendy C. Rodriguez et al. 2 cass. (Running Time: 2 hrs. 2 min.). 1986. pap. bk. 55.00 set, incl. binder & 2 user's guides. (978-0-938540-17-5(3)) CIS.
Designed to help non-Spanish speakers gain sufficient proficiency for conducting clinical interviews & physical exams with Spanish-speaking patients. Covers: single words & short phrases, phrases & short sentences, physical exam, & history.

Spanish in Just One Week: Answer Keys & Tapescript. Mark Frobose. (SPA., 2002. per. 67.00 (978-1-893564-72-5(X)); per. 23.00 (978-1-893564-73-2(8)) Macmill Audio.

Spanish in Review. 2nd ed. John B. Dalbor & H. Tracy Sturcken. (ENG.). (C). 1992. 66.95 (978-0-471-54568-2(6), JWiley) Wiley US.

Spanish in the Field, Carmen P. Clough et al. 4 cass. (Running Time: 4 hrs.). 1990. pap. bk. 59.95 incl. dictionary. Ag Access.
Teaches practical Spanish for ranchers, farmers or vintners, with extensive vocabulary, phrases & sentences that are basic to the subject of each chapter, & helpful exercises. Everything is presented in both Spanish & English.

Spanish in the Field, Set. Carmen P. Clough et al. 4 cass. 1990. 35.95 Pub: Ag Access. Dist(s): Fertile Ground Bks

Spanish in Three Months, Courses 1-6. unabr. ed. Joseph N. Granados & Mary P. Granados. 48 cass. (Running Time: 41 hrs. 16 min.). (SPA & ENG.). 1990. pap. bk. 690.00 (978-1-879090-05-7(8), S100) Granados Schl.
6 volume comprehensive Spanish language course for the English-speaker. Course work covers basic, intermediate & advanced levels.

Spanish in Three Months: Basic Spanish I. unabr. ed. 8 cass. (Running Time: 60 min. per cass.). (Granados School of Languages Ser.). bk. 95.00 Books on Tape.
The emphasis of this course is the mastery of the basic recurring structures of Spanish which allows the student to absorb vocabulary quickly. Exercises are programmed so that the student is speaking & thinking in Spanish immediately. Includes 60 page text.

Spanish In Three Months: Basic Spanish Two. unabr. ed. 8 cass. (Running Time: 8 hrs.). 95.00 (GS2) Books on Tape.
This course is designed for those who have completed Basic Spanish I, or students who have knowledge of Spanish, such as basic Spanish courses in high school or college.

Spanish in Three Months: Intermediate Spanish I. unabr. ed. 8 cass. (Running Time: 8 hrs.). (Granados School of Languages Ser.). bk. 100.00 (GSI1) Books on Tape.
The emphasis of this course is the mastery of the more advanced tenses which gives our student a complete knowledge of simple as well as compound tenses, such as the Present, Past, Future & Conditional Perfects. This course also gives the student an indepth study of the usage of Prepositions, Conjunctions, as well as Special Verbs in their Relationship to certain prepositions & prepositional phrases. The student is introduced to more advanced vocabulary. Also, throughout the whole course & especially in the review tapes, there is a constant review of all that has been learned from the beginning with Basic Spanish I. Includes 79 page text.

Spanish in Three Months: Course 1: Basic Spanish One. unabr. ed. Joseph N. Granados & Mary P. Granados. 8 cass. (Running Time: 7 hrs. 22 min.). (SPA & ENG.). 1982. pap. bk. 105.00 (978-1-879090-06-4(6), S101) Granados Schl.
Comprehensive basic Spanish language course for self-instruction.

Spanish in Three Months: Course 2: Basic Spanish Two. unabr. ed. Joseph N. Granados & Mary P. Granados. 8 cass. (Running Time: 7 hrs. 28 min.). (SPA & ENG.). 1983. pap. bk. 105.00 (978-1-879090-07-1(4), S102) Granados Schl.
Comprehensive basic level 2, Spanish language course for self-instruction.

Spanish in Three Months: Course 3: Intermediate Spanish One. unabr. ed. Joseph N. Granados & Mary P. Granados. 8 cass. (Running Time: 7 hrs. 7 min.). (SPA & ENG.). 1985. pap. bk. 115.00 (978-1-879090-08-8(2), S103) Granados Schl.
Comprehensive intermediate level Spanish language course for self-instruction.

Spanish in Three Months: Course 4: Intermediate Spanish Two. unabr. ed. Joseph N. Granados & Mary P. Granados. 8 cass. (Running Time: 6 hrs. 27 min.). (SPA & ENG.). 1986. pap. bk. 115.00 (978-1-879090-09-5(0), S104) Granados Schl.
Comprehensive intermediate level 2 Spanish language course for self-instruction.

Spanish in Three Months, Course 5: Advanced Spanish: Idioms One. unabr. ed. Joseph N. Granados & Mary P. Granados. 8 cass. (Running Time: 6 hrs. 36 min.). (SPA & ENG.). 1990. pap. bk. 125.00 (978-1-879090-10-1(4), S105) Granados Schl.
Comprehensive study of advanced Spanish grammar, vocabulary & idioms for self-instruction.

Spanish in Three Months, Course 6: Advanced Spanish: Idioms Two. unabr. ed. Joseph N. Granados & Mary P. Granados. 8 cass. (Running Time: 6 hrs. 16 min.). (SPA & ENG.). 1990. pap. bk. 125.00 (978-1-879090-11-8(2), S106) Granados Schl.
Comprehensive study of advanced Spanish grammar, vocabulary & idioms, level 2 for self-instruction.

***Spanish in 10 Minutes a Day.** Kristine K. Kershul. ([i]10 minutes a day[/i][sup]R[/sup] AUDIO CD Ser.). (ENG.). 2007. audio compact disk 42.95 (978-1-931873-28-4(3)) Pub: Bilingual Bks. Dist(s): Midpt Trade

Spanish in 30 Days. 2nd rev. abr. ed. Created by Berlitz Guides. (Berlitz in 30 Days Ser.). 2007. audio compact disk 19.95 (978-981-268-225-3(2)) Pub: APA Pubns Serv SGP. Dist(s): Langenscheidt

Spanish Indispensables. unabr. ed. 1 cass. (Running Time: 25 min.). 1996. 11.95 (978-0-88432-947-3(X), CSP104) J Norton Pubs.
50 useful phrases for foreign travel.

Spanish Inquisition, unabr. ed. Cecil Roth. Read by Nadia May. 6 cass. (Running Time: 8 hrs. 30 mins.). 1995. 44.95 (978-0-7861-0880-0(0), 1543) Blckstn Audio.
In 1478 Pope Sixtus IV issued the fatal Bull empowering the Spanish sovereigns to establish tribunals to exterminate heresy from within their realms. For the 356 years which followed, the Inquisition ruthlessly pursued a course of blood, whose goal was no less than the annihilation of all people who were not sincere Roman Catholic Christians. In the beginning their sights were set upon Jews, but the Holy Office later expanded its range of victims to include Protestants, mystics & non-conformists of every type.

Spanish Is Fun Book A Audio Program Bk. A: Lively Lessons for Beginners. Heywood Wald. 4 CDs with script. (J). 2004. (978-0-87720-145-8(5), N529CD) AMSCO Sch.

***Spanish IV, Comprehensive: Learn to Speak & Understand Spanish with Pimsleur Language Programs.** Pimsleur. (Running Time: 160 hrs. 0 mins. 0 sec.). (Comprehensive Ser.). (ENG.). 2010. audio compact disk 345.00 (978-0-671-31796-6(2), Pimsleur) Pub: S&S Audio. Dist(s): S and S Inc

Spanish Language. 2005. 44.99 (978-1-59895-000-7(2)) Find a World.

Spanish Language Study Level 2. George Holod. 1 CD. (Running Time: 60 mins). 2003. audio compact disk 16.00 (978-0-923586-54-6(7)) Data Syst CA.

Spanish (Latin American) for Speakers of English, One. rev. ed. 16 cass. (Running Time: 15 hrs.). (Pimsleur Tapes Ser.). (SPA.). 1996. 345.00 set. (18367, Pimsleur) S&S Audio.
Spoken foreign-language proficiency training. Thirty, half-hour, intensive, spoken-language lesson units to be completed at the rate of one lesson per day for 30 days. By achieving eighty-percent correct answers to the questions in each unit, the Pimsleur Spoken Language Programmed Instructional Method will enable the learner to achieve the ACTFL Intermediate-Low Spoken Proficiency Level.

Spanish (Latin American) for Speakers of English, Three. unabr. ed. 16 cass. (Running Time: 15 hrs.). (Pimsleur Tapes Ser.). (SPA.). 1994. 345.00 set. (18371, Pimsleur) S&S Audio.
An additional thirty-lesson-unit program, for a total of ninety lesson units. Will allow the learner to achieve the ACTFL Intermediate-High Spoken Proficiency Level.

Spanish (Latin American) for Speakers of English, Two. 2nd ed. 16 cass. (Running Time: 15 hrs.). (Pimsleur Tapes Ser.). (SPA.). 1996. 345.00 set. (18369, Pimsleur) S&S Audio.
An additional thirty-lesson unit program, accomplished at the same rate as a Pimsleur I. Will enable the learner to achieve the ACTFL Intermediate-Mid Spoken Proficiency Level.

Spanish Living Language Course for Young People. 2 cass. (Running Time: 2 hrs.). (SPA.). (J). bk. 24.95 (AFS410) J Norton Pubs.

Spanish Mastery. Valette Staff. (J). (gr. 7-8). 1984. (978-0-669-06176-5(X)) HM Schl Div.

Spanish Music of the Golden Age. 1 cass. 11.95 J Norton Pubs.
Rustic songs by the most distinguished poet-musicians of the Golden Age (late 15th to 17th centuries), & selections from the cancioneros.

Spanish New American Standard Bible NASB - New Testament (Spoken Word) Read by Samuel Montoya. 12 cass. 1994. 29.97 (1860A) Chrstn Dup Intl.

Spanish New Testament. 1 cass. 1984. 79.90 Am Bible.

Spanish New Testament. Narrated by Samuel Montoya. 12 cass. (Running Time: 18 hrs.). (SPA.). 1994. 29.98 (978-7-902031-54-7(2)) Chrstn Dup Intl.

Spanish New Testament. Read by Samuel Montoya. 12 cass. (Running Time: 18 hrs.). (SPA.). 1994. 29.98 (978-7-902032-10-0(7)) Chrstn Dup Intl.

Spanish New Testament. Narrated by Samuel Montoya. 12 cass. (Running Time: 18 hrs.). (SPA.). 1994. 39.99 (978-7-902031-68-4(2)) Chrstn Dup Intl.

Spanish New Testament. Narrated by Samuel Montoya. 16 CDs. (Running Time: 24 hrs.). (SPA.). 1999. audio compact disk 59.98 (978-7-902031-56-1(9)) Chrstn Dup Intl.

Spanish New Testament, Narrated by Bruno Tokarz. 14 cass. (Running Time: 14 hrs.). (SPA.). 25.95 (978-1-55503-574-7(4), 520047) Covenant Comms.

Spanish Old Testament, 48 cass. (Running Time: 48 hrs.). 1984. 179.90 (978-0-00-620424-4(4)) Am Bible.

Spanish Old Testament. Narrated by Samuel Montoya. 36 cass. (Running Time: 54 hrs.). (SPA.). 1994. 79.98 (978-7-902032-03-2(4)) Chrstn Dup Intl.

Spanish Old Testament. Narrated by Samuel Montoya. 45 CDs. (Running Time: 67 hrs. 30 mins.). (SPA.). 1999. audio compact disk 169.98 (978-7-902031-98-1(4)) Chrstn Dup Intl.

Spanish on Location. Susana Chiabrando & Angels Valgro. 1 cass. (Languages on Location Ser.). (SPA & ENG., 1992. pap. bk. 10.95 (978-0-8120-7901-2(9)) Barron.

Spanish on the Go. 2 cass. (On the Go Ser.). (SPA.). 1992. pap. bk. 13.95 (978-0-8120-7829-9(2)) Barron.

Spanish on the Go. 2nd unabr. ed. William Lawton. 2 cass. (Running Time: 3 hrs.). (On the Go Ser.). 2001. 14.95 (978-0-7641-7349-3(9)) Barron.
Features updated dialogue that closely reflect the contemporary scene in Spanish-speaking countries.

Spanish on the Go: A Level One Language Program. 3rd ed. W. Lawton. (On the Go/Level 1 Ser.). (ENG & SPA., 2004. bk. 16.95 (978-0-7641-7757-6(5)) Barron.

Spanish Phrasebook & Dictionary. HarperCollins Publishers Ltd. Staff. (SPA & ENG., pap. bk. 19.99 (978-0-00-768270-6(0)) Pub: HarpC GBR. Dist(s): Trafalgar

Spanish Platiquemos Course Levels 1-4: Multilingual Books Language Course. 2nd ed. Don Casteel. 29 CDs. (Multilingual Books Intensive Language Courses). (SPA.). (C). 2004. per. 349.00 (978-1-58214-141-1(X)) Language Assocs.

Spanish Plus Program: Learn to Speak & Understand Spanish. Pimsleur Staff. 5 CDs. (Running Time: 500 hrs. 0 mins. NaN sec.). (Pimsleur Language Program Ser.). (KOR & ENG.). 2001. audio compact disk 115.00 (978-0-7435-0503-1(4), Pimsleur) Pub: S&S Audio. Dist(s): S and S Inc

Spanish Pocahontas Soundtrack. 1 cass. (SPA.). 1995. 12.98 (978-1-55723-772-9(7)); 22.50 (978-1-55723-774-3(3)) W Disney Records.

Spanish Programmatic Course. C. Cleland Harris. 40 dual track cass. Incl. Vol. 1. Spanish Programmatic Course. 24 dual track cass. C. Cleland Harris. (Spoken Language Ser.). (J). (gr. 9-12). 1975. pap. bk. & stu. ed. 110.00 incl. bk. (978-0-87950-359-8(9)); Vol. 1. Spanish Programmatic Course. 24 dual track cass. C. Cleland Harris. (Spoken Language Ser.). (J). (gr. 9-12). 1975. 90.00 (978-0-87950-358-1(0)); Vol. 2. Spanish Programmatic Course. 16 dual track cass. C. Cleland Harris. (Spoken Language Ser.). (J). (gr. 9-12). 1975. pap. bk. & stu. ed. 90.00 incl. bk. (978-0-87950-361-1(0)); Vol. 2. Spanish Programmatic Course. 16 dual track cass. C. Cleland Harris. (Spoken Language Ser.). (SPA.). 70.00 (978-0-87950-360-4(2)); (Spoken Language Ser.). (J). (gr. 9-12). 1975. 200.00 Set, incl. bk. (978-0-87950-362-8(9)) Spoken Lang Serv.

Spanish Programmatic Course, Vol. 2. 16 CDs. (Running Time: 12 hrs.). (Foreign Service Institute Language Ser.). (SPA.). 2005. audio compact disk 185.00 (978-1-57970-209-0(0), AFS121D) J Norton Pubs.

Spanish Pronunciation: Theory & Practice. 3rd ed. John B. Dalbor. (SPA.). 1997. (978-0-03-020082-3(2)) Harcourt Coll Pubs.

Spanish Proverbs 1960. Narrated by Samuel Montoya. 2 cass. 8.98 (2021A) Chrstn Dup Intl.

Spanish Psalms 1909. Narrated by Samuel Montoya. 4 cass. 9.98 (2009A) Chrstn Dup Intl.

Spanish Psalms 1960. Narrated by Samuel Montoya. 4 cass. 12.98 (2020A) Chrstn Dup Intl.

Spanish Rush Hour Express Cd Berlitz. (RUSH HOUR EXPRESS Ser.). 2008. audio compact disk 9.95 (978-981-268-239-0(2)) Pub: Berlitz Pubng. Dist(s): Langenscheidt

Spanish Savvy Traveler: Business CDs & Booklet. 2 CDs. (Running Time: 1 hr. 50 mins.). (SPA.). 2005. audio compact disk 21.95 (978-1-57970-144-4(2), SSP575) J Norton Pubs.

Spanish Savvy Traveler: Food & Dining CDs & Booklet. 2 CDs. (Running Time: 1 hr. 30 mins.). (SPA.). 2005. audio compact disk 21.95 (978-1-57970-145-1(0), SSP580) J Norton Pubs.

Spanish Savvy Traveler: Shopping CD & Booklet. 1 CD. (Running Time: 1 hr.). (SPA.). 2005. audio compact disk 14.95 (978-1-57970-146-8(9), SSP585) J Norton Pubs.

Spanish Savvy Traveler: Travel CD & Booklet. 1 CD. (Running Time: 1 hr.). (SPA.). 2005. audio compact disk 14.95 (978-1-57970-147-5(7), SSP590D) J Norton Pubs.

Spanish Savvy Traveler 4-vol. set CDs & Booklets. 6 CDs. (Running Time: 5 hrs. 30 min.). (SPA.). 2005. audio compact disk 59.96 (978-1-57970-149-9(3), SSP600D) J Norton Pubs.

Spanish Say Hello. 2nd rev. ed. Louis Aarons. 4 cass. (Running Time: 3 hrs. 75 min.). (WordMate Ser.). (SPA.). (gr. 9 up). 1996. pap. bk., stu. ed., spiral bd. 39.95 (978-1-887447-00-3(8)) WordMate.
Basic Spanish for native speakers of English includes pronunciation guide, word lists, study & review tests, interactive dialogs for communication, essential grammar, & glossary with correlated workbook. Requires stereo headphones.

Spanish Short Stories. Short Stories. 1 cass. (Running Time: 90 mins.). (SPA.). 1994. 16.95 (978-0-88432-512-3(1), SSP240) J Norton Pubs.
For the advanced listener. Includes notes.

Spanish Short Stories CD & Booklet. ed. Gustavo Adolfo Bécquer & Pedro Antonio de Alarcón. Read by Jorge Juan Rodriguez. 1 CD. (Running Time: 60 mins.). (SPA.). 2006. audio compact disk 16.95 (978-1-57970-391-2(7), SSP240D, Audio-For) J Norton Pubs.
Short stories of Gustavo Adolfo Bécquer and Pedro Antonio de Alarcóon are read in Spanish by Jorge Juan Rodriguez.

Spanish Simplified Language Learning Program: A Short Self-Directed Program for Beginners or As a Refresher. Gail Lebow. 4 cass. 2001. pap. bk. 40.00 (978-0-9710972-0-9(8)) JRI Pr.

Spanish Simply Fast & Easy: Complete 200 Page Illustrated Text/Tapescript/Answer Keys. Mark Frobose. 8 CDs. (Running Time: 8 hrs). (YA). 2003. audio compact disk 49.00 (978-1-893564-62-6(2)) Macmill Audio.

Spanish Songs for Children. 1 cass. (Running Time: 90 mins.). (J). 1994. 14.95 (978-0-88432-485-0(0), SSP120) J Norton Pubs.
Twelve delightful songs, most of which have been sung for hundreds of years by Spanish children. Includes lyric sheet.

Spanish Songs for Children CD & Booklet. ed. Perf. by Eva Llorens & Alberto Castilla. 1 CD. (Running Time: 44 mins.). (SPA.). (J). 2006. audio compact disk 14.95 (978-1-57970-387-5(9), SSP120D, Audio-For) J Norton Pubs.
12 delightful songs, most of which have been sung for hundreds of years by Spanish children. Printed lyrics in Spanish.

Spanish Songs for the Guitar, Volume 1. Contrib. by Rogelio Maya. (Running Time: 55 mins.). 2006. 19.95 (978-5-558-09190-8(8)) Mel Bay.

Spanish Songs for the Guitar, Volume 2. Contrib. by Rogelio Maya. (Running Time: 57 mins.). 2006. 19.95 (978-5-558-09189-2(4)) Mel Bay.

Spanish Speakers: Learning the Sounds of American English. unabr. ed. 4 cass. (Running Time: 4 hrs.). (Accent English Ser.). bk. 89.50 (SEN180) J Norton Pubs.

Spanish Speed. Mark Frobose. 3 cass. (Running Time: 3 hrs.). (SPA.). 2000. 19.99 (978-1-893564-71-8(1)) Macmill Audio.

Spanish Speed Immersion? Tapescript & Answer Keys. Mark Frobose. 8 cds. (SPA.). 2002. per. 79.00 (978-1-893564-91-6(6)) Macmill Audio.

Spanish Speed Immersion? Tapescript & Answer Keys. Mark Frobose. (SPA.). 2002. per. 24.99 (978-1-893564-89-3(4)) Macmill Audio.

Spanish Teaching Set. unabr. ed. University of Iowa, CEEDE Staff. 5 cass. (Tales of Marvel & Wonder Ser.). (SPA.). 1988. tchr. ed. 99.00 (978-0-7836-1093-1(9), 9993) Triumph Learn.
Twenty-three Indochinese fables.

Spanish, Think: Levels 1 & 2. 2 cass. 21.95 ea. J Norton Pubs.
Build your vocabulary & enhance your ability to think in Spanish by answering questions of native speaker.

Spanish to Brazilian Portuguese, Foreign Service Institute Staff. 2 cass. (Running Time: 2 hrs.). 1994. pap. bk. 45.00 (AFSP50) J Norton Pubs.
Designed for those who already have a good command of Spanish. Focuses on pronunciation, grammar & vocabulary which have similar but not always identical counterparts in Spanish.

Spanish Vocabulary, 4 cass. (Running Time: 4 hrs.). (Learn While You Drive Ser.). (SPA.). 1995. bk. 47.95 (5059-AMR) Olivia & Hill.
A wealth of words not covered in the basic courses (2000 words). Specifically designed to increase vocabulary without opening a book.

Spanish Vocabulary, AMR Staff. 4 cass. (Running Time: 4 hrs.). (Foreign Language Vocabulary Builder Ser.). 1980. 43.95 Oasis Audio.

Spanish Vocabulary Builder. unabr. ed. 1 cass. 12.95 (SSP010) J Norton Pubs.
Dictionary providing 101 essential words & phrases for the traveler.

Spanish Vocabulary Builders for Dental Personnel. (ENG.). 2007. audio compact disk 11.95 (978-0-9793655-3-9(8)) R Language.

Spanish Vol. 1 FSI Programmatic Course CDs, text & Manual. 24 CDs. (Running Time: 17 hrs.). (Foreign Service Institute Language Ser.). (SPA.). 2005. audio compact disk 225.00 (978-1-57970-142-0(6), AFS101D) J Norton Pubs.

Spanish with Ease see Nuovo Spagnolo Senza Sforzo

Spanish with Ease see Spanisch Ohne Muhe Heute

Spanish with Michel Thomas. (Delux Language Ser.). 2000. 69.95 (978-0-658-00772-9(6), 007726) M-H Contemporary.

Spanish 1 audio Cassettes - 12. 1993. 105.00 (978-1-57924-165-0(4)) BJUPr.

Spanish 1 CD Set (grades 9-12) audio compact disk 105.00 (978-1-59166-252-5(4)) BJUPr.

Spanish 2 audio Cassettes - 6. 1996. 56.00 (978-1-57924-166-7(2)) BJUPr.

Spanish 2 CD Set (12 CDs) audio compact disk 60.00 (978-1-59166-373-7(3)) BJUPr.

Spanish/Chinese. Vocabulearn. 2 cass. (Running Time: 90 mins. ea.). (VocabuLearn Ser.). (SPA, CHI & ENG.). 1995. 15.95 (978-957-9330-85-5(9)) Penton Overseas.

Spanish/Chinese Level II, Level 2. Vocabulearn. 2 cass. (Running Time: 3 hrs.). (VocabuLearn Ser.). (SPA & CHI.). 1995. pap. bk. 15.95 (978-957-9330-84-8(0)) Penton Overseas.

Spanish/Cinderella Classic Read along Audio Book. Prod. by PC Treasures Staff. (J). 2007. (978-1-60072-068-0(4)) PC Treasures.

Spanish/English Fluency Kit Audio CD's: Levels F-M (9-28) Benchmark Education Staff. (J). 2006. audio compact disk 20.00 (978-1-4108-7703-1(5)) Benchmark Educ.

Spanish/English Fluency Kit Audio CD's: Levels N-U (30-50) Benchmark Education Staff. (J). 2006. audio compact disk 20.00 (978-1-4108-7704-8(3)) Benchmark Educ.

Spanish/Goldilocks & the Three Bears Classic Read along Audio Book. Prod. by PC Treasures Staff. (SPA.). (J). 2007. (978-1-60072-061-1(7)) PC Treasures.

Spanish/Hansel & Gretel Classic Read along Audio Book. Prod. by PC Treasures Staff. (SPA.). (J). 2007. (978-1-60072-064-2(1)) PC Treasures.

Spanish/Little Red Riding Hood Classic Read along Audio Book. Prod. by PC Treasures Staff. (SPA.). (J). 2007. (978-1-60072-062-8(5)) PC Treasures.

Spanish/the Gingerbread Man Classic Read along Audio Book. Prod. by PC Treasures Staff. (SPA.). (J). 2007. (978-1-60072-065-9(X)) PC Treasures.

Spanish/the Little Mermaid Classic Read along Audio Book. Prod. by PC Treasures Staff. (SPA.). (J). 2007. (978-1-60072-066-6(8)) PC Treasures.

Spanish/the Three Little Pigs Classic Read along Audio Book. Prod. by PC Treasures Staff. (SPA.). (J). 2007. (978-1-60072-067-3(6)) PC Treasures.

Spanish/the Ugly Duckling Classic Read along Audio Book. Prod. by PC Treasures Staff. (SPA.). (J). 2007. (978-1-60072-063-5(3)) PC Treasures.

Spanking Shakespeare. unabr. ed. Jake Wizner. Read by Mike Chamberlain. 6 CDs. (Running Time: 6 hrs. 35 mins.). (YA). (gr. 10 up). 2007. audio compact disk 45.00 (978-0-7393-6325-6(5), Listening Lib) Pub: Random Audio Pubg. Dist(s): Random
Shakespeare Shapiro has always hated his name. His parents bestowed it on him as some kind of sick joke when he was born, and since then his life has been one embarrassing incident after another. As he enters his senior year of high school, Shakespeare's love life is nonexistent, his younger brother is maddeningly popular, and his best friend talks nonstop about his bowel movements. But Shakespeare will have the last laugh. He is chronicling every mortifying detail in his memoir, the writing project each senior must complete. And he is doing it brilliantly. For as much as he hates his name, Shakespeare is a good writer. And just maybe a prizewinning memoir will bring him respect, admiration, and a girlfriend?.?.?.? or at least a prom date. In his debut novel, Shakespeare Shapiro takes a humorous look at one popularity-challenged boy's journey to self-respect and sexual fulfillment.

Spanning Silos. abr. unabr. ed. David Aaker. Read by Phil Gigante. 1 MP3-CD. (Running Time: 7 hrs.). 2008. 39.25 (978-1-4233-7589-0(0), 9781423375890, Brinc Audio MP3 Lib); 24.95 (978-1-4233-7588-3(2), 9781423375883, Brilliance MP3); audio compact disk 92.25 (978-1-4233-7587-6(4), 9781423375876, BriAudCD Unabrid); audio compact disk 29.95 (978-1-4233-7586-9(6), 9781423375869, Bril Audio CD Unabri) Brilliance Audio.

Spanning Silos. unabr. abr. ed. David Aaker. (Running Time: 7 hrs.). 2008. 39.25 (978-1-4233-7591-3(2), 9781423375913, BADLE) Brilliance Audio.

Spanning Silos. unabr. abr. ed. David Aaker. Read by Phil Gigante. (Running Time: 7 hrs.). 2008. 24.95 (978-1-4233-7590-6(4), 9781423375906, BAD) Brilliance Audio.

Spare Change. unabr. ed. Robert B. Parker. 4 cass. (Running Time: 6 hrs.). (Sunny Randall Ser.: No. 6). 2007. 50.00 (978-1-4159-3893-5(8)) Books on Tape.

Spare Change. unabr. ed. Robert B. Parker. Read by Robert B. Parker. 5 CDs. (Running Time: 6 hrs.). (Sunny Randall Ser.: No. 6). 2007. audio compact disk 50.00 (978-1-4159-3638-2(2)) Books on Tape.

Spare Change. unabr. ed. Robert B. Parker. Read by Kate Burton. 5 CDs. (Running Time: 21600 sec.). (Sunny Randall Ser.: No. 6). (ENG.). 2007. audio compact disk 29.95 (978-0-7393-1871-3(3)) Pub: Random Audio Pubg. Dist(s): Random

Spare Parts. unabr. ed. Sally Rogers-Davidson. Read by Suzi Dougherty. 6 cass. (Running Time: 9 hrs. 30 mins.). 2002. (978-1-74030-481-8(0)) Bolinda Pubng AUS.

***spare Room.** Helen Garner. Read by Heather Bolton. (Running Time: 4 hrs. 15 mins.). 2009. 59.99 (978-1-74214-560-0(4), 9781742145600) Pub: Bolinda Pubng AUS. Dist(s): Bolinda Pub Inc

Spare Room. abr. ed. Mordecai Richler & Morris Surdin. Prod. by Esse Ljungh. (Running Time: 1 hr.). (Stage Ser.). 2004. audio compact disk 14.99 (978-1-894003-25-4(X)) Pub: Scenario Prods CAN. Dist(s): PerseuPGW

Spare Room. unabr. ed. Helen Garner. Read by Heather Bolton. (Running Time: 4 hrs. 15 mins.). 2009. audio compact disk 57.95 (978-1-74214-013-1(0), 9781742140131) Pub: Bolinda Pubng AUS. Dist(s): Bolinda Pub Inc

Spare Wife. unabr. ed. Alex Witchel. Read by Laural Merlington. (Running Time: 9 hrs.). 2008. 39.25 (978-1-4233-4296-0(8), 9781423342960, BADLE); 24.95 (978-1-4233-4295-3(X), 9781423342953, BAD); 87.25 (978-1-4233-4290-8(9), 9781423342908, BrilAudUnabridg); audio compact disk 92.25 (978-1-4233-4292-2(5), 9781423342922, BriAudCD Unabrid); audio compact disk 39.25 (978-1-4233-4294-6(1), 9781423342946, Brinc Audio MP3 Lib); audio compact disk 24.95 (978-1-4233-4293-9(3), 9781423342939, Brilliance MP3); audio compact disk 34.95 (978-1-4233-4291-5(7), 9781423342915, Bril Audio CD Unabri) Brilliance Audio.

Spark: The Breakthrough Plan for Losing Weight, Getting Fit, & Transforming Your Life. Chris Downie. 2010. audio compact disk 24.95 (978-1-4019-2647-2(9)) Hay House.

Spark: The Revolutionary New Science of Exercise & the Brain. unabr. ed. John J. Ratey. Read by Walter Dixon. Told to Eric Hagerman. (Running Time: 9 hrs. 30 mins.). (ENG.). 2008. 29.98 (978-1-59659-269-8(9), GildAudio) Pub: Gildan Media. Dist(s): HachBkGrp

Spark: The Revolutionary New Science of Exercise & the Brain. unabr. ed. John J. Ratey. Read by Walter Dixon. Told to Eric Hagerman. (Running Time: 9 hrs. 30 mins.). (ENG.). 2009. audio compact disk 39.98 (978-1-59659-283-4(4), GildAudio) Pub: Gildan Media. Dist(s): HachBkGrp

Spark Your Love Life. 1 cass. 10.00 (978-1-58506-028-3(3), 58) New Life Inst OR.
Put new life in your marriage or love relationship.

Sparkle-Tude: Women in Business. Sheryl L. Roush. (ENG.). 2003. audio compact disk 15.95 (978-1-880878-07-1(0)) Sparkle Present.

Sparklers Body Moves. DRG Publishing. (Running Time: 1 hr. 0 mins. 0 sec.). (Sparklers Body Moves Ser.). (ENG.). (J). (ps-k). 2008. audio compact disk 16.99 (978-0-237-53680-0(3), Evans Bros) Pub: Evans GBR. Dist(s): IPG Chicago

Sparkles the Fire Safety Dog. Read by Firefighter Glenn Trembley. Based on a book by Firefighter Dayna Hilton. Firefighter Dayna Hilton. Engineer Michael Post. Music by Michael Post. (ENG.). (J). 2008. audio compact disk 5.99 (978-0-9814977-1-6(3)) Firehouse Dog.

Sparkling Cyanide. Agatha Christie. Narrated by Robin Bailey. (Running Time: 22980 sec.). (Audio Editions Mystery Masters Ser.). (ENG.). 2007. audio compact disk 29.95 (978-1-57270-568-5(X)) Pub: AudioGO. Dist(s): Perseus Dist

Sparkling Cyanide. unabr. ed. Agatha Christie. Read by Robin Bailey. 5 cass. (Running Time: 6 hrs. 23 mins.). 2002. 27.95 (978-1-57270-263-9(X)) Pub: Audio Partners. Dist(s): PerseuPGW
At her birthday party, Rosemary Barton imbibes a celebratory glass of sparkling champagne and promptly keels over dead, of cyanide poisoning. The coroner's verdict is death by suicide. But was it really? Despite the coroner's conclusion, Rosemary's husband, George, receives anonymous letters informing him that his wife's death was a case of murder. In an effort to trap the perpetrator, George calls the original party together on the anniversary of Rosemary's death.

***Sparks: Reader to Energize Writing Cd.** rev. ed. Donna Barnard. (ENG.). 2010. audio compact disk 63.00 (978-0-7575-7091-9(7)) Kendall-Hunt.

Sparks on Flags: Traditional Dance Music from Ireland. Contrib. by Bridge Ceili Band. (ENG.). 1999. audio compact disk 20.95 (978-0-8023-8138-5(3)) Pub: Clo Iar-Chonnachta IRL. Dist(s): Dufour

***Sparks on Flags: Traditional Dance Music from Ireland.** Bridge Ceili Band. (ENG.). 1999. 13.95 (978-0-8023-7138-6(8)) Pub: Clo Iar-Chonnachta IRL. Dist(s): Dufour

Sparring with Charlie. Christopher Hunt. Read by Tom Parker. 8 CDs. (Running Time: 8 hrs. 30 mins.). 2003. audio compact disk 64.00 (978-0-7861-9804-7(4), 2663) Blckstn Audio.

Sparring with Charlie: Motorbiking down the Ho Chi Minh Trail. Christopher Hunt. Read by Tom Parker. 6 cass. (Running Time: 9 hrs.). 2000. 44.95 (2663); audio compact disk 79.99 (z2663) Blckstn Audio.
Captures the color & complexity of Vietnam today.

Sparring with Shadows. unabr. ed. Archimede Fusillo. 5 cass. (Running Time: 6 hrs. 45 mins.). 2003. 40.00 (978-1-74093-001-7(0)) Pub: Bolinda Pubng AUS. Dist(s): Bolinda Pub Inc

Sparrow. unabr. ed. Mary Doria Russell. Read by David Colacci. (Running Time: 15 hrs.). 2008. 39.25 (978-1-4233-5632-5(2), 9781423356325, BADLE); 24.95 (978-1-4233-5631-8(4), 9781423356318, BAD); audio compact disk 117.25 (978-1-4233-5628-8(4), 9781423356288, BriAudCD Unabrid); audio compact disk 39.25 (978-1-4233-5630-1(6), 9781423356301, Brinc Audio MP3 Lib); audio compact disk 38.95 (978-1-4233-5627-1(6), 9781423356271, Bril Audio CD Unabri); audio compact disk 24.95 (978-1-4233-5629-5(2), 9781423356295, Brilliance MP3) Brilliance Audio.

Sparrow & the Phoenix see Chinese Fairy Tales

Sparrow Falls. Wilbur Smith. Read by Tim Pigott-Smith. 4 cass. (Running Time: 6 hrs.). (ENG., 2001. 17.99 (978-0-333-90277-6(7)) Pub: Macmillan UK GBR. Dist(s): Trafalgar
From the bloody trenches of northern France, Gen. Sean Courtney returns to South Africa and a new life of fame, fortune and a seat in the government. But for Mark Anders, the young South African whom he has come to regard as his son, the return home is an empty and painful experience - with his grandfather murdered and his property seized, he has lost everything.

Sparrow Falls. unabr. ed. Wilbur Smith. Read by Stephen Thorne. 16 cass. (Running Time: 20 hrs. 09 min.). 2001. 41.95 (978-0-7540-0599-5(2), CAB2022) Pub: Chivers Audio Bks GBR. Dist(s): AudioGO
From the trenches of France, General Sean Courtney comes back to fame, fortune & a seat in the Government. Mark Anders, the courageous young South African whom he has come to regard as his own son, returns to nothing, his grandfather murdered, his property seized by an unknown company.

Sparrow Falls, Pt. 1. unabr. collector's ed. Wilbur Smith. Read by Richard Brown. 8 cass. (Running Time: 12 hrs.). (Courtney Novels). 1989. 64.00 (978-0-7366-1475-7(3), 2353-A) Books on Tape.
Ten years of peace were shattered by WWI.

Sparrow Falls, Pt. 2. unabr. collector's ed. Wilbur Smith. Read by Richard Brown. 8 cass. (Running Time: 12 hrs.). (Courtney Novels). 1989. 64.00 (978-0-7366-1476-4(1), 2353-B) Books on Tape.
Ten years of peace were shattered by WWI. Sean Courtney is once more in uniform, this time in France.

Sparrow Hawk Red, unabr. ed. Ben Mikaelsen. Narrated by Robert Ramirez. 4 cass. (Running Time: 5 hrs. 30 mins.). (gr. 5 up). 1997. 35.00 (978-0-7887-0827-5(9), 94868E7) Recorded Bks.
Eighth-grader Ricky Diaz & his dad, an ex-DEA agent, love to fly loops over the desert in their Baby Great Lakes biplane. But when Ricky learns that his

mother's fatal auto crash the year before wasn't an accident, he decides to put his flying talents to a real test. Disguised as a ragged street kid, he travels to Mexico & into the compound of the drug smugglers who were responsible for his mother's death.

Sparrows in the Scullery. unabr. ed. Barbara Brooks Wallace. Narrated by Steven Crossley. 4 pieces. (Running Time: 5 hrs. 30 mins.). (gr. 3 up). 2000. 37.00 (978-0-7887-3521-9(7), 95913E7) Recorded Bks.
This suspenseful book transports youngsters to the England of 100 years ago. One night, 10-year-old Colley wakes up wrapped tightly in a rough blanket. The next thing he knows, he is in London at the dreadful Broggin Home for Boys. Why is this happening to him?.

Sparrows in the Scullery. unabr. ed. Barbara Brooks Wallace. Read by Steven Crossley. 4 cass. (Running Time: 5 hrs. 30 mins.). (J). 2000. pap. bk. & stu. ed. 49.75 (978-0-7887-3842-5(9), 41053X4) Recorded Bks.

Sparrows in the Scullery. unabr. ed. Barbara Brooks Wallace. Narrated by Steven Crossley. 5 CDs. (Running Time: 5 hrs. 30 mins.). (gr. 3 up). 2000. audio compact disk 48.00 (978-0-7887-4651-2(0), C1198E7) Recorded Bks.

Sparrows in the Scullery, Class Set. unabr. ed. Barbara Brooks Wallace. Read by Steven Crossley. 4 cass. (Running Time: 5 hrs. 30 mins.). (J). (gr. 3). 1999. 102.80 (978-0-7887-3843-2(7), 47047) Recorded Bks.

Spartan Gold. Clive Cussler & Grant Blackwood. (Running Time: 6 hrs.). No. 1. (ENG.). (gr. 12 up). 2009. audio compact disk 29.95 (978-0-14-314568-4(1), PengAudBks) Penguin Grp USA.

Spartan Gold. unabr. ed. Clive Cussler & Grant Blackwood. Read by Dick Hill. 10 CDs. (Running Time: 13 hrs.). No. 1. (ENG.). (gr. 12 up). 2009. audio compact disk 39.95 (978-0-14-314567-7(3), PengAudBks) Penguin Grp USA.

Spartans, lecture 7. Teaching Co.

Spartans: The World of the Warrior-Heroes of Ancient Greece, from Utopia to Crisis & Collapse. unabr. ed. Paul Cartledge. Read by John Lee. (Running Time: 30600 sec.). 2007. 19.95 (978-1-4332-0498-2(3)) Blckstn Audio.

Spartans: The World of the Warrior-Heroes of Ancient Greece, from Utopia to Crisis & Collapse. unabr. ed. Paul Cartledge. (Running Time: 30600 sec.). 2007. 44.95 (978-1-4332-0496-8(7)); audio compact disk 55.00 (978-1-4332-0497-5(5)) Blckstn Audio.

Spartans: The World of the Warrior-Heroes of Ancient Greece, from Utopia to Crisis & Collapse. unabr. ed. Paul Cartledge. Read by John Lee. (Running Time: 30600 sec.). 2007. audio compact disk 29.95 (978-1-4332-0500-2(9)) Blckstn Audio.

Spartans: The World of the Warrior-Heroes of Ancient Greece from Utopia to Crisis & Collapse. unabr. ed. Paul Cartledge. Read by John Lee. (Running Time: 30600 sec.). 2007. audio compact disk 19.95 (978-1-4332-0499-9(1)) Blckstn Audio.

Spatial Archetypes. Mimi Lobell. 4 cass. 36.00 (OC153) Sound Horizons AV.

Spawn of Skull Island. Read by Michael H. Price. 5 CDs. 2006. audio compact disk 25.00 (978-1-887664-65-3(3)) Pub: Midnght Marquee Pr. Dist(s): Distributors

Speak. Laurie Halse Anderson. Read by Mandy Siegfried. 4 CDs. (Running Time: 5 hrs. 1 min.). (J). (gr. 8 up). 2004. audio compact disk 35.00 (978-1-4000-8998-7(0), Listening Lib) Random Audio Pubg.

Speak. unabr. ed. Laurie Halse Anderson. Read by Mandy Seigfried. 3 vols. (Running Time: 5 hrs. 1 min.). (J). (gr. 8 up). 2004. 36.00 (978-0-8072-8404-9(1), Listening Lib); 30.00 (978-0-8072-8403-2(3), YA195CX, Listening Lib) Random Audio Pubg.
After calling the cops to an end-of-summer party, Melinda is a friendless outcast at Merryweather High. Through her work on an art project, she is finally able to face what really happened to her at that terrible party: she was raped by an upperclassman who is still a threat to her. It will take another violent encounter with him to make Melinda fight back.

Speak. unabr. ed. Laurie Halse Anderson. Read by Mandy Siegfried. (Running Time: 18060 sec.). (ENG.). (J). (gr. 7-12). 2006. audio compact disk 30.00 (978-0-7393-3672-4(X), Listening Lib) Pub: Random Audio Pubg. Dist(s): Random

Speak & Grow Rich. Dottie Walters. Read by Dottie Walters. 6 cass. (Running Time: 6 hrs.). 1989. 89.95 (978-0-934344-29-6(9)) Royal Pub.
Insider's tips, how-to's, where-to-finds, trade secrets, valuable information for paid professional speakers. Discloses many ways to earn big money in the speaking world.

Speak & Money Will Follow. 3 cass. 39.95 Set. (978-1-882306-13-8(9)) Planned Mktg.
Educational/training.

Speak & Read Essential German. (Pimsleur Language Program Ser.). 295.00 (978-0-7612-0869-3(0), 70059) AMACOM.
This method will give you: a high-utility vocabulary; a bank of practical, basic sentences; the ability to express yourself creatively in new situations; fluency without drills, memorization, grammar instruction, or reading or writing assignments. Offers guaranteed results.

Speak & Sing: The Developing Child. Featuring Shari Tallon & Jerry Tallon. 1 CD. (Running Time: 40 mins.). (J). (ps-1). 2007. audio compact disk (978-0-9799996-4-8(0)) Narroway ProCN CAN.

Speak Arabic. 2 cass. (Running Time: 2 hrs.). (ARA.). bk. 180.00 J Norton Pubs.

Speak Arabic: Arabic Script Version. 2 cass., 1 video. (Running Time: 3 hrs.). (YA). pap. bk. 180.00 (978-0-88432-519-2(9), SAR202) J Norton Pubs.
Designed for beginners & filmed on location in the Arab word; produced to broadcast standards & the accompanying books are fully illustrated with everyday scenes & information on local customs.

Speak Arabic: Transliterated Version. 2 cass. (Running Time: 3 hrs.). (YA). pap. bk. 180.00 incl. 1 video cass., texts. (978-0-88432-518-5(0), SAR201) J Norton Pubs.
Designed for beginners & filmed on locationin the Arab world; the video & audio tapes have been produced to broadcast standars, & the accompanying books are fully illustrated with everyday scenes & information on local customs.

Speak Business English Like an American: Learn the Idioms & Expressions You Need to Succeed on the Job. Amy Gillett. Illus. by Evgeny Kran. 1 CD. (Running Time: 40 mins). Dramatization. 2005. pap. bk. 29.95 (978-0-9725300-6-4(1)) Language Success Pr.

Speak Cantonese, Bk. 1. rev. ed. Po-Fei Huang & Gerard P. Kok. 19 cass. 1960. 7.95 ea. (incl. supp. materials) Set. (978-0-88710-095-6(3)) Yale Far Eastern Pubns.

Speak Cantonese, Bk. 2. Po-Fei Huang. 7 cass. 1982. 7.95 ea. (incl. supp. materials) Set. (978-0-88710-097-0(X)) Yale Far Eastern Pubns.

Speak Cantonese, Bk. 3. rev. ed. Po-Fei Huang. 9 cass. 1967. 7.95 ea. (incl. supp. materials) Set. (978-0-88710-099-4(6)) Yale Far Eastern Pubns.

Speak Chinese: Supplementary Materials. 8 cass. 1985. 7.95 ea. (incl. supp. materials) Set. (978-0-88710-105-2(4)) Yale Far Eastern Pubns.

Speak Easy Umati. Sarah K. Silverson et al. Illus. by Ellen Eagle. Intro. by Joe Hambrook. (Video Course Through Mime Sketches Ser.). 1984. 55.00 (978-0-582-79837-3(X), 75112) Longman.

Speak Effectively. Betty L. Randolph. Read by Betty L. Randolph. Read by Leonard Baron. Ed. by Success Education Institute International Staff. 1 cass. (Running Time: 60 min.). (Educational Ser.). 1989. bk. 14.98 (978-1-55909-251-7(3), 390P) Randolph Tapes.
60,000 messages left-right brain. Male-female voice tracks with Megafonic Subliminals. Ocean (P) & Music (PM).

Speak English Like an American: For Native Speakers of Any Language. 2nd ed. Scripts. Amy Gillett. Illus. by Manny Jose. 1 CD. (Running Time: 30 minutes). Dramatization. 2006. pap. bk. 24.95 (978-0-9725300-3-3(7)) Language Success Pr.
An ESL book & CD set for intermediate to advanced students of English from any language background. Designed for self-study. "A highly recommended self-teaching tool for those who are familiar with the English language, yet who seek to take their fluency to new heights by mastering common English idioms." - Midwest Book Review.

Speak English Like an American for Native Japanese Speakers. Amy Gillett. Illus. by Manny Jose. 1 CD. (Running Time: 30 minutes). (JPN & ENG.). 2004. pap. bk. 24.95 (978-0-9725300-2-6(9)) Language Success Pr.

Speak English Like an American for Native Russian Speakers. Scripts. Amy Gillett. Tr. by Larisa Keselman. Illus. by Manny Jose. 1 CD. (Running Time: 30 minutes). Dramatization. (RUS & ENG.). 2003. per. 24.95 (978-0-9725300-0-2(2)) Language Success Pr.

Speak English Like an American for Native Spanish Speakers. Amy Gillett. Illus. by Manny Jose. Dramatization. (SPA & ENG.). 2003. pap. bk. 24.95 (978-0-9725300-1-9(0)) Language Success Pr.

Speak for Me. Perf. by Jaci Velasquez. 1 cass. 1998. 7.98 HiLo Plus. (978-0-7601-2571-7(6)) Brentwood Music.

Speak for the Dead. abr. ed. Rex Burns. Read by Charlton Griffin. 2 vols. No. 2. 2003. (978-1-58807-666-3(0)) Am Pubng Inc.

Speak for the Dead. unabr. ed. Elizabeth Lord & Margaret Yorke. Read by Elizabeth Proud. 6 cass. (Running Time: 9 hrs.). (Isis Ser.). (J). 2000. 54.95 (978-0-7531-0921-2(2), 001010) Pub: ISIS Lrg Prnt GBR. Dist(s): Ulverscroft US

Speak for Yourself. unabr. ed. Robert Montgomery. 2 CDs. (Smart Tapes Ser.). 2004. audio compact disk 19.99 (978-1-58926-051-1(1)) Oasis Audio.

Speak for Yourself. unabr. ed. Robert L. Montgomery & Robert Montgomery. Read by Robert L. Montgomery. 2 cass. (Running Time: 2 hrs. 49 min.). (Smart Tapes Ser.). (gr. 10-12). 1994. pap. bk. 19.99 Set. (978-1-55678-052-3(4), 3235) Oasis Audio.
Now you can be self-assured & confident every time you speak-whether it's one-on-one or in front of a crowd. You'll learn to excel in meeting, negotiation, conversations & interviews, & you'll discover how to prepare & deliver exceptional speeches & presentations.

Speak French for Beginners with Michel Thomas, 10-Hour Complete Course. Michel Thomas. (Michel Thomas Ser.). 2006. 79.95 (978-0-07-147982-0(1), 9780071479820) McGraw.

Speak French with Confidence. 2nd ed. Jean-Claude Arragon. (TY: Conversation Ser.). (ENG.). 2010. audio compact disk 19.95 (978-0-07-166460-8(2), 0071664602) McGraw.

Speak French with Michel Thomas. (Speak... with Michel Thomas Ser.). 2000. 22.95 (978-0-658-00796-5(3), 007963) M-H Contemporary.

Speak from the Heart: Be Yourself & Get Results. Steve Adubato. 2004. 10.95 (978-0-7435-4607-2(5)) Pub: S&S Audio. Dist(s): S and S Inc

Speak German with Confidence. 2nd ed. Paul Coggle & Heiner Schenke. (TY: Conversation Ser.). (ENG.). 2010. audio compact disk 19.95 (978-0-07-166459-2(9), 0071664599) McGraw.

Speak German with Michel Thomas. Kenneth W. Thomas. (Speak... with Michel Thomas Ser.). 2000. 22.95 (978-0-658-00744-6(0), 007440) M-H Contemporary.

Speak Greek with Confidence. 2nd ed. Howard Middle & Hara Garoufalia-Middle. (TY: Conversation Ser.). (ENG.). 2010. audio compact disk 19.95 (978-0-07-166461-5(0), 0071664610) McGraw.

Speak Ill of the Dead. abr. ed. Peter Chambers. Read by John Keyworth. 4 cass. (Running Time: 6 hrs.). (Sound Ser.). 2004. 44.95 (978-1-85496-262-1(0), 62620) Pub: UlverLrgPrint GBR. Dist(s): Ulverscroft US

Speak in a Week Flash! English. 2008. audio compact disk 14.95 (978-1-59125-938-1(X)) Penton Overseas.

Speak Italian with Confidence. 2nd ed. Maria Guarnieri & Federica Sturani. (TY: Conversation Ser.). (ENG.). 2010. audio compact disk 19.95 (978-0-07-166462-2(9), 0071664629) McGraw.

Speak Italian with Michel Thomas. (Speak... with Michel Thomas Ser.). 2000. 22.95 (978-0-658-00824-5(2), 008242) M-H Contemporary.

Speak Japanese with Confidence. 2nd ed. Helen Gilhooly. (TY: Conversation Ser.). (ENG.). 2010. audio compact disk 19.95 (978-0-07-166463-9(7), 0071664637) McGraw.

Speak Like a CEO: Secrets for Commanding Attention & Getting Results. abr. ed. Suzanne Bates. Read by Bernadette Dunne. (Running Time: 16200 sec.). 2006. audio compact disk 28.00 (978-1-933309-09-5(1)) Pub: A Media Intl. Dist(s): Natl Bk Netwk

Speak Like a CEO Toolkit. 2005. audio compact disk 199.00i (978-0-9767156-0-3(0)) Bates Comm Inc.

Speak Like a Thai: Volume 2: Thai Slang & Idioms. Benjawan Poomsan Becker. (Speak Like a Thai Ser.). 2007. audio compact disk 15.00 (978-1-887521-73-4(9)) Paiboon Pubng.

Speak Like a Thai: Volume 3: Thai Proverbs & Sayings. Benjawan Poomsan Becker. (Speak Like a Thai Ser.). 2007. audio compact disk 15.00 (978-1-887521-74-1(7)) Paiboon Pubng.

Speak Mandarin. 185.00 (1975, Lrn Inc) Oasis Audio.
Features methods in learning a second language.

Speak Mandarin. 7 cass. 1985. 7.95 ea. (incl. supp. materials) Set. (978-0-88710-145-8(3)) Yale Far Eastern Pubns.

Speak Mandarin. unabr. ed. Henry C. Fenn et al. 7 cass. (Running Time: 5 hrs. 30 mins.). (CHI.). (YA). (gr. 10-12). 1967. pap. bk. 225.00 (978-0-88432-027-2(8), AFM201) J Norton Pubs.
Presents the basic structure patterns of colloquial Mandarin using a vocabulary that would be heard in everyday Chinese conversations. Since the Yale romanization is used throughout the text, you are not required to learn Chinese characters; attention is concentrated on new sounds, words & language patterns. Presented in 20 lessons, each containing a dialog (or narrative), vocabulary, sentence patterns, notes & a translation of the introductory dialog.

Speak Mandarin CDs & Books. 7 CDs. (Running Time: 5 hrs. 30 mins.). (CHI.). 2005. audio compact disk (978-1-57970-195-6(7)) J Norton Pubs.

***Speak, Memory.** unabr. ed. Vladimir Nabokov. Read by Stefan Rudnicki. (Running Time: 11 hrs.). 2010. 39.97 (978-1-4418-7264-7(7), 9781441872647, BADLE); 24.99 (978-1-4418-7262-3(0), 9781441872623, Brilliance MP3); 39.97 (978-1-4418-7263-0(9), 9781441872630, Brinc Audio MP3 Lib); audio compact disk 29.99 (978-1-4418-7260-9(4), 9781441872609, Bril Audio CD Unabri); audio compact disk 74.97 (978-1-4418-7261-6(2), 9781441872616, BriAudCD Unabrid) Brilliance Audio.

Speak, Memory: An Autobiography Revisited. unabr. collector's ed. Vladimir Nabokov. Read by John McDonald. 7 cass. (Running Time: 10 hrs. 30 mins.). 1987. 56.00 (978-0-7366-1124-4(X), 2047) Books on Tape.
Autobiography of the novelist (author of "Lolita" & "Pale Fire"), covering the years 1903-1940.

Speak Navajo CDs & Text. Alan Wilson. 2 CDs. (Running Time: 2 hrs.). (NAV.). 2005. audio compact disk 49.00 (978-1-57970-198-7(1), AFNV20D) J Norton Pubs.

Speak No Evil. Martyn Waites. 2009. 69.95 (978-0-7531-4257-8(0)); audio compact disk 84.95 (978-0-7531-4258-5(9)) Pub: Isis Pubng Ltd GBR. Dist(s): Ulverscroft US

Speak Out!, Vol. 2. Hal Kornell. Read by Hal Kornell. 1 cass. (Running Time: 42 min.). (Sounds of U.S. English Ser.). 1998. bk. 19.95 Snds US English.
Contains exercises to improve articulation & delivery of U.S. speech. Helps with grammar & conversational skills, quells nervousness in public speaking situations.

Speak Portuguese with Confidence. 2nd ed. Sue Tyson-Ward. (TY: Conversation Ser.). (ENG.). 2010. audio compact disk 19.95 (978-0-07-166464-6(5), 0071664645) McGraw.

Speak Russian. 1 cass. (Running Time: 30 mins.). (YA). (gr. 10-12). 1990. pap. bk. 34.95 (978-1-57970-014-0(4), SRU100) J Norton Pubs.
Emphasizes active communication, both listening & speaking & is intended for those who have already acquired an elementary knowledge of Russian. Structured around real life situations you might encounter in Russia.

Speak Softly, Love Loudly: Uncommon Sense for Raising Healthy & Successful Kids. William Allen Baughman. 2007. audio compact disk 40.99 (978-1-60247-696-7(9)) Tate Pubng.

Speak Spanish Naturallly, Fast & Fun. Mark A. Frobose. 2004. audio compact disk 69.00 (978-1-893564-82-4(7)) Macmill Audio.

Speak Spanish with Confidence. 2nd ed. Juan Kattan-Ibarra & Angela Howkins. (TY: Conversation Ser.). (ENG.). 2010. audio compact disk 19.95 (978-0-07-166465-3(3), 0071664653) McGraw.

Speak Spanish with Michel Thomas. (Speak... with Michel Thomas Ser.). 2000. 22.95 (978-0-658-00771-2(8), 007718) M-H Contemporary.

Speak Standard, Too: Add Mainstream American English to Your Talking Style. Mary I. Berger. Read by Mary I. Berger. 4 cass. (Running Time: 6 hrs.). 1991. pap. bk. 35.00 (978-0-9630778-1-3(3)) Orchrd Bks IL.
Accompanies paperback text which is a bi-dialectic program that teaches nonstandard English speakers to switch between their primary dialects & standard English - for school & career.

Speak the Language of Healing. Read by Meredith McRae. 4 cass. (Running Time: 6 hrs.). 2001. 25.00 (978-1-59040-106-4(9), Phoenix Audio) Pub: Amer Intl Pub. Dist(s): PerseuPGW

Speak, Think & Understand Essential German Two. 16 cass. (Pimsleur System Ser.). 345.00 Incl. user's guide. (4025) SyberVision.

Speak, Think & Understand Essential Spanish Two. unabr. ed. 16 cass. (Pimsleur System Ser.). 1989. 345.00 (4024) SyberVision.
Learn to speak intermediate Spanish in 30 days.

Speak to Influence. Braun Media Services. (ENG.). 2007. audio compact disk 17.95 (978-1-59987-629-0(9)) Braun Media.

Speak to Influence/Write to Influence Audio Book Set. Braun Media Services. (ENG.). 2007. audio compact disk 23.95 (978-1-59987-631-3(0)) Braun Media.

Speak to My Heart! Carla Person's Step-by-Step Method for Shamanic Animal Communication. Created by Carla Person. 2004. video 34.95 (978-0-9744145-2-2(2)) Coccora Pr.

Speak to Sell: Using Public Speaking As a Marketing Tool. 2002. audio compact disk 34.95 (978-0-9716089-0-0(3)) Sullivan Speaker.

Speak to Win. Bert Decker. Read by Bert Decker. 6 cass. 59.95 Set. (122A) Nightingale-Conant.
Speak up & gain the winner's edge.

Speak to Win: How to Present with Power in Any Situation. unabr. ed. Brian Tracy. Read by Brian Tracy. 6 CDs. (Running Time: 5 hrs.). (ENG.). 2009. audio compact disk 29.98 (978-1-59659-215-5(X), GildAudio) Pub: Gildan Media. Dist(s): HachBkGrp

Speak Up. abr. ed. Robert A. Monroe. Read by Robert A. Monroe. (Running Time: 30 min.). (Human Plus Ser.). 1980. 14.95 (978-1-56102-041-6(9)) Inter Indus.
Address groups for individual with ease.

Speak Up: Say What You Want to Say. Dick Sutphen. 1 cass. (Running Time: 1 hr.). (RX17 Ser.). 1986. 14.98 (978-0-87554-314-7(6), RX123) Valley Sun.
You now speak up & say what you want to say. You find it easy to say what needs to be said. You stand up for yourself & increase your self-esteem. You always act in a manner you respect. You are assertive about your human rights, & show consideration & respect for the feelings & rights of others. You will not tolerate manipulation. "Speak up" are your key words for conditioned response.

Speak Up & Stand Out! Lisa Contini. 3 cass. (Running Time: 3 hrs.). 1995. 29.95 incl. script. (978-1-57294-039-0(5), 11-0303) SkillPath Pubns.
Insights, tips & tricks from a professional seminar leader.

Speak up Audio Programme: Banish the fear of public Speaking. Gavin Ingham. 1 cd. (Running Time: 73 min). 2005. audio compact disk 147.00 (978-1-59971-679-4(8)) AardGP.

Speak up Sing Out, Bk. 2. Rebecca W. Bushnell. 1 cass. 12.00 (978-0-8325-0361-0(4), Natl Textbk Co) M-H Contemporary.
Features 12 songs to help reinforce the basic strutures of English.

Speak up with Confidence. Jack Valenti. Read by Jack Valenti. (Playaway Adult Nonfiction Ser.). (ENG.). 2009. 44.99 (978-1-60775-730-6(3)) Find a World.

Speak up with Confidence. unabr. abr. ed. Jack Valenti. Read by Jack Valenti. 5 CDs. (Running Time: 4 hrs. 45 mins.). (ENG.). 2002. audio compact disk 29.95 (978-1-56511-739-6(5), 1565117395) Pub: HighBridge. Dist(s): Workman Pub

Speak with an Accent. Speeches. 1. (Running Time: 69:40). Dramatization. 2006. audio compact disk (978-0-9703652-3-1(3)) Daily Plnt.

Speak Without Fear: How to Give a Speech Like a Pro. Jan D'Arcy. Read by Jan D'Arcy. 6 cass. (Running Time: 6 hrs.). 59.95 (444AD) Nightingale-Conant.
Public speaking made worry-free.

Speak Yiddish. Scripts. 1 cass. (Running Time: 55 min.). 2000. (19204-4); audio compact disk (978-1-890095-22-2(2), 19204-2) Nesak Intl.

Speak 5001 Easy Phrases in Spanish, French, Italian, & German. Mark Frobose. 8 cass. (Running Time: 8 hrs.). (FRE, SPA, ITA & GER.). 1999. 69.00 (978-1-893564-49-7(5)) Macmill Audio.

Speaker for the Dead. Orson Scott Card. Read by David Birney & Stefan Rudnicki. (Ender Ser.: Bk. 2). 2005. audio compact disk 110.95 (978-0-7927-3807-7(1)) AudioGO.

Speaker for the Dead. Orson Scott Card. Read by Ray Verna. 9 cass. (Running Time: 13 hrs. 10 min.). (Ender Ser.: Bk. 2). 1993. 63.40 Set. (978-1-56544-044-9(7), 550002); Rental 11.40 Set, 30-day. (550002) Literate Ear.
Sequel to "Ender's Game." Ender Wiggin, who had been tricked into becoming the greatest criminal in the history of mankind, vanished immediately after the first terrible war. Three thousand years after the Xenocide of the Buggers by the monstrous Ender, human space colonists find a second species of intelligent aliens. With this discovery begins resumption of extermination.

Speaker for the Dead. Orson Scott Card. Read by David Birney & Stefan Rudnicki. (Ender Ser.: Bk. 2). 2004. 29.95 (978-1-59397-477-0(9)) Pub: Macmill Audio. Dist(s): Macmillan

Speaker for the Dead. Orson Scott Card. Read by David Birney & Stefan Rudnicki. (Ender Ser.: Bk. 2). 2005. audio compact disk 49.95 (978-0-7927-3848-0(9)) Pub: Macmill Audio. Dist(s): Macmillan

Speaker for the Dead. unabr. ed. Orson Scott Card. Read by David Birney & Stefan Rudnicki. 12 CDs. (Running Time: 14 hrs. 0 mins. 0 sec.). (Ender Quartet Ser.). (ENG.). 2005. audio compact disk 49.95 (978-1-59397-476-3(0)) Pub: Macmill Audio. Dist(s): Macmillan

Speaker of Mandarin. unabr. ed. Ruth Rendell. Read by Michael Bryant. 6 cass. (Running Time: 9 hrs.). (Inspector Wexford Mystery Ser.: Bk. 12). 2000. 49.95 (978-0-7451-6239-3(8), CAB 108) Pub: Chivers Audio Bks GBR. Dist(s): AudioGO
The Chinese government wants advice on crime prevention and detection, so Scotland Yard assembles a team that includes the best detection experts. Inspector Wexford is sent to the conference, staying an extra two weeks for his annual vacation. But upon his return, word arrives that a woman Wexford met while in China has been murdered. Now Wexford must figure out who killed her and why.

Speakers: Generating Back-of-the Room Sales. Gordon Burgett. 1. (Running Time: 60 mins.). 1996. 9.95 (978-0-910167-11-6(7)) Comm Unltd CA.

Speakers: How to Earn Happily Ever after with One Speech. unabr. ed. Gordon Burgett. Read by Gordon Burgett. 1 cass. (Running Time: 1 hr.). 1994. 9.95 (978-0-910167-26-0(5)) Comm Unltd CA.
Shows how to build a speaking career from one speech.

Speakers: Using Your Book to Penetrate Your Niche Market. Gordon Burgett. 1 cass. (Running Time: 45 min.). 1996. 9.95 (978-0-910167-19-2(2)) Comm Unltd CA.
Shows professionals how to get in control, in demand, & in clover.

Speaker's Voice. unabr. ed. David A. Stern. Read by David A. Stern. 3 cass. (Running Time: 3 hrs.). 1993. 29.95 Set.; 29.95 Set. (978-0-926862-92-0(8)) Dialect Accent.
Course in accent reduction for all speakers of English as a second language.

Speaking: 90 minute audiotape/CD for the Speaking Text. Elaine Kirn. 1998. audio compact disk 12.00 (978-1-891077-25-8(2)) Authors Editors.

Speaking & Listening Skills in the Workplace. 1 cass. (Running Time: 90 mins.). (Essential Business Skills Ser.). 1999. pap. bk. & wbk. ed. 30.00 (80209CHDG); pap. bk. & wbk. ed. 129.00 Incl. multiple choice tests. AMACOM.
Will help staff overcome barriers to effective communication, build rapport & handle difficult communication tasks. The Institute for Certification, a department of Professional Secretaries International, will grant points towards CPS recertification to qualified individuals who successfully complete this course. 1 CEU.

Speaking & Social Interaction. 2nd ed. Susan M. Reinhart & Ira Fisher. (ENG., 2000. 17.00 (978-0-472-00300-6(3), 00300) U of Mich Pr.

Speaking & Writing with Confidence. Shad Helmstetter. 1 cass. (Self-Talk Cassettes Ser.). 10.95 (978-0-937065-11-2(0)) Grindle Pr.

Speaking Chinese about China, Vol. 1. Helen T. Lin & Du Rong. 1 cass. (Running Time: 1 hr. 30 mins.). (CHI.). (978-7-80052-194-2(X)) Sinolingua CHN.

Speaking Chinese about China, Vol. 2. Helen T. Lin & Du Rong. 1 cass. (Running Time: 1 hr. 30 mins.). (978-7-80052-195-9(8)) Sinolingua CHN.

Speaking Chinese in China. Hsu Ying & J. Marvin Brown. 6 cass. (Running Time: 5 hrs.). (YA). (gr. 10-12). 1983. pap. bk. 175.00 (978-0-88432-150-7(9), AFM320) J Norton Pubs.
Conversation course suitable for anyone who has completed the first-year study of Chinese. Pinyin & Yale transcriptions are used throughout the text, but correspondence tables are given between Wades-Giles romanization & Pinyin so the text can be used regardless of the romanization system learned previously. Both full & simplified characters are provided.

peaking Chinese in China CDs & Text. Hsu Ying & J. Marvin Brown. 6 CDs. (Running Time: 5 hrs.). (CHI.). 2005. audio compact disk 155.00 (978-1-57970-279-3(1), AFM320D, Audio-For) J Norton Pubs.
This second-year conversation course teachese Chinese the way it is :urretnly being used in China. This program of lively and colloquial dialogs is uitable for anyone who has completed the first-year study of Chinese. inyin and Yale romanization are used, but correspondence tables are given tween Wade-Giles romanzation and pinyin so the text can be used ardless of the romanization system learned previously. Both full and lified characters are provided.

g Clearly: Pronunciation & Listening Comprehension for Learners glish. Pamela Rogerson & Judy B. Gilbert. 2 cass. (Running Time: ins.). (ENG., 1990. 45.00 (978-0-521-32187-7(5)) Cambridge U Pr.

Clearly Audio CDs (3) Pronunciation & Listening hension for Learners of English. Pamela Rogerson & Judy B. Running Time: 2 hrs. 48 mins.). (ENG.). 2010. audio compact disk '8-0-521-14220-5(2)) Cambridge U Pr.

fective English! Your Guide to Acquiring New Confidence in & Professional Communication. Bettye Zoller et al. Read by r. Frwd. by Edward Asner. 2004. 10.95 (978-0-7435-1943-4(4),) Pub: S&S Audio. Dist(s): S and S Inc

tive English! Your Guide to Acquiring New Confidence in rofessional Communication. abr. ed. Hugh Lampman et al. e Zoller. Frwd. by Edward Asner. (Running Time: 2 hrs. 0 ENG.). 2006. audio compact disk 19.95 12-0(X)) Pub: S&S Audio. Dist(s): S and S Inc

Resource Book of Multi-Level Skills Activities. Mick bridge Copy Collection). (ENG.). 2004. audio compact -521-75465-1(8)) Cambridge U Pr.

: How to Communicate Substance with Passion. T. J. compact disk 39.00 (978-1-932642-00-1(5)) Media

Speaking for Themselves: The Personal Letters of Winston & Clementine Churchill. Winston L. S. Churchill & Clementine Churchill. Narrated by Helen Bourne. Adapted by Penny Leicester. 2004. audio compact disk 29.95 (978-0-563-52443-4(X)) AudioGO.

Speaking Freely. Interview with Ayn Rand. 1 cass. (Running Time: 55 min.). 12.95 (978-1-56114-016-9(3), AR07C) Second Renaissance.
NBC newsman Edwin Newman interviews Ayn Rand on such topics as feminism, environmentalism, drug use & the cultural influence of Immanuel Kant.

Speaking Globally: English in an International Context. William Grohe & Christine B. Root. 2002. 22.05 (978-0-13-460361-2(3)) Longman.

Speaking God's Word. Speeches. Henry Neufeld & Linda Smith. 4 CDs. 2004. audio compact disk 20.00 (978-1-893729-06-3(0)) Energion Pubns.
Conference presentation on the spiritual gifts of prophecy, teaching and exhortation presented at Pine Forest United Methodist Church in the fall of 1999. The four CDs each contain one session between 40 and 60 minutes.

Speaking Greek CD. 2nd ed. Joint Association of Classical Teachers' Greek Course. (Reading Greek Ser.). (ENG.). (C). 2008. audio compact disk 33.99 (978-0-521-72896-6(7)) Cambridge U Pr.

Speaking High Frequency French: Complete Learning Guide & Tapescript. Mark Frobose. 8 cass. (Running Time: 8 hrs.). (FRE.). 1993. stu. ed. 69.00 (978-1-893564-02-2(9)) Macmill Audio.

Speaking High Frequency German: Complete Learning Guide & Tapescript. Mark Frobose. 6 cass. (Running Time: 6 hrs.). (GER.). 1993. stu. ed. 49.00 (978-1-893564-06-0(1)) Macmill Audio.

Speaking High Frequency Italian Course. Mark Frobose. 6 CDs. 2004. audio compact disk 49.00 (978-1-893564-04-6(5)) Macmill Audio.

Speaking High Frequency Spanish: Complete Learning Guide & Tapescript. Mark Frobose. 8 cass. (Running Time: 8 hrs.). (SPA.). 1993. stu. ed. 69.00 (978-1-893564-00-8(2)) Macmill Audio.

Speaking in Public: Buckley's Techniques for Winning Arguments & Getting Your Point Across. Reid Buckley. Read by Thomas Andrews. (Running Time: 32400 sec.). 2007. audio compact disk 72.00 (978-1-4332-0388-6(X)) Blckstn Audio.

Speaking in Public: Buckley's Techniques for Winning Arguments & Getting Your Point Across. unabr. ed. Read by Thomas Andrews. (Running Time: 32400 sec.). 2007. audio compact disk 29.95 (978-0-7861-5906-2(5)); audio compact disk 72.00 (978-0-7861-5905-5(7)) Blckstn Audio.

Speaking in Public: Buckley's Techniques for Winning Arguments & Getting Your Point Across, unabr. ed. Reid Buckley. Read by Reid Buckley. 7 cass. (Running Time: 10 hrs.). 1992. 49.95 (978-0-7861-0051-4(6), 1049) Blckstn Audio.
Topics included are: defeating nervousness; building a formidable case that will crush the opposition; developing a speech; how to gesture; one common mistake of public speakers; how to cope with a hostile press & how to dress.

Speaking in the Strike Zone: How to Get in Front of a Buying Audience. 2002. audio compact disk 34.95 (978-0-9716089-1-7(1)) Sullivan Speaker.

Speaking in Tongues. Jeffery Deaver. Read by Grover Gardner. 2000. 56.00 (978-0-7366-5928-4(5)) Books on Tape.

Speaking in Tongues. John MacArthur, Jr. 7 cass. (John MacArthur's Bible Studies). 22.25 (HarperThor) HarpC GBR.

Speaking in Tongues. abr. ed. Jeffery Deaver. Read by Dennis Boutsikaris. 2006. 17.95 (978-0-7435-6424-3(3)) Pub: S&S Audio. Dist(s): S and S Inc

Speaking in Tongues. unabr. ed. Jeffery Deaver. Read by Grover Gardner. 7 cass. (Running Time: 10 hrs. 30 min.). 2000. 56.00 Books on Tape.
Tate Collier & his ex-wife Bett reunite in a desperate attempt to save their daughter from a psychopathic psychologist.

Speaking in Tongues: Logos Jan. 31,1999. Ben Young. 1999. 4.95 (978-0-7417-6117-0(3), B0117) Win Walk.

Speaking My Mind. unabr. ed. Ronald Reagan. Read by Ronald Reagan. 6 cass. (Running Time: 6 hrs.). 1989. pap. bk. 79.95 set. (978-0-671-69472-2(3)) S&S Audio.

Speaking My Mind: Selected Speeches with Personal Reflections. Ronald Reagan. Read by Ronald Reagan. 5 CDs. (Running Time: 5 hrs. 30 mins. 0 sec.). (ENG.). 1999. audio compact disk 32.00 (978-0-7435-0033-3(4), Audioworks) Pub: S&S Audio. Dist(s): S and S Inc

Speaking Naturally. 1 cass. bk. 29.50 (SEN158) J Norton Pubs.
For intermediate & high intermediate students interested in using American English in social interaction. Uses short recorded dialogs in a wide range of accents & different levels of formality.

Speaking Naturally: Communication Skills in American English. Bruce Tillitt & Mary Newton Bruder. (Running Time: 43 mins.). (ENG., 1985. 24.00 (978-0-521-25007-8(2)) Cambridge U Pr.

Speaking Naturally: Communication Skills in American English. Bruce Tillitt & Mary Newton Bruder. 1 cass. 19.95 Midwest European Pubns.
Each unit focuses on a language function such as asking for information, thanking, complimenting, & inviting.

Speaking Naturally Audio Sampler: Communication Skills in American English. Bruce Tillitt & Mary Newton Bruder. 1 cass. (Running Time: 1 hr.). Cambridge U Pr.
For students learning to make appropriate linguistic choices in a variety of situations. Each unit focuses on a language function, such as asking for information thanking, complimenting, and inviting. Readings explain the cultural "rules" students need to know in real-life situations. Short recorded dialogs expose students to a range of American accents. Structured exercises as well as freer role plays, often involving pairs or small groups, encourage interaction in the classroom.

Speaking of Faith. unabr. ed. Krista Tippett. Read by Krista Tippett. (Running Time: 24300 sec.). (ENG.). 2007. audio compact disk 29.95 (978-1-59887-083-1(1), 1598870831) Pub: HighBridge. Dist(s): Workman Pub

Speaking of Freedom: The Collected Speeches. abr. ed. George H. W. Bush. Read by George H. W. Bush. (Running Time: 6 hrs. 0 mins. 0 sec.). (ENG.). 2009. audio compact disk 29.99 (978-0-7435-8305-3(1)) Pub: S&S Audio. Dist(s): S and S Inc

Speaking of Life pt. 1: The Beggining. Short Stories. Perf. by Kevin Sharp. Prod. by Kevin Sharp. Prod. by Paul E. Jones. 1 CD. (Running Time: 58 Min). (J). 2004. audio compact disk 15.45 (978-0-9758512-2-7(5), 00124) ZassCo Pub.
Platinum Selling Recording artist Kevin Sharp is know world wide for such #1 hits as "Know Body Knows" and "If You Love Somebody", he is also know as a Cancer Survivor. Listen as Kevin tells his story in his own words about growing up, the diagnoses and his journey with Cancer. This is a 4 part series that will include Music tracks picked by Kevin that have special meaning to him.

Speaking of Radio: Jack Benny. (Running Time: 6 hrs.). 2004. audio compact disk 29.95 (978-1-57816-196-6(7)) Audio File.

Speaking of Shakespeare's Verse. Read by Ronald Watkins et al. 10.95 (978-0-8045-1022-6(9), SAC 1022) Spoken Arts.

Speaking of Survival. Daniel B. Freeman. 1993. 17.50 (978-0-88336-197-9(3)) OUP.

Speaking of Your Garden, Set. abr. ed. Robert Smaus. 2 cass. (Running Time: 2 hrs.). (Discovery Ser.). 1992. pap. bk. 15.95 (978-1-56015-208-8(7)) Penton Overseas.
Guides listeners through the design, planting & maintenance of an attractive garden.

Speaking Out. Steck-Vaughn Staff. 2003. (978-0-7398-8431-7(X)) SteckVau.

Speaking Pain Free French the Natural Way: Complete Learning Guide & Tapescript. Mark Frobose. 6 cass. (Running Time: 6 hrs.). (ITA.). 1999. stu. ed. 69.00 (978-1-893564-64-0(9)) Macmill Audio.

Speaking Pain Free German the Natural Way: Complete Learning Guide & Tapescript. Mark Frobose. 6 cass. (Running Time: 6 hrs.). (GER.). 1999. stu. ed. 49.00 (978-1-893564-66-4(5)) Macmill Audio.

Speaking Pain Free Italian the Natural Way: Complete Learning Guide & Tapescript. Mark Frobose. 6 cass. (Running Time: 6 hrs.). (ITA.). 1999. stu. ed. 59.00 (978-1-893564-65-7(7)) Macmill Audio.

Speaking Pain Free Spanish. Mark Frobose. 8 CDs. (Running Time: 8 hrs.). (SPA., 2002. pap. bk. 69.00 (978-1-893564-47-3(9)) Macmill Audio.

Speaking Pain Free Spanish the Natural Way: Complete Learning Guide & Tapescript. Mark Frobose. 8 cass. (Running Time: 8 hrs.). (SPA.). 1999. stu. ed. 69.00 (978-1-893564-63-3(0)) Macmill Audio.

Speaking Peace. Marshall Rosenberg. 2003. audio compact disk 24.95 (978-1-59179-077-8(8)) Sounds True.

Speaking Polish in Poland. Oscar E. Swan. 3 cass. (Running Time: 3 hrs. 30 mins.). 1993. pap. bk. 49.95 (978-0-88432-693-9(4), AFP650) J Norton Pubs.
Essential phrases & vocabulary for the traveler or business person are arranged topically & presented first in English, then in Polish.

Speaking Polish in Poland CDs & Text. Oscar E. Swan. 3 CDs. (Running Time: 3 hrs. 30 min.). (POL.). 2005. audio compact disk 49.95 (978-1-57970-137-6(X), AFP650D) J Norton Pubs.

Speaking Solutions: Interaction, Presentation, Listening, & Pronunciation Skills, Set. Candace Matthews. 2002. 43.85 (978-0-13-100611-9(8)) Longman.

Speaking the Lost Language of God: Awakening the Forgotten Wisdom of Prayer, Prophecy, & the Dead Sea Scrolls. Gregg Braden. 4 CDs. 2005. audio compact disk 23.95 (978-1-4019-0764-8(4)) Hay House.

Speaking the Right Words. Speeches. Joel Osteen. 1 Cass. (Running Time: 30 Mins.). 2002. 6.00 (978-1-59349-150-5(6), JA0150) J Osteen.

Speaking to the Neshoma: The Critical Difference Between Discipline & Tochacha. Elimelech Gottlieb. 1 cass. (Running Time: 90 mins.). 1999. 6.00 (W60SB) Torah Umesorah.

Speaking up & Speaking Out! Created by Louise LeBrun. (Women & Power Ser.: Vol. 1). 1999. 10.95 (978-0-9685566-0-3(4)) Par3tners Renewal CAN.

Speaking with One Heart: The Mayan Languages of Mexico. Robert Laughlin. Read by Robert Laughlin. 1 cass. (Running Time: 30 min.). 1996. 10.95 (978-1-57511-012-7(1)) Pub Mills.
A radio documentary of the Smithsonian Institution & Soundprint. The ancient language of the Mayans, Tzotzil, preserves valuable knowledge of plants useful in food, medicine, & even construction. It is a living, beautiful language, spoken by thousands in the Chiapas region of present-day Mexico. But it has been, until now, an unwritten language. Smithsonian anthropologist Robert Laughlin is working with Mayans living in Mexico to write a Tzotzil dictionary, insuring the preservation of the language & of the knowledge that it carries. With the power of words, a renewed sense of self-respect has led some Mayans working with Laughlin to new insights on questions of the meaning of cultural identity.

Speaking with Your Guardian Angel. unabr. ed. Gary Arnold. 1 cass. (Running Time: 1 hr.). 1997. pap. bk. 12.95 Windhorse Corp.
A practical guide to contacting & communications with your guardian angel.

Speaking Without Fear or Nervousness: How to Be Effective Whenever You Make Presentations, Lead Meetings or Join Group Discussions. Helen Sutton. 2 cass. (Running Time: 3 hrs.). 1997. 15.95 (978-1-55977-675-2(7)) CareerTrack Pubns.

Speaking Your Client's Language see Hablar el Idioma de Su Cliente, A Spanish Course for Patient Registration, Student Edition: Speaking your Client's Language

Speaking 4: Advanced. Joanne Collie & Stephen Slater. Contrib. by Adrian Doff. (Running Time: 55 mins.). (Cambridge Skills for Fluency Ser.). (ENG., 1993. stu. ed. 25.20 (978-0-521-39973-9(4)) Cambridge U Pr.

Spear. James Herbert. 9 cass. (Isis Cassettes Ser.). (J). 2005. 76.95 (978-0-7531-2143-6(3)); audio compact disk 89.95 (978-0-7531-2392-8(4)) Pub: ISIS Lrg Prnt GBR. Dist(s): Ulverscroft US

Spear of Destiny. unabr. ed. Trevor Ravenscroft. 1 cass. (Running Time: 1 hr. 29 min.). 1978. 11.00 (12501) Big Sur Tapes.
Tracing the mythic history of the Spear of Destiny through Roman times into the Middle Ages, when it disappears from sight, through its re-emergence in the 20th Century in conjunction with Hitler's rise to power.

Spear Throwing Contest: Scripts for Young Readers. Read by Patrick Feehan. Retold by Heather McDonald. (J). 2009. 9.95 (978-1-60184-159-9(0)) Primry Concpts.

Special Children/Special Solutions. Created by Samahria Kaufman. (ENG.). 2006. audio compact disk 59.00 (978-1-887254-24-3(2)) Epic Century.

Special Christmas Gift: The New Life Community Choir Featuring John P. Kee. 1 cass., 1 CD. Provident Mus Dist.

Special Circumstances. unabr. ed. Sheldon Siegel. Narrated by Frank Muller. 10 cass. (Running Time: 14 hrs. 30 mins.). 2000. 91.00 (978-0-7887-4849-3(1), 96449E7) Recorded Bks.
Placed in the center of an explosive murder trial where politics & greed clash with truth & justice. Fired by Simpson & Gates, one of San Francisco's most prestigious law firms, lawyer Mike Dailey quietly opens his practice on the wrong side of town. He takes on his first client, a partner at Simpson & Gates, for a brutal double murder. As Mike frantically digs for evidence, he discovers the firm has a lot to hide & his friend conceals a dirty secret, too.

Special Circumstances. unabr. ed. Sheldon Siegel. Narrated by Frank Muller. 13 CDs. (Running Time: 14 hrs. 30 mins.). 2001. audio compact disk 124.00 (978-0-7887-6183-6(8), C1408) Recorded Bks.
Crackling with energy & suspense, Special Circumstances places you in the center of an explosive murder trial where politics & greed clash with truth & justice. Fired by Simpson & Gates, one of San Francisco's most prestigious law firms, lawyer Mike Dailey quietly opens his own practice on the wrong side of town. He takes on his first client when police arrest his best friend, a partner at Simpson & Gates, for a brutal double murder. As Mike frantically digs for evidence, he discovers the firm has a lot to hide & his friend conceals a dirty secret, too. In this brilliantly paced, sharp-witted thriller, Sheldon Siegel reveals both the pitfalls & safeguards in our criminal justice

system. Frank Muller's dramatic pacing keeps you on the edge of your chair from the intriguing first chapter to the stunning conclusion.

Special Days / Lullabies & Quiet Time: Songs for Children & Lullabies & Quiet Time. Perf. by Myrna Cohen. Prod. by George Fogelman. Arranged by George Fogelman. Executive Producer Randee Friedman. (Running Time: 70 mins.). (HEB.). (J). 2002. audio compact disk 15.95 (978-1-890161-49-1(7), 0606261700125) Sounds Write.
Now available together on one CD, are SPECIAL DAYS and LULLABIES & QUIET TIME, the popular children?s recordings by Cantorial Soloist, Myrna Cohen. SPECIAL DAYS is a collection of 21 upbeat, Hebrew and English songs, and Jewish holiday music, that highlight the special days of our people and special portions of a young child?s day - wakeup, school, home, the neighborhood, and beyond. LULLABIES & QUIET TIME features 10 English, Hebrew and Yiddish songs for nap or bedtime, and songs for quiet time or quiet play.

Special Deception. Alexander Fullerton. (Soundings (CDs) Ser.). (J). 2006. audio compact disk 99.95 (978-1-84559-298-1(0)) Pub: ISIS Lrg Prnt GBR. Dist(s): Ulverscroft US

Special Deception. Alexander Fullerton. Read by Terry Wale. 10 cass. (Soundings Ser.). (J). 2006. 84.95 (978-1-84559-126-7(7)) Pub: ISIS Lrg Prnt GBR. Dist(s): Ulverscroft US

Special Deliverance. unabr. ed. Alexander Fullerton. 10 cass. (Soundings Ser.). (J). 2006. 84.95 (978-1-84559-125-0(9)); audio compact disk 99.95 (978-1-84559-148-9(8)) Pub: ISIS Lrg Prnt GBR. Dist(s): Ulverscroft US

Special Delivery. Zoe Barnes. 2008. 76.95 (978-0-7531-3041-4(6)); audio compact disk 89.95 (978-0-7531-3042-1(4)) Pub: ISIS Audio GBR. Dist(s): Ulverscroft US

Special Dynamic. unabr. ed. Alexander Fullerton. Read by Terry Wale. 10 CDs. (Running Time: 11 hrs.). (Soundings (CDs) Ser.). (J). 2006. audio compact disk 89.95 (978-1-84559-215-8(8)) Pub: ISIS Lrg Prnt GBR. Dist(s): Ulverscroft US

Special Dynamic. unabr. ed. Alexander Fullerton. Read by Terry Wale. 9 cass. (Soundings Ser.). (J). 2006. 76.95 (978-1-84559-124-3(0)) Pub: ISIS Lrg Prnt GBR. Dist(s): Ulverscroft US

Special Education Law. Salomone et al. 1 cass. (Running Time: 1 hr.). 1986. 7.95 Ed Law Assn.

Special for Fundraisers. Julian Padowicz. Read by Julian Padowicz. 3 cass. 1993. 34.95 set. (978-1-881288-07-7(2), BFI AudioBooks) BusnFilm Intl.
Instructional cassettes: Soliciting the Major Gift, Stalking the Corporate Dollar, Public Relations in Support of Development.

Special Libraries & Information Centers: An Introductory Text. 4th ed. Ellis Mount & Renee Massoud. 1 cass. 1999. bk. 49.00 (978-0-87111-501-0(8)) SLA.

Special Meditation: Healing the Past. Paul Chivington. Voice by Paul Chivington. 1 CD. (Running Time: 90 mins.). 1983. 10.00 (978-0-9791360-8-5(3)) Gentle Living.
Paul Chivington leading the meditation for healing the past and experiencing your Anima or Animus.

Special Meditation: Healing the Past. Paul Chivington. Voice by Paul Chivington. 1 CD. (Running Time: 90 mins.). 2006. audio compact disk 10.00 (978-0-9791360-7-8(5)) Gentle Living.

Special Moments with the Message for Women. unabr. ed. Eugene H. Peterson. Narrated by Rebecca St. James. (Running Time: 2 hrs. 0 mins. 0 sec.). (ENG.). 2006. 6.99 (978-1-60814-395-5(3)) Oasis Audio.

Special Moments with the Message for Women. unabr. ed. Eugene H. Peterson. Narrated by Brooke Sanford & Rebecca St. James. (Running Time: 2 hrs. 0 mins. 0 sec.). (ENG.). 2008. audio compact disk 12.99 (978-1-59859-464-5(8)) Oasis Audio.

Special Music from Special Kids. Perf. by Kids of Widney High. 1 cass. (Running Time: 41 min.). (Family Ser.). (J). (gr. 1-9). 1989. 9.98 (8014); audio compact disk 14.98 (8014) Rounder Records.
This remarkable recording results from a songwriting class at Widney High, where Michael Monagan was teaching severely handicapped students. The students poured their efforts into the writing & performing of the songs.

Special Needs Trusts: Administering, Advising, & Representing the Trustee. 2 cass. (Running Time: 2 hrs.). 1997. 25.00 Set; incl. study outline. (M208) Am Law Inst.
Advanced program reviews techniques, offers important tax tips, & identifies practical approaches from the teleseminar series, "Counseling the Older Clients on Trusts & Nursing Home Issues".

Special Operations. unabr. collector's ed. W. E. B. Griffin. Read by Michael Rossotto. 8 cass. (Running Time: 12 hrs.). (Badge of Honor Ser.: Vol. 2). 1993. 64.00 (978-0-7366-2492-3(9), 3251) Books on Tape.
Police face desperate public & hostile press when kidnapping spree terrifies city.

Special Operations DVD. International Association of Fire Chiefs Staff & National Fire Protection Association. 2005. 315.95 (978-0-7637-3613-2(9)) Jones Bartlett.

Special Ops. W. E. B. Griffin. Read by Scott Brick. (Brotherhood of War Ser.: Bk. 9). 2001. 88.00 (978-0-7366-6306-9(1)) Books on Tape.

Special Ops. W. E. B. Griffin. Read by Scott Brick. (Brotherhood of War Ser.: No. 9). 2001. 64.00 (978-0-7366-6307-6(X)) Books on Tape.

Special Order & the Canterville Ghost. 1 CD. (Running Time: 1 hr.). 2001. audio compact disk 15.95 (ARTC008) Lodestone Catalog.
A very strange client places an unusual order with a mall bookstore: When an American family moves into the British Canterville manor, to scare the ghosts away.

Special Powers. unabr. ed. Mary Hoffman. Read by Helen Lederer. 4 cass. (Running Time: 4 hrs.). (J). (gr. 1-8). 1999. 32.95 (CCA 3500, Chivers Child Audio) AudioGO.

Special Reading Problems: Some Helps Training Module - Trainer's Guide. Susanne Miller. 1 cass. 1983. 132.00 (978-0-930713-47-8(8)) Lit Vol Am.

Special Relationships. Kenneth Wapnick. 1 CD. (Running Time: 19 hrs. 38 mins. 25 secs.). 2006. 94.00 (978-1-59142-256-3(6), 3m9&10) Foun Miracles.

Special Relationships, Part 1. Kenneth Wapnick. 10 CDs. 2006. audio compact disk 62.00 (978-1-59142-254-9(X), CD9) Foun Miracles.

Special Relationships, Part 2. Kenneth Wapnick. 7 CDs. 2006. audio compact disk 49.00 (978-1-59142-255-6(8), CD10) Foun Miracles.

Special Relationships: The Home of Guilt. Kenneth Wapnick. 3CDs. 2006. audio compact disk 20.00 (978-1-59142-227-3(2), CD68) Foun Miracles.

Special Relationships: The Home of Guilt. Kenneth Wapnick. 2009. 16.00 (978-1-59142-377-5(5)) Foun Miracles.

Special Settings Kit. 1998. bk. 24.95 (978-0-664-50050-4(1)) Pub: Presbyterian Pub. Dist(s): Westminster John Knox

Special Student Series: Practice Dictation Recordings. National Shorthand Reporters Association. 3 cass. (SS Ser. A). 20.00 SS-110-1, SS-120-1, SS-130-1. (CT-74); 20.00 SS-140-1, SS-150-1, SS-160-1. (CT-75); 7.00 SS-170-1. (CT-76) Natl Ct Report.
Prepared specifically for the professional of the future. There are seven recordings in all, recorded in studios under exacting conditions. They are offered at student speeds of 110, 120, 130, 140, 150, & 160 wpm. Each cassette tape provides 12 five-minute selections. Please note each set is priced independently.

Special Tax-Planning Techniques for Small Businesses & Individuals. Melvyn Poswolsky. 4 cass. (Running Time: 10 hrs.). 1995. wbk. ed. 129.00 (753462EZ) Am Inst CPA.
This advanced course will guide you in such areas as choice of accounting methods, changes of accounting methods, depreciation, the problems of survivors, executors & administrators, tax penalties, bankruptcy, & educational expenses.

Special Techniques for Working with Older Adults: Tapes & Exam. Elinor Waters. 4 cass. (Running Time: 4 hrs.). 94.00 (74217) Am Coun Assn.
This program includes a discussion of the advantages & limitations of group counseling with older adults, & the special value of peer counseling with this population.

***Special Words for Special People: Offering Grace to the Weary.** Charles R. Swindoll. 2009. audio compact disk 34.00 (978-1-57972-856-4(1)) Insight Living.

Specially Special Songs. 1998. 21.95 (978-0-7673-3482-2(5)); audio compact disk 24.95 (978-0-7673-3481-5(7)) LifeWay Christian.

Specialty Bugler: An Eclectic Survey of Diverse American Bugling Traditions Co-Ordinated with Recordings. Mark Johnson. (Complete Bugler Ser.). (J). (gr. 4-12). 1995. pap. bk. 13.99 (978-1-883988-19-7(5)) RSV Prods.

Specialty Review in Critical Care, Vol. A192. unabr. ed. 25 cass. (Running Time: 32 hrs.). 1995. 695.00 set. (978-1-57664-360-0(3)) CME Info Svcs.
Continuing medical education home-study. Complete package contains audiotapes, syllabus, self-assessment examination to earn CME Category 1 credit.

Specialty Review in Gastroenterology, Vol. A191. unabr. ed. 31 cass. (Running Time: 35 hrs.). 1995. 695.00 set. (978-1-57664-359-4(X)) CME Info Svcs.

Specialty Series No. 3: Medical. National Shorthand Reporters Association. 1 cass. 9.00 (CT-39) Natl Ct Report.
Practice dictation testimony dealing with orthopedics, gynecology, proctology, general medicine, cardiology, pediatrics, obstetrics, neurology & internal medicine. (150 & 160 wpm).

Specialty Series No. 4: Medical. National Shorthand Reporters Association. 1 cass. 9.00 (CT-40) Natl Ct Report.
Practice dictation testimony dealing with pathology, neurology, orthopedics, gynecology, internal medicine, chiropractics, radiology, gastroentrology & neurosurgey. (170 & 180 wpm.).

Specialty Series No. 5: Medical. National Shorthand Reporters Association. 1 cass. 9.00 (CT-41) Natl Ct Report.
Practice dictation testimony dealing with orthopedics, internal medicine, radiology, obstetrics, pathology, neurosurgey, general surgery . (190 & 200 wpm.).

Species: A Novel. abr. ed. Yvonne Navarro. Read by Alfred Molina. Contrib. by Dennis Feldman. 2 cass. 1995. 17.00 Set. (978-1-56876-039-1(6)) Soundlines Ent.
An outer space transmission leads to a female human/alien hybrid. And when the hybrid escapes, they must put together a task force to track her. Their only lead is a growing trail of dead bodies. When the team determines that she intends to propagate her species, their desperate search intensifies. Audie Award winner 1996.

Species Extinction & Tax Deductions. Hosted by Nancy Pearlman. 1 cass. (Running Time: 29 min.). 10.00 (601) Educ Comm CA.

Specimen Days. Michael Cunningham. Read by Alan Cumming. 2005. 20.95 (978-1-59397-715-3(8)) Pub: Macmill Audio. Dist(s): Macmillan

Specimen Days. abr. ed. Michael Cunningham. Read by Alan Cumming. 2005. 14.95 (978-1-59397-714-6(X)) Pub: Macmill Audio. Dist(s): Macmillan

Specimen Days. unabr. ed. Michael Cunningham. 2005. 29.95 (978-0-7927-3659-2(1), CMP 809); 54.95 (978-0-7927-3657-8(5), CSL 809); audio compact disk 79.95 (978-0-7927-3658-5(3), SLD 809) AudioGO.

Specimen Days. unabr. ed. Michael Cunningham. Read by Alan Cumming. 9 CDs. (Running Time: 11 hrs. 0 mins. 0 sec.). (ENG.). 2005. audio compact disk 39.95 (978-1-59397-689-7(5)) Pub: Macmill Audio. Dist(s): Macmillan

Specimen Days Journal: Walt Whitman. abr. ed. Read by Jeff Riggenbach. 2 cass. 1995. 17.95 set. (8480Q) Filmic Archives.
An intimate glimpse of nineteenth century America as seen through the personal reflections of its most representative poet. This is Whitman's autobiography in journal from a prosaic account of his life as a poet, nurse, & sage. It is a portrayal of Whitman's Civil War ministrations & the subsequent years he spent in creative contemplation traces the growth of the poet's soul.

Speckled Band see Adventures of Sherlock Holmes

Speckled Band see Famous Cases of Sherlock Holmes

***Specky Magee & the Great Footy Contest.** unabr. ed. Felice Arena & Gary Lyon. Read by Felice Arena & Gary Lyon. (Running Time: 3 hrs. 20 mins.). (YA). 2003. audio compact disk 24.00 (978-1-74093-035-2(5)) Pub: Bolinda Pubng AUS. Dist(s): Bolinda Pub Inc

Spectacle of Corruption. abr. ed. David Liss. Read by Michael Page. (Running Time: 6 hrs.). 2004. audio compact disk 74.25 (978-1-59355-657-0(8), 1593556578) Brilliance Audio.
Benjamin Weaver, the quick-witted pugilist turned private investigator, who was first introduced in the Edgar Award-winning novel, THE CONSPIRACY OF PAPER, returns. While inquiring into some threatening notes sent to a Church of England priest, Weaver is arrested for the murder of a dockworker. After his conviction, engineered by a crooked judge who has blatantly instructed the jury to disregard the truth, Weaver escapes from prison, intent upon proving his innocence. Meanwhile, Great Britain is reeling from a financial scandal that has sent the economy into a downward spiral; it is also preparing for a general parliamentary election - an event that happens only every seven years. Not generally someone to get caught up in politics, Benjamin Weaver finds himself caught in the crossfire of election trickery as he attempts to clear his name. The question remains, however: What good is proving his innocence, again, when having done so once only resulted in conviction? Instead, he is determined to work against his enemies and learn their secrets to try to discover why he has been singled out for this prosecution. The most likely engineer of his ruin is Dennis Dogmill, a tobacco importer and the election agent of the Whig candidate for the Westminster Parliamentary seat. Dogmill's opponent, and Weaver's unlikely ally, is Griffin Melbury, the Tory candidate and the husband of his cousin's widow, Miriam, whom Weaver once sought to marry. To discover the truth about the plot against him, Weaver disguises himself as a newly returned West Indian plantation owner. He must integrate himself with London society and political manipulators in order to learn the truth.

Spectacle of Corruption. unabr. ed. David Liss. Read by Michael Page. (Running Time: 14 hrs.). 2004. 97.25 (978-1-59355-655-6(1), 1593556551); 34.95 (978-1-59355-654-9(3), 1593556543) Brilliance Audio.

Spectacle of Corruption. unabr. ed. David Liss. Read by Michael Page. (Running Time: 14 hrs.). (Benjamin Weaver Ser.). 2004. 39.25 (978-1-59335-543-2(2), 1593355432, Brinc Audio MP3 Lib); 24.95 (978-1-59335-284-4(0), 1593352840, Brilliance MP3) Brilliance Audio.

Spectacle of Corruption. unabr. ed. David Liss. Read by Michael Page. (Running Time: 14 hrs.). 2004. 39.25 (978-1-59710-735-8(2), 1597107352, BADLE); 24.95 (978-1-59710-734-1(4), 1597107344, BAD) Brilliance Audio.

Spectacular Moves of the Spirit: Contending for the End-Time Outpouring. Lynne Hammond. 4 CDs. 2006. audio compact disk 20.00 (978-1-57399-354-8(9)) Mac Hammond.

Spectacular Now. unabr. ed. Tim Tharp. Read by MacLeod Andrews. (Running Time: 8 hrs.). 2009. 24.99 (978-1-4233-9964-3(1), 9781423399643, Brilliance MP3); 39.97 (978-1-4233-9965-0(X), 9781423399650, Brinc Audio MP3 Lib); 24.99 (978-1-4233-9966-7(8), 9781423399667, BAD); 39.97 (978-1-4233-9967-4(6), 9781423399674, BADLE); audio compact disk 29.99 (978-1-4233-9962-9(5), 9781423399629) Brilliance Audio.

Spectacular Now. unabr. ed. Tim Tharp. Read by MacLeod Andrews. 7 CDs. (Running Time: 8 hrs.). (YA). (gr. 9 up). 2009. audio compact disk 87.97 (978-1-4233-9963-6(3), 9781423399636, BriAudCD Unabrid) Brilliance Audio.

Spectacular Sins: And Their Global Purpose in the Glory of Christ. unabr. ed. John Piper. (Running Time: 3 hrs. 30 mins. 0 sec.). (ENG.). 2009. audio compact disk 15.98 (978-1-59644-765-3(6), Hovel Audio) christianaud.

***Spectacular Sins: And Their Global Purpose in the Glory of Christ.** unabr. ed. John Piper. Narrated by Arthur Morey. (ENG.). 2009. 9.98 (978-1-59644-766-0(4), Hovel Audio) christianaud.

Spectacular Stone Soup. unabr. ed. Patricia Reilly Giff. 1 cass. (Running Time: 48 min.). (New Kids at the Polk Street School Ser.). (J). (gr. 1-2). 1990. pap. bk. 15.98 (978-0-8072-0175-6(8), FTR 139 SP, Listening Lib) Random Audio Pubg.

Spectacular Support Centers: The Companion CD. Kristin E. Robertson. (ENG.). 2008. audio compact disk 56.95 (978-0-9713406-8-8(4)) Cust Service Pr.

Spectator Bird. unabr. ed. Wallace Stegner. Read by Edward Herrmann. (Running Time: 8 hrs. 0 mins.). 2010. 29.95 (978-1-4417-2494-6(X)); 54.95 (978-1-4417-2490-8(7)); audio compact disk 76.00 (978-1-4417-2491-5(5)) Blckstn Audio.

Spectator Bird & Crossing to Safety. Wallace Stegner. Read by Wallace Stegner. 1 cass. (Running Time: 70 min.). 1987. 13.95 (978-1-55644-198-1(3), 7081) Am Audio Prose.
This marvelous reading performance will delight the late Stegner's many, many fans.

Specter Bridegroom see Selected American Short Stories

Spectral Ship see Flying Dutchman

Spectre. William Shatner. (Star Trek Ser.). 2004. 10.95 (978-0-7435-4681-2(4)) Pub: S&S Audio. Dist(s): S and S Inc

Spectre. William Shatner et al. Read by William Shatner. (Running Time: 4 hrs.). 2002. 19.95 (978-1-60083-434-9(5), Audiofy Corp) Iofy Corp.

Spectre Bride see Classic Ghost Stories, Vol. 2, A Collection

Spectrum: A Communicative Course in English, Level 1. Diane Warshawsky et al. 6 cass. 2002. 132.30 (978-0-13-328931-2(1)); 63.00 (978-0-13-829938-5(2)); 63.00 (978-0-13-829953-8(6)) Longman.

Spectrum: A Communicative Course in English, Level 2, 2B. Diane Warshawsky et al. (Spectrum Ser.). 2002. 63.00 (978-0-13-830050-0(X)) Longman.

Spectrum: A Communicative Course in English, Level 3. Diane Warshawsky et al. 6 cass. 2002. 132.30 (978-0-13-830548-2(X)) Longman.

Spectrum: A Communicative Course in English, Level 3, 3A. Diane Warshawsky et al. 2002. 63.00 (978-0-13-830100-2(X)) Longman.

Spectrum: A Communicative Course in English, Level 3, 3B. Diane Warshawsky et al. 2002. 63.00 (978-0-13-830142-2(5)) Longman.

Spectrum: A Communicative Course in English, Level 4. Diane Warshawsky et al. 2002. bk. 63.00 (978-0-13-830761-5(X)); 132.30 (978-0-13-830811-7(X)); 63.00 (978-0-13-830183-5(2)) Longman.

Spectrum: A Communicative Course in English, Level 5. Diane Warshawsky et al. 5 cass. 2002. 111.60 (978-0-13-830225-2(1)) Longman.

Spectrum: A Communicative Course in English, Level 6. Diane Warshawsky et al. 5 cass. 2002. bk. 111.60 (978-0-13-830266-5(9)) Longman.

Spectrum: A Scientifically Proven Program to Feel Better, Live Longer, Lose Weight, & Gain Health. abr. ed. Dean Omish. Read by Dean Omish. Read by Anne Omish. (Running Time: 12600 sec.). (ENG.). 2007. audio compact disk 24.95 (978-0-7393-2909-2(X), Random Hse Audible) Pub: Random Audio Pubg. Dist(s): Random

Spectrum Audio Program: A Communicative Course in English, Level 2, Bk. 2A. 2nd ed. Diane Warshawsky et al. 2002. pap. bk. 63.00 (978-0-13-830019-7(4)) Longman.

Spectrum of Techniques. Harvey Jackins. 1 cass. 10.00 (978-1-58429-014-8(5)) Rational Isl.
Lecture describing techniques used in counseling clients.

Spectrum Suite. Music by Steven Halpern. 1 cass. 9.95 (LA127); audio compact disk 14.95 compact disc. (LA127D) Lghtwrks Aud & Vid.
Ascending through the color spectrum & corresponding chakras, you can feel the relaxing effects of this simple yet elegant album. "Spectrum Suite" is an ideal choice for a wide variety of listening situations. As soon as you hea it, you'll know why it ushered in a whole new genre of contemporary music a whole new dimension for creating a meditative & healing environment.

Spectrum 2: A Communicative Course in English, Level 2. Diane Warshawsky et al. 6 cass. 1994. 160.00 (978-0-13-832882-5(X)) Longmar

Speech A, Tape 3. abr. ed. Robert A. Monroe. Read by Robert A. Monroe. 6 cass. (Stroke Recovery Ser.). 1983. 69.00 Set. (978-1-56102-708-8(1)); Inter Indus.
Assists in progressive recovery of speech skills.

Speech at Sunshine Gardens. unabr. ed. Terence McKenna. 2 cass. 1984 18.00 Set. (978-1-56964-039-5(4), A0195-84) Sound Photosyn.

Speech B, Tape 4. abr. ed. Robert A. Monroe. Read by Robert A. Monroe. cass. (Stroke Recovery Ser.). 1983. 69.00 Set. (978-1-56102-709-5(X)) Inter Indus.
Assists in continued recovery of speech skills.

Speech C, Tape 5. abr. ed. Robert A. Monroe. Read by Robert A. Monro cass. (Stroke Recovery Ser.). 1983. 69.00 Set. (978-1-56102-710-1(3 Inter Indus.
Assists in more healing techniques.

Speech Communication Made Simple: A Multicultural Approach. 2n Paulette Dale & James C. Wolf. 2002. 20.95 (978-0-13-026603-3(5)) Longman.

Speech D, Tape 6. abr. ed. Robert A. Monroe. Read by Robert A. Monroe. 6 cass. (Stroke Recovery Ser.). 1983. 69.00 Set. (978-1-56102-711-8(1)); Inter Indus.
Hemi-Sync for overall physical healing.

Speech Effective. 94th ed. Holt, Rinehart and Winston Staff. 1994. 9.60 (978-0-03-098356-6(8)) Holt McDoug.

Speech for Effective Communication: Audiovisual Resource Binder. 94th ed. Holt, Rinehart and Winston Staff. 1994. 61.60 (978-0-03-098333-7(9)) Holt McDoug.

Speech Improvement: Do It Yourself CDs & Booklet. Phyllis Rooder Weiss. 3 CDs. (Running Time: 2 hrs.). 2005. audio compact disk 39.50 (978-1-57970-153-6(1), S23720D) J Norton Pubs.

Speech Improvement Vol. 1: Do It Yourself. Phyllis R. Weiss. 3 cass. (Running Time: 3 hrs.). pap. bk. 39.50 (978-0-88432-075-3(8), S23720) J Norton Pubs.
This is designed to correct the most outstanding causes of unpleasant American speech. Beginning with voice diagnosis & nasality correction, the course moves on to voice drills & building resonance.

Speech Interactive: Student Speeches for Critique & Analysis. Wadsworth. (C). 2000. audio compact disk 9.95 (978-0-534-52999-4(2)) Pub: Wadsworth Pub. Dist(s): CENGAGE Learn

Speech of Oedipus at Colonus see Dylan Thomas Reads the Poetry of W. B. Yeats & Others

Speech on the Weather see Best of Mark Twain

Speech Power. Preston Miles. Ed. by Mario A. Pei. 12 cass. (Running Time: 30 min. per cass.). (J). (gr. 10-12). 1983. pap. bk. 99.95 incl. wkbk. (978-1-55678-024-0(9), 1804, Lrn Inc) Oasis Audio.
Dramatizes real-life situations & lets you listen to the speech of famous personalities to show you how to quickly break through the barriers to effective communication.

Speech Power. Preston H. Miles. Ed. by Mario Pei. Hosted by Vivian Lyons & Frank Simms. 11 cass. 99.95 Set incl. wkbk. & practice tape. (729PAM) Nightingale-Conant.
Now learn how to take control & influence the direction of any conversation...like "verbal hypnosis." Become a more effective, more persuasive - more hypnotic - speaker. Speech Power provides 22 half-hour lessons, each addressing a specific phase of verbal communication.

Speechcraft: Discourse Pronunciation for Advanced Learners. Laura D. Hahn & Wayne B. Dickerson. (Michigan Series in English for Academic & Professional Purposes). (C). 1999. 20.00 (978-0-472-00295-5(3)) U of Mich Pr.

Speechcraft: Workbook for Academic Discourse. Laura D. Hahn & Wayne B. Dickerson. (Michigan Series in English for Academic & Professional Purposes). (C). 1999. 10.00 (978-0-472-00297-9(X)) U of Mich Pr.

Speechcraft: Workbook for International TA Discourse. Laura D. Hahn & Wayne B. Dickerson. (Michigan Series in English for Academic & Professional Purposes). (C). 1999. 10.00 (978-0-472-00296-2(1)) U of Mich Pr.

Speechercize 1 And 2. unabr. ed. Twin Sisters Productions. Read by Twin Sisters. (J). 2007. 44.99 (978-1-60252-629-7(X)) Find a World.

Speeches by Frederick Douglass. Frederick Douglass. 1 cass. (Running Time: 60 mins.). 1999. 12.95 (FH-5528) African Am Imag.

Speeches of Barack Obama. Barack Obama. (JPN., 2008. pap. bk. 24.00 (978-4-255-00451-8(X)) Asahi Shu JPN.

Speeches That Shaped A Century. AudioVille Staff. (Running Time: 1 hr.). 2005. 16.95 (978-1-59912-935-8(3)) Iofy Corp.

Speechless. Perf. by Steven Curtis Chapman. 1 cass. 1999. 7.98 (978-0-7601-2883-1(9)) Provident Music.

Speechless. Perf. by Sandi Patty. 1 cass. 1999. 7.98 (978-0-7601-2802-2(2)) Brentwood Music.

Speechless, Set. abr. ed. Harriet Greenberg. Read by Bonnie Bedelia. 2 cass. (Running Time: 3 hrs.). 1994. 16.95 (978-1-56876-034-6(5), 391624) Soundlines Ent.
An enlightening romantic comedy which sets off fireworks when two complete opposites try to fight off magnetic attraction. The sparks fly when these two political speech writers meet, both unaware they share the same profession & work for opposite candidates. When the truth is discovered, romance gives way to rivalry.

Speechphone: Advanced Course. Hazel P. Brown. 3 cass. (Running Time: 3 hrs.). 2001. 39.50 (S23709) J Norton Pubs.

Speechphone: Elementary Course. Hazel P. Brown. 3 cass. (Running Time: 3 hrs.). bk. 39.50 (978-0-88432-061-6(8), S23701) J Norton Pubs.
Planned for the foreign-born student who can read & understand simple English but who is unable to make himself-herself understood because of incorrect stress & faulty rhythmic pattern.

Speechphone: Intermediate Course. Hazel P. Brown. 3 cass. (Running Time: 3 hrs.). pap. bk. 39.50 (S23705) J Norton Pubs.
Planned for the American student & for the advanced foreign-born student. Differ from the Elementary only in that the vocabulary & sound combinations increase in difficulty. In the Intermediate & Advanced courses, contrasting combinations have been introduced when the contrast serves to reinforce the sound beign presented.

Speechphone: Spoken Word List, Hazel P. Brown. 3 cass. (Running Time: 3 hrs.). 1989. pap. bk. 39.50 (978-0-88432-064-7(2), S23713) J Norton Pubs.
Consists of 3,000 American English words which are frequently mispronounced or are likely to be confusing because of various spellings & pronunciations. A unique feature of this spoken word list is that the division of the words has been changed from the traditional form so that the eye sees what the ear hears.

Speechphone Advanced CDs & Text: American Speech Sounds & Rhythm, Advanced course CDs & Text. Hazel P. Brown. Dorothy Mulgrave & Evelyn Konigsberg. Frwd. by John Carr Duff. 3 CDs. (Running Time: 2 hrs. 15 mins.). (Speechphone Ser.). 2006. audio compact disk 49.95 (978-1-57970-426-1(3), S23709D, Audio-For) J Norton Pubs.
These materials are intended primarily for the non-US-born learner who can read and understand simple English but who is unable to be understood because of incorrect stress and faulty rhythmic patterns. They will also be useful for native English speakers who wish to attain greater clarity, smoothness of speech, and rounder, fuller tones, or who lack self-confidence in speaking and in oral reading because they are not sure of their pronunciation. Professional people who wish to improve their speech for business or social reasons, or who do not wish to be misjudged or misunderstood because of incorrect pronunciation of frequently mispronounced words will also find the program helpful. Finally, the Advanced course is useful for teachers who are interested in their own pronunciation, both socially and professionally, who wish to check the pronunciation of their students, or who are preparing for speech examinations.

Speechphone Intermediate CDs & Text: American Speech Sounds & Rhythm, Intermediate course CDs & Text. Hazel P. Brown. 3 CDs. (Running Time: 2 hrs.). (Speechphone Ser.). 2006. audio compact disk 49.95 (978-1-57970-424-7(7), S23701D, Audio-For) J Norton Pubs.
These materials are intended primarily for the non-US-born learner who can read and understand simple English but who is unable to make himself or herself understood because of incorrect stress and faulty rhythmic patterns. In the Elementary course there are no combinations of contrasting sounds.

Speechphone Spoken Word List CDs & Text: American Speech Sounds & Rhythms. Hazel Brown. 3 CDs. (Running Time: 2 hrs. 20 mins.). (Speechphone Ser.). (ENG.). 2006. audio compact disk 49.95 (978-1-57970-427-8(1), S23705D, Audio-For) J Norton Pubs.
These materials are intended primarily for the non-US-born learner who can read and understand simple English, but who is unable to make himself or herself understood because of incorrect stress and faulty rhythmic patterns. They will also be useful for US-born learners who wish to attain greater clarity, smoothness of speech and rounder, fuller tones, or who lack self-confidence in speaking and in oral reading, because they are not sure of their pronunciation. Professional people who wish to improve their speech for business or social reasons, or who do not wish to be misjudged or misunderstood because of incorrect pronunciations of frequently mispronounced words, will also find these materials helpful.

Speed see May Swenson

Speed. unabr. ed. Mark Harris. Narrated by Norman Dietz. 9 cass. (Running Time: 12 hrs. 45 mins.). 1991. 78.00 (978-1-55690-490-5(8), 91315E7) Recorded Bks.
Speed was the handsome second son, a great athlete, a brilliant writer. But an incurable stammer keeps him from achieving his older brother's easy success. A humorous tale of coming-of-age, of irreparable choice & tender, half-forgotten joys.

Speed & Accuracy at Your Keyboard. unabr. ed. 3 cass. (Running Time: 4 hrs.). 1994. pap. bk. 34.50 (978-0-88432-751-6(5), S17085) J Norton Pubs.

Speed-b-b-b-bumps: And Other Poems for Kids & Families. Darrell House. 1 CD. (Running Time: 27 mins.). (J). (ps-5). 2009. audio compact disk 16.95 (978-0-615-31853-0(3)) Pub: MagMusic. Dist(s): Super D

Speed Building Series. National Shorthand Reporters Association. 22 cass. Incl. Speed Building Series: SB-130-A & B; Speed Building Series: SB-140-A & B; Speed Building Series: SB-150-A & B; Speed Building Series: SB-160-A & B; Speed Building Series: SB-180-A & B; Speed Building Series: SB-190-A & B; Speed Building Series: SB-200-A & B; Speed Building Series: SB-225-A & B; Speed Building Series: SB-240-A & B; Speed Building Series: SB-260-A & B; Speed Building Series: SB-270-A & B; Speed Building Series. National Shorthand Reporters Association.; (SB Ser.). 17.00 ea. Natl Ct Report.
This series advances in increments of 10 wpm which will give you the chance to work out on one-minute takes at increasing speeds, with a repetition of the five-minute take at a control speed for accuracy. The number of the tape indicates the speed at which the testimony is dictated. The jury charge & literary selections are dictated at slower speeds.

Speed Building Series: SB-130-A & B see Speed Building Series

Speed Building Series: SB-140-A & B see Speed Building Series

Speed Building Series: SB-150-A & B see Speed Building Series

Speed Building Series: SB-160-A & B see Speed Building Series

Speed Building Series: SB-180-A & B see Speed Building Series

Speed Building Series: SB-190-A & B see Speed Building Series

Speed Building Series: SB-200-A & B see Speed Building Series

Speed Building Series: SB-225-A & B see Speed Building Series

Speed Building Series: SB-240-A & B see Speed Building Series

Speed Building Series: SB-260-A & B see Speed Building Series

Speed Building Series: SB-270-A & B see Speed Building Series

Speed Development Series: Jury Charge Tapes. National Shorthand Reporters Association. 3 cass. 9.00 ea. SD-120-J. (CT-62) Natl Ct Report.
Side 1 on each of these tapes contains speed development. Each minute is dictated three times at increasing speeds of ten words a minute. The entire selection is dictated at the control speed. Side 2 contains four five-minute selections & one ten-minute selection at the control speed.

Speed Development Series: Literary Tapes. National Shorthand Reporters Association. 6 cass. 9.00 ea. SD-100-L. (CT-56) Natl Ct Report.
Side 1 of each of these tapes contains speed development. Each minute is dictated three times at increasing speeds of ten words a minute. The entire selection is dictated at the control speed. Side 2 contains six five-minute selections at the control speed.

Speed English. 2nd rev. ed. Louis Aarons. 4 cass. (Running Time: 4 hrs. 50 min.). (WordMate Say Hello Ser.). (JPN.). (YA). (gr. 7-12). 1996. bk. & stu. ed. 59.95 Set. (978-1-887447-02-7(4)) WordMate.
Program of basic English for native speakers of Japanese includes pronunciation guide, word lists, study & review tests, interactive dialogs for communication, essential grammar, & glossary with correlated workbook. Proven & patented learning system requires stereo headphones. Both sides of the brain are used to automatically speed up language learning.

Speed German. Mark Frobose. 2003. audio compact disk 39.00 (978-1-893564-86-2(X)) Macmill Audio.

Speed Italian: 4 One Hour CDs. Mark A. Frobose. 8 CDs. (Running Time: 8 hrs.). 2004. audio compact disk 69.00 (978-1-893564-61-9(4)) Macmill Audio.

Speed Learning. unabr. ed. 4 cass. (Running Time: 6 hrs.). 2001. pap. bk. Oasis Audio.
Master new information in minutes. Speed Learning will double your "reading intelligence" in just 24 hours.

Speed Learning: Medical Edition. 154.00 (1164, Lrn Inc) Oasis Audio.

Speed Learning: Science & Engineering Edition. Learn Inc. Staff. bk. & stu. ed. 154.00 (978-1-55678-035-6(4), 3083, Lrn Inc) Oasis Audio.

Speed Learning - Data Processing. 4 cass. 145.00 incl. 3 textbooks & 5 practice bks. (S1940) J Norton Pubs.
The basic Speed Learning course in a professional edition with Data Processing-related reading.

Speed Learning - Finance & Accounting. 4 cass. 145.00 incl. 3 textbooks & 5 practice bks. (S1955) J Norton Pubs.
The basic Speed Learning Course in a professional edition with Finance & Accounting-related reading.

Speed Learning - Management. 4 cass. 145.00 incl. 3 textbooks & 5 practice bks. (S1950) J Norton Pubs.
The basic Speed Learning Course in a professional edition with Management-related reading.

Speed Learning - Medical. 4 cass. 145.00 incl. 3 textbooks & 5 practice bks. (S1935) J Norton Pubs.
The basic Speed Learning Course in a professional edition with medical-related reading.

Speed Learning - Science & Engineering. 4 cass. 145.00 incl. 3 textbooks & 5 practice bks. (S1945) J Norton Pubs.
The basic Speed Learning Course in a professional edition with Science & Engineering-related reading.

Speed Learning Accounting. 154.00 (1328, Lrn Inc) Oasis Audio.

Speed Learning for a Better Memory. 1 cass. 7.95 (3042, Lrn Inc) Oasis Audio.

Speed Learning for a Higher IQ. 1 cass. 7.95 (1864, Lrn Inc) Oasis Audio.

Speed Learning for a Winning Vocabulary. 1 cass. 7.95 (1863, Lrn Inc) Oasis Audio.

Speed of Balance: A Musical Adventure for Emotional & Mental Regeneration. Doc Childre. 2000. 9.95 (978-1-879052-50-5(4)); audio compact disk 15.95 (978-1-879052-49-9(0)) HeartMath.

Speed of Dark. collector's unabr. ed. Elizabeth Moon. Read by Grover Gardner. 9 cass. (Running Time: 10 hrs. 30 min.). (YA). 2003. 72.00 (978-0-7366-9131-4(6)) Books on Tape.

***Speed of Dark.** unabr. ed. Elizabeth Moon. Read by Jay Snyder. (Running Time: 14 hrs.). 2010. 39.97 (978-1-4418-7510-5(7), 9781441875105, BADLE); 24.99 (978-1-4418-7508-2(5), 9781441875082, Brilliance MP3); 39.97 (978-1-4418-7509-9(3), 9781441875099, Brlnc Audio MP3 Lib); audio compact disk 29.99 (978-1-4418-7506-8(9), 9781441875068, Bril Audio CD Unabri); audio compact disk 79.97 (978-1-4418-7507-5(7), 9781441875075, BriAudCD Unabrid) Brilliance Audio.

Speed of Darkness see Poetry & Voice of Muriel Rukeyser

Speed of Darkness. Rodney Morales. 1 cass. 1993. pap. bk.; 8.00 SELECTIONS FROM PAP. BK. (978-0-910043-30-4(2)) Bamboo Ridge Pr.

Speed of Sound. unabr. ed. Scott Eyman & Adams Morgan. 2007. audio compact disk 29.95 (978-0-7861-6023-5(3)) Blckstn Audio.

Speed of Sound: Hollywood & the Talkie Revolution, 1926-1930. unabr. ed. Scott Eyman. (Running Time: 48600 sec.). 2007. audio compact disk 99.00 (978-0-7861-6022-8(5)) Blckstn Audio.

Speed of Sound: Hollywood & the Talkie Revolution 1926-1930. unabr. ed. Scott Eyman. Read by Adams Morgan. 10 cass. (Running Time: 14 hrs. 30 mins.). 1997. 69.95 (978-0-7861-1205-0(0), 1974) Blckstn Audio.
Epic story of the transition from silent films to talkies - that moment when movies were totally transformed & the American public cemented its love affair with Hollywood.

Speed of Trust: Live from L. A. - The One Thing That Changes Everything. unabr. ed. Stephen M. R. Covey. 3 CDs. (Running Time: 3 hrs. 45 mins. 0 sec.). (ENG.). 2009. audio compact disk 29.99 (978-1-933976-90-7(X)) Pub: Franklin Covey. Dist(s): S and S Inc

Speed of Trust: The One Thing That Changes Everything. abr. ed. Stephen M. R. Covey. Read by Stephen M. R. Covey. 2006. 8.98 (978-0-7435-6198-3(8)) Pub: S&S Audio. Dist(s): S and S Inc

Speed of Trust: The One Thing That Changes Everything. abr. ed. Stephen M. R. Covey & Rebecca R. Merrill. Read by Stephen M. R. Covey & Rebecca R. Merrill. (Running Time: 1 hr. 15 mins. 0 sec.). 2006. audio compact disk 14.00 (978-0-7435-6469-4(3), Sound Ideas) Pub: S&S Audio. Dist(s): S and S Inc

Speed of Trust: The One Thing That Changes Everything. unabr. ed. Stephen M. R. Covey. (Running Time: 12 hrs. 0 mins. 0 sec.). (ENG.). 2009. audio compact disk 44.99 (978-1-933976-79-2(9)) Pub: Franklin Covey. Dist(s): S and S Inc

Speed Portuguese. Mark Frobose. 4 CDs. (Running Time: 4 hrs.). 2006. audio compact disk 39.00 (978-1-893564-50-3(9)) Macmill Audio.

Speed Reading. 1 cass. 10.00 (978-1-58506-003-0(8), 04) New Life Inst OR.
Release the barriers that hold back reading, speed & comprehensi on.

Speed Reading. Graham Mallett. 2 cass. (YA). (gr. 9-12). 14.95 (978-1-55569-256-8(7), EDU-6023) Great Am Audio.
Teaches techniques that produce rapid reading with increased comprehension.

Speed Reading. Steve Moidel. 6 cass. 99.95 incl. workbook. (C10076) CareerTrack Pubns.
Sharp reading skills are essential for every professional. You know that it's easy to get overwhelmed by all the information you must process - just to keep up. Along with more speed, this program shows you how to get more out of what you read. You'll improve your comprehension, concentration & retention.

Speed Reading. Steve Moidel. 2 cass. (Running Time: 111 min.). 1996. 15.95 (978-1-55977-490-1(8)) CareerTrack Pubns.

Speed Reading. Read by Mary Richards. (Subliminal Impact Ser.). 12.95 (621) Master Your Mind.
Discusses how to extract ideas & concepts from what was before a mass of words.

Speed Reading. Dick Sutphen. 1 cass. (Running Time: 1 hr.). (RX17 Ser.). 1986. 14.98 (978-0-87554-324-6(3), RX133) Valley Sun.
You are a highly accomplished speed reader. You skim the lines, fixating less & less. You read faster & faster through daily practice. You vertically eye sweep a column of type. You vertically eye sweep the page of a book. There is no limit to your reading speed & comprehension. You retain & recall everything important you read. "Speed reading access" are your key words for conditioned response.

Speed Reading for Accountants. Melvin B. Seiden. 4 cass. bk. 159.00 (CPE4040) Bisk Educ.
Get practical techniques to increase your on-the-job reading speed, plus understand & remember more of what you read. Learn three different reading styles & when to use each - & how to apply what you've learned when reading business reports, financial statements, technical bulletins, leisure material, & more.

Speed Sleep. abr. ed. Frank A. Prince. Read by Frank A. Prince. 1 cass. (Running Time: 25 mins.). 2000. (978-1-893013-06-3(5)); audio compact disk (978-1-893013-05-6(7)) Unleash Your Mind.
Prince walks you through the deep sleep process.

Speed Spanish. Mark Frobose. 4 CDs. (Running Time: 4 hrs.). 2003. audio compact disk 39.00 (978-1-893564-51-0(7)) Macmill Audio.

Speed Spanish the Simple Way: 207 Page Illustrated Text/Complete Tapescript & Answer Keys. Mark Frobose. 8 CDs. (Running Time: 8 hrs.). (YA). 2003. audio compact disk 49.00 (978-1-893564-74-9(6)) Macmill Audio.

Speed-the-Plow. David Mamet. Perf. by Adam Arkin et al. 2 CDs. (Running Time: 1 hr. 21 mins.). 2005. audio compact disk 25.95 (978-1-58081-278-8(3), CDTPT189) Pub: L A Theatre. Dist(s): NetLibrary CO

Speed Typing. abr. ed. Roger W. Breternitz. 1 cass. (Running Time: 45 min.). 1985. pap. bk. 9.95 (978-1-893417-19-9(0)) Vector Studios.
Hypnosis: Implants belief system that one can really type faster & with greater accuracy. Increases sight recognition of words & phrases.

Speed up Collections: (Tips & Tricks That Work) Jane K. Cleland. 1 cass. (Running Time: 60 min.). (Improving Accounts Receivable Collections: Tape 1). 1991. 39.50 (978-1-877680-07-6(9)) Tiger Pr.
Tape 1 Reviews the four stages of collections & offers tips to speed up the process at each stage. Lots of real world examples are given.

Speedwriting Exercise. 1 cass. (Running Time: 1 hr.). 2000. 15.95 Prof Pride.
Recording names, addresses, phonetic, skill building. Difficult.

Speedy. unabr. ed. Max Brand. Read by Dick Hill. (Running Time: 7 hrs.). 2007. 39.25 (978-1-4233-3534-4(1), 9781423335344, BADLE); 24.95 (978-1-4233-3533-7(3), 9781423335337, BAD) Brilliance Audio.

Speedy. unabr. ed. Max Brand. Read by Dick Hill. (Running Time: 25200 sec.). 2007. audio compact disk 24.95 (978-1-4233-3531-3(7), 9781423335313, Brilliance MP3); audio compact disk 39.25 (978-1-4233-3532-0(5), 9781423335320, Brlnc Audio MP3 Lib) Brilliance Audio.

Speedy. unabr. ed. Max Brand. Read by Dick Hill. (Running Time: 8 hrs.). 2010. audio compact disk 19.99 (978-1-4418-0493-8(5), 9781441804938) Brilliance Audio.

***Speedy.** unabr. ed. Max Brand. Read by Dick Hill. (Running Time: 8 hrs.). 2010. audio compact disk 59.97 (978-1-4418-0494-5(3), 9781441804945, BriAudCD Unabrid) Brilliance Audio.

Speedy Medical - Nursing Spanish Audio. unabr. ed. T. L. Hart. Read by T. L. Hart. Read by Anna Jones. 1 cass. (Running Time: 1 hr. 30 min.). (SPA.). 1988. 16.95 (978-0-9615829-9-9(5)) Baja Bks.
Cassette pack contains 2 phrasebooks: Speedy Spanish for Medical Personnel & Speedy Spanish for Nursing Personnel which are reproduced on the cassette.

Speer Morgan. Interview. Interview with Speer Morgan & Kay Bonetti. 1 cass. (Running Time: 70 min.). 13.95 (978-1-55644-022-9(7), 1122) Am Audio Prose.
Articulate discussion of the use of history in contemporary fiction, the turn away from the psychological novel, & a wide range of issues surrounding the business of writing.

Speer Morgan. unabr. ed. Speer Morgan. Read by Speer Morgan. 1 cass. (Running Time: 29 min.). 1989. 10.00 New Letters.
Morgan reads from his thriller novel The Assemblers & is interviewed.

Speers: First Family of Gospel Music. Contrib. by Speers. (Gospel Legacy Ser.). 2007. audio compact disk 13.99 (978-5-557-60925-8(3)) Pt of Grace Ent.

Spell It Right!, 4 cass. (Running Time: 5 hrs. 15 mins.). 1992. pap. bk. 39.50 (978-0-88432-454-6(0), SO2095) J Norton Pubs.
Created specifically for the adult learner, 300 commonly misspelled words & guidelines to spell accurately hundreds of others.

Spell It Right. Prod. by Audio-Forum. (ENG.). 1992. audio compact disk 39.50 (978-1-57970-490-2(5), Audio-For) J Norton Pubs.

Spell My Name with an 'S' see Science Fiction Favorites of Isaac Asimov

Spell of the Highlander. unabr. ed. Karen Marie Moning. Read by Phil Gigante. (Running Time: 11 hrs.). (Highlander Ser.). 2008. 24.95 (978-1-4233-4170-3(8), 9781423341703, Brilliance MP3); 39.25 (978-1-4233-4171-0(6), 9781423341710, Brlnc Audio MP3 Lib); 39.25 (978-1-4233-4173-4(2), 9781423341734, BADLE); 24.95 (978-1-4233-4172-7(4), 9781423341727, BAD); audio compact disk 29.95 (978-1-4233-4168-0(6), 9781423341680, Bril Audio CD Unabri); audio compact disk 102.25 (978-1-4233-4169-7(4), 9781423341697, BriAudCD Unabrid) Brilliance Audio.

Spell of the Yukon see Poetry of Robert W. Service

Spell of the Yukon see Favorite American Poems

Spell of Winter. unabr. ed. Helen Dunmore. Read by Janet Maw. 8 cass. (Running Time: 12 hrs.). 1999. 69.95 (978-0-7531-0296-1(X), 980107) Pub: ISIS Audio GBR. Dist(s): Ulverscroft US
Catherine & her brother Rob do not know why they have been abandoned by their parents. In the house of their grandfather, "the man from nowhere", they make a passionate refuge for themselves against the terror of family secrets. While the world outside moves to the brink of war, their sibling love becomes fraught with dangers but as Catherine fights free of the past the spell of winter that has held her in its grasp begins to break.

Spell of Winter. unabr. ed. Helen Dunmore. Read by Janet Maw. 10 CDs. (Running Time: 11 hrs. 45 min.). (Isis Ser.). (J). 2000. audio compact disk 89.95 (978-0-7531-0716-4(3), 107163) Pub: ISIS Lrg Prnt GBR. Dist(s): Ulverscroft US

Spell Power. Jeanie Eller. Read by Jeanie Eller. 2 cass. (Running Time: 2 hrs.). 1995. (978-1-928606-25-3(3)) Action Readg.
A spelling enhancement instructional program.

Spella-Ho. unabr. ed. H. E. Bates. Read by Gordon Griffin. 9 cass. (Running Time: 13 hrs. 30 mins.). 2001. (978-1-85496-418-2(6)) ISIS Audio GBR.
The Desolate empty house on the bar Northampton hillside. In the Winter of 1873 Bruno had been here three times hunting for coal,, but his mother had made him rturn it. Drawn to every room began to realise that somewhere, something was terribly wrong.

Spellbinder. unabr. ed. L. J. Smith. (Running Time: 6 hrs.). (Night World Ser.: Vol. 3). 2009. 19.99 (978-1-4418-0451-8(X), 9781441804518, BAD); 39.97 (978-1-4418-0452-5(8), 9781441804525, BADLE) Brilliance Audio.

Spellbinder. unabr. ed. L. J. Smith. Read by Jeannie Stith. (Running Time: 6 hrs.). (Night World Ser.: Vol. 3). 2009. 19.99 (978-1-4418-0449-5(8), 9781441804495, Brilliance MP3); 39.97 (978-1-4418-0450-1(1), 9781441804501, Brlnc Audio MP3 Lib); audio compact disk 19.99 (978-1-4418-0447-1(1), 9781441804471, Bril Audio CD Unabri) Brilliance Audio.

Spellbinder. unabr. ed. L. J. Smith. Read by Jeannie Stith. (Running Time: 6 hrs.). (Night World Ser.: Vol. 3). 2009. audio compact disk 59.97 (978-1-4418-0448-8(X), 9781441804488, BriAudCD Unabrid) Brilliance Audio.

***Spellbound.** unabr. ed. Nancy Holder & Debbie Viguié. Read by Cassandra Morris. (Running Time: 8 hrs.). (Wicked Ser.). 2010. 24.99 (978-1-4418-3545-1(8), 9781441835451, Brilliance MP3); 39.97 (978-1-4418-3546-8(6), 9781441835468, Brlnc Audio MP3 Lib); audio compact disk 24.99 (978-1-4418-3543-7(1), 9781441835437); audio compact disk 54.97 (978-1-4418-3544-4(X), 9781441835444, BriAudCD Unabrid) Brilliance Audio.

***Spellbound.** unabr. ed. Nora Roberts. (Running Time: 3 hrs.). 2010. 19.99 (978-1-4418-6730-8(9), 9781441867308, Brilliance MP3); 14.99 (978-1-4418-6732-2(5), 9781441867322, BAD); 39.97 (978-1-4418-6731-5(7), 9781441867315, Brlnc Audio MP3 Lib); 39.97 (978-1-4418-6733-9(3), 9781441867339, BADLE) Brilliance Audio.

***Spellbound.** unabr. ed. Nora Roberts. Read by Jeffrey Cummings. (Running Time: 3 hrs.). 2010. audio compact disk 14.99 (978-1-4418-6728-5(7), 9781441867285, Bril Audio CD Unabri); audio compact disk 62.97 (978-1-4418-6729-2(5), 9781441867292, BriAudCD Unabrid) Brilliance Audio.

***Spellbound.** unabr. ed. Debbie Viguié & Nancy Holder. Read by Cassandra Morris. (Running Time: 8 hrs.). (Wicked Ser.). 2010. 39.97 (978-1-4418-3547-5(4), 9781441835475, BADLE) Brilliance Audio.

Spelling: Syllabus. 2nd ed. Delpha Hurlburt. (J). (gr. 7-12). 1980. 134.10 (978-0-89420-185-1(9), 187900) Natl Book.

Spelling Advantage. unabr. ed. 1 cass. (Running Time: l hr.). 2000. (978-1-931187-20-6(7), SA); audio compact disk (978-1-931187-05-3(3), CDSA) Word Success.

Spelling Basics. 2 cass. (Running Time: 2 hrs.). 1993. 36.00 (978-1-56118-090-5(4), 81098) Paradigm MN.

Spelling Connections 2007. Richard Gentry. (Spelling Connections Ser.). (gr. 3). 2007. audio compact disk 62.63 (978-0-7367-4769-1(9)) Zaner-Bloser.

Spelling Connections 2007: Grade 1 Audio CD. Richard Gentry. (Spelling Connections Ser.). (gr. 1). 2007. audio compact disk 62.63 (978-0-7367-4767-7(2)) Zaner-Bloser.

Spelling Connections 2007: Grade 2 Audio CD. Richard Gentry. (Spelling Connections Ser.). (gr. 2). 2007. audio compact disk 62.63 (978-0-7367-4768-4(0)) Zaner-Bloser.

Spelling Connections 2007: Grade 4 Audio CD. Richard Gentry. (Spelling Connections Ser.). (gr. 4). 2007. audio compact disk 62.63 (978-0-7367-4770-7(2)) Zaner-Bloser.

Spelling Connections 2007: Grade 5: Audio CD. Richard Gentry. (Spelling Connections Ser.). (gr. 5). 2007. audio compact disk 62.63 (978-0-7367-4771-4(0)) Zaner-Bloser.

Spelling Connections 2007: Grade 6 Audio CD. Richard Gentry. (Spelling Connections Ser.). (gr. 6). 2007. audio compact disk 62.63 (978-0-7367-4772-1(9)) Zaner-Bloser.

Spelling Connections 2007: Grade 7 Audio CD. Richard Gentry. (Spelling Connections Ser.). (gr. 7). 2007. audio compact disk 62.63 (978-0-7367-4773-8(7)) Zaner-Bloser.

Spelling Connections 2007: Grade 8 Audio CD. Richard Gentry. (Spelling Connections Ser.). (gr. 8). 2007. audio compact disk 62.63 (978-0-7367-4774-5(5)) Zaner-Bloser.

Spelling Songs. 1 cass. (Running Time: 1 hr.). (J). 2001. wbk. ed. 10.95 (THR 102C) Kimbo Educ.
Let the mighty I-N-G & the powerful silent E entertain you as they sing about the rules of spelling. Includes Change Y to I, E-S-T's the Best, I Before E & more. Reproducible workbook & lyrics included.

Spelling Songs: Language Arts Skills. Kidzup Productions Staff. 1 CD. (Running Time: 20 min.). (Learning Beat Ser.). (J). 2002. wbk. ed. 13.99 (978-1-894677-32-5(3)) Pub: Kidzup Prodns. Dist(s): Penton Overseas
Children will learn spelling and language arts skills such as changing 'y' to 'i' before adding 'er', 'est', or 'es'...etc.

***Spelling Success System Audio Companion: Chronic Spelling Struggles Will Be Transformed into Spelling Success with SSS.** Joan Ripley. 2010. 9.99 (978-1-60645-052-9(2)) BkWise Pubng.

***Spelling Success System CDs: Chronic Spelling Struggles Will Be Transformed into Spelling Success with SSS.** Joan Ripley. (ENG.). 2010. 21.99 (978-1-60645-053-6(0)) BkWise Pubng.

Spelling Workbook Set: English As a Second Language. tchr. ed. 55.00 (978-1-57970-017-1(9), SEN120) J Norton Pubs.

Spellman Files. abr. ed. Lisa Lutz. (Izzy Spellman Mystery Ser.: Bk. 1). 2007. 17.95 (978-0-7435-6435-9(9)) Pub: S&S Audio. Dist(s): S and S Inc

Spellman Files. abr. ed. Lisa Lutz. Read by Ari Graynor. (Running Time: 6 hrs. 0 mins. 0 sec.). Bk. 1. (ENG.). 2008. audio compact disk 14.99 (978-0-7435-7135-7(5)) Pub: S&S Audio. Dist(s): S and S Inc

Spellman Files. unabr. ed. Lisa Lutz. Read by Christina Moore. 8 cass. (Running Time: 9 hrs. 45 mins.). (Izzy Spellman Mystery Ser.: Bk. 1). 2007. 92.75 (978-1-4281-4221-3(5)); audio compact disk 123.75 (978-1-4281-4223-7(1)) Recorded Bks.

***Spells.** unabr. ed. Aprilynne Pike. Read by Mandy Siegfried. (ENG.). 2010. (978-0-06-199309-1(3)); (978-0-06-198397-9(7)) HarperCollins Pubs.

Spells & Sleeping Bags. unabr. ed. Sarah Mlynowski. Read by Ariadne Meyers. 7 CDs. (Running Time: 8 hrs. 43 mins.). (YA). (gr. 6-9). 2009. audio compact disk 55.00 (978-0-7393-7946-2(1), Listening Lib) Pub: Random Audio Pubg. Dist(s): Random

Spence & Lila. Bobbie Ann Mason. Read by Bobbie Ann Mason. 2 cass. (Running Time: 90 min. per cass.). 1990. 15.95 HarperCollins Pubs.

Spencer Johnson Audio Collection: Including Who Moved My Cheese? & Peaks & Valleys. unabr. ed. Spencer Johnson. Read by Spencer Johnson. Read by Tony Roberts et al. (Running Time: 3 hrs. 30 mins. 0 sec.). (ENG.). 2009. audio compact disk 39.99 (978-0-7435-9782-1(6)) Pub: S&S Audio. Dist(s): S and S Inc

Spencer MacCallum: Lessons Learned from the Atlantis Experiment. 1983. (FL1) Freeland Pr.

Spencer's Hospital. unabr. ed. Alex Stuart. 5 cass. (Sound Ser.). 2004. 49.95 (978-1-85496-532-5(8)) Pub: UlverLrgPrint GBR. Dist(s): Ulverscroft US

***Spencerville.** unabr. ed. Nelson DeMille. Read by Scott Brick. (Running Time: 22 hrs. 30 mins.). (ENG.). 2010. 24.98 (978-1-60941-162-6(5)) Pub: Hachet Audio. Dist(s): HachBkGrp

Spend Each Moment Doing Most Productive Thing. unabr. ed. Dick Sutphen. Read by Dick Sutphen. 1 cass. (Running Time: 30 min.). (Quick Fix Meditations Ser.). 1998. 10.98 (978-0-87554-622-3(6), QF104) Valley Sun.
The way to get what you want is to focus your energy.

Spend Game. Jonathan Gash. Narrated by Christopher Kay. 7 CDs. (Running Time: 8 hrs. 15 mins.). audio compact disk 73.00 (978-1-84197-171-1(5)) Recorded Bks.

Spend Game. unabr. ed. Jonathan Gash. Narrated by Christopher Kay. 6 cass. (Running Time: 8 hrs. 15 mins.). (Lovejoy Mystery Ser.). 2000. 53.00 (978-1-84197-045-5(X), H1050E7) Recorded Bks.
Lovejoy isn't a master antique dealer, but he is a master at being in the wrong place at the wrong time. Leaving a mundane auction for an amorous assignation, he witnesses the calculated murder of a fellow dealer. The question is why. After searching the victim's car, the killers leave empty-handed. Lovejoy is tracking down just what sparked their interest, unofficially & anonymously of course, when he's given a letter written by the victim shortly before he died. Suffice it to say that Lovejoy's cover has been blown.

Spend Game. unabr. ed. Jonathan Gash. Narrated by Christopher Kay. 7 CDs. (Running Time: 8 hrs. 15 min.). 2000. audio compact disk 73.00 (C1306E7, Clipper Audio) Recorded Bks.

Spenser Collection Vol. 2: Back Story; Widow's Walk. unabr. ed. Robert B. Parker. Read by Joe Mantegna. (Running Time: 43200 sec.). (Spenser Ser.). (ENG.). 2006. audio compact disk 29.95 (978-0-7393-4021-9(2), Random AudioBks) Pub: Random Audio Pubg. Dist(s): Random

Spenser's Ireland see Twentieth-Century Poetry in English, No. 2, Recordings of Poets Reading Their Own Poetry

Sphere Center see Centro de la Esfera

Sphere of Influence. Kyle Mills. (New Core Collections). 2003. audio compact disk 88.00 (978-0-7366-8818-5(8)) Books on Tape.

Sphinx. 1979. (N-2) Jimcin Record.

Sphinx. unabr. ed. Robin Cook. Read by Donada Peters. 7 cass. (Running Time: 10 hrs. 30 min.). 1993. 56.00 (978-0-7366-2545-6(3), 3296) Books on Tape.
Searching for a pharoah's unplundered tomb, a young Egyptologist finds a web of corruption & murder.

Spice: The Unauthorized Biography of the Spice Girls. Tim Footman. (Maximum Ser.). (ENG.). 2001. audio compact disk 14.95 (978-1-84240-011-1(8)) Pub: Chrome Dreams GBR. Dist(s): IPG Chicago

Spider & the Crows: A Story from Nelson Mandela's Favorite African Folktales. Read by Don Cheadle. Compiled by Nelson Mandela. (Running Time: 10 mins.). (ENG.). 2009. 1.99 (978-1-60788-007-3(5)) Pub: Hachet Audio. Dist(s): HachBkGrp

Spider & the Fly. Mary Howitt. Narrated by David Porter. (Running Time: 15 mins.). (gr. k up). 10.00 (978-1-4025-3416-4(7)) Recorded Bks.

Spider Bones. abr. ed. Kathy Reichs. Read by Linda Emond. (Running Time: 6 hrs. 0 mins. 0 sec.). (ENG.). 2010. audio compact disk 29.99 (978-1-4423-0434-5(0)) Pub: S&S Audio. Dist(s): S and S Inc

Spider Bones. unabr. ed. Kathy Reichs. Read by Linda Emond. 8 CDs. (Running Time: 9 hrs. 30 mins. 0 sec.). 2010. audio compact disk 39.99 (978-1-4423-0436-9(7)) Pub: S&S Audio. Dist(s): S and S Inc

Spider for Loco Shoat. unabr. ed. Douglas C. Jones. Narrated by Ed Sala. 7 cass. (Running Time: 10 hrs. 15 mins.). 1998. 60.00 (978-0-7887-1764-2(2), 95242 E7) Recorded Bks.
One night, when a young boy finds a naked corpse in an Arkansas riverside graveyard, no one takes the death seriously, until former Deputy Federal Marshall Oscar Schiller rouses himself from retirement.

Spider-man the lizard Sanction. Diane Duane. 2004. 7.95 (978-0-7435-4228-9(2)) Pub: S&S Audio. Dist(s): S and S Inc

Spider Mountain. abr. ed. P. T. Deutermann. Read by Dick Hill. (Running Time: 21600 sec.). 2007. audio compact disk 14.99 (978-1-59737-675-4(2), 9781597376754, BCD Value Price) Brilliance Audio.

Spider Mountain. abr. ed. P. T. Deutermann. (Running Time: 6 hrs.). 2008. audio compact disk 26.95 (978-1-4233-3631-0(3), 9781423336310, BACD) Brilliance Audio.

Spider Mountain. abr. ed. P. T. Deutermann. Read by Dick Hill. (Running Time: 6 hrs.). (Cam Richter Ser.). 2009. audio compact disk 14.99 (978-1-4233-3632-7(1), 9781423336327, BCD Value Price) Brilliance Audio.

Spider Mountain. abr. unabr. ed. P. T. Deutermann. Read by Dick Hill. (Running Time: 50400 sec.). 2006. audio compact disk 112.25 (978-1-59600-076-6(7), 9781596000766, BACDLib Ed) Brilliance Audio.
Please enter a Synopsis.

Spider Mountain. unabr. ed. P. T. Deutermann. Read by Dick Hill. (Running Time: 14 hrs.). 2006. 39.25 (978-1-59710-865-2(0), 9781597108652, BADLE); 24.95 (978-1-59710-864-5(2), 9781597108645, BAD); audio compact disk 24.95 (978-1-59335-791-7(5), 9781593357917, Brilliance MP3); audio compact disk 39.25 (978-1-59335-925-6(X), 9781593359256, Brlnc Audio MP3 Lib); audio compact disk 39.95 (978-1-4233-0651-1(1), 9781423306511, Bril Audio CD Unabri); 97.25 (978-1-59600-073-5(2), 9781596000735, BrilAudUnabridg) Brilliance Audio.

Spider-Orchid, Set. unabr. ed. Celia Fremlin. 6 cass. 1998. 69.95 Set. (978-1-85903-009-7(2)) Pub: Magna Story GBR. Dist(s): Ulverscroft US

Spider Sparrow. unabr. ed. Dick King-Smith. Read by Christian Rodska. 3 vols. (Running Time: 3 hrs. 26 mins.). (J). (gr. 5-9). 2004. pap. bk. 36.00 (978-0-8072-8407-0(6), Listening Lib); 30.00 (978-0-8072-8406-3(8), Listening Lib) Random Audio Pubg.
Spider Sparrow has always been different form other children. He can't walk like them, he can't talk like them, he can't learn like them. But Spider has a very special gift: he can perfectly imitate the sounds of animals, drawing them to him, soothing them & he amazes everyone when he uses this gift to save a life.

Spiders. 1 cass. (Running Time: 35 min.). (J). (ps-4). 2001. bk. 15.95 (VX-587C) Kimbo Educ.
Some of the 30,000 species of spiders are described & assorted webs are superbly illustrated. Includes book.

Spiders. 9.95 (978-1-59112-177-0(9)) Live Oak Media.

Spiders. Gail Gibbons. Illus. by Gail Gibbons. 11 vols. (Running Time: 15 mins.). 1999. bk. 28.95 (978-1-59519-086-4(4)); pap. bk. 39.95 (978-1-59519-085-7(6)) Live Oak Media.

Spiders. Gail Gibbons. Illus. by Gail Gibbons. 11 vols. (Running Time: 15 mins.). (J). 1999. pap. bk. 18.95 (978-1-59519-084-0(8)) Pub: Live Oak Media. Dist(s): AudioGO

Spiders. Gail Gibbons. Illus. by Gail Gibbons. (Running Time: 15 mins.). (J). (gr. k-3). 1999. 9.95 (978-0-87499-586-2(8)); audio compact disk 12.95 (978-1-59519-083-3(X)) Live Oak Media.

Spiders. unabr. ed. Gail Gibbons. Illus. by Gail Gibbons. Read by Suzanne Toren. 11 vols. (Running Time: 15 mins.). (Gail Gibbons' Creatures Great & Small Ser.). (J). (gr. 1-6). 1999. pap. bk. 16.95 (978-0-87499-587-9(6)) AudioGO.
Describes some of the 30,000 species of spiders, meanwhile illustrating assorted webs.

Spiders. unabr. ed. Gail Gibbons. Read by Suzanne Toren. 11 vols. (Running Time: 15 mins.). (Gail Gibbons' Creatures Great & Small Ser.). (J). 1999. bk. 25.95 (978-0-87499-588-6(4)) Live Oak Media.

Spiders. unabr. ed. Gail Gibbons. Illus. by Gail Gibbons. Read by Suzanne Toren. 14 vols. (Running Time: 15 mins.). (Gail Gibbons' Creatures Great & Small Ser.). (J). (gr. 1-6). 1999. pap. bk. & tchr. ed. 37.95 Reading Chest. (978-0-87499-585-5(X)) Live Oak Media.

Spiders & Insects: Includes Cassette. unabr. ed. Brad Caudle & Melissa Caudle. Illus. by Anthony Guerra. 1 cass. (Running Time: 30 min.). (Rock 'n Learn Ser.). (J). (gr. 2-6). 1999. pap. bk. 12.99 (978-1-878489-55-5(0), RL955) Rock N Learn.
Catchy songs & beautifully detailed illustrations teach awesome facts: their body parts, colors, life cycles, eating habits & more.

Spiders & Milk: Four Stories Read by the Author. unabr. ed. Donald R. Burleson. Read by Donald R. Burleson. 1 cass. (Running Time: 1 hr. 30 min.). (C). 1996. 9.95 (978-0-940884-84-7(4)) Necronomicon.
The following four stories written & read by Burleson, a popular author of horror & the macabre: "Uncle Neddy's Chair", "Milk", "Brownie", & "One-Night Strand".

Spider's House. unabr. ed. Sarah Diamond. 10 cass. (Running Time: 14 hrs. 14 mins.). (Isis Cassettes Ser.). (J). 2005. 84.95 (978-0-7531-2148-1(4)) Pub: ISIS Lrg Prnt GBR. Dist(s): Ulverscroft US

Spiders in the Hairdo. Perf. by David Holt & Bill Mooney. 1 cass. (Running Time: 60 mins.). 1997. 9.98 (978-0-942303-13-1(X)) Pub: High Windy Audio. Dist(s): August Hse

Weirdest tales to delight everyone from older children to adults. Hear such favorites as "Spiders in the Hairdo," "The Hook," "The Vanishing Hitchhiker," "The Cement-Filled Cadillac" & many more.

Spiders in the Hairdo: Modern Urban Legends. unabr. ed. Perf. by David Holt & Bill Mooney. 1 cass. (Running Time: 55 mins.). (gr. 7-12). 1999. 12.00 (978-0-87483-573-1(9)) Pub: August Hse. Dist(s): Natl Bk Netwk

Folktales are not a thing of the past. Urban legends are the tabloids of living folklore.

Spider's Web. unabr. ed. Agatha Christie. Read by Hugh Fraser. Adapted by Charles Osborne. 3 cass. (Running Time: 4 hrs. 18 mins.). 2000. 22.95 (978-1-57270-204-2(4), N31204u, Audio Edits Mystry) Pub: Audio Partners. Dist(s): PerseuPGW

Spider's Web. unabr. ed. Agatha Christie. Read by Hugh Fraser. Adapted by Charles Osborne. 4 CDs. (Running Time: 4 hrs. 18 mins.). (Mystery Masters Ser.). (ENG.). 2000. audio compact disk 29.95 (978-1-57270-205-9(2), N45205u) Pub: AudioGO. Dist(s): Perseus Dist

Spider's Web. unabr. ed. Nigel McCrery. Read by Paddy Glynn. 8 cass. (Running Time: 12 hrs.). 2001. 69.95 (978-0-7531-0600-6(0), 000309) Pub: ISIS Audio GBR. Dist(s): ISIS Pub

A teenage boy is killed in a joy-riding accident & the results of the post mortem seem clear. But the boy's parents beg Dr. Sam Ryan for a second opinion. Something in the file persuades her to go ahead & what she finds convinces her that this was no ordinary accident. Determined to prove her case, Sam begins her own investigation & begins to unravel a bizarre series of murders that has her searching the Internet for the killer as she realizes, to her horror, that her own nephew could be in terrible danger.

Spider's Web. unabr. ed. Nigel McCrery. Read by Paddy Glynn. 8 CDs. (Running Time: 9 hrs. 15 mins.). (Isis (CDs) Ser.). (J). 2004. audio compact disk 79.95 (978-0-7531-2275-4(8)) Pub: ISIS Lrg Prnt GBR. Dist(s): Ulverscroft US

Spider's Web. unabr. ed. Howard L. Peterson. Read by Maynard Villers. 6 cass. (Running Time: 6 hrs. 42 min.). (Sheriff Burley Grantham Ser.). 1996. 39.95 Set. (978-1-55686-707-1(7)) Books in Motion.

Sheriff Burley Grantham of Canyon County, Oregon investigates a murder that takes place behind the backdrop at the Summit-Littlefield Community Theater during a stage play.

Spiderweb. unabr. ed. Penelope Lively. Read by Diana Bishop. 6 cass. (Running Time: 8 hrs.). (Sound Ser.). 2001. 54.95 (978-1-86042-512-7(7), 25127) Pub: UlverLrgPrint GBR. Dist(s): Ulverscroft US

Spiderweb for Two: A Melendy Maze. Elizabeth Enright. Narrated by Pamela Dillman. 4 CDs. (Running Time: 5 Hrs.). (J). 2004. audio compact disk 27.95 (978-1-59316-034-0(8)) Listen & Live.

The fourth in the Melendys family series! Mona, Rush, Miranda and Oliver all live with their father, who is a writer, and Cuffy, their beloved housekeeper. This story tells about how when everyone else leaves for school, Randy and Oliver are left to solve a mystery.

Spiderweb for Two - A Melendy Maze. unabr. ed. Elizabeth Enright. Read by Pamela Dillman. (J). 2007. 34.99 (978-1-59895-945-1(X)) Find a World.

Spiderweb for Two: A Melendy Maze: A Melendy Maze. Elizabeth Enright. Read by Pamela Dillman. (Running Time: 5 hrs.). 2005. 19.95 (978-1-59912-906-8(X)) Iofy Corp.

Spiderwoman: A Celebration of Women Heroes. Short Stories. Read by Justice Jennifer. 1 cass. (Running Time: 1 hr.). (J). (gr. 3 up). 1990. 9.95 (978-0-938756-43-9(5), 080) Yellow Moon.

A collection of traditional tales that present new & positive images of women.

Spies. Michael Frayn. Read by Martin Jarvis. 6 cass. (Running Time: 9 hrs.). 2002. 54.95 (978-0-7540-0882-8(7)) Pub: Chivers Audio Bks GBR. Dist(s): AudioGO

Spies! Real People, Real Stories. (High Five Reading - Green Ser.). (ENG.). (gr. 3-4). 2007. audio compact disk 5.95 (978-1-4296-1443-6(9)) CapstoneDig.

Spies & Agents. 2004. 29.95 (978-1-57019-762-8(8)) Radio Spirits.

Spies & Agents. Radio Spirits Staff. 2005. audio compact disk 29.95 (978-1-57019-761-1(X)) Radio Spirits.

Spies for Hire: The Secret World of Intelligence Outsourcing. unabr. ed. Tim Shorrock. Read by Dick Hill. Narrated by Dick Hill. (Running Time: 15 hrs. 30 mins. 0 sec.). (ENG.). 2008. audio compact disk 39.99 (978-1-4001-0772-8(5)); audio compact disk 79.99 (978-1-4001-3772-5(1)); audio compact disk 29.99 (978-1-4001-5772-3(2)) Pub: Tantor Media. Dist(s): IngramPubServ

Spies, Inc. unabr. ed. Jack D. Hunter. Read by Tom Weiner. (Running Time: 7 hrs. 0 mins.). 2010. 29.95 (978-1-4332-1977-1(8)); 44.95 (978-1-4332-1973-3(5)); audio compact disk 69.00 (978-1-4332-1974-0(3)) Blckstn Audio.

Spies of the Balkans. unabr. ed. Alan Furst. Read by Daniel Gerroll. 8 CDs. (Running Time: 9 hrs. 30 mins. 0 sec.). 2010. audio compact disk 39.99 (978-1-4423-0605-9(X)) Pub: S&S Audio. Dist(s): S and S Inc

Spies of Warsaw. unabr. ed. Alan Furst. Read by Daniel Gerroll. 9 CDs. (Running Time: 10 hrs. 0 mins. 0 sec.). (ENG.). 2008. audio compact disk 39.95 (978-0-7435-3387-4(9), Audioworks) Pub: S&S Audio. Dist(s): S and S Inc

Spies! Real People, Real Stories. (High Five Reading Ser.). (ENG.). (gr. 4 up). 2003. audio compact disk 5.95 (978-0-7368-2850-5(8)) CapstoneDig.

Spike Jones & His City Slickers: The Radio Years. Featuring Boris Karloff & Peter Lorre. 1 CD. (Running Time: 1 hr. 30 mins.). 2001. audio compact disk 11.98 (R2 71156) Rhino Enter.

Spike Lee. 1 cass. (Running Time: 1 hr. 30 mins.). (SmartReader Ser.). (J). 1999. pap. bk. & tchr. ed. 19.95 (978-0-7887-0120-7(7), 79308T3) Recorded Bks.

Through his controversial subjects & innovative techniques, filmmaker Spike Lee has changed the way African American culture is seen. Follow this award-winning director through his early works & later successes.

[illegible]ke Milligan: Vivat Milligna! abr. ed. Russell Davies. 4 cass. (Running [illegible]me: 3600 sec.). (BBC Radio Collections). 2003. audio compact disk 29.95 [illegible]8-0-563-52400-7(6)) AudioGO.

[illegible]he Rebel! / ¡Púa, el Rebelde! ed. Carl Sommer. Illus. by Enrique [illegible]. (Another Sommer-Time Story Bilingual Ser.). (ENG & SPA.). (J). [illegible] 26.95 (978-1-57537-192-4(8)) Advance Pub.

[illegible]vel. Michael Griffith. Narrated by L. J. Ganser. 7 cass. (Running [illegible]s.). 65.00 (978-0-7887-9433-9(7)) Recorded Bks.

[illegible]l. unabr. ed. Michael Griffith. Narrated by L. J. Ganser. 9 CDs. [illegible]: 10 hrs.). 2004. audio compact disk 89.00 [illegible]93-8(X)) Recorded Bks.

[illegible] Brian Schwan is already a washed-up professional golfer. [illegible]s managed only $19,000 in winnings. His wife is [illegible]d is pressuring him to start a family. His golf-obsessed [illegible]him. But when Brian decides to throw his life away, he [illegible]o easier than keeping it all together.

Spilled Water. Sally Grindley. Read by Liz Sutherland. (Running Time: 16200 sec.). (J). (gr. 3-7). 2001. audio compact disk 34.95 (978-0-7540-6756-6(4)) AudioGo GBR.

***Spilling Ink: A Young Writer's Handbook.** Anne Mazer & Ellen Potter. Read by Anne Mazer & Ellen Potter. (ENG.). (J). 2010. audio compact disk 45.00 (978-1-936223-43-5(0)) Full Cast Audio.

Spillover Effect: How to Create the Most Sensational Email Marketing Phenomenon. Speeches. 1. (Running Time: 1 hr.). 2002. 19.99 (978-0-9717222-7-9(7)) Idea Delivery Systems.

***Spilt Milk: Devotions for Moms.** Linda Vujnov. (Running Time: 4 hrs. 23 mins. 0 sec.). (ENG.). 2009. 12.99 (978-0-310-77313-9(X)) Zondervan.

Spin & Die. Stella Whitelaw. Read by Julia Franklin. 6 cass. (Soundings Ser.). (J). 2006. 54.95 (978-1-84559-287-5(5)) Pub: ISIS Lrg Prnt GBR. Dist(s): Ulverscroft US

Spin Cycle: Inside the Clinton Propaganda Machine. Howard Kurtz. 1998. 18.00 (978-0-684-85273-7(X), Free Pr) S and S.

Spin Cycle: Inside the Clinton Propaganda Machine. Howard Kurtz. 2004. 10.95 (978-0-7435-4606-5(7)) Pub: S&S Audio. Dist(s): S and S Inc

Spin Cycles. Compiled by Ira Basen. (ENG.). 2007. audio compact disk 49.95 (978-0-660-19739-5(1)) Canadian Broadcasting CAN.

Spin Injection & Transport in Magnetoelectronics. Ed. by P. Vincenzini & D. Fiorani. (Advances in Science & Technology Ser.: Vol. 52). audio compact disk 113.00 (978-3-908158-08-0(7)) Trans T Pub CHE.

Spin Me. Perf. by Jenny Gullen et al. 1 cass. 1993. audio compact disk Brentwood Music.

This Australian-born band features the unique lead vocals of Jenny Gullen & the talented guitar playing of her husband Andrew Horst. Hoi Polloi is not just their band name, but their mission, meaning "reach out to the masses".

Spin Me a Tale. unabr. ed. Read by Cynthia Changaris. 1 cass. (Running Time: 44 min.). (J). (gr. 1-7). 1995. 10.00 (978-1-887828-26-0(5)); audio compact disk 15.00 CD. (978-1-887828-27-7(3)) Roots & Dreams.

Folktales & stories that cross cultures; stories that touch, tickle, teach on side 2 & shivery stories on side 1. Story titles: Side I - Black Bubblegum; Ghost with One Black Eye; Monkeys Heart. Side II - Epaminondas; Bettys Butter; The Rice Field's Burning; Bird in Hand; God's Well; Spin Me a Tale.

SPIN Selling. abr. ed. Neil Rackham. Read by Bob Kalomer. 3 CDs. (Running Time: 3 hrs.). 2000. audio compact disk 24.95 HighBridge.

Using wit & authority, real-world examples, informative cases, effective & powerful techniques are unfolded to outsell the competition.

Spin Selling. abr. unabr. ed. Neil Rackham & Bob Kalomeer. 3 CDs. (Running Time: 3 hrs.). (ENG.). 2000. audio compact disk 24.95 (978-1-56511-420-3(5), 1565114205) Pub: HighBridge. Dist(s): Workman Pub

Spin, Spider, Spin: Songs for a Greater Appreciation of Nature. Patty Zeitlin. (J). 1974. 11.95 Ed Activities.

Spinal & Bulbar Muscular Atrophy - A Bibliography & Dictionary for Physicians, Patients, & Genome Researchers. Compiled by Icon Group International, Inc. Staff. 2007. ring bd. 28.95 (978-0-497-11383-4(X)) Icon Grp.

Spinal Cord Healing. Steven Gurgevich. (ENG.). 2005. audio compact disk 19.95 (978-1-932170-33-7(2), HWH) Tranceformation.

Spinal Muscular Atrophy - A Bibliography & Dictionary for Physicians, Patients, & Genome Researchers. Compiled by Icon Group International, Inc. Staff. 2007. ring bd. 28.95 (978-0-497-11295-0(7)) Icon Grp.

Spindrift. abr. unabr. ed. Brian Hancock. 2 cass. (Running Time: 3 hrs.). (YA). 2000. 17.95 (978-0-929071-75-6(1)) B-B Audio.

Join sailor/adventurer Brian Hancock for a fun-filled trip traveling around the world. You will sail across the Atlantic, hike through Africa, climb mountains in South America, round Cape Horn under sail in a full gale, and spend some quiet time with t.

Spindrift. unabr. ed. Phyllis A. Whitney. Read by Shelley Thompson. 10 cass. (Running Time: 10 hrs.). 2001. 84.95 (978-0-7540-0645-9(X), CAB2067) Pub: Chivers Audio Bks GBR. Dist(s): AudioGO

Christy Moreland never believed her father committed suicide at Spindrift. She was certain that her wealthy & powerful mother-in-law Theo was behind his death, but she had no way of proving it. Until now, for she was back at the huge old mansion where she could discover the truth.

Spine Chillers: Five Radio Dramas Based on the Stories of M. R. James. unabr. ed. M. R. James. Narrated by Full Cast. (Running Time: 1 hr. 0 mins. 0 sec.). (ENG.). 2010. audio compact disk 24.95 (978-1-60283-854-3(2)) Pub: AudioGO. Dist(s): Perseus Dist

***Spine Chillers Mysteries 3-in-1.** unabr. ed. Fred E. Katz. Narrated by Kirby Heyborne. (Running Time: 8 hrs. 20 mins. 49 sec.). (ENG.). 2010. 18.19 (978-1-60814-755-7(X)); audio compact disk 25.99 (978-1-59859-801-8(5)) Oasis Audio.

Spine Chilling Tales of Horror: A Caedmon Collection. abr. ed. Various. 4 CDs. (Running Time: 6 hrs.). 2002. audio compact disk 29.95 (978-0-06-051187-6(7)) HarperCollins Pubs.

Spine Fractures - What to Do? Interdisciplinary Panel Discussion. Moderated by Sanford J. Larson. 2 cass. (Neurological Surgery Ser.: NS-3). 1986. 19.00 (8649) Am Coll Surgeons.

Spineless Wonders: Strange Tales from the Invertebrate World. unabr. ed. Richard Conniff. Narrated by Richard M. Davidson. 5 cass. (Running Time: 7 hrs. 30 mins.). 1998. 46.00 (978-0-7887-2178-6(X), 95474E7) Recorded Bks.

With humor & sophistication, Conniff depicts the idiosyncratic habits of invertebrates - from moths to leeches - & the extraordinary contributions they make to our survival.

Spineless Wonders Set: Strange Tales from the Invertebrate World. unabr. ed. Richard Conniff. Narrated by Richard M. Davidson. 5 cass. (Running Time: 7 hrs. 5 min.). 1999. 44.00 (95474) Recorded Bks.

This funny & sophisticated exploration of invetebrates, from leeches to tarantulas, will have you groaning with delight.

Spinning a Web. Sundance/Newbridge, LLC Staff. (Early Science Ser.). (gr. k-3). 2007. audio compact disk 12.00 (978-1-4007-6235-4(9)); audio compact disk 12.00 (978-1-4007-6237-8(5)); audio compact disk 12.00 (978-1-4007-6236-1(7)) Sund Newbrdge.

Spinning into Butter. unabr. ed. Rebecca Gilman. Contrib. by Jordan Baker et al. 2 CDs. (Running Time: 5880 sec.). (L. A. Theatre Works). 2003. audio compact disk 25.95 (978-1-58081-270-2(8), CDTPT176) Pub: L A Theatre. Dist(s): NetLibrary CO

What happens when conflicting emotions inhabit the same space? When a new vocabulary is devised to disguise the same old thoughts? In this barbed satire of political correctness, Rebecca Gilman?s provocative characters spin a web of their own, revealing the latent racism that may lurk beneath the porcelain veneer of a liberated conscience.

Spinning Jenny. unabr. ed. Ruth Hamilton. Read by Marlene Sidaway. 16 cass. (Running Time: 21 hrs.). 2000. 104.95 (978-0-7531-0514-6(4), 990913) Pub: ISIS Audio GBR. Dist(s): Ulverscroft US

At eighteen Jennifer Crawley leads a strange & lonely life, her days in the cotton mill & her nights with her strange Aunt Mavis. Then comes work at Skipton Hall & a chance to better herself. But this household is just as strange as the one she has left, containing Henry Skipton, an embittered, solitary man who never visits his invalid wife & bed-ridden Louise Skipton, a beautiful woman plotting vengeance on the man she married. Jenny seems the perfect weapon for revenge.

Spinning-Wheel Stories, Set. unabr. ed. Louisa May Alcott. Read by Flo Gibson. 5 cass. (Running Time: 6 hrs. 30 min.). (J). (gr. 4-7). 1997. 20.95 (978-1-55685-444-6(7), 444-7) Audio Bk Con.

These homespun tales are full of old time values, simple pleasures & caring.

Spinoza in 90 Minutes. Paul Strathern. Read by Robert Whitfield. (Running Time: 1 hr. 30 mins.). 2004. 15.95 (978-0-7861-2782-5(1), 3315); audio compact disk 17.00 (978-0-7861-8533-7(3), 3315) Blckstn Audio.

Spinoza in 90 Minutes. unabr. ed. Paul Strathern. Read by Robert Whitfield. (Running Time: 1 hr. 30 mins.). (Philosophers in 90 Minutes Ser.). 2004. reel tape 14.95 (978-0-7861-2787-0(2)); audio compact disk 14.95 (978-0-7861-8532-0(5)) Blckstn Audio.

Spinoza of Market Street see Isaac Bashevis Singer Reader

Spinsters in Jeopardy. Ngaio Marsh. Narrated by Nadia May. (Running Time: 10 hrs.). 2000. 30.95 (978-1-59912-607-4(9)) Iofy Corp.

Spinsters in Jeopardy. unabr. ed. Ngaio Marsh. Read by Nadia May. 7 cass. (Running Time: 10 hrs.). 2001. 49.95 (978-0-7861-2097-0(5), 2859); audio compact disk 64.00 (978-0-7861-9677-7(7), 2859) Blckstn Audio.

En route to a family vacation on the French Riviera, Inspector Roderick Alleyn glimpses from the train a shocking tableau. In a moonlit window, a white-robed figure raises a knife to a woman's shadow. Thus begins his incognito exploration of the Chateau of the Silver Goat... where a jet-set cult's "Way of Life" could spell death for a maiden lady of a certain age?and even for Alleyn's own young son, unless he can unveil its illicit mysteries.

Spiral Dance: A Rebirth of the Ancient Religion of the Great Goddess. Starhawk. Read by Starhawk. 1 cass. (Running Time: 60 min.). 1990. 9.95 HarperCollins Pubs.

Spiral Dynamics Integral: Sounds True Audio Learning Course: Learn to Master the Memetric Codes of Human Behavior. Don Beck. 6 CDs. (Running Time: 443:57). 2006. audio compact disk 69.95 (978-1-59179-425-7(0), AF01009D) Sounds True.

Spiral Staircase: My Climb Out of Darkness. abr. ed. Karen Armstrong. Read by Karen Armstrong. 2004. audio compact disk 29.95 (978-0-06-059438-1(1)) HarperCollins Pubs.

Spirals. Barry Bernstein. 1 cass. (Running Time: 1 hr.). 9.95 (978-1-55961-503-7(6), Ellipsis Arts) Relaxtn Co.

Spirals. Harry Berstein. 1 CD. (Running Time: 1 hr.). 1998. audio compact disk 14.95 (978-1-55961-500-6(1)) Relaxtn Co.

SpiralUp Overview. Compiled by Benchmark Education Staff. 2006. audio compact disk 10.00 (978-1-4108-6368-3(9)) Benchmark Educ.

***Spire.** unabr. ed. Richard North Patterson. Read by Holter Graham. 1 Playaway. (Running Time: 11 hrs.). 2009. 89.95 (978-0-7927-6759-6(4)); 54.95 (978-0-7927-6683-4(0)); audio compact disk 89.95 (978-0-7927-6614-8(8)) AudioGO.

Spire. unabr. ed. Richard North Patterson. Read by Holter Graham. (Running Time: 11 hrs. 0 mins. 0 sec.). (ENG.). 2009. audio compact disk 39.99 (978-1-4272-0807-1(7)) Pub: Macmill Audio. Dist(s): Macmillan

Spirit, Set. abr. ed. R. A. Salvatore. Read by Bill Mumy. 4 cass. (Running Time: 6 hrs.). (Demon Wars Ser.: Bk. 1). 1997. 24.95 (978-1-57511-026-4(1), 695318) Pub Mills.

A young man discovers his true heritage when his village is destroyed by goblins & he is called upon to battle a horrific beast. In a volcanic cavern an evil beast awakens & wrecks terror on the enchanted land of Corona. Meanwhile, on a far-off island, magic gems fall to the beach, carrying with them all that is good in the world & all that is evil. Pray they do not fall into the beast's hands.

Spirit: How to Confidently Discern Between Soul & Spirit. 5. (Running Time: 5 hrs.). (Soul Control Ser.: 3). 2002. 5.00 (978-1-57399-109-4(0)); audio compact disk 25.00 (978-1-57399-160-5(0)) Mac Hammond.

In this third volume of Mac Hammond's Soul Control series, he talks about the real you-your spirit-and its operation in the process of making decisions for life and blessing. Begin to remove the clouds between you and your potential by learning how to confidently discern between soul and spirit so you can walk out the will of God on a daily basis.

Spirit: The Work of the Holy Spirit in the Life of a Disciple. Douglas Jacoby. 1 cass. 1998. 16.99 (978-1-57782-061-1(4)) Discipleshp.

A discussion of how the Holy Spirit works in the life of a disciple in practical terms.

Spirit - Soul - Body. James A. Crook. Read by James A. Crook. 1 cass. (Running Time: 1 hr.). 2000. 5.00 (978-0-939399-33-8(4)) Bks of Truth.

Explains functions of each part & how to protect the spirit from false doctrine.

Spirit & Nature. adpt. ed. Interview with Bill Moyers et al. Music by Paul Winter Consort. 1 cass. (Running Time: 89 min.). 1994. 10.95 (978-1-56176-904-9(5)) Mystic Fire.

Explores the ethical & spiritual issues of ecology & the need to re-examine our traditional viewpoints.

Spirit & Soul (the Ultimate Healer Subliminal Series, 6 Of 6) Blend spirit & soul together to live life in a state of Grace. Kyrah Malan. 1 CD. (Running Time: 26 mins). 2006. audio compact disk 39.95 (978-0-9787324-6-2(4), SPS6) K Malan.

The ultimate in subliminal affirmations. Music, messages and binaural beats are specifically designed to work together to help you begin living a life of unlimited joy and grace. Feel the power of your soul as you think, feel, and act in higher ways.What you hear is beautiful music that has been proven in university studies or harmonize and organize your energy field, putting you in a calm, receptive state quickly and easily.What your subconscious hears are specially designed affirmations and suggestions, designed to rewrite subconscious beliefs and change behavior faster and more effectively than any subliminal program available today.The Foundation set is designed to be used in order, each CD building on the effects of the previous CDs, and includes Love Your Life, Release & Relax, Energy & Power, Manifest & Magnetize, Live Your Life, and Spirit & Soul. Can be used independently. Unlike typical subliminal programs which recommend you listen to them for at least 30 days, Ultimate healer CDs help create positive results in only 17 days; some people report results in as little as 2 or 3 days!You can play them during everyday activities, while driving, reading, or at work, or listen to them with headphones. You have freedom and flexibility with The Ultimate Healer Subliminal Series.

Spirit & the Bride. Derek Prince. 1 cass. (B-3015) Derek Prince.

Spirit & the Church. Vincent M. Walsh. (Running Time: 15 hrs.). 1986. 50.00 incl. album Set. Key of David.

Spirit Bound. unabr. ed. Richelle Mead. Contrib. by Emily Shaffer. 8 CDs. (Running Time: 10 hrs.). (Vampire Academy Ser.: Bk. 5). (ENG.). (YA). 2010. audio compact disk 39.95 (978-0-14-314527-1(4), PengAudBks) Penguin Grp USA.

Spirit Calls. . . Rejoice. 1999. audio compact disk 32.00 (978-0-933173-75-0(X)) Chging Church Forum.

Spirit Centered Life. Patricia Fosarelli. 2007. audio compact disk 59.95 (978-0-9795255-1-3(9)) Now You Know.

Spirit Come Down. Barbara Stone. Read by Barbara Stone. 1 cass. (Running Time: 42 min.). 1994. bk. 9.95 (978-1-893129-02-3(0), 003) Stonepower.
Each side has repetitions of the theme song "Spirit Come Down" from the cassette "Initiation I," relaxation & chakra attunement for the 7th chakra, the crown chakra.

***Spirit Eater.** unabr. ed. Rachel Aaron. Read by Luke Daniels. (Running Time: 13 hrs.). (Legend of the Eli Monpress Ser.). 2010. 19.99 (978-1-4418-8667-5(2), 9781441886675, BAD); 39.97 (978-1-4418-8668-2(0), 9781441886682, BADLE); 19.99 (978-1-4418-8665-1(6), 9781441886651, Brilliance MP3); 39.97 (978-1-4418-8666-8(4), 9781441886668, Brinc Audio MP3 Lib); audio compact disk 19.99 (978-1-4418-8663-7(X), 9781441886637, Bril Audio CD Unabri); audio compact disk 64.97 (978-1-4418-8664-4(8), 9781441886644, BriAudCD Unabrid) Brilliance Audio.

Spirit Empowered Evangelism. Marc Estes. 4 cass. (Running Time: 6 hrs.). 2000. (978-1-886849-21-1(8)) CityChristian.

Spirit Fruits. Ed. by Strang Communications Company Staff. 1 cass. (Running Time: 1 hr.). (J). (gr. k-7). 1997. 10.99 (978-1-57405-040-0(0), SPFRCA) CharismaLife Pub.
At last music and praise songs just perfect for kids. These are the best songs from our KIDS Church programs. For classrooms and presentations, these songs teach as well as touch the heart. 15 inspirational songs that help kids understand the nature of God living in them.

Spirit Gives Life. Neville Goddard. 1 cass. (Running Time: 62 min.). 1964. 8.00 (13) J & L Pubns.
Neville taught Imagination Creates Reality. He was a powerfully influential teacher of God as Consciousness.

Spirit Guide Contact. Bruce Goldberg. (ENG.). 2005. audio compact disk 17.00 (978-1-57968-057-2(7)) Pub: B Goldberg. Dist(s): Baker Taylor

Spirit Guide Contact. Bruce Goldberg. Read by Bruce Goldberg. 1 cass. (Running Time: 25 min.). 2006. 13.00 (978-1-885577-65-8(6)) Pub: B Goldberg. Dist(s): Baker Taylor
Through self-hypnosis safely establish a two-way communication with one's master & guides from the spirit realms.

Spirit Guides Meditation. 1 cass. (Tara Sutphen Meditation Tapes Ser.). 11.98 (978-0-87554-568-4(8), TS206) Valley Sun.

Spirit Heals: Core Teachings & Practices. 2nd rev. ed. Read by Meredith L. Young-Sowers. (Running Time: 16080 sec.). (ENG., 2008. audio compact disk 24.95 (978-1-57731-618-3(5)) Pub: New Wrld Lib. Dist(s): PerseuPGW

Spirit in the Bottle: The Nature of Spirit & the Spirit of Nature. Read by Barry Williams. 1 cass. (Running Time: 90 min.). (Fairytales Ser.: No. 2). 1987. 10.95 (978-0-7822-0327-1(2), 228) C G Jung IL.

Spirit in the Theater. unabr. ed. Roni S. Denholtz. 1 cass. (Running Time: 20 min.). (Adventure Abounds Ser.). (J). (gr. 3-6). 1984. bk. 16.99 (978-0-934898-66-9(9)); pap. bk. 9.95 (978-0-934898-79-9(0)) Jan Prods.
Julie is very excited when she lands a part in a local play. They are rehearsing in a old barn that's being converted to a theater. But things begin to go wrong; some believe a mischievous spirit is haunting the theater.

***Spirit in the Woods: A Jennifer Caldwell Family Adventure.** Paula Jean Chretien. (YA). 2010. 12.00 (978-1-4276-4589-0(2)) AardGP.

Spirit Instrumental. Jerry Barnes. 1998. audio compact disk 14.95 (978-0-8198-1876-8(3), 332-071) Pauline Bks.

Spirit Knee. Donald Clayton Porter. Read by Lloyd James. 4 vols. 2004. 25.00 (978-1-58807-231-3(2)) Am Pubng Inc.

Spirit Knee. Donald Clayton Porter. Read by Lloyd James. 4 vols. No. 15. 2004. (978-1-58807-748-6(9)); audio compact disk 30.00 (978-1-58807-415-7(3)); audio compact disk (978-1-58807-879-7(5)) Am Pubng Inc.

Spirit-Led Ministry. Larry Randolph. 1 cass. (Running Time: 90 mins.). (Church in Transition Ser.: Vol. 2). 2000. 5.00 (LR01-002) Morning NC.
Larry prepares us for the needed changes we must accept in order to receive our bridegroom.

Spirit of a Finisher Series, Set. Elbert Willis. 4 cass. 13.00 Fill the Gap.

Spirit of Abundance, Having It All Together with Abundance & Finances. Narrated by Suzie Humphreys. 6 cass. 2001. vinyl bd. 54.95 (978-0-9715637-1-1(3)) Abund Resource.

Spirit of America: A Tribute & Celebration of the American Spirit. Created by Carl Mays. 1 CD. (Running Time: 13 min. 28 sec.). 2002. audio compact disk 7.98 (978-1-879111-00-4(4), LB7101) Lincoln-Bradley.

Spirit of Brokeness. Contrib. by Bradley T. Cooke. 1997. 24.95 (978-0-7601-2046-0(3), 75700135) Pub: Brentwood Music. Dist(s): H Leonard

Spirit of Christmas. Mormon Tabernacle Choir. 1 CD. audio compact disk 8.98 (3333140) Covenant Comms.

Spirit of Christmas. Mormon Tabernacle Choir. 1 cass. 4.98 (3111431) Covenant Comms.

Spirit of Christmas. unabr. ed. Nancy Tillman. Read by Jim Dale. 1 CD. (Running Time: 1 hr. 0 mins. 0 sec.). (ENG.). (J). (ps-3). 2009. audio compact disk 14.99 (978-1-4272-0811-8(5)) Pub: Macmill Audio. Dist(s): Macmillan

Spirit of Christmas: A History of Best-Loved Carols. Virginia Reynolds. (BookNotes with CDs Ser.). 2000. bk. 14.99 (978-0-88088-414-3(2)) Peter Pauper.

Spirit of Counsel. Featuring Bill Winston. 4. 2002. audio compact disk Rental 32.00 (978-1-59544-067-9(4)) B Winston Min.
The Spirit of Councel is divine information from God. It is advise and direction to help you to conduct your affairs.Proverbs 3:5-6 says, "Trust in the Lord with all thine heart;and lean not unto thine own understanding. In all thy ways acknowledge Him, and he shall direct thy paths.".

Spirit of Division. Kenneth Copeland. Perf. by Kenneth Copeland. 1 cass. (Anointed & His Anointing Ser.: Tape 6). 1995. cass. & video 5.00 (978-1-57562-033-6(2)) K Copeland Pubns.
Biblical teaching on the anointing.

Spirit of Enterprise. unabr. ed. George Gilder. Read by Joe Vincent. 8 cass. (Running Time: 11 hrs. 30 mins.). 1989. 56.95 (978-0-7861-0053-8(2), 1051) Blckstn Audio.
This is an ode to that risk-taking breed of Americans who stake their reputations, mortgages & sundry assets so they can live out their visions. Explores the impact of enterprise on business & technology.

Spirit of Excellence. Alfred D. Harvey, Jr. 1 Cass. 2003. 5.00 (978-1-932508-31-4(7)) Doers Pub.

Spirit of Faith. Kenneth Copeland. 7 CDs. 2006. audio compact disk 20.00 (978-1-57562-837-0(6)) K Copeland Pubns.

Spirit of Faith: Reaching into the Glory Realm. Kenneth Copeland. 4 cass. 1991. 20.00 Set incl. study guide. (978-0-88114-838-1(5)) K Copeland Pubns.
Biblical teaching on faith.

Spirit of Flame. E. Allison Peers. 6 cass. 24.95 (726) Ignatius Pr.
Life of the great Spanish mystic, St. John of the Cross.

Spirit of Giving. Glenn Hass. Read by Glenn Hass. Read by Brenda Neth et al. 1 cass. (Running Time: 1 hr. 07 min.). (J). (ps-4). 1993. 10.00 (978-0-9639615-0-1(0)) Life & Peace.
A collection of original poems, stories, & songs sharing a message of love, listening, honesty, communication, friendship & sharing through bears, teddy bears, butterflies, children, Christmas & frogs.

Spirit of God. Michael Ballam. 1 cass. 9.95 (978-1-55503-431-3(4), 1100432); audio compact disk 14.95 (978-1-55503-458-0(6), 110521) Covenant Comms.
Includes "Love at Home" & Oh, How Lovely Was the Morning".

Spirit of God Unleashed: The Choral Music of Richard Proulx: A Retrospective. Richard Proulx. Perf. by Cathedral Singers. 1997. 10.95 (405) GIA Pubns.

Spirit of God Unleashed: The Choral Music of Richard Proulx: A Retrospective. Richard Proulx & Cathedral Singers. 1997. audio compact disk 15.95 (405) GIA Pubns.

Spirit of India. (Running Time: 60 mins.). 2002. audio compact disk 15.99 (978-1-904972-59-4(4)) Global Jrny GBR GBR.

Spirit of Inner Renunciation. Swami Amar Jyoti. 1 cass. 1982. 9.95 (K-52) Truth Consciousness.
Courage to renounce the values of bondage. Truth shines by itself. Not East vs. West, but Truth vs. untruth. The Himalayan wisdom.

Spirit of Jesus. Neville Goddard. 1 cass. (Running Time: 62 min.). 1963. 8.00 (28) J & L Pubns.
Neville taught Imagination Creates Reality. He was a powerfully influential teacher of God as Consciousness.

Spirit of Jezebel. Francis Frangipane. 1 cass. (Running Time: 90 mins.). (Pulling down Strongholds Ser.: Vol. 7). 2000. 5.00 (FF05-007) Morning NC.
Some of Francis' most famous life-changing messages are contained in this comprehensive 10-tape series.

Spirit of Jungian Analysis. Read by Anthony Stevens. 1 cass. (Running Time: 1 hr.). 1989. 9.95 (978-0-7822-0300-4(0), 383) C G Jung IL.

Spirit of Knowledge. Featuring Bill Winston. 3. 2002. audio compact disk 24.00 (978-1-59544-063-1(1)) Pub: B Winston Min. Dist(s): Anchor Distributors
Learn to operate on Knowledge from God and not just information. The knowledge from God is called "Revelation."Revelation knowledge causes you to operate at a level that the worldis unfamiliar with and this knowledge will certainly set you apart.

Spirit of Leadership. Bill Winston. 3 cass. (Running Time: 3hr.39min.). (C). 2000. 15.00 (978-1-931289-27-6(1)) Pub: B Winston Min. Dist(s): Anchor Distributors

Spirit of Leonardo: Seven Steps to Self-Realization from History's Greatest Genius. Michael J. Gelb. 6 CDs. (Running Time: 21600 sec.). 2007. audio compact disk 69.95 (978-1-59179-568-1(0), AF01143D) Sounds True.

Spirit of Malia. Marty Haugen et al. 1997. 10.95 (414); audio compact disk 15.95 (414) GIA Pubns.

Spirit of Martyrdom: For the Love of Muslims. David Witt & Mujahid El Masih. Narrated by Bill Witt. (ENG.). 2007. audio compact disk 14.99 (978-1-930034-50-1(4)) Casscomm.

Spirit of Motherhood: Returning to Our Senses. 1 CD. (Running Time: 50 mins.). 2006. audio compact disk 15.00 (978-0-9785388-0-4(3)) Captiv8ting Bks.

Spirit of Murder. 1 cass. (Running Time: 1 hr. 30 mins.). 1999. 6.00 (978-1-58602-051-4(X)) E L Long.

Spirit of Now. unabr. ed. Excerpts. Peter Russell. 4 cass. (Running Time: 2 hrs.). (YA). 1997. 25.00 (978-1-928586-04-3(X)) Elf Rock Prodns.
Four recent speeches by futurist Russell include: "The Great Awakening," "Science & Spirituality," "The Evolution of Consciousness" & "The Redemption of the Executive".

Spirit of Offense. Mark Hanby. 3 cass. 1995. 24.00 Set. (978-1-56043-886-1(X)) Destiny Image Pubs.

Spirit of Poverty. Thomas Merton. 1 cass. 1995. 8.95 (AA2807) Credence Commun.
The will of God, not just our own ability, determines whether we should have a thing or not. Private ownership is relative.

Spirit of Prayer. Edward Hays. 2 cass. (Running Time: 60 min. per cass.). 14.95 set in vinyl album. (For Peace Pubng) Ave Maria Pr.
Four conferences on the Spirit of Prayer & on how "naturally" you can cultivate a spirit of being prayerful. Introduces such innovative prayer allies as prayer horns & prayer flags to help you keep your prayer alive in a computerized, mechanized world.

Spirit of Prophecy. Rick Joyner. 1 cass. (Running Time: 90 mins.). (Prophetic Ministry & Gifts Ser.: Vol. 2). 2000. 5.00 (RJ06-002) Morning NC.
These messages contain advanced teaching on the prophetic ministry, including discussion of strongholds & hindrances.

Spirit of Prophecy. Steve Thompson. 1 cass. (Running Time: 90 mins.). (Prophetic Ministry Ser.: Vol. 5). 2000. 5.00 (ST01-005) Morning NC.
Now updated & expanded, this popular series combines insights from the Scriptures & personal experience to explain how we can more effectively hear from God & minister prophetically.

Spirit of Racism. Stephen Mansfield. 1 cass. (Running Time: 90 mins.). (Studies in Church History Ser.: Vol. 1). 2000. 5.00 (SM02-001) Morning NC.
An in-depth look at different philosophies that have influenced church history, this series provides excellent keys for understanding how to effectively confront the important issues of our times.

Spirit of Seeking. Swami Amar Jyoti. 1 cass. 1989. 9.95 (M-79) Truth Consciousness.
Making mind spacious enough to allow growth toward God in our own life situation. Aspiration to awaken.

Spirit of St. Francis. Richard Rohr. 2 cass. (Running Time: 2 hrs.). 16.95 Set. (AA2407) Credence Commun.
Introduction to St. Francis, his spirit & the tradition he began.

***Spirit of Success: Consciousness & the Economy.** abr. ed. Marianne Williamson & Deepak Chopra. Read by Marianne Williamson & Deepak Chopra. (Running Time: 2 hrs. 0 mins. 0 sec.). (ENG.). 2010. audio compact disk 19.99 (978-1-4423-4016-9(9), Nightgale) Pub: S&S Audio. Dist(s): S and S Inc

Spirit of the Age. 1 CD. 2006. audio compact disk 11.00 (978-1-933207-14-8(0)) Ransomed Heart.

Spirit of the American Revolution. unabr. ed. David Barton. Read by David Barton. 1 cass. (Running Time: 1 hr.). 1993. 4.95 (978-0-925279-39-2(0), A02) Wallbuilders.
What was the spirit behind the American Revolution? Investigate the Founders words & their actions & witness their strong reliance upon God for wisdom & direction.

Spirit of the American Voice. unabr. ed. 1 cass. (Running Time: 1 hr. 12 mins.). 2001. 12.95 (978-1-58807-076-0(X)); audio compact disk 12.95 (978-1-58807-077-7(8)) Am Pubng Inc.
Spirit of the American Voice offers a spectacular collection of prose, poetry, and music that recounts the overwhelming faith and fortitude that Americans hold close to their heart. With interludes of patriotic anthems and hymns of faith woven through the fabric of the spoken word, the pride that has carried our great nation forward in times of peril and celebration will come alive.

Spirit of the Ancestors. (Running Time: 60 mins.). 2002. audio compact disk 15.99 (978-1-904972-18-1(7)) Global Jrny GBR GBR.

Spirit of the Body Politic. Thomas Berry et al. 4 cass. 1992. 36.00 set. (OC293-65) Sound Horizons AV.

Spirit of the Border. Zane Grey. Read by Michael Prichard. (Playaway Adult Fiction Ser.). (ENG.). 2009. 64.99 (978-1-60775-777-1(X)) Find a World.

Spirit of the Border. Zane Grey. Read by Michael Prichard. (Ohio River Trilogy). (ENG.). 2004. audio compact disk 34.99 (978-1-4001-0133-7(6)); audio compact disk 22.99 (978-1-4001-5133-2(3)) Pub: Tantor Media. Dist(s): IngramPubServ

Spirit of the Border. Zane Grey. Narrated by Michael Prichard. (Ohio River Trilogy). (ENG.). 2005. audio compact disk 69.99 (978-1-4001-3133-4(2)) Pub: Tantor Media. Dist(s): IngramPubServ

Spirit of the Border. unabr. ed. Zane Grey. Read by Robert Morris. 7 cass. (Running Time: 14 hrs.). 1995. 49.95 (978-0-7861-0896-1(7), 1672) Blckstn Audio.
The U. S. frontier in the 1700s produced some men of utter ruthlessness, & Jim Girty was one of the worst. Living among the Delaware Indians in the Ohio Valley, Girty & his brothers incited acts of savagery & war against the white settlers. Lewis Wetzel, a lonely, taciturn hunter whose family had been the victim of Delaware atrocities, swore revenge on Girty. The intrepid Wetzel, called "Deathwind" by the Delawares, had saved Fort Henry from Indian attack, but was he any match for the odious Girty?.

Spirit of the Border. unabr. ed. Zane Grey. Read by Gene Engene. 8 cass. (Running Time: 10 hrs. 30 min.). 2001. 49.95 (978-1-55686-944-0(4)) Books in Motion.
The frontier settlers in 1777 dealt with danger from both Native Americans and marauding white men who perpetrated fiendish cruelties upon the settlers. But Wetzel, a great frontiersman, became protector to the settlers, known to his enemies as the "Spirit of the Border".

Spirit of the Border. unabr. ed. Zane Grey. Narrated by Michael Prichard. (Running Time: 10 hrs. 30 mins. 0 sec.). (Ohio River Ser.). (ENG.). 2009. 22.99 (978-1-4001-5927-7(X)); lab manual ed. 65.99 (978-1-4001-3927-9(9)); audio compact disk 32.99 (978-1-4001-0927-2(2)) Pub: Tantor Media. Dist(s): IngramPubServ

Spirit of the Border, Set. unabr. ed. Zane Grey. Read by Robert Morris. 7 cass. 1999. 49.95 (FS9-26025) Highsmith.

Spirit of the Cowboy. Cliff Erickson. 1 cass. (Running Time: 20 min.). Dramatization. 1993. 1.95 incl. script. (978-1-885527-13-4(6)) Feather Fables.
Based on the poem "Spirit of the Cowboy," narrative & song for the Old West. A Kenny Rogers look-a-like performs.

***Spirit of the Disciplines: Understanding How God Changes Lives.** unabr. ed. Dallas Willard. Narrated by Robertson Dean. (ENG.). 2007. 16.98 (978-1-59644-497-3(5), Hovel Audio) christianaud.

Spirit of the Disciplines: Understanding How God Changes Lives. unabr. ed. Dallas Willard. Narrated by Robertson Dean. (Running Time: 10 hrs. 0 mins. 0 sec.). (ENG.). 2007. audio compact disk 26.98 (978-1-59644-496-6(7), Hovel Audio) christianaud.

Spirit of the Great Auk. Jay O'Callahan. Perf. by Jay O'Callahan. 1 cass. (Running Time: 1 hrs. 2 min.). (J). (gr. 7 up). 1997. 10.00 (978-1-877954-25-2(X)) Pub: Artana Prodns. Dist(s): Yellow Moon
Story of Richard Wheeler's kayak voyage from Newfoundland to Buzzard's Bay, in which the migratory journey of the Great Auk bird is recreated. He discovers the depth of the sea's plight & decides he must tell us - for it's our plight too.

Spirit of the Great Auk. Jay O'Callahan. Perf. by Jay O'Callahan. 1 CD. (Running Time: 1 hr. 2 mins.). Dramatization. 2002. audio compact disk 15.00 (978-1-877954-31-3(4)) Pub: Artana Prodns. Dist(s): High Windy Audio
Richard Wheeler 's kayak voyage from Newfoundland to Buzzard's Bay, in which the migratory journey of the Great Auk bird is recreated. He discovers the depth of the sea's plight and decides he must tell us, for it's our plight too.

Spirit of the Laws. unabr. ed. Baron De Montesquieu. Read by Nadia May. 16 cass. (Running Time: 23 hrs. 30 mins.). 1990. 99.95 (978-0-7861-0105-4(9), 1098) Blckstn Audio.
Originally published in 1748, this is possibly the most masterful & influential book ever written on the subject of liberty & justice. Accordingly, it is a work which profoundly influenced America's Founding Fathers. Montesquieu discusses numerous topics including the general functions of government, relations between the sexes, the morals & customs of the nation, economics & religion & the theory of law & legislative practice.

Spirit of the Leopard. Ingwe. Read by Ingwe. Ed. by Jay Sullivan et al. 1 cass. (Running Time: 1 hr. 30 min.). 1996. 12.95 (978-0-9649842-0-2(2)) Red Hawk Prodns.
Through his story as a boy of British descent, that ran barefoot with boys of an African tribe, Ingwe reveals the wisdom, joy & spirituality found by living close to the earth.

Spirit of the Lord. Featuring Bill Winston. 3. 2002. audio compact disk Rental 24.00 (978-1-59544-068-6(2)) B Winston Min.
Are you different? Are you tired of living the same old lifestyle? If you are no longer content with the way things are,then you need the Spirit of The Lord!

Spirit of the Mind: How to Change Your Life by Renewing Your Mind. Mac Hammond. 1 cass. 1996. 12.00 (978-1-57399-022-6(1)) Mac Hammond.
Teaching on the importance of controlling the thought process of the minc

Spirit of the Mountain Man. William W. Johnstone. 4 cass. (Running Time hrs.). (Mountain Man Ser.: No. 16). 2001. 24.95 (978-1-890990-69-5(8)) Audio.
With a bitter hatred for Smoke Jensen, the man who landed him in jail Ralph Tinsdale manages to escape & gathers a posse for the purpos getting even. His first act is to kidnap Jensen's wife.

Spirit of the Upanishads. Pandit Rajmani Tigunait. (Running Time: 1 h mins.). audio compact disk 16.95 (978-0-89389-253-1(X), CD271M Himalayan Inst.

Spirit of the Upanishads. unabr. ed. Pandit Rajmani Tigunait. 1 cass. (Running Time: 1 hr. 20 mins.). 2004. 8.95 (978-0-89389-225-8(4)) Himalayan Inst.

Spirit of the Vedas. unabr. ed. Pandit Rajmani Tigunait. 1 cass. (Running Time: 1 hr. 3 mins.). 2004. 8.95 (978-0-89389-224-1(6)) Himalayan Inst.

Spirit of Truth. Lynne Hammond. 1 cass. (Running Time: 1 hr.). 2005. 5.00 (978-1-57399-255-8(0)) Mac Hammond.

Spirit of Truth. Lynne Hammond. 1 CD. 2006. audio compact disk 5.00 (978-1-57399-359-3(X)) Mac Hammond.

Spirit of Understanding. Featuring Bill Winston. 2. 2002. audio compact disk 16.00 (978-1-59544-066-2(6)) Pub: B Winston Min. Dist(s): Anchor Distributors
Learn to skillfully use the laws of God by operating in the anointing of God. The Spirit of Understanding is one of the characteristics of the anointing and you need to leam how theanointing works and how you are to operate under this anointing. Get bettter organized mentally by getting understanding.

Spirit of Wisdom. Featuring Bill Winston. 3. 2002. audio compact disk 24.00 (978-1-59544-065-5(8)) Pub: B Winston Min. Dist(s): Anchor Distributors
Receive the Wisdom of God Which is the Word of God. Thisawesome teaching on The Spirit of Wisdom will cause you to operate in God's class because the Word of God will direct your path, it will guide you into all truth.

Spirit of Zen. Instructed by Manly P. Hall. 8.95 (978-0-89314-263-6(8), C800105) Philos Res.

Spirit Possession. Stephen Hawley Martin. 2008. 2.95 (978-1-892538-25-3(3)) Pub: Oaklea Pr. Dist(s): Midpt Trade

***Spirit Rebellion.** unabr. ed. Rachel Aaron. Read by Luke Daniels. (Running Time: 13 hrs.). (Legend of the Eli Monpress Ser.). 2010. 19.99 (978-1-4418-8659-0(1), 9781441886590, Brilliance MP3); 19.99 (978-1-4418-8661-3(3), 9781441886613, BAD); 39.97 (978-1-4418-8660-6(5), 9781441886606, Brinc Audio MP3 Lib); 39.97 (978-1-4418-8662-0(1), 9781441886620, BADLE); audio compact disk 19.99 (978-1-4418-8657-6(5), 9781441886576, Bril Audio CD Unabri); audio compact disk 64.97 (978-1-4418-8658-3(3), 9781441886583, BriAudCD Unabrid) Brilliance Audio.

Spirit Seeker, unabr. ed. Joan Lowery Nixon. Narrated by Christina Moore. 4 pieces. (Running Time: 4 hrs. 45 mins.). (gr. 7 up). 2000. 36.00 (978-0-7887-3527-1(6), 95916E7) Recorded Bks.
Holly Campbell's world has suddenly been turned upside down. Her best friend stands accused of murdering his parents. She knows he's innocent, but the only person willing to help her prove it is a weird psychic. And the things she's asking Holly to do are frightening.

Spirit Seeker, unabr. ed. Joan Lowery Nixon. Read by Christina Moore. 4 cass. (Running Time: 4 hrs. 45 mins.). (YA). 2000. pap. bk. & stu. ed. 48.75 (978-0-7887-3654-4(X), 41020X4) Recorded Bks.

Spirit Seeker, Class Set. unabr. ed. Joan Lowery Nixon. Read by Christina Moore. 4 cass. (Running Time: 4 hrs. 45 mins.). (YA). 1999. 101.80 (978-0-7887-3683-4(3), 46987) Recorded Bks.

Spirit Sickness. unabr. ed. Kirk Mitchell. Read by Stefan Rudnicki. (Running Time: 12 hrs. 0 mins.). 2009. 29.95 (978-1-4332-9595-9(4)); 72.95 (978-1-4332-9591-1(1)); audio compact disk 105.00 (978-1-4332-9592-8(X)) Blckstn Audio.

Spirit Sings. 1 cass. (Running Time: 60 min.). 1994. audio compact disk 15.95 CD. (2604, Creativ Pub) Quayside.
Indian flute. Harmonic sounds of nature highlight original flute music by native Ojibwa artist, Anakwad.

Spirit Sings. 1 cass. (Running Time: 60 min.). 1994. 9.95 (2602, NrthWrd Bks) TandN Child.

Spirit Song: The Introduction of No-Eyes. abr. ed. Mary S. Rain. Read by Nancy Fish. 2 cass. (Running Time: 3 hrs.). 1997. 17.95 (978-1-57453-173-2(5)) Audio Lit.
Meet No-Eyes, a blind-from-birth Chippewa visionary who lives alone in the Colorado mountains. No-Eyes teaches her the song of the shaman, guides her in the use of medicinal herbs & becomes her beloved friend.

Spirit Songs: Gong Music for Meditation. 1994. audio compact disk 16.00 (978-0-9700967-1-5(2)) Khalsa Con.

Spirit, Soul & Body. 1999. 25.00 (978-1-881541-66-0(5)) A Wommack.

Spirit, Soul & Body. 4. 2004. audio compact disk 28.00 (978-1-881541-97-4(5)) A Wommack.

Spirit, Soul, & Body. Kenneth E. Hagin. 6 cass. 24.00 (11H) Faith Lib Pubns.

Spirit, Soul & Body. Gary V. Whetstone. 9 cass. (Running Time: 13 hrs. 30 mins.). (Theology Ser.: TH103). 1996. 170.00 (978-1-58866-089-3(3), BT 103 A00) Gary Whet Pub.
Gain a clear understanding of the nature, operations & positions of influence your spirit, soul & body have in your life. Learn how to develop your human spirit.

Spirit, Soul & Body Connection. Henry W. Wright. (ENG.). 2007. audio compact disk 17.95 (978-1-934680-16-2(8)) Be in Hlth.

Spirit, Soul & Society. Richard Rohr. 5 cass. (Running Time: 6 hrs.). 1993. 39.95 set. (AA2623) Credence Commun.
An integrated spirituality for serious inner work. This is not beginner's material; it is an in-depth analysis of what needs to be done to integrate our body, soul & spirit.

Spirit Style, Pt. 1. unabr. ed. Read by Gayle D. Erwin. 1 cass. (Running Time: 1 hr.). 1992. 4.95 (978-1-56599-514-7(7), C-14) Yahshua Pub.
Joy in the Holy Spirit.

Spirit Style, Pt. 2. unabr. ed. Read by Gayle D. Erwin. 1 cass. (Running Time: 1 hr.). 1992. 4.95 (978-1-56599-515-4(5), C-15) Yahshua Pub.

Spirit Style, Vol. 1. Gayle D. Erwin. Read by Gayle D. Erwin. 4 cass. (Running Time: 4 hrs.). 1994. bk. 15.00 Set. (978-1-56599-093-7(5), AB3) Yahshua Pub.
God's activity in our life & the Holy Spirit as is evidenced through Jesus.

***Spirit Thief.** unabr. ed. Rachel Aaron. Read by Luke Daniels. (Running Time: 8 hrs.). (Legend of the Eli Monpress Ser.). 2010. 19.99 (978-1-4418-8289-9(8), 9781441882899, Brilliance MP3); 19.99 (978-1-4418-8291-2(X), 9781441882912, BAD); 39.97 (978-1-4418-8290-5(1), 9781441882905, Brinc Audio MP3 Lib); 39.97 (978-1-4418-8292-9(8), 9781441882929, BADLE); audio compact disk 19.99 (978-1-4418-8287-5(1), 9781441882875, Bril Audio CD Unabri); audio compact disk 64.97 (978-1-4418-8288-2(X), 9781441882882, BriAudCD Unabrid) Brilliance Audio.

Spirit to Spirit. Perf. by Lori Wilke. 1 cass. 1988. 9.98 (978-1-891916-16-8(5)) Spirit To Spirit.

Spirit Trail. abr. ed. Johnny Quarles. Read by Charlie Dickerson. 4 cass. (Running Time: 6 hrs.). 1998. Rental 24.95 (978-1-890990-16-9(7)) Otis Audio.

Spirit Walker. unabr. ed. Michelle Paver. Read by Ian McKellen. 5 CDs. (Running Time: 6 hrs. 30 mins.). (Chronicles of Ancient Darkness: Bk. 2). (YA). (gr. 5-9). 2006. audio compact disk 49.75 (978-1-4193-9379-2(0), C3724); 39.75 (978-1-4193-9374-7(X), 98369) Recorded Bks.
From nationally best-selling author Michelle Paver comes this thrilling sequel to the popular Wolf Brother. A terrible sickness has come to the forest where Torak lives. Sufferers are covered in putrid scabs and blisters - and eventually lose their minds. Nobody knows whatژs causing it, but Torak believes the dreaded Soul-Eaters are responsible - and it is his destiny to fight them.

Spirit Within-the Spirit Upon, Vol. 1. Kenneth E. Hagin. 6 cass. 24.00 (60H) Faith Lib Pubns.

Spirit Within-the Spirit Upon, Vol. 2. Kenneth E. Hagin. 6 cass. 24.00 (61H) Faith Lib Pubns.

Spirit Woman. unabr. ed. Margaret Coel. Read by Stephanie Brush. 8 cass. (Running Time: 8 hrs. 42 min.). (Wind River Ser.). 2001. 39.95 (978-1-58116-137-3(9)); 45.50 (978-1-58116-138-0(7)) Books in Motion.
A historian arrives in Wind River country convinced that the memoirs of the 19th century Shoshone heroine Sacajawea are stashed somewhere on the reservation. And when the historian turns up missing, Father John and Vicky Holden become convinced that someone has come between the researcher and the memoirs - if they exist.

Spirit World: Underworld of Departed Spirits, Heaven, Hell. Finis J. Dake, Sr. (J). (gr. k up). 5.95 (978-1-55829-037-2(0)) Dake Publishing.
Bible study.

Spirit World of the Neanderthals. Engineer Bob E. Flick. Music by Bob E. Flick. Des. by Adam Mayefsky. 1 CD. (Running Time: 1 hr. 7 mins.). 2002. audio compact disk 15.00 (978-1-884214-26-4(6)) Ziggurat Prods.
[Instrumental]: A unique & powerful rhythmic journey through time, space...and history.The Neanderthals survived over200,000 years. The Paleolithicworld in which they lived wasthe size and shape of the GreatRoman Empire. The Ice-Ageconditions in which they existedproved extremely harsh...the lastGlacial Maximum. But now, theywere on the threshold of extinction.

Spirit World Realities. Henry W. Wright. (ENG.). 2007. audio compact disk 42.95 (978-1-934680-05-6(2)) Be in Hlth.

Spiritalkin' Valjahna Hill-Cox. Ed. by Valjahna Hill-Cox. 2002. 12.00 (978-0-9705358-1-8(3)); audio compact disk 12.00 (978-0-9705358-5-6(6)) Darby Hill.

***Spirited.** unabr. ed. Rebecca Rosen & Samantha Rose. Read by Rebecca Rosen. (ENG.). 2010. (978-0-06-199168-4(6), Harper Audio) HarperCollins Pubs.

***Spirited: Connect to the Guides All Around You.** unabr. ed. Rebecca Rosen & Samantha Rose. Read by Rebecca Rosen. (ENG.). 2010. (978-0-06-199054-0(X), Harper Audio) HarperCollins Pubs.

Spirited Yarns, Vols. I & II. Charles Dickens et al. 2 cass. (Running Time: 2 hrs.). 2001. 19.95 (SMPD012) Lodestone Catalog.
Humorous ghost stories that rattle your funny bones with great characterizations, spine chilling sounds & original music.

Spirited Yarns Vol. 2: Classic Humorous Ghost Stories. unabr. ed. Ed. by Pent. 1 cass. (Running Time: 60 min.). 1999. 12.95 (978-1-896617-00-8(X), SMA001) Pub: Stuffed Moose CAN. Dist(s): Hushion Hse
Includes: The Lawyer and the Ghost, Selecting a Ghost, and Buggam Grange.

Spirited Yarns Vol. 2: Classic Humorous Ghost Stories. unabr. ed. Ed. by Pent. 1 cass. (Running Time: 60 mins.). 2001. 12.95 (978-1-896617-01-5(8), SMA002) Stuffed Moose CAN.
Includes: The Canterville Ghost, The Third Person, The Transferred Ghost, and The Ghost Ship.

Spirits! Poetry of Edgar A. Poe & James Whitcomb Riley. Edgar Allan Poe & James Whitcomb Riley. Music by Leonard Carpenter & Mary Daily. Narrated by Ross Ballard. (ENG.). 2002. audio compact disk 14.95 (978-0-9717801-2-5(9)) Mtn Whispers Pubng.

Spirits & Spooks for Halloween. unabr. ed. Perf. by William Conrad. 1 cass. Incl. Belinda & the Swab. Ian Serraillier. (J). (CPN 1344); Fereyel & Debbo the Witch. Ian Serraillier. (J). (CPN 1344); Hag. Ian Serraillier. (J). (CPN 1344); How a Witch Tried to Kill a King. Ian Serraillier. (J). (CPN 1344); Merry Night of Halloween. Hans Christian Andersen. (J). (CPN 1344); Secret Commonwealth. Ian Serraillier. (J). (CPN 1344); Strange Visitor. Ian Serraillier. (J). (CPN 1344); Suppose You Met a Witch. Ian Serraillier. (J). (CPN 1344); (J). 1984. 9.95 (978-0-89845-754-4(8), CPN 1344) HarperCollins Pubs.

Spirits in the Wires: A Novel of Myth & Magic-on the Streets & on the Net. Charles de Lint. Narrated by Christine Marshall & William Dufris. 1 CD. (Running Time: 16 hrs. 42 mins.). 2004. audio compact disk 18.45 (978-1-58439-000-8(X)) Pbk Dig Inc.
Ancient magic and the Internet weave a spell in the latest Newford novel from urban fantasy master Charles de Lint.Charles de Lint's "Newford" novels, loosely-linked tales with overlapping characters set in an imaginery modern North American city, are the gold standard of modern urban fantasy.De Lint tells tales of magic and myth afoot on today's city streets, but at the center of every de Lint story is the miracle of the human heart. And at the heart of Spirits in the Wires are Saskia Madding and Christiana Tree, both of whom are tied to a perennial Newford character, the writer Christy Riddell.Are either Saskia or Christiana real? Christy's girlfriend, Saskia, believes she was born in a Web site, while Christiana is Christy's "shadow-self" - all the parts of him that he cast out when he was seven years old.At a popular Newford online research and library Web site called the Wordwood, a mysterious "crash" occurs. Everyone visiting the site at the moment of the crash vanishes from where they were sitting in front of their computers. Saskia disappears right before Christy's eyes, along with countless others.Now Christy and his companions must journey into Newford's otherworld, where the Wordwood, it transpires, has a physical presence of its own - to rescue their missing friends and loved ones and to set this viral spirit right before it causes further harm. - - - - - - - - - - - - - - - - This MP3-CD Audiobook can only be played on an MP3 compatible CD player or an MP3 device like an Apple iPod. Please make sure that your CD player is MP3 compatible before you purchase this audiobook.

Spirits of Defiance: National Prohibition & Jazz Age Literature, 1920-1933. Kathleen Morgan Drowne. 2005. audio compact disk 9.95 (978-0-8142-9075-0(2)) Pub: Ohio St U Pr. Dist(s): Chicago Distribution Ctr

Spirits of the Wild: The World's Great Nature Myths. unabr. ed. Gary Ferguson. Read by Gary Ferguson. 2 cass. (Running Time: 2 hrs. 30 mins.). 2000. 18.00; audio compact disk 20.00 Pub Mills.

Spirits of the Wild: The World's Great Nature Myths. unabr. ed. Gary Ferguson. 2 CDs. (Running Time: 3 hrs.). 2001. audio compact disk 20.00 (978-1-57511-085-1(7)) Pub: Pub Mills. Dist(s): TransVend
Many of these enchanting myths are hundreds, even thousands, of years old. Tales explain why tulips rock in the breeze (Ireland), why spiders have small waists (Liberia), & how rainbows came into being (Philippines).

Spirits of the Wild: The World's Great Nauture Myths. unabr. ed. Gary Ferguson. 2 cass. (Running Time: 3 hrs.). 2001. 18.00 (978-1-57511-084-4(9)) Pub: Pub Mills. Dist(s): TransVend

Spirits Walk: Chilling Tales for Teenagers & Adults. Connie Regan-Blake. 1 cass., 1 CD. (Running Time: 1 hr. 03 min.). 1999. 10.99 (978-1-929415-05-2(2)) StoryWindow Prodns.

Spirits Walk: Chilling Tales for Teenagers & Adults. Connie Regan-Blake. 1 cass., 1 CD. (Running Time: 1 hr. 03 min.). (YA). (gr. 7 up). 1999. audio compact disk 15.99 CD. (978-1-929415-06-9(0)) StoryWindow Prodns.

Spiritual Activation: Why Each of Us Does Make the Difference. Julia Butterfly Hill. 2 CDs. (Running Time: 2 hrs. 30 mins.). 2002. audio compact disk 24.95 (978-1-59179-015-0(8), AW00650D) Sounds True.
Representing the highest spiritual principles, the author has attracted the attention of the world with her living example of how one person can truly alter the course of world events. This book shares the author's hope-giving message for a more sacred world, a place where we consciously consider the impact of our choices and act from a center of "power, responsibility, and love." Distilled from the best moments captured at her standing room only appearances across the country, here is a wellspring of simple, useful practices and moving insights to help us activate our spiritual selves, while cultivating a more sustainable lifestyle, today and tomorrow.

Spiritual Adventurism. Jack Marshall. 1 cass. 3.95 (978-1-57734-390-5(5), 34441301) Covenant Comms.

Spiritual Adventurism. unabr. ed. Jack Marshall. Read by Jack Marshall. 1 cass. (Running Time: 60 min.). (YA). 1993. 7.98 (978-1-55503-587-7(6), 06004822) Covenant Comms.
Youth motivation talk.

Spiritual Alchemy Set: The Seven Processes of Spiritual Awakening. unabr. ed. Jacquelyn Small. 2 cass. (Running Time: 2 hrs.). 1998. 16.00 (978-0-939344-07-9(6)) Eupsychian.
Describes the seven alchemical processes & their effect on our body & soul as we "cook" in the chasm of the heart when we are undergoing a transformational cycle. Includes a potent guided imagery exercise.

Spiritual Anarchy in Colonial America. Peter L. Wilson. 2 cass. 1992. 18.00 set. (OC281-62) Sound Horizons AV.

Spiritual Arts: Mastering the Disciplines for a Rich Spiritual Life. unabr. ed. Jill Briscoe. (Running Time: 6 hrs. 16 mins. 0 sec.). (ENG.). 2009. 13.99 (978-0-310-77193-7(5)) Zondervan.

Spiritual Assessment: A Case Example of the Seven by Seven. 1 cass. (Care Cassettes Ser.: Vol. 22, No. 3). 1995. 10.80 Assn Prof Chaplains.

Spiritual Authority. 6 cass. (Running Time: 5 hrs. 30 min.). bk. set. (978-1-881541-24-0(X), 1017) A Wommack.
Understanding Spiritual Authority is an indispensable ingredient. Failure to understand this critical issue causes many to passively wait on the Lord to move in their life when in actuality, God is waiting on them to exercise their authority.

Spiritual Authority. Created by AWMI. (ENG.). 2001. audio compact disk 35.00 (978-1-59548-033-0(1)) A Wommack.

Spiritual Authority. unabr. ed. Watchman Nee. 6 CDs. (Running Time: 6 hrs. 0 mins. 0 sec.). (ENG.). 2005. audio compact disk 24.98 (978-1-59644-124-8(0), Hovel Audio) christianaud.

***Spiritual Authority.** unabr. ed. Watchman Nee. Narrated by Michael Kramer. (ENG.). 2005. 14.98 (978-1-59644-908-4(X), Hovel Audio) christianaud.

Spiritual Authority Series. George Bloomer. 5. audio compact disk Whitaker Hse.

Spiritual Authority Series. unabr. ed. George Bloomer. 5 CDs. (Running Time: 6 hrs.). 2003. audio compact disk 59.99 (978-0-88368-966-0(9)) Whitaker Hse.
Authority: At its best, it's a blessing, a representation of the Lord's gracious guidance and leading of His sheep. However, when tainted by sin and selfishness, authority can turn into a curse. It doesn't matter where this authority comes into play - the classroom, the church, the home, or the workplace. What matters is that God-given authority is in alignment with the Lord's perfect provision for leadership. In this dynamic series, George Bloomer explores principles that can ensure the proper exercise of authority in every area of our lives.

Spiritual Awakening. Ram Dass. 5 cass. (Running Time: 4 hrs.). 1993. 49.95 set incl. meditation cass. (685A) Nightingale-Conant.

Spiritual Awakening & Group Dynamics. 1 cass. (Recovery - The New Life Ser.). 8.95 (1595G) Hazelden.

Spiritual Awareness. James R. Dolan. 2 cass. (Running Time: 2 hrs. 5 min.). 1994. 17.95 Set. (TAH324) Alba Hse Comns.
Fr. Dolan uses stories from life & experience along with a vast repertoire of De Mello stories to help you experience that God loves you all the time & unconditionally, how prayer & holiness flow naturally & how reconciliation truly sets you free.

Spiritual Awareness. unabr. ed. Judith L. Powell. Read by Judith L. Powell. 1 cass. (Running Time: 40 min.). (Successful Living Ser.). 1987. pap. bk. 12.95 (978-0-914295-31-0(4)) Top Mtn Pub.
Side A presents exercises designed to awaken spiritual awareness. Side B presents subliminal suggestions hidden in New Age Music.

Spiritual Balance & Attunement: Cultivate & Resotre Spiritual Balance & Integration. Mark Bancroft. Read by Mark Bancroft. 1 CD, 1 bklet. (Running Time: 1 hr.). (Spirituality & Consciousness Ser.). 2006. audio compact disk 20.00 (978-1-58522-050-2(7)) EnSpire Pr.
Two complete sessions plus printed instructionmanual/guidebook. With healing music soundtrack.

Spiritual Balance & Attunement: Cultivate & Restore Spiritual Balance & Integration. Mark Bancroft. Read by Mark Bancroft. 1 cass., bklet. (Running Time: 1 hr.). (Spirituality & Consciousness Ser.). 1999. 12.95 (978-1-58522-016-8(7), 707, EnSpire Aud) EnSpire Pr.
Two complete sessions plus printed instruction manual/guidebook. With healing music soundtrack.

Spiritual Blindness - Cause & Curse. Derek Prince. 1 cass. (I-4068) Derek Prince.

Spiritual Boot Camp (Activating the Power of God) No. 2: Ephesians 6:18. Ed Young. 1980. 4.95 (978-0-7417-1136-6(2), A036) Win Walk.

Spiritual Boot Camp (How To Study The Bible) Vol. 1: 1 Peter 2:1-2. Ed Young. (J). 1980. 4.95 (978-0-7417-1134-2(6), A0134) Win Walk.

Spiritual Bootcamp. 4 cass. 15.95 incl. study guide. (2035, HarperThor) HarpC GBR.

Spiritual Brain. unabr. ed. Mario Beauregard & Denyse O'Leary. Read by Patrick G. Lawlor. (YA). 2008. 59.99 (978-1-60514-509-9(2)) Find a World.

Spiritual Brain: A Neuroscientist's Case for the Existence of the Soul. unabr. ed. Mario Beauregard. Read by Patrick G. Lawlor. (Running Time: 13 hrs. 0 mins. 0 sec.). (ENG.). 2007. audio compact disk 37.99 (978-1-4001-0538-0(2)); audio compact disk 24.99 (978-1-4001-5538-5(X)); audio compact disk 75.99 (978-1-4001-3538-7(9)) Pub: Tantor Media. Dist(s): IngramPubServ

Spiritual Calisthenics: The Inner Workout That Affects Your Outer Life. unabr. ed. Eric A. Braun. Read by Eric A. Braun. 1 cass. 1990. 9.95 (978-0-9625268-1-7(9)) Applied Wisdom.

Spiritual Canticle As the Story of Human Desire. Constance Fitzgerald. 4 cass. 1988. 32.95 (TAH218) Alba Hse Comns.
By exploring the symbolism & language of desire in the Spiritual Canticle, this workshop develops a new interpretive framework for understanding John of the Cross' writings so that his teaching can actually function as a resource for self-understanding, for spiritual direction & for ministry.

Spiritual Canticle of John of the Cross As the Story of Human Desire. Constance FitzGerald. Read by Constance FitzGerald. 4 cass. (Running Time: 5 hrs. 40 min.). 32.95 set. (TAH218) Alba Hse Comns.

Spiritual Care of the Aging; Family Consideration in Ministry to Aging. Harold Nelson. 1986. 10.80 (0211) Assn Prof Chaplains.

Spiritual Centering. 1 cass. (Running Time: 39 min.). (Guided Meditation Ser.: No. 1). 11.95 (978-1-57025-002-6(2), SPC) Whole Person.
Side A: Tap into spiritual depth on this inward journey of renewal. Guided imagery & deep breathing help wandering thoughts come to rest, & let the listener emerge in touch with his or her inner strength. Side B: The same powerful meditative encounter with your inner advisor with female narration.

Spiritual Challenge of Our Time. David Steindl-Rast. 1 cass. 9.00 (OC45) Sound Horizons AV.
Enables us to accept threats as oppurtunites when challenges are approached with a fearlessness.

Spiritual Child-Raising Series. 6 cass. 44.95 (LS-9) Crystal Clarity.
Discusses: The Why & How of Spiritual Education; Bringing Out the Best in Children (by Michael Nitai Deranja, former principal, Ananda How-to-Love Schools); The Art of Loving Discipline; Creative Visualizations for Children; Childhood As a Stage on the Spiritual Path.

Spiritual Cleansing. Read by Mary Richards. (Subliminal - Self Hypnosis Ser.). 12.95 (809) Master Your Mind.
Encourages you to cleanse yourself of that which is not your highest good.

Spiritual Cleansing. Read by Mary Richards. 1 cass. (Running Time: 45 min.). (Series Two Thousand). 2007. audio compact disk 19.95 (978-1-56136-099-4(6)) Master Your Mind.

Spiritual Conflict, Album 1: Lucifer Challenges God. Derek Prince. 6 cass. 29.95 (I-SC1) Derek Prince.

Spiritual Conflict, Album 2: God's Secret Plan Unfolds. Derek Prince. 6 cass. 29.95 (I-SC2) Derek Prince.

Spiritual Conflict, Album 3: God's People Triumphant. Derek Prince. 6 cass. 29.95 (I-SC3) Derek Prince.

Spiritual Conflict, Album 4: Strategy for Conquest. Derek Prince. 4 cass. 19.95 (I-SC4) Derek Prince.

Spiritual Conflict, Album 5: Weapons that Prevail. Derek Prince. 4 cass. 19.95 (I-SC5) Derek Prince.

Spiritual Connection CD. Tarot by Tracey. 2001. audio compact disk (978-0-9714181-8-9(7)) Tarot By Tracey.

Spiritual Connections: How to Find Spirituality Throughout All the Relationships in Your Life. abr. ed. Sylvia Browne. Read by Sylvia Browne. 2 CDs. 2007. audio compact disk 18.95 (978-1-4019-0883-6(7)) Hay House.

***Spiritual Cycles That Drive Our Life.** Louis Gates. 2009. audio compact disk 10.00 (978-0-578-00105-0(5)) Red Candy.

Spiritual Death of Jesus: The Great Plan. Kenneth Copeland. Perf. by Kenneth Copeland. 3 cass. (Running Time: 3 hrs.). 1995. cass. & video 25.00 Set. (978-1-57562-021-3(9)) K Copeland Pubns.
Biblical teaching on spiritual death of Jesus.

Spiritual Deception in the Church: Romans 16:17-20. Ben Young. 1997. 4.95 (978-0-7417-6039-5(8), B0039) Win Walk.

Spiritual Development. Scripts. Marjorie Baker Price. Narrated by Marjorie Baker Price. 3 cassettes. (Running Time: 90 minutes). 1992. 26.95 (978-0-9713013-3-7(6)) Centering Pubns.
Powerfully explore and experience spiritual developement and beingness through this 3 tape set, which includes: " Connecting With Your Higher Self", " Finding Your Guide", "Shamanism-Spiritual Journey of Empowerment". Transformational guided imagery tht moves you to the deepest truths of your being, where you can recieve higher guidance and find answers to your deepest questions for healing, power, guidance and transformation.

Spiritual Dimensions of Alternative Medicine. 1 cass. (Care Cassettes Ser.: Vol. 22, No. 5). 1995. 10.80 Assn Prof Chaplains.

Spiritual Dimensions of Pastoral Leadership. 1 cass. (Care Cassettes Ser.: Vol. 18, No. 2). 1991. 10.80 Assn Prof Chaplains.

Spiritual Direction. 1 cass. (Care Cassettes Ser.: Vol. 19, No. 3). 10.80 Assn Prof Chaplains.

Spiritual Direction. Thomas Merton. 1 cass. 8.95 (AA2137) Credence Commun.

Spiritual Direction, Vol. 1. Chester P. Michael. 1985. 24.00 (978-0-940136-12-0(0)) Open Door Inc.

Spiritual Direction, Vol. 2. Chester P. Michael. 1985. 24.00 (978-0-940136-13-7(9)) Open Door Inc.

Spiritual Direction in the Letters of St. John of the Cross. Kevin Culligan. 1 cass. (Running Time: 61 min.). 8.95 I C S Pubns.
Fr. Kevin Culligan, O.C.D. provides a glimpse into St. John of the Cross's own application of his principles in guiding others to union with God.

Spiritual Discernment. Niel T. Anderson. Read by Niel T. Anderson. 1 cass. (Running Time: 1 hr.). (ICEL Three Ser.). 1996. 6.00 (978-1-57838-024-4(3)) CrossLife Express.
Christian living.

***Spiritual Disciplines for the Christian Life.** unabr. ed. Donald Whitney. Narrated by Grover Gardner. (ENG.). 2008. 16.98 (978-1-59644-590-1(4), Hovel Audio) christianaud.

Spiritual Disciplines for the Christian Life. unabr. ed. Donald S. Whitney. Read by Grover Gardner. Frwd. by J. I. Packer. (Running Time: 9 hrs. 15 mins. 0 sec.). (ENG.). 2008. audio compact disk 26.98 (978-1-59644-589-5(0)) christianaud.

Spiritual Disciplines 101. Daniel Stolebarger & Joe Frocht. 5 Audio CD's. 2006. audio compact disk 34.95 (978-1-57821-357-3(6)) Koinonia Hse.
SD 101 Introduction to Spiritual DisciplinesDiscipleship, Prayer, The Text & Small GroupsSpiritual Disciplines begins with the call to discipleship. The first session gives us a look at our Jewish roots, zeroing in on what it meant to be a telmidin and what it means to follow in the dust of your Rabbi. The session ends with a study of the Sh?ma.Session two is given to Prayer. This class will hopefully be more of a ?lab,? with the emphasis on the experiential element. Our desire is for our students to spend as much time praying as they do in study.Session three deals with one?s commitment to the study of God?s Word. The fourth session speaks to the importance of Community and where Small Groups fit into The Fellowship. The fifth session is by Joe Focht, Pastor of Calvary Chapel Philadelphia, teaching on the purity of God?s Word.Contains 5 individual audio CD's plus the fully automated MP3 CD-ROM with 4 multimedia presentations and 5 MP3 files.

Spiritual Emergence & Addiction. unabr. ed. Jacquelyn Small. 1 cass. (Running Time: 1 hr. 30 min.). (C). 1995. 11.00 (978-0-939344-13-0(0)) Eupsychian.
A lecture & guided imagery exercise for therapists & healers concerning the limits of traditional therapies for carrying us through the process of spiritual awakenings. Levels beyond the ego are explained.

Spiritual Energy Crisis. 2007. audio compact disk (978-0-937249-44-4(0)) Aetherius Soc.

Spiritual Enlightenment: The Enlightenment Trilogy Book One: the Damnedest Thing Audio. Jed McKenna. 8 CDs. 2005. audio compact disk 39.95 (978-0-9714352-1-6(9)) Wisefool Pr.
FROM A SPIRITUAL MASTER unlike any, a spiritual masterpiece like no other. A masterpiece of illuminative writing, Spiritual Enlightenment: The Damnedest Thing is mandatory reading for anyone following a spiritual path. From Jed McKenna, author of Spiritually Incorrect Enlightenment. AUDIOBOOK ON 8 CDs "Absolutely marvelous, splendid, perfect book!" Shri Acharyaji.

Spiritual Evolution & Healing. Kyriacos Markides. 3 cass. 24.00 (OC83W) Sound Horizons AV.

Spiritual Exercises. unabr. ed. Ignatius of Loy. (Running Time: 3 hrs. 0 mins. 0 sec.). (ENG.). 2009. audio compact disk 18.98 (978-1-59644-815-5(6), Hovel Audio) christianaud.

***Spiritual Exercises.** unabr. ed. St. Ignatius of Loyola. Narrated by Geoffrey Silver. (ENG.). 2009. 10.98 (978-1-59644-816-2(4), Hovel Audio) christianaud.

Spiritual Exploration of the Human Suffering. 1 cass. (Care Cassettes Ser.: Vol. 21, No. 8). 1994. 10.80 Assn Prof Chaplains.

Spiritual Food for the Soul. Alphonse Curry, Sr. 1 cass. 1998. Pub & Prof Ghost Writers.

Spiritual Foundation of Life. Swami Amar Jyoti. 1 dolby cass. 1986. 9.95 (A-33) Truth Consciousness.
Keeping in touch with the Divine in all aspects of life. Coming back to our roots & moorings.

Spiritual Freedom. Robert Wicks. 1 cass. (Running Time: 1 hr.). 1995. Credence Commun.
Spiritual freedom begins with self-knowledge, but not just information, the kind of self-knowledge that comes in prayer.

Spiritual Friendship & Intimate Community: The Joy of Being Unconditionally Committed to Each Other's Liberation. abr. ed. Scott Morrison. 1 cass. (Running Time: 1 hr.). 1998. 7.50 (978-1-882496-25-9(6)) Twnty Frst Cntry Ren.
Living the art of unconditional openness, honesty & intimacy with each other; the transformative power of undefended kindness.

Spiritual Gifts. Chuck Missler. 2 cass. (Running Time: 2.5 hours plus). (Briefing Packages by Chuck Missler). 1994. vinyl bd. 14.95 (978-1-880532-59-1(X)) Koinonia Hse.
Are the gifts for today? What does the Bible say about the gift of tongues? How do you validate the reality of God the Holy Spirit in a Christian's life?The Holy Spirit is given to unite, not divide, the Body. There are two common errors: One is to ignore the Spiritual Gifts, the other is to over-emphasize one gift above another. There are many controversial topics associated with the mysterious Gifts of the Holy Spirit.This study focuses in on the Apostle Paul, who addresses the controversial topics associated with the mysterious "Gifts of the Holy Spirit".

Spiritual Gifts. Chuck Missler. 2 CDs. (Running Time: 120 mins.). (Briefing Packages by Chuck Missler). 1994. audio compact disk 19.95 (978-1-57821-302-3(9)) Koinonia Hse.

Spiritual Gifts & Levels of Revelation. Rick Joyner. 1 cass. (Running Time: 90 mins.). (Prophetic Ministry & Gifts Ser.: Vol. 7). 2000. 5.00 (RJ06-007) Morning NC.
These messages contain advanced teaching on the prophetic ministry, including discussion of strongholds & hindrances.

Spiritual Gifts of Your Childhood Pain. John E. Bradshaw. (Running Time: 30600 sec.). 2008. audio compact disk 199.00 (978-1-57388-162-3(7)) J B Media.

Spiritual Growth. Dan Corner. 1 cass. 3.00 (107) Evang Outreach.

Spiritual Growth: Footprints into the Self - Starlight. Diana Keck. Read by Diana Keck. 1 cass. 1985. 9.95 (978-0-929653-10-5(6), TAPE 500) Mntn Spirit Tapes.

Spiritual Growth: Soul Images of Woman - Woman Spirit. Diana Keck. Read by Diana Keck. 1 cass. 1985. 9.95 (978-0-929653-11-2(4), TAPE 501) Mntn Spirit Tapes.

Spiritual Growth: Tread Lightly upon the Earth - The Wisdom of the Soul. Diana Keck. Read by Diana Keck. 1 cass. 1985. 9.95 (978-0-929653-12-9(2), TAPE 502) Mntn Spirit Tapes.

Spiritual Growth Experience Cassette Album, Set. Bruce Goldberg. Read by Bruce Goldberg. 6 cass. (Running Time: 3 hrs.). (ENG.). 2006. 65.00 (978-1-885577-74-0(5)) Pub: B Goldberg. Dist(s): Baker Taylor
Self-hypnosis program training to protect oneself from negativity from invisible forces, and how to safely leave the body and find karmic purpose.

Spiritual Growth Experience CD Album. Bruce Goldberg. (ENG.). 2005. audio compact disk 75.00 (978-1-57968-055-8(0)) Pub: B Goldberg. Dist(s): Baker Taylor

Spiritual Growth for Contemporary Males. Martin W. Pable. 3 cass. (Running Time: 3 hrs. 41 min.). 1998. 29.95 Set. (TAH396) Alba Hse Comns.
For the male, contemporary culture is defined by the struggles for success & achievement, many times at the times of a developing spirituality. The search for wholeness is a search for the reintegration of life which embraces God.

Spiritual Guidance: The Carmelite Tradition. Kevin Culligan et al. 13 cass. 79.95 Set. I C S Pubns.

Spiritual Healing. George King. 2005. audio compact disk 12.50 (978-0-937249-22-2(X)) Aetherius Soc.

Spiritual Healing. George King. 2007. audio compact disk (978-0-937249-46-8(7)) Aetherius Soc.

Spiritual Healing. Stanley Krippner. 1 cass. 1993. 9.00 (OC349-73) Sound Horizons AV.

Spiritual Healing. Eldon Taylor. 1 cass. (Running Time: 62 min.). (Inner Talk Ser.). 16.95 incl. script. (978-1-55978-008-7(8), 5408C) Progress Aware Res.
Soundtrack - Musical Themes with underlying subliminal affirmations.

Spiritual Healing. Stuart Wilde. 1 cass. (Running Time: 1 hr.). 11.95 (978-0-930603-08-3(7)) White Dove NM.
A subliminal tape. Relaxing musical background. Your conscious mind hears only the music while your subconscious mind, accepts the powerful affirmations.

Spiritual Healing: Babbling Brook. Eldon Taylor. 1 cass. 16.95 (978-1-55978-536-5(5), 5408F) Progress Aware Res.

Spiritual Healing & Meditation. Elizabeth Joyce. 1 cass. (Running Time: 1 hr.). 1992. 12.00 (978-1-57124-008-8(X)) Creat Seminars.
Self healing techniques with guided meditations.

Spiritual Healing (Hypnosis), Vol. 6. Jayne Helle. 1 cass. (Running Time: 56 min.). 1996. 15.00 (978-1-891826-05-4(0)) Introspect.
Helps the body heal itself mentally, physically & emotionally. Not a medical replacement.

Spiritual Healing Series: The Sexual Addict. Vol. 1. 2001. audio compact disk 149.99 (978-0-9621127-5-1(5)) Daly Consulting.

Spiritual Healing-series 2000. (ENG.). 2007. audio compact disk 19.95 (978-1-56136-127-4(5)) Master Your Mind.

Spiritual Hunger, Set. Mac Hammond. 4 cass. (Running Time: 4 hrs.). 1995. Mac Hammond.
What do you do when you seem to have lost your appetite for the things of God? Mac reveals some simple, yet powerful steps you can take.

Spiritual Immune System; A Look at Lent. Jonathan Murro & Ann Ree Colton. 1 cass. 7.95 A R Colton Fnd.

Spiritual Intent. 2005. audio compact disk 12.98 (978-5-559-33141-6(4)) Pub: Pt of Grace Ent. Dist(s): STL Dist NA

Spiritual Intimacy: Drawing Closer to God. Carole Riley. 2 cass. (Running Time: 2 hrs.). 2001. vinyl bd. 16.95 (A6440) St Anthony Mess Pr.
Looks at human intimacy and the manner of our heart's longing.

Spiritual Investments: Wall Street Wisdom from the Career of Sir John Templeton. Gary Moore. 2 CDs. (Running Time: 76 Minutes). 2005. audio compact disk 12.95 (978-1-932031-80-5(4)) Pub: Templeton Pr. Dist(s): Chicago Distribution Ctr

Spiritual Issues in Mental Illness. 1 cass. (Care Cassettes Ser.: Vol. 16, No. 8). 1989. 10.80 Assn Prof Chaplains.

Spiritual Journey. unabr. ed. Ram Dass. Read by Ram Dass. 3 CDs. (Running Time: 3 hrs. 0 mins. 0 sec.). (ENG.). 2005. audio compact disk 19.95 (978-1-59397-672-9(0)) Pub: Macmill Audio. Dist(s): Macmillan

Spiritual Journeys. Perf. by Rhiannon Waits. (ENG.). 2003. 12.99 (978-0-9779502-2-5(0)) R Waits Co.

Spiritual Justice: A New Dawn Is Rising. Speeches. Created by John Dennison. 2 CDs. (ENG.). 2007. audio compact disk 24.95 (978-1-932986-03-7(0)) WhisperZone.

Spiritual Leadership. Scott Green & Lynne Green. 1 cass. 1998. 16.99 (978-1-57782-062-8(2)) Disciplesho.
Leadership in the Kingdom of God is critical. Nothing great happens on any level without effective leadership. Exposes God's unique & powerful message about leadership, especially as it is found in the letters of 1 & 2 Timothy.

Spiritual Leadership: Principles of Excellence for Every Believer. unabr. ed. J. Oswald Sanders. 4 CDs. (Running Time: 5 hrs. 0 mins. 0 sec.). (ENG.). 2006. audio compact disk 21.98 (978-1-59644-180-4(1), Hovel Audio) christianaud.

***Spiritual Leadership: Principles of Excellence for Every Believer.** unabr. ed. J. Oswald Sanders. Narrated by Grover Gardner. (ENG.). 2006. 12.98 (978-1-59644-181-1(X), Hovel Audio) christianaud.

Spiritual Lessons, No. 1. Swami Jyotirmayananda. 1 cass. (Running Time: 1 hr.). 1990. 12.99 Yoga Res Foun.

Spiritual Lessons, No. 2. Swami Jyotirmayananda. 1 cass. (Running Time: 1 hr.). 1990. 12.99 Yoga Res Foun.

Spiritual Lessons from the Forests, Set. Ben Mathes. Read by Ben Mathes. 2 cass. (Running Time:). 1995. 12.95 (978-1-886463-23-3(9)) Oasis Audio.
Takes you along as he encounters some of the most remarkable, fascinating & courageous people in the world. From a tribe waiting for a word from the unknown God, to a father who tied his family to the tops of trees to save their lives in a typhoon.

Spiritual Liberation: Fulfilling Your Soul's Potential. unabr. ed. Michael Bernard Beckwith. Read by Michael Bernard Beckwith. (Running Time: 8 hrs. 0 mins. 0 sec.). (ENG.). 2008. audio compact disk 39.99 (978-0-7435-7133-3(9)) Pub: S&S Audio. Dist(s): S and S Inc

Spiritual Life. Swami Amar Jyoti. 1 dolby cass. 1985. 9.95 (A-31) Truth Consciousness.
What is the spiritual life & what is its purpose. Consciously connecting our life with the spiritual. Refining of human nature.

Spiritual Life & Scriptural Healing. Kenneth W. Hagin, Jr. 6 cass. 24.00 (13J) Faith Lib Pubns.

SpiritualL Life in the Rosary. 1 cass. (Running Time: 60 min.). (Mother Angelica Live Ser.). 10.00 (978-1-55794-068-1(1), T19) Eternal Wrd TV.

Spiritual Life of a Chaplain. Angela Blackburn. 1986. 10.80 (0903) Assn Prof Chaplains.

Spiritual Life of Children, unabr. ed. Robert Coles. Narrated by Nelson Runger. 11 cass. (Running Time: 16 hrs.). 91.00 (978-1-55690-732-6(X), 92317E7) Recorded Bks.
Robert Coles, psychiatrist & professor at Harvard University, gives his insights on the religious & spiritual lives of children as gleaned from interaction with dozens of children from every walk of life; this work completes a trilogy of studies that also includes "The Moral Life of Children" & "The Political Life of Children". Available to libraries only.

Spiritual Life of the Theologian. Rosemary L. Haughton. 1 cass. (Running Time: 1 hrs.). 1997. 9.95 (TAH390) Alba Hse Comns.
In this descriptive discourse the author makes a concise exploration of the sources of spirituality, demonstrating how theology issues of our spiritual experience & ultimately feeds back into it.

Spiritual Light Journey. Richard Gordon. 1 cass. 1994. pap. bk. 10.00 (978-0-931892-82-0(1)) B Dolphin Pub.

Spiritual Light of Ralph Waldo Emerson. unabr. ed. Read by Richard Kiley. 2 cass. (Running Time: 3 hrs.). 1995. 16.95 (978-0-944993-59-0(1)) Audio Lit.

Spiritual Literacy: Reading the Sacred in Everyday Life. Frederic Brussat. 2004. 10.95 (978-0-7435-4613-3(X)) Pub: S&S Audio. Dist(s): S and S Inc

Spiritual Lives: John Bunyan. unabr. ed. John Brown. Read by Nadia May. 6 cass. (Running Time: 8 hrs. 30 mins.). 1999. 44.95 (978-0-7861-1638-6(2), 2466) Blckstn Audio.
A traveling tinker, Bunyan accepted long imprisonment rather than give up preaching the Gospel. He explained the life of the Spirit in language the common people could understand, & in pictures that stuck in the mind. When he wrote "Pilgrim's Progress," his fame spread rapidly, & the book was reputed to be found in most English homes within fifty years of his death.

Spiritual Living: Cultivate Spiritual Living in Daily Life. Mark Bancroft. Read by Mark Bancroft. 1 cass., 1 bklet. (Running Time: 1 hr.). (Spirituality & Consciousness Ser.). 1999. wbk. ed. 12.95 (978-1-58522-015-1(9), 715) EnSpire Pr.
Two complete sessions plus printed instructionmanual/guidebook. With healing music soundtrack.

Spiritual Living: Cultivate Spiritual Living in Daily Life. Mark Bancroft. 1 CD, bklet. (Running Time: 1 hr.). (Spirituality & Consciousness Ser.). 2006. audio compact disk 20.00 (978-1-58522-042-7(6)) EnSpire Pr.

Spiritual Madness: The Necessity of Meeting God in Darkness. Caroline Myss. 2 CDs. (Running Time: 2 hrs. 30 mins.). 2002. audio compact disk 24.95 (978-1-56455-902-9(5), AW00550D) Sounds True.
This classic session describes a contemporary path open to all who seek direct mystical experience. Modern mystics are faced with conflicts no medieval monk ever faced, the author says, leading to a "dark night" unique to our age, and a deep and rich "madness" that is an inescapable part of the mystical journey today.

Spiritual Makeover. 1 cass. 1997. 20.00 (978-1-57855-017-3(3)) T D Jakes.

Spiritual Man & the Divine Man, Side 1; Enthusiasm - God Within, Side 2. unabr. ed. Ann Ree Colton & Jonathan Murro. 1 cass. (Running Time: 55 min.). 1994. 7.95 (978-0-917189-22-7(1), 104) A R Colton Fnd.
Side 1: Discusses initiation into the nature-related, biological, psychological, metaphysical, spiritual & divine dimensions of being; Side 2: Discusses the spiritual dynamics of obtaining & maintaining an enthusiastic love for God.

Spiritual Marriage. Brother Anandamoy. 1984. 8.50 (2506) Self Realization.
Discusses the principles & ideals of marriage as taught by Paramahansa Yogananda & explains how to apply them to gain the greatest spiritual benefit & fulfillment from married life.

Spiritual Message of the New Testament: Acts, Major Letters & Revelation, Vols. 5-9. Joseph A. Grassi. 16 cass. 1981. 92.95 Set, Vol. 5-9. (TAH082); 20.75 Vol. 5, Acts of the Apostles. (TAH077); 26.95 Vol. 6, Letters of St. Paul. (TAH078); 20.75 Vol. 7, Pauline Letters. (TAH079); 20.75 Vol. 8, Pauline Letters (cont.). (TAH080); 20.75 Vol. 9, Letter to the Hebrews, Revelation & the Letter of John. (TAH081) Alba Hse Comns.
Examines & explores the spiritual nuances of the New Testament & shares findings & observations.

Spiritual Message of the New Testament: The Complete New Testament, Vol. 1-9. Joseph A. Grassi. 34 cass. 192.90 (TAH083) Alba Hse Comns.

Spiritual Message of the New Testament: The Gospels, Vols. 1-4. Joseph A. Grassi. 18 cass. 99.95 Set, Vols. 1-4. (TAH009); 32.95 Vol. 1, Gospel of Mark. (TAH005); 26.95 Vol. 2, Gospel of Matthew. (TAH006); 26.95 Vol. 3, Gospel of Luke. (TAH007); 32.95 Vol. 4, Gospel of John. (TAH008) Alba Hse Comns.
Argues that the message of the Good News is there for all who would open themselves to receive & experience it.

Spiritual Motherhood: Every Woman's Call. George Pearsons. (ENG.). 2008. audio compact disk 5.00 (978-1-57562-968-1(2)) K Copeland Pubns.

Spiritual Nearsightedness. Dan Comer. 1 cass. 3.00 (84) Evang Outreach.

Spiritual Needs of Patients with Eating Disorders. 1 cass. (Care Cassettes Ser.: Vol. 17, No. 9). 1990. 10.80 Assn Prof Chaplains.

Spiritual Needs of the Terminally Ill. E. Ronal Mudd. 1986. 10.80 (0808A) Assn Prof Chaplains.

Spiritual Notebook. unabr. ed. Scripts. Paul Twitchell. 6 cass. (Running Time: 7 hrs. 31 mins.). 1992. 28.00 (978-1-57043-036-7(5), 160041) Pub: Eckankar. Dist(s): Hushion Hse

Spiritual or Survival Astrology. Beverly J. Farrell. 1 cass. 8.95 (404) Am Fed Astrologers.

***Spiritual Parenting: An Awakening for Today's Families.** unabr. ed. Michelle Anthony. Narrated by Michelle Anthony. (ENG.). 2010. 12.98 (978-1-61045-090-4(6)); audio compact disk 21.98 (978-1-61045-089-8(2)) christianaud.

***Spiritual Partnership.** unabr. ed. Gary Zukav. Read by Gary Zukav. (ENG.). 2010. (978-0-06-199300-8(X), Harper Audio) HarperCollins Pubs.

***Spiritual Partnership: The Journey to Authentic Power.** unabr. ed. Gary Zukav. Read by Gary Zukav. (ENG.). 2010. (978-0-06-198865-3(0), Harper Audio) HarperCollins Pubs.

Spiritual Partnership & Marriage: Create a Soulful, Loving Relationship. Mark Bancroft. Read by Mark Bancroft. 1 cass. (Running Time: 1 hr.). (Relationships/Family/Parenting Ser.). 1999. wbk. ed. 12.95 (978-1-58522-035-9(3)) EnSpire Pr.
Contains two complete holistic self-hypnosis sessions.

Spiritual Partnership & Marriage: Create a Soulful, Loving Relationship. Mark Bancroft. Read by Mark Bancroft. 1 CD, 1 bklet. (Running Time: 1 hr.). (Relationships/Family/Parenting Ser.). 2006. audio compact disk 20.00 (978-1-58522-052-6(3)) EnSpire Pr.
Two complete sessions plus printed instructionmanual/guidebook. With healing music soundtrack.

Spiritual Passivity. Lee Lefebre. 1 cass. (Running Time: 1 hr. 20 min.). 1992. 6.00 (978-1-57838-080-0(4)) CrossLife Express.
Christian living.

Spiritual Path. Swami Jyotirmayananda. 1 cass. (Running Time: 45 min.). 1990. 10.00 Yoga Res Foun.

Spiritual Path Exploration: Discover & Explore Your Spiritual Path in Life. Mark Bancroft. Read by Mark Bancroft. 1 cass., bklet. (Running Time: 1 hr.). (Spirituality & Consciousness Ser.). 1999. 12.95 (978-1-58522-009-0(4), 706, EnSpire Aud) EnSpire Pr.
Two complete sessions plus printed instruction manual/guidebook. With healing music soundtrack.

Spiritual Path Exploration: Discover & Explore Your Spiritual Path in Life. Mark Bancroft. Read by Mark Bancroft. 1 CD, 1 bklet. (Running Time: 1 hr.). (Spirituality & Consciousness Ser.). 2006. audio compact disk 20.00 (978-1-58522-051-9(5)) EnSpire Pr.
Two complete sessions plus printed instructionmanual/guidebook. With healing music soundtrack.

Spiritual Path to Success see Unleash Your Potential: The Quest Life Trilogy

Spiritual Power of Storytelling. Jose Hobday. Read by Jose Hobday. 2 cass. (Running Time: 1 hr. 45 min.). 19.95 incl. vinyl album. Credence Commun.
Explains how you can reflect on your own lifestory & relate to those of your family, community & Jesus.

Spiritual Power, Spiritual Practice. Read by Caroline Myss. 2 cass. (Running Time: 3 hrs.). 1999. 18.95 (83-0071) Explorations.
Daily practice of meditations & other techniques to tap the wellsprings of love, faith & trust that energize spiritual potential.

Spiritual Power, Spiritual Practice. Caroline Myss. 2 CDs. (Running Time: 2 hrs. 30 min.). 2000. stu. ed. 24.95 (978-1-56455-797-1(9), AE00498) Sounds True.
Prayers, reflections & other teachings Dr. Caroline Myss developed in her own spiritual practice. Includes two 40-minute meditations, one for morning & one for evening.

***Spiritual Practice: A Meditation CD.** David Elliott. (ENG.). 2005. 15.00 (978-0-9753910-5-1(4)) Hawk Pr CA.

Spiritual Practices in Our Life. Swami Amar Jyoti. 1 cass. 1989. 9.95 (P-52) Truth Consciousness.
Practical instructions for modification & regulation of life necessary for spiritual growth.

Spiritual Preparation for Earth Changes. Swami Amar Jyoti. 1 cass. (Satsangs of Swami Amar Jyoti Ser.). 1996. 9.95 (K-155) Truth Consciousness.
With faith & reliance on the Lord, "Fasten your seat belt & relax." Changing ourselves before earth changes take over.

Spiritual Principles. Marianne Williamson. 4 CDs. 2004. audio compact disk 23.95 (978-1-4019-0416-6(5)) Hay House.

Spiritual Principles. abr. ed. Marianne Williamson. 4 cass. (Running Time: 4 hrs.). 1997. 30.00 (978-1-56170-272-5(2), M775) Hay House.
Lectures based on "A Course in Miracles" include: All Things Are Lessons/I Am As God Created Me (Tape 1); Celebrating Yourself/Spiritual Practice (Tape 1); Basic ACIM Principles/Only the Love Is Real (Tape 3) & The Living Temple (Tape 4).

Spiritual Progress Through Regression. Brian L. Weiss. 2008. audio compact disk 15.00 (978-1-4019-2234-4(1)) Hay House.

Spiritual Protection & Healing. William L. Rand. Illus. by Craig Maher. 1 cass. (Running Time: 65 min.). pap. bk. (978-1-886785-00-7(7)) Vision Pub.
Hypnosis self-help.

Spiritual Purpose & Life's Work: Cultivate Meaning & Purpose in Your Life's Work. Mark Bancroft. Read by Mark Bancroft. 1 cass., bklet. (Running Time: 60 min.). (Spirituality & Consciousness Ser.). 1999. 12.95 (978-0-9665539-6-3(9), 703, EnSpire Aud) EnSpire Pr.
Two complete sessions plus printed instructionmanual/guidebook. With healing music soundtrack.

Spiritual Purpose & Life's Work: Cultivate Meaning & Purpose in Your Life's Work. Mark Bancroft. Read by Mark Bancroft. 1 CD, bklet. (Running Time: 60 min.). (Spirituality & Consciousness Ser.). 2006. audio compact disk 20.00 CD & bklet. (978-0-9665539-7-0(7)) EnSpire Pr.

Spiritual Quest. Swami Amar Jyoti. 2 cass. 1981. 12.95 (M-21) Truth Consciousness.
The spiritual quest does not lead away from the world, it justifies it. Knowing our True Identity, the perfect answer to everything.

Spiritual Quotient. Eldon Taylor. 1 cass. (Running Time: 62 min.). (Inner Talk Ser.). 16.95 incl. script. (978-1-55978-788-8(0), SQ1) Progress Aware Res.
Soundtrack - Musical Themes with underlying subliminal affirmations.

Spiritual Regression Methodology: Life Between Lives Methodology. Michael Newton. 2 CDs. (Running Time: 45 min each). 2003. audio compact disk 35.00 (978-1-929661-03-9(7)) Pub: Transpersonal Pubng. Dist(s): New Leaf Dist

Spiritual Resolves & How to Keep Them. 1 cass. (Running Time: 1 hr.). 12.99 (173) Yoga Res Foun.

Spiritual Revolution. unabr. ed. Perf. by Eknath Easwaran. 1 cass. (Running Time: 1 hr.). 1992. 7.95 (978-1-58638-610-8(7)) Nilgiri Pr.

Spiritual Revolution... & the Law of Attraction: Spirituality As a Practical Everyday Experience. Esther Hicks & Jerry Hicks. 5 CDs. (ENG.). 2011. audio compact disk 49.95 (978-1-4019-1879-8(4)) Hay House.

***Spiritual Rhythm: Being with Jesus Every Season of Your Soul.** Zondervan. (Running Time: 11 hrs. 20 mins. 54 sec.). (ENG.). 2010. 17.99 (978-0-310-41330-1(3)) Zondervan.

Spiritual Safeguards. Dan Comer. 1 cass. 3.00 (DC2) Evang Outreach.

Spiritual Savvy! Laurie Morse. 2006. audio compact disk 29.95 (978-0-9767262-2-7(X)) L Morse.

Spiritual Self Healing. Speeches. Edward Strachar. 1 cass. (Running Time: 50 mins.). 2002. 14.95 (978-0-9719358-2-2(3)) InGenius Inc.

Spiritual Self Healing. Speeches. Edward Strachar. 2 CDs. (Running Time: 90 mins.). 2002. audio compact disk 24.95 (978-0-9726941-7-9(X)) InGenius Inc.

Spiritual Songs of Hildegard. Perf. by Mimi Dye. 1 cass. 1995. 13.95 (MoreHse Pubng); audio compact disk 16.95 CD. (MoreHse Pubng) Church Pub Inc.
Performance of solo viola creates an environment of sound that soothes, inspires & comforts.

Spiritual Stories of the East. Justin Stone. (ENG.). 2008. audio compact disk 19.95 (978-1-882290-10-9(0)) Good Karma.

Spiritual Stories of the East, Vol. 1 & 2. unabr. ed. Justin F. Stone. Read by Justin F. Stone. 2 cass. (Running Time: 2 hrs.). 1990. bk. 19.95 Set. (978-1-882290-04-8(6)) Good Karma.
Little-known stories from Zen, Sufic, Indian traditions containing universal insights from author's/reader's vast personal experience.

Spiritual Study of the Tarot: Including the Kabalah, Numerology & Astrology. Louise Fimlaid. Read by Louise Fimlaid. 6 cass. (Running Time: 9 hrs.). 1997. 40.00 Set. (978-0-9630409-4-7(4)) Galaxy Pub.

Spiritual Success, Set. Mark Victor Hansen. 2 cass. 1997. 16.95 (978-1-879323-57-5(5)) Hay House.

Spiritual Survival. William Wait. 1 cass. 2004. 3.95 (978-1-57734-410-0(3), 34441522) Covenant Comms.

Spiritual Survival & the Joy of Service. William Wait. 1 cass. 7.98 (978-1-55503-051-3(3), 0600308) Covenant Comms.
Timely topics, typical Wait humor & wisdom.

Spiritual Techniques to Heal Body, Mind & Soul. Elizabeth Clare Prophet. 1 cass. (Running Time: 1 hr.). 2001. 8.95 (978-0-922729-59-3(X)) Pub: Summit Univ. Dist(s): Natl Bk Netwk

Spiritual Things. Bobby Hilton. 4 cass. 2000. 22.00 (978-1-930766-13-6(0)) Pub: Bishop Bobby. Dist(s): STL Dist NA

Spiritual Training of Children. James C. Dobson. 1 cass. (Life-Lifter Ser.). 1985. 10.99 Nelson.
States that parents must be models of Christian values, taking the time to point their children's hearts toward Christ.

Spiritual Training of Children. unabr. ed. Elisabeth Elliot. Read by Elisabeth Elliot. 2 cass. (Running Time: 1 hr. 45 min.). 1990. 9.95 (978-0-8474-2021-6(3)) Back to Bible.
Elisabeth & her sister-in-law discuss ideas on raising children to love God, to pray & to live for Him.

Spiritual Transformation. Swami Jyotirmayananda. 1 cass. (Running Time: 45 min.). 1990. 10.00 Yoga Res Foun.

Spiritual Truth: Using the Enneagram. Read by Alan Fensin. 2 cass. (Running Time: 1 hr. 30 mins.). 12.95 (978-1-57867-064-2(0)); audio compact disk 16.95 (978-1-57867-065-9(9)) Windhorse Corp.

Spiritual Tune Up. Lynne Hammond. 1 cass. (Running Time: 1 hr.). 2005. 5.00 (978-1-57399-253-4(4)) Mac Hammond.

Spiritual Value of Conflict. Swami Jyotirmayananda. Read by Swami Jyotirmayananda. 1 cass. (Running Time: 60 min.). 12.99 (729) Yoga Res Foun.

Spiritual Value of Life. Swami Jyotirmayananda. 1 cass. (Running Time: 1 hr.). 1990. 12.99 Yoga Res Foun.

Spiritual Values. Swami Amar Jyoti. 1 cass. 1976. 9.95 (K-73) Truth Consciousness.
The meaning of Divine Life. The basis of morality. Test of spiritual values.

Spiritual Verses, Bk. 1. Rumi Jellaludin. Read by Anton Lesser. 4 . 2007. audio compact disk 28.98 (978-962-634-466-8(0), Naxos AudioBooks) Naxos.

Spiritual Victory. Swami Amar Jyoti. 1 cass. 1988. 9.95 (K-152) Truth Consciousness.
Victory over one's own self defeats no one. On love & attachment. Our link with angels & natural forces. In tune with all Nature, mankind as protector.

Spiritual Victory/Power of Forgiveness. Marianne Williamson. Read by Marianne Williamson. 1 cass. (Running Time: 90 mins.). (Lectures on a Course in Miracles). (ENG.). 1998. 10.00 (978-1-56170-622-8(1), M859) Hay House.

Spiritual Warfare. David T. Demola. 10 cass. 40.00 (S-1084) Faith Fellow Min.

Spiritual Warfare. Derek Prince. 3 cass. 17.85 Set. (036-037-038) Derek Prince.
Headquarters - the heavenlies; the battlefield - our minds! All Bible-believing Christians are involved in this battle whether they realize it or not.

Spiritual Warfare. Bill Winston. 4 cass. (C). 2000. 20.00 (978-1-931289-76-4(X)) Pub: B Winston Min. Dist(s): Anchor Distributors

Spiritual Warfare. unabr. ed. Neal Pirolo & Yvonne Pirolo. 10 cass. (Running Time: 9 hrs. 7 min.). 1988. pap. bk. 35.00 Set. (978-1-880185-02-5(4)) Emmaus Rd Intl.
Nine lessons on spiritual warfare includes 19 pages of student notes & assignments & a 22-page study guide for group leader.

Spiritual Warfare. unabr. ed. Dean Sherman. Read by Dean Sherman. 5 cass. (Running Time: 3 hrs. 40 min.). 1999. 24.95 (978-0-935779-04-2(3), SWA-2) Crown Min.
Features a biblically based teaching on how christians can stand the forces of spiritual darkness & develop an overcoming lifestyle.

Spiritual Warfare, Pt. 2. Rick Joyner. 1 cass. (Running Time: 90 mins.). (Spiritual Warfare Ser.: Vol. 2). 2000. 5.00 (RJ15-002) Morning NC.
God has designed spiritual weapons of warfare for Christians to use & the insightful teaching in this five-part series will encourage, strengthen & prepare you to wage war against the enemy.

Spiritual Warfare, Pt. 4. Rick Joyner. 1 cass. (Running Time: 90 mins.). (Spiritual Warfare Ser.: Vol. 4). 2000. 5.00 (RJ15-004) Morning NC.

Spiritual Warfare: Fighting to Win. John MacArthur, Jr. 4 cass. (John MacArthur's Bible Studies). 16.25 (HarperThor) HarpC GBR.

Spiritual Warfare - a Word Filled Life of VictoryAgainst the Powers of Darkness: Fighting & Winning the Battle for Our Mind. 2005. 15.00 (978-1-933561-08-0(4)) BFM Books.

***Spiritual Warfare Audio: The Enlightenment Trilogy Book Three.** Jed McKenna. (ENG.). 2010. cd-rom 39.95 (978-0-9801848-1-5(9)) Wisefool Pr.

Spiritual Warfare Manual. Carol Crook. Read by Carol Crook. 6 cass. (Running Time: 8 hr. 30 min.). (YA). (gr. 10 up). 1998. 30.00 (978-0-939399-26-0(1)) Bks of Truth.
To equip the saints of God to do battle against their arch enemy - Satan. Teaches methods of protection as well as offensive methods of battle in the spirit realm.

Spiritual Warfare Series. Rick Joyner. 5 cass. (Running Time: 7 hrs. 30 mins.). 2000. 25.00 (RJ15-000) Morning NC.
God has designed spiritual weapons of warfare for Christians to use & the insightful teaching in this five-part series will encourage, strengthen & prepare you to wage war against the enemy.

Spiritual Warrior. Swami Amar Jyoti. 1 cass. (Satsangs of Swami Amar Jyoti Ser.). (C). 1996. 9.95 (M-105) Truth Consciousness.
Spiritual warriors do not fight; they keep going on the path. Remembrance - consistency - selflessness. Reaching the ultimate Goal of life.

Spiritual Warrior: The Secret Power Within - Self Discovery Program. Edward A. Wacks. Read by Edward A. Wacks. 1 cass. (Running Time: 45 mins.). 1999. 11.95 (978-1-929843-29-9(1)) Map Pubs.
Based on Martial Arts Philosophy & Zen wisdom, it's your pathway to spiritual wealth, happiness & success in the 21st Century.

Spiritualism vs. Spirituality. 1 cass. (Running Time: 1 hr.). 12.99 (124) Yoga Res Foun.

Spirituality. R. Leslie & A. Bickel. 1986. 10.80 (0104B) Assn Prof Chaplains.

Spirituality: Teachings from a World Beyond. Bill Ferguson. Read by Bill Ferguson. 2 cass. 1990. 18.00 Set. (978-1-878410-11-5(3)) Return Heart.
Several years ago, some profound teachings were received through a form of meditation. Since then, thousands of people have had their lives deeply altered. Through these teachings, you will discover the essence of spirituality. You will experience a oneness with God & will discover a truth that will profoundly alter your life.

Spirituality - It's a Lifestyle, Set. unabr. ed. Featuring Peter T. Motika. Interview with Althea S. Gonzalez. 4 cass. (Running Time: 4 hrs.). 1999. 39.95 (978-0-9678454-0-1(8)) Total Freedom Intl.
Topics include: "Your Purpose in Being," "Creating Great Relationships," "Healthy Mind/Healthy Body" & "Money, Prosperity & You.".

Spirituality & Divorce. Carole Riley. 2 cass. (Running Time: 2 hrs. 33 min.). 1996. 17.95 (TAH357) Alba Hse Comns.
Sr. Riley gently leads those broken by divorce through the stages of grief that are so much a part of separation, allowing the spirit to bring healing through acceptance, forgiveness, & ultimately through a stronger union with God.

Spirituality & Healing. Sogyal Rinpoche. 2 cass. 18.00 set. (A0242-87) Sound Photosyn.
The right man with the right talk at the Art of Healing conference.

Spirituality & Healthcare: Reaching Toward a Holistic Future. John Shea. 3 cass. (Running Time: 6 hrs.). 2001. 19.95 (978-0-945482-04-8(3)) Park Ridge Ctr.
Six topics related to spirituality & healthcare.

Spirituality & Human Growth. Robert F. Morneau. Read by Robert F. Morneau. 8 cass. (Running Time: 10 hrs. 45 min.). Incl. Spirituality & Human Growth: Courage-Longing. 1 cass. 1982. (TAH097); Spirituality & Human Growth: Creativity. 1 cass. 1982. (TAH097); Spirituality & Human Growth: Intimacy. 1 cass. 1982. (TAH097); Spirituality & Human Growth: Joy-Contemplation. 1 cass. 1982. (TAH097); Spirituality & Human Growth: Loneliness-Growth. 1 cass. 1982. (TAH097); Spirituality & Human Growth: Person-Meaning. 1 cass. 1982. (TAH097); Spirituality & Human Growth: Suffering-Death. 1 cass. 1982. (TAH097); Spirituality & Human Growth: Weakness-Time. 1 cass. 1982. (TAH097); 1982. 59.95 incl. outline. (TAH097); 9.95 ea. cass. set. Alba Hse Comns.
A program recorded at a three-week workshop at St. Norbert College brings a blending of deep spirituality, fine literary awareness & sensitivity & a theological-historical awareness.

Spirituality & Human Growth: Courage-Longing see Spirituality & Human Growth

Spirituality & Human Growth: Creativity see Spirituality & Human Growth

Spirituality & Human Growth: Intimacy see Spirituality & Human Growth

Spirituality & Human Growth: Joy-Contemplation see Spirituality & Human Growth

An Asterisk (*) at the beginning of an entry indicates that the title is appearing for the first time.

Spirituality & Human Growth: Loneliness-Growth see Spirituality & Human Growth

Spirituality & Human Growth: Person-Meaning see Spirituality & Human Growth

Spirituality & Human Growth: Suffering-Death see Spirituality & Human Growth

Spirituality & Human Growth: Weakness-Time see Spirituality & Human Growth

Spirituality & Pastoral Care. 1 cass. (Care Cassettes Ser.: Vol. 10, No. 2). 1983. 10.80 Assn Prof Chaplains.

Spirituality & Politics. abr. ed. Marianne Williamson. 2 cass. (Running Time: 1 hr. 30 min.). 1997. 16.95 (978-1-56170-425-5(3), M817) Hay House.

Spirituality & Psychological Type. James Christopher & Carole Christopher. Read by James Christopher & Carole Christopher. 3 cass. (Running Time: 3 hrs. 20 min.). 1997. 24.95 Set. (978-0-7822-0535-0(6), 602) C G Jung IL.
Spirituality is the state we enter when we are in the presence of a greater universal reality that defies rational explanation. Recognizing that spirituality is a very individual matter, the framework developed by the Christophers links it with psychological type to explore preferred spiritual practices.

Spirituality & Sexuality. Kriyananda, pseud. (Running Time: 90 min.). (Relationships Ser.). 9.95 (ST-37) Crystal Clarity.
For spiritual aspirants, sex is neither shameful nor a "regrettable concession to human nature." We spiritualize sex by seeing the act as one of love, of serving & of inner communion.

Spirituality & Sexuality. Pia Mellody. Read by Pia Mellody. 2 cass. 18.00 Set. (A15) Featuka Enter Inc.
Pia shares her ideas about both of these relationship issues & how they are related to one another.

Spirituality & Social Accountability. 1 cass. (Care Cassettes Ser.: Vol. 19, No. 6). 1992. 10.80 Assn Prof Chaplains.

Spirituality & Social Justice. Robert F. Morneau. 7 cass. 1983. 53.95 incl. outlines & shelf-case. (TAH130) Alba Hse Comns.
Illustrates how spirtuality & social justice are inextricably intertwined. Includes topics: Twin Circles; To Act Justly; To Love Tenderly; To Walk Humbly with God; the Portrait of a Just Person; Mater Et Magistra; plus more.

Spirituality & Suffering: The Essence of Teshuva - Why Do Bad Things Happen to Good People? unabr. ed. Shmuel Irons. Read by Shmuel Irons. 2 cass. (Running Time: 3 hrs.). 19.95 Set. (978-1-889648-14-9(0)) Jwish Her Fdtn.
Timeless truths found in the Bible & Talmud to gain knowledge, peace of mind, & the practical tools to live a happier life.

***Spirituality & the Oil Spill.** unabr. ed. Marianne Williamson. 1 CD. (Running Time: 1 hr.). 2010. audio compact disk 12.95 (978-1-61544-097-9(6)) Better Listen.

Spirituality for the Marketplace. Robert F. Morneau. Read by Robert F. Morneau. 1 cass. (Running Time: 60 min.). 7.95 (TAH122) Alba Hse Comns.

Spirituality in Alcohol Treatment & Recovery. 1 cass. (Care Cassettes Ser.: Vol. 16, No. 2). 1989. 10.80 Assn Prof Chaplains.

Spirituality in Management: Implications for Health Care Institutions. 1 cass. (Care Cassettes Ser.: Vol. 16, No. 7). 1989. 10.80 Assn Prof Chaplains.

Spirituality in Patient Care: Who, How, When, & What. Harold G. Koenig. 4 CDs. (Running Time: 3 hrs., 30 mins.). 2005. audio compact disk 14.95 (978-1-932031-86-7(3)) Pub: Templeton Pr. Dist(s): Chicago Distribution Ctr

Spirituality in the Priesthood. Ronald D. Witherup. 3 cass. (Running Time: 4 hrs. 15 min.). 1996. 28.95 Set. (TAH372) Alba Hse Comns.
Focuses on the essential dimensions of spirituality in the priesthood today. Fr. Witherup helps clarify the relationship between personality & prayer, priestly identity & the life of the spirit, the role of the Bible in spirituality.

Spirituality in the West. Chogyam Trungpa. 1 cass. 1975. 10.00 Vajradhatu.
The authors representing Tibetan Buddhism, Zen, Judaism & Christianity, address themselves to questions concerning their spiritual practices.

Spirituality Insight & Meditation. Sally Fisher. 1 cass. 1996. 11.95 (978-1-881451-44-0(5)) Brain Sync.

Spirituality is Scientific see Letting Go

Spirituality of Diocesan Priesthood, Set. George Aschenbrenner. 4 cass. (Running Time: 6 hrs.). (Diocesan Priestly Spirituality Ser.). 1998. 35.95 INCL. SCRIPT. (TAH404) Alba Hse Comns.
Clarifies some of the defining elements of spirituality by studying the religious experiences of Christian spiritual history.

Spirituality of Diocesan Priesthood Series, Set. George Aschenbrenner. 11 cass. (Running Time: 15 hrs. 7 min.). 1998. 89.95 INCL. SCRIPTS. (TAH408) Alba Hse Comns.

Spirituality of Human Wholeness. Martin Padovani. 3 cass. (Running Time: 2 hrs. 41 min.). 1996. 27.95 Set. (TAH364) Alba Hse Comns.
Human wholeness is an image of incarnational spirituality, & demands that we reflect on & come to know healthy, human feelings to arrive at the sense of integration that is a reflection of Christ living in us. An effective, enlightening study of the integration of psychology & religion for the clinician or individual study.

Spirituality of Imperfection. Richard Rohr. 1 cass. (Running Time: 1 hr.). 2001. 8.95 (A6711) St Anthony Mess Pr.
Imperfection is the framework in which God calls us to himself.

Spirituality of Renewal Within the Prophecy of Isaiah. Carroll Stuhlmueller & Timothy Lenchak. 5 cass. (Running Time: 6 hrs. 58 min.). 1994. 40.95 Set. (TAH302) Alba Hse Comns.
We are shown how prophecy is edited, reworked, & organized to give us the bigger picture of God's enduring presence. We experience, through the guidance of a skilled biblical scholar, how the book of Isaiah was redacted & edited by several people who were able to adapt the prophecy of the original Isaiah to new situations which really represented a new creation.

Spirituality of Struggle: Living As a Disciple. Patricia Livingston. 1 cass. (Running Time: 1 hr.). 2001. 6.95 (A6411) St Anthony Mess Pr.
She trusts that her touching stories which are filled with uproariously funny moments will remind us of our own lives and lead to an everyday spirituality.

Spirituality of the Our Father. Thomas Merton. 1 cass. 8.95 (AA2259) Credence Commun.

Spirituality of the Psalms: The Schola Cantorum of St. Peter the Apostle. Directed By J. Michael Thompson. 2005. audio compact disk 16.95 (978-0-8146-7952-4(8)) Liturgical Pr.

Spirituality of Waiting: Being Alert to God's Presence in Our Lives. abr. ed. 2 CDs. (Running Time: 5040 sec.). 2006. audio compact disk 24.95 (978-1-59471-080-3(5)) Ave Maria Pr.
A brilliant description of an important element of the spiritual life: how we wait for God, and how God waits for his people. God's love is a waiting love, depending completely on our response to it. Nouwen presents as examples the figures of the Israelites, of Jesus the God-man, and of people he has met in his own ministry.

Spiritualizing the Arts. Kriyananda, pseud. 1 cass. 9.95 (ST-69) Crystal Clarity.
Explores the difference between art & religion; today's music as a reflection of our world; how the ego obstructs the creation of true art; the need for clarity & feeling in creating art; art as a means of attuning ourselves to God.

Spiritually Incorrect Enlightenment Audio: The Enlightenment Trilogy Book Two. Jed McKenna. 9 CDs. 2005. audio compact disk 39.95 (978-0-9714352-0-9(0)) Wisefool Pr.
Jed McKenna is a one-man spiritual revolution. His first book, SPIRITUAL ENLIGHTENMENT: THE DAMNEDEST THING, was an instant classic and established him as a spiritual teacher of startling depth and clarity. Now, his second book, SPIRITUALLY INCORRECT ENLIGHTENMENT, takes readers on a fascinating tour of the enlightened state as it's never been seen before. (9 AUDIO CDs).

Spiritually Prepared. Bernell Christensen. 1 cass. 7.98 (978-1-55503-423-8(3), 06004660) Covenant Comms.
Winning on the spiritual battlefront.

Spirituals & Gospel Songs for SAB Voices: Accompaniment/Performance. Composed by Mark Hayes. (ENG.). 2004. audio compact disk 50.00 (978-0-7390-3521-4(5)) Alfred Pub.

Spirituals & Gospel Songs for SAB Voices: Listening. Composed by Mark Hayes. (ENG.). 2004. audio compact disk 10.00 (978-0-7390-3522-1(3)) Alfred Pub.

Spirituals for Solo Singers (10 Spirituals for Solo Voice & Piano for Recitals, Concerts, & Contests) Medium High Voice. Ed. by Andy Beck. (For Solo Singers Ser.). (ENG.). 2006. audio compact disk 12.95 (978-0-7390-3840-6(0)) Alfred Pub.

Spirituals for Solo Singers (10 Spirituals for Solo Voice & Piano for Recitals, Concerts, & Contests) Medium Low Voice. Ed. by Andy Beck. (For Solo Singers Ser.). (ENG.). 2006. audio compact disk 12.95 (978-0-7390-3844-4(3)) Alfred Pub.

Spirituals of Harry T. Burleigh. Created by Alfred Publishing. (ENG.). 2007. audio compact disk 24.95 (978-0-7390-4527-5(X)) Alfred Pub.

Spirituals of Harry T. Burleigh: High Voice, 2 CDs. Composed by Harry T. Burleigh. (ENG.). 2007. audio compact disk 24.99 (978-0-7390-4525-1(3)) Alfred Pub.

Spiritwalker: Messages from the Future. abr. ed. Hank Wesselnman. Read by Michael Tucker. 2 cass. (Running Time: 3 hrs.). 1995. 17.95 (978-1-57453-008-7(9)) Audio Lit.

Spiritwalker Teachings: Journeys for the Modern Mystic. Jill Kuykendall. (ENG.). (YA). 2008. audio compact disk 149.95 (978-0-9821238-0-5(9)) IAO Prod.

Spirtual Discernment. Jack Deere. 1 cass. (Running Time: 90 mins.). (Hearing God's Voice Ser.: Vol. 5). 2000. 5.00 (JD04-005) Morning NC.
These messages are an outstanding collection that lay a solid & practical foundation for discerning God's voice.

Spirtual Warfare, Pt. 3. Rick Joyner. 1 cass. (Running Time: 90 mins.). (Spiritual Warfare Ser.: Vol. 3). 2000. 5.00 (RJ15-003) Morning NC.
God has designed spiritual weapons of warfare for Christians to use & the insightful teaching in this five-part series will encourage, strengthen & prepare you to wage war against the enemy.

Spite Fences. unabr. ed. Trudy B. Krisher. Narrated by Kate Forbes. 6 pieces. (Running Time: 8 hrs. 30 mins.). (gr. 7 up). 2001. 54.00 (978-0-7887-8971-7(6)) Recorded Bks.
Kinship, Georgia in 1960 is just a sleepy Southern town. Thirteen-year-old Maggie Pugh knows how things work: the rich live on one side of town; the poor live on another. Pretty girls get love; plain ones don't. Black and white don't mix. When the winds of civil rights start blowing through Kinship, Maggie sees violence boil to the surface. Through her camera, a gift from a black friend, Maggie focuses first on the injustice in her own family, then on the cruelty accepted by the town. She wonders if anything can change the hatred that has built so many fences between people.

Spitfire Wingman Audio Set: Col. Haun Reads His Story. Based on a book by James Robert Haun, Sr. (ENG.). 2009. audio compact disk 49.95 (978-0-9790002-3-2(8)) Stormwatch Pr.

Spitfire Wingman from Tennessee: My love affair with Flight, Vol.1. Read by James Robert Haun, Sr. Comment by James Robert Haun, Jr. Voice by David Joseph Hoffman. (ENG.). 2009. audio compact disk 24.97 (978-0-9790002-1-8(1)) Stormwatch Pr.

Spitting Image. unabr. ed. Shutta Crum. 5 cass. (Running Time: 6 hrs.). (J). (gr. 5-8). 2004. 45.75 (978-1-4025-7341-5(3)) Recorded Bks.

Spitting Image Pt. 1: Hebrews 1:1-3. Ed Young. 1991. 4.95 (978-0-7417-1873-0(1), 873) Win Walk.

Spitting Image Pt. 2: Hebrews 1:1-3. Ed Young. 1991. 4.95 (978-0-7417-1874-7(X), 874) Win Walk.

Spitze. Isobel Drummond. 1989. pap. bk. 22.61 (978-0-582-33207-2(9), 72076) Longman.

Splash I Audio Cd. Ed. by Pacific Learning Staff. (Splash Ser.). (ps-2). 2006. audio compact disk 33.00 (978-1-86970-319-6(7), HeinemannNZL) Pearson EdNZL NZL.

Splash of Red: A Jemina Shore Mystery. unabr. ed. Antonia Fraser. Read by Patricia Hodge. 6 cass. (Running Time: 9 hrs.). (Jemima Shore Mystery Ser.: Bk. 3). 2000. 49.95 (CAB 101) Pub: Chivers Audio Bks GBR. Dist(s): AudioGO
Since her arrival in London, Chloe Fontaine had a series of admirers, lovers and husbands. Exquisitely pretty, her fragile looks hid a considerable talent as a novelist. This latest Jemima Shore mystery centers around the strange and sudden disappearance of Chloe, leaving Jemima in charge of solving her disappearance.

Splash Zone: Singable Sea Songs Just for Kids. Linda Arnold. Prod. by Linda Arnold. Perf. by Justin Mayer. Prod. by John Lee Saunders. 1CD. (Running Time: 1 hr). 2000. audio compact disk 13.98 (978-1-57471-747-1(2)) Youngheart Mus.
Fun educational lyrics set to lively Caribbean, Cuban & South African rhythms which will inspire audiences of all ages to discover & celebrate the wonders of the sea.

Splash Zone: Singable Sea Songs Just for Kids. Linda Arnold. Tr. by Linda Arnold. Perf. by Justin Mayer. Prod. by John Lee Saunders. 1 cass. (Running Time: 1 hr.). 2000. 10.98 (978-1-57471-749-5(9), 130 CN) Youngheart Mus.

Splashdance. 1 cass. (Retro Mickey Ser.). (J). 7.99 Norelco. (978-1-55723-951-8(7)); audio compact disk 13.99 CD. (978-1-55723-952-5(5)) W Disney Records.

Splatball Square-off: Or... Nose to Knee with a Defiant Giant. Contrib. by Mickey Rooney, Jr. Created by Integrity Music. (Running Time: 50 mins.). (God Rocks! Ser.). (J). (ps-3). 2005. 9.99 (978-5-558-52632-5(7)) Integrity Music.

Spleen de Paris. Poems. Charles Baudelaire. Read by Dominiue Daguier. 1 cass. (FRE.). 1995. 21.95 (1719-LQP) Olivia & Hill.
Famous collection of "poemes en prose.".

Spleen de Paris: With Maupassant "Menuet" Charles Baudelaire. 1 cass. (Running Time: 60 min.). (FRE.). 1996. pap. bk. 19.50 (978-1-58085-364-4(1)) Interlingua VA.
Includes dual language French-English transcription. The combination of written text & clarity & pace of diction will open the door for intermediate & advanced students to genuine comprehension & the use of literary texts for advancement in rapid understanding of written & oral language materials. The audio text plus written text concept makes foreign languages accessible to a much wider range of students than books alone.

Splendid Animal: Genesis 25:34. Ed Young. 1979. 4.95 (978-0-7417-1035-2(8), A0035) Win Walk.

Splendid Exchange: How Trade Shaped the World. William J. Bernstein. Read by Mel Foster. (Playaway Adult Nonfiction Ser.). 2008. 69.99 (978-1-60640-873-5(9)) Find a World.

Splendid Exchange: How Trade Shaped the World. unabr. ed. William J. Bernstein. Read by Mel Foster. (Running Time: 17 hrs. 0 mins. 0 sec.). (ENG.). 2008. audio compact disk 39.99 (978-1-4001-0669-1(9)) Pub: Tantor Media. Dist(s): IngramPubServ

Splendid Exchange: How Trade Shaped the World from Prehistory to Today. unabr. ed. William J. Bernstein. Read by Mel Foster. (Running Time: 17 hrs. 0 mins. 0 sec.). (ENG.). 2008. audio compact disk 79.99 (978-1-4001-3669-8(5)); audio compact disk 29.99 (978-1-4001-5669-6(6)) Pub: Tantor Media. Dist(s): IngramPubServ

Splendid Outcast. Beryl Markham. Read by Francis Sternhagen. 6 cass. (Running Time: 7 hrs.). 1989. 55.00 (PCC 79) Spoken Arts.
Eight wonderful stories of Africa by the magnificent aviatrix who wrote the bestselling autobiography Straight on Till Morning.

Splendid Outcast. unabr. collector's ed. Beryl Markham. Read by Penelope Dellaporta. 6 cass. (Running Time: 6 hrs.). 1991. 36.00 (978-0-7366-1903-5(8), 2729) Books on Tape.
Readers of Beryl Markham's lyrical autobiography, West with the Night, will enjoy The Splendid Outcast, a collection of her short stories originally published in magazines. The stories reflect her interests: horses, aviation, Africa. Several spring from real events - bidding at a horse auction, flying through a violent storm, a lion's attack. Others are romances & adventures typical of the war years when they were written. All are set against the backdrop of an Africa with which she was on intimate terms.

Splendid Solution: Jonas Salk & the Conquest of Polio. unabr. ed. Jeffrey Kluger. Narrated by Michael Prichard. 11 CDs. (Running Time: 13 hrs. 30 mins. 0 sec.). (ENG.). 2005. audio compact disk 37.99 (978-1-4001-0149-8(2)) Pub: Tantor Media. Dist(s): IngramPubServ

Splendid Solution: Jonas Salk & the Conquest of Polio. unabr. ed. Jeffrey Kluger. Narrated by Michael Prichard. (Running Time: 13 hrs. 30 mins. 0 sec.). (ENG.). 2005. audio compact disk 75.99 (978-1-4001-3149-5(9)) Pub: Tantor Media. Dist(s): IngramPubServ

Splendid Solution: Jonas Salk & the Conquest of Polio. unabr. ed. Jeffrey Kluger. Read by Michael Prichard. (Running Time: 13 hrs. 30 mins. 0 sec.). (ENG.). 2005. audio compact disk 22.99 (978-1-4001-5149-3(X)) Pub: Tantor Media. Dist(s): IngramPubServ

***Splendor: A Luxe Novel.** unabr. ed. Anna Godbersen. Read by Nina Siemaszko. (ENG.). 2009. (978-0-06-196727-6(0)); (978-0-06-170962-3(X)) HarperCollins Pubs.

Splendor & Honor: Selected Canticles from the Hymnal 1982. Church Publishing. (ENG.). audio compact disk 18.00 (978-0-89869-349-2(7)) Church Pub Inc.

Splendor & Tragedy of King Arthur in Each of Us: The Many Faces of the Child. Read by John Giannini. 1 cass. (Running Time: 1 hr.). 1988. 9.95 (978-0-7822-0072-0(9), 358) C G Jung IL.

Splendor of Irish Literature: A Light & Enlightening Lecture, Featuring Elliot Engel. 2001. bk. 15.00 (978-1-890123-41-3(2)) Media Cnslts.

Splendor of Silence. unabr. ed. Indu Sundaresan. Read by Sneha Mathan. 9 cass. (Running Time: 57600 sec.). 2006. 29.95 (978-0-7861-4604-8(4)); 65.95 (978-0-7861-4771-7(7)); audio compact disk 29.95 (978-0-7861-6895-8(1)); audio compact disk 29.95 (978-0-7861-7501-7(X)) Blckstn Audio.

Splendor of Silence. unabr. ed. Indu Sundaresan. Read by Marguerite Gavin. (Running Time: 57600 sec.). 2006. audio compact disk 81.00 (978-0-7861-6333-5(X)) Blckstn Audio.

Splinter. unabr. ed. Michael MacConnell. Read by Sean Mangan. (Running Time: 10 hrs. 25 mins.). 2009. audio compact disk 93.95 (978-1-74214-017-9(3), 9781742140179) Pub: Bolinda Pubng AUS. Dist(s): Bolinda Pub Inc

***Splish, Splash!** unabr. ed. Sarah Weeks. (ENG.). 2008. (978-0-06-169489-9(4)); (978-0-06-172960-7(4)) HarperCollins Pubs.

Splish! Splash!/Splish! Splash! A Book about Rain/un Libro Sobre la Lluvia. abr. ed. Josepha Sherman. Tr. by Sol Robledo. Illus. by Jeff Yesh. (Amazing Science Ser.). (SPA.). (gr. k). 2008. audio compact disk 14.60 (978-1-4048-4478-0(3)) CapstoneDig.

Split. Tara Moss. Read by Tara Moss. (Running Time: 7 hrs. 30 mins.). 2009. 74.99 (978-1-74214-272-2(9), 9781742142722) Pub: Bolinda Pubng AUS. Dist(s): Bolinda Pub Inc

Split. unabr. ed. Swati Avasthi. Read by Joshua Swanson. (ENG.). (J). (gr. 9). 2010. audio compact disk 37.00 (978-0-307-57994-2(8), Listening Lib) Pub: Random Audio Pubg. Dist(s): Random

Split. unabr. ed. Tara Moss. Read by Tara Moss. 7 CDs. (Running Time: 27000 sec.). (Makedde Vanderwall Ser.: Bk. 2). 2005. audio compact disk 83.95 (978-1-74093-080-2(0)) Pub: Bolinda Pubng AUS. Dist(s): Bolinda Pub Inc

***Split.** unabr. ed. Tara Moss. Read by Tara Moss. (Running Time: 7 hrs. 30 mins.). 2009. 43.95 (978-1-74214-139-8(0), 9781742141398) Pub: Bolinda Pubng AUS. Dist(s): Bolinda Pub Inc

Split Ends. Zoe Barnes. 10 cass. (Isis Cassettes Ser.). (J). 2005. 84.95 (978-0-7531-2118-4(2)) Pub: ISIS Lrg Prnt GBR. Dist(s): Ulverscroft US

Split Ends. unabr. ed. Zoe Barnes. Read by Trudy Harris. 12 CDs. (Running Time: 13 hrs. 40 mins.). (Isis (CDs) Ser.). (J). 2006. audio compact disk 99.95 (978-0-7531-2507-6(2)) Pub: ISIS Lrg Prnt GBR. Dist(s): Ulverscroft US

Split Image. unabr. ed. Robert B. Parker. Read by James Naughton. 2010. audio compact disk 32.00 (978-0-7393-5748-4(4), Random AudioBks) Pub: Random Audio Pubg. Dist(s): Random

***Split Images.** unabr. ed. Elmore Leonard. Read by George Guidall. (ENG.). 2010. (978-0-06-199374-9(3), Harper Audio); (978-0-06-206264-2(6), Harper Audio) HarperCollins Pubs.

Split Images, unabr. ed. Elmore Leonard. Narrated by George Guidall. 6 cass. (Running Time: 7 hrs. 45 mins.). 51.00 (978-0-7887-0510-6(5), 94703E7) Recorded Bks.
A wealthy young playboy decides that money can buy him everything, including the right to murder. Available to libraries only.

Split Images. unabr. collector's ed. Elmore Leonard. Read by Alexander Adams. 5 cass. (Running Time: 7 hrs. 30 min.). 1996. 40.00 (978-0-7366-3374-1(X), 4024) Books on Tape.
Murder is his plan & his joy. When Angela smokes it, she races to spoil Daniels' fun & save his prey.

Split Infinitive, Adverbial Advice see World of James Thurber

Split Second. John Hulme & Michael Wexler. Read by Oliver Wyman. (Seems (Playaway) Ser.). (ENG.). (J). 2009. 64.99 (978-1-60775-611-8(0)) Find a World.

Split Second. abr. ed. David Baldacci. Read by Ron McLarty. (Sean King & Michelle Maxwell Ser.: No. 1). (ENG.). 2005. 14.98 (978-1-59483-297-0(8)) Pub: Hachet Audio. Dist(s): HachBkGrp

Split Second. abr. ed. David Baldacci. Read by Ron McLarty. 5 CDs. (Running Time: 6 hrs.). (Replay Edition Ser.). (ENG.). 2007. audio compact disk 14.98 (978-1-60024-091-1(7)) Pub: Hachet Audio. Dist(s): HachBkGrp

Split Second. unabr. ed. David Baldacci. Read by Scott Brick. 8 cass. (Running Time: 12 hrs.). (Sean King & Michelle Maxwell Ser.: No. 1). 2003. 80.00 (978-0-7366-9389-9(0)); audio compact disk 86.40 (978-0-7366-9390-5(4)) Books on Tape.

Split Second. unabr. ed. David Baldacci. Read by Scott Brick. (Sean King & Michelle Maxwell Ser.: No. 1). (ENG.). 2005. 16.98 (978-1-59483-298-7(6)) Pub: Hachet Audio. Dist(s): HachBkGrp

Split Second. unabr. ed. David Baldacci. Read by Scott Brick. (Running Time: 11 hrs. 30 mins.). No. 1. (ENG.). 2007. audio compact disk 29.98 (978-1-60024-134-5(4)) Pub: Hachet Audio. Dist(s): HachBkGrp

Split Second. unabr. ed. David Baldacci. Read by Scott Brick. (Running Time: 11 hrs. 30 mins.). (ENG.). 2009. 44.98 (978-1-60024-988-4(4)) Pub: Hachet Audio. Dist(s): HachBkGrp

Split Second. unabr. ed. John Hulme. Narrated by Oliver Wyman. 6 CDs. (Running Time: 7 hrs 43 mins.). (Seems Ser.: Bk. 2). (ENG.). (J). (gr. 4-7). 2008. audio compact disk 64.95 (978-0-545-09105-3(5)) Scholastic Inc.

Split Second. unabr. ed. John Hulme & Michael Wexler. Read by Oliver, Wyman and Company Staff. Narrated by Oliver Wyman. (Seems Ser.: No. 2). (J). (gr. 4-7). 2008. audio compact disk 29.95 (978-0-545-09103-9(9)) Scholastic Inc.

Split Shadow & the Father-Son Relationship. Read by Donald Sandner. 1 cass. (Running Time: 90 min.). 1987. 10.95 (978-0-7822-0242-7(X), 258) C G Jung IL.

Splitting. unabr. ed. Fay Weldon. Narrated by Jenny Sterlin. 6 cass. (Running Time: 9 hrs.). 1997. 56.00 (978-0-7887-0825-1(2), 94828E7) Recorded Bks.
Chronicling an ill fated marriage from beginning to end, this story of a shattering divorce takes a surreal life of its own as a woman splits into three personalities.

Splitting Heirs: Giving an Inheritance to Your Children Without Ruining Their Lives. Ron Blue. 2004. 16.99 (978-0-8024-1372-7(2)); audio compact disk 16.99 (978-0-8024-1371-0(4)) Moody.

Splitting the Licks. Steve Kaufman. 1999. pap. bk. 31.95 (978-0-7866-5061-3(3), 93998CDP) Mel Bay.

Spock vs. Q. Leonard Nimoy & John De Lancie. Read by Leonard Nimoy & John De Lancie. (Running Time: 2 hrs.). 2003. 19.95 (978-1-60083-431-8(0), Audiofy Corp) Iofy Corp.

Spock vs. Q. Perf. by Leonard Nimoy & John De Lancie. 1 cass. (Running Time: 1 hr.). 2001. 12.95 (ALEN013); audio compact disk 15.95 (ALEN014) Lodestone Catalog.
Ambassador Spock travels back in time to our era to warn us that an asteroid is hurling toward Earth & the impact will destroy all life on the planet.

Spock vs. Q. abr. ed. Alien Voices Staff & Alien Voices. Read by Leonard Nimoy et al. 1 CD. (Running Time: 10 hrs. 0 mins. 0 sec.). (Star Trek Ser.). (ENG.). 2000. audio compact disk 15.00 (978-0-7435-0703-5(7), Audioworks) Pub: S&S Audio. Dist(s): S and S Inc
THE BATTLE OF WITS AND LOGIC IS JOINED AGAIN! STAR TREK® SPOCK VS. Q THE SEQUEL AN ALIEN VOICES® PRODUCTION STARRING LEONARD NIMOY AND JOHN de LANCIE Written by Cecelia Fannon Following their debate over the fate of mankind, Spock and Q have continued their discussions over a meal. After dining, the two return to the stage to recount their repast, which included encounters with several of Spock's former shipmates. However, at the moment the two verbal sparring partners shake hands, a power surge places them in total darkness. Suddenly, Spock and Q are no longer on stage, but somewhere in deep space. As they struggle to determine what has happened, a curious personality change takes hold. Spock is overcome with giddy delight. Q is much more serious, even...logical. Masterfully performed by Leonard Nimoy and John de Lancie, Star Trek® Spock vs. Q: The Sequel is a fascinating and often hilarious role reversal that reveals previously unknown sides of Spock and Q. It is a program so original it could only come from Alien Voices®.

Spock vs. Q. abr. ed. Alien Voices Staff & John De Lancie. Read by Leonard Nimoy. 1 CD. (Running Time: 10 hrs. 0 mins. 0 sec.). (Star Trek Ser.). (ENG.). 1999. audio compact disk 15.00 (978-0-671-04583-8(0), Audioworks) Pub: S&S Audio. Dist(s): S and S Inc

Spock vs. Q, Set. unabr. gif. ed. Alien Voices et al. 2 CDs. (Running Time: 2 hrs.). (ENG.). 2001. audio compact disk 19.95 (978-0-7435-0946-6(3), Audioworks) Pub: S&S Audio. Dist(s): S and S Inc
Star Trek's most popular characters convene for two hours of adventure and banter!.

Spoiled Earth. unabr. ed. Jessica Stirling. Read by Vivien Heilbron. 12 cass. (Running Time: 12 hrs.). (Stalker Trilogy: Vol. 1). 1997. 96.95 Set. (978-0-7540-0035-8(4), CAB 1458) AudioGO.

Spoiled Parents, Spoiled Children. Created by Sally Atman. 2006. audio compact disk 12.95 (978-1-928843-34-4(4)) Ad Lib Res.

***Spoiled Rotten America.** abr. ed. Larry Miller. Read by Larry Miller. (ENG.). 2006. (978-0-06-113485-2(6), Harper Audio); (978-0-06-113484-5(8), Harper Audio) HarperCollins Pubs.

Spoiled Rotten America: Outrages of Everyday Life. abr. ed. Larry Miller. Read by Larry Miller. (Running Time: 12600 sec.). 2007. audio compact disk 14.95 (978-0-06-137418-0(0), Harper Audio) HarperCollins Pubs.

Spoilers, unabr. ed. Rex Ellingwood Beach. Read by Grover Gardner. 6 cass. (Running Time: 9 hrs.). (gr. 8 up). 1990. 24.95 (978-1-55685-187-2(1)) Audio Bk Con.
A rollicking, fast-paced western concerning double-crossing mayhem set against the colorful background of the Yukon gold rush. This 1907 classic is perfect for teens as well as older readers.

Spoilers. unabr. ed. Rex Ellingwood Beach. Read by Jack Sondericker. 8 cass. (Running Time: 8 hrs. 30 min.). Dramatization. 1989. 49.95 (978-1-55686-323-3(3), 323) Books in Motion.
Made into a film several years ago. This story is about small claim miners & gold panners fighting big interests trying to sieze their gold claims in Alaska through corrupt legal manipulations.

Spoils of Poynton, Set. unabr. ed. Henry James. Read by Flo Gibson. 5 cass. (Running Time: 7 hrs.). (gr. 9 up). 1991. 20.95 (978-1-55685-204-6(5)) Audio Bk Con.
Mrs. Gereth's passion for precious antiques causes many maneuverings & battles with her son, Owen, while the charming Fleda Vetch & the crass Mona Brigstock vie for his love.

Spoils of War. Catrin Collier. Read by Helen Griffin. 12 cass. (Running Time: 18 hrs.). 2002. 96.95 (978-0-7540-0782-1(0), CAB 2204) AudioGO.

Spokane Falls Falcon: Mysteries of the Brothers Hood-Children's Fiction. Karen Jean Matsko Hood. (J). 2006. 29.95 (978-1-59434-225-7(3)); audio compact disk 24.95 (978-1-59434-224-0(5)) Whsprng Pine.

Spoken. Contrib. by Spoken. Prod. by Travis Wyrick. 2007. audio compact disk 13.99 (978-5-557-59356-4(X)) Tooth & Nail.

Spoken Albanian. 6 cass. (Running Time: 4 hrs.). pap. bk. 135.00 (AFAL10) J Norton Pubs.
The majority of the lesson units contain dialogs, an analysis of language functions in the dialog, a section on pronunciation & pronunciation practice, supplementary vocabulary & new conversations. Dialogs & conversations of Lessons 1-12 are recorded. The end-of-text alphabetical vocabulary list is Albanian-English.

Spoken Albanian. Leonard Newmark et al. 6 dual track cass. 1980. bk. 75.00 (978-0-87950-007-8(7), AFAL10) Spoken Lang Serv.

Spoken Albanian. 2nd rev. ed. Leonard I. Newmark. 1886. 75.00 (978-0-87950-012-2(3)) Spoken Lang Serv.

Spoken Albanian. 2nd rev. ed. Leonard I. Newmark. 1997. pap. bk. 90.00 (978-0-87950-013-9(1)) Spoken Lang Serv.

Spoken Amharic, Bk. 1. Serge Obolensky et al. 26 cass. (Spoken Language Ser.). (AMH.). 1980. pap. bk. 190.00 incl. bk. (978-0-87950-654-4(7)) Spoken Lang Serv.

Spoken Amharic, Bk. 1, Units 1-50. Serge Obolensky et al. 26 cass. (Spoken Language Ser.). (AMH.). 1980. pap. bk. 145.00 (978-0-87950-652-0(0)) Spoken Lang Serv.

Spoken Amharic, Bk. 2, Units 51-60. Serge Obolensky et al. 5 cass. (Spoken Language Ser.). (AMH.). 1980. pap. bk. 110.00 (978-0-87950-655-1(5)); 65.00 (978-0-87950-653-7(9)) Spoken Lang Serv.

Spoken Amharic, Set. Serge Obolensky et al. (Spoken Language Ser.). (AMH.). 1980. pap. bk. 300.00 (978-0-87950-656-8(3)) Spoken Lang Serv.

Spoken Amoy Hokkien. Nicholas C. Bodman. 16 dual track cass. (Spoken Language Ser.). 1987. bk. 125.00 (978-0-87950-451-9(X)); pap. bk. 170.00 (978-0-87950-452-6(8)) Spoken Lang Serv.

Spoken Arabic: Iraqi. Merrill Y. Van Wagoner. 6 dual track cass. (Spoken Language Ser.). (J). (gr. 9-12). 1975. bk. 75.00 (978-0-87950-016-0(6)); pap. bk. & stu. ed. 90.00 (978-0-87950-017-7(4)) Spoken Lang Serv.

Spoken Arabic: Saudi. Merrill Y. Van Wagoner et al. 5 dual track cass. (Spoken Language Ser.). 1979. pap. bk. & stu. ed. 90.00 incl. bk. (978-0-87950-412-0(9)) Spoken Lang Serv.

Spoken Arabic: Saudi. Merrill Y. Van Wagoner et al. 5 dual track cass. (Spoken Language Ser.). (J). (gr. 9-12). 1979. bk. 75.00 (978-0-87950-411-3(0)) Spoken Lang Serv.

Spoken Armenian: East. Gordon H. Fairbanks & Earl W. Stevick. 6 dual track cass. (Spoken Language Ser.). (C). (gr. 9-12). 1975. bk. 75.00 (978-0-87950-421-2(8)) Spoken Lang Serv.

Spoken Armenian: East. Gordon H. Fairbanks & Earl W. Stevick. 6 dual track cass. (Spoken Language Ser.). (C). (gr. 9-12). 1975. pap. bk. & stu. ed. 95.00 (978-0-87950-422-9(6)) Spoken Lang Serv.

Spoken Arts Introduction to American Folk Songs. Perf. by Ed McCurdy. 1 cass. (Music Ser.). 1987. 10.95 (SAC 224) Spoken Arts.
Includes: Chilly Winds, On Top of Old Smokey, Jesse James.

Spoken Arts Treasury: 100 Modern American Poets Reading Their Poems, Vol. 3. unabr. ed. 6 cass. (Running Time: 5 hrs. 15 mins.). 2007. 51.75 (978-1-4281-5243-4(1)) Recorded Bks.

Spoken Arts Treasury: 100 Modern American Poets Reading Their Poems, Vol. 3. unabr. ed. 6 CDs. (Running Time: 7 hrs. 25 mins.). (Spoken Arts Treasury Ser.: Bk. 3). 2007. audio compact disk 72.75 (978-1-4281-5245-8(8)) Recorded Bks.

Spoken Arts Treasury: 100 Modern American Poets Reading Their Poetry. unabr. ed. Read by Theodore Roethke et al. 6 CDs. (Running Time: 6 hrs.). 2007. audio compact disk 75.75 (978-1-4281-4282-4(7)) Recorded Bks.

Spoken Arts Treasury: 100 Modern American Poets Reading Their Poetry. unabr. ed. Read by Theodore Roethke et al. 6 cass. (Running Time: 6 hrs.). (Spoken Arts Treasury Ser.: Bk. 2). 2007. 51.75 (978-1-4281-4280-0(0)) Recorded Bks.

Spoken Arts Treasury Vol. 1: 100 Modern American Poets Reading Their Poems. unabr. ed. 6 cass. (Running Time: 7 hrs.). 2007. 51.75 (978-1-4281-1861-4(6)); audio compact disk 72.75 (978-1-4281-1863-8(2)) Recorded Bks.

Spoken Bulgarian. Carleton T. Hodge. 19 dual track cass. 1980. bk. 125.00 (978-0-87950-660-5(1)); pap. bk. 170.00 (978-0-87950-662-9(8)) Spoken Lang Serv.

Spoken Burmese. 6 cass. (Running Time: 4 hrs.). bk. 115.00 (AFBU10) J Norton Pubs.
The text uses Roman transcription & Contains 12 lesson units which provide all the basic structures of the language & grammatical explanations.

Spoken Burmese, Bk. I. William S. Cornyn. 6 dual track cass. (Spoken Language Ser.). (J). (gr. 9-12). 1979. bk. 75.00 (978-0-87950-025-2(5)) Spoken Lang Serv.

Spoken Burmese, Bk. 1. William S. Cornyn. 6 dual track cass. (Spoken Language Ser.). (J). (gr. 9-12). 1979. pap. bk. 90.00 (978-0-87950-026-9(3)) Spoken Lang Serv.

Spoken Cambodian. Franklin E. Huffman. 14 cass. (Spoken Language Ser.). 1985. pap. bk. 130.00 incl. bk. (978-0-87950-473-1(0)) Spoken Lang Serv.

Spoken Cambodian. Franklin E. Huffman & F. E. Huffman. 14 cass. (Spoken Language Ser.). 1985. bk. 105.00 (978-0-87950-472-4(2)) Spoken Lang Serv.

Spoken Cantonese. Elisabeth L. Boyle & Pauline N. Delbridge. 30 dual track cass. Incl. Bk I. Spoken Cantonese. 15 dual track cass. Elisabeth L. Boyle & Pauline N. Delbridge. 1980. 105.00 (978-0-87950-677-3(6)); Bk. I. Spoken Cantonese. 15 dual track cass. Elisabeth L. Boyle & Pauline N. Delbridge. 1980. pap. bk. 130.00 (978-0-87950-679-7(2)); Bk. II. Spoken Cantonese. 15 dual track cass. Elisabeth L. Boyle & Pauline N. Delbridge. 1980. 105.00 (978-0-87950-678-0(4)); Bk. 2. Spoken Cantonese. 15 dual track cass. Elisabeth L. Boyle & Pauline N. Delbridge. pap. bk. 140.00 (978-0-87950-680-3(6)); 1980. Set pap. bk. 250.00 Set, incl. bk. (978-0-87950-681-0(4)) Spoken Lang Serv.

Spoken Chinese. Charles F. Hockett & Chaoying Fang. 6 dual track cass. (Spoken Language Ser.). (J). (gr. 9-12). 1976. bk. 75.00 (978-0-87950-036-8(0)) Spoken Lang Serv.

Spoken Chinese, Bk. 1. Charles F. Hockett & Chaoying Fang. 6 dual track cass. (Spoken Language Ser.). (J). (gr. 9-12). 1976. pap. bk. 90.00 (978-0-87950-037-5(9)) Spoken Lang Serv.

Spoken Czech: Czech Fast Course. Radovan Pletka. 12 cass. (Spoken Language Ser.). 1995. pap. bk. 135.00 (978-0-87950-632-2(6)); 105.00 (978-0-87950-631-5(8)) Spoken Lang Serv.
Self instructional Czech course.

Spoken Danish, Bk. I. Jeannette Dearden & Karin Stig-Nielsen. 6 dual track cass. (J). (gr. 9-12). 1976. pap. bk. 90.00 incl. bk. (978-0-87950-051-1(4)); 75.00 (978-0-87950-050-4(6)) Spoken Lang Serv.

Spoken Dutch. Leonard Bloomfield. 5 dual track cass. (Spoken Language Ser.). (J). (gr. 9-12). 1975. bk. 75.00 (978-0-87950-060-3(3)); pap. bk. & stu. ed. 90.00 (978-0-87950-061-0(1)) Spoken Lang Serv.

Spoken East Armenian. 6 cass. (Running Time: 3 hrs.). bk. 115.00 (AFAR10) J Norton Pubs.
With the exception of the review lessons, each of the lesson units contains basic sentences, useful expressions, grammatical notes, exercises, & new conversations.

Spoken Egyptian Arabic. 12 cass. (Running Time: 12 hrs.). 185.00 (AFA400) J Norton Pubs.
Spoken Egyptian Arabic is designed to bridge the gap that exists between the highly technical Arabic grammars, meant only for the specialized student of Arabic & the simple phrase-books of basic sentences that are unsatisfactory for the purpose of real communication.

Spoken Egyptian Arabic. Samia Mehrez. 12 cass. (Running Time: 9 hrs. 30 mins.). (YA). (gr. 10-12). 1985. pap. bk. 225.00 (978-0-88432-131-6(2), AFA400) J Norton Pubs.
Designed to bridge the gap that exists between the highly technical Arabic grammars, meant for the specialized student of Arabic & the simple phrase-books of basic sentences that are unsatisfactory for the purpose of real communication.

Spoken Egyptian Arabic CDs & Text. Samia Mehrez. 13 CDs. (Running Time: 9 hrs. 30 mins.). (ARA.). 2005. audio compact disk 225.00 (978-1-57970-255-7(4), AFA400D, Audio-For) J Norton Pubs.
This self-instructional course is primarily concerned with developing oral skills. The entire text is in transliteration; ARabic script is not introduced, so your attention is focused exclusively on mastering a new and intricate phonetic system. The course is designed to bridge the gap that exists between the highly technical Arabic grammars, meant for the specialized student of Arabic, and the simple phrasebooks of basic sentences that are unsatisfactory of the purpose of real communication. Th eocurse has been tested with a group of foreign engineers/businesspeople in Cairo, and the audio has been used in the language lab with foreign university students.

Spoken Finnish. Thomas A. Sebeok. 3 dual track cass. (Spoken Language Ser.). (J). (gr. 9-12). 1977. bk. 55.00 (978-0-87950-075-7(1)); pap. bk. 70.00 (978-0-87950-076-4(X)) Spoken Lang Serv.

Spoken French. Francois Denoeu et al. 6 dual track cass. (Spoken Language Ser.). (J). (gr. 9-12). 1973. bk. 75.00 (978-0-87950-085-6(9)); pap. bk. 90.00 (978-0-87950-086-3(7)) Spoken Lang Serv.

Spoken from the Heart. abr. ed. Laura Bush. Read by Laura Bush. 7 CDs. (Running Time: 8 hrs.). 2010. audio compact disk 29.99 (978-1-4423-0520-5(7)) Pub: S&S Audio. Dist(s): S and S Inc

Spoken German. William G. Moulton & Jenni K. Moulton. 6 dual track cass. (Spoken Language Ser.). 1971. bk. 75.00 (978-0-87950-096-2(4)); pap. bk. 90.00 (978-0-87950-097-9(2)) Spoken Lang Serv.

Spoken Greek. Henry Kahane et al. (Spoken Language Ser.). (J). (gr. 9-12). 1976. 75.00 (978-0-87950-105-1(7)) Spoken Lang Serv.

Spoken Hausa, Vol. 1. J. Ronayne Cowan et al. 6 dual track cass. (Spoken Language Ser.). (J). (gr. 9-12). 1976. bk. 75.00 (978-0-87950-402-1(1)); pap. bk. 90.00 (978-0-87950-403-8(X)) Spoken Lang Serv.

Spoken Hausa, Vol. 2. J. Ronayne Cowan et al. 16 dual track cass. (Spoken Language Ser.). (J). (gr. 9-12). 1976. bk. 105.00 (978-0-87950-404-5(8)) Spoken Lang Serv.

Spoken Hindi. unabr. rev. ed. Surendra K. Gambhir. 10 cass. (Running Time: 5 hrs.). (HIN & ENG.). (J). (gr. 10-12). 1993. pap. bk. 175.00 (978-0-88432-699-1(3), AFH100) J Norton Pubs.
Intermediate-level course in Hindi emphasizes natural conversation interspersed with cultural information. text presupposes a knowledge of the Hindi alphabet & does not include translations. Pauses are provided in all drills for the learner to repeat material recorded by native speakers.

Spoken Hindi CDs & Text. Surendra K. Gambhir. 5 CDs. (Running Time: 5 hrs.). (HIN.). 2005. audio compact disk 175.00 (978-1-57970-188-8(4), AFH100D) J Norton Pubs.

Spoken Hindustani. Henry Hoenigswald. 6 dual track cass. (Spoken Language Ser.). (J). (gr. 9-12). 1976. bk. 75.00 (978-0-87950-115-0(4)) Spoken Lang Serv.

Spoken Hindustani. Henry Hoenigswald. 6 dual track cass. (Spoken Language Ser.). (YA). (gr. 9-12). 1976. pap. bk. 90.00 (978-0-87950-116-7(2)) Spoken Lang Serv.

Spoken Hungarian. Thomas A. Sebeok. 6 dual track cass. (Spoken Language Ser.). (J). (gr. 9-12). 1983. bk. 75.00 (978-0-87950-126-6(X)) Spoken Lang Serv.

Spoken Hungarian. Thomas A. Sebeok. 6 dual track cass. (Spoken Language Ser.). (YA). (gr. 9-12). 1983. pap. bk. 90.00 (978-0-87950-127-3(8)) Spoken Lang Serv.

Spoken Korean. Fred Lukoff. 6 dual track cass. (Spoken Language Ser.). (J). (gr. 9-12). 1975. bk. 75.00 (978-0-87950-155-6(3)) Spoken Lang Serv.

Spoken Korean, Bk. 1. Fred Lukoff. 6 dual track cass. (Spoken Language Ser.). (J). (gr. 9-12). 1975. pap. bk. 90.00 (978-0-87950-156-3(1)) Spoken Lang Serv.

Spoken Lebanese. Maksoud N. Feghali. 1999. pap. bk. 34.95 (978-1-887905-14-5(6)) Pkway Pubs.

Spoken Malay, Bk. I. Isidore Dyen et al. 6 dual track cass. (J). (gr. 9-12). 1971. 75.00 (978-0-87950-165-5(0)); 90.00 incl. bk. (978-0-87950-166-2(9)) Spoken Lang Serv.

Spoken Modern Hebrew. Joseph A. Reif & Hanna Levinson. 31 dual track cass. (Spoken Language Ser.). 1980. bk. 190.00 (978-0-87950-684-1(9)); pap. bk. 220.00 (978-0-87950-685-8(7)) Spoken Lang Serv.

Spoken Norwegian, Bk. 1. Einar Ingvald Haugen. 6 dual track cass. (Spoken Language Ser.). (J). (gr. 9-12). 1976. pap. bk. 90.00 (978-0-87950-176-1(6)) Spoken Lang Serv.

Spoken Norwegian, Bk. I. Einar Ingvald Haugen. 6 dual track cass. (Spoken Language Ser.). (J). (gr. 9-12). 1976. bk. 75.00 (978-0-87950-175-4(8)) Spoken Lang Serv.

Spoken Peretz: The Collected Works of I. L. Peretz, Father of Yiddish Literature. unabr. ed. I. L. Peretz. 3 cass. (Running Time: 4 hrs.). 2001. 29.95 Jewish Contempry Classics.
Peretz is the acknowledged father of Yiddish literature. This collection, edited by Prof. Ruth Wisse of Harvard, includes his greatest stories & his autobiography.

Spoken Persian. S. Obolensky et al. 5 dual track cass. (Running Time: 8 hrs.). (J). (gr. 9-12). 1973. 100.00 (978-0-87950-297-3(5)); 120.00 incl. bk. (978-0-87950-299-7(1)) Spoken Lang Serv.

Spoken Polish. Alexander M. Schenker. 19 dual track cass. (Spoken Language Ser.). 1981. bk. 130.00 (978-0-87950-041-2(7)); pap. bk. 165.00 (978-0-87950-042-9(5)) Spoken Lang Serv.

Spoken Portuguese, Bk. I. Margarida F. Reno et al. 6 dual track cass. (ENG & POR.). (J). (gr. 9-12). 1978. pap. bk. 90.00 (978-0-87950-186-0(3)); 75.00 (978-0-87950-185-3(5)) Spoken Lang Serv.

Spoken Romanian. 6 cass. (Running Time: 4 hrs.). pap. bk. 135.00 (AFRM10) J Norton Pubs.
Consists of dialogs, pattern practices, sections on grammar, pronunciation, comprehension & additional conversations. Each part ends with a Romanian-English vocabulary.

Spoken Romanian. Frederick Browning Agard. 6 dual track cass. (Spoken Language Ser.). (J). (gr. 9-12). 1976. bk. 75.00 (978-0-87950-317-8(3)) Spoken Lang Serv.

Spoken Romanian. Frederick Browning Agard. 6 dual track cass. (Spoken Language Ser.). (YA). (gr. 9-12). 1976. pap. bk. 95.00 (978-0-87950-314-7(9)) Spoken Lang Serv.

Spoken Russian, Bk. I. Leonard Bloomfield et al. (J). (gr. 9-12). 1971. pap. bk. 95.00 (978-0-87950-197-6(9)) Spoken Lang Serv.

Spoken Russian, Pt. 1. Leonard Bloomfield et al. Incl. Bk. IE. Spoken Russian. 15 dual track cass. Leonard Bloomfield et al. (J). (gr. 9-12). 1971. pap. bk. 135.00 incl. bk. incl. bk. (978-0-87950-202-7(9)); Bk. IIE. Spoken Russian. 11 dual track cass. Leonard Bloomfield et al. (J). (gr. 9-12). 1971. pap. bk. 130.00 incl. bk. incl. bk. (978-0-87950-203-4(7)); Bks. I & II. Spoken Russian. 26 dual track cass. Leonard Bloomfield et al. (J). (gr. 9-12). 1971. pap. bk. 265.00 incl. bk. (978-0-87950-204-1(5)); Pt. 1E. Spoken Russian. 15 dual track cass. Leonard Bloomfield et al. (J). (gr. 9-12). 1971. 115.00 15 dual track cass. (978-0-87950-200-3(2)); Pt. 2E. Spoken Russian. 11 dual track cass. Leonard Bloomfield et al. (J). (gr. 9-12). 1971. 110.00 (978-0-87950-201-0(0)); (J). (gr. 9-12). 1971. 75.00 (978-0-87950-196-9(0)) Spoken Lang Serv.

Spoken Serbo-Croatian. Carleton T. Hodge. 6 dual track cass. (Spoken Language Ser.). (J). (gr. 9 up). 1973. bk. 75.00 (978-0-87950-215-7(0)) Spoken Lang Serv.

Spoken Serbo-Croatian, Bk. 1. Carleton T. Hodge. 6 dual track cass. (Spoken Language Ser.). (J). (gr. 9 up). 1973. pap. bk. 90.00 . (978-0-87950-216-4(9)) Spoken Lang Serv.

Spoken Sinhalese, Bks. I, II & Cassettes I, II. Gordon H. Fairbanks et al. 34 dual track cass. Incl. Set. Spoken Sinhalese. 21 dual track cass. Gordon H. Fairbanks et al. (Spoken Language Ser.). (J). (gr. 9-12). 1968. pap. bk. 160.00 incl. bk. incl. bk. (978-0-87950-444-1(7)); Set. Spoken Sinhalese. 13 dual track cass. Gordon H. Fairbanks et al. (Spoken Language Ser.). (J). (gr. 9-12). 1968. pap. bk. 140.00 incl. bk. incl. bk. (978-0-87950-445-8(5)); Bk. 1. Spoken Sinhalese. 21 dual track cass. Gordon H. Fairbanks et al. (Spoken Language Ser.). (J). (gr. 9-12). 1968. 135.00 21 dual track cass. (978-0-87950-441-0(2)); Bk. 2. Spoken Sinhalese. 13 dual track cass. Gordon H. Fairbanks et al. (Spoken Language Ser.). (J). (gr. 9-12). 1968. 115.00 (978-0-87950-443-4(9)); (Spoken Language Ser.). (J). (gr. 9-12). 1980. Set pap. bk. 300.00 Set, incl. bk. (978-0-87950-446-5(3)) Spoken Lang Serv.

Spoken Spanish. S. N. Trevino. 6 dual track cass. (Spoken Language Ser.). (J). (gr. 9-12). 1975. bk. 75.00 (978-0-87950-225-6(8)); pap. bk. & stu. ed. 90.00 (978-0-87950-226-3(6)) Spoken Lang Serv.

Spoken Standard Chinese, Vol. 2. Hugh M. Stimson & Huang P. Po-Fei. 10 cass. 1976. 7.95 ea. (incl. supp. materials) Set. (978-0-88710-111-3(9)) Yale Far Eastern Pubns.

Spoken Swahili. Anthony J. Vitale. 6 dual track cass. (J). (gr. 9-12). 1979. pap. bk. 90.00 (978-0-87950-365-9(3)); 75.00 (978-0-87950-364-2(5)) Spoken Lang Serv.

Spoken Swedish. Fritz Frauchiger & William R. Van Buskirk. 24 cass. (Spoken Language Ser.). 1980. bk. 145.00 (978-0-87950-705-3(5)); pap. bk. 160.00 (978-0-87950-706-0(3)) Spoken Lang Serv.

Spoken Tagalog Bk. 1: Dialogues. J. Donald Bowen. 6 cass. (Spoken Language Ser.). (C). (gr. 9-12). 1982. pap. bk. 135.00 (978-0-87950-407-6(2)) Spoken Lang Serv.

Spoken Tagalog Bk. 1: Dialogues, No. I, Units 1-12. J. Donald Bowen. 6 cass. (Spoken Language Ser.). (C). (gr. 9-12). 1982. bk. 95.00 (978-0-87950-466-3(8)) Spoken Lang Serv.

Spoken Tagalog Bk. 2: Notes, Exercises, Drills. J. Donald Bowen. 18 cass. (Spoken Language Ser.). (C). (gr. 9-12). 1982. pap. bk. 245.00 (978-0-87950-469-4(2)) Spoken Lang Serv.

Spoken Tagalog Bk. 2: Notes, Exercises, Drills, No. II, Exercise Tests. J. Donald Bowen. 18 cass. (Spoken Language Ser.). (C). (gr. 9-12). 1982. bk. 110.00 (978-0-87950-468-7(4)) Spoken Lang Serv.

Spoken Taiwanese. Nicholas C. Bodman & Wu Su-Chu. 13 dual track cass. (Spoken Language Ser.). (CHI.). 1980. bk. 105.00 (978-0-87950-461-8(7)); pap. bk. 120.00 (978-0-87950-462-5(5)) Spoken Lang Serv.

Spoken Telugu, Vol. 1. Leigh Lisker. 6 cass. (Spoken Language Ser.). (J). (gr. 9-12). 1976. bk. 100.00 (978-0-87950-377-2(7)) Spoken Lang Serv.

Spoken Telugu, Vol. 1. Leigh Lisker. 6 cass. (Spoken Language Ser.). (YA). (gr. 9-12). 1976. pap. bk. 120.00 (978-0-87950-378-9(5)) Spoken Lang Serv.

Spoken Telugu, Vol. 2. Leigh Lisker. 5 cass. (Spoken Language Ser.). (YA). (gr. 9-12). 1976. bk. 55.00 (978-0-87950-379-6(3)) Spoken Lang Serv.

Spoken Thai. Mary R. Haas & Heng R. Subhanka. 6 dual track cass. (Spoken Language Ser.). (J). (gr. 9-12). 1978. bk. 75.00 (978-0-87950-235-5(5)) Spoken Lang Serv.

Spoken Thai. Mary R. Haas & Heng R. Subhanka. 6 dual track cass. (Spoken Language Ser.). (YA). (gr. 9-12). 1978. pap. bk. 90.00 (978-0-87950-236-2(3)) Spoken Lang Serv.

Spoken Turkish. Norman A. McQuown & Sadi Kaylan. 6 dual track cass. (Spoken Language Ser.). (J). (gr. 9-12). 1971. bk. 75.00 (978-0-87950-245-4(2)) Spoken Lang Serv.

Spoken Turkish, Bk. 1. Norman A. McQuown & Sadi Kaylan. 6 dual track cass. (Spoken Language Ser.). (J). (gr. 9-12). 1971. pap. bk. 95.00 (978-0-87950-246-1(0)) Spoken Lang Serv.

Spoken Urdu, Bks. 1 & 2. Muhammad A. Barker et al. 12 dual track cass. Incl. Bk. 1. Spoken Urdu. 6 dual track cass. Muhammad A. Barker et al. (Spoken Language Ser.). (YA). (gr. 9-12). 1975. 100.00 6 dual track cass. (978-0-87950-344-4(0)); Bk. 1. Spoken Urdu. 6 dual track cass. Muhammad A. Barker et al. (Spoken Language Ser.). (YA). (gr. 9-12). 1975. pap. bk. 120.00 incl. bk. incl. bk. (978-0-87950-347-5(5)); Bk. 2. Spoken Urdu. 6 dual track cass. Muhammad A. Barker et al. (Spoken Language Ser.). (YA). (gr. 9-12). 1975. 85.00 6 dual track cass. Set, incl. bk. (978-0-87950-345-1(9)); Bk. 2. Spoken Urdu. 6 dual track cass. Muhammad A. Barker et al. (Spoken Language Ser.). (YA). (gr. 9-12). 1975. pap. bk. 105.00 incl. bk. incl. bk. (978-0-87950-348-2(3)); (Spoken Language Ser.). (YA). (gr. 9-12). 1975. Set pap. bk. 225.00 (978-0-87950-349-9(1)) Spoken Lang Serv.

Spoken Vietnamese. Robert B. Jones & Huynh S. Thong. 6 dual track cass. (Spoken Language Ser.). (J). (gr. 9-12). 1976. bk. 75.00 (978-0-87950-372-7(6)) Spoken Lang Serv.

Spoken Vietnamese. Robert B. Jones & Huynh S. Thong. 6 dual track cass. (Spoken Language Ser.). (YA). (gr. 9-12). 1976. pap. bk. 90.00 incl. bk. (978-0-87950-373-4(4)) Spoken Lang Serv.

Spoken Vietnamese for Beginners. Nguyen Long & Marybeth Clark. Prod. by Nguyen Bich Thuan. 3 cass. (C). 1994. audio compact disk 12.00 (978-1-877979-33-0(3)) SE Asia.

Spoken Vietnamese for Beginners. Nguyen Long et al. 3 cass. (Running Time: 4 hrs. 30 mins.). (Southeast Asian Language Text Ser.). (C). 1994. pap. bk. 42.95 (978-1-877979-45-3(7)) SE Asia.

Spoken Vietnamese for Beginners. Le Pham Thuy-Kim. 3 cass. 1996. pap. bk., wbk. ed., act. bk. ed. 27.95 (978-1-877979-30-9(9)); act. bk. ed. 20.00 (978-1-877979-26-2(0)) SE Asia.

Spoken Vietnamese for Beginners, Bk. 1. Le Pham Thuy-Kim. Illus. by Vivian Nguyen. 4 cass. (C). 1996. pap. bk., wbk. ed., act. bk. ed. 29.95 (978-1-877979-27-9(9)) SE Asia.

Spoken Vietnamese for Beginners, Bk. 2. Le Pham Thuy-Kim. 3 cass. (C). 1996. act. bk. ed. 15.00 (978-1-877979-29-3(5)) SE Asia.

Spoken Word. Mumia Abu-Jamal. 1 CD. (AK Press Audio Ser.). (ENG.). 2000. audio compact disk 14.98 (978-1-902593-07-4(3)) Pub: AK Pr GBR. Dist(s): Consort Bk Sales

Spoken Word. W. H. Auden et al. (British Library - British Library Sound Archive Ser.). (ENG.). 2009. audio compact disk 25.00 (978-0-7123-0535-8(1)) Pub: Britis Library GBR. Dist(s): Chicago Distribution Ctr

Spoken Word. British Library Staff & Vrej Nersessian. (British Library - British Library Sound Archive Ser.). (ENG.). 2009. audio compact disk 15.00 (978-0-7123-0548-8(3)) Pub: Britis Library GBR. Dist(s): Chicago Distribution Ctr

Spoken Word. Graham Greene Staff et al. (British Library - British Library Sound Archive Ser.). 2009. audio compact disk 15.00 (978-0-7123-0539-6(4)) Pub: Britis Library GBR. Dist(s): Chicago Distribution Ctr

Spoken Word. George Bernard Shaw & Vrej Nersessian. (British Library - British Library Sound Archive Ser.). (ENG.). 2009. audio compact disk 25.00 (978-0-7123-0531-0(9)) Pub: Britis Library GBR. Dist(s): Chicago Distribution Ctr

Spoken Word. The British Library. (British Library - British Library Sound Archive Ser.). (ENG.). 2009. audio compact disk 25.00 (978-0-7123-0549-5(1)) Pub: Britis Library GBR. Dist(s): Chicago Distribution Ctr

Spoken Word. Evelyn Waugh et al. (British Library - British Library Sound Archive Ser.). (ENG.). 2009. audio compact disk 15.00 (978-0-7123-0546-4(7)) Pub: Britis Library GBR. Dist(s): Chicago Distribution Ctr

Spoken Word. H. G. Wells et al. (British Library - British Library Sound Archive Ser.). (ENG.). 2009. audio compact disk 15.00 (978-0-7123-0532-7(7)) Pub: Britis Library GBR. Dist(s): Chicago Distribution Ctr

Spoken Word. 2nd ed. British Library Sound Archive Staff & Vrej Nersessian. (British Library - British Library Sound Archive Ser.). (ENG.). 2009. audio compact disk 15.00 (978-0-7123-0591-4(2)) Pub: Britis Library GBR. Dist(s): Chicago Distribution Ctr

Spoken Word, Set. Richard L. Evans. 2 cass. 2004. 11.98 (978-1-55503-194-7(3), 0700746) Covenant Comms.
More than 50 sermonettes delivered with Tabernacle Choir Broadcasts.

Spoken Word, Set. Richard Ranft et al. (Running Time: 3 hrs. 57 mins. 0 sec.). (British Library - British Library Sound Archive Ser.). 2008. audio compact disk 35.00 (978-0-7123-0541-9(6)) Pub: Britis Library GBR. Dist(s): Chicago Distribution Ctr

***Spoken Word: Aldous Huxley.** The British Library. (British Library - British Library Sound Archive Ser.). (ENG.). 2010. audio compact disk 15.00 (978-0-7123-5103-4(5)) Pub: Britis Library GBR. Dist(s): Chicago Distribution Ctr

***Spoken Word: American Poets.** The British Library. (British Library - British Library Sound Archive Ser.). (ENG.). 2010. audio compact disk 35.00 (978-0-7123-5106-5(X)) Pub: Britis Library GBR. Dist(s): Chicago Distribution Ctr

***Spoken Word: British Poets.** The British Library. (British Library - British Library Sound Archive Ser.). (ENG.). 2010. audio compact disk 35.00 (978-0-7123-5105-8(1)) Pub: Britis Library GBR. Dist(s): Chicago Distribution Ctr

Spoken Word on Behalf of the Feminine. Judith Barr. 4 cass. Vol.s 1 through 4. 1994. 45.00 (978-1-886264-05-2(8)) Mysteries of Life.
Women's spirituality - psychology.

Spoken Word Project: Poet. Poems. Based on a book by Angela Williamston. 1 CD. (Running Time: 59 mins). 2002. audio compact disk 14.95 (978-0-9674984-8-5(1)) Freeverse Pubng.
Poet On Watch, The Spoken Word Project, is a mix between conscious poetry, soulful vocals, neofunk, hip-hop, acid jazz, and R&B. It belongs in the category of spoken word music. It's based on the self-entitled book Poet On Watch written by Angela Williamston. ISBN 0-9674984-9-X.

***Spoken Word: Sylvia Plath.** Vrej Nersessian & British Library Staff. (British Library - British Library Sound Archive Ser.). 2010. audio compact disk 15.00 (978-0-7123-5102-7(7)) Pub: Britis Library GBR. Dist(s): Chicago Distribution Ctr

Spondyloepiphyseal Dysplasia Congenita - A Bibliography & Dictionary for Physicians, Patients, & Genome Researchers. Compiled by Icon Group International, Inc. Staff. 2007. ring bd. 28.95 (978-0-497-11297-4(3)) Icon Grp.

Spondyloperipheral Dysplasia - A Bibliography & Dictionary for Physicians, Patients, & Genome Researchers. Compiled by Icon Group International, Inc. Staff. 2007. ring bd. 28.95 (978-0-497-11298-1(1)) Icon Grp.

SpongBob Square Pants Typing. (J). 2006. audio compact disk 4.99 (978-1-59987-473-9(3)) Braun Media.

SpongeBob AirPants: The Lost Episode, Vol. 8. Kitty Richards. Read by Denis Lawrence. (Running Time: 33 mins.). (J). (gr. 2-5). 2004. pap. bk. 17.00 (978-1-4000-8631-3(0), Listening Lib) Random Audio Pubg.

Spongebob NaturePants, Vol. 7. Terry Collins. Read by Denis Lawrence. (Running Time: 40 mins.). (J). (gr. 2-5). 2004. pap. bk. 17.00 (978-1-4000-8630-6(2), Listening Lib) Random Audio Pubg.

SpongeBob Squarepants Chapter Books. Annie Auerbach & Terry Collins. Read by Denis Lawrence. 2 cass. (Running Time: 2 hrs. 8 mins.). (J). (gr. 2-5). 2004. 23.00 (978-0-8072-1884-6(7), Listening Lib) Random Audio Pubg.

SpongeBob SquarePants Chapter Books, Vol. 2. Annie Auerbach et al. Read by Denis Lawrence. 2 cass. (Running Time: 2 hrs. 31 mins.). (J). (gr. 2-5). 2004. 23.00 (978-1-4000-8607-8(8), Listening Lib) Random Audio Pubg.

Spongebob Superstar, Vol. 5. Annie Auerbach. Read by Denis Lawrence. (Running Time: 44 mins.). (J). (gr. 2-5). 2004. pap. bk. 17.00 (978-1-4000-8628-3(0), Listening Lib) Random Audio Pubg.

Sponono see Tales from a Troubled Land

Spon's Mechanical & Electrical Services Price Book 2008. Davis Langdon Mott Green Staff. 2007. audio compact disk 240.00 (978-0-415-42443-1(7)) Taylor and Fran.

Sponsorship, Vol. 1. Ed. by Ames Sweet & Ann Warner. 1 cass. (Running Time: 1 hr. 30 min.). Dramatization. 1992. 6.50 (978-0-933685-22-2(X), TP-16) A A Grapevine.
Personal experience of individual AA members on the topic of AA Sponsorship.

Sponsorship, Vol. 2. Ed. by Ames Sweet & Ann Warner. 1 cass. (Running Time: 1 hr. 30 min.). Dramatization. 1992. 6.50 (978-0-933685-23-9(8), TP-17) A A Grapevine.

Spontaneous Awakening. Adyashanti. 6 CDs. (Running Time: 27900 sec.). 2005. audio compact disk 69.95 (978-1-59179-291-8(6), F916D) Sounds True.
The buzz about this earnest, clear-minded, Northern California Zen teacher is growing louder. Adyashanti's retreats have become known as profoundly liberating events that open the heart of realization and true understanding. Now, in his first national audio release, listeners can join this sought-after spiritual teacher on retreat in their own homes with Spontaneous Awakening. For those who are seeking a path of simplicity, not bound by the trappings of spiritual practice, Adyashati brings a fresh and humble approach to Zen wisdom. "Don't think that awakening is the end," teaches Adyashanti. "Awakening is the end of seeking, the end of the seeker, but it is the beginning of a life lived from your true nature.".

Spontaneous Descriptions, Bk. 2. Harris Winitz & Douglas Moore. Illus. by Sydney M. Baker. 1985. pap. bk. 40.00 (978-0-939990-42-9(3)) Intl Linguistics.

Spontaneous Evolution: Our Positive Future & How to get There from Here. Bruce Lipton & Steve Bhaerman. 2008. audio compact disk 34.95 (978-1-59179-964-1(3)) Sounds True.

Spontaneous Fulfillment of Desire: Harnessing the Infinite Power of Coincidence to Create Miracles. unabr. ed. Read by Deepak Chopra. 5 CDs. (Running Time: 6 hrs.). (Deepak Chopra Ser.). (ENG.). 2003. audio compact disk 29.95 (978-0-7393-0644-4(8), RH-Aud Dim) Pub: Random Audio Pubg. Dist(s): Random

Spontaneous Healing: How to Discover & Enhance Your Body's Natural Ability to Maintain & Heal Itself. unabr. ed. Andrew Weil. Read by Barrett Whitener. 9 cass. (Running Time: 13 hrs. 30 min.). 1998. 72.00 (978-0-7366-4222-4(6), 4722) Books on Tape.

Spontaneous Healing of Belief: Shattering the Paradigm of False Limits. abr. ed. Gregg Braden. 4 CDs. 2008. audio compact disk 23.95 (978-1-4019-1731-9(3)) Hay House.

Spontaneous Optimism. abr. ed. Michael Mercer & Maryann Troiani. Read by Michael Mercer & Maryann Troiani. 2 cass. (Running Time: 3 hrs.). 1998. 16.95 (978-1-885408-21-1(8), LL014) Listen & Live.
Simple techniques to quickly develop an optimistic attitude & lifestyle. Discover the secrets to becoming an extraordinary individual.

Spook: Science Tackles the Afterlife. unabr. ed. Mary Roach. Read by Bernadette Quigley. (Running Time: 8 hrs.). 2005. 39.25 (978-1-59737-886-4(0), 9781597378864, BADLE); 24.95 (978-1-59737-885-7(2), 9781597378857, BAD); 74.25 (978-1-59737-880-2(1), 9781597378802, BrilAudUnabridg); 29.95 (978-1-59737-879-6(8), 9781597378796, BAU); audio compact disk 39.25 (978-1-59737-884-0(4), 9781597378840, Brlnc Audio MP3 Lib); audio compact disk 87.25 (978-1-59737-882-6(8), 9781597378826, BriAudCD Unabrid); audio compact disk 32.95 (978-1-59737-881-9(X), 9781597378819, Bril Audio CD Unabri); audio compact disk 24.95 (978-1-59737-883-3(6), 9781597378833, Brilliance MP3) Brilliance Audio.
"What happens when we die? Does the light just go out and that's that - the million-year nap? Or will some part of my personality, my me-ness persist? What will that feel like? What will I do all day? Is there a place to plug in my laptop?" In an attempt to find out, Mary Roach brings her tireless curiosity to bear on an array of contemporary and historical soul-searchers: scientists, schemers, engineers, mediums, all trying to prove (or disprove) that life goes on after we die. She begins the journey in rural India with a reincarnation researcher and ends up in a University of Virginia operating room where cardiologists have installed equipment near the ceiling to study out-of-body near-death experiences. Along the way, she enrolls in an English medium school, gets electromagnetically haunted at a university in Ontario, and visits a Duke University professor with a plan to weigh the consciousness of a leech. Her historical wanderings unearth soul-seeking philosophers who rummaged through cadavers and calves' heads, a North Carolina lawsuit that established legal precedence for ghosts, and the last surviving sample of "ectoplasm" in a Cambridge University archive.

Spook Country. unabr. ed. William Gibson. Read by Robertson Dean. 9 CDs. (Running Time: 11 hrs.). 2007. audio compact disk 110.00 (978-1-4159-4176-8(9)) Random.

Spook House. Don Whittington. Read by John Durand. 2 cass. (Running Time: 2 hrs.). (Forging of the Key Ser.). (J). (gr. 4-9). 1995. 12.95 (978-1-886392-11-3(0), Parrot Bks) Walberg Pubng.
The third book in the Forging of the Key Series, Don Whittington is the Dean Koontz of young adult fiction with his marvelous blend of science & horror.

Spooky Book. Steve Patschke. Illus. by Matthew McElligott. 1 cass. (Running Time: 9 min.). (J). (gr. k-3). 2001. bk. 26.90 (978-0-8045-6871-5(5), 6871) Spoken Arts.
Lightning cracks, thunder rumbles, the wind howls and shadows creep, creep, creep up the walls in this most inventive of spooky books. From the moment the cover is first opened to the turn of the last page, readers will be held in playful suspense as they follow the adventures of Andrew and Zo Zo, two children reading spooky books on a dark and stormy night.

Spooky Classics for Children. As told by Jim Weiss. 1 cass. (Running Time: 1 hr.). Dramatization. (Storyteller's Version Ser.). (YA). 1997. 10.95 (978-1-882513-18-5(5), 1124-18); audio compact disk 14.95 (978-1-882513-43-7(6), 1124-018) Greathall Prods.
Spooky Classics from Wilde, Hawthorne and Kipling in which chills and laughter are mixed together. Includes: "The Canterville Ghost," "Dr. Heidegger's Experiment" and "The Sending of Dana Da".

Spooky Classics for Children. Read by Jim Weiss. 1 cass., 1 CD. (Running Time: 1 hr.). (J). 1999. (GHP18) NewSound.

Spooky Night in Disney's Haunted Mansion: A Thrilling Story Adventure Featuring the Chilling Sounds of the Famous Disney Ride. Prod. by Walt Disney Records Staff. 1 cass. (J). 1998. 5.98 (978-0-7634-0489-5(6)) W Disney Records.

Spooky Songs. 1 CD. (Running Time: 30 min.). (Halloween Party Ser.). (J). (gr. k-5). 2001. pap. bk. 5.98 (9688-2) Peter Pan.
Spooky songs, sounds and stories with holiday spirit. Includes Halloween Party Tip Guide.

Spooky Stickers. (Art Rom Create Your Own... Ser.). (J). 2004. pap. bk. 9.99 (978-1-84229-738-4(4)) Top That GBR.

Spoon River Anthology. abr. ed. Edgar Lee Masters. Perf. by Julie Harris. 1 cass. (Running Time: 90 min.). 1984. 12.95 (978-0-694-50113-7(1), SWC 1152) HarperCollins Pubs.

Spoon River Anthology. unabr. ed. Edgar Lee Masters. Read by Patrick Fraley et al. 4 cass. (Running Time: 5 hrs.). 2002. 24.95 (978-1-57270-278-3(8)) Pub: Audio Partners. Dist(s): PerseuPGW
The dead speak the truths about their lives from a cemetery. Some speak of hardships and sordidness; others, of their simple, honest, happy lives. As the spoon river residents examine their lives, they invite us to do the same.

Spoon River Anthology. unabr. ed. Edgar Lee Masters. Read by Edward Asner. Narrated by Patrick Fraley & Emily Woo Zeller. 4 CDs. (Running Time: 5 hrs.). (Audio Editions Ser.). (ENG.). 2002. audio compact disk 25.95 (978-1-57270-279-0(6)) Pub: AudioGO. Dist(s): Perseus Dist
The dead speak the truth about their lives from a cemetery. Some speak of hardships and sordidness; others of their simple, honest, happy lives. As the spoon river residents examine their lives, they invite us to do the same.

Spoonbill Swamp. unabr. ed. Brenda Z. Guiberson. 1 cass. (Running Time: 10 min.). (J). (gr. k-4). 1994. pap. bk. 17.90 (978-0-8045-6820-3(0), 6820) Spoken Arts.
On a typical day in the swamp, an alligator mother and a spoonbill mother tend to their young. Learn the similarities and differences between these two who live in the same environment.

Sporran Connection. Peter Kerr. 2008. 69.95 (978-1-84559-986-7(1)); audio compact disk 84.95 (978-1-84559-987-4(X)) Pub: Soundings Ltd GBR. Dist(s): Ulverscroft US

Sport. Louise Fitzhugh. Read by Anne Bobby. 3 cass. (Running Time: 4 hrs. 25 mins.). (J). (gr. 3-7). 2004. 30.00 (978-0-8072-1024-6(2), Listening Lib) Random Audio Pubg.

Sport, the Philosophy Of. George Leonard & Ira Berkow. 1 cass. (Running Time: 56 min.). 10.95 (40211) J Norton Pubs.
With Heywood Hale Broun, the authors ponder unrestricted play; the need for rules in both life & games; & the terrible price demanded by current professional sport. At the same time they lament the lack of real risk & excitement in our lives.

Sporting Chance. Based on a book by Elizabeth Moon. (Serrano Legacy Ser.: Bk. 2). 2008. 12.99 (978-1-59950-544-2(4)) GraphicAudio.

Sporting Chance. Based on a book by Elizabeth Moon. (Serrano Legacy Ser.: Bk. 2). 2008. 12.99 (978-1-59950-545-9(2)) GraphicAudio.

Sporting Chance Part 1. Elizabeth Moon. (Serrano Legacy Ser.: Bk. 2). 2008. audio compact disk 19.99 (978-1-59950-451-3(0)) GraphicAudio.

Sporting Chance Part 2. Elizabeth Moon. (Serrano Legacy Ser.: Bk. 2). 2008. audio compact disk 19.99 (978-1-59950-459-9(6)) GraphicAudio.

Sporting Goods in Australia: A Strategic Reference 2007. Compiled by Icon Group International, Inc. Staff. 2007. ring bd. 195.00 (978-0-497-35812-9(3)) Icon Grp.

Sporting Goods in Hong Kong: A Strategic Reference 2007. Compiled by Icon Group International, Inc. Staff. 2007. ring bd. 195.00 (978-0-497-36002-3(0)) Icon Grp.

Sporting Laughs. 2 cass. (Running Time: 2 hrs.). 1998. 16.85 Set. (978-0-563-55773-9(7)) BBC WrldWd GBR.
A compilation of Sporting Comedy clips.

Sportman's Best: Inshore Fishing. Mike Holliday. Ed. by Joe Richard. Illus. by Joe Suroviec. (ENG.). 2005. pap. bk. 19.95 (978-0-936240-32-9(6), FlaSports) InterMedia Outdrs.

Sports. Eldon Taylor. Read by Eldon Taylor. Interview with XProgress Aware Staff. 1 cass. (Running Time: 62 min.). 16.95 incl. script. (978-1-55978-294-4(3), 020108) Progress Aware Res.
Verbal coaching soundtrack with underlying subliminal affirmations & sound matrix frequencies for brain entrainment.

Sports Classic. Created by Radio Spirits. (Running Time: 10800 sec.). 2004. 9.98 (978-1-57019-764-2(4)) Radio Spirits.

Sports Classics. Created by Radio Spirits. (Running Time: 10800 sec.). 2004. audio compact disk 9.98 (978-1-57019-763-5(6)) Radio Spirits.

Sports from Hell: My Search for the World's Dumbest Competition. unabr. ed. Rick Reilly. Read by Mike Chamberlain. (ENG.). 2010. audio compact disk 30.00 (978-0-307-57794-8(5), Random AudioBks) Pub: Random Audio Pubg. Dist(s): Random

Sports Heroes Collection 1-3. unabr. ed. (J). 2006. 39.99 (978-1-59895-622-1(1)) Find a World.

Sports Heroes Collection 3-5. unabr. ed. (J). 2006. 39.99 (978-1-59895-719-8(8)) Find a World.

Sports Illustrated Moments of Glory: Unforgettable Games. unabr. ed. Sports Illustrated Staff. (ENG.). 2006. 9.99 (978-1-59483-723-4(6)) Pub: Hachet Audio. Dist(s): HachBkGrp

Sports in America, Pt. 1. unabr. ed. James A. Michener. Read by Larry McKeever. 9 cass. (Running Time: 13 hrs. 30 min.). 1995. 72.00 (978-0-7366-2986-7(6), 3676-A) Books on Tape.
Corruption, greed & vice plague American sports. Why do we still love the games? Comprehensive & provoking.

Sports in America, Pt. 2. James A. Michener. Read by Larry McKeever. 9 cass. (Running Time: 13 hrs. 30 min.). 1995. 72.00 (3676-B) Books on Tape.

Sports Law. 2nd rev. ed. Ray Yasser. 2 cass. (Running Time: 3 hrs.). (Outstanding Professors Ser.). 1997. 63.00 (978-1-57793-023-5(1), 28427, West Lglwrks) West.
Introduction to Sports Law; Structure of Sports in America; Amateur Sports-Organizations & Issue of State Action; Private Associational Law; Constitutional Law; Antitrust Law; Professional Sports; Traditional Player Restraints & the Antitrust Law; The Draft; "Rozelle" Rule & Limits on Free Agency; Decisional Law; Labor Law Exemption to the Antitrust Law; Significance of Collective Bargaining; Powell v. NFL; Baseball's Exemption to Antitrust Law; Teams "In League", Franchise Sale or Relocation; Raiders' Case; Fledgling League v. Established League; Commissioner Power, Representation of Professional Athletes; Issues Common to Amateur & Professional Sports; Tort Liability; Liability of One Participant to Another, Spectator as Plaintiff; Medical Malpractice; Products Liability; Defamation; Invasion of Privacy; Drug Testing.

Sports Marketing: Create Extensive Media Coverage. Kermit Pemberton. 1 cass. 49.95 (978-0-9656421-4-9(3)) Sports Servs.
Sports celebrities & media attention.

Sports Marketing: Increase Profits, Motivate Customers, Distributors & Employers Through Sports. Kermit Pemberton. 1 cass. 49.95 (978-0-9656421-5-6(1)) Sports Servs.

***Sports Math Complete Program.** EDCON Publishing Group Staff. 2004. 189.00 (978-1-55576-485-2(1)) EDCON Pubng.

Sports: Mentally Fit. Eldon Taylor. 2 cass. 29.95 Set. (978-1-55978-743-7(0), 4408) Progress Aware Res.

Sports Minded-Sports Psychology: Program from the Award Winning Public Radio Series. Hosted by Fred Goodwin. Comment by John Hockenberry. Contrib. by Jack Raglin et al. Photos by Philip Glass. Contrib. by Surya Das et al. 1 cass. (Running Time: 1 hr.). (Infinite Mind Ser.). 1998. audio compact disk 21.95 (978-1-888064-31-5(5), LCM 31) Lichtenstein Creat.
The psychology and brain science of athletic performance. Hear about the secret mind-body techniques used by top athletes, from the sports psychologist for the U.S. Olympic ski team and Ohio State's football team, five-time American league batting champ Wade Boggs, and sportswriter extraordinare George Plimpton.

Sports Performance. 1 cass. 10.00 (978-1-58506-049-8(6), 94) New Life Inst OR.
Relax, concentrate & get in the groove - whatever your sport.

Sports Performance. 1 cass. (Running Time: 45 min.). (Sports Ser.). 9.98 (978-1-55909-035-3(9), 39S); 9.98 90 min. extended length stereo music. (978-1-55909-036-0(7), 39X) Randolph Tapes.
Works on concentration, coordination & control for any sport. Subliminal messages are heard 3-5 minutes before becoming ocean sounds or music.

Sports Performance. Barry Tesar. 1 cass. (Running Time: 1 hr.). (Subliminal Inspiration Ser.). 1992. 9.98 (978-1-56470-011-7(9)) Success Cass.
Subliminal program.

Sports Power. (Sports Ser.). 14.98 (978-1-55909-216-6(5), 110PM) Randolph Tapes.

Sports Radio. (Stereo Boom Box Ser.: Vol. 2). (J). (gr. 1-6). 1998. ring bd. 164.99 (978-1-57405-049-3(4)) CharismaLife Pub.

Sports Rock: For Alto Sax. Created by Hal Leonard Corporation Staff. 2009. pap. bk. 12.99 (978-1-4234-6203-3(3), 1423462033) H Leonard.

Sports Rock: For Cello. Created by Hal Leonard Corporation Staff. 2009. pap. bk. 12.99 (978-1-4234-6210-1(6), 1423462106) H Leonard.

Sports Rock: For Clarinet. Created by Hal Leonard Corporation Staff. 2009. pap. bk. 12.99 (978-1-4234-6202-6(5), 1423462025) H Leonard.

Sports Rock: For Flute. Created by Hal Leonard Corporation Staff. 2009. pap. bk. 12.99 (978-1-4234-6201-9(7), 1423462017) H Leonard.

Sports Rock: For Tenor Sax. Created by Hal Leonard Corporation Staff. 2009. pap. bk. 12.99 (978-1-4234-6204-0(1), 1423462041) H Leonard.

Sports Rock: For Viola. Created by Hal Leonard Corporation Staff. 2009. pap. bk. 12.99 (978-1-4234-6209-5(2), 1423462092) H Leonard.

Sports Rock: For Violin. Created by Hal Leonard Corporation Staff. 2009. pap. bk. 12.99 (978-1-4234-6208-8(4), 1423462084) H Leonard.

Sports Rules on File. Facts on File, Inc. Staff. (C). (gr. 6-12). 2000. audio compact disk 149.95 (978-0-8160-4445-0(7)) Facts On File.

Sports World. Patricia Snyder. 1 cass. 8.95 (325) Am Fed Astrologers.
Influence of Astrology on athletes & coaches.

Sportsman's Best: Dolphin Book & DVD. Rick Ryals. Ed. by Florida Sportsman Staff. (Sportsman's Best Ser.). (ENG., 2008. pap. bk. (978-1-892947-33-8(1), FlaSports) InterMedia Outdrs.

Sportsman's Life: How I Built Orvis by Mixing Business & Sport. abr. ed. Leigh Perkins. Read by Doug Ordunio. 4 cass. (Running Time: 6 hrs.). 2001. 25.00 (978-1-59040-114-9(X), Phoenix Audio) Pub: Amer Intl Pub. Dist(s): PerseuPGW

Sportsman's Life: How I Built Orvis by Mixing Business & Sport. collector's ed. L. Perkins & G. Norman. Read by Michael Kramer. 5 cass. (Running Time: 7 hrs. 30 min.). 1999. 40.00 (978-0-7366-4750-2(3), 5088) Books on Tape.
Leigh Perkins tells a vivid & passionate story about how he turned Orvis into one of the country's most noted fly fishing & sporting companies. A pioneer in the mail order business, Perkins boosted sales of the Manchester, Vermont, company from $500,000 annually to nearly $200 million. Perkins believes he succeeded by building a superior product & selling a lifestyle in his catalogs, an appreciation of fishing, bird hunting & country living. It is also the story of how his love for the outdoors made him one of America's leading converstationists.

Sportswriter. Richard Ford. Read by Richard Ford. 1 cass. 1985. 13.95 (978-1-55644-151-6(7), 6031) Am Audio Prose.
Ford reads the first chapter of "The Sportwriter" & a short story, "Rock Springs," about a man on the run in a stolen car with his girl friend & young daughter.

Sportswriter. unabr. ed. Richard Ford. Read by Richard Ford. 1 cass. (Running Time: 29 min.). 1987. 10.00 (110687) New Letters.
Ford discusses his work & reads from "The Sportswriter".

Spot in the Dark. Gylys Beth. (Osu journal award Poetry Ser.). 2004. audio compact disk 9.95 (978-0-8142-9057-6(4)) Pub: Ohio St U Pr. Dist(s): Chicago Distribution Ctr

Spot of Bother. unabr. ed. Mark Haddon. Read by Simon Vance. (Running Time: 43200 sec.). (ENG.). 2006. audio compact disk 39.95 (978-0-7393-4264-0(9), Random AudioBks) Pub: Random Audio Pubg. Dist(s): Random

Spot of Bother: A Novel. unabr. ed. Mark Haddon. 7 cass. (Running Time: 10 hrs.). 2006. 63.00 (978-1-4159-3502-6(5)); audio compact disk 68.85 (978-1-4159-3503-3(3)) Pub: Books on Tape. Dist(s): NetLibrary CO

Spot of Decorating see Paddington Dissappearing

Spotlight on Flute. (Vox - Turnabout Classical Ser.). 3.98 (CTX 4815); audio compact disk (ACD 8746) VOX Music Grp.

Spotlight on Guitar. 1 cass. (Vox - Turnabout Classical Ser.). 3.98 (CTX 4806); audio compact disk (ACD 8742) VOX Music Grp.

Spotlight on Piano: Concertos. 1 cass. (Vox - Turnabout Classical Ser.). 3.98 (CTX 4810); audio compact disk (ACD 8714) VOX Music Grp.

Spotlight on Two-Word Verb Idioms: Skits & Exercises to Develop Listening, Speaking, & Context-Use Skills. Charlotte Perkins Gilman. 1 Cassette. (ENG.). (gr. 10-12). 1998. suppl. ed. 14.95 (978-1-882483-55-6(3), AL3553) Alta Bk Ctr Pubs.

Spotlight on Violin: Concertos. 1 cass. (Vox - Turnabout Classical Ser.). 3.98 (CTX 4811); audio compact disk (ACD 8715) VOX Music Grp.

Spotlighting Your Reflected Image - Solstice Points. Alice Q. Reichard. 1 cass. 8.95 (292) Am Fed Astrologers.
An AFA Convention workshop tape.

Spotting Price Swings & Seasonal Patterns: Techniques for precisely timing Major Market Moves. Speeches. Jake Bernstein. (Running Time: 90 mins.). (Trade Secrets Audio Ser.). 2002. 19.95 (978-1-59280-002-5(5)) Marketplace Bks.
What if you could know a simple price pattern for trading on Monday? Or how about a price pattern that signals a powerful trend is about to get underway? With Jake Bernstein's new video, now you can! President of MBH Commodity Advisors Inc. and Bernstein Investments Inc., Bernstein provides the viewer with one of his favorite price patterns for trading S&P futures on Monday based on the price action on Friday.

Spousal Rights & Marital Agreements in Estate Planning. unabr. ed. Contrib. by Linda B. Hirschson. 4 cass. (Running Time: 4 hrs. 30 min.). 1989. 50.00 course handbk. (T7-9200) PLI.

***Spousonomics: Using Economics to Master Love, Marriage, & Dirty Dishes.** unabr. ed. Paula Szuchman & Jenny Anderson. (ENG.). 2011. audio compact disk 30.00 (978-0-307-87677-5(2), Random AudioBks) Pub: Random Audio Pubg. Dist(s): Random

Spqr I: The Kings Gambit. unabr. ed. John Maddox Roberts. Read by Simon Vance. (Running Time: 7.5 hrs. 0 mins.). 2008. 29.95 (978-1-4332-2753-0(3)); 54.95 (978-1-4332-2749-3(5)); audio compact disk 60.00 (978-1-4332-2750-9(9)) Blckstn Audio.

Spqr II: The Catiline Conspiracy. unabr. ed. John Maddox Roberts. (Running Time: 7 hrs. NaN mins.). 2009. 29.95 (978-1-4332-2761-5(4)); audio compact disk 60.00 (978-1-4332-2758-5(4)); audio compact disk 54.95 (978-1-4332-2757-8(6)) Blckstn Audio.

Sprachbruecke: Cassette zu den Einsprchigen Arbeitshefte. Gudula Mebus et al. 1 cass. (GER.). (C). 1989. 34.25 (978-3-12-557151-8(0)) Intl Bk Import.

Sprachbruecke: Cassetten zum Lehrbuch. Gudula Mebus et al. 1 cass. (GER.). (C). 1988. 49.25 (978-3-12-557170-9(7)) Intl Bk Import.

Sprachbruecke Level 2: Lehrbuch. A. Pauldrach et al. (GER.). (C). 1990. 45.00 (978-3-12-557215-7(0)) Pub: Klett Ernst Verlag DEU. Dist(s): Intl Bk Import

Sprachkurs Deutsch 1. Ulrich Haussermann et al. (GER.). 1995. 90.00 (978-3-425-05941-9(6)) Pub: Verlag Moritz Diesterweg DEU. Dist(s): Intl Bk Import

Sprachkurs Deutsch 3. Ulrich Haussermann & Georg Dietrich. (GER.). (C). 1991. 76.00 (978-3-425-05943-3(2)) Pub: Verlag Moritz Diesterweg DEU. Dist(s): Intl Bk Import

Sprachkurs Deutsch 5. Ulrich Haussermann & Georg Koller. (GER., (C). 1993. 72.00 (978-3-425-05945-7(9)) Pub: Verlag Moritz Diesterweg DEU. Dist(s): Intl Bk Import

Sprachkurs Deutsch 6. Ulrich Haussermann & Georg Koller. (GER., (C). 1994. 72.00 (978-3-425-05946-4(7)) Pub: Verlag Moritz Diesterweg DEU. Dist(s): Intl Bk Import

Sprdsht Dec Aid Cd T/A Mngrl Acctg. V. Balachandran & Rajiv D. Banker. (C). 2006. audio compact disk 15.95 (978-0-03-031917-4(X)) Pub: South-West. Dist(s): CENGAGE Learn

Spread Eagle. unabr. ed. George Brooks & Walter Lister. Perf. by Edward Asner et al. 2 cass. (Running Time: 1 hr. 36 mins.). 1999. 23.95 (978-1-58081-139-2(6), TPT133) L A Theatre.
Commerce & heroism clash when a titan of American business orchestrates a U. S. invasion of Mexico.

Spread the News Cassette Promo Pak. Greg Skipper. 1997. 8.00 (978-0-7673-3988-9(6)) LifeWay Christian.

Spread the News Choral Cassette. Greg Skipper. 1997. 11.98 (978-0-7673-3990-2(8)) LifeWay Christian.

Spread the News Stereo/Split Acc Cassette. Greg Skipper. 1997. 40.00 (978-0-7673-3989-6(4)) LifeWay Christian.

Spread the Word. Ed. by Strang Communications Company Staff. 1 cass. (Running Time: 1 hr.). (J). (gr. k-7). 1997. 10.99 (978-1-57405-041-7(9), SPREAD) CharismaLife Pub.
At last music and praise songs just perfect for kids. These are the best songs from our KIDS Church programs. For classrooms and presentations, these songs teach as well as touch the heart. 15 exciting songs about living and loving God's Word.

Spread the Word: Introduction to Planet X And 2012. Narrated by Marshall Masters. (ENG.). 2007. audio compact disk 8.00 (978-1-59772-080-9(1), Your Own Wrld Bks) Your Own Wrld.

Spread Your Wings. 2000. audio compact disk (978-0-9776545-1-2(6)) Ken Smith.

Spreading "You Know" see World of James Thurber

Sprechen wir Deutsch! 2nd ed. Kathryn A. Corl et al. (GER., (C). 1989. bk. (978-0-318-64064-8(3)) Harcourt Coll Pubs.

Sprig Muslin. unabr. ed. Georgette Heyer. Read by Sian Phillips. 8 cass. (Running Time: 12 hrs.). 2000. 59.95 (978-0-7451-4134-3(X), CAB 817) Pub: Chivers Audio Bks GBR. Dist(s): AudioGO
Finding young Amanda wandering unattended, Sir Gareth Ludlow feels obligated to restore her to her family. His task proves difficult, however, when he learns that Amanda also has a runaway imagination.

Spriggan: Original Soundtrack. 1 CD. 2003. audio compact disk 14.98 (978-1-57813-379-6(3), CSP/001, ADV Music) A D Vision.

Spring. abr. unabr. ed. Garrison Keillor. 1 CD. (Running Time: 1 hr.). (ENG.). 1998. audio compact disk 13.95 (978-1-56511-250-6(4), 1565112504) Pub: HighBridge. Dist(s): Workman Pub

Spring: Classics for all Seasons. 1 cass., 1 CD. (J). 7.98 (TA 30321); audio compact disk 8.78 CD Jewel box. (TA 80321) NewSound.

Spring: Stories from the Collection. abr. ed. Garrison Keillor. 1 cass. (Running Time: 1 hr.). (ENG.). 1991. 11.00 (978-0-942110-19-7(6)) Pub: HighBridge. Dist(s): Workman Pub
Original best-selling collection of 20 Lake Wobegon monologues.

Spring: Where Can the Heart Be Hidden in the Ground see Poetry of Edna St. Vincent Millay

Spring A. D. see George Seferis

Spring Affair. Milly Johnson. 2009. 84.95 (978-0-7531-4378-0(X)); audio compact disk 99.95 (978-0-7531-4379-7(8)) Pub: Isis Pubng Ltd GBR. Dist(s): Ulverscroft US

Spring & All see Twentieth-Century Poetry in English, No. 4, Recordings of Poets Reading Their Own Poetry

Spring Audio CD. Adapted by Benchmark Education Company Staff. Based on a work by Francisco Blane. (My First Reader's Theater Ser.). (J). (gr. k-1). 2008. audio compact disk 10.00 (978-1-60634-085-1(9)) Benchmark Educ.

Spring Broke. unabr. ed. Melody Carlson. Narrated by Pam Turlow. (Running Time: 8 hrs. 27 mins. 4 sec.). (86 Bloomberg Place Ser.). (ENG.). 2009. 18.19 (978-1-60814-524-9(7)); audio compact disk 25.99 (978-1-59859-495-9(8)) Oasis Audio.

Spring Cleaning: Biblical Instruction for Freshening up the Christian Home. Matt Whitling & Douglas Wilson. (ENG.). 2008. audio compact disk 28.00 (978-1-59128-599-1(2)) Canon Pr ID.

Spring Emergence. Marina Bokelman. Read by Marina Bokelman. 1 cass. (Running Time: 1 hr.). (Seasonal Medicine Wheel Ser.). 1992. 9.95 (978-1-886139-01-5(6), SMW-1) Sacred Paw.
Attunement with seasonal energy, Spring healing issues, transformational process work.

Spring Forest Qigong: For Health, Set. Chunyi Lin & Paul R. Scheele. Read by Chunyi Lin & Paul R. Scheele. 6 cass. (Running Time: 7 hrs.). 2000. pap. bk. 245.00 (978-0-925480-33-0(9), 9QLC) Learn Strategies.
Eliminate pain & sickness through controlled breathing, focused concentration & simple movement. Includes video & CD.

Spring Forest Qigong Level One for Health Active Exercises. 1 CD. (Running Time: 60 mins). (C). 2003. audio compact disk 11.00 (978-0-9740944-4-1(7)) Spring Frst Qig.

Spring Forest Qigong Level One for Health Sitting Meditations. 1 CD. (Running Time: 60 mins). (C). 2003. audio compact disk 11.00 (978-0-9740944-5-8(5)) Spring Frst Qig.

Spring Music. unabr. ed. Elvi Rhodes. Read by Diana Bishop. 11 cass. (Running Time: 12 hrs.). (Sound Ser.). 2001. 89.95 (978-1-86042-494-6(5)) Pub: UlverLrgPrint GBR. Dist(s): Ulverscroft US
Naomi had been contentedly and, she thought, happily married for nearly all of her adult life when her husband, Edward, explained kindly to her one day that he had fallen in love with a twenty-six-year-old and wanted a divorce. Forced to leave the comfortable home she had shared with Edward and their three children, the dramatic change in her life threatened to overwhelm her. But gradually Naomi began to appreciate the changes, and even enjoy them.

Spring of the Tiger. unabr. ed. Victoria Holt. Read by Eva Haddon. 10 cass. (Running Time: 10 hrs.). 1993. bk. 84.95 (978-0-7451-6034-4(4), CAB 596) AudioGO.

Spring Pools see Robert Frost in Recital

Spring Rain. Perf. by Hennie Bekker. 1 cass. (Running Time: 50 min.). 1994. audio compact disk 15.95 CD. (2354, Creativ Pub) Quayside.
Original solo piano by one of Northern America's finest composers. Features piano artistry without nature sounds.

Spring Rain. Perf. by Hennie Bekker. 1 cass. (Running Time: 50 min.). 1994. 9.95 (2352, NrthWrd Bks) TandN Child.

***Spring Running: A Story from the Jungle Books.** Rudyard Kipling. 2009. (978-1-60136-512-5(8)) Audio Holding.

Spring Stars. 1 cass. (Running Time: 27 min.). 14.95 (23322) MMI Corp.
Spring constellations are discussed including Polaris, Large & Small Dippers, etc.

Spring Thunder see Gathering of Great Poetry for Children

Spring Tone. unabr. ed. Kazumi Yumoto. Read by Christina Moore. Tr. by Cathy Hirano. 3 cass. (Running Time: 4 hrs. 15 mins.). (YA). 2000. pap. bk. & stu. ed. 52.00 (978-0-7887-4189-0(6), 41112) Recorded Bks.
At night, Tomomi dreams she is a monster. Awake, she is horrified by how fast her body is growing. The safe world of childhood seems to be falling apart before her eyes. A sensitive portrait of a Japanese girl as she confronts the demons of adolescence.

Spring Tone. unabr. ed. Kazumi Yumoto. Tr. by Cathy Hirano. Narrated by Christina Moore. 3 pieces. (Running Time: 4 hrs. 15 mins.). (gr. 7 up). 2000. 29.00 (978-0-7887-4024-4(5), 96145E7) Recorded Bks.

Spring Tone, Class Set. unabr. ed. Kazumi Yumoto. Read by Christina Moore. Tr. by Cathy Hirano. 3 cass. (Running Time: 4 hrs. 15 mins.). (YA). 2000. 197.30 (978-0-7887-4190-6(X), 47105) Recorded Bks.

Spring Up, Oh Well. Read by Chris Thomas. 1 cass. (Running Time: 1 hr. 38 min.). (ICEL Three Ser.). 1996. 6.00 (978-1-57838-061-9(8)) CrossLife Express.
Christian living.

Springboard. Jack C. Richards. 1998. audio compact disk 22.75 (978-0-19-435197-3(1)) OUP.

Springboard. Jack C. Richards. 1999. audio compact disk 22.75 (978-0-19-435198-0(X)) OUP.

SpringBoard Marketing: Leverging Your Expertise into an Empire. 2004. (978-0-9716089-5-5(4)) Sullivan Speaker.

Springboard to Success: Communication Strategies for the Classroom & Beyond. Patricia J. Skillman & Cheiron S. McMahill. 2002. 22.00 (978-0-13-461393-2(7)) Longman.

Springing Voices: Really Happy Birds. Created by Thomas W. Gustin. 1 CD. (Running Time: 1 hr, 19 mins, 30 secs). 2004. audio compact disk 8.00 (978-0-9761848-5-0(0), EC5) Gustech.
Features 2 extremely high quality recordings made 31 Mar 03 & 11 Apr 03 here at the Emerald Cave. EC2 was so popular that by many requests, a second "Birds" volume has been added. You'll hear the flapping of wings as geese fly through your ears, & you'll enjoy this great escape along with the many other winged voices in the woods as they all express their delight with Nature.

Spring's Gentle Promise. Janette Oke. Read by Marguerite Gavin. 1 CD. (Running Time: 1 hr. 30 mins.). (Seasons of the Heart Ser.: Vol. 4). 2000. audio compact disk 19.95 (PZM2724) Blckstn Audio.
The farm belonged to Joshua Chadwick Jones. Grandpa & Uncle Charlie had signed all the official papers to make the farm his. Sobering down a bit, he realized the big responsibility it would be, for he had to support Grandpa, Uncle Charlie & himself. Adding to the challenge was a desire for a family of his own.

Spring's Gentle Promise. unabr. ed. Janette Oke. Read by Marguerite Gavin. 5 cass. (Running Time: 7 hrs.). (Seasons of the Heart Ser.: Vol. 4). 2001. 39.95 (978-0-7861-1953-0(5), 2724); audio compact disk 48.00 (978-0-7861-9768-2(4), 2724) Blckstn Audio.

***Spring's Renewal.** unabr. ed. Shelley Shepard Gray. (Running Time: 10 hrs. 30 mins.). (Seasons of Sugarcreek Ser.: Bk. 2). 2010. 29.95 (978-1-4417-7074-5(7)); 65.95 (978-1-4417-7071-4(2)); audio compact disk 100.00 (978-1-4417-7072-1(0)) Blckstn Audio.

Springtime a la Carte see Favorite Stories by O. Henry

Springtime Ghost. unabr. ed. Beverly Swerdlow Brown & Kate Brown. 1 cass. (Running Time: 8 min.). (Kate & Tracy Series: We Love a Mystery!). (J). (gr. 4-8). 1989. bk. 16.99 (978-0-87386-059-8(4)); pap. bk. 9.95 (978-0-87386-063-5(2)) Jan Prods.
In this adventure, Kate & Tracy visit a ghost town. Once again their active imaginations bring the "ghosts" to life until they figure out who their springtime ghost really is.

***Springtime of the Soul.** (ENG.). 2010. audio compact disk (978-0-9788646-2-0(X)) Daffodil Hill.

Springwater Wedding. Linda Lael Miller. Read by Kate Forbes. 9 CDs. (Springwater Seasons Ser.). 2004. audio compact disk 44.95 (978-0-7927-3246-4(4), SLD 389, Chivers Sound Lib) AudioGO.

Springwater Wedding. Linda Lael Miller. Read by Jenna Stern. (Springwater Seasons Ser.). 2004. 15.95 (978-0-7435-1944-1(2)) Pub: S&S Audio. Dist(s): S and S Inc

Springwater Wedding. unabr. ed. Linda Lael Miller. Read by Kate Forbes. 8 vols. (Running Time: 12 hrs.). (Springwater Seasons Ser.). 2001. bk. 69.95 (978-0-7927-2500-8(X), CSL 389, Chivers Sound Lib) AudioGO.
Once a frontier stagecoach stop, tiny Springwater has grown and changed and entered the twenty-first century. Heartbreak is still heartbreak, and love still love, and Springwater still boasts a rich legacy of joy, sorrow and second chances-as two childhood sweethearts discover when they rekindle a long-ago passion in the place they will always call home.

Sprituality of Diocesan Priesthood, Set. unabr. ed. George Aschenbrenner. 11 cass. (Running Time: 15 hrs. 7 min.). 1998. 89.95 (TAH408) Alba Hse Comns.
Includes "Diocesan Priestly Spirituality," "A Discerning Presence in the Midst of the People," "Administering the Inner Journey of God's Forgiveness" & "Evangelical Imperatives in Diocesan Priestly Spirituality.".

***Spud Gun Chronicles, Earthshine, the V. I. P., Lethal Words & Other Short Stories (Audio)** Colleen Hitchcock. (ENG.). (C). 2011. 19.95 (978-0-9723441-3-5(6), Leop Spot Pr) Leopard Spot.

Spur Fuhrt Nach Bayern. 3 cass. (Running Time: 3 hrs.). (Mystery Thrillers in German Ser.). (GER.). 2001. pap. bk. 49.95 (SGE114) J Norton Pubs.
Recorded by native professional actors in a radio-play format, these short-episode thrillers on an intermediate level were especially created to develop listening comprehension skills. Book provides a transcripts of the recording, exercises & vocabulary.

***Spur of the Moment.** (ENG.). 2010. audio compact disk (978-1-59171-253-4(X)) Falcon Picture.

Spurgeon Live Comfort Series. Speeches. 6 CDs. (Running Time: 4 hrs. 30 min.). Dramatization. 2004. audio compact disk 34.95 (978-0-9753214-0-9(4)) EarSightBible.

Spurgeon Live Newness Series. Speeches. 6 CDs. (Running Time: 4.5 hrs.). Dramatization. 2004. audio compact disk 34.95 (978-0-9753214-1-6(2)) EarSightBible.

***Spurious Glitter of Pantheism.** Featuring Ravi Zacharias. 1991. audio compact disk 9.00 (978-1-61256-044-1(X)) Ravi Zach.

Sputnik: The Shock of the Century. Paul Dickson. Narrated by Jerry Carrier. 2007. audio compact disk 33.95 (978-1-60031-024-9(9)) Spoken Books.

Spy. Ted Bell. Read by John Shea. (Hawke Ser.). 2008. 109.99 (978-1-60640-605-2(1)) Find a World.

Spy. James Fenimore Cooper. Read by Jim Killavey. 5 cass. (Running Time: 7 hrs.). 1989. 29.00 incl. album. (C-74) Jimcin Record.
Revolutionary war drama.

Spy. abr. ed. Ted Bell. Read by John Shea. (Running Time: 21600 sec.). (Hawke Ser.). 2007. audio compact disk 14.99 (978-1-59737-386-9(9), 9781597373869, BCD Value Price) Brilliance Audio.
Please enter a Synopsis.

Spy. abr. ed. Clive Cussler & Justin Scott. Contrib. by Richard Ferrone. (Running Time: 6 hrs.). (Isaac Bell Ser.: No. 3). (ENG.). 2010. audio compact disk 29.95 (978-0-14-242778-1(0), PengAudBks) Penguin Grp USA.

Spy. unabr. ed. Ted Bell. Read by John Shea. (Running Time: 16 hrs.). (Hawke Ser.). 2006. 39.25 (978-1-59737-390-6(7), 9781597373906, BADLE); 24.95 (978-1-59737-389-0(3), 9781597373890, BAD); 107.25 (978-1-59737-382-1(6), 9781597373821, BriAudUnabridg); audio compact disk 122.25 (978-1-59737-384-5(2), 9781597373845, BriAudCD Unabrid); audio compact disk 39.25 (978-1-59737-388-3(5), 9781597373883, Brlnc Audio MP3 Lib); audio compact disk 24.95 (978-1-59737-387-6(7), 9781597373876, Brilliance MP3); audio compact disk 39.95 (978-1-59737-383-8(4), 9781597373838, Bril Audio CD Unabri) Brilliance Audio.

Spy. unabr. ed. James Fenimore Cooper. Read by Flo Gibson. 10 cass. (Running Time: 14 hrs. 30 min.). 1993. 44.95 (978-1-55685-297-8(5)) Audio Bk Con.
At the time of the Revolutionary War, a peddler makes use of the suspicions that he is in league with the British in order to procure information for General Washington.

Spy. unabr. ed. Clive Cussler & Justin Scott. Contrib. by Scott Brick. 10 CDs. (Running Time: 13 hrs.). (Isaac Bell Ser.: No. 3). (ENG.). 2010. audio compact disk 39.95 (978-0-14-242779-8(9), PengAudBks) Penguin Grp USA.

Spy. unabr. collector's ed. James Fenimore Cooper. Read by Jim Roberts. 7 cass. (Running Time: 7 hrs.). (J). 1982. 42.00 (978-0-7366-3867-8(9), 9074) Books on Tape.
The theme is the American Revolutionary War & describes the conflicting interests of British & Americans. Harvey Birch is the hero, a true American & patriot.

Spy at the Heart of the Third Reich: He Extraordinary Life of Fritz Kolbe, America's Most Important Spy in World War II. unabr. ed. Lucas Delattre. Narrated by Michael Prichard. (Running Time: 10 hrs. 0 mins. 0 sec.). (ENG.). 2005. audio compact disk 19.99 (978-1-4001-5147-9(3)); audio compact disk 69.99 (978-1-4001-3147-1(2)) Pub: Tantor Media. Dist(s): IngramPubServ

Spy at the Heart of the Third Reich: The Extraordinary Life of Fritz Kolbe, America's Most Important Spy in World War II. unabr. ed. Lucas Delattre. Narrated by Michael Prichard. 8 CDs. (Running Time: 10 hrs. 0 mins. 0 sec.). (ENG.). 2005. audio compact disk 34.99 (978-1-4001-0147-4(6)) Pub: Tantor Media. Dist(s): IngramPubServ

Spy by Nature. unabr. ed. Charles Cumming. Narrated by Simon Vance. (Running Time: 12 hrs. 0 mins. 0 sec.). (ENG.). 2007. audio compact disk 29.99 (978-1-4001-5517-0(7)); audio compact disk 79.99 (978-1-4001-3517-2(6)) Pub: Tantor Media. Dist(s): IngramPubServ

Spy by Nature. unabr. ed. Charles Cumming. Read by Simon Vance. (Running Time: 12 hrs. 0 mins. 0 sec.). (ENG.). 2007. audio compact disk 39.99 (978-1-4001-0517-5(X)) Pub: Tantor Media. Dist(s): IngramPubServ

Spy for the Redeemer. Candace Robb. Read by Stephen Thorne. 10 cass. (Running Time: 11 hrs.). 2001. (978-1-84283-104-5(6)) Soundings Ltd GBR.

Spy in Chancery. unabr. ed. Paul C. Doherty. Narrated by Paul Matthews. 5 cass. (Running Time: 6 hrs. 30 mins.). 2000. 48.00 (978-1-84197-204-6(5), H1209L8) Recorded Bks.
During the war, King Edward I suspects that his enemy, Philip IV of France, is being aided by a spy in the English court. He commissions his chancery clerk, Hugh Corbett, to trace & destroy the traitor. Corbett soon finds himself in serious danger from a spy who will stop at nothing, not even murder, to keep his identity secret.

Spy in Petticoats. Katrina Wright. Read by Margaret Holt. 2 cass. (Running Time: 3 hrs.). 1999. 24.95 (62140) Pub: Soundings Ltd GBR. Dist(s): Ulverscroft US

Spy in Question, unabr. ed. Tim Sebastian. Narrated by Simon Prebble. 7 cass. (Running Time: 10 hrs.). 1992. 60.00 (978-1-55690-733-3(8), 92221E7) Recorded Bks.
Over 20 years ago Dmitry Kalyagin was the Communist Party's golden boy, a young, rising star in an aging & effete Kremlin. But someone had singled Kalyagin out for an entirely different future & one night in a Moscow discotheque, he danced with a girl named ira & came face-to-face with an irreversible fate.

Spy Killer. 20th anniv. unabr. ed. L. Ron Hubbard. Read by Roddy McDowell. 2 CDs. (Running Time: 2 hrs.). (Stories from the Golden Age Ser.). 2008. audio compact disk 9.95 (978-1-59212-166-3(7)) Gala Pr LLC.

Spy Meeting. (Sails Literacy Ser.). (gr. 2 up). 10.00 (978-0-7578-2673-3(3)) Rigby Educ.

Spy Next Door: The Extraordinary Secret Life of Robert Philip Hanssen, the Most Damaging FBI Agent in U. S. History. abr. ed. Elaine Shannon & Ann Blackman. 4 cass. (Running Time: 4 hrs. 30 min.). 2002. 24.98 (978-1-58621-250-6(8)) Hachet Audio.
Two veterans of Time magazine's Washington bureau, with years of experience covering crime, espionage & national affairs, uncover how one man almost single-handedly devised & operated a 15-year spying operation from within the ranks of one of the most exclusive, sophisticated & carefully guarded counter-espionage organizations in the world.

Spy Next Door: The Extraordinary Secret Life of Robert Philip Hanssen, the Most Damaging FBI Agent in U. S. History. unabr. ed. Elaine Shannon & Ann Blackman. Read by Barbara Daniels Korsen. 8 vols. (Running Time: 12 hrs.). 2002. bk. 69.95 (978-0-7927-2538-1(7), CSL 427, Chivers Sound Lib); audio compact disk 94.95 (978-0-7927-9866-8(X), SLD 117, Chivers Sound Lib) AudioGO.
Robert Hanssen was a trusted and loyal FBI agent. he had almost total access to the most sensitive material and her was in a position to betray more valuable secrets than almost anyone else. And he did. Now veteran Time reporters reveal the truth about Robert Hanssen and his 15 years of exceptionally destructive espionage.

Spy Shadow, unabr. ed. Tim Sebastian. Narrated by Simon Prebble. 8 cass. (Running Time: 11 hrs.). 1992. 70.00 (978-1-55690-766-1(4), 92413E7) Recorded Bks.
Secret Service agent James Tristram links the death of an Underground leader in Poland with the murder of an old man in London's King's Cross. With the leadership crumbling in Moscow & the Polish Underground gaining momentum, Tristram feels the time is ripe to send someone back to finish the job he left undone. When he discovers that the Underground uprising will be used as the pretext for the Soviet Union to intervene, Tristram has to confront a past destined to repeat itself.

Spy Story. unabr. ed. Len Deighton. Read by Robert Whitfield. 1 CD. (Running Time: 6 hrs. 30 mins.). 2001. audio compact disk 19.95 (zm2596) Blckstn Audio.
Cocky, sardonic Charles Schlegel the third, Colonel U.S. Marine Corps Air Wing (retired), with the iron handshake & a flat refusal to let anything stand in his way, is brought in to run London's Strategic War Game Studies Centre. Under a joint Anglo-American naval warfare committee, military computers match NATO defense strategies against theoretical Russian strike threats. Schlegel appoints Deighton's spy hero his personal assistant.

Spy Who Came for Christmas. unabr. ed. David Morrell. Read by David Colacci. 1 MP3-CD. (Running Time: 6 hrs.). 2008. 24.95 (978-1-4233-6172-5(5), 9781423361725, Brilliance MP3); 39.25 (978-1-4233-6175-6(X), 9781423361756, BADLE); 39.25 (978-1-4233-6173-2(3), 9781423361732, Brlnc Audio MP3 Lib); 24.95 (978-1-4233-6174-9(1), 9781423361749, BAD); audio compact disk 74.25 (978-1-4233-6171-8(7), 9781423361718, BriAudCD Unabrid); audio compact disk 26.99 (978-1-4233-6170-1(9), 9781423361701, Bril Audio CD Unabri) Brilliance Audio.

Spy Who Came in from the Cold. John le Carré. Read by John le Carré. 2 cass. (George Smiley Ser.). 34.95 Inc. Transcript & leaner's guide. (S23911) J Norton Pubs.

Spy Who Came in from the Cold. unabr. ed. John le Carré. Read by Simon Russell Beale. 2009. audio compact disk 19.95 (978-1-60283-658-7(2)) AudioGO.

Spy Who Came in from the Cold, unabr. ed. John le Carré. Narrated by Frank Muller. 5 cass. (Running Time: 6 hrs. 15 mins.). (George Smiley Novels Ser.). 1987. 44.00 (978-1-55690-491-2(6), RD805) Recorded Bks.
Alec Leamas, a burned-out secret agent is put into the field for one last mission.

Spy Who Came in from the Cold. unabr. collector's ed. John le Carré. Read by Chris Winfield. 6 cass. (Running Time: 6 hrs.). (George Smiley Novels Ser.). 1977. 36.00 (978-0-7366-2929-4(7), 3625) Books on Tape.
Too long in the service, a tired British spy gears up for one final assignment.

Spy Who Came North from the Pole Vol. III: Mr. Pin. unabr. ed. Mary Elise Monsell. Narrated by John McDonough. 1 cass. (Running Time: 1 hr.). (gr. 2 up). 1997. 10.00 (978-0-7887-1344-6(2), 95193E7) Recorded Bks.
When a penguin is seen smashing a stone gargoyle, the Chicago police blame Mr. Pin. The feathered detective must find the culprit, quickly, or lose his reputation forever. As he munches his way through the chocolate clues in two puzzling cases, the lovable penguin from the South teaches that appearances can be misleading.

Spy Who Died of Boredom. unabr. ed. George Mikes. Read by Dan Lazar. 8 cass. (Running Time: 8 hrs.). 48.00 (978-0-7366-2930-0(0), 1028) Books on Tape.
Posted to London, a young Russian undercover agent determines that British secrets will fall to him from the lips of British secretaries whom he seduces. He sets for himself a prodigious pace & we are treated to a humorous interpretation of coexistence.

Spy Who Loved Me. unabr. ed. Ian Fleming. Read by Rula Lenska. 4 cass. (Running Time: 6 hrs.). 1990. 39.95 set. (978-0-7451-5934-8(6), CAB 406) AudioGO.
James Bond has never before met a woman quite like the magnetic Vivienne Michel. Captivated by her fascinating sensual past, he learns too late that Vivienne's history also contains some deadly elements: for some reason, she is being pursued by several sadistic killers.

Spy Who Loved Me. unabr. ed. Ian Fleming. 5 CDs. (Running Time: 5 hrs. 30 mins.). 2001. audio compact disk 40.00 (978-0-7861-9718-7(8), 2783) Blckstn Audio.
For the first time in a James Bond adventure, we see Agent 007 as he appears through the eyes of a beautiful woman... a woman who, in the midst of brutality and terror, meets Bond and recognizes him for what he is. A handsome and appealing killer. But only a killer can help her now.

Spy Who Loved Me. unabr. ed. Ian Fleming. Read by Nadia May. 4 cass. (Running Time: 5 hrs. 30 mins.). 2001. 32.95 (978-0-7861-2015-4(0), 2783) Blckstn Audio.

Spy Who Loved Me. unabr. ed. Ian Fleming. Read by Nadia May. (Running Time: 5 hrs. 0 mins.). (James Bond Ser.: No. 10). 2009. audio compact disk 19.95 (978-1-4332-6133-6(2)) Blckstn Audio.

Spy Who Loved Me: James Bond Series #10. unabr. ed. Ian Fleming. Read by Nadia May. (Running Time: 1 hr. 0 mins.). (ENG.). 2009. 29.95 (978-1-4332-9037-4(5)) Blckstn Audio.

Spy Wore Red, unabr. ed. Aline, Countess of Romanones. Read by Grace Conlin. 8 cass. (Running Time: 11 hrs. 30 mins.). 1995. 56.95 (978-0-7861-0753-7(7), 1604) Blckstn Audio.
When Aline Griffith was born in Pearl River, New York, in 1923, one might have guessed that a career as an actress or a model might be in her future. Few would have imagined that twenty-one years later, she would find herself in Spain, as a deep-cover OSS agent, infiltrating the highest levels of Spanish society; or that five years later still, she would marry a Spanish grandee & become one of the most watched, most admired, most fascinating women of international society. This is the story of Aline, Countess of Romanones, a story of courage, beauty & success that is far more exciting than any fictionalized thriller.

Spy Wore Red. unabr. ed. Aline, Countess of Romanones. Read by Grace Conlin. 9 CDs. (Running Time: 13 hrs. 30 min.). 2000. audio compact disk 72.00 (z1604) Blckstn Audio.
When Aline Griffith was born in Pearl River, New York, in 1923, one might have guessed from her exceptional beauty that a career as an actress or a

model would be in her future. Few would have imagined that twenty-one years later, she would find herself in Spain as a deep-cover OSS agent, infiltrating the highest levels of Spanish society; or that five years later still, she would marry a Spanish grandee & become one of the most watched, most admired, most fascinating women of international society.

Spy Wore Red. unabr. ed. Aline Countess of Romanones Staff. Read by Grace Conlin. 9 CDs. (Running Time: 11 hrs. 30 mins.). 2001. audio compact disk 72.00 (978-0-7861-9803-0(6), 1604) Blckstn Audio.

Spy Wore Shades. unabr. ed. Martha Freeman. Narrated by Carine Montbertrand. 4 pieces. (Running Time: 5 hrs. 15 mins.). (gr. 4 up). 2002. 37.00 (978-1-4025-1453-1(0)) Recorded Bks.
This fantasy teams together two delightful characters: Varloo, from the secret underground Druid caves known as Hek, and Dougie, from the lands above this civilization, suburban California. These two unlikely heroes realize that a plan to build a development on the land above the caves must be stopped in order to preserve their existence. Luckily, Dougie's mom is an attorney who tries to keep the developers at bay for environmental reasons. Can they stop the construction and save the day before it's too late?.

Spycatcher. unabr. ed. Peter Wright. Read by Bill Kelsey. 12 cass. (Running Time: 18 hrs.). 1990. 96.00 (978-0-7366-1725-3(6), 2566) Books on Tape.
Peter Wright has been called the real-life model for John le Carre's George Smiley. A top professional, he left British Intelligence in 1976 when the government repeatedly refused to pursue his inquiries into the infamous "Fifth Man" in the Burgess-Maclean-Philby-Blunt KGB spy ring. The document he prepared for the original investigation forms the basis for this incredible book: an uncensored account of the business of spying & of the behavior of British & American spies - a work so revealing it could not be published in Britain.

Spycraft: The Secret History of the CIA's Spytechs from Communism to Al-Qaeda. Robert Wallace & H. Keith Melton. Read by David Drummond. Told to Henry Robert Schlesinger. Frwd. by George J. Tenet. (Playaway Adult Nonfiction Ser.). 2008. 89.99 (978-1-60640-876-6(3)) Find a World.

Spycraft: The Secret History of the CIA's Spytechs from Communism to Al-Qaeda. unabr. ed. Robert Wallace et al. Narrated by David Drummond. (Running Time: 19 hrs. 30 mins. 0 sec.). (ENG.). 2008. audio compact disk 49.99 (978-1-4001-0714-8(8)); audio compact disk 34.99 (978-1-4001-5714-3(5)); audio compact disk 99.99 (978-1-4001-3714-5(4)) Pub: Tantor Media. Dist(s): IngramPubServ

Spyder Web. Tom Grace. Read by Michael Kramer. 1999. audio compact disk 72.00 (978-0-7366-5166-0(7)) Books on Tape.

Spyder Web. Tom Grace. 2000. (978-1-57042-935-4(9)) Hachet Audio.

Spyder Web. abr. ed. Tom Grace. (ENG.). 2006. 14.98 (978-1-59483-724-1(4)) Pub: Hachet Audio. Dist(s): HachBkGrp

Spyder Web. unabr. ed. Tom Grace. Read by Michael Kramer. 8 cass. (Running Time: 12 hrs.). 1999. 64.00 (978-0-7366-4461-7(X), 4906) Books on Tape.
Nolan Kilkenny is a former Navy SEAL now pursuing his doctorate in advanced computer technology. While investigating a seemingly harmless technical problem in a complex, highly secured computer network, he becomes involved in the CIA & FBI's fierce hunt for three computer-age information pirates. The ruthless, brilliant thieves have stolen SPYDER - the CIA's ultra-secret electronic intelligence gathering project that can pry open the most heavily-guarded computer networks in existence - & the United States government will do anything to get it back. Suddenly, Kilkenny is leading the search for SPYDER...& is in sharp focus in the crosshairs of those who will stop at nothing to possess the ultimate spy weapon.

Spyder Web. unabr. ed. Tom Grace. Read by Michael Kramer. 9 CDs. (Running Time: 13 hrs. 30 mins.). (Men at War Ser.). 2001. audio compact disk 72.00 Books on Tape.
A former Navy SEAL becomes involved in the CIA and FBI's hunt to recover SPYDER - the CIA's ultra-secret electronic intelligence project.

Spyder Web, Set. abr. ed. Tom Grace. Read by Gregory Harrison. 4 cass. 1999. 22.00 (FS9-43333) Highsmith.

Spyhole Secrets. Zilpha Keatley Snyder. Narrated by Christina Moore. 4 CDs. (Running Time: 4 hrs. 15 mins.). (J). (gr. 6 up). audio compact disk 39.00 (978-1-4025-1489-0(1)) Recorded Bks.

Spyhole Secrets. unabr. ed. Zilpha Keatley Snyder. Narrated by Christina Moore. 3 pieces. (Running Time: 4 hrs. 15 mins.). (J). (gr. 6 up). 2001. 29.00 (978-0-7887-8970-0(8), 96699) Recorded Bks.
Hallie Meredith is having a tough time adjusting to her new life and new surroundings. It all started with the death of her father in a car crash. Hallie mother had to find a job in a new town, and they moved into a small apartment in a dreary old mansion far away from her friends and without her beloved pets. Now three months later, nothing has improved for Hallie. Her new middle school has been horrible. Feeling the need to get away from everything, especially her own misery, Hallie begins exploring the mansion's dusty and forbidden attic.

Spy's Wife. Reginald Hill. 2009. 49.95 (978-0-7531-3920-2(0)); audio compact disk 71.95 (978-0-7531-3921-9(9)) Pub: Isis Pubng Ltd GBR. Dist(s): Ulverscroft US

Spytime: The Undoing of James Jesus Angleton. unabr. ed. William F. Buckley, Jr. Read by Raymond Todd. 6 cass. (Running Time: 8 hrs. 30 mins.). 2001. 44.95 (978-0-7861-1967-7(5), 2737); audio compact disk 56.00 (978-0-7861-9758-3(7), 2737) Blckstn Audio.
From his early involvement in the World War II underground to the waning days of the Cold War in Washington, D.C., Angleton pursued his enemies, real & imagined, with a cool, calculating intelligence & an unwillingness to take anything at face value. Convinced that there was a turncoat within the CIA itself, he confused his enemy by misleading acts & deceptive feints to distort his real objective - to capture & expose a traitor. The making & tragic unmaking of a man without peer & at the end, a man without a country to serve.

Squadron Airborne. unabr. collector's ed. Elleston Trevor. Read by Christopher Hurt. 6 cass. (Running Time: 9 hrs.). 1986. 48.00 (978-0-7366-0754-4(4), 1707) Books on Tape.
The story of the young men who fought the Battle of Britain in the skies over England during the summer of 1940.

Squandering Aimlessly: My Adventures in the American Marketplace. David Brancaccio. 2004. 10.95 (978-0-7435-1884-0(5)) Pub: S&S Audio. Dist(s): S and S Inc

Squanto. Matthew G. Grant. (J). 1974. 7.95 Creat Teach Pr.

Square Dance Fun for Everyone. Instructed by Rudy Franklin. 2 cass. 2001. pap. bk. 18.95 (KEA 1138C) Kimbo Educ.
The basic fundamentals of American square dance. Traveling Minstrel Man, Early Morning Rain, Briar Patch & more. Includes manual.

Square Dancing: The American Way. 2 LPs. (J). 2001. pap. bk. 20.95 (KIM 4061); pap. bk. 24.95 (KIM 4061CD); 18.95 (KIM 4061C) Kimbo Educ.
Contains all basics & features swing & grand square. Country western music includes Real Madrid, Sugar Blues, God Bless America, Happy Days Are Here Again & more. Includes manual.

Square Dancing Made Easy. 1 CD. (Running Time: 1 hr.). (J). 2001. bk. 14.95 (EA 680CD); pap. bk. 11.95 (EA 680C) Kimbo Educ.
A follow-up to Get Ready to Square Dance, easy-to-follow square dances. Flop-Eared Mule, Old Dan Tucker, Yee-Ha!, Basketball Square Dance, Cowboy, Whoopin' It Up & more. Includes guide.

Square Rigger Round the Horn. unabr. collector's ed. C. Ray Wilmore. Read by Jonathan Reese. 8 cass. (Running Time: 8 hrs.). 1976. 48.00 (978-0-7366-0010-1(8), 1020) Books on Tape.
Wilmore sailed the last of the wind ships.

Square Root of Murder. unabr. ed. 2 cass. (Running Time: 3 hrs.). (YA). (gr. 5-9). 2003. 19.00 (978-1-4025-1812-6(9)) Recorded Bks.
High school sleuths P.C. Hawke and Mackenzie Riggs quickly regret their decision to take a difficult calculus class from a tough instructor at Columbia University. But even though she¿s mean, Professor Dunaway certainly seems an unlikely candidate for murder. Though there are plenty of suspects, a lot of things about this case just don¿t add up.

Squashed, unabr. ed. Joan Bauer. Narrated by C. J. Critt. 5 pieces. (Running Time: 6 hrs.). (gr. 6 up). 1997. 44.00 (978-0-7887-0683-7(7), 94857E7) Recorded Bks.
Sixteen-year-old Ellie Morgan wants to become the first teenager to win the Rock River Pumpkin Weigh-In. Can she beat the obnoxious four-time defending champion Cyril Pool?.

Squashed in the Middle. Elizabeth Winthrop. Read by Robin Miles. Illus. by Pat Cummins. 1 cass. (Running Time: 8 mins.). (J). (gr. k-4). 2008. bk. 25.95 (978-1-4301-0440-7(6)); bk. 28.95 (978-1-4301-0443-8(0)) Live Oak Media.

Squawk! How to Stop Making Noise & Start Getting Results. Travis Bradberry. Read by Lloyd James. (Playaway Adult Nonfiction Ser.). (ENG.). 2009. 40.00 (978-1-60775-626-2(9)) Find a World.

Squawk! How to Stop Making Noise & Start Getting Results. unabr. ed. Travis Bradberry. Narrated by Lloyd James. (Running Time: 2 hrs. 30 mins. 0 sec.). (ENG.). 2008. audio compact disk 19.99 (978-1-4001-0766-7(0)); audio compact disk 39.99 (978-1-4001-3766-4(7)); audio compact disk 19.99 (978-1-4001-5766-2(8)) Pub: Tantor Media. Dist(s): IngramPubServ

***Squeaky Wheel: Complaining the Right Way to Get Results, Improve Your Relationships, & Enhance Self-Esteem.** unabr. ed. Guy Winch. Read by Sean Runnette. Renaissance Books Staff. (Running Time: 9 hrs. 0 mins. 0 sec.). (ENG.). 2011. audio compact disk 29.99 (978-1-4272-1197-2(3)) Pub: Macmill Audio. Dist(s): Macmillan

Squeeze Play. unabr. ed. Jane Leavy. 10 cass. (Running Time: 14 hrs. 30 mins.). 2003. 69.95 (978-0-7861-2586-9(1), 3187) Blckstn Audio.
Reporter A. B. Berkowitz finds herself "alone with a locker room full of naked men" as she tries to write about the game of baseball amidst players who only want to gross her out, in this funny, raunchy, authentic tale by a former Washington Post sportswriter. Sure to offend some people who cried during Field of Dreams - and that's good enough for me." -.

Squeeze Play. unabr. ed. Jane Leavy. Read by Anna Fields. 12 CDs. (Running Time: 14 hrs. 30 mins.). 2003. audio compact disk 96.00 (978-0-7861-8980-9(0), 3187) Blckstn Audio.

Squiggle & Squirm: Moon-Star Records. Sandi Johnson. Narrated by Lynette Louise. 1 cass., 1 CD. (J). (ps-6). 1996. 4.99 (978-1-929063-23-9(7), 123); audio compact disk 9.99 CD. (978-1-929063-24-6(5), 124) Moons & Stars.
Two worms help cultivate the soil & get ready for Spring. Includes song.

Squire. Tamora Pierce. Read by Bernadette Dunne. 9 CDs. (Running Time: 10 hrs. 49 mins.). (Protector of the Small Ser.: No. 3). (YA). (gr. 7-9). 2007. audio compact disk 65.00 (978-0-7393-6165-8(1), Listening Lib) Pub: Random Audio Pubg. Dist(s): Random
When Keladry of Mindelan is chosen by the legendary Lord Raoul to be his squire, the conservatives of the realm hardly think she's up to the job. Kel quickly proves her ability as a jouster, warrior, and guardian of a fiery griffin, ultimately earning respect and admiration among the men, as well as the affection of a fellow squire. In addition to coping with the challenges of a new romance and a life in the royal guard, Kel must also prepare for the infamous "Ordeal," the last challenge that stands between her and her dream of knighthood.

Squire. unabr. ed. Tamora Pierce. Read by Bernadette Dunne. (Protector of the Small Ser.: No. 3). (ENG.). (J). (gr. 5). 2009. audio compact disk 44.00 (978-0-7393-6183-2(X), Listening Lib) Pub: Random Audio Pubg. Dist(s): Random

Squirrel Cage, Set. Dorothy Canfield Fisher. Read by Flo Gibson. 8 cass. (Running Time: 12 hrs.). 1990. 26.95 (978-1-55685-156-8(1)) Audio Bk Con.
The quest for social standing & financial advancement blurs communications & perceptions of Lydia's parents & her husband. Only Rankin dares to seek the true values of life that she longs for.

Squirrel Nutkin see Favorite Children's Stories: A Collection

***Squirrel Seeks Chipmunk: A Modest Bestiary.** unabr. ed. David Sedaris. Read by David Sedaris. Read by Dylan Baker et al. (Running Time: 3 hrs.). (ENG.). 2010. 21.98 (978-1-60788-646-4(4)) Pub: Hachet Audio. Dist(s): HachBkGrp

Squirrel Seeks Chipmunk: A Modest Bestiary. unabr. ed. David Sedaris. Read by David Sedaris. Read by Dylan Baker et al. 3 CDs. (Running Time: 3 hrs.). 2010. audio compact disk 24.98 (978-1-60024-499-5(8)) Pub: Hachet Audio. Dist(s): HachBkGrp

Squirrels All Year Long. Sundance/Newbridge, LLC Staff. (Early Science Ser.). (gr. k-3). 2007. audio compact disk 12.00 (978-1-4007-6406-8(8)); audio compact disk 12.00 (978-1-4007-6408-2(4)); audio compact disk 12.00 (978-1-4007-6407-5(6)) Sund Newbrdge.

Squirt. 1 CD. (Running Time: 20 min.). (Good to Grow Ser.). (J). (ps-3). 2001. pap. bk. & act. bk. ed. 8.95 (978-1-929962-02-0(9)) Write BIG.
A lighthearted look at a neighborhood water fight. Listeners learn that friendships are important and that "hate" should be avoided.

Squonks, Moskittos & Gillygaloos & Rattlers & Rollers. abr. ed. Adrien Stoutenburg. Read by Ed Begley. 1 cass. (Running Time: 90 min.). (J). 1984. 9.95 (978-0-89845-520-5(0), CDL5 1317) HarperCollins Pubs.

Sraight Talk about Sex. 2003. audio compact disk 6.95 (978-1-932631-06-7(2)) Ascensn Pr.

Sredni Vashtar see Saki: Strange Tales

Sredni Vashtar, Vol. 5. unabr. ed. Saki. Narrated by Amato Petale. 1 cass. (Running Time: 44 min.). Incl. After Twenty Years. O. Henry. (J). 1984.; Dr. Heidegger's Experiment. Nathaniel Hawthorne. (J). 1984.; (Fantasies Ser.). (J). 1984. 17.95 Incl. holder, scripts, lesson plans, & tchr's. guide. (978-0-86617-046-8(4)) Multi Media TX.
Comprehensive lesson plans that use classic short stories to develop skills in listening, reading, vocabulary, following details, making inferences, visualization, drawing conclusions, critical appreciation & comparison. This module's objective is to compare different stories by the same writer, pointing out what appears to be typical subjects, purposes, values, recurring characters or themes.

Sri Brahma Samhita. 1 cass.; 1 CD. 4.95 (CD-4); audio compact disk 14.95 CD. Bhaktivedanta.

Sri Caitaya-Caritamrta. Krsnadasa Kaviraja. Tr. by Srila Prabhupada. 32 cass,. 60.00 Album. Bhaktivedanta.

Sri Isopanisad. Tr. by Srila Prabhupada. 4 cass. 18.00 Set, incl. 1 vinyl album. Bhaktivedanta.
The most confidential of the Upanisads, these eighteen jewel-like mantras of Sri Isopanisad can release us from the bleak, unsatisfying conceptions of impersonalism & bring us in touch with the primeval original Personality, who is the fountainhead of all energies. Provides insights into the nature of the supreme intelligence that governs the universe.

Sri Rama. Sivananda Radha. 1 cass. 1993. 9.95 (978-0-931454-44-8(1)) Timeless Bks.
Swami Radha chants traditional ancient Mantra. Effective in keeping the mind centered while working, or for meditation.

Sri Sri Gurvastakam. 1 cass.; 1 CD. 4.95 (CD-10); audio compact disk 14.95 CD. Bhaktivedanta.

Sri Sri Siksastakam. 1 cass.; 1 CD. 4.95 (CD-11); audio compact disk 14.95 CD. Bhaktivedanta.

Sriking Out at Stress. Harold H. LeCrone. 2 cass. 21.95 Self-Control Sys.
Learn to reduce stress & tension in your life.

Srila Prabhupada Bhajans. 35 cass. (Running Time: 1 hr. 30 min. per cass.). 85.00 set. Prabhupada Inst.
Original unedited bhajans.

Srila Prabhupada Kirtans. Perf. by Srila Prabhupada. (Running Time: 60 min.). 3.95 Prabhupada Inst.

Srimad-Bhagavatam: The Science of Knowing God. Tr. by Srila Prabhupada. 16 cass. 60.00 Album. Bhaktivedanta.

SS Francais. 1 cass. (FRE.). 1995. 16.95 (1741-RF) Olivia & Hill.
In 1943 almost 8,000 Frenchmen joined the elite Nazi troops: the SS. Three among them tell their story without remorse.

Ssm Intro Math Mod Discr Dyn. (C). 2005. audio compact disk 30.95 (978-0-495-01746-2(9)) Pub: Brooks-Cole. Dist(s): CENGAGE Learn

St Albans Fire. Archer Mayor. Read by Christopher Graybill. 6 cass. (Joe Gunther Ser.). 54.95 (978-0-7927-3798-8(9), CSL 865); audio compact disk 74.95 (978-0-7927-3799-5(7), SLD 865) AudioGO.

St. Anselm: Reasonable Faith. Thomas Merton. 1 cass. (Running Time: 62 min.). 1993. 8.95 (AA2618) Credence Commun.
Merton explores the creative theology of the period in which Anselm lived & shows how Anselm demonstrated the existence of God by the persistent use of reason.

St. Augustine. Thomas Merton. 1 cass. (Running Time: 60 min.). (Church Fathers Ser.). 8.95 (AA2236) Credence Commun.
Commentary on St. Augustine - church father.

St. Augustine. R. J. O'Connell. Read by Charlton Heston. (Running Time: 7200 sec.). (Audio Classics Ser.). 2006. audio compact disk 25.95 (978-0-7861-6933-7(8)) Pub: Blckstn Audio. Dist(s): NetLibrary CO

St. Augustine, unabr. ed. Read by Charlton Heston. 2 cass. (Giants of Philosophy Ser.). 17.95 (K119) Blckstn Audio.
See how one of the world's most important philosophers created a complete system of thought, including his views on ethics, metaphysics, politics & aesthetics. Learn about his epistemology - how we know what we know.

St. Augustine: Its History & Attractions. unabr. ed. Read by Joyce Jerden & Michael Emerson. 1 cass. (Running Time: 1 hr. 20 min.). 4.95 (978-0-9630499-0-2(9)) B J Fitz.
Side 1 tells of St. Augustine's colorful history as our country's oldest, continuously inhabited, European city. Side 2 details its museums & other attractions.

St. Augustine in 90 Minutes. unabr. ed. Paul Strathern. Read by Robert Whitfield. (Running Time: 2 hrs. NaN mins.). 2009. audio compact disk 22.95 (978-0-7861-3679-7(0)); audio compact disk 27.00 (978-1-4332-6798-7(5)) Blckstn Audio.

St. Augustine Stories. Prod. by Richard Wall. 2 CDs. (Running Time: 2 hrs. 25 mins.). Dramatization. 2003. audio compact disk (978-0-9749321-0-1(8)) Walk Ab St Aug.
The history of St. Augustine, Florida, from 1565 to the present told in stories by 21 people from the town's past (portrayed by actors) and one contemporary resident.

St. Augustine's Confessions, I-II. Instructed by William Cook & Ronald Herzman. 12 cass. (Running Time: 12 hrs.). bk. 54.95 (978-1-56585-875-6(1), 6627) Teaching Co.

St. Augustine's Confessions, Vol. I-II. Instructed by William Cook & Ronald Herzman. 12 CDs. (Running Time: 12 hrs.). 2004. bk. 69.95 (978-1-56585-877-0(8), 6627) Teaching Co.

St. Barts Breakdown. unabr. ed. Don Bruns. Read by Paul Michael Garcia. (Running Time: 8.5 hrs. NaN mins.). 2008. 29.95 (978-1-4332-3153-7(0)); audio compact disk 70.00 (978-1-4332-3150-6(6)); audio compact disk 54.95 (978-1-4332-3149-0(2)) Blckstn Audio.

St. Benedict, Hero of the Hills. Mary F. Windeatt. 4 cass. (J). 18.95 (512) Ignatius Pr.
The life of the founder of the Benedictine Order.

St. Dale. unabr. ed. Sharyn McCrumb. Read by Anna Fields. 6 cass. (Ballad Ser.: No. 8). 2005. 54.95 (978-0-7927-3465-9(3), CSL 756); audio compact disk 74.95 (978-0-7927-3466-6(1), SLD 756) AudioGO.

St. Dominic & the Rosary. Catherine Beebe. 5 cass. (J). 22.95 (509) Ignatius Pr.
Dramatic account of the vocation & life of St. Dominic.

St. Dominic Savior. John Bosco. 5 cass. (J). 22.95 (502) Ignatius Pr.
Story for young people of St. Dominic Savio by the Saint who was his teacher & confessor.

St. Faustina's Way of The Cross. Dave Maroney. audio compact disk 14.95 (978-1-59614-120-9(4)) Marian Pr.

St. Francis Dane Disaster. Kenneth Bruce. 1 cass. (Running Time: 1 hr.). Dramatization. (Excursions in History Ser.). 12.50 Alpha Tape.

St. Francis of Assisi. G. K. Chesterton. Read by Paul Rogers. 4 cass. (Running Time: 6 hrs.). 1995. 19.95 (711-C) Ignatius Pr.
A classic life of Saint Francis by one of this century's greatest Catholic authors.

St. Francis of Assisi. unabr. ed. G. K. Chesterton. Read by Bernard Mayes. 4 cass. (Running Time: 5 hrs. 30 mins.). 1992. 32.95 (978-0-7861-0128-3(8), 1114) Blckstn Audio.
This biography examines the life of a pure artist, a man whose whole life was a poem. Yet St. Francis also aknowledges the mystic responsibility to communicate his divine experience.

St. Francis of Assisi: A New Way of Being Christian. Br. Bill Short. 2008. audio compact disk 59.95 (978-0-9795255-5-1(1)) Now You Know.

St. Francis of Paola. Gino Simi & Mario Segreti. 8 cass. 32.95 (729) Ignatius Pr.
God's miracle worker supreme who cured the sick & raised the dead.

St. Francis of the Seven Seas. Albert Nevins. 4 cass. (J). 18.95 (505) Ignatius Pr.
Francis Xavier travels to India & Japan to bring the Gospel to the East.

St. Gemma Galgani. Leo Prosperio. 9 cass. 36.95 (756) Ignatius Pr.
A young mystic who advised peasants & Popes.

St. George & the Dragon. Theo S. Brown & Toby Brown. Read by Theo S. Brown. Contrib. by Patty Forbes. 1 cass. (J). (ps-5). 1993. cass. & video 150.00 Incl. audio tape & bklt. (978-1-884151-00-2(0)) Manitou WA.
The video is of a live stage performance of "St. George & the Dragon." There is an abundance of audience participation in which the video viewer may take part. The audio tape contains background information for the teacher plus all the songs from the play with & without the lyrics. The music has been rekeyed for children's voices & is in the booklet as well as information about the play.

St. George & the Dragon. Manuel Media. (J). 1985. bk. 44.43 (978-0-676-31261-4(6)) RandomHse Pub.

St. Helena. Christopher Knight. 1999. 10.00 (978-1-893699-01-4(3)) AudioCraft.

St. Jerome, God's Grouch. 1 cass. (Running Time: 60 min.). (Church Fathers Ser.). 8.95 (978-7-900781-28-4(5), AA2237) Credence Commun.
Commentary on St. Jerome.

St. Joan of Arc. John Beevers. 7 cass. 28.95 (716) Ignatius Pr.
A modern portrait of the warrior maiden, patroness of France.

St. John Fisher. E. E. Reynolds. 7 cass. 28.95 (724) Ignatius Pr.
English Bishop & martyr during the reign of Henry VIII.

St. John of the Cross. Gregory Elmer. Perf. by Gregory Elmer. 10 cass. (Running Time: 10 hrs.). 1996. pap. bk. (AA2992) Credence Commun.
Exploration of mystical prayer.

St. John of the Cross: A Retreat with Ernest Larkin, O. Carm. Redemptorist Pastoral Communications Staff. 4 cass. (Running Time: 60 min. per cass.). 1992. 29.95 set. (978-0-89243-459-6(7)) Liguori Pubns.
This retreat is based on the life & writings of St. John of the Cross, with special attention to his poetry. John's teaching concentrates on inner renewal & union with God. Listeners will learn how the journey to his union relates to contemporary spirituality.

St. John of the Cross: The Person, His Times, His Wisdom. Michael Dodd. Read by Michael Dodd. 1 cass. (Running Time: 62 min.). 8.95 I C S Pubns.
Fr. Michael Dodd, O.C.D. presents a verbal biography of St. John of the Cross showing what influence his family & his life within the Carmelite Order had upon his not so easy to understand writings.

St. John of the Cross: Thomas Merton & American Responses. Steven Payne. 1 cass. (Running Time: 73 min.). 8.95 I C S Pubns.
Fr. Steven Payne, O.C.D. reveals the unexpected influence of St. John of the Cross on Thomas Merton, Dorothy Day, Isaac Hecker, the founder of the Paulists & many others.

St. John of the Cross for Carpenters: The Ordinary Way of the Dark Night of Faith. Denis Read. Read by Denis Read. 1 cass. (Running Time: 62 min.). 8.95 I C S Pubns.
Fr. Denis Read, O.C.D. speaks of the common way in which the purification St. John of the Cross speaks about occurrences in people's ordinary lives.

St. John of the Cross on Love & Kenosis in Prayer. Kevin Culligan. 1 cass. (Running Time: 41 min.). 8.95 I C S Pubns.
Shows how St. John teaches that prayer is our loving response to the complete self-emptying of Jesus Christ.

St. John's Gospel. Stephen Doyle. 5 cass. (Running Time: 7 hrs. 25 min.). 1997. 42.95 Set. (TAH387) Alba Hse Comns.
Fr. Doyle shows in this series of conferences the many unique aspects of St. John's Gospel, the definitive faces of discipleship, the temptation of Christ & his works.

St. Joseph in the Teaching of Pope John Paul the Second. Frederick L. Miller. Read by Frederick L. Miller. 1 cass. (Running Time: 1 hr. 23 min.). 2.50 (978-1-56036-020-9(8), 361914) AMI Pr.
Explores the special relationship of St. Joseph to Jesus & Mary & his role in the Redemption as taught by Pope John Paul II.

St. Joseph Pignatelli. unabr. ed. D. A. Hanly. Read by William Nelson. 7 cass. 28.95 set. (715) Ignatius Pr.
18th Century Spanish Jesuit who worked tirelessly for the restoration of the Society of Jesus.

***St. Louis Woman Dance Suite.** Perf. by R. A. Zuckerman. (ENG.). 2010. 12.95 (978-1-891083-20-4(1)) ConcertHall.

St. Margaret of Cortona. Francois Mauriac. 6 cass. 24.95 (748) Ignatius Pr.
This relates the stern spectacle of a soul laid bare & purified by penance.

St. Mark's Basilica, Basilica di San Marco. Scripts. Laura Pytlik. Narrated by Christopher Kent. 1 CD. (Running Time: 2 hrs. 28 mins.). (Great Discoveries Personal Audio Guides: Venice Ser.). 2005. 19.95 (978-1-59971-133-1(8)); audio compact disk 24.95 (978-1-59971-104-1(4)) AardGP.
Two hours and twenty-eight minutes of playtime provide today's independent traveler with an unparalleled audio tour of St. Mark's Basilica. St. Mark's has majestically dominated Venice's grand square, the Piazza San Marco, for over 900 years. Throughout the centuries, countless numbers of pilgrims and tourists alike have been awestruck by the golden magnificence of this, the largest and most lavishly decorated church of the 11th century. You can only imagine what it would have meant to an ancient pilgrim, weary from his long and dreary travels, to stand in the Piazza and view the Basilica's exotic beauty. Professional narrators delight, inform and amuse as they guide the listener through a spell binding tour of the basilica, discussing its unique history, the life of St. Mark and its ancient but spectacular mosaics. Over the centuries, some of the greatest Italian, European and Eastern artists have worked in this glorious studio creating exotic, ornate, and utterly breathtaking art. Some 8,000 square meters of mediaeval mosaics, made from gold, semi precious stones and Venetian glass, covers the walls, vaults, and cupolas. Eight centuries of artisans and craftsmen have contributed to these wondrous decorations that characterize the evolution of Venetian art. The mosaics are virtual storybooks revealing the history of Venice and illustrating events from the Bible. They depict stories from the Old and New Testaments including events in the lives of Christ, the Virgin Mary, Saint Mark, and other saints. St. Mark's Basilica is a martyrium, a sacred burial place for the mortal remains of martyrs. It has been a very significant holy place since the arrival of St. Mark's body in 828 A.D. Countless pilgrims have traveled to visit the holy relics, including a Holy Roman Emperor. Angelo Fiorenzuola once wrote; "In Venice, St. Mark was honored more highly than God Himself." This 29 track audio tour is in standard CD format, on 3 CD's, ready for play on any CD player. Not for use on MP3 players.

St. Martin De Porres. Giuliana Cavallini. 9 cass. 36.95 (727) Ignatius Pr.
Great Apostle of Charity in South America.

St. Mawr, unabr. ed. D. H. Lawrence. Narrated by Davina Porter. 5 cass. (Running Time: 6 hrs. 30 mins.). 1988. 44.00 (978-1-55690-492-9(4), 88190E7) Recorded Bks.
Lou Witt, the future Lady Carrington if she behaved herself, was 24 & in her mother's words, "beyond management." When Lou's family bought the splendid stallion named St. Mawr & moved to Arizona, Lou learned quite a lot about horses, men & herself.

St. Mawr. unabr. ed. D. h. Lawrence. Narrated by Flo Gibson. 4 cass. (Running Time: 6 hrs.). 2003. 19.95 (978-1-55685-700-3(4)) Audio Bk Con.
The novella, set in England and Arizona, is about a magnificent stallion in whom the heroine finds qualities missing in her relationships.

St Patrick. unabr. ed. Michael J. McHugh. Read by Fred Williams. 3 cass. (Running Time: 4 hrs.). 2004. 23.95 (978-0-7861-2482-4(2), 3135) Blckstn Audio.

St Patrick: Pioneer Missionary to Ireland. unabr. ed. Michael J. McHugh. Read by Fred Williams. 4 CDs. (Running Time: 4 hrs.). 2003. audio compact disk 32.00 (978-0-7861-8792-8(1), 3135) Blckstn Audio.

***St. Patrick of Ireland: A Biography.** Philip Freeman. Read by Alan Sklar. (Playaway Adult Nonfiction Ser.). (ENG.). 2010. 59.99 (978-1-61587-795-9(9)) Find a World.

St. Patrick of Ireland: A Biography. unabr. ed. Philip Freeman. Narrated by Alan Sklar. (Running Time: 6 hrs. 6 mins. 0 sec.). (ENG.). 2004. audio compact disk 27.99 (978-1-4001-0111-5(5)); audio compact disk 19.99 (978-1-4001-5111-0(2)) Pub: Tantor Media. Dist(s): IngramPubServ

St. Paul, Apostle of Nations. Henri Daniel-Rops. 7 cass. 28.95 (707) Ignatius Pr.
Penetrating account of St. Paul's life & preaching during the birth of Christianity.

St. Paul at the Altar of the Unknown God. Manly P. Hall. 8.95 (978-0-89314-240-7(9), C870913) Philos Res.
Teaching of the bible & christianity.

St. Paul, the Initiate Apostle. Manly P. Hall. 8.95 (978-0-89314-241-4(7), C880403) Philos Res.

St. Peter Eymard: Champion of the Blessed Sacrament. Martin Dempsey. 7 cass. 28.95 (749) Ignatius Pr.
A saint who served Jesus in a most special way.

St. Peter's Fair. unabr. ed. Ellis Peters. Read by Johanna Ward. 6 cass. (Running Time: 8 hrs. 30 mins.). (Chronicles of Brother Cadfael Ser.: Vol. 4). 1997. 44.95 (978-0-7861-1238-8(7), 1985) Blckstn Audio.
A grand, festive event, attracting merchants from across England & beyond. There is a pause in the civil war racking the country in the summer of 1139, & the fair promises to bring some much-needed gaiety to the town of Shrewsbury. Until the body of a wealthy merchant is found murdered in the river Severn.

St. Peter's Fair. unabr. ed. Ellis Peters, pseud. Read by Stephen Thorpe. 8 cass. (Running Time: 12 hrs.). (Chronicles of Brother Cadfael Ser.: Vol. 4). 2000. 59.95 (CAB 550) Pub: Chivers Audio Bks GBR. Dist(s): AudioGO
The great annual fair of Saint Peter at Shrewsbury attracts merchants from far and wide to do business. But when a quarrel breaks out between the locals and the monks from the Benedictine monastery over who shall benefit from the levies the fair provides, a riot ensues. Afterwards, a merchant is found dead, and Brother Cadfael is summoned from his peaceful herb-garden to test his skills as a detective once more.

St. Peter's Fair. unabr. ed. Ellis Peters, pseud. Narrated by Patrick Tull. 7 cass. (Running Time: 9 hrs. 30 mins.). (Chronicles of Brother Cadfael Ser.: Vol. 4). 1992. 60.00 (978-1-55690-726-5(5), 92109E7) Recorded Bks.
King Stephen's bloody siege against the town of Shrewsbury has reduced many of its stores & homes to rubble. The townspeople, busy preparing for the annual St. Peter's Fair, complain that the Shrewsbury monks have not shouldered their fair share of the burden. Cadfael, hoping to assuage flaring tempers, is drawn into a worse kind of violence on the eve of the festival.

***St. Peter's Fair: The Fourth Chronicle of Brother Cadfael.** unabr. ed. Ellis Peters. Read by Johanna Ward. (Running Time: 8 hrs.). (Chronicles of Brother Cadfael Ser.). 2010. 29.95 (978-1-4332-6481-8(1)); audio compact disk 76.00 (978-1-4332-6478-8(1)) Blckstn Audio.

St. Roach see Poetry & Voice of Muriel Rukeyser

St. Teresa: The Book of Her Life. unabr. ed. Teresa of Avila. Read by Mary Doyle. Tr. by Kieran Kavanaugh & Otilio Rodriguez. 12 cass. 47.95 set. (930) Ignatius Pr.
This unusual & detailed autobiography serves as an excellent devotional guide to holiness in one's daily life.

St. Teresa: The Interior Castle. unabr. ed. Teresa of Avila. Read by Al Covaia. Tr. by Kieran Kavanaugh & Otilio Rodriguez. 5 cass. 22.95 set. (932) Ignatius Pr.
This work, perhaps her best known, provides an absorbing account of the soul's journey through the "crystal globe" & its seven mansions, beset by dangers & temptations, to its final ecstatic union & marriage with God.

St. Teresa: The Way of Perfection. unabr. ed. Teresa of Avila. Read by Al Covaia. Tr. by Kieran Kavanaugh & Otilio Rodriguez. 5 cass. 22.95 set. (931) Ignatius Pr.
The Way of Perfection affords an excellent & inspiring guide to the life of prayer, written by Teresa at the request of her community of discalced Carmelites for their instruction.

St. Teresa of Avila & the Gifts of the Holy Spirit. Denis Read. 1 cass. (Running Time: 55 min.). 8.95 I C S Pubns.
Fr. Denis Read, O.C.D. gives an overview on the Spirit's centrality in St. Teresa's writings. He then reflects on the pivotal importance of the Spirit in Karl Rahner & Bernard Lonergan, concluding with a new definition of mystical experience.

St. Teresa of the Andes: American Sanctity. Michael Dodd. 1 cass. (Running Time: 53 min.). 8.95 I C S Pubns.
Fr. Michael Dodd, O.C.D. relates the life story of the young Carmelite novice who became the first Chilean & the first New World Carmelite to be canonized. Fr. Dodd draws many lessons from her life that touch our experience, in particular, issues with regard to family.

St. Therese: Her Mission Today 1897-1997. Kieran Kavanaugh et al. 7 cass. 44.95 Set. I C S Pubns.
To celebrate the centenary of St. Therese of Lixieux's death, deals with various aspects of her life & mission.

St. Therese & the Roses. Helen Walker Homan. 4 cass. (J). 18.95 (508) Ignatius Pr.
The life of the Little Flower.

St. Therese of Lisieux: A Triduum. Patrick Ahern. Read by Patrick Ahern. 2 cass. (Running Time: 1 hr. 45 min.). 1985. 16.95 set. (TAH162) Alba Hse Comns.
Argues that a spirituality that is practical, tender, courageous, & profound can be obtained through following the path of St. Therese of Lisieux.

St. Therese of Lisieux: From Her Heart to Your Heart. unabr. ed. Debra-Therese Carroll. Read by Debra-Therese Carroll. 1 cass. Dramatization. 19.95 (978-0-8198-6997-5(X)) Pauline Bks.
Hear the narrated voice of St. Therese herself, speaking to you as a close friend. These unique first person accounts explore in depth Therese's spirituality of confidence in God's love & mercy.

St. Therese of Lisieux: Light & Darkness. Benedict J. Groeschel. 1 cass. (Running Time: 43 min.). 1998. 9.95 (TAH394) Alba Hse Comns.
In this earthy, unaffected presentation, a picture is painted of the saint in human, realistic terms that reflect the age in which she lived. She is a saint in which we can find some measure of strength.

St. Therese of Lisieux: The Experience of Love & Mercy. Margaret Dorgan. 4 cass. 1988. 32.95 (TAH208) Alba Hse Comns.
In a world where our human fragility can seem overwhelmed, St. Therese of Lisieux shows how the experience of weakness is a claim on divine power to take over & direct our lives... even to heights of sanctity. Therese is the apostle of hope & confidence.

St. Therese of Lisieux & the Meaning of Grace in Our Lives: A Spiritual & Theological Exploration. Margaret Dorgan. 2 cass. (Running Time: 3 hrs. 8 min.). 1998. 19.95 Set. (TAH392) Alba Hse Comns.
Therese helps us understand our God as the three divine persons who dwell within us, permeating our being & all that happens to us with merciful love.

St. Thomas Aquinas. G. K. Chesterton. 8 cass. 32.95 (714) Ignatius Pr.
Biography of the Angelic Doctor.

St. Thomas Aquinas, unabr. ed. G. K. Chesterton. Read by Frederick Davidson. 2 cass. (Giants of Philosophy Ser.). 2002. 17.95 (K120) Blckstn Audio.
See how one of the world's philosophers created a complete system of thought, including his views on ethics, metaphysics, politics & aesthetics. Learn about his epistemology - how we know what we know.

St. Thomas Aquinas: Italy (1224-1274) Kenneth L. Schmitz. Read by Charlton Heston. (Running Time: 7200 sec.). (Audio Classics: the Giants of Philosophy Ser.). 2006. audio compact disk 25.95 (978-0-7861-6932-0(X)) Pub: Blckstn Audio. Dist(s): NetLibrary CO

St. Thomas Aquinas: Italy (1224-1274) unabr. ed. Kenneth L. Schmitz. Read by Charlton Heston. Ed. by George H. Smith & Wendy McElroy. 2 cass. (Running Time: 3 hrs.). Dramatization. (Giants of Philosophy Ser.). 1990. 17.95 (978-0-938935-20-9(8), 10304) Pub: Knowledge Prod. Dist(s): APG
St. Thomas Aquinas produced a momentous summation, called the "Summa Theologica," of the facts of Christian faith & knowledge. He offered proofs of the existence of God & set limits to the power of reason; he gave an account of the nature & constitution of the world, & outlined the soul's road to blessedness.

St. Thomas Aquinas, the Dumb Ox. unabr. ed. G. K. Chesterton. Read by Frederick Davidson. 5 cass. (Running Time: 7 hrs.). 1992. 39.95 (978-0-7861-0129-0(6), 1115) Blckstn Audio.
Perhaps the best book ever written on St. Thomas Aquinas.

St. Thomas More. Thomas Morrow. 1 cass. (Inspiring Presentations from the National Rosary Congress Ser.). 2.50 (978-1-56036-099-5(2)) AMI Pr.

St. Vincent Ferrer. Henri Gheon. 5 cass. 22.95 (755) Ignatius Pr.
Biography of this zealous Dominican priest.

Stab in the Dark. unabr. ed. Lawrence Block. Read by William Roberts. 6 vols. (Running Time: 9 hrs.). (Matthew Scudder Mystery Ser.: No. 4). 2000. bk. 54.95 (978-0-7927-2249-6(3), CSL 138, Chivers Sound Lib) AudioGO.
Nine years have passed since the killer last struck: eight helpless young women were slaughtered with an ice-pick. Now ex-cop Matthew Scudder has been hired to bring the slayer to justice. Scudder sets out on a bloody trail of death almost a decade cold, searching for a psycho who's either long gone, long dead, or patiently waiting to kill again.

Stab in the Dark. unabr. ed. Lawrence Block. Read by William Roberts. 6 CDs. (Running Time: 9 hrs.). (Matthew Scudder Mystery Ser.: No. 4). 2001. audio compact disk 64.95 (978-0-7927-9974-0(7), SLD 025, Chivers Sound Lib) AudioGO.

Stab in the Dark. unabr. ed. Carter Brown. Read by Sean Mangan. 2005. audio compact disk 54.95 (978-1-74093-692-7(2)) Pub: Bolinda Pubng AUS. Dist(s): Bolinda Pub Inc

Stabbing in the Stables. Simon Brett & Simon Brett. (Isis (CDs) Ser.). 2006. audio compact disk 79.95 (978-0-7531-2554-0(4)) Pub: ISIS Lrg Prnt GBR. Dist(s): Ulverscroft US

Stabbing in the Stables. unabr. ed. Simon Brett & Simon Brett. 7 cass. (Running Time: 9 hrs.). (Isis Cassettes Ser.). 2006. 61.95 (978-0-7531-3541-9(8)) Pub: ISIS Lrg Prnt GBR. Dist(s): Ulverscroft US

Stabbing in the Stables: A Fethering Mystery. unabr. ed. Simon Brett & Ralph Cosham. (Running Time: 10 hrs. NaN mins.). 2008. 29.95 (978-1-4332-2713-4(4)); 65.95 (978-1-4332-2709-7(6)); audio compact disk 80.00 (978-1-4332-2710-3(X)) Blckstn Audio.

Stability Analysis & Modelling of Underground Excavations in Fractured Rocks. Weishen Zhu & Jian Zhao. Ed. by John A. Hudson. (Elsevier Geo Engineering Book Ser.: Vol. 1). (ENG., 2003. 170.00 (978-0-08-043012-6(0), ElseSci) Sci Tech Bks.

Stabilization & Transport. Joseph E. Simon. (Pediatric Emergencies: The National Conference for Practioners Ser.). 1986. 9.00 (978-0-932491-68-8(5)) Res Appl Inc.

Stabilizers for Love. Elbert Willis. 1 cass. (Developing Ability to Love Ser.). 4.00 Fill the Gap.

Stable Loft Songs (Welsh Music) 1 cass. 10.95 J Norton Pubs.
Authentic farming folk songs of the 50's & 60's recorded "in the field.".

Staci's Dilemma. (Paws & Tales Ser.: Vol. 19). (J). 2001. audio compact disk 5.99 (978-1-57972-423-8(X)) Insight Living.

Staci's Dilemma. (Paws & Tales Ser.: Vol. 19). (J). 2002. 3.99 (978-1-57972-422-1(1)) Insight Living.

Stacked Zodiac - Forty-Five Degree Graph Ephemeris. Roxanne Muise. 1 cass. 8.95 (570) Am Fed Astrologers.

Stacking the Deck in Favor of the Mentally Ill: A Supportive Ministry. 1 cass. (Care Cassettes Ser.: Vol. 17, No. 9). 1990. 10.80 Assn Prof Chaplains.

Stacks of Stories. Geraldine McCaughrean et al. Read by Jan Francis & Richard Briers. Illus. by Colin Hawkins. 2 cass. (Running Time: 3 hrs.). (J). 1999. 15.99 (978-1-85998-940-1(3), HoddrStoughton) Pub: Hodder General GBR. Dist(s): Trafalgar

Stacy Says Good-Bye. unabr. ed. Patricia Reilly Giff. 1 cass. (Running Time: 50 min.). (New Kids at the Polk Street School Ser.). (J). (gr. 1-2). 1990. 15.98 incl. pap. bk. & guide. (978-0-8072-0181-7(2), FTR 141 SP, Listening Lib) Random Audio Pubg.

Staff Orientation & In-Service Training. Dora C. Fowler. 1 cass. (Running Time: 60 min.). 1990. 9.95 (978-1-57323-027-8(8)) Natl Inst Child Mgmt.
Staff training material for child care.

Stalking the Angel. abr. ed. Robert Crais. Read by David Stuart. (Running Time: 6 hrs.). (Elvis Cole Ser.). 2006. 24.95 (978-1-4233-0219-3(2), 9781423302193, BAD) Brilliance Audio.

Stalking the Angel. abr. ed. Robert Crais. Read by David Stuart. (Running Time: 21600 sec.). (Elvis Cole Ser.). 2006. audio compact disk 16.99 (978-1-4233-1944-3(3), 9781423319443, BCD Value Price) Brilliance Audio.

Stalking the Angel. unabr. ed. Robert Crais. Read by Patrick G. Lawlor. (Running Time: 7 hrs.). (Elvis Cole Ser.). 2008. 39.25 (978-1-4233-5626-4(8), 9781423356264, BADLE); 24.95 (978-1-4233-5625-7(X), 9781423356257, BAD); audio compact disk 39.25 (978-1-4233-5624-0(1), 9781423356240, Brinc Audio MP3 Lib); audio compact disk 82.25 (978-1-4233-5622-6(5), 9781423356226, BriAudCD Unabrid); audio compact disk 29.95 (978-1-4233-5621-9(7), 9781423356219, Bril Audio CD Unabri); audio compact disk 24.95 (978-1-4233-5623-3(3), 9781423356233, Brilliance MP3) Brilliance Audio.

Stalking the Corporate Dollar: A Guide to Fundraising from the Corporate Sector. unabr. ed. Julian Padowicz. Read by Julian Padowicz. 1 cass. (Running Time: 50 min.). 1996. 15.95 (978-1-881288-14-5(5), BFI AudioBooks) BusnFilm Intl.
Discussion of principles, techniques, & ideas for fundraising from corporations.

Stalking the Renegade. unabr. ed. John D. Heisner. Read by Maynard Villers. 4 cass. (Running Time: 5 hrs. 36 min.). (Chinook Ser.: Bk. 3). 1996. 26.95 Set. (978-1-55686-690-6(9)) Books in Motion.
Jackson Kane "Chinook" hunts down the infamous 'Patch', a vicious one-eyed killer of kids, old ladies & anyone else who gets in his way.

***Stalking the Vampire: A Fable of Tonight.** Mike Resnick. Narrated by Mike Resnick. Narrated by Bypeter Ganim. (Playaway Adult Fiction Ser.). (ENG.). 2009. 69.99 (978-1-61545-765-6(8)) Find a World.

Stalky & Co. Rudyard Kipling. Read by Shelly Frasier. (Running Time: 7 hrs. 30 mins.). 2001. 27.95 (978-1-60083-597-1(X), Audiofy Corp) Iofy Corp.

Stalky & Co. Rudyard Kipling. Read by Shelly Frasier. (ENG.). 2005. audio compact disk 78.00 (978-1-4001-3025-2(5)) Pub: Tantor Media. Dist(s): IngramPubServ

Stalky & Co. unabr. ed. Rudyard Kipling. Narrated by Shelly Frasier. 1 CD (MP3). (Running Time: 7 hrs. 19 mins.). (ENG.). 2001. audio compact disk 20.00 (978-1-4001-5025-0(6)) Pub: Tantor Media. Dist(s): IngramPubServ

Stalky & Co. unabr. ed. Rudyard Kipling. Narrated by Shelly Frasier. 7 CDs. (Running Time: 7 hrs. 19 mins.). (ENG.). 2001. audio compact disk 39.00 (978-1-4001-0025-5(9)) Pub: Tantor Media. Dist(s): IngramPubServ

Stalky & Co. unabr. ed. Rudyard Kipling. Narrated by Shelly Frasier. (Running Time: 7 hrs. 30 mins. 0 sec.). (ENG.). 2009. audio compact disk 19.99 (978-1-4001-6099-0(5)); audio compact disk 27.99 (978-1-4001-1099-5(8)); audio compact disk 55.99 (978-1-4001-4099-2(4)) Pub: Tantor Media. Dist(s): IngramPubServ

Stallcup's Complete Code Changes, 2008 Edition. James Stallcup. (C). 2008. audio compact disk 83.95 (978-0-7637-5150-0(2)) Jones Bartlett.

Stallcup's(r) Illustrated Code Changes DVD. National Fire Protection Association & James G. Stallcup. 2008. 240.95 (978-0-7637-5949-0(X)) Jones Bartlett.

Stallion. unabr. ed. Harold Robbins. Read by Jonathan Marosz. 9 cass. (Running Time: 13 hrs. 30 min.). 1996. 72.00 (978-0-7366-3528-8(9), 4166) Books on Tape.
The sequel of "The Betsy," in which Angelo Perino helped Loren Hardeman I wrest his control of Bethlehem Motors from his grandson, Loren III & it cost him. Loren III had thugs beat up Perino & Loren I fired him for knowing too much. Perino fled to New York, married & settled down.

Stallion Gate. unabr. ed. Martin Cruz Smith. Narrated by Frank Muller. 6 cass. (Running Time: 9 hrs.). 1986. 51.00 (978-1-55690-493-6(2), 86310E7) Recorded Bks.
An Indian army sergeant uncovers an attempt to disrupt the first test of the atomic bomb in Los Alamos.

Stallion Gate. unabr. collector's ed. Martin Cruz Smith. Read by Wolfram Kandinsky. 8 cass. (Running Time: 12 hrs.). 1989. 64.00 (978-0-7366-1605-8(5), 2466) Books on Tape.
In a New Mexico blizzard, four men cross a barbed-wire fence at Stallion Gate to select a test site for the first atomic weapon. They are Oppenheimer, the physicist; Groves, the general; Fuchs, the spy. The fourth man is Sergeant Joe Pena, an Indian & a man of great complexity - warrior, musician, hero & informer. Los Alamos lies on a mesa surrounded by vast Indian reservations. It is the most secret installation of the war, the future encompassed by the past. It is also a magnet to soldiers, roughnecks & scientists, including Anna Weiss, a beautiful & talented refugee with whom Joe falls deeply in love.

Stamboul Train. abr. ed. Graham Greene. Read by Roddy McDowell. 2 cass. (Running Time: 3 hrs.). (J). 1986. 15.95 (978-1-55994-087-0(5), CPN 2099) HarperCollins Pubs.
Greene's menage of witty & sophisticated characters on board the Orient Express as they speed from Ostend to Constantinople, leaving a trail of lust, murder, revolution, & intrigue.

Stamboul Train. unabr. ed. Graham Greene. Read by Michael Maloney. 8 CDs. (Running Time: 26520 sec.). 2001. 79.95 (978-0-7540-5417-7(9), CCD 108) Pub: Chivers Audio Bks GBR. Dist(s): AudioGO
A spy thriller aboard the majestic Orient Express as it cross Europe. A disturbing relationship between Myatt, the pragmatic Jew & a naive chorus girl, Coral Musker, as they engage in an angst-ridden pas de deux before a chilling turn of events spells an end to the unlikely interlude.

Stamford, Our Pride: Millenium Edition. Julian Pudowicz. 1 cass. (Running Time: 1 hr.). 1999. 8.95 (978-1-881288-25-1(0)) BusnFilm Intl.
History of Stamford, Connecticut.

Stan Freberg Presents: The United States of America, Vols. 1 & 2. Stan Freberg. 2 cass. (Running Time: 2 hrs.). (Stan Freberg Presents Ser.). 1996. 16.98 (978-1-56826-716-6(9)) Rhino Enter.
Hilarious original 1961 classic coupled with belated but welcome 1996 sequel.

Stan Freberg Presents Vols. 1 & 2: The United States of America. Stan Freberg. 2 CDs. (Running Time: 3 hrs.). 1996. audio compact disk 31.98 (978-1-56826-715-9(0), R2 72476) Rhino Enter.

Stan Freberg Presents the United States of America Vol. 1: The Early Years. Stan Freberg. 2 CDs. (Running Time: 2 hrs.). 2001. audio compact disk 24.95 Lodestone Catalog.
Hilarious musical comedy skewers Columbus & Our Founding Fathers & now reveals never before heard laughs generated by the Civil War, the Industrial Revolution & World War I.

Stan Freberg Presents the United States of America Vol. II: The Middle Years. Stan Freberg. 2 CDs. (Running Time: 2 hrs.). 2001. audio compact disk 24.95 Lodestone Catalog.

Stan Freberg Show: The First 7 Shows, collector's ed. Perf. by June Foray et al. Frwd. by Stan Freberg. 4 cass. (Running Time: 4 hrs.). (Smithsonian Historical Performances Ser.). 1996. bk. 12.49 (978-1-57019-052-0(6), 4107) Radio Spirits.
The first seven, uncut radio broadcasts from the famed 1957 CBS radio series. Booklet contains insightful commentary about the shows. Digitally restored and remastered.

Stan Getz: A Life in Jazz. Donald L. Maggin. Read by Fred Williams. 11 cass. (Running Time: 16 hrs.). 2000. 76.95 (978-0-7861-1774-1(5), 2577) Blckstn Audio.
From Getz's recording of "Early Autumn" with the Woody Herman band, which catapulted him to stardom in 1949 at age twenty-two, to the 1961 jazz/classical masterpiece "Focus," to the 1990 release of "Apasionado," Maggin chronicles a forty-nine-year career of enduring artistic success in the midst of a troubled life. Getz struggled with heroin addiction until the age of twenty-seven & violent alcoholism until the last decade of his life, which led him into trouble with the law & marred his relationships with family & friends. Despite his self-destructive behavior, he was still creating gorgeous music at the time of his death from cancer in 1991.

***Stan Musial: An American Life.** unabr. ed. George Vecsey. (ENG.). 2011. audio compact disk 30.00 (978-0-307-93440-6(3), Random AudioBks) Pub: Random Audio Pubg. Dist(s): Random

Stan Musial Plays the Harmonica. Stan Musial. 1994. pap. bk. 16.95 (978-0-7866-0536-1(7), 95288P) Mel Bay.

Stand. unabr. ed. Stephen King. Read by Grover Gardner. 23 cass. (Running Time: 34 hrs. 30 mins.). 184.00 (978-0-7366-1248-7(3), 2163A/B) Books on Tape.
Describes how the "good" survivors restructure society after almost all of humanity has been wiped out by a superflu. An epic struggle with the "evil" survivors takes on apocalyptic symbolism.

Stand. unabr. ed. Stephen King. 11 cass. (Running Time: 16 hrs. 30 mins.). 1987. 88.00 (2163-A) Books on Tape.

Stand: Victory in Praise Music & Arts Seminar Mass Choir. Perf. by John P. Kee & Victory in Praise Music and Arts Seminar Mass Choir. 1 cass., 1 CD. Provident Mus Dist.

Stand a Little Taller. Curtis Jacobs. 2004. 9.95 (978-1-57734-703-3(X)); audio compact disk 10.95 (978-1-57734-704-0(8)) Covenant Comms.

Stand Alone - Blues. 1993. 12.95 (978-0-88284-547-0(0), 4447) Alfred Pub.

Stand Alone Blues. Robert Brown. (Alfred's Handy Guide Ser.). (YA). 1992. pap. bk. 9.95 (978-0-88284-543-2(8), 4428) Alfred Pub.

Stand Alone Classic Rock. Robert Brown. 1 cass. (Alfred HandyGuide Ser.). 1994. pap. bk. 9.95 (978-0-88284-638-5(8), 4492) Alfred Pub.

Stand Alone Fusion. Mark Dziuba. (Alfred Handy Guide Ser.). 1992. pap. bk. 9.95 (978-0-88284-542-5(X), 4429) Alfred Pub.

Stand Alone Jazz. Robert Brown. 1 cass. (Alfred HandyGuide Ser.). 1994. pap. bk. 9.95 (978-0-88284-640-8(X), 4491) Alfred Pub.

Stand Alone Rockabilly. Robert Brown. 1 cass. (Alfred HandyGuide Ser.). 1994. pap. bk. 9.95 (978-0-88284-639-2(6), 4493) Alfred Pub.

Stand-Alone 2-CD set t/a Experience Music. 2nd ed. Katherine Charlton. (ENG.). (C). 2008. audio compact disk 40.00 (978-0-07-727041-4(X), 007727041X, Mc-H Human Soc) Pub: McGrw-H Hghr Educ. Dist(s): McGraw

Stand & Deliver: Method to Public Speaking. unabr. ed. Dale Carnegie. (Running Time: 6 hrs. 0 mins. 0 sec.). (ENG.). 2008. audio compact disk 29.95 (978-0-7435-7103-6(7), Nightgale) Pub: S&S Audio. Dist(s): S and S Inc

Stand as a Witness. 2 cass. 2004. 14.95 (978-1-57734-749-1(8)) Covenant Comms.

Stand Aside & Watch Yourself Go By. Instructed by Manly P. Hall. 1 cass. 8.95 (978-0-89314-264-3(6), C830327) Philos Res.

Stand Fast! In the Storms of Life. Kenneth W. Hagin, Jr. 12.00 (C8131) Faith Lib Pubns.
As Christians encounter storms in life, they must realize that God is right there with them.

Stand for Something: The Battle for America's Soul. abr. ed. John Kasich. (Running Time: 3 hrs.). (ENG.). 2006. 14.98 (978-1-59483-514-8(4)) Pub: Hachet Audio. Dist(s): HachBkGrp

Stand for Something: The Battle for America's Soul. abr. ed. John Kasich. (Running Time: 3 hrs.). (ENG.). 2009. 39.98 (978-1-60788-124-7(1)) Pub: Hachet Audio. Dist(s): HachBkGrp

Stand into Danger, unabr. ed. Alexander Kent, pseud. Narrated by Steven Crossley. 8 cass. (Running Time: 11 hrs.). (Richard Bolitho Ser.: Bk. 2). 2000. 72.00 (978-0-7887-3123-5(8), 95620E7) Recorded Bks.
In 1774, aboard the 28-gun frigate "Destiny," Lt. Richard Bolitho wonders why the mission has been kept a secret. As the swift British ship enters the warm seas around Rio, Bolitho sails into an adventure that will alter his career & his heart.

Stand-off at Tinajas Atlas. Tim Champlin. (Running Time: 0 hr. 24 mins.). 2000. 10.95 (978-1-60083-528-5(7)) Iofy Corp.

Stand on Your Chair: Managing Change Through Creativity. unabr. ed. 1 cass. (Running Time: 1 hr.). 2000. (978-0-9700349-7-7(0)) Mayfield Present.

Stand or Fall. Kenneth Copeland. 3 cass. 1988. 15.00 Set. (978-0-88114-910-4(1)) K Copeland Pubns.
Biblical teaching on victorious living.

Stand Out Rob Jenkins & Staci Lyn Sabbagh. 1 CD. (Running Time: 1 hr.). 2002. audio compact disk 26.95 (978-0-8384-2768-2(5)) Heinle.

Stand Out. Contrib. by Tye Tribbett. Prod. by Dana Sorey & Thaddaeus Tribbett. 2008. audio compact disk 13.99 (978-5-557-43247-4(7)) Integrity Music.

Stand Out Level 1. Staci Lyn Sabbagh & Rob Jenkins. 1 cass. (Running Time: 1 hr.). (ENG.). (C). 2002. 27.95 (978-0-8384-2216-8(0)) Pub: Heinle. Dist(s): CENGAGE Learn

Stand Out Level 2. Rob Jenkins & Staci Lyn Sabbagh. 2002. bk. 38.95 (978-0-8384-4214-2(5)); audio compact disk 26.95 (978-0-8384-2746-0(4)) Heinle.

Stand Out Level 2. Rob Jenkins & Staci Lyn Sabbagh. 1 cass. (Running Time: 1 hr.). (ENG.). (C). 2002. 34.95 (978-0-8384-2219-9(5)) Pub: Heinle. Dist(s): CENGAGE Learn

Stand Out Level 2. Rob Jenkins & Staci Lyn Sabbagh. 1 CD. (Running Time: 1 hr.). 2002. audio compact disk 26.95 (978-0-8384-2766-8(9)) Heinle.

Stand Out: Live. Contrib. by Tye Tribbett & G A et al. Prod. by Mark Brown. 2008. 14.98 (978-5-557-39785-8(X)) Columba Pub.

***Stand Out L4-Audiotape.** Geraint H. Jenkins. (ENG.). (C). 2002. 34.95 (978-0-8384-2238-0(1)) Pub: Heinle. Dist(s): CENGAGE Learn

Stand Proud. abr. ed. Elmer Kelton. Read by Ronald Wilcox. Ed. by Stephen Holland. 4 cass. (Running Time: 6 hrs.). (Texas Tradition Ser.: No. 13). 1994. 24.95 Set. (978-1-883268-02-2(8)) Spellbinders.
A novel about the heyday of the open-range, cattlemen & cowboys.

Stand Tall. unabr. ed. Joan Bauer. 3 cass. (Running Time: 4 hrs. 9 mins.). (J). (gr. 5-9). 2004. 30.00 (978-0-8072-1674-3(7), Listening Lib) Random Audio Pubg.

Stand Tall. unabr. ed. Joan Bauer. Read by Ron McLarty. 4 CDs. (Running Time: 4 hrs. 9 mins.). (J). (gr. 5-9). 2004. audio compact disk 35.00 (978-0-8072-1772-6(7), Listening Lib) Random Audio Pubg.

Stand Tall, Molly Lou Melon. Patty Lovell. 1 cass. (Running Time: 7 mins.). (J). (gr. k-3). 2002. bk. 25.95 (978-0-8045-6891-3(X)) Spoken Arts.
Molly Lou Melon is short and clumsy, has buckteeth and a voice that sound like a bullfrog being squeezed by a boa constrictor. Her grandmother has always told her to walk proud, smile big and sing loud. When a bully picks on her at school, she knows what to do.

Stand the Storm. unabr. ed. Breena Clarke. Narrated by Richard Allen. (Running Time: 10 hrs. 30 mins. 0 sec.). (ENG.). 2008. audio compact disk 34.99 (978-1-4001-0878-7(0)); audio compact disk 24.99 (978-1-4001-5878-2(8)); audio compact disk 69.99 (978-1-4001-3878-4(7)) Pub: Tantor Media. Dist(s): IngramPubServ

Stand Up! Music by Judy Rogers. 1 cass. (Running Time: 1 hr.). (YA). (gr. 8-12). 2002. 8.50 (JR00004) Christian Liberty.
Challenging young Christians to stand strong for Christ. It deals with many issues facing young people today. Such topics as peer pressure, boy/girl relationships, friendship, temptation, worship and witnessing are addressed.

Stand up & Be Counted. Gloria Steinem. 1 cass. 9.00 (A0290-88) Sound Photosyn.
From the Women in the World conference.

Stand up for Amnesty. abr. ed. 1 cass. 1998. 15.00 (978-1-897774-94-6(X)) LaughStockProd GBR.

Stand up for Your Life: Develop the Courage, Confidence, & Character to Fulfill Your Greatest Potential. Cheryl Richardson. 1 CD. 2002. audio compact disk 10.95 (978-1-4019-0163-9(8), 1638) Hay House.

Stand-up Reagan. abr. ed. Ronald Reagan. 1 CDs. (Running Time: 45 mins.). 2005. audio compact disk 16.98 (978-1-929243-65-5(0)) Uproar Ent.

Stand Up! Speak Out! 1 CD. (Running Time: 1 hr.). (J). (gr. 3-8). 2001. pap. bk. & tchr. ed. 14.95 (SM1005CD) Soozaroo Music.
Twelve original songs designed to raise awareness of prejudice and bullying. Encourages kids to have the moral courage to "do the right thing" as they face challenges.

Standard American Diction. Geoffrey G. Forward. Read by Geoffrey G. Forward. Read by Elisabeth Howard. 2 cass. (Running Time: 2 hrs.). 24.95 set. (978-0-944200-03-2(6)) Perfom Arts Global.
How to pronounce the speech sounds of Standard American Speech. How to link them together in words & sentences.

Standard & Poor: Show Me the Money. Michael Lattiboudeaire. 8 cass. (Running Time: 18 hrs.). 1998. pap. bk. 85.00 Set. (978-1-889448-19-0(2)) Great Hse Pub.
Economics within the body of Christ.

Standard Arabic: An Advanced Course, Set. James Dickins & Janet Watson. 2 cass. (Running Time: 2 hrs. 43 mins.). (ENG., (C). 1999. 23.99 (978-0-521-63531-8(4)) Cambridge U Pr.

Standard Arabic: An Elementary-Intermediate Course. Eckehard Schulz et al. 1 cass. (Running Time: 2 hrs. 14 mins.). (ARA & ENG., (C). 2000. 43.99 (978-0-521-78739-0(4)) Cambridge U Pr.

Standard Audio Tape Series. Milady Publishing Company Staff. 29 cass. 1995. 270.95 (978-1-56253-269-7(3), Milady) Pub: Delmar. Dist(s): CENGAGE Learn

Standard Ballads - Men's Edition: Cabaret Arrangements for Singer & Trio (Piano, Bass, Drums) 1 CD. (Running Time: 90 mins.). 2000. pap. bk. 19.95 (00740089) H Leonard.
Fantastic songs in fantastic renditions, in comfortable keys for pop singing. Includes: "All the Things You Are," "Autumn Leaves," "Call Me Irresponsible," "East of the Sun," "I Left My Heart in San Francisco" & more.

Standard Ballads - Women's Edition: Cabaret Arrangements for Singer & Trio (Piano, Bass, Drums) 1 CD. (Running Time: 90 mins.). 2000. pap. bk. 19.95 (00740088) H Leonard.

Standard Book of Mormon. Narrated by Rex Campbell. 17 cass. 25.95 (050016) Covenant Comms.

Standard British see Acting with an Accent

Standard Chinese Modular Approach Module 4. FSI Staff. 15 cass. (Multilingual Books Intensive Language Courses). (CHI.). 2005. per. 199.00 (978-1-58214-338-5(2)) Language Assocs.

Standard Chinese Modular Approach Module 8: Traveling in China. FSI Staff. 10 CDs. (Multilingual Books Intensive Language Courses). (CHI.). 2006. per. 199.00 (978-1-58214-327-9(7)) Language Assocs.

Standard Chinese Module 4 CD: Multilingual Books Language Course. FSI Staff. 15 CD's. (Multilingual Books Intensive Language Courses). (CHI.). 2005. per. 239.00 (978-1-58214-339-2(0)) Language Assocs.

Standard Comprehensive Training for Esthet. 2002. audio compact disk 34.95 (978-1-56253-807-1(1), Milady) Pub: Delmar. Dist(s): CENGAGE Learn

Standard Doctrine & Covenants, Pearl of Great Price. Narrated by Rex Campbell. 10 cass. 17.95 (050024) Covenant Comms.

Standard Lesson Commentary: NIV Standard Lesson Commentary(r) Soft Cover. bk. 17.99 (978-0-7847-1306-8(5)) Standard Pub.

Standard Lesson Commentary: Standard Lesson Commentary(r) (KJV) Soft Cover. bk. 17.99 (978-0-7847-1305-1(7)) Standard Pub.

***Standard Lesson Commentary (Complete 2010-2011 Year)** abr. ed. Oasis Audio Staff & Standard Lesson Commentary Staff. Read by Marquis Laughlin. Narrated by Lucille Cole & Bob Souer. (Running Time: 16 hrs. 23 mins. 56 sec.). (ENG.). 2010. audio compact disk 64.99 (978-1-59859-752-3(3)) Oasis Audio.

***Standard Lesson Commentary (Fall 2010)** abr. ed. Oasis Audio Staff & Standard Lesson Commentary Staff. Read by Marquis Laughlin. Narrated by Lucille Cole & Bob Souer. (Running Time: 4 hrs. 12 mins. 22 sec.). (ENG.). 2010. 13.99 (978-1-60814-696-3(0)); audio compact disk 19.99 (978-1-59859-748-6(5)) Oasis Audio.

***Standard Lesson Commentary Spring 2011.** abr. ed. Oasis Audio Staff & Standard Lesson Commentary Staff. Read by Marquis Laughlin. Narrated by Lucille Cole & Bob Souer. (Running Time: 4 hrs. 0 mins. 7 sec.). (ENG.). 2010. 13.99 (978-1-60814-699-4(5)); 13.99 (978-1-60814-698-7(7)) Oasis Audio.

***Standard Lesson Commentary (Spring 2011)** abr. ed. Oasis Audio Staff & Standard Lesson Commentary Staff. Read by Marquis Laughlin. Narrated by Lucille Cole & Bob Souer. (Running Time: 4 hrs. 5 mins. 30 sec.). (ENG.). 2010. audio compact disk 19.99 (978-1-59859-750-9(7)) Oasis Audio.

***Standard Lesson Commentary (Summer 2011)** abr. ed. Oasis Audio Staff & Standard Lesson Commentary Staff. Read by Marquis Laughlin. Narrated by Lucille Cole & Bob Souer. (Running Time: 4 hrs. 0 mins. 7 sec.). (ENG.). 2010. audio compact disk 19.99 (978-1-59859-751-6(5)) Oasis Audio.

***Standard Lesson Commentary (Winter 2010-2011)** abr. ed. Oasis Audio Staff & Standard Lesson Commentary Staff. Read by Marquis Laughlin. Narrated by Lucille Cole & Bob Souer. (Running Time: 4 hrs. 5 mins. 57 sec.). (ENG.). 2010. audio compact disk 19.99 (978-1-59859-749-3(3)) Oasis Audio.

***Standard Lesson Commentary Winter 2010-2011.** abr. ed. Oasis Audio Staff & Standard Lesson Commentary Staff. Read by Marquis Laughlin. Narrated by Lucille Cole & Bob Souer. (Running Time: 4 hrs. 5 mins. 57 sec.). (ENG.). 2010. 13.99 (978-1-60814-697-0(9)) Oasis Audio.

Standard Methods for the Examination of Water & Wastewater. 2004. cd-rom & audio compact disk 285.00 (978-0-87553-239-4(X)); cd-rom & audio compact disk 437.00 (978-0-87553-240-0(3)) Am Pub Health.

Standard New Testament (King James) Narrated by Rex Campbell. 12 cass. 21.95 (050032) Covenant Comms.

Standard of Excellence: Full Score, Bk. 1. Bruce Pearson. 1994. audio compact disk 12.95 (978-0-614-03108-9(7), W22CD1) Kjos.

Standard of Excellence: Full Score, Bk. 2. Bruce Pearson. 1994. audio compact disk 12.95 (978-0-318-72755-4(2), W22CD2) Kjos.

Standard of Excellence Bk. 1: Full Score. Bruce Pearson. 1994. 8.95 (978-0-614-03107-2(9)) Kjos.

Standard of Excellence Bk. 2: Full Score. Bruce Pearson. 1994. 8.95 (978-0-614-03111-9(7)) Kjos.

Standard of Excellence Jazz Ensemble Method: For Group or Individual Instruction - Baritone Saxophone. Dean Sorenson & Bruce Pearson. 1998. bk. & stu. ed. 14.95 (978-0-8497-5744-0(4), W31XR) Kjos.

Standard of Excellence Jazz Ensemble Method: For Group or Individual Instruction - Bass. Dean Sorenson & Bruce Pearson. 1998. bk. & stu. ed. 17.95 (978-0-8497-5756-3(8), W31B) Kjos.

Standard of Excellence Jazz Ensemble Method: For Group or Individual Instruction - Drums. Dean Sorenson & Bruce Pearson. 1998. bk. & stu. ed. 17.95 (978-0-8497-5755-6(X), W31D) Kjos.

Standard of Excellence Jazz Ensemble Method: For Group or Individual Instruction - Piano. Dean Sorenson & Bruce Pearson. 1998. bk. & stu. ed. 17.95 (978-0-8497-5754-9(1), W31P) Kjos.

Standard of Excellence Jazz Ensemble Method: For Group or Individual Instruction - Vibes & Auxiliary Percussion. Dean Sorenson & Bruce Pearson. 1998. bk. & stu. ed. 17.95 (978-0-8497-5757-0(6), W31A) Kjos.

Standard of Excellence Jazz Ensemble Method: For Group or Individual Instruction - 1st Alto Saxophone. Dean Sorenson & Bruce Pearson. 1998. bk. & stu. ed. 14.95 (978-0-8497-5740-2(1), W31XE1) Kjos.

Standard of Excellence Jazz Ensemble Method: For Group or Individual Instruction - 1st Tenor Saxophone. Dean Sorenson & Bruce Pearson. 1998. bk. & stu. ed. 14.95 (978-0-8497-5742-6(8), W31XB1) Kjos.

Standard of Excellence Jazz Ensemble Method: For Group or Individual Instruction - 1st Trumpet. Dean Sorenson & Bruce Pearson. 1998. bk. & stu. ed. 14.95 (978-0-8497-5745-7(2), X31TP1) Kjos.

Standard of Excellence Jazz Ensemble Method: For Group or Individual Instruction - 2nd Alto Saxophone. Dean Sorenson & Bruce Pearson. 1998. bk. & stu. ed. 14.95 (978-0-8497-5741-9(X), W31XE2) Kjos.

Standard of Excellence Jazz Ensemble Method: For Group or Individual Instruction - 2nd Tenor Saxophone. Dean Sorenson & Bruce Pearson. 1998. bk. & stu. ed. 14.95 (978-0-8497-5743-3(6), W31XB2) Kjos.

Standard of Excellence Jazz Ensemble Method: For Group or Individual Instruction - 2nd Trumpet. Dean Sorenson & Bruce Pearson. 1998. bk. & stu. ed. 14.95 (978-0-8497-5746-4(0), W31TP2) Kjos.

Standard of Excellence Jazz Ensemble Method: For Group or Individual Instruction - 3rd Trumpet. Dean Sorenson & Bruce Pearson. 1998. bk. & stu. ed. 14.95 (978-0-8497-5747-1(9), W31TP3) Kjos.

Standard Old Testament. Narrated by Charles Freed. 42 cass. 79.95 (978-1-55503-278-4(8), 0200434) Covenant Comms.

Standard Operating Procedure: A War Story. Philip Gourevitch & Errol Morris. (Running Time: 10 hrs.). (ENG.). (YA). (gr. 12). 2008. audio compact disk 34.95 (978-0-14-314268-3(2), PengAudBks) Penguin Grp USA.

Standard Series: Introduction. Milady Publishing Company Staff. 1 cass. 1995. 6.95 (978-1-56253-299-4(5), Milady) Delmar.

Standard System Hairdressing Support Tools CD-ROM. 2001. audio compact disk 260.95 (978-1-56253-665-7(6), Milady) Pub: Delmar. Dist(s): CENGAGE Learn

Standard Turn-Arounds. Duane Shinn. 1 cass. 19.95 (CP-15) Duane Shinn.
Turn-arounds are chord progressions which are used at the end of a phrase to get one launched into the next phrase.

Standardized Testing. 2 cass. (Running Time: 1 hr. per cass.). 9.00 Pts I & II. (D032AB090, HarperThor); 9.00 Pts III & IV. (OE-81-07-13, HarperThor) HarpC GBR.

Standardized Testing Differs from Informal Testing, How. Shelley C. Stone. 1 cass. (Running Time: 20 min.). 1968. (29235) J Norton Pubs.
A discussion of the basic differences between standardized & the more familiar, teacher-made informal tests, & the ways they resemble each other.

Standards are Not Enough: Essential Transformations for Successful Schools. Douglas B. Reeves. 2003. video & audio compact disk 14.00 (978-0-9709455-2-5(3)) LeadplusLrn.
Presents the latest research on student achievement. leadership strategies, and effective teaching practices.

Standards Are Not Enough: Essential Transformations for Successful Schools. Douglas B. Reeves. 2002. audio compact disk 15.00 (978-0-9709455-7-0(4)) LeadplusLrn.

Standards for Guitar: Intermediate-Advanced Level. John Griggs & Carlos Barbosa-Lima. 1998. pap. bk. 19.95 (978-0-7866-2079-1(X), 95988BCD) Mel Bay.

Standards for Solo Singers (12 Contemporary Settings of Favorites from the Great American Songbook for Solo Voice & Piano) Medium High Voice. Composed by Jay Althouse. (For Solo Singers Ser.). (ENG.). 2007. audio compact disk 13.95 (978-0-7390-4716-3(7)) Alfred Pub.

Standards for Solo Singers (12 Contemporary Settings of Favorites from the Great American Songbook for Solo Voice & Piano) Medium Low Voice. Composed by Jay Althouse. (For Solo Singers Ser.). (ENG.). 2007. audio compact disk 13.95 (978-0-7390-4717-0(5)) Alfred Pub.

Standards of Leadership. Paul Cain. 1 cass. (Running Time: 90 mins.). (next move of God Ser.: Vol. 2). 2000. 5.00 (PC02-002) Morning NC.
"The Face of the Next Move of God" & "Standards of Leadership." The requirements to be part of the next move of God are examined in these powerful messages.

Standards Reprints. Ed. by Marco A. V. Bitetto. 1 cass. 2000. (978-1-58578-062-4(6)) Inst of Cybernetics.

Standhaftige Tinsoldat see Steadfast Tin Soldier

Standin' Tall Cleanliness. Janeen Brady. Illus. by Neil Galloway. (J). (ps-6). 1984. pap. bk. 12.95 (978-0-944803-55-4(5)) Brite Music.

Standin' Tall Courage. Janeen Brady. Illus. by Grant Wilson. (J). (ps-6). 1982. pap. bk. 11.95 (978-0-944803-45-5(8)) Brite Music.

Standin' Tall Forgiveness. Janeen Brady. Illus. by Grant Wilson & Neil Galloway. (J). (ps-6). 1981. pap. bk. 11.95 (978-0-944803-40-0(7)) Brite Music.

Standin' Tall Gratitude. Janeen J. Brady & Diane Woolley. Illus. by Grant Wilson. (J). (ps-6). 1982. pap. bk. 11.95 (978-0-944803-49-3(0)) Brite Music.

Standin' Tall Happiness. Janeen J. Brady & Diane Woolley. Illus. by Grant Wilson. (J). (ps-6). 1982. pap. bk. 11.95 (978-0-944803-47-9(4)) Brite Music.

Standin' Tall Honesty. Janeen Brady. Illus. by Grant Wilson & Neil Galloway. (J). (ps-6). 1981. pap. bk. 11.95 (978-0-944803-38-7(5)) Brite Music.

Standin' Tall Self-Esteem. Janeen J. Brady & Diane Woolley. Illus. by Grant Wilson. (J). (ps-6). 1984. pap. bk. 11.95 (978-0-944803-57-8(1)) Brite Music.

Standin' Tall Service. Janeen J. Brady & Diane Woolley. Illus. by Grant Wilson. (J). (ps-6). 1984. pap. bk. 11.95 (978-0-944803-53-0(9)) Brite Music.

Standin' Tall Work. Janeen Brady. Illus. by Grant Wilson & Neil Galloway. (J). (ps-6). 1981. pap. bk. 11.95 (978-0-944803-42-4(3)) Brite Music.

Standing Against the Enemy: Ephesians 6:10-18. Ed Young. 1983. 4.95 (978-0-7417-1310-0(1), 310) Win Walk.

Standing Alone. 1 cass. 10.00 Esstee Audios.
After the fall of France in 1940, England stood between Hitler & the fall of civilization.

Standing Alone. (Paws & Tales Ser.: Vol. 6). 2001. 3.99 (978-1-57972-396-5(9)); audio compact disk 5.99 (978-1-57972-397-2(7)) Insight Living.

Standing for Something: Ten Neglected Virtues That Will Heal Our Hearts & Homes. Gordon B. Hinckley. Read by George Grizzard. 2004. 15.95 (978-0-7435-1945-8(0)) Pub: S&S Audio. Dist(s): S and S Inc

Standing in the Rainbow. unabr. ed. Fannie Flagg. Read by Kate Reading. 11 cass. (Running Time: 16 hrs. 30 mins.). 2002. 117.00 (978-0-7366-8668-6(1)); audio compact disk 135.00 (978-0-7366-8669-3(X)) Books on Tape.
World War Two has ended, and in the bucolic realms of Elmwood Springs, Missouri, peace has broken out all over. Bobby Smith, ten, is the effervescent son of the well-known radio hostess Neighbor Dorothy, who broadcasts every day from her living room, via the tower in her backyard, to an eager, at times lonely audience. We come to know the Oatman Family Southern Gospel Singers; a super-salesman everyone likes and trusts who soon sells all of Missouri; and the phenomena known as the Sunset Club, Dinner on the Ground, and the Funeral King. By novel's end, we see how these characters, and many more, deal with the wonders of a changing America, and we wish that we had been there, too, standing in the rainbow with th.

Standing in the Shadows. unabr. ed. Michelle Spring. Read by Rachel Atkins. 8 cass. (Running Time: 9 hrs.). (Isis Ser.). (J). 2003. 69.95 (978-0-7531-0377-7(X)) Pub: ISIS Lrg Prnt GBR. Dist(s): Ulverscroft US
Laura Principle investigates the case of an eleven-year-old boy who has murdered his foster mother. Not the sort of crime one would expect in Cambridge. The child, Daryll, has confessed to the killing: now his elder brother wants to find out what has turned him into an apparently ruthless killer. But as Laura becomes increasingly involved in Daryll's background, she is forced to confront some disturbing questions. And that's not all. Someone is standing in the shadows, watching Laura's every move.

Standing Like a Stone Wall: The Life of General Thomas J. Jackson. unabr. ed. James I. Robertson, Jr. Narrated by Jack Garrett. 6 pieces. (Running Time: 7 hrs. 15 mins.). (gr. 7 up). 2002. 54.00 (978-1-4025-1729-7(7)) Recorded Bks.
The story of Jackson's life.

Standing on Fishes. NorthWord Books for Young Readers Editors. 2 cass. (Running Time: 2 hrs.). 1995. 16.95 (978-0-939643-62-2(6), NrthWrd Bks) TandN Child.

Standing on the Promises. Mark Hayes. 2000. audio compact disk 19.95 (978-0-7390-1371-7(8), 19870) Alfred Pub.

Standing on the Word. Gloria Copeland. 1 cass. 1985. 5.00 (978-0-88114-748-3(6)) K Copeland Pubns.
How to use God's word for victorious living.

Standing on the Word. Gloria Copeland. (ENG.). 2009. audio compact disk 5.00 (978-1-57562-989-6(5)) K Copeland Pubns.

Standing Right Here Next to Me. Karla Bonhoff. 1 cass. 1999. pap. bk. 7.98 (978-0-7601-2885-5(5)) Brentwood Music.

Standing Room Only. 10.98 (978-1-57908-365-6(X), 1419); audio compact disk 15.98 CD. (978-1-57908-364-9(1), 1419) Platinm Enter.

***Standing Strong.** unabr. ed. Donna Fleisher. (Running Time: 10 hrs. 27 mins. 0 sec.). (Homeland Heroes Ser.). (ENG.). 2009. 14.99 (978-0-310-77187-6(0)) Zondervan.

Standing Strong: Stories of Changed Lives. Promise Keepers Staff. 1 cass. (Running Time: 1 hrs. 30 mins.). 1999. bk. 12.99 (978-0-8499-5501-3(7)) Nelson.

Standing Strong in Difficult Times. Speeches. Told to Joel Osteen. 1 Cass. (Running Time: 30 Mins). 2002. 6.00 (978-1-59349-139-0(5), JA0139) J Osteen.

Standing Strong in Difficult Times. Speeches. Joel Osteen. 6 audio cass. (J). 2002. 24.00 (978-1-931877-18-3(1), JAS014); audio compact disk 24.00 (978-1-931877-35-0(1), JCS014) J Osteen.

Standing Strong in the Trial of Your Faith. Speeches. Joel Osteen. 1 Cass. (Running Time: 30 Mins.). 2000. 6.00 (978-1-59349-085-0(2), JA0085) J Osteen.

Standing Tall: A Memoir of Tragedy & Triumph. abr. ed. C. Vivian Stringer & Laura Tucker. Read by C. Vivian Stringer et al. 5 CDs. (Running Time: 6 hrs.). (ENG.). 2008. audio compact disk 29.95 (978-0-7393-2911-5(1), Random AudioBks) Pub: Random Audio Pubg. Dist(s): Random

Standing Tall: A Memoir of Tragedy & Triumph. unabr. ed. C. Vivian Stringer & Laura Tucker. 8 CDs. (Running Time: 10 hrs.). 2008. audio compact disk 80.00 (978-1-4159-4992-4(1)) Random.

Standing Tall: Daniel 12:13. Ben Young. 2000. 4.95 (978-0-7417-6217-7(X), B0217) Win Walk.

Standing up in a Fallen World. Chuck Smith. 4 cass. (Running Time: 3 hrs.). 2001. 12.95 (978-0-936728-89-6(2), TPSUI01) Word For Today.
A collection of Bible study messages going through the book of Daniel.

Standoff. unabr. ed. Sandra Brown. Read by Enid Graham. 6 cass. (Running Time: 9 hrs.). 2000. 54.95 (CSL 329, Chivers Sound Lib) AudioGO.
T.V. reporter Tiel McCoy is on her way to New Mexico for a well-earned vacation. She hears on the radio that the daughter of well-known Fort Worth multimillionaire Russell Dendy has been kidnapped. Tiel abandons her holiday plans in favor of pursuing the story.

Standoff. unabr. ed. Sandra Brown. Read by Enid Graham. 6 CDs. (Running Time: 9 hrs.). 2000. audio compact disk 64.95 (978-0-7927-9981-8(X), SLD 032, Chivers Sound Lib) AudioGO.

Standoff. unabr. ed. Sandra Brown. Read by Enid Graham. (Running Time: 63 hrs. 0 mins. 0 sec.). 2003. audio compact disk 14.95 (978-0-7435-3262-4(7), S&S Encore) Pub: S&S Audio. Dist(s): S and S Inc

***Standoff at Tinajas Altas.** Tim Champlin. 2009. (978-1-60136-463-0(6)) Audio Holding.

Stanley & the Women. unabr. collector's ed. Kingsley Amis. Read by Richard Green. 6 cass. (Running Time: 9 hrs.). 1986. 48.00 (978-0-7366-0816-9(8), 1765) Books on Tape.
Stanley Duke, attractive, prosperous & happily remarried, leads a life that is positively enviable - that is, until it becomes apparent that his teenage son, Steve, is going mad. Stanley's confrontation with his son's madness gives Amis the opportunity to pull off a comic masterpiece.

Stanley Easter. Donald Davis. Read by Donald David. 1 cass. (Running Time: 57 mins.). 1996. 12.00 (978-0-87483-505-2(4)) Pub: August Hse. Dist(s): Natl Bk Netwk
This story of accepting one's roots endears anyone who has ever thought twice about admitting where they came from. Davis, in his sly narration, acknowledges that a whole lifetime of thoughts & attitudes can be rearranged in a single moment.

Stanley Elkin. Interview with Stanley Elkin. 1 cass. (Running Time: 25 min.). 1981. 11.95 (L021) TFR.
Elkin talks about his novels, "The Franchiser" & "The Dick Gibson Show." He says he knows of no subject that is too painful for humor, including his own struggle with muscular dystrophy.

Stanley Elkin. unabr. ed. Stanley Elkin. 1 cass. (Running Time: 29 min.). 1985. 10.00 New Letters.
A talk with the winner of the 1982 National Book Award & a reading from "The Dick Gibson Show".

Stanley Elkin, No. 11. unabr. ed. Stanley Elkin. Read by Stanley Elkin. 1 cass. (Running Time: 29 min.). 1988. 10.00 (120288) New Letters.
Elkin won the National Book Critics Circle Award for "George Mills." Here he reads an essay about his father, a salesman who inspired the novel "Franchiser".

Stanley Elkin: Interview. Interview. Interview with Stanley Elkin & Lyn Ballard. 1 cass. (Running Time: 1 hr. 6 min.). 13.95 (978-1-55644-011-3(1), 1062) Am Audio Prose.
Full of Elkin's wit & wisdom on a variety of topics concerning the teaching & craft of writing, with marvelous anecdotes.

Stanley Ellin: Die Spezialitat des Hauses. 1 cass. (Running Time: 1 hr.). (GER.). 18.95 (CGE345) J Norton Pubs.
The macabre story of an exquisite restaurant & the special dish that hides a hair-raising secret.

Stanley Karnow: History of Vietnam. Narrated by Stanley Karnow. 1 cass. (Running Time: 60 min.). 10.95 (K0210B090, HarperThor) HarpC GBR.

Stanley Kunitz. Interview with Stanley Kunitz. 1 cass. (Running Time: 25 min.). 1978. 11.95 (L041) TFR.
The Pulitzer prize winning poet talks about his fascination with nature & the similarities between a poem & a garden.

Stanley Kunitz, Vol. II. unabr. ed. Ed. by Jim McKinley. Prod. by Rebekah Presson. 1 cass. (Running Time: 29 min.). (New Letters on the Air Ser.). 1994. 10.00 (012293) New Letters.
This is the balance of the interview broadcast in December, featuring the 87 year old Pulitzer Prize winner, who is also the Poet Laureate of New York state. Kunitz reads poems & talks about gardening, which he sees as an activity equal to that of writing poems. He also talks about his feeling of connection to the natural world, saying that humans are no different than any other animals or growing things, even stones.

Stanley Kunitz One, Two. unabr. ed. Poems. Stanley Kunitz. Ed. by James McKinley. Prod. by Rebeah Presson. 1 cass. (Running Time: 29 min.). (On the Air Ser.). 1993. 10.00 New Letters.
Pulitzer-Prize winner & New York Poet Laureate reads poems, & interview.

Stanley Meets Mutesa see Poems from Black Africa

Stanley Park. abr. ed. Timothy L. Taylor. Contrib. by Betty Quan. Betty Quan. 2 CDs. (Running Time: 2 hrs.). (ENG.). 2004. audio compact disk 19.95 (978-0-86492-389-9(9)) Pub: BTC Audiobks CAN. Dist(s): U Toronto Pr
Alessandro Juliani stars as Jeremy Papier, a brilliant, young Parisian-trained chef, who will do almost anything to keep his high-end Vancouver restaurant, Monkey's Paw Bistro, afloat. Jeremy, who views the cooking industry in terms of gang warfare, is a self-styled "Blood," a believer in preparing unpretentious dishes from fresh, local ingredients. He has nothing but contempt for the "Crips" who bow to every passing food fad. But when his latest financial scam fails, Jeremy is forced to strike a deal with the devil in the form of Dante Beale (played by Scott Hylands), the owner of an undeniably "Crip" chain of gourmet coffee shops.

Stanley Plumly. unabr. ed. Read by Stanley Plumly & Rebekah Presson. Ed. by James McKinley. 1 cass. (Running Time: 29 min.). (New Letters on the Air Ser.). 1994. 10.00 (102494); 18.00 2-sided cass. New Letters.
Plumly is interviewed by Rebekah Presson & reads from his work.

Stanley the Christmas Tree, A Wish Come True Audio Book. adpt. ed. R. E. Hughes. Perf. by Nickels Pennie. Narrated by Mackenzie Paul. Music by Williams Maynard. Saunders Anita. (ENG.). (J). 2008. audio compact disk 14.95 (978-0-9820328-1-7(1)) Pennie Rich.

Stansfield Career Advancement System. Richard H. Stansfield. Read by Richard Gebhart. 4 cass. 1989. 29.95 (3030) SyberVision.
Discusses how to spell out what one has accomplished in your career so that your prospective employer can clearly see your worth.

Stanway Cameo Mystery see Martin Hewitt, Investigator

Stanway Cameo Mystery. unabr. ed. Arthur Morrison. Read by Walter Covell. 1 cass. (Running Time: 50 min.). Dramatization. 1981. 7.95 (S-13) Jimcin Record.
Martin Hewitt on the trail of missing art treasures.

Stanzas for Music see Treasury of George Gordon, Lord Byron

Stapled Anastomosis: Indications; Technical Problems; & Complications. 2 cass. (Colon & Rectal Surgery Ser.: C84-CR4). 1984. 15.00 (8431) Am Coll Surgeons.

Staples for Success. Thomas G. Stemberg & David D. Busch. 1 cass. (Running Time: 1 hr.). 1996. pap. bk. 12.00 (978-1-888232-25-7(0)) Pub: Spurge ink. Dist(s): Natl Bk Netwk

***Star: How Warren Beatty Seduced America.** unabr. ed. Peter Biskind. Narrated by David Drummond. (Running Time: 23 hrs. 30 mins. 0 sec.). (ENG.). 2010. 39.99 (978-1-4001-6574-2(1)); 25.99 (978-1-4001-8574-0(2)); audio compact disk 109.99 (978-1-4001-4574-4(0)); audio compact disk 54.99 (978-1-4001-1574-7(4)) Pub: Tantor Media. Dist(s): IngramPubServ

Star & Other Stories. unabr. ed. H. G. Wells. Read by Walter Covell. 1 cass. (Running Time: 110 min.). Dramatization. Incl. Crystal Egg. 1981. (S-3); Red Room. 1981. (S-3); 1981. 7.95 (S-3) Jimcin Record.

Star & Snow: Christmas Songs for Solo Piano. Christopher Leonard. 1 cass. 1991. 9.95 (978-1-887756-04-4(3)) Richmnd Hill.
Musical recording.

Star Beast. unabr. ed. Robert Heinlein. Read by Full Cast Production Staff. (J). 2007. 44.99 (978-1-60252-703-4(2)) Find a World.

Star Called Henry. Roddy Doyle. Narrated by Gerard Doyle. 11 CDs. (Running Time: 12 hrs. 45 mins.). audio compact disk 111.00 (978-0-7887-5200-1(6)) Recorded Bks.

Star Called Henry. unabr. ed. Roddy Doyle. Narrated by Gerard Doyle. 9 cass. (Running Time: 12 hrs. 45 mins.). 2000. 81.00 (978-0-7887-4402-0(X), 96100E7) Recorded Bks.
The life of a young man, born in the Dublin slums in 1901, who became a soldier in the Irish Rebellion by the time he is 14. The Dublin accents & Gaelic phrases create a man & an Ireland you will not soon forget.

Star Called Wormwood: Rev. 8:1-13. Ed Young. 1986. Rental 4.95 (978-0-7417-1564-7(3), 564) Win Walk.

Star Child: David Haas & Friends. David Haas. 1 cass. 1999. 10.95 (CS-471); audio compact disk 15.95 (CD-471) GIA Pubns.

Star Comes Home. Caroline Stutson. Read by Tom Chapin. 1 cass. (Running Time: 12 min.). (Humane Society of the United States Animal Tales Ser.). (J). (gr. 1-4). 1998. pap. bk. 19.95 Incl. plush animal. (978-1-58021-050-8(3)) Benefactory.
In 1995, a truckful of horses, illegally bound for Canada, was stopped just in time. A tiny Shetland pony, found sheltered beneath a giant draft horse, heals slowly & finds a loving home.

Star Comes Home. Caroline Stutson. Read by Tom Chapin. 1 cass. (Running Time: 12 min.). (Humane Society of the United States Animal Tales Ser.). (J). (gr. 1-4). 1999. pap. bk. 9.95 (978-1-58021-048-5(1)) Benefactory.

Star Crusaders of the Earthian Foundation Vol. 1: First Crusade: Entombment on Vultrex. Bob E. Flick & Adam Mayefsky. 2 cass. (Running Time: 1 hr. 45 min.). Dramatization. (Star Crusaders of the Earthian Foundation Ser.: Vol. 1). 1999. 16.99 (978-1-884214-04-2(5)) Ziggurat Prods.
All new original science-fiction series: an aging group of earth-born scientists attempt to save mankind by finding another planet to inhabit. Will they overcome all the obstacles & dangers in time?.

Star Crusaders of the Earthian Foundation Vol. 1: First Crusade: Entombment on Vultrex. unabr. ed. Bob E. Flick & Adam Mayefsky. Created by Bob E. Flick. 2 CDs. (Running Time: 1hr. 45 min.). Dramatization. (Star Crusaders of the Earthian Foundation Ser.: Vol. 1). 1999. audio compact disk 19.99 (978-1-884214-05-9(3)) Ziggurat Prods.

Star Crusaders of the Earthian Foundation Vol. 2: Second Crusade: Mass Extinction. abr. ed. Bob E. Flick & Adam Mayefsky. Created by Bob E. Flick. 1 CD. (Running Time: 68 mins.). Dramatization. (Star Crusaders of the Earthian Foundation Ser.: Vol. 2). 2000. audio compact disk 15.99 (978-1-884214-09-7(6)) Ziggurat Prods.

Star Crusaders of the Earthian Foundation Vol. 2: Second Crusade: Mass Extinction. abr. ed. Bob E. Flick & Adam Mayefsky. Created by Bob E. Flick. 1 Cass. (Running Time: 68 min.). Dramatization. (Star Crusaders of the Earthian Foundation Ser.: Vol. 2). 2000. 12.99 (978-1-884214-20-2(7)) Ziggurat Prods.

Star Dreamer. Perf. by Priscilla Herdman. (J). 9.98 (2136) MFLP CA.
Beautiful arrangements with accordions, cellos, mandolins, piano, fiddles & rich harmonies - a great selection of 15 timeless tunes.

Star Flight. unabr. ed. Phyllis A. Whitney. Read by Anna Fields. 6 cass. (Running Time: 8 hrs. 30 mins.). 1997. 44.95 (978-0-7861-1211-1(5), 1991) Blckstn Audio.
It has been two years since Lauren's filmmaker husband died mysteriously. Now Lauren has received a warning that her husband was murdered. What deadly secret had he uncovered in this scenic idyll? To find her answers, Lauren must face her own past & delve into the dark truths of a place shrouded in terrifying secrets.

Star Flight. unabr. ed. Phyllis A. Whitney. Read by Anna Fields. (Running Time: 8 hrs. 30 mins.). 2010. 29.95 (978-1-4417-0713-0(1)); audio compact disk 76.00 (978-1-4417-0710-9(7)) Blckstn Audio.

Star Garden. unabr. ed. Nancy E. Turner. Read by Laura Hicks. (YA). 2008. 94.99 (978-1-60514-515-0(7)) Find a World.

Star Husband. 1 cass. (Kiowa, Star Lore Ser.). 12.95 (C19204) J Norton Pubs.
Native American myths.

Star Is Born. Perf. by Judy Garland & Walter Pidgeon. 1 cass. Dramatization. 7.95 (DD6800) Natl Recrd Co.

***Star Island.** unabr. ed. Carl Hiaasen. Read by Stephen Hoye. 9 CDs. (Running Time: 11 hrs. 30 mins.). 2010. audio compact disk 40.00 (978-0-7393-8512-8(7), Random AudioBks) Pub: Random Audio Pubg. Dist(s): Random

Star Journey. 1 CD. (Running Time: 35 min.). (J). 2001. audio compact disk 80.00 (MU-9274T) Lillenas.
Meet Quasar, Venus & Polaris "star" characters in this imaginative kids' musical. Along with Moon, their adult adviser, these heavenly characters interact with earth & relate their views of present-day Christmas & the original Christmas event. Original songs & an intriguing arrangement of "O Little Town of Bethlehem" combine with a highly creative, humorous script, giving solo & dramatic opportunities for lots of kids. The trax are especially fresh-sounding, utilizing "live" instruments. A strong, biblical message of God's love & concern for us is woven throughout, offering a uniquely evangelistic message from children.

Star Journey: A Most Heavenly Children's Christmas Musical. 1 cass. (Running Time: 35 min.). (J). 2001. 80.00 (MU-9274C) Lillenas.
Meet Quasar, Venus & Polaris - "star" characters in this imaginative kids' musical. Along with Moon, their adult adviser, these heavenly characters interact with earth & relate their views of present-day Christmas & the original Christmas event. Original songs & an intriguing arrangement of "O Little Town of Bethlehem" combine with a highly creative, humorous script, giving solo & dramatic opportunities for lots of kids. The trax are especially fresh-sounding, utilizing "live" instruments. A strong, biblical message of God's love & concern for us is woven throughout, offering a uniquely evangelistic message from children. Accompaniment cassette with side 1, split-channel & side 2, stereo trax.

Star Lake Saloon & Housekeeping Cottages. abr. ed. Sara Rath. Read by Jim Fleming. (ENG.). 2006. audio compact disk 34.95 (978-0-299-22100-3(8)) Pub: U of Wis Pr. Dist(s): Chicago Distribution Ctr

Star of Bethlehem. (J). (ps-3). 2000. 7.98 (978-1-887729-31-4(3)) Toy Box Prods.

Star of Bethlehem. Elizabeth Gauerke. 1 cass. 8.95 (525) Am Fed Astrologers.
What did it really mean?.

Star of Bethlehem. abr. ed. Joe Loesch. Ed. by Cheryl J. Hutchinson. Illus. by Ott Denney. 1 CD. (CD Bible Stories for Kids Ser.: Vol. 4). (J). (ps-3). 1996. pap. bk. 16.95 (978-1-887729-13-0(5)) Toy Box Prods.
The animals tell the story of Mary & Joseph's travel to Bethlehem, the Three Wise Men, King Herod & the blessed birth of Jesus.

Star of Bethlehem. unabr. ed. Joe Loesch. Ed. by Cheryl J. Hutchinson. Illus. by Ott Denney. 1 cass. (Bible Stories for Kids Ser.: Vol. 4). (J). (gr. 1-5). 1996. pap. bk. 14.95 (978-1-887729-12-3(7)) Toy Box Prods.

Star of Kazan. unabr. ed. Eva Ibbotson. Read by Patricia Conolly. 7 cass. (Running Time: 10 hrs. 25 mins.). 2005. 61.75 (978-1-4193-2001-9(7), 94937) Recorded Bks.
In early 20th-century Vienna, Annika is raised by Ellie and Sigrid, a cook and housemaid for a household of three professors. Abandoned when she was a baby, Annika dreams of the day her mother will come back to claim her. Then one day, it happens. A glamorous woman arrives and sweeps Annika away to a crumbling castle in Germany. But there is much more to this new woman than meets the eye and none of it is good.

Star of the Sea. unabr. ed. Joseph O'Connor. Read by Peter Marinker. 11 cass. 2005. 89.95 (978-0-7927-3439-0(4), CSL 767); audio compact disk 112.95 (978-0-7927-3440-6(8), SLD 767) AudioGO.

Star of Wonder. Monica Ballard. 1 CD. (Running Time: 1hour 27min 35sec). 2005. pap. bk. 12.95 (978-1-932226-37-9(0)) Pub: Wizard Acdmy. Dist(s): Baker Taylor
The four Evangelists serve you at the museum snack bar? the gift shop is run by the Magi and a ragged shepherd ? and the planetarium show features the constellation of - the Buick? So goes the strange dream of a widow as she jets home after an uncomfortable visit with family and considers their reaction to her husband?s death. But it?s also the answer to her unspoken question, ?What next?? A story for all seasons, Star of Wonder is about recovery, reclamation and renewal. Anyone who has suffered setbacks or second-guessed their abilities will find guidance and illumination in this Journey Back to Creativity. Make your way to the Observation Deck of this museum, see age-old characters in a new light and come to appreciate how ?Each day is a gift.? ?The perfect remedy for anyone who feels ?stuck? and needs that nod from the Universe. Ms. Ballard has struck the perfect harmony between what you might hear from the pulpit and what you can use in the real world.? Roxanne Walker Cordonier, Columnist, MetroBeat MagazineIncludes:1hour 27min 35sec on 2 Audio CDs63 page booklet.

Star of Wonder, Star of Light the Christ Church Choir of New York City CD. 2005. audio compact disk 15.00 (978-0-687-33134-5(X)) Abingdon.

***Star Principle: How It Can Make You Rich.** Richard Koch. Read by Richard Aspel. (Running Time: 7 hrs. 10 mins.). 2010. 69.99 (978-1-74214-598-3(1), 9781742145983) Pub: Bolinda Pubng AUS. Dist(s): Bolinda Pub Inc

Star Principle: How It Can Make You Rich. unabr. ed. Richard Koch. Read by Richard Aspel. (Running Time: 7 hrs. 10 mins.). 2009. audio compact disk 77.95 (978-1-74214-120-6(X), 9781742141206) Pub: Bolinda Pubng AUS. Dist(s): Bolinda Pub Inc

Star Principle: How It Can Make You Rich. unabr. ed. Richard Koch. Read by Richard Aspel. (Running Time: 7 hrs. 10 mins.). 2009. 43.95 (978-1-74214-499-3(3), 9781742144993) Pub: Bolinda Pubng AUS. Dist(s): Bolinda Pub Inc

Star Quality. Pamela Evans. Read by Annie Aldington. 11 CDs. (Running Time: 12 hrs. 30 mins.). (Soundings (CDs) Ser.). (J). 2004. audio compact disk 99.95 (978-1-84283-784-9(2)) Pub: ISIS Lrg Prnt GBR. Dist(s): Ulverscroft US

Star Quality. unabr. ed. Pamela Evans. Read by Annie Aldington. 10 cass. (Running Time: 12 hrs. 40 mins.). (Sound Ser.). 2002. 84.95 (978-1-84283-004-8(X)) Pub: UlverLrgPrint GBR. Dist(s): Ulverscroft US
Meeting at a Saturday night dance, Tess and Max are instantly attracted, soon discovering they share the same dreams. But Max's ambitions drive them apart. Betrayed by the man she loves, Tess tries to find fulfillment in marriage, and her successful fineware shop. Then Tess's nineteen-year-old daughter, Judy, meets and falls in love with a musician: it is Max Bentley.

Star Quality: A Collection of Short Stories. unabr. ed. Noel Coward. Read by Derek Jacobi & Denholm Elliott. 6 cass. (Running Time: 8 hrs. 41 min.). (Cassette Library). 1987. 44.98 (978-0-8072-3113-5(4), CXL 536CX, Listening Lib) Random Audio Pubg.
From the volume of short stories that was recently featured on TV's "Masterpiece Theatre" under the title of Star Quality, the stories featured in this collection are works of the man Harpers magazine called "The Master." Presented here is a World unto itself... "A world spinning happily on the fingertip of its creator, in all its mad, charming, frivolous glory".

Star-Scape over Europe, Vols. 1-3. 3 cass. 8.98 Vol. 1. (KGOC19); 8.98 Vol. 2. (KGOC20); 8.98 Vol. 3. (KGOC21) Ken Mills Found.
Kenneth G. Mills conducts The Star-Scape Singers live on tour in Europe, also available on LP.

Star Search (A Light Musical for Unison & 2-Part Voices) SoundTrax. Composed by Janet Gardner & Jay Althouse. (ENG.). 2003. audio compact disk 59.95 (978-0-7390-3102-5(3)) Alfred Pub.

Star Ship Technology Handbook. Ed. by Marco A. V. Bitetto. 1 cass. 2000. (978-1-58578-298-7(X)) Inst of Cybernetics.

Star Spangled: Songs of America. 1 cass., 1 CD. 7.18 (CMH 6285); audio compact disk 9.58 CD Jewel box. (CMH 6285) NewSound.

Star Spangled Banner. 2004. pap. bk. 38.75 (978-1-55592-644-1(4)); pap. bk. 14.95 (978-0-7882-0310-7(X)) Weston Woods.

Star-Spangled Banner. 2004. bk. 24.95 (978-0-7882-0563-7(3)); pap. bk. 32.75 (978-1-55592-625-0(8)); 8.95 (978-1-56008-332-0(8)); cass. & flmstrp 30.00 (978-1-56008-766-3(8)) Weston Woods.

Star-Spangled Banner. Peter Spier. 1 cass. (Running Time: 12 mins.). (J). (ps-6). 2004. pap. bk. 14.95 (978-1-55592-160-6(4)); pap. bk. 18.95 (978-1-55592-144-6(2)); pap. bk. 14.95 (978-1-55592-161-3(2)); pap. bk. 18.95 (978-1-55592-143-9(4)); 8.95 (978-1-55592-829-2(3)); audio compact disk 12.95 (978-1-55592-896-4(X)) Weston Woods.
Classic interpretation of our national anthem.

Star Spangled Banner. unabr. ed. Ingri Parin D'Aulaire & Edgar Parin D'Aulaire. 1 cass. (Running Time: 6 min.). (J). (gr. 3-5). 1992. pap. bk. 20.00 (6512-C) Spoken Arts.

Star Spangled Banner in Translation: What It Really Means. Elizabeth Raum. Contrib. by Amy Stockhaus & Scott Combs. (Kids' Translations Ser.). (ENG.). (gr. 3-4). 2008. audio compact disk 17.32 (978-1-4296-3218-8(6)) CapstoneDig.

Star-Spangled Stories. Focus on the Family & AIO Team Staff. (Running Time: 1 hr. 0 mins.). (Adventures in Odyssey Ser.). (ENG.). (J). (gr. 1). 2007. audio compact disk 1.99 (978-1-58997-459-3(X), Tyndale Ent) Tyndale Hse.

Star Spangled Stories. Prod. by Focus on the Family Staff. 6 cass. (Running Time: 360 min.). (Adventures in Odyssey Classics Ser.: Vol. 6). (J). (gr. 3-7). 2000. 24.99 (978-1-56179-873-5(8)) Bethany Hse.

Star Spangled Stories of American History. Prod. by Focus on the Family Staff. (Running Time: 6 hrs.). (Adventures in Odyssey Classics Ser.: No. 6). 2000. audio compact disk 24.99 (978-1-56179-874-2(6)) Pub: Focus Family. Dist(s): Nelson
Here's an Adventures in Odyssey Classics Album chock-full of American History! From Christopher Columbus's grand voyage, throught the colonists' struggle for independence from England, to the writing of The Star-Spangled Banner, as well as the Underground Railroad, Abraham Lincoln, the attack on Pearl Harbor and stories from World War II, this collection has something for everyone.

Star Still Shines: A Diamond Rio Christmas. Contrib. by Diamond Rio. Prod. by Michael D. Clute & Jimmy Olander. 2007. audio compact disk 18.99 (978-5-557-59241-3(5), Word Records) Word Enter.

Star-Stone Tribes - Soul Sounds of World Birth. Ani Lea & Mary Saint-Marie. 1 cass. 9.95 (978-0-9645725-0-8(8)) Numina.

Star Strategy: The Comprehensive Guide to Personal & Financial Success. 1998. (978-0-9705107-0-9(5)) Star Strategy.

Star Struck. Val McDermid & Val Mcdermid. (Isis (CDs) Ser.). (J). 2005. audio compact disk 89.95 (978-0-7531-2397-3(5)) Pub: ISIS Lrg Prnt GBR. Dist(s): Ulverscroft US

Star Struck. unabr. ed. Val McDermid. Read by Laura Brattan. 8 cass. 1999. 69.95 (978-0-7531-0543-6(8), 990403) Pub: ISIS Audio GBR. Dist(s): Ulverscroft US
Manchester PI Kate Brannigan is hired to play nursemaid to a paranoid soap star. Soon offstage dramas overshadow the fictional story-lines, culminating in unscripted murder & Kate finds herself with more questions than answers. What's more, her tame hacker has found virtual love & the ever-reliable Dennis has had the timerity to get himself charged with murder.

Star Team. Norman Whitney. 2005. audio compact disk 37.50 (978-0-19-448061-1(5)) OUP.

Star Team Starter. Norman Whitney. 2005. audio compact disk 37.50 (978-0-19-448054-3(2)) OUP.

Star Team 2. Norman Whitney. 2005. audio compact disk 37.50 (978-0-19-448068-0(2)) OUP.

Star Team 3: Audio CDs (2) Norman Whitney. 2005. audio compact disk 37.50 (978-0-19-448075-8(5)) OUP.

Star, the Crystal Egg & the Red Room. H. G. Wells. 1 cass. 1989. 7.95 (S-3) Jimcin Record.
Science fiction & the supernatural.

Star Tracks: Sir Bernard Lowell on Listening to the Universe. 1 cass. (Running Time: 26 min.). 14.95 (35284) MMI Corp.
Discusses theories of creation, optical & radio telescopes, quasars & discoveries he has made.

Star Trap. unabr. ed. Simon Brett. Read by Simon Brett. 6 cass. (Running Time: 6 hrs.). 1995. 54.95 Set. (978-0-7451-6481-6(1), CAB 1097) AudioGO.
A nervous Gerald Venables hires Charles Paris for a part in the musical, "She Stoops to Conquer," in order to keep an eye on things. Tension comes from the brilliant but egomaniacal star, Christopher Milton. Soon, accidents begin & it's obvious that someone is trying to sabotage the show.

Star Trap. unabr. ed. Simon Brett. Read by Geoffrey Howard. 4 cass. (Running Time: 5 hrs. 30 mins.). 2000. 32.95 (978-0-7861-1750-5(8), 2554); audio compact disk 40.00 (978-0-7861-9901-3(6), 2554) Blckstn Audio.
Charles Paris has landed a dual role in a lavish West End musical, onstage as a bit player, offstage as an undercover sleuth. The production's nervous backers fear that someone is trying to kill the play. The ultimate showstopper would be to eliminate the star.

Star Trap. unabr. ed. Simon Brett. Narrated by Simon Prebble. 5 cass. (Running Time: 6 hrs. 45 mins.). (Charles Paris Mystery Ser.: Vol. 3). 1997. 44.00 (978-0-7887-1146-6(6), 95084E7) Recorded Bks.
When suspicious accidents plague the company, Charles discovers the glamorous make-believe hides a cast teemed with dangerous, dirty secrets & bizarre accidents.

Star Trek. 1 cass. (Star Trek Ser.). (978-0-7921-2101-5(5)); CD. (978-0-7921-2100-8(7)) Paramount Pictures.

Star Trek. movie tie-in unabr. ed. Alan Dean Foster. Read by Zachary Quinto. 7 CDs. (Running Time: 8 hrs. 30 mins. 0 sec.). (Star Trek: the Original Ser.). (ENG.). 2009. audio compact disk 29.99 (978-0-7435-9834-7(2)) Pub: S&S Audio. Dist(s): S and S Inc

***Star Trek.** unabr. movie tie-in ed. Alan Dean Foster. Read by Zachary Quinto. (Running Time: 8 hrs. 30 mins. 0 sec.). (Star Trek: the Original Ser.). (ENG.). 2010. audio compact disk 14.99 (978-1-4423-3642-1(0)) Pub: S&S Audio. Dist(s): S and S Inc

Star Trek: The Twenty-Fifth Anniversary Collection. abr. ed. Read by James Doohan et al. 4 CD's. (Running Time: 4 hrs. 30 min.). (Star Trek Ser.). audio compact disk 29.95 S&S Audio.

Star Trek Deep Space Nine: The 34th Rule. Armin Shimerman & David R. George, III. Read by Armin Shimerman. 2 cass. (Running Time: 3 hrs.). (Star Trek Ser.: No. 23). 1999. 16.85 (978-0-671-03358-3(1)) S and S Inc.
For once, business is going well for Quark, until he suddenly finds himself right in the middle of a major dispute between Bajor & the Ferengi Alliance. Then he finds himself losing both his bar & his freedom with only his cunning left to help him.

Star Trek, Deep Space Nine: the 34th Rule. Armin Shimerman & David R. George, III. 2004. 10.95 (978-0-7435-4624-9(5)) Pub: S&S Audio. Dist(s): S and S Inc

Star trek deep space nine Warped. K. W. Jeter. 2004. 10.95 (978-0-7435-4621-8(0)) Pub: S&S Audio. Dist(s): S and S Inc

Star Trek Deep Space 9: Millenium. Judith Reeves-Stevens & Garfield Reeves-Stevens. Read by Joe Morton. 2004. 10.95 (978-0-7435-1956-4(6)) Pub: S&S Audio. Dist(s): S and S Inc

Star Trek IX: Insurrection. Read by Joe Morton. 2 cass. (Running Time: 3 hrs.). (Star Trek Ser.). 1999. 15.00 (978-0-671-03344-6(1)) S and S Inc.

Star Trek Klingon Set. gif. ed. Marc Okrand et al. Read by Michael Dorn. 3 cass. (Running Time: 3 hrs.). 1999. 29.95 (978-0-671-75754-0(7), Audioworks) S&S Audio.

***Star trek Memories.** abr. ed. William Shatner. Read by William Shatner. (ENG.). 2006. (978-0-06-113917-8(3), Harper Audio); (978-0-06-113916-1(5), Harper Audio) HarperCollins Pubs.

Star Trek Memories. unabr. ed. William Shatner & Chris Kreski. Read by Larry McKeever. 8 cass. (Running Time: 12 hrs.). 1997. 64.00 (978-0-7366-3502-8(5), 4142) Books on Tape.
When Star Trek debuted in 1966, it seemed like an odd TV show for prime-time. The shaky ratings over the next few seasons confirmed that.

***Star trek movie Memories.** abr. ed. William Shatner. Read by William Shatner. (ENG.). 2006. (978-0-06-113915-4(7), Harper Audio); (978-0-06-113914-7(9), Harper Audio) HarperCollins Pubs.

Star Trek Movie Memories. unabr. ed. William Shatner & Chris Kreski. Read by Larry McKeever. 10 cass. (Running Time: 15 hrs.). 1997. 80.00 (978-0-7366-3625-4(0), 4285) Books on Tape.
Anecdotes & trivia that will take Trekkers where no man - or woman - has gone before.

Star Trek: Nemesis Movie-tie In. abr. ed. J. M. Dillard. 2004. 11.95 (978-0-7435-4781-9(0)) Pub: S&S Audio. Dist(s): S and S Inc

Star Trek: the Next Generation: IQ. John de Lancie. Read by John de Lancie. 2004. 10.95 (978-0-7435-1958-8(2)) Pub: S&S Audio. Dist(s): S and S Inc

Star Trek Time for Yesterday. A. C. Crispin. 2004. 7.95 (978-0-7435-4539-6(7)) Pub: S&S Audio. Dist(s): S and S Inc

Star trek transformations a captain sulu Adventure (cst) Dave Stern. 2004. 7.95 (978-0-7435-4250-0(9)) Pub: S&S Audio. Dist(s): S and S Inc

Star trek VI. J. M. Dillard. 2004. 7.95 (978-0-7435-4232-6(0)) Pub: S&S Audio. Dist(s): S and S Inc

Star Trek Voyager: Pathways. Jeri Taylor. Read by Robert Picardo. 4 cass. (Star Trek Voyager Ser.). 1999. 24.35 (978-0-671-01115-4(4)) S and S Inc.
A life-threatening injury to Capt. Janeway leads the crew members to reflect upon the circumstances which led them to serve on the U.S.S. Voyager.

Star trek 5:the final Frontier. J. M. Dillard. 2004. 7.95 (978-0-7435-4249-4(5)) Pub: S&S Audio. Dist(s): S and S Inc

Star Wars. Matthew Stover. 2005. 49.99 (978-1-59895-040-3(1)) Find a World.

Star Wars. unabr. ed. George Lucas. Read by Full Cast Production Staff. (YA). 2008. 84.99 (978-1-60514-827-4(X)) Find a World.

Star Wars: A New Hope. 1 cass. (Read Along Star Wars Ser.). (J). bk. 7.99 (978-0-7634-0195-5(1)) W Disney Records.

Star Wars: A New Hope. Characters created by George Lucas. 1 cass. (Running Time: 1 hr.). (Play Pack Star Wars Ser.). (J). bk. 14.99 (978-0-7634-0197-9(8)) W Disney Records.

Star Wars: The Clone Wars. unabr. ed. Karen Traviss. (ENG.). 2008. audio compact disk 34.95 (978-0-7393-7681-2(0), Random AudioBks) Pub: Random Audio Pubg. Dist(s): Random

Star Wars: The Complete Trilogy. unabr. ed. George Lucas. Created by Workman Publishing Company. (Running Time: 46800 sec.). (ENG.). 2007. audio compact disk 99.95 (978-1-59887-580-5(9), 1598875809) Pub: HighBridge. Dist(s): Workman Pub

Star Wars: The Original Radio Drama. unabr. abr. ed. Lucasfilm Ltd. Staff & National Public Radio Staff. Perf. by Mark Hamill et al. Based on a story by George Lucas. 7 CDs. (Running Time: 6 hrs. 30 mins.). Dramatization. (ENG.). 1993. audio compact disk 64.95 (978-1-56511-005-2(6), 1565110056) Pub: HighBridge. Dist(s): Workman Pub

Star Wars - Agents of Chaos II: Jedi Eclipse. abr. ed. James Luceno. 2 cass. (Running Time: 3 hrs.). 2000. 18.00 (Random AudioBks) Random Audio Pubg.

Star Wars - Return of the Jedi. unabr. ed. George Lucas. Read by Full Cast Production Staff. (YA). 2008. 39.99 (978-1-60514-828-1(8)) Find a World.

Star Wars - the Complete Trilogy. unabr. ed. George Lucas. Read by Full Cast Production Staff. (YA). 2008. 119.99 (978-1-60514-829-8(6)) Find a World.

Star Wars - the Empire Strikes Back. unabr. ed. George Lucas. Read by Full Cast Production Staff. (YA). 2008. 79.99 (978-1-60514-830-4(X)) Find a World.

Star Wars - The New Jedi Order: Balance Point. abr. ed. Kathy Tyers. 2 cass. (Running Time: 3 hrs.). 2000. 18.00 (Random AudioBks) Random Audio Pubg.

Star Wars: Clone Wars Gambit: Siege. unabr. ed. Karen Miller. Read by Jeff Gurner. (ENG.). 2010. audio compact disk 40.00 (978-0-7393-7685-0(3), Random AudioBks) Pub: Random Audio Pubg. Dist(s): Random

Star Wars: Episode I: The Phantom Menace. Read by Liam Neeson et al. Ed. by Rhino Records Staff. Based on a story by George Lucas. 1 CD. (Running Time: 30 mins.). (Star Wars Ser.). (J). 1999. bk. 9.98 (R2 75642) Rhino Enter.

Star Wars: Episode I: The Phantom Menace. Read by Liam Neeson et al. Ed. by Rhino Records Staff. Based on a story by George Lucas. 1 cass. (Running Time: 30 mins.). (Star Wars Ser.). 1999. bk. 5.98 (978-1-56826-996-2(X), R4 75642) Rhino Enter.

Star Wars: Episode II: Attack of the Clones. unabr. ed. Patricia C. Wrede. Based on a story by George Lucas. 3 cass. (Running Time: 4 hrs. 15 mins.). (Star Wars Ser.). (J). (gr. 3-7). 2002. 30.00 (978-0-8072-0827-4(2), LyA 369 CX, Listening Lib) Random Audio Pubg.
Anakin Skywalker is now age nineteen and facing temptations of love, violence, betrayal, honor, and above all, the dark side of the Force.

Star Wars: Episode II: Attack of the Clones. unabr. ed. Patricia C. Wrede. Based on a story by George Lucas. 3 cass. (Running Time: 3 hrs. 50 mins.). (YA). (gr. 3 up). 2002. pap. bk. 35.00 (978-0-8072-0857-1(4), LYA 369 SP, Listening Lib) Random Audio Pubg.

***Star Wars: Heir to the Empire: 20th Anniversary Edition.** unabr. ed. Timothy Zahn. (ENG.). 2011. audio compact disk 45.00 (978-0-307-93355-3(5), Random AudioBks) Pub: Random Audio Pubg. Dist(s): Random

***Star Wars: Red Harvest.** unabr. ed. Joe Schreiber. (ENG.). 2010. audio compact disk 30.00 (978-0-307-87935-6(6), Random AudioBks) Pub: Random Audio Pubg. Dist(s): Random

Star Wars: the Clone Wars 3. unabr. ed. Karen Traviss. (ENG.). 2009. audio compact disk 30.00 (978-0-7393-7683-6(7), Random AudioBks) Pub: Random Audio Pubg. Dist(s): Random

***Star Wars: the Old Republic: Deceived.** unabr. ed. Paul S. Kemp. (ENG.). 2011. audio compact disk 40.00 (978-0-307-87932-5(1), Random AudioBks) Pub: Random Audio Pubg. Dist(s): Random

Star Wars Trilogy: Star Wars; The Empire Strikes Back; Return of the Jedi. 1 cass. (J). 9.98 (2102) MFLP CA.
This instrumental soundtrack of one of the most incredible epics of all time is the perfect backdrop for inspiring youngsters' imaginary space adventures.

Star Wars Trilogy: Star Wars; The Empire Strikes Back; Return of the Jedi. Based on a story by George Lucas. Directed By George Lucas. 1 CD. (Running Time: 1 hr.). (J). audio compact disk 14.98 (D2102) MFLP CA.

Star Within: Self-Esteem. Roxanne E. Daleo. 1 cass. (J). 1999. 12.95 Hlth Jrnys.

Star Within: Self-Esteem. unabr. ed. Roxanne E. Daleo. Read by Roxanne E. Daleo. 1 cass. (Running Time: 28 min.). (MindWorks for Children Ser.: Vol. 2). (J). (ps-6). 1988. 12.95 (978-1-889447-12-4(9)) Mindwrks Chldrn.
Designed to give children the tools they need to relax body & mind. Regular use of these tapes will help children develop self-confidence & a healthy mental attitude, improve concentration & problem-solving abilities, & stimulate creativity.

Star Witness. unabr. ed. D. W. Buffa. Read by Buck Schirner. 10 cass. (Running Time: 14 hrs.). (Joseph Antonelli Ser.: Vol. 5). 2003. 34.95 (978-1-59086-792-1(0), 1590867920, BAU); 97.25 (978-1-59086-793-8(9), 1590867939, Unabridge Lib Edns) Brilliance Audio.
Star Witness is about a man on trial for murder - a man recognized as one of the film industry's most successful writers/directors, a man of almost mythic drive and talent, and someone who looks more guilty with every passing witness. Attorney Joseph Antonelli - suave, philosophical, fearless, and cagey - takes up the director's defense for the murder of his wife, the actress every woman wants to be and every man wants to possess. Despite Antonelli's flawless examination of the prosecution's witnesses, the jury finds fewer and fewer reasons to doubt. Then the director shows Antonelli the script he considers his masterpiece - a re-imagining of Orson Welles's Citizen Kane - with a visionary film director as its hero. In this story-within-a-story, the accused reveals his version of the tragedy - the secrets of his marriage, and the ominous events that led to his wife's death. In it we see the way art can imitate life - and unmask a killer even the court can't find. Star Witness is a breath-taking novel about the nature of fame and the ever-confusing intersection of truth and fantasy, dream and desire.

Star Witness. unabr. ed. D. W. Buffa. Read by Buck Schirner. (Running Time: 14 hrs.). (Joseph Antonelli Ser.). 2004. 39.25 (978-1-59335-400-8(2), 1593354002, Brlnc Audio MP3 Lib) Brilliance Audio.

Star Witness. unabr. ed. D. W. Buffa. Read by Buck Schirner. (Running Time: 14 hrs.). (Joseph Antonelli Ser.). 2004. 39.25 (978-1-59710-736-5(0), 1597107360, BADLE); 24.95 (978-1-59710-737-2(9), 1597107379, BAD) Brilliance Audio.

Star Witness. unabr. ed. D. W. Buffa. Read by Buck Schirner. (Running Time: 14 hrs.). (Joseph Antonelli Ser.). 2004. 24.95 (978-1-59335-170-0(4), 1593351704) Soulmate Audio Bks.

Starbucks Experience: 5 Principles for Turning Ordinary into Extraordinary. abr. ed. Joseph A. Michelli. Narrated by Dick Hill. (Running Time: 16200 sec.). 2007. audio compact disk 28.00 (978-1-933309-64-4(4)) Pub: A Media Intl. Dist(s): Natl Bk Netwk

Starburst. unabr. ed. Robin Pilcher. Read by John Lee. (Running Time: 13 hrs. 30 mins. 0 sec.). (ENG.). 2007. audio compact disk 39.95 (978-1-4272-0131-7(5)) Pub: Macmill Audio. Dist(s): Macmillan

Starcarbon: A Meditation on Love. unabr. collector's ed. Ellen Gilchrist. Read by Mary Peiffer. 8 cass. (Running Time: 12 hrs.). 1994. 64.00 (978-0-7366-2894-5(0), 3594) Books on Tape.
After a year away at college, a young woman confronts the mystery of her identity & her Cherokee heritage.

***Starclimber.** Kenneth Oppel. Narrated by David Kelly. (ENG.). (YA). 2010. audio compact disk 65.00 (978-1-934180-95-2(5)) Full Cast Audio.

***Star/Cross: An Entrance MeditationTM Reading.** Ira Progoff. 2010. audio compact disk 15.00 (978-1-935859-01-7(3)) Dialogue Assoc.

Starcross: An Intergalactic Adventure of Spies & Time Travel. unabr. ed. Philip Reeve. Narrated by Greg Steinbruner. 7 cass. (Running Time: 8 hrs.). (YA). (gr. 6-10). 2008. 56.75 (978-1-4281-8302-5(7)); audio compact disk 44.95 (978-1-4361-2491-1(3)); audio compact disk 77.75 (978-1-4281-8307-0(8)) Recorded Bks.
Winner of the Gold Nestlé Smarties Book Prize, Philip Reeve received five starred reviews for Larklight. The extraordinary adventure of that book continues in Starcross, as Art and Myrtle receive an ominous warning from an ancient superhuman (their mum). The solar system is on the brink of invasion - from highly intelligent hats from the future!.

Starcycles: The Myths & Signs of the Zodiac. unabr. ed. Georgia Stathis. Read by Georgia Stathis. 12 cass. (Running Time: 9 hrs. 45 min.). 1995. 79.95 Set. (978-1-881229-30-8(0)) Starcycles.
Studio-produced collection of stories of astrological signs & their myths.

Starcycles Vol. 9: Synodic Cycles. unabr. ed. Georgia Stathis. Read by Georgia Stathis. 3 cass. (Running Time: 3 hrs.). 1995. 25.00 Set. (978-1-881229-39-1(4)) Starcycles.
Different planets have periodic alignments. These tapes explain this phenomenon as it pertains to your horoscope.

Starcycles Vol. 10: The Saturn-Jupiter Career Cycle. unabr. ed. Georgia Stathis. Read by Georgia Stathis. 3 cass. (Running Time: 3 hrs.). 1995. 25.00 Set. (978-1-881229-40-7(8)) Starcycles.
There is a twelve year career development cycle that can be plotted in the horoscope & using transiting Jupiter to natal Saturn. This tape explains their procedure.

Starcyles Vol. 1: The Planets. Georgia Stathis. Read by Georgia Stathis. 12 cass. (Running Time: 12 hrs.). 1995. 79.95 Set. (978-1-881229-31-5(9)) Starcycles.
Classroom teaching tapes of the planets & their astrological explanations.

Starcyles Vol. 2: Basic Interpretation. unabr. ed. Georgia Stathis. Read by Georgia Stathis. 12 cass. (Running Time: 13 hrs.). 1995. 79.95 Set. (978-1-881229-32-2(7)) Starcycles.
Classroom teaching tapes of interpretation techniques used in astrological analysis.

Starcyles Vol. 3: Advanced Interpretation. unabr. ed. Georgia Stathis. Read by Georgia Stathis. 12 cass. (Running Time: 13 hrs.). 1995. 79.95 Set. (978-1-881229-33-9(5)) Starcycles.
Classroom teaching tapes of advanced interpretation techiques used in astrological analysis.

Starcyles Vol. 4: Business Astrology. unabr. ed. Georgia Stathis. Read by Georgia Stathis. 12 cass. (Running Time: 12 hrs.). 1995. 79.95 Set. (978-1-881229-34-6(3)) Starcycles.

Starcyles Vol. 6: Eclipses & Prediction. unabr. ed. Georgia Stathis. Read by Georgia Stathis. 3 cass. (Running Time: 2 hrs. 30 min.). 1995. 25.00 Set. (978-1-881229-36-0(X)) Starcycles.
How eclipses strike the astrological horoscope & how to predict events.

Starcyles Vol. 7: Aspects. unabr. ed. Georgia Stathis. Read by Georgia Stathis. 3 cass. (Running Time: 3 hrs.). 1995. 25.00 Set. (978-1-881229-37-7(8)) Starcycles.
The distances that the planets are from each other are called aspects. This tape analyzes their meanings.

Starcyles Vol. 8: The Houses. unabr. ed. Georgia Stathis. Read by Georgia Stathis. 3 cass. 1995. 25.00 Set. (978-1-881229-38-4(6)) Starcycles.
There are twelve houses in a horoscope. These tapes explain their meaning & how they apply to a natal horoscope.

Starcyles Vol. 11: Business Astrology Weekend. unabr. ed. Georgia Stathis. Read by Georgia Stathis. 6 cass. (Running Time: 8 hrs. 30 min.). 1995. 49.95 Set. (978-1-881229-41-4(6)) Starcycles.
A compilation of different astrological techniques used in business, business timing, economic cycles, real estate transactions & city charts, as well as incorporation charts.

Stardance. unabr. ed. Spider Robinson & Jeanne Robinson. Read by Spider Robinson. (Running Time: 28800 sec.). 2008. 54.95 (978-1-4332-4481-0(0)); audio compact disk 29.95 (978-1-4332-4483-4(7)); audio compact disk & audio compact disk 70.00 (978-1-4332-4482-7(9)) Blckstn Audio.

Stardom on a Shoestring! unabr. ed. Bettye P. Zoller et al. Read by Bettye P. Zoller et al. 2 cass. (Running Time: 2 hrs. 50 min.). (YA). (gr. 8-12). 2003. 25.00 (978-1-884643-15-6(9)) Voicesvoices.
From headshots to costumes to demo tapes to building an act, show business pros share valuable secrets on realizing your dreams. Excellent for actors, singers, commercial talents, song writers, filmmakers - everyone who has stars in their eyes & a shoestring budget.

Stardust. abr. ed. Joseph Kanon. Read by Boyd Gaines. 6 CDs. (Running Time: 6 hrs. 30 mins. 0 sec.). (ENG.). 2009. audio compact disk 29.99 (978-0-7435-9793-7(1)) Pub: S&S Audio. Dist(s): S and S Inc

Stardust. unabr. ed. Neil Gaiman. Read by Neil Gaiman. 5 CDs. (Running Time: 6 hrs.). 2006. audio compact disk 29.95 (978-0-06-115392-1(3), Harper Audio) HarperCollins Pubs.

***Stardust.** unabr. ed. Neil Gaiman. Read by Neil Gaiman. (ENG.). 2006. (978-0-06-133622-5(X), Harper Audio); (978-0-06-133623-2(8), Harper Audio) HarperCollins Pubs.

***Stardust.** unabr. ed. Joseph Kanon. Narrated by T. Ryder Smtih. 1 Playaway. (Running Time: 18 hrs. 15 mns.). 2009. 64.75 (978-1-4407-5816-4(6)); 113.75 (978-1-4407-5813-3(1)); audio compact disk 123.75 (978-1-4407-5814-0(X)) Recorded Bks.

***Stardust.** unabr. collector's ed. Joseph Kanon. Narrated by T. Ryder Smith. 15 CDs. (Running Time: 18 hrs. 15 mins.). 2009. audio compact disk 72.95 (978-1-4407-5815-7(8)) Recorded Bks.

Stardust. unabr. collector's ed. Robert B. Parker. Read by Michael Prichard. 6 cass. (Running Time: 6 hrs.). (Spenser Ser.). 1990. 48.00 (978-0-7366-1840-3(6), 2673) Books on Tape.
When a Hollywood-based TV series schedules filming in Boston, Spenser smells trouble. When he signs up to protect the show's star, Jill Joyce, he knows it's on its way. First, there's Jill herself. She's spoiled, arrogant, drugged out - made worse by fear. Someone is out to get her - does she imagine it, or is it real? Spenser monitors her neurosis, but finds evidence of harassment. It escalates to murder. Now begins the dangerous part - while the act may have ended, the murderer lingers on.

Stare Back & Smile. unabr. ed. Joanna Lumley. Read by Joanna Lumley. 7 cass. (Running Time: 7 hrs. 10 min.). 1994. 61.95 (978-1-85089-874-0(X), 92056) Pub: ISIS Audio GBR. Dist(s): Ulverscroft US
This is the story of Joanna Lumley's childhood & how she shot to fame. Born in the hills of Kashmir, growing up in Malaya with her army parents, she was finally sent back to Kent & Sussex to finish her schooling. During the sixties she was a top model & later went on to become an actress. Joanna recalls with affection the people & events which made up her early life.

Starfish & the Spider: The Unstoppable Power of Leaderless Organizations. unabr. ed. Ori Brafman & Rod A. Beckstrom. Read by Sean Pratt. 5 CDs. (Running Time: 5 hrs. 30 mins.). (ENG.). 2008. audio compact disk 29.98 (978-1-59659-151-6(X), GildAudio) Pub: Gildan Media. Dist(s): HachBkGrp

Starfish Sisters. unabr. ed. J. C. Burke. Read by Edwina Wren. (Running Time: 8 hrs. 5 mins.). (YA). 2008. audio compact disk 83.95 (978-1-74214-037-7(8), 9781742140377) Pub: Bolinda Pubng AUS. Dist(s): Bolinda Pub Inc

Starfishing. Perf. by Green Chili Jam Band. 1 cass. (J). (ps-5). 1993. 9.98 (978-0-9638680-1-5(2), GC020); audio compact disk 14.98 CD. (978-0-9638680-2-2(0), GC021) Squeaky Wheel.
Self esteem & imagination.

Stargate. abr. ed. Dean Devlin. Read by Erick Avari. 4 cass. (Running Time: 6 hrs.). 1994. 22.95 (978-1-56876-028-5(0)) Soundlines Ent.
In 1928 a series of cover stones are found buried over a giant metallic ring, both containing complicated hieroglyphics. After decades of secrecy, the government recruits an unorthodox egyptologist , Dr. Daniel Jackson, who manages to decipher the tablets. He identifies the ring as a Stargate - portal to another world. They are soon on their way to this mysterious unknown world.

Stargate Set: Rebellion. unabr. ed. Bill McCay. Read by David Fox. 6 cass. 1999. 57.25 (FS9-34488) Highsmith.

Stargate Set: Reconnaissance. unabr. ed. Bill McCay. Read by John Kenneth. 6 cass. 1999. 57.25 (FS9-43180) Highsmith.

Stargate Set: Resistance. unabr. ed. Bill McCay. Read by John Kenneth. 6 cass. 1999. 57.25 (FS9-51025) Highsmith.

Stargate Set: Retaliation. unabr. ed. Bill McCay. Read by John Kenneth. 6 cass. 1999. 57.25 (FS9-34489) Highsmith.

Stargate Set: Retribution. unabr. ed. Bill McCay. Read by John Kenneth. 6 cass. 1999. 57.25 (FS9-34491) Highsmith.

Stargate Atlantis. Scott Andrews. 2009. audio compact disk 15.95 (978-1-84435-403-0(2)) Pub: Big Finish GBR. Dist(s): Natl Bk Netwk

Stargate Sg-1. Sally Malcolm. 2009. audio compact disk 15.95 (978-1-84435-344-6(3)) Pub: Big Finish GBR. Dist(s): Natl Bk Netwk

Stargate Sg 1. Sally Malcolm. 2009. audio compact disk 15.95 (978-1-84435-348-4(6)) Pub: Big Finish GBR. Dist(s): Natl Bk Netwk

Stargate Sg-1. James Swallow. 2009. audio compact disk 15.95 (978-1-84435-402-3(4)) Pub: Big Finish GBR. Dist(s): Natl Bk Netwk

Stargate SG-1: Pathogen. Sharon Gosling. 2009. audio compact disk 15.95 (978-1-84435-404-7(0)) Pub: Big Finish GBR. Dist(s): Natl Bk Netwk

Stargazer. Patrick Carman. Narrated by Ellen Archer. (Land of Elyon Ser.: Bk. 5). (J). (gr. 4-7). 2008. audio compact disk 28.95 (978-0-545-09109-1(8)) Scholastic Inc.

Stargazer. unabr. ed. Patrick Carman. Narrated by Ellen Archer. 6 CDs. (Running Time: 6 hrs. 38 mins.). (Land of Elyon Ser.: Bk. 5). (ENG.). (J). (gr. 4-7). 2008. audio compact disk 64.95 (978-0-545-09136-7(5)) Scholastic Inc.

Stargazey. Martha Grimes. Read by Donada Peters. (Richard Jury Novel Ser.). 1999. audio compact disk 80.00 (978-0-7366-5167-7(5)) Books on Tape.

Stargazey. unabr. ed. Martha Grimes. Read by Donada Peters. 8 cass. (Running Time: 12 hrs.). (Richard Jury Novel Ser.). 1999. 64.00 (978-0-7366-4463-1(6), 4908) Books on Tape.
In a bleak November, a bleak Richard Jury takes an aimless ride on one of London's icons, the old double-decker bus, a number 14 traveling the Fulham Road. His attention is caught by a woman "with hair so gossamer-pale you could see the moon through it" leaving a pub called the Stargazey. Her behavior intrigues him, as she leaves, reboards & leaves the bus again at Fulham Palace Road. Jury follows her to the gates of Fulham Palace, but only to the gates. There he stops. He wonders if the death in the Palace's walled garden could have been averted if he had gone in. The answer he settles for is "Fate, I guess. It wasn't in the stars".

Stargazey. unabr. ed. Martha Grimes. Read by Donada Peters. 10 CDs. (Running Time: 15 hrs.). (Richard Jury Novel Ser.). 2001. audio compact disk 80.00 Books on Tape.

Stargirl. unabr. ed. Jerry Spinelli. Read by John Ritter. 4 CDs. (Running Time: 4 hrs. 25 mins.). (Young Adult Cassette Librariestm Ser.). (J). (gr. 7 up). 2004. audio compact disk 32.30 (978-0-8072-1048-2(X), S YA 323 CD, Listening Lib); 30.00 (978-0-8072-0572-3(9), Listening Lib); pap. bk. 40.00 (978-0-8072-0855-7(8), LYA 323 SP, Listening Lib) Random Audio Pubg.
Leo Borlock follows the unspoken rule at Mica Area High School. Don't stand out, under any circumstances. Then Stargirl arrives at Mica High and everything changes. After 15 years of home schooling, Stargirl bursts into tenth grade in an explosion of color and a clatter of ukulele music, enchanting the Mica student body. But the delicate scales of popularity suddenly shift, and Stargirl is shunned for everything that makes her different. Somewhere in the midst of Stargirl's arrival and rise and fall, normal Leo Borlock has tumbled into love with her.

Stargirl. unabr. ed. Jerry Spinelli. Read by John Ritter. (Running Time: 15900 sec.). (ENG.). (J). (gr. 5-8). 2007. audio compact disk 25.00 (978-0-7393-3897-1(8), Listening Lib) Pub: Random Audio Pubg. Dist(s): Random

Starhawk. abr. ed. Mack Maloney. Read by Charlton Griffin. 2 vols. No. 1. 2003. (978-1-58807-548-2(6)) Am Pubng Inc.

Starhawk. abr. ed. Mack Maloney. Read by Charlton Griffin. 4 cass. (Running Time: 6 hrs.). (Starhawk Ser.: No. 1). 2003. 25.00 (978-1-58807-136-1(7)) Am Pubng Inc.
Earth is the center of a vast galactic empire - a militaristic state governed by stern repression. The Specials, an extended family that has wielded power for nearly two thousand years, control the galazy with ironfisted zeal; and, after generations of genetic manipulation they are virtually immortal, as is their rule. Meanwhile, on an isolated planet at the fringe of the galazy lives a pilot named Hawk Hunter, who designs his own ships, using strange technology; however, he cannot explain his abilities or his knowledge. His past is a mystery, even to himself. But, now Hawk's talents have been discovered. And in the Earth Race - a state-sponsored gladiatorial contest that pits pilot against pilot, and earns both winner and sponsor unimaginable wealth - he will not only test the limits of his endurance, but begin to learn the truth of his identity.

Staring at the Light. unabr. ed. Frances Fyfield. Read by Nathaniel Parker. 10 CDs. (Attorney Sarah Fortune Ser.). 2000. audio compact disk 94.95 (978-0-7540-5313-2(X), CCD 004) Pub: Chivers Audio Bks GBR. Dist(s): AudioGO
John Smith's twin has disappeared. Cannon, a gifted artist, goes into hiding to avoid John's destructive behavior. Attorney Sarah Fortune shields Cannon & more importantly, his wife, the real target. But is Cannon really telling the truth about John?.

Staring at the Light, Set. unabr. ed. Frances Fyfield. Read by Nathaniel Parker. 8 cass. (Running Time: 12 hrs.jr). 1999. 69.95 (978-0-7540-0364-9(7), CAB1787) AudioGO.
John Smith is a man with a corrupted conscience: his twin, Cannon, has disappeared. Cannon, a gifted artist, goes into hiding to avoid Johnny's destructive behavior. Attorney Sarah Fortune, who has made a habit of helping people, shields Cannon & more importantly, his wife, the real target. But is he really telling the truth about Johnny?.

Stark Realities. Alexander Fullerton. (Soundings Ser.). (J). 2005. 69.95 (978-1-84559-059-8(7)); audio compact disk 79.95 (978-1-84559-079-6(1)) Pub: ISIS Lrg Prnt GBR. Dist(s): Ulverscroft US

Starlight see Asimov's Mysteries

Starlight. unabr. ed. Erin Hunter. Read by Nanette Savard. (Running Time: 28800 sec.). (Warriors Ser.: Bk. 4). (J). (gr. 5-9). 2006. audio compact disk 25.95 (978-0-06-089736-9(8)) HarperCollins Pubs.

Starlight Like Intuition Pierced the Twelve see Twentieth-Century Poetry in English, No. 9, Recordings of Poets Reading Their Own Poetry

Starlight Wishlist. Perf. by Glisten. 1 cass. 1999. 10.99 (978-5-551-85483-8(3), KMGC8692); audio compact disk 16.99 (978-5-551-85501-9(5), KMGD8692) Provident Mus Dist.
Beautiful & creative music that celebrates Christ in praise & worship like lyrics. They do all this without losing the hard rock edge that made them one of Dallas' most popular bands.

Starlust: The Price of Fame. Jesse Cutler. 2008. 59.95 (978-1-60037-419-7(0)) Pub: Morgan James Pubng. Dist(s): IngramPubServ

Starman Jones. unabr. ed. Robert A. Heinlein & Paul Michael Garcia. (Running Time: 8.5 hrs. NaN mins.). 2008. 29.95 (978-1-4332-3041-7(0)); 54.95 (978-1-4332-3037-0(2)); audio compact disk 70.00 (978-1-4332-3038-7(0)) Blckstn Audio.

Starmind. unabr. ed. Jeanne Robinson & Spider Robinson. Read by Spider Robinson. (Running Time: 8 hrs. 0 mins.). 2009. 54.95 (978-1-4332-4780-4(1)) Blckstn Audio.

Starmind. unabr. ed. Jeanne Robinson & Spider Robinson. Read by Spider Robinson. (Running Time: 8 hrs. 0 mins.). 2010. audio compact disk 70.00 (978-1-4332-4781-1(X)) Blckstn Audio.

Starmind. unabr. ed. Jeanne Robinson & Spider Robinson. Read by Spider Robinson. (Running Time: 8 hrs. 0 mins.). 2011. 29.95 (978-1-4332-4783-5(6)) Blckstn Audio.

Starr Report Vol. 1: Nature of President Clinton's Relationship with Monica Lewinsky. unabr. ed. Narrated by Judi Barton. 2 cass. (Running Time: 3 hr.). 1998. 16.95 (978-1-879755-07-9(6)) Recorded Pubns.
Tells the public what it deserves to know about the affair that led to the President's impeachment.

Starr Report Vol. 2: Nature of President Clinton's Relationship with Monica Lewinsky. unabr. ed. Narrated by Judi Barton. 2 cass. (Running Time: 3 hr.). 1998. 16.95 (978-1-879755-08-6(4)) Recorded Pubns.

Starring First Grade. Miriam Cohen. (Miriam Cohen Ser.). (J). (ps-6). 1988. bk. 13.90 (SAC 6515-D) Spoken Arts.

Starring Grace. Mary Hoffman. Narrated by Andrea Johnson. 2 CDs. (Running Time: 2 hrs.). (gr. 1 up). 2000. audio compact disk 22.00 (978-1-4025-1493-7(X), C1618) Recorded Bks.
Grace is a delightful as ever in this beginning chapter book, a perfect companion to Amazing Grace. School's out for the summer, and every day the gang is meeting at her house to play act. They go on a ghost hunt, play circus and even go on safari in the back yard.

Starring Grace. Mary Hoffman. Narrated by Andrea Johnson. 2 pieces. (Running Time: 2 hrs.). (gr. 1 up). 2001. 19.00 (978-0-7887-5034-2(8), 96493E7) Recorded Bks.
School's out for the summer & every day the gang is meeting at Grace's house to play act. They go on a ghost hunt, play circus & even go on a safari in the back yard. Grace learns lessons about privacy, compassion & friendship.

Starring in Your Own Life/Being Sweet. Marianne Williamson. Read by Marianne Williamson. 1 cass. (Running Time: 90 mins.). (Lectures on a Course in Miracles). 1999. 10.00 (978-1-56170-265-7(X), M768) Hay House.

***Starring Prima!** abr. ed. Jacquelyn Mitchard. Read by Jacquelyn Mitchard. (ENG.). 2004. (978-0-06-081373-4(3), Harper Audio) HarperCollins Pubs.

***Starring Prima!** abr. ed. Jacquelyn Mitchard. Read by Jacquelyn Mitchard. (ENG.). 2004. (978-0-06-078271-9(4), Harper Audio) HarperCollins Pubs.

Starring Prima! The Mouse of the Ballet Jolie. unabr. ed. Jacquelyn Mitchard. Read by Jacquelyn Mitchard. 3 CDs. (Running Time: 4 hrs. 30 mins.). (J). 2004. audio compact disk 22.00 (978-0-06-074742-8(0), HarperChildAud) HarperCollins Pubs.

***Starring Sally J. Freedman as Herself.** unabr. ed. Judy Blume. Read by Judy Blume. Read by Laura Hamilton. (ENG.). (J). 2011. audio compact disk 34.00 (978-0-307-74569-9(4), Listening Lib) Pub: Random Audio Pubg. Dist(s): Random

Starring Sally J. Freedman As Herself. unabr. collector's ed. Judy Blume. Read by Judy Blume. 4 cass. (Running Time: 6 hrs. 30 mins.). (J). (gr. 4-7). 2005. 35.00 (978-1-4000-9932-0(3), BksonTape); audio compact disk 42.50 (978-0-307-20741-8(2), BksonTape) Pub: Random Audio Pubg. Dist(s): NetLibrary CO
When Sally's family moves to Miami Beach for the winter of 1947, she is excited and nervous at the same time. What will school be like in Florida? Will she make any friends? Will she fit in so far away from home? But these worries don't stop Sally from having her own wonderful adventures. One minute she's a famous movie star or a brilliant detective; the next she's found the Latin lover of her dreams - her classmate Peter Hornstein. And what about the Freedmans' neighbor, old Mr. Zavodsky, who looks suspiciously like Hitler in disguise? Miami Beach has so many things to worry and wonder about, Sally is in for one unforgettable winter!.

Starry Messenger: A Book Depicting the Life of a Famous Scientist, Mathematician, Astronomer, Philosopher, Physicist Galileo Galilei. unabr. ed. Peter Sis. Narrated by Barbara Caruso & John McDonough. 1 cass. (Running Time: 15 mins.). (gr. 3 up). 1997. 10.00 (978-0-7887-0904-3(6), 95042E7) Recorded Bks.
Provides a clear view of galileo's life & times & his far-reaching discoveries.

Starry Night-Music. 2007. audio compact disk 16.95 (978-1-56136-433-6(9)) Master Your Mind.

Starry Sea. Bernie Krause. 1 cass. (Running Time: 60 min.). (Nature's Lullabyes Ser.). 1994. 7.95 (2662, NrthWrd Bks) TandN Child.
Features the calming sounds of ocean waves sweeping onto a beach with the delicate voices of shore birds.

Stars. Compiled by Benchmark Education Staff. 2006. audio compact disk 10.00 (978-1-4108-6698-1(X)) Benchmark Educ.

Stars. Read by James Pickering. 1 cass. (Running Time: 36 min.). 14.95 (13527) MMI Corp.
Discusses stars, variable stars, types, life & death of stars, reasons for variability of stars, physical composition, etc.

Stars. abr. ed. Kathryn Harvey. Read by Paula Prentiss. 2 cass. (Running Time: 3 hrs.). 2000. 7.95 (978-1-57815-057-1(4), 1030, Media Bks Audio) Media Bks NJ.
Every woman's ultimate fantasy - entices you to go beyond the ectasy.

Stars. abr. ed. Kathryn Harvey. Read by Paula Prentiss. 2 cass. (Running Time: 3 hrs.). 1992. 15.95 Set. (978-1-879371-27-9(8), 40110) Pub Mills.
This is the sequel to the runaway bestseller "Butterfly.".

Stars & Dice. Frank R. Kegan. 1 cass. 8.95 (617) Am Fed Astrologers.
An AFA Convention workshop tape.

***Stars & Galaxies: CD add-on Set.** Perf. by Millmark Education Staff. (ConceptLinks Ser.). 2009. audio compact disk 50.00 (978-1-61618-351-6(9)) Millmark Educ.

***Stars & Galaxies Audio CD.** Perf. by Millmark Education Staff. (ConceptLinks Ser.). 2008. audio compact disk 28.00 (978-1-4334-0235-7(1)) Millmark Educ.

***Stars & Galaxies SB1 Audio CD Light from Far Away.** Perf. by Millmark Education Staff. (Content Literacy Libraries Ser.). 2008. audio compact disk (978-1-4334-0444-3(3)) Millmark Educ.

***Stars & Galaxies SB2 Audio CD Our Universe.** Perf. by Millmark Education Staff. (Content Literacy Libraries Ser.). 2008. audio compact disk (978-1-4334-0445-0(1)) Millmark Educ.

***Stars & Galaxies SB3 Audio CD Changing over Time.** Perf. by Millmark Education Staff. (Content Literacy Libraries Ser.). 2008. audio compact disk (978-1-4334-0446-7(X)) Millmark Educ.

***Stars & Galaxies SB4 Audio CD Exploring with Technology.** Perf. by Millmark Education Staff. (Content Literacy Libraries Ser.). 2008. audio compact disk (978-1-4334-0447-4(8)) Millmark Educ.

Stars & Stripes. unabr. ed. Adam Rutledge. Read by Charlie O'Dowd. 6 vols. No. 6. 2003. (978-1-58807-568-0(0)) Am Pubng Inc.

Stars & Stripes. unabr. ed. Adam Rutledge. Read by Charlie O'Dowd. 6 vols. (Running Time: 6 hrs.). (Patriots Ser.: No. 6). 2003. 30.00 (978-1-58807-090-6(5)) Am Pubng Inc.

Stars & Stuff. Meatball Fulton. Music by Tim Clark. 6 cass. (Running Time: 8 hrs.). 37.50 set. (S&S) ZBS Ind.
Twenty stories in all.

Stars & Stuff. unabr. ed. Short Stories. Meatball Fulton. Read by Laura Esterman & Tim Clark. 6 cass. (Running Time: 8 hrs.). (J). 1977. 35.00 set. (978-1-881137-14-6(7)) ZBS Found.
A series of twenty short stories by Meatball Fulton.

Stars for a Light: Cheney Duvall. unabr. ed. Lynn Morris & Gilbert Morris. Narrated by Kate Forbes. 8 cass. (Running Time: 11 hrs.). 1999. 70.00 (978-0-7887-3779-4(1), 95996E7) Recorded Bks.
In 1865 New York City, beautiful, young Cheney Duvall has gone against the odds by becoming a medical doctor. For her first position, she is planning to become the physician & chaperone for a shipload of women traveling to Seattle to become brides. As the ship prepares to weigh anchor, Cheney wonders if she can really handle the responsibility.

Stars in Orion. 1 cass. (Running Time: 25 min.). 14.95 (23317) MMI Corp.
Discusses this most conspicuous constellation including magnitude of stars, parts of Orion, importance of Orion to early navigators.

Stars in Their Courses. unabr. ed. Gilbert Morris. Read by Maynard Villers. 8 cass. (Running Time: 10 hrs. 36 min.). (Appomattox Ser.: Bk. 8). 2001. 49.95 (978-1-55686-847-4(2)) Books in Motion.
Actor, turned Union soldier, Frank Rocklin accepts a spy mission, and takes an acting troupe south. But the woman he loves could pose Frank's greatest danger.

Stars of Discovery Music. Read by Joanie Bartels et al. 1 cass. (Magic Ser.). (J). (978-1-881225-25-6(9)) Discov Music.
Discovery Music's stars team up for a compilation tape with the best in kids' music, from storytelling songs, silly tunes & music with a touch of magic.

Stars of Fall. 1 cass. (Running Time: 29 min.). 14.95 (23343) MMI Corp.
Discusses Autumn constellations including Cassiopeia, how ancient civilizations used stars to form calendars.

Stars of Radio Comedy: Kraft Music Hall. Perf. by Original Radio Broadcasts. (ENG.). 2008. audio compact disk 18.95 (978-1-57019-854-0(3)) Radio Spirits.

Stars on Suspense. 6 CDs. (Running Time: 6 hrs.). 2004. audio compact disk 29.95 (978-1-57816-212-3(2)) Audio File.

Stars on Suspense. Perf. by Eve Arden et al. 6 cass. 24.95 Set. (978-1-57816-032-7(4), 1001SS) Audio File.
A dozen programs from the Golden Age of Radio featuring a dozen of Hollywood's most popular stars in outstanding mystery dramas. Other performers are Red Skelton & James Stewart.

Stars over Hollywood: Ask Thyself & Dead on Arrival. Perf. by Brenda Joyce & G. Raymond. 1 cass. (Running Time: 1 hr.). 2001. 6.98 (2407) Radio Spirits.

Stars Shine Down. unabr. ed. Sidney Sheldon. Read by Alexander Adams. 6 cass. (Running Time: 9 hrs.). 1994. 48.00 (978-0-7366-2648-4(4), 3385) Books on Tape.
Lisa Cameron, young & beautiful, rises phoenix-like from a past she burns to hide. She creates a business empire & both admired & envied, surveys her work. In that moment, fortune turns. Everything she's built - her wealth, achievements & marriage - everything - seems ready to melt. What's gone wrong?.

Stars Shine Down, Set. unabr. ed. Sidney Sheldon. Read by Roddy McDowall. 12 cass. 1999. 49.95 (FS9-34533) Highsmith.

Stars! Stars! Stars! (J). 2005. bk. 29.95 (978-0-439-80468-4(X)); bk. 24.95 (978-0-439-80462-2(0)) Weston Woods.
In this lively story, children take a colorful ride through outer space to visit distant planets and dazzling stars. With simple rhyming text and colorful collage-style animation, aspiring stargazers will rocket right out of this world!.

Starseed. unabr. ed. Spider Robinson. Read by Spider Robinson. (Running Time: 8.5 hrs. 0 mins.). 2008. 29.95 (978-1-4332-4556-5(6)); cass. & audio compact disk 70.00 (978-1-4332-4555-8(8)) Blckstn Audio.

Starseed. unabr. ed. Spider Robinson & Jeanne Robinson. Read by Spider Robinson. (Running Time: 8.5 hrs. 0 mins.). 2008. 54.95 (978-1-4332-4554-1(X)) Blckstn Audio.

Starseed Awakening: Channeled Meditations from the Sirians. Patricia Cori. (ENG.). 2009. audio compact disk 12.95 (978-1-55643-782-3(X)) Pub: North Atlantic. Dist(s): Random

Starship Titanic. abr. ed. Terry Jones. 2 cass. (Running Time: 3 hrs.). 1997. 22.00 S&S Audio.

Starship Troopers. unabr. ed. Robert A. Heinlein. Read by Lloyd James. 1 CD. (Running Time: 10 hrs.). 2001. audio compact disk 19.95 (978-0-7861-9562-6(2), zm1977) Blckstn Audio.
A recruit of the future goes through the toughest boot camp in the Universe & into battle with the Terran Mobile Infantry against mankind's most alarming enemy!.

Starship Troopers. unabr. ed. Robert A. Heinlein. Read by Lloyd James. 7 cass. (Running Time: 10 hrs. 30 mins.). 1997. 49.95 (978-0-7861-1231-9(X), 895604) Blckstn Audio.

Starship Troopers. unabr. ed. Robert A. Heinlein. Read by Lloyd James. 9 CDs. (Running Time: 11 hrs. 20 min.). 2000. audio compact disk 72.00 (978-0-7861-9946-4(6), z1977) Blckstn Audio.

Starship Troopers. unabr. ed. Robert A. Heinlein. Read by Lloyd James. (Running Time: 36000 sec.). 2007. audio compact disk 24.95 (978-0-7861-6142-3(6)) Blckstn Audio.

Starship Troopers. unabr. ed. Robert A. Heinlein. Narrated by George Wilson. 7 cass. (Running Time: 9 hrs. 45 mins.). 1998. 60.00 (978-0-7887-2023-9(6), 95398E7) Recorded Bks.
Life on the planet is peaceful when Johnny Rico enlists. But, after communist aliens attack, he heads for the frontlines in a violent struggle for survival.

Starswarm. unabr. ed. Jerry Pournelle. Read by Lloyd James. 7 cass. (Running Time: 10 hrs.). 2000. 49.95 (978-0-7861-1829-8(6), 2628) Blckstn Audio.
Kip, a young boy who lives with his uncle at Starswarm Station research outpost on planet Paradise, has heard a voice in his head which guides him through situations with useful information & helpful insight. Kip discovers that his computer scientist parents implanted an artificial intelligence chip in his skull, connecting with a computer via satellite & learns that his parents died under suspicious circumstances & that he is a well-kept secret that will soon come to light, putting his own life & the whole of outpost Starswarm in grave danger.

***Starswarm.** unabr. ed. Jerry Pournelle. Read by Lloyd James. (Running Time: 10 hrs. NaN mins.). (Jupiter Ser.). (ENG.). 2011. 29.95 (978-1-4417-8508-4(6)); audio compact disk 90.00 (978-1-4417-8506-0(X)) Blckstn Audio.

Start Dreaming! Perf. by Ray Andersen. 1 CD. (Running Time: 39 min.). (J). (gr. k-2). 2001. audio compact disk 12.98 (978-1-888795-21-9(2)) Sugar Beats.
Twelve original songs in a pop/rock style by Mr. Ray.

Start Dreaming! unabr. ed. Perf. by Ray Andersen. 1 cass. (Running Time: 39 min.). (gr. k-2). 2001. 9.98 (978-1-888795-22-6(0)) Sugar Beats.

Start Here: Doing Hard Things Right Where You Are. unabr. ed. Alex Harris et al. Read by Alex Harris & Brett Harris. (ENG.). 2010. 20.00 (978-0-307-71405-3(5), Random AudioBks) Pub: Random Audio Pubg. Dist(s): Random

Start in Life. unabr. ed. Alan Sillitoe. Read by Richard Green. 9 cass. (Running Time: 13 hrs. 30 min.). 1977. 72.00 (978-0-7366-0073-6(6), 1083) Books on Tape.
The story chronicles the young manhood of a vigorous non-conformist, Michael Cullen. Born a bastard, Cullen refuses to stand in the working class ranks & batters his way up. In the course of his picaresque adventures he makes a great deal of money & a great deal of love.

Start Kidding Yourself! A Practical Guide to Smashing Success. Will Pemble. 6 CDs. 2007. audio compact disk 89.95 (978-0-9790875-1-6(1)) Pemblecom.

Start Late, Finish Rich: A No-Fail Plan for Achieving Financial Freedom at Any Age. unabr. abr. ed. David Bach. Read by David Bach. 4 cass. (Running Time: 6 hrs.). (ENG.). 2005. audio compact disk 25.00 (978-0-7393-1509-5(9)) Pub: Random Audio Pubg. Dist(s): Random

Start Meditating Now: How to Stop Thinking. Barry Long. 2 cass. (Running Time: 3 hrs.). (ENG.). 1996. audio compact disk 17.95 (978-1-899324-05-7(4)) Pub: B Long Bks. Dist(s): AtlasBooks
How to meditate, release tension & resentment, dissolve negative emotion, deal with worry & banish unnecessary thought.

Start Meditatng Now: How to Stop Thinking. Barry Long. (ENG.). 2007. 24.95 (978-1-899324-20-0(8)) Pub: B Long Bks. Dist(s): AtlasBooks

Start of a New Business see Creacion de Empresas

Start of A New Business. Basilio Balli Morales et al. Read by Basilio Balli Morales et al. (Running Time: 1 hr.). 2003. 14.95 (978-1-60083-302-1(0), Audiofy Corp) Iofy Corp.

Start Over, Finish Rich: 10 Steps to Get You Back on Track in 2010. unabr. ed. David Bach. Read by David Bach. (ENG.). 2009. audio compact disk 9.99 (978-0-307-70757-4(1), Random AudioBks) Pub: Random Audio Pubg. Dist(s): Random

Start Playing Acoustic Blues Guitar. Gerry Hendricks. (Start Playing... Ser.). 2004. audio compact disk 17.95 (978-0-8256-1788-1(X), AM962445) Pub: Music Sales. Dist(s): H Leonard

Start Playing Blues Guitar. 1 CD. (Running Time: 90 mins.). (Start Playing. . .Ser.). 2000. pap. bk. 11.95 (978-0-8256-1791-1(X)) Music Sales.

Start Playing Blues Guitar Licks. (Start Playing. . .Ser.). 2000. pap. bk. 11.95 (978-0-8256-1784-3(7)) Music Sales.

Start Playing Country Guitar Licks. Alan Warner. (Start Playing... Ser.). 2004. pap. bk. 14.95 (978-0-8256-1786-7(3), AM962423) Pub: Music Sales. Dist(s): H Leonard

Start Playing Folk Guitar. 1 CD. (Running Time: 90 mins.). (Start Playing. . .Ser.). 2000. pap. bk. 11.95 (978-0-8256-1792-8(8)) Music Sales.

Start Playing Hard Rock Guitar Licks. (Start Playing. . .Ser.). 2000. pap. bk. 11.95 (978-0-8256-1787-4(1)) Music Sales.

Start Playing Rock Guitar. (Start Playing... Ser.). 2000. pap. bk. 11.95 (978-0-8256-1790-4(1)) Music Sales.

Start the Bidding: A Floor Traders Inside Secrets to Buying & Selling on the New York Stock Exchange. 1997. bk. 19.95 HDG Unltd.
Describes the stock market.

Start up Basics Audio Guide. Excerpts. 2 CDs. (Running Time: 2 hrs). 2003. audio compact disk 69.00 (978-1-932156-28-7(3)) Entrepreneur Pr.

Start up French. unabr. ed. Howard Beckerman. (Berlitz Audio for Kids Ser.). (FRE & ENG., 2007. audio compact disk 12.95 (978-981-268-076-1(4)) Pub: Berlitz Pubng. Dist(s): Langenscheidt

Start up Italian. unabr. ed. Howard Beckerman. (Berlitz Audio for Kids Ser.). (ITA & ENG., 2007. audio compact disk 12.95 (978-981-268-078-5(0)) Pub: Berlitz Pubng. Dist(s): Langenscheidt

Start-up Nation: The Story of Israel's Economic Miracle. unabr. ed. Saul Singer. Read by Sean Pratt. (Running Time: 8 hrs. 30 mins.). (ENG.). 2009. 29.98 (978-1-59659-471-5(3), GildAudio) Pub: Gildan Media. Dist(s): HachBkGrp

Start up Poetry. ed. Compiled by Benchmark Education Staff. (Phonics Ser.). (J). 2004. audio compact disk 12.00 (978-1-4108-1493-7(9)) Benchmark Educ.

Start up Song & Rhyme. ed. Compiled by Benchmark Education Staff. (Phonics Ser.). (J). 2004. audio compact disk 12.00 (978-1-4108-1492-0(0)) Benchmark Educ.

Start up Song & Rhyme/Poetry, Set. ed. Compiled by Benchmark Education Staff. (Phonics Ser.). (J). 2004. audio compact disk 20.00 (978-1-4108-1494-4(7)) Benchmark Educ.

Start up Spanish. unabr. ed. Howard Beckerman. (Berlitz Audio for Kids Ser.). (SPA & ENG., 2007. audio compact disk 12.95 (978-981-268-079-2(9)) Pub: Berlitz Pubng. Dist(s): Langenscheidt

Start Where You Are. Rick Joyner. 1 cass. (Running Time: 90 mins.). (Vision Ser.: Vol. 1). 2000. 5.00 (R16-001) Morning NC.
This tape series will help to impart new vision or restore lost vision in the church.

***Start Where You Are.** abr. ed. Chris Gardner & Mim E. Rivas. Read by Andre Blake. (ENG.). 2009. (978-0-06-190182-9(2), Harper Audio); (978-0-06-190183-6(0), Harper Audio) HarperCollins Pubs.

Start Where You Are: A Guide to Compassionate Living. unabr. ed. Pema Chödrön. Read by Joanna Rotte. (ENG.). 2008. audio compact disk 21.95 (978-1-59030-582-9(5)) Pub: Shambhala Pubns. Dist(s): Random

Start Where You Are: Life Lessons in Getting from Where You Are to Where You Want to Be. abr. ed. Chris Gardner & Mim E. Rivas. Read by Andre Blake. 2009. audio compact disk 29.99 (978-0-06-171468-9(2), Harper Audio) HarperCollins Pubs.

Start Where You Find Yourself. Voice by Eddie Long. (ENG.). 2008. audio compact disk 25.00 (978-1-58602-370-6(5)) Pub: E L Long. Dist(s): Anchor Distributors

Start with Hello. 1 cass. 1985. 12.95; 18.90 incl. bk. & cass. Alemany Pr.
Eighteen recorded conversations telling the story of a young woman who changes jobs & moves from New York to San Francisco. Conversations contain all the elements of authentic discourse - hesitations, reductions, false starts, variations in formality - without slang or uncommon idioms.

Start with Listening. Patricia A. Dunkel & Christine Gorder. 6 cass. (J). (gr. 9 up). 1987. mass mkt. 12.50 (978-0-8384-2820-7(7), Newbury) Heinle.
Provides a high-interest context for developmental skills building.

Start with Listening. Patricia A. Dunkel & Christine Gorder. 6 cass. (YA). (gr. 9 up). 1987. 75.00 incl. script. (Newbury) Heinle.

Startbahn: Multimedia CD-ROM for Beginner Learners of German. Katalin Somlo & Tamas Gal. (ENG & GER.). 2000. audio compact disk 45.00 (978-963-05-7653-6(8)) Pub: Akade Kiado HUN. Dist(s): Intl Spec Bk

***Started Early, Took My Dog: A Novel.** unabr. ed. Kate Atkinson. (Running Time: 11 hrs.). (ENG.). 2011. 24.98 (978-1-60788-679-2(0)); audio compact disk 34.98 (978-1-60788-678-5(2)) Pub: Hachet Audio. Dist(s): HachBkGrp

Starter Collection, Set. unabr. ed. Evelyn Anthony et al. 84 cass. 543.38 AudioGO.
Includes "Exposure" by Evelyn Anthony, "Darkwater" By Dorothy Eden, "High Stakes" By Dick Francis, "Venetia" by Georgette Heyer, "The Road to Paradise Island" by Victoria Holt, "Night Without End" by Alistair MacLean, "The Mugger" by Ed McBain, "Someone in the House" by Barbara Micheals, "Treasures" by Belva Plain, "Feather on the Moon" by Phyllis A. Whitney.

Starter Wife. abr. ed. Gigi Levangie Grazer. Read by Susan Ericksen. (Running Time: 21600 sec.). 2006. audio compact disk 16.99 (978-1-59737-624-2(8), 9781597376242) Brilliance Audio.
When her husband Kenny dumps her (by cell phone) mere months before their ten-year wedding anniversary, Gracie Pollock finds herself reeling. Though her role as the wife of a semifamous Hollywood studio executive often left her cold, Gracie had grown accustomed to the unique privileges extended to Tinseltown's power elite: reservations at Spago on a Friday night; beauty treatments by dermatologists (Arnie), manicurists (Jessica), and colorists (Christophe) to the stars; line-jumping at Disneyland with her daughter and Ugg-wearing celebrity offspring. And despite consenting to naming their daughter Jaden in a (failed) attempt to lure Will Smith into one of Kenny's productions, Gracie believed she and Kenny were different from other Hollywood couples. She never thought she'd be a starter wife. But now that her marriage is over, she's a social pariah, and it's only through a faux pas by her world-class florist that she learns her husband has upgraded: Kenny is dating a pop tartlet. With images of the 'tween queen everywhere she turns, Gracie seeks refuge at her best friend's Malibu mansion for some much-needed divorce therapy. Soon she's associating with all the wrong people, including a mysterious hunk who saves her from drowning, the security guard at her gated community, and - God forbid - Kenny's boss, one of Hollywood's better-known Lotharios. With her signature wit, sassy style, and cameos of the rich and famous - and wannabe rich and famous - Gigi Grazer tackles the most delicious and dastardly details of a divorce and recovery, Hollywood style.

Starter Wife. unabr. ed. Gigi Levangie Grazer. Read by Susan Ericksen. (Running Time: 11 hrs.). 2005. 39.25 (978-1-59737-622-8(1), 9781597376228, BADLE); 24.95 (978-1-59737-621-1(3), 9781597376211, BAD); 82.25 (978-1-59737-616-7(7), 9781597376167, BrilAudUnabridg); 32.95 (978-1-59737-615-0(9), 9781597376150, BAU); audio compact disk 97.25 (978-1-59737-618-1(3), 9781597376181, BriAudCD Unabrid); audio compact disk 39.25 (978-1-59737-620-4(5), 9781597376204, Brinc Audio MP3 Lib); audio compact disk 24.95 (978-1-59737-619-8(1), 9781597376198, Brilliance MP3); audio compact disk 36.95 (978-1-59737-617-4(5), 9781597376174, Bril Audio CD Unabri) Brilliance Audio.
When Gracie's husband unceremoniously dumps her (by cell phone) mere months before their ten-year anniversary and takes up with a famous pop starlet, she finds herself reeling. Though somewhat uncomfortable in the role of "Wife Of" her semi-famous husband, she has grown accustomed to the privileges of power and wealth afforded by Hollywood. And of course there's her beloved daughter Jaden - who might now call a tween queen "stepmom." Suddenly stripped of quasi-celebrity status, Gracie seeks refuge at her best friend's Malibu mansion for some much needed "divorce therapy." Soon she's associating with all the wrong people, including a mysterious hunk who saves her from drowning, the security guard at the gated community, and - God forbid - her ex-husband's boss, one of Tinseltown's better-known womanizers. Filled with the most delicate and dastardly Hollywood details, cameos of the rich and famous and wannabe rich and famous, and Gigi Grazer's trademark wit and sassy style, Malibu Shocker is a hilarious tale about life out of the spotlight.

***Starting an E-Bay Business for Dummies.** abr. ed. Marsha Collier. Read by Brett Barry. (ENG.). 2008. (978-0-06-176390-8(X), Harper Audio); (978-0-06-176389-2(6), Harper Audio) HarperCollins Pubs.

Starting an eBay Business. 2nd abr. ed. Barbara Weltman & Malcolm Katt. Narrated by Rebecca Gallagher. (Running Time: 5 hrs. 0 mins. 0 sec.). (Complete Idiot's Guide Ser.). (ENG.). 2008. audio compact disk 19.99 (978-1-59859-331-0(5)) Oasis Audio.

Starting an eBay Business for Dummies. 3rd abr. ed. Marsha Collier. Read by Brett Barry. (Playaway Adult Nonfiction Ser.). (ENG.). 2009. 39.99 (978-1-60812-578-4(5)) Find a World.

***Starting Blues Harmonica.** Stuart "Son" Maxwell. (ENG.). 2007. pap. bk. 9.99 (978-0-8256-3732-2(5), 0825637325) Pub: Music Sales. Dist(s): H Leonard

Starting English with a Smile. Barbara Zaffran & David Krulik. (English with a Smile Ser.: Bk. 1). 1995. 20.00 (978-0-8442-0586-1(9)) M-H Contemporary.

Starting from Glasgow. Rosemary Trollope. Read by Nicolette McKenzie. 4 cass. (Running Time: 6 hrs.). 2001. 44.95 (000816) Pub: ISIS Audio GBR. Dist(s): Ulverscroft US

Starting from Scratch: How to Start a Business When You Don't Have Money. 10th unabr. ed. Gary G. Schoeniger. Read by Gary G. Schoeniger. 3 cass. (Running Time: 1 hr. 45 min.). 2001. 24.95 (978-0-9713059-0-8(0)) ELIPr.
Self-help program designed to teach anyone how to start and succeed in virtually any business, regardless of the circumstances.

Starting on a Shoestring: Building a Business Without a Bankroll. Arnold S. Goldstein. 2 cass. (Running Time: 2 hrs.). 1998. cass. & cass. 15.95 (978-0-471-63712-7(2)) Wiley US.

Starting Out in Arabic. Created by Living Language Staff. (Playaway Adult Nonfiction Ser.). (ARA & ENG.). 2009. 60.00 (978-1-60775-601-9(3)) Find a World.

Starting Out in Arabic. unabr. l.t. ed. Living Language Staff. (ENG.). 2008. audio compact disk 15.95 (978-1-4000-2467-4(6), LivingLang) Pub: Random Info Grp. Dist(s): Random

Starting Out in French. Created by Living Language Staff. (Playaway Adult Nonfiction Ser.). (ENG & FRE.). 2009. 60.00 (978-1-60775-603-3(X)) Find a World.

Starting Out in German. Created by Living Language Staff. (Playaway Adult Nonfiction Ser.). (ENG & GER.). 2009. 60.00 (978-1-60775-604-0(8)) Find a World.

Starting Out in German. abr. unabr. l.t. ed. Living Language Staff. (Starting Out In... Ser.). (ENG.). 2008. audio compact disk 15.95 (978-1-4000-2465-0(X), LivingLang) Pub: Random Info Grp. Dist(s): Random

Starting Out in Italian. Created by Living Language Staff. (Playaway Adult Nonfiction Ser.). (ENG & ITA.). 2009. 60.00 (978-1-60775-605-7(6)) Find a World.

Starting Out in Italian. unabr. l.t. ed. Living Language Staff. Created by Living Language Staff. (Starting Out In Ser.). (ENG.). 2008. audio compact disk 15.95 (978-1-4000-2464-3(1)) Pub: Random Info Grp. Dist(s): Random

Starting Out in Spanish. Created by Living Language Staff. (Starting Out In... Ser.). (ENG.). 2009. 60.00 (978-1-60775-606-4(4)) Find a World.

Starting Point for Truth. Swami Amar Jyoti. 1 cass. 1988. 9.95 (F-15) Truth Consciousness.
The symbolic physical world, our make-believe reality & sophisticated excuses. Facing our first action, the main issue. Giving up untruth, choosing freedom. The real cause of crime.

Starting Point Starter Kit Leader's Notes. 2009. 49.99 (978-0-310-94806-3(1)) Zondervan.

Starting the Day. Steven Halpern. 1 cass. (Soundwave Two Thousand, the Audio Active Subliminal Ser.). 1990. (2011) Inner Peace Mus.
Relaxing, beautiful music with subliminal affirmations.

Starting with the Right Premise. Swami Amar Jyoti. 1 cass. 1992. 9.95 (M-89) Truth Consciousness.
How can we live without God? The answer is not within dualism. Seeking our full glory.

Starting Your Day Right/Ending Your Day Right Set: Devotions to Begin & End Each Day. unabr. abr. ed. Joyce Meyer. Read by Sandra McCollom. (Running Time: 5 hrs.). (ENG.). 2007. 19.98 (978-1-60024-096-6(8)) Pub: Hachet Audio. Dist(s): HachBkGrp

Starting Your Day Right/Ending Your Day Right Box Set: Devotions to Begin & End Each Day. unabr. abr. ed. Joyce Meyer. Read by Sandra McCollom. (Running Time: 5 hrs.). (ENG.). 2007. audio compact disk 24.98 (978-1-60024-095-9(X)) Pub: Hachet Audio. Dist(s): HachBkGrp

Starting Your Own Business: An Easy-to-Follow Guide for the New Entrepreneur. Joan Sotkin. Read by Joan Sotkin. 2 cass. (Running Time: 1 hr. 57 min.). (Build Your Business Tape Ser.). 1992. 19.95 Set. (978-1-881002-88-8(8)) Build Your Busn.
Includes a business planning/marketing guide. Topics include: establishing a values base for your business, the importance of a business & marketing plan, how to develop an effective, low-cost business/marketing strategy, how to develop a better relationship with money.

Startled by His Furry Shorts. Louise Rennison. Read by Louise Rennison. 4. (Running Time: 4 hrs. 75 mins.). (Confessions of Georgia Nicolson Ser.: No. 7). 2007. 30.75 (978-1-4281-3477-5(8)); audio compact disk 46.75 (978-1-4281-3482-9(4)) Recorded Bks.

Startup Business Chinese. Jane C. M. Kuo. 2006. audio compact disk (978-0-88727-524-1(9)) Cheng Tsui.

StartUp Phonics Skill Bags. Compiled by Benchmark Education Staff. 2006. audio compact disk 10.00 (978-1-4108-6976-0(8)) Benchmark Educ.

StarWreck. 1 cass. (Running Time: 60 min.). (At the Sound of the Beep Ser.). 1989. 6.95 (978-1-55569-336-7(9), 6150) Great Am Audio.
Features pre-recorded answering machine messages. Spoofs on the voyages of the Spaceship Free Enterprise.

Stash Envy & Other Quilting Confessions & Adventures. Lisa Boyer. Read by Lisa Boyer. (Running Time: 10800 sec.). 2007. audio compact disk 19.95 (978-1-56148-582-6(9)) Good Bks PA.

State Against Blacks. Walter Williams. 1 cass. (Running Time: 60 min.). 1987. 9.95 (978-0-945999-27-0(5)) Independent Inst.
The Economic & Social Development of Blacks Is Undermined by Government, While Unrestricted Neighborhood & Business Enterprises Create Substantial Advancement in the Quality of Life.

State & Local Taxation: Corporate Income Tax & Related Tax Topics. Kirk M. Linford & Karl Eschelback. 6 cass. bk. 159.00 set. (CPE0520) Bisk Educ.
This authoritative overview summarizes recent changes in state & local taxation of corporations & includes the impact of major cases, key rulings, legislative & regulatory developments & the necessary changes in tax planning techniques that result.

State & Local Taxation: Sales & Use Tax & Special Tax Topics. Dennis C. Neilson & Amy Eisenstadt. 6 cass. 1994. 159.00 set incl. wkbk. & quizzer set, incl. textbk. & quizzer. (CPE0515); 65.00 extra textbks. & quizzers. (CPE0516) Bisk Educ.
Here's the latest information on sales & use tax issues involving interstate transactions, including common problems & possible solutions. Covers recent judicial, legislative, & administrative activities, & the planning & refund opportunities that have resulted. An overview of UISUTA a proposed uniform state tax law is provided.

State & Ruling Class in Corporate America. G. William Domhoff. 1 cass. (Running Time: 1 hr. 6 min.). 11.95 (423) J Norton Pubs.
Domhoff gives his ideas on how a ruling class dominates American government. Defines the processes by which they protect their special interests.

State Birds. 1 cass. Dramatization. (J). pap. bk. 6.95 (978-0-86545-098-1(6)) Spizzirri.
Features the state birds of all fifty states.

State Board Review. Leigh Beekman et al. 16 cass. 1987. 69.95 SCE Prod & List & Lrn.
Review material for chiropractic state licensing board exam.

State Flowers. unabr. ed. Ed. by Linda Spizzirri. 48 cass. (Running Time: 15 min.). Dramatization. (Educational Coloring Book & Cassette Package Ser.). (J). (gr. k-8). 1989. pap. bk. 6.95 (978-0-86545-163-6(X)) Spizzirri.
Explains which particular flower each state has chosen to be especially representative of their state.

State Intervention in the Family & Parental Rights: A Legal Assessment see State Intervention in the Family & Parental Rights, Pt. 2, A Psychological Assessment

State Intervention in the Family & Parental Rights Pt. 1: A Psychological Assessment. Read by Roger Rinn. (123) ISI Books.

State Intervention in the Family & Parental Rights Pt. 2: A Psychological Assessment. Read by Roger Rinn. 1 cass. Incl. Parental Rights & Education Panel Discussion. Read by Craig A. Stern & Joseph Cascarelli. (124); State Intervention in the Family & Parental Rights: A Legal Assessment. Read by Robert J. D'Agostino. (124); Pt. 1. State Intervention in the Family & Parental Rights Panel Discussion. Read by Claire D'Agostino & Onalee McGraw. (124); 3.00 (124) ISI Books.

State Intervention in the Family & Parental Rights Panel Discussion see State Intervention in the Family & Parental Rights, Pt. 2, A Psychological Assessment

State Intervention in the Family & Parental Rights Panel Discussion, Pt. 2. Read by Craig A. Stern et al. 1 cass. 3.00 (125) ISI Books.

State of American Defense. Zumwalt. 1 cass. (Running Time: 47 min.). 10.95 (322) J Norton Pubs.

State of Chan. Contrib. by Hua. (978-0-88139-603-4(6)) Buddhist Text.

State of Denial Pt. 3: Bush at War. unabr. ed. Bob Woodward. Read by Adam Grupper. 18 cass. (Running Time: 21 hrs. 30 mins.). 2007. 113.75 (978-1-4281-3548-2(0)); audio compact disk 123.75 (978-1-4281-3550-5(2)) Recorded Bks.
Bob Woodward examines how the Bush administration avoided telling the truth about Iraq to the public, to the Congress, and often to themselves in State of Denial. Woodward's third book on President Bush is a sweeping narrative from the first days George W. Bush thought seriously about running for president, through the recruitment of his national security team, the war in Afghanistan, the invasion and occupation of Iraq, and the struggle for political survival in the second term.

State of Emergency. unabr. ed. Steve Peiczenik. Read by Adams Morgan. (Running Time: 11 hrs. 30 mins.). 2010. 29.95 (978-1-4417-1922-5(9)); audio compact disk 100.00 (978-1-4417-1919-5(9)) Blckstn Audio.

State of Emergency. unabr. ed. Steve Pieczenik. Read by Adams Morgan. 8 cass. (Running Time: 11 hrs. 30 mins.). 1998. 56.95 (978-0-7861-1317-0(0), 2241) Blckstn Audio.
In Nevada, a man bulldozes a new forest road, to the cheers of his neighbors & the local police. Waiting for him on the other side are three nervous forest rangers & a handful of ATF agents. In Arizona, the governor finds thousands of citizens evacuating a town under the watchful eye of officials from the Federal Emergency Management Agency. He is baffled by the fact that no National Guardsmen, state troopers, or local police are anywhere in sight. It is July Fourth weekend, & the governor of Utah is getting angrier by the minute. With the leaders of three other Western states - Colorado, Wyoming, & Arizona - he threatens to secede from the Union. Their bargaining tool: the mighty Glen Canyon Dam in Page, Arizona. If the president does not give in to their demands within seventy-two hours, they will destroy the dam, & the lives of thousands will be at risk. Their ultimatum: accession of all constitutional rights & full military control of their borders.

***State of Fear.** abr. ed. Michael Crichton. Read by John Bedford Lloyd. (ENG.). 2004. (978-0-06-081779-4(8), Harper Audio); (978-0-06-081777-0(1), Harper Audio) HarperCollins Pubs.

State of Fear. abr. ed. Michael Crichton. Read by John Bedford Lloyd. (Running Time: 25200 sec.). 2008. audio compact disk 14.95 (978-0-06-157121-3(0), Harper Audio) HarperCollins Pubs.

State of Fear. unabr. ed. Michael Crichton. Read by George Wilson & John Bedford Lloyd. 16 CDs. (Running Time: 18.5 Hours). 2004. audio compact disk 49.95 (978-0-06-078601-4(9)) HarperCollins Pubs.

State of Fear. unabr. ed. Michael Crichton. Read by George Wilson. 2004. audio compact disk 34.95 (978-0-06-079745-4(2)) HarperCollins Pubs.

***State of Fear.** unabr. ed. Michael Crichton. Read by John Bedford Lloyd. (ENG.). 2004. (978-0-06-081775-6(5), Harper Audio); (978-0-06-081776-3(3), Harper Audio) HarperCollins Pubs.

State of Fear. unabr. ed. Michael Crichton. Narrated by George Wilson. 16 CDs. (Running Time: 18 hrs. 30 mins.). 2005. audio compact disk 109.75 (978-1-4193-2044-6(0), C2923); 99.75 (978-1-4193-2042-2(4), 97937) Recorded Bks.
Michael Crichton, the number one best-selling author of Prey and Jurassic Park, has done it again! His latest novel is full of electrifying suspense and provides a compelling commentary on the information age. This spellbinding techno-thriller takes listeners on an unforgettable journey from Paris to Antarctica to the Solomon Islands and back.

State of Jones: The Small Southern County That Seceded from the Confederacy. abr. ed. John Stauffer & Sally Jenkins. Read by Don Leslie. (ENG.). 2009. audio compact disk 29.95 (978-0-7393-8281-3(0), Random AudioBks) Pub: Random Audio Pubg. Dist(s): Random

***State of Jones: The Small Southern County That Seceded from the Confederacy.** unabr. ed. John Stauffer & Sally Jenkins. Read by Don Leslie. 11 CDs. (Running Time: 13 hrs.). 2009. audio compact disk 100.00 (978-1-4159-6294-7(4), BksonTape) Pub: Random Audio Pubg. Dist(s): Random

State of Mind: Program from the Award Winning Public Radio Serie. Interview. Hosted by Fred Goodwin. Comment by John Hockenberry. 1 CD. (Running Time: 1 hr.). 2004. audio compact disk 21.95 (978-1-932479-95-9(3), LCM 326) Lichtenstein Creat.
State of Mind: America 2004 is The Infinite Mind's third annual examination of the state of the nation's mental health care system, taped before a live audience. This special one-hour public radio broadcast features discussions about the state of the nation's mental health care system, thrilling musical performances from smash Broadway musicals, and groundbreaking research and developments in the treatment of manic-depressive illness. Join host Dr. Goodwin and his guests for this unprecedented program, recorded at New York's historic Radio City Music Hall before a live audience of 3,000 public radio listeners. Joining The Infinite Mind's host Dr. Goodwin on stage at Radio City are: Actress and writer Carrie Fisher, who will read from and discuss her newest novel, ?The Best Awful.?A. Kathryn Power, Director, U.S. Center for Mental Health Services. Ms. Power is charged with transforming our nation?s system of mental health care and putting into action the recommendations of the President?s New Freedom Commission on Mental Health. Robert Post, M.D., Chief, Biological Psychiatry Branch, National Institute of Mental Health. His work on the ?kindling model? of bipolar disorder is widely recognized as a foundation of current understanding and treatment of the illness.Dominic Lam, Ph.D., Institute of Psychiatry, King?s College, London, who pioneered research into the use of cognitive techniques to help bipolar patients identify the early signs of potential relapses and improve their quality of life.Stephan Heckers, M.D., Director, Schizophrenia and Bipolar Disorder Program, McLean Hospital, Belmont, Massachusetts. And special commentary from The Infinite Mind?s John Hockenberry.Special performances by the casts of the hit Broadway shows performing "The Musical Mind on Broadway":Wicked: (10 Tony Award nominations and named "Best Musical on Broadway" by Time Magazine). "The Wizard and I" performed by Eden Espinosa (as "Elphaba," the Wicked Witch of the West.) Avenue Q (2004 Tony Award winner "Best Musical") "Schadenfreude," performed by Natalie Venetia Belcon, (Gary Coleman), Rick Lyon, (Nicky) and Jennifer Barnhart (Nicky). Highlighted on State of Mind: America 2004 will be the President?s New Freedom Commission on Mental Health report, released in July 2003. The report, the most significant Presidential initiative in 50 years, aims to transform health care for those with mental illness through the implementation of six goals: o Americans understand that mental health is essential to overall health, with mental illness and physical illness being treated equally. o Mental health is consumer and family driven, with people affected and their families having greater control of their health care.o Disparities in mental health services be eliminated, particularly among racial and ethnic minorities. o Early mental health screening, assessment, and referral to services be common practice to assist proper diagnosis and treatment of young people. o Excellent mental health care is delivered and research is accelerated in order to close the gap, currently as much as seven years, between scientific research and new medical treatments. o Technology is used to access mental health care and information, allowing Internet technology to make mental information and care more widely available to all Americans.

State of Mind: Program from the Award Winning Public Radio Series. Interview. Hosted by Fred Goodwin & John Hockenberry. 1CD. (Running Time: 1 hr). (Infinite Mind Ser.). 2002. audio compact disk 21.95 (978-1-888064-90-2(0), LCM 205) Lichtenstein Creat.
This landmark event two-hour live radio broadcast explores the mental health and emotional well-being of Americans as the nation heads out of the turmoil of 2001 and into a challenging 2002. Recorded live in front of an audience of 600. Guests include former First Lady, Rosalynn Carter, leading trauma researchers Dr. Dennis Charney and Dr. Carol North, pollster Richard Rockwell, Dr. Marilyn Benoit, president of the American Academy of Child and Adolescent Psychiatry, Marian Wright Edelman, executive director of the Children's Defense Fund, Dr. Rosemarie Truglio, psychologist and consultant to Sesame Street, researcher Dr. David Spiegel, comedian Al Franken, Tipper Gore and author Dr. Peter Kramer. Plus, journalist Robert Krulwich presents an exclusive interview with U.S. Surgeon General David Satcher, and actor David Strathaim reads a commentary on religion by the noted civil rights and peace activist William Sloane Coffin. Pollster Robert Boorstin discusses the results of The Infinite Mind/American Psychological Association poll on America's recovery from 9/11, and singers Jessye Norman and Judy Collins perform.Co-hosted by Dr. Fred Goodwin, host of The Infinite Mind in Washington and John Hockenberry in New York. Produced in association with WAMU/Washington, D.C. and WNYC/New York.

State of Our Union. Alan Bock et al. 1 cass. (Running Time: 1 hr. 47 min.). 12.50 (420) J Norton Pubs.

State of Siege. abr. ed. Created by Tom Clancy & Steve Pieczenik. 4 cass. (Op-Center Ser.: No. 6). 1999. 24.00 (FS9-50938) Highsmith.

State of Siege. unabr. collector's ed. Eric Ambler. Read by Richard Brown. 7 cass. (Running Time: 7 hrs.). 1989. 42.00 (978-0-7366-1606-5(3), 2467) Books on Tape.
Set in Southeast Asia, State of Siege covers 24 critical hours in a military coup d'etat. Fraser, an oil technician on leave & caught up in this explosive whirlwind tries to extricate himself & pursue his pleasures - namely an Eurasian beauty. But he is hopelessly entangled in the conspiracy & the final outbreak of violence which ends the day.

State of Stony Lonesome. unabr. ed. Jessamyn West. Read by Roses Prichard. 5 cass. (Running Time: 5 hrs.). 1986. 30.00 (978-0-7366-1049-0(9), 1977) Books on Tape.
Zen is a gambler, drinker & womanizer. Ginerva is a lovely girl, still in her teens. But in the theatre of her imagination, romance & propriety frequently clash. The problem is Zen, with whom she is secretly & most improperly in love. Zen is not only old enough to be her father, but in fact, is her uncle.

State of the Art. 1 cass. (Care Cassettes Ser.: Vol. 11, No. 4). 1984. 10.80 Assn Prof Chaplains.

State of the Art, Pt. 1. unabr. ed. Pauline Kael. Read by Ruth Stokesberry. 8 cass. (Running Time: 12 hrs.). 1989. 64.00 (978-0-7366-1623-2(3), 2483-A) Books on Tape.
Praising Pauline Kael at this stage of her career is like announcing that the world is round. As film critic of The New Yorker, & in a succession of books that began in 1965 with I Lost It at the Movies, she has established an unshakable claim to preeminence. She is a rarity, a marvelous writer who is also a marvelous critic. In this collection, she takes on movies released from 1983-1985. Flashdance, Terms of Endearment, Yentl, Under Fire, Bizet's Carmen, Purple Rain, The Purple Rose of Cairo, Amadeus, The Killing Fields, Stranger than Paradise, The Makioka Sisters, Greystoke, Prizzi's Honor, Rambo.

State of the Art, Pt. 2. Pauline Kael. Read by Ruth Stokesberry. 7 cass. (Running Time: 10 hrs. 30 min.). 1989. 56.00 (2483-B) Books on Tape.

State-of-the-Art Selling, Set. Barry Farber. 6 cass. 39.95 (10490AX) Nightingale-Conant.
Selling is a natural, non-manipulative act based on developing relationships, building trust & - most importantly - solving customer problems. In this high-power program, Barry Farber reveals the Management Account Profile & unique customer profile techniques that will assure you spectacular results: more leads, better leads & increase sales. Includes guidebook.

State of the Economy: A Panel Discussion. unabr. ed. Contrib. by John Allison et al. 1 cass. (Running Time: 1 hrs. 35 min.). 1997. 14.95 (978-1-56114-424-2(X), DX48C) Second Renaissance.
Illuminating insights into the workings of our economy.

State of the Nation: Government & the Quest for a Better Society. unabr. ed. Derek C. Bok. 1999. 24.95 (978-0-9660180-1-1(X)) Scholarly Audio.
An assessment of how America has fared economically, in terms of quality of life, in providing equal opportunity, in providing security, & on societal values over the last five decades.

State of the Union. abr. ed. Brad Thor. Read by George Guidall. (Running Time: 6 hrs. 0 mins. 0 sec.). (ENG.). 2009. audio compact disk 14.99 (978-0-7435-8036-6(2)) Pub: S&S Audio. Dist(s): S and S Inc

State of the Union. unabr. ed. Howard Lindsey & Russel Crouse. Perf. by Lindsay Crouse et al. 1 cass. (Running Time: 2 hrs. 2 min.). 1996. 22.95 (978-1-58081-016-6(0)) L A Theatre.
The 1996 presidential election provides the backdrop to celebrate the 50th anniversary of the Pulitzer Prize winning play. By Special permission of the authors, famed political correspondent Sidney Blumenthal has updated the campaign issues & mores in the play for today. This classic political comedy has all the ingredients needed to give it accuracy - including a candidate with integrity & principles, an inconvenient mistress & an estranged wife who must be wooed back so he can win the election.

State of Vermont. Robert W. Magee. Read by Grover Gardner & Kimberly Schraf. 1 cass. (Running Time: 90 min.). (Ride with Me Ser.). 1994. 10.95 (978-0-942649-29-1(X)) RWM Assocs.
Anecdotal discussion on Vermont history, geography & trivia.

State of War: The Secret History of the CIA & the Bush Administration. abr. ed. James Risen. Read by Boyd Gaines. 2006. 17.95 (978-0-7435-5586-9(4)) Pub: S&S Audio. Dist(s): S and S Inc

***State of Wonder: A Novel.** unabr. ed. Ann Patchett. Read by Tbd. 2011. audio compact disk 39.99 (978-0-06-207247-4(1), Harper Audio) HarperCollins Pubs.

State v. Justice, Set. unabr. ed. Gallatin Warfield. 11 cass. 1998. 103.95 (978-1-85903-130-8(7)) Pub: Magna Story GBR. Dist(s): Ulverscroft US

Statecraft As Soulcraft. unabr. ed. George F. Will. Read by Robin Lawson. 4 cass. (Running Time: 5 hrs. 30 mins.). 1991. 32.95 (978-0-7861-0277-8(2), 1243) Blckstn Audio.
Urges us to reconsider some of our most fundamental beliefs, for he concludes that they have contributed to producing a society that is deeply troubled & in very real danger.

Stately Home Murder. unabr. ed. Catherine Aird. Read by Robin Bailey. 4 cass. (Running Time: 5 hrs. 30 min.). (C. D. Sloan Mystery Ser.). 2001. 24.95 (978-1-57270-162-5(5), N41162u) Pub: Audio Partners. Dist(s): PerseuPGW

Stately Pursuits. Katie Fforde. Read by Roe Kendall. 8 cass. (Running Time: 11 hrs. 30 mins.). 2000. 56.95 (978-0-7861-1575-4(0), 2404) Blckstn Audio.
Hettie Longden, freshly dumped & broken-hearted, agrees to look after her great-uncle's long-abandoned mansion in the countryside. She is at something of a life-time low: no job, no lover, no prospects, & no particular talent for resuscitating crumbling estates. Then she finds a couple of sensitive New Age guys & ever-present neighbors.

Stately Pursuits. unabr. ed. Katie Fforde. Narrated by Jenny Sterlin. 8 cass. (Running Time: 11 hrs. 30 mins.). 1998. 70.00 (978-0-7887-2608-8(0), 95446E7) Recorded Bks.
Freshly dumped by her dashing lover, Hetty Longden agrees to look after an aging relative's abandoned mansion in the countryside. She is hoping for a place to hide out with her broken heart. Instead she is forced to deal with a cast of ever present, quirky neighbors & a crumbling house, all demanding constant attention.

Statement. unabr. ed. Brian Moore. Read by Andrew Sachs. 6 cass. (Running Time: 6 hrs. 23 mins.). 2003. 29.95 (978-1-57270-332-2(6)); audio compact disk 29.95 (978-1-57270-333-9(4)) Pub: Audio Partners. Dist(s): PerseuPGW
Paul Touvier was a Vichy functionary in France during World War II. Judged guilty of wartime crimes, including the murder of seven Jews, he was sentenced to death in absentia after the war. Thanks to Church sympathizers and highly placed government officials, he eluded capture until 1989. Acclaimed novelist Brian Moore reinvented this true-life case into a gripping tale of crime, pursuit, and punishment. Since the Allied victory, Pierre Brossard has been on the run for his war crimes, successfully protected by powerful friends in the French government and the Church. However, time is running out for Brossard - those who once saved him may now betray him - and his future grows increasingly uncertain. In The Statement, evil wears a disturbingly human face. Reader Andrew Sachs captures the essence of Moore's storytelling in this complex literary thriller.

Statement, unabr. ed. Brian Moore. Narrated by Steven Crossley. 5 cass. (Running Time: 7 hrs. 15 mins.). 1998. 44.00 (978-0-7887-1311-8(6), 95085E7) Recorded Bks.
War criminal, Pierce Brossard is wanted for killing Jews in southern France during WWII. He has avoided capture for almost 50 years, but now his allies are growing old. How much is Brossard willing to risk for protection?.

Statement Vol. 4: Yves Netzhammer Opiate Mouse on Mars to Rococo Rot. 2 vols. (ENG & GER.). 2002. pap. bk. 42.00 (978-3-936919-41-7(0)) Pub: C Keller Revolver DEU. Dist(s): RAM Publications

States & Capitals. Penton Overseas, Inc. Staff. 1 cass. (Running Time: 1 hr.). (J). 2001. wbk. ed. 12.95 (TS 406C); wbk. ed. 14.95 (KIM9112) Kimbo Educ.
Patriotic melodies teach about our 50 states, the capital of each state & fascinating facts about our nation. 48 page reproducible workbook includes puzzles, graphs, maps & creative writing activities.

States & Capitals. Penton Overseas, Inc. Staff. 1 cass. (Social Studies Ser.). (J). bk. Incl. 24p. bk., maps, graphs, sheet music & activities. (TWIN 406) NewSound.
Learn the 50 states & their capitals as well as interesting facts about each state.

States & Capitals. Penton Overseas, Inc. Staff. 1 CD. (Running Time: 1 hr.). (J). 2000. audio compact disk 12.99 (TWIN106CD) Twin Sisters.
Learning our 50 states & capitals has never been more fun! Children travel through each state learning important facts & trivia while singing "I want to learn about my country & learn about each state." All states are sung in alphabetical order to the old favorite song "Turkey in the Straw".

States & Capitals. Kim Mitzo Thompson & Karen Mitzo Hilderbrand. Arranged by Hal Wright. (J). 1993. pap. bk. 13.99 (978-1-57583-296-8(8), Twin 406CD); audio compact disk 12.99 (978-1-57583-236-4(4), TWIN 106CD) Twin Sisters.

States & Capitals. Kim Mitzo Thompson & Karen Mitzo Hilderbrand. Illus. by Goran Kozjak. 1 cass. (Running Time: 40 min.). (Rhythm, Rhyme & Read Ser.). (J). (gr. 3-6). 1993. bk. & stu. ed. 9.98 (978-1-882331-24-6(9), TWIN 406) Twin Sisters.
States & their capitals as well as interesting facts about each state are presented in a wide array of instantly recognizable patriotic melodies.

States & Capitals. unabr. ed. Twin Sisters Productions. Read by Twin Sisters. (J). 2008. 44.99 (978-1-60514-610-2(2)) Find a World.

States & Capitals Rap. unabr. ed. Brad Caudle & Richard Caudle. Perf. by D. J. Doc Roc and the Get Smart Crew Staff. 1 cass. (Running Time: 30 min.). (J). (gr. 4 up). 1993. audio compact disk 12.95 CD Set. (978-1-878489-16-6(X), RL916) Rock N Learn.
"Top 40" type rap songs with educational lyrics teach states & capitals. Includes reproducible, illustrated book with fun facts on each state.

States & Capitals Rap. unabr. ed. Brad Caudle & Richard Caudle. Perf. by D. J. Doc Roc and the Get Smart Crew Staff. Illus. by Bart Harlan. 1 cass. (Running Time: 30 min.). (Rock 'N Learn Ser.). (J). (gr. 4-12). 1993. bk. 12.99 (978-1-878489-15-9(1), RL915) Rock N Learn.

States & Capitals Songs. 1 CD. (Running Time: 1 hr.). 2001. pap. bk. & tchr. ed. 12.95 (3CD) Audio Memory.
Easy sing-along songs teach names and locations of the 50 states and their capitals. Includes 25"x36" black and white poster map of the US to label and color.

States & Capitals Songs. 2004. audio compact disk 12.95 (978-1-883028-14-5(0)) Audio Memory.

States & Capitals Songs, Grades K-5. Larry Troxel & Kathy Troxel. 1 cass. (Running Time: 1 hr.). (J). 1994. pap. bk. & tchr. ed. 9.95 (978-1-883028-00-8(0), 3) Audio Memory.
U. S. Geography.

States & Capitals Workbook & Music CD. Twin Sisters Productions Staff. 2009. pap. bk. & wbk. ed. 10.99 (978-1-57583-891-5(5)) Twin Sisters.

States & Strategies. John Grinder & Robert Dilts. Read by John Grinder & Robert Dilts. 8 cass. (Running Time: 12 hrs.). (Syntax of Behavior One Ser.: Vol. I). 1988. 99.95 set. Metamorphous Pr.
Robert & John begin this seminar with advocacy positions regarding the advantages of state vs. strategy approaches to change. The sharpening of these initial positions yields a new relationship between state/strategy approaches resulting in a layered format, integrating these core NLP principles.

States of Campaign Finance Reform. Donald A. Gross & Robert K. Goidel. 2003. audio compact disk 9.95 (978-0-8142-9003-3(5)) Pub: Ohio St U Pr. Dist(s): Chicago Distribution Ctr

States/Capitals Songs. 2001. 9.95 (1861, Hewitt Homeschl Res) Hewitt Res Fnd.

***Static.** (ENG.). 2010. audio compact disk (978-1-59171-269-5(6)) Falcon Picture.

Static. unabr. ed. Ron Martoia. Narrated by Kelly Ryan Dolan. (ENG.). 2007. 9.09 (978-1-60814-396-2(1)) Oasis Audio.

Stationary Ark. unabr. collector's ed. Gerald Durrell. Read by Stuart Courtney. 7 cass. (Running Time: 7 hrs.). 1983. 42.00 (978-0-7366-0551-9(7), 1525) Books on Tape.
On one level this is about zoos. More profoundly, however, it is about the misuse of wild animals in captivity.

Stationary Bike. unabr. ed. Stephen King. Read by Ron McLarty. 2 CDs. (Running Time: 1 hr. 30 mins.). 2007. audio compact disk 30.75 (978-1-4281-3554-3(5)); 20.75 (978-1-4281-3552-9(9)) Recorded Bks.
This imaginative work recounts the unfortunate story of an obese man named Richard Sifkitz. Finally caving-in to his doctor's advice, Richard decides to change his life for the better. So in a bid to lose weight after years of muscle neglect and persistent self-indulgence he begins taking daily rides on his stationary exercise bike. Soon his laborious journeys become increasingly obsessive - and then, maddeningly desperate. Now reality and fantasy commingle as Richard begins to fear that something is following him - something terrible - and it's getting closer by the minute.

Stationary Bike. unabr. ed. Stephen King. Read by Ron McLarty. 2006. 12.95 (978-0-7435-6525-7(8), Audioworks) Pub: S&S Audio. Dist(s): S and S Inc

Stationary Bike. unabr. ed. Stephen King. Read by Ron McLarty. 2 CDs. (Running Time: 1 hr. 30 mins. 0 sec.). (ENG.). 2006. audio compact disk 20.00 (978-0-7435-5561-6(9), Audioworks) Pub: S&S Audio. Dist(s): S and S Inc

Stationary Man. Gilbert Highet. Read by Gilbert Highet. 1 cass. (Running Time: 30 min.). 10.95 (23291-A) J Norton Pubs.

Stationary Planets As Timers. Stephanie Ennis. 1 cass. 8.95 (109) Am Fed Astrologers.
An AFA Convention workshop tape.

Stations of the Cross. Illus. by Sheldon Cohen. 1 cass. (Running Time: 45 mins.). 2004. 8.95 (978-0-914070-32-0(0), 304) ACTA Pubns.
Meditations for each station were written by Rev. James Killgallon, author of the popular catechism "Life in Christ".

Stations of the Cross. Megan McKenna. 2 cass. (Running Time: 2 hrs.). 1992. 17.95 (AA2589) Credence Commun.
Meditations on the stations of the cross that are more challenging than you are used to. Both pious & political.

***Stations of the Cross: A Family Devotional Audio CD.** Kenneth L. Davison, Jr.. Kenneth L. Davison, Jr. Narrated by Jim Morlino. Prod. by Jim Morlino. (ENG.). (J). 2009. audio compact disk 15.00 (978-0-9801121-4-6(1)) Holy Heroes.

Stations of the Cross & the Gospel of the Passion. Narrated by Owen F. Campion. 1 cass. (Running Time: 1 hr. 30 mins.). 7.95 (978-0-87973-229-5(6), 229) Our Sunday Visitor.
After a brief introduction, Father Campion recites original meditations for each of the 14 stations. Following is a narration of the Passion of Our Lord Jesus Christ according to St. Mark.

Statistical Sampling Procedures. John Wragge. 3 cass. 99.00 incl. wkbk. & quizzer. (CPE0050) Bisk Educ.
Designed to help understand & apply statistical sampling techniques to your audit work.

Statistics. Norman H. Crowhurst. (J). 1981. 103.95 (978-0-89420-202-5(2), 413000) Natl Book.

Statistics Lecture Series. Terance D. Miethe & Timothy C. Hart. (C). 2009. audio compact disk (978-1-61623-937-4(9)) Indep Pub IL.

Statue of Liberty: Early Explorers Early Set B Audio CD. Danielle S. Hammelef. Adapted by Benchmark Education Staff. (J). 2007. audio compact disk 10.00 (978-1-4108-8233-2(0)) Benchmark Educ.

Stature of Christ. Jack Deere. 1 cass. (Running Time: 90 mins.). (Intimacy with God & the End-Time Church Ser.: Vol. 3). 2000. 5.00 (JD09-003) Morning NC.
Oneness with the Father is essential for every believer in these last days & the teaching in this six-tape series will impart a heartfelt hunger for intimate fellowship with Him.

Status Anxiety. abr. unabr. ed. Alain de Botton. Read by Simon Vance. 8 cass. (Running Time: 23400 sec.). 2006. 29.95 (978-0-7861-4464-8(5)); audio compact disk 29.95 (978-0-7861-7288-7(6)) Blckstn Audio.

Status Anxiety. abr. unabr. ed. Alain de Botton. Read by Simon Vance. (Running Time: 23400 sec.). 2006. audio compact disk 29.95 (978-0-7861-7710-3(1)) Blckstn Audio.

Status Anxiety. unabr. ed. Alain de Botton. Read by Simon Vance. (Running Time: 23400 sec.). 2006. 44.95 (978-0-7861-4696-3(6)); audio compact disk 45.00 (978-0-7861-6781-4(5)) Blckstn Audio.

Status, Application & Progressive Development of International & National Space Law: Proceedings - United Nations/Ukraine Workshop on Space Law (CD-ROM) United Nations. (ENG.). 2008. audio compact disk 25.00 (978-92-1-101171-5(X)) Untd Nat Pubns.

Status for Sale: The Complete Guide to Instant Prestige. Wayne Yeager. 1992. 8.95 (978-1-881248-02-6(X)) Charter Pubns.

Status Unknown. Howard B. Lyman. 1 cass. (Running Time: 21 min.). (Single Again Ser.). 10.95 (35024) J Norton Pubs.

Statutory Close Corporations - Important but Unused Vehicles. Read by Mark Witzig. 1 cass. 1990. 20.00 (AL-96) PA Bar Inst.

Statutory Construction: Capitol Learning Audio Course. Todd Tatelman. Prod. by TheCapitol.Net. (ENG.). 2008. 47.00 (978-1-58733-078-0(4)) TheCapitol.

***Stay.** unabr. ed. Allie Larkin. Read by Julia Whelan. (Running Time: 10 hrs.). 2010. 24.99 (978-1-4418-4279-4(9), 9781441842794, Brilliance MP3); 24.99 (978-1-4418-4281-7(0), 9781441842817, BAD); 39.97 (978-1-4418-4282-4(9), 9781441842824, BADLE); 39.97 (978-1-4418-4280-0(2), 9781441842800, Brlnc Audio MP3 Lib); audio compact disk 29.99 (978-1-4418-4271-8(3), 9781441842718, Bril Audio CD Unabri); audio compact disk 79.97 (978-1-4418-4272-5(1), 9781441842725, BriAudCD Unabrid) Brilliance Audio.

***Stay a Little Longer.** Dorothy Garlock. Narrated by Susan Boyce. (Running Time: 8 hrs. 49 mins. 0 sec.). (ENG.). 2011. audio compact disk 29.95 (978-1-60998-155-6(3)) Pub: AudioGO. Dist(s): Perseus Dist

Stay after School: The Bugville Critters. unabr. ed. Robert Stanek, pseud. Narrated by Ginny Westcott. (Running Time: 19 mins.). (ENG.). (J). 2008. 5.95 (978-1-57545-359-0(2), RP Audio Pubng) Pub: Reagent Press. Dist(s): OverDrive Inc

Stay as Sweet as You Are, Set. unabr. ed. Joan Jonker. 12 cass. (Running Time: 59100 sec.). (Eve Duncan Ser.). 2000. 96.95 (978-0-7540-0429-5(5), CAB 1852) Pub: Chivers Audio Bks GBR. Dist(s): AudioGO

Lucy Mellor is a daughter who'd make any parents proud. However, Lucy only knows cruelty from her mother. Although her father tries to protect her, he is no match for a wife who has no love for him or his daughter. One day, Irene from next door, decides she can no longer stand back, so she takes Lucy under her wing & into a loving house.

Stay Awake. abr. ed. Robert A. Monroe. Read by Robert A. Monroe. (Running Time: 30 min.). (Human Plus Ser.). 1989. 14.95 (978-1-56102-042-3(7)) Inter Indus.

Obtain immediate restoration of full alertness.

Stay Away from That City... They Call It Cheyenne. abr. ed. Stephen A. Bly. 2 cass. (Running Time: 3 hrs.). (Code of the West Ser.: No. 4). 2001. 17.99 (978-1-58926-014-6(7)) Oasis Audio.

Married life for Tap and Pepper isn't turning out quite the way they planned. Tap has found a job that uses his strengths, integrity, nerves of steel, and a fast draw. Those things come in handy for a deputy marshal.

Stay Away from That City... They Call It Cheyenne. unabr. ed. Stephen A. Bly. Read by Jerry Sciarrio. 6 cass. (Running Time: 6 hrs. 18 min.). (Code of the West Ser.: Bk. 4). 2001. 39.95 (978-1-58116-050-5(X)) Books in Motion.

Married life for Tap and Pepper isn't turning out quite the way they planned. The ranch is gone and they've moved to Cheyenne where Tap finds himself a job as acting marshall in a town that has little regard for the law.

Stay Filled with the Fire. Lynne Hammond. 1 cass. (Running Time: 1 hr.). 2005. 5.00 (978-1-57399-254-1(2)); audio compact disk 5.00 (978-1-57399-271-8(2)) Mac Hammond.

Stay Fit & Healthy until You're Dead. unabr. ed. Dave Barry. Read by Arte Johnson. 2 cass. (Running Time: 2 hrs.). 1996. 16.95 (978-1-57270-022-2(X), C21022) Pub: Audio Partners. Dist(s): PerseuPGW

Laugh with Barry as he de-bunks, de-motivates, & de-lights on the subject of fitness.

Stay Hard. Wendi Friesen. 2 CDs. (Running Time: 4 sessions). 2002. audio compact disk 69.00 (978-1-929058-04-4(7)) Wendicom.

Many of you are probably very skeptical about how hypnosis could actually enlarge breasts. It seems odd, but once you understand how the mind works, and how easy it is to reprogram the cells with hypnosis, you will find that you actually have a lot of control in the area of making changes in your body.

Stay Healthy. Maritha Pottenger. 1 cass. 1992. 8.95 (1084) Am Fed Astrologers.

Stay in the Lifeboat: Don't Let the World Pull You Under. Read by Brad Wilcox. 2007. audio compact disk 13.95 (978-1-59038-879-2(8)) Deseret Bk.

Stay in the White Light, & Dream. Scripts. Martin Brofman. 1 CD. (Running Time: 50 mins.). (ENG.). 2004. audio compact disk 17.99 (978-1-84409-023-5(X)) Pub: Findhorn Pr GBR. Dist(s): IPG Chicago

These meditations were conceived by Martin Brofman, healer, author, and teacher, to help you get in contact with the nature of your being, and to enhance the quality of your life. The brilliant musical accompaniment was composed for this meditation by popular Danish musician Mikkel Nords?.?Stay in the White Light? is a progressive relaxation through your body. As each part of your body relaxes, you can imagine it glowing with White Light. When your entire body is glowing, you can experience yourself being centered, enjoying a deep state of relaxation known to enhance the generation of beneficial alpha brain waves, and listening to affirmations encouraging self expression and self acceptance. The second meditation, ?Dream,? guides you to an experience of being a single point of consciousness, able to see your life as a dream, as the product of what is happening in your consciousness, as you see yourself moving toward the fulfillment of your goals. Excellent for lending stability to those going through an extreme lifestyle change.

Stay in Your Own Backyard. unabr. ed. Joan Jonker. Read by Maggie Ollerenshaw. 10 cass. (Running Time: 10 hrs.). 1997. 84.95 Set. (978-0-7540-0007-5(9), CAB 1430) AudioGO.

In her home in Liverpool, Molly Bennett struggles to raise four children on her husband's meager wage. Although she can't complain, she has a home filled with love. Her eldest daughter, Jill, manages to get a job while going to night school. When Molly & her best friend, Nellie, discover that a neighbor is being beaten by her violent husband, the friends move into action.

Stay of Execution. unabr. ed. Quintin Jardine. 12 cass. (Running Time: 13 hrs. 19 mins.). (Isis Cassettes Ser.). (J). 2004. 94.95 (978-0-7531-2018-7(6)); audio compact disk 99.95 (978-0-7531-2341-6(X)) Pub: ISIS Lrg Prnt GBR. Dist(s): Ulverscroft US

Stay Out of My Nightmare, Set. abr. ed. Louis L'Amour. Read by Charles Dean. 2 cass. (Running Time: 3 hrs.). 1999. (978-0-931969-38-6(7), 391678) Book of the Rd.

There are two things you need to make a murder: a corpse & a killer. Packed with fatal suspense & mystery.

Stay Out of My Nightmare; Street of Lost Corpses. abr. ed. Louis L'Amour. 2 cass. (Running Time: 3 hrs.). (Louis L'Amour Collector Ser.:). 2000. 7.95 (978-1-57815-103-5(1), 1074, Media Bks Audio) Media Bks NJ.

The brave men & women who settled the American frontier.

Stay Sane Through Change: How to Rise above the Challenges of Life's Complex Transitions. 9 discs. (Running Time: 10:36:17). 2006. audio compact disk 33.95 (978-1-60031-008-9(7)) Spoken Books.

Stay sane through Change: How to rise above the challenges of life's complex Transitions. rev. ed. F. David Webster & Tolulope A. Adeleye. (ENG.). 2009. audio compact disk 44.95 (978-1-936001-00-2(4)) Comtemp Life.

Stay under the Blood: Live in Baton Rouge, LA. Perf. by Slim and the Supreme Angels. 1 cass. 1995. audio compact disk 15.98 CD. (978-1-57908-052-5(9), 9144) Platinm Enter.

Classic gospel quartet music with the added dimension of The Voices of Praise Gospel choir. Gospel fans will be familiar with the traditional quartet harmonies in the style made famous by groups like the Mighty Clouds of Joy. Recipients of a Gold Record & a Stellar nomination, Slim & the Supreme Angels have been performing their quartet style gospel music for thousands of fans across the country since 1958.

***Stay with Me.** Jessica Blair. Read by Anne Dover. 2010. 84.95 (978-1-84652-710-4(4)); audio compact disk 89.95 (978-1-84652-711-1(2)) Pub: Magna Story GBR. Dist(s): Ulverscroft US

Stay with Me. Perf. by John Gerighty et al. 1 cass., 1 CD. (Running Time: 45 min.). 1997. 11.95 (978-0-86347-158-2(7), MoreHse Pubng); audio compact disk 16.95 CD. (978-0-86347-159-9(5), MoreHse Pubng) Church Pub Inc.

Songs from the French ecumenical youth center, Taize, plus some other songs suited for meditation & prayer. Pan pipes, classical guitar, flutes, etc.

Stay Young, Start Now: A Family Doctor's Guide to More Energy, Less Stress & Better Sex. abr. ed. Alan Bonsteel. Read by Scott Brick. 4 cass. (Running Time: 6 hrs.). 2001. 25.00 (978-1-57453-386-6(X)) Audio Lit.

Stayin' Over. Perf. by Peter Alsop. 1 cass. (J). (ps-7). 9.98 (2115) MFLP CA.

Songs include: "You're Okay," "I Cried," "Juice," "I Wanna Try It," "Where Will I Go," "No Excuse T'Use Booze," "Us Kids Brush Our Teeth," "Dear Mr. President" & more.

Stayin' Over. Perf. by Peter Alsop. 1 CD. (Running Time: 47 min.). (J). (gr. k-6). audio compact disk (MS502) Moose Schl Records.

Grab your toothbrush & stay overnight with Peter & the gang. Includes exercise & discussion questions to use with the songs. Best Children's Album - Naird. Parent's Choice - Honors Award.

Stayin' Over. Perf. by Peter Alsop. 1 cass. (Running Time: 47 min.). (J). (gr. k-6). 1987. 11.00 (MS 502) Moose Schl Records.

Staying Alive. Alexander Fullerton. 2007. audio compact disk 99.95 (978-1-84559-586-9(6)) Pub: ISIS Audio GBR. Dist(s): Ulverscroft US

Staying Alive. Alexander Fullerton. Read by Nicolette McKenzie. 10 cass. 2007. 84.95 (978-1-84559-414-5(2)) Pub: ISIS Audio GBR. Dist(s): Ulverscroft US

Staying Alive Inside: How to Get Close Again. Bruce A. Baldwin. Read by Bruce A. Baldwin. (Running Time: 60 min.). (Personal Development Ser.). 1983. 8.95 (978-0-933583-15-3(X), PDC839) Direction Dynamics.

Book on Tape: Chapter from "It's All in Your Head." Discusses betrayal patterns & how to rebuild closeness to your special person.

Staying at Daisy's. unabr. ed. Jill Mansell. Read by Penelope Freeman. 12 cass. (Isis Cassettes Ser.). (J). 2005. 94.95 (978-0-7531-1506-0(9)) Pub: ISIS Lrg Prnt GBR. Dist(s): Ulverscroft US

Staying Evergreen. 1 cass. 11.95 (978-1-57025-010-1(3)) Whole Person.

Warm & uplifting observations on the importance of personal refueling emphasize the need to build & maintain self-care habits.

Staying Faithful in Adversity. Short Stories. Joel Osteen. 1 Cass. (Running Time: 30 Mins.). 2002. 6.00 (978-1-59349-164-2(6), JA0164) J Osteen.

Staying Faithful in the Tough Times to Life. Speeches. Joel Osteen. 1 Cass. (Running Time: 30 MINS). 2001. 6.00 (978-1-59349-095-9(X), JA0095) J Osteen.

Staying Fat for Sarah Byrnes. unabr. ed. Chris Crutcher. Narrated by Johnny Heller. 5 pieces. (Running Time: 6 hrs. 30 mins.). (YA). (gr. 9 up). 2002. 47.00 (978-1-4025-2280-2(0)) Recorded Bks.

Staying Healthy with Nutrition. Elson M. Haas. 2 cass. 1993. 18.00 set. (OC352-73) Sound Horizons AV.

Staying in the Right Lane. (Power Tool Box Ser.: Vol. 4). (J). (gr. 1-6). 1998. ring bd. 164.99 (978-1-57405-046-2(X)) CharismaLife Pub.

Staying Motivated. Pat Sladey. Read by Pat Sladey. 1 cass. (Running Time: 60 min.). 1988. 9.95 P Sladey.

Self-help program designed to build confidence & self-motivation.

Staying Nine. unabr. ed. Pam Conrad. Narrated by Kate Forbes. 1 cass. (Running Time: 1 hr. 15 mins.). (gr. 2 up). 2000. 10.00 (978-0-7887-3162-4(9), 95835E7) Recorded Bks.

Heather doesn't want to turn 10. She thinks her life is perfect just the way it is. She & her mom decide to give an unbirthday party. But when things don't go quite as planned, Heather finally realizes that staying nine may not be such a good idea.

Staying Nine. unabr. ed. Pam Conrad. Read by Kate Forbes. 1 cass. (Running Time: 1 hr. 15 mins.). (YA). (gr. 2 up). 2000. pap. bk. & stu. ed. 22.50 (978-0-7887-3184-6(X), 40919X4) Recorded Bks.

Staying Nine, Class Set. Pam Conrad. Read by Kate Forbes. 1 cass. (Running Time: 1 hr. 15 mins.). (YA). (gr. 2 up). 1999. 73.30 (978-0-7887-3230-0(7), 46886) Recorded Bks.

Heather doesn't want to turn ten so her mother throws her an unbirthday party. But things don't go quite as planned & Heather decides that staying nine may not be such a good idea.

Staying On. unabr. collector's ed. Paul Scott. Read by Richard Brown. 7 cass. (Running Time: 10 hrs. 30 min.). 1992. 56.00 (978-0-7366-2159-5(8), 2958) Books on Tape.

Postscript to Scott's masterful Raj Quartet.

Staying on Course. Elbert Willis. 1 cass. (Increasing Spiritual Assurance Ser.). 4.00 Fill the Gap.

Staying on the Path. Wayne W. Dyer. One CD. 2005. audio compact disk 10.95 (978-1-4019-0657-3(5)) Hay House.

Staying on the Path. unabr. ed. Wayne W. Dyer. Read by Wayne W. Dyer. Ed. by Jill Kramer. 1 cass. (Running Time: 1 hr.). 1995. 10.95 (978-1-56170-127-8(0), 352) Hay House.

Dr. Dyer's insights help you stay on the path...or will help you get there!.

Staying on Top: The Power of Natural Hair Growth. Robert I. Berrick. 1 cass. (Running Time: 60 min.). 1989. 29.95 Inner Visions.

A self-help program utilizing mental imagery to stop hair loss and promote hair growth.

Staying Positive in a Negative World. Short Stories. Joel Osteen. 1 Cass. (Running Time: 30 Mins.). 2000. 6.00 (978-1-59349-093-5(3), JA0093) J Osteen.

Staying Power. unabr. ed. Judith Cutler. Narrated by Patricia Gallimore. 7 cass. (Running Time: 9 hrs. 30 mins.). 2000. 63.00 (978-1-84197-142-1(1), H1136E7) Recorded Bks.

Detective Sergeant Kate Power, recovered from her knee injury, is back to work. While on holiday in Florence, Kate met a man on her flight & now she finds him hanging from the canal bridge.

Staying Street Smart in the Internet Age. abr. ed. Mark H. McCormack. Read by David Ackroyd. 4 cass. (Running Time: 6 hrs.). 2004. 25.00 (978-1-931056-04-5(8), N Millennium Audio) New Millenn Enter.

Increasing complexity of technology has brought both perils & opportunities to business. In spite of the hype, the cyber age is not really revolutionary: personal touch ultimately seals the deal. Technology & the Internet are no substitute for the old-fashioned business lunch & experience & human contact are the most important products.

Staying Street Smart in the Internet Age. unabr. ed. Mark H. McCormack. Read by David Ackroyd. 8 cass. (Running Time: 9 hrs.). 2004. 39.95 (978-1-931056-05-2(6), N Millennium Audio) New Millenn Enter.

Staying the Course. unabr. ed. Donald S. McClure et al. 10 cass. (Running Time: 7 hrs. 30 mins.). 2001. 21.99 (978-0-936728-98-8(1), tdstc03) Calvar ChalPub.

A collection of workshops taught by Landus Calvary pastors. Taken from this years pastors conference.

Staying the Course. unabr. ed. Chuck Smith & Lewis Nealy. 10 cass. (Running Time: 7 hrs. 30 mins.). 2001. 21.99 (978-0-936728-96-4(5)) Calvar ChalPub.

A collection of teachings at this years pastors conference.

Staying the Course. unabr. ed. Wayne Taylor et al. 10 cass. (Running Time: 7 hrs. 30 mins.). 2001. 21.99 (978-0-936728-97-1(3)) Calvar ChalPub.

Various workshops given by various pastors.

Staying Together, Level 4. Judith Wilson. Contrib. by Philip Prowse. (Running Time: 2 hrs. 56 mins.). (Cambridge English Readers Ser.). (ENG.). 2001. 15.75 (978-0-521-79849-5(3)) Cambridge U Pr.

Staying True. unabr. ed. Jenny Sanford. Read by Jenny Sanford. 5 CDs. (Running Time: 5 hrs. 30 mins.). (ENG.). 2010. audio compact disk 25.00 (978-0-307-73628-4(8), Random AudioBks) Pub: Random Audio Pubg. Dist(s): Random

Staying up, up, up in a down, down World: Daily Hope for the Daily Grind. unabr. ed. Zig Ziglar. Narrated by Zig Ziglar. (ENG.). 2004. 12.59 (978-1-60814-397-9(X)); audio compact disk 17.99 (978-1-58926-617-9(X)) Oasis Audio.

Staying Well. American Institute for Preventive Medicine Staff. (For Your Information Ser.). 1993. 16.00 (978-1-56420-028-0(0)) New Readers.

Staying Young: The Owner's Manual for Extending Your Warranty. Michael F. Roizen & Mehmet C. Oz. 2007. audio compact disk 34.99 (978-1-60252-235-0(9)) Find a World.

Staying Young: The Owner's Manual for Extending Your Warranty. abr. ed. Michael F. Roizen & Mehmet C. Oz. Read by Michael F. Roizen & Mehmet C. Oz. 5 CDs. (Running Time: 5 hrs. 0 mins. 0 sec.). (ENG.). 2007. audio compact disk 29.95 (978-0-7435-6938-5(5)) Pub: S&S Audio. Dist(s): S and S Inc

STDs (Sexually Transmitted Deceptions) George Bloomer. audio compact disk Whitaker Hse.

STDs (Sexually Transmitted Deceptions) Speeches. Perf. by George Bloomer. 1 CD. (Running Time: 60 min.). 2004. audio compact disk 14.99 (978-0-88368-747-5(X)) Pub: Whitaker Hse. Dist(s): Anchor Distributors

Stds9 legends of the ferengi Cassette. Ira Steven Behr. Based on a work by Robert Hewitt Wolfe. 2004. 7.95 (978-0-7435-4229-6(0)) Pub: S&S Audio. Dist(s): S and S Inc

Stdt Sprd Temp Mgmt Acc the Cornerstone of Business Decision. Mowen & Hansen. (C). 2005. audio compact disk 10.95 (978-0-324-18980-3(X)) Pub: South-West. Dist(s): CENGAGE Learn

Stdt Tool Cd-Prin Physics. 3rd ed. Serway. (C). 2001. audio compact disk 27.95 (978-0-03-031748-4(7)) Pub: Brooks-Cole. Dist(s): CENGAGE Learn

Stdy Wizard Ny Real Est Sales. 3rd ed. Spada. (C). 2004. audio compact disk 43.95 (978-0-324-27487-5(4)) Pub: South-West. Dist(s): CENGAGE Learn

Steadfast Christianity. (AFR.). 2002. 20.95 (978-1-57972-455-9(8)); audio compact disk 29.00 (978-1-57972-456-6(6)) Insight Living.

Steadfast Christianity: A Study of 2 Thessalonians. 1998. 20.95 (978-1-57972-267-8(9)) Insight Living.

Steadfast Tin Soldier see Emperor's New Clothes & Other Tales

Steadfast Tin Soldier see Soldadito de Plomo

Steadfast Tin Soldier. Hans Christian Andersen et al. Read by Jeremy Irons. (Running Time: 47 min.).Tr. of Standhaftige Tinsoldat. (J). 1988. 10.00 (WHO702) Windham Hill.

Story of love between a one-legged soldier & a paper ballerina.

***Steadfast Tin Soldier.** Anonymous. 2009. (978-1-60136-602-3(7)) Audio Holding.

Steadfast Tin Soldier. I.t. ed. Short Stories. Illus. by Graham Percy. 1 cass. (Running Time: 10 mins.). Dramatization. (J). (ps-3). 2001. bk. 8.99 (978-84-86154-59-2(6)) Pub: Peralt Mont ESP. Dist(s): imaJen

Steadfast Tin Soldier; The Princess & the Pea; Little Green Ones. unabr. ed. Hans Christian Andersen. Narrated by Aurora Wetzel. 1 cass. (J). 1993. 9.95 (978-1-887393-04-1(8)) Aurora Audio.

Three delightful stories - two well-known & one surprise.

Steadiness. 1 cass. (Running Time: 1 hr.). 12.99 (710) Yoga Res Foun.

Steadiness in Wisdom. Swami Jyotirmayananda. 1 cass. (Running Time: 1 hr.). 1990. 12.99 Yoga Res Foun.

Steal Away. unabr. ed. Jennifer Armstrong. Narrated by C. Moore et al. 4 cass. (Running Time: 5 hrs. 30 mins.). (gr. 5 up). 2000. 37.00 (978-0-7887-3246-1(3), 95850E7) Recorded Bks.

In 1863, two brave young women flee from a Virginia plantation. One is the master's niece, the other is her slave girl. As they tell their story through alternating chapters, they share the dangers they face on their perilous journey north to freedom.

Steal Away. unabr. ed. Jennifer Armstrong. Read by C. Moore et al. 4 cass. (Running Time: 5 hrs. 30 mins.). (J). 2000. pap. bk. & stu. ed. 49.75 (978-0-7887-4349-8(X), 41143) Recorded Bks.

Steal Away. unabr. ed. Jennifer Armstrong. Read by C. Moore et al. 4 cass. (Running Time: 5 hrs. 30 mins.). (YA). 2000. 102.80 (978-0-7887-4449-5(6), 47140) Recorded Bks.

Steal Away. unabr. ed. Katharine Clark. Read by Multivoice Production Staff. (Running Time: 12 hrs.). 2008. 24.95 (978-1-4233-5935-7(6), 9781423359357, Brilliance MP3); 24.95 (978-1-4233-5937-1(2), 9781423359371, BAD); 39.25 (978-1-4233-5936-4(4), 9781423359364, Brlnc Audio MP3 Lib); 39.25 (978-1-4233-5938-8(0), 9781423359388, BADLE) Brilliance Audio.

Steal Away to Jesus CD: Spirituals. Compiled by GBGMusik. Executive Producer S. T. Kimbrough. (ENG.). 2006. audio compact disk 12.95

(978-1-933663-10-4(3), GBGMusik) Pub: Gnl Brd Glbl Minis. Dist(s): Cokesbury

Stealer of Souls. 2 cass. (Running Time: 2 hrs.). 2001. 19.95 Lodestone Catalog.

Stealer of Souls. unabr. ed. Larry Weiner. Perf. by Radio Repertory Company Staff & Katey Sagal. 2 cass. (Running Time: 2 hrs.). Dramatization. (C). 1997. 17.95 (978-0-9660392-0-7(3), RRCA002) Pub: Radio Repertory. Dist(s): Penton Overseas
A guardian of lost souls has become disenchanted with his job, & after being unceremoniously fired, has taken to roaming the world & robbing innocent people of their souls.

Stealing Buddha's Dinner. unabr. ed. Bich Minh Nguyen. Read by Alice H. Kennedy. (Running Time: 8 hrs.). 2009. 39.97 (978-1-4233-9113-5(6), 9781423391135, BADLE); 24.99 (978-1-4233-9112-8(8), 9781423391128, BAD); 24.99 (978-1-4233-9110-4(1), 9781423391104, Brilliance MP3); 39.97 (978-1-4233-9111-1(X), 9781423391111, Brlnc Audio MP3 Lib); audio compact disk 28.99 (978-1-4233-9108-1(X), 9781423391081); audio compact disk 92.97 (978-1-4233-9109-8(8), 9781423391098, BriAudCD Unabrid) Brilliance Audio.

Stealing from God: Malachi 3:8. Ed Young. 1985. 4.95 (978-0-7417-1438-1(8), 438) Win Walk.

***Stealing Home.** unabr. ed. Sherryl Woods. Read by Janet Metzger. (Running Time: 11 hrs.). (Sweet Magnolias Ser.). 2010. 19.99 (978-1-4418-6454-3(7), 9781441864543, Brilliance MP3); 19.99 (978-1-4418-6456-7(3), 9781441864567, BAD); 39.97 (978-1-4418-6455-0(5), 9781441864550, Brlnc Audio MP3 Lib); 39.97 (978-1-4418-6457-4(1), 9781441864574, BADLE); audio compact disk 19.99 (978-1-4418-6452-9(0), 9781441864529, Bril Audio CD Unabri); audio compact disk 79.97 (978-1-4418-6453-6(9), 9781441864536, BriAudCD Unabrid) Brilliance Audio.

Stealing Myspace: The Battle to Control the Most Popular Website in America. unabr. ed. Julia Angwin. (Running Time: 10 hrs. 5 mins.). 2009. 29.95 (978-1-4332-5890-9(0)); audio compact disk 29.95 (978-1-4332-5889-3(7)); audio compact disk 90.00 (978-1-4332-5887-9(0)); audio compact disk 65.95 (978-1-4332-5886-2(2)) Blckstn Audio.

Stealing Princes. unabr. ed. Read by Nicky Talacko. 7 CDs. (Running Time: 29700 sec.). (Calypso Chronicles). (YA). (gr. 8-12). 2007. audio compact disk 83.95 (978-1-74093-961-4(1), 9781740939614) Pub: Bolinda Pubng AUS. Dist(s): Bolinda Pub Inc

Stealing Second. Contrib. by Chris Thile. Prod. by Sam Bush. 2000. audio compact disk 15.98 (978-0-7866-3538-2(X), 97173CD) Mel Bay.

Stealing Shadows. Kay Hooper. Narrated by Cristine McMurdo-Wallis. 8 cass. (Running Time: 11 hrs. 45 mins.). 74.00 (978-0-7887-8860-4(4)) Recorded Bks.
Cassie Neill has a powerful but troubling gift. She can see inside the minds of serial killers as they are planning their crimes. Tormented by her ability, she takes refuge in a secluded North Carolina town. But there¿s no escaping her visions, and when a body surfaces just where she predicted, Cassie is suddenly a suspect.

***Stealing the Mystic Lamb: The True Story of the World's Most Coveted Masterpiece.** unabr. ed. Noah Charney. Narrated by John Allen Nelson. (Running Time: 11 hrs. 30 mins.). 2010. 24.99 (978-1-4526-5033-3(0)); 34.99 (978-1-4526-0033-8(3)); 83.99 (978-1-4526-3033-5(X)); 17.99 (978-1-4526-7033-1(1)) Tantor Media.

***Stealing the Mystic Lamb (Library Edition) The True Story of the World's Most Coveted Masterpiece.** unabr. ed. Noah Charney. Narrated by John Allen Nelson. (Running Time: 11 hrs. 30 mins.). 2010. 34.99 (978-1-4526-2033-6(4)) Tantor Media.

Stealing Time. Leslie Glass. Read by Jane E. Lawder. 4 cass. (Running Time: 360 min.). (April Woo Detective Ser.: No. 5). 2000. 25.00 (978-1-58807-055-5(7)) Am Pubng Inc.

Stealing Time. abr. ed. Leslie Glass. Read by Jane E. Lawder. 4 vols. No. 5. 2003. (978-1-58807-611-3(3)) Am Pubng Inc.

Stealing Time. unabr. ed. Leslie Glass. Read by Kathy Hsieh. 8 vols. (Running Time: 12 hrs.). (April Woo Mystery Ser.). 2000. bk. 69.95 (978-0-7927-2384-4(8), CSL 273, Chivers Sound Lib) AudioGO.
April finds herself caught between New York city powerhouse politics & ethnic expectations when a young Chinese-American mother is beaten unconscious & her newborn son is gone. The woman's domineering husband wants to control the whole investigation, the mayor wants the case solved yesterday & April's boss is just waiting for her to make a career-killing mistake. April must find the missing child & the motive behind this mystery, before someone decides to make this her last case.

Stealing Your Life: The Ultimate Identity Theft Prevention Plan. unabr. ed. Frank W. Abagnale. Read by Raymond Todd. (Running Time: 27000 sec.). 2007. 24.95 (978-0-7861-4871-4(3)); audio compact disk 24.95 (978-0-7861-6083-9(7)) Blckstn Audio.

Stealing Your Life: The Ultimate Identity Theft Prevention Plan. unabr. ed. Frank W. Abagnale. (Running Time: 27000 sec.). 2007. audio compact disk 55.00 (978-0-7861-6918-4(4)) Blckstn Audio.

Stealing Your Life: The Ultimate Identity Theft Prevention Plan. unabr. ed. Frank W. Abagnale. Read by Raymond Todd. (Running Time: 27000 sec.). 2007. 54.95 (978-0-7861-6919-1(2)); audio compact disk 29.95 (978-0-7861-7161-3(8)) Blckstn Audio.

Stealth. unabr. ed. Karen Miller. Read by Jeff Gurner. (ENG.). 2010. 40.00 (978-0-7393-7689-8(6), Random AudioBks) Pub: Random Audio Pubg. Dist(s): Random

Stealth Jihad: How Radical Islam Is Subverting America Without Guns or Bombs. unabr. ed. Robert Spencer. Read by Lloyd James. (Running Time: 9 hrs. 30 mins. 0 sec.). (ENG.). 2008. audio compact disk 19.99 (978-1-4001-5757-0(9)); audio compact disk 59.99 (978-1-4001-3757-2(8)); audio compact disk 29.99 (978-1-4001-0757-5(1)) Pub: Tantor Media. Dist(s): IngramPubServ

Steam Heat (from The Pajama Game) - ShowTrax. Arranged by Mac Huff. 1 CD. (Running Time: 90 mins.). 2000. audio compact disk 19.95 (08621155) H Leonard.
Shirley MacLaine rocketed to fame after she filled in for the lead in this 1954 Broadway smash. Simply sizzling for pop & show groups!.

Steambath. unabr. ed. Bruce J. Friedman. Perf. by Jason Alexander et al. 1 cass. (Running Time: 1 hr. 33 min.). 1994. 19.95 (978-1-58081-017-3(9), TPT41) L A Theatre.
A parade of unforgettable characters emerge from the steam, in this hilarious, supernatural bathhouse. There is Tandy, fresh from teaching art appreciation at the Police Academy; Merideth, whose last memory involves buying a micro-mini skirt; Biberman, a karate silver-belt who masquerades as a paraplegic; not to mention the Puerto Rican janitor, a mysterious man given to omniscient musings & munipulating the fate of mankind.

Steamboats Come True: American Inventors in Action. unabr. collector's ed. James Thomas Flexner. Read by Jonathan Reese. 11 cass. (Running Time: 16 hrs. 30 min.). 1995. 88.00 (978-0-7366-2923-2(8), 3621) Books on Tape.
Celebratory account of "the first American invention of world-shattering importance" - the steamboat.

Steamer Demons. unabr. ed. Stephen Axelsen. Read by Stanley McGeagh. (Running Time: 9180 sec.). (Piccolo & Annabelle Ser.). (J). (gr. 2). 2008. audio compact disk 43.95 (978-1-74093-948-5(4), 9781740939485) Pub: Bolinda Pubng AUS. Dist(s): Bolinda Pub Inc

Steaming to Bamboola: The World of a Tramp Freighter. unabr. collector's ed. Christopher Buckley. Read by Justin Hecht. 6 cass. (Running Time: 9 hrs.). 1984. 48.00 (978-0-7366-0729-2(3), 1686) Books on Tape.
A young man's first hand story of his time on a commercial steamer, with typhoons, cargoes, smuggling, mid-ocean burials, rescues, stowaways, hard places, hard drinking & hard romance.

Stedman's Endocrinology Words: Multi-User License. 2nd ed. Stedman's Staff. 2005. (978-0-7817-7164-1(1)) Lppncott W W.

***Steel.** (ENG.). 2010. audio compact disk (978-1-59171-303-6(X)) Falcon Picture.

***Steel Bridge Songs: Saving an Old Bridge, Creating New Ones.** Prod. by pat mAcdonald & Chris Aaron. (ENG.). (C). 2010. audio compact disk 10.00 (978-1-891609-08-4(4)) Pub: Home Brew Pr. Dist(s): Chicago Distribution Ctr

***Steel Bridge Songs, Vol. 5.** Prod. by pat mAcdonald. (ENG.). 2010. audio compact disk 10.00 (978-1-891609-12-1(2)) Pub: U of Wis Pr. Dist(s): Chicago Distribution Ctr

***Steel Bridge Songs Year 4: Even more songs that owe their life to that bridge in Sturgeon Bay.** Compiled by pat mAcdonald. (ENG.). (C). 2010. audio compact disk 10.00 (978-1-891609-09-1(2)) Pub: Home Brew Pr. Dist(s): Chicago Distribution Ctr

***Steel Bridge Songs Years 2 And 3 Vol. 2: More Songs Inspired by Sturgeon Bay's Historic Bridge.** 2nd ed. Prod. by pat mAcdonald. (C). 2010. audio compact disk 15.00 (978-1-891609-10-7(6)) Pub: Home Brew Pr. Dist(s): Chicago Distribution Ctr

Steel Cables: Love Poems from Adam Rib. unabr. ed. Poems. Brod Bagert. Read by Brod Bagert. 1 cass. (Running Time: 41 min.). 1994. 9.00 (978-1-887746-00-7(5)); audio compact disk 9.00 CD. (978-1-887746-03-8(X)) Juliahouse Pubs.
Poems about love beyond romance - the poetry of permanent love.

Steel Dragonfly: Dance of the Tao. unabr. ed. Joey Bond. Perf. by Joey Bond. 1 CD. (Running Time: 1 hr.). 1995. audio compact disk 19.95 CD Jewel case. (978-0-9668495-1-6(5)) Tai Chi INNERWAVE.
Descriptive relaxation & meditation technique.

Steel Guitar. unabr. ed. Linda Barnes. Narrated by C. J. Critt. 5 cass. (Running Time: 7 hrs. 15 mins.). (Carlotta Carlyle Mystery Ser.). 1993. 44.00 (978-1-55690-787-6(7), 93102E7) Recorded Bks.
Private investigator Carlotta Carlyle finds overdose & suicide aren't what they seem in the fast-paced world of rock & roll & Boston's night life.

Steel Remains. unabr. ed. Richard K. Morgan. (Running Time: 15 hrs. 0 mins. 0 sec.). (ENG.). 2009. audio compact disk 79.99 (978-1-4001-3963-7(5)) Pub: Tantor Media. Dist(s): IngramPubServ

Steel Remains. unabr. ed. Richard K. Morgan. Narrated by Simon Vance. (Running Time: 15 hrs. 0 mins. 0 sec.). (ENG.). 2009. audio compact disk 29.99 (978-1-4001-5963-5(6)) Pub: Tantor Media. Dist(s): IngramPubServ

Steel Remains. unabr. ed. Morgan Richard & Richard K. Morgan. Narrated by Simon Vance. (Running Time: 15 hrs. 0 mins. 0 sec.). (ENG.). 2009. audio compact disk 39.99 (978-1-4001-0963-0(9)) Pub: Tantor Media. Dist(s): IngramPubServ

Steel Tears. Eldon Taylor. Music by Brueggeman Staff. 1 cass. (Running Time: 62 min.). (Inner Talk Ser.). 16.95 incl. script. (978-0-940699-99-1(0), 53816C) Progress Aware Res.
Soundtrack with underlying subliminal affirmations.

***Steel Trapp: the Academy.** Ridley Pearson. Contrib. by William Dufris. (Playaway Children Ser.). (ENG.). (J). 2010. 54.99 (978-1-4418-3772-1(8)) Find a World.

Steel Wave: A Novel of World War II. abr. ed. Jeff Shaara. Read by Anthony Heald. (Running Time: 21600 sec.). (ENG.). 2008. audio compact disk 29.95 (978-0-7393-3465-2(4), Random AudioBks) Pub: Random Audio Pubg. Dist(s): Random

Steep Approach to Garbadale. unabr. ed. Iain Banks, pseud. Read by Peter Kenny. (Running Time: 12 hrs.). (ENG., 2007. audio compact disk 39.95 (978-1-4055-0125-5(1)) Pub: Little BrownUK GBR. Dist(s): IPG Chicago

Steering Clear of Satan. Victor Harris. 1 cass. 9.98 (978-1-57734-151-2(1), 06005659) Covenant Comms.
How to avoid Satan's road hazards along the straight & narrow path.

Steering Through Chaos: Mapping a Clear Direction for Your Church in the Midst of Transition & Change. Scott Wilson. (Running Time: 7 hrs. 20 mins. 0 sec.). (ENG.). 2010. 18.99 (978-0-310-57608-2(3)) Zondervan.

Stefan Grossman's Complete Fingerpicking Guide Exercises & Hot Licks. Stefan Grossman. 1994. 10.98 (978-0-7866-0099-1(3), 95216C) Mel Bay.

Stefan Grossman's Complete Fingerpicking Guitar Exercises & Hot Licks. Stefan Grossman. 1994. bk. 24.95 (978-0-7866-1229-1(0), 95216P) Mel Bay.

Stegosaurus. Angela Shenan. (Angela Shenan Ser.). (J). (ps-6). 1988. bk. 25.95 (6513-B) Spoken Arts.

Stein on Writing. Sol Stein. Read by Christopher Lane. (Running Time: 11 hrs.). (C). 2003. 34.95 (978-1-59912-609-8(5)) Iofy Corp.

Stein on Writing. unabr. ed. Sol Stein. Read by Christopher Lane. 9 CDs. (Running Time: 11 hrs. 30 mins.). 2003. audio compact disk 72.00 (978-0-7861-9149-9(X), 3144); 56.95 (978-0-7861-2511-1(X), 3144) Blckstn Audio.
Provides immediately useful advice for writers of fiction and nonfiction, whether newcomers or accomplished professionals.

Steinbeck: A Life in Letters. Read by Heywood Hale Broun et al. 1 cass. (Running Time: 56 min.). (Broun Radio Ser.). 10.95 (40215) J Norton Pubs.
A conversation with Mrs. Steinbeck & Robert Wallsten.

Steinbeck's Ghost. Lewis Buzbee. Read by Christopher Lee. (Playaway Children Ser.). (ENG.). (J). (gr. k). 2008. 44.99 (978-1-60640-892-6(5)) Find a World.

Steinbeck's Ghost. unabr. ed. Lewis Buzbee. Read by Christopher Lane. 1 MP3-CD. (Running Time: 7 hrs.). 2008. 24.95 (978-1-4233-6944-8(0), 9781423369448, Brilliance MP3); 39.25 (978-1-4233-6947-9(5), 9781423369479, BADLE); 39.25 (978-1-4233-6945-5(9), 9781423369455, Brlnc Audio MP3 Lib); 24.95 (978-1-4233-6946-2(7), 9781423369462, BAD); audio compact disk 60.97 (978-1-4233-6943-1(2), 9781423369431, BriAudCD Unabrid); audio compact disk 29.95 (978-1-4233-6942-4(4), 9781423369424, Bril Audio CD Unabri) Brilliance Audio.

***Steinbrenner: The Last Lion of Baseball.** unabr. ed. Bill Madden. Read by Kerin Mccue. (ENG.). 2010. (978-0-06-199310-7(7), Harper Audio); (978-0-06-198874-5(X), Harper Audio) HarperCollins Pubs.

Steiner Series: Reincarnation & Karma. Paul Margulies. 2 cass. 1993. 18.00 set. (OC339-72) Sound Horizons AV.

Steiner's Life As Path of Initiation. Robert McDermott. 2 cass. 1992. 18.00 set. (OC315-68) Sound Horizons AV.

Steiner's Social Ideas & Relevance. Christopher Schaefer. 2 cass. 1992. 18.00 set. (OC316-68) Sound Horizons AV.

Stella Etc: Sweet Talking Tj. unabr. ed. Karen McCombie. Read by Jennifer Bryce. 4 CDs. (Running Time: 4 hrs. 35 mins.). (YA). (gr. 5-8). 2007. audio compact disk 34.95 (978-1-4056-5540-8(2), Chivers Child Audio) AudioGO.

Stella in Heaven: Almost a Novel. Art Buchwald. 4 cass. (Running Time: 6 hrs.). 2001. 25.00 New Millenn Enter.
When 61-year-old Roger loses his wife, Stella, he expects to spend his time grieving. But Stella's spirit returns posthaste & continues to chat with her husband in the privacy of the home they shared for many years. Stella worries that Roger may be lonely & decides to find him a new wife.

Stella in Heaven: Almost a Novel. abr. ed. Art Buchwald. Read by Elliott Gould. 4 cass. (Running Time: 6 hrs.). 2004. 25.00 (978-1-931056-23-6(4), N Millennium Audio) New Millenn Enter.

Stellaluna. Janell Cannon. Read by David Holt. 1 CD. (Running Time: 30 mins.). 1995. audio compact disk 15.98 (978-0-942303-12-4(1)) Pub: August Hse. Dist(s): Natl Bk Netwk
Story of a young lost bat who finally finds her way home to her mother and friends. Includes "Hattie the Backstage Bat," "Why the Bat Flies at Night" and "Amazing Bat Facts".

Stellaluna. Janell Cannon. Read by David Holt. 1 cass. (Running Time: 30 mins.). (ENG.). (J). 9.98 (978-0-942303-11-7(3)) Pub: High Windy Audio. Dist(s): Penton Overseas

Stellaluna. Janell Cannon. Perf. by David Holt. 1 cass. (Running Time: 35 min.). (J). 1997. 15.98 (978-0-942303-17-9(2)) Pub: High Windy Audio. Dist(s): Penton Overseas
Recording of Stellaluna & other bat stories. Includes finger puppet.

Stellaluna. Janell Cannon. Narrated by David Holt. 1 cass., 1 CD. (J). 7.98 (HIGH 1211); audio compact disk 12.78 NewSound.
A lost young bat finally finds her way safely home to her mother & friends.

Stellaluna. abr. ed. Janell Cannon. Perf. by David Holt. 1 cass. (Running Time: 34 min.). (J). (ps-k). 1996. 12.00 (978-0-87483-574-8(7)) August Hse.

Stellaluna. abr. ed. Janell Cannon. Read by David Holt. 1 cass. (J). S&S Audio.

Stellen, Legen und Setzen: German Put, Place, Set. Sigrid S. Hildebrand & Eckart Hildebrand. Ed. by Josef Rohrer. Illus. by Sydney M. Baker. Intro. by Harris Winitz. (GER.). (YA). (gr. 7 up). 1990. bk. 25.00 (978-0-939990-65-8(2)) Intl Linguistics.

Stelliums. Henrietta Cramton. 1 cass. (Running Time: 90 min.). 1984. 8.95 (070) Am Fed Astrologers.

Stendhal's Scarlet & Black. Read by Martin Jarvis. 1 cass. 1994. 12.00 (978-1-878427-34-2(2), XC428) Cimino Pub Grp.
"Scarlet & Black" is now a major BBC TV series & U.S. film. One of the most shocking & outstanding novels in French literature, it is a tale of obsessions, betrayal & seduction relating the "liaisons dangere uses" of young Julien Sorel, a provincial carpenter's son.

Stenotype Text Entry: Package. George P. Andrews & Beverly L. Ritter. 1 cass. (Running Time: 90 mins.). (Realtime Machine Shorthand Ser.). (C). 1993. pap. bk. & stu. ed. 39.00 (978-0-938643-62-3(2), 905) Stenotype Educ.

Stenotype Text Entry: Stenoscription Manual. George P. Andrews. 1 cass. (Running Time: 90 mins.). (Realtime Machine Shorthand Ser.). (C). 1993. pap. bk. & stu. ed. 12.00 (978-0-938643-61-6(4), 904) Stenotype Educ.

Step Aside. Contrib. by Yolanda Adams. (Soundtraks Ser.). 2007. audio compact disk 8.99 (978-5-557-56228-7(1)) Christian Wrld.

Step-Ball-Change. unabr. ed. Jeanne Ray. Read by Jeanne Ray. (Running Time: 6 hrs.). 2004. 39.25 (978-1-59335-605-7(6), 1593356056, Brlnc Audio MP3 Lib) Brilliance Audio.
With a ringing phone, Jeanne Ray's charming and amusing novel gets off to a rollicking start that never lets up. Not for a minute. On the other end of the phone is Caroline's daughter, Kay, a public defender like her father, sobbing at the improbably good news that the richest, most eligible boy in Raleigh, North Carolina, has asked her to marry him. While Caroline and Tom are trying to digest this, the other phone, the "children's line," rings and it is Caroline's sister, Taffy, hysterical over her husband's decision to leave her for a woman two years younger than her daughter. Soon Taffy is wending her way up from Atlanta to seek solace in her sister's home, even though the two have been separated by more than just geography for the past forty years. With her is her little dog, Stamp, who has a penchant for biting ankles and stealing hearts. Tom and Caroline quickly realize that the wedding their future son-in-law's family is envisioning for nine hundred-plus guests is their fiscal responsibility and, to top it all off, the foundation of their home is in danger of collapsing and their contractor and his crew have all but moved in. It's a thundering whirlwind of emotion that finally boils down to Who is in love with whom? and Who's going to get the next dance?.

Step-Ball-Change. unabr. ed. Jeanne Ray. Read by Jeanne Ray. (Running Time: 6 hrs.). 2004. 39.25 (978-1-59710-739-6(5), 1597107395, BADLE); 24.95 (978-1-59710-738-9(7), 1597107387, BAD) Brilliance Audio.

Step-Ball-Change. unabr. ed. Jeanne Ray. Read by Jeanne Ray. (Running Time: 6 hrs.). 2004. 24.95 (978-1-59335-168-7(2), 1593351682) Soulmate Audio Bks.

Step-Ball-Change: A Novel. unabr. ed. Jeanne Ray. Read by Jeanne Ray. 4 cass. Library ed. (Running Time: 6 hrs.). 2002. 62.25 (978-1-59086-083-0(7), 1590860837, Unabridge Lib Edns) Brilliance Audio.

Step by Step. (J). 1998. 9.95 (978-1-887028-23-3(4)) Slim Goodbody.

Step by Step. June Francis. (Story Sound Ser.). (J). 2005. 76.95 (978-1-85903-759-1(3)) Pub: Mgna Lrg Print GBR. Dist(s): Ulverscroft US

Step by Step: A Memoir of Hope, Friendship, Perserverance & Living the American Dream. unabr. ed. Bertie Bowman. Narrated by Bob Stewart. (Running Time: 8 hrs. 30 mins. 0 sec.). (ENG.). 2008. 19.59 (978-1-60814-398-6(8), SpringWater) Oasis Audio.

Step by Step: A Memoir of Hope, Friendship, Perseverance, & Living the American Dream. unabr. ed. Bertie Bowman. Read by Bertie Bowman. Narrated by Bob Stewart. (Running Time: 8 hrs. 30 mins. 0 sec.). (ENG.). 2008. audio compact disk 27.99 (978-1-59859-356-3(0)) Oasis Audio.

Step by Step Computed Tomography. Kartikeyan. 2004. cd-rom 30.00 (978-81-8061-327-2(5)) Jaypee Brothers IND.

Step-by-Step Hiring. Dora C. Fowler. 1 cass. (Running Time: 60 min.). 9.95 (4001) Natl Inst Child Mgmt.
Review of the hiring process to insure deciding on the most qualified person for the job.

Step by Step Massage. Diana Abatecola. 2010. audio compact disk 19.99 (978-1-60604-190-1(8)) Tate Pubng.

Step by Step or Direct Jump. Swami Amar Jyoti. 1 cass. 1981. 9.95 (P-40) Truth Consciousness.
Ways of approach to the spiritual Goal. Meditating upon Light, we become Light.

Step by Step Pediatric Echocardiography. Gera. 2005. audio compact disk 15.00 (978-81-8061-371-5(2)) Jaypee Brothers IND.

Step by Step Ultrasound in Obstetrics. Singh. 2004. audio compact disk 15.00 (978-81-8061-203-9(1)) Jaypee Brothers IND.

Step by Step Wound Healing. Teot. 2005. audio compact disk 15.00 (978-81-8061-382-1(8)) Jaypee Brothers IND.

Step by Step 1A - an Introduction to Successful Practice for Violin: With instructions in English, French, & Spanish. Composed by Kerstin Wartberg. (FRE.). 2004. audio compact disk 12.95 (978-1-58951-206-1(5)) Alfred Pub.

Step by Step 1B - an Introduction to Successful Practice for Violin: With instructions in English, French, & Spanish. Composed by Kerstin Wartberg. (FRE.). 2004. audio compact disk 12.95 (978-1-58951-207-8(3)) Alfred Pub.

Step by Step 2A - an Introduction to Successful Practice for Violin: With instructions in English, French, & Spanish. Composed by Kerstin Wartberg. (FRE.). 2006. audio compact disk 12.95 (978-0-7390-4104-8(5)) Alfred Pub.

Step by Step 2B - an Introduction to Successful Practice for Violin: With instructions in English, French, & Spanish. Composed by Kerstin Wartberg. (FRE.). 2006. audio compact disk 12.95 (978-0-7390-4221-2(1)) Alfred Pub.

Step Eleven & Step Twelve. 1 cass. (Twelve Steps to Recovery Ser.). 8.95 (1585G) Hazelden.

Step Five & Steps Six & Seven. 1 cass. (Twelve Steps to Recovery Ser.). 8.95 (1583G) Hazelden.

Step Forward, No. 1. Jane Spigarelli. Contrib. by Jayme Adelson-Goldstein. (Step Forward Ser.). 2006. audio compact disk 54.95 (978-0-19-439240-2(6)) OUP.

Step Forward, No. 4. Barbara Denman. Contrib. by Jayme Adelson-Goldstein. (Step Forward Ser.). 2006. audio compact disk 54.95 (978-0-19-439243-3(0)) OUP.

Step Forward Introductory Level: Class Cassette. Jenni Currie Santamaria & Jayme Adelson-Goldstein. (Step Forward Ser.). 2007. 54.95 (978-0-19-439875-6(7)) OUP.

Step Forward 1: Language for Everyday Life Class Cassettes. Jane Spigarelli. Contrib. by Jayme Adelson-Goldstein. (Step Forward Ser.). 2006. 54.95 (978-0-19-439236-5(8)) OUP.

Step Forward 2: Language for Everyday Life Class Cassettes. Ingrid Wisniewska. Contrib. by Jayme Adelson-Goldstein. (Step Forward Ser.). 2006. 54.95 (978-0-19-439237-2(6)) OUP.

Step Forward 3: Language for Everday Life. Jane Spigarelli. Contrib. by Jayme Adelson-Goldstein. (Step Forward Ser.: Vol. 3). 2007. audio compact disk 54.95 (978-0-19-439242-6(2)) OUP.

Step Forward 3: Language for Everyday Life Class Cassettes. Jane Spigarelli. Contrib. by Jayme Adelson-Goldstein. (Step Forward Ser.). 2006. 54.95 (978-0-19-439238-9(4)) OUP.

Step Forward 4: Language for Everyday Life Class Cassettes. Barbara Denman. Contrib. by Jayme Adelson-Goldstein. (Step Forward Ser.). 2006. 54.95 (978-0-19-439239-6(2)) OUP.

Step Four (Stewardship) Malachi 3:3-10. Ed Young. 1995. 4.95 (978-0-7417-2049-8(3), 1049) Win Walk.

Step from Heaven. Read by Jina Oh. 3 vols. (Running Time: 4 hrs. 14 mins.). (J). (gr. 6 up). 2004. pap. bk. 36.00 (978-0-8072-2287-4(9), Listening Lib) Random Audio Pubg.

Step from Heaven. unabr. ed. An Na. 3 cass. (Running Time: 4 hrs. 14 mins.). (J). (gr. 6 up). 2004. 30.00 (978-0-8072-0722-2(5), Listening Lib) Random Audio Pubg.

Step from Heaven. unabr. ed. An Na. Read by Jina Oh. 4 CDs. (Running Time: 4 hrs. 14 mins.). (J). (gr. 6 up). 2004. audio compact disk 35.00 (978-0-8072-1612-5(7), S YA 362 CD, Listening Lib) Random Audio Pubg.

Step in the Dark. unabr. ed. Elizabeth Lemarchand. Read by Gordon Griffin. 5 cass. (Running Time: 6 hrs.). (Sound Ser.). 2004. 49.95 (978-1-85496-694-0(4), 66944) Pub: UlverLrgPrint GBR. Dist(s): Ulverscroft US
What more unlikely a setting for violent death than the sleepy historic premises of the Ramsden Literary & Scientific Society? Yet it is here that a corpse with a fractured skull is found in highly peculiar circumstances. How did anyone enter the Society's library after its doors were locked for the night? Andy why has the shy unhappy woman who has devoted herself to writing a history of the Society suddenly left town? This is more than enough for Detective Superintendent Pollard to cope with.

Step into the Frame: Your 21-Day Journey of Self-Optimization, Movement Two. Melody Ivory. Ed. by Lynda McDaniel. Des. by Maggie Flynn. Photos by Allum Ross Ndiaye. (ENG.). 2009. pap. bk. 9.95 (978-0-9795504-1-6(6)) Melody Ivory.

Step It Down. Perf. by Bessie Jones. 1 cass. (Running Time: 42 min.). (Family Ser.). (J). (gr. 1-7). 1979. 9.98 (8004) Rounder Records.
Here is a recording full of games & songs, with children lending enthusiastic support & participation. Many of these songs date back before the Civil War, & have been kept alive through oral tradition.

Step on a Crack. abr. ed. James Patterson & Michael Ledwidge. Read by John Slattery & Reg Rogers. (Running Time: 6 hrs.). (Michael Bennett Ser.: No. 1). (ENG.). 2007. 14.98 (978-1-59483-624-4(8)) Pub: Hachet Audio. Dist(s): HachBkGrp

Step on a Crack. abr. unabr. ed. James Patterson & Michael Ledwidge. Read by John Slattery & Reg Rogers. (Running Time: 8 hrs.). (Michael Bennett Ser.: No. 1). (ENG.). 2008. audio compact disk 14.98 (978-1-60024-279-3(0)) Pub: Hachet Audio. Dist(s): HachBkGrp

Step on a Crack. unabr. ed. James Patterson & Michael Ledwidge. Read by John Slattery & Reg Rogers. (Running Time: 8 hrs.). (Michael Bennett Ser.: No. 1). (ENG.). 2007. 14.98 (978-1-59483-626-8(4)) Pub: Hachet Audio. Dist(s): HachBkGrp

Step One: Play Alto Sax. Sue Terry. 1 cd. (Step One Ser.). 2004. audio compact disk 7.95 (978-0-8256-2725-5(7), AM974336) Pub: Music Sales. Dist(s): H Leonard

Step One: Play Piano. Ernest Lubin. (Step One Ser.). 1998. audio compact disk 7.95 (978-0-8256-1610-5(7), AM943162) Pub: Music Sales. Dist(s): H Leonard

Step One: Play Tenor Sax. Sue Terry. 1 cd. (Step One Ser.). 2004. audio compact disk 9.99 (978-0-8256-2772-9(9), AM976668) Pub: Music Sales. Dist(s): H Leonard

Step One: Playing Bass Guitar. Peter Pickow. (Step One Ser.). 1997. audio compact disk 9.95 (978-0-8256-1592-4(5)) Pub: Music Sales. Dist(s): H Leonard

Step One: Playing Blues Guitar. Darryl Winston. (Step One Ser.). 1997. audio compact disk 9.95 (978-0-8256-1591-7(7)) Pub: Music Sales. Dist(s): H Leonard

Step One: Playing Guitar. Artie Traum. (Step One Ser.). 1997. pap. bk. 9.95 (978-0-8256-1589-4(5), Schirmer Trade Bks) Pub: Music Sales. Dist(s): H Leonard

Step One: Playing Guitar Scales. Peter Pickow. (Step One Ser.). 1997. audio compact disk 9.95 (978-0-8256-1590-0(9)) Pub: Music Sales. Dist(s): H Leonard

Step One: Playing Harmonica. Peter Pickow & Jason A. Shulman. (Step One Ser.). 1997. pap. bk. 9.95 (978-0-8256-1594-8(1), Schirmer Trade Bks) Pub: Music Sales. Dist(s): H Leonard

Step One: Teach Yourself Violin Course. 3 CDs. 2004. DVD & audio compact disk 29.95 (978-0-8256-2959-4(4), AM979693, Schirmer Trade Bks) Pub: Music Sales. Dist(s): H Leonard

Step One & Step Two. 1 cass. (Twelve Steps to Recovery Ser.). 8.95 (1581G) Hazelden.

Step Out on Nothing: How Faith & Family Helped Me Conquer Life's Challenges. abr. ed. Byron Pitts. (Running Time: 6 hrs. 0 mins. 0 sec.). (ENG.). 2009. audio compact disk 29.99 (978-1-4272-0828-6(X)) Pub: Macmill Audio. Dist(s): Macmillan

Step Three & Step Four. 1 cass. (Twelve Steps to Recovery Ser.). 8.95 (1582G) Hazelden.

Step up & Reap. Gary V. Whetstone. 5 cass. (Running Time: 7 hrs. 30 mins.). (Empowerment Ser.). 1998. pap. bk. 40.00 (978-1-58866-202-6(0), VH410A) Gary Whet Pub.
Jesus said , it is harvest time. Do you know how to reap the ripe fields of souls, your personal dreams & visions, family, finances, workplace, city, country?.

Step up to IELTS. Vanessa Jakeman & Clare McDowell. (Running Time: 2 hrs. 34 mins.). (ENG.). 2004. audio compact disk 44.00 (978-0-521-54470-2(X)) Cambridge U Pr.

Step up to IELTS. Vanessa Jakeman & Clare McDowell. (Running Time: 2 hrs. 34 mins.). (ENG., 2004. 44.00 (978-0-521-53303-4(1)) Cambridge U Pr.

Step up to Success in Business & in Life: You Can Achieve Your Dreams! unabr. rev. ed. Nido R. Qubein. Read by Nido R. Qubein. (Running Time: 4 hrs.). (ENG.). 2007. audio compact disk 19.98 (978-1-59659-083-0(1), GildAudio) Pub: Gildan Media. Dist(s): HachBkGrp

Step-up to the Bedside Audio Mp3 File. Nalin Mehta. 2007. audio compact disk 49.95 (978-0-7817-6660-9(5)) Lppncott W W.

Step up with the Son. Jon VonSeggen. Perf. by Jon VonSeggen. Executive Producer One Way Street Staff. (YA). 2003. audio compact disk 15.00 (978-1-58302-250-4(3)) One Way St.
This album celebrates sons...Dale and Liz VonSeggen proudly present the original music of Jon VonSeggen, their son. Jon brings you a comtemporary Christian sound for easy listening ro performances. Jon takes this special opportunity to reflect on watching his own young son, Pkoe, in the song "In Your Eyes." Take time to reflect on your family. Relationships are what make the difference in our lives, but the greatest relationship is to know Jesus, the greatest. SON.

Stepfamilies in Therapy: Understanding Systems, Assessment & Intervention. Don Martin et al. (Social & Behavioral Science Ser.). 1992. bk. 41.50 (978-1-55542-453-4(8), Jossey-Bass) Wiley US.

Stepfamily Journey. Elizabeth A. Einstein. Read by Elizabeth A. Einstein. 1 cass. (Running Time: 1 hr.). (Stepfamily Living Ser.: No. 2). 1992. 9.95 (978-1-884944-08-6(6)) E Einstein.
Remarriage can be challenging when people don't understand two realities: Making a stepfamily is a process & it takes time.

Stepfamily Living: The Couple's Spiritual Challenge. Elizabeth A. Einstein. Read by Elizabeth A. Einstein. 1 cass. (Stepfamily Living Ser.: No. 4). 1997. 9.95 (978-1-884944-10-9(8)) E Einstein.
A remarried couple's ability to build a strong remarriage determines the strength of the stepfamily.

***Stephanie.** unabr. ed. Debbie Macomber. Read by Tanya Eby. (Running Time: 5 hrs.). (Orchard Valley Ser.: Bk. 2). 2010. 14.99 (978-1-4418-6128-3(9), 9781441861283, Brilliance MP3); 14.99 (978-1-4418-6129-0(7), 9781441861290, BAD); audio compact disk 14.99 (978-1-4418-6127-6(0), 9781441861276, Bril Audio CD Unabri) Brilliance Audio.

Stephanie Pearl-McPhee Casts Off: The Yarn Harlot's Guide to the Land of Knitting. Stephanie Pearl-McPhee. Read by Stephanie Pearl-McPhee. (Playaway Adult Nonfiction Ser.). 2008. 54.99 (978-1-60640-526-0(8)) Find a World.

Stephanie Pearl-McPhee Casts Off! The Yarn Harlot's Guide to the Land of Knitting. unabr. ed. Stephanie Pearl-McPhee. Read by Stephanie Pearl-McPhee. (Running Time: 16200 sec.). (ENG.). 2007. audio compact disk 24.95 (978-1-59887-519-5(1), 1598875191) Pub: HighBridge. Dist(s): Workman Pub

Stephanie winston's best organizing tips quick simple ways to get organized Cs: Quick, Simple Ways to Get Organized & Get on with Your Life. Stephanie Winston. 2004. 7.95 (978-0-7435-4542-6(7)) Pub: S&S Audio. Dist(s): S and S Inc

Stephen Ambrose. Stephen E. Ambrose. 8 cass. 1998. 45.00 Gift Set. S&S Audio.

Stephen Ambrose World War II Audio Collection. unabr. ed. Stephen E. Ambrose. Read by Cotter Smith. 6 CDs. (Running Time: 8 hrs.). (ENG.). 2004. audio compact disk 49.95 (978-0-7435-3857-2(9), Audioworks) Pub: S&S Audio. Dist(s): S and S Inc
Stephen Ambrose draws from more than 1,400 interviews with American, British, Canadian, French, and German veterans to create the preeminent chronicle of the most important day in the twentieth century. Ambrose reveals how the original plans for the invasion were abandoned, and how ordinary soldiers and officers acted on their own initiative.

Stephen Coonts: America, Liberty, Liars & Thieves. abr. ed. Stephen Coonts. Read by John Kenneth & Guerin Barry. (Running Time: 18 hrs.). (Jake Grafton Novel Ser.). 2007. audio compact disk 34.95 (978-1-4233-3425-5(6), 9781423334255, BACD) Brilliance Audio.

Stephen Coonts Deep Black CD Collection 2: Deep Black: Payback, Deep Black: Jihad, Deep Black: Conspiracy. abr. ed. Stephen Coonts & Jim DeFelice. (Running Time: 13 hrs.). 2009. audio compact disk 34.99 (978-1-4418-0152-4(9), 9781441801524, BACD) Brilliance Audio.

Stephen Covey. Stephen R. Covey. 1 cass. 1997. 1062.00 (978-1-883219-52-9(3)); 1000.50 CD. (978-1-883219-54-3(X)) Franklin Covey.

Stephen Dobyns. unabr. ed. Stephen Dobyns. Read by Stephen Dobyns. 1 cass. (Running Time: 29 min.). Incl. Cemetry Nights; 1987. 10.00 New Letters.
The poet & novelist reads from his sixth poetry book.

Stephen Dunn. unabr. ed. Read by Stephen Dunn. 1 cass. (Running Time: 29 min.). 1985. 10.00 New Letters.
One of a weekly half-hour radio program with authors talking & presenting their own works.

Stephen Dunn, No. II. Stephen Dunn. Read by Stephen Dunn. 1 cass. (Running Time: 29 min.). 1988. 10.00 (052788) New Letters.
Interview with award-winning poet. Dunn reads from his book, "Local Time".

Stephen F. Austin & the Founding of Texas. unabr. ed. James Haley. Read by Benjamin Becker. (Running Time: 2 hrs.). (Library of American Lives & Times Ser.). 2009. 19.99 (978-1-4233-9452-5(6), 9781423394525, Brilliance MP3); 39.97 (978-1-4233-9453-2(4), 9781423394532, Brinc Audio MP3 Lib); 39.97 (978-1-4233-9454-9(2), 9781423394549, BADLE); audio compact disk 19.99 (978-1-4233-9450-1(X), 9781423394501, Bril Audio CD Unabri); audio compact disk 39.97 (978-1-4233-9451-8(8), 9781423394518, BriAudCD Unabrid) Brilliance Audio.

Stephen Foster for Acoustic Guitar. Steven Zdenek Eckels. 1996. pap. bk. 17.95 (978-0-7866-0503-3(0), 95475BCD) Mel Bay.

Stephen J. Cannell CD Collection: The Tin Collectors, the Viking Funeral. abr. ed. Stephen J. Cannell. (Running Time: 10 hrs.). 2005. audio compact disk 29.95 (978-1-59737-706-5(6), 9781597377065, BACD) Brilliance Audio.
The Tin Collectors: L.A. police detective Shane Scully, comes under investigation by Internal Affairs (derisively known as "the tin collectors") after he kills his ex-partner who was one of the mayor's bodyguards. Temporarily reassigned, so that he can remain under the department's watchful eye, Scully finds that more than his badge is at stake when he is set up to take the rap in a deadly plot of corruption and conspiracy that reaches to the highest levels of the LAPD. The Viking Funeral: Driving along the freeway, LAPD Sergeant Shane Scully glances over and sees at the wheel of a neighboring car his oldest friend and LAPD colleague, Jody Dean. Why is Scully so surprised? Because it's been two years since Jody committed suicide. Now Shane is confronted by the bizarre truth: Jody and five other cops thought to be dead are anything but. Originally sent deep undercover to bust an extremely violent international criminal network, they've gone bad. Calling themselves the Vikings, they are LAPD's worst nightmare: dangerous rogue cops who know how the system works.

Stephen King Collection. unabr. ed. Stephen King. 10 CDs. (Running Time: 12 hrs.). 2005. audio compact disk 90.00 (978-0-4159-1652-0(7)); 72.00 (978-1-4159-1565-3(2)) Books on Tape.
This collection of three bone-chilling dramatic audio productions includes 16 unabridged classic stories from Stephen King's bestseller NIGHT SHIFT. In GRAY MATTER, a group of old codgers who gather around the Reliable at Henry's Nite-Owl discover one stormy night the gruesome fate of an old crony. In THE GRAVEYARD SHIFT, a dropout drifter Hall working the graveyard shift in a decrepit Massachusetts mill thinks it just another stop in his journey - that is until he meets the Rat Queen. In THE LAWNMOWER MAN, Harold Parkette disposes of his lawnmower after a neighbor's cat dies a gruesome death and hires a peculiar lawnmower man to the job, and more.

Stephen King Collection: Stories from Night Shift. unabr. ed. Stephen King. Read by John Glover. 10 CDs. (Running Time: 11 hrs.). (ENG.). 2005. audio compact disk 35.00 (978-0-7393-1736-5(9)) Pub: Random Audio Pubg. Dist(s): Random

Stephen King Value Collection, Set. abr. ed. Stephen King. Read by John Glover. 6 cass. (Running Time: 9 hrs.). 2000. 34.95 (Random AudioBks) Random Audio Pubg.
A valued collection of books including "Gray Matter," "The Graveyard Shift" & "The Lawnmower Man.".

Stephen Mitchell. unabr. ed. Ed. by Jim McKinley. Prod. by Rebekah Presson. 1 cass. (Running Time: 29 min.). (New Letters on the Air Ser.). 1994. 10.00 (101593) New Letters.
Mitchell is much celebrated as the premier translator of spiritual texts including the "Tao te Ching," "The Book of Job," "The Gospels According to Jesus" & the recently published "Book of Psalms." Mitchell talks about these texts, which he translates from their original languages & about the universal truths found in them. He also reads from his own poetry.

Stephen Pollan's Complete Book of Money: Unconventional Wisdom about Everything from Annuities to Zero Coupon Bonds. abr. ed. Stephen M. Pollan. Read by Stephen M. Pollan. 4 cass. (Running Time: 6 hrs.). 2000. 25.95 HarperCollins Pubs.

***Stephen Prina: Modern Movie Pop.** Stephen Prina. (ENG.). 2010. 15.00 (978-0-9777528-8-1(7)) Pub: CAMSL. Dist(s): Dist Art Pubs

Stephen R. Covey Collection. 20th abr. anniv. ed. Stephen R. Covey. (Running Time: 6 hrs. 0 mins. 0 sec.). (ENG.). 2008. audio compact disk 49.99 (978-0-7435-7802-8(3)) Pub: S&S Audio. Dist(s): S and S Inc

Stephen Richards: A Solo Collection. 2007. pap. bk. 24.95 (978-0-8074-0972-5(3), 993288) URJ Pr.

Stephen Spender. Stephen Spender. 1 cass. (Author Speaks Ser.). 1991. 14.95 J Norton Pubs.
Archival recordings of 20th-century authors.

Stephen W. Hawking's Life Works: The Cambridge Lectures. unabr. ed. Stephen W. Hawking. Read by Stephen W. Hawking. 4 cass. (Running Time: 6 hrs.). 2002. 25.00 (978-1-57453-509-9(9)) Audio Lit.
Professor Hawking, who transformed our view of the universe in his landmark book, A Brief History of Time, reviews great ideas of the past from Aristotle to Newton, Einstein's theory of gravity, the Big Bang, and black holes. He goes on to apply the principle of quantum mechanics to the Big Bang theory and the origin of the universe.

Stephen White CD Collection 1: Missing Persons; Kill Me; Dry Ice. abr. ed. Stephen White. Read by Dick Hill. (Running Time: 18 hrs.). (Dr. Alan Gregory Ser.). 2008. audio compact disk 34.95 (978-1-4233-5242-6(4), 9781423352426, BACD) Brilliance Audio.

Stephen White CD Collection 2: Privileged Information; Private Practices; Higher Authority. abr. ed. Stephen White. Read by Dick Hill. (Running Time: 19 hrs.). (Dr. Alan Gregory Ser.). 2008. audio compact disk 34.95 (978-1-4233-6212-8(8), 9781423362128, BACD) Brilliance Audio.

***Stephen White CD Collection 3: Harm's Way - Remote Control - Critical Conditions.** abr. ed. Stephen White. Read by Dick Hill. (Running Time: 18 hrs.). (Dr. Alan Gregory Ser.). 2010. audio compact disk 29.99 (978-1-4418-6167-2(X), 9781441861672, BACD) Brilliance Audio.

Stephenie Meyer: Twilight/New Moon/Eclipse/Breaking Dawn CD Ppk. unabr. ed. Stephenie Meyer. Read by Ilyana Kadushin. (ENG.). (J). 2008. audio compact disk, audio compact disk, audio compact disk 200.99 (978-0-7393-5235-9(0), Listening Lib) Pub: Random Audio Pubg. Dist(s): Random

Stepmother. unabr. ed. Diana Diamond, pseud. Read by Susannah Birney. 2005. 29.95 (978-0-7927-3691-2(5), CMP 822); 59.95 (978-0-7927-3689-9(3), CSL 822); audio compact disk 89.95 (978-0-7927-3690-5(7), SLD 822) AudioGO.

Steppenwolf see Lobo Estepario

Steppenwolf. Hermann Hesse. Read by Daniel Quintero. (Running Time: 3 hrs.). (C). 2006. 16.95 (978-1-60083-274-1(1), Audiofy Corp) Iofy Corp.

Steppenwolf. unabr. ed. Hermann Hesse. Narrated by Peter Weller. 6 CDs. (Running Time: 7 hrs. 30 mins.). (ENG.). 2008. audio compact disk 29.95 (978-1-60283-351-7(6)) Pub: AudioGO. Dist(s): Perseus Dist

Steppin' Out. Perf. by Braxton Brothers Staff. 1 cass., 1 CD. 8.78 (WH 11318); audio compact disk 13.58 CD Jewel box. (WH 11318) NewSound.

Steppin' Out. Perf. by Braxton Brothers. 1 cass., 1 CD. 8.78 (WH 11318); audio compact disk 13.58 CD Jewel box. (WH 11318) NewSound.

Steppin' Out with Jazzercise. 1 cass. (Running Time: 60 min.). 1989. 9.95 Peter Pan.

***Steppin' Razor, the Life of Peter Tosh.** unabr. ed. John Masouri. (Running Time: 10 hrs. 0 mins.). 2011. 29.95 (978-1-4417-5251-2(X)); 65.95 (978-1-4417-5247-5(1)); audio compact disk 29.95 (978-1-4417-5250-5(1)); audio compact disk 100.00 (978-1-4417-5248-2(X)) Blckstn Audio.

Stepping in the Breach. Read by Basilea Schlink. 1 cass. (Running Time: 30 min.). 1985. (0219) Evang Sisterhood Mary.
Talks about the power of intercessory prayer & practical steps for difficult times.

Stepping into English, Levels I-VI. bk. 39.50 Level I; 2 bks. & 2 audio cass.; The City Mouse & the Country Mouse/The Lion & the Mouse. (AFE441); bk. 39.50 Level II; 2 bk. & 2 audio cass.; The Rabbit & the Turtle/The Boy Who Cried Wolf. (AFE442); bk. 39.95 Level III; 2 bks. & 2 audio cass.; Belling the Cat/The Milkmaid & Her Pail. (AFE443); bk. 19.95 Level IV; 1 bk. & 1 audio cass.; Goldilocks & the Three Bears. (AFE444); bk. 19.95 Level V; 1 bk. & 1 audio cass.; The Little Red Hen. (AFE445); bk. 19.95 Level VI; 1 bk. & 1 audio cass.; The Boy & His Donkey. (AFE446) J Norton Pubs.

Stepping into Your Destiny. Perf. by Various Speakers. (Running Time: 4 hrs. 42 mins.). 2007. 29.99 (978-1-4245-0686-6(7)) Tre Med Inc.

Stepping into Your Destiny: N/a. Rick Joyner. 2005. audio compact disk 29.99 (978-1-929371-66-2(7)) Pub: Morning NC. Dist(s): Destiny Image Pubs

Stepping It Up. Jamie Borden. 2006. 14.95 (978-5-558-29144-5(3)) Omnibus Press GBR.

Stepping Out. Rita Abrams. (J). 1991. 12.95 (978-0-938971-75-7(1)) JTG Nashville.

Stepping Out: Broad-based community Instruction. 2005. spiral bd. 159.00 (978-1-57861-526-1(7), IEP Res) Attainment.

Stepping Out of Line: Lessons for Women Who Want It Their Way... in Life, in Love, & at Work. unabr. ed. Nell Merlino. Read by Laural Merlington. 1 MP3-CD. (Running Time: 6 hrs.). 2009. 22.99 (978-1-4233-9170-8(5), 9781423391708, Brilliance MP3); 22.99 (978-1-4233-9172-2(1), 9781423391722, BAD); 39.97 (978-1-4233-9171-5(3), 9781423391715, Brinc Audio MP3 Lib); 39.97 (978-1-4233-9173-9(X), 9781423391739, BADLE); audio compact disk 22.99 (978-1-4233-9168-5(3), 9781423391685, Bril Audio CD Unabri); audio compact disk 74.97 (978-1-4233-9169-2(1), 9781423391692, BriAudCD Unabrid) Brilliance Audio.

Stepping Out on the World of God. David T. Demola. 1 cass. 4.00 (2-106) Faith Fellow Min.

Stepping Stones Stories for Children 4-10. Retold by Mary Hamilton. 1 cass. (Running Time: 58 min.). (J). (gr. k-6). 1992. 10.00 (978-1-885556-03-5(9)) Hidden Sprng.
Five stories including "The Bun" - the Gingerbread Man of Russian folklore; "Jack & the Wishgiver" - a tale of wise wishing; "Drakestail" - a French fairytale; "Wishing Star" adapted from Bethany Roberts' Waiting for Spring Stories; & "Vasilisa the Beautiful" - a classic Russian fairytale.

Stepping Through an Open Doorway. Osel Tendzin. Read by Osel Tendzin. 6 cass. 1977. 58.50 (A052) Vajradhatu.
Six talks: 1) Mindfulness Practice; 2) Aspects of Shamatha Practice; 3) Attributes of Vipashyana; 4) The Practice of Vipashyana; 5) Vipashyana & Mahayana Path; 6) Open Doorway to the Bodhisattva Path.

Stepping up Audio CDs: A Journey Through the Psalms of Ascent. Beth Moore. 2007. audio compact disk 39.95 (978-1-4158-5836-3(5)) LifeWay Christian.

Steppingstones One. J. Johnston. 1981. stu. ed. (978-0-201-04656-4(3)) AddisonWesley.

Steps along the Diamond Way - Stages of Meditation. Ole Nydahl. 2 cass. 18.00 set. (A0410-89) Sound Photosyn.
Ole's Buddhist meditation centers around the world teach the Diamond Way in terms that Westerners can understand & enjoy. He's a character who has been around. We like our thoughts after we've been with Ole.

Steps Eight & Nine & Step Ten. 1 cass. (Twelve Steps to Recovery Ser.). 8.95 (1584G) Hazelden.

Steps of a Righteous Man. Evelyn Murray. Read by Evelyn Murray. 6 cass. (Running Time: 6 hrs.). 1997. 24.00 Set. (978-1-893072-01-5(0)) Evelyn Murray.
Bill comes home from the Army a changed man (born again), he had made a commitment with the Lord. He opened a chain of clubs for young men & big brothers, he was jilted at the alter.

Steps to a Successful Transformation. Innovation Groups Staff. 1 cass. (Transforming Local Government Ser.). Alliance Innov.

Steps to Christ. 1. (Running Time: 4 hours). 2002. (978-0-9767533-2-2(4)) T Harriman.

Steps to Christ. 2nd ed. Narrated by Tony J. Harriman. 3 CDs. (Running Time: 4 hrs). 2003. audio compact disk (978-0-9767533-0-8(8)) T Harriman.

Steps to English. 2nd ed. Kernan. 1982. 29.36 Listing Comp. Ex. (978-0-07-033165-5(0)) McGraw.

Steps to English, Grade 5. 2nd ed. Doris Kernan. 1984. 220.20 cassettes. (978-0-07-033145-7(6)) McGraw.

Steps to Healing Set: Wisdom from the Sages, the Rosemarys & the Times. abr. ed. Dana Ullman. Read by Dana Ullman. 2 cass. (Running Time: 3 hrs.). 2000. 18.95 (978-1-56170-772-0(4), 4071) Hay House.

Steps to Inner Peace. Swami Amar Jyoti. 1 cass. 1978. 9.95 (P-24) Truth Consciousness.
Revealing inner peace; remedies for our blocks. On genuine humility. Digging out the roots of disturbance. Many methods, one Goal.

Steps to Resolving Conflict. abr. ed. Ed. by Keith Lynch. 8 cass. (Running Time: 8 hrs.). 1994. 39.95 Set. (978-1-57229-035-8(8)) FamilyLife.

Steps to Self Hypnosis. abr. ed. Instructed by C. Alexander Simpkins & Annellen M. Simpkins. (Running Time: 55 mins.). 2001. 14.95 (978-0-9679113-3-5(8)) Radiant Dolphin Pr.

Steps Toward Utopia. unabr. ed. George Leonard. 1 cass. (Running Time: 90 min.). 1966. 11.00 (03801) Big Sur Tapes.

Stepsister from Planet Weird. unabr. ed. Francess L. Lantz. Narrated by Christina Moore & Julie Dretzin. 4 cass. (Running Time: 4 hrs. 30 mins.). (YA). 2001. pap. bk. & stu. ed. 53.24 Recorded Bks.
Megan Larsen doesn't want Ariel Cola for a stepsister, because Ariel's too perfect to be from planet Earth. But that's just it. Ariel is from Zircalon-6, where she was a gaseous creature.

Stepsister from the Planet Weird. Francess L. Lantz. Narrated by Julie Dretzin. 4 CDs. (Running Time: 4 hrs. 30 mins.). (gr. 5 up). audio compact disk 39.00 (978-0-7887-6157-7(9)) Recorded Bks.

Stepsister from the Planet Weird. Francess L. Lantz. Narrated by Julie Dretzin et al. 8 CDs. (Running Time: 12 hrs.). audio compact disk 40.00 Recorded Bks.
The last thing in the world Megan Larsen wants is to have Ariel Cola for a stepsister. With her golden hair, violet-blue eyes & musical voice, Ariel is a magnet for all the cutest schoolboys. She's too perfect to be from planet Earth but that's just it. Ariel is from Zircalon-g, where she was a gaseous creature horribly solid like human beings, unfortunately, her father prefers being solid. He enjoys American television & can't get enough of human food. Most importantly, he loves Megan's mother & they plan to get married. If Mega & Ariel want to avoid becoming stepsisters, they'll need to team up & split their parents apart before it's too late.

Stepsister from the Planet Weird. unabr. ed. Francess L. Lantz. Narrated by Julie Dretzin. 4 CDs. (Running Time: 4 hrs.). (YA). (gr. 5-8). 2001. audio compact disk 39.00 (C1381) Recorded Bks.
The last thing in the world Megan Larsen wants is to have Ariel Cola for a stepsister. With her golden hair, violet-blue eyes & musical voice, Ariel is a magnet for all the cutest schoolboys. She's too perfect to be from planet Earth. But that's just it. Ariel is from Zircalon-6, where she was a gaseous creature, not horribly solid like human beings. Unfortunately, her father prefers being solid, enjoys American television & can't get enough of human food. Most importantly, he loves Megan's mother & they plan to get married. If Megan & Ariel want to avoid becoming stepsisters, they'll need to team up & split their parents apart before it's too late.

Stepsister from the Planet Weird. unabr. ed. Francess L. Lantz & George Wilson. Narrated by Christina Moore et al. 8 CDs. (Running Time: 8 hrs. 45 mins.). (gr. 5 up). 2001. audio compact disk 78.00 (978-0-7887-4920-9(X), 96456E7) Recorded Bks.
Megan Larsen doesn't want Ariel Cola for a stepsister, because Ariel's too perfect to be from planet Earth. But that's just it. Ariel is from Zircalon-6, where she was a gaseous creature.

Stereo Boom Box Full Year, Vols. 1-4. (Stereo Boom Box Ser.). (J). (gr. 1-6). 1997. bk. & ring bd. 619.99 (978-1-57405-047-9(8)) CharismaLife Pub.

Stereo Headphones. (J). 2007. 19.95 (978-1-56911-341-7(6)) Lrning Res.

Stereo Headphones with Microphone. (J). 2007. 38.95 (978-1-56911-339-4(4)) Lrning Res.

Stern. abr. ed. Adam Grupper & Bruce Jay Friedman. 3 cass. (Running Time: 4 hrs. 30 mins.). 2000. 29.95 (978-1-893079-05-2(8), JCCAUDIOBOOKS) Jewish Contempry Classics.
Hilarious dark comedy about a sweet guy who moves to the suburbs & meets anxiety & bigotry, gets an ulcer, has a nervous breakdown & recovers to win the day. (Interview with the author included).

Stern Men. unabr. ed. Elizabeth Gilbert. Contrib. by Allyson Ryan. (Running Time: 12 hrs.). (ENG.). 2009. audio compact disk 39.95 (978-0-14-314334-5(4), PengAudBks) Penguin Grp USA.

Sterner Stuff Set: A Detective Tansey Mystery. unabr. ed. John Penn. Read by Alexander John. 6 cass. 1999. 54.95 (978-0-7540-0328-1(0), CAB1751) Pub: Chivers Audio Bks GBR. Dist(s): AudioGO
Who would want to kill a harmless priest in the quiet Cotswold town of Colombury? Surprisingly, it transpires that there are a variety of suspects: a brigadier whom has quarreled with the priest; a vagrant whom he befriended; & a thief who stole a chalice from the church. With the discovery of a second body, Detective Tansey finds himself on the trail of a murderer.

Stess Talk. 1 cass. 11.95 (978-1-57025-011-8(1)) Whole Person.
A single-session do-it-yourself workshop on audiocassette for individuals or groups who want to learn to manage stress.

Steve Adelson: Concert on the Chapman Stick. Steve Adelson. 2008. 24.95 Mel Bay.

Steve Allen's Meeting of Minds. (978-1-57453-546-4(3)) Mar Co Prods.

Steve Allen's Meeting of Minds, Vol. II. unabr. ed. Steve Allen. Read by Steve Allen. 8 cass. (Running Time: 8 hrs.). 2002. 32.00 (978-1-59040-549-9(8)) Audio Lit.

Steve Baughman - Celtic Fingerstyle Guitar Solos. Steven A. Baughman. 1998. pap. bk. 17.95 (978-0-7866-3851-2(6), 97259BCD) Mel Bay.

Steve Cabot's Blueprint for Union Avoidance. 2006. audio compact disk (978-0-9777803-0-3(9)) Cabot Inst for Labor.

Steve Curtis Chapman: the Early Years. Contrib. by Steven Curtis Chapman. Prod. by Phil Naish. (Early Years (EMI-Cmg) Ser.). 2006. audio compact disk 7.99 (978-5-558-24619-3(7)) Pt of Grace Ent.

Steve Deal Band. Steve Deal Band Staff. 2005. audio compact disk 14.99 (978-0-88368-845-8(X)) Whitaker Hse.

Steve Gadd: Up Close. Steve Gadd & Bobby Cleall. Ed. by Dan Thress. Contrib. by Ricardo Betancourt. 1 cass. (Video Transcription Ser.). pap. bk. 21.95 incl. 2 pullout drum solo charts. (BD073) DCI Music Video.
Steve Gadd, world famous drummer focuses on three main topics: drum corps/rudiments, jazz/studio playing. Also includes five-page solo transcription.

Steve Heller. unabr. ed. Read by Steve Heller. 1 cass. (Running Time: 29 min.). Incl. Railroad Feast. 1987. (22); 1987. 10.00 (22) New Letters.
Heller reads a story set in the Depression concerning a young boy's encounter with a rough group of railroad men who offer him contraband food.

Steve Jobs, Steve Wozniak, & the Personal Computer. Donald B. Lemke. Illus. by Tod Smith & Al Milgrom. (Inventions & Discovery Ser.). (ENG.). (gr. 3-4). 2007. audio compact disk 6.95 (978-1-4296-1120-6(0)) CapstoneDig.

Steve Jobs, Steve Wozniak, & the Personal Computer (INK Audiocassette) (Inventions & Discovery Ser.). (ENG.). 2007. audio compact disk 5.95 (978-0-7368-7993-4(5)) CapstoneDig.

Steve Kaufman's Favorite 50 Flatpicking Guitar, Vol. 1 A-F: Traditional American Fiddle Tunes. Steve Kaufman. 2008. pap. bk. 19.95 (978-0-7866-7582-1(9)) Mel Bay.

Steve Kaufman's Favorite 50 Mandolin, Tunes S-W: Traditional American Fiddle Tunes. Steve Kaufman. 2008. pap. bk. 19.95 (978-0-7866-5382-9(5)) Mel Bay.

Steve Martin: The Magic Years. Morris Walker. Read by Barrett Whitener. 6 cass. (Running Time: 9 hrs.). 1999. 29.95 (978-0-7861-1704-8(4)) Pub: Blckstn Audio. Dist(s): Penton Overseas
This is no ordinary celebrity biography pieced together by an outsider. Martin & the author had a close relationship growing up.

Steve Martin: The Magic Years. unabr. ed. Morris Walker. Read by Barrett Whitener. 6 cass. (Running Time: 8 hrs. 30 mins.). 2003. 44.95 (978-0-7861-1572-3(6), 2401) Blckstn Audio.
Will take you through the more serious side of Steve's youth including his loss of virginity & the terrifying moments he spent at the wrong end of a shotgun. Also, shows the funny side & the pranks he used to play.

Steve Martin: The Magic Years, Set. unabr. ed. Morris Walker. Read by Barrett Whitener. 6 cass. 1999. 44.95 (FS9-51040) Highsmith.

Steve Moore: Integrating Two Different Analytical Approaches in Two Different Time Frames into a Unified Trading Style. Read by Steve Moore. 1 cass. 30.00 Dow Jones Telerate.
Steve will focus on the following topics: how to integrate two different analytical approaches in two different time frames into a unified trading style; & how to prepare, like a professional trader, for each day's trading session. From this presentation you will gain a new appreciation of historical analysis, short-term market tendencies, the compatibility between the two, & the value & techniques of daily preparation.

Steve Smith & Vital Information - Visualization. Steve Smith. 2007. audio compact disk 17.95 (978-1-4234-2859-6(5), 1423428595) Pub: Hudson Music. Dist(s): H Leonard

Steven B. Stevens NASB Bible. Narrated by Steven11/2007 Stevens. (ENG.). 2007. audio compact disk 79.99 (978-1-930034-48-8(2)) Casscomm.

Steven B. Stevens NASB New Testament. Narrated by Steven Stevens. (ENG.). 2007. audio compact disk 34.99 (978-1-930034-49-5(0)) Casscomm.

Steven Spielberg. unabr. ed. Joseph McBride. Read by David Hilder. 15 cass. (Running Time: 22 hrs.). 1998. 95.95 (978-0-7861-1254-8(9), 2170) Blckstn Audio.
The most successful director in movie history has been responsible for many box-office blockbusters. And yet throughout much of his career, Spielberg's work has been undervalued by critics who have questioned his emotional maturity & intellectual seriousness. It was not until he made "Schindler's List" in 1993 that he was widely recognized as a serious filmmaker.

Stevenson Vol. 1: Short Stories. unabr. ed. 3 cass. (Running Time: 4 hrs. 30 mins.). 2002. 24.00 (978-1-929718-03-0(9), 1401-4) Audio Conn.
Includes Markheim, A Lodging for the Night, The Body Snatcher, Essay by Edmond Gosse.

SteveSongs: Marvelous Day! Steve Roslonek. (J). 2006. audio compact disk 11.99 (978-1-57940-154-2(6)) Rounder Records.
Every day is a Marvelous Day with SteveSongs' blend of musicality and imagination. Smart and sassy, catchy and fun, these jazzy rock songs reach out to the heart of kids and their families. Steve blends participatory songs, clever stories and great melodies into an experience that leads young listeners on what the Boston Globe calls "not just a musical journey but an entertaining, interactive and educational one." The Los Angeles Times applauds Steve's "warmth, gentle humor and well-crafted, quirky wordplay." His songs are tested and approved by the toughest audience on the planet - kids.

Stevie. pap. bk. 18.95 (978-1-59519-352-0(9)) Pub: Live Oak Media. Dist(s): AudioGO

Stevie. John Steptoe. Narrated by Lawrence Wrentz. (J). (gr. k-3). 1987. audio compact disk 12.95 (978-1-59519-351-3(0)) Live Oak Media.

Stevie. John L. Steptoe. 1 read-along cass. (Running Time: 8 min.). (J). 1987. 9.95 Live Oak Media.
When his mother temporarily boards Stevie as a favor to a friend, a young black boy takes exception to the younger child's intrusion into his household & daily routine - & then misses him greatly when his stay ends.

Stevie. John L. Steptoe. Illus. by John L. Steptoe. (Running Time: 8 mins.). (J). (gr. k-3). 1987. 9.95 (978-1-59112-124-4(8)) Live Oak Media.

Stevie. John L. Steptoe. (J). 1989. 12.95 (978-0-676-87187-6(9)) McGraw.

Stevie. unabr. ed. John L. Steptoe. Illus. by John L. Steptoe. Read by Lawrence Wrentz. 11 vols. (Running Time: 8 mins.). (J). (gr. 1-3). 1987. bk. 24.95 (978-0-87499-050-8(5)); pap. bk. 16.95 (978-0-87499-049-2(1)) Live Oak Media.

Stevie, Grades 1-3. John L. Steptoe. Illus. by John L. Steptoe. Read by Lawrence Wrentz. 14 vols. (Running Time: 8 mins.). (J). 1987. pap. bk. & tchr. ed. 37.95 Reading Chest. (978-0-87499-051-5(3)) Live Oak Media.

Stevie Smith. 2nd ed. British Library Sound Archive Staff & Vrej Nersessian. (British Library - British Library Sound Archive Ser.). (ENG.). 2009. audio compact disk 15.00 (978-0-7123-0592-1(0)) Pub: Britis Library GBR. Dist(s): Chicago Distribution Ctr

Stewardship. David T. Demola. 10 cass. 40.00 (S-1073) Faith Fellow Min.

Stewardship: A Ministers Guide to Managing & Ministering on Money. Mac Hammond. 2008. audio compact disk 24.00 (978-1-57399-347-0(6)) Mac Hammond.

Stewardship: Choosing Service over Self-Interest. abr. ed. Peter Block. Read by Peter Block. Read by Michael Toms et al. 2 cass. (Running Time: 3 hrs.). (Right Livelihood Ser.). 1997. 17.95 (978-1-57453-147-3(6)) Audio Lit.
Accepting ownership & accountability for the well-being of the larger organization while, at the same time, giving up the need to control & take care of others.

Stewardship: Key to Maturity. Dudley Hall. 1 cass. (Running Time: 90 mins.). (Keys to the Kingdom Ser.: Vol. 2). 2000. 5.00 (DH01-002) Morning NC.
These messages outline three essentials for successful Christian living.

Stewardship: The Key to Wealth. Creflo A. Dollar. 2008. audio compact disk 14.00 (978-1-59944-715-5(0)) Creflo Dollar.

Stewardship & Bureaucracy. Read by T. Kenneth Cribb, Jr. 1 cass. 2.50 (108) ISI Books.

Stewardship & Bureaucracy. Read by William Dennis. 1 cass. 2.50 (109) ISI Books.

Stewardship & Bureaucracy. Read by Charles L. Heatherly. 1 cass. 2.50 (110) ISI Books.

Stewardship & Bureaucracy. Read by Robert R. Reilly. 1 cass. 2.50 (111) ISI Books.

Stewardship & Bureaucracy. Read by Robert A. Schadler. 1 cass. 2.50 (112) ISI Books.

Stewardship As a Way of Life Thematic. 1999. pap. bk. 35.00 (978-0-933173-85-9(7)) Chging Church Forum.

Stewardship of Education. Read by Harry Jaffa. 1 cass. 2.50 (103) ISI Books.

Stewardship of Education. Read by Paul Craig Roberts & Lawrence Uzzell. 1 cass. 2.50 (102) ISI Books.

Stewardship of the Heart. Richard M. Eyre. 2 cass. 11.95 Set. (Bkcraft Inc) Deseret Bk.

Stewardship of Western Civilization. Read by Richard V. Allen. 1 cass. 2.50 (105) ISI Books.

Stewardship of Western Civilization. Read by Gerhart Niemeyer. 1 cass. 2.50 (104) ISI Books.

Stewardship of Western Civilization. Read by Erik Von Kuehnelt-Leddihn. 1 cass. 2.50 (106) ISI Books.

Stewart's Calculus: Early Transcendentals. 5th ed. (C). 2003. stu. ed. 19.95 (978-0-534-39329-8(2)) Pub: Brooks-Cole. Dist(s): CENGAGE Learn

Sthita Prigna: Established in Pure Intelligence. unabr. ed. Swami Amar Jyoti. 1 cass. (Running Time: 90 mins.). (Satsangs of Swami Amar Jyoti Ser.). 1999. 9.95 (978-0-933572-46-1(8), R-117) Truth Consciousness.
Sthita Prigna transcends intellect, gives the higher answers. The power of Faith. Heaven on Earth.

***Stick.** unabr. ed. Elmore Leonard. Read by Frank Muller. (ENG.). 2010. (978-0-06-199376-3(X), Harper Audio); (978-0-06-206265-9(4), Harper Audio) HarperCollins Pubs.

Stick, unabr. ed. Elmore Leonard. Narrated by Frank Muller. 6 cass. (Running Time: 8 hrs. 15 mins.). 51.00 (978-0-7887-0359-1(5), 94551E7) Recorded Bks.
In this sequel to "Swag," Ernest Stickley, Jr. is back after seven years of hard time in a Michigan prison. As the chauffeur to an investment whiz, he's suddenly surrounded by underworld figures & fools with money. Will a golden opportunity to run a profitable sweet-revenge scam be too much to pass up? Available to libraries only.

Stick. unabr. collector's ed. Elmore Leonard. Read by Alexander Adams. 6 cass. (Running Time: 9 hrs.). 1996. 48.00 (978-0-7366-3360-4(X), 4010) Books on Tape.
Prison should reform the criminal, & Ernest Stickly thinks he's a new man. But after serving seven years for armed robbery in Michigan, "Stick" heads for Miami, where he finds the easy money hard to ignore. When Stick nearly gets iced by some of the crazies, he goes on the run, but leaves a trail that's easy to follow. Why doesn't he cover his tracks? Maybe that's part of the perfect scam that he plans with a beautiful blonde, an expert on money & men. The target is a drug czar. The sting: sweet revenge.

Stick Figure: A Diary of My Former Self. unabr. ed. Lori Gottlieb. 4 cass. (Running Time: 360 mins.). 2001. 24.95 (978-1-57511-089-9(X)) Pub Mills.
Based on her childhood diaries, Lori Gottlieb's book chronicles her preteen battle with anorexia nervosa. A precocious chess-loving student with a straight A average, young Lori aspires to supermodel thinness in an attempt to reconcile society's conflicting messages & to gain her parents' attention.

Stick Fly. Lydia R. Diamond. Contrib. by Dule Hill et al. (Running Time: 6600 sec.). 2008. audio compact disk 25.95 (978-1-58081-380-8(1)) Pub: L A Theatre. Dist(s): NetLibrary CO

Stick Like Glue. Colin Wells. Narrated by Larry A. McKeever. (Mystery Ser.). (J). 2000. audio compact disk 14.95 (978-1-58659-278-3(5)) Artesian.

Stick Like Glue. unabr. ed. Colin Wells. Narrated by Larry A. McKeever. 1 cass. (Running Time: 40 min.). (Mystery Ser.). (J). 2000. 10.95 (978-1-58659-009-3(X), 54104) Artesian.

Stick to Drawing Comics, Monkey Brain! Cartoonist Ignores Helpful Advice. Scott Adams. Read by William Dufris. (Playaway Adult Fiction Ser.). 2008. 64.99 (978-1-60640-142-2(4)) Find a World.

Stick to Drawing Comics, Monkey Brain! Cartoonist Ignores Helpful Advice. unabr. ed. Scott Adams. Read by William Dufris. (Running Time: 10 hrs. 0 mins. 0 sec.). (ENG.). 2007. audio compact disk 34.99 (978-1-4001-0549-6(8)); audio compact disk 24.99 (978-1-4001-5549-1(5)); audio compact disk 69.99 (978-1-4001-3549-3(4)) Pub: Tantor Media. Dist(s): IngramPubServ

Stick Tricks. Contrib. by Chip Ritter. 2007. 24.95 (978-5-557-47318-7(1)) Mel Bay.

Stickeen. John Muir. Narrated by Salisbury. Prod. by Purl. 1 Cassette. (Running Time: 62 minutes). 1999. 9.95 (978-1-58436-600-3(1)) Haven Bks CA.
The unabridged audio book of the classic John Muir tale of man...and man's best friend, beautifully narrated with haunting music and recorded-live sound effects. One of John Muir's favorite adventures took place across the face of an Alaskan glacier, and in the company of the little dog Stickeen, whose cunning and bravery made him of the famed naturalist's most treasured companions. As you hear the unbridled power of an Arctic storm unleashed, and the haunting strains of inspiring music, travel with them beyond the bounds of wisdom, into the soul of courage.

Stickeen - Audio CDs. John Muir. Read by Purl. Narrated by Salisbury. 1 CD. (Running Time: 62 minutes). 2002. audio compact disk 14.95 (978-1-58436-601-0(X)) Haven Bks CA.
The playwrights and their process:Two modern women writers became fascinated by a woman writer from the past. After extensive research through the author's published and unpublished works, Mara Purl & Sydney Swire honor Mary Shelley by presenting her thoughts in her own words.

Stickeen & Other John Muir Animal Adventures. John Muir. Retold by Garth Gilchrist. 1 cass. (Running Time: 45 mins.). (John Muir: Audio Stories with Garth Gilchrist Ser.). (YA). (gr. k-6). 2004. 9.95 (978-1-58469-021-4(6)); audio compact disk 16.95 (978-1-58469-022-1(4)) Dawn CA.
Tells the memorable story of Muir's glacier crossing with the dog Stickeen, as well as a delightful collection of true stories Muir had with his "fellow mortals.".

Sticking Point Solution: 9 Ways to Move Your Business from Stagnation to Stunning Growth in Tough Economic Times. unabr. ed. Jay Abraham. Read by Jay Abraham. 1 MP3-CD. (Running Time: 9 hrs.). 2009. 39.97 (978-1-4233-9346-7(5), 9781423393467, Brlnc Audio MP3 Lib); 24.99 (978-1-4233-9345-0(7), 9781423393450, Brilliance MP3); 39.97 (978-1-4233-9348-1(1), 9781423393481, BADLE); 24.99 (978-1-4233-9347-4(3), 9781423393474, BAD); audio compact disk 29.99 (978-1-4233-9343-6(0), 9781423393436, Bril Audio CD Unabri); audio compact disk 97.97 (978-1-4233-9344-3(9), 9781423393443) Brilliance Audio.

Sticking to My Diet. Paul Babiak. 2 cass. (Running Time: 2 hrs.). 1988. 14.95 (978-0-924135-00-2(X)) LDNCWIP.
Training program designed to help people stick to their diet by strengthening willpower, building self-confidence, & managing stress. Contains voice narrative, self-hypnosis, & subliminal messages beneath sounds of ocean.

Stickler Syndrome - A Bibliography & Dictionary for Physicians, Patients, & Genome Researchers. Compiled by Icon Group International, Inc. Staff. 2007. ring bd. 28.95 (978-0-497-11299-8(X)) Icon Grp.

Sticks. Karl E. Wagner & Craig K. Strete. 1 cass. (Running Time: 60 min.). 9.95 (SBS) ZBS Ind.

Sticks, unabr. ed. Joan Bauer. Narrated by Andy Paris. 4 pieces. (Running Time: 4 hrs. 45 mins.). (gr. 3 up). 1997. 35.00 (978-0-7887-0600-4(4), 94786E7) Recorded Bks.
Mickey Vernon, a ten-year-old pool player, wants to win the ten-to-thirteen-year-old's nine-ball tournament. No matter how good he gets, Buck Pender is always better. Even Mickey's math-whiz best friend Arlen can't find Buck's weakness.

Sticks - Bleeding Man. unabr. ed. Karl E. Wagner & Craig K. Strete. Read by Laura Esterman & Steven Keats. Ed. by Tom Lopez. 1 cass. (Running Time: 60 min.). Dramatization. 1984. 10.00 (978-1-881137-17-7(1)) ZBS Found.
An old abandoned farmhouse, set on top of an ancient burial chamber, is the setting of "Sticks." "The Bleeding Man" is the story of an Indian who has been bleeding from his chest his whole life, building up destructive power.

Sticks & Scones. unabr. ed. Diane Mott Davidson. Narrated by Barbara Rosenblat. 8 cass. (Running Time: 10 hrs. 30 mins.). (Goldy Schulz Culinary Mysteries Ser.: No. 10). 2001. 78.00 (978-0-7887-5316-9(9)) Recorded Bks.
Catering Elizabethan fare to Aspen Meadow's elite at an authentic castle brought from England is a dream come true for Goldy. But the day of the luncheon, Goldy is rudely awakened by a shotgun blast through her living room window. As the day goes on, she finds a murder victim floating in a stream on castle property, watches someone close to her get shot, and begins to see the ghost that haunts the castle. Instead of a welcome opportunity, this job has suddenly become a waking nightmare.

***Sticks & Stones: Using Your Words as a Positive Force.** Ace Collins. (Running Time: 5 hrs. 51 mins. 0 sec.). (ENG.). 2009. 16.99 (978-0-310-30260-5(9)) Zondervan.

Sticky Beak. unabr. ed. Morris Gleitzman. Read by Mary-Anne Fahey. 2 cass. (Running Time: 2 hrs. 15 mins.). (J). 2003. 24.00 (978-1-74093-009-3(6)) Pub: Bolinda Pubng AUS. Dist(s): Bolinda Pub Inc

Sticky Beak. unabr. ed. Morris Gleitzman. Read by Mary-Anne Fahey. 2 CDs. (Running Time: 2 hrs. 15 mins.). (J). 2003. audio compact disk 43.95 (978-1-74093-130-4(0)) Pub: Bolinda Pubng AUS. Dist(s): Bolinda Pub Inc

Sticky Teams: Keeping Your Leadership Team & Staff on the Same Page. Larry Osborne. (Running Time: 6 hrs. 30 mins. 0 sec.). (ENG.). 2010. 15.99 (978-0-310-57616-7(4)) Zondervan.

***Stieg Larsson Millennium Trilogy CD Bundle: The Girl with the Dragon Tattoo, the Girl Who Played with Fire, the Girl Who Kicked the Hornet's Nest.** Stieg Larsson. (ENG.). 2010. audio compact disk, audio compact disk, audio compact disk 114.95 (978-0-7393-5275-5(X), Random AudioBks) Pub: Random Audio Pubg. Dist(s): Random

Stiff: The Curious Lives of Human Cadavers. Mary Roach. Read by Shelly Frasier. (Running Time: 8 hrs.). 2003. 27.95 (978-1-60083-662-6(3), Audiofy Corp) Iofy Corp.

Stiff: The Curious Lives of Human Cadavers. unabr. ed. Mary Roach. Read by Shelly Frasier. (Running Time: 8 hrs. 4 mins. 12 sec.). (ENG.). 2003. audio compact disk 59.99 (978-1-4001-3097-9(2)); audio compact disk 29.99 (978-1-4001-0097-2(6), 890585); audio compact disk 19.99 (978-1-4001-5097-7(3)) Pub: Tantor Media. Dist(s): IngramPubServ
An oddly compelling, often hilarious exploration of the strange lives of our bodies postmortem. For two thousand years, cadavers?some willingly, some unwittingly?have been involved in science's boldest strides and weirdest undertakings. They've tested France's first guillotines, ridden the NASA Space Shuttle, been crucified in a Parisian laboratory to test the authenticity of the Shroud of Turin, and helped solve the mystery of TWA Flight 800. For every new surgical procedure, from heart transplants to gender reassignment surgery, cadavers have been there alongside surgeons, making history in their quiet way.In this fascinating, ennobling account, Mary Roach visits the good deeds of cadavers over the centuries?from the anatomy labs and human-sourced pharmacies of medieval and nineteenth-century Europe to a human decay research facility in Tennessee, to a plastic surgery practice lab, to a Scandinavian funeral directors' conference on human composting. In her droll, inimitable voice, Roach tells the engrossing story of our bodies when we are no longer with them."Uproariously funny ...informative and respectful...irreverent and witty...impossible to put down.? ~ Publishers Weekly?Not grisly but inspiring, this work considers the many valuable scientific uses of the body after death.? ~ Library Journal"One of the funniest and most unusual books of the year." ~ Entertainment WeeklyNew York Times National Best-Seller.

Stiff News. Catherine Aird. Read by Bruce Montague. 4 CDs. 2000. audio compact disk 39.95 (CAB1686) AudioGO.

***Stiff Upper Lip, Jeeves.** P. G. Wodehouse. Narrated by Richard Briers & Michael Hordern. (Running Time: 3 hrs. 0 mins. 0 sec.). (ENG., 2010. audio compact disk 29.95 (978-0-563-51007-9(2)) Pub: AudioGO. Dist(s): Perseus Dist

Stiff Upper Lip, Jeeves. unabr. ed. P. G. Wodehouse. Read by Jonathan Cecil. (Jeeves & Wooster Ser.). 2005. 27.95 (978-1-57270-483-1(7)) Pub: Audio Partners. Dist(s): PerseuPGW
Bertie Wooster's blissful bachelorhood is in dire peril: unless he can patch things up between Gussie Fink-Nottle and the horrifying Madeline Bassett, Bertie must wed the heiress of Totleigh Towers. Disaster looms as Gussie rebels against his new vegetarian diet, and a furtive supply of meat pies from a pretty cook lead him further astray. Only Jeeves can save Bertie from entombment at Totleigh, but Jeeves so strongly disapproves of his young master's new hat that Bertie may have to rely on his own wits for once.

Stiff Upper Lip, Jeeves. unabr. ed. P. G. Wodehouse. Narrated by Jonathan Cecil. (Running Time: 18840 sec.). (Jeeves & Wooster Ser.). (ENG.). 2005. audio compact disk 27.95 (978-1-57270-484-8(5)) Pub: AudioGO. Dist(s): Perseus Dist

Stiff Upper Lip, Jeeves. unabr. ed. P. G. Wodehouse. Read by Frederick Davidson. 5 cass. (Running Time: 7 hrs.). (Jeeves & Wooster Ser.). 1991. 39.95 (978-0-7861-0279-2(9), 1245) Blckstn Audio.
The feather-brained Bertie Wooster complicates his life by interceding with the predatory Madeline Bassett on behalf of his friend Gussie Fink-Nottle & finds himself entangled in terrifying misunderstandings. In the mounting storm clouds on the Wooster horizon there is but one ray of comfort - the presence of Jeeves, steadfast & reassuring.

Stiff Upper Lip, Jeeves. unabr. ed. P. G. Wodehouse. Read by Frederick Davidson. (Running Time: 6 hrs. 0 mins.). 2010. 29.95 (978-1-4417-2010-8(3)); audio compact disk 55.00 (978-1-4417-2007-8(3)) Blckstn Audio.

Stig of the Dump. Clive King. Read by Martin Jarvis. 3 cass. (Running Time: 3 hrs. 45 min.). (J). (gr. 1-4). (CC/006) C to C Cassettes.
Stig is a resourceful Stone-Age man who lives at the bottom of a chalk pit. Barney is his young friend. Together they enjoy a series of funny & exciting adventures.

Stigma: Program from the Award Winning Public Radio Serie. Interview. Hosted by Fred Goodwin. 1 CD. (Running Time: 1 hr.). 2003. audio compact disk 21.95 (978-1-932479-96-6(1), LCM 283) Lichtenstein Creat.
n this hour, we tackle the stigma of mental illness. Guests include Isaac Brown, director of advocacy and housing services for Baltic Street Mental Health Services; Dr. Patrick Corrigan, principal investigator for the Chicago Consortium for Stigma Research and the executive director of the University of Chicago Center for Psychiatric Rehabilitation; Dr. Michael Hogan, chair of the President's New Freedom Commission on Mental Health and director of the Ohio Department of Mental Health; Tom Johnson, the former president and CEO of CNN; and Bill Lichtenstein and June Peoples, the senior executive producer and executive producer of The Infinite Mind and the co-producers and co-directors of a new documentary film about mental illness called West 47th Street.

Stigmata. collector's ed. Phyllis Alesia Perry. Read by Mary Peiffer. 5 cass. (Running Time: 7 hrs. 30 min.). 2000. 40.00 (978-0-7366-5103-5(9)) Books on Tape.
The story of a young woman, Lizzie, whose life is changed when she inherits a trunk from her grandmother. In the trunk is a diary written by an ancestor, Ayo, while on passage to America on a slave ship & a guilt into which the grandmother has stitched the family's history & dreams. Slowly Lizzie begins to believe that she is possessed by the reincarnated figures of Ayo's story. When stigmata marks, apparently made by iron chains, appear on her wrists & legs, her family commits her to an asylum, wondering whether she made the marks herself or has made a frighteningly real connection to the past.

Still a Gypsy. unabr. ed. Toni Lamond. Read by Toni Lamond. (Running Time: 36900 sec.). 2007. audio compact disk 93.95 (978-1-74093-985-0(9), 9781740939850) Pub: Bolinda Pubng AUS. Dist(s): Bolinda Pub Inc

***Still Alice.** unabr. ed. Lisa Genova. Read by Lisa Genova. 7 CDs. (Running Time: 8 hrs.). 2010. audio compact disk 19.99 (978-1-4423-3620-9(X)) Pub: S&S Audio. Dist(s): S and S Inc

Still Amazed: Live. Contrib. by B. J. Davis & Luke Gambill. 2007. audio compact disk 10.00 (978-5-557-61405-4(2), Brentwood-Benson Music) Brentwood Music.

Still Amazed: Live. Directed By Dale Mowery. Contrib. by Luke Gambill & B. J. Davis. 2007. audio compact disk 16.98 (978-5-557-61407-8(9), Brentwood-Benson Music) Brentwood Music.

Still Amazed: Live: Alto. Contrib. by Johnathan Crumpton et al. Prod. by Luke Gambill & B. J. Davis. 2007. audio compact disk 5.00 (978-5-557-61403-0(6), Brentwood-Benson Music) Brentwood Music.

Still Amazed: Live: Bass. Contrib. by Jonathan Crumpton et al. Prod. by Luke Gambill & B. J. Davis. 2007. audio compact disk 5.00 (978-5-557-61401-6(X), Brentwood-Benson Music) Brentwood Music.

Still Amazed: Live: Satb. Contrib. by B. J. Davis & Luke Gambill. 2007. audio compact disk 90.00 (978-5-557-61406-1(0), Brentwood-Benson Music) Brentwood Music.

Still Amazed: Live: Soprano. Contrib. by Luke Gambill. Prod. by Luke Gambill & B. J. Davis. Prod. by B. J. Davis. 2007. audio compact disk 5.00 (978-5-557-61404-7(4), Brentwood-Benson Music) Brentwood Music.

Still Amazed: Live: Tenor. Contrib. by Jonathan Crumpton et al. Prod. by Luke Gambill & B. J. Davis. 2007. audio compact disk 5.00 (978-5-557-61402-3(8), Brentwood-Benson Music) Brentwood Music.

Still Falls the Rain see Caedmon Treasury of Modern Poets Reading Their Own Poetry

Still Going: The Added Years. Donna Henson. Read by Donna Henson. 1 cass. (Running Time: 90 min.). 1994. 8.95 (1162) Am Fed Astrologers.

Still Just Grace. unabr. ed. Charise Mericle Harper. Narrated by Michele O. Medlin. 2 cass. (Running Time: 1 hr. 46 mins.). (Just Grace Ser.). (J). (gr. 2-4). 2008. 25.75 (978-1-4281-9628-5(5)); audio compact disk 25.75 (978-1-4281-9633-9(1)) Recorded Bks.

Still Life. abr. ed. Joy Fielding. Read by Kymberly Dakin. (Running Time: 6 hrs.). 2010. audio compact disk 14.99 (978-1-4233-6266-1(7), 9781423362661, BCD Value Price) Brilliance Audio.

Still Life. abr. unabr. ed. Louise Penny. Read by Ralph Cosham. 8 cass. (Running Time: 34200 sec.). (Chief Inspector Armand Gamache Ser.: BK. 1). 2006. 29.95 (978-0-7861-4536-2(6)) Blckstn Audio.

Still Life. abr. unabr. ed. Louise Penny. Read by Ralph Cosham. 9 CDs. (Running Time: 34200 sec.). (Chief Inspector Armand Gamache Ser.: Bk. 1). 2006. audio compact disk 29.95 (978-0-7861-7142-2(1)); audio compact disk 29.95 (978-0-7861-7605-2(9)) Blckstn Audio.

Still Life. unabr. ed. Joy Fielding. Read by Kymberly Dakin. (Running Time: 11 hrs.). 2009. 39.97 (978-1-4233-6264-7(0), 9781423362647, BADLE); 39.97 (978-1-4233-6262-3(4), 9781423362623, Brlnc Audio MP3 Lib); 24.99 (978-1-4233-6263-0(2), 9781423362630, BAD); 24.99 (978-1-4233-6261-6(6), 9781423362616, Brilliance MP3); audio compact disk 97.97 (978-1-4233-6260-9(8), 9781423362609, BriAudCD Unabrid); audio compact disk 36.99 (978-1-4233-6259-3(4), 9781423362593, Bril Audio CD Unabri) Brilliance Audio.

Still Life. unabr. ed. Louise Penny. Read by Ralph Cosham. (Running Time: 34200 sec.). (Chief Inspector Armand Gamache Ser.: Bk. 1). 2006. 72.95 (978-0-7861-4636-9(2)); audio compact disk 90.00 (978-0-7861-6832-3(3)) Blckstn Audio.

Still Life with Crows. abr. ed. Douglas Preston & Lincoln Child. Read by Rene Auberjonois. (Pendergast Ser.: No. 4). (ENG.). 2005. 14.98 (978-1-59483-286-4(2)) Pub: Hachet Audio. Dist(s): HachBkGrp

Still Life with Crows. abr. ed. Douglas Preston & Lincoln Child. Read by Rene Auberjonois. (Running Time: 6 hrs.). (ENG.). 2009. 49.98 (978-1-60024-975-4(2)) Pub: Hachet Audio. Dist(s): HachBkGrp

Still Lives. unabr. ed. Anne Cato. Read by Patricia Gillimore. 9 cass. (Running Time: 13 hrs.). 1998. 79.95 (978-1-86042-395-6(7), 23957) Pub: Soundings Ltd GBR. Dist(s): Ulverscroft US
When Louise's French cousin Pierre visits her, it is almost inevitable that he will become the catalyst for a reappraisal of a marriage already at risk. As he lays siege to Louise's heart, she forms an unlikely friendship with a visiting American professor, tends her beloved garden & tries to remain a good wife.

Still Me: A Life. abr. ed. Christopher Reeve. Read by Christopher Reeve. 2 cass. (Running Time: 3 hrs.). 1998. 16.85 Set. (978-0-00-105538-4(0)) Zondervan.
On the third jump of a riding competition, Reeve was thrown head first from his horse in an accident that broke his neck & left him unable to move or breathe. Reeve has not only survived, he has fought for h imself, & for his family.

Still Me: A Life, Set. abr. ed. Christopher Reeve. Read by Christopher Reeve. 2 cass. 1999. 18.95 (FS9-43193) Highsmith.

***Still Midnight.** Denise Mina. Narrated by Jane MacFarlane. (Running Time: 10 hrs. 30 mins. 0 sec.). (ENG.). 2010. audio compact disk 29.95 (978-1-60283-909-0(3)) Pub: AudioGO. Dist(s): Perseus Dist

***Still Midnight.** unabr. ed. Denise Mina. Narrated by Jane McFarlane. 1 Playaway. (Running Time: 11 hrs.). 2010. 89.95 (978-0-7927-7063-3(3)); 54.95 (978-0-7927-7062-6(5)); audio compact disk 89.95 (978-0-7927-6307-9(6)) AudioGO.

***Still Missing.** unabr. ed. Chevy Stevens. (Running Time: 11 hrs.). 2010. 24.99 (978-1-4418-4323-4(X), 9781441843234, BAD); 39.97 (978-1-4418-4322-7(1), 9781441843227, Brlnc Audio MP3 Lib); 39.97 (978-1-4418-4324-1(8), 9781441843241, BADLE) Brilliance Audio.

***Still Missing.** unabr. ed. Chevy Stevens. Read by Angela Dawe. (Running Time: 11 hrs.). 2010. 24.99 (978-1-4418-4321-0(3), 9781441843210, Brilliance MP3); audio compact disk 79.97 (978-1-4418-4320-3(5), 9781441843203, BriAudCD Unabrid); audio compact disk 29.99 (978-1-4418-4319-7(1), 9781441843197, Bril Audio CD Unabri) Brilliance Audio.

Still of the Night. Meagan McKinney. Narrated by George Guidall. 8 cass. (Running Time: 10 hrs. 30 mins.). 74.00 (978-1-4025-3249-8(0)) Recorded Bks.

Still on the Journey. Perf. by Sweet Honey in the Rock. 1 cass. (Running Time: 61 min.). 1993. 9.98 (978-1-56628-023-5(0), EB2525/WB4-42536) MFLP CA.
A capella songs in the African-American traditions gospel, congregational, jazz, folk, R & B, & rap. Messages of love & positive social change.

Still Practising: From Country Vet to the Animal Hospital. David Grant. 8 vols. (Running Time: 12 hrs.). 2003. audio compact disk 79.95 (978-0-7540-5589-1(2)) Pub: Chivers Audio Bks GBR. Dist(s): AudioGO

Still Practising: From Country Vet to the Animal Hospital. David Grant. 2003. 69.95 (978-0-7540-0974-0(2)) Pub: Chivers Audio Bks GBR. Dist(s): AudioGO

Still Ranting after All These Years. abr. ed. Dennis Miller. Read by Dennis Miller. 1 CD. (Running Time: 1 hr. 30 mins.). 2004. audio compact disk 22.00 (978-0-06-053100-3(2)) HarperCollins Pubs.

***Still Ranting after All These Years.** abr. ed. Dennis Miller. Read by Dennis Miller. (ENG.). 2004. (978-0-06-078263-4(3), Harper Audio); (978-0-06-081393-2(8), Harper Audio) HarperCollins Pubs.

Still Standing. Perf. by Stevie Wonder & Williams Brothers. 1 cass. 1997. audio compact disk 15.99 CD. (D5212) Diamante Music Grp.
The Brothers promise that this album will give you more of the brothers of old, the sounds, styles, harmonies & messages that helped propel them to the top & make them one of the most consistent record sellers of all time.

Still Summer. abr. ed. Jacquelyn Mitchard. Read by Susan Ericksen. (Running Time: 6 hrs.). (ENG.). 2007. 24.98 (978-1-60024-192-5(1)) Pub: Hachet Audio. Dist(s): HachBkGrp

Still Surprised: A Memoir of a Life in Leadership. unabr. ed. Warren Bennis. Read by Sean Pratt & Erik Synnestvedt. (Running Time: 8 hrs.). (ENG.). 2010. audio compact disk 29.98 (978-1-59659-451-7(9), GildAudio) Pub: Gildan Media. Dist(s): HachBkGrp

Still the Mind: An Introduction to Meditation. unabr. ed. Alan Watts. Read by Alan Watts. 2 CDs. (Running Time: 1 hr. 30 mins. 0 sec.). (ENG.). 2005. audio compact disk 17.95 (978-1-57731-495-0(6)) Pub: New Wrld Lib. Dist(s): PerseuPGW
During the last decade of his life, Alan Watts lectured extensively as he traveled across the country. He often accompanied his talks with guided meditation sessions & contemplative rituals designed to instruct his audiences in the art of meditation. Features thoughts on the purity of everyday experiences & the path of soulful contemplation.

Still the Mind: Simple Breathing Practices for Inner Peace. unabr. ed. Bodhipaksa. 2009. audio compact disk 19.95 (978-1-59179-683-1(0)) Sounds True.

Still the Same Me. 1 CD. (Running Time: 42 min.). 2000. audio compact disk 14.98 Rounder Kids Mus Dist.
A spirited collection of songs centered around the experiences of children everywhere.

Still the Same Me. 1 cass. (Running Time: 42 min.). (J). (gr. k-4). 2000. 9.98 Rounder Kids Mus Dist.

***Still Valley.** 2010. audio compact disk (978-1-59171-182-7(7)) Falcon Picture.

Still Voices. Maria Barrett. Read by Anna Bentinck. 11 CDs. (Running Time: 12 hrs. 57 mins.). (Isis (CDs) Ser.). (J). 2004. audio compact disk 99.95 (978-0-7531-2330-0(4)) Pub: ISIS Lrg Prnt GBR. Dist(s): Ulverscroft US

Still Voices. unabr. ed. Maria Barrett. Read by Anna Bentinck. 9 cass. (Running Time: 12 hrs. 57 min.). (Isis Ser.). (J). 2003. 76.95 (978-0-7531-1754-5(1)) Pub: ISIS Lrg Prnt GBR. Dist(s): Ulverscroft US
Young history professor Charles Meredith may be researching a book about a Victorian crime of passion, but passion is something lacking in his own life. Student Claire Thompson is a loner, who fills the gaps where her friends should be with fantasy. And on the night she boasts that her professor Charles Meredith is taking her to supper, she disappears . . .As Charles searches for the woman who can prove his innocence, as the police-hunt for Claire intensifies help comes from a silent voice, a voice that speaks from the grave.

Still Water Saints. unabr. ed. Alex Espinoza. (Running Time: 8.5 hrs. NaN mins.). 2009. 29.95 (978-1-4332-3501-6(3)); audio compact disk 70.00 (978-1-4332-3498-9(X)); audio compact disk 54.95 (978-1-4332-3497-2(1)) Blckstn Audio.

Still Waters. Judith Cutler. 2008. 54.95 (978-0-7531-2985-2(X)); audio compact disk 79.95 (978-0-7531-2986-9(8)) Pub: Isis Pubng Ltd GBR. Dist(s): Ulverscroft US

Still Waters. Stanton Lanier. (Running Time: 52 mins.). 2002. audio compact disk 15.00 (978-0-9746289-0-5(5)) S Lanier.

Still Waters. abr. ed. Tami Hoag. Read by Joyce Bean. 4 cass. (Running Time: 6 hrs.). 2001. 53.25 (978-1-58788-629-4(4), 1587886294, Lib Edit) Brilliance Audio.

Still Waters. abr. ed. Tami Hoag. Read by Joyce Bean. (Running Time: 6 hrs.). 2006. 39.25 (978-1-4233-0222-3(2), 9781423302223, Brlnc Audio MP3 Lib); 24.95 (978-1-4233-0221-6(4), 9781423302216, Brilliance MP3); 39.25 (978-1-4233-0224-7(9), 9781423302247, BADLE); 24.95 (978-1-4233-0223-0(0), 9781423302230, BAD) Brilliance Audio.

Still Waters. unabr. ed. Claudia K. Allen. Perf. by Deanna Dunagan et al. 1 cass. (Running Time: 1 hr. 40 min.). 1992. 19.95 (978-1-58081-100-2(0)) L A Theatre.
The setting is rural Michigan in the 1940's, the situation is a soft spoken woman who wants to keep her right to preach. Rev. Myrtle took over the pulpit of her church when the men went off to World War II. But when the men come back, they take Myrtle's ministry away from her. It seems she was good enough to inspire the congregation in wartime but peace is different "Rosie the Riveter" should go quietly back to the kitchen. But Myrtle won't be "defrocked" without a fight.

Still Waters. unabr. ed. John Harvey. Narrated by Ron Keith. 8 cass. (Running Time: 10 hrs. 45 mins.). (Charlie Resnick Mystery Ser.: Vol. 9). 2000. 70.00 (978-0-7887-3057-3(6), 95751E7) Recorded Bks.
When the battered body of a young woman is found floating in a city canal, police suspect a serial killer. When a second body is found, detective Resnick begins to think otherwise. His girlfriend knew this woman had a jealous, abusive husband.

Still Waters. unabr. ed. Judith Saxton. Read by Carole Boyd. 16 cass. (Running Time: 24 hrs.). 2000. 99.95 (978-0-7540-0034-1(6), CAB 1457) Pub: Chivers Audio Bks GBR. Dist(s): AudioGO
Tess Delamere yearns to discover more about her dead mother, but her father will not divulge the secrets of the past. As Tess grows up, she begins to put together the pieces of the puzzle herself. She is both helped and hindered by the two men in her life: Andy, her childhood companion, and Ashley, who falls in love with her as a young woman.

Stillness at Appomattox. abr. ed. Bruce Catton. Read by Dan Lazar. 3 cass. 17.85 (E-202) Audio Bk.

Stillness in Motion: Tranquil Music from Emmy Winning Artist. Jim Oliver. 1 cass. (Running Time: 1 hr.). (Art of Relaxation Ser.). 9.95 (978-1-55961-110-7(3)) Relaxtn Co.

Stillness Shall Be the Dancing: Feminine & Masculine in Emerging Balance. Marion Woodman. 2 cass. (Carolyn & Ernest Fay Series in Analytical Psychology: No. 4). (ENG.). 1994. 19.95 (978-0-89096-605-1(2)) Tex AM Univ Pr.
Psychology.

Stillness Speaks. Eckhart Tolle. Read by Eckhart Tolle. (Playaway Adult Nonfiction Ser.). (ENG.). 2009. 40.00 (978-1-60775-592-0(0)) Find a World.

Stillness Speaks. unabr. ed. Eckhart Tolle. Read by Eckhart Tolle. 3 CDs. (Running Time: 1 hr. 30 mins. 0 sec.). (ENG.). 2003. audio compact disk 21.95 (978-1-57731-419-6(0)) Pub: New Wrld Lib. Dist(s): PerseuPGW
Illuminates the fundamental elements of his teaching. He continues to address the spiritual needs of our generation by drawing from the essence of spiritual truths at the core of all spiritual traditions, while also advancing this wisdom for our generation. As such, this book is paradoxically both ancient and contemporary.

Stillness, Time & the Brain, Set. unabr. ed. J. Krishnamurti & David Bohm. Read by J. Krishnamurti & David Bohm. Ed. by Krishnamurti Foundation of America Staff. 3 cass. (Running Time: 90 min. per cass.). 1991. 29.00 Boxed Set. (ASTB65) Krishnamurti.
This early recording of Krishnamurti & Dr. David Bohm recorded in Gestad, Switzerland in 1965 offers an in-depth exploration of how the brain cells work, & whether stillness has any movement in time.

Stillwater Smith. unabr. ed. Frank Roderus. Read by Jack Sondericker. 4 cass. (Running Time: 5 hrs.). 2001. 26.95 (978-1-55686-999-0(1)) Books in Motion.
Civil War veteran Stillwater Smith is pushed into action when a wealthy landowner launches a scheme to control area water rights.

Stilwell & the American Experience in China, 1911-45. unabr. ed. Barbara W. Tuchman. Read by Pam Ward. (Running Time: 28 hrs. 0 mins.). (ENG.). 2009. 44.95 (978-1-4332-9297-2(1)); 72.95 (978-1-4332-9330-6(7)); 85.95 (978-1-4332-9293-4(9)); audio compact disk 160.00 (978-1-4332-9294-1(7)) Blckstn Audio.

Stilwell & the American Experience in China, 1911-45, Pts. A & B. unabr. ed. Barbara W. Tuchman. Read by Walter Zimmerman. 10 cass. (Running Time: 15 hrs.). 1987. 80.00 (978-0-7366-1238-6(0), 2156-A) Books on Tape.
An examination of America's relationship with China from 1911 to 1945, & a personal portrait of General Stilwell. Part 1 of 2.

Stimuli. unabr. ed. Ronald Knox & Jo Tomalin. 6 cass. 24.95 set. (941) Ignatius Pr.
A collection of very short sermons which first appeared in The London Times. The seventy-one witty pieces focus on liturgical themes, saints, & details of day to day life. At one a day, ten weeks of spiritual enjoyment.

Stingy Witch Vol. 1: Stories & Songs That Encourage Children to Listen & Join in. unabr. ed. Charlotte Rivera. Read by Charlotte Rivera. Perf. by Dennis O'Hanlon. 1 cass. (Running Time: 30 min.). (J). (ps-1). 1997. 10.00 (978-0-9671654-1-7(5)) Charlotte Rivera.
Three stories & eight songs, both traditional & original.

Stink: The Incredible Shrinking Kid. unabr. ed. Prod. by Listening Library Staff. 1 cass. (Running Time: 41 mins.). 2005. 15.00 (978-0-307-20668-8(8), Listening Lib); audio compact disk 17.00 (978-0-307-20669-5(6), Listening Lib) Pub: Random Audio Pubg. Dist(s): NetLibrary CO

Stink & the Incredible Super-Galactic Jawbreaker. unabr. ed. Megan McDonald. Read by Nancy Cartwright. 1 CD. (Running Time: 41 mins.). (Stink Ser.). (J). 2006. audio compact disk 17.00 (978-0-7393-3589-5(8), Listening Lib); 15.00 (978-0-7393-3588-8(X), Listening Lib) Pub: Random Audio Pubg. Dist(s): Random
Stink Moody can't believe it - he gets a ten-pound box of 21,280 jawbreakers (for FREE!), just for writing a letter to the candy company! Soon, he's writing more letters... and the packages of free stuff just keep coming. Among all the packages, it's easy to miss a small envelope with scribbly writing. But one thing Stink doesn't miss is that his best friend, Webster, is looking as mad as a hornet!.

Stink & the Incredible Super-Galactic Jawbreaker. unabr. ed. Megan McDonald. Read by Nancy Cartwright. 1 CD. (Running Time: 3060 sec.). (Stink Ser.). (ENG.). (J). (gr. 1-3). 2006. audio compact disk 15.95 (978-0-7393-3555-0(3), ImaginStudio) Pub: Random Audio Pubg. Dist(s): Random

Stink & the World's Worst Super-Stinky Sneakers / Stink & the Great Guinea Pig Express. unabr. ed. Megan McDonald. Read by Nancy Cartwright. 2 CDs. (Running Time: 1 hr. 37 mins.). (Stink Ser.). (J). (gr. 2-4). 2008. audio compact disk 24.00 (978-0-7393-6387-4(5), Listening Lib) Pub: Random Audio Pubg. Dist(s): Random

Stink & the World's Worst Super-Stinky Sneakers / Stink & the Great Guinea Pig Express. unabr. ed. Megan McDonald. Read by Nancy Cartwright. (Running Time: 5820 sec.). (ENG.). (J). (gr. 1-3). 2008. audio compact disk 19.95 (978-0-7393-6386-7(7), Listening Lib) Pub: Random Audio Pubg. Dist(s): Random

***Stink: Solar System Superhero.** unabr. ed. Megan McDonald. Read by Nancy Cartwright. (ENG.). (J). 2010. audio compact disk 15.00 (978-0-307-73848-6(5), Listening Lib) Pub: Random Audio Pubg. Dist(s): Random

Stinkers in the Church. 18.3. 2006. 12.00 (978-1-59128-596-0(8)); 12.00 (978-1-59128-598-4(4)) Canon Pr ID.

Stinking Great Lie. unabr. ed. Catherine Jinks. Read by Soula Alexandra. 2 cass. (Running Time: 2 hrs. 30 mins.). 2002. (978-1-74030-216-6(8)) Bolinda Pubng AUS.

Stinky Cheese Gypsies. unabr. ed. Stephen Axelsen. Read by Stanley McGeagh. (Running Time: 7200 sec.). (Piccolo & Annabelle Ser.). (J). 2007. audio compact disk 43.95 (978-1-74093-878-5(X)) Pub: Bolinda Pubng AUS. Dist(s): Bolinda Pub Inc

Stinky Feet & Other Unpleasant Items. Karen Jean Matsko Hood. 2010. audio compact disk 24.95 (978-1-59210-916-6(0)) Whspmg Pine.

Stir of Echoes. unabr. ed. Richard Matheson. (Running Time: 7 hrs. NaN mins.). 2009. 29.95 (978-1-4332-6748-2(9)); audio compact disk 44.95 (978-1-4332-6744-4(6)) Blckstn Audio.

Stir of Echoes. unabr. ed. Richard Matheson. Read by Scott Brick. 6 CDs. (Running Time: 7 hrs.). 2009. audio compact disk 60.00 (978-1-4332-6745-1(4)) Blckstn Audio.

Stir Yourself Up. Kenneth Copeland. 1 cass. 1990. 5.00 (978-0-88114-828-2(8)) K Copeland Pubns.
Biblical teaching on powerful living.

Stirring It Up: How to Make Money & Save the World. abr. unabr. ed. Gary Hirshberg. Read by Gary Hirshberg. (Running Time: 21600 sec.). 2008. audio compact disk 29.95 (978-1-4013-8890-4(6), Hyperion Audio) Pub: Hyperion. Dist(s): HarperCollins Pubs

Stitch 'n Bitch: The Knitter's Handbook. Debbie Stoller. 2007. audio compact disk 19.95 (978-0-9796073-2-5(9)) Knitting Out.

Stitch 'n Bitch: The Knitter's Handbook. abr. ed. Debbie Stoller. Read by Debbie Stoller. (YA). 2008. 54.99 (978-1-60514-924-0(1)) Find a World.

Stitches in Time. abr. ed. Barbara Michaels, pseud. Read by Barbara Rosenblat. 2 cass. (Running Time: 3 hrs.). 1995. 17.00 (978-0-694-51553-0(1)) HarperCollins Pubs.

***Stitches in Time.** abr. ed. Barbara Michaels, pseud. Read by Barbara Rosenblat. (ENG.). 2005. (978-0-06-088899-2(7), Harper Audio); (978-0-06-089397-2(4), Harper Audio) HarperCollins Pubs.

Stitches in Time. unabr. ed. Barbara Michaels, pseud. Read by Frances Cassidy. 9 cass. (Running Time: 13 hrs. 30 min.). 1995. 72.00 (978-0-7366-3084-9(8), 3764) Books on Tape.
The evil aura woven into an antique bridal quilt possesses the thoughts & deeds of a superstitious woman. Friends may suffer.

Stitches in Time, unabr. ed. Barbara Michaels, pseud. Narrated by Barbara Rosenblat. 10 cass. (Running Time: 13 hrs. 30 mins.). 85.00 (978-0-7887-0339-3(0), 94531E7) Recorded Bks.
Rachel Grant has never been able to resist the allure of finely crafted quilts & clothes from centuries past. So when an antique bridal quilt mysteriously appears in the vintage clothing store where she works, Rachel is instantly fascinated. But woven into the quilt's stitches is a sinister legacy of revenge & deception that Rachel is powerless to escape. Available to libraries only.

S.T.O., Set. Henri Amouroux. 2 cass. (Francais sous l'occupation Ser.). (FRE.). 1991. 26.95 (1234-RF) Olivia & Hill.
Pursuit of the Jews.

Stock Brokers & Investment Bankers. Narrated by Louis Rukeyser. 2 cass. (Running Time: 2 hrs. 30 mins.). (Secrets of the Great Investors Ser.: Vol. 12). 2003. 17.95 (978-1-56823-064-1(8)) Pub: Knowledge Prod. Dist(s): APG
Learn about the timeless strategies, tactics, judgments, & principles that have produced great wealth. Hear history's great figures & personalities - in their own words - describe their techniques & achievements in finance & investing. Now you can listen to these great lessons while commuting, traveling, walking...anytime your hands are busy, but your mind is not.

Stock Car Racing. Tom Greve. (Rourke Discovery Library (CD-ROM) Ser.). (J). (gr. 3-7). 2008. 24.95 (978-1-60472-774-6(8)) Rourke FL.

Stock Frauds, Manipulations & Insider Trading. Narrated by Louis Rukeyser. 2 cass. (Running Time: 2 hrs. 30 mins.). (Secrets of the Great Investors Ser.: Vol. 11). 2003. 17.95 (978-1-56823-062-7(1)) Pub: Knowledge Prod. Dist(s): APG

Stock Frauds, Manipulations, & Insider Trading. unabr. abr. ed. Read by Louis Rukeyser. (Running Time: 10800 sec.). (Secrets of the Great Investors Ser.). 2006. audio compact disk 25.95 (978-0-7861-6526-1(X)) Pub: Blckstn Audio. Dist(s): NetLibrary CO

Stock Investing. 2nd abr. ed. Paul Mladjenovic. Read by Brett Barry. (Running Time: 12600 sec.). (For Dummies Ser.). 2007. audio compact disk 14.95 (978-0-06-117584-8(6)) HarperCollins Pubs.

***Stock Investing for Dummies 2nd Ed.** abr. ed. Paul Mladjenovic. Read by Brett Barry. (ENG.). 2006. (978-0-06-128731-2(8), Harper Audio); (978-0-06-128732-9(6), Harper Audio) HarperCollins Pubs.

Stock Investing for Everyone. unabr. ed. David K. Luhman. Read by David K. Luhman. 1 cass. (Running Time: 1 hr. 30 min.). (Personal Finance for Everyone Ser.: Vol. 6). 1996. 9.00 (978-1-889297-16-3(X)) Numen Lumen.
History of stock investing, indicators of a stock's value, what stocks really represent, why stocks increase in value over time, the Tokyo crash of the 1990s, buying stocks on margin, IPOs, types of stocks & exchanges, ways to invest in stocks, buying through a broker, stock buying techniques, stock investment techniques, foreign stocks.

Stock Market, Vol. 32. Tracy Herrick. 1 cass. (Running Time: 45 min.). (Money Talk Ser.). 1986. 7.95 B & H Comm.
Examines new information about the stock market that every investor must know to avoid costly trading errors. Explores Key questions & essentials all investors should know before opening an account or trading a share.

Stock Market Crash of 1929. unabr. ed. Aron Abrams. 1 CD. (Running Time: 90 min.). 2002. audio compact disk 12.95 (978-0-929071-78-7(6)) B-B Audio.

Stock Market Crash of 1929. unabr. ed. Aron Abrams. Read by Huey James. 1 cass. (Running Time: 1 hr.). 1994. 7.95 (978-1-882071-22-7(0), 024) B-B Audio.
Taken from the actual newspaper reports written in 1929 and the 1930s, this captures the sense of immediacy thats missing from present-day historical perspectives. Covers causes, results, and short-term effects on individuals.

Stockbroker's Clerk see Memoirs of Sherlock Holmes

Stockbroker's Clerk. 1981. (S-39) Jimcin Record.

Stockholm Syndicate. unabr. ed. Colin Forbes. Read by Sean Barrett. 8 cass. (Running Time: 11 hrs.). 2001. 69.95 (978-1-85089-690-6(9), 91104) Pub: ISIS Audio GBR. Dist(s): Ulverscroft US
Jules Beaurain is the commander of Telescope; unofficial, unauthorized & utterly effective, it's the toughest strike force in the world. Now Telescope is confronted by its most deadly enemy so far - The Syndicate. Helped by contacts in the twilight world of security & intelligence, Beaurain aims to locate & eliminate his enemy's mysterious leaders.

Stockley's Drug Interactions 8 CD-ROM (Personal User) Ed. by Karen Baxter. 2007. audio compact disk 250.00 (978-0-85369-755-8(8)) Pub: Pharmaceutical Pr GBR. Dist(s): SmithFulServ

Stocks, Bonds, Bills & Inflation Valuation Edition 2004 Data CD. ValuSource Staff. (ValuSource Accounting Software Products Ser.). 2004. audio compact disk 65.00 (978-0-471-67772-7(8), Valu-Source) Wiley US.

Stocks for the Long Run: The Definitive Guide to Financial Market Returns & Long-Term Investment Strategies. abr. ed. Jeremy J. Siegel. 4 CDs. (Running Time: 4 hrs. 30 mins.). (McGraw Hill Audiobks.). 2003. audio compact disk 28.00 (978-0-9724889-1-4(X)); 24.00 (978-0-9724462-3-5(0)) Pub: A Media Intl. Dist(s): Natl Bk Netwk
This book combines a compelling and timely portrait of today's turbulent stock market with the strategies, tools,and techniques investors need to maintain their focus and achieve meaningful stock returns over time.

Stoics & Epicureans. unabr. ed. Daryl Hale. Read by Lynn Redgrave. Ed. by John Lachs & Wendy McElroy. Prod. by Pat Childs. (Running Time: 9000 sec.). (World of Philosophy Ser.). 2006. audio compact disk 25.95 (978-0-7861-6625-1(8)) Pub: Blckstn Audio. Dist(s): NetLibrary CO

***Stokes Field Guide to Bird Songs: Eastern & Western Box Set.** abr. ed. Donald Stokes et al. Read by Donald Stokes et al. (Running Time: 8 hrs.). (ENG.). 2010. 29.98 (978-1-60941-255-5(9)) Pub: Hachet Audio. Dist(s): HachBkGrp

***Stokes Field Guide to Bird Songs: Eastern & Western Box Set.** abr. unabr. ed. Donald Stokes et al. Read by Donald Stokes et al. (Running Time: 8 hrs.). (ENG.). 2010. audio compact disk 39.98 (978-1-60788-763-8(0)) Pub: Hachet Audio. Dist(s): HachBkGrp

Stokes Field Guide to Bird Songs: Eastern Region. abr. unabr. ed. Donald Stokes et al. Read by Lang Elliot. (Running Time: 4 hrs.). (ENG.). 2009. 19.98 (978-1-60788-442-2(9)) Pub: Hachet Audio. Dist(s): HachBkGrp

***Stokes Field Guide to Bird Songs: Eastern Region.** abr. unabr. ed. Donald Stokes et al. Read by Lillian Stokes & Lang Elliot. (Running Time: 4 hrs.). (ENG.). 2010. audio compact disk 24.98 (978-1-60788-783-6(5)) Pub: Hachet Audio. Dist(s): HachBkGrp

Stokes Field Guide to Bird Songs: Western Region. abr. unabr. ed. Lang Elliot et al. Read by Lang Elliot. (Running Time: 3 hrs.). (ENG.). 2009. 24.98 (978-1-60788-444-6(5)) Pub: Hachet Audio. Dist(s): HachBkGrp

***Stokes Field Guide to Bird Songs: Western Region.** abr. unabr. ed. Lang Elliot et al. Read by Lang Elliot et al. (Running Time: 4 hrs.). (ENG.). 2010. audio compact disk 24.98 (978-1-60788-784-3(3)) Pub: Hachet Audio. Dist(s): HachBkGrp

Stolen Arrows. Don Pendleton. (Mack Bolan Ser.: No. 96). 2006. audio compact disk (978-1-59950-169-7(4)) GraphicAudio.

Stolen Bacillus. 1977. (N-9) Jimcin Record.

Stolen Blessings. Lawrence Sanders. 2004. 10.95 (978-0-7435-4682-9(2)) Pub: S&S Audio. Dist(s): S and S Inc

Stolen Child. unabr. ed. Keith Donohue. Read by Andy Paris & Jeff Woodman. 8 cass. (Running Time: 12 hrs.). 2006. 79.75 (978-1-4193-8922-1(X), 98341); audio compact disk 119.75 (978-1-4193-8924-5(6), C3692) Recorded Bks.

This critically acclaimed debut by breakout author Keith Donohue flawlessly blends fantasy and realism into an utterly unique fable - inspired by a W.B. Yeats poem - that has been described as a bedtime story for adults. Seven-year-old Henry Day is kidnapped and renamed "Aniday" by changelings, ageless beings who inhabit the woods near his home. The changelings also leave behind one of their own, who flawlessly impersonates Henry except for one noteworthy detail - the new Henry is a prodigiously talented pianist. Both Aniday and Henry settle comfortably enough into their new existences, but both are haunted by vague memories of their former lives.

Stolen Child. unabr. ed. Keith Donohue. 10 CDs. (Running Time: 43200 sec.). 2006. audio compact disk 34.99 (978-1-4193-7171-4(1)) Recorded Bks.

Stolen Cigar Case see Classic Detective Stories, Vol. II, A Collection

Stolen Cigar Case. Bret Harte. Jimcin Record.

Stolen from Gypsies. unabr. ed. Noble Smith. Read by Frederick Davidson. 6 cass. (Running Time: 8 hrs. 30 mins.). 2000. 44.95 (978-0-7861-1836-6(9), 2635) Blckstn Audio.

Stolen from Gypsies. unabr. ed. Noble Smith. Read by Frederick Davidson. 7 cass. (Running Time: 10 hrs.). 2000. 49.95 (978-0-7861-1936-3(5), 2707); audio compact disk 56.00 (978-0-7861-9836-8(2), 2635) Blckstn Audio.

During the era of the Napoleonic Wars, the backdrop of the story, you will meet the character Ambrogio Smythe, a hypochondriacal British nobleman, who leaves his ancestral estate in Warwickshire & makes his way to Italy, during the Peace of Amiens. He meets a wandering storyteller who spins him a magical yarn about a Gypsy babe kidnapped by a demon.

Stolen from Gypsies. unabr. ed. Noble Smith. Read by Frederick Davidson. 6 cass. (Running Time: 9 hrs.). 2001. 29.95 (978-0-7861-1912-7(8)) Blckstn Audio.

The listener is treated to a comedic tour de force that is on par with the works of other great comedic writers such as Shakespeare.

Stolen from Gypsies. unabr. ed. Noble Smith. Read by Frederick Davidson. 1 CD. (Running Time: 8 hrs.). 2001. audio compact disk 19.95 (2635) Blckstn Audio.

During the era of the Napoleonic Wars, the backdrop of the story, you will meet the character Ambrogio Smythe, a hypochondriacal British nobleman, who leaves his ancestral estate in Warwickshire & makes his way to Italy, during the Peace of Amiens. He meets a wandering storyteller who spins him a magical yarn about a Gypsy babe kidnapped by a demon.

Stolen Gods. unabr. ed. Jake Page. Read by Jonathan Marosz. 8 cass. (Running Time: 8 hrs.). 1993. 48.00 (978-0-7366-2546-3(1), 3297) Books on Tape.

Missing Hopi deities are linked to Santa Fe art dealer's death. Renowned sculptor & his Hopi girlfriend seek answers.

Stolen Innocence: My Story of Growing up in a Polygamous Sect, Becoming a Teenage Bride, & Breaking Free of Warren Jeffs. unabr. ed. Elissa Wall & Lisa Pulitzer. Narrated by Renée Raudman. (Running Time: 16 hrs. 0 mins. 0 sec.). (ENG.). 2008. audio compact disk 79.99 (978-1-4001-3790-9(X)) Pub: Tantor Media. Dist(s): IngramPubServ

Stolen Innocence: My Story of Growing up in a Polygamous Sect, Becoming a Teenage Bride, & Breaking Free of Warren Jeffs. unabr. ed. Elissa Wall & Lisa Pulitzer. Read by Renée Raudman. 12 CDs. (Running Time: 16 hrs. 0 mins. 0 sec.). (ENG.). 2008. audio compact disk 39.99 (978-1-4001-0790-2(3)); audio compact disk 29.99 (978-1-4001-5790-7(0)) Pub: Tantor Media. Dist(s): IngramPubServ

***Stolen Lives.** unabr. ed. Jassy Mackenzie. Read by To be announced. (Running Time: 8.5 hrs. NaN mins.). (Jade de Jong Investigations Ser.). (ENG.). 2011. 29.95 (978-1-4417-8186-4(2)) Blckstn Audio.

***Stolen Lives.** unabr. ed. Jassy Mackenzie. Read by To be Announced. (Running Time: 8.5 hrs. NaN mins.). (Jade de Jong Investigations Ser.). (ENG.). 2011. 54.95 (978-1-4417-8183-3(8)) Blckstn Audio.

***Stolen Lives.** unabr. ed. Jassy Mackenzie. Read by To be announced. (Running Time: 8.5 hrs. NaN mins.). (Jade de Jong Investigations Ser.). 2011. audio compact disk 29.95 (978-1-4417-8185-7(4)) Blckstn Audio.

***Stolen Lives.** unabr. ed. Jassy Mackenzie. Read by To be Announced. (Running Time: 8.5 hrs. NaN mins.). (Jade de Jong Investigations Ser.). (ENG.). 2011. audio compact disk 76.00 (978-1-4417-8184-0(6)) Blckstn Audio.

Stolen Lives: Twenty Years in a Desert Jail. Malika Oufkir.Tr. of Prisonniere. 2007. 19.98 (978-1-4013-8503-3(6)) Pub: Hyperion. Dist(s): HarperCollins Pubs

Stolen Lives: Twenty Years in a Desert Jail. abr. ed. Malika Oufkir & Michele Fitoussi. Read by Edita Brychta. (Running Time: 21600 sec.).Tr. of Prisonniere. 2006. audio compact disk 19.98 (978-1-4013-8493-7(5), Hyperion Audio) Pub: Hyperion. Dist(s): HarperCollins Pubs

***Stolen One.** unabr. ed. Suzanne Crowley. Read by Sarah Coomes. (ENG.). 2009. (978-0-06-190247-5(0), GreenwillowBks); (978-0-06-180954-5(3), GreenwillowBks) HarperCollins Pubs.

Stolen Season. abr. ed. Steve Hamilton. Read by Jim Bond. (Running Time: 14400 sec.). (Alex Mcknight Ser.). 2007. audio compact disk 14.99 (978-1-4233-1236-9(8), 9781423312369, BCD Value Price) Brilliance Audio.

Stolen Season. unabr. ed. Steve Hamilton. Read by Jim Bond. (Running Time: 9 hrs.). (Alex Mcknight Ser.). 2006. 39.25 (978-1-4233-0718-1(6), 9781423307181, BADLE); 24.95 (978-1-4233-0717-4(8), 9781423307174, BAD); 74.25 (978-1-4233-0712-9(7), 9781423307129, BrilAudUnabridg); audio compact disk 92.25 (978-1-4233-0714-3(3), 9781423307143, BriAudCD Unabrid); audio compact disk 39.25 (978-1-4233-0716-7(X), 9781423307167, Brlnc Audio MP3 Lib); audio compact disk 29.95 (978-1-4233-0713-6(5), 9781423307136, Bril Audio CD Unabri); audio compact disk 24.95 (978-1-4233-0715-0(1), 9781423307150, Brilliance MP3) Brilliance Audio.

Alex and his sometimes-partner Leon are waiting for the Fourth of July fireworks to begin when an antique boat runs into a line of railroad pilings, the only remains of an old lumber mill. Alex and Leon go out to rescue the passengers - three men, who are not seriously injured. Alex figures he'll never see the men again. But when they show up at the Glasgow Inn the next day, Alex discovers they've a connection to his friend Vinnie, and that they mean trouble. Five-hundred miles away, Alex's girlfriend, Natalie Reynaud, has her own problems. She's working undercover, part of a special task force dealing with the recent influx of illegal handguns in Toronto's inner-city. It's a dangerous job and now Alex has to worry about both her and Vinnie. The unthinkable happens, and Alex must decide how far he'll go to get revenge.

Stolen Secrets. unabr. ed. Jerry B. Jenkins. (Red Rock Mystery Ser.: No. 2). 2005. audio compact disk 14.99 (978-1-58926-887-6(3), 6887) Oasis Audio.

Stolen Secrets. unabr. ed. Jerry B. Jenkins & Chris Fabry. Read by Dramatized. (Red Rock Mystery Ser.). (J). 2007. 34.99 (978-1-60252-786-7(5)) Find a World.

Stolen Secrets. unabr. ed. Jerry B. Jenkins & Chris Fabry. (Running Time: 10800 sec.). (Red Rock Mystery Ser.: No. 2). (J). 2005. 11.99 (978-1-58926-886-9(5), 6886) Pub: Oasis Audio. Dist(s): TNT Media Grp

Stolen Secrets. unabr. ed. Jerry B. Jenkins & Chris Fabry. (Red Rock Mysteries Ser.). (ENG.). 2005. 10.49 (978-1-60814-356-6(2)) Oasis Audio.

***Stolen Throne.** unabr. ed. David Gaider. Narrated by Stephen Hoye. (Running Time: 13 hrs. 0 mins. 0 sec.). (Dragon Age Ser.). (ENG.). 2010. audio compact disk 69.99 (978-1-4001-4621-5(6)) Pub: Tantor Media. Dist(s): IngramPubServ

Stolen White Elephant see Classic Detective Stories, Vol. II, A Collection

Stolen White Elephant see Selected American Short Stories

Stolen White Elephant. unabr. ed. Mark Twain. 1 cass. (Running Time: 56 min.). Dramatization. 1977. 7.95 (D-3); 9.95 incl. follow along script. Jimcin Record.

Two hilarious parodies of the detective story.

Stolen Years, Set. unabr. ed. Elizabeth Lord. Read by Tanya Myers. 10 cass. (Running Time: 13 hrs. 15 min.). 1999. 98.95 (978-1-85903-283-1(4)) Pub: Magna Story GBR. Dist(s): Ulverscroft US

Arthur Bancroft is ambitious for his three daughters & his plans are well on course when his two eldest make good matches. Letty, the youngest, has an eligible suitor in David Baron when Arthur's wife dies, & he changes his mind, refusing to allow her to marry. He turns Letty into a domestic drudge, tied to house & shop while her sisters find joy in their marriages. As the First World War breaks out, Letty's passionate love for David can no longer be denied. As her lover sets off for the trenches, she realises that he has left a lasting legacy behind him.

Stomach Problems. Barrie Konicov. 1 cass. 11.98 (978-0-87082-367-1(1), 122) Potentials.

Author Barrie Konicov tells how & why your stomach hurts, how to deal with the situation without suffering further.

Stomp the Elephant in the Office (Book on CD) Craig W. Ross & Steven W. Vannoy. (ENG.). 2008. (978-0-9793768-1-8(5)) Wister Willows.

Stone Angel. abr. ed. Margaret Laurence. Adapted by James W. Nichol. Prod. by CBC Radio Staff. 3 cass. (Running Time: 3 hrs.). Dramatization. (Between the Covers Classics). (J). (gr. 9-12). 2003. 19.95 (978-0-86492-243-4(4)) Pub: Goose Ln Eds CAN. Dist(s): U Toronto Pr

Stone Angel. abr. ed. Margaret Laurence et al. Contrib. by James W. Nichol. 3 CDs. (Running Time: 3 hrs.). (ENG.). 2004. audio compact disk 24.95 (978-0-86492-393-6(7)) Pub: BTC Audiobks CAN. Dist(s): U Toronto Pr

Stone Angel. unabr. ed. Carol O'Connell. Read by Laural Merlington. (Running Time: 12 hrs.). 2009. 24.99 (978-1-4233-9070-1(9), 9781423390701, Brilliance MP3); 39.97 (978-1-4233-9071-8(7), 9781423390718, Brlnc Audio MP3 Lib); 24.99 (978-1-4233-9072-5(5), 9781423390725, BAD); 39.97 (978-1-4233-9073-2(3), 9781423390732, BADLE) Brilliance Audio.

***Stone Angel.** unabr. ed. Carol O'Connell. Read by Laural Merlington. (Running Time: 12 hrs.). 2010. audio compact disk 89.97 (978-1-4418-4058-5(3), 9781441840585, BriAudCD Unabrid); audio compact disk 29.99 (978-1-4418-4057-8(5), 9781441840578, Bril Audio CD Unabri) Brilliance Audio.

***Stone Arch Books (Audio CD - Complete Set Spring 2008)** (SAB-Marketing Ser.). (ENG.). 2008. audio compact disk 263.70 (978-1-4342-0655-8(6)) CapstoneDig.

Stone by Stone. Music by Michael John Poirier. 1990. 11.00 (978-1-58459-112-2(9), 002674); audio compact disk 16.00 (978-1-58459-113-9(7), 002678) Wrld Lib Pubns.

Stone by Stone. Mae Robertson. 2000. audio compact disk 15.00 Lyric Prtnrs.

Stone Carvers. abr. ed. Jane Urquhart. Narrated by Nicky Guadagni. 3 CDs. (Running Time: 4 hrs.). (ENG.). 2003. audio compact disk 24.95 (978-0-86492-366-0(X)) Pub: BTC Audiobks CAN. Dist(s): U Toronto Pr

Sweeping across three countries and two war-torn centuries, Jane Urquhart's mesmerizing fifth novel interweaves the stories of long-estranged siblings Klara and Tilman Becker with that of a visionary German priest and the obsessive real-life sculptor who created Canada's Vimy Ridge memorial.

Stone Circle: Guided Shamanic Journey. Perf. by Alexander Alich. Prod. by Alexander Alich. Tr. by Regina Revermann from ENG. Kati Meden. 1 CD. (Running Time: 66 Minutes). (GER.). 2002. audio compact disk 17.00 (978-0-9710275-0-3(1), FoxTales) FoxFire Institute.

Guided Shamanic Journey with S. Alexander Alich, Director of FoxFire Institute of Shamanic Studies.

Stone Cold. David Baldacci. (Camel Club Ser.: No. 3). 2007. audio compact disk 49.99 (978-1-60252-232-9(4)) Find a World.

Stone Cold. abr. ed. David Baldacci. Read by Ron McLarty. (Running Time: 6 hrs.). (Camel Club Ser.: No. 3). (ENG.). 2007. 14.98 (978-1-60024-049-2(6)) Pub: Hachet Audio. Dist(s): HachBkGrp

Stone Cold. abr. ed. David Baldacci. Read by Ron McLarty. (Running Time: 6 hrs.). (ENG.). 2008. audio compact disk 14.98 (978-1-60024-460-5(2)) Pub: Hachet Audio. Dist(s): HachBkGrp

Stone Cold. unabr. ed. David Baldacci. Read by Ron McLarty. (Running Time: 10 hrs. 30 mins.). (Camel Club Ser.: No. 3). (ENG.). 2007. 32.98 (978-1-60024-051-5(8)); audio compact disk 49.98 (978-1-60024-052-2(6)) Pub: Hachet Audio. Dist(s): HachBkGrp

Stone Cold. unabr. ed. David Baldacci. Read by Ron McLarty. 9 CDs. (Running Time: 10 hrs. 30 mins.). (Camel Club Ser.: No. 3). 2007. audio compact disk 110.00 (978-1-4159-4490-5(3), BksonTape) Pub: Random Audio Pubg. Dist(s): Random

Oliver Stone, the leader of the mysterious group that calls itself the Camel Club, is both feared and respected by those who've crossed his path. Keeping a vigilant watch over our leaders in Washington, D.C., the Camel Club has won over some allies, but it has also earned formidable enemies - including those in power who will do anything to prevent Stone and his friends from uncovering the hidden, secret work of the government. Annabelle Conroy, an honorary member of the Camel Club, is also the greatest con artist of her generation. She has swindled forty million dollars from casino king Jerry Bagger, the man who murdered her mother. Now he's hot on her trail with only one goal in mind: Annabelle's death. But as Stone and the Camel Club circle the wagons to protect Annabelle, a new opponent, who makes Bagger's menace pale by comparison, suddenly arises. One by one, men from Stone's shadowy past are turning up dead. Behind this slaughter stands one man: Harry Finn. To almost all who know him, Finn is a doting father and loving husband who uses his skills behind the scenes to keep our nation safe. But the other face of Harry Finn is that of an unstoppable killer who inevitably sets his lethal bull's-eye on Oliver Stone. And with Finn, Stone may well have met his match.

Stone Cold. unabr. ed. Robert B. Parker. Perf. by Robert Forster. 6 CDs. (Running Time: 7 hrs. 30 mins.). (Jesse Stone Ser.: No. 4). 2004. audio compact disk 34.95 (978-1-59007-432-9(7)) Pub: New Millenn Enter. Dist(s): PerseuPGW

Stone Cold. unabr. ed. Robert B. Parker. 4 cass. (Running Time: 6 hrs.). (Jesse Stone Ser.: No. 4). 2003. 47.00 (978-1-4025-0734-2(8)) Recorded Bks.

Stone Cold. unabr. abr. ed. Robert B. Parker. Perf. by Robert Forster. 8 cass. (Running Time: 7 hrs. 30 mins.). (Jesse Stone Ser.: No. 4). 2004. 24.95 (978-1-59007-431-2(9)) Pub: New Millenn Enter. Dist(s): PerseuPGW

Stone Cold Heart. Stephen L. Hill. Read by Stephen L. Hill. 1 cass. 1998. 10.00 (978-0-9637090-8-0(9)) Togthr Hrvest.

Stone Diaries. abr. ed. Carol Shields. Read by Sara Botsford. 4 CDs. (Running Time: 18000 sec.). (ENG.). 2006. audio compact disk 29.95 (978-0-86492-468-1(2)) Pub: BTC Audiobks CAN. Dist(s): U Toronto Pr

Stone Diaries. unabr. ed. Carol Shields. Narrated by Alyssa Bresnahan. 10 cass. (Running Time: 13 hrs. 30 mins.). 1999. 85.00 (978-0-7887-0465-9(6), 94658E7) Recorded Bks.

Celebrates an ordinary woman's extraordinary journey through the 20th century.

Stone Fox. John Reynolds Gardiner. Narrated by George Guidall. 1 CD. (Running Time: 1 hr.). (gr. 3 up). 1980. audio compact disk 12.00 (978-0-7887-4640-6(5), C1214) Recorded Bks.

Children will be captivated by the adventurous tale of 10-year-old Willy, who enters the National Dogsled Race. He is determined to win the race and use the prize money to save his family's farm from the tax collector. But also competing is Stone Fox, the legendary Shoshone Indian who has never lost a race.

Stone Fox. unabr. ed. John Reynolds Gardiner. Read by B. D. Wong. (J). 2008. 34.99 (978-1-60514-975-2(6)) Find a World.

***Stone Fox.** unabr. ed. John Reynolds Gardiner. Read by B. D. Wong. (ENG.). 2007. (978-0-06-143281-1(4)); (978-0-06-143282-8(2)) HarperCollins Pubs.

Stone Fox. unabr. ed. John Reynolds Gardiner. Read by Jerry Terheyden. 1 cass. (Running Time: 17 mins.). (Follow the Reader Ser.). (J). (gr. 3-6). 1986. pap. bk. 17.00 (978-0-8072-0129-9(4), FTR121SP, Listening Lib) Random Audio Pubg.

To help his ailing grandfather keep his farm going, Willy & his dog enter a dog-sled race against the legendary Stone Fox in hopes of winning the big money prize.

Stone Fox. unabr. ed. John Reynolds Gardiner. Narrated by George Guidall. 1 cass. (Running Time: 1 hr.). (gr. 3 up). 1997. 10.00 (978-0-7887-0433-8(8), 94625E7) Recorded Bks.

Adventurous tale of ten-year-old Willy, who enters the National Dogsled Race. Willy is determined to win the race & use the prize money to save his family's farm from the tax collector. But also competing in the race is Stone Fox, the legendary Shoshone Indian who has never lost a race.

Stone Fox & Top Secret. unabr. ed. John Reynolds Gardiner. Contrib. by B. D. Wong. (Running Time: 9000 sec.). (J). (gr. 4-7). 2006. audio compact disk 17.95 (978-0-06-089786-4(4)) HarperCollins Pubs.

***Stone Fox & Top Secret.** unabr. ed. John Reynolds Gardiner. Read by B. D. Wong. (ENG.). 2006. (978-0-06-122920-6(2)); (978-0-06-122919-0(9)) HarperCollins Pubs.

Stone Gullets see May Swenson

Stone King see Coven of Witches' Tales

Stone Kiss. abr. ed. Faye Kellerman. Read by Dennis Boutsikaris. (Peter Decker & Rina Lazarus Novel Ser.). (ENG.). 2005. 14.98 (978-1-59483-365-6(6)) Pub: Hachet Audio. Dist(s): HachBkGrp

Stone Kiss. abr. ed. Faye Kellerman. Read by Dennis Boutsikaris. (Running Time: 6 hrs.). (ENG.). 2009. 49.98 (978-1-60788-093-6(8)) Pub: Hachet Audio. Dist(s): HachBkGrp

Stone Kiss. unabr. ed. Faye Kellerman. Narrated by Julia Gibson & George Guidall. 9 cass. (Running Time: 13 hrs.). (Peter Decker & Rina Lazarus Novel Ser.). 2002. 102.00 (978-1-4025-2570-4(2)) Recorded Bks.

Stone Kiss. unabr. ed. Faye Kellerman. 9 cass. (Running Time: 13 hrs.). (Peter Decker & Rina Lazarus Novel Ser.). 2002. 44.95 (978-1-4025-2571-1(0), RG135) Recorded Bks.

Murder hits close to home as the brother-in-law of Decker's half-brother is found dead in a seedy hotel room. Missing from the scene is the dead man's 15-year old niece. Pete finds the girl in the last place anyone could think to look, and soon devastating family secrets emerge.

Stone Kiss. unabr. ed. Faye Kellerman. Narrated by Julia Gibson & George Guidall. 11 CDs. (Running Time: 13 hrs.). (Peter Decker & Rina Lazarus Novel Ser.). 2002. audio compact disk 111.00 (978-1-4025-2900-9(7), C1812) Recorded Bks.

Stone Mistress. Anita Burgh. Read by Anne Dover. 16 cass. (Running Time: 19 hrs. 30 mins.). (Soundings Ser.). (J). 2004. 104.95 (978-1-84283-327-8(8)) Pub: ISIS Lrg Prnt GBR. Dist(s): Ulverscroft US

Stone Mistress. unabr. ed. Anita Burgh. Read by Anne Dover. 16 CDs. (Sound Ser.). (J). 2003. audio compact disk 109.95 (978-1-84283-367-4(7)) Pub: ISIS Lrg Prnt GBR. Dist(s): Ulverscroft US

Stone Monkey. abr. ed. Jeffery Deaver. 2 cass. (Running Time: 2 hrs.). (Lincoln Rhyme Ser.: No. 4). 2002. (978-1-84032-458-7(9), HoddrStoughton) Hodder General GBR.

Stone Monkey. abr. ed. Jeffery Deaver. (Lincoln Rhyme Ser.: No. 4). 2005. 15.95 (978-0-7435-5169-4(9)) Pub: S&S Audio. Dist(s): S and S Inc

Stone of Destiny. Perf. by Steve McDonald. 1 cass., 1 CD. 7.98 (EC 7602); audio compact disk 12.78 CD Jewel box. (EC 7602) NewSound.

Stone of Sorrow. unabr. ed. John Ward. Read by Colin Moody. 7 CDs. (Running Time: 25200 sec.). (Fate of the Stone Ser.). (YA). (gr. 7-13). 2005. audio compact disk 83.95 (978-1-74093-664-4(7)) Pub: Bolinda Pubng AUS. Dist(s): Bolinda Pub Inc

Stone of Tears. unabr. ed. Terry Goodkind. Read by Jim Bond. (Running Time: 39 hrs.). (Sword of Truth Ser.). 2004. 167.25 (978-1-59355-556-6(3), 1593555563, BrilAudUnabridg); 39.95 (978-1-59355-555-9(5), 1593555555, BAU) Brilliance Audio.

In Wizard's First Rule, Richard Cypher's world was turned upside down. Once a simple woods guide, Richard was forced to become the Seeker of Truth, to save the world from the vile dominance of Darken Rahl, the most viciously savage and powerful wizard the world had ever seen. He was joined on this epic quest by his beloved Kahlan, the only survivor among the Confessors, who brought a powerful but benevolent justice to the land before Rahl's evil scourge. Aided by Zedd, the last of the wizards who opposed Rahl, they were able to cast him into the underworld, saving the world from the living hell of life under Rahl. But the veil to the underworld has been torn, and Rahl, from beyond the veil, begins to summon a sinister power more dreadful than any he has wielded before. Horrifying creatures escape through the torn veil, wreaking havoc on the unsuspecting world above. If Rahl isn't stopped, he will free the Keeper itself, an evil entity whose power is so vast and foul that once freed, it can never again be contained.

Stone of Tears. unabr. ed. Terry Goodkind. Read by Jim Bond. (Running Time: 39 hrs.). (Sword of Truth Ser.). 2004. 49.25 (978-1-59335-533-3(5), 1593355335, Brlnc Audio MP3 Lib); 34.95 (978-1-59335-300-1(6), 1593353006, Brilliance MP3) Brilliance Audio.

Stone of Tears. unabr. ed. Terry Goodkind. Read by Jim Bond. (Running Time: 39 hrs.). (Sword of Truth Ser.). 2004. 49.25 (978-1-59710-743-3(3), 1597107433, BADLE); 34.95 (978-1-59710-742-6(5), 1597107425, BAD) Brilliance Audio.

Stone of Tears. unabr. ed. Terry Goodkind. Read by Jim Bond. (Running Time: 39 hrs.). (Sword of Truth Ser.). 2006. audio compact disk 112.25 (978-1-4233-2166-8(9), 9781423321668, BriAudCD Unabrid); audio compact disk 44.95 (978-1-4233-2165-1(0), 9781423321651, Bril Audio CD Unabri) Brilliance Audio.

Stone Quarry: A Bill Smith/Lydia Chin Mystery. unabr. ed. S. J. Rozan. Read by William Dufris. 8 vols. (Running Time: 9 hrs. 30 min.). 2000. bk. 69.95 (978-0-7927-2349-3(X), CSL 238, Chivers Sound Lib) AudioGO.
For the past twelve years that private investigator Bill Smith has owned his cabin in upstate New York, he has used it as a place of refuge. This changes when Eva Colgate, a local farmer, asks him to quietly recover some stolen possessions that could expose her dark past. As Bill & his sometime-partner, Lydia Chin, begin searching, the usual quiet of this rural country is abruptly shattered.

Stone Soup see Sopa de Piedras

Stone Soup. 1 cass. (Running Time: 35 min.). (J). (ps-4). 2001. 15.95 (VX-75C) Kimbo Educ.
The classic tale of three hungry soldiers who overcome the distrust of peasant villagers by cooking a large pot of stone soup & inviting the villagers to participate.

Stone Soup. 2004. bk. 24.95 (978-0-89719-687-1(2)); pap. bk. 18.95 (978-0-7882-0311-4(8)); pap. bk. 32.75 (978-1-55592-311-2(9)); pap. bk. 14.95 (978-1-56008-075-6(2)); 8.95 (978-1-56008-333-7(6)); cass. & flmstrp 30.00 (978-0-89719-546-1(9)); audio compact disk 12.95 (978-0-7882-0314-5(2)) Weston Woods.

Stone Soup. Judi Barrett. Read by Peter Fernandez. 1 cass. (Running Time: 30 mins.). (J). 2000. pap. bk. 19.97 (978-0-7366-9217-5(7)) Books on Tape.
Three hungry soldiers outwit greedy villagers into providing them with a feast, in this classic based on an old French tale.

Stone Soup. Marcia Brown. Illus. by Marcia Brown. 14 vols. (Running Time: 13 mins.). 1987. pap. bk. 39.95 (978-1-59112-737-6(8)); 9.95 (978-1-59112-125-1(6)); audio compact disk 12.95 (978-1-59112-734-5(3)) Live Oak Media.

Stone Soup. Marcia Brown. Illus. by Marcia Brown. Read by Peter Fernandez. 14 vols. (Running Time: 13 mins.). (J). (gr. k-3). 1987. pap. bk. & tchr. ed. 37.95 Reading Chest. (978-0-87499-054-6(8)) Live Oak Media.

Stone Soup. Marcia Brown. Illus. by Marcia Brown. 11 vols. (Running Time: 13 mins.). (J). 2005. pap. bk. 18.95 (978-1-59112-735-2(1)) Pub: Live Oak Media. Dist(s): AudioGO

Stone Soup. Marcia Brown. (J). 1989. bk. 53.32 (978-0-676-87183-8(6)) SRA McGraw.

Stone Soup. Marcia Brown. 1 cass., 5 bks. (Running Time: 10 min.). (J). pap. bk. 32.75; 8.95 (RAC007) Weston Woods.
One side with page turn signals, one side without.

Stone Soup. Marcia Brown. 1 cass. (Running Time: 10 min.). (J). bk. 24.95; pap. bk. 12.95 (PRA007) Weston Woods.

Stone Soup. Marcia Brown. Tr. by Teresa Mlawer. (J). 2004. 8.95 (978-1-56008-428-0(6)) Weston Woods.

Stone Soup. Ann McGovern. 1 cass. (J). 1986. 5.95 incl. bk. Scholastic Inc.

Stone Soup. unabr. ed. Marcia Brown. Illus. by Marcia Brown. Read by Peter Fernandez. 11 vols. (Running Time: 13 mins.). (J). (gr. k-3). 1987. bk. 25.95 (978-0-87499-053-9(X)); pap. bk. 16.95 (978-0-87499-052-2(1)) Pub: Live Oak Media. Dist(s): AudioGO

Stone Soup (A Mini-Musical for Unison Voices) SoundTrax. Composed by Sally K. Albrecht & Jay Althouse. (ENG.). 2005. audio compact disk 54.95 (978-0-7390-3679-2(3)) Alfred Pub.

Stone Soup for the World Set: Life-Changing Stories of Kindness & Courageous Acts of Service. Read by Susan Anspach et al. Compiled by Marianne Larned. 2 cass. (Running Time: 3 hrs.). 1999. 18.00 (978-1-57453-343-9(6)) Audio Lit.
These heartwarming stories show that greatness can grow out of simple acts of giving.

Stone Soup; Sopa de Piedras. unabr. ed. Marcia Brown. Illus. by Marcia Brown. Tr. by Teresa Mlawer. 22 vols. (Running Time: 17 mins.). (ENG & SPA.). (J). (gr. 1-3). 1999. pap. bk. 33.95 (978-0-87499-571-8(X)) Live Oak Media.

***stone Testament.** Celia Rees. Read by Colin Moody. (Running Time: 11 hrs. 30 mins.). (YA). 2009. 89.99 (978-1-74214-555-6(8), 9781742145556) Pub: Bolinda Pubng AUS. Dist(s): Bolinda Pub Inc

Stone Testament. unabr. ed. Celia Rees. Read by Colin Moody. 10 CDs. (Running Time: 11 hrs. 30 mins.). (YA). (gr. 9 up). 2009. audio compact disk 98.95 (978-1-74214-130-5(7), 9781742141305) Pub: Bolinda Pubng AUS. Dist(s): Bolinda Pub Inc

Stone Water: Voices of Second Tuesday. Poems. 200. (Running Time: 50 minutes). 2004. audio compact disk 10.00 (978-0-9747001-2-0(6)) Edinboro Bk Arts.

Stone Work: Reflections on Serious Play & Other Aspects of Country Life, unabr. ed. John Jerome. Narrated by Ed Sala. 5 cass. (Running Time: 7 hrs. 15 mins.). 1997. 44.00 (978-0-7887-0857-2(0), 95003E7) Recorded Bks.
Describes the back-breaking but soul-strengthening task of reconstructing a stone wall on his New England farm.

Stonebreakers. Philip Hook. Narrated by Steven Crossley. 12 CDs. (Running Time: 14 hrs. 15 mins.). 2001. audio compact disk 120.00 (978-1-84197-202-2(9), C1347E7) Recorded Bks.
Excitement stirs the art world when eminent art dealer Oswald Ginn is allowed to discover a secret, one to which forgotten dreams of the past are of great importance. A disillusioned, war-weary art historian & two captains of the British & Soviet Intelligence Services are linked to a 19th century masterpiece, said to have been destroyed in Dresden's bombing. Yet a modern photograph of the painting is sent to Oswald 50 years later. Three people embark on a worldwide search for it, unaware that someone is surveying their efforts, someone who's very interested indeed.

Stonebreakers. unabr. ed. Philip Hook. Narrated by Steven Crossley. 10 cass. (Running Time: 14 hrs. 15 mins.). 1999. 89.00 (978-1-84197-037-0(9), H1037E7) Recorded Bks.
Excitement stirs the art world when eminent art dealer Oswald Ginn is allowed to discover a secret. A disillusioned, war-weary art historian & two captains of the British & Soviet Intelligence Services are linked to a 19th century masterpiece, said to have been destroyed in Dresden's bombing. Yet a modem photograph of the painting is sent to Oswald 50 years later. Three people embark on a worldwide search for it, unaware that someone is surveying their efforts, someone who's very interested indeed.

Stonecutter. 2004. pap. bk. 32.75 (978-1-55592-312-9(7)); 8.95 (978-1-56008-334-4(4)); cass. & flmstrp 30.00 (978-1-56008-767-0(6)) Weston Woods.

Stonecutter: A Japanese Folk Tale. Gerald McDermott. 1 cass., 5 bks. (Running Time: 7 min.). (J). pap. bk. 32.75 Weston Woods.
A lonely stonecutter, tempted by a nobleman's wealth, longs foolishly for powe.

Stonecutter: A Japanese Folk Tale. Gerald McDermott. 1 cass. (Running Time: 7 min.). (J). (ps-4). 1990. pap. bk. 14.95 (978-1-56008-027-5(2), PRA178); 8.95 (978-1-56008-104-3(X), RAC178) Weston Woods.
A lonely stonecutter, tempted by a nobleman's wealth, longs foolishly for power.

Stoneflowers. abr. ed. Sue Chance. 4 cass. (Running Time: 6 hrs.). 1994. 22.95 set. (978-0-9638398-7-9(X)) Bonne Chance.

Stoneheart. Charlie Fletcher. Read by Jim Dale. (Running Time: 35760 sec.). (Stoneheart Trilogy: Bk. 1). (ENG.). (J). (gr. 4-7). 2007. audio compact disk 39.95 (978-0-545-00365-0(2)) Scholastic Inc.

Stoneheart. unabr. ed. Charlie Fletcher. Read by Jim Dale. (J). 2007. 64.99 (978-1-60252-862-8(4)) Find a World.

Stonehenge: A Novel. Bernard Cornwell. 2001. 88.00 (978-0-7366-6349-6(5)) Books on Tape.

Stonehenge: A Novel. Bernard Cornwell. Read by Frederick Davidson. (C). 2000. 40.95 (978-1-59912-610-4(9)) Iofy Corp.

Stonehenge: A Novel. Bernard Cornwell. Read by George Guidall. 10 Cass. (Running Time: 17.25 Hrs). 39.95 (978-1-4025-5852-8(X)) Recorded Bks.

Stonehenge: A Novel. unabr. ed. Bernard Cornwell. Read by Sean Barrett. 14 cass. (Running Time: 14 hrs.). 2000. 110.95 (978-0-7540-0507-0(0), CAB1930) AudioGO.
This is the story of three brothers & their great rivalry that creates the temple that we know as Stonehenge. One summer's day, a stranger carrying great wealth in gold comes to Ratharryn. He is killed in the temple & the people assume that the gold is a gift from the gods. The three sons of Ratharryn's chief each perceive the gift in different ways. It is one son's love for a sorceress that finally brings the rivalries of the brothers to a head.

Stonehenge: A Novel. unabr. ed. Bernard Cornwell. Read by Frederick Davidson. 12 cass. (Running Time: 17 hrs. 30 mins.). 2001. 83.95 (978-0-7861-1952-3(7), 2723); audio compact disk 120.00 (978-0-7861-9769-9(2), 2723) Blckstn Audio.
Four thousand years ago, a stranger's death at the Old Temple of Fatharryn & his ominous "gift" of gold precipitates the building of what for centuries to come will be known as one of mankind's most singular & remarkable achievements. This epic catapults us into a powerful & vibrant world of ritual & sacrifice at once timeless & wholly original, a tale of patricide, betrayal & murder; of bloody brotherly rivalry; & of the neverending pursuit of power, wealth & spiritual fulfillment.

Stonehenge: A Novel. unabr. ed. Bernard Cornwell. Read by Geoffrey Howard. 12 cass. (Running Time: 18 hrs.). 2001. 34.95 (978-0-7366-6744-9(X)) Books on Tape.
An epic tale of the powerful & vibrant world of ritual & sacrifice that constructed the mysterious Stonehenge.

Stonehenge: A Novel. unabr. ed. Bernard Cornwell. Read by Sean Barrett. 14 CDs. (Running Time: 21 hrs.). 2000. audio compact disk 115.95 (978-0-7540-5383-5(0), CCD 074) Pub: Chivers Audio Bks GBR. Dist(s): AudioGO
Three brothers & their great rivalry that creates the temple that we know as Stonehenge. One summer's day, a stranger carrying great wealth in gold come to Ratharryn. He is killed in the temple & the people assume that the gold is a gift in different ways.

Stonehenge: A Novel. unabr. ed. Bernard Cornwell. Narrated by George Guidall. 12 cass. (Running Time: 17 hrs. 15 mins.). 2000. 101.00 (978-0-7887-4868-4(8), 96257E7) Recorded Bks.
A dramatic saga of how one of the greatest wonders of the prehistoric world came to be built. Framed by the story of three brothers, this story draws the listener into the struggles, the mystic visions & the sacrifices surrounding the creation of the giant temple.

Stonehenge Gate. unabr. ed. Jack Williamson. Read by Harlan Ellison. (Running Time: 32400 sec.). 2006. 59.95 (978-0-7861-4655-0(9)); audio compact disk 63.00 (978-0-7861-6778-4(5)); audio compact disk 29.95 (978-0-7861-7411-9(0)) Blckstn Audio.

Stonehenge Landscapes. Vincent Gaffney et al. Ed. by Sally Exon. 2000. pap. bk. 70.00 (978-0-9539923-0-0(6)) Pub: Archaeopress GBR. Dist(s): David Brown

Stonehill: Thirst. Perf. by Randy Stonehill. Prod. by Rick Elias. 1 cass., 1 CD. 1998. 10.98 (978-0-7601-2138-2(9)); audio compact disk 16.98 CD. (978-0-7601-2139-9(7)) Provident Mus Dist.
Randy Stonehill dedicated this album to those men & women who have given their lives to feeding the hungry, clothing the naked, caring for the sick & bringing Christ to a lost world.

***Stoner.** unabr. ed. John Williams. (Running Time: 9 hrs. 30 mins.). 2010. 29.95 (978-1-4417-4831-7(8)); 59.95 (978-1-4417-4827-0(X)); audio compact disk 26.95 (978-1-4417-4830-0(X)); audio compact disk 90.00 (978-1-4417-4828-7(8)) Blckstn Audio.

Stones Are Hatching. unabr. ed. Geraldine McCaughrean. Read by Christian Rodska. 4 cass. (Running Time: 5 hrs. 45 mins.). (J). (gr. 5-9). 2004. 32.00 (978-0-8072-0521-1(4), Listening Lib); pap. bk. 38.00 (978-0-8072-0866-3(3), LYA 318 SP, Listening Lib) Random Audio Pubg.
After centuries of undisturbed slumber, the Stoor Worm, the World Eater, is waking. A creature from monstrous proportions and unimaginable evil, the Stoor Worm must be destroyed. Already its murderous hatchlings are bringing terror and destruction to every corner of Britain. And an odd trio, a Fool, a Maiden, and a Horse, is desperately trying to convince one quite ordinary boy that he alone can save the world.

Stones, Bones, & Brains: Program from the Award Winning Public Radio Serie. Interview. Hosted by Fred Goodwin. Comment by John Hockenberry. 1 CD. (Running Time: 1 hr.). 1999. audio compact disk 21.95 (978-1-932479-97-3(X), LCM 87) Lichtenstein Creat.
The skulls of early humans and our pre-human ancestors hold important clues to human evolution. We'll look at what scientists are learning from recent discoveries, and what the field of "paleoneurology" can tell us about our own brains. With commentary by John Hockenberry.

Stone's Fall. abr. unabr. ed. Iain Pears. Read by Roy Dotrice et al. (ENG.). 2009. audio compact disk 45.00 (978-0-7393-5437-7(X), Random AudioBks) Pub: Random Audio Pubg. Dist(s): Random

Stones for Ibarra. unabr. ed. Harriet Doerr. Narrated by Barbara Rosenblat. 6 cass. (Running Time: 8 hrs.). 1993. 51.00 (978-1-55690-829-3(6), 93129E7) Recorded Bks.
An American husband & wife abandon their comfortable life in California to pursue the dream of reopening a copper mine deep in the Mexican wilderness.

Stones for Ibarra. unabr. collector's ed. Harriet Doerr. Read by Frances Cassidy. 6 cass. (Running Time: 9 hrs.). 1997. 48.00 (978-0-7366-3652-0(8), 1766) Books on Tape.
Richard & Sara Everton leave friends & country to settle in the Mexican village of Ibarra. They intend to spend the rest of their lives here & their dream is to reopen Richard's grandfather's abandoned copper mine. Then Richard learns he has six years to live. His determination to make the mine & village prosper matches Sara's effort to deny the diagnosis. While Richard measures time, she rejects its passage.

Stones from the River. Ursula Hegi. 3 CDs. (Running Time: 3 hrs.). 2000. audio compact disk 15.99 (978-0-7435-0572-7(7), Audioworks) S&S Audio.
Trudi Montag is a Zwerg - a dwarf - short, undesirable, different, the voice of anyone who has ever tried to fit in. Eventually she learns that being different is a secret that all humans share - from her mother who flees into madness, to her friend Georg whose parents pretend he's a girl, to the Jews Trudi harbors in her cellar.

Stones from the River. Ursula Hegi. 2004. 15.95 (978-0-7435-4880-9(9)) Pub: S&S Audio. Dist(s): S and S Inc

Stones from the River. unabr. ed. Ursula Hegi. Read by Kim Edwards-Fukei. 16 vols. (Running Time: 24 hrs.). 2001. bk. 124.95 (978-0-7927-2433-9(X), CSL 322, Chivers Sound Lib) AudioGO.
A daring, dramatic & complex novel of life in Germany. It is set in Burgdorf, a small German town, between 1915 & 1951. Trudi Montag is a Zwerg, the German word for dwarf woman. As a dwarf she is set apart, the outsider whose physical "otherness" has a corollary in her refusal to be a part of Burgdorf's silent complicity during & after World War II. Trudi establishes her status & power, not through beauty, marriage or motherhood, but rather as the town's librarian & relentless collector of stories.

Stones from the River. unabr. ed. Ursula Hegi. Read by Kim Edwards-Fukei. 2 CDs. 2002. audio compact disk 49.95 (978-0-7927-2767-5(3), CMP 322, Chivers Sound Lib) AudioGO.
Trudi Montag is a Zwerg, a dwarf, short, squat, undesirable, different. Through two world wars, she yearns to stretch and grow to be like everyone else. But as the town's librarian and unofficial historian, conscience, and purveyor of gossip, she comes to learn that being different is a secret everyone shares. A "moving, elegiac" novel.

Stones into Schools: Promoting Peace with Books, Not Bombs, in Afghanistan & Pakistan. unabr. ed. Greg Mortenson. (Running Time: 12 hrs. 0 mins.). 2009. 29.95 (978-1-4332-7718-4(2)); 72.95 (978-1-4332-9826-4(0)); audio compact disk 105.00 (978-1-4332-9827-1(9)) Blckstn Audio.

Stones into Schools: Promoting Peace with Books, Not Bombs, in Afghanistan & Pakistan. unabr. ed. Greg Mortenson & Mike Bryan. Contrib. by Atossa Leoni. 10 CDs. (Running Time: 12 hrs.). (ENG.). (gr. 12 up). 2009. audio compact disk 39.95 (978-0-14-314496-0(0), PengAudBks) Penguin Grp USA.

Stones of Green Knowe. L. M. Boston. Read by Simon Vance. (Running Time: 5 hrs.). 2006. 21.95 (978-1-60083-125-6(7)) Iofy Corp.

Stones of Green Knowe. L. M. Boston. Read by Simon Vance. (Running Time: 18000 sec.). (Green Knowe Chronicles). (J). (ps-7). 2006. audio compact disk 27.95 (978-1-59316-065-4(8)) Listen & Live.

Stones of Green Knowe. unabr. ed. L. M. Boston. Read by Simon Vance. (J). 2007. 39.99 (978-1-60252-930-4(2)) Find a World.

Stones of Muncaster Cathedral, unabr. ed. Robert Westall. Narrated by Ron Keith. 2 pieces. (Running Time: 3 hrs.). (gr. 7 up). 1994. 19.00 (978-0-7887-0014-9(6), 94213E7) Recorded Bks.
Steeplejack Joe Clarke, restoring the southwest tower of Muncaster Cathedral finds an evil force concentrated in a grotesquely carved gargoyle. When the force claims two victims, Joe starts a hunt through the cathedral's past to lay the evil to rest.

Stones of Remembrance Series, Charles R. Swindoll. 2 cass. (Running Time: 4 hrs.). 1994. 11.95 (978-1-57972-031-5(5)) Insight Living.
Bible study highlighting God's sovereignty, mercy, faithfulness & holiness.

Stones of Summer. unabr. ed. Dow Mossman. 28 CDs. 2003. audio compact disk 29.95 (978-0-7607-5215-9(X)) Barnes & Noble Inc.

Stonewall: A Biography of General Thomas J. Jackson. unabr. ed. Byron Farwell. Read by Bill Kelsey. 15 cass. (Running Time: 22 hrs. 30 mins.). 1993. 120.00 (978-0-7366-2547-0(X), 3298) Books on Tape.
Stonewall Jackson's hidden side...obsessive, dark, radically different from the legend.

Stonewall Jackson. unabr. ed. Donald A. Davis. Read by Stefan Rudnicki. Frwd. by Wesley K. Clark. (Running Time: 25200 sec.). (Great Generals Ser.). 2007. 19.95 (978-1-4332-0352-7(9)); audio compact disk 19.95 (978-1-4332-0353-4(7)); audio compact disk 29.95 (978-1-4332-0354-1(5)); audio compact disk 55.00 (978-1-4332-0351-0(0)) Blckstn Audio.

Stonewall Jackson, Pt. C. unabr. ed. James I. Robertson. 10 cass. (Running Time: 18 hrs. 30 mins.). 2002. 80.00 (978-0-7366-8742-3(4)) Books on Tape.
A distinguished Civil War historian unravels the complex character of the Confederacy's greatest general. Drawing on previously untapped manuscript sources, the author refutes such long-standing myths as Stonewall Jackson's obsessive eating of lemons and gives a three-dimensional account of the profound religious faith frequently caricatured as grim Calvinism. He also shows him as a brilliant strategist who had a well-deserved reputation for bravery under fire, which earned him the nickname "Stonewall." He was also a bundle of contradictions, which, however, he never let slow him down. While covering the battles that made Jackson a legend - Sharpsburg, Fredericksburg, Antietam, Chancellorsville - the author emphasizes "the life story of an extraordinary man.

Stonewall Jackson, Pt. A. unabr. ed. James I. Robertson. 13 cass. (Running Time: 19 hrs. 30 mins.). 2002. 104.00 (978-0-7366-8713-3(0)) Books on Tape.
Stonewall Jackson's had an obsession with eating lemons and there's a three-dimensional account of the profound religious faith frequently caricatured as grim Calvinism. This shows him as a brilliant strategist who had a well-deserved reputation for bravery under fire, which earned him the nickname "Stonewall." There's a bundle of contradictions, which, however, he never let slow him down. While covering the battles that made Jackson a legend - Sharpsburg, Fredericksburg, Antietam, Chancellorsville, this is "the life story of an extraordinary man." The result is a biography that will fascinate even those allergic to military history.

Stonewall Jackson, Pt. B. unabr. ed. James I. Robertson. 14 cass. (Running Time: 18 hrs. 30 mins.). 2002. 112.00 (978-0-7366-8741-6(6)) Books on Tape.
A distinguished Civil War historian unravels the complex character of the Confederacy's greatest general. Drawing on previously untapped manuscript sources, the author refutes such long-standing myths as Stonewall Jackson's obsessive eating of lemons and gives a three-dimensional account of the profound religious faith frequently caricatured as grim Calvinism. He also shows him as a brilliant strategist who had a well-deserved reputation for bravery under fire, which earned him the nickname "Stonewall." He was also a bundle of contradictions, which, however, he never let slow him down. While covering the battles that made Jackson a legend - Sharpsburg, Fredericksburg, Antietam, Chancellorsville - the author emphasizes "the life story of an extraordinary man.

Stonewall Jackson: A Biography. unabr. ed. Donald A. Davis. Read by Stefan Rudnicki. Frwd. by Wesley K. Clark. (Running Time: 25200 sec.). (Great Generals Ser.). 2007. 54.95 (978-1-4332-0350-3(2)) Blckstn Audio.

Stonewall's Gold. unabr. ed. Robert J. Mrazek. Narrated by Jeff Woodman. 6 cass. (Running Time: 7 hrs. 45 mins.). 2000. 53.00 (978-0-7887-3119-8(X), 95685E7) Recorded Bks.
A Civil War adventure in which teenager Jamie Lockhart discovers a mysterious map & embarks on a quest through Virginia that will test his courage & could cost him his life.

Stony Man 1: Doctrine. Based on a novel by Don Pendleton. (Stony Man Ser.: No. 89). 2008. audio compact disk 19.99 (978-1-59950-401-8(4)) GraphicAudio.

Stony Man 2. Don Pendleton. (Stony Man Ser.: No. 2). 2008. audio compact disk 19.99 (978-1-59950-425-4(1)) GraphicAudio.

Stony Man 3. Don Pendleton. (Stony Man Ser.: No. 3). 2008. audio compact disk 19.99 (978-1-59950-427-8(8)) GraphicAudio.

Stony Man 39: Breach of Trust. Don Pendleton. (Stony Man Ser.: No. 39). 2006. audio compact disk 19.99 (978-1-59950-110-9(4)) GraphicAudio.

Stony Man 4. Based on a novel by Don Pendleton. 2008. audio compact disk 19.99 (978-1-59950-446-9(4)) GraphicAudio.

Stony Man 40: Betrayal. Don Pendleton. (Stony Man Ser.: No. 40). 2006. audio compact disk 19.99 (978-1-59950-133-8(3)) GraphicAudio.

Stony Man 41: Silent Invader. Don Pendleton. (Stony Man Ser.: No. 41). 2006. audio compact disk 19.99 (978-1-59950-172-7(4)) GraphicAudio.

Stony Man 42: Edge of Night. Don Pendleton. (Stony Man Ser.: No. 42). 2006. audio compact disk 19.99 (978-1-59950-183-3(X)) GraphicAudio.

Stony Man 43: Zero Hour. Don Pendleton. (Stony Man Ser.: No. 43). 2007. audio compact disk 19.99 (978-1-59950-201-4(1)) GraphicAudio.

Stony Man 44: Thirst for Power. Don Pendleton. (Stony Man Ser.: No. 44). 2007. audio compact disk 19.99 (978-1-59950-212-0(7)) GraphicAudio.

Stony Man 45: Star Venture. Don Pendleton. (Stony Man Ser.: No. 45). 2007. audio compact disk 19.99 (978-1-59950-314-1(X)) GraphicAudio.

Stony Man 46: Hostile Instinct. Don Pendleton. (Stony Man Ser.: No. 46). 2007. audio compact disk 19.99 (978-1-59950-331-8(X)) GraphicAudio.

Stony Man 47: Command Force. Don Pendleton. (Stony Man Ser.: No. 47). 2007. audio compact disk 19.99 (978-1-59950-349-3(2)) GraphicAudio.

Stony Man 48: Conflict Imperative. Based on a novel by Don Pendleton. (Stony Man Ser.: No. 48). 2007. audio compact disk 19.99 (978-1-59950-384-4(0)) GraphicAudio.

Stony Man 5. Based on a novel by Don Pendleton. 2008. audio compact disk 19.99 (978-1-59950-467-4(7)) GraphicAudio.

Stony Man 6. Alex Pendleton. 2008. audio compact disk 19.99 (978-1-59950-506-0(1)) GraphicAudio.

Stony Man 68: Outbreak. Don Pendleton. (Stony Man Ser.: No. 68). 2004. audio compact disk 19.99 (978-1-933059-54-9(0)) GraphicAudio.

Stony Man 69: Day of Decision. Don Pendleton. (Stony Man Ser.: No. 69). 2004. audio compact disk 19.99 (978-1-933059-59-4(1)) GraphicAudio.

Stony Man 7. Don Pendleton. 2009. audio compact disk 19.99 (978-1-59950-536-7(3)) GraphicAudio.

Stony Man 70: Ramrod Intercept. Don Pendleton. (Stony Man Ser.: No. 70). 2005. audio compact disk 19.99 (978-1-933059-67-9(2)) GraphicAudio.

Stony Man 72: Rolling Thunder. Don Pendleton. (Stony Man Ser.: No. 72). 2005. audio compact disk 19.99 (978-1-933059-83-9(4)); audio compact disk 19.99 (978-1-933059-99-0(0)) GraphicAudio.

Stony Man 73: Cold Objective. Don Pendleton. (Stony Man Ser.: No. 73). 2005. audio compact disk 19.99 (978-1-933059-91-4(5)) GraphicAudio.

Stony Man 75: Silent Arsenal. Don Pendleton. (Stony Man Ser.: No. 75). 2005. audio compact disk 19.99 (978-1-59950-003-4(5)) GraphicAudio.

Stony Man 76: Gathering Storm. Don Pendleton. (Stony Man Ser.: No. 76). 2005. audio compact disk 19.99 (978-1-59950-010-2(8)) GraphicAudio.

Stony Man 77: Full Blast. Don Pendleton. (Stony Man Ser.: No. 77). 2005. audio compact disk 19.99 (978-1-59950-016-4(7)) GraphicAudio.

Stony Man 78: Maelstrom. Don Pendleton. (Stony Man Ser.: No. 78). 2006. audio compact disk 19.99 (978-1-59950-022-5(1)) GraphicAudio.

Stony Man 79: Promise to Defend. Don Pendleton. (Stony Man Ser.: No. 79). 2006. audio compact disk 19.99 (978-1-59950-028-7(0)) GraphicAudio.

Stony Man 80: Doomsday Conquest. Don Pendleton. (Stony Man Ser.: No. 80). 2006. audio compact disk 19.99 (978-1-59950-033-1(7)) GraphicAudio.

Stony Man 81: Sky Hammer. Don Pendleton. (Running Time: 25200 sec.). (Stony Man Ser.). 2006. audio compact disk 19.99 (978-1-59950-074-4(4)) GraphicAudio.

Stony Man 82: Vanishing Point. Don Pendleton. (Stony Man Ser.: No. 82). 2006. audio compact disk 19.99 (978-1-59950-090-4(6)) GraphicAudio.

Stony Man 83: Doom Prophecy. Don Pendleton. (Stony Man Ser.: No. 83). 2006. audio compact disk 19.99 (978-1-59950-125-3(2)) GraphicAudio.

Stony Man 84: Sensor Sweep. Don Pendleton. (Mack Bolan Ser.: No. 94). 2006. audio compact disk 19.99 (978-1-59950-143-7(0)) GraphicAudio.

Stony Man 85: Hell Dawn. Don Pendleton. (Stony Man Ser.: No. 85). 2006. audio compact disk 19.99 (978-1-59950-193-2(7)) GraphicAudio.

Stony Man 86: Oceans of Fire. Don Pendleton. (Stony Man Ser.: No. 86). 2007. audio compact disk 19.99 (978-1-59950-223-6(2)) GraphicAudio.

Stony Man 87: Extreme Arsenal. Don Pendleton. (Stony Man Ser.: No. 87). 2007. audio compact disk 19.99 (978-1-59950-323-3(9)) GraphicAudio.

Stony Man 88: Starfire. Don Pendleton. (Stony Man Ser.: No. 88). 2007. audio compact disk 19.99 (978-1-59950-340-0(9)) GraphicAudio.

Stony Man 89: Neutron Force. Don Pendleton. (Stony Man Ser.: No. 89). 2007. audio compact disk 19.99 (978-1-59950-358-5(1)) GraphicAudio.

Stony Man 90: Red Frost. Don Pendleton. 2009. audio compact disk 19.99 (978-1-59950-519-0(3)) GraphicAudio.

Stony Man 91: China Crisis. Don Pendleton. 2009. audio compact disk 19.99 (978-1-59950-565-7(7)) GraphicAudio.

Stony Man 92: Capital Offensive. Don Pendleton. 2009. audio compact disk 19.99 (978-1-59950-593-0(2)) GraphicAudio.

Stonybridges for Children (German) Veronica Foster. Read by Veronica Foster. Read by Sadie & Sydney. 3 cass. (Running Time: 60 min.). (J). (gr. k-4). 1989. 24.95 Set. (978-0-88432-248-1(3), SGR125) J Norton Pubs.
Six familiar stories retold using German words & phrases which are repeated by the children on the tapes as well as the children listening.

Stop Acting Rich: How to Live Like a Millionaire. unabr. ed. Thomas J. Stanley. Read by Fred Stella. (Running Time: 8 hrs.). 2009. 24.99 (978-1-4233-9812-7(2), 9781423398127, Brilliance MP3); 39.97 (978-1-4233-9813-4(0), 9781423398134, Brlnc Audio MP3 Lib); 24.99 (978-1-4233-9814-1(9), 9781423398141, BAD); 39.97 (978-1-4233-9815-8(7), 9781423398158, BADLE); audio compact disk 99.97 (978-1-4233-9811-0(4), 9781423398110, BriAudCD Unabrid) Brilliance Audio.

Stop Acting Rich: How to Live Like a Millionaire. unabr. ed. Thomas J. Stanley & Finance Personal. Read by Fred Stella. (Running Time: 8 hrs.). 2009. audio compact disk 29.99 (978-1-4233-9810-3(6), 9781423398103) Brilliance Audio.

Stop AIDS... The Right Way. Cary Savitch. 1 cass. (Running Time: 43 min.). 1997. bk. 25.00 (978-1-58111-031-9(6)) Contemporary Medical.
Discusses AIDS as a public health issue. Also discussed are various medical aspects of AIDS & HIV; current information regarding the transmission of this disease.

Stop & Smell the Roses. Perf. by Sally Harmon. 1 cass., 1 CD. 7.98 (SO 120); audio compact disk 12.78 CD Jewel box. (SO 120) NewSound.

Stop & Think. Dottie Waddell. 1 cass. (Running Time: 36 min.). (J). (ps-6). 1993. 9.99 (978-0-9643681-0-1(2)); audio compact disk 12.99 CD. (978-0-9643681-1-8(0)) Apple Core.
"Stop & Think" is sung by "The Right Choice Kids," ages 6-12. The 12 song collection has upbeat lyrics & melodies & are fun to sing-along with. Common sense is the key theme in this album, aiming to help children grow up in today's fast-paced, pressured world.

***Stop at Willoughby.** 2010. audio compact disk (978-1-59171-157-5(6)) Falcon Picture.

Stop Bad Dreams. Betty L. Randolph. Read by Betty L. Randolph. Read by Leonard Baron. Ed. by Success Education Institute International. 1 cass. (Running Time: 45 min.). (Health Ser.). 1989. bk. 9.98 (978-1-55909-074-2(X), 61X) Randolph Tapes.
Helps in changing unwanted dreams into dreams with positive benefits. Subliminal messages are heard 3-5 minutes before becoming ocean sounds or music.

Stop Bed-Wetting. Barrie Konicov. 1 cass. (J). 11.98 (978-0-87082-368-8(X), 123) Potentials.
Suggests how to prevent bed-wetting by playing this program for the individual or child at bedtime.

Stop Being Angry. Barrie Konicov. 1 cass. 11.98 (978-0-87082-369-5(8), 124) Potentials.
Discusses how not to blow your cool, turn into that negative "other" person, in which events, situations & people respond to you in a similiar manner.

Stop Being Angry. Barrie Konicov. 1 CD. 2003. audio compact disk 19.98 (978-0-87082-970-3(X)) Potentials.
When you feel angry, people respond to you in a similar manner. There is a better way. Learn how to let go of angry thoughts. You will find the self-hypnosis on track 1 and the subliminal on track 2. The easy-listening music of the subliminal, together with the self-hypnosis, is the original format which most people love and with which they are most familiar.

Stop Being Angry. Barrie Konicov. 2 CDs. 2003. audio compact disk 27.98 (978-1-56001-991-6(3)) Potentials.

***Stop Being Your Symptoms & Start Being Yourself.** abr. ed. Arthur J. Barsky. (ENG.). 2006. (978-0-06-123522-1(9), Harper Audio) HarperCollins Pubs.

***Stop Being Your Symptoms & Start Being Yourself: The 6-Week Mind-Body Program to Ease Your Chronic Symptoms.** abr. ed. Arthur J. Barsky. (ENG.). 2006. (978-0-06-123498-9(2), Harper Audio) HarperCollins Pubs.

Stop by Here. Perf. by Praise II Choir. 1 cass. 10.98 (978-1-57908-261-1(0), 1314); audio compact disk 15.98 CD. (978-1-57908-260-4(2), 1314) Platinm Enter.

Stop Clutter from Stealing Your Life: Discover Why You Clutter & How You Can Stop. Mike Nelson. Read by David Elias. (Running Time: 3 hrs. 30 mins.). (C). 2005. 21.95 (978-1-60083-124-9(9)) Iofy Corp.

Stop Clutter from Stealing Your Life: Discover Why You Clutter & How You Can Stop. abr. ed. Mike Nelson. 2 cass. (Running Time: 3 hrs. 30 mins.). 2002. 17.95 (978-1-885408-91-4(9)) Listen & Live.

Stop Clutter from Stealing Your Life: Discover Why You Clutter & How You Can Stop. abr. ed. Mike Nelson. Read by David Elias. 3 CDs. (Running Time: 12600 sec.). 2006. audio compact disk 19.95 (978-1-59316-073-9(9), LL165) Listen & Live.

Stop Disfunctional Relationships (Hypnosis), Vol. 11. Jayne Helle. 1 cass. (Running Time: 28 min.). 1997. 15.00 (978-1-891826-10-8(7)) Introspect.
Develop the confidence you need to let go of a no-win relationship that's harming your productivity & hurting you emotionally.

Stop Drinking. 2 CDs. 1982. audio compact disk 27.98 (978-1-56001-964-0(6)) Potentials.
Drinking is one problem that most health care officials feel cannot be cured. That does not have to be the case. Drinking is a sympton, not a cause. This program could quickly get to the cause of the problem; a cause which exists in the mind. Change the mind, eliminate the cause, ansd its sympton could be eliminated too. It all depends on your desire.This 2-CD program from our Super Consciousness series is our newest, most powerful format. On the self-hypnosis CD, SC programs have the Subliminal Persuasion soundtrack added under Barrie?s voice. And the 17th Century Baroque music on the Subliminal CD has the same beat as your body's natural rhythm, thereby allowing the suggestions to enter deeply and effortlessly.

Stop Drinking. Rick Brown. Read by Rick Brown. Ed. by John Quatro. 1 cass. (Running Time: 30 min.). (Subliminal - Easy Listening Ser.). 1993. 10.95 (978-1-57100-011-8(9), E130); 10.95 (978-1-57100-035-4(6), J130); 10.95 (978-1-57100-059-0(3), N130); 10.95 (978-1-57100-083-5(6), S130); 10.95 (978-1-57100-107-8(7), W130); 10.95 (978-1-57100-131-3(X), H130) Sublime Sftware.
Stop drinking substitutes pride & accomplishment.

Stop Drinking. Barrie Konicov. 1 cass. 11.98 (978-0-87082-315-2(9), 022) Potentials.
Subliminal suggestions for dealing with the underlying causes of prolem drinking.

Stop Drinking. Barrie Konicov. 1 CD. 2004. audio compact disk 19.98 (978-1-56001-670-0(1)) Potentials.
Drinking is a sympton, not a cause. This program quickly gets to the cause of the problem, a cause which exists in your mind. Change your mind, eliminate the cause, and its symptom is eliminated too.You will find the self-hypnosis on track 1 and the subliminal on track 2. The easy-listening music of the subliminal, together with the self-hypnosis, is the original format which most people love and with which they are most familiar.

Stop Drinking. Betty L. Randolph. Read by Betty L. Randolph. Read by Leonard Baron. Ed. by Success Education Institute International. 1 cass. (Running Time: 45 min.). (Health Ser.). 1989. 9.98 (978-1-55909-203-6(3), 75M) Randolph Tapes.
Use mind power for self-control, you grow stronger, more confident. Subliminal messages are heard 3-5 minutes before becoming ocean sounds or music.

Stop Drinking. Dick Sutphen. 1 cass. (Running Time: 1 hr.). (RX17 Ser.). 14.98 (978-0-87554-399-4(5), RX163) Valley Sun.

Stop Drinking: Dejar de Beber. Barrie Konicov. 1 cass. (Running Time: 1 hr. 30 min.). (Spanish-Language Audios Ser.). (SPA.). 1995. 11.98 (978-1-56001-397-6(4), 022) Potentials.
This tape can help you get to the cause of the problem which leads to drinking - a cause which exists in the mind. Change the mind, eliminate the cause & the drinking could be eliminated, too. If you are truly motivated for change, this tape could help you.

Stop Drinking (Hypnosis), Vol. 10. Jayne Helle. 1 cass. (Running Time: 28 min.). 1997. 15.00 (978-1-891826-09-2(3)) Introspect.
Rediscover a life of happiness & good health.

Stop Drop & Roll. Margery Cuyler. Illus. by Arthur Howard. 11 vols. bk. 25.95 (978-1-59112-976-9(1)); bk. 28.95 (978-1-59112-980-6(X)); pap. bk. 16.95 (978-1-59112-975-2(3)); pap. bk. (978-1-59112-977-6(X)); pap. bk. 18.95 (978-1-59112-979-0(6)); pap. bk. (978-1-59112-981-3(8)); 9.95 (978-1-59112-974-5(5)); audio compact disk 12.95 (978-1-59112-978-3(8)) Live Oak Media.

Stop, Drop & Roll: Learn Not to Burn Self Reader. Lyn Hester. Narrated by Lyn Hester. (J). (ps-2). 1982. pap. bk. 12.95 (978-0-9676006-0-4(X)) Mktg Dyn Inc.

STOP... Drowning in Debt. PUEI. 2007. audio compact disk 24.95 (978-1-934147-31-3(1), Fred Pryor) P Univ E Inc.

Stop Drugs. Dick Sutphen. 1 cass. (Running Time: 1 hr.). (RX17 Ser.). 14.98 (978-0-87554-400-7(2), RX164) Valley Sun.

Stop Hiding Behind Your Weight. Shad Helmstetter. 1 cass. (Self-Talk Cassettes Ser.). 10.95 (978-0-937065-41-9(2)) Grindle Pr.

***Stop in the Name of Pants!** unabr. ed. Louise Rennison. Narrated by Stina Nielsen. 1 Playaway. (Running Time: 6 hrs. 30 mins.). (Confessions of Georgia Nicolson Ser.: Bk. 9). (YA). (gr. 8-10). 2010. 59.75 (978-1-4407-7781-3(0)); 51.75 (978-1-4407-7770-7(5)); audio compact disk 66.75 (978-1-4407-7774-5(8)) Recorded Bks.

***Stop in the Name of Pants!** unabr. collector's ed. Louise Rennison. Narrated by Stina Nielsen. 6 CDs. (Running Time: 6 hrs. 30 mins.). (Confessions of Georgia Nicolson Ser.: Bk. 9). (YA). (gr. 8-10). 2010. audio compact disk 41.95 (978-1-4407-7778-3(0)) Recorded Bks.

STOP IRS Headaches. Adrian Van Zelfdan. 2007. audio compact disk 12.95 (978-1-932226-57-7(5)) Wizard Acdmy.

Stop Living Paycheck to Paycheck: How you can learn to make more money & create all the wealth you Want. Created by Jim Donovan. (ENG.). 2008. audio compact disk 197.00 (978-0-9786891-8-6(6)) Austin Bay.

Stop Mood Swings. 1 cass. (Health Ser.). 12.98 (106) Randolph Tapes.
This tape helps alleviate some of the ups & downs of the body. An aid to help you cope with monthly changes.

Stop 'n' Go Girls. unabr. ed. Tom E. Neet. Read by Lynda Evans. 6 cass. (Running Time: 8 hrs. 12 min.). (Mel Tippet Mystery Ser.: Bk. 2). 1996. 39.95 (978-1-55686-645-6(3)) Books in Motion.
Mel is hired to watch over a teen-age debutante working as a clerk in the Stop 'N Go Market. Like previous clerks, the teen-ager disappears.

Stop Nail-Biting. Barrie Konicov. 1 cass. (YA). 11.98 (978-0-87082-371-8(X), 126) Potentials.
According to the editors, the results of this program are guaranteed to be immediate, safe & permanent, regardless of your age.

Stop Nail Biting. Barrie Konicov. 1 CD. 2004. audio compact disk 19.98 (978-1-56001-675-5(2)) Potentials.
If someone in your family is a habitual nail-biter, order this program. Regardless of age, the results are guaranteed to be immediate, safe and permanent. You will find the self-hypnosis on track 1 and the subliminal on track 2. The easy-listening music of the subliminal, together with the self-hypnosis, is the original format which most people love and with which they are most familiar.

Stop Nail-Biting Now. Norman J. Caldwell. Read by Norman J. Caldwell. Ed. by Achieve Now Institute Staff. 1 cass. (Running Time: 20 min.). (Self-Directed Improvement Ser.). 1988. 9.97 (978-1-56273-059-8(2)) My Mothers Pub.
Long nails become a reality!.

Stop Obsessing. Edna B. Foa & Reid Wilson. Read by Reid Wilson. 3 cass. (Running Time: 2 hrs. 6 min.). 1994. 24.95 set. (978-0-9630683-1-6(8)) Pathway Systs.
Self-help for those suffering from obsessions or compulsions. Supplement to the book Stop Obsessing! (Bantam).

Stop Pain; Pain Management. Christopher Love. Read by Christopher Love. 1 cass. (Running Time: 30 min.). 1997. 10.95 (978-1-891820-15-1(X)) World Sangha Pubg.
Self-hypnosis meditation for healing, self-improvement & realizing our full & powerful potential as spiritual beings.

Stop Procrastinating. Rick Brown. Read by Rick Brown. Ed. by John Quatro. 1 cass. (Running Time: 30 min.). (Subliminal - Easy Listening Ser.). 1993. 10.95 (978-1-57100-016-3(X), E137); 10.95 (978-1-57100-040-8(2), J137); 10.95 (978-1-57100-064-4(X), N137); 10.95 (978-1-57100-088-0(7), S137); 10.95 (978-1-57100-112-2(3), W137); 10.95 (978-1-57100-136-8(0), H137) Sublime Sftware.
Stop procrastinating gets them up & going strong.

Stop Procrastinating. Richard Jafolla & Mary-Alice Jafolla. Read by Richard Jafolla & Mary-Alice Jafolla. (Overcoming Ser.). 1986. 12.95 (150) Stppng Stones.
Motivational tapes that work on the subconscious mind (subliminal) & conscious mind to bring about self-improvement.

Stop Procrastinating. Read by Mary Richards. (Subliminal Impact Ser.). 12.95 (626) Master Your Mind.
Experience the total satisfaction of prioritzing & completing projects on time.

Stop Procrastinating: Do It Now! Edwin C. Bliss. 2 cass. (Running Time: 2 hrs.). vinyl bd. 19.95 (978-0-88432-184-2(3), S01850) J Norton Pubs.
Analyzes the reasons for procrastination & provides a step-by-step guide that shows how to overcome it.

Stop Procrastinating: Do It Now! Edwin C. Bliss. 2 CDs. 2005. audio compact disk 19.95 (978-1-57970-270-0(8), S01850D, Audio-For) J Norton Pubs.
Chronic procrastination can be cured. This program tells you how to do it by using a 5-minute plan and 12 specific techniques guaranteed to increase your productivity.

Stop Procrastinating - Do It! James R. Sherman. 1 cass. 10.00 (SP100045) SMI Intl.
If you are a confirmed procrastinator, don't put off getting this one. Here's a simple, four-step plan to break the procrastination habit & get a better start toward professional & personal success. Get it now!.

Stop Procrastinating - Do it. James R. Sherman. 1 cass. (Running Time: 1 hr. 1 min.). 11.00 (978-0-89811-170-5(6), 9413) Meyer Res Grp.
Offers a simple, 4-step plan to break the procrastination habit & get a better start toward professional & personal success.

Stop Procrastination. 1 cass. (Running Time: 45 min.). (Success Ser.). 9.98 (978-1-55909-037-7(5), 40S); 9.98 90 min. extended length stereo music. (978-1-55909-038-4(3), 40X) Randolph Tapes.
"Get it done now!" This tape helps you get going. Subliminal messages are heard for 3-5 minutes before becoming ocean sounds or music.

Stop Procrastination. Prod. by Betty L. Randolph. 1 cass. (Power Weight Loss Works! Ser.). 19.95 (430) Randolph Tapes.

An Asterisk (*) at the beginning of an entry indicates that the title is appearing for the first time.

Stop Procrastination. Betty L. Randolph. Read by Betty L. Randolph. Read by Leonard Baron. Ed. by Success Education Institute International Staff. 1 cass. (Success Ser.). 1989. bk. 14.98 (978-1-55909-255-5(6), 430P) Randolph Tapes.
60,000 messages left-right brain. Male-females voice tracks with Megafonic Subliminals. Ocean (P) & Music (PM).

Stop Procrastination: Take Action Now & Succeed. Jonathan Parker. 2 cass. (Running Time: 1 hr. 45 min.). 1992. 17.00 Set. (978-1-58400-014-3(7)) QuantumQuests Intl.

Stop Procrastination (Subliminal), Vol. 30. Jayne Helle. 1 cass. (Running Time: 28 min.). 1995. 15.00 (978-1-891826-29-0(8)) Introspect.
Enjoy the tasks you once avoided. Be a can-do person.

Stop Punishing Yourself. Dick Sutphen. 1 cass. (Running Time: 1 hr.). (RX17 Ser.). 14.98 (978-0-87554-391-8(X), RX155) Valley Sun.

Stop screaming at the Microwave! How to Connect Your Disconnected Life. Mary LoVerde. 2004. 7.95 (978-0-7435-4543-3(5)) Pub: S&S Audio. Dist(s): S and S Inc

Stop Selling & Start Listening! Marketing Strategies That Create Top Producers. Read by Chip Cummings. 5 CDs. (Running Time: 7 hrs.). 2005. audio compact disk 69.00 (978-0-9746975-2-9(4)) Northwind Financial.

Stop Shoplifting: Music. Betty L. Randolph. Read by Betty L. Randolph. Read by Leonard Baron. Ed. by Success Education Institute International Staff. 1 cass. (Running Time: 60 min.). (Educational Ser.). 1989. bk. 14.98 (978-1-55909-215-9(7), 90PM) Randolph Tapes.
60,000 messages left-right brain. Male-females voice tracks with Megafonic Subliminals. Ocean (P) & Music (PM).

Stop Sitting on Your Assets: How to safely leverage the equity trapped in your home & transform it into a constant flow of wealth & Security. Marian Snow. Read by Hana Haatainen Caye. Prod. by Les Lingle Productions. 8 CDs. (Running Time: 7 hrs. 40 mins.). (ENG.). 2007. audio compact disk 37.95 (978-0-9790142-2-2(0)) E Madison Pub.

Stop Smoking. 1 cass. (Running Time: 33 min.). 1985. L M Hersh.

Stop Smoking. 1 cass. 10.00 (978-1-58506-006-1(2), 12) New Life Inst OR.
Now you can quit smoking the easy way - quickly, automatically & painlessly.

Stop Smoking. Rick Brown. Read by Rick Brown. Ed. by John Quatro. 1 cass. (Running Time: 30 min.). (Subliminal - Easy Listening Ser.). 1993. 10.95 (978-1-57100-002-6(X)); 10.95 (978-1-57100-026-2(7), J105); 10.95 (978-1-57100-050-7(X), N105); 10.95 (978-1-57100-074-3(7), S105); 10.95 (978-1-57100-098-9(4), W105); 10.95 (978-1-57100-122-1(0), H105) Sublime Sftware.
Stop smoking with hypnotic suggestions to quit!.

Stop Smoking. Pat Carroll. Read by Pat Carroll. Ed. by Tony Carroll. 1 cass. (Running Time: 30 min.). 10.00 Inner-Mind Concepts.
Explains that smoking is a conditioned habit one can end.

Stop Smoking! Read by Bob Griswold. 1 cass. 1992. 10.95 (978-1-55848-047-6(1)) EffectiveMN.
It takes little or no time to quit smoking with this tape because it's designed to help you eliminate the desire to smoke.

Stop Smoking. Bob Griswold. Read by Bob Griswold. 1 CD. (Running Time: 75 mins). (Love Tapes Ser.). 2005. audio compact disk 15.98 (978-1-55848-155-8(9), Love Tapes) EffectiveMN.
This highly-effective and enjoyable CD will help you quit smoking quickly, easily, and permanently. You'll feel healthier, more energetic, attractive and confident as you take control and overcome the smoking habit once and for all. Comes complete with a 100% satisfaction guarantee.This CD contains 3 programs. The first is a guided meditation with powerful imagery and techniques for becoming smoke-free. It also includes two excellent subliminal programs, one with the sound of ocean waves and the other with relaxing original music.

Stop Smoking. Read by Steven Halpern. 1 cass. 7.98 (HAL 2030); 7.98 (HAL 2030); audio compact disk 12.78 Jewel box. (HAL 2030); audio compact disk 12.78 CD Jewel box. (HAL 2030) NewSound.

Stop Smoking. Richard Jafolla & Mary-Alice Jafolla. Read by Richard Jafolla & Mary-Alice Jafolla. (Overcoming Ser.). 1986. 12.95 (120) Stppng Stones.
Motivational tapes that work on the subconscious mind (subliminal) & conscious mind to bring about self-improvement.

Stop Smoking. Barrie Konicov. 1 CD. 2003. audio compact disk 19.98 (978-0-87082-959-8(9)) Potentials.
Cut your habit off immediately! This program contains the techniques and procedures that have helped thousands of people, over the years, to stop smoking, forever.You will find the self-hypnosis on track 1 and the subliminal on track 2. The easy-listening music of the subliminal, together with the self-hypnosis, is the original format which most people love and with which they are most familiar.

Stop Smoking. Barrie Konicov. 2 CDs. 2003. audio compact disk 27.98 (978-1-56001-992-3(1)) Potentials.

Stop Smoking. Christopher Love. Read by Christopher Love. 1 cass. (Running Time: 30 min.). 1997. 10.95 (978-1-891820-18-2(4)) World Sangha Pubg.
Self-hypnosis meditation for healing, self-improvement & realizing our full & powerful potential as spiritual beings.

Stop Smoking. Narrated by Dick Lutz. 1 cass. (Running Time: 15 min.). 1984. 7.95 (978-0-931625-10-7(6), 10) DIMI Pr.
Describes steps for you to take to quit completely. Relaxation narration on reverse helps your subconscious work with your conscious mind to eliminate your habit.

Stop Smoking. Michael P. Marshall. Read by Michael P. Marshall. Ed. by Jonathan C. Renaud. Music by Ted Crook. 1 cass. (Running Time: 52 min.). 1995. 9.00 (978-0-912403-18-2(7)) Prod Renaud.
A fresh, positive approach, not revealed by any other methodology. We recommend that you also purchase "Basis of Addiction".

Stop Smoking. Lee Pulos. 2 cass. (Running Time: 60 min. per cass.). (Self Hypnosis & Subliminal Reinforcement Ser.). 14.95 (978-1-55569-227-8(3), SUB-8003) Great Am Audio.
Presents tools for positive self-change.

Stop Smoking. Lee Pulos. Read by Lee Pulos. 1 cass. (Running Time: 60 min.). 9.95 (978-1-55569-424-1(1), 4013) Great Am Audio.
Subliminal self-help.

Stop Smoking. Betty L. Randolph. 1 stereo cass. (Running Time: 45 min.). (Self-Hypnosis Ser.). 1989. bk. 9.98 (978-1-55909-266-1(1), 802) Randolph Tapes.
The 10-day method.

Stop Smoking. Read by Mary Richards. 12.95 (202) Master Your Mind.
Explains ways to reinforce your desire to stop smoking or cut down by making a firm decision while relaxed.

Stop Smoking. Read by Mary Richards. 1 cass. (Running Time: 63 min.). (Series Two Thousand). 2007. audio compact disk 19.95 (978-1-56136-094-9(5)) Master Your Mind.

Stop Smoking. Dick Sutphen. 1 cass. (Running Time: 1 hr.). (Only Subliminals Ser.). 1990. 12.98 (978-0-87554-445-8(2), T205) Valley Sun.
One hour of soothing, digitally mastered stereo music with positive subliminal suggestions phrased for maximum acceptance by your subconscious mind.

Stop Smoking. Eldon Taylor. 2 cass. (Running Time: 62 min. per cass.). (Omniphonics Ser.). 29.95 incl. script Set. (978-1-55978-815-1(1), 4016) Progress Aware Res.
3-D soundtrack with underlying subliminal affirmations, night & day versions.

Stop Smoking. Scripts. Eldon Taylor. Read by Eldon Taylor. Interview with Progress Aware Staff. 1 cass. (Running Time: 62 min.). 16.95 (978-1-55978-291-3(9), 020105) Progress Aware Res.
Verbal coaching soundtrack with underlying subliminal affirmations & sound matrix frequencies for brain entrainment.

Stop Smoking. Eldon Taylor. Read by Eldon Taylor. Interview with XProgress Aware Staff. 1 cass. (Running Time: 1 hr. 30 min.). (Power Imaging Ser.). 16.95 incl. script. (978-1-55978-182-4(3), 8002) Progress Aware Res.
Hypnosis & soundtrack with underlying subliminal affirmations.

Stop Smoking. Eldon Taylor. 1 CD. (Running Time: 52 min.). (Whole Brain Innertalk Ser.). 1998. audio compact disk (978-1-55978-855-7(0)) Progress Aware Res.

Stop Smoking. Eldon Taylor. 1 CD. (Running Time: 52 min.). (Whole Brain Innertalk Ser.). 1999. audio compact disk (978-1-55978-917-2(4)) Progress Aware Res.

Stop Smoking, Set. Barrie Konicov. 1 cass., 1 video. (Video-Audio System Ser.). cass. & video 24.98 (978-0-87082-452-4(X), SYS 127); 16.98 (978-1-56001-298-6(6), SCII 127) Potentials.
This program can cut your habit off immediately. This is basically the same technique & procedure that the author, Barrie Konicov, has used to help literally thousands of people over the years to stop smoking.

Stop Smoking: Become smoke Free. Kelly Howell. 1 cass. (Running Time: 1 hr.). (Brain Wave Subliminal Ser.). 1996. 9.95 (978-1-881451-32-7(1)) Brain Sync.
The subconscious mind easily absorbs subliminal messages that give you the desire and motivation to terminate self-destructive patterns.

Stop Smoking: Creative Visualizations into Self Empowerment & Spiritual Identity. (ENG.). 2009. 15.95 (978-0-9758866-3-2(0)) Awakening Pubns Inc.

Stop Smoking: Dejar de Fumar. Barrie Konicov. 1 cass. (Running Time: 1 hr. 16 min.). (Spanish-Language Audios Ser.). (SPA.). 1995. 11.98 (978-0-87082-801-0(0), 127) Potentials.
This tape can help cut your habit off immediately, using the same techniques & procedures I have used to help thousands of people, over the years, to stop smoking.

Stop Smoking: Free Yourself from Smoking, Once & for All. Kelly Howell. 1 CD. (Running Time: 60 mins.). (ENG.). 2004. audio compact disk 14.95 (978-1-881451-87-7(9)) Brain Sync.
No matter how many times you've tried to quit, you can do it now! And this time you'll succeed. Precision-engineered brain wave frequencies induce a state of hyper-receptivity where subliminal messages get down to the very root of self-sabotage. Specially designed trigger phrases curb cravings, bolster resolve, and re-build a new sense of self that is healthy, vibrant and free from the grip of nicotine addiction.

Stop Smoking: Lose All Desire Once & for All. 1 cass. 10.49 (978-0-87554-425-0(8), SS102) Valley Sun.
There is no easier, more convenient way to program your mind, any time, any place. No distracting ocean waves or music, Silent Subliminals contain just pure subliminals that bypass your conscious hearing to go directly to your brain.

Stop Smoking: SuccessWorld Hypnotic & Subliminal Learning. David P. Illig. 2001. audio compact disk 19.99 (978-0-86580-048-9(0)) Success World.

Stop Smoking - Sleep Tape. Read by Mary Richards. 12.95 (302) Master Your Mind.
Presents suggestions that support the decision to become an ex-smoker.

Stop Smoking - Start Living. Norman J. Caldwell. Read by Norman J. Caldwell. Ed. by Achieve Now Institute Staff. 1 cass. (Running Time: 20 min.). (Self-Directed Improvement Ser.). 1988. 9.97 (978-1-56273-055-0(X)) My Mothers Pub.
If you're now at the point of wanting to become a permanent non-smoker, this tape will complete your success.

Stop Smoking / You Can Do It Today! Created by Anne H. Spencer-Beacham. 1. 2003. audio compact disk (978-1-932163-70-4(0)) Infinity Inst.

Stop Smoking Forever. Glenn Harrold. 1 cass. (Running Time: 1 hr. 30 mins.). 2002. 11.95 (978-1-901923-04-9(5)) Pub: Divinit Pubing GBR. Dist(s): Bookworld

Stop Smoking Forever. Glenn Harrold. 2 CDs. (Running Time: 3 hrs.). 2002. audio compact disk Rental 17.95 (978-1-901923-24-7(X)) Divinit Pubing GBR.

Stop Smoking Forever. Michael P. Kelly. 1 cass. 1992. 14.95 (978-1-883700-02-7(7)) ThoughtForms.
Self help.

Stop Smoking Forever. Dick Sutphen. 5 cass. (Self-Change Programming Ser.). cass. & video 59.95 Set, incl. 4 audio cass. & 1 video cass. (978-0-87554-335-2(9), PK108) Valley Sun.
Includes: Stop Smoking Forever Video Hypnosis; Instruction - Motivation Tape; The 25 Best Ways to Stop Smoking; Cutting Down on Smoking; Quitting Smoking; Stop Smoking Forever 5-tape Power Package.

Stop Smoking Forever. Eldon Taylor. Read by Eldon Taylor. Ed. by Leslie Brice. 1 cass. (Running Time: 1 hr.). 1992. 12.95 (978-1-56705-020-2(4)) Gateways Inst.
Self improvement.

Stop Smoking Forever - For Women: Subliminal Self Help. abr. ed. Audio Activation Staff. 1 CD. (Running Time: 1 hr.). (ENG.). 2003. audio compact disk 9.99 (978-0-7393-0960-5(9)) Pub: Random Audio Pubg. Dist(s): Random

Stop Smoking Forever with Mind Power, Vol. 36, Set. Jonathan Parker. Read by Jonathan Parker. 2 CDs. (Running Time: 2 hrs.). (Success Ser.: Vol. 3). 1999. audio compact disk (978-1-58400-035-8(X)) QuantumQuests Intl.
Disc 1 contains several guided visualizations. Disc 2 contains audible & subliminal positive affirmations with music.

Stop Smoking (Hypnosis), Vol. 24. Jayne Helle. 1 cass. 1995. 15.00 (978-1-891826-23-8(9)) Introspect.
Helps to become a relaxed non-smoker, without weight gain.

Stop Smoking in One Hour. Susan Hepburn. 2001. audio compact disk (978-0-00-710406-2(5), HarperThor) HarpC GBR.

Stop Smoking in Ten Days. Richard Harte. 1 cass. (Running Time: 1 hr.). (Self-Help Ser.). 1987. 9.95 (978-1-55569-196-7(X), SFH-6300) Great Am Audio.
Learn the proven method of self-hypnosis that has been successfully used by thousands of people to stop smoking.

Stop Smoking Kit. Betty L. Randolph. 2 cass. 19.95 (802S; 30S) Randolph Tapes.
Ten day program which includes goal setting target, subliminal program messages plus secrets of success & information.

Stop Smoking Naturally. 2005. audio compact disk (978-1-932086-22-5(6)) L Lizards Pub Co.

Stop Smoking Naturally: An HSR Trance Formation Tape. Dean A. Montalbano. 3. (Running Time: 3hrs). 2002. 49.95 (978-1-932086-02-7(1)) L Lizards Pub Co.

Stop Smoking Now! Gil Boyne. Read by Gil Boyne. 1 cass. (Running Time: 45 min.). (Hypnosis Motivation Cassettes Ser.). 1977. 9.95 (114) Westwood Pub Co.
Your need & desire to smoke are eliminated through powerful subconscious suggestions, so you act automatically to control this hazardous habit, without painful "psychological withdrawal".

Stop Smoking Now! Mel Gilley. Ed. by Steven C. Eggleston. 1 cass. (World of Hypnosis Ser.). 1987. 6.95 SCE Prod & List & Lrn.
Self-hypnosis to stop smoking.

Stop Smoking Now: Echotech. Eldon Taylor. Read by Eldon Taylor. Ed. by Leslie Brice. 1 cass. (Running Time: 1 hr.). 1992. 19.95 (978-1-56705-004-2(2)) Gateways Inst.
Self improvement.

Stop Smoking Now: OZO. Eldon Taylor. Read by Eldon Taylor. Ed. by Leslie Brice. 1 cass. (Running Time: 1 hr.). 1992. 19.95 (978-1-56705-015-8(8)) Gateways Inst.

Stop Smoking Permanently, Vol. 8. Jonathan Parker. Read by Jonathan Parker. 1 CD. (Running Time: 1 hr.). (Subliminal Ser.: Vol. 4). 1999. audio compact disk (978-1-58400-049-5(X)) QuantumQuests Intl.
1 compact disc with subliminal affirmations & classical music.

Stop Smoking Permanently, Vol. 24. Jonathan Parker. 2 cass. (Running Time: 1 hr. 45 min.). 1992. 17.00 Set. (978-1-58400-023-5(6)) QuantumQuests Intl.

Stop Smoking Program: The Revolutionary Manhattan Hypnosis Approach. Kurt Ostergaard. (ENG.). 2009. DVD & audio compact disk 127.00 (978-0-615-28451-4(5)) Man Hyp.

Stop Smoking Program (Hypnosis & Subliminal) Stop Smoking Subliminal - Stress Related to Quit Smoking & Prevent Weight Gain, Vol. 2. Jayne Helle. 4 cass. (Running Time: 3 hrs. 45 min.). 1995. 49.00 Set. (978-1-891826-01-6(8)) Introspect.

Stop Smoking (Subliminal), Vol. 25. Jayne Helle. 1 cass. 1995. 15.00 (978-1-891826-24-5(7)) Introspect.
Helps to become a relaxed non-smoker, without weight gain. Can be used anywhere.

Stop Smoking the Positive Changes Way. Patrick K. Porter. 4 cass. 1995. 16.00 Set. (978-0-9637611-0-1(2)) Positive Chngs Hypnosis.
Self-help guided imagery.

Stop Smoking Today Reinforcement. Ormond McGill. 2000. (978-1-933332-13-0(1)) Hypnotherapy Train.

Stop Smoking with Self-Hypnosis: Better Health in Thirty Days. unabr. ed. Clark Redwoods. Read by Clark Redwoods. 1 cass. (Running Time: 60 min.). 1994. 10.99 (978-1-892654-00-7(8), BET010) FutureLife.
Self-hypnosis techniques & exercises to break smoking habit.

Stop Smoking/Start Living. 1998. 24.95 (978-1-58557-013-3(3)) Dynamic Growth.

Stop Smoking/Start Living: You're at the point of wanting to become a non smoker. This CD will complete your Success. Scripts. Norm Caldwell. 1 CD. (Running Time: 20 Minutes). (ENG.). 1988. 14.95 (978-1-56273-034-5(7)) My Mothers Pub.

S.T.O.P. Stay Thin on Purpose. Betty L. Randolph. Read by Betty L. Randolph. Read by Leonard Baron. Ed. by Success Education Institute International. 4 cass. (Health Ser.). 1989. 39.95 Set. (978-1-55909-264-7(5), PACS) Randolph Tapes.
Eight weight loss programs (4 audible, 4 subliminal). Side 1 - Spoken word with music visual imagery plus behavior modification & healthy nutrition. Side 2 - Subliminal reinforcement of program, ocean background.

Stop Stuttering. Barrie Konicov. 1 cass. (YA). 11.98 (978-0-87082-456-2(2), 128) Potentials.
The author explains that post-hypnotic suggestions can keep speech clear & stop stuttering.

Stop Substance Abuse. Betty L. Randolph. Read by Betty L. Randolph. Read by Leonard Baron. Ed. by Success Education Institute International. 1 cass. (Running Time: 45 min.). (I Can Ser.). 1989. bk. 9.98 (978-1-55909-195-4(9), 62M) Randolph Tapes.
Helps you take control of your life & kick the habit. Subliminal messages are heard 3-5 minutes before becoming ocean sounds or music.

Stop the Drugs in the Black Community! Jawanza Kunjufu. 1 cass. (Running Time: 60 mins.). 1999. 5.95 (AT9) African Am Imag.

Stop the Investing Rip-off: How to Avoid Being a Victim & Make More Money. abr. ed. David B. Loeper. Read by Erik Synnestvedt. (Running Time: 6 hrs.). (ENG.). 2009. 24.98 (978-1-59659-404-3(7), GildAudio) Pub: Gildan Media. Dist(s): HachBkGrp

Stop the Investing Rip-off: How to Avoid Being a Victim & Make More Money. unabr. abr. ed. David B. Loeper. Read by Walter Dixon. (Running Time: 5 hrs.). (ENG.). 2009. audio compact disk 29.98 (978-1-59659-344-2(X), GildAudio) Pub: Gildan Media. Dist(s): HachBkGrp

Stop the Press: Tales of Reporters on the Radio. Perf. by Fred Mac Murry et al. 2008. audio compact disk 31.95 (978-1-57019-864-9(0)) Radio Spirits.

Stop the Press! Tales of Reporters on the Radio. unabr. ed. Anthony Tollin. 8 CDs. (Running Time: 8 hrs.). 2006. audio compact disk 26.95 (978-0-9770819-7-4(4), 8197) Choice Vent.

Stop the Retirement Rip-off: How to Avoid Hidden Fees & Keep More of Your Money. unabr. ed. David B. Loeper. Read by Erik Synnestvedt. (Running Time: 4 hrs.). (ENG.). 2009. 24.98 (978-1-59659-394-7(6), GildAudio) Pub: Gildan Media. Dist(s): HachBkGrp

Stop the Retirement Rip-off: How to Avoid Hidden Fees & Keep More of Your Money. unabr. abr. ed. David B. Loeper. Read by Walter Dixon & Erik Synnesvetd. (Running Time: 4 hrs.). (ENG.). 2009. audio compact disk 29.98 (978-1-59659-340-4(7), GildAudio) Pub: Gildan Media. Dist(s): HachBkGrp

Stop the Train! unabr. ed. Geraldine McCaughrean. Read by Full Cast Production Staff. (J). 2007. 44.99 (978-1-59895-882-9(8)) Find a World.

Stop the Ward... I Want to Get Off!, Set. Joni Hilton. 2 cass. (As the Ward Turns Ser.). 1999. 13.95 (978-1-57734-439-1(1), 07002025) Covenant Comms.
"As the Ward Turns" series.

Stop the Whining. unabr. ed. Contrib. by Pat Wagner & Alan Dumas. 1 cass. (Running Time: 55 min.). 1999. 12.95 (978-0-9642678-9-3(6)) Pattern Res.
How to complain effectively.

Stop the World, I Want to Get On: Fulton J. Sheen, Vol. I. unabr. ed. Fulton J. Sheen. 7 cass. (Running Time: 30 min.). (Life Is Worth Living Ser.: 0002). 1985. 29.95 F Sheen Comm.
The late Bishop Sheen explains how we connect events to life. Our private vision to a reality within our hearts.

Stop-Time. unabr. ed. Frank Conroy. Narrated by Frank Muller. 8 cass. (Running Time: 10 hrs. 45 mins.). 1999. 70.00 (978-0-7887-0220-4(3), 94445E7) Recorded Bks.
His own passage from childhood to adolescence & beyond.

***Stop Whining, Start Living.** unabr. ed. Laura Schlessinger. Read by Lily Lobianco. (ENG.). 2008. (978-0-06-157960-8(2)) HarperCollins Pubs.

***Stop Whining, Start Living.** unabr. ed. Laura Schlessinger. Read by Lily Lobianco. (ENG.). 2008. (978-0-06-157961-5(0)) HarperCollins Pubs.

Stop Whining, Start Living: Turning Hurt into Happiness. abr. ed. Laura Schlessinger. 2008. audio compact disk 24.95 (978-0-06-145913-9(5), Harper Audio) HarperCollins Pubs.

Stop Whining, Start Living: Turning Hurt into Happiness. unabr. ed. Laura Schlessinger & L. Schlessinger. Read by Lily Lobianco. 5 CDs. (Running Time: 5 hrs.). 2008. audio compact disk 29.95 (978-0-06-145637-4(3), Harper Audio) HarperCollins Pubs.

***Stopover in a Quiet Town.** (ENG.). 2010. audio compact disk (978-1-59171-264-0(5)) Falcon Picture.

Stopping by Woods on a Snowy Evening see Robert Frost in Recital

Stopping by Woods on a Snowy Evening see Twentieth-Century Poetry in English, No. 6, Recordings of Poets Reading Their Own Poetry

Stopping Identity Theft: 10 Easy Steps to Security. rev. ed. Scott Mitic. (ENG.). 2009. audio compact disk 19.99 (978-1-4133-0980-5(1)) Nolo.

Stopping Procrastination. Shad Helmstetter. 1 cass. (Self-Talk Cassettes). 10.95 (978-0-937065-04-4(8)) Grindle Pr.

Stopping Smoking. Shad Helmstetter. 1 cass. (Self-Talk Cassettes Ser.). 10.95 (978-0-937065-19-8(6)) Grindle Pr.

Stopping Smoking: Creative Visualizations for Creating a New Reality. Created by Stanley Haluska. 1 CD. (Running Time: 70 mins). 2004. audio compact disk 15.00 (978-0-9668872-3-5(9), AP108) Awakening Pubns Inc.

***Stopping Stress Before It Stops You: A Game Plan for Every Mom.** unabr. ed. Kevin Leman. Narrated by Wayne Shepherd. (Running Time: 6 hrs. 0 mins. 0 sec.). (ENG.). 2011. audio compact disk 22.99 (978-1-59859-857-5(0)) Oasis Audio.

Stopping Tollroads - New Highways Through Natural Habitat in Orange County, California. Hosted by Nancy Pearlman. 1 cass. (Running Time: 29 min.). 10.00 (1313) Educ Comm CA.

Stopping Violent Crime: New Directions for Reduction & Prevention. Arthur R. Miller. (Running Time: 57 mins.). (ENG.). 2004. 9.95 (978-0-945999-94-2(1)) Pub: Independent Inst. Dist(s): IPG Chicago

Stopwatch & an Ordinance Map see Twentieth-Century Poetry in English, No. 9, Recordings of Poets Reading Their Own Poetry

Stor Amhran. unabr. ed. Perf. by Noirin Ni Riain. 1 CD. (Running Time: 53 min.). 1995. audio compact disk 16.98 (978-1-56455-345-4(0), MM00270D) Sounds True.
Presents 18 traditional songs, including: Eamann Mhagaine; Le hAis na Siuire; Sliabh Geal gCua; A Bhurcaigh Bhui on g Ceim; & More.

Storage & Systems Management Leadership Conference: The World's Top CEOs on Best Practices & Strategies for Success. Speeches. ReedLogic Conference Staff. (Running Time: 4 hrs). 2006. audio compact disk 249.95 (978-1-59701-055-9(3)) Aspatore Bks.
The Storage and Systems Management Leadership Conference features nine speeches totaling more than four hours of authoritative, insider?s perspectives on the best practices of the world?s top storage and systems management companies. Featuring executives representing some of the nation's top companies, this conference provides a broad yet comprehensive overview of implementing dynamic storage business strategies to provide customers with superior storage management solutions and service level agreements. Each speaker shares their insight for thriving business practices and industry expertise in a format similar to a radio address, with graphics displayed in the background. Simply insert the CD-ROM into your computer, sit back, and watch and learn from the top professionals in the field as they discuss their specific storage and systems management processes for working with clients and ensuring success. The breadth of perspectives presented enable attendees to get inside some of the great minds of the storage world without leaving the office. The Conference has been produced on CD-ROM and can be viewed in PowerPoint by any PC-based computer.The conference features speeches by:1. Noel Barnard, Chairman, President & CEO, HyPerformix, Inc. ? ?Predictive Rather Than Reactive?2. Chris Broderick, Senior Vice President and General Manager of Computer Associates?s Storage Management Business Unit, ?Integration?3. Robert Cramer, President & CEO LiveVault Corporation ? ?Data Protection Made Simple?4. Gary Doan, CEO ,Intradyn, Inc. ? ?Back-up Versus Archive?5. E. Alexander Goldstein, CEO, Configuresoft, Inc. ? ?Compelling Product?6. Michael Grove, CEO, Open Country, Inc. ? ?Going From ?Blah? To What Makes A Difference?7. Yoram Novick, CEO, Topio, Inc. ? ?Listen To The Customer?8. Howard Reisman, Chairman & CEO, Heroix Corporation ? ?Technical And Customer Care?9. Alfred Zollar ? General Manager IBM Tivoli Software, IBM Corporation ? ?Storage and System Management Best Practices.?In this CD you will learn:? Crucial mistakes and pitfalls to avoid when implementing storage best practices? The financial benefit of implementing an organized storage management system? How rapidly the storage industry has changed and grown? An insider?s view of what of storage systems and software might exist 5-10 years down the road.

Storage Area Network in Belgium: A Strategic Reference 2006. Compiled by Icon Group International, Inc. Staff. 2007. ring bd. 195.00 (978-0-497-35829-7(8)) Icon Grp.

Storage Area Networks (SAN) in Brazil: A Strategic Reference 2006. Compiled by Icon Group International, Inc. Staff. 2007. ring bd. 195.00 (978-0-497-35843-3(3)) Icon Grp.

Storage Area Networks (SAN) in Germany: A Strategic Reference 2006. Compiled by Icon Group International, Inc. Staff. 2007. ring bd. 195.00 (978-0-497-35986-7(3)) Icon Grp.

Storage Tank Litigation. 1995. bk. 99.00 (ACS-1012) PA Bar Inst.
There is a gray line between who is liable & who is not when it comes to cleanup of storage tank spills & leaks. Because there is so much uncertainty in these cases, a legal battle can tie up the court system for years at a time.

Stori Telling. abr. ed. Tori Spelling. Read by Tori Spelling. 5 CDs. (Running Time: 6 hrs. 0 mins. 0 sec.). (ENG.). 2008. audio compact disk 29.99 (978-0-7435-8239-1(X)) Pub: S&S Audio. Dist(s): S and S Inc

Storiau Pum Munud. Catherine Aran & Tympan. 2005. audio compact disk 11.99 (978-0-9546025-2-9(8)) Tympan GBR.

Stories. Short Stories. Perf. by Gioia Timpanelli. 1 cass. (Running Time: 60 min.). (YA). (gr. 7 up). 1990. 9.95 (978-0-938756-29-3(X), 070) Yellow Moon.
In this studio recorded tape the noted storyteller Gioia Timpanelli, who has appeared often with Robert Bly around the US, shares personal stories, two Sicilian folktales & three Grimm Brothers tales. Includes a marvelous telling of "Cinderella," taken from the original & as you've probably never heard it. This is an equally wonderful tape for both adults & children. The stories show a reverence for the natural world & honor how the extraordinary things are made of the ordinary.

***Stories.** unabr. ed. Neil Gaiman & Al Sarrantonio. Read by Anne Bobby et al. 2010. (978-0-06-201621-8(0), Harper Audio); (978-0-06-198879-0(0), Harper Audio) HarperCollins Pubs.

Stories. unabr. ed. Zora Neale Hurston. Read by Renee Joshua-Porter. 3 CDs. (Running Time: 3 hrs.). 1996. audio compact disk 29.95 (978-1-883332-53-2(2)) Audio Bkshelf.
Seven of Hurston's best-loved stories dance & soar.

Stories: An Audio Collection. abr. unabr. ed. Garrison Keillor. Read by Garrison Keillor. 3 CDs. (Running Time: 3 hrs.). (ENG.). 1993. audio compact disk 29.95 (978-1-56511-009-0(9), 1565110099) Pub: HighBridge. Dist(s): Workman Pub

***Stories: An Audio Collection.** unabr. ed. Garrison Keillor. Read by Garrison Keillor. (ENG.). 2010. audio compact disk 24.95 (978-1-61573-078-0(8), 1615730788) Pub: HighBridge. Dist(s): Workman Pub

Stories: Old as the World Fresh as the Rain. Short Stories. As told by Laura Simms. Music by Steve Gorn. 1 cass. (Running Time: 45 mins.). 1999. 9.95 (978-0-938756-54-5(0)) Yellow Moon.
For this collection, Laura Simms has gathered together six timeless tales that she breathes new life into with her vibrant storytelling. Music by Steve Gorn creates a vivid backdrop for each story. The stories Laura has included on this tape are all traditional tales that remain fresh and enchanting in today's world.

Stories - Old as the World, Fresh as the Rain. Read by Laura Simms. 1 cass. (Running Time: 51 min.). (J). (gr. k-8). 1981. 8.95 (978-0-89719-935-3(9), WW712C) Weston Woods.
Collection includes "a Single Grain of Rice," "the Woodcutter," "Magoolie," "the Magic Crystal," "Superman" & "The Wooden Box".

Stories about Divorce to Aid Children Understand the Situation. unabr. ed. Perf. by Julie Harris & Joseph Wiseman. 1 cass. (Running Time: 90 mins.). (J). 1987. 8.98 (CDL5 1362) HarperCollins Pubs.
Includes " A visit to Daddy's House," "Secret" & "Where Is Daddy?".

Stories about Kids Like Us. 1999th ed. Perf. by Ethel Barrett. 1 cass. (J). 1999. 7.99 Gospel Lght.
Eleven contemporary stories & one Bible story play.

Stories about the West. Elizabeth R. Montgomery. Read by Laurie Klein. 3 cass. (Running Time: 4 hrs.). Dramatization. 1990. 21.95 (978-1-55686-096-6(X), 096) Books in Motion.
Three short stories, historical & simplified for children. Included are: When Pioneers Pushed West to Oregon, Chief Joseph, Lewis & Clark.

Stories & Sea Songs by Jay O'Callahan & John Langstaff. Jay O'Callahan. Perf. by Jay O'Callahan. Perf. by John Langstaff. 1 CD. (Running Time: 50 min. 40 sec). Dramatization. (YA). 2004. audio compact disk 15.00 (978-1-877954-47-4(0)) Pub: Artana Prodns. Dist(s): Yellow Moon
Jay O'Callahan and John Langstaff, longtime friends, came together on a Sunday afternoon for a concert of Stories and Sea Songs. John, famed baritone and founder of The Revels, sang marvelous sea songs and Jay told his story "The Herring Shed." This is a live recording of Act I of that concert.

Stories & Songs. unabr. ed. Eve Ilsen. Read by Eve Ilsen. 1 cass. 1996. 11.00 (31101) Big Sur Tapes.
Uses songs to create sacred space & stories to convey a sense of the inexplicable & extraordinary - the points at which sparks of realization break through the patterns of everyday life. Her compelling renditions bring forth the mystical dimensions of the stories, most of which are selected from Jewish sources.

Stories & Songs for Little Children. Perf. by Pete Seeger. 1 cass. (Running Time: 36 min.). (ps up). 1995. audio compact disk 15.98 (978-0-942303-08-7(3), HW 1207D) Pub: August Hse. Dist(s): Natl Bk Netwk
Nine songs & stories for young listeners, including such classics as "Green Grass Grew All Around," "Skip to My Lou," "Frog Went A-Courting," & "Abiyoyo." Naird award winner.

Stories & Songs for Little Children. Perf. by Pete Seeger. 1 cass. (Running Time: 36 min.). (J). (ps up). 1992. 9.95 (978-0-942303-05-6(9), HW 1207C) Pub: High Windy Audio. Dist(s): August Hse

Stories & Songs for Little Children. Perf. by Pete Seeger. 1 cass. (J). (ps-5). 9.98 (2114) MFLP CA.
In this wonderful collection story & song come together to create the intimate atmosphere of a campfire circle. Songs include: "Foolish Frog," "Abiyoyo," "Skip to My Lou," "Racoon's Got a Bushy Tail" & more.

Stories & Songs from Ananda. 1 cass. (Running Time: 40 min.). (J). 9.95 (MP-30) Crystal Clarity.
Stories & songs conveying timeless spiritual values, including "A Special Victory" & "A Letter to God," adapted from "Stories of Mukunda" by Sri Kriyananda: "Two Frogs & the Bucket," "The Birds of the Air," "Crystal in Your Eyes," & "Little Kathy".

Stories & Songs of Jesus. Christopher C. Walker & Paule Freeburg, Sr. Read by Christopher C. Walker & Paule Freeburg, Sr. 1 cass. (J). (gr. k-3). 1997. 12.95 (9404); audio compact disk 24.95 (10610) OR Catholic.
22 stories from the life of Jesus with a song for each story.

Stories at the Tipi. Read by Joe Hayes. 1 cass. (J). (gr. k-6). 1989. 10.95 (978-0-939729-17-3(2)) Trails West Pub.
Joe Hayes live at the Wheelwright Museum of the American Indian.

***Stories Behind Men of Faith.** Ace Collins. (Running Time: 6 hrs. 49 mins. 0 sec.). (ENG.). 2009. 16.99 (978-0-310-77281-1(8)) Zondervan.

Stories Behind the Best-Loved Songs of Christmas. unabr. ed. Ace Collins. (Running Time: 4 hrs. 18 mins. 0 sec.). (ENG.). 2008. 15.99 (978-0-310-29352-1(9)) Zondervan.

***Stories Behind the Greatest Hits of Christmas.** unabr. ed. Ace Collins. (Running Time: 5 hrs. 33 mins. 16 sec.). (ENG.). 2010. 15.99 (978-0-310-59752-0(8)) Zondervan.

***Stories Behind the Traditions & Songs of Easter.** Ace Collins. (Running Time: 4 hrs. 40 mins. 0 sec.). (ENG.). 2008. 15.99 (978-0-310-30528-6(4)) Zondervan.

Stories by Beatrix Potter: The Tale of Peter Rabbit, the Tale of Mr. Jeremy Fisher, & the Tailor of Gloucester. unabr. ed. Beatrix Potter & Rabbit Ears Books Staff. Read by Meryl Streep. (Running Time: 2820 sec.). (Rabbit Ears Ser.). (ENG.). (J). (gr. 1). 2007. audio compact disk 11.95 (978-0-7393-3871-1(4), Listening Lib) Pub: Random Audio Pubg. Dist(s): Random

Stories by Ethel Wilson - Shaw Festival. Christopher Newton. 1 CD. (Running Time: 1 hr. 30 mins.). 2005. audio compact disk 12.95 (978-0-660-18813-3(9)) Pub: Canadian Broadcasting CAN. Dist(s): Georgetown Term

Stories by Grimm see Cuentos de Grimm

Stories by Mordecai Richler. unabr. ed. Read by Louis Negin. 2 cass. (Running Time: 2 hrs. 12 mins.). (Stage Ser.). (gr. 9-12). 2004. 18.99 (978-1-894003-30-8(6)) Pub: Scenario Prods CAN. Dist(s): Baker Taylor

Stories by Stuhlman: Vol. 1: My Own Pesah Story & other Jewish Stories. Daniel D. Stuhlman. 1. (Running Time: 64). (ENG.). 2006. audio compact disk 11.00 (978-0-934402-31-6(0)) BYLS Pr.

Stories by Stuhlman Vol. 1 & 2: My Own Hanukah Story & other Jewish Stories. Short Stories. Daniel D. Stuhlman. 1. (Running Time: 64). Dramatization. 2006. audio compact disk 11.00 (978-0-934402-32-3(9)) BYLS Pr.
Jewish stories for adults and children. Including My Own Hanukah Story.

Stories Children Love to Hear. abr. ed. Ed. by Charlotte Harrison. 2 cass. (Running Time: 57 min.). Incl. Beauty & the Beast. (J). (837); Jack & the Beanstalk. (J). (837); Rumpelstiltskin. (J). (837); Sleeping Beauty. (J). (837); Snow White & the Seven Dwarfs. (J). (837); (J). 12.95 (978-0-89926-149-2(3), 837) Audio Bk.

Stories for Children. unabr. ed. Alicia Aspenwall. Read by Jean DeBarbieris. 2 cass. (Running Time: 2 hrs. 30 min.). Dramatization. (J). 1990. 16.95 (978-1-55686-095-9(1), 095) Books in Motion.
Short stories included are: The Echo-Maid & The Land of the Wee-Uns.

Stories for Heroes - Arthur Celebrity Audiobook. Short Stories. Marc Brown. Executive Producer Vinodh Bhat. Arranged by Little. Executive Producer Neal Shenoy. Voice by Clay Aiken et al. Des. by Jeff Smith. 1. (Running Time: 80 mins.). Dramatization. (J). 2004. audio compact disk 19.99 (978-0-9754049-0-4(3)) Two Twelve MEDIA.
Notable personalities in media and entertainment such as Clay Aiken, Kevin Bacon, Marcia Gay Harden and Kelly Ripa read stories from the Arthur Adventure series. The proceeds will benefit 3 charities: Elizabeth Glaser Pediatric AIDS Foundation, the National Education Association and the Bubel/Aiken Foundation.

Stories for Small Angels. Gary W. Cook. (J). 2007. audio compact disk 14.99 (978-1-60247-135-1(5)) Tate Pubng.

Stories for the Road. Connie Regan-Blake & Barbara Freeman. 1 cass. (Running Time: 40 min.). 1992. 10.99 (978-1-929415-01-4(X)) StoryWindow Prodns.
Traditional, literary & original stories for all ages - perfect for traveling & family vacations.

Stories for the Road & to Grow On: The Folktellers Award Winning Classics. Connie Regan-Blake & Barbara Freeman. Photos by Connie Regan-Blake & Barbara Freeman. (J). (gr. k-6). 2006. audio compact disk 12.99 (978-1-929415-07-6(9)) StoryWindow Prodns.

Stories for the Telling. abr. ed. Alma Flor Ada. (Libros para Contar / Stories for the Telling Ser.). (ENG.). (J). (ps-3). 2008. audio compact disk 15.95 (978-1-60396-347-3(2), Alfaguara) Santillana.

Stories for Young Readers & the Wizard of the Wood. unabr. collector's ed. Elleston Trevor & Jonquil Trevor. Read by Gary Martin & Donada Peters. 5 cass. (Running Time: 5 hrs.). (Woodlander Ser.). (J). (gr. 4 up). 1992. 30.00 (978-0-7366-2092-5(3), 2898) Books on Tape.
Strange & wonderful things are happening in Deep Wood plus stories by Jonquil Trevor.

Stories from American History. Myrtis Mixon. 2 cass. (Running Time: 3 hrs.). 2000. 34.94 (P1793-X) M-H Contemporary.
Collection of high-interest original stories about famous people & events in American history such as Ponce de Leon. Chief Joseph & Susan B. Anthony, the 1849 Gold Rush, the San Francisco Earthquake, the Vietnam War Protests & many more.

Stories from an Irish Fireside. Read by Eamon Kelly. 1 cass. 10.95 (SAC 46-3) Spoken Arts.

Stories from Han Andersen see Cuentos de Andersen

Stories from Home, Vols.I & II. unabr. ed. Mitch Jayne. Read by Mitch Jayne. 2 cass. (Running Time: 2 hrs.). 15.00 Set. (978-1-882467-02-0(7)) Wildstone Media.
Mitch Jayne is a writer, humorist, & storyteller from the Missouri Ozarks. These tapes feature the wit & wisdom of Mitch in such stories as "Mother Nature", "The Ozark Language", "Yard Sales" & many more.

Stories from Lake Wobegon. Garrison Keillor. pap. bk. 59.95 (978-0-88432-995-4(X), SEN265) J Norton Pubs.

Stories from Many Lands. 1 cass. (Running Time: 41 min.). (Picture Book Parade Ser.). (J). (ps-4). 1986. 8.95 (978-0-89719-932-2(4), WW736C) Weston Woods.
Includes "The Silver Cow," "The Stonecutter," "The Treasure," "Tikki, Tikki Tembo," "The Hole in the Dike" & "One Fine Day".

Stories from Shakespeare. David Timson. Read by Juliet Stevenson & Michael Sheen. 3 CDs. (Running Time: 14270 sec.). (Junior Classics Ser.). (J). (ps-7). 2005. audio compact disk 22.98 (978-962-634-351-7(6)) Naxos UK GBR.

Stories from Shakespeare 2. David Timson. Read by Juliet Stevenson & Alex Jennings. (Classic Literature with Classical Music Ser.). (J). 2006. audio compact disk 22.98 (978-962-634-409-5(1), Naxos AudioBooks) Naxos.

Stories from Shakespeare 3. abr. ed. David Timson. Read by Juliet Stevenson & Simon Russell Beale. (Running Time: 13947 sec.). (Classic Fiction Ser.). (J). (gr. 3-8). 2008. audio compact disk 22.98 (978-962-634-873-4(9), Naxos AudioBooks) Naxos.

Stories from Starlight, Set. John Shea. 2 cass. (Running Time: 3 hrs.). 1993. 15.95 (978-0-87946-087-7(3), 324) ACTA Pubns.
Stories & reflections on Christmas.

Stories from Superior Heartland. Based on a book by Fred Rydholm. (ENG.). 2003. audio compact disk 14.95 (978-0-9823000-2-2(6)) TopWater Prod.

Stories from Tanglewood Tales. unabr. ed. Nathaniel Hawthorne. Read by Mary Starkey. 3 cass. (Running Time: 4 hrs.). Dramatization. 1990. 21.95 (978-1-55686-098-0(6), 098) Books in Motion.
Several stories. Included are: Pandora & the Mysterious Box, The Miraculous Pitcher, The Pomegranate Seeds, The Golden Touch, The Pygmies.

Stories from the Bible. unabr. ed. Read by Jane Webb. 4 cass. (J). 23.80 (E-307) Audio Bk.

Stories from the Enchanted Loom. Perf. by Marcia Lane. (J). 1999. audio compact disk 14.95 (978-0-939065-79-0(7)) Gentle Wind.

Stories from the Enchanted Loom. Read by Marcia Lane. 1 cass. (Running Time: 56 min.). (J). (gr. k-7). 1987. 9.95 (978-0-939065-36-3(3), GW 1040) Gentle Wind.
Enchanting stories & songs including 'Rumplestiltskin,' 'The Mouse Bride,' & Edward Lear's 'The Jumblies'.

Stories from the Golden Age Display W/ Out Audio. L. Ron Hubbard. 358.20 (978-1-59212-248-6(5)); 348.25 (978-1-59212-363-6(5)) Gala Pr LLC.

Stories from the Hearth World Folk Stories, Vol. 2. unabr. ed. Maureen Pedone. Read by Maureen Pedone. Read by Kathryn Hurd et al. Ed. by Joanna Sales. 2 cass. (Running Time: 65 min.). (J). (gr. k-6). 1995. 12.95 Set. (978-1-886088-03-0(9)); audio compact disk 14.95 CD. (978-1-886088-04-7(7)) Stories Hearth.
Folk stories, with music & sound effects, from Russia, Greece, Persia, Japan & Arctic tundra.

Stories from the Italian Country Table: Exploring the Culture of Italian Farmhouse Cooking. Lynne Rossetto Kasper. 2004. 7.95 (978-0-7435-4886-1(8)) Pub: S&S Audio. Dist(s): S and S Inc

Stories from the Jungle Book. Rudyard Kipling. 2009. (978-1-60136-049-6(5)) Audio Holding.

Stories from the Jungle Book. unabr. ed. Rudyard Kipling. Read by Laurie Klein. 3 cass. (Running Time: 3 hrs.). Dramatization. (J). 1990. 21.95 (978-1-55686-097-3(8), 097) Books in Motion.
Four short stories from the Jungle Book included: Mowgli's Brothers; Rikki Tikki Tavi; Kaa's Hunting; The White Seal.

Stories from the Jungle Books. Rudyard Kipling. Narrated by Stephan Cox. (Running Time: 16200 sec.). (Unabridged Classics in MP3 Ser.). (ENG.). (J). 2008. audio compact disk 14.95 (978-1-58472-604-3(0), In Aud); audio compact disk 24.00 (978-1-58472-601-2(6), In Aud) Sound Room.

Stories from the Jungle Books. unabr. ed. Joseph Rudyard Kipling. Read by Ralph Cosham. 4 cds. (Running Time: 4 hrs 24 mins). (J). 2002. audio compact disk 26.95 (978-1-58472-330-1(0), 021, In Aud) Pub: Sound Room. Dist(s): Baker Taylor
The adventures of Mowgli, the boy who was raised by wolves.

Stories from the Jungle Books. unabr. ed. Rudyard Kipling. Read by Ralph Cosham. (J). 2006. 34.99 (978-1-59895-183-7(1)) Find a World.

Stories from the Spirit World: Legends of Native Americans Pt. 1: The Old Ways Are Gone. 1 cass. (Running Time: 90 min.). 11.95 (F004AB090, HarperThor) HarpC GBR.

Stories from the Spirit World: Legends of Native Americans Pt. 2: The Legend of the Sun. 1 cass. (Running Time: 60 min.). 10.95 (F004BB090, HarperThor) HarpC GBR.

Stories from the Spirit World: Legends of Native Americans Pt. 3: December's Child. 1 cass. (Running Time: 60 min.). 10.95 (F004CB090, HarperThor) HarpC GBR.

Stories from the Spirit World: Legends of Native Americans Pt. 4: Confrontation of Mythologies. 1 cass. (Running Time: 30 min.). 9.95 (F004DB090, HarperThor) HarpC GBR.

Stories from the States. 2005. pap. bk. 44.95 (978-1-86015-476-8(X)) Ulverscroft US.

Stories from under the Redwoods. unabr. ed. Bret Harte. Read by Mark St. John. 6 cass. (Running Time: 5 hrs. 30 min.). Dramatization. 1989. 36.95 Set. (978-1-55686-337-0(3), 337) Books in Motion.
Fine collection of the ten best western short stories from Bret Harte's book entitled Under the Redwoods.

Stories from Wildwood, Collection 1: A Good Foundation. 2004. 19.00 (978-1-57972-598-3(8)); audio compact disk 17.00 (978-1-57972-597-6(X)) Insight Living.

Stories from Wildwood, Collection 1: A Good Foundation. 2003. 19.00 (978-1-57972-538-9(4)) Insight Living.

Stories from Wildwood, Collection 1: A Good Foundation. 2003. audio compact disk 17.00 (978-1-57972-537-2(6)) Insight Living.

Stories from Wildwood, Collection 2: Character Counts. 2004. audio compact disk 17.00 (978-1-57972-603-4(8)); audio compact disk 19.00 (978-1-57972-604-1(6)) Insight Living.

Stories from Wildwood, Collection 2: Character Counts. 2003. 19.00 (978-1-57972-540-2(6)); audio compact disk 17.00 (978-1-57972-539-6(2)) Insight Living.

Stories from Xenophon - Excerpts. unabr. ed. Xenophon. Narrated by Nelson Runger. 3 cass. (Running Time: 4 hrs. 30 mins.). 1992. 26.00 (978-1-55690-752-4(4), 92119E7) Recorded Bks.
A contemporary account of the Peloponnesian war & the withdrawal of the Greek armies from Persia.

Stories Hollywood Never Tells. Howard Zinn. (ENG.). 2000. audio compact disk 13.98 (978-1-902593-36-4(7)) Pub: AK Pr GBR. Dist(s): Consort Bk Sales

Stories in My Pocket: Tales Kids Can Tell. Martha Hamilton & Mitch Weiss. 1998. 9.95 (978-1-55591-996-2(0)) Fulcrum Pub.

Stories Just Right for Kids. Read by Laura Simms. Music by Steve Gorn. 1 cass. (Running Time: 45 mins.). (J). 2000. 9.95 Yellow Moon.

Stories of Edgar Allen Poe. 2 cass. (J). 16.95 (MOSW013, Monterey SoundWorks) Monterey Media Inc.

Stories of Edgar Allen Poe. Prod. by Monterey SoundWorks. 2 cass. (Running Time: 1 hr. 16 mins.). 2001. 16.95 (MOSW013) Lodestone Catalog.
Famous tales from a master storyteller: "The Gold Bug, "The Cask of Amontillado, "The Fall of the House of Usher" to name a few to chill you & thrill you.

Stories of Ernest Hemingway. unabr. ed. Short Stories. Ernest Hemingway. Read by Alexander Scourby. 6 cass. (Running Time: 5 hrs. 33 mins.). 44.95 (L143) Blckstn Audio.
Includes "The Short Happy Life of Francis Macomber"; "The Snows of Kilimanjaro"; "The Capital of the World"; "The Killers"; "The Undefeated"; "A Clean, Well-Lighted Place"; "The Gambler"; "The Nun & the Radio" & "Fifty Grand.".

Stories of Ernest Hemingway. unabr. ed. Ernest Hemingway. Read by Alexander Scourby. 6 cass. (Running Time: 5 hrs. 34 min.). Incl. Capital of the World. 1977. (CXL 504CX); Clean, Well-Lighted Place. 1977. (CXL 504CX); Fifty Grand. 1977. (CXL 504CX); Gambler, the Nun & the Radio. 1977. (CXL 504CX); Killers. 1977. (CXL 504CX); Short Happy Life of Francis Macomber. 1977. (CXL 504CX); Snows of Kilimanjaro. Ernest Hemingway. 1977. (CXL 504CX); Undefeated. 1977. (CXL 504CX); Stories of Ernest Hemingway. Ernest Hemingway. Read by Alexander Scourby. 1977. (CXL 504CX); 1977. 44.98 (978-0-8072-2921-7(0), CXL 504CX, Listening Lib) Random Audio Pubg.
The eight stories in this collection are classic examples of Hemingway's shorter pieces.

Stories of Ernest Hemingway, Set unabr. ed. Ernest Hemingway. Read by Alexander Scourby. 6 cass. 1999. 44.98 (LL 0022) AudioGO.

Stories of F. Scott Fitzgerald. unabr. ed. F. Scott Fitzgerald. Read by Robert Sean Leonard et al. 6 cass. (Running Time: 9 hrs.). (gr. 9-12). 2001. 34.95 (978-0-694-52446-4(8)) HarperCollins Pubs.

Stories of Faith for Christmas: Guideposts for the Spirit. unabr. ed. (Running Time: 4 hrs. 23 mins. 13 sec.). (ENG.). 2008. 13.99 (978-1-60814-399-3(6)); audio compact disk 19.99 (978-1-59859-438-6(9)) Oasis Audio.

Stories of Hans Christian Andersen. unabr. ed. Hans Christian Andersen. 6 cass. (J). 35.70 (C-310) Audio Bk.
14 stories by the master.

Stories of I. L. Peretz. Short Stories. I. L. Peretz. Narrated by George Guidall & Suzanne Toren. 5 CDs. (Running Time: 6 hrs). 2002. audio compact disk 44.95 (978-1-893079-14-4(7), JCCAUDIOBOOKS) Jewish Contempry Classics.
Classic short stories by the "Father of Yiddish Literature" in English translation.

Stories of I. L. Peretz. unabr. ed. 4 cass. (Running Time: 6 hrs.). 2001. 34.95 (978-1-893079-10-6(4), JCCAUDIOBOOKS) Jewish Contempry Classics.
I.L. Peretz is considered the Father of Yiddish Literature. He wrote of the magical quality of kindness and the bitter truths of blind faith. Collection of short stories includes some of his classics.

Stories of John Cheever. abr. ed. John Cheever. Contrib. by Barry Cooper. 2 cass. (Running Time: 2 hrs. 16 min.). 12.95 (978-0-89926-176-8(0), 864) Audio Bk.
Here are the collected stories of one of America's greatest writers.

Stories of John Cheever, Pt. 1. unabr. collector's ed. John Cheever. Read by Michael Prichard. 11 cass. (Running Time: 16 hrs. 30 min.). 1988. 88.00 (978-0-7366-1387-3(0), 2278-A) Books on Tape.
Cheever, in 61 stories, recaptures a world when New York was filled with river light, when Benny Goodman was king. Europe meant ship travel. Love & happiness were elusive & nostalgic & the gods were ancient, not fresh-cut.

Stories of John Cheever, Pt. 2. collector's unabr. ed. John Cheever. Read by Michael Prichard. 11 cass. (Running Time: 16 hrs. 30 min.). 1988. 88.00 (978-0-7366-1388-0(9), 2278-B) Books on Tape.

Stories of Lake Superior Shipwrecks, Vol. 1. Julius F. Wolff. 2 cass. 1994. (978-0-9660402-1-0(X)) Superior Prodn.
Stirring tales of heroism & tragedy, told by Lake Superior's foremost historian & storyteller. With authentic sounds of the lake.

Stories of Lake Superior Shipwrecks, Vol. 2. Julius F. Wolff. 2 cass. 1994. (978-0-9660402-2-7(8)) Superior Prodn.

Stories of Lead - Stories of Gold. Donna R. O'Toole. Contrib. by Sauni Wood. 2003. audio compact disk (978-1-878321-29-9(3)) Compassion Bks.

Stories of Magical Animals. Carol Watson. Read by Melinda Walker. (Young Reading CD Packs Ser.). (J). (gr. k-3). 2006. pap. bk. 9.99 (978-0-7945-0946-0(0), UsborneU) EDC Pubng.

Stories of Men. Anton Chekhov. Tr. by Paula P. Ross from RUS. (Literary Classics Ser.). (ENG.). 1997. 20.98 (978-1-57392-135-0(1), Pyr Bks) Prometheus Bks.

Stories of Muriel Spark, Vol. I. unabr. ed. Muriel Spark. Read by Derek Jacobi & Eleanor Bron. 6 cass. (Running Time: 5 hrs. 46 min.). (Cassette Library). 1991. 44.98 set. (978-0-8072-3193-7(2), CXL 551 CX, Listening Lib) Random Audio Pubg.

Stories of Mythical Creatures & Legendary Heroes. unabr. ed. Dale Bulla. 1 cass. (Running Time: 53 min.). Dramatization. (YA). (gr. 4-12). 1997. 9.95 (978-1-884197-08-6(6)) N Horizon Educ.
Storyteller Dale Bulla tells five stories: Wylie & the Hairy Man, The Legend of Baba Yaga, The Legend of Montezuma, The Legend of Beowulf & Grendel, Sir Dwaine & the Choice (adapted from Chaucer's Wife of Bath Tale).

Stories of New England: Then & Now. unabr. ed. Short Stories. James Thurber et al. 4 CDs. (Running Time: 5 hrs.). 1997. audio compact disk 39.95 (978-1-883332-52-5(4)) Audio Bkshelf.

Stories of New England: Then & Now. unabr. ed. Short Stories. James Thurber et al. Read by Terry Bregy et al. 4 cass. (Running Time: 5 hrs.). 1997. 24.95 (978-1-883332-30-3(3)) Audio Bkshelf.

Stories of Our Days. Jay Speyerer. 2006. audio compact disk 23.95 (978-0-9764729-3-3(7)) Legacy Rd.

Stories of People Who Changed America. Christine Farris et al. Read by Joan Allen. Narrated by Nikki Giovanni & Lynn Whitfield. (Playaway Children Ser.). (ENG.). (J). 2009. 44.99 (978-1-60812-601-9(3)) Find a World.

Stories of Pirates. rev. ed. Russell Punter. Illus. by Christyan Fox. (Young Reading CD Packs Ser.). (J). (gr. 4-7). 2007. bk. 9.99 (978-0-7945-1542-3(8), UsborneU) EDC Pubng.

Stories of Raffles, Set. unabr. ed. E. W. Hornung. Read by Richard Brown. 2 cass. (Running Time: 3 hrs.). (gr. 8 up). 1989. 14.95 (978-1-55685-152-0(9)) Audio Bk Con.
The Debonair criminal hero is featured in "A Costume Piece," "Le Premier Pas," "The Return March," & "The Gift of the Emperor".

Stories of Robots. Russell Punter. (Usborne Young Reading: Series One Ser.). (J). 2006. pap. bk. 9.99 (978-0-7945-1153-1(8), UsborneU) EDC Pubng.

Stories of Saint John Bosco. Peter Lappin. 7 cass. (J). 28.95 (503) Ignatius Pr.
True accounts for young people of the exciting events of the life of St. John Bosco.

Stories of Sherlock Holmes. Arthur Conan Doyle. Perf. by Basil Rathbone. 2 cass. Incl. Redheaded League. 1970. 12.95 (978-0-694-50158-8(1)); 8.98 ea. HarperCollins Pubs.

Stories of Suspence. Nathaniel Hawthorne. Retold by Gina Clemen. (Reading & Training, Elementary Ser.). (J). (gr. 4-7). 2005. pap. bk. 21.95 (978-88-530-0160-3(7)) Cideb ITA.

Stories of the Jungle. unabr. ed. Rudyard Kipling. Read by Ralph Cosham. 2 cass. (Running Time: 2 hrs. 35 min.). 1994. lib. bdg. 18.95 set incl. vinyl case with notes, author's picture & biography. (978-1-883049-29-4(6)) Sound Room.
A collection of stories from "The Jungle Books": "The King's Ankus", "Red Dog", "Rikki Tikki Tavi" & "Tomai of the Elephants".

Stories of the Jungle, Set. unabr. ed. Short Stories. Rudyard Kipling. Read by Ralph Cosham. 6 cass. (Running Time: 9 hrs.). (Timeless Treasures Collection). (J). 1999. 34.95 (978-1-883049-54-6(7), Commuters Library) Sound Room.
The very best of "The Jungle Book's" stories: Mowgli's Brothers," "Tiger-Tiger," "Letting in the Jungle," "The King's Ankus," "Kaa's Hunting," "Red Dog," "The Undertakers," "Toomai of the Elephants," "Rikki-Tikki-Tavi".

Stories of the Jungle, Set. unabr. ed. Rudyard Kipling. Read by Ralph Cosham. 2 cass. (Running Time: 2 hrs. 30 mins.). (Rudyard Kipling Ser.). (J). 1994. bk. 16.95 (978-1-883049-10-2(5), 390242, Commuters Library) Sound Room.
More intriguing stories from the original Jungle Books: "The King's Ankus," "Red Dog," "Toomai of the Elephants" & the classic, "Rikki-Tikki-Tavi.".

Stories of the Macabre. unabr. ed. Edgar Allan Poe. Read by Ralph Cosham. 2 CDs. (Running Time: 2 hrs. 30 mins.). 2000. audio compact disk 25.00 (978-1-58472-094-2(8), Commuters Library) Sound Room.

Stories of the Northwest Coast. Johnny Moses. 2 cass. 1993. 18.00 set. (OC326-70) Sound Horizons AV.

Stories of the Old Duck Hunters Audio, Vol. 1. abr. ed. Gordon MacQuarrie. Read by Karl Schmidt. 2 cass. (Running Time: 2 hrs. 30 min.). (Gordon MacQuarrie Trilogy). 1994. bk. 16.95 set. (978-1-57223-014-9(2), 0142) Willow Creek Pr.
Entertaining stories from the pages of the Gordon MacQuarrie trilogy. Classic hunting & fishing yarns from a master storyteller. Winner of the 1995 Ben Franklin award - Best Audio.

Stories of the Pilgrims. unabr. ed. Margaret B. Pumphrey. Narrated by Marguerite Gavin. 3 cass. (Running Time: 4 hrs.). 2002. 23.95 (978-0-7861-2169-4(6), 2919) Blckstn Audio.
Written especially for children, this is a delightful and interesting account of the Pilgrims. The book explores their religious oppression in England, their escape to Holland and eventual crossing to America on the Mayflower, and their early days in New England. Based on historical fact, the stories are filled with details of everyday life and vivid characterizations of Pilgrim families as they struggle to maintain their faith in the New World.

***Stories of the Pilgrims.** unabr. ed. Margaret B. Pumphrey. Read by Marguerite Gavin. (Running Time: 4 hrs. NaN mins.). (ENG.). 2011. 19.95 (978-1-4417-8366-0(0)); audio compact disk 30.00 (978-1-4417-8364-6(4)) Blckstn Audio.

Stories of the Stone Age see Tales of Space & Time

Stories of the Supernatural. abr. ed. Nostradamus. Narrated by Valentine Dyall. 2 cass. (Running Time: 1 hr. 28 min.). 12.95 (978-0-89926-146-1(9), 834) Audio Bk.
"Nostradamus - The Man Who Foretold the Future" leaves the listener with a disquieting & most uncomfortable sense of unease.

Stories of the Unusual. unabr. ed. H. G. Wells. 2 CDs. (Running Time: 2 hrs. 15 mins.). (YA). (gr. 7 up). 2002. audio compact disk 25.00 (978-1-58472-098-0(0), Commuters Library) Sound Room.

Stories of the Unusual. unabr. ed. Short Stories. H. G. Wells. Read by Ralph Cosham. 2 cds. (Running Time: 2 hrs 8 mins). (YA). 2002. audio compact disk 18.95 (978-1-58472-334-9(3), 011, In Aud) Pub: Sound Room. Dist(s): Baker Taylor
Contains The Door in the Wall, Aepyomis Island, The Purple Pileus, The Truth About Pyecraft, and The Strange Orchid.

***Stories of Vladimir Nabokov.** unabr. ed. Vladimir Nabokov. (Running Time: 32 hrs.). 2010. 29.99 (978-1-4418-7283-8(3), 9781441872838, Brilliance MP3); 29.99 (978-1-4418-7285-2(X), 9781441872852, BAD); 44.97 (978-1-4418-7284-5(1), 9781441872845, Brinc Audio MP3 Lib); 44.97 (978-1-4418-7286-9(8), 9781441872869, BADLE); audio compact disk 39.99 (978-1-4418-7281-4(7), 9781441872814, Bril Audio CD Unabri) Brilliance Audio.

***Stories of Vladimir Nabokov.** unabr. ed. Vladimir Nabokov. Read by Arthur Morey. (Running Time: 32 hrs.). 2010. audio compact disk 99.97 (978-1-4418-7282-1(5), 9781441872821, BriAudCD Unabrid) Brilliance Audio.

Stories Plus Readings & Activities for Language Skills: High Beginning. Ann Gianola. 2001. 17.00 (978-1-56420-210-9(0)); audio compact disk 18.00 (978-1-56420-232-1(1)) New Readers.

Stories That Educate, Entertain, Inspire & Inform - Ten Stories. Story Time Staff. 2 cass. (Running Time: 2 hrs.). (J). (gr. 4-8). 1992. 40.00 Set. (37SOR304CT) Sell Out Recordings.
Stories that have characters such as plants, animals, & knick-knacks. Ranging from educational, entertaining, inspirational & informative.

Stories That Ignite Healing, Volume 1: Generational Stories That Inspire & Enhance Healing. John Patrick Gatton. Read by John Patrick Gatton. (ENG.). 2009. audio compact disk 14.99 (978-1-930034-44-0(X)) Casscomm.

Stories That Make Children Happy. Cassette Enterprises Staff. (Running Time: 1 hr. 28 min.). (J). L & L Mgmt.
Snow White, Jack & the Bean Stalk, The Little Boy Who Cried Wolf, The Princess & the Pea, Sleeping Beauty, The Emperor's New Clothes, Pinocchio, Rumpelstiltskin, Little Red Ridding Hood, Peter Rabbit, Cinderella & The Shoemaker & the Elves.

Stories That Rhyme Every Time - 20 Stories. Poet's Workshop Staff. 1 cass. (J). (gr. 3-7). 1991. 76.00 (37SOR999) Sell Out Recordings.
Children's educational stories.

Stories the Year 'Round. abr. ed. Alma Flor Ada. (Cuentos para Todo el Ano / Stories the Year Round Ser.). (J). (ps-3). 2008. audio compact disk 24.95 (978-1-60396-349-7(9), Alfaguara) Santillana.

Stories This Spring! Telling, Listening, Living. 7 cass. Incl. Stories This Spring! Telling, Listening, Living: Baal Shem Tov: Master of the Good Name. Eugenia Friedman. 1985.; Stories This Spring! Telling, Listening, Living: Examples from Reality: Sufi Wisdom, Stories, & Teachings. Jonathan Granoff. 1985.; Stories This Spring! Telling, Listening, Living: Stories from the Black Oral Tradition. Linda Goss & Marian Barnes. 1985.; Stories This Spring! Telling, Listening, Living: Storytime-Storyspace. Ed Stivender. 1985.; Stories This Spring! Telling, Listening, Living: Tell the Next Generation (Psalm 48) Mark W. Bailey. 1985.; Stories This Spring! Telling, Listening, Living: The Kingdom of Heaven Is Like a Party. Ed Stivender. 1985.; Stories This Spring! Telling, Listening, Living: Vital Lessons from a Welsh Fairy Tale. David Hart. 1985.; 1985. 24.50 Set.; 4.50 ea. Pendle Hill.

Stories This Spring! Telling, Listening, Living: Baal Shem Tov: Master of the Good Name see Stories This Spring! Telling, Listening, Living

Stories This Spring! Telling, Listening, Living: Examples from Reality: Sufi Wisdom, Stories, & Teachings see Stories This Spring! Telling, Listening, Living

Stories This Spring! Telling, Listening, Living: Stories from the Black Oral Tradition see Stories This Spring! Telling, Listening, Living

Stories This Spring! Telling, Listening, Living: Storytime-Storyspace see Stories This Spring! Telling, Listening, Living

Stories This Spring! Telling, Listening, Living: Tell the Next Generation (Psalm 48) see Stories This Spring! Telling, Listening, Living

Stories This Spring! Telling, Listening, Living: The Kingdom of Heaven Is Like a Party see Stories This Spring! Telling, Listening, Living

Stories This Spring! Telling, Listening, Living: Vital Lessons from a Welsh Fairy Tale see Stories This Spring! Telling, Listening, Living

Stories to Celebrate (English Audio) see Cuentos para celebrar (English Audio)

Stories to Celebrate (Spanish Audio) see Cuentos para Celebrar /Stories to Celebrate

Stories to Grow On. Timmy Abell. Music by Steven Heller. 1 cass., 1 CD. (YA). (gr. 5 up). 1998. 10.00; 16.00 CD. Upstream Prodns.
Highly recommended for listeners of all age, it includes "Cumberland Mountain," "The White Horse Girl & the Blue Wind Boy,".

Stories to Remember: Here Comes Jesus. Peter Enns. Illus. by Terry Ligon. (J). (ps-5). 1987. 5.98 (978-0-943593-14-2(X)) Kids Intl Inc.

Stories to Remember "Music" Gift Set. Perf. by Judy Collins et al. 4 cass. (Running Time: 4 hrs.). (Stories to Remember Ser.). (J). 23.98 Set. (978-1-56896-126-2(X), 54164-4) Lightyear Entrtnmnt.
The best music, poetry, lullabies, nursery rhymes & stories for children.

Stories to Remember "Story" Gift Set. Narrated by Kevin Klein et al. 4 cass. (Running Time: 3 hrs.). (Stories to Remember Ser.). (J). 23.98 Set. (978-1-56896-127-9(8), 54165-4) Lightyear Entrtnmnt.
Contains some of the most well-known children's stories.

Stories to Stir the Imagination, Album No. 1. unabr. ed. Allan Kelley. Read by Frances Kelley. 1 cass. (Running Time: 60 min.). Dramatization. (Little People Ser.). (J). (gr. k-6). 1993. 9.95 (978-1-884428-00-5(2), 428002) Eye Ear.
With the inspired dramatizations of renowned storyteller Frances Kelley, these revitalized classics spring to life with a new spirit of excitement. Album No. 1 contains the following stories: The Emperor's New Clothes; Toads & Diamonds; The Story of William Tell; & The Golden Touch.

Stories to Stir the Imagination, No. 2. unabr. ed. Allan Kelley. Read by Frances Kelley. 1 cass. (Running Time: 60 min.). Dramatization. (Little People Ser.). (J). (gr. k-6). 1993. (978-1-884428-01-2(0), 42810) Eye Ear.

Stories to Stir the Imagination, No. 3. unabr. ed. Allan Kelley. Read by Frances Kelley. 1 cass. (Running Time: 60 min.). Dramatization. (Little People Ser.). (J). (gr. k-6). 1993. 11.95 (978-1-884428-02-9(9), 428029) Eye Ear.

Stories to Stir the Imagination: The Elephant's Child; Rip Van Winkle; The Princess & the Pea, Vol. 4. adpt. ed. Rudyard Kipling et al. 1 cass. (Running Time: 1 hr.). Dramatization. (J). (gr. k-6). 1991. 9.95 Eye-In-The-Ear.
Album #4 of "Stories to Stir the Imagination" continues our effort to truly stir the imagination of children whose imaginations have been numbed by too much television...to stimulate & enliven the child's magical mind's eye at a time when the outer eye is so dominated by the overwhelming - & often unpleasant - present. The four stories on Album #4 have been adapted & revitalized for dramatized audio presentation, enhanced by original music & sound effects...all of which can be shared with the child's parents & grandparents.

Stories to Stir the Imagination Vol. 1: The Emperor's New Clothes; Toad & Diamonds; The Story of William Tell; The Golden Touch. 1 CD. (Running Time: 1 hr.). audio compact disk 14.95 (978-0-944168-11-0(6)) Eye-In-The-Ear.

Stories to Stir the Imagination Vol. 1: The Emperor's New Clothes; Toad & Diamonds; The Story of William Tell; The Golden Touch. adpt. ed. 1 cass. (Running Time: 1 hr.). Dramatization. (J). (gr. k-6). 11.95 (978-0-944168-03-5(5)) Eye-In-The-Ear.
The goal of this series of dramatized stories on audiocassettes is to truly stir the imagination of children whose imaginations have been numbed by too much television...to stimulate & enliven the child's magical mind's eye at a time when the outer eye is so dominated by the overwhelming - & often unpleasant - present. All the stories have been adapted & revitalized for dramatic audio presentation, enhanced by original music & sound effects...all of which can be shared with the child's parents & grandparents.

Stories to Stir the Imagination Vol. 2: Androcles & the Lion; The Ugly Duckling; The Mad Tea Party; The Dutch Boy & the Dike. 1 CD. (Running Time: 1 hr.). 2003. audio compact disk 14.95 (978-0-944168-12-7(4)) Eye-In-The-Ear.

Stories to Stir the Imagination Vol. 2: Androcles & the Lion; The Ugly Duckling; The Mad Tea Party; The Dutch Boy & the Dike. adpt. ed. 1 cass. (Running Time: 1 hr.). Dramatization. (J). (gr. k-6). 11.95 (978-0-944168-04-2(3)) Eye-In-The-Ear.

Stories to Stir the Imagination Vol. 3: Pandora's Box; The Fisherman & His Wife; The Boy Who Cried Wolf; The Nutcracker & the Mouse King. 1 CD. (Running Time: 1 hr.). 2003. audio compact disk 14.95 (978-0-944168-13-4(2)) Eye-In-The-Ear.

Stories to Stir the Imagination Vol. 3: Pandora's Box; The Fisherman & His Wife; The Boy Who Cried Wolf; The Nutcracker & the Mouse King. adpt. ed. 1 cass. (Running Time: 1 hr.). Dramatization. (J). (gr. k-6). 11.95 (978-0-944168-05-9(1)) Eye-In-The-Ear.

Stories to Tell: Slan le Loch Eirne. Gary Hastings. Contrib. by Seamus Quinn. (ENG.). 2002. audio compact disk 23.95 (978-0-8023-8152-1(9)) Pub: Clo Iar-Chonnachta IRL. Dist(s): Dufour

Stories with a Twist. Natalie Hess. (ENG.). 2000. audio compact disk 15.25 (978-1-882483-84-6(7)) Alta Bk Ctr Pubs.

Stories with Music - A Collection for Children: Mortimer the Very Rich Mouse, The Kingfisher & the Catfish, Eudora May. Dixon DeVore, II. Read by Dixon DeVore, II. Illus. by Al Reida. 1 CD. (Running Time: 70 mins.). (J). (gr. k-4). 1999. audio compact disk (978-0-9614998-3-9(4)) Cricket Power.
Mortimer the Very Rich Mouse, the story of a flute playing mouse, teaches the lesson of friendship. The Kingfisher & the Catfish is based on the classic fairy tale, "The Fisherman & His Wife" with the moral - be thankful for what you have. Endora May tells the story of a budding young concert artist who finds a surprise inside her piano & it has wings!.

***Stork.** unabr. ed. Wendy Delsol. (Running Time: 9 hrs.). 2010. 19.99 (978-1-4418-8986-7(8), 9781441889867, Candlewick Bril); 39.97 (978-1-4418-8987-4(6), 9781441889874, Candlewick Bril) Brilliance Audio.

***Stork.** unabr. ed. Wendy Delsol. Read by Julia Whelan. (Running Time: 9 hrs.). 2010. audio compact disk 24.99 (978-1-4418-8982-9(5), 9781441889829, Candlewick Bril); audio compact disk 19.99 (978-1-4418-8984-3(1), 9781441889843, Candlewick Bril); audio compact disk 54.97 (978-1-4418-8983-6(3), 9781441889836, Candlewick Bril); audio compact disk 39.97 (978-1-4418-8985-0(X), 9781441889850, Candlewick Bril) Brilliance Audio.

Stork Club. unabr. ed. Iris Rainer Dart. Read by Sandra Burr. (Running Time: 12 hrs.). 2009. 39.97 (978-1-4418-1854-6(5), 9781441818546, Brinc Audio MP3 Lib); 24.99 (978-1-4418-1853-9(7), 9781441818539, Brilliance MP3); 39.97 (978-1-4418-1856-0(1), 9781441818560, BADLE); 24.99 (978-1-4418-1855-3(3), 9781441818553, BAD) Brilliance Audio.

Storm. Hearn. (J). 1984. Multi Media TX.

Storm. Cynthia Rylant. Narrated by Mark Nelson. (Running Time: 45 mins.). (Lighthouse Family Ser.). (J). 2002. 10.75 (978-1-4193-1717-0(2)) Recorded Bks.

Storm: Stories of Survival from Land, Sea & Sky. unabr. ed. Sebastian Junger et al. Ed. by Clint Willis. Narrated by Nick Sampson et al. 4 cass. (Running Time: 6 hrs.). (Adrenaline Ser.). 2001. 24.95 (978-1-885408-56-3(0), LL048) Listen & Live.
Reminds us of what happens when people find that treacherous weather - or when it finds them - & we are reminded of the fragility of life, the capriciousness of nature's will & how little we can do when both cross paths.

Storm & Conquest: The Clash of Empires in the Eastern Seas 1809. unabr. ed. Stephen Taylor. Read by James Adams. (Running Time: 43200 sec.). 2008. 29.95 (978-1-4332-0854-6(7)); audio compact disk 29.95 (978-1-4332-0855-3(5)) Blckstn Audio.

Storm & Conquest: The Clash of Empires in the Eastern Seas 1809. unabr. ed. Stephen Taylor. Read by James Adams. (Running Time: 43200 sec.). 2008. 72.95 (978-1-4332-0857-7(1)); audio compact disk & audio compact disk 29.95 (978-1-4332-0856-0(3)); audio compact disk & audio compact disk 99.00 (978-1-4332-0858-4(X)) Blckstn Audio.

Storm at Daybreak. unabr. ed. B. J. Hoff. Read by Jean DeBarbieris. 6 cass. (Running Time: 6 hrs. 12 min.). (Daybreak Mystery Ser.: Bk. 1). 1998. 39.95 (978-1-55686-830-6(8)) Books in Motion.
A former singer hired at a radio station, helps solve the mystery of threatening phone calls her new boss is recieving. The two suddenly falls helplessly in love.

Storm Canvas: John Paul Jones, Fighting Sailor & Amazon: River Sea of Brazil. unabr. collector's ed. Armstrong Sperry. Read by Paul Shay. 9 cass. (Running Time: 13 hrs. 30 mins.). 1989. 72.00 (978-0-7366-1607-2(1), 2468) Books on Tape.
Amazon: River Sea of Brazil is a survey of that region before it was changed by our post-WW II civilization. Sperry knew it when the Indians traveled by dugouts, when few white men had been to its headwaters & when mystery lay in every bayou. Storm Canvas is a story of the sea, set in the War of 1812. This story of a young man aboard a fighting ship is a stirring evocation of those times. John Paul Jones, Fighting Sailor is an adventurous life of the father of the U. S. Navy. Jones was everything he is remembered for...decisive, quick-tempered, tempestuous.

Storm Chasers: On the Trail of Deadly Tornadoes. Matt White. (High Five Reading - Red Ser.). (ENG.). (gr. 2-3). 2007. audio compact disk 5.95 (978-1-4296-1417-7(X)) CapstoneDig.

Storm Cycle. abr. ed. Iris Johansen & Roy Johansen. Read by Tanya Eby. (Running Time: 6 hrs.). 2009. audio compact disk 26.99 (978-1-4233-2966-4(X), 9781423329664, BACD) Brilliance Audio.

Storm Cycle. abr. ed. Iris Johansen & Roy Johansen. Read by Tanya Eby. 5 CDs. (Running Time: 6 hrs.). 2010. audio compact disk 14.99 (978-1-4233-2967-1(8), 9781423329671, BCD Value Price) Brilliance Audio.

Storm Cycle. unabr. ed. Iris Johansen & Roy Johansen. (Running Time: 10 hrs.). 2009. 39.97 (978-1-4233-2965-7(1), 9781423329657, BADLE) Brilliance Audio.

Storm Cycle. unabr. ed. Iris Johansen & Roy Johansen. Read by Tanya Eby. 1 MP3-CD. (Running Time: 10 hrs.). 2009. 24.99 (978-1-4233-2962-6(7), 9781423329626, Brilliance MP3); 24.99 (978-1-4233-2964-0(3), 9781423329640, BAD); 39.97 (978-1-4233-2963-3(5), 9781423329633, Brinc Audio MP3 Lib); audio compact disk 36.99 (978-1-4233-2960-2(0), 9781423329602, Bril Audio CD Unabri); audio compact disk 97.97 (978-1-4233-2961-9(9), 9781423329619, BriAudCD Unabrid) Brilliance Audio.

***Storm Cycle.** unabr. ed. Iris Johansen & Roy Johansen. Narrated by Tanya Eby. 1 Playaway. (Running Time: 10 hrs. 30 mins.). 2009. 69.99 (978-1-61545-531-7(0)) Find a World.

Storm from the Shadows. unabr. ed. David Weber. Read by Jay A. Snyder. 2 MP3-CDs. (Running Time: 31 hrs.). (Honorverse Ser.). 2009. 29.99 (978-1-4233-9160-9(8), 9781423391609, Brilliance MP3); 44.97 (978-1-4233-9161-6(6), 9781423391616, Brinc Audio MP3 Lib); 44.97 (978-1-4233-9162-3(4), 9781423391623, BADLE) Brilliance Audio.

Storm from the Shadows. unabr. ed. David Weber. Read by Kevin Pariseau & Jay A. Snyder. 25 CDs. (Running Time: 31 hrs.). (Honorverse Ser.). 2009. audio compact disk 49.99 (978-1-4233-9158-6(6), 9781423391586, Bril Audio CD Unabri) Brilliance Audio.

Storm from the Shadows. unabr. ed. David Weber. Read by Jay A. Snyder. 25 CDs. (Running Time: 31 hrs.). (Honorverse Ser.). 2009. audio compact disk 99.97 (978-1-4233-9159-3(4), 9781423391593, BriAudCD Unabrid) Brilliance Audio.

Storm Front. Jim Butcher. Read by James Marsters. 8 CDs. (Running Time: 10 hrs.). (Dresden Files Ser.: Bk. 1). 2002. audio compact disk 47.95 (978-0-9657255-0-7(2), 19) Buzzy Multimed.

Storm Front: Book 1 of the Dresden Files. 2005. 34.95 (978-0-9657255-6-9(1), Buzzy Audio) Buzzy Multimed.

Storm Gathering. unabr. ed. Rene Gutteridge. 2004. 27.99 (978-1-58926-838-8(5), 6838); audio compact disk 29.99 (978-1-58926-839-5(3), 6839) Pub: Oasis Audio. Dist(s): TNT Media Grp

Storm in the Mountains. unabr. ed. Nancy Buckingham. Read by Margaret Holt. 4 cass. (Running Time: 6 hrs/). 1999. 44.95 (65131) Pub: Soundings Ltd GBR. Dist(s): Ulverscroft US

Storm in the Village & the Fairacre Festival. Read by Miss Read & June Barrie. 2002. 69.95 (978-0-7540-0889-7(4), CAB 2311) Pub: Chivers Audio Bks GBR. Dist(s): AudioGO

Storm Knight. unabr. ed. Frederick E. Smith. 6 cass. (Running Time: 28800 sec.). (Story Sound Ser.). 2006. 54.95 (978-1-85903-962-5(6)) Pub: Mgna Lrg Print GBR. Dist(s): Ulverscroft US

Storm Knight. unabr. ed. Frederick E Smith & Jeff Harding. Contrib. by Jeff Harding. 7 CDs. (Story Sound CD Ser.). 2006. audio compact disk 71.95 (978-1-84652-035-8(5)) Pub: Mgna Lrg Print GBR. Dist(s): Ulverscroft US

***Storm of the Century: A Hurricane Katrina Story.** Stephanie True Peters & Jorge Maese. Illus. by Aburtov. (Historical Fiction Ser.). (ENG.). 2010. audio compact disk 14.60 (978-1-4342-2582-5(8)) CapstoneDig.

Storm over Burracombe. Lilian Harry. 2008. audio compact disk 99.95 (978-1-84559-996-6(9)) Pub: Soundings Ltd GBR. Dist(s): Ulverscroft US

Storm over Burracombe. Lillian Harry. 2008. 89.95 (978-1-84559-995-9(0)) Pub: Soundings Ltd GBR. Dist(s): Ulverscroft US

Storm over Rhanna. unabr. ed. Christine Marion Fraser. Read by Vivien Heilbron. 10 cass. (Running Time: 41400 sec.). (Rhanna Ser.: Vol. 6). 1997. 84.95 Set. (978-0-7451-6729-9(2), CAB 1345) AudioGO.
Mark James, the island minister, has lost his family to tragedy. But he finds solace with Rhanna's new doctor, Megan Jenkins, unknowing of her mysterious past. And when a fearsome storm hits Rhanna, the lifeboats take to the sea in response to distress signals from a luxury yacht. On board is a man from Megan's past, & her heart will soon be torn between him & the minister who needs her so much.

Storm over Saturn. abr. ed. Mack Maloney. 4 cass. (Running Time: 6 hrs.). (Starhawk Ser.: No. 5). 2004. 25.00 (978-1-58807-351-8(3)) Am Pubng Inc.

***Storm Prey.** John Sandford, pseud. Read by Richard Ferrone. (Running Time: 6 hrs.). (ENG.). 2011. audio compact disk 14.95 (978-0-14-242907-5(4), PengAudBks) Penguin Grp USA.

Storm Prey. abr. ed. John Sandford, pseud. Contrib. by Richard Ferrone. 5 CDs. (Running Time: 6 hrs.). (Prey Ser.). (ENG.). 2010. audio compact disk 29.95 (978-0-14-242775-0(6), PengAudBks) Penguin Grp USA.

Storm Prey. unabr. ed. John Sandford, pseud. Read by Richard Ferrone. 9 CDs. (Running Time: 11 hrs.). (Prey Ser.). (ENG.). 2010. audio compact disk 39.95 (978-0-14-242776-7(4), PengAudBks) Penguin Grp USA.

Storm Runner. unabr. ed. Tara K. Harper. Read by Karen White. (Tales of Wolves Ser.: Vol. 3). 2001. 80.00 (978-0-7366-8330-2(5)) Books on Tape.
Dion, the healer and Wolfwalker, is back home with her friends, and they are preparing for war against Longear. There's trouble with the wolves in the enemy counties. Many of them are fleeing in droves. The rest appear to have broken their generations-long pact with the humans, and are hunting down refugees for the enemy. Dion can no longer communicate with their packsong, and must find out why they have fled and turned. But that means her venturing into dangerous enemy territory without the help of Gray Hishn. The only possible hope is her learning and mastering an ancient ceremony.

Storm Runners. Ed. by T. Jefferson Parker. 2007. audio compact disk 29.95 (978-0-06-122717-2(X)) HarperCollins Pubs.

Storm Runners. abr. ed. T. Jefferson Parker. Read by Christopher Lane. (Running Time: 21600 sec.). 2007. audio compact disk 14.99 (978-1-4233-0594-1(9), 9781423305941, BCD Value Price) Brilliance Audio.

Storm Runners. unabr. ed. T. Jefferson Parker. Read by Christopher Lane. (Running Time: 9 hrs.). 2007. 39.25 (978-1-4233-0592-7(2), 9781423305927, BADLE); 24.95 (978-1-4233-0591-0(4), 9781423305910, BAD); 74.25 (978-1-4233-0586-6(8), 9781423305866, BrilAudUnabridg); audio compact disk 92.25 (978-1-4233-0588-0(4), 9781423305880, BriAudCD Unabrid); audio compact disk 39.25 (978-1-4233-0590-3(6), 9781423305903, Brinc Audio MP3 Lib); audio compact disk 24.95 (978-1-4233-0589-7(2), 9781423305897, Brilliance MP3); audio compact disk 34.95 (978-1-4233-0587-3(6), 9781423305873, Bril Audio CD Unabri) Brilliance Audio.

***Storm Runners - Audio.** Roland Smith. (ENG.). 2011. audio compact disk 25.99 (978-0-545-28285-7(3)) Scholastic Inc.

***Storm Runners - Audio Library Edition.** Roland Smith. (ENG.). 2011. audio compact disk 39.99 (978-0-545-28293-2(4)) Scholastic Inc.

Storm Swept. 1 cass. (Running Time: 60 min.). 1994. audio compact disk 15.95 CD. (2610, Creativ Pub) Quayside.
Thunderstorms mixed with contemporary music.

Storm Swept. 1 cass. (Running Time: 60 min.). 1994. 9.95 (2609, NrthWrd Bks) TandN Child.

Storm Testament, Set. Lee Nelson. 2 cass. 1999. 11.95 (978-1-57734-267-0(4), 07001665) Covenant Comms.
The epic begins.

Storm Testament II, Set. Lee Nelson. 2 cass. 1999. 12.95 (978-1-57734-349-3(2), 07001975) Covenant Comms.

Storm the Gates of Hell. Contrib. by Demon Hunter. 2007. 29.99 (978-5-557-56809-8(3)) Solid State MO.

Storm the Gates of Hell. Contrib. by Demon Hunter. Prod. by Aaron Sprinkle. 2007. audio compact disk 13.99 (978-5-557-56811-1(5)) Solid State MO.

STORM Tough Questions DVD. Prod. by City on a Hill Productions. 2006. audio compact disk 99.99 (978-0-7847-2071-4(1)) Standard Pub.

Storm Track. unabr. ed. Margaret Maron. Narrated by C. J. Critt. 6 cass. (Running Time: 8 hrs.). (Deborah Knott Mystery Ser.: No. 7). 2000. 57.00 (978-0-7887-4866-0(1), 96463E7) Recorded Bks.
When the wife of one of Colleton County's lawyers is found dead in a low-budget hotel, the news comes as a thunderclap. People begin looking around suspiciously for the culprit & Judge Deborah Knott learns her own cousin possesses a mighty powerful motive.

Storm Track. unabr. ed. Margaret Maron. Narrated by C. J. Critt. 7 CDs. (Running Time: 8 hrs.). (Deborah Knott Mystery Ser.: No. 7). 2001. audio compact disk 69.00 (978-0-7887-6180-5(3), C1405) Recorded Bks.
Swirling dark clouds of illicit affairs & brutal murder threaten Colleton County, North Carolina. No one worries much about the scantily clad woman found strangled in the Orchid Motel. She must be a tourist. But when the victim turns out to be the wife of one of Colleton County's up-&-coming lawyers, the news comes as a thunderclap. People begin looking suspiciously among themselves for the culprit & Judge Deborah Knott learns her own handsome cousin possesses a mighty powerful motive. While Deborah searches for the vicious killer, a deadly hurricane rages up the Carolina coast, bringing destruction & its own kind of justice.

Storm Warning. Graham. 1 cass. 1992. 15.99 (978-0-8499-6071-0(1), 6189) Nelson.

Storm Warning. abr. ed. Jack Higgins. Read by Stefan Rudnicki. 2 cass. (Running Time: 3 hrs.). 2004. 18.00 (978-1-59007-196-0(4)) Pub: New Millenn Enter. Dist(s): PerseuPGW
During World War II, a group of German expatriates trapped in Brazil must sail across five thousand miles of tempestuous water to reach their homeland-and face the deadly barricade of American and British military power.

***Storm Warning.** unabr. ed. Jack Higgins. Read by Michael Page. (Running Time: 8 hrs.). 2011. audio compact disk 29.99 (978-1-4418-4483-5(X), 9781441844835, Bril Audio CD Unabri) Brilliance Audio.

Storm Warning, Bk. 9. Linda Sue Park. Illus. by David Pittu. (ENG.). (J). 2010. audio compact disk 49.99 (978-0-545-22600-4(7)) Scholastic Inc.

Storm Warning, Bk. 9. Linda Sue Park. Narrated by David Pittu. (Running Time: 4 hrs.). (ENG.). (J). 2010. audio compact disk 19.99 (978-0-545-22481-9(0)) Scholastic Inc.

***Storm Warning: Whether Global Recession, Terrorist Threats, or Devastating Natural Disasters, These Ominous Shadows Must Bring Us Back to the Gospel.** unabr. ed. Billy Graham. Read by Don Leslie. (Running Time: 10 hrs. 30 mins.). 2010. 29.95 (978-1-4417-6638-0(3)); 65.95 (978-1-4417-6635-9(9)); audio compact disk 29.95 (978-1-4417-6637-3(5)); audio compact disk 90.00 (978-1-4417-6636-6(7)) Blckstn Audio.

Storm World: Hurricanes, Politics, & the Battle over Global Warming. unabr. ed. Christopher Cole Mooney. Read by Lloyd James. (Running Time: 10 hrs. 30 mins. 0 sec.). (ENG.). 2007. audio compact disk 34.99 (978-1-4001-0508-3(0)); audio compact disk 24.99 (978-1-4001-5508-8(8)); audio compact disk 69.99 (978-1-4001-3508-0(7)) Pub: Tantor Media. Dist(s): IngramPubServ

Storm 4. 0 for Windows: Quantitative Modeling for Decision Support. Hamilton Emmons et al. 2000. per. 40.00 (978-1-933403-01-4(2)) Crown Custom.

Stormalong see American Tall Tales

Stormbreaker. Anthony Horowitz. Read by Nathaniel Parker. 3 vols. (Running Time: 4 hrs. 44 mins.). (Alex Rider Ser.: Bk. 1). (J). (gr. 4-7). 2004. pap. bk. 38.00 (978-0-8072-2277-5(1), Listening Lib) Random Audio Pubg.

Stormbreaker. unabr. ed. Anthony Horowitz. Read by Nathaniel Parker. 3 cass. (Running Time: 4 hrs. 44 mins.). (Alex Rider Ser.: Bk. 1). (J). (gr. 4-7). 2004. 30.00 (978-0-8072-0500-6(1), Listening Lib) Random Audio Pubg.

Stormbreaker. unabr. ed. Anthony Horowitz. Read by Nathaniel Parker. (Running Time: 16620 sec.). (Alex Rider Ser.: Bk. 1). (ENG.). (J). (gr. 5-6). 2006. audio compact disk 30.00 (978-0-7393-3535-2(9), Listening Lib) Pub: Random Audio Pubg. Dist(s): Random

Stormchaser. unabr. ed. Paul Stewart & Chris Riddell. Read by John Lee. 5 cass. (Running Time: 8 hrs. 15 mins.). (Edge Chronicles Ser.: Bk. 2). (J). (gr. 4-7). 2005. 40.00 (978-0-307-28371-9(2), Listening Lib); audio compact disk 46.75 (978-0-307-28372-6(0), Listening Lib) Pub: Random Audio Pubg. Dist(s): NetLibrary CO

Stormchild. collector's ed. Bernard Cornwell. Read by David Case. 9 cass. (Running Time: 13 hrs. 30 min.). 2000. 72.00 (978-0-7366-5573-6(5), 5387) Books on Tape.
Tim Blackburn, famous solo round-the-world yachtsman, must now use all the skills that brought him world renown to discover the fate of his impulsive, brilliant, but wayward daughter, Nicole. She has disappeared in the company of Casper von Rellsteb, an environmental activist & leader of the Genesis Community.

Stormchild. unabr. ed. Bernard Cornwell. Read by Stephen Pacy. 8 cass. (Running Time: 8 hrs. 10 min.). 1999. 61.95 (978-1-85695-495-2(1), 92115) Pub: ISIS Audio GBR. Dist(s): Ulverscroft US

Stormchild. unabr. ed. Bernard Cornwell. Read by Steven Pacey. 10 CDs. (Running Time: 15 hrs.). 2001. audio compact disk 89.95 (978-0-7531-1134-5(9), 11349) Pub: ISIS Audio GBR. Dist(s): Ulverscroft US
Tim Blackburn begins his search for his daughter with the help of Jackie Potten; a young American who disapproves of his methods, and his elder brother, who disapproves of Jackie Potten. However, his most valuable aid is the Stormchild, in which he became famous as a solo round the world yachtsman.

Storming Heaven. Kyle Mills. Read by Michael Kramer. 1998. audio compact disk 80.00 (978-0-7366-8286-2(4)) Books on Tape.

Storming Heaven. abr. ed. Dale Brown. Read by Robert Foxworth. 4 cass. (Running Time: 6 hrs.). 2004. 25.00 (978-1-59007-170-0(0)) Pub: New Millenn Enter. Dist(s): PerseuPGW

Storming Heaven. unabr. ed. Kyle Mills. Read by Michael Kramer. 8 cass. (Running Time: 12 hrs.). 1999. 64.00 (978-0-7366-4278-1(1), 4776) Books on Tape.
Mark Beamon, a maverick FBI agent now shunted to a no-action office in the remote southwestern desert, is told to "play it by the book." Unfortunately crime doesn't follow any rules & so when a teenage girl disappears & her parents are murdered, Beamon scraps the rules & goes to work on his own.

Storming Intrepid. Payne Harrison. Read by Allison Green. 12 cass. (Running Time: 18 hrs.). 1993. 78.60 Set. (978-1-56544-004-3(8), 250019); Rental 11.30 30 day rental Set. (250019) Literate Ear.
The American space shuttle Intrepid lifts off with the final components to make "Star Wars" a working defense system. An onboard fire during its first orbit knocks out the radio transmission. As the U.S. begins rescue operations, a radio signal is discovered between Intrepid & an earth station deep within the Soviet Union.

Storming Las Vegas: How a Cuban-Born, Soviet-Trained Commando Took down the Strip to the Tune of Five World-Class Hotels, Three Armored Cars, & Millions of Dollars. unabr. ed. John Huddy. Read by Stefan Rudnicki. (Running Time: 48600 sec.). 2008. 79.95 (978-1-4332-3368-5(1)); audio compact disk & audio compact disk 99.00 (978-1-4332-3369-2(X)); audio compact disk & audio compact disk 29.95 (978-1-4332-3372-2(X)) Blckstn Audio.

Storming the Magic Kingdom. unabr. collector's ed. John Taylor. Read by Walter Zimmerman. 8 cass. (Running Time: 12 hrs.). 1990. 64.00 (978-0-7366-1841-0(4), 2674) Books on Tape.
When Wall Street mercenaries attacked the Walt Disney Company a fierce fight followed.

Stormjammers: The Extraordinary Story of Electronic Warfare Operations in the Gulf War. unabr. ed. Robert Stanek, pseud. Narrated by Ron Knowles. (Running Time: 11 hrs. 2 mins.). (ENG.). 2008. 28.95 (978-1-57545-360-6(6), RP Audio Pubng) Pub: Reagent Press. Dist(s): OverDrive Inc

Stormrider. David Gemmell. Narrated by Christopher Kay. 13 cass. (Running Time: 19 hrs.). 2002. 111.00 (978-1-84197-476-7(5)) Recorded Bks.

Storms - Rain - Rainbows. Excerpts. Based on a book by Martha Wood. 1. (Running Time: 50 mins). 2004. 15.00 (978-0-9651906-2-6(5)) Lily Pubns.
A companion C D to Set Free - A Caregivers Daily Devotional Journal, with healing scripture passages prayerfully read over newly composed worship music to bring hope and comfort, cleansing rain, and the promise of the rainbow. For anyone in the midst of a storm of illness, divorce, depression, financial difficulty or a painful relationship.

Storms of My Grandchildren: The Truth about the Coming Climate Catastrophe & Our Last Chance to Save Humanity. unabr. ed. James Hansen. Narrated by John Allen Nelson. (Running Time: 12 hrs. 30 mins.). 2009. 18.99 (978-1-4001-8524-5(6)); 24.99 (978-1-4001-6524-7(5)); audio compact disk 34.99 (978-1-4001-1524-2(8)); audio compact disk 69.99 (978-1-4001-4524-9(4)) Pub: Tantor Media. Dist(s): IngramPubServ

Storms over Africa. unabr. ed. Beverley Harper. Read by Jerome Pride. 7 cass. (Running Time: 12 hrs. 30 mins.). 2001. (978-1-74030-167-1(6), 500955) Bolinda Pubng AUS.

Storms over Africa. unabr. ed. Beverly Harper. Read by Jerome Pride. (Running Time: 45000 sec.). 2006. audio compact disk 103.95 (978-1-74093-792-4(9)) Pub: Bolinda Pubng AUS. Dist(s): Bolinda Pub Inc

Stormswift. unabr. ed. Madeline Brent. Read by Judith Porter. 8 cass. (Running Time: 12 hrs.). 2001. 69.95 (62825) Pub: Soundings Ltd GBR. Dist(s): Ulverscroft US

Stormy: Misty's Foal. Marguerite Henry. Narrated by John McDonough. 5 CDs. (Running Time: 5 hrs. 30 mins.). (gr. 3 up). 2000. audio compact disk 48.00 (978-0-7887-4941-4(2), C1304E7) Recorded Bks.
In the midst of a raging storm, "Misty," the famous mare of Chincoteague, is about to give birth. Will "Misty" & her colt survive? The story of the hurricane that destroyed the wild herds of Assateague & how strength & love helped rebuild them. Available to libraries only.

Stormy: Misty's Foal, unabr. ed. Marguerite Henry. Narrated by John McDonough. 4 pieces. (Running Time: 5 hrs. 30 mins.). (gr. 3 up). 37.00 (978-0-7887-2969-0(1), 95741E7) Recorded Bks.

Stormy: Misty's Foal. unabr. ed. Marguerite Henry. Read by John McDonough. 4 cass. (Running Time: 5 hrs. 15 mins.). (J). 1999. stu. ed. 49.20 (978-0-7887-2999-7(3), 40881) Recorded Bks.

Stormy: Misty's Foal, unabr. ed. Marguerite Henry. Read by John McDonough. 4 cass. (Running Time: 5 hrs. 15 mins.). (J). (gr. 3). 1999. 97.30 (978-0-7887-3029-0(0), 46846) Recorded Bks.

Stormy Weather. unabr. ed. Carl Hiaasen. Narrated by George Wilson. 12 CDs. (Running Time: 14 hrs. 30 mins.). 1999. audio compact disk 109.00 (978-0-7887-3414-4(8), C1020E7) Recorded Bks.
During the aftermath of Hurricane Andrew, crowds of con artists & impostors move in to prey on storm-shocked victims, but these predators arouse a bizarre hero: a hoary ex-governor who lives on road kill.

Stormy Weather, unabr. ed. Carl Hiaasen. Narrated by George Wilson. 10 cass. (Running Time: 14 hrs. 30 mins.). 1997. 85.00 (978-0-7887-0669-1(1), 94846E7) Recorded Bks.

Stormy Weather. unabr. ed. Paulette Jiles. Read by Colleen Delany. 10 CDs. (Running Time: 11 hrs. 30 mins.). 2007. audio compact disk 39.95 (978-0-06-125646-2(3), Harper Audio) HarperCollins Pubs.

***Stormy Weather.** unabr. ed. Paulette Jiles. Read by Colleen Delany. (ENG.). 2007. (978-0-06-144998-7(9), Harper Audio); (978-0-06-144997-0(0), Harper Audio) HarperCollins Pubs.

Stormy Weather: A Charlotte Justice Novel. Paula L. Woods. Narrated by Patricia R. Floyd. 8 cass. (Running Time: 10 hrs. 45 mins.). 72.00 (978-1-4025-0982-7(0)) Recorded Bks.

Stormy Weather Vol. 2: And Other Grins, Grabbers & Great Getaways. Created by Focus on the Family Staff. 4 CDs. (Running Time: 6 hrs.). (Adventures in Odyssey Ser.: Vol. 2). (ENG.). (J). 2005. audio compact disk 24.99 (978-1-58997-071-7(3)) Pub: Focus Family. Dist(s): Tyndale Hse

Story. Zondervan Publishing Staff. 2006. audio compact disk 29.99 (978-0-310-93451-6(6)) Zondervan.

***Story: Style, Structure, Substance, & the Pri.** abr. ed. Robert Mckee. Read by Robert Mckee. (ENG.). 2006. (978-0-06-114653-4(6), Harper Audio); (978-0-06-114652-7(8), Harper Audio) HarperCollins Pubs.

Story: Substance, Structure, Style, & the Principles of Screenwriting. abr. ed. Robert McKee. Read by Robert McKee. (Running Time: 21600 sec.). 2006. audio compact disk 29.95 (978-0-06-085618-2(1)) HarperCollins Pubs.

Story, a Story. (J). 2004. bk. 24.95 (978-1-56008-211-8(9)); pap. bk. 32.75 (978-1-55592-315-0(1)); pap. bk. 14.95 (978-1-56008-212-5(7)); 8.95 (978-1-56008-437-2(5)); cass. & flmstrp 30.00 (978-1-56008-769-4(2)) Weston Woods.

Story, a Story. Gail E. Haley. 1 cass., 5 bks. (Running Time: 10 min.). (J). pap. bk. 32.75 Weston Woods.
Anansi the Spider Man climbs up to the sky to buy stories from the Sky God.

Story, a Story. Gail E. Haley. 1 cass. (Running Time: 10 min.). (J). (gr. k-4). bk. 24.95 Weston Woods.

Story, a Story. Gail E. Haley. 1 cass. (Running Time: 10 min.). (J). (gr. k-4). 1993. pap. bk. 12.95 (978-1-56008-036-7(1), PRA123); 8.95 (978-1-56008-117-3(1), RAC123) Weston Woods.
From the book by Gail E. Haley. Anansi the Spider Man climbs up to the sky to buy stories from the Sky God.

Story, a Story. Gail E. Haley. 1 cass. (Running Time: 10 min.). (J). (ps-3). 2000. pap. bk. 12.95 Weston Woods.
Ananse the Spider Man climbs up the sky to buy stories from the Sky God in this folktale from Africa.

Story-A Story, A, Pigs & Pirates; Tomten & the Fox, the; Great Big Enormous Turnip, the; Three Poor Tailors. 2004. (978-0-89719-831-8(X)); cass. & flmstrp (978-0-89719-739-7(9)) Weston Woods.

Story about Ping see Historia Del Patito Ping

Story about Ping. 2004. bk. 24.95 (978-0-89719-688-8(0)); pap. bk. 32.75 (978-1-55592-313-6(5)); pap. bk. 32.75 (978-1-55592-314-3(3)); pap. bk. 14.95 (978-1-56008-076-3(0)); 8.95 (978-1-56008-335-1(2)); cass. & flmstrp 30.00 (978-1-56008-768-7(4)) Weston Woods.

Story about Ping. (J). 2004. pap. bk. 14.95 (978-1-55592-857-5(9)) Weston Woods.

Story about Ping. Marjorie Flack. 1 read-along cass. (Running Time: 11 min.). (J). 1978. 9.95 Live Oak Media.
The adventures that befall a young duckling during an evening on the Yangtze River.

Story about Ping. Marjorie Flack. Read by Jerry Terheyden. 14 vols. (Running Time: 11 mins.). (J). 1982. pap. bk. & tchr. ed. 33.95 (978-0-670-67225-7(4)) Live Oak Media.

Story about Ping. Marjorie Flack. Illus. by Marjorie Flack. 11 vols. (Running Time: 11 mins.). 1982. bk. 28.95 (978-1-59519-090-1(2)); pap. bk. 18.95 (978-1-59519-088-8(0)); pap. bk. 35.95 (978-1-59519-089-5(9)); 9.95 (978-1-59112-126-8(4)); audio compact disk 12.95 (978-1-59519-087-1(2)) Live Oak Media.

Story about Ping. Marjorie Flack. (J). 1989. bk. 37.26 (978-0-394-76396-5(3)) SRA McGraw.

Story about Ping. Marjorie Flack. 1 read-along cass. (Running Time: 9 min.). (J). 8.95 (RAC008) Weston Woods.
One side with page turn signals, one side without.

Story about Ping. Marjorie Flack. Illus. by Kurt Wiese. 1 cass., 5 bks. (Running Time: 9 min.). (J). pap. bk. 32.75 Weston Woods.
A duck suffers the loneliness of abandonment before he is befriended by a little boy who returns him to his family.

Story about Ping. Marjorie Flack. Illus. by Kurt Wiese. 1 cass. (Running Time: 9 min.). (J). bk. 24.95; pap. bk. 12.95 (PRA008) Weston Woods.
One side with page turn signals, one side without.

Story about Ping. Marjorie Flack. (J). 2004. 8.95 (978-1-56008-429-7(4)) Weston Woods.

Story about Ping. unabr. ed. Marjorie Flack. Read by Jerry Terheyden. 11 vols. (Running Time: 11 mins.). (J). (gr. k-3). 1982. bk. 25.95 (978-0-670-67226-4(2)); pap. bk. 16.95 (978-0-670-67230-1(0)) Live Oak Media.
The adventures that befall a young duckling during an evening on the Yangtze River.

Story & Songs from the Wizard of Oz. 1 cass. 1998. 10.98 (978-1-56826-976-4(5)); audio compact disk 16.98 (978-1-56826-977-1(3)) Rhino Enter.

Story Bridges: French. 3 cass. (J). (ps-4). 19.98 Set. (313) MFLP CA.
An absolutely delightful way to introduce your children to another language. Familiar fairy tales were reworded in a nonviolent way, creating solutions to the often scary climaxes.

Story Bridges: German. 3 cass. (J). (ps-4). 19.98 Set. (361) MFLP CA.
An absolutely delightful way to introduce your children to another language. Familiar fairy tales are reworded in a nonviolent way, creating solutions to the often scary climaxes.

Story Bridges: Spanish. 3 cass. (J). (ps-4). 19.98 Set. (335) MFLP CA.

Story Classics - Volume 1. Short Stories. Arranged by Rich Herman. (J). 2004. audio compact disk 9.95 (978-0-9765630-3-7(7)) Family Bks N CDs.
Story Classics Volume 1 - Contains six fun and exciting classic stories. Stories include: Little Red Riding Hood, Read and You Will Know, The Boy and the Robbers, The Gingerbread Man, The Little Half-Chick, and The Little Red Hen. Your children will love these story CDs. Great music and voice talent make these stories come to life!http://www.FamilyBooksandCDs.com.

Story Classics - Volume 2. Short Stories. Arranged by Rich Herman. (J). 2004. audio compact disk 9.95 (978-0-9765630-4-4(5)) Family Bks N CDs.
Story Classics Volume 2 - Contains six fun and exciting classic stories. Stories include: The Boy Who Cried Wolf, The Little Fir Tree, The Country Mouse and the City Mouse, The Emperor's New Clothes, The Frog King, and The Little Jackal and the Alligator. Your children will love these story CDs. Great music and voice talent make these stories come to life!http://www.FamilyBooksandCDs.com.

Story Classics - Volume 3. Short Stories. Arranged by Rich Herman. (J). 2004. audio compact disk 9.95 (978-0-9765630-5-1(3)) Family Bks N CDs.
Story Classics Volume 3 - Contains six fun and exciting classic stories. Stories include: The Adventures of the Little Field Mouse, The Three Little Pigs, The Sun and the Wind, The Leap-Frog, The Sleeping Beauty, and Try, Try, Again. Your children will love these story CDs. Great music and voice talent make these stories come to life!http://www.FamilyBooksandCDs.com.

Story Girl. unabr. ed. L. M. Montgomery. Read by Grace Conlin. 7 cass. (Running Time: 10 hrs. 30 min.). (J). 1997. 49.95 (1893) Blckstn Audio.
When two city boys are sent to spend the summer on a rural island, they discover a very different world & a very different, though special, person, Sara Stanley, the Story Girl. Their vacation becomes a time for magic & mischief as they spend their days with Sara & the eccentric local people, with a mysterious blue treasure chest & intrepid cat & experience an ordeal that may cost a friend his life.

Story Girl. unabr. ed. L. M. Montgomery. Read by Grace Conlin. 7 cass. (Running Time: 10 hrs.). 2001. 49.95 (978-0-7861-1128-2(3), 1893) Blckstn Audio.

Story Girl, Set. unabr. ed. L. M. Montgomery. Read by Grace Conlin. 7 cass. (J). 1999. 49.95 (FS9-34409) Highsmith.

***story House.** Vivian French. Read by Stanley McGeagh. (Running Time: 5 hrs. 15 mins.). (J). 2009. 44.99 (978-1-74214-173-2(0), 9781742141732) Pub: Bolinda Pubng AUS. Dist(s): Bolinda Pub Inc

Story House: 52 New Stories to Share, One for Every Week of the Year. unabr. ed. Vivian French. Read by Stanley McGeagh. Illus. by Selina Young. (Running Time: 18900 sec.). (J). 2008. audio compact disk 63.95 (978-1-921334-90-0(8), 9781921334900) Pub: Bolinda Pubng AUS. Dist(s): Bolinda Pub Inc

Story Knife. unabr. ed. Brad Reynolds. Read by Kevin Foley. 8 cass. (Running Time: 9 hrs. 30 mins.). (Father Mark Townsend Mystery Ser.). 2000. 49.95 (978-1-55686-975-4(4)) Books in Motion.
It begins with a murder, in Seattle, that takes amateur sleuth Father Mark Townsend into the frozen tundra of Alaska. He is joined by a Seattle detective that will be his first murder case. They will encounter a librarian who could hold the key to the killings & also an environmentalist who will go to any length to protect the tundra & a hot-headed priest who resents the intruders from Seattle. Father Townsend will be forced to make some difficult decisions in order to save the lives of those around him.

Story Knife. unabr. ed. Brad Reynolds. Read by Kevin Foley. 8 CDs. (Running Time: 9 hrs. 30 min.). (Father Mark Townsend Mystery Ser.). 2001. audio compact disk 52.00 (978-1-58116-178-6(6)) Books in Motion.
Father Mark Townsend helps the Seattle police with the murder of a crooked lawyer who was slain with a distinctive Eskimo knife.

Story Lady. Read by Jackie Torrence. 1 cass. (J). (gr. 4 up). 1989. 10.00 (WW720) Earwig.

Story Library of the Saints. Joan Wyndham. 8 cass. (J). 32.95 (510) Ignatius Pr.
Brief portraits of the saints whose names we still hear though often in a disguised form.

Story Meditation: Living in the Present. 2005. audio compact disk 19.99 (978-0-9764358-3-9(7)) Oh Mind.

Story of a Bad Boy. Thomas Bailey Aldrich. Read by Anais 9000. 2008. 27.95 (978-1-60112-149-3(0)) Babblebooks.

Story of a Fierce Bad Rabbit. (Running Time: 15 mins.). (Beatrix Potter's Tales Ser.). (ps up). 10.00 (978-1-4025-1655-9(X)) Recorded Bks.

Story of a Girl. unabr. ed. Sara Zarr. Read by Sara Zarr. 4 CDs. (Running Time: 4 hrs. 48 mins.). (YA). (gr. 9 up). 2008. audio compact disk 38.00 (978-0-7393-7133-6(9), Listening Lib) Pub: Random Audio Pubg. Dist(s): Random
I was thirteen when my dad caught me with Tommy Webber in the back of Tommy's Buick, parked next to the old Chart House down in Montara at eleven o'clock on a Tuesday night. Tommy was seventeen and the supposed friend of my brother, Darren. I didn't love him. I'm not sure I even liked him. In a moment, Deanna Lambert's teenage life is changed forever. Struggling to overcome the lasting repercussions and the stifling role of "school slut," Deanna longs to escape a life defined by her past. With subtle grace, complicated wisdom, and striking emotion, Story of a Girl reminds us of our human capacity for resilience, epiphany, and redemption.

Story of a Girl. unabr. ed. Sara Zarr. Read by Sara Zarr. (ENG.). (J). (gr. 9). 2009. audio compact disk 30.00 (978-0-307-70604-1(4), Listening Lib) Pub: Random Audio Pubg. Dist(s): Random

Story of a Hundred Operas. unabr. ed. Felix Mendelssohn. Narrated by Flo Gibson. 5 cass. (Running Time: 7 hrs. 34 mins.). 2004. 20.95 (978-1-55685-755-3(1)) Audio Bk Con.
100 famous, not-so-famous and infamous operas.

Story of a Marriage. unabr. ed. Andrew Sean Greer. Read by S. Epatha Merkerson. 6 CDs. (Running Time: 7 hrs. 0 mins. 0 sec.). (ENG.). 2008. audio compact disk 29.95 (978-1-4272-0462-2(4)) Pub: Macmill Audio. Dist(s): Macmillan

Story of a Million Years. unabr. ed. David Huddle. 5 cass. (Running Time: 6 hrs. 30 mins.). 1999. 48.00 (978-0-7887-4376-4(7), 96134E75) Recorded Bks.
He examines the complex mixture of longing & contentment that makes up relationships. As the layers of stories we tell ourselves & others are gently stripped away, we find the strengths & weaknesses of people who could easily be our friends, our spouses, or ourselves.

Story of a Soul. Read by Cynthia Splatt. Tr. by John Beevers. 5 cass. 1995. 22.95 Set. (701-C) Ignatius Pr.
Autobiography of Saint Therese of Lisieux. One of the greatest spiritual classics of modern times which reveals the saint's "Little Way" to sanctity.

***Story of a Soul.** St. Thérèse of Lisieux. (ENG.). 2009. audio compact disk 19.95 (978-1-936231-15-7(8)) Cath Audio.

Story of a Soul: The Autobiography of St. Therese of Lisieux. unabr. ed. John Clarke. 9 cass. (Running Time: 9 hrs.). 1997. 49.95 Set. (978-0-8198-6995-1(3)) Pauline Bks.
Fr. John Clarke's acclaimed translation, accepted as the standard throughout the English speaking world, is a faithful & unaffected rendering of Therese's own words, from the original manuscript.

Story of Adolph Ochs. 10.00 Esstee Audios.
The story of how Ochs founded The New York Times.

Story of Albert Einstein. 1 cass. (Running Time: 27 min.). 14.95 (12579) MMI Corp.
Life & work of this great mathematician.

Story of America. 1 cass. (Running Time: 1 hr.). 2002. 19.95 Listen & Live.

Story of America: The Pilgrims, the American Revolution, the Star-Spangled Banner. unabr. ed. 2 cass. (Running Time: 3 hrs.). (Full-Cast Productions Ser.). (J). (gr. 4-8). 2002. 19.95 (978-1-931953-10-8(4), AA104) Listen & Live.
In this original production you'll learn about three pivitol periods in our nation's history: The Pilgrims, who sowed the seeds of what would become

America; The American Revolution and our battle for independence; and The War of 1812, which yielded our beloved national anthem - TheStar-Spangled Banner.

Story of an Hour see Women in Literature, the Short Story: A Collection

Story of an Hour see White Heron

Story of an Hour & Others. unabr. ed. Kate Chopin. Read by Marilyn Langbehn. 2 cass. (Running Time: 2 hrs. 30 min.). Dramatization. 1992. 16.95 (978-1-55686-380-6(2), 380) Books in Motion.
Included: The Story of an Hour, A Vocation & a Voice, An Egyptian Cigarette, Lilacs, & Her Letters.

Story of Anne Frank. Alan Venable. (Step into History Ser.). 2000. audio compact disk 18.95 (978-1-4105-0161-5(2)) D Johnston Inc.

Story of Anne Frank. Alan Venable. Illus. by Jeff Ham. Narrated by Jennifer Morrison. (J). (gr. 5-6). 2001. audio compact disk 200.00 (978-1-58702-518-1(3)) D Johnston Inc.

Story of Anne Frank. Alan Venable. Ed. by Jerry Stemach et al. Illus. by Jeff Ham. Narrated by Jennifer Morrison. Contrib. by Ted S. Hasselbring. (Start-to-Finish Books). (J). (gr. 2-3). 2002. 100.00 (978-1-58702-947-9(2)) D Johnston Inc.

Story of Anne Frank, Vol. 7. unabr. ed. Alan Venable. Ed. by Jerry Stemach et al. Illus. by Jeff Ham. Narrated by Jennifer Morrison. Contrib. by Ted S. Hasselbring. (Start-to-Finish Books). (J). (gr. 2-3). 2001. 35.00 (978-1-58702-519-8(1)) D Johnston Inc.
Anne Frank was only thirteen years old when she started writing the diary that would become the most famous book ever written about World War II. Anne Frank and her family were Jews living occupied Amsterdam. Facing Nazi persecution, Anne frank's family went into hiding in the attic of the building where Otto has his business, Sharing the hideout with the Frank family wan another family with a young girl.

Story of Anne-Therese. Beatrice Hoberg & Brendan Harvey. Illus. by Adelaide Ortegel. 1 cass. (Running Time: 20 min.). (J). (gr. k-3). 1997. pap. bk. 8.95 (978-1-893789-05-0(5)) Sists Prov.

Story of Babar. (Babar Ser.). (J). (ps-3). 1975. bk. 31.98 (978-0-394-03903-9(3)) SRA McGraw.

Story of Bad Little Boy see Best of Mark Twain

***Story of Beautiful Girl.** unabr. ed. Rachel Simon. (Running Time: 9 hrs.). (ENG.). 2011. 24.98 (978-1-60941-112-1(9)); audio compact disk & audio compact disk 29.98 (978-1-60941-108-4(0)) Pub: Hachet Audio. Dist(s): HachBkGrp

Story of Britain: A People's History. unabr. ed. Roy Strong. Read by Stephen Thorne. 14 cass. (Running Time: 21 hrs. 15 mins.). 1999. 99.95 (978-0-7531-0554-2(3), 990103) Pub: ISIS Audio GBR. Dist(s): Ulverscroft US
Tells the story from the very earliest recorded Celtic times to the era of Margaret Thatcher. The monarchy, parliament, the law, the church - all the great institutions whose fortunes are so much part of the fabric of British history are here seen in perspective, effecting the everyday lives of men & women against ever-changing social, cultural, & economic backgrounds.

Story of Britain: A People's History. unabr. ed. Roy Strong. Read by Stephen Thorne. 18 CDs. (Running Time: 20 hrs. 19 mins.). (Isis Ser.). (J). 2002. audio compact disk 116.95 (978-0-7531-1494-0(1)) Pub: ISIS Lrg Prnt GBR. Dist(s): Ulverscroft US
The story of Britain from the very earliest recorded Celtic times to the era of Margaret Thatcher. The story is an exciting one, peopled with great characters, huge events, turbulent dramas affecting the Monarchy, Parliament, the law and the Church. All the great institutions whose fortunes are so much a part of the fabric of British history are seen in perspective, relating the everyday lives of men and women to the ever-changing social, cultural, and economic backgrounds.

Story of Chicago May. unabr. ed. Nuala O'Faolain. Read by Terry Donnelly. 8 cass. (Running Time: 11 hrs.). 2006. 89.75 (978-1-4193-6931-5(8), 98252) Recorded Bks.
Award-winning memoirist and New York Times best-selling author Nuala O'Faolain branches into new territory with her biography of the infamous Irish-American prostitute and thief, Chicago May. O'Faolain uses May's autobiography, primary sources from the turn of the 19th century and her own experience as an Irishwoman to bring May - and all her heartache, deception and violence - to life.

Story of Christmas. Lois Duncan. Music by Robin Arquette. 1 cass. (Running Time: 40 min.). (J). (gr. k up). 1989. 9.95 RDA Enter.

Story of Christmas. Prod. by JLP International Inc & Paulist Press. 1996. 7.95 (978-0-8091-8221-3(1)) Paulist Pr.
Tells the story of Christmas through narrations, best-loved Christmas carols, scripture and sacred classical music.

Story of Cirrus Flux. unabr. ed. Matthew Skelton. Read by Jon Smith. (ENG.). (J). (gr. 4). 2010. audio compact disk 34.00 (978-0-307-70635-5(4), Listening Lib) Pub: Random Audio Pubg. Dist(s): Random

Story of Civilization: The Age of Faith. unabr. ed. Will Durant & Ariel Durant. Read by Alexander Adams. 37 cass. (Story of Civilization Ser.: Vol. 4). 2000. 89.95 (978-0-7366-5543-9(3)) Books on Tape.
An integrated, detailed and picturesque history of three great religions during the Middle Ages.

Story of Civilization: The Age of Louis XIV. Will Durant & Ariel Durant. Read by Alexander Adams. 23 cass. (Running Time: 34 hrs.). (Story of Civilization Ser.: Vol. 8). 2000. 79.95 (978-0-7366-5546-0(8)) Books on Tape.
The Durants explore an apex of modern European culture, the years 1648 to 1715, the era of Louis XIV.

Story of Civilization: The Age of Louis XIV, Pt. 1. unabr. collector's ed. Will Durant & Ariel Durant. Read by Alexander Adams. 10 cass. (Running Time: 15 hrs.). (Story of Civilization Ser.). 1997. 104.00 (978-0-7366-3795-4(8), 4468-A) Books on Tape.
Explore the apex of European civilization to that time, the years 1648 - 1715. It is the era of the "Sun King," Louis XIV, one of the most powerful rulers in Western history. It is also the pinnacle of Dutch culture, the heyday of Vermeer & William of Orange, later King of England.

Story of Civilization: The Age of Louis XIV, Pt. 2. unabr. collector's ed. Will Durant & Ariel Durant. Read by Alexander Adams. 13 cass. (Running Time: 19 hrs. 30 mins.). (Story of Civilization Ser.). 1997. 80.00 (978-0-7366-3794-7(X), 4468-B) Books on Tape.

Story of Civilization: The Age of Napoleon. Will Durant & Ariel Durant. Read by Alexander Adams. 32 cass. (Running Time: 48 hrs.). (Story of Civilization Ser.: Vol. 11). 2001. 89.95 (978-0-7366-5549-1(2)) Books on Tape.
The Durants conclude their epic series with the volatile age of Napoleon, from the French Revolution to the Industrial Revolution.

Story of Civilization: The Age of Napoleon. unabr. collector's ed. Will Durant & Ariel Durant. Read by Alexander Adams. 13 cass. (Running Time: 19 hrs. 30 min.). (Story of Civilization Ser.). 2000. 104.00 (978-0-7366-5102-8(0), 5291-C) Books on Tape.
Takes us from a feudal peasantry in revolt to the beginnings of the Industrial Revolution.

Story of Civilization: The Age of Reason Begins. unabr. ed. Will Durant & Ariel Durant. Read by Alexander Adams. 21 cass. (Running Time: 32 hrs.). (Story of Civilization Ser.: Vol. 7). 2001. 79.95 (978-0-7366-5545-3(X)) Books on Tape.
The Durants take on the linchpin of modern European history, the religious strife & scientific progress between the 1550's & 1650's.

Story of Civilization: The Age of Voltaire. unabr. ed. Will Durant & Ariel Durant. Read by Alexander Adams. 26 cass. (Running Time: 39 hrs.). (Story of Civilization Ser.: Vol. 9). 2000. 79.95 (978-0-7366-5547-7(6)) Books on Tape.
A biography of a great man as well as the story of ideas and events that culminated in the French Revolution.

Story of Civilization: The Reformation. unabr. ed. Will Durant & Ariel Durant. Read by Alexander Adams. 10 cass. (Running Time: 15 hrs.). (Story of Civilization Ser.). 1997. 80.00 (978-0-7366-3621-6(8), 4279-C) Books on Tape.
At the beginning of the sixteenth century, a movement began to sweep through Western Europe, shaking the stability of every state & institution in its path - the Reformation.

Story of Civilization: The Reformation. unabr. ed. Will Durant & Ariel Durant. Read by Alexander Adams. 32 cass. (Running Time: 48 hrs.). (Story of Civilization Ser.: Vol. 6). 2001. 89.95 (978-0-7366-5539-2(5)) Books on Tape.

Story of Civilization Pt. 1: Our Oriental Heritage. Will Durant & Ariel Durant. Read by Alexander Adams. 26 cass. (Running Time: 39 hrs.). (Story of Civilization Ser.: Vol. 1). 2000. 79.95 (978-0-7366-5540-8(9)) Books on Tape.
First volume in The Story of Civilization, traces history of Egypt & Middle East, India, China & Japan.

Story of Civilization Pt. 1: Rousseau & Revolution. Will Durant & Ariel Durant. Read by Alexander Adams. 36 vols. (Running Time: 240 min.). (Story of Civilization Ser.: Vol. 10). 2001. 89.95 (978-0-7366-5548-4(4)) Books on Tape.
With Rousseau as his focal point, the Durants present a dramatic exploration of the events leading up to the French Revolution.

Story of Civilization Pt. 1: Rousseau & Revolution. collector's ed. Will Durant & Ariel Durant. Read by Alexander Adams. 14 cass. (Running Time: 21 hrs.). (Story of Civilization Ser.). 1999. 112.00 (978-0-7366-4756-4(2), 5079-A) Books on Tape.
A history of Europe during much of the eighteenth century that concentrates on the French Revolution & the beginnings of the Romantic movement.

Story of Civilization Pt. 1: The Life of Greece. Will Durant & Ariel Durant. Read by Alexander Adams. 20 cass. (Running Time: 30 hrs.). (Story of Civilization Ser.: Vol. 2). 1994. 80.00 (978-0-7366-5541-5(7), 3464-B) Books on Tape.
Re-creates Greek civilization from the prehistoric culture of Crete to the Roman conquest.

Story of Civilization Pt. 1: The Life of Greece. unabr. collector's ed. Will Durant & Ariel Durant. Read by Alexander Adams. 10 cass. (Running Time: 15 hrs.). (Story of Civilization Ser.). 1994. 80.00 (978-0-7366-2737-5(5), 3464-A) Books on Tape.

Story of Civilization Pt. 2: The Renaissance. Will Durant & Ariel Durant. Read by Alexander Adams. 24 cass. (Running Time: 36 hrs.). (Story of Civilization Ser.: Vol. 5). 2000. 79.95 (978-0-7366-5544-6(1)) Books on Tape.
A colorful pageant of princes & kings, painters & philosophers, scientists & architects comes to life in Will Durant's study of the Italian Renaissance. He sets the stage in Florence for the opening act of a magnificent cultural flowering spread across Europe & continued through time.

Story of Civilization Pt. 2: The Renaissance. unabr. collector's ed. Will Durant & Ariel Durant. Read by Alexander Adams. 12 cass. (Running Time: 18 hrs.). (Story of Civilization Ser.). 1995. 96.00 (978-0-7366-3159-4(3), 3830-B) Books on Tape.

Story of Civilization Pt. 2: The Renaissance. unabr. collector's ed. Will Durant & Ariel Durant. Read by Alexander Adams. 12 cass. (Running Time: 18 hrs.). (Story of Civilization Ser.: Vol. 5). 1995. 96.00 (978-0-7366-3158-7(5), 3830-A) Books on Tape.

Story of Civilization Pt. 3: The Age of Faith. unabr. collector's ed. Ariel Durant & Will Durant. Read by Alexander Adams. 12 cass. (Running Time: 18 hrs.). (Story of Civilization Ser.). 1995. 96.00 (978-0-7366-3090-0(2), 3768-A); 96.00 (978-0-7366-3092-4(9), 3768-C) Books on Tape.
Here's a look at the Middle Ages through a wide angle lens. Will Durant blends stories of saints, martyrs, kings, knights, popes & poets to tell the story of three cultures: Christian, Islamic & Judaic. Christian civilization, rooted in Jewish philosophy, sits against the backdrop of a complex Islamic tradition.

Story of Civilization Pt. A: Caesar & Christ. Will Durant & Ariel Durant. Read by Alexander Adams. 22 cass. (Running Time: 33 hrs.). (Story of Civilization Ser.: Vol. 3). 2000. 79.95 (978-0-7366-5542-2(5)) Books on Tape.
The Roman age, from infancy to empire, with an account of the advent of Jesus of Nazareth.

Story of Civilization Pt. A: Caesar & Christ. unabr. collector's ed. Will Durant & Ariel Durant. Read by Alexander Adams. 11 cass. (Running Time: 16 hrs. 30 min.). (Story of Civilization Ser.). 1994. 88.00 (978-0-7366-2855-6(X), 3563-A) Books on Tape.
The Roman age, from infancy to empire, with an account of the advent of Jesus of Nazareth. The Story of Civilization.

Story of Classical Music. Darren Henley. Read by Marin Alsop. 4 x CDs. (Junior Classics Ser.). (J). 2004. cd-rom & audio compact disk 22.98 (978-962-634-310-4(9), Naxos AudioBooks) Naxos.

Story of Creation. 1 cass. (Beginner's Bible Ser.). (J). 5.58 Blisterpack. (SME 67808) NewSound.

***Story of Dianetics & Scientology.** L. Ron Hubbard. (SWE.). 2010. audio compact disk 15.00 (978-1-4031-7706-3(6)); audio compact disk 15.00 (978-1-4031-7702-5(3)); audio compact disk 15.00 (978-1-4031-7696-7(5)); audio compact disk 15.00 (978-1-4031-7700-1(7)); audio compact disk 15.00 (978-1-4031-7704-9(X)); audio compact disk 15.00 (978-1-4031-7703-2(1)); audio compact disk 15.00 (978-1-4031-7692-9(2)); audio compact disk 15.00 (978-1-4031-7698-1(1)); audio compact disk 15.00 (978-1-4031-7693-6(0)); audio compact disk 15.00 (978-1-4031-7705-6(8)); audio compact disk 15.00 (978-1-4031-7699-8(X)); audio compact disk 15.00 (978-1-4031-7694-3(9)); audio compact disk 15.00 (978-1-4031-7695-0(7)); audio compact disk 15.00 (978-1-4031-7707-0(4)); audio compact disk 15.00 (978-1-4031-7701-8(5)); audio compact disk 15.00 (978-1-4031-7697-4(3)); audio compact disk 15.00 (978-1-4031-0378-9(X)) Bridge Pubns Inc.

Story of Doctor Dolittle. Hugh Lofting. Read by Flo Gibson. 2 cass. (Running Time: 2 hrs. 30 min.). (Doctor Dolittle Ser.). (J). (gr. 4-6). 1996. 14.95 (978-1-55685-451-4(X)) Audio Bk Con.
Polynesia the parrot, Jip the dog, Too-Too the owl, Dab-Dab the duck, Gub-Gub the pig, Chee-Chee the monkey & many other animals accompany kind Dr. Doolittle on his rounds & adventures in England, Africa & on the high seas. Parental guidance may be needed due to certain unfortunate racial insensitivities that may serve to remind us that many have come a long way.

Story of Doctor Dolittle. Hugh Lofting. Narrated by Nadia May. (Running Time: 2 hrs. 30 mins.). (YA). 1995. 17.95 (978-1-59912-718-7(0)) Iofy Corp.

Story of Doctor Dolittle. Hugh Lofting. Read by David Case. (ENG.). 2004. audio compact disk 16.99 (978-1-4001-5100-4(7)) Pub: Tantor Media. Dist(s): IngramPubServ

Story of Doctor Dolittle. Hugh Lofting. Read by David Case. (ENG.). 2005. audio compact disk 39.99 (978-1-4001-3100-6(6)) Pub: Tantor Media. Dist(s): IngramPubServ

Story of Doctor Dolittle. unabr. ed. Hugh Lofting. Read by Martin Short. 2 cass. (Running Time: 3 hrs.). (Doctor Dolittle Ser.). (J). (gr. 4-6). 1997. 14.95 (978-1-885608-18-5(7)) Airplay.
Doctor Dolittle has an extraordinary gift: he can understand the language of the animals! As word of his kindness spreads around the world he is called away on the first of his many extraordinary adventures.

Story of Doctor Dolittle. unabr. ed. Hugh Lofting. Narrated by Martin Short. 2 cass. (Running Time: 2 hrs.). (Doctor Dolittle Ser.). (J). (gr. 4-6). 2000. audio compact disk 15.00 (978-1-885608-37-6(3)) Airplay.

Story of Doctor Dolittle. unabr. ed. Hugh Lofting. Narrated by Bobbie Frohman. Music by David Thorn. B. J. Bedford. 3 Cds. (Running Time: 2 3/4 hours). (J). 2007. audio compact disk (978-0-9787553-6-2(7)) Alcazar AudioWorks.

Story of Doctor Dolittle. unabr. ed. Hugh Lofting. Read by Nadia May. 2 cass. (Running Time: 2 hrs. 30 mins.). (Doctor Dolittle Ser.). (gr. 4-6). 1996. 17.95 (978-0-7861-0946-3(7), 1698) Blckstn Audio.
Hugh Lofting was an officer in the Irish Guards during World War I when he found that writing illustrated letters to his children eased the terrific strain of the war which he felt so keenly. These letters became "The Story of Dr. Dolittle," published in 1920. Since then, children all over the world have been reading the adventures of the animals' own doctor. Lofting's stories have been translated into almost every language & excerpts from them are used in standard textbooks as examples of good writing for children.

Story of Doctor Dolittle. unabr. ed. Hugh Lofting. Read by Nadia May. 2 CDs. (Running Time: 2 hrs. 30 mins.). (Doctor Dolittle Ser.). (gr. 4-6). 2000. audio compact disk 16.00 (978-0-7861-9920-4(2), 1698) Blckstn Audio.

Story of Doctor Dolittle. unabr. ed. Hugh Lofting. Read by David Case. 3 cass. (Running Time: 3 hrs.). (Doctor Dolittle Ser.). (J). (gr. 4-6). 1995. 18.00 Set. (3795) Books on Tape.
You will recall that Doctor Dolittle had a singular ability to talk with animals. Through them, he learns of an epidemic among the monkeys & - true to his Hippocratic oath - sails away to contain the outbreak. His adventures there remind us of the unusual nature of the "Dark Continent".

Story of Doctor Dolittle. unabr. collector's ed. Hugh Lofting. Read by David Case. 3 cass. (Running Time: 3 hrs.). (Doctor Dolittle Ser.). (J). (gr. 4-6). 1995. 28.00 (978-0-7366-3119-8(4), 3795) Books on Tape.
Doctor Dolittle, Hugh Lofting's wonderful creation, comes to life in David Case's exquisite reading of this timeless classic. Each character has its own voice & we finally feel connected to the Dolittle menage - Polynesia the parrot, Gub-Gub the pig, Dab-Dab the duck & Jip the dog. You will recall that Doctor Dolittle had a singular ability to talk with animals. Through them, he learns of an epidemic among the monkeys true to his Hippocratic oath - sails away to Africa to contain the outbreak. His adventures there remind us of the unusual nature of the Dark Continent.

Story of Dona Chila. (Greetings Ser.: Vol. 3). (gr. 3-5). 10.00 (978-0-7635-1776-2(3)) Rigby Educ.

Story of Dr. Dolittle. unabr. ed. Hugh Lofting. Read by David Case. (J). 2006. 34.99 (978-1-59895-674-0(4)) Find a World.

Story of Dr. Dolittle, with eBook. unabr. ed. Hugh Lofting. Narrated by David Case. (Running Time: 2 hrs. 30 mins. 0 sec.). (ENG.). (J). 2009. audio compact disk 17.99 (978-1-4001-0895-4(0)); audio compact disk 35.99 (978-1-4001-3895-1(7)); audio compact disk 17.99 (978-1-4001-5895-9(8)) Pub: Tantor Media. Dist(s): IngramPubServ

***Story of Dr. Doolittle.** Hugh Lofting. Narrated by Flo Gibson. (ENG.). (J). 2010. audio compact disk 16.95 (978-1-60646-103-7(6)) Audio Bk Con.

***Story of Dr. Kildare, Volume 1.** RadioArchives.com. (Running Time: 600). (ENG.). 2004. audio compact disk 29.98 (978-1-61081-018-0(X)) Radio Arch.

***Story of Dr. Kildare, Volume 2.** RadioArchives.com. (ENG.). 2006. audio compact disk 29.98 (978-1-61081-048-7(1)) Radio Arch.

Story of Druva. Swami Jyotirmayananda. 1 cass. (Running Time: 45 min.). 1990. 10.00 Yoga Res Foun.

Story of Easter. 1 cass. (Beginner's Bible Ser.). (J). 5.58 Blisterpack. (SME 67806) NewSound.

Story of Edgar Sawtelle. unabr. ed. David Wroblewski. Narrated by Richard Poe. (Running Time: 21 hrs. 45 mins.). 2008. 61.75 (978-1-4361-6508-2(3)) Recorded Bks.

Story of Edgar Sawtelle. unabr. ed. David Wroblewski. Read by Richard Poe. 18 cass. (Running Time: 21 hrs. 45 mins.). 2008. 113.75 (978-1-4361-4956-3(8)); audio compact disk 123.75 (978-1-4361-4958-7(4)) Recorded Bks.

Story of Edgar Sawtelle. unabr. ed. David Wroblewski. Read by Richard Poe. 18 CDs. (Running Time: 21 hrs. 30 mins.). 2008. audio compact disk 39.99 (978-1-4361-6030-8(8)) Recorded Bks.

Story of Electricity. unabr. ed. Jack Sanders. Read by Edwin Newman. (Running Time: 10800 sec.). (Audio Classics: Science & Discovery Ser.). 2006. audio compact disk 25.95 (978-0-7861-6496-7(4)) Pub: Blckstn Audio. Dist(s): NetLibrary CO

Story of Electricity. unabr. ed. John T. Sanders. Read by Edwin Newman. Ed. by Jack Sommer & Mike Hassell. 2 cass. (Running Time: 2 hrs. 45 min.). Dramatization. (Science & Discovery Ser.). (YA). (gr. 11 up). 1993. 17.95 set. (978-1-56823-000-9(1), 10410) Knowledge Prod.
In the 19th century, scientists working with chemistry & magnetism began discovering a rich variety of electrical phenomena. These were to be applied later in inventions including motors, alternating current, radio, batteries, the telephone, & much more. This is the story of a new branch of science that changed the way the world does physical work & the way it controls information, spurring the Industrial Revolution & then the Information Age.

Story of Esther. 2003. 15.00 (978-1-57972-533-4(3)) Insight Living.

Story of Esther: A Girl Who Became Queen to Save Her People. 2004. audio compact disk 14.00 (978-1-57972-607-2(0)) Insight Living.

Story of Esther: A Girl Who Became Queen to Save Her People. 2003. audio compact disk 14.00 (978-1-57972-534-1(1)) Insight Living.

Story of Esther: A Girl Who Became Queen to Saver Her People. 2004. 15.00 (978-1-57972-608-9(9)) Insight Living.

Story of Ferdinand see Cuento de Ferdinando

Story of Ferdinand see Cuento de Ferdinando, Grades K-3

Story of Ferdinand. Munro Leaf. (J). 1985. 29.95 (978-0-941078-80-1(9)) Live Oak Media.

Story of Ferdinand. Munro Leaf. Illus. by Robert Lawson. 11 vols. (Running Time: 10 mins.). 1989. bk. 28.95 (978-1-59519-094-9(5)); pap. bk. 18.95 (978-1-59519-092-5(9)); pap. bk. 39.95 (978-1-59519-093-2(7)); 9.95 (978-1-59112-127-5(2)); audio compact disk 12.95 (978-1-59519-091-8(0)) Live Oak Media.

Story of Ferdinand. Munro Leaf. Illus. by Robert Lawson. (J). (ps-3). 1988. 6.95 (978-0-318-37106-1(5), PufBks) Penguin Grp USA.

Story of Ferdinand. Munro Leaf. Illus. by Robert W. Lawson. (Story Tapes Ser.). (J). (ps-6). 1988. pap. bk. 6.95 (PufBks) Penguin Grp USA.

Story of Ferdinand. unabr. ed. Munro Leaf. Read by Larry Robinson. Illus. by Robert Lawson. 1 read along cass. (Running Time: 10 min.). (J). (gr. k-3). 1978. pap. bk. 15.95 Live Oak Media.
The tale of the bull who preferred to sit & smell flowers rather than fight.

Story of Ferdinand. unabr. ed. Munro Leaf. Read by Larry Robinson. Illus. by Robert Lawson. 11 vols. (Running Time: 10 mins.). (J). (gr. k-3). 1978. bk. 25.95 incl. cloth bk. in bag. (978-0-670-67427-5(3)) Live Oak Media.

Story of Ferdinand. unabr. ed. Munro Leaf. Illus. by Robert Lawson. 11 vols. (Running Time: 10 mins.). (J). 1989. pap. bk. 16.95 (978-0-670-67431-2(1)) Live Oak Media.

Story of Ferdinand, Set. unabr. ed. Munro Leaf. Read by Larry Robinson. Illus. by Robert Lawson. 14 vols. (Running Time: 10 mins.). (J). (gr. k-3). 1982. pap. bk. & tchr. ed. 37.95 incl. 4 pap. bks. & guide. (978-0-670-67426-8(5)) Live Oak Media.

Story of Ferdinand: El Cuento de Ferdinando. Munro Leaf. Tr. by Pura Belpré. Illus. by Robert Lawson. 2 cass. (J). 1999. pap. bk. 29.95 Set. Live Oak Media.

Story of Ferdinand: El Cuento de Ferdinando. unabr. ed. Ed. by Munro Leaf. Tr. by Pura Belpré. Illus. by Robert Lawson. 22 vols. (Running Time: 11 mins.). (ENG & SPA.). (J). (gr. 1-3). 1999. pap. bk. 33.95 (978-0-87499-567-1(1)) Live Oak Media.

Story of Ferdinand Bilingual Pack. Munro Leaf. Illus. by Robert Lawson. 22 vols. (Running Time: 22 mins.). pap. bk. (978-1-59519-155-7(0)) Live Oak Media.

Story of Forgetting. Stefan Merrill Block. Read by Patrick G. Lawlor. (Playaway Adult Fiction Ser.). 2008. 64.99 (978-1-60640-693-9(0)) Find a World.

Story of Forgetting. unabr. ed. Stefan Merrill Block. Narrated by Patrick G. Lawlor. (Running Time: 10 hrs. 30 mins. 0 sec.). (ENG.). 2008. audio compact disk 24.99 (978-1-4001-5717-4(X)) Pub: Tantor Media. Dist(s): IngramPubServ

Story of Forgetting. unabr. ed. Stefan Merrill Block. Read by Patrick G. Lawlor. 9 CDs. (Running Time: 10 hrs. 30 mins. 0 sec.). (ENG.). 2008. audio compact disk 34.99 (978-1-4001-0717-9(2)); audio compact disk 69.99 (978-1-4001-3717-6(9)) Pub: Tantor Media. Dist(s): IngramPubServ

Story of Freemasonry. W. G. Sibley. Ed. by Michael R. Poll. 2005. 9.50 (978-1-887560-52-8(1), Cstone Bk Pubs) M Poll Pub.

Story of Henri Tod. William F. Buckley, Jr. Read by Bushnell James. 7 cass. (Running Time: 10 hrs.). (Blackford Oakes Mystery Ser.). 2004. 49.95 (978-0-7861-2752-8(X), 3285); audio compact disk 72.00 (978-0-7861-8645-7(3), 3285) Blckstn Audio.

Story of Henri Tod. unabr. collector's ed. William F. Buckley, Jr. Read by Michael Prichard. 6 cass. (Running Time: 9 hrs.). (Blackford Oakes Mystery Ser.). 1984. 48.00 (978-0-7366-1003-2(0), 1936) Books on Tape.
Berlin before the wall. Khruschev issues President Kennedy an ultimatum. Kennedy stalls, but directs the CIA to contact a secret group of German dissidents: the Bruderschaft. Blackford Oakes, senior U.S. field operative & the author's alter ego, leads the charge. While Kennedy confers with de Gaulle & MacMillan, Oakes penetrates the Bruderschaft. He meets their leader, Henri Tod & finds him ready with a master plan.

Story of Henry Ford. Kenneth Bruce. 1 cass. (Running Time: 1 hr.). Dramatization. (Excursions in History Ser.). 12.50 Alpha Tape.

Story of Human Language, I-III. Instructed by John McWhorter. 18 cass. (Running Time: 18 hrs.). 2004. bk. 79.95 (978-1-56585-945-6(6), 1600); bk. 99.95 (978-1-56585-947-0(2), 1600) Teaching Co.

Story of Jesus. Created by AWMI. (ENG.). 2007. audio compact disk 15.00 (978-1-59548-097-2(8)) A Wommack.

Story of Jesus. unabr. ed. David Angus. Read by Kerry Shale. 2 CDs. (Running Time: 8472 sec.). 2006. audio compact disk 17.98 (978-962-634-408-8(3), Naxos AudioBooks) Naxos.

Story of Jesus for Adults. Eric Martin. 4 CDs. 2004. audio compact disk 10.99 (978-0-88368-835-9(2)) Whitaker Hse.

Story of Jesus for Kids. 4 CDs. (J). 2004. audio compact disk 10.99 (978-0-88368-834-2(4)) Whitaker Hse.

Story of Jesus for Kid's-CEV. Created by Casscom Media. (J). (ps-k). 2003. audio compact disk 14.99 (978-1-930034-23-5(7)) Casscomm.

***Story of Jonah.** Created by Karen Heimbuch. Narrated by Karen Heimbuch. Illus. by Burt Medall. Music by Steve Wilkinson. Created by Revelation Media International. (ENG.). (J). 2010. bk. (978-0-9843304-4-7(5)) HeuleGordon.

Story of Joseph. Perf. by Diane Wolkstein. (Running Time: 54 min.). (J). (gr. 1-12). 10.00 (978-1-879846-08-1(X)) Cloudstone NY.
A tale of transformation Joseph passes from dreamer to a man of action; from slave to ruler of Egypt, from arrogant son to one who rebinds, reunites & carries forward the traditions of his ancesters. Parents' Choice.

***Story of Joseph.** unabr. ed. Zondervan Publishing Staff. (Running Time: 0 hr. 14 mins. 44 sec.). (Best-Loved Stories of the Bible, NIrV Ser.). (ENG.). (J). 2010. 1.99 (978-0-310-86497-4(6)) Pub: Zondkidz. Dist(s): Zondervan

Story of King Arthur & His Knights. Read by David Thorn. Howard Pyle. 10 CDs. (Running Time: 11 Hrs. 30 mins.). (J). 2006. audio compact disk (978-0-9787553-2-4(4)) Alcazar AudioWorks.
Howard Pyle (who also wrote The Merry Adventures of Robin Hood) weaves the tales of chivalrous Knights, the magic sword of Excalibur, the Magician Merlin the Wise...and the legendary Arthur...later to become King of Britain. Pyle resorts to his often ponderousw language describing bouts of jousting...and knightly jealousies played out in grand style.

Story of King Arthur & His Knights. unabr. ed. Howard Pyle. Narrated by Flo Gibson. 7 cass. (Running Time: 9 hrs. 30 min.). (YA). (gr. 10 up). 1999. 25.95 (978-1-55685-629-7(6)) Audio Bk Con.
The stories of the chivalry & courage of King Arthur & the Knights of the Round Table, the Sword Excalibur, the beautiful Lady Guinevere, Merlin the Magician, Sir Gawaine & the Lady of the Lake are vividly told.

Story of King Arthur & His Knights. unabr. ed. Howard Pyle. Read by Stuart Langston. 8 cass. (Running Time: 11 hrs. 30 mins.). 2002. 56.95 (978-0-7861-2248-6(X), 2971); audio compact disk 72.00 (978-0-7861-9491-9(X), 2971) Blckstn Audio.
The first volume of the four, is the true spirit of the England of that time, when Arthur, son of Uther-Pendragon, was overlord of Britain and Merlin was a powerful enchanter, when the sword Excalibur was forged and won, when the Round Table came into being.

Story of Kwanzaa. unabr. ed. Donna L. Washington. Narrated by Graham Brown. 1 cass. (Running Time: 15 mins.). (gr. 1 up). 1998. 10.00 (978-0-7887-1790-1(1), 95262E7) Recorded Bks.
Features the celebration of African history & culture of Kwanzaa; the special food, decorations & traditions associated with it.

Story of Lady Jacqueline. unabr. ed. 1 cass. (Running Time: 20 min.). Dramatization. (Magic Looking Glass Ser.). (J). (gr. 2-6). 1989. 9.95 (978-0-7810-0036-9(X), NIM-CW-129-1-C) NIMCO.
A Dutch folk tale.

Story of Liberty. Charles C. Coffin. Narrated by Edward Lewis. (Running Time: 10 hrs.). 2001. 30.95 (978-1-59912-719-4(9)) Iofy Corp.

Story of Liberty. unabr. ed. Charles Carleton Coffin. Narrated by Edward Lewis. 7 cass. (Running Time: 10 hrs.). 2001. 49.95 (978-0-7861-2142-7(4), 2893) Blckstn Audio.
Does America still have a rendezvous with destiny? Is there yet a generation to come forth from this nation which will turn the hearts of not only its countrymen back to the living God, but the heart of the world as well? The Story of Liberty, originally published in 1879, reaches back into the records of history to observe the hand of the Great Author and give a direction for the days ahead. As we look at that which preceded our nation's history and led to its founding, we will begin to have an idea of what liberty cost those who love the truth and how much still is at stake.

Story of Little Tree. 1 cass. (J). 9.95 (ASLT) Brdgstn Multimed Grp.
Little Tree wonders if he'll amount to anything in this Easter fable.

Story of Little Tree. Bridgestone Staff. 2004. audio compact disk 7.98 (978-1-56371-031-5(5)) Brdgstn Multimed Grp.

Story of Lucy Gault. William Trevor. Narrated by Terry Donnelly. 6 cass. (Running Time: 8 hrs. 45 mins.). 2002. 64.00 (978-1-4025-4207-7(0)) Recorded Bks.

Story of Mankind. unabr. ed. Hendrik Willem Van Loon. Read by Sneha Mathan. 10 cass. (Running Time: 14 hrs. 30 mins.). 2001. 69.95 (978-0-7861-2110-6(6), 2872) Blckstn Audio.
Van Loon recounts history as living news, relating everything in the past to the present.

***Story of Mankind.** unabr. ed. Hendrik Willem Van Loon. Read by Sneha Mathan. (Running Time: 14 hrs. 5 mins.). (ENG.). 2011. 29.95 (978-1-4417-8349-3(0)); audio compact disk 118.00 (978-1-4417-8347-9(4)) Blckstn Audio.

Story of Mary Magdalene: He's Waiting for You. 2 cass. (Running Time: 2 hrs.). Dramatization. 2000. 12.99 HARK Ent.
The story of Mary takes you into the life of one of history's most radically changed women. From the wrenching emotions of her troubled past to her overwhelming joy in discovering Christ.

Story of Mickey Mouse. Disney Staff. 1 CD. (Running Time: 1 hr.). (ENG., (J). (ps-3). 2004. audio compact disk 100.00 (978-1-55709-352-3(0)) Pub: Applewood. Dist(s): IngramPubServ
Highlighting some of Disney's more popular characters.

Story of Minikin & Manikin see Pony Engine & Other Stories for Children

Story of Miss Moppet. 1 cass. (Running Time: 15 mins.). (Beatrix Potter's Tales Ser.). (ps up). 10.00 (978-1-4025-1647-4(9)) Recorded Bks.

Story of Mohammed the Muallim see Tales of the Desert

Story of Moses. 1 cass. (Beginner's Bible Ser.). (J). 5.58 (SME 67807) NewSound.

Story of My Disappearance: A Novel. unabr. ed. Paul Watkins. Narrated by Richard Poe. 6 cass. (Running Time: 8 hrs. 15 mins.). 1998. 53.00 (978-0-7887-2179-3(8), 95475E7) Recorded Bks.
Seeing a man brutally murdered in his local hangout on the docks of Newport sends Paul Wedekind into a torturous reverie of his violent past. Even more disturbingly, Paul is convinced that he recognizes the killer as Ingo Budde, a black marketering East German friend he left for dead in a Mujahideen prison camp.

Story of My Life. Helen Keller. Narrated by Flo Gibson. (ENG.). 2008. audio compact disk 19.95 (978-1-60646-040-5(4)) Audio Bk Con.

Story of My Life. Helen Keller. Read by Mary Woods. 7 CDs. (Running Time: 7 hrs.). 2000. audio compact disk 56.00 (978-0-7861-9846-7(X), 2629) Blckstn Audio.
A serious illness destroyed Helen Keller's sight & hearing before she reached the age of two. Beginning at seven, she was helped by Ann Sullivan, her beloved teacher & friend. Through sheer determination & resolve, she learned to speak & prepared herself for entry into prep school by age sixteen. Later she enrolled at Radcliffe & graduated with honors. Her motto: "There are no handicaps, only challenges".

Story of My Life. Helen Keller. Narrated by Cindy Hardin. (Running Time: 4 hrs.). 2006. 22.95 (978-1-59912-818-4(7)) Iofy Corp.

Story of My Life. Helen Keller. Read by Frances Cassidy. (ENG.). 2005. audio compact disk 16.99 (978-1-4001-5129-5(5)) Pub: Tantor Media. Dist(s): IngramPubServ

Story of My Life, unabr. ed. Helen Keller. Read by Flo Gibson. 3 cass. (Running Time: 4 hrs.). 1987. (978-1-55685-077-6(8)) Audio Bk Con.
The inspiring autobiography of Helen Keller as a young girl experiencing the joys of discovery of the world around her & literature.

Story of My Life. unabr. ed. Helen Keller. Read by Cindy Hardin. 5 cass. (Running Time: 7 hrs. 30 min.). 2000. 39.95 (978-0-7861-0599-1(2), 2629) Blckstn Audio.
A serious illness destroyed Helen Keller's sight & hearing before she reached the age of two. At seven, she was helped by Ann Sullivan, her beloved teacher & friend. Through sheer determination & resolve, she learned to speak & prepared herself for entry into prep school by age sixteen. Later she enrolled at Radcliffe & graduated with honors. Her motto: "There are no handicaps, only challenges.".

Story of My Life. unabr. ed. Helen Keller. Read by Mary Woods. 5 cass. (Running Time: 7 hrs.). 2000. 39.95 (978-0-7861-1830-4(X), 2629) Blckstn Audio.
A serious illness destroyed Helen Keller's sight & hearing before she reached the age of two. Beginning at seven, she was helped by Ann Sullivan, her beloved teacher & friend. Through sheer determination & resolve, she learned to speak & prepared herself for entry into prep school by age sixteen. Later she enrolled at Radcliffe & graduated with honors. Her motto: "There are no handicaps, only challenges".

Story of My Life. unabr. ed. Helen Keller. Read by Frances Cassidy. (J). 2006. 39.99 (978-1-59895-733-4(3)) Find a World.

Story of My Life. unabr. ed. Helen Keller. Read by Cindy Hardin. 4 cass. (Running Time: 4 hrs 30 min.). 1984. 26.00 (C-109) Jimcin Record.
Before she was 2 years old a serious illness destroyed her sight & hearing. At 7, alone & withdrawn, she was rescued by Anne Sullivan, her teacher & friend. By the time she was 16, Helen could speak well enough to attend preparatory school. Later she went to Radcliffe, from which she graduated with honors in 1904.

Story of My Life. unabr. ed. Helen Keller. Narrated by Alyssa Bresnahan. 3 cass. (Running Time: 4 hrs. 15 mins.). 1993. 26.00 (978-1-55690-870-5(9), 93312E7) Recorded Bks.
Her own account of her triumph over deafness & blindness, written when she was 21 & first published in 1902.

Story of My Life. unabr. collector's ed. Helen Keller. Read by Frances Cassidy. 4 cass. (Running Time: 4 hrs.). 1994. 24.00 (978-0-7366-2840-2(1), 3548) Books on Tape.
Inspirational classic & an example of what we can overcome & accomplish, given fortitude & purpose.

Story of My Life: An Afghan Girl on the Other Side of the Sky. abr. ed. Farah Ahmedi. Read by Masuda Sultan. Told to Tamim Ansary. 2005. 17.95 (978-0-7435-5168-7(0)) Pub: S&S Audio. Dist(s): S and S Inc

Story of My Life, with EBook. unabr. ed. Helen Keller. Narrated by Frances Cassidy. (Running Time: 3 hrs. 30 mins. 0 sec.). (ENG.). 2009. 17.99 (978-1-4001-5893-5(1)); audio compact disk 17.99 (978-1-4001-0893-0(4)) Pub: Tantor Media. Dist(s): IngramPubServ

Story of My Life, with eBook. unabr. ed. Helen Keller. Narrated by Frances Cassidy. (Running Time: 3 hrs. 30 mins. 0 sec.). (ENG.). 2009. audio compact disk 35.99 (978-1-4001-3893-7(0)) Pub: Tantor Media. Dist(s): IngramPubServ

***Story of Nehemiah.** unabr. ed. Zondervan. (Running Time: 0 hr. 15 mins. 1 sec.). (Best-Loved Stories of the Bible, NIrV Ser.). (ENG.). (J). 2010. 1.99 (978-0-310-86515-5(8)) Pub: Zondkidz. Dist(s): Zondervan

Story of O see Histoire d'O

Story of Old Ram see Best of Mark Twain

Story of Paul Bigsby: Father of the Modern Electric Solidbody Guitar. deluxe collector's ed. Andy Babiuk. (ENG., 2009. lthr. 150.00 (978-0-615-25407-4(1)) Pub: FG Publng. Dist(s): H Leonard

Story of Paul J. Meyer. Lois S. Strain & Gladys W. Hudson. 1 cass. 10.00 (SP100071) SMI Intl.
The story of the founder & Chairman of the Board of SMI International is more than just the usual success story, for the rewards earned by his achievements have provided for literally thousands of others the true "abundance of life." A truly fascinating, inspirational story.

Story of Peter Pan. abr. ed. J. M. Barrie. Perf. by Glynis Johns. Music by Dick Hyman. 1 cass. (Running Time: 53 min.). (J). (ps-3). 1992. 11.00 (978-1-55994-655-1(5), HarperChildAud) HarperCollins Pubs.
Close your eyes, & Wendy, Michael, John, their dog Nana, & of course Peter Pan himself will have you in Never-Never-Land in this delightful version of the coziest, most comforting story ever written.

Story of Peter Pan. abr. ed. Perf. by Glynis Johns. 1 cass. (J). 1984. 9.95 (978-0-89845-822-0(6), CPN 1395) HarperCollins Pubs.

Story of Philosophy. unabr. ed. Will Durant. Read by Frederick Davidson. 16 cass. (Running Time: 24 hrs.). 2003. 99.95 (978-0-7861-0287-7(X), 1252) Blckstn Audio.
An endlessly inspiring & instructive chronicle of the world's great thinkers, from Socrates to Santayana. It gives not only the ideas and philosophical systems of the world-famous "monarchs of the mind," such as Plato, Aristotle, Francis Bacon, Spinoza, Kant, Voltaire, Locke and others of similar stature, but their flesh and blood biographies.

Story of Philosophy. unabr. ed. Will Durant. Narrated by Robert Sevra. 8 cass. (Running Time: 10 hrs. 45 mins.). 1994. 70.00 (978-0-7887-0042-2(1), 94241E7) Recorded Bks.
Durant chronicles the ideas of five thinkers, the economic & intellectual environments which influenced them & the personal traits & adventures out of which each philosophy grew. Begins with the Greeks & moves through Voltaire & the French Enlightenment.

Story of Philosophy. unabr. ed. Will Durant. Narrated by Robert Sevra. 8 cass. (Running Time: 11 hrs. 30 mins.). 1999. 70.00 (978-0-7887-0304-1(8), 94497E7) Recorded Bks.
Begins with Voltaire & continues through contemporary European & American philosophers like William James & John Dewey.

Story of Philosophy: From Kant to William James & the American Pragmatists. unabr. ed. Will Durant. Read by Grover Gardner. 9 CDs. (Running Time: 11 hrs.). (ENG.). 2004. audio compact disk 37.95 (978-1-57270-420-6(9)) Pub: AudioGO. Dist(s): Perseus Dist

Story of Philosophy: From Plato to the American Pragmatists. unabr. ed. Will Durant & Grover Gardner. 3 CDs. (Running Time: 22 hrs.). (ENG.). 2004. audio compact disk 29.95 (978-1-57270-421-3(7)) Pub: AudioGO. Dist(s): Perseus Dist
Will Durant's classic Story of Philosophy has stood the test of time, setting millions of wisdom seekers on the path to greater understanding for nearly 80 years. His sparkling, vibrant prose, infused with warmth and humor, brings to life the lives and ideas of the great Western philosophers, from Plato to Bertrand Russell. Durant provides compelling historical and intellectual context as well as clear, in-depth explanations for each concept.

Story of Philosophy: From Plato to Voltaire & the French Enlightenment. unabr. ed. Will Durant. Narrated by Grover Gardner. 9 CDs. (Running Time: 11 hrs.). (ENG.). 2004. audio compact disk 34.95 (978-1-57270-419-0(5)) Pub: AudioGO. Dist(s): Perseus Dist
The first volume of this engaging survey covers Plato, Aristotle, Francis Bacon, Spinoza, Voltaire, and Rousseau. As well as offering historical context and a cogent explanation for each school of thought, Durant provides biographical information, a gentle reminder that philosophers are people as well as thinkers.

***Story of Philosophy: The Lives & Opinions of the Greater Philosophers.** unabr. ed. Will Durant. Read by Grover Gardner. (Running Time: 23 hrs. NaN mins.). (ENG.). 2010. 44.95 (978-1-4417-7350-0(9)); audio compact disk 39.95 (978-1-4417-7349-4(5)) Blckstn Audio.

***Story of Philosophy: The Lives & Opinions of the Greater Philosophers.** unabr. ed. Will Durant. Read by Grover Gardner. (Running Time: 23 hrs. NaN mins.). 2010. 109.95 (978-1-4417-7347-0(9)); audio compact disk 123.00 (978-1-4417-7348-7(7)) Blckstn Audio.

Story of Pluto & Proserpina see Tanglewood Tales

Story of Prahlad. Swami Jyotirmayananda. 1 cass. (Running Time: 45 min.). 1990. 10.00 Yoga Res Foun.

Story of Punxsutawney Phil, "The Fearless Forecaster" Julia F. Spencer. Illus. by Marsha L. Dubnansky. (Adventures of Punxsutawney Phil Ser.). (J). (ps-5). 1987. 10.95 (978-0-9617819-3-4(9)) Lit Pubns.

Story of Rama. 1 cass. (Running Time: 1 hr.). 12.99 (608) Yoga Res Foun.

Story of Silent Night. Perf. by Vienna Boys Choir, The. 1 cass. (Running Time: 35 min.). 2001. cass. & video 12.99 (2828) Vision Vid PA.

Story of Sir Galahad see Tales of King Arthur & His Knights

Story of Sir Galahad see King Arthur

Story of Sir Lancelot see King Arthur

Story of Sir Launcelot see Tales of King Arthur & His Knights

Story of Sleeping Beauty. Read by Claire Bloom. Music by Peter Illich Tchaikovsky. 1 cass. (J). 9.98 (332) MFLP CA.
Introduces children to the classics through lively storytelling interwoven with beautiful orchestral music.

Story of Speech see Sampler of American Humor

Story of Studs Lonigan. James T. Farrell. 1 cass. (Running Time: 30 min.). 1954. 11.95 (23056) J Norton Pubs.
The author reflects on the evolution & meaning of his classic trilogy.

Story of Stuff: How Our Obsession with Stuff Is Trashing the Planet, Our Communities, & Our Health - & a Vision for Change. unabr. ed. Annie Leonard. Read by Annie Leonard. 2 MP3-CDs. (Running Time: 12 hrs.). 2010. 26.00 (978-0-7435-9915-3(2)) Pub: S&S Audio. Dist(s): S and S Inc

Story of Swan Lake. Read by Claire Bloom. Music by Peter Illich Tchaikovsky. 1 cass. (J). 9.98 (334) MFLP CA.
Introduces children to the classics through lively storytelling interwoven with beautiful orchestral music.

Story of the Amulet. Edith Nesbit. Read by Anna Bentinck. 2. (Running Time: 9468 sec.). (Junior Classics Ser.). (J). (gr. 3-8). 2007. audio compact disk 17.98 (978-962-634-461-3(X), Naxos AudioBooks) Naxos.

Story of the Amulet, Set. unabr. ed. E. Nesbit. Read by Flo Gibson. 5 cass. (Running Time: 7 hrs. 30 min.). (J). (gr. 3-5). 1986. 20.95 (978-1-55685-067-7(0)) Audio Bk Con.
In this sequel to "Five Children & It", the Psammead (Sand Fairy) returns with half an amulet. In the search for the other half it's magic takes them to ancient Egypt, Babylon, Atlantis & a meeting with Julius Caesar.

Story of the Bad Little Boy see Man That Corrupted Hadleyburg & Other Stories

Story of the Bad Little Boy see Favorite Stories by Mark Twain

Story of the Bagman's Uncle see Classic Ghost Stories, Vol. 2, A Collection

Story of the Bagman's Uncle. Charles Dickens. Read by Walter Zimmerman. 1 cass. (Running Time: 54 min.). 1989. 7.95 (S-44) Jimcin Record.
Hilarious story of a ghostly ride.

Story of the Bible. Matthew Arnold. 2001. audio compact disk 11.95 (978-1-57058-362-9(5)) Pub: St Joseph Communs. Dist(s): STL Dist NA

Story of the Bible. Instructed by Luke Timothy Johnson. 12 CDs. (Running Time: 12 hrs.). 2006. 69.95 (978-1-59803-249-9(6)); 129.95 (978-1-59803-248-2(8)) Teaching Co.

Story of the Blues. Friedman-Fairfax and Sony Music Staff. 1 cass. (CD Ser.). 1994. pap. bk. 15.98 (978-1-56799-075-1(4), Friedman-Fairfax) M Friedman Pub Grp Inc.

Story of the Creation. unabr. ed. Robert A. Monroe. Read by Robert A. Monroe. (Running Time: 45 min.). (Explorer Ser.). 1983. 12.95 (978-1-56113-017-7(6), 18) Monroe Institute.
The created as the Creator & unity of all things.

Story of the Days to Come see Tales of Space & Time

Story of the Gateway Arch. Narrated by Joseph Campanella. 1 cass. (C). 1993. 8.95 (978-0-931056-08-6(X)) Jefferson Natl.

Story of the Good Little Boy. (J). 1980. (N-33) Jimcin Record.

Story of the Grail. (Running Time: 57:52). 2004. audio compact disk (978-0-9759559-0-1(X)) E Warren AZ.
The Story of the Grail has captivated people for hundreds of years, and the questions it poses are as relevant today as they were when it was written. With its roots in the Celtic oral tradition of heroes and magical cauldrons, the story emerged in 12th century Europe at a time of great cultural, technological and spiritual change - a time not unlike our own. In this new recorded version, storyteller Liz Warren brings this powerful and timeless story into the present.

Story of the Little Tree. 1 cass. (Running Time: 1 hr.). (J). 2000. 6.99 HARK Ent.
Will fill your home with fun-filled praise of the Lord. Provides wholesome messages that are sure to last a lifetime.

Story of the Messiah. Short Stories. 6 CD's. (Running Time: 7 hrs. 30 mins.). Dramatization. 2005. audio compact disk 59.95 (978-0-9774447-1-7(6)) Sine Ministries.

Story of the Nutcracker. Read by Claire Bloom. Perf. by Orchestra de la Suisse Romada. (Running Time: 60 min.). (J). 9.98 (333) MFLP CA.
Children are treated to the lovely interweaving of stirring narration & magical Nutcracker music, making this recording a spellbinding gift for all.

***Story of the Nutcracker Audio.** abr. ed. E. T. A. Hoffman. (ENG.). 2006. (978-0-06-114320-5(0), Harper Audio); (978-0-06-114321-2(9), Harper Audio) HarperCollins Pubs.

Story of the Old Ram see Sampler of American Humor

Story of the Old Testament: From Adam to Moses Volume I. (ENG.). 2005. audio compact disk 29.95 (978-1-885224-66-8(4), Bristol Bks) Bristol Hse.

Story of the Oregon Trail. unabr. ed. Mike Trinklein & Steve Boettcher. 1 cass. (Running Time: 1 hr. 30 min.). 1993. 9.95 (978-1-883691-03-5(6)) Trinklein Pub.
History of the Oregon trail.

Story of the Other Wiseman. Based on a story by Henry Van Dyke. (ENG.). 2007. 5.00 (978-1-60339-101-6(0)) Listenr Digest.

Story of the Other Wiseman. Based on a story by Henry Van Dyke. (ENG.). (YA). 2007. audio compact disk 5.00 (978-1-60339-102-3(9)) Listenr Digest.

Story of the Physician & the Saratoga Trunk see Suicide Club & Other Stories

Story of the Princess of the Roses see Tales of the Desert

Story of the Red Cross. Clara Barton. Read by S. Patricia Bailey. 3 cass. (Running Time: 4 hrs.). 2000. 23.95 (978-0-7861-1770-3(2), 2573) Blckstn Audio.
Clara Barton was one of the diminutive New England women of the nineteenth century who was determined to make the world a better place. In 1881, she founded the American Red Cross; she served as its president from 1882 to 1904. The Red Cross of today stands as a living memorial to the lifelong efforts of this valiant woman.

Story of the Red Cross. Clara Barton. Narrated by S. Patricia Bailey. (Running Time: 4 hrs.). 1999. 22.95 (978-1-59912-398-1(3)) Iofy Corp.

Story of the Red Cross. unabr. ed. Clara Barton. Read by S. Patricia Bailey. (Running Time: 4 hrs. 30 mins.). 2003. 29.95 (978-0-7861-8423-1(X), 2573); audio compact disk 36.00 (978-0-7861-8129-2(X), 2573) Blckstn Audio.

ory of the Renaissance. unabr. ed. W. H. Hudson. Read by Robert Whitfield. 6 cass. (Running Time: 8 hrs. 30 mins.). 1997. 44.95 978-0-7861-1235-7(2), 1982) Blckstn Audio.
his history offers a perceptive analysis of the splendid Renaissance, written a man who contributed to this remarkable movement.

of the Renaissance. unabr. ed. Read by Robert Whitfield. (Running e: 28800 sec.). 2007. audio compact disk 29.95 (978-0-7861-5950-5(2)); o compact disk 63.00 (978-0-7861-5924-6(3)) Blckstn Audio.

f the Shadow. Perf. by Bret Morrison & Walter Gibson. 2010. audio act disk 18.95 (978-1-57019-931-8(0)) Radio Spirits.

Story of the Statue of Liberty. unabr. ed. Betsy Maestro & Giulio Maestro. 1 cass. (Running Time: 7 min.). (J). (gr. 2-5). 1993. pap. bk. 17.90 (978-0-8045-6666-7(6), 6666) Spoken Arts.
Frederic Bartholdi created the huge statue that France gave to the United States as a symbol of liberty.

Story of the Three Bears see Favorite Children's Stories: A Collection

Story of the Three Kings. abr. ed. John Hildesheim. Read by George Rose. Retold by Margaret Freeman. 1 cass. 1984. 8.98 (978-0-89845-143-6(4), CP 1724) HarperCollins Pubs.

Story of the Treasure Seekers, unabr. ed. E. Nesbit. Read by Flo Gibson. 4 cass. (Running Time: 5 hrs. 30 min.). (Classic Books on Cassettes Ser.). (J). (gr. 2-5). 1988. 19.95 (978-1-55685-113-1(8)) Audio Bk Con.
The five Bastable children seek their fortunes in sometimes amazing & always amusing ways.

Story of the Treasure Seekers: Complete & Unabridged. unabr. ed. E. Nesbit. 4 cass. (Running Time: 5 hrs. 30 mins.). 1997. 32.95 (978-0-7861-0450-5(3), 1402) Blckstn Audio.
Story of the extraordinary adventures of the incorrigible Bastible children & their attempts to restore the family fortunes. Their escapades begin with the simple idea of digging in the back garden & lead to many more novel approaches, such as writing poetry & selling it to a Fleet Street editor.

Story of the Treasure Seekers: Complete & Unabridged. unabr. ed. E. Nesbit. Narrated by Simon Prebble. 4 pieces. (Running Time: 5 hrs. 15 mins.). (gr. 3 up). 37.00 (978-1-4025-0708-3(9), 96930) Recorded Bks.
All six Bastable children - Dora, Oswald, Dicky, Alice, Noel and Horace Octavius - are ambitious adventurers, digging detectives and intrepid treasure seekers by nature. Unfortunately, the Bastable family is currently facing an uncertain financial future. When father takes ill, and his business partners abandon him, the six children team up in an effort to restore their family's wealth. Although they devise some ingenious escapades, their efforts usually end up unprofitable but fun - and sometimes their digging gets downright dangerous. But one day their adventure leads them to completely unexpected results. Available to libraries only.

Story of the Typewriter. 1 cass. 10.00 Esstee Audios.
How a new machine changed business.

Story of the World: History for the Classical Child. Susan Wise Bauer & Jim Weiss. Read by Barbara Allen Johnson. 8 CDs. (Running Time: 10 hrs.). 2004. audio compact disk 49.95 (978-0-9742391-1-8(9)) Pub: Open Texture. Dist(s): Natl Bk Netwk

Story of the World: History for the Classical Child. unabr. ed. Susan Wise Bauer & Barbara Allen Johnson. 10 CDs. (Running Time: 12 hrs.). 2005. audio compact disk 55.95 (978-0-9742391-2-5(7)) Pub: Open Texture. Dist(s): Natl Bk Netwk

Story of the Young Man with the Cream Tarts see Suicide Club & Other Stories

Story of Theseus see Tanglewood Tales

Story of Tracy Beaker, unabr. ed. Jacqueline Wilson. Read by Sandi Toksvig. 2 cass. (Running Time: 2 hrs.). (J). (gr. 1-8). 1999. 18.95 (CTC 788, Chivers Child Audio) AudioGO.

Story of Tracy Beaker. unabr. ed. Jacqueline Wilson. Read by Sandi Toksvig. 3 CDs. (Running Time: 4 hrs. 30 mins.). (J). 2002. audio compact disk 29.95 (978-0-7540-6562-3(6), CHCD 062) AudioGO.
Tracy is ten years old. She lives in a Children's Home but would like a real home one day, with a real family. Meet Tracy, follow her story, and share her hopes for the future in this beautifully observed, touching, and often very funny tale, all told in Tracy's own words.

Story of West Asheville: People, Places, Events. 2003. audio compact disk 9.95 (978-1-56664-251-4(5), Land Sky Bks) WorldComm.

Story of You: And How to Create a New One. unabr. ed. Steve Chandler. (Running Time: 18960 sec.). (ENG.). 2007. audio compact disk 29.95 (978-1-60283-033-2(9)) Pub: AudioGO. Dist(s): Perseus Dist

Story of Your Life: Your Testimony & Creating Miracles in Your Life. Short Stories. Steven Edwards. 1 CD. (Running Time: 70 Minutes). 2006. audio compact disk 17.95 (978-0-9778654-2-0(8)) Creative Innov.
A wonderful and inspirational message that looks back on your life and plans for your future as you begin to write your own life's story. This beautiful and powerful message will help you look at where you were in the past, how to create a wonderful life for yourself and create miracles everyday of your life!.

Story Play: Costumes, Cooking, Music & More for You. Joyce Harlow. 1 cass. (J). (ps-1). 1992. 10.00 (X370, TIP) Libs Unl.

***Story Reader with Toy Story Storybook.** Ed. by Publications International Staff. (J). 2009. 32.98 (978-1-4127-1909-4(7)) Pubns Intl Ltd.

***Story Reader 3-Book ni Hao, Kai-Lan Library: Dragon Boat Race; the Music Show; Let's Fly A Kite.** Ed. by Publications International Staff. (J). 2009. 32.98 (978-1-4127-1916-2(X)) Pubns Intl Ltd.

Story Rhyme Journey - Fifteen Stories. Story Time Staff. 2 cass. (Running Time: 2 hrs. 30 min.). (J). (gr. 4-8). 1992. 60.00 Set. (37SOR300CT) Sell Out Recordings.
Stories that rhyme on various subjects. These stories also educate, inform, inspire & entertain.

Story Rhyme Kids Program. unabr. ed. Alfreda C. Doyle. Read by Alfreda C. Doyle. 1 cass. (Running Time: 45 min.). (YA). (gr. 7-12). 1994. 12.95 (978-1-56820-109-2(5)) Story Time.
Stories that educate, entertain, & rhyme.

Story Rhyme Radio Programs. Story Time Staff. 1 cass. (J). (gr. 4-10). 1992. 79.95 (978-1-56820-089-7(7)) Story Time.

Story Rhymes That Educate, Entertain & Inform. unabr. ed. Alfreda C. Doyle. Read by Alfreda C. Doyle. 2 cass. (Running Time: 1 hr. 30 min.). (YA). (gr. 3-12). 1993. 18.00 set. (978-1-56820-091-0(9)) Story Time.
Nine stories, tales & fables of 100 percent silk creativity imported from a galaxy of muses.

Story Songs, Collections 4-6. PUEI. 2006. audio compact disk 24.95 (978-1-934147-02-3(8), CareerTrack) P Univ E Inc.

Story Songs Set, 1-6. PUEI. 2006. audio compact disk 44.95 (978-1-934147-05-4(2), CareerTrack) P Univ E Inc.

Story Songs, 1-3. PUEI. 2006. audio compact disk 24.95 (978-1-934147-01-6(X), CareerTrack) P Univ E Inc.

Story Sticks/How to Make a Lion Mask. Created by Steck-Vaughn Staff. (Running Time: 428 sec.). (Primary Take-Me-Home Books Level A Ser.). 1998. 9.80 (978-0-8172-8663-7(2)) SteckVau.

Story-Teller see Selected European Short Stories

Story-Teller see Gathering of Great Poetry for Children

Story Teller. unabr. ed. Margaret Coel. Read by Stephanie Brush. 8 cass. (Running Time: 8 hrs. 12 min.). (Wind River Ser.). 1999. 49.95 (978-1-55686-891-7(X)) Books in Motion.
A museum is ordered by the courts to return a rare book to its rightful owners, the Arapaho people. Museum employees claim to have never seen the book, which is worth millions, & Vicki Holden suspects foul play. When Vicki discovers that an Arapaho student died while studying the text, she & Father O'Malley begin a search for the sacred treasure & the killer.

Story Teller. unabr. ed. Perf. by Dylan Pritchett. 1 cass. (Running Time: 1 hr.). Dramatization. (J). (gr. 4 up). 1991. 19.95 incl. looseleaf study guide for teachers. (978-1-56817-005-3(X)) Pepper Bird.
Twenty short dramatized narratives. Unique stories of unusual achievers from African-American history.

Story the Soldiers Wouldn't Tell: Sex in the Civil War. unabr. collector's ed. Thomas Lowry. Read by Michael Kramer. 6 cass. (Running Time: 9 hrs.). 1995. 48.00 (978-0-7366-3034-4(1), 3716) Books on Tape.
How soldiers sought action behind the front lines. Informative & entertaining.

Story Theater: How to Market & Sell Yourself & Your Speeches. unabr. ed. Doug Stevenson. 2 cass. (Running Time: 3 hrs.). 2001. 29.95 (978-0-9713440-1-3(9)) Cornelia Pr.
Live tele-seminar covering how to take a story, make great, create a speech or keynote around it and market it. Lots of step by step information for the new or seasoned speaker about the business.

Story Theater - Advanced Drama & Comedy Performance Skills. unabr. ed. Doug Stevenson. 2 cass. (Running Time: 3 hrs.). 2001. 29.95 (978-0-9713440-2-0(7)) Cornelia Pr.
Live tele-seminar focusing on performance of stories. Covers how to make stories more visual, dramatic and funny. Contains specific exercises to apply to your stories and numerous performance tips.

Story Theater - Make the Move from Training to Keynotes. unabr. ed. Doug Stevenson. 2 cass. (Running Time: 3 hrs.). 2001. 29.95 (978-0-9713440-0-6(0)) Cornelia Pr.
Describes the differences of trainers and keynoters and helps listener decide if keynoting is for them. Covers types of keynotes, what clients expect, working with bureaus, marketing and keynote templates.

Story Theater Audio CD Six Pack: The Science of the Art of Storytelling & Humor in Business. 2003. audio compact disk 77.00 (978-0-9713440-8-2(6)) Cornelia Pr.

Story Theater Audio Six Pack: The Science of the Art of Storytelling & Humor in Business. unabr. ed. Doug Stevenson. 6 cass. (Running Time: 6 hrs.). 2001. 67.00 (978-0-9713440-6-8(X)) Cornelia Pr.
Comprehensive "how-to" guide to using stories in business presentations and Keynotes. Covers how and why stories work, how to choose stories, branding, crafting, rehearsal, humor, drama, and performance skills.

Story Theater Live: The Science of the Art of Storytelling & Humor in Business. unabr. ed. Doug Stevenson. 2 cass. (Running Time: 2 hrs.). 1999. 20.00 (978-0-9713440-3-7(5)) Cornelia Pr.
Live presentation about storytelling to make a point in business presentations and keynotes. Covers 8 steps of story structure, acting tips to make your content come alive, creating humor and drama.

Story Therapy 1: The Wide-Open Meadow. 2005. audio compact disk 19.99 (978-0-9764358-0-8(2)) Oh Mind.

Story Therapy 2: The Beauty Behind the Mask. 2005. audio compact disk 19.99 (978-0-9764358-1-5(0)) Oh Mind.

Story Therapy 3: The Fall to Freedom. 2005. audio compact disk 19.99 (978-0-9764358-2-2(9)) Oh Mind.

Story Time. Edward Bloor. Narrated by Julie Dretzin. 9 CDs. (Running Time: 10 hrs. 15 mins.). (YA). 2004. audio compact disk 89.75 (978-1-4193-1813-9(6)) Recorded Bks.

Story Time. unabr. ed. 7 cassettes. (Running Time: 10:15 hrs). (J). 2004. 61.75 (978-1-4025-9929-3(3)) Recorded Bks.

Story Time Stories That Rhyme. Alfreda C. Doyle. Read by Alfreda C. Doyle. 1 cass. (Running Time: 27 min.). (YA). (gr. 4-12). 1989. 14.95 (37 SOR 900CT) Sell Out Recordings.
Features children's stories that rhyme. Titles include: Fish Convention, Clouds, Rye the Rhyming Detective in the Missing Hammer Oyster Shell, Tennis Shoes, Terry the Ferry, Amp the Lamp in the Myna Bird Story.

Story Time Stories That Rhyme. unabr. ed. Frieda Carrol. 1 cass. (Running Time: 27 min.). (J). (gr. 5-7). 1989. 16.95 (37 SOR 900) Prosperity & Profits.
Children's stories that rhyme. Titles include: Fish Convention, Clouds, Rye the Rhyming Detective in the Missing Hammer Oyster Shell, Tennis Shoes, Terry the Ferry, Amp the Lamp in the Myna Bird Story.

Story to Tell. Perf. by Lamelle. 1 CD. (Running Time: 60 mins.). 2000. audio compact disk (978-0-7601-2899-2(5)) Brentwood Music.
Songs include: "A Story to Tell," "I Love to Tell the Story," "All Creatures Medley," "Creation Medley," He Gives Joy" & more.

Story Tree: Tales to Read Aloud. Hugh Lupton. Narrated by Hugh Lupton. 1 CD. (Running Time: 1 min. 32 sec.). (ENG., (J). (ps-2). 2001. audio compact disk 15.99 (978-1-84148-417-4(2)) BarefootBksMA.
Seven stories from around the world, including "The Little Red Hen," "The Sweetest Song" and "The Blue Coat." Includes leaflet.

***Story We Find Ourselves In: Further Adventures of a New Kind of Christian.** unabr. ed. Brian McLaren. Narrated by Paul Michael. (ENG.). 2006. 14.98 (978-1-59644-321-1(9), Hovel Audio) christianaud.

Story We Find Ourselves In Bk. 2: Further Adventures of a New Kind of Christian. unabr. ed. Brian D. McLaren. 8 CDs. (Running Time: 10 hrs. 0 mins. 0 sec.). (ENG.). 2006. audio compact disk 26.98 (978-1-59644-320-4(0), Hovel Audio) christianaud.
After many years as a successful pastor, Brian McLaren has found, as more and more Christians are finding, that none of the current strains of Christianity fully describes his own faith. In The Story We Find Ourselves In a?? the much anticipated sequel to his award-winning book A New Kind of Christiana?? McLaren captures a new spirit of a relevant Christianity, where traditional divisions and doctrinal differences give way to a focus on God and the story of God's love for this world. If you are searching for a deeper life with Goda?? one that moves beyond the rhetoric of denominational and theological categoriesa?? this delightful and inspiring fictional tale will provide a picture of what it could mean to recapture a joyful spiritual life.

Story We Find Ourselves In Bk. 2: Further Adventures of a New Kind of Christian. unabr. ed. Brian D. McLaren. Narrated by Paul Michael. 1 MP3CD. (Running Time: 10 hrs. 0 mins. 0 sec.). (ENG.). 2006. lp 19.98 (978-1-59644-319-8(7), Hovel Audio) christianaud.

Story Without an End see $30,000 Bequest & Other Stories

Storybook Party. unabr. ed. Dennis Scott. 1 cass. (Running Time: 30 min.). (J). (ps-5). 1992. 7.95 (978-1-880578-01-8(8)) Kidoodle Music.
Traditional children's fairy tales sung & told & told in an upbeat contemporary style: Fun & lively.

Storybridges for Young Children (French) Veronica Foster. 3 cass. (Running Time: 18 min. per cass.). (ENG & FRE.). (J). (gr. 1-9). 1990. 24.95 Incl. Goldilocks & The Three Bears & Little Red Riding Hood, Cass. 1; The Turtle's Music & The Nightingale, Cass. 2 & The Shoemakers & the Elves & Peter & the Wolf, Cass. 3. (978-0-88432-247-4(5), SFR125) J Norton Pubs.
Children become participants in the actual telling of the story, as they join the storyteller's young helpers, Sadie & Sydney in repeating the French words & phrases spoken in the context of the story.

Storybridges to French for Children. 3 cass. (Running Time: 53 mins.). (J). 29.95 (SFR125) J Norton Pubs.
Using the art of storytelling, this charming bilingual program is as entertaining as it is instructive. Young children become participants as they join the storyteller's young helpers, Sadie & Sydney, in repeating the French words & phrases spoken in the context of familiar stories.

Storybridges to German for Children. 3 cass. (Running Time: 3 hrs.). (J). 2001. 29.95 (SBE125) J Norton Pubs.
Using the art of storytelling, this charming program is as entertaining as it is instructive. Young children become participants as they join the young helpers, Sadie & Sydney, in repeating the German words & phrases spoken in the context of familiar stories such as "Little Red Riding Hood".

Storyline, Plot, & Characterization. Brenda Wilbee. 1 cass. (Running Time: 45 min.). (Writing for Publication: Fiction that Sells Ser.: No. 2). 1987. 7.95 (978-0-943777-02-3(X)) byBrenda.
The main elements of fiction.

Storysinger. Chris Holder. (J). 1999. audio compact disk 14.95 (978-0-939065-84-4(3)) Gentle Wind.

Storysinger: Tunes & Tales Both Tall & True. Chris Holder. Read by Chris Holder. 1 cass. (Running Time: 50 min.). (J). (gr. k-6). 1982. 9.95 (978-0-939065-14-1(2), GW 1014) Gentle Wind.
Meet Johnny Appleseed, Paul Bunyon, Nellie Bly & other incredible characters from our country's history & folklore.

Storyteller. Read by Wayne Monbleau. 3 cass. (Running Time: 4 hrs.). 1993. 15.00 Set. (978-0-944648-22-3(3), LGT-1188) Loving Grace Pubns.
Religious.

Storyteller. Music by Michael John Poirier. 1998. 11.00 (978-1-58459-110-8(2), 002663); audio compact disk 16.00 (978-1-58459-111-5(0), 002662) Wrld Lib Pubns.

Storyteller. Andy Wilkinson. 1 CD. 1998. audio compact disk 20.00 CD. (978-1-888609-06-6(0)) Grey Hrse Pr.

Storyteller Complete Library: CD Version. Contrib. by Lakeshore Learning Materials Staff. (J). 2007. bk. 99.50 (978-1-59746-019-4(2)) Lkeshore Learn Mats.

***Storyteller of Marrakesh.** Joydeep Roy-Bhattacharya. 2011. audio compact disk 39.99 (978-1-61120-017-1(2)) Dreamscap OH.

***Storyteller's Daughter.** abr. ed. Saira Shah. Read by Saira Shah. (ENG.). 2005. (978-0-06-089042-1(8), Harper Audio); (978-0-06-078378-5(8), Harper Audio) HarperCollins Pubs.

Storyteller's Daughter. unabr. abr. ed. Saira Shah. Read by Saira Shah. 4 CDs. (Running Time: 6 hrs.). 2003. audio compact disk 27.50 (978-0-06-050515-8(X)) HarperCollins Pubs.

Storytelling. 1 cass. (Running Time: 30 min.). (J). 9.95 (F0300B090, HarperThor) HarpC GBR.

Storytelling. Juergen Kremer. 1 cass. (J). 9.00 (A0361-88) Sound Photosyn.
ICSS '88 with Jean Millay.

Storytelling. B. Lane. 1 cass. 1993. 32.99 Chalice Pr.

Storytelling. Lewis Mehl. 1 cass. (J). 9.00 (A0377-88) Sound Photosyn.
American Indian tales are told around the fire. Felicitas Goodman is featured on this tape from ICSS '88.

Storytelling: Imagination & Faith. William Bansch. Read by William Bansch. Read by Jack Van Bemmel et al. 3 cass. (Running Time: 3 hrs.). Dramatization. (YA). (gr. 9 up). 1987. 24.95 (978-0-89622-342-4(6)) Twenty-Third.
Emphasizes the use of story in order to understand the mystery of life.

Storytelling: Program from the Award Winning Public Radio Series. Interview. Hosted by Fred Goodwin. Comment by John Hockenberry. 1 CD. (Running Time: 1 hr). 2000. audio compact disk 21.95 (978-1-932479-98-0(8), LCM 131) Lichtenstein Creat.
The magic words "once upon a time" transport us to other worlds and other times. Storytelling is the primary technology of a preliterate age and has traveled through time to make its mark on history. Our brain constructs images and puts them into a narrative flow; our body projects those images onto an audience in front of the hearth, around a fire, sitting in the kitchen or on a stage. Guests include Diane Wolkstein, a master storyteller from New York City; Dr. Joseph Sobol, director of the Storytelling Graduate Program at East Tennessee State University and author of "The Storytellers' Journey: An American Revival;" Donald Davis, one of the nation's foremost storytellers; and Linda Blackman, founder and director of The Mothers' Living Stories Project. With commentary by John Hockenberry.

Storytelling, Education & Rhyme: Stories for the Classroom. Alfreda C. Doyle. Read by Alfreda C. Doyle. 1 cass. (Running Time: 45 min.). 1993. 15.95 (978-1-56820-112-2(5)) Story Time.
Stories that educate, inform & rhyme.

Storytelling Enchantment. 1 cass. 1986. 32.95 (978-0-00-656238-2(8)) Chalice Pr.

***Storytelling for Kids.** Mary Jo Huff. Music by James Coffey. (ENG.). (J). 2009. 15.00 (978-0-9722213-8-2(7)) Storytellin Time.

Storytelling in the Courtroom. Paul M. Lisnek. Read by Paul M. Lisnek. Ed. by Robert L. Sandidge. 1 cass. (Running Time: 1 hr.). 1993. 16.95 (978-1-57654-207-1(6), CPA109) Creat Core.
Helps to identify common facts & issues in a case based on a storytelling model.

Storytelling Treasury. Ed. by Carol Birch. 5 cass. (Running Time: 5 hrs.). (J). 1993. 39.98 set. (978-1-879991-11-8(X)) Natl Storytlng Network.
Tales told at the 20th Anniversary National Storytelling Festival.

Storytelling Treasury. Short Stories. Perf. by Kathryn Windham et al. Prod. by National Storytelling Press Staff. 4 CDs. (Running Time: 4hrs. 41 mins.). 1993. audio compact disk 39.95 (978-1-879991-25-5(X)) Natl Storytlng Network.
In October 1992 thousands came to tiny Jonesborough, Tennessee, to hear more than 80 of America's best-loved storytellers share their tales at the 20th National Storytelling Festival. This five-volume collection, A Storytelling Treasury, captures that celebration with nearly five hours of contemporary storytelling that reverberates with thousands of years of memories and dreams and history. You'll hear stories from Africa, the Orient, and Europe. You'll also discover a wealth of tales from cultures closer to home - stories whose origins are Native American, Appalachian, African-American, Western, and Southern. Listen now, as we share with you the richness and wonder of this world's storytelling traditions.

Storytime Classics. Perf. by James 'D Train' Williams & LaJuan Carter. 1 cass. (Running Time: 90 mins.). (J). 2000. 7.98; audio compact disk 9.98 Peter Pan.
Peter Pan dipped into his magical library to present songs from classic stories like "Snow White," "Alice in Wonderland," "The Boy Who Never Grew up" & others.

Storytime Favorites. 1 cass. (Running Time: 90 mins.). (J). 2000. 3.98; audio compact disk 6.98 MFLP CA.
Features classic children's stories & rhymes in song.

Storytime Favorites. abr. ed. Ed. by Jane Webb. 2 cass. (Running Time: 1 hr. 44 min.). Incl. Emperor's New Clothes. Hans Christian Andersen. (J). (817); Little Red Riding Hood. (J). (817); Princess & the Pea. Based on a story by Hans Christian Andersen. (J). (817); Puss in Boots. (J). (817); Three Little Pigs. (J). (817); (J). 12.95 (978-0-89926-129-4(9), 817) Audio Bk.

Storytime Songs. 1 cass. (Running Time: 62m). (J). 2002. audio compact disk 14.95 (978-1-58467-015-5(0), GW1064) Gentle Wind.

***Storytime Songs for Storytellers Everywhere: CD with Performance Guide, Vol. 101.** Perf. by (Missus Z). Text by (Missus Z). Text by R. A. Zuckerman. Music by R. A. Zuckerman. (ENG., 2010. 12.95 (978-1-891083-03-7(1)) ConcertHall.

Storytime with Barney: 3 Billy Goats Gruff. 1 cass. ea. (Running Time: 54 min.). (Barney Ser.). (J). (ps-k). 1997. 7.95 ea. Lyrick Studios.
Spoken-word stories narrated Barney-style.

Storytime with Bob & Larry, Volume 1. Contrib. by VeggieTales. (VeggieTales (Word Audio) Ser.). (J). (ps-3). 2007. audio compact disk 10.99 (978-5-557-57927-8(3)) Big Idea.

Storytime with Bob & Larry, Volume 2. Contrib. by VeggieTales. (VeggieTales (Word Audio) Ser.). (J). (ps-3). 2007. audio compact disk 10.99 (978-5-557-57926-1(5)) Big Idea.

***Storyville Presents Duke Ellington: The Original Piano Transcriptions.** Composed by Duke Ellington. (ENG.). 2011. pap. bk. 19.99 (978-1-4234-9810-0(0), 1423498100) Pub: Music Sales. Dist(s): H Leonard

***Storyville Presents Earl Hines: The Original Piano Transcriptions.** Earl Hines. (ENG.). 2011. pap. bk. 19.99 (978-1-4234-9809-4(7), 1423498097) Pub: Music Sales. Dist(s): H Leonard

***Storyville Presents Teddy Wilson: The Original Piano Transcriptions.** Teddy Wilson. (ENG.). 2011. pap. bk. 19.99 (978-1-4234-9811-7(9), 1423498119) Pub: Music Sales. Dist(s): H Leonard

Stout Gentleman see Great American Short Stories, Vol. III, A Collection

Stout Gentleman. unabr. ed. Washington Irving. Perf. by David Ely. 1 cass. (Running Time: 80 min.). Dramatization. 1986. 7.95 (S-73) Jimcin Record.
Strange stories of the imagination.

Stout Gentleman & the Phantom Island. Washington Irving. 1 cass. 1989. 8.95 (S-73) Jimcin Record.

Stout-Hearted Seven. unabr. ed. Neta Frazier. Read by Laurie Klein. 3 cass. (Running Time: 4 hrs. 24 min.). 21.95 (978-1-55686-181-9(8), 181) Books in Motion.
True story of the seven Sager children. They loose two sets of parents in three years on the long & dangerous journey west & still manage to pick up & go on with their lives.

Stover at Yale. unabr. ed. Owen Johnson. Read by Flo Gibson. 7 cass. (Running Time: 10 hrs.). 1995. 25.95 (978-1-55685-349-4(1)) Audio Bk Con.
The all-American boy, Dink Stover, after numerous escapades & pitfalls, grows into a man as he searches for the real values.

Stowaway. unabr. ed. Karen Hesse. Read by David Cale. 6 cass,. (Running Time: 8 hrs. 30 min.). (J). 2000. 30.00 (Random AudioBks) Random Audio Pubg.
In 1767, 11-year-old Nicholas Young stowed away on Captain James Cook's "Endeavour." Cook's three year mission was secret, he was charged by the British Navy to search for a lost continent, believed to be located between the southern tip of South American & New Zealand. Young's journal charts the voyage & with every port of call a new adventure awaits. This is the story of a great voyage of discovery seen through the eyes of a boy who was actually there.

Stowaway. unabr. ed. Karen Hesse. Read by David Cale. 6 cass. (Running Time: 8 hrs. 1 min.). (J). (gr. 5-9). 2004. 40.00 (978-0-8072-8759-0(8), YA259CX, Listening Lib); pap. bk. 48.00 (978-0-8072-8760-6(1), LYA 259 SP, Listening Lib) Random Audio Pubg.
In 1767, 11 year old Nicholas Young stowed away on Captain james Cook's Endeavour. Cook's three year mission was secret. he was charged by the British Navy to search for a lost continent believed to be located between the southern tip of South American and New Zealand. Young's journal charts the voyage, and with every port of call a new adventure awaits.

Stowaway & Milk Run: Two Stories from Mary Higgins Clark. unabr. ed. Mary Higgins Clark. Read by Jan Maxwell. 2004. 7.95 (978-0-7435-1952-6(3)) Pub: S&S Audio. Dist(s): S and S Inc

Stracyles Vol. 5: Teachings. unabr. ed. Georgia Stathis. Read by Georgia Stathis. 12 cass. (Running Time: 12 hrs.). 1995. 79.95 Set. (978-1-881229-35-3(1)) Starcycles.
Designed for the general public. Special collection explaining various aspects of planetary movements & how they correlate to events on earth. Myths, stories, & their connection to history.

Straeon Cymru: 10 o Chwedlau Cyfarwydd. Esyllt Nest et al. 2005. audio compact disk 9.50 (978-88-88046-55-6(0)) Scuola Istruzione ITA.

Straeon Hud a Lledrith. Iwan John & Fflach. 2005. 4.99 (978-0-00-067981-9(X)) Zondervan.

Straeon Sam Tan. Sain. 2005. audio compact disk 12.98 (978-88-88046-77-8(1)) Scuola Istruzione ITA.

Straeon Sion Corn. Angharad Tomos & Sain. 2005. audio compact disk 9.99 (978-88-88039-33-6(3)) Il Calamo ITA.

Stragglers Reef. unabr. ed. Elaine Forrestal. 2 cass. (Running Time: 2 hrs. 30 mins.). 2002. (978-1-74030-587-7(6)) Bolinda Pubng AUS.

Straight. abr. ed. Dick Francis. 2 cass. (Running Time: 3 hrs.). (J). 1989. 15.95 (978-1-55994-118-1(9), CPN 2128) HarperCollins Pubs.

Straight. unabr. ed. Dick Francis. Narrated by Simon Prebble. 8 cass. (Running Time: 11 hrs.). 1994. 70.00 (978-1-55690-993-1(4), 94132E7) Recorded Bks.
Thirty-four-year-old Derek Franklin, recovering from a race injury, is thrown into familial chaos when his older brother Greville dies from a bizarre, seemingly random accident. With little more to go on than his brother's expensive toys & a few vague diary entries, Derek becomes more & more convinced that his very straight brother was brought down by some crooked men.

Straight Ahead: Digitally Remastered. Contrib. by Amy Grant. Prod. by Brown Bannister. 2007. audio compact disk 13.99 (978-5-557-62608-8(5)) Pt of Grace Ent.

***Straight-Ahead Jazz for Banjo Book/CD Set.** Patrick Cloud. 2010. lib. bdg. Rental 19.99 (978-0-7866-8164-8(0)) Mel Bay.

Straight down a Crooked Path Set: A Christian Response to Homosexuality. Instructed by Gregory Koukl & Thomas Schmidt. 2 cass. (Running Time: 4 hrs.). 1999. 12.95 (978-0-9673584-4-4(2)) Stand to Reason.

Straight from the Dragon's Mouth. 5 compact discs. (Running Time: 5 hrs. +). Dramatization. (J). 2002. audio compact disk 24.95 (978-0-9724995-1-4(2)) Alcazar AudioWorks.
Full Cast Production of traditional Fairy Tales and other stories for children. Includes: Cinderella, Rumplestiltskin, The Froh Prince, Beauty and the Beast, East of the Sun and West of the Moon, Land of the Blue Flower by Frances Hodgson Burnett (author of the Secret Garden and Little Lord Fauntleroy), and Dollypogs by David Thorn (a contemporary tale of 3 very smart dogs who live on Chula Lane), and Selections from Beatrix Potter.

Straight from the Heart. unabr. ed. Tami Hoag. Read by Staci Snell. (Running Time: 21600 sec.). (ENG.). 2007. audio compact disk 29.95 (978-0-7393-5772-9(7), Random AudioBks) Pub: Random Audio Pubg. Dist(s): Random

Straight from the Heart, Set. George Verwer. Read by George Verwer. 2 cass. (Running Time: 2 hr. 45 mins.). 1999. 15.95 (978-1-886463-49-3(2)) Oasis Audio.
Four days of high-energy teaching on topics like spiritual warfare & revival, the power of prayer & God's plan for sexual expression.

***Straight from the Hip.** unabr. ed. Susan Mallery. Read by Julie E. Francis. (Running Time: 9 hrs.). (Lone Star Sisters Ser.). 2010. 19.99 (978-1-4418-7089-6(X), 9781441870896, Brilliance MP3); 39.97 (978-1-4418-7091-9(1), 9781441870919, BADLE); 39.97 (978-1-4418-7090-2(3), 9781441870902, Brinc Audio MP3 Lib); audio compact disk 19.99 (978-1-4418-7087-2(3), 9781441870872, Bril Audio CD Unabri); audio compact disk 79.97 (978-1-4418-7088-9(1), 9781441870889, BriAudCD Unabrid) Brilliance Audio.

Straight into Darkness. abr. ed. Faye Kellerman. Read by Paul Michael. (ENG.). 2005. 14.98 (978-1-59483-248-2(X)) Pub: Hachet Audio. Dist(s): HachBkGrp

Straight into Darkness. abr. ed. Faye Kellerman. Read by Paul Michael. (Running Time: 6 hrs.). (ENG.). 2009. 49.98 (978-1-60788-056-1(3)) Pub: Hachet Audio. Dist(s): HachBkGrp

Straight Man: My Life in Comedy. Nicholas Parsons. 16.95 (978-1-85998-274-7(3), HoddrStoughton) Pub: Hodder General GBR. Dist(s): Trafalgar

Straight Talk about Sex. 2003. 6.95 (978-1-932631-03-6(8)) Ascensn Pr.

***Straight Talk, No Chaser.** unabr. ed. Steve Harvey. (ENG.). 2010. (978-0-06-206466-0(5), Harper Audio); (978-0-06-206467-7(3), Harper Audio); audio compact disk 29.99 (978-0-06-200696-7(7), Harper Audio) HarperCollins Pubs.

Straight Talk on Raising Kids, Set 4. unabr. ed. Curt Shreiner & Douglas Powell. 4 cass. (Running Time: 3 hrs.). 1988. pap. bk. 49.95 (978-1-55678-007-3(9), 2091, Lrn Inc) Oasis Audio.
Presents help for concerned parents of school-age children.

Straight Talk on Raising Young Children. Lendon H. Smith & Curt Shreiner. 4 cass. 49.95 set, incl. 106p. guide bk. (S02055) J Norton Pubs.
You'll discover how to use your natural parenting instincts to clear the hurdles in raising a child between the ages of 1 & 6. This program gives down-to-earth advice - the kind that is based on years of observing what works & what doesn't when raising young children.

Straight Talk on Raising Young Children. unabr. ed. Lendon H. Smith & Curt Shreiner. 4 cass. (Running Time: 3 hrs.). (Straight Talk Ser.). (J). (gr. 10-12). 1989. pap. bk. 49.95 (978-1-55678-011-0(7), 3020, Lrn Inc) Oasis Audio.
Explains how to plan discipline, without punishment.

Straight Talk on Regulatory Compliance for Today's Advisors. Instructed by Brian S. Hamburger. (Running Time: 90 mins.). 2004. audio compact disk 19.95 (978-1-59280-117-6(X)) Marketplace Bks.
Whether you're in the process of setting up a new practice, or part of one that's already established, you'll benefit from the tips and insights industry expert Brian Hamburger shares in his straight-talking overview of the regulatory and compliance net. Join Hamburger as he addresses the most critical compliance issues that financial professionals today - and methods for avoiding serious missteps that could mean trouble for you or your firm.You'll walk away from this in-depth session with the knowledge and insight needed to steer clear of compliance slip-ups, as Hamburger covers it all, including ? -The most important compliance issues for setting up a new practice-How to navigate through the ever changing regulatory environment -The top 10 regulatory mistakes - and how to avoid them-The cost of compliance foul-ups vs. cost of effective compliance programs-New SEC custody rules, and dozens more critical issues-The statistics are startling: Over 70% of all investigations conducted by the SEC's Office of Compliance, Inspections and Examinations find that a firm has failed to disclose material facts. Now, broker dealers, advisors, insurance agents and all financial professionals can find the protection and peace of mind they need, in this important new presentation.

Straight Talk to Men & Their Wives. James C. Dobson. 1 cass. (FRE.). (J). 1981. 10.99 (978-2-01-014273-4(X)) Nelson.
Looking for God's leadership in human relationships with questions such as: What makes a man a man? A woman a woman? What does the Bible say about roles? Where do the boundaries fall between male chauvinism & being an effective, forceful leader? And many other relevant topics for today's marriages!.

Straight Talk to Teens about Sex & Morality. Marcellino D'Ambrosio. 2004. audio compact disk 7.95 (978-1-932927-11-5(5)) Ascensn Pr.

Straight to Bethlehem: Luke 2:1-20. Ed Young. 1989. 4.95 (978-0-7417-1771-9(9), 771) Win Walk.

Straight Way. Thomas Merton. 1 cass. 1995. 8.95 (AA2801) Credence Commun.
To search for God, we begin by accepting what is real. This doesn't mean passivity, it means prayer & discernment. Merton makes brilliant use of insights from the Koran to support his thought.

***Strain.** unabr. ed. Guillermo del Toro & Chuck Hogan. Read by Ron Perlman. (Strain Trilogy: Bk. 1). 2009. (978-0-06-190205-5(5), Harper Audio); (978-0-06-190206-2(3), Harper Audio) HarperCollins Pubs.

***Strain.** unabr. ed. Guillermo del Toro & Chuck Hogan. Read by Ron Perlman. (Strain Trilogy: Bk. 1). 2010. audio compact disk 19.99 (978-0-06-201093-3(X), Harper Audio) HarperCollins Pubs.

Straken. unabr. ed. Terry Brooks. Read by Paul Boehmer. 11 cass. (Running Time: 15 hrs.). (High Druid of Shannara Ser.: Bk. 3). 2005. 81.00 (978-1-4159-2417-4(1)); audio compact disk 84.15 (978-1-4159-2418-1(X)) Pub: Books on Tape. Dist(s): NetLibrary CO

Strand of Dreams, Set. unabr. ed. Audrey Howard. Read by Carole Boyd. 14 cass. 1999. 110.95 (978-0-7540-0297-0(7), CAB 1720) AudioGO.

Strand of Dreams, Set. unabr. ed. Audrey Howard. Read by Carole Boyd. 14 cass. 1999. 110.95 (CAB 1720) AudioGO.

Stranded. unabr. ed. V. L. McDermid. Read by V. Sylvester & G. Griffin. 5 cass. (Running Time: 6 hrs.). (Isis Cassettes Ser.). (J). 2005. 49.95 (978-0-7531-3457-3(8)) Pub: ISIS Lrg Prnt GBR. Dist(s): Ulverscroft US

Stranded. unabr. ed. Val McDermid. Read by V. Sylvester & G. Griffin. 6 CDs. (Running Time: 6 hrs. 5 mins.). (Isis (CDs) Ser.). (J). 2005. audio compact disk 64.95 (978-0-7531-2474-1(2)) Pub: ISIS Lrg Prnt GBR. Dist(s): Ulverscroft US

Stranded. unabr. ed. Ben Mikaelsen. Narrated by Christina Moore. 6 pieces. (Running Time: 7 hrs. 45 mins.). (gr. 5 up). 1997. 51.00 (978-0-7887-0682-0(9), 94854E7) Recorded Bks.
When Koby discovers a stranded mother whale & her baby, she must overcome her physical disability to help them survive. Alone with them in tl. ocean, night is falling fast & help is nowhere in sight.